ETYMOLOGY KEY

<	descended from, derived from, from
<<	descended, derived from, through intermediate stages not shown
>	whence
?	origin unknown, perhaps
*	hypothetical
abbr.	abbreviation
abl.	ablative
acc.	accusative
adj.	adjective
adv.	adverb
alter.	alteration
aph.	aphetic
appar.	apparently
assoc.	association
aug.	augmentative
b.	blend of, blended
c.	cognate with
cf.	compare
comb. form	combining form
comp.	comparative
contr.	contraction
decl.	declension
dial.	dialect, dialectal
dat.	dative
deriv.	derivative
dim.	diminutive
eccl.	ecclesiastical
equiv. to	equivalent to
etc.	etcetera
etym.	etymology, etymological
fem.	feminine
fig.	figurative
freq.	frequentative
fut.	future
gen.	genitive
ger.	gerund, gerundive
i.e.	that is
imit.	imitative
impv.	imperative
indic.	indicative
inf.	infinitive
irreg.	irregularly
lit.	literally
m.	modification of
masc.	masculine
mod.	modern
n.	noun
nom.	nominative
north.	northern
obl.	oblique
obs.	obsolete
orig.	origin, originally
pass.	passive
perh.	perhaps
pl.	plural
prep.	preposition
pres.	present
prob.	probably
prp.	present participle
ptp.	past participle
r.	replacing
redupl.	reduplication
repr.	representing
s.	stem
sing.	singular
sp.	spelling
subj.	subjunctive
superl.	superlative
syll.	syllable
trans.	translation
transit.	transitive
ult.	ultimate, ultimately
uncert.	uncertain
v.	verb, verbal
var.	variant
voc.	vocative

LANGUAGES

AF	Anglo-French
Afr	African
AInd	Anglo-Indian
AL	Anglo-Latin
Amer	American
AmerInd	American Indian
AmerSp	American Spanish
Ar	Arabic
Aram	Aramaic
Arm	Armenian
Austral	Australian
Bulg	Bulgarian
CanF	Canadian French
Celt	Celtic
Chin	Chinese
D	Dutch
Dan	Danish
E	English
EGmc	East Germanic
Egypt	Egyptian
F	French
Finn	Finnish
Flem	Flemish
Fris	Frisian
G	German
Gael	Gaelic
Gk	Greek
Gmc	Germanic
Goth	Gothic
Heb	Hebrew
HG	High German
Hind	Hindustani
Hung	Hungarian
Icel	Icelandic
IE	Indo-European
Ind	Indian
Ir	Irish
IrGael	Irish Gaelic
It	Italian
Jap	Japanese
L	Latin
LaF	Louisiana French
LG	Low German
LGk	Late Greek
Lith	Lithuanian
LL	Late Latin
ME	Middle English
Mex	Mexican
MexSp	Mexican Spanish
MF	Middle French
MGk	Medieval Greek
MHG	Middle High German
MPers	Middle Persian
ML	Medieval Latin
ModGk	Modern Greek
ModHeb	Modern Hebrew
NL	Neo-Latin
Norw	Norwegian
OBulg	Old Bulgarian
OCS	Old Church Slavonic
ODan	Old Danish
OE	Old English
OF	Old French
OFris	Old Frisian
OG	Old German
OHG	Old High German
OIcel	Old Icelandic
OIr	Old Irish
OIt	Old Italian
OL	Old Latin
OLG	Old Low German
ON	Old [illegible]
ONF	Old [illegible] Fr[illegible]
OPers	Old [illegible]
OPg	Old Portuguese
OPr	Old Provençal
OPruss	Old Prussian
ORuss	Old Russian
OS	Old Saxon
OSlav	Old Slavic
OSerb	Old Serbian
OSp	Old Spanish
OSw	Old Swedish
PaG	Pennsylvania German
Pers	Persian
Pg	Portuguese
Pol	Polish
Pr	Provençal
Pruss	Prussian
Rom	Romance
Rum	Rumanian
Russ	Russian
SAfrD	South African Dutch (Afrikaans)
Scand	Scandinavian
Scot	Scottish
ScotGael	Scots Gaelic
Sem	Semitic
[illegible]	[illegible]rit
[illegible]	[illegible]
[illegible]	[illegible]sh
[illegible]	[illegible]sh Arabic
[illegible]	[illegible]ish
SwissF	Swiss French
Turk	Turkish
VL	Vulgar Latin
WFlem	West Flemish
WGmc	West Germanic

D1165789

Webster's Encyclopedic Unabridged Dictionary of the English Language

Webster's Encyclopedic Unabridged Dictionary of the English Language

The dictionary entries are based on the First Edition of *The Random House Dictionary of the English Language*

GRAMERCY BOOKS
NEW YORK

ACKNOWLEDGMENTS AND PERMISSIONS

The "A dictionary of the English Language" section of this book *(Webster's Encyclopedic Unabridged Dictionary)* is based on the first edition of The *Random House Dictionary of the English Language, the Unabridged Edition*, copyright © 1983.

A Manual of Style, copyright © 1986 by Crown Publishers, Inc. Excerpted and reprinted by arrangement with Crown Publishers, Inc.

Stein, Jess, Ed.—*Rhyming Dictionary*, copyright © 1960 by Random House, Inc. Reprinted by arrangement with Random House, Inc.

Copyright © 1996 by Gramercy Books
All rights reserved under International and Pan-American
Copyright Conventions.

No part of the book may be reproduced or transmitted in any form or by any means electronic or mechanical including photocopying, recording, or by any information storage and retrieval system, without permission in writing from the publisher.

This 1996 edition is published by Gramercy Books,
a division of Random House Value Publishing, Inc.,
201 East 50th Street, New York, N. Y. 10022.

Gramercy Books and colophon are trademarks of
Random House Value Publishing, Inc.

Random House
New York • Toronto • London • Sydney • Auckland
http://www.randomhouse.com/
Printed and bound in the United States

Library of Congress Cataloging-in-Publication
Webster's encyclopedic unabridged dictionary of the English language.
1. English language—Dictionaries.
PE1625.W46 1989
423—dc19 89-3785
CIP

Special Value Edition: ISBN: 0-517-15141-3
Original ISBN: 0-517-11864-5

10 9 8 7 6 5

CONTENTS

INTRODUCTION

THE ENGLISH LANGUAGE AND THE DICTIONARY

Although not everyone may realize it, the origin of the English language can be dated with relative precision. The term ''English'' goes back to the name of one of the Germanic tribes—the Angles—who, according to the Venerable Bede, began to invade Britain in the year 449. ''English'' derives from ''Angle-ish,'' and both the name of the tribe, the ''Angles,'' and the ''-ish'' suffix are entered in this *Dictionary*—as are the name ''Bede'' and, of course, the word ''English'' itself, where the etymology just outlined is given.

The Angles, and also the Saxons and the Jutes, who, according to Bede, joined in the invasion of Britain, all spoke dialects of a language scholars call West Germanic, no contemporary records of which are extant. Other current West Germanic languages, along with English, are Dutch and German. West Germanic was closely related to North Germanic, which survives today in the Scandinavian languages such as Norwegian, Swedish, and Danish. Originally, both West Germanic and North Germanic were the same language, called Germanic, before its speakers split up and in time evolved their own distinctive speech. Germanic, in turn, is related to a number of other ancient languages in both Europe and Asia, such as Greek, Latin, Slavic, Celtic, Hittite, and Indic. Some of these ancient languages, such as Hittite, have no surviving descendants; others, such as Latin, have many, e.g., French, Italian, Spanish, and Portuguese. As with the branches of Germanic, all these ancient languages stem from the same prehistoric language, which scholars call ''Indo-European.'' Attempts have long been made to relate the Indo-European family of languages—now spoken by half the people in the world—to the many other known language families, such as Semitic, which includes the current languages Hebrew and Arabic, or Ural-Altaic, which includes Finnish and Hungarian.

The oldest stage of the English language is called Anglo-Saxon or Old English. Its period lasted until the Norman Conquest of 1066, when William the Conqueror imposed a new government, and tried, with some, but far from total success, to impose on Britain the conquerors' French. From then until about 1475, the language is called Middle English, and from then to now, Modern English. The earliest Old English records date from about the year 650. Most surviving Old English manuscripts, however, are from the tenth and eleventh centuries, including the single surviving manuscript of the epic poem *Beowulf.* The English of these early times is much different from that of today. Here is the Lord's Prayer as written in the southwest of England about the year 1000:

> Faeder ure, thu the eart on heofenum, si thin nama gehalgod. To-becume thin rice. Geweorthe thin willa on eorthan, swa swa on heofenum. Urne daeghwamlican hlaf syle us to-daeg. And forgyf us ure gyltas, swa swa we forgifath urum gyltendum. And ne gelaede thu us on costnunge, ac alys us of yfle: Sothlice.

Almost all of the eleven words of the opening sentence, for instance, are recognizable, but barely. Some of them have changed simply in pronunciation, and thus in spelling, but still have essentially the same form, e.g., *faeder*/''father'' and *thu*/''thou.'' Other words have also changed in inflection. An ''inflection'' is a sound (and hence, in writing, one or more letters) added to a word to show how that word is being used. So, for instance, *heofenum* in the Old English is the noun *heofen* (''heaven'') plus the *-um* inflection, which indicated ''dative plural.'' That is, the noun is plural here, and in the dative case, which is the case of the indirect object. Thus the form *heofenum* by itself means ''in (the) heavens.''

Yet in this first sentence of the Lord's Prayer, the Old English also uses a preposition with the dative noun: *on heofenum.* This is redundant, as both the preposition *on* (here meaning ''in'') and the inflection *-um* show how the noun *heofen* is being used in, or relates to the rest of, the sentence. Because of such redundancies, many inflections used in Old English have died out. So, whereas in Old English a singular noun can have special inflections for any of four cases—nominative (subject), genitive (possessive), dative, and accusative (direct object)—today only one case, the possessive, has any inflection: we say ''heaven'' for subject or object, but ''heaven's'' for possessive. And whereas in Old English a plural noun can likewise have special inflections for the same four cases, today in the plural, nouns are not inflected at all: we say ''heavens,'' plural subject or object, and also ''heavens','' plural possessive. In writing we use apostrophes to show the singular and plural possessives, but there is no difference in pronunciation between ''heavens,'' ''heaven's,'' and ''heavens'.''

Verbs, pronouns, and adjectives also have far more inflections in Old English than in later stages of the language. In fact, adjectives in current English do not have any inflections at all, and have not had any for over five hundred years. Verbs and pronouns still inflect, but not so much as previously, and some pronouns have been lost or are now little used, such as the *thu*/''thou'' and *thin*/''thine'' of the Lord's Prayer for second person singular. Today we say ''you'' or ''your'' whether the reference is to one other person or more than one. The opening sentence of the Lord's Prayer also happens to show how some Old English verbal inflections have coalesced or been lost. The last word in the sentence, *gehalgod*, meaning ''hallowed,'' is a past participle, and this is shown by the distinctive inflection *-od*. (The *ge-* prefix occurs here, too, but this prefix was not restricted to past participles in Old English.) The past tense forms of this verb in Old English are *gehalgode*, singular, and *gehalgodon*, plural. Thus Old English has three distinct inflections— *-od*, *-ode* (pronounced as two syllables), and *-odon*—which have all coalesced into ''-ed'': we use ''hallowed'' not only as a past participle, but also in the past tense singular and past tense plural. The distinctive *o* vowel in the Old English inflection was reduced in pronunciation to an undifferentiated ''e'' sound (called ''schwa'') early in the Middle English period, the final *-n* was lost from past plural inflections (but not always from past participles: note, e.g., the current past participles ''ridden'' and driven''), and, around the year 1400, the unstressed final *-e* was lost.

By the time of Chaucer, who wrote during the Middle English period (and died in the year 1400), the English is much more easily recognizable as the language we speak today. There are still more inflections than we use, but not so many more, and, equally important, the vocabulary has already taken in many of the now familiar loan words from French. In the famous opening couplet of Chaucer's *Canterbury Tales*, for instance, the main verb, *perced* (''pierced''), is a French loan word:

> Whan that Aprille with his shoures sote,
> The droghte of Marche hath perced to the rote.

The names of the months in this couplet are also from French (see the etymologies for ''March'' and ''April'' in this *Dictionary*), but the rest of the words come from Anglo-Saxon, even if, as with *sote*, a variant form of ''sweet,'' we no longer use them. Chaucer's couplet is obviously not free from inflections, but most of them simply consist of final *-e*. This inflection was by now pronounced with very little stress and was soon lost, as its function had become minimal. In these first two lines of the *Canterbury Tales*, for instance, none of the five final *-e*'s conveys any information not already provided by a preposition or by the word order.

Chaucer lived 600 years ago, but he spoke and wrote in the London dialect of English—the dialect from which descend the standard varieties of English used today in both North America and Britain. This makes Chaucer much easier for us to read than he otherwise would be, as can be seen by comparing his language with the opening two lines of the poem *Sir Gawain and the Green Knight*, also from the late fourteenth century, but from the northwest of England, near Liverpool:

> Sithen the sege and the assaut watz sesed at Troye,
> The borg brittened and brent to brondez and askez
> (''Since the siege and the assault was céased at Troy,
> The city destroyed and burnt to brands and ashes'')

Not only is the language less familiar to us, but so also is the style. Chaucer wrote in rhymed verse, in imitation of French and Italian models; the Gawain poet used alliteration, in the tradition of Anglo-Saxon poetry.

Shakespeare, like Chaucer, lived and wrote in London (though he came from Stratford), as did most of the writers from the sixteenth and seventeenth centuries we now read. The works of these writers need progressively less respelling and glossing as we move toward our own time. It is important to realize, however, that most current editions of Shakespeare do not keep the original spellings. Here is a famous line from *Hamlet* as found in an edition printed in 1604 (the Second Quarto edition):

> O that this too too sallied flesh would melt

Another early edition of Shakespeare, the so-called First Folio of 1623, has ''too too solid flesh,'' but this does not mean that ''sallied'' is an error. It may well be exactly what Shakespeare intended: his way of spelling (reflecting his pronunciation of) the word ''sullied.'' The entry for the verb *sully* in this *Dictionary* explains that it descends from Old English *soli(an)*, and in pronunciation the *o* can develop as easily into an *a* (Shakespeare's ''sallied'') as into a *u* (''sullied'').

Shakespeare may have brought the form ''sallied'' to London from his native Stratford, or it may have been used widely in London in his time and since died out. We do not know. What is known, however, is that the English language continues to have regional dialects. They developed in Britain during the Middle Ages, and they likewise sprang up and have persisted in North America. Benjamin Franklin, writing to Noah Webster in December 1789, remembers his own native New England dialect of the 1720s and 1730s:

> When I left New England in the year 23, the word *improved* had never been used among us, as far as I know, but in the sense of *ameliorated* or *made better*, except once in a very old book of Dr. Mather's entitled, *Remarkable Providences.* As that eminent man wrote a very obscure hand, I remember that when I read that word in his book, used instead of the word *imployed*, I conjectured that it was an error of the printer. . . . But when I returned to Boston in 1733, I found this change had obtained favor, and was then become common; for I met with it often in perusing the newspapers, where it frequently made an appearance rather ridiculous: Such, for instance, as the advertisement of a country-house to be sold, which had been many years improved as a tavern . . .

First note that in Franklin's time, the choice between the forms ''imployed'' and ''employed'' had still not been settled; I have also lower-cased the nouns throughout the passage, for it was then common to capitalize them. But Franklin's main assertion, of course, is that the use of the verb *improve* with the meaning ''employ'' is a local feature of the New England dialect of English—and is a deplorable error. The first part of the assertion, that this use of *improve* is a local feature, may be correct, though the usage is now known to antedate Mather's book. The second part of the assertion, however, the prescriptive part, is another matter. Many words change in meaning through time, usually imperceptibly, and have always done so. The half-dozen current meanings distinguished in the *Dictionary* for the verb *improve* have all evolved from an earlier, simpler meaning for the word in French.

This fine *Dictionary* continues, in magnificent form, the noble tradition exemplified by Benjamin Franklin of describing and reporting the English language.

David Yerkes
B.A. Yale; B.A., D.Phil. Oxford
Professor of English, Columbia University

A

A, a (ā), *n., pl.* **A's** or **As, a's** or **as.** **1.** the first letter of the English alphabet, a vowel. **2.** any spoken sound represented by the letter *A* or *a*, as in *ate, tall, animal*, etc. **3.** something having the shape of an A. **4.** a written or printed representation of the letter *A* or *a*. **5.** a device, as a printer's type, for reproducing the letter *A* or *a*. **6. from A to Z,** from beginning to end; completely: *He knows the Bible from A to Z.* **7. not know from A to B,** to know nothing; be ignorant.

a[1] (ə; *when stressed* ā), *indefinite article.* **1.** not any particular or certain one of a class or group: *a man; a chemical; a house.* **2.** another; typically representing: *a Cicero in eloquence; a Jonah.* **3.** one; a certain; a particular: *one at a time; two of a kind; a Miss Johnson.* **4.** (used before plural nouns that are preceded by a quantifier singular in form): *a hundred men* (compare *hundreds of men*); *a dozen times* (compare *dozens of times*). **5.** indefinitely or nonspecifically (used with adjectives expressing number): *a great many years; a few stars.* **6.** any; a single: *not a one.* [ME; phonetic var. of AN[1]]

a[2] (ə; *when stressed* ā), *prep.* each; every; per: *ten cents a dance; three times a day.* [orig. *a*, prep. var. of ON (see A-[1]); confused with A[1]]

a[3] (ə), *prep. Informal or Eye Dialect.* of (often written as an unhyphenated element): *cloth a gold; time a day; kinda; sorta.* [var. of OF[1]]

a' (ä, ô), *adj. Scot.* all: *for a' that.* Also, **a.**

A, **1.** *Elect.* ampere. **2.** *Physics.* angstrom. **3.** answer.

A, **1.** the first in order or in a series. **2.** (*sometimes l.c.*) (in some grading systems) a grade or mark, as in school or college, indicating the quality of a student's work as excellent or superior. **3.** (*sometimes l.c.*) (in some school systems) a symbol designating the first semester of a school year. **4.** a major blood group or type usually enabling a person whose blood is of this group to donate blood to persons of group A or AB and to receive blood from persons of O or A. **5.** *Music.* **a.** the sixth tone in the scale of C major or the first tone in the relative minor scale, A minor. **b.** a string, key, or pipe tuned to this tone. **c.** a written or printed note representing this tone. **d.** (in the fixed system of solmization) the sixth tone of the scale of C major, called *la.* **e.** the tonality having A as the tonic note. **6.** (*sometimes l.c.*) the medieval Roman numeral for 50 or 500. Cf. **Roman numerals.** **7.** *Chem.* argon. **8.** *Chem., Physics.* See **mass number.** **9.** *Logic.* See **universal affirmative.** **10.** *Brit.* **a.** (on public telephones) a designation on a button that must be pushed to permit the caller to be heard by the person being called. **b.** a designation for a film recommended for adults only. Cf. **U** (def. 4), **X** (def. 7). **11.** a proportional shoe width size, narrower than B and wider than AA. **12.** a proportional brassiere cup size, smaller than B and larger than AA. **13.** (in men's pajama sizes) small.

a, **1.** are; ares. **2.** See **universal affirmative.**

Å, *Physics.* See **angstrom unit.**

A-, atomic (used in combination): *A-plant; A-ship.*

a-[1], a reduced form of Old English prep. *on*, meaning "on," "in," "into," "to," "towards," preserved before a noun in a prepositional phrase, forming a predicate adjective or an adverbial element (*afoot; abed; ashore; aside*), and in archaic and dialectal use before a present participle in *-ing* (*set the bells aringing*). [ME, late OE]

a-[2], a reduced form of Old English prep. *of: akin; afresh; anew.* [ME]

a-[3], an old point-action prefix, not referring to an act as a whole, but only to the beginning or end: *She awoke* (became awake). *They abided by these conclusions* (remained faithful to the end). [ME; OE *ā-*; in some cases confused with A-[5], as in ABRIDGE]

a-[4], var. of **ab-** before *p* and *v: aperient; avert.* [ME < L *ā-, a-* (var. of *ab-* AB-); in some words < F *a-* < L *ab-*, as in ABRIDGE]

a-[5], var. of **ad-**, used: (1) before *sc, sp, st* (*ascend*) and (2) in words of French derivation (often with the sense of increase, addition): *amass.* [ME, in some words < MF *a-* < L *ad-* prefix or *ad* prep. (see AD-), as in ABUT; in others < L *a-* (var. of *ad-* AD-), as in ASCEND]

a-[6], var. of **an-**[1] before a consonant: *achromatic.*

-a, a plural ending of nouns borrowed from Greek and Latin: *phenomena; criteria; data; errata.*

A., **1.** Absolute. **2.** Academy. **3.** acre. **4.** America. **5.** American. **6.** See **angstrom unit.** **7.** year. [< L *annō*, abl. of *annus*] **8.** answer. **9.** before. [< L *ante*] **10.** April. **11.** Artillery.

a., **1.** about. **2.** acre; acres. **3.** active. **4.** adjective. **5.** alto. **6.** ampere. **7.** year. [< L *annō*, abl. of *annus*] **8.** anonymous. **9.** answer. **10.** before. [< L *ante*] **11.** *Metric System.* are. **12.** *Baseball.* assist; assists.

A-1, See **A one.**

a·a (ä′ä), *n.* basaltic lava having a rough surface. Cf. **pahoehoe.** [< Hawaiian *a′ā*]

AA, **1.** See **Alcoholics Anonymous.** **2.** See **author's alteration.**

AA, **1.** a proportional shoe width size, narrower than A and wider than AAA. **2.** the smallest proportional brassiere cup size.

a̅a̅, (in prescriptions) of each. [< Gk *aná*] Also, **āa**

A.A., **1.** Alcoholics Anonymous. **2.** antiaircraft. **3.** antiaircraft artillery. **4.** Associate in Accounting. **5.** Associate of Arts or Associate in Arts. **6.** See **author's alteration.**

AAA, **1.** Agricultural Adjustment Administration. **2.** Amateur Athletic Association. **3.** American Automobile Association. **4.** antiaircraft artillery. **5.** Automobile Association of America.

AAA, a proportional shoe width size, narrower than AA and wider than AAAA.

A.A.A., **1.** Amateur Athletic Association. **2.** American Automobile Association. **3.** Automobile Association of America.

AAAA, Amateur Athletic Association of America.

AAAA, a proportional shoe width size, narrower than AAA and wider than AAAAA.

AAAAA, a proportional shoe width size, narrower than AAAA and wider than AAAAAA.

AAAAAA, a proportional shoe width size, narrower than AAAAA and wider than AAAAAAA.

AAAAAAA, the narrowest proportional shoe width size.

A.A.A.L., American Academy of Arts and Letters.

A.A.A.S., American Association for the Advancement of Science. Also, **AAAS**

Aa·chen (ä′kən; *Ger.* ä′KHən), *n.* a city in W Germany: coronation city of German kings 936–1531. 242,000. French, **Aix-la-Chapelle.**

A.A.E., American Association of Engineers.

A.Ae.E., Associate in Aeronautical Engineering.

A.A.E.E., American Association of Electrical Engineers.

AAF, *U.S.* Army Air Forces.

A.A.G., Assistant Adjutant General.

A.Agr., Associate in Agriculture.

Aal·borg (ôl′bôrg), *n.* Alborg.

Aa·le·sund (ô′lə so͞on′), *n.* Ålesund.

aa·li·i (ä lē′ē), *n.* a bushy shrub, *Dodonaea viscosa*, of Australia, Hawaii, Africa, and tropical America, having sticky foliage. [< Hawaiian]

Aalst (älst), *n.* Flemish name of **Alost.**

Aal·to (äl′tô), *n.* **Al·var** (äl′vär), 1898–1976, Finnish architect and furniture designer.

AAM, air-to-air missile.

a & h, *Insurance.* accident and health.

A and M, **1.** Agricultural and Mechanical. **2.** (of hymns) Ancient and Modern.

A. and M., Agricultural and Mechanical.

A & R, artists and repertory. Also, **A. & R., A-and-R, a. and r., a-&-r**

A.A.P.S.S., American Academy of Political and Social Sciences.

Aar (är), *n.* a river in central Switzerland, flowing N to the Rhine. 175 mi. long.

Aar·au (är′ou), *n.* a town in and capital of Aargau, in N Switzerland. 17,045 (1960).

Aardvark
(2 ft. high at shoulder; total length 5½ ft.; tail to 2½ ft.)

aard·vark (ärd′värk′), *n.* a large, nocturnal, burrowing mammal, *Orycteropus afer*, of Africa, feeding on ants and termites and having a long, extensile tongue, strong claws, and long ears. [< obs. SAfrD (replaced by *erdvark*), equiv. to *aarde* EARTH + *vark* pig; see FARROW[1]]

aard·wolf (ärd′wo͝olf′), *n., pl.* **-wolves.** a striped, hyenalike African mammal, *Proteles cristatus*, that feeds chiefly on insects. [< SAfrD, equiv. to *aarde* EARTH + *wolf* WOLF]

Aar·gau (är′gou), *n.* a canton in N Switzerland. 360,940 (1960); 542 sq. mi. *Cap.:* Aarau. French, **Argovie.**

Aar·hus (*Dan.* ôʀ′; ôr′ho͞os′), *n.* Århus.

Aar·on (âr′ən, ar′-), *n.* **1.** the brother of Moses, usually regarded as the first high priest of the Hebrews. Ex. 28; 40:13–16. **2.** Also, **Aron.** a boy's given name.

Aa·ron·ic (â ron′ik), *adj.* **1.** of or pertaining to Aaron. **2.** pertaining or belonging to the order of Jewish priests descended from Aaron. **3.** of the second, or lesser, order of priesthood among the Mormons. Also, **Aaronical.** [AARON + -IC]

Aa·ron·i·cal (â ron′i kəl), *adj.* **1.** Aaronic. **2.** of or like a high priest; pontifical. [AARONIC + -AL[1]]

Aa·ron·ite (âr′ə nīt′), *n.* one of the priestly descendants of Aaron. [AARON + -ITE] —**Aar·on·it·ic** (âr′ə nit′ik), *adj.*

Aa·ron's-beard (âr′ənz bērd′), *n.* See **rose of Sharon** (def. 2).

Aar′on's rod′, **1.** a rod, inscribed with the name of Aaron, that miraculously blossomed and yielded almonds, Num. 17:8. **2.** any of various plants having a tall, flowering stem, as the goldenrod, mullein, etc. **3.** a smooth-stemmed herb, *Thermopsis caroliniana*, found from North Carolina to Georgia, having yellow flowers in stiffly erect clusters and hoary pods. **4.** *Archit.* a convex molding having regularly spaced representations of leaves or scrollwork.

A.A.S., **1.** Fellow of the American Academy. [< L *Acadēmiae Americānae Socius*] **2.** American Academy of Sciences. **3.** Associate in Applied Science.

A.A.Tech., Associate in Automotive Technology.

A.A.U., Amateur Athletic Union.

A.A.U.P., **1.** American Association of University Professors. **2.** American Association of University Presses. Also, **AAUP**

A.A.U.W., American Association of University Women.

A.Av.Tech., Associate in Aviation Technology.

A-ax·is (ā′ak′sis), *n., pl.* **A-ax·es** (ā′ak′sēz). *Crystall.* the horizontal crystallographic axis passing from front to back. Cf. **B-axis, C-axis.**

Ab (ôv; *Heb.* äv), *n.* the eleventh month of the Jewish calendar. Also, **Av.** Cf. **Jewish calendar.** [< Heb *ābh*]

Ab (ab), *n.* a boy's given name.

AB, a major blood group or type usually enabling a person whose blood is of this group to donate blood to persons of group AB and to receive blood from persons of group O, A, B, or AB.

Ab, *Chem.* alabamine.

ab-, a formal element occurring in loan words from Latin, where it meant "away from": *abdicate; abolition.* Also, **a-, abs-.** [< L *ab* prep. and prefix, from, away, c. Gk *apó*, Skt *apa*, G *ab*, E OF[1], OFF]

ab., **1.** about. **2.** *Baseball.* (times) at bat.

A.B., **1.** *Naut.* See **able seaman.** **2.** See **Bachelor of Arts.** [< L *Artium Baccalaureus*]

a·ba (ə bä′, ä′bə), *n.* **1.** a fabric woven of camel's or goat's hair. **2.** a sleeveless outer garment made of this fabric or silk, worn by Arabs. Also, **abba.** [< Ar *′abā′(ah)*]

A.B.A., **1.** American Bar Association. **2.** American Basketball Association. **3.** American Booksellers Association. **4.** Associate in Business Administration.

a·ba·ca (ä′bä kä′, ä′bə-), *n.* **1.** a Philippine plant, *Musa textilis.* **2.** the fiber of this plant, used in making rope. [< Sp < Tagalog *abaká*]

ab·a·cis·cus (ab′ə sis′kəs, -kis′-), *n., pl.* **-cis·ci** (-sis′ī, -kis′kī). **1.** *Archit.* a small abacus. **2.** a tessera. Also, **abaculus.** [< NL < Gk *abakískos*, equiv. to *abak-* (s. of *ábax*; see ABACUS) + *-iskos* dim. suffix]

ab·a·cist (ab′ə sist), *n.* a person who uses an abacus. [< ML *abacist(a)* (L *abac(us)* ABACUS + *-ista* -IST)]

a·back (ə bak′), *adv.* **1. taken aback,** disconcerted; surprised: *I was quite taken aback at their bad manners.* **2.** *Naut.* so that the wind presses against the forward side of the sail or sails: *a sail laid aback; a yard braced aback; a schooner caught aback.* **3.** toward the back. **—***adj. Naut.* **4.** (of a sail) in such a position that the wind presses against the forward side. **5.** (of a yard) in such a position that its sail is laid aback. [ME *abak,* OE *on bæc* to the rear. See ON, BACK[1]]

Ab·a·co (ab′ə kō′), *n.* two islands (**Great Abaco** and **Little Abaco**) in the N Bahamas. 3407 (1953); 776 sq. mi.

a·bac·u·lus (ə bak′yə ləs), *n., pl.* **-li** (-lī′). abaciscus. [< L; see ABACUS, -ULE]

ab·a·cus (ab′ə kəs, ə-bak′əs), *n. pl.* **ab·a·cus·es, ab·a·ci** (ab′ə sī′, -kī′, ə bak′ī). **1.** a device for making arithmetic calculations, consisting of a frame set with rods on which balls or beads are moved. **2.** *Archit.* a slab forming the top of the capital of a column. See diag. under **volute.** [< L; re-formed < Gk *ábax* board, counting board]

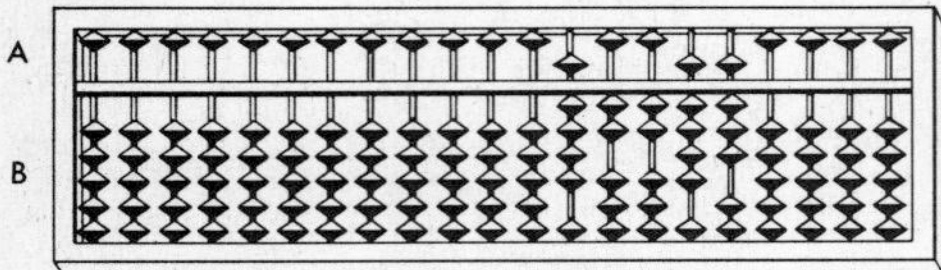

Abacus (Japanese)
Each vertical column=one integer: each bead in group A=5 when lowered; each bead in group B=1 when raised; value of this setting is 922,980,000

A·ba·dan (ä′bä dän′), *n.* a city in SW Iran, on the Shatt-al-Arab: oil refineries. 226,103 (1956).

A·bad·don (ə bad′ən), *n.* **1.** a place of destruction; the depths of hell. **2.** Apollyon. Rev. 9:11. [< Heb *'abhaddōn,* lit., destruction]

ab ae·ter·no (äb′ ī ter′nō; *Eng.* ab′ ē tûr′nō), *Latin.* down the ages; from the most remote antiquity; without an assignable origin or beginning date.

a·baft (ə baft′, ə bäft′), *Naut.* **—***prep.* **1.** to the rear of; aft of: *the fife rail abaft the mainmast.* **—***adv.* **2.** in the direction of the stern; astern; aft. [ME *on baft, abaft,* equiv. to *on* ON + *baft,* OE *bæftan.* See BY, AFT]

A·bag·tha (ə bag′thə), *n.* one of the seven eunuchs who served in the court of King Ahasuerus. Esther 1:10. Also, *Douay Bible,* **Abgatha.**

A·bai·lard (A bā lar′), *n.* **Pierre** (pyer). See **Abélard.**

a·baised (ə bāst′), *adj. Heraldry.* abased.

ab·a·lo·ne (ab′ə lō′nē), *n.* a large snail of the genus *Haliotis,* having a bowllike shell bearing a row of respiratory holes, the flesh of which is used for food and the shell for ornament and as a source of mother-of-pearl. Also called **ear shell, sea-ear.** [< AmerSp, var. of *abulón* < ?]

ab·amp (ab′amp′), *n. Elect.* abampere. [by shortening]

ab·am·pere (ab am′pēr, ab′am pēr′), *n. Elect.* the centimeter-gram-second unit of electromagnetic current, equivalent to 10 amperes. [*ab-* (prefix used for a cgs. electromagnetic unit) + AMPERE]

a·ban·don[1] (ə ban′dən), *v.t.* **1.** to leave completely and finally; forsake utterly; desert: *to abandon one's home; to abandon a child; to abandon a sinking ship.* **2.** to give up; discontinue; withdraw from: *to abandon the cares of empire; to abandon a research project.* **3.** to give up the control of: *to abandon a city to a conqueror.* **4.** to yield (oneself) without restraint or moderation; give (oneself) over to natural impulses, usually without self-control: *to abandon oneself to grief.* **5.** *Law.* to cast away, leave, or desert, as property or a child. **6.** *Insurance.* to relinquish (insured property) to the underwriter in case of partial loss, thus enabling the insured to claim a total loss. **7.** *Obs.* to banish. [ME *abando(u)ne* < MF *abandon(er)* for OF (*mettre*) *a bandon* (put) under ban, equiv. to *a* at, to (< L *ad;* see AD-) + *bandon* < LL *bandum,* var. of *bannum* interdict < Gmc; see BAN[2]] **—a·ban′don·a·ble,** *adj.* **—a·ban′don·er,** *n.* **—a·ban′donment,** *n.*
—Syn. 2. ABANDON, RELINQUISH, RENOUNCE mean to give up all concern in something. ABANDON means to give up or discontinue any further interest in something because of discouragement, weariness, distaste, or the like: *to abandon one's efforts.* RELINQUISH implies being or feeling compelled to give up something one would prefer to keep: *to relinquish a long-cherished desire.* RENOUNCE implies making (and perhaps formally stating) a voluntary decision to give something up: *to renounce worldly pleasures.* See also **desert**[2]. **3.** yield, surrender, resign, waive, abdicate. **—Ant. 3.** keep.

a·ban·don[2] (ə ban′dən), *n.* a complete surrender to natural impulses without restraint or moderation; freedom from constraint or conventionality: *to dance with reckless abandon.* [< F, back formation from *abandonner* to ABANDON[1]]
—Ant. restraint, constraint.

a·ban·doned (ə ban′dənd), *adj.* **1.** forsaken; deserted: *an abandoned cabin; an abandoned kitten.* **2.** unrestrained; uncontrolled: *She danced with abandoned enthusiasm.* **3.** utterly lacking in moral restraints; shameless; wicked: *an abandoned and dissolute woman.* [ME; see ABANDON[1], -ED[2]] **—a·ban′doned·ly,** *adv.*
—Syn. 1. discarded, rejected. **3.** See **immoral.**

A·ban·tes (ə ban′tēz), *n.* (*construed as pl.*) (in the *Iliad*) a warlike tribe from the island of Euboea, allies of the Greeks in the Trojan War.

ab·ap·tis·ton (ab′ap tis′tən), *n. Surg.* a trephine with a cone-shaped saw. [< Gk (*trýpanon*) *abáptiston* (trepan) not dipped, neut. of *abáptistos,* equiv. to *a-* A-[6] + *baptis-,* var. s. of *baptízein* to immerse (see BAPTIZE) + *-tos* verbal adj. suffix]

A·bar·bar·e·a (ə bär bar′ē ə), *n.* (in the *Iliad*) a fountain nymph.

Ab·a·ris (ab′ər is), *n. Class. Myth.* a Greek sage known for his miraculous cures.

à bas (A bä′), *French.* down with. [lit., to the bottom]

A·bas (ā′bəs), *n. Class. Myth.* **1.** a son of Celeus and Metanira who was changed into a lizard for mocking Demeter. **2.** a king of Argolis and the father of Acrisius and Proetus who was protected from all enemies by a magic shield in his possession. **3.** (in the *Iliad*) a son of Eurydamas who was slain by Diomedes in the Trojan War. **4.** a youth who was changed into a bird for trying to protect his companion, Diomedes, from the revenge of Aphrodite.

a·base (ə bās′), *v.t.,* **a·based, a·bas·ing. 1.** to reduce or lower, as in rank, office, reputation, or estimation; humble; degrade. **2.** *Archaic.* to lower; put or bring down: *He abased his head.* [A-[5] + BASE[2]; r. late ME *abaisse, abesse* < MF *abaiss(ier),* equiv. to *a-* A-[5] + *baissier* to make low; see BASS[1]] **—a·base′ment,** *n.* **—a·bas′er,** *n.*
—Syn. 1. humiliate. **—Ant. 1.** elevate, exalt.

a·based (ə bāst′), *adj. Heraldry.* (of a charge) lower on an escutcheon than is usual: *a bend abased.* Also, **abaised.** [ABASE + -ED[2]]

a·bash (ə bash′), *v.t.* to destroy the self-possession of; disconcert; make ashamed or embarrassed: *to abash someone by sneering.* [ME *aba(i)sshe* < AF *abaiss-,* var. of MF *esbaiss-,* long s. of *esbair* (F *ébahir*) to be surprised (*es-* EX-[1] + *bair* to gape)] **—a·bash·ed·ly** (ə bash′id lē), *adv.* **—a·bash′ed·ness,** *n.* **—a·bash′ment,** *n.*
—Syn. shame, discompose.

a·ba·sia (ə bā′zhə, -zhē ə, -zē ə), *n. Med.* inability to walk due to a limitation or absence of muscular coordination. Cf. **astasia.** [< NL; see A-[6], BASIS, -IA] **—a·ba·sic** (ə bā′zik, -sik), **a·bat·ic** (ə bat′ik), *adj.*

a·ba·tage (ä bə täzh′), *n.* abattage.

a·bate (ə bāt′), *v.,* **a·bat·ed, a·bat·ing. —***v.t.* **1.** to reduce in amount, degree, intensity, worth, etc.; lessen; diminish: *to abate a tax; to abate one's enthusiasm.* **2.** *Law.* **a.** to put an end to or suppress (a nuisance). **b.** to suspend or extinguish (an action). **c.** to annul (a writ). **3.** to deduct or subtract: *to abate part of the cost.* **4.** to omit: *to abate all mention of names.* **5.** to remove, as in stone carving, or hammer down, as in metalwork, (a portion of a surface) in order to produce a figure or pattern in low relief. **—***v.i.* **6.** to decrease or diminish in intensity, violence, amount, worth, etc.: *The storm has abated. The pain in his shoulder finally abated.* [late ME < MF *abat(re),* equiv. to *a-* A-[5] + *batre* < LL *batere* for L *batuere* to beat] **—a·bat′a·ble,** *adj.* **—a·bat′er;** *Law.* **a·ba′tor,** *n.*
—Syn. 6. subside. **—Ant. 1, 6.** increase, intensify.

a·bate·ment (ə bāt′mənt), *n.* **1.** the act or state of abating or the state of being abated; reduction; decrease; alleviation; mitigation. **2.** suppression or termination: *abatement of a nuisance.* **3.** an amount deducted or subtracted, as from the usual price, the full tax, etc. **4.** *Law.* **a.** a wrongful entry on land made by a stranger, after the owner's death and before the owner's heir or devisee has obtained possession. **b.** a decrease in the legacies of a will when the assets of an estate are insufficient to pay all general legacies in full. **c.** a reduction of a tax assessment. **d.** the termination of a nuisance. **5.** Also called **rebatement.** *Heraldry.* a charge or mark that, when introduced into a coat of arms, indicates the owner's disgrace. [< MF, or ABATE + -MENT]
—Syn. 1. lessening, letup, diminution. **2.** end, cessation. **—Ant. 1.** intensification, increase.

ab·a·tis (ab′ə tē′, -tis, ə bat′ē, ə bat′is), *n., pl.* **ab·a·tis** (ab′ə tēz′, ə bat′ēz), **ab·a·tis·es** (ab′ə tis′iz, ə bat′i siz). an obstacle of trees with bent or sharpened branches directed toward the enemy, now often interlaced with barbed wire. [< F; OF *abateis* < LL* *abatetīcius*]

a·bat-jour (A bA zhoor′), *n., pl.* **-jours** (-zhoor′). **1.** a device, as a skylight or reflector, for diverting light into a building. **2.** a sloping screen for cutting off the view between an interior or porch and a lower area in front of a building. [< F: lit., it throws down (*abat*) the daylight (*jour*). See ABATE, JOURNEY]

a·bat·tage (ä′bə tazh′), *n.* the slaughter of animals, esp. the slaughter of diseased animals to prevent the infection of others. Also, **abatage.** [< F; see ABATE, -AGE]

A battery, *Electronics.* an electric battery for heating the filament or cathode heater of an electron tube. Cf. **B battery, C battery.**

ab·at·toir (ab′ə twär′), *n.* a slaughterhouse. [< F, equiv. to *abatt(re)* (to) slaughter (see ABATE) + *-oir* -ORY[2]]

ab·ax·i·al (ab ak′sē əl), *adj.* being or situated away from the axis: *the abaxial surface of a leaf.* [AB- + AXIAL]

abb (ab), *n.* **1.** low-grade wool from the edges of a fleece. **2.** yarn made from this wool. [OE *ab, aweb, oweb;* see WOOF]

ab·ba (ä bä′, ä′bə), *n.* aba.

Ab·ba (ab′ə), *n.* (*sometimes l.c.*) **1.** a title of reverence for bishops and patriarchs in certain Eastern churches. **2.** *New Testament.* a title of reverence for God, used esp. in prayers; Father. Mark 14:36; Rom. 8:15; Gal. 4:6. [< Aram *abbā* father]

ab·ba·cy (ab′ə sē), *n., pl.* **-cies. 1.** the rank, rights, privileges, or jurisdiction of an abbot. **2.** the term of office of an abbot. [< LL *abbātia,* equiv. to *abbāt-* (see ABBOT) + *-ia* -IA]

Ab·bai (ä bī′), *n.* the part of the Blue Nile above Lake Tana.

Ab·bas·id (ab′ə sid, ə bas′id), *n.* a member of a dynasty of caliphs ruling at Baghdad, A.D. 750–1258, and claiming descent from Abbas, uncle of Muhammad. Also, **Ab′bas·sid, Ab·bas·side** (ab′ə sīd′, ə bas′īd).

ab·ba·tial (ə bā′shəl), *adj.* of or pertaining to an abbot, abbess, or abbey. [< LL *abbātiāl(is).* See ABBACY, -AL[1]]

ab·bé (a bā′, ab′ā; *Fr.* A bā′), *n., pl.* **ab·bés** (a bāz′, ab′āz; *Fr.* A bā′). (esp. in France) **1.** an abbot. **2.** a title of respect for any ecclesiastic or clergyman. [< F < LL *abbāt-* ABBOT]

Ab·be (ab′ē), *n.* a girl's given name, form of **Abigail.** Also, **Abbey, Abbie, Abby.**

Ab′be condens′er (ä′bə, ab′ē), *Optics.* a combination of two or three lenses, having a large aperture and used as a condenser for a compound microscope. [named after Ernst *Abbe* (1840–1905), German physicist]

Ab′be num′ber, *Optics.* the reciprocal of the dispersive power of a substance. Also called **nu-value, relative dispersion.** [see ABBE CONDENSER]

Ab′be sine′ condi′tion, *Optics.* the condition for an optical system to be free of coma. Also, **Ab′be's sine′ condi′tion.** [see ABBE CONDENSER]

ab·bess (ab′is), *n.* the female superior of a convent of nuns. [ME *abbesse* < OF *abbesse, abaesse* < LL *abbātissa,* fem. of *abbāt-* ABBOT]

Ab·be·ville (ab′ē vil), *n.* **1.** a town in N France, on the Somme River. 22,816 (1962). **2.** a town in NW South Carolina. 5436 (1960). **3.** a town in SE Alabama. 2524 (1960).

Abbe·vill·i·an (ab vil′ē ən, -vil′yən, ab′ə vil′-), *adj.* of, pertaining to, or characteristic of a Paleolithic culture lasting in Europe from the first glacial epoch through the second interglacial epoch and marked by the use of crude stone hand axes; Chellean. Also, **Abbe·vil′e·an.** [ABBEVILLE (France) + -IAN]

ab·bey (ab′ē), *n., pl.* **-beys. 1.** a monastery under the supervision of an abbot or a convent under the supervision of an abbess. **2.** the group of buildings comprising such a monastery or convent. **3.** the church of an abbey. **4.** *Brit.* **a.** a country residence that was formerly an abbatial house: *Newstead Abbey.* **b. the Abbey.** See **Westminster Abbey.** [ME < OF *abeie* < LL *abbātia* ABBACY]

Ab·bey (ab′ē), *n.* **1. Edwin Austin,** 1852–1911, U.S. painter. **2.** Also, **Abbe, Abbie, Abby.** a girl's given name, form of **Abigail.**

ab·bey·stead (ab′ē sted′), *n.* the site of an abbey. Also, **ab′bey·stede′.** [ABBEY + STEAD]

Ab′bey The′atre, a theater in Dublin associated with the Irish National Theatre Society (founded 1901) and the dramas of Synge, Yeats, and Lady Gregory.

Ab·bie (ab′ē), *n.* a girl's given name, form of **Abigail.** Also, **Abbe, Abbey, Abby.**

ab·bot (ab′ət), *n.* the head or superior of a monastery. [ME, var. of *abbat* < L *abbāt-* (s. of *abbās*) < Gk < Aram *abbā* ABBA; r. ME, OE *abbod* < LL *abbād-* for L *abbāt-*] **—ab′bot·cy, ab′bot·ship′,** *n.*

Ab·bot (ab′ət), *n.* **1. Charles Greeley,** born 1872, U.S. astrophysicist. **2.** Also, **Abbott.** a boy's given name.

Ab·bots·ford (ab′əts fərd), *n.* Sir Walter Scott's residence from 1812 to 1832, near Melrose, in SE Scotland.

Ab·bott (ab′ət), *n.* **1. Edith,** 1876–1957, and her sister **Grace,** 1878–1939, U.S. social reformers. **2. Ed·ville Ger·hardt** (ed′vil gâr′härt), 1871–1938, U.S. orthopedist. **3. George,** born 1889, U.S. playwright and producer. **4. Jacob,** 1803–79, and his son, **Ly·man** (lī′mən), 1835–1922, U.S. clergyman and writer. **5.** Also, **Abbot.** a boy's given name.

Ab·boud (ä bood′), *n.* **Ib·ra·him** (ib rä hēm′), born 1900, Sudanese army general and statesman: president of the Supreme Council of the Armed Forces and prime minister since 1958.

abbr., abbreviation. Also, **abbrev.**

ab·bre·vi·ate (ə brē′vē āt′), *v.t.,* **-at·ed, -at·ing. 1.** to shorten (a word or phrase) by omitting letters, substituting shorter forms, etc., as *ft.* for *foot, ab.* for *about, R.I.* for *Rhode Island, NW* for *Northwest,* or *Xn* for *Christian.* **2.** to reduce (anything) in length, duration, etc.; make briefer: *to abbreviate a sermon.* [< L *abbreviāt(us)* shortened (ptp. of *abbreviāre*), equiv. to *ad-* AD- + *breviātus* (*brevi(s)* short + *-ātus* -ATE[1])] **—ab·bre′vi·a′tor,** *n.*
—Syn. See **shorten.**

ab·bre·vi·at·ed (ə brē′vē ā′tid), *adj.* **1.** shortened; made briefer. **2.** (of clothing) scanty; barely covering the body: *an abbreviated costume.* **3.** constituting a shorter version of: *The stool had steps, forming an abbreviated ladder.* [ABBREVIATE + -ED[2]]

ab·bre·vi·a·tion (ə brē′vē ā′shən), *n.* **1.** a shortened or contracted form of a word or phrase, used to represent the whole. **2.** act of abbreviating; state or result of being abbreviated; reduction in length, duration, etc.; abridgment. **3.** *Music.* any of several signs or symbols used to abbreviate musical notation, as those indicating repetition of a phrase or a note. [< L *abbreviātiōn-* (s. of *abbreviātiō*). See ABBREVIATE, -ION]

Ab·by (ab′ē), *n.* a girl's given name, form of **Abigail.** Also, **Abbe, Abbey, Abbie.**

ABC, (ā′bē′sē′), *n., pl.* **ABC's, ABCs. 1.** the basic or elementary facts, principles, etc. (of a subject): *the ABC of electricity.* **2. ABC's,** the alphabet.

ABC, atomic, biological, and chemical: *ABC warfare.*

A.B.C., Alcoholic Beverage Control.

ab·cou·lomb (ab koo′lom, ab′koo lom′), *n. Elect.* the centimeter-gram-second unit of quantity of electricity, equivalent to 10 coulombs. [AB(AMPERE) + COULOMB]

ABC Powers, Argentina, Brazil, and Chile, usually with reference to their mediation between the U.S. and Mexico in 1914.

abd., abdicated.

Abd-el-Ka·dir (äb′del kä′dēr), *n.* 1807?–83, Algerian leader. Also, **Abd-al-Ka·dir** (äb′dal kä′dēr).

Abd-el Krim (äb′del krēm′, krim′), born 1881?, Moroccan chief: leader of the Riffian revolts 1921, 1924.

Ab·der·hal·den (äp′dər häl′dən), *n.* **E·mil** (ā′mēl), 1877–1950, Swiss chemist and physiologist.

Abd-er-Rah·man Khan (äb′dər rə män′ кнän′), 1830?–1901, amir of Afghanistan 1880–1901. Also, **Abdurrahman Khan.**

Ab·de·rus (ab dēr′əs), *n. Class. Myth.* a son of Hermes who was killed by the man-eating mares of Diomedes.

Ab·di·as (ab dī′əs), *n. Douay Bible.* Obadiah (defs. 1, 2).

ab·di·cant (ab′də kənt), *adj.* **1.** abdicating, forsaking, or deserting: *to be abdicant of one's responsibilities.* **—***n.* **2.** a person who abdicates; abdicator. [< L *abdicant-* (s. of *abdicāns*), prp. of *abdicāre.* See ABDICATE, -ANT]

ab·di·cate (ab′də kāt′), *v.,* **-cat·ed, -cat·ing. —***v.i.* **1.** to renounce or relinquish a throne, right, power, claim, or the like, esp. in a formal manner: *He decided to abdicate.* **2.** *Poker Informal.* to withdraw from the play, forfeiting all money or chips put in the pot. **—***v.t.* **3.** to give up or renounce (authority, duties, an office, etc.), esp. in a voluntary, public, or formal manner: *King Edward VIII of England abdicated the throne in 1936.* [< L *abdicāt(us)* renounced (ptp. of *abdicāre*), equiv. to *ab-* AB- + *dicātus* dedicated (*dic-* (see DICTUM) + *-ātus* -ATE[1])] **—ab·di·ca·ble** (ab′də kə bəl), *adj.* **—ab·di·ca·tive** (ab′də kā′tiv, -kə-), *adj.* **—ab′di·ca′tor,** *n.*
—Syn. 3. abandon, repudiate.

ab·di·ca·tion (ab′də kā′shən), *n.* the act or state of abdicating; renunciation. [< L *abdicātiōn-* (s. of *abdicātiō*). See ABDICATE, -ION]

ab·do·men (ab′də mən, ab dō′-), *n.* **1.** *Anat., Zool.* **a.** the part of the body of a mammal between the thorax and the pelvis; belly. **b.** the cavity of this part of the body containing most of the digestive organs. **2.** (in vertebrates below mammals) a region of the body corresponding to, but not coincident with, this part or cavity. **3.** *Entomol.* the posterior section of the body of an arthropod, behind the thorax or the cephalothorax. See diag. under **insect.** [< L: belly < ?]

ab·dom·i·nal (ab dom′ə nəl), *adj.* of, in, on, or for the abdomen: *abdominal muscles; an abdominal support.*

CONCISE ETYMOLOGY KEY: <, descended or derived from; >, whence; b., blend of, blended; c., cognate with; deriv., derivative; equiv., equivalent; imit., imitative; m., modification of; obl., oblique; r., replacing; s., stem; sp., spelling; trans., translation; ?, origin unknown, perhaps; *, hypothetical. See the full key inside the front cover.

[< L *abdomin-* (s. of *abdōmen*) ABDOMEN + -AL[1]] —**ab·dom′i·nal·ly,** *adv.*

ab·dom·i·nous (ab dom′ə nəs), *adj.* having a large belly; potbellied. [< L *abdomin-* (see ABDOMINAL) + -OUS]

Ab·don (ab′don), *n.* **1.** one of the minor judges of Israel. Judges 12:13–15. **2.** a courtier of Josiah. II Chron. 34:20.

ab·duce (ab do͞os′, -dyo͞os′), *v.t.*, **-duced, -duc·ing.** to draw or take away; abduct. [< L *abdūce(re)*, equiv. to *ab-* AB- + *dūcere* to lead]

ab·du·cens (ab do͞o′senz, -sənz, -dyo͞o′-), *n.*, *pl.* **ab·du·cen·tes** (ab′do͞o sen′tēz, -dyo͞o-). See **abducens nerve.** [< L, prp. of *abdūcere* to ABDUCE]

abdu′cens nerve′, *Anat.* either one of the sixth pair of cranial nerves composed of motor fibers that innervate the lateral rectus muscle of the eye. Also called **abdu′cent nerve′.**

ab·du·cent (ab do͞o′sənt, -dyo͞o′-), *adj. Physiol.* drawing away, as by the action of a muscle; abducting. [< L *abdūcent-* (s. of *abdūcens*). See ABDUCENS]

ab·duct (ab dukt′), *v.t.* **1.** to carry off or lead away (a person) illegally and in secret or by force, esp. to kidnap. **2.** *Physiol.* to move or draw away from the axis of the body or from one of its parts (opposed to *adduct*). [< L *abduct(us)*, ptp. of *abdūcere* to ABDUCE]

ab·duc·tion[1] (ab duk′shən), *n.* **1.** act of abducting. **2.** the state of being abducted. [< F < L *abduct(us)* (see ABDUCT) + F *-ion* -ION]

ab·duc·tion[2] (ab duk′shən), *n. Logic.* a syllogism whose major premise is certain but whose minor premise is probable. [< NL *abductiōn-* (s. of *abductiō*; trans. of Gk *apagōgē*). See ABDUCT, -ION]

ab·duc·tor[1] (ab duk′tər), *n.* any muscle which abducts (opposed to *adductor*). [< NL; see ABDUCT, -OR[2]]

ab·duc·tor[2] (ab duk′tər), *n.* a person who abducts. [ABDUCT + -OR[2]]

Ab·dul-A·ziz (äb′do͝ol ä zēz′), *n.* 1830–76, sultan of Turkey 1861–76 (brother of Abdul-Mejid).

Ab·dul-Ha·mid II (äb′do͝ol hä mēd′), 1842–1918, sultan of Turkey 1876–1909.

Ab·dul-Me·jid I (äb′do͝ol me jēd′), *n.* 1823–61, sultan of Turkey 1839–61 (brother of Abdul-Aziz). Also **Ab′dul-Me·djid′ I.**

Abd·ur·rah·man Khan (äb′dər RƏ män′ KHän′), See **Abd-er-Rahman Khan.**

Abe (āb), *n.* a boy's given name, form of **Abraham.**

a·beam (ə bēm′), *adv. Naut., Aeron.* at right angles to the fore-and-aft line: *The vessel was sailing with the wind directly abeam.* [A-[1] + BEAM]

a·be·ce·dar·i·an (ā′bē sē dâr′ē ən), *n.* **1.** a person who is learning the letters of the alphabet. **2.** a beginner in any field of learning. —*adj.* **3.** of or pertaining to the alphabet. **4.** in alphabetical order. **5.** rudimentary; elementary; primary. Also, **abecedary.** [< ML *abecedāriān(us)*. See ABECEDARY, -AN]

a·be·ce·dar·i·um (ā′bē sē dâr′ē əm), *n.*, *pl.* **-dar·i·a** (-dâr′ē ə). a primer, esp. for teaching the alphabet. [< ML]

a·be·ce·da·ry (ā′bē sē′də rē), *n.*, *pl.* **-ries,** *adj.* —*n.* **1.** abecedarian. **2.** abecedarium. —*adj.* **3.** abecedarian. [< LL *abecedāri(us)* (*a be ce d(e)* + *-ārius* -ARY)]

a·bed (ə bed′), *adv.* **1.** in bed: *to stay abed late on Sundays.* **2.** confined to bed. [A-[1] + BED]

A.B.Ed., Bachelor of Arts in Education.

A·bed·ne·go (əbed′nə gō′), *n.* a companion of Daniel. Cf. **Shadrach.**

A·bel (ā′bəl; *for 4 also Norw.* ä′bəl), *n.* **1.** the second son of Adam and Eve, slain by his brother, Cain. Gen. 4. **2. Sir Frederick Augustus,** 1827–1902, English chemist. **3. I. W.,** born 1908, U.S. labor leader: president of the United Steelworkers of America since 1965. **4. Niels Hen·rik** (nēls hen′rik), 1802–29, Norwegian mathematician. **5.** a boy's given name.

Ab·e·lard (ab′ə lärd′), *n.* a boy's given name.

Ab·é·lard (ab′ə lärd′; *Fr.* A bā lAR′), *n.* **Pierre** (pē âr′; *Fr.* pyer), (*Peter Abelard*), 1079–1142, French scholastic philosopher, teacher, and theologian. His love affair with Héloïse is one of the famous romances of history. Also, **Abailard.**

a·bele (ə bēl′, ā′bəl), *n.* the white poplar tree, *Populus alba.* [< D *abeel* < north F *a(u)biel* < LL *albell(us)*, equiv. to L *alb(us)* white + *-ellus* dim. suffix]

A·bel·i·an (ə bē′lē ən, ə bēl′yən), *adj. Math.* **1.** of or pertaining to Niels Henrik Abel or his theorems. **2.** pertaining to an algebraic system in which an operation is commutative: *an Abelian group.* **3.** pertaining to such an operation. [ABEL + -IAN]

Abe′ Lin′coln in Illinois′, a play (1938) by Robert E. Sherwood.

A·bel-me·ho·lah (ā′bəl mi hō′lə), *n.* a city in ancient Palestine, east of the Jordan River: the home of Elisha. Judges 7:22; I Kings 4:12; 19:16.

a·bel·mosk (ā′bəl mosk′), *n.* a tropical, malvaceous plant, *Hibiscus Abelmoschus,* cultivated for its musky seeds, which yield ambrette-seed oil. [< NL *abelmosch(us)* < Ar *abu'l misk* father of musk]

A·be·nez·ra (ä′bə nez′rə, ab′ə-), *n.* a crater in the fourth quadrant of the face of the moon: about 27 miles in diameter.

A·be·o·ku·ta (ä′bā ō′ko͝o tä), *n.* a city in SW Nigeria. 187,292 (1963).

ABEPP, American Board of Examiners in Professional Psychology. Also, **A.B.E.P.P.**

Ab·er·crom·bie (ab′ər krom′bē, -krum′-), *n.* **Sir (Leslie) Patrick,** 1879–1957, English architect and town planner.

Ab·er·dare (ab′ər dâr′), *n.* a city in Glamorganshire, in S Wales. 39,044 (1961).

Ab·er·deen (ab′ər dēn′; *also, for 1, 2,* ab′ər dēn′), *n.* **1.** Also called **Aberdeenshire.** a county in NE Scotland. 298,503 (1961); 1974 sq. mi. **2.** its county seat, a seaport on the North Sea. 185,034 (est. 1964). **3.** a city in NE South Dakota. 23,073. (1960). **4.** a seaport in W Washington. 18,741 (1960). **5.** a town in NE Maryland. 9679 (1960). **6.** a town in E Mississippi. 6450 (1960). **7.** a fishhook having an extended bend. —**Ab·er·do·ni·an** (ab′ər dō′nē ən), *adj.*, *n.*

Ab′erdeen An′gus, one of a breed of hornless beef cattle raised originally in Scotland and having a smooth, black coat.

Ab·er·deen·shire (ab′ər dēn′shēr, -shər), *n.* Aberdeen (def. 1).

Ab′erdeen ter′rier. See **Scottish terrier.**

A·ber·glau·be (ä′bər glou′bə), *n. German.* belief beyond what is known or proved by experience; superstition. [lit., misbelief]

ab·er·rant (ə ber′ənt, ab′ər-), *adj.* **1.** straying from the right, normal, or usual course. **2.** deviating from the ordinary, usual, or normal type; exceptional; abnormal. [< L *aberrant-* (s. of *aberrāns,* prp. of *aberrāre* to deviate). See AB-, ERRANT] —**ab·er′rance, ab·er′ran·cy,** *n.*
—**Syn. 1.** wandering. **2.** divergent, unusual.

ab·er·ra·tion (ab′ə rā′shən), *n.* **1.** the act of straying from the right, normal, or usual course. **2.** the act of deviating from the ordinary, usual, or normal type. **3.** deviation from truth or moral rectitude. **4.** mental irregularity or disorder, esp. of a minor nature; lapse from a sound mental state. **5.** *Astron.* apparent displacement of a heavenly body, owing to the motion of the earth in its orbit. **6.** *Optics.* any disturbance of the rays of a pencil of light such that they can no longer be brought to a sharp focus or form a clear image. [< L *aberrātiōn-* (s. of *aberrātiō*), equiv. to *aberrāt(us)* (ptp. of *aberrāre;* see ABERRANT) + *-iōn-* -ION] —**ab′er·ra′tion·al,** *adj.*
—**Syn. 1.** wandering; deviation, divergence. **4.** abnormality, eccentricity, illusion, delusion, hallucination.

ab es·se (äb es′se; *Eng.* ab es′ē), *Latin.* absent.

ab·es·sive (a bes′iv), *Gram.* —*adj.* **1.** noting a case, as in Finnish, whose distinctive function is to indicate absence or lack. —*n.* **2.** the abessive case. [< L *abess(e)* (to) be absent + -IVE]

a·bet (ə bet′), *v.t.*, **a·bet·ted, a·bet·ting.** to encourage, support, or countenance by aid or approval, usually in wrongdoing: *to abet a swindler; to abet a crime.* [ME *abette* (whence OF *abeter*), OE **abǣtan* to hound on, equiv. to *ā-* A-[3] + *bǣtan* to bait, akin to BITE] —**a·bet′ment, a·bet′tal,** *n.*
—**Syn.** help, aid, assist; promote. —**Ant.** hinder.

a·bet·tor (ə bet′ər), *n.* a person who abets. Also, **a·bet′ter.** [< AF *abettour.* See ABET, -OR[2]]

ab ex·tra (äb ek′strä; *Eng.* ab ek′strə), *Latin.* from the outside.

a·bey·ance (ə bā′əns), *n.* **1.** temporary inactivity, cessation, or suspension: *Let's hold that problem in abeyance for a short while.* **2.** *Law.* a state or condition of real property in which title is not as yet vested in a known titleholder: *an estate in abeyance.* [< AF (equiv. to OF *abeance*) aspiration, lit., a gaping towards. See A-[5], BAY[2], -ANCE]

a·bey·ant (ə bā′ənt), *adj.* temporarily inactive or suspended. [ABEY(ANCE) + -ANT]

ab·far·ad (ab far′ad, -əd), *n. Elect.* the centimeter-gram-second unit of capacitance, equivalent to 10^9 farads. [*ab-* (see ABAMPERE) + FARAD]

A.B.F.M., American Board of Foreign Missions.

Ab·ga·tha (ab′gə thə), *n. Douay Bible.* Abagtha.

ab·hen·ry (ab hen′rē), *n.*, *pl.* **-ries.** *Elect.* the centimeter-gram-second unit of inductance, equivalent to 10^{-9} henry. [*ab-* (see ABAMPERE) + HENRY]

Ab′hi·dham·ma Pit′aka (ub′i dum′ə), *Buddhism.* See under **Pali Canon.**

ab·hom·i·na·ble (ab hom′ə nə bəl), *adj. Obs.* abominable. [< ML *abhominābil(is)*, alter. of L *abōminābilis* ABOMINABLE, by assoc. with phrase *ab homine* from man, inhuman]

ab·hor (ab hôr′), *v.t.*, **-horred, -hor·ring.** to regard with extreme repugnance; detest utterly; loathe; abominate. [< L *abhorr(ēre)* (to) shrink back from, shudder at, equiv. to *ab-* AB- + *horrēre* to bristle, tremble] —**ab·hor′rer,** *n.*
—**Syn.** despise. See **hate.** —**Ant.** love.

ab·hor·rence (ab hôr′əns, -hor′-), *n.* **1.** a feeling of extreme repugnance or aversion; utter loathing; abomination. **2.** something or someone extremely repugnant or loathsome. [ABHORR(ENT) + -ENCE]
—**Syn. 1.** execration, detestation.

ab·hor·rent (ab hôr′ənt, -hor′-), *adj.* **1.** feeling extreme repugnance or aversion (usually fol. by *of*): *abhorrent of waste.* **2.** utterly opposed or in conflict (usually fol. by *to*): *abhorrent to reason.* **3.** causing repugnance; detestable; loathsome: *an abhorrent deed.* **4.** remote in character (usually fol. by *from*): *abhorrent from the principles of law.* [< L *abhorrent-* (s. of *abhorrēns,* prp. of *abhorrēre*). See ABHOR, -ENT] —**ab·hor′rent·ly,** *adv.*
—**Syn. 3.** shocking, abominable.

Ab·i·a (ab′ē ə), *n. Class. Myth.* a nurse who founded a temple of Hercules in Messenia.

A·bi·a·thar (ə bī′ə thər), *n.* a priest of Israel and a companion of David. I Sam. 22:20; II Sam. 15:24–36.

A·bib (ā′bib; *Heb.* ä vēv′), *n. Chiefly Biblical.* the month equivalent to Nisan of the modern Jewish calendar. Ex. 34:18. [< Heb *ābhībh,* lit., ear of grain]

a·bid·ance (ə bīd′ᵊns), *n.* **1.** the act or state of abiding. **2.** conformity; compliance (usually fol. by *by*): *abidance by rules.* [ABIDE + -ANCE]

a·bide (ə bīd′), *v.*, **a·bode** or **a·bid·ed, a·bid·ing.** —*v.i.* **1.** to remain; continue; stay: *Abide with me.* **2.** to have one's abode; dwell; reside: *to abide in a little Scottish village.* **3.** to continue in a particular condition, attitude, relationship, etc.; last. —*v.t.* **4.** to wait for; await: *to abide the coming of the Lord.* **5.** to endure, sustain, or withstand without yielding or submitting: *to abide a vigorous onslaught.* **6.** to put up with; tolerate; stand: *I can't abide such a person.* **7.** to accept without opposition or question: *to abide the verdict of the judges.* **8.** to pay the price or penalty of; suffer for. **9. abide by, a.** to act in accord with. **b.** to submit to; agree to. **c.** to remain steadfast or faithful to: *If you make a promise, abide by it.* [ME *abide(n),* OE *ābīdan.* See A-[3], BIDE] —**a·bid′er,** *n.*
—**Syn. 1.** tarry. **2.** live. **3.** persevere, endure. **6.** bear, endure, brook; support.

a·bid·ing (ə bī′ding), *adj.* continuing without change; enduring; steadfast; lasting: *an abiding faith in God.* [ME; see ABIDE, -ING[2]] —**a·bid′ing·ly,** *adv.* —**a·bid′ing·ness,** *n.*

Ab·i·djan (ab′i jän′; *Fr.* A bē jäN′), *n.* a seaport in and the capital of the Ivory Coast. 180,000 (est. 1960).

A·bie (ā′bē), *n.* a boy's given name, form of **Abraham.**

ab·i·ent (ab′ē ənt), *adj. Psychol.* tending to remove an organism from a stimulus or situation. Cf. **adient.** [< L *abient-* (s. of *abiēns,* prp. of *abīre*), equiv. to *ab-* AB- + *-i-* go + *-ent-* -ENT]

ab·i·e·tate (ab′ē i tāt′), *n. Chem.* a salt or ester of abietic acid. [ABIET(IC ACID) + -ATE[2]]

ab′i·et′ic ac′id (ab′ē et′ik, ab′-), *Chem.* a yellow, crystalline, water-insoluble acid, $C_{19}H_{29}COOH$, obtained from the resin of a species of pine: used chiefly in driers, varnishes, and soaps. Also called **sylvic acid.** [< L *abiet-* (s. of *abiēs*) fir + -IC]

ab·i·gail (ab′ə gāl′), *n.* a lady's maid. [after *Abigail,* name of attendant in play *The Scornful Lady* (1610), by Francis Beaumont and John Fletcher]

Ab·i·gail (ab′ə gāl′), *n.* **1.** the wife of Nabal and later of David. I Sam. 25. **2.** a girl's given name.

A·bi·hu (ə bī′hyo͞o), *n.* a son of Aaron who, with Nadab, was destroyed by fire from heaven for disobeying the Lord. Lev. 10:1–5. Also, *Douay Bible,* **Abiu.**

Ab·i·lene (ab′ə lēn′), *n.* **1.** a city in central Texas. 90,368 (1960). **2.** a town in central Kansas. 6746 (1960).

a·bil·i·ty (ə bil′i tē), *n.*, *pl.* **-ties. 1.** power or capacity to do or act physically, mentally, legally, morally, financially, etc. **2.** competence in an activity or occupation because of one's skill, capacity, means, or other qualification: *the ability to write well.* **3. abilities,** talents; special skills or aptitudes: *Composing music is beyond his abilities.* [ME *(h)abilite* < MF < L *habilitās* aptitude, equiv. to *habili(s)* handy (see ABLE) + *-tās* -TY[2]; r. ME *ablete* < F < L]
—**Syn. 1.** capability; proficiency, expertness, dexterity. **2.** ABILITY, FACULTY, TALENT denote mental qualifications or powers. ABILITY is a general word for mental power, native or acquired, enabling one to do things well: *a person of great ability; ability in mathematics.* FACULTY denotes a natural ability for a particular kind of action: *a faculty of saying what he means.* TALENT is often used to mean a native ability or aptitude in a special field: *a talent for music or art.*

-ability, a combination of **-able** and **-ity,** used to form nouns from stems in **-able:** *capability.* [ME *-abilite* << L *-abilitās*]

Ab·i·lyne (ab′ə lin), *n.* a girl's given name.

A·bim·e·lech (ə bim′ə lek′), *n.* either of two kings of Gerar. Gen. 20:1–18; 26:1–33.

A·bi·ne·ri (ä′bə nâr′ē), *n.* a walled plain in the first quadrant of the face of the moon, in the libration area: about 35 miles in diameter.

Ab·ing·don (ab′ing dən), *n.* **1.** a town in SW Virginia. 4758 (1960). **2.** a town in central Illinois. 3469 (1960). **3.** a town in N Berkshire, in S England, on the Thames: site of Benedictine abbey founded 7th century A.D. 14,283 (1961).

Ab·in·ger (ab′ən jər), *n.* a village in S central Surrey, in S England: governmental magnetic observation station.

Ab·ing·ton (ab′ing tən), *n.* a town in SE Pennsylvania. 55,831 (1960).

ab in·i·ti·o (äb i nit′ē ō′; *Eng.* ab i nish′ē ō′), *Latin.* from the beginning.

A·bin·o·am (ə bin′ō əm), *n.* the father of Barak. Judges 4:6; 12; 5:1. Also, *Douay Bible,* **A·bin·o·em** (ə bin′ō em′).

ab in·tra (äb in′trä; *Eng.* ab in′trə), *Latin.* from inside; from within.

a·bi·o·gen·e·sis (ā′bī ō jen′i sis, ab′ē ō-), *n. Biol.* the production of living organisms from inanimate matter; spontaneous generation. [< NL; see A-[6], BIOGENESIS] —**a·bi·og·e·nist** (ā′bīoj′ə nist, ab′ē-), *n.*

a·bi·o·ge·net·ic (ā′bī ō jə net′ik, ab′ē ō-), *adj. Biol.* of or pertaining to abiogenesis. Also, **a′bi·o·ge·net′i·cal.** [< NL *abiogenetic(us).* See ABIOGENESIS, -TIC] —**a′bi·o·ge·net′i·cal·ly,** *adv.*

a·bi·o·sis (ā′bī ō′sis, ab′ē-), *n.* the absence or lack of life; a nonviable state. [A-[6] + -BIOSIS]

a·bi·ot·ic (ā′bī ot′ik), *adj.* pertaining to or characterized by the absence of life or living organisms. Also, **a′bi·ot′i·cal.** [A-[6] + BIOTIC] —**a′bi·ot′i·cal·ly,** *adv.*

a·bi·ot·ro·phy (ab′ē o′trə fē), *n. Pathol.* the loss of vitality in or the degeneration of certain cells or tissues. [A-[6] + BIO- + -TROPHY] —**ab·i·o·troph·ic** (ab′ē ə trof′ik), *adj.*

ab·ir·ri·tant (ab ir′i tᵊnt), *Med.* —*n.* **1.** a soothing agent. —*adj.* **2.** relieving or allaying irritability. [AB- + IRRITANT]

ab·ir·ri·tate (ab ir′i tāt′), *v.t.*, **-tat·ed, -tat·ing.** *Med.* to make less irritable. [AB- + IRRITATE] —**ab·ir′ri·ta′tion,** *n.* —**ab·ir′ri·ta′tive,** *adj.*

Ab·i·shag (ab′ə shag′), *n.* a young maiden brought to comfort David in his old age. I Kings 1:1–4. Also, *Douay Bible,* **Ab·i·sag** (ab′i sag′).

A·bi·u (ə bī′yo͞o), *Douay Bible.* Abihu.

ab·ject (ab′jekt, ab jekt′), *adj.* **1.** utterly hopeless, humiliating, or wretched: *abject poverty.* **2.** contemptible; despicable; base-spirited: *an abject coward.* **3.** shamelessly servile. **4.** *Obs.* cast aside. [< L *abject(us)* thrown down (ptp. of *abicere, abjicere*), equiv. to *ab-* AB- + *-jec-* throw + *-tus* ptp. suffix] —**ab·jec′tion,** *n.* —**ab·ject·ly** (ab jekt′lē, ab′jekt lē), *adv.* —**ab·ject′ness, ab·ject′ed·ness,** *n.*
—**Syn. 1.** debasing, degrading; miserable. **2.** base, mean, low, vile.
—**Ant.** exalted.

ab·jec·tive (ab jek′tiv), *adj.* tending to degrade, humiliate, or demoralize: *the abjective influences of his early life.* [ABJECT + -IVE]

ab·junc·tion (ab jungk′shən), *n. Bot.* abstriction. [AB- + JUNCTION]

ab·ju·ra·tion (ab′jo͝o rā′shən), *n.* **1.** the act of abjuring. **2.** renunciation upon oath. [< ML *abjūrātiōn-* (s. of *abjūrātiō*), equiv. to *abjūrāt(us)* denied on oath (ptp. of *abjūrāre;* see ABJURE, -ATE[1]) + *-iōn-* -ION]

ab·jure (ab jo͝or′), *v.t.*, **-jured, -jur·ing. 1.** to renounce, repudiate, or retract, esp. with solemnity; recant: *to abjure one's errors.* **2.** to renounce or give up under oath; forswear: *to abjure allegiance.* **3.** to avoid or shun. [late ME < L *abjūr(āre)* (to) deny on oath, equiv. to *ab-* AB- + *jūrāre* to swear; see JURY[1]] —**ab·jur′a·to·ry,** *adj.* —**ab·jur′er,** *n.*

Ab·kha·zi·a (ab kä′zhə, -zē ə; *Russ.* ub KHä′zyi yə), *n.* an autonomous republic in the Georgian Republic, on the E coast of the Black Sea. 506,000; 3360 sq. mi. *Cap.:* Sukhumi. Also, **Ab·kha′si·a.** Formerly, **Abkhaz′ Auton′omous So′viet So′cialist Repub′lic.**

CONCISE PRONUNCIATION KEY: *act, āble, dâre, ärt; ebb, ēqual; if, īce; hot, ōver, ôrder, oil, bo͝ok, o͞oze, out; up, ûrge; chief; sing; shoe; thin, that;* zh *as in measure.* ə = *a* as in *alone, e* as in *system, i* as in *easily, o* as in *gallop, u* as in *circus;* ᵊ as in *button* (but′ᵊn), *fire* (fīᵊr), *cradle* (krād′ᵊl). See the full key inside the front cover.

Ab·kha·zi·an (ab kä′zē ən, -zhən), *n.* a North Caucasian language of Abkhazia, best known for its rich consonantism. Also, **Ab·kha′si·an.** [ABKHAZI(A) + -AN]

abl., ablative.

ab·lac·tate (ab lak′tāt), *v.t.,* **-tat·ed, -tat·ing.** to wean. [< LL *ablactāt(us)* weaned (ptp. of *ablactāre*), equiv. to *ab-* AB- + *lact-* (s. of *lac*) milk + *-ātus* -ATE[1]] —**ab′lac·ta′tion,** *n.*

ab·late (a blāt′), *v.,* **-lat·ed, -lat·ing.** —*v.t.* **1.** to remove or dissipate by melting, vaporization, erosion, etc.: *to ablate a metal surface with intense heat.* —*v.i.* **2.** to become ablated; undergo ablation. [< L *ablāt(us)* carried away (ptp. of *auferre*), equiv. to *ab-* AB- + *lātus* (ptp. of *ferre* to bear); see -ATE[1]]

ab·la·tion (ab lā′shən), *n.* **1.** removal, esp. of organs, abnormal growths, or harmful substances, from the body by mechanical means, as by surgery. **2.** reduction in volume of glacial ice, snow, or névé by the combined processes of melting, evaporation, and calving. Cf. **alimentation** (def. 3). **3.** *Rocketry.* removal or falling away of the parts of a nose cone that are melted by the heat generated by hypersonic reentry speeds. [< LL *ablātiōn-* (s. of *ablātiō*). See ABLATE, -ION]

ab·la·tive[1] (ab′lə tiv), *Gram.* —*adj.* **1.** (in some inflected languages) noting a case which has among its functions the indication of place from which, or, as in Latin, place in which, manner, means, instrument, agent, etc. —*n.* **2.** the ablative case. **3.** a word in that case, as *Troiā* in Latin *Æneas Troiā vēnit,* "Aeneas came from Troy." [< L *ablātīv(us).* See ABLATE, -IVE] —**ab·la·ti·val** (ab′lə tī′vəl), *adj.*

ab·la·tive[2] (ab lā′tiv), *adj.* capable of or susceptible to ablation; tending to ablate: *the ablative nose cone of a rocket.* [ABLATE + -IVE]

ab′lative ab′solute, *Latin Gram.* a construction not dependent upon any other part of the sentence, consisting of a noun and a participle, noun and adjective, or two nouns, in which both members are in the ablative case, as Latin *viā factā,* "the road having been made."

ab·laut (äb′lout, ab′-; *Ger.* äp′lout), *n. Gram.* (in Indo-European languages) regular alternation in the internal phonological structure of a word element, esp. alternation of a vowel, that is coordinated with a change in grammatical function or combination, as in English *sing, sang, sung, song;* apophony. [< G, equiv. to *ab-* off + *Laut* sound]

a·blaze (ə blāz′), *adj.* **1.** burning; on fire: *They set the logs ablaze.* **2.** gleaming with bright lights, bold colors, etc. **3.** excited; eager; zealous; ardent. **4.** very angry. [A-[1] + BLAZE[1]]

a·ble (ā′bəl), *adj.,* **a·bler, a·blest,** *n.* —*adj.* **1.** having necessary power, skill, resources, or qualifications; qualified: *able to lift a trunk; able to write music; able to travel widely; able to vote.* **2.** having unusual or superior intelligence, skill, etc.: *an able minister.* **3.** showing talent, skill, or knowledge: *an able speech.* —*n.* **4.** a code word used in communications to represent the letter *A.* [ME < MF < L *habil(is)* handy, equiv. to *hab(ēre)* (to) have, hold + *-ilis* -ILE]

—**Syn. 1.** fit, fitted. ABLE, CAPABLE, COMPETENT all mean possessing adequate power for doing something. ABLE implies power equal to effort required: *able to finish in time.* CAPABLE implies power to meet or fulfill ordinary, usual requirements: *a capable workman.* COMPETENT suggests power to meet demands in a completely satisfactory manner: *a competent nurse.* **2.** talented; skilled, clever, ingenious. **3.** apt. —**Ant. 1.** incompetent.

-able, a suffix, associated in meaning with the word **able,** occurring in loan words from Latin (*laudable*); used in English as a highly productive suffix to form adjectives by addition to stems of any origin (*teachable; photographable*). Also, **-ble, -ible.** [ME < OF < L *-ābilis* adj. suffix]

a·ble-bod·ied (ā′bəl bod′ēd), *adj.* having a strong, healthy body; physically fit. —**a′ble-bod′ied·ness,** *n.*

ab·le·gate (ab′lə gāt′), *n.* a papal envoy to a newly appointed church dignitary. [< L *ablēgāt(us)* sent away (ptp. of *ablēgāre*), equiv. to *ab-* AB- + *-lēg-* send (on a mission) + *-ātus* -ATE[1]]

a·bleph·a·rous (ā blef′ər əs), *adj. Ophthalm.* having no eyelids. [< NL *ablepharus.* See A-[6], BLEPHAR-, -OUS]

a·blep·si·a (ə blep′sē ə), *n. Ophthalm.* blindness. Also, **a·blep′sy.** [< LL < Gk, equiv. to *a-* A-[6] + *blep-* (s. of *blépein* to look) + *-s-* v. suffix + *-ia* -IA] —**a·blep·ti·cal** (ə blep′ti kəl), *adj.* —**a·blep′ti·cal·ly,** *adv.*

a′ble sea′man, a member of the deck department of a merchant vessel, certified to have certain skills. *Abbr.:* A.B. Also called **a′ble-bodied sea′man.**

a·blins (ā′blinz), *adv. Scot.* perhaps. Also, **a′blings, aiblins.** [ABLE + -LING[2] + -S[1]]

a·block (ə blok′), *adv.* chock-a-block (def. 1).

a·bloom (ə blōōm′), *adv., adj.* in blossom; blooming; flowering. [A-[1] + BLOOM[1]]

A.B.L.S., Bachelor of Arts in Library Science.

ab·lu·ent (ab′lōō ənt), *adj.* **1.** serving to cleanse. —*n.* **2.** a cleansing agent. [< L *abluent-* (s. of *abluēns,* prp. of *abluere*), equiv. to *ab-* AB- + *-lu-* wash + *-ent-* -ENT]

a·blush (ə blush′), *adj.* blushing; reddened. [A-[1] + BLUSH]

ab·lu·tion (ab lōō′shən, ə blōō′-), *n.* **1.** a cleansing with water or other liquid, esp. as a religious ritual. **2.** the liquid used. **3.** a washing of the hands, body, etc. **4. ablutions,** *Brit.* **a.** (*construed as pl.*) the bathing and toilet facilities at a military camp. **b.** (*construed as sing.*) Also called **ablu′tion room′.** a room or building housing such facilities. [ME < L *ablūtiōn-* (s. of *ablūtiō*), equiv. to *ablūt(us)* washed away, ptp. of *abluere* (*ab-* AB- + *-lu-* wash + *-tus* ptp. suffix) + *-iōn-* -ION] —**ab·lu′tion·ar′y,** *adj.*

a·bly (ā′blē), *adv.* in an able manner; with skill or ability; competently. [ABLE + -LY]

-ably, a combination of **-able** and **-ly** used to form adverbs by addition to stems in **-able:** *probably.* Also, **-bly, -ibly.**

ABM, antiballistic missile.

ab·mho (ab′mō), *n., pl.* **-mhos.** *Elect.* the centimeter-gram-second unit of conductance, equivalent to 10^9 mhos. [AB(AMPERE) + MHO]

ab·mo·dal·i·ty (ab′mō dal′i tē), *n., pl.* **-ties.** *Statistics.* the differing of a measurable trait in an individual case from the mean for a population. [AB- + MODALITY]

Ab·na·ki (ab nä′kē), *n., pl.* **-kis,** (*esp. collectively*) **-ki. 1.** a member of an American Indian people of Maine, New Brunswick, and Quebec. **2.** the language of the Abnaki, an Algonquian language.

ab·ne·gate (ab′nə gāt′), *v.t.,* **-gat·ed, -gat·ing. 1.** to refuse or deny oneself (some rights, conveniences, etc.); reject; renounce. **2.** to relinquish; give up. [< L *abnegāt(us)* denied (ptp. of *abnegāre*). See AB-, NEGATE] —**ab′ne·ga′tion,** *n.* —**ab′ne·ga′tor,** *n.*

Ab·ner (ab′nər), *n.* **1.** the commander of the Israelite army and a cousin of Saul. I Sam. 14:50; 26:5. **2.** a boy's given name.

Ab′ney lev′el (ab′nē), *Survey.* a hand level for determining elevations and angles of slope.

ab·nor·mal (ab nôr′məl), *adj.* **1.** not average, typical, or usual; deviating from a standard: *abnormal powers of concentration; a school for abnormal children.* **2.** extremely or excessively large: *abnormal profit.* [AB- + NORMAL; r. *anormal* < ML *anōrmāl(us),* var. of *anōmalus* ANOMALOUS] —**ab·nor′mal·ly,** *adv.* —**ab·nor′mal·ness,** *n.*

—**Syn. 1.** anomalous, aberrant, irregular, deviant, unnatural, odd. See **irregular.**

ab·nor·mal·cy (ab nôr′məl sē), *n., pl.* **-cies.** abnormality. [ABNORMAL + -CY]

ab·nor·mal·ise (ab nôr′mə līz′), *v.t.,* **-ised, -is·ing.** *Chiefly Brit.* abnormalize.

ab·nor·mal·i·ty (ab′nôr mal′i tē), *n., pl.* **-ties. 1.** an abnormal thing or event. **2.** an abnormal condition, state, or quality; irregularity; deviation. Also, **abnormalcy.** [ABNORMAL + -ITY]

—**Syn.** anomaly, aberration, peculiarity.

ab·nor·mal·ize (ab nôr′mə līz′), *v.t.,* **-ized, -iz·ing.** to make abnormal. [ABNORMAL + -IZE]

abnor′mal psychol′ogy, the branch of psychology that deals with modes of behavior, mental phenomena, etc., that deviate widely from the average.

ab·nor·mi·ty (ab nôr′mi tē), *n., pl.* **-ties. 1.** an abnormal condition, quality, etc.; abnormality; irregularity. **2.** something abnormal; a malformation or monstrosity. [< LL *abnōrmitās,* equiv. to *abnōrm(is)* (*ab-* AB- + *nōrm(a)* rule + *-is* adj. suffix) + *-itās* -ITY]

ab·o (ab′ō), *n., pl.* **ab·os,** *adj. Australian.* —*n.* **1.** an aborigine. —*adj.* **2.** aboriginal. [by shortening]

Å·bo (ô′bōō), *n.* Swedish name of **Turku.**

a·board (ə bōrd′, ə bôrd′), *adv.* **1.** on board; on, in, or into a ship, railroad car, airplane, bus, etc.: *to step aboard.* **2.** alongside; to the side. **3.** *Baseball Slang.* on base: *a homer with two aboard.* **4. all aboard!** (as a warning to passengers entering or planning to enter a conveyance just before starting) Step in! Hurry! —*prep.* **5.** on board of; on, in, or into: *to come aboard a ship.* [A-[1] + BOARD]

a·board·age (ə bōr′dij, ə bôr′-), *n. Naut.* collision between two vessels meeting side-on or at a slight angle. [ABOARD + -AGE]

a·bode[1] (ə bōd′), *n.* **1.** a place in which one resides; dwelling; habitation; home. **2.** an extended stay in a place. [ME *abood* a waiting, delay, stay; akin to ABIDE]

a·bode[2] (ə bōd′), *v.i., v.t.* a pt. and pp. of **abide.**

ab·ohm (ab ōm′, ab′ōm′), *n. Elect.* the centimeter-gram-second unit of electrical resistance, equivalent to 10^{-9} ohm. [*ab-* (see ABAMPERE) + OHM]

a·bol·ish (ə bol′ish), *v.t.* **1.** to do away with; put an end to; annul; make void: *to abolish slavery.* **2.** to destroy (a person, thing, etc.) totally. [late ME < MF *aboliss-* (long s. of *abolir*) < L *abolēsc(ere)* (to) wither, equiv. to *abolē(re)* (to) efface (*ab-* AB- + *-ol-* grow + *-sc-* inchoative suffix)] —**a·bol′ish·a·ble,** *adj.* —**a·bol′ish·er,** *n.* —**a·bol′ish·ment,** *n.*

—**Syn.** suppress, nullify, cancel; annihilate, obliterate, extinguish; exterminate, extirpate, eliminate. ABOLISH, ERADICATE, STAMP OUT mean to do away completely with something. To ABOLISH is to cause to cease, often by a summary order: *to abolish a requirement.* STAMP OUT, stronger though less formal, implies forcibly making an end to something considered undesirable or harmful: *to stamp out the opium traffic.* ERADICATE (literally, *to tear out by the roots*), a formal word, suggests extirpation, leaving no vestige or trace: *to eradicate the dandelions in the lawn.* —**Ant.** establish.

ab·o·li·tion (ab′ə lish′ən), *n.* **1.** the act of abolishing: *the abolition of disease.* **2.** the state of being abolished; annulment; abrogation: *the abolition of unjust laws; the abolition of unfair taxes.* **3.** the legal prohibition and ending of slavery, esp. of Negro slavery in the U.S. [< L *abolitiōn-* (s. of *abolitiō*), equiv. to *abolit(us)* effaced, destroyed, ptp. of *abolēre* (*ab-* -AB + *-ol-* grow + *-itus* -ITE[2]) + *-iōn-* -ION] —**ab′o·li′tion·ar′y,** *adj.*

—**Syn. 2.** annihilation, eradication, elimination, extinction; nullification, invalidation, revocation, repeal. —**Ant.** establishment.

ab·o·li·tion·ise (ab′ə lish′ə nīz′), *v.t.,* **-ised, -is·ing.** *Chiefly Brit.* abolitionize.

ab·o·li·tion·ism (ab′ə lish′ə niz′əm), *n.* the principle or policy of abolition, esp. of Negro slavery in the U.S. [ABOLITION + -ISM] —**ab′o·li′tion·ist,** *n.*

ab·o·li·tion·ize (ab′ə lish′ə nīz′), *v.t.,* **-ized, -iz·ing.** *Chiefly U.S.* (esp. prior to the Civil War) to convert (persons, a region, a state, etc.) to abolitionism. Also, *esp. Brit.,* **abolitionise.** [ABOLITION + -IZE]

a·bol·la (ə bol′ə), *n., pl.* **a·bol·lae** (ə bol′ē). a woolen cloak worn by men in ancient Rome. [< L < Gk *ambolé,* syncopated var. of *anabolé* a throwing back (and about). See ANABOLISM]

ab·o·ma·sum (ab′ə mā′səm), *n., pl.* **-sa** (-sə). the fourth or true stomach of cud-chewing animals, lying next to the omasum. See diag. under **ruminant.** [< NL; see AB-, OMASUM]

ab·o·ma·sus (ab′ə mā′səs), *n., pl.* **-si** (-sī). abomasum.

A-bomb (ā′bom′), *n.* See **atomic bomb.**

a·bom·i·na·ble (ə bom′ə nə bəl), *adj.* **1.** repugnantly hateful; detestable; loathsome. **2.** very unpleasant; disagreeable: *The weather was abominable last week.* **3.** very bad, poor, or inferior: *She has abominable taste in clothes.* [late ME < L *abōminābil(is),* equiv. to *abōminā(rī)* (to) loathe as of ill omen (see AB-, OMEN) + *-bilis* -BLE] —**a·bom′i·na·ble·ness,** *n.* —**a·bom′i·na·bly,** *adv.*

—**Syn. 1.** abhorrent, horrible, revolting, foul. —**Ant. 1.** likable.

Abom′inable Snow′man, a large, hairy, manlike creature reported to inhabit the Himalayas. Also called **yeti.** [trans. of Tibetan *metohkangmi,* equiv. to *metoh* foul + *kangmi* snowman]

a·bom·i·nate (ə bom′ə nāt′), *v.t.,* **-nat·ed, -nat·ing. 1.** to regard with intense aversion or loathing; abhor. **2.** to dislike strongly. [< L *abōmināt(us)* loathed, ptp. of *abōminārī.* See ABOMINABLE, -ATE[1]] —**a·bom′i·na′tor,** *n.*

—**Syn. 1.** loathe, execrate. See **hate.** —**Ant. 1.** like, love.

a·bom·i·na·tion (ə bom′ə nā′shən), *n.* **1.** anything abominable; anything greatly disliked or abhorred. **2.** intense aversion or loathing; detestation. **3.** a vile, shameful, or detestable action, condition, habit, etc. [< LL *abōminātiōn-* (s. of *abōminātiō*). See ABOMINATE, -ION]

—**Syn. 2.** hatred. **3.** corruption, depravity.

à bon mar·ché (A bôN MAR shā′), *French.* for a good price; cheap; at a bargain. [lit., at good market]

a·boon (ə bōōn′), *adv., prep. Scot. and Brit. Dial.* above. [ME *abone, abowne*]

ab·o·rad (ab ōr′ad, -ôr′-), *adv. Anat., Zool.* away from the mouth. [AB- + L *or-* (s. of *ōs*) mouth + *ad* to, toward]

ab·o·ral (ab ōr′əl, -ôr′-), *adj. Anat., Zool.* opposite to or away from the mouth. [AB- + ORAL]

ab·o·rig·i·nal (ab′ə rij′ə nəl), *adj.* **1.** of or pertaining to aborigines; primitive: *aboriginal customs.* **2.** native; indigenous; original. —*n.* **3.** an aborigine. [ABORIGINE + -AL[1]] —**ab′o·rig′i·nal′i·ty,** *n.* —**ab′o·rig′i·nal·ly,** *adv.*

ab o·rig·i·ne (äb ō rig′i ne′; *Eng.* ab ō rij′ə nē′, -ô-rij′-), *Latin.* from the very first; from the source or origin.

ab·o·rig·i·ne (ab′ə rij′ə nē), *n.* **1.** one of the original or earliest known inhabitants of a country or region. **2. aborigines,** the original fauna or flora of a region. [< L, based on phrase AB ORIGINE]

a·born·ing (ə bôr′ning), *adv.* **1.** in birth; before being carried out: *The scheme died a-borning.* —*adj.* **2.** being born; coming into being, fruition, realization, etc.: *A new era of architecture is a-borning.* [A-[1] + BORN + -ING[2]]

a·bort (ə bôrt′), *v.i.* **1.** to bring forth a fetus from the uterus before the fetus is viable; miscarry. **2.** to develop incompletely; remain in a rudimentary or undeveloped state. **3.** to fail, cease, or stop at an early or premature stage. **4.** *Mil.* (of an aircraft or missile) to fail to accomplish its purpose for any reason other than enemy action. **5.** *Rocketry.* (of a missile) to stop before the scheduled flight is completed. —*v.t.* **6.** to cause to bring forth a fetus from the uterus before the fetus is viable. **7.** to cause to cease or end at an early or premature stage: *to abort a cold.* **8.** to terminate (a missile flight) before completion. **9.** to put down or quell in the early stages: *Troops aborted the uprising.* —*n.* **10.** *Rocketry.* a missile, rocket, etc., that has aborted. **11.** any aborted flight. [< L *abort(us)* miscarried (ptp. of *aborīrī* to disappear, miscarry, equiv. to *ab-* AB- + *-or-* come into being + *-tus* ptp. suffix)]

a·bor·ti·cide (ə bôr′ti sīd′), *n.* **1.** destruction of a fetus in the uterus; feticide. **2.** an agent that causes abortion; an abortifacient. [ABORT + -I- + -CIDE]

a·bor·ti·fa·cient (ə bôr′tə fā′shənt), *adj.* **1.** causing abortion. —*n.* **2.** a drug or other agent used to cause abortion. [ABORT + -I- + -FACIENT]

a·bor·tion (ə bôr′shən), *n.* **1.** the expulsion of a human fetus within the first 12 weeks of pregnancy, before it is viable. Cf. **miscarriage** (def. 3). **2.** an immature and nonviable fetus. **3.** any malformed or monstrous person, thing, etc. **4.** *Biol.* the arrested development of an embryo or an organ at a more or less early stage. **5.** anything that fails to develop, progress, or mature, as a design or project. **6.** the stopping of an illness, infection, etc., at a very early stage. [< L *abortiōn-* (s. of *abortiō*). See ABORT, -ION] —**a·bor′tion·al,** *adj.*

a·bor·tion·ist (ə bôr′shə nist), *n.* a person who performs or induces abortions illegally. [ABORTION + -IST]

a·bor·tive (ə bôr′tiv), *adj.* **1.** failing to succeed; unsuccessful: *an abortive rebellion; an abortive scheme.* **2.** born prematurely. **3.** imperfectly developed; rudimentary. **4.** *Med.* **a.** producing or intended to produce abortion; abortifacient. **b.** acting to halt progress of a disease. **5.** *Pathol.* (of the course of a disease) short and mild without the usual, pronounced clinical symptoms. **6.** *Bot.* (of seeds or pollen grains) imperfect; unable to germinate. [< L *abortīv(us).* See ABORT, -IVE] —**a·bor′tive·ly,** *adv.* —**a·bor′tive·ness,** *n.*

a·bor·tus (ə bôr′təs), *n., pl.* **-tus·es. 1.** a miscarriage. **2.** *Med.* **a.** immature placental or fetal tissue prematurely passed or curetted. **b.** an aborted fetus. [< NL, L. See ABORT]

à bouche ou·verte (A bōōsh ōō vert′), *French.* gaping; eager; gullible. [lit., with open mouth]

a·bou·dik·ro (ä′bōō dē′krō), *n.* the wood of a sapele. [< native WAfr name]

a·bought (ə bôt′), *v.* pt. and pp. of **aby.**

A·bou·kir (ä′bōō kēr′, ə bōō′kər), *n.* Abukir.

a·bou·li·a (ə bōō′lē ə), *n.* abulia. —**a·bou′lic,** *adj.*

a·bound (ə bound′), *v.i.* **1.** to occur or exist in great quantities or numbers: *a stream in which trout abound.* **2.** to be rich or well supplied (usually fol. by *in*): *Some languages abound in figurative expressions. Resort areas abound in tourists.* **3.** to be filled; teem (usually fol. by *with*): *The ship abounds with rats.* [late ME *abounde* < L *abund(āre)* (to) overflow, equiv. to *ab-* AB- + *undāre* to move in waves; see UNDULATE] —**a·bound′ing·ly,** *adv.*

a·bout (ə bout′), *prep.* **1.** of; concerning; in regard to: *to talk about committee plans; instructions about the work; a movie about Pasteur.* **2.** connected or associated with: *There was an air of mystery about her.* **3.** in or somewhere near: *He is about the house.* **4.** near; close to: *about my height.* **5.** on every side of; around: *the railing about the tower.* **6.** on or near (one's person): *They had lost all they had about them.* **7.** so as to be of use to: *Keep your wits about you.* **8.** on the verge or point of (usually fol. by an infinitive): *about to leave.* **9.** here or there; in or on: *to wander about the place.* **10.** concerned with; engaged in doing: *Tell me what it's about. Bring me the other book while you're about it.* —*adv.* **11.** near in time, number, degree, etc.; approximately: *to drive about a hundred miles.* **12.** nearly; almost: *He is about ready.* **13.** nearby; not far off: *He is somewhere about.* **14.** on every side; in every direction; around: *Look about and see if you can find it.* **15.** halfway around; in the opposite direction: *to turn a car about.* **16.** from one place to another; in this place or that: *to move furniture about; his papers strewn about.* **17.** in rotation or succession; alternately: *Turn about is fair play.* **18.** in circumference: *a wheel two inches about.* —*adj.* **19.** moving around; astir: *He was up and about while the rest of us still slept.* **20.** in existence; current; prevalent: *Smallpox is about.* **21.** *Naut.* **a.** onto a new tack. **b.** onto a new course. **22. at about,** nearly; approximately; in the neighborhood of: *The sun set at about six o'clock.* [ME *aboute(n)*, OE *abūtan, onbūtan* on the outside of (*on* + *b(e)* BY + *ūtan*, c. Icel *ūtan*, OHG *ūzan(a)* outside)]

about′ face′, *U.S.* a military command to face to the rear in a prescribed manner while standing. Also called, *Brit.*, **about′ turn′.**

a·bout-face (*n.* ə bout′fās′, ə bout′fās′; *v.* ə bout′fās′), *n., v.,* **-faced, -fac·ing.** —*n.* **1.** a complete, sudden change in position, direction, principle, attitude, etc.: *They've done an about-face in their foreign policy.* —*v.i.* **2.** to turn in the opposite direction, switch to an opposite opinion, etc.

about′ ship′, (as a command) put the ship on a new tack.

a·bout-ship (ə bout′ship′), *v.i.,* **-shipped, -ship·ping.** *Naut.* to tack.

a·bove (ə buv′), *adv.* **1.** in or to a higher place; overhead: *the blue sky above; the floor above.* **2.** higher in rank, authority, or power: *appeal to the courts above.* **3.** higher in quantity or number: *books with 100 pages and above.* **4.** before or earlier, esp. in a book or other piece of writing; foregoing: *the remark quoted above.* Cf. **below** (def. 5). **5.** in or to heaven: *gone to her eternal rest above.* **6.** *Zool.* on the upper or dorsal side. **7.** *Theat.* upstage. Cf. **below** (def. 7). —*prep.* **8.** in or to a higher place than; over: *to fly above the earth; the floor above ours.* **9.** more in quantity or number than; in excess of: *The weight is above a ton. All boys above 12 years of age.* **10.** superior in rank, authority, or standing to: *A captain is above a lieutenant.* **11.** not subject or liable to; not capable of (some undesirable action, thought, etc.): *to be above suspicion; to be above bad behavior.* **12.** averse or opposed to: *He is not above such trickery.* **13.** rather than; in preference to: *to favor one child above the other.* **14.** north of: *six miles above Baltimore.* **15.** *Theat.* upstage of. **16. above all,** most important of all; principally: *charity above all.* —*adj.* **17.** said, mentioned, or written above; foregoing: *the above explanation.* —*n.* **18.** that which was said, mentioned, or written above: *to refer to the above.* **19.** the person or persons previously indicated: *The above will all stand trial.* **20.** heaven: *truly a gift from above.* [ME *above(n)*, OE *abufan, onbufan* (*on* + *b(e)* BY + *ufan*, c. Icel *ofan*, G *oben* above)]

a·bove·board (ə buv′bōrd′, -bôrd′), *adv., adj.* in open sight; without tricks or disguise: *An honest man deals aboveboard. His actions are open and aboveboard.* [ABOVE + BOARD; so called from the requirement of keeping the hands above the table or board in order to discourage possible cheating at cards]

a·bove·ground (ə buv′ground′), *adj.* situated on or above the ground. [ABOVE + GROUND¹]

above′ stairs′, *Chiefly Brit.* upstairs.

above′ the line′, *Bridge.* See under **line**¹ (def. 31).

ab o·vo (äb ō′wō; *Eng.* ab ō′vō), *Latin.* from the beginning. [lit., from the egg]

a·box (ə boks′), *adj.* *Naut.* (of the yards of a square-rigged vessel) braced in opposite directions on different masts in order to halt the vessel. [A-¹ + BOX¹]

abp., archbishop.

A.B.P.C., American Book Publishers Council. Also, **ABPC**

abr., **1.** abridge. **2.** abridged. **3.** abridgment.

ab·ra·ca·dab·ra (ab′rə kə dab′rə), *n.* **1.** a mystical word used in incantations, on amulets, etc., as a magical means of warding off misfortune, harm, or illness. **2.** any charm or incantation using nonsensical or supposedly magical words. **3.** gibberish; jargon; nonsense. [< L]

a·bra·dant (ə brād′ənt), *adj.* **1.** having an abrasive property or quality; abrading. —*n.* **2.** an abrasive. [ABRADE + -ANT]

a·brade (ə brād′), *v.t., v.i.,* **a·brad·ed, a·brad·ing.** **1.** to wear off or down by friction; erode. **2.** to scrape off. [< L *abrādere*, equiv. to *ab-* AB- + *rādere* to scrape] —**a·brad′er,** *n.*

A·bra·ham (ā′brə ham′, -həm), *n.* **1.** the first of the great postdiluvian patriarchs, father of Isaac, and traditional founder of the ancient Hebrew nation. **2.** a boy's given name.

A′braham's bos′om, heaven, considered as the reward of the righteous. Luke 16:22.

A·bram (ā′brəm), *n.* **1.** an earlier name of Abraham. Gen. 17:5. **2.** a boy's given name, form of **Abraham.**

a·bran·chi·ate (ā brang′kē it, -āt′), *adj.* *Zool.* having no gills. Also, **a·bran·chi·al** (ā brang′kē əl). [A-⁶ + Gk *bránchi(a)* (neut. pl.) gills + -ATE¹]

a·bra·ser (ə brā′sər), *n.* a machine for testing the abrasion resistance of a material. [*abrase* (< L *abrās(us)*; see ABRASION) + -ER¹]

a·bra·sion (ə brā′zhən), *n.* **1.** a scraped spot or area; the result of rubbing or abrading: *abrasions on his leg caused by falling on the gravel.* **2.** the act or process of abrading. [< ML *abrāsiōn-* (s. of *abrāsiō*), equiv. to *abrās(us)* scraped off (ptp. of *abrādere*; see ABRADE) + *-iōn-* -ION]
—**Syn. 1.** sore, scrape. **2.** rubbing, erosion.

a·bra·sive (ə brā′siv, -ziv), *n.* **1.** any material or substance used for grinding, polishing, lapping, etc., as emery, pumice, or sandpaper. —*adj.* **2.** tending to abrade; causing abrasion; abrading. [< L *abrās(us)* (see ABRASION) + -IVE]
—**Syn. 2.** harsh, rough, rasping.

à bras ou·verts (A BRA zōō VER′), *French.* cordially; gladly. [lit., with arms open]

a·brax·as (ə brak′səs), *n.* (in many parts of the ancient world) a word, often engraved on a gem, used as a charm. [< L < Gk: name used in magic]

a·bra·zo (ä brä′thō, -sō; *Eng.* ə brä′sō), *n., pl.* **-zos** (-thōs, -sōs; *Eng.* -sōz). *Spanish.* an embrace, used in greeting someone.

ab·re·act (ab′rē akt′), *v.t.* *Psychoanal.* to remove by abreaction. [AB- + REACT, modeled on G *abreagieren*]

ab·re·ac·tion (ab′rē ak′shən), *n.* *Psychoanal.* the release of psychic tension through verbalizing or acting out an adequate resolution of a repressed traumatic experience, with the appropriate emotion or affect. [AB- + REACTION, modeled on G *Abreagierung*]

a·breast (ə brest′), *adv., adj.* **1.** side by side; beside each other in a line: *They walked two abreast down the road.* **2.** equal to or alongside in progress, attainment, or awareness (usually fol. by *of* or *with*): *to keep abreast of scientific developments; keeping abreast with the times.* [A-¹ + BREAST]

a·bri (a brē′, ä brē′; *Fr.* A BRĒ′), *n., pl.* **a·bris** (a brēz′, ä brēz′; *Fr.* A BRĒ′). a shelter or place of refuge, esp. a dugout. [< F < L *apri(cum)* open place, neut. of *apricus* open, exposed]

a·bridge (ə brij′), *v.t.,* **a·bridged, a·bridg·ing.** **1.** to shorten by condensation or omission while retaining the basic contents: *to abridge a long novel.* **2.** to reduce or lessen in duration, scope, etc.; diminish; curtail: *to abridge a visit; to abridge one's freedom.* **3.** to deprive; cut off. [ME *abregge, abrigge* < MF *abreg(i)er* < LL *abbreviāre* to shorten. See ABBREVIATE] —**a·bridg′a·ble;** *esp. Brit.*, **a·bridge′a·ble,** *adj.* —**a·bridged′,** *adj.* —**a·bridg′er,** *n.*
—**Syn. 1.** cut down; epitomize; condense, abstract, digest. See **shorten. 2.** contract, reduce. **3.** divest.
—**Ant. 1.** lengthen. **2.** expand.

a·bridg·ment (ə brij′mənt), *n.* **1.** a shortened or condensed form of a book, speech, etc., that still retains the basic contents: *an abridgment of Tolstoy's* War and Peace. **2.** the act or process of abridging. **3.** the state of being abridged. Also, *esp. Brit.*, **a·bridge′ment.** [late ME *abrygement* < MF *abregement.* See ABRIDGE, -MENT]
—**Syn. 1.** digest, epitome; compendium, synopsis, abstract, summary, précis, conspectus; syllabus, brief, outline. **2.** reduction, shortening, contraction, compression.
—**Ant. 1, 2.** expansion, enlargement.

a·broach (ə brōch′), *adv., adj.* **1.** opened or tapped so that the contents can flow out; broached: *The cask was set abroach.* **2.** astir; in circulation. [late ME *abroche.* See A-¹, BROACH]

a·broad (ə brôd′), *adv.* **1.** in or to a foreign country or countries: *a trip abroad; to live abroad; famous at home and abroad.* **2.** *Chiefly U.S.* to or in Europe: *We're saving to go abroad next summer. She went to school abroad.* **3.** out of doors; from one place to another; about: *No one is abroad in the noonday heat. The owl ventures abroad at night.* **4.** spread around; in circulation: *Rumors of disaster are abroad.* **5.** broadly; widely; far and wide. **6.** wide of the mark; astray; in error. [ME *abrod.* See A-¹, BROAD]
—**Syn. 1.** overseas. **3.** out, outside. **4.** everywhere.
—**Ant. 1.** at home.

ab·ro·gate (ab′rə gāt′), *v.t.,* **-gat·ed, -gat·ing.** **1.** to abolish by formal or official means; annul by an authoritative act; repeal: *to abrogate a law.* **2.** to put aside; put an end to. [< L *abrogāt(us)* repealed (ptp. of *abrogāre*). See AB-, ROGATION, -ATE¹] —**ab·ro·ga·ble** (ab′rə gə bəl), *adj.* —**ab′ro·ga′tion,** *n.* —**ab′ro·ga′tive,** *adj.* —**ab′ro·ga′tor,** *n.*
—**Syn. 1.** cancel, revoke, rescind, nullify, void, invalidate. —**Ant. 1.** ratify, establish.

ab·rupt (ə brupt′), *adj.* **1.** sudden; unexpected: *an abrupt departure.* **2.** curt or brusque in speech, manner, etc.: *an abrupt reply.* **3.** terminating or changing suddenly: *an abrupt turn in a road.* **4.** having many sudden changes from one subject to another; lacking in continuity or smoothness: *an abrupt literary style.* **5.** steep; precipitous: *an abrupt descent.* **6.** *Bot.* truncate (def. 3). [< L *abrupt(us)* broken off (ptp. of *abrumpere*), equiv. to *ab-* AB- + *-rup-* break + *-tus* ptp. suffix] —**ab·rupt′ly,** *adv.* —**ab·rupt′ness,** *n.*
—**Syn. 1, 3.** quick, sharp. See **sudden. 2.** short, hurried, hasty, blunt. **4.** discontinuous, broken, uneven.
—**Ant. 1, 3.** gradual. **2.** deliberate.

ab·rup·tion (ə brup′shən), *n.* a sudden breaking off. [< L *abruptiōn-* (s. of *abruptiō*). See ABRUPT, -ION]

abrupt′ly pin′nate, paripinnate.

A·bruz·zi (ä brōōt′tsē), *n.* **Duke of the** (*Prince Luigi Amedeo of Saxony-Aosta*), 1873–1933, Italian naval officer, mountain climber, and arctic explorer.

A·bruz·zi e Mo·li·se (ä brōōt′tsē e mô lē′ze), a region in central Italy. 1,584,777 (1961); 5881 sq. mi. *Cap.:* Aquilla.

abs-, var. of **ab-**: *absent; abscond.*

abs., **1.** absent. **2.** absolute. **3.** abstract.

A.B.S., **1.** American Bible Society. **2.** American Bureau of Shipping.

Ab·sa·lom (ab′sə ləm), *n.* **1.** the third son of David, who rebelled against his father and was slain by Joab. II Sam. 13–18. **2.** a boy's given name.

Ab′salom, Ab′salom!, a novel (1936) by William Faulkner.

Ab′salom and A·chit′o·phel (ə kit′ə fel′), a satirical poem (1681) by Dryden.

Ab·sa′ro·ka Moun′tains, (ab sär′ə kə), a range in S Montana and NW Wyoming: part of the Rocky Mountains. Highest peak, 13,140 ft.

ab·scess (ab′ses), *n.* *Pathol.* a localized collection of pus in the tissues of the body, often accompanied by swelling and inflammation and often caused by bacteria. [< L *abscess(us)* a going away, abscess, n. use of ptp. of *abscēdere*, equiv. to *abs-* ABS- + *cessus* (see CEDE)] —**ab′scessed,** *adj.*

ab·scind (ab sind′), *v.t.* to cut off; sever. [< L *abscind(ere)*, equiv. to *ab-* AB- + *scindere* to divide, tear]

ab·scise (ab sīz′), *v.i.,* **-scised, -scis·ing.** *Bot.* to separate by abscission, as a leaf from a stem. [< L *abscīs(us)* cut off (ptp. of *abscīdere*), equiv. to *abs-* ABS- + *-cīdere* (for *caedere* to cut)]

ab·scis·sa (ab sis′ə), *n., pl.* **-scis·sas, -scis·sae** (-sis′ē). *Math.* (in plane Cartesian coordinates) the x-coordinate of a point: its distance from the y-axis measured parallel to the x-axis. Cf. **ordinate.** [fem. of L *abscissus* (ptp. of *abscindere* to ABSCIND)]

Abscissa
(P, any point; AP or OB, abscissa of P; XX, axis of abscissa; YY, axis of the ordinate

ab·scis·sion (ab sizh′ən, -sish′-), *n.* **1.** the act of cutting off; sudden termination. **2.** *Bot.* the normal separation of flowers, fruit, and leaves from plants, usually caused by the development of the abscission layer. [< L *abscissiōn-* (s. of *abscissiō*). See ABSCISSA, -ION]

abscis′sion lay′er, *Bot.* the layer of specialized, cutinized parenchyma cells that develops in the abscission zone, the disintegration of which causes abscission. Also called **ab′sciss lay′er** (ab′sis).

abscis′sion zone′, *Bot.* the zone at the base of a leaf petiole, fruit stalk, or branch in which the abscission layer develops.

ab·scond (ab skond′), *v.i.* to depart in a sudden and secret manner, esp. to avoid detection or capture: *The cashier absconded from Detroit with the bonds.* [< L *abscond(ere)* (to) hide or stow away, equiv. to *abs-* ABS- + *condere* to stow (*con-* CON- + *-dere* to put; see DO¹)] —**ab·scond′er,** *n.*
—**Syn.** decamp, bolt.

Ab·se·con (ab sē′kən), *n.* a town in SE New Jersey. 4320 (1960).

ab·seil (äp′zīl), *Mountain Climbing.* —*n.* **1.** a method of descent in which the climber slides down a rope looped over or fastened to an overhead projection. —*v.i.* **2.** to descend by an abseil. [< G *abseil(en)* (*ab-* down + *seilen* to rope)]

ab·sence (ab′səns), *n.* **1.** state of being away or not being present: *Speak ill of no one in his absence.* **2.** period of being away: *an absence of several weeks.* **3.** failure to attend or appear when expected. **4.** lack; deficiency: *the absence of proof.* [late ME < MF < L *absentia.* See ABSENT, -IA]
—**Ant. 1.** presence.

ab′sence flag′, a rectangular blue flag flown at the starboard main spreader or main yardarm of a yacht to indicate that the owner is away. Also, **ab′sent flag′.**

ab′sence of mind′, absent-mindedness.

ab′sence without′ leave′, *Mil.* See **A.W.O.L.**

ab·sent (*adj.* ab′sənt; *v.* ab sent′), *adj.* **1.** not in a certain place at a given time; away; missing; not present. **2.** lacking; nonexistent: *Revenge is absent from his mind.* **3.** not attentive; preoccupied; absent-minded. —*v.t.* **4.** to take or keep (oneself) away: *to absent oneself from home.* [late ME < L *absent-* (s. of *absēns*, prp. of *abesse* to be away (*ab-* AB- + *-s-* be (see IS) + *-ent-* -ENT))] —**ab·sen·ta·tion** (ab′sən tā′shən), *n.* —**ab·sent′er,** *n.* —**ab′sent·ness,** *n.*
—**Syn. 1.** out, off. —**Ant. 1.** present.

ab·sen·tee (ab′sən tē′), *n.* **1.** a person who is absent. **2.** a person who absents himself from his own place, duty, etc., as a landowner who does not live on his own estate or a voter who is permitted to cast his ballot by mail. [ABSENT + -EE] —**ab′sen·tee′ism,** *n.*

ab′sentee bal′lot, the ballot used for an absentee vote.

ab′sentee land′lord, a landlord who lives in a place other than that in which his property is located.

ab′sentee vote′, a vote cast by a person who, because of illness, military service, or the like, has been permitted to vote by mail. —**ab′sentee vot′er.**

ab·sen·te re·o (ab sen′tē rē′ō), *Law.* in the absence of the defendant. *Abbr.:* abs. re. [< L: lit., the party being away]

ab·sent·ly (ab′sənt lē), *adv.* inattentively. [ABSENT + -LY]

ab·sent-mind·ed (ab′sənt mīn′did), *adj.* so lost in thought that one does not realize what one is doing, what is happening, etc.; preoccupied to the extent of being unaware of one's immediate surroundings. —**ab′sent-mind′ed·ly,** *adv.* —**ab′sent-mind′ed·ness,** *n.*
—**Syn.** withdrawn, musing, daydreaming, dreamy. ABSENT-MINDED, ABSTRACTED, OBLIVIOUS all mean inattentive to immediate surroundings. ABSENT-MINDED suggests an unintentional wandering of the mind from the present: *an absent-minded professor.* ABSTRACTED implies that the mind has been drawn away from the immediate present by reflection upon some engrossing subject: *wearing an abstracted air.* OBLIVIOUS implies absorption in some thought which causes one to be completely forgetful of or unaware of one's surroundings: *oblivious of danger.* —**Ant.** attentive.

ab′sent without′ leave′, *Mil.* See **A.W.O.L.**

ab·sinthe (ab′sinth), *n.* **1.** a strong, bitter, green-colored, aromatic liqueur that is 68 percent alcohol, is made with wormwood and other herbs, and has an aromatic, predominantly licorice flavor. **2.** wormwood (def. 2). **3.** *U.S.* sagebrush. Also, **ab′sinth.** [< F < L *absinth(ium)* wormwood < Gk *apsínthion*] —**ab·sin′thi·al, ab·sin′thi·an,** *adj.*

ab·sinth·ism (ab′sin thiz′əm), *n.* a diseased condition due to the excessive use of absinthe. [ABSINTHE + -ISM]

ab·sit o·men (äb′sit ō′men; *Eng.* ab′sit ō′men), *Latin.* may it bear no ill omen. [lit., may omen be wanting]

ab·so·lute (ab′sə lōōt′), *adj.* **1.** free from imperfection; complete; perfect: *absolute liberty.* **2.** not mixed or adulterated; pure. **3.** complete; outright: *an absolute lie; an absolute denial; an absolute loss.* **4.** free from restriction or limitation; not limited in any way: *absolute command; absolute freedom.* **5.** unrestrained in the exercise of governmental power, esp. when arbitrary or despotic: *An absolute monarch rules with an iron hand.* **6.** viewed independently; not comparative or relative; ultimate; intrinsic: *absolute knowledge.* **7.** positive; certain: *absolute in opinion; absolute evidence.* **8.** *Gram.* **a.** relatively independent syntactically. The construction *It being Sunday* in *It being Sunday, the family went to church* is an absolute construction. **b.** (of a usually transitive verb) used without an object, as the verb *give* in *The solicitors for the community chest asked him to give.* **c.** (of an adjective) having its noun understood, not expressed, as *poor* in *The poor are always with us.* **d.** characterizing the phonological form of a word or phrase occurring by itself, not influenced by surrounding forms (distinguished from *sandhi*), as *not* in *is not* (as opposed to *isn't*), or *will* in *they will* (as opposed to *they'll*). **9.** *Physics.* **a.** independent of arbitrary standards or of particular properties of substances or systems: *absolute humidity.* **b.** pertaining to a system of units, as the centimeter-gram-second system, based on some primary units, esp. units of length, mass, and time. **c.** pertaining to a measurement based on an absolute zero or unit: *absolute temperature.* **10.** *Educ.* noting or pertaining to the scale of a grading system based solely on an individual's performance considered as representing his personal knowledge of a given subject regardless of the performance of others in a group: *The math department always marks on an absolute scale.* Cf. **curve** (def. 9). **11.** *Climatology.* noting or pertaining to the highest or lowest value of a meteorological quantity recorded during a given, usually long, period of time: *absolute maximum temperature.* **12.** *Math.* (of an inequality) indicating that the expression is true for all values of the variable, as $x^2 + 1 > 0$ for all real

numbers *x;* unconditional. Cf. **conditional** (def. 4). **13.** *Computer Technol.* written in machine language: *absolute coding; absolute address.* —*n.* **14.** something that is not dependent upon external conditions for existence or for its specific nature, size, etc. (opposed to *relative*). **15. the absolute, a.** something that is free from any restriction or condition. **b.** something that is independent of some or all relations. **c.** something that is perfect or complete. **d.** (in Hegelianism) the world process operating in accordance with the absolute idea. [< L *absolūt(us)* free, unrestricted, unconditioned (ptp. of *absolvere* to ABSOLVE), equiv. to *ab-* AB- + *solū-* loose + *-tus* ptp. suffix] —**ab′so·lute′ness,** *n.*
—**Syn. 2.** unadulterated, sheer, unqualified. **4.** total, unconditional. ABSOLUTE, UNQUALIFIED, UTTER all mean unmodified. ABSOLUTE implies an unquestionable finality: *an absolute coward.* UNQUALIFIED means without reservations or conditions: *an unqualified success.* UTTER expresses totality or entirety: *an utter failure.* **5.** autocratic, dictatorial, totalitarian. **6.** categorical. **7.** unequivocal, definite, sure. —**Ant. 1.** imperfect. **2.** mixed. **4.** qualified. **6.** relative.

ab′solute al′cohol, ethyl alcohol containing less than one percent by weight of water.

ab′solute al′titude, *Aeron.* the vertical distance between a flying aircraft, rocket, etc., and the point on the earth's surface directly below it.

ab′solute ceil′ing, *Aeron.* the maximum height above sea level at which an aircraft can maintain horizontal flight.

ab′solute com′plement, *Math.* complement (def. 8).

ab′solute conver′gence, *Math.* **1.** the property of an infinite series in which the series formed by replacing each term in the original series with its absolute value converges. Cf. **conditional convergence. 2.** the property of a sequence of functions in which the series whose terms are the successive differences of the elements of the sequence exhibits absolute convergence. **3.** the property of an improper integral in which the integral formed by replacing the integrand by its absolute value converges. Also called **unconditional convergence.**

ab′solute e′go, (in the philosophy of Fichte) a transcendental and impersonal ego dividing itself into the personal ego and the nonego in order to attain self-knowledge.

ab′solute humid′ity, the ratio of the mass of water vapor to the volume of moist air within which it is contained. Cf. **relative humidity.**

ab′solute ide′a, *Hegelianism.* the spiritual principle, independent of all historical necessity, of which the world process is the progressive expression and fulfillment.

ab′solute ide′alism, *Philos.* a doctrine asserting the existence of an absolute having the form of an idea, experience, or principle. —**ab′solute ide′alist.**

ab′solute imped′iment, *Law.* a fact or circumstance that disqualifies a person from lawful marriage.

ab′solute in′dex of refrac′tion, *Optics.* See under **index of refraction.**

ab·so·lute·ly (ab′sə lo͞ot′lē, ab′sə lo͞ot′-), *adv.* **1.** completely; wholly; fully: *He is absolutely wrong.* **2.** positively; certainly. **3.** (of a transitive verb) without an object. —*interj.* **4.** (used to express complete agreement or unqualified assent): *Do you think it will work? Absolutely!* [ABSOLUTE + -LY]
—**Syn. 1.** entirely, totally, unqualifiedly. **2.** unquestionably, unequivocally, definitely.

ab′solute mag′nitude, *Astron.* the magnitude of a star as it would appear to a hypothetical observer at a distance of 10 parsecs or 32.6 light years. Cf. **apparent magnitude.**

ab′solute major′ity, 1. a number of votes constituting more than half of the number cast. **2.** a number of voters constituting more than half of the number registered. Cf. **simple majority.**

ab′solute max′imum, *Math.* the largest value a given function assumes on a specified set. Cf. **maximum** (def. 2).

ab′solute min′imum, *Math.* the smallest value a given function assumes on a specified set. Cf. **minimum** (def. 4).

ab′solute mon′archy, a monarchy that is not limited by laws or a constitution.

ab′solute mu′sic, music whose patterns in sound are not illustrative of or dependent on a text or program.

ab′solute pitch′, *Music.* **1.** the exact pitch of a tone in terms of vibrations per second. **2.** Also called **perfect pitch.** the ability to sing or recognize the pitch of a tone by ear.

ab′solute scale′, *Physics.* any temperature scale in which zero corresponds to absolute zero. Cf. **Kelvin** (def. 2), **Rankine** (def. 2).

ab′solute spir′it, *Hegelianism.* spirit in a state of identity with the absolute idea through attainment of perfect consciousness of its true nature.

ab′solute tem′perature, *Physics.* temperature measured on an absolute scale.

ab′solute val′ue, *Math.* **1.** the magnitude of a quantity, irrespective of sign; the distance of a quantity from zero. The absolute value of a number is symbolized by two parallel lines, as $|3|$ or $|-3|$ is 3. **2.** the square root of the sum of the squares of the real and imaginary parts of a given complex number, as $|a + bi|$ is equal to $\sqrt{a^2 + b^2}$. Also called **modulus.**

ab′solute ze′ro, *Physical Chem.* the lowest possible temperature that the nature of matter admits; the temperature at which the particles whose motion constitutes heat would be at rest, being a hypothetical point 273° below the zero of the Celsius scale. Cf. **absolute** (def. 9c).

ab·so·lu·tion (ab′sə lo͞o′shən), *n.* **1.** act of absolving; release from consequences, obligations, or penalties. **2.** state of being absolved. **3.** *Rom. Cath. Theol.* **a.** a remission of sin or of the punishment due to sin, which the priest, on the ground of authority received from Christ, makes in the sacrament of penance. **b.** the formula declaring such remission. **4.** *Prot. Theol.* a declaration or assurance of divine forgiveness to penitent believers, made after confession of sins. [ME *absolucion* < L *absolūtiōn-* (s. of *absolūtiō*) acquittal. See ABSOLUTE, -ION]

ab·so·lut·ism (ab′sə lo͞o tiz′əm), *n.* **1.** the principle or the exercise of complete and unrestricted power in government. **2.** *Philos.* the doctrine of an absolute or nonrelative being. [ABSOLUTE + -ISM] —**ab′so·lut′ist,** *n.* —**ab′so·lu·tis′tic,** *adj.* —**ab′so·lu·tis′ti·cal·ly,** *adv.*
—**Syn. 1.** totalitarianism.

ab·sol·u·to·ry (ab sol′yə tôr′ē, -tōr′ē), *adj.* giving absolution. [< L *absolūtōri(us).* See ABSOLUTE, -ORY[1]]

ab·solve (ab zolv′, -solv′), *v.t.,* **-solved, -solv·ing. 1.** to free from the consequences or penalties resulting from actions (usually fol. by *from*): *to absolve a person from moral blame.* **2.** to set free or release, as from some duty, obligation, or responsibility (usually fol. by *from*): *to be absolved from one's oath.* **3.** to grant pardon for. **4.** *Eccles.* **a.** to grant or pronounce remission of sins to. **b.** to remit (a sin) by absolution. **c.** to declare (censure, as excommunication) removed. [< L *absolve(re),* equiv. to *ab-* AB- + *solvere* to loosen] —**ab·solv′a·ble,** *adj.* —**ab·sol′vent,** *adj., n.* —**ab·solv′er,** *n.*
—**Syn. 1.** exculpate, excuse, forgive, pardon, clear. ABSOLVE, ACQUIT, EXONERATE all mean to free from blame. ABSOLVE is a general word for this idea. To ACQUIT is to release from a specific and usually formal accusation: *The court must acquit the accused if there is enough evidence of innocence.* To EXONERATE is to consider a person clear of blame or consequences for an act (even when the act is admitted), or to justify him for having done it: *to exonerate one for a crime committed in self-defense.* **2.** liberate, exempt. **3.** excuse, forgive. —**Ant. 1.** blame.

ab·so·nant (ab′sə nənt), *adj.* dissonant; discordant (usually fol. by *from* or *to*): *behavior that is absonant to nature.* [AB- + *-sonant,* as in *consonant*]

ab·sorb (ab sôrb′, -zôrb′), *v.t.* **1.** to suck up or drink in (liquid): *A sponge absorbs water.* **2.** to swallow up the identity or individuality of; incorporate: *The empire absorbed all the small nations.* **3.** to engross or engage wholly: *so absorbed in a book that he did not hear the bell.* **4.** to occupy or fill: *This job absorbs all of my time.* **5.** to take up or receive by chemical or molecular action: *Carbonic acid is formed when water absorbs carbon dioxide.* **6.** to take in without echo, recoil, or reflection: *to absorb sound and light; to absorb shock.* **7.** to take in or utilize: *The market absorbed all the automobiles we could build.* **8.** to pay for: *The company will absorb all the research costs.* **9.** *Archaic.* to swallow up. [< L *absorb(ēre),* equiv. to *ab-* AB- + *sorbēre* to suck in, swallow] —**ab·sorb′a·ble,** *adj.* —**ab·sorb′a·bil′i·ty,** *n.*
—**Syn. 2.** assimilate, consume, devour, engulf; destroy.

ab·sorb·ance (ab sôr′bəns, -zôr′-), *n.* *Physics.* the common logarithm of the reciprocal of the internal transmittance of a given substance. [ABSORB(ENT) + -ANCE]

ab·sorbed (ab sôrbd′, -zôrbd′), *adj.* deeply engrossed; preoccupied: *absorbed in his book.* [ABSORB + -ED[2]] —**ab·sorb·ed·ly** (ab sôr′bid lē, -zôr′-), *adv.* —**ab·sorb′ed·ness,** *n.*

ab·sor·be·fa·cient (ab sôr′bə fā′shənt, -zôr′-), *adj.* causing absorption. [ABSORB + *-e-* (as in *liquefy, liquefaction*) + -FACIENT]

ab·sorb·ent (ab sôr′bənt, -zôr′-), *adj.* **1.** capable of absorbing; tending to absorb: *absorbent material.* —*n.* **2.** a thing, material, etc., that absorbs. [< L *absorbent-* (s. of *absorbēns,* prp. of *absorbēre*). See ABSORB, -ENT] —**ab·sorb′en·cy,** *n.*

absorb′ent cot′ton, cotton for surgical dressings, cosmetic purposes, etc., made absorbent by removing the natural wax.

ab·sorb·er (ab sôr′bər, -zôr′-), *n.* **1.** one who or that which absorbs. **2.** See **shock absorber. 3.** *Physics.* a material in a nuclear reactor which absorbs, but does not reproduce, neutrons. [ABSORB + -ER[1]]

ab·sorb·ing (ab sôr′biŋg, -zôr′-), *adj.* extremely interesting; deeply engrossing: *an absorbing drama.* [ABSORB + -ING[2]] —**ab·sorb′ing·ly,** *adv.*

absorb′ing well′, a well for draining off surface water and conducting it to absorbent earth underground. Also called **dry well, waste well.**

ab·sorp·tance (ab sôrp′təns, -zôrp′-), *n.* *Physics, Optics.* the ratio of the amount of radiation absorbed by a surface to the amount of radiation incident upon it. Cf. **reflectance, transmittance** (def. 2). [trans. of G *Absorptionsvermögen.* See ABSORPTION, -ANCE]

ab·sorp·ti·om·e·ter (ab sôrp′shē om′i tər, -zôrp′-), *n.* a photoelectric instrument for measuring the concentration of a substance, as a transparent solution, by its absorption of monochromatic light. [ABSORPTIO(N) + -METER] —**ab·sorp·ti·o·met·ric** (ab sôrp′shē ə me′trik, -zôrp′-), *adj.*

ab·sorp·tion (ab sôrp′shən, -zôrp′-), *n.* **1.** the act of absorbing. **2.** the state or process of being absorbed. **3.** assimilation; incorporation: *the absorption of small farms into one big one.* **4.** passage of substances to the blood, lymph, and cells, as from the alimentary canal or from the tissues. **5.** a taking in or reception by molecular or chemical action, as of gases or liquids. **6.** *Physics.* the reduction of energy in the form of electromagnetic radiation by a medium or by a reflecting surface. **7.** complete attention or preoccupation; deep engrossment: *absorption in one's work.* [< L *absorptiōn-* (s. of *absorptiō*), equiv. to *absorpt(us)* (ptp.) (*absorb-;* see ABSORB + *-tus* ptp. suffix) + *-iōn-* -ION] —**ab·sorp′tive,** *adj.* —**ab·sorp′tive·ness,** *n.*

absorp′tion band′, *Physics.* a dark band in the absorption spectrum of a substance, corresponding to a range of wavelengths for which the substance absorbs more strongly than at adjacent wavelengths.

absorp′tion coeffi′cient, *Physics, Optics.* a measure of the rate of decrease in the intensity of electromagnetic radiation, as light, as it passes through a given substance.

absorp′tion dynamom′eter, *Elect.* a device for measuring the torque or power of an engine in a process in which the energy supplied to the device by the engine is absorbed.

absorp′tion edge′, *Physics.* a discontinuity in the graph of the absorption coefficient of a substance plotted against the wavelength of x-rays being absorbed, representing the minimum energy necessary to free electrons from particular shells of the atoms of the substance. Also called **absorp′tion discontinu′ity, absorp′tion lim′it.**

absorp′tion spec′trum, *Physics.* the spectrum formed by electromagnetic radiation that has passed through a medium in which radiation of certain frequencies was absorbed.

ab·sorp·tiv·i·ty (ab′sôrp tiv′i tē, -zôrp-), *n.* *Physics.* the property of a body that determines the fraction of incident radiation absorbed or absorbable by the body. [< L *absorpt-* (s. of *absorptus* absorbed; see ABSORPTION) + -IVE + -ITY]

abs. re., *Law.* See **absente reo.**

ab·stain (ab stān′), *v.i.* to refrain or hold (oneself) back voluntarily, esp. from doing or enjoying something (usually fol. by *from*): *to abstain from eating meat; a referendum in which two delegates abstained.* [late ME *abste(i)ne* < MF *absten(ir)* < L *abstinēre,* equiv. to *abs-* ABS- + *tinēre,* comb. form of *tenēre* to hold, keep] —**ab·stain′er,** *n.*
—**Syn.** forbear; desist, cease.

ab·ste·mi·ous (ab stē′mē əs), *adj.* **1.** sparing or moderate in eating and drinking; temperate in diet. **2.** characterized by abstinence: *an abstemious life.* **3.** sparing: *an abstemious diet.* [< L *abstēmius,* equiv. to *abs-* ABS- + *tēm-* (root of *tēmētum* intoxicating drink) + *-ius* -IOUS] —**ab·ste′mi·ous·ly,** *adv.* —**ab·ste′mi·ous·ness,** *n.*

ab·sten·tion (ab sten′shən), *n.* **1.** holding off or refraining; abstinence from action. **2.** withholding of one's vote. [< LL *abstentiōn-* (s. of *abstentiō*), equiv. to L *abstent(us)* (ptp.) (see ABSTAIN) + *-iōn-* ION] —**ab·sten′tious,** *adj.*

ab·sterge (ab stûrj′), *v.t.,* **-sterged, -sterg·ing. 1.** *Med.* to purge. **2.** to clean by wiping. [< L *absterg(ēre),* equiv. to *abs-* ABS- + *tergēre* to wipe]

ab·ster·gent (ab stûr′jənt), *adj.* **1.** cleansing. —*n.* **2.** a cleansing agent, as a detergent or soap. [< L *abstergent-* (s. of *abstergēns* (prp.) wiping off). See ABSTERGE, -ENT]

ab·ster·sion (ab stûr′shən), *n.* the act of absterging. [< ML *abstersiōn-* (s. of *abstersiō*), equiv. to L *absters(us)* (ptp. of *abstergēre* to ABSTERGE) + *-iōn-* -ION]

ab·ster·sive (ab stûr′siv), *adj.* abstergent. [< L *absters(us)* (see ABSTERSION) + -IVE] —**ab·ster′sive·ness,** *n.*

ab·sti·nence (ab′stə nəns), *n.* **1.** forbearance from any indulgence of appetite, esp. from the use of alcoholic liquors: *total abstinence.* **2.** self-restraint; self-denial; forbearance. **3.** *Eccles.* the refraining from certain kinds of food on certain days, as from flesh on Fridays. **4.** *Econ.* the conserving of current income in order to build up capital or savings. Also, **ab′sti·nen·cy.** [ME < MF < L *abstinentia.* See ABSTAIN, -ENCE] —**ab′sti·nent,** *adj.* —**ab′sti·nent·ly,** *adv.*
—**Syn. 1.** abstemiousness, sobriety, teetotalism.

ab′stinence the′ory, *Econ.* the theory that interest is payment for conserving current income.

abstr., 1. abstract. **2.** abstracted.

ab·stract (*adj.* ab′strakt, ab strakt′; *n.* ab′strakt; *v.* ab strakt′ *for 12–15,* ab′strakt *for 16*), *adj.* **1.** conceived apart from concrete realities, specific objects, or actual instances: *an abstract idea.* **2.** expressing a quality or characteristic apart from any specific object or instance, as *justice, poverty,* and *speed.* **3.** theoretical; not applied or practical: *abstract science.* **4.** difficult to understand; abstruse: *abstract speculations.* **5.** *Fine Arts.* **a.** of or pertaining to the formal aspect of art, emphasizing lines, colors, generalized or geometrical forms, etc., esp. with reference to their relationship to one another. **b.** (*often cap.*) pertaining to the nonrepresentational art styles of the 20th century. —*n.* **6.** a summary of a statement, document, speech, etc.; epitome. **7.** something that concentrates in itself the essential qualities of anything more extensive or more general, or of several things; essence. **8.** an idea or term considered apart from some material basis or object. **9.** an abstract work of art. **10. in the abstract,** without reference to practical considerations or applications; in theory: *beauty in the abstract.* **11. the abstract,** something that exists only as an idea: *justice in the abstract.* —*v.t.* **12.** to draw or take away; remove. **13.** to divert or draw away the attention of. **14.** to steal. **15.** to consider as a general quality or characteristic apart from specific objects or instances: *to abstract the notions of time, space, and matter.* **16.** to make an abstract, summary, or epitome of; summarize. [< L *abstract(us)* drawn off (ptp. of *abstrahere*). See ABS-, TRACT[1]] —**ab·stract′er,** *n.* —**ab′stract·ly,** *adv.* —**ab′stract·ness,** *n.*

ab′stract al′gebra, the branch of mathematics that deals with the extension of algebraic concepts usually associated with the real number system to other, more general systems.

ab·stract·ed (ab strak′tid), *adj.* lost in thought; deeply engrossed or preoccupied; absent-minded. [ABSTRACT + -ED[2]] —**ab·stract′ed·ly,** *adv.* —**ab·stract′ed·ness,** *n.*
—**Syn.** See **absent-minded.**

Ab′stract Expres′sionism, (*sometimes l.c.*) *Fine Arts.* a style of painting in which paint is applied in an apparently random manner producing images that may or may not have reference to forms exterior to the picture: thought to be derived from Surrealism and Expressionism.

ab·strac·tion (ab strak′shən), *n.* **1.** an abstract or general idea or term. **2.** an impractical idea; something visionary and unrealistic. **3.** the act of considering something as a general quality or characteristic, apart from concrete realities, specific objects, or actual instances. **4.** the act of taking away or separating; withdrawal: *The sensation of cold is due to the abstraction of heat from our bodies.* **5.** absent-mindedness; inattention; mental absorption. **6.** *Fine Arts.* **a.** the abstract qualities or characteristics of a work of art. **b.** a work of art, esp. nonrepresentational, stressing formal relationships. [< LL *abstractiōn-* (s. of *abstractiō*) separation. See ABSTRACT, -ION] —**ab·strac′tion·al,** *adj.*

ab·strac·tion·ism (ab strak′shə niz′əm), *n.* *Fine Arts.* the practice and theory of abstract art. [ABSTRACTION + -ISM]

ab·strac·tion·ist (ab strak′shə nist), *n.* **1.** a person who produces abstract paintings. —*adj.* **2.** tending toward or showing abstract characteristics in art. [ABSTRACTION + -IST]

ab·strac·tive (ab strak′tiv), *adj.* **1.** having the power of abstracting. **2.** pertaining to an abstract or summary. [< ML *abstractīv(us).* See ABSTRACT, -IVE] —**ab·strac′tive·ly,** *adv.* —**ab·strac′tive·ness,** *n.*

ab′stract noun′, *Gram.* **1.** a noun having an abstract meaning as opposed to a concrete meaning, or grammatical coverage associated with such a meaning, as *dread.* **2.** a noun formed with a suffix whose grammatical role imparts such a meaning, as *witness.* Cf. **concrete noun.**

ab′stract of ti′tle, *Law.* an outline history of the title to a parcel of real estate, showing the original grant, subsequent conveyances, mortgages, etc.

ab′stract space′, *Math.* a space whose elements are not geometric points, esp. a function space.

ab·stric·tion (ab strik′shən), *n. Bot.* a method of spore formation in fungi in which successive portions of the sporophore are cut off through the growth of septa; abjunction. [AB- + STRICTION]

ab·struse (ab stro͞os′), *adj.* **1.** hard to understand; recondite; esoteric: *abstruse theories.* **2.** *Obs.* secret; hidden. [< L *abstrūs(us)* thrust away, concealed (ptp. of *abstrūdere*), equiv. to *abs-* ABS- + *trūd-* thrust + *-tus* ptp. suffix] —**ab·struse′ly,** *adv.* —**ab·stru′si·ty, ab·struse′ness,** *n.*

ab·surd (ab sûrd′, -zûrd′), *adj.* ridiculously senseless, illogical, or untrue; contrary to all reason or common sense; laughably foolish or false: *an absurd explanation.* [< L *absurd(us)* dissonant. See AB-, SURD] —**ab·surd′ly,** *adv.* —**ab·surd′ness,** *n.*
—**Syn.** irrational. ABSURD, RIDICULOUS, PREPOSTEROUS all mean inconsistent with reason or common sense. ABSURD means glaringly opposed to manifest truth or reason: *an absurd claim.* RIDICULOUS implies that something is fit only to be laughed at, perhaps contemptuously or derisively: *a ridiculous suggestion.* PREPOSTEROUS implies an amazing extreme of foolishness: *a preposterous proposal.*

ab·surd·i·ty (ab sûr′di tē, -zûr′-), *n., pl.* **-ties. 1.** the state or quality of being absurd. **2.** something absurd. [late ME *absurdite* (< MF) < L *absurditāt-* (s. of *absurditās*). See ABSURD, -ITY]

Ab·syr·tus (ab sûr′təs), *n. Class. Myth.* Apsyrtus.

abt., about.

A·bu-Bekr (ə bo͞o′bek′ər), *n.* A.D. 573–634, Muhammad's father-in-law and successor: first caliph of Mecca 632–634. Also, **A·bu-Bakr** (ə bo͞o′bak′ər).

A·bu Dha·bi (ä′bo͞o dä′bē, dab′ē). **1.** a sheikdom on the S coast of the Persian Gulf in N United Arab Emirates. 235,662. **2.** the capital of this sheikdom. 95,000. **3.** the capital of United Arab Emirates.

A·bu·kir (ä′bo͞o kēr′, ə bē′kər), *n.* a bay in N Egypt, at the mouth of the Nile: French fleet defeated here by British fleet 1798. Also, **Aboukir.**

a·bu·li·a (ə byo͞o′lē ə), *n. Psychiatry.* a form of mental disorder in which volition is impaired or lost. Also, **aboulia.** [< NL < Gk *aboulía* irresolution. See A-[6], -BULIA] —**a·bu′lic,** *adj.*

A·bu·na (ə bo͞o′nə), *n.* (*often l.c.*) the title of the chief bishop of the Ethiopian Church. [< Ar < *abū* father + *-na* our]

a·bun·dance (ə bun′dəns), *n.* **1.** an extremely plentiful or oversufficient quantity or supply: *an abundance of grain.* **2.** overflowing fullness: *abundance of the heart.* **3.** affluence; wealth: *the enjoyment of abundance.* [ME < MF < L *abundantia.* See ABUNDANT, -ANCE]
—**Syn. 1.** copiousness, plenteousness. See **plenty. 2.** generosity. —**Ant. 1.** scarcity.

a·bun·dant (ə bun′dənt), *adj.* **1.** present in great quantity; more than adequate; oversufficient: *an abundant supply of water.* **2.** having in great quantity; abounding (usually fol. by *in*): *a river abundant in salmon.* **3.** richly supplied: *an abundant land.* [late ME (< MF) < L *abundant-* (s. of *abundāns*) overflowing. See ABOUND, -ANT] —**a·bun′dant·ly,** *adv.*
—**Syn. 1.** copious, profuse, overflowing. See **plentiful. 2.** profuse, overflowing, teeming. —**Ant. 1, 2.** sparse, scarce.

abun′dant num′ber, *Math.* a positive number that is less than the sum of all positive integers which are submultiples of it, as 12, which is less than the sum of 1, 2, 3, 4, and 6. Cf. **deficient number, perfect number.**

abun′dant year′. See under **Jewish calendar.**

a·bu·ra (ə byo͝or′ə), *n.* **1.** a West African tree, *Mitragyna stipulosa.* **2.** the pinkish-brown wood of this tree, used for veneers. [< Yoruba]

ab ur·be con·di·ta (äb o͝or′be kōn′di tä′; *Eng.* ab ûr′bē kon′di tə), *Latin.* from the founding of the city (Rome, ab. 753 B.C.). *Abbr.:* A.U.C. [lit., from the built city]

A·bur·y (ā′bə rē), *n.* Avebury (def. 2).

A.Bus., Associate in Business.

a·bus·age (ə byo͞o′sij), *n.* improper use of words; unidiomatic or ungrammatical language. [ABUSE + -AGE]

a·buse (*v.* ə byo͞oz′; *n.* ə byo͞os′), *v.,* **a·bused, a·bus·ing,** *n.* —*v.t.* **1.** to use wrongly or improperly; misuse: *to abuse one's rights or authority.* **2.** to treat in a harmful, injurious, or offensive way: *to abuse a horse; to abuse one's eyesight.* **3.** to speak insultingly, harshly, and unjustly to or about; revile; malign. **4.** to commit indecent assault upon. **5.** *Obs.* to deceive; cheat. **6. abuse oneself,** to masturbate. —*n.* **7.** wrong or improper use; misuse: *the abuse of privileges.* **8.** harshly or coarsely insulting language: *The officer heaped abuse on his men.* **9.** bad or improper treatment; maltreatment: *The child was subjected to cruel abuse.* **10.** a corrupt or improper practice or custom: *the abuses of bad government.* **11.** rape or indecent assault. **12.** *Obs.* deception; misrepresentation. [late ME < MF *abuse(r)* < L *abūs(us)* misused (ptp. of *abūtī*). See AB-, USE] —**a·bus′a·ble,** *adj.* —**a·bus′er,** *n.*
—**Syn. 1.** misapply, mistreat. **2.** ill-use, maltreat, injure, harm, hurt. **3.** vilify, vituperate, berate, scold; slander, defame, calumniate, traduce. **7.** misapplication. **8.** slander, aspersion. ABUSE, CENSURE, INVECTIVE all mean strongly expressed disapproval. ABUSE implies an outburst of harsh and scathing words against another (often one who is defenseless): *abuse directed against an opponent.* CENSURE implies blame, adverse criticism, or hostile condemnation: *severe censure of acts showing bad judgment.* INVECTIVE applies to strong but formal denunciation in speech or print, often in the public interest: *invective against graft.* —**Ant. 3, 8.** praise.

A·bu Sim·bel (ä bo͞o′ sim′bel, -bəl), a village in S Egypt, on the Nile: site of two temples of Rameses II. Also, **Abu Sim·bil** (sim′bil). Also called **Ipsambul.**

a·bu·sive (ə byo͞o′siv), *adj.* **1.** using, containing, or characterized by harshly or coarsely insulting language: *an abusive author; abusive remarks.* **2.** treating badly or injuriously; mistreating, esp. physically: *his abusive handling of the horse.* **3.** wrongly used; corrupt: *an abusive exercise of power.* [< L *abūsīv(us).* See ABUSE, -IVE] —**a·bu′sive·ly,** *adv.* —**a·bu′sive·ness,** *n.*

a·but (ə but′), *v.,* **a·but·ted, a·but·ting.** —*v.i.* **1.** to be adjacent; touch or join at the edge or border (often fol. by *on, upon,* or *against*): *This piece of land abuts on a street.* —*v.t.* **2.** to be adjacent to; border on; end at. **3.** to support by an abutment. [late ME < MF *about(er)* (to) join end to end (*a-* A-[5] + *bout* end) and *abut(er)* (to) touch at one end (*a-* A-[5] + *but* end)]

a·bu·ti·lon (ə byo͞ot′əlon′), *n.* a shrub of the genus *Abutilon,* comprising the flowering maples. [< NL < Ar *awbūtīlūn*]

a·but·ment (ə but′mənt), *n.* **1.** *Archit., Civ. Eng.* **a.** a masonry mass supporting and receiving the thrust of part of an arch or vault. **b.** a mass, as of masonry, receiving the arch, beam, truss, etc., at each end of a bridge. **c.** a mass or structure for resisting the pressure of water on a bridge, pier, or the like. **d.** each of the parts of a canyon or the like receiving the thrusts of an arch dam. **e.** a structure for absorbing tensions from reinforcing strands for concrete being prestressed. **2.** the place where projecting parts meet; junction. **3.** *Dentistry.* a tooth or tooth root that supports or stabilizes a bridge, a denture, or other prosthetic appliance. [ABUT + -MENT]

A, Abutment

a·but·tal (ə but′əl), *n.* **1. abuttals,** those parts of one piece of land that abut on adjacent lands; boundaries. **2.** act or state of abutting. [ABUT + -AL[2]]

a·but·tals (ə but′əlz), *n. pl. Law.* the boundary lines of a piece of land in relation to adjacent lands. Also, **buttals.** [see ABUTTAL]

a·but·ter (ə but′ər), *n.* a person who owns adjacent land. [ABUT + -ER[1]]

a·but·ting (ə but′ing), *adj.* that abuts; adjoining; adjacent. [ABUT + -ING[2]]
—**Syn.** joining, touching, bordering.

a·buzz (ə buz′), *adj.* **1.** buzzing. **2.** bursting or alive with activity. [A-[1] + BUZZ[1]]

abv., above.

ab·volt (ab vōlt′), *n. Elect.* the centimeter-gram-second unit of electromotive force, equivalent to 10^{-8} volt. [*ab-* (see ABAMPERE) + VOLT[1]]

ab·watt (ab wot′), *n. Elect.* the centimeter-gram-second unit of electrical power, equivalent to 10^{-7} watt. [*ab-* (see ABAMPERE) + WATT]

a·by (ə bī′), *v., pt. and pp.* **a·bought.** —*v.t.* **1.** *Archaic.* to pay the penalty of. —*v.i. Obs.* **2.** to endure; continue. **3.** to undergo suffering as a penalty. Also, **abye.** [ME *abye(n),* OE *ābycgan.* See A-[3], BUY]

A·by·dos (ə bī′dos), *n.* **1.** an ancient ruined city in central Egypt, near Thebes: temples and necropolis. **2.** an ancient town in NW Asia Minor, at the narrowest part of the Hellespont.

a·bye (ə bī′), *v.t., v.i., pt. and pp.* **a·bought.** aby.

Ab·y·la (ab′ə lə), *n.* ancient name of **Jebel Musa.**

a·bysm (ə biz′əm), *n.* an abyss. [ME *abi(s)me* < VL **abyssim(us),* a superl. of LL *abyssus* ABYSS]

a·bys·mal (ə biz′məl), *adj.* of or like an abyss; immeasurably deep or great: *abysmal ignorance; abysmal poverty.* [ABYSM + -AL[1]] —**a·bys′mal·ly,** *adv.*

a·byss (ə bis′), *n.* **1.** a deep, immeasurable space, gulf, or cavity; vast chasm. **2.** anything profound, unfathomable, or infinite: *the abyss of time.* **3.** (in ancient cosmogony) **a.** the primal chaos before Creation. **b.** the infernal regions; hell. **c.** a subterranean ocean. [< LL *abyss(us)* < Gk *ábyssos* bottomless, equiv. to *a-* A-[6] + *byssós* bottom of the sea]

Abyss., **1.** Abyssinia. **2.** Abyssinian.

a·byss·al (ə bis′əl), *adj.* **1.** of or like an abyss; immeasurable; unfathomable. **2.** of or pertaining to the lowest depths of the ocean, esp. the stratum of bottom waters. [< ML *abyssāl(is).* See ABYSS, -AL[1]]

Ab·ys·sin·i·a (ab′i sin′ē ə), *n.* former name of **Ethiopia.** —**Ab′ys·sin′i·an,** *adj., n.*

Abyssin′ian banan′a, a large, treelike herb, *Musa Ensete,* of Ethiopia, having leaves from 10 to 20 feet long, whitish flowers with reddish-brown bracts, and inedible, dry fruit.

Ab′yssin′ian cat′, a breed of domesticated cat originating in Africa: typically having grayish or brownish fur with a reddish undercoat, giving it a ticked appearance similar to that of a rabbit.

Ab′yssin′ian Church′. See **Ethiopian Church.**

Ab′yssin′ian well′, a perforated pipe driven into the ground for pumping out collected ground water; wellpoint.

ac-, var. of **ad-** before *c* and *qu: accede; acquire.*

-ac, a suffix used in forming adjectives: *elegiac; cardiac.* [comb. form repr. L *-acus,* Gk *-akos,* r. *-ikos* -IC when the base ended in *-i-*]

AC, 1. *Chem.* actinium. **2.** Also, **A.C., ac, a-c, a.c.** *Elect.* alternating current: an electric current that reverses direction at regular intervals, having a magnitude that varies continuously in a sinusoidal manner. Cf. **DC** (def. 2).

Ac, *Chem.* **1.** actinium. **2.** acetate. **3.** acetyl.

A/C, *Bookkeeping.* **1.** account. **2.** account current. Also, **a/c**

A.C., 1. ante Christum. **2.** Army Corps. **3.** Associate in Commerce. **4.** See **AC** (def. 2).

a.c., 1. (in prescriptions) before meals. [< L *ante cibum*] **2.** See **AC** (def. 2).

ACAA, Agricultural Conservation and Adjustment Administration.

A·ca·cal·lis (ə kə kal′is), *n. Class. Myth.* the mother of Amphithemis by Apollo.

a·ca·cia (ə kā′shə), *n.* **1.** any mimosaceous tree or shrub of the genus *Acacia,* of warm regions. **2.** one of several other plants, as the locust tree. **3.** See **gum arabic.** [< L < Gk *akakía* Egyptian thorn]

Aca′cia Av′enue, *Brit. Facetious.* any middle-class suburban street.

acad., 1. academic. **2.** academy.

ac·a·deme (ak′ə dēm′), *n.* **1.** (*cap.*) the public grove in Athens in which Plato taught. **2.** (*sometimes cap.*) any place of instruction; a school. **3.** the environment of a college or university: *the lethal rivalries of academe.* **4.** a person living in, accustomed to, or preferring the environment of a university. [< L *Acadēm(us)* < Gk *Akádēmos* ACADEMUS]

ac·a·de·mi·a (ak′ə dē′mē ə, -dēm′yə, -dem′ē ə, -dem′yə), *n.* the milieu or interests of a university, college, or academy; academe. [< NL: university]

ac·a·dem·ic (ak′ə dem′ik), *adj.* **1.** of or pertaining to a college, academy, school, or other educational institution, esp. one for higher education: *the academic curriculum.* **2.** *U.S.* pertaining to areas of study that are not vocational or applied, as the humanities, pure mathematics, etc. **3.** theoretical; not practical, realistic, or directly useful: *an academic discussion of a matter already decided.* **4.** learned or scholarly but lacking in worldliness, common sense, or practicality. **5.** conforming to set rules, standards, or traditions; conventional: *academic painting.* **6.** acquired by formal education, esp. at a college or university: *excellent academic preparation for the ministry.* —*n.* **7.** a student or teacher at a college or university. [< L *Acadēmic(us)* < Gk *Akadēmeikós.* See ACADEMY, -IC]
—**Syn. 2.** humanistic, liberal. **5.** See **formal.**

ac·a·dem·i·cal (ak′ə dem′i kəl), *adj.* **1.** academic. —*n.* **2. academicals.** See **cap and gown.** [ACADEMIC + -AL[1]] —**ac′a·dem′i·cal·ly,** *adv.*

ac′adem′ic cos′tume, the ceremonial costume of the students and faculty in schools, colleges, and universities, consisting of a mortarboard, a long, wide-sleeved gown, and sometimes a hood, worn esp. at commencement exercises.

ac′adem′ic free′dom, 1. freedom of a teacher to discuss any social, economic, or political problems without interference or penalty from officials, organized groups, etc. **2.** freedom of a student to explore any field or hold any belief without interference from the teacher.

a·cad·e·mi·cian (ə kad′ə mish′ən, ak′ə də-), *n.* **1.** a member of an association or institution for the advancement of arts, sciences, or letters. **2.** a follower or promoter of the traditional trends in philosophy, art, or literature: *Reforms were instituted over the protests of the academicians.* [< F *académicien,* equiv. to *académic-* ACADEMIC + *-ien* -IAN]

ac·a·dem·i·cism (ak′ə dem′i siz′əm), *n.* traditionalism or conventionalism in art, literature, etc. Also **academism.** [ACADEMIC + -ISM]

ac′adem′ic year′, the customary annual schedule of courses at a college, university, etc., running approximately from September to June. Also called **school year.**

A·ca·dé·mie Fran·çaise (A KA dā mē frän sez′), *French.* See **French Academy.**

A·ca·dé·mie Gon·court (A KA dā mē gôn ko͞or′). See under **Goncourt** (def. 2).

a·cad·e·mise (ə kad′ə mīz′), *v.t.,* **-mised, -mis·ing.** *Chiefly Brit.* academize.

a·cad·e·mism (ə kad′ə miz′əm), *n.* **1.** academicism. **2.** *Philos.* the philosophy of the school founded by Plato. [ACADEM(E) + -ISM]

a·cad·e·mize (ə kad′ə mīz′), *v.t.,* **-mized, -miz·ing.** to reduce (a subject) to a rigid set of rules, principles, precepts, etc.: *futile attempts to academize the visual arts.* [ACADEM(Y) + -IZE]

Ac·a·de·mus (ak′ə dē′məs), *n. Class. Myth.* an Arcadian whose estate became a meeting place for Athenian philosophers.

a·cad·e·my (ə kad′ə mē), *n., pl.* **-mies. 1.** a secondary or high school, esp. a private one. **2.** a school or college for special instruction or training in a subject: *a military academy.* **3.** an association or institution for the advancement of art, literature, or science: *the National Academy of Arts and Letters.* **4.** a group of persons who are acknowledged as authorities and leaders in a field of scholarship, art, etc., and are often permitted to dictate standards, prescribe methods, and criticize new ideas. **5. the Academy, a.** the Platonic school of philosophy or its adherents. **b.** academe (def. 1). **c.** See **French Academy. d.** See **Royal Academy.** [< L *acadēmīa* < Gk *akadémeia,* equiv. to *Akádēm(os)* ACADEMUS + *-eia* adj. suffix]

acad′emy fig′ure, *Fine Arts.* a representation of a nude human figure, executed for purposes of study and usually about one half life-size.

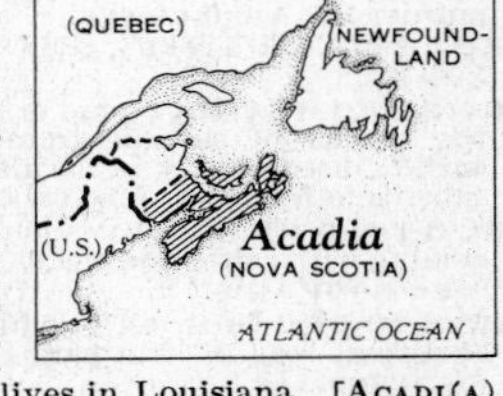

A·ca·di·a (ə kā′dē ə), *n.* a former French colony in SE Canada: ceded to Great Britain, 1713. French, **A·ca·die** (A KA dē′).

A·ca·di·an (ə kā′dē ən), *adj.* **1.** of or pertaining to Acadia or its inhabitants. —*n.* **2.** a native or inhabitant of Acadia or a descendant of such natives or inhabitants who lives in Louisiana. [ACADI(A) + -AN]

Aca′dia Na′tional Park′, a national park in Maine, on Mount Desert Island. 44 sq. mi.

a·cal·cu·li·a (ā′kal kyo͞o′lē ə), *n. Psychiatry.* inability to perform arithmetic operations. [< NL, equiv. to *a-* A-[6] + *calcul-* (see CALCULATE) + *-ia* -IA]

ac·a·leph (ak′ə lef′), *n.* (in former classifications) any coelenterate of the group *Acalephae,* including the sea nettles and jellyfishes. Also, **ac·a·lephe** (ak′ə lēf′). [< NL *acaleph(a)* < Gk *akalḗphē* stinging nettle, sea anemone]

Ac·a·mas (ak′ə məs), *n. Class. Myth.* **1.** a son of Theseus and Phaedra who entered Troy in the Trojan Horse. **2.** (in the *Iliad*) **a.** the companion of Aeneas who killed Promachus to avenge the murder of his brother Archelochus. **b.** a captain of the Thracian allies of Troy.

ac·an·tha·ceous (ak′ən thā′shəs), *adj.* **1.** having prickly growths. **2.** belonging to the *Acanthaceae,* or acanthus family of plants. [< NL *Acanthace(ae)* (see ACANTHUS, -ACEAE) + -OUS]

a·can·thite (ə kan′thīt), *n. Mineral.* the orthorhombic form of silver sulfide. Cf. **argentite.** [ACANTH- + -ITE[1]]

acantho-, a learned borrowing from Greek meaning "spiny," used in the formation of compound words: *acanthocephalan.* Also, *esp. before a vowel,* **acanth-.** [< Gk *akantho-,* comb. form of *ákantha* thorn]

a·can·tho·car·pous (ə kan′thə kär′pəs), *adj. Bot.* having prickly or spiny fruit. [ACANTHO- + -CARPOUS]

a·can·tho·ceph·a·lan (ə kan′thə sef′ə lən), *n.* **1.** any parasitic worm of the phylum or class *Acanthocephala,* having a protrusible proboscis covered with recurved hooks and a hollow body without a digestive tract, found in the intestine of vertebrates. —*adj.* **2.** belonging or pertaining to the *Acanthocephala.* [ACANTHO- + CEPHAL- + -AN]

ac·an·thoc·la·dous (ak′ən thok′lə dəs), *adj. Bot.* having spiny stems or branches. [ACANTHO- + CLAD- + -OUS]

ac·an·tho·di·an (ak′ən thō′dē ən), *n.* any small, spiny-finned, sharklike fish of the extinct order *Acanthodii,* from the Paleozoic era. [*acanthode* (see ACANTH-, -ODE¹) + -IAN]

a·can·thoid (ə kan′thoid), *adj.* spiny; spinous. [ACANTH- + -OID]

ac·an·thop·ter·yg·i·an (ak′ən thop′tə rij′ē ən), *adj.* **1.** belonging or pertaining to the *Acanthopterygii* (*Acanthopteri*), the group of spiny-finned fishes, including the bass and perch. —*n.* **2.** an acanthopterygian fish. [< NL *Acanthopterygi*(ī) (*acantho-* ACANTHO- + Gk *pterýgi*(*on*) small wing, fin + L -ī masc. pl. ending) + -AN]

ac·an·tho·sis (ak′ən thō′sis), *n., pl.* **-ses** (-sēz). *Pathol.* a thickening of the germinative layer of the epidermis due to hyperplasia of the cells. [ACANTH- + -OSIS] —**ac·an·thot·ic** (ak′ən thot′ik), *adj.*

a·can·thous (ə kan′thəs), *adj.* spinous. [ACANTH- + -OUS]

a·can·thus (ə kan′thəs), *n., pl.* **-thus·es, -thi** (-thī). **1.** any of several herbs of the genus *Acanthus,* of the Mediterranean region, having spiny or toothed leaves. **2.** an architectural ornament, as in the Corinthian capital, resembling the leaves of this plant. [< L < Gk *ákanthos* bearsfoot] —**a·can·thine** (ə kan′thin, -thīn), *adj.*

A B

Acanthus
A, Leaf of plant, *Acanthus mollis;* B, Architectural ornament, front and side views

a ca·pi·te ad cal·cem (ä kä′pi te′ äd käl′kem; *Eng.* ā kap′i tē ad kal′sem), *Latin.* from top to bottom. [lit., from head to heel]

a·cap·ni·a (ə kap′nē ə, ā kap′-), *n. Med.* a deficiency of carbon dioxide in the blood and tissues. [< NL < Gk *ákapn*(*os*) smokeless (*a-* A-⁶ + *kapnós* smoke) + *-ia* -IA; NL sense from the fact that smoke contains carbon dioxide] —**a·cap′ni·al,** *adj.*

a cap·pel·la (ä′ kə pel′ə; *It.* ä′ käp pel′lä), *Music.* **1.** without instrumental accompaniment. **2.** in the style of church or chapel music. [< It: according to chapel]

a ca·pric·cio (ä′ kä prēt′chō), *Music.* freely; at the whim of the performer (a musical direction). [< It: according to caprice]

A·ca·pul·co (ak′ə pōōl′kō; *Sp.* ä′kä pōōl′kō), *n.* a seaport in SW Mexico, on the Pacific. 27,913 (1950).

a·car·di·a (ā kär′dē ə), *n. Pathol.* congenital absence of the heart. [A-⁶ + Gk *kardía* heart] —**a·car·di·ac** (ā kär′dē ak′), *adj.*

ac·a·ri·a·sis (ak′ə rī′ə sis), *n. Pathol.* **1.** infestation with acarids, esp. mites. **2.** a skin disease caused by such infestation. [< NL; see ACARUS, -IASIS]

a·car·i·cide (ə kar′i sīd′, ak′ər i-), *n.* a substance or preparation for killing acarids. [ACAR(US) + -I- + -CIDE] —**a·car′i·cid′al,** *adj.*

ac·a·rid (ak′ə rid), *n.* **1.** an acarine, esp. of the family *Acaridae.* —*adj.* **2.** of or pertaining to an acarid. [ACAR(US) + -ID²]

a·car·i·dan (ə kar′i dᵊn), *adj.* **1.** belonging or pertaining to the family *Acarina.* —*n.* **2.** an acarine. [ACARID + -AN]

ac·a·rine (ak′ə rīn′, -rēn′, -rin), *n.* **1.** any of numerous arachnids of the order *Acarina,* comprising the mites and ticks. —*adj.* **2.** belonging or pertaining to the order *Acarina.* [< NL *Acarina* name of the order, equiv. to *Acar*(*us*) name of the genus (see ACARUS) + *-ina* -INE¹]

A·car·nan (ə kär′nən), *n. Class. Myth.* an infant who, with his brother, was enabled by Zeus to grow to manhood in a single day in order to avenge his father's murder Cf. **Amphoterus.**

ac·a·roid (ak′ə roid′), *adj.* resembling a mite or tick. [ACAR(US) + -OID]

ac′aroid res′in, a red or yellow resin obtained from the trunks of several grass trees, esp. *Xanthorrhoea hastilis,* used chiefly in varnishes and lacquers and as a substitute for rosin. Also called **accroides gum.**

ac·a·rol·o·gy (ak′ə rol′ə jē), *n.* the branch of zoology dealing with mites and ticks. [ACAR(US) + -O- + -LOGY] —**ac′a·rol′o·gist,** *n.*

ac·a·ro·pho·bi·a (ak′ər ə fō′bē ə), *n. Psychiatry.* an abnormal fear of skin parasites. [< NL; see ACARUS, -O-, -PHOBIA]

a·car·pel·ous (ā kär′pə ləs), *adj. Bot.* having no carpels. Also, **a·car′pel·lous.** [A-⁶ + CARPEL + -OUS]

a·car·pous (ā kär′pəs), *adj. Bot.* not producing fruit; sterile; barren. [< Gk *ákarpos,* equiv. to *a-* A-⁶ + *karpós* fruit; see -OUS]

ac·a·rus (ak′ər əs), *n., pl.* **-a·ri** (-ə rī′). a mite, esp. of the genus *Acarus.* [< NL < Gk *akarí* mite]

A·cas·tus (ə kas′təs), *n. Class. Myth.* an Argonaut, the son of Pelias and brother of Alcestis.

a·cat·a·lec·tic (ā kat′ᵊlek′tik), *Pros.* —*adj.* **1.** not catalectic; complete. —*n.* **2.** a verse having the complete number of syllables in the last foot. Cf. **catalectic, hypercatalectic.** [< LL *acatalectic*(*us*). See A-⁶, CATALECTIC]

a·cau·dal (ā kôd′ᵊl), *adj. Zool.* tailless. Also, **a·cau·date** (ā kô′dāt). [A-⁶ + CAUDAL]

ac·au·les·cent (ak′ô les′ənt), *adj. Bot.* not caulescent; stemless; without visible stem. Also, **a·cau·line** (ā kô′lin), **a·cau·lose** (ā kô′lōs), **a·cau·lous** (ā kô′ləs). [A-⁶ + CAULESCENT] —**ac′au·les′cence,** *n.*

acc., **1.** accelerate. **2.** acceleration. **3.** accept. **4.** acceptance. **5.** accompanied. **6.** accompaniment. **7.** accordant. **8.** according. **9.** account. **10.** accountant. **11.** accusative.

Ac·cad (ak′ad, ä′käd), *n.* one of the four cities of Nimrod's kingdom. Gen. 10:10. Also, **Akkad;** *Douay Bible,* **Achad.**

Ac·ca·di·an (ə kā′dē ən, ə kä′-), *n., adj. Obs.* Sumerian. [ACCAD + -IAN]

Ac·ca La·ren·ti·a (ak′ə lə ren′shē ə), an ancient Roman goddess, identified either with the wife of Faustulus or with a wealthy prostitute who bequeathed her money to the state.

acce., acceptance.

ac·cede (ak sēd′), *v.i.,* **-ced·ed, -ced·ing. 1.** to give consent, approval, or adherence; agree; assent: *to accede to a request; to accede to terms.* **2.** to attain or assume (an office, title, or dignity); arrive at or succeed to (usually fol. by *to*): *to accede to the throne.* **3.** *Internat. Law.* to become a party to by way of accession. [< L *accēde*(*re*) (to) approach, assent, equiv. to *ac-* AC- + *cēdere* to go] —**ac·ced′ence,** *n.* —**ac·ced′er,** *n.* —**Syn. 1.** See **agree.**

accel., accelerando.

ac·cel·er·an·do (ak sel′ə rän′dō; *It.* ät che′le rän′dô), *adv., adj. Music.* gradually increasing in speed. [< It < L *accelerandus,* gerundive of *accelerāre* to speed up. See ACCELERATE]

ac·cel·er·ant (ak sel′ər ənt), *n. Chem.* accelerator (def. 5). [< L *accelerant-* (s. of *accelerāns*) hastening (prp. of *accelerāre*). See ACCELERATE]

ac·cel·er·ate (ak sel′ə rāt′), *v.,* **-at·ed, -at·ing.** —*v.t.* **1.** to cause faster or greater activity, progress, advancement, etc., in: *to accelerate economic growth.* **2.** to hasten the occurrence of: *to accelerate the fall of a government.* **3.** to increase or otherwise change the velocity of (a body) or the rate of (motion); cause to undergo acceleration. **4.** to reduce the time required for (a course of study) by intensifying the work, eliminating detail, etc. —*v.i.* **5.** to move or go faster; increase in speed. [< L *accelerāt*(*us*) speeded up (ptp. of *accelerāre*), equiv. to *ac-* AC- + *celer* swift + *-ātus* -ATE¹] —**ac·cel′er·a·ble,** *adj.* —**ac·cel′er·at′ed·ly,** *adv.*

ac·cel·er·a·tion (ak sel′ə rā′shən), *n.* **1.** the act of accelerating; increase of speed or velocity. **2.** a change in velocity. **3.** the time rate of change of velocity with respect to magnitude or direction; the derivative of velocity. [< L *accelerātiōn-* (s. of *accelerātiō*). See ACCELERATE, -ION]

accelera′tion coeffi′cient, *Econ.* the ratio of change in capital investment to the change in consumer spending. Also called **accelerator, coefficient of acceleration.** Cf. **acceleration principle.**

accelera′tion of grav′ity, *Physics.* the acceleration of a falling body in the earth's gravitational field, inversely proportional to the square of the distance from the body to the center of the earth, and varying somewhat with latitude: approximately 32 feet per second per second. *Symbol:* g

accelera′tion prin′ciple, *Econ.* the principle that an increase in the demand for a finished product will create a greater percentage of change in the demand for capital goods.

ac·cel·er·a·tive (ak sel′ə rā′tiv, -ər ə tiv), *adj.* tending to accelerate; increasing the velocity of. Also, **ac·cel·er·a·to·ry** (ak sel′ər ə tôr′ē, -tōr′ē). [ACCELERATE + -IVE]

ac·cel·er·a·tor (ak sel′ə rā′tər), *n.* **1.** one who or that which accelerates. **2.** *Auto.* a device, usually operated by the foot, for controlling the speed of an engine. **3.** *Brit.* any two- or three-wheeled motor vehicle, as a motorcycle or motor scooter. **4.** *Photog.* a chemical, usually an alkali, added to a developer to increase the rate of development. **5.** *Chem.* any substance that increases the speed of a chemical change, as one that increases the rate of vulcanization of rubber, that hastens the setting of concrete, mortar, plaster, or the like, etc. **6.** *Anat.* any muscle, nerve, or activating substance that quickens a movement. **7.** Also called **atom smasher, particle accelerator.** *Physics.* an electrostatic or electromagnetic device, as a cyclotron, that produces high-energy particles and focuses them on a target. **8.** *Econ.* See **acceleration coefficient.** [ACCELERATE + -OR²]

accel′erator glob′ulin, *Biochem.* a protein, found in blood plasma, that during coagulation accelerates the conversion of prothrombin to thrombin. Also called **ac-globulin, proaccelerin.**

ac·cel·er·om·e·ter (ak sel′ə rom′i tər), *n.* an instrument for measuring acceleration, as of aircraft or guided missiles. [ACCELER(ATION) + -O- + -METER]

ac·cent (*n.* ak′sent; *v.* ak′sent, ak sent′), *n.* **1.** prominence of a syllable in terms of differential loudness, or of pitch, or length, or of a combination of these. **2.** degree of prominence of a syllable within a word and sometimes of a word within a phrase: *primary accent; secondary accent.* **3.** a mark indicating stress (′, ′), vowel quality (as French grave `, acute ´, circumflex ^), or form (as French *la* "the" versus *là* "there"). **4.** any similar mark. **5.** *Pros.* **a.** regularly recurring stress. **b.** a mark indicating stress or some other distinction in pronunciation or value. **6.** a musical tone or pattern of pitch inherent in a particular language either as a feature essential to the identification of a vowel or a syllable or to the general acoustic character of the language. Cf. **pitch**¹ (def. 28), **tone** (def. 7). **7.** Usually, **accents.** the unique speech patterns, inflections, choice of words, etc., that identify a particular individual: *We recognized his accents immediately. She addressed the garden club in mellifluous accents.* **8.** a mode of pronunciation, as pitch or tone, emphasis pattern, or intonation, characteristic of or peculiar to the speech of a particular person, group, or locality: *foreign accent; regional accent.* Cf. **tone** (def. 5). **9.** a foreign accent: *He still speaks with an accent.* **10.** *Music.* **a.** a stress or emphasis given to certain notes. **b.** a mark noting this. **c.** stress or emphasis regularly recurring as a feature of rhythm. **11.** *Math.* **a.** a symbol used to distinguish similar quantities which differ in value, as in b′, b″, b‴ (called *b prime, b second* or *b double prime, b third* or *b triple prime,* respectively). **b.** a symbol used to indicate a particular unit of measure, as feet (′) or inches (″), minutes (′) or seconds (″). **c.** a symbol used to indicate the order of a derivative of a function in calculus, as *f′* (called *f prime*) is the first derivative of a function *f.* **12.** words or tones expressive of some emotion. **13. accents,** words; language; speech: *He spoke in accents bold.* **14.** distinctive character or tone: *an accent of whining complaint.* —*v.t.* **15.** to pronounce with prominence (a syllable within a word or a word within a phrase): *to accent the first syllable of "into"; to accent the first word of "White House."* **16.** to mark with a written accent or accents: *There's an acute accent on the "e" in "passé."* **17.** to give emphasis or prominence to; accentuate. [< L *accent*(*us*) speaking tone, equiv. to *ac-* AC- + *-centus,* comb. form of *cantus* song (see CANTO); trans. of Gk *prosōidía* PROSODY] —**ac′cent·less,** *adj.* —**ac·cen·tu·a·ble** (ak sen′chōō ə bəl), *adj.*

Ac·cent (ak′sent), *n. Trademark.* See **monosodium glutamate.**

ac′cent mark′, a mark used to indicate an accent, stress, etc., as for pronunciation or in musical notation. Cf. **diacritic** (def. 1).

ac·cen·tor (ak sen′tər, ak′sen-), *n.* any oscine bird of the family *Prunellidae,* of Europe and Asia, resembling sparrows but having more finely pointed bills, as the hedge sparrow. [< NL, ML: one who sings with, equiv. to L *ac-* AC- + ML *-centor* singer; see ACCENT, -OR²]

ac·cen·tu·al (ak sen′chōō əl), *adj.* **1.** of or pertaining to accent or stress; rhythmical. **2.** *Pros.* of or pertaining to poetry based on the number of stresses, as distinguished from poetry depending on the number of syllables or quantities. [< L *accentu*(*s*) (see ACCENT) + -AL¹] —**ac·cen′tu·al′i·ty,** *n.* —**ac·cen′tu·al·ly,** *adv.*

ac·cen·tu·ate (ak sen′chōō āt′), *v.t.,* **-at·ed, -at·ing. 1.** to give emphasis or prominence to; emphasize. **2.** to mark or pronounce with an accent. [< ML *accentuāt*(*us*) intoned (ptp. of *accentuāre*). See ACCENT, -ATE¹]

ac·cen·tu·a·tion (ak sen′chōō ā′shən), *n.* **1.** act of accentuating. **2.** that which is accentuated. [< ML *accentuātiōn-* (s. of *accentuātiō*) intoning. See ACCENTUATE, -ION]

ac·cen·tu·a·tor (ak sen′chōō ā′tər), *n.* **1.** *Electronics.* a circuit or network inserted to provide less loss or greater gain to certain frequencies in an audio spectrum, as a preemphasis spectrum. **2.** one who or that which accentuates. [ACCENTUATE + -OR²]

ac·cept (ak sept′), *v.t.* **1.** to take or receive (something offered); receive with approval or favor: *to accept a present; to accept a proposal.* **2.** to agree or consent to; accede to: *to accept a treaty; to accept an apology.* **3.** to respond or answer affirmatively to: *to accept an invitation.* **4.** to undertake the duties, honors, etc., of: *to accept the office of president.* **5.** to receive or admit formally, as to a college or club. **6.** to accommodate or reconcile oneself to: *to accept the situation.* **7.** to regard as true or sound; believe: *to accept a fact; to accept Catholicism.* **8.** to regard as normal, suitable, or usual. **9.** to receive as to meaning; understand. **10.** *Com.* to acknowledge, by signature, as calling for payment, and thus to agree to pay, as a draft. **11.** (in a deliberative body) to receive as an adequate performance of the duty with which an officer or a committee has been charged; receive for further action: *The report of the committee was accepted.* **12.** to receive or contain (something attached, inserted, etc.): *This socket won't accept a three-pronged plug.* —*v.i.* **13.** to accept an invitation, gift, position, etc. (sometimes fol. by *of*). [late ME *accepte* < L *accept*(*āre*), equiv. to *ac-* AC- + *-cep-* take + *-t-* freq. suffix] —**Syn. 2.** concede. **7.** acknowledge. —**Ant. 1.** reject. —**Usage.** ACCEPT and EXCEPT are sometimes confused as verbs because of their similarities in speech. ACCEPT means "to take or receive" (*I accept this trophy*), while EXCEPT means "to exclude" (*They excepted him from the membership list*).

ac·cept·a·ble (ak sep′tə bəl), *adj.* **1.** capable or worthy of being accepted. **2.** pleasing to the receiver; satisfactory; agreeable; welcome. **3.** meeting only minimum requirements; barely adequate: *acceptable applicants.* [late ME < L *acceptābil*(*is*). See ACCEPT, -ABLE] —**ac·cept′a·bil′i·ty, ac·cept′a·ble·ness,** *n.* —**ac·cept′a·bly,** *adv.*

ac·cept·ance (ak sep′təns), *n.* **1.** the act of taking or receiving something offered. **2.** favorable reception; approval; favor. **3.** the act of assenting or believing: *acceptance of a theory.* **4.** the fact or state of being accepted or acceptable. **5.** *Com.* **a.** an engagement to pay an order, draft, or bill of exchange when it becomes due, as by the person on whom it is drawn. **b.** an order, draft, etc., which a person has accepted as calling for payment and has thus promised to pay. [ACCEPT + -ANCE]

accept′ance race′, *Brit.* See **allowance race.**

accept′ance sam′pling, *Com.* a procedure by which a decision is made to accept or reject a lot of articles on the basis of the results of the inspection of one or more samples of articles from the lot.

ac·cept·an·cy (ak sep′tən sē), *n., pl.* **-cies. 1.** act of accepting; acceptance. **2.** willingness to accept or receive; receptiveness. [ACCEPT + -ANCY]

ac·cept·ant (ak sep′tənt), *adj.* willingly accepting or receiving; receptive. [ACCEPT + -ANT]

ac·cep·ta·tion (ak′sep tā′shən), *n.* **1.** favorable regard; approval. **2.** belief; conviction. **3.** the usual or accepted meaning of a word, phrase, etc. [late ME < MF. See ACCEPT, -ATION]

ac·cept·ed (ak sep′tid), *adj.* generally approved; usually regarded as normal, right, etc.: *an accepted pronunciation.* [ACCEPT + -ED²] —**ac·cept′ed·ly,** *adv.*

accept′ed ma′sons, *Hist.* See under **Freemason** (def. 2b).

ac·cept·ee (ak′sep tē′), *n.* a person who is accepted, as for military service. [ACCEPT + -EE]

ac·cept·er (ak sep′tər), *n.* one who or that which accepts. [ACCEPT + -ER¹]

ac·cep·tor (ak sep′tər), *n.* **1.** accepter. **2.** *Finance.* a person who accepts a draft or bill of exchange, esp. the drawee who signs the draft or bill, confirming his willingness to pay it when due. **3.** Also called **accep′tor at′om, accep′tor impu′rity.** *Physics.* an atom of impurity in a semiconducting crystal such that the atom can capture an electron, creating a hole in a filled electron shell thereby changing the electric conductivity of the crystal. [< L; see ACCEPT, -OR²]

ac·cess (ak′ses), *n.* **1.** ability or permission to approach, enter, speak with, or use; admittance: *They have access to the files.* **2.** state or quality of being approachable: *The house was difficult of access.* **3.** a way or means of approach. **4.** *Theol.* approach to God through Jesus Christ. **5.** an attack or onset, as of a disease. **6.** a sudden and strong emotional outburst. **7.** accession. —*v.t.* **8.** to gain access to or retrieve. [late ME *accesse* < L *access*(*us*) an approach, n. use of ptp. of *accēdere* to ACCEDE: ME *acces* attack (of illness, anger, etc.) < MF < L *access*(*us*), as above]

ac·ces·sa·ry (ak ses′ə rē), *n., pl.* **-ries,** *adj. Chiefly Law.* accessory. —**ac·ces′sa·ri·ly,** *adv.* —**ac·ces′sa·ri·ness,** *n.*

ac·ces·si·ble (ak ses′ə bəl), *adj.* **1.** easy to approach, enter, speak with, or use. **2.** that can be used, entered, reached, etc.: *an accessible road; accessible ruins.* **3.** obtainable; attainable: *accessible evidence.* **4.** open to the influence of (usually fol. by *to*): *accessible to bribery.* [< L *accessibil*(*is*). See ACCESS, -IBLE] —**ac·ces′si·bil′i·ty,** *n.* —**ac·ces′si·bly,** *adv.*

ac·ces·sion (ak sesh′ən), *n.* **1.** act of coming into the possession of a right, title, office, etc.: *accession to the* throne. **2.** an increase by something added: *an accession of territory.* **3.** something added: *a list of accessions to the college library.* **4.** *Law.* addition to property by growth or improvement. **5.** consent; agreement; approval: *accession to a demand.* **6.** *Internat. Law.* formal acceptance of a treaty, international convention, or other agreement between states. **7.** act of coming near; approach. **8.** attack or onset, as of a disease. —*v.t.* **9.** *Library Science.* **a.** to make a record of (a book, painting, etc.) in the order of acquisition. **b.** to acquire (a book, pamphlet, etc.), esp. for a permanent collection. [< L *accessiōn-* (s. of *accessiō*) an approach, addition. See ACCESS, -ION] —**ac·ces′sion·al,** *adj.*

acces′sion num′ber, the individual number or serial designation identifying specifically any of the items, as books, records, etc., acquired by a library, collection, or the like. Cf. **serial number.**

ac·ces·so·ri·al (ak′si sôr′ē əl, -sōr′-), *adj.* accessory; supplementary. [ACCESSORY + -AL¹]

ac·ces·so·ri·us (ak′si sôr′ē əs, -sōr′-), *n., pl.* **-so·ri·i** (-sôr′ē ī′, -sōr′-). *Anat.* any muscle, nerve, gland, etc., that reinforces the action of another. [< NL, ML: ACCESSORY]

ac·ces·so·rize (ak ses′ə rīz′), *v.t.,* **-rized, -riz·ing.** to fit or equip with accessories. [ACCESSOR(Y) + -IZE]

ac·ces·so·ry (ak ses′ə rē), *n., pl.* **-ries,** *adj.* —*n.* **1.** a subordinate or supplementary part, object, etc., used mainly for convenience, attractiveness, safety, etc., as a spotlight on an automobile or a lens cover on a camera. **2.** an article or set of articles of dress, as gloves, earrings, a scarf, or the like, that adds completeness, convenience, attractiveness, etc., to one's basic outfit. **3.** *Law.* **a.** Also called **acces′sory before′ the fact′.** a person who, though not present during the commission of a felony, is guilty of having aided and abetted another, who committed the felony. **b.** Also called **acces′sory af′ter the fact′.** a person who knowingly conceals or assists another who has committed a felony. Cf. **principal** (def. 9b). **4.** *Anat.* See **accessory nerve. 5.** Also called **corner accessory.** *Survey.* a natural feature forming part of a monument or forming a reference point from which a monument can be reestablished. —*adj.* **6.** contributing to a general effect; supplementary; subsidiary: *accessory sounds in music.* **7.** *Law.* giving aid as an accessory. **8.** *Petrog.* noting any mineral present in relatively small amounts in a rock and not mentioned in its definition, as zircon in granite. [< ML *accessōri(us).* See ACCESS, -ORY¹] —**ac·ces′so·ri·ly,** *adv.* —**ac·ces′so·ri·ness,** *n.*
—**Syn. 1.** See **addition. 3.** accomplice.

acces′sory nerve′, *Anat.* either one of the eleventh pair of cranial nerves, consisting of motor fibers from the spinal cord that innervate the pharyngeal, trapezius, and sternocleidomastoid muscles, and motor fibers from the brain that join the vagus to innervate the thoracic and abdominal viscera. Also called **spinal accessory nerve.**

ac′cess time′, *Computer Technol.* **1.** the elapsed time from the instant that information is called from a storage unit to the instant it is received. **2.** the elapsed time from the instant that information is ready for storage to the instant it is stored. Cf. **word time.**

Written Played

A B

Acciaccatura (def. 1)
A, Grace note
B, Principal note

ac·ciac·ca·tu·ra (ä chä′kə to͝or′ə; *It.* ät chäk′kä to͞o′rä), *n., pl.* **-tu·ras, -tu·re** (-to͝or′ə, -to͝or′ē; *It.* -to͞o′re). *Music.* **1.** a short appoggiatura. **2.** a short grace note one half step below, and struck at the same time as, a principal note. [< It: lit., a pounding, crushing, equiv. to *acciaccat(o)* (*acciacc-* crush, pound < ? + *-ato* -ATE¹) + *-ura* -URE]

ac·ci·dence (ak′si dəns), *n.* **1.** the rudiments or essentials of a subject. **2.** *Gram.* **a.** the study of inflection and word order as grammatical devices. **b.** the devices so studied. **c.** a property shown by such inflection. [< L *accidentia,* neut. pl. of *accidēns* (prp. of *accidere* to fall, befall). See ACCIDENT]

ac·ci·dent (ak′si dənt), *n.* **1.** an undesirable or unfortunate happening, unintentionally caused and usually resulting in harm, injury, damage, or loss; casualty; mishap: *automobile accidents.* **2.** any event that happens unexpectedly, without a deliberate plan or cause. **3.** chance; fortune; luck: *I was there by accident.* **4.** a nonessential circumstance, quality, or characteristic. **5.** *Philos.* any entity or event contingent upon the existence of something else. **6.** *Geol.* a surface irregularity, usually on a small scale, the reason for which is not apparent. [< L *accident-* (s. of *accidēns* happening, prp. of *accidere* to befall), equiv. to *ac-* AC- + *-cid-,* var. of *-cad-* fall + *-ent-* -ENT]
—**Syn. 1.** mischance, misfortune, misadventure, contingency; disaster. —**Ant. 3.** design, intent.

ac·ci·den·tal (ak′si den′tᵊl), *adj.* **1.** happening by chance or accident; unexpected: *an accidental meeting.* **2.** nonessential; incidental; subsidiary: *accidental benefits.* **3.** *Music.* relating to or indicating sharps, flats, or naturals. —*n.* **4.** a nonessential or subsidiary circumstance, characteristic, or feature. **5.** *Music.* a sign placed before a note indicating a change of its pitch. [< ML *accidentāl(is).* See ACCIDENT, -AL¹] —**ac′ci·den′tal·ly,** *adv.* —**ac′ci·den′tal·ness, ac′ci·den·tal′i·ty,** *n.*
—**Syn. 1.** undesigned, unplanned, contingent. ACCIDENTAL, CASUAL, FORTUITOUS all describe something outside the usual course of events. ACCIDENTAL implies occurring unexpectedly or by chance: *an accidental blow.* CASUAL describes a passing event of slight importance: *a casual reference.* FORTUITOUS is applied to events occurring without known cause: *a fortuitous shower of meteors.* —**Ant. 1.** planned.

ac·ci·den·tal·ism (ak′si den′tᵊliz′əm), *n.* **1.** a system of medicine based on the symptoms of a disease, disregarding its origin or cause. **2.** *Philos.* any theory holding that some events have no causes. [ACCIDENTAL + -ISM] —**ac′ci·den′tal·ist,** *n., adj.*

ac′cident boat′, *Naut.* a boat kept suspended outboard so that it can be lowered immediately if someone falls overboard.

ac′cident insur′ance, insurance providing for loss resulting from accidental bodily injury.

ac′cident prone′, tending to have more accidents or mishaps than the average person.

ac′cident tout′, *Brit. Slang.* See **ambulance chaser.**

ac·ci·die (ak′si dē), *n.* acedia. [ME < ML *accīdia* (alter. of L *acēdia* ACEDIA); r. ME *accide* < OF]

ac·cip·i·ter (ak sip′i tər), *n.* any hawk of the genus *Accipiter,* of the family *Accipitridae,* that has short, rounded wings and a long tail and that feeds chiefly on small mammals and birds. [< L: hawk]

ac·cip·i·tral (ak sip′i trəl), *adj.* accipitrine. [< L *accipitr-* (s. of *accipiter*) ACCIPITER + -AL¹]

ac·cip·i·trine (ak sip′i trin, -trīn′), *adj.* **1.** of, pertaining to, or belonging to the family *Accipitridae,* comprising the hawks, Old World vultures, kites, harriers, and eagles. **2.** raptorial; like or related to the birds of prey. [< L *accipitr-* (see ACCIPITRAL) + -INE¹]

Ac·ci·us (ak′shē əs), *n.* **Lucius,** c170–c90 B.C., Roman poet and prose writer. Also, **Attius.**

ac·claim (ə klām′), *v.t.* **1.** to salute with shouts or sounds of joy and approval; applaud: *to acclaim the conquering heroes.* **2.** to announce or proclaim by acclamation: *to acclaim the new king.* —*v.i.* **3.** to make acclamation; applaud. —*n.* **4.** acclamation (defs. 1, 2). [< L *acclām(āre).* See AC-, CLAIM] —**ac·claim′er,** *n.*

ac·cla·ma·tion (ak′lə mā′shən), *n.* **1.** a loud shout or other demonstration of welcome, good will, or applause. **2.** act of acclaiming. **3.** an oral vote, often unanimous, expressing approval by shouts, hand-clapping, etc., rather than by formal ballot. **4.** *Liturgy.* a brief responsive chant in antiphonal singing. **5.** *Eccles.* response (def. 3a). [< L *acclāmātiōn-* (s. of *acclāmātiō*) a shouting, equiv. to *acclāmāt(us)* (ptp. of *acclāmāre;* see ACCLAIM, -ATE¹) + *-iōn-* -ION] —**ac·clam·a·to·ry** (ə klam′ə tôr′ē, -tōr′ē), *adj.*

ac·cli·mate (ə klī′mit, ak′lə māt′), *v.t., v.i.,* **-mat·ed, -mat·ing.** to accustom or become accustomed to a new climate or environment; adapt. [< F *acclimat(er).* See AC-, CLIMATE] —**ac·cli·mat·a·ble** (ə klī′mi tə bəl), *adj.* —**ac·cli·ma·tion** (ak′lə mā′shən), *n.*

ac·cli·ma·tise (ə klī′mə tīz′), *v.t., v.i.,* **-tised, -tis·ing.** *Chiefly Brit.* acclimatize. —**ac·cli′ma·tis′a·ble,** *adj.* —**ac·cli′ma·ti·sa′tion,** *n.* —**ac·cli′ma·tis′er,** *n.*

ac·cli·ma·tize (ə klī′mə tīz′), *v.t., v.i.,* **-tized, -tiz·ing.** to acclimate. [ACCLIMATE + -IZE] —**ac·cli′ma·tiz′a·ble,** *adj.* —**ac·cli′ma·ti·za′tion,** *n.*

ac·cliv·i·ty (ə kliv′i tē), *n., pl.* **-ties.** an upward slope, as of ground; an ascent (opposed to *declivity*). [< L *acclīvitās,* equiv. to *acclīv(is)* steep (*ac-* AC- + *-clīvis,* alter. of *clīvus* slope) + *-itās* -ITY] —**ac·cliv′i·tous, ac·cli·vous** (ə klī′vəs), *adj.*

ac·co·lade (ak′ə lād′; ak′ə läd′), *n.* **1.** any award, honor, or laudatory notice: *The play received accolades from the press.* **2.** a ceremony used in conferring knighthood, consisting at one time of an embrace but afterward of giving the candidate a light blow upon the shoulder with the flat of a sword. **3.** the blow itself. **4.** *Music.* a brace joining several staves. **5.** *Archit.* **a.** an archivolt or hood molding having more or less the form of an ogee arch. **b.** a decoration having more or less the form of an ogee arch, cut into a lintel or flat arch. [< F < It *accollat(a),* fem. of *accollato* (ptp. of *accollāre* to hug round the neck). See AC-, -COLLAR, -ATE¹] —**ac·co·lad·ed** (ak′ə lā′did, -lä′-), *adj.*

ac·co·lat·ed (ak′ə lā′tid), *adj.* (of portraits on a coin, medal, or escutcheon) overlapping and facing in the same direction; conjoined. [< F *accol(er)* (to) embrace (see ACCOLADE) + -ATE¹ + -ED²]

ac·com·mo·date (ə kom′ə dāt′), *v.,* **-dat·ed, -dat·ing.** —*v.t.* **1.** to do a kindness or a favor to; oblige; *to accommodate a friend.* **2.** to provide suitably; supply (usually fol. by *with*): *to accommodate a friend with money.* **3.** to lend money to: *Can you accommodate him?* **4.** to provide with room and sometimes with food and entertainment. **5.** to make suitable or consistent; adapt: *to accommodate oneself to circumstances.* **6.** to bring into harmony; adjust; reconcile: *to accommodate differences.* **7.** to furnish with accommodations. **8.** to have or make room for: *Will this elevator accommodate 10 people?* —*v.i.* **9.** to become or be conformable; act conformably; agree. [< L *accommodāt(us)* adjusted (ptp. of *accommodāre*), equiv. to *ac-* AC- + *commod(us)* fitting, suitable (*com-* COM- + *modus* measure, manner) + *-ātus* -ATE¹] —**ac·com′mo·da·ble,** *adj.* —**ac·com′mo·da′tor,** *n.*
—**Syn. 1.** serve, aid, assist, help, abet. See **oblige. 5.** fit, suit. **6.** compose, harmonize. **8.** See **contain.** —**Ant. 1.** inconvenience.

ac·com·mo·dat·ing (ə kom′ə dā′ting), *adj.* easy to deal with; eager to help or please; obliging. [ACCOMMODATE + -ING²] —**ac·com′mo·dat′ing·ly,** *adv.*

ac·com·mo·da·tion (ə kom′ə dā′shən), *n.* **1.** the act of accommodating; state or process of being accommodated; adaptation. **2.** adjustment of differences; reconciliation. **3.** *Sociol.* a process of mutual adaptation between persons or groups, usually achieved by eliminating or reducing hostility, as by compromise, arbitration, etc. **4.** anything that supplies a need, want, convenience, etc. **5.** Usually, **accommodations. a.** lodging. **b.** food and lodging. **c.** a seat, berth, or other facilities for a passenger on a train, plane, etc. **6.** readiness to aid others; obligingness. **7.** a loan. **8.** *Ophthalm.* the automatic adjustment by which the eye adapts itself to distinct vision at different distances. **9.** an accommodation bill, draft, note, etc. [< L *accommodātiōn-* (s. of *accommodātiō*) adjustment. See ACCOMMODATE, -ION] —**ac·com′mo·da′tion·al,** *adj.*

accommoda′tion bill′, a bill, draft, or note made, drawn, accepted, or endorsed by one person for another without consideration, to enable the second person to obtain credit or raise money.

accommoda′tion lad′der, a portable flight of steps suspended at the side of a vessel to give access to and from boats, a wharf, etc.

accommoda′tion line′, insurance which, by itself, would not be acceptable to an insurer but is written in connection with other policies as an accommodation to an agent or broker.

accommoda′tion train′, a local train.

ac·com·mo·da·tive (ə kom′ə dā′tiv), *adj.* tending to accommodate; adaptive. [ACCOMMODATE + -IVE] —**ac·com′mo·da′tive·ness,** *n.*

ac·com·pa·ni·ment (ə kum′pə ni mənt, ə kump′ni-), *n.* **1.** something incidental or added for ornament, symmetry, etc. **2.** a portion of the musical text designed to serve as background and support for more important parts. [ACCOMPANY + -MENT]

ac·com·pa·nist (ə kum′pə nist, ə kump′nist), *n. Music.* a person who plays an accompaniment. Also, **ac·companyist** [ACCOMPAN(Y) + -IST]

ac·com·pa·ny (ə kum′pə nē), *v.t.,* **-nied, -ny·ing. 1.** to go along or in company with; join in action: *to accompany a friend on a walk.* **2.** to be or exist in company with: *Thunder accompanies lightning.* **3.** to put in company with; cause to be or go along; associate (usually fol. by *with*): *He accompanied his speech with gestures.* **4.** *Music.* to play or sing an accompaniment to: *Anne Murphy will accompany me on the piano.* [late ME *accompanye* < MF *accompagni(er).* See AC-, COMPANY] —**ac·com′pa·ni·er,** *n.*
—**Syn. 1.** ACCOMPANY, ATTEND, CONVOY, ESCORT mean to go along with someone (or something). To ACCOMPANY is to go along as an associate on equal terms: *to accompany a friend on a shopping trip.* ATTEND implies going along with, usually to render service or perform duties: *to attend one's employer on a business trip.* To CONVOY is to accompany (esp. ships) with an armed guard for protection: *to convoy a fleet of merchant vessels.* To ESCORT is to accompany in order to protect, guard, honor, or show courtesy: *to escort a visiting dignitary.*

ac·com·pa·ny·ist (ə kum′pə nē ist), *n.* accompanist.

ac·com·plice (ə kom′plis), *n.* a person who helps another in a crime or wrongdoing, often as a subordinate. [AC- + late ME *complice* < MF < ML *complici-* (s. of *complex*) partner; see COMPLEX]

ac·com·plish (ə kom′plish), *v.t.* **1.** to bring to its goal or conclusion; carry out; perform; finish: *to accomplish one's mission.* **2.** to complete (a distance or period of time). [late ME, earlier *accomplice* < MF *accompliss-* (s. of *acomplir*), equiv. to *a-* AC- + L *complē(re)* (to) fill up (*com-* COM- + *plere* to FILL) + *-sc-* -ISH²] —**ac·com′plish·a·ble,** *adj.* —**ac·com′plish·er,** *n.*
—**Syn. 1.** complete, fulfill; execute, effect. See **do**¹.

ac·com·plished (ə kom′plisht), *adj.* **1.** completed; effected: *an accomplished fact.* **2.** perfected; expert: *an accomplished scholar.* **3.** having all the social graces, manners, and other attainments of polite society. [ACCOMPLISH + -ED²]

ac·com·plish·ment (ə kom′plish mənt), *n.* **1.** the act or an instance of carrying into effect; fulfillment: *the accomplishment of our desires.* **2.** anything accomplished; achievement: *the accomplishments of scientists.* **3.** Often, **accomplishments. a.** a grace, skill, or knowledge expected in polite society. **b.** any acquired ability or knowledge. [late ME; see ACCOMPLISH, -MENT. Cf. F *accomplissement*]
—**Syn. 1.** completion, effecting, execution. **2.** consummation. **3.** acquisition, proficiency. —**Ant. 1.** failure.

ac·compt (ə kount′), *n., v.i., v.t. Archaic.* account.

ac·cord (ə kôrd′), *v.i.* **1.** to be in agreement or harmony; agree. —*v.t.* **2.** to make to agree or correspond; adapt. **3.** to grant; bestow: *to accord due praise.* **4.** *Archaic.* to settle; reconcile. —*n.* **5.** proper relationship or proportion; harmony. **6.** a harmonious union of sounds. **7.** consent or concurrence of opinions or wills; agreement. **8.** an international agreement; settlement of questions outstanding among nations. **9. of one's own accord,** voluntarily: *We signed up for the protest march of our own accord.* [late OE *ācordian* < VL **accordāre,* equiv. to L *ac-* AC- + *cord-* heart, mind + *-āre* inf. suffix (translated *-ian* in OE)] —**ac·cord′a·ble,** *adj.* —**ac·cord′er,** *n.*
—**Syn. 1.** harmonize, concur. See **correspond. 2.** reconcile. —**Ant. 1.** conflict.

ac·cord·ance (ə kôr′dᵊns), *n.* **1.** agreement; conformity: *in accordance with the rules.* **2.** act of according or granting: *the accordance of all rights and privileges.* [ME *acordance* < OF. See ACCORD, -ANCE]

ac·cord·ant (ə kôr′dᵊnt), *adj.* agreeing; comformable. [ME *acordant* < OF. See ACCORD, -ANT] —**ac·cord′ant·ly,** *adv.*

ac·cor·da·tu·ra (ə kôr′də to͝or′ə; *It.* äk kôr′dä to͞o′rä), *n., pl.* **-tu·ras,** *It.* **-tu·re** (-to͞o′re). *Music.* the notes to which a stringed instrument is tuned. [< It: lit., a tuning, equiv. to *accordat(o)* (ptp. of *accordare*) < VL **accordāre* (see ACCORD) + *-ura* -URE]

ac·cord·ing (ə kôr′ding), *adj.* **1.** agreeing. **2.** *Informal.* depending: *It's all according what you want to do.* Cf. **according as, according to.** [ME; see ACCORD, -ING²]

accord′ing as′, 1. to the extent that; proportionately as. **2.** on the condition that; if: *According as I have the money, I'll stay.*

ac·cord·ing·ly (ə kôr′ding lē), *adv.* **1.** in accordance; correspondingly. **2.** therefore; so; in due course. [ME; see ACCORDING, -LY]
—**Syn. 1, 2.** consequently, hence, thus. See **therefore.**

accord′ing to′, 1. in accordance or accord with: *according to his judgment.* **2.** consistent with; in conformity with: *to pay according to experience.* **3.** on the authority of; as stated by: *According to her, they have gone.* **4.** in proportion to: *He'll be charged according to his ability to pay.* **5.** contingent on: *According to the number of winners, the judges will award duplicate prizes.*

Accordion

ac·cor·di·on (ə kôr′dē ən), *n. Music.* **1.** Also called **piano accordion.** a portable wind instrument having a large bellows for forcing air through small metal reeds, a keyboard for the right hand, and buttons for sounding single bass notes or chords for the left hand. **2.** a similar instrument having single-note buttons instead of a keyboard. —*adj.* **3.** having folds like the bellows of an accordion: *accordion pleat; accordion panel.* [ACCORD + -ION, modeled on *clarion*] —**ac·cor′di·on·ist,** *n.*

ac·cost (ə kôst′, ə kost′), *v.t.* **1.** to approach, esp. with a greeting or remark. **2.** to confront boldly: *The beggar accosted me for money.* **3.** (of prostitutes, procurers, etc.) to solicit for immoral sexual purposes. —*n.* **4.** a greeting. [< LL *accost(āre)* (to) be or put side by side. See AC-, COAST] —**ac·cost′a·ble,** *adj.*

ac·cost·ed (ə kô′stid, ə kos′tid), *adj. Heraldry.* (of animals) represented as side by side: *two dolphins accosted.* [ACCOST + -ED²]

ac·couche·ment (A ko͞osh mäN′; *Eng.* ə ko͞osh′mänt, -mənt), *n., pl.* **-ments** (-mäN′; *Eng.* -mänts, -mənts). *French.* period of confinement in childbirth. [lit., a going to bed]

ac·cou·cheur (A ko͞o shœr′), *n., pl.* **-cheurs** (-shœr′). *French.* a man who assists during childbirth; obstetrician. [lit., he who is present at the bedside]

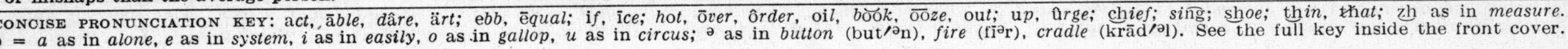

ac·cou·cheuse (A kōō shœz′), *n., pl.* **-cheuses** (-shœz′). *French.* a midwife. [lit., she who is present at the bedside]

ac·count (ə kount′), *n.* **1.** a verbal or written description of particular transactions or events; narrative: *an account of the meetings; an account of the trip.* **2.** an explanatory statement of conduct, as to a superior. **3.** a statement of reasons, causes, etc., explaining some event. **4.** reason; basis; consideration: *On this account I'm refusing your offer.* **5.** importance; worth; value; consequence: *things of no account.* **6.** estimation; judgment: *In his account it was an excellent piece of work.* **7.** an amount of money deposited with a bank, as in a checking or savings account: *My account is now with Third National.* **8.** an accommodation or service extended by a business establishment to a customer and usually permitting the charging of purchases, the returning for credit of unsatisfactory merchandise, etc.; charge account: *Do you have an account at this store? My account with the men's club is past due.* **9.** a statement of pecuniary transactions. **10.** *Bookkeeping.* **a.** a formal record of the debits and credits relating to the person named, or caption placed, at the head of the ledger account. **b.** a balance of a specified period's receipts and expenditures. **11.** *Com.* **a.** a business relation in which credit is used. **b.** any customer or client. **c.** Also called **advertising account.** the business assigned to an advertising agency by a client: *The toothpaste account was awarded to a new agency last year.* **12. call to account,** to hold accountable; blame; reprimand: *Call them to account for having endangered their lives.* **13. give a good (bad, etc.) account of,** to conduct oneself in a certain manner: *She gave a good account of herself in the tennis tournament.* **14. on account of, a.** by reason of; because of. **b.** for the sake of: *She saw it through on account of me.* **15. on all accounts,** in any case; under any circumstances. Also, **at all accounts. 16. on no account,** under no circumstances; absolutely not: *On no account should you buy that painting without having it appraised.* **17. on (someone's) account,** in the interest of a person; for the sake of someone: *She left her native land on her husband's account.* **18. take account of,** to make allowance for; consider: *One must take account of the difficult circumstances. Taking account of the high overhead, the price is not excessive.* Also, **take into account. 19. turn to account,** to derive profit or use from; turn to advantage: *She has turned her misfortune to account.* —*v.i.* **20.** to give an explanation (usually fol. by *for*): *to account for the accident.* **21.** to answer concerning one's conduct, duties, etc. (usually fol. by *for*): *to account for shortages.* **22.** to provide a report on money received, kept, and spent. **23.** to cause (usually fol. by *for*): *The humidity accounts for the discomfort. His reckless driving accounted for the accident.* —*v.t.* **24.** to count; consider as: *I account myself well paid.* **25.** to assign or impute (usually fol. by *to*): *the many virtues accounted to him.* [ME *acunt(en)* < OF *acunt(er).* See AC-, COUNT[1]]
—**Syn. 1.** report, chronicle. See **narrative. 2.** justification. **5, 6.** consideration.

ac·count·a·ble (ə koun′tə bəl), *adj.* **1.** subject to having to report, explain, or justify; responsible; answerable. **2.** that can be explained; explicable. [ACCOUNT + -ABLE] —**ac·count′a·bil′i·ty, ac·count′a·ble·ness,** *n.* —**ac·count′a·bly,** *adv.*

ac·count·an·cy (ə koun′tᵊn sē), *n.* the art or practice of an accountant. [ACCOUNTAN(T) + -CY]

ac·count·ant (ə koun′tᵊnt), *n.* a person whose profession is inspecting and auditing personal or commercial accounts. [ACCOUNT + -ANT; r. late ME *accomptant* < MF; OF *acuntant,* prp. of *acunter* to ACCOUNT] —**ac·count′ant·ship′,** *n.*

account′ book′, a book in which personal or commercial accounts are recorded; ledger.

account′ cur′rent, *pl.* **ac·counts cur·rent. 1.** a personal account providing for periodic settlements, esp. such an account that is not overdue; current account. **2.** the periodic statement or transcript of such an account.

account′ exec′utive, (in an advertising agency or other service business) the manager of a client's account.

ac·count·ing (ə koun′ting), *n.* the theory and system of setting up, maintaining, and auditing the books of a firm; art of analyzing the financial position and operating results of a business house from a study of its sales, purchases, overhead, etc. (distinguished from *bookkeeping*). [ME; see ACCOUNT, -ING[1]]

account′ing pe′riod, a regular period of time, as a month or a year, for which an operative statement is drawn up. Also called **fiscal period.**

account′ pay′able, *pl.* **accounts payable.** a liability to a creditor, carried on open account, usually for purchases of goods and services.

account′ receiv′able, *pl.* **accounts receivable.** a claim against a debtor, carried on open account, usually limited to debts due from the sale of goods and services.

ac·cou·ple·ment (ə kup′əl mənt), *n.* **1.** act of coupling. **2.** that which couples, esp. a tie or brace in building. **3.** *Archit.* the coupling of columns or pilasters. [late ME, equiv. to *accouple* (< MF *accopler;* see AC-, COUPLE) + *-ment* -MENT]

ac·cou·ter (ə kōō′tər), *v.t.* to equip or outfit, esp. with military accouterments. Also, *esp. Brit.,* **accoutre.** [earlier *accou(s)tre* < MF *accoustre(r)* (*ac-* AC- + *coustre* attendant who robes clergy in vestry)]

ac·cou·ter·ment (ə kōō′tər mənt), *n.* **1.** equipage; trappings. **2.** the equipment, excluding arms and clothing, of a soldier. Also, *esp. Brit.,* **ac·cou·tre·ment** (ə kōō′tər mənt, -trə-). [< MF *accou(s)trement.* See ACCOUTER, -MENT]

ac·cou·tre (ə kōō′tər), *v.t.,* **-tred, -tring.** *Chiefly Brit.* accouter.

ac·cra (ak′rə, ə krä′), *n.* the wood of a sapele. [after *Accra,* a people of Ghana whence it comes]

Ac·cra (ak′rə, ə krä′), *n.* a seaport in and the capital of Ghana, on the Gulf of Guinea. 388,231 (1960). Also, **Akkra.**

accrd. int., accrued interest.

ac·cred·it (ə kred′it), *v.t.* **1.** to ascribe or attribute to (usually fol. by *with*): *He was accredited with having said it.* **2.** to attribute; consider as belonging: *a discovery accredited to Edison.* **3.** to provide or send with credentials: *to accredit an envoy.* **4.** to certify (a school, college, or the like) as meeting all formal official requirements of academic excellence, curriculum, facilities, etc. **5.** to make authoritative, creditable, or reputable; sanction. **6.** to believe. [earlier *acredit* < MF *acredit(er).* See AC-, CREDIT] —**ac·cred′i·ta′tion, ac·cred′it·ment,** *n.*

ac·cres·cent (ə kres′ənt), *adj.* increasing; growing, as floral parts that increase in size after flowering has occurred. [< L *accrēscent-* (s. of *accrēscēns,* prp. of *accrēscere* to grow). See AC-, CRESCENT]

ac·crete (ə krēt′), *v.,* **-cret·ed, -cret·ing,** *adj.* —*v.i.* **1.** to grow together; adhere (usually fol. by *to*). —*v.t.* **2.** to add, as by growth. —*adj.* **3.** *Bot.* grown together. [back formation from ACCRETION]

ac·cre·tion (ə krē′shən), *n.* **1.** an increase by natural growth or by gradual external addition; growth in size or extent. **2.** the result of this process. **3.** an extraneous addition: *The last part of the legend is a later accretion.* **4.** the growing together of separate parts into a single whole. **5.** *Law.* increase of property by gradual natural additions, as of land by alluvion. [< L *accrētiōn-* (s. of *accrētiō*), equiv. to *accrēt(us)* increased, ptp. of *accrēscere* to grow (*ac-* AC- + *crē-* grow + *-tus* ptp. suffix) + *-iōn-* -ION] —**ac·cre′tive, ac·cre′tion·ar·y,** *adj.*

ac·croach (ə krōch′), *v.t.* to assume to oneself without right or authority; usurp. [ME *acroche* < MF *acroch(i)e(r),* from phrase *a croc* on (the) hook, equiv. to *a* (< L *ad* to) + *croc* < Gmc; see CROOK[1]] —**ac·croach′ment,** *n.*

ac·croi′des gum′ (ə kroi′dēz, ak roi′-). See **acaroid resin.** [alter. of NL *acaroides.* See ACAROID]

ac·cru·al (ə krōō′əl), *n.* **1.** the act or process of accruing. **2.** something accrued; accretion. [ACCRUE + -AL[2]]

accru′al ba′sis, a method of recording income and expenses, in which each item is reported as earned or incurred, without regard to when actual payments are received or made. Cf. **cash basis.**

ac·crue (ə krōō′), *v.i.,* **-crued, -cru·ing. 1.** to happen or result as a natural growth, addition, etc. **2.** to be added as a matter of periodic gain or advantage, as interest on money. **3.** *Law.* to become a present and enforceable right or demand. [late ME *acrewe* < MF *acreue* growth. See AC-, CREW[1]] —**ac·crue′ment,** *n.*

accrued′ div′idend, accumulated unpaid dividend on preferred stock.

accrued′ in′terest, interest accumulated at a given time but not yet due or paid.

accrued′ liabil′ity, the amount of liability accumulated at a given time but not yet paid.

acct., account.

ac·cul·tur·ate (ə kul′chə rāt′), *v.t., v.i.,* **-at·ed, -at·ing.** to alter by acculturation. [back formation from ACCULTURATION] —**ac·cul′tur·a′tive,** *adj.*

ac·cul·tur·a·tion (ə kul′chə rā′shən), *n.* **1.** *Sociol.* the process of adopting the cultural traits or social patterns of another group. **2.** the result of this process. [AC- + CULTURE + -ATION] —**ac·cul′tur·a′tion·al,** *adj.*

ac·cul·tur·a·tion·ist (ə kul′chə rā′shə nist), *n.* a person who studies the process of acculturation. [ACCULTURATION + -IST]

ac·cul·tur·ize (ə kul′chə rīz′), *v.t.,* **-ized, -iz·ing.** to cause (a nation, tribe, or other ethnic group) to adopt the culture of another people: *A series of invasions from the North had slowly acculturized his people.* [ACCULTUR(ATION) + -IZE]

accum., accumulative.

ac·cum·bent (ə kum′bənt), *adj.* **1.** reclining: *accumbent posture.* **2.** *Bot.* lying against something. [< L *accumbent-* (s. of *accumbēns,* prp. of *accumbere*), equiv. to *ac-* AC- + *cumb-* (nasalized var. of *cub-* lie, recline; see COVEY) + *-ent-* -ENT] —**ac·cum′ben·cy,** *n.*

ac·cu·mu·late (ə kyōō′myə lāt′), *v.,* **-lat·ed, -lat·ing.** —*v.t.* **1.** to heap up; gather, as into a mass; collect: *to accumulate wealth.* —*v.i.* **2.** to grow into a heap or mass; form an increasing quantity: *Public evils accumulate.* [< L *accumulāt(us)* heaped up (ptp. of *accumulāre*), equiv. to *ac-* AC- + *cumul(us)* heap + *-ātus* -ATE[1]] —**ac·cu′mu·la·ble,** *adj.*

ac·cu·mu·la·tion (ə kyōō′myə lā′shən), *n.* **1.** act or state of accumulating; state of being accumulated. **2.** that which is accumulated; an accumulated amount, number, or mass. **3.** growth by continuous additions, as of interest to principal. [< L *accumulātiōn-* (s. of *accumulātiō*). See ACCUMULATE, -ION]

accumula′tion point′, *Math.* a point such that every neighborhood of the point contains at least one point in a given set other than the given point. Also called **cluster point, limit point, weak accumulation point.** Cf. **derived set, strong accumulation point.**

ac·cu·mu·la·tive (ə kyōō′myə lā′tiv, -lə tiv), *adj.* tending to or arising from accumulation; cumulative. [ACCUMULATE + -IVE] —**ac·cu′mu·la′tive·ly,** *adv.* —**ac·cu′mu·la′tive·ness,** *n.*

ac·cu·mu·la·tor (ə kyōō′myə lā′tər), *n.* **1.** one who or that which accumulates. **2.** a register or electric device on an arithmetic machine, as an adding machine, cash register, digital computer, etc., that receives a number and produces and stores the results of arithmetic operations of the given number with other numbers. **3.** *Brit.* a storage battery or storage cell. **4.** an apparatus which stores fluid at approximately the working pressure of the hydraulic or pneumatic system in which it will be employed, so that a supply of fluid is always immediately available to the system. **5.** *Mach.* **a.** (in a boiler) a vessel for storing hot fluid, ready to flash into steam. **b.** (in a hydraulic system) a vessel in which air is trapped and compressed by the liquid, thus storing energy to supply liquid under pressure when the demand of the system is greater than the pump can momentarily supply. [< L *accumulātor.* See ACCUMULATE, -OR[2]]

ac·cu·ra·cy (ak′yər ə sē), *n., pl.* **-cies. 1.** condition or quality of being true, correct, or exact; freedom from error or defect; precision or exactness; correctness. **2.** *Chem., Physics.* the extent to which a given measurement agrees with the standard value for that measurement. Cf. **precision** (def. 6). **3.** *Math.* the degree of correctness of a quantity, expression, etc. Cf. **precision** (def. 5). [ACCUR(ATE) + -ACY]

ac·cu·rate (ak′yər it), *adj.* **1.** conforming to truth; consistent with a standard, rule, or model; free from error or defect; precise; exact; correct. **2.** careful or meticulous; not making mistakes: *an accurate typist.* [< L *accūrāt(us)* carefully prepared (ptp. of *accūrāre*), equiv. to *ac-* AC- + *cūr(a)* care + *-ātus* -ATE[1]] —**ac′cu·rate·ly,** *adv.* —**ac′cu·rate·ness,** *n.*
—**Syn. 1.** true, unerring. See **correct.**

ac·curs·ed (ə kûr′sid, ə kûrst′), *adj.* **1.** subject to a curse; ruined. **2.** worthy of curses; detestable. Also, **ac·curst** (ə kûrst′). [ME *acursed,* OE *ācursod,* ptp. of *ācursian.* See A-[3], CURSE] —**ac·curs·ed·ly** (ə kûr′sid lē), *adv.* —**ac·curs′ed·ness,** *n.*

ac·cu·sa·tion (ak′yŏŏ zā′shən), *n.* **1.** a charge of wrongdoing; imputation of guilt or blame. **2.** the specific offense charged: *the accusation is murder.* **3.** the act of accusing or charging. Also, **ac·cus·al** (ə kyōō′zəl). [late ME *accusacion* < L *accūsātiōn-* (s. of *accūsātiō*), equiv. to *accūsāt(us)* (ptp.) called to account (see ACCUSE, -ATE[1]) + *-iōn-* -ION]

ac·cu·sa·ti·val (ə kyōō′zə tī′vəl), *adj.* pertaining to the accusative case. [ACCUSATIVE + -AL[1]]

ac·cu·sa·tive (ə kyōō′zə tiv), *Gram.* —*adj.* **1.** (in certain inflected languages, as Latin, Greek, Russian) noting a case whose distinctive function is to indicate the direct object of a verb. **2.** similar to such a case form in function or meaning. **3.** accusatory. —*n.* **4.** the accusative case. **5.** a word in the accusative case. **6.** a form or construction of similar meaning. [< L *accūsātīv(us),* equiv. to *ac-* AC- + *cūsātīvus,* var. of *causātīvus;* see CAUSATIVE (*accūsātīvus* is a loan-translation of Gk *aitiatikḗ,* in the sense of causing, effecting)] —**ac·cu′sa·tive·ly,** *adv.*

ac·cu·sa·to·ri·al (ə kyōō′zə tôr′ē əl, -tôr′-), *adj.* pertaining to an accuser. [ACCUSATORY + -AL[1]] —**ac·cu′sa·to′ri·al·ly,** *adv.*

ac·cu·sa·to·ry (ə kyōō′zə tôr′ē, -tōr′ē), *adj.* containing an accusation; accusing: *He looked at the jury with an accusatory expression.* Also, **accusative.** [< L *accūsātōri(us),* equiv. to *accūsāt(us)* (ptp. of *accūsāre* to ACCUSE) + *-ōrius* -ORY[1]]

ac·cuse (ə kyōōz′), *v.,* **-cused, -cus·ing.** —*v.t.* **1.** to bring a charge against; charge with the fault, offense, or crime (usually fol. by *of*): *He accused him of murder.* **2.** to blame. —*v.i.* **3.** to make an accusation. [ME *ac(c)use* < OF *acuse(r)* < L *accūsār(e)* (to) call to account (*ac-* AC- + *cūs-,* var. of *caus-;* see CAUSE)] —**ac·cus′a·ble,** *adj.* —**ac·cus′a·bly,** *adv.* —**ac·cus′er, ac·cus′ant,** *n.* —**ac·cus′ing·ly,** *adv.*
—**Syn. 1.** arraign, indict; incriminate, impeach. —**Ant. 1, 2.** exonerate.

ac·cused (ə kyōōzd′), *adj.* **1.** charged with a crime, fault, etc.: *the accused boy.* —*n.* **2.** the defendant or defendants in a court of law; the person or persons charged with a crime, offense, etc. [ACCUSE + -ED[2]]

ac·cus·tom (ə kus′təm), *v.t.* to familiarize by custom or use; habituate: *to accustom oneself to cold weather.* [late ME < MF *acoustume(r).* See AC-, CUSTOM]

ac·cus·tomed (ə kus′təmd), *adj.* **1.** customary; habitual: *in their accustomed manner.* **2.** in the habit of: *He is accustomed to staying up late.* [ME; see ACCUSTOM, -ED[2]] —**ac·cus′tomed·ly,** *adv.* —**ac·cus′tomed·ness,** *n.*
—**Syn. 1.** usual, characteristic. **2.** used (to). —**Ant. 2.** unused (to).

AC/DC (ā′sē′dē′sē), *adj.* *Slang.* tending to respond sexually to both men and women; bisexual.

AC/DC, *Elect.* alternating current or direct current. Also, **A.C./D.C., ac/dc, a-c/d-c, a.c.-d.c.**

ace (ās), *n., v.,* **aced, ac·ing,** *adj.* —*n.* **1.** a single spot or mark on a card or die. **2.** (in tennis, badminton, handball, etc.) **a.** Also called **service ace.** a placement made on a service. **b.** any placement. **c.** a serve which the opponent fails to touch. **d.** the point thus scored. **3.** a playing card or die marked with a single spot: *He dealt me four aces in the first hand.* **4.** a very skilled person; expert; adept: *an ace at tap dancing.* **5.** a fighter pilot credited with destroying a prescribed number or more of enemy aircraft, usually five, in flight. **6.** *Slang.* a one-dollar bill. **7.** *Golf.* **a.** Also called **hole in one.** a shot in which the ball is driven from the tee into the hole in one stroke: *He hit a 385-yard ace on the first hole.* **b.** a score of one stroke made on such a shot: *to card an ace.* **8.** *Rare.* a very small quantity, amount, or degree; a particle: *not worth an ace.* **9. easy aces,** *Auction Bridge.* aces equally divided between opponents. **10. have** or **keep an ace up one's sleeve,** to be in possession of the most important information, argument, etc. **11. within an ace of,** within a narrow margin of; close to: *He came within an ace of winning.* —*v.t.* **12.** (in tennis, badminton, handball, etc.) to win a point against (one's opponent) by an ace. **13.** *Golf.* to make an ace on (a hole). —*adj.* **14.** excellent; first in quality; outstanding. [ME *as, aas* < OF *as* < L *as* the whole, a unit, perh. < dial. Gk *ás* one (Gk *heîs*)]

Ace (ās), *n.* a boy's given name.

-acea, *Zool.* a learned borrowing from Latin, used in the formation of names of classes and orders: *Crustacea.* [< L, neut. pl. of *-āceus.* See -ACEOUS]

-aceae, *Bot.* a learned borrowing from Latin, used in the formation of names of families: *Rosaceae.* [< L, fem. pl. of *-āceus.* See -ACEOUS]

a·ce·di·a (ə sē′dē ə), *n.* **1.** sloth. Cf. **deadly sins. 2.** laziness or indifference in religious matters. [< LL < Gk *akḗdeia,* equiv. to *akēdé(s)* (*a-* A-[6] + *-kēdes,* var. of *kêdos* care, anxiety) + *-ia* -IA]

ace′ in the hole′, an advantage or a resource kept back until the proper opportunity presents itself: *His strength in a crisis is an ace in the hole.* [from the strategic advantage of having an ace as a hole card in five-card stud]

A·cel·da·ma (ə sel′də mə), *n.* **1.** the place near Jerusalem purchased with the bribe Judas took for betraying Jesus. Acts 1:18, 19. **2.** any place of slaughter and bloodshed. Also, **Akeldama.** [< L < Gk *Akeldamá* < Aram *ḥăqēl dəmā* field of blood]

a·ce·nes·the·sia (ā′sē nis thē′zhə), *n.* *Psychiatry.* loss of the physical awareness of one's body. Also, **acoenaesthesia.** [A-[6] + CENESTHESIA]

a·cen·tric (ā sen′trik), *adj.* not centered; having no center. [A-[6] + CENTRIC]

-aceous, a suffix of adjectives, used in scientific terminology and in the formation of adjectives to stems in **-acea** and **-aceae:** *cretaceous; herbaceous.* [< L *-āceus* of the nature of]

a·ceph·a·lous (ā sef′ə ləs), *adj.* **1.** headless; lacking a distinct head. **2.** without a leader or ruler. [A-[6] + -CEPHALOUS]

ace′ point′, the first point in backgammon.

a·ce·quia (ə sā′kyə; *Sp.* ä se′kyä), *n., pl.* **-quias** (-kyəz; *Sp.* -kyäs). *Southwestern U.S.* an irrigation ditch. [< Sp < Ar *as sāqiyah* the irrigating stream]

ac·er·ate (as′ə rāt′, -ər it), *adj.* acerose[1]. [< L *ācer* sharp + -ATE[1]]

a·cerb (ə sûrb′), *adj.* **1.** sour or astringent in taste. **2.** harsh or severe, as of temper or expression. Also, **a·cer·bic** (ə sûr′bik). [< L *acerb(us)* bitter, morose]

A·cer·bas (ə sûr′bəs), *n.* (in the *Aeneid*) Sychaeus.

ac·er·bate (*v.* as′ər bāt′; *adj.* ə sûr′bit), *v.*, **-bat·ed, -bat·ing,** *adj.* —*v.t.* **1.** to make sour or bitter. **2.** to exasperate. —*adj.* **3.** embittered. [< L *acerbāt(us)* (ptp. of *acerbāre*). See ACERB, -ATE[1]]

a·cer·bi·ty (ə sûr′bi tē), *n.* **1.** sourness, with roughness or astringency of taste. **2.** harshness or severity, as of temper or expression. [< L *acerbitās.* See ACERB, -ITY]

ac·er·dol (as′ər dōl′, -dôl′, -dol′), *n. Chem.* See **calcium permanganate.** [*acerd(ese),* earlier name of manganite (< Gk *akerdḗs* unprofitable, equiv. to *a-* A-[6] + *kérd(os)* profit, value) + -OL[1]]

ac·er·ose[1] (as′ə rōs′), *adj. Bot.* needle-shaped, as the leaves of the pine. Also, **acerate, acerous.** [special sense of ACEROSE[2], by confusion of *acer-* with L *acus* needle]

ac·er·ose[2] (as′ə rōs′), *adj.* **1.** resembling chaff. **2.** mixed with chaff. [< L *acerōs(us),* equiv. to *acer-* (s. of *acus*) chaff + *-ōsus* -OSE[1]]

ac·er·ous[1] (as′ər əs), *adj. Bot.* acerose[1].

a·ce·rous[2] (ā sēr′əs), *adj. Zool.* **1.** having no antennae. **2.** having no horns. [< Gk *akerōs,* equiv. to *a-* A-[6] + *kér(as)* horn + *-os* adj. suffix]

a·cer·vate (ə sûr′vit, -vāt), *adj. Bot.* heaped; growing in heaps, or in closely compacted clusters. [< L *acervāt(us)* heaped up (ptp. of *acervāre*), equiv. to *acerv(us)* heap + *-ātus* -ATE[1]] —**a·cer′vate·ly,** *adv.*

a·cer·vu·lus (ə sûr′vyə ləs), *n., pl.* **-li** (-lī′). *Bot.* (in certain fungi) an asexual fructification consisting of a mat of hyphae that give rise to short-stalked conidiophores. [< L *acerv(us)* heap + *-ulus* dim. suffix]

a·ces·cent (ə ses′ənt), *adj.* turning sour; slightly sour; acidulous. [< L *acēscent-* (s. of *acēscēns* souring, prp. of *acēscere*), equiv. to *ac-* sharp + *-ēscent-* -ESCENT] —**a·ces′cence, a·ces′cen·cy,** *n.*

A·ces·i·us (ə ses′ē əs), *n. Class. Myth.* an epithet of Apollo, meaning "healer."

a·ces·o·dyne (ə ses′ə dīn′), *adj.* mitigating pain; anodyne. [< Gk *akesṓdyn(os),* equiv. to *akes-* (var. s. of *akeîsthai* to heal) + *ōdyn-* (s. of *odýnē* pain) + *-os* adj. suffix] —**ac·e·sod·y·nous** (as′i sod′ᵊnəs), *adj.*

A·ces·sa·me·nus (ə ses′ə mē′nəs), *n.* (in the *Iliad*) a Thracian king.

a·ces·to·ma (as′i stō′mə), *n.* the granulated tissue that forms over a wound and later contracts into scar tissue. [< NL < Gk *akes-* (see ACESODYNE) + *tomḗ* -TOME]

acet-, var. of **aceto-,** esp. before a vowel.

ac·e·tab·u·li·form (as′i tab′yə lə fôrm′), *adj. Bot.* saucer-shaped, as the fructifications of certain lichens. [< NL; see ACETABULUM, -I-, -FORM]

ac·e·tab·u·lum (as′i tab′yə ləm), *n., pl.* **-la** (-lə). **1.** *Anat.* the socket in the hipbone which receives the head of the thighbone. See illus. under **pelvis. 2.** *Zool.* any of the suction appendages of a leech, octopus, etc. [< L: vinegar cup, equiv. to *acēt(um)* vinegar + *-abulum* suffix denoting instrument or vessel] —**ac′e·tab′u·lar,** *adj.*

ac·e·tal (as′i tal′), *n. Chem.* **1.** Also called **ethylidene diethyl ether, diethylacetal.** a colorless, volatile, sparingly water-soluble liquid, $CH_3CH(OC_2H_5)_2$, having a nutlike aftertaste, obtained from acetaldehyde and ethyl alcohol: used chiefly as a solvent, in perfumery, in organic synthesis, and in medicine as a hypnotic. **2.** any of a class of compounds of aldehydes with alcohols. [ACET- + -AL[3]]

ac·et·al·de·hyde (as′i tal′də hīd′), *n. Chem.* a volatile, colorless, water-soluble liquid, CH_3CHO, having a pungent, fruitlike odor: used chiefly in the silvering of mirrors and in organic synthesis. [ACET- + ALDEHYDE]

ac·e·tal·dol (as′i tal′dōl, -dôl, -dol), *n. Chem.* aldol (def. 1). [ACETALD(EHYDE) + -OL[1]]

ac′etal phos′phatide, *Biochem.* plasmalogen.

ac·et·am·ide (as′i tam′īd, -id; ə set′ə mīd′, -mid), *n. Chem.* a white, water-soluble, crystalline solid, CH_3CONH_2, the amide of acetic acid: used chiefly in organic synthesis. Also, **ac·et·am·id** (as′i tam′id, ə set′ə mid). Also called **acetic acid amide, ethanamide.** [ACET- + AMIDE]

ac·et·an·i·lide (as′i tan′ᵊlīd′, -ᵊlid), *n. Chem., Pharm.* a white, crystalline, odorless, organic powder, $CH_3CONHC_6H_5$, produced by the action of glacial acetic acid on aniline: used chiefly in organic synthesis and in medicine in the treatment of fever, headache, and rheumatism. Also, **ac·et·an·i·lid** (as′i tan′ᵊlid). Also called **acetylaniline, antifebrin, acetylaminobenzene.** [ACET- + ANILIDE]

ac·et·a·nis·i·dine (as′i tə nis′i dēn′, -din), *n. Pharm.* methacetin. [ACET- + ANISE + -IDE + -INE[2]]

ac·e·tate (as′i tāt′), *n.* **1.** *Chem.* a salt or ester of acetic acid. **2.** a synthetic filament, yarn, or fabric composed of a derivative of the acetic ester of cellulose, differing from viscose rayon in having greater strength when wet and greater sensitivity to high temperatures. **3.** *Print.* a sheet of clear plastic film fastened over the front of artwork for protection, as an overlay or the like. [ACET- + -ATE[2]] —**ac′e·tat′ed,** *adj.*

ac′etate ray′on, (formerly) acetate (def. 2).

ac·et·a·zol·a·mide (as′i tə zol′ə mīd′, -mid), *n. Pharm.* a white or yellowish, crystalline, slightly water-soluble powder, $C_4H_6N_4O_3S_2$: used as a diuretic chiefly in edematous or heart conditions. [ACET- + AZOLE + AMIDE]

A·ce·tes (ə sē′tēz), *n. Class. Myth.* a Lydian helmsman who, realizing that a youth captured by his crew was actually Dionysus in disguise, protected the god from the crew and eventually became his follower.

a·ce·tic (ə sē′tik, ə set′ik), *adj.* pertaining to, derived from, or producing vinegar or acetic acid. [ACET- + -IC]

ace′tic ac′id, *Chem.* a colorless, pungent, water-miscible liquid, CH_3COOH, the essential constituent of vinegar, produced by oxidation of acetaldehyde, bacterial action on ethyl alcohol, the reaction of methyl alcohol with carbon monoxide, and other processes: used chiefly in the manufacture of acetate fibers and in the production of numerous esters that are solvents and flavoring agents. Cf. **glacial acetic acid.**

ace′tic ac′id am′ide, acetamide.

ace′tic anhy′dride, *Chem.* a colorless, pungent liquid, $(CH_3CO)_2O$, the anhydride of acetic acid: used chiefly as a reagent and in the production of plastics, film, and fabrics derived from cellulose.

a·cet·i·fy (ə set′ə fī′), *v.t., v.i.,* **-fied, -fy·ing.** to turn into vinegar; make or become acetous. [ACET- + -IFY] —**a·cet′i·fi·ca′tion, ac·e·ta·tion** (as′i tā′shən), *n.* —**a·cet′i·fi′er,** *n.*

ac·e·tim·e·ter (as′i tim′i tər), *n. Chem.* acetometer. —**ac·e·ti·met·ric** (as′i tə me′trik), *adj.* —**ac′e·tim′e·try,** *n.*

ac·e·tin (as′i tin), *n. Chem.* a colorless, thick, hygroscopic liquid, $CH_3COOC_3H_5(OH)_2$: used chiefly in the manufacture of explosives. Also called **glyceryl monoacetate, monacetin, monoacetin.** [ACET- + -IN[2]]

aceto-, a combining form indicating the presence of acetic acid or the acetyl group (*acetophenetidin*), used esp. before a consonant. Also, *esp. before a vowel,* **acet-.** [< L *acēt(um)* vinegar + -O-]

a·ce·to·bac·ter (ə sē′tə bak′tər, as′i tō-, ə set′ə bak′tər), *n. Bacteriol.* any of several ellipsoidal or rod-shaped aerobic bacteria of the genus *Acetobacter,* certain species of which are used in making vinegar. [ACETO- + *-bacter,* comb. form of BACTERIUM]

a·cet·o·in (ə set′ō in), *n. Chem.* a yellowish, pleasant-smelling liquid, $CH_3CH(OH)COCH_3$, obtained from various carbohydrates, as glucose, by fermentation: used chiefly in the manufacture of flavors and essences. Also called **acetylmethylcarbinol, dimethylketol.** [ACETO- + -IN[2]]

ac·e·tom·e·ter (as′i tom′i tər), *n. Chem.* an instrument for measuring the amount of acetic acid present in a solution. Also, **acetimeter.** [ACETO- + -METER] —**ac·e·to·met·ri·cal** (as′i tə me′tri kəl), **ac·e·to·met·ric** (as′i tə me′trik), *adj.* —**ac′e·to·met′ri·cal·ly,** *adv.* —**ac′e·tom′e·try,** *n.*

ac·e·tone (as′i tōn′), *n. Chem.* a colorless, volatile, water-soluble, flammable liquid, $(CH_3)_2CO$, usually derived by oxidation of isopropyl alcohol or by bacterial fermentation of carbohydrates: used chiefly in paints and varnishes, as a general solvent, and in organic synthesis. Also called **dimethylketone.** [ACET- + -ONE] —**ac·e·ton·ic** (as′i ton′ik), *adj.*

ac′etone bod′y, *Biochem.* See **ketone body.**

ac·e·to·ni·trile (as′i tō nī′tril, -trēl, -tril, ə sē′tō-, ə set′ō-), *n. Chem.* a colorless, poisonous, water-soluble liquid, CH_3CN, having an etherlike odor: used chiefly in organic synthesis and as a solvent. Also called **methyl cyanide.** [ACETO- + NITRILE]

ac·e·to·phe·net·i·din (as′i tō fə net′i din, ə sē′tō-), *n. Pharm.* a white, slightly water-soluble, crystalline solid, $CH_3CONHC_6H_4OC_2H_5$: used in medicine chiefly as an agent for checking or preventing fever or for relieving pain. Also, **ac·e·to·phe·net·i·dine** (as′i tō fə net′i dēn′, -din, ə sē′tō-). Also called **phenacetin.** [ACETO- + PHENETIDIN]

ac·e·to·phe·none (as′i tō fə nōn′, ə sē′tō-), *n. Chem.* a colorless liquid, $C_6H_5COCH_3$, having a sweet odor: used chiefly as a scent in the manufacture of perfume. Also called **acetylbenzene, hypnone, phenyl methyl ketone.** [ACETO- + PHEN- + -ONE]

ac·e·to·ste·a·rin (as′i tō stē′ə rin, -stēr′in, ə sē′tō-), *n. Chem.* a waxlike, nongreasy solid, $CH_3(CH_2)_{16}COOCH_2CHOHCH_2OOCCH_3$: used chiefly as a food preservative and as a plasticizer. [ACETO- + STEARIN]

ac·e·tous (as′i təs, ə sē′-), *adj.* **1.** containing or producing acetic acid. **2.** sour; producing or resembling vinegar; vinegary. Also, **ac·e·tose** (as′i tōs′). [< LL *acētōs(us),* equiv. to *acēt(um)* vinegar + *-ōsus* -OSE[1]]

a·ce·tum (ə sē′təm), *n.* a preparation having vinegar or dilute acetic acid as the solvent. [< L: vinegar]

a·ce·tyl (ə sēt′ᵊl, ə set′-, as′i tᵊl), *adj. Chem.* containing the acetyl group. [ACET- + -YL]

a·ce·tyl·am·i·no·ben·zene (ə sēt′ᵊl ə mē′nō ben′zēn, -ben zēn′, -am′ə nō-, ə set′-, as′i tᵊl-), *n. Chem.* acetanilide. [ACETYL + AMINO- + BENZENE]

a·ce·tyl·an·i·line (ə sēt′ᵊl an′ᵊlin, -ᵊlīn′, ə set′-, as′i-tᵊl-), *n. Chem.* acetanilide. [ACETYL + ANILINE]

a·cet·y·late (ə set′ᵊlāt′), *v.,* **-lat·ed, -lat·ing.** *Chem.* —*v.t.* **1.** to introduce one or more acetyl groups into (a compound). —*v.i.* **2.** to become acetylated. Also, **acetylize.** [ACETYL + -ATE[1]] —**a·cet′y·la′tion,** *n.*

a·ce·tyl·ben·zene (ə sēt′ᵊl ben′zēn, -ben zēn′, ə set′-, as′i tᵊl-), *n. Chem.* acetophenone. [ACETYL + BENZENE]

a·ce·tyl·cho·line (ə sēt′ᵊl kō′lēn, -lin, -kol′ēn, -in, as′i tᵊl-), *n.* **1.** *Biochem.* the acetic acid ester of choline, $(CH_3)_3N(OH)(CH_2)_2OCOCH_3$, released and hydrolyzed during nerve conduction and causing muscle action by transmitting nerve impulses across synapses. **2.** *Pharm.* a commercial form of this compound, obtained from ergot or prepared from choline and acetic anhydride, used chiefly as its hydrochloride or hydrobromide to decrease blood pressure or initiate peristalsis. [ACETYL + CHOLINE]

a·cet·y·lene (ə set′ᵊlēn′, -ᵊlin), *n. Chem.* a colorless gas, $HC{\equiv}CH$, having an etherlike odor, produced usually by the action of water on calcium carbide or by pyrolesis of natural gas: used esp. in metal cutting and welding, as an illuminant, and in organic synthesis. Also called **ethine, ethyne.** [ACETYL + -ENE] —**a·cet·y·len·ic** (ə set′ᵊlen′ik), *adj.*

acet′ylene se′ries, *Chem.* See **alkyne series.**

a·cet·y·le·no·gen (ə set′ᵊlē′nə jən, -ᵊlin′ə-), *n.* See **calcium carbide.** [ACETYLENE + -O- + -GEN]

a·ce′tyl·for′mic ac′id (ə sēt′ᵊl fôr′mik, ə set′-, as′i-tᵊl-), *Chem.* See **pyruvic acid.** [ACETYL + FORMIC ACID]

ace′tyl group′, *Chem.* the univalent group, CH_3CO-, derived from acetic acid. Also called **ace′tyl rad′ical.**

ac·e·tyl·ic (as′i til′ik), *adj.* of, pertaining to, or characteristic of the acetyl group. [ACETYL + -IC]

a·cet·y·lide (ə set′ᵊlīd′), *n. Chem.* **1.** any compound derived from acetylene by the replacement of one or both of its hydrogen atoms by a metal, as silver acetylide, Ag_2C_2. **2.** any of a class of compounds having the general formula RC–CM, where R is an organic group and M is a metal. [ACETYL + -IDE]

a·cet·y·lize (ə set′ᵊlīz′), *v.t., v.i.,* **-lized, -liz·ing.** acetylate. [ACETYL + -IZE] —**a·cet′y·li·za′tion,** *n.* —**a·cet′y·liz′er,** *n.*

a·ce·tyl·meth·yl·car·bi·nol (ə sēt′ᵊl meth′il kär′bə nōl′, -nôl′, -nol′, ə set′-, as′i tᵊl-), *n. Chem.* acetoin. [ACETYL + METHYL + CARBINOL]

a·ce′tyl·sal·i·cyl′ic ac′id (ə sēt′ᵊl sal′i sil′ik, ə set′-, as′i tᵊl-), *Pharm.* aspirin. [ACETYL + SALICYLIC ACID]

ace·y-deuc·y (ā′sē dōō′sē, -dyōō′-), *n.* **1.** a form of backgammon. —*adj.* **2.** *Slang.* A-O.K.; great. [ACE + -Y[2] + DEUCE[1] + -Y[2]]

ac-glob·u·lin (ā′sē′glob′yə lin, ak′-), *n. Biochem.* See **accelerator globulin.**

A·chab (ā′kab), *n. Douay Bible.* Ahab.

A·chad (ā′kad), *n. Douay Bible.* Accad.

A·chae·a (ə kē′ə), *n.* an ancient district in S Greece, on the Gulf of Corinth. Also, **A·cha·ia** (ə kā′ə, ə kī′ə).

A·chae·an (ə kē′ən), *adj.* **1.** of or pertaining to Achaea or the Achaeans. **2.** Greek. —*n.* **3.** an inhabitant of Achaea. **4.** a Greek, esp. a member of the Achaean League. **5.** a member of one of the four main divisions of prehistoric Greeks, believed to have occupied the Peloponnesus and to have produced the Mycenaean culture. Cf. **Aeolian** (def. 2), **Dorian** (def. 2), **Ionian** (def. 3). Also, **A·cha·ian** (ə kā′ən, ə kī′ən). [< L *Achae(us)* (< Gk *Achaiós*) + -AN]

Achae′an League′, a political confederation of Achaean and other Greek cities, established in the late 3rd century B.C. and dissolved by the Romans in 146 B.C.

A·chae·me·nes (ə kē′mə nēz′, ə kem′ə-), *n.* fl. 7th century B.C., Persian king: traditional founder of the Achaemenid dynasty.

Ach·ae·me·ni·an (ak′ə mē′nē ən), *adj.* of or pertaining to the Achaemenids or their language, as recorded in cuneiform inscriptions. [< L *Achaemeni(us)* (< Gk *Achaimén(ēs)* ACHAEMENES + L *-ius* adj. suffix) + -AN]

A·chae·me·nid (ə kē′mə nid, ə kem′ə-), *n., pl.* **A·chae·me·nids, Ach·ae·men·i·dae** (ak′ə men′i dē′), **Ach·ae·men·i·des** (ak′ə men′i dēz′). a member of the dynasty of kings in ancient Persia that ruled from c550 B.C. to 331 B.C. [ACHAEMEN(ES) + -ID[2]]

A·chae·us (ə kē′əs), *n. Class. Myth.* the eponymous founder of Achaea.

ach·a·la·sia (ak′ə lā′zhə, -zhē ə, -zē ə), *n. Med.* inability of a circular muscle or a group of circular muscles, esp. of the esophagus or stomach, to relax. [A-[6] + Gk *chálas(is)* (*chala-* (s. of *chalân* to loosen) + *-sis* -SIS) + -IA]

A·chan (ā′kan), *n.* a member of the tribe of Judah who, with his family, was stoned to death for stealing forbidden spoils. Josh. 7:19–26.

a·char (ä chär′, ā′chär), *n. Anglo-Indian.* a salt relish or condiment. [< Pers]

A·char·ni·ans, The (ə kär′nē ənz), a comedy (425 B.C.) by Aristophanes.

A·cha·tes (ə kā′tēz), *n.* **1.** (in the *Aeneid*) the companion and friend of Aeneas. **2.** a faithful friend or companion.

A·chaz (ā′kaz), *n. Douay Bible.* Ahaz.

ache (āk), *v.,* **ached, ach·ing,** *n.* —*v.i.* **1.** to have or suffer a continuous, dull pain: *His whole body ached.* **2.** to feel sympathy, pity, or the like: *Her heart ached for the starving animals.* **3.** *Informal.* to feel eager; yearn; long: *She ached to be near him. He's just aching to get even.* [ME *ake(n),* OE *acan*] —*n.* **4.** a continuous, dull pain, in contrast to a sharp, sudden, or sporadic pain. [late ME *ake* < v.; r. ME *ache, eche,* OE *æce, ece*] —**ach′ing·ly,** *adv.*
—**Syn. 1.** hurt. **4.** See **pain.**

a·chech (a chek′), *n. Egyptian Myth.* a creature having the body of a lion and the wings of a bird. [< Egypt]

a·chei·la·ry (ə kī′lə rē), *adj. Bot.* achilary.

Ach·e·lo·us (ak′ə lō′əs), *n. Class. Myth.* a river god, defeated by Hercules in a struggle over Deianira.

a·chene (ā kēn′), *n. Bot.* a small, dry, hard, one-seeded, indehiscent fruit. Also, **akene.** [< NL *achaen(ium),* equiv. to *a-* A-[6] + Gk *chain-* (s. of *chaínein* to gape) + NL *-ium* n. suffix] —**a·che·ni·al** (ā kē′nē əl), *adj.*

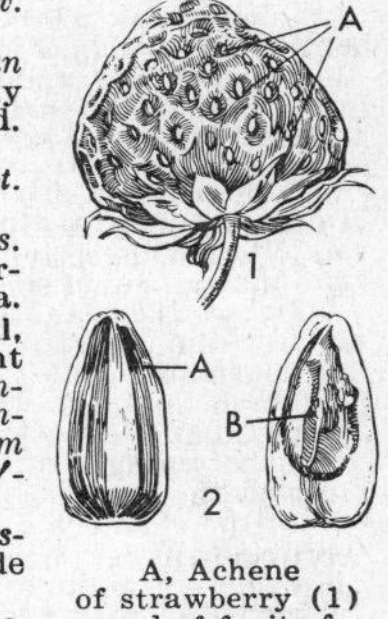

A, Achene of strawberry (1) and of fruit of sunflower (2); B, Seed

A·cher·nar (ā′kər när′), *n. Astron.* a star of the first magnitude in the constellation Eridanus.

Ach·er·on (ak′ə ron′), *n.* **1.** *Class. Myth.* a river in Hades over which Charon ferried the souls of the dead. **2.** the infernal regions; hell; Hades.

Ach·e·son (ach′i sən), *n.* **1. Dean Good·er·ham** (gŏŏd′ər ham′, -əm), born 1893, U.S. statesman: Secretary of State 1949–53. **2. Edward Good·rich** (gŏŏd′rich), 1856–1931, U.S. chemist.

A·cheu·le·an (ə shōō′lē ən), *adj.* of, pertaining to, or characteristic of the Lower Paleolithic Age, lasting from the second to the third interglacial epoch and marked by the use of finely made bifacial tools with multiple cutting edges. Also, **A·cheu′li·an.** [< F *Acheuléen,* named after *St. Acheul* (where remains were found) + *-é* (see -EE) + *-en* -AN]

à che·val (A shə VAL′), *French.* by horse; on horseback.

a·chieve (ə chēv′), *v.* **a·chieved, a·chiev·ing.** —*v.t.* **1.** to bring to a successful end; carry through; accomplish: *They achieved the purpose of their strike.* **2.** to get or attain by effort; gain; obtain: *to achieve victory.* —*v.i.* **3.** to bring about an intended result; accomplish some purpose or effect. [ME *acheve(n)* < OF *achever* to finish, from phrase *a chef* to (the) head (i.e., to conclusion). See CHIEF] —**a·chiev′a·ble,** *adj.* —**a·chiev′er,** *n.*
—**Syn. 1.** consummate, complete; effect, execute; realize, reach. See **do**[1]. **2.** realize, win.

a·chieve·ment (ə chēv′mənt), *n.* **1.** something accomplished, esp. by superior ability, special effort, great valor, etc.; a great or heroic deed. **2.** act of achieving; accomplishment: *the achievement of one's object.* **3.** *Heraldry.* the full display of the armorial bearings of an individual or corporation, consisting of an escutcheon, usually with a crest, helmet, mantling, and motto, and often with supporters and a badge; coat of arms. [late ME < MF *achevement* conclusion. See ACHIEVE, -MENT]
—**Syn. 1.** ACHIEVEMENT, EXPLOIT, FEAT are terms for a noteworthy act. ACHIEVEMENT connotes final accomplishment of something noteworthy, after much effort and often in spite of obstacles and discouragements: *a scientific achievement.* EXPLOIT connotes boldness, bravery, and usually ingenuity: *the famous exploit of an aviator.* FEAT connotes the performance of something difficult, generally demanding skill and strength: *a feat of horsemanship.* **2.** attainment, realization.

achieve′ment age′, *Psychol.* the level of educational development of an individual as determined by an achievement test and based on a comparison of his score with the average score of individuals of the same chronological age. Cf. **mental age.**

achieve′ment quo′tient, *Psychol.* achievement age divided by chronological age, usually expressed as a multiple of 100. The achievement quotient of a ten-year-old child whose achievement age equals that of the average twelve-year-old is 1.2, or 120. *Abbr.:* AQ Cf. **intelligence quotient.**

achieve′ment test′, *Psychol.* a test designed to measure the knowledge or proficiency of an individual in something that has been learned or taught, as arithmetic or typing. Cf. **intelligence test.**

a·chi·la·ry (ə kī′lə rē), *adj. Bot.* having no labellum or lip, or one that is undeveloped, as in the flower of certain orchids. Also, **acheilary.** [A-[6] + CHIL- + -ARY]

Ach·ill (ak′əl), *n.* an island off the coast of NW Ireland. 14 mi. long; 11 mi. wide.

A·chil·les (ə kil′ēz), *n. Class. Myth.* the greatest Greek warrior in the Trojan War and hero of Homer's *Iliad*, killed when Paris wounded him in the heel, his one vulnerable spot. —**Ach·il·le·an** (ak′ə lē′ən), *adj.*

Achil′les heel′, a portion, spot, area, etc., that is especially or solely vulnerable: *The enemy's Achilles heel was his harbor defenses. Her Achilles heel is her tallness.* Also, **Achil′les' heel.**

Achil′les re′flex. See **ankle jerk.** Also, **Achil′les' re′flex.**

Achil′les ten′don, *Anat.* the tendon joining the calf muscles to the heelbone. Also, **Achil′les' ten′don.**

A·chim·a·as (ə kim′ē as′), *n. Douay Bible.* Ahimaaz.

A·chim·e·lech (ə kim′ə lek′), *n. Douay Bible.* Ahimelech.

a·chim·e·nes (ə kim′ə nēz′), *n., pl.* **-nes.** any of several tropical American herbs of the genus *Achimenes*, cultivated for their showy, tubular flowers. [< NL, alter. of L *achaemenis* < Gk *achaimenís*]

A·chish (ā′kish), *n.* the king of the Philistine city of Gath, who twice gave refuge to David. I Sam. 21:10–15.

A·chit·o·phel (ə kit′ə fel′), *n. Douay Bible.* Ahithophel.

ach·kan (ach′kən), *n.* a close-fitting, high-necked coat, slightly flared below the waist and reaching almost to the knee, worn by men in India. [< Hindi *ackan*]

a·chlam·y·date (ā klam′i dāt′, -dit), *adj. Zool.* not chlamydate; having no mantle or pallium. [A-[6] + CHLAMYDATE]

ach·la·myd·e·ous (ak′lə mid′ē əs), *adj. Bot.* not chlamydeous; having no calyx and corolla. [A-[6] + CHLAMYDEOUS]

a·chlor·hy·dri·a (ā′klôr hī′drē ə, ā′klôr-), *n. Med.* absence of hydrochloric acid in the gastric juice. [< NL; see A-[6], CHLOR-[2], HYDR-[2], -IA] —**a′chlor·hy′dric,** *adj.*

a·chlo·ro·phyl·lous (ā klôr′ə fil′əs, ā klôr′-), *adj. Bot.* containing no chlorophyll. [A-[6] + CHLOROPHYLLOUS]

a·cho·li·a (ā kō′lē ə), *n. Pathol.* lack of a secretion of bile. [< Gk *ácholo(s)* (a- A-[6] + *chol-* CHOL- + -*os* adj. suffix) + -IA] —**a·chol·ic** (ā kol′ik), **a·cho·lous** (ā kō′ləs, -kol′əs, ak′ə ləs) *adj.*

ach·o·lu·ri·a (ak′ə lŏŏr′ē ə), *n. Med.* the absence of bile pigments in the urine. [< NL < Gk *ácholo(s)* (see ACHOLIA) + NL -*uria* -URIA] —**ach′o·lu′ric,** *adj.*

a·chon·drite (ā kon′drīt), *n.* a meteorite containing no chondrules. [A-[6] + CHONDRITE] —**a·chon·drit·ic** (ā′kon drit′ik), *adj.*

a·chon·dro·pla·sia (ā kon′drə plā′zhə, -zhē ə, -zē ə), *n. Pathol.* defective conversion of cartilage into bone, producing dwarfism. [A-[6] + CHONDRO- + -PLASIA] —**a·chon·dro·plas·tic** (ā kon′drə plas′tik), *adj.*

ach·ro·ite (ak′rō īt′), *n.* the colorless or white variety of tourmaline, often used as a gem. [< Gk *áchro(os)* colorless (*a-* A-[6] + -*chroos* colored) + -ITE[1]]

ach·ro·mat (ak′rə mat′), *n.* See **achromatic lens.** [by shortening]

ach·ro·mate (ak′rə māt′), *n. Ophthalm.* a person unable to perceive color. [back formation from ACHROMATIC]

ach·ro·mat·ic (ak′rə mat′ik), *adj.* **1.** *Optics.* **a.** free from color. **b.** able to emit, transmit, or receive light without separating it into colors. **2.** *Biol.* **a.** containing or consisting of achromatin. **b.** (of a cell structure) difficult to stain. **3.** *Music.* without accidentals or changes in key. [A-[6] + CHROMATIC] —**ach′ro·mat′i·cal·ly,** *adv.*

ach·ro·ma·tic·i·ty (ak′rō mə tis′i tē, ā krō′-), *n. Optics.* achromatism. [ACHROMATIC + -ITY]

ach′romat′ic lens′, *Optics.* a system of two or more lenses that is substantially free from chromatic aberration and in which the lenses are made of different substances so that the focal length of the system is the same for two or three wavelengths of light. Also called **achromat.** Cf. **crown lens, flint glass.**

ach′romat′ic prism′, *Optics.* a system of two or more prisms made from different substances, which deviates but does not disperse a beam of light.

a·chro·ma·tin (ā krō′mə tin), *n. Biol.* the nonstainable portion of the nucleus of a cell. [A-[6] + CHROMATIN]

a·chro·ma·tise (ā krō′mə tīz′), *v.t.,* **-tised, -tis·ing.** *Chiefly Brit.* achromatize. —**a·chro′ma·ti·sa′tion,** *n.*

a·chro·ma·tism (ā krō′mə tiz′əm), *n. Optics.* **1.** freedom from color. **2.** freedom from chromatic aberration, as in an achromatic lens. Also, **achromaticity.** [ACHROMAT(IC) + -ISM]

a·chro·ma·tize (ā krō′mə tīz′), *v.t.,* **-tized, -tiz·ing.** to make achromatic; deprive or free of color. Also, *esp. Brit.,* **achromatise.** [ACHROMAT(IC) + -IZE] —**a·chro′ma·ti·za′tion,** *n.*

a·chro·mat·o·phil (ā′krə mat′ə fil, ak′rə-, ā krō′mə tə-), *Biol.* —*adj.* **1.** Also, **a·chro·mat·o·phil·ic** (ā′krə mat′ə fil′ik, ak′rə-, ā krō′mə tə-). having little or no affinity for stains. —*n.* **2.** an achromatophil cell or tissue. [ACHROMAT(IC) + -O- + -PHIL]

a·chro·mat·o·phil·i·a (ā′krə mat′ə fil′ē ə, -fēl′yə, ak′rə-, ā krō′mə tə-), *n. Biol.* the property of having little or no affinity for stains. [ACHROMATOPHIL + -IA]

a·chro·ma·tous (ā krō′mə təs), *adj.* **1.** without color. **2.** having little or inadequate color; lighter in color than normal. [ACHROMAT(IC) + -OUS]

a·chro·mic (ā krō′mik), *adj.* colorless; without coloring matter. Also, **a·chro′mous.** [A-[6] + CHROMIC]

a·chro·mo·bac·ter (ā krō′mə bak′tər), *n. Bacteriol.* any of several rod-shaped bacteria of the genus *Achromobacter*, found in soil and water. [< NL < Gk *áchrōmo(s)* colorless (*a-* A-[6] + *chrômos* color) + NL -*bacter* BACTER-]

Ach·ro·my·cin (ak′rō mī′sin), *n. Pharm., Trademark.* tetracycline.

a·chron·y·chous (ə kron′ə kəs), *adj. Rare.* acronychous.

Ach·sah (ak′sə), *n.* the daughter of Caleb who was promised in marriage to the conqueror of the city of Debir. Josh. 15:16–19; Judges 1:12–15. Also, *Douay Bible,* **Axa.**

a·cic·u·la (ə sik′yə lə), *n., pl.* **-lae** (-lē′). a needlelike part; spine, bristle, or needlelike crystal. [< NL, LL: small pin for a headdress, equiv. to L *aci-* (var. s. of *acus*) needle + -*cula* -CULE]

a·cic·u·lar (ə sik′yə lər), *adj.* **1.** needle-shaped. **2.** *Metall.* **a.** (of cast iron) containing ferrite in a needlelike form. **b.** (of an alloy) having a microstructure of needlelike components. [ACICUL(A) + -AR[1]] —**a·cic·u·lar·i·ty** (ə sik′yə lar′i tē), *n.* —**a·cic′u·lar·ly,** *adv.*

a·cic·u·late (ə sik′yə lit, -lāt′), *adj.* **1.** having aciculae. **2.** marked as with needle scratches. **3.** needle-shaped; acicular. Also, **a·cic′u·lat′ed.** [ACICUL(A) + -ATE[1]]

a·cic·u·lum (ə sik′yə ləm), *n., pl.* **-lums, -la** (-lə). **1.** an acicula. **2.** *Zool.* one of the slender, sharp stylets embedded in the parapodia of certain annelids, as the polychaetes. [alter. of ACICULA]

ac·id (as′id), *n.* **1.** *Chem.* a compound usually having a sour taste and capable of neutralizing alkalis and reddening blue litmus paper, containing hydrogen that can be replaced by a metal or an electropositive group to form a salt, or containing an atom that can accept a pair of electrons from a base. Acids are proton donors that yield hydronium ions in water solution, or electron-pair acceptors that combine with electron-pair donors or bases. **2.** a substance with a sour taste. **3.** something, as a remark, piece of writing, etc., that is sharp, sour, or ill-natured: *He has nothing but acid to offer as criticism.* **4.** *U.S. Slang.* **LSD** (def. 2). —*adj.* **5.** *Chem.* **a.** belonging or pertaining to acids or the anhydrides of acids. **b.** having only a part of the hydrogen of an acid replaced by a metal or its equivalent: *an acid phosphate.* **6.** sharp or biting to the taste; tasting like vinegar; sour: *acid fruits.* **7.** sharp, biting, or ill-natured in mood, manner, etc.: *an acid remark; an acid wit.* **8.** Also, **acidic.** *Geol.* containing much silica. **9.** *Metall.* noting, pertaining to, or made by a process in which the lining of the furnace, or the slag that is present, functions as an acid in high-temperature reactions in taking electrons from oxide ions: usually a siliceous material, as sand or ganister. Cf. **basic** (def. 3). **10. put on the acid,** *Australian Slang.* to pilfer for one's own use. [< L *acid(us)* sour, akin to *ācer* sharp, *acētum* vinegar, ACICULA] —**ac′id·ly,** *adv.* —**ac′id·ness,** *n.*
—**Syn. 7.** tart. ACID, ASTRINGENT are terms used figuratively of wit or humor. ACID suggests a sharp, biting, or ill-natured quality: *an acid joke about an opponent.* ASTRINGENT connotes severity but usually also a bracing quality, as of something applied with curative intent: *much-needed astringent criticism.*

Ac·i·dal·i·um (as′i dal′ē əm), *n.* **Mare.** See **Mare Acidalium.**

ac′id anhy′dride, *Chem.* See under **anhydride** (def. 1).

Ac·i·dan·the·ra (as′i dan′thər ə), *n.* a genus of bulbous, African herbs having sword-shaped leaves and long-tubed flowers. [< NL < Gk *akid-* (s. of *akís*) needle + NL -*anthera;* see ANTHER]

ac′id cell′, **1.** *Elect.* a cell using an acid electrolyte. **2.** See **parietal cell.**

ac′id drop′, *Brit.* a tart candy, as a sourball.

ac′id dye′, *Chem.* any of a class of dyes containing one or more acidic groups, as the sulfo group: used in acid solution chiefly for dyeing wool and silk.

ac·i·de·mi·a (as′i dē′mē ə), *n. Pathol.* an abnormal acidity of the blood; acidosis. [ACID + -EMIA]

ac·id-fast (as′id fast′, -fäst′), *adj.* resistant to decolorizing by acidified alcohol after staining. —**ac′id-fast′ness,** *n.*

ac·id-form·ing (as′id fôr′ming), *adj.* **1.** yielding acid in chemical reaction; acidic. **2.** (of food) containing a large amount of acid ash after complete oxidation.

ac·id-head (as′id hed′), *n. Slang.* a person who habitually takes the drug LSD. [ACID (in sense of def. 4) + HEAD]

a·cid·ic (ə sid′ik), *adj.* **1.** *Geol.* acid (def. 7). **2.** acid-forming (def. 1). [ACID + -IC]

a·cid·i·fy (ə sid′ə fī′), *v.t., v.i.,* **-fied, -fy·ing.** to make or become acid; convert into an acid. [ACID + -IFY] —**a·cid′i·fi′a·ble,** *adj.* —**a·cid′i·fi·ca′tion,** *n.* —**a·cid′i·fi′er,** *n.*

ac·i·dim·e·ter (as′i dim′i tər), *n. Chem.* an instrument for measuring the amount of acid in a solution. [ACID + -I- + -METER]

ac·i·dim·e·try (as′i dim′i trē), *n. Chem.* the process of measuring the amount of acid in a solution, as with an acidimeter or by titration. [ACID + -I- + -METRY] —**ac·i·di·met·ric** (as′i də me′trik), **ac′i·di·met′ri·cal,** *adj.* —**ac′i·di·met′ri·cal·ly,** *adv.*

a·cid·i·ty (ə sid′i tē), *n.* **1.** the quality or state of being acid. **2.** sourness; tartness. **3.** excessive acid quality, as of the gastric juice. [< LL *aciditās.* See ACID, -ITY]

ac·id·ize (as′i dīz′), *v.,* **-ized, -iz·ing.** —*v.t.* **1.** to impregnate with acid; acidify. —*v.i.* **2.** to become acidified. [ACID + -IZE]

ac′id metapro′tein, *Biochem.* a metaprotein derived by means of a hydrolytic acid.

ac′id num′ber, *Chem.* a number expressing the acidity of a substance, equal to the number of milligrams of potassium hydroxide needed to neutralize the free fatty acids present in one gram of the substance.

ac·i·do·gen·ic (as′i dō jen′ik, ə sid′ə-), *adj. Biochem.* producing acid, as bacteria, or causing acidity, as of the urine. [ACID + -O- + -GENIC]

ac·i·dol·y·sis (as′i dol′i sis), *n. Chem.* decomposition resulting from the interaction of a compound and an acid. [< NL; see ACID, -O-, -LYSIS]

ac·i·do·phil (as′i dō fil′, ə sid′ə-), *Biol.* —*adj.* **1.** acidophilic. —*n.* **2.** an acidophilic cell, tissue, organism, or substance. Also, **ac·i·do·phile** (as′i dō fīl′, ə sid′ə-). [ACID + -O- + -PHIL]

ac·i·do·phil·ic (as′i dō fil′ik, ə sid′ə-), *adj.* **1.** *Biol.* having an affinity for acid stains. **2.** (of bacteria) thriving in or having an affinity for an acid environment; aciduric. Also, **ac·i·doph·i·lus** (as′i dof′ə ləs). [ACIDOPHIL + -IC]

acidoph′ilus milk′, a fermented milk produced by growing the bacterium *Lactobacillus acidophilus* in milk, used in medicine to alter the microbial flora of the intestinal tract under certain conditions. [< NL; see ACID, -O-, -PHILOUS]

ac·i·do·sis (as′i dō′sis), *n. Pathol.* a blood condition in which the bicarbonate concentration is below normal; acidemia. [< NL; see ACID, -OSIS] —**ac·i·dot·ic** (as′i dot′ik), *adj.*

ac′id phos′phate, superphosphate (def. 1).

ac′id rain′, rain containing large amounts of acid-bearing chemicals, such as the pollutants from coal smoke, vehicle exhaust, or chemical manufacturing, that have been released into the atmosphere and combined with water vapor: regarded as harmful to the environment.

ac′id soil′, a soil of acid reaction or having a predominance of hydrogen ions, tasting sour in solution.

ac′id test′, a severe and conclusive test to establish genuineness, worth, etc.

ac′id test′ ra′tio, a ratio of cash, receivables, and marketable securities to current liabilities, used by banks and other lending agencies in determining credit risks.

a·cid·u·lant (ə sij′ə lənt, ə sid′yə-), *n. Chem.* an acidulating substance. Also, **acidulent.** [< F, n. use of prp. of *aciduler* < L *acidul(us).* See ACIDULOUS, -ANT]

a·cid·u·late (ə sij′ə lāt′, ə sid′yə-), *v.t.,* **-lat·ed, -lat·ing.** **1.** to make somewhat acid. **2.** to sour; embitter. [ACIDUL(OUS) + -ATE[1]] —**a·cid′u·la′tion,** *n.*

a·cid·u·lent (ə sij′ə lənt, ə sid′yə-), *n.* **1.** *Chem.* acidulant. —*adj.* **2.** acidulous.

a·cid·u·lous (ə sij′ə ləs, ə sid′yə-), *adj.* **1.** slightly sour. **2.** sharp; caustic. **3.** moderately acid or tart; subacid. Also, **acidulent.** [< L *acidulus.* See ACID, -ULOUS]

ac·i·du·ric (as′i dŏŏr′ik, -dyŏŏr′-), *adj.* (of bacteria) capable of growth in an acid environment. [ACID + L *dūr(āre)* (to) last + -IC]

ac·id·y (as′i dē), *adj.* of the nature of or resembling acid; sharp; sour: *an acidy taste.* [ACID + -Y[1]]

ac·i·er·ate (as′ē ə rāt′), *v.t.,* **-at·ed, -at·ing.** to convert (iron) into steel. [< F *acier* steel (< VL **aciār(ium),* equiv. to L *aci(ēs)* sharpness + -*ārium* -ARY) + -ATE[1]] —**ac′i·er·a′tion,** *n.*

ac·i·form (as′ə fôrm′), *adj.* needle-shaped; acicular. [< L *ac-* (s. of *acus* (needle) + -I- + -FORM]

ac·i·na·ceous (as′ə nā′shəs), *adj. Bot.* having many small seeds, as a grape. [ACIN(US) + -ACEOUS]

a·cin·a·ci·fo·li·ous (ə sin′ə sə fō′lē əs), *adj. Bot.* having scimitar-shaped leaves. Also, **a·cin·a·ci·fo·li·ate** (ə sin′ə sə fō′lē it, -āt′). [< L *acinaci-* (see ACINACIFORM) + -I- + -FOLIOUS]

ac·i·nac·i·form (as′ə nas′ə fôrm′), *adj. Bot.* scimitar-shaped, as a leaf. [< L *acīnac-* (s. of *acīnacēs* < Gk *akinákēs* short sword) + -I- + -FORM]

Acinaciform leaf

ac·i·nar·i·ous (as′ə nâr′ē əs), *adj. Bot.* covered with globose vesicles resembling grape seeds, as certain algae. [prob. < F *acinaire* < L *acin(us)* ACINUS + F -*aire* -ARIOUS]

a·cin·i·form (ə sin′ə fôrm′), *adj.* **1.** clustered like grapes. **2.** acinous. [ACIN(US) + -I- + -FORM]

ac·i·nous (as′ə nəs), *adj.* consisting of acini. Also, **ac·i·nose** (as′ə nōs′). [< L *acinōs(us)*]

ac·i·nus (as′ə nəs), *n., pl.* **-ni** (-nī′). **1.** *Bot.* one of the small drupelets or berries of an aggregate, baccate fruit, as the blackberry. **2.** a berry, as a grape, currant, etc. **3.** *Anat.* **a.** a minute rounded lobule. **b.** the smallest secreting portion of a gland. [< L: grape, berry, seed of a berry] —**a·cin·ic** (ə sin′ik), *adj.*

-acious, a form resulting from the addition of the adjectival suffix **-ous** to stems in **-acity** or **-acy:** *audacious; fallacious.* [< L -*āci-* (s. of -*ax*) adj. suffix + -OUS]

A·cis (ā′sis), *n. Class. Myth.* the lover of Galatea, killed by Polyphemus out of jealousy.

-acity, a formal element meaning "quality of" or "abounding in," appearing in loan words from Latin: *tenacity.* [ME -*acite* << L -*ācitāt-* (s. of -*ācitās*)]

ack., **1.** acknowledge. **2.** acknowledgment.

ack-ack (ak′ak′), *n. Slang.* **1.** antiaircraft fire. **2.** antiaircraft arms. Also, **Ack′-Ack′.** [for A.A. (abbreviation) as said by British signalmen, by assoc. with *aircraft* and *attack*]

ack·ey (ak′ē), *n., pl.* **-eys.** **1.** a silver coin minted in England in the late 18th and early 19th centuries for use in western Africa. **2.** *Metall.* a mixture of nitric and sulfuric acids used in electroplating. [< Liberian *akee,* tree with a seed that served as a unit of weight]

ac·knowl·edge (ak nol′ij), *v.t.,* **-edged, -edg·ing.** **1.** to admit to be real or true; recognize the existence, truth, or fact of; confess to: *to acknowledge belief in God.* **2.** to show or express recognition or realization of: *to acknowledge an acquaintance by bowing.* **3.** to recognize the authority, validity, or claims of: *The member nations acknowledged the powers of the President.* **4.** to show or express appreciation or gratitude for: *to acknowledge a favor.* **5.** to indicate or make known the receipt of: *to acknowledge a letter.* **6.** to take notice of or reply to: *to acknowledge a greeting.* **7.** *Law.* to confirm as binding or of legal force: *to acknowledge a deed.* [late ME *acknowleche,* equiv. to *acknow* (OE *oncnāwan* to recognize; see A-[3], KNOW[1]) + -*leche*] —**ac·knowl′edge·a·ble,** *adj.* —**ac·knowl′edged·ly,** *adv.* —**ac·knowl′edg·er,** *n.*
—**Syn. 1.** concede, grant. ACKNOWLEDGE, ADMIT, CONFESS agree in the idea of declaring something to be true. ACKNOWLEDGE implies making a statement reluctantly, often about something previously denied: *to acknowledge a fault.* ADMIT especially implies acknowledging something under pressure: *to admit a charge.* CONFESS usually means stating somewhat formally an admission of wrongdoing, crime, or shortcoming: *to confess guilt; to confess an inability to understand.* —**Ant. 1.** deny.

ac·knowl·edg·ment (ak nol′ij mənt), *n.* **1.** act of acknowledging or admitting. **2.** recognition of the existence or truth of anything: *the acknowledgment of a sovereign power.* **3.** an expression of appreciation. **4.** a thing done or given in appreciation or gratitude. **5.** *Law.* **a.** declaration by a person before an official that he executed a legal document. **b.** an official certificate of a formal acknowledging. **c.** public recognition by a man of an illegitimate child as his own. Also, *esp. Brit.,* **ac·knowl′edge·ment.** [ACKNOWLEDGE + -MENT]

ack·ton (ak′tən), *n. Armor.* acton.

ac·le (ak′lē), *n.* the hard, durable wood of a Philippine leguminous tree, *Albizzia acle,* used for making fine furniture. [< Tagalog *akle*]

a·cleis·to·car·di·a (ə klī′stə kär′dē ə, ā klī′-), *n.* *Pathol.* failure of the foramen ovale of the heart to close. [< Gk *ákleisto(s)* (*a-* A-[6] + *kleis-,* var. s. of *kleíein* to close + *-tos* verbal adj. suffix) + *kardiā* heart]

a·clin′ic line′ (ā klin′ik), an imaginary line on the surface of the earth, close and approximately parallel to the equator, connecting all those points over which a magnetic needle shows no inclination from the horizontal. Also called **magnetic equator.** [< Gk *aklin(ḗs)* not bending (*a-* A-[6] + *klin-,* var. s. of *klínein* to bend) + -IC]

A.C.L.S., American Council of Learned Societies.

A.C.L.U., American Civil Liberties Union.

ac·me (ak′mē), *n.* the highest point; summit. [< Gk *akmḗ* point, highest point, extremity] —**ac·mic** (ak′mik), **ac·mat·ic** (ak mat′ik), *adj.*

ac·mes·the·sia (ak′mis thē′zhə, -zhē ə, -zē ə), *n.* *Psychol.* awareness of sharp points through the sense of touch without experiencing pain. Also, **ac′maes·the′sia.** [< Gk *akm(ḗ)* point, edge + ESTHESIA]

ac·mite (ak′mīt), *n.* a rare pyroxene mineral, sodium-ferric iron silicate, $NaFe(Si_2O_6)$, found in feldspathoid rocks. [< Gk *akm(ḗ)* sharp point + -ITE[1]]

Ac·mon (ak′mən), *n.* *Class. Myth.* a companion of Diomedes who was changed into a bird for defying Aphrodite.

ac·ne (ak′nē), *n.* *Pathol.* an inflammatory disease of the sebaceous glands, characterized by an often pustular eruption of the skin, esp. of the face. [< Gk *aknḗ* facial eruption, orig. var. of *akmḗ;* see ACME]

ac·ne·mi·a (ak nē′mē ə), *n.* **1.** *Pathol.* a condition characterized by atrophy of the muscles of the calf of the leg. **2.** congenital absence of the legs. [A-[6] + *cnem-* (< Gk *knḗm(ē)* shin) + -IA]

ac·node (ak′nōd), *n.* *Math. Rare.* a point that is an element of a set but is isolated from the other elements. [< L *ac(us)* needle + NODE] —**ac·no′dal,** *adj.*

ac·o·asm (ak′ō az′əm), *n.* acouasm.

a·cock (ə kok′), *adv., adj.* cocked. [A-[1] + COCK[2]]

a·cock·bill (ə kok′bil′), *adj.* *Naut.* pointed upward, as the flukes of an anchor. [ACOCK + BILL[3]]

ac·o·cotl (ak′ə kot′əl), *n.* clarin. [< Nahuatl]

a·coe·lo·mate (ā sē′lə māt′, ā′sē lō′mit), *adj.* *Zool.* having no coelom. Also, **a·coe·lom·a·tous** (ā′sē lom′ə təs, -lō′mə-), **a·coe′lo·mous.** [A-[6] + COELOMATE[1]]

a·coe·lous (ā sē′ləs), *adj.* **1.** without a true alimentary canal. **2.** acoelomate. [A-[6] + COEL(UM) + -OUS]

A·coe·me·ti (ä kē′mē tē, ə sem′i tī′), *n.pl.* *Eastern Ch.* (in the 5th and 6th centuries) a group of monks or nuns maintaining perpetual worship through uninterrupted recitation of the divine office. Also, **A·coe′me·tae.** [< ML < LGk *akoímētoi* (n. pl.), Gk: sleepless, n. pl. use of *akoímētos* (adj.), equiv. to *a-* A-[6] + **koimētos* verbal of *koimân* to go to sleep]

a·coe·naes·the·sia (ā′sē nis thē′zhə), *n.* *Psychiatry.* acenesthesia. [A-[6] + COENESTHESIA]

a·cold (ə kōld′), *adj.* *Archaic.* being cold or chilled. [ME *acolde,* OE *ācōlod,* ptp. of *ācōlian* to grow cold. See A-[3], COOL]

ac·o·lyte (ak′ə līt′), *n.* **1.** an altar attendant in public worship; altar boy. **2.** *Rom. Cath. Ch.* **a.** a member of the highest-ranking of the four minor orders. **b.** the order itself. Cf. **exorcist** (def. 2), **lector** (def. 2), **ostiary** (def. 1). **3.** any attendant, assistant, or follower. [< ML *acolyt(us)* < Gk *akólouthos* follower, attendant, equiv. to *a-* prefix denoting association + *-kolouthos,* var. of *kéleuthos* road, journey]

à compte (A kôNt′), *French.* on account; in partial payment.

A·con·ca·gua (ä′kông kä′gwä), *n.* a mountain in W Argentina, in the Andes: the highest peak in the Western Hemisphere. 22,834 ft.

ac·o·nite (ak′ə nīt′), *n.* any ranunculaceous plant of the genus *Aconitum,* including species with poisonous and medicinal properties. Also, **a·con·i·tum** (ak′ə nī′təm). Cf. **monkshood, wolfsbane.** [< L *aconīt(um)* < Gk *akóniton* leopard's bane, wolf's bane] —**ac·o·nit·ic** (ak′ə nit′ik), *adj.*

a·corn (ā′kôrn, ā′kərn), *n.* **1.** the typically ovoid fruit or nut of an oak, enclosed at the base by a cupule. **2.** a finial or knop, as on a piece of furniture, in the form of an acorn. [ME *acorne,* r. *akern,* OE *æcern, æcren* mast, oak-mast; c. Icel *akarn,* Goth *akran* fruit, yield] —**a′corned,** *adj.*

A, Acorn
C, Cupule

a′corn bar′nacle. See under **barnacle**[1] (def. 1).

a′corn chair′, *Eng. Furniture.* a Jacobean chair having a crossrail with acorn-shaped pendants.

a′corn clock′, a mantel clock used in New England in the first half of the 19th century, having the upper part of the case shaped with a double ogee curve to resemble an acorn.

a′corn spoon′, a spoon having an acornlike ornament at the end of its stem.

a′corn squash′, **1.** an acorn-shaped variety of winter squash, having a dark-green to orange-yellow skin. **2.** the plant bearing this fruit.

a′corn sug′ar, *Chem.* quercitol.

a′corn tube′, *Electronics.* a vacuum tube, resembling an acorn in size and shape, used chiefly in ultrahigh-frequency electronic devices.

a′corn worm′, any of several wormlike, burrowing hemichordates of the class *Enteropneusta,* having an acorn-shaped proboscis. Also called **tongue worm.**

à corps per·du (A kôR peR dY′), *French.* desperately; with abandon. [lit., with body lost]

a·cos·mism (ā koz′miz əm), *n.* *Philos.* any theory that denies the existence of a physical world. [A-[6] + COSMISM] —**a·cos′mist,** *n.* —**a′cos·mis′tic,** *adj.*

a·cot·y·le·don (ā′kot′əl ēd′ən, ā kot′-), *n.* a plant without cotyledons, therefore one belonging to a group lower than the seed plants. [A-[6] + COTYLEDON] —**a·cot·y·le·don·ous** (ā′kot′əlēd′ənəs, ā kot′əlēd′-; ā′kot′əled′ənəs, ā kot′əled′-).

a·cou·asm (ə ko͞o′az əm, ak′o͞o az′-), *n.* *Psychiatry.* a nonverbal auditory hallucination, as a ringing or hissing. Also, **acoasm, acousma.** [< Gk *ákousma,* equiv. to *akoas-* (var. of *akoúzesthai* to listen) + *-ma,* n. suffix]

a·cous·ma (ə ko͞oz′mə), *n., pl.* **-mas, -ma·ta** (-mə tə). acouasm.

a·cous·tic (ə ko͞o′stik *or, esp. Brit.,* ə kou′-), *adj.* Also, **a·cous′ti·cal.** **1.** pertaining to the sense or organs of hearing, to sound, or to the science of sound. **2.** (of a building material) designed for controlling sound: *acoustic tile.* —*n.* **3.** a remedy for deafness or imperfect hearing. [< Gk *akoustik(ós).* See ACOUASM, -TIC] —**a·cous′ti·cal·ly,** *adv.*

acous′tical cloud′, one of a number of acoustical panels installed near the ceiling of a concert hall to reflect sound for the purpose of improving the acoustical quality of music.

ac·ous·ti·cian (ak′o͞o stish′ən *or, esp. Brit.,* ak′ou-), *n.* an acoustic engineer. [ACOUST(ICS) + -ICIAN]

acous′tic imped′ance, *Acoustics.* the total reaction of a medium to the transmission of sound through it, expressed as the ratio of sound pressure to particle velocity at a given point in the medium.

acous′tic inert′ance, *Acoustics.* inertance. Also called **acous′tic mass′.**

acous′tic mine′, a naval mine designed to be exploded by the vibration of the propeller of a passing ship or by the sound of water along the hull. Also called **sonic mine.** Cf. **contact mine, magnetic mine.**

acous′tic nerve′. See **auditory nerve.**

acous′tic ohm′, *Acoustics.* the unit of acoustic impedance, equal to the impedance of a medium in which a sound pressure of one dyne per square centimeter produces a velocity of one centimeter per second.

acous′tic phonet′ics, **1.** the study or branch of science dealing with the sounds of speech in terms of their acoustic properties, as loudness, pitch, duration, etc., esp. as now analyzed by means of instruments like the sound spectrograph, oscillograph, etc. Cf. **articulatory phonetics.** **2.** a composite branch of physics and linguistics which treats sound proper as it relates to speech. **3.** the branch of phonetics dealing with the preotic transmission of the sounds of speech and with their otic, but preneural, reception. Cf. **auditory phonetics.**

acous′tic react′ance, *Acoustics.* acoustic impedance caused by the inertia and elasticity of the transmitting medium. Also called **reactance.**

acous′tic resist′ance, *Acoustics.* acoustic impedance caused by the internal friction of the transmitting medium.

a·cous·tics (ə ko͞o′stiks *or, esp. Brit.,* ə kou′-), *n.* **1.** (*construed as sing.*) *Physics.* the branch of physics that deals with sound and sound waves. **2.** (*construed as pl.*) the qualities or characteristics of a room, auditorium, stadium, etc., that determine the audibility or fidelity of sounds in it. [see ACOUSTIC, -ICS]

à cou·vert (A ko͞o veR′), *French.* under cover.

A.C.P., American College of Physicians.

acpt., acceptance.

ac·quaint (ə kwānt′), *v.t.* **1.** to make more or less familiar or conversant (usually fol. by *with*): *to acquaint the mayor with our plan.* **2.** to furnish with knowledge; inform (usually fol. by *with*): *to acquaint a friend with one's efforts.* **3.** to bring into social contact; introduce (usually fol. by *with*): *She acquainted her roommate with my cousin.* [ME *acointe(n)* < OF *acoint(i)er* < ML *accognitāre,* deriv. of L *accognitus* made known to (ptp. of *accognoscere*), equiv. to *ac-* AC- + *co-* CO- + *gni-* know + *-tus* ptp. suffix]

ac·quaint·ance (ə kwān′təns), *n.* **1.** a person known to one, usually a person with whom one is not on terms of great intimacy. **2.** state of being acquainted. **3.** personal knowledge: *a good acquaintance with French wines.* Also, **ac·quaint′ance·ship′** (for defs. 2, 3). [ME *acoyntaunce* < OF *acointance.* See ACQUAINT, -ANCE]
—**Syn. 1.** ACQUAINTANCE, ASSOCIATE, COMPANION, FRIEND refer to a person with whom one is in contact. An ACQUAINTANCE is someone recognized by sight or someone known, though not intimately: *a casual acquaintance.* An ASSOCIATE is a person who is often in one's company, usually because of some work, enterprise, or pursuit in common: *a business associate.* A COMPANION is a person who shares one's activities, fate, or condition: *a traveling companion; companion in despair.* A FRIEND is a person with whom one is on intimate terms and for whom one feels a warm affection: *a trusted friend.*

ac·quaint·ed (ə kwān′tid), *adj.* **1.** having personal knowledge; informed (usually fol. by *with*): *to be acquainted with law.* **2.** brought into social contact; made familiar: *people acquainted through mutual friends.* [ME; see ACQUAINT, -ED[2]] —**ac·quaint′ed·ness,** *n.*

ac·quest (ə kwest′), *n.* *Law.* property acquired other than by inheritance, as by purchase or gift. [< obs. F < VL **acquaesit(um)* that which has been acquired, n. use of *acquaesitus* (ptp. of *acquaerere* to acquire, alter. of L *acquīrere* to ACQUIRE)]

ac·qui·esce (ak′wē es′), *v.i.,* **-esced, -esc·ing.** to assent tacitly; submit or comply quietly; agree; consent (often fol. by *in*): *to acquiesce in an opinion.* [< L *acquiēsc(re)* (to) find rest in, equiv. to *ac-* AC- + *quiēt-* (see QUIET[1]) + *-sce* inchoative suffix] —**ac′qui·esc′ing·ly,** *adv.*
—**Syn.** accede, comply, concur, submit. —**Ant.** protest.

ac·qui·es·cence (ak′wē es′əns), *n.* **1.** act or condition of acquiescing or giving tacit assent; silent submission; compliance (usually fol. by *to* or *in*): *acquiescence to his boss' demands.* **2.** *Law.* such neglect to take legal proceedings for such a long time as to imply the abandonment of a right. [ACQUIESCE + -ENCE]

ac·qui·es·cent (ak′wē es′ənt), *adj.* disposed to acquiesce or yield; submissive; compliant. [< L *acquiēscent-* (s. of *acquiēscēns,* prp. of *acquiēscere*). See ACQUIESCE, -ENT] —**ac′qui·es′cent·ly,** *adv.*

ac·quire (ə kwīər′), *v.t.,* **-quired, -quir·ing.** **1.** to come into possession of; get as one's own: *to acquire property, a title etc.* **2.** to gain for oneself through one's actions or efforts: *to acquire learning, a reputation, etc.* [< L *acquīre(re)* (to) get besides (*ac-* AC- + *quīr-,* var. of *quaer-* get); r. late ME *aquere* < MF *aquer(re)* < L] —**ac·quir′a·bil′i·ty,** *n.* —**ac·quir′a·ble,** *adj.* —**ac·quir′er,** *n.*
—**Syn. 1.** See **get. 2.** win, earn, attain; appropriate.

acquired′ char′acter, *Genetics.* a noninheritable character that results from certain environmental influences.

ac·quire·ment (ə kwīər′mənt), *n.* **1.** act of acquiring, esp. the gaining of knowledge or mental attributes. **2.** Often, **acquirements.** that which is acquired; attainment. [ACQUIRE + -MENT]

ac·qui·si·tion (ak′wi zish′ən), *n.* **1.** act of acquiring or gaining possession: *the acquisition of property.* **2.** something acquired: *a recent acquisition to the library.* [< L *acquīsītiōn-* (s. of *acquīsītiō*), equiv. to *acquīsīt(us)* gotten (ptp. of *acquīrere* to ACQUIRE) + *-iōn-* -ION]

ac·quis·i·tive (ə kwiz′i tiv), *adj.* tending or seeking to acquire and own, often greedily; eager to get wealth, land, etc.: *our acquisitive impulses; acquisitive societies.* [ACQUISIT(ION) + -IVE] —**ac·quis′i·tive·ly,** *adv.* —**ac·quis′i·tive·ness,** *n.*

ac·quit (ə kwit′), *v.t.,* **-quit·ted, -quit·ting.** **1.** to relieve from a charge of fault or crime; pronounce not guilty: *They acquitted him of the crime. The jury acquitted her even though she was guilty.* **2.** to release or discharge (a person) from an obligation. **3.** to settle or satisfy (a debt, obligation, claim, etc.). **4.** to bear or conduct (oneself); behave: *He acquitted himself well in battle.* **5.** to free or clear (oneself): *He acquitted himself of suspicion.* [ME *aquit(en)* < OF *aquite(r),* equiv. to *a-* (< L *ac-* AC-) + *quiter* to QUIT] —**ac·quit′ter,** *n.*
—**Syn. 1.** exculpate. See **absolve. 2.** free. —**Ant. 1.** convict.

ac·quit·tal (ə kwit′əl), *n.* **1.** the act of acquitting; discharge. **2.** the state of being acquitted; release. **3.** discharge or settlement of a debt, obligation, etc. **4.** *Law.* judicial deliverance from a criminal charge on a verdict or finding of not guilty. [ACQUIT + -AL[2]]

ac·quit·tance (ə kwit′əns), *n.* **1.** the act of acquitting. **2.** discharge of or from debt or obligation. **3.** a document or receipt as evidence of the discharge of debt, obligation, etc. [late ME *aquitance* < OF. See ACQUIT, -ANCE]

acr-, var. of **acro-** before a vowel: *acronym.*

A·crae·a (ə krē′ə), *n.* *Class. Myth.* an epithet of Aphrodite as goddess of the heavens, meaning "of the height."

a·cral·de·hyde (ə kral′də hīd′), *n.* *Chem.* acrolein. [< L *ācr-* (s. of *ācer*) sharp + ALDEHYDE]

a·cre (ā′kər), *n.* **1.** a common variable unit of land measure, now equal in the U.S. and Great Britain to 43,560 square feet or 1/640 square mile. **2. acres, a.** fields; estate; land in general: *His ranch is fifty acres.* **b.** *Informal.* large quantities: *a library with acres of books.* **3.** *Archaic.* a plowed or sown field. [ME *aker,* OE *æcer;* c. Icel *akr,* Goth *aker(s),* OHG *ackar* (G *Acker*), L *ager,* Gk *agró(s),* Skt *ájra-*]

A·cre (ä′krə *for 1;* ä′kər, ā′kər *for 2*), *n.* **1.** a state in W Brazil. 160,208 (1960); 58,899 sq. mi. *Cap.:* Rio Branco. **2.** a seaport in NW Israel: besieged and captured by Crusaders 1191. 20,000 (est. 1956).

a·cre·age (ā′kər ij), *n.* extent or area in acres; acres collectively. [ACRE + -AGE]

A·cre′a moth′ (ə krē′ə), a tiger moth, *Estigmene acrea,* having black spots on its wings and abdomen. [< L *acraea,* fem. of *acraeus* < Gk *akraîos* living high up; see ACRO-]

a·cred (ā′kərd), *adj.* owning many acres of land; landed. [ACRE + -ED[3]]

a·cre-foot (ā′kər fo͝ot′), *n.* a unit of volume of water in irrigation: the amount covering one acre to a depth of one foot, equal to 43,560 cubic feet.

a·cre-inch (ā′kər inch′), *n.* one-twelfth of an acre-foot.

ac·rid (ak′rid), *adj.* **1.** sharp or biting to the taste or smell; bitterly pungent; irritating to the eyes, nose, etc.: *acrid smoke from the burning rubber.* **2.** extremely or sharply stinging or bitter; exceedingly caustic: *acrid remarks.* [< L *ācr-* (s. of *ācer*) sharp, sour + -ID[4], perh. through influence of ACID] —**a·crid·i·ty** (ə krid′i tē), **ac′rid·ness,** *n.* —**ac′rid·ly,** *adv.*

ac·ri·dine (ak′ri dēn′, -din), *n.* *Chem.* a colorless, crystalline solid, $C_{13}H_9N$, usually obtained from the anthracine fraction of coal tar: used chiefly in the synthesis of dyes and drugs. [ACRID + -INE[2]]

ac·ri·fla·vine (ak′rə flā′vin, -vēn), *n.* *Chem.* an orange-brown, granular solid, $C_{14}H_{14}N_3Cl$, usually in mixture with another acridine derivative, proflavine, from which it differs in molecular structure by a methyl group: used chiefly in medicine as an antiseptic. Also called **neutral acriflavine, euflavine, trypaflavine neutral.** [ACRI(DINE) + -FLAVIN]

acrifla′vine hydrochlo′ride, *Chem.* the reddish-brown, crystalline, water-soluble hydrochloride of acriflavine, used similarly. Also called **trypaflavine, flavine.**

Ac·ri·lan (ak′rə lan′), *n.* *Trademark.* an acrylic fiber used in textiles, characterized chiefly by softness, strength, and wrinkle-resistant properties.

ac·ri·mo·ni·ous (ak′rə mō′nē əs), *adj.* caustic, stinging, or bitter in nature, speech, behavior, etc.: *an acrimonious answer; an acrimonious dispute.* [< ML *ācrimōniōs(us).* See ACRIMONY, -OUS] —**ac′ri·mo′ni·ous·ly,** *adv.* —**ac′ri·mo′ni·ous·ness,** *n.*

ac·ri·mo·ny (ak′rə mō′nē), *n.* sharpness, harshness, or bitterness of nature, speech, disposition, etc.: *The speaker attacked him with great acrimony.* [< L *ācrimōnia,* equiv. to *ācri-* (s. of *ācer*) sharp, sour + *-mōnia* -MONY]

A·cris·i·us (ə kris′ē əs), *n.* *Class. Myth.* a king of Argos, the father of Danae and grandfather of Perseus, by whom he was killed.

a·crit·i·cal (ā krit′i kəl), *adj.* **1.** not critical. **2.** *Med.* (of a disease) not showing a crisis. [A-[6] + CRITICAL]

acro-, a learned borrowing from Greek meaning "extremity" or "height," used in the formation of compound words: *acrophobia.* Also, *esp. before a vowel,* **acr-.** [< Gk *ákro(s)* topmost, highest; akin to L *ācer* sharp. Cf. ACME, EAR[2]]

ac·ro·bat (ak′rə bat′), *n.* **1.** a skilled performer of gymnastic feats, such as walking on a tightrope, swinging on a trapeze, etc. **2.** a person who with remarkable ease makes sudden changes or reversals in his opinions, relationships, etc. [back formation from NL *acrobatēs* rope-dancers < Gk *akrobátos* going aloft, equiv. to *akro-* ACRO- + *-batos,* verbal adj. of *baínein* to go]

ac·ro·bat·ic (ak′rə bat′ik), *adj.* of or pertaining to an acrobat or acrobatics. Also, **ac′ro·bat′i·cal.** [< Gk *akrobatik(ós).* See ACROBAT, -IC] —**ac′ro·bat′i·cal·ly,** *adv.*

ac·ro·bat·ics (ak′rə bat′iks), *n.* **1.** (*construed as pl.*) the feats of an acrobat; gymnastics. **2.** (*construed as sing.*) the art or practice of acrobatic feats. **3.** (*construed as pl.*) any actions performed with remarkable agility and ease: *the verbal acrobatics of a habitual liar.* Also, **ac′ro·bat′ism.** [see ACROBATIC, -ICS]

CONCISE PRONUNCIATION KEY: act, āble, dâre, ärt; ebb, ēqual; if, īce; hot, ōver, ôrder, oil, bo͝ok, o͞oze, out; up, ûrge; chief; sing; shoe; thin, that; zh as in *measure.* ə = *a* as in *alone, e* as in *system, i* as in *easily, o* as in *gallop, u* as in *circus;* ə as in *button* (but′ən), *fire* (fīər), *cradle* (krād′əl). See the full key inside the front cover.

ac·ro·car·pous (ak′rə kär′pəs), *adj.* *Bot.* having the fruit at the end of the primary axis. [< NL *acrocarpus* < Gk *akrókarpos.* See ACRO-, -CARPOUS]

ac·ro·ceph·a·ly (ak′rə sef′ə lē), *n.* *Pathol.* a malformation in which the head is somewhat pointed, caused by premature closure of the skull sutures. Also, **ac·ro·ce·pha·lia** (ak′rō sə fāl′yə). Also called **hypsicephaly, oxycephaly.** [ACRO- + -CEPHALY] —**ac′ro·ce·phal′ic** (ak′rō sə fal′ik), *adj., n.* —**ac′ro·ceph′a·lous,** *adj.*

Ac·ro·cor·inth (ak′rə kôr′inth, -kor′-), *n.* the citadel of ancient Corinth: strategic in the control of the Isthmus of Corinth; extensive ruins.

ac·ro·cy·a·no·sis (ak′rō sī′ə nō′sis), *n.* *Pathol.* cyanosis of the extremities, characterized by blueness and coldness of the fingers and toes. [< NL; see ACRO-, CYANOSIS]

ac·ro·dont (ak′rə dont′), *adj.* *Anat., Zool.* having rootless teeth fastened to the alveolar ridge of the jaws. [ACR- + -ODONT] —**ac′ro·dont′ism,** *n.*

ac·ro·drome (ak′rə drōm′), *adj.* *Bot.* running to a point: said of a nervation with the nerves terminating in or curving inward to the point of a leaf. Also, **a·crod·ro·mous** (ə krod′rə məs). [ACRO- + -DROME]

ac·ro·dyn·i·a (ak′rə din′ē ə, -dī′nē ə), *n.* *Pathol.* a condition of infants characterized by swelling, itching, and pinkness of the hands and feet, restlessness, and sensitivity to light. Also called **erythredema polyneuropathy, pink disease, Swift's disease.** [ACR- + -ODYNIA]

ac·ro·gen (ak′rə jən), *n.* *Bot.* a flowerless plant growing and producing its reproductive structures at the apex only, as ferns and mosses. [ACRO- + -GEN] —**ac·ro·gen·ic** (ak′rə jen′ik), **a·crog·e·nous** (ə kroj′ə nəs), *adj.* —**a·crog′e·nous·ly,** *adv.*

a·crog·ra·phy (ə krog′rə fē), *n.* a process for producing designs in relief on metal by tracing on chalk, for stereotype or electrotype plates. [ACRO- + -GRAPHY]

a·crog·y·nous (ə kroj′ə nəs), *adj.* *Bot.* having the archegonia arising from the apical cell of the stem, thereby terminating its growth, as certain liverworts. Cf. **anacrogynous.** [ACRO- + -GYNOUS]

a·cro·le·in (ə krō′lē in), *n.* *Chem.* a yellow, flammable liquid, $CH_2{=}CHCHO$, having a stifling odor, usually obtained by the decomposition of glycerol: used chiefly in the synthesis of commercial and pharmaceutical products. Also called **acraldehyde, acrylaldehyde, acrylic aldehyde.** [< L *ācr-* (s. of *ācer*) sharp + *ole(re)* (to) smell + -IN[2]]

ac·ro·lith (ak′rə lith), *n.* a sculptured figure having only the head and extremities made of marble or other stone. [< L *acrolith(us)* < Gk *akrólithos.* See ACRO-, -LITH] —**ac′ro·lith′ic,** *adj.*

a·crol·o·gy (ə krol′ə jē), *n., pl.* **-gies.** acrophony. [< F *acrologie.* See ACRO-, -LOGY] —**ac·ro·log·ic** (ak′rə loj′ik), *adj.* —**ac′ro·log′i·cal·ly,** *adv.*

ac·ro·me·gal·ic (ak′rō mə gal′ik), *adj.* **1.** pertaining to or suffering from acromegaly. —*n.* **2.** a person suffering from acromegaly. [ACROMEGAL(Y) + -IC]

ac·ro·meg·a·ly (ak′rə meg′ə lē), *n.* *Pathol.* a chronic disease characterized by enlargement of the bones of the head, the soft parts of the feet and hands, and sometimes other structures, due to dysfunction of the pituitary gland. [< NL *acromegalia.* See ACRO-, -MEGALY]

ac·ro·mic·ri·a (ak′rə mik′rē ə, -mī′krē ə), *n.* abnormal smallness of the head and extremities. [< NL; see ACRO-, MICRO-, -IA]

a·cro·mi·on (ə krō′mē ən), *n., pl.* **-mi·a** (-mē ə). *Anat.* the outward end of the spine of the scapula or shoulder blade. See diag. under **shoulder.** [< NL < Gk *akrṓmion,* equiv. to *akro-* ACRO- + *ôm(os)* shoulder + *-ion* dim. suffix] —**a·cro′mi·al,** *adv.*

ac·ron (ak′ron, -rən), *n.* the unsegmented, preoral portion of the body of an arthropod. [< NL < Gk *ákron,* neut. sing. of *ákros;* see ACRO-] —**ac·ro·nal** (ak′rə nᵊl), *adj.*

a·cron·i·cal (ə kron′i kəl), *adj.* *Rare.* occurring at sunset, as the rising or setting of a star. Also, **a·cron′y·cal.** [alter. of *acronychal* < Gk *akrónych(os)* vespertine (*akro-* ACRO- + *nych-,* var. s. of *nýx* night + *-os* adj. suffix) + -AL[1]] —**a·cron′i·cal·ly, a·cron′y·cal·ly,** *adv.*

a·cron·y·chous (ə kron′ə kəs), *adj.* *Rare.* having nails, claws, or hooves. Also, **achronychous.** [ACR- + Gk *onych-* (s. of *ónyx*) fingernail, claw + -OUS]

ac·ro·nym (ak′rə nim), *n.* **1.** a word formed from the initial letters or groups of letters of words in a set phrase, as *WAC* from *Women's Army Corps* or *loran* from *long-range navigation.* **2.** an acrostic. [ACR- + -ONYM] —**ac′ro·nym′ic, a·cron·y·mous** (ə kron′ə məs), *adj.*

a·cron·y·mize (ə kron′ə mīz′), *v.i., v.t.,* **-mized, -miz·ing.** to form into an acronym. [ACRONYM + -IZE]

a·crop·a·thy (ə krop′ə thē), *n.* *Pathol.* any disease of the extremities. [ACRO- + -PATHY]

a·crop·e·tal (ə krop′i tᵊl), *adj.* *Bot.* (of an inflorescence) developing upwards, towards the apex. [ACRO- + -PETAL] —**a·crop′e·tal·ly,** *adv.*

ac·ro·pho·bi·a (ak′rə fō′bē ə), *n.* *Psychiatry.* a pathological dread of high places. [< NL; see ACRO-, -PHOBIA]

a·croph·o·ny (ə krof′ə nē), *n., pl.* **-nies. 1.** the use of what was originally a logogram as a phonetic symbol for the initial sound of the word the logogram represented, as, in Semitic writing, the use of a picture of a shepherd's crook to represent the sound *l,* the first sound of *lamed,* the Hebrew word for a shepherd's crook. **2.** the use of a word as the name of the alphabetical symbol representing the initial sound of that word. Also, **acrology.** [ACRO- + -PHONY] —**ac·ro·phon·ic** (ak′rə fon′ik), **ac·ro·pho·net·ic** (ak′rə fə net′ik), *adj.* —**ac′ro·phon′i·cal·ly,** *adv.*

a·crop·o·lis (ə krop′ə lis), *n.* **1.** a fortified hilltop in ancient Greek cities. **2. the Acropolis,** the citadel of Athens on whicl the Parthenon was built. [< Gk *akrópolis.* See ACRO-, -POLIS] —**ac·ro·pol·i·tan** (ak′rə pol′i tᵊn), *adj.*

ac·ro·spire (ak′rə spīᵊr′), *n.* *Bot.* the first sprout appearing in the germination of grain; the developed plumule of the seed. [ACRO- + SPIRE[1]; r. *akerspire,* equiv. to *aker* (OE *æchir* ear of grain) + *spire*]

ac·ro·spore (ak′rə spōr′, -spôr′), *n.* *Bot.* a spore borne at the tip of a sporophore, as a basidiospore. [< F; see ACRO-, SPORE] —**ac·ro·spo·rous** (ak′rə spōr′əs, -spôr′-; ə kros′pər əs), *adj.*

a·cross (ə krôs′, ə kros′), *prep.* **1.** from one side to the other of: *a bridge across a river.* **2.** on or to the other side of: *across the sea.* **3.** into contact with; into the presence of, usually by accident: *to come across an old friend; to run across a first edition of Byron.* **4.** crosswise of or transversely to the length of something; athwart: *coats across the bed; standing across the boundary line.* —*adv.* **5.** from one side to another. **6.** on the other side: *We'll soon be across.* **7.** crosswise; transversely: *with arms across.* **8.** so as to be understood or learned: *He couldn't get the idea across to the class.* **9.** into a desired or successful state: *to put a business deal across.* [A-[1] + CROSS]

a·cross-the-board (ə krôs′thə bōrd′, -bôrd′, ə kros′-), *adj.* **1.** applying to each of several categories; general: *The corporation's across-the-board pay increase results in a raise for all employees of every department.* **2.** noting or pertaining to a radio or television program scheduled for the same hour Monday through Friday. **3.** (of a bet) covering all possibilities of winning on a given result, esp. by placing a combination bet on one horse in a race for win, place, and show.

a·cros·tic (ə krô′stik, ə kros′tik), *n.* **1.** a series of lines or verses in which the first, last, or other particular letters form a word, phrase, the alphabet, etc. —*adj.* **2.** Also, **a·cros′ti·cal.** of, like, or forming an acrostic. [< Gk *akrostich(is),* equiv. to *ákro(s)* ACRO- + *stích(os)* STICH + *-is* dim. suffix] —**a·cros′ti·cal·ly,** *adv.*

ac·ro·sto·li·um (ak′rə stō′lē əm), *n., pl.* **-li·a** (-lē ə). acroterium (def. 2).

ac·ro·ter (ak′rə tər), *n.* acroterium.

ac·ro·te·ri·on (ak′rə tēr′ē on′, -ē ən), *n., pl.* **-te·ri·a** (-tēr′ē ə). acroterium. [< Gk *akrōtḗrion* topmost part, extremity, equiv. to *akrō-* ACRO- + *-tērion* suffix designating a place for]

ac·ro·te·ri·um (ak′rə tēr′ē əm), *n., pl.* **-te·ri·a** (-tēr′ē ə). **1.** *Archit.* a pedestal for a sculpture or ornament at each base or at the apex of a pediment. **2.** Also called **acrostolium.** *Naut.* an ornamental termination to the stem or stern of any of various ancient Mediterranean vessels. Cf. **aplustre.** Also, **acroterion.** [Latinization of ACROTERION] —**ac′ro·te′ral, ac′ro·te′ri·al,** *adj.*

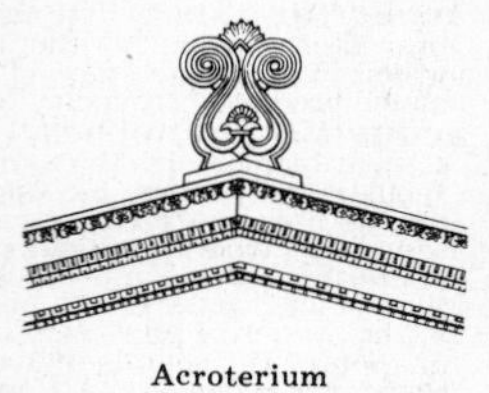

Acroterium

ac·ro·tism (ak′rə tiz′əm), *n.* *Pathol.* absence or weakness of the pulse. [A-[6] + Gk *krót(os)* beating or rhythmical sound + -ISM] —**a·crot·ic** (ə krot′ik), *adj.*

A·crux (ā′kruks), *n.* *Astron.* a star of the first magnitude in the constellation Southern Cross.

ac·ryl·al·de·hyde (ak′ril al′də hīd′), *n.* *Chem.* acrolein. Also called **acryl′ic al′dehyde.** [ACRYL(IC) + ALDEHYDE]

ac·ry·late (ak′rə lāt′, -lit), *n.* *Chem.* a salt or ester of an acrylic acid. [ACRYL(IC) + -ATE[2]]

a·cryl·ic (ə kril′ik), *adj.* **1.** of or derived from acrylic acid. —*n.* **2.** See **acrylic fiber. 3.** See **acrylic resin.** [ACR(OLEIN) + -YL + -IC]

acryl′ic ac′id, *Chem.* a colorless, corrosive liquid, $CH_2{=}CHCOOH$, having an acrid odor, usually derived from acrolein by oxidation: used esp. in the synthesis of acrylic resins.

acryl′ic es′ter, any of a series of esters derived from the acrylic acids.

acryl′ic fi′ber, *Chem.* any of the group of synthetic textile fibers, as Orlon, made by the polymerization of acrylonitrile as the principal component with one or more other monomers.

acryl′ic res′in, *Chem.* any of a group of thermoplastic resins formed by polymerizing the esters of amides of acrylic or methacrylic acid: used chiefly where transparency is desired, as in the methacrylate resins Lucite and Plexiglas. Also called **ac′rylate res′in.**

ac·ry·lo·ni·trile (ak′rə lō nī′tril, -trēl, -trīl), *n.* *Chem.* a colorless, flammable, poisonous liquid, $CH_2{=}CHCN$, used chiefly in the polymerization or copolymerization of rubber, textile fibers, and plastics. [ACRYL(IC) + -O- + NITRILE]

ac·ryl·yl (ak′rə lil), *adj.* *Chem.* containing the acrylyl group. [ACRYL(IC) + -YL]

ac′rylyl group′, *Chem.* the univalent group, $CH_2{=}CHCO{-}$, derived from acrylic acid. Also called **ac′rylyl rad′ical.**

A.C.S., 1. American Cancer Society. **2.** American Chemical Society. **3.** Associate in Commercial Science.

A/cs pay., accounts payable. Also, **a/cs pay.**

A/cs rec., accounts receivable. Also, **a/cs rec.**

act (akt), *n.* **1.** anything done, being done, or to be done; performance; deed. **2.** the process of doing: *caught in the act.* **3.** a formal decision, law, or the like, by a legislature, ruler, court, or other authority; decree or edict; statute; judgment, resolve, or award: *an act of Congress.* **4.** an instrument or document stating something done or transacted. **5.** one of the main divisions of a play or opera: *the second act of* Hamlet. **6.** a short performance by one or more entertainers, usually part of a variety show, radio program, etc. **7.** the personnel of such a group: *The act broke up after 30 years.* **8.** a piece of insincere conduct, pretended manner, or the like: *Her tearful farewell was all an act.* **9.** (in British universities) a degree candidate's formal defense of his thesis before a faculty committee. **10.** *Philos.* (in scholasticism) **a.** activity in process; operation. **b.** the principle or power of operation. **c.** form as determining essence. **d.** a state of realization, as opposed to potentiality. —*v.i.* **11.** to do something; exert energy or force; be employed or operative: *His mind acts sluggishly.* **12.** to reach, make, or issue a decision on some matter: *I am required to act before tomorrow noon.* **13.** to operate or function in a particular way; perform specific duties or functions: *to act as chairman.* **14.** to produce an effect; perform a function: *The medicine failed to act.* **15.** to behave or conduct oneself in a particular fashion: *to act well under all conditions.* **16.** to pretend; feign: *Act interested.* **17.** to perform on a stage as an actor: *He acted in three plays by Molière.* **18.** to be capable of being performed on the stage: *His plays don't act well.* **19.** to serve or substitute (usually fol. by *for*): *In my absence the assistant manager will act for me.* **20.** to perform on stage: *They will act in* Oedipus Rex. —*v.t.* **21.** to represent (a fictitious or historical character) with one's person: *to act* Macbeth. **22.** to feign; counterfeit: *to act outraged virtue.* **23.** to behave as: *He acted the fool.* **24.** *Obs.* to actuate. **25. act on** or **upon, a.** to act in accordance with; follow: *He acted on my advice.* **b.** to bring about a change in; affect: *The stirring music acted on the emotions of the audience.* **26. act one's age,** to behave in a manner appropriate to one's maturity: *Elderly women who dress as young girls are not acting their age.* **27. act out,** to demonstrate or illustrate by pantomime or by words and gestures: *Everyone roared when George acted out the episode with the plumber.* **28. act up,** *Informal.* **a.** to exhibit unusual or unexpected behavior: *Every time she used the vacuum cleaner the television would act up.* **b.** to behave willfully: *The children always act up in school the day before a holiday.* [< L *āct(a)* (pl.) things done, and *āct(us)* a doing, n. use of ptp. of *agere* to do (*āg-* ptp. s. + *-tus* ptp. suffix); r. late ME *acte* < MF] —**Syn. 1.** feat, exploit; achievement; transaction; accomplishment. See **action. 2.** deed. **4.** record. **6.** turn, routine. **11–15.** perform, function, work. **17, 18.** play.

Ac·ta (ak′tə), *n.pl.* official records, as of acts, deeds, proceedings, transactions, or the like. [< L, neut. pl. of *āctus,* ptp. of *agere* to do]

act·a·ble (ak′tə bəl), *adj.* **1.** capable of being acted on the stage. **2.** (of a play or parts of a play) providing roles of effectiveness and substance. [ACT + -ABLE] —**act′a·bil′i·ty,** *n.*

Ac·tae·on (ak tē′ən), *n.* *Class. Myth.* a hunter who, for having seen Diana bathing, was changed by her into a stag and was torn to pieces by his own hounds.

Ac′ta Sanc·to′rum (äk′tə säṅgk tōr′əm, -tôr′-), the collection of the biographies of the Christian saints and martyrs, edited by the Bollandists and arranged according to the ecclesiastical calendar.

act′ call′, *Theat.* **1.** Also called **act warning.** a call or order from the stage manager summoning performers onstage for the beginning of a performance or act. **2.** a signal summoning the audience to their seats for the beginning of a performance or act.

act′ cur′tain, *Theat.* a curtain for closing the proscenium opening between acts or scenes. Also called **act′ drop′, house curtain.**

actg., acting.

ACTH, 1. *Biochem.* a polypeptide hormone, produced by the anterior lobe of the pituitary gland, which stimulates the cortical substance of human adrenal glands. **2.** *Pharm.* this substance, extracted from the pituitary glands of hogs and other species, in the form of its white, water-soluble powder, used in the treatment of rheumatic fever, rheumatoid arthritis, and various allergic disorders. Also called **adrenocorticotropic hormone.** [*a(dreno)c(ortico)t(ropic) h(ormone)*]

ac·tin (ak′tən), *n.* *Biochem.* a globulin that is present in muscle plasma and that in connection with myosin plays an important role in muscle contraction. [ACT + -IN[2]]

actin-, var. of **actino-** before a vowel: *actinism.*

ac·ti·nal (ak′tə nᵊl, ak tīn′ᵊl), *adj.* *Zool.* **1.** having tentacles or rays. **2.** pertaining to the oral area from which the arms or tentacles radiate. [ACTIN- + -AL[1]] —**ac′ti·nal·ly,** *adv.*

act·ing (ak′ting), *adj.* **1.** serving temporarily, esp. as a substitute during another's absence; not permanent: *the acting mayor.* **2.** that acts; functioning. **3.** designed, adapted, or suitable for stage performance. **4.** provided with stage directions: *an acting version of a play.* —*n.* **5.** the art, profession, or activity of those who perform in stage plays, motion pictures, etc. [ACT + -ING[2], -ING[1]]

act′ing ar′ea, *Theat.* the part of the stage used for acting: *Confine the acting area for this scene to downstage.*

ac·tin·i·a (ak tin′ē ə), *n., pl.* **-tin·i·ae** (-tin′ē ē′), **-tin·i·as.** a sea anemone, esp. of the genus *Actinia.* [< NL; see ACTIN-, -IA]

ac·tin·i·an (ak tin′ē ən), *adj.* **1.** belonging or pertaining to the order or suborder *Actiniaria,* comprising the sea anemones. —*n.* **2.** any sea anemone. [< NL *Actīni(a)* ACTINIA + -AN]

ac·tin·ic (ak tin′ik), *adj.* pertaining to actinism. [ACTIN- + -IC] —**ac·tin′i·cal·ly,** *adv.*

actin′ic ray′, *Physics.* a ray of light of short wavelengths, as ultraviolet or violet, which produces photochemical effects.

ac′ti·nide se′ries (ak′tə nīd′), *Chem.* the series of radioactive elements that starts with actinium and ends with lawrencium. [ACTIN- + -IDE]

ac·tin·i·form (ak tin′ə fôrm′), *adj.* *Zool.* having a radiate form. [ACTIN- + -I- + -FORM]

ac·tin·ism (ak′tə niz′əm), *n.* the property of radiation by which chemical effects are produced. [ACTIN- + -ISM]

ac·tin·i·um (ak tin′ē əm), *n.* *Chem.* a radioactive chemical element, an isotope of mesothorium occurring in pitchblende, resembling the rare earths in chemical behavior and valence. *Symbol:* Ac; *at. no.:* 89; *at. wt.:* 227; *half life:* 13.5 years. [ACTIN- + -IUM]

actin′ium emana′tion, *Chem.* actinon.

actin′ium se′ries, *Chem.* the radioactive series that starts with actinouranium and ends with a stable isotope of lead of mass number 207. Also called **actinouranium series.**

actino-, 1. *Physical Chem.* a combining form indicating actinic radioactivity, used esp. before a consonant: *actinotherapy.* **2.** a combining form meaning "radiate in structure," "actinian": *actinozoan.* Also, *esp. before a vowel,* **actin-.** [< Gk, comb. form of *aktíno(s),* s. of *aktís* ray]

ac·ti·no·bac·il·lo·sis (ak′tə nō bas′ə lō′sis), *n.* *Vet. Pathol.* an infectious disease of cattle, domestic animals, and occasionally man, resembling actinomycosis and caused by the bacterium *Actinobacillus lignieresi.* Also called **wooden tongue.** [< NL *actinobacill(us)* (see ACTINOBACILLUS) + -OSIS] —**ac·ti·no·bac·il·lot·ic** (ak′tə nō bas′ə lot′ik), *adj.*

ac·ti·no·ba·cil·lus (ak′tə nō bə sil′əs), *n., pl.* **-cil·li** (-sil′ī). *Bacteriol.* any of several spherical or rod-shaped, aerobic, parasitic bacteria of the genus *Actinobacillus,* certain species of which, as *A. mallei,* are pathogenic for animals. [< NL; see ACTINO-, BACILLUS]

ac·ti·no·chem·is·try (ak′tə nō kem′i strē), *n.* the branch of chemistry dealing with actinism; photochemistry. [ACTINO- + CHEMISTRY] —**ac·ti·no·chem·i·cal** (ak′tə nō kem′i kəl), *adj.*

ac·ti·no·der·ma·ti·tis (ak′tə nō dûr′mə tī′tis), *n.* *Pathol.* inflammation of the skin caused by sunlight or other radiation. [ACTINO- + DERMATITIS]

ac·ti·no·drome (ak tin′ə drōm′), *adj.* (of a leaf) palmately veined. Also, **ac·ti·nod·ro·mous** (ak′tə nod′rə məs). [ACTINO- + -DROME]

ac·tin·o·gram (ak tin′ə gram′), *n.* the record produced by the action of an actinograph. [ACTINO- + -GRAM[1]]

ac·tin·o·graph (ak tin′ə graf′, -gräf′), *n.* a recording actinometer. [ACTINO- + -GRAPH] —**ac·tin·o·graph·ic** (ak tin′ə graf′ik), *adj.* —**ac·ti·nog·ra·phy** (ak′tə nog′rə fē), *n.*

ac·ti·noid (ak′tə noid′), *adj.* raylike; radiate. [ACTIN- + -OID]

ac·tin·o·lite (ak tin′ᵊlīt′), *n. Mineral.* a variety of amphibole, occurring in greenish bladed crystals or in masses. [ACTINO- + -LITE] —**ac·tin·o·lit·ic** (ak′ti nᵊlit′ik, ak tin′ᵊlit′-), *adj.*

ac·ti·nol·o·gy (ak′tə nol′ə jē), *n.* the science that deals with actinism. [ACTINO- + -LOGY]

ac·ti·nom·e·ter (ak′tə nom′i tər), *n.* a device for measuring intensity of radiation, usually by the photochemical effect. Cf. **actinograph.** [ACTINO- + -METER] —**ac·ti·no·met·ric** (ak′tə nō me′trik), **ac′ti·no·met′ri·cal,** *adj.* —**ac′ti·nom′e·try,** *n.*

ac·ti·no·mor·phic (ak′tə nō môr′fik), *adj.* **1.** *Biol.* having radial symmetry. **2.** *Bot.* (of certain flowers, as the buttercup) divisible vertically into similar halves by each of a number of planes. Also, **ac′ti·no·mor′phous.** [ACTINO- + -MORPHIC] —**ac′ti·no·mor′phy,** *n.*

ac·ti·no·my·ces (ak′tə nō mī′sēz), *n., pl.* **-ces.** *Bacteriol.* any of several saprophytic, filamentous, anaerobic bacteria of the genus *Actinomyces,* certain species of which are pathogenic for man and animals. [< NL, equiv. to *actīno-* ACTINO- + *mycēs* < Gk: fungus]

ac·ti·no·my·cete (ak′tə nō mī sēt′), *n. Bacteriol.* any of several rod-shaped or filamentous, aerobic or anaerobic bacteria of the family *Actinomycetaceae,* of the order *Actinomycetales,* certain species of which are pathogenic for man and animals. [prob. back formation from NL *actinomycētes;* pl. of ACTINOMYCES] —**ac′tin·o·my·cet′ous,** *adj.*

ac·ti·no·my·co·sis (ak′tə nō mī kō′sis), *n. Vet. Pathol., Pathol.* an infectious, inflammatory disease of cattle and other animals and of man, due to certain parasites and causing lumpy, often suppurating tumors, esp., about the jaws. Also called **lumpy jaw.** [ACTINOMYC(ES) + -OSIS] —**ac·ti·no·my·cot·ic** (ak′tə nō mī kot′ik), *adj.*

ac·ti·non (ak′tə non′), *n. Chem.* a chemically inert, gaseous, radioactive element isotopic with radon. It is a member of the actinium series. *Symbol:* An; *at. no.:* 86; *at. wt.:* 219. Also called **actinium emanation.** [< NL; see ACTINIUM, -ON²]

ac·tin·o·pod (ak tin′ə pod′), *n.* any protozoan of the subclass *Actinopoda,* including the heliozoans and radiolarians, having stiff, rodlike, radiating pseudopodia. [ACTINO- + -POD]

ac·ti·nop·te·ryg·i·an (ak′tə nop′tə rij′ē ən), *adj.* **1.** belonging or pertaining to the *Actinopterygii,* a group of bony fishes. —*n.* **2.** an actinopterygian fish. [< NL *actinopterygi(ī)* (pl.) (*actīno-* ACTINO- + Gk *pterýgi(on)* fin, equiv. to *pteryg-* (s. of *ptéryx* wing) + *-ion* dim. suffix) + -AN]

ac·ti·no·ther·a·py (ak′tə nō ther′ə pē), *n. Med.* radiotherapy. [ACTINO- + THERAPY]

ac·ti·no·u·ra·ni·um (ak′tə nō yŏŏ rā′nē əm), *n. Chem.* a radioactive isotope of uranium having an atomic mass of 235. [ACTINO- + URANIUM]

actinoura′nium se′ries, *Chem.* See **actinium series.**

ac·ti·no·zo·an (ak′tə nə zō′ən), *n., adj. Zool.* anthozoan. [ACTINO- + -ZO(A) + -AN]

ac·tion (ak′shən), *n.* **1.** the process or state of acting or of being active: *The machine is not now in action.* **2.** something performed; an act; deed. **3.** an act that one consciously wills and which may be characterized by physical or mental activity (contrasted with *passion*): *a crisis that demands action instead of debate; hoping for constructive action by the landlord.* **4. actions,** habitual or usual acts; conduct: *He is responsible for his actions.* **5.** energetic activity: *a man of action.* **6.** an exertion of power or force: *the action of wind upon a ship's sails.* **7.** effect or influence: *the action of morphine.* **8.** *Physiol.* a change in organs, tissues, or cells leading to performance of a function, as in muscular contraction. **9.** way or manner of moving: *the action of a machine or of a horse.* **10.** the mechanism by which something is operated, as that of a breechloading rifle or a piano. **11.** a military encounter or engagement. **12.** actual engagement in fighting an enemy. **13.** military and naval combat: *He saw action in the South Pacific.* **14.** *Slang.* **a.** an active gambling game: *Where can I find some action?* **b.** profits, esp. quick profits: *Cut me in for a piece of the action.* **15.** *Poetry, Theater.* the main subject or story, as distinguished from an incidental episode. **16.** *Theater.* **a.** an event or series of events that form part of a dramatic plot: *the action of a scene.* **b.** one of the three unities. Cf. **unity** (def. 9). **17.** the gestures or deportment of an actor or speaker. **18.** *Fine Arts.* the appearance of animation, movement, or emotion given to figures by their attitude, position, or expression. **19.** *Law.* **a.** a proceeding instituted by one party against another. **b.** the right of bringing it. **20.** *Eccles.* **a.** a religious ceremony, esp. a Eucharistic service. **b.** the canon of the Mass. **c.** those parts of a service of worship in which the congregation participates. [< L *āctiōn-* (s. of *āctiō*), equiv. to *āct(us)* (see ACT) + *-iōn-* -ION; r. late ME *accioun* < AF] —**ac′tion·less,** *adj.*

—**Syn. 1.** movement, operation. **2.** ACTION, ACT, DEED mean something done. ACTION applies esp. to the doing; ACT to the result of the doing. An ACTION usually lasts through some time and consists of more than one act: *to take action on a petition.* An ACT is single and of slight duration: *an act of kindness.* DEED emphasizes the finished or completed quality of an act; it may imply an act of some note, good or bad: *an irrevocable deed; a deed of daring.* **4.** behavior. **12.** brush, encounter, fight, skirmish. See **battle. 15.** plot. —**Ant. 1.** rest.

ac·tion·a·ble (ak′shə nə bəl), *adj.* **1.** furnishing ground for a lawsuit. **2.** liable to a law suit. [ACTION + -ABLE] —**ac′tion·a·bly,** *adv.*

Ac′tion Paint′ing, (*sometimes l.c.*) *Fine Arts.* a development of Abstract Expressionism characterized chiefly by a calligraphic quality or by broad, vigorous brushstrokes.

ac′tion ser′mon, the sermon preached before the administration of the Lord's Supper in Presbyterian churches in Scotland.

Ac·tis (ak′tis), *n. Class. Myth.* a son of Rhoda and Helius who, when banished from his home for fratricide, fled to Egypt, where he taught astrology. The Colossus of Rhodes was built in his honor.

Ac·ti·um (ak′tē əm, -shē əm), *n.* a promontory in NW ancient Greece: Antony and Cleopatra were defeated by Octavian and Agrippa in a naval battle near here in 31 B.C.

ac·ti·vate (ak′tə vāt′), *v.t.,* **-vat·ed, -vat·ing. 1.** to make active. **2.** *Physics.* **a.** to render more reactive; excite: *to activate a molecule.* **b.** to induce radioactivity. **3.** to aerate (sewage) in order to accelerate decomposition of impure organic matter by microorganisms. **4.** *Chem.* **a.** to make (carbon, a catalyst, molecules, etc.) more active. **b.** to hasten (reactions) by various means, such as heating. **5.** *Mil.* **a.** to create (a military unit or station). **b.** to place (a military unit or station) on an active status in an assigned capacity. [ACTIVE + -ATE¹] —**ac′ti·va′tion,** *n.*

ac′tivated sludge′, sludge (def. 8).

ac·ti·va·tor (ak′tə vā′tər), *n.* **1.** *Chem., Biochem.* a catalyst. **2.** any impurity in a mineral that causes luminescence. Cf. **inhibitor** (def. 2). [ACTIVATE + -OR²]

ac·tive (ak′tiv), *adj.* **1.** constantly engaged in action; busy: *an active life.* **2.** in a state of action; in actual existence, progress, or motion: *active hostilities.* **3.** involving physical effort and action: *active sports.* **4.** having the power of quick motion; nimble: *an active gazelle.* **5.** characterized by considerable or current action, motion, volume, use, participation, etc.: *an active market in wheat; an active list of subscribers.* **6.** causing change; capable of exerting influence (opposed to *passive*): *active treason.* **7.** effective (opposed to *inert*): *active ingredients.* **8.** *Gram.* noting or pertaining to a voice of verbal inflection in which typically the subject of the sentence is represented as performing the action expressed by the verb (opposed to *passive*): *Writes* in *He writes a letter every day* is an active verb. **9.** requiring or giving rise to action; practical: *the intellectual and the active mental powers.* **10.** (of a volcano) in eruption. **11.** *Accounting.* profitable; busy: *active accounts.* **12.** interest-bearing: *active paper.* **13.** *Med.* acting quickly; producing immediate effects: *active remedies.* **14.** *Sociol.* (of a crowd) engaging in purposeful activity, often of a violent nature. Cf. **expressive** (def. 4). **15.** *Rocketry.* able to transmit signals: *an active communications satellite.* **16.** *Mil.* serving on active duty. —*n.* **17.** *Gram.* **a.** the active voice. **b.** a form or construction in the active voice. [< L *āctīv(us)* (see ACT, -IVE); r. ME *actif* < MF] —**ac′tive·ly,** *adv.* —**ac′tive·ness,** *n.*

—**Syn. 1.** acting; working; operative. **3.** ACTIVE, ENERGETIC, STRENUOUS, VIGOROUS imply a liveliness and briskness in accomplishing something. ACTIVE suggests quickness and diligence as opposed to laziness or dilatory methods: *an active and useful person.* ENERGETIC suggests forceful and intense, sometimes nervous, activity: *conducting an energetic campaign.* STRENUOUS implies eager and zealous activity with a sense of urgency: *making a strenuous effort.* VIGOROUS suggests strong, effective activity: *using vigorous measures to accomplish an end.* **4.** agile, sprightly. —**Ant. 1, 4.** lazy. **5.** sluggish.

ac′tive du′ty, *Mil.* **1.** the status of full duty: *on active duty.* **2.** full duty. Also called **ac′tive serv′ice.**

ac′tive immu′nity, *Immunol.* immunity resulting from the production of antibodies within an organism.

ac′tive lay′er, the layer of soil, above the permafrost, that thaws during the summer.

ac′tive list′, a list of military personnel on active duty.

ac′tive prin′ciple, *Med.* the component or components of a crude drug, usually extracted, responsible for the characteristic medicinal effect.

ac′tive rea′son, *Aristotelianism.* an activity of intellect, embodying universal truth, potentially present in the mind of every individual, and when present, forming the only immortal part of the individual. Cf. **passive reason.**

ac·tiv·ism (ak′tə viz′əm), *n.* **1.** *Philos.* **a.** a theory that the essence of reality is an act or process of some sort. **b.** a theory that the relationship between the mind and the reality outside the mind is one involving continuous activity on the part of the mind. **2.** the doctrine or practice of vigorous action or involvement as a means of achieving political goals. [< G *Aktivism(us).* See ACTIVE, -ISM]

ac·tiv·ist (ak′tə vist), *n.* an especially active, vigorous advocate of a political cause. [ACTIVE + -IST]

ac·tiv·i·ty (ak tiv′i tē), *n., pl.* **-ties. 1.** the state or quality of being active; the state of action; doing. **2.** the quality of acting promptly; energy. **3.** a specific deed, action, function, or sphere of action: *social activities.* **4.** work, esp. in elementary grades at school, that involves direct experience by the student rather than textbook study. **5.** a use of energy or force; an active movement or operation. **6.** normal mental or bodily power, function, or process. **7.** liveliness, alertness, or vigorous action: *The movie is full of activity and noise.* **8.** *Physical Chem.* the capacity of a substance to react corrected for the loss of reactivity due to the interaction of its constituents. **9.** *Physics.* **a.** the number of atoms of a radioactive substance that disintegrate per unit of time, usually expressed in curies. **b.** radioactivity. **10.** *U.S.* an organizational unit or the function it performs. [< ML *activitāt-* (s. of *activitās*). See ACTIVE, -ITY]

ac·tiv·ize (ak′tə vīz′), *v.t.,* **-ized, -iz·ing.** to make active; activate. [ACTIVE + -IZE]

act′ of faith′, an act that demonstrates or tests the strength of a person's convictions, as an important personal sacrifice. Cf. **auto-da-fé.**

act′ of God′, *Law.* a direct, sudden, and irresistible action of natural forces, such as could not reasonably have been foreseen or prevented.

Act′ of Par′liament clock′, a weight-driven pendulum wall clock of the late 18th century, usually having an unglazed black dial with gilt numbers and a trunk below it to accommodate the end of the pendulum (originally installed in English taverns because of the lack of private clocks due to a burdensome tax).

Act′ of Tolera′tion, *Eng. Hist.* the statute (1689) granting religious freedom to dissenting Protestants upon meeting certain conditions, as the rejection of the doctrine of transubstantiation.

Act′ of Uniform′ity, *Eng. Hist.* any of the three statutes (1549, 1559, 1662) regulating public worship services in the Anglican Church, esp. the act of 1662 requiring the use of the Book of Common Prayer.

act′ of war′, an illegal act of aggression by a country against another with which it is nominally at peace.

ac·to·my·o·sin (ak′tə mī′ə sin), *n. Biochem.* a complex protein, consisting of myosin and actin, that is the major constituent of skeletal muscle and is thought to interact with ATP to cause muscle contraction. [ACT(IN) + -O- + MYOSIN]

ac·ton (ak′tən), *n. Armor.* a quilted garment worn under mail in the 13th and 14th centuries; gambeson. Also, **ackton, aketon, haqueton.** [ME < AF *aketoun,* OF *a(u)queton* < OPr *alcoton* << Ar *al qutum* the cotton]

Ac·ton (ak′tən), *n.* **1. Lord** (*John Emerich Edward Dalberg-Acton,* 1st Baron), 1834–1902, English historian. **2.** a city in SE England, near London: center of Puritanism at time of Cromwell. 67,274 (1961).

ac·tor (ak′tər), *n.* **1.** a person who acts in stage plays, motion pictures, television broadcasts, etc., esp. professionally. **2.** a person who does something; doer; participant. [< L *āctor.* See ACT, -OR²]

Ac·tor (ak′tər), *n. Class. Myth.* **1.** a brother of King Augeas, sometimes believed to be the father, by Molione, of Eurytus and Cteatus. Cf. **Moliones. 2.** a son of Myrmidon and Pasidice who became king of Phthia.

Ac·tor·i·dae (ak tôr′i dē′), *n.pl. Class. Myth.* Moliones.

ac·tor-proof (ak′tər prōōf′), *adj. Theat.* (of a role or script) effective even if poorly acted. [ACTOR + -PROOF]

Ac′tors' Eq′uity Associa′tion, a labor union for actors, founded in 1912 and affiliated with the AFL-CIO.

ac·tress (ak′tris), *n.* a female actor. [ACT(O)R + -ESS]

Acts′ of the Apos′tles, a book of the New Testament. Also called **Acts.**

act′ tune′, a musical piece played between the acts of a play in 17th- or early 18th-century England. Cf. **entr'acte** (def. 3).

ac·tu·al (ak′chōō əl), *adj.* **1.** existing in act or fact; real: *an actual case of treason; actual expenses; an actual hardship.* **2.** existing now; present; current: *the actual position of the moon.* **3.** *Obs.* pertaining to or involving acts or action. [< LL *āctuāl(is),* equiv. to L *āctu-* (s. of *āctus;* see ACT) + *-ālis* -AL¹; r. ME *actuel* < MF] —**ac′tu·al·ness,** *n.*

—**Syn. 1.** genuine, veritable. See **real.** —**Ant. 1.** unreal.

ac′tual cost′, the cost of a product based on incurred costs of material and labor required in its production. Cf. **standard cost.**

ac′tual grace′, *Rom. Cath. Ch.* supernatural help given by God to enlighten the mind and strengthen the will to do good and avoid evil.

ac·tu·al·ise (ak′chōō ə līz′), *v.t.,* **-ised, -is·ing.** *Chiefly Brit.* actualize. —**ac′tu·al·i·sa′tion,** *n.*

ac·tu·al·ism (ak′chōō ə liz′əm), *n. Philos.* the doctrine that all reality is animate or in motion. [ACTUAL + -ISM] —**ac′tu·al·ist,** *n., adj.* —**ac′tu·al·is′tic,** *adj.*

ac·tu·al·i·ty (ak′chōō al′i tē), *n., pl.* **-ties. 1.** actual existence; reality. **2. actualities,** actual conditions or circumstances; facts: *He had to adjust to the actualities of life.* **3.** *Brit.* a television or radio broadcast, or a film or sound recording, of an actual event; documentary. [late ME *actualite* < ML *actuālitāt-* (s. of *actuālitās*). See ACTUAL, -ITY]

ac·tu·al·ize (ak′chōō ə līz′), *v.t.,* **-ized, -iz·ing.** to make actual; realize in action or fact. Also, *esp. Brit.,* **actualise.** [ACTUAL + -IZE] —**ac′tu·al·i·za′tion,** *n.*

ac·tu·al·ly (ak′chōō ə lē), *adv.* as an actual or existing fact; really. [ACTUAL + -LY]

ac′tual sin′, *Theol.* any sin committed by an individual of his free will, as contrasted with original sin.

ac·tu·ary (ak′chōō er′ē), *n., pl.* **-ar·ies. 1.** *Insurance.* a person who computes premium rates, dividends, risks, etc., according to probabilities based on statistical records. **2.** (formerly) a registrar or clerk. [< L *āctuāri(us)* shorthand writer, clerk, var. (with *u* of *āctus* ACT) of *āctārius* (*āct(a)* deeds, documents + *-ārius* -ARY)] —**ac·tu·ar·i·al** (ak′chōō âr′ē əl), **ac′tu·ar′i·an,** *adj.* —**ac′tu·ar′i·al·ly,** *adv.*

ac·tu·ate (ak′chōō āt′), *v.t.,* **-at·ed, -at·ing. 1.** to incite to action; impel; motivate: *actuated by selfish motives.* **2.** to put into action; start a process; turn on: *to actuate a machine.* [< ML *actuāt(us)* reduced to action (ptp. of *actuāre*), equiv. to L *āctu(s)* (see ACT) + *-ātus* -ATE¹] —**ac′tu·a′tion,** *n.* —**ac′tu·a′tor,** *n.*

act-wait (akt′wāt′), *n. Theat. Chiefly Brit.* an interval between the acts of a play; an intermission; entr'acte.

act′ warn′ing, *Theat.* **1.** notification from the manager advising the performers of the amount of time left before they must appear onstage. **2.** See **act call** (def. 1).

ac·u·ate (ak′yōō it, -āt′), *adj.* sharpened; pointed. [late ME < L *acu(s)* needle + -ATE¹]

a·cu·i·ty (ə kyōō′i tē), *n.* sharpness; acuteness; keenness: *acuity of vision.* [< ML *acūitāt-* (s. of *acūitās*) (L *acū(men)* ACUMEN + *-itāt-* -ITY)]

a·cu·le·ate (ə kyōō′lē it, -lē āt′), *adj.* **1.** *Biol.* having or being any sharp-pointed structure. **2.** having a slender ovipositor or sting, as the hymenopterous insects. **3.** pointed; stinging. Also, **a·cu′le·at′ed.** [< L *acūleāt(us).* See ACULEUS, -ATE¹]

a·cu·le·us (ə kyōō′lē əs), *n., pl.* **-le·i** (-lē ī′). **1.** Also, **acus.** the modified ovipositor or sting of certain hymenopterous insects. **2.** prickle (def. 2). [< L, equiv. to *acu(s)* needle + *-leus* dim. suffix]

a·cu·men (ə kyōō′mən, ak′yə-), *n.* superior mental acuteness and discernment; keen and penetrating insight: *remarkable acumen in business matters.* [< L: sharpness, equiv. to *acū-* (ptp. s. of *acuere* to sharpen; see ACUTE) + *-men* n. suffix] —**a·cu·mi·nous** (ə kyōō′mə nəs), *adj.*

a·cu·mi·nate (*adj.* ə kyōō′mə nit, -nāt′; *v.* ə kyōō′mə nāt′), *adj., v.,* **-nat·ed, -nat·ing.** —*adj.* **1.** *Bot., Zool.* pointed; tapering to a point. —*v.t.* **2.** to make sharp or keen. [< L *acūmināt(us)* (ptp. of *acūmināre*), equiv. to *acūmin-* (s. of *acūmen*) ACUMEN + *-ātus* -ATE¹] —**a·cu′mi·na′tion,** *n.*

Acuminate leaf

ac·u·punc·ture (*n.* ak′yōō pungk′chər; *v.* ak′yōō pungk′chər), *n., v.,* **-tured, -tur·ing.** —*n.* **1.** a Chinese medical practice that attempts to cure illness by puncturing specified areas of the skin with needles. **2.** *Med.* the puncture of a tissue with a needle, as for drawing off fluids or relieving pain. —*v.t.* **3.** to perform an acupuncture on. [< L *acū-* (s. of *acus*) needle + PUNCTURE]

a·cus (ā′kəs), *n., pl.* **a·cus.** **1.** *Surg.* a needle, esp. one used in a surgical operation. **2.** aculeus (def. 1). [< L]

ac·u·sec·tor (ak′yə sek′tər), *n. Surg.* (in electrosurgery) a needle for cutting tissue by means of a high-frequency current. [< NL; see ACUS, SECTOR] —**ac′u·sec′tion,** *n.*

a·cut·ance (ə kyōōt′ᵊns), *n.* a measure of the sharpness with which a film can reproduce the edge of an object. [ACUTE + -ANCE]

a·cute (ə kyōōt′), *adj.* **1.** sharp at the end; ending in a point; not blunt or obtuse. **2.** sharp or severe in effect; intense; poignant: *acute sorrow.* **3.** extremely great or severe; crucial; sharp: *an acute shortage.* **4.** (of disease) brief and severe (opposed to *chronic*). **5.** sharp or penetrating in intellect, insight, or perception: *an acute observer.* **6.** extremely sensitive even to slight details or impressions: *acute eyesight.* **7.** *Geom.* **a.** (of an angle) less than 90°. See diag. under **angle. b.** (of a triangle) containing only acute angles. See diag. under **triangle. 8.** consisting of, indicated by, or bearing the mark ´, placed over vowel symbols in some languages to show that the vowels or the syllables they are in are pronounced in a certain way, as in French that the quality of an *e* so marked is close; in Hungarian that the vowel is long; in Spanish that the marked syllable bears the word accent; in Ibo that it is pronounced with high tones; or in classical Greek, where the mark originated, that the syllable bears the word accent and is pronounced, according to the ancient grammarians, with raised pitch (opposed to *grave*): *the acute accent; an acute e.* —*n.* **9.** the acute accent. [< L *acūt(us)* sharpened, ptp. of *acuere* (*acū-*, ptp. s., akin to *acus* needle, *ācer* sharp + *-tus* ptp. suffix)] —**a·cute′ly,** *adv.* —**a·cute′ness,** *n.*
—**Syn. 3.** critical. **4.** sudden, distressing, violent. **5.** keen, astute, discerning, perceptive, intelligent, perspicacious; sharp-witted, clever, smart, bright, ingenious, brilliant; knowing, wise, sage, sagacious, sapient. ACUTE, PENETRATING, SHREWD imply a keenness of understanding, perception, or insight. ACUTE suggests particularly a clearness of perception and a realization of related meanings: *an acute intellect.* PENETRATING adds the idea of depth of perception and a realization of implications: *a wise and penetrating judgment.* SHREWD adds the idea of knowing how to apply practically (or to one's own advantage) what one perceives and understands: *wary and shrewd.* **6.** keen. —**Ant. 1, 2, 5, 6.** dull.

acute′ al′coholism, *Pathol.* a temporary state resulting from excessive consumption of alcohol; drunkenness; intoxication. Cf. **chronic alcoholism.**

acute′ ante′rior poliomyeli′tis, *Pathol.* poliomyelitis.

acute′ bisec′trix, *Crystall.* See under **bisectrix** (def. 1).

a·cu·ti·lin·gual (ə kyōōt′ᵊlĭng′gwəl), *adj. Zool.* having a sharply pointed tongue or mouth, as certain bees. [< L *acūt(us)* ACUTE + -I- + LINGUAL]

ACW, *Radio.* alternating continuous waves.

ACWA, Amalgamated Clothing Workers of America.

-acy, a suffix of nouns of quality, state, office, etc., many of which accompany adjectives in *-acious* or nouns or adjectives in *-ate: fallacy; papacy; legacy; delicacy; piracy.* [< L *-ācia*, ML *-ācia* (L *-ātia*), ML *-ātia*. Cf. -CRACY]

a·cy·clic (ā sī′klik, ā sik′lik), *adj.* not cyclic: *an acyclic flower; acyclic compounds.* [A-[6] + CYCLIC]

acy′clic ter′pene, *Chem.* See under **terpene** (def. 2).

ac·yl (as′il, -ēl), *adj. Chem.* containing the acyl group. [AC(ID) + -YL]

ac·yl·ate (as′ə lāt′), *v.t.,* **-at·ed, -at·ing.** *Chem.* to introduce the acyl group into (a compound). [ACYL + -ATE[1]] —**ac′yl·a′tion,** *n.*

ac′yl group′, *Chem.* the univalent group, RCO–, where R is any organic group attached to one bond of the carbonyl group. Also called **ac′yl rad′ical.**

a·cyl·o·in (ə sil′ō in, as′ə loin′, as′ə lō′in), *n. Chem.* a hydroxy ketone of the general formula, RCOCHOHR, where R is an element or group. [ACYL + (BENZ)OIN]

ad[1] (ad), *n.* **1.** advertisement. **2.** advertising: *an ad director.* [by shortening]
—**Usage.** AD, a clipped form of *advertisement,* is not used in formal writing or speech. There is no objection generally to its use in informal contexts.

ad[2] (ad), *n. Tennis.* **1.** advantage (def. 5). **2. ad in,** the advantage being scored by the server. **3. ad out,** the advantage being scored by the receiver. [by shortening]

ad[3] (ad), *prep.* (in prescriptions) to; up to. [< L]

Ad (ad), *n.* a boy's given name.

ad-, a formal element occurring in loan words from Latin, where it meant "toward" and indicated direction, tendency, or addition; attached chiefly to stems not found as words themselves: *adjective.* [< L *ad, ad-* (prep. and prefix) to, toward, at, about; c. AT[1]]

-ad[1], **1.** a suffix occurring in loan words from Greek denoting a numerical group: *dyad; triad.* **2.** a suffix meaning "derived from," "related to," introduced in loan words from Greek (*Olympiad*), used sporadically in imitation of Greek models, as *Dunciad,* after *Iliad.* [comb. form repr. Gk *-ad-*, specialization of adjective-forming suffix, often used substantively]

-ad[2], var. of **-ade**[1]: *ballad.*

ad., **1.** adverb. **2.** advertisement.

A.D., in the year of our Lord; since Christ was born: *From 20* B.C. *to* A.D. *50 is 70 years.* [< L *annō Domini*]

a.d., **1.** after date. **2.** before the day. [< L *ante diem*] **3.** autograph document.

A·da (ā′də), *n.* **1.** a city in central Oklahoma. 14,347 (1960). **2.** a town in central Ohio. 3918 (1960). **3.** *Douay Bible.* Adah (defs. 1, 2). **4.** Also, **Adie.** a girl's given name.

A.D.A., **1.** American Dental Association. **2.** Americans for Democratic Action. Also, **ADA**

A·da·bel (ā′də bel′), *n.* a girl's given name. Also, **A′da·belle′.**

a·dac·ty·lous (ā dak′tᵊləs), *adj. Zool.* having no fingers or toes. [A-[6] + DACTYL + -OUS]

ad·age (ad′ij), *n.* a traditional saying expressing a common experience or observation; proverb. [< F < L *adag(ium),* equiv. to *ad-* AD- + *agi-* (for **agi-*, s. of *āio* I say) + *-um* n. suffix] —**a·da·gi·al** (ə dā′jē əl), *adj.*

a·da·giet·to (ə dä′jē et′ō, -zhē-; *It.* ä′dä jet′tô), *adj., adv., n., pl.* **-tos.** *Music.* —*adj., adv.* **1.** slightly faster than adagio. —*n.* **2.** a short adagio. [< It, equiv. to *adagi(o)* ADAGIO + *-etto* dim. suffix; see -ET]

a·da·gio (ə dä′jō, -zhē ō′; *It.* ä dä′jô), *adv., adj., n., pl.* **-gios.** *Music.* —*adv.* **1.** in a leisurely manner; slowly. —*adj.* **2.** slow. —*n.* **3.** an adagio movement or piece. **4.** **a.** *Dance.* a sequence of well-controlled, graceful movements performed as a display of skill. **b.** *Dance.* a duet by a man and a woman or mixed trio emphasizing difficult technical feats. **c.** *Ballet.* a love-duet sequence in the pas de deux. [< It, for *ad agio* at ease < L *ad-* AD- + Pr *aize;* see EASE]

a·da·gis·si·mo (ä′dä jēs′ə mō′, -jis′ə-; *It.* ä′dä jēs′sē mô), *adv., adj. Music.* very slow. [< It, equiv. to *adag(io)* ADAGIO + *-issimo* < L *-issimus* superl. suffix]

A·dah (ā′də), *n.* **1.** one of the two wives of Lamech. Gen. 4:19. **2.** the wife of Esau, and the mother of Eliphaz. Gen. 36:2, 4, 10, 12, 16. **3.** a girl's given name. Also, *Douay Bible,* **Ada** (for defs. 1, 2).

A·dair (ə dâr′), *n.* a boy's given name.

A·dal (ə dal′), *n.* a boy's given name. Also, **Adel.**

Ad·al·bert (ad′ᵊl bərt, ə dal′bərt; *Ger.* ä′däl bert′), *n.* a boy's given name. Also, **Adelbert.**

Ad·am (ad′əm *for 1, 2, 4, 6–9;* A DÄN′ *for 3, 5*), *n.* **1.** the name of the first man: progenitor of the human race. Gen. 2:7; 5:1–5. **2.** man. **3.** **Adolphe Charles** (A dôlf′ SHARL), 1803–56, French composer of comic opera and ballet music. **4.** **James,** 1730–94, and his brother **Robert,** 1728–92, English architects and furniture designers. **5.** **Lam·bert Si·gis·bert** (läN beR′ sē zhēz beR′), 1700–59, and his brother **Ni·cho·las Sé·bas·tien** (nē kō lä′ sā bäs tyaN′), 1705–78, French sculptors. **6.** a boy's given name. **7. not know someone from Adam,** to be unacquainted with a person: *He greeted us every morning, but we didn't know him from Adam.* **8. the old Adam,** the unregenerate nature of man; disposition to evil: *He attributed his wild outburst to the old Adam in him.* —*adj.* **9.** noting or pertaining to the style of architecture, decoration, or furnishings associated with Robert and James Adam, characterized by free adaptation of ancient Roman forms, by façades of refined simplicity, by interiors lavishly treated with shallow, delicate ornament generally painted in light, vivid colors, and by furnishings designed as an integral part of the decorative schemes of the various interiors, generally with slender lines and ornamentation in low relief, and with much use of unpainted wood with a dark finish. [< Heb: man]

Adam pedestal with urn

Ad·a·ma (ad′ə mə), *n. Douay Bible.* Admah.

Ad·am-and-Eve (ad′əm ən ēv′, -ənd-), *n. U.S.* the puttyroot.

ad·a·mant (ad′ə mənt, -mant′), *n.* **1.** *Archaic.* an impenetrably hard substance, formerly sometimes identified with the diamond. **2.** any impenetrably or unyieldingly hard substance. —*adj.* **3.** impenetrably or unyieldingly hard; adamantine. **4.** utterly unyielding in attitude or opinion in spite of all appeals, urgings, etc. [< L *adamant-* (s. of *adamas*) < Gk, equiv. to *a-* A-[6] + *-damant-* verbal adj. of *damân* to conquer; r. OE *athamans* (< ML) and ME *aymont* < MF *aimant* < VL **adimant-*]

ad·a·man·tine (ad′ə man′tin, -tēn, -tīn), *adj.* **1.** impenetrably or unyieldingly hard. **2.** utterly unyielding or firm in attitude or opinion. **3.** like a diamond in luster. [late ME < L *adamantin(us)* < Gk *adamántinos.* See ADAMANT, -INE[1]]

Ad·a·mas (ad′ə məs), *n.* (in the *Iliad*) a Trojan ally who was killed when his attempt to slay Antilochus was thwarted by Poseidon.

Ad′am Bede′ (bēd), a novel (1859) by George Eliot.

A·dam de la Halle (A däN′ də lA Al′), c1240–87, French troubadour: composer of what is reputedly the earliest French comic opera. Also, **A·dam′ de la Hale′.**

Ad·am·ic (ad′ə mik), *adj.* pertaining to or suggestive of Adam. Also, **A·dam·i·cal** (ə dam′i kəl). [ADAM + -IC] —**A·dam′i·cal·ly,** *adv.*

A·dam·ic (ə dam′ik, ad′ə mik), *n.* **Louis,** 1899–1951, U.S. novelist, born in Yugoslavia.

Ad·am·ite (ad′ə mīt′), *n.* **1.** a descendant of Adam; human being. **2.** a nudist. [ADAM + -ITE[1]] —**Ad·am·it·ic** (ad′ə mit′ik), **Ad′am·it′i·cal,** *adj.*

Ad·ams (ad′əmz), *n.* **1. Charles Francis,** 1807–86, U.S. statesman: minister to Great Britain 1861–68 (son of John Quincy Adams). **2. Franklin Pierce** ("*F.P.A.*"), 1881–1960, U.S. author and columnist. **3. Henry (Brooks),** 1838–1918, U.S. historian, writer, and teacher (son of Charles Francis Adams). **4. James Trus·low** (trus′lō), 1878–1949, U.S. historian. **5. John,** 1735–1826, 2nd president of the U.S. 1797–1801: a leader in the American Revolution. **6. John Quin·cy** (kwin′zē, -sē), 1767–1848, 6th president of the U.S. 1825–29; Secretary of State 1817–25 (son of John Adams). **7. Lé·o·nie Fuller** (lā ō′nē), born 1899, U.S. poet. **8. Maude** (*Maude Kiskadden*), 1872–1953, U.S. actress. **9. Roger,** born 1889, U.S. chemist. **10. Samuel,** 1722–1803, American statesman: a leader in the American Revolution. **11. Samuel Hopkins,** 1874–1958, U.S. journalist and novelist. **12. Mount.** a mountain in SW Washington, in the Cascade Range. 12,307 ft. **13.** a mountain in N New Hampshire, in the White Mountains. 5798 ft. **14.** a crater in the fourth quadrant of the face of the moon: about 36 miles in diameter.

Ad′am's ale′, *Facetious.* water.

Ad′am's ap′ple, **1.** a projection of the thyroid cartilage at the front of the neck, more prominent in men. **2.** See **crape jasmine.**

ad·ams·ite (ad′əm zīt′), *n. Chem., Mil.* a yellow irritant smoke, containing a poisonous form of arsenic, used as a harassing agent. Also called **phenarsazine chloride, diphenylaminechlorarsine, DM** [named after R. ADAMS; see -ITE[1]]

Ad′am's-nee′dle (ad′əmz nēd′ᵊl), *n. U.S.* a yucca, *Yucca filamentosa,* grown as an ornamental.

Ad′ams-Stokes′ syn′drome (ad′əmz stōks′), *Pathol.* See **Stokes-Adams syndrome.** Also called **Ad′ams-Stokes′ disease′.**

A·da·na (ä′dä nä′), *n.* a city in S Turkey. 750,803 (1960). Also called **Seyhan.**

A·da·pa (ä′dä pä′), *n.* a legendary Akkadian sage who unwittingly rejected on behalf of mankind the food and water of immortality offered by Anu.

a·dapt (ə dapt′), *v.t.* **1.** to make suitable to requirements or conditions; adjust or modify fittingly: *They adapted themselves to the change quickly.* —*v.i.* **2.** to adjust oneself to different conditions, environment, etc.: *She lacked the ability to adapt easily.* [< L *adapt(āre)* (to) fit, adjust. See AD-, APT] —**a·dapt′ed·ness,** *n.*
—**Syn. 1.** fit, accommodate, suit, compose, reconcile, conform, qualify. See **adjust.**

a·dapt·a·ble (ə dap′tə bəl), *adj.* **1.** capable of being adapted. **2.** able to adjust oneself readily to different conditions: *an adaptable person.* [ADAPT + -ABLE] —**a·dapt′a·bil′i·ty, a·dapt′a·ble·ness,** *n.*

ad·ap·ta·tion (ad′əp tā′shən), *n.* **1.** the act of adapting. **2.** the state of being adapted; adjustment. **3.** something produced by adapting: *an adaptation of an opera for television.* **4.** *Biol.* **a.** any alteration in the structure or function of an organism or any of its parts that results from natural selection and by which the organism becomes better fitted to survive and multiply in its environment. **b.** a form or structure modified to fit changed environment. **5.** *Physiol.* the decrease in response of sensory receptor organs, as those of vision, touch, temperature, olfaction, audition, and pain, to changed, constantly applied, environmental conditions. **6.** *Ophthalm.* the regulating by the pupil of the quantity of light entering the eye. **7.** Also, **a·dap·tion** (ə dap′shən). *Sociol.* a slow, usually unconscious modification of individual and social activity in adjustment to cultural surroundings. [< LL *adaptātiōn-* (s. of *adaptātiō*), equiv. to L *adaptāt(us)* fitted (ptp. of *adaptāre* to ADAPT; see -ATE[1]) + *-iōn-* -ION] —**ad′ap·ta′tion·al,** *adj.* —**ad′ap·ta′tion·al·ly,** *adv.*

a·dapt·er (ə dap′tər), *n.* **1.** one who or that which adapts. **2.** a device to connect parts having different sizes or designs, enabling them to be fitted together. **3.** an accessory to convert a machine, tool, etc., to a new or modified use. Also, **a·dap·tor.** [ADAPT + -ER[1]]

a·dap·tive (ə dap′tiv), *adj.* serving or able to adapt; showing or contributing to adaptation: *adaptive coloring of a chameleon.* [ADAPT + -IVE] —**a·dap′tive·ly,** *adv.* —**a·dap′tive·ness,** *n.*

A·dar (ə där′; *Heb.* ä däR′), *n.* a month of the Jewish calendar. Cf. **Jewish calendar.** [< Heb]

ad ar·bi·tri·um (äd är bi′tRē ŏŏm′; *Eng.* ad är bi′trē əm), *Latin.* at pleasure; at will. [lit., at (one's) control or decision]

Adar′ She′ni (shā′nē; *Heb.* shā nē′), Veadar. [< Heb: Adar the Second]

ad a·stra per a·spe·ra (äd ä′strä peR ä′spe Rä′; *Eng.* ad as′trə pər as′pər ə), *Latin.* to the stars through difficulties: motto of Kansas.

a·dat (ä′dät), *n.* the native law traditional in Indonesia. [< Javanese < Ar *'adālat* (court of) equity]

a da·tu (ä dä′tōō), *Latin.* from the date.

ad·ax·i·al (ad ak′sē əl), *adj. Bot.* situated on the side toward the axis or stem. [AD- + AXIAL]

A.D.C., aide-de-camp.

ad cap·tan·dum vul·gus (äd käp tän′dŏŏm wŏŏl′gŏŏs; *Eng.* ad kap tan′dəm vul′gəs), *Latin.* in order to please the mob. [lit., for courting the crowd]

Ad′cock anten′na (ad′kok), *Electronics.* an antenna used for direction-finding, consisting of a pair of vertical dipoles. [named after its inventor]

add (ad), *v.t.* **1.** to unite or join so as to increase the number, quantity, size, or importance: *to add another stone to the pile.* **2.** to find the sum of (often fol. by *up*): *adding the grocery bill up.* **3.** to say or write further. **4.** to include (usually fol. by *in*). —*v.i.* **5.** to perform the arithmetic operation of addition: *children learning to add and subtract.* **6. add to,** to be or serve as an addition: *His illness added to the family's troubles.* **7. add up, a.** to make the desired or expected total: *These figures don't add up right.* **b.** to seem reasonable or consistent; be in harmony or accord: *There were aspects of the story that didn't add up.* **8. add up to,** to signify; indicate: *The evidence adds up to a case of murder.* —*n. Journalism.* **9.** copy added to a completed story. [< L *add(ere),* equiv. to *ad-* AD- + *-dere* to put (see DO[1])] —**add′a·ble, add′i·ble,** *adj.* —**add′ed·ly,** *adv.*
—**Syn. 1.** affix, append, attach, adjoin. **2.** total, sum.

add., **1.** (in prescriptions) **a.** add. [< L *adde*] **b.** let there be added. [< L *addāntur*] **2.** addenda. **3.** addition. **4.** additional. **5.** address.

Ad·dams (ad′əmz), *n.* **1. Charles Samuel,** born 1912, U.S. cartoonist. **2. Jane,** 1860–1935, U.S. social worker and writer: Nobel peace prize 1931.

ad·dax (ad′aks), *n.* a large, pale-colored antelope, *Addax nasomaculatus,* of North Africa, with loosely spiral horns. [< L < some language of ancient North Africa]

Addax
(3½ ft. high at shoulder; horns 3½ ft.; length 6½ ft.)

ad·dend (ad′end, ə dend′), *n. Math.* a number that is added to another in forming a sum. Cf. **augend.** [shortening of ADDENDUM]

ad·den·dum (ə den′dəm), *n., pl.* **-da** (-də) for 1, 2; **-dums** for 3. **1.** a thing to be added; an addition. **2.** an appendix to a book. **3.** *Mach.* **a.** the radial distance between the tip of a gear tooth and either the pitch circle of a gear or the pitch line of a rack. Cf. **dedendum. b.** Also called **adden′dum cir′cle.** an imaginary circle touching the tips of the teeth on a gear. [neut. sing. of L *addendus* to be added, gerundive of *addere* to ADD]

ad·der[1] (ad′ər), *n.* **1.** the common European viper, *Vipera berus.* **2.** any of various other venomous or harmless snakes resembling the viper. [late ME; r. ME *nadder* (*a nadder* becoming *an adder*), OE *nǣdre;* c. OHG *nātara* (G *Natter*), Icel *nathr(a),* Goth *nadr(s),* OIr *nathir*]

CONCISE ETYMOLOGY KEY: <, descended or derived from; >, whence; b., blend of, blended; c., cognate with; deriv., derivative; equiv., equivalent; imit., imitative; m., modification of; obl., oblique; r., replacing; s., stem; sp., spelling; trans., translation; ?, origin unknown, perhaps; *, hypothetical. See the full key inside the front cover.

add·er[2] (ad′ər), *n.* one who or that which adds. [ADD + -ER[1]]

ad·der's-mouth (ad′ərz mouth′), *n., pl.* **-mouths** (-mouthz′). **1.** any of several North American, terrestrial orchids of the genus *Malaxis*, having tiny, white or greenish flowers. **2.** the snakemouth.

ad·der's-tongue (ad′ərz tung′), *n.* **1.** a fern of the genus *Ophioglossum*, having a fruiting spike. **2.** *U.S.* any of several American dogtooth violets.

ad′der's vi′olet, the rattlesnake plantain, *Goodyera pubescens*.

ad·dict (*n.* ad′ikt; *v.* ə dikt′), *n.* **1.** a person who is addicted to a practice or habit: *a drug addict.* —*v.t.* **2.** to give (oneself) over, as to a habit or pursuit; apply or devote habitually (usually fol. by *to*): *to addict oneself to stimulants.* [< L *addict(us)* assigned, surrendered (ptp. of *addīcere*, equiv. to *ad-* AD- + *dic-* (ptp. s. of *dīcere* to fix, determine) + *-tus* ptp. suffix]

ad·dict·ed (ə dik′tid), *adj.* devoted or given up to a practice or habit or to something habit-forming, as a narcotic, cigarettes, etc. (usually fol. by *to*): *to be addicted to drugs.* [ADDICT + -ED[2]] —**ad·dict′ed·ness,** *n.*

ad·dic·tion (ə dik′shən), *n.* the state of being given up or having yielded to a habit or practice or to something that is habit-forming, as narcotics, to such an extent that its cessation causes severe trauma. [< L *addictiōn-* (s. of *addictiō*) a giving over, surrender. See ADDICT, -ION]

ad·dic·tive (ə dik′tiv), *adj.* producing, causing, or marked by addiction, as a narcotic drug. [ADDICT + -IVE]

Ad·die (ad′ē), *n.* a girl's given name, form of **Adeline.**

add′ing machine′, a business machine, typically for adding, but often also capable of subtracting, multiplying, and dividing.

Ad·ding·ton (ad′ing tən), *n.* **Henry, Viscount Sidmouth** (sid′məth), 1757–1844, British statesman: prime minister 1801–04.

Ad·dis A·ba·ba (äd′dis ä′bə bä′; *Eng.* ad′is ab′ə bə), a city in and the capital of Ethiopia, in the central part. 504,900 (est. 1964).

Ad·di·son (ad′i sən), *n.* **1. Joseph,** 1672–1719, English essayist and poet. **2. Thomas,** 1793–1860, English physician. **3.** a town in NE Illinois. 6741 (1960).

Ad·di·so·ni·an (ad′i sō′nē ən), *adj.* **1.** of, pertaining to, or characteristic of Joseph Addison or his works. **2.** characterized or marked by purity and flawlessness of literary style. —*n.* **3.** one who studies the works of Addison. [ADDISON + -IAN]

Ad′dison's disease′, *Pathol.* a disease characterized by asthenia, low blood pressure, and a brownish coloration of the skin, due to disturbance of the suprarenal glands. [named after T. ADDISON, who described it]

ad·dit·a·ment (ə dit′ə mənt), *n.* something added; an addition. [< L *additāment(um)*, equiv. to *addit(us)* (ptp.) added (see ADDITION) + *-ā-* + *-mentum* -MENT] —**ad·dit·a·men·ta·ry** (ə dit′ə men′tə rē), *adj.*

ad·di·tion (ə dish′ən), *n.* **1.** the act or process of adding or uniting. **2.** the process of uniting two or more numbers into one sum, represented by the symbol +. **3.** the result of adding; anything added. **4.** *U.S.* a wing, room, etc., added to a building, or abutting land added to real estate already owned. **5.** *Chem.* a reaction in which two or more substances combine to form another compound. **6.** *Obs. exc. Law.* a particularizing designation added to a person's name, as *Plaintiff* in *John Doe, Plaintiff.* **7. in addition to,** as well as; besides: *He rides well, in addition to being a fine marksman.* [< L *additiōn-* (s. of *additiō*), equiv. to *addit(us)* added, ptp. of *addere* to ADD (*ad-* AD- + *di-* put + *-tus* ptp. suffix)]
—**Syn. 1.** joining. **3.** increase, enlargement; increment; accession, supplement; appendix. ADDITION, ACCESSORY, ADJUNCT, ATTACHMENT mean something joined onto or used with something else. ADDITION is the general word, carrying no implication of size, importance, or kind, but merely that of being joined to something previously existing: *an addition to an income, to a building, to one's cares.* An ACCESSORY is a subordinate addition to a more important thing, for the purpose of aiding, completing, ornamenting, etc.: *accessories to a costume.* An ADJUNCT is a subordinate addition that aids or assists a main thing or person but is often separate: *a second machine as an adjunct to the first.* An ATTACHMENT is an accessory part which may be easily connected and removed: *a sewing machine attachment for pleating.*

ad·di·tion·al (ə dish′ə nəl), *adj.* added; supplementary: *additional information.* [ADDITION + -AL[1]] —**ad·di′tion·al·ly,** *adv.*

addi′tion pol′ymer, *Chem.* a polymer formed by the direct reaction of two or more monomers, and with no resulting water or other by-product.

addi′tion polymeriza′tion, *Chem.* See under **polymerization** (def. 2).

ad·di·tive (ad′i tiv), *adj.* **1.** characterized or produced by addition; cumulative: *an additive process.* **2.** *Math.* (of a function) having the property that the function of the union or sum of two quantities is equal to the sum of the functional values of each quantity; linear. —*n.* **3.** something that is added, as one substance to another, to alter or improve the general quality or to counteract undesirable properties: *an additive in foodstuffs to retard spoilage; an additive to thin paint.* **4.** a substance added to food as a preservative, coloring agent, or the like. [< LL *additīv(us)*. See ADDITION, -IVE] —**ad′di·tive·ly,** *adv.*

ad′ditive col′or, *Photog.* red, green, or blue-violet, as used in the additive process of color photography. Also called **ad′ditive pri′mary.**

ad′ditive group′, *Math.* a group in which the operation of the group is addition.

ad′ditive proc′ess, a process of color photography in which the colors are formed by the combination of red, green, and blue-violet lights. Cf. **subtractive process.**

ad·di·to·ry (ad′i tôr′ē, -tōr′ē), *adj.* capable of or tending to make an addition; additional; supplementary. [ADDIT(ION) + -ORY[1]]

ad·dle (ad′əl), *v.,* **-dled, -dling,** *adj.* —*v.t., v.i.* **1.** to make or become muddled or confused. **2.** to make or become spoiled or rotten, as eggs. —*adj.* **3.** mentally confused; muddled. **4.** rotten: *addle eggs.* [ME *adel*, OE *adel(a)* liquid, filth; c. G *Adel* liquid manure, OSw *adel* urine]

ad·dle·brained (ad′əl brānd′), *adj.* having a muddled or confused mind; illogical; harebrained. [ADDLE + BRAIN + -ED[3]]

ad·dle·pat·ed (ad′əl pā′tid), *adj.* foolish; silly; addlebrained. [ADDLE + PATE + -ED[3]]

ad·dorsed (ə dôrst′), *adj. Heraldry.* (of charges or emblems) back to back; endorsed: *two wings addorsed.* Also, **adorsed, adorsé.** [AD- + L *dors(um)* back + -ED[2], modeled on F *adossé*]

ad·dress (*n.* ə dres′, ad′res; *v.* ə dres′), *n., v.,* **-dressed** or **-drest, -dress·ing.** —*n.* **1.** a formal speech or written statement directed to a person or group of persons: *the President's address on the national economy.* **2.** a direction as to intended recipient, written on or attached to a letter, package, etc. **3.** the place or the name of the place where a person, organization, or the like is located or may be reached: *What is your address when you're in Des Moines?* **4.** manner of speaking to persons; personal bearing in conversation. **5.** skillful and expeditious management; ready skill; dispatch: *to handle a matter with address.* **6.** *Computer Technol.* a label, as an integer, symbol, or other set of characters, designating a location, register, etc., where information is stored. **7.** *Govt.* a request to the executive by the legislature to remove a judge for unfitness. **8.** Usually, **addresses.** attentions paid by a lover; courtship. **9.** (*usually cap.*) the reply to the King's speech in the English Parliament. **10.** *Obs.* preparation. —*v.t.* **11.** to direct a speech or written statement to: *to address an assembly.* **12.** to use a specified form or title in speaking or writing to: *How does one address the governor?* **13.** to direct to the ear or attention: *to address a warning to someone.* **14.** to apply in speech (used reflexively, usually fol. by *to*): *He addressed himself to the chairman.* **15.** to put the directions for delivery on: *to address a letter.* **16.** *Com.* to consign or entrust to the care of another, as agent or factor. **17.** to direct the energy or force of (used reflexively, usually fol. by *to*): *He addressed himself to the task.* **18.** to woo; court. **19.** to direct (data) to a specified location in an electronic computer. **20.** *Golf.* to take a stance and place the head of the club behind (the ball) preparatory to hitting it. **21.** *Obs.* to give direction to; aim. **22.** *Obs.* to prepare. —*v.i. Obs.* **23.** to make an appeal. **24.** to make preparations. [late ME *adresse(n)* (to) adorn < MF *adresse(r)*. See AD-, DRESS] —**ad·dress′er, ad·dres′sor,** *n.*
—**Syn. 1.** discourse, lecture. See **speech. 3.** residence, domicile, dwelling, house, lodging. **5.** adroitness, cleverness, ingenuity, tact.

ad·dress·ee (ad′re sē′, ə dre sē′), *n.* a person, company, or the like, to whom a letter, package, etc., is addressed. [ADDRESS + -EE]

address′ing machine′, a machine for printing addresses on letters, packages, etc., for mailing.

Ad·dres·so·graph (ə dres′ə graf′, -gräf′), *n. Trademark.* a machine designed for the rapid, automatic addressing of mail in large quantities.

Address′ to the Deil′, a poem (1786) by Burns.

ad·duce (ə do͞os′, ə dyo͞os′), *v.t.,* **-duced, -duc·ing.** to bring forward in argument or as evidence; cite as pertinent or conclusive: *to adduce reasons in support of one's case.* [< L *addūce(re)* (to) bring into, equiv. to *ad-* AD- + *dūcere* to lead] —**ad·duce′a·ble, ad·duc′i·ble,** *adj.* —**ad·duc′er,** *n.*

ad·du·cent (ə do͞o′sənt, ə dyo͞o′-), *adj. Physiol.* drawing toward, as by the action of a muscle; adducting. [< L *addūcent-* (s. of *addūcēns*), prp. of *addūcere.* See ADDUCE, -ENT]

ad·duct (ə dukt′), *v.t. Physiol.* to move or draw toward the axis of the body or one of its parts (opposed to *abduct*). [< L *adduct(us)* drawn to, ptp. of *addūcere*; see ADDUCE] —**ad·duc′tive,** *adj.*

ad·duc·tion (ə duk′shən), *n.* **1.** *Physiol.* the action of an adducent muscle. **2.** act of adducing. [< ML *adductiōn-* (s. of *adductiō*). See ADDUCT, -ION]

ad·duc·tor (ə duk′tər), *n.* any muscle which adducts (opposed to *abductor*). [< NL, LL: conductor. See ADDUCT, -OR[2]]

Ade (ād), *n.* **George,** 1866–1944, U.S. writer of humorous prose.

-ade[1], **1.** a suffix found in nouns denoting action or process or a person or persons acting, appearing in loan words from French and sometimes from Spanish (*cannonade; fusillade; renegade*), often irregularly attached: *blockade; escapade; masquerade.* **2.** a noun suffix indicating a drink made of a particular fruit: *lemonade.* [< F < (It or) L *-āta* (fem. of *ātus*); < Sp *-ado* < L *-ātus* -ATE[1]]

-ade[2], a collective suffix like **-ad**[1]: *decade.* [< F < Gk *-ada*, acc. to nom. *-ás*]

A·dee (ad′ē), *n.* a girl's given name, form of **Adelaide.**

A·del (ə del′), *n.* **1.** a town in S Georgia. 4321 (1960). **2.** Also, **Adal.** a boy's given name.

A·del·a (ə del′ə, ad′ələ), *n.* a girl's given name. Also, **Adele.**

Ad·e·laide (ad′əlād′), *n.* **1.** a city in and the capital of South Australia, in Australia. 587,957 with suburbs (1961). **2.** a girl's given name.

a·de·lan·ta·do (ad′əlän tä′dō; *Sp.* ä′the län tä′thō), *n., pl.* **-dos** (-dōz; *Sp.* -thōs). *Hist.* **1.** a governor of a province in Spain or of a Spanish colonial province. **2.** any of the early explorers, conquerors, or colonizers in Spanish America. [< Sp n. use of ptp. of *adelantar* to go forward, deriv. of *adelante* in front (*a-* (< L *ad-* AD-) + *delante* before, for *denante* < LL *dē in ante*)]

Ad·el·bert (ad′əl bərt, ə del′bərt; *Ger.* äd′əl bert′), *n.* a boy's given name. Also, **Adalbert.**

A·dele (ə del′), *n.* a girl's given name. Also, **Adela.**

Ad·el·heid (ad′əl hīd′; *Ger.* äd′əl hīt′), *n.* a girl's given name.

A·dé·lie Coast′ (ə dā′lē; *Fr.* A dā lē′), a coastal region of Antarctica, south of Australia: claimed by France.

Adé′lie pen′guin, a penguin, *Pygoscelis adeliae*, occurring in large colonies in Antarctica. Also called **Adélie, Ade′lie pen′guin.**

Ad·e·line (ad′əlīn′; *Dan.* ä′də lē′nə; *Fr.* adə lēn′; *Ger.* ä dā lē′nə), *n.* a girl's given name. Also, **Ad·e·li·na** (ad′əlē′nə, ad′əlī′nə).

A·del·phe (ə del′fē), *n.* a girl's given name.

-adelphous, *Bot.* a word element meaning "having stamens growing together in bundles," of the number specified by the prefix: *monadelphous.* [< Gk *adelph(ós)* brother + -OUS]

a·demp·tion (ə demp′shən), *n. Law.* the failure of a specific legacy because the subject matter no longer belongs to the testator's estate at his death. [< L *ademptiōn-* (s. of *ademptiō*) a taking away, equiv. to *adempt(us)* (*ad-* AD- + *em(p)-*, s. of *emere* to take + *-tus* ptp. suffix) + *-iōn-* -ION]

A·den (äd′ən, ād′ən), *n.* **1.** a seaport in SW South Yemen: formerly the center of a British colony. 230,000 (est. 1966). **2. Colony of.** Also called **State of Aden.** a former British colony on the Gulf of Aden and a member of the Federation of South Arabia, now part of South Yemen. 75 sq. mi. **3. Protectorate of,** former name, until 1962, of the Protectorate of South Arabia. **4. Gulf of,** an arm of the Arabian Sea between the E tip of Africa and the Arabian Peninsula.

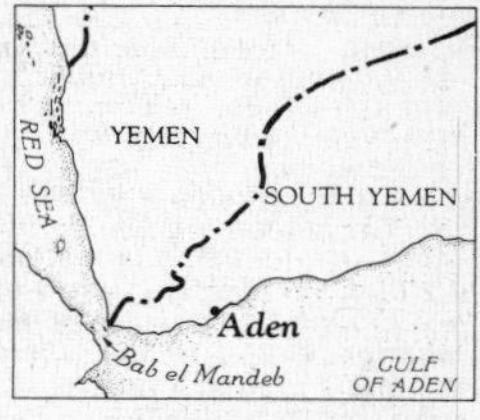

aden-, var. of **adeno-** before a vowel: *adenitis.*

ad·e·nal·gia (ad′ənal′jə, -jē ə), *n. Pathol.* pain in a gland. [ADEN- + -ALGIA]

A·de·nau·er (ad′ənou ər, ad′ənou′-; *Ger.* äd′ənou′ər), *n.* **Kon·rad** (kon′rad; *Ger.* kōn′rät), 1876–1967 chancellor of the West German Federal Republic 1949–63.

ad·e·nec·to·my (ad′ənek′tə mē), *n., pl.* **-mies.** *Surg.* excision of a gland. [ADEN- + -ECTOMY]

ad·e·nine (ad′ənin, -ənēn′, -ənīn′), *n. Chem.* a white, finely crystalline alkaloid, usually obtained from tea by extraction or from uric acid by synthesis: used chiefly in medicine. [ADEN- + -INE[2]]

ad·e·ni·tis (ad′ənī′tis), *n. Pathol.* inflammation of the lymph nodes or glands. [ADEN- + -ITIS]

adeno-, a learned borrowing from Greek meaning "gland," used in the formation of compound words: *adenovirus.* Also, *esp. before a vowel,* **aden-.** [< Gk, comb. form of *adḗn*; akin to L *inguen* groin]

ad·e·no·car·ci·no·ma (ad′ənō kär′sə nō′mə), *n., pl.* **-mas, -ma·ta** (-mə tə). *Pathol.* **1.** a malignant tumor arising in a secretory gland. **2.** a malignant tumor of glandlike structure. [ADENO- + CARCINOMA] —**ad·e·no·car·ci·nom·a·tous** (ad′ənō kär′sə nom′ə təs, -nō′mə-), *adj.*

ad′e·no·hy·poph·y·se′al luteotro′pin (ad′ənō hī pof′i sē′əl, -zē′-, ad′-), *Biochem.* luteotropin. [ADENO- + HYPOPHYS(IS) + *-eal*, alter. of -IAL]

ad·e·noid (ad′ənoid′), *n.* **1.** Usually, **adenoids.** an enlarged mass of lymphoid tissue in the upper pharynx, often obstructing breathing through the nasal passages. See diag. under **tonsil.** —*adj.* **2.** Also, **ad′e·noi′dal. a.** of or pertaining to the lymph glands. **b.** of or pertaining to the adenoids. [< Gk *adenoeid(ḗs)*. See ADEN-, -OID]

ad·e·noid·ec·to·my (ad′ənoi dek′tə mē), *n., pl.* **-mies.** *Surg.* the operation of removing the adenoids. [ADENOID + -ECTOMY]

ad·e·nol·o·gy (ad′ənol′ə jē), *n. Med.* the branch of medicine dealing with the development, structure, function, and diseases of glands. [ADENO- + -LOGY] —**ad·e·no·log·i·cal** (ad′ənəloj′i kəl), *adj.*

ad·e·no·ma (ad′ənō′mə), *n., pl.* **-mas, -ma·ta** (-mə tə). *Pathol.* **1.** a benign tumor originating in a secretory gland. **2.** a benign tumor of glandlike structure. [< NL; see ADEN-, -OMA] —**ad·e·nom·a·tous** (ad′ənom′ə təs, -ənō′mə-), *adj.*

a·den·o·phore (ə den′ə fôr′, -fōr′), *n. Bot.* the stalk of a nectary. [ADENO- + -PHORE]

ad·e·no·phyl·lous (ad′ənō fil′əs), *adj. Bot.* having gland-bearing leaves. [ADENO- + -PHYLLOUS]

ad·e·no·sar·co·ma (ad′ənō sär kō′mə), *n., pl.* **-mas, -ma·ta** (-mə tə). *Pathol.* a complex neoplasm, containing both glandular and connective tissues. Also called **sarcoadenoma.** [ADENO- + SARCOMA]

a·den·o·sine (ə den′ə sēn′, -sin), *n. Chem.* a white, crystalline, water-soluble powder, $C_{10}H_{13}N_5O_4$, obtained from the nucleic acid of yeast, which upon hydrolysis produces adenine and ribose. [irreg. b. ADENINE and RIBOSE]

aden′osine diphos′phate, *Biochem.* See **ADP** (def. 1). Also called **a·den′o·sine·di·phos·phor′ic ac′id** (ə den′ə sēn dī′fos fôr′ik, -for′-, -sin-).

aden′osine phos′phate, *Biochem.* See **adenylic acid.**

aden′osine tri·phos′pha·tase (trī fos′fə tās′), *Biochem.* an enzyme that catalyzes the hydrolysis of ATP.

aden′osine triphos′phate, *Biochem.* See **ATP.** Also called **a·den′o·sine·tri·phos·phor′ic ac′id** (ə den′ə sēn trī′fos fôr′ik, -for′-, -sin-). [TRIPHOSPHATE + -ASE]

ad·e·no·vi·rus (ad′ənō vī′rəs), *n., pl.* **-rus·es.** a virus which attacks the mucosa of the upper respiratory tract and the lymph nodes. [ADENO- + VIRUS]

ad′e·nyl′ic ac′id (ad′ənil′ik, ad′-), *Biochem.* a white, crystalline, water-soluble nucleotide, $C_{10}H_{12}N_5O_3H_2PO_4$, obtained by the partial hydrolysis of ATP or of ribonucleic acid, yielding on hydrolysis adenine, ribose, and orthophosphoric acid. Also called **adenosine phosphate, AMP** [ADEN(INE) + -YL + -IC]

a·de·nyl·py·ro·phos·phate (ad′ənil pī′rō fos′fāt), *n. Biochem.* See **ATP.** Also called **ad′e·nyl·py·ro·phos·phor′ic ac′id** (ad′ənil pī′rō fos fôr′ik, -for′-). [ADEN(INE) + -YL + PYROPHOSPH(ORIC ACID) + -ATE[2]]

A·de·od·a·tus I (ā′dē od′ə təs), Deusdedit.

Adeodatus II, Saint, died A.D. 676, pope 672–676.

ad·e·pha·gia (ad′ə fā′jə, -jē ə), *n. Pathol.* bulimia. [< Gk *adēphagía*, equiv. to *hádē(n)*, *ádē(n)* to satiety + *-phagia* -PHAGIA]

ad·ept (*adj.* ə dept′; *n.* ad′ept, ə dept′), *adj.* **1.** very skilled; proficient; expert. —*n.* **2.** a very skilled or proficient person; expert. [< ML *adept(us)* one who has attained (the secret of transmuting metals), n. use of L ptp. of *adipiscī* to attain to (*ad-* AD- + *-ep-*, var. of *apin aptus* APT + *-tus* ptp. suffix)] —**a·dept′ly,** *adv.* —**a·dept′ness,** *n.*

ad·e·qua·cy (ad′ə kwə sē), *n.* the state or quality of being adequate; sufficiency for a particular purpose. [ADEQU(ATE) + -ACY]

ad·e·quate (ad′ə kwit), *adj.* **1.** equal to the requirement or occasion; commensurate; fully sufficient, suitable, or fit (often fol. by *to* or *for*): *This car is adequate to our needs.* **2.** barely sufficient or suitable: *The violinist gave only an adequate performance.* **3.** *Law.* reasonably sufficient for starting legal action: *adequate grounds.* [< L *adaequāt(us)* matched (ptp. of *adaequāre*). See AD-, EQUAL, -ATE[1]] —**ad′e·quate·ly,** *adv.* —**ad′e·quate·ness,** *n.*
—**Syn. 1.** satisfactory, competent, sufficient, enough; capable.

a·der·min (ā dûr′min), *n.* pyridoxine. Also, **a·der·mine** (ā dûr′mēn, -min). [A-[6] + *derm-* (short s. of Gk *dérma* skin) + -IN[2]]

-ades, a formal element appearing in loan words from Greek: *Hyades; Pleiades.* [< Gk *-ades* descendant of (nom. pl.). See -AD[1]]

ad es·se (äd es′se; *Eng.* ad es′ē), *Latin.* present; in attendance.

ad·es·sive (ad es′iv), *Gram.* —*adj.* **1.** locative. —*n.* **2.** the adessive case. [< L *adess(e)* (to) be present (*ad-* AD- + *esse* to be) + -IVE]

à deux (A dœ′), *French.* of or for two; two at a time.

ad ex·tre·mum (äd ek strā′mŏŏm; *Eng.* ad ek strē′məm), *Latin.* to the extreme; at last; finally.

ad fin., *Latin.* to, toward, or at the end. [< *ad fīnem*]

ad·freeze (ad frēz′), *v.t.,* **-froze, -fro·zen, -freez·ing.** to adhere through the binding power of ice. [AD- + FREEZE]

ad glo·ri·am (äd glō′ri äm′; *Eng.* ad glōr′ē am′, -glôr′-), *Latin.* for glory.

ad·here (ad hēr′), *v.i.,* **-hered, -her·ing. 1.** to stick fast; cleave; cling (usually fol. by *to*): *The mud adhered to his shoes.* **2.** *Physics.* (of two or more dissimilar substances) to be united by a molecular force acting in the area of contact. **3.** to be devoted; be attached as a follower or upholder (usually fol. by *to*): *to adhere to a party.* **4.** to hold closely or firmly (usually fol. by *to*): *to adhere to a plan.* **5.** *Obs.* to be consistent. [< ML *adhēr(ēre)* for L *adhaerēre* (*ad-* AD- + *haerēre* to stick, cling)] —**ad·her′er,** *n.*
—**Syn. 1.** See **stick.** —**Ant. 1.** part, loosen.

ad·her·ence (ad hēr′əns), *n.* **1.** quality of adhering; fidelity; steady attachment: *adherence to a party; rigid adherence to rules.* **2.** act or state of adhering; adhesion. [< ML *adhērentia.* See ADHERE, -ENCE]

ad·her·end (ad hēr′ənd, ad′hi rend′), *n.* *Chem.* any substance bonded to another by an adhesive. [ADHERE + -end (< L *-end(um)* ger. suffix)]

ad·her·ent (ad hēr′ənt), *n.* **1.** a person who follows or upholds a leader, cause, etc.; supporter; follower (usually fol. by *of*). —*adj.* **2.** sticking; clinging; adhering: *an adherent substance like peanut butter.* **3.** *Bot.* adnate. **4.** *Gram.* standing before and modifying a noun. [< ML *adhērent-* for L *adhaerent-* (s. of *adhaerēns,* prp. of *adhaerēre*). See ADHERE, -ENT] —**ad·her′ent·ly,** *adv.*
—**Syn. 1.** disciple, devotee, fan. See **follower.**

ad·he·sion (ad hē′zhən), *n.* **1.** the act or state of adhering; state of being adhered or united: *the adhesion of parts united by growth.* **2.** steady attachment of the mind or feelings; adherence. **3.** assent; concurrence. **4.** *Physics.* the molecular force of attraction in the area of contact between unlike bodies that acts to hold them together. Cf. **cohesion** (def. 2). **5.** *Pathol.* **a.** the abnormal union of adjacent tissues. **b.** the tissue involved. **6.** *Bot.* the union of normally separate parts. **7.** *Railroads.* **a.** the frictional resistance of rails to the tendency of driving wheels to slip. **b.** See **factor of adhesion.** [< ML *adhēsiōn-* for L *adhaesiōn-* (s. of *adhaesiō*) a clinging, equiv. to *adhaes(us)* clung (*ad-* AD- + *haes-,* perf. s. of *haerēre* to cling + *-sus* ptp. suffix) + *-iōn-* -ION] —**ad·he′sion·al,** *adj.*

ad·he·sive (ad hē′siv), *adj.* **1.** clinging; tenacious; sticking fast. **2.** adhering; gummed; sticky: *an adhesive surface; an adhesive substance.* **3.** *Physics.* of or pertaining to the molecular force that exists in the area of contact between unlike bodies and that acts to unite them. —*n.* **4.** adhesive material, such as adhesive tape. **5.** a substance that causes something to adhere, such as glue, rubber cement, etc. **6.** *Philately.* a postage stamp with a gummed back, as distinguished from one embossed or printed on an envelope or card. [ADHES(ION) + -IVE] —**ad·he′sive·ly,** *adv.* —**ad·he′sive·ness,** *n.*

adhe′sive cell′, colloblast.

adhe′sive fac′tor, *Railroads.* See **factor of adhesion.**

adhe′sive plas′ter, adhesive tape, esp. in wide sheets.

adhe′sive tape′, cotton or other fabric coated with an adhesive substance, used for covering slight injuries on the skin, holding a bandage in place, etc.

ad·hib·it (ad hib′it), *v.t.* **1.** to take or let in; admit. **2.** to use or apply. **3.** to attach. [< L *adhibit(us)* brought (ptp. of *adhibēre* to bring to), equiv. to *ad-* AD- + *hibi-* (var. s. of *habēre* to hold, have) + *-tus* ptp. suffix] —**ad·hi·bi·tion** (ad′hə bish′ən), *n.*

ad hoc (ad hok′; *Lat.* äd hōk′), for this (special purpose); with respect to this (subject or thing).

ad ho·mi·nem (äd hō′mi nem′; *Eng.* ad hom′ə nem′), **1.** *Latin.* appealing to a person's prejudices, emotions, or special interests rather than to his intellect or reason. **2.** attacking an opponent's character rather than answering his argument. [lit., to the man]

ad·i·a·bat (ad′ē ə bat′), *n.* a line on a thermodynamic chart relating the pressure and temperature of a substance undergoing an adiabatic change. [back formation from ADIABATIC]

ad·i·a·bat·ic (ad′ē ə bat′ik, ā′dī ə-), *adj.* occurring without gain or loss of heat: *an adiabatic process.* [< Gk *adiábat(os)* incapable of being crossed (*a-* A-[6] + *dia-* DIA- + *ba-* (s. of *bainein* to cross) + *-tos* verbal adj. suffix) + -IC] —**ad′i·a·bat′i·cal·ly,** *adv.*

ad′iabat′ic chart′, a graph for the analysis of adiabatic processes. Also called **ad′iabat′ic di′agram.**

a·di·ac·tin·ic (ā′dī ak tin′ik), *adj.* *Obs.* (of a medium) not capable of transmitting actinic rays. [A-[6] + DIACTINIC]

ad·i·ad·o·cho·ki·ne·sia (ad′ē ad′ə kō ki nē′zhə, -zhē ə, -zē ə, -kī nē′-), *n.* *Med.* the inability to perform rapidly alternating muscular movements as flexion and extension. Also, **ad′i·ad′o·cho·ki·ne′sis, ad′i·ad′o·ko·ki·ne′sia, ad′i·ad′o·ko·ki·ne′sis.** Cf. **diadochokinesia.** [A-[6] + Gk *diádocho(s)* successor (*dia-* DIA- + *doch-,* var. s. of *déchesthai* to receive + *-os* adj. suffix) + *kīnēs(is)* motion (*kīnē-,* s. of *kinein* to move + *-sis* -SIS) + *-ia* -IA]

ad·i·aph·o·re·sis (ad′ē af′ə rē′sis, ə dī′ə fə-), *n.* *Med.* absence or reduction of perspiration. [A-[6] + DIAPHORESIS]

ad·i·aph·o·ret·ic (ad′ē af′ə ret′ik, ə dī′ə fə-), *Med.* —*adj.* **1.** preventing or reducing perspiration. —*n.* **2.** an adiaphoretic agent. [A-[6] + DIAPHORETIC]

ad·i·aph·or·ism (ad′ē af′ə riz′əm), *n.* tolerance of actions or beliefs not specifically prohibited in the Scriptures; indifferentism. [ADIAPHOR(OUS) + -ISM] —**ad′i·aph′o·rist,** *n.* —**ad′i·aph′o·ris′tic,** *adj.*

ad·i·aph·o·rous (ad′ē af′ər əs), *adj.* doing neither good nor harm, as a medicine. [< Gk *adiáphoros,* equiv. to *a-* A-[6] + *diáphoros* different (*dia-* DIA- + *phor-* (var. s. of *phérein* to carry, bring) + *-os* adj. suffix)]

A·die (ā′dē), *n.* a girl's given name. Also, **Ada.**

ad·i·ent (ad′ē ənt), *adj.* *Psychol.* tending to expose an organism to a stimulus. Cf. **abient.** [< L *adient-* (s. of *adiēns* approaching, prp. of *adīre*), equiv. to *ad-* AD- + *-i-* go + *-ent-* -ENT]

a·dieu (ə do͞o′, ə dyo͞o′; *Fr.* A dyœ′), *interj., n., pl.* **a·dieus, a·dieux** (ə do͞oz′, ə dyo͞oz′; *Fr.* A dyœ′). —*interj.* **1.** good-by; farewell. —*n.* **2.** act of leaving or departing; farewell. [late ME < MF, equiv. to *a* (< L *ad* to) + *dieu* (< L *deum,* acc. of *deus* god)]

A·di·ge (ä′dē je), *n.* a river in N Italy, flowing SE to the Adriatic Sea. 220 mi. long.

A·di·ghe (ä′də gā′), *n.* Adygei.

A·di·granth (ä′di grunt′), *n.* Granth.

A·din (ā′din, ad′ən), *n.* a boy's given name.

A·di·na (ə dē′nə), *n.* a girl's given name. Also, **A·de′na.**

ad inf., ad infinitum. Also, **ad infin.**

ad in·fi·ni·tum (ad in′fə nī′təm), to infinity; endlessly; without limit. [< L: lit., to the endless]

ad init., ad initium.

ad i·ni·ti·um (ad i nish′ē əm), at the beginning. [< L]

ad int., ad interim.

ad in·te·rim (ad in′tə rim), in the meantime. [< L: lit., for the time between]

a·di·ós (ad′ē ōs′, ä′dē-; *Sp.* ä thyôs′), *interj.* good-by; farewell. [< Sp: lit., to God]

ad·i·pate (ad′ə pāt′), *n.* *Chem.* **1.** a salt or ester of adipic acid. **2.** an alkyd resin derived from adipic acid. [*adip-* (see ADIPOSE) + -ATE[2]]

a·diph·e·nine (ə dif′ə nēn′, -nin′), *n.* *Pharm.* a compound, $C_{20}H_{25}NO_2$, used in the form of its crystalline, water-soluble hydrochloride chiefly as an antispasmodic in the treatment of peptic ulcer and gastritis. [*adip-* (see ADIPOSE) + PHEN- + -INE[2]]

a·dip′ic ac′id (ə dip′ik), *Chem.* a white, crystalline, slightly water-soluble solid, $HOOC(CH_2)_4COOH$, used chiefly in the synthesis of nylon. Also called **hexanedioic acid.** [*adip-* (see ADIPOSE) + -IC]

ad·i·po·cere (ad′ə pō sēr′), *n.* a waxy substance produced by the decomposition of dead animal bodies in moist burial places or under water. [ADIPO(SE) + *cere,* as in *cerecloth*] —**ad·i·poc·er·ous** (ad′ə pos′ər əs), *adj.*

ad·i·poc·er·ite (ad′ə pos′ə rīt′), *n.* hatchettite. [ADIPOCERE + -ITE[1]]

ad·i·po·ni·trile (ad′ə pō nī′tril, -trēl, -trīl), *n.* *Chem.* a colorless liquid, $NC(CH_2)_4CN$, used chiefly as an intermediate in the manufacture of nylon. [*adip-* (see ADIPOSE) + -O- + NITRILE]

ad·i·po·pex·i·a (ad′ə pō pek′sē ə), *n.* *Biochem.* lipopexia. Also, **ad·i·po·pex·is** (ad′ə pō pek′sis). [*adip-* (see ADIPOSE) + -O- + *-pex(is)* < Gk *pēg(nýnai)* (to) solidify, fix, make fast + *-ia* -IA] —**ad′i·po·pec′tic, ad′i·po·pex′ic,** *adj.*

ad·i·pose (ad′ə pōs′), *adj.* **1.** fatty; consisting of, resembling, or having relation to fat: *adipose tissue.* —*n.* **2.** animal fat stored in the fatty tissue of the body. [< NL *adipōs(us)* (L *adip-* (s. of *adeps*) fat, suet + *-ōsus* -OSE[1])] —**ad′i·pose′ness, ad·i·pos·i·ty** (ad′ə pos′i tē), **ad′i·po′sis,** *n.*

ad′ipose fin′, a small, fleshy fin, usually lacking rays, behind the main dorsal fin in trouts, catfishes, and other bony fishes.

Ad·i·ron·dack (ad′ə ron′dak), *n., pl.* **-dacks,** (*esp. collectively*) **-dack. 1.** a member of an Algonquian people living mainly north of the St. Lawrence River. **2. Adirondacks.** See **Adirondack Mountains.**

Adiron′dack chair′, a chair for use out of doors, having a sloping back, seat, and arms made of wooden slats.

Ad′iron′dack Moun′tains, a mountain range in NE New York: a part of the Appalachian Mountains. Highest peak, Mt. Marcy, 5344 ft. Also called **Adirondacks.**

Adiron′dack skiff′, a light, double-ended skiff used on the lakes of northern New York for hunting and fishing.

ad·it (ad′it), *n.* **1.** an entrance or a passage. **2.** *Mining.* a nearly horizontal passage leading into a mine. **3.** access. [< L *adit(us)* an approach, equiv. to *ad-* AD- + *-i-* (s. of *īre* to go) + *-tus* suffix marking n. denoting action or the means of action]

A·dit·ya (ä′dit yə), *n.* *Hinduism.* one of the Vedic gods. Cf. **Asura.** [< Skt: lit., son of *Aditi* (goddess of heaven)]

ADIZ (ā′diz), *n.* *U.S. Air Force.* Air Defense Identification Zone.

adj., **1.** adjacent. **2.** adjective. **3.** adjoining. **4.** adjourned. **5.** adjudged. **6.** adjunct. **7.** *Banking.* adjustment. **8.** adjutant.

Adj.A., Adjunct in Arts.

ad·ja·cence (ə jā′səns), *n.* adjacency (def. 1).

ad·ja·cen·cy (ə jā′sən sē), *n., pl.* **-cies. 1.** Also, **adjacence.** state of being adjacent. **2.** Usually, **adjacencies.** things, places, etc., which are adjacent. **3.** *Radio and Television.* a broadcast or announcement immediately preceding or following another. [< LL *adjacentia.* See ADJACENT, -ENCY]

ad·ja·cent (ə jā′sənt), *adj.* **1.** lying near, close, or contiguous; adjoining; neighboring: *a field adjacent to the highway.* **2.** just before, after, or facing: *a map on an adjacent page.* [< L *adjacent-* (s. of *adjacēns,* prp. of *adjacēre* to adjoin), equiv. to *ad-* AD- + *jac-* lie + *-ent-* -ENT] —**ad·ja′cent·ly,** *adv.*
—**Syn. 1.** abutting, juxtaposed, touching. See **adjoining.** —**Ant.** distant.

adja′cent an′gles, *Geom.* two angles having the same vertex and having a common side between them.

ad·jec·ti·val (aj′ik tī′vəl), *adj.* **1.** of, pertaining to, or used as an adjective. **2.** describing by means of many adjectives; depending for effect on intensive qualification of subject matter, as a writer, style, essay, etc. [ADJECTIVE + -AL[1]] —**ad′jec·ti′val·ly,** *adv.*

ad·jec·tive (aj′ik tiv), *n.* **1.** *Gram.* any member of a class of words that in many languages are distinguished in form, as partly in English by having comparative and superlative endings, or by functioning as modifiers of nouns, as *good, wise, perfect.* —*adj.* **2.** pertaining to or functioning as an adjective; adjectival: *the adjective use of a noun.* **3.** not able to stand alone; dependent. **4.** *Law.* concerning methods of enforcement of legal rights, as pleading and practice (opposed to *substantive*). **5.** (of dye colors) requiring a mordant or the like to render them permanent (opposed to *substantive*). [late ME < LL *adjectīv(um),* neut. of *adjectīvus,* equiv. to *adject(us)* added to, ptp. of *adicere,* (*ad-* AD- + *jec-* lay + *-tus* ptp. suffix) + *-īvus* -IVE] —**ad′jec·tive·ly,** *adv.*

ad·join (ə join′), *v.t.* **1.** to be close to or in contact with; abut on: *His house adjoins the lake.* —*v.i.* **2.** to be in connection or contact: *the point where the estates adjoin.* [late ME *a(d)joine(n)* < MF *ajoindre.* See AD-, JOIN]

ad·join·ing (ə joi′ning), *adj.* being in contact at some point or line; bordering; contiguous: *the adjoining room.* [ADJOIN + -ING[2]]
—**Syn.** ADJOINING, ADJACENT, BORDERING all mean near or close to something. ADJACENT implies being nearby or next to: *adjacent angles.* ADJOINING implies touching, having a common point or line: *an adjoining yard.* BORDERING means having a common boundary with: *the farm bordering on the river.* —**Ant.** separated.

ad·joint (ə joint′), *n.* *Math.* **1.** Also called **adjugate.** a square matrix obtained from a given square matrix and having the property that its product with the given matrix is equal to the determinant of the given matrix times the identity matrix. **2.** Also called **associate, Hermitian conjugate, transposed conjugate.** the matrix obtained from a given matrix by interchanging rows and columns and by replacing each element by its complex conjugate. [AD- + JOINT]

adjoint′ differen′tial equa′tion, *Math.* a differential equation obtained from a given differential equation and having the property that any solution of one equation is an integrating factor of the other.

ad·journ (ə jûrn′), *v.t.* **1.** to suspend the meeting of (a club, legislature, committee, etc.) to a future time or to another place: *to adjourn the court.* **2.** to defer or postpone (a matter) to a future meeting of the same body. **3.** to defer or postpone (a matter) to some future time, either specified or not specified. —*v.i.* **4.** to postpone, suspend, or transfer proceedings. **5.** to go to another place: *to adjourn to the dining room.* [ME *ajo(u)rn(en)* < MF *ajo(u)rn(er),* equiv. to *a-* AD- + *jorn-* < L *diurn(us)* daily; see JOURNAL, JOURNEY]

ad·journ·ment (ə jûrn′mənt), *n.* act or state of adjourning; state or period of being adjourned. [< AF (legal) *adjournement,* MF. See ADJOURN, -MENT]

adjt., adjutant.

ad·judge (ə juj′), *v.t.,* **-judged, -judg·ing. 1.** to pronounce formally; decree: *The will was adjudged void.* **2.** to award judicially; assign: *The prize was adjudged to him.* **3.** to decide by a judicial opinion or sentence: *to adjudge a case.* **4.** to sentence or condemn: *He was adjudged to die.* **5.** to deem; consider; think: *It was adjudged wise to avoid war.* [late ME *ajuge* < MF *ajug(i)e(r)* < L *adjūdicāre.* See ADJUDICATE]

ad·ju·di·cate (ə jo͞o′də kāt′), *v.,* **-cat·ed, -cat·ing.** —*v.t.* **1.** to pronounce or decree by judicial sentence; settle judicially; pass judgment on; determine (an issue or dispute) judicially. —*v.i.* **2.** to sit in judgment (usually fol. by *upon*). [< L *adjūdicāt(us)* (ptp. of *adjūdicāre*). See AD-, JUDGE, -ATE[1]] —**ad·ju·di·ca·tive** (ə jo͞o′də kā′tiv, -kə tiv), *adj.* —**ad·ju′di·ca′tor,** *n.*

ad·ju·di·ca·tion (ə jo͞o′də kā′shən), *n.* **1.** act of adjudicating. **2.** *Law.* **a.** act of a court in making an order, judgment, or decree. **b.** a judicial decision or sentence. [< LL *adjūdicātiōn-* (s. of *adjūdicātiō*). See ADJUDICATE, -ION]

ad·ju·gate (aj′o͝o git, -gāt′), *n.* *Math.* adjoint (def. 1). [AD- + *-jugate,* as in *conjugate*]

ad·junct (aj′ungkt), *n.* **1.** something added to another thing but not essentially a part of it. **2.** a person joined to another in some duty or service; assistant. **3.** *Gram.* a modifying form, word, phrase, etc., depending on some other form, word, phrase, etc. —*adj.* **4.** joined or associated, esp. in an auxiliary or subordinate relationship. **5.** attached or belonging without full or permanent status: *an adjunct surgeon on the hospital staff.* [< L *adjunct(us)* joined to (ptp. of *adjungere*), equiv. to *ad-* AD- + *jung-* (nasal var. of *jug-* YOKE[1]) + *-tus* ptp. suffix] —**ad·junct′ly,** *adv.*
—**Syn. 1.** appendix, supplement. See **addition. 2.** aide, attaché.

ad·junc·tion (ə jungk′shən), *n.* addition of an adjunct. [< L *adjunctiōn-* (s. of *adjunctiō*). See ADJUNCT, -ION]

ad·junc·tive (ə jungk′tiv), *adj.* forming an adjunct. [< LL *adjunctīv(us).* See ADJUNCT, -IVE] —**ad·junc′tive·ly,** *adv.*

ad·jure (ə jo͝or′), *v.t.,* **-jured, -jur·ing. 1.** to charge, bind, or command earnestly and solemnly, often under oath or the threat of a curse. **2.** to entreat or request earnestly. [late ME < L *adjūr(āre).* See AD-, JURY] —**ad·ju·ra·tion** (aj′o͝o rā′shən), *n.* —**ad·jur·a·to·ry** (ə jo͝or′ə tôr′ē, -tōr′ē), *adj.* —**ad·jur′er, ad·ju′ror,** *n.*

ad·just (ə just′), *v.t.* **1.** to fit, as one thing to another; make correspondent or conformable; adapt; accommodate: *to adjust expenses to income.* **2.** to put in working order; regulate; bring to a proper state or position: *to adjust an instrument.* **3.** to settle or bring to a satisfactory state, so that parties are agreed in the result: *to adjust differences.* **4.** *Insurance.* to determine the amount to be paid in settlement of (a claim). **5.** to systematize. **6.** *Mil.* to correct the elevation or deflection of (a gun) or the height at which its projectile bursts. —*v.i.* **7.** to adapt oneself; become adapted. [< ML *adjust(āre),* alter. of LL *adjuxtāre.* See AD-, JUXTA-] —**ad·just′a·ble,** *adj.* —**ad·just′a·bly,** *adv.* —**ad·just′er, ad·jus′tor,** *n.*
—**Syn. 2.** set; repair, fix. ADJUST, ADAPT, ALTER in their literal meanings imply making necessary or desirable changes (as in position, shape, or the like). To ADJUST is to move into proper position for use: *to adjust the eye-*

piece of a telescope. To ADAPT is to make a change in character, to make something useful in a new way: *to adapt a paper clip for a hairpin.* To ALTER is to change the appearance but not the use: *to alter the height of a table.* **3.** arrange; rectify; reconcile.

ad·just·a·ble-pitch (ə jus′tə bəl pich′), *adj.* (of a marine or aircraft propeller) having blades whose pitch can be changed while the propeller is stationary, chiefly to suit various conditions of navigation or flight. Cf. **controllable-pitch.**

adjust′able span′ner, *Brit.* See **monkey wrench** (def. 1).

ad·just·ment (ə just′mənt), *n.* **1.** the act of adjusting; adaptation to a particular purpose. **2.** the state of being adjusted; orderly relation of parts or elements. **3.** a knob, lever, or other means of adjusting: *the adjustments on a microscope.* **4.** the act of bringing something into conformity with external requirements: *the adjustment of one's view of reality.* **5.** harmony achieved by modification or alteration of a position: *They worked out an adjustment of their conflicting ideas.* **6.** *Sociol.* a process of modifying, adapting, or altering individual or collective patterns of behavior so as to bring them into conformity with other such patterns, as with those provided by a cultural environment. **7.** *Insurance.* act of ascertaining the amount of indemnity which the party insured is entitled to receive under the policy, and of settling the claim. **8.** a settlement of a disputed account or claim. **9.** a change or concession, as in price or other terms, in view of special circumstances. [ADJUST + -MENT] —**ad·just·ment·al** (ə just men′təl), *adj.*

ad·ju·tant (aj′ə tənt), *n.* **1.** *Mil.* a staff officer who assists the commanding officer in issuing orders. **2.** *Mil. Brit.* an executive officer. **3.** an assistant. **4.** See **adjutant stork.** [< L *adjūtant-* (s. of *adjūtāns*, prp. of *adjūtāre*), equiv. to *ad-* AD- + *jū-* (perf. s. of *juvāre* to help) + *-t-* freq. suffix + *-ant-* -ANT] —**ad′ju·tan·cy,** *n.*

ad′jutant gen′eral, *pl.* **adjutants general.** **1.** *U.S. Army.* **a.** the **Adjutant General,** the chief administrative officer of the Army. **b.** an adjutant of a unit having a general staff, usually an officer of the Adjutant General's Corps. **2.** a high, often the highest, officer of the National Guard of a State or Territory.

ad′jutant stork′, a large East Indian stork, *Leptoptilus dubius.* Also called **ad′jutant bird′, ad′jutant crane′.**

ad·ju·vant (aj′ə vənt), *adj.* **1.** serving to help or assist; auxiliary. —*n.* **2.** one who or that which aids or helps. **3.** anything that aids in removing or preventing a disease, esp. a substance added to a prescription to aid the effect of the main ingredient. [< L *adjuvant-* (s. of *adjuvāns*, prp. of *adjuvāre*), equiv. to *ad-* AD- + *juv-* (s. of *juvāre* to help) + *-ant-* -ANT]

ad Ka·len·das Grae·cas (äd kä len′däs grī′käs; *Eng.* ad kə len′dəs grē′kəs), *Latin.* at no time; never: from the fact that the Greeks did not reckon dates by calends. [lit., at the Greek Calends]

Ad·lai (ad′lē, -lā, -lī), *n.* a boy's given name. Also, **Adley.**

Ad·ler (ad′lər), *n.* **1. Alfred,** 1870–1937, Austrian psychiatrist and psychologist. **2. Felix,** 1851–1933, U.S. educator, reformer, and writer. **3. Kurt Herbert,** born 1905, U.S. orchestra conductor, born in Austria. **4. Mortimer Jerome,** born 1902, U.S. philosopher and educator. **5. Peter Hermann,** born 1899, U.S. orchestra conductor, born in Czechoslovakia.

Ad·le·ri·an (ad lēr′ē ən), *adj.* of or pertaining to Alfred Adler or his doctrines, esp. in respect to the belief that behavior is determined by compensation for feelings of inferiority. [ADLER + -IAN]

Ad·ley (ad′lē), *n.* a boy's given name. Also, **Adlai.**

ad lib (ad lib′, ad′), **1.** something ad-libbed. —*adv.* **2.** at one's pleasure; without restriction: *The matching stole can be worn ad lib.* [see AD LIBITUM]

ad-lib (ad lib′, ad′-), *v.*, **-libbed, -lib·bing,** *adj.* —*v.t.* **1.** to improvise (a speech, music, etc.). —*v.i.* **2.** to act, speak, etc., without preparation: *He has had to ad-lib constantly.* —*adj.* **3.** impromptu; makeshift; extemporaneous: *an ad-lib organization.* [v. use of AD LIB]

ad lib., ad libitum.

ad lib·i·tum (ad lib′i təm; *Lat.* äd lib′i to͝om′), **1.** at one's pleasure. **2.** *Music.* not obligatory or indispensable; not so important that it cannot be omitted (opposed to *obbligato*). *Abbr.:* **ad lib.** [< L]

ad li·tem (ad′ lī′təm), *Law.* for the particular action or proceeding: *a guardian ad litem.* [< L]

ad lit·te·ram (äd lit′te räm′; *Eng.* ad lit′ə ram′), *Latin.* to the letter; exactly.

ad loc., at or to the place. [< L *ad locum*]

Adm., **1.** Admiral. **2.** Admiralty.

adm., **1.** administration. **2.** administrator. **3.** admission.

Ad·mah (ad′mə), *n.* one of the cities that was destroyed along with Sodom and Gomorrah. Deut. 29:23. Also, *Douay Bible,* **Adama.**

ad ma·jo·rem De·i glo·ri·am (äd mä yō′rem dā′ē glō′rē äm′), *Latin.* for the greater glory of God.

ad·man (ad′man′, -mən), *n., pl.* **-men** (-men′, -mən). **1.** Also called **advertising man.** one whose profession is writing, designing, or selling advertisements. **2.** a printer or compositor who specializes in setting advertisements. [AD[1] + MAN[1]]

ad·mass (ad′mas′), *Chiefly Brit.* —*n.* **1.** the segment of the public strongly or easily influenced by mass media, advertising, etc. —*adj.* **2.** of, pertaining to, characterized by, or comprised of such a populace: *admass culture; admass life.* [AD[1] + MASS]

ad·meas·ure (ad mezh′ər), *v.t.*, **-ured, -ur·ing.** **1.** to measure off or out; apportion. **2.** *Naut.* to measure the dimensions and capacity of a vessel, as for official registration. [late ME *amesure* < MF *amesure(r).* See AD-, MEASURE] —**ad·meas′ur·er,** *n.*

ad·meas·ure·ment (ad mezh′ər mənt), *n.* **1.** process of measuring. **2.** number, dimensions, or measure of anything. **3.** apportionment. [ADMEASURE + -MENT]

Ad·me·te (ad mē′tē), *n.* *Class. Myth.* a daughter of Eurystheus for whom Hercules took the golden girdle of Ares from Hippolyte.

Ad·me·tus (ad mē′təs), *n.* *Class. Myth.* a Thessalian king, one of the Argonauts and husband of Alcestis.

ad·min·i·cle (ad min′i kəl), *n.* an aid; auxiliary. [< L *adminicul(um)* prop, support (*ad-* AD- + *min(ae)* projecting points, pinnacles of walls + *-i-* -I- + *-culum* -CLE)] —**ad·mi·nic·u·lar** (ad′mə nik′yə lər), **ad·mi·nic·u·lar·y** (ad′mə nik′yə ler′ē), *adj.*

ad·min·is·ter (ad min′i stər), *v.t.* **1.** to manage (affairs, a government, etc.); have executive charge of: *to administer laws.* **2.** to bring into use or operation; dispense: *to administer justice.* **3.** to make application of; give: *to administer medicine.* **4.** to tender or impose: *to administer an oath.* **5.** *Law.* to manage or dispose of, as a decedent's estate by an executor or administrator or a trust estate by a trustee. —*v.i.* **6.** to contribute assistance; bring aid or supplies (usually fol. by *to*): *to administer to the needs of the poor.* **7.** to perform the duties of an administrator. [< L *administrāre* (see AD-, MINISTER); r. late ME *amynistre* < MF *aministre(r)*] —**ad·min·is·tra·ble** (ad min′i strə bəl), *adj.* —**ad·min·is·trant** (ad min′i strənt), *adj.*
—**Syn. 1.** conduct, control, execute; direct, superintend, supervise, oversee. See **rule. 2.** distribute, supply, furnish. **3.** apply.

ad·min·is·trate (ad min′i strāt′), *v.t.*, **-trat·ed, -trat·ing.** to administer. [< L *administrāt(us)*, ptp. of *administrāre* to ADMINISTER; see -ATE[1]]

ad·min·is·tra·tion (ad min′i strā′shən), *n.* **1.** the management of any office, employment, or organization; direction. **2.** the function of a political state in exercising its governmental duties. **3.** the duty or duties of an administrator in exercising his executive functions. **4.** the management by an administrator of such duties. **5.** a body of administrators, esp. governmental administrators. **6.** the period of service of a governmental administrator or body of governmental administrators. **7.** *U.S.* any group entrusted with executive or administrative powers: *the administration of a college.* **8.** *Law.* management of a decedent estate by an executor or administrator, or of a trust estate by a trustee. **9.** act of dispensing, esp. formally: *administration of the sacraments.* **10.** act of tendering: *the administration of an oath.* **11.** application, as of a salve, medicine, etc. [late ME *administracio(u)n* < L *administrātiōn-* (s. of *administrātiō*) service. See ADMINISTRATE, -ION] —**ad·min′is·tra′tion·al,** *adj.*

ad·min·is·tra·tive (ad min′i strā′tiv, -strə-), *adj.* pertaining to administration; executive: *administrative ability.* [< L *administrātīv(us).* See ADMINISTRATE, -IVE] —**ad·min′is·tra′tive·ly,** *adv.*

ad·min·is·tra·tor (ad min′i strā′tər), *n.* **1.** a person who directs or manages affairs of any kind. **2.** a person with a talent for managing or organizing. **3.** *Law.* a person appointed by a court to take charge of the estate of a decedent, but not appointed in the decedent's will. [< L *administrātor.* See ADMINISTRATE, -OR[2]] —**ad·min′is·tra′tor·ship′,** *n.*

admin′istrator with the will′ annexed′, *Law.* one appointed to administer the estate of a deceased person who named no executor in his will or named executors who refused to act, were incompetent, or had died.

ad·min·is·tra·trix (ad min′i strā′triks, ad′min i-), *n., pl.* **-is·tra·tri·ces** (-i strā′tri sēz′, -i strə trī′sēz). *Law.* a female administrator. [< ML; fem. of ADMINISTRATOR; see -TRIX]

ad·mi·ra·ble (ad′mər ə bəl), *adj.* worthy of admiration; exciting approval, reverence, or affection; excellent. [< L *admīrābil(is).* See ADMIRE, -ABLE] —**ad′mi·ra·ble·ness, ad′mi·ra·bil′i·ty,** *n.* —**ad′mi·ra·bly,** *adv.*
—**Syn.** estimable, praiseworthy.

Ad′mirable Crich′ton, The (krīt′ən), a comedy (1902) by Sir James M. Barrie.

ad·mi·ral (ad′mər əl), *n.* **1.** the commander in chief of a fleet. **2.** a naval officer of the highest rank. **3.** a naval officer of a high rank: the grades in the U.S. Navy are fleet admiral, admiral, vice-admiral, and rear admiral. **4.** *Obs.* the flagship of an admiral. **5.** *Brit.* a master who directs a fishing fleet. **6.** any of several often brightly colored butterflies of the family *Nymphalidae,* as *Vanessa atalanta* (**red admiral**). [ME, var. of *amiral* < OF < Ar *amīr al* commander of; *-d-* < ML *admīrābilis mundi* for Ar *amīr al mūminīn* commander of the faithful] —**ad′mi·ral·ship′,** *n.*

Ad·mi·ral (ad′mər əl), *n.* a boy's given name.

Ad′miral of the Fleet′, an officer of the highest rank in the British navy.

ad·mi·ral·ty (ad′mər əl tē), *n., pl.* **-ties,** *adj.* —*n.* **1.** the office or jurisdiction of an admiral. **2.** the officials or the department of state having charge of naval affairs, as in Great Britain. **3.** a court dealing with maritime questions, offenses, etc. **4.** maritime law. **5. the Admiralty,** the offical building, in London, of the British commissioners for naval affairs. —*adj.* **6.** of or pertaining to admiralty law. [ME *amiralty* < MF. See ADMIRAL, -TY[2]]

ad′miralty cloth′, *Brit. Slang.* melton cloth, used in the manufacture of coats and jackets, esp. for the naval service.

Ad′miralty Is′lands, a group of islands in the SW Pacific, N of New Guinea: under Australian administration. 19,017 (1964); ab. 800 sq. mi.

ad′miralty met′al, an alloy of not less than 70 percent copper, about 1 percent tin, small amounts of other elements, and the balance zinc; tin brass. Also called **ad′miralty brass′, ad′miralty bronze′.**

Ad′miralty Range′, a mountain range in Antarctica, NW of the Ross Sea.

ad·mi·ra·tion (ad′mə rā′shən), *n.* **1.** a feeling of wonder, pleasure, and approbation. **2.** act of looking on or contemplating with pleasure: *admiration of a pretty girl.* **3.** an object of wonder or approbation: *She was the admiration of everyone.* **4.** *Archaic.* wonder; astonishment. [< L *admīrātiōn-* (s. of *admīrātiō*). See ADMIRE, -ATION] —**ad·mi·ra·tive** (ad mī′rə tiv, ad′mə-rā′-), *adj.* —**ad·mi′ra·tive·ly,** *adv.*
—**Syn. 1.** approval; esteem, regard; affection. —**Ant. 1.** condemnation.

ad·mire (ad mīər′), *v.*, **-mired, -mir·ing.** —*v.t.* **1.** to regard with wonder, pleasure, and approval. **2.** to regard with wonder or surprise (usually used ironically or sarcastically): *I admire your audacity.* —*v.i.* **3.** to feel or express admiration. **4.** *Chiefly Southern and Midland U.S.* to take pleasure; like or desire: *I would admire to go.* [< L *admīr(ārī)*, equiv. to *ad-* AD- + *mīrārī* (in ML *mīrāre*) to wonder at, admire] —**ad·mir′er,** *n.* —**ad·mir′ing·ly,** *adv.*
—**Syn. 1.** esteem, revere, venerate. —**Ant. 1.** despise.

ad·mis·si·ble (ad mis′ə bəl), *adj.* **1.** that may be allowed or conceded; allowable: *an admissible plan.* **2.** capable or worthy of being admitted: *an admissible piece of evidence.* [< LL *admissibil(is)*, equiv. to L *admiss-* (see ADMISSION) + *-ibilis* -IBLE] —**ad·mis′si·bil′i·ty, ad·mis′si·ble·ness,** *n.* —**ad·mis′si·bly,** *adv.*

ad·mis·sion (ad mish′ən), *n.* **1.** act of allowing to enter; entrance granted by permission, by provision or existence of pecuniary means, or by the removal of obstacles: *the admission of aliens into a country.* **2.** right or permission to enter: *to grant a person admission.* **3.** the price paid for entrance, as to a theater, ball park, etc. **4.** act or condition of being received or accepted in a position or office; appointment: *admission to the practice of law.* **5.** confession of a charge, an error, or a crime; acknowledgment: *His admission of the theft solved the mystery.* **6.** an acknowledgment of the truth of something. **7.** a point or statement admitted; concession. [< L *admission-* (s. of *admissiō*), equiv. to *admiss(us)* admitted, ptp. of *admittere* (*ad-* AD- + *mitt-* let go + *-tus* ptp. suffix) + *-iōn-* -ION]
—**Syn. 1.** See **entrance**[1]. **2.** access.

Admis′sion Day′, *U.S.* a legal holiday in some States commemorating the day of admission into the Union.

ad·mis·sive (ad mis′iv), *adj.* tending to admit. [< L *admiss(us)* (see ADMISSION) + -IVE]

ad·mit (ad mit′), *v.*, **-mit·ted, -mit·ting.** —*v.t.* **1.** to allow to enter; grant or afford entrance to: *to admit a student to college.* **2.** to give right or means of entrance to: *This ticket admits two people.* **3.** to permit to exercise a certain function or privilege: *admitted to the bar.* **4.** to permit; allow. **5.** to allow as valid: *to admit the force of an argument.* **6.** to acknowledge; confess: *He admitted his guilt.* **7.** to grant in argument; concede: *The fact is admitted.* **8.** to have capacity for the admission of at one time: *This passage admits two abreast.* —*v.i.* **9.** to permit entrance; give access: *This key admits to the garden.* **10.** to grant opportunity or permission (usually fol. by *of*): *Circumstances do not admit of this.* [< L *admitt(ere)*, equiv. to *ad-* AD- + *mittere* to send, let go; r. late ME *amitte,* with *a-* (instead of *ad-*) < MF *amettre*] —**ad·mit′ta·ble, ad·mit′ti·ble,** *adj.* —**ad·mit′ter,** *n.*
—**Syn. 1.** receive. **6.** own, avow. See **acknowledge.**

ad·mit·tance (ad mit′əns), *n.* **1.** permission to enter; the power or right of entrance: *admittance into the exhibit room.* **2.** act of admitting. **3.** actual entrance. **4.** *Elect.* the measure of the ability of a circuit to conduct an alternating current, consisting of two components, conductance and susceptance; the reciprocal of impedance, expressed in mhos. *Symbol:* Y [ADMIT + -ANCE]
—**Syn. 1.** access. See **entrance**[1].

ad·mit·ted·ly (ad mit′id lē), *adv.* by acknowledgment; by his own admission; confessedly: *He was admittedly the one who had lost the documents.* [ADMITTED + -LY]

ad·mix (ad miks′), *v.t., v.i.* to mingle with or add to something else. [AD- + MIX, modeled on L *admiscēre* (*admixtus* ptp.)]

ad·mix·ture (ad miks′chər), *n.* **1.** act or state of mixing; state of being mixed. **2.** anything added; any alien element or ingredient. **3.** a compound containing an admixture. [< L *admixt(us).* See ADMIX, -URE]

ad·mon·ish (ad mon′ish), *v.t.* **1.** to caution, advise, or counsel against something. **2.** to reprove or scold, esp. in a mild and good-willed manner: *The teacher admonished him about excessive noise.* **3.** to urge to duty; remind: *to admonish someone about his obligations.* [alter. of late ME *amonyssche* (with *ad-* for *a-*), itself alter. of ME *amoneste* < MF *amoneste(r).* See AD-, MONISH] —**ad·mon′ish·er,** *n.* —**ad·mon′ish·ing·ly,** *adv.* —**ad·mon′ish·ment,** *n.*
—**Syn. 1.** See **warn. 2.** rebuke, censure. **3.** notify, jog, apprise.

ad·mo·ni·tion (ad′mə nish′ən), *n.* **1.** act of admonishing. **2.** counsel, advice, or caution. **3.** gentle and good-willed reproof. **4.** a warning or reproof given by an ecclesiastical authority. [< L *admonitiōn-* (s. of *admonitiō*); see AD-, MONITION; r. late ME *amonicioun* < AF]

ad·mon·i·tor (ad mon′i tər), *n.* an admonisher. [< L; see AD-, MONITOR] —**ad·mon·i·to·ri·al** (ad mon′i tôr′ē əl, -tōr′-), *adj.*

ad·mon·i·to·ry (ad mon′i tōr′ē, -tôr′ē), *adj.* tending or serving to admonish; warning: *an admonitory gesture.* [< ML *admonitōri(us).* See AD-, MONITORY] —**ad·mon′i·to′ri·ly,** *adv.*

admov., (in prescriptions) **1.** apply. **2.** let it be applied. [< L *admovē*] [< L *admoveātur*]

Ad·nah (ad′nə), *n.* **1.** a Manassite deserter from Saul's to David's army. I Chron. 12:20. **2.** a commander in King Jehosaphat's army. II Chron. 17:14. Also, *Douay Bible,* **Ednas.**

ad·nate (ad′nāt), *adj.* *Biol.* grown fast to something; congenitally attached. [< L *adnāt(us)*, var. of *agnātus* AGNATE]

A, Adnate stipule

ad·na·tion (ad nā′shən), *n.* adnate condition. [< L *adnātiōn-*, var. of *agnātiōn-* AGNATION]

ad nau·se·am (ad nô′shē əm, -am′, -zhē-, -sē-, -zē-), to a sickening or disgusting degree. [< L: lit., to seasickness]

a·do (ə do͞o′), *n.* busy activity; bustle; fuss. [ME (north) *at do,* equiv. to *at* to (< Scand) + *do* DO[1]]
—**Syn.** flurry; confusion, upset, excitement; hubbub, noise, turmoil. ADO, TO-DO, COMMOTION, STIR, TUMULT suggest a great deal of fuss and noise. ADO implies a confused bustle of activity, a considerable emotional upset, and a great deal of talking: *Much Ado About Nothing.* TO-DO, now more commonly used, may mean merely excitement and noise and may be pleasant or unpleasant: *a great to-do over a movie star.* COMMOTION suggests a noisy confusion and babble: *commotion at the scene of an accident.* STIR suggests excitement and noise, with a hint of emotional cause: *The report was followed by a tremendous stir in the city.* TUMULT suggests disorder with noise and violence: *a tumult as the mob stormed the Bastille.*

a·do·be (ə dō′bē), *n.* **1.** the sun-dried brick in common use in countries having little rainfall. **2.** a yellow silt or clay, deposited by rivers, used to make bricks. **3.** a building constructed of adobe. **4.** a dark, heavy soil, containing clay. [< Sp < Ar *aṭ-ṭōb*, by assimilation from *al ṭōb* the brick < Coptic *tōb* brick]

ado′be flat′, a plain consisting of adobe deposited by short-lived rainfall or thaw streams, usually having a smooth or unmarked surface.

ad·o·les·cence (ad′əles′əns), *n.* **1.** the transitional period between puberty and adulthood in human development, extending mainly over the teen years and

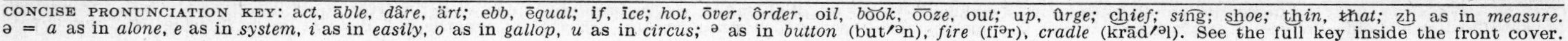
CONCISE PRONUNCIATION KEY: act, āble, dâre, ärt; ebb, ēqual; if, īce; hot, ōver, ôrder, oil, bo͝ok, o͞oze, out; up, ûrge; chief; sing; shoe; thin, that; zh as in *measure.* ə = *a* as in *alone,* *e* as in *system,* *i* as in *easily,* *o* as in *gallop,* *u* as in *circus;* ə as in *button* (but′ən), *fire* (fīər), *cradle* (krād′əl). See the full key inside the front cover.

terminating legally when the age of majority is reached; youth. **2.** quality or state of being adolescent; youthfulness. [late ME < MF < L *adolēscentia.* See ADOLESCENT, -ENCE]

ad·o·les·cent (ad/ᵊles/ənt), *adj.* **1.** growing to manhood or womanhood; youthful. **2.** having the characteristics of adolescence or of an adolescent. —*n.* **3.** an adolescent person. [< L *adolēscent-* (s. of *adolēscēns* growing up, prp. of *adolēscere*), equiv. to *adol-* (see ADULT) + *-ēsc-* -ESCE + *-ent-* -ENT] —**ad/o·les/cent·ly,** *adv.*
—**Syn. 1.** immature, young. **3.** youth, teen-ager, minor.

Ad·olf (ad/olf, ā/dolf; *Ger.* ä/dôlf), *n.* a boy's given name. Also, **Ad/olph, Ad/olphe, A·dol·phus** (ə dol/fəs).

A·do·nai (ä/dō nī/, -noi/), *n.* **1.** (*italics*) Also, **A·do·noy** (ä/dō noi/). *Hebrew.* a title of reverence for God, serving also as a substitute pronunciation of the Tetragrammaton. **2.** *Liturgy.* the second person of the Trinity; Christ. [lit., my Lord; spoken in place of the ineffable name YAHWEH]

Ad·o·na·is (ad/ᵊnā/is), *n.* (*An Elegy on the Death of John Keats*) a poem (1821) by Shelley.

A·do·ni·a (ə dō/nē ə), *n.* (*sometimes construed as pl.*) an ancient festival in honor of the death and resurrection of Adonis, held in Greece, Rome, and the Middle East.

Ad·o·ni·as (ad/ᵊnī/əs), *n.* *Douay Bible.* Adonijah.

A·don·ic (ə don/ik), *adj.* **1.** *Pros.* noting a verse consisting of a dactyl (—⏑⏑) followed by a spondee (— —) or trochee (—⏑). **2.** of or like Adonis. —*n.* **3.** *Pros.* an Adonic verse or line. [< ML *Adōnic(us).* See ADONIS, -IC]

Ad·o·ni·jah (ad/ᵊnī/jə), *n.* a son of David, put to death at the order of Solomon. II Sam. 3:4; I Kings 2:19–25. Also, *Douay Bible,* **Adonias.**

A·do·nis (ə don/is, ə dō/nis), *n.* **1.** *Class. Myth.* a favorite of Aphrodite, slain by a wild boar, but permitted by Zeus to pass four months every year in the lower world with Persephone, four with Aphrodite, and four wherever else he chose. In another account he spent half the year on earth and thus symbolically represented the vegetation cycle. **2.** a very handsome young man. **3.** a boy's given name.

A·don O·lam (ä dōn/ ō läm/), *Judaism.* a liturgical prayer or hymn expressing the faith of Israel in God, often sung in unison usually at the close of a service. [< Heb: Lord of the world]

a·dopt (ə dopt/), *v.t.* **1.** to choose for or take to oneself; make one's own by selection or assent: *to adopt a name.* **2.** to take as one's own child, specifically by a formal legal act. **3.** to vote to accept: *The House adopted the report.* **4.** to select as a basic or required textbook or series of textbooks in a course. **5.** to take or receive into any kind of new relationship: *to adopt a person as an heir.* **6.** *Brit.* to nominate a candidate for office, esp. for political office. [< L *adopt(āre),* equiv. to *ad-* AD- + *optāre* to OPT] —**a·dopt/a·bil/i·ty,** *n.* —**a·dopt/a·ble,** *adj.* —**a·dopt/er,** *n.* —**a·dop/tion,** *n.* —**a·dop/tion·al,** *adj.*

a·dopt·ee (ə dop tē/, ad/op-), *n.* a person who is adopted.

a·dop·tive (ə dop/tiv), *adj.* **1.** of or involving adoption. **2.** acquired or related by adoption: *an adoptive father or son.* **3.** tending to adopt. [< L *adoptīv(us);* see ADOPT -IVE; r. late ME *adoptife* < MF *adoptif*] —**a·dop/tive·ly,** *adv.*

a·dor·a·ble (ə dōr/ə bəl, ə dôr/-), *adj.* **1.** worthy of being adored. **2.** very delightful; charming: *What an adorable hat!* [< L *adōrābil(is).* See ADORE, -ABLE] —**a·dor/a·ble·ness, a·dor/a·bil/i·ty,** *n.* —**a·dor/a·bly,** *adv.*

ad·o·ra·tion (ad/ə rā/shən), *n.* **1.** act of paying honor, as to a divine being; worship. **2.** reverent homage. **3.** fervent and devoted love. [< L *adōrātiōn-* (s. of *adōrātiō*) worship. See ADORE, -ATION]

a·dore (ə dōr/, ə dôr/), *v.,* **a·dored, a·dor·ing.** —*v.t.* **1.** to regard with the utmost esteem, love, and respect; honor. **2.** to pay divine honor to; worship: *to adore God.* **3.** to like very much: *I simply adore the way your hair is done!* —*v.i.* **4.** to worship. [< L *adōr(āre)* (to) speak to, pray, worship, equiv. to *ad-* AD- + *ōrāre* to speak, beg (see ORAL); r. ME *aour(i)e* < OF *aourer*] —**a·dor/er,** *n.* —**a·dor/ing·ly,** *adv.*
—**Syn. 1.** idolize; reverence, revere, venerate. —**Ant. 1.** abhor.

a·dorn (ə dôrn/), *v.t.* **1.** to decorate or add beauty to, as by ornaments: *garlands of flowers adorning her hair.* **2.** to make pleasing, more attractive, more impressive, etc.; enhance: *the piety which adorns his character.* [late ME *adorne* < L *adōrnāre,* equiv. to *ad-* AD- + *ōrnāre* to dress (see ORNATE); r. late ME *aourne* < MF] —**a·dorn/er,** *n.* —**a·dorn/ing·ly,** *adv.*
—**Syn. 1.** beautify; deck, bedeck; bedizen, array.

a·dorn·ment (ə dôrn/mənt), *n.* **1.** an ornament; accessory: *the adornments and furnishings of a room.* **2.** ornamentation; embellishment: *personal adornment.* [ADORN + -MENT; r. late ME *aournement* < MF]

a·dor·no (ə dôr/nō), *n., pl.* **-nos.** *Ceram.* relief ornament applied to a piece. [< Sp, equiv. to *adorn(ar)* (< L *adōrnāre* to ADORN) + *-o* masc. n. suffix]

a·dorsed (ə dôrst/), *adj.* *Heraldry.* addorsed. Also, **a·dor·sé** (ə dôr sā/, ə dôr/sē).

A·dou·la (ä do͞o/lə), *n.* **Cy·rille** (sē ril/), 1922–78, African statesman: premier of the Democratic Republic of the Congo 1961–66.

A·do·wa (ä/do͝o wä/), *n.* Aduwa.

a·down (ə doun/), *adv., prep.* *Archaic.* down. [ME *adoun,* OE *of dūne* off the hill. See A-², DOWN²]

ADP, 1. Also called **adenosine diphosphate, adenosinediphosphoric acid.** *Biochem.* an ester of adenosine and pyrophosphoric acid, $C_{10}H_{12}N_5O_3H_3P_2O_7$, derived from ATP, and serving to transfer energy during glycolysis. **2.** See **automatic data processing.**

ad part. dolent., (in prescriptions) to the painful parts. [< L *ad partēs dolentēs*]

ad pa·tres (äd pä/trēs; *Eng.* ad pā/trēz), *Latin.* dead. [lit., to the fathers]

ad quem (äd kwem/; *Eng.* ad kwem/), *Latin.* at or to which; the goal or extremity toward which something tends.

A·dram·me·lech (ə dram/ə lek/), *n.* **1.** one of the gods worshiped by the Sepharvites. II Kings 17:31. Cf. **Anammelech. 2.** a son of Sennacherib. II Kings 19:37. Also, *Douay Bible,* **A·dram/e·lech/.**

Ad·ras·te·a (ad/ra stē/ə), *n.* *Class. Myth.* **1.** Nemesis (def. 1). **2.** a daughter of Melisseus entrusted by Rhea with the rearing of the infant Zeus.

A·dras·tus (ə dras/təs), *n.* *Class. Myth.* a king of Argos and leader of the Seven against Thebes. Also, **A·dras/tos.**

ad rem (äd rem/; *Eng.* ad rem/), *Latin.* **1.** relevant; pertinent: *an ad rem remark.* **2.** without digressing; in a straightforward manner: *to reply ad rem.* [lit., to the thing]

ad·re·nal (ə drēn/ᵊl), *Anat., Zool.* —*adj.* **1.** situated near or on the kidneys; suprarenal. **2.** of or produced by the adrenal glands. —*n.* **3.** See **adrenal gland.** [AD- + L *ren-* (s. of *rēnēs* kidneys) + -AL¹]

ad·re·nal·ec·to·mize (ə drēn/ᵊlek/tə mīz/), *v.t.,* **-mized, -miz·ing.** *Surg.* to perform an adrenalectomy on. [ADRENALECTOM(Y) + -IZE]

ad·re·nal·ec·to·my (ə drēn/ᵊlek/tə mē), *n., pl.* **-mies.** *Surg.* the removal of one or both adrenal glands. [ADRENAL + -ECTOMY]

adre/nal gland/, *Anat., Zool.* one of a pair of ductless glands, located above the kidneys, consisting of a cortex and a medulla. Also called **suprarenal gland.** See diag. under **kidney.**

A·dren·al·in (ə dren/ᵊlin), *n.* *Pharm., Trademark.* epinephrine (def. 2).

a·dren·a·line (ə dren/ᵊlin, -ᵊlēn/), *n.* epinephrine. [ADRENAL + -INE¹]

a·dre·nin (ə drē/nin, ə dren/in), *n.* epinephrine. Also, **a·dre·nine** (ə drē/nin, ə dren/in, -ēn). [ADREN(AL) + -IN²]

a·dre·no·cor·ti·co·trop·ic (ə drē/nō kôr/tə kō trop/ik), *adj.* stimulating the adrenal cortex. Also, **a·dre·no·cor·ti·co·troph·ic** (ə drē/nō kôr/tə kō trof/ik). [ADREN(AL) + -O- + *cortic-* (see CORTICAL) + -O- + -TROPIC]

adre/nocorticotrop/ic hor/mone, *Biochem.* See **ACTH.**

A·dres·tus (ə dres/təs), *n.* (in the *Iliad*) **1.** the son of Merops who was a Trojan ally killed by Diomedes. **2.** a Trojan ally captured by Menelaus and killed by Agamemnon.

a·dret (a drā/), *n.* a side of a mountain receiving direct sunlight. [< F for *a dret,* dial. var. of *à droit* on the right (side) << L *ad-* AD- + *dīrectus* DIRECT]

A·dri·an (ā/drē ən), *n.* **1. Edgar Douglas,** 1889–1977, English physiologist: Nobel prize for medicine 1932. **2.** Hadrian. **3.** a city in SE Michigan. 20,347 (1960). **4.** a boy's given name.

Adrian I, died A.D. 795, pope 772–795. Also, **Hadrian I.**

Adrian II, Italian ecclesiastic: pope A.D. 867–872. Also, **Hadrian II.**

Adrian III, Saint, Italian ecclesiastic: pope A.D. 884–885. Also, **Hadrian III.**

Adrian IV, (*Nicholas Breakspear*), c1100–59, only Englishman to become pope, 1154–59. Also, **Hadrian IV.**

Adrian V, died 1276, Italian ecclesiastic: pope 1276. Also, **Hadrian V.**

Adrian VI, 1459–1523, Dutch ecclesiastic: pope 1522–23. Also, **Hadrian VI.**

A·dri·an·o·ple (ā/drē ə nō/pəl), *n.* Edirne.

A/driano/ple red/, a medium red color. Also called **Levant red, Turkey red.**

A·dri·an·op·o·lis (ā/drē ə nop/ə lis), *n.* former name of **Edirne.**

A·dri·at·ic (ā/drē at/ik, ad/rē-), *adj.* **1.** of or pertaining to the Adriatic Sea. —*n.* **2.** See **Adriatic Sea.**

A/driat/ic Sea/, an arm of the Mediterranean between Italy and Yugoslavia. Also called **Adriatic.**

A·dri·enne (ā/drē en/; *Fr.* A drē en/), *n.* a girl's given name.

a·drift (ə drift/), *adj., adv.* **1.** not fastened by any kind of mooring; without anchor; drifting. **2.** swaying from one idea or course of action to another; without direction or stability. [A-¹ + DRIFT]

a·droit (ə droit/), *adj.* **1.** expert or nimble in the use of the hands. **2.** cleverly skillful, resourceful, or ingenious: *an adroit debater.* [< F, orig. phrase *à droit* rightly << L *ad* according to + *dīrectum,* neut. of *dīrectus* right; see DIRECT] —**a·droit/ly,** *adv.* —**a·droit/ness,** *n.*
—**Syn. 1.** dexterous; skillful, clever; deft, apt, adept. —**Ant. 1.** clumsy.

à droite (A DRWAT/), *French.* to the right.

A·dron (ā/drən), *n.* a boy's given name, form of **Adrian.**

ads., advertisements.

a.d.s., autograph document, signed.

ad·sci·ti·tious (ad/si tish/əs), *adj.* added or derived from without; supplemental; additional. [< L *adscīt(us)* derived, assumed, foreign (ptp. of *asciscī*), equiv. to *ad-* AD- + *scī-* (s. of *scīre* to know) + *-t(us)* ptp. suffix + -ITIOUS] —**ad/sci·ti/tious·ly,** *adv.*

ad·script (ad/skript), *adj.* **1.** written after (distinguished from *superior, subscript*). —*n.* **2.** an adscript character. Cf. **inferior** (def. 10), **superior** (def. 13). [< L *a(d)script(us)* (ptp. of *ascrībere* to ASCRIBE), equiv. to *ad-* AD- + *scrīptus* written; see SCRIPT]

ad·scrip·tion (ad skrip/shən), *n.* ascription.

ad·sorb (ad sôrb/, -zôrb/), *Physical Chem.* to gather (a gas, liquid, or dissolved substance) on a surface in a condensed layer, as when charcoal adsorbs gases. [AD- + (AB)SORB] —**ad·sorb/a·bil/i·ty,** *n.* —**ad·sorb/a·ble,** *adj.* —**ad·sorb/ent,** *adj., n.* —**ad·sorp·tion** (ad sôrp/shən, -zôrp/-), *n.* —**ad·sorp/tive,** *adj., n.* —**ad·sorp/tive·ly,** *adv.*

ad·sorb·ate (ad sôr/bāt, -bit, -zôr/-), *n.* the substance adsorbed. [ADSORB + -ATE¹]

adst. feb., (in prescriptions) when fever is present. [< L *adstānte febre*]

ad·su/ki bean/ (ad so͞o/kē, -zo͞o/-). See **adzuki bean.**

ad·sum (äd/so͝om; *Eng.* ad/sum), *interj.* *Latin.* I am present.

a du·e (ä do͞o/ā; *It.* ä do͞o/e), *Music.* **1.** together; in unison. **2.** divisi. [< It: lit., by two]

ad·u·la·res·cent (aj/ə lə res/ənt), *adj.* (of certain gemstones, esp. the adularia) having a milky, bluish luster. [ADULAR(IA) + -ESCENT] —**ad/u·la·res/cence,** *n.*

ad·u·lar·i·a (aj/ə lâr/ē ə), *n.* *Mineral.* a sometimes opalescent variety of orthoclase formed at a low temperature. [< It < F *adulaire,* named after *Adula* name of a mountain group in Switzerland; see -ARY]

ad·u·late (aj/ə lāt/), *v.t.,* **-lat·ed, -lat·ing.** to show excessive devotion to; flatter or admire servilely. [back formation from *adulation* < L *adūlātiōn-* (s. of *adūlātiō*) a fawning, equiv. to *adūlāt(us),* ptp. of *adūlārī, -āre* (*ad-* AD- + *-ūl-* fawn (<?) + *-ātus* -ATE¹) + *-iōn-* -ION] —**ad/u·la/tion,** *n.* —**ad/u·la/tor,** *n.* —**ad·u·la·to·ry** (aj/ə lə tôr/ē, -tōr/ē), *adj.*

a·dult (ə dult/, ad/ult), *adj.* **1.** having attained full size and strength; grown up; mature: *an adult person, animal, or plant.* **2.** of or for adults: *adult education; adult movies.* —*n.* **3.** a person who is grown up or of age. **4.** a full-grown animal or plant. **5.** a person who has attained the legal age of majority, in the common law generally 21 years for males. [< L *adult(us)* grown (ptp. of *adolēre* to make grow), equiv. to *ad-* AD- + *ul-* (identical with root *al-* in ALIMENT, *ol-* in PROLIFIC) + *-tus* ptp. suffix] —**a·dult/hood,** *n.* —**a·dult/ness,** *n.*

adult/ educa/tion, an educational program, esp. one offering special schedules, courses, etc., for adults who have not completed high school, college, or the like, at the usual age. Cf. **postgraduate.**

a·dul·ter·ant (ə dul/tər ənt), *n.* **1.** a substance that adulterates. —*adj.* **2.** adulterating. [< L *adulterant-* (s. of *adulterāns,* prp. of *adulterāre*), equiv. to *ad-* AD- + *ulter* (see ADULTERATE) + *-ant-* -ANT]

a·dul·ter·ate (*v.* ə dul/tə rāt/; *adj.* ə dul/tər it, -tə rāt/), *v.,* **-at·ed, -at·ing,** *adj.* —*v.t.* **1.** to debase by adding inferior materials or elements; make impure by admixture; use cheaper, inferior, or less desirable goods in the production or marketing of (any professedly genuine article): *to adulterate food.* —*adj.* **2.** adulterated. **3.** adulterous (def. 1). [< L *adulterāt(us)* altered (ptp. of *adulterāre*), equiv. to *ad-* AD- + *ulter* (var. of *alter* other; see ALTER) + *-ātus* -ATE¹] —**a·dul/ter·a/tor,** *n.*

a·dul·ter·a·tion (ə dul/tə rā/shən), *n.* **1.** the act or process of adulterating. **2.** state of being adulterated. **3.** something adulterated. [< L *adulterātiōn-* (s. of *adulterātiō*), equiv. to *adulterāt(us)* (see ADULTERATE) + *-iōn-* -ION]

a·dul·ter·er (ə dul/tər ər), *n.* a person, esp. a man, who commits adultery. [earlier *adulter* adulterer (< L, akin to *adulterāre* to defile; see ADULTERATE) + -ER¹]

a·dul·ter·ess (ə dul/tər is, -tris), *n.* a woman who commits adultery. [ADULTER(ER) + -ESS]

a·dul·ter·ine (ə dul/tər in, -tə rēn/, -tə rīn/), *adj.* **1.** characterized by adulteration; spurious. **2.** born of adultery. **3.** of or involving adultery. [< L *adulterī-n(us),* equiv. to *adulter* adulterer, counterfeiter (see ADULTERER) + *-īnus* -INE¹]

a·dul·ter·ous (ə dul/tər əs), *adj.* **1.** characterized by or given to adultery; illicit. **2.** spurious (def. 1). [ADULTER(Y) + -OUS] —**a·dul/ter·ous·ly,** *adv.*

a·dul·ter·y (ə dul/tə rē), *n., pl.* **-ter·ies.** voluntary sexual intercourse between a married person and someone other than his or her lawful spouse. [< L *adulteri(um),* equiv. to *adulter* (see ADULTERER) + *-ium* -Y³]

ad·um·bral (ad um/brəl), *adj.* shadowy; shady. [AD- + L *umbr(a)* shade, shadow + -AL¹]

ad·um·brate (ad um/brāt, ad/əm brāt/), *v.t.,* **-brat·ed, -brat·ing.** **1.** to give a faint shadow or resemblance of; to outline or sketch. **2.** to foreshadow; prefigure. **3.** to darken or conceal partially; overshadow. [< L *adumbrāt(us)* shaded (ptp. of *adumbrāre*), equiv. to *ad-* AD- + *umbr(a)* shade, shadow + *-ātus* -ATE¹] —**ad/um·bra/tion,** *n.*

ad·um·bra·tive (ad um/brə tiv, ad/əm brā/tiv), *adj.* foreshadowing; sketchy; faintly indicative. [ADUMBRATE + -IVE] —**ad·um/bra·tive·ly,** *adv.*

a·dunc (ə dungk/), *adj.* curved inward; hooked. [< L *adunc(us),* equiv. to *ad-* AD- + *uncus* hook, barb] —**a·dun·ci·ty** (ə dun/si tē), *n.*

Ad·u·rol (aj/ə rōl/, -rōl/, aj/ə-), *n.* *Trademark.* chlorohydroquinone.

a·dust (ə dust/), *adj.* **1.** dried or darkened as by heat; burned; scorched. **2.** gloomy in appearance or mood. [< L *adust(us)* (ptp. of *adūrere*), equiv. to *ad-* AD- + *us-* (var. s. of *ūrere* to burn) + *-tus* ptp. suffix]

ad u·trum·que pa·ra·tus (äd o͞o tro͞om/kwe pä rä/to͞os; *Eng.* ad yo͞o trum/kwē pə rā/təs), *Latin.* ready for either alternative.

A·du·wa (ä/do͞o wä/), *n.* a town in N Ethiopia: Italians defeated 1896. 15,712 (est. 1970). Also, **Adowa.**

Adv., 1. Advent. **2.** Advocate.

adv., 1. ad valorem. **2.** advance. **3.** adverb. **4.** adverbial. **5.** adverbially. **6.** adversus. **7.** advertisement.

Ad·vai·ta (əd vī/tə), *n.* *Hinduism.* one of the two principal Vedantic schools, asserting the existence of Brahman alone, whose appearance as the world is an illusion resulting from ignorance. Cf. **dvaita** (def. 2). [< Skt, equiv. to *a-* A-⁶ + *dvai-* (var. s. of *dvau* two) + *-ta* n. suffix]

ad val., ad valorem.

ad va·lo·rem (ad və lōr/əm, -lôr/-), in proportion to the value (applied esp. to duties on imports which are fixed at a percentage of the value as stated on the invoice). [< L: lit., according to the worth]

ad·vance (ad vans/, -väns/), *v.,* **-vanced, -vanc·ing,** *n., adj.* —*v.t.* **1.** to move or bring forward: *The general advanced his troops to the new position.* **2.** to bring into consideration or notice; suggest; propose: *to advance reasons for a tax cut.* **3.** to improve; further: *to advance one's interests.* **4.** to raise in rank; promote. **5.** to raise in rate; increase: *to advance the price.* **6.** to bring forward in time; accelerate: *to advance growth.* **7.** to supply beforehand; furnish on credit or before goods are delivered or work is done. **8.** to furnish as part of a stock or fund. **9.** to supply or pay in expectation of reimbursement. **10.** *Archaic.* to raise, as a banner. —*v.i.* **11.** to move or go forward; proceed: *The troops advanced.* **12.** (of a color, form, etc., on a flat surface) to move toward or be perceived as moving toward an observer, esp. as giving the illusion of space. Cf. **recede**¹ (def. 3). **13.** to improve or make progress; grow or rise in importance, status, etc.: *to advance in knowledge or rank.* **14.** to increase in quantity, value, price, etc.: *His stock advanced three points.* —*n.* **15.** a forward movement; progress in space: *the advance of the troops to the border.* **16.** promotion; improvement in importance, rank, etc.: *his advance to the position of treasurer.* **17.** a step forward; actual progress in any course of action: *the advance of knowledge.* **18.** Usually, **advances.** an effort to bring about acquaintance, accord, understanding, etc. **19.** addition to price; rise in price: *an advance on cottons.* **20.** *Com.* **a.** a giving beforehand; a furnishing of something before an equivalent is received: *An advance on salary permitted him to pay his debt on time.* **b.** the money or goods thus furnished: *He received $100 as an advance against future delivery.* **21.** *Journalism.* **a.** copy prepared before the event it describes has occurred: *The morning papers carried advances on the ceremony, which will take place tonight.* **b.** a press release, wire-service dispatch, or the like, as one containing the text or partial text of a speech, sent to arrive in advance of the event to which it is related. Cf. **release copy. 22.** *U.S.* the leading body of an army. **23.** *Mil.* (formerly) the order or a signal to advance. **24.** *Naut.* the distance traveled by a turning vessel in the direction of the original course before proceeding on a new course. **25. in advance, a.** in front; before: *They walked on in advance of the king.* **b.** ahead of time; beforehand: *It will be necessary to get tickets well in advance.* —*adj.* **26.** going or placed before: *an advance section of a train.* **27.** made or given ahead of time: *an advance payment on a loan.* **28.** issued ahead of time: *an advance copy of the President's speech.* **29.** having gone beyond others or beyond the average. [ME *avaunce(n)* < OF *avanc(i)e(r)* < VL **abanteāre*, equiv. to LL *abante* away before (see AB-, ANTE-) + *-āre* v. and inf. suffix; *ad-* by confusion of prefixes] —**ad·vanc′er,** *n.* —**ad·vanc′ing·ly,** *adv.*

—**Syn. 2.** adduce, propound; offer. **3.** forward, promote. **6.** force; quicken, hasten, speed up. **9.** lend, loan. **11.** ADVANCE, MOVE ON, PROCEED all imply movement forward. ADVANCE applies to forward movement, esp. toward an objective: *to advance to a platform.* PROCEED emphasizes movement, as from one place to another, and often implies continuing after a halt: *to proceed on one's journey.* MOVE ON, a more informal expression, is similar in meaning to proceed; it does not, however, imply a definite goal: *The crowd was told to move on.* **13.** thrive, flourish; prosper. **14.** rise. **16, 17.** improvement, rise. **18.** overture, proposal; offer, tender. **22.** spearhead. **28.** prepublication. —**Ant. 1, 2, 11.** withdraw. **11.** retreat. **14.** decrease.

ad·vanced (ad vanst′, -vänst′), *adj.* **1.** placed ahead or forward: *with one foot advanced.* **2.** ahead or further along in progress, knowledge, etc.: *an advanced class in French.* **3.** pertaining to or embodying ideas, practices, attitudes, etc., taken as being more enlightened or liberal than the standardized, established, or traditional: *advanced theories of child care; the more advanced members of the artistic community.* **4.** far on in time: *the advanced age of most senators.* [ME; see ADVANCE, -ED²]

advanced′ degree′, an academic degree conferred for completion of requirements beyond the college level, as M.S., Ph.D., etc.

advanced′ stand′ing, 1. credit for studies completed elsewhere, granted to a student by the college or university to which he has been admitted. **2.** the higher academic status of a student granted such credit.

advance′ fee′. See **front money** (def. 2).

advance′ guard′, a body of troops going before the main force to clear the way, guard against surprise, etc.

ad·vance·ment (ad vans′mənt, -väns′-), *n.* **1.** act of moving forward. **2.** promotion in rank or standing; preferment: *His hopes of advancement failed.* **3.** *Law.* money or property given during his lifetime by a person subsequently dying intestate and deducted from the intestate share of the recipient. [ME *avauncement* < OF *avancement.* See ADVANCE, -MENT]

ad·vanc·er (ad van′sər, -vän′-), *n.* **1.** one who or that which advances. **2.** the second branch of the antlers of a buck. [ME; see ADVANCE, -ER¹]

ad·van·tage (ad van′tij, -vän′-), *n., v.,* **-taged, -tag·ing.** —*n.* **1.** any state, circumstance, opportunity, or means specially favorable to success, interest, or any desired end: *the advantage of a good education.* **2.** benefit; gain; profit: *It is to his advantage.* **3.** superiority or ascendancy (often fol. by *over* or *of*): *His height gave him an advantage over his opponent.* **4.** a position of superiority (often fol. by *over* or *of*): *their advantage in experienced players.* **5.** *Tennis.* the first point scored after deuce. **6. have the advantage of,** to be in a superior or advantageous position; possess an advantage over: *By virtue of independent wealth, he has the advantage of his opponents.* **7. take advantage of, a.** to make use of for gain: *to take advantage of an opportunity.* **b.** to impose upon, esp. unfairly, as by exploiting a weakness: *to take advantage of someone.* **8. to advantage,** to good effect; advantageously: *The paintings were arranged to advantage on one wall.* —*v.t.* **9.** to be of service to; yield profit or gain to; benefit. **10.** to cause to advance or progress; further; promote: *Such action will advantage our cause.* **11.** to improve the position of; prove beneficial to; profit: *It would advantage him to work harder.* [late ME *avantage* < MF *avant* before (< LL *abante;* see ADVANCE) + *-age* -AGE]

—**Syn. 2.** ADVANTAGE, BENEFIT, PROFIT all mean something that is of use or value. ADVANTAGE is anything that places one in an improved position, esp. in coping with competition or difficulties: *It is to one's advantage to have traveled widely.* BENEFIT is anything that promotes the welfare or improves the state of a person or group: *a benefit to society.* PROFIT is any valuable, useful, or helpful gain: *profit from trade or experience.* **9.** serve, avail, help, aid.

ad·van·taged (ad van′tijd, -vän′-), *adj.* having advantage or advantages: *She is more advantaged than her sister. They are one of the world's most advantaged peoples.* [ADVANTAGE + -ED³]

ad·van·ta·geous (ad′vən tā′jəs), *adj.* providing an advantage; furnishing convenience or opportunity; profitable; useful; beneficial: *an advantageous position, an advantageous treaty.* [ADVANTAGE + -OUS; cf. F *avantageux,* It *avantaggioso*] —**ad′van·ta′geous·ly,** *adv.* —**ad′van·ta′geous·ness,** *n.*

adv. chgs., advance charges.

ad·vec·tion (ad vek′shən), *n.* **1.** *Meteorol.* the horizontal transport of atmospheric properties (distinguished from *convection*). **2.** the movement of air horizontally. [< L *advectiōn-* (s. of *advectiō*), equiv. to *advect(us),* ptp. of *advehere* (*ad-* AD- + *vec-* (var. s. of *vehere* to carry, bring) + *-tus* ptp. suffix) + *-iōn-* -ION] —**ad·vec′tive,** *adj.*

advec′tion fog′, *Meteorol.* fog caused by the movement of warm, moist air over a cold surface.

ad·ve·na (äd′we nä′), *n., pl.* **-ve·nae** (-we nī′). *Latin.* foreigner or alien; stranger.

ad·vent (ad′vent), *n.* **1.** a coming into place, view, or being; arrival: *the advent of the holiday season.* **2.** (*usually cap.*) the coming of Christ into the world. **3.** (*cap.*) the period beginning four Sundays before Christmas, observed in commemoration of the coming of Christ into the world. **4.** (*usually cap.*) Also called **Second Advent, Second Coming.** the coming of Christ on Judgment Day. [early ME < L *advent(us)* a coming to, equiv. to *ad-* AD- + *ven-* (s. of *venīre* to come) + *-tus* suffix-making n. denoting action]

Ad·vent·ist (ad′ven tist, ad ven′-), *n.* **1.** Also called **Second Adventist.** a member of any of certain Christian denominations which maintain that the Second Advent of Christ is imminent. —*adj.* **2.** of or pertaining to Adventists or Adventism. [ADVENT + -IST] —**Ad′vent·ism,** *n.*

ad·ven·ti·ti·a (ad′ven tish′ē ə, -tish′ə), *n.* *Anat.* the external covering of an organ or other structure, derived from connective tissue, esp. the external covering of a blood vessel. [< L *adventīcia,* neut. pl. of *adventīcius* ADVENTITIOUS] —**ad′ven·ti′tial,** *adj.*

ad·ven·ti·tious (ad′vən tish′əs), *adj.* **1.** associated with something by chance rather than as an integral part; extrinsic; foreign: *Ivy gives an adventitious charm to the undistinguished architecture of the campus.* **2.** *Bot., Zool.* appearing in an abnormal or unusual position or place, as a root. [< L *adventīcius* coming from outside, equiv. to *ad-* AD- + *ven-* (s. of *venīre* to come) + *-t(us)* ptp. suffix + *-īcius* -ITIOUS] —**ad′ven·ti′tious·ly,** *adv.* —**ad′ven·ti′tious·ness,** *n.*

ad·ven·tive (ad ven′tiv), *Bot., Zool.* —*adj.* **1.** not native and usually not yet well established, as exotic plants or animals. —*n.* **2.** an adventive plant or animal. [< L *advent(us)* (ptp. of *advenīre;* see ADVENT) + -IVE] —**ad·ven′tive·ly,** *adv.*

Ad′vent Sun′day, the first Sunday in Advent.

ad·ven·ture (ad ven′chər), *n., v.,* **-tured, -tur·ing.** —*n.* **1.** an undertaking of uncertain outcome; a hazardous enterprise. **2.** an exciting or very unusual experience. **3.** participation in exciting undertakings or enterprises: *the spirit of adventure.* **4.** a commercial or financial speculation of any kind; venture. **5.** *Obs.* **a.** peril; danger; risk. **b.** chance; fortune; luck. —*v.t.* **6.** to risk or hazard. **7.** to take the chance of; dare. **8.** to venture to say or utter: *to adventure an opinion.* —*v.i.* **9.** to take the risk involved. **10.** to venture; hazard. [partly Latinized from ME *aventure* < OF < L (*rēs*) *adventūra* (thing) about to happen (to someone), fem. fut. participle of *advenīre* to arrive. See ADVENT, -URE] —**ad·ven′ture·ful,** *adj.*

ad·ven·tur·er (ad ven′chər ər), *n.* **1.** one who adventures. **2.** a seeker of fortune in daring enterprises; soldier of fortune. **3.** one who undertakes any great commercial risk; speculator. **4.** one who seeks power or wealth by underhand or questionable means. [ADVENTURE + -ER¹]

ad·ven·ture·some (ad ven′chər səm), *adj.* bold; daring; adventurous. [ADVENTURE + -SOME¹] —**ad·ven′ture·some·ly,** *adv.* —**ad·ven′ture·some·ness,** *n.*

ad·ven·tur·ess (ad ven′chər is), *n.* **1.** a female adventurer. **2.** a woman who schemes to win social position, wealth, etc., by unscrupulous or questionable means. [ADVENTUR(ER) + -ESS]

ad·ven·tur·ism (ad ven′chə riz′əm), *n.* defiance or disregard of accepted standards of behavior. [ADVENTURE + -ISM]

ad·ven·tur·ous (ad ven′chər əs), *adj.* **1.** inclined or willing to engage in adventures. **2.** full of risk; requiring courage; hazardous: *an adventurous undertaking.* [late ME *aventurous* < MF *aventur(e)os.* See ADVENTURE, -OUS] —**ad·ven′tur·ous·ly,** *adv.* —**ad·ven′tur·ous·ness,** *n.*

—**Syn. 1.** daring, venturous, venturesome.

ad·verb (ad′vûrb), *n.* *Gram.* any member of a class of words that in many languages are distinguished in form, as *partly* in English by the ending *-ly,* or by functioning as modifiers of verbs, and in some languages, as Latin and English, also as modifiers of adjectives or other adverbs or adverbial phrases, as *very, well, quickly.* Adverbs typically express some relation of place, time, manner, attendant circumstance, degree, cause, inference, result, condition, exception, concession, purpose, or means. [< L *adverb(ium),* equiv. to *ad-* AD- + *verb(um)* word, verb, + *-ium* n. suffix; loan trans. of Gk *epírrhēma*] —**ad·ver·bi·al** (ad vûr′bē əl), *adj.* —**ad·ver′bi·al·ly,** *adv.* —**ad′verb·less,** *adj.*

ad ver·bum (äd wer′bŏŏm; *Eng.* ad vûr′bəm), *Latin.* to the word; exact in wording according to an original.

ad·ver·sa (äd wer′sä; *Eng.* ad vûr′sə), *n.pl.* *Latin.* things noted.

ad·ver·sa·ri·a (äd′wer sä′ri ä; *Eng.* ad′vər sâr′ē ə), *n. pl.* (*construed as sing. or pl.*) *Latin.* **1.** notes; brief written comments or remarks. **2.** a commonplace book. **3.** things written on a facing page. **4.** annotations; commentaries.

ad·ver·sar·y (ad′vər ser′ē), *n., pl.* **-sar·ies. 1.** a person or group that opposes or attacks another; opponent; enemy; foe. **2.** an opponent in a contest; contestant. **3. the Adversary,** the devil; Satan. [late ME *adversarie* < L *adversāri(us),* equiv. to *advers(us)* (see ADVERSE) + *-ārius* -ARY; r. ME *adversere* < AF]

—**Syn. 1.** ADVERSARY, ANTAGONIST mean a person, a group, or a personified force, contending against another. ADVERSARY suggests an enemy who fights determinedly, continuously, and relentlessly: *a formidable adversary.* ANTAGONIST suggests one who, in hostile spirit, opposes another, often in a particular contest or struggle: *a duel with an antagonist.* —**Ant. 1.** ally.

ad·ver·sa·tive (ad vûr′sə tiv), *adj.* **1.** expressing contrariety, opposition, or antithesis: *"But" is an adversative conjunction.* —*n.* **2.** an adversative word or proposition. [< LL *adversātīv(us),* equiv. to *adversāt(us)* (ptp. of *adversārī* to resist; see ADVERSE, -ATE¹) + *-īvus* -IVE] —**ad·ver′sa·tive·ly,** *adv.*

adver′sative asyn′deton, *Rhet.* a staccato effect produced by omitting adversative connectives from between two or more items forming a group, as in "Look out for yourselves . . . stop treating me considerately." Cf. **copulative asyndeton.**

ad·verse (ad vûrs′, ad′vûrs), *adj.* **1.** antagonistic in purpose or effect: *adverse criticism; opinions adverse to slavery.* **2.** opposing one's interests or desire: *adverse fate; adverse circumstances.* **3.** being or acting in a contrary direction; opposed or opposing: *adverse winds.* **4.** opposite; confronting: *the adverse page.* **5.** *Bot.* turned toward the axis, as a leaf (opposed to *averse*). [late ME < L *advers(us)* hostile (ptp. of *advertere*), equiv. to *ad-* AD- + *vert-* turn + *-tus* ptp. suffix] —**ad·verse′ly,** *adv.* —**ad·verse′ness,** *n.*

—**Syn. 1.** hostile, inimical, unfriendly. **2.** unfavorable; unlucky, unfortunate; disastrous, calamitous, catastrophic. See **contrary.** —**Ant. 1–3.** favorable.

ad·ver·si·ty (ad vûr′si tē), *n., pl.* **-ties. 1.** adverse fortune or fate; a condition marked by misfortune, calamity, or distress: *his struggles with adversity.* **2.** an unfortunate event or circumstance: *the prosperities and adversities of this life.* [ME *adversite* < L *adversitāt-* (s. of *adversitās*). See ADVERSE, -ITY]

—**Syn. 1.** catastrophe, disaster; trouble, misery. **2.** See **affliction.** —**Ant. 1.** prosperity.

ad·vert[1] (ad vûrt′), *v.i.* **1.** to remark or comment about or in relation to; refer (usually fol. by *to*): *He adverted briefly to the news of the day.* **2.** to turn the attention (usually fol. by *to*). [late ME < L *advert(ere)* (to) pay attention, equiv. to *ad-* AD- + *vertere* to turn]

—**Syn. 1.** allude.

ad·vert[2] (ad′vərt), *n.* *Chiefly Brit. Informal.* advertisement. [by shortening]

ad·vert·ent (ad vûr′tᵊnt), *adj.* attentive; heedful. [< L *advertent-* (s. of *advertēns,* prp. of *advertere*), equiv. to *ad-* AD- + *vert-* turn + *-ent-* -ENT] —**ad·vert′ence, ad·vert′en·cy,** *n.* —**ad·vert′ent·ly,** *adv.*

ad·ver·tise (ad′vər tīz′, ad′vər tīz′), *v.,* **-tised, -tis·ing.** —*v.t.* **1.** to give information to the public about; announce publicly in a newspaper, on the radio, etc.: *to advertise a reward.* **2.** to praise the good qualities of (a product, service, etc.) in order to induce people to buy or use it. **3.** to call attention to, in a boastful or ostentatious manner: *Stop advertising yourself!* **4.** *Obs.* to give notice, advice, or information to; inform: *I advertised him of my intention.* **5.** *Obs.* to admonish; warn. —*v.i.* **6.** to ask for by a notice in a newspaper, over the radio, etc.: *to advertise for a house to rent.* **7.** to offer goods for sale or rent, solicit funds, etc., by means of advertisements: *It pays to advertise.* **8.** *Cards.* **a.** *Poker.* to bluff so as to make the bluff obvious. **b.** *Rummy.* to discard a card in order to induce an opponent to discard one of the same suit or denomination. Also, **advertize.** [late ME < MF *avertiss-,* var. s. of *avertir* << L *advertere* to ADVERT¹] —**ad·ver·tis·a·ble** (ad′vər tī′zə bəl, ad′vər-tī′-), *adj.* —**ad′ver·tis′er,** *n.*

ad·ver·tise·ment (ad′vər tīz′mənt, ad vûr′tis mənt, -tiz-), *n.* **1.** an announcement, as of goods for sale, in newspapers or magazines, on the radio, etc. **2.** a public notice, esp. in print. **3.** the action of making generally known; a calling to the attention of the public: *The news of this event will receive wide advertisement.* Also, **ad′ver·tize′ment.** [late ME < MF *avertissement.* See ADVERTISE, -MENT]

ad·ver·tis·ing (ad′vər tī′zing), *n.* **1.** the act or practice of calling public attention to one's product, service, need, etc., esp. by paid announcements in newspapers and magazines, over radio or television, on billboards, etc.: *to get more customers by advertising.* **2.** paid announcements; advertisements. **3.** the profession of planning, designing, and writing advertisements. Also, **ad′ver·tiz′ing.** [ADVERTISE + -ING¹]

ad′vertising account′, account (def. 11c).

ad′vertising a′gency, an agency employed by advertisers to plan, design, place, and supervise their advertisements or advertising campaigns.

ad′vertising man′, adman (def. 1).

ad·ver·tize (ad′vər tīz′, ad′vər tīz′), *v.t., v.i.,* **-tized, -tiz·ing.** advertise. —**ad·ver·tiz·a·ble** (ad′vər tī′zə bəl, ad′vər tī′-), *adj.* —**ad′ver·tiz′er,** *n.*

ad·vice (ad vīs′), *n.* **1.** an opinion or recommendation offered as a guide to action, conduct, etc.: *I shall act on your advice.* **2.** a communication, esp. from a distance, containing information: *Advice from abroad informs us that the government has fallen.* [late ME *advise;* r. ME *avis* < OF *a vis* (in phrase *ce m'est a vis* that is my impression) < L *ad* (see AD-) + *vīs(us)* (see VISAGE)]

—**Syn. 1.** admonition, warning, caution; guidance; urging. ADVICE, COUNSEL, SUGGESTION, RECOMMENDATION, PERSUASION, EXHORTATION refer to opinions urged with more or less force as worthy bases for thought, opinion, conduct, or action. ADVICE is a practical recommendation as to action or conduct: *advice about purchasing land.* COUNSEL is weighty and serious advice, given after careful deliberation: *counsel about one's career.* RECOMMENDATION is weaker than advice and suggests an opinion that may or may not be acted upon: *Do you think that he'll follow my recommendation?* SUGGESTION implies something more tentative than a recommendation: *He did not expect his suggestion to be taken seriously.* PERSUASION suggests a stronger form of advice, urged at some length with appeals to reason, emotion, self-interest, or ideals: *His persuasion changed their minds.* EXHORTATION suggests an intensified persuasion or admonition, often in the form of a discourse or address: *an impassioned exhortation.* **2.** intelligence, notice, notification, word.

advice′ boat′, a fast boat for conveying messages; dispatch boat.

ad·vis·a·ble (ad vī′zə bəl), *adj.* **1.** proper to be advised or recommended; desirable or wise, as a course of action: *Is it advisable for me to write to him?* **2.** open to or desirous of advice. [ADVISE + -ABLE] —**ad·vis′a·bil′i·ty, ad·vis′a·ble·ness,** *n.* —**ad·vis′a·bly,** *adv.*

—**Syn. 1.** expedient, politic, proper, fit, suitable, prudent, sensible, judicious.

ad·vise (ad vīz′), *v.,* **-vised, -vis·ing.** —*v.t.* **1.** to give counsel to; offer an opinion or suggestion as worth following: *I advise you to be cautious.* **2.** to recommend as wise, prudent, etc.: *He advised secrecy.* **3.** to give (a person, group, etc.) information or notice (often fol. by *of*): *The investors were advised of the risk. They advised him that this was their final notice.* —*v.i.* **4.** to take counsel (usually fol. by *with*): *I shall advise with my friends.* **5.** to offer counsel; give advice: *I shall act as you advise.* [late ME; r. ME *avise(n)* < OF *aviser* < VL **advisāre,* equiv. to *ad-* AD- + **vīsāre,* alter. of L *vīsere* to view, freq. of *vidēre* to see]

—**Syn. 1.** counsel, admonish, caution. **2.** suggest. **3.** inform, notify, apprise, acquaint. **4.** confer, deliberate, discuss, consult.

ad·vised (ad vīzd′), *adj.* **1.** considered (usually used in combination): *ill-advised; well-advised.* **2.** informed: *kept thoroughly advised.* [ME; see ADVISE, -ED²] —**ad·vis·ed·ness** (ad vī′zid nis), *n.*

ad·vis·ed·ly (ad vī′zid lē), *adv.* after due consideration; deliberately. [ADVISED + -LY]

ad·vis·ee (ad vī zē′, ad′-), *n.* *Educ.* one of a group of students assigned to a faculty adviser for help in selection of a course of studies. [ADVISE + -EE]

ad·vise·ment (ad vīz′mənt), *n.* careful deliberation or consideration; consultation: *The application was taken under advisement.* [ADVISE + -MENT; r. ME *avisement* < OF]

ad·vis·er (ad vī′zər), *n.* **1.** one who gives advice. **2.** *Educ.* a teacher who helps students select their courses of study and offers career guidance. Also, **ad·vi′sor.** [ADVISE + -ER¹] —**ad·vis′er·ship′,** *n.*

ad·vi·so·ry (ad vī′zə rē), *adj.* **1.** of, giving, or containing advice: *an advisory letter from a stockbroker.* **2.** having the power or duty to advise: *an advisory council.* [ADVISE + -ORY¹] —**ad·vi′so·ri·ly,** *adv.*

advi′sory opin′ion, a formal opinion that is given on a point of law by a court, judge, or judges on request from a legislature or government official, contrasted with an opinion in a case at law where the point is being adjudicated.

ad vi·tam (äd wē′täm; *Eng.* ad vī′tam), *Latin.* for life.

ad vi·vum (äd wē′wŏŏm; *Eng.* ad vī′vəm), *Latin.* to that which is alive.

ad·vo·caat (ad′vō kät′), *n.* a Dutch liqueur made with brandy, sugar, and eggs. [< D, short for *advocatenborrel* drink for lawyers, equiv. to *advocaten* (see ADVOCATE) + *borrel* < ?]

ad·vo·ca·cy (ad′və kə sē), *n., pl.* **-cies.** act of pleading for, supporting, or recommending; active espousal. [late ME *advocacye* < ML *advocātia.* See ADVOCATE, -ACY]

ad·vo·cate (*v.* ad′və kāt′; *n.* ad′və kit, -kāt′), *v.,* **-cat·ed, -cat·ing,** *n.* —*v.t.* **1.** to plead in favor of; support or urge by argument; recommend publicly: *He advocated higher salaries for teachers.* —*n.* **2.** one who defends, vindicates, or espouses a cause by argument; upholder; defender (usually fol. by *of*): *an advocate of peace.* **3.** one who pleads for or in behalf of another; intercessor. **4.** one who pleads the cause of another in a court of law. [< L *advocāt(us)* legal counselor (orig. ptp. of *advocāre* to call to one's aid), equiv. to *ad-* AD- + *voc-* (s. of *vox* voice) + *-ātus* -ATE¹; r. ME *avocat* < MF]

ad·vo·ca·tion (ad′və kā′shən), *n.* **1.** *Law.* (in papal or Scottish courts) the calling of an action before itself by a superior court. **2.** *Obs.* **a.** advocacy. **b.** act of summoning. [late ME < L *advocātiōn-* (s. of *advocātiō*), equiv. to *advocāt(us)* (see ADVOCATE) + *-iōn-* -ION]

ad·voc·a·to·ry (ad vok′ə tôr′ē, -tôr′ē), *adj.* of or pertaining to an advocate or his functions. [ADVOCATE + -ORY¹]

ad·vo·ca·tus di·a·bo·li (äd′vō kä′tŏŏs dē ä′bə lē′), *Medieval Latin.* See **devil's advocate** (def. 2).

ad·vow·son (ad vou′zən), *n.* *Eng. Eccles. Law.* the right of presentation to a benefice or church office. [< AF; r. ME *avoweisoun* < AF, OF *avoeson* << L *advocātiōn-.* See ADVOCATION]

advt., advertisement.

A·dy·gei (ä′də gā′, ä′də gā′; *Russ.* u di gyā′), *n.* **1.** Official name, **A′dygei Auton′omous Re′gion.** an autonomous region in the Russian Federation, part of the Krasnodar territory, in the NW Caucasus Mountains. 410,000; 1505 sq. mi. *Cap.:* Maikop. **2.** a Circassian language spoken in the Adygei Autonomous Region. Also, **Adighe, A′dy·ghe.**

A·dy·ghe (ä′də gā′, ä′də gā′, ä di ge′), *n.* **1.** Circassian (def. 1). **2.** Adygei.

a·dy·na·mi·a (ad′ᵊnā′mē ə), *n.* *Pathol.* weakness; debility; asthenia. [< NL < Gk, equiv. to *a-* A-⁶ + *dýnam(is)* force, power + *-ia* -IA]

a·dy·nam·ic (ad′ᵊnam′ik, ā′dī nam′-), *adj.* *Pathol.* lacking strength; asthenic. [ADYNAM(IA) + -IC, prob. by assoc. with DYNAMICS]

ad·y·tum (ad′i təm), *n., pl.* **-ta** (-tə). **1.** (in ancient worship) a sacred place which the public might not enter; an inner shrine. **2.** the most sacred or reserved part of any place of worship. [< L < Gk *ádyton* (place) not to be entered, equiv. to *a-* A-⁶ + *dy-* (s. of *dýein* to enter) + *-ton* adj. suffix]

adz (adz), *n.* a heavy, curved steel tool, for dressing timbers roughly, with a broad, chisellike end mounted on a wooden handle. Also, **adze.** [ME *ad(e)se,* OE *adesa* < ?]

Adzes
A, Cooper's adz
B, Carpenter's adz

A·dzhar·i·stan (ə jär′ə stan′; *Russ.* u jə ryi stän′), *n.* an autonomous republic in the Georgian republic, in Transcaucasia. 355,000; 1080 sq. mi. *Cap.:* Batumi. Formerly, **A·dzhar′ Auton′omous So′viet So′cialist Repub′lic** (ə jär′; *Russ.* u jär′).

ad·zu′ki bean′ (ad zōō′kē), an annual, bushy bean, *Phaseolus angularis,* grown chiefly in Asia, the seeds of which are used for food. Also, **adsuki bean.** [< Jap]

ae (ā), *adj.* *Scot.* one. [ME (Scot) *ā-,* OE *ān* ONE]

Æ, pen name of George William Russell. Also, **A.E.**

æ, an early English ligature representing a vowel sound like that of *a* in modern *bad.* The long *ǣ* continued in use until about 1250, but was finally replaced by *e.* The short *æ* was given up by 1150, being replaced usually by *a* but sometimes by *e.*

ae, a digraph or ligature appearing in Latin and Latinized Greek words. In English words of Latin or Greek origin, *ae* is now usually reduced to *e,* except generally in proper names (*Caesar*), in words belonging to Roman or Greek antiquities (*aegis*), and in modern words of scientific or technical use (*aecium*). Also, **æ.**

ae-, for words with initial **ae-,** see also **e-.**

AE, account executive.

ae., at the age of; aged. [< L *aetātis*]

A.E., 1. Aeronautical Engineer. **2.** Agricultural Engineer. **3.** Associate in Education. **4.** Associate in Engineering.

a.e., *Math.* See **almost everywhere.**

-aea, var. of **-ea:** *Athenaea.*

A.E.A., Actors' Equity Association.

Ae·ac·i·des (ē as′i dēz′), *n., pl.* **-dae** (-dē′). *Class. Myth.* a patronymic for any of the descendants of Aeacus, as Achilles, Peleus, and Telamon.

Ae·a·cus (ē′ə kəs), *n.* *Class. Myth.* a judge in Hades, a son of Zeus and grandfather of Achilles.

Ae·ae·a (ē ē′ə), *n.* *Class. Myth.* **1.** the island inhabited by Circe. **2.** Circe (def. 1).

-aean, a combination of **-aea** and **-an:** *Athenaean.*

A.E. and P., Ambassador Extraordinary and Plenipotentiary.

AEC, See **Atomic Energy Commission.**

Aech·mag·o·ras (ēk mag′ər əs), *n.* *Class. Myth.* a son of Hercules and Phialo.

ae·cid·i·um (ē sid′ē əm), *n., pl.* **ae·cid·i·a** (ē sid′ē ə). *Bot.* an aecium in which the spores are always formed in chains and enclosed in a cup-shaped peridium. [< NL; see AECIUM, -IDIUM]

ae·ci·o·spore (ē′sē ə spôr′, -spôr′), *n.* *Bot.* a spore borne by an aecium. [AECI(UM) + -O- + SPORE]

ae·ci·um (ē′shē əm, ē′sē-), *n., pl.* **ae·ci·a** (ē′shē ə, ē′sē ə). *Bot.* the sorus of rust fungi which arises from the haploid mycelium, commonly accompanied by spermogonia and bearing chainlike or stalked spores. [< NL < Gk *aik(ía)* assault, injury; see -IUM] —**ae·ci·al** (ē′shē əl, ē′sē-), *adj.*

A.Ed., Associate in Education.

ae·de·a·gus (ē dē′ə gəs), *n., pl.* **-gi** (-gī′, -jī′). the intromittent organ of a male insect. Also, **aedoeagus.** [< NL < Gk *aidoîa* genitals + *agós* leader (deriv. of *ágein* to lead)] —**ae·de′a·gal,** *adj.*

a·e·des (ā ē′dēz), *n.* **1.** See **yellow-fever mosquito. 2.** any mosquito of the genus *Aedes.* Also, **a·ë′des.** [< NL < Gk *aēdḗs* distasteful, unpleasant, equiv. to *a-* A-⁶ + *-ēdēs,* akin to *hêdos* pleasure, *hēdýs* sweet, *hēdonḗ* pleasure. See SWEET]

ae·dic·u·la (ē dik′yə lə), *n., pl.* **-lae** (-lē′). aedicule.

ae·di·cule (ē′də kyōōl′, ed′ə-), *n.* **1.** a small building. **2.** a small construction, as a shrine, imitating the form of a building. Also, **aedicula, edicule.** [< L *aedicul(a),* equiv. to *aedi-* (s. of *aedēs*) temple, shrine (akin to Gk *aíthein* to blaze, *aithḗr* bright upper sky, ETHER) + *-cula* -CULE]

Æ·dil·berct (a′dil berkt), *n.* old spelling of **Ethelbert.**

ae·dile (ē′dīl), *n.* *Rom. Hist.* one of a board of magistrates in charge of public buildings, streets, markets, games, etc. Also, **edile.** [< L *aedīl(is),* equiv. to *aedi-* (s. of *aedēs;* see AEDICULE) + *-īlis* -ILE] —**ae′dile·ship′,** *n.* —**ae·dil·i·tian** (ēd′ᵊlish′ən, ē′dī lish′-), *adj.*

ae·doe·a·gus (ē dē′ə gəs), *n., pl.* **-gi** (-gī′, -jī′). aedeagus.

A·ë·don (ā ēd′ᵊn), *n.* *Class. Myth.* a daughter of Pandareus who mistakenly killed her son. Zeus took pity on her and turned her into a nightingale.

Ae.E., Aeronautical Engineer.

Ae·ë·tes (ē ē′tēz), *n.* *Class. Myth.* a king of Colchis, father of Medea and custodian of the Golden Fleece.

A.E.F., American Expeditionary Forces.

Ae·ga′di·an Is′lands (i gā′dē ən), Egadi. Also, **Ae·ga′de·an Is′lands.**

Ae·gae·on (i jē′on), *n.* *Class. Myth.* Briareus.

Ae·ga·tes (i gā′tēz), *n.* ancient name of **Egadi.**

Ae·ge·an (i jē′ən), *adj.* **1.** of, pertaining to, or denoting the prehistoric civilization which preceded the historic Hellenic period and which flourished on the various islands and nearby regions of the Aegean Sea, as at Crete and Argolis. —*n.* **2.** See **Aegean Sea.** [< L *Aegae(us)* (< Gk *Aigaîos*) + -AN]

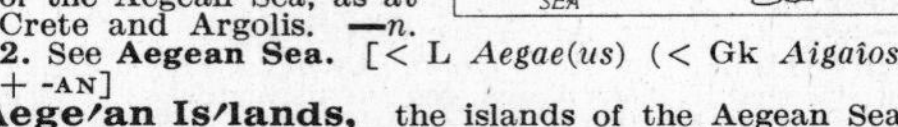

Aege′an Is′lands, the islands of the Aegean Sea, including the Dodecanese, Cyclades, and Sporades.

Aege′an Sea′, an arm of the Mediterranean Sea between Greece and Turkey. Also called **Aegean.**

Ae·ge·ri·a (i jēr′ē ə), *n.* *Rom. Legend.* Egeria (def. 1).

Ae·ges·ta (i jes′tə), *n.* *Class. Myth.* Egesta.

Ae·ge·us (ē′jē əs, ē′jōōs), *n.* *Class. Myth.* a king of Athens and the father of Theseus.

Ae·gi·a (i jī′ə), *n.* *Class. Myth.* a daughter of Adrastus and the wife of Polynices. Also, **Argia.**

Ae·gi·a·leus (i jī′ə lōōs′), *n.* *Class. Myth.* a son of Adrastus who was the only one of the Epigoni killed in the second attack against Thebes.

Ae·gi·a·li·a (ē′jē ə lī′ə), *n.* (in the *Iliad*) the wife of Diomedes who took Cometes as her lover when Nauplius falsely convinced her that her husband was deceiving her. Also, **Ae·gi·a·le** (i jē′ə lē′).

Ae·gi·co·res (ē′jə kôr′ēz, -kôr′-), *n.* *Class. Myth.* a son of Ion.

Ae·gim·i·us (i jim′ē əs), *n.* *Class. Myth.* a son of Dorus who was king of the Dorians.

Ae·gi·na (i jī′nə), *n.* **1.** *Class. Myth.* a daughter of Asopus and Metope who was abducted by Zeus and who bore him a son, Aeacus. **2. Gulf of,** a gulf of the Aegean Sea, in SE Greece. **3.** an island in this gulf. 11,000 (est. 1948); 32 sq. mi. **4.** a seaport on this island. 6000 (est. 1948). —**Ae·gi·ne·tan** (ē′jə nēt′ᵊn), *adj.*

Ae·gi·nae·a (ē′jə nē′ə), *n.* *Class. Myth.* an epithet of Artemis, meaning "goat-goddess."

Ae·gi·o·chus (i jī′ə kəs), *n.* *Class. Myth.* an epithet of Zeus, meaning "aegis-bearer."

Ae·gi·pan (ē′jə pan′), *n.* *Class. Myth.* a goatlike god, often identified with Pan or regarded as being related to him.

Ae·gir (e′jir), *n.* *Scand. Myth.* the sea-god, the husband of Ran.

ae·gir·ite (ā′gə rīt′, ē′jə-), *n.* a mineral, mainly sodium-ferric iron silicate, $NaFe·(Si_2O_6)$, occurring in feldspathoid rocks in slender prismatic crystals. Also, **ae·gir·ine** (ā′gə rēn′, ē′jə-). [AEGIR + -ITE²]

ae·gis (ē′jis), *n.* **1.** *Class. Myth.* the shield or breastplate of Zeus or Athena, bearing at its center the head of the Gorgon. **2.** protection; sponsorship: *under the imperial aegis.* Also, **egis.** [< L < Gk *aigís* shield of Zeus or Athena, prob. from *aig-* (s. of *aíx* goat) + *-is* n. suffix, from a type of shield made of goatskin]

Ae·gis·thus (i jis′thəs), *n.* *Class. Myth.* a cousin of Agamemnon who seduced Clytemnestra, Agamemnon's wife, and was later killed by Orestes, Clytemnestra's son.

Ae·gi·um (ē′jē əm), *n.* a town in ancient Achaea, on the Gulf of Corinth: Achaean League met here.

Aeg·le (eg′lē), *n.* *Class. Myth.* **1.** one of the Hesperides. **2.** a naiad often identified as the mother of the Graces. **3.** one of the Heliades.

Ae·gos·pot·a·mi (ē′gəs pot′ə mī′), *n.* a river in ancient Thrace, flowing into the Hellespont: near its mouth the Athenian fleet was defeated by Lysander, 405 B.C., in the last battle of the Peloponnesian War.

ae·gro·tat (ē′grō tat′, ē grō′tat), *n.* *Brit.* **1.** an official note certifying that a university student is too ill to attend lectures or examinations. **2.** the unclassified degree granted a university student who has fulfilled all requirements for graduation but was prevented by illness from attending the final examinations. [< L: lit., he is sick (pres. 3rd sing. of *aegrōtāre*), equiv. to *aegrōt(us)* sick (*aeg(e)r* sick + *-ōtus* adj. suffix) + *-at* 3rd sing. ending]

Ae·gyp·tus (ē jip′təs), *n.* *Class. Myth.* a king of Egypt and twin brother of Danaüs.

Æl·fric (al′frik), *n.* ("*Ælfric Grammaticus*") A.D. c955–c1020, English abbot and writer.

A·el·la (ā el′ə), *n.* *Class. Myth.* an Amazon, noted for her swiftness, who was slain by Hercules.

A·el·lo (ā el′ō), *n.* *Class. Myth.* one of the Harpies.

-aemia, var. of **-emia:** *anaemia.*

-aena, var. of **-ena:** *hyaena.*

Ae·ne·as (i nē′əs), *n.* *Class. Myth.* a Trojan hero, the son of Anchises and Venus, and reputed ancestor of the Romans.

Aene′as Sil′vi·us (sil′vē əs), **1.** Also, **Aene′as Syl′vius.** literary name of **Pius II. 2.** *Rom. Legend.* a king of Alba Longa.

Ae·ne·id (i nē′id), *n.* a Latin epic poem by Vergil, recounting the adventures of Aeneas after the fall of Troy.

A·e·ne·o·lith·ic (ā ē′nē ō lith′ik), *adj.* Chalcolithic. Also, **Eneolithic.** [AENE(OUS) + -O- + -LITHIC]

a·e·ne·ous (ā ē′nē əs), *adj.* bronze-colored: *an aeneous beetle.* Also, **a·ë′ne·ous.** [< L *aēneus,* equiv. to *aēn(us)* of bronze (*ae(s)* bronze + *-n-* adj. suffix) + *-eus* -EOUS]

A.Eng., Associate in Engineering.

Ae·ni·us (ē′nē əs), *n.* (in the *Iliad*) a Paeonian ally of the Trojans who was slain by Achilles.

Ae·o·li·a (ē ō′lē ə), *n.* Aeolis.

Ae·o·li·an (ē ō′lē ən), *adj.* **1.** Also, **Aeolic.** belonging to a branch of the Greek race named after Aeolus, its legendary founder. —*n.* **2.** a member of one of the four main divisions of the prehistoric Greeks. Cf. **Achaean** (def. 5), **Dorian** (def. 2), **Ionian** (def. 4). **3.** Aeolic. Also, **Eolian.** [< L *Aeoli(i)* (< Gk *Aioleîs* the Aeolians, with change of suffix) + -AN]

Ae·o·li·an (ē ō′lē ən), *adj.* **1.** pertaining to Aeolus, or to the winds in general. **2.** (*usually l.c.*) of or caused by the wind; wind-blown. **3.** (*l.c.*) *Geol. Obs.* Eolian (def. 1). [AEOL(US) + -IAN]

aeo′lian harp′, a box over which are stretched a number of strings of equal length, tuned in unison and sounded by the wind. Also called **aeo′lian lyre′, wind harp.**

Aeo′lian mode′, *Music.* an authentic church mode represented on the white keys of a keyboard instrument by an ascending scale from A to A.

Ae·ol·ic (ē ol′ik), *n.* **1.** the Greek dialect of ancient Aeolis and Thessaly. —*adj.* **2.** *Archit.* noting or pertaining to a capital used in the Greek territories of the eastern Aegean in the 7th and 6th centuries B.C., having two volutes rising from a shaft in opposite directions, and often having below them two convex rings of leaf ornament in the form of water-lily buds. **3.** Aeolian (def. 1). Also, **Eolic.** [< L *Aeolic(us)* < Gk *Aiolikós,* equiv. to *Aiol(eus),* pl. *Aioleîs,* + *-ikos* -IC]

Ae·o·li·des (ē ō′li dēz′), *n.pl.* *Class. Myth.* an epithet applied to descendants of Aeolus.

ae·ol·i·pile (ē ol′ə pīl′), *n.* **1.** a round vessel caused to rotate by the force of tangentially escaping steam: an early example of jet propulsion. **2.** a device for injecting the vapors of heated alcohol into a laboratory furnace. Also, **ae·ol′i·pyle′.** [< L *aeolipilae* balls of AEOLUS, alter. of *aeolipylae* gates of AEOLUS, equiv. to *Aeolī* (gen. sing. of AEOLUS) + *pylae,* pl. of *pyla* < Gk *pýlē* gate]

Ae·o·lis (ē′ə lis), *n.* an ancient coastal region and Greek colony in NW Asia Minor: settled by Aeolians. Also, **Aeolia.**

ae·o·lo·trop·ic (ē′ə lō trop′ik), *adj.* *Physics.* not isotropic; anisotropic. [< Gk *aiólo(s)* fickle, changeful, + -TROPIC] —**ae·o·lot·ro·py** (ē′ə lo′trə pē), **ae′o·lot′ro·pism,** *n.*

Ae·o·lus (ē′ə ləs), *n.* *Class. Myth.* **1.** the ruler of the winds. **2.** the eponymous founder of the Aeolian nation.

ae·on (ē′ən, ē′on), *n.* **1.** Also, **eon.** an indefinitely long period of time; age. **2.** (in Gnosticism) one of a class of powers or beings conceived as emanating from the Supreme Being and performing various functions in the operations of the universe. **3.** *Geol.* eon (def. 1). [< LL < Gk *aiṓn* space of time, age]

ae·o·ni·an (ē ō′nē ən), *adj.* eternal; everlasting. Also, **eonian.** [< Gk *aiṓni(os)* (*aiṓn* AEON + *-ios* adj. suffix) + -AN]

Ae·py·or·nis (ē′pē ôr′nis), *n.* an extinct genus of ratite birds, best known from the Pleistocene epoch of Madagascar, having massive legs, rudimentary wings, and growing to a height of eight feet. [< NL < Gk *aipý(s)* steep, lofty, + *órnis* bird]

Ae·py·tus (ē′pi təs), *n.* *Class. Myth.* **1.** a son of Elatus who reared Evadne. **2.** the grandson of Hercules who, with his mother, killed Polyphontes. **3.** an Arcadian king. **4.** father of Cypselus and king of Arcadia. He was blinded when he entered a sanctuary of Poseidon forbidden to mortals.

ae·quo a·ni·mo (ī′kwō ä′ni mō′; *Eng.* ē′kwō an′ə-mō′), *Latin.* with an even mind; with composure.

aer-, var. of **aero-** before a vowel: *aerate.*

ae·rar·i·an (ē râr′ē ən), *Rom. Hist.* —*adj.* **1.** of or pertaining to the aerarium. —*n.* **2.** a member of the lowest class of Roman citizens, who paid a poll tax but did not vote. [< L *aerāri(us)* (adj. for *aerārium* AERARIUM) + -AN]

ae·rar·i·um (ē râr′ē əm), *n., pl.* **ae·rar·i·a** (ē râr′ē ə). the state treasury in ancient Rome. [< L, equiv. to *aer-* (s. of *aes* bronze, money) + *-ārium* -ARY]

aer·ate (âr′āt, ā′ə rāt′), *v.t.,* **-at·ed, -at·ing. 1.** to expose to the action or effect of air: *to aerate milk in* order to remove odors. **2.** to charge or treat with air or a gas, esp. with carbon dioxide. **3.** *Physiol.* to expose (a medium or tissue) to air, as in the oxygenation of the blood in respiration. Also, **aër′ate.** [< L *āer* AER- + -ATE[1]] —**aer·a′tion,** *n.*

aer·a·tor (âr′ā tər, ā′ə rā′tər), *n.* **1.** an apparatus for aerating water or other fluids. **2.** a device for introducing air into a bin of wheat or other grain in order to prevent the accumulation of moisture, keeping it free of fungi and insects. Also, **aër′a·tor.** [AERATE + -OR[2]]

aer·en·chy·ma (â reng′kə mə, -ren′-), *n.* *Bot.* a tissue in certain aquatic plants, consisting of thin-walled cells having large, intercellular spaces adapted for the circulation of air within the plant. [< NL; see AER-, PARENCHYMA]

ae·re per·en·ni·us (ī′re pe ren′ni o͝os′; *Eng.* ēr′ē pə ren′ē əs), *Latin.* more lasting than bronze.

aeri-, var. of **aero-** before an element of Latin origin: *aeriferous.*

Aer·i·a (ēr′ē ə), *n.* an area in the northern hemisphere of Mars.

aer·i·al (*adj.* âr′ē əl, ā ēr′ē əl; *n.* âr′ē əl), *adj.* **1.** of, in, or produced by the air: *aerial currents.* **2.** inhabiting or frequenting the air: *aerial creatures.* **3.** operating above ground on an elevated track or cable: *an aerial ski lift up the mountainside.* **4.** reaching far into the air; high; lofty: *aerial spires.* **5.** partaking of the nature of air; airy. **6.** unsubstantial; visionary: *aerial fancies.* **7.** having a light and graceful beauty; ethereal: *aerial music.* **8.** *Biol.* growing in the air, as the adventitious roots of some trees. **9.** pertaining to or used for, against, or in aircraft. **10.** supplied or performed by means of aircraft: *aerial support; aerial reconnaissance.* —*n.* **11.** *Radio.* an antenna. **12.** *Football Informal.* See **forward pass.** Also, **aër′i·al.** [< L *āeri(us)* of the air (< Gk *āérios,* equiv. to *āer-* (s. of *āēr* AIR[1]) + *-ios* adj. suffix) + -AL[1]] —**aer′i·al·ly, aër′i·al·ly,** *adv.* —**aer′i·al·ness, aër′i·al·ness,** *n.*

aer′ial bomb′, a bomb designed to be dropped from an aircraft.

aer·i·al·ist (âr′ē ə list, ā ēr′ē ə-), *n.* a trapeze artist. Also, **aër′i·al·ist.** [AERIAL + -IST]

aer·i·al·i·ty (âr′ē al′i tē, ā ēr′-), *n.* unsubstantiality. Also, **aër′i·al′i·ty.** [AERIAL + -ITY]

aer′ial lad′der, an extensible ladder used for reaching heights, esp. from a hook and ladder truck.

aer′ial mine′, **1.** *Mil.* a mine designed to be dropped from the air, esp. into water. **2.** Also called **land mine.** a bomb designed to be dropped by parachute, used in World War II.

aer′ial mosa′ic, *Survey.* mosaic (def. 4).

aer′ial perspec′tive, a technique of rendering depth or distance in painting by modifying the tone or hue of objects perceived as receding from the picture plane, esp. by reducing distinctive local colors and contrasts of light and dark to a uniform light, bluish-gray color. Also called **atmospheric perspective.**

aer′ial pho′tograph, a photograph taken from an aircraft or other vehicle in flight. Also called **aerophoto, air photograph.** —**aer′ial photog′raphy.**

aer′ial rail′way, an apparatus consisting of cars suspended from cables or rails, used for transportation over canyons, between mountain peaks, etc. Also called **aerial tramway.**

aer′ial sur′vey, **1.** a survey made from above, as from an aircraft, a high point, etc. **2.** a survey which maps an area by means of aerial photography, photogrammetry, and the like.

aer′ial torpe′do, a torpedo designed to be launched from an airplane.

aer′ial tram′way, tramway (def. 4).

aer·ie (âr′ē, ēr′ē), *n.* **1.** the nest of a bird of prey, as an eagle or a hawk. **2.** a lofty nest of any large bird. **3.** an elevated habitation or situation. **4.** *Rare.* the brood in a nest, esp. of a bird of prey. Also, **aery, eyrie, eyry.** [< ML *aeria* < OF *aire* < L *ātrium* ATRIUM]

aer·if·er·ous (â rif′ər əs), *adj.* conveying air, as the bronchial tubes. Also, **aër·if′er·ous.** [AERI- + -FEROUS]

aer·i·fi·ca·tion (âr′ə fə kā′shən, ā ēr′-), *n.* **1.** act of combining with air. **2.** state of being filled with air. Also, **aër′i·fi·ca′tion.** [AERI- + -FICATION]

aer·i·form (âr′ə fôrm′, ā ēr′-), *adj.* **1.** having the form or nature of air; gaseous. **2.** unsubstantial; unreal. Also, **aër′i·form′.** [AERI- + -FORM]

aer·i·fy (âr′ə fī′, ā ēr′-), *v.t.,* **-fied, -fy·ing.** **1.** to aerate. **2.** to make aeriform; convert into vapor. Also, **aër′i·fy′.** [AERI- + -FY]

aer·o (âr′ō), *adj.* **1.** of or for aircraft. **2.** of or pertaining to aeronautics. [AERO- used as free form]

aero-, a learned borrowing from Greek meaning "air," used in formation of compound words: *aerodrome.* Also, **aer-, aeri-.** [comb. form < Gk, equiv. to *āer-* (s. of *āēr* AIR[1]) + *-o-* -O-]

aer·o·bac·te·ri·ol·o·gy (âr′ō bak tēr′ē ol′ə jē), *n.* the branch of aerobiology dealing with bacteria. [AERO- + BACTERIOLOGY] —**aer·o·bac·te·ri·o·log·i·cal** (âr′ō bak tēr′ē ə loj′i kəl), *adj.* —**aer′o·bac·te′ri·o·log′i·cal·ly,** *adv.* —**aer′o·bac·te′ri·ol′o·gist,** *n.*

aer·o·bal·lis·tics (âr′ō bə lis′tiks), *n.* (*construed as sing.*) the science of ballistics combined with that of aerodynamics and dealing primarily with the motion through the atmosphere of rockets, guided missiles, and other projectiles. [AERO- + BALLISTICS] —**aer′o·bal·lis′tic,** *adj.*

aer·o·bat·ics (âr′ə bat′iks), *n.* **1.** (*construed as pl.*) stunts performed in flight by an airplane, glider, or the like. **2.** (*construed as sing.*) the art or technique of performing such stunts. [AERO- + (ACRO)BATICS] —**aer′o·bat′ic,** *adj.*

aer·obe (âr′ōb), *n.* an organism, esp. a bacterium, that requires air or free oxygen for life (opposed to *anaerobe*). [AERO- + *-be* (< Gk *bíos* life) as in MICROBE]

aer·o·bic (â rō′bik), *adj.* **1.** (of an organism or tissue) requiring the presence of air or free oxygen for life. **2.** pertaining to or caused by the presence of oxygen. **3.** of or utilizing the principles of aerobics: *aerobic dancing.* [AEROBE + -IC] —**aer·o′bi·cal·ly,** *adv.*

aer·o·bics (â rō′biks), *n.* **1.** Also called **aero′bic ex′ercises.** (*construed as pl.*) any of various sustained exercises, as jogging, rowing, swimming, or cycling, that stimulate and strengthen the heart and lungs, thereby improving the body's utilization of oxygen. **2.** (*construed as sing.*) a physical fitness program based on such exercises.

aer·o·bi·ol·o·gy (âr′ō bī ol′ə jē), *n.* the branch of biology dealing with airborne particles and organisms, as bacteria, dust, pollen, and spores. [AERO- + BIOLOGY] —**aer·o·bi·o·log·ic** (âr′ō bī′ə loj′ik), **aer′o·bi′o·log′i·cal,** *adj.* —**aer′o·bi′o·log′i·cal·ly,** *adv.* —**aer′o·bi·ol′o·gist,** *n.*

aer·o·bi·o·sis (âr′ō bī ō′sis), *n.* *Biol.* life in an environment containing oxygen or air. [< NL; see AERO-, -BIOSIS] —**aer·o·bi·ot·ic** (âr′ō bī ot′ik), *adj.* —**aer′o·bi·ot′i·cal·ly,** *adv.*

aer·o·bi·um (â rō′bē əm), *n., pl.* **-bi·a** (-bē ə). *Biol.* an aerobe. [< NL; see AEROBE, modeled after *microbium*]

aer·o·car (âr′ə kär′), *n.* a vehicle that can be converted for use as an automobile or airplane. [AERO- + CAR[1]]

aer·o·do·net·ics (âr′ō də net′iks), *n.* (*construed as sing.*) *Rare.* the study and practice of gliding flight. [< Gk *āerodónēt(os)* air-tossed (*āero-* AERO- + *donē-* (s. of *donein* to shake) + *-tos* adj. suffix) + -ICS] —**aer′o·do·net′ic,** *adj.*

aer·o·don·tal·gia (âr′ō don tal′jə, -jē ə), *n.* *Dentistry.* a toothache caused by a lowered barometric pressure, as in high-altitude flight. [AER- + ODONTALGIA]

aer·o·don·tia (âr′ə don′chə, -chē ə), *n.* the branch of dentistry dealing with dental problems that result from flying. [AER- + ODONT- + -IA]

aer·o·drome (âr′ə drōm′), *n.* *Chiefly Brit.* airdrome.

aer·o·dy·nam·i·cist (âr′ō dī nam′i sist), *n.* an expert in aerodynamics. [AERODYNAMIC + -IST]

aer·o·dy·nam·ics (âr′ō dī nam′iks), *n.* (*construed as sing.*) the branch of mechanics that deals with the motion of air and other gases and with the effects of such motion on bodies in the medium. Cf. **aerostatics** (def. 1). [AERO- + DYNAMICS] —**aer′o·dy·nam′ic, aer′o·dy·nam′i·cal,** *adj.* —**aer′o·dy·nam′i·cal·ly,** *adv.*

aer′odynam′ic trajec′tory, *Rocketry.* the path of an object, as a rocket, where the air is dense enough to modify the course of flight significantly.

aer′odynam′ic wave′ drag′, *Aeron.* the restraining force on a supersonic aircraft, caused by shock waves. Also called **wave drag.**

aer·o·dyne (âr′ə dīn′), *n.* any heavier-than-air craft. [back formation from AERODYNAMIC; see DYNE]

aer·o·e·las·tic (âr′ō i las′tik), *adj.* *Aeron.* (of an airframe) deformable by aerodynamic forces. [AERO- + ELASTIC] —**aer·o·e·las·tic·i·ty** (âr′ō i la stis′i tē, -ē′las-), *n.*

aer·o·e·las·tics (âr′ō i las′tiks), *n.* (*construed as sing.*) *Aeron.* the study of aeroelastic phenomena. [see AEROELASTIC, -ICS]

aer·o·em·bo·lism (âr′ō em′bə liz′əm), *n.* *Pathol.* a condition caused by substantial decrease in atmospheric pressure, as in high-altitude flying, and characterized by the formation of nitrogen bubbles in the blood, by pains in the lungs, etc. Cf. **caisson disease.** [AERO- + EMBOLISM]

aer·o·gen·ic (âr′ə jen′ik), *adj.* producing gas, as certain bacteria. Also, **aer·og·e·nous** (â roj′ə nəs). [AERO- + -GENIC] —**aer′o·gen′i·cal·ly,** *adv.*

aer·o·gram (âr′ə gram′), *n.* **1.** a radiogram. **2.** a message carried by aircraft; an air-mail letter. **3.** *Meteorol.* **a.** a diagram for analyzing thermodynamic processes in the atmosphere. **b.** the record of an aerograph. **4.** aërogramme. [AERO- + -GRAM[1]]

aér·o·gramme (âr′ə gram′, ā′ər ə-), a sheet of lightweight paper, bearing an official postal stamp imprint, that is folded to form its own envelope and can be sent via air mail at a special, low rate because of its standard size, light weight, and lack of enclosures. Also, **aerogram, aer′o·gramme′.** Cf. **air letter.** [< F]

aer·o·graph (âr′ə graf′, -gräf′), *n.* *Meteorol.* any automatic recording instrument that is airborne. [AERO- + -GRAPH]

aer·og·ra·phy (â rog′rə fē), *n.* description of the air or atmosphere. [AERO- + -GRAPHY] —**aer·og′ra·pher,** *n.* —**aer·o·graph·ic** (âr′ə graf′ik), **aer′o·graph′i·cal,** *adj.*

Aer·ol (âr′ōl, -ol), *n.* a boy's given name.

aer·o·lite (âr′ə līt′), *n.* a meteorite consisting mainly of stony matter. Also, **aer·o·lith** (âr′ə lith). [AERO- + -LITE] —**aer·o·lit·ic** (âr′ə lit′ik), *adj.*

aer·o·lit·ics (âr′ə lit′iks), *n.* (*construed as sing.*) the study of aerolites. [AEROLITE + -ICS]

aer·ol·o·gy (â rol′ə jē), *n.* **1.** *Obsolesc.* the branch of meteorology involving the observation of the atmosphere by means of balloons, airplanes, etc. **2.** (in former use by the U.S. Navy) meteorology. [AERO- + -LOGY] —**aer·o·log·ic** (âr′ə loj′ik), **aer′o·log′i·cal,** *adj.* —**aer·ol′o·gist,** *n.*

aer·o·man·cy (âr′ə man′sē), *n.* the prediction of future events from observation of weather conditions. [AERO- + -MANCY] —**aer′o·man′cer,** *n.* —**aer′o·man′tic,** *adj.*

aer·o·ma·rine (âr′ō mə rēn′), *adj.* *Aeron.* relating to navigation of aircraft above the ocean. [AERO- + MARINE]

aer·o·me·chan·ic (âr′ō mə kan′ik), *n.* **1.** an aviation mechanic. —*adj.* **2.** of or pertaining to aeromechanics. [AERO- + MECHANIC]

aer·o·me·chan·ics (âr′ō mə kan′iks), *n.* (*construed as sing.*) the mechanics of air or gases. [AERO- + MECHANICS] —**aer′o·me·chan′i·cal,** *adj.*

aer·o·med·i·cal (âr′ə med′i kəl), *adj.* of or pertaining to the science or practice of aviation medicine. [AERO- + MEDICAL]

aer·o·med·i·cine (âr′ə med′i sən), *n.* See **aviation medicine.** [AERO- + MEDICINE]

aer·o·me·te·or·o·graph (âr′ə mē′tē ər ə graf′, -gräf′, -mē′tē ôr′ə-, -or′ə-), *n.* a meteorograph for use in aircraft. [AERO- + METEOROGRAPH]

aer·om·e·ter (â rom′i tər), *n.* an instrument for determining the weight, density, etc., of air or other gases. [AERO- + -METER] —**aer·o·met·ric** (âr′ə me′trik), *adj.* —**aer·om·e·try** (â rom′i trē), *n.*

aeron., aeronautics.

aer·o·naut (âr′ə nôt′, -not′), *n.* **1.** the pilot of a balloon or other lighter-than-air craft. **2.** a traveler in an airship. [AERO- + (ARGO)NAUT; cf. F *aéronaute*]

aer·o·nau·tic (âr′ə nô′tik, -not′ik), *adj.* of aeronautics or aeronauts. Also, **aer′o·nau′ti·cal.** [AERONAUT + -IC] —**aer′o·nau′ti·cal·ly,** *adv.*

aer·o·naut·ics (âr′ə nô′tiks, -not′iks), *n.* (*construed as sing.*) the science or art of flight. [AERONAUT + -ICS]

aer·o·neu·ro·sis (âr′ō no͝o rō′sis, -nyo͝o-), *n.* *Psychiatry.* a psychoneurotic condition that occurs in aviators and airmen and is characterized by worry, loss of self-confidence, mild depression, and usually various physical symptoms. [AERO- + NEUROSIS]

aer·on·o·my (â ron′ə mē), *n.* the study of chemical and physical phenomena in the upper stratosphere. [AERO- + -NOMY]

aer′o·o·ti′tis me′dia (âr′ō ō tī′təs, âr′-), *Med.* inflammation of the middle ear due to trauma occurring as a result of a difference between the atmospheric pressure and the pressure in the tympanic cavity. Also, **aerotitis media.**

aer·o·pause (âr′ə pôz′), *n.* *Aeron.* (not used scientifically) the region beyond the earth's atmosphere marking the present limit of manned flight. [AERO- + PAUSE]

A·ër·o·pe (ā er′ə pē), *n.* *Class. Myth.* the wife of Atreus, seduced by her brother-in-law Thyestes.

aer·o·pha·gia (âr′ə fā′jə, -jē ə), *n.* *Psychiatry.* swallowing of air due to neurotic gastric disturbances. [AERO- + -PHAGIA] —**aer·oph·a·gist** (â rof′ə jist), *n.*

aer·o·phi·lat·e·ly (âr′ō fi lat′ə lē), *n.* the study or collection of air-mail stamps, cancellations, etc. [AERO- + -PHILATELY] —**aer·o·phil·a·tel·ic** (âr′ō fil′ə tel′ik), *adj.* —**aer′o·phi·lat′e·list,** *n.*

aer·o·pho·bi·a (âr′ə fō′bē ə), *n.* *Psychiatry.* an abnormal fear of drafts of air, gases, and airborne noxious influences. [AERO- + -PHOBIA] —**aer·o·pho·bic** (âr′ə fō′bik, -fob′ik), *adj.*

aer·o·phone (âr′ə fōn′), *n.* any musical wind instrument. [AERO- + -PHONE]

aer·o·phore (âr′ə fōr′, -fôr′), *n.* a portable device filled with compressed air and used in cases of asphyxia or the like. [AERO- + -PHORE]

aer·o·pho·to (âr′ō fō′tō), *n., pl.* **-tos.** See **aerial photograph.** [AERO- + PHOTO] —**aer·o·pho·tog·ra·phy** (âr′ō fə tog′rə fē), *n.*

aer·o·phyte (âr′ə fīt′), *n.* *Bot.* epiphyte. [AERO- + -PHYTE]

aer·o·plane (âr′ə plān′), *n.* *Chiefly Brit.* airplane.

aer·o·plank·ton (âr′ō plangk′tən), *n.* minute living organisms collectively, that are carried in the air. [AERO- + PLANKTON]

aer·o·pulse (âr′ə puls′), *n.* See **pulsejet engine.** [AERO- + PULSE]

aer·o·scep·sy (âr′ə skep′sē), *n.* (in insects and other invertebrate animals) sensitivity to atmospheric conditions, as the perception of odors by the antennae of insects. Also, **aer·o·scep·sis** (âr′ō skep′sis). [AERO- + *-scepsy* < Gk *sképsis* observation, perception, equiv. to *skep-* (s. of *sképtesthai* to observe, examine) + *-sis* -SIS]

aer·o·scope (âr′ə skōp′), *n.* an apparatus for collecting microscopic objects from the air. [AERO- + -SCOPE] —**aer·o·scop·ic** (âr′ə skop′ik), *adj.* —**aer′o·scop′i·cal·ly,** *adv.*

aer·o·si·nus·i·tis (âr′ō sī′nə sī′tis), *n.* *Med.* inflammation of the nasal sinuses caused by the effect on the sinuses of changes in atmospheric pressure. Also called **barosinusitus.** [AERO- + SINUSITIS]

aer·o·sol (âr′ə sōl′, -sôl′, -sol′), *n.* **1.** *Physical Chem.* a system of colloidal particles dispersed in a gas; smoke or fog. **2.** a liquid substance, as a disinfectant, deodorant, etc., sealed in a metal container under pressure with an inert gas or other activating agent and released through a push-button valve or nozzle: *a new type of aerosol for coating silverware.* **3.** the container for such a substance. **4.** See **aerosol bomb.** [AERO- + SOL[4]]

aer′osol bomb′, a metal container that sprays an insecticide, disinfectant, or the like, when its gas pressure is released.

aer·o·space (âr′ə spās′), *n.* **1.** the atmosphere and the space beyond considered as a whole. —*adj.* **2.** of, pertaining to, or concerned with the design and manufacture of vehicles, missiles, and the like that operate in aerospace. [AERO- + SPACE]

aer·o·sphere (âr′ə sfēr′), *n.* *Aeron.* (not used scientifically) the region above the earth's atmosphere where manned flight is possible at present. [AERO- + -SPHERE]

aer·o·stat (âr′ə stat′), *n.* any lighter-than-air craft as a balloon or dirigible. [AERO- + -STAT]

aer·o·stat·ic (âr′ə stat′ik), *adj.* **1.** of or pertaining to aerostatics. **2.** of, or capable of supporting, aerostats. Also, **aer′o·stat′i·cal.** [AERO- + STATIC]

aer·o·stat·ics (âr′ə stat′iks), *n.* (*construed as sing.*) **1.** the branch of statics that deals with gases in equilibrium and with gases and bodies in the gases in equilibrium with each other. Cf. **aerodynamics.** **2.** the science of lighter-than-air craft. [see AEROSTATIC, -ICS]

aer·o·sta·tion (âr′ə stā′shən), *n.* *Aeron.* the science or art of operating aerostats. [AEROSTAT + -ION]

aer·o·ther·a·peu·tics (âr′ō ther′ə pyo͞o′tiks), *n.* (*construed as sing.*) the branch of therapeutics that deals with the curative use of air or of artificially prepared atmospheres. Also, **aer·o·ther·a·py** (âr′ō ther′ə pē). [AERO- + THERAPEUTICS]

aer·o·ther·mo·dy·nam·ics (âr′ō thûr′mō dī nam′iks), *n.* (*construed as sing.*) aerodynamics dealing with conditions where there are significant heat exchanges in gases or significant thermal effects between gas and solid surfaces, as in very high-speed, generally supersonic flight. [AERO- + THERMODYNAMICS] —**aer′o·ther′mo·dy·nam′ic,** *adj.*

aer′o·ti′tis me′dia (âr′ō tī′tis, âr′-). See **aero-otitis media.**

aer·o·tow (âr′ə tō′), *v.t.* **1.** to tow (an aircraft) through the air. —*n.* **2.** act of aerotowing. [AERO- + TOW[1]]

aer·o·trop·ic (âr′ə trop′ik), *adj.* *Biol.* taking a particular direction under the influence of air. [AERO- + -TROPIC]

aer·ot·ro·pism (â ro′trə piz′əm), *n.* *Biol.* aerotropic tendency or growth. [AERO- + -TROPISM]

ae·ru·gi·nous (i ro͞o′jə nəs, ī ro͞o′-), *adj.* bluish-green; like verdigris. [< L *aerūginōs(us),* equiv. to *aerūgin-* (s. of *aerūgō*) AERUGO + *-ōsus* -OUS]

ae·ru·go (i ro͞o′gō, ī ro͞o′-), *n.* verdigris. [< L, equiv. to *aer-* (s. of *aes* copper, bronze) + *-ūgō* suffix used in forming names of rusts and surface growths; see FERRUGINOUS, LANUGO]

aer·y[1] (âr′ē, ā′ə rē), *adj.* ethereal; aerial. Also, **aër′y.** [< L *āeri(us)* < Gk *āérios*, equiv. to *āer-* AER- + *-ios* adj. suffix]

aer·y[2] (âr′ē, ēr′ē), *n., pl.* **aer·ies.** aerie.

aes-. for words with initial **aes-,** see also **es-.**

Ae·sa·cus (ē′sə kəs), *n. Class. Myth.* one of the 50 sons of Priam.

æsc (ash), *n.* ash[1] (def. 6).

Aes·chi·nes (es′kə nēz′ *or, esp. Brit.,* ēs′-), *n.* 389–314 B.C., Athenian orator: rival of Demosthenes.

Aes·chy·lus (es′kə ləs *or, esp. Brit.,* ē′skə-), *n.* 525–456 B.C., Greek poet and dramatist. —**Aes·chy·le·an** (es′kə lē′ən *or, esp. Brit.,* ēs′-), *adj.*

Aes·cu·la·pi·an (es′kyə lā′pē ən *or, esp. Brit.,* ēs′-), *adj.* **1.** pertaining to Aesculapius. **2.** medical; medicinal. —*n.* **3.** a physician; doctor. Also, **Esculapian.** [AESCULAPI(US) + -AN]

Aes·cu·la·pi·us (es′kyə lā′pē əs *or, esp. Brit.,* ēs′-), *n.* the ancient Roman god of medicine and healing, identified with the Greek Asclepius.

aes·cu·lin (es′kyə lin), *n. Chem.* esculin.

Ae·se·pus (i sē′pəs), *n.* (in the *Iliad*) a son of Abarbarea who, with his twin brother Pedasus, fought in the Trojan War and was slain by Euryalus.

Ae·sir (e′sir), *n.* (*often l.c.*) (*construed as pl.*) *Scand. Myth.* a superior race of gods, led by Odin and living at Asgard. Also, **Asar.** Cf. **Vanir.** [< Icel, pl. of *āss* god; c. OE *ōs* god, *Os-* in proper names (as *Oswald*), OHG *Ans-* in proper names (as *Anselm*); akin to Skt *asura* lord, etc.]

Ae·sop (ē′səp, ē′sop), *n.* c620–c560 B.C., Greek writer of fables. —**Ae·so·pi·an** (ē sō′pē ən), **Ae·sop·ic** (ē sop′ik), *adj.*

Ae·sta·tis (ā stä′tis), *n.* **Mare.** See **Mare Aestatis.**

aes·the·sia (es thē′zhə, -zhē ə, -zē ə), *n.* esthesia. Also, **aes·the·sis** (es thē′sis).

aes·thete (es′thēt *or, esp. Brit.,* ēs′-), *n.* **1.** one who has or professes to have a high degree of sensitivity toward the beauties of art or nature. **2.** one who affects great love of art, music, poetry, etc., and indifference to practical matters. Also, **esthete.** [< Gk *aisthētēs* one who perceives, equiv. to *aisthē-* (var. s. of *aisthánesthai* to perceive) + *-tēs* n. suffix denoting agent]
—**Syn. 1.** connoisseur. **2.** dilettante.

aes·thet·ic (es thet′ik *or, esp. Brit.,* ēs-), *adj.* **1.** pertaining to a sense of the beautiful or to the science of aesthetics. **2.** having a sense of the beautiful; characterized by a love of beauty. **3.** pertaining to, involving, or concerned with pure emotion and sensation as opposed to pure intellectuality. —*n.* **4.** aesthetics. **5.** a philosophical theory or idea of what is aesthetically valid at a given time and place: *the clean lines, bare surfaces, and sense of space that bespeak the machine-age aesthetic.* **6.** *Archaic.* the study of the nature of sensation. Also, **esthetic.** [< NL *aesthētic(us)* < Gk *aisthētikós*, equiv. to *aisthē-* (var. s. of *aisthánesthai* to perceive) + *-tikos* -TIC]

aes·thet·i·cal (es thet′i kəl *or, esp. Brit.,* ēs-), *adj.* of or relating to aesthetics. Also, **esthetical.** [AESTHETIC + -AL[1]]

aes·thet·i·cal·ly (es thet′ik lē *or, esp. Brit.,* ēs-), *adv.* **1.** according to aesthetics or its principles. **2.** in an aesthetic manner. Also, **esthetically.** [AESTHETICAL + -LY]

aesthet′ic dis′tance, a degree of detachment from or nonidentification with the characters or circumstances of a work of art, permitting the formation of judgments based on aesthetic rather than extra-aesthetic criteria.

aes·the·ti·cian (es′thi tish′ən *or, esp. Brit.,* ēs′-), *n.* one versed in aesthetics. Also, **esthetician.** [AESTHETIC + -IAN; see -ICIAN]

aes·thet·i·cism (es thet′i siz′əm *or, esp. Brit.,* ēs-), *n.* **1.** the acceptance of artistic beauty and taste as a fundamental standard, ethical and other standards being secondary. **2.** an exaggerated or excessive devotion to art, music, or poetry, with indifference to practical matters. Also, **estheticism.** [AESTHETIC + -ISM]

aes·thet·ics (es thet′iks *or, esp. Brit.,* ēs-), *n.* (*construed as sing.*) **1.** *Philos.* the branch of philosophy dealing with such notions as the beautiful, the ugly, the sublime, the comic, etc., as applicable to the fine arts, with a view to establishing the meaning and validity of critical judgments concerning works of art, and the principles underlying or justifying such judgments. **2.** the study of the mind and emotions in relation to the sense of beauty. Also, **esthetics.** [see AESTHETIC, -ICS]

aes·ti·val (es′tə vəl, e stī′- *or, esp. Brit.,* ē′stə-, ē stī′-), *adj.* estival.

aes·ti·vate (es′tə vāt′ *or, esp. Brit.,* ēs′-), *v.i.,* **-vat·ed, -vat·ing.** estivate. —**aes′ti·va′tion,** *n.* —**aes′ti·va′tor,** *n.*

A.-E. Sud., Anglo-Egyptian Sudan.

Ae·sy·e·tes (ē′sē ē′tēz), *n.* (in the *Iliad*) the father of Antenor.

aet., at the age of. [< L *aetātis*]

A.E.T., Associate in Electrical Technology.

ae·ta·tis su·ae (ī tä′tis sōō′ī; *Eng.* ē tā′tis sōō′ē), *Latin.* in a certain year of one's age.

Ae·ter·ni Pa·tris (ā târ′nē pä′trēs), *Latin. Of the Eternal Father* (opening words and the title of an encyclical of Pope Leo XIII issued in 1879 on the philosophy of St. Thomas Aquinas).

Ae·thal·i·des (i thal′i dēz′), *n. Class. Myth.* a son of Hermes who was one of the Argonauts and who was endowed with infallible memory.

Æth·el·bert (ath′əl bərt), *n.* old spelling of **Ethelbert.**

ae·ther (ē′thər), *n.* **1.** ether (defs. 3–5). **2.** (*cap.*) the ancient Greek personification of the clear upper air of the sky. —**ae·the·re·al** (i thēr′ē əl), **ae·ther·ic** (i ther′ik), *adj.*

Ae·the·ri·a (i thēr′ē ə), *n.* **1.** (*italics*) Etheria. **2.** *Class. Myth.* a daughter of Helius and Clymene who, with her sisters, was one of the Heliades.

ae·thon (ē′thon), *n. Chem.* See **triethyl orthoformate.** [< L < Gk *aíthōn* burning]

Ae·thra (ē′thrə), *n. Class. Myth.* **1.** the mother, by Aegeus, of Theseus. **2.** an Oceanid.

Ae·thyl·la (i thil′ə), *n. Class. Myth.* a sister of Priam.

aetio-, var. of **etio-.**

ae·ti·ol·o·gy (ē′tē ol′ə jē), *n., pl.* **-gies.** etiology. —**ae·ti·o·log·i·cal** (ē′tē ə loj′i kəl), *adj.* —**ae′ti·o·log′i·cal·ly,** *adv.* —**ae′ti·ol′o·gist,** *n.*

Aet·na (et′nə), *n.* **1.** *Class. Myth.* a Sicilian nymph. **2.** Mount. See **Etna, Mount.**

Ae·to·li·a (ē tō′lē ə), *n.* an ancient district in W Greece. See map under **Delphi.** —**Ae·to′li·an,** *adj.*

Ae·to·lus (ēt′ələs), *n. Class. Myth.* son of Endymion and founder of Aetolia.

af-, var. of **ad-** before *f*: *affect.*

AF, 1. Air Force. **2.** Anglo-French.

Af., 1. Africa. **2.** African.

A.F., 1. Air Force. **2.** Anglo-French. **3.** audio frequency.

a.f., audio frequency.

A.F.A., Associate in Fine Arts.

A.F.A.M., Ancient Free and Accepted Masons.

a·far (ə fär′), *adv.* **1.** from, at, or to a distance; far away (usually fol. by *off*): *He saw the police afar off.* —*n.* **2. from afar,** from a long way off: *She saw him riding toward her from afar.* [ME *a fer.* See A-[1], FAR]

A·fars′ and Is′sas Ter′ritory (ə färz′ and ē′säz), a former overseas territory of France, in E Africa, on the Gulf of Aden. See **Djibouti** (def. 1). Formerly, **French Somaliland.**

AFB, Air Force Base.

A.F.B., American Federation for the Blind.

AFC, 1. automatic flight control. **2.** automatic frequency control.

a·feard (ə fērd′), *adj. Brit. and Southern Coastal U.S. Dial.* afraid. Also, **a·feared′.** [ME *afered,* OE *afǣred* frightened (ptp. of *afǣran*). See A-[3], FEAR, -ED[2]]

a·fe·brile (ā fē′brəl, ā feb′rəl), *adj.* without fever; feverless. [A-[6] + FEBRILE]

aff (af), *prep., adv. Scot.* off.

af·fa·ble (af′ə bəl), *adj.* **1.** pleasantly easy to talk to; friendly; cordial; warmly polite: *an affable and courteous gentleman.* **2.** showing warmth and friendliness; benign; pleasant: *an affable countenance.* [< L *affābil(is)* that can be spoken to, courteous, equiv. to *af-* AF- + *fā-* speak (see FATE) + *-bilis* -BLE] —**af′fa·bil′i·ty, af′fa·ble·ness,** *n.* —**af′fa·bly,** *adv.* —**Syn. 1.** See **civil.**

af·fair (ə fâr′), *n.* **1.** anything done or to be done; anything requiring action or effort; business; concern: *an affair of great importance.* **2. affairs,** matters of commercial or public interest or concern; the transactions of public or private business: *affairs of state; Put your affairs in order.* **3.** an event or a performance; a particular action, operation, or proceeding: *When did this affair happen?* **4.** thing; matter (applied to anything made or existing, usually with a descriptive or qualifying term): *This machine is a complicated affair.* **5.** a private or personal concern; a special function, business, or duty: *That is none of your affair.* **6.** a romantic or amorous relationship of brief duration, esp. an illicit one. **7.** an event or happening that occasions or arouses notoriety, dispute, and often public scandal; incident: *the Mason-Slidell affair of 1861.* [earlier *affaire* < MF, OF *afaire* for *a faire* to do, equiv. to *a* (see AD-) + *faire* < L *facere*; r. ME *afere* < OF]

af·faire (A fer′), *n., pl.* **-faires** (-fer′). *French.* **1.** See **affaire d'amour. 2.** See **affaire de coeur.**

af·faire d'a·mour (A fer′ dA mōōr′), *pl.* **af·faires d'a·mour** (A fer′ dA mōōr′). *French.* a love affair. Also called **affaire.**

af·faire de coeur (A fer′ də kœr′), *pl.* **af·faires de coeur** (A fer′ də kœr′). *French.* a love affair. Also called **affaire.** [lit., affair of heart]

af·faire d'hon·neur (A fer′ dô nœr′), *pl.* **af·faires d'hon·neur** (A fer′ dô nœr′). *French.* a duel. [lit., affair of honor]

af·fect[1] (*v.* ə fekt′; *n.* af′ekt, ə fekt′), *v.t.* **1.** to act on; produce an effect or change in: *Cold affects the body.* **2.** to impress the mind or move the feelings: *The poetry affected him deeply.* **3.** (of pain, disease, etc.) to attack or lay hold of. —*n.* **4.** *Psychol.* feeling or emotion. **5.** *Obs.* affection; passion; sensation; inclination; inward disposition or feeling. [< L *affect(us)* acted upon, subjected to (ptp. of *afficere*), equiv. to *af-* AF- + *fec-* (var. s. of *facere* to make, do) + *-tus* ptp. suffix]
—**Syn. 1.** influence, sway; modify, alter. AFFECT, EFFECT agree in the idea of exerting influence. TO AFFECT is to concern, be of interest or importance to; to produce an effect in or upon something: *to affect one's conduct or health.* TO EFFECT is to accomplish or bring about something: *to effect a reconciliation.* **2.** touch, stir.

af·fect[2] (ə fekt′), *v.t.* **1.** to give the appearance of; pretend; feign: *to affect ignorance.* **2.** to display a fondness for; imitate: *to affect a Southern accent.* **3.** to use or adopt by preference; choose; prefer: *the peculiar costume which he affected.* **4.** to assume the character or attitude of: *to affect the freethinker.* **5.** to tend toward habitually or naturally; gravitate: *a substance which affects colloidal form.* **6.** (of animals and plants) to occupy or inhabit; live in or on: *Lions affect Africa. Moss affects the northern slopes.* **7.** *Archaic.* **a.** to have affection for; fancy. **b.** to aim at; aspire to. —*v.i.* **8.** *Obs.* to incline, tend, or favor (usually fol. by *to*): *He affects to the old ways.* [late ME < L *affect(āre)* (to) strive after, feign (freq. of *afficere* to do to), equiv. to *af-* AF- + *fec-* (see AFFECT[1]) + *-t-* freq. suffix] —**af·fect′er,** *n.*
—**Syn. 1.** See **pretend.**

af·fec·ta·tion (af′ek tā′shən), *n.* **1.** a striving for the appearance of a quality not really or fully possessed; the pretense of actual possession: *an affectation of wit; affectation of great wealth.* **2.** conspicuous artificiality of manner or appearance; effort to attract notice by pretense, assumption, or any assumed peculiarity. **3.** a trait or action characterized by such artificiality: *a man of a thousand affectations.* **4.** *Obs.* **a.** strenuous pursuit, desire, or aspiration. **b.** affection; fondness: *his affectation of literature.* [< L *affectātiōn-* (s. of *affectātiō*) a striving after, equiv. to *affectāt(us),* ptp. of *affectāre* to AFFECT[2] (*af-* AF- + *fec-* do + *-t-* freq. suffix + *-ātus* -ATE[1]) + *-iōn-* -ION] —**Syn. 2.** pretension, airs, mannerisms, pose, insincerity. —**Ant. 2.** simplicity, sincerity.

af·fect·ed[1] (ə fek′tid), *adj.* **1.** acted upon; influenced. **2.** influenced injuriously; impaired; attacked, as by climate or disease. **3.** (of the mind or feelings) impressed; moved; touched: *She was deeply affected by the performance.* [AFFECT[1] + -ED[2]]

af·fect·ed[2] (ə fek′tid), *adj.* **1.** assumed artificially; unnatural; feigned: *affected airs; an affected Oxonian accent.* **2.** assuming or pretending to possess that which is not natural: *Her affected wealth and social pedigree are so obviously false that it's embarrassing.* **3.** inclined or disposed: *well affected toward the speaker's cause.* **4.** held in affection; fancied: *a novel much affected by our grandparents.* [AFFECT[2] + -ED[2]] —**af·fect′ed·ly,** *adv.* —**af·fect′ed·ness,** *n.*

af·fect·ing (ə fek′ting), *adj.* moving or exciting the feelings or emotions. [AFFECT[1] + -ING[2]] —**af·fect′ing·ly,** *adv.* —**Syn.** touching, pathetic, piteous, stirring.

af·fec·tion[1] (ə fek′shən), *n.* **1.** fond attachment, devotion, or love: *the affection of a parent for his child.* **2.** emotion; feeling; sentiment: *over and above our reason and affections.* **3.** *Pathol.* a disease, or the condition of being diseased; abnormal state of body or mind: *a gouty affection.* **4.** act of affecting; act of influencing or acting upon. **5.** the state of being affected. **6.** *Philos.* a contingent, alterable, and accidental state or quality of being. **7.** the affective aspect of a mental process. **8.** bent or disposition of mind. **9.** *Obs.* bias; prejudice. [ME < L *affectiōn-* (s. of *affectiō*) disposition or state of mind or body, equiv. to *affect(us),* ptp. of *afficere* (see AFFECT[1]) + *-iōn-* -ION]
—**Syn. 1.** liking, friendliness, amity, fondness, friendship. See **love. 3.** See **disease.** —**Ant. 1.** dislike.

af·fec·tion[2] (ə fek′shən), *n. Obs.* affectation (defs. 1–3). [AFFECT[2] + -ION]

af·fec·tion·al (ə fek′shə nəl), *adj.* relating to or implying affection. [AFFECTION[1] + -AL[1]] —**af·fec′tion·al·ly,** *adv.*

af·fec·tion·ate (ə fek′shə nit), *adj.* **1.** showing, indicating, or characterized by affection or love; tender: *an affectionate embrace.* **2.** having great affection or love; warmly attached; loving: *your affectionate brother.* **3.** *Obs.* **a.** strongly disposed or inclined. **b.** passionate; headstrong. **c.** biased; partisan. [AFFECTION[1] + -ATE[1], modeled after *passionate*] —**af·fec′tion·ate·ly,** *adv.* —**af·fec′tion·ate·ness,** *n.* —**Syn. 1.** loving, fond.

af·fec·tive (ə fek′tiv), *adj.* **1.** of, caused by, or expressing emotion or feeling; emotional. **2.** causing emotion or feeling. **3.** *Psychol.* pertaining to feeling or emotion, esp. to pleasurable or unpleasurable aspects of a mental process. [< ML *affectīv(us),* equiv. to L *affect(us)* (ptp.; see AFFECT[1]) + *-īvus* -IVE] —**af·fec·tiv·i·ty** (af′ek tiv′i tē), *n.*

af·fen·pin·scher (af′ən pin′shər), *n.* one of a breed of toy dogs having a dense, wiry, red or gray coat with tufts of hair around the eyes, nose, and chin, cropped ears, and a docked tail. Also called **monkey pinscher, monkey dog.** [< G, equiv. to *Affen* (inflected form of *Affa* APE) + *Pinscher* breed of dogs]

af·fer·ent (af′ər ənt), *adj. Physiol.* bringing to or leading toward an organ or part, as a nerve or vein (opposed to *efferent*). [< L *afferent-* (s. of *afferēns,* prp. of *afferre*), equiv. to *af-* AF- + *fer-* (s. of *ferre* to carry) + *-ent-* -ENT]

af·fet·tuo·so (a fech′ōō ō′sō; *It.* äf′fet twô′zô), *adj. adv., n., pl.* **-sos.** *Music.* —*adj., adv.* **1.** with affection and tenderness (a musical direction). —*n.* **2.** a composition or movement of gentle, tender character. [< It: affecting, moving < L *affectuōsus,* equiv. to *affectu(s)* AFFECT[1] + *-ōsus* -OUS]

af·fi·ance (ə fī′əns), *v.,* **-anced, -anc·ing,** *n.* —*v.* **1.** to pledge by promise of marriage; betroth: *to affiance a daughter.* —*n. Archaic.* **2.** a pledging of faith, as a marriage contract. **3.** trust; confidence; reliance. [ME < MF *afiance,* equiv. to *afi(er)* (to) trust to (< LL *affidāre,* equiv. to *ad-* AD- + **fidāre,* alter. of L *fīdere* to trust; see CONFIDE) + *-ance* -ANCE]

af·fi·anced (ə fī′ənst), *adj.* betrothed; engaged.

af·fi·ant (ə fī′ənt), *n. Law.* one who makes an affidavit. [obs. v. *affy* (< MF *afi(er)*; see AFFIANCE) + -ANT]

af·fiche (A fēsh′), *n., pl.* **af·fiches** (A fēsh′). *French.* a notice posted in a public place; poster. [lit., something affixed]

af·fi·da·vit (af′i dā′vit), *n. Law.* a written declaration upon oath made before an authorized official. [< ML: he has made oath (perf. 3rd sing. of *affidāre*), equiv. to *af-* AF- + *fīd-* (s. of *fīdere* to trust) + *-ā-* + *-v-* suffix or perf. tense + *-it* suffix of 3rd pers. sing.]

af·fil·i·ate (*v.* ə fil′ē āt′; *n.* ə fil′ē it, -āt′), *v.,* **-at·ed, -at·ing,** *n.* —*v.t.* **1.** to bring into close association or connection: *Both schools are affiliated with the university.* **2.** to attach or unite on terms of fellowship; associate (usually fol. by *with* in U.S. usage, by *to* in Brit. usage): *to affiliate with the church; to affiliate to the church.* **3.** to trace the descent, derivation, or origin of: *to affiliate a language.* **4.** to adopt. **5.** *Law.* to fix the paternity of, as a bastard child: *The mother affiliated her child upon John Doe.* —*v.i.* **6.** to associate oneself; be intimately united in action or interest. —*n.* **7.** *U.S.* a branch organization. **8.** *Com.* **a.** a business concern owned or controlled in whole or in part by another concern. **b.** a subsidiary. **9.** one who is affiliated; associate; auxiliary. [< L *affiliāt(us)* adopted as son (ptp. of *affiliāre*), equiv. to *af-* AF- + *fīli(us)* son + *-ātus* -ATE[1]] —**af·fil·i·a·ble** (ə fil′ē ə bəl), *adj.*

af·fil·i·a·tion (ə fil′ē ā′shən), *n.* act of affiliating; state of being affiliated or associated. [< ML *affiliātiōn-* (s. of *affiliātiō* adoption), equiv. to *affiliāt(us)* (see AFFILIATE) + *-iōn-* -ION]

af·fi·nal (ə fīn′əl, ə fīn′-), *adj.* related by or concerning marriage. [< L *affīn(is)* a relative + AL[1]. See AFFINITY]

af·fine (ə fīn′, ə fīn′, af′īn), *adj. Math.* **1.** assigning finite values to finite quantities. **2.** of or pertaining to a transformation that maps parallel lines to parallel lines and finite points to finite points. [< F *affin* related < L *affīn(is)*; see AFFINAL] —**af·fine′ly,** *adv.*

af·fined (ə fīnd′), *adj.* **1.** closely related, associated, or connected. **2.** bound; obligated. [AFFINE + -ED[3]]

af′fine geom′etry, the branch of geometry dealing with affine transformations.

af′fine group′, *Math.* the group of all affine transformations of a finite-dimensional vector space.

af·fin·i·tive (ə fin′i tiv), *adj.* characterized by affinity; closely related or associated. [AFFINIT(Y) + -IVE]

af·fin·i·ty (ə fin′i tē), *n., pl.* **-ties. 1.** a natural liking for or attraction to a person or thing. **2.** a person or thing for whom such a natural liking or attraction is felt. **3.** relationship by marriage or by ties other than those of blood (distinguished from *consanguinity*). **4.** inherent likeness or agreement; close resemblance or connection. **5.** *Biol.* the phylogenetic relationship between two organisms or groups of organisms resulting in a resemblance in general plan or structure, or in the essential structural parts. **6.** *Chem.* the force by which atoms are held together in chemical compounds. [ME *affinite* < MF < L *affinitāt-* (s. of *affinitās*) connection by marriage. See AFFINE, -ITY]

CONCISE ETYMOLOGY KEY: <, descended or derived from; <, whence; b., blend of, blended; c., cognate with; deriv., derivative; equiv., equivalent; imit., imitative; m., modification of; obl., oblique; r., replacing; s., stem; sp., spelling; translation; ?, origin unknown, perhaps; *, hypothetical. See the full key inside the front cover.

af·firm (ə fûrm′), *v.t.* **1.** to state or assert positively; maintain as true: *to affirm one's loyalty to one's country.* **2.** to confirm or ratify: *The appellate court affirmed the judgment of the lower court.* —*v.i.* **3.** to declare positively; assert solemnly: *He affirmed that all was well.* **4.** *Law.* **a.** to declare solemnly before a court or magistrate, but without oath. **b.** to ratify and accept (a voidable transaction). **c.** (of an appellate court) to determine (that the action of the lower court shall stand). [< L *affirm(āre)*, equiv. to *af-* AF- + *firmāre* to make firm (see FIRM[1]); r. late ME *aferme* < MF *afermer* < L] —**af·firm′a·ble,** *adj.* —**af·firm′a·bly,** *adv.* —**af·firm′er,** *n.* —**af·firm′ing·ly,** *adv.*
—**Syn. 1.** aver, asseverate, depose, testify. See **declare. 2.** approve, endorse. —**Ant. 1.** deny.

af·firm·ant (ə fûr′mənt), *n.* one who affirms. [AFFIRM + -ANT]

af·fir·ma·tion (af′ər mā′shən), *n.* **1.** the act or state of affirming; state of being affirmed. **2.** the assertion that something exists or is true. **3.** that which is affirmed; a statement or proposition that is declared to be true. **4.** confirmation or ratification of the truth or validity of a prior judgment, decision, etc. **5.** *Law.* a solemn declaration accepted instead of a statement under oath. Also, **af·firm·ance** (ə fûr′məns). [< L *affirmātiōn-* (s. of *affirmātiō*), equiv. to *affirmāt(us)* (ptp. of *affirmāre* to AFFIRM) + *-iōn-* -ION]

af·firm·a·tive (ə fûr′mə tiv), *adj.* **1.** affirming or assenting; asserting the truth, validity, or fact of something; positive; not negative: *an affirmative reply.* **2.** *Logic.* noting a proposition in which a property is affirmed of a subject, as "All men are happy." —*n.* **3.** that which affirms or asserts; a positive statement or proposition: *Two negatives make an affirmative.* **4.** an affirmative response, as *Yes* or *I do.* **5.** the side, as in a debate, which affirms or defends a statement that the opposite side denies or attacks: *to speak for the affirmative.* [< L *affirmātīv(us)*, equiv. to *affirmāt-* (see AFFIRMATION) + *-īvus* -IVE; r. late ME *affirmatyff* < MF] —**af·firm′a·tive·ly,** *adv.*

affirm′ative ac′tion, encouragement for increased representation of women and minority-group members, esp. in employment. —**af·firm′a·tive-ac′tion,** *adj.*

affirm′ative flag′, *Naut.* a flag having five horizontal stripes, blue, white, red, white, and blue, from top to bottom, signifying "yes": letter C in the International Code of Signals.

af·firm·a·to·ry (ə fûr′mə tôr′ē, -tōr′ē), *adj.* affirmative. [AFFIRMAT(ION) + -ORY[1]]

affirm′ing gun′. See **informing gun.**

af·fix (*v.* ə fiks′; *n.* af′iks), *v.t.* **1.** to fasten, join, or attach (usually fol. by *to*): *to affix stamps to a letter.* **2.** to put or add on; append: *to affix a signature to a contract.* **3.** to impress (a seal or stamp). **4.** to attach (blame, reproach, ridicule, etc.). —*n.* **5.** that which is joined or attached. **6.** *Gram.* a bound inflectional or derivational element, as a prefix, infix, or suffix, added to a base or stem to form a fresh stem or a word, as *-ed* added to *want* to form *wanted*, or *im-* added to *possible* to form *impossible*, or *un-* to *-kempt* to form *unkempt.* [< L *affix(us)* fastened to (ptp. of *affīgere*), equiv. to *af-* AF- + *fīg-* fasten + *-sus*, var. of *-tus* ptp. suffix] —**af·fix·al** (af′ik səl), **af·fix·i·al** (a fik′sē əl), *adj.* —**af·fix′er,** *n.*

af·fix·a·tion (af′ik sā′shən), *n.* **1.** affixture. **2.** *Gram.* the process of inflection or derivation which consists in the addition of an affix. [AFFIX + -ATION]

af·fix·ture (ə fiks′chər), *n.* act of affixing; attachment. Also, **affixation.** [b. obs. *affixion* (see AFFIX, -ION) and FIXTURE]

af·flat·ed (ə flā′tid), *adj.* having inspiration; inspired. [obs. *afflate* (< L *afflāt(us)*; see AFFLATUS) + -ED[2]]

af·fla·tus (ə flā′təs), *n.* **1.** inspiration; an impelling mental force acting from within. **2.** divine communication of knowledge. [< L: a breathing on, equiv. to *af-* AF- + *flā-* (s. of *flāre* to blow) + *-tus* n. suffix, r. *-tus* ptp. suffix]

af·flict (ə flikt′), *v.t.* **1.** to distress with mental or bodily pain; trouble greatly or grievously: *to be afflicted with the gout.* **2.** *Obs.* **a.** to overthrow; defeat. **b.** to humble. [< L *afflīct(us)* distressed, ptp. of *afflīgere* to cast down (*af-* AF- + *flīg-* knock + *-tus* ptp. suffix); r. late ME *aflight* < MF *aflit* < L. See INFLICT] —**af·flict′ed·ness** *n.* —**af·flict′er,** *n.*
—**Syn. 1.** vex, harass, torment, plague.

af·flic·tion (ə flik′shən), *n.* **1.** a state of pain, distress, or grief: *They sympathized with us in our affliction.* **2.** a cause of continued mental or bodily pain, as sickness, loss, calamity, persecution, etc. [ME *afliccioun* < L *afflictiōn-* (s. of *afflictiō*). See AFFLICT, -ION] —**af·flic′tion·less,** *adj.*
—**Syn. 1.** mishap, trouble, tribulation, calamity, catastrophe, disaster. AFFLICTION, ADVERSITY, MISFORTUNE, TRIAL refer to an event or circumstance which is hard to bear. A MISFORTUNE is any seriously adverse or unfavorable occurrence: *He had the misfortune to break his leg.* AFFLICTION suggests not only a misfortune but the emotional effect of this: *Blindness is one kind of affliction.* ADVERSITY suggests one of a succession of mishaps and afflictions: *Job remained patient despite all his adversities.* TRIAL emphasizes the testing of one's character in undergoing misfortunes, trouble, etc.: *His son's conduct was a great trial to him.* **2.** misery, woe; plague, scourge. —**Ant. 1.** relief.

af·flic·tive (ə flik′tiv), *adj.* characterized by or causing pain; distressing. [AFFLICT + -IVE] —**af·flic′tive·ly,** *adv.*

af·flu·ence (af′lo͞o əns, *sometimes* ə flo͞o′əns), *n.* **1.** abundance of money, property, and other material goods; wealth: *to live in affluence.* **2.** an abundant supply, as of thoughts, words, etc.; profusion. **3.** a flowing to or toward; afflux. [late ME < MF < L *affluentia*, equiv. to *af-* AF- + *flu-* flow + *-entia* -ENCE]

af·flu·ent (af′lo͞o ənt, *sometimes* ə flo͞o′ənt), *adj.* **1.** prosperous; wealthy; rich: *an affluent person.* **2.** abounding in anything; abundant. **3.** flowing freely: *an affluent fountain.* —*n.* **4.** a tributary stream. [late ME < L *affluent-* (s. of *affluēns* rich; orig. prp. of *affluere*), equiv. to *af-* AF- + *flu-* flow + *-ent* -ENT] —**af′flu·ent·ly,** *adv.*
—**Syn. 1.** See **rich. 2.** teeming.

af·flux (af′luks), *n.* **1.** that which flows to or toward a point: *an afflux of blood to the head.* **2.** act of flowing to or toward; flow. [< ML *afflux(us)*, equiv. to *af-* AF- + *fluxus* FLUX]

af·ford (ə fōrd′, ə fôrd′), *v.t.* **1.** to be able to do, manage, or bear without serious consequence or adverse effect: *She can't afford to miss any more days at work.* **2.** to be able to meet the expense of; have or spare the price of: *He still can't afford a car.* **3.** to be able to give or spare: *He can afford the loss of a day.* **4.** to furnish; supply: *The transaction afforded him a good profit.* **5.** to be capable of yielding or providing: *The records afford no explanation.* **6.** to give or confer upon: *to afford great pleasure to someone.* [ME *aforthen, iforthen*, OE *geforthian* to further, accomplish, equiv. to *ge-* Y- + *forth* FORTH + *-ian* inf. suffix] —**af·ford′a·ble,** *adj.*

af·for·est (ə fôr′ist, ə for′-), *v.t.* to convert (bare or cultivated land) into forest, originally for the purpose of providing hunting grounds. [< ML *afforest(āre)*, equiv. to *af-* AF- + *forest(is)* FOREST + *-āre* inf. suffix] —**af·for′est·a′tion, af·for′est·ment,** *n.*

af·fran·chise (ə fran′chīz), *v.t.*, **-chised, -chis·ing.** to free from a state of dependence, servitude, or obligation. [late ME < MF *afranchiss-* (long s. of *afranchir*), equiv. to *a-* A-[5] + *franch-* free (see FRANK[1]) + *-iss-* -ISE[2]] —**af·fran′chise·ment,** *n.*

af·fray (ə frā′), *n.* **1.** a public fight; a noisy quarrel; brawl. **2.** *Law.* the fighting of two or more persons in a public place. —*v.t.* **3.** *Archaic.* to frighten. [ME < AF *afray* (n.), *afray(er)* (v.), OF *esfrei* (n.), *esfreer* (v.) < VL **exfridāre* to break the peace, equiv. to *ex-* EX-[1] + *-frid-* peace (< Gmc; cf G *Friede*) + *-āre* inf. suffix]

af·fray·er (ə frā′ər), *n.* one who engages in an affray; brawler. [AFFRAY + -ER[1]]

af·freight (ə frāt′), *v.t.* to charter (a ship) as a freight carrier. [< F *affrét(er)* (m. by influence of *freight*), equiv. to *a-* (< L *ad-* AD-) + *frêter* to hire a ship, deriv. of *fret* FREIGHT < OF < MD] —**af·freight′er,** *n.* —**af·freight′ment,** *n.*

af·fri·cate (af′rə kit), *n.* *Phonet.* a speech sound comprising occlusion, plosion, and frication, as either of the *ch*-sounds in *church*, the *j*-sound in *joy*, the *ts*-sound in *cats*, and, for many speakers, the *tr*-sound in *tree* and the *dr*-sound in *dry*. Also called **affricative.** [< L *affricāt(us)* rubbed against (ptp. of *affricāre*), equiv. to *af-* AF- + *fric-* (see FRICTION) + *-ātus* -ATE[1]]

af·fri·ca·tion (af′rə kā′shən), *n.* **1.** *Phonet.* act or process of changing a stop sound to an affricate. **2.** the result of such a change, as *pf-* in German. [AFFRICATE + -ION]

af·fric·a·tive (ə frik′ə tiv, af′rə kā′-), *Phonet.* —*n.* **1.** affricate. —*adj.* **2.** of or pertaining to an affricate. **3.** articulated as an affricate. [AFFRICATE + -IVE]

af·fright (ə frīt′), *Archaic.* —*v.t.* **1.** to frighten. —*n.* **2.** sudden fear or terror; fright. **3.** a source of terror. **4.** act of terrifying. [ME *afright(en)*, OE *āfyrhtan*, equiv. to *ā-* A-[3] + *fyrhtan* to FRIGHT]

af·front (ə frunt′), *n.* **1.** a personally offensive act or word; deliberate act or display of disrespect; intentional slight; insult: *an affront to the king.* **2.** an offense to one's dignity or self-respect. —*v.t.* **3.** to offend by an open manifestation of disrespect or insolence: *His speech affronted all of us.* **4.** to make ashamed or confused; embarrass. **5.** to meet or encounter face to face; confront. **6.** *Archaic.* to front; face; look on. [ME *afrounte(n)* < MF *afronter*, *affronter* to strike in the face < VL **affrontāre*, deriv. of L phrase *ad frontem* at the face. See AD-, FRONT] —**af·front′ed·ly,** *adv.* —**af·front′ed·ness,** *n.* —**af·front′er,** *n.* —**af·front′ing·ly,** *adv.*
—**Syn. 1.** impertinence; contumely, scorn; indignity, abuse, outrage. See **insult. 3.** insult, slight, abuse.

af·fron·té (af′rən tā′, ə frun′tē), *adj.* *Heraldry.* (of a beast or helmet) represented as facing outward toward the spectator: *a stag affronté.* [< F, n. use of ptp. of *affronter*; see AFFRONT]

af·fron·tive (ə frun′tiv), *adj.* *Archaic.* insulting; offensive. [AFFRONT + -IVE] —**af·fron′tive·ness,** *n.*

af·fu·sion (ə fyo͞o′zhən), *n.* the pouring on of water or other liquid, as in the rite of baptism. [< LL *affūsiōn-* (s. of *affūsiō* a pouring upon), equiv. to *affūs(us)* (ptp. of *affundere*; see AF-, FUSE[2]) + *-iōn-* -ION]

Afgh., Afghanistan. Also, **Afg.**

Af·ghan (af′gən, -gan), *n.* **1.** a native of Afghanistan. **2.** Pashto. **3.** (*l.c.*) a woolen blanket, knitted, crocheted, or woven, usually in a geometric pattern. **4.** Also called **Af′ghan hound′.** one of a breed of hounds having a long, narrow head and a long, silky coat. —*adj.* **5.** of Afghanistan or its people.

af·ghan·ets (af′gan its), *n.* a strong, gusty, dust-bearing wind of Turkestan. [< Turkic: lit., Afghan wind]

af·ghan·i (af gan′ē, -gä′nē), *n.* a coin and monetary unit of Afghanistan, equal to 100 puls and equivalent to about .022 of a U.S. dollar. *Abbr.:* Agh. [< Pushtu]

Af·ghan·i·stan (af gan′i stan′), *n.* a republic in S Asia, NW of India, E of Iran, and S of the Soviet Union. 13,150,000 (est. 1959); 250,000 sq. mi. *Cap.:* Kabul.

a·fi·cio·na·da (ə fish′yə nä′də; *Sp.* ä fē′thyô nä′thä), *n.*, *pl.* **-das** (-dəz; *Sp.* -thäs). a female aficionado. [< Sp]

a·fi·cio·na·do (ə fish′yə nä′dō; *Sp.* ä fē′thyô nä′thô), *n.*, *pl.* **-dos** (-dōz; *Sp.* -thôs). an ardent devotee. [< Sp: lit., affectionate, equiv. to *afición* AFFECTION[1] + *-ado* -ATE[1]]

a·field (ə fēld′), *adv.* **1.** abroad; away from home. **2.** off the beaten path; far and wide: *to stray far afield in one's reading.* **3.** in or to the field or countryside. **4.** beyond the range or field of one's experience, knowledge, acquaintanceship, etc.: *a philosophy far afield of previous philosophical thought.* [ME *afelde*, OE *on felda.* See A-[1], FIELD]

a·fi·ko·men (ä′fē kō′mən), *n.* *Hebrew.* a piece of matzo broken off by the leader of a Seder from the center one of the three matzoth set before him: it is hidden by the leader and later searched for by the children, with the youngest, usually by prearrangement, receiving a reward.

a·fire (ə fīər′), *adj.* on fire: *to set a house afire.* [ME; see A-[1], FIRE]

Alc, airman, first class.

A.F.L., See **American Federation of Labor.** Also, **A.F. of L.**

a·flame (ə flām′), *adj.* **1.** on fire; ablaze: *The house was all aflame.* **2.** glowing: *I was aflame with curiosity.*

AFL-CIO, American Federation of Labor and Congress of Industrial Organizations.

a·float (ə flōt′), *adv.*, *adj.* **1.** borne on the water; in a floating condition: *The ship was set afloat.* **2.** on board ship; at sea: *cargo afloat and ashore.* **3.** covered with water; flooded; awash: *The main deck was afloat.* **4.** moving without guide or control; drifting: *afloat from place to place.* **5.** passing from place to place; in circulation: *A rumor is afloat.* **6.** financially solvent: *to keep a venture afloat; to stay afloat.* [ME, OE *on flote.* See A-[1], FLOAT]

a·flut·ter (ə flut′ər), *adj.* in a flutter. [A-[1] + FLUTTER]

AFM, American Federation of Musicians.

a·fo·cal (ā fō′kəl), *adj.* *Optics.* pertaining to or having no finite focal point, as a telescope. [A-[6] + FOCAL]

à fond (A fôN′), *French.* to or toward the bottom; thoroughly; fully.

a·foot (ə fo͝ot′), *adv.*, *adj.* **1.** on foot; walking: *I came afoot.* **2.** astir; in progress: *There is mischief afoot.* [ME *a fote, on fote.* See A-[1], FOOT]

a·fore (ə fōr′, ə fôr′), *adv.*, *prep.*, *conj.* *Dial.* before. [late ME; ME *aforne, aforen*, OE *on foran.* See A-[1], FORE[1]]

a·fore·men·tioned (ə fōr′men′shənd, ə fôr′-), *adj.* cited or mentioned earlier or previously. [AFORE + MENTION + -ED[2]]

a·fore·said (ə fōr′sed′, ə fôr′-), *adj.* said or mentioned earlier or previously. [AFORE + SAID[1]]

a·fore·thought (ə fōr′thôt′, ə fôr′-), *adj.* **1.** thought of previously; premeditated (usually used predicatively): *with malice aforethought.* —*n.* **2.** premeditation; forethought. [AFORE + THOUGHT[2]]

a·fore·time (ə fōr′tīm′, ə fôr′-), *adv.* **1.** in time past; in a former time; previously. —*adj.* **2.** former; previous.

a for·ti·o·ri (ä fôR′ti ō′Rē; *Eng.* ā fōr′shē ōr′ē, ā fôr′shē ôr′ē), *Latin.* for a still stronger reason; even more certain; all the more.

a·foul (ə foul′), *adv.*, *adj.* **1.** in a state of collision or entanglement: *a ship with its shrouds afoul.* **2. run afoul of, a.** to come into conflict with: *to run afoul of the law.* **b.** to become entangled with: *The ship ran afoul of the floating seaweed.* [A-[1] + FOUL]

Afr-, var. of **Afro-** before a vowel: *Afric.*

Afr., 1. Africa. 2. African. Also, **Afr**

A.-Fr., Anglo-French.

a·fraid (ə frād′), *adj.* **1.** feeling fear; filled with apprehension: *afraid to go.* **2.** feeling regret, unhappiness, etc.: *I'm afraid we can't go on Monday.* **3.** feeling reluctance, unwillingness, distaste, etc.: *He seemed afraid to show his own children a little kindness.* [var. sp. of *affrayed*, ptp. of AFFRAY to disturb, frighten]
—**Syn. 1.** scared, fearful, disquieted, apprehensive, timid, timorous. AFRAID, ALARMED, FRIGHTENED, TERRIFIED all indicate a state of fear. AFRAID implies inner apprehensive disquiet: *afraid of* (or *in*) *the dark.* ALARMED implies that the feelings are aroused through realization of some imminent or unexpected danger to oneself or others: *alarmed by* (or *about*) *someone's illness.* FRIGHTENED means shocked with sudden, but usually short-lived, fear, esp. that arising from apprehension of physical harm: *frightened by* (or *about*) *an accident.* TERRIFIED suggests the emotional reaction when one is struck with a violent, overwhelming fear: *terrified by an earthquake.* —**Ant. 1.** bold, confident.

A-frame (ā′frām′), *n.* any upright, rigid supporting frame in the form of a triangle or an inverted V, as Λ.

Af·ra·sia (af rā′zhə, -shə), *n.* *Chiefly Geol.* N Africa and SW Asia considered together. [AFR- + ASIA]

Af·ra·sian (af rā′zhən, -shən), *adj.* **1.** of Afrasia. **2.** of mixed African and Asian descent. —*n.* **3.** the offspring of an African and an Asian. [AFRASI(A) + -AN]

af·reet (af′rēt, ə frēt′), *n.* *Arabian Myth.* a powerful evil demon or monster. Also, **afrit.** [< Ar *'ifrīt*]

a·fresh (ə fresh′), *adv.* anew; again: *to start afresh.* [A-[2] + FRESH]

Af·ric (af′rik), *adj.* African. [< L *Afric(us).* See AFR-, -IC]

Af·ri·ca (af′ri kə), *n.* a continent S of Europe and between the Atlantic and Indian oceans. 248,652,500 (latest censuses and estimates 1955–60); ab. 11,700,000 sq. mi.

Af·ri·can (af′ri kən), *adj.* of or from Africa; belonging to the black race of Africa; Negro. Also, **Afric.** [< L *Africān(us)*, equiv. to *Afric(us)* AFRIC + *-ānus* -AN]

Af·ri·can-A·mer·i·can (af′ri kən ə mer′i kən), *n.* **1.** a black American of African descent. —*adj.* **2.** of or pertaining to African-Americans. Also, **Afro-American, Aframerican.**

Af′rican cher′ry-or·ange (cher′ē ôr′inj, -or′-), a shrub or small tree, *Citropsis Schweinfurthi*, of Africa, having limelike, but sweet, fruit.

Af′rican dai′sy, any of several showy, African, composite herbs of the genera *Arctotis, Dimorphotheca, Gerbera*, and *Gazania*, having daisylike flowers.

Af·ri·can·der (af′ri kan′dər), *n.* Afrikander.

Af·ri·can·der·ism (af′ri kan′də riz′əm), *n.* Afrikanderism.

Af′rican dom′inoes, *Slang.* dice.

Af′rican el′ephant, any elephant of the genus *Loxodonta*, of Africa. Cf. **elephant** (def. 1).

Af′rican gray′. See **gray parrot.**

Af·ri·can·ist (af′ri kə nist), *n.* a person who specializes in and studies the culture of Africa. [AFRICAN + -IST] —**Af′ri·can·ism,** *n.*

Af·ri·can·ize (af′ri kə nīz′), *v.t.*, **-ized, -iz·ing. 1.** to replace the European or white staff of (an organization in Africa) with African Negroes. **2.** to bring under African, esp. African Negro, influence or to adapt to African needs. [AFRICAN + -IZE] —**Af′ri·can·i·za′tion,** *n.*

Af′rican lil′y, agapanthus.

Af′rican mar′igold, a bushy herb, *Tagetes erecta*, of Mexico, having yellow or orange flower heads from two to four inches wide. Also called **Aztec marigold, big marigold.**

Af′rican mil′let, 1. a grass, *Eleusine coracana*, of Asia and Africa, having round fruit with a loose husk, grown as a cereal and as an ornamental. **2.** See **pearl millet.**

Af′rican sleep′ing sick′ness, *Pathol.* See **sleeping sickness** (def. 1).

Af·ri·can·thro·pus (af′ri kan′thrə pəs, -kan thrō′pəs), *n.* a proposed genus of hominids from the Pleistocene of East Africa, assumed from a number of now lost skull fragments to have been similar in physical type to Rhodesia man. [< NL, equiv. to *Afric(a)* + Gk *ánthrōpos* man, human being]

Af′rican trypanosomi′asis, *Pathol.* See **sleeping sickness** (def. 1).

Af′rican vi′olet, a popular house plant, *Saintpaulia ionantha,* having violet, pink, or white flowers.

Af′rican yel′lowwood, a tree, *Podocarpus elongatus,* of tropical Africa and the mountains of South Africa, having globe-shaped fruit, grown as an ornamental.

Af·ri·kaans (af′rə käns′, -känz′), *n.* a language of South Africa, developed out of the speech of 17th-century settlers from Holland and still very like Dutch; South African Dutch. Also called **the Taal.** [var. sp. of D *Afrikaansch,* equiv. to *Afrikaan* AFRICAN + *-sch* -ISH[1]]

Af·ri·kan·der (af′rə kan′dər), *n.* **1.** Also, **Afrikaner.** an Afrikaans-speaking native of Cape Province or the neighboring regions of Africa who is born of white, esp. Dutch or Huguenot parents. **2.** one of a breed of red beef cattle, raised originally in southern Africa, well adapted to high temperatures. Also, **Africander.** [by alter. from SAfrD *Afrikaander,* deriv. of *Africaaner* (*Afrikaan* AFRICAN + *-er* -ER[1]) with *-d-* of *Hollander*]

Af·ri·kan·der·ism (af′rə kan′də riz′əm), *n.* a word, usage, etc., peculiar to or originating among Afrikanders. Also, **Africanderism.** [AFRIKANDER + -ISM]

Af·ri·ka·ner (af′rə kä′nər, -kan′ər), *n.* Afrikander (def. 1).

af·rit (af′rēt, ə frēt′), *n.* afreet.

Af·ro (af′rō), *adj.* **1.** of or pertaining to Afro-Americans or to black traditions, culture, etc.: *Afro societies; Afro hair styles.* —*n.* **2.** a hair style of black persons in which the hair is allowed to grow naturally and to acquire a bushy appearance.

Afro-, a combining form of **Africa:** *Afro-American; Afro-Asiatic.* Also, *esp. before a vowel,* **Afr-.** [< L *Afr-* (s. of *Afer* an African) + -o-]

Af·ro-A·sian (af′rō ā′zhən, -shən), *adj.* of or pertaining to the nations of Africa and Asia or their peoples.

Af·ro-A·si·at·ic (af′rō ā′zhē at′ik, -ā′shē-), *adj.* **1.** of, belonging to, or pertaining to Afro-Asiatic; Hamito-Semitic. —*n.* **2.** Also called **Hamito-Semitic.** a family of languages including as subfamilies Semitic, Egyptian, Berber, Cushitic, and Chad. Cf. **family** (def. 11). Also, **Af′ro·a′si·at′ic.**

Af·ro·cen·tric (af′rō sen′trik), *adj.* centered on Africa or on African-derived cultures, as those of Brazil, Cuba, and Haiti: *Afrocentric art.* —**Af′ro·cen′trism,** *n.* —**Af′ro·cen′trist,** *n.*

A.F.S., American Field Service.

aft (aft, äft), *Naut., Aeron.* —*adv.* **1.** at, close to, or toward the stern or tail: *The men ran aft.* —*adj.* **2.** situated toward or at the stern: *The aft sail was luffing.* [OE *æft(an)* from behind, equiv. to *æf-* OFF + *-t-* superl. suffix + *-an* suffix marking motion from; c. Goth *aftana,* Icel *aptan*]

aft., afternoon.

A.F.T., American Federation of Teachers.

af·ter (af′tər, äf′-), *prep.* **1.** behind in place or position; following behind: *men lining up one after another.* **2.** later in time than; in succession to; at the close of: *Tell me after supper. Time after time I saw him.* **3.** subsequent to and in consequence of: *After what has happened, I can never return.* **4.** below in rank or excellence; nearest to: *Milton is usually placed after Shakespeare among English poets.* **5.** in imitation of or in imitation of the style of: *to make something after a model; fashioned after Raphael.* **6.** in pursuit or search of; with or in desire for: *I'm after a decent job. Run after him!* **7.** concerning; about: *to inquire after a person.* **8.** with the name of; for: *He was named after his uncle.* **9.** in proportion to; in accordance with: *He was a man after the hopes and expectations of his father.* **10.** according to the nature of; in conformity to; in agreement or unison with: *He was a man after my own heart. He swore after the manner of his faith.* —*adv.* **11.** behind; in the rear: *Jill came tumbling after.* **12.** later in time; afterward: *three hours after; happily ever after.* —*adj.* **13.** later in time; next; subsequent; succeeding: *In after years we never heard from him.* **14.** *Naut., Aeron.* **a.** farther aft. **b.** located closest to the stern or tail; aftermost: *after hold; after mast.* **c.** including the stern or tail: *the after part of a hull.* —*conj.* **15.** subsequent to the time that: *after the boys left.* —*n.* **16. afters,** *Brit. Informal.* the final course of a meal, as pudding, ice cream, or the like, similar to the U.S. dessert. [ME; OE *æfter,* equiv. to *æf-* OFF + *-ter* comp. suffix (c. Gk *-teros*)]
—**Syn. 1.** See **behind.**

af·ter·birth (af′tər bûrth′, äf′-), *n.* the placenta and fetal membranes expelled from the uterus after childbirth. [AFTER + BIRTH]

af·ter·bod·y (af′tər bod′ē, äf′-), *n., pl.* **-bod·ies. 1.** *Naut.* the portion of a ship's hull aft of the middle body. **2.** *Rocketry.* the part of a guided missile behind the nose cone, usually unprotected against reentry heat. [AFTER + BODY]

af·ter·brain (af′tər brān′, äf′-), *n.* the metencephalon. [AFTER + BRAIN]

af·ter·burn·er (af′tər bûr′nər, äf′-), *n.* **1.** *Aeron.* a device placed within, or attached to the exit of, a jet-engine exhaust pipe to produce afterburning. **2.** a device for burning exhaust fumes from an internal-combustion engine, as of an automobile. [AFTER + BURNER]

af·ter·burn·ing (af′tər bûr′ning, äf′-), *n.* **1.** *Aeron.* combustion in an afterburner that results from the injection of fuel into the exhaust gases of a jet engine to produce additional thrust with more efficient fuel consumption. **2.** *Rocketry.* an irregular burning of residual fuel in some rocket motors after the cessation of the main burning. [AFTER + BURNING]

af·ter·care (af′tər kâr′, äf′-), *n.* *Med.* the care and treatment of a convalescent patient. [AFTER + CARE]

af·ter·cast (af′tər kast′, äf′tər käst′), *n.* *Foundry.* **1.** a casting made from a mold that was itself made from an original casting. **2.** an exact impression, usually in plaster, made of a permanent mold or die after the production of castings is finished. [AFTER + CAST[1]]

af·ter·clap (af′tər klap′, äf′-), *n.* an unexpected repercussion. [late ME; cf. LG *achterklap*]

af·ter·cool·er (af′tər ko͞o′lər, äf′-), *n.* a device for cooling compressed air or gases to reduce their volume or temperature. [AFTER + COOLER]

af·ter·damp (af′tər damp′, äf′-), *n.* an irrespirable mixture of gases, consisting chiefly of carbon dioxide and nitrogen, left in a mine after an explosion or fire. [AFTER + DAMP]

af·ter·deck (af′tər dek′, äf′-), *n.* *Naut.* the weather deck of a vessel abaft the bridge house or midship section. [AFTER + DECK]

af·ter-din·ner (af′tər din′ər, äf′-), *adj.* following dinner: *an after-dinner speech.*

af·ter·ef·fect (af′tər i fekt′, äf′-), *n.* **1.** a delayed effect; an effect that follows at some interval after the stimulus that produces it. **2.** *Med.* a result appearing after the first effect due to an agent, usually a drug, has gone. [AFTER + EFFECT]

af·ter·glow (af′tər glō′, äf′-), *n.* **1.** the glow frequently seen in the sky after sunset. **2.** a second or secondary glow, as in heated metal before it ceases to become incandescent. **3.** the pleasant remembrance of a past experience, glory, etc.: *She basked in the afterglow of her triumph.* **4.** phosphorescence (def. 3). [AFTER + GLOW]

af·ter·growth (af′tər grōth′, äf′-), *n.* a second growth, as of crops, timber, or the like, after one harvesting, cutting, etc.; second crop. [AFTER + GROWTH]

af·ter·guard (af′tər gärd′, äf′-), *n.* *Naut. Slang.* **1.** the owner of a yacht or his guests. **2.** the officers quartered in the stern of a vessel. [AFTER + GUARD]

af·ter·heat (af′tər hēt′, äf′-), *n.* *Physics.* the heat generated by radioactivity remaining in a nuclear reactor after it has been shut down. [AFTER + HEAT]

af·ter·im·age (af′tər im′ij, äf′-), *n.* *Psychol.* a visual image or other sense impression that persists after the stimulus that caused it is no longer operative. [trans. of G *Nachbild;* see AFTER, IMAGE]

af·ter·life (af′tər līf′, äf′-), *n.* **1.** Also called **future life.** the life after death. **2.** the part of one's life subsequent to an earlier part: *In afterlife he became a teacher.* [AFTER + LIFE]

af′ter mast′, the aftermost mast of a sailing vessel.

af·ter·math (af′tər math′, äf′-), *n.* **1.** that which results or follows from an event, esp. one of a disastrous or violent nature; consequence: *the aftermath of war; the aftermath of the flood.* **2.** a new growth of grass following one or more mowings, which may be grazed, mowed, or plowed under. [AFTER + *math* a mowing, OE *mǣth,* c. OHG *mād* (G *mahd*); akin to MOW[1]]

af·ter·most (af′tər mōst′, äf′- *or, esp. Brit.,* äf′tər məst), *adj.* **1.** *Naut.* farthest aft; aftmost: *The aftermost sail is called a spanker.* **2.** hindmost; last. [AFTER + -MOST; r. ME *aftemest,* itself r. OE *æftemest,* equiv. to *æfte* (see AFT) + *-m-* superl. suffix + *-est* -EST[1]]

af·ter·noon (*n.* af′tər no͞on′, äf′-; *adj.* af′tər no͞on′, äf′-, af′-, äf′-), *n.* **1.** the time from noon until evening. **2.** the latter part: *the afternoon of life.* —*adj.* **3.** pertaining to the latter part of the day. [ME; see AFTER, NOON]

Afternoon′ of a Faun′, The. See **L'Après-midi d'un Faune.**

af·ter·noons (af′tər no͞onz′, äf′-), *adv.* in or during the afternoon regularly: *He slept late and worked afternoons.* [AFTERNOON + -S[1]]

af′ternoon tea′, 1. light refreshments served late in the afternoon. **2.** an afternoon social gathering.

afternoon′ watch′, *Naut.* the watch from noon until 4 P.M.

af·ter·pain (af′tər pān′, äf′-), *n.* *Med.* **1.** pain that occurs after a definite period following the stimulus. **2. afterpains,** pains following childbirth, due to contractions of the uterus. [AFTER + PAIN]

af·ter·peak (af′tər pēk′, äf′-), *n.* *Naut.* the extreme after part of the interior of a hull, esp. that part below the water immediately forward of the sternpost (opposed to *forepeak*). [AFTER + PEAK[1]]

af·ter·piece (af′tər pēs′, äf′-), *n.* a short dramatic piece performed after a featured play. [AFTER + PIECE]

af·ter·sen·sa·tion (af′tər sen sā′shən, äf′-), *n.* *Psychol.* an afterimage. [AFTER + SENSATION]

af·ter·shaft (af′tər shaft′, af′tər shäft′), *n.* *Ornith.* **1.** a supplementary feather, usually small, arising from the underside of the base of the shafts of certain feathers in many birds. **2.** the shaft of such a feather. [AFTER + SHAFT] —**af′ter·shaft′ed,** *adj.*

af·ter·shock (af′tər shok′, äf′-), *n.* any small earthquake or tremor that follows a major earthquake. [AFTER + SHOCK[1]]

af·ter·taste (af′tər tāst′, äf′-), *n.* **1.** a taste remaining after the substance causing it is no longer in the mouth. **2.** the remaining sensation following an unpleasant experience, incident, etc.: *the aftertaste of a bad marriage.* [AFTER + TASTE]

af·ter·thought (af′tər thôt′, äf′-), *n.* **1.** a later or second thought; reconsideration. **2.** reflection after an act; an appropriate explanation, answer, expedient, or the like, conceived of too late for the occasion. **3.** something added, as a part or feature, that was not included in the original plan or design: *The vestry was added to the church as an afterthought.* [AFTER + THOUGHT[1]]

af·ter·time (af′tər tīm′, äf′-), *n.* future time. [AFTER + TIME]

af·ter·treat·ment (af′tər trēt′mənt, äf′-), *n.* a chemical treatment to which a fabric is subjected immediately after being dyed, for increasing the fastness of the color. [AFTER + TREATMENT]

af·ter·ward (af′tər wərd, äf′-), *adv.* in later or subsequent time; subsequently. Also, **af′ter·wards.** [ME; OE *æfterweard,* alter. (with *-r-* of *æfter* AFTER) of *æfteweard,* equiv. to *æfte-, æftan* AFT + *-weard* -WARD]

af·ter·word (af′tər wûrd′, äf′-), *n.* a concluding section, commentary, etc., as of a book, treatise, or the like; closing statement. Cf. **foreword.** [AFTER + WORD]

af·ter·world (af′tər wûrld′, äf′-), *n.* the future world, esp. the world believed to exist after death. [AFTER + WORLD]

af·ter·years (af′tər yērz′, äf′-), *n.pl.* the years following a specified event: *Often, in afteryears, I have regretted my hasty decision.* [AFTER + YEAR + -S[3]]

aft·most (aft′mōst′, -məst, äft′-), *adj.* *Naut.* aftermost (def. 1).

AFTRA, American Federation of Television and Radio Artists. Also, **A.F.T.R.A.**

A·fyon (ä fyôn′), *n.* a city in W Turkey. 43,646 (1965). Also called **Afyon′ Ka·ra·hi·sar′** (kär′ə hi sär′).

ag-, var. of **ad-** before *g: agglutinate.*

Ag., August.

ag., agriculture.

A.G., 1. Adjutant General. **2.** Attorney General.

Ag, *Chem.* silver. [< L *argentum*]

a·ga (ä′gə), *n.* (in Turkey) **1.** a title of honor, usually implying respect for age. **2.** a general. Also, **agha.** [< Turk *ağa* lord]

Ag·a·bus (ag′ə bəs), *n.* a Christian prophet who predicted a great famine. Acts 11:28.

Ag·a·cles (ag′ə klēz′), *n.* (in the *Iliad*) a king of the Myrmidons.

A·ga·dir (ä′gä dēr′), *n.* a seaport in SW Morocco: destroyed by earthquake in 1960; new town rebuilt S of original site.

A·gag (ā′gag), *n.* an Amalekite king who was captured and spared by Saul but later killed by Samuel. I Sam. 15.

a·gain (ə gen′ *or, esp. Brit.,* ə gān′), *adv.* **1.** once more; another time; anew; in addition: *Will you spell your name again, please?* **2.** in an additional case or instance; moreover; besides; furthermore. **3.** on the other hand: *It might happen, and again it might not.* **4.** back; in return; in reply: *to answer again.* **5.** in the opposite direction; to the same place or person: *to return again.* **6. again and again,** with frequent repetition; often: *They went over the same arguments again and again.* **7. as much again,** twice as much: *She earns as much again as I do.* [ME *agayn, ageyn,* OE *ongegn* opposite (to), equiv. to *on,* in + *gegn* straight; c. OHG *ingagan, ingegin* (G *entgegen*), Icel *ígegn*]

a·gainst (ə genst′ *or, esp. Brit.,* ə gānst′), *prep.* **1.** in opposition to; adverse or hostile to: *twenty votes against ten; against reason.* **2.** in resistance to or defense from: *protection against burglars.* **3.** in an opposite direction to, so as to meet; toward; upon: *to ride against the wind; The rain beats against the window.* **4.** in contact with: *to lean against the wall.* **5.** in preparation for; in provision for: *money saved against a rainy day.* **6.** having as background: *a design of flowers against a dark wall.* **7.** in exchange for; in return for; as a balance to: *to draw against merchandise shipped.* **8.** in competition with: *a race horse running against his own record time.* **9.** in comparison or contrast with: *a matter of reason as against emotion.* **10.** beside; near; before: *The car is over against the building.* —*conj.* **11.** *Archaic.* before; by the time that. [late ME; ME *agens, ageynes,* equiv. to *ageyn* AGAIN + *-es* -S[1]; for *-t* cf. WHILST, AMONGST]

A·ga Khan III (ä′gə kän′), 1877–1957, leader of the Ismaili sect of Muslims in India 1885–1957.

Aga Khan IV, (*Shah Karim al-Husainy*) born 1936, leader of the Ismaili sect of Muslims in India since 1957 (grandson of Aga Khan III).

a·gal (ə gäl′), *n.* a cord wound around a kaffiyeh to hold it in place. [< Ar *'iqāl* cord, rope]

ag·a·lite (ag′ə līt′), *n.* *Mineral.* a fibrous variety of talc. [< Gk *aga-* (< ?) + -LITE]

a·gal·loch (ə gal′ək, ag′ə lok′), *n.* the fragrant, resinous wood of an East Indian thymelaeaceous tree, *Aquilaria Agallocha,* used as incense in the Orient. Also called **a·gal·lo·chum** (ə gal′ə kəm), **agalwood, agilawood, aloes, aloeswood, eaglewood, lignaloes.** [< LL *agallochon* < Gk (m. by influence of *agállein* to decorate); of Dravidian origin]

ag·al·mat·o·lite (ag′əl mat′ᵊlīt′, ə gal mat′-), *n.* pagodite. [< NL *agalmatolith(us)* < Gk *agalmat-* (s. of *agalma* statue) + NL *litus* -LITE]

ag·al·wood (ag′əl wo͝od′), *n.* agalloch. [*agal* (deriv. of AGALLOCH) + WOOD[1]]

ag·a·ma (ag′ə mə), *n.* any of numerous agamid lizards of the genus *Agama,* many of which are brilliantly colored and have the ability to change the color of the skin. [< Carib]

A·ga·ma (ä′gə mə), *n.* *Hinduism.* any of the Tantric writings. [< Skt *āgama* arrival, acquisition of knowledge, equiv. to *ā* toward + *gama* coming, akin to COME, L *venire*]

Ag·a·me·de (ag′ə mē′dē), *n.* *Class. Myth.* a daughter of Augeas noted for her skill at using herbs for healing.

Ag·a·me·des (ag′ə mē′dēz), *n.* *Class. Myth.* a son of Erginus who, with his brother Trophonius, built the temple of Apollo at Delphi.

Ag·a·mem·non (ag′ə mem′non, -nən), *n.* **1.** *Class. Myth.* a king of Mycenae, a son of Atreus and brother of Menelaus, who led the Greeks in the Trojan War and who was murdered by Clytemnestra, his wife, upon his return from Troy. **2.** (*italics*) a tragedy (458 B.C.) by Aeschylus. Cf. **Oresteia.**

ag·am·ete (ā gam′ēt, ā′gə mēt′), *n.* *Biol.* an asexual reproductive cell, as a spore, which forms a new organism without fusion with another cell. [< Gk *agámet(os)* unmarried, equiv. to *a-* A-[6] + *-gametos* married, deriv. of *gamétēs;* see GAMETE]

a·gam·ic (ə gam′ik), *adj.* **1.** *Biol.* **a.** asexual. **b.** occurring without sexual union; germinating without impregnation; not gamic. **2.** *Bot.* cryptogamic. Also, **ag·a·mous** (ag′ə məs). [< Gk *ágam(os)* unwed (*a-* A-[6] + *gámos* marriage) + -IC] —**a·gam′i·cal·ly,** *adv.*

ag·a·mid (ag′ə mid), *n.* **1.** any of numerous Old World lizards of the family *Agamidae,* related to the iguanids. —*adj.* **2.** belonging or pertaining to the *Agamidae.* [< NL *Agam(a)* genus name + -ID[2]]

a·gam·ma·glob·u·li·ne·mi·a (ā′gam ə glob′yə lə nē′mē ə), *n.* *Pathol.* a condition of the blood, either congenital or acquired, in which there is near or complete absence of gamma globulin and the failure of the body to form antibodies, resulting in a frequent occurrence of infectious disease. [A-[6] + GAMMA GLOBULIN + -EMIA]

ag·a·mo·gen·e·sis (ag′ə mō jen′i sis), *n.* *Biol.* asexual reproduction by buds, offshoots, cell division, etc. [< Gk *ágamo(s)* (see AGAMIC) + -GENESIS] —**ag·a·mo·ge·net·ic** (ag′ə mō jə net′ik), *adj.* —**ag′a·mo·ge·net′i·cal·ly,** *adv.*

ag·a·my (ag′ə mē), *n.* absence or nonrecognition of marriage in a social group. [< Gk *agamía,* equiv. to *ágam(os)* (see AGAMIC) + *-ia* -Y[3]]

A·ga·ña (ä gä′nyä), *n.* a seaport in and the capital of Guam. 1642 (1960).

Ag·a·nip·pe (ag′ə nip′ē), *n.* *Class. Myth.* a fountain near Helicon, in Greece, sacred to the Muses in ancient times and believed to inspire those who drank from it.

Ag·a·nus (ag′ə nəs), *n.* *Class. Myth.* a son of Helen and Paris.

ag·a·pan·thus (ag′ə pan′thəs), *n., pl.* **-thus·es.** any of several African, liliaceous plants of the genus *Agapanthus,* having umbels of blue or white flowers. Also called **African lily.** [< NL < Gk *agap(ē)* love + *ánthos* flower]

a·gape[1] (ə gāp′, ə gap′), *adv., adj.* **1.** with the mouth wide open; in an attitude of wonder or eagerness. **2.** wide open: *his mouth agape.* [A-[1] + GAPE]

a·ga·pe[2] (ä gä′pā, ä′gə pā′, ag′ə-), *n., pl.* **-pae** (-pī, -pī′, -pē′), **-pai** (-pī, -pī′) for 3. **1.** the love of God or Christ for mankind. **2.** the brotherly or spiritual love of one Christian for another, corresponding to the love of God for man. Cf. **Eros** (def. 5). **3.** unselfish love of one person for another without sexual implications; brotherly love. **4.** See **love feast** (defs. 1, 2). [< Gk *agápē* love]

Ag·a·pe·tus I (ag′ə pē′təs), **Saint,** died A.D. 536, Italian ecclesiastic: pope 535–536.

Agapetus II, died A.D. 955, Italian ecclesiastic: pope 946–955.

a·gar (ä′gär, ag′ər), *n.* **1.** Also, **a′gar-a′gar.** Also called **Chinese gelatin, Chinese isinglass, Japanese gelatin, Japanese isinglass.** a gelatinlike product of certain seaweeds: used for solidifying certain culture media, as a thickening agent for ice cream and other foods, as a substitute for gelatin, in adhesives, as an emulsifier, and as a sizing for paper and silk. **2.** *Biol.* a culture medium having an agar base. [short for AGAR-AGAR < Malay]

A·gar (ā′gär), *n. Douay Bible.* Hagar (def. 1).

ag·a·ric (ag′ə rik, ə gar′ik), *n.* an agaricaceous fungus; mushroom. [< NL *Agaric(us)* genus name < Gk *agarikós* (adj.) pertaining to *Agaria,* a town in Sarmatis; neut. *agarikón* used as n., name of some fungi]

a·gar·i·ca·ceous (ə gar′ə kā′shəs), *adj.* belonging to the *Agaricaceae,* a family of fungi including mushrooms having blade-shaped gills on the underside of the cap. [< NL *agaricace(ae)* (*agaric(us)* AGARIC + -ACEAE) with -ACEOUS r. *-aceae*]

ag′aric ac′id, *Chem.* a white, microcrystalline, water-soluble powder, $C_{19}H_{36}OH(COOH)_3 \cdot 1\frac{1}{2}H_2O$: formerly used in medicine to stop excessive perspiration. Also, **ag′a·ric′ic ac′id** (ag′ə ris′ik, ag′-).

a·gar·i·cin (ə gar′i sin, -sən), *n. Chem.* an impure form of agaric acid: formerly used in medicine as an agent for stopping excessive perspiration. [AGARIC + -IN[2]]

ag′aric min′eral. See **rock milk.**

ag·a·ri·ta (ag′ə rē′tə, ä′gə-), *n.* a tall shrub, *Mahonia trifoliolata,* of southwestern North America, having a red fruit used in jelly. Also, **algerita.** [< MexSp *agrito,* prob. < Sp *agri(o)* bitter < OSp *agro* < L *acr-* (s. of *acer* sharp)]

Ag·as·siz (ag′ə sē; *for 2 also Fr.* A GA sē′), *n.* **1. Alexander,** 1835–1910, U.S. oceanographer and marine zoologist, born in Switzerland. **2.** his father, **(Jean) Louis (Ro·dolphe)** (zhäN lwē rô dôlf′), 1807–73, Swiss zoologist and geologist, in the U.S. after 1846.

A·gas·tro·phus (ə gas′trə fəs), *n.* (in the *Iliad*) a son of Paeon who was slain by Diomedes.

A·gas·tya (ä′gəs tyə), *n.* the legendary Aryan sage who introduced the Vedas to southern India.

ag·a·ta (ag′ə tə), *n.* an American art glass having a mottled, glossy, white and rose surface. [< It: AGATE < L *achates*]

ag·ate (ag′it), *n.* **1.** a variegated chalcedony showing curved, colored bands or other markings. **2.** a playing marble made of this substance, or of glass in imitation of it. **3.** *Print.* a 5½-point type of a size between pearl and nonpareil. Cf. **ruby** (def. 5). [earlier *agat,* appar. < It *agat(a)* (initial stress) << L *achātēs* < Gk *achátēs*] —**ag′ate·like′, ag′a·toid′,** *adj.*

ag′ate line′, a measure of advertising space, $^1/_{14}$ of an inch deep and one column wide.

ag·ate·ware (ag′it wâr′), *n.* **1.** steel or iron household ware enameled in an agatelike pattern. **2.** pottery variegated to resemble agate. [AGATE + WARE[1]]

Ag·a·tha (ag′ə thə), *n.* a girl's given name.

Ag·a·thar·chi·des (ag′ə thär′ki dēz′), *n.* a ring formation in the third quadrant of the face of the moon: about 33 miles in diameter.

Ag·a·tho (ag′ə thō′), *n.* **Saint,** died A.D. 681, Sicilian ecclesiastic: pope 678–681.

A·gath·o·cles (ə gath′ə klēz′), *n.* 361–289 B.C., tyrant of Syracuse 317–289.

Ag·a·thon (ag′ə thon′), *n.* **1.** c450–c400 B.C., Greek poet and dramatist. **2.** (in the *Iliad*) one of the 50 sons of Priam.

Ag·a·thyr·sus (ag′ə thûr′səs, -thēr′-), *n. Class. Myth.* a son of Hercules.

ag·at·ize (ag′ə tīz′), *v.t.,* **-ized, -iz·ing.** to change into or make like agate. [AGATE + -IZE]

à gauche (A gōsh′), *French.* on or to the left-hand side.

a·ga·ve (ə gä′vē, ə gä′-), *n.* any of numerous American, amaryllidaceous plants of the genus *Agave,* species of which are cultivated for economic or ornamental purposes. Cf. **century plant, maguey, sisal.** [< NL < Gk *agauē,* fem. of *agauós* noble, brilliant]

A·ga·ve (ə gā′vē), *n. Class. Myth.* a daughter of Cadmus and Harmonia and the wife of Echion who, in a bacchanalian frenzy, tore her son Pentheus to pieces.

a·gaze (ə gāz′), *adj.* staring intently; gazing: *The children were agaze at the Christmas tree.* [A-[1] + GAZE]

ag·ba (ag′bə), *n.* **1.** a tropical, leguminous tree, *Gossweilerodendron balsamiferum.* **2.** the hard, strong, mahoganylike wood of this tree, used for veneers. [< native Afr name]

AGC, automatic gain control.

AGCA, See **Automatic Ground Control Approach.**

AGCT, Army General Classification Test.

agcy., agency.

age (āj), *n., v.,* **aged, ag·ing** or **age·ing.** —*n.* **1.** the length of time during which a being or thing has existed; length of life or existence to the time spoken of or referred to: *trees of unknown age; His age is 20 years.* **2.** the average life expectancy of an individual or of the individuals of a class or species: *The age of the horse is from 25 to 30 years.* **3.** a period of human life, measured by years from birth, usually marked by a certain stage or degree of mental or physical development and involving legal responsibility and capacity: *the age of discretion; the age of consent.* **4.** the particular period of life at which one becomes naturally or conventionally qualified or disqualified for anything: *He was over age for conscription.* **5.** one of the periods or stages of human life: *a person of middle age.* **6.** advanced years; old age: *His eyes were dim with age.* **7.** a particular period of history, as distinguished from others; a historical epoch: *the age of Pericles; the Stone Age; the age of atomic science.* **8.** the period of history contemporary with the span of an individual's life: *He was the leader of the age. Obsession with speed is the curse of the age.* **9.** a generation or a succession of generations: *ages yet unborn.* **10.** a great length of time: *I haven't seen you for an age. He's been gone for ages.* **11.** *Psychol.* the level of mental, emotional, or educational development of an individual as determined by various tests and based on a comparison of his score with the average score of individuals of the same chronological age. **12.** *Geol.* **a.** a period of the history of the earth distinguished by some special feature: *Ice Age.* **b.** a period during which one particular stage of rock formation takes place: shorter than an epoch. **13.** any of the successive periods in the history of man divided, according to Hesiod, into the golden, silver, bronze, heroic, and iron ages. **14.** *Cards.* **a.** *Poker.* the first player at the dealer's left. Cf. **edge** (def. 11a). **b.** See **eldest hand. 15. of age,** *Law.* **a.** being any of several ages, usually 21 or 18, at which certain legal rights, as voting, marriage, etc., are acquired. **b.** *U.S.* being 21 years old, in possession of full legal rights and responsibilities. —*v.i.* **16.** to grow old: *He is aging rapidly.* **17.** to mature, as wine, cheese, wood, etc.: *a heavy port that ages slowly.* —*v.t.* **18.** to make old; cause to grow or seem old: *Fear aged him overnight.* **19.** to bring to maturity or a state fit for use: *to age wine.* **20.** to store (a permanent magnet, a capacitor, or other similar device) so that its electrical or magnetic characteristics become constant. [ME < OF *aage, eage* < VL **aetāticum* < L *ae(vi)tāt-* (s. of *ae(vi)tās*), equiv. to *aev(um)* lifetime (akin to AY[1]) + *-itāt-* -ITY + *-icum* neut. of *-icus* -IC]

—**Syn. 7.** AGE, EPOCH, ERA, PERIOD all refer to an extent of time. AGE usually implies a considerable extent of time, esp. one associated with a dominant personality, influence, characteristic, or institution: *the age of chivalry.* EPOCH and ERA are often used interchangeably, but an ERA is an extent of time characterized by changed conditions and new undertakings: *an era of invention.* An EPOCH is properly the beginning of an era: *an epoch of armed aggression.* A PERIOD may be long or short, but usually has a marked condition or feature: *the glacial period; a period of expansion.* **17.** mature, ripen.

-age, a formal element meaning "pertaining to", occurring in loan words from French: (*language; voyage*); used also as a noun-forming suffix to stems of native origin (*fruitage; bondage; postage*). [ME < OF < L *-āticum,* neut. of *-āticus* adj. suffix]

Ag.E., Agricultural Engineer.

A.G.E., Associate in General Education.

a·ged (ā′jid *for 1, 2, 5, 6;* ājd *for 1, 3, 4*), *adj.* **1.** having lived or existed long; of advanced age; old: *an aged man; an aged tree.* **2.** pertaining to or characteristic of old age: *aged wrinkles.* **3.** of the age of: *a man aged 40 years.* **4.** brought to maturity or mellowness, as wine, cheese, wood, etc.: *aged whiskey.* **5.** *Phys. Geog.* old; approaching the state of peneplain. —*n.* **6.** (*construed as pl.*) old persons collectively (usually prec. by *the*): *Medical care for the aged is one aspect of social security.* [AGE + -ED[2]] —**a′ged·ly,** *adv.* —**a′ged·ness,** *n.*

—**Syn. 1.** ancient. See **old.** —**Ant. 1.** young.

a·gee (ə jē′), *adv. Brit. Dial.* to one side; awry. Also, **ajee.** [A-[1] + GEE]

A·gee (ā′jē), *n.* **James,** 1909–55, U.S. author, scenarist, and film critic.

age-group (āj′grōōp′), *n.* persons of approximately the same age and often of the same sex, nationality, social background, and scholastic ability, as of a nation, school system, community, etc.

age·less (āj′lis), *adj.* never growing old or outdated: *an ageless piece of sculpture.* [AGE + -LESS] —**age′less·ness,** *n.*

age·long (āj′lông′, -long′), *adj.* lasting for an age. [AGE + LONG]

A·ge·na (ə jē′nə), *n. U.S.* an upper stage for a rocket, usually a Thor or Atlas, for launching satellites.

A·ge·nais (Azhə ne′), *n.* an ancient region of SW France. Also, **A·ge·nois** (Azhə nwA′).

a·gen·cy (ā′jən sē), *n., pl.* **-cies. 1.** an organization, company, or bureau that provides some service for another: *a welfare agency.* **2.** a company having a franchise to represent another. **3.** a governmental bureau, or an office that represents it. **4.** the place of business of an agent. **5.** See **Indian agency. 6.** an administrative division of a government. **7.** the duty or function of an agent. **8.** the relationship between a principal and his agent. **9.** state of being in action or of exerting power; action; operation: *the agency of Providence.* **10.** a means of exerting power or influence; instrumentality: *nominated by the agency of friends.* [< ML *agentia* < L *ag-* (root of *agere* to do) + *-entia* -ENCY]

—**Syn. 10.** intercession, means, good offices.

A′gency for Interna′tional Devel′opment. See **AID.**

a′gency shop′, a shop in which the union represents all workers in the bargaining unit and collects dues and fees from nonunion as well as union members.

a·gen·da[1] (ə jen′də), *n., formally a pl. of* **agendum,** *but usually used as a sing. with pl.* **-das** *or* **-da.** a list, plan, outline, or the like, of things to be done, matters to be acted or voted upon, etc.: *The chairman says we have a lengthy agenda this afternoon.* [< L, pl. of *agendum* that which is to be done, ger. of *agere* to do]

a·gen·dum (ə jen′dəm), *n., pl.* **-da** (-də), **-dums.** an agenda. [< L, ger. of *agere* to do]

a·gen·e·sis (ā jen′i sis), *n. Med.* **1.** defective development or absence, as of a limb; aplasia. **2.** sterility; impotence; barrenness. Also, **a·ge·ne·sia** (ā′jə nē′zhə, -zhē ə -sē ə). [< NL; see A-[6], GENESIS] —**a·ge·net·ic** (ā′jə net′ik), *adj.*

A·ge·nor (ə jē′nôr, -nər), *n. Class. Myth.* **1.** a son of Poseidon and Libya who became king of Phoenicia. **2.** (in the *Iliad*) a son of Antenor and Theano who was noted for his bravery.

a·gent (ā′jənt), *n.* **1.** a person authorized by another to act on his behalf: *My agent has power to sign my name.* **2.** one who or that which acts or has the power to act. **3.** a natural force or object producing or used for obtaining specific results: *Many insects are agents of fertilization.* **4.** an active cause; an efficient cause. **5.** one who works for or manages an agency. **6.** one who acts in an official capacity, as a policeman, guard, detective, spy, etc.: *an FBI agent; the secret agents of a foreign power.* **7.** See **Indian agent. 8.** a representative of a business firm, esp. a traveling salesman; a canvasser; solicitor. **9.** *Chem.* a substance which causes a reaction. **10.** *Brit.* a campaign manager; an election agent. —*adj.* **11.** *Rare.* acting; exerting power (opposed to *patient*). [< L *agent-* (s. of *agēns* (prp.) doing), equiv. to *ag-* (root of *agere* to do) + *-ent-* -ENT]

—**Syn. 1.** representative, deputy. **3.** means.

a·gen·tial (ā jen′shəl), *adj.* **1.** pertaining to an agent or agency. **2.** *Gram.* agentive. [AGENT + -IAL]

a·gen·ti·val (ā′jən tī′vəl), *adj.* agentive. [AGENTIVE + -AL[1]]

a·gen·tive (ā′jən tiv), *adj. Gram.* pertaining to, or productive of, a form which indicates an agent or agency. [AGENT + -IVE]

A′gent Or′ange, a powerful herbicide and defoliant, containing a toxic impurity, dioxin, and used by U.S. armed forces during the Vietnam War to defoliate jungles concealing enemy troops and supply bases and now believed to cause serious health damage, including cancer, to those exposed to it and birth defects in their offspring.

a·gent pro·vo·ca·teur (A zhäN′ prô vô kA tœr′), *pl.* **a·gents pro·vo·ca·teurs** (A zhäN′ prô vô kA tœr′). *French.* a secret agent hired to incite suspected persons to some illegal action, outbreak, etc., that will make them liable to punishment.

age′ of consent′, the age at which one, esp. a female, is considered by law to be able to give consent, to marriage or illegal sexual intercourse.

age′ of discre′tion, *Law.* the age at which a person becomes legally responsible for certain acts and competent to exercise certain powers.

Age′ of Rea′son, any period in history characterized by a critical approach to religious, social, and philosophical matters that seeks to repudiate beliefs or systems not based on or justifiable by reason.

Age′ of Rea′son, The, a pamphlet (1795) by Thomas Paine.

age-old (āj′ōld′), *adj.* ancient; traditional.

ag·er·a·tum (aj′ə rā′təm, ə jer′ə-), *n.* **1.** any of several composite plants of the genus *Ageratum,* esp. *A. Houstonianum,* having small, dense, blue or white flower heads, often grown in gardens. **2.** any of various other composite plants, as the mistflower, having blue or white flowers. [< NL < L *agēraton* < Gk *agḗraton,* neut. of *agḗratos* unaging, equiv. to *a-* A-[6] + *gērat-* (s. of *gêras*) old age + *-os* adj. suffix]

a·geu·si·a (ə gyōō′zē ə, -sē ə, -zhə, -shə), *n. Pathol.* loss or impairment of the sense of taste. Also, **a·geu·sti·a** (ə gyōō′stē ə). [< NL, equiv. to A-[6] + *geus-* (var. s. of Gk *geúesthai* to taste) + *-ia* -Y[3]] —**a·geu·sic** (ə gyōō′zik, -sik), *adj.*

Ag·ga·da (ä gä dä′, ə gä′də), *n., pl.* **-doth** (-dôt′, -dōt). Aggadah.

Ag·ga·dah (ä gä dä′, ə gä′də), *n., pl.* **-doth** (-dôt′, -dōt). the nonlegal or narrative material, as parables, maxims, or anecdotes, in the Talmud and other rabbinical literature, serving either to illustrate the meaning or purpose of the law, custom, or Biblical passage being discussed or to introduce a different, unrelated topic. Also, **Aggada.** [< Heb *haggādhāh,* deriv. of *higgīdh* to narrate] —**Ag·gad·ic, ag·gad·ic** (ə gad′ik, ə gä′dik), *adj.*

ag·ger (aj′ər), *n.* **1.** a high tide in which the water rises to a certain level, recedes, then rises again. **2.** a low tide in which the water recedes to a certain level, rises slightly, then recedes again. **3.** (in ancient Roman building) an earthen mound or rampart, esp. one having no revetment. Also called **double tide** (for defs. 1, 2). [< L: heap, pile, equiv. to *ag-* AG- + *ger-* root of *gerere* to carry, bring]

Ag·ge·us (ə jē′əs), *n. Douay Bible.* Haggai.

ag·gie[1] (ag′ē), *n.* agate (def. 2).

ag·gie[2] (ag′ē), *n. Slang.* a student at an agricultural college. [*ag-* (from *agricultural*) + -IE]

Ag·gie (ag′ē), *n.* a girl's given name, form of **Agatha** or **Agnes.**

ag·gior·na·men·to (äd jôr′nä men′tô), *n., pl.* **-ti** (-tē). *Italian.* the act of bringing something up to date to meet current needs.

ag·glom·er·ate (*v.* ə glom′ə rāt′; *adj., n.* ə glom′ər it, -ə rāt′), *v.,* **-at·ed, -at·ing,** *adj., n.* —*v.t., v.i.* **1.** to collect or gather into a cluster or mass. —*adj.* **2.** gathered together into a cluster or mass. **3.** *Bot.* crowded into a dense cluster, but not cohering. —*n.* **4.** a mass of things clustered together. **5.** rock composed of rounded or angular volcanic fragments. [< L *agglomerāt(us)* (ptp. of *agglomerāre*), equiv. to *ag-* AG- + *glomer-* (s. of *glomus* ball of yarn) + *-ātus* -ATE[1]] —**ag·glom·er·a·tive** (ə glom′ə rā′tiv, -ər ə tiv), *adj.* —**ag·glom′er·a′tor,** *n.*

ag·glom·er·a·tion (ə glom′ə rā′shən), *n.* **1.** a jumbled cluster or mass of varied parts. **2.** the act or process of agglomerating. [AGGLOMERATE + -ION]

—**Syn. 1.** cluster, conglomeration, aggregation, conglomerate, agglomerate, aggregate.

ag·glu·ti·nant (ə glōōt′ənənt), *adj.* **1.** uniting, as glue; causing adhesion. —*n.* **2.** an agglutinating agent. [< L *agglūtinant-* (s. of *agglūtināns,* prp. of *agglūtināre*), equiv. to *agglūtin-* (see AGGLUTINATE) + *-ant* -ANT]

ag·glu·ti·nate (*v.* ə glōōt′ənāt′; *adj.* ə glōōt′ənit, -ənāt′), *v.,* **-nat·ed, -nat·ing,** *adj.* —*v.t., v.i.* **1.** to unite or cause to adhere, as with glue. **2.** *Ling.* to form by agglutination. —*adj.* **3.** united by or as by glue. **4.** agglutinative. [< L *agglūtināt(us)* (ptp. of *agglūtināre*), equiv. to *ag-* AG- + *glūtin-* (s. of *glūten* glue) + *-ātus* -ATE[1]] —**ag·glu·tin·a·bil·i·ty** (ə glōōt′ənə bil′i tē), *n.* —**ag·glu′tin·a·ble,** *adj.*

ag·glu·ti·nat·ing (ə glōōt′ənā′ting), *adj.* characterized by agglutination: *an agglutinating language.*

ag·glu·ti·na·tion (ə glōōt′ənā′shən), *n.* **1.** the act or process of uniting by glue or other tenacious substance. **2.** state of being thus united; adhesion of parts. **3.** that which is united; a mass or group cemented together. **4.** *Immunol.* the clumping of bacteria, erythrocytes, or other cells, due to the introduction of an antibody. **5.** *Ling.* a process of word formation in which morphemes, each having one relatively constant shape, are combined without fusion or morphophonemic change, and in which each grammatical category is typically represented by a single morpheme in the resulting word, esp. such a process involving the addition of one or more affixes to a base, as in Turkish, in which *ev* means "house," *ev-den* means "from a house," and *ev-ler-den* means "from houses." [AGGLUTINATE + -ION]

ag·glu·ti·na·tive (ə glōōt′ənā′tiv, ə glōōt′ənə-), *adj.* **1.** tending or having power to agglutinate or unite: *an agglutinative substance.* **2.** *Ling.* (of a language or construction) characterized by agglutination. [AGGLUTINATE + -IVE]

ag·glu·ti·nin (ə glo͞ot′ənin), *n.* *Immunol.* an antibody which causes agglutination. [AGGLUTIN(ATE) + -IN[2]]

ag·glu·tin·o·gen (ag′lo͞o tin′ə jən), *n.* *Immunol.* an antigen present in a bacterial body which when injected into an animal causes the production of agglutinins. [AGGLUTIN(ATE) + -O- + -GEN] —**ag·glu·tin·o·gen·ic** (ag′lo͞o tin′ə jen′ik, ə glo͞ot′ənə-), *adj.*

ag·grade (ə grād′), *v.t.*, **-grad·ed, -grad·ing.** *Phys. Geog.* to raise the grade or level of (a river valley, a stream bed, etc.) by depositing detritus, sediment, or the like. [AG- + GRADE] —**ag·gra·da·tion** (ag′rə dā′shən), *n.* —**ag′gra·da′tion·al,** *adj.*

ag·gran·dise (ə gran′dīz, ag′rən dīz), *v.t.*, **-dised, -dis·ing.** *Chiefly Brit.* aggrandize. —**ag·gran·dise·ment** (ə gran′diz mənt), *n.* —**ag·gran′dis′er,** *n.*

ag·gran·dize (ə gran′dīz, ag′rən dīz′), *v.t.*, **-dized, -diz·ing.** **1.** to widen in scope; increase in size or intensity; enlarge; extend. **2.** to make great or greater in power, wealth, rank, or honor. **3.** to make (something) appear greater. Also, *esp. Brit.*, **aggrandise.** [< MF *aggrandiss-* (long s. of *aggrandir* to magnify), equiv. to *ag-* AG- + *grand* (see GRAND) + *-iss* irregularly equated with -IZE[1]] —**ag·gran·dize·ment** (ə gran′diz mənt), *n.* —**ag·gran′diz′er,** *n.*
—**Syn. 2.** exalt. **3.** magnify. —**Ant. 1.** reduce. **3.** minimize.

ag·gra·vate (ag′rə vāt′), *v.t.*, **-vat·ed, -vat·ing. 1.** to make worse or more severe; intensify, as anything evil, disorderly, or troublesome: *to aggravate a grievance; to aggravate an illness.* **2.** to annoy; irritate; exasperate: *His questions aggravate her.* **3.** to cause to become irritated or inflamed: *The child's constant rubbing aggravated the rash.* [< L *aggravāt(us)* (ptp. of *aggravāre*), equiv. to *ag-* AG- + *grav-* (see GRAVE[2]) + *-ātus* -ATE[1]] —**ag′gra·vat′ing·ly,** *adv.* —**ag′gra·va′tive,** *adj.* —**ag′gra·va′tor,** *n.*
—**Syn. 1.** heighten, increase. AGGRAVATE, INTENSIFY both mean to increase in degree. To AGGRAVATE is to make more serious or more grave: *to aggravate a danger, an offense, a wound.* To INTENSIFY is perceptibly to increase intensity, force, energy, vividness, etc.: *to intensify heat, color, rage.* —**Ant. 1.** alleviate.
—**Usage.** AGGRAVATE, in the sense of "to annoy, provoke, or irritate," is usually avoided in formal contexts. In informal usage, it is widespread and generally unobjectionable.

ag·gra·va·tion (ag′rə vā′shən), *n.* **1.** an increase in intensity, seriousness, or severity; act of making worse: *an aggravation of pain.* **2.** state of being aggravated. **3.** something that increases the intensity, degree, or severity of something. **4.** irritation; annoyance: *Johnny causes me so much aggravation!* **5.** a source of irritation or annoyance: *Johnny's such an aggravation to her!* [< ML *aggravātiōn-* (s. of *aggravātiō*), deriv. of *aggravāt(us)*. See AGGRAVATE, -ION]
—**Usage.** AGGRAVATION, in the sense of def. 5, follows the same usage pattern as AGGRAVATE.

ag·gre·gate (*adj., n.* ag′rə git, -gāt′; *v.* ag′rə gāt′), *adj., n., v.,* **-gat·ed, -gat·ing.** —*adj.* **1.** formed by the conjunction or collection of particulars into a whole mass or sum; total; combined: *the aggregate amount of indebtedness.* **2.** *Bot.* **a.** (of a flower) formed of florets collected in a dense cluster but not cohering, as in composite plants. **b.** (of a fruit) composed of a cluster of carpels belonging to the same flower, as the raspberry. —*n.* **3.** a sum, mass, or assemblage of particulars; a total or gross amount: *the aggregate of all past experience.* **4.** a cluster of soil granules not larger than a small crumb. **5.** *Geol.* a mixture of different mineral substances separable by mechanical means, as granite. **6.** any of various hard, inert materials, as sand, gravel, or pebbles, added to a cementing agent to make concrete, plaster, etc. —*v.t.* **7.** to bring together; collect into one sum, mass, or body. **8.** to amount to (the number of): *The guns captured will aggregate five or six hundred.* —*v.i.* **9.** to combine and form a collection or mass. [< L *aggregāt(us)* (ptp. of *aggregāre*), equiv. to *ag-* AG- + *greg-* (s. of *grex* flock) + *-ātus* -ATE[1]] —**ag·gre·ga·ble** (ag′rə gə bəl), *adj.* —**ag′gre·gate·ly,** *adv.* —**ag′gre·gate·ness,** *n.* —**ag·gre·ga·tive** (ag′rə gā′tiv), *adj.* —**ag·gre·ga·to·ry** (ag′rə gə tôr′ē, -tōr′ē), *adj.*
—**Syn. 1.** added, complete, whole. **7.** assemble, amass, accumulate, gather.

ag·gre·ga·tion (ag′rə gā′shən), *n.* **1.** a group or mass of distinct or varied things, persons, etc.: *an aggregation of complainants.* **2.** collection into an unorganized whole. **3.** state of being so collected. **4.** *Biol., Ecol.* a group of organisms of the same or different species living closely together but less integrated than a society. [< ML *aggregātiōn-* (s. of *aggregātiō*), deriv. of *aggregāt(us)*. See AGGREGATE, -ION]

ag·gress (ə gres′), *v.i.* **1.** to commit the first act of hostility or offense; attack first. **2.** to begin to quarrel. [< ML *aggress(āre)* (to) attack < L *aggress(us)* (ptp. of *aggredī* to attack), equiv. to *ag-* AG- + *gred-* (see GRADE) + *-tus* ptp. suffix]

ag·gres·sion (ə gresh′ən), *n.* **1.** the action of a state in violating by force the rights of another state, particularly its territorial rights; an unprovoked offensive, attack, invasion, or the like. **2.** any offensive action or procedure; an inroad or encroachment: *an aggression upon one's rights.* **3.** the practice of making assaults or attacks; offensive action in general. **4.** *Psychol.* outwardly or inwardly directed, overt or suppressed hostility either innate or resulting from continued frustration. [< L *aggressiōn-* (s. of *aggressiō*), equiv. to *aggress(us)* (see AGGRESS) + *-iōn-* -ION]

ag·gres·sive (ə gres′iv), *adj.* **1.** characterized by or tending toward unprovoked offensives, attacks, invasions, or the like; militantly forward or menacing: *aggressive acts against Hungary.* **2.** vigorously energetic, esp. in the use of initiative and forcefulness; boldly assertive and forward: *an aggressive salesman.* [AGGRESS(ION) + -IVE] —**ag·gres′sive·ly,** *adv.* —**ag·gres′sive·ness,** *n.*
—**Syn. 1.** pugnacious, militant. **2.** pushing, enterprising, assertive. —**Ant. 2.** retiring.

ag·gres·sor (ə gres′ər), *n.* one who attacks first or initiates hostilities; an assailant or invader. [< LL, L *aggress(us)* (see AGGRESS) + *-or* -OR[2]]

ag·grieve (ə grēv′), *v.t.*, **-grieved, -griev·ing. 1.** to oppress or wrong grievously; injure by injustice (usually used passively). **2.** to afflict with pain, anxiety, etc.; trouble sorely. [ME *agreve(n)* < MF *agrever* < L *aggravāre* to make heavy, worsen, equiv. to *ag-* AG- + *grav-* (see GRAVE[2]) + *-āre* inf. suffix]

ag·grieved (ə grēvd′), *adj.* **1.** wronged, offended, or injured: *He felt himself aggrieved.* **2.** *Law.* deprived of legal rights or claims. **3.** troubled; worried; disturbed; unhappy. [AGGRIEVE + -ED[2]] —**ag·griev·ed·ly** (ə grē′vid lē), *adv.* —**ag·griev′ed·ness,** *n.*
—**Syn. 1.** abused, harmed, wounded.

Agh., afghani.

a·gha (ä′gə), *n.* aga.

a·ghast (ə gast′, ə gäst′), *adj.* struck with overwhelming shock or amazement; filled with sudden fright or horror: *They stood aghast at this unforeseen disaster.* [ME *agast* frightened, ptp. of *agasten*, equiv. to *a-* A-[3] + *gasten*, deriv. of OE *gǣstan* to frighten]

ag·i·la·wood (ag′ə lə wo͝od′), *n.* agalloch. [< Pg *agila* (see AGALLOCH) + WOOD[1]]

ag·ile (aj′əl *or, esp. Brit.*, aj′īl), *adj.* **1.** quick and well-coordinated in movement; lithe: *an agile leap.* **2.** active; lively: *an agile person.* **3.** marked by an ability to think quickly; mentally acute or aware. [earlier *agil* < L *agil(is)*, equiv. to *ag-* (root of *agere* to do) + *-ilis* -ILE] —**ag′ile·ly,** *adv.* —**ag′ile·ness,** *n.*
—**Syn. 1.** nimble, sprightly. **2.** brisk, spry. —**Ant. 1.** awkward. **2.** sluggish.

a·gil·i·ty (ə jil′i tē), *n.* **1.** the power of moving quickly and easily; nimbleness: *agility of the body.* **2.** the ability to think and draw conclusions quickly; intellectual acuity. [late ME *agilite* < MF < L *agilitāt-* (s. of *agilitās*). See AGILE, -ITY]

Ag·in·court (aj′in kōrt′, -kôrt′; *Fr.* A zhan ko͞or′), *n.* a village in N France, near Calais: victory of the English over the French 1415. 207 (1962).

ag·i·o (aj′ē ō′), *n., pl.* **-os. 1.** a premium on money in exchange. **2.** an allowance for the difference in value of two currencies. **3.** an allowance given or taken on bills of exchange from other countries, as to balance exchange expenses. **4.** agiotage. [< It *a(g)gio* exchange, premium < ?]

ag·i·o·tage (aj′ē ə tij), *n.* **1.** the business of dealing in foreign exchange. **2.** *Rare.* speculative dealing in securities. [< F, equiv. to *agiot(er)* to speculate (*agiot* exchange < It *aggio* AGIO) + *-age* -AGE]

a·gist (ə jist′), *v.t.* *Obs.* to feed or pasture (livestock) for a fee. [< AF, MF *agist(er)* (to) give lodgings to, equiv. to *a-* A-[5] + *gister* to lodge, lie < Gmc; cf. OE *giestian* to lodge, deriv. of *giest* GUEST]

a·gist·er (ə jis′tər), *n.* *Obs.* one who agists. Also, **a·gis′tor.** [ME < AF *agistour*, equiv. to *agist(er)* (see AGIST) + *-our* -ER[1]]

a·gist·ment (ə jist′mənt), *n.* *Obs.* **1.** the act of agisting. **2.** a contract or an agreement to agist. **3.** the fee paid or the profit made in agisting. [AGIST + -MENT]

agit., (in prescriptions) shake, stir. [< L *agitā*]

ag·i·tate (aj′i tāt′), *v.,* **-tat·ed, -tat·ing.** —*v.t.* **1.** to move or force into violent, irregular action: *The wind agitates the sea.* **2.** to shake or move briskly: *The machine agitated the mixture.* **3.** to move to and fro; impart regular motion to: *to agitate a fan.* **4.** to disturb or excite emotionally; arouse; perturb: *a crowd agitated to a frenzy by impassioned oratory; a man agitated by disquieting news.* **5.** to call attention to by speech or writing; discuss; debate: *to agitate the question.* **6.** to consider on all sides; revolve in the mind; plan. —*v.i.* **7.** to arouse or attempt to arouse public interest, as in some political or social question: *to agitate for the repeal of a tax.* [< L *agitāt(us)* (ptp. of *agitāre* to set in motion), equiv. to *ag-* (root of *agere* to drive) + *-it-* freq. suffix + *-ātus* -ATE[1]] —**ag·i·ta·ble** (aj′i tə bəl), *adj.* —**ag′i·tat′ed·ly,** *adv.* —**ag′i·ta′tive,** *adj.*
—**Syn. 1.** disturb, toss. **3.** wave. **4.** ruffle, fluster. **5.** dispute. —**Ant. 1.** calm.

ag·i·ta·tion (aj′i tā′shən), *n.* **1.** act or process of agitating; state of being agitated: *She left in great agitation.* **2.** persistent urging of a political or social question before the public. [< L *agitātiōn-* (s. of *agitātiō*), deriv. of *agitāt(us)*. See AGITATE, -ION] —**ag′i·ta′tion·al,** *adj.*
—**Syn. 1.** tumult, storm; unrest, disquiet; struggle, conflict; perturbation, ado. AGITATION, DISTURBANCE, EXCITEMENT, TURMOIL imply inner unrest, uneasiness or apprehension. AGITATION implies a shaken state of emotions, usually perceptible in the face or movements: *With evident agitation she opened the telegram.* DISTURBANCE implies an inner disquiet caused by worry, indecision, apprehension, and the like: *Long-continued mental disturbance is a cause of illness.* EXCITEMENT implies a highly emotional state caused by either agreeable or distressing circumstances: *excitement over a proposed trip, unexpected good news, a fire.* TURMOIL suggests such a struggle or conflict of emotions that one is unable to think consecutively: *Her thoughts were in a hopeless turmoil.* **2.** debate, discussion, argument.

a·gi·ta·to (aj′i tä′tō; *It.* ä′jē tä′tô), *adj.* *Music.* agitated; restless or hurried in movement or style. [< It < L *agitāt(us)*. See AGITATE]

ag·i·ta·tor (aj′i tā′tər), *n.* **1.** a person who stirs up others in order to strengthen his own cause or that of his party, church, union, etc. **2.** a machine or device for agitating and mixing. [< L: one who sets in motion, deriv. to *agitāt(us)*. See AGITATE, -OR[2]] —**ag·i·ta·to·ri·al** (aj′i tə tôr′ē əl, -tōr′-), *adj.*

ag·it·prop (aj′it prop′), *n.* **1.** agitation and propaganda, esp. for the cause of communism. **2.** (*often cap.*) an agency or department, as of a government, that directs and coordinates agitation and propaganda. **3.** one who is trained or takes part in such activities. —*adj.* **4.** of or pertaining to agitprop. [short for Russ *Agitpropbyuro*, equiv. to *agit(atsiya)* agitation + *prop(aganda)* propaganda + *byuro* bureau] —**ag′it·prop′ist,** *n.*

A·gla·ia (ə glā′ə), *n.* *Class. Myth.* **1.** one of the Graces. **2.** the mother of Acrisius and Proteus. [< Gk: splendor, beauty]

A·gla′o·phon of Tha′sos (ə glou′ə fon′), fl. 6th to 5th centuries B.C., Greek painter: father and teacher of Polygnotus.

A·glau·ros (ā glôr′os), *n.* *Class. Myth.* Agraulos.

A·gla·us (ə glā′əs), *n.* *Class. Myth.* a son of Thyestes and a naiad, slain by Atreus in revenge for Thyestes' adultery with the wife of Atreus.

a·gleam (ə glēm′), *adj.* gleaming; bright; radiant: *a city agleam with lights.* [A-[1] + GLEAM]

ag·let (ag′lit), *n.* **1.** a metal tag or sheath at the end of a lace used for tying, as of a shoelace. **2.** (in the 16th and 17th centuries) an ornament at the end of a point or other ribbon used to secure a garment. **3.** aiguillette (def. 1). Also, **aiglet.** [late ME < MF *aiguillette*, equiv. to *aiguille* needle (see AIGUILLE) + *-ette* -ET]

a·gley (ə glē′, ə glī′), *adv.* *Chiefly Scot. and North Eng.* off the right line; awry; wrong. [A-[1] + *gley* GLEE[2]]

a·glim·mer (ə glim′ər), *adj.* glimmering; shining faintly or unsteadily. [A-[1] + GLIMMER]

a·glint (ə glint′), *adj.* displaying bright points of light, as by reflection; glittering: *a diamond tiara aglint under the ballroom lights.* [A-[1] + GLINT]

a·glis·ten (ə glis′ən), *adj.* refulgent; glistening: *a young lieutenant with shoes aglisten.* [A-[1] + GLISTEN]

a·glit·ter (ə glit′ər), *adj.* glittering; sparkling. [A-[1] + GLITTER]

a·glos·si·a (ə glô′sē ə, ə glos′ē ə), *n.* **1.** *Pathol.* absence of the tongue, esp. congenital absence of the tongue. **2.** inability to speak. [< Gk: want of eloquence, equiv. to *a-* A-[6] + *gloss(a)* tongue + *-ia* -Y[3]]

a·glow (ə glō′), *adj.* glowing: *a house aglow with lights; a face aglow with happiness.* [A-[1] + GLOW]

a·glu·con (ə glo͞o′kon), *n.* *Biochem.* an aglycon, esp. one combined with glucose to form a glycoside. Also, **a·glu·cone** (ə glo͞o′kōn). [< Gk *a-* together + *gluk-* (var. sp. of *glyk-*, s. of *glykýs*) sweet + *-on*; see -ONE]

a·gly (ə glē′, ə glī′), *adv.* *Chiefly Scot. and North Eng.* agley.

a·gly·con (ə glī′kon), *n.* *Biochem.* a noncarbohydrate group, usually an alcohol or phenol, combined with a sugar to form a glycoside. Also, **a·gly·cone** (ə glī′kōn). Cf. **aglucon.** [see AGLUCON]

AGM, air-to-ground missile.

ag·ma (ag′mə), *n.* **1.** (in Latin and Greek) the velar nasal consonant sound, esp. in those forms where it was represented by the letter *g* or by *gamma.* **2.** eng. [< LGk; Gk: fracture]

AGMA, American Guild of Musical Artists. Also, **A.G.M.A.**

ag·mi·nate (ag′mə nit, -nāt′), *adj.* aggregated or clustered together. Also, **ag′mi·nat′ed.** [< L *agmin-* (s. of *agmen*) army on march, throng, crowd + -ATE[1]]

ag·nail (ag′nāl′) *n.* **1.** hangnail. **2.** whitlow. [ME; OE *angnægl*, equiv. to *ang-* tight, hard, painful + *nægl* corn (on foot), NAIL]

ag·nate (ag′nāt), *n.* **1.** a kinsman whose connection is traceable exclusively through males. **2.** any male relation on the father's side. —*adj.* **3.** related or akin through males or on the father's side. **4.** allied or akin. [< L *agnāt(us)* paternal kinsman, var. of *ad(g)nātus* born to (ptp. of *adgnāscī*), equiv. to *ad-* AD- + *-gnā* be born + *-tus* ptp. suffix] —**ag·nat·ic** (ag nat′ik), **ag·nat′i·cal,** *adj.* —**ag·nat′i·cal·ly,** *adv.* —**ag·na·tion** (ag nā′shən), *n.*

Ag·na·tha (ag′nə thə), *n.* the class of vertebrates comprising the lampreys, hagfishes, and several extinct forms, having no jaws or paired appendages. [< NL, equiv. to *a-* A-[6] + Gk *gnáth(os)* jaw + *-a* L neut. pl. ending]

ag·na·thous (ag′nə thəs), *adj.* *Zool.* **1.** having no jaws. **2.** belonging or pertaining to the family *Agnatha.* [A-[6] + -GNATHOUS]

ag·nel (A nyel′), *n., pl.* **ag·neaux** (A nyō′). a gold coin of France of the 13th–16th centuries, bearing the figure of a lamb. [< F < MF: lit., lamb < L *agnell(us)*, dim. of *agn(us)* lamb]

Ag·nes (ag′nis), *n.* **1. Saint,** A.D. 292?–304?, Roman Catholic child martyr. **2.** a girl's given name.

Ag·new (ag′no͞o, -nyo͞o), *n.* **1. Spi·ro T(heodore)** (spēr′ō), born 1918, U.S. politician: vice-president 1969–73 (resigned). **2.** a boy's given name.

Ag·ni (ug′nē; *Eng.* ag′nē), *n.* **1.** *Hindu Myth.* the god of fire, one of the three chief divinities of the Vedas. **2.** a boy's given name. [< Skt: fire, the fire-god; akin to L *ignis*, Russ *ogon′* fire]

ag·nize (ag nīz′, ag′nīz), *v.t.,* **-nized, -niz·ing.** *Archaic.* to recognize; acknowledge; own. [< L *agn(ōscere)* (to) recognize (*a(d)-* AD- + *(g)nōscere* to come to know, equiv. to *gnō-* know + *-scere* -ESCE) + -IZE, modeled on COGNIZE, RECOGNIZE]

ag·noi·ol·o·gy (ag′noi ol′ə jē), *n.* *Archaic.* the branch of philosophy which investigates the nature and extent of human ignorance. [< Gk *ágnoia* (*a-* A-[6] + **gnoia* -NOIA) + -O- + -LOGY]

ag·no·men (ag nō′mən), *n., pl.* **-nom·i·na** (-nom′ə nə). **1.** an additional, fourth name given to a person by the ancient Romans in allusion to some achievement or other circumstance, as *Africanus* in *Publius Cornelius Scipio Africanus.* **2.** a nickname. [< LL, equiv. to *ad-* AD- + *nōmen* name, with alter. to *ag-* through influence of *agnōscere*; see AGNIZE] —**ag·nom·i·nal** (ag nom′ə nəl), *adj.*

ag·no·sia (ag nō′zhə, -zhē ə, -zē ə), *n.* *Psychiatry.* partial or total inability to recognize objects by use of the senses. [< NL < Gk *agnōsía*, equiv. to *a-* A-[6] + *gnō-* (s. of *gignṓskein* to KNOW) + -S(IS) + *-ia* -Y[3]]

ag·nos·tic (ag nos′tik), *n.* **1.** one who holds that the ultimate cause (God) and the essential nature of things are unknown and unknowable, or that human knowledge is limited to experience. **2.** *Philos.* one who denies or doubts the possibility of ultimate knowledge in some area of study. —*adj.* **3.** of or pertaining to agnostics or agnosticism. **4.** asserting the uncertainty of all claims to knowledge. [< Gk *agnōst(ós)* not known, incapable of being known (*a-* A-[6] + *gnōs-*, var. of *gnō-*; see AGNOSIA + *-tos* adj. suffix) + *-tic*, after GNOSTIC] —**ag·nos′ti·cal·ly,** *adv.* —**Syn. 1.** See **atheist.**

ag·nos·ti·cism (ag nos′ti siz′əm), *n.* **1.** the doctrine or belief of an agnostic. **2.** an intellectual doctrine or attitude affirming the uncertainty of all claims to ultimate knowledge. [AGNOSTIC + -ISM]

Ag·nus De·i (ag′nəs dē′ī, ä′nyo͞os de′ē), **1.** *Eccles.* **a.** a figure of a lamb as emblematic of Christ. **b.** such a representation with the nimbus inscribed with the cross about its head, and supporting the banner of the cross. **2.** *Rom. Cath. Ch.* **a.** a wax medallion stamped with this figure and blessed by the pope, or a fragment of such a medallion. **b.** a triple chant preceding the communion in the Mass. **c.** the music accompanying this prayer. **3.** (*italics.*) *Anglican Ch.* **a.** an invocation beginning "O Lamb of God," said or sung in the communion service. **b.** a musical setting for this. [< L]

a·go (ə gō′), *adj.* **1.** gone; gone by; past (usually prec. by a noun): *five days ago.* —*adv.* **2.** in past time: *It happened long ago.* [ME *ago, agoon,* OE *āgān,* ptp. of *āgān* to go by, pass, equiv. to *ā-* A-[3] + *gān* to GO[1]]

a·gog (ə gog′), *adj.* **1.** highly excited by eagerness, curiosity, anticipation, etc. —*adv.* **2.** in a state of eager desire; excitedly. [var. of *on gog* (in phrase *set on gog* rouse, stir up); *gog* perh. akin to GOGGLE]

-agog, var. of **-agogue.**

a·gog′ic ac′cent (ə goj′ik, ə gō′jik), *Music.* stress given to a note through prolonged duration. [< Gk *agōg(ē)* course + -IC (modeled on G *agogisch*)]

a·gog·ics (ə goj′iks, ə gō′jiks), *n.* (*usually construed as sing.*) *Music.* the theory that accent within a musical phrase can be produced by modifying the duration of certain notes rather than by increasing dynamic stress. [see AGOGIC ACCENT, -ICS]

à go·go (ä gō′gō′), as much as you like; to your heart's content; galore (used esp. in the names of cabarets, discothèques, etc.): *They danced all night at the Mistral à Gogo.* Also, **à Gogo, à go-go.** [< F]

-agogue, a suffix occurring in loan words from Greek where it meant "leading," "leader," "course," "withdrawing agent." Also, **-agog.** [< Gk *-agōg(ós),* -ē, -on, akin to *ágein* to lead, c. L *agere* to lead, drive, Icel *aka* to carry, convey]

ag·on (ag′ōn, -on), *n., pl.* **a·go·nes** (ə gō′nēz). **1.** (in ancient Greece) a contest in which prizes were awarded in any of a number of events, as athletics, dramatics, music, poetry, and painting. **2.** (*italics*) *Greek.* (in ancient Greek drama) a formalized debate or argumentation, esp. in comedy: usually following the *proagon* and preceding the *parabasis.* **3.** *Literature.* conflict, esp. between the protagonist and the antagonist. [< Gk *agṓn* struggle, contest]

Ag·on (ag′on), a ballet (1953–57) by Stravinsky.

ag·o·nal (ag′ə nəl), *adj.* of, pertaining to, or symptomatic of agony, esp. paroxysmal distress, as the death throes. [AGON(Y) + -AL[1]]

a·gone (ə gôn′, ə gon′), *adv., adj. Archaic.* ago.

a·gon·ic (ā gon′ik), *adj.* not forming an angle. [< Gk *ágōn(os)* (*a-* A-[6] + *gōn-* s. of *gōnía* angle + *-os* adj. suffix) + -IC]

agon′ic line′, an imaginary line on the surface of the earth connecting all points at which the declination of the magnetic field of the earth is zero.

ag·o·nise (ag′ə nīz′), *v.i., v.t.,* **-nised, -nis·ing.** *Chiefly Brit.* agonize. —**ag′o·nis′ing·ly,** *adv.*

ag·o·nist (ag′ə nist), *n.* **1.** one engaged in a contest, conflict, struggle, etc., esp. the protagonist in a literary work. **2.** one who is torn by inner conflict. **3.** *Physiol.* a contracting muscle whose action is opposed by another muscle. Cf. **antagonist** (def. 3). [< LL *agōnist(a)* < Gk *agōnistḗs* contestant, equiv. to *agṓn* AGON + *-istēs* -IST]

ag·o·nis·tic (ag′ə nis′tik), *adj.* **1.** combative; striving to overcome in argument. **2.** straining for effect: *agonistic humor.* **3.** *Gk. Antiq.* of or pertaining to athletic contests. Also, **ag′o·nis′ti·cal.** [< Gk *agōnistik(ós),* equiv. to *agonist(ḗs)* AGONIST + *-ikos* -IC] —**ag′o·nis′ti·cal·ly,** *adv.*

ag·o·nize (ag′ə nīz′), *v.,* **-nized, -niz·ing.** —*v.i.* **1.** to suffer extreme pain or violent anguish; be in agony. **2.** to put forth great effort of any kind. —*v.t.* **3.** to distress with extreme pain; torture. Also, *esp. Brit.,* **agonise.** [< ML *agōniz(āre)* < Gk *agōnízesthai* (to) struggle (for a prize), equiv. to *agōn-* AGON + *-ize(sthai)* -IZE] —**ag′o·niz′ing·ly,** *adv.*

ag·o·nized (ag′ə nīzd′), *adj.* involving or accompanied by agony or severe struggle: *an agonized effort.* [AGONIZE + -ED[2]] —**ag·o·niz·ed·ly** (ag′ə nī′zid lē), *adv.*

ag·o·niz·ing (ag′ə nī′zing), *adj.* resulting in agony. [AGONIZE + -ING[2]]

ag·o·ny (ag′ə nē), *n., pl.* **-nies.** **1.** extreme and generally prolonged pain; intense suffering. **2.** a display or outburst of intense mental or emotional excitement: *an agony of utter joy.* **3.** the struggle preceding natural death: *mortal agony.* **4.** a violent struggle. **5.** (*often cap.*) *Theol.* the sufferings of Christ in the garden of Gethsemane. [ME *agonye* < LL *agōnia* < Gk, equiv. to *agṓn* AGON + *-ia* -Y[3]]
—**Syn. 1.** distress, throe, paroxysm, pang; ache. See **pain. 2.** anguish, torment, torture. —**Ant. 1, 2.** comfort.

ag′ony col′umn, *Informal.* a section or column in a newspaper containing advertisements by individuals seeking missing relatives or lost pets or possessions, announcing the end of a marriage, etc.

ag·o·ra[1] (ag′ər ə), *n., pl.* **-o·rae** (-ə rē′). (in ancient Greece) **1.** a popular political assembly. **2.** the place where such an assembly met, originally a marketplace or public square. [< Gk *agorá* marketplace, equiv. to *agor-* (var. s. of *ageírein* to gather together) + *-ā* n. suffix]

a·go·ra[2] (ä gō rä′, -gôr′ə; *Heb.* ä gō rä′), *n., pl.* **a·go·roth** (ä gôr′ōt, -gôr′-; *Heb.* ä gō rôt′). an aluminum coin of Israel, the 100th part of a pound, equivalent to about .003 of a U.S. dollar: replaced the prutah as the fractional unit in 1960. Also, **agura.** [< Heb]

Ag·o·rae·a (ag′ə rē′ə), *n. Class. Myth.* an epithet of Athena, meaning "of the market place."

Ag·o·rae·us (ag′ə rē′əs), *n. Class. Myth.* an epithet of Zeus and Hermes, meaning "of the market place."

ag·o·ra·pho·bi·a (ag′ər ə fō′bē ə), *n. Psychiatry.* an abnormal fear of being in an open space. [AGORA + -PHOBIA]

a·gou·ta (ə gōō′tə), *n. Zool.* the Haitian solenodon, *Solenodon paradoxus.* [< F < Sp *aguta* < Taino]

a·gou·ti (ə gōō′tē), *n., pl.* **-tis, -ties.** **1.** any of several short-haired, short-eared, rabbitlike rodents of the genus *Dasyprocta,* of South and Central America and the West Indies, destructive to sugar cane. **2.** an irregularly barred pattern of the fur of certain rodents. **3.** an animal having fur of this pattern. [< F < Sp *agutí* < Guarani *acutí*]

Agouti
Dasyprocta aguti
(Length 20 in.)

a·gou·ty (ə gōō′tē), *n., pl.* **-ties.** agouti.

agr., **1.** agricultural. **2.** agriculture.

A·gra (ä′grə), *n.* a city in W Uttar Pradesh, in N India: site of the Taj Mahal. 462,000 (1961).

A·grae·us (ə grē′əs), *n. Class. Myth.* an epithet of Apollo, meaning "hunter."

a·graffe (ə graf′), *n.* **1.** a small cramp iron. **2.** a clasp, often richly ornamented, for clothing or armor. **3.** a device, as a hook, for preventing vibration in the section of a piano string between the pin and the bridge. **4.** (in classical architecture) a sculptural relief on the face of a keystone. Also, **a·grafe** (ə graf′). [< F, var. of *agrafe,* back formation from *agrafer* to hook, equiv. to *a-* A-[5] + *grafe* hook, cramp iron, prob. < Gmc; see GRAPE]

A·gram (ä′gräm), *n.* German name of **Zagreb.**

a·gram·ma·tism (ā gram′ə tiz′əm), *n. Pathol.* a type of aphasia, usually caused by cerebral disease, characterized by an inability to construct a grammatical or intelligible sentence while retaining the ability to speak single words. Also called **a·gram·ma·pha·sia** (ə gram′ə-fā′zhə, -zē ə), **ag·ram·mat·i·ca** (ag′rə mat′i kə), **a·gram·ma·to·lo·gi·a** (ə gram′ə tə lō′jē ə). [< Gk *agrámmat(os)* (*a-* A-[6] + *grammat-* (s. of *grámma* letter) + *-os* adj. suffix) + -ISM]

à grands frais (A GRÄN FRE′), *French.* at great cost or expense.

a·gran·u·lo·cy·to·sis (ə gran′yə lō sī tō′sis), *n. Pathol.* a serious, often fatal blood disease, characterized by a great reduction of the leucocytes. [A-[6] + GRANULOCYTE + -OSIS]

ag·ra·pha (ag′rə fə), *n.* (*construed as sing. or pl.*) the sayings of Jesus as recorded in the writings of the early Christians and in those parts of the New Testament other than the Gospels. [< Gk, neut. pl. of *ágraphos,* equiv. to *a-* A-[6] + *graph-* (s. of *gráphein* to write) + *-os* adj. suffix]

a·graph·i·a (ā graf′ē ə), *n. Pathol.* a cerebral disorder characterized by total or partial inability to write. [< NL; see A-[6], -GRAPHY] —**a·graph′ic,** *adj.*

a·grar·i·an (ə grâr′ē ən), *adj.* **1.** relating to land, land tenure, or the division of landed property: *agrarian laws.* **2.** pertaining to the advancement of agricultural groups: *an agrarian movement.* **3.** rural; agricultural. **4.** growing in fields; wild: *an agrarian plant.* —*n.* **5.** one who favors the equal division of landed property and the advancement of agricultural groups. [< L *agrāri(us)* (*agr-* s. of *ager* field + *-ārius* -ARY) + -AN] —**a·grar′i·an·ism,** *n.* —**a·grar′i·an·ly,** *adv.*

A·grau·los (ə grô′ləs), *n. Class. Myth.* the wife of Cecrops. Also, **Aglauros.**

Agrau′los the Young′er, *Class. Myth.* a daughter of Cecrops and Agraulos who was changed into stone for inciting the wrath of Hermes.

a·grav·ic (ə grav′ik, ā grav′-), *adj.* pertaining to a state or region in which the effect of gravity is zero. [A-[6] + GRAV(ITY) + -IC]

a·gré·a·tion (*Fr.* A GRĀ A SYÔN′), *n., pl.* **-tions** (*Fr.* -SYÔN′). the procedure followed by a government for determining the acceptability to a foreign government of a proposed envoy. [< F, equiv. to *agré(er)* (to) AGREE + *-ation* -ATION]

a·gree (ə grē′), *v.,* **a·greed, a·gree·ing.** —*v.i.* **1.** to be of one mind; harmonize in opinion or feeling (often fol. by *with*): *I don't agree with you.* **2.** to give consent; assent (often fol. by *to*): *He agreed to accompany the ambassador. Do you agree to the conditions?* **3.** to live in concord or without contention; harmonize in action. **4.** to come to one opinion or mind; come to an arrangement or understanding; arrive at a settlement: *They have agreed on the terms of the surrender.* **5.** to be consistent; harmonize (usually fol. by *with*): *This story agrees with hers.* **6.** to correspond; conform; resemble (usually fol. by *with*): *The play does not agree with the book.* **7.** to be suitable; comply with a preference or an ability to assimilate (usually fol. by *with*): *The same food does not agree with every person.* **8.** *Gram.* to correspond in inflectional form, as in number, case, gender, or person; to show agreement. In *The boy runs, boy* is a singular noun and *runs* agrees with it in number. —*v.t.* **9.** to concede; grant (usually fol. by a noun clause): *I agree that he is the ablest of us.* **10.** *Chiefly Brit.* to consent to or concur with: *We agree the stipulations. I must agree your plans.* [late ME *agre* < MF *agre(e)r* from phrase *a gre* at pleasure. See A-[5], GREE[2]] —**a·gree′ing·ly,** *adv.*
—**Syn. 1.** AGREE, CONSENT, ACCEDE, ASSENT, CONCUR all imply complying with the idea, sentiment, or action of someone. AGREE, the general term, suggests compliance in response to any degree of persuasion or opposition: *to agree to go; to agree to a meeting, to a wish, request, demand, an ultimatum.* CONSENT, applying to rather important matters, conveys an active and positive idea; it implies making a definite decision to comply with someone's expressed wish: *to consent to become engaged.* ACCEDE, a more formal word, also applies to important matters and implies a degree of yielding to conditions: *to accede to terms.* ASSENT conveys a more passive idea; it suggests agreeing intellectually or merely verbally with someone's assertion, request, etc.: *to assent to a speaker's theory, to a proposed arrangement.* To CONCUR is to show accord in matters of opinion, as of minds independently running along the same channels: *to concur in a judgment about an art exhibit.* **5.** See **correspond.** —**Ant. 2, 5.** disagree.

a·gree·a·ble (ə grē′ə bəl), *adj.* **1.** to one's liking; pleasing: *agreeable manners.* **2.** willing or ready to agree or consent: *Are you agreeable to my plans for Saturday?* **3.** suitable; conformable (usually fol. by *to*): *practice agreeable to theory.* [late ME *agreable* < MF. See AGREE, -ABLE] —**a·gree′a·bil′i·ty, a·gree′a·ble·ness,** *n.* —**a·gree′a·bly,** *adv.*
—**Syn. 1.** pleasant, likable, accommodating, gracious, amiable. **3.** concordant, harmonious.

a·greed (ə grēd′), *adj.* arranged or set by common consent: *They met at the agreed time.* [AGREE + -ED[2]]

a·gree·ment (ə grē′mənt), *n.* **1.** act of agreeing or of coming to a mutual arrangement; state of being in accord. **2.** the arrangement itself. **3.** unanimity of opinion; harmony in feeling: *agreement among the members.* **4.** *Gram.* correspondence in number, case, gender, person, or some other formal category between syntactically connected words, esp. between one or more subordinate words and the word or words upon which they depend; selection by one word of the matching formal subclass, or category, in another word syntactically construed with the first. **5.** See **collective agreement. 6.** *Law.* **a.** an expression of assent by two or more parties to the same object. **b.** the phraseology, written or oral, of an exchange of promises. [late ME *agrement* < MF. See AGREE, -MENT]
—**Syn. 2.** understanding. AGREEMENT, BARGAIN, COMPACT, CONTRACT all suggest a binding arrangement between two or more parties. AGREEMENT ranges in meaning from mutual understanding to binding obligation. BARGAIN applies particularly to agreements about buying and selling. COMPACT applies to treaties or alliances between nations or to solemn personal pledges. CONTRACT is used especially in law and business for such agreements as are legally enforceable. **3.** concord. **6.** settlement, treaty, pact.

a·gré·gé (ä′gre zhā′; *Fr.* A GRĀ ZHĀ′), *n., pl.* **-gés** (-zhāz′; *Fr.* -ZHĀ′). a degree awarded by a French university, based on a competitive examination given by the state and qualifying the recipient for the highest teaching positions in a lycée or for the rank of professor in a school of law or medicine. [< F: lit., aggregated; i.e., admitted to membership]

a·gré·ment (ä′grā mänt′; *Fr.* A GRĀ MÄN′), *n., pl.* **-ments** (-mänts′; *Fr.* -MÄN′). **1.** *Music.* ornament (def. 8). **2. agréments.** Also, **a·gré·mens** (A GRĀ MÄN′). agreeable qualities or circumstances. **3.** the official approval by a government of a proposed envoy from a foreign government. [< F: lit., pleasure; see AGREEMENT]

a·gres·tic (ə gres′tik), *adj.* **1.** rural; rustic. **2.** unpolished; awkward: *agrestic behavior.* [< L *agrest(is),* equiv. to *agr-* (s. of *ager* field) + *-estis* adj. suffix + -IC]

ag·ri·busi·ness (ag′rə biz′nis), *n.* farming and related food-processing and marketing businesses operated as a large-scale industry. [AGRI(CULTURE) + BUSINESS]

agric., **1.** agricultural. **2.** agriculture.

A·gric·o·la (ə grik′ə lə), *n.* **1. Geor·gi·us** (jôr′jē əs, jē ôr′-), (*Georg Bauer*), 1494–1555, German historian, physician, and pioneer in mineralogy. **2. Gnae·us Julius** (nē′əs), A.D. 37–93, Roman general: governor of Britain.

agricul′tural a′gent, *U.S.* See **county agent.**

agricul′tural ant′. See **harvester ant.**

agricul′tural chem′ical, any chemical used in agriculture to enhance the yield or the quality of crops.

ag·ri·cul·ture (ag′rə kul′chər), *n.* **1.** the science or art of cultivating land in the raising of crops; tillage; husbandry; farming. **2.** the production of crops, livestock, or poultry. **3.** agronomy. [< L *agricultūra,* equiv. to *agrī* (gen. sing. of *ager*) field + *cultūra* CULTURE] —**ag′ri·cul′tur·al,** *adj.* —**ag′ri·cul′tur·al·ly,** *adv.*

ag·ri·cul·tur·ist (ag′rə kul′chər ist), *n.* **1.** a farmer. **2.** an expert in agriculture. Also, **ag·ri·cul·tur·al·ist** (ag′rə kul′chər ə list). [AGRICULTURE + -IST]

A·gri·gen·to (ä′grē jen′tô), *n.* a city in S Italy. 47,094 (1961). Formerly, **Girgenti.**

ag·ri·mo·ny (ag′rə mō′nē), *n., pl.* **-nies.** **1.** any rosaceous plant of the genus *Agrimonia,* esp. the perennial *A. Eupatoria,* having pinnate leaves and small, yellow flowers. **2.** any of certain other plants, as hemp agrimony or bur marigold. [late ME < L *agrimōnia,* metathetic var. of *argemōnia* < Gk *argemṓnē* poppy; r. ME *egremoyne* < MF *aigremoine*]

A·gri·nion (ä grē′nyôn), *n.* a city in W Greece. 21,752 (1951).

ag·ri·ol·o·gy (ag′rē ol′ə jē), *n.* the comparative study of primitive tribal customs. [< Gk *ágrio(s)* uncultivated, wild (*agr(ós)* field + *-ios* adj. suffix) + -LOGY] —**ag·ri·o·log·i·cal** (ag′rē ə loj′i kəl), *adj.* —**ag′ri·ol′o·gist,** *n.*

A·gri·o·pe (ə grī′ə pē′), *n. Class. Myth.* Eurydice.

A·grip·pa (ə grip′ə), *n.* **1. Marcus Vip·sa·ni·us** (vip-sā′nē əs), 63–12 B.C., Roman statesman, general, and engineer: defeated Antony and Cleopatra at Actium. **2.** a walled plain in the first quadrant of the face of the moon: about 28 miles in diameter.

Ag·rip·pi·na II (ag′rə pī′nə), A.D. 16?–59?, mother of the Roman emperor Nero.

A·gri·us (ā′grē əs), *n. Class. Myth.* **1.** one of the Gigantes. **2.** a centaur who attacked Hercules. **3.** a son of Circe and Odysseus. **4.** the father of Thersites.

agro-, a learned borrowing from Greek meaning "soil," "crop production," used in the formation of compound words: *agronomy.* [comb. form of Gk *agrós* tilled land. See ACRE]

ag·ro·bi·ol·o·gy (ag′rō bī ol′ə jē), *n.* the quantitative science of plant life and plant nutrition. [AGRO- + BIOLOGY] —**ag·ro·bi·o·log·ic** (ag′rō bī′ə loj′ik), **ag′ro·bi′o·log′i·cal,** *adj.* —**ag′ro·bi′o·log′i·cal·ly,** *adv.* —**ag′ro·bi·ol′o·gist,** *n.*

a·grol·o·gy (ə grol′ə jē), *n.* the branch of soil science dealing esp. with the production of crops. [AGRO- + -LOGY] —**ag·ro·log·ic** (ag′rə loj′ik), **ag′ro·log′i·cal,** *adj.*

ag·ro·ma·ni·a (ag′rə mā′nē ə, -mān′yə), *n. Psychiatry.* an abnormal desire to live in open areas or in isolation. [AGRO- + -MANIA]

agron., agronomy.

ag·ro·nom·ics (ag′rə nom′iks), *n.* (*construed as sing.*) the art or science of managing land or crops. [AGRONOM(Y) + -ICS]

a·gron·o·my (ə gron′ə mē), *n.* the science of soil management and the production of field crops. [AGRO- + -NOMY] —**ag·ro·nom·ic** (ag′rə nom′ik), **ag′ro·nom′i·cal,** *adj.* —**a·gron′o·mist,** *n.*

ag·ros·tog·ra·phy (ag′rə stog′rə fē), *n., pl.* **-phies.** a treatise on grasses. [< Gk *ágrōst(is)* (see AGROSTOLOGY), + -O- + -GRAPHY] —**ag′ros·tog′ra·pher,** *n.* —**a·gros·to·graph·ic** (ə gros′tə graf′ik), **a·gros′to·graph′i·cal,** *adj.*

ag·ros·tol·o·gy (ag′rə stol′ə jē), *n.* the branch of botany dealing with grasses. [< Gk *ágrōst(is)* name of certain grasses + -O- + -LOGY] —**a·gros·to·log·ic** (ə gros′tə loj′ik), **a·gros′to·log′i·cal,** *adj.* —**ag′ros·tol′o·gist,** *n.*

A·gro·te·ra (ə grō′tər ə), *n. Class. Myth.* an epithet of Artemis, meaning "the huntress."

a·ground (ə ground′), *adv., adj.* on or onto the ground; in a stranded condition or state: *The ship ran aground.* [A-[1] + GROUND]

A.G.S., Associate in General Studies.

agst., against.

Agt., agent. Also, **agt.**

A·gua·dil·la (ä′gwə dē′ə; *Sp.* ä′gwä ᵺē′yä), *n.* a seaport in NW Puerto Rico. 15,943 (1960).

A·guas·ca·lien·tes (ä′gwäs kä lyen′tes), *n.* **1.** a state in central Mexico. 236,574 (1960); 2499 sq. mi. **2.** a city in and the capital of this state. 122,809 (1960).

a·gue (ā′gyōō), *n.* **1.** *Pathol.* a malarial fever characterized by regularly returning paroxysms, marked by successive cold, hot, and sweating fits. **2.** a fit of fever or shivering or shaking chills, accompanied by malaise, pains in the bones and joints, etc.; chill. [late ME < MF, short for *fievre ague* acute fever < L *febris acūta.* See ACUTE] —**a′gue·like′,** *adj.*

a·gue·weed (ā′gyo͞o wēd′), *n. U.S.* **1.** a boneset, *Eupatorium perfoliatum.* **2.** a gentian, *Gentiana quinquefolia.* [AGUE + WEED¹]

A·gui·nal·do (ä′gē näl′dô), *n.* **E·mi·lio** (e mē′lyô), 1869–1964, Filipino leader during the Spanish-American war: opposed to U.S. occupation.

a·gu·ish (ā′gyo͞o ish), *adj.* **1.** producing, resembling, or resulting from ague. **2.** easily affected by or subject to fits of ague. **3.** shaking; quivering. —**a′gu·ish·ly,** *adv.*

a·gu·jon (ä′go͞o hōn′), *n.* a needlefish, *Strongylura acus,* found in the western Atlantic Ocean. [< Sp, equiv. to *aguj(a)* kind of fish (< VL **acūcula;* see AIGUILLE) + *-on* aug. suffix]

A·gul·has (ə gul′əs; *Port.* ä go͞o′lyəsh), *n.* **Cape,** the southernmost point of Africa.

Agul′has Cur′rent, a warm ocean current flowing S along the SE coast of Africa. Also called **Mozambique Current.**

A·gung (ä′go͝ong), *n.* a volcano on NE Bali, in Indonesia: erupted 1963. 10,300 ft.

a·gu·ra (ä go͝or′ə), *n., pl.* **a·gu·roth** (ä go͝or′ōt). agora².

A·gus·tín I (ä′go͞os tēn′). See **Iturbide, Agustín de.**

A·gy·ieus (ə jī′yo͞os), *n. Class. Myth.* an epithet of Apollo, meaning "god of the streets."

ah (ä), *interj.* (an exclamation expressing pain, surprise, pity, complaint, dislike, joy, etc., according to the manner of utterance.) [ME *a!* which survives in dial. *eh!, ay!*]

Ah, ampere-hour. Also, **a.h.**

A.H., in the year of the Hegira (A.D. 622). [< L *annō Hejirae*]

a·ha (ä hä′), *interj.* (an exclamation expressing triumph, mockery, contempt, irony, surprise, etc., according to the manner of utterance.) [var. of HA. Cf. AHEM, AHOY]

A.H.A., **1.** American Historical Association. **2.** American Hospital Association.

A·hab (ā′hab), *n.* a king of Israel and husband of Jezebel, reigned 874?–853? B.C. I Kings 16–22. Also, *Douay Bible,* **Achab.**

A·had Ha·am (*Heb.* ä κнäd′ hä äm′), pen name of Asher Ginzberg.

a·han·ka·ra (ə hung kär′ə), *n. Hinduism, Buddhism.* the false identification of the purusha, or true inner self, with the body, the mind, or the outside world. [< Skt, equiv. to *aham* I + *kāra* making, cause]

A·has·u·e·rus (ə haz′yo͞o ēr′əs, ə has′-, ə hazh′o͞o-), *n.* the king of ancient Persia, known to the Greeks as Xerxes: the husband of the Biblical Esther. Also, *Douay Bible,* **Assuerus.**

à haute voix (A ōt′ VWA′), *French.* aloud; in a loud voice.

A·haz (ā′haz), *n.* a king of Judah, 735?–715? B.C. II Kings 16; II Chron. 28:9. Also, *Douay Bible,* **Achaz.**

A·ha·zi·ah (ā′ə zī′ə), *n.* **1.** a son of Ahab and his successor as king of Israel, reigned 853?–852? B.C. I Kings 22:40. **2.** a king of Judah, 846? B.C. II Kings 8:24. Also called, *Douay Bible,* **Ochozias.**

ah·choo (ä cho͞o′), *interj.* (used to represent the sound of a person sneezing.) Also, **achoo, kerchoo.**

A.H.E., Associate in Home Economics.

a·head (ə hed′), *adv.* **1.** in or to the front; in advance of; before: *Walk ahead of us.* **2.** in a forward direction; onward; forward: *The line of cars moved ahead slowly.* **3.** into or for the future: *Plan ahead.* **4.** so as to register a later time: *to put a clock ahead.* **5.** at or to a different time, either earlier or later: *to push a deadline ahead one day from Tuesday to Monday; to push a deadline ahead one day from Tuesday to Wednesday.* **6.** onward toward success; to a more advantageous position; upward in station: *There's a young man who is sure to get ahead.* **7. ahead of, a.** in front of; before: *He ran ahead of me.* **b.** superior to; beyond: *materially ahead of other countries.* **c.** in advance of; at an earlier time than: *We got there ahead of the other guests.* **8. be ahead,** *U.S. Informal.* to be in a position of advantage; be winning or benefiting: *His score in mathematics may be poor, but he will surely be ahead in foreign languages.* [A-¹ + HEAD]

a·hem (ə hem′), *interj.* (an utterance designed to attract attention, express doubt, etc.) [var. of HEM! Cf. AHA, AHOY]

Ah·hi·ya·wa (ä hē yä′wä), *n.* **1.** a kingdom mentioned in ancient Hittite writings, possibly identical with Achaia. **2.** the people inhabiting this kingdom. Also, **Ah·hi·ya′wa.**

A·hid·jo (ä ē jō′), *n.* **Ah·ma·dou** (ä mä do͞o′), born 1922, African statesman: president of the Republic of Cameroun since 1960.

A·hi·e·zer (ā′hī ē′zər), *n.* **1.** a Danite who assisted Moses with the census and was head of the tribe of Dan in the wilderness. Num. 1:12; 2:35; 10:25. **2.** a Benjaminite chief of a body of archers who came to David's aid while he was hiding from Saul. I Chron. 12:3.

A·him·a·az (ə him′ē az′), *n.* a priest who supported David during the revolt of Absalom. II Sam. 18:19–32. Also, *Douay Bible,* **Achimaas.**

A·him·e·lech (ə him′ə lek′), *n.* a priest who was killed by Saul for helping David. I Sam. 21:1–9; 22:9–23. Also, *Douay Bible,* **Achimelech.**

a·him·sa (ə him′sä, ə hiṅg′sä), *n. Hinduism.* the principle of nonviolence. [< Skt, equiv. to *a-* not, without (c. A-⁶) + *hiṁsā* injury, akin to *hanti* he slays, Gk *phónos* murder]

A·hir (ə hēr′), *n.* a member of the caste of cowherds and milkmen in India. [< Hindi < Skt *Abhīra*]

A·hi·ra (ə hī′rə), *n.* a Naphtalite who assisted Moses with the census in the wilderness. Num. 1:15; 2:29.

A·hi·shar (ə hī′shär), *n.* a chamberlain in Solomon's household. I Kings 4:6. Also, *Douay Bible,* **A·hi·sar** (ə hī′sär).

a·his·tor·ic (ā′hi stôr′ik, -stor′-), *adj.* without concern for history or historical development; indifferent to tradition. Also, **a′his·tor′i·cal.** [A-⁶ + HISTORIC]

A·hith·o·phel (ə hith′ə fel′), *n.* an advisor to David who joined the rebellion of Absalom. II Sam. 15–17. Also, *Douay Bible,* **Achitophel.**

Ah·ma·di (ä′mə dē′), *n. Islam.* a member of the Ahmadiya.

Ah·ma·di·ya (ä′mə dē′yə), *n. Islam.* a modern sect, divided into an older group **(Qadianis)** and a newer group **(Lahore party),** occupied with a number of specific theological questions. [< Ar: lit., followers of *Ahmad,* i.e., Muhammad]

Ah·med·a·bad (ä′məd ä bäd′), *n.* a city in E Gujarat, in W India, N of Bombay. 1,149,900 (1961). Also, **Ah′mad·a·bad′.**

Ah·med·na·gar (ä′məd nug′ər), *n.* a city in W Maharashtra, in W India, E of Bombay. 119,000 (1961). Also, **Ah′mad·na′gar.**

Ah·mose I (ä′mōs), 1580–1557 B.C., founder of the New Kingdom of ancient Egypt.

Ahn′felt's sea′weed (än′felts), a red alga, *Ahnfeltia plicata,* found along the coasts of North America and Europe, characterized by brownish, bushlike branches. [named after N. *Ahnfelt* (1801–37), Swedish botanist]

a·hold (ə hōld′), *n.* **1.** *Informal.* a hold (often fol. by *of*): *He grabbed ahold of my lapel.* —*adv.* **2.** *Naut. Archaic.* close to the wind and on a single tack: *to keep a vessel ahold.* [A-¹ + HOLD¹ (n.)]

a·holt (ə hōlt′), *n. Chiefly Dial.* ahold.

A·hom (ä′hōm), *n.* an extinct Thai language of Assam.

A horizon, *Geol.* the topsoil in a soil profile. Cf. **B horizon, C horizon.**

a·horse (ə hôrs′), *adj., adv.* mounted on a horse: *The king was ahorse; to escape ahorse.* [A-¹ + HORSE]

A·hos·kie (ə hos′kē), *n.* a town in NE North Carolina. 4583 (1960).

a·hoy (ə hoi′), *interj. Naut.* (a call used in hailing). [var. of HOY. Cf. AHA, AHEM]

AHQ, 1. Air Headquarters. **2.** Army Headquarters.

Ah·ri·man (ä′ri mən), *n. Zoroastrianism.* See **Angra Mainyu.**

AHSA, American Horse Shows Association.

a·hu (ä′ho͞o), *n.* a stone heap or platform used by the Polynesians as a marker or a memorial. [< Hawaiian]

a·hue·hue·te (ä′wē wā′tē), *n.* See **Montezuma cypress.** [< Sp < Nahuatl *ahuehueton,* lit., (the) old one of the water, equiv. to *atl* water + *hueton* old one, deriv. of *huehue* old]

a·hull (ə hul′), *adj. Naut.* **1.** (of a sailing vessel) with all sails furled and the helm lashed to head into the wind, as in heavy weather. **2.** abandoned, with decks awash. [A-¹ + HULL²]

a·hun·gered (ə hung′gərd), *adj. Archaic.* very hungry. [late ME *ahungred,* equiv. to *a-* A-² + *hungred* (ptp. of *hungren* to HUNGER), modeled on ATHIRST]

A·hu·ra Maz·da (ä′ho͝o rə maz′də), *Zoroastrianism.* the supreme creative deity, the creator of Gayomart and the opponent of Angra Mainyu. Also called **Mazda, Ohrmazd, Ormazd, Ormuzd.**

A·huz·zath (ə huz′ath), *n.* a friend of Abimelech with whom he journeyed from Gerar to make a covenant with Isaac in Beersheba. Gen. 26:26–31. Also, *Douay Bible,* **Ochozath.**

Ah·ve·nan·maa (äκн′ve nän mä′), *n.* (*construed as pl.*) Finnish name of the **Åland Islands.**

Ah·waz (ä wäz′), *n.* a city in W Iran. 155,054 (est. 1963). Also, **Ah·vaz′.**

Ah! Wil′derness, a comedy (1933) by Eugene O'Neill.

a·i¹ (ä′ē), *n., pl.* **a·is** (ä′ēz). a large sloth, *Bradypus tridactylus,* of Central and South America, having three toes on each forelimb. [< Pg < Tupi]

ai² (ī), *interj.* (an utterance expressing pity, pain, anguish, etc.)

A.I., artificial insemination.

A.I.A., See **American Institute of Architects.**

A·ias (ā′yas), *n.* Ajax.

ai·blins (ā′blinz), *adv. Scot.* ablins.

A.I.C., American Institute of Chemists.

aid (ād), *v.t.* **1.** to provide support for or relief to; help: *to aid the new nations.* **2.** to promote the progress or accomplishment of; facilitate. —*v.i.* **3.** to give help or assistance. —*n.* **4.** help; support; assistance. **5.** one who or that which aids or furnishes assistance; helper; auxiliary. **6. aids,** *Manège.* **a.** Also called **natural aids.** the means by which a rider communicates with and controls a horse, as the hands, legs, voice, and shifts in weight. **b.** Also called **artificial aids.** the devices by means of which a rider increases his control of a horse, as spurs, whip, and martingale. **7.** *U.S.* aide-de-camp. **8.** See **foreign aid. 9.** a payment made by feudal vassals to their lord on special occasions. **10.** *Eng. Hist.* (after 1066) any of several revenues received by a king in the Middle Ages from his vassals and other subjects, limited by the Magna Charta to specified occasions. [late ME *ayde* < MF *aid(i)er* < L *adjūtāre* to help (freq. of *adjuvāre*), equiv. to *ad-* AD- + *-jū-* help + *-tā-* freq. suffix + *-re* inf. suffix] —**aid′er,** *n.* —**aid′ful,** *adj.* —**aid′less,** *adj.*
—**Syn. 1.** See **help. 2.** abet, back. **4.** succor; relief; subsidy; subvention. —**Ant. 2.** hinder.

AID (ād), *n. U.S. Govt.* the division of the Department of State which coordinates the various foreign aid programs with U.S. foreign policy: established in 1961. [*A*(*gency for*) *I*(*nternational*) *D*(*evelopment*)]

AID, 1. American Institute of Decorators. **2.** American Institute of Interior Designers. **3.** *Brit.* artificial insemination donor.

A.I.D., *Brit.* artificial insemination donor.

A·ï·da (ä ē′də), *n.* **1.** (*italics*) an opera (1871) by Giuseppe Verdi. **2.** a girl's given name.

aid-de-camp (ād′də kamp′), *n., pl.* **aids-de-camp.** *Chiefly U.S.* aide-de-camp.

aide (ād), *n.* **1.** an aide-de-camp. **2.** See **nurse's aide. 3.** any official, confidential assistant.

aide-de-camp (ād′də kamp′), *n., pl.* **aides-de-camp.** a subordinate military or naval officer acting as a confidential assistant to a superior, usually to a general officer or admiral. Also, **aid-de-camp.** [< F: lit. camp helper; see AID, DE, CAMP]

aide-mé·moire (ād′mem wär′; *Fr.* ed mā mwar′), *n., pl.* **aides-mé·moire** (ādz′mem wär′; *Fr.* ed mā-mwar′). *French.* a memorandum of discussion, agreement, or action. [lit., memory-helper]

AIDS (ādz), *n.* an immune-system disease, caused by a virus, in which the resistance of the body to certain infections and cancers is lowered. [*a*(*cquired*) *i*(*mmune*) *d*(*eficiency*) *s*(*yndrome*)]

aid′ sta′tion, *Mil.* a medical installation located in a forward or isolated position in the field for providing routine or emergency medical treatment to the troops.

A·i·e·a (ä′ē ä′ä), *n.* a town on S Oahu, in Hawaii. 11,826 (1960).

A.I.E.E., American Institute of Electrical and Electronic Engineers. Also, **AIEEE**

ai·glet (ā′glit), *n.* aglet.

ai·grette (ā′gret, ā gret′), *n.* **1.** a plume or tuft of feathers, esp. the back plume of any of various herons, arranged as a head ornament. **2.** a copy in jewelry of such a plume. [< F, equiv. to *aigr-* (< Gmc; cf. OHG *heiger* heron) + *-ette* -ETTE. See EGRET, HERON]

ai·guille (ā gwēl′, ā′gwēl), *n.* a needlelike rock mass or mountain peak. [< F < VL **acūcula* (r. *acicula*), equiv. to *ac(us)* needle + *-cula* -CULE]

ai·guil·lette (ā′gwi let′), *n.* **1.** an ornamental tagged cord or braid on a uniform; aglet. **2.** a long thin slice or slices of cooked meat, esp. narrow strips of meat cut lengthwise from the breast of a fowl. [< F; see AIGUILLE, -ETTE] —**ai′guil·let′ted,** *adj.*

Ai·ken (ā′kən), *n.* **1. Conrad (Potter),** born 1889, U.S. poet. **2.** a boy's given name.

Ai′ken South′, a town in W South Carolina. 2980 (1960).

Ai′ken West′, a town in W South Carolina. 2602 (1960).

ai·ki·do (ī′kē dô, ī kē′dō), *n.* a Japanese form of self-defense utilizing wrist, joint, and elbow grips to immobilize or throw one's opponent. [< Jap equiv. to *ai* to coordinate + *ki* breath control + *do* way]

ai·ku·chi (ī′ko͞o chē′), *n., pl.* **-chi.** a Japanese knife without a guard, used under the Tokugawas to indicate status and to commit suicide. [< Jap]

ail (āl), *v.t.* **1.** to cause pain, uneasiness, or trouble to. —*v.i.* **2.** to be unwell; feel pain; be ill. [ME *ail, eilen,* OE *eglan* to afflict (c. Goth *-agljan*), deriv. of *egle* painful; akin to Goth *agls* shameful]

ai·lan·thus (ā lan′thəs), *n., pl.* **-thus·es.** any simaroubaceous tree of the genus *Ailanthus,* esp. *A. altissima.* Cf. **tree of heaven.** [< NL < Amboinese *ai lanto,* lit., tree (of) the gods] —**ai·lan′thic,** *adj.*

ailan′thus silk′worm, a green silkworm, *Samia walkeri,* introduced into the U.S. from China, which feeds on the leaves of the ailanthus.

Ai·leen (ā lēn′; *Irish* ī lēn′), *n.* a girl's given name, form of **Helen.** Also, **Alene, Eileen.**

ai·ler·on (ā′lə ron′), *n.* **1.** *Aeron.* a movable surface, usually near the trailing edge of a wing, that controls the roll of the airframe or effects maneuvers, as banks and the like. **2.** a wall at the end of a roof with a single slope, as that of a church aisle. [< F, equiv. to *ail(e)* (see AISLE) + *-eron* dim. suffix]

ai′leron roll′, *Aeron.* a roll consisting of one or more rotations, usually controlled by the use of ailerons.

ai·lette (ā let′), *n. Armor.* either of two standing pieces of metal or cuir-bouilli, attached to the shoulders as an ornament or as a means of displaying the wearer's arms: used c1275–c1350. [< F < OF, dim. of *aile* wing. See AISLE, -ETTE]

ail·ing (ā′ling), *adj.* sickly; unwell. [AIL + -ING²]
—**Syn.** See **sick**¹.

ail·ment (āl′mənt), *n.* a physical disorder or illness, sometimes of a chronic nature. [AIL + -MENT]

ai·lu·ro·phile (ī lo͝or′ə fīl′), *n.* a person who likes cats; cat fancier. [< NL < Gk *ailouro(s)* cat + -PHILE] —**ai·lu·ro·phil·ic** (ī lo͝or′ə fil′ik), *adj.*

ai·lu·ro·phil·i·a (ī lo͝or′ə fil′ē ə), *n.* a liking for cats, as by cat fanciers. [< NL < Gk *ailouro(s)* cat + *-philia* -PHILIA]

ai·lu·ro·phobe (ī lo͝or′ə fōb′), *n.* **1.** a person who has an abnormal fear of cats. **2.** a person who detests cats. [< NL < Gk *ailouro(s)* cat + -PHOBE] —**ai·lu′ro·pho′bic,** *adj.*

ai·lu·ro·pho·bi·a (ī lo͝or′ə fō′bē ə), *n. Psychiatry.* an abnormal fear of cats. [< NL < Gk *ailouro(s)* cat + *-phobia* -PHOBIA]

aim (ām), *v.t.* **1.** to position (a firearm, ball, arrow, etc.) so that, on firing or release, the discharged projectile will hit the target. **2.** to intend or direct for a particular effect or purpose: *to aim a satire at snobbery.* —*v.i.* **3.** to strive; try (usually fol. by *to* or *at*): *We aim to please. They aim at saving something every month.* **4.** *Chiefly Dial.* to intend: *She aims to go tomorrow.* **5.** to direct efforts toward an object: *The book was aimed at the intelligentsia.* **6.** *Obs.* to estimate; guess. —*n.* **7.** act of aiming or directing anything at or toward a particular point or target. **8.** the direction in which a weapon or missile is pointed; the line of sighting: *within the cannon's aim.* **9.** the point intended to be hit; thing or person aimed at: *to miss one's aim.* **10.** something intended or desired to be attained by one's efforts; purpose: *I can't understand what his aim in life may be.* **11.** *Obs.* conjecture; guess. **12. take aim,** to sight a weapon or missile at a target: *to take aim and fire.* [late ME *aime(n)* < MF *aesmer* < LL *adaestimāre,* equiv. to L *ad-* AD- + *aestimāre* (see ESTIMATE); r. ME *ame(n)* < OF (dial.) *amer* < L *aestimāre*] —**aim′er,** *n.* —**aim′ful,** *adj.* —**aim′ful·ly,** *adv.*
—**Syn. 1.** point. **7.** sighting. **9.** target, objective. **10.** goal; intent, design. AIM, END, OBJECT all imply something which is the goal of one's efforts. AIM implies that toward which one makes a direct line, refusing to be diverted from it: *a nobleness of aim; one's aim in life.* END emphasizes the goal as a cause of efforts: *the end for which one strives.* OBJECT emphasizes the goal as that toward which all efforts are directed: *the object of years of study.*

ai·mak (ī′mak, ā′mak), *n.* a clanlike group among Mongolian peoples. [< Mongolian]

A.I.M.E., 1. American Institute of Mining Engineers. **2.** Association of the Institute of Mechanical Engineers.

Ai·mee (ā′mē), *n.* a girl's given name. Also, **Amy.**

aim′ing point′, the point at which a gun or bombsight is actually aimed in order to strike a desired target.

aim·less (ām′lis), *adj.* without aim; purposeless. [AIM + -LESS] —**aim′less·ly,** *adv.* —**aim′less·ness,** *n.*

ain (ān), *adj. Scot.* own. [OE *ǣgen*]

Ain (AN), *n.* a department in E France. 327,146 (1962); 2249 sq. mi. *Cap.:* Bourg.

′ain (īn, ān), *n.* **1.** the 18th letter of the Arabic alphabet. **2.** the voiced pharyngeal constrictive consonant represented by this letter. [< Ar]

AInd, Anglo-Indian (def. 4).

aî·né (e nā′), *adj. French.* elder; eldest. Also, *referring to a woman,* **aî·née′.** [lit., born before]

ain't (ānt), **1.** *Nonstandard in U.S. except in some dialects; informal in Brit.* am not. **2.** *Nonstandard.* are not, is not, have not, or has not. [var. of *amn't* (contr. of AM NOT) by loss of *m* and raising with compensatory lengthening of *a*]
—Usage. AIN'T is so traditionally and widely regarded as a nonstandard form that it should be shunned by all who prefer to avoid being considered illiterate. AIN'T occurs occasionally in the informal speech of some educated users, especially in self-consciously or folksy or humorous contexts (*Ain't it the truth! She ain't what she used to be!*), but it is completely unacceptable in formal writing and speech. Although the expression *ain't I?* is perhaps defensible—and it is considered more logical than *aren't I?* and more euphonious than *amn't I?*—the well-advised person will avoid any use of AIN'T.

Ain·tab (īn täb′), *n.* former name of **Gaziantep.** Also, **Antep, Ayntab.**

Ai·nu (ī′no͞o), *n., pl.* **-nus,** (*esp. collectively*) **-nu. 1.** a member of an aboriginal race of the northernmost islands of Japan, having Caucasoid or Australoid features, light skin, and hairy bodies. **2.** the language of the Ainus, of uncertain relationship.

air[1] (âr), *n.* **1.** a mixture of oxygen, nitrogen, and other gases which surrounds the earth and forms its atmosphere. **2.** a stir in the atmosphere; a light breeze. **3.** circulation; publication; publicity: *to give air to one's theories.* **4.** the general character or complexion of anything; appearance: *His early work bore an air of freshness and originality.* **5.** the peculiar look, appearance, and bearing of a person: *There is an air of mystery about him.* **6. airs,** affected manner; manifestation of pride or vanity; assumed haughtiness: *She acquired airs that proved insufferable to her friends.* **7.** *Music.* **a.** a tune; melody. **b.** the soprano or treble part. **c.** an aria. **d.** Also, **ayre.** an Elizabethan art song. **8.** *Radio.* the medium through which radio waves are transmitted. **9.** *Obs.* breath. **10. clear the air,** to eliminate dissension, ambiguity, or tension from a discussion, situation, etc.: *The general staff meeting was intended to help clear the air.* **11. get the air,** *Slang.* **a.** to be rejected, as by a lover. **b.** to be dismissed, as by an employer: *He had worked only a few days when he got the air.* **12. give oneself airs,** to assume an affected or haughty manner: *She had few friends because she gave herself such airs.* **13. give someone the air, a.** to reject, as a lover: *He was bitter because she gave him the air.* **b.** to dismiss, as an employee. **14. in the air,** in circulation; current: *There is a rumor in the air that we are moving to a new location.* **15. into thin air,** completely or entirely out of sight or reach: *He vanished into thin air.* **16. off the air, a.** not broadcasting: *He goes off the air at midnight.* **b.** no longer being broadcast: *The program went off the air years ago.* **c.** (of a computer) not in operation. **17. on the air, a.** in the act of broadcasting; being broadcast: *The program will be going on the air in a few seconds.* **b.** (of a computer) in operation. **18. put on airs,** to assume an affected or haughty manner: *As their fortune increased, they began to put on airs.* **19. take the air, a.** to go out-of-doors; take a short walk or ride. **b.** *Slang.* to leave, esp. hurriedly. **c.** *Radio.* to begin broadcasting. **20. tread** or **walk on air,** to feel very happy; be elated: *Since her engagement she has been walking on air.* **21. up in the air, a.** Also, **in the air.** undecided or unsettled: *The contract is still up in the air.* **b.** *Informal.* angry; perturbed: *There is no need to get so up in the air over a simple mistake.* —*v.t.* **22.** to expose to the air; give access to the open air; ventilate. **23.** to expose ostentatiously; bring into public notice; display: *to air one's opinions; to air one's theories.* **24.** to broadcast or televise. [ME *eir* < OF *air* < L *āer-* < Gk *āer-* (s. of *āḗr*) the lower atmosphere, akin to *áein* to blow] —**air′less,** *adj.*
—Syn. 2. See **wind**[1]. **4, 5.** impression, aspect, look. **5.** demeanor, attitude. See **manner.**

air[2] (âr), *Scot.* —*adj.* **1.** early. —*adv.* **2.** *Obs.* before; previously. [var. of ERE]

A·ïr (ä′ēr), *n.* a region in N Niger, in the Sahara: low massif and oases. ab. 30,000 sq. mi. Also called **Asben.**

air′ alert′, 1. act of flying while waiting for combat orders or for enemy airplanes to appear. **2.** the signal to take stations for such action.

air′ attaché′, a commissioned officer or warrant officer of an air force serving on the staff of an ambassador or minister.

air′ bag′, a bag that inflates automatically upon impact in order to protect automobile passengers from injury in a collision.

air′ base′, 1. an operations center for units of an air force. **2.** *Aerial Photogrammetry.* **a.** a line joining two camera stations. **b.** the length of this line. **3.** (in aerial photography) the distance between the points on the ground over which a photograph is taken.

air′ bed′, a bed made by inflating a mattresslike bag.

air′ bell′, *Glassmaking.* an air bubble formed in glass during blowing and often retained as a decorative element.

air·bill (âr′bil′), *n.* See **air waybill.**

air′ blad′der, 1. a vesicle or sac containing air. **2.** Also called **gas bladder, swim bladder.** *Ichthyol.* a gas-filled sac located against the roof of the body cavity of most bony fishes, originally functioning only as a lung, now serving in many higher fishes to regulate hydrostatic pressure.

air′ blast′, a jet of air produced mechanically.

air·borne (âr′bōrn′, -bôrn′), *adj.* **1.** carried by the air, as pollen or dust. **2.** in flight; aloft: *The plane was airborne by six o'clock.* **3.** *Mil.* (of ground forces) carried in airplanes or gliders: *airborne infantry.* **4.** *Aeron.* (of an aircraft) supported entirely by the atmosphere; flying. [AIR[1] + BORNE]

air-bound (âr′bound′), *adj.* stopped up by air. [AIR[1] + -BOUND[1]]

air′ brake′, 1. a brake or system of brakes operated by compressed air. **2.** *Aeron.* (not used scientifically) a device for reducing the air speed of an aircraft by increasing its drag. **3.** a device for stopping the sails of a windmill by disrupting the flow of air around them.

air·bra·sive (âr′brā′siv, -ziv), *Dentistry.* —*n.* **1.** an instrument for cutting tooth structure by means of a stream of abrasive particles under gas or air pressure. —*adj.* **2.** noting or pertaining to the technique employed in the use of this instrument. [AIR[1] + (A)BRASIVE]

air-breathe (âr′brēth′), *v.i.,* **-breathed** (-brētht′), **-breath·ing.** (of an engine, aircraft, missile, etc.) to take in air from the atmosphere to oxidize the fuel for combustion. [AIR[1] + BREATHE]

air-breath·er (âr′brē′thər), *n.* an aircraft, missile, or submarine engine that requires air from the atmosphere for the combustion of its fuel. Also, **air′ breath′er.**

air′ brick′, a ceramic or metal unit the size of a brick, open at the sides for admitting air to a building interior.

air·brush (âr′brush′), *n.* an atomizer for spraying paint. [AIR[1] + BRUSH[1]]

air·burst (âr′bûrst′), *n.* the explosion of a bomb or shell in midair. [AIR[1] + BURST]

air′ bus′, *Informal.* an airplane that carries passengers.

air′ car′go, cargo transported or to be transported by an air carrier.

air′ car′rier, 1. a commercial carrier utilizing aircraft as its means of transport; an air line, as for passengers, freight, etc. **2.** an aircraft meeting the requirements, as of type, safety inspection, etc., for use by an air line.

air′ cas′ing, a casing for the funnel of a powered vessel, large enough to provide an air space all around the funnel.

air′ cas′tle. See **castle in the air.**

air′ cell′, *Anat., Zool., Bot.* a cavity or receptacle containing air.

air′ cham′ber, 1. a chamber containing air, as in a pump, lifeboat, or organic body. **2.** Also called **air cushion.** a compartment of a hydraulic system containing air which by its elasticity equalizes the pressure and flow of liquid within the system.

air′ coach′, a class or category of passenger transportation offered by some airlines, usually having less luxurious accommodations and lower fare than first class.

air′ cock′, *Mach.* a special type of valve for controlling the flow of air.

air′ command′, *U.S. Air Force.* a unit of command that is higher than an air force.

air-con·di·tion (âr′kən dish′ən), *v.t.* **1.** to furnish with an air-conditioning system. **2.** to treat (air) with such a system.

air′ condi′tioner, an air-conditioning device.

air′ condi′tioning, 1. a system or process for controlling the temperature, humidity, and sometimes the purity of the air in an interior, as of an office, theater, laboratory, house, or the like. **2.** an air-conditioning system or unit: *Turn on the air conditioning.* —**air′-con·di′tion·ing,** *adj.*

air′ conduc′tion, *Med.* transmission of sound vibrations to the eardrum through the external auditory meatus (opposed to *bone conduction*).

air′ consign′ment note′, *Chiefly Brit.* See **air waybill.**

air-cool (âr′ko͞ol′), *v.t.* **1.** *Mach.* to remove the heat of combustion, friction, etc., from, as by air streams flowing over an engine jacket. **2.** (loosely) to air-condition.

air-core (âr′kōr′, -kôr′), *adj.* *Elect.* having a nonmagnetic core, as one of fiber or plastic, encircled by a coil (**air′-core coil′**), or containing one or more such coils: *air-core transformer.*

Air′ Corps′, *U.S. Army.* **1.** (before July 26, 1947) a branch of the U.S. Army concerned with military aviation. **2.** (before May 1, 1942) the name for the Army Air Forces.

air′ course′, *Naut.* (in a wooden vessel) a fore-and-aft passage between timbers, for circulation of air.

air·craft (âr′kraft′, -kräft′), *n., pl.* **-craft.** any machine supported for flight in the air by buoyancy or by the dynamic action of air on its surfaces, esp. powered airplanes, gliders, and helicopters. [AIR[1] + CRAFT]

Aircraft carrier

air′craft car′rier, a warship equipped with a deck for the taking off and landing of aircraft and with storage space for aircraft.

air·craft·man (âr′kraft′mən, -kräft′-), *n., pl.* **-men.** *Brit.* aircraftsman.

air′craft observ′er, *U.S. Army.* observer (def. 3).

air·crafts·man (âr′krafts′mən, -kräfts′-), *n., pl.* **-men.** *Brit.* a man holding the rank of noncommissioned officer in the RAF. Also, **aircraftman.** [AIRCRAFT + 's[1] + MAN[1]]

air·crafts·wom·an (âr′krafts′wo͝om′ən, -kräfts′-), *n., pl.* **-wom·en.** *Brit.* a woman holding a noncommissioned rank in the RAF. [AIRCRAFT + 's[1] + WOMAN]

air·crew (âr′kro͞o′), *n.* *U.S. Air Force.* the crew of an aircraft. Also, **air′ crew′.** [AIR[1] + CREW]

air·crew·man (âr′kro͞o′mən), *n., pl.* **-men.** a member of an aircrew. [AIRCREW + MAN]

air′ cur′tain, compressed air directed, usually downward, across a doorway so as to form a shield to exclude drafts, insects, etc.

air′ cush′ion, 1. an inflatable, airtight cushion. **2.** See **air chamber** (def. 2).

air′ cyl′inder, a cylinder containing air, esp. one equipped with a piston and used as a device for checking the recoil of a gun.

air′ dis′charge, a lightning discharge that occurs within a cloud and the volume of air beneath it and that does not reach the ground.

air′ divi′sion, *U.S. Air Force.* a unit of command, within an air force, usually composed of two or more wings.

air′ drain′, any of various passages for conducting air to foundation walls, the back of woodwork, etc.

Air·drie (ᴀʀ′drē), *n.* a city in central Scotland, near Glasgow. 33,620 (1961).

air′ drill′, a pneumatic drill.

air·drome (âr′drōm′), *n.* a landing field for airplanes which has extensive buildings, equipment, shelters, etc. Also, *esp. Brit.,* **aerodrome.** [AIR[1] + -DROME]

air·drop (âr′drop′), *v.,* **-dropped, -drop·ping,** *n.* —*v.t.* **1.** to drop (persons, equipment, etc.) by parachute from an aircraft in flight. —*n.* **2.** the act or process of airdropping. [AIR[1] + DROP]

air-dry (âr′drī′), *v.,* **-dried, -dry·ing,** *adj.* —*v.t.* **1.** to dry by exposure to the air. —*adj.* **2.** dry beyond further evaporation.

air′-earth′ cur′rent (âr′ûrth′), the net electric current from the positively charged atmosphere to the negatively charged earth.

Aire·dale (âr′dāl′), *n.* one of a breed of large terriers having a wiry, black-and-tan coat and a docked tail.

Airedale (23 in. high at shoulder)

air·field (âr′fēld′), *n.* a level area, usually equipped with hard-surfaced runways, on which airplanes take off and land. [AIR[1] + FIELD]

air′ fleet′, a group of military aircraft, usually under one commander.

air·flow (âr′flō′), *n.* air currents caused by a moving aircraft, automobile, etc. [AIR[1] + FLOW]

air·foil (âr′foil′), *n.* *Aeron.* any surface, as a wing, aileron, or stabilizer, designed to aid in lifting or controlling an aircraft by making use of the air currents through which it moves. [AIR[1] + FOIL[2]]

Air′ Force′, 1. *U.S.* the department consisting of practically all military aviation forces, established July 26, 1947. **2.** (*l.c.*) a similar department in any military organization. **3.** (*l.c.*) *U.S.* (formerly) the largest unit in the Army Air Forces. **4.** (*l.c.*) *U.S.* a unit of Air Force command between an air division and an air command. **5.** (*sometimes l.c.*) the military unit of a nation charged with carrying out military operations in the air. **6.** *Brit.* Royal Air Force.

air·frame (âr′frām′), *n.* the framework and external covering of an airplane, rocket, etc. [AIR[1] + FRAME]

air′ freight′, 1. a system of transporting freight by aircraft: *Ship it by air freight.* **2.** freight transported by aircraft.

air′ gap′, *Elect.* the space between two objects magnetically related, as between the rotor and the stator in a dynamo, or between two objects electrically related, as between the electrode and the tip of a spark plug.

air′ gas′, *Chem.* See **producer gas.**

air′ gauge′, a gauge for measuring air pressure.

air·glow (âr′glō′), *n.* a nighttime glow from the upper atmosphere, occurring over middle and low latitudes. [AIR[1] + GLOW]

air·graph (âr′graf′, -gräf′), *Brit.* —*n.* **1.** a letter written on paper of a particular size, transferred to film which is sent by air, and enlarged before delivery: similar to the U.S. V-mail. —*v.t.* **2.** to send or mail (such a letter). [AIR[1] + -GRAPH]

air′ gun′, a gun operated by compressed air.

air′ ham′mer, a pneumatic hammer, usually portable.

air′ har′bor, a harbor for hydroplanes, esp. seaplanes.

air-hard·en·ing (âr′här′dᵊning), *adj.* *Metall.* noting any metal, esp. alloy steel, that can be hardened from above its transformation point by cooling in air.

air·head (âr′hed′), *n.* an area in enemy territory or in threatened friendly territory, seized by airborne troops for bringing in supplies and additional troops by airdrop or landing. [AIR[1] + HEAD]

air′ hoist′, a pneumatic hoist.

air′ hole′, 1. an opening to admit or discharge air. **2.** a natural opening in the frozen surface of a river or pond. **3.** See **air pocket.**

air·i·ly (âr′ə lē), *adv.* **1.** in a gay or breezy manner; jauntily. **2.** lightly; delicately. [AIRY + -ILY]

air·ing (âr′ing), *n.* **1.** an exposure to the air, as for drying. **2.** a walk, drive, etc., in the open air. [AIR[1] + -ING[1]]

air′ injec′tion, injection of liquid fuel into the cylinder of an internal-combustion engine, esp. a diesel, by means of a jet of compressed air. Cf. **solid injection.**

air′ jack′et, 1. an envelope of enclosed air about part of a machine, as for checking the transmission of heat. **2.** *Brit.* See **life belt.**

air′ lance′, *Mach.* a lance using an air blast.

air-lance (âr′lans′, -läns′), *v.t.,* **-lanced, -lanc·ing.** to clean with an air lance.

air′ lane′, a route regularly used by airplanes; airway.

air·less (âr′lis), *adj.* **1.** lacking air. **2.** without fresh air; stuffy: *a dark, airless hallway.* **3.** still. [AIR[1] + -LESS]

air′ let′ter, 1. an air-mail letter. **2.** a sheet of very lightweight stationery for use in air mail. Cf. **aérogramme.**

air·lift (âr′lift′), *n.* Also, **air′ lift′. 1.** a system for transporting persons or cargo by aircraft, esp. in an emergency. **2.** the persons or cargo so transported. **3.** act or process of transporting such a load. **4.** a pump for raising liquids by the pressure of air forced into the pump chamber. —*v.t.* **5.** to transport (persons or cargo) by airlift. [AIR[1] + LIFT]

air·light (âr′līt′), *n.* light scattered, or diffused, in the air by dust, haze, etc., esp. as it limits the visibility of distant, dark objects by causing them to blend with the background sky. [AIR[1] + LIGHT[1]]

air·like (âr′līk′), *adj.* like or resembling air. [AIR[1] + -LIKE]

air-line (âr′līn′), *adj.* **1.** *Chiefly U.S.* direct. **2.** via airplane: *the air-line distance between Detroit and Washington.* **3.** *Chiefly U.S.* straight; direct.

air·line (âr′līn′), *n.* **1.** *Aeron.* **a.** a system usually furnishing scheduled air transport between specified points. **b.** the airplanes, airports, etc., of such a system. **c.** Often, **air′lines′** (*usually construed as sing.*). a company that owns or operates such a system. **2.** *Chiefly U.S.* a direct line; a line as direct as a beeline. **3.** a tube or hose used to pipe air to a deep-sea diver, pneumatic drill, etc. [AIR[1] + LINE[1]]

air·lin·er (âr′lī′nər), *n.* *Aeron.* a passenger aircraft operated by an airlines. Also, **air′ lin′er.** [AIR[1] + LINER[1]]

air′ lock′, 1. *Civ. Eng.* an airtight chamber permitting passage to or from a space, as in a caisson, in which the air is kept under pressure. **2.** the impedance in the functioning of a pump or a system of piping caused by the presence of an air bubble; vapor lock.

air′ log′, 1. *Aeron.* a device for recording the distance traveled by an aircraft, relative to the air through which it moves. **2.** *Rocketry.* a device for regulating the range of a guided missile.

air-logged (âr′lôgd′, -logd′), *adj.* (of a pump or system of piping) hindered in its functioning by an air lock; air-bound.

air′ mail′, 1. the system of transmitting mail by airplane. 2. mail transmitted by airplane.

air-mail (âr′māl′), *adj.* 1. of or pertaining to air mail. —*n.* 2. an air-mail letter. 3. an air-mail stamp. —*adv.* 4. by air mail: *Send all the letters air-mail.* —*v.t.* 5. to send via air mail: *I air-mailed your letter yesterday.* Also, **air′mail′.**

air·man (âr′mən), *n., pl.* **-men.** 1. an aviator. 2. *U.S. Air Force.* an enlisted man of one of the four lowest ranks (**basic airman, air′man third′ class′, air′man sec′ond class′,** and **air′man first′ class′**). 3. a member of a military aircrew. 4. *U.S. Navy.* an enlisted man with duties relating to aircraft. 5. (in other countries) an enlisted man in the air force. [AIR[1] + MAN[1]] —**air′man·ship′,** *n.*

air′ map′, a map constructed from aerial photographs.

air′ mass′, 1. a body of air covering a relatively wide area, exhibiting approximately uniform properties through any horizontal section. 2. Also called **optical air mass.** *Astron.* the relative distance through the atmosphere of light from a certain object in space, expressed as the ratio of the actual distance to the distance if the object were in the zenith.

air-mass show·er (âr′mas′ shou′ər), a shower of rain, hail, or snow caused by local convection within an air mass rather than being associated with a front or instability line.

air′ med′al, *U.S.* a decoration awarded for meritorious achievement in aerial duty.

air′ me′ter, a small, sensitive anemometer of the windmill type.

air′ mile′, mile (def. 1c).

air-mind·ed (âr′mīn′did), *adj.* 1. interested in aviation or aeronautics. 2. favoring increased use of aircraft. —**air′-mind′ed·ness,** *n.*

Air′ Min′istry, (in England) the department of government administering all civil and military matters concerning aviation.

Air′ Na′tional Guard′, a national guard organization similar to and coordinate with the U.S. Air Force.

air′ observ′er, *U.S. Army.* observer (def. 3).

air′ pas′sage, 1. a space occupied or traversed by air. 2. travel by air. 3. accommodations for an air trip: *to book air passage for Hong Kong.*

air′ pho′tograph. See **aerial photograph.** —**air′ photog′raphy.**

air·plane (âr′plān′), *n.* 1. a heavier-than-air aircraft kept aloft by the upward thrust exerted by the passing air on its fixed wings and driven by propellers, jet propulsion, etc. 2. any similar heavier-than-air craft, as a glider or helicopter. Also, *esp. Brit.*, **aeroplane.** [< late Gk *āer(ó)plan(os)* wandering in air, equiv. to *āero-* AERO- + *plan-* (s. of *planâsthai* to wander) + *-os* adj. suffix; see PLANET]

air′plane car′rier, an aircraft carrier.

air′plane cloth′, 1. a cotton fabric of plain weave formerly used as a covering for the wings and fuselages of airplanes. 2. a similar, lighter weight fabric for shirts and pajamas.

air′plane spin′, *Professional Wrestling.* a maneuver in which a wrestler takes his opponent by the head and crotch, lifts him crosswise onto the back at the shoulders, spins around, and throws him overhead to the mat.

air′ plant′, 1. an epiphyte. 2. Also called **life plant.** a tropical, perennial herb, *Bryophyllum pinnatum*, having drooping clusters of red flowers and new plants sprouting at the leaf-notches.

air′ plot′, 1. *Aeron.* the calculation of the ground position of an aircraft by first determining its air position from its speed in the air and heading information, and then correcting for wind effects. 2. the room or rooms from which aircraft are directed aboard an aircraft carrier. Also, **air′plot′.**

air′ plug′, a plug making an airtight seal to a vent.

air′ pock′et, (not in technical use) a nearly vertical air current which can cause an aircraft to experience a sudden change in altitude, usually a decrease. Also called **air hole.**

air′ police′, (*often cap.*) an organization of personnel in the U.S. Air Force or Air National Guard serving as police. *Abbr.:* AP, A. P.

air·port[1] (âr′pōrt′, -pôrt′), *n.* a tract of land or water with facilities for the landing, take-off, shelter, supply, and repair of aircraft, esp. one used for receiving or discharging passengers and cargo at regularly scheduled times. [AIR[1] + PORT[1]]

air·port[2] (âr′pōrt′, -pôrt′), *n.* *Naut.* a porthole designed to be opened to the outside air. [AIR[1] + PORT[4]]

Air·port (âr′pōrt′, -pôrt′), *n.* a town in central California. 3689 (1960).

air′ post′, *Brit.* See **air mail.**

air′ pota′to, a vine, *Dioscorea bulbifera*, of southeastern Asia, having tubers from 8 to 12 inches long, weighing several pounds, and growing in the leaf axils.

air′ pow′er, the aggregate military capabilities of a nation for operations involving the use of aircraft.

air′ pres′sure. See **atmospheric pressure.**

air·proof (âr′pro͞of′), *adj.* 1. impervious to air. —*v.t.* 2. to make impervious to air. [AIR[1] + -PROOF]

air′ pump′, 1. an apparatus for drawing in, compressing, or exhausting air. 2. (*caps.*) *Astron.* the constellation Antlia.

air′ raid′, a raid by aircraft, esp. for bombing a particular area. —**air′-raid′,** *adj.* —**air′ raid′er.**

air′-raid shel′ter, an area specifically designated as a shelter during an air raid.

air′-raid ward′en, a civilian having police duties during an air-raid alert.

air′ ri′fle, an air gun with rifled bore.

air′ right′, 1. a right of way in the airspace owned by a person over his land, including as much of the airspace as can be occupied by his immovable property on the land, and subject to the public right of air navigation above the property at a legally prescribed altitude. 2. such a right sold or leased for use or occupation, esp. on a support elevated above an immovable property, as for the erection of an office building over a railroad track.

air′ route′, a designated route for aircraft flying between particular ground locations at specified minimum altitudes.

air′ sac′, 1. a sac containing air. 2. any of certain cavities in a bird's body connected with the lungs. 3. a saclike dilation of the wall of a trachea in many insects.

air·screw (âr′skro͞o′), *n.* *Brit.* an airplane propeller. [AIR[1] + SCREW]

air′ serv′ice, 1. the services performed by an airline, as the transportation of passengers, freight, and mail. 2. (*caps.*) (formerly) the air arm of the U.S. military forces.

air′ shaft′, a ventilating shaft. Also called **air well.**

air·ship (âr′ship′), *n.* a self-propelled, lighter-than-air craft with means of controlling the direction of flight, usually classed as rigid, semirigid, or nonrigid. [AIR[1] + SHIP]

air·sick (âr′sik′), *adj.* ill with airsickness. [AIR[1] + SICK]

air·sick·ness (âr′sik′nis), *n.* a feeling of nausea and dizziness, sometimes accompanied by vomiting, as a result of the motion of the aircraft in which one is traveling. Cf. **motion sickness.** [AIR[1] + SICKNESS]

air-slake (âr′slāk′), *v.t.,* **-slaked, -slak·ing.** to slake (lime or the like) with moist air.

air′ sleeve′, windsock.

air′ sock′, windsock.

air′ space′, 1. a space occupied by air. 2. the amount of breathing air in a room or other enclosed space. 3. Also, **air′space′.** the region of the atmosphere above a plot of ground, municipality, state, or nation.

air·speed (âr′spēd′), *n.* the forward speed of an aircraft relative to the air through which it moves. Also, **air′ speed′.** Cf. **ground speed.** [AIR[1] + SPEED]

air′speed in′dicator, *Aeron.* a flight instrument showing the air speed of an aircraft.

air-spray (âr′sprā′), *adj.* pertaining to compressed-air spraying devices or to liquids used in them. —**air′-sprayed′,** *adj.*

air′ spray′er, a pneumatic sprayer.

air′ spring′, *Mach.* a springlike support utilizing the compressibility of air confined behind a piston in a cylinder.

air′ stack′, stack (def. 12).

air′ sta′tion, an airfield having facilities for sheltering and servicing aircraft.

air·strip (âr′strip′), *n.* *Aeron.* runway (def. 2). [AIR[1] + STRIP[2]]

air′ switch′, *Elect.* a switch in which the interruption of the circuit occurs in air.

air′ sys′tem, 1. a system of refrigeration utilizing air as a coolant. 2. any group of devices operated or controlled by air under pressure or vacuum.

airt (ârt; *Scot.* ĕrt), *Chiefly Scot.* —*n.* 1. a direction. —*v.t.* 2. to point out the way; direct; guide. Also, **airth** (ârth; *Scot.* ĕrth). [< Gael *aird* a high point, quarter of the compass]

air′ tee′. See **wind tee.**

air·tight (âr′tīt′), *adj.* 1. preventing the entrance or escape of air. 2. having no weak points or openings of which an opponent may take advantage: *an airtight contract.* [AIR[1] + TIGHT] —**air′tight′ly,** *adv.* —**air′-tight′ness,** *n.*

air-to-air (âr′to͞o âr′, -tə-), *adj.* 1. operating between airborne objects, esp. aircraft: *air-to-air missiles; air-to-air communication.* —*adv.* 2. from one aircraft, missile, or the like, to another while in flight: *They refueled air-to-air.*

air-to-sur·face (âr′tə sûr′fəs), *adj.* 1. operating or directed from a flying aircraft to the surface: *air-to-surface missiles.* —*adv.* 2. from a flying aircraft to the surface of the earth: *They released the rockets air-to-surface.* Also called **air-to-ground** (âr′tə ground′).

air′ train′. See **sky train.**

air′ trap′, trap[1] (def. 4).

air′ tur′bine, a turbine operated by air under pressure.

air′ twist′, a serpentine motif within the stem of a goblet, produced by extending and twisting an air bubble during glass blowing. —**air′-twist′ed,** *adj.*

air′ valve′, a device for controlling the flow of air, as from a pipe or tank.

air va·rié (âr′ vâr′ē ā′; *Fr.* er va ryā′), *Music.* a melody with variations. [F: lit., varied air]

air′ ves′icle, *Bot.* a large, air-filled pocket, chiefly in plants which float on water, as kelps.

air′ war′, 1. military operations by combatants involving the use of aircraft. 2. those phases or aspects of a war in which aircraft play a part.

air·wash (âr′wosh′, -wôsh′), *v.t.* 1. to cool (a roof or the like) with a current of air. —*n.* 2. a current of air for cooling a roof or the like. [AIR[1] + WASH]

air·waves (âr′wāvz′), *n. pl.* the media of radio and television broadcasting: *The airwaves were filled with references to this important development.* [AIR[1] + *waves* (pl. of WAVE)]

air·way (âr′wā′), *n.* 1. an air route fully equipped with emergency landing fields, beacon lights, radio beams, etc. 2. any passage in a mine used for purposes of ventilation; an air course. 3. **airways, a.** the band of frequencies, taken collectively, used by radio broadcasting stations: *The news is sent out over the airways as soon as it is received.* **b.** airline (def. 1c). [AIR[1] + WAY]

air′ way′bill, a nonnegotiable shipping document evidencing the contract between shipper and air carrier for transportation and delivery of cargo. *Abbr.:* AWB Also, **air′way′bill′.** Also called **airbill, waybill;** *esp. Brit.,* **air consignment note, consignment note.**

air′ well′. See **air shaft.**

air·wom·an (âr′wo͝om′ən), *n., pl.* **-wom·en.** an aviatrix. [AIR[1] + WOMAN]

air′ wood′, timber dried naturally by contact with the open air.

air·wor·thy (âr′wûr′thē), *adj.* *Aeron.* meeting accepted standards for safe flight; equipped and maintained in condition to fly. [AIR[1] + WORTHY] —**air′-wor′thi·ness,** *n.*

air·y (âr′ē), *adj.,* **air·i·er, air·i·est.** 1. open to a free current of air; breezy: *airy rooms.* 2. consisting of or having the character of air; immaterial: *airy phantoms.* 3. light in appearance; thin: *airy garments.* 4. light in manner; sprightly; lively: *airy songs.* 5. light in movement; graceful; delicate: *an airy step.* 6. light as air; unsubstantial; unreal; imaginary: *airy dreams.* 7. visionary; speculative. 8. performed in the air; aerial. 9. lofty; high in the air. [late ME *ayery;* see AIR[1], -Y[1]] —**air′i·ness,** *n.*

Air·y (âr′ē), *n.* a crater in the fourth quadrant of the face of the moon: about 22 miles in diameter.

Air′y disc′ (âr′ē), *Optics.* the bright central part of the diffraction pattern of light from a point source which is diffracted by a circular aperture. [after Sir George Biddel *Airy* (1801–92) + DISC]

A·i·sha (ä′ē shä′), *n.* A.D. 613?–678, favorite wife of Muhammad (daughter of Abu-Bekr). Also, **Ayesha.**

AISI, American Iron and Steel Institute.

AISI steel, any steel made to conform to the standard chemical compositions generally accepted by the U.S. steel industry and its principal customers.

aisle (īl), *n.* 1. *Archit.* **a.** a longitudinal division of an interior area, as in a church, separated from the main area by an arcade or the like. **b.** any of the longitudinal divisions of a church or the like. 2. **in the aisle,** (of an audience) convulsed with laughter. [alter. (with *ai* < F *aile* wing) of earlier *isle, ile;* r. ME *ele* < MF < L *āla* wing. See ALA] —**aisled,** *adj.*

Aisne (ān; *Fr.* en), *n.* 1. a river in N France, flowing NW and W to the Oise. 175 mi. long. See map under **Compiègne.** 2. a department in N France. 503,000 (est. 1958); 2868 sq. mi. *Cap.:* Laon.

ait (āt), *n.* *Brit. Dial.* a small island, esp. in a river. Also, **eyot.** [ME *eyt* < OE *ȳgett,* dim. of *īeg* island, c. Icel *ey.* See ISLAND]

aitch (āch), *n.* the letter *H, h.* [ME *ache* < OF *ache* < LL **hacca* or **accha;* r. *ha*]

aitch·bone (āch′bōn′), *n.* 1. the rump bone, as of beef. 2. the cut of beef which includes this bone. Also, **edgebone.** [late ME *hach-boon* (with spurious *h-*); (*h*)*ach* var. of *nache* rump < MF < VL **natica,* fem. of **naticus* of the rump < L *nati(s)* rump + *-cus* adj. suffix]

Ait·ken (āt′kən), *n.* 1. **Robert Grant,** 1864–1951, U.S. astronomer. 2. **William Maxwell.** See **Beaverbrook, William Maxwell Aitkin.**

A·i·us Lo·cu·tius (ā′ē əs lō kyo͞o′shəs), *Rom. Legend.* a disembodied voice that warned the Romans of a coming invasion by the Gauls.

Aix-en-Pro·vence (eks äN prô väNs′), *n.* a city in SE France, N of Marseilles. 72,696 (1962). Also called **Aix.**

Aix-la-Cha·pelle (eks lA shA pel′; *Eng.* āks′lä shä-pel′), *n.* French name of **Aachen.**

Aix-les-Bains (eks lā baN′; *Eng.* āks′lā bānz′, āks′lə-pānz′), *n.* a town in SE France, N of Chambéry.

A·jac·cio (ä yät′chô), *n.* a seaport in and the capital of Corsica: the birthplace of Napoleon I. 32,997 (1954).

A·jan·ta (ə jun′tə), *n.* a village in central Maharashtra, in S central India: caves and shrines containing Buddhist frescoes and sculptures.

a·jar[1] (ə jär′), *adj., adv.* neither entirely open nor entirely shut; partly open: *The door was ajar.* [ME *on char* on the turn; see CHAR[3]]

a·jar[2] (ə jär′), *adv., adj.* in contradiction to; at variance with: *ajar with the facts.* [for *at jar* at discord; cf. JAR[3] (n.)]

A·jax (ā′jaks), *n.* *Class. Myth.* 1. Also called **Great Ajax, Telamonian Ajax.** a Greek hero in the Trojan War who rescued the body of Achilles and killed himself out of jealousy when Odysseus was awarded the armor of Achilles. 2. Also called **A′jax the Less′er, Locrian Ajax, Oilean Ajax.** a Locrian king, noted for his fighting during the Trojan War, who was said to have been killed in a shipwreck as a punishment for violating a shrine of Athena. 3. (*italics*) a tragedy (c440 B.C.) by Sophocles. Also, **Aias.**

a·jee (ə jē′), *adv.* *Brit. Dial.* agee.

a·ji·va (ə jē′və), *n.* *Jainism.* all in the universe that is not jiva, as space, time, matter, and those things by which rest and motion are possible to objects. [< Skt *ajīva* without life, equiv. to *a-* A-[6] + *jīva* living]

A·ji·vi·ka (ä jē′vi kə), *n.* a member of a former Indian sect, originated in the 5th century B.C. as a heretical offshoot of Jainism, which maintained that each individual must have passed through 84,000 existences, gradually evolving in mental capacity until his final and predestined liberation, which no spiritual exercises or discipline can hasten: a disciple of Gosala. [< Skt *ājīvika:* lit., observing certain rules about living (*ājīva* way of life, deriv. of *ājīvati* he continues living, equiv. to *ā-* toward + *jīvati* he lives)]

Aj·mer (uj mēr′), *n.* a city in central Rajasthan, in NW India. 231,200 (1961).

Aj·mer-Mer·wa·ra (uj mēr′mer wär′ə), *n.* a former province in NW India. 2400 sq. mi.

A·jo (ä′hō), *n.* a town in SW Arizona. 7049 (1960).

A·jodh·ya (ə yōd′yə), *n.* a city in central Uttar Pradesh, in N India; a suburb of Fyzabad: one of the seven most sacred Hindu centers.

à jour (ä′ zho͝or′; *Fr.* A zhōōr′), of or pertaining to objects that are pierced, perforated, or decorated with an openwork pattern. Also, **a·jou·ré** (ä zho͝o rā′; *Fr.* A zho͞o rā′). [< F: lit., (open) to daylight]

A·ju·ga (aj′ə gə), *n.* a genus of plants comprising the bugles. [< NL, equiv. to *a-* A-[6] + *juga* < L *jug(um)* yoke + *-a* fem. n. suffix]

a·ka·la (ə kä′lə), *n.* a Hawaiian shrub or climber, *Rubus Macraei,* bearing a large, red, edible raspberry. [< Hawaiian]

a·ka·sha (ä kä′shə), *n.* (in the philosophies of India) the ether, regarded as including material and nonmaterial entities in a common medium. [< Skt *ākāśa*]

Ak·bar (ak′bär), *n.* ("*the Great*") (*Jalal-ud-Din Mohammed*) 1542–1605, Mogul emperor of India 1556–1605.

A.K.C., American Kennel Club.

ake (āk), *v.i.,* **aked, ak·ing,** *n.* *Obs.* ache.

a·ke·a·ke (ä′kē ä′kē), *n.* aalii. [< Maori]

ak·e·bi (ak′ə bē), *n.* a climbing vine, *Akebia quinata,* of eastern Asia, bearing purple, edible berries, grown as an ornamental in the U.S. [< Jap]

a·kee (ə kē′), *n.* a tropical, sapindaceous tree, *Blighia sapida,* cultivated for the edible aril of its seeds. [< Kwa]

a·ke·la (ə kē′lə), *n.* (in the Cub Scouts) a pack leader. [after *Akela,* leader of the wolfpack in the *Jungle Book* by Kipling]

A·kel·da·ma (ə kel′də mə), *n.* Aceldama.

Ake·ley (āk′lē), *n.* **Carl Ethan,** 1864–1926, U.S. naturalist, explorer, and sculptor.

a·kene (ā kēn′), *n.* achene.

ake·ton (ak′tən), *n.* *Armor.* acton.

Akh (äk), *n.* *Egyptian Myth.* the transfigured and beatified spirit of a dead person. [< Egypt]

Akh·e·ta·ton (ä′kə tät′ən), *n.* the capital of ancient Egypt under the reign of Amenhotep IV: its excavated site is at the modern village of Tell el Amarna.

Ak·hi·sar (äk′hi sär′), *n.* a town in W Turkey, NE of Izmir. 104,744 (1960). Ancient, **Thyatira.**

Akh·na·ton (äk nät′ən), *n.* See **Amenhotep IV.**

A·ki·ba ben Jo·seph (ä kē′bä ben jō′zəf, -səf, ə kē′və), A.D. c50–c135, Hebrew scholar: compiler of Jewish oral law on which the Mishnah is based. Also called **A·ki′ba.**

A·ki·hi·to (ä kē′hē tô′), *n.* born 1933, crown prince of Japan (son of Hirohito).

A·kim (ä′kim; *Pol.* ä′kēm; *Russ.* ä kēm′), *n.* a boy's given name.

a·kim·bo (ə kim′bō), *adj., adv.* with hand on hip and elbow bent outward: *to stand with arms akimbo.* [late ME *in kenebowe,* appar., in keen bow, in a sharp bent]

a·kin (ə kin′), *adj.* **1.** of kin; related by blood (usually used predicatively): *cousins that were too closely akin for marriage.* **2.** allied by nature; having the same properties: *Something akin to vertigo was troubling her.* **3.** having or showing an affinity; kindred: *They are emotionally but not intellectually akin.* [A-² + KIN] **—Syn. 2.** cognate; similar, analogous.

a·ki·ne·sia (ā′ki nē′zhə, -kī-), *n.* *Pathol.* absence, loss, or impairment of the power of voluntary movement. Also, **a·ki·ne·sis** (ā kin′i sis, ā′kī nē′sis). [< NL < Gk *akinēsía,* equiv. to *a-* A-⁶ + *kīnēs(is)* (*kīnē-,* s. of *kīnein* to move + *-sis*) + *-iā* -Y³] **—a·ki·net·ic** (ā′ki net′ik, -kī-), *adj.*

ak·i·nete (ak′ə nēt′, ā kī′nēt), *n.* (in certain algae) a nonmotile, asexual spore formed within a cell, the wall of which is fused to that of the parent cell. Cf. **aplanospore.** [< Gk *akínēt(os)* without movement, equiv. to *a-* A-⁶ + *kīnētos* moving, deriv. of *kīn(ein)* (to) move]

A·kins (ā′kinz), *n.* **Zo·ë** (zō′ē), 1886–1958, U.S. playwright.

A·ki·ta (ä′kē tä′), *n.* a seaport on N Honshu, in N Japan, on the Sea of Japan. 190,202 (1955).

Ak·kad (ak′ad, ä′käd), *n.* **1.** Accad. **—*adj.* 2.** Akkadian.

Ak·ka·di·an (ə kā′dē ən, ə kä′-), *n.* **1.** the eastern Semitic language, now extinct, of Assyria and Babylonia, written with a cuneiform script. **2.** one of the Akkadian people. **3.** *Obs.* Sumerian. **—*adj.* 4.** of or belonging to Accad. **5.** of or pertaining to the eastern Semitic language called Akkadian. **6.** *Obs.* Sumerian. Also, Accadian. [AKKAD + -IAN]

Ak·ker·man (ä′kər män′), *n.* former name of **Belgorod-Dnestrovski.**

Ak·kra (ak′rə, ə krä′), *n.* Accra.

Ak·mo·linsk (äk′mə linsk′; *Russ.* uk mô′lyinsk), *n.* former name of **Tselinograd.**

Ak·ron (ak′rən), *n.* **1.** a city in NE Ohio. 290,351 (1960). **2.** a town in W New York. 2841 (1960).

ak·ro·ter (ak′rə tər), *n.* acroter.

ak·ro·te·ri·on (ak′rə tēr′ē on′, -ən), *n., pl.* **-te·ri·a** (-tēr′ē ə). acroterium.

Ak·sum (äk′so͞om), *n.* the capital of an ancient Ethiopian kingdom, ruled by Himyaritic emigrants from Arabia. Also, **Axum.**

A·ku·ta·ga·wa (ä ko͞o′tä gä′wä), *n.* **Ryu·no·su·ke** (ryo͞o nô′so͞o ke′), 1892–1927, Japanese short-story writer and essayist.

ak·va·vit (äk′vä vēt′), *n.* a dry, Scandinavian, ginlike distilled spirit made from redistilled neutral spirits flavored with caraway seeds. Also, **aquavit.** [< Scand < L *aqua vīt(ae)* water of life]

Ak·yab (ak yab′, ak′yab), *n.* a seaport in W Burma. 42,329 (1953).

Al (al), *n.* a boy's given name, form of **Albert, Alfred, Aloysius.**

à l′, form of **à la** used for either gender before a vowel or *h.*

al-, var. of **ad-** before *l: allure.*

-al¹, an adjectival suffix occurring in loan words from Latin (*regal; equal*); on this model, used in the formation of adjectives from other sources (*typical*). [< L *-ālis, -āle* pertaining to; often r. ME *-el* < OF]

-al², a suffix forming nouns from verbs of French or Latin origin: *denial; refusal.* [< L *-āle* (sing.), *-ālia* (pl.), neut. of *-ālis* -AL¹; often r. ME *-aille* < OF]

-al³, *Chem.* a suffix indicating that a compound contains an aldehyde group: *chloral.* [short for ALDEHYDE]

AL, Anglo-Latin. Also, **AL., A.L.**

Al, *Chem.* aluminum.

al., **1.** other things. [< L *alia*] **2.** other persons. [< L *alii*]

A.L., **1.** *Baseball.* American League. **2.** American Legion. **3.** Anglo-Latin.

a.l., autograph letter.

à la (ä′ lä, ä′ lə; *Fr.* A lA), **1.** according to; in the manner of: *a poetic tragedy à la Maxwell Anderson.* **2.** *Cookery.* prepared with, as in, or by: *à la jardinière; à la Boston; à la Ritz.* Also, **a la.** [< F: short for *à la mode de* in the style of]

a·la (ā′lə), *n., pl.* **a·lae** (ā′lē). **1.** a wing. **2.** a winglike part, process, or expansion, as of a bone, shell, seed, stem, etc. **3.** one of the two side petals of a papilionaceous flower. **4.** (in an ancient Roman house) a small room, as an alcove, opening into a larger room or courtyard. [< L: wing, armpit, shoulder < *ax-* (see AXIS) + *-la* dim. suffix]

A·la (ä′lä), *n.* **Hus·sein** (ho͞o sān′), 1888–1964, Iranian statesman and diplomat premier 1951 and 1955–57.

Ala., Alabama.

A.L.A., **1.** American Library Association. **2.** Associate in Liberal Arts. **3.** Authors League of America. **4.** Automobile Legal Association.

Al·a·bam·a (al′ə bam′ə), *n.* **1.** a State in the SE United States. 3,266,740 (1960); 51,609 sq. mi. *Cap.:* Montgomery. *Abbr.:* Ala. **2.** a river flowing SW from central Alabama to the Mobile River. 315 mi. long. **—Al·a·bam·i·an** (al′ə bam′ē ən), **Al′a·bam′an,** *adj., n.*

Al′abam′a Claims′, claims of the U.S. against England for damages caused in the American Civil War by the warship Alabama and by other vessels fitted out in British ports for the Confederacy. The claims were arbitrated at Geneva (1871–72) and a monetary settlement made to the U.S.

al·a·bam·ine (al′ə bam′ēn, -in), *n.* *Chem.* (formerly) astatine. *Symbol:* Ab [ALABAM(A) + -INE²]

al·a·ban·dite (al′ə ban′dīt), *n.* a rare mineral, manganese sulfide, MnS, occurring in a massive form and having a cubical lattice structure. [named after *Alaband(a)* town in Turkey, + -ITE¹]

à l′a·ban·don (A lA bäN dôN′), *French.* carelessly; recklessly. [lit., in lack of restraint]

al·a·bas·ter (al′ə bas′tər, -bä′stər), *n.* **1.** a finely granular variety of gypsum, often white and translucent, used for ornamental objects or work, such as lamp bases, figurines, etc. **2.** Also called **Oriental alabaster.** a variety of calcite, often banded, used or sold as alabaster. **—*adj.*** Also, **al·a·bas·trine** (al′ə bas′trin). **3.** made of alabaster: *an alabaster column.* **4.** resembling alabaster; smooth and white as alabaster: *her alabaster throat.* [< L < Gk *alábastros;* r. late ME *alabastre* < MF < L]

al·a·bas·tos (al′ə bas′tos, -təs, -bä′ stos, -stəs), *n., pl.* **-bas·toi** (-bas′toi, -bä′stoi). alabastron.

al·a·bas·tron (al′ə bas′tron, -trən; -bä′stron, -strən), *n., pl.* **-bas·tra** (-bas′trə, -bä′strə), **-trons.** *Gk. and Rom. Antiq.* an oil jar characteristically having an elongated shape, narrow neck, flat-rimmed mouth, and rounded base requiring a stand or support, chiefly used for fragrant ointments. Also, **alabastos, alabastrum.** Cf. **aryballos, askos, lekythos.** [< Gk: alabaster vase]

al·a·bas·trum (al′ə bas′trəm, -bä′strəm), *n., pl.* **-bas·tra** (-bas′trə, -bä′strə), **-trums.** alabastron.

à la boi·telle (A lA bwA tel′), *French.* cooked with mushrooms.

à la bonne heure (A lA bô nœr′), *French.* **1.** at the right moment. **2.** just right; excellent; very well. [lit., at the good hour]

à la broche (A lA brôsh), *French.* cooked on a skewer.

à la carte (ä′ lə kärt′, al′ə; *Fr.* A lA KART′), with a stated price for each dish offered: *dinner à la carte.* Cf. **prix fixe, table d'hôte.** [< F: according to the card; see CARTE²]

a·lack (ə lak′), *interj.* *Archaic.* an exclamation of sorrow, regret, or dismay. Also, **a·lack·a·day** (ə lak′ə dā′). [var. of old exclamation *lack!* Cf. AHA, AHEM, and OE *lǣccung* reproach]

a·lac·ri·ty (ə lak′ri tē), *n.* **1.** cheerful readiness, promptness, or willingness. **2.** liveliness; briskness. [< L *alacritāt-* (s. of *alacritās*), equiv. to *alacri(s)* lively + *-tāt-* -TY²] **—a·lac′ri·tous,** *adj.*

A·la Dagh (ä′lä däkh′), **1.** a mountain range in S Turkey: highest peak, ab. 11,000 ft. **2.** a mountain range in E Turkey: highest peak, ab. 11,500 ft.

A·lad·din (ə lad′ən), *n.* (in *The Arabian Nights' Entertainments*) the son of a poor widow in China. He becomes the possessor of a magic lamp and ring with which he commands two jinns who gratify all his wishes.

a·lae (ā′lē), *n.* pl. of **ala.**

à la fran·çaise (A lA fräN sez′), *French.* in or according to the French manner or style.

A·la·gez (*Armenian.* u′lə gyôs′), *n.* **Mount.** See **Aragats, Mount.**

A·la·go·as (ä′lə gō′əs), *n.* a state in NE Brazil. 1,271,062 (1960); 10,674 sq. mi. *Cap.:* Maceió.

A·la·göz (ä′lä gœz′), *n.* Turkish name of Mount Aragats.

A·lai′ Moun′tains (ä lī′), a mountain range in the SW Soviet Union in Asia, in the Kirghizia: part of the Tien Shan Mountains; highest peak, ab. 19,000 ft.

A·lain (ə lān′), *n.* a girl's given name, form of **Helen.** Also, **Alayne, Elaine, Elena.**

à la king (ä′ lə king′, al′ə), (of a dish of diced, cooked fowl, fish, etc.) creamed with pimiento or green pepper: *chicken à la king.*

Al·al·co·me′ne·an Athe′na (al′al kə mē′nē ən), *n.* *Class. Myth.* Athena: so called because she was reared by Alalcomeneus.

Al·al·co·me·neus (al′al kə mēn′yəs), *n.* *Class. Myth.* the first man.

a·la·li·a (ə lā′lē ə, ə lāl′yə), *n.* *Pathol.* an inability to speak. [A-⁶ + Gk *laliá* talk, chatter, equiv. to *lal(ein)* (to) talk, chatter + *-iā* -Y³]

Al·a·man·ni (al′ə man′ī), *n.pl.* Alemanni.

Al·a·man·nic (al′ə man′ik), *n., adj.* Alemannic.

al·a·me·da (al′ə mā′də), *n.* *Chiefly Southwestern U.S.* a public walk shaded with poplar or other trees. [< Sp, equiv. to *álam(o)* poplar + *-eda* < L *-ētum* suffix marking provision]

Al·a·me·da (al′ə mē′də, -mā′-), *n.* a city in W California. 63,855 (1960).

A·la·mein (al′ə mān′), *n.* See **El Alamein.**

al·a·mi·qui (al′ə mə kē′), *n.* almique (def. 3).

al·a·mo (al′ə mō′, al′ə-), *n., pl.* **-mos.** *Southwestern U.S.* a cottonwood. [< Sp: poplar < ?]

Al·a·mo (al′ə mō′), *n.* **1.** a Franciscan mission in San Antonio, Texas, besieged by Mexicans on February 23, 1836, during the Texan war for independence and taken on March 6, 1836, with its entire garrison killed. **2.** a town in S Texas. 4121 (1960).

à la mode (ä′ lə mōd′, al′ə-; *Fr.* A lA môd′), **1.** in or according to the fashion. **2.** *Cookery.* **a.** (of pie or other dessert) served with a portion of ice cream. **b.** (of beef) larded and braised or stewed with vegetables, herbs, etc., and served with a rich brown gravy. Also, **a′ la mode′, a′la·mode′.** [< F: in the manner]

al·a·mode (al′ə mōd′), *n.* a lightweight, glossy silk fabric used in the manufacture of scarfs, hoods, etc. [from À LA MODE]

Al·a·mo·gor·do (al′ə mə gôr′dō), *n.* a city in S New Mexico: first atomic bomb exploded in the desert ab. 50 mi. NW of here, July 16, 1945. 21,723 (1960).

Al′amo Heights′, a town in Texas. 7552 (1960).

à la mort (A lA môr′), *French.* **1.** mortally ill. **2.** melancholy; dispirited. **3.** grievously; fatally. [lit., to the death]

Al·a·mo·sa (al′ə mō′sə, -mo͞o′sə), *n.* a town in S Colorado. 6205 (1960).

Al·an (al′ən), *n.* a boy's given name. Also, **Allan, Allen, Allyne.**

Al·an-a-dale (al′ən ə dāl′), *n.* Allan-a-dale.

à l′an·cienne (A läN syen′), *French.* in or according to the old-fashioned manner or style.

Å′land Is′lands (ä′lənd, ō′lənd; *Swed.* ō′länd′), a group of Finnish islands in the Baltic Sea, between Sweden and Finland. 22,000 (est. 1958); 572 sq. mi. Finnish, **Ahvenanmaa.**

à l′an·glaise (A läN glez′), *French.* in or according to the English manner or style.

al·a·nine (al′ə nēn′, -nin), *n.* *Chem., Biochem.* any of several isomers of a colorless, crystalline, water-soluble amino acid, $CH_3CH(NH_2)COOH$, found in many proteins and produced synthetically: used chiefly in biochemical research. [AL(DEHYDE) + *-an-* (arbitrarily inserted) -INE²]

al′ant starch′ (al′ənt, ə lant′), *Chem.* inulin. [< G < OHG < VL **iluna,* alter. of L *inula* (see INULIN)]

a·lap·a (ə lap′ə), *n.* *Rom. Cath. Ch., Anglican Ch.* the light blow on the cheek delivered by the bishop in a confirmation service. [< L: a slap]

a·lar (ā′lər), *adj.* **1.** pertaining to or having wings; alary. **2.** winglike; wing-shaped. **3.** *Anat., Bot.* axillary. [< L *ālār(is)* < *āl(a)* ALA + *-āris* -AR¹]

A·lar·cón (ä′lär kôn′), *n.* **Pe·dro An·to·nio** (pe′thrô än tô′nyô), (*Pedro Antonio Alarcón y Ariza*), 1833–91, Spanish novelist, short-story writer, and diplomat.

A la Re·cherche du Temps Per·du (*Fr.* A lA rə shersh′ dY täN per dY′). See **Remembrance of Things Past.**

Al·a·ric (al′ər ik), *n.* **1.** A.D. c370–410, king of the Visigoths: captured Rome 410. **2.** a boy's given name.

à la ri·gueur (A lA rē gœr′), *French.* to the fullest extent; literally. [lit., in strictness]

a·larm (ə lärm′), *n.* **1.** a sudden fear or distressing suspense excited by an awareness of danger; apprehension; fright. **2.** any sound, outcry, or information intended to warn of approaching danger: *He ran through the town raising the alarm that the enemy was coming.* **3.** an automatic device that serves to call attention, rouse from sleep, warn of danger, etc. **4.** a warning sound; signal for attention. **5.** a call to arms. **6.** *Fencing.* an appeal or a challenge made by a step or stamp on the ground with the advancing foot. **—*v.t.* 7.** to make fearful or apprehensive; distress. **8.** to warn of danger; rouse to vigilance and swift measures for safety. [ME *alarme* < MF < It *allarme,* deriv. of *all'arme* to (the) arms. See ARM²] **—a·larm′a·ble,** *adj.* **—a·larm·ed·ly** (ə lär′mid lē), *adv.* **—a·larm′ing·ly,** *adv.*
—Syn. 1. consternation; terror, panic. See **fear. 7.** See **frighten.**

alarm′ clock′, a clock with a bell or buzzer which can be set to sound at a particular time, used esp. to awaken oneself.

a·larm·ist (ə lär′mist), *n.* **1.** a person who tends to raise alarms, esp. without sufficient reason, as by exaggerating dangers, prophesying calamities, etc. **—*adj.* 2.** of or like an alarmist. [ALARM + -IST] **—a·larm′ism,** *n.*

alarm′ reac′tion, *Physiol.* the first stage of the general adaptation syndrome, in which the body responds to stress by exhibiting shock.

a·lar·um (ə lar′əm, ə lär′-), *n.* *Archaic.* alarm. [ME *alarom*]

alar′ums and excur′sions, (in early modern English drama) military action, as representative fragments of a battle, sound effects of trumpets, clash of arms, etc.: used as a stage direction.

a·la·ry (ā′lə rē, al′ə-), *adj.* **1.** of or pertaining to wings. **2.** *Biol.* wing-shaped. [< L *ālāri(us),* equiv. to *āl(a)* ALA + *-ārius* -ARY]

a·las (ə las′, ə läs′), *interj.* an exclamation expressing sorrow, grief, pity, concern, or apprehension of evil. [ME < OF *(h)a las!,* equiv. to *(h)a* AH + *las* wretched < L *lass(us)* weary]

Alas., Alaska.

A·las·ka (ə las′kə), *n.* **1.** a State of the United States in NW North America. 226,167 (1960); 586,400 sq. mi. *Cap.:* Juneau. *Abbr.:* Alas. **2. Gulf of,** a gulf of the Pacific, on the coast of S Alaska. **—A·las′kan,** *adj., n.*

Alas′ka ce′dar, **1.** an evergreen, coniferous tree, *Chamaecyparis nootkatensis,* of northwestern North America. **2.** the hard, yellow wood of this tree, used in shipbuilding and in making furniture. Also called **Nootka cypress, Sitka cypress, yellow cedar, yellow cypress.**

Alas′ka cod′, a cod, *Gadus macrocephalus.*

Alas′ka cot′ton, a cotton grass, esp. *Eriophorum angustifolium.*

Alas′ka cur′rent, an ocean current flowing counterclockwise in the Gulf of Alaska.

Alas′ka High′way, a highway in NW Canada and Alaska, extending from E British Columbia to Fairbanks: built as a U.S. military supply route 1942. 1523 mi. long. Also called **Alcan Highway.**

Alas′kan mal′amute, one of an Alaskan breed of large dogs having a dense, coarse coat, raised originally for drawing sleds. Also, **Alas′kan Mal′amute.**

Alas′kan or′chis, a North American fringed orchis, *Habenaria unalascensis,* having green flowers.

Alas′ka Penin′sula, a peninsula in SW Alaska. 500 mi. long.

Alas′ka pol′lock. See **walleye pollock.**

Alas′ka Range′, a mountain range in S Alaska. Highest peak, Mt. McKinley, 20,300 ft.

Alas′ka time′. See under **standard time.**

Al·as·tair (al′ə stər, -stâr′), *n.* a boy's given name. Also, **Al·as·ter** (al′ə stər), **Alastor, Alister.**

A·las·tor (ə las′tər *for 1, 2;* al′ə stər *for 3*), *n. Class. Myth.* **1.** an epithet of Zeus, meaning "avenger." **2.** an epithet of any avenging god or demon. **3.** a boy's given name.

al·as·trim (al′ə strim), *n. Pathol.* mild smallpox. Also called **glass pox.** [< Pg, equiv. to *alastr(ar)* (to) cover, spread on (*a-* A-[5] + *lastro* covering, load < Gmc; see LAST[4]) + *-im* n. suffix]

a·late (ā′lāt), *adj.* **1.** having wings; winged. **2.** having membranous expansions like wings. Also, **a′lat·ed.** [< L *ālāt(us),* equiv. to *āl(a)* ALA + *-ātus* -ATE[1]]

à la va·peur (A lA vA pœr′), *French.* steamed.

A·layne (ə lān′), *n.* a girl's given name, form of **Helen.** Also, **Alain, Elaine, Elena.**

alb (alb), *n. Eccles.* a close-sleeved linen vestment, worn chiefly by priests, now invariably white in the Western Church but any color in the Eastern Church. [ME, OE *albe* < L *alba* (*vestis*) white (garment)]

Alb

Alb., **1.** Albania. **2.** Albanian. **3.** Albany. **4.** Alberta.

alb., (in prescriptions) white. [< L *albus*]

al·ba (al′bə, al′-), *n.* a Provençal troubadour poem or love song, typically about the parting of lovers at dawn. [< OPr: dawn < L, fem. of *albus* white]

Al·ba (al′bə; *Sp.* äl′vä), *n.* **Duke of.** See **Alva, Fernando, Álvarez.**

Alba., Alberta.

Al·ba·ce·te (äl′bä the′te), *n.* a city in SE Spain. 79,875 (est. 1960).

al·ba·core (al′bə kōr′, -kôr′), *n., pl.* **-cores,** (*esp. collectively*) **-core. 1.** a long-finned edible tuna, *Germa alalunga,* found in all warm or temperate seas, the flesh of which is valued for canning. **2.** any of various tunalike fishes. [< Pg *albacor(a)* < Ar *al bakūrah* the tuna]

Al·ba Lon·ga (al′bə lông′gə, long′-), a city of ancient Latium, SE of Rome: legendary birthplace of Romulus and Remus.

Al·ba·my·cin (al′bə mī′sin), *n. Pharm., Trademark.* novobiocin.

Al·ban (ôl′bən, al′-), *n.* **1. Saint,** 3rd century A.D., first English martyr. **2.** Also, **Alben, Albin.** a boy's given name.

Al·ba·ne·se (al′bə nā′zə, -sə, äl′-; *It.* äl′bä ne′ze), *n.* **Li·cia** (lē′chē ə; *It.* lē′chä), born 1913, Italian operatic soprano.

Al·ba·ni·a (al bā′nē ə, -bān′yə), *n.* **1. a republic in S Europe, in the Balkan Peninsula, W of Macedonia and NW of Greece. 2,400,000; 10,632 sq. mi.** *Cap.:* **Tirana. 2.** *Obs.* **Scotland.**

Al·ba·ni·an (al bā′nē ən, -bān′yən), *adj.* **1.** pertaining to Albania, its inhabitants, or their language. —*n.* **2.** a native or inhabitant of Albania or Albany, N.Y. **3.** the Indo-European language of Albania in the Balkan Peninsula. [ALBANI(A) + -AN]

Al·ba·ny (ôl′bə nē), *n.* **1.** a city in and the capital of New York, in the E part, on the Hudson. 129,726 (1960). **2.** a city in SW Georgia. 55,890 (1960). **3.** a city in W California, on San Francisco Bay. 14,804 (1960). **4.** a city in W Oregon. 12,929 (1960). **5.** a seaport in SW Australia: resort. 8265 (1954). **6.** a river in central Canada, flowing E from W Ontario to James Bay. 610 mi. long.

Al′bany Con′gress, *Amer. Hist.* a meeting of delegates from seven American colonies, held in 1754 at Albany, New York, at which Benjamin Franklin proposed a plan (**Al′bany Plan′ of Un′ion**) for unifying the colonies.

al·ba·rel·lo (al′bə rel′ō), *n., pl.* **-rel·los, -rel·li** (-rel′ē). a majolica jar of the 15th and 16th centuries, cylindrical with a waist slightly narrower than the ends, used in Spain and Italy for keeping dry drugs. [< It, prob. dim. of *albero* poplar << L *alb(us)* white]

al·bar·i·um (al bâr′ē əm), *n.* a stucco used in ancient times, made from powdered marble and lime mortar and often polished. [< L: white stucco, neut. sing. of *albārius* pertaining to whitening of walls, equiv. to *alb(us)* white + *-ārius* -ARY]

al·ba·ta (al bā′tə), *n.* See **German silver.** [< NL < L, fem. sing. of *albāt(us),* equiv. to *alb(us)* white + *-ātus* -ATE[1]]

Al·ba·teg·ni·us (äl′bə teg′nē əs), *n.* a walled plain in the fourth quadrant of the face of the moon: about 80 miles in diameter.

al·ba·tross (al′bə trôs′, -tros′), *n.* **1.** any of several large, web-footed sea birds of the family *Diomedeidae,* which have the ability to remain aloft for long periods. Cf. **wandering albatross. 2.** *Textiles.* **a.** a lightweight worsted fabric with a crepe or pebble finish. **b.** a plain-weave cotton fabric with a soft nap surface. [var. of *algatross* frigate bird < Pg or Sp *alcatraz* pelican; *-b-* for *-g-* perh. by assoc. with L *alba* white (the bird's color)]

Albatross, *Diomedea exulans* (Length 4 ft.; wingspread 12 ft.)

Al·bay (äl bī′), *n.* former name of **Legaspi.**

al·be·do (al bē′dō), *n. Astron.* the ratio of the light reflected by a planet or satellite to that received by it. < LL: whiteness, equiv. to *alb(us)* white + *-ēdō* n. suffix as in TORPEDO]

al·be·dom·e·ter (al′bi dom′i tər), *n.* an instrument that measures the albedo of a surface. [ALBEDO + -METER]

Al·bee (ôl′bē), *n.* **Edward,** born 1928, U.S. playwright.

al·be·it (ôl bē′it), *conj.* although; even if: *a peaceful, albeit inglorious retirement.* [ME *al be it* al(though) it be]

Al·be·marle (al′bə märl′), *n.* a city in central North Carolina. 12,261 (1960).

Al′bemarle Sound′, an inlet of the Atlantic Ocean, in NE North Carolina. 60 mi. long.

Al·ben (al′bən), *n.* a boy's given name. Also, **Alban, Albin.**

Al·bé·niz (äl ve′nēth; *Eng.* äl bā′nēs, al-), *n.* **I·sa·ac** (ē′sä äk′; *Eng.* ī′zək), 1860–1909, Spanish composer and pianist.

al·ber·go (äl beʀ′gô), *n., pl.* **-ghi** (-gē). *Italian.* an inn; hotel; tavern.

Al·ber·ich (äl′bər ikh), *n. Teutonic Legend.* a king of the dwarfs, the possessor of the tarnkappe and of the treasure of the Nibelungs.

Al·be·ro·ni (äl′be rô′nē), *n.* **Giu·lio** (jōō′lyô), 1664–1752, Italian cardinal and statesman: prime minister of Spain 1715–19.

Al·bert (al′bərt), *n.* **1. Prince** (*Albert Francis Charles Augustus Emanuel, Prince of Saxe-Coburg-Gotha*), 1819–61, consort of Queen Victoria. **2. Lake.** Also called **Albert Nyanza.** a lake in central Africa, between Uganda and the Republic of the Congo: a source of the Nile. 100 mi. long; 2064 sq. mi.; 2030 ft. above sea level. **3.** a boy's given name.

Albert I, 1875–1934, king of the Belgians 1909–34.

Al·ber·ta (al bûr′tə), *n.* **1.** a province in W Canada. 1,398,464 (1956); 255,285 sq. mi. *Cap.:* Edmonton. *Abbr.:* Alta. **2.** a girl's given name, form of **Albertine.**

Al·bert, d′ (dal′bərt; *Ger.* däl′bert; *Fr.* dal beʀ′), **Eu·gen** (*Ger.* oi gān′) or **Eu·gène** (*Fr.* œ zhen′) **Francis Charles,** 1864–1932, German-French pianist and composer, born in Scotland.

Al′bert Ed′ward, a mountain in SE New Guinea, in the Owen Stanley Range. 13,030 ft.

Al·ber·ti (äl beʀ′tē), *n.* **1. Le·on Bat·ti·sta** (le ôn′ bät tē′stä), 1404–72, Italian architect, artist, musician, and poet. **2. Ra·fa·el** (rä fä el′), born 1902, Spanish poet.

Al·ber′ti bass′ (al bûr′tē bās′, äl ber′-), *Music.* a reiterated broken-chord figure used as an accompaniment, esp. in 18th-century rococo keyboard music. [named after Domenico *Alberti,* 18th-century Italian musician]

Alberti bass

Al·ber·tine (al′bər tēn′; *Fr.* Al beʀ tēn′; *Ger.* äl′ber tē′nə), *n.* a girl's given name. Also, **Al·ber·ti·na** (al′bər tē′nə).

al·bert·ite (al′bər tīt′), *n.* an asphalt from the Albert mine in New Brunswick, Canada. [*Albert* + -ITE[1]]

Al′bert Lea′, a city in S Minnesota. 17,108 (1960).

Al′bert Ny·an′za (nī an′zə, nyän′zä). See **Albert, Lake.**

Al·ber·tus Mag·nus (al bûr′təs mag′nəs), **Saint** (*Albert von Böllstadt*) ("*Albert the Great*", "*the Universal Doctor*"), 1193?–1280, German scholastic philosopher: teacher of Saint Thomas Aquinas. —**Al·ber·tist** (al bûr′tist, al′bər-), *n.*

Al·bert·ville (*Fr.* Al beʀ vēl′ *for 1;* al′bərt vil *for 2*), *n.* **1.** a city in the E Republic of the Congo, on Lake Tanganyika. 29,488 (est. 1958). **2.** a town in NE Alabama. 8250 (1960).

al·ber·type (al′bər tīp′), *n. Print.* collotype. [after Joseph *Albert* (1825–86), Austrian photographer + -TYPE]

al·bes·cent (al bes′ənt), *adj.* becoming white; whitish. [< L *albēscent-* (s. of *albēscēns,* prp. of *albēscere*), equiv. to *alb(us)* white + *-ēscent-* -ESCENT] —**al·bes′cence,** *n.*

Al·bi (Al bē′), *n.* a city in and the capital of Tarn, in S France: center of the Albigenses. 41,268 (1962).

Al·bi·a (al′bē ə), *n.* a town in S Iowa. 4582 (1960).

Al·bi·gen·ses (al′bi jen′sēz), *n.pl.* members of a Catharistic sect in the south of France that arose in the 11th century and was exterminated in the 13th century by a crusade (**Albigen′sian Crusade′**) and the Inquisition. [< L *Albig(a)* ALBI + *-enses* -ESE] —**Al·bi·gen·si·an** (al′bi jen′sē ən, -shən), *adj., n.* —**Al′bi·gen′si·an·ism,** *n.*

Al·bin (al′bin), *n.* a boy's given name. Also, **Alban, Alben.**

Al·bi·na (al bī′nə, -bē′-), *n.* a girl's given name.

al·bi·nism (al′bə niz′əm), *n.* the state or condition of being an albino. [ALBIN(O) + -ISM] —**al′bi·nis′tic,** *adj.*

al·bi·no (al bī′nō *or, esp. Brit.,* -bē′-), *n., pl.* **-nos. 1.** a person with a pale, milky skin, light hair, and pink eyes, resulting from congenital absence of pigmentation. **2.** an animal or plant with a marked deficiency in pigmentation. **3.** *Philately.* an embossed stamp accidentally left without ink. [< Pg, equiv. to *alb(o)* white (L *albus*) + *-ino* -INE[1]] —**al·bin·ic** (al bin′ik), **al·bi·nal** (al′bə nəl), *adj.*

Al·bi·nus (al bī′nəs), *n.* Alcuin.

Al·bi·on (al′bē ən), *n.* **1.** a town in W New York. 5182 (1960). **2.** *Archaic.* Britain. **3.** Alebion.

al·bite (al′bīt), *n. Mineral.* the sodium end member of the plagioclase feldspar group, light-colored and found in alkali rocks. [< L *alb(us)* white + -ITE[1]] —**al·bit·ic** (al bit′ik), *adj.*

Al·bi·zu Cam·pos (äl bē′sōō käm′pôs), **Pe·dro** (pe′thrô), 1891–1964, Puerto Rican political leader.

ALBM, *Rocketry.* air-launched ballistic missile.

Al·boin (al′boin, -bō in), *n.* died A.D. 573?, king of the Langobards 561?–573?.

Ål·borg (ôl′bôrg), *n.* a seaport in NE Jutland, in Denmark. 96,438 (1960). Also, **Aalborg.**

al·bronze (al′bronz′), *n.* See **aluminum bronze.**

al·bum (al′bəm), *n.* **1.** a book consisting of blank leaves, pockets, envelopes, etc., for entering or storing photographs, stamps, autographs, phonograph records, or the like. **2.** a long-playing phonograph record or set of records containing several musical selections, a complete play, opera, etc.: *Her album of folk songs will be out next month.* **3.** the package or container for such record or records: *The album has separate pockets for each of the records.* **4.** a visitor's register; visitor's book. [< L: neut. sing. of *albus* white]

al·bu·men (al byōō′mən), *n.* **1.** the white of an egg. **2.** *Bot.* the nutritive matter about the embryo in a seed. **3.** *Biochem.* albumin. [< L, equiv. to *alb(us)* white + *-ū-* connective + *-men* n. suffix]

al·bu·me·nise (al byōō′mə nīz′), *v.t.,* **-nised, -nis·ing.** *Chiefly Brit.* albumenize. —**al·bu′me·ni·sa′tion,** *n.* —**al·bu′me·nis′er,** *n.*

al·bu·me·nize (al byōō′mə nīz′), *v.t.,* **-nized, -niz·ing.** to treat with an albuminous solution. [ALBUMEN + -IZE] —**al·bu′me·ni·za′tion,** *n.* —**al·bu′me·ni·iz′er,** *n.*

albu′men plate′, a flexible zinc or aluminum printing plate coated with a photosensitive compound, used in offset printing of usually fewer than 50,000 copies. Also called **surface plate.** Cf. **deep-etch plate.**

al·bu·min (al byōō′mən), *n. Biochem.* any of a class of water-soluble proteins composed of nitrogen, carbon, hydrogen, oxygen, and sulfur, occurring in animal and vegetable juices and tissues. Also, **albumen.** [ALBUM(EN) + -IN[2]]

al·bu·mi·nate (al byōō′mə nāt′), *n. Biochem.* a compound resulting from the action of an alkali or an acid upon albumin. [ALBUMIN + -ATE[2]]

albu′min col′or, (in textile printing) a color fixed to a fabric by an albuminous mordant.

al·bu·mi·nise (al byōō′mə nīz′), *v.t.,* **-nised, -nis·ing.** *Chiefly Brit.* albuminize.

al·bu·mi·nize (al byōō′mə nīz′), *v.t.,* **-nized, -niz·ing.** albumenize.

al·bu·mi·noid (al byōō′mə noid′), *Biochem.* —*n.* **1.** any of a class of simple proteins, as keratin, gelatin, collagen, etc., that are insoluble in all neutral solvents. **2.** scleroprotein. —*adj.* **3.** resembling albumen or albumin. [ALBUMIN + -OID] —**al·bu′mi·noi′dal,** *adj.*

al·bu·mi·nous (al byōō′mə nəs), *adj.* of, containing, or resembling albumen. Also, **al·bu·mi·nose** (al byōō′mə nōs′). [ALBUMIN + -OUS]

al·bu·mi·nu·ri·a (al byōō′mə nŏŏr′ē ə, -nyŏŏr′-), *n. Pathol.* the presence of albumin in the urine. [ALBUMIN + -URIA] —**al·bu′mi·nu′ric,** *adj.*

al·bu·mose (al′byə mōs′), *n. Biochem.* any of a class of compounds derived from proteins, as albumin, by the action of proteolytic enzymes. [ALBUM(IN) + -OSE[2]]

Al·bu·ne·a (al byōō′nē ə), *n. Rom. Legend.* a fountain nymph noted for her prophetic powers. Also, **Al·bu·na** (al byōō′nə).

Al·bu·quer·que (al′bə kûr′kē; *for 1 also Port.* ôl′bŏŏ-keʀ′kə), *n.* **1. Af·fon·so de** (ə fōN′sōō də), 1453–1515, founder of the Portuguese empire in the East. **2.** a city in central New Mexico. 201,189 (1960).

al·bur·num (al bûr′nəm), *n. Bot.* sapwood. [< L, equiv. to *alb(us)* white + *-urnum* neut. n. suffix] —**al·bur′nous,** *adj.*

Al·cae·us (al sē′əs), *n.* **1.** fl. c600 B.C., Greek poet of Mytilene. **2.** *Class. Myth.* a son of Androgeus and a grandson of Minos.

al·ca·hest (al′kə hest′), *n.* alkahest.

Al·ca·ic (al kā′ik), *adj.* **1.** pertaining to Alcaeus or to certain meters or a form of strophe or stanza used by, or named after, him. —*n.* **2. Alcaics,** Alcaic verses or strophes. [< LL *Alcaic(us)* < Gk *Alkaïkós,* equiv. to *Alka(íos)* ALCAEUS + *-ikos* -IC]

al·cai·de (al kī′dē; *Sp.* äl kī′the), *n., pl.* **-caides** (-kī′dēz; *Sp.* -kī′thes). (in Spain, Portugal, Southwestern U.S., etc.) **1.** a commander of a fortress. **2.** a jailer; the warden of a prison. Also, **alcayde.** [< Sp < Ar *al-qā'id* the chief]

Al·ca·ids (al kā′idz), *n.pl. Class. Myth.* the descendants of Alcaeus.

al·cal·de (al kal′dē; *Sp.* äl käl′de), *n., pl.* **-des** (-dēz; *Sp.* -des). (in Spain and Southwestern U.S.) a mayor having judicial powers. Also, **al·cade** (al kād′). [< Sp < Ar *al qāḍī* the judge]

al·ca·lig·e·nes (al′kə lij′ə nēz′), *n., pl.* **-nes.** *Bacteriol.* any of several rod-shaped, aerobic or facultatively anaerobic bacteria of the genus *Alcaligenes,* found in the intestinal tract of man and other vertebrates and in dairy products. [< NL < F *alcali-* ALKALI + Gk *-genēs;* see -GEN]

Al·can·dre (al kan′drē), *n.* (in the *Odyssey*) the wife of Polybus who received Helen and Menelaus on their way home from Troy.

Al′can High′way (al′kan). See **Alaska Highway.**

al·cap·ton (al kap′ton, -tən), *n. Biochem.* alkapton.

al·cap·ton·u·ri·a (al kap′tə nŏŏr′ē ə, -nyŏŏr′-), *n. Pathol.* alkaptonuria.

Al·cath·o·us (al kath′ō əs), *n. Class. Myth.* **1.** a son of Pelops and Hippodamia who married Euachme and became king of Megara. **2.** (in the *Iliad*) a Trojan chieftain slain by Idomeneus.

Al·ca·traz (al′kə traz′), *n.* an island in W California, in San Francisco Bay: former site of a U.S. penitentiary.

al·cay·de (al kī′dē; *Sp.* äl kī′the), *n., pl.* **-cay·des** (-kī′dēz; *Sp.* -kī′thes). alcaide.

Al·ca·zar (al′kə zär′, al kaz′ər; *Sp.* äl kä′thär), *n.* **1.** the palace of the Moorish kings at Seville. **2.** (*l.c.*) a castle or fortress of the Spanish Moors. [< Sp < Ar *al* the + *qaṣr* < L *castr(um)* CASTLE, stronghold]

Al·ceste (al sest′), *n.* an opera (1767) by Christoph Willibald Gluck.

Al·ces·tis (al ses′tis), *n.* **1.** *Class. Myth.* the wife of Admetus who gave up her life in order that the Fates might save the life of Admetus and later was brought back from Hades by Hercules. **2.** (*italics*) a tragedy (438 B.C.) by Euripides.

alchem., alchemy.

al·che·mise (al′kə mīz′), *v.t.*, **-mised, -mis·ing.** *Chiefly Brit.* alchemize.

al·che·mist (al′kə mist), *n.* one who is versed in or practices alchemy. [prob. < ML *alchymist(a)*, equiv. to *alchym(ia)* ALCHEMY + *-ista* -IST]

Alchemist, The, a comedy (1610) by Ben Jonson.

al·che·mize (al′kə mīz′), *v.t.*, **-mized, -miz·ing.** to change by alchemy; transmute, as metals. Also, *esp. Brit.*, **alchemise.** [ALCHEM(Y) + -IZE]

al·che·my (al′kə mē), *n., pl.* **-mies** for 2. **1.** an art, practiced in the Middle Ages and the Renaissance, concerned principally with discovering methods for transmuting baser metals into gold and with finding a universal solvent and an elixir of life. **2.** any magical power or process of transmuting a common substance, usually of little value, into a substance of great value. [earlier *alchimie* < ML *alchymia* < Ar *al* the + *kīmiyā′* < Gk *kēmeía* transmutation; r. ME *alconomye*, equiv. to *alk(imie)* + *(astr)onomye* ASTRONOMY] —**al·chem·ic** (al kem′ik), **al·chem′i·cal, al·che·mis·tic** (al′kə mis′tik), **al′che·mis′ti·cal,** *adj.* —**al·chem′i·cal·ly,** *adv.*

al·che·rin·ga (al′chə ring′gə), *n.* *Anthropol.* the never-ending period of the creation of all things, as conceived in the mythology of the Arunta people of Australia. Also called **dreamtime.** [< native Austral name]

Al·chuine (al′kwin), *n.* Alcuin.

Al·ci·bi·a·des (al′sə bī′ə dēz′), *n.* 450?–404 B.C., Athenian politician and general. —**Al′ci·bi′a·de′an,** *adj.*

al·cid (al′sid), *adj.* **1.** Also, **al·ci·dine** (al′si dīn′). of, pertaining, or belonging to the family *Alcidae*, comprising the auks, murres, puffins, etc. —*n.* **2.** a bird of the family *Alcidae*. [< NL *Alcid(ae)* name of the family, equiv. to *alca* auk + *-idae* -ID²]

Al·ci·des (al sī′dēz), *n.* Hercules (def. 1).

Al·cid·i·ce (al sid′i sē′), *n.* *Class. Myth.* the wife of Salmoneus and the mother of Tyro.

Al·cim·e·de (al sim′i dē′), *n.* *Class. Myth.* the mother of Jason.

Al·ci·me·des (al′sə mē′dēz), *n.* *Class. Myth.* a son of Jason and Medea.

Al·cim·e·don (al sim′i don′), *n.* *Class. Myth.* **1.** an Arcadian hero whose daughter, Philao, was seduced by Hercules. **2.** (in the *Iliad*) a son of Laerces who was a captain of the Myrmidons under Patroclus.

Al·cin·o·üs (al sin′ō əs), *n.* (in the *Odyssey*) king of the Phaeacians and father of Nausicaä and Laodamas.

Al·cis (al′sis), *n.* *Class. Myth.* a daughter of Antipoenus, who, with her sister Androclea, gladly committed suicide to insure a victory against the attacking Erginus, king of the Minyans.

Al·cith·o·ë (al sith′ō ē′), *n.* *Class. Myth.* a daughter of Minyas who was driven mad for mocking Dionysus.

al·clad (al′klad), *adj.* noting any of various wire and sheet-metal products coated with pure or alloyed aluminum. [formerly a trademark]

Alc·mae·on (alk mē′ən), *n.* *Class. Myth.* a son of Amphiaraus and Eriphyle who commanded the second expedition against Thebes.

Alc·ma·on (alk′mā ən), *n.* (in the *Iliad*) the son of Thestor who wounded Glaucus and was slain by Sarpedon.

Alc·me·ne (alk mē′nē), *n.* *Class. Myth.* the mother of Hercules.

Al·co·a (al kō′ə), *n.* a town in E Tennessee. 6395 (1960).

al·co·hol (al′kə hôl′, -hol′), *n.* **1.** Also called **ethyl alcohol, grain alcohol, ethanol, fermentation alcohol, spirits of wine, Cologne spirit.** a colorless, limpid, volatile, flammable, water-miscible liquid, C_2H_5OH, having an etherlike odor and pungent, burning taste, the intoxicating principle of fermented liquors, produced by yeast fermentation of certain carbohydrates, as grains, molasses, starch, or sugar, or obtained synthetically by hydration of ethylene or as a by-product of certain hydrocarbon syntheses: used chiefly as a solvent in the extraction of specific substances, in beverages, medicines, organic synthesis, lotions, tonics, colognes, rubbing compounds, as an automobile radiator antifreeze, and as a rocket fuel. **2.** any intoxicating liquor containing this spirit. **3.** *Chem.* any of a class of chemical compounds having the general formula ROH, where R represents an alkyl group and –OH a hydroxyl group, as in methyl alcohol, CH_3OH, or ethyl alcohol, C_2H_5OH. [< NL < ML < Ar *al-kuḥul* the powdered antimony, the distillate]

al·co·hol·ate (al′kə hô lāt′, -ho-; al′kə hô′lit, -hol′it), *n.* *Chem.* **1.** any of a class of compounds, analogous to hydrates, containing chemically combined alcohol, as chloral alcoholate, $CCl_3CHO{\cdot}C_2H_5OH$. **2.** alkoxide. [ALCOHOL + -ATE²]

al·co·hol·ic (al′kə hô′lik, -hol′ik), *adj.* **1.** of, pertaining to, or of the nature of alcohol. **2.** containing or using alcohol. **3.** caused by alcohol. **4.** suffering from alcoholism. **5.** preserved in alcohol. —*n.* **6.** *Pathol.* a person suffering from alcoholism. **7.** one addicted to intoxicating drinks. [ALCOHOL + -IC] —**al′co·hol′i·cal·ly,** *adv.*

al·co·hol·ic·i·ty (al′kə hô lis′i tē, -ho-), *n.* alcoholic quality or strength. [ALCOHOLIC + -ITY]

Alcohol′ics Anon′ymous, a fellowship formed for the purpose of helping alcoholics achieve sobriety. *Abbr.:* AA, A.A.

al·co·hol·ise (al′kə hô līz′, -ho-), *v.t.*, **-ised, -is·ing.** *Chiefly Brit.* alcoholize. —**al′co·hol′i·sa′tion,** *n.*

al·co·hol·ism (al′kə hô liz′əm, -ho-), *n.* *Pathol.* a diseased condition due to the excessive use of alcoholic beverages. Cf. **acute alcoholism, chronic alcoholism.** [ALCOHOL + -ISM]

al·co·hol·ize (al′kə hô līz′, -ho-), *v.t.*, **-ized, -iz·ing.** *Chem.* **1.** to convert into an alcohol. **2.** to treat or saturate with an alcohol. **3.** to place under the influence of alcoholic beverages; make drunk; besot. Also, *esp. Brit.*, **alcoholise.** [ALCOHOL + -IZE] —**al′co·hol′i·za′tion,** *n.*

al·co·hol·om·e·ter (al′kə hô lom′i tər, -ho-), *n.* an instrument for finding the percentage of alcohol in a liquid. [ALCOHOL + -O- + -METER] —**al·co·hol·o·met·ric** (al′kə hô′lə me′trik, -hol′ə-), **al′co·hol′o·met′ri·cal,** *adj.* —**al′co·hol·om′e·try,** *n.*

al·co·hol·y·sis (al′kə hol′i sis, -hô′li-), *n.* *Chem.* chemical decomposition resulting from the interaction of a compound and an alcohol. [ALCOHOL + -LYSIS] —**al·co·hol·yt·ic** (al′kə hô lit′ik, -ho-), *adj.*

Al·con (al′kon), *n.* *Class. Myth.* **1.** a noted archer who helped Hercules abduct the cattle of Geryon. **2.** a Trojan warrior who wounded Odysseus while trying to seize the body of Achilles and who was later killed by Odysseus.

Al·cor (al kôr′), *Astron.* the fifth-magnitude companion of Mizar in the handle of the Big Dipper; 80 Ursae Majoris.

Al·co·ran (al′kō răn′, -ran′, -kô-), *n.* Alkoran. —**Al′co·ran′ic,** *adj.*

Al·co·ran·ist (al′kō rä′nist, -ran′ist, -kô-), *n.* *Islam.* one who believes in an absolutely literal interpretation of the Koran. [ALCORAN + -IST]

Al·cott (ôl′kət, -kot), *n.* **1. (Amos) Bron·son** (bron′sən), 1799–1888, U.S. educator and philosopher. **2.** his daughter **Louisa May,** 1832–88, U.S. author. **3.** a boy's given name.

al·cove (al′kōv), *n.* **1.** a recess adjacent to or opening out of a room: *a dining alcove.* **2.** a recess in a room for a bed, bookcases, or the like. **3.** any recessed space, as in a garden. [< F *alcôve* < Sp *alcoba* < Ar *al* the + *qobbah*, var. of *qubbah* arch, vault, vaulted room]

Al·cuin (al′kwin), *n.* (*Ealhwine Flaccus*) A.D. 735–804, English theologian and scholar: teacher and adviser of Charlemagne. Also, **Alchuine.** Also called **Albinus.**

al·cy·o·nar·i·an (al′sē ə nâr′ē ən), *n.* **1.** any anthozoan coelenterate of the subclass *Alcyonaria*, having the body parts in groups of eight. —*adj.* **2.** belonging or pertaining to the *Alcyonaria*. [< NL *alcyonāri(a)* < Gk *alkyón(ion)* a type of coral named from its resemblance to the nest of the kingfisher (Gk *alkyṓn*) + *-āria* -ARY + -AN]

Al·cy·o·ne (al sī′ə nē′), *n.* **1.** a third-magnitude star in the constellation Taurus; the brightest star in the Pleiades. **2.** Also, **Halcyon.** *Class. Myth.* a daughter of Aeolus who, with her husband, Ceyx, was transformed into a kingfisher.

Al·cy·o·neus (al sī′ə nōōs′, -nyōōs′, -nəs), *n.* *Class. Myth.* **1.** a giant who threw a stone at Hercules and was killed when Hercules hit the stone back with his club. **2.** a giant who, invulnerable in his own country, was dragged by Hercules to another country and there killed.

Ald., Alderman. Also, **ald.**

Al·da (äl′də, ôl′-, al′-), *n.* **1. Frances,** 1885–1952, U.S. operatic singer. **2.** a boy's or girl's given name.

Al·dan (*Russ.* äl dän′ *for 1;* ôl′dᵊn, -dən *for 2*), *n.* **1.** a river in the Soviet Union in Asia, flowing NE from the Yabloni Mountains to the Lena. ab. 1500 mi. long. **2.** a town in SE Pennsylvania. 4324 (1960).

Al·deb·a·ran (al deb′ər ən), *n.* a first-magnitude star, orange in color, in the constellation Taurus. [< Ar *al* the + *dabarān* follower (of the Pleiades)]

al·de·hyde (al′də hīd′), *n.* *Chem.* any of a class of organic compounds containing the group –CHO, which yields acids when oxidized and alcohols when reduced. [< NL *al(cohol) dehyd(rogenātum)* dehydrogenated alcohol] —**al′de·hy′dic,** *adj.*

Al·den (ôl′dᵊn, -dən), *n.* **1. John,** 1599?–1687, Pilgrim settler in Plymouth, Massachusetts, 1620. **2.** a boy's or girl's given name.

al·der (ôl′dər), *n.* **1.** any betulaceous shrub or tree of the genus *Alnus*, growing in moist places in northern temperate or colder regions. **2.** any of various trees or shrubs resembling an alder. [ME *alder, aller*, OE *alor, al(e)r*; akin to OHG *elira, erila* (G *Erle*), Russ *ólícha*, L *alnus*]

Al·der (äl′dər; *Ger.* äl′dəʀ), *n.* **Kurt** (kûrt; *Ger.* kōōrt), 1902–58, German chemist: Nobel prize 1950.

al′der buck′thorn, a shrub or small tree, *Rhamnus Frangula*, of Eurasia and northern Africa, having red fruit that turns black.

al·der·fly (ôl′dər flī′), *n., pl.* **-flies.** any of several dark-colored neuropterous insects of the family *Sialidae*, the larvae of which are aquatic and predacious on other aquatic insects. [ALDER + FLY²]

al′der fly′catcher, a North American flycatcher, *Empidonax traillii*, of alder thickets and other moist areas, having greenish-brown upper parts and whitish underparts. Also called **Traill's flycatcher.**

al·der·man (ôl′dər mən), *n., pl.* **-men. 1.** *U.S.* a member of a municipal legislative body; councilman. **2.** (in England) one of the members, chosen by the elected councilors, in a borough or county council. **3.** *Early Eng. Hist.* **a.** a chief. **b.** (later) the chief magistrate of a county or group of counties. [ME; OE *(e)aldormann*, equiv. to *ealdor* chief, patriarch (*eald* OLD + *-or* n. suffix) + *mann* MAN¹] —**al′der·man·cy, al′der·man·ship′,** *n.*

al·der·man·ic (ôl′dər man′ik), *adj.* of or characteristic of an alderman or aldermen. [ALDERMAN + -IC]

al·der·man·ry (ôl′dər mən rē), *n., pl.* **-ries.** the district, office, or rank of an alderman. [ME *aldermanrie*. See ALDERMAN, -RY]

Al·der·ney (ôl′dər nē), *n.* **1.** one of the Channel Islands in the English Channel. 1350 (1956); 3 sq. mi. **2.** any of several breeds of cattle raised originally in the Channel Islands, as the Jersey or Guernsey.

Al·der·shot (ôl′dər shot′), *n.* **1.** a city in NE Hampshire, in S England, SW of London. 33,690 (est. 1964). **2.** a large military training center there.

Al·dine (ôl′dīn, -dēn), *adj.* **1.** of or from the press of Aldus Manutius and his family in Venice, c1490–1597, chiefly noted for compactly printed editions of the classics. —*n.* **2.** an Aldine or other early edition. **3.** any of several styles of printing types modeled on those designed by Aldus, esp. italic. [< It *aldin(o)*, named after ALD(O MANUZIO); see *Manutius, Aldus* + *-ino* -INE¹]

Al·ding·ton (ôl′ding tən), *n.* **Richard,** 1892–1962, English poet, novelist and composer.

Al·dis (ôl′dis), *n.* a boy's given name. Also, **Aldous.**

Aldm., Alderman. Also, **aldm.**

Al·do (äl′dō, ôl′-, al′-), *n.* a boy's given name.

al·do·hex·ose (al′dō hek′sōs), *n.* *Chem.* any of several hexoses in which one carbon atom is part of an aldehyde structure. [ALD(EHYDE) + -O- + HEXOSE]

al·dol (al′dôl), *n.* *Chem.* **1.** Also called **acetaldol.** a colorless, syrupy, water-soluble liquid, $CH_3CHOHCH_2CHO$, formed by the condensation of acetaldehyde: used chiefly in the manufacture of rubber vulcanizers and accelerators, and in perfumery. **2.** any of a class of compounds containing the group, –CHOH(–C–)CHO, formed from aldehydes. [ALD(EHYDE) + -OL]

al·dose (al′dōs), *n.* *Chem.* a sugar containing the aldehyde group or its hemiacetal equivalent. [ALD(EHYDE) + -OSE²]

al·do·ste·rone (al′dō sti rōn′, al′dō sti rōn′, al dos′tə rōn′), *n.* *Biochem.* a hormone produced by the cortex of the adrenal gland, instrumental in the regulation of sodium and potassium reabsorption by the cells of the tubular portion of the kidney. [ALD(EHYDE) + -O- + STER(OL) + -ONE]

Al·dous (ôl′dəs), *n.* a boy's given name. Also, **Aldis.**

Al·drich (ôl′drich), *n.* **Thomas Bailey,** 1836–1907, U.S. short-story writer, poet, and novelist.

al·drin (ôl′drin), *n.* *Chem.* a brown, water-insoluble, toxic solid consisting of more than 95 percent of the chlorinated hydrocarbon $C_{12}H_8Cl_6$: used as an insecticide. [named after Kurt ALDER; see -IN²]

Al·dus Ma·nu·ti·us (ôl′dəs mə nōō′shē əs, -nyōō′, al′dəs). See **Manutius, Aldus.**

ale (āl), *n.* a malt beverage, darker, heavier, and more bitter than beer, containing about 6 percent alcohol by volume. [ME; OE *(e)alu*; c. OS *alu*, Icel *öl*]

A·le·a (ā′lē ə), *n.* **1.** *Class. Myth.* an epithet of Athena referring to a sanctuary built in her honor by Aleus. **2.** an ancient city on the E border of Arcadia, near Argolis.

A·le·ar·di (ä′le äʀ′dē), *n.* **Count A·le·ar·do** (ä′le äʀ′dō), 1812–78, Italian poet and patriot.

a·le·a·to·ry (ā′lē ə tôr′ē, -tōr′ē), *adj.* **1.** *Law.* depending on a contingent event: *an aleatory contract.* **2.** of or pertaining to accidental causes; of luck or chance; unpredictable: *an aleatory element.* **3.** *Music.* employing the element of chance in the choice of notes. [< L *āleātōri(us)*, equiv. to *āleātōr-* (s. of *āleātor*) gambler (*ālea* game of dice + *-āt-* -ATE¹ + *-ōr-* -OR²) + *-ius* adj. suffix]

A·le·bi·on (ə lē′bē on′), *n.* *Class. Myth.* a son of Poseidon who, with his brother Dercynus, was killed by Hercules while attempting to steal the cattle that Hercules had taken from Geryon. Also, **Albion.**

Al·ec (al′ik), *n.* a boy's given name, form of **Alexander.** Also, **Al′eck, Alex, Alick.**

a·lec·i·thal (ā les′ə thəl), *adj.* *Embryol.* having little or no yolk in the cytoplasm of the egg or ovum. Also, **a·le·cith·ic** (ā′li sith′ik). [A-⁶ + Gk *lékith(os)* + -AL¹]

A·lec·to (ə lek′tō), *n.* *Class. Myth.* one of the Furies.

a·lec·try·o·man·cy (ə lek′trē ə man′sē), *n.* an ancient form of divination, using a rooster to select grains of food placed on letters of the alphabet. Also called **a·lec·to·ro·man·cy** (ə lek′tə rō man′sē). [< Gk *alektryṓ(n)* cock + -MANCY]

A·le·do (ə lē′dō), *n.* a town in NW Illinois. 3080 (1960).

a·lee (ə lē′), *adv., adj.* *Naut.* upon or toward the lee side of a vessel; away from the wind (opposed to *aweather*). [A-¹ + LEE¹]

al·e·gar (al′ə gər, ā′lə-), *n.* *Brit. Informal.* ale vinegar; sour ale. [ALE + (VIN)EGAR]

A·le·gre·te (ô li gʀe′ti), *n.* a city in SW Brazil. 19,560 (1950).

ale·house (āl′hous′), *n., pl.* **-hous·es** (-hou′ziz). a tavern where ale is sold. [ALE + HOUSE]

A·lei·chem (ä lā′ḵhem), *n.* **Sho·lom** (shō′ləm) or **Sho·lem** (shō′lem, -ləm) or **Sha·lom** (shä lōm′), pen name of Solomon Rabinowitz.

a·lei·chem sha·lom (ä lā ḵhem′ shä lôm′), *Hebrew.* a conventional Jewish expression, meaning "peace to you": used as a greeting in reply to the greeting *shalom aleichem.*

A·lei·xan·dre (ä′lā ksän′dʀe), *n.* **Vi·cen·te** (bē then′te), born 1900, Spanish poet.

A·le·ksan·dra Fyo·do·rov·na (*Russ.* ä′le ksän′dʀä fyô′do ʀov′nä). See **Alexandra Feodorovna.**

A·le·ksan·dro·pol (*Russ.* ä le′ksän dʀô′pol), *n.* former name of **Leninakan.**

A·le·ksan·drovsk (*Russ.* ä′le ksän′dʀofsk), *n.* former name of **Zaporozhe.**

A·le·mán (ä′le män′), *n.* **1. Ma·te·o** (mä te′ō), 1547?–1610, Spanish novelist. **2. Mi·guel** (mē gel′), born 1902, president of Mexico 1946–52.

Al·e·man·ni (al′ə man′ī), *n.* (*construed as pl.*) a confederation of Germanic tribes, first recorded in the 3rd century A.D., which settled in the area between the Rhine, Main, and Danube rivers, and made harassing attacks against the Roman Empire. Also, **Alamanni.** [< L, of Gmc orig.; c. Goth *alamans* totality of mankind]

Al·e·man·nic (al′ə man′ik), *n.* **1.** the high German speech of Switzerland, Alsace, and southwestern Germany. Cf. **Bavarian** (def. 3). —*adj.* **2.** of, pertaining to, or belonging to Alemannic or the Alemanni. Also, **Alamannic.** [< L *Alamannic(us)*: see ALEMANNI, -IC]

A·lem·bert, d′ (dal′əm bâr′; *Fr.* dᴀ lāɴ beʀ′), **Jean Le Rond** (zhäɴ lə ʀôɴ′), 1717?–83, French mathematician, philosopher, and writer: associate of Diderot.

a·lem·bic (ə lem′bik), *n.* **1.** a vessel with a beaked cap or head, formerly used in distilling. **2.** anything that transforms, purifies, or refines. [ME, var. of *alambic* < ML *alambic(us)* < Ar *al* the *anbīq* still < Gk *ámbix* cup]

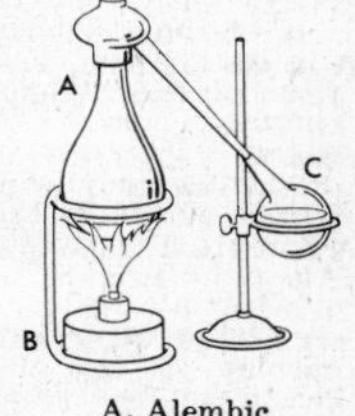

A, Alembic
B, Lamp
C, Receiver

A·len·çon (ᴀ läɴ sôɴ′; *Eng.* ə len′sən, -son), *n.* a city in and the capital of Orne, in NW France: lace manufacture. 27,024 (1962).

Alen′çon lace′, **1.** Also called **point d'Alençon.** a delicate, needle-point lace having a solid design outlined with twisted yarn on a background of hexagonal mesh. **2.** a machine reproduction of this lace, with a cordlike outline.

A·lene (ā lēn′), *n.* a girl's given name, form of **Helen.** Also, **Aileen, Eileen.**

a·leph (ä′lif; *Heb.* ä′lef), *n.* **1.** the first letter of the Hebrew alphabet. **2.** the glottal stop consonant or, alternatively, long vowel represented by this letter. [< Heb, prob. var. of *eleph* ox]

a·leph-null (ä′lef nul′, ä′lif-), *n.* *Math.* the cardinal number of the set of all positive integers; the smallest infinite cardinal number. *Symbol:* $\aleph_0$ Also called **a·leph-ze·ro** (ä′lef zēr′ō, ä′lif-).

A·lep·po (ə lep′ō), *n.* a city in NW Syria. 425,000 (est. 1960). French, **A·lep** (ᴀ lep′).

Alep′po gall′, a nutlike gall produced by gall wasps on certain oaks in Western Asia and eastern Europe.

Alep′po grass′. See **Johnson grass.**

a·ler·ce (ə ler′sə), *n.* **1.** the wood of the sandarac tree. **2.** a Chilean evergreen tree, *Fitzroya cupressoides*, having furrowed, reddish bark and overlapping leaves. 3. an incense cedar, *Libocedrus chilensis*, of Chile. Also called **Chilean arborvitae** (for defs. 1, 2). [< Sp < Ar *al* the + L *laric-* (s. of *larix*) LARCH]

a·le·ri·on (ə lēr′ē ən, -on′), *n.* *Heraldry.* an eagle displayed, usually represented without a beak or legs. [< MF *alérion* < ML *ālāriōn-* (s. of *ālāriō*), big eagle, ? equiv. to L *ālār(is)* of the wing (see ALAR) + *-iōn-* n. suffix]

a·lert (ə lûrt′), *adj.* **1.** vigilantly attentive; wide-awake; keen: *an alert mind.* **2.** swift; agile; nimble. —*n.* **3.** an attitude of vigilance or caution, as before an expected attack. **4.** an air-raid alarm. **5.** the period during which an air-raid alarm is in effect. **6. on the alert,** on guard against danger; in readiness; vigilant: *The state police are on the alert for an escaped convict who is believed to be in the area.* —*v.t.* **7.** to warn (troops, ships, etc.) to prepare for action. **8.** to warn of an impending raid, attack, storm, etc.: *The radio alerted coastal residents to prepare for the hurricane.* **9.** to advise or warn; cause to be on guard: *to alert a community to the dangers of inflation.* [< It *all'erta*, equiv. to *all(a)* to the *erta* lookout, watchtower, orig. fem. of *erto*, ptp. of *ergere* < L *ērigere* to ERECT] —**a·lert′ly,** *adv.* —**a·lert′ness,** *n.*
—**Syn. 1.** aware, wary, observant. ALERT, VIGILANT, WATCHFUL imply a wide-awake attitude, as of someone keenly aware of his surroundings. ALERT describes a ready and prompt attentiveness together with a quick intelligence: *The visitor to the city was alert and eager to see the points of interest.* VIGILANT suggests some immediate necessity for keen, active observation, and for continuing alertness: *Knowing the danger, the scout was unceasingly vigilant.* WATCHFUL suggests carefulness and preparedness: *watchful waiting.* **2.** brisk, lively, quick, active, sprightly, spirited. —**Ant. 1.** unaware.

-ales, *Bot.* a suffix of names of orders: *Cycadales.* [< L pl. of *-ālis* -AL¹]

A·le·si·a (ə lē′zhē ə, -zhə), *n.* an ancient city and fortress in Gaul: Caesar captured Vercingetorix here 52 B.C.

Al·es·san·dra (al′i san′drə, -sän′-; *It.* ä′les sän′drä), *n.* a girl's given name, Italian form of **Alexandra.**

A·les·san·dri (ä′le sän′drē), *n.* **1. Jor·ge** (hôr′he), born 1896, Chilean engineer and statesman: president 1958–64. **2. Pal·ma Ar·tu·ro** (päl′mä är to͞o′rô), 1868–1950, Chilean lawyer and statesman: president of Chile 1920–24, 1925, 1932–38.

A·les·san·dri·a (ä′les sän′drē ä), *n.* a city in NW Italy, in Piedmont. 92,291 (1961).

Al·es·san·dro (al′i san′drō), *n.* **Victor Nicholas,** born 1915, U.S. orchestra conductor.

Å·le·sund (ô′lə so͞on′), *n.* a seaport in W Norway. 18,527 (est. 1959). Also, **Aalesund.**

A·le·tes (ə lē′tēz), *n.* *Class. Myth.* **1.** a son of Clytemnestra and her lover Aegisthus. He became ruler of Mycenae after the death of his parents. **2.** a descendant of Hercules who conquered Corinth.

Al·e·the·a (al′ə thē′ə), *n.* a girl's given name.

Al·e·thi·a (al′ə thē′ə), *n.* the ancient Greek personification of truth.

a·le·thi·ol·o·gy (ə lē′thē ol′ə jē), *n.* the branch of logic dealing with truth and error. [< Gk *alḗthei(a)* truth (*alēthḗ(s)* true + *-ia* -IA) + -o- + -LOGY] —**a·le·thi·o·log·ic** (ə lē′thē ə loj′ik), **a·le′thi·o·log′i·cal,** *adj.* —**a·le′thi·ol′o·gist,** *n.*

A·let·ta (ə let′ə), *n.* a girl's given name. Also, **A·lette** (ə let′).

a·lette (ə let′), *n.* **1.** (in classical architecture) a part of a pier, flanking a pilaster or engaged column and supporting either impost of an arch. **2.** a small wing of a building. **3.** either jamb of a doorway. [< F, var. of AILETTE]

à l'étuvée (A lā ty vā′), *French.* stewed.

a·leu·ro·man·cy (ə lo͞or′ə man′sē), *n.* the use of flour as a means of divination. [< F *aleuromancie* (see ALEURONE, -MANCY), alter. of Gk *aleuromanteíon* divination by meal]

al·eu·rone (al′yə rōn′, ə lo͞or′ōn), *n.* (in the seeds of cereal plants) protein granules (**al′eurone grains′**) found in a single layer of cells (**al′eurone lay′er**) in the outermost portion of the endosperm. Also, **al·eu·ron** (al′yə ron′, ə lo͞or′on). [< Gk *áleuron* flour, meal] —**al′eu·ron·ic** (al′yo͞o ron′ik), *adj.*

A·le·us (ā′lē əs), *n.* *Class. Myth.* a king of Tegea and the father of Amphidamas, Auge, Cepheus, and Lycurgus.

Al·eut (ə lo͞ot′, al′ē o͞ot′), *n.* **1.** Also, **Aleutian.** a native of the Aleutian Islands. **2.** either of two related languages spoken by the Aleuts.

A·leu·tian (ə lo͞o′shən), *adj.* **1.** of or pertaining to the Aleutian Islands. —*n.* **2.** Aleut (def. 1).

Aleutian Islands

Aleu′tian cur′rent, a current in the Pacific Ocean that flows eastward between latitudes 40° and 50° N. Also called **subarctic current.**

Aleu′tian Is′lands, an archipelago extending SW from the Alaska Peninsula: part of Alaska. Also called **A·leu′tians.**

Aleu′tian low′, a semipermanent atmospheric low-pressure area located in the vicinity of the Aleutian Islands.

ale·wife¹ (āl′wīf′), *n., pl.* **-wives.** a North American fish, *Pomolobus* (or *Alosa*) *pseudoharengus*, resembling a small shad. [?]

ale·wife² (āl′wīf′), *n., pl.* **-wives.** a woman who owns or operates an alehouse. [ALE + WIFE]

Al·ex (al′iks), *n.* **1.** Also, **Alec, Al′eck, Alix.** a boy's given name, form of **Alexander. 2.** a girl's given name.

A·lex·a (ə lek′sə), *n.* a girl's given name, form of **Alexandra.** Also, **Alexine.**

al·ex·an·der (al′ig zan′dər, -zän′-), *n.* (*often cap.*) a cocktail made with crème de cacao, gin or brandy, and cream. [prob. after the proper name]

Al·ex·an·der (al′ig zan′dər, -zän′-), *n.* **1.** See **Alexander the Great. 2. Franz** (frants, franz, fränts), 1891–1964, U.S. psychoanalyst, born in Hungary. **3. Sir Harold R. L. G.,** born 1891. English field marshal: governor general of Canada 1946–52; minister of defense 1952–54. **4. Hartley Burr,** 1873–1939, U.S. philosopher, writer, and educator. **5. Samuel,** 1859–1938, British philosopher. **6. William,** 1726–83, general in the American Revolution. **7.** a walled plain in the first quadrant of the face of the moon: about 60 miles in diameter. **8.** a boy's given name.

Alexander I, 1. Saint, pope A.D. 106?–115. **2.** (*Aleksandr Pavlovich*) 1777–1825, czar of Russia 1801–25. **3.** (*Alexander Obrenovich* or *Aleksandar Obrenović*) 1876–1903, king of Serbia 1889–1903. **4.** 1888–1934, king of Yugoslavia 1921–34 (son of Peter I of Serbia).

Alexander I Island, an island off the coast of Antarctica, in the Bellingshausen Sea.

Alexander II, 1. died 1073, Italian ecclesiastic: pope 1061–1073. **2.** (*Aleksandr Nikolaevich*) 1818–81, czar of Russia 1855–81.

Alexander III, 1. died 1181, Italian ecclesiastic: pope 1159–81. **2.** (*Aleksandr Aleksandrovich*) 1845–94, czar of Russia 1881–94 (son of Alexander II).

Alexander IV, (*Rinaldo Conti*) died 1261, Italian ecclesiastic: pope 1254–61.

Alexander V, 1340?–1410, Cretan ecclesiastic: pope 1409–10.

Alexander VI, (*Roderigo Lanzol y Borgia*) 1431?–1503, Italian ecclesiastic: pope 1492–1503 (father of Cesare and Lucrezia Borgia).

Alexander VII, (*Fabio Chigi*) 1599–1667, Italian ecclesiastic: pope 1655–67.

Alexander VIII, (*Pietro Ottoboni*) 1610–91, Italian ecclesiastic: pope 1689–91.

Alexan′der Archipel′ago, an archipelago off the coast of SE Alaska.

Al′exan′der Cit′y, a city in E Alabama. 13,140 (1960).

Alexan′der Nev′ski (nev′skē, nef′-), 1220?–63, Russian prince, national hero, and saint.

Alexan′der Se·ve′rus (sə vēr′əs), A.D. 208?–235, Roman emperor 222–235.

Alexan′der's Feast′, an ode (1697) by Dryden, written for St. Cecilia's Day.

Al·ex·an·der·son (al′ig zan′dər sən), *n.* **Ernst F. W.** (ûrnst), born 1878, U.S. engineer and inventor.

Alexan′der the Great′, 356–323 B.C., king of Macedonia 336–323: conqueror of Greek city-states and of the Persian empire from Asia Minor and Egypt to India.

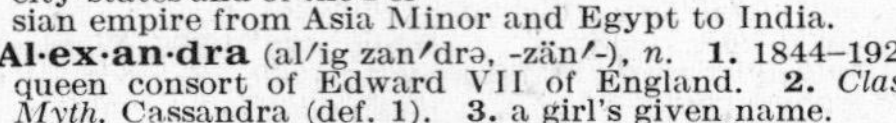

Empire of Alexander, Fourth Century B.C.

Al·ex·an·dra (al′ig zan′drə, -zän′-), *n.* **1.** 1844–1925, queen consort of Edward VII of England. **2.** *Class. Myth.* Cassandra (def. 1). **3.** a girl's given name.

A·le·xan·dra Feo·do·rov·na (ä′le ksän′drä fyô′do rôv′nä), 1872–1918, empress of Russia (wife of Nicholas II). Also, **Aleksandra Fyodorovna.**

Al·ex·an·dret·ta (al′ig zan dret′ə, -zän-), *n.* former name of **Iskenderun.**

Al·ex·an·dri·a (al′ig zan′drē ə, -zän′-), *n.* **1.** Arabic, **Al-Iskandariyah.** a seaport in the N United Arab Republic, in the Nile delta: founded in 332 B.C. by Alexander the Great; ancient center of learning. 1,513,000 (est. 1960). **2.** a city in NE Virginia, S of the District of Columbia. 91,023 (1960). **3.** a city in central Louisiana, on the Red River. 40,272 (1960). **4.** a town in W Minnesota. 6713 (1960). **5.** a town in central Indiana. 5582 (1960).

Al·ex·an·dri·an (al′ig zan′drē ən, -zän′-), *adj.* **1.** of Alexandria, Egypt. **2.** of or pertaining to the schools of philosophy, literature, and science in ancient Alexandria. **3.** Alexandrine. —*n.* **4.** a native or inhabitant of Alexandria, Egypt. [ALEXANDRI(A) + -AN]

Alexan′dria sen′na. See under **senna** (def. 2).

Alexan′dria Southwest′, a town in central Louisiana. 2782 (1960).

Al·ex·an·drine (al′ig zan′drin, -drēn, -zän′-), *Pros.* —*n.* **1.** (*often l.c.*) a verse or line of poetry of twelve syllables. —*adj.* **2.** (*often l.c.*) of or pertaining to such a verse or line. [< MF *alexandrin*, after *Alexandre*, from the use of this meter in an Old French poem on Alexander the Great; see -INE¹]

Al·ex·an·drine (al′ig zan′drin, -drēn, -zän′-), *adj.* of or pertaining to Alexandria, Egypt. [ALEXANDR(IA) + -INE¹]

Alexan′drine rat′. See **roof rat.**

Al·ex·an·dri·nus (al′ig zan drē′nəs, -drī′-, -zän-), *n.* the Greek uncial codex, dating from the early 5th century A.D., originally containing the complete text of the Greek Old and New Testaments. Cf. **codex.** [< L: lit., of ALEXANDRIA (Egypt); so called from its origin; see -INE¹]

al·ex·an·drite (al′ig zan′drīt, -zän′-), *n.* a variety of chrysoberyl, green by daylight and red-violet by artificial light, used as a gem. [named after ALEXANDER I of Russia; see -ITE¹]

A·le·xan·drou·po·lis (ä′le ksän dro͞o′pô lēs), *n.* a seaport in W Thrace, in NE Greece. 18,453 (1950). Formerly, **Dede Agach.**

a·lex·i·a (ə lek′sē ə), *n.* *Psychiatry.* a cerebral disorder marked by inability to understand written speech. [A-⁶ + Gk *léx(is)* speech (*lég-* s. of *légein* to speak + *-sis* -SIS) + -IA; altered meaning by assoc. of *-lex-* with LEXICON, etc.]

A·lex·i·an (ə lek′shən, -sē ən), *n.* *Rom. Cath. Ch.* a member of a congregation of brothers founded for the care of sick people at Mechlin, Brabant, in the 15th century. [named after Saint *Alexius* of Edessa, 5th-century Christian; see -AN]

A·lex·i·ar·es (ə lek′sē âr′ēz), *n.* *Class. Myth.* a son of Hercules and Hebe.

A·lex·i·ca·cus (ə lek′sə kā′kəs), *n.* *Class. Myth.* an epithet of Apollo, meaning "averter of evil," in reference to his dispelling a plague that afflicted the Athenian forces in the Peloponnesian War.

a·lex·in (ə lek′sin), *n.* *Immunol.* complement (def. 10). [< Gk *aléx(ein)* to ward off + -IN²] —**al·ex·in·ic** (al′ek sin′ik), *adj.*

A·lex·ine (ə lek′sēn), *n.* a girl's given name, form of **Alexandra.** Also, **Alexa.**

a·lex·i·phar·mic (ə lek′sə fär′mik), *Med.* —*adj.* **1.** warding off poisoning or infection; antidotal; prophylactic. —*n.* **2.** an alexipharmic agent, esp. an internal antidote. [obs. *alexipharm(ac)* antidote (< Gk *alexiphármakon*, equiv. to *alexi-* averter (see ALEXIN) + *phármakon* poison, drug) + -IC; see PHARMACY]

A·lex·is (ə lek′sis), *n.* a boy's or girl's given name.

A·lex·is I Mi·khai·lo·vich (ə lek′sis, mə kī′lə vich; *Russ.* mi khī′lo vich), 1629–76, czar of Russia 1645–76 (father of Peter I).

A·lex·is Ni·ko·la·ye·vich (ə lek′sis nik′ə lī′ə vich; *Russ.* ni ko lä′yə vich), 1904–18, son of Nicholas II of Russia, heir apparent to the Russian throne: executed in the Russian Bolshevik Revolution.

A·lex·i·us I (ə lek′sē əs), (*Alexius Comnenus*) 1048–1118, emperor of the Byzantine Empire 1081–1118.

ale·yard (āl′yärd′), *n.* yard-of-ale. [ALE + YARD¹]

Alf (alf; *Nor.* älf), *n.* a boy's given name, form of **Alfred.**

ALFA (al′fə), *n.* a word used in communications to represent the letter *A.* [var. spelling of alpha]

Al·fa·dir (al′fä dər), *n.* *Scand. Myth.* an epithet of Odin. [< Icel *alfathir.* See ALL, FATHER]

al·fal·fa (al fal′fə), *n.* a European leguminous plant, *Medicago sativa*, having bluish-purple flowers, grown for forage in the U.S. Also called **Burgundy trefoil, lucerne, Spanish trefoil.** [< Sp, var. of *alfalfez* < SpAr *al* the + *faṣfaṣah* lucerne]

alfal′fa but′terfly, a sulfur butterfly, *Colias eurytheme*, having orange wings edged with black, the larvae of which feed on alfalfa and other legumes. Also called **orange sulfur.**

alfal′fa valve′, a means of closing the end of a vertical pipe, consisting of a plate mounted on a threaded shaft that screws into a socket inside the end of the pipe.

Al Fa·ra·bi (al′ fä rä′bē), died A.D. 950, Arab philosopher. Also called **Al·fa·ra·bi·us** (al′fə rā′bē əs).

Alf·heim (alv′hām′), *n.* *Scand. Myth.* the domain of elves living above ground. [< Icel *Alfheimr*, equiv. to *alf-* (s. of *alfr*) ELF + *heimr* world, HOME]

Al·fie (al′fē), *n.* a boy's given name, form of **Alfred.**

Al·fie·ri (äl fye′rē), *n.* **Count Vit·to·rio** (vēt tô′ryô), 1749–1803, Italian dramatist and poet.

al·fil·a·ri·a (al fil′ə rē′ə), *n.* a European geraniaceous herb, *Erodium cicutarium*, grown for forage in the U.S. [< Sp *alfilerillo*, equiv. to *alfiler* pin (< Ar *al khilāl* the thorn) + *-illo* dim. suffix]

al fi·ne (al′ fē′nā; *It.* äl fē′ne), *Music.* to the end (a direction, as after a *da capo* or *dal segno*, to continue to *fine*, the indicated end). [< It]

Al·fon·so X (al fon′sō, -zō; *Sp.* äl fôn′sô), ("*Alfonso the Wise*") 1221–84, king of Castile 1252–84.

Alfonso XII, 1857–85, king of Spain 1874–85.

Alfonso XIII, 1886–1941, king of Spain 1886–1930.

Al·fon·son (al fon′sən), *n.* a boy's given name, form of **Alphonso.**

al·for·ja (al fôr′jə; *Sp.* äl fôr′hä), *n., pl.* **-jas** (-jəz; *Sp.* -häs). *Southwestern U.S.* **1.** a leather bag; saddlebag. **2.** a cheek pouch. [< Sp < Ar *al* the + *khorj*, var. of *khurj* pair of saddlebags]

Al·fra·ga·nus (al′frə gā′nəs), *n.* a crater in the fourth quadrant of the face of the moon: about 12 miles in diameter.

Al·fred (al′fred, -frid), *n.* **1.** a town in W New York. 2807 (1960). **2.** a boy's given name.

Al·fre·da (al frē′də), *n.* a girl's given name.

Al′fred the Great′, A.D. 849–899, king of the West Saxons 871–899.

al·fres·co (al fres′kō), *adv., adj.* out-of-doors; open air: *to dine alfresco; an alfresco café.* Also, **al fres′co.** [< It: in the cool. See FRESH]

Al·fur (al′fo͝or, -fyo͝or), *n.* a member of an aboriginal people of eastern Indonesia, esp. of the Moluccas, whose features show both Malayan and Papuan characteristics.

al-Fus·tat (al fo͞o stät′), *n.* an ancient city in N Egypt, near the modern city of Cairo, founded in the 7th century A.D. Also, **El Fostat, el-Fustat.** Also called **Old Cairo.**

Alg., 1. Algerian. **2.** Algiers.

alg., algebra.

al·ga (al′gə), *n., pl.* **-gae** (-jē). any of numerous motile or nonmotile, chlorophyll-containing plants of the *phylum Thallophyta*, ranging from unicellular, usually microscopic, forms to multicellular forms sometimes 100 feet or more in length, occurring in fresh or salt water, on or in other organisms or the soil, on rocks, trees, etc. [< L: sea-weed] —**al′gal,** *adj.*

Al·ga·lene (al′gə lēn′), *n.* a girl's given name.

Al·gar (al′gər), *n.* a boy's given name. Also, **Alger.**

Al′ga·roth pow′der (al′gə rôth′, -roth′). See **antimony oxychloride.** [part trans. of F *poudre d'algaroth* powder of algaroth < It *algarotto*, named after Vittorio *Algarotto* (d. 1604), Italian physician]

al·gar·ro·ba (al′gə rō′bə), *n.* **1.** any of certain mesquites, esp. *Prosopis juliflora.* **2.** the beanlike pod of this plant. **3.** the carob tree or fruit. Also, **al′ga·ro′ba.** [< Sp < Ar *al* the + *kharrūba* CAROB]

Al-Ga·zel (al′gə zel′), *n.* Ghazzali. Also, **Al′ga·zel′.**

al·ge·bra (al′jə brə), *n.* **1.** the branch of mathematics that deals with general statements of relations, utilizing letters and other symbols to represent specific sets of numbers, values, vectors, etc., in the description of such relations. **2.** any of several algebraic systems, esp. a ring in which elements can be multiplied by real or complex numbers (**linear algebra**) as well as by other elements of the ring. **3.** any special system of notation adapted to the study of a special system of relationship: *algebra of classes.* [< ML < Ar *al* the + *jebr*, var. of *jabr* bone-setting, (algebraic) reduction]

al·ge·bra·ic (al′jə brā′ik), *adj.* **1.** of, occurring in, or utilizing algebra. **2.** *Math.* of or pertaining to an element that is the root of a polynomial equation with coefficients from some given field: $\sqrt{2}$ *is algebraic over the field of real numbers.* **3.** using arbitrary letters or symbols in place of the letters, symbols, or numbers of an actual application. Also, **al′ge·bra′i·cal.** [ALGEBRA + -IC] —**al′ge·bra′i·cal·ly,** *adv.*

algebra′ically closed′ field′, *Math.* a field in which every polynomial equation with coefficients that are elements of the field has at least one root in the field, as the field of complex numbers. Cf. **fundamental theorem of algebra.**

al′gebra′ic con′jugate, *Math.* See **dual space** (def. 2).

algebra′ic equa′tion, *Math.* an equation in the form of a polynomial having a finite number of terms and equated to zero, as $3x^3 + 2x^2 + x = 0$.

algebra′ic exten′sion, *Math.* a field containing a given field such that every element in the first field is algebraic over the given field. Cf. **extension field.**

al′gebra′ic num′ber, *Math.* **1.** a root of an algebraic equation with integral coefficients. **2.** root[1] (def. 10b).

algebra′ic topol′ogy, *Math.* the branch of mathematics that deals with the application of algebraic methods to topology.

al·ge·bra·ist (al′jə brā′ist), *n.* an expert in algebra. [ALGEBRA + -IST]

al′gebra of sets′, *Math.* a nonempty collection of sets having the property that the union of two sets of the collection is a set of the collection and the complement of each set of the collection is a set in the collection. Cf. **Boolean ring, sigma-ring.**

Al·ge·ci·ras (al′ji sir′əs; *Sp.* äl′he the′räs), *n.* a seaport in S Spain, on the Strait of Gibraltar. 42,728 (est. 1960).

Al·ger (al′jər), *n.* **1. Horatio,** 1834–99, U.S. novelist. **2.** Also, **Algar.** a boy's given name.

Al·ge·ri·a (al jēr′ē ə), *n.* a republic in NW Africa: formerly comprised 13 departments of France; gained independence July 3, 1962. 11,240,000 (est. 1965); 919,352 sq. mi. *Cap.:* Algiers.

Al·ge·ri·an (al jēr′ē ən), *adj.* **1.** of or pertaining to Algeria or its inhabitants. —*n.* **2.** a native or inhabitant of Algeria. Also, **Algerine.** [ALGERI(A) + -AN]

Alge′rian stripe′, a fabric woven with alternate stripes of coarse cotton and silk, usually cream-colored.

al·ge·ri·enne (al jēr′ē en′), *n.* a fabric with brightly colored stripes, used for curtains, awnings, etc. Also, **Algerine.** [< F *algérienne,* fem. of *algérien* ALGERIAN, from the fact that the fabric is made in Algeria]

Al·ge·rine (al′jə rēn′), *adj.* **1.** Algerian. —*n.* **2.** Algerian. **3.** (*l.c.*) a pirate. **4.** (*l.c.*) algerienne. [ALGER(IA) + -INE[1]]

al·ge·ri·ta (al′gə rē′tə), *n.* agarita.

Al·ger·non (al′jər nən), *n.* a boy's given name.

al·ge·si·a (al jē′zē ə, -sē ə), *n.* *Med.* sensitivity to pain; hyperesthesia. [< NL < Gk *álgēs(is)* feeling of pain + NL *-ia* -IA] —**al·ge·sic** (al jē′zik, -sik), *adj.*

al·ge·sim·e·ter (al′ji sim′i tər), *n.* an instrument for determining the sensitiveness of the skin to a painful stimulus. Also, **al·ge·si·om·e·ter** (al jē′sē om′i tər, -zē-). [ALGESI(A) + -METER]

al·ge·si·re·cep·tor (al jē′zə ri sep′tər, -sə-), *n.* *Physiol., Biol.* a receptor stimulated by pain. [ALGESI(A) + RECEPTOR]

al·get·ic (al jet′ik), *adj.* *Med.* pertaining to or causing pain; painful. [< Gk *algē-* (verbid s. of *algeîn* to suffer pain) + -TIC]

Al·ghe·ro (äl gâr′ō), *n.* a seaport in W Sardinia. 26,666 (1961).

-algia, var. of **algo-** as final element of a compound word: *neuralgia.* Also, **-algy.** [< NL < Gk; see ALGO-, -IA]

al·gi·cide (al′ji sīd′), *n.* a substance or preparation for killing algae. [ALG(A) + -I- + -CIDE]

al·gid (al′jid), *adj.* cold; chilly. [< L *algid(us)* cold] —**al·gid′i·ty, al′gid·ness,** *n.*

Al·giers (al jērz′), *n.* **1.** a seaport in and the capital of Algeria, in the N part. 883,879 with suburbs (1960). **2.** one of the former Barbary States in N Africa: now modern Algeria.

al·gin (al′jin), *n.* *Chem.* any hydrophilic, colloidal substance found in or obtained from various kelps, esp. from *Macrocystis pyrifera.* [ALG(A) + -IN[2]]

al·gi·nate (al′jə nāt′), *n.* a salt of alginic acid. [ALGIN + -ATE[2]]

al′gin fi′ber, *Chem.* an alkali-soluble fiber produced by injecting a fine stream of alkaline algin into an aqueous solution of a metallic salt, used chiefly in the manufacture of fine threads.

al·gin′ic ac′id (al jin′ik), *Chem.* an insoluble, colloidal acid, $(C_6H_8O_6)_n$, found in the cell walls of various kelps, esp. brown kelps, known chiefly in the form of its salts, and used esp. for sizing paper. [ALGIN + -IC + ACID]

algo-, a learned borrowing from Greek meaning "pain," used in the formation of compound words: *algophobia.* [comb. form repr. Gk *álgos*]

al·goid (al′goid), *adj.* like algae. [ALG(A) + -OID]

Al·gol (al′gol), *n.* a star of the second magnitude in the constellation Perseus: the first known and most famous eclipsing binary star. [< Ar < *al* the + *ghūl* GHOUL]

ALGOL (al′gol, -gôl), *n.* *Computer Technol.* a type of computer language in which information is expressed in algebraic notation and according to the rules of Boolean algebra. [*Algo(rithmic) L(anguage)*]

al·go·lag·ni·a (al′gə lag′nē ə), *n.* *Psychiatry.* sexual pleasure derived from enduring or inflicting pain, as in masochism or sadism. [< NL, equiv. to *algo-* ALGO- + Gk *lagneía* lust] —**al′go·lag′nic,** *adj.* —**al′go·lag′nist,** *n.*

al·gol·o·gy (al gol′ə jē), *n.* the branch of botany dealing with algae. [ALG(A) + -O- + -LOGY] —**al·go·log·i·cal** (al′gə loj′i kəl), *adj.* —**al·gol′o·gist,** *n.*

Al·go·ma (al gō′mə), *n.* a town in E Wisconsin. 3855 (1960).

Al·go·man (al gō′mən), *adj.* *Geol.* of or pertaining to the orogeny and the accompanying intrusions of the early Proterozoic. [named after *Algoma,* a district in Ontario, Canada, + -AN]

al·gom·e·ter (al gom′i tər), *n.* a device for determining sensitiveness to pain due to pressure. [ALGO- + -METER] —**al·go·met·ric** (al′gə me′trik), **al′go·met′ri·cal,** *adj.* —**al′go·met′ri·cal·ly,** *adv.* —**al·gom′e·try,** *n.*

Al·go·na (al gō′nə), *n.* a town in N Iowa. 5702 (1960).

Al·go·nac (al′gō nak′), *n.* a town in E Michigan. 3190 (1960).

Al·gon·ki·an (al goŋ′kē ən), *adj.* **1.** *Geol.* Proterozoic (def. 1). **2.** Algonquian. —*n.* **3.** *Geol.* Proterozoic (def. 3). **4.** Algonquian.

Al·gon·kin (al goŋ′kin), *n., pl.* **-kins,** (*esp. collectively*) **-kin,** *adj.* —*n.* **1.** Algonquin. **2.** Algonquian. —*adj.* **3.** Algonquian. **4.** Algonquin.

Al·gon·qui·an (al goŋ′kē ən, -kwē ən), *n., pl.* **-ans,** (*esp. collectively*) **-an** for 2, *adj.* —*n.* **1.** a family of languages spoken now or formerly by American Indians in an area extending from Labrador westward to the Rocky Mountains, westsouthwestward through Michigan and Illinois, and southwestward along the Atlantic coast to Cape Hatteras, including esp. Arapaho, Blackfoot, Cheyenne, Cree, Fox, Massachuset, Micmac, Ojibwa, and Powhatan. Cf. **family** (def. 11). **2.** a member of an Algonquian tribe. —*adj.* **3.** of or pertaining to Algonquian. Also, **Algonkian, Algonkin, Algonquin.** [ALGONQUI(N) + -AN]

Al·gon·quin (al goŋ′kin, -kwin), *n., pl.* **-quins,** (*esp. collectively*) **-quin** for 1, 3, *adj.* —*n.* **1.** a member of a group of North American Indian tribes formerly along the Ottawa River and the northern tributaries of the St. Lawrence. **2.** their speech, a dialect of Ojibwa, of the Algonquian family of languages. **3.** Algonquian. —*adj.* **4.** Algonquian. Also, **Algonkin.** [< F, var. of *algoumaqin* after native place-name; cf. Micmac *algūmaking* fishing-place]

Algon′quin Park′, a national park in S Canada, in SE Ontario. 2741 sq. mi.

al·goph·a·gous (al gof′ə gəs), *adj.* feeding on algae, as certain insects. [ALG(A) + -O- + -PHAGOUS]

al·go·pho·bi·a (al′gə fō′bē ə), *n.* *Psychiatry.* an abnormal dread of pain. [ALGO- + -PHOBIA]

al·gor (al′gôr), *n.* *Pathol.* coldness or chill, esp. at the onset of fever. [< L: coldness, equiv. to *alg-* (base of *algidus* algid) + -OR[1]]

al·go·rism (al′gə riz′əm), *n.* **1.** the Arabic system of arithmetical notation (with the figures 1, 2, 3, etc.). **2.** the art of computation with the Arabic figures, one to nine, plus the zero; arithmetic. **3.** algorithm. [< ML *algorism(us)* < Ar *al* the + *kh(u)wārizmī* (surname of a 9th-century Muslim mathematician), equiv. to *khwārizm* KHIVA + *-ī* -AN; r. ME *augrim,* etc. < MF] —**al′go·ris′mic,** *adj.*

al·go·rithm (al′gə rith′əm), *n.* any particular procedure for solving a certain type of problem, as the rule for finding the greatest common denominator. Also, **algorism.** [var. of ALGORISM, by assoc. with Gk *arithmós* number. See ARITHMETIC] —**al′go·rith′mic,** *adj.*

al′gorith′mic lan′guage, *Computer Technol.* See **ALGOL.** [ALGORITHM + -IC + LANGUAGE]

al·gra·phy (al′grə fē), *n.* *Print.* (formerly) an offset process employing an aluminum plate instead of a stone. Also, **aluminography.** [AL(UMINUM) + -GRAPHY] —**al·graph·ic** (al graf′ik), *adj.*

Al·gren (ôl′grin), *n.* **Nelson,** born 1909, U.S. novelist and short-story writer.

al·gum (al′gəm, ôl′-), *n.* a Biblical tree, possibly the red sandalwood. II Chron. 2:8. Cf. **almug.** [< Heb *algumm(īm)* (pl.), var. of *almuggīm*]

Al·gy (al′jē), *n.* a boy's given name, form of **Algernon.**

-algy, var. of **-algia:** *coxalgy.*

Al·ham·bra (al ham′brə), *n.* **1.** a palace of the Moorish kings in Granada, Spain: completed in the 14th century. **2.** a city in SW California, near Los Angeles. 54,807 (1960). [< Sp < Ar *al hamrā′* the red (house)]

Al·ham·bresque (al′ham bresk′), *adj.* resembling the fanciful style of ornamentation of the Spanish Alhambra. [ALHAMBR(A) + -ESQUE]

Al·ha·zen (al hā′zən), *n.* a walled plain in the first quadrant of the face of the moon: about 20 miles in diameter.

Al Hu·fuf (al hŏŏ fōōf′), Hofuf.

A·li (ä′lē, ä lē′), *n.* **1.** (*Ali ibn-abu-Talib*) ("*the Lion of God*") A.D. c600–661, Arab caliph (cousin and son-in-law of Muhammad). **2.** See **Mehemet Ali. 3. Mohammed,** 1909–63, Pakistani statesman and diplomat. **4.** See **Mohammed Ali, Maulana. 5. Muhammad** (*Cassius Marcellus Clay, Jr.*), born 1942, U.S. boxer: world heavyweight champion 1964–67, 1974–78, 1978–79.

A·li·a·cen·sis (ä′lē ə sen′sis), *n.* a crater in the fourth quadrant of the face of the moon: about 52 miles in diameter.

a·li·as (ā′lē əs), *n., pl.* **-as·es,** *adv.* —*n.* **1.** an assumed name; another name: *The files indicate that Smith is an alias for Simpson.* —*adv.* **2.** at another time; in another place; in other circumstances; otherwise. "Simpson *alias* Smith" means that Simpson in other circumstances has called himself Smith. [< L (adv.): at another time] —**Syn. 1.** nom de guerre; nom de plume.

a·li·as dic·tus (ā′lē äs dik′tōōs; *Eng.* ā′lē əs dik′ təs), *Latin.* otherwise called; alias.

A·li Ba·ba (ä′lē bä′bä, al′ē bab′ə), the poor woodchopper, hero of a tale in *The Arabian Nights' Entertainments,* who uses the magic words "Open sesame" to open the door to the hidden treasure-cave of the Forty Thieves.

al·i·bi (al′ə bī′), *n., pl.* **-bis,** *v.* —*n.* **1.** *Law.* the defense by an accused person that he was elsewhere at the time the offense with which he is charged was committed. **2.** *U.S. Informal.* an excuse. —*v.i.* **3.** *Informal.* to give an excuse; offer a defense: *to alibi for being late.* —*v.t.* **4.** *Informal.* to provide an alibi for (someone): *He alibied his friend out of a fix.* [< L (adv.): in or at another place] —**Usage.** Careful users of English limit ALIBI to its formal meaning in law, but it is commonly used in informal contexts to mean "excuse or reason" with a connotation of dishonesty or evasiveness.

al·i·ble (al′ə bəl), *adj.* nutritive; nourishing. [< L *alibil(is),* equiv. to *al(ere)* (to) feed + *-ibilis* -BLE] —**al′i·bil′i·ty,** *n.*

Al·i·can·te (al′ə kan′tē; *Sp.* ä′lē kän′te), *n.* a seaport in SE Spain, on the Mediterranean. 111,875 (est. 1960).

Al·ice (al′is), *n.* **1.** a city in S Texas. 20,861 (1961). **2.** Also, **Alyce, Alys.** a girl's given name.

Al′ice blue′, a pale grayish-blue color. [named after *Alice* Longworth (daughter of Theodore Roosevelt)]

Al′ice's Adven′tures in Won′derland, a story for children (1865) by Lewis Carroll. Also called **Al′ice in Won′derland.**

Al′ice's fern′. See **Hartford fern.**

Al·ice·ville (al′is vil′), *n.* a town in W Alabama. 3194 (1960).

A·li·cia (ə lish′ə, ə lish′ē ə, ə lē′shə, -shē ə), *n.* a girl's given name, form of **Alice.**

Al·ick (al′ik), *n.* a boy's given name, form of **Alexander.** Also, **Alec, Aleck, Alex.**

al·i·cy·clic (al′i sī′klik, -sik′lik), *adj.* *Chem.* of or noting organic compounds essentially aliphatic in chemical behavior but differing structurally in that the essential carbon atoms are connected in a ring instead of a chain. [ALI(PHATIC) + CYCLIC]

al·i·dade (al′i dād′), *n.* *Survey.* **1.** (in plane-tabling) a straightedge having a telescopic sight or other means of sighting parallel to the straightedge. **2.** *U.S.* the entire upper part of a theodolite or transit, including the telescope, its supports, the level vials, the circle-reading device, and the spindle. Also, **al·i·dad** (al′i dad′). [var. of *alhidade* < ML *alhidada* < Ar *al* the + *'idadah* turning radius (like a clock hand) of a circle; r. late ME *allydatha* (? < Sp *alhidada*)]

al·ien (āl′yən, ā′lē ən), *n.* **1.** one born in or belonging to another country who has not acquired citizenship by naturalization (distinguished from *citizen*). **2.** a foreigner. **3.** one who has been estranged or excluded. **4.** a nonterrestrial being. —*adj.* **5.** residing under a government or in a country other than that of one's birth without having or obtaining rights of citizenship there. **6.** belonging or relating to aliens: *alien property.* **7.** foreign; strange; not belonging to one: *alien speech.* **8.** adverse; hostile; opposed (usually fol. by *to* or *from*): *ideas alien to our way of thinking.* **9.** nonterrestrial. [ME < L *aliēn(us),* equiv. to *ali(us)* other + *-ēnus* adj. suffix; see -ENE]
—**Syn. 1.** immigrant. **2.** See **stranger. 3.** outcast.

al·ien·a·ble (āl′yə nə bəl, ā′lē ə-), *adj.* *Law.* capable of being sold or transferred. [ALIEN + -ABLE] —**al′ien·a·bil′i·ty,** *n.*

al·ien·age (āl′yə nij, ā′lē ə-), *n.* **1.** state of being an alien. **2.** the legal status of an alien. Also called **alienism.** [ALIEN + -AGE]

al·ien·ate (āl′yə nāt′, ā′lē ə-), *v.t.,* **-at·ed, -at·ing.** **1.** to make indifferent or averse; estrange: *He has alienated his entire family.* **2.** to turn away; transfer or divert: *to alienate funds from their intended purpose.* **3.** *Law.* to transfer or convey, as title, property, or other right, to another: *to alienate lands.* [late ME < L *aliēnāt(us)* (ptp. of *aliēnāre*), equiv. to *aliēn(us)* ALIEN + *-ātus* -ATE[1]] —**al′ien·a′tor,** *n.*

al·ien·a·tion (āl′yə nā′shən, ā′lē ə-), *n.* **1.** act of alienating. **2.** state of being alienated. **3.** *Law.* a transfer of the title to property by one person to another; conveyance. **4.** *Psychiatry.* **a.** mental or psychiatric illness. **b.** legal insanity. **5.** *Statistics.* the lack of correlation in the variation of two measurable variates over a population. [late ME < L *aliēnātiōn-* (s. of *aliēnātiō*), equiv. to *aliēnāt(us)* (see ALIENATE) + *-iōn-* -ION]

aliena′tion of affec′tions, *Law.* the estrangement by a third person of one spouse from the other.

al·ien·ee (āl′yə nē′, ā′lē ə-), *n.* *Law.* one to whom property is alienated. [obs. *alien* (v.) < ME *aliene(n)* + -EE]

a·li·e·ni ge·ne·ris (ä′li ā′nē ge′ne ris; *Eng.* ā′lē ē′nī jen′ər is), *Latin.* of another kind.

al·i·e·ni ju·ris (al′i ē′nī jŏŏr′is), *Law.* under the control of another, as a lunatic or infant. Cf. **sui juris.** [< L: lit., of another's law]

al·ien·ism (āl′yə niz′əm, ā′lē ə-), *n.* **1.** alienage. **2.** the study or treatment of mental diseases, esp. in their relation to legal problems. [ALIEN + -ISM]

al·ien·ist (āl′yə nist, ā′lē ə-), *n.* a physician who treats mental disorders; esp. one who specializes in related legal matters. [ALIEN(ATION) + -IST; cf. F *aliéniste* in same sense]

al·ien·or (āl′yə nər, ā′lē ə-, āl′yə nôr′, ā′lē ə-), *n.* *Law.* one who transfers property. Also, **al·ien·er** (āl′yə nər, ā′lē ə-). [obs. *alien* (v.) < ME *aliene(n)* + -OR[2]; r. *alienour* < AF (c. F *aliéneur*) < L *aliēnātor.* See ALIENATE, -OR[2]]

a·lif (ä′lif), *n.* **1.** the first letter of the Arabic alphabet. **2.** the glottal stop consonant or, alternatively, long vowel represented by this letter. [< Ar; see ALEPH]

al·i·form (al′ə fôrm′, ā′lə-), *adj.* wing-shaped; winglike; alar. [AL(A) + -I- + -FORM]

A·li·garh (ä′lē gur′, al′ə gär′), *n.* a city in W Uttar Pradesh, in N India. 185,000 (1961).

a·light[1] (ə līt′), *v.i.,* **a·light·ed** or **a·lit, a·light·ing.** **1.** to dismount from a horse, descend from a vehicle, etc. **2.** to settle or stay after descending: *A bird alights on a tree.* **3.** to encounter or notice something accidentally or without design. [ME *alighte(n),* OE *ālīhtan,* equiv. to *ā-* A-[3] + *līhtan* to relieve of weight, descend (deriv. of *lēoht, līht* LIGHT[2])]

a·light[2] (ə līt′), *adv., adj.* provided with light; lighted up; burning. [now taken as A-[1] + LIGHT[1]; orig. ptp. of *alight* to light up (ME *alihte(n),* OE *onlīhtan,* equiv. to *on* A-[1] + *līhtan* to LIGHT[1])]

a·lign (ə līn′), *v.t.* **1.** to arrange in a straight line; adjust according to a line. **2.** to bring into a line. **3.** to ally (oneself) with a group, party, cause, etc.: *He aligned himself with the liberals.* **4.** to adjust (two or more components of an electronic circuit) to improve the response over a frequency band, as to align the tuned circuits of a radio receiver for proper tracking throughout its frequency range, or a television receiver for appropriate wide-band responses. —*v.i.* **5.** to fall or come into line; be in line. **6.** to join with others in a cause. Also, **aline.** [< F *align(er),* equiv. to *a-* A-[5] + *ligner* < L *līneāre,* deriv. of *līnea* LINE[1]] —**a·lign′er,** *n.*
—**Syn. 1, 2.** straighten.

align′ing punch′, a drift for aligning rivet holes.

a·lign·ment (ə līn′mənt), *n.* **1.** an adjustment to a line; arrangement in a straight line. **2.** the line or lines so formed. **3.** the proper adjustment of the components of an electronic circuit, machine, etc., for coordinated functioning: *This radio is out of alignment.* **4.** a ground plan of a railroad or highway. **5.** *Archaeol.* a line or an arrangement of parallel or converging lines of upright stones or menhirs. Also, **alinement.** [ALIGN + -MENT; r. earlier *alignement* < F]

align′ment chart′, *Math.* nomogram.

a·like (ə līk′), *adv.* **1.** in the same manner, form, or degree; in common; equally: *known to treat all customers alike.* —*adj.* **2.** having resemblance or similarity; having or showing no marked or important difference: *He thinks all politicians are alike.* [late ME *alyke* < Scand; cf.

Icel *ālíkr*, c OE *onlīc*; r. ME *ilich*, OE *gelīc*, c. G *gleich*, Icel *glīkr*] —**a·like′ness,** *n.*
—**Syn. 1.** similarly. **2.** similar, akin. —**Ant. 1.** differently.

al·i·ment (*n.* al′ə mənt; *v.* al′ə ment′), *n.* **1.** that which nourishes; nutriment; food. **2.** that which sustains; support. —*v.t.* **3.** to sustain; support. [< L *aliment(um)*, equiv. to *al(ere)* to feed + *-i-* -I- + *-mentum* -MENT] —**al′i·men′tal,** *adj.* —**al′i·men′tal·ly,** *adv.*
—**Syn. 1.** nourishment. **1, 2.** sustenance.

al·i·men·ta·ry (al′ə men′tə rē), *adj.* **1.** concerned with the function of nutrition; nutritive. **2.** pertaining to food. **3.** providing sustenance or maintenance. [< L *alimentāri(us)*. See ALIMENT, -ARY]

alimen′tary canal′, a tubular passage functioning in the digestion and absorption of food, in man and most animals, beginning at the mouth and terminating at the anus.

al·i·men·ta·tion (al′ə men tā′shən), *n.* **1.** nourishment; nutrition. **2.** maintenance; support. **3.** addition to the volume of a glacial mass, chiefly by the accumulation of ice, snow, or névé. Cf. **ablation** (def. 2). [< ML *alimentātiōn-* (s. of *alimentātiō*). See ALIMENT, -ATION]

al·i·men·ta·tive (al′ə men′tə tiv), *adj.* nourishing; nutritive. [ALIMENT + -ATIVE] —**al′i·men′ta·tive·ly,** *adv.* —**al′i·men′ta·tive·ness,** *n.*

al·i·mo·ny (al′ə mō′nē), *n.* **1.** *Law.* an allowance paid to a woman by her husband or former husband for her maintenance, granted by a court upon a legal separation or a divorce or while action is pending. In exceptional cases, in some States, a husband may receive alimony. **2.** supply of the means of living; maintenance. [< L *alimōnia* nourishment, sustenance, equiv. to *ali-* (see ALIMENT) + *-mōnia* -MONY] —**al′i·mo′nied,** *adj.*

à l'im·pro·viste (A lan prō vēst′), *French.* all of a sudden; unexpectedly; unawares. [lit., at the unprovided for]

A′li Muham′mad of Shiraz′. See **Bab ed-Din.**

a·line (ə līn′), *v.t., v.i.,* **a·lined, a·lin·ing.** align. —**a·line′ment,** *n.* —**a·lin′er,** *n.*

A·line (ə lēn′, al′ēn), *n.* a girl's given name, form of **Adeline.**

A-line (ā′līn′), *n.* **1.** (esp. in women's clothing) a cut of garment consisting basically of two A-shaped panels for the front and back, designed to give increasing fullness toward the hemline. **2.** a garment having such a cut. —*adj.* **3.** being of such design or cut: *an A-line coat; an A-line dress.*

a·li·no·tum (ā′lə nō′təm, al′ə-), *n., pl.* **-ta** (-tə). the plate to which the wings are attached on the notum of an insect. [< NL; AL(A) + -I- + *nōtum* < Gk *nôton* back]

Al·i·oth (al′ē oth′), *n.* *Astron.* a star of the second magnitude in the constellation Ursa Major. [< Ar < ?]

A·li Pa·sha (ä′lē pä shä′), *(Arslan)* 1741–1822, Turkish pasha and ruler of Albania 1787?–1820.

al·i·ped (al′ə ped′), *Zool.* —*adj.* **1.** having the toes connected by a winglike membrane, as a bat. —*n.* **2.** an aliped animal. [< L *ālliped-* (s. of *ālipēs* wing-footed). See ALA, -PED]

al·i·phat·ic (al′ə fat′ik), *adj.* *Chem.* noting organic compounds in which the carbon atoms form open chains, as the paraffins or olefins. [< Gk *aleiphat-* (s. of *áleiphar* oil, fat) + -IC]

al·ip·te·ri·on (al′ip tēr′ē on), *n., pl.* **-te·ri·a** (-tēr′ē ə). (in an ancient Roman bath) a room for anointment. Also called **elaeothesium, unctuarium.** [< Gk *aleiptḗrion* < *aleipt(ēs)* anointer + *-ērion* place for]

al·i·quant (al′ə kwənt), *adj.* *Math.* contained in a number or quantity, but not dividing it evenly: *An aliquant part of 16 is 5.* [< L *aliquant(us)* more or less great, equiv. to *ali-* differently + *quantus* great]

Al·i·quip·pa (al′ə kwip′ə), *n.* a borough in W Pennsylvania. 26,369 (1960).

al·i·quot (al′ə kwət), *adj.* **1.** *Math.* forming an exact proper divisor: *An aliquot part of 15 is 5.* **2.** *Chem.* comprising a definite part of a whole: *an aliquot quantity of acid for analysis.* —*n.* **3.** an aliquot part. [< L, equiv. to *ali-* some other + *quot* as many as]

-alis, a suffix occurring in scientific names from Latin: *borealis.* [< L *-ālis;* see -AL[1]]

Al-Is·kan·da·ri·yah (al is kan da rē′yə, -ya), *n.* Arabic name of **Alexandria.**

Al·i·son (al′i sən), *n.* a girl's given name, form of **Alice.** Also, **Allison, Alyson.**

A·lis·sa (ə lis′ə), *n.* a girl's given name, form of **Alice.** Also, **A·li·sa** (ə lē′sə).

a·list (ə list′), *adj.* *Naut.* (of a vessel) inclined to one side; heeling or listing. [A-[1] + LIST[1]]

Al·is·ter (al′i stər), *n.* a boy's given name. Also, **Alastair, Alaster, Alastor.**

a·lis vo·lat pro·pri·is (ä′lis wō′lät prō′prē is; *Eng.* ā′lis vō′lat prō′prē is), *Latin.* she flies with her own wings (motto of Oregon).

a·lit (ə lit′), *v.* a pt. and pp. of **alight**[1].

a·li·tur·gi·cal (ā′li tûr′ji kəl), *adj.* designating those days on which the celebration of certain liturgies, esp. the Eucharist, is forbidden. Also, **a′li·tur′gic.** [A-[6] + LITURGICAL]

a·li·un·de (ā′lē un′dē), *adv., adj.* *Chiefly Law.* not part of or derivable from the document or instrument itself: *evidence aliunde.* [< L: from another person or place, equiv. to *ali(us)* other + *unde* whence]

a·live (ə līv′), *adj.* **1.** having life; existing; not dead or lifeless. **2.** living (used for emphasis): *the proudest man alive.* **3.** in a state of action; in force or operation; active: *to keep hope alive.* **4.** full of life; lively: *She's more alive than most of her contemporaries.* **5.** having the quality of life; full of verve; vivid; vibrant: *The room was alive with color.* **6.** *Elect.* live[2] (def. 13). **7. alive to,** alert or sensitive to; aware of: *City planners are alive to the necessity of finding better ways of revitalizing deteriorating neighborhoods.* **8. alive with,** filled with living things; swarming; teeming: *The room was alive with mosquitoes.* **9. look alive!** pay attention! move quickly!: *Look alive! We haven't got all day.* [ME; OE *on līfe* in LIFE] —**a·live′ness,** *n.*
—**Syn. 4.** active. —**Ant. 1.** dead. **3.** defunct. **4.** lifeless.

a·li·yah (ä lē′ō, ä′lē ä′), *n., pl.* **a·li·yahs, a·li·yos** (ä lē′ōs), **a·li·yoth** (ä′lē ōt′). *Hebrew.* (in a Jewish service) act of proceeding to the reading table on the bimah of a synagogue to recite the blessings before and after the chanting or reading of a portion of the Torah. [lit., act of going up]

A·li·za (ə lī′zə), *n.* a girl's given name.

a·liz·a·rin (ə liz′ər in), *n.* *Chem.* a solid appearing reddish-orange as crystals and brownish-yellow as powder, $C_6H_4(CO)_2C_6H_2(OH)_2$, one of the earliest known dyes, formerly obtained in its natural state from madder and now derived from anthraquinone: used chiefly in the synthesis of other dyes. Also, **a·liz·a·rine** (ə liz′ə rin, -rēn′). [< F *alizarine*, equiv. to *alizar(i)* (< Sp < Ar *al* the + *'aṣārah* juice) + *-ine* -INE[1]]

aliz′arin crim′son, a pigment used in painting, derived from anthraquinone and characterized by its red color and transparency.

alk-, var. of **alka-,** esp. before a vowel.

alk., alkali.

alka-, a combining form of the alkane series, used esp. before a consonant: *alkadiene.*

al·ka·hest (al′kə hest′), *n.* the universal solvent sought by the alchemists. Also, **alcahest.** [< late ML; prob. coinage of PARACELSUS] —**al′ka·hes′tic, al′ka·hes′ti·cal,** *adj.*

al·ka·le·mi·a (al′kə lē′mē ə), *n.* *Pathol.* a condition of abnormal alkalinity of the blood. [ALKAL(I) + -EMIA]

al·ka·les·cent (al′kə les′ənt), *adj.* tending to become alkaline; slightly alkaline. [ALKAL(I) + -ESCENT] —**al′ka·les′cence, al′ka·les′cen·cy,** *n.*

al·ka·li (al′kə lī′), *n., pl.* **-lis, -lies,** *adj.* —*n.* **1.** *Chem.* **a.** any of various bases, the hydroxides of the alkali metals and of ammonium, which neutralize acids to form salts and turn red litmus paper blue. **b.** any of various other more or less active bases, as calcium hydroxide. **c.** *Obs.* any of various other compounds, as the carbonates of sodium and potassium. **2.** *Agric.* a soluble mineral salt or a mixture of soluble salts, present in some soils, esp. in arid regions, and detrimental to the growing of most crops. —*adj.* **3.** *Chem.* alkaline. [late ME *alkaly* < MF *alcali* < Ar *al* the + *qalīy*, var. of *qilīy* saltwort ashes]

al′kali blue′, *Chem.* any of the class of blue pigments having the highest tinting strength, by weight, of all known blue pigments: used chiefly in the manufacture of printing inks.

al′kali disease′, *Vet. Pathol.* botulism in wild ducks.

al·ka·li·fy (al′kə lə fī′, al kal′ə-), *v.,* **-fied, -fy·ing.** *Chem.* —*v.t.* **1.** to alkalize. —*v.i.* **2.** to become alkaline. [ALKALI + -FY] —**al·ka·li·fi·a·ble** (al′kə lə fī′ə bəl, al kal′ə-), *adj.*

al′kali grass′, a perennial herb, *Zygadenus elegans,* of central and western North America, having tough, wiry, bluish-green leaves and greenish flowers.

al′kali met′al, *Chem.* any of the group of univalent metals including potassium, sodium, lithium, rubidium, cesium, and francium, whose hydroxides are alkalis.

al′kali metapro′tein, *Chem.* a metaprotein derived by means of a hydrolytic alkali.

al·ka·lim·e·ter (al′kə lim′i tər), *n.* *Physical Chem.* an instrument for determining the quantity of carbon dioxide. [ALKALI + -METER] —**al·ka·li·met·ric** (al′kə lə me′trik), **al′ka·li·met′ri·cal,** *adj.* —**al′ka·li·met′ri·cal·ly,** *adv.* —**al′ka·lim′e·try,** *n.*

al·ka·line (al′kə līn′, -lin), *adj.* of, containing, or like an alkali; having the properties of an alkali. [ALKALI + -INE[1]]

al′kaline earth′, *Chem.* any of the oxides of barium, strontium, calcium, and, sometimes, magnesium.

al′ka·line-earth′ met′al (al′kə līn′ûrth′, -lin-), *Chem.* any of the group of bivalent metals including barium, strontium, calcium, and, usually, magnesium, the hydroxides of which are alkalis but less soluble than those of the alkali metals.

al·ka·lin·ise (al′kə li nīz′), *v.t.,* **-ised, -is·ing.** *Chiefly Brit.* alkalinize. —**al′ka·lin′i·sa′tion,** *n.*

al·ka·lin·i·ty (al′kə lin′i tē), *n.* *Chem.* alkaline condition; the quality which constitutes an alkali. [ALKALINE + -ITY]

al·ka·lin·ize (al′kə li nīz′), *v.t.,* **-ized, -iz·ing.** to make alkaline; change into an alkali. [ALKALINE + -IZE] —**al′ka·lin′i·za′tion,** *n.*

al′kali rock′, *Mineral.* any igneous rock with a marked preponderance of alkali and a low percentage of silica.

al·ka·lise (al′kə līz′), *v.t.,* **-lised, -lis·ing.** *Chiefly Brit.* alkalize. —**al′ka·lis′a·ble,** *adj.* —**al′ka·li·sa′tion,** *n.* —**al′ka·lis′er,** *n.*

al′kali soil′, soil that has either a high degree of alkalinity or a high percentage of sodium, or both, so that most crops cannot be grown in it profitably.

al·ka·lize (al′kə līz′), *v.t.,* **-lized, -liz·ing.** *Chem.* alkalinize. [ALKAL(I) + -IZE] —**al′ka·liz′a·ble,** *adj.* —**al′ka·li·za′tion,** *n.* —**al′ka·liz′er,** *n.*

al·ka·loid (al′kə loid′), *Biochem., Chem., Pharm.* —*n.* **1.** any of a large class of organic, nitrogen-containing ring compounds of vegetable origin and sometimes synthesized, some of which are liquid but most of which are solid, that have a bitter taste, that are usually water-insoluble and alcohol-soluble, that combine with acids without the loss of a water molecule to form water-soluble hydrochlorides, hydrobromides, or the like, and that usually exhibit pharmacological action, as nicotine, morphine, or quinine. —*adj.* **2.** resembling an alkali; alkaline. [ALKAL(I) + -OID]

al·ka·loi·dal (al′kə loid′əl), *adj.* of, pertaining to, or derived from alkaloids. [ALKALOID + -AL[1]]

al·ka·lo·sis (al′kə lō′sis), *n.* *Pathol.* a condition of the blood and other body fluids in which the bicarbonate concentration is above normal, tending toward alkalemia. [ALKAL(I) + -OSIS]

al·kane (al′kān), *n.* *Chem.* any member of the alkane series. [ALK(YL) + -ANE]

al′kane se′ries, *Chem.* the homologous series of saturated, aliphatic hydrocarbons having the general formula, C_nH_{2n+2}, as methane, CH_4, or ethane, C_2H_6. Also called **methane series, paraffin series.**

al·ka·net (al′kə net′), *n.* **1.** a European, boraginaceous plant, *Alkanna tinctoria.* **2.** the root of this plant, yielding a red dye. **3.** the dye itself. **4.** any of several similar plants, as the bugloss, *Anchusa officinalis,* or a puccoon of the genus *Lithospermum.* [ME < Sp *alcanet(a)*, equiv. to *alcan(a)* henna (plant) (< ML *alchanna* < Ar *al* the + *hinnā'* henna) + *-eta* dim. suffix]

al·kane·thi·ol (al′kān thī′ōl, -ôl, -ol), *n.* *Chem.* any compound containing an alkyl group joined to a mercapto group, as methyl mercaptan or methanethiol, CH_3SH. [ALKANE + THIOL]

al·kan·nin (al kan′in), *n.* *Chem.* a dark red, amorphous, water-insoluble powder, $C_{16}H_{16}O_5$, obtained from the root of the alkanet: used chiefly for coloring fats, oils, and pharmaceuticals. [< NL *alkann(a)* < ML *alchanna* (see ALKANET) + -IN[2]]

al·kap·ton (al kap′ton, -tən), *n.* *Biochem.* See **homogentisic acid.** Also, **alcapton.** [AL(KALI) + Gk *kápt(ein)* (to) gulp + -ON]

al·kap·to·nu·ri·a (al kap′tə nŏŏr′ē ə, -nyŏŏr′-), *n.* *Pathol.* a condition characterized by the excretion of alkapton in the urine, caused by the faulty metabolism of tyrosine and phenylalanine. Also, **alcaptonuria.** [ALKAPTON + -URIA]

al·kar·gen (al kär′jən), *n.* *Chem.* See **cacodylic acid.** [ALK(ALI) + AR(SENIC) + -GEN]

al·ke·ken·gi (al′kə ken′jē), *n.* the winter cherry plant or fruit. [late ME < ML < Ar *al* the + *kākenj*, var. of *kākanj* ground cherry < Pers]

al·kene (al′kēn), *n.* *Chem.* any member of the alkene series. [ALK(YL) + -ENE]

al′kene se′ries, *Chem.* the homologous series of unsaturated, aliphatic hydrocarbons containing one double bond and having the general formula C_nH_{2n}, as ethylene, $H_2C{=}CH_2$. Also called **ethylene series, olefin series.**

al·ker·mes (al kûr′mēz), *n.* a Mediterranean liqueur made from brandy flavored with nutmeg, cinnamon, cloves, and other spices, and colored red with kermes or cochineal. [< Sp *alkermes* < Ar *al* the + *qirmiz* KERMES]

al·kine (al′kīn), *n.* *Chem.* alkyne.

Alk·maar (älk′mär), *n.* a city in the W Netherlands. 41,330 (est. 1956).

Al·ko·ran (al′kō rän′, -ran′, -kō-), *n.* the Koran. Also, **Alcoran.** [< Ar *al* the + *qor'ān*, var. of *qur'ān* reading (aloud); r. ME *alkaro(u)n* < MF or ML]

alk·ox·ide (al kok′sīd, -sid), *n.* *Chem.* a compound formed from an alcohol by the replacement of the hydrogen of the hydroxyl group with a metal, as sodium methoxide, CH_3ONa, from methyl alcohol, CH_3OH. Also called **alcoholate.** [ALK(YL) + OX(Y)-[2] + -IDE]

Al Ku·fa (al kōō′fə, -fa), Kufa.

al′kyd res′in (al′kid), *Chem.* any of a group of sticky resins derived from dicarboxylic acids, as phthalic or maleic acids, in reaction with glycols or glycerol: used chiefly in adhesives and paints. Also called **alkyd.** [ALKY(L + ACI)D + RESIN]

al·kyl (al′kil, -kēl), *adj.* *Chem.* containing an alkyl group. [< G < *Alk(ohol)* ALC(OHOL) + *-yl* -YL]

al·kyl·a·tion (al′kə lā′shən), *n.* *Chem.* **1.** the replacement of a hydrogen atom in an organic compound by an alkyl group. **2.** the addition of a paraffin to an olefin, done in the manufacture of gasoline. [ALKYL + -ATION]

al′kyl group′, *Chem.* any of a series of univalent groups of the general formula C_nH_{2n+1}, derived from aliphatic hydrocarbons, as the methyl group, CH_3–, or ethyl group, C_2H_5–. Also called **al′kyl rad′ical.**

al′kyl hal′ide, *Chem.* a compound with the type formula RX, where R is an alkyl group and X is a halogen.

al·kyl·ic (al kil′ik), *adj.* of, pertaining to, or characteristic of an alkyl group. [ALKYL + -IC]

al·kyne (al′kīn), *n.* *Chem.* any member of the alkyne series. Also, **alkine.** [ALK(YL) + -INE[2], altered to *-yne*]

al′kyne se′ries, *Chem.* the homologous series of unsaturated, aliphatic hydrocarbons containing one triple bond and having the general formula, C_nH_{2n-2}, as acetylene, $HC{\equiv}CH$. Also called **acetylene series.**

all (ôl), *adj.* **1.** the whole of (used in referring to quantity, extent, or duration): *all the cake; all the way; all year.* **2.** the whole number of (used in referring to individuals or particulars, taken collectively): *all men.* **3.** the greatest possible (used in referring to quality or degree): *with all due respect; with all speed.* **4.** every: *all kinds; all sorts; all manner of men.* **5.** any; any whatever: *beyond all doubt.* **6.** *Dial.* all gone; consumed; finished: *The pie is all.* —*pron.* **7.** the whole quantity or amount: *He ate all of the peanuts. All are gone.* **8.** the whole number: *all of us.* **9.** everything: *Is that all you want to say? All is lost.* —*n.* **10.** *(often cap.)* everything; all matter; the universe. **11.** one's whole interest, energy, or property: *to give one's all; to lose one's all.* **12. above all,** before everything else; chiefly: *Above all, the little girl wanted a giant teddy bear.* **13. after all,** in spite of the circumstances; notwithstanding: *He came in time after all.* **14. all in all, a.** everything considered; in general: *All in all, her condition is greatly improved.* **b.** altogether: *There were twelve absentees all in all.* **c.** everything in one: *Painting became his all in all.* **15. all in hand,** *Print., Journ.* (of the copy for typesetting a particular article, book, issue, etc.) in the possession of the compositor. **16. and all,** together with every other associated or connected attribute or object: *What with the snow and all, we may be a little late. You sure you have enough gas and all?* **17. at all, a.** in the slightest degree: *I wasn't surprised at all.* **b.** for any reason: *Why bother at all?* **c.** in any way: *no offense at all.* **18. for all (that),** in spite of; notwithstanding: *For all that, it was a good year.* **19. in all,** all included; all together: *a hundred guests in all.* **20. once and for all,** for the last time; finally: *The case was settled once and for all when the appeal was denied.* —*adv.* **21.** wholly; entirely; completely: *all alone.* **22.** only; exclusively: *He spent his income all on pleasure.* **23.** each; apiece: *The score was one all.* **24.** *Archaic.* even; just. **25. all at once.** See **once** (def. 14). **26. all in,** *U.S. Informal.* tired; exhausted: *We were all in at the end of the day.* **27. all in the wind,** *Naut.* too close to the wind. **28. all standing,** *Naut.* **a.** in such a way and so suddenly that sails or engines are still set to propel a vessel forward: *The ship ran aground all standing.* **b.** fully clothed: *The crew turned in all standing.* **c.** fully equipped, as a vessel. **29. all the better,** more advantageous; so much the better: *If the sun shines it will be all the better for our excursion.* **30. all the more so,** the more reason for (doing, saying, believing, etc., something): *all the more so to think well of him.* **31. all up, a.** *Print., Journ.* (of copy) completely set in type. **b.** *Informal.* no vestige of hope remains: *It's all up with George—they've*

caught him. **32. be not all there,** *Informal.* **a.** to be feeble-minded. **b.** to be insane: *He's not all there, but his family refuses to have him committed to an institution.* [ME; OE (*e*)*all*; c. Goth *all*(*s*), Icel *all*(*r*), OHG *all* (>G *all*)]
—**Usage.** Such expressions as ALL THE FARTHER (*This is all the farther the elevator goes*) and ALL THE FASTER (*This is all the faster I can run*) are generally avoided in informal English in favor of AS FAR AS (*This is as far as the elevator goes*) and AS FAST AS (*This is as fast as I can run*). They are almost always avoided in formal English. Although some object to ALL OF (*All of the students will attend*), preferring to drop OF (*All students will attend*), both forms are so commonly met in educated usage that there need be no hesitation in using ALL OF. See also **altogether, alright, already.**

all-, var. of **allo-** before a vowel: *allonym.*

Al·la (al′ə), *n.* a girl's given name, form of **Alexandra.**

al·la bre·ve (ä′lə brev′ā; *It.* äl′lä brе′ve), *Music.* using the half note as the basic time unit; 2/2 time. *Symbol:* ₵ Also called **cut time.** [< It: lit., to the short (time). See BRIEF]

al·la·ches·the·sia (al′ə kes thē′zhə), *n.* a condition in which tactile sensation is referred to a point other than the point of stimulation. [< Gk *allach*(*ē*) elsewhere + ESTHESIA]

Al·lah (al′ə, ä′lə), *n.* *Islam.* the Supreme Being. [< Ar < *al* the + *ilāh* God, akin to Heb *elōah*]

Al·lah·a·bad (al′ə hə bad′, ä′lə hä bäd′), *n.* a city in SE Uttar Pradesh, in N India, on the Ganges. 430,700 (1961).

al·la mar·cia (ä′lə mär′chə; *It.* äl′lä mär′chä), *Music.* like a march; in the manner of a march. [< It: lit., to the march (time). See MARCH]

all-A·mer·i·can (ôl′ə mer′i kən), *adj.* **1.** representing the entire United States. **2.** composed exclusively of American members or elements. **3.** representing the best in any field of U.S. sport. —*n.* **4.** an all-American player or performer.

Al·lan (al′ən), *n.* a boy's given name. Also, **Alan, Allen, Allyne.**

Al·lan-a-Dale (al′ən ə dāl′), *n.* (in English balladry) a member of Robin Hood's band who carried off his bride just before she was to be forced into marriage with an aged knight. Also, **Alan-a-dale.**

al·lan·ite (al′ə nīt′), *n.* a mineral, a silicate of calcium, cerium, aluminum, and iron, occurring chiefly in brown-to-black masses or prismatic crystals. [named after Thomas *Allan* (1777–1833), English mineralogist + -ITE[1]] —**al·la·nit·ic** (al′ə nit′ik), *adj.*

al·l'an·ti·ca (äl′län tē′kä), *adv.* *Italian.* in the manner of the ancients.

al·lan·to·ic (al′ən tō′ik), *adj.* of or pertaining to the allantois. [ALLANTO(IS) + -IC]

al·lan·toid (ə lan′toid), *adj.* **1.** Also, **al·lan·toi·dal** (al′ən toid′əl). allantoic. —*n.* **2.** the allantois. [< Gk *allantoeid*(*ēs*), equiv. to *allant-* (s. of *allās* sausage) + *-oeidēs* -OID]

al·lan·to·is (ə lan′tō is, -tois), *n.* *Embryol., Zool.* a vascular, extraembryonic membrane of birds, reptiles, and certain mammals, which develops as a sac or diverticulum from the ventral wall of the hindgut. [< NL < Gk *allantoeidēs*, wrongly taken for pl. and given a sing., on model of words like *hērōis* (sing.), *hērōides* (pl.)]

al·la pri·ma (ä′lə prē′mə), *Fine Arts.* a painting technique in which a canvas is completed in one session, often having a thickly applied impasto. [< It: lit., at the first]

al·lar·gan·do (ä′lär gän′dō; *It.* äl′lär gän′dô), *adj.* *Music.* becoming slower and broader. [< It: *al* to the + *largando* broadening. See LARGE]

all-a·round (ôl′ə round′), *adj.* **1.** versatile: *an all-around player.* **2.** able to do many things; broadly applicable; not specialized: *all-around education.* **3.** inclusive; comprehensive; complete: *an all-around failure.*

al-Lat (äl lät′), *n.* a pre-Islamic Arabian goddess personifying the sun and considered to be a daughter of Allah.

al·la·tive (al′ə tiv), *Gram.* —*adj.* **1.** noting a case, as in Finnish, whose distinctive function is to indicate place to or toward which. —*n.* **2.** the allative case. [< L *allāt*(*us*) (*al-* AL- + *lātus* suppletive ptp. of *ferre* to bring) + -IVE]

al·la vos·tra sa·lu·te (äl′lä vôs′trä sä lo͞o′te), *Italian.* to your health (used as a toast).

al·lay (ə lā′), *v.t.*, **-layed, -lay·ing. 1.** to put (fear, doubt, suspicion, anger, etc.) to rest; calm; quiet. **2.** to lessen or relieve; mitigate; alleviate: *to allay pain.* [ME *aleye*(*n*), OE *ālecgan* to put down, allay (*ā-* A-[3] + *lecgan* to LAY[1]); sp. *-ll-* shows influence of the now obs. *allege* (< F *alléger*) to alleviate, allay] —**al·lay′er,** *n.*
—**Syn. 1.** soften, assuage. ALLAY, MODERATE, SOOTHE mean to reduce excitement or emotion. To ALLAY is to lay to rest or lull to a sense of security, possibly by making the emotion seem unjustified: *to allay suspicion, anxiety, fears.* To MODERATE is to tone down any excess and thus to restore calm: *to moderate the expression of one's grief.* To SOOTHE is to exert a pacifying or tranquilizing influence: *to soothe a terrified child.* **2.** lighten, mollify, temper, ease. —**Ant. 1.** excite.

all′ clear′, the signal that an air raid or air-raid drill is over.

all-day (ôl′dā′), *adj.* taking up, extending through, lasting for, or occurring continually during a day, esp. the hours of daylight; daylong: *an all-day tour of the city; an all-day sucker.* Cf. **all-night.**

al·le·cret (al′ə kret′), *n.* a half suit of light plate armor. [< MF *halecret*, perh. < G *Hals* neck]

Al·le·gan (al′ə gan′), *n.* a town in SW Michigan. 4822 (1960).

al·le·ga·tion (al′ə gā′shən), *n.* **1.** act of alleging; affirmation. **2.** a statement offered as a plea, excuse, or justification. **3.** an assertion made without substantial proof. **4.** an assertion made by a party in a legal proceeding, which he undertakes to prove. [late ME < L *allēgātiōn-* (s. of *allēgātiō*), equiv. to *allēgāt*(*us*) adduced (ptp. of *allēgāre*; *al-* AL- + *lēg-* ordain by law (see *lex*) + *-ātus* -ATE[1] + *-iōn-* -ION]

al·lege (ə lej′), *v.t.*, **-leged, -leg·ing. 1.** to declare with positiveness; affirm; assert: *to allege a fact.* **2.** to declare before a court or elsewhere as if under oath. **3.** to assert without proof. **4.** to plead in support of; urge as a reason or excuse. **5.** *Archaic.* to cite or quote in confirmation. [ME *alegge*(*n*) < AF *alegier* (<< VL **exlītigāre*; see EX-, LITIGATE) with sense of L *allēgāre* to adduce] —**al·lege′a·ble,** *adj.* —**al·leg′er,** *n.*
—**Syn. 1.** state, asseverate, aver. **2.** attest. —**Ant. 1.** deny.

al·leged (ə lejd′), *adj.* **1.** declared or stated to be as described; asserted: *The alleged murderer could not be located for questioning.* **2.** doubtful; suspect; supposed: *The alleged cure-all produced no results when it was tested.* [ALLEGE + -ED[2]] —**al·leg′ed·ly,** *adv.*

Al·le·ghe·ny (al′ə gā′nē), *n.* a river flowing S from SW New York through W Pennsylvania, joining the Monongahela at Pittsburgh to form the Ohio River. 325 mi. long. —**Al′le·ghe′ni·an, Al′le·gha′ni·an,** *adj.*

Al′leghe′ny bar′berry, a shrub, *Berberis canadensis*, of North America, resembling the common barberry of Europe, but having leaves with grayish undersides. Also called **Canada barberry.**

Al′leghe′ny Moun′tains, a mountain range in Pennsylvania, Maryland, West Virginia, and Virginia: a part of the Appalachian Mountains. Also called **Al′le·ghe′nies.**

Al′leghe′ny spurge′, a low perennial herb, *Pachysandra procumbens*, of the southeastern U.S., having spikes of white or purplish flowers.

Al′leghe′ny vine′. See **climbing fumitory.**

al·le·giance (ə lē′jəns), *n.* **1.** the loyalty of a citizen to his government or of a subject to his sovereign. **2.** loyalty or devotion to some person, group, cause, or the like. [late ME *aliegiaunce*, equiv. to *a-* (< ?) + *liege* LIEGE + *-aunce* -ANCE; cf. MF *ligeance*]
—**Syn.** See **loyalty.** —**Ant. 1.** treason. **2.** treachery.

al·le·giant (ə lē′jənt), *adj.* loyal; faithful. [ALLEGI(ANCE) + -ANT]

al·le·gor·i·cal (al′ə gôr′i kəl, -gor′-), *adj.* consisting of or pertaining to allegory; of the nature of or containing allegory; figurative: *an allegorical poem; an allegorical meaning.* Also, **al′le·gor′ic.** [< L *allēgoric*(*us*) (< Gk *allēgorikós*; see ALLEGORY, -IC) + -AL[1]] —**al′le·gor′i·cal·ly,** *adv.* —**al′le·gor′i·cal·ness,** *n.*

al·le·go·rise (al′ə gə rīz′), *v.t., v.i.*, **-rised, -ris·ing.** *Chiefly Brit.* allegorize. —**al′le·gor′i·sa′tion,** *n.* —**al′le·go·ris′er,** *n.*

al·le·go·rist (al′ə gōr′ist, -gôr′-, al′ə gər ist), *n.* one who uses or writes allegory. [ALLEGOR(IZE) + -IST]

al·le·go·ris·tic (al′ə gə ris′tik), *adj.* writing or using allegory; interpreting in an allegorical sense. [ALLEGORIST + -IC]

al·le·go·rize (al′ə gə rīz′), *v.*, **-rized, -riz·ing.** —*v.t.* **1.** to make into an allegory; narrate allegorically. **2.** to understand in an allegorical sense; interpret allegorically. —*v.i.* **3.** to use allegory. Also, *esp. Brit.*, **allegorise.** [< LL *allēgorizāre*; see ALLEGORY, -IZE] —**al′le·gor′i·za′tion,** *n.* —**al′le·go·riz′er,** *n.*

al·le·go·ry (al′ə gōr′ē, -gôr′ē), *n., pl.* **-ries. 1.** a representation of an abstract or spiritual meaning through concrete or material forms; figurative treatment of one subject under the guise of another. **2.** a symbolical narrative: *the allegory of* Piers Plowman. **3.** emblem (def. 3). [late ME *allegorie* < L *allēgoria* < Gk *allēgoría*, deriv. of *allēgorein* so to speak as to imply something other. See ALLO-, AGORA]

Al·le·gra (ə leg′rə; *It.* äl le′grä), *n.* a girl's given name.

al·le·gret·to (al′ə gret′ō; *It.* äl′le gret′tô), *adj., n., pl.* **-tos.** *Music.* —*adj.* **1.** light, graceful, and moderately fast in tempo. —*n.* **2.** an allegretto movement. [< It, equiv. to *allegr*(*o*) cheerful + *-etto* -ET]

al·le·gro (ə lā′grō, ə leg′rō; *It.* äl le′grô), *adj., n., pl.* **-gros.** *Music.* —*adj.* **1.** brisk or rapid in tempo. —*n.* **2.** an allegro movement. [< It < L *alacer* brisk. See ALACRITY]

Al·le·gro, L' (lä lā′grō, la-). See **L'Allegro.**

al·lele (ə lēl′), *n.* *Genetics.* any of several forms of a gene, usually arising through mutation, that are responsible for hereditary variation. [short for ALLELOMORPH] —**al·lel·ic** (ə lē′lik), *adj.* —**al·lel′ism,** *n.*

al·le·lo·morph (ə lē′lə môrf′, ə lel′ə-), *n.* *Genetics.* allele. [< *allelo-* (s. of Gk *allēlōn* of one another, equiv. to *áll*(*os*) other + *állōn*, gen. pl. of *állos*) + -MORPH] —**al·le′lo·mor′phic,** *adj.* —**al·le′lo·mor′phism,** *n.*

al·le·lu·ia (al′ə lo͞o′yə), *interj.* **1.** praise ye the Lord; hallelujah. —*n.* **2.** a song of praise to God. [< LL < Gk *allēloúia* < Heb *hallēlūyāh* praise ye Yahweh] —**al·le·lu·iat·ic** (al′ə lo͞o yat′ik), *adj.*

al·le·mande (al′ə mand′, -mänd′, al′ə mand′, -mänd′; *Fr.* alᵊ mäɴd′), *n., pl.* **-mandes** (-mandz′, -mändz′, -mandz′, -mändz′; *Fr.* -mäɴd′). **1.** a 17th- and 18th-century dance in slow duple time. **2.** a piece of music based on its rhythm, often following the prelude in the classical suite. **3.** a figure performed in a quadrille. **4.** a German folk dance in triple meter, similar to the ländler. [< F, short for *danse allemande* German dance]

al′lemande sauce′, a velouté thickened and enriched with egg yolk. Also, **Al′lemande sauce′.**

all-em·brac·ing (ôl′em brā′sing), *adj.* covering or applying to all; exhaustive; all-inclusive; blanket: *an all-embracing definition; He dismissed all criticism with an all-embracing charge of the critics' ignorance.*

al·le·mont·ite (al′ə mon′tīt), *n.* a mineral, arsenic antimony, AsSb, occurring in reniform masses. [named after *Allemont* (place in France where found) + -ITE[1]]

Al·len (al′ən), *n.* **1. (Charles) Grant (Blair·fin·die)** (blâr fin′dē), ("*Cecil Power*", "*J. Arbuthnot Wilson*"), 1848–99, British philosophical writer and novelist. **2. Ethan,** 1738–89, American soldier in the Revolutionary War: leader of the "Green Mountain Boys" of Vermont. **3. Frederick Lewis,** 1890–1954, U.S. historian and editor. **4. (William) Her·vey** (hûr′vē), 1889–1949, U.S. novelist, poet, and biographer. **5.** Also, **Alan, Allan, Allyne.** a boy's given name.

Al·len·by (al′ən bē), *n.* **Edmund Henry Hyn·man** (hin′mən), **1st Viscount,** 1861–1936, British field marshal: commander of British forces in Palestine and Syria in World War I.

Al·len·dale (al′ən dāl′), *n.* **1.** a town in NE New Jersey. 4092 (1960). **2.** a town in SW South Carolina. 3114 (1960).

Al·len·de Gos·sens (ä yen′de gô′sens), **Salvador,** 1908–73, Chilean political leader: president 1970–73.

Al′len Park′, a city in SE Michigan. 37,052 (1960).

Al′len screw′, a screw turned by means of an axial hexagonal hole in its head. [formerly a trademark]

Al·len·town (al′ən toun′), *n.* a city in E Pennsylvania. 108,347 (1960).

Al′len wrench′, a wrench for Allen screws, formed from a piece of hexagonal bar stock bent to a right angle. [formerly a trademark]

al·ler·gen (al′ər jen′), *n.* *Immunol.* any substance which might induce an allergy. [ALLER(GY) + -GEN]

al·ler·gen·ic (al′ər jen′ik), *adj.* causing allergic sensitization. [ALLERGEN + -IC] —**al·ler·gen·ic·i·ty** (al′ər jə nis′i tē), *n.*

al·ler·gic (ə lûr′jik), *adj.* **1.** of or pertaining to allergy: *an allergic reaction to wool.* **2.** having an allergy. **3.** excessively sensitive; responding antipathetically; susceptible: *allergic to criticism.* [ALLERG(Y) + -IC]

al·ler·gist (al′ər jist), *n.* a physician specializing in the diagnosis and treatment of allergies. [ALLERG(Y) + -IST]

al·ler·gy (al′ər jē), *n., pl.* **-gies. 1.** a state of hypersensitivity, as hay fever or asthma, to certain things, as pollen, food, animals, etc., usually characterized by difficult respiration, skin rashes, etc. **2.** altered susceptibility due to a first inoculation, treatment, or the like, as exhibited in reaction to a subsequent one of the same nature. Cf. **anaphylaxis. 3.** *Informal.* an antipathy, as toward a person or activity: *He has an allergy to hard work.* [< Gk *áll*(*os*) other + *-ergy*, deriv. of *-ergia*, equiv. to *érg*(*on*) activity + *-ia* -Y[3]]

al·le·thrin (al′ə thrin), *n.* *Chem.* a clear, amber, viscous liquid, $C_{19}H_{26}O_3$, used as an insecticide. [ALL(YL) + (*pyr*)*ethrin*, equiv. to *pyrethr*(*um*) name of a genus of composite plants + -IN[2]]

al·le·vi·ant (ə lē′vē ənt), *n.* something that alleviates a condition. [ALLEVI(ATE) + -ANT]

al·le·vi·ate (ə lē′vē āt′), *v.t.*, **-at·ed, -at·ing.** to make easier to endure; lessen; mitigate: *to alleviate sorrow; to alleviate pain.* [< LL *alleviāt*(*us*) (ptp. of *alleviāre*), equiv. to *al-* AL- + *levi*(*s*) light, not heavy + *-ātus* -ATE[1]]
—**Syn.** lighten, diminish, abate, relieve, assuage.

al·le·vi·a·tion (ə lē′vē ā′shən), *n.* **1.** act of alleviating. **2.** that which alleviates or palliates. [< ML *alleviātiōn-* (s. of *alleviātiō*), equiv. to *alleviāt*(*us*) (see ALLEVIATE) + *-iōn-* -ION]

al·le·vi·a·tive (ə lē′vē ā′tiv, -ə tiv), *adj.* **1.** Also, **alleviatory.** serving to alleviate; palliative. —*n.* **2.** *Obs.* alleviation (def. 2). [ALLEVIATE + -IVE]

al·le·vi·a·tor (ə lē′vē ā′tər), *n.* **1.** one who or that which alleviates. **2.** (in a pipeline) an airtight box, having a free liquid surface, for cushioning the shock of water hammer. [ALLEVIATE + -OR[2]]

al·le·vi·a·to·ry (ə lē′vē ə tōr′ē, -tôr′ē), *adj.* alleviative; palliative. [ALLEVIATE + -ORY[1]]

all-ex·pense (ôl′ik spens′), *adj.* including all necessary or usual expenses, as the price of a trip, tour, or the like; not requiring a purchaser, participant, etc., to pay extra or incidental charges; package: *an all-expense vacation plan.* Also called **all-ex·pens·es-paid** (ôl′ik-spen′siz pād′).

al·ley[1] (al′ē), *n., pl.* **-leys. 1.** a narrow back street. **2.** a walk, as in a garden, enclosed with hedges or shrubbery. **3.** a passage, as through a continuous row of houses, permitting access from the street to back yards, garages, etc. **4.** *Bowling.* **a.** a long, narrow, wooden lane or floor along which the ball is rolled. **b.** See **bowling green. 5.** *Tennis.* the space on each side of a tennis court between the doubles sideline and the service or singles sideline. **6.** *Rare.* an aisle. **7. up one's alley,** *Slang.* in keeping with one's natural abilities or interests: *Doing a book on sailing would be right up his alley.* [ME *al*(*e*)*y* < MF *alee* walk, passage, deriv. of fem. of *ale*, ptp. of *aler* to walk < ?]
—**Syn. 1.** See **street.**

al·ley[2] (al′ē), *n., pl.* **-leys.** a choice, large playing marble. [short for ALABASTER]

al′ley cat′, a homeless, usually mongrel, cat that scavenges for food in alleys, streets, etc.

al·ley·way (al′ē wā′), *n.* **1.** an alley or lane. **2.** a narrow passageway. [ALLEY[1] + WAY]

all-fired (ôl′fīᵊrd′), *adj., superl.* **-fired·est,** *adv.* *Chiefly U.S. Informal.* —*adj.* **1.** tremendous; extreme; excessive: *He had the all-fired gall to quit in the middle of the job.* —*adv.* **2.** Also, **all-fired·ly** (ôl′fīᵊrd′lē, -fīr′id-). extremely; excessively: *Don't be so all-fired sure of yourself.*

All′ Fools′ Day′. See **April Fools' Day.**

All′ for Love′, a drama in blank verse (1678) by Dryden.

all′ fours′, 1. all four limbs or extremities; the four legs of an animal or both arms and both legs of a man: *to land on all fours.* **2.** (*construed as sing.*) Also called **high-low-jack, old sledge, pitch, seven-up.** *Cards.* a game for two or three players or two partnerships in which a 52-card pack is used, the object being to win special scoring values for the highest trump, the lowest trump, the jack, the ace, the ten, and the face cards. **3. on all fours, a.** in conformity with; corresponding exactly with. **b.** (of a person) on the hands and feet, or the hands and knees: *It was necessary to go on all fours to squeeze through the opening.* **c.** (of a four-legged animal) with all four feet on the ground: *My dog can stand and beg for five minutes before going back down on all fours.*

all′ get′-out (get′out′), *Slang.* possible; imaginable: *The wind was as cold as all get-out.* Also, **all′ get′ out′.**

All′ God's Chil′lun Got Wings′ (chil′ən), a play (1924) by Eugene O'Neill.

all′ hail′, *Archaic.* a salutation of greeting or welcome.

All·hal·low·mas (ôl′hal′ō məs), *n.* *Archaic.* Allhallows. [ME *alhalwemesse*, OE *ealra hālgena mæsse* mass of all saints]

All·hal·lows (ôl′hal′ōz), *n.* See **All Saints' Day.**

Allhal′lows eve′, Halloween. Also called **All′ Hal′low E′ven.**

All·hal·low·tide (ôl′hal′ō tīd′), *n.* *Archaic.* the time or season of Allhallows. [ALLHALLOW(S) + TIDE[1]]

all·heal (ôl′hēl′), *n.* **1.** valerian (def. 1). **2.** a selfheal. [ALL + HEAL]

al·li·a·ceous (al′ē ā′shəs), *adj.* **1.** *Bot.* belonging to the genus *Allium*, comprising the garlic, onion, leek, etc. **2.** having the odor or taste of garlic, onion, etc. [< L *alli*(*um*) garlic + -ACEOUS]

al·li·ance (ə lī′əns), *n.* **1.** the act of allying or state of being allied. **2.** marriage or the relationship created by marriage between the families of the bride and bridegroom. **3.** a formal agreement or treaty between two or more nations to cooperate for specific purposes. **4.** a merging of efforts or interests by persons, families, states, or organizations: *an alliance between church and state.* **5.** the persons or entities so allied. **6.** correspondence in basic characteristics; affinity: *the alliance between logic and metaphysics* [ME *aliance* < OF, equiv. to *ali(er)* (to) ALLY + *-ance* -ANCE]

—Syn. 1. association; coalition, combination, bloc; partnership; affiliation. ALLIANCE, CONFEDERATION, LEAGUE, UNION all mean the joining of states for mutual benefit or to permit the joint exercise of functions. An ALLIANCE may apply to any connection entered into for mutual benefit. LEAGUE usually suggests closer combination or a more definite object or purpose. CONFEDERATION applies to a permanent combination for the exercise in common of certain governmental functions. UNION implies an alliance so close and permanent that the separate states or parties become essentially one. **3.** treaty, pact, compact.

Al·li·ance (ə lī′əns), *n.* **1.** a city in NE Ohio. 28,362 (1960). **2.** a town in NW Nebraska. 7845 (1960).

al·lied (ə līd′, al′īd), *adj.* **1.** joined by treaty: *allied nations.* **2.** related; kindred: *allied species.* **3.** (*cap.*) of or pertaining to the Allies. [ME; see ALLY, -ED²]

Al·lier (A lyā′), *n.* **1.** a river flowing N from S France to the Loire. ab. 250 mi. long. **2.** a department in central France. 380,221 (1962); 2850 sq. mi. *Cap.:* Moulins.

al·lies (al′īz, ə līz′), *n.* pl. of **ally. 2.** (*cap.*) (in World War I) the powers of the Triple Entente (Great Britain, France, Russia), with the nations allied with them (Belgium, Serbia, Japan, Italy, etc., not including the United States), or loosely, with all the nations (including the United States) allied or associated with them as opposed to the Central Powers. **3.** (*cap.*) the 26 nations that fought against the Axis in World War II and which, with subsequent additions, signed the charter of the United Nations in San Francisco in 1945. **4.** (*cap.*) the member nations of NATO.

al·li·gate (al′ə gāt′), *v.t.*, **-gat·ed, -gat·ing.** *Obs.* to attach; bind. [< L *alligāt(us)* (ptp. of *alligāre*), equiv. to *al-* AL- + *lig-* bind (see LIGATURE) + *-ātus* -ATE¹]

al·li·ga·tor (al′ə gā′tər), *n.* **1.** either of two broad-snouted crocodilians of the genus *Alligator*, found in the southeastern U.S. and eastern China. **2.** (loosely) any broad-snouted crocodilian, as a caiman. **3.** Also called **al′ligator squeez′er.** *Metall.* a machine for bringing the balls of iron from a puddling furnace into compact form so that they can be handled. **4.** *Jazz.* an enthusiastic fan of swing. **—***v.i.* **5.** (of paint, varnish, or the like) to crack and acquire the appearance of alligator hide, as from weathering or improper application to a surface. **—***v.i.* **6.** *Metalworking.* (of a rolled metal slab) to split and curl up and down at one end; to fishmouth. [< Sp *el lagarto* the lizard << L *lacertus*, lizard]

Alligator,
Alligator mississipiensis
(Length 11 ft.)

al′ligator clip′, *Elect.* a type of terminal for making temporary electrical connections, consisting of a cliplike device with long, narrow jaws that resemble those of an alligator.

al·li·ga·tor·fish (al′ə gā′tər fish′), *n., pl.* (*esp. collectively*) **-fish,** (*esp. referring to two or more kinds or species*) **-fish·es.** any of several slender, marine fishes of the family *Agonidae*, having the body covered with overlapping plates, esp. *Aspidophoroides monopterygius*, found in the Atlantic Ocean. [ALLIGATOR + FISH]

al′ligator liz′ard, any of several lizards of the genus *Gerrhonotus*, of Mexico and the southwestern U.S., having the body covered with scales that resemble those of an alligator.

al′ligator pear′, avocado (def. 1). [*alligator*, alter. by folk etym. of Sp *avocado, abogado* or AmerSp *aguacate* (see AVOCADO) + PEAR]

al′ligator shear′, a heavy shear for cutting metal slabs.

al′ligator snap′ping tur′tle, a large, American snapping turtle, *Macroclemys temmincki*, having three prominent ridges on its shell and a wormlike process on the floor of the mouth used to attract prey. Also called **al′ligator snap′per.**

al′ligator wam·pee′ (wom pē′), pickerelweed. [< Algonquian *wampee*]

al′ligator wrench′, *Mach.* a wrench having a V-shaped pair of serrated jaws set at right angles to the shank for turning cylindrical or irregularly shaped parts.

all-im·por·tant (ôl′im pôr′tᵊnt), *adj.* very important; essential.

all-in (ôl′in′), *adj.* **1.** *Brit.* with extras included; inclusive: *at the all-in rate.* **2.** *Wrestling.* without restrictions; with virtually every type of hold permitted. **3.** *Jazz.* performed by all members of the group; played ensemble: *An all-in chorus followed the solos.*

all-in·clu·sive (ôl′in klo͞o′siv), *adj.* wholly inclusive; comprehensive.

al·li·sion (ə lizh′ən), *n.* *Law.* the striking of one ship by another. [< LL *allisiōn-* (s. of *allisiō*), equiv. to *allis(us)* struck at, ptp. of *allidere* (*al-* AL- + *lid-* strike (var. of *laed-*; see LESION) + *-tus* ptp. suffix) + *-iōn-* -ION]

Al·li·son (al′i sən), *n.* a girl's given name, form of **Alice.** Also, **Alison, Alyson.**

al·lit·er·ate (ə lit′ə rāt′), *v.*, **-at·ed, -at·ing.** **—***v.i.* **1.** to show alliteration: *The "h" in "harp" does not alliterate with the "h" in "honored."* **2.** to use alliteration: *Swinburne often alliterates.* **—***v.t.* **3.** to compose or arrange with alliteration: *He alliterates the "w's" in that line.* [back formation from ALLITERATION] **—al·lit′er·a′tor,** *n.*

al·lit·er·a·tion (ə lit′ə rā′shən), *n.* **1.** the commencement of two or more stressed syllables of a word group either with the same consonant sound or sound group (**consonantal alliteration**), as in *from stem to stern*, or with a vowel sound that may differ from syllable to syllable (**vocalic alliteration**), as in *each to all.* Cf. **consonance** (def. 4a). **2.** the commencement of two or more words of a word group with the same letter, as in *apt alliteration's artful aid.* [< ML *alliterātiōn-*, s. of *alliterātiō*, equiv. to *al-* AL- + *literātiō*, modeled after *obliterātiō* OBLITERATION]

al·lit·er·a·tive (ə lit′ə rā′tiv, -ər ə tiv), *adj.* pertaining to or characterized by alliteration: *alliterative verse.* [ALLITERAT(ION) + -IVE] **—al·lit′er·a′tive·ly,** *adv.* **—al·lit′er·a′tive·ness,** *n.*

al·li·um (al′ē əm), *n.* any bulbous, liliaceous plant of the genus *Allium*, including the onion, leek, shallot, garlic, and chive. [< L: garlic]

all·mouth (ôl′mouth′), *n., pl.* **-mouths** (-mouthz′). angler (def. 2). [ALL + MOUTH; i.e., big mouth]

all·ness (ôl′nis), *n.* quality or state of universality or totality. [ALL + -NESS]

all-night (ôl′nīt′), *adj.* **1.** taking up, extending through, or occurring continually during a night; nightlong: *an all-night vigil.* **2.** open all night, as for business; providing services, accommodations, etc., at all hours of the night: *an all-night drug store.*

allo-, a learned borrowing from Greek meaning "other," used in the formation of compound words (*allotrope*) and in chemistry to denote the more stable of two geometric isomers. Also (except in chemistry), *esp. before a vowel*, **all-.** [< Gk, comb. form of *állos* other; c. L *alius*, ELSE]

al·lo·bar·ic (al′ə bar′ik), *adj.* *Meteorol.* of or pertaining to change in atmospheric pressure: *allobaric wind.* [ALLO- + BARIC²]

al·lo·ca·ble (al′ə kə bəl), *adj.* that can be allocated. [ALLOC(ATE) + -ABLE]

al·lo·cate (al′ə kāt′), *v.t.*, **-cat·ed, -cat·ing.** **1.** to set apart for a particular purpose; assign or allot: *to allocate funds for new projects.* **2.** to fix the place of; locate. [< ML *allocāt(us)* (ptp. of *allocāre*), equiv. to *al-* AL- + *loc(us)* place + *-ātus* -ATE¹]
—Syn. 1. See **assign.**

al·lo·ca·tion (al′ə kā′shən), *n.* **1.** act of allocating; apportionment. **2.** state of being allocated. **3.** the share or portion allocated. **4.** *Accounting.* a system of dividing expenses and incomes among the various branches, departments, etc., of a business. [< ML *allocātiōn-* (s. of *allocātiō*), equiv. to *allocāt(us)* (see ALLOCATE) + *-iōn-* -ION]

al·lo·chro·mat·ic (al′ə krə mat′ik, -krō-), *adj.* **1.** *Physical Chem.* pertaining to or having photochemical properties resulting from an impurity or from exposure to radiation. **2.** *Mineral.* (of a mineral) having no color in itself but bearing colored impurities. [ALLO- + CHROMATIC]

al·loch·thon (ə lok′thən, -thon), *n.* *Geol.* a geological formation formed elsewhere than in the region where found and moved to its present location by tectonic forces. Cf. **autochthon** (def. 3). [back formation from ALLOCHTHONOUS]

al·loch·tho·nous (ə lok′thə nəs), *adj.* *Geol.* (of rocks, minerals, etc.) formed elsewhere than in the region where found. Cf. **autochthonous** (def. 4). [ALLO- + *-chthonous*, modeled after AUTOCHTONOUS]

al·lo·cu·tion (al′ə kyo͞o′shən), *n.* **1.** a formal speech, esp. one of an incontrovertible or hortatory nature. **2.** a pronouncement delivered by the pope to a secret consistory, esp. on a matter of policy or of general importance. [< L *allocūtiōn-* (s. of *allocūtiō*), equiv. to *allocūt(us)*, ptp. of *alloquī* (*al-* AL- + *locū-* (s. of *loquī* to speak) + *-tus* ptp. suffix) + *-iōn-* -ION]

al·lo·di·al (ə lō′dē əl), *adj.* free from the tenurial rights of a feudal overlord. Also, **alodial.** [< ML *allodiāl(is)*, equiv. to *allōdi(um)*, ALLODIUM + *-ālis* -AL¹] **—al·lo′di·al′i·ty,** *n.* **—al·lo′di·al·ly,** *adv.*

al·lo·di·um (ə lō′dē əm), *n., pl.* **-di·a** (-dē ə). land owned absolutely; land owned and not subject to any rent, service, or other tenurial right of an overlord. Also, **alodium.** Also called **allod, alod.** [< ML < OG *allōd* (*all* ALL + *-ōd* patrimony, c. Icel *ōth-*, OE *ēth-* in *ēthel*, akin (by gradation) to *ath-* of ATHELING)]

al·log·a·my (ə log′ə mē), *n.* cross-fertilization in plants. [ALLO- + -GAMY] **—al·log′a·mous,** *adj.*

al·lo·gen·ic (al′ə jen′ik), *adj.* *Geol.* (of a constituent of a rock) formed elsewhere than in the rock where it is found. Cf. **authigenic.** [ALLO- + GENIC] **—al′lo·gen′i·cal·ly,** *adv.*

al·lo·graph (al′ə graf′, -gräf′), *n.* **1.** writing or a signature inscribed by one person for another, as distinguished from autograph. **2.** a deed or other legal document not in the writing of any of the persons who are party to it. **3.** *Ling.* a variant form of a grapheme that is in complementary distribution or free variation with another form of the same grapheme; an orthographic contextual variant. [ALLO- + -GRAPH]

al·lom·er·ism (ə lom′ə riz′əm), *n.* *Chem.* variability in chemical constitution without change in crystalline form. [ALLO- + -MER + -ISM] **—al·lom′er·ous,** *adj.*

al·lom·er·ize (ə lom′ə rīz′), *v.i.*, **-ized, -iz·ing.** *Chem.* to undergo allomerism. [ALLO- + -MER + -IZE] **—al·lom′er·i·za′tion,** *n.*

al·lom·e·try (ə lom′i trē), *n.* *Biol.* **1.** growth of a part of an organism in relation to the growth of the whole organism or some part of it. **2.** the measurement or study of this growth. Also, **al·loi·om·e·try** (al′oi om′i trē). [ALLO- + -METRY] **—al·lo·met·ric** (al′ə me′trik), **al·loi·o·met·ric** (ə loi′ə me′trik), *adj.*

al·lo·morph (al′ə môrf′), *n.* **1.** any of two or more different forms of the same chemical compound. **2.** *Ling.* one of the alternate contextually determined phonological shapes of a morpheme, as *en* in *oxen*, which is an allomorph of the English plural morpheme. Cf. **morph.** [ALLO- + -MORPH] **—al′lo·mor′phic,** *adj.*

al·lo·mor·phism (al′ə môr′fiz əm), *n.* *Chem.* variability in crystalline form without change in chemical constitution. [ALLOMORPH + -ISM]

all′ on′, *Fox Hunting.* the cry uttered by a whipper-in to signify that all the hounds are accounted for.

al·longe (ə lunj′; *Fr.* A lôɴzh′), *n., pl.* **al·long·es** (ə lun′jiz; *Fr.* A lôɴzh′). *Law.* a paper annexed to a negotiable instrument, for endorsements too numerous or lengthy to be contained in the original. [< F: lengthening; see LUNGE¹]

al·lon·gé (*Fr.* A lôɴ zhā′), *adj.* *Ballet.* performed with the body and one arm stretched forward: *an arabesque allongé.* [< F: lit., extended, lengthened, ptp. of *allonger*]

al·lo·nym (al′ə nim), *n.* **1.** the name of another person taken by an author as a pen name. Cf. **pseudonym. 2.** a work published under a name that is not that of the author. [ALL(O)- + *-onym* < Gk *-ōnymos* comb. form of *ónoma* name. Cf. HOMONYM, PSEUDONYM] **—al·lon·y·mous** (ə lon′ə məs), *adj.* **—al·lon′y·mous·ly,** *adv.*

al·lo·path (al′ə path′), *n.* one who practices or favors allopathy. Also, **al·lop·a·thist** (ə lop′ə thist). [< G, back formation from *Allopathie* ALLOPATHY]

al·lop·a·thy (ə lop′ə thē), *n.* the method of treating disease by the use of agents, producing effects different from those of the disease treated (opposed to *homeopathy*). [< G *Allopathie.* See ALLO-, -PATHY] **—al·lo·path·ic** (al′ə path′ik), *adj.* **—al′lo·path′i·cal·ly,** *adv.*

al·lo·pat·ric (al′ə pa′trik), *adj.* *Biol., Ecol.* originating in or occupying different geographical areas. [ALLO- + Gk *pátr(iā)* fatherland (*patēr* father + *-iā* n. suffix) + -IC] **—al′lo·pat′ri·cal·ly,** *adv.*

al·lo·pe·lag·ic (al′ō pə laj′ik), *adj.* (of a marine organism) living or growing at different depths. [< G *allopelagisch.* See ALLO-, PELAGIC]

al·lo·phane (al′ə fān′), *n.* a mineral, an amorphous hydrous silicate of aluminum, occurring in blue, green, or yellow, resinous to earthy masses. [< Gk *allophan(ḗs)*, equiv. to *allo-* ALLO- + *phan-* (s. of *phainesthai* to appear) + *-ēs* adj. suffix]

al·lo·phone (al′ə fōn′), *n.* *Phonet.* **1.** a speech sound constituting one of the phonetic variants of a given phoneme. **2.** any member of a phoneme, regardless of phonetic variances. **3.** any of the members of a class of speech sounds which, taken together, are commonly felt to be a phoneme, as the *t*-sounds of *toe, stow, tree, hatpin, catcall, cats, catnip, button, metal, city*, etc.; a phonetic manifestation of a particular phoneme. [ALLO- + PHONE²] **—al·lo·phon·ic** (al′ə fon′ik), *adj.* **—al′lo·phon′i·cal·ly,** *adv.*

al·lo·phyl·i·an (al′ə fil′ē ən, -fil′yən), *adj.* *Archaic.* **1.** (of languages, esp. those of Europe and Asia) neither Indo-European nor Semitic. **—***n.* **2.** Turanian (defs. 3, 4). [< LL *allophyl(us)* (< Gk *allóphylos*, equiv. to *allo-* ALLO- + *phŷl(ē)* tribe + *-os* adj. suffix) + -IAN]

al·lo·plasm (al′ə plaz′əm), *n.* *Biol.* a part of protoplasm that is differentiated to perform a special function, as that of the flagellum. [ALLO- + -PLASM] **—al′lo·plas·mat′ic, al′lo·plas′mic,** *adj.*

al·lo·poly·ploid (al′ə pol′ə ploid′), *Biol.* **—***adj.* **1.** having more than two haploid sets of chromosomes that are dissimilar and derived from different species. **—***n.* **2.** an allopolyploid cell or organism. Cf. **autopolyploid.** [ALLO- + POLYPLOID] **—al·lo·pol·y·ploi·dy** (al′ə pol′ə ploi′dē), *n.*

all′-or-none′ law′ (ôl′ər nun′), *Physiol.* the principle that under given conditions the response of a nerve or muscle fiber to a stimulus at any strength above the threshold is the same.

al·lo·saur (al′ə sôr′), *n.* a carnivorous dinosaur of the genus *Allosaurus*, from the late Jurassic period of North America, growing to a length of more than 30 feet. [ALLO- + -SAUR]

al·lot (ə lot′), *v.t.*, **-lot·ted, -lot·ting.** **1.** to divide or distribute by lot or as if by lot; distribute or parcel out; apportion: *to allot portions.* **2.** to appropriate for a special purpose: *to allot money for a park.* **3.** to assign as a portion; set apart; dedicate. [earlier *alot* < MF *aloter*, equiv. to *a-* A-⁵ + *lot* LOT + *-er* inf. suffix] **—al·lot′ta·ble,** *adj.* **—al·lot′ter,** *n.*
—Syn. 1. See **assign.**

al·lot·ment (ə lot′mənt), *n.* **1.** act of allotting. **2.** that which is allotted. **3.** a portion or thing allotted; a share granted. **4.** (in U.S. military use) the portion of the pay of an officer or enlisted person that he authorizes to be paid directly to another person, as a dependent, or an institution, as an insurance company. **5.** *Brit.* a plot of land rented to a gardener. [ALLOT + -MENT; cf. F *allotement*]

al·lot·ri·o·mor·phic (ə lo′trē ə môr′fik), *adj.* *Petrog.* xenomorphic (def. 1). [< Gk *allótrio(s)* strange + -MORPHIC]

al·lo·trope (al′ə trōp′), *n.* *Chem.* one of two or more existing forms of an element: *Charcoal, graphite, and diamond are allotropes of carbon.* [ALLO- + -TROPE]

al·lo·trop·ic (al′ə trop′ik), *adj.* pertaining to or characterized by allotropy. Also, **al′lo·trop′i·cal.** [ALLOTROP(Y) + -IC] **—al′lo·trop′i·cal·ly,** *adv.* **—al·lo·tro·pic·i·ty** (al′ə trə pis′i tē), *n.*

al·lot·ro·py (ə lo′trə pē), *n.* *Chem.* a property of certain elements, as carbon, sulfur, and phosphorus, of existing in two or more distinct forms; allomorphism. Also, **al·lot′ro·pism.** [ALLO- + -TROPY]

all′ ot·ta·va (äl′ ə tä′və; *It.* äl′lôt tä′vä), *Music.* a direction (8va), placed above or below the staff to indicate that the passage covered is to be played one octave higher or lower respectively. [< It: lit., at the octave]

al·lot·tee (ə lot ē′), *n.* one to whom something is allotted. [ALLOT + -EE]

al·lo·type (al′ə tīp′), *n.* *Biol.* a type specimen of the sex opposite to that of the holotype. [ALLO- + TYPE] **—al·lo·typ·ic** (al′ə tip′ik), *adj.*

all-out (ôl′out′), *adj.* using all one's resources; complete; total: *an all-out effort.*

all·ov·er (*adj.* ôl′ō′vər; *n.* (ôl′ō′vər), *adj.* **1.** extending or repeated over the entire surface, as a decorative pattern on embroidered or lace fabrics. **—***n.* **2.** fabric with an allover pattern. [ALL + OVER]

al·low (ə lou′), *v.t.* **1.** to give permission to or for; permit: *to allow a student to be absent.* **2.** to let have; give as one's share; grant as one's right: *to allow a person $100 for expenses.* **3.** to permit by neglect, oversight, or the like: *to allow a door to remain open.* **4.** to admit; acknowledge; concede: *to allow a claim.* **5.** to take into consideration, as by adding or subtracting; set apart: *to allow an hour for changing trains.* **6.** *U.S. Dial.* to say; think. **7.** *Archaic.* to approve; sanction. **—***v.i.* **8.** to permit; admit (sometimes fol. by *of*): *more than her budget allows; a premise that allows of only one conclusion.* **9. allow for,** to make concession or provision for: *to allow for breakage; Allowing for her faults, she makes a fair actress.* [ME *alowe(n)* < MF *alouer* to assign (< LL *allocāre*; see AL-, LOCUS), in sense to praise highly (< L *adlaudāre*; see AD-, LAUD)]

—Syn. 1. ALLOW, LET, PERMIT imply granting or conceding the right of someone to do something. ALLOW and PERMIT are often interchangeable, but PERMIT is the more positive. ALLOW implies complete absence of an attempt, or even an intent, to hinder. PERMIT suggests formal or implied assent or authorization. LET is the familiar, conversational term for both ALLOW and PERMIT. **—Ant. 1.** forbid.

al·low·a·ble (ə lou′ə bəl), *adj.* that may be allowed; legitimate; permissible: *an allowable tax deduction.* [late ME < MF *alouable.* See ALLOW, -ABLE] —**al·low′a·ble·ness,** *n.* —**al·low′a·bly,** *adv.*

al·low·ance (ə lou′əns), *n., v.,* **-anced, -anc·ing.** —*n.* **1.** act of allowing. **2.** an amount or share allotted or granted. **3.** a sum of money allotted or granted for a particular purpose, as for expenses: *Her allowance for groceries was $25.* **4.** an addition or deduction based on an extenuating or qualifying circumstance: *an allowance for profit; an allowance for depreciation.* **5.** acknowledgment; concession: *the allowance of a claim.* **6.** sanction; tolerance: *the allowance of slavery.* **7.** *Coining.* tolerance (def. 7). **8.** *Mach.* a prescribed difference in dimensions of two closely fitting mating parts with regard to minimum clearance or maximum interference. Cf. **tolerance** (def. 6a). **9. make allowance** or **allowances (for), a.** to take mitigating factors or circumstances into consideration. **b.** to pardon; excuse. **c.** to allow for: *Make allowance for souvenirs on the return trip.* —*v.t.* **10.** to place on a fixed allowance, as of food or drink. **11.** to allocate (supplies, rations, etc.) in fixed or regular amounts. [late ME *alouance* < MF. See ALLOW, -ANCE] —**Syn. 2.** allotment. **3.** stipend. **6.** permission, authorization, approval, sufferance.

allow′ance race′, *Horse Racing.* a race in which each horse is assigned a specified weight according to age, record of performance, sex, etc.

Al·lo·way (al′ə wā′), *n.* a hamlet in SW Scotland, near Ayr: birthplace of Robert Burns.

al·lowed (ə loud′), *adj.* *Physics.* involving a change in quantum numbers, permitted by the selection rules: *allowed transition.* [ALLOW + -ED[2]]

al·low·ed·ly (ə lou′id lē), *adv.* admittedly; permissibly. [ALLOWED + -LY]

allowed′ time′, the time permitted a worker to spend cleaning his machine, attending to personal needs, etc., without loss of pay.

al·loy (*n.* al′oi, ə loi′; *v.* ə loi′), *n.* **1.** a substance composed of two or more metals, or of a metal or metals with a nonmetal, intimately mixed as by fusion, electrodeposition, etc. **2.** a less costly metal mixed with a more valuable one. **3.** standard; quality; fineness. **4.** admixture, as of good with evil. **5.** anything added which serves to reduce quality or purity. —*v.t.* **6.** to mix (metals or metal with nonmetal) so as to form an alloy. **7.** to reduce in value by an admixture of a less costly metal. **8.** to debase, impair, or reduce by admixture; adulterate. [< MF *aloi* < OF *alei,* back formation from *aleier* to combine < L *alligāre* to bind up, equiv. to *al-* AL- + *ligāre* to bind. See LIGAMENT]

al′loy steel′, carbon steel to which various elements, as chromium, cobalt, copper, manganese, molybdenum, nickel, tungsten, or vanadium, have been added to obtain desirable properties otherwise available only for steel made in small quantities or under special conditions.

all-pass (ôl′pas′, -päs′), *adj.* *Radio.* (of a network, transducer, etc.) transmitting signals without significant attenuation of any frequencies.

all-pow·er·ful (ôl′pou′ər fəl), *adj.* having or exercising exclusive and unlimited authority; omnipotent.

all-pur·pose (ôl′pûr′pəs), *adj.* for every purpose: *an all-purpose detergent.*

All′ Qui′et on the West′ern Front′, a novel (1929) by Erich Maria Remarque.

all′ right′, 1. safe; sound: *Are you all right?* **2.** yes; very well; okay: *All right, I'll go with you.* **3.** satisfactory; acceptable: *His performance was all right, but I've seen better.* **4.** satisfactorily; acceptably: *His work is coming along all right.* **5.** without fail; certainly: *You'll hear about this, all right!* **6.** *Informal.* reliable; good: *an all right fellow.* **7. (a) bit of all right,** *Brit.* quite satisfactory (used as an understatement): *The way he saved that girl's life was a bit of all right.* —**Usage.** See **alright.**

all-round (ôl′round′), *adj.* all-around. Also, **all′-round′.** —**all′-round′er,** *n.*

All′ Saints′ Day′, a church festival celebrated November 1 in honor of all the saints; Allhallows.

all·seed (ôl′sēd′), *n.* any of various many-seeded plants, as a goosefoot, *Chenopodium polyspermum,* and the knotgrass, *Polygonum aviculare.* [ALL + SEED]

All′ Souls′ Day′, a day of solemn prayer for all dead persons, observed by Roman Catholics and certain Anglicans, usually on November 2.

all·spice (ôl′spīs′), *n.* **1.** Also **all′spice tree′.** an aromatic, myrtaceous tree, *Pimenta officinalis,* of tropical America, having leathery foliage and white flowers. **2.** the brown berry of this tree. **3.** a mildly sharp spice made from this berry, its scent resembling that of the combination of cloves, cinnamon, and nutmeg; pimento. [ALL + SPICE]

all-star (ôl′stär′), *adj.* **1.** consisting entirely of star performers: *an all-star cast.* —*n.* **2.** *Sports.* a player selected for an all-star team.

All·ston (ôl′stən), *n.* **Washington,** 1799–1843, U.S. painter, novelist, and poet.

All's′ Well′ That Ends′ Well′, a comedy (1602?) by Shakespeare.

All′ the King's′ Men′, a novel (1946) by Robert Penn Warren.

all-time (ôl′tīm′), *adj.* of, from, or in terms of the entire history or knowledge of events of a specified type: *Production will reach an all-time high.*

al·lude (ə lo͞od′), *v.i.,* **-lud·ed, -lud·ing. 1.** to make an allusion; refer casually or indirectly (usually fol. by *to*): *He often alluded to his poverty.* **2.** to contain a casual or indirect reference (usually fol. by *to*): *The letter alludes to something now forgotten.* [< L *allūde(re),* equiv. to *al-* AL- + *lūdere* to play]

al·lure[1] (ə lo͝or′), *v.,* **-lured, -lur·ing,** *n.* —*v.t.* **1.** to attract by the offer of something having real or seemingly real value; tempt by something flattering or desirable. **2.** to fascinate; charm. —*n.* **3.** fascination; charm; appeal. [late ME *alure* < MF *alure(r),* equiv. to *a-* A-[5] + *lurer* to LURE] —**al·lur′er,** *n.* —**Syn. 1.** entice, lure. **2.** enchant, entrance, captivate.

al·lure[2] (al′yo͝or), *n.* alure.

al·lure·ment (ə lo͝or′mənt), *n.* **1.** fascination; charm. **2.** the means of alluring. **3.** act or process of alluring. [ALLURE[1] + -MENT]

al·lur·ing (ə lo͝or′ing), *adj.* **1.** tempting; enticing; seductive. **2.** fascinating; charming. [ALLURE[1] + -ING[2]] —**al·lur′ing·ly,** *adv.* —**al·lur′ing·ness,** *n.*

al·lu·sion (ə lo͞o′zhən), *n.* **1.** a passing or casual reference; an incidental mention of something, either directly or by implication: *an allusion to Shakespeare.* **2.** *Obs.* a metaphor; parable. [< LL *allūsiōn-* (s. of *allūsiō*), equiv. to *allūs(us)* played with, ptp. of *allūdere* to ALLUDE (*al-* AL- + *lūd-* play + *-tus* ptp. suffix) + *-iōn-* -ION]

al·lu·sive (ə lo͞o′siv), *adj.* **1.** having reference to something implied or inferred; containing, abounding in, or characterized by allusions. **2.** *Obs.* metaphorical; symbolic; figurative. [ALLUS(ION) + -IVE] —**al·lu′sive·ly,** *adv.* —**al·lu′sive·ness,** *n.*

al·lu·vi·al (ə lo͞o′vē əl), *adj.* **1.** of or pertaining to alluvium. —*n.* **2.** alluvial soil. **3.** *Australia.* gold-bearing alluvial soil. [ALLUVI(UM) + -AL[1]]

allu′vial fan′, *Phys. Geog.* a fan-shaped alluvial deposit formed by a stream where its velocity is abruptly decreased, as at the mouth of a ravine or at the foot of a mountain. Also called **allu′vial cone′.**

al·lu·vi·on (ə lo͞o′vē ən), *n.* **1.** alluvium. **2.** *Law.* a gradual increase of land on a shore or a river bank by the action of water, whether from natural or artificial causes. **3.** overflow; flood. [< L *alluviōn-* (s. of *alluviō* an overflowing), equiv. to *al-* AL- + *luv-* (s. of *luere* to wash) + *-iōn-* -ION]

al·lu·vi·um (ə lo͞o′vē əm), *n., pl.* **-vi·ums, -vi·a** (-vē ə). **1.** a deposit of sand, mud, etc., formed by flowing water. **2.** the sedimentary matter deposited thus within recent times, esp. in the valleys of large rivers. Also, **alluvion.** [< L, n. use of neut. of *alluvius* washed against, equiv. to *alluv-* (see ALLUVION) + *-ius, -ium* adj. suffix]

all′ways′ fuze′ (ôl′wāz′), an impact fuze on a bomb or missile, designed to function at any angle of impact with the target.

all-weath·er (ôl′weth′ər), *adj.* **1.** designed to operate or be usable in any type of weather: *an all-weather boat; an all-weather shelter.* **2.** capable of resisting damage from exposure to any climatic conditions; weatherproof: *an all-weather paint.* **3.** in or including all types of weather: *years of all-weather experience in the Arctic.*

al·ly (*v.* ə lī′; *n.* al′ī, ə lī′), *v.,* **-lied, -ly·ing,** *n., pl.* **-lies.** —*v.t.* (used passively or reflexively) **1.** to unite formally, as by treaty, league, marriage, or the like (usually fol. by *to* or *with*): *two countries allied by trade agreements; a country that allied itself with a more powerful nation.* **2.** to associate or connect by some mutual relationship, as resemblance or friendship. —*v.i.* **3.** to enter into an alliance; join; unite. —*n.* **4.** one who or that which is united with another, esp. by treaty or league, as an allied nation, kingdom, sovereign, or the like. **5.** something akin to or resembling another: *a cucumber is an ally of a watermelon.* **6.** one who associates or cooperates with another; supporter. [ME *alie(n)* < OF *alier,* var. of *aleier* < L *alligāre* to bind to. See ALLOY] —**al·li′a·ble,** *adj.*
—**Syn. 1.** unify, join, combine, wed. **4.** partner, confederate. **6.** friend, aide, accomplice, accessory, assistant, abettor; colleague, coadjutor, auxiliary, helper. —**Ant. 4, 6.** enemy, foe, adversary.

-ally, an adverbial suffix attached to certain adjectives with stems in *-ic* which have no forms ending in *-ical*: *terrifically.* [-AL[1] + -LY]

all-year (ôl′yēr′), *adj.* **1.** taking up, extending through, or occurring continually during a year: *an all-year activity.* **2.** open all year, as for business, occupancy, etc.: *an all-year resort.* **3.** usable or productive during all parts of a year: *all-year pasture; all-year fishing grounds.*

al·lyl (al′il), *adj.* *Chem.* containing the allyl group. [< L *all(ium)* garlic + -YL]

al′lyl al′cohol, *Chem.* a colorless liquid, $CH_2{=}CHCH_2OH$, having a pungent, mustardlike odor irritating to the skin and mucous membranes, usually obtained from allyl chloride by hydrolysis: used chiefly in organic synthesis in the manufacture of resins, plasticizers, and pharmaceuticals. Also called **propenyl alcohol.**

al′lyl cap′roate, *Chem.* a colorless to pale yellow liquid, $CH_3(CH_2)_4COOCH_2CH{=}CH_2$, having a pineapple odor: used chiefly as a scent in the manufacture of flavorings and perfume.

al′lyl chlo′ride, *Chem.* a colorless, volatile, flammable liquid, $CH_2{=}CHCH_2Cl$, having a pungent odor, derived from propylene by chlorination: used chiefly in the synthesis of allyl alcohol, resins, and pharmaceuticals.

al′lyl group′, *Chem.* the univalent group, $CH_2{=}CHCH_2{-}$, derived from propylene. Also called **al′lyl rad′ical.**

al·lyl·ic (ə lil′ik), *adj.* of, pertaining to, or characteristic of the allyl group. [ALLYL + -IC]

al′lyl mercap′tan, *Chem.* a colorless liquid, $CH_2{=}CHCH_2SH$, having a strong, garlicky odor, used chiefly as a flavoring agent in cookery.

al′lyl res′in, *Chem.* any of a class of thermosetting resins made from allyl alcohol and a dibasic acid, used chiefly as adhesives for laminated materials.

al′lyl sul′fide, *Chem.* a colorless or pale yellow, water-insoluble liquid, $(CH_2{=}CHCH_2)_2S$, having a garliclike odor, used chiefly in flavoring. Also called **diallyl sulfide, thioallyl ether.**

al·lyl·thi·o·u·re·a (al′il thī′ō yo͝o rē′ə, -yo͝or′ē ə), *n.* *Chem.* thiosinamine. [< NL; see ALLYL, THIOUREA]

Al·lyn (al′in), *n.* a girl's given name.

Al·lyne (al′in), *n.* a boy's given name. Also, **Alan, Allan, Allen.**

Al·ma (al′mə), *n.* **1.** a town in central Michigan. 8978 (1960). **2.** a town in central Georgia. 3515 (1960). **3.** a girl's given name.

Al·ma-A·ta (äl′mä ä′tä), *n.* a city in and the capital of Kazakhstan, in the S Soviet Union in Asia. 455,000 (1959). Formerly, **Vyernyi.**

Al·ma·dén (äl′mä then′), *n.* a town in Spain: mercury mines. 12,998 (1950).

Al·ma·gest (al′mə jest′), *n.* **1.** (*italics*) a Greek work on astronomy by Ptolemy. **2.** (*l.c.*) any of various medieval works of a like kind, as on astrology or alchemy. [late ME *almageste* < MF < Ar *al* the + *majistī* < Gk *megístē* greatest (composition)]

al·mah (al′mə), *n.* (in Egypt) a girl who dances or sings professionally. Also, **al′ma, alme, almeh.** [< Ar *ʿalmah* trained (lit., knowledgeable)]

al·ma ma·ter (äl′mə mä′tər, al′-; al′mə mā′tər), a school, college, or university at which one has studied and, usually, from which one has graduated. [< L: nourishing (i.e., dear) mother]

al·ma·nac (ôl′mə nak′), *n.* **1.** an annual publication containing a calendar for the coming year, the times of such events and phenomena as anniversaries, sunrises and sunsets, phases of the moon, tides, etc., and other statistical information and related topics. **2.** a publication containing astronomical or meteorological information, usually including future positions of celestial objects, star magnitudes, and culmination dates of constellations. **3.** a compendium of useful and interesting facts relating to countries of the world, sports, entertainment, etc. [late ME *almenak* < ML *almanac(h)* < SpAr *al* the + *ʿmanākh* calendar < ?]

Al·ma·nach de Go·tha (ôl′mə nak′ də goth′ə; *Ger.* äl′mä näkh′ də gō′tä; *Fr.* al ma na′ də gō tä′), a publication giving statistical information on European royalty.

Al Ma·nam·ah (al mə nam′ə), Manama.

al·man·dine (al′mən dēn′, -dīn′, -din), *n.* a mineral, red iron aluminum garnet. [late ME *alabandina* < L, equiv. to *Alaband(a)* town in Turkey + *-ina* -INE[1]]

al·man·dite (al′mən dīt′), *n.* almandine. [ALMAND(INE) + -ITE[1]]

Al·ma·non (al′mə non′), *n.* a walled plain in the fourth quadrant of the face of the moon: about 28 miles in diameter.

Al·ma-Tad·e·ma (al′mə tad′ə mə), *n.* **Sir Lawrence,** 1836–1912, English painter, born in the Netherlands.

al·me (al′me), *n.* almah. Also, **al′meh.**

al·me·mar (al mē′mär), *n.* bimah. [< Heb < Ar *al* the + *minbar* stand, platform]

Al·me·ri·a (al mēr′ē ə), *n.* a girl's given name. Also, **Almira.**

Al·me·rí·a (äl′me rē′ä), *n.* a seaport in S Spain, on the Mediterranean. 73,715 (est. 1960). —**Al·me·ri·an** (al′mə rē′ən), *adj., n.*

alm·er·y (äm′ə rē), *n., pl.* **-er·ies.** *Rare.* ambry.

Al·mer·ic (al′mər ik, al mer′ik), *n.* a boy's given name.

al·might·y (ôl mī′tē), *adj.* **1.** having unlimited power; omnipotent, as God or a deity. **2.** having very great power, influence, etc.; overpowering: *the almighty power of the press.* **3.** *Informal.* extreme; terrible: *He's in an almighty fix.* —*adv.* **4.** *Slang.* extremely: *It's almighty hot.* —*n.* **5. the Almighty,** God. [ME; OE *ælmihtig, ealmihtig,* equiv. to *æl-, eal-* ALL + *mihtig* (*miht, meaht* MIGHT[2] + *-ig* -Y[1])] —**al·might′i·ly,** *adv.* —**al·might′i·ness,** *n.*

almight′y dol′lar, *Informal.* money as the basis of power: *Love of the almighty dollar has ruined many a man.*

al·mi·que (al′mə kē′), *n.* **1.** a West African, sapotaceous tree, *Manilkara albescens.* **2.** the hard, reddish-brown wood of this tree, used for making furniture. **3.** Also, **alamiqui.** a Cuban solenodon, *Solenodon cubanus.* [< AmerSp *almiquí*]

Al·mi·ra (al mī′rə), *n.* a girl's given name. Also, **Almeria.**

al·mi·rah (al mī′rə), *n.* *Anglo-Indian.* a wardrobe, cabinet, or cupboard. [<< Pg *almario* < L *armārium* closet, chest; akin to *arma* armor, arms]

Al·mo·had (al′mə had′), *n.* a member of a Muslim dynasty ruling in Spain and northern Africa during the 12th and 13th centuries. Also, **Al·mo·hade** (al′mə hād′, -had′).

al·mon (al′mōn, am′ən), *n.* **1.** a Philippine, dipterocarpaceous tree, *Shorea eximia.* **2.** the hard, yellowish-white wood of this tree, used for making furniture. [< Visayan]

al·mond (ä′mənd, am′ənd; *spelling pron.* al′mənd), *n.* **1.** the nutlike stone or kernel of the fruit of a tree, *Amygdalus Prunus,* of warm temperate regions. **2.** the tree itself. **3.** a delicate, pale tan. **4.** anything shaped like an almond, esp. an ornament. —*adj.* **5.** of the color, taste, or shape of an almond. **6.** made or flavored with almonds: *almond cookies.* [ME *almande* < MF, OF *alemandle,* equiv. to *al-* (< Ar *al* the) + *emandle* < Pr *amandola* << L *amygdala* < Gk *amygdálē;* r. OE *amygdal* < L] —**al′mond·like′, al′mond·y,** *adj.*

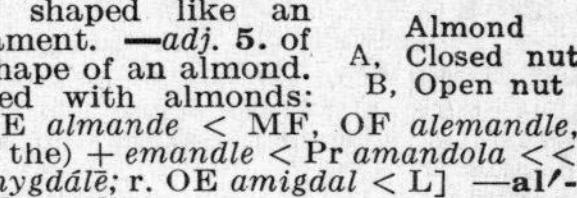

Almond
A, Closed nut
B, Open nut

al′mond cake′, *Chem.* the residue of almonds from which oil has been expressed.

al·mond-eyed (ä′mənd īd′, am′ənd-; *spelling pron.* al′mənd īd′), *adj.* having long or narrow, oval-shaped eyes.

al′mond meal′, *Chem.* the meal obtained by pulverizing blanched almonds, used chiefly in the manufacture of perfume and cosmetics.

al′mond milk′, a creamy mixture of blanched almonds, sugar, and water, blended to a smooth paste and sieved.

al′mond oil′, *Chem.* **1.** Also called **sweet almond oil, expressed almond oil.** a colorless to pale yellow fatty oil expressed from the seeds of the sweet almond, used chiefly as a lubricant for delicate mechanisms. **2.** Also called **bitter almond oil.** a colorless to yellow, poisonous oil obtained by steam distillation from the almond meal of bitter almond seeds: used chiefly in the manufacture of cosmetics, medicine, and perfume.

al·mond-shaped (ä′mənd shāpt′, am′ənd-; *spelling pron.* al′mənd shāpt′), *adj.* having an oblong shape conventionally pointed at both ends.

al·mon·er (al′mə nər, ä′mə-), *n.* **1.** a person whose function or duty is the distribution of alms in behalf of an institution, a royal personage, a monastery, etc. **2.** *Brit.* **a.** a hospital official who determines the amount due for a patient's treatment. **b.** a social worker in a hospital. [ME *aumoner* < OF << LL *eleēmosynār(ius)* ELEEMOSYNARY]

al′moner's cup′board. See **livery cupboard.**

al·mon·ry (al′mən rē, ä′mən-), *n., pl.* **-ries.** the place where an almoner resides or where alms are distributed. [ALMON(ER) + -RY; r. late ME *almonesrie* (? mistake for *almonerrie*)]

Al·mo·ra·vid (al′mə rä′vid, al mōr′ə-, -môr′-), *n.* a member of a Muslim dynasty that ruled in Spain and northern Africa from 1056 to 1147. Also, **Al·mo·ra·vide** (al mōr′ə vīd′, -môr′-, al′mə rä′vid). [< Ar *al-murābiṭ;* lit., the occupant of a fortified convent]

al·most (ôl′mōst, ôl mōst′), *adv.* very nearly; all but: *almost every house; almost the entire symphony; to pay* *almost nothing for a car; almost twice as many books.* [ME; OE (*e*)*al māst,* var. of *æl mǣst* nearly]

—Syn. ALMOST (MOST), NEARLY, WELL-NIGH all mean within a small degree of or short space of. ALMOST implies very little short of: *almost exhausted; almost home.* MOST is colloquial for ALMOST. NEARLY implies a slightly greater distance or degree than ALMOST: *nearly well; nearly to the city.* WELL-NIGH, a more literary word, implies a barely appreciable distance or extent: *well-nigh forgotten; well-nigh home.*

al′most ev′erywhere, *Math.* everywhere in a given set except on a subset with measure zero. *Abbr.:* a.e.

al′most period′ic func′tion, *Math.* a function that repeats its values approximately at almost equally spaced intervals of its domain.

al·mous (ä′məs, ô′məs), *n.* (*construed as pl.*) *Brit. Dial.* alms. [ME *almus* < Scand; cf. Icel *almusa* ALMS]

alms (ämz), *n.* (*construed as sing. or pl.*) money, food, or other donations given to the poor or needy; anything given as charity: *The hands of the beggars were outstretched for alms.* [ME *almes,* OE *ælmysse* << LL *eleēmosyna* < Gk *eleēmosýnē* compassion, alms. See ELEEMOSYNARY]

alms·giv·er (ämz′giv′ər), *n.* a person who gives alms. [ALMS + GIVER] **—alms′giv′ing,** *n.*

alms·house (ämz′hous′), *n., pl.* **-hous·es** (-hou′ziz). *Chiefly Brit.* a poorhouse. [ALMS + HOUSE]

alms·man (ämz′mən), *n., pl.* **-men. 1.** a person supported by or receiving alms. **2.** *Archaic.* a person who gives alms. [ALMS + MAN[1]]

alms·wom·an (ämz′wo͝om′ən), *n., pl.* **-wom·en. 1.** a woman supported by alms. **2.** *Archaic.* a woman who gives alms. [ALMS + WOMAN]

al·mu·can·tar (al′myo͞o kan′tər), *n.* *Astron.* a circle on the celestial sphere parallel to the horizon; the locus of all points of a given altitude. Also called **parallel of altitude.** [prob. < ML *almucantarath* < Ar *al-muqanṭarāt* the almucantars, equiv. to *al-* the + *muqanṭarāt* sundial, deriv. of *qanṭarah* arch; r. *almicanter* < ME *almicanteras* (pl.) < MF *almicantarath* < ML, as above]

al·muce (al′myo͞os), *n.* a furred hood or hooded cape with long ends hanging down in front, formerly worn by the clergy. Also, **amice.** [< OF *almuce, aumuce.* See AMICE[2]]

al·mug (al′məg, ôl′-), *n.* *Bible.* a tree, possibly the red sandalwood. I Kings 10:12. Cf. **algum.** [var. of ALGUM]

Al·ni·co (al′ni kō′), *n.* *Trademark.* a permanent-magnet alloy having aluminum, nickel, and cobalt as its principal ingredients.

a·lo·di·um (ə lō′dē əm), *n., pl.* **-di·a** (-dē ə). allodium. Also called **al·od** (al′od). **—a·lo′di·al,** *adj.* **—a·lo′di·al′i·ty,** *n.* **—a·lo′di·al·ly,** *adv.*

al·oe (al′ō), *n., pl.* **-oes. 1.** any chiefly African, liliaceous plant of the genus *Aloes,* certain species of which yield a drug and a fiber. **2.** Often, **aloes.** (*construed as sing.*) *Pharm.* a bitter purgative drug, the inspissated juice of several species of *Aloe.* **3.** See **century plant. 4. aloes,** (*construed as sing.*) agalloch. [ME; OE *alu*(*w*)*e* < L *aloē* < Gk *alóē*] **—al·o·et·ic** (al′ō et′ik), *adj.*

al·oes·wood (al′ōz wo͝od′), *n.* agalloch.

A·lo·e·us (ə lō′ē əs, ə lō′yo͞os), *n.* *Class. Myth.* a son of Poseidon, husband of Iphimedia, and foster father of Otus and Ephialtes. Cf. **Aloidae.**

a·loft (ə lôft′, ə loft′), *adv.* **1.** high up; in or into the air; far above the ground. **2.** *Naut.* on the masts; in the rigging; overhead. [A-[1] + LOFT; cf. Icel *ā lopt* in the air]

A·lo·gi (ā lō′gī), *n.* (*construed as sing. or pl.*) a group of Christians in the 2nd century A.D. who rejected the doctrine of the Logos. [< ML < Gk *álogoi,* pl. of *álogos,* equiv. to *a-* A-[6] + *lógos* speech, word, the Word]

a·lo·gia (ə lō′jə, -jē ə), *n.* *Pathol.* aphasia. [< NL < Gk *álog*(*os*) (< *a-* A-[6] + *lógos* speech, akin to *légein* to speak) + NL *-ia* -IA]

a·lo·ha (ə lō′ə, ä lō′hä), *n., interj.* **1.** greetings; a greeting. **2.** farewell. [< Hawaiian]

A·lo·ha (ə lō′ə, ä lō′hä), *n.* a girl's given name.

Al·o·i·dae (al′ō ī′dē), *n. pl.* *Class. Myth.* Ephialtes and Otus, the sons of Poseidon and Iphimedia, raised by Aloeus.

al·o·in (al′ō in), *n.* *Pharm.* an intensely bitter, crystalline, water-soluble powder composed of the active principles of and obtained from aloe, used chiefly as a purgative. [ALOE + -INE[2]]

a·lone (ə lōn′), *adj.* (used predicatively) **1.** separate, apart or isolated from another or others: *I want to be alone.* **2.** to the exclusion of all others or all else: *Man shall not live by bread alone.* **3.** unique; unequaled; unexcelled: *He is alone among his peers in devotion to duty.* **4. leave alone, a.** to allow (someone) to be by himself: *Leave him alone, for he wants to rest.* **b.** *Informal.* to refrain from annoying or interfering with: *The youngsters wouldn't leave the dog alone, and he finally turned on them.* **5. let alone, a.** to refrain from annoying or interfering with. **b.** not to mention: *He was too tired to walk, let alone run.* **6. let well enough alone,** to be satisfied with the existing situation; refrain from attempting to change conditions: *Marriages are often destroyed by relatives who will not let well enough alone.* **—adv. 7.** solitarily; solely. **8.** only; exclusively. **9.** without aid or help: *The baby let go of his mother's hands and stood alone.* [ME *al one* ALL (wholly) ONE] **—a·lone′ness,** *n.*

—Syn. 1. single, solitary, isolated. ALONE, LONE, LONELY, LONESOME all imply being without companionship or association. ALONE is colorless unless reinforced by ALL; it then suggests solitariness or desolation: *alone in the house; all alone on an island.* LONE is somewhat poetic or is intended humorously: *a lone sentinel, widow.* LONELY implies a sad or disquieting feeling of isolation. LONESOME connotes emotion, a longing for companionship. **—Ant. 1.** accompanied.

a·long (ə lông′, ə long′), *prep.* **1.** through, on, beside, over, or parallel to the length or direction of; from one end to the other of: *to walk along a highway; to run a border along a shelf.* **2.** during; in the course of: *Somewhere along the journey I lost my hat.* **3.** in conformity or accordance with: *Along the lines just stated, I suggest we start the new project.* **—adv. 4.** by the length; lengthwise; parallel to or in a line with the length or direction: *He ran along beside me.* **5.** with a progressive motion; onward: *The police ordered the line to move along.* **6.** *U.S. Informal.* (of time) some way on: *along toward evening.* **7.** in company; in agreement (usually fol. by *with*): *I'll go along with you. He planned the project along with his associates.* **8.** *Chiefly U.S.* as a companion; with one: *He took his sister along.* **9.** from one person or place to another: *The order was passed along from the general to the captain and from the captain to a private.* **10.** at or to an advanced place or state: *Work on the new ship is quite far along.* **11.** as an accompanying item; on hand: *Bring along your umbrella.* **12. all along,** all the time; throughout: *He knew all along that it was a lie.* **13. be along,** *Informal.* to arrive at a place; come: *He will be along soon.* [ME; OE *andlang,* equiv. to *and-* (c. OS, Icel *and-,* Goth *and*(*a*)-, OHG *ant-,* prefix) + *lang* LONG[1]]

along′ of′, *Dial.* **1.** owing to; because of: *We weren't invited, along of your rudeness.* **2.** in company with: *You come along of me to the store.* [ME *along on,* alter. of *ilong on,* OE *gelang on* (*ge-* + *lang* LONG[1])]

a·long·ships (ə lông′ships′, ə long′-), *adj., adv.* *Naut.* in the fore-and-aft line of a vessel. [ALONG + SHIP + -S[1]]

a·long·shore (ə lông′shôr′, -shōr′, ə long′-), *adv., adj.* by or along the shore or coast. [ALONG + SHORE[1]]

a·long·side (ə lông′sīd′, ə long′-), *adv.* **1.** along, by, at, or to the side of something: *We brought the boat alongside.* **—prep. 2.** beside; by the side of: *The dog ran alongside me all the way.* [ALONG + SIDE[1]]

A·lon·so (ə lon′zō; *Sp.* ä lôn′sō), *n.* **1. Alicia** (*Alicia Ernestina de la Caridad del Cobre Martínez Hoyo*), born 1921, Cuban ballerina. **2. Dá·ma·so** (dä′mä sō′), born 1898, Spanish poet, critic, and philologist. **3.** Also, **Alonzo, Alphonso.** a boy's given name.

A·lon·zo (ə lon′zō), *n.* a boy's given name. Also, **Alonso, Alphonso.**

a·loof (ə lo͞of′), *adv.* **1.** at a distance, esp. in feeling or interest: *He stood aloof from their arguments.* **—adj. 2.** reserved or reticent; indifferent; disinterested: *Because of her shyness, she had the reputation of being aloof.* [A-[1] + *loof* LUFF windward] **—a·loof′ly,** *adv.* **—a·loof′ness,** *n.*

—Syn. 1. apart. **2.** withdrawn, removed, impartial, uninvolved. **—Ant. 1.** near. **2.** involved.

Al·o·pe (al′ō pē′), *n.* *Class. Myth.* a daughter of Cercyon who was attacked by Poseidon and who bore a son, Hippothous.

al·o·pe·ci·a (al′ə pē′shē ə), *n.* *Pathol.* loss of hair; baldness. [late ME < L < Gk *alōpekíā* mange in foxes, equiv. to *alōpek-* (s. of *alṓpēx*) fox + *-iā* -IA] **—al·o·pe·cic** (al′ə pē′sik), *adj.*

alope′cia ar·e·a′ta (ar′ē ā′tə, -ä′tə), *Pathol.* a scalp condition characterized by baldness in circumscribed patches. Also called **alope′cia cel′si** (sel′sī), **alope′cia cir·cum·scrip′ta** (sur′kəm skrip′tə). [< NL: circumscribed alopecia]

A·lo·pe·cus (ə lō′pə kəs), *n.* *Class. Myth.* a Spartan prince.

Al·or·ton (ə lôr′tᵊn), *n.* a town in SW Illinois. 3282 (1960).

A·lost (*Fr.* A lôst′), *n.* a city in central Belgium, NW of Brussels. 42,939 (1947). Flemish, **Aalst.**

a·loud (ə loud′), *adv.* **1.** with the natural tone and volume of the speaking voice, as distinguished from whisperingly: *They could not speak aloud in the library.* **2.** vocally, as distinguished from mentally: *He read the book aloud.* **3.** with a loud voice; loudly: *to cry aloud.* [ME; see A-[1], LOUD]

a·lou·ette (A lwet′ *or, for 2,* A lo͞oe′tə; *Eng.* al′o͞o et′ə, ä′lo͞o-), *n., pl.* **a·lou·et·tes** (A lwet′; *Eng.* al′o͞o et′əz, ä′lo͞o-) for 1.) **1.** *French.* a lark. **2.** (*cap.*) a French children's song for group singing.

a·low[1] (ə lō′), *adv.* *Naut.* **1.** near the deck; in the lower rigging. **2. alow and aloft,** everywhere. [A-[1] + LOW[1]]

a·low[2] (ə lō′), *adj., adv.* *Dial.* ablaze; aflame. Also, **a·lowe′.** [A-[1] + LOW[3]]

Al·o·y·sius (al′ō ish′əs), *n.* a boy's given name.

alp (alp), *n.* a high mountain. [back formation from ALPS]

A.L.P., American Labor Party. Also, **ALP**

al·pac·a (al pak′ə), *n.* **1.** a domesticated, South American animal of the genus *Lama,* having long, soft, silky hair or wool, related to the camels, resembling a llama, and believed to be a variety of the guanaco. **2.** the hair of this animal. **3.** a fabric made of it. **4.** a glossy, wiry, commonly black woolen fabric with cotton warp. **5.** a rayon crepe made in imitation of an alpaca fabric. [< Sp < Aymara]

Alpaca, *Lama pacos* (3½ ft. high at shoulder; total height 5 ft.; length 3½ ft.)

Al·pe·na (al pē′nə), *n.* a city in NE Michigan, on Lake Huron. 14,682 (1960).

al·pen·glow (al′pən glō′), *n.* a reddish glow often seen on the summits of mountains just before sunrise or just after sunset. [< G *Alpenglühen,* with GLOW r. G *glühen*]

al·pen·horn (al′pən hôrn′), *n.* a long, powerful horn of wood or bark, with a cupped mouthpiece and a curved bell at opposite ends, used by Swiss herdsmen and mountaineers. Also called **alphorn.** [< G, equiv. to *Alpen* ALP(s) + *Horn* HORN]

al·pen·stock (al′pən stok′), *n.* a strong staff with an iron point, used by mountain climbers. [< G, equiv. to *Alpen* ALP(s) + *Stock* staff]

Alpes-Ma·ri·times (alp′ma rē tēm′), *n.* a department in SE France. 618,265 (1962); 1527 sq. mi. *Cap.:* Nice.

al·pes·trine (al pes′trin), *adj.* *Bot.* subalpine (def. 2). [< ML *alpestr*(*is*) (*Alp*(*ēs*) the Alps + *-estris* adj. suffix; see TERRESTRIAL) + -INE[1]]

Al·pet·ra·gi·us (äl′pə trā′jē əs), *n.* a crater in the third quadrant of the face of the moon: about 27 miles in diameter.

al·pha (al′fə), *n.* **1.** the first letter of the Greek alphabet (A, α). **2.** the vowel sound represented by this letter. **3.** the first; beginning. **4.** (*cap.*) *Astron.* the brightest star in a constellation: *the brightest star in the Southern Cross is Alpha Crucis.* **5.** *Chem.* **a.** one of the possible positions of an atom or group in a compound. **b.** one of two or more isomeric compounds. **6.** *Chiefly Brit.* a grade or mark showing that a student is in the highest or best of three scholastic sections in his class. Cf. **beta** (def. 5), **gamma** (def. 9). [< L < Gk < a Phoenician word; cf. Heb *āleph* ox]

Al·pha (al′fə), *n.* a boy's or girl's given name.

al′pha and ome′ga, the beginning and the end. Rev. 1:8.

al·pha·bet (al′fə bet′), *n.* **1.** the letters of a language in their customary order. **2.** any system of characters or signs with which a language is written: *the Greek alphabet.* **3.** any such system for representing the sounds of a language: *the phonetic alphabet.* **4.** first elements; basic facts; simplest rudiments: *the alphabet of radio.* **5. the alphabet,** a system of writing, developed in the ancient Near East and transmitted from the northwest Semites to the Greeks, in which each symbol ideally represents one sound unit in the spoken language, and from which most alphabetical scripts are derived. [< LL *alphabēt*(*um*), alter. of Gk *alphábētos.* See ALPHA, BETA]

al′pha·be′ta brass′ (al′fə bā′tə, -bē′-), an alloy of from 55 to 61 percent copper with from 39 to 45 percent zinc. Also called **Muntz metal.**

al′phabet code′, a list of easily distinguishable words, each representing a letter of the alphabet, used in radio and telephonic communications.

al·pha·bet·i·cal (al′fə bet′i kəl), *adj.* **1.** in the order of the letters of the alphabet: *alphabetical arrangement.* **2.** pertaining to, expressed by, or using an alphabet: *alphabetical writing.* Also, **al′pha·bet′ic.** [ALPHABET + -ICAL] **—al′pha·bet′i·cal·ly,** *adv.*

al·pha·bet·ise (al′fə bi tīz′), *v.t.,* **-ised, -is·ing.** *Chiefly Brit.* alphabetize. **—al·pha·bet·i·sa·tion** (al′fə bet′i zā′shən), *n.* **—al′pha·bet·is′er,** *n.*

al·pha·bet·ize (al′fə bi tīz′), *v.t.,* **-ized, -iz·ing. 1.** to put or arrange in alphabetical order. **2.** to express by or furnish with an alphabet. [ALPHABET + -IZE] **—al·pha·bet·i·za·tion** (al′fə bet′i zā′shən), *n.* **—al′pha·bet·iz′er,** *n.*

al′phabet soup′, a soup containing small noodles in the shapes of letters.

al′pha brass′, any alloy of copper and zinc, a homogeneous solid solution containing more than 64 percent copper.

Al′pha Centau′ri, a first magnitude star 4.3 light-years from the sun; Rigil Kentaurus: the star closest to the sun.

al′pha decay′, *Physics.* a radioactive process in which an alpha particle is emitted from the nucleus of an atom, decreasing its atomic number by two.

Al·phae·a (al fē′ə), *n.* *Class. Myth.* an epithet of Artemis alluding to her rejection of Alpheus.

al·pha-hy·poph·a·mine (al′fə hī pof′ə mēn′), *n.* *Biochem.* oxytocin. [ALPHA + HYPOPH(YSIS) + AMINE]

al′pha i′ron, *Metall.* the magnetic allotrope of iron, stable below 910°C and having a body-centered cubic space lattice. Also called **ferrite.**

al·pha·mer·ic (al′fə mer′ik), *adj.* *Computer Technol.* alphanumeric. Also, **al′pha·mer′i·cal.** [ALPHA(BET + NU)MERIC] **—al′pha·mer′i·cal·ly,** *adv.*

al·pha-naph·thol (al′fə naf′thōl, -thôl, -thol, -nap′-), *n.* *Chem.* naphthol (def. 1).

al′pha-naph′thyl group′ (al′fə naf′thil, -nap′-, al′-), *Chem.* See **naphthyl group** (def. 1). Also called **al′pha-naph′thyl rad′ical.**

al·pha-naph·thyl·thi·o·u·re·a (al′fə naf′thil thī′ō-yo͞o rē′ə, -yo͝or′ē ə, -nap′-), *n.* *Chem.* See **ANTU.**

al·pha·nu·mer·ic (al′fə no͞o mer′ik, -nyo͞o-), *adj.* *Computer Technol.* (of a set of characters) including both letters and numbers: *alphanumeric code.* Also, **alphameric, alphamerical, al′pha·nu·mer′i·cal.** [ALPHA(BET) + NUMERIC(AL)] **—al′pha·nu·mer′i·cal·ly,** *adv.*

al′pha par′ticle, *Physics.* a positively-charged particle consisting of two protons and two neutrons, emitted in radioactive decay or nuclear fission; the nucleus of a helium atom.

al′pha-par′ti·cle scat′tering (al′fə pär′ti kəl), *Physics.* See **Rutherford scattering.**

al′pha ray′, *Physics.* a stream of alpha particles.

al′pha-stan′nic ac′id (al′fə stan′ik). *Chem.* See under **stannic acid.**

al′pha test′, *Psychol.* a set of mental tests designed to measure the general intelligence of individuals able to read and write, used by the U.S. Army in World War I. Cf. **beta test.**

Al·phe·si·boe·a (al′fi sə bē′ə), *n.* *Class. Myth.* **1.** a nymph who rejected the attentions of Dionysus. **2.** Arsinoë. **3.** the mother, by Phoenix, of Adonis. **4.** a daughter of Bias.

Al·phe·us (al fē′əs), *n.* **1.** *Class. Myth.* a river god, son of Oceanus and Tethys, who fell in love with the nymph Arethusa and, when she became a spring to escape him, changed into a river and mingled with her. **2.** a boy's given name.

al·phit·o·man·cy (al fit′ə man′sē), *n.* the use of barley meal as a means of divination. [< Gk *álphito*(*n*) barley + -MANCY, prob. influenced by Gk *alphitómantis* one who divines from barley meal]

Al·phon·so (al fon′sō, -zō), *n.* a boy's given name. Also, **Alonso, Alonzo.**

Al·phon·sus (al fon′səs), *n.* a crater in the third quadrant of the face of the moon: about 70 miles in diameter; site of the third U.S. lunar probe (1965). Also, **Al·phons** (al′fons).

alp·horn (alp′hôrn′), *n.* alpenhorn.

al·pho·sis (al fō′sis), *n.* *Pathol.* lack of pigment in the skin, as in albinism. [< Gk *alph*(*ós*) white leprosy (cf. L *albus* white) + -OSIS]

al·pine (al′pīn, -pin), *adj.* **1.** of, pertaining to, on, or part of any lofty mountain. **2.** very high; elevated. **3.** (*cap.*) of, pertaining to, on, or part of the Alps. **4.** *Bot.* growing on mountains above the limit of tree growth: *alpine plants.* **5.** *Anthropol.* having the racial characteristics of an Alpine. **—n. 6.** (*cap.*) *Anthropol.* a Caucasoid racial type found in Europe and characterized by heavy body build, considerable hairiness, and brachycephaly. [< L *Alpīn*(*us*), equiv. to *Alp*(*ēs*) (pl.) the ALPS + *-īnus* -INE[1]] **—al′pine·ly,** *adv.*

Al·pine (al′pīn), *n.* a town in W Texas. 4740 (1960).

al′pine bis′tort. See under **bistort** (def. 2).

Al′pine catch′fly, a low, spreading, perennial herb, *Silene alpestris,* of the mountainous regions of Europe, having sticky stems and satiny-white flowers.

Al′pine cur′rant. See **mountain currant.**

al′pine fir′, a fir, *Abies lasiocarpa,* of the Rocky Mountains, yielding a soft, brittle wood used for making boxes, crates, etc.

al′pine gar′den, a rock garden.

Al′pine i′bex, an ibex, *Capra ibex*, of the Alps and Apennines, having long, heavy horns with transverse ridges.

Al′pine pop′py, a hardy, perennial herb, *Papaver alpinum*, of the Alps, having fragrant, white or yellow flowers.

Al′pine sa′vory, a shrubby, perennial herb, *Satureia alpina*, of the Mediterranean region, having purple flowers in terminal spikes.

al′pine tun′dra, a tundra that is treeless because of high elevation rather than high latitude.

Al′pine Val′ley, a gorge in the lunar Alps, in the first quadrant of the face of the moon: about 80 miles long, and as wide as about 6 miles in places.

Al′pine wall′flower, a perennial herb, *Erysium linifolium* of Spain, having grayish foliage and mauve or lilac-colored flowers.

al·pin·ism (al′pə niz′əm), *n.* (*often cap.*) mountain climbing, esp. in the Alps. [ALPINE + -ISM] —**al′pin·ist, Al′pin·ist,** *n.*

Alps (alps), *n.* (*construed as pl.*) **1.** a mountain range in S Europe, extending from France through Switzerland and Italy into Austria, Slovenia, and Croatia. Highest peak, Mont Blanc, 15,781 ft. **2.** a mountain range in the northern hemisphere of the face of the moon, and forming a border of the Mare Imbrium.

al·read·y (ôl red′ē), *adv.* **1.** by this or that time; previously; prior to or at some specified or implied time: *When we came in, we found they had already arrived.* **2.** now; so soon; so early: *Is it noon already?* [ME *alredy* ALL READY]

—**Usage.** ALREADY is sometimes confused with ALL READY, although they are far apart in meaning. ALREADY means "previously" (*The plane had already left the airport*), while ALL READY means "completely prepared or ready" (*The troops were all ready to attack*).

al·right (ôl rīt′), *adv.* all right.

—**Usage.** The form ALRIGHT is occasionally seen as a variant of ALL RIGHT, probably by analogy with ALREADY and ALTOGETHER, but it is not considered acceptable in standard English.

a.l.s., autograph letter, signed.

Al·sace (al sās′, al′sas; *Fr.* AL ZAS′), *n.* a region and former province of France between the Vosges and the Rhine. Cf. **Alsace-Lorraine.**

Al·sace-Lor·raine (al′sās lō rān′, -lô-, -sas-; *Fr.* AL ZAS lô REN′), *n.* a region in NE France, including the former provinces of Alsace and Lorraine: part of Germany 1871–1917, 1940–44. 1,986,969 (1954); 5607 sq. mi. —**Al′sace-Lorrain′er,** *n.*

al-Sa·hih (äl sä hē′), *n. Islam.* a compilation of hadith deemed to be authentic (A.D. c850). [< Ar: lit., the right]

Al·sa·tia (al sā′shə), *n.* **1.** a former cant name given to the Whitefriars district in London, England, because of the lawless characters and libertines who sought privileges of sanctuary at the monastery there. **2.** ancient name of **Alsace.**

Al·sa·tian (al sā′shən), *adj.* **1.** of or pertaining to Alsace or its inhabitants. **2.** of or pertaining to Alsatia. —*n.* **3.** a native or inhabitant of Alsace. **4.** a resident or native of Alsatia. **5.** Also called **Alsa′tian dog′.** *Brit.* the German shepherd dog. [< ML *Alsati(a)* Alsace + -AN]

al′sike clo′ver, (al′sīk, -sik, ôl′-), a European clover, *Trifolium hybridum*, having whitish or pink flowers, grown in the U.S. for forage. Also called **al′sike.** [after *Alsike*, near Uppsala, Sweden]

al·si·na·ceous (al′sə nā′shəs), *adj. Bot.* **1.** caryophyllaceous. **2.** relating to or resembling the chickweed. [< L *alsin(ē)* a plant (< Gk *alsínē*) + -ACEOUS]

Al·sip (ôl′sip), *n.* a town in NE Illinois. 3770 (1960).

Al Si·rat (al si rät′), *Islam.* **1.** the correct path of religion. **2.** the bridge, fine as a razor's edge, over which all who enter paradise must pass. [< Ar, equiv. to *al* the + *ṣirāṭ* road < L (*via*) *strāta* paved (way). See STREET]

al·so (ôl′sō), *adv.* **1.** in addition; too; besides; as well: *He was thin, and he was also tall.* **2.** likewise; in the same manner: *Since you're having another cup of coffee, I'll also have one.* —*conj.* **3.** and: *He was mean, also ugly.* [ME; OE (*e*)*alswā* ALL (wholly or quite) SO[1]]

—**Syn. 1.** moreover.

Al·son (al′sən), *n.* a boy's given name.

al·so-ran (ôl′sō ran′), *n.* **1.** *Sports.* **a.** (in a race) a contestant who fails to win or to place among the first three finishers. **b.** an athlete or team whose performance in competition is rarely, if ever, a winning or near-winning one. **2.** *Informal.* one who is defeated in any competition; one who attains little or no success: *For every great artist there are a thousand also-rans.*

Al·so Sprach Za·ra·thus·tra (*Ger.* äl′zō shpräkh tsä′rä tōōs′trä). See **Thus Spake Zarathustra.**

Al·ston (ôl′stən), *n.* a boy's given name.

alt (alt) *Music.* —*adj.* **1.** high. —*n.* **2. in alt,** in the first octave above the treble staff. [< Pr < L *alt*(*um*), n. use of neut. of *altus* high]

alt-, var. of **alti-** before a vowel: *altazimuth.*

alt., 1. alternate. **2.** altitude. **3.** alto.

Al·ta (al′tə), *n.* a girl's given name.

Alta., Alberta.

Al·ta·de·na (al′tə dē′nə), *n.* a town in SW California, near Los Angeles. 40,568 (1960).

Al·tai (al tī′, äl-; al′tī, äl′-), *n.* a territory of the RSFSR, in the S Soviet Union in Asia. 101,000 sq. mi. *Cap.:* Barnaul. Also, **Altay.**

Al·ta·ic (al tā′ik), *n.* **1.** a family of languages made up of the Turkic, Mongolian, Tungusic, and Korean subfamilies. —*adj.* **2.** of or belonging to Altaic. **3.** of or pertaining to the Altai Mountains. Also, **Al·ta·ian** (al tā′ən, -tī′-). [ALTA(I) + -IC]

Al′tai Moun′tains, 1. Also, **Altay Mountains.** a mountain range in central Asia, mostly in Outer Mongolia and the S Soviet Union. Highest peak, Belukha, 15,157 ft. **2.** a mountain range in the fourth quadrant of the face of the moon: about 315 miles long.

Al·ta·ir (al tä′ir), *n.* a first-magnitude star in the constellation Aquila. [< Ar, equiv. to *al* the + *ṭā'ir* bird (lit., flyer)]

Al·ta·mi·ra (al′tə mēr′ə; *Sp.* äl′tä mē′rä), *n.* a cave in N Spain, near Santander, noted for its Stone Age color drawings of animals.

al·tar (ôl′tər), *n.* **1.** an elevated place or structure, as a mound or platform, at which religious rites are performed or on which sacrifices are offered to gods, ancestors, etc. **2.** *Eccles.* See **communion table. 3.** (*cap.*) *Astron.* the constellation Ara. **4.** (in a dry dock) a ledge for supporting the feet of shorings. **5. lead to the altar,** *Informal.* to marry: *After a five-year courtship, he led her to the altar.* [ME, OE *alter* (OE also *altar*) < L *altāria* (pl.), equiv. to *alt*(*us*) high + *-āria*, pl. of *-āre* -AR[2]]

al·tar·age (ôl′tər ij), *n.* **1.** *Eccles.* **a.** offerings made upon an altar of a church. **b.** offerings made to a church. **2.** an honorarium paid to a priest for services at the altar from offerings and gifts. **3.** endowments for the saying of Masses for deceased persons, often at a particular altar. [ME *awterage* < AF, OF *auterage.* See ALTAR, -AGE]

al′tar board′, *Coptic Church.* an elaborately carved wooden panel, placed in a recess on top of an altar during the Mass, on which the chalice and paten rest.

al′tar boy′, acolyte (def. 1).

al′tar bread′, bread for use in a Eucharistic service.

al′tar card′, *Rom. Cath. Ch.* one of three cards having certain portions of the Mass printed on them, placed upright on the altar to assist the memory of the celebrant.

al′tar cloth′, a cloth covering for an altar. [ME]

al·tar·piece (ôl′tər pēs′), *n.* a painted or carved screen behind or above the altar or communion table in Christian churches; reredos. [ALTAR + PIECE]

al′tar rail′, the rail in front of an altar, separating the sanctuary from those parts of the church that are in front of it.

al′tar stand′. See **missal stand.**

al′tar stone′, mensa. Also called **al′tar slab′.** [ME *awterston*]

al′tar wine′. See **sacramental wine.**

Al·ta·vis·ta (al′tə vis′tə), *n.* a town in central Virginia. 3299 (1960).

Al·tay (al tī′, äl-; al′tī, äl′-), *n.* Altai.

Al′tay Moun′tains. See **Altai Mountains.**

alt·az·i·muth (al taz′ə məth), *n. Astron.* an instrument for determining both the altitude and the azimuth of a heavenly body. [ALT(ITUDE) + AZIMUTH]

altaz′imuth mount′ing, a mounting with two axes, to allow movement in both horizontal and vertical planes, used with telescopes, antennas, and precise surveying instruments.

Alt·dorf (ält′dôrf′), *n.* a town in and the capital of Uri, in central Switzerland, near Lucerne: legendary home of William Tell. 6576 (1950).

Alt·dor·fer (ält′dôr′fər; *Ger.* ält′dôR′fəR), *n.* **Albrecht** (äl′bReKHt), c1480–1538, German painter.

al·ter (ôl′tər), *v.t.* **1.** to make different in some particular, as size, style, course, or the like; modify: *to alter a coat; to alter a will; to alter course.* **2.** to castrate or spay. —*v.i.* **3.** to change; become different or modified. [late ME < OF *alter*(*er*) < LL *alterāre* to change, worsen, deriv. of L *alter* other]

—**Syn. 1.** See **adjust, change.**

alter., alteration.

al·ter·a·ble (ôl′tər ə bəl), *adj.* capable of being altered. [ALTER + -ABLE] —**al′ter·a·bil′i·ty, al′ter·a·ble·ness,** *n.* —**al′ter·a·bly,** *adv.*

al·ter·ant (ôl′tər ənt), *adj.* **1.** producing alteration. —*n.* **2.** something that produces alteration. [< L *alterant-* (s. of *alterāns* changing, prp. of *alterāre*), equiv. to *alter* other + *-ant-* -ANT]

al·ter·a·tion (ôl′tə rā′shən), *n.* **1.** the act or state of altering; or the state of being altered: *The alteration improved the dress.* **2.** a change; modification: *There has been an alteration in our plans.* [late ME < ML *alterātiōn-* (s. of *alterātiō*). See ALTER, -ATION]

al·ter·a·tive (ôl′tə rā′tiv, -tər ə tiv), *adj.* **1.** tending to alter. **2.** *Med. Obs.* gradually restoring healthy bodily functions. —*n.* **3.** *Med. Obs.* an alterative remedy. [< ML *alterātīv*(*us*). See ALTER, -ATIVE]

al·ter·cate (ôl′tər kāt′, al′-), *v.i.*, **-cat·ed, -cat·ing.** to argue with zeal, heat, or anger; wrangle: *They altercated in the Senate for days on end.* [< L *altercāt*(*us*) (ptp. of *altercārī* to quarrel), equiv. to **alterc*(*us*) a disputing (*alter* other + *-cus* formative suffix) + *-ātus* -ATE[1]]

al·ter·ca·tion (ôl′tər kā′shən, al′-), *n.* a heated or angry dispute; noisy argument or controversy. [< L *altercātiōn-* (s. of *altercātiō*). See ALTERCATE, -ION]

—**Syn.** quarrel, contention.

al′tered chord′, *Music.* a chord in which at least one tone has been changed from its normal pitch in the key.

al·ter e·go (ôl′tər ē′gō, eg′ō, al′-), **1.** a second self; a perfect substitute or deputy: *The adviser of the president acts as his alter ego during his absence.* **2.** an inseparable friend. [< L]

al·ter i·dem (äl′teR ē′dem; *Eng.* ôl′tər ī′dem, al′-), *Latin.* another exactly the same.

al·tern (ôl′tərn, al′-), *adj. Archaic.* alternate; following one another. [< L *altern*(*us*) interchangeable, alternating, equiv. to *alter* the other (see ALTER) + *-nus* adj. suffix]

al·ter·nant (ôl′tûr nənt, al′- *or, esp. Brit.*, ôl tûr′nənt, al-), *adj.* **1.** alternating; alternate. —*n.* **2.** *Ling.* an orthographic or phonetic variant that does not affect the meaning of a word. [< L *alternant-* (s. of *alternāns*, prp. of *alternāre*). See ALTERN, -ANT]

al·ter·nate (*v.* ôl′tər nāt′, al′-; *adj.*, *n.* ôl′tər nit, al′-), *v.*, **-nat·ed, -nat·ing,** *adj.*, *n.* —*v.i.* **1.** to interchange repeatedly and regularly with one another in time or place; rotate (usually fol. by *with*): *Day alternates with night.* **2.** to change back and forth between conditions, states, actions, etc.: *He alternates between hope and despair.* **3.** *Elect.* to reverse direction or sign periodically. —*v.t.* **4.** to perform in succession or one after another: *to alternate vaudeville acts.* **5.** to interchange successively or regularly: *to alternate hot and cold compresses.* —*adj.* **6.** being in a constant state of succession or rotation; interchanged repeatedly one for another: *Winter and summer are alternate seasons.* **7.** reciprocal; mutual: *alternate acts of kindness.* **8.** every second one of a series: *Read only the alternate lines.* **9.** alternative (def. 4). **10.** *Bot.* **a.** placed singly at different heights on the axis, on each side in succession, or at definite angular distances from one another, as leaves. **b.** opposite to the intervals between other organs: *petals alternate with sepals.* —*n.* **11.** *U.S.* a person authorized to fill the position, exercise the duties, etc., of another in his absence; substitute. **12.** *Theat.* **a.** either of two actors who take turns playing the same role. **b.** an understudy. **13.** alternative. [< L *alternāt*(*us*) (ptp. of *alternāre*). See ALTERN, -ATE[1]] —**al′ter·nate·ness,** *n.* —**al′ter·nat′ing·ly,** *adv.*

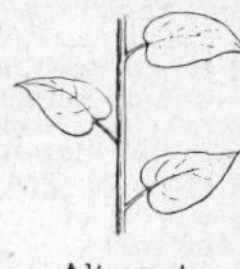

Alternate leaves

al′ternate an′gles, *Geom.* two nonadjacent angles made by the crossing of two lines by a third line, both angles being either interior or exterior, and being on opposite sides of the third line.

al·ter·nate·ly (ôl′tər nit lē, al′-), *adv.* **1.** in alternate order; by rotation: *He alternately worked and slept.* **2.** in alternate position: *Dark stripes were spaced alternately with light ones.* [ALTERNATE + -LY]

al′ternate plum′age, *Ornith.* (of birds having more than one plumage in their usually annual cycle of molts) the plumage assumed at the second molt, which is often but not always brighter than the basic plumage. Cf. **basic plumage, supplemental plumage.**

al′ternate straight′, *Poker.* See **skip straight.**

al′ternating cur′rent. See AC (def. 2).

al′ternating group′, *Math.* the subgroup consisting of all even permutations, of the group of all permutations of a finite set. Cf. **symmetric group.**

al′ternating light′, *Navig.* a beacon showing different colors in succession.

al′ternating personal′ity, *Psychol.* a type of multiple personality in which two or more distinct personalities appear consecutively within the same individual.

al′ternating se′ries, *Math.* a series, usually infinite, in which successive terms have opposite signs, as $1 - \frac{1}{2} + \frac{1}{4} - \frac{1}{8} + \ldots$.

al′ternating volt′age, *Elect.* a voltage that reverses direction in regular cycles.

al·ter·na·tion (ôl′tər nā′shən, al′-), *n.* **1.** the act or state of alternating or the state of being alternated. **2.** alternate succession; repeated rotation: *the alternation of the seasons.* **3.** *Elect.* a single fluctuation in the absolute value of an alternating current or voltage from zero to a maximum and back to zero, being equal to one half cycle. [< LL *alternātiōn-* (s. of *alternātiō*). See ALTERNATE, -ION]

alterna′tion of genera′tions, *Biol.* the alternation in the life cycle of an organism of forms produced in a different manner, esp. the alternation of sexual with asexual generations.

al·ter·na·tive (ôl tûr′nə tiv, al-), *n.* **1.** a choice limited to one of two or more possibilities, as of things, courses of action, propositions, etc., the selection of which precludes any other possibility: *You have the alternative of riding or walking.* **2.** one of the things, propositions, or courses which can be chosen: *The alternative to riding is walking.* **3.** a necessary or remaining course or choice: *There was no alternative but to walk.* —*adj.* **4.** affording a choice of two or more things, propositions, or courses. **5.** (of two things, propositions, or courses) mutually exclusive so that if one is chosen the other must be rejected: *The alternative possibilities are neutrality or war.* **6.** *Logic.* (of a proposition) asserting two or more choices, at least one of which is true. Also, **alternate** (for defs. 1–4). [ALTERNATE + -IVE] —**al·ter′na·tive·ly,** *adv.* —**al·ter′na·tive·ness, al·ter′na·tiv′i·ty,** *n.*

—**Syn. 1.** option, selection. See **choice.**

al·ter·na·tor (ôl′tər nā′tər, al′-), *n. Elect.* a generator of alternating current. [ALTERNATE + -OR[2]]

Al·tes (al′tēz), *n.* (in the *Iliad*) a king of the Leleges and the father of Laothoë.

Alt·geld (ôlt′geld), *n.* **John Peter,** 1847–1902, governor of Illinois 1892–96.

Al·thae·a (al thē′ə), *n. Class. Myth.* wife of Oeneus and mother of Toxeus, Tydeus, Meleager and Deianira.

Al·thae·me·nes (al thē′mə nēz′), *n. Class. Myth.* a son of Catreus who mistakenly killed his father, thus fulfilling a prophecy that Catreus would die by the hand of one of his children.

al·the·a (al thē′ə), *n.* **1.** any plant of the genus *Althaea*, comprising the hollyhocks, marsh mallows, etc. **2.** the rose of Sharon, *Hibiscus syriacus.* Also, **al·thae′a.** [< L *althaea* < Gk *althaía* marsh mallow]

Al·the·a (al thē′ə), *n.* a girl's given name.

Al·thing (äl′thing, ôl′-), *n.* the parliament of Iceland, consisting of an upper and a lower house. [< Icel; see ALL, THING[2]]

alt·horn (alt′hôrn′), *n.* a valved brass instrument that is the alto member of the cornet family. Also called **alto horn.** [ALT + HORN]

Althorn

al·though (ôl thō′), *conj.* in spite of the fact that; even though; though. Also, **al·tho′.** [ME *al thogh* ALL (adv.) even + THOUGH]

—**Syn.** though, notwithstanding (that), even if, albeit (that).

alti-, a prefix occurring in loan words from Latin where it meant "high" (*altitude*); used in the formation of compound words: *altigram.* Also, *esp. before a vowel,* **alt-.** [ME < L, equiv. to *alt*(*us*) + *-i-* -I-]

al·ti·graph (al′tə graf′, -gräf′), *n.* an altimeter equipped with a device for recording its measurements on a graph. [ALTI- + -GRAPH]

al·tim·e·ter (al tim′i tər, al′tə mē′tər), *n.* **1.** a sensitive aneroid barometer that is graduated and calibrated, used chiefly in aircraft for finding distance above sea level, terrain, or some other reference point by a comparison of air pressures. **2.** any device used for the same purpose which operates by some other means, as by radio waves. [ALTI- + -METER]

al·tim·e·try (al tim′i trē), *n.* the science of measuring altitudes, as by altimeters. [ALTI- + -METRY] —**al·ti·met·ri·cal** (al′tə me′tri kəl), *adj.* —**al′ti·met′ri·cal·ly,** *adv.*

al·tis·si·mo (al tis′ə mō′; *It.* äl tēs′sē mô′), *Music.* —*adj.* **1.** very high. —*n.* **2. in altissimo,** in the second octave above the treble staff. [< It: lit., highest, equiv. to *alt(o)* high + *-issimo* superl. suffix]

al·ti·tude (al′ti to͞od′, -tyo͞od′), *n.* **1.** the height above sea level of any point on the earth's surface or in the atmosphere. **2.** extent or distance upward; height: *The buildings of Paris are not of great altitude.* **3.** *Astron.* the angular distance of a heavenly body above the horizon. **4.** *Geom.* **a.** the perpendicular distance from the vertex of a figure to the side opposite the vertex. **b.** the line through the vertex of a figure perpendicular to the base. **5.** Usually, **altitudes.** a high point or region; *mountain altitudes.* **6.** high or exalted position, rank, etc. [< L *altitūd(ō),* equiv. to *alt(us)* high + *-i-* -I- + *-tūdō* -TUDE] —**Syn. 2.** See **height.** —**Ant. 2.** depth.

al′titude di′al, an adjustable sundial utilizing the altitude of the sun, at a given latitude and time of year, as a means of telling the time. Cf. **direction dial.**

al·ti·tu·di·nal (al′ti to͞od′ᵊnəl, -tyo͞od′-), *adj.* relating to altitude or height. [< L *altitūdin-* (s. of *altitūdō*) ALTITUDE + -AL[1]]

al·to (al′tō), *n., pl.* **-tos,** *adj. Music.* —*n.* **1.** the lowest female voice; contralto. **2.** the highest male voice; counter-tenor. **3.** a singer with such a voice. **4.** a musical part for such a voice. **5.** the second highest of the four parts of a mixed vocal chorus, or the voices or persons singing this part. **6.** the second highest instrument in a family of musical instruments, as the viola in the violin family or the althorn in the cornet family. —*adj.* **7.** of, noting, pertaining to, or having the tonal range of the alto. **8.** (of a musical instrument) second highest in a family of musical instruments: *alto saxophone.* [< It *alto* < L *alt(us)* high]

alto-, var. of **alti-:** *altostratus.*

al′to clef′, *Music.* a sign locating middle C on the third line of the staff. Also called **viola clef.** See illus. under **clef, C clef.**

al·to·cu·mu·lus (al′tō kyo͞o′myə ləs), *n., pl.* **-lus.** *Meteorol.* a cloud of a class characterized by globular masses or rolls in layers or patches, the individual elements being larger and darker than those of cirrocumulus and smaller than those of stratocumulus: of medium altitude, about 8000–20,000 feet. [ALTO- + CUMULUS]

al′tocu′mulus castella′nus, *pl.* **altocumulus castellanus.** *Meteorol.* an altocumulus cloud having its summit shaped like a crenelated tower. Also, **al′to·cu′mulus castella′tus.**

al′tocu′mulus floc′cus, *pl.* **altocumulus floccus.** *Meteorol.* an altocumulus cloud having its summit in the shape of small cumuliform tufts or masses.

al′tocu′mulus lenticular′is, *pl.* **altocumulus lenticularis.** *Meteorol.* an altocumulus cloud having at its summit sharply outlined lenticular shapes and sometimes showing irisation.

al′tocu′mulus stratifor′mis, *pl.* **altocumulus stratiformis.** *Meteorol.* an altocumulus cloud consisting chiefly of one or more horizontal layers.

al·to·geth·er (ôl′tə geth′ər; ôl′tə geth′ər), *adv.* **1.** wholly; entirely; completely; quite. **2.** with all or everything included: *The debt amounted altogether to twenty dollars.* **3.** with all or everything considered; on the whole: *Altogether, I'm glad it's over.* —*n.* **4. in the altogether,** *Informal.* nude: *When the phone rang she had just stepped out of the bathtub and was in the altogether.* [var. of ME *altogeder.* See ALL, TOGETHER]
—**Usage.** ALTOGETHER and ALL TOGETHER are sometimes confused. As an adverb, ALTOGETHER means "wholly, completely, entirely" (*an altogether confused report*) while ALL TOGETHER, as an adjective phrase, means "in a group" (*They were all together in the kitchen*).

al′to horn′, althorn.

Al·ton (ôl′tᵊn), *n.* **1.** a city in SW Illinois. 43,047 (1960). **2.** a boy's given name.

Al·to·na (äl′tō nä), *n.* a metropolitan district of Hamburg, West Germany: formerly an independent city.

Al·too·na (al to͞o′nə), *n.* a city in central Pennsylvania. 69,407 (1960).

Al′to Park′, a town in NW Georgia. 2526 (1960).

al·to-re·lie·vo (al′tō ri lē′vō), *n., pl.* **-vos.** See **high relief.** Italian, **alto-rilievo.**

al·to-ri·lie·vo (äl′tô rē lye′vô), *n., pl.* **al·ti-ri·lie·vi** (äl′tē rē lye′vē). *Italian.* See **high relief.**

al·to·stra·tus (al′tō strā′təs), *n., pl.* **-tus.** *Meteorol.* a cloud of a class characterized by a generally uniform gray sheet or layer, lighter in color than nimbostratus and darker than cirrostratus: of medium altitude, about 8000–20,000 feet. [ALTO- + STRATUS]

al·tri·cial (al trish′əl), *adj. Ornith.* helpless at hatching and requiring parental care for a period of time. Cf. **precocial.** [< NL *altriciāl(is),* L *altrīci-* (s. of *altrix*) nourisher, equiv. to *al-* feed (see ALIMENT) + *-trīci-* fem. suffix of agency + *-ālis* -AL[1]]

al·tru·ism (al′tro͞o iz′əm), *n.* the principle or practice of unselfish concern for or devotion to the welfare of others (opposed to *egoism*). [< F *altruisme,* equiv. to It *altrui* others (alter. of L *alterī*) + F *-isme* -ISM]

al·tru·ist (al′tro͞o ist), *n.* a person unselfishly concerned for or devoted to the welfare of others (opposed to *egoist*). [back formation from ALTRUISTIC]

al·tru·is·tic (al′tro͞o is′tik), *adj.* unselfishly concerned for or devoted to the welfare of others (opposed to *egoistic*). [ALTRU(ISM) + -ISTIC] —**al′tru·is′ti·cal·ly,** *adv.*
—**Syn.** charitable, generous, philanthropic; disinterested, unselfish.

Al·tu·ras (al to͝or′əs), *n.* a town in NE California. 2819 (1960).

Al·tus (al′təs), *n.* a city in SW Oklahoma. 21,225 (1960).

al·u·del (al′yo͝o del′), *n. Chem.* one of a series of pear-shaped vessels of earthenware or glass, open at both ends and fitted one above the other, for recovering the sublimates produced during sublimation. [< MF < Sp < Ar *al* the + *uthāl,* var. of *ithāl,* pl. of *athla* piece of apparatus]

al·u·la (al′yə lə), *n., pl.* **-lae** (-lē′). **1.** Also called **bastard wing, spurious wing.** the group of three to six small, rather stiff feathers growing on the first digit, pollex, or thumb of a bird's wing. **2.** a membranous lobe at the base of each wing of a dipterous insect. [< NL, equiv. to L *āl(a)* wing + *-ula* -ULE] —**al′u·lar,** *adj.*

al·um (al′əm), *n. Chem.* **1.** Also called **aluminum potassium sulfate, common alum, potash alum, potassium alum.** a colorless, odorless, crystalline, water-soluble solid, $K_2SO_4 \cdot Al_2(SO_4)_3 \cdot 24H_2O$, a double sulfate of aluminum and potassium, used in medicine as an astringent and styptic, in dyeing and tanning, and in many technical processes. **2.** one of a class of double sulfates analogous to the potassium alum, having the general formula $R_2SO_4 \cdot X_2(SO_4)_3 \cdot 24H_2O$, where R is a univalent alkali metal or ammonium, and X one of a number of trivalent metals. **3.** (not in technical use) aluminum sulfate, $Al_2(SO_4)_3$. [ME < MF < L *alūm(en);* r. OE *ælefne* for **alūmne* < L *alūmini-* (s. of *alūmen*)]

alum., *Chem.* aluminum.

alumin-, var. of **alumino-,** esp. before a vowel.

a·lu·mi·na (ə lo͞o′mə nə), *n.* the natural or synthetic oxide of aluminum, occurring in nature in a pure crystal form as corundum. Also called **aluminum oxide.** [pl. of L *alūmen* alum]

alu′mina cement′, a quick-setting cement with a large bauxite content.

a·lu·mi·nate (ə lo͞o′mə nāt′), *n.* **1.** *Chem.* a salt of the acid form of aluminum hydroxide, containing the group AlO_2^- or AlO_3^{-3}. **2.** *Mineral.* a metallic oxide combined with alumina. [ALUMIN- + -ATE[2]]

alu′mina trihy′drate, *Chem.* a white, crystalline, water-insoluble solid, $Al_2O_3 \cdot 3H_2O$ used chiefly in the synthesis of aluminum salts.

a·lu·mi·nif·er·ous (ə lo͞o′mə nif′ər əs), *adj.* containing or yielding aluminum. [ALUMIN- + -I- + -FEROUS]

a·lu·mi·nise (ə lo͞o′mə nīz′), *v.t.,* **-nised, -nis·ing.** *Chiefly Brit.* aluminize.

a·lu·mi·nite (ə lo͞o′mə nīt′), *n.* a mineral, hydrous aluminum sulfate, occurring in white, chalky masses. Also called **websterite.** [ALUMIN- + -ITE[1]]

al·u·min·i·um (al′yə min′ē əm), *n., adj. Chiefly Brit.* aluminum.

a·lu·mi·nize (ə lo͞o′mə nīz′), *v.t.,* **-nized, -niz·ing.** to treat with aluminum. [ALUMIN- + -IZE]

alumino-, a combining form of **aluminum,** used esp. before a consonant: *aluminosilicate.* Also, *esp. before a vowel,* **alumin-.**

a·lu·mi·nog·ra·phy (ə lo͞o′mə nog′rə fē), *n. Print.* algraphy. [ALUMIN- + -O- + -GRAPHY] —**a·lu·mi·no·graph·ic** (ə lo͞o′mə nə graf′ik), *adj.*

a·lu·mi·no·sil·i·cate (ə lo͞o′mə nō sil′ə kit, -kāt′), *n.* any naturally occurring or synthetically produced aluminum silicate containing alkali-metal or alkaline-earth-metal ions, as a feldspar, zeolite, or ultramarine. [ALUMINO- + SILICATE]

a·lu·mi·no·ther·my (ə lo͞o′mə nō thûr′mē), *n. Metall.* a process of producing high temperatures by causing finely divided aluminum to react with the oxygen from another metallic oxide. Also, **a·lu′mi·no·ther′mics.** [ALUMINO- + -THERMY]

a·lu·mi·nous (ə lo͞o′mə nəs), *adj.* of the nature of or containing alum or alumina. [< L *alūminōs(us),* equiv. to *alūmin-* (s. of *alūmen* ALUM) + *-ōsus* -OUS] —**a·lu·mi·nos·i·ty** (ə lo͞o′mə nos′i tē), *n.*

a·lu·mi·num (ə lo͞o′mə nəm), *n.* **1.** *Chem.* a silver-white metallic element, light in weight, ductile, malleable, and not readily corroded or tarnished, occurring combined in nature in igneous rock, shale, clay, and most soil: used in alloys and for lightweight utensils, castings, airplane parts, etc. *Abbr.:* alum.; *Symbol:* Al; *at. wt.:* 26.98; *at. no.:* 13; *sp. gr.:* 2.70 at 20°C. —*adj.* **2.** of, pertaining to, made of, or containing aluminum: *an aluminum frying pan.* Also, *Brit.,* **aluminium.** [< NL, alter. of *alumium.* See ALUMINA, -IUM] —**al·u·min·ic** (al′yə min′ik), *adj.*

alu′minum ac′etate, *Chem.* a compound which in the form of its normal salt, $Al(C_2H_3O_2)_3$, obtained as a white, water-soluble, amorphous powder, is used chiefly in medicine as an astringent and as an antiseptic, and which in the form of its basic salt, $Al(C_2H_3O_2)_2OH$, obtained as a white, crystalline, water-insoluble powder, is used chiefly in the textile industry as a waterproofing agent, as a fireproofing agent, and as a mordant.

alu′minum ammo′nium sul′fate, *Chem.* a colorless, crystalline, water-insoluble solid, $AlNH_4(SO_4)_2 \cdot 12H_2O$, used chiefly as a size in the manufacture of paper; alum. Also called **ammonium alum, ammonia alum.**

alu′minum bo′rate, *Chem.* a white, granular, water-insoluble powder, $2Al_2O_3 \cdot B_2O_3 \cdot 3H_2O$, used chiefly in the manufacture of crown glass.

alu′minum borohy′dride, *Chem.* a volatile liquid, $Al(BH_4)_3$, that ignites spontaneously in air and reacts vigorously with water to form hydrogen, used chiefly in organic synthesis.

alu′minum brass′, an alloy of about 75 percent copper, 2 percent aluminum, small amounts of other elements, and the balance zinc.

alu′minum bronze′, any of several alloys containing a high percentage of copper with from 5 to 11 percent aluminum and varying amounts of iron, nickel, manganese, and other elements. Also called **albronze.**

alu′minum car′bide, *Chem.* a yellow, crystalline solid, Al_4C_3, that reacts with water to form methane.

alu′minum chlo′ride, *Chem.* a yellow-white, crystalline, water-soluble solid which in its white hydrated form, $AlCl_3 \cdot 6H_2O$, is used chiefly as a wood preservative and in its yellow-white anhydrous form, $AlCl_3$, chiefly as a catalyst.

alu′minum fluosil′icate, *Chem.* a white, water-soluble powder, $Al_2(SiF_6)_3$, used in the manufacture of optical glass and of synthetic sapphires and rubies.

alu′minum hydrox′ide, *Chem.* a white, crystalline, tasteless, water-insoluble powder, $Al(OH)_3$ or $Al_2O_3 \cdot H_2O$, obtained chiefly from bauxite: used in the manufacture of glass, ceramics, and printing inks, in dyeing, and in medicine as an antacid and in the treatment of ulcers. Also called **alu′minum hy′drate, hydrated alumina.**

alu′minum monoste′arate, *Chem.* a white, water-insoluble powder, $Al(OH)_2[O_2C(CH_2)_{16}CH_3]$, used as a drier in paints and as a thickener in lubricating oils.

alu′minum ni′trate, *Chem.* a white, crystalline, water-soluble solid, $Al(NO_3)_3 \cdot 9H_2O$, used chiefly as a mordant in dyeing cotton.

alu′minum ox′ide, alumina.

alu′minum potas′sium sul′fate, *Chem.* alum (def. 1).

alu′minum sil′icate, any of a group of naturally occurring, water-insoluble substances, obtained from clay or synthesized, containing varying amounts of oxides of aluminum and silicon, Al_2O_3 and Si_2O_3, and used in the manufacture of glass, ceramics, paints, printing inks, rubber, and plastics. Cf. **mullite.**

alu′minum sul′fate, *Chem.* a white, crystalline, water-soluble solid, $Al_2(SO_4)_3$, used chiefly as a water-purifying agent, as a mordant, and as a size in the manufacture of paper.

a·lum·na (ə lum′nə), *n., pl.* **-nae** (-nē). a girl or woman who is a graduate or former student of a specific school, college, or university. [< L: foster daughter, pupil; fem. of ALUMNUS]
—**Usage.** See **alumnus.**

a·lum·nus (ə lum′nəs), *n., pl.* **-ni** (-nī). a graduate or former student of a specific school, college, or university. [< L: foster son, pupil, equiv. to *al-* (s. of *alere* to feed, support) + *-u-* + *-mnus,* orig. passive participial suffix, akin to Gk *-menos;* see PHENOMENON]
—**Usage.** A male graduate is an ALUMNUS (plural ALUMNI) and a female graduate is an ALUMNA (plural ALUMNAE). When referring to male and female graduates together, the masculine form ALUMNI is used.

al·um·root (al′əm ro͞ot′, -ro͝ot′), *n.* **1.** any of several North American, saxifragaceous herbs of the genus *Heuchera,* esp. *H. americana.* **2.** the root of any of these plants, used as an astringent. **3.** Also called **chocolate-flower.** a perennial herb, *Geranium maculatum,* of the eastern U.S., having rose-purple flowers. [ALUM + ROOT[1]]

A·lun·dum (ə lun′dəm), *n. Trademark.* a substance consisting of fused alumina, used chiefly as an abrasive and as a refractory.

al·u·nite (al′yə nīt′), *n.* a mineral, a hydrous sulfate of potassium and aluminum, $KAl_3(SO_4)_2(OH)_6$, commonly occurring in fine-grained masses. [< F *alun* (< L *alūmen* ALUM) + -ITE[1]]

a·lu·no·gen (ə lo͞o′nə jən), *n.* a mineral, hydrous sulfate of aluminum, $Al_2(SO_4)_3 \cdot 18H_2O$, occurring as a white, fibrous crust on quarry or mine walls. [< F *alun* (see ALUNITE) + -O- + -GEN]

al·ure (al′yər, ə lo͝or′), *n.* a passageway, as the walk along one side of a cloister. Also, **allure.** [ME *al(o)ur* < OF *aleor* passage, equiv. to *ale* walk (see ALLEY[1]) + *-or* -URE]

al·u·ta·ceous (al′yə tā′shəs), *adj.* **1.** *Zool.* covered with minute cracks or wrinkles and having a pale, leathery-brown color. **2.** having the color of soft brown leather. [< LL *alūtācius,* equiv. to L *alūt(a)* leather softened with alum + *-ācius* -ACIOUS (altered to -ACEOUS)]

al-Uz·za (äl o͝oz′zä), *n.* a pre-Islamic Arabian goddess personifying the planet Venus and considered to be a daughter of Allah.

Al·va (al′və; *Sp.* äl′vä), *n.* **1.** Also, **Alba. Fer·nan·do Ál·va·rez de To·le·do** (fer nän′dô äl′vä reth′ the tō le′thô), **Duke of,** 1508–82, Spanish general who suppressed a Protestant rebellion in the Netherlands in 1567. **2.** a town in NW Oklahoma. 6258 (1960). **3.** a boy's or girl's given name.

Al·vah (al′və), *n.* a boy's given name.

Al·van (al′vən), *n.* a boy's given name.

Al·var (äl′vär), *n.* (*sometimes l.c.*) *Hinduism.* (in southern India) a holy person of the Vaishnava sect. [< Tamil *Āṟvār,* deriv. of *āṟ-* to be deep in contemplation]

Al·va·ra·do (äl′vä rä′thô), *n.* **1. A·lon·so de** (ä lôn′sô the), c1490–1554, Spanish soldier in the conquests of Mexico and Peru: governor of Cuzco 1552?–54. **2. Pe·dro de** (pe′thrô the), 1495–1541, Spanish soldier: chief aide of Cortés in conquest of Mexico; governor of Guatemala 1530–34.

Ál·va·rez Quin·te·ro (äl′vä reth′ kēn te′rô), **Joa·quín** (hwä kēn′), 1873–1944, and his brother **Se·ra·fín** (se′rä fēn′), 1871–1938, Spanish dramatists and coauthors.

Al·va·ro (äl vä′rô), *n.* **Cor·ra·do** (kôr rä′thô), c1890–1956, Italian journalist and novelist.

al·ve·at·ed (al′vē ā′tid), *adj.* having the vaulted shape of a beehive. [< L *alveāt(us)* (*alve(us)* concave vessel, trough, equiv. to *alv(us)* belly + *-eus* + *-ātus* -ATE[1]) + -ED[2]]

alveol-, var. of **alveolo-** before a vowel.

al·ve·o·la (al vē′ə lə), *n., pl.* **-lae** (-lē′). *Bot., Zool.* **1.** a small cavity, cell, or pit on the surface of an organ. **2.** an alveolus. [< NL; L *alveolus;* see ALVEOLUS]

al·ve·o·lar (al vē′ə lər), *adj.* **1.** *Anat., Zool.* of or pertaining to an alveolus or to alveoli. **2.** *Phonet.* articulated with the tongue touching or close to the alveolar ridge, as *t, d, n;* gingival. —*n.* **3.** *Phonet.* an alveolar sound. [ALVEOL- + -AR[1]] —**al·ve′o·lar·ly,** *adv.*

alve′olar arch′, the part of the upper or lower jawbone in which the teeth are set.

alve′olar ridge′, the ridgelike border of the upper and lower jaws containing the sockets of the teeth. Also called **alve′olar proc′ess.** See diag. under **mouth.**

al·ve·o·late (al vē′ə lit, -lāt′), *adj.* having alveoli; deeply pitted, as a honeycomb. Also, **al·ve′o·lat′ed.** [< L *alveolāt(us).* See ALVEOL-, -ATE[1]] —**al·ve′o·la′tion,** *n.*

alveolo-, a combining form of **alveolus:** *alveolodental.* Also, *esp. before a vowel,* **alveol-.**

al·ve·o·lus (al vē′ə ləs), *n., pl.* **-li** (-lī′). *Anat., Zool.* **1.** a little cavity, pit, or cell, as a cell of a honeycomb. **2.** an air cell of the lungs, formed by the terminal dilation of tiny air passageways. **3.** one of the terminal secretory units of a racemose gland. **4.** the socket within the jawbone in which the root or roots of a tooth are set. [< L, equiv. to *alve(us)* concave vessel + *-olus,* var. of *-ulus* -ULE]

Al·ve·ra (al vēr′ə), *n.* a girl's given name, form of **Elvira.** Also, **Alvira.**

Al·vin (al′vin), *n.* **1.** a town in S Texas. 5643 (1960). **2.** Also, **Alwin, Alwyn.** a boy's given name.

Al·vi·na (al vī′nə), *n.* a girl's given name.

al·vine (al′vin, -vīn), *adj. Med. Obs.* of or pertaining to the belly; intestinal. [< L *alvīn(us),* equiv. to *alv(us)* belly + *-īnus* -INE[1]]

Al·vi·no (al vē′nō), *n.* a boy's given name, form of **Alvin.**

Al·vi·ra (al vī′rə, -vẽr′ə), *n.* a girl's given name, form of Elvira. Also, **Alvera.**

Al·vis (al′vis), *n.* a boy's given name.

al·way (ôl′wā), *adv.* *Archaic.* always. [ME; OE *ealneweg,* equiv. to *ealne* (acc. sing. masc. of *eal* ALL) + *weg* WAY]

al·ways (ôl′wāz, -wēz), *adv.* **1.** every time; on every occasion; without exception: *He always works on Saturday.* **2.** forever: *Will you love me always?* **3.** in any event; if necessary: *She can always move back with her parents.* **4.** all the time; continually; uninterruptedly: *Nearer, always nearer, he came.* [ME *alles weis,* gen. of *all wei.* See ALL, WAY]
—**Syn. 2, 4.** perpetually, everlastingly, forever, continually. Both ALWAYS and EVER refer to uniform or perpetual continuance. ALWAYS often expresses or implies repetition as producing the uniformity or continuance: *The sun always rises in the east.* EVER implies an unchanging sameness throughout: *Natural law is ever to be reckoned with.*

Al·win (al′win), *n.* a boy's given name. Also, **Alvin, Al′wyn.**

al·wite (ôl′wīt), *adj.* *Armor.* white (def. 14).

Al·y·at·tes (al′ē at′ēz), *n.* king of Lydia c617–560 B.C.

Al·yce (al′is), *n.* a girl's given name. Also, **Alice, Al′ys.**

Al·y·son (al′i sən), *n.* a girl's given name. Also, **Alison, Allison.**

a·lys·sum (ə lis′əm), *n.* **1.** any of several brassicaceous herbs of the genus *Alyssum,* having small, yellow or white, racemose flowers. **2.** See **sweet alyssum.** [< L *alysson* < Gk, neut. of *ályssos* curing (canine) madness, equiv. to *a-* A-[6] + *lýss(a)* madness + *-os* adj. suffix]

Alz′hei·mer's disease′ (älts′hī′mərz), *Pathol.* presenile dementia usually occurring in a middle-aged person and associated with sclerosis and nerve degeneration. [named after A. *Alzheimer* (fl. c1900) German physician]

am (am; *unstressed* əm, m), *v.* 1st pers. sing. pres. indic. of **be.** [ME; OE *am, eam, eom;* c. Goth *im,* Icel *em,* Ir *am,* Gk *eimí,* Skt *asmi*]

AM, *Radio.* See **amplitude modulation.**

Am, *Chem.* americium.

Am., **1.** America. **2.** American.

A/m, ampere per meter.

A.M., Master of Arts. [< L *Artium Magister*]

a.m., **1.** before noon. **2.** the period from 12 midnight to 12 noon, esp. the period of daylight prior to noon: *Shall we meet Saturday a.m.?* **3.** a morning newspaper, sometimes issued shortly before midnight. Also, **A.M.** Cf. **p.m.** [< L *ante meridiem*]

A.M.A., **1.** American Management Association. **2.** American Medical Association.

Am·a·belle (am′ə bel′), *n.* a girl's given name. Also, **Am·a·bel·la** (am′ə bel′ə).

am·a·dan (ä′mə thôn′), *n.* (in Irish folklore) a fairy who kills or deforms people by his touch. [< IrGael]

am·a·da·vat (am′ə də vat′), *n.* avadavat.

Am·a·de·o (am′ə dē′ō), *n.* a boy's given name.

Am·a·dis (am′ə dis), *n.* *Medieval Romance.* a knight-errant, model of the chivalric hero.

Am′a·dis of Gaul′, a Spanish romance of the second half of the 15th century by García de Montalvo, possibly based on Portuguese and French material of the late medieval period. Spanish, **A·ma·dís de Gau·la** (ä′mä-thēs′ de gou′lä).

am·a·dou (am′ə do͞o′), *n.* a spongy substance prepared from fungi, *Polyporus* (*Fomes*) *fomentarius,* and allied species, growing on trees, used as tinder and in surgery. [< F < ?]

A·ma·ga·sa·ki (ä′mä gä sä′kē), *n.* a city on SW Honshu, in S Japan. 335,513 (1955).

a·mah (ä′mə, am′ə), *n.* (used among Europeans in India and the Orient) **1.** a nurse, esp. a wet nurse. **2.** a maidservant. [< Pg *ama* nurse, governess < ML *amma* wet nurse, perh. alter. of L *mamma* breast]

a·main (ə mān′), *adv.* *Archaic.* **1.** with full force. **2.** at full speed. **3.** suddenly; hastily. **4.** exceedingly; greatly. [A-[1] + MAIN[1]]

amal., **1.** amalgamate. **2.** amalgamated. Also, **amalg.**

a·ma·la·ka (ä mul′ə kə), *n.* (in Hindu architecture) the bulbous finial of a sikhara. [< Skt *āmalaka* the myrobalan tree]

Am·a·lek (am′ə lek′), *n.* the son of Eliphaz and grandson of Esau. Gen. 36:12; I Chron. 1:36.

Am·a·lek·ite (am′ə lek′īt, ə mal′ə kīt′), *n.* **1.** a member of a tribe descended from Esau. Gen. 36:12. —*adj.* **2.** of or pertaining to the Amalekites. [< Heb *'Amālēq(ī)* (alter. of *'Amālēq* AMALEK) + -ITE[1]]

a·mal·gam (ə mal′gəm), *n.* **1.** an alloy of mercury with another metal or metals. **2.** a rare mineral, an alloy of silver and mercury, occurring as silver-white crystals or grains. **3.** a mixture or combination: *His character is a strange amalgam of contradictory traits.* [late ME *amalgam(a)* (in pl. *amalgamē*) < ML < Ar *al* the + Gk *málagma* softening agent, equiv. to *malak-* (s. of *malássein* to soften) + *-ma* n. suffix]

a·mal·gam·ate (ə mal′gə māt′), *v.,* **-at·ed, -at·ing.** —*v.t.* **1.** to mix or merge so as to make a combination; blend; unite; combine: *to amalgamate two companies.* **2.** *Metall.* to mix or alloy (a metal) with mercury. —*v.i.* **3.** to combine, unite, merge, or coalesce. **4.** to blend with another metal, as mercury. [AMALGAM + -ATE[1]] —**a·mal′gam·a·ble,** *adj.* —**a·mal′gam·a′tive,** *adj.* —**a·mal′gam·a′tor,** *n.*
—**Syn. 1.** mingle, commingle, unify.

a·mal·gam·a·tion (ə mal′gə mā′shən), *n.* **1.** the act or state of amalgamating; or the state or united result of being amalgamated. **2.** *Com.* a consolidation of two or more corporations. **3.** *Ethnol.* the biological fusion of diverse racial stocks. **4.** *Metall.* the extraction of the precious metals from their ores by treatment with mercury. [AMALGAM + -ATION]

amal′gam gild′ing. See **fire gilding.**

A·mal·ia (ə māl′yə, am′ə lē′ə), *n.* a girl's given name. Also, **Amelia.**

Am·al·thae·a (am′əl thē′ə), *n.* *Class. Myth.* a nymph who brought up the infant Zeus on the milk of a goat: in some versions she is the goat rather than a nymph. Also, **Am′al·the′a.**

A·man (ā′mən), *n.* *Douay Bible.* Haman.

A·man′a Church′ Soci′ety (ə man′ə). See under **Amanist.**

A·man·da (ə man′də), *n.* a girl's given name.

a·man·dine (ä′mən dēn′, am′ən-), *adj.* (of food) served or prepared with almonds: *trout amandine.* [< F; see ALMOND, -INE[2]]

A·man·ist (ə man′ist), *n.* a member of a religious group (**Amana Church Society**), which was founded in Germany in 1714, moved to New York State in 1843, and then to Iowa in 1855, where its communal villages have flourished as cooperative corporations since 1932. [AMAN(A CHURCH SOCIETY) + -IST]

am·a·ni·ta (am′ə nī′tə), *n.* any agaricaceous fungus of the genus *Amanita,* comprised chiefly of poisonous species. [< Gk *amānîtai* (pl.) kind of fungi]

a·man·u·en·sis (ə man′yo͞o en′sis), *n., pl.* **-ses** (-sēz). a person employed to write what another dictates or to copy what has been written by another; secretary. [< L, equiv. to *ā-* A-[4] + *manū,* abl. of *manus* hand + *-ēnsis* -ESE]

A·ma·pá (ä′mä pä′), *n.* a federal territory in N Brazil. 68,889 (1960); 51,177 sq. mi. *Cap.:* Macapá.

A·mar·a (ə mär′ə), *n.* a girl's given name.

am·a·ranth (am′ə ranth′), *n.* **1.** an imaginary, undying flower. **2.** any plant of the genus *Amaranthus,* certain species of which are cultivated for their showy flowers, as the love-lies-bleeding, or their colored foliage. **3.** *Chem.* a purplish-red, water-soluble powder, $C_{20}H_{11}N_2O_{10}Na_3$, an azo dye used chiefly to color pharmaceuticals, food, and garments. **4.** purpleheart. [< L *amarant(us),* alter. of Gk *amáranton* unfading flower, n. use of neut. sing. of *amárantos,* equiv. to *a-* A-[6] + *maran-* (s. of *maraínein* to fade) + *-tos* verbal adj. suffix]

am·a·ran·tha·ceous (am′ə ran thā′shəs), *adj.* belonging to the family *Amaranthaceae* (or *Amarantaceae*), comprising mostly herbaceous or shrubby plants, as the cockscomb, pigweed, amaranth, etc. [< NL *amaranthāce(ae)* (L *amarant(us)* AMARANTH + *-āceae* -ACEAE) + -OUS]

am·a·ran·thine (am′ə ran′thin, -thīn), *adj.* **1.** of or like the amaranth. **2.** unfading; everlasting: *a woman of amaranthine loveliness.* **3.** of purplish-red color. [AMARANTH + -INE[1]]

am·a·relle (am′ə rel′), *n.* any variety of the sour cherry, *Prunus Cerasus,* having colorless juice. [< G < ML *amārell(um),* equiv. to L *amār(us)* bitter + *-ellum* dim. suffix]

Am·a·ril·lo (am′ə ril′ō), *n.* a city in NW Texas. 137,969 (1960).

A·mar·na (ə mär′nə), *adj.* (*sometimes l.c.*) of, pertaining to, or belonging to the period in ancient Egyptian history described on cuneiform tablets (**Amar′na tab′lets**) that were found in 1887 at Tell el Amarna and contain the correspondence (**Amar′na let′ters**) from neighboring kings and governors to Amenhotep IV and his father Amenhotep III.

am·a·ryl·li·da·ceous (am′ə ril′i dā′shəs), *adj.* belonging to the *Amaryllidaceae,* or amaryllis family of plants, which includes the amaryllis, narcissus, snowdrop, agave, etc. [< NL *amaryllidāce(ae)* (*amaryllid-,* s. of *amaryllis* AMARYLLIS, + *-āceae* -ACEAE) + -OUS]

am·a·ryl·lis (am′ə ril′is), *n.* **1.** Also called **belladonna lily.** a bulbous plant, *Amaryllis Belladonna,* having large, lilylike, usually rose-colored flowers. **2.** any of several related plants formerly included in the genus *Amaryllis.* **3.** (*cap.*) a shepherdess or country girl, esp. in classical and later pastoral poetry. [< L: name of a shepherdess in Vergil's *Eclogues*]

Amaryllis, *Amaryllis Belladonna*

Am·a·ryl·lis (am′ə ril′is), *n.* a girl's given name.

A·mar·yn·ceus (ə mar′in so͞os′), *n.* (in the *Iliad*) a king of Messene who ruled Elis with Augeas and who was slain by Nestor in a war against the Pylians.

A·ma·sa (ə mā′sə), *n.* the commander of Absalom's army and later of David's army. II Sam. 17:25; 19:13.

Am·a·si·as (am′ə sī′əs), *n.* *Douay Bible.* Amaziah.

a·mass (ə mas′), *v.t.* **1.** to gather for oneself; collect as one's own: *to amass a fortune.* **2.** to collect into a mass or pile; accumulate; gather: *He amassed his papers for burning.* —*v.i.* **3.** to come together; assemble: *The people amassed for the parade.* [< F *amass(er),* equiv. to *a-* A-[5] + *mass(e)* MASS + *-er* inf. suffix] —**a·mass′a·ble,** *adj.* —**a·mass′er,** *n.* —**a·mass′ment,** *n.*
—**Syn. 1.** accumulate. **2.** assemble, aggregate.

A·ma·ta (ə mā′tə), *n.* *Rom. Legend.* the mother, by Latinus, of Lavinia.

a·mate[1] (ə māt′), *v.t.,* **a·mat·ed, a·mat·ing.** *Archaic.* to dismay; daunt. [ME < MF *amat(ir),* equiv. to *a-* A-[5] + *matir* to subdue, deriv. of *mat* subdued, dull. See MAT[3]]

a·mate[2] (ə māt′), *v.t.,* **a·mat·ed, a·mat·ing.** *Obs.* to be a mate to. [A-[1] + MATE[1]]

A·ma·te·ra·su (ä′mä te rä′so͞o), *n.* the Japanese Shinto goddess personifying the sun.

am·a·teur (am′ə cho͝or′, -tyo͝or′, am′ə tûr′), *n.* **1.** a person who engages in a study, sport, or other activity for pleasure rather than for financial benefit or professional reasons. Cf. **professional.** **2.** an athlete who has never competed for payment or for a monetary prize. **3.** a superficial or unskillful worker; dabbler: *Portrait painting is not for amateurs.* **4.** one who admires; devotee; fan: *an amateur of the cinema.* —*adj.* **5.** characteristic of an amateur; nonprofessional: *an amateur painter; amateur writing.* [< F, alter. of L *amātor* lover, equiv. to *amā-* (s. of *amāre* to love) + *-t-* ptp. suffix + *-or* -OR[2]]
—**Syn. 2.** nonprofessional. **3.** dilettante, tyro, novice.

am·a·teur·ish (am′ə cho͝or′ish, -tyo͝or′-, -tûr′-), *adj.* characteristic of an amateur; having the faults or deficiencies of an amateur: *Though an excellent violinist, he gave an amateurish performance.* [AMATEUR + -ISH[1]] —**am′a·teur′ish·ly,** *adv.* —**am′a·teur′ish·ness,** *n.*

am·a·teur·ism (am′ə cho͝o riz′əm, -tyo͝o-, am′ə tûr′iz əm), *n.* the practice, quality, or character of an amateur or amateurish performance. [AMATEUR + -ISM]

Am·a·thi (am′ə thī′), *n.* *Douay Bible.* Amittai.

A·ma·ti (ä mä′tē), *n.* **1. Ni·co·lò** (nē′kô lô′), 1596–1684, Italian violinmaker, one of a famous family of 16th and 17th century violinmakers: teacher of Antonio Stradivari. **2.** a violin made by a member of this family.

am·a·tive (am′ə tiv), *adj.* disposed to love; amorous. [< ML *amātīv(us),* equiv. to *amāt(us)* (ptp. of *amāre* to love) + *-īvus* -IVE] —**am′a·tive·ly,** *adv.* —**am′a·tive·ness,** *n.*

A·ma·to (ə mä′tō; *It.* ä mä′tô), *n.* **Pa·squa·le** (pə-skwä′lē, -lā; *It.* päs kwä′le), 1879–1942, Italian operatic baritone.

am·a·tol (am′ə tol′, -tôl′, -tōl′), *n.* *Chem.* an explosive mixture of ammonium nitrate and TNT. [AM(MONIUM) + connective *-a-* + (TRINITRO)TOL(UENE)]

am·a·tory (am′ə tôr′ē, -tōr′ē), *adj.* of or pertaining to lovers or love-making, or expressive of love: *amatory poems; an amatory look.* Also, **am′a·to′ri·al.** [< L *amātōri(us),* equiv. to *amāt(us)* (ptp. of *amāre* to love) + *-ōrius* -ORY[1]] —**am′a·to′ri·al·ly,** *adv.*

am·a·tun·gu·la (am′ə tung′gyə lə), *n.* See **Natal plum.** [< Zulu *amatungulu* (pl.)]

am·au·ro·sis (am′ô rō′sis), *n.* partial or total loss of sight. [< Gk: darkening, hindrance to sight, equiv. to *amaur(ós)* dim, dark + *-ōsis* -OSIS] —**am·au·rot·ic** (am′ô rot′ik), *adj.*

A·may·a (ə mī′ə), *n.* a girl's given name.

a·maze (ə māz′), *v.,* **a·mazed, a·maz·ing,** *n.* —*v.t.* **1.** to overwhelm with surprise or wonder; astonish greatly. **2.** *Obs.* to bewilder; perplex. —*n.* **3.** *Archaic.* amazement. [ME *amase(n),* OE *āmasian* to confuse, stun, astonish. See A-[3], to MAZE]
—**Syn. 1.** astound, dumfound. See **surprise.**

a·mazed (ə māzd′), *adj.* surprised; astounded; filled with wonder: *The magician made the dove disappear before our amazed eyes.* [ME; see AMAZE, -ED[2]] —**a·maz·ed·ly** (ə mā′zid lē), *adv.* —**a·maz′ed·ness,** *n.*

a·maze·ment (ə māz′mənt), *n.* **1.** overwhelming surprise or astonishment. **2.** *Obs.* **a.** stupefaction; frenzy. **b.** perplexity. **c.** consternation. [AMAZE + -MENT]

Am·a·zi·ah (am′ə zī′ə), *n.* a son and successor of Joash as king of Judah. II Kings 14. Also, *Douay Bible,* **Amasias.**

a·maz·ing (ə mā′zing), *adj.* causing great surprise or wonder. [AMAZE + -ING[2]] —**a·maz′ing·ly,** *adv.*

Am·a·zon (am′ə zon′, -zən), *n.* **1.** a river in N South America, flowing E from the Peruvian Andes through N Brazil to the Atlantic Ocean: the largest river in the world in volume of water carried. 3900 mi. long. **2.** *Class. Myth.* one of a race of female warriors said to dwell near the Black Sea. **3.** one of a fabled tribe of female warriors in South America. **4.** (*often l.c.*) a tall, powerful, aggressive woman. **5.** See **Amazon ant.** **6.** any of several green parrots of the genus *Amazona,* of tropical America, often kept as pets. [< L *Amazōn* < Gk, uncertain etymology]

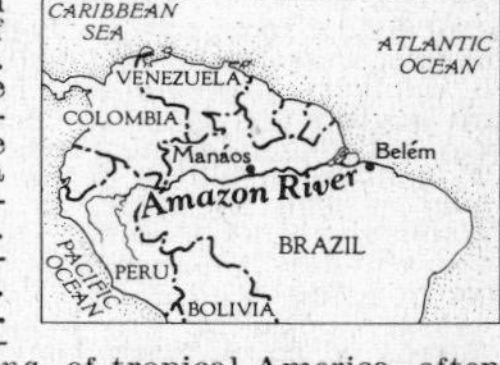

Am′azon ant′, any of several ants of the genus *Polyergus* that raid the nests of other species, carrying off and enslaving the young.

A·ma·zo·nas (am′ə zō′nəs), *n.* a state in NW Brazil. 721,215 (1960); 601,769 sq. mi. *Cap.:* Manaus.

Am·a·zo·ni·an (am′ə zō′nē ən), *adj.* **1.** (of a woman) characteristic of or like an Amazon; warlike; powerful and aggressive; masculine. **2.** pertaining to the Amazon river or the country adjacent to it. [AMAZON + -IAN]

Am·a·zo·nis (am′ə zō′nis), *n.* an area on the equator of Mars.

am·a·zon·ite (am′ə zə nīt′), *n.* *Mineral.* a green feldspar, a variety of microcline, used as an ornamental material. Also called **Am′azon stone′.** [AMAZON (river) + -ITE[1]]

Am·a·zon·o·mach·i·a (am′ə zon′ə mak′ē ə), *n.* **1.** a battle between Amazons and Greeks. **2.** a representation of this in art. [< Gk *Amazonomachía.* See AMAZON, -MACHY]

Amb., Ambassador.

am·ba (am′bə), *n.* anba.

am·ba·ges (am bā′jēz), *n.* *Archaic.* (*construed as pl.*) winding, roundabout paths or ways. [late ME < L *ambāgēs* (pl.) circuits, equiv. to *amb(i)-* AMBI- + *-āg-* (var. s. of *agere* to move) + *-ēs* pl. ending]

am·ba·gious (am bā′jəs), *adj.* roundabout; circuitous: *ambagious reasoning.* [< L *ambāgiōs(us),* equiv. to *ambāgi-* (s. of *ambāgēs* AMBAGES) + *-ōsus* -OUS] —**am·ba′gious·ly,** *adv.* —**am·ba′gious·ness,** *n.*

Am·ba·la (əm bä′lə), *n.* a city in E Punjab, in N India. 76,200 (1961).

am·ba·rel·la (am′bə rel′ə), *n.* See **Otaheite apple.** [< Sinhalese *æmbarælla* < Skt *āmravāṭaka* a kind of tree, equiv. to *āmra* mango (deriv. of *amla* bitter) + *vāṭaka* garden, deriv. of *vāṭa* enclosed]

am·ba·ry (am bär′ē), *n.* **1.** an East Indian plant, *Hibiscus cannabinus,* yielding a useful fiber. **2.** the fiber itself, used in canvas and cordage. Also, **am·ba′ri.** Also called **kenaf.** [< Hindi *ambāṛī*]

am·bas·sa·dor (am bas′ə dər), *n.* **1. a.** a diplomatic official of the highest rank, sent by one sovereign or state to another as its resident representative (**ambas′sador extraor′dinary and plenipoten′tiary**). **b.** a diplomatic official of the highest rank representing his government on a temporary mission, as for negotiating a treaty. **c.** a diplomatic official serving as permanent head of his country's mission to the United Nations or some other international organization. **2.** an authorized messenger or representative. *Abbr.:* Amb. Also, **embassador.** [late ME *am-, embass(i)adour, imbassadore,* etc. < MF *ambassadeur* < Pr *ambassador* < *ambass-* (see EMBASSY) + *-ador* < L *-ātor* (see -ATE[1], -OR[2])] —**am·bas·sa·do·ri·al** (am bas′ə dôr′ē əl, -dōr′-), *adj.* —**am·bas′sa·do′ri·al·ly,** *adv.* —**am·bas′sa·dor·ship′,** *n.*

am·bas·sa·dor-at-large (am bas′ə dər ət lärj′), *n., pl.* **am·bas·sa·dors-at-large.** an ambassador who is not assigned to a particular diplomatic post but is appointed on a special mission.

Ambassadors, The, a novel (1903) by Henry James.

am·bas·sa·dress (am bas′ə dris), *n.* **1.** a female ambassador. **2.** the wife of an ambassador. [AMBASSAD(O)R + -ESS]

am·batch (am′bach), *n.* an Egyptian, leguminous tree, *Aeschynomene elaphroxylon*, having a light-colored, spongy wood. [< Amharic *ambatcho*]

Am·bed·kar (äm bed′kär), *n.* **Bhim·rao Ram·ji** (bēm′rou räm′jē), 1893–1956, Indian politician and jurist.

am·ber (am′bər), *n.* **1.** a pale yellow, sometimes reddish or brownish, fossil resin of vegetable origin, translucent, brittle, and capable of gaining a negative electrical charge by friction and of being an excellent insulator. **2.** the yellowish-brown color of resin. —*adj.* **3.** of the color of amber; yellowish-brown. [ME *ambra* < ML < Ar *'anbar* ambergris] —**am′ber-like′, am′ber·y, am′ber·ous,** *adj.*

am·ber·fish (am′bər fish′), *n., pl.* (*esp. collectively*) **-fish,** (*esp. referring to two or more kinds or species*) **-fish·es.** amberjack. [AMBER + FISH]

am·ber·gris (am′bər grēs′, -gris), *n.* a morbid secretion of the sperm whale intestine, an opaque, ash-colored substance which is fragrant when heated, usually found floating on the ocean or cast ashore: used in perfumery. [< F *ambre gris* gray amber (see AMBER); r. late ME *imbergres*]

Am′ber Is′lands, (in ancient geography) a name given by the Greeks in later times to the islands in the North Sea. Cf. **Electrides, Glessariae.**

am·ber·i·na (am′bə rē′nə), *n.* an American art glass having transparent colors ranging from pale amber to ruby. [formerly trademark]

am·ber·jack (am′bər jak′), *n., pl.* (*esp. collectively*) **-jack,** (*esp. referring to two or more kinds or species*) **-jacks.** any of several carangoid fishes of the genus *Seriola*, as *S. dumerili*, a game fish found in warmer waters of the Atlantic Ocean. Also called **amberfish.** [AMBER (color) + *jack* (kind of fish)]

Am·ber·ley (am′bər lē), *n.* a town in SW Ohio. 2951 (1960).

am·ber·oid (am′bə roid′), *n.* synthetic amber made by compressing pieces of various resins at a high temperature. Also, **ambroid.** [AMBER + -OID]

ambi-, a prefix occurring in loan words from Latin where it meant "both" (*ambiguous*); used in the formation of compound words: *ambitendency.* [< L; akin to OE *ymb(e)-* around. Cf. AMPHI-]

am·bi·ance (am′bē əns; *Fr.* äɴ byäɴs′), *n., pl.* **-bi·anc·es** (-bē ən siz; *Fr.* -byäɴs′). ambience.

am·bi·dex·ter (am′bi dek′stər), *adj.* **1.** *Archaic.* ambidextrous. —*n.* **2.** *Obs.* an ambidextrous person. [< LL; see AMBI-, DEXTER] —**am′bi·dex′tral,** *adj.*

am·bi·dex·ter·i·ty (am′bi dek ster′i tē), *n.* **1.** ambidextrous ease, skill, or facility. **2.** unusual cleverness. **3.** duplicity; deceitfulness. [AMBIDEXTER + -ITY]

am·bi·dex·trous (am′bi dek′strəs), *adj.* **1.** able to use both hands equally well: *an ambidextrous surgeon.* **2.** unusually skillful; facile: *an ambidextrous painter, familiar with all media.* **3.** double-dealing; deceitful. [AMBIDEXT(E)R + -OUS] —**am′bi·dex′trous·ly,** *adv.* —**am′bi·dex′trous·ness,** *n.*

am·bi·ence (am′bē əns; *Fr.* äɴ byäɴs′), *n., pl.* **-bi·enc·es** (-bē ən siz; *Fr.* -byäɴs′). **1.** that which surrounds or encompasses; environment. **2.** the mood, character, quality, tone, atmosphere, etc., particularly of an environment or milieu: *Her salon had a delightful ambience.* Also, **ambiance.** [< F; see AMBIENT, -ENCE]

am·bi·ent (am′bē ənt), *adj.* **1.** completely surrounding; encompassing: *ambient noises.* **2.** moving freely; circulating: *ambient air.* [< L *ambient-* (s. of *ambiēns*, prp. of *ambīre* to go around), equiv. to *amb-* AMBI- + *-i-* go + *-ent-* -ENT]

am·bi·gu·i·ty (am′bə gyōō′i tē), *n., pl.* **-ties. 1.** doubtfulness or uncertainty of meaning or intention: *to speak with ambiguity; an ambiguity of manner.* **2.** an equivocal or ambiguous word, expression, meaning, etc.: *a contract free of ambiguities; the ambiguities of modern poetry.* [late ME *ambiguite* < L *ambiguitāt-* (s. of *ambiguitās*), equiv. to *ambigu-* (see AMBIGUOUS) + *-itāt-* -ITY]
—**Syn. 1.** vagueness, deceptiveness. **2.** equivocation.
—**Ant. 1.** explicitness.

am·big·u·ous (am big′yōō əs), *adj.* **1.** open to various interpretations; having several possible meanings or interpretations; equivocal: *an ambiguous answer.* **2.** *Ling.* (of an expression) exhibiting constructional homonymity; having two or more structural descriptions, as the sound sequence *Flying planes can be dangerous.* **3.** of doubtful or uncertain nature; difficult to comprehend, distinguish, or classify: *a rock of ambiguous character.* **4.** lacking clearness or definiteness; obscure; indistinct: *an ambiguous future; an ambiguous shape.* [< L *ambigu(us)* (*ambig(ere)*, equiv. to *amb-* AMBI- + *-igere*, var. of *agere* to drive, lead, act, + *-uus* adj. suffix) + -OUS] —**am·big′u·ous·ly,** *adv.* —**am·big′u·ous·ness,** *n.*
—**Syn. 1.** AMBIGUOUS, EQUIVOCAL describe that which is not clear in meaning. That which is AMBIGUOUS leaves the intended sense doubtful; it need not be purposely deceptive. That which is EQUIVOCAL is equally capable of two or more interpretations, and is usually intended to be so for the purpose of mystifying or confusing. **3.** dubious, vague, indeterminate, unclassifiable, anomalous. **4.** puzzling, enigmatic, problematic. —**Ant. 1.** explicit. **3.** certain. **4.** clear.

am·bil-a·nak (am′bəl ä′nək), *adj.* of or pertaining to a Malayan marriage arrangement in which the husband joins the wife's family, instead of paying a bride price, and loses his property rights in his wife and children. [< Malay, equiv. to *ambil* adjusting + *anak* child]

am·bi·lat·er·al (am′bə lat′ər əl), *adj.* of, pertaining to, or affecting both sides. [AMBI- + LATERAL] —**am′bi·lat′er·al′i·ty,** *n.* —**am′bi·lat′er·al·ly,** *adv.*

am·bi·sex·u·al (am′bi sek′shōō əl), *adj., n.* bisexual (defs. 2, 3). [AMBI- + SEXUAL]

am·bi·sin·is·ter (am′bə sin′i stər), *adj.* clumsy or unskillful with both hands. Also, **am·bi·sin·is·trous** (am′bē sin′is trəs, -si nis′trəs). [AMBI- + SINISTER]

am·bi·syl·lab·ic (am′bē si lab′ik), *adj. Phonet.* (of a single speech sound or cluster) shared phonetically by two contiguous syllables, as the single *n*-sound of *any* or the *pl*-cluster of *grappling.* [AMBI- + SYLLABIC]

am·bit (am′bit), *n.* **1.** circumference; circuit. **2.** boundary; limits. [ME < L *ambit(us)* a going around, equiv. to *amb-* AMBI- + *itus* a going (*-i-* (s. of *īre* to go) + *-tus* verbal n. suffix)]

am·bi·tend·en·cy (am′bi ten′dən sē), *n., pl.* **-cies.** *Psychol.* ambivalence, esp. when acted out; a tendency to contradictory behavior arising from conflicting impulses. [AMBI- + TENDENCY]

am·bi·tion (am bish′ən), *n.* **1.** an earnest desire for some type of achievement or distinction, as power, fame, wealth, etc., and the willingness to strive for its attainment: *It was his ambition to be an actor.* **2.** the object, state, or result desired or sought after: *The crown was his ambition.* **3.** desire for work or activity; energy: *He has plenty of drive and ambition.* —*v.t.* **4.** to seek after earnestly; aspire to. [ME *ambicion* < L *ambitiōn-* (s. of *ambitiō*), equiv. to *amb-* AMBI- + *-i-* go + *-t-* ptp. suffix + *-iōn-* -ION] —**am·bi′tion·less,** *adj.* —**am·bi′tion·less·ly,** *adv.*
—**Syn. 1.** aspiration, yearning, longing. **2.** goal, aim. **3.** drive, force.

am·bi·tious (am bish′əs), *adj.* **1.** having ambition; eagerly desirous of achieving or obtaining power, superiority, or distinction: *ambitious students.* **2.** showing or caused by ambition: *an ambitious attempt.* **3.** strongly desirous; eager: *ambitious of love and approval.* **4.** requiring exceptional effort, ability, etc.: *an ambitious program for eliminating all slums.* [< L *ambitiōs(us)*, equiv. to *ambiti(ō)* AMBITION + *-ōsus* -OUS] —**am·bi′tious·ly,** *adv.* —**am·bi′tious·ness,** *n.*
—**Syn. 1.** AMBITIOUS, ASPIRING, ENTERPRISING describe one who wishes to rise above his present position or condition. The AMBITIOUS man wishes to attain worldly success, and puts forth effort toward this end: *ambitious for social position.* The ENTERPRISING man, interested especially in wealth, is characterized by energy and daring in undertaking projects. The ASPIRING man wishes to rise (mentally or spiritually) to a higher level or plane, or to attain some end that he feels to be above his ordinary expectations.

am·biv·a·lence (am biv′ə ləns), *n.* **1.** uncertainty or fluctuation, esp. when caused by inability to make a choice or a simultaneous desire to say or do two opposite things. **2.** *Psychol.* the coexistence within an individual of positive and negative feelings toward the same person, object, or action, simultaneously drawing him in opposite directions. [AMBI- + VALENCE] —**am·biv′a·lent,** *adj.*

am·bi·ver·sion (am′bə vûr′zhən, -shən), *n. Psychol.* a state intermediate between extroversion and introversion. [AMBI- + *-version*, as in EXTROVERSION, INTROVERSION]

am·bi·vert (am′bə vûrt′), *n. Psychol.* one whose personality type is intermediate between extravert and introvert. [AMBI- + *-vert*, as in EXTROVERT, INTROVERT]

am·ble (am′bəl), *v.,* **-bled, -bling,** *n.* —*v.i.* **1.** to go at an easy pace; stroll; saunter: *He ambled around the town.* **2.** (of a horse) to go at a slow pace with the legs moving in lateral pairs and usually having a four-beat rhythm. —*n.* **3.** an ambling gait. **4.** an easy walk or gentle pace. **5.** a stroll. [late ME < MF *amble(r)* < L *ambulāre* to walk, equiv. to *amb-* AMBI- + *-ulāre* to step (< ?)] —**am′bler,** *n.* —**am′bling·ly,** *adv.*

Am·bler (am′blər), *n.* a town in SE Pennsylvania. 6765 (1960).

am·blyg·o·nite (am blig′ə nīt′), *n.* a mineral, a lithium aluminum fluophosphate, $Li(AlF)PO_4$. [< Gk *amblygōn(ios)* (*amblý(s)* blunt, obtuse + *gōni(a)* angle + *-os* adj. suffix) + -ITE[1]]

am·bly·o·pi·a (am′blē ō′pē ə), *n. Ophthalm.* dimness of sight, without apparent organic defect. [< NL < Gk *amblyōpía*, equiv. to *amblý(s)* dull + *-ōpia* -OPIA] —**am·bly·op·ic** (am′blē op′ik), *adj.*

am·bly·o·scope (am′blē ə skōp′), *n.* an instrument used to train an amblyopic eye to function properly. [< Gk *amblý(s)* dull, dim-sighted + -o- + -SCOPE]

am·bly·pod (am′blə pod′), *n.* one of the primitive ungulate mammals of the extinct order *Pantodonta*, from the Paleocene and Eocene epochs, having a massive body and short legs. [< NL *amblypod(a)* < Gk *amblý(s)* blunt + *-poda* -PODA]

am·bo (am′bō), *n., pl.* **-bos.** (in an early Christian church) a raised desk, or either of two such desks, from which the Gospels or Epistles were read or chanted. Also, **ambon.** [< ML < Gk *ámbō(n)* edge, rim, pulpit]

am·bo·cep·tor (am′bə sep′tər), *n. Immunol.* a substance which develops during infection in the blood, believed to have affinities for both the bacterial cell or erythrocytes and the complement. [< L *ambō* both (akin to AMBI-) + (RE)CEPTOR]

Am·boi·na (am boi′nə), *n.* **1.** an island in the central Moluccas, in E Indonesia. 64,486 (est. 1954); 314 sq. mi. **2.** Also, **Am·bon** (äm′bôn). a seaport on this island. 55,263 (est. 1961). —**Am·boi·nese** (am′boi nēz′, -nēs′), *adj., n.*

Amboi′na wood′. See **padouk wood.** Also, **Amboy′na wood′.**

Am·boise (äɴ bwäz′), *n.* a town in central France, E of Tours: castle. 8192 (1962).

am·bon (am′bon), *n., pl.* **am·bo·nes** (am bō′nēz). ambo.

ambrette′ seed′ (am bret′), the seed of the abelmosk. [< F *ambrette.* See AMBER, -ETTE]

am·brette′-seed oil′ (am bret′sēd′), a yellow oil expressed from ambrette seeds, used as a fixative in the manufacture of perfume.

am·bret·to·lide (am bret′əlīd′), *n. Chem.* a colorless liquid, $C_{16}H_{28}O_2$, having a strong musky odor, used as a fixative in the manufacture of perfume. [AMBRETTE + -OLE + -IDE]

am·broid (am′broid), *n.* amberoid.

Am·brose (am′brōz), *n.* **1. Saint,** A.D. 340?–397, bishop of Milan 374–397. **2.** a boy's given name.

Am′brose Chan′nel, a ship channel at the entrance to New York harbor, near Sandy Hook. 7½ mi. long.

am·bro·sia (am brō′zhə), *n.* **1.** *Class. Myth.* the food, drink, or perfume of the gods. Cf. **nectar** (def. 2). **2.** anything imparting the sense of divinity, as poetic inspiration, music, etc. **3.** something especially delicious to taste or smell. [< L < Gk: immortality, food of the gods, n. use of fem. of *ambrósios*, equiv. to *a-* A-[6] + *-mbros-* (var. s. of *brotós* mortal; akin to L *mortuus* dead) + *-ios* adj. suffix]

am·bro·si·a·ceous (am brō′zē ā′shəs), *adj. Bot.* belonging to the *Ambrosiaceae*, or ragweed family of plants, which includes the ragweed, marsh elder, etc. [< NL *ambrosiāce(ae)* (see AMBROSIA, -ACEAE) + -OUS]

am·bro·sial (am brō′zhəl), *adj.* **1.** exceptionally pleasing to taste or smell; especially delicious or fragrant. **2.** worthy of the gods; divine. Also, **am·bro′sian.** [AMBROSI(A) + -AL[1]] —**am·bro′sial·ly,** *adv.*

Ambro′sian chant′, the liturgical chant, established by St. Ambrose, characterized by ornamented, often antiphonal, singing. Also called **Milanese chant.**

am·bro·type (am′brə tīp′), *n. Photog., Obs.* a picture made by placing a glass negative against a dark background. [< Gk *ámbro(tos)* immortal (see AMBROSIA) + -TYPE]

am·bry (am′brē), *n., pl.* **-bries. 1.** a storeroom; closet. **2.** a pantry. **3.** Also called **armarium.** *Eccles.* a recess in the wall of a church or a cupboard in the sacristy where sacred vessels, books, vestments, etc., are kept. **4.** *Obs.* any of various types of closet or cupboard with doors and shelves. Also, **aumbry.** [late ME *almerie, almarie* (also *armarie*) < ML *almāri(um)*, dissimilated var. of *armārium* < L. See ARM[2], -ARY]

ambs·ace (āmz′ās′, amz′-), *n.* **1.** the lowest throw at dice, the double ace. **2.** bad luck; misfortune. **3.** the smallest amount or distance. Also, **amesace.** [ME *ambes as* < OF < L *ambas* both + *as* unit; see ACE]

ambulac′ral foot′. See **tube foot.**

am·bu·lac·rum (am′byə lak′rəm, -lā′krəm), *n., pl.* **-lac·ra** (-lak′rə, -lā′krə). one of the radial areas in an echinoderm, bearing the tubular protrusions by which locomotion is accomplished. [< NL, L: alley, walking place, equiv. to *ambulā-* (s. of *ambulāre* to walk) + *-crum* n. suffix denoting means] —**am′bu·lac′ral,** *adj.*

am·bu·lance (am′byə ləns), *n.* a wheeled vehicle, airplane, etc., equipped for carrying sick, injured, or wounded people, usually to a hospital. [< F, equiv. to (*hôpital*) *ambul(ant)* walking (hospital) + *-ance* -ANCE. See AMBULANT]

am′bulance chas′er, *U.S. Informal.* **1.** a lawyer who seeks accident victims as clients and encourages them to sue for damages. **2.** any unduly aggressive lawyer. —**am′bulance chas′ing.**

am·bu·lant (am′byə lənt), *adj.* **1.** moving from place to place; shifting. **2.** *Med.* ambulatory (def. 4). [< L *ambulant-* (s. of *ambulāns*, prp. of *ambulāre* to walk). See AMBLE]

am·bu·lante (am′byə länt′; *Fr.* äɴ by läɴt′), *n., pl.* **-lantes** (-länts′; *Fr.* -läɴt′). a portable tea table, used in 18th century France. [< F: lit., walking, fem. of *ambulant*, prp. of *ambuler* < L *ambulāre.* See AMBLE]

am·bu·late (am′byə lāt′), *v.i.,* **-lat·ed, -lat·ing.** to walk about or move from place to place. [< L *ambulāt(us)* (ptp. of *ambulāre* to walk), equiv. to *ambul-* (see AMBLE) + *-ātus* -ATE[1]] —**am′bu·la′tion,** *n.*

am·bu·la·tor (am′byə lā′tər), *n.* **1.** one who or that which ambulates. **2.** *Survey.* perambulator (def. 2). [AMBULATE + -OR[2]]

am·bu·la·to·ry (am′byə lə tōr′ē, -tôr′ē), *adj., n., pl.* **-ries.** —*adj.* **1.** of, pertaining to, or capable of walking: *an ambulatory exploration of the countryside.* **2.** adapted for walking, as the limbs of many animals. **3.** moving about; not stationary: *an ambulatory tribe.* **4.** Also, **ambulant.** *Med.* not confined to bed; able or strong enough to walk: *an ambulatory patient.* **5.** *Law.* not fixed; alterable or revocable: *ambulatory will.* —*n.* **6.** Also called **deambulatory.** *Archit.* **a.** an aisle surrounding the end of the choir or chancel of a church. **b.** the covered walk of a cloister. [< L *ambulātōri(us)*, equiv. to *ambulāt(us)* (see AMBULATE) + *-ōrius* -ORY[1]]

am·bus·cade (am′bə skād′), *n., v.,* **-cad·ed, -cad·ing.** —*n.* **1.** an ambush. —*v.i.* **2.** to lie in ambush. —*v.t.* **3.** to attack from a concealed position; ambush. [< F < Pg *embuscada* (or Sp *emboscada*), equiv. to *embusc-* (see AMBUSH) + *-ada* -ADE[1]] —**am′bus·cad′er,** *n.*

am·bus·ca·do (am′bə skā′dō), *n., pl.* **-dos.** *Obs.* ambuscade. [pseudo-Sp alter. of AMBUSCADE]

am·bush (am′bŏŏsh), *n.* Also, **am′bush·ment. 1.** the act or an instance of lying concealed so as to attack by surprise: *The highwaymen waited in ambush near the road.* **2.** the act or an instance of attacking unexpectedly from a concealed position. **3.** the concealed position itself: *A clump of bushes and trees was their ambush.* **4.** those who attack suddenly and unexpectedly from a concealed position: *The ambush was a dozen well-armed men.* —*v.t.* **5.** to attack from ambush. [ME *enbuss(h)e* < MF *embusch(ier)* (to) set in the woods, equiv. to *em-* IM-[1] + *busch-* < LL *bosc(um)* wood (< Gmc; see BUSH[1]) + *-ier* verbal and inf. suffix] —**am′bush·er,** *n.* —**am′bush·like′,** *adj.*

am′bush bug′, any of several carnivorous bugs of the family *Phymatidae*, that lie concealed in flowers to prey on insects.

Am·chit·ka (am chit′kə), *n.* an island off the coast of SW Alaska, in the W part of the Aleutian Islands: site of U.S. air base during World War II. 40 mi. long.

A.M.D.G., to the greater glory of God. [< L *ad majorem Dei gloriam*] Also, **AMDG**

A.M.E., 1. Advanced Master of Education. **2.** African Methodist Episcopal.

a·me·ba (ə mē′bə), *n., pl.* **-bas, -bae** (-bē). amoeba.

a·me·bic (ə mē′bik), *adj.* amoebic.

a·me·bo·cyte (ə mē′bə sīt′), *n. Zool.* amoebocyte.

a·me·boid (ə mē′boid), *adj.* amoeboid. —**a·me′boid·ism,** *n.*

âme dam·née (äm′ dä nā′), *pl.* **âmes dam·nées** (äm′ dä nā′). *French.* one who is willingly the tool of another person. [lit., damned soul]

AMEDS, Army Medical Service. Also, **AMedS**

a·meer (ə mēr′), *n.* amir.

a·meer·ate (ə mēr′it, -āt), *n.* amirate.

a·mei·o·sis (ā′mī ō′sis), *n. Biol.* aberrant meiosis in which only an equational division occurs, as in parthenogenesis. [< NL; see A-[6], MEIOSIS] —**a·mei·ot·ic** (ā′mī ot′ik), *adj.*

A·mel·ia (ə mēl′yə), *n.* a girl's given name. Also, **Amalia.**

a·mel·io·rate (ə mēl′yə rāt′), *v.t., v.i.,* **-rat·ed, -rat·ing.** to make or become better; improve; meliorate. [A-[5] + MELIORATE] —**a·mel·io·ra·ble** (ə mēl′yər ə bəl), *adj.* —**a·mel′io·ra·ble·ness,** *n.* —**a·mel·io·rant** (ə mēl′yər ənt), *n.* —**a·mel·io·ra·tive** (ə mēl′yə rā′tiv, -yər ə tiv), *adj.* —**a·mel′io·ra′tor,** *n.*
—**Syn.** amend, better. See **improve.** —**Ant.** worsen.

a·mel·io·ra·tion (ə mēl′yə rā′shən), *n.* **1.** the act or an instance of ameliorating; improvement. **2.** that which is ameliorated. [AMELIORATE + -ION]

A·me·li·ta (am′ə lē′tə; *Sp., It.* ä′me lē′tä), *n.* a girl's given name.

am·e·lo·blast (am′ə lō blast′), *n. Anat.* one of a layer of cells which covers the dentin of a developing tooth and secretes enamel. [ME *amel* < MF *esmal* (see ENAMEL) + -O- + -BLAST] —**am·e·lo·blas·tic** (am′ə lō-blas′tik), *adj.*

a·men (ā′men′, ä′men′), *interj.* **1.** it is so; so be it (used after a prayer, creed, or other formal statement to express solemn ratification or agreement). —*adv.*

2. verily; truly. —*n.* 3. an utterance of the interjection "Amen." 4. a musical setting for such an utterance. 5. an expression of concurrence or assent: *The committee gave its amen to the proposal.* [ME, OE < LL < Gk < Heb. *āmēn* certainty, certainly]

A·men (ä′mən), *n.* *Egyptian Myth.* a primeval deity worshiped esp. at Thebes, the personification of air or breath represented either as a ram or a goose (later identified with Amen-Ra). Also, **Amon.**

a·me·na·ble (ə mē′nə bəl, ə men′ə-), *adj.* 1. ready or willing to answer, act, agree, or yield; agreeable; submissive; tractable: *an amenable servant.* 2. liable to be called to account; answerable; legally responsible: *You are amenable for this debt.* 3. capable of or agreeable to being tested, tried, analyzed, etc. [< AF, equiv. to MF *amen(er)* (to) lead to (*a-* A-⁵ + *mener* < L *mināre* to drive) + *-able* -ABLE] —**a·me′na·bil′i·ty, a·me′na·ble·ness,** *n.* —**a·me′na·bly,** *adv.*
—**Syn. 1.** manageable, docile, easy. **3.** open, subject.
—**Ant. 1.** stubborn.

a′men′ cor′ner, *U.S.* 1. a place in a church, usually at one side of the pulpit, once occupied by those worshipers who led the responsive amens during the service. 2. any special place in a church occupied by zealous worshipers.

a·mend (ə mend′), *v.t.* 1. to alter, modify, rephrase, or add to or subtract from (a motion, bill, constitution, etc.) by formal procedure: *Congress may amend the proposed tax bill.* 2. to change for the better; improve: *to amend one's ways.* 3. to remove or correct faults in; rectify. —*v.i.* 4. to grow or become better by reforming oneself: *He amends day by day.* [ME *amende(n)* < OF *amende(r)* < L *ēmendāre* to correct, equiv. to *ē-* E- + *menda* blemish] —**a·mend′a·ble,** *adj.* —**a·mend′er,** *n.*
—**Syn. 2.** ameliorate, better. **3.** AMEND, EMEND both mean to improve by correcting or by freeing from error. AMEND is the general term, used of any such correction in detail: *to amend spelling, punctuation, grammar.* EMEND usually applies to the correction of a text in the process of editing or preparing for publication; it implies improvement in the sense of greater accuracy: *He emended the text of the play by restoring the original reading.* **4.** improve, ameliorate. —**Ant. 2, 4.** worsen.

a·mend·a·tory (ə men′də tōr′ē, -tôr′ē), *adj.* *U.S.* serving to amend; corrective. [< LL *ēmendātōri(us)* (with *e-* for *a-* from AMEND). See EMENDATOR, -Y¹]

a·mende ho·no·ra·ble (ə mend′ on′ər ə bəl; *Fr.* A mäN dô nô RA′blᵊ), *pl.* **a·mendes ho·no·ra·bles** (ə mendz′ on′ər ə bəl; *Fr.* A mäNd zô nô RA′blᵊ). a formal apology to a person whose honor has been offended. [< F; see AMENDS, HONORABLE]

a·mend·ment (ə mend′mənt), *n.* 1. the act or state of amending or the state of being amended. 2. an alteration of or addition to a motion, bill, constitution, etc. 3. a change made by correction, addition, or deletion: *The editors made few amendments to the manuscript.* [ME < OF *amendement.* See AMEND, -MENT]

a·mends (ə mendz′), *n.* (*construed as sing. or pl.*) 1. reparation or compensation for a loss, damage, or injury of any kind; recompense: *The court ordered that amends be made to the widow.* 2. *Obs.* improvement; recovery, as of health. 3. **make amends,** to attempt to compensate for a personal slight, insult, fit of temper, etc., by making an apology or being exceptionally kind; to attempt to get back into the good graces of a person one has insulted or slighted. [ME *amendes* < MF, pl. of *amende* reparation, deriv. of *amender* to AMEND]

A′men′ glass′ (ā′men′, ä′men′), a British glass of the mid-18th century, having engraved on it a sentiment favoring the cause of the Old Pretender, concluded with the word "Amen."

A·men·ho·tep III (ä′mən hō′tep, am′ən-), king of Egypt 1411?–1375 B.C. Also called **Amenophis III.**

Amenhotep IV, died 1357? B.C., king of Egypt 1375?–1357?: reformer of ancient Egyptian religion (son of Amenhotep III). Also called **Amenophis IV, Akhnaton, Ikhnaton.**

a·men·i·ty (ə men′i tē, ə mē′ni-), *n., pl.* **-ties.** 1. **amenities,** agreeable ways or manners; courtesies; civilities: *the graceful amenities of society.* 2. the quality of being pleasing or agreeable in situation, prospect, disposition, etc.; pleasantness: *the amenity of the climate.* [late ME *amenite* < L *amoenitāt-* (s. of *amoenitās*), equiv. to *amoen(us)* pleasing + *-itāt-* -ITY]

a·men·or·rhe·a (ā men′ə rē′ə), *n.* *Pathol.* absence of the menses. Also, **a·men′or·rhoe′a.** [A-⁶ + MENO- + -RRHEA] —**a·men′or·rhe′al, a·men′or·rhoe′al, a·men′or·rhe′ic, a·men′or·rhoe′ic,** *adj.*

A·men-Ra (ä′mən rä′), *n.* *Egyptian Myth.* a god in whom Amen and Ra were combined: the god of the universe and the supreme Egyptian god during the period of Theban political supremacy. Also, **Amon-Ra.**

a men·sa et tho·ro (ā men′sə et thōr′ō, thôr′ō), *Law.* pertaining to or noting a divorce that forbids husband and wife to live together but does not dissolve the marriage bond: *a divorce a mensa et thoro.* [< L: lit., from board and bed. See MENSAL², TORUS]

am·ent¹ (am′ənt, ā′mənt), *n.* *Bot.* a spike of unisexual, apetalous flowers having scaly, usually deciduous bracts; catkin. [< L *ament(um)* strap, thong]

a·ment² (ā′ment, ā′mənt), *n.* one who has amentia. [< L *āment-* (s. of *āmēns* out of one's mind, mad), equiv. to *ā-* A-⁴ + *ment-*; see MENTAL] —**a·men·tal** (ā men′tᵊl), *adj.*

am·en·ta·ceous (am′ən tā′shəs), *adj.* *Bot.* 1. consisting of an ament. 2. bearing aments. [AMENT¹ + -ACEOUS]

a·men·tia (ā men′shə), *n.* *Psychiatry.* lack of intellectual development; imbecility; idiocy. [< L, equiv. to *āment-* (see AMENT²) + -ia -IA]

A, Ament

am·en·tif·er·ous (am′ən tif′ər əs), *adj.* *Bot.* bearing aments or catkins. [AMENT¹ + -I- + -FEROUS]

a·men·ti·form (ə men′tə fôrm′), *adj.* ament-shaped. [AMENT¹ + -I- + -FORM]

Amer., 1. America. 2. Also, **Amer** American.

a·merce (ə mûrs′), *v.t.,* **a·merced, a·merc·ing.** 1. to punish by imposing a fine not fixed by statute. 2. to punish by inflicting any discretionary or arbitrary penalty. [late ME *amercy* < AF *amerci(er)* (to) fine, repr. (*estre*) *a merci* (to be) at (someone's) mercy. See A-⁵, MERCY] —**a·merce′a·ble,** *adj.* —**a·merce′ment,** *n.* —**a·merc′er,** *n.*

A·mer·i·ca (ə mer′i kə), *n.* 1. See **United States.** 2. See **North America.** 3. See **South America.** 4. Also called **the Americas.** North and South America, considered together. [named after *Americus* Vespucius. See VESPUCCI]

Amer′ica First′ Par′ty, *U.S.* a political party formed in 1942, advocating isolationism, racism, etc.

A·mer·i·can (ə mer′i kən), *adj.* 1. of or pertaining to the United States of America or its inhabitants: *an American citizen.* 2. of or pertaining to North or South America: *the American continents.* 3. of or pertaining to the aboriginal Indians of North and South America, usually excluding the Eskimos, regarded as being a subdivision of the Mongolians, and marked generally by reddish to brownish skin, black hair, dark eyes, and prominent cheekbones. —*n.* 4. a citizen of the United States of America. 5. a native or an inhabitant of the western hemisphere. 6. an Indian of North or South America. 7. a steam locomotive having a four-wheeled front truck, four driving wheels, and no rear truck. [AMERIC(A) + -AN] —**A·mer′i·can·ly,** *adv.*

American, The, a novel (1877) by Henry James.

A·mer·i·ca·na (ə mer′i kan′ə, -kä′nə, -kā′nə), *n.* 1. (*often construed as pl.*) books, papers, maps, etc., relating to America, esp. to its history and geography. 2. (*construed as sing.*) a collection of such materials. [AMERIC(A) + -ANA]

Amer′ican ab′scess·root (ab′ses ro͞ot′, -ro͝ot′), bluebell (def. 3). [ABSCESS + ROOT¹]

Amer′ican al′oe. See **century plant.**

Amer′ican ap′ple, *Brit.* any large, well-shaped eating apple.

Amer′ican Beau′ty, an American variety of rose, periodically bearing large crimson blossoms.

Amer′ican bi′son, bison (def. 1).

Amer′ican bit′tern. See under **bittern** (def. 1).

Amer′ican bond′, a brickwood bond having a course of headers between five or six courses of stretchers. Also called **common bond.** See illus. under **bond.**

Amer′ican brook′lime. See under **brooklime.**

Amer′ican buf′falo, bison (def. 1).

Amer′ican chair′, *Brit.* See **Hitchcock chair.**

Amer′ican chame′leon. See under **chameleon** (def. 2).

Amer′ican cheese′, a type of Cheddar, esp. a mild processed cheese, made in America.

Amer′ican chest′nut. See under **chestnut** (def. 2).

Amer′ican Civ′il War′, the war in the U.S. between the North and the South, 1861–65.

Amer′ican cloth′, *Brit.* oilcloth.

Amer′ican cock′roach, a large, reddish-brown cockroach, *Periplaneta americana,* found originally in the southern U.S. but now widely distributed.

Amer′ican cop′per. See under **copper**¹ (def. 7).

Amer′ican cot′ton. See **upland cotton.** Also called **Amer′ican up′land cot′ton.**

Amer′ican cow′slip. See **shooting star** (def. 2).

Amer′ican crab′, a twiggy, stiff-branched tree, *Malus coronaria,* of southern central North America, having small fruit and rose-colored flowers that change to white. Also called **garland crab apple, sweet crab apple.**

Amer′ican cran′berry. See under **cranberry** (def. 1).

Amer′ican Directoire′, a style of American furniture making and related crafts from c1805 to c1815, corresponding to the French Directoire and English Regency styles.

Amer′ican ea′gle, the bald eagle, esp. as depicted on the coat of arms of the United States.

Amer′ican elm′, an elm, *Ulmus americana,* of North America, cultivated for shade and ornament: State tree of Massachusetts, Nebraska, and North Dakota.

Amer′ican Em′pire, a style of American furniture making and related crafts from c1815 to c1840, corresponding to the French Empire and late English Regency.

Amer′ican Eng′lish, the English language as used in the U.S.

Amer′ican Expedi′tionary Forc′es, troops sent to Europe by the U.S. Army during World War I. *Abbr.:* A.E.F.

Amer′ican Farm′ Bu′reau Federa′tion, an organization founded in 1920 to promote the interests of farmers, esp. in state and national legislation.

Amer′ican Federa′tion of La′bor, a federation of trade unions organized in 1886; united with C.I.O., 1955. *Abbr.:* A.F.L., A.F. of L.

Amer′ican flag′fish, flagfish (def. 1).

Amer′ican Fork′, a town in central Utah. 6373 (1960).

Amer′ican globe′flower, a perennial herb, *Trollius laxus,* of the northeastern and Great Lakes coastal areas of the U.S., having solitary, yellowish-green flowers.

Amer′ican hol′ly. See under **holly** (def. 1).

Amer′ican horn′beam. See under **hornbeam.**

Amer′ican In′dian, Indian (def. 1).

Amer′ican In′stitute of Ar′chitects, the principal association of architects in the U.S., founded in 1857. *Abbr.:* A.I.A.

Amer′ican ip′ecac, an herb, *Gillenia stipulata,* of the eastern coast of the U.S., having white flowers.

A·mer·i·can·ise (ə mer′i kə nīz′), *v.t., v.i.,* **-ised, -is·ing.** *Chiefly Brit.* Americanize. —**A·mer′i·can·i·sa′tion,** *n.* —**A·mer′i·can·is′er,** *n.*

A·mer·i·can·ism (ə mer′i kə niz′əm), *n.* 1. devotion to or preference for the United States of America and its institutions. 2. a custom, trait, or thing peculiar to the U.S. or its citizens. 3. a word, phrase, or other language feature that is especially characteristic of the English language as spoken in the U.S. [AMERICAN + -ISM]

A·mer·i·can·ist (ə mer′i kə nist), *n.* 1. a student of America, esp. of its history and geography. 2. a specialist in the cultures or languages of American Indians. 3. one who favors the U.S., its policies, etc. [AMERICAN + -IST] —**A·mer′i·can·is′tic,** *adj.*

Amer′ican i′vy. See **Virginia creeper.**

A·mer·i·can·ize (ə mer′i kə nīz′), *v.t., v.i.,* **-ized, -iz·ing.** to make or become American in character; assimilate to the customs and institutions of the U.S. Also, *esp. Brit.,* **Americanise.** [AMERICAN + -IZE] —**A·mer′i·can·i·za′tion,** *n.* —**A·mer′i·can·iz′er,** *n.*

Amer′ican La′bor par′ty, *U.S.* a former political party (1936–1956) organized in New York to gain independent political status for the labor and liberal factions of the Democratic Party.

Amer′ican lan′guage, English as spoken and written in the U.S. (usually prec. by *the*).

Amer′ican Le′gion, a society, organized in 1919, now composed of veterans of the armed forces of the U.S. in World Wars I and II and the Korean War.

Amer′ican leop′ard, (not used scientifically) a jaguar.

Amer′ican lin′den. See under **linden** (def. 1).

Amer′ican lo′tus. See **water chinquapin** (def. 1).

Amer′ican lung′wort. See **Virginia cowslip.**

Amer′ican mar′ten. See **pine marten** (def. 2).

Amer′ican mul′berry. See under **mulberry** (def. 2).

A·mer·i·ca·no (ə mer′i kan′ō, -kä′nō), *n., pl.* **-nos.** a cocktail made with bitters and sweet vermouth, and containing soda water. Also called **Amer′ica′no cock′tail.** [< Sp: American]

Amer′ican or′gan, a reed organ having a suction bellows that draws the air in through the reeds.

Amer′ican os′trich, (not used scientifically) a **rhea,** as distinguished from the true ostrich.

Amer′ican par′ty. See under **know-nothing** (def. 3). Also called **Know-Nothing party.**

Amer′ican plan′, (in hotels) a system of paying a single fixed rate that includes both room and meals.

Amer′ican Revised′ Ver′sion, a revision of the Bible, based chiefly on the Revised Version of the Bible, published in the U.S. in 1901. Also called **American Standard Version.**

Amer′ican Revolu′tion, the war between Great Britain and her American colonies, 1775–83, by which the colonies won their independence.

Amer′ican rig′, a rig for drilling oil and gas wells by using a chisel bit dropped from a considerable height.

Amer′ican sa′ble, 1. the pine marten, *Martes americana,* of the U.S. and Canada. 2. the fur of this animal.

Amer′ican sad′dle horse′, one of a breed of horses, raised originally in the U.S., that have high-stepping gaits and are bred to the three-gaited or five-gaited type. Also called **saddle horse.**

Amer′ican Samo′a, the part of Samoa belonging to the U.S., comprising mainly Tutuila and the Manua Islands. 20,051 (est. 1960); 76 sq. mi. *Cap.:* Pago Pago. Cf. **Samoa, Western Samoa.**

Amer′ican sen′na. See **wild senna.**

Amer′ican smoke′ tree′, a small tree, *Cotinus obovatus,* of the central southern U.S., having yellowish flowers and clusters of fleshy fruit with silky plumes. Also called **chittamwood.**

Amer′ican Span′ish, Spanish as used in Latin America.

Amer′ican Stand′ard Ver′sion. See **American Revised Version.**

Amer′ican star′, *Heraldry.* mullet².

Amer′ican Stock′ Exchange′, the second largest stock exchange in the U.S., located in New York City. Former name, **New York Curb Exchange.** Cf. **New York Stock Exchange.**

Amer′ican Trag′edy, An, a novel (1925) by Dreiser.

Amer′ican trypanosomi′asis, *Pathol.* See **Chagas' disease.**

Amer′ican twist′, *Tennis.* a service in which the ball is spun so as to bounce high and to the left of the receiver.

Amer′ican wa′ter span′iel, one of an American breed of medium-sized water spaniels having a thick, curly, chocolate-colored or liver-colored coat.

Amer′ican way′faring tree′, hobblebush.

Amer′ican white′ hel′lebore. See under **hellebore** (def. 2).

Amer′ican wood′bine. See under **woodbine** (def. 2).

Amer′ican worm′seed. See **Mexican tea.**

am·er·i·ci·um (am′ə rish′ē əm), *n.* *Chem.* a radioactive element, one of the products of high-energy helium bombardment of uranium and plutonium. *Symbol:* Am; *at. no.:* 95. [AMERIC(A) + -IUM]

A·me·ri·go Ves·puc·ci (ə mer′ə gō′ ve spo͞o′chē, -spyo͞o′-; *It.* ä′me RĒ′gô ves po͞ot′chē). See **Vespucci, Amerigo.**

Am·er·ind (am′ə rind), *n.* 1. a member of any of the aboriginal Indian or Eskimo peoples of North or South America. 2. any of the indigenous languages of the American Indians. [AMER(ICAN) + IND(IAN)] —**Am′er·in′dian,** *adj., n.* —**Am′er·in′dic,** *adj.*

AmerInd, Amerind (def. 2).

am·er·is·tic (am′ə ris′tik, ā′me ris′-), *adj.* *Bot.* not divided into parts; having no meristem. [< Gk *amérist-(os)* undivided (*a-* A-⁶ + *meristós* divided) + -IC] —**am′er·ism,** *n.*

A·mers·foort (ä′mərz fōrt′, -fôrt′, -mərs-), *n.* a city in the central Netherlands. 67,658 (1959).

AmerSp, American Spanish.

Ames (āmz), *n.* a city in central Iowa. 27,003 (1960).

ames·ace (āmz′ās′, amz′-), *n.* ambsace.

Ames·bur·y (āmz′ber′ē, -bə rē), *n.* a town in NE Massachusetts. 9625 (1960).

A·me·sha Spen·ta (ä′me shə spen′tə), *Zoroastrianism.* any of the personified attributes of Ahura Mazda. Also called **Spenta Amesha.** [< Avestan, equiv. to *amesha* angel + *spenta* good]

a·met·a·bol·ic (ā′met ə bol′ik), *adj.* *Zool.* undergoing slight or no metamorphosis. Also, **a·me·tab·o·lous** (ā′mə tab′ə ləs). [A-⁶ + METABOLIC]

am·e·thyst (am′i thist), *n.* 1. a coarsely crystallized purple or violet quartz, used as a gem. 2. a purplish tint. —*adj.* 3. having the color of amethyst. 4. containing or set with an amethyst or amethysts: *an amethyst brooch.* [ME *ametist* < L *amethyst(us)* < Gk *améthystos* not intoxicating, not intoxicated (so called from a belief that it prevented drunkenness), equiv. to *a-* A-⁶ + *methys-* (var. s. of *methýein* to intoxicate; see METHYLENE) + *-tos* verbal adj. suffix] —**am·e·thys·tine** (am′i this′tin, -tīn), *adj.* —**am′e·thyst·like′,** *adj.*

am·e·tro·pi·a (am′i trō′pē ə), *n. Ophthalm.* an abnormal condition of the eye causing faulty refraction of light rays, as in astigmatism, myopia, etc. [< Gk *ámetr(os)* unmeasured (*a-* A-⁶ + *métr(on) measure* + *-os* adj. suffix) + -OPIA] —**am·e·trop·ic** (am′i trop′ik), *adj.*

Am·ha·ra (äm här′ə), *n.* a former kingdom in E Africa: now a province in NW Ethiopia. *Cap.:* Gondar.

Am·har·ic (am har′ik, äm här′ik), *n.* **1.** the Semitic language which is the official language of Ethiopia. —*adj.* **2.** of or pertaining to this language. [AMHAR(A) + -IC]

Am·herst (am′ərst), *n.* **1. Jeffrey, Baron,** 1717–97, British field marshal: governor general of British North America 1760–63. **2.** a town in N Ohio. 6750 (1960).

a·mi (A mē′), *n., pl.* **a·mis** (A mē′). *French.* **1.** friend. **2.** *Slang.* (on the continent of Europe) a citizen of the U.S.; American.

a·mi·a·ble (ā′mē ə bəl), *adj.* **1.** having or showing agreeable personal qualities; kind; pleasant: *an amiable disposition.* **2.** friendly; sociable: *an amiable greeting; an amiable gathering.* **3.** agreeable; willing to accept the wishes, decisions, or suggestions of another or others. **4.** *Obs.* lovable or lovely. [ME < MF < L *amīcābil(is)* AMICABLE] —**a′mi·a·bil′i·ty, a′mi·a·ble·ness,** *n.* —**a′mi·a·bly,** *adv.*
—**Syn. 1.** gracious, agreeable. **2.** amicable. —**Ant. 2.** unfriendly; rude.

am·i·an·thus (am′ē an′thəs), *n. Mineral.* a fine variety of asbestos, with delicate, flexible filaments. [< L *amiantus* < Gk *amíantos,* equiv. to *a-* A-⁶ + *mian-* (s. of *miaínein* to defile, make impure) + *-tos* verbal adj. suffix] —**am·i·an·thine** (am′ē an′thən, -thin), *adj.* —**am′i·an′thoid, am′i·an·thoi′dal,** *adj.*

am·ic (am′ik), *adj. Chem.* of or pertaining to an amide or amine. [AM(IDE) or AM(INE) + -IC]

am·i·ca·ble (am′ə kə bəl), *adj.* characterized by or exhibiting good will; friendly; peaceable: *an amicable settlement.* [< LL *amīcābil(is),* equiv. to *amīc(us)* friend, friendly + *-ābilis* -ABLE] —**am′i·ca·bil′i·ty, am′i·ca·ble·ness,** *n.* —**am′i·ca·bly,** *adv.*
—**Syn.** agreeable.

am′icable num′ber, *Math.* either of a pair of positive integers in which each member is equal to the sum of the submultiples of the other, as 220 and 284.

am·ice¹ (am′is), *n. Eccles.* an oblong vestment, usually of white linen, worn about the neck and shoulders and partly under the alb. [late ME *amyse,* perh. < MF *amis,* pl. of *amit* < L *amict(us)* wrap, equiv. to *amic-,* base of *amicīre* to wrap around (*am-* AMBI- + *-ic-,* var. s. of *iacere* to throw) + *-tus* n. suffix, 4th decl.]

am·ice² (am′is), *n.* almuce. [late ME *amisse* < MF *aumusse, aumuce* < Sp *almucio,* equiv. to *al* the (< Ar) + *mucio* (< Gmc; cf. G *Mütze* cap]

A·mi′ci prism′ (ə mē′chē), *Optics.* a reflecting prism having an isosceles, right-triangle shape, the hypotenuse of which has been ground and polished, deviating a beam of light by 90° and producing an image that is upside down and inverted from left to right. Also called **Ami′ci direct′-vision′ prism′, Ami′ci prism′ sys′tem, Ami′ci roof′ prism′, roof prism.** [named after G. B. *Amici* (1784–1863), Italian astronomer]

a·mi·cus cu·ri·ae (ə mī′kəs kyŏŏr′ē ē′), *pl.* **a·mi·ci cu·ri·ae** (ə mī′kī kyŏŏr′ē ē′). *Law.* a person, not a party to the litigation, who volunteers or is invited by the court to give advice upon some matter pending before it. Also called **friend of the court.** [< L]

a·mi·cus hu·ma·ni ge·ne·ris (ä mē′kŏŏs hŏŏ mä′nē gen′e ris; *Eng.* ə mī′kəs hyŏŏ mā′nī jen′ə ris), *Latin.* a philanthropist. [lit., friend of the human race]

a·mi·cus us·que ad a·ras (ä mē′kŏŏs ŏŏs′kwe äd ä′räs; *Eng.* ə mī′kəs us′kwē ad ā′rəs), *Latin.* a friend to the last degree.

a·mid (ə mid′), *prep.* **1.** in the midst of or surrounded by; among. **2.** during; in or throughout the course of. Also, **amidst.** [ME *amidde,* OE *amidd(an)* for *on middan* in (the) middle. See MID¹]
—**Syn. 1.** See **among.**

amid-, var. of **amido-** before a vowel: *amidase.*

A·mi·da (ä′mē dä′), *n. Buddhism.* See under **Pure Land.** Sanskrit, **Amitabha.**

A·mi·dah (ä mē′dä), *n. Judaism.* a liturgical prayer that is recited in standing position at each of the three daily services and consists of three opening blessings, three closing blessings, and one intermediate blessing on the Sabbath and holy days and 13 intermediate blessings on other days. [< Heb *ʿamīdhāh* a standing]

am·i·dase (am′i dās′), *n. Biochem.* an enzyme that catalyzes the hydrolysis of an acid amide. [AMID- + -ASE]

am·i·date (am′i dāt′), *v.t.,* **-dat·ed, -dat·ing.** *Chem.* to convert into an amide. [AMID- + -ATE¹] —**am′i·da′tion,** *n.*

am·ide (am′īd, -id), *n. Chem.* **1.** a metallic derivative of ammonia in which the $-NH_2$ group is retained, as potassium amide, KNH_2. **2.** an organic compound obtained by replacing the –OH group in acids by the $-NH_2$ group. **3.** an organic compound formed from ammonia by replacing a hydrogen atom by an acyl group. [AM(MONIA) + -IDE] —**a·mid·ic** (ə mid′ik), *adj.*

am·i·din (am′i din), *n.* the soluble matter of starch. [< ML *amid(um)* starch (alter. of L *amylum;* see AMYL) + -IN²]

am·i·dine (am′i dēn′, -din), *n. Chem.* any of a group of compounds containing the $-C(-NH_2)=NH$ group, some of which have marked pharmacological action. [AMID- + -INE²]

amido-, 1. a combining form of the amido group, used esp. before a consonant: *amidogen.* **2.** (erroneously) **amino-.** Also, *esp. before a vowel,* **amid-.** [AMIDE + -O-]

a·mi·do·cy·an·o·gen (ə mē′dō sī an′ə jən, am′i dō-), *n. Chem.* cyanamide. [AMIDO- + CYANOGEN]

a·mi·do·gen (ə mē′də jən, ə mid′ə-), *n. Chem. Obs.* (esp. of inorganic compounds) the NH_2- group. [AMIDO- + -GEN]

am·i·dol (am′i dōl′, -dôl′, -dol′), *n. Chem.* a colorless, crystalline powder, $HOC_6H_4(NH_2)_2·2HCl$, derived from phenol, used chiefly as a photographic developer. [AMID- + -OL¹]

a·mi·do·py·rine (ə mē′dō pī′rēn, am′i dō-), *n. Pharm.* aminopyrine.

a·mid·ships (ə mid′ships), *Naut., Aeron.* —*adv.* **1.** in or toward the middle part of a vessel or aircraft; midway between the ends. **2.** along the central fore-and-aft line of a vessel or aircraft. —*adj.* **3.** of, pertaining to, or located in the middle part of a ship or aircraft. Also, **a·mid′ship.** [AMID + SHIP + -S¹]

a·midst (ə midst′), *prep.* amid. [ME *amiddes;* see AMID, -S¹; for *-t* see AGAINST, etc.]

a·mie (A mē′), *n., pl.* **a·mies** (A mē′). *French.* fem. form of **ami.**

A·mi·el (ā′mē əl, am′ē-), *n.* a boy's given name.

Am·i·ens (am′ē ənz; *Fr.* A myaN′), *n.* a city in and the capital of Somme, in N France: cathedral; battles 1914, 1918, 1944. 109,869 (1962).

a·mi·ga (ə mē′gə; ä mē′-; *Sp.* ä mē′gä), *n., pl.* **-gas** (-gəz; *Sp.* -gäs). a female friend. [< Sp; fem. of AMIGO]

Am·i·gen (am′i jən), *n. Trademark.* a protein prepared by predigesting hog pancreas and milk with various enzymes, used intravenously in the treatment of malnutrition and widespread burns and as an aid to surgical convalescence.

a·mi·go (ə mē′gō, ä mē′-; *Sp.* ä mē′gô), *n., pl.* **-gos** (-gōz; *Sp.* -gôs). **1.** a friend. **2.** a native of a Spanish-speaking country who is friendly toward Americans. [< Sp < L *amīcus.* See AMI]

a·mim·i·a (ā mim′ē ə), *n. Med.* the inability to express ideas by means of gestures or signs. [< NL, equiv. to *a-* A-⁶ + Gk *mîm(os)* actor, mimic + *-ia* -IA]

amin-, var. of **amino-** before a vowel.

am·i·nase (am′ə nās′), *n. Biochem.* any of a group of enzymes that catalyze the hydrolysis of amino compounds, releasing the amino group and liberating nitrogen. [AMIN- + -ASE]

am·i·nate (am′ə nāt′), *v.t.,* **-nat·ed, -nat·ing.** *Chem.* to introduce an amino group into (a compound). [AMINE + -ATE¹] —**am′i·na′tion,** *n.*

a·mine (ə mēn′, am′in), *n. Chem.* any of a class of compounds derived from ammonia by replacement of one or more hydrogen atoms with organic groups. [AM(MONIUM) + -INE²] —**a·min·ic** (ə mē′nik, ə min′ik), *adj.* —**a·min·i·ty** (ə min′i tē), *n.*

-amine, var. of **amino-** as final element of a compound word: *Dramamine.*

a·mi·no (ə mē′nō, am′ə nō′), *adj. Chem.* containing the amino group. [independent use of AMINO-]

amino-, a combining form of the amino group, used esp. before a consonant: *aminobenzene.* Also, **-amine;** *esp. before a vowel,* **amin-.** [AMINE + -O-]

a·mi′no·a·ce′tic ac′id (ə mē′nō ə sē′tik, am′ə nō-, ə mē′nō-, am′ə nō-), *Chem.* glycine. [AMINO- + ACETIC ACID]

ami′no ac′id, *Chem.* any of a class of organic compounds that contains at least one carboxyl group and one amino group: the alpha-amino acids, $RCH(NH_2)COOH$, are the building blocks from which proteins are constructed.

a·mi·no·ben·zene (ə mē′nō ben′zēn, -ben zēn′, am′ə nō-), *n. Chem.* aniline (def. 1). [AMINO- + BENZENE]

a·mi′no·ben·zo′ic ac′id (ə mē′nō ben zō′ik, am′ə nō-, ə mē′nō-, am′ə nō-), *Chem.* any of three isomers having the formula $H_2NC_6H_4COOH$, derived from benzoic acid, esp. the para isomer, para-aminobenzoic acid. [AMINO- + BENZOIC]

ami′no group′, *Chem.* the univalent group, $-NH_2$. Also called **ami′no rad′ical.**

am·i·noph·er·ase (am′ə nof′ə rās′), *n. Biochem.* an enzyme which catalyzes transamination; transaminase. [AMINO- + Gk *phér(ein)* (to) bear + -ASE]

a·mi·no·phyl·line (ə mē′nō fil′in, -ēn, am′ə nō-), *n. Pharm.* a white or yellowish, water-soluble powder or granules, $(C_7H_8N_4O_2)_2·C_2H_4(NH_2)_2·2H_2O$, having a slight ammoniacal odor and bitter taste: used in medicine chiefly to relieve bronchial spasm in asthma, in the treatment of certain heart conditions, and as a diuretic. Also called **theophylline ethylenediamine.** [AMINO- + (THEO)PHYLLINE]

a·mi·no·plast (ə mē′nə plast′, am′ə nō-), *n. Chem.* See **amino resin.** [AMINO- + PLAST(IC)]

a·mi·no·py·rine (ə mē′nə pī′rēn, am′ə nō-), *n. Pharm.* a white, water-soluble, crystalline solid, $C_{13}H_{17}N_3O$, used chiefly to reduce or prevent fever and to relieve pain. Also, **amidopyrine.** [(DIMETHYL)AMINE + -O- + (ANTI)PYRINE]

a·mi·no·quin naph·tho·ate (ə mē′nō kwin naf′thō āt′, am′ə nō-), *Pharm.* pamaquine. [AMINO- + (PAMA)QUIN(E) + NAPHTO- + -ATE²]

ami′no res′in, *Chem.* any of the class of thermosetting resins formed by the interaction of an amine, as urea, and an aldehyde, as formaldehyde: used chiefly as adhesives for laminated materials and as coatings for paper and textiles. Also called **aminoplast.**

a·mi′no·suc·cin′ic ac′id (ə mē′nō sək sin′ik, am′ə nō-, ə mē′nō-, am′ə nō-), *Biochem.* See **aspartic acid.** [AMINO- + SUCCINIC]

a·mir (ə mēr′), *n.* **1.** a Muslim prince, lord, or nobleman. **2.** Also called **sharif, sherif.** a title of honor of the descendants of Muhammad. **3.** (*cap.*) the former title of the ruler of Afghanistan. **4.** a title of certain Turkish officials. Also, **ameer.** [< Ar: commander; see EMIR]

a·mir·ate (ə mēr′it, -āt), *n.* the office or rank of an amir. Also, **ameerate.** [AMIR + -ATE¹]

A·mis (ā′mis), *n.* **Kingsley,** born 1922, English novelist.

A·mish (ä′mish, am′ish), *adj.* **1.** of or pertaining to any of the strict Mennonite groups in Pennsylvania, Ohio, Indiana, and Canada, descended from the followers of Jakob Ammann, a Swiss Mennonite bishop of the 17th century. —*n.* **2.** the Amish people. [< G *amisch,* after Jakob *Ammann;* see -ISH¹]

a·miss (ə mis′), *adv.* **1.** out of the proper course, order, or condition; improperly; wrongly; astray: *She certainly went amiss in quitting school. Did I speak amiss?* **2. take amiss,** to be offended at; misunderstand; resent: *I couldn't think of a way to present my view so that no one would take it amiss.* —*adj.* (usually used predicatively) **3.** improper; wrong; faulty: *I think something is amiss in your calculations.* [ME *amis,* equiv. to *a-* A-¹ + *mis* wrong. See MISS¹]

A·mi·ta·bha (u′mi tä′bə), *n. Sanskrit.* Amida.

am·i·tate (am′i tāt′, -tit), *n. Anthropol.* a close social relationship between a paternal aunt and her niece. [< L *amit(a)* paternal aunt + -ATE¹]

A·mite′ Cit′y (ə mēt′), a town in SE Louisiana. 3316 (1960).

am·i·to·sis (am′i tō′sis), *n. Biol.* the direct method of cell division, characterized by simple cleavage of the nucleus without the formation of chromosomes. [A-⁶ + MITOSIS] —**am·i·tot·ic** (am′i tot′ik), *adj.* —**am′i·tot′i·cal·ly,** *adv.*

A·mit·tai (ə mit′ī), *n.* the father of Jonah. II Kings 14:25. Also, *Douay Bible,* **Amathi.**

am·i·ty (am′i tē), *n.* friendship; peaceful harmony; mutual understanding and a peaceful relationship, esp. between nations; peace; accord. [late ME *amit(i)e* < MF *amitie,* OF *amiste(t)* < VL **amicitāt-.* See AMI, -ITY]

Am·i·ty (am′i tē), *n.* a girl's given name.

Am·i·ty·ville (am′i tē vil), *n.* a town in SE New York. 8318 (1960).

A.M.L.S., Master of Arts in Library Science.

Am·man (äm′män), *n.* a city in and the capital of Jordan, in the W part. 103,304 (1952). Also called **Rabbath Ammon.**

Am·ma·na·ti (äm′mä nä′tē; *It.* äm′mä nä′tē), *n.* **Bar·to·lom·me·o** (bär′tô lôm me′ô), 1511–92, Italian architect and sculptor.

am·me·ter (am′mē′tər), *n. Elect.* an instrument for measuring current in amperes. [AM(PERE) + -METER]

am·mi·a·ceous (am′ē ā′shəs), *adj. Bot.* apiaceous; umbelliferous. [< NL *Ammi* genus name (L *ammi* < Gk: kind of umbelliferous plant) + -ACEOUS]

Am·mi·a·nus (am′ē ā′nəs), *n.* **Mar·cel·li·nus** (mär′sə lī′nəs), A.D. c325–c398, Roman historian.

am·mine (am′ēn, ə mēn′), *n. Chem.* **1.** a compound containing one or more ammonia molecules in coordinate linkage. **2.** any coordination compound containing one or more ammonia molecules bonded to a metal ion. [AMM(ONIA) + -INE²]

Am·mi·shad·dai (am′i shad′ī), *n.* the father of Ahiezer, the Danite. Num. 1:12; 2:25. Also, *Douay Bible,* **Am·mi·sad·dai** (am′i sad′ī, -sad′ā ī′).

am·mo (am′ō), *n. Informal.* ammunition. [AMM(UNITION) + *-o* n. suffix as in AUTO]

am·mo·cete (am′ə sēt′), *n.* the larval stage of a lamprey. Also, **am′mo·coete′.** [< NL *ammocoetē(s),* lit. something bedded in sand < Gk *ámmo(s)* sand + *koítē* bed]

Am·mon (am′ən), *n.* **1.** the classical name of the Egyptian divinity Amen, whom the Greeks identified with Zeus, the Romans with Jupiter. **2.** the ancient country of the Ammonites, east of the Jordan River.

am·mo·nal (am′ə nal′), *n.* a high explosive consisting chiefly of powdered aluminum, ammonium nitrate, and TNT. [AMMON(IUM) + AL(UMINUM)]

am·mo·nate (am′ə nāt′), *n. Chem.* ammoniate (def. 2). —**am′mo·na′tion,** *n.*

ammoni-, var. of **ammonio-,** esp. before a vowel.

am·mo·nia (ə mōn′yə, ə mō′nē ə), *n. Chem.* **1.** a colorless, pungent, suffocating, highly water-soluble, gaseous compound, NH_3, usually produced by the direct combination of nitrogen and hydrogen gases: used chiefly for refrigeration and in the manufacture of commercial chemicals and laboratory reagents. **2.** Also called **ammonia solution, ammonia water, aqua ammoniae, aqueous ammonia.** this gas dissolved in water; ammonium hydroxide. [< NL, so called as being obtained from sal *ammoniac.* See AMMONIAC]

ammo′nia al′um, *Chem.* See **aluminum ammonium sulfate.**

am·mo·ni·ac (ə mō′nē ak′), *n.* **1.** Also, **am·mo·ni·a·cum** (am′ə nī′ə kəm). See **gum ammoniac.** —*adj.* **2.** ammoniacal. [< L *ammōniac(um)* < Gk *ammōniakón* (neut. of *ammōniakós* of AMMON; see -I-, -AC), applied to a salt and a gum resin said to come from near the Shrine of Ammon in Libya]

am·mo·ni·a·cal (am′ə nī′ə kəl), *adj.* **1.** consisting of, containing, or using ammonia. **2.** like ammonia. Also, **ammoniac.** [AMMONIAC + -AL¹]

ammo′nia liq′uor, *Chem.* a concentrated solution of ammonia, ammonium compounds, and sulfur compounds, obtained as a by-product in the destructive distillation of bituminous coal. Also, **ammoni′acal liq′uor.** Also called **gas liquor.**

ammo′nia solu′tion, *Chem.* ammonia (def. 2).

am·mo·ni·ate (ə mō′nē āt′), *v.,* **-at·ed, -at·ing,** *n. Chem.* —*v.t.* **1.** to treat or cause to unite with ammonia. —*n.* **2.** Also, **ammonate.** a compound formed by adding ammonia in stoichiometric proportions to another compound, as $CaCl_2·8NH_3$ or $CuSO_4·4NH_3$. [AMMONI(A) + -ATE¹] —**am·mo′ni·a′tion,** *n.*

ammo′nia wa′ter, *Chem.* ammonia (def. 2).

am·mon·ic (ə mon′ik, ə mō′nik), *adj.* of or pertaining to ammonia or ammonium. Also, **am·mon′i·cal.** [AMMON(IA) + -IC]

am·mon·i·fi·ca·tion (ə mon′ə fə kā′shən, ə mō′nə-), *n.* **1.** the act of impregnating with ammonia, as in the manufacture of fertilizer. **2.** the state of being so impregnated. **3.** the formation of ammonia or its compounds, as in soil by soil organisms. [AMMONI(A) + -FICATION]

am·mon·i·fy (ə mon′ə fī′, ə mō′nə-), *v.,* **-fied, -fy·ing.** —*v.t.* **1.** to combine or impregnate with ammonia. **2.** to form into ammonia or ammonium compounds. —*v.i.* **3.** to become ammonified; produce ammonification. [AMMONI(A) + -FY]

ammonio-, a combining form of **ammonia** or **ammonium,** used esp. before a consonant: *ammonioferric.* Also, *esp. before a vowel,* **ammoni-.**

am·mo′ni·o·fer′ric ox′alate (ə mō′nē ō fer′ik, ə mō′-), *Chem.* See **ferric ammonium oxalate.** [AMMONIO- + FERRIC]

am·mo·nite¹ (am′ə nīt′), *n.* one of the coiled, chambered fossil shells of a cephalopod mollusk of the extinct order *Ammonoidea.* [< NL *Ammōnītes* < ML (*cornū*) *Ammōn(is)* (lit., horn of Ammon) + *-ites* -ITE¹; fossil so called from resemblance to horn of Jupiter AMMON] —**am·mo·nit·ic** (am′ə nit′ik), *adj.* —**am·mon·i·toid** (ə mon′i toid′), *adj.*

Ammonite

am·mo·nite² (am′ə nīt′), *n.* a nitrogenous mixture consisting chiefly of dried animal fats, usually obtained from livestock carcasses, and used as a fertilizer. [AMMO(NIUM) + NIT(RAT)E]

Am·mon·ite (am′ə nīt′), *n.* **1.** an inhabitant of Ammon. **—***adj.* **2.** of or pertaining to the Ammonites. [AMMON + -ITE[1]] **—Am′mon·it′ish,** *adj.*

am·mo·ni·um (ə mō′nē əm), *n. Chem.* the univalent ion, NH_4^+, or group, NH_4, which plays the part of a metal in the salt formed when ammonia reacts with an acid. [< NL; see AMMONIA, -IUM]

ammo′nium ac′etate, *Chem.* a white, crystalline, deliquescent, water-soluble solid, $NH_4(C_2H_3O_2)$, used chiefly in the manufacture of dyes and meat preservatives.

ammo′nium al′um, *Chem.* See **aluminum ammonium sulfate.**

ammo′nium bicar′bonate, *Chem.* a white, crystalline, water-soluble solid, NH_4HCO_3, used chiefly in the manufacture of baking powder.

ammo′nium biflu′oride, *Chem.* a white, crystalline, water-soluble, poisonous solid, NH_4HF_2, used chiefly for cleaning and sterilizing brewing and dairying equipment.

ammo′nium binox′alate, *Chem.* a colorless, crystalline, water-soluble, poisonous solid, $NH_4HC_2O_4 \cdot H_2O$, used chiefly for removing ink stains from fabrics.

ammo′nium car′bamate, *Chem.* a white, crystalline, water-soluble, extremely volatile powder, $H_2NCOONH_4$, used as a fertilizer.

ammo′nium car′bonate, *Chem.* a water-soluble mixture of ammonium bicarbonate and ammonium carbamate, occurring either as a white powder or in colorless, hard, crystalline masses: used chiefly in the manufacture of smelling salts and baking powder.

ammo′nium chlo′ride, *Chem., Pharm.* a white, crystalline, water-soluble powder, NH_4Cl, which produces a cooling sensation to the tongue, used chiefly in the manufacture of dry cells, in electroplating, and in medicine as an expectorant. Also called **sal ammoniac.**

ammo′nium chrome′ al′um, *Chem.* See **chrome alum** (def. 1).

ammo′nium chro′mic sul′fate, *Chem.* See **chrome alum** (def. 1).

ammo′nium hydrox′ide, *Chem.* a basic compound, NH_4OH, existing only in solution, formed by dissolving ammonia gas in water. Cf. **ammonia.**

ammo′nium lac′tate, *Chem.* a colorless to yellow, water-soluble, syrupy liquid, $CH_3CHOHCOONH_4$, used chiefly in electroplating.

ammo′nium ni′trate, *Chem.* a white, crystalline, water-soluble powder, NH_4NO_3, usually produced by reacting nitric acid with vaporous ammonia: used chiefly in explosives, fertilizers, freezing mixtures, and in the manufacture of nitrous oxide.

ammo′nium pur′pu·rate (pûr′pyə rit, -rāt′), *Chem.* murexide. [PURPUR(IC) + -ATE[2]]

ammo′nium salt′, *Chem.* any salt containing the NH_4^+ ion, formed by the neutralization of ammonium hydroxide by an acid.

ammo′nium sel′enate, *Chem.* a colorless, crystalline, water-soluble solid, $(NH_4)_2SeO_4$, used as a mothproofing agent.

ammo′nium ste′arate, *Chem.* a tan, waxlike, water-insoluble solid, $CH_3(CH_2)_{16}COONH_4$, used chiefly in the manufacture of cosmetics.

ammo′nium sul′fate, *Chem.* a white, crystalline, water-soluble solid, $(NH_4)_2SO_4$, used chiefly as a fertilizer.

ammo′nium thiocy′anate, *Chem.* a colorless, crystalline, deliquescent, water-soluble solid, NH_4SCN, used chiefly as a herbicide, and as a fixative in textile printing.

ammo′nium thiosul′fate, *Chem.* a white, crystalline, water-soluble solid, $(NH_4)_2S_2O_3$, used chiefly in the manufacture of cleaning compounds for alloys having a tin or lead base.

am·mo·no (am′ə nō′), *adj. Chem.* of, containing, or derived from ammonia. [independent use of AMMONO-]

ammono-, a combining form of **ammonia:** *ammonolysis.*

am·mo·noid (am′ə noid′), *n.* any cephalopod mollusk of the extinct order *Ammonoidea,* from the Devonian to the Cretaceous periods, having a coiled, chambered shell. [< NL *Ammonoid(ea),* equiv. to *Ammon(ites)* name of the order + *-oidea* -OIDEA; see AMMONITE[2]]

am·mo·nol·y·sis (am′ə nol′i sis), *n., pl.* **-ses** (-sēz′). *Chem.* decomposition in which ammonia is resolved into other compounds by being a source of H^+ and NH_2. [AMMONO- + -LYSIS] **—am·mo·no·lit·ic** (ə mōn′ᵊlit′ik, am′ə nᵊlit′-), *adj.*

am·mo·no·lyze (ə mōn′ᵊlīz′), *v.,* **-lyzed, -lyz·ing.** *Chem.* **—***v.t.* **1.** to subject to ammonolysis. **—***v.i.* **2.** to undergo ammonolysis. [AMMONOL(YSIS) + -IZE]

am·moph·i·lous (ə mof′ə ləs), *adj. Biol.* living or growing in sand. [< Gk *ámmo(s)* sand + -PHILOUS]

am·mu·ni·tion (am′yə nish′ən), *n.* **1.** all the material used in discharging all types of firearms or any weapon that throw projectiles; powder, shot, shrapnel, bullets, cartridges, and the means of igniting and exploding them, as primers and fuzes. Chemicals, bombs, grenades, missiles, pyrotechnics, and rockets are also ammunition. **2.** any material, means, weapons, etc. used in any conflict: *a crude ammunition of stones.* **3.** *Informal.* information, advice, or supplies to help win one's point or support one's argument: *Give me some ammunition for the debate.* **4.** *Obs.* military supplies generally. [< F *amunition* (now obs.) for *la munition* the munition, wrongly analyzed as *l'amunition*]

am·ne·sia (am nē′zhə), *n.* loss of a large block of interrelated memories; complete or partial loss of memory. [< NL < Gk *amnēsía,* var. of *amnēstía* oblivion. See AMNESTY] **—am·nes·tic** (am nes′tik), *adj.*

am·ne·si·ac (am nē′zhē ak′, -zē-), *n.* **1.** a person affected by amnesia. **—***adj.* **2.** Also, **am·ne·sic** (am nē′sik, -zik). displaying the symptoms of amnesia. [AMNESI(A) + -AC, after such pairs as *mania, maniac*]

am·nes·ty (am′ni stē), *n., pl.* **-ties,** *v.,* **-tied, -ty·ing.** **—***n.* **1.** a general pardon for offenses against a government. **2.** the granting of immunity for past offenses against the laws of war. **3.** *Law.* an act of forgiveness for past offenses, esp. to a class of persons as a whole. **4.** a forgetting or overlooking of any past offense: *Agreeing to a mutual amnesty, they renewed their friendship.* **—***v.t.* **5.** to grant amnesty to; pardon. [< Gk *amnēstía* oblivion, equiv. to *ámnēst(os)* forgetting (*a-* A-[6] + *mnēs-* remember + *-tos* verbal suffix) + *-ia* -Y[3]]

am·ni·o·cen·te·sis (am′nē ō sen tē′sis), *n.* a surgical procedure for obtaining a sample of amniotic fluid from the uterus of a pregnant woman by inserting a hollow needle through the abdominal wall, used in diagnosing possible obstetric complications or genetic defects. [AMNIO(N) + NL *centesis,* puncture]

am·ni·on (am′nē ən), *n., pl.* **-ni·ons, -ni·a** (-nē ə). **1.** *Anat., Zool.* the innermost of the embryonic or fetal membranes of reptiles, birds, and mammals; the sac in which the embryo is suspended. **2.** *Zool.* a similar membrane of insects and other invertebrates. [< Gk, equiv. to *amn(ós)* lamb + *-ion* dim. suffix]

am·ni·ote (am′nē ōt′), *n.* any vertebrate of the group *Amniota,* comprising the reptiles, birds, and mammals, characterized by having an amnion during the embryonic stage. Cf. **anamniote.** [back formation from AMNIOTIC, parallel to NL *amniota* (neut. pl.)]

am·ni·ot·ic (am′nē ot′ik), *adj. Anat., Zool.* of, pertaining to, or having an amnion. Also, **am·ni·on·ic** (am′nē on′ik), **am·nic** (am′nik). [*amnio(s)* (pseudo-Gk var. of AMNION) + -TIC]

amniot′ic flu′id, *Anat., Zool.* the watery fluid in the amniotic sac, in which the embryo is suspended.

amn't (ant, am′ənt), *Dial.* am not. **—Usage.** See **ain't.**

am·o·bar·bi·tal (am′ō bär′bi tal′, -tōl′), *n. Pharm.* a colorless, crystalline barbiturate, $C_{11}H_{18}N_2O_3$, used chiefly as a sedative. [AM(YL) + -O- + BARBITAL]

a·moe·ba (ə mē′bə), *n., pl.* **-bae** (-bē), **-bas.** *Zool.* **1.** a microscopic, one-celled animal consisting of a naked mass of protoplasm constantly changing in shape as it moves and engulfs food. **2.** a protozoan of the genus *Amoeba.* Also, **ameba.** [< NL < Gk *amoibḗ* change, alternation, akin to *ameíbein* to exchange] **—a·moe′ba·like′,** *adj.*

Amoeba
A, Pseudopodia; B, Food vacuole; C, Nucleus; D, Contractile vacuole

am·oe·bae·an (am′ə bē′ən), *adj. Pros.* alternately responsive, as verses in dialogue. Also, **am′oe·be′an.** [< L *amoebae(us)* antiphonal (< Gk *amoibaîos* interchanging, equiv. to *amoib(ḗ)* alternation + *-aios* adj. suffix) + -AN]

a·moe·bic (ə mē′bik), *adj.* **1.** of, pertaining to, or resembling an amoeba. **2.** characterized by or due to the presence of amoebae, as certain diseases. Also, **amebic.** [AMOEB(A) + -IC]

amoe′bic dys′entery, a variety of dysentery caused by a protozoan, *Endamoeba histolytica,* characterized esp. by intestinal ulceration.

a·moe·bo·cyte (ə mē′bə sīt′), *n. Zool.* a migratory, amoeboid cell found in many invertebrates, which functions in excretion, assimilation, etc. Also, **amebocyte.** [AMOEB(A) + -O- + -CYTE]

a·moe·boid (ə mē′boid), *adj. Biol.* resembling or related to amoebae. Also, **ameboid.** [AMOEB(A) + -OID] **—a·moe′boid·ism,** *n.*

a·mok (ə muk′, ə mok′), *n.* **1.** (among Malays) a psychic disturbance characterized by depression followed by an overwhelming desire to murder. **—***adv.* **2. run amok.** See **amuck** (def. 1). Also, **amuck.** [< Malay *amoq*]

a·mo·le (ə mō′lā; *Sp.* ä mô′le), *n., pl.* **-les** (-lāz; *Sp.* -les). *Southwestern U.S.* **1.** the root of any of several plants, as Mexican species of agaves, used as a substitute for soap. **2.** any such plant. [< Sp < Nahuatl *amolli* soap]

A·mon (ä′mən), *n. Egyptian Myth.* Amen.

a·mong (ə mung′), *prep.* **1.** in, into, or through the midst of; in association or connection with; surrounded by: *He was among friends.* **2.** with a share for each of: *Divide the cigars among you.* **3.** in the number, class, or group of; of or out of: *That is among the things we must do.* **4.** by all or with the whole of; by most or with many of: *popular among the people.* **5.** by the joint or reciprocal action of: *Settle it among yourselves.* **6.** each with the other; mutually: *They quarreled among themselves.* [ME; OE *amang, onmang* for *on gemang* in (the) group (of); akin to MINGLE]
—Syn. AMONG and BETWEEN suggest a relationship that is not necessarily physical: *among the crowd; between two pillars; They don't have much sense among them. Between you and me, I don't like any of them.* AMID, a more literary word, implies being in the middle of a place or surrounded by something: *to stand amid ruins.*
—Usage. Precise users of English tend to use AMONG when more than two persons or things are involved (*The winnings were divided among the six men*) and to use BETWEEN chiefly when only two persons or things are involved (*to decide between tea and coffee*). This distinction is not very widely maintained in the case of BETWEEN, which is often used when more than two persons or things are involved in individual or reciprocal relationships (*a contract between five companies; between you, me, and the gatepost*).

a·mongst (ə mungst′), *prep.* among. [earlier *amongs,* ME *amonges,* equiv. to *among* AMONG + *-es* adv. gen. suffix; excrescent *-t* as in AGAINST]

A·mon-Ra (ä′mən rä′), *n. Egyptian Myth.* Amen-Ra.

a·mon·til·la·do (ə mon′tᵊlä′dō; *Sp.* ä môn′tē lyä′thō), *n.* a pale, dry Spanish sherry. [< Sp, equiv. to *a* to, near (< L *ad*) + *Montill(a)* (see MONTILLA) + *-ado* -ATE[1]]

A·mo·pa·on (ə mō′pā ən), *n.* (in the *Iliad*) a Trojan warrior slain by Teucer.

A·mor (ā′môr), *n.* Cupid. [< L: love; see AMOROUS]

a·mo·ra (ə môr′ə, ə mōr′ə), *n., pl.* **a·mo·ra·im** (ä′mō-rä′im, ä′mō-). (*often cap.*) *Judaism.* one of a group of Jewish scholars, active in the rabbinical academies of Palestine and Babylonia from the 3rd to the 6th centuries A.D., whose commentaries on and interpretations of the Mishnah comprise the Palestinian and Babylonian Gemaras. Cf. **sabora, tanna.** [< Heb *amōrā'* interpreter]

a·mor·al (ā môr′əl, a môr′-, ā mor′-, a mor′-), *adj.* **1.** without moral quality; neither moral nor immoral. **2.** having no moral standards, restraints, or principles: *a completely amoral person.* [A-[6] + MORAL] **—a·mo·ral·i·ty** (ā′mə ral′i tē, am′ə-), *n.* **—a·mor′al·ly,** *adv.*
—Syn. 1, 2. See **immoral.**

AMORC, Ancient Mystic Order Rosae Crucis.

Am·o·rette (am′ə ret′), *n.* a girl's given name. Also, **Am′o·ret′.**

Am·o·ret·ti (am′ə ret′ē, ä′mō-), *n.* a sonnet sequence (1595) by Edmund Spenser.

am·o·ret·to (am′ə ret′ō; *It.* ä′mô ret′tô), *n., pl.* **-ret·ti** (-ret′ē; *It.* -ret′tē). a little cupid. [< It, equiv. to *amor(e)* love (< L *amor*) + *-etto* -ET]

a·mo·ri·no (ä′mô rē′nō), *n., pl.* **-ni** (-nē). *Fine Arts.* a putto represented as an infant cupid. [< It, equiv. to *amor(e)* love (< L *amor*) + *-ino* dim. suffix (< L *-īnus* adj. suffix)]

am·o·rist (am′ə rist), *n.* **1.** a lover; gallant. **2.** one who writes about love. [< L *amor* love + -IST] **—am′o·ris′tic,** *adj.*

a·mo·ro·so (ä′mə rō′sō; *Sp.* ä′mô rô′sô), *n.* a medium dry sherry of Spain. [< Sp: amorous]

am·o·rous (am′ər əs), *adj.* **1.** inclined or disposed to love, esp. sexual love: *an amorous disposition.* **2.** being in love; enamored: *One look, and he became amorous of her.* **3.** showing or expressing love: *an amorous sigh.* **4.** of or pertaining to love: *amorous poetry.* [ME < MF < L *amōrōs(us),* equiv. to *amor* love + *-ōsus* -OSE[1], -OUS] **—am′o·rous·ly,** *adv.* **—am′o·rous·ness, am·o·ros·i·ty** (am′ə ros′i tē), *n.*
—Syn. 1. loving; amatory. **3.** passionate, impassioned; fond, tender. **4.** erotic. **—Ant. 1.** indifferent, cold.

a·mor pa·tri·ae (ä′mōr pä′trē ī′; *Eng.* ā′môr pā′trē ē′), *Latin.* love of country; patriotism.

a·mor·phism (ə môr′fiz əm), *n.* **1.** state or quality of being amorphous. **2.** *Obs.* nihilism (def. 3). [< G *Amorphism(us)* < Gk *ámorph(os)* AMORPHOUS + *-ismos* -ISM]

a·mor·phous (ə môr′fəs), *adj.* **1.** lacking definite form; having no specific shape; formless: *the amorphous clouds.* **2.** of no particular kind or character; indeterminate; having no pattern or structure; unorganized: *an amorphous style; an amorphous personality.* **3.** *Petrog.* occurring in a mass, as without stratification or crystalline structure. **4.** *Chem.* not crystalline. **5.** *Biol.* having structural components that are not clearly differentiated, as the nuclear material in certain bacteria. [< Gk *ámorphos* shapeless. See A-[6], -MORPH, -OUS] **—a·mor′phous·ly,** *adv.* **—a·mor′phous·ness,** *n.*

a·mort (ə môrt′), *adj. Archaic.* spiritless; lifeless. [< F *à mort* at (the point of) death. See A-[5], MORT]

am·or·ti·za·tion (am′ər ti zā′shən, ə môr′-), *n.* **1.** the act or an instance of amortizing a debt or other obligation. **2.** the sums devoted to this purpose. Also, **amortizement, amortissement;** *esp. Brit.,* **am′or·ti·sa′tion.** [< ML *a(d)mortizātiōn-* (s. of *admortizātiō*). See AMORTIZE, -ATION]

am·or·tize (am′ər tīz′, ə môr′tīz), *v.t.,* **-tized, -tiz·ing.** **1.** *Finance.* to liquidate or extinguish (a mortgage, debt, or other obligation), esp. by periodic payments to the creditor or to a sinking fund. **2.** *Old Eng. Law.* to convey to a corporation or church group; alienate in mortmain. Also, **am′or·tise′.** [< ML *a(d) mortiz (āre)* (to) bring to death < MF *amortiss-* (var. s. of *amortir;* see AMORT) + *-āre* inf. suffix; r. ME *amortisse(n)* < MF] **—am′or·tiz′a·ble,** *adj.*

am·or·tize·ment (am′ər tīz′mənt, ə môr′tiz-), *n.* **1.** a sloping top on a buttress, pillar, etc. **2.** an architectural feature, as a gable, at the top of a façade. **3.** amortization. Also, **a·mor·tisse·ment** (ə môr′tiz mənt). [AMORTIZE + -MENT, after MF *amortissement*]

A·mo·ry (ā′mə rē), *n.* **1.** a town in E Mississippi. 6474 (1960). **2.** a boy's or girl's given name.

A·mos (ā′məs), *n.* **1.** a minor Prophet of the 8th century B.C. **2.** a book of the Bible bearing his name. **3.** a boy's given name.

am·o·site (am′ə sīt′), *n. Mineral.* an asbestos variety of anthophyllite rich in iron, used as a heat-resistant material. [*A(sbestos) M(ine) O(f) S(outh Africa)* + -ITE[1]]

a·mount (ə mount′), *n.* **1.** the sum total of two or more quantities or sums; aggregate: *The amount of 7 and 9 is 16.* **2.** the sum of the principal and interest of a loan. **3.** quantity; measure: *a great amount of resistance.* **4.** the full effect, value, or significance. **—***v.i.* **5.** to reach, extend, or be equal in number, quantity, effect, etc.; be equivalent (usually fol. by *to*): *It is stated differently but amounts to the same thing.* **6.** to total; add (usually fol. by *to*): *The repair bill amounts to $300.* **7.** to develop into; become (usually fol. by *to*): *With his intelligence, he should amount to something when he grows up.* [ME *amount(en)* < OF *amonte(r)* (to) go up, deriv. of *amont* upward for *a mont* < L *ad montem* to the mount]

amount′ at risk′, *Insurance.* the difference between the reserve of a life-insurance policy and its face amount.

a·mour (ə mŏŏr′), *n.* **1.** a love affair. **2.** an illicit love affair. [ME < MF < L *amōr-* (s. of *amor*) love, akin to *amāre* to love]

a·mour-pro·pre (A mōōr prô′prᵊ), *n. French.* self-esteem; self-respect. [lit., self-love]

A·moy (ä moi′), *n.* **1.** an island near the Chinese mainland in the Formosa Strait. **2.** a seaport on this island. 224,300 (1953).

amp[1] (amp), *n. Elect.* ampere. [by shortening]

amp[2] (amp), *n. Informal.* amplifier. [by shortening]

AMP, *Biochem.* See **adenylic acid.** [A(DENOSINE) + M(ONO)- + P(HOSPHATE)]

amp., **1.** amperage. **2.** ampere; amperes.

AMPAS, Academy of Motion Picture Arts and Sciences.

am·pe·lite (am′pə līt′), *n. Mineral.* any black carbonaceous shale. [< F < L *ampelīt(is)* < Gk *ampelîtis* (*gê*) (earth) of the vine < *ámpel(os)* vine + *-ītis* -ITIS] **—am·pe·lit·ic** (am′pə lit′ik), *adj.*

am·pe·lop·sis (am′pə lop′sis), *n.* any climbing, woody vine or shrub of the genus *Ampelopsis.* [< NL < Gk *ámpel(os)* vine + *ópsis* -OPSIS]

Am·pe·los (am′pə los′), *n. Class. Myth.* a satyr who was placed among the stars by Dionysus.

am·per·age (am′pər ij, am pēr′-), *n. Elect.* the strength of an electric current measured in amperes. [AMPERE + -AGE]

am·pere (am′pēr, am pēr′), *n. Elect.* the meter-kilogram-second unit of electric current, equal to the current produced by an electromotive force of one volt acting through a resistance of one ohm, and equivalent to one coulomb per second. *Abbr.:* A, amp Also, **am′père.** [named after A. M. AMPÈRE]

Am·père (am′pēr; *Fr.* äN per′), *n.* **An·dré Ma·rie** (äN drā′ mə rē′; *Fr.* äN drā′ mA rē′), 1775–1836, French physicist. **—Am·per·i·an** (am pēr′ē ən, -per′-), *adj.*

am·pere-hour (am′pēr our′, -ou′ər), *n. Elect.* a unit of electric charge noting the amount of electricity transferred by a current of one ampere in one hour, equal to 3600 coulombs. *Abbr.:* Ah, amp-hr

Am/père's law/, *Physics.* the law that a magnetic field induced by an electric current is, at any point, directly proportional to the product of the current intensity and the length of the current conductor, inversely proportional to the square of the distance between the point and the conductor, and perpendicular to the plane joining the point and the conductor. [named after A. M. AMPÈRE]

am·pere-turn (am/pēr turn/), *n. Elect.* **1.** one complete convolution of a conducting coil, through which one ampere of current passes. **2.** the magnetomotive force produced by one ampere passing through one complete turn or convolution of a coil. *Abbr.:* At

am·per·o·met·ric (am/pēr ə me/trik, am pēr/ə-), *adj. Elect.* pertaining to or involving the measurement of an electric current. [AMPERE + -O- + METRIC[1]]

amperomet/ric titra/tion, *Chem.* titration in which the end point is determined by measuring the amperage of an electric current of given voltage that is passed through the solution.

am·per·sand (am/pər sand/, am/pər sand/), *n.* a character or symbol (& or &) for *and.* [contr. of *and per se and,* lit., (the symbol) & by itself (stands for) and; see PER SE]

am·phe·rot·o·ky (am/fə rot/ə kē), *n.* parthenogenesis in which both males and females are produced. Also, **amphitoky.** [< Gk *amph(ót)ero(s)* both + *tók(os)* child + -Y[3]] —**am/pher·ot/o·kous,** *adj.*

am·phet·a·mine (am fet/ə mēn/, -min), *n. Pharm.* a racemic drug, $C_6H_5CH_2CH(NH_2)CH_3$, which stimulates the central nervous system: used in medicine, usually in the form of its sulfate, chiefly to lift the mood in depressive states and to control the appetite in cases of obesity. [A(LPHA) + M(ETHYL) + PH(ENYL) + ET(HYL) + AMINE]

amphi-, a prefix occurring in loan words from Greek (*amphibious*); on this model, used with the meaning "two," "both," "on both sides," in the formation of compound words: *amphiaster.* [< Gk, comb. form of *amphí* on both sides; akin to Skt *abhitas,* G *-um,* OE *ymb(e)-* around. Cf. AMBI-]

Am·phi·a·ra·us (am/fē ə rā/əs), *n. Class. Myth.* a hero who joined the Seven against Thebes, although he knew that his death was fated: deified after death.

am·phi·ar·thro·sis (am/fē är thrō/sis), *n., pl.* **-ses** (-sēz). *Anat.* an articulation permitting only slight motion, as that between the vertebrae. [AMPHI- + Gk *árthrōsis* articulation. See ARTHRO-, -OSIS] —**am/phi·ar·thro/di·al,** *adj.*

am·phi·as·ter (am/fē as/tər), *n. Biol.* the achromatic spindle with two asters that forms during mitosis. [AMPHI- + -ASTER[2]]

Am·phib·i·a (am fib/ē ə), *n.* the class comprising the amphibians. [< NL < Gk *amphíbia* (*zôia*) (animals) living a double life, neut. pl. of *amphíbios.* See AMPHIBIOUS]

am·phib·i·an (am fib/ē ən), *n.* **1.** any cold-blooded vertebrate of the class *Amphibia,* comprising the frogs, salamanders, and caecilians, the larva of which are typically aquatic, breathing by gills, and the adult of which are terrestrial, breathing by lungs and through the moist, glandular skin. **2.** an amphibious plant. **3.** an airplane designed for taking off from and landing on both land and water. **4.** a person or thing having a twofold nature. **5.** Also called **amtrac.** a flat-bottomed, armed, military vehicle equipped to move on land or water on tracks equipped with fins, used chiefly for landing assault troops. —*adj.* **6.** belonging or pertaining to the *Amphibia.* **7.** amphibious (def. 2). [< L *amphibi(a),* neut. pl. of *amphibius* (adj.) (see AMPHIBIOUS) + -AN]

am·phi·bi·ot·ic (am/fə bī ot/ik), *adj. Zool.* living on land during the adult stage and in water during a larval stage. [AMPHI- + BIOTIC]

am·phib·i·ous (am fib/ē əs), *adj.* **1.** living or able to live both on land and in water; belonging to both land and water. **2.** Also, **amphibian.** capable of operating on both land and water: *amphibious vehicles.* **3.** of a twofold nature. **4.** of or pertaining to military operations by both land and naval forces against the same object, esp. to a military attack by troops landed by naval ships. **5.** trained or organized to fight, or fighting, on both land and sea. [< L *amphibius* < Gk *amphíbios* living a double life. See AMPHI-, BIO-, -OUS] —**am·phib/i·ous·ly,** *adv.* —**am·phib/i·ous·ness,** *n.*

am·phi·bole (am/fə bōl/), *n. Mineral.* any of a complex group of hydrous silicate minerals, containing chiefly calcium, magnesium, sodium, iron, and aluminum, and including hornblende, tremolite, asbestos, etc., occurring as important constituents of many rocks. [< F < LL *amphibol(us)* AMPHIBOLOUS]

am·phi·bol·ic (am/fə bol/ik), *adj.* equivocal; uncertain; changing; ambiguous. [AMPHIBOL(Y) + -IC]

am·phib·o·lite (am fib/ə līt/), *n. Petrog.* a metamorphic rock composed basically of an amphibole, usually hornblende. [AMPHIBOLE + -ITE[1]] —**am·phib·o·lit·ic** (am fib/ə lit/ik), *adj.*

am·phi·bol·o·gy (am/fə bol/ə jē), *n., pl.* **-gies.** ambiguity of speech, esp. from uncertainty of the grammatical construction rather than of the meaning of the words, as in *The Duke yet lives that Henry shall depose.* Also called **amphiboly.** [ME *amphibologie* < LL *amphibologia.* See AMPHIBOLY, -LOGY] —**am·phib·o·log·i·cal** (am fib/ə loj/i kəl), *adj.* —**am·phib/o·log/i·cal·ly,** *adv.*

am·phib·o·lous (am fib/ə ləs), *adj. Logic.* ambiguous; equivocal; susceptible of two interpretations. [< L *amphibolus* < Gk *amphíbolos* thrown on both sides ambiguous, equiv. to *amphi-* AMPHI- + *-bol-* (var. s. of *bállein* to throw) + *-os* -OUS]

am·phib·o·ly (am fib/ə lē), *n., pl.* **-lies.** amphibology. [< L *amphibolia* < Gk. See AMPHIBOLOUS, -Y[3]]

am·phi·brach (am/fə brak/), *n. Pros.* a trisyllabic foot, the arrangement of the syllables of which is short, long, short in quantitative meter, or unstressed, stressed, unstressed in accentual meter. Thus, *together* is an accentual amphibrach. [< L *amphibrach(us)* < Gk *amphíbrachys* short before and after (*amphi-* AMPHI- + *brachýs* short)] —**am/phi·brach/ic,** *adj.*

am·phi·car·pous (am/fi kär/pəs), *adj. Bot.* producing two kinds of fruit that differ either in form or in time of ripening. Also, **am/phi·car/pic.** [AMPHI- + -CARP + -OUS]

am·phi·chro·ic (am/fə krō/ik), *adj. Chem.* giving either of two colors, one with acids and one with alkalis. Also, **am·phi·chro·mat·ic** (am/fi krō mat/ik, -krə-). [AMPHI- + -CHROIC]

am·phi·coe·lous (am/fi sē/ləs), *adj. Anat., Zool.* concave on both sides, as the bodies of the vertebrae of fishes. [< Gk *amphíkoilos* hollow at both ends. See AMPHI-, -COELE, -OUS]

am·phi·cra·ni·a (am/fə krā/nē ə), *n. Pathol.* pain in both sides of the head. Cf. **hemicrania.** [< NL; see AMPHI-, CRANIA]

am·phic·ty·on (am fik/tē ən), *n.* a deputy to the council of an amphictyony. [back formation from *amphictyons* < Gk *amphiktýones,* orig. *amphiktíones* neighbors, equiv. to *amphi-* AMPHI- + *-kti-* inhabit + *-ones* n. suffix (pl.)]

Am·phic·ty·on (am fik/tē ən), *n. Class. Myth.* a son of Deucalion and Pyrrha who seized the throne of Attica and who, in devising a plan for avoiding disputes at his council meetings, became the first man to mix water with wine.

am·phic·ty·on·ic (am fik/tē on/ik), *adj.* of or pertaining to an amphictyon or an amphictyony. [< Gk *Amphiktyonik(ós)* of, for the amphictyons. See AMPHICTYON, -IC]

am·phic·ty·o·ny (am fik/tē ə nē), *n., pl.* **-nies.** (in ancient Greece) any of the leagues of states, esp. the league at Delphi, united for mutual protection and the worship of a common deity. [< Gk *Amphiktyonía.* See AMPHICTYON, -Y[3]]

Am·phid·a·mas (am fid/ə məs), *n. Class. Myth.* **1.** a son of Aleus who, with his brother Cepheus, joined the Argonauts. **2.** (in the *Iliad*) a king of Cythera.

am·phi·dip·loid (am/fi dip/loid), *n. Biol.* a plant having the sum of the chromosome numbers of two parental species, owing to the doubling of the chromosomes in a hybrid of two species. [AMPHI- + DIPLOID]

am·phi·dro·mi·a (am/fi drō/mē ə), *n.* a family festival in ancient Athens in honor of the birth of a child, during which the child received its name. [< Gk, equiv. to *amphídrom(os)* running about (see AMPHI-, -DROME) + *-ia* -IA]

am·phig·e·nous (am fij/ə nəs), *adj.* (of certain parasitic fungi) growing on both sides of leaves. [AMPHI- + -GENOUS] —**am·phig/e·nous·ly,** *adv.*

am·phi·go·ry (am/fə gôr/ē, -gōr/ē), *n., pl.* **-ries.** a meaningless rigamarole, as of nonsense verses; a nonsensical parody. Also, **amphigouri.** [< F *amphigouri,* equiv. to *amphi-* AMPHI- + *gouri* < ?] —**am·phi·gor·ic** (am/fə gôr/ik, -gor/-), *adj.*

am·phi·gou·ri (am/fə go͝or/ē), *n., pl.* **-ris.** amphigory.

am·phi·kar·y·on (am/fə kar/ē on/, -ē ən), *n. Biol.* a diploid nucleus. Cf. **hemikaryon.** [AMPHI- + Gk *káryon* nut] —**am/phi·kar/y·ot/ic,** *adj.*

Am·phil·o·chus (am fil/ə kəs), *n. Class. Myth.* a seer, the son of Amphiaraus and Eriphyle, and the brother of Alcmaeon.

am·phim·a·cer (am fim/ə sər), *n. Pros.* a trisyllabic foot, the arrangement of the syllables of which is long, short, long in quantitative meter, or stressed, unstressed, stressed in accentual meter, as *anodyne,* an accentual amphimacer. [< L *amphimacr(us)* < Gk *amphímakros* long at both ends. See AMPHI-, MACRO-]

Am·phim·a·chus (am fim/ə kəs), *n.* (in the *Iliad*) a chief of the Epeans, slain by Hector.

Am·phim·a·rus (am fim/ər əs), *n. Class. Myth.* a son of Poseidon, sometimes believed to be the father, by Urania, of the poet Linus.

am·phi·mix·is (am/fə mik/sis), *n., pl.* **-mix·es** (-mik/sēz). **1.** *Biol.* the merging of the germ plasm of two organisms in sexual reproduction. **2.** *Embryol., Genetics.* the combining of paternal and maternal hereditary substances. **3.** *Psychoanal.* the combining of anal and genital erotism in the development of sexuality. [AMPHI- + Gk *míxis* a mingling, equiv. to *mig-* (s. of *mígnynai* to mix) + *-sis* -SIS]

Am·phin·o·me (am fin/ə mē/), *n. Class. Myth.* a maiden who, along with her sister Evadne, was deceived by Medea into murdering their father Pelias.

Am·phin·o·mus (am fin/ə məs), *n.* (in the *Odyssey*) Penelope's favorite suitor.

Am·phi·on (am fī/on), *n. Class. Myth.* a son of Antiope by Zeus, and the husband of Niobe. With his twin brother, Zethus, he built the walls of Thebes, charming the stones into place with his lyre. —**Am·phi·on·ic** (am/fī on/ik), *adj.*

am·phi·ox·us (am/fē ok/səs), *n., pl.* **-ox·i** (-ok/sī), **-ox·us·es.** a lancelet of the genus *Branchiostoma,* having such vertebrate characteristics as a notochord and a dorsal cord of nerve tissue. [< NL: lit., sharp at both ends < Gk *amphi-* AMPHI- + *oxýs* pointed]

am·phi·pneus·tic (am/fə no͞o/stik, -nyo͞o/-), *adj. Entomol.* having only the prothoracic and last abdominal spiracles open, as the tracheal system of certain dipterous larvae. [AMPHI- + Gk *pneustik(ós)* pertaining to breathing, equiv. to **pneust(os)* (verbid of *pneîn* to breathe) + *-ikos* -IC]

am·phi·pod (am/fə pod/), *n.* **1.** any of numerous small crustaceans of the group *Amphipoda,* including the beach fleas, sand hoppers, etc. —*adj.* **2.** of or pertaining to the amphipods. [AMPHI- + -POD]

am·phip·ro·style (am fip/rə stīl/, am/fə prō/stīl), *adj.* (of a classical temple) prostyle on both fronts. [< L *amphiprostȳl(us)* < Gk *amphipróstȳlos.* See AMPHI-, PROSTYLE] —**am·phip/ro·sty/lar,** *adj.*

am·phi·sar·ca (am/fi sär/kə), *n. Bot.* a many-seeded, indehiscent fruit, as a gourd, having a pulpy interior and a hard, woody rind. [< NL; see AMPHI-, SARC-]

am·phis·bae·na (am/fis bē/nə), *n., pl.* **-nae** (-nē), **-nas.** **1.** any of numerous worm lizards of the genus *Amphisbaena.* **2.** *Class. Myth.* a serpent having a head at each end of its body and the ability to move forward or backward. [< L < Gk *amphísbaina* a serpent that moves forward or backward, equiv. to *amphís* both ways + *bain(ein)* (to) go + *-a* n. suffix] —**am/phis·bae/ni·an, am/phis·bae/nic, am/phis·bae/noid, am/phis·bae/nous,** *adj.*

am·phis·bae·nid (am/fəs bē/nid), *n.* any of numerous lizards of the family *Amphisbaenidae,* comprising the worm lizards. [< NL *Amphisbaenid(ae)* name of the family. See AMPHISBAENA, -ID[2]]

am·phis·ci·ans (am fish/ē ənz, -fish/ənz), *n.pl. Archaic.* inhabitants of the tropics. Also, **am·phis·ci·i** (am fish/ē ī/). [< ML *Amphisci(ī)* (< Gk *amphískioi,* pl. of *amphískios* (adj.) casting a shadow both ways, equiv. to *amphi-* AMPHI- + *ski(á)* shadow + *-os* adj. suffix) + *-ans,* pl. of -AN]

Am·phis·sa (am fis/ə), *n. Class. Myth.* **1.** a daughter of Echetus, blinded by her father in punishment for being ravished and bearing a child. **2.** a granddaughter of Aeolus, loved by Apollo.

Am·phis·sus (am fis/əs), *n. Class. Myth.* a son of Apollo and the nymph Dryope.

am·phi·sty·lar (am/fi stī/lər), *adj. Archit.* **1.** (of a classical temple) having columns on both fronts. **2.** having columns at both sides. [AMPHI- + Gk *stŷl(os)* pillar + -AR[1]]

am·phi·tene (am/fi tēn/), *n. Biol.* zygotene. [AMPHI- + *-tene,* var. of TAENIA]

am·phi·thal·a·mus (am/fə thal/ə məs), *n., pl.* **-mi** (-mī/). (in an ancient Greek house) a room adjoining the thalamus. [< L < Gk *amphithálamos.* See AMPHI-, THALAMUS]

am·phi·the·a·ter (am/fə thē/ə tər, -thēə/tər), *n.* **1.** a building with tiers of seats around a central area, as those used in ancient Rome for gladiatorial contests. **2.** any similar place for public contests, games, performances, exhibitions, etc.; an arena, stadium, or auditorium. **3.** a room having tiers of seats arranged around a central area, in which students and other observers can view surgery, hear lectures, etc. **4.** *Brit.* **a.** the first section of seats in the gallery of a theater. **b.** a designated section of seats in any part of a theater. **5.** a level area of oval or circular shape surrounded by rising ground. Also, **am/phi·the/a·tre.** [< L *amphitheātr(um)* < Gk *amphithéātron.* See AMPHI-, THEATER] —**am·phi·the·at·ric** (am/fə thē a/trik), **am/phi·the·at/ri·cal,** *adj.* —**am/phi·the·at/ri·cal·ly,** *adv.*

am·phi·the·ci·um (am/fə thē/shē əm), *n., pl.* **-ci·a** (-shē ə). *Bot.* the layer or one of the layers of cells in the capsule of a moss surrounding the spores. [< NL < Gk *amphi-* AMPHI- + *thēkíon* (*thḗkē* case, cover + *-ion* dim. suffix)] —**am·phi·the·cial** (am/fə thē/shəl, -shē əl, -sē-əl), *adj.*

Am·phith·e·mis (am fith/ə mis), *n. Class. Myth.* a son of Apollo and Acacallis. Also called **Garamas.**

am·phi·thu·ron (am/fə tho͞or/on), *n., pl.* **-thu·ra** (-tho͞or/ə), **-thu·rons.** amphithyra (def. 1).

am·phi·thy·ra (äm fē/thē rä; *Eng.* am fith/ər ə), *n.* **1.** Also, **amphithyron, am·phi·thu·ra** (am/fə tho͞or/ə), **amphithuron.** *Gk. Orth. Ch.* a divided curtain in front of the door of the iconostasis. **2.** pl. of **amphithyron.** [< LGk, equiv. to *amphi-* AMPHI- + *thýra* door]

am·phi·thy·ron (äm fē/thē ron; *Eng.* am fith/ə ron/), *n., pl.* **-phi·thy·ra** (-fē/thē rä; *Eng.* -fith/ər ə), **-phi·thy·rons.** amphithyra (def. 1). Also, **amphithuron.**

am·phit·o·ky (am fit/ə kē), *n.* amphetotoky. [AMPHI- + Gk *tók(os)* bringing forth + -Y[3]] —**am·phit/o·kal, am·phit/o·kous,** *adj.*

am·phit·ri·chate (am fi/trə kit), *adj.* (of bacteria) having a single flagellum at each end. Also, **am·phit/ri·chous.** [< NL *amphitricha* name of the genus < Gk *amphi-* AMPHI- + *trich-* (s. of *thríx* hair) + -ATE[1]]

Am·phi·tri·te (am/fə trī/tē), *n.* an ancient Greek sea goddess, a daughter of Nereus and the wife of Poseidon.

am·phit·ro·pous (am fi/trə pəs), *adj. Bot.* (of an ovule) inverted so that the funicle is in the middle of one side. [AMPHI- + -TROPOUS]

Am·phit·ru·o (am fi/tro͞o ō/), *n.* a comedy (c200 B.C.) by Plautus.

Am·phit·ry·on (am fi/trē ən), *n. Class. Myth.* the husband of Alcmene killed in a war against Erginus.

Amphitryon 38, a play (1938) by Jean Giraudoux.

am·phi·u·ma (am/fē yo͞o/mə), *n.* an aquatic, eellike salamander of the genus *Amphiuma,* of the southeastern U.S., having two pairs of very small feet. [< NL *Amphiuma* name of the genus, prob. irreg. formation. See AMPHI-, PNEUMA]

Am·phi·us (am/fē əs), *n.* (in the *Iliad*) a Trojan ally.

am·pho·gen·ic (am/fə jen/ik), *adj. Biol.* producing both male and female offspring. Also, **am·phog·e·nous** (am foj/ə nəs). [*ampho-* (< Gk *ampho-* (see AMPHI-) + GENIC] —**am·phog·e·ny** (am foj/ə nē), *n.*

am·pho·lyte (am/fə līt/), *n. Chem.* an ampholytic substance. [AMPHO(TERIC + ELECTRO)LYTE]

am·pho·lyt·ic (am/fə lit/ik), *adj. Chem.* capable of ionizing into both anions and cations; amphoteric. [AMPHOLYTE + -IC]

am·pho·ra (am/fər ə), *n., pl.* **-pho·rae** (-fə rē/), **-pho·ras.** *Gk. and Rom. Antiq.* a large two-handled storage jar having an oval body, usually tapering to a point at the base, with a pair of handles extending from immediately below the lip to the shoulder: used chiefly for oil, wine, etc., and, set on a foot, as a commemorative vase awarded the victors in contests such as the Panathenaic games. Cf. **pelike, stamnos.** [< L < Gk *amphor(eús),* equiv. to *am(phi)-* AMPHI- + *phoreús* bearer (i.e., handle), akin to *phérein* to bear] —**am/pho·ral,** *adj.*

Amphora

am·phor·ic (am fôr/ik, -for/-), *adj.* resembling the deep, hollow sound made by blowing across the mouth of a large, narrow-necked, empty bottle: *amphoric breathing.* [< NL *amphoric(us).* See AMPHORA, -IC] —**am·pho·ric·i·ty** (am/fə ris/i tē), *n.*

am·pho·ris·kos (am/fə ris/kəs), *n., pl.* **-koi** (-koi). *Gk. and Rom. Antiq.* a miniature amphora. [< Gk, equiv. to *amphor(eús)* AMPHORA + *-iskos* dim. suffix]

am·pho·ter·ic (am/fə ter/ik), *adj. Chem.* capable of functioning either as an acid or as a base. [< Gk *amphóter(os)* (comp. of *ámphō* both; c. L *ambō*) + -IC]

Am·pho·te·rus (am fō/tər əs), *n. Class. Myth.* a son of Alcmaeon and Callirrhoë, and the brother of Acarnan. The two brothers grew to manhood in a single day and avenged the murder of their father by the sons of Phegeus.

am·ple (am/pəl), *adj.,* **-pler, -plest.** **1.** of adequate or more than adequate extent, size, or amount; large; spacious. **2.** of sufficient or abundant measure; liberal; copious: *an ample reward.* **3.** fully sufficient or more than adequate for the purpose or needs; plentiful enough: *an ample supply of water; ample time to finish.* [late ME < L *ampl(us)* wide] —**am/ple·ness,** *n.*

—Syn. 1. extensive, vast, great, capacious, roomy. **2.** generous, free, abounding, lavish, plenteous, overflowing. AMPLE, LIBERAL, COPIOUS, PROFUSE describe degrees of abundant provision. AMPLE implies a plentiful provision: *to give ample praise.* LIBERAL implies provision from a generous supply (more than AMPLE but less than COPIOUS): *Liberal amounts of food were distributed to the needy.* COPIOUS implies an apparently inexhaustible and lavish abundance: *a copious flow of tears.* PROFUSE implies a still more unrestrained abundance of provision or flow: *profuse in his apologies.* **3.** See **plentiful.** —**Ant. 2.** scanty, meager.

am·plec·tant (am plek′tənt), *adj. Bot.* twining around or clasping some other body, as a tendril. [< L *amplect-* twine around, surround (s. of *amplectī*) + -ANT]

am·plex·i·caul (am plek′sə kôl′), *adj. Bot.* clasping the stem, as some leaves do at their base. [< NL *amplexicaul(is)*, equiv. to *amplexi-* (comb. form of L *amplexus* a clasping, n. use of ptp. of *amplectī* to clasp) + *caulis* stem (see COLE)]

Amplexicaul leaf

am·plex·i·fo·li·ate (am′plek sə fō′lē it, -āt′, am plek′-), *adj. Bot.* having amplexicaul leaves. [*amplexi-* (comb. form of L *amplexus* embracing, ptp. of *amplectī*) + FOLIATE]

am·pli·ate (am′plē it, -āt′), *adj.* **1.** enlarged; dilated. **2.** *Rare.* (of the wing of an insect) having a thick outer edge. [< L *ampliāt(us)* extended (ptp. of *ampliāre*). See AMPLE, -I-, -ATE[1]]

am·pli·a·tion (am′plē ā′shən), *n. Archaic.* enlargement; amplification. [< L *ampliātiōn-* (s. of *ampliātiō*) an extending. See AMPLIATE, -ION]

am·pli·dyne (am′pli dīn′), *n. Elect.* a direct-current generator with a rotating armature, capable of magnifying a small amount of power supplied to the field winding of the device and using the amplified power to operate an attached, direct-current motor. [AMPLI(FIER) + DYNE]

am·pli·fi·ca·tion (am′plə fə kā′shən), *n.* **1.** the act or state of amplifying or the state of being amplified. **2.** expansion of a statement, narrative, etc., as for rhetorical purposes: *In its next revision, the story underwent considerable amplification.* **3.** a statement, narrative, etc., so expanded: *The text of the next edition was an amplification.* **4.** the matter or substance used to expand an idea, statement, or the like: *He added an anecdote to his speech, as an amplification.* **5.** *Elect.* increase in the strength of current, voltage, or power. [< L *amplificātiōn-* (s. of *amplificātiō*). See AMPLE, -I-, -FICATION]

am·plif·i·ca·to·ry (am plif′ə kə tôr′ē, -tōr′ē), *adj.* of the nature of enlargement or extension, as of a statement, narrative, etc. [< L *amplificātor* amplifier (see AMPLE, -I-, -FIC, -ATE[1], -OR[2]) + -Y[1]]

am·pli·fi·er (am′plə fī′ər), *n.* one who or that which amplifies or enlarges, esp. an electronic component or circuit for amplifying power, current, or voltage. [AMPLIFY + -ER[1]]

am·pli·fy (am′plə fī′), *v.,* **-fied, -fy·ing.** —*v.t.* **1.** to make larger or greater; enlarge; extend. **2.** to expand in stating or describing, as by details, illustrations, etc.; to clarify by expanding. **3.** to exaggerate. **4.** *Elect.* to increase the amplitude of; to produce amplification. —*v.i.* **5.** to discourse at length; expatiate or expand one's remarks, speech, etc. (usually fol. by *on*): *The preacher amplified on the theme of brotherly love.* [late ME *amplifye* < MF *amplifie(r)* < < L *amplificāre* to extend. See AMPLE, -IFY] —**am′pli·fi′a·ble,** *adj.*
—**Syn. 2.** widen, broaden, develop. —**Ant. 1.** contract. **2.** condense.

am·pli·tude (am′pli to͞od′, -tyo͞od′), *n.* **1.** the state or quality of being ample, esp. as to breadth or width; largeness; greatness of extent. **2.** large or full measure; abundance; copiousness. **3.** *Physics.* the absolute value of the maximum displacement from a zero value during one period of an oscillation. **4.** *Elect.* the maximum deviation of an alternating current from its average value during its cycle. **5.** *Astron.* the arc of the horizon measured from the east or west point to the point where a vertical circle through a heavenly body would intersect the horizon. **6.** *Math.* argument (def. 8b). [< L *amplitūdō.* See AMPLE, -I-, -TUDE]

am′plitude modula′tion, **1.** *Electronics.* a method of impressing a signal on a radio carrier wave by varying its amplitude (distinguished from *frequency modulation*). **2.** a radio broadcasting network or station using such a broadcasting method. —*adj.* **3.** (of a radio network or station) broadcasting or capable of broadcasting by this method. **4.** (of a radio program) broadcast by this method. *Abbr.:* AM

am·ply (am′plē), *adv.* in an ample manner; sufficiently: *He apologized amply for his error. They were amply supplied with food.* [AMP(LE) + -LY]

am·pule (am′pyo͞ol), *n. Med.* a sealed glass or plastic bulb containing solutions for hypodermic injection. Also, **am′pul, am′poule.** [< F < L *ampull(a)* AMPULLA; r. ME *ampulle* < OF < L *ampull(a)*]

am·pul·la (am pul′ə, -po͝ol′ə), *n., pl.* **-pul·lae** (-pul′ē, -po͝ol′ē). **1.** *Anat.* a dilated portion of a canal or duct, esp. of the semicircular canals of the ear. **2.** *Eccles.* **a.** a vessel for the wine and water used at the altar. **b.** a vessel for holding consecrated oil. **3.** a two-handled bottle having a somewhat globular shape, made of glass or earthenware, used by the ancient Romans for holding oil, wine, or perfumes. [< L, equiv. to *amp(hora)* AMPHORA + *-ulla* dim. suffix]

am·pul·la·ceous (am′pə lā′shəs), *adj.* like an ampulla; bottle-shaped. Also, **am·pul·lar** (am pul′ər, -po͝ol′-), **am·pul·la·ry** (am pul′ə rē, -po͝ol′-, am′pə ler′ē). [< L *ampullāceus.* See AMPULLA, -ACEOUS]

am·pul·lu·la (am pul′yə lə, -po͝ol′-), *n., pl.* **-lae** (-lē′). *Anat.* a small ampulla. [< NL; see AMPULLA, -ULE]

am·pu·tate (am′pyo͝o tāt′), *v.t.,* **-tat·ed, -tat·ing.** **1.** to cut off (all or part of a limb or digit of the body), as by surgery. **2.** to prune, lop off, remove: *If you amputate a dozen pages you'll have a better essay; it's too long now.* **3.** *Obs.* to prune, as branches of trees. [< L *amputāt(us)* pruned, trimmed (ptp. of *amputāre*), equiv. to *am(bi)* around + *put-* trim + *-ātus* -ATE[1]] —**am′pu·ta′tion,** *n.* —**am′pu·ta′tive,** *adj.* —**am′pu·ta′tor,** *n.*

am·pu·tee (am′pyo͝o tē′), *n.* a person who has lost an arm, hand, leg, etc., by amputation. [AMPUT(ATED) + -EE, modeled on F *amputé*, ptp. of *amputer* to amputate]

Am·py·ci·des (am pī′si dēz′), *n. Class. Myth.* an epithet of Mopsus, meaning "son of Ampycus."

Am·py·cus (am′pə kəs), *n. Class. Myth.* a son of Pelias, husband of Chloris, and father of Mopsus. Also called **Am·pyx** (am′piks).

Am·ram (am′ram), *n.* the father of Aaron and Moses. Ex. 6:20.

Am·ra·tian (am rā′shən), *adj.* of, pertaining to, or belonging to the predynastic aeneolithic culture that flourished in Upper Egypt about 3800 B.C., characterized by the working of raw gold, the use of copper, and the burial of the dead in shallow graves. [named after (El) *Amra*, site of archaeological discoveries in Upper Egypt; see -IAN (*-t-* is hiatus-filling)]

Am·ri (am′rī), *n. Douay Bible.* Omri.

am·ri·ta (əm rē′tə), *n. Hindu Myth.* **1.** the beverage of immortality. **2.** the immortality conferred by this beverage. Also, **am·ree′ta.** [< Skt, equiv. to *a-* not (see A-[6]) + *mṛta* dead (*-mr* die + *-ta* verbid suffix); akin to Gk *ámbrotos* IMMORTAL]

Am·rit·sar (əm rit′sər), *n.* a city in NW Punjab, in NW India. 376,300 (1961).

A.M.S., Army Medical Staff.

Am·ster·dam (am′stər dam′; *Du.* äm′stər däm′), *n.* **1.** a city in and the nominal capital of the Netherlands. 869,602 (est. 1960). Cf. **Hague, The. 2.** a city in E New York. 28,772 (1960).

A.M.S.W., Master of Arts in Social Work.

amt (amt, ämt), *n.* an administrative division in Denmark. [< Dan < G; OHG *ambaht* service]

amt., amount.

A.M.T., **1.** Associate in Mechanical Technology. **2.** Associate in Medical Technology. **3.** Master of Arts in Teaching.

Am·torg (am′tôrg), *n.* a trading company established and operated in the U.S. by the Soviet Union. [*Am(erican) t(rade) org(anization)*]

am·trac (am′trak′), *n.* amphibian (def. 5). Also, **am′track′.** [AM(PHIBIOUS) + TRAC(TOR)]

amu, See **atomic mass unit.**

a·muck (ə muk′), *adv.* **1. run amuck, a.** to rush about in a murderous frenzy: *The maniac ran amuck in the crowd, shooting at random.* **b.** to rush about wildly; lose control: *When the night club caught fire the patrons ran amuck, blocking the exits.* —*n.* **2.** amok. [var. of AMOK]

A·mu Dar·ya (ä mo͞o′ där′yä), a river in central Asia, flowing NW from the Pamirs to the Aral Sea. ab. 1400 mi. long. Also called **Oxus.**

a·mu·gis (ä mo͞o′gēs), *n.* **1.** a Philippine, anacardiaceous tree, *Koordersiodendron pinnatum.* **2.** the hard, reddish wood of this tree, used in the construction of houses, ships, etc. [< Tagalog]

am·u·let (am′yə lit), *n.* an object superstitiously worn to ward off evil; protecting charm. [< L *amulēt(um)*]
—**Syn.** talisman.

A·mu·li·us (ə myo͞o′lē əs), *n. Rom. Legend.* a son of Proca who revolted against his brother Numitor and seized the throne of Alba Longa.

A·mund·sen (ä′mənd sən; *Norw.* ä′mo͝on sən), *n.* **1. Ro·ald** (rō′äl), 1872–1928, Norwegian explorer: discovered the South Pole in 1911. **2.** a ring formation in the fourth quadrant of the face of the moon, in the libration area and near South Pole.

A·mur (ä mo͝or′), *n.* a river in E Asia, forming most of the boundary between N Manchuria and the SE Soviet Union, flowing into the Sea of Okhotsk. ab. 2700 mi.

a·mur·ca (ə mûr′kə), *n.* the lees or sediment of olive oil. [< L < Gk *amórgē*]

Amur′ cork′ tree′, an Asiatic cork tree, *Phellodendron amurense*, having a deeply ridged, corky bark.

Amur′ li′lac, a small tree, *Syringa amurensis*, of eastern Asia, having clusters of whitish-yellow flowers nearly six inches long.

Amur′ priv′et, a shrub, *Ligustrum amurense*, of northern China, having hairy leaves and white flowers.

A.Mus., Associate in Music.

A.Mus.D., Doctor of Musical Arts.

a·muse (ə myo͞oz′), *v.t.,* **a·mused, a·mus·ing.** **1.** to hold the attention of (someone) agreeably; entertain or divert in a pleasant or cheerful manner: *She was amused by the children's conversation.* **2.** to excite mirth, laughter, or the like, in: *The joke amused them highly.* **3.** to cause (time, leisure, etc.) to pass agreeably. **4.** *Archaic.* to keep in expectation by flattery, pretenses, etc. **5.** *Obs.* **a.** to engross; absorb. **b.** to puzzle; distract. [late ME < MF *amuse(r)* (to) cause to MUSE; see A-[5]] —**a·mus′a·ble,** *adj.* —**a·mus′er,** *n.*
—**Syn. 1.** please, charm, cheer. AMUSE, DIVERT, ENTERTAIN mean to occupy the attention with something pleasant. That which AMUSES dispels the tedium of idleness or pleases the fancy. DIVERT implies turning the attention from serious thoughts or pursuits to something light, amusing, or lively. That which ENTERTAINS usually does so because of a plan or program which engages and holds the attention by being pleasing and sometimes instructive.

a·mused (ə myo͞ozd′), *adj.* **1.** pleasurably occupied; entertained; diverted. **2.** displaying amusement: *an amused expression on Enid's face.* **3.** aroused to mirth. [AMUSE + -ED[2]] —**a·mus·ed·ly** (ə myo͞o′zid lē), *adv.*

a·muse·ment (ə myo͞oz′mənt), *n.* **1.** that which amuses; pastime; entertainment. **2.** the act of amusing. **3.** the state of being amused; enjoyment. [< MF; see AMUSE, -MENT]
—**Syn. 1.** diversion, game. **3.** recreation, frolic, pleasure, merriment.

amuse′ment park′, a park equipped with such recreational devices as a Ferris wheel, roller coaster, etc., and usually having vendors of toys, food, and beverages.

amuse′ment tax′, a tax levied on such forms of entertainment as motion pictures, the theater, etc., and paid on admission. Cf. **cabaret tax.**

a·mu·si·a (ā myo͞o′zē ə), *n. Med.* the inability to produce or comprehend music or musical sounds. [< NL < Gk *amousía* state of being without the Muses, especially song. See A-[6], MUSE, -IA]

a·mus·ing (ə myo͞o′zing), *adj.* **1.** pleasantly entertaining or diverting: *an amusing speaker.* **2.** exciting laughter or mirth; delighting the fancy: *an amusing joke.* [AMUSE + -ING[2]] —**a·mus′ing·ly,** *adv.* —**a·mus′ing·ness,** *n.*
—**Syn. 1.** charming, cheering, lively. **2.** laughable, delightful, funny. AMUSING, COMICAL, DROLL describe that which causes mirth. That which is AMUSING is quietly humorous or funny in a gentle, good-humored way: *The baby's attempts to talk were amusing.* That which is COMICAL causes laughter by being incongruous, witty, or ludicrous: *His huge shoes made the clown look comical.* DROLL adds to COMICAL the idea of strange or peculiar, and sometimes that of sly or waggish humor: *droll antics of a kitten; a droll imitation.* —**Ant. 1, 2.** boring, tedious.

a·mu·sive (ə myo͞o′ziv), *adj. Rare.* affording amusement or entertainment; amusing. [AMUSE + -IVE] —**a·mu′sive·ly,** *adv.* —**a·mu′sive·ness,** *n.*

A·my (ā′mē), *n.* a girl's given name. Also, **Aimee.**

A·my·clas (ə mī′klas, -kləs), *n. Class. Myth.* **1.** a son of Lacedaemon and Sparta. **2.** a son of Niobe and Amphion.

Am·y·cus (am′ə kəs), *n. Class. Myth.* a son of Poseidon and the nymph Melia, known for his ruthlessness and his skill at boxing.

am·y·e·li·a (am′ī ē′lē ə, -el′ē ə, am′ē-), *n. Med.* congenital absence of the spinal cord. [< NL < Gk *amyel(os)* marrowless (see A-[6], MYEL-) + *-ia* -IA] —**am·y·el·ic** (am′ī el′ik, am′ē-), **a·my·e·lous** (ə mī′ə ləs), *adj.*

a·myg·da·la (ə mig′də lə), *n., pl.* **-lae** (-lē′). **1.** an almond. **2.** *Anat.* **a.** an almond-shaped part. **b.** a tonsil. [< ML: almond, tonsil, L: almond < Gk *amygdálē*; r. ME *amygdal*, OE *amigdal* almond < L *amygdal(on)* < Gk *amýgdalon*]

a·myg·da·la·ceous (ə mig′də lā′shəs), *adj.* belonging or pertaining to the *Amygdalaceae*, a family of plants bearing fruit containing a single hard seed. [< NL *Amygdalāce(ae)* plant family name (see AMYGDALA, -ACEAE) + -OUS]

a·myg·da·late (ə mig′də lit, -lāt′), *adj.* pertaining to, resembling, or made of almonds. [< L *amygdal-* ALMOND + -ATE[1]]

am·yg·dal·ic (am′ig dal′ik), *adj.* **1.** of almonds. **2.** *Chem.* of or derived from amygdalin or amygdalic acid. [< L *amygdal-* ALMOND + -IC]

am′ygdal′ic ac′id, *Chem.* See **mandelic acid.**

a·myg·da·li·form (ə mig′də lə fôrm′), *adj. Rare.* almond-shaped. [*amygdali-* (comb. form of L *amygdala* ALMOND) + -FORM]

a·myg·da·lin (ə mig′də lin), *n. Chem., Pharm.* a white, bitter-tasting, water-soluble, glycosidic powder, $C_6H_5CHCNOC_{12}H_{21}O_{10}$, usually obtained from bitter almond seeds and the leaves of plants of the genus *Prunus* and related genera: used chiefly in medicine as an expectorant. [< L *amygdal-* ALMOND + -IN[2]]

a·myg·da·line (ə mig′də lin, -līn′), *adj.* **1.** of, pertaining to, or resembling an almond. **2.** of or pertaining to a tonsil. [< L *amygdalin(us)* < Gk *amygdálinos* of almonds. See AMYGDALA, -INE[1]]

a·myg·da·loid (ə mig′də loid′), *n. Petrog.* **1.** an igneous rock in which rounded cavities formed by the expansion of steam have later become filled with deposits of various minerals. —*adj.* Also, **a·myg′da·loi′dal.** **2.** (of rocks) containing amygdules. **3.** almond-shaped. [< L *amygdal-* ALMOND + -OID]

a·myg·dule (ə mig′do͞ol, -dyo͞ol), *n. Petrog.* one of the mineral nodules in amygdaloid. [AMYGD(ALA) + -ULE]

am·yl (am′il), *adj. Chem.* containing an amyl group; pentyl. [< Gk *ám(ylon)* starch (see AMYLO-) + -YL]

amyl-, var. of **amylo-,** esp. before a vowel.

am·y·la·ceous (am′ə lā′shəs), *adj.* of the nature of starch; starchy. [AMYL- + -ACEOUS]

am′yl ac′etate, *Chem.* See **banana oil** (def. 1). Also called **am′yl·a·ce′tic e′ther** (am′il ə sē′tik, -set′ik, am′-).

am′yl al′cohol, *Chem.* a colorless liquid, $C_5H_{11}OH$, consisting of a mixture of two or more isomeric alcohols, derived from the pentanes, and used as a solvent and intermediate for organic synthesis.

am·yl·ase (am′ə lās′), *n. Biochem.* **1.** a starch-splitting enzyme that hydrolyzes complex sugars to glucose, present in the blood and in certain plants. **2.** any of several digestive enzymes, as amylopsin or ptyalin, which break down starches. [AMYL- + -ASE]

am·yl·ene (am′ə lēn′), *n. Chem.* any of five unsaturated isomeric hydrocarbons having the formula C_5H_{10}. [AMYL + -ENE]

am′yl group′, *Chem.* any of several univalent, isomeric groups having the formula $C_5H_{11}-$, esp. $CH_3CH_2C(CH_3)_2-$ whose derivatives are found in fusel oil, fruit extracts, etc. Also called **amyl radical.**

a·myl·ic (ə mil′ik), *adj.* of, pertaining to, or characterized by the amyl group. [AMYL + -IC]

am′yl ni′trite, *Pharm.* a yellowish, fragrant, flammable liquid, $(CH_3)_2CHCH_2CH_2ONO$, used in medicine, by inhalation, chiefly as a vasodilator, esp. in the treatment of angina pectoris. Also called **isoamyl nitrite.**

amylo-, a combining form of **amylum,** used esp. before a consonant: *amylolysis.* Also, *esp. before a vowel,* **amyl-.** [comb. form of Gk *ámylon* starch, n. use of neut. of *ámylos* not milled (*a-* A-[6] + *mýl(ē)* mill + *-os* adj. suffix)]

a·myl·o·gen (ə mil′ə jən), *n. Chem.* the water-soluble part of a starch granule. [AMYLO- + -GEN]

am·y·loid (am′ə loid′), *n.* **1.** *Pathol.* a hard, homogeneous, glossy substance deposited in tissues in certain diseases. **2.** *Chem.* any gelatinous hydrate formed by the interaction of sulfuric acid and cellulose. **3.** a nonnitrogenous food consisting esp. of starch. —*adj.* **4.** Also, **am′y·loi′dal.** of, resembling, or containing amylum. [AMYL- + -OID]

am·y·loi·do·sis (am′ə loi dō′sis), *n., pl.* **-ses** (-sēz). *Pathol.* **1.** a deposit of amyloid in tissues or organs. **2.** the diseased state resulting from this deposit. [AMYLOID + -OSIS]

am·y·lol·y·sis (am′ə lol′i sis), *n. Biochem.* the conversion of starch into sugar. [AMYLO- + -LYSIS] —**am·y·lo·lyt·ic** (am′ə lō lit′ik), *adj.*

am·y·lo·pec·tin (am′ə lō pek′tin), *n.* the insoluble or gel component of starch which forms a paste with water, but does not solidify, and which turns red in iodine. Cf. **amylose.** [AMYLO- + PECTIN]

am·y·lo·plast (am′ə lō plast′), *n. Bot.* a starch-forming granule in plants; leucoplast. [AMYLO- + -PLAST]

am·y·lop·sin (am′ə lop′sin), *n. Biochem.* an enzyme of the pancreatic juice, capable of converting starch into sugar. [AMYLO(LYSIS + PE)PSIN]

am·yl·ose (am′ə lōs′), *n.* the soluble or sol component of starch which forms a stiff gel at ordinary temperatures and turns blue in iodine. Cf. **amylopectin.** [AMYL- + -OSE[2]]

am′yl pro′pionate, *Chem.* a colorless liquid, $CH_3CH_2COOC_5H_{11}$, having an applelike odor, used chiefly as a scent in the manufacture of flavorings and perfume.

am′yl rad′ical, *Chem.* See **amyl group.**
am′yl sul′fide, *Chem.* See **diamyl sulfide.**
am·y·lum (am′ə ləm), *n.* starch (def. 1). [< L < Gk *ámylon* starch. See AMYLO-]
Am·y·mo·ne (am′ə mō′nē), *n.* *Class. Myth.* one of the fifty daughters of Danaus and mother of Nauplius by Poseidon.
Am·yn·tor (am′in tôr′), *n.* *Class. Myth.* a king of Ormenium who refused to give his daughter Astydamia to Hercules and who was slain by Hercules.
a·my·o·to·ni·a (ā′mī ə tō′nē ə, ā mī′-), *n.* *Pathol.* myatonia. [< NL; see A-[6], MYATONIA] **—a·my·a·ton·ic** (ā′mī ə ton′ik, ā mī′-), *adj.*
Am·y·tal (am′i tôl′, -tal′), *n.* *Pharm., Trademark.* amobarbital.
Am·y·tha·on (am′ə thā′on), *n.* *Class. Myth.* the son of Cretheus and Tyro who supported Jason's claim to the throne of Iolcus.
a·myx·or·rhe·a (ā mik′sə rē′ə), *n.* *Med.* the absence of the normal secretion of mucus. Also, **a·myx′or·rhoe′a.** [< NL; see A-[6], MYXO-, -RRHEA]
an[1] (ən; *when stressed* an), *indefinite article.* the form of **a** before an initial vowel sound and sometimes, esp. in British English, before an *h* that is normally pronounced in American English: *an arch; an event; an honor; an historian.* Cf. **a**[1]. [ME; OE *ān* ONE]
an[2] (ən; *when stressed* an), *conj.* **1.** *Informal.* and. **2.** *Archaic.* if. Also, **an′, ′n′.**
An (än), *n.* the Sumerian god of heaven: the counterpart of the Akkadian Anu.
an-[1], a prefix occurring in loan words from Latin or Greek where it meant "not," "without," "lacking" (*anarchy; anecdote*); used in the formation of compound words: *anelectric.* Also, *esp. before a consonant,* **a-.** [< L, Gk. See A-[6], UN-[1]]
an-[2], var. of **ad-** before *n: announce.*
an-[3], var. of **ana-** before a vowel: *anaerobe.*
-an, a suffix occurring in adjectives borrowed from Latin (*republican*); on this model, used as an adjective-forming suffix: *American; Elizabethan.* [< L *-ānus, -āna, -ānum;* in some words r. *-ain, -en* < OF]
AN, Anglo-Norman. Also, **A.-N.**
An, *Chem.* actinon.
an., in the year. [< L *anno*]
A.N., **1.** Anglo-Norman. **2.** Associate in Nursing.
a·na[1] (ā′nə, ä′nə), *n.* **1.** a collection of miscellaneous information about a particular subject, person, place, or thing. **2.** an item in such a collection, as an anecdote, a memorable saying, etc. [independent use of -ANA]
an·a[2] (an′ə), *adv.* (of ingredients in pharmaceutical prescriptions) in equal quantities; of each. *Symbol:* āā. [< ML < Gk *aná* of each]
ana-, a first element in loan words from Greek where it meant "up," "against": *anabasis;* used in the formation of compound words: *anacardiaceous.* [< Gk, comb. form of *aná;* akin to Skt *ā-,* L *an-;* cf. ON]
-ana, a noun suffix denoting a collection of material on a certain subject: *Americana.* [< L, neut. pl. of *-ānus* -AN]
an·a·bae·na (an′ə bē′nə), *n.* any of the fresh-water algae of the genus *Anabaena,* commonly occurring in masses and often contaminating drinking water, giving it a fishy odor and taste. [< NL < Gk *anabain(ein)* (to) go up (*ana-* ANA- + *baínein* to go) + L *-a* n. suffix]
an·a·ban·tid (an′ə ban′tid), *n.* **1.** any of several fishes of the family *Anabantidae,* comprising the labyrinth fishes. **—*adj.*** **2.** belonging or pertaining to the family *Anabantidae.* [< NL *Anabantid(ae)* < *anabant-* (s. of ANABAS) + *-idae* -ID[2]]
An·a·bap·tist (an′ə bap′tist), *n.* **1.** a member of any of various Protestant sects, formed in Europe after 1520, that denied the validity of infant baptism, baptized believers only, and advocated social and economic reforms as well as the complete separation of church and state. **2.** *Archaic.* Baptist (def. 1). **—*adj.*** **3.** of or pertaining to Anabaptists or Anabaptism. [< NL *anabaptist(a)* < ML *anabapt(izāre)* (to) re-baptize (< LGk *anabaptízein;* see ANA-, BAPTIZE) + *-ista* -IST] **—An′a·bap′tism,** *n.* **—An′a·bap·tis′ti·cal·ly,** *adv.*
an·a·bas (an′ə bas′), *n.* any fish of the genus *Anabas,* found in Africa and southeastern Asia. Cf. **climbing perch.** [< NL < Gk, aorist participle of *anabaínein* to go up. See ANABAENA]
A·na·base (*Fr.* A NA bäz′), *n.* a poem (1924) by St.-John Perse.
a·nab·a·sine (ə nab′ə sēn′, -sin), *n.* *Chem.* a colorless, poisonous liquid, $C_{10}H_{14}N_2$, used as an insecticide. [< NL *Anabas(is)* genus name (see ANA-, BASIS) + -INE[2]]
a·nab·a·sis (ə nab′ə sis), *n., pl.* **-ses** (-sēz′). **1.** a march from the coast into the interior, as that of Cyrus the Younger against Artaxerxes II, described by Xenophon in his historical work *Anabasis* (379–371 B.C.). **2.** *Literary.* any military expedition. Cf. **katabasis.** [< Gk: a stepping up. See ANA-, BASIS]
an·a·bat·ic (an′ə bat′ik), *adj.* *Meteorol.* **1.** pertaining to an uphill wind produced by the effects of local heating. Cf. **katabatic.** **2.** (formerly) pertaining to any upward-moving air current. [< Gk *anabatik(ós)* pertaining to climbing or to a climber, equiv. to *anaba-* (s. of *anabaínein;* see ANABAENA) + *-tikos* -TIC]
an·a·bi·o·sis (an′ə bī ō′sis), *n.* a bringing back to consciousness; reanimation after apparent death. [< NL < Gk *anabíōsis* a coming back to life, equiv. to *anabi-* (s. of *anabióein* to return to life; see ANA-, BIO-) + *-ōsis* -OSIS] **—an·a·bi·ot·ic** (an′ə bī ot′ik), *adj.*
a·nab·o·lism (ə nab′ə liz′əm), *n.* *Biol., Physiol.* constructive metabolism; the synthesis in living organisms of more complex substances from simpler ones (opposed to *catabolism*). [ANA- + (META)BOLISM] **—an·a·bol·ic** (an′ə bol′ik), *adj.*
a·nab·o·lite (ə nab′ə līt′), *n.* *Biol., Physiol.* a product of anabolic action. [ANABOL(ISM) + -ITE[1]]
an·a·branch (an′ə branch′, -bränch′), *n.* a stream branching off from a river and rejoining it further downstream. [short for *anastomotic branch.* See ANASTOMOSIS]
an·a·can·thous (an′ə kan′thəs), *adj.* *Bot.* having no spines or thorns. [< Gk *anákanthos* thornless. See AN-[1], ACANTHOUS]
an·a·car·di·a·ceous (an′ə kär′dē ā′shəs), *adj.* belonging to the *Anacardiaceae,* a family of trees and shrubs including the cashew, mango, pistachio, sumac, etc. [< NL *Anacardiāce(ae)* plant family name (see ANA-, CARDI-, -ACEAE) + -OUS]
a·nach·ro·nism (ə nak′rə niz′əm), *n.* **1.** something or someone remaining or appearing after its own time; an obsolete or archaic form: *contemporary monarchy is an anachronism.* **2.** a chronological error in which a person, event, etc., is assigned a date or period other than the correct one: *To assign Michelangelo to the 14th century is an anachronism.* Cf. **parachronism, prochronism.** [< L *anachronism(us)* < Gk *anachronismós* a wrong time reference, equiv. to *anachron(ízein)* (to) make a wrong time reference (see ANA-, CHRON-, -IZE) + *-ismos* -ISM] **—an·a·chron·i·cal·ly** (an′ə kron′ik lē), *adv.*
a·nach·ro·nis·tic (ə nak′rə nis′tik), *adj.* pertaining to or containing an anachronism. Also, **a·nach′ro·nis′ti·cal.** [ANACHRON(ISM) + -ISTIC] **—a·nach′ro·nis′ti·cal·ly,** *adv.*
a·nach·ro·nous (ə nak′rə nəs), *adj.* misplaced in time; anachronistic. [ANACHRON(ISM) + -OUS] **—a·nach′ro·nous·ly,** *adv.*
an·a·cid·i·ty (an′ə sid′i tē), *n.* *Med.* the abormal absence of hydrochloric acid in the stomach. [AN-[1] + ACIDITY]
an·a·clas·tic (an′ə klas′tik), *adj.* *Optics Obs.* of or pertaining to refraction. [< Gk *anáklast(os)* bent back (verbid of *anakláein* to refract, equiv. to *ana-* ANA- + *kláein* to break) + -IC]
An·a·cle·tus (an′ə klē′təs), *n.* fl. 1st century A.D., pope 76–88. Also called **Cletus.**
an·a·cli·nal (an′ə klīn′əl), *adj.* *Geol.* descending in a direction opposite to the dip of the surrounding strata. Cf. **cataclinal.** [< Gk *anaklín(ein)* (to) lean (something) upon (see ANACLISIS) + -AL[1]]
an·a·cli·sis (an′ə klī′sis), *n.* *Psychoanal.* the choice of an object of libidinal attachment on the basis of a resemblance to early childhood protective and parental figures. [< Gk *anáklisis* a reclining, equiv. to *anakli-,* var. s. of *anaklínein* to lean (something) upon (*ana-* ANA- + *klínein* to lean) + *-sis* -SIS]
an·a·clit·ic (an′ə klit′ik), *adj.* *Psychoanal.* exhibiting or pertaining to anaclisis. [< Gk *anaklit(os)* for reclining (*anakli-* (see ANACLISIS) + *-tos* verbid suffix) + -IC]
an·a·coe·no·sis (an′ə si nō′sis), *n., pl.* **-ses** (-sēz). *Rhet.* a figure of speech in which an appeal is made to one's listeners or opponents for their opinion or judgment as to the subject under discussion. [< ML < Gk *anakoínōsis,* equiv. to *anakoinō(ein)* (to) impart (*ana-* ANA- + *koinóein* to make common, deriv. of *koinós* CENO-[2]) + *-sis* -SIS]
an·a·co·lu·thi·a (an′ə kə lo͞o′thē ə), *n.* *Rhet.* lack of grammatical sequence or coherence, esp. in a sentence. [< L < Gk *anakolouthía.* See ANACOLUTHON, -IA] **—an′a·co·lu′thic,** *adj.* **—an′a·co·lu′thi·cal·ly,** *adv.*
an·a·co·lu·thon (an′ə kə lo͞o′thon), *n., pl.* **-tha** (-thə). *Rhet.* a construction involving a break in grammatical sequence; a case of anacoluthia. [< Gk *anakólouthon,* neut. of *anakólouthos* not following, equiv. to *an-* AN-[1] + *akólouthos* marching together (*a* together + *kolouth-,* gradative var. of *keleuth-* road, march + *-os* adj. suffix)]
an·a·con·da (an′ə kon′də), *n.* **1.** a South American boa, *Eunectes murinus,* that often grows to a length of more than 20 feet. **2.** any large boa. **3.** *Cards.* a variety of poker in which each player is dealt seven cards, discards two, and turns up one of the remaining five before each betting round. [? < Singhalese *henakandayā* kind of snake, equiv. to *hena* lightning + *kanda* stem + *-yā* suffix]
An·a·con·da (an′ə kon′də), *n.* a city in SW Montana: largest copper smelter in the world. 12,054 (1960).
An·a·cor·tes (an′ə kôr′tis), *n.* a town in NW Washington. 8414 (1960).
An·a·cos·ti·a (an′ə kôs′tē ə, -kos′-), *n.* a section of the District of Columbia, in the SE part.
Anacos′tia Riv′er, a river in the District of Columbia flowing into the Potomac River. ab. 24 mi. long.
A·nac·re·on (ə nak′rē ən), *n.* c570–c480 B.C., Greek writer, esp. of love poems and drinking songs.
A·nac·re·on·tic (ə nak′rē on′tik), *adj.* **1.** (*sometimes l.c.*) of or in the manner of Anacreon. **2.** (*sometimes l.c.*) convivial; amatory. **—*n.*** **3.** (*l.c.*) an Anacreontic poem. [< L *Anacreontic(us),* equiv. to *Anacreont-* (< Gk *Anakreont-,* s. of *Anakréōn*) ANACREON + *-icus* -IC] **—A·nac′re·on′ti·cal·ly,** *adv.*
an·a·crog·y·nous (an′ə kroj′ə nəs), *adj.* *Bot.* having the archegonia arising from any cell of the stem below the apical cell, thereby not terminating its growth, as certain liverworts. Cf. **acrogynous.** [AN-[1] + ACROGYNOUS]
an·a·cru·sis (an′ə kro͞o′sis), *n., pl.* **-cru·ses** (-kro͞o′sēz). **1.** *Pros.* an unstressed syllable or syllable group which begins a line of verse but is not counted as part of the first foot. **2.** *Music.* the note or notes preceding a downbeat; upbeat. [< L < Gk *anákrousis,* equiv. to *anakroú(ein)* (to) strike up, push back (*ana-* ANA- + *kroúein* to strike, push) + *-sis* -SIS] **—an·a·crus·tic** (an′ə krus′tik), *adj.* **—an′a·crus′ti·cal·ly,** *adv.*
an·a·cu·sia (an′ə kyo͞o′zhə, -zhē ə, -zē ə), *n.* *Med.* total deafness. [< NL; see AN-[3], ACOUSTIC, -IA] **—an·a·cu·sic** (an′ə kyo͞o′sik), *adj.*
an·a·dam′a bread′ (an′ə dam′ə), a yeast-raised bread having corn meal and molasses among its ingredients. [?]
An·a·dar·ko (an′ə där′kō), *n.* a town in central Oklahoma. 6299 (1960).
an·a·dem (an′ə dem′), *n.* *Literary.* a garland or wreath for the head. [< L *anadēm(e)* headband < Gk, equiv. to *anadē(ein)* (to) bind up (*ano-* ANO- + *déein* to bind) + *-ēma* -EME]
an·a·de·ni·a (an′ə dē′nē ə, -dēn′yə), *n.* *Pathol.* **1.** deficient glandular activity. **2.** absence of glands. [< NL; see AN-[1], ADEN-, -IA]
an·a·di·plo·sis (an′ə di plō′sis), *n.* *Rhet.* repetition in the first part of a clause or sentence of a prominent word from the latter part of the preceding clause or sentence, usually with a change or extension of meaning. [< L < Gk, equiv. to *anadiplō(esthai)* (to) be doubled back + *-ōsis* -OSIS. See ANA-, DIPLOSIS]
a·nad·ro·mous (ə nad′rə məs), *adj.* (of fish) migrating from the sea up a river to spawn (opposed to *catadromous*). [< Gk *anádromos* running upward. See ANA-, -DROME, -OUS]
An·a·dy·om·e·ne (an′ə dī om′ə nē′), *n.* Aphrodite: so called because of her birth from the sea. [< Gk: rising (from the sea), fem. prp. of *anadýesthai* to come up, esp. from the sea]
A·na·dyr′ Range′ (ä′nə dēr′, an′ə-; *Russ.* u nu dir′), a mountain range in NE Siberia in the Russian Federation: a part of the Kolyma Range.
a·nae·mi·a (ə nē′mē ə), *n.* *Pathol.* anemia.
a·nae·mic (ə nē′mik), *adj.* *Pathol.* anemic.
an·aer·obe (an âr′ōb), *n.* an organism, esp. a bacterium, that does not require air or free oxygen to live (opposed to *aerobe*). [AN-[1] + AEROBE]
an·aer·o·bic (an′â rō′bik, an′ə-), *adj.* **1.** (of an organism or tissue) living in the absence of air or free oxygen. **2.** pertaining to or caused by the absence of oxygen. [ANAEROBE + -IC] **—an′aer·o′bi·cal·ly,** *adv.*
an·aer·o·bi·o·sis (an′ə rō bī ō′sis, an′âr ō-), *n.* *Biol.* life in an environment without oxygen or air. [< NL; see AN-[1], AEROBIOSIS] **—an·aer·o·bi·ot·ic** (an′ə rō bī ot′ik), *adj.* **—an′aer·o·bi·ot′i·cal·ly,** *adv.*
an·aer·o·bi·um (an′ə rō′bē əm, an′ə-), *n., pl.* **-bi·a** (-bē ə). *Biol.* an anaerobe. [< NL; see AN-[1], AEROBIUM]
an·aes·the·sia (an′is thē′zhə), *n.* *Med., Pathol.* anesthesia. **—an·aes·thet·ic** (an′is thet′ik), *adj., n.* **—an·aes·the·tist** (ə nes′thi tist), *n.*
an·aes·the·si·ol·o·gy (an′is thē′zē ol′ə jē), *n.* anesthesiology. **—an′aes·the′si·ol′o·gist,** *n.*
an·aes·the·tize (ə nes′thi tīz′), *v.t.,* **-tized, -tiz·ing.** anesthetize.
an·a·gen·e·sis (an′ə jen′i sis), *n.* **1.** *Biol.* the progressive evolution of a species. Cf. **catagenesis.** **2.** *Physiol.* the regeneration of tissue. [< NL; see ANA-, GENESIS] **—an·a·ge·net·ic** (an′ə jə net′ik), **an′a·ge·net′i·cal,** *adj.*
an·a·glyph (an′ə glif), *n.* **1.** an ornament sculptured or embossed in low relief, as a cameo. **2.** *Optics.* a composite picture printed in two colors that produces a three-dimensional image when viewed through spectacles having lenses of corresponding colors. [< Gk *anáglyph(os)* wrought in low relief. See ANA-, GLYPH] **—an′a·glyph′ic, an′a·glyph′i·cal, an·a·glyp·tic** (an′ə glip′tik), **an′a·glyp′ti·cal,** *adj.* **—a·nag·ly·phy** (ə nag′-lə fē, an′ə glif′ē), *n.*
an·a·glyph·o·scope (an′ə glif′ə skōp′), *n.* *Optics.* a pair of spectacles for viewing an anaglyph.
an·ag·no·ri·sis (an′ag nôr′i sis, -nōr′-), *n., pl.* **-ses** (-sēz′). (in ancient Greek tragedy) the critical moment of recognition or discovery, esp. preceding peripeteia. [< L < Gk, equiv. to *anagnōrí(zein)* (to) know again (*ana-* ANA- + *gnōr-,* c. L *-gnōr-* in *ignōrāre* to IGNORE, + *-izein* -IZE) + *-sis* -SIS]
an·a·go·ge (an′ə gō′jē, an′ə gō′jē), *n.* **1.** a spiritual interpretation or application of words, as of Scriptures. **2.** a form of allegorical interpretation of Scripture which seeks hidden meanings regarding the future life. [< LL < Gk *anagōgḗ* an uplifting, equiv. to *an-* AN-[3] + *agōgḗ,* fem. of *agōgós* leading, deriv. of *ágein* to lead, c. L *agere* to do]
an·a·gog·ic (an′ə goj′ik), *adj.* **1.** of or pertaining to an anagoge. **2.** *Psychol.* deriving from, pertaining to, or reflecting the moral or idealistic striving of the unconscious: *anagogic image; anagogic interpretation.* Also, **an′a·gog′i·cal.** [ME < ML *anagogic(us).* See ANAGOGE, -IC] **—an′a·gog′i·cal·ly,** *adv.*
an·a·gram (an′ə gram′), *n.* **1.** a transposition of the letters of a word or sentence to form a new word or sentence. **2.** the new word or sentence so formed: "*Galenus*" *is an anagram of* "*angelus.*" **3. anagrams,** (*construed as sing.*) a game in which the players build words by transposing or adding letters. [< NL *anagramm(a).* See ANA-, -GRAM[1]] **—an·a·gram·mat·ic** (an′ə grə mat′ik), **an′a·gram·mat′i·cal,** *adj.* **—an′a·gram·mat′i·cal·ly,** *adv.*
an·a·gram·ma·tise (an′ə gram′ə tīz′), *v.t.,* **-tised, -tis·ing.** *Chiefly Brit.* anagrammatize.
an·a·gram·ma·tize (an′ə gram′ə tīz′), *v.t.,* **-tized, -tiz·ing.** to transpose into an anagram. [< Gk *anagrammatíz(ein)* (to) transpose letters, equiv. to *ana-* ANA- + *grammat-* (s. of *grámma*) letter + *-izein* -IZE] **—an·a·gram·ma·tism** (an′ə gram′ə tiz′əm), *n.* **—an′a·gram′ma·tist,** *n.*
An·a·heim (an′ə hīm′), *n.* a city in SW California, SE of Los Angeles. 104,184 (1960).
An·a·kim (an′ə kim), *n.pl.* tall people or giants who lived in S Palestine and were destroyed or scattered after the arrival of the Hebrews. Num. 13:28, 31; Deut. 2:21; 9:2.
a·nal (ān′əl), *adj.* **1.** of, pertaining to, involving, or near the anus. **2.** *Psychoanal.* **a.** of or pertaining to the second stage of libidinal development in which attention is centered on the anal region and gratification is derived from the retention or expulsion of feces. **b.** of or pertaining to the sublimation of feelings experienced during the anal stage of childhood: *anal personality traits.* **c.** of or pertaining to gratification derived from stimulation of the anus. [< NL *ānāl(is).* See ANUS, -AL[1]] **—a′nal·ly,** *adv.*
anal., **1.** analogous. **2.** analogy. **3.** analysis.
a·nal·cite (ə nal′sīt, an′əl sīt′), *n.* a white or slightly colored zeolite mineral, generally found in crystalline form. Also, **a·nal·cime** (ə nal′sēm, -sīm, -sim). [< Gk *análk(imos)* weak (*an-* AN-[1] + *álkimos* strong) + -ITE[1]]
an·a·lects (an′əlekts′), *n.pl.* selected passages from the writings of an author or of different authors. Also, **an·a·lec·ta** (an′əlek′tə). [< L *analect(a)* < Gk *análekta,* neut. pl. of *análektos* (ptp. of *analégein* to pick up, gather up), equiv. to *ana-* ANA- + *-lek-* gather (var. of *-leg-*) + *-tos* ptp. suffix] **—an′a·lec′tic,** *adj.*
An′alects of Confu′cius, The, a compilation of the discourses, maxims, and aphorisms of Confucius, dating from the 4th century B.C. Chinese, **Lun Yü.**
an·a·lem·ma (an′əlem′ə), *n., pl.* **-a·lem·mas, -a·lem·ma·ta** (-əlem′ə tə). a scale shaped like the figure 8, showing the declination of the sun and the equation of time for each day of the year. [< L: pedestal of a sundial, sundial < Gk *análēmma* support] **—an·a·lem·mat·ic** (an′əle mat′ik), *adj.*
an·a·lep·tic (an′əlep′tik), *Med.* **—*adj.*** **1.** restoring; invigorating; giving strength after disease. **2.** awakening, esp. from drug stupor. **—*n.*** **3.** an analeptic remedy. [< NL *analēptic(us)* < Gk *analēptikós* restorative, equiv. to *analēp-,* var. s. of *analambánein* to restore (*ana-* ANA- + *lambánein* to take) + *-tikos* -TIC]
a′nal fin′, the median, unpaired fin on the ventral margin between the anus and the caudal fin in fishes.
an·al·ge·si·a (an′əl jē′zē ə, -sē ə), *n.* *Med.* absence of sense of pain. [< NL < Gk *analgēsía* painlessness, equiv. to *analgḗs* painless (see AN-[1], -ALGIA) + *-ia* -IA]

CONCISE ETYMOLOGY KEY: <, descended or derived from; >, whence; b., blend of, blended; c., cognate with; deriv., derivative; equiv., equivalent; imit., imitative; m., modification of; obl., oblique; r., replacing; s., stem; sp., spelling; trans., translation; ?, origin unknown, perhaps; *, hypothetical. See the full key inside the front cover.

an·al·ge·sic (an′ᵊl jē′zik, -sik), *Med.* —*n.* **1.** a remedy that relieves or allays pain. —*adj.* **2.** of, pertaining to, or causing analgesia. [ANALGES(IA) + -IC]

an·a·log (an′ᵊlôg′, -ᵊlog′), *n.* analogue.

an′alog comput′er, a computer that solves a given mathematical problem by using physical analogues, as electric voltages or shaft rotations, of the numerical variables occurring in the problem. Cf. **digital computer.**

an·a·log·i·cal (an′ᵊloj′i kəl), *adj.* based on, involving, or expressing an analogy. Also, **an′a·log′ic.** [< L *analogic(us)* (< Gk *analogikós*; see ANALOGY, -IC) + -AL[1]] —**an′a·log′i·cal·ly,** *adv.* —**an′a·log′i·cal·ness,** *n.*

a·na·lo·gi·on (ä′nä lô′yē ôn; *Eng.* an′ᵊlō′jē on′), *n., pl.* **-gi·a** (-yē ä; *Eng.* -jē ə), **-gi·ons** • *Gk. Orth. Ch.* a lectern. [< Gk *analogeîon,* deriv. of *analégesthai* to read through (*ana-* ANA- + *légein* to gather, collect, speak)]

a·nal·o·gise (ə nal′ə jīz′), *v.i., v.t.,* **-gised, -gis·ing.** *Chiefly Brit.* analogize.

a·nal·o·gism (ə nal′ə jiz′əm), *n.* reasoning or argument by analogy. [ANALOG(Y) + -ISM]

a·nal·o·gist (ə nal′ə jist), *n.* **1.** a person who employs or argues from analogy. **2.** a person who seeks analogies. [ANALOG(IZE) + -IST] —**a·nal′o·gis′tic,** *adj.*

a·nal·o·gize (ə nal′ə jīz′), *v.,* **-gized, -giz·ing.** —*v.i.* **1.** to make use of analogy in reasoning, argument, etc. **2.** to be analogous; exhibit analogy: *Light traditionally analogizes with intellectual brilliance.* —*v.t.* **3.** to make analogous; show an analogy between: *to analogize a dog to a cat.* Also, *esp. Brit.,* **analogise.** [ANALOG(Y) + -IZE]

a·nal·o·gous (ə nal′ə gəs), *adj.* **1.** having analogy; corresponding in some particular: *The works of Keats and Schubert are somewhat analogous in mood.* **2.** *Biol.* corresponding in function, but not evolved from corresponding organs, as the wings of a bee and those of a hummingbird. [< L *analogus* < Gk *análogos* proportionate, equiv. to *ana-* ANA- + *lóg(os)* ratio + *-os* adj. suffix; see -OUS] —**a·nal′o·gous·ly,** *adv.* —**a·nal′o·gous·ness,** *n.*
—**Syn. 1.** similar, alike, like, comparable, akin. —**Ant. 1.** dissimilar.

an·a·logue (an′ᵊlôg′, -ᵊlog′), *n.* **1.** something having analogy to something else: *As a great dramatist, Racine is the French analogue of Shakespeare.* **2.** *Biol.* an organ or part analogous to another. Also, **analog.** [< F < Gk *análog(on),* neut. of *análogos* ANALOGOUS; r. earlier *analog(on)* < Gk]

an′alogue comput′er. See **analog computer.**

a·nal·o·gy (ə nal′ə jē), *n., pl.* **-gies. 1.** a partial similarity between like features of two things, on which a comparison may be based: *the analogy between the heart and a pump.* **2.** agreement; similarity: *I see no analogy between your problem and mine.* **3.** *Biol.* an analogous relationship. **4.** *Ling.* **a.** the process by which words or phrases are created or re-formed according to existing patterns in the language, as when *shoon* was re-formed as *shoes,* when *-ize* is added to nouns such as *winter* to form verbs, or when a child says *foots* for *feet.* **b.** a form resulting from such a process. **5.** *Logic.* a form of reasoning in which one thing is inferred to be similar to another thing in a certain respect, on the basis of the known similarity between the things in other respects. [< L *analogia* < Gk. See ANALOGOUS, -Y[3]]
—**Syn. 1.** comparison, kinship. **2.** correspondence.

an·al·pha·bet·ic (an′al fə bet′ik, an al′-), *adj.* **1.** not alphabetic: *an analphabetic arrangement of letters.* **2.** unable to read or write; illiterate: *analphabetic peoples.* **3.** *Phonet.* of or constituting a system of phonetic transcription, as the one devised by Otto Jespersen, which for each sound indicates by separate sets of symbols the articulator, the point of articulation, and the size and shape of the mouth opening. —*n.* **4.** a person who cannot read or write; illiterate. [< Gk *analphábēt(os)* not knowing the alphabet (*an-* AN-[1] + *alphábēt(os)* ALPHABET + *-os* adj. suffix) + -IC]

a′nal vein′, one of several veins in the rear portion of the wing of an insect.

a·nal·y·sand (ə nal′i sand′, -zand′), *n.* *Psychiatry.* a person undergoing psychoanalysis. [ANALYSE + *-and* as in MULTIPLICAND]

an·a·lyse (an′ᵊlīz′), *v.t.,* **-lysed, -lys·ing.** *Chiefly Brit.* analyze. —**an′a·lys′a·bil′i·ty,** *n.* —**an′a·lys′a·ble,** *adj.* —**an′a·ly·sa′tion,** *n.* —**an′a·lys′er,** *n.*

a·nal·y·sis (ə nal′i sis), *n., pl.* **-ses** (-sēz′). **1.** the separating of any material or abstract entity into its constituent elements (opposed to *synthesis*). **2.** this process as a method of studying the nature of something or of determining its essential features and their relations: *the grammatical analysis of a sentence.* **3.** a presentation, usually in writing, of the results of this process: *The paper published an analysis of the political situation.* **4.** *Math.* **a.** an investigation based on the properties of numbers. **b.** the discussion of a problem by algebra, as opposed to geometry. **c.** the branch of mathematics consisting of calculus and its higher developments. **d.** a system of calculation, as combinatorial analysis or vector analysis. **5.** *Chem.* **a.** intentionally produced decomposition or separation of materials into their ingredients or elements, as to find their kind or quantity. **b.** the ascertainment of the kind or amount of one or more of the constituents of materials, whether obtained in separate form or not. Cf. **qualitative analysis, quantitative analysis. 6.** psychoanalysis. [< ML < Gk, equiv. to *analý(ein)* (to) loosen up (*ana-* ANA- + *lýein* to loosen) + *-sis* -SIS]

anal′ysis of var′iance, *Statistics.* a procedure for resolving the total variance of a set of variates into component variances which are associated with defined factors affecting the variates. Also called **variance analysis.**

anal′ysis si′tus, *Math.* topology.

an·a·lyst (an′ᵊlist), *n.* **1.** a person who analyzes or who is skilled in analysis. **2.** a psychoanalyst. [ANALY(ZE) + -(I)ST]

analyt., analytical.

an·a·lyt·ic (an′ᵊlit′ik), *adj.* **1.** pertaining to or proceeding by analysis (opposed to *synthetic*). **2.** skilled in or habitually using analysis. **3.** (of a language) characterized by a relatively frequent use of function words, auxiliary verbs, and changes in word order to express syntactic relations, rather than of inflected forms. Cf. **synthetic** (def. 3), **polysynthetic** (def. 1). **4.** *Logic.* (of a proposition) necessarily true because its denial involves a contradiction, as "All spinsters are unmarried." **5.** *Math.* **a.** (of a function of a complex variable) having a first derivative at all points of a given domain; holomorphic; regular. **b.** (of a curve) having parametric equations that represent analytic functions. **c.** (of a proof) using analysis. Also, **an′a·lyt′i·cal.** [< ML *analytic(us)* < Gk *analytikós,* equiv. to *analy-* (see ANALYSIS) + *-tikos* -TIC] —**an′a·lyt′i·cal·ly,** *adv.*

Analyt′ical Cub′ism, (*sometimes l.c.*) *Fine Arts.* the early phase of Cubism, chiefly characterized by a pronounced use of geometric shapes and by a tendency toward a monochromatic use of color. Cf. **Synthetic Cubism.**

analyt′ic continua′tion, *Math.* **1.** a method of finding a function that coincides with a given analytic function in a domain and that remains analytic in a larger domain. **2.** any function found by this method.

analyt′ic geom′etry, a branch of mathematics in which algebraic procedures are applied to geometry and position is represented analytically by coordinates.

an·a·lyt·ics (an′ᵊlit′iks), *n.* (*construed as sing.*) *Logic.* the science of logical analysis. [see ANALYTIC, -ICS]

an·a·ly·tique (an′ᵊli tēk′), *n.* *Archit.* an elevation drawing of a façade, surrounded by a decorative arrangement composed of drawings of the important details and sometimes a plan or section of the façade. [< F: ANALYTIC]

an·a·lyze (an′ᵊlīz′), *v.t.,* **-lyzed, -lyz·ing. 1.** to separate (a material or abstract entity) into constituent parts or elements; determine the elements or essential features of (opposed to *synthesize*): *to analyze an argument.* **2.** to examine critically, so as to bring out the essential elements or give the essence of: *to analyze a poem.* **3.** to subject to mathematical, chemical, grammatical, etc., analysis. Also, *esp. Brit.,* **analyse.** [back formation from ANALYSIS] —**an′a·lyz′a·bil′i·ty,** *n.* —**an′a·lyz′a·ble,** *adj.* —**an′a·ly·za′tion,** *n.*
—**Syn. 1.** separate, reduce, break down. **2.** explicate. —**Ant. 1.** synthesize.

an′alyzed rhyme′, *Pros.* the use of assonance and consonance in a complex pattern at the ends of alternate lines of a quatrain, as in *head, mat, met, had.*

an·a·lyz·er (an′ᵊlī′zər), *n.* **1.** one who or that which analyzes. **2.** *Optics.* a polarizing device, often a Nicol prism, that indicates the direction of vibration of light by selecting and transmitting only the component of linearly polarized light in that direction. Also, *esp. Brit.,* **analyser.** [ANALYZE + -ER[1]]

A·nam (ə nam′), *n.* Annam.

A·nam·mel·ech (ə nam′ə lek′), *n.* one of the gods worshiped by the Sepharvites. II Kings 17:31. Also, *Douay Bible,* **A·nam′el·ech′.** Cf. **Adrammelech** (def. 1).

an·am·ne·sis (an′am nē′sis), *n., pl.* **-ses** (-sēz). **1.** the recollection or remembrance of the past; reminiscence. **2.** *Platonism.* recollection of the Ideas, which the soul had known in a previous existence, esp. by means of reasoning. **3.** *Psychiatry.* a case history. **4.** (*often cap.*) a prayer in a Eucharistic service, recalling the Passion, Resurrection, and Ascension of Christ. [< NL < Gk *anámnēsis* remembrance, equiv. to *ana(mi)mnḗ(skein)* (to) remember (*ana-* ANA- + *mimnḗskein* to call to mind) + *-sis* -SIS] —**an·am·nes·tic** (an′am nes′tik), *adj.* —**an′am·nes′ti·cal·ly,** *adv.*

an·am·ni·ote (an am′nē ōt′), *n.* any of the vertebrates of the group *Anamnia* (*Anamniota*), comprising the cyclostomes, fishes, and amphibians, characterized by the absence of an amnion during the embryonic stage. Cf. **amniote.** [< NL *Anamniot(a).* See AN-[1], AMNIOTE]

an·a·mor·phic (an′ə môr′fik), *adj.* **1.** *Optics.* having or producing unequal magnifications along two axes perpendicular to each other. **2.** of, pertaining to, or created by anamorphosis or anamorphism. [ANAMORPH(ISM) + -IC]

an′amor′phic lens′, *Optics.* a compound lens or system of lenses that produces greater magnification in one direction than in another, usually at right angles to the first, used for compressing wide-screen motion pictures onto conventional film and for projecting such compressed images onto a wide screen.

an·a·mor·phism (an′ə môr′fiz əm), *n.* *Geol.* metamorphism, usually occurring deep under the earth's surface, which changes simple minerals to complex minerals. Cf. **katamorphism.** [ANA- + -MORPHISM]

an·a·mor·pho·scope (an′ə môr′fə skōp′), *n.* a curved mirror or other optical device for giving a correct image of a picture or the like distorted by anamorphosis. [ANAMORPHO(SIS) + -SCOPE]

an·a·mor·pho·sis (an′ə môr′fə sis, -môr fō′sis), *n., pl.* **-ses** (-sēz′, -sēz). **1.** a drawing presenting a distorted image which appears in natural form under certain conditions, as when viewed at a raking angle or reflected from a curved mirror. **2.** the method of producing such a drawing. **3.** *Zool., Entomol.* the gradual change in form from one type to another during the evolution of a group of plants or animals. **4.** (in certain arthropods) metamorphosis in which body parts or segments are added to those already present. [< Gk, equiv. to *anamorphō-* (verbid s. of *anamorphóein* to transform; see ANA-, MORPHO-) + *-sis* -SIS]

An·a·mo·sa (an′ə mō′sə), *n.* a town in E Iowa. 4616 (1960).

A·nand (ä′nənd), *n.* a boy's given name.

a·nan·da (ä′nən də), *n.* *Hinduism.* perfect bliss. Cf. **Sat-cit-ananda.** [< Skt, equiv. to *a-* intensive prefix + *nānda,* var. of *nāndī* joy]

A·nan·da (ä′nən də), *n.* fl. early 5th century B.C., favorite disciple of Gautama Buddha.

an·an·drous (ə nan′drəs, an an′-), *adj.* *Bot.* having no stamens. [< Gk *ánandros* manless, equiv. to *an-* AN-[1] + *andr-* (s. of *anḗr*) man + *-os;* see -OUS]

An·a·ni·as (an′ə nī′əs), *n.* a man who was struck dead for lying. Acts. 5:1–5.

an·an·thous (ə nan′thəs, an an′-), *adj.* *Bot.* having no flowers. [< Gk *ananth(ḗs)* without flowers (*an-* AN-[1] + *anth(os)* flower + *-ēs* adj. suffix) + *-(OUS)*]

an·a·pest (an′ə pest′), *n.* *Pros.* a foot of three syllables, two short followed by one long in quantitative meter, and two unstressed followed by one stressed in accentual meter, as in *for the nonce.* Also, **an′a·paest′.** [< L *anapaest(us)* < Gk *anápaistos* struck back, reversed (as compared with a dactyl), equiv. to *ana-* ANA- + *pais-* (verbid s. of *paíein* to strike) + *-tos* ptp. suffix] —**an′a·pes′tic, an′a·paes′tic,** *adj.* —**an′a·pes′ti·cal·ly, an′a·paes′ti·cal·ly,** *adv.*

an·a·phase (an′ə fāz′), *n.* *Biol.* the stage in mitosis following metaphase in which the daughter chromosomes move away from each other to opposite ends of the cell. [ANA- + PHASE]

a·naph·o·ra (ə naf′ər ə), *n.* **1.** Also called **epanaphora.** *Rhet.* repetition of a word or words at the beginning of two or more successive verses, clauses, or sentences. Cf. **epistrophe** (def. 1), **symploce. 2.** *Gram.* the use of a word as a regular grammatical substitute for a preceding word or group of words, as the use of *it* and *do* in *I know it and he does too.* **3.** (*sometimes cap.*) *Eastern Ch.* **a.** the prayer of oblation and consecration in the Divine Liturgy during which the Eucharistic elements are offered. **b.** the part of the ceremony during which the Eucharistic elements are offered as an oblation. [< L < Gk: a bringing back, repeating, equiv. to *ana-* ANA- + *-phora,* akin to *phérein* to carry, bring] —**a·naph′o·ral,** *adj.*

an·aph·ro·dis·i·ac (an af′rə diz′ē ak′), *Med.* —*adj.* **1.** capable of diminishing sexual desire. —*n.* **2.** an anaphrodisiac agent. [AN-[1] + APHRODISIAC]

an·a·phy·lax·is (an′ə fə lak′sis), *n.* *Pathol.* increased susceptibility to a foreign protein resulting from previous exposure to it, as in serum treatment. [ANA- + (PRO)-PHYLAXIS] —**an·a·phy·lac·tic** (an′ə fə lak′tik), *adj.* —**an′a·phy·lac′ti·cal·ly,** *adv.*

an·a·plas·mo·sis (an′ə plaz mō′sis), *n.* *Vet. Pathol.* a disease of cattle caused by a blood-infecting protozoan parasite, transmitted by bloodsucking flies and ticks. [< NL *Anaplasm(a)* genus name (see ANA-, PLASMA) + -OSIS]

an·a·plas·tic (an′ə plas′tik), *adj.* **1.** *Surg.* replacing lost tissue or parts, or remedying natural defects, as by transplanting. **2.** *Pathol.* **a.** (of cells) having reverted to a more primitive form. **b.** (of tumors) having a high degree of malignancy. [ANAPLAST(Y) + -IC]

an·a·plas·ty (an′ə plas′tē), *n.* See **plastic surgery.** [< Gk *anáplast(os)* remolded (see ANA-, -PLAST) + -Y[3]]

an·a·ple·ro·sis (an′ə plə rō′sis), *n., pl.* **-ses** (-sēz). plastic surgery involving the transplantation of tissue to fill a wound, lesion, or the like. [< NL < Gk *anaplḗrōsis* a filling up, equiv. to *anaplērō(ein)* (to) fill up (*ana-* ANA- + *plēróein* to fill, deriv. of *plḗrēs* full) + *-ōsis* -OSIS]

A·ná·po·lis (ä nä′po͝o lis), *n.* a city in central Brazil. 51,169 (1960).

an·ap·o·phys·i·al (an′ə pə fiz′ē əl, ə nap′ə-), *adj.* of or pertaining to an anapophysis. [ANAPOPHYSI(S) + -AL[1]]

an·a·poph·y·sis (an′ə pof′i sis), *n., pl.* **-ses** (-sēz′). *Anat.* a small process of a vertebra, esp. of a lumbar or thoracic vertebra. [AN-[3] + APOPHYSIS]

an·ap·tot·ic (an′ap tot′ik), *adj.* (of languages) tending to become uninflected, in accordance with a theory that languages evolve from uninflected to inflected and back. [AN-[3] + *aptote* (< Gk *áptōton,* n. use of neut. of *áptōtos* uninflected, not falling, equiv. to *a-* A-[6] + *ptōtós* falling, verbid of *píptein* to fall) + -IC]

an·ap·tyx·is (an′əp tik′sis), *n., pl.* **-tyx·es** (-tik′sēz). epenthesis of a vowel. [< NL < Gk, equiv. to *anaptyk-* (verbid s. of *anaptýssein* to unfold, equiv. to *ana-* ANA- + *ptýssein* to fold) + *-sis* -SIS] —**an·ap·tyc·tic** (an′ap tik′tik), **an′ap·tyc′ti·cal,** *adj.*

an·arch (an′ärk), *n.* *Archaic.* anarchist. [back formation from ANARCHY]

an·ar·chic (an är′kik), *adj.* **1.** of, like, or tending to anarchy. **2.** advocating anarchy. **3.** not regulated by law; lawless: *Anarchic bands pillaged the countryside.* Also, **an·ar′chi·cal.** [ANARCH(Y) + -IC] —**an·ar′chi·cal·ly,** *adv.*

an·ar·chism (an′ər kiz′əm), *n.* **1.** a doctrine urging the abolition of government or governmental restraint as the indispensable condition for full social and political liberty. **2.** the methods or practices of anarchists. [ANARCH(Y) + -ISM]

an·ar·chist (an′ər kist), *n.* **1.** a person who advocates anarchism as a political doctrine; a believer in voluntary association as the most satisfactory means of organizing society. **2.** a person who seeks to overturn by violence all constituted forms and institutions of society and government, with no purpose of establishing any other system of order in the place of that destroyed. **3.** a person who promotes disorder or excites revolt against any established rule, law, or custom. [ANARCH(Y) + -IST] —**an′ar·chis′tic,** *adj.*

an·ar·chy (an′ər kē), *n.* **1.** a state of society without government or law. **2.** political and social disorder due to absence of governmental control: *The death of the king was followed by a year of anarchy.* **3.** a theory that regards the absence of all direct or coercive government as a political ideal and that proposes the cooperative and voluntary association of individuals and groups as the principal mode of organized society. **4.** confusion; chaos; disorder: *Intellectual and moral anarchy followed his loss of faith.* [< ML *anarchia* < Gk, equiv. to *ánarch(os)* leaderless (*an-* AN- + *arch(ós)* leader + *-os* adj. suffix) + *-ia* -Y[3]]

an·ar·thri·a (an är′thrē ə), *n.* *Pathol.* loss of articulate speech. [< NL; see AN-[1], ARTHR-, -IA] —**an·ar·thric** (an är′thrik), *adj.*

an·ar·throus (an är′thrəs), *adj.* **1.** *Zool.* having no joints or articulated limbs. **2.** (esp. in Greek grammar) used without the article. [< Gk *ánarthros* jointless. See AN-[1], ARTHR-, -OUS] —**an·ar′throus·ly,** *adv.* —**an·ar′throus·ness,** *n.*

an·a·sar·ca (an′ə sär′kə), *n.* *Pathol.* a pronounced, generalized dropsy. [< NL; see ANA-, SARC-] —**an′a·sar′cous,** *adj.*

A·na·sa·zi (ä′nə sä′zē), *n., pl.* **-zis,** (*esp. collectively*) **-zi** for 2. **1.** a Basket Maker-Pueblo culture of the plateau region of northern Arizona and New Mexico and of southern Utah and Colorado, dating probably from A.D. 100–1300. **2.** a member of the people producing this culture. [< Navaho *'anaasázi* outsider from of old]

an·as·pid (ə nas′pid), *n.* *Paleontol.* any of several ostracoderms of the order *Anaspida,* from the Silurian and Devonian periods, having the body covered with small scales. [< NL *Anaspid(a)* name of the order, equiv. to *an-* ANA- + Gk *aspid-* (s. of *aspís* shield) + *-a* neut. pl. n. ending]

An·a·sta·sia (an′ə stā′zhə, än′ə stä′shə), *n.* **1. Ni·ko·la·iev·na Ro·ma·nov** (ni ko lä′yəv nə ro mä′nof), **Grand Duchess,** 1901–?, daughter of Nicholas II: believed executed by the Bolsheviks in 1918 with other members of the Romanov family. **2.** a girl's given name.

a·nas·ta·sis (ə nas′tə sis), *n., pl.* **-ses** (-sēz′). a representation, in Byzantine art, of Christ harrowing hell. [< Gk *anástasis* a raising up, removal. See ANA-, STASIS]

An·as·ta·sius I (an′ə stä′shəs, -shē əs), A.D. c430–518, emperor of the Eastern Roman Empire 491–518.

an·as·tig·mat (ə nas′tig mat′, an′ə stig′mat), *n. Optics.* a compound lens corrected for the aberrations of astigmatism and curvature of field. [< G, back formation from *anastigmatisch* ANASTIGMATIC]

an·as·tig·mat·ic (an′ə stig mat′ik, a nas′tig-), *adj. Optics.* (of a lens) not having astigmatism; forming point images of a point object located off the axis of the lens; stigmatic. [AN-[1] + ASTIGMATIC]

a·nas·to·mose (ə nas′tə mōz′), *v.t., v.i.,* **-mosed, -mos·ing.** *Physiol., Anat.* to communicate or connect by anastomosis. [back formation from ANASTOMOSIS]

a·nas·to·mo·sis (ə nas′tə mō′sis), *n., pl.* **-ses** (-sēz). **1.** *Anat.* communication between blood vessels by means of collateral channels. **2.** *Biol.* connection between parts of any branching system. **3.** *Surg., Pathol.* communication between two organs or spaces which normally are not connected. [< NL < Gk: opening. See ANA-, STOMA, -OSIS] —**a·nas·to·mot·ic** (ə nas′tə mot′ik), *adj.*

a·nas·tro·phe (ə nas′trə fē), *n. Rhet.* inversion of the usual order of words. [< Gk: a turning back. See ANA-, STROPHE]

anat., **1.** anatomical. **2.** anatomy.

a·nat·a·bine (ə nat′ə bēn′, -bin), *n. Chem.* a liquid alkaloid, $C_{10}H_{12}N_2$, obtained from tobacco. [ANA- + Sp *tab(aco)* TOBACCO + -INE[2]]

an·a·tase (an′ə tās′), *n. Mineral.* a form of titanium dioxide, TiO_2, occurring as tetragonal crystals. Also called **octahedrite.** [< F < Gk *anátasis*, equiv. to *ana-* ANA- + *ta-* (var. s. of *teinein* to stretch) + *-sis* -SIS]

an·a·tex·is (an′ə tek′sis), *n., pl.* **-tex·es** (-tek′sēz). *n. Geol.* the process by which igneous rock remelts into magma. [< NL < Gk *anátēxis* a melting, equiv. to *anatḗk(ein)* (to) melt down (*ana-* ANA- + *tḗkein* to thaw) + *-sis* -SIS]

a·nath·e·ma (ə nath′ə mə), *n., pl.* **-mas.** **1.** a formal ecclesiastical curse involving excommunication. **2.** any imprecation of divine punishment. **3.** a curse; execration: *His misbehavior brought upon him his father's anathema.* **4.** a person or thing accursed or consigned to damnation or destruction. **5.** a person or thing detested or loathed. [< L < Gk: a thing accursed, devoted to evil, orig. devoted, equiv. to *ana(ti)thé(nai)* to set up + *ma* n. suffix]

a·nath·e·mat·ic (ə nath′ə mat′ik), *adj.* loathesome; disgusting; hateful. Also, **a·nath′e·mat′i·cal.** [< Gk *anathemat-* (s. of *anáthema*; see ANATHEMA) + -IC] —**a·nath′e·mat′i·cal·ly,** *adv.*

a·nath·e·ma·tise (ə nath′ə mə tīz′), *v.t., v.i.,* **-tised, -tis·ing.** *Chiefly Brit.* anathematize. —**a·nath′e·ma·ti·sa′tion,** *n.* —**a·nath′e·ma·tis′er,** *n.*

a·nath·e·ma·tize (ə nath′ə mə tīz′), *v.,* **-tized, -tiz·ing.** —*v.t.* **1.** to pronounce an anathema against; denounce; curse. —*v.i.* **2.** to pronounce anathemas; curse. [< LL *anathematiz(āre)* (to) put under the ban, curse, detest < Gk *anathematíz(ein)* (to) bind by a curse, make accursed, equiv. to *anathemat-* (s. of *anáthema*) + *-izein* -IZE] —**a·nath′e·ma·ti·za′tion,** *n.* —**a·nath′e·ma·tiz′er,** *n.*

an·a·tine (an′ə tīn′, -tin), *adj.* **1.** of or pertaining to the family *Anatidae*, comprising the swans, geese, and ducks, esp. to the subfamily *Anatinae*, comprising the ducks. **2.** ducklike. [< L *anatīn(us)* of, pertaining to a duck, equiv. to *anat-* (s. of *anas*) duck + *-īnus* -INE[1]]

a·nat·man (ə nät′mən), *n. Sanskrit.* anatta.

An·a·tol (an′ə tōl′), *n.* a boy's given name. Also, **Anatole, Annatol.**

An·a·tole (an′ə tōl′; *Fr.* A NA tôl′), *n.* a boy's given name. Also, **Anatol, Annatol.**

An·a·to·li·a (an′ə tō′lē ə), *n.* a vast plateau between the Black and the Mediterranean seas: in ancient usage, synonymous with the peninsula of Asia Minor; in modern usage, applied to Turkey in Asia. Cf. **Asia Minor.**

An·a·to·li·an (an′ə tō′lē ən), *adj.* **1.** of or pertaining to Anatolia, its inhabitants, or their language. **2.** of, pertaining to, or belonging to a group or family of languages that includes cuneiform Hittite and its nearest congeners. —*n.* **3.** a native or inhabitant of Anatolia. **4.** any of various Turkish dialects spoken in Anatolia. **5.** a group or family of extinct languages that includes cuneiform Hittite and its nearest congeners. **6.** a variety of Turkish rug woven in Anatolia. [ANATOLI(A) + -AN]

An·a·tol·ic (an′ə tol′ik), *adj., n.* Anatolian. [ANATOL(IA) + -IC]

an·a·tom·i·cal (an′ə tom′i kəl), *adj.* of or pertaining to anatomy. Also, **an′a·tom′ic.** [< LL *anatomic(us)* (< Gk *anatomikós*; see ANATOMY, -IC) + -AL[1]] —**an′a·tom′i·cal·ly,** *adv.*

anatom′ical pathol′ogy, the branch of pathology dealing with the morphologic changes in the tissues, both gross and microscopic; pathological anatomy. —**an·a·tom·i·co·path·o·log·i·cal** (an′ə tom′i kō path′ə loj′i kəl), *adj.*

a·nat·o·mise (ə nat′ə mīz′), *v.t.,* **-mised, -mis·ing.** *Chiefly Brit.* anatomize. —**a·nat′o·mis′a·ble,** *adj.* —**a·nat′o·mi·sa′tion,** *n.* —**a·nat′o·mis′er,** *n.*

a·nat·o·mist (ə nat′ə mist), *n.* a specialist in anatomy. [ANATOM(IZE) + -IST]

a·nat·o·mize (ə nat′ə mīz′), *v.t.,* **-mized, -miz·ing.** **1.** to cut apart (an animal or plant) to show or examine the position, structure, and relation of the parts; display the anatomy of; dissect. **2.** to examine to the slightest detail; analyze minutely: *The two women anatomized the new neighbor.* Also, *esp. Brit.,* **anatomise.** [< ML *anatomīz(āre)*. See ANATOMY, -IZE] —**a·nat′o·miz′a·ble,** *adj.* —**a·nat′o·mi·za′tion,** *n.* —**a·nat′o·miz′er,** *n.*

a·nat·o·my (ə nat′ə mē), *n., pl.* **-mies.** **1.** the science dealing with the structure of animals and plants. **2.** the structure of an animal or plant, or of any of its parts. **3.** dissection of all or part of an animal or plant in order to study its structure. **4.** a plant or animal that has been or will be dissected, or a model of such a dissected organism. **5.** a skeleton. **6.** *Informal.* the human body. **7.** an analysis or minute examination. [< L *anatomia* < Gk *anatom(ḗ)* a cutting up (*ana-* ANA- + *tom-* cut, var. of *tem-*, + *-ē* n. suffix) + *-ia* -Y[3]]

Anat′omy of Mel′ancholy, The, a long, philosophical treatise (1621) by Robert Burton.

a·nat·ro·pous (ə na′trə pəs), *adj. Bot.* (of an ovule) inverted at an early stage of growth, so that the micropyle is turned toward the funicle, the chalaza being situated at the opposite end. [ANA- + -TROPOUS]

an·at·ta (un′ət tä′), *n. Buddhism.* the doctrine asserting the nonexistence of a personal and immortal soul. Sanskrit, **anatman.** Cf. **Three Signs of Being.** [< Pali: lit., breathless]

a·nat·to (ə nat′ō, ä nä′tō), *n., pl.* **-tos.** annatto.

An·ax (an′aks), *n. Class. Myth.* one of the Gigantes and father of Asterius.

An·ax·ag·o·ras (an′ak sag′ər əs), *n.* **1.** 500?–428 B.C., Greek philosopher. **2.** a crater in the second quadrant of the face of the moon near the North Pole: about 32 miles in diameter. —**An·ax·ag·o·re·an** (an′ak sag′ə rē′ən), *adj.*

An·ax·ar·e·te (an′ak sar′i tē′), *n. Class. Myth.* a princess turned to stone for scorning the love of a commoner.

An·ax·ib·i·a (an′ak sib′ē ə), *n. Class. Myth.* **1.** a daughter of Atreus and Aërope, and the sister of Agamemnon and Menelaus. **2.** the wife of Nestor.

A·nax·i·man·der (ə nak′sə man′dər), *n.* **1.** 611?–547? B.C., Greek astronomer and philosopher. **2.** a walled plain in the second quadrant of the face of the moon, in the libration area and near the North Pole: about 54 miles in diameter. —**A·nax·i·man·dri·an** (ə nak′sə man′drē ən), *adj.*

An·ax·im·e·nes (an′ak sim′ə nēz′), *n.* **1.** fl. 6th century B.C., Greek philosopher at Miletus. **2.** a walled plain in the second quadrant of the face of the moon, in the libration area and near the North Pole: about 65 miles in diameter.

A·nax·o (ə nak′sō), *n. Class. Myth.* a daughter of Alcaeus who was the mother, by Electryon, of Alcmene.

an·ba (an′bə), *n.* father: a title of a clergyman or saint in the Coptic Church. Also, **amba.** [< Ar < Coptic *apa, abba* < Syriac *abbā* father]

ANC, Army Nurse Corps.

anc., ancient.

An·cae·us (an sē′əs), *n. Class. Myth.* **1.** a son of Poseidon who joined the Argonauts and became helmsman of the *Argo.* **2.** a descendant of Lycurgus who, among the Argonauts, was second in strength only to Hercules.

-ance, a suffix used to form nouns either from adjectives in *-ant* or from verbs: *brilliance; appearance.* [ME < OF < L *-antia* -ANCY]

an·ces·tor (an′ses tər), *n.* **1.** one from whom a person is descended; forefather; progenitor. **2.** *Biol.* the actual or hypothetical form or stock from which an organism has developed or descended. **3.** an object, idea, style, or occurrence serving as a prototype, forerunner, or inspiration to a later one: *the ancestor of the modern bicycle.* **4.** a person who serves as an influence or model for another; one from whom mental, artistic, spiritual, etc., descent is claimed: *Montaigne is his spiritual ancestor.* **5.** *Law.* one from whom an heir derives an inheritance. [ME *ancestre* < OF < L *antecēssor* ANTECESSOR]

an·ces·tral (an ses′trəl), *adj.* **1.** pertaining to ancestors; descending or claimed from ancestors: *an ancestral home.* **2.** serving as a forerunner, prototype, or inspiration. [earlier *ancestrel* < MF, equiv. to *ancestre* ANCESTOR + *-el* -AL[1]] —**an·ces′tral·ly,** *adv.*

an·ces·tress (an′ses tris), *n.* a female ancestor; a woman from whom a person is descended. [ANCEST(O)R + -ESS]

an·ces·try (an′ses trē), *n., pl.* **-tries.** **1.** ancestral descent; lineage. **2.** honorable or distinguished descent: *famous by title and ancestry.* **3.** a series of ancestors: *His ancestry settled the state.* **4.** the inception or origin of a phenomenon, object, idea, or style. **5.** the history or developmental process of a phenomenon, object, idea, or style. [late ME, equiv. to *ancestre* ANCESTOR + -Y[3]; r. ME *aunce(s)trie* < AF]
—**Syn. 1.** pedigree, genealogy, stock. **3.** family, line.

An·ches·mi·us (an kes′mē əs), *n. Class. Myth.* Zeus: so called because of a shrine to him on Mount Anchesmus, near Athens.

An·chi·a·le (an kī′ə lē′, -kē′-), *n. Class. Myth.* a nymph.

An·chin·o·ë (an kin′ō ē′), *n. Class. Myth.* a daughter of Nilus who was the mother, by Belus, of Aegyptus and Danaus.

An·chi·ses (an kī′sēz), *n. Class. Myth.* a prince of Troy, crippled as a punishment for boasting of his intimacy with Aphrodite, and later carried away from burning Troy by their son Aeneas.

an·chor (aŋ′kər), *n.* **1.** any of various devices dropped by a chain, cable, or rope to the bottom of a body of water for preventing or restricting the motion of a vessel or other floating object, typically having broad, hooklike arms that bury themselves in the bottom to provide a firm hold. **2.** any similar device for holding fast or checking motion: *an anchor of stones.* **3.** any device for securing a suspension or cantilever bridge at either end. **4.** any of various devices, as a metal tie, for binding one part of a structure to another. **5.** a means of stability: *Hope is his only anchor.* **6.** *Mil.* a key position in defense lines. **7.** *Sports.* **a.** Also, **anchor man.** the person on a team, esp. a relay team, who performs his assignment last. **b.** the person farthest to the rear on a tug-of-war team. **8. at anchor,** held in place by its anchor: *The new luxury liner is at anchor in the harbor.* **9. cast** or **drop anchor,** to let a vessel's anchor take hold to stay in place: *They dropped anchor in a bay to escape the storm.* **10. drag anchor,** (of a vessel) to move with a current or wind because an anchor has failed to hold. **11. weigh anchor,** to take up the anchor: *We will weigh anchor at dawn.* —*v.t.* **12.** to hold fast by an anchor. **13.** to fix or fasten; affix firmly: *The button was anchored to the cloth with heavy thread.* **14.** *Sports.* to serve as the anchor for: *He anchored the winning team in the mile relay.* —*v.i.* **15.** to drop anchor; lie or ride at anchor: *The ship anchored at dawn.* **16.** to keep hold or be firmly fixed: *The insect anchored fast to its prey.* [ME *anker, ancre,* OE *ancor* < L *ancora* < Gk *ánkyra*] —**an′chor·a·ble,** *adj.* —**an′chor·less,** *adj.* —**an′chor·like′,** *adj.*

STOCKLESS ANCHOR MUSHROOM ANCHOR

Anchor
A, Stock; B, Shank; C, Arm; D, Fluke; E, Palm; F, Bill

an·chor·age (aŋ′kər ij), *n.* **1.** a place for anchoring. **2.** a charge for occupying such a place. **3.** the act of anchoring; state of being anchored. **4.** that to which anything is fastened. **5.** a means of anchoring or making fast. **6.** that which can be relied on: *The Bible is her anchorage.* **7.** (in a suspension bridge) a massive masonry or concrete construction securing a cable at each end. **8.** *Dentistry.* **a.** an abutment. **b.** the locking in of a tooth filling by means of an undercut. [ANCHOR + -AGE]

An·chor·age (aŋ′kər ij), *n.* a seaport in S Alaska: earthquake 1964. 44,237 (1960).

an′chor ball′, *Naut.* a day shape consisting of a black ball not less than two feet in diameter, displayed in the fore rigging of a vessel at anchor.

an′chor bed′, *Naut.* a sloping, slightly projecting platform on the forecastle of a ship, for supporting an anchor when not in use. Also called **billboard.**

an′chor bell′, a bell rung in foggy weather by a vessel at anchor.

an′chor bend′. See **fisherman's bend.**

an′chor bolt′, any of several kinds of bolts inserted and fixed in masonry as a hold for timbers, shelves, etc.

an′chor buoy′, a buoy used to indicate the location of an underwater anchor.

an′chor deck′, *Naut.* a small forecastle housing the machinery for operating the anchors of a ship.

an′chor escape′ment, *Horol.* an escapement in which wedge-shaped pallets engage with an escape wheel having pointed teeth, usually facing in the direction of revolution, so that the escape wheel recoils slightly at every release. Also called **recoil escapement.** See diag. under **escapement.**

an·cho·ress (aŋ′kər is), *n.* a female anchorite. [ME *ankres,* equiv. to *ancre* ANCHORITE + *-es* -ESS]

an·cho·ret (aŋ′kər it, -kə ret′), *n.* anchorite. [earlier *anchorete,* syncopated var. of *anachorete* < L *anachōrēta* < Gk *anachōrētḗs,* equiv. to *anachōrḗ(ein)* (to) retire (*ana-* ANA- + *chōrein* to withdraw) + *-tēs* agent suffix] —**an·cho·ret·ic** (aŋ′kə ret′ik), *adj.* —**an′cho·ret′ism,** *n.*

an′chor ice′, ice formed below the surface of a body of water that attaches either to a submerged object or to the bottom. Also called **bottom ice, ground ice.**

an·cho·rite (aŋ′kə rīt′), *n.* one who has retired to a solitary place for a life of religious seclusion; hermit. Also, **anchoret.** [late ME *ancorite* < ML *anachōrīta,* var. of *anachōrēta* ANCHORET] —**an·cho·rit·ic** (aŋ′kə rit′ik), *adj.* —**an·cho·rit·ism** (aŋ′kə rī tiz′əm), *n.*

an′chor knot′. See **fisherman's bend.**

an′chor light′, *Naut.* a 32-point light, visible from at least two miles away, shown at night near the bow and not more than 20 feet above the deck of a vessel lying at anchor. Also called **riding light.**

an′chor man′, **1.** *Sports.* anchor (def. 7a). **2.** a person upon whose reliable performance an organization, business, activity, etc., depends; mainstay. **3.** *Radio and Television.* an announcer or newscaster at a central station who introduces and integrates a broadcast, as of an election, consisting of coverage coming from several different locations.

an·chor·man (aŋ′kər man′), *n., pl.* **-men.** See **anchor man** (def. 3).

an′chor plant′, a South American shrub, *Colletia cruciata,* having flattened, green branches and yellowish-white flowers.

an′chor pock′et, *Naut.* a recess in the bow of a vessel, for housing a stockless anchor.

an′chor ring′, *Geom.* torus (def. 2a).

an′chor shot′, *Naut.* See **grapple shot.**

an′chor span′, (on a suspension or cantilever bridge) a span from an anchorage to the nearest pier or tower.

an′chor watch′, *Naut.* a deck watch maintained by the crew of a vessel at anchor.

an·chor·y (aŋ′kə rē, aŋ′krē), *adj. Heraldry.* ancré. [m. F *ancré* by influence of *anchor*]

an·cho·vet·a (an′chō vet′ə), *n.* an anchovy, *Cetengraulis mysticetus,* found along the Pacific coast from British Columbia to Lower California, used for bait. [< Sp, equiv. to *anchov(a)* ANCHOVY + *-eta* < L *-itta* dim. suffix]

an·cho·vy (an′chō vē, -chə vē, an chō′vē), *n., pl.* **-vies.** any small, marine, herringlike fish of the family *Engraulidae,* esp. *Engraulis encrasicholus,* found in the Mediterranean Sea, used as food. [< Sp *ancho(v)a* < Genoese *anciòa* < ?]

an′chovy pear′, **1.** the fruit of a West Indian tree, *Grias cauliflora,* somewhat resembling the mango. **2.** the tree.

an·chu·sin (aŋ kyōō′sin), *n.* a red coloring matter obtained from the root of the alkanet, *Alkanna tinctoria.* [< NL *Anchus(a)* genus name (L *anchūsa* < Gk *ánchousa* alkanet) + -IN[2]]

anchylo-, var. of **ancylo-.**

an·chy·lose (aŋ′kə lōs′), *v.t., v.i.,* **-losed, -los·ing.** ankylose. —**an′chy·lo′sis,** *n.* —**an·chy·lot·ic** (aŋ′kə lot′ik), *adj.*

an·cienne no·blesse (äN syen′ nô bles′), *French.* the ancient nobility, esp. of the *ancien régime.*

an·cien ré·gime (äN syaN′ Rā zhēm′), *pl.* **an·ciens ré·gimes** (äN syaN′ Rā zhēm′). *French.* **1.** the political and social system of France before the revolution of 1789. **2.** the system of government during this period.

an·cient[1] (ān′shənt), *adj.* **1.** of or in time long past, esp. before the end of the Western Roman Empire A.D. 476: *ancient history.* **2.** dating from a remote period; of great age: *ancient rocks; ancient trees.* **3.** old; aged. **4.** being old in wisdom and experience; venerable. **5.** old-fashioned or antique. —*n.* **6.** a person who lived in ancient times, esp. one of the ancient Greeks, Romans, or Hebrews. **7.** one of the classical writers of antiquity. **8.** a very old or aged person, esp. if venerable or patriarchal. **9. ancients,** the civilized peoples, nations, or cultures of antiquity (usually prec. by *the*). [ME *auncien* < AF; OF *ancien* < VL *antiān(us),* equiv. to L *ante(ā)* before + *-ānus* -AN] —**an′cient·ness,** *n.*
—**Syn. 2.** ANCIENT, ANTIQUATED, ANTIQUE, OLD-

FASHIONED refer to something dating from the past. ANCIENT implies existence or first occurrence in a distant past: *an ancient custom.* ANTIQUATED connotes something too old or no longer useful: *an antiquated building.* ANTIQUE suggests a curious or pleasing quality in something old: *antique furniture.* OLD-FASHIONED may disparage something as being out of date or may approve something as being superior: *an old-fashioned hat; old-fashioned courtesy.* —**Ant. 2.** new.

an·cient² (ān′shənt), *n. Obs.* **1.** the bearer of a flag. **2.** a flag, banner, or standard; ensign. [var. of ENSIGN by confusion with ANCIENT¹]

An′cient Ar′abic Or′der of No′bles of the Mys′tic Shrine′. See under **Shriner.**

an′cient his′tory, 1. the study or a course of study of history before the end of the Western Roman Empire A.D. 476. **2.** *Informal.* information or events of the recent past which are common knowledge or are no longer pertinent: *Last week's news is ancient history.*

an·cient·ly (ān′shənt lē), *adv.* in ancient times; of old: *customs observed anciently.* [ANCIENT¹ + -LY]

An′cient Mys′tic Or′der Ro′sae Cru′cis (rō′zē krōō′sis). See under **Rosicrucian** (def. 2). *Abbr.:* AMORC

An′cient of Days′, the Supreme Being; God.

An′cient of Days′, The, a hand-colored print by William Blake, the frontispiece of his poem *Europe* (1794).

an·cient·ry (ān′shən trē), *n.* **1.** *Archaic.* **a.** ancient character or style. **b.** ancient times. **2.** *Obs.* **a.** ancient lineage. **b.** old people. [ANCIENT¹ + -RY]

an·ci·le (an sī′lē, äng kē′lā), *n., pl.* **an·cil·i·a** (an sil′ē ə, äng kil′-). *Rom. Religion.* **1.** a shield given by Mars to Numa Pompilius as the palladium of Rome. **2.** any of 11 counterfeits of this shield, carried with it on ceremonial occasions. [< L, equiv. to *an-* (var. of *ambi-* AMBI-) + *-cīle*, akin to *caedere* to cut]

an·cil·la (an sil′ə), *n., pl.* **-las. 1.** an accessory; auxiliary or adjunct. **2.** *Archaic.* a maidservant. [see ANCILLARY]

an·cil·lar·y (an′sə ler′ē *or, esp. Brit.,* an sil′ə rē), *adj.* accessory; auxiliary: *an ancillary function.* [< L *ancillāri(us)* relating to maidservants, equiv. to *ancill(a)* maidservant (*anc(ula)* maidservant + *-illa* dim. suffix) + *-ārius* -ARY (r. *-āris* -AR¹)]

an·cip·i·tal (an sip′i tᵊl), *adj. Bot., Zool.* two-edged: *ancipital stems.* [< L *ancipit-* (s. of *anceps*) two-headed, two-sided (*an-*, var. of *ambi-* AMBI- + *-cipit-*, var. of *caput* head) + -AL¹]

An·ci·us (an′shē əs, -shəs), *n. Class. Myth.* a centaur.

An·co·hu·ma (äng′kō ōō′mä), *n.* a peak of Mount Sorata. Cf. **Sorata, Mount.**

an·con (ang′kon), *n., pl.* **an·co·nes** (ang kō′nēz). **1.** the elbow. **2.** *Arch.* a bracket or console, as one supporting part of a cornice. [< L < Gk *ankṓn* elbow] —**an·co·nal** (ang kō′nᵊl), **an·co·ne·al** (ang kō′nē əl), *adj.* —**an′con·oid,** *adj.*

A, Ancon

An·cón (ang′kon; *Sp.* äng kōn′), *n.* a town in the Canal Zone, near the city of Panama: medical center of the Canal Zone. 1946 (1950).

an·co·na (än kô′nä; *Eng.* ang kō′nə), *n., pl.* **-ne** (-ne), *Eng.* **-nas.** *Italian.* an altarpiece, usually consisting of a painted panel or panels, reliefs, or statues set in an elaborate frame.

An·co·na (än kô′nä), *n.* **1.** a seaport in E Italy, on the Adriatic Sea. 99,678 (1961). **2.** one of a Mediterranean breed of chickens having mottled black-and-white plumage.

an·cré (ang′krā), *adj. Heraldry.* (of a cross) having the end of each limb divided and carved outward like the flukes of an anchor; moline: *a cross ancré.* Also, **anchory.** [< F, equiv. to *anchre* ANCHOR + *é* (< L *-atus* -ATE¹)]

An·cus Mar·ci·us (ang′kəs mär′shē əs, -shəs), *Rom. Legend.* a king of Rome, during whose reign the first bridge across the Tiber is believed to have been constructed.

-ancy, a combination of **-ance** and **-y,** used to form nouns denoting state or quality: *brilliancy.* [< L *-antia*, equiv. to *-ā-* thematic vowel + *-nt-* prp. suffix + *-ia* -Y³]

ancylo-, a learned borrowing from Greek meaning "hook," "joint," used in the formation of technical terms: *ancylostomiasis.* Also, **anchylo-, ankylo-.** [< Gk *ankylo-* (s. of *ankýlos*) crooked, curved, equiv. to *ánk(os)* bend (c. L *uncus* bent, E *angle* to fish with hook and line) + *-ylos* adjective-forming suffix]

an·cy·lo·sto·mi·a·sis (an′sə los′tə mī′ə sis), *n. Pathol.* hookworm (def. 2). Also, **ankylostomiasis.** [< NL, equiv. to *Ancylostom(a)* a genus of hookworms (see ANCYLO-, STOMA) + *-iasis* -IASIS]

and (and; *unstressed* ənd, ən), *conj.* **1.** (used to connect grammatically coordinate words, phrases, or clauses) with; along with; together with; added to; in addition to; besides; also; moreover: *pens and pencils.* **2.** as well as: *nice and warm.* **3.** then: *He read for an hour and went to bed.* **4.** also, at the same time: *to sleep and dream.* **5.** then again, repeatedly: *He coughed and coughed.* **6.** as opposed to different examples of the same kind: *There are dogs and dogs, some mean, some friendly.* **7.** (used to introduce a sentence, implying continuation) also; then: *And he said unto Moses.* **8.** to (used between two finite verbs): *Try and do it.* **9.** *Archaic or Dial.* if: *and you please.* Cf. **an².** **10. and so forth,** and so on; and others; et cetera: *We discussed traveling, sightseeing, and so forth.* **11. and so on,** and more of a similar kind; and further in the same way: *It was a summer filled with parties, picnics, and so on.* —*n.* **12.** an added condition or stipulation: *He accepted the job, no and about it.* **13.** Often, **ands.** an additional detail or particular: *It was a long story, with many ands.* **14.** conjunction (def. 4). [ME; OE *and, ond;* c. OS, OHG *ant,* OFris. Goth *and,* Icel *and-;* akin to G *und,* D *en* Skt *anti,* etc.]
—**Usage.** Since ETC. is an abbreviation for ET CETERA which means "and others," the form AND ETC. is condemned as being redundant. Use ETC. or AND OTHERS or AND SO FORTH instead.

and., *Music.* andante.

An·da·lu·sia (an′dᵊlōō′zhə, -shē ə), *n.* a region in S Spain, bordering on the Atlantic Ocean and the Mediterranean Sea. 33,712 sq. mi. Spanish, **An·da·lu·cí·a** (än′dä lōō thē′ä). —**An′da·lu′sian,** *adj. n.*

FRANCE
SPAIN
Madrid
PORTUGAL
Seville
Andalusia
MEDITERRANEAN SEA
Gibraltar
ATLANTIC OCEAN
MOROCCO
ALGERIA

an·da·lu·site (an′dᵊlōō′sīt), *n. Mineral.* an orthorhombic form of aluminum silicate, Al_2SiO_5, found in schistose rocks. [named after ANDALUSIA, where it was first found; see -ITE¹]

An·da·man (an′də mən), *adj.* **1.** Also, **Andamanese.** of or pertaining to the Andaman Islands, their inhabitants, or the inhabitants' language. —*n.* **2.** Andamanese (def. 1).

An′daman and Nic′o·bar Is′lands (nik′ə bär′, nik′ə bär′), a centrally administered territory of India, comprising two groups of islands in the E part of the Bay of Bengal, SW of Burma. 63,548 (1961); 3143 sq. mi. *Cap.:* Port Blair.

An·da·man·ese (an′də mə nēz′, -nēs′), *n., pl.* **-ese,** *adj.* —*n.* **1.** Also, **Andaman.** Also called **An′daman Is′lander.** a member of a Negrito people of the Andaman Islands. **2.** the language of the Andamanese, not known to be related to any other language despite attempts to connect it with Dravidian and with the aboriginal languages of Australia. —*adj.* **3.** Andaman (def. 1).

An′daman Is′lands, a group of islands in the E part of the Bay of Bengal, W of the Malay Peninsula. 18,939 (1951); 2508 sq. mi.

An′daman Sea′, a part of the Bay of Bengal, E of the Andaman and Nicobar islands. 300,000 sq. mi.

an·da·men·to (an′də men′tō; *It.* än′dä men′tô), *n., pl.* **-tos,** *It.* **-ta** (-tä). *Music.* **1.** an extended fugue subject. **2.** an episode in a fugue. [< It, equiv. to *anda(re)* to walk, proceed + *-mento* -MENT]

an·dan·te (an dan′tē, än dän′tā; *It.* än dän′te), *adj., adv., n., pl.* **-tes.** *Music.* —*adj., adv.* **1.** moderately slow and even. —*n.* **2.** an andante movement or piece. *Abbr.:* and. [< It: lit., walking (prp. of *andare* to walk); see -ANT]

an·dan·ti·no (an′dan tē′nō, än′dän-; *It.* än′dän tē′nô), *adj., adv., n., pl.* **-nos,** *It.* **-ni** (-nē). *Music.* —*adj., adv.* **1.** slightly faster than andante. —*n.* **2.** an andantino movement or piece. [< It, equiv. to *andan(te)* walking + *-ino* dim. suffix]

and′ cir′cuit, a circuit in an electronic computer that is energized only when all of its inputs are energized.

An·de·an (an dē′ən, an′dē-), *adj.* of or like the Andes.

Ande′an con′dor. See under **condor** (def. 1).

Ande′an deer′, huemul.

An·děl (an del′, an′del), *n.* a walled plain in the fourth quadrant of the face of the moon: about 19 miles in diameter.

An·de·lee (an′dᵊlē′), *n.* a girl's given name.

An·der·lecht (än′dər lekht′), *n.* a city in central Belgium, near Brussels. 99,485 (est. 1964).

An·der·sen (an′dər sən), *n.* **Hans Christian** (hanz), 1805–75, Danish author, esp. of fairy tales.

An·der·sen Nex·ö (ä′nər sən nik′sœ). See **Nexö, Martin Andersen.**

An·der·son (an′dər sən), *n.* **1. Carl David,** born 1905, U.S. physicist; discoverer of the positron: Nobel prize 1936. **2. Dame Judith,** born 1898, Australian actress in the U.S. **3. John (Bayard),** born 1922, U.S. political leader: member of the House of Representatives since 1961. **4. Marian,** born 1908, U.S. contralto. **5. Maxwell,** 1888–1959, U.S. dramatist. **6. Sherwood,** 1876–1941, U.S. novelist and short-story writer. **7.** a city in central Indiana. 49,061 (1960). **8.** a city in NW South Carolina. 41,316 (1960). **9.** a town in N California. 4492 (1960).

An′derson East′ Side′, a town in central Indiana. 3778 (1960).

An·der·son·ville (an′dər sən vil′), *n.* a village in SW Georgia: site of a Confederate military prison. 263 (1960).

An·des (an′dēz), *n.* (*construed as pl.*) a mountain range in W South America, extending ab. 4500 mi. from N Colombia and Venezuela S to Cape Horn. Highest peak, Aconcagua, 22,834 ft.

an·de·sine (an′di zēn′), *n.* a mineral, intermediate in the plagioclase feldspar group, having a play of colors and usually found as crystals in igneous rocks. [named after ANDES; see -INE²]

an·des·ite (an′di zīt′), *n.* a volcanic rock composed essentially of plagioclase feldspar, resembling trachyte in appearance. [named after ANDES; see -ITE¹] —**an·de·sit·ic** (an′di zit′ik), *adj.*

An′des light′ning, an electrical discharge of the corona type, occurring over mountains when the area is electrically disturbed. Also called **An′des glow′, An′des lights′.**

An·dhra Pra·desh (än′drə prə dāsh′), a state in SE India, formed from portions of Madras and Hyderabad states 1956. 35,983,447 (1961); 105,963 sq. mi. *Cap.:* Hyderabad.

An·die (an′dē), *n.* a boy's or girl's given name. Also, **Andy.**

An·di·ki·thi·ra (an′də ki thēr′ə; *Gk.* än′dē kē′thē rä) *n.* Antikythera.

and·i·ron (and′ī′ərn), *n.* one of a pair of metal stands, usually of iron or brass, for supporting logs in a fireplace. [ME *aundyr(n)e* < OF *andier,*? < Gaulish **andera* heifer (through use of cows' heads as decorations on andirons); *-iron* by assoc. with IRON]

Andirons

An·di·zhan (än′di zhän′), *n.* a city in E Uzbekistan, in the SW Soviet Union in Asia. 154,000 (est. 1964).

and/or, (used to imply that any or all of the things named may be affected): *insurance covering fire and/or wind damage.*

an·do·ro·ba (an′də rō′bə), *n.* carapa. [< Tupi < Sp or Pg]

An·dor·ra (an dôr′ə, -dor′ə; *Sp.* än dôr′rä), *n.* a republic in the E Pyrenees between France and Spain, under the joint suzerainty of France and the Spanish Bishop of Urgel. 11,000 (est. 1963). 191 sq. mi. *Cap.:* Andorra. French, **An·dorre** (äN dôr′). —**An·dor′ran,** *adj., n.*

andr-, var. of **andro-** before a vowel: *androecium.*

An·dra·da e Sil·va (äN drä′də e sēl′və), **Jo·sé Bo·ni·fa·cio de** (zhō ze′ bō′nē fä′syōō dĭ), 1763–1838, Brazilian statesman and scientist.

an·dra·dite (an′drə dīt′), *n.* a mineral, calcium-iron garnet, $Ca_3Fe_2Si_3O_{12}$, occurring in brown, green, or black crystals. [named after J. B. de ANDRADA E SILVA; see -ITE¹]

An·drás·sy (an dras′ē; *Hung.* on′drä shē), *n.* **1. Count Julius,** 1823–90, Hungarian statesman. **2.** his son, **Count Julius** (*Gyula*), 1860–1929, Hungarian statesman.

An·dré (än′drā *or, for 1,* an′drē; *for 2 also Fr.* äN drā′), *n.* **1. John,** 1751–80, British major hanged as a spy by the Americans in the Revolutionary War. **2.** a boy's given name, French form of **Andrew.**

An·dre·a (an′drē ə, än′-, än drā′ə), *n.* a boy's or girl's given name.

An·dre·a del Sar·to (än drā′ə del sär′tō; *It.* än dre′ä del sär′tô), **1.** (*Andrea Domenico d'Annolo di Francesco*) 1486–1531, Italian painter. **2.** (*italics*) a dramatic monologue (1855) by Robert Browning.

An·dre·a′nof Is′lands (an′drē an′of; *Russ.* än dre-ä′nof), a group of islands in the W part of the Aleutian Islands. 1432 sq. mi.

An·dre·ev (än dre′yəf), *n.* **1. An·drei An·dre·e·vich** (än drā′ än dre′yə vich), 1895–1971, Russian statesman. **2.** See **Andreyev, Leonid Nikolaevich.**

An·drew (an′drōō), *n.* **1.** one of the 12 apostles of Jesus. Mark 3:18; John 1:40–42. **2.** a boy's given name.

An·drewes (an′drōōz), *n.* **Lancelot,** 1555–1626, English theologian: one of the translators of the Authorized Version of the Bible.

An′drew of Crete′, A.D. c650–730, Greek Orthodox archbishop of Crete; poet; reputed inventor of the musical canon.

An·drews (an′drōōz), *n.* **1. Charles Mc·Lean** (mə klān′), 1863–1943, U.S. historian and author. **2. Roy Chapman,** 1884–1960, U.S. naturalist, explorer, and author. **3.** a town in E South Carolina. 2995 (1960).

An·dre·yev (än dre′yəf), *n.* **Le·o·nid Ni·ko·la·e·vich** (le o nēt′ ni ko lä′yə vich), 1871–1919, Russian novelist, short-story writer, and playwright. Also, **Andreev.**

An·drić (än′drich), *n.* **I·vo** (ē′vô), 1892–1975, Yugoslavian poet, novelist, and short-story writer: Nobel prize 1961.

andro-, a learned borrowing from Greek meaning "male," used in the formation of compound words: *androsterone.* Also, **andr-, -androus.** [< Gk *andrō(s)*, gen. of *anḗr* old man; akin to Skt *nara-,* L *Nero*]

an·dro·cen·tric (an′drə sen′trik), *adj.* dominated by males or by masculine interests: *an androcentric society.* [ANDRO- + CENTRIC]

An·dro·cle·a (an′drō klē′ə), *n. Class. Myth.* a daughter of Antipoenus of Thebes. Cf. **Alcis.**

An·dro·cles (an′drə klēz′), *n.* a legendary Roman slave who was spared in the arena by a lion from whose foot he had long before extracted a thorn. Also, **An·dro·clus** (an′drə kləs).

An′drocles and the Li′on, a comedy (1913) by G. B. Shaw.

an·dro·clin·i·um (an′drə klin′ē əm), *n., pl.* **-clin·i·a** (-klin′ē ə). *Bot.* clinandrium. [< NL, equiv. to *andro-* ANDRO- + *-clinium* < Gk *klīníon*, dim. of *klīnē* bed; see -CLIN]

an·dro·co·ni·um (an′drə kō′nē əm), *n., pl.* **-ni·a** (-nē ə). a scale on the forewing of certain male butterflies from which an odor attractive to females is emitted. [< NL, equiv. to *andro-* ANDRO- + *-conium* < Gk *kónion*, neut. of *kónios* dusty (*kóni(s)* dust + *-os* adj. suffix)]

an·droc·ra·cy (an drok′rə sē), *n.* social rule by men. [ANDRO- + -CRACY] —**an·dro·crat·ic** (an′drə krat′ik), *adj.*

An·droc·ra·tes (an drok′rə tēz′), *n. Class. Myth.* the hero who founded Plataea.

an·dro·di·oe·cious (an′drō dī ē′shəs), *adj. Bot.* having staminate and monoclinous flowers on separate plants of the same species. [ANDRO- + DIOECIOUS] —**an·dro·di·oe·cism** (an′drō dī ē′siz əm), *n.*

an·droe·ci·um (an drē′shē əm), *n., pl.* **-ci·a** (-shē ə). *Bot.* the stamens of a flower collectively. [< NL < Gk *andr-* ANDR- + *oikíon*, dim. of *oîkos* house] —**an·droe·cial** (an drē′shəl), *adj.*

an·dro·gam·one (an′drə gam′ōn), *n. Biochem.* a gamone liberated by a male gamete. [ANDRO- + GAMONE]

an·dro·gen (an′drə jən), *n. Biochem.* any substance, natural or synthetic, that promotes masculine characteristics. [ANDRO- + -GEN] —**an·dro·gen·ic** (an′drə-jen′ik), *adj.*

An·drog·e·us (an droj′ē əs), *n. Class. Myth.* a son of Minos and Pasiphaë who fell victim to Athenian King Aegeus: in revenge, Minos waged war on the Athenians and forced them to send a tribute of seven maidens and seven youths to the Minotaur every nine years.

an·dro·gyne (an′drə jīn′), *n.* an androgynous organism. [< MF < L *androgyn(us)* < Gk *andrógynos* hermaphrodite, equiv. to *andro-* ANDRO- + *gyn-* GYN- + *-os* masc. n. suffix]

an·drog·y·nous (an droj′ə nəs), *adj.* **1.** *Bot.* having staminate and pistillate flowers in the same inflorescence. **2.** being both male and female; hermaphroditic. [ANDROGYNE + -OUS] —**an·drog′y·ny,** *n.*

an·droid (an′droid), *n.* an automaton in the form of a human being. [ANDR- + -OID]

An·drom·a·che (an drom′ə kē′), *n.* **1.** *Class. Myth.* the wife of Hector and mother of Astyanax. **2.** (*italics.*) a tragedy (c419 B.C.) by Euripides.

An·dro·maque (äN drô mak′), *n.* a tragedy (1667) by Racine.

an·drom·e·da (an drom′i də), *n.* See **Japanese andromeda.** [special use of ANDROMEDA]

An·drom·e·da (an dromʹi də), *n., gen.* **-dae** (-dēʹ) for 2. **1.** *Class Myth.* the daughter of Cassiopeia and wife of Perseus, by whom she was rescued from a sea monster. **2.** *Astron.* the Chained Lady, a northern constellation between Pisces and Cassiopeia, containing within its borders the external stellar system known as the Great Nebula in Andromeda.

an·dro·mo·noe·cious (anʹdrō mə nēʹshəs), *adj. Bot.* having staminate and monoclinous flowers on the same plant. [ANDRO- + MONOECIOUS] —**an·dro·mo·noe·cism** (anʹdrō mə nēʹsiz əm), *n.*

an·dron (anʹdron), *n.* **1.** (in an ancient Greek house) an apartment for men, esp. one for banqueting. **2.** (in an ancient Roman house) a passage between two peristyles. [< Gk, equiv. to *andr-* ANDR- + *-ōn* n. suffix]

An·dron (anʹdron), *n. Class. Myth.* a son of Anius who was given the power of prophecy by Apollo. Also, **Andrus.**

an·dro·pet·a·lous (anʹdrō petʹᵊləs), *adj. Bot.* having petaloid stamens, or petals with a small anther at the apex, as certain double flowers. [ANDRO- + PETALOUS]

An·droph·o·nos (an drofʹə nos/), *n. Class. Myth.* an epithet of Aphrodite, meaning "manslayer."

an·dro·phore (anʹdrə fōrʹ, -fôrʹ), *n.* (in certain flowers) a stalk or column supporting the stamens, formed by the fusion of their filaments. [ANDRO- + -PHORE]

An·dro·pov (än drôʹpof), *n.* **Yu·ri** (yo͞oʹri), born 1914, Soviet political leader: general secretary of the Communist party since 1982.

An·dros (anʹdrəs), *n.* **1. Sir Edmund,** 1637–1714, British governor in the American Colonies, 1686–89, 1692–98. **2.** an island in the Bahamas, in the N West Indies. 7852 (est. 1955); 1600 sq. mi.

An·dros·cog·gin (anʹdrə skogʹin), *n.* a river flowing from NE New Hampshire through SW Maine into the Kennebec River. 171 mi. long.

an·dro·sphinx (anʹdrə sfingksʹ), *n., pl.* **-sphinx·es, -sphin·ges** (-sfinʹjēz). a sphinx with the head of a man. [< Gk; see ANDRO-, SPHINX]

an·dro·spore (anʹdrə spōrʹ, -spôrʹ), *n. Bot.* the zoospore of certain algae, which develops into a small male plant producing antherozoids. [ANDRO- + SPORE]

an·dros·ter·one (an drosʹtə rōnʹ), *n. Biochem.* a sex hormone, $C_{19}H_{30}O_2$, usually present in male urine. [ANDRO- + STER(OL) + -ONE]

An·drou·et du Cer·ceau (äN dro͞o eʹ dy ser sōʹ), **1. Jacques** (zhäk), (*Jacques Androuet*), c1510–84, architect, author, and illustrator of architectural books. **2.** his sons, **Bap·tiste** (ba tēstʹ), c1544–1602, and **Jacques,** died 1614, French architects. **3. Jean** (zhäN), died c1650, architectural designer (son of Baptiste Androuet du Cerceau).

-androus, a word element meaning "male," occurring as final element of a compound word: *polyandrous.* [< NL *-andrus.* See ANDR-, -OUS]

An·drus (anʹdrəs), *n. Class. Myth.* Andron.

-andry, a word element referring to males, occurring as final element of a compound word: *polyandry.* [< Gk *-andria.* See ANDR-, -Y³]

An·dva·ri (änʹdwä rē), *n. Scand. Legend.* a dwarf from whom Loki extorted a treasure, including a magic ring, to give to Hreidmar as wergild for the killing of Otter: Andvari then cursed all those who would possess the treasure. Also, **An·dvar** (änʹdwär), **Anʹdva·re.**

An·dy (anʹdē), *n.* a boy's or girl's given name. Also, **Andie.**

ane (ān), *adj., n., pron. Dial.* one. [ME *an,* var. of *on* ONE]

-ane, *Chem.* a suffix used in names of hydrocarbons of the methane or paraffin series: *propane.* [< L *-ānus* -AN]

A·neale (ə nēlʹ), *n.* a boy's given name.

a·near (ə nērʹ), *adv., prep. Dial.* near. [A-² + NEAR]

an·ec·dot·age¹ (anʹik dōʹtij), *n.* anecdotes collectively. [ANECDOTE + -AGE]

an·ec·dot·age² (anʹik dōʹtij), *n.* the state of being advanced in age and strongly inclined to tell reminiscent anecdotes: *Grandfather is in his anecdotage.* [b. ANECDOTE and DOTAGE]

an·ec·do·tal (anʹik dōtʹᵊl, anʹik dōtʹᵊl), *adj.* **1.** pertaining to, marked by, or consisting of anecdotes: *an anecdotal history of jazz.* **2.** (of the treatment of subject matter in representational art) pertaining to the relationship of figures or to the arrangement of elements in a scene so as to emphasize the story content of a subject. Cf. **narrative** (def. 5). Also, **anecdotic, anecdotical.** [ANECDOTE + -AL¹] —**anʹec·doʹtal·ism,** *n.* —**anʹec·doʹtal·ist,** *n.* —**anʹec·doʹtal·ly,** *adv.*

an·ec·dote (anʹik dōtʹ), *n.* a short narrative concerning a particular incident or event of an interesting or amusing nature. [earlier *anecdota* (pl.) < ML < Gk *anékdota* things unpublished, neut. pl. of *anékdotos,* equiv. to *an-* AN-¹ + *ékdotos* given out, ptp. of *ekdídonai* to give out, publish (*ek-* EC- + *didónai* to give)]

an·ec·dot·ic (anʹik dotʹik), *adj.* **1.** anecdotal. **2.** given to relating anecdotes. Also, **anʹec·dotʹi·cal.** [ANECDOTE + -IC] —**anʹec·dotʹi·cal·ly,** *adv.*

an·ec·dot·ist (anʹik dōʹtist), *n.* a relator of anecdotes. [ANECDOTE + -IST]

an·e·cho·ic (anʹe kōʹik), *adj.* (of a recording chamber, television studio, or the like) characterized by an unusually low degree of reverberation. [AN-¹ + ECHOIC]

an·e·lace (anʹᵊlāsʹ), *n.* a short sword having a double-edged blade tapering sharply to a point: worn by civilians from the 13th to the 16th centuries. Also, **anlace.** [ME *an(e)las* < OF *ale(s)naz* (by methathesis), deriv. of *alesne* awl < OHG *alasna.* See AWL]

an·e·las·tic·i·ty (anʹi la stisʹi tē, an ēʹla stisʹ-), *n. Physics.* the property of a solid in which the deformation of the solid depends on the time rate of change of stress as well as on the stress itself. [AN¹ + ELASTICITY] —**an·e·las·tic** (anʹi lasʹtik), *adj.*

a·nele (ə nēlʹ), *v.t.,* **a·neled, a·nel·ing.** *Archaic.* to administer extreme unction to. [ME *anelien,* equiv. to *an-* ON + *elien* to oil, equiv. to *el-* (OE *ele* oil < L *oleum*) + *-i-* thematic vowel + *-en* (OE *-an*) inf. ending]

an·e·lec·tric (anʹi lekʹtrik), *adj. Elect.* not capable of acquiring an electric charge when subjected to friction. [AN-¹ + ELECTRIC]

a·ne·mi·a (ə nēʹmē ə), *n.* **1.** *Pathol.* a quantitative deficiency of the hemoglobin, often accompanied by a reduced number of red blood cells, and causing pallor, weakness, and breathlessness. **2.** a lack of power, vigor, vitality, or colorfulness: *His writing suffers from anemia.* Also, **anaemia.** [< NL < Gk *anaimía* want of blood. See AN-¹, -EMIA]

a·ne·mic (ə nēʹmik), *adj.* **1.** *Pathol.* suffering from anemia. **2.** lacking power, vigor, vitality, or colorfulness: *an anemic novel.* Also, **anaemic.** [ANEM(IA) + -IC]

anemo-, a learned borrowing from Greek meaning "wind": *anemograph.* [< Gk, comb. form of *ánemos;* akin to Skt *anilas,* L *animus* breath]

a·nem·o·chore (ə nemʹə kōrʹ, -kôrʹ), *n.* an anemochorous plant, seed, or spore. [ANEMO- + Gk *chorē(ein)* (to) spread]

an·e·moch·o·rous (anʹə mokʹər əs), *adj.* **1.** (of a fruit, seed, or spore) adapted for dispersion by wind. **2.** (of a plant) having anemochorous fruits, seeds, or spores, as the dandelion. Also, **a·ne·mo·cho·ric** (ə nēʹmə-kōrʹik, -kôrʹ-). [ANEMOCHORE + -OUS]

a·nem·o·gram (ə nemʹə gramʹ), *n.* an anemographic record. [ANEMO- + -GRAM¹]

a·nem·o·graph (ə nemʹə grafʹ, -gräfʹ), *n.* a recording anemometer. [ANEMO- + -GRAPH] —**a·nem·o·graph·ic** (ə nemʹə grafʹik), *adj.* —**a·nemʹo·graphʹi·cal·ly,** *adv.*

an·e·mog·ra·phy (anʹə mogʹrə fē), *n. Meteorol. Rare.* anemometry. [ANEMO- + -GRAPHY]

an·e·mom·e·ter (anʹə momʹi tər), *n. Meteorol.* any instrument for measuring the speed of the wind. [ANEMO- + -METER] —**an·e·mo·met·ric** (anʹə mō meʹtrik), **anʹe·mo·metʹri·cal,** *adj.* —**anʹe·mo·metʹri·cal·ly,** *adv.*

an·e·mom·e·try (anʹə momʹi trē), *n. Meteorol.* the science of measuring the speed of the wind. [ANEMO- + -METRY]

a·nem·o·ne (ə nemʹə nēʹ), *n.* **1.** any ranunculaceous plant of the genus *Anemone,* esp. *A. quinquefolia,* a spring wild flower having a slender stem and delicate whitish blossoms. **2.** See **sea anemone.** [< L < Gk: lit., daughter of the wind, equiv. to *ánem(os)* wind + *-ōnē* fem. patronymic suffix; see -ONE]

an·e·moph·i·lous (anʹə mofʹə ləs), *adj.* (of seed plants) pollinated by wind-borne pollen. [ANEMO- + -PHILOUS] —**anʹe·mophʹi·ly,** *n.*

a·nem·o·scope (ə nemʹə skōpʹ), *n. Meteorol.* any device showing the existence and direction of the wind. [ANEMO- + -SCOPE]

an·e·mo·sis (anʹə mōʹsis), *n., pl.* **-ses** (-sēz). See **wind shake.** [ANEMO- + -OSIS]

an·e·mo·tax·is (anʹə mō takʹsis), *n.* oriented movement in response to a current of air. [ANEMO- + -TAXIS]

A·nem·o·tis (ə nemʹə tis), *n. Class. Myth.* an epithet of Athena, meaning "of the winds," referring to her ending violent windstorms in Messenia.

an·e·mot·ro·pism (anʹə moʹtrə pizʹəm), *n. Biol.* orientation in response to a current of air. [ANEMO- + TROPISM] —**an·e·mo·trop·ic** (anʹə mə tropʹik), *adj.*

an·en·ce·pha·lia (anʹən sə fālʹyə), *n. Med.* congenital absence of part or all of the brain. [< NL; see AN-¹, ENCEPHAL-, -IA] —**an·en·ce·phal·ic** (anʹən sə falʹik), **an·en·ceph·a·lous** (anʹən sefʹə ləs), *adj.*

an-end (an endʹ), *adj. Naut.* upright in its customary position, as an upper mast when fidded. [*an-* ON + END¹]

a·nenst (ə nenstʹ), *prep. Brit. Dial.* anent (def. 2). [ME *anenist,* equiv. to *anen* (see ANENT) + *-is* adv. gen. suffix + excrescent *-t*]

a·nent (ə nentʹ), *prep.* **1.** in regard to; concerning. **2.** *Brit.* Also, **anenst.** beside; in line with. [ME var. (with excrescent *-t*) of *anen,* OE *on emn, on efen* on EVEN¹ (ground), with, beside]

an·ep·i·graph·ic (an epʹə grafʹik), *adj.* (of a coin, artifact, etc.) without a legend or inscription. Also, **an·e·pig·ra·phous** (anʹə pigʹrə fəs). [AN-¹ + EPIGRAPHIC]

an·er·gy (anʹər jē), *n.* **1.** *Pathol.* deficiency of energy. **2.** *Immunol.* lack of immunity to an antigen. [< NL *anergia.* See AN-¹, ERGO-¹, -Y³] —**a·ner·gic** (a nûrʹjik, anʹər-), *adj.*

an·er·oid (anʹə roidʹ), *adj.* **1.** using no fluid. —*n.* **2.** See **aneroid barometer.** [A-⁶ + Gk *nēr(ós)* wet, fluid (akin to *náein* to flow) + -OID]

anʹeroid barʹograph, *Meteorol.* aneroid barometer equipped with an automatic recording mechanism. Also called **aneroidograph.**

anʹeroid baromʹeter, a device for measuring atmospheric pressure, often specially calibrated for use as an altimeter, consisting of a box or chamber partially exhausted of air, having an elastic top and a pointer to indicate the degree of compression of the top caused by the external air. Cf. **mercury barometer.**

anʹeroid capʹsule, *Meteorol.* a box or chamber of thin metal, partially evacuated of air, used in the aneroid barometer and pressure altimeter.

an·er·oid·o·graph (anʹə roiʹdə grafʹ, -gräfʹ), *n.* See **aneroid barograph.** [ANEROID + -O- + -GRAPH]

anes (ānz), *adv. Dial.* once. [ME, OE, equiv. to *ān* ONE + *-es* adv. gen. suffix]

A·nes·i·dor·a (ə nesʹi dôrʹə), *n. Class. Myth.* an epithet of Demeter, meaning "sender-up of gifts."

an·es·the·sia (anʹis thēʹzhə), *n.* **1.** *Med.* general or local insensibility, as to pain and other sensation, induced by certain drugs. **2.** *Pathol.* general loss of the senses of feeling, such as pain, heat, cold, touch, and other less common varieties of sensation. Also, **anaesthesia.** [< NL < Gk *anaisthēsía* want of feeling. See AN-¹, ESTHESIA]

an·es·the·sim·e·ter (ə nesʹthi simʹi tər), *n. Med.* **1.** a device for measuring the amount of anesthetic given by inhalation. **2.** an esthesiometer. Also, **an·es·the·si·om·e·ter** (anʹis thēʹzē omʹi tər). [ANESTHESI(A) + -METER]

an·es·the·si·ol·o·gist (anʹis thēʹzē olʹə jist), *n.* a physician who specializes in anesthesiology. Also, **anaesthesiologist.** [ANESTHESIOLOG(Y) + -IST]

an·es·the·si·ol·o·gy (anʹis thēʹzē olʹə jē), *n.* the science of administering anesthetics. Also, **anaesthesiology.** [ANESTHESI(A) + -O- + -LOGY]

an·es·thet·ic (anʹis thetʹik), *n.* **1.** a substance that produces anesthesia, as ether, chloroform, cocaine, etc. —*adj.* **2.** pertaining to or causing physical insensibility: *an anesthetic gas.* **3.** physically insensitive: *Chloroform is used to produce an anesthetic state.* Also, **anaesthetic.** [< Gk *anaísthēt(os)* without feeling, senseless. See AN-¹, ESTHETIC] —**anʹes·thetʹi·cal·ly,** *adv.*

an·es·the·tist (ə nesʹthi tist), *n.* a person who administers anesthetics, usually a specially trained doctor or nurse. Also, **anaesthetist.** [ANESTHET(IZE) + -IST]

an·es·the·tize (ə nesʹthi tīzʹ), *v.t.,* **-tized, -tiz·ing.** to render physically insensible, as by an anesthetic. Also, **anaesthetize.** [< Gk *anaísthēt(os)* (see ANESTHETIC) + -IZE] —**a·nesʹthe·ti·zaʹtion,** *n.*

an·e·thole (anʹə thōlʹ), *n. Chem., Pharm.* a white, crystalline powder, $CH_3CH{=}CHC_6H_4OCH_3$, having a sweet taste, obtained from anise or fennel oils or synthesized: used chiefly in perfumes, flavoring, and in medicine as an antiseptic and carminative. Also called **anise camphor.** [< Gk *ánēth(on)* dill, anise + -OLE]

A·ne·to (ä neʹtō), *n.* **Pi·co de** (pēʹkō de), Spanish name of **Pic de Nethou.**

a·neuch (ə no͞okhʹ), *adj., n., adv., interj. Scot.* enough.

a·neu·ri·a (ə no͝orʹē ə, ə nyo͝orʹ-), *n. Med., Pathol.* neurasthenia. [< NL; see AN-¹, NEUR-, -IA] —**a·neuʹric,** *adj.*

an·eu·rin (anʹyə rin), *n. Biochem.* thiamine. Also, **an·eu·rine** (anʹyə rēnʹ). [AN-¹ + -NEUR- + -IN²]

A·neu·rin (ə nīʹrin), *n.* a boy's given name.

an·eu·rysm (anʹyə rizʹəm), *n. Pathol.* a permanent cardiac or arterial dilatation usually caused by weakening of the vessel wall by diseases such as syphilis or arteriosclerosis. Also, **anʹeu·rism.** [< Gk *aneúrysma* dilation, equiv. to *aneurys-* (var. s. of *aneurýnein* to dilate; see AN-³, EURY-) + *-ma* n. suffix] —**anʹeu·rysʹmal, an/eu·risʹmal,** *adj.* —**anʹeu·rysʹmal·ly, anʹeu·risʹmal·ly,** *adv.*

a·new (ə no͞oʹ, ə nyo͞oʹ), *adv.* **1.** over again; once more: *to play the tune anew.* **2.** in a new form or manner: *to write the story anew.* [ME *onew,* OE *of niowe;* r. OE *edniwe* once more]

an·frac·tu·os·i·ty (an frakʹcho͞o osʹi tē), *n.* **1.** the state or quality of being anfractuous. **2.** a channel, crevice, or passage full of windings and turnings. [< L *anfrāctuōs(us)* winding (*anfrāctu(s)* a bend (see AMBI-, FRACTO-) + *-ōsus* -OSE¹) + -ITY]

an·frac·tu·ous (an frakʹcho͞o əs), *adj.* characterized by windings and turnings; sinuous; circuitous: *an anfractuous path.* [back formation from ANFRACTUOSITY]

ANG, Air National Guard.

an·ga (ungʹgə), *n.* any of the eight practices of Yoga, including the abstentions, mandatory actions, posture, breath control, control of the senses, concentration, meditation, and contemplation. Cf. **antaranga.** [< Skt: discipline]

an·ga·kok (angʹgə kokʹ), *n.* a shaman in Eskimo society. Also, **anʹge·kokʹ.** [< Eskimo]

An·gang (änʹgängʹ), *n. German.* divination based on the first man or animal met on a journey. [< G: advance, approach]

An·ga·ra (änʹgä räʹ), *n.* a river in the S Soviet Union in Asia, flowing NW from Lake Baikal to the Yenisei River: called Upper Tunguska in its lower course. 1151 mi. long.

An·garsk (än gärskʹ), *n.* a city in the S RSFSR, in the S Soviet Union in Asia, near Lake Baikal. 160,000.

an·ga·ry (angʹgə rē), *n. Internat. Law.* the right of a belligerent state to seize and use the property of neutrals for purposes of warfare, subject to payment of full compensation. [< LL *angaria* service to a lord < Gk *angareía* couriership, equiv. to *ángaros* official courier (< Pers) + *-eia* -Y³]

an·gel (ānʹjəl), *n.* **1.** one of a class of spiritual beings; a celestial attendant of God. In medieval angelology, angels constituted the lowest of the nine celestial orders (seraphim, cherubim, thrones, dominations or dominions, virtues, powers, principalities or princedoms, archangels, and angels). **2.** a conventional representation of such a being, in human form, with wings. **3.** a messenger, esp. of God. **4.** a person, esp. a woman, having such qualities attributed to an angel as beauty, kindliness, etc.: *an angel of mercy.* **5.** an attendant or guardian spirit. **6.** a deceased person whose soul is regarded as having been accepted into heaven. **7.** one who provides financial backing for some undertaking, as a play, political campaign, etc. **8.** an English gold coin issued from 1470 to 1634, varying in value from 6s. 8d. to 10s. and bearing on its obverse a figure of St. Michael killing the dragon. **9.** *Slang.* an image on a radar screen caused by a low-flying object, often a bird. **10.** *Naut. Slang.* See **jolly jumper.** —*v.t.* **11.** *Informal.* to provide financial backing for. [ME, OE < L *angel(us)* < eccl. Gk *ángelos* messenger of God, special use of Gk *ángelos,* messenger; r. OE *engel* < L, as above]

An·gel (ānʹjəl), *n.* a boy's or girl's given name. Also, **Anʹgell.**

An·ge·la (anʹjə lə), *n.* a girl's given name.

An·ge·la Me·ri·ci (änʹje lä me rēʹchē), **Saint,** 1474–1540, Italian ecclesiastic, founder of the Ursuline order.

anʹgel bed/, **1.** *Fr. Furniture.* a bed having a suspended or bracketed canopy of less than full length. Cf. **duchesse bed. 2.** *U.S. Furniture.* a bed without posts, as a truckle bed.

anʹgel dustʹ, *Slang.* a powerful hallucinogenic drug made from phencyclidine, widely used as an illicit narcotic, often causing bizarre behavior.

An·ge·le·no (anʹjə lēʹnō), *n., pl.* **-nos. 1.** a Los Angeleno. —*adj.* **2.** of or pertaining to Los Angeles.

an·gel·fish (ānʹjəl fishʹ), *n., pl.* (*esp. collectively*) **-fish,** (*esp. referring to two or more kinds or species*) **-fish·es. 1.** any of several brightly colored, spiny-headed butterflyfishes of the genera *Holocanthus* and *Pomacanthus,* which have a compressed body and are found in tropical shore waters. **2.** See **angel shark.** [ANGEL + FISH]

anʹgel foodʹ cake/, a white sponge cake with a light, delicate texture obtained by using stiffly beaten egg whites and cream of tartar. Also called **anʹgel cakeʹ.** [after the white color of the cake]

an·gel·hood (ānʹjəl ho͝odʹ), *n.* **1.** the state or condition of being an angel; angelic nature. **2.** angels collectively: *the angelhood of heaven.* **3.** an angelic being.

an·gel·ic (an jelʹik), *adj.* **1.** of or belonging to angels: *the angelic host.* **2.** like or befitting an angel; saintly: *angelic sweetness.* Also, **an·gelʹi·cal.** [late ME *angelyk* < LL *angelic(us)* < eccl. Gk *angelikós.* See ANGEL, -IC] —**an·gelʹi·cal·ly,** *adv.* —**an·gelʹi·cal·ness,** *n.*

An·gel·ic (an jelʹik), *n.* a girl's given name. Also, **Angelica.**

an·gel·i·ca (an jelʹə kə), *n.* **1.** Also called **archangel.** any umbelliferous plant of the genus *Angelica,* esp. *A. Archangelica,* cultivated in Europe for its aromatic odor and medicinal root and for its stalks, which are candied and eaten. **2.** the candied stalks of this plant. **3.** (*cap.*) a sweet white California wine. [< ML (*herba*) *angelica* ANGELIC (herb)]

CONCISE ETYMOLOGY KEY: <, descended or derived from; <, whence; b., blend of, blended; c., cognate with; deriv., derivative; equiv., equivalent; imit., imitative; m., modification of; obl., oblique; r., replacing; s., stem; sp., spelling; translation; ?, origin unknown, perhaps; *, hypothetical. See the full key inside the front cover.

An·gel·i·ca (an jel′ə kə), *n.* a girl's given name, Latin form of **Angelic.**

angel′ica tree′, **1.** *U.S.* Hercules'-club (def. 2). **2.** See **prickly ash** (def. 1).

An·ge·li·co (an jel′ə kō′; *It.* än je′lē kō), *n.* **Fra** (frä; *It.* frä), (*Giovanni da Fiesole*), 1387–1455, Italian painter. —**An·gel·i·can** (an jel′ə kən), *adj.*

An·ge·li·na (an′jə lē′nə, -lī′-), *n.* a girl's given name, form of **Angela.** Also, **An·ge·line** (an′jə lēn′), **Angelyn.**

an·gé·lique (an′jə lēk′), *n.* **1.** a South American, leguminous tree, *Dicorynia paraensis.* **2.** the hard, reddish-brown wood of this tree, used in shipbuilding. [< F: plant of *Angelica* genus. See ANGELIC]

An·gé·lique (an′jə lēk′; *Fr.* äN zhā lēk′), *n.* a girl's given name, French form of **Angelic.**

An·gell (ān′jəl), *n.* **1. James Row·land** (rō′lənd), 1869–1949, U.S. educator. **2. Norman** (*Sir Ralph Norman Angell Lane*), 1874–1967, English pacifist, economist, and writer: Nobel peace prize 1933. **3.** Also, **Angel.** a boy's or girl's given name.

an′gel light′, *Archit.* (in an English Perpendicular window) a compartment, approximately triangular, formed by the arch of the window, an arch of a lower tier of tracery, and a mullion of an upper tier of tracery.

An·ge·lo (an′jə lō′), *n.* a boy's given name.

angelo-, a combining form of **angel:** *angelology.*

an·gel·ol·o·gy (ān′jə lol′ə jē), *n.* doctrine on theory concerning angels. [ANGELO- + -LOGY]

an′gel's foot′stool, *Naut. Slang.* See **jolly jumper.**

an′gel shark′, any shark of the genus *Squatina,* found in warm and temperate shore waters, having a depressed, flat body and large, winglike pectoral fins.

an′gel shot′, (formerly, in naval gunnery) a compound shot used against the rigging of an enemy, consisting of two hemispherical pieces linked to a disklike central piece.

an·gel's-trum·pet (ān′jəlz trum′pit), *n.* either of two South American, solanaceous plants of the genus *Datura, D. arborea* or *D. suaveolens,* having large, trumpet-shaped flowers.

An·ge·lus (an′jə ləs), *n. Rom. Cath. Ch.* **1.** a devotion in memory of the Annunciation. **2.** Also called **An′gelus bell′.** the bell tolled in the morning, at noon, and in the evening to indicate the time when the Angelus is to be recited. Also, **an′ge·lus.** [< LL, from the first word of the service: *Angelus (domini nuntiavit Mariae).* See ANGEL]

Angelus, The a painting (1857?–59?) by Jean François Millet.

An′gelus Si·le′si·us (si lē′shē əs, -zhē əs, sī), (*Johannes Scheffler*) 1627–77, German poet.

An·ge·lyn (an′jə lin), *n.* a girl's given name. Also, **Angelina, Angeline.**

an·ger (ang′gər), *n.* **1.** a strong feeling of displeasure and belligerence aroused by a real or supposed wrong; wrath; ire. **2.** *Dial.* pain or smart, as of a sore. **3.** *Obs.* grief; trouble. —*v.t.* **4.** to excite to anger or wrath. **5.** *Dial.* to cause to smart; inflame. —*v.i.* **6.** to become angry: *He angers with little or no provocation.* [ME < Scand; cf. Icel *angr* sorrow, grief, akin to OHG *angust* (G *Angst* fear), L *angor* anguish]
—**Syn. 1.** resentment, exasperation; choler, bile, spleen. ANGER, FURY, INDIGNATION, RAGE imply deep and strong feelings aroused by injury, injustice, wrong, etc. ANGER is a sudden violent displeasure accompanied by an impulse to retaliate: *a burst of anger.* INDIGNATION, a more formal word, implies deep and justified anger: *indignation at cruelty or against corruption.* RAGE is vehement anger: *rage at being frustrated.* FURY is rage so great that it resembles insanity: *the fury of a woman scorned.* **4.** displease, vex, irritate, exasperate, infuriate, enrage, incense, madden.

An·ger·bo·da (äng′gər bō′də), *n. Scand. Myth.* a giantess who was the mother of Loki's children, Fenrir and Hel, and also of the Midgard serpent. Also, **Angrbodha, Angurboda.**

an·ger·ly (ang′gər lē), *adv.* **1.** *Archaic.* angrily. **2.** *Obs.* hurtfully; painfully. [ME; see ANGER, -LY]

An·ge·ro·na (an′jə rō′nə), *n.* the ancient Roman goddess of anguish. Also, **An·ge·ro·ni·a** (an′jə rō′nē ə).

An·gers (an′jərz, ang′gərz; *Fr.* äN zhā′), *n.* a city in and capital of Maine-et-Loire, in W France. 122,269 (1962).

An·ge·vin (an′jə vin), *adj.* **1.** of or pertaining to Anjou or its inhabitants. **2.** relating to the counts of Anjou or their descendants, esp. those who ruled in England, or to the period during which they ruled. —*n.* **3.** an inhabitant of Anjou. **4.** a member of an Angevin royal house, esp. that of the Plantagenets in England. Also, **An·ge·vine** (an′jə vin, -vīn′).

angi-, var. of **angio-** before a vowel.

An·gie (an′jē), *n.* a boy's or girl's given name, form of **Angel.**

an·gi·na (an jī′nə; *in Med. often* an′jə nə), *n. Pathol.* **1.** any inflammatory affection of the throat or fauces, as quinsy, croup, mumps, etc. **2.** See **angina pectoris.** [< L: quinsy, equiv. to *ang(ere)* (to) throttle, torture (see ANGER) + *-ina* n. use of fem. of *-inus* adj. suffix]

an·gi·nal (an jīn′əl, an′jə nəl), *adj.* of, noting, or pertaining to angina, esp. angina pectoris. Also, **an·gi·nous** (an jī′nəs), **an·gi·nose** (an′jə nōs′, an jī′nōs). [ANGIN(A) + -AL¹]

angi′na pec′to·ris (pek′tə ris), *Pathol.* a syndrome characterized by paroxysmal, constricting pain below the sternum, most easily precipitated by exertion or excitement and caused by ischemia of the heart muscle, usually due to a coronary artery disease, such as arteriosclerosis. [< NL: angina of the chest]

angio-, a learned borrowing from Greek meaning "vessel," "container," used in the formation of compound words: *angiosperm.* Also, *esp. before a vowel,* **angi-.** [< Gk, comb. form repr. *angeîon,* equiv. to *ángos* vessel, vat, shell + *-eion* dim. suffix]

an·gi·o·blast (an′jē ə blast′), *n. Embryol.* one of several mesenchymal cells capable of developing into the endothelium of the blood vessels. [ANGIO- + -BLAST] —**an′gi·o·blas′tic,** *adj.*

an·gi·o·car·di·og·ra·phy (an′jē ō kär′dē og′rə fē), *n., pl.* **-phies.** x-ray examination of the heart and its blood vessels following intravenous injection of radiopaque fluid. [ANGIO- + CARDIOGRAPHY] —**an·gi·o·car·di·o·graph·ic** (an′jē ō kär′dē ə graf′ik), *adj.*

an·gi·o·carp (an′jē ə kärp′), *n.* a plant bearing an angiocarpous fruit. [ANGIO- + -CARP]

an·gi·o·car·pous (an′jē ō kär′pəs), *adj.* **1.** (of a fruit) partially or wholly enclosed in a shell, involucre, or husk. **2.** (of a fungus or lichen) having the ascocarp immersed or enclosed in the thallus. Also, **an′gi·o·car′pic.** Cf. **gymnocarpous.** [ANGIO- + -CARPOUS]

an·gi·ol·o·gy (an′jē ol′ə jē), *n.* the branch of anatomy dealing with blood vessels and lymphatics. [ANGIO- + -LOGY]

an·gi·o·ma (an′jē ō′mə), *n., pl.* **-mas, -ma·ta** (-mə tə). *Pathol.* a tumor consisting chiefly of dilated or newly formed blood vessels (**hemangioma**), or lymph vessels (**lymphangioma**). [ANGI- + -OMA] —**an·gi·om·a·tous** (an′jē om′ə təs, -ō′mə-), *adj.*

an·gi·o·plas·ty (an′jē ə plas′tē), *n., pl.* **-ties.** the surgical repair of a blood vessel, as by inserting a balloon to widen a blocked artery. [ANGIO- + -PLASTY]

an·gi·o·sperm (an′jē ə spûrm′), *n.* a plant having its seeds enclosed in an ovary; a flowering plant. Cf. **gymnosperm.** [ANGIO- + -SPERM]

an·gi·o·sper·mous (an′jē ō spûr′məs), *adj.* of or pertaining to an angiosperm; having enclosed seeds. [ANGIOSPERM + -OUS]

an·gi·ot·o·nase (an′jē ot′ənās′), *n. Biochem.* hypertensinase. [ANGIO- + TON(IC) + -ASE]

an·gi·o·to·nin (an′jē ə tō′nin, an′jē ot′ənin), *n. Biochem.* hypertensin. [ANGIO- + TON(IC) + -IN²]

an·gi·o·tribe (an′jē ə trīb′), *n. Surg.* a hemostat in the form of a large forceps used to arrest hemorrhage by crushing an artery with the tissue in which it is embedded. Also called **vasotribe.** [ANGIO- + *-tribe* < Gk *tríbein* to rub]

Ang·kor (ang′kōr, -kôr), *n.* a vast assemblage of ruins of the Khmer empire, near the modern city of Siem Reap in NW Cambodia: many elaborately carved and decorated temples, stone statues, gateways, and towers.

Ang′kor Thom′ (tōm), the site of the ruined capital city of the Khmer empire, at Angkor.

Ang′kor Wat′ (wät, vät), the largest and best preserved Khmer temple in the Angkor complex of ruins. Also, **Ang′kor Vat′** (vät).

Angl., **1.** Anglican. **2.** Anglicized.

an·glaise (äng glāz′, -glez′), *n.* **1.** an old English country-dance. **2.** a dance form in quick duple time, occasionally constituting part of an 18th-century instrumental suite. [< F, fem. of *anglais* English]

an·gle¹ (ang′gəl), *n., v.,* **-gled, -gling.** —*n.* **1.** *Geom.* **a.** the space within two lines or three or more planes diverging from a common point, or within two planes diverging from a common line. **b.** the figure so formed. **c.** the amount of rotation needed to bring one line or plane into coincidence with another. **2.** an angular projection; a projecting corner: *the angles of a building.* **3.** a viewpoint; standpoint: *He looked at the problem only from his own angle.* **4.** *Journalism.* **a.** slant (def. 11). **b.** the point of view from which copy is written, esp. when the copy is intended to interest a particular audience: *A political reporter wrote the main story and the financial editor added a sidebar from the investor's angle.* **5.** an aspect of an event or situation, as of one forming the basis of a news report; side; phase: *The yellow press played up the sex angle.* **6.** *Informal.* opportunity for gain; advantage: *What was his angle in buying up penny stocks?* **7.** See **angle iron** (def. 2). —*v.t.* **8.** to move or bend in an angle. **9.** to set, fix, direct, or adjust at an angle: *to angle a spotlight.* **10.** *Journalism.* to write or edit in such a way as to appeal to a particular audience; slant: *She angled her column of chitchat toward teen-agers.* —*v.i.* **11.** to turn sharply in a different direction: *The road angles to the right.* **12.** to move or go in angles or at an angle: *The trout angled downstream.* [ME < MF < L *angulus;* akin to ANKLE, ANGLE²]

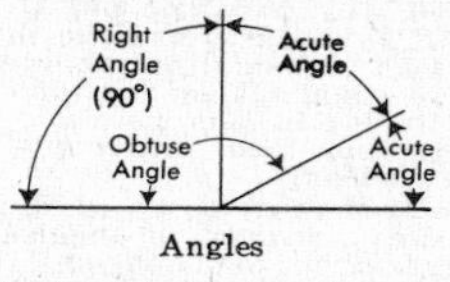

Angles

an·gle² (ang′gəl), *v.,* **-gled, -gling,** *n.* —*v.i.* **1.** to fish with hook and line. **2.** to attempt to get something by sly or artful means; fish: *to angle for a compliment.* —*n.* **3.** *Archaic.* a fishhook or fishing tackle. [ME *angel,* OE *angul;* c. G *Angel,* Icel *öngull.* See ANGLE¹]

an′gle bar′. See **angle iron** (def. 2).

an′gle board′, a board serving as a gauge for an angle planed across the end of other boards.

an′gle cleat′, a short length of angle iron used as a bracket. Also called **seat angle.**

an′gle col′lar, stapling.

an·gled (ang′gəld), *adj.* **1.** having an angle or angles. **2.** *Heraldry.* **a.** noting an interrupted partition line having the two parts offset and a line at right angles connecting them. **b.** (of an ordinary) having an edge or edges so formed. [ANGLE¹ + -ED³]

an′gle i′ron, **1.** an iron or steel bar, brace, or cleat in the form of an angle. **2.** Also called **angle, angle bar, L bar, L beam.** a piece of structural iron or steel having a cross section in the form of an L. See illus. under **shape.**

an′gle of attack′, the acute angle between the chord of an aircraft wing or other airfoil and the direction of the relative wind. Also called, *esp. Brit.,* **angle of incidence.**

an′gle of climb′, *Aeron.* the angle between the axis of motion of a climbing aircraft and the horizontal plane.

an′gle of devia′tion, *Optics.* the angle equal to the difference between the angle of incidence and the angle of refraction of a ray of light passing through the surface between one medium and another of different refractive index. Also called **deviation.**

an′gle of dip′, dip (def. 30).

an·gle-off (ang′gəl ôf′, -of′), *n.* **1.** the angle formed by the line of flight of an aerial target and the line of sight on a gun of an attacking aircraft. **2.** the angle formed by the line of flight of an attacking aircraft and that of an aerial target. [ANGLE¹ + OFF]

an′gle of in′cidence, **1.** Also called **incidence.** the angle that a straight line, ray of light, etc., meeting a surface, makes with a normal to the surface at the point of meeting. **2.** (on an airplane) the angle, usually fixed, between a wing or tail root chord and the axis of the fuselage. **3.** *Brit. Aeron.* See **angle of attack.**

ECD, Angle of incidence on surface AB; CD, Perpendicular; E′CD, Angle of reflection

an′gle of lag′, *Physics, Elect.* the phase difference, expressed in degrees, by which one sinusoidal function moves behind a second having the same period, as alternating current moving behind the alternating voltage.

an′gle of lead′ (lēd), *Physics, Elect.* the phase difference, expressed in degrees, by which one sinusoidal function is moving ahead of a second having the same period, as alternating voltage moving ahead of the alternating current.

an′gle of pitch′, *Aeron.* the acute angle between the longitudinal axis of an aircraft or spacecraft and the direction of the wind relative to the vehicle.

an′gle of polariza′tion, *Obs.* Brewster angle. See under **Brewster's law.**

an′gle of reflec′tion, the angle that a ray of light or the like, reflected from a surface, makes with a normal to the surface at the point of reflection. See diag. under **angle of incidence.**

an′gle of refrac′tion, *Physics, Optics.* the angle between a refracted ray and a line drawn normal to the interface between two media at the point of refraction. See diag. under **refraction.**

an′gle of roll′, *Aeron.* the acute angle between the lateral axis of an aircraft or spacecraft and a horizontal plane.

an′gle of view′, *Optics.* the angle formed at a nodal point of a lens by the intersection of two lines drawn from the opposite ends of an image produced by the lens.

an′gle of yaw′, *Aeron.* the acute angle between the longitudinal axis of an aircraft or spacecraft and a given reference direction, as viewed from above.

an′gle plate′, an angular metal plate or casting for clamping and supporting work in metalworking machines.

an·gle·pod (ang′gəl pod′), *n.* an asclepiadaceous plant, *Vincetoxicum* (or *Gonolobus*) *Gonocarpas,* of southern and central U.S. [ANGLE¹ + POD¹; so called from its shape]

an·gler (ang′glər), *n.* **1.** a person who angles. **2.** Also called **goosefish.** any large pediculate fish of the family *Lophiidae,* esp. *Lophius americanus,* found along the Atlantic coast of America, having an immense mouth and a large, depressed head to which is attached a wormlike filament for luring prey. **3.** any of various related fishes of the order *Pediculati.* [ANGLE² + -ER¹]

An·gles (ang′gəlz), *n. pl.* a West Germanic people that migrated from Sleswick to Britain in the 5th century A.D. and founded the kingdoms of East Anglia, Mercia, and Northumbria. As early as the 6th century their name was extended to all the Germanic inhabitants of Britain. [OE *Angle* pl. (var. of *Engle*) tribal name of disputed orig.]

An·gle·sey (ang′gəl sē), *n.* an island and county in NW Wales. 51,700 (1961); 276 sq. mi. *Co. seat:* Holyhead.

an·gle·site (ang′gəl sīt′), *n.* a mineral, lead sulfate, $PbSO_4$, found in massive deposits and in colorless or variously tinted crystals: a minor ore of lead. [named after ANGLESEY where it was first found; see -ITE¹]

an·gle·smith (ang′gəl smith′), *n.* a blacksmith skilled in forging angle irons, beams, etc., into various forms used in shipbuilding. [ANGLE¹ + SMITH]

An·gle·ton (ang′gəl tən), *n.* a town in S Texas. 7312 (1960).

an·gle·wing (ang′gəl wing′), *n.* any of several butterflies, esp. of the genus *Polygonia,* having angular notches on the outer edges of the forewings. [ANGLE¹ + WING]

an·gle·worm (ang′gəl wûrm′), *n.* an earthworm, as used for bait in angling. [ANGLE² + WORM]

An·gli·a (ang′glē ə), *n.* Latin name of **England.**

An·gli·an (ang′glē ən), *adj.* **1.** Also, **Anglic.** of or relating to the Angles or to East Anglia. —*n.* **2.** a member of the Angles. **3.** the northern and central group of Old English dialects, spoken in Northumbria and Mercia. [< L *Angli* the ANGLES + -AN]

An·glic (ang′glik), *n.* **1.** the English language in a simplified spelling devised by R. E. Zachrisson (1880–1937), a Swedish philologist, to make English easier to use as an auxiliary language. About 40 of the most frequent words are kept in their usual spellings; the rest of the vocabulary is spelled phonetically with letters of the traditional 26-letter alphabet. —*adj.* **2.** Anglian (def. 1). [< ML *anglic(us)* English, equiv. to L *Angl(ī)* the English (see ANGLES) + *-icus* -IC]

An·gli·can (ang′glə kən), *adj.* **1.** of or pertaining to the Church of England. **2.** related in origin to and in communion with the Church of England, as various Episcopal churches in other parts of the world. **3.** *Chiefly U.S.* English (def. 1). —*n.* **4.** a member of the Church of England or of a church in communion with it. **5.** one who upholds the system or teachings of the Church of England. [< ML *Anglicān(us).* See ANGLIC, -AN] —**An′gli·can·ly,** *adv.*

An′glican chant′, *Music.* a harmonized, strictly metrical chant to which canticles, psalms, and other liturgical texts are sung in the Anglican Church.

An′glican Church′, the Church of England and those churches that are in communion with it and each other and that share essentially its doctrines and order, as the Church of Ireland, the Episcopal Church of Scotland, the Church of Wales, and the Protestant Episcopal Church in the U.S.

An·gli·can·ism (ang′glə kə niz′əm), *n.* the doctrines, principles, or system of the Anglican Church. [ANGLICAN + -ISM]

An·gli·ce (ang′gli sē), *adv.* in English; as the English would say it; according to the English way: *Córdoba, Anglice "Cordova."* [< ML, equiv. to *anglic(us)* English (see ANGLIC) + *-ē* adv. suffix]

An·gli·cise (ang′gli sīz′), *v.t., v.i.,* **-cised, -cis·ing.** *Chiefly Brit.* Anglicize. Also, **an′gli·cise′.** —**An′gli·ci·sa′tion, an′gli·ci·sa′tion,** *n.*

An·gli·cism (ang′gli siz′əm), *n.* **1.** an English idiom. **2.** *U.S.* a Briticism. **3.** the state of being English; characteristic English quality. **4.** a word, idiom, or characteristic feature of the English language occurring in or borrowed by another language. **5.** any custom, manner, idea, etc., characteristic of the English people. [< ML *anglic(us)* English + -ISM]

An·gli·cist (ang′gli sist), *n.* an authority on the English language or English literature. [< ML *anglic(us)* English + -IST]

An·gli·cize (ang′gli sīz′), *v.t., v.i.,* **-cized, -ciz·ing.** to make or become English in form or character: *to Anglicize the pronunciation of a Russian name.* Also, **an′gli·cize′;** *esp. Brit.,* **Anglicise, anglicise.** [< ML *anglic(us)* English + -IZE] —**An′gli·ci·za′tion, an′gli·ci·za′tion,** *n.*

An·gli·fy (ang′glə fī′), *v.t.,* **-fied, -fy·ing.** to Anglicize. [< L *Anglī* the English + -FY] —**An′gli·fi·ca′tion,** *n.*

an·gling (ang′gling), *n.* the act or art of fishing with a hook and line, usually attached to a rod. [ANGLE[2] + -ING[1]]

An·glist (ang′glist), *n.* an authority on England, its language, or its literature. [< G < ML *Angl(ia)* England + G *-ist* -IST]

Ang·lis·tics (ang glis′tiks), *n.* (*construed as sing.*) the study of the English language and of literature written in English. [< G *Anglistik,* equiv. to *Anglist* ANGLIST + *-ik* -ICS]

An·glo (ang′glō), *n., pl.* **-glos.** (among Spanish-speaking people in the southwest U.S.) an English-speaking American of north-European ancestry. [separate use of ANGLO-]

Anglo-, a combining form of **English:** *Anglo-Norman; Anglo-Catholic.* [< L *Angl(ī)* + -o-]

An·glo-A·mer·i·can (ang′glō ə mer′i kən), *adj.* **1.** belonging to, relating to, or involving England and America, esp. the United States, or the peoples of the two countries: *the Anglo-American policy toward Russia.* **2.** of or pertaining to Anglo-Americans. —*n.* **3.** a native or descendant of a native of England, who has settled in or become a citizen of America, esp. of the United States. —**An′glo-A·mer′i·can·ism,** *n.*

An·glo-Aus·tral·ian (ang′glō ô strāl′yən), *adj.* **1.** belonging, relating to, or involving England and Australia, or the people of the two countries. —*n.* **2.** a native or descendant of a native of England who has settled in Australia.

An·glo-Cath·o·lic (ang′glō kath′ə lik, -kath′lik), *n.* **1.** one who emphasizes the Catholic character of the Anglican Church, opposing a Protestant designation. **2.** an Anglican Catholic, as opposed to a Roman or Greek Catholic. —*adj.* **3.** of or pertaining to Anglo-Catholicism or Anglo-Catholics. —**An·glo-Ca·thol·i·cism** (ang′glō-kə thol′i siz′əm), *n.*

An′glo-E·gyp′tian Sudan′ (ang′glō i jip′shən), former name of **Sudan.**

An·glo-French (ang′glō french′), *adj.* **1.** belonging to, relating to, or involving England and France, or the people of the two countries. **2.** of or pertaining to the Anglo-French dialect. —*n.* **3.** Also called **Anglo-Norman.** the dialect of French current in England from the Norman Conquest to the end of the Middle Ages.

An·glo-Gal·lic (ang′glō gal′ik), *adj.* *Numis.* noting or pertaining to the coins or series of coins issued by the English kings from Henry II to Henry VIII for their French domains.

An·glo-In·di·an (ang′glō in′dē ən), *adj.* **1.** belonging to, relating to, or involving England and India, esp. as politically associated: *Anglo-Indian treaties.* **2.** of or pertaining to Anglo-Indians or their speech. —*n.* **3.** a person of English and Indian ancestry. **4.** the speech of such persons, characterized by the Anglicizations of Indian words. *Abbr.:* AInd **5.** a person of English birth or citizenship living in India.

Anglo-Irish (ang′glō ī′rish), *adj.* Hiberno-Saxon.

Anglo-Latin (ang′glō lat′ᵊn, -in), *n.* Medieval Latin as used in England. *Abbr.:* AL

An·glo·ma·ni·a (ang′glə mā′nē ə, -mān′yə), *n.* an excessive devotion to, interest in, or tendency to imitate English institutions, manners, customs, etc. [ANGLO- + MANIA]

An·glo·ma·ni·ac (ang′glə mā′nē ak′), *n.* a person having Anglomania. [< NL; see ANGLOMANIA, -AC] —**An·glo·ma·ni·a·cal** (ang′glō mə nī′ə kəl), *adj.*

An·glo-Nor·man (ang′glō nôr′mən), *adj.* **1.** pertaining to the period, 1066–1154, when England was ruled by Normans. **2.** of or pertaining to Anglo-Normans or the Anglo-Norman dialect. —*n.* **3.** a Norman who settled in England after 1066, or one of his descendants. **4.** Anglo-French (def. 2).

An·glo·phile (ang′glə fīl′, -fil), *n.* one who is friendly to or admires England or English customs, institutions, etc. Also, **An·glo·phil** (ang′glə fil). [ANGLO- + -PHILE] —**An·glo·phil·i·a** (ang′glə fil′ē ə, -fēl′yə), *n.* —**An·glo·phil·i·ac** (ang′glə fil′ē ak′, -fēl′yak), **An·glo·phil·ic** (ang′glə fil′ik), *adj.*

An·glo·phobe (ang′glə fōb′), *n.* one who hates or fears England or anything English. [ANGLO- + -PHOBE]

An·glo·pho·bi·a (ang′glə fō′bē ə), *n.* an intense hatred or fear of England or anything English. [ANGLO- + -PHOBIA] —**An·glo·pho·bi·ac** (ang′glə fō′bē ak′), **An·glo·pho·bic** (ang′glə fō′bik), *adj.*

An·glo-Sax·on (ang′glō sak′sən), *n.* **1.** a person whose native language is English. **2.** an Englishman of the period before the Norman Conquest. **3.** a person of English descent. **4.** *U.S.* a person of colonial descent or British origin. **5.** See **Old English** (def. 1). **6.** plain and simple English. **7.** the original Germanic element in the English language. —*adj.* **8.** of, pertaining to, or characteristic of the Anglo-Saxons. **9.** pertaining to Anglo-Saxon. [< NL *Anglo-Saxonēs* (pl.) the English people (i.e., Angles and Saxons taken as one), ML *Anglī Saxonēs,* Latinizations of OE *Angle* ANGLES and OE *Seaxan* SAXONS]

An′glo-Ve·ne′tian glass′ (ang′glō və nē′shən), glassware made in England from the late 16th to the late 17th centuries in imitation of Venetian models.

An·go·la (ang gō′lə), *n.* a republic in SW Africa: former overseas province of Portugal; gained independence 1975. 5,500,000; 481,226 sq. mi. *Cap.:* Luanda. Formerly, **Portuguese West Africa.** —**An·go′lan,** *adj., n.*

An·go·lese (ang′gō lēz′, -lēs′, -gə-), *n., pl.* **-lese.** a member of any of the Bantu tribes residing in Angola. [ANGOL(A) + -ESE]

an·gor (ang′gər), *n.* *Med.* **1.** extreme distress or mental anguish, usually of physical origin. **2.** See **angina pectoris.** [< L: suffocation. See ANGER]

An·go·ra (ang gôr′ə, -gōr′ə, an- *for 1–3, 5–7;* ang gôr′ə, -gōr′ə, ang′gər ə *for 4*), *n.* **1.** See **Angora cat. 2.** Also, **Angora wool.** the hair of the Angora goat or of the Angora rabbit. **3.** yarn, fabric, or a garment made from this hair. **4.** Ankara. **5.** See **Angora goat. 6.** See **Angora rabbit.** —*adj.* **7.** made from a yarn or fabric of the hairs of the Angora goat or Angora rabbit: *an Angora sweater.* [dial. var. of ANKARA]

Ango′ra cat′, a long-haired variety of the domestic cat, raised originally in Angora, having a long body, pointed head, and bushy tail. Also called **Angora.**

Ango′ra goat′, a variety of domestic goat, raised originally in Angora, having long, silky hair called mohair. Also called **Angora.**

Ango′ra rab′bit, one of a breed of rabbits raised chiefly in Europe for its long, silky hair. Also called **Angora.**

Ango′ra wool′, Angora (def. 2).

an·gos·tu·ra bark′ (ang′gə stŏŏr′ə, -styŏŏr′ə), the bitter, aromatic bark of either of two South American, rutaceous trees, *Galipea officinalis* or *G. cusparia,* used in medicine and in the preparation of liqueurs and bitters. Also called **an′gos·tu′ra.** [after *Angostura* (now Ciudad Bolívar), town in central Venezuela]

An·gou·mois (äng′gōōm wä′; *Fr.* äN gōō mwa′), *n.* a region and former province of W France: famous as source of cognac.

Angoumois′ grain′ moth′, a gelechiid moth, *Sitotroga cerealella,* the larvae of which feed on stored corn and other grains. [after ANGOUMOIS]

An·gra do He·ro·is·mo (*Port.* äng′grə dōō e′rōō-ēzh′mōō), a seaport on and the capital of the island of Terceira in the Azores: former capital of the Azores. 10,296 (1950).

An·gra Main·yu (ang′rə mīn′yōō), *Zoroastrianism.* the evil spirit who contends against Spenta Mainyu. Also called **Ahriman.** [Avestan]

An·gr·bo·dha (äng′gər bō′də), *n.* *Scand. Myth.* Angerboda.

an·gry (ang′grē), *adj.,* **-gri·er, -gri·est. 1.** feeling or showing anger or resentment (usually fol. by *at, with,* or *about*): *to be angry at the dean; to be angry about the snub.* **2.** characterized by anger; wrathful: *angry words.* **3.** *Med.* inflamed, as a sore; exhibiting inflammation. **4.** (of an object or phenomenon) exhibiting a characteristic or creating a mood associated with anger or danger, as by color, sound, force, etc.: *an angry sea; the boom of angry guns.* [ME *angry.* See ANGER, -Y[1]] —**an′gri·ly,** *adv.* —**an′gri·ness,** *n.*

—**Syn. 1.** irate, incensed, enraged, infuriated, furious, mad; provoked, irritated. —**Ant. 1.** calm.

an′gry young′ man′, 1. (*often cap.*) one of a group of British writers since the late 1950's whose works reflect strong dissatisfaction with, frustration by, and rebellion against tradition and society. **2.** any author writing in this manner. **3.** any frustrated, rebellious person. Also, *referring to a woman,* **an′gry young′ wom′an.**

angst (ängkst), *n., pl.* **äng·ste** (engk′stə). a feeling of dread, anxiety, or anguish. [< G: fear, anxiety, OHG *angust* (c. MLG *angest,* MD *anxt*), equiv. to *ang-* (akin to *eng* narrow, constricted) + *-st* abstract nominal suffix]

Ång·ström (ang′strəm; *Swed.* ông′strœm), *n.* **An·ders Jo·nas** (an′dərz jō′nəs; *Swed.* än′dərs yōō′näs), 1814–74, Swedish astronomer and physicist.

Ång·ström (ang′strəm), *n.* a crater in the second quadrant of the face of the moon: about 6 miles in diameter.

ang′strom u′nit (ang′strəm), a unit of length, equal to one tenth of a millimicron; or one ten millionth of a millimeter, primarily used to express electromagnetic wavelengths. *Abbr.:* Å, A., Å Also, **Ang′strom u′nit, angstrom, Angstrom.** [named after A. J. ÅNGSTRÖM]

An·guier (äN gyā′), *n.* **Fran·çois** (fräN swa′), 1604–69, and his brother **Mi·chel** (mē shel′), 1614–86, French sculptors.

An·guil·la (ang gwil′ə), *n.* an island in the N Leeward Islands, in the E West Indies: a British colony. 34 sq. mi. Cf. **St. Kitts-Nevis-Anguilla.**

an·guil·li·form (ang gwil′ə fôrm′), *adj.* having the shape or form of an eel. [< L *anguill(a)* eel (*angu(is)* snake + *-illa* dim. suffix) + -I- + -FORM]

an·guine (ang′gwin), *adj.* pertaining to or resembling a snake. [< L *anguīn(us)* pertaining to a snake, equiv. to *angu(is)* snake, serpent + *-īnus* -INE[1]]

An·guis (ang′gwis), *n.* **Mare.** See **Mare Anguis.**

an·guish (ang′gwish), *n.* **1.** excruciating or acute pain, suffering, or distress: *the anguish of grief.* —*v.t.* **2.** to inflict with pain, suffering, or distress. [ME *anguisse* < OF < L *angustia* tight place, equiv. to *angust(us)* narrow + *-ia* -IA; akin to ANGER]

—**Syn. 1.** agony, torment, torture. See **pain.** —**Ant. 1.** delight.

an·guished (ang′gwisht), *adj.* **1.** feeling, showing, or accompanied by anguish. **2.** resulting from or produced by anguish. [ME; see ANGUISH, -ED[3]]

an·gu·lar (ang′gyə lər), *adj.* **1.** having an angle or angles. **2.** consisting of, situated at, or forming an angle. **3.** of, pertaining to, or measured by an angle. **4.** *Physics.* pertaining to quantities related to a revolving body that are measured in reference to its axis of revolution. **5.** bony, gaunt: *a tall, angular man.* **6.** acting or moving awkwardly. **7.** stiff in manner; unbending. Also, **angulose, angulous.** [< L *angulār(is)* having corners or angles, equiv. to *angul(us)* ANGLE[1] + *-āris* -AR[1]] —**an′gu·lar·ly,** *adv.* —**an′gu·lar·ness,** *n.*

—**Ant. 1.** curved. **5.** rotund. **6.** graceful.

an′gular accelera′tion, *Physics.* the time rate of change of angular velocity of a rotating body.

an′gular disper′sion, *Optics.* a measure of the angular separation of light rays of different wavelength or color traversing a prism or diffraction grating, equal to the rate of change of the angle deviation with respect to the change in wavelength.

an′gular displace′ment, *Physics.* the amount of rotation of a point, line, or body in a specified direction about an axis.

an′gular fre′quency, *Physics.* a measure of the frequency of an object varying sinusoidally equal to 2π times the frequency in cycles per second and expressed in radians per second. *Symbol:* π

an·gu·lar·i·ty (ang′gyə lar′i tē), *n., pl.* **-ties. 1.** the quality of being angular. **2. angularities,** sharp corners; angular outlines: *the angularities of the coastline.* [ANGULAR + -ITY]

an′gular leaf′ spot′, *Plant Pathol.* a disease of plants, characterized by angular, watery spots on the leaves and fruit, caused by any of several bacteria, as *Pseudomonas lachrymans* or *Xanthomonas malvacearum.*

an′gular magnifica′tion, *Optics.* the ratio of the angle subtended at the eye by the image formed by an optical instrument to the angle subtended at the eye by the object being viewed.

an′gular momen′tum, *Physics.* the product of the moment of inertia of a body about an axis and its angular velocity with respect to the same axis. Also called **moment of momentum.**

an′gular momen′tum quan′tum num′ber, *Physics.* the quantum number that represents the quantized vector sum of the orbital angular momentum and the spin. Also called **total angular momentum quantum number.**

an′gular veloc′ity, *Physics.* the time rate of change of angular position of a rotating body, usually expressed in radians per second or radians per minute.

an·gu·late (ang′gyə lit, -lāt′), *adj.* of angular form; angled: *angulate stems.* Also, **an′gu·lat′ed.** [< L *angulāt(us)* having angles. See ANGLE[1], -ATE[1]] —**an′gu·late·ly,** *adv.* —**an′gu·late·ness,** *n.*

an′gulated sail′, *Naut.* any of various jib-headed sails composed of two cloths running in different directions and joined in a miter. Also called **mitered sail.**

an·gu·la·tion (ang′gyə lā′shən), *n.* **1.** an angular formation. **2.** the exact measurement of angles. [ANGULATE + -ION]

an·gu·lous (ang′gyə ləs), *adj.* angular. Also, **an·gu·lose** (ang′gyə lōs′). [< L *angulōs(us).* See ANGLE[1], -OUS] —**an·gu·los·i·ty** (ang′gyə los′i tē), *n.*

An·gur·bo·da (äng′gər bô′də), *n.* *Scand. Myth.* Angerboda.

An·gus (ang′gəs), *n.* **1.** Formerly, **Forfar.** a county in E Scotland. 278,370 (est. 1961); 873 sq. mi. *Co. seat:* Forfar. **2.** See **Aberdeen Angus. 3.** a boy's given name.

An′gus Og′ (ōg), *Irish Myth.* the god of love and beauty, the patron deity of young men and women.

an·haem·a·to·poi·e·sis (an hem′ə tō poi ē′sis, -hē′-mə-), *n.* *Med.* anhematopoiesis.

An·halt (än′hält), *n.* a former state in central Germany.

an·har·mon·ic (an′här mon′ik), *adj.* *Physics.* of or pertaining to an oscillating system that is not undergoing simple harmonic motion. [AN-[1] + HARMONIC; modeled on F *anharmonique*]

an′harmon′ic ra′tio, *Math.* See **cross ratio.**

an·he·do·ni·a (an′hē dō′nē ə), *n.* *Psychol.* lack of pleasure or of the capacity to experience it. [< Gk *an-* AN-[1] + *hēdon(ḗ)* pleasure + *-ia* -IA] —**an·he·don·ic** (an′hē don′ik), *adj.*

an·he·dral (an hē′drəl), *adj.* *Petrog.* xenomorphic (def. 1). [AN-[1] + -HEDRAL]

an·hem·a·to·poi·e·sis (an hem′ə tō poi ē′sis, -hē′-mə-), *n.* *Med.* the defective formation of blood. Also, **anhaematopoiesis.** Also called **anhematosis.** [< NL; see AN-[1], HEMATOPOESIS]

an·he·ma·to·sis (an hē′mə tō′sis, -hem′ə-), *n.* *Med.* anhematopoiesis. [AN-[1] + HEMATO- + -SIS]

an·hem·i·ton·ic (an hem′ē ton′ik), *adj.* (of a musical scale) having no semitones. [AN-[1] + HEMI- + TONIC]

an·hi·dro·sis (an′hi drō′sis, -hī-), *n.* *Med.* the deficiency or absence of perspiration; adiaphoresis. Also, **anhydrosis.** [< NL; see AN-[1], HIDROSIS] —**an·hi·drot·ic** (an′hi drot′ik, -hī-), *adj.*

an·hin·ga (an hing′gə), *n.* snakebird. [< Pg < Tupi]

An·hwei (än′hwā′), *n.* a province in E China. 33,560,000 (est. 1957); 54,015 sq. mi. *Cap.:* Hofei. Also, **Nganhwei.**

an·hy·dre·mi·a (an′hī drē′mē ə), *n.* *Med.* an abnormal decrease in the volume of the blood, due to loss of water. [ANHYDR- + -EMIA] —**an′hy·dre′mic,** *adj.*

anhydr-, var. of **anhydro-** before a vowel.

an·hy·dride (an hī′drīd, -drid), *n.* *Chem.* **1.** a compound formed by removing water from a more complex compound: an oxide of a nonmetal **(acid anhydride)** or a metal **(basic anhydride)** which forms an acid or a base, respectively, when united with water. **2.** a compound from which water has been abstracted. [ANHYDR- + -IDE]

an·hy·drite (an hī′drīt), *n.* a mineral, calcium sulfate, $CaSO_4$, usually occurring in whitish or slightly colored masses. [ANHYDR- + -ITE[1]]

anhydro-, *Chem.* combining form of **anhydride:** *anhydroglucose.* Also, *esp. before a vowel,* **anhydr-.**

an·hy·dro·sis (an′hi drō′sis, -hī-), *n.* *Med.* anhidrosis. —**an·hy·drot·ic** (an′hi drot′ik, -hī-), *adj.*

an·hy·drous (an hī′drəs), *adj.* *Chem.* with all water removed, esp. water of crystallization. [< Gk *ánydros* waterless (with etym. *h* put in). See AN-[1], HYDRO-[1], -OUS]

a·ni (ä′nē), *n., pl.* **a·nis.** any of several black, tropical American cuckoos of the genus *Crotophaga,* having a compressed, bladelike bill. [< Sp or Pg < Tupi]

a·nic·ca (ə nik′ə), *n.* *Buddhism.* the cycle of birth, growth, decay, and death through which every living thing must pass. Cf. **Three Signs of Being.** [< Pali < Skt *anitya* not everlasting, equiv. to *a-* A-[6] + *nitya* eternal]

An·i·ce·tus (an′i sē′təs), *n.* **1. Saint,** pope A.D. 155?–166?. **2.** *Class. Myth.* a son of Hercules and Hebe.

an·i·con·ic (an′ī kon′ik), *adj.* **1.** not employing or permitting images, idols, etc.: *an aniconic religion.* **2.** not forming an image. **3.** of or pertaining to aniconism. [AN-[1] + ICONIC]

an·i·con·ism (an ī′kə niz′əm), *n.* **1.** opposition to the use of idols or images. **2.** the worship of objects symbolic of but not depicting a deity. [AN- + ICONISM]

an·il (an′il), *n.* **1.** a fabaceous shrub, *Indigofera suffruticosa,* of the West Indies, yielding indigo. **2.** indigo; deep blue. [< Pg < Ar *an-nīl,* equiv. to *al* the + *nīl* indigo < Skt *nīlī* indigo (*nīl(a)* dark blue + *-ī* n. suffix)]

an·ile (an′īl, ā′nīl), *adj.* of or like a weak old woman: *anile ideas.* [< L *anīl(is)* pertaining to an old woman, equiv. to *an(us)* old woman + *-īlis* -ILE]

an·i·lide (an′ᵊlid, -ᵊlīd′), *n.* *Chem.* any compound containing the univalent group, C_6H_5NH-, derived from aniline, as acetanilide, $CH_3CONHC_6H_5$. [< G *Anilid.* See ANIL, -IDE] —**an·i·lid·ic** (an′ə lid′ik), *adj.*

an·i·line (an′əlin, -əlīn′), *n.* **1.** Also called **an′iline oil′, aminobenzine, phenylamine.** *Chem.* a colorless, oily, slightly water-soluble liquid, $C_6H_5NH_2$, usually derived from nitrobenzene by reduction: used chiefly in the synthesis of dyes and drugs. —*adj.* **2.** pertaining to or derived from aniline: *aniline colors.* Also, **an·i·lin** (an′əlin). [ANIL + -INE[2]]

an′iline black′, *Chem.* the black dye obtained by the oxidation of aniline hydrochloride, used for dyeing textiles, esp. cotton.

an′iline dye′, *Chem.* any of a large number of synthetic dyes derived from aniline, usually obtained from coal tar.

an′iline hydrochlo′ride, *Chem.* a white, crystalline, water-soluble solid, $C_6H_5NH_2 \cdot HCl$, used chiefly as an intermediate in the manufacture of dyes, esp. aniline black.

a·nil·i·ty (ə nil′i tē), *n., pl.* **-ties. 1.** the state of being anile. **2.** an anile notion or procedure. [< L *anīlitās* the old age of a woman. See ANILE, -ITY]

anim., *Music.* animato.

an·i·ma (an′ə mə), *n.* **1.** soul; life. **2.** (in the psychology of C. G. Jung) **a.** the inner personality that is turned toward the unconscious of the individual (contrasted with *persona*). **b.** the feminine principle, esp. as present in men (contrasted with *animus*). [< L: lit., that which blows (i.e., wind) or is breathed (i.e., air)]

an·i·mad·ver·sion (an′ə mad vûr′zhən, -shən), *n.* **1.** a censorious remark; criticism or adverse comment: *to make animadversions on someone's conduct.* **2.** the act or fact of criticizing. [< L *animadversiōn-* (s. of *animadversiō*) a heeding, censure, equiv. to *animadvers(us)* (ptp. of *animadvertere* to heed, censure; see ANIMADVERT) + *-iōn-* -ION] —**an′i·mad·ver′sion·al,** *adj.*

—**Syn. 1.** aspersion, reflection, derogation.

an·i·mad·vert (an′ə mad vûrt′), *v.i.* **1.** to comment critically; make remarks by way of criticism or censure (usually fol. by *on* or *upon*): *to animadvert at length upon a shortcoming.* **2.** *Obs.* to take cognizance or notice. [< L *animadvert(ere)* (to) heed, censure, equiv. to *anim(um),* acc. of *animus* (see ANIMUS) + *advertere* to ADVERT] —**an′i·mad·vert′er,** *n.*

an·i·mal (an′ə məl), *n.* **1.** any living thing typically having certain characteristics distinguishing it from a plant, as the ability to move voluntarily, the presence of a nervous system and a greater ability to respond to stimuli, the need for complex organic materials for nourishment obtained by eating plants or other animals, and the delimitation of cells usually by a membrane rather than a cellulose wall. **2.** any animal other than man. **3.** a mammal, as opposed to a fish, bird, etc. **4.** the physical or carnal nature of man: *the animal in every man.* **5.** an inhuman person; brutish or beastlike person: *She married an animal.* **6.** *Facetious.* something, esp. an object or phenomenon, that is dangerous or challenging: *The new airplane was a fast animal.* —*adj.* **7.** of, pertaining to, or derived from animals: *animal life; animal fats.* **8.** pertaining to the physical or carnal nature of man, rather than his spiritual or intellectual nature: *animal needs.* [< L *animāl(e),* neut. of *animālis* living (lit., breathing), equiv. to *anim(a)* air, breath + *-ālis* -AL[1]] —**an·i·mal·ic** (an′ə mal′ik), **an·i·ma·li·an** (an′ə mā′lē ən, -māl′yən), *adj.*

—**Syn. 1, 2.** ANIMAL, BEAST, BRUTE refer to sentient creatures as distinct from minerals and plants; figuratively, they usually connote qualities and characteristics below the human level. ANIMAL is the general word; figuratively, it applies merely to the body or to animal-like characteristics: *An athlete is a magnificent animal.* BEAST refers to four-footed animals; figuratively, it suggests a base, sensual nature: *A glutton is a beast.* BRUTE implies absence of ability to reason; figuratively, it connotes savagery as well: *a drunken brute.* **5.** monster. **8.** fleshly, physical; beastly, brutal.

an′imal black′, any of various black pigments, as boneblack or ivory black, obtained from calcined animal matter.

an′imal crack′er, a small cookie in the shape of an animal.

an·i·mal·cule (an′ə mal′kyo͞ol), *n.* **1.** a minute or microscopic animal, nearly or quite invisible to the naked eye, as an infusorian or rotifer. **2.** *Rare.* a tiny animal, as a mouse, fly, etc. [< NL *animalcul(um)* a small animal. See ANIMAL, -CULE] —**an·i·mal·cu·lar** (an′ə mal′kyə lər), **an·i·mal·cu·line** (an′ə mal′kyə lin′, -lin), **an′i·mal′cu·lous,** *adj.*

an·i·mal·cu·lum (an′ə mal′kyə ləm), *n., pl.* **-la** (-lə). animalcule.

an′imal faith′, nonrational belief in the existence of a fully knowable world outside the mind.

An′imal Farm′, a satire on dictatorship (1945) by George Orwell.

an′imal heat′, *Physiol.* heat produced in a living animal by any of various metabolic activities.

an′imal hus′bandry, the science of breeding, feeding, and tending domestic animals, esp. farm animals. —**an′imal hus′bandman.**

an·i·mal·ise (an′ə mə līz′), *v.t.,* **-ised, -is·ing.** *Chiefly Brit.* animalize. —**an′i·mal·i·sa′tion,** *n.*

an·i·mal·ism (an′ə mə liz′əm), *n.* **1.** preoccupation with or motivation by sensual, physical, or carnal appetites rather than moral, spiritual, or intellectual forces. **2.** the theory that human beings lack a spiritual nature. [ANIMAL(IZE) + -ISM]

an·i·mal·ist (an′ə mə list), *n.* **1.** a person driven by animal appetites; sensualist. **2.** an advocate of the theory of animalism. [ANIMAL + -IST] —**an′i·mal·is′tic,** *adj.*

an·i·mal·i·ty (an′ə mal′i tē), *n.* **1.** the state of being an animal. **2.** the animal nature in man. **3.** See **animal kingdom.** [ANIMAL + -ITY, modeled on *carnality*]

an·i·mal·ize (an′ə mə līz′), *v.t.,* **-ized, -iz·ing. 1.** to excite the animal passions of; brutalize; sensualize. **2.** *Fine Arts.* to represent in animal form or endow with animal features. Also, *esp. Brit.,* **animalise.** [ANIMAL + -IZE] —**an′i·mal·i·za′tion,** *n.*

an′imal king′dom, the animals of the world collectively. Cf. **plant kingdom.**

an·i·mal·ly (an′ə mə lē), *adv.* physically. [ANIMAL + -LY]

an′imal mag′netism, 1. the indefinite power, presumably innate in some persons, which enables one to induce hypnosis. **2.** appeal for members of the opposite sex by virtue of one's physical attributes. Also called **biomagnetism.**

an′imal pole′, *Biol.* the formative part of an ovum, having the greatest amount of cytoplasm and containing the nucleus. Cf. **vegetal pole.**

an′imal spir′its, exuberance arising from an excess of energy; vivacity and good humor: *The children romped on the lawn, full of animal spirits.*

an′imal starch′, *Biochem.* glycogen.

an·i·mate (*v.* an′ə māt′; *adj.* an′ə mit), *v.,* **-mat·ed, -mat·ing,** *adj.* —*v.t.* **1.** to give life to; make alive: *God animated the dust.* **2.** to make lively, vivacious, or vigorous; give zest or spirit to: *Her presence animated the party.* **3.** to encourage: *to animate weary troops.* **4.** to move to action; actuate: *animated by religious zeal.* —*adj.* **5.** alive; possessing life: *animate creatures.* **6.** lively: *an animate expression of joy.* **7.** of or relating to animal life. **8.** able to move voluntarily. [< L *animāt(us)* filled with breath or air, quickened, animated (ptp. of *animāre*). See ANIMA, -ATE[1]] —**an′i·mate·ly,** *adv.* —**an′i·mate·ness,** *n.* —**an′i·mat′ing·ly,** *adv.*

—**Syn. 1.** vivify, quicken, vitalize. **2.** energize, fortify. ANIMATE, INVIGORATE, STIMULATE mean to enliven. To ANIMATE is to create a liveliness: *Health and energy animated his movements.* To INVIGORATE means to give physical vigor, to refresh, to exhilarate: *Mountain air invigorates.* To STIMULATE is to arouse a latent liveliness on a particular occasion: *Alcohol stimulates.* **3.** inspire, inspirit, hearten, arouse, exhilarate. **4.** excite, incite, fire, urge, kindle, prompt. —**Ant. 1.** kill. **5.** dead.

an·i·mat·ed (an′ə mā′tid), *adj.* **1.** full of life, action, or spirit; lively; vigorous: *an animated debate.* **2.** made or equipped to move or give the appearance of moving in an animallike fashion: *animated puppet.* **3.** containing representations of animals or mechanical objects that appear to move as real ones do: *an animated window display.* [ANIMATE + -ED[2]] —**an′i·mat′ed·ly,** *adv.*

an′imated cartoon′, a motion picture consisting of a sequence of drawings, each so slightly different that when filmed and run through a projector the figures seem to move.

an′imated oat′, an oat, *Avena sterilis,* of the Mediterranean region, having spikelets which twist or move when exposed to sudden moisture, due to the hygroscopic action of its awns.

an·i·ma·tion (an′ə mā′shən), *n.* **1.** animated quality; liveliness; vivacity; spirit: *to talk with animation.* **2.** the act or an instance of animating or enlivening. **3.** the state or condition of being animated. **4.** the process of preparing animated cartoons. [< L *animātiōn-* (s. of *animātiō*) a bestowing of life). See ANIMATE, -ION]

—**Syn. 1.** vigor, energy; enthusiasm, ardor; exhilaration, sprightliness. —**Ant. 1.** sluggishness.

an·i·ma·tism (an′ə mə tiz′əm), *n.* the attribution of consciousness to inanimate objects and natural phenomena. [ANIMATE + -ISM] —**an′i·ma·tis′tic,** *adj.*

a·ni·ma·to (ä′nə mä′tō, an′ə-; *It.* ä′nē mä′tô), *adj. Music.* animated (def. 1). *Abbr.:* anim. [< It]

an·i·ma·tor (an′ə mā′tər), *n.* **1.** one who or that which animates. **2.** an artist who draws animated cartoons. Also, **an′i·mat′er.** [< LL; see ANIMATE, -OR[2]]

a·nime (ə nēm′), *n. Armor.* an articulated cuirass of the 16th century, composed of horizontal lames joined by rivets and concealed thongs. [< MF, n. use of ptp. of *animer* to animate]

an·i·mé (an′ə mā′, -mē), *n.* any of various resins or copals, esp. that from *Hymenaea Courbaril,* a tree of tropical America, used in making varnish, scenting pastilles, etc. Also, **a·ni·mi** (ə nē′mē). [< F < Sp or Pg *anime* < Tupi *an(an)im* resin + excrescent *-e*]

an·i·mism (an′ə miz′əm), *n.* **1.** the belief that natural objects, natural phenomena, and the universe itself possess souls. **2.** the belief that natural objects have souls which may exist apart from their material bodies. **3.** the doctrine that the soul is the principle of life and health. **4.** belief in spiritual beings or agencies. [< L *anim(a)* air, the breath of life, spirit, soul + -ISM] —**an′i·mist,** *adj.* —**an′i·mis′tic,** *adj.*

a·ni·mis o·pi·bus·que pa·ra·ti (ä′ni mis ō′pi bo͝os′kwe pä rä′tē; *Eng.* an′ə mis ō′pə bus′kwē pə rā′tī), *Latin.* prepared in mind and resources.

an·i·mos·i·ty (an′ə mos′i tē), *n., pl.* **-ties.** a feeling of ill will or enmity that determines conduct or tends to display itself in action (usually fol. by *between* or *against*): *a deep-seated animosity between two sisters; animosity against one's neighbor.* [late ME *animosite* < LL *animōsitās.* See ANIMUS, -OSE[1], -ITY]

—**Syn.** hostility, unfriendliness, opposition, antagonism, animus, hatred.

an·i·mus (an′ə məs), *n.* **1.** hostile feeling or attitude; antagonism; animosity. **2.** purpose; intention; animating spirit. **3.** (in the psychology of C. G. Jung) the masculine principle, esp. as present in women (contrasted with *anima*). [< L: soul, feeling, spirit, courage, passion, wrath; akin to ANIMA]

an·i·on (an′ī′ən), *n. Physical Chem.* **1.** a negatively charged ion, as one attracted to the anode in electrolysis. **2.** any negatively charged atom or group of atoms (opposed to *cation*). [< Gk, neut. of *aniṓs* going up (prp. of *aniénai* to go up), equiv. to *an-* AN-[3] + *-i-* go + *-os* adj. suffix] —**an·i·on·ic** (an′ī on′ik), *adj.*

an′ion′ic deter′gent, *Chem.* any of a class of synthetic compounds whose anions are alkali salts, as soap, or whose ions are ammonium salts.

An I′rish Air′man Foresees′ His Death′, a poem (1919) by W. B. Yeats.

an·is (ä′nēs), *n.* a variety of anisette made esp. in Spain and Latin America. [< Sp: lit., anise]

an·is·al·de·hyde (an′i sal′də hīd′), *n. Chem.* a colorless, oily, aromatic liquid, the para form of $CH_3OC_6H_4CHO$, having a vanillalike odor: used chiefly in the manufacture of cosmetics and perfume, and as an intermediate in organic synthesis. Also called **anisic aldehyde.** [ANISE + ALDEHYDE]

an·ise (an′is), *n.* **1.** a herbaceous plant, *Pimpinella Anisum,* of Mediterranean regions, yielding aniseed. **2.** aniseed. [ME *anis* < OF < L *anisum* < Gk *ánison*] —**a·nis·ic** (ə nis′ik), *adj.*

an′ise cam′phor, anethole.

an·i·seed (an′i sēd′, an′is sēd′), *n.* the aromatic seed of the anise, used in medicine, in cookery, etc., for its licoricelike flavor. [late ME *annes sede.* See ANISE, SEED]

an·is·ei·ko·ni·a (an′ī sī kō′nē ə), *n. Ophthalm.* a defect of vision in which the images at the retinas are unequal in size. Also, **anisoiconia, anisokonia.** [< Gk; see ANISO-, EIKON, -IA] —**an·is·ei·kon·ic** (an′ī sī kon′ik), *adj.*

an·i·sette (an′i set′, -zet′, an′i set′, -zet′), *n.* a cordial or liqueur flavored with aniseed. [< F, short for *anisette de Bordeaux.* See ANISE, -ETTE]

anis′ic al′cohol, *Chem.* See **anisyl alcohol.**

anis′ic al′dehyde, *Chem.* anisaldehyde.

aniso-, a learned borrowing from Greek meaning "unequal," "uneven," used in the formation of compound words: *anisogamous.* [< Gk *ániso(s)*]

an·i·so·car·pic (an ī′sə kär′pik, an′ī-), *adj. Bot.* (of a flower) having a lower number of carpels than of other floral parts. [AN-[1] + ISOCARPIC]

an·i·so·co·ri·a (an ī′sə kôr′ē ə, -kōr′-, an′ī-), *n. Ophthalm.* inequality in the size of the pupils. [ANISO- + Gk *kór(ē)* pupil + -IA]

an·i·so·dac·ty·lous (an ī′sə dak′təl əs, an′ī-), *adj.* **1.** *Zool.* having the toes unlike, or unequal in number. **2.** *Ornith.* having three toes directed forward and one backward. Also, **an·i′so·dac′tyl.** [ANISO- + Gk *dáktyl(os)* finger, toe + -OUS]

an·i·so·dont (an ī′sə dont′), *adj.* having teeth which vary abnormally in height. [ANIS(O)- + -ODONT]

an·i·so·ga·mete (an ī′sō gə mēt′, -gam′ēt, an′ī-), *n. Biol.* either of a pair of unlike gametes, usually differing in size. [ANISO- + GAMETE] —**an·i·so·ga·met·ic** (an ī′sō gə met′ik, an′ī-), *adj.*

an·i·sog·a·mous (an′ī sog′ə məs), *adj. Biol.* reproducing by the fusion of dissimilar gametes or individuals, usually differing in size. Also, **an·i·so·gam·ic** (an ī′sə gam′ik, an′ī-). [ANISO- + -GAMOUS] —**an·i·sog·a·my** (an′ī sog′ə mē), *n.*

an·i·so·i·co·ni·a (an ī′sō ī kō′nē ə, an′ī-), *n. Ophthalm.* aniseikonia. Also, **an·i·so·ko·ni·a** (an ī′sə kō′nē ə, an′ī-).

an·i·sole (an′i sōl′), *n. Chem.* a colorless, water-insoluble liquid, $C_6H_5OCH_3$, having a pleasant, aromatic odor, used chiefly in perfumery and organic synthesis, and as a vermicide. Also called **methyl phenyl ether, methoxybenzene.** [ANISE + -OLE]

an·i·som·er·ous (an′ī som′ər əs), *adj. Bot.* unsymmetrical: applied to flowers which do not have the same number of parts in each circle. [AN-[1] + -ISOMEROUS]

an·i·so·met·ric (an ī′sə me′trik, an′ī-), *adj.* **1.** not isometric; of unequal measurement. **2.** (of a crystal) having axes of different lengths. [AN-[1] + ISOMETRIC]

an·i·so·me·tro·pi·a (an ī′sə mə trō′pē ə, an′ī-), *n. Ophthalm.* inequality in the power of the two eyes to refract light. [AN-[1] + ISOMETROPIA] —**an·i·so·me·trop·ic** (an ī′sə mə trop′ik, an′ī-), *adj.*

an·i·so·phyl·lous (an ī′sə fil′əs, an′ī-), *adj. Bot.* having leaves of different shapes or sizes. [ANISO- + -PHYLLOUS] —**an·i′so·phyl′ly,** *n.*

an·i·sop·ter·an (an′ī sop′tər ən), *adj.* belonging or pertaining to the suborder *Anisoptera,* comprising the dragonflies. [< NL *Anisopter(a)* (see ANISO-, -PTEROUS) + -AN]

an·i·so·trop·ic (an ī′sə trop′ik, an′ī-), *adj.* **1.** *Physics.* of unequal physical properties along different axes. Cf. **isotropic.** (def. 1). **2.** *Bot.* of different dimensions along different axes. [AN-[1] + ISOTROPIC] —**an·i·sot·ro·py** (an′ī so′trə pē), *n.*

an′i·syl ac′etate (an′i sil), *Chem.* a colorless liquid, the para form of $CH_3OC_6H_4CH_2OCOCH_3$, having a lilaclike odor, used chiefly as a scent in the manufacture of perfume. [ANISE + -YL]

an′isyl al′cohol, *Chem.* a colorless liquid, the para form of $CH_3OC_6H_4CH_2OH$, having a hawthornlike odor, used chiefly as a scent in the manufacture of perfume. Also, **anisic alcohol.**

A·ni·ta (ə nē′tə), *n.* a girl's given name, form of **Anna.**

An·i·us (an′ē əs), *n. Class. Myth.* the son of Apollo and Rhoeo who became king of Delos.

An·ja·nette (an′jə net′), *n.* a girl's given name.

An·jou (an′jo͞o; *Fr.* äN zho͞o′), *n.* a region and former province in W France, in the Loire Valley.

An·ka·ra (ang′kər ə, äng′kä rä′), *n.* a city in and the capital of Turkey, in the central part. 1,321,380 (1960). Also, **Angora.**

An′ka·ra′tra Moun′tains (äng′kə rä′trä, -trə, ang′-), a mountain range in central Madagascar: highest peak, 8675 ft.

An·ke·ny (ang′kə nē), *n.* a town in central Iowa. 2964 (1960).

an·ker·ite (ang′kə rīt′), *n.* a rhomboidal carbonate mineral related to dolomite but with iron replacing part of the magnesium. [named after M. J. *Anker,* (d. 1843), Austrian mineralogist; see -ITE[1]]

ankh (angk), *n. Egyptian Art.* a tau cross with a loop at the top, used as a symbol of generation or enduring life. [< Egypt]

Ankh

An·king (än′king′), *n.* a city in E China, on the Yangtze River: former capital of Anhwei.

an·kle (ang′kəl), *n.* **1.** the joint between the foot and the leg, in which movement occurs in two planes. **2.** the slender part of the leg above the foot. [ME *ankel,* perh. < Scand. (cf. Dan, Sw *ankel;* c. MLG *enkel,* OHG *anchal, enchil*); r. ME *anclowe,* OE *anclēow(e)* ankle, c. OHG *anchlāo*]

an·kle·bone (ang′kəl bōn′), *n.* the talus. [ME; see ANKLE, BONE[1]]

an·kle-deep (ang′kəl dēp′), *adj.* **1.** high enough to reach or cover the ankles: *Ankle-deep dust accumulated in the cave. The rising tide was already ankle-deep.* —*adv.* **2.** as high as the ankles: *Rain water ran ankle-deep.*

an′kle jerk′, a reflex extension of the foot, caused by contraction of the muscles of the calf, resulting from a sharp tap on the Achilles tendon; Achilles reflex.

an·klet (ang′klit), *n.* **1.** a sock that reaches just above the ankle. **2.** an ornamental circlet worn around the ankle. [ANKLE + -LET, modeled on *bracelet*]

an·klung (ang′klung), *n.* a southeast Asian rhythm instrument consisting of a set of bamboo tubes that are tuned in octaves and slide in the grooves of a frame shaken by the performer. [< Malay]

an·kus (ang′kəs, ung′kəsh), *n., pl.* **-kus, -kus·es.** (in India) an elephant goad with a spike and a hook at one end. [< Hindi; akin to ANGLE[2]]

ankylo-, var. of **ancylo-:** *ankylosis.*

an·ky·lo·glos·si·a (ang′kə lō glô′sē ə, -glos′ē ə), *n.* *Pathol.* tongue-tie. [ANKYLO- + Gk *glôss(a)* tongue + -IA]

an·ky·lo·saur (ang′kə lō sôr′), *n.* any of several herbivorous dinosaurs of the suborder *Ankylosauria,* from the Cretaceous period, having the body covered with thick, bony plates. Also called **armored dinosaur.** [< NL *Ankylosaur(ia)* name of the suborder. See ANKYLO-, -SAUR, -IA]

an·ky·lose (ang′kə lōs′), *v.t., v.i.,* **-losed, -los·ing.** to unite or grow together, as the bones of a joint or the root of a tooth and its surrounding bone. Also, **anchylose.** [back formation from ANKYLOSIS]

an·ky·lo·sis (ang′kə lō′sis), *n.* **1.** *Pathol.* abnormal adhesion of the bones of a joint. **2.** *Anat.* the union or consolidation of two or more bones or other hard tissues into one. Also, **anchylosis.** [< Gk: a stiffening of the joints. See ANKYLO-, -OSIS] —**an·ky·lot·ic** (ang′kə lot′ik), *adj.*

an·ky·los·to·mi·a·sis (ang′kə los′tə mī′ə sis), *n.* *Pathol.* hookworm (def. 2). Also, **ancylostomiasis.**

an·lace (an′lis), *n.* anelace.

an·la·ge (än′lä gə), *n., pl.* **-gen** (-gən), **-ges.** (*sometimes cap.*) *Embryol.* primordium. [< G: setup, layout, equiv. to *an-* ON + *lage* position, akin to LAY¹]

Ann (an), *n.* a girl's given name, form of **Anna.** Also, **Anne.**

ann., **1.** annual. **2.** annuity. **3.** years. [< L *annī*]

an·na (an′ə), *n.* **1.** a former cupronickel coin of Pakistan, the 16th part of a rupee: last issued in 1960. **2.** a former cupronickel coin of India, the 16th part of a rupee. [< Hindi *ānā*]

An·na (an′ə), *n.* **1.** *Douay Bible.* Hannah. **2.** *Class. Myth.* the sister of Dido, supposed to have drowned herself in Italy. **3.** a town in S Illinois. 4280 (1960). **4.** a girl's given name.

An·na·bel (an′ə bel′), *n.* a girl's given name.

an·na·berg·ite (an′ə bûr′gīt), *n.* a mineral, hydrous nickel arsenate, $Ni_3As_2O_8{\cdot}8H_2O$, occurring in apple-green masses. [named after *Annaberg* town in central East Germany, where found; see -ITE¹]

An′na Chris′tie (kris′tē), a play (1921) by Eugene O'Neill.

An Na·fud (an′ na fo͞od′). See **Nefud Desert.**

An·na I·va·nov·na (ä′nä ē vä′nov nə), 1693–1740, empress of Russia 1730–40.

An·na Ka·ren·i·na (an′ə kə ren′ə nə; *Russ.* ä′nä kä-re′ni nä), a novel (1875–76) by Leo Tolstoy.

an·nal (an′ᵊl), *n.* *Archaic.* a record, as annals, esp. of a single year, people, etc. [back formation from ANNALS]

an·nal·ist (an′ᵊlist), *n.* a chronicler of yearly events. [*annal* (v., now obs.) + -IST] —**an′nal·is′tic,** *adj.* —**an′nal·is′ti·cal·ly,** *adv.*

an·nals (an′ᵊlz), *n.* (*construed as pl.*) **1.** a record of events, esp. a yearly record, usually in chronological order. **2.** historical records generally: *the annals of war.* **3.** a periodical publication containing the formal reports of an organization. [< L *annālēs* (*librī*), lit., yearly (books), pl. of *annālis* continuing for a year, annual, equiv. to *ann(us)* a year + *-ālis* -AL¹]

An·nam (ə nam′), *n.* a former kingdom and French protectorate along the E coast of French Indochina: now part of Vietnam. Also, **Anam.**

An·na·mese (an′ə mēz′, -mēs′), *adj., n., pl.* **-mese.** —*adj.* **1.** of or pertaining to Annam, its people, or their language. —*n.* Also, **An·nam·ite** (an′ə mīt′). **2.** a native of Annam. **3.** former name of the language **Vietnamese.** [ANNAM + -ESE]

An′na Pe·ren′na (pə ren′ə), an ancient Roman goddess of longevity: later identified with Anna, the sister of Dido.

An·nap·o·lis (ə nap′ə lis), *n.* a seaport in and the capital of Maryland, in the central part, on Chesapeake Bay: U.S. Naval Academy. 23,385 (1960).

Annap′olis Roy′al, a town in W Nova Scotia, in SE Canada, on an arm of the Bay of Fundy: the first settlement in Canada 1605. 800 (1961). Formerly, **Port Royal.**

An·na·pur·na (an′ə po͝or′nə, -pûr′-; *also, for 1, Skt.* un′nə po͞or′nä), *n.* **1.** *Hinduism.* Devi (def. 2). **2.** a mountain in N Nepal, in the Himalayas. 26,503 ft.

Ann Ar·bor (an är′bər), a city in SE Michigan. 67,340 (1960).

an·nates (an′āts, -its), *n.* (*construed as sing. or pl.*) *Eccles. Hist.* the first year's revenue of a benefice, payable to the one presenting the benefice, as the pope. Also, **an·nats** (an′ats, -its). [< ML *annāta,* equiv. to L *ann(us)* year + *-āta,* neut. pl. of *-ātus* -ATE¹]

An·na·tol (an′ə tōl′), *n.* a boy's given name. Also, **Anatol, Anatole.**

an·nat·to (ə nat′ō, ə nä′tō), *n., pl.* **-tos.** **1.** a small tree, *Bixa Orellana,* of tropical America. **2.** Also, **arnatto.** a yellowish-red dye obtained from the pulp enclosing the seeds of this tree, used for coloring fabrics, butter, varnish, etc. Also, **anatto.** [< Carib]

Anne (an), *n.* **1.** 1665–1714, queen of England 1702–14 (daughter of James II of England). **2.** Also, **Ann.** a girl's given name, form of **Anna.**

an·neal (ə nēl′), *v.t.* **1.** to heat (glass, earthenware, metals, etc.) to remove or prevent internal stress. **2.** to free from internal stress by heating and gradually cooling. **3.** to toughen or temper: *to anneal the mind.* **4.** *Obs.* to fuse colors onto (a vitreous or metallic surface) by heating. [ME *anele(n),* OE *anǣlan* to kindle, equiv. to *an-* ON + *ǣlan* to burn, akin to *āl* fire] —**an·neal′er,** *n.*

Anne′ Bol·eyn′ (bo͝o lin′, bo͝ol′in). See **Boleyn, Anne.**

an·nec·tent (ə nek′tənt), *adj.* *Zool.* connecting or linking, as a group of animals transitional between two other species, families, classes, etc. Also, **an·nec′tant.** [< L *annectent-* (s. of *annectēns* tying to, prp. of *annectere*), equiv. to *an-* AN-² + *nect-* bind + *-ent-* -ENT]

An·ne·cy (anᵊ sē′), *n.* a city in and the capital of Haute-Savoie, in SE France. 45,715 (1962).

Anne de Beau·jeu (*Fr.* an′ də bō zhœ′). See **Anne of France.**

an·ne·lid (an′ᵊlid), *n.* **1.** any segmented worm of the phylum *Annelida,* including the earthworms, leeches, and various marine forms. —*adj.* **2.** belonging or pertaining to the *Annelida.* Also, **an·nel·i·dan** (ə nel′i dᵊn). [back formation from ANNELIDA]

An·nel·i·da (ə nel′i də), *n.* the phylum comprising the annelids. [< NL, equiv. to *annel-* (< F *annel(és),* lit., ringed ones, pl. ptp. of *anneler* to ring, deriv. of OF *an(n)el* ring < L *annell(us),* dim. of *anus* anus, orig. ring) + *-ida* -ID²]

Anne·ma·rie (an′mə rē′), *n.* a girl's given name.

An·nen·sky (ä nen′ski), *n.* **In·no·ken·ty Fyo·do·ro·vich** (i no ken′ti fyô′do rô′vich), 1856–1909, Russian poet. Also, **An·nen′ski.**

Anne′ of Aus′tria, 1601–66, queen consort of Louis XIII of France: regent during minority of her son Louis XIV.

Anne′ of Bohe′mia, 1366–94, queen consort of Richard II of England.

Anne′ of Brit′tany, 1477–1514, wife of Maximilian I of Austria 1490–91; queen consort of Charles VIII of France 1491–98; queen consort of Louis XII of France 1499–1514. French, **Anne de Bre·tagne** (an də brə-tan′yə).

Anne′ of Cleves′, 1515–57, fourth wife of Henry VIII of England.

Anne′ of Den′mark, 1574–1619, queen consort of James I of England.

Anne′ of France′, (*Anne de Beaujeu*) 1460–1522, daughter of Louis XI of France: regent during the minority of her brother Charles VIII 1483–91.

An·nette (ə net′; *Fr.* a net′), *n.* a girl's given name, form of **Anne.**

an·nex (*v.* ə neks′; *n.* an′eks), *v.t.* **1.** to attach, subjoin, append, or add, esp. to something larger or more important: *Germany annexed part of Czechoslovakia.* **2.** to attach as an attribute, concomitant, or consequence. —*n.* Also, *esp. Brit.,* **an′nexe.** **3.** something annexed. **4.** a subsidiary building or an addition to a building. **5.** something added to a document; appendix; supplement: *an annex to a treaty.* [late ME < ML *annex(āre),* deriv. of L *annexus* tied to, ptp. of *annectere.* See ANNECTENT] —**an·nex′a·ble,** *adj.*

an·nex·a·tion (an′ək sā′shən, -ek-), *n.* **1.** the act or an instance of annexing, esp. new territory. **2.** the fact of being annexed. **3.** something annexed. [< ML *annexātiōn-* (s. of *annexātiō*), equiv. to *annexāt(us)* joined to (ptp. of *annexāre;* see ANNEX, -ATE¹) + *-iōn-* -ION] —**an′nex·a′tion·al,** *adj.* —**an′nex·a′tion·ism,** *n.* —**an′nex·a′tion·ist,** *n.*

an·nex·ment (ə neks′mənt), *n.* *Rare.* that which is annexed. [ANNEX + -MENT]

Ann·fwn (än′fo͞on), *n.* *Welsh Myth.* a land of perpetual beauty and happiness where death is unknown, often thought to be an island in the sea. Also, **Annwn.**

An·nie (an′ē), *n.* a girl's given name, form of **Ann, Anna, or Anne.**

An′nie Oak′ley (ōk′lē), *Slang.* a free ticket of admittance, as to a theater. [after similarity between a punched ticket and a playing card shot through by Annie Oakley (1860–1926), American sharpshooter]

an·ni·hi·la·ble (ə nī′ə lə bəl), *adj.* susceptible of annihilation. [ANNIHIL(ATE) + -ABLE] —**an·ni′hi·la·bil′i·ty,** *n.*

an·ni·hi·late (ə nī′ə lāt′), *v.t.,* **-lat·ed, -lat·ing.** **1.** to reduce to utter ruin or nonexistence; destroy utterly: *The bombing annihilated the city. We annihilated the opposition.* **2.** to destroy the collective existence or main body of; decimate: *to annihilate an army.* **3.** to annul; make void: *to annihilate a law.* **4.** to cancel the effect of; nullify. **5.** *Informal.* to defeat completely; vanquish: *The home basketball team annihilated the visiting team.* [< LL *annihilāt(us)* brought to nothing, annihilated (ptp. of *annihilāre*) (L *an-* AN-² + *nihil* nothing + *-ātus* -ATE¹)] —**an·ni·hi·la·tive** (ə nī′ə lā′tiv, -ə lə-), **an·ni·hi·la·to·ry** (ə nī′ə lə tôr′ē, -tōr′ē), *adj.*
—**Syn.** **1.** ravage, devastate, desolate. **1, 2.** smash, obliterate, demolish.

an·ni·hi·la·tion (ə nī′ə lā′shən), *n.* **1.** the act or an instance of annihilating. **2.** state of being annihilated; extinction; destruction. **3.** *Physics.* **a.** Also called **pair annihilation.** the process in which a particle and antiparticle unite, annihilate each other, and produce one or more photons. Cf. **positronium.** **b.** the conversion of rest mass into energy in the form of electromagnetic radiation. [< LL *annihilātiōn-* (s. of *annihilātiō*). See ANNIHILATE, -ION]

an·ni·hi·la·tion·ism (ə nī′ə lā′shə niz′əm), *n.* *Theol.* the belief that the souls of the wicked are annihilated after death. [ANNIHILATION + -ISM] —**an·ni′hi·la′tion·ist,** *n.* —**an·ni′hi·la′tion·is′tic, an·ni′hi·la′tion·is′ti·cal,** *adj.*

annihila′tion radia′tion, *Physics.* electromagnetic radiation produced by the coalescence and mutual annihilation of a positron and an electron, each pair forming two photons having a minimum energy of .5 million electron volts each.

an·ni·hi·la·tor (ə nī′ə lā′tər), *n.* **1.** one who or that which annihilates. **2.** *Math.* the set of all linear functionals which map to zero all elements of a given subset of a vector space. [ANNIHILATE + -OR²]

An·nis·ton (an′i stən), *n.* a city in E Alabama. 33,657 (1960).

anniv., anniversary.

an·ni·ver·sa·ry (an′ə vûr′sə rē), *n., pl.* **-ries,** *adj.* —*n.* **1.** the yearly recurrence of the date of a past event. **2.** the celebration or commemoration of such a date. —*adj.* **3.** returning or recurring each year; annual. **4.** pertaining to an anniversary: *an anniversary gift. Abbr.:* anniv. [ME < L *anniversāri(us)* returning every year, equiv. to *anni-* (comb. form of *annus* year) + *vers(us)* turned, ptp. of *vertere* (*vert-* turn + *-tus* ptp. suffix) + *-ārius* -ARY]

an·no ae·ta·tis su·ae (än′nō ī tä′tis so͞o′ī; *Eng.* an′ō ē tā′tis so͞o′ē), *Latin.* in the year of his age; in the year of her age.

an·no Dom·i·ni (an′ō dom′ə nī′, -nē′, ä′nō). See **A.D.**

An·no He·ji·rae (an′ō hi jī′rē, hej′ə rē′, ä′nō). See **A.H.**

an·no mun·di (än′nō mo͝on′dē; *Eng.* an′ō mun′dī), *Latin.* in the year of the world.

an·no reg·ni (än′nō reg′nē; *Eng.* an′ō reg′nī), *Latin.* in the year of the reign.

annot., **1.** annotated. **2.** annotation. **3.** annotator.

an·no·tate (an′ō tāt′), *v.,* **-tat·ed, -tat·ing.** —*v.t.* **1.** to supply with critical or explanatory notes; remark upon in notes: *to annotate the works of Bacon.* —*v.i.* **2.** to make annotations or notes. [< L *annotāt(us)* noted down (ptp. of *annotāre*), equiv. to *an-* AN-² + *notātus* noted, marked; see NOTE, -ATE¹] —**an′no·ta′tive, an·no·ta·to·ry** (an′ə tā′tə rē, -tə tôr′ē, -tōr′ē, ə nō′tə-tôr′ē, -tōr′ē), *adj.* —**an′no·ta′tor,** *n.*

an·no·tat·ed (an′ō tā′tid), *adj.* supplied with or containing explanatory notes, textual comments, etc.: *an annotated edition of Milton's poetry.* [ANNOTATE + -ED²]

an·no·ta·tion (an′ō tā′shən), *n.* **1.** the act of annotating. **2.** a critical or explanatory note added to a text. **3.** note (def. 1). *Abbr.:* annot. [< L *annotātiōn-* (s. of *annotātiō*). See ANNOTATE, -ION]

an·not·i·nous (ə not′ᵊnəs, a not′-), *adj.* *Bot.* one year old. [< L *annotinus,* equiv. to *ann(us)* year + *-tinus* affix of time]

an·nounce (ə nouns′), *v.,* **-nounced, -nounc·ing.** —*v.t.* **1.** to make known publicly or officially; proclaim; give notice of: *to announce a special sale.* **2.** to state the approach or presence of: *to announce guests; to announce dinner.* **3.** to make known to the mind or senses. **4.** to serve as an announcer of: *The mayor announced the program.* **5.** to state; declare. **6.** to state in advance; declare beforehand. **7.** to write, or have printed, and send a formal declaration of an event, esp. a social event, as a wedding. —*v.i.* **8.** to be employed or serve as an announcer, esp. of a radio or television broadcast: *He announces for the local radio station.* **9.** to declare one's candidacy, as for a public office (usually fol. by *for*): *We are hoping that he will announce for governor.* [late ME *anounce* < MF *anoncer* < L *annūntiāre,* equiv. to *an-* AN-² + *nūntiāre* to announce, deriv. of *nūntius* messenger] —**an·nounce′a·ble,** *adj.*
—**Syn.** **1.** declare, report, promulgate. ANNOUNCE, PROCLAIM, PUBLISH, mean to communicate something in a formal or public way. To ANNOUNCE is to give out news, often of something expected in the future: *to announce a lecture series.* To PROCLAIM is to make a widespread and general announcement of something of public interest: *to proclaim a holiday.* To PUBLISH is to make public in an official way, now esp. by printing: *to publish a book.*

an·nounce·ment (ə nouns′mənt), *n.* **1.** public or formal notice announcing something: *The announcement appeared in the newspapers.* **2.** the act of announcing. **3.** a short message or commercial, esp. a commercial spoken on radio or television. **4.** a card or piece of formal stationery containing a formal declaration of an event, as a wedding. [< MF *anoncement.* See ANNOUNCE, -MENT]

an·nounc·er (ə noun′sər), *n.* a person who announces, esp. one who introduces programs, presents news items, reads advertisements, and does other similar assignments over radio or television. [ANNOUNCE + -ER¹]

an·no ur·bis con·di·tae (än′nō o͞or′bis kōn′di tī′; *Eng.* an′ō ûr′bis kon′di tē′), *Latin.* See **A.U.C.** (def. 2).

an·noy (ə noi′), *v.t.* **1.** to disturb (a person) in a way that displeases, troubles, or slightly irritates. **2.** *Mil.* to molest; harm. —*v.i.* **3.** to be hateful or troublesome. —*n.* **4.** *Archaic.* an annoyance. [ME *anui* < OF, var. of *enui* < L phrase *in odiō* in ill-will; see IN-², ODIUM, ENNUI] —**an·noy′er,** *n.*
—**Syn.** **1.** harass, pester. See **bother, worry.** —**Ant.** **1.** comfort.

an·noy·ance (ə noi′əns), *n.* **1.** one who or that which annoys; a nuisance: *Some visitors are an annoyance.* **2.** the act or an instance of annoying. **3.** the feeling of being annoyed. [ME < MF; see ANNOY, -ANCE]

an·noy·ing (ə noi′ing), *adj.* causing annoyance: *annoying delays.* [ME; see ANNOY, -ING²] —**an·noy′ing·ly,** *adv.* —**an·noy′ing·ness,** *n.*

an·nu·al (an′yo͞o əl), *adj.* **1.** of, for, or pertaining to a year; yearly: *the annual enrollment in high schools.* **2.** occurring or returning once a year: *an annual celebration.* **3.** *Bot.* living only one growing season, as beans or corn. **4.** performed or executed during a year: *the annual course of the sun.* **5.** *Entomol.* living or lasting but one season or year, as certain insects or colonies of insects. —*n.* **6.** a plant living only one year or season. **7.** a book, report, etc. published annually. [< LL *annuāl(is),* equiv. to L *annu(us)* yearly (deriv. of *annus* circuit of the sun, year) + *-ālis* -AL¹; r. ME *annuel* < MF] —**an′nu·al·ly,** *adv.*

an′nual par′allax. See under **parallax** (def. 2).

an′nual ring′, an annual formation of wood in plants, consisting of two concentric layers, one of springwood and one of summerwood. Also called **growth ring.**

an′nual wage′. See **guaranteed annual wage.**

an·nu·i·tant (ə no͞o′i tᵊnt, ə nyo͞o′-), *n.* one who receives an annuity. [ANNUIT(Y) + -ANT]

an·nu·it coep·tis (än′no͞o it koip′tis; *Eng.* an′yo͞o it sep′tis), *Latin.* He (God) has favored our undertakings: a motto on the reverse of the great seal of the U.S. (adapted from Vergil's *Aeneid* IX: 625).

an·nu·i·ty (ə no͞o′i tē, ə nyo͞o′-), *n., pl.* **-ties.** **1.** a specified income payable at stated intervals for a fixed or a contingent period, often for the recipient's life, in consideration of a stipulated premium paid either in prior installment payments or in a single payment. **2.** the right to receive such an income, or the duty to make such a payment or payments. [late ME *annuitee* < MF *annuite* < ML *annuitāt-* (s. of *annuitās*) < L *annu(us)* yearly + *-itāt-* -ITY]

annu′ity cer′tain, *pl.* **annuities certain.** an annuity payable for a certain number of years regardless of any contingency.

an·nul (ə nul′), *v.t.,* **-nulled, -nul·ling.** **1.** (esp. of laws or other established rules, usages, etc.) to make void or null; abolish; invalidate: *to annul a marriage.* **2.** to reduce to nothing; obliterate. [late ME < LL *annul(āre),* equiv. to *an-* AN-² + *nullāre* to reduce to nothing, deriv. of L *nūllum* nothing, neut. of *nūllus* none] —**an·nul′la·ble,** *adj.*

an·nu·lar (an′yə lər), *adj.* **1.** having the form of a ring. **2.** (of a carpenter's nail) having a series of concentric grooves to improve holding power. [< L *annulār(is),* equiv. to *annul(us)* ring (var. of *ānulus*) + *-āris* -AR¹] —**an·nu·lar·i·ty** (an′yə lar′i tē), *n.* —**an′nu·lar·ly,** *adv.*

an′nular clock′, a clock in the form of a vase, ball, etc., having the hours painted on a ring rotating beneath a pointer.

an′nular eclipse′, *Astron.* an eclipse of the sun in which a portion of its surface is visible as a ring surrounding the dark moon. Cf. **total eclipse.**

an′nular lig′ament, *Anat.* the ligamentous envelope surrounding a part, as the joints of the wrist or ankle or the head of the radius.

an·nu·late (an′yə lit, -lāt′), *adj.* **1.** formed of ringlike segments, as an annelid worm. **2.** having rings or ringlike bands. Also, **an′nu·lat′ed.** [< L *annulāt(us),* var. of *ānulātus* ringed, equiv. to *ānul(us)* ring + *-ātus* -ATE[1]]

an·nu·la·tion (an′yə lā′shən), *n.* **1.** formation with or into rings. **2.** a ringlike formation or part. [ANNULATE + -ION]

an·nu·let (an′yə lit), *n.* **1.** Also called **bandelet, bandlet, square and rabbet.** *Archit.* an encircling band, molding, or fillet, as on the shaft of a column. **2.** *Entomol.* a ring, usually colored, around or on the surface of an organ. **3.** *Heraldry.* a ring, represented as a voided roundel, used esp. as the cadence mark of a fifth son. [< L *annul(us)* ring + -ET; r. earlier *anlet* < MF *anelet,* dim. of OF *anel* ring < L *anell(us)* ring]

an·nul·ment (ə nul′mənt), *n.* **1.** the act of annulling, esp. the formal declaration that annuls a marriage. **2.** *Psychoanal.* a mental process by which unpleasant or painful ideas are abolished from the mind. [ANNUL + -MENT]

an·nu·lose (an′yə lōs′), *adj.* furnished with or composed of rings: *annullose animals.* [< NL *annulōs(us).* See ANNULUS, -OSE[1]]

an·nu·lus (an′yə ləs), *n., pl.* **-li** (-lī′), **-lus·es. 1.** a ring; a ringlike part, band, or space. **2.** *Geom.* the space between two concentric circles on a plane. [< L, var. of *ānulus,* equiv. to *ān(us)* ring + *-ulus* -ULE]

An·nun·cia·ta (ə nun′shē ā′tə; *It.* än′no͞on chä′tä), *n.* a girl's given name. Also, **Annunziata.**

an·nun·ci·ate (ə nun′sē āt′, -shē-), *v.t.,* **-at·ed, -at·ing.** to announce. [< ML *annunciātus,* sp. var. of L *annuntiātus,* ptp. of *annuntiāre* to make known. See ANNOUNCE, -ATE[1]] —**an·nun′ci·a·ble,** *adj.* —**an·nun′ci·a′tive, an·nun·ci·a·to·ry** (ə nun′sē ə tôr′ē, -tōr′ē), *adj.*

an·nun·ci·a·tion (ə nun′sē ā′shən, -shē-), *n.* **1.** (*often cap.*) the announcement by the angel Gabriel to the Virgin Mary of the incarnation of Christ. **2.** (*cap.*) a representation of this in art. **3.** (*cap.*) Also called **Lady Day.** the church festival on March 25 in memory of this. **4.** the act or an instance of announcing; proclamation: *the annunciation of a new foreign policy.* [late ME < eccl. L *annunciātiōn-* (s. of *annunciātiō*). See ANNUNCIATE, -ION]

Annuncia′tion lil′y. See **Madonna lily.**

an·nun·ci·a·tor (ə nun′sē ā′tər, -shē-), *n.* **1.** an announcer. **2.** *U.S.* a signaling apparatus, generally used in conjunction with a buzzer, which displays a visual indication when energized by electric current. [ANNUNCIATE + -OR[2]; r. earlier *annuntiator* < L]

An·nun·zia·ta (ə nun′zē ä′tə; *It.* än′no͞on tsä′tä), *n.* a girl's given name. Also, **Annunciata.**

An·nun·zio, d′ (dän no͞on′tsyō), **Ga·bri·e·le** (gä′brē e′le). See **D'Annunzio, Gabriele.**

an·nus mi·ra·bi·lis (än′no͝os mi rä′bi lis; *Eng.* an′əs mə rab′ə lis), *pl.* **an·ni mi·ra·bi·les** (än′nē mi rä′bi les′; *Eng.* an′ī mə rab′ə lēz′). *Latin.* year of wonders; wonderful year.

Ann·ville (an′vil), *n.* a town in central Pennsylvania. 4264 (1960).

An·nwn (än′no͞on), *n.* *Welsh Myth.* Annfwn.

ano-[1], a combining form of **anus** or **anal:** *anorectal.*

ano-[2], a learned borrowing from Greek meaning "up," "upper," "upward": *anoopsia.* [< Gk, comb. form of *ánō*]

a·no·ci·as·so·ci·a·tion (ə nō′sē ə sō′sē ā′shən, -shē-ā′shən), *n.* *Surg.* a method for preventing shock and other harmful effects resulting from an operation, consisting principally in giving general and local anesthesia and in avoiding all unnecessary trauma during the operation. Also called **a·no·ci·a·tion** (ə nō′sē ā′shən, -shē-), **a·no·ci·the·sia** (ə nō′sə thē′zhə, -zhē ə, -zē ə). [A-[6] + L *noc(ēre)* (to) do harm, injure + -I- + ASSOCIATION]

an·ode (an′ōd), *n.* **1.** the positive electrode, that emits positive ions and attracts negative ions, within a voltaic cell or other such device. **2.** the positive terminal or pole of a battery (opposed to *cathode*). **3.** a positively charged plate in an electron tube. [< Gk *ánod(os)* way up, equiv. to *an-* AN-[3] + *hodós* a way, path, road]

an′ode dark′ space′, *Physics.* the dark region between the anode glow and the anode in a vacuum tube, occurring when the pressure is low.

an′ode glow′, *Physics.* the luminous region between the positive column and the anode dark space in a vacuum tube, occurring when the pressure is low.

an′ode ray′, *Physics.* See **canal rays.**

an′ode resist′ance, *Electronics.* (of a vacuum tube at a given level of output) the ratio of a small change in voltage of the anode to the corresponding small change in anode current. Also called **plate resistance.**

an·od·ic (an od′ik), *adj.* pertaining to an anode or the phenomena in its vicinity. [ANODE + -IC] —**an·od′i·cal·ly,** *adv.*

an·o·dize (an′ə dīz′), *v.t.,* **-dized, -diz·ing.** *Chem.* to coat a metal, esp. magnesium or aluminum, with a protective film by chemical or electrolytic means. [ANODE + -IZE]

an·o·don·tia (an′ə don′chə), *n.* *Dentistry.* absence of the teeth. [AN-[1] + -ODONT + -IA]

an·o·dyne (an′ə dīn′), *n.* **1.** a medicine that relieves or allays pain. **2.** anything that relieves distress or pain: *The music was an anodyne to his grief.* —*adj.* **3.** relieving pain. **4.** soothing to the mind or feelings. [< L *anōdyn(us)* < Gk *anṓdynos* painless, equiv. to *an-* AN-[1] + *ōdyn-* (akin to *odýnē* pain) + *-os* adj. suffix]

an·o·e·sis (an′ō ē′sis), *n.* a state of mind consisting of pure sensation or emotion without cognitive content. [A-[6] + NOESIS] —**an·o·et·ic** (an′ō et′ik), *adj.*

a·noi·a (ə noi′ə), *n.* extreme mental deficiency, esp. idiocy. Also called **an·o·e·sia** (an′ō ē′shə, -shē ə, -zē ə). [< Gk, equiv. to *ánoos* not understanding (*a-* A-[6] + *nó(os)* mind + *-os* adj. suffix) + *-ia* -IA]

a·noint (ə noint′), *v.t.* **1.** to put oil on; apply an unguent or oily liquid to. **2.** to smear with any liquid. **3.** to consecrate by applying oil: *He anointed the new high priest.* **4.** to dedicate to the service of God. [ME *anoynte(n),* deriv. of *anoynt,* var. of *enoynt* (ptp.) < F *enoint* < L *inunct(us)* anointed (ptp. of *inungere*), equiv. to *in-* IN-[2] + *ung-* smear with oil + *-tus* ptp. suffix] —**a·noint′er,** *n.* —**a·noint′ment,** *n.*

a·no·le (ə nō′lē), *n.* any of numerous chiefly insectivorous iguanid lizards of the genus *Anolis,* of North, Central, and South America, that have the ability to change the color of their skin. [var. of *anoli* < Carib]

an·o·lyte (an′əlīt′), *n.* (in electrolysis) the portion of the electrolyte in the immediate vicinity of the anode. [ANO(DE) + (ELECTRO)LYTE]

a·nom·a·lism (ə nom′ə liz′əm), *n.* *Rare.* **1.** the state or quality of being anomalous. **2.** an anomaly. [*anomal-* (see ANOMALOUS) + -ISM]

a·nom·a·lis·tic (ə nom′ə lis′tik), *adj.* of or pertaining to an anomaly. [*anomal-* (see ANOMALOUS) + -ISTIC] —**a·nom′a·lis′ti·cal·ly,** *adv.*

anom′alis′tic month′, *Astron.* See under **month** (def. 5).

anom′alis′tic year′, *Astron.* the average interval between consecutive passages of the earth through the perihelion, equivalent to 365.26 days.

a·nom·a·lous (ə nom′ə ləs), *adj.* **1.** deviating from the common rule, type, or form; abnormal; irregular. **2.** peculiar; strange; unusual; odd: *He held an anomalous position in the world of art.* **3.** incongruous or contradictory. [< L *anōmalus* < Gk *anṓmalos* irregular, equiv. to *an-* AN-[1] + *homalós* even; see HOMO-, -OUS] —**a·nom′a·lous·ly,** *adv.* —**a·nom′a·lous·ness,** *n.*

anom′alous zee′man effect′, *Physics, Optics.* See under **zeeman effect.**

a·nom·a·ly (ə nom′ə lē), *n., pl.* **-lies. 1.** a deviation from the common rule, type, or form. **2.** someone or something anomalous: *With his quiet nature, he was an anomaly in his exuberant family.* **3.** an odd, peculiar, or strange condition, situation, quality, etc. **4.** an incongruity or inconsistency. **5.** *Astron.* a quantity measured in degrees, defining the position of an orbiting body with respect to the point at which it is nearest to or farthest from its primary. **6.** *Meteorol.* **a.** the value deviation of a meteorological element at a specific location from the mean value of the element for that parallel of latitude. **b.** the value deviation of a meteorological element at a specific location for a specified time from the mean value of that element for the same location at all other times. [< L *anōmalia* < Gk *anōmalía,* equiv. to *anṓmal-* (see ANOMALOUS) + *-ia* -IA]
—**Syn. 1, 2.** abnormality, exception, peculiarity.

a·no·mi·a (ə nō′mē ə), *n.* *Med.* the inability to name objects or to recognize the written or spoken names of objects. [< NL, irreg. < Gk *a-* A-[6] + L *nōm(en)* name + *-ia* -IA]

an·o·mie (an′ə mē′), *n.* *Sociol.* a state or condition of individuals or society characterized by a breakdown or absence of social norms and values, as in the case of uprooted people. [< F < Gk *anomía* lawlessness. See A-[6], -NOMY] —**a·nom·ic** (ə nom′ik), *adj.*

an·o·mite (an′ə mīt′), *n.* *Mineral.* a variety of mica, similar to biotite but differing in optical orientation. [< Gk *ánom(os)* lawless (*a-* A-[6] + *nóm(os)* law + *-os* adj. suffix) + -ITE[1]]

a·non (ə non′), *adv.* *Archaic.* **1.** in a short time; soon. **2.** at another time. **3.** at once; immediately. **4. ever and anon,** now and then; occasionally: *Ever and anon she thought back to those difficult times.* [ME *anon, anoon,* OE *on āne* in ONE (course) i.e., straightway]

anon., anonymous.

an·o·nych·i·a (an′ə nik′ē ə), *n.* *Med.* congenital absence of the nails. [< NL < Gk *an-* AN-[1] + *onych-* (s. of *ónyx* nail; see ONYX) + *-ia* -IA]

an·o·nym (an′ə nim), *n.* **1.** an assumed or false name. **2.** an anonymous person or publication. [back formation from ANONYMOUS]

a·non·y·mous (ə non′ə məs), *adj.* **1.** without any name acknowledged, as that of author, contributor, or the like: *an anonymous pamphlet.* **2.** of unknown name; whose name is withheld: *an anonymous author.* **3.** lacking individuality, unique character, or distinction: *an endless row of drab, anonymous houses.* [< L *anōnymus* < Gk *anṓnymos,* equiv. to *an-* AN-[1] + *ónym(a)* -ONYM + *-os* adj. suffix; see -OUS] —**an·o·nym·i·ty** (an′ə nim′i tē), **a·non′y·mous·ness,** *n.* —**a·non′y·mous·ly,** *adv.*

an·o·op·si·a (an′ō op′sē ə), *n.* *Ophthalm. Rare.* strabismus in which one or both eyes are turned upward. Also, **an′o·öp′si·a, anopia, a·nop·si·a** (ə nop′sē ə). [< NL; see ANO-[2], OPSIS, -IA]

a·noph·e·les (ə nof′ə lēz′), *n., pl.* **-les.** any mosquito of the genus *Anopheles,* certain species of which are vectors of the parasite causing malaria in man. [< NL < Gk *anōphelḗs* useless, hurtful, harmful, equiv. to *an-* AN-[1] + *ōphelē(ein)* (to) help + *-ēs* adj. suffix]

Anopheles, *Anopheles punctipennis* (Length ¼ in.)

an·o·pi·a (an ō′pē ə), *n.* *Ophthalm.* **1.** absence of sight, esp. when due to a structural defect in or absence of an eye. **2.** anoopsia. [< NL < Gk *an-* AN-[1] + *ōp-* (s. of *ṓps*) eye + *-ia* -IA]

an·o·pis·tho·graph (an′ə pis′thə graf′, -gräf′), *n.* a manuscript, parchment, or book having writing on only one side of the leaves. Cf. **opisthograph.** [AN-[1] + OPISTHOGRAPH] —**an′o·pis′tho·graph′ic,** *adj.* —**an′o·pis′tho·graph′i·cal·ly,** *adv.*

a·no·rak (ä′nə räk′), *n.* a jacket with a hood, as worn in the arctic. [< Eskimo *anoraq*]

an·o·rec·tal (an′ō rek′təl), *adj.* of, pertaining to, or associated with the anus and rectum. [ANO-[1] + RECTAL]

an·o·rec·tic (an′ə rek′tik), *adj.* **1.** Also, **an′o·rec′tous,** having no appetite. **2.** causing a loss of appetite. —*n.* **3.** an anorectic substance, as a drug; anorexiant. Also, **an·o·ret·ic** (an′ə ret′ik). [AN-[1] + ORECTIC]

an·o·rex·i·a (an′ə rek′sē ə), *n.* *Psychiatry.* **1.** lack of appetite and inability to eat, often based on abnormal psychological attitudes. **2.** See **anorexia nervosa.** [< NL < Gk, equiv. to *an-* AN-[1] + *órex(is)* longing (*oreg-* reach after + *-sis* -SIS) + *-ia* -IA]

anorex′ia ner·vo′sa (nər vō′sə), *Psychiatry.* a hysterical condition characterized by loss of appetite and aversion to food, typically accompanied by deficiency symptoms and emaciation. [< NL: nervous anorexia]

an·o·rex·i·ant (an′ō rek′sē ənt, an′ə-), *n.* *Med.* a substance, as a drug, for causing loss of appetite. [ANOREXI(A) + -ANT]

an·or·thic (an ôr′thik), *adj.* *Crystall.* triclinic. [AN-[1] + ORTH- + -IC]

an·or·thite (an ôr′thīt), *n.* *Mineral.* the calcium end member of the plagioclase group, a rare mineral that alters easily. [AN-[1] + ORTH- + -ITE[1]] —**an·or·thit·ic** (an′ôr thit′ik), *adj.*

an·or·tho·clase (an ôr′thə klās′, -klāz′), *n.* *Mineral.* a variety of microcline, rich in sodium and sometimes having a play of color: sometimes considered a variety of orthoclase. [AN-[1] + ORTHOCLASE]

an·or·tho·site (an ôr′thə sīt′), *n.* *Petrog.* a granular igneous rock composed largely of labradorite or a more calcic feldspar. [< F *anorthose* anorthoclase (*an-* AN-[1] + Gk *orthós* straight) + -ITE[1]]

a·no·scope (ā′nə skōp′), *n.* *Med.* an instrument for rectal and anal examination. [ANO-[2] + -SCOPE]

an·os·mi·a (an oz′mē ə, -os′-), *n.* *Pathol.* loss of the sense of smell. [< NL < Gk *an-* AN-[1] + *osm(ḗ)* smell (akin to *ózein* to smell) + *-ia* -IA] —**an·os·mat·ic** (an′əz mat′ik), **an·os′mic,** *adj.*

an·o·sog·no·sia (an′ə sog nō′zhə, -shə), *n.* *Psychiatry.* refusal to acknowledge sensory or motor defects. [< NL; see A-[6], NOSO-, -GNOSIS, -IA]

an·oth·er (ə nuth′ər), *adj.* **1.** a second; a further; an additional: *another piece of cake.* **2.** a different; a distinct; of a different kind: *at another time; another man.* —*pron.* **3.** one more; an additional one: *Try another.* **4.** a different one; something different: *going from one house to another.* **5.** one like the first: *one copy for her and another for him.* **6. one another,** one (person or thing) in relation to another; each other: *Love one another.* [ME; see AN[1], OTHER]

an·oth·er-guess (ə nuth′ər ges′), *adj.* *Archaic.* of another kind.

A·nouilh (A no͞o′yə), *n.* **Jean** (zhäN), born 1910, French dramatist.

an·our·ous (ə no͝or′əs), *adj.* anurous.

an·ox·e·mi·a (an′ok sē′mē ə), *n.* *Med.* a deficiency of oxygen in the arterial blood. Also, **an′ox·ae′mi·a.** [AN-[1] + OX(YGEN) + -EMIA] —**an′ox·e′mic, an′ox·ae′mic,** *adj.*

an·ox·i·a (an ok′sē ə, ə nok′-), *n.* *Med.* **1.** an abnormally low amount of oxygen in the body tissues. **2.** the mental and physical disturbances that occur as a result of hypoxia. [AN-[1] + OX(YGEN) + -IA] —**an·ox′ic,** *adj.*

ANPA, American Newspaper Publishers Association. Also, **A.N.P.A.**

ans., answer.

an·sa (an′sə), *n., pl.* **-sae** (-sē). *Archaeol.* a looped handle, esp. of a vase. [< L]

An·sar (an′sär), *n.* (*sometimes l.c.*) (*construed as pl.*) **1.** the first inhabitants of Medina to accept Islam. **2.** any of those who helped Muhammad after he began his preaching. [< Ar *Anṣār,* pl. of *nāṣir* helper] —**An·sar′i·an,** *adj.*

an·sate (an′sāt), *adj.* having a handle or handlelike part. [< L *ansātus* having a handle. See ANSA, -ATE[1]]

an′sate cross′, ankh.

An·schau·ung (än′shou o͝ong′, -əng), *n.* *Philos.* direct or immediate intuition or perception of sense data with little or no rational interpretation. [< G: view, equiv. to *anschau(en)* (to) view (*an-* on, at + *schauen* to look) + *-ung* -ING[1]]

An·schluss (än′shlo͝os), *n.* union, esp. the political union of Austria with Germany in 1938. [< G: consolidation, joining together, equiv. to *an-* on, to + *Schluss* a closing]

Anse (ans), *n.* a boy's given name, form of **Anselm.**

An·sel (an′sel), *n.* a boy's given name. Also, **Anselm.**

An·selm (an′selm), *n.* **1. Saint,** 1033–1109, archbishop of Canterbury: scholastic theologian and philosopher. **2.** Also, **Ansel.** a boy's given name.

an·ser·ine (an′sə rīn′, -rin), *adj.* **1.** of or pertaining to the subfamily *Anserinae,* of the family *Anatidae,* comprising the true geese. **2.** resembling a goose; gooselike. **3.** stupid; foolish; silly. Also, **an′ser·ous.** [< L *anserīn(us)* of, pertaining to geese, equiv. to *anser* a goose + *-īnus* -INE[1]]

An·ser·met (äN ser mā′), *n.* **Er·nest** (er nest′), born 1883, Swiss symphony orchestra conductor.

Ans·gar·i·us (ans gâr′ē əs), *n.* a crater in the fourth quadrant of the face of the moon, in the libration area: about 50 miles in diameter.

An·son (an′sən), *n.* **1.** a town in central Texas. 2890 (1960). **2.** a boy's given name.

An·so·ni·a (an sō′nē ə, -sōn′yə), *n.* a city in SW Connecticut. 19,819 (1960).

an·stoss (än′shtōs), *n., pl.* **-stös·se** (-shtœ sə). (in the philosophy of Fichte) any of the six successive steps by which the absolute ego attains self-knowledge. [< G: impetus, collision]

an·swer (an′sər, än′-), *n.* **1.** a spoken or written reply or response to a question, request, letter, etc.: *What is your answer?* **2.** a correct response to a question asked to test one's knowledge. **3.** an action serving as a reply or response: *The answer was a volley of fire.* **4.** a solution to a problem, esp. in mathematics. **5.** a reply to a charge or accusation. **6.** *Law.* a pleading of facts by a defendant in opposition to those stated in the plaintiff's declaration. **7.** *Music.* the entrance of a fugue subject, usually on the dominant, either slightly altered or transposed exactly after each presentation in the tonic. —*v.i.* **8.** to make answer; reply. **9.** to respond by a word or act: *to answer with a nod.* **10.** to act or suffer in consequence of (usually fol. by *for*). **11.** to be or declare oneself responsible or accountable (usually fol. by *for*): *I will answer for his safety.* **12.** to be satisfactory or serve (usually fol. by *for*): *to answer for a purpose.* **13.** to conform; correspond (usually fol. by *to*): *to answer to a description.* —*v.t.* **14.** to make answer to; reply or respond to: *to answer a person; to answer a question.* **15.** to act in reply or response to: *to answer the bell.* **16.** to solve or present a solution of. **17.** to serve or fulfill: *This will answer the purpose.* **18.** to discharge (a responsibility, claim, debt, etc.). **19.** to conform or correspond to; be similar or equivalent to: *to answer a description.* **20.** to atone for; make amends for. **21.** to reply or respond favorably to: *I would like to answer your request but am unable to do so.* **22. answer back,** to reply impertinently or rudely: *Well-behaved children do not answer back when scolded.* **23. answer the helm,** *Naut.* (of a vessel) to maneuver or remain steady according to the position of the rudder. [ME *andswerien,* OE *andswerian, andswarian* deriv. of *andswaru* an answer] —**an′swer·er,** *n.* —**an′swer·less,** *adj.* —**an′swer·less·ly,** *adv.*
—**Syn. 1.** riposte. ANSWER, REJOINDER, REPLY, RESPONSE, RETORT, all mean words used to meet a question,

remark, charge, etc. An ANSWER is a return remark: *an answer giving the desired information.* A REJOINDER is a quick, usually clever answer or remark made in reply to another's comment, not to a question. REPLY is somewhat more formal than ANSWER: *a reply to a letter.* A RESPONSE often suggests an answer to an appeal, exhortation, etc., or an expected or fixed reply: *a response to inquiry; a response in a church service.* A RETORT implies a keen, prompt answer, esp. one that turns a remark upon the person who made it: *a sharp retort.* **6.** defense, plea.

an·swer·a·ble (an′sər ə bəl, än′-), *adj.* **1.** liable to be asked to give account; responsible, as to a person, for an act, etc.: *He is answerable to me for all his acts.* **2.** capable of being answered: *a question answerable by mail.* **3.** proportionate; correlative (usually fol. by *to*). **4.** corresponding; suitable (usually fol. by *to*): *The amount is not answerable to my needs.* [ANSWER + -ABLE] **—an′swer·a·bil′i·ty,** *n.* **—an′swer·a·ble·ness,** *n.* **—an′swer·a·bly,** *adv.*

an′swering pen′nant, *Naut.* one of the flags of the International Code of Signals, a pennant of three red and two white vertical stripes, flown at the dip while a message is being interpreted and close up when it is understood. Also called **code flag.**

ant (ant), *n.* **1.** any hymenopterous insect of the family *Formicidae*, comprising thousands of widely distributed species, all of which exhibit some degree of social organization. **2. have ants in one's pants,** *Slang.* to be impatient or eager to act or speak: *She's had ants in her pants ever since she won that ticket to Bermuda.* [ME *am(e)te*, OE *ǣmette*; c. MLG *āmete*, OHG *āmeiza* (*ā-* prefix + *meizan* to beat, cut), G *Ameise*] **—ant′like′,** *adj.*

Ant, *Monomorium minimum*
A, Male; B, Female

an't (ant, änt, ānt), **1.** *Chiefly Brit. Dial.* contraction of *am not.* **2.** *Dial.* ain't.

ant-, var. of **anti-** before a vowel or *h*: *antacid; anthelmintic.*

-ant, a suffix appearing in adjectives formed from verbs of Latin origin and in nouns formed from those adjectives (when the adjective form may not survive): *pleasant; constant; servant.* [< L *-ant-*, prp. s. of verbs in *-āre*; in many words < F *-ant* < L *-ant-* or *-ent-* (see -ENT); akin to ME, OE *-and-*, *-end-*, prp. suffix]

ant., antonym.

an·ta (an′tə), *n., pl.* **-tae** (-tē). *Archit.* a rectangular pier or pilaster, esp. one formed by thickening the end of a masonry wall. Cf. **in antis.** [deduced < L *antae* pilasters (in pl. only); akin to ANTE-]

A, Anta

ANTA (an′tə), *n.* a privately supported organization, chartered by Congress in 1935, for the encouragement and advancement of professional and nonprofessional theater. [*A(merican) N(ational) T(heatre and) A(cademy)*]

Ant·a·buse (an′tə byo͞os′), *n. Pharm., Trademark.* disulfiram. [ANT- + ABUSE]

ant·ac·id (ant as′id), *adj.* **1.** preventing, neutralizing, or counteracting acidity, as of the stomach. **—***n.* **2.** an antacid agent. [ANT- + ACID]

An·tae·a (an tē′ə), *n. Class. Myth.* an epithet variously applied to Rhea, Cybele, and Demeter, the goddesses to whom men prayed. [< Gk *antaia* besought with prayers]

An·tae·us (an tē′əs), *n. Class. Myth.* an African giant who was invincible when in contact with the earth, but was lifted into the air by Hercules and crushed. **—An·tae′an,** *adj.*

an·tag·o·nise (an tag′ə nīz′), *v.t., v.i.,* **-nised, -nis·ing.** *Chiefly Brit.* antagonize. **—an·tag′o·nis′a·ble,** *adj.* **—an·tag′o·ni·sa′tion,** *n.*

an·tag·o·nism (an tag′ə niz′əm), *n.* **1.** an active hostility or opposition, as between unfriendly or conflicting groups. **2.** an opposing force, principle, or tendency: *Her plan to become an actress met with the antagonism of her family.* [< Gk *antagōnism(a).* See ANTAGONIZE, -ISM]
—Syn. 1, 2. hostility. **2.** animosity.

an·tag·o·nist (an tag′ə nist), *n.* **1.** one who is opposed to or strives with another; opponent; adversary. **2.** the adversary of the hero or of the protagonist of a drama or other literary work: *Iago is the antagonist of Othello.* **3.** *Physiol.* a muscle which acts in opposition to another. Cf. **agonist** (def. 3). **4.** *Dentistry.* a tooth in one jaw that articulates during mastication or occlusion with a tooth in the opposing jaw. **5.** *Pharm.* a drug that counteracts the effects of another drug. [< LL *antagōnist(a)* < Gk *antagōnistḗs.* See ANTAGONIZE, -IST]
—Syn. 1. contestant, enemy, foe. See **adversary.**
—Ant. 1. ally, friend.

an·tag·o·nis·tic (an tag′ə nis′tik), *adj.* **1.** acting in opposition; mutually opposing. **2.** hostile; unfriendly. [ANTAGONIST + -IC] **—an·tag′o·nis′ti·cal·ly,** *adv.*

an·tag·o·nize (an tag′ə nīz′), *v.,* **-nized, -niz·ing.** **—***v.t.* **1.** to make hostile; make an enemy or antagonist of: *His speech antagonized many voters.* **2.** to act in opposition to; oppose. **—***v.i.* **3.** *Rare.* to act antagonistically. Also, *esp. Brit.,* **antagonise.** [< Gk *antagōniz(esthai)* contend against, dispute with. See ANT-, AGONIZE] **—an·tag′o·niz′a·ble,** *adj.* **—an·tag′o·ni·za′tion,** *n.*

An·tag·o·ras (an tag′ər əs), *n. Class. Myth.* a shepherd from the island of Cos who challenged Hercules to a wrestling match.

An·ta·ki·ya (än′tä kē′yä), *n.* Arabic name of **Antioch.**

ant·al·ka·li (ant al′kə lī′), *n., pl.* **-lis, -lies.** something that neutralizes alkalis or counteracts alkalinity. Also, **antalkaline.** [ANT- + ALKALI]

ant·al·ka·line (ant al′kə lin′, -lin), *adj.* **1.** preventing, neutralizing, or counteracting alkalinity. **—***n.* **2.** antalkali. [ANT- + ALKALINE]

An·tal·ya (än′täl yä′), *n.* a seaport in SW Turkey. 35,923 (1955).

An·ta·na·na·ri·vo (än′tə nä′nə rē′vō, an′-), *n.* Tananarive.

ant·a·pex (ant ā′peks), *n., pl.* **-a·pex·es, -ap·i·ces** (-ap′i sēz′, -ā′pi-). *Astron.* the point exactly opposite in direction to the solar apex; the point away from which the solar system is moving and toward which the stars appear to be converging, located in the constellation Columba. [ANT- + APEX]

an·ta·ra·la (un′tə rä′lə), *n.* a vestibule of a Brahman temple. [< Skt: entrance; see INTER-]

an·tar·an·ga (un′tər uṅ′gə), *n.* (*construed as pl.*) *Yoga.* the three angas pertaining to the mind: dharana or concentration, dhyana or meditation, and samadhi or contemplation. [< Skt: inner discipline]

ant·arc·tic (ant ärk′tik, -är′-), *adj.* **1.** of, at, or near the S Pole. **—***n.* **2. the Antarctic,** the Antarctic Ocean and Antarctica. [< L *antarctic(us)* < Gk *antarktikós* (see ANT-, ARCTIC); r. ME *antartik* < ML *antartic(us)*]

Ant·arc·ti·ca (ant ärk′ti kə, -är′-), *n.* the continent surrounding the South Pole: almost entirely covered by an ice sheet. ab. 5,000,000 sq. mi. Also called **Antarctic Continent.**

Antarc′tic Cir′cle, an imaginary line drawn parallel to the equator, at 23° 28′ N of the South Pole: between the South Frigid Zone and the South Temperate Zone. See diag. under **zone.**

antarc′tic circumpo′lar cur′rent, an ocean current flowing from west to east around the antarctic continent. Also called **west wind drift.**

Antarc′tic Con′tinent, Antarctica.

Antarc′tic O′cean, the waters surrounding Antarctica, comprising the southernmost parts of the Pacific, Atlantic, and Indian oceans.

Antarc′tic Penin′sula, a peninsula in Antarctica, S of South America. Also called **Graham Land.** Formerly, **Palmer Peninsula.**

Antarc′tic Zone′, the section of the earth's surface lying between the Antarctic Circle and the South Pole. See diag. under **zone.**

An·tar·es (an târ′ēz), *n. Astron.* a red supergiant giant star of the first magnitude in the constellation Scorpius. [< Gk, equiv. to *ant-* ANT- (in the sense of simulating) + *Ares* (Gk name of planet Mars); so called because it is like Mars in color]

ant·ar·thrit·ic (ant′är thrit′ik), *Med.* **—***adj.* **1.** relieving the pain of arthritis or of gout. **—***n.* **2.** an antarthritic agent. [ANT- + ARTHRITIC]

ant·asth·mat·ic (ant′az mat′ik, -as-), *Med.* **—***adj.* **1.** relieving or preventing asthma or an asthmatic paroxysm. **—***n.* **2.** an antasthmatic agent. [ANT- + ASTHMATIC]

ant·a·troph·ic (ant′ə trof′ik), *Med.* **—***adj.* **1.** preventing or curing atrophy. **—***n.* **2.** an antatrophic agent. [ANT- + ATROPHIC]

ant′ bear′, **1.** Also called **great anteater.** a large, terrestrial, tropical American edentate, *Myrmecophaga jubata*, feeding on ants and termites, and having a long, tapering snout and extensile tongue, powerful front claws, and a shaggy gray coat marked with a conspicuous black band. **2.** the aardvark.

Ant bear
(2 ft. high at shoulder; total length 6 ft.; tail about 2 ft.)

ant·bird (ant′bûrd′), *n.* any of numerous passerine birds of the family *Formicariidae*, of the New World tropics, many species of which feed on ants and other insects. [ANT + BIRD]

an·te (an′tē), *n., v.,* **-ted** or **-teed, -te·ing.** **—***n.* **1.** *Poker.* a fixed but arbitrary stake put into the pot by each player before the deal. **2.** an amount of money paid in advance to insure an individual's share in a joint business venture. **3.** *Informal.* an individual's share of the total expenses incurred by a group. **4.** *Slang.* the price or cost of something. **—***v.t.* **5.** *Poker.* to put (one's initial stake) into the pot. **6.** to produce or pay (one's share) (usually fol. by *up*): *He anted up his half of the bill.* **—***v.i.* **7.** *Poker.* to put one's initial stake into the pot. **8.** *Informal.* to pay (usually fol. by *up*). [< ANTE-]

ante-, a learned borrowing from Latin meaning "before," used in the formation of compound words: *anteroom; antebellum; antedate.* [< L, comb. form of prep. and adv. *ante*; akin to Gk *antí*, OE *and-* against, toward, opposite. See ANTI-]

ant·eat·er (ant′ē′tər), *n.* **1.** any of several mammals, esp. certain tropical American edentates feeding chiefly on ants and termites. Cf. **ant bear, silky anteater, tamandua. 2.** the aardvark. **3.** a pangolin. **4.** an echidna. **5.** See **banded anteater.** [ANT + EATER]

an·te·bel·lum (an′tē bel′əm), *adj.* **1.** before the war. **2.** *U.S.* before or existing before the American Civil War. **3.** before or existing before World War I. [< L *ante bellum*: before the war]

an·te·cede (an′ti sēd′), *v.t.,* **-ced·ed, -ced·ing.** to go before, in time, order, etc.; precede: *Shakespeare antecedes Milton.* [< L *antecēd(ere)* (to) go before, precede, excel, surpass. See ANTE-, CEDE]

an·te·ced·ence (an′ti sēd′əns), *n.* **1.** the act of going before; precedence. **2.** priority. **3.** *Astron. Rare.* (of a planet) apparent retrograde motion. [ANTECED(ENCY) + -ENCE]

an·te·ced·en·cy (an′ti sēd′ən sē), *n.* the quality or condition of being antecedent. [< L *antecēdentia.* See ANTECEDE, -ENCY]

an·te·ced·ent (an′ti sēd′ənt), *adj.* **1.** existing, being, or going before; preceding; prior: *an antecedent event.* **—***n.* **2.** a preceding circumstance, event, object, style, phenomenon, etc. **3. antecedents, a.** ancestors. **b.** the history, events, characteristics, etc., of one's earlier life: *Little is known about his birth and antecedents.* **4.** *Gram.* a word, phrase, or clause, usually a substantive, which is replaced by a pronoun or other substitute later, or occasionally earlier, in a sentence or in a subsequent sentence. In *Jack lost a hat and he can't find it, Jack* is the antecedent of *he,* and *hat* is the antecedent of *it.* **5.** *Math.* **a.** the first term of a ratio; the first or third term of a proportion. **b.** the first of two vectors in a dyad. **6.** *Logic.* the conditional element in a proposition, as "Caesar conquered Gaul," in "If Caesar conquered Gaul, he was a great general." [ME < L *antecēdent-* (s. of *antecēdēns*) going before, prp. of *antecēd(ere)* (to) ANTECEDE; see -ENT] **—an·te·ce·den·tal** (an′ti sē den′tᵊl), *adj.* **—an′te·ced′ent·ly,** *adv.*

an·te·ces·sor (an′ti ses′ər), *n.* one who goes before; predecessor. [late ME *antecessour* < L *antecessor* he who goes before, a predecessor, equiv. to *antecess(us)* (ptp. of *antecēdere*) gone before, preceded (*ante-* ANTE- + *cēd-* go + *-tus* ptp. suffix) + *-or* -OR²]

an·te·cham·ber (an′tē chām′bər), *n.* a chamber or room which serves as a waiting room and entrance to a larger room or an apartment. [earlier *antichamber* < MF *antichambre* < It *anticamera*, equiv. to *anti-* (< L *anti-*, var. of *ante-* ANTE-) + *camera* CHAMBER]

an·te·chap·el (an′tē chap′əl), *n.* a room or hall before the entrance to a chapel. [ANTE- + CHAPEL]

an·te·choir (an′tē kwīᵊr′), *n.* an enclosed space in front of the choir of a church. Also called **forechoir.** [ANTE- + CHOIR]

an·te-Chris·tum (an′tē kris′təm), *adj. Latin.* before Christ. *Abbr.:* A.C.

an·te·court (an′tē kōrt′, -kôrt′), *n. Rare.* a forecourt. [ANTE- + COURT]

an·te·date (*v.* an′ti dāt′, an′ti dāt′; *n.* an′ti dāt′), *v.,* **-dat·ed, -dat·ing,** *n.* **—***v.t.* **1.** to be of older date than; precede in time: *The Peruvian empire antedates the Mexican empire.* **2.** predate (def. 1). **3.** to assign to an earlier date: *to antedate a historical event.* **4.** to cause to return to an earlier time: *to antedate one's thoughts by remembering past events.* **5.** to cause to happen sooner; accelerate: *The cold weather antedated their departure from the country.* **6.** to take or have in advance; anticipate: *The children antedated Christmas by talking about it continually.* **—***n.* **7.** a prior date. [ANTE- + DATE¹]

an·te·di·lu·vi·an (an′tē di lo͞o′vē ən), *adj.* **1.** belonging to the period before the Flood. Gen. 7, 8. **2.** antiquated; primitive: *antediluvian ideas.* **—***n.* **3.** a person who lived before the Flood. **4.** a very old or old-fashioned person. [ANTE- + L *dīluvi(um)* a flood, deluge (see DILUVIUM) + -AN]

ante′dilu′vian pa′triarch. See under **patriarch** (def. 1).

an·te·fix (an′tə fiks′), *n., pl.* **-fix·es, -fix·a** (-fik′sə). *Archit.* **1.** an upright ornament at the eaves of a tiled roof, to conceal the foot of a row of convex tiles which cover the joints of the flat tiles. **2.** an ornament above the top molding of a cornice. [< L *antefix(a)*, neut. pl. of *antifixus* fastened in front, equiv. to *ante-* ANTE- + *fixus* ptp. of *fīgere* to FIX] **—an′te·fix′al,** *adj.*

an·te·flex·ion (an′tə flek′shən), *n. Pathol.* a bending forward, esp. of the body of the uterus. [ANTE- + L *flexiōn-* (s. of *flexiō*) a bending; see FLEXION]

ant′ egg′, the white pupa or larva of an ant, sold in dried quantities as food for pet fish, birds, turtles, etc.

an·te·hall (an′tē hôl′), *n.* a room or hall serving as a waiting room and entrance to a larger hall. [ANTE- + HALL]

an·te·lope (an′tᵊlōp′), *n., pl.* **-lopes,** (*esp. collectively*) **-lope. 1.** any of several ruminants of the family *Bovidae*, found chiefly in Africa and Asia, having permanent, hollow, unbranched horns. **2.** leather made from the hide of such an animal. **3.** *U.S.* pronghorn. [late ME *antelop* < MF < ML *antalopus* < Gk *anthólops* fabulous beast] **—an′te·lo′pi·an, an·te·lo·pine** (an′tᵊlō′pin, -pīn), *adj.*

an·te·me·rid·i·an (an′tē mə rid′ē ən), *adj.* **1.** occurring before noon. **2.** of or pertaining to the forenoon. [ANTE- + MERIDIAN]

an·te me·rid·i·em (an′tē mə rid′ē em′, -əm). See **a.m.**

an·te-mor·tem (an′tē môr′təm), *adj. Latin.* before death: *an ante-mortem confession.*

an·te·mun·dane (an′tē mun′dān), *adj.* before the creation of the world. [ANTE- + MUNDANE]

an·te·na·tal (an′tē nāt′ᵊl), *adj.* prenatal. [ANTE- + NATAL]

an·te·nave (an′tē nāv′), *n.* a porch or narthex before the nave of a church. [ANTE- + NAVE¹]

an·te-Ni·cene (an′tē nī sēn′, -nī′sēn), *adj.* of or pertaining to the Christian church or period before the Nicene Council of A.D. 325. Also, **an·te-Ni·cae·an** (an′tē nī sē′ən).

an·ten·na (an ten′ə), *n., pl.* **-ten·nas** for 1; **-ten·nae** (-ten′ē) for 2. **1.** *Radio.* a conductor by which electromagnetic waves are sent out or received, consisting commonly of a wire or set of wires; aerial. **2.** *Zool.* one of the jointed, movable, sensory appendages occurring in pairs on the heads of insects and most other arthropods. See diag. under **insect.** [< L: a sailyard] **—an·ten′nal,** *adj.*

anten′na array′, a directional antenna or system of antennas for radio transmission or reception.

anten′nal gland′. See **green gland.**

an·ten·na·ry (an ten′ə rē), *adj. Zool.* **1.** of, pertaining to, or resembling an antenna. **2.** bearing antennae; antennate. [ANTENNA + -ARY¹]

an·ten·nate (an′tə nit, -nāt′), *adj. Zool.* having antennae. [ANTENNAE + -ATE¹]

an·ten·ni·fer (an ten′ə fər), *n. Zool.* a pivotlike projection that articulates with the antenna, located on the rim of an antennal socket. [ANTENN(A) + -I- + -FER]

an·ten·ni·form (an ten′ə fôrm′), *adj.* shaped like an antenna. [ANTENN(A) + -I- + -FORM]

an·ten·nule (an ten′yo͞ol), *n. Zool.* a small antenna, esp. one of the anterior pair of a crustacean. [ANTENN(A) + -ULE] **—an·ten·nu·lar** (an ten′yə lər), **an·ten·nu·lar·y** (an ten′yə ler′ē), *adj.*

An·te·nor (an tē′nôr), *n. Class. Myth.* a counselor who advised Priam to return Helen to Menelaus.

an·te·num·ber (an′tē num′bər), *n.* a number that immediately precedes another: *Three is the antenumber of four.* [ANTE- + NUMBER]

an·te·nup·tial (an′tē nup′shəl), *adj.* before marriage: *an antenuptial agreement.* [ANTE- + NUPTIAL]

an·te·or·bit·al (an′tē ôr′bi tᵊl), *adj. Anat.* situated in front of the eye. [ANTE- + ORBITAL]

An·tep (än tep′), *n.* Aintab.

an·te par·tum (an′tē pär′təm), *Obstet.* of or noting the period prior to childbirth; before delivery. Also, **an′te·par′tum, an′te-par′tum.** Cf. **post partum.** [< L]

an·te·past (an′ti past′), *n. Archaic.* a foretaste; appetizer. [ANTE- + L *pāstus* food (orig. ptp. of *pāscere* to feed), equiv. to *pās-* feed + *-tus* ptp. suffix]

CONCISE ETYMOLOGY KEY: <, descended or derived from; >, whence; b., blend of, blended; c., cognate with; deriv., derivative; equiv., equivalent; imit., imitative; m., modification of; obl., oblique; r., replacing; s., stem; sp., spelling; trans., translation; ?, origin unknown, perhaps; *, hypothetical. See the full key inside the front cover.

an·te·pen·di·um (an′ti pen′dē əm), *n., pl.* **-di·a** (-dē ə). the decoration of the front of an altar, as a covering of silk or a painted panel. [< ML < L *ante* before + *pend(ere)* hang, suspend + *-ium* -IUM]

an·te·pe·nult (an′tē pē′nult, -pi nult′), *n.* the last syllable but two in a word, as *te* in *antepenult.* [< L *(syllaba) antepaenult(ima)* the second (syllable) from the last, fem. of *antepaenultimus* standing before the penult. See ANTE-, PENULT] —**an·te·pe·nul·ti·mate** (an′tē pi-nul′tə mit), *adj., n.*

an·te·porch (an′tē pōrch′, -pôrch′), *n.* an outer porch. [ANTE- + PORCH]

an·te·port (an′tē pōrt′, -pôrt′), *n. Obs.* an outer door or gate. [< It *antiporta* < L *anti-* (var. of *ante-* ANTE-) + *porta* gate; see PORT⁴]

an·te·por·ti·co (an′tē pōr′tə kō′, -pôr′-), *n., pl.* **-coes, -cos.** a lesser portico preceding a main portico. [ANTE- + PORTICO]

an·te·pran·di·al (an′tē pran′dē əl), *adj.* preprandial. [ANTE- + PRANDIAL]

an·te·pro·hi·bi·tion (an′tē prō′ə bish′ən), *adj.* before prohibition. [ANTE- + PROHIBITION]

an·te·ri·or (an tēr′ē ər), *adj.* **1.** placed before; situated in or toward the front (opposed to *posterior*). **2.** going before in time; preceding; earlier: *an anterior age.* [< L, comp. of *ante* before, formed on model of POSTERIOR] —**an·te·ri·or·i·ty** (an tēr′ē ôr′i tē, -or′-), *n.* —**an·te′ri·or·ly,** *adv.*

ante′rior pitu′itary luteotro′pin, *Biochem.* luteotropin.

ante′rior tooth′, *Dentistry.* a tooth in the front of the mouth; an incisor or cuspid.

antero-, a learned borrowing from Latin meaning "front," "fore": *anteroparietal.* [< L **anter(us)* assumed positive of *anterior* + -o-; cf. ANTE-]

an·te·room (an′tē rōōm′, -rŏŏm′), *n.* **1.** a room which admits to a larger room. **2.** a waiting room. [ANTE- + ROOM]

an·ter·o·pa·ri·et·al (an′tə rō pə rī′i tᵊl), *adj. Anat.* situated in an anterior and parietal position. [ANTERO- + PARIETAL]

An·te·ros (an′tə ros′), *n.* **1.** *Class. Myth.* a brother of Eros, most often regarded as the avenger of unrequited love. **2.** Anterus.

An·ter·us (an′tər əs), *n.* **Saint,** pope A.D. 235–236. Also, **Anteros.**

an·te·type (an′tē tīp′), *n.* an earlier form; prototype. [ANTE- + TYPE]

an·te·ver·sion (an′tē vûr′zhən, -shən), *n. Pathol.* a tipping forward of the uterus with its fundus directed toward the pubis. [ANTE- + VERSION]

an·te·vert (an′tē vûrt′), *v.t. Pathol.* to displace (the uterus) by tipping forward. [< L *antevert(ere)* (to) go before, precede, equiv. to *ante* ANTE- + *vert(ere)* (to) turn]

An·te·vor·ta (an′tə vôr′tə), *n. Class. Myth.* a nymph, one of the Camenae, having knowledge of the future. Also called **Porrima, Pronsa.** Cf. **Postvorta.**

anth-, var. of **antho-** esp. before a vowel.

An·thas (an′thəs), *n. Class. Myth.* a son of Poseidon and Alcyone.

An·the·a (an thē′ə), *n.* **1.** *Class. Myth.* an epithet of Hera, meaning "flowery." **2.** a girl's given name. [< Gk *Ántheia;* akin to *ántheion* flower]

An·theil (an′tīl), *n.* **George,** 1900–59, U.S. composer.

anthel′ic arcs′, a rare halo occurring at the sun's elevation but in the opposite part of the sky. [ANTHEL(ION) + -IC]

ant·he·li·on (ant hē′lē ən, an thē′-), *n., pl.* **-li·a** (-lē ə). a luminous, white spot occasionally appearing at the sun's elevation but in the opposite part of the sky. [< LGk *anthḗlion,* neut. of *anthḗlios* opposite the sun, equiv. to *ant-* ANT- + *hḗli(os)* the sun + *-os* adj. suffix]

an·thel·min·tic (an′thel min′tik), *Med.* —*adj.* **1.** destroying or expelling intestinal worms. —*n.* **2.** an anthelmintic drug or medicine. [ANT- + HELMINT(H)IC]

an·them (an′thəm), *n.* **1.** a hymn, as of praise, devotion, or patriotism: *the national anthem of Spain.* **2.** a piece of sacred vocal music, usually with words taken from the Scriptures. **3.** a hymn sung in alternate parts. —*v.t.* **4.** to celebrate with or in an anthem. [ME *antem,* OE *antemn(e), antefne* < VL *antefna* < LL *antifona* < Gk *antiphōna* ANTIPHON]

an·the·ma (an thē′mə, an′thə-), *n., pl.* **an·the·ma·ta** (an thē′mə tə, -them′ə tə), **-the·mas.** *Pathol.* **1.** exanthema. **2.** an eruption of the skin. [< Gk *ánthēma* efflorescence, equiv. to *ánth(os)* flower + *-ēma* -EME]

an·the·mi·on (an thē′mē ən), *n., pl.* **-mi·a** (-mē ə). an ornament of floral forms in a flat radiating cluster, as in architectural decoration, vase painting, etc. Also called **honeysuckle ornament.** [< Gk *anthémion,* equiv. to *ánthem(on)* flower + *-ion* dim. suffix; see ANTHO-]

an·ther (an′thər), *n. Bot.* the pollen-bearing part of a stamen. See diag. under **flower.** [< NL *anthēr(a)* < L < Gk, fem. of *anthērós* flowery; see ANTHESIS] —**an′ther·al,** *adj.* —**an′ther·less,** *adj.*

an·ther·id·i·um (an′thə rid′ē əm), *n., pl.* **-ther·id·i·a** (-thə rid′ē ə). *Bot.* a male reproductive organ containing motile male gametes. [< NL; see ANTHER, -IDIUM] —**an′ther·id′i·al,** *adj.*

an·ther·o·zo·id (an′thər ə zō′id, an′thər ə zoid′), *n. Bot.* the motile male gamete produced in an antheridium. [ANTHER + -O- + Z(O)OID]

an·the·sis (an thē′sis), *n. Bot.* the period or act of expansion in flowers, esp. the maturing of the stamens. [< NL < Gk *ánthēsis* full bloom < *anthē(ein)* to bloom + *-sis* -SIS]

An·thes·te·ri·a (an′thi stēr′ē ə), *n.* (*sometimes construed as pl.*) one of the ancient Athenian festivals composing the Dionysia; a spring festival celebrating flowers and new wine. —**An·thes·te·ri·ac** (an′thi stēr′ē ak′), *adj.*

An·the·us (an′thē əs), *n. Class. Myth.* a son of Antenor, accidentally killed by Paris.

ant′ hill′, a mound of earth, leaves, etc., formed by a colony of ants in constructing their habitation.

antho-, a formal element of no assignable meaning, occurring in loan words from Greek (*anthology*); used with the meaning "flower" to form compound words (*anthotaxy*). [< Gk, comb. form of *ánthos* flower; akin to Skt *andha-,* OIr *ainder* maiden]

an·tho·bi·an (an thō′bē ən), *n.* any scarabeid beetle that feeds on flowers. [ANTHO- + BIO-² + -AN]

an·tho·car·pous (an′thə kär′pəs), *adj.* (of a fruit) having accessory or enlarged tissue, as the apple or strawberry. [ANTHO- + -CARPOUS]

an·tho·cy·a·nin (an′thə sī′ə nin), *n. Biochem.* any of a class of water-soluble pigments, including most of those that give red and blue flowers their colors. Also, **an·tho·cy·an** (an′thə sī′ən). [ANTHO- + CYANIN(E)]

an·tho·di·um (an thō′dē əm), *n., pl.* **-di·a** (-dē ə). *Bot.* a flower head or capitulum, esp. the head of a composite plant. See illus. under **inflorescence.** [< NL < Gk *anthṓd(ēs)* flowerlike (*ánth(os)* a flower + *-ṓdēs* like) + L *-ium* -IUM]

anthol., anthology.

an·thol·o·gise (an thol′ə jīz′), *v.i., v.t.,* **-gised, -gis·ing.** *Chiefly Brit.* anthologize.

an·thol·o·gize (an thol′ə jīz′), *v.,* **-gized, -giz·ing.** —*v.i.* **1.** to compile an anthology. —*v.t.* **2.** to include in an anthology. [ANTHOLOG(Y) + -IZE]

an·thol·o·gy (an thol′ə jē), *n., pl.* **-gies. 1.** a book or other collection of selected writings by various authors, usually in the same literary form or on the same subject: *an anthology of Elizabethan drama; an anthology of modern philosophy.* **2.** a collection of selected writings by one author. [< L *anthologia* < Gk: collection of poems, lit., one of flowers. See ANTHO-, -LOGY] —**an·tho·log·i·cal** (an′thə loj′i kəl), *adj.* —**an′tho·log′i·cal·ly,** *adv.* —**an·thol′o·gist,** *n.*

An·tho·ny (an′tə nē, -thə- *for 1, 2;* an′thə nē *for 3, 4;* an′thə nē *or, esp. Brit.,* -tə- *for 5*), *n.* **1.** See **Antony, Mark. 2. Saint,** A.D. 251?–356?, Egyptian hermit: founder of Christian monasticism. **3. Susan Brow·nell** (brou′nel), 1820–1906, U.S. reformer and suffragist. **4.** a town in S Kansas. 2744 (1960). **5.** Also, **Antony.** a boy's given name.

An′thony Ad′verse, a novel (1933) by William Hervey Allen.

An·tho·ny of Pad′ua (an′tə-nē, -thə-), **Saint,** 1195–1231, Franciscan monk and preacher in Italy and France.

an·thoph·i·lous (an thof′ə ləs), *adj.* having an affinity for or feeding on flowers. [ANTHO- + -PHILOUS]

an·tho·phore (an′thə fōr′, -fôr′), *n. Bot.* a form of floral stipe, produced by the elongation of the internode between the calyx and the corolla, and bearing the corolla, stamens, and pistil. [< Gk *anthophóros* flower-bearing, blooming. See ANTHO-, -PHORE]

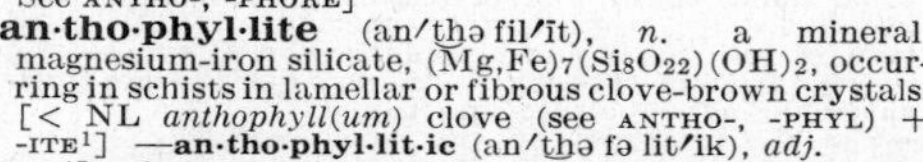
A, Anthophore (Within the calyx of flower of wild pink *Silene caroliniana*)

an·tho·phyl·lite (an′thə fil′īt), *n.* a mineral, magnesium-iron silicate, $(Mg,Fe)_7(Si_8O_{22})(OH)_2$, occurring in schists in lamellar or fibrous clove-brown crystals. [< NL *anthophyll(um)* clove (see ANTHO-, -PHYL) + -ITE¹] —**an·tho·phyl·lit·ic** (an′thə fə lit′ik), *adj.*

an·tho·tax·y (an′thə tak′sē), *n. Bot.* the arrangement of flowers on the axis of growth; inflorescence. [ANTHO- + -TAXY]

-anthous, var. of **antho-** as final element in a compound word: *monanthous.* [< Gk *ánth(os)* flower + -OUS]

An·tho·zo·a (an′thə zō′ə), *n.* the class comprising the corals, sea anemones, sea pens, etc. [NL; see ANTHO-, -ZOA]

an·tho·zo·an (an′thə zō′ən), *n.* **1.** any marine coelenterate of the class *Anthozoa,* comprising colonial and solitary polyps and including corals, sea anemones, sea pens, etc. —*adj.* **2.** Also, **an′tho·zo′ic.** belonging or pertaining to the *Anthozoa.* [< NL; see ANTHOZOA, -AN]

anthrac-, a learned borrowing from Greek meaning "coal," "carbon," "carbuncle," used in the formation of compound words: *anthracosis; anthracnose; anthracoid.* Also, *esp. before a consonant,* **anthraco-.** [< L *anthrac-* < Gk *anthrak-* (s. of *ánthrax*). See ANTHRAX]

an·thra·cene (an′thrə sēn′), *n. Chem.* a colorless, crystalline powder, $C_6H_4(CH_2)C_6H_4$, obtained from coal tar and having a violet fluorescence: used chiefly as a source of anthraquinone and alizarin, and in the process of measuring radioactive materials. [ANTHRAC- + -ENE]

an·thra·cite (an′thrə sīt′), *n.* a mineral coal containing little of the volatile hydrocarbons and burning almost without flame; hard coal. Also called **an′thracite coal′.** [< L *anthracītes* a kind of bloodstone < Gk *anthrakítēs,* lit., coallike. See ANTHRAC-, -ITE¹] —**an·thra·cit·ic** (an′thrə sit′ik), **an·thra·cit·ous** (an′thrə sī′təs), *adj.*

an·thrac·nose (an thrak′nōs), *n. Plant. Pathol.* a disease of plants, characterized by restricted, discolored lesions, caused by a fungus. [< F; see ANTHRAC-, NOS(O)-]

anthraco-, var. of **anthrac-** before a consonant.

an·thra·coid (an′thrə koid′), *adj.* **1.** resembling anthrax. **2.** resembling coal or charcoal; carbonlike. [ANTHRAC- + -OID]

an·thra·co·sil·i·co·sis (an′thrə kō sil′ə kō′sis), *n. Pathol.* a form of pneumoconiosis occurring in miners, caused by the inhalation of coal and siliceous particles. Also, **anthrasilicosis.** [< NL; see ANTHRACO-, SILICOSIS]

an·thra·co·sis (an′thrə kō′sis), *n. Pathol.* a form of pneumoconiosis in which the lungs become darkened from the inhalation of coal dust. [< NL; see ANTHRAC-, -OSIS] —**an·thra·cot·ic** (an′thrə kot′ik), *adj.*

an·thra·qui·none (an′thrə kwə nōn′, -kwē′nōn, -kwin′ōn), *n. Chem.* a yellow, water-insoluble, crystalline powder, $C_6H_4(CO_2)_2C_6H_4$, usually derived from anthracene or phthalic anhydride: used chiefly in the manufacture of anthraquinone dyes. [ANTHRA(CENE) + QUINONE]

an′thraquinone′ dye′, *Chem.* any of the class of dyes derived from anthraquinone, used for dyeing textiles, esp. cotton, rayon, and silk.

an·thra·sil·i·co·sis (an′thrə sil′ə kō′sis), *n. Pathol.* anthracosilicosis.

an·thrax (an′thraks), *n., pl.* **-thra·ces** (-thrə sēz′). *Pathol.* **1.** a malignant infectious disease of cattle, sheep, and other mammals, including man, caused by *Bacillus anthracis.* **2.** a malignant carbuncle that is the diagnostic lesion of anthrax disease in man. [< L *anthrax* carbuncle < Gk *ánthrax* (live) coal, carbuncle]

anthrop., **1.** anthropological. **2.** anthropology.

anthropo-, a learned borrowing from Greek meaning "human," used in the formation of compound words: *anthropometry.* [< Gk *ánthrōpo(s)* man]

an·thro·po·cen·tric (an′thrə pō sen′trik), *adj.* **1.** regarding man as the central fact of the universe. **2.** assuming man to be the final aim and end of the universe. **3.** viewing and interpreting everything in terms of human experience and values. [ANTHROPO- + CENTRIC]

an·thro·po·cen·trism (an′thrə pō sen′triz əm), *n.* an anthropocentric theory or view. [ANTHROPOCENTR(IC) + -ISM]

an·thro·po·gen·e·sis (an′thrə pō jen′i sis), *n.* the genesis or development of the human race, esp. as a subject of scientific study. Also, **an·thro·pog·e·ny** (an′thrə poj′ə nē). [ANTHROPO- + GENESIS] —**an·thro·po·ge·net·ic** (an′thrə pō jə net′ik), **an′thro·po·gen′ic,** *adj.*

an·thro·po·ge·og·ra·phy (an′thrə pō jē og′rə fē), *n.* a branch of anthropology dealing with the geographical distribution of mankind and the relationship between man and his environment. [ANTHROPO- + GEOGRAPHY] —**an′thro·po·ge·og′ra·pher,** *n.* —**an·thro·po·ge·o·graph·ic** (an′thrə pō jē′ə graf′ik), **an′thro·po·ge′o·graph′i·cal,** *adj.*

an·thro·pog·ra·phy (an′thrə pog′rə fē), *n.* the branch of anthropology that describes the varieties of mankind and their geographical distribution. [ANTHROPO- + -GRAPHY] —**an·thro·po·graph·ic** (an′thrə pə graf′ik), *adj.*

an·thro·poid (an′thrə poid′), *adj.* **1.** resembling man. —*n.* **2.** See **anthropoid ape.** [< Gk *anthropoeidḗs* in the shape of a man. See ANTHROP(O)-, -OID] —**an′thro·poi′dal,** *adj.*

an′thropoid ape′, any tailless ape of the family *Pongidae,* anatomically resembling man, comprising the gorillas, chimpanzees, orangutans, and gibbons.

anthropol., anthropology.

an·thro·pol·a·try (an′thrə pol′ə trē), *n.* the worship of a human being conceived as a god. [ANTHROPO- + -LATRY] —**an′thro·pol′a·ter,** *n.* —**an′thro·pol′a·tric,** *adj.*

an·thro·pol·o·gist (an′thrə pol′ə jist), *n.* one who specializes in anthropology. [ANTHROPOLOG(Y) + -IST]

an·thro·pol·o·gy (an′thrə pol′ə jē), *n.* **1.** the science that deals with the origins, physical and cultural development, racial characteristics, and social customs and beliefs of mankind. **2.** the study of man's similarity to and divergence from other animals. **3.** the science of man and his works. **4.** Also called **philosophical anthropology.** the study of the nature and essence of man. [ANTHROPO- + -LOGY] —**an·thro·po·log·i·cal** (an′thrə pə loj′i kəl), **an′thro·po·log′ic,** *adj.* —**an′thro·po·log′i·cal·ly,** *adv.*

an·thro·pom·e·ter (an′thrə pom′i tər), *n. Anthropol.* an instrument that consists of a calibrated, vertical rod to which are attached two horizontal arms, one fixed and one movable, for measuring the human trunk and limbs. [ANTHROPO- + -METER]

an·thro·pom·e·try (an′thrə pom′i trē), *n.* the measurement of the size and proportions of the human body. [ANTHROPO- + -METRY] —**an·thro·po·met·ric** (an′thrə-pə me′trik, -pō-), **an′thro·po·met′ri·cal,** *adj.* —**an′thro·po·met′ri·cal·ly,** *adv.* —**an′thro·pom′e·trist,** *n.*

an·thro·po·mor·phic (an′thrə pə môr′fik, -pō-), *adj.* **1.** ascribing human form or attributes to a being or thing not human, esp. to a deity. **2.** resembling or made to resemble a human form: *an anthropomorphic carving.* Also, **anthropomorphous.** [ANTHROPO- + -MORPHIC] —**an′thro·po·mor′phi·cal·ly,** *adv.*

an·thro·po·mor·phise (an′thrə pə môr′fīz, -pō-), *v.t., v.i.,* **-phised, -phis·ing.** *Chiefly Brit.* anthropomorphize. —**an′thro·po·mor′phi·sa′tion,** *n.*

an·thro·po·mor·phism (an′thrə pə môr′fiz əm, -pō-), *n.* an anthropomorphic conception or representation, as of a deity. [ANTHROPO- + -MORPHISM] —**an′thro·po·mor′phist,** *n.*

an·thro·po·mor·phize (an′thrə pə môr′fīz, -pō-), *v.t., v.i.,* **-phized, -phiz·ing.** to ascribe human form or attributes to (an animal, plant, material object, etc.). Also, *esp. Brit.,* **anthropomorphise.** [ANTHROPOMORPH(OUS) + -IZE] —**an′thro·po·mor′phi·za′tion,** *n.*

an·thro·po·mor·pho·sis (an′thrə pə môr′fə sis, -pō-), *n.* transformation into human form. [ANTHROPO- + (META)MORPHOSIS]

an·thro·po·mor·phous (an′thrə pə môr′fəs, -pō-), *adj.* anthropomorphic. [< Gk *anthrōpómorphos* shaped like a man. See ANTHROPO-, -MORPHOUS] —**an′thro·po·mor′phous·ly,** *adv.*

an·thro·pon·o·my (an′thrə pon′ə mē), *n. Rare.* the science dealing with the laws regulating the development of the human organism in relation to other organisms and to environment. Also, **an·thro·po·nom·ics** (an′-thrə pə nom′iks). [ANTHROPO- + -NOMY] —**an·thro·po·nom·i·cal** (an′thrə pə nom′i kəl), *adj.* —**an′thro·pon′o·mist,** *n.*

an·thro·pop·a·thy (an′thrə pop′ə thē), *n.* ascription of human passions or feelings to a being or beings not human, esp. to a deity. Also, **an′thro·pop′a·thism.** [< ML *anthropopatheia* < Gk *anthrōpopátheia* humanness. See ANTHROPO-, -PATHY] —**an·thro·po·path·ic** (an′-thrə pə path′ik), *adj.*

an·thro·poph·a·gi (an′thrə pof′ə jī′), *n.pl., sing.* **-a·gus** (-ə gəs). man-eaters; cannibals. [< L, pl. of *anthrōpophagus* cannibal < Gk *anthrōpophágos* man-eating. See ANTHROPO-, -PHAGE, -PHAGOUS]

an·thro·poph·a·gite (an′thrə pof′ə jīt′), *n.* a man-eater; cannibal. [< L *anthrōpophag(us)* (see ANTHROPOPHAGI) + -ITE¹]

an·thro·poph·a·gy (an′thrə pof′ə jē), *n.* the eating of human flesh; cannibalism. [< Gk *anthrōpophagía.* See ANTHROPO-, -PHAGY] —**an·thro·po·phag·ic** (an′-thrə pə faj′ik), **an′thro·po·phag′i·cal, an′thro·poph·a·gous** (an′thrə pof′ə gəs), *adj.* —**an′thro·poph′a·gous·ly,** *adv.*

an·thro·pos·co·py (an′thrə pos′kə pē), *n.* physiognomy (def. 2). [ANTHROPO- + -SCOPY]

an·thro·pos·o·phy (an′thrə pos′ə fē), *n.* a philosophy based on the teachings of Rudolf Steiner (1861–1925) which maintains that, by virtue of a prescribed method of self-discipline, cognitional experience of the spiritual world can be achieved. [ANTHROPO- + -SOPHY] —**an·thro·po·soph·i·cal** (an′thrə pə sof′i kəl), **an′thro·po·soph′ic,** *adj.*

an·thu·ri·um (an tho͝or′ē əm), *n.* any tropical American, araceous plant of the genus *Anthurium,* certain species of which are cultivated for their showy leaves and flowers. [< NL *Anthurium,* equiv. to *anth-* ANTH- + *-urium* < Gk *our(á)* tail + NL *-ium* n. suffix]

an·ti (an′tī, an′tē), *n., pl.* **-tis.** *Informal.* one who is opposed to a particular practice, party, policy, action, etc. [< ANTI-]

anti-, a learned borrowing from Greek meaning "against," "opposite of," used in the formation of compound words (*anticline*); used freely in combination with elements of any origin (*antibody; antifreeze; antiknock*). Also, *before a vowel,* **ant-.** [ME < L < Gk, comb. form of *antí;* akin to Skt *anti,* L *ante,* E *an-* in *answer.* Cf. ANTE-]

An·ti·a (an tī′ə), *n. Class. Myth.* the wife of Proetus who slandered Bellerophon and demanded his death when he rejected her advances. Also called **Stheneboea.**

an·ti·air·craft (an′tē âr′kraft′, -kräft′, an′tī-), *adj.* **1.** designed for or used in defense against enemy aircraft. —*n.* **2.** artillery used against enemy aircraft. **3.** a military organization operating and servicing antiaircraft artillery. **4.** shellfire from antiaircraft artillery: *The planes flew through heavy antiaircraft but were untouched.* Also, **an′ti-air′craft′.** [ANTI- + AIRCRAFT]

an·ti·al·co·hol·ism (an′tē al′kə hô liz′əm, -ho-, an′tī-), *n.* opposition to excessive use of alcohol or alcoholic beverages. [ANTI- + ALCOHOLISM] —**an′ti·al′co·hol′ic,** *adj.* —**an′ti·al′co·hol·ist,** *n.*

an·ti-A·mer·i·can (an′tē ə mer′i kən, an′tī-), *adj.* **1.** opposed or hostile to America, its principles, and its policies. —*n.* **2.** an anti-American person. [ANTI + AMERICAN] —**An′ti-A·mer′i·can·ism,** *n.*

an·ti·ar (an′tē är′), *n.* **1.** the upas tree. **2.** Also, **an·ti·a·rin** (an′tē ər in). an arrow poison prepared from the sap of the upas tree. [< Javanese]

an·ti·aux·in (an′tē ôk′sin, an′tī-), *n. Biochem.* a substance that inhibits the growth-regulating function of an auxin. [ANTI- + AUXIN]

an·ti·bac·chi·us (an′ti bə kī′əs), *n., pl.* **-chi·i** (-kī′ī). *Pros.* a foot of three syllables that in quantitative meter consists of two long syllables followed by a short one, and that in accentual meter consists of two stressed syllables followed by an unstressed one. Cf. **bacchius.** [< L < Gk *antibákcheios.* See ANTI-, BACCHIUS] —**an·ti·bac·chic** (an′ti bak′ik), *adj.*

an·ti·bac·te·ri·al (an′tē bak tēr′ē əl, an′tī-), *adj.* destructive to or inhibiting the growth of bacteria. [ANTI- + BACTERIAL]

an·ti·bal·lis·tic (an′tē bə lis′tik, an′tī-), *adj. Mil.* designed for use against ballistic missiles: *antiballistic missile.* [ANTI- + BALLISTIC]

An·tibes (äɴ tēb′), *n.* a seaport in SE France, SW of Nice: preserved ruins of 4th century B.C. Roman town. 35,976 (1962).

an·ti·bil·ious (an′tē bil′yəs, an′tī-), *adj.* serving to prevent or cure biliousness. [ANTI- + BILIOUS]

an·ti·bi·o·sis (an′tē bī ō′sis, an′tī-), *n. Biol.* an association between organisms which is injurious to one of them. [ANTI- + -BIOSIS]

an·ti·bi·ot·ic (an′ti bī ot′ik, -bē-, an′tē-, -tī-), *n.* **1.** *Biochem.* any of a large group of chemical substances, as penicillin or streptomycin, produced by various microorganisms and fungi, having the capacity in dilute solutions to inhibit the growth of or to destroy bacteria and other microorganisms, used chiefly in the treatment of infectious diseases. —*adj.* **2.** of or involving antibiotics. [ANTI- + BIOTIC] —**an′ti·bi·ot′i·cal·ly,** *adv.*

an·ti·blas·tic (an′tē blas′tik, an′tī-), *adj. Biol.* antagonistic to growth. [ANTI- + -BLAST + -IC]

an′tiblas′tic immu′nity, immunity resulting from the presence of substances in the body of a host that inhibit the growth of parasitic microorganisms.

an·ti·bod·y (an′ti bod′ē, an′tē-), *n., pl.* **-bod·ies.** a protein naturally existing in blood serum, or produced by an animal in response to stimulation by an antigen, which reacts to overcome the toxic effects of a specific antigen. [ANTI- + BODY]

an·tic (an′tik), *n., adj., v.,* **-ticked, -tick·ing.** —*n.* **1.** Usually, **antics. a.** a playful trick or prank; caper. **b.** a grotesque, fantastic, or ludicrous gesture or posture. **2.** *Archaic.* **a.** an actor in a grotesque or ridiculous presentation. **b.** a buffoon; clown. **3.** *Obs.* **a.** a grotesque theatrical presentation; ridiculous interlude. **b.** a grotesque or fantastic sculptured figure, as a gargoyle. —*adj.* **4.** *Archaic.* fantastic; odd; grotesque: *an antic disposition.* —*v.i.* **5.** to perform antics; to caper. [earlier *antike* < L *antīc(us)* primitive, equiv. to *anti-* (var. of *ante* before) + *-icus* -IC. See ANTIQUE]

an·ti·car·i·ous (an′tē kâr′ē əs, -kar′-, an′tī-), *adj. Dentistry.* preventing or retarding caries. [ANTI- + CARIOUS]

an·ti·cat·a·lase (an′tē kat′ᵊlās′, an′tī-), *n. Biochem.* a substance that inhibits the enzymatic action of a catalase. [ANTI- + CATALASE]

an·ti·cat·a·lyst (an′tē kat′ᵊlist, an′tī-), *n. Chem.* an inhibitor. [ANTI- + CATALYST]

an·ti·ca·tarrh·al (an′tē kə tär′əl, an′tī-), *Med.* —*adj.* **1.** relieving or preventing catarrh. —*n.* **2.** an anticatarrhal agent. [ANTI- + CATARRHAL]

an·ti·ca·thex·is (an′tē kə thek′sis, an′tī-), *n. Psychoanal.* a change from one emotion to its opposite, as from hate to love. [ANTI- + CATHEXIS]

an·ti·cath·ode (an′tē kath′ōd, an′tī-), *n.* the positive plate of an x-ray or other electron tube serving as the target for electrons coming from the cathode, which cause it to emit high-frequency radiations. [ANTI- + CATHODE]

an·ti·chlor (an′ti klōr′, -klôr′), *n. Chem.* any of various substances, esp. sodium thiosulfate, used for removing excess chlorine from paper pulp, textile, fiber, etc., after bleaching. [ANTI- + CHLOR(INE)] —**an·ti·chlo·ris·tic** (an′ti klō ris′tik, -klô-), *adj.*

an·ti·cho·lin·er·gic (an′ti kō′li nûr′jik), *Med.* —*adj.* **1.** preventing the action of acetylcholine. —*n.* **2.** an anticholinergic substance, as a drug. [ANTI- + *cholinergic,* equiv. to CHOLIN(E) + ERG- + -IC]

An·ti·christ (an′ti krīst′), *n. Theol.* **1.** a particular personage or power, variously identified or explained, who is conceived of as appearing in the world as the principal antagonist of Christ. **2.** (*sometimes l.c.*) an opponent of Christ; a person or power antagonistic to Christ. [< LL *Antichrīst(us)* < LGk *Antíchrīstos* the Antichrist. See ANTI-, CHRIST] —**an·ti·chris·tian** (an′tē kris′chən, an′tī-), *adj., n.* —**an′ti·chris′tian·ly,** *adv.*

an·tich·thon (an tik′thon, -thən), *n., pl.* **-tho·nes** (-thə nēz′). counterearth. [< L *antichthones* < Gk *antíkhthon(es)* the antipodes, equiv. to *anti* ANTI- + *chthon-* (s. of *chthṓn*) earth + L *-ēs* pl. n. suffix]

an·tic·i·pant (an tis′ə pənt), *adj.* **1.** anticipative (usually fol. by *of*): *We were eagerly anticipant of her arrival.* —*n.* **2.** one who anticipates. [< L *anticipant-* (s. of *anticipāns;* prp. of *anticipāre*) taking before, equiv. to *anti-* (var. of *ante* before) + *-cip-* (var. of *cap-* take) + *-ant-* -ANT]

an·tic·i·pate (an tis′ə pāt′), *v.t.,* **-pat·ed, -pat·ing.** **1.** to realize beforehand; foretaste or foresee: *to anticipate pleasure.* **2.** to expect; be sure of: *to anticipate a favorable decision.* **3.** to perform (an action) before another has had time to act. **4.** to answer (a question), obey (a command), or satisfy (a request) before it is made. **5.** to nullify, prevent, or forestall by taking countermeasures in advance: *to anticipate a blow.* **6.** to consider or mention before the proper time: *to anticipate more difficult questions.* **7.** *Finance.* **a.** to expend (funds) before they are legitimately available for use. **b.** to discharge (an obligation) before it is due. —*v.i.* **8.** to think, speak, act, or feel an emotional response in advance. [< L *anticipāt(us)* taken before, anticipated (ptp. of *anticipāre*), equiv. to *anti-* (var. of *ante* before) + *-cip-* (var. of *cap-* take) + *-ātus* -ATE[1]] —**an·tic′i·pat′a·ble,** *adj.* —**an·tic′i·pa′tor,** *n.*
—**Syn. 1.** See **expect. 5.** preclude, obviate.

an·tic·i·pa·tion (an tis′ə pā′shən), *n.* **1.** the act of anticipating; state of being anticipated. **2.** realization in advance; foretaste. **3.** expectation or hope. **4.** previous notion; slight previous impression. **5.** intuition, foreknowledge, or prescience. **6.** *Law.* a premature withdrawal or assignment of money from a trust estate. **7.** *Music.* a tone introduced in advance of its harmony so that it sounds against the preceding chord. [< L *anticipātiōn-* (s. of *anticipātiō*), equiv. to *anticipāt(us)* (ptp.; see ANTICIPATE) + *-iōn-* -ION]

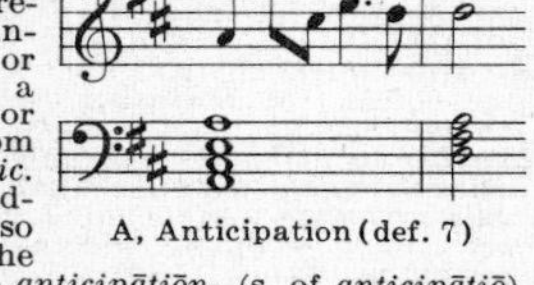

A, Anticipation (def. 7)

an·tic·i·pa·tive (an tis′ə pā′tiv, -pə tiv), *adj.* anticipating or tending to anticipate; containing anticipation: *an anticipative action; an anticipative look.* [< L *anticipāt-* (see ANTICIPATE) + -IVE] —**an·tic′i·pa′tive·ly,** *adv.*

an·tic·i·pa·to·ry (an tis′ə pə tōr′ē, -tôr′ē), *adj.* of, showing, or expressing anticipation. [< L *anticipātor* (see ANTICIPATE, -OR[2]) + -Y[1]; see -ORY[1]] —**an·tic′i·pa·to′ri·ly,** *adv.*

an·ti·clas·tic (an′tē klas′tik, an′tī-), *adj. Math.* (of a surface) having principal curvatures of opposite sign at a given point. Cf. **synclastic.** [ANTI- + CLASTIC]

an·ti·cler·i·cal (an′tē kler′i kəl, an′tī-), *adj.* opposed to the influence and activities of the clergy in public affairs. [ANTI- + CLERICAL] —**an′ti·cler′i·cal·ism,** *n.* —**an′ti·cler′i·cal·ist,** *n.*

an·ti·cli·mac·tic (an′tē klī mak′tik), *adj.* of, pertaining to, or expressing anticlimax. [ANTI + CLIMACTIC] —**an′ti·cli·mac′ti·cal·ly,** *adv.*

an·ti·cli·max (an′ti klī′maks), *n.* **1.** a noticeable or ludicrous descent in discourse from lofty ideas or expressions to banalities or commonplace remarks: *We were amused by the anticlimax of the company's motto: "For God, for country, and for Acme Gasworks."* **2.** an abrupt descent in dignity, quality, power, etc.; a weak, inglorious, or disappointing conclusion. [ANTI- + CLIMAX]

an·ti·cli·nal (an′ti klīn′ᵊl), *adj.* **1.** inclining in opposite directions from a central axis. **2.** *Geol.* **a.** inclining downward on both sides from a median line or axis, as a fold of rock strata. **b.** pertaining to such a fold. [< Gk *antiklín(ein)* (to) lean against each other (*anti-* ANTI- + *klínein* to lean) + -AL[1]]

AXIS

Anticlinal fold (Cross section)

an·ti·cline (an′ti klīn′), *n. Geol.* an anticlinal rock structure. [back formation from ANTICLINAL]

an·ti·cli·no·ri·um (an′ti klī nōr′ē əm, -nôr′-), *n., pl.* **-no·ri·a** (-nōr′ē ə, -nôr′-). *Geol.* a compound anticline, consisting of a series of subordinate anticlines and synclines, the whole having the general contour of an arch. [< NL; see ANTICLINE, -ORIUM]

an·tic·ly (an′tik lē), *adv.* in an antic or grotesque manner; ludicrously. [ANTIC + -LY]

an·ti·co·ag·u·lant (an′tē kō ag′yə lənt, an′tī-), *Med.* —*adj.* **1.** Also, **an·ti·co·ag·u·la·tive** (an′tē kō ag′yə lā′tiv, an′tī-). preventing coagulation, esp. of blood. —*n.* **2.** an anticoagulant agent, as heparin. [ANTI- + COAGULANT]

An′ti-Com′in·tern Pact′ (an′tē kom′in tûrn′, -kom′in tûrn′, an′tī-), an agreement in 1936 between Germany, Japan, and Italy, to oppose the Comintern.

an·ti·com·mu·ta·tive (an′tē kə myo͞o′tə tiv, -kom′yə tā′-, an′tī-), *adj. Math.* **1.** (of a binary operation) having the property that one term operating on a second is equal to the negative of the second operating on the first, as $ab = -ba$. **2.** (of two matrices) defined by an anticommutative operation. [ANTI- + COMMUTATIVE]

an·ti·co·ro·na (an′tē kə rō′nə), *n.* a luminous edging around the shadow of an observer or the point where his shadow would fall, as thrown by the sun upon a cloud or fog bank. Also called **Brocken bow, glory.** [ANTI- + CORONA]

an·ti·cor·ro·sive (an′tē kə rō′siv, an′tī-), *n.* **1.** that which prevents or counteracts corrosion. —*adj.* **2.** preventing or counteracting corrosion. [ANTI- + CORROSIVE] —**an′ti·cor·ro′sive·ly,** *adv.* —**an′ti·cor·ro′sive·ness,** *n.*

An·ti·cos·ti (an′tə kô′stē, -kos′tē), *n.* an island at the head of the Gulf of St. Lawrence in E Canada, in E Quebec province. 135 mi. long; 3043 sq. mi.

an·ti·cre·pus′cu·lar arch′ (an′tē kri pus′kyə lər, an′tī-, an′tē-, an′tī-). See **antitwilight arch.** [ANTI- + CREPUSCULAR]

an·ti·cryp·tic (an′tē krip′tik, an′tī-), *adj. Zool.* serving to conceal an animal from its prey. Cf. **procryptic.** [ANTI- + CRYPTIC] —**an′ti·cryp′ti·cal·ly,** *adv.*

an·ti·cum (an tī′kəm), *n., pl.* **-ca** (-kə). pronaos. [< L, neut. of *anticus* foremost, equiv. to *anti* (var. of *ante* before) + *-icus* -IC]

an·ti·cy·clo·gen·e·sis (an′tē sī′klō jen′i sis, an′tī-), *n. Meteorol.* the intensification or development of an anticyclone. Cf. **anticyclolysis.** [ANTICYCLO(NE) + GENESIS]

an·ti·cy·clol·y·sis (an′tē sī klol′i sis, an′tī-), *n. Meteorol.* the weakening or extinction of an anticyclone. Cf. **anticyclogenesis.** [ANTICYCLO(NE) + -LYSIS]

an·ti·cy·clone (an′ti sī′klōn), *n. Meteorol.* a circulation of winds around a central region of high atmospheric pressure, clockwise in the Northern Hemisphere, counterclockwise in the Southern Hemisphere. Cf. **cyclone** (def. 1), **high** (def. 40). [ANTI- + CYCLONE] —**an·ti·cy·clon·ic** (an′tē sī klon′ik, an′tī-), *adj.*

an·ti·de·pres·sant (an′tē di pres′ənt, an′tī-), *n. Med.* any of a class of drugs used in the treatment of mental depression for raising the spirits; psychic energizer. Also, **an′ti-de·pres′sant.** [ANTI- + DEPRESSANT]

an·ti·de·riv·a·tive (an′tē də riv′ə tiv, an′tī-), *n.* See **indefinite integral.** [ANTI- + DERIVATIVE]

an·ti·diph·the·rit·ic (an′tē dif′thə rit′ik, an′tī-), *Med.* —*adj.* **1.** curing or preventing diphtheria. —*n.* **2.** an antidiphtheritic remedy. [ANTI- + DIPHTHERITIC]

an·ti·dis·es·tab·lish·men·tar·i·an·ism (an′tē dis′e stab′lish mən târ′ē ə niz′əm, an′tī-), *n.* opposition to the withdrawal of state support or recognition from an established church, esp. the Anglican church in 19th-century England. [ANTI- + DISESTABLISHMENT + -ARIAN + -ISM]

an′ti·ag·glu′ti·nant, *adj., n.*
an′ti·ag·glu′ti·na′tion, *adj.*
an′ti·ag·glu′ti·na′tive, *adj.*
an′ti·ag·gres′sion, *adj.*
an′ti·ag·gres′sive, *adj.;* **-ly,** *adv.;* **-ness,** *n.*
an′ti·an′nex·a′tion, *adj.*
an′ti·an′nex·a′tion·ist, *n., adj.*
an′ti·aph′ro·dis′i·ac, *adj., n.*
an′ti-Ar′ab, *adj., n.*
an′ti·ar′is·toc′ra·cy, *adj., n., pl.* **-cies.**
an′ti·a·ris′to·crat′ic, *adj.*
an′ti·a·ris′to·crat′i·cal, *adj.;* **-ly,** *adv.*
an′ti-Ar′is·to·te′lian, *adj., n.*
an′ti-Ar′is·to·te′lian·ism, *n.*
an′ti·a′the·ism, *adj., n.*
an′ti·a′the·ist, *n., adj.*
an′ti·a′the·is′tic, *adj.*
an′ti·a′the·is′ti·cal, *adj.;* **-ly,** *adv.*
an′ti-Aus·tral′ian, *adj., n.*
an′ti-Aus′tri·a, *adj.*
an′ti-Aus′tri·an, *adj., n.*
an′ti-Bi′ble, *adj.*
an′ti-Bib′li·cal, *adj.;* **-ly,** *adv.*
an′ti-Bol′she·vik, *n., adj.*
an′ti-Bol′she·vism, *n.*
an′ti-Bol′she·vist, *n., adj.*
an′ti-Bol′she·vis′tic, *adj.*
an′ti-Brit′ish, *adj., n.*
an′ti-Cal′vin·ism, *n.*
an′ti-Cal′vin·ist, *n., adj.*
an′ti-Cal′vin·is′tic, *adj.*
an′ti-Cal′vin·is′ti·cal, *adj.*
an′ti·cap′i·tal·ism, *n.*
an′ti·cap′i·tal·ist, *n., adj.*
an′ti·cap′i·tal·is′tic, *adj.*
an′ti·cap′i·tal·is′ti·cal·ly, *adv.*
an′ti·caste′, *adj.*
an′ti·cat′a·lyt′ic, *adj., n.*
an′ti·cat′a·lyt′i·cal·ly, *adv.*
an′ti-Cath′o·lic, *adj., n.*
an′ti-Ca·thol′i·cism, *n.*
an′ti·cen·so′ri·al, *adj.*
an′ti·cen·so′ri·ous, *adj.;* **-ly,** *adv.;* **-ness,** *n.*
an′ti·cen′sor·ship′, *n.*
an′ti·cen′tral·ism, *n.*
an′ti·cen′tral·ist, *n., adj.*
an′ti·cen′tral·i·za′tion, *adj., n.*
an′ti·cer′e·mo′ni·al, *adj., n.;* **-ly,** *adv.*
an′ti·cer′e·mo′ni·al·ism, *n.*
an′ti·cer′e·mo′ni·al·ist, *n., adj.*
an′ti·cer′e·mo′ni·ous, *adj.;* **-ly,** *adv.;* **-ness,** *n.*
an′ti·church′, *adj.*
an′ti·civ′ic, *adj.*
an′ti·civ′il, *adj.*
an′ti·ci·vil′ian, *adj., n.*
an′ti·clas′si·cal, *adj.;* **-ly,** *adv.;* **-ness,** *n.*
an′ti·clas′si·cal·ism, *n.*
an′ti·clas′si·cal·ist, *n., adj.*
an′ti·clas′si·cism, *n.*
an′ti·clas′si·cist, *n., adj.*
an′ti·cler′gy, *adj.*
an′ti·clog′ging, *adj.*
an′ti·co·ag′u·lat′ing, *adj.*
an′ti·co·ag′u·la′tion, *n., adj.*
an′ti·co·ag′u·la′tor, *n.*
an′ti·com·mer′cial, *adj.;* **-ly,** *adv.;* **-ness,** *n.*
an′ti·com·mer′cial·ism, *n.*
an′ti·com·mer′cial·ist, *n., adj.*
an′ti·com·mer′cial·is′tic, *adj.*
an′ti·com·mer′ci·al′i·ty, *n.*
an′ti·com′mu·nism, *n.*
an′ti·com′mu·nist, *n., adj.*
an′ti·com′mu·nis′tic, *adj.*
an′ti·com′mu·nis′ti·cal, *adj.;* **-ly,** *adv.*
an′ti·con·fed′er·a′tion·ism, *n.*
an′ti·con·fed′er·a′tion·ist, *n., adj.*
an′ti·con·fed′er·a′tive, *adj.*
an′ti·con·form′ist, *n.*
an′ti·con·form′i·ty, *n., pl.* **-ties.**
an′ti·con·scrip′tion, *n.*
an′ti·con·serv′a·tism, *n.*
an′ti·con·serv′a·tive, *adj., n.;* **-ly,** *adv.;* **-ness,** *n.*
an′ti·con′sti·tu′tion, *adj.*
an′ti·con′sti·tu′tion·al, *adj.;* **-ly,** *adv.*
an′ti·con′sti·tu′tion·al·ism, *n.*
an′ti·con′sti·tu′tion·al·ist, *adj., n.*
an′ti·con·ta′gious, *adj.;* **-ly,** *adv.;* **-ness,** *n.*
an′ti·con·ven′tion, *adj.*
an′ti·con·ven′tion·al, *adj.;* **-ly,** *adv.*
an′ti·con·ven′tion·al·ism, *n.*
an′ti·con·ven′tion·al·ist, *n., adj.*
an′ti·cor·ro′sion, *adj.*
an′ti·cos·met′ics, *adj.*
an′ti·cre·a′tion, *adj.*
an′ti·cre·a′tion·al, *adj.*
an′ti·cre·a′tion·ism, *n.*
an′ti·cre·a′tion·ist, *n., adj.*
an′ti·cre·a′tive, *adj.;* **-ly,** *adv.;* **-ness,** *n.*
an′ti·cre′a·tiv′i·ty, *n.*
an′ti·crit′i·cal, *adj.;* **-ly,** *adv.;* **-ness,** *n.*
an′ti·cy′clic, *adj.*
an′ti·cy′cli·cal, *adj.;* **-ly,** *adv.*
an′ti·cyn′ic, *n., adj.*
an′ti·cyn′i·cal, *adj.;* **-ly,** *adv.*
an′ti·cyn′i·cism, *n.*
an′ti·danc′ing, *adj.*
an′ti-Dar′win, *adj.*
an′ti-Dar·win′i·an, *n., adj.*
an′ti-Dar′win·ism, *n.*
an′ti-Dar′win·ist, *n., adj.*
an′ti·de·moc′ra·cy, *n., pl.* **-cies,** *adj.*
an′ti·dem′o·crat′, *n.*
an′ti·dem′o·crat′ic, *adj.*
an′ti·dem′o·crat′i·cal, *adj.;* **-ly,** *adv.*

an·ti·do·ron (än dē′thô rôn; *Eng.* an′tē dōr′on, -dôr′-), *n.* **1.** Also called **holy bread.** *Gk. Orth. Ch.* bread blessed and distributed to the congregation at the end of the liturgy. **2.** *Eastern Ch.* eulogia (def. 1). [< LGk *antídōron* return gift, equiv. to *anti-* ANTI- + *dōron* gift, deriv. of *didónai* to give]

an·ti·dote (an′ti dōt′), *n.* **1.** a medicine or other remedy for counteracting the effects of poison, disease, etc. **2.** something that prevents or counteracts injurious effects: *Hard work is the best antidote to mischief.* [< L *antidotum* < Gk *antídoton* something given against (i.e., for counteracting), equiv. to *anti-* ANTI- + *dotón* (akin to DATUM), neut. of *dotós* given, verbid of *didónai* to give] —**an′ti·dot′al, an·ti·dot·i·cal** (an′ti dot′i kəl), *adj.* —**an′ti·dot′al·ly, an′ti·dot′i·cal·ly,** *adv.*

an·ti·drom·ic (an′ti drom′ik), *adj.* *Physiol.* conducting nerve impulses in a direction opposite to the usual one. [ANTI- + -DROME + -IC] —**an′ti·drom′i·cal·ly,** *adv.*

an·ti·en·er·gis·tic (an′tē en′ər jis′tik, an′tī-), *adj.* opposing or resisting applied energy. [ANTI- + ENERG(IZE) + -ISTIC]

an·ti·en·zyme (an′tē en′zīm, an′tī-), *n.* *Biochem.* **1.** an agent that inhibits or prevents the action of an enzyme. **2.** an antibody produced by an animal or plant to counteract the effect of a foreign enzyme. [ANTI- + ENZYME] —**an·ti·en·zy·mat·ic** (an′tē en′zī mat′ik, -zi-, an′tī-), **an·ti·en·zy·mic** (an′tē en zī′mik, -zim′ik, an′tī-), *adj.*

An·tie·tam (an tē′təm), *n.* a creek flowing from S Pennsylvania through NW Maryland into the Potomac: Civil War battle fought near here at Sharpsburg, Maryland, in 1862.

an·ti·fe·brile (an′tē fē′brəl, -feb′rəl, an′tī-), *Med.* —*adj.* **1.** efficacious against fever; febrifuge; antipyretic. —*n.* **2.** an antifebrile agent. [ANTI- + FEBRILE]

an·ti·fe·brin (an′tē fē′brin, -feb′rin, an′tī-), *n.* *Chem.* acetanilide. [ANTI- + FEBR(ILE) + -IN[2]]

An·ti·fed·er·al·ist (an′tē fed′ər ə list, -fed′rə-, an′tī-), *n.* **1.** *U.S. Hist.* a member or supporter of the Antifederal party. **2.** (*l.c.*) an opponent of federalism. [ANTI- + FEDERALIST] —**An′ti·fed′er·al·ism,** *n.*

An′ti·fed′er·al par′ty (an′tē fed′ər əl, -fed′rəl, an′tī-, an′tē-, an′tī-), *U.S. Hist.* the party which, before 1789, opposed the adoption of the proposed Constitution and after that favored its strict construction. Cf. **States' rights.**

an·ti·fer·ro·mag·net (an′tē fer′ō mag′nit, an′tī-), *n.* *Physics.* an antiferromagnetic substance. [ANTI- + FERROMAGNET]

an·ti·fer·ro·mag·net·ic (an′tē fer′ō mag net′ik, an′tī-), *adj.* *Physics.* noting or pertaining to a substance in which, at sufficiently low temperatures, the magnetic moments of adjacent atoms point in opposite directions. Cf. **diamagnetic, ferromagnetic, paramagnetic.** [ANTI- + FERROMAGNETIC] —**an·ti·fer·ro·mag·ne·tism** (an′tē fer′ō mag′ni tiz′əm, an′tī-), *n.*

an·ti·foam·ing (an′tē fō′ming, an′tī-), *adj.* preventing the development of or reducing foam. [ANTI- + FOAM + -ING[2]]

an·ti·fog·gant (an′tē fog′ənt, -fô′gənt, an′tī-), *n.* *Photog.* a chemical that prevents or minimizes fogging. [*antifog* (ANTI- + FOG) + -ANT]

an·ti·foul·ing (an′tē fou′ling, an′tī-), *adj.* (of a coating, process, or the like) having the property of preventing the accumulation of barnacles, algae, etc., on underwater surfaces: *The makers now use an antifouling chemical on all marine hulls.* [ANTI- + FOUL + -ING[1]]

antifoul′ing paint′, *Naut.* paint applied to the portion of a hull below the waterline to poison or discourage marine animals and plants that would otherwise cling to it.

an·ti·freeze (an′ti frēz′, an′tē-), *n.* a liquid used in the radiator of an internal-combustion engine to lower the freezing point of the cooling medium. [ANTI- + FREEZE]

an·ti·fric·tion (an′tē frik′shən, an′tī-), *n.* **1.** something that prevents or reduces friction; lubricant. —*adj.* **2.** tending to prevent or reduce friction. [ANTI- + FRICTION] —**an′ti·fric′tion·al,** *adj.*

an·ti·fric′tion bear′ing, *Mach.* See **rolling-element bearing.**

an·ti·gen (an′ti jən, -jen′), *n.* **1.** *Biochem.* any of a class of substances, produced by the body, that stimulate production of antibodies. **2.** *Pharm.* any commercial substance that, when injected or absorbed into animal tissues, stimulates the production of antibodies. [ANTI(BODY) + -GEN] —**an·ti·gen·ic** (an′ti jen′ik), *adj.* —**an·ti·ge·nic·i·ty** (an′ti jə nis′i tē), *n.*

An·ti·go (an′ti gō′), *n.* a town in NE Wisconsin. 9691 (1960).

An·tig·o·ne (an tig′ə nē′), *n.* **1.** *Class. Myth.* a daughter of Oedipus and Jocasta who defied her uncle, King Creon, by performing funeral rites over her brother, Polynices, and was condemned to be immured alive in a cave. **2.** (*italics.*) a tragedy (c440 B.C.) by Sophocles.

An·tig·o·nus I (an tig′ə nəs), (*Cyclops*), 382?–301 B.C., Macedonian general under Alexander the Great.

Antigonus II, (*Gonatus*) c319–239 B.C., king of Macedonia 283–239 (son of Demetrius I).

an·tig·o·rite (an tig′ə rīt′), *n.* *Mineral.* a variety of serpentine occurring in a brownish-green lamellar form. [named after *Antigor(io)* valley in N Italy where first found + -ITE[1]]

an·ti·grav·i·ty (an′tē grav′i tē, an′tī-), *n.* **1.** *Physics.* the antithesis of gravity; a hypothetical force by which a body of positive mass would repel a body of negative mass. **2.** (not in technical use) a controllable force that can be made to act against the force of gravity. —*adj.* **3.** (not in technical use) counteracting the force of gravity: *The antigravity drive in this spaceship will enable us to reach Polaris.* [ANTI- + GRAVITY]

an·ti-G′ suit′ (an′tē jē′, an′tī-), *Aeron.* a garment for fliers, designed to exert pressure on the abdomen and thighs to prevent or retard the pooling of blood below the heart under the influence of excessive head-to-toe acceleration forces. Also called **G-suit.**

An·ti·gua (an tē′gwə, -gə), *n.* one of the Leeward Islands, in the E West Indies: a member of the West Indies Associated States; formerly a British colony. 54,304 (est. 1964); 108 sq. mi. *Cap.:* St. John's. —**An·ti′guan,** *adj., n.*

an·ti·ha·la·tion (an′tē hā lā′shən, -ha-, an′tī-), *Photog.* —*n.* **1.** the process of treating a film base with a light-absorbing substance to prevent refraction of light from the rear of the film. —*adj.* **2.** resistant to halation. [ANTI- + HALATION]

an·ti·he·lix (an′tē hē′liks, an′tī-), *n., pl.* **-hel·i·ces** (-hel′i sēz′), **-he·lix·es.** *Anat.* the inward curving ridge of the auricle of the ear. See diag. under **ear.** [ANTI- + HELIX; r. *anthelix* < Gk, equiv. to *ant(i)-* ANTI- + *hélix* HELIX]

an·ti·he·ro (an′tē hēr′ō, an′tī-), *n.* a protagonist who lacks the attributes that would make him a heroic figure, as nobility of mind and spirit, a life or attitude marked by action or purpose, and the like. [ANTI- + HERO]

an·ti·he·ro·ic (an′tē hi rō′ik, an′tī-), *adj.* **1.** (of a protagonist) possessing the characteristics of an antihero. **2.** (of a literary work) having an anti-hero as its protagonist. [ANTI- + HEROIC]

an·ti·his·ta·mine (an′ti his′tə mēn′, -min), *n.* *Med.* any of certain compounds or medicines that neutralize or inhibit the effect of histamine in the body, used chiefly in the treatment of allergic disorders and colds. [ANTI- + HISTAMINE]

an·ti·his·ta·min·ic (an′tē his′tə min′ik, an′tī-), *adj.* **1.** of or pertaining to an antihistamine or its effect. —*n.* **2.** an antihistaminic agent, as a drug. [ANTIHISTAMINE + -IC]

an·ti·ic·er (an′tē ī′sər), *n.* **1.** a device used to prevent the forming of ice, as on an airplane propeller. Cf. **slinger ring.** **2.** a fluid used in such a device.

an·ti·im·pe·ri·al·ist (an′tē im pēr′ē ə list, an′tī-), *n.* **1.** an opponent of imperialism. —*adj.* **2.** opposed to imperialism. —**an′ti-im·pe′ri·al·ism,** *n.* —**an′ti-im·pe′ri·al·is′tic,** *adj.*

an·ti·in·tel·lec·tu·al (an′tē in′təlek′cho͞o əl, an′tī-), *n.* **1.** a person hostile toward intellectuals and the modern academic, artistic, social, religious, etc., theories associated with them. **2.** a person who believes that intellect and reason are less important than actions and emotions in solving practical problems and understanding reality. —*adj.* **3.** of, pertaining to, or characteristic of anti-intellectuals or their beliefs. Also, **an′ti-in′tel·lec′tu·al·ist.** —**an′ti-in′tel·lec′tu·al·ism,** *n.*

an·ti·ke·to·gen·e·sis (an′ti kē′tə jen′i sis), *n.* *Med.* prevention of the excessive formation of acetone bodies in the body, such as occurs in diabetes. [ANTI- + KETOGENESIS] —**an′ti·ke′to·gen′ic,** *adj.*

an·ti·knock (an′tē nok′, an′tī-), *adj.* noting or pertaining to any material added to fuel for an internal-combustion engine to eliminate or minimize knock. [ANTI- + KNOCK]

An·ti·ky·ther·a (an′tə ki thēr′ə; *Gk.* än′dē kē′thē rä), *n.* an island in the E Mediterranean, NW of Crete: archaeological site. 8½ sq. mi. Also, **Andikithira.**

an·ti-Lea·guer (an′tē lē′gər, an′tī-), *n.* *Hist.* a person who opposed the League of Nations or the U.S. entry into it.

An·ti-Leb·a·non (an′tē leb′ə nən), *n.* a mountain range in SW Asia, between Syria and Lebanon, E of the Lebanon Mountains.

an·ti·le·gom·e·na (an′ti lə gom′ə nə), *n.* (*construed as sing.*) a group of books in the New Testament, generally held to be uncanonical by the early church. Cf. **homologumena.** [< Gk: things spoken against, neut. pl. of *antilegómenos* (pass. prp. of *antilégein* to speak against), equiv. to *anti-* ANTI- + *lego-* speak + *-menos* pass. prp. suffix]

An·til·les (an til′ēz), *n.* (*construed as pl.*) a chain of islands in the West Indies, divided into two parts, the one including Cuba, Hispaniola, Jamaica, and Puerto Rico (**Greater Antilles**), the other including a group of smaller islands to the SE (**Lesser Antilles**). —**An·til·le·an** (an′tə lē′ən, an til′ē-), *adj.*

Antil′les Cur′rent, a warm ocean current flowing NW along the N coast of the Greater Antilles and joining the Florida Current off the SW coast of Florida.

An·til·o·chus (an til′ə kəs), *n.* *Class. Myth.* a son of Nestor and a trusted friend of Achilles.

antilog (an′ti lôg′, -log), *n.* antilogarithm.

an·ti·log·a·rithm (an′ti lô′gə rith′əm, -log′ə-), *n.* *Math.* the number of which a given number is the logarithm. *Symbol:* antilog [ANTI- + LOGARITHM] —**an′ti·log′a·rith′mic,** *adj.*

an·til·o·gism (an til′ə jiz′əm), *n.* *Logic.* a group of three inconsistent propositions, two of which are premises of a syllogism that contradicts the third. [< LGk *antilogism(ós),* equiv. to *anti-* ANTI- + *logismós* calculation, deriv. of *logíz(esthai)* (to) calculate, deriv. of *lógos* reasoning] —**an·til′o·gis′tic,** *adj.* —**an·til′o·gis′ti·cal·ly,** *adv.*

an·til·o·gy (an til′ə jē), *n., pl.* **-gies.** a contradiction in terms or ideas. [< Gk *antilogía* controversy, discussion. See ANTI-, -LOGY]

an·ti·ma·cas·sar (an′ti mə kas′ər), *n.* a covering, usually ornamental, placed on the backs and arms of upholstered furniture to prevent wear or soiling; a tidy. [ANTI- + MACASSAR (OIL)]

An·tim·a·chus (an tim′ə kəs), *n.* **1.** Also called **the Colophonian.** fl. c410 B.C. Greek poet. **2.** (in the *Iliad*) a chieftain who believed that the Trojans should not return Helen to Menelaus.

an·ti·mag·net·ic (an′tē mag net′ik, an′tī-), *adj.* **1.** resistant to magnetization. **2.** (of a precision instrument, watch, etc.) having the critical parts composed of antimagnetic materials, and hence not seriously affected in accuracy by exposure to magnetic fields. [ANTI- + MAGNETIC]

an·ti·ma·lar·i·al (an′tē mə lâr′ē əl, an′tī-), *Med.* —*adj.* **1.** preventive of or efficacious against malaria. —*n.* **2.** an antimalarial agent. [ANTI- + MALARIAL]

An·ti-Ma·son (an′tē mā′sən, an′tī-), *n.* *U.S.* a member of the Anti-Masonic party or a supporter of its principles. —**An·ti-Ma·son·ic** (an′tē mə son′ik, an′tī-), *adj.* —**An′ti-Ma′son·ry,** *n.*

An′ti-Mason′ic par′ty, *U.S.* a former political party (1826–35) that opposed Freemasonry in civil affairs.

an·ti·masque (an′ti mask′, -mäsk′), *n.* a comic or grotesque performance, as a dance, presented before or between the acts of a masque. Also, **an′ti·mask′.** [ANTI- + MASQUE; r. *antemask;* see ANTE-, MASK] —**an′ti·mas′quer, an′ti·mask′er,** *n.*

an·ti·mat·ter (an′tē mat′ər, an′tī-), *n.* *Physics.*

an′ti·di′u·ret′ic, *adj., n.*
an′ti·di·vorce′, *adj.*
an′ti·dog·mat′ic, *adj.*
an′ti·dog·mat′i·cal, *adj.*; **-ly,** *adv.*
an′ti·dog′ma·tism, *n.*
an′ti·dog′ma·tist, *n., adj.*
an′ti·do·mes′tic, *adj.*
an′ti·do·mes′ti·cal·ly, *adv.*
an′ti·draft′, *adj.*
an′ti·drug′, *n., adj.*
an′ti·dy·nas′tic, *adj.*
an′ti·dy·nas′ti·cal, *adj.*; **-ly,** *adv.*
an′ti·dy′nas·ty, *adj.*
an′ti·ec·cle′si·as′tic, *n., adj.*
an′ti·ec·cle′si·as′ti·cal, *adj.*; **-ly,** *adv.*
an′ti·ec·cle′si·as′ti·cism, *n.*
an′ti·ed′u·ca′tion, *adj.*
an′ti·ed′u·ca′tion·al, *adj.*; **-ly,** *adv.*
an′ti·ed′u·ca′tion·al·ist, *n.*
an′ti·ed′u·ca′tion·ist, *n., adj.*
an′ti·e′go·ism, *n.*
an′ti·e′go·ist, *n.*
an′ti·e′go·is′tic, *adj.*
an′ti·e′go·is′ti·cal, *adj.*; **-ly,** *adv.*
an′ti·e′go·tism, *n.*
an′ti·e′go·tist, *n., adj.*
an′ti·e′go·tis′tic, *adj.*
an′ti·e′go·tis′ti·cal, *adj.*; **-ly,** *adv.*
an′ti·em·pir′ic, *n., adj.*
an′ti·em·pir′i·cal, *adj.*; **-ly,** *adv.*
an′ti·em·pir′i·cism, *n.*
an′ti·em·pir′i·cist, *n., adj.*
an′ti-Eng′lish, *adj.*
an′ti·en·thu′si·asm, *n.*
an′ti·en·thu′si·ast, *n.*
an′ti·en·thu′si·as′tic, *adj.*
an′ti·en·thu′si·as′ti·cal·ly, *adv.*
an′ti·e·ro′sion, *adj.*
an′ti·e·ro′sive, *adj.*
an′ti-Eu′rope, *adj.*
an′ti-Eu′ro·pe′an, *adj., n.*
an′ti-Eu′ro·pe′an·ism, *n.*
an′ti·ev′o·lu′tion, *adj.*
an′ti·ev′o·lu′tion·al, *adj.*; **-ly,** *adv.*
an′ti·ev′o·lu′tion·ar′y, *adj.*
an′ti·ev′o·lu′tion·ist, *n., adj.*
an′ti·ev′o·lu′tion·is′tic, *adj.*
an′ti·ex·pan′sion, *adj.*
an′ti·ex·pan′sion·ism, *n.*
an′ti·ex·pan′sion·ist, *n., adj.*
an′ti·ex·pres′sion·ism, *n.*
an′ti·ex·pres′sion·ist, *n., adj.*
an′ti·ex·pres′sion·is′tic, *adj.*
an′ti·ex·pres′sive, *adj.*; **-ly,** *adv.*; **-ness,** *n.*
an′ti·fas′cism, *n.*
an′ti·fas′cist, *n., adj.*
an′ti·fem′i·nism, *n.*
an′ti·fem′i·nist, *n., adj.*
an′ti·fem′i·nis′tic, *adj.*
an′ti·feu′dal, *adj.*
an′ti·feu′dal·ism, *n.*
an′ti·feu′dal·ist, *n.*
an′ti·feu′dal·is′tic, *adj.*
an′ti·feu′dal·i·za′tion, *adj., n.*
an′ti-France′, *adj.*
an′ti-French′, *adj.*
an′ti-Freud′, *adj.*
an′ti-Freud′i·an, *adj., n.*
an′ti-Freud′i·an·ism, *n.*
an′ti·fun′da·men′tal·ism, *n.*
an′ti·fun′da·men′tal·ist, *n., adj.*
an′ti·fun′gal, *adj.*
an′ti·gam′bling, *adj., n.*
an′ti-Ger′man, *n., adj.*
an′ti-Ger·man′ic, *adj.*
an′ti-Ger′man·ism, *n.*
an′ti-Ger′man·i·za′tion, *adj., n.*
an′ti·gnos′tic, *adj., n.*
an′ti·gnos′ti·cal, *adj.*
an′ti·gov′ern·ment, *adj.*
an′ti·gov′ern·men′tal, *adj.*; **-ly,** *adv.*
an′ti·graft′, *adj.*
an′ti·gram·mat′i·cal, *adj.*; **-ly,** *adv.*; **-ness,** *n.*
an′ti·grav′i·ta′tion, *adj.*
an′ti·grav′i·ta′tion·al, *adj.*; **-ly,** *adv.*
an′ti-Greece′, *adj.*
an′ti-Greek′, *adj., n.*
an′ti·hi′er·ar′chal, *adj.*
an′ti·hi′er·ar′chic, *adj.*
an′ti·hi′er·ar′chi·cal, *adj.*; **-ly,** *adv.*
an′ti·hi′er·ar′chism, *n.*
an′ti·hi′er·ar′chy, *n., pl.* **-chies,** *adj.*
an′ti·hu′man, *adj.*
an′ti·hu′man·ism, *n.*
an′ti·hu′man·ist, *n., adj.*
an′ti·hu′man·is′tic, *adj.*
an′ti·hunt′ing, *n., adj.*
an′ti·hy·gi·en′ic, *adj.*
an′ti·hy·gi·en′i·cal·ly, *adv.*
an′ti·hyp·not′ic, *adj., n.*
an′ti·hyp·not′i·cal·ly, *adv.*
an′ti·hys·ter′ic, *n., adj.*
an′ti-i·de′al, *adj.*
an′ti-i·de′al·ism, *n.*
an′ti-i·de′al·ist, *n., adj.*
an′ti-i·de′al·is′tic, *adj.*
an′ti-i·de′al·is′ti·cal·ly, *adv.*
an′ti·im′mi·gra′tion, *adj.*
an′ti·in·dem′ni·ty, *adj.*
an′ti-in·duc′tion, *adj.*
an′ti-in·duc′tive, *adj.*; **-ly,** *adv.*; **-ness,** *n.*
an′ti-in′tel·lec′tu·al′i·ty, *n.*
an′ti-I′rish, *adj., n., pl.* **-I·rish.**
an′ti-i′so·la′tion, *adj.*
an′ti-i′so·la′tion·ism, *n.*
an′ti-i′so·la′tion·ist, *n., adj.*
an′ti-I·tal′ian, *adj., n.*
an′ti-I·tal′ian·ism, *n.*
an′ti-Jap′a·nese′, *adj., n., pl.* **-nese.**
an′ti-Jes′u·it, *n., adj.*
an′ti-Jes′u·it′ic, *adj.*
an′ti-Jes′u·it′i·cal, *adj.*; **-ly,** *adv.*
an′ti-Jes′u·it·ism, *n.*
an′ti-Jes′u·it·ry, *n.*
an′ti-Jew′ish, *adj.*
an′ti-Ju·da′ic, *adj.*
an′ti-Ju′da·ism, *n.*
an′ti-Ju′da·ist, *n., adj.*
an′ti-Ju′da·is′tic, *adj.*
an′ti·la′bor, *adj.*
an′ti-Lat′in, *adj.*
an′ti-Lat′in·ism, *n.*
an′ti·league′, *adj.*
an′ti·lev′el·ing, *adj.*
an′ti·lev′el·ling, *adj.*
an′ti·lib′er·al, *adj., n.*; **-ly,** *adv.*; **-ness,** *n.*
an′ti·lib′er·al·ism, *n.*
an′ti·lib′er·al·ist, *n., adj.*
an′ti·lib′er·al·is′tic, *adj.*
an′ti·liq′uor, *adj.*
an′ti·li·tur′gic, *adj.*
an′ti·li·tur′gi·cal, *adj.*; **-ly,** *adv.*
an′ti·lit′ur·gist, *n.*
an′ti·lit′ur·gy, *adj.*
an′ti·lot′ter·y, *adj.*
an′ti·mach′i·na′tion, *adj.*
an′ti·ma·chine′, *adj.*
an′ti·ma·chin′er·y, *adj.*
an′ti-Mal·thu′si·an, *adj., n.*
an′ti-Mal·thu′si·an·ism, *n.*
an′ti·ma·te′ri·al·ism, *n.*
an′ti·ma·te′ri·al·ist, *n., adj.*
an′ti·ma·te′ri·al·is′tic, *adj.*
an′ti·ma·te′ri·al·is′ti·cal·ly, *adv.*
an′ti·mech′an·ism, *n.*
an′ti·mech′an·ist, *n., adj.*
an′ti·mech′a·nis′tic, *adj.*
an′ti·mech′a·nis′ti·cal·ly, *adv.*
an′ti·mech′a·ni·za′tion, *adj.*
an′ti·med′i·cal, *adj.*; **-ly,** *adv.*
an′ti·med′i·ca′tion, *adj.*

matter composed of particles which are analogous to but have charges opposite to those of common particles of matter, as positrons which are analogous to electrons but are positively charged. Cf. **annihilation** (def. 3). [ANTI- + MATTER]

an·ti·men·si·on (än/dē mēn/sē ôn; *Eng.* an/ti men/sē on/), *n., pl.* **-si·a** (-sē ä; *Eng.* -sē ə). *Gk. Orth. Ch.* a consecrated linen or silk cloth, kept on an altar, to which is sewn a linen or silk bag containing relics of saints. Also, **antimensium.** [< ML *antimensium* < MGk *antimínsion, antimḗsion* < Gk *anti-* ANTI- + L *mens(a)* table + Gk *-ion* n. suffix]

an·ti·men·si·um (an/ti men/sē əm), *n., pl.* **-si·a** (-sē ə). antimension.

an·ti·mere (an/tə mēr/), *n.* *Zool.* a segment or division of the body in the direction of one of the secondary or transverse axes, as either half of a bilaterally symmetrical animal or a radiating part of a radially symmetrical animal. [ANTI- + -MERE] —**an·ti·mer·ic** (an/tə mer/ik), *adj.* —**an·tim·er·ism** (an tim/ə riz/əm), *n.*

an·ti·mi·cro·bi·al (an/tē mī krō/bē əl, an/tī-), *Biochem.* —*adj.* **1.** inhibiting the growth of or destroying microbes. —*n.* **2.** an antimicrobial agent. [ANTI- + MICROBIAL]

an·ti·mis·sile (an/tē mis/əl, an/tī- *or, esp. Brit.,* -mis/īl), *Mil.* —*adj.* **1.** designed or used in defense against guided missiles. —*n.* **2.** a ballistic device for seeking and destroying enemy missiles. Also, **an/ti·mis/sile.** [ANTI- + MISSILE]

an/timis/sile mis/sile, a ballistic missile for seeking and destroying missiles in flight.

an·ti·mo·nate (an/tə mə nāt/), *n.* *Chem.* a salt containing pentavalent antimony and oxygen, as potassium antimonate, $KSb(OH)_6$. Also, **an·ti·mo·ni·ate** (an/tə mō/nē āt/, -it). [ANTIMON(Y) + -ATE[2]]

an·ti·mo·nic (an/tə mō/nik, -mon/ik), *adj.* *Chem.* of or containing antimony, esp. in the pentavalent state. [ANTIMON(Y) + -IC]

an/timo/nic ac/id, *Chem.* See **antimony pentoxide.**

an·ti·mo·nide (an/tə mə nīd/, -nid), *n.* *Chem.* a binary compound containing antimony and a second element, usually a metal. [ANTIMON(Y) + -IDE]

an·ti·mo·nous (an/tə mə nəs, an/tə mō/nəs), *adj.* *Chem.* of or containing antimony, esp. in the trivalent state. Also, **an·ti·mo·ni·ous** (an/tə mō/nē əs). [ANTIMON(Y) + -OUS]

an/timonous hy/dride, *Chem.* stibine.

an·ti·mon·soon (an/tē mon sōōn/), *n.* *Meteorol.* a current of air lying above a monsoon and moving in an opposite direction. [ANTI- + MONSOON]

an·ti·mo·ny (an/tə mō/nē), *n.* *Chem.* a brittle, lustrous, white metallic element occurring in nature free or combined, used chiefly in alloys and in compounds in medicine. *Symbol:* Sb; *at. no.:* 51; *at. wt.:* 121.75. [late ME < ML *antimōni(um)*] —**an/ti·mo/ni·al,** *adj., n.*

antimony 124, *Chem.* the radioactive isotope of antimony having a mass number of 124 and a half life of 60 days, used chiefly as a tracer.

an/timony glance/, *Obs.* stibnite.

an/timony hy/dride, *Chem.* stibine.

an·ti·mo·nyl (an/tə mə nil, an tim/ə-), *n.* *Chem.* the univalent group, –SbO, believed to exist in certain compounds, as antimony potassium tartrate, $K(SbO)C_4H_4O_6$. [ANTIMON(Y) + -YL]

an/timony oxychlo/ride, *Chem.* a white, water-insoluble powder, SbOCl, used chiefly in the manufacture of antimony salts. Also called **Algaroth powder.**

an/timony pen·ta·sul/fide (pen/tə sul/fīd), *Chem.* a deep-yellow, water-insoluble powder, Sb_2S_5, used chiefly as a pigment in oil and water colors.

an/timony pent·ox/ide (pen tok/sīd), *Chem.* a white or yellowish, water-insoluble powder, Sb_2O_5, used chiefly in the synthesis of antimonates. Also called **antimonic acid.**

an/timony potas/sium tar/trate, *Chem.* See **tartar emetic.** Also, **an/timonyl potas/sium tar/trate.**

an/timony sul/fate, *Chem.* a white, crystalline, deliquescent, water-insoluble solid, $Sb_2(SO_4)_3$, used chiefly in the manufacture of explosives.

an/timony sul/fide, *Chem.* **1.** See **antimony pentasulfide. 2.** See **antimony trisulfide.**

an/timony triflu/oride, *Chem.* a white to grayish-white, crystalline, hygroscopic, water-soluble, poisonous solid, SbF_3, used chiefly in dyeing textiles.

an/timony trisul/fide, *Chem.* a black or orange-red, crystalline, water-insoluble solid, Sb_2S_3, used chiefly as a pigment in paints and in the manufacture of fireworks and matches.

an/timony yel/low. See **Naples yellow.** —**an/ti·mo/ny-yel/low,** *adj.*

an·ti·neu·ral·gic (an/tē nōō ral/jik, -nyōō-, an/tī-), *Med.* —*adj.* **1.** preventing or relieving neuralgia. —*n.* **2.** an antineuralgic substance. [ANTI- + NEURALGIC]

an·ti·neu·rit·ic (an/tē nōō rit/ik, -nyōō-, an/tī-), *Med.* —*adj.* **1.** relieving or preventing neuritis. —*n.* **2.** an antineuritic agent. [ANTI- + NEURITIC]

an·ti·neu·tri·no (an/tē nōō trē/nō, -nyōō-, an/tī-), *n., pl.* **-nos.** *Physics.* the antiparticle of the neutrino. [ANTI- + NEUTRINO]

an·ti·neu·tron (an/tē nōō/tron, -nyōō/-, an/tī-), *n.* *Physics.* an elementary particle having no charge and having a mass and spin equal to that of the neutron but with magnetic moment opposite to that of the neutron; the antiparticle of the neutron. [ANTI- + NEUTRON]

ant·ing (an/ting), *n.* the placing by certain birds of ants among their feathers, apparently to kill parasites. [ANT + -ING[1]]

an·ti·node (an/ti nōd/), *n.* *Physics.* the region of maximum amplitude between two adjacent nodes in a standing wave. [ANTI- + NODE] —**an/ti·nod/al,** *adj.*

an·ti·no·mi·an (an/ti nō/mē ən), *n.* one who maintains that Christians are freed from the moral law by virtue of grace as set forth in the gospel. [< ML *Antinomi* name of sect (pl. of *Antinomus* opponent of (the moral) law < Gk *anti* ANTI- + *nómos* law) + -AN] —**an/ti·no/mi·an·ism,** *n.*

an·tin·o·my (an tin/ə mē), *n., pl.* **-mies. 1.** opposition between one law, principle, rule, etc., and another. **2.** *Philos.* a contradiction between two statements, both apparently obtained by correct reasoning. [< L *antinomia* < Gk *antinomía* a contradiction between laws. See ANTI-, -NOMY] —**an·ti·nom·ic** (an/ti nom/ik), **an/ti·nom/i·cal,** *adj.*

An·tin·o·us (an tin/ō əs), *n.* *Class. Myth.* the chief suitor of Penelope, killed by Odysseus upon his return from Troy.

an·ti·nov·el (an/tē nov/əl, an/tī-), *n.* a literary work in which the author rejects the use of traditional elements of novel structure, esp. in regard to development of plot. —**an/ti·nov/el·ist,** *n.*

an·ti·nu·cle·on (an/tē nōō/klē on/, -nyōō/-, an/tī-), *n.* *Physics.* an antiproton or an antineutron. [ANTI- + NUCLEON]

An·ti·och (an/tē ok/), *n.* a city in S Turkey: capital of the ancient kingdom of Syria, 300–64 B.C. 37,484 (1955). Arabic, **Antakiya.** —**An·ti·o·chi·an** (an/tē ō/kē ən), *n., adj.*

An·ti·o·chus (an tī/ə kəs), *n.* *Class. Myth.* a son of Hercules and Meda.

Antiochus III, ("*the Great*") 241?–187 B.C., king of Syria 223–187.

Antiochus IV, (*Antiochus Epiphanes*) died 164? B.C., king of Syria 175–164?.

an·ti·o·don·tal·gic (an/tē ō don tal/jik, an/tī-), *Dentistry.* —*adj.* **1.** relieving the pain of a toothache. —*n.* **2.** a toothache remedy. Also, **antodontalgic.** [ANTI- + ODONTALGIC]

An·ti·o·pe (an tī/ə pē), *n.* *Class. Myth.* **1.** an Amazon, the sister of Hippolyte, mistress of Theseus, and mother of Hippolytus. **2.** the mother of Amphion and Zethus.

an·ti·ox·i·dant (an/tē ok/si dənt, an/tī-), *n.* *Chem.* **1.** any substance inhibiting oxidation. **2.** any of a group of substances that inhibit deterioration of rubber, gasoline, soaps, etc. [ANTI- + *oxidant* (OXID(IZE) + -ANT)]

an·ti·o·zon·ant (an/tē ō/zō nənt, an/tī-), *n.* *Chem.* an admixture to natural or synthetic rubber for preventing ozonolysis. [ANTI- + *ozonant* (OZON(IZE) + -ANT)]

an·ti·par·a·be·ma (an/ti par/ə bē/mə), *n., pl.* **-ma·ta** (-mə tə). either of two chapels at the west end of an Armenian or Byzantine church. [ANTI- + NGk *parabêma* < Gk *para-* PARA-[1] + LGk *bêma* BEMA]

an·ti·par·al·lel (an/tē par/ə lel/, an/tī-), *adj.* *Math.* (of two vectors) varying in direction by 180°. [ANTI- + PARALLEL]

an·ti·par·ti·cle (an/tē pär/ti kəl, an/tī-), *n.* *Physics.* either of two particles, one of matter and one of antimatter, that annihilate each other upon collision, as an electron and a positron. [ANTI- + PARTICLE]

an·ti·pas·to (an/ti pä/stō, -pas/tō; *It.* än/tē päs/tô), *n., pl.* **-pas·tos, -pas·ti** (-pä/stē, -pas/tē; *It.* -päs/tē). *Italian Cookery.* a course of appetizers or hors d'oeuvres, consisting of an assortment of foods, as olives, anchovies, sliced sausage, artichoke hearts, etc. [< It: lit., before-food, equiv. to *anti-* (< L, var. of *ante-* ANTE-) + *pasto* < L *pāst(us)* food; see PASTOR]

An·tip·a·ter (an tip/ə tər), *n.* 398?–319 B.C., Macedonian statesman and general: regent of Macedonia 334–323.

an·ti·pa·thet·ic (an/ti pə thet/ik, an tip/ə-), *adj.* **1.** having antipathy for or a basic aversion to something or someone: *He was antipathetic to any change.* **2.** causing or likely to cause antipathy: *The new house was antipathetic to all of us.* Also, **an/ti·pa·thet/i·cal.** [< Gk *antipathḗ(s)* opposed in feeling (*antipathḗ(ein)* (to) have feelings of aversion, equiv. to *anti-* ANTI- + *pathe-,* var. s. of *páthos* feeling) + -TIC] —**an/ti·pa·thet/i·cal·ly,** *adv.* —**an/ti·pa·thet/i·cal·ness,** *n.*

an·tip·a·thy (an tip/ə thē), *n., pl.* **-thies. 1.** a natural, basic, or habitual repugnance; aversion. **2.** an instinctive contrariety or opposition in feeling. **3.** an object of natural aversion or habitual dislike. [< L *antipathīa* < Gk *antipátheia.* See ANTI-, -PATHY] —**an·tip/a·thist,** *n.*
—**Syn. 1.** disgust, abhorrence, detestation, hatred. See **aversion.** —**Ant. 1.** attraction.

an·ti·pe·dal (an/ti pēd/əl), *adj.* (in a mollusk) located opposite to the foot. [ANTI- + PEDAL]

an·ti·pe·ri·od·ic (an/tē pēr/ē od/ik, an/tī-), *adj.* **1.** efficacious against periodic diseases, as intermittent fever. —*n.* **2.** an antiperiodic agent. [ANTI- + PERIODIC]

an·ti·per·i·stal·sis (an/tē per/i stôl/sis, -stal/-, an/tī-), *n.* *Physiol.* reversed peristaltic action of the intestines, by which their contents are carried upward. [ANTI- + PERISTALSIS] —**an·ti·per·i·stal·tic** (an/tē per/i stal/tik, an/tī-), *adj.*

an/ti·per·ni/cious ane/mia fac/tor (an/tē pər nish/əs, an/tī-, an/tē-, an/tī-), *Biochem.* See **vitamin** B_{12}. [ANTI- + PERNICIOUS ANEMIA]

an·ti·per·son·nel (an/tē pûr/sə nel/, an/tī-), *adj.* *Mil.* used against enemy personnel rather than against mechanized vehicles, materiel, etc.: *antipersonnel bombs.* [ANTI- + PERSONNEL]

an·ti·per·spi·rant (an/ti pûr/spər ənt), *n.* any preparation for retarding perspiration. [ANTI- + PERSPIRE + -ANT]

an·ti·pet·al·ous (an/ti pet/əl əs), *adj.* *Bot.* having the stamens inserted opposite to the petals, as in the flower of the buckthorn. [ANTI- + PETALOUS]

An·ti·phas (an/tə fəs), *n.* *Class. Myth.* one of the twin sons of Laocoön.

An·tiph·a·tes (an tif/ə tēz/), *n.* *Class. Myth.* **1.** a son of Melampus. **2.** (in the *Odyssey*) a chieftain of the Laestrygones, the man-eating giants of Italy. **3.** (in the *Iliad*) a Trojan warrior, slain by Leonteus.

an·ti·phlo·gis·tic (an/ti flō jis/tik, an/tī-), *adj.* **1.** acting against inflammation. —*n.* **2.** an antiphlogistic agent; antipyrotic. [ANTI- + PHLOGISTIC]

an·ti·phon (an/tə fon/), *n.* **1.** a verse or song to be chanted or sung in response. **2.** *Eccles.* **a.** a psalm, hymn, or prayer sung in alternate parts. **b.** a verse or a series of verses sung as a prelude or conclusion to some part of the service. [< ML *antiphōna* responsive singing < Gk (*tà*) *antíphōna,* neut. pl. of *antíphōnos* sounding in answer, equiv. to *anti-* ANTI- + *phōn(ḗ)* sound + *-os* adj. suffix]

an·tiph·o·nal (an tif/ə nəl), *adj.* **1.** pertaining to antiphons or antiphony; responsive. —*n.* **2.** an antiphonary. [ANTIPHON + -AL[1]] —**an·tiph/o·nal·ly,** *adv.*

an·tiph·o·nar·y (an tif/ə ner/ē), *n., pl.* **-nar·ies.** a book of antiphons. [< ML *antiphōnāri(um).* See ANTIPHON, -ARY]

an·tiph·o·ny (an tif/ə nē), *n., pl.* **-nies. 1.** alternate or responsive singing by a choir in two divisions. **2.** a psalm, verse, etc., so sung; an antiphon. **3.** a responsive musical utterance. [ANTIPHON + -Y[3], modeled on *symphony*] —**an·ti·phon·ic** (an/tə fon/ik), *adj.* —**an/ti·phon/i·cal·ly,** *adv.*

an·tiph·ra·sis (an tif/rə sis), *n.* *Rhet.* the use of a word in a sense opposite to its proper meaning. [< L < Gk *antíphrasis,* equiv. to *antiphráz(ein)* (to) speak the opposite (*anti-* ANTI- + *phrázein* to speak) + *-sis* -SIS; see PHRASE] —**an·ti·phras·tic** (an/ti fras/tik), **an/ti·phras/ti·cal,** *adj.* —**an/ti·phras/ti·cal·ly,** *adv.*

An·ti·phus (an/tə fəs), *n.* *Class. Myth.* **1.** (in the *Iliad*) a Trojan ally, the son of Talaemenes and a nymph. **2.** one of the 50 sons of Priam. **3.** a Greek commander who sailed from Troy with Odysseus and was devoured by Polyphemus.

an·ti·plas·tic (an/tē plas/tik, an/tī-), *adj.* allaying or preventing the growth of new tissue. [ANTI- + PLASTIC]

an·tip·o·dal (an tip/ə dəl), *adj.* **1.** *Geog.* on the opposite side of the globe; pertaining to the antipodes. **2.** diametrically opposite: *twin brothers with antipodal personalities.* [ANTIPODE + -AL[1]]

an·ti·pode (an/ti pōd/), *n.* a direct or exact opposite. [back formation from ANTIPODES]

an·tip·o·des (an tip/ə dēz/), *n.pl.* **1.** places diametrically opposite to each other on the globe. **2.** those who dwell there. [ME < L < Gk (*hoi*) *antípodes* (those) with the feet opposite (pl. of *antípous*), equiv. to *anti-* ANTI- + *-podes,* nom. pl. of *poûs* foot] —**an·tip·o·de·an** (an tip/ə dē/ən), *adj., n.*

an/ti·med/i·ca/tive, *adj.*
an/ti·med/i·cine, *adj.*
an/ti·me/di·ae/val, *adj.;* **-ly,** *adv.*
an/ti·me/di·ae/val·ism, *n.*
an/ti·me/di·ae/val·ist, *n., adj.*
an/ti·me/di·e/val, *adj.;* **-ly,** *adv.*
an/ti·me/di·e/val·ism, *n.*
an/ti·me/di·e/val·ist, *n., adj.*
an/ti·merg/er, *adj.*
an/ti·merg/ing, *adj.*
an/ti·meth/od, *adj.*
an/ti·me·thod/ic, *adj.*
an/ti·me·thod/i·cal, *adj.;* **-ly,** *adv.;* **-ness,** *n.*
an/ti-Mex/i·can, *n., adj.*
an/ti·mil/i·ta·rism, *n.*
an/ti·mil/i·ta·rist, *n., adj.*
an/ti·mil/i·ta·ris/tic, *adj.*
an/ti·mil/i·ta·ris/ti·cal·ly, *adv.*
an/ti·mil/i·tar/y, *adj.*
an/ti·min/is·te/ri·al, *adj.;* **-ly,** *adv.*
an/ti·min/is·te/ri·al·ist, *n., adj.*
an/ti·mod/ern, *adj.. n.;* **-ly,** *adv.;* **-ness,** *n.*
an/ti·mod/ern·ism, *n.*
an/ti·mod/ern·ist, *n., adj.*
an/ti·mod/ern·is/tic, *adj.*
an/ti·mod/ern·i·za/tion, *adj.*
an/ti·mon/arch, *adj., n.*
an/ti·mo·nar/chal, *adj.;* **-ly,** *adv.*
an/ti·mo·nar/chi·al, *adj.*
an/ti·mo·nar/chic, *adj.*
an/ti·mo·nar/chi·cal, *adj.;* **-ly,** *adv.*
an/ti·mon/ar·chism, *n.*
an/ti·mon/ar·chist, *n., adj.*
an/ti·mon/ar·chis/tic, *adj.*
an/ti·mon/ar·chy, *adj.*
an/ti·mo·nop/o·lism, *n.*
an/ti·mo·nop/o·list, *n., adj.*
an/ti·mo·nop/o·lis/tic, *adj.*
an/ti·mo·nop/o·li·za/tion, *adj.*
an/ti·mo·nop/o·ly, *adj.*
an/ti·mor/al, *adj.*
an/ti·mor/al·ism, *n.*
an/ti·mor/al·ist, *n., adj.*
an/ti·mor/al·is/tic, *adj.*
an/ti·mo·ral/i·ty, *adj.*
an/ti·mu/si·cal, *adj.;* **-ly,** *adv.;* **-ness,** *n.*
an/ti·mys/tic, *adj., n.*
an/ti·mys/ti·cal, *adj.;* **-ly,** *adv.;* **-ness,** *n*
an/ti·mys/ti·cism, *n.*
an/ti·nar·cot/ic, *adj., n.*
an/ti·na/tion·al, *adj.;* **-ly,** *adv.*
an/ti·na/tion·al·ism, *n.*
an/ti·na/tion·al·ist, *n., adj.*
an/ti·na/tion·al·is/tic, *adj.*
an/ti·na/tion·al·is/ti·cal·ly, *adv.*
an/ti·na/tion·al·i·za/tion, *adj.*
an/ti·nat/u·ral, *adj.;* **-ly,** *adv.;* **-ness,** *n.*
an/ti·nat/u·ral·ism, *n.*
an/ti·nat/u·ral·ist, *n., adj.*
an/ti·nat/u·ral·is/tic, *adj.*
an/ti-Ne/gro, *adj., n., pl.* **-groes.**
an/ti-Ne/gro·ism, *n.*
an/ti·neu/tral, *adj., n.;* **-ly,** *adv.*
an/ti·neu/tral·ism, *n.*
an/ti·neu·tral/i·ty, *n.*
an/ti·ni/hil·ism, *n.*
an/ti·ni/hil·ist, *n., adj.*
an/ti·ni/hil·is/tic, *adj.*
an/ti·noise/, *adj.*
an/ti-Nor/dic, *adj.*
an/ti·nor/mal, *adj.;* **-ness,** *n.*
an/ti·nor·mal/i·ty, *n.*
an/ti·o/pen-shop/, *n.*
an/ti·op/ti·mism, *n.*
an/ti·op/ti·mist, *n., adj.*
an/ti·op/ti·mis/tic, *adj.*
an/ti·op/ti·mis/ti·cal, *adj.;* **-ly,** *adv.*
an/ti-O/ri·en/tal, *adj., n.*
an/ti-O/ri·en/tal·ism, *n.*
an/ti-O/ri·en/tal·ist, *n., adj.*
an/ti·or/tho·dox/, *adj.;* **-ly,** *adv.*
an/ti·or/tho·dox/y, *n.*
an/ti·ox/i·diz/er, *n.*
an/ti·ox/i·diz/ing, *adj.*
an/ti·ox/y·gen·at/ing, *adj.*
an/ti·ox/y·gen·a/tion, *n.*
an/ti·ox/y·gen·a/tor, *n.*
an/ti·pac/i·fism, *n.*
an/ti·pac/i·fist, *n., adj.*
an/ti·pac/i·fis/tic, *adj.*
an/ti·pa/pa·cy, *adj.*
an/ti·pa/pal, *adj.*
an/ti·pa/pal·ist, *n., adj.*
an/ti·pa/pism, *n.*
an/ti·pa/pist, *n., adj.*
an/ti·pa·pis/tic, *adj.*
an/ti·pa·pis/ti·cal, *adj.*
an/ti·par/a·sit/ic, *adj.*
an/ti·par/a·sit/i·cal, *adj.;* **-ly,** *adv.*
an/ti·par/lia·ment, *adj.*
an/ti·par/lia·men/ta·ry, *adj.*
an/ti·path/o·gen, *n.*
an/ti·path/o·gene/, *n.*
an/ti·path/o·gen/ic, *adj.*
an/ti·pa/tri·arch/, *n.*
an/ti·pa/tri·ar/chal, *adj.;* **-ly,** *adv.*
an/ti·pa/tri·ar/chy, *n.*
an/ti·pa/tri·ot, *n.*
an/ti·pa/tri·ot/ic, *adj.*
an/ti·pa/tri·ot/i·cal·ly, *adv.*
an/ti·pa/tri·ot·ism, *n.*
an/ti·pes/ti·lence, *adj.*
an/ti·pes/ti·lent, *adj.;* **-ly,** *adv.*
an/ti·pes/ti·len/tial, *adj.*
an/ti·phil/o·soph/ic, *adj.*
an/ti·phil/o·soph/i·cal, *adj.;* **-ly,** *adv.*
an/ti·phi·los/o·phism, *n.*
an/ti·phi·los/o·phy, *adj., n.., pl.* **-phies.**
an/ti·phys/i·cal, *adj.;* **-ly,** *adv.;* **-ness,** *n.*
an/ti-Pla/to, *adj.*
an/ti-Pla·ton/ic, *adj.*
an/ti-Pla·ton/i·cal·ly, *adv.*
an/ti-Pla/to·nism, *n.*
an/ti-Pla/to·nist, *n., adj.*

An·tip·o·des (an tip′ə dēz′), *n.* (*construed as pl.*) a group of islands SE of and belonging to New Zealand. 24 sq. mi.

An·ti·poe·nus (an′tə pē′nəs), *n.* *Class. Myth.* a Theban descendant of the Sparti who refused to give his life for his city. Cf. **Alcis.**

an·ti·pole (an′ti pōl′), *n.* the opposite pole. [ANTI- + POLE]

an·ti·pope (an′ti pōp′), *n.* one who is elected pope in opposition to another held to be canonically chosen. [ANTI- + POPE; r. *antipape* < ML *antipāpa*, modeled on *Antichrīstus* Antichrist]

an·ti·pov·er·ty (an′tē pov′ər tē, an′tī-), *adj.* directed against poverty (used esp. in describing certain governmental programs intended to reduce or eliminate poverty). [ANTI- + POVERTY]

an·ti·pro·ton (an′tē prō′ton, an′tī-), *n.* *Physics.* an elementary particle having negative charge equal in magnitude to that of the electron and having the same mass and spin as a proton; the antiparticle of the proton. [ANTI- + PROTON]

an·ti·pru·rit·ic (an′tē pro͞o rit′ik, an′tī-), *Med.* —*adj.* **1.** relieving or preventing itching. —*n.* **2.** an antipruritic agent. [ANTI- + PRURITIC]

an·ti·py·ret·ic (an′tē pī ret′ik, an′tī-), *Med.* —*adj.* **1.** checking or preventing fever. —*n.* **2.** an antipyretic agent. [ANTI- + PYRETIC] —**an·ti·py·re·sis** (an′tē pī rē′sis, an′tī-), *n.*

an·ti·py·rine (an′tē pī′rin, an′tī-), *n.* *Pharm.* a white powder, $C_{11}H_{12}N_2O$, used as a sedative, antipyretic, antirheumatic, and antineuralgic. [< G *Antipyrin* a trademark. See ANTI-, PYR-, -INE[2]]

an·ti·py·rot·ic (an′tē pī rot′ik, an′tī-), *Med.* —*adj.* **1.** antiphlogistic. **2.** relieving the pain and stimulating the healing of burns. —*n.* **3.** an antipyrotic agent. **4.** antiphlogistic. [ANTI- + Gk *pyrōtik(ós)* burning, equiv. to *pyró(ein)* (to) burn + *-tikos* -TIC]

antiq., antiquity.

an·ti·quar·i·an (an′tə kwâr′ē ən), *adj.* **1.** pertaining to antiquaries or to the study of antiquities. **2.** dealing in or pertaining to old or rare books. —*n.* **3.** an antiquary. **4.** a size of drawing and writing paper, 31 × 53 or 29 × 52 inches. [< L *antīquāri(us)* (see ANTIQUARY) + -AN] —**an′ti·quar′i·an·ism,** *n.*

an·ti·quar·y (an′tə kwer′ē), *n., pl.* **-quar·ies. 1.** an expert on or student of antiquities. **2.** a collector of antiquities. [< L *antīquāri(us)* of, belonging to antiquity, equiv. to *antīqu(us)* ancient, old (see ANTIQUE) + *-ārius* -ARY]

an·ti·quate (an′tə kwāt′), *v.t.,* **-quat·ed, -quat·ing. 1.** to make obsolete by replacing with something newer or better: *This new device antiquates the ice-cube tray.* **2.** to design or create in an antique style. [< L *antīquāt(us)* (ptp. of *antīquāre*) made old. See ANTIQUE, -ATE[1]] —**an′ti·qua′tion,** *n.*

an·ti·quat·ed (an′tə kwā′tid), *adj.* **1.** obsolete or obsolescent: *The spinning wheel is an antiquated machine.* **2.** aged; old: *several antiquated lexicographers.* **3.** continued from, resembling, or adhering to the past; old-fashioned: *antiquated attitudes.* [ANTIQUATE + -ED[2]] —**an′ti·qua′ted·ness,** *n.*
—**Syn. 2.** See **ancient**[1].

an·tique (an tēk′), *adj., n., v.,* **-tiqued, -ti·quing.** —*adj.* **1.** of or belonging to the past; not modern. **2.** dating from an early period: *antique furniture.* **3.** in the tradition, fashion, or style of an earlier period; old-fashioned; antiquated. **4.** (of paper) neither calendered nor coated and having a rough surface. **5.** ancient. —*n.* **6.** any work of art, piece of furniture, decorative object, or the like, created or produced in a former period, usually over 100 years ago or, according to U.S. customs laws, before 1830. **7.** the antique style, usually Greek or Roman, esp. in art. **8.** *Print.* a style of type. —*v.t.* **9.** to make (something) appear antique. **10.** to emboss (an image, design, letters, or the like) on paper or fabric. [< MF < L *antīqu(us)* (var. of *anticus* old, primitive; see ANTIC); r. *antike* < L] —**an·tique′ly,** *adv.* —**an·tique′ness,** *n.*
—**Syn. 1.** bygone, archaic. **2.** old, obsolete, obsolescent. See **ancient**[1]. **6.** bibelot, curio.

an′tique crown′, *Heraldry.* See **eastern crown.**

an′tique glass′. See **pot metal** (def. 3).

an·ti·quer (an tē′kər), *n.* **1.** one who takes a special interest in antiques; a collector of antiquities; antiquary. **2.** one who simulates antique furniture by using processes which give an appearance of age, wear, etc., to recently manufactured pieces. [ANTIQUE + -ER[1]]

an·tiq·ui·ty (an tik′wi tē), *n., pl.* **-ties. 1.** the quality of being ancient; ancientness: *a family of great antiquity.* **2.** ancient times; former ages: *the splendor of antiquity.* **3.** the time before the Middle Ages. **4.** the ancients collectively; the peoples, nations, tribes, or cultures of ancient times. **5.** Usually, **antiquities.** something belonging to or remaining from ancient times, as monuments, relics, customs, etc. [ME *antiquite* < MF < L *antīquitāt-* (s. of *antīquitās*), equiv. to *antīqu(us)* old (see ANTIQUE) + *-itāt-* -ITY]

an·ti·ra·chit·ic (an′tē rə kit′ik, an′tī-), *adj.* pertaining to the prevention or cure of rickets. [ANTI- + RACHITIC] —**an′ti·ra·chit′i·cal·ly,** *adv.*

an·ti·re·flex·ive (an′tē ri flek′siv, an′tī-), *adj.* *Math.* noting a relation in which no element is in relation to itself, as "less than." [ANTI- + REFLEXIVE]

an·ti·re·mon·strant (an′tē ri mon′strənt, an′tī-), *n.* **1.** one opposed to remonstrance or to those who remonstrate. **2.** (*cap.*) a member or supporter of that party in the Dutch Calvinistic Church which opposed the Remonstrants or Arminians. [ANTI- + REMONSTRANT]

an·ti·rent (an′tē rent′, an′tī-), *adj.* noting or pertaining to a political party (1839–47) in New York that opposed the payment of rents to patroons. [ANTI + RENT[1]] —**an′ti·rent′er,** *n.* —**an′ti·rent′ism,** *n.*

an·ti·res·o·nance (an′tē rez′ə nəns, an′tī-), *n.* *Physics.* a phenomenon in an electric, acoustic, or other such system in which the impedance is tending to infinity. [ANTI- + RESONANCE]

an·ti·rheu·mat·ic (an′tē ro͝o mat′ik, an′tī-), *Med.* —*adj.* **1.** preventing or relieving rheumatic pain. —*n.* **2.** an antirheumatic substance. [ANTI- + RHEUMATIC]

an·tir·rhi·num (an′tə rī′nəm), *n.* any plant of the genus *Antirrhinum,* comprising the snapdragons. [< NL < Gk *antírrīn(on)* calf's snout, lit., noselike object. See ANTI-, RHINO-]

an·ti·rust (an′tē rust′, an′tī-, an′ti rust′), *adj.* **1.** preventing or resisting rust. **2.** rustproof. —*n.* **3.** something that prevents or resists rust. [ANTI- + RUST]

An·ti-sa·loon′ League′ of Amer′ica (an′tē sə lo͞on′, an′tī-), a national organization, founded in 1893 in Ohio, advocating the prohibition of the manufacture and sale of alcoholic beverages.

An·ti·sa·na (än′tē sä′nä), *n.* **Mount,** an active volcano in N central Ecuador, near Quito. 18,885 ft.

an·ti·scor·bu·tic (an′tē skôr byo͞o′tik, an′tī-), *Med.* —*adj.* **1.** efficacious against scurvy. —*n.* **2.** an antiscorbutic agent. [ANTI- + SCORBUTIC]

an·ti-Sem·ite (an′tē sem′īt, an′tī- *or, esp. Brit.,* -sē′mit), *n.* a person who is hostile to Jews. —**an·ti-Se·mit·ic** (an′tē sə mit′ik, an′tī-), *adj.* —**an′ti-Se·mit′i·cal·ly,** *adv.* —**an·ti-Sem·i·tism** (an′tē sem′i tiz′əm, an′tī-), *n.*

an·ti·sep·al·ous (an′ti sep′ə ləs), *adj.* *Bot.* having the stamens inserted opposite to the sepals, as in the flower of the lady's-mantle. [ANTI- + -SEPALOUS]

an·ti·sep·sis (an′ti sep′sis), *n.* destruction of the microorganisms that produce sepsis or septic disease. [ANTI- + SEPSIS]

an·ti·sep·tic (an′ti sep′tik), *adj.* **1.** pertaining to or affecting antisepsis. **2.** free from or cleaned of germs and other microorganisms. **3.** exceptionally clean or neat. —*n.* **4.** an antiseptic agent. [ANTI- + SEPTIC]

an·ti·sep·ti·cal·ly (an′ti sep′tik lē), *adv.* with the aid of antiseptics. [ANTISEPTIC + -AL[1] + -LY]

an·ti·sep·ti·cise (an′ti sep′ti sīz′), *v.t.,* **-cised, -cis·ing.** *Chiefly Brit.* antisepticize.

an·ti·sep·ti·cize (an′ti sep′ti sīz′), *v.t.,* **-cized, -ciz·ing.** to treat with antiseptics. [ANTISEPTIC + -IZE]

an·ti·se·rum (an′ti sēr′əm), *n., pl.* **-se·rums, -se·ra** (-sēr′ə). a serum containing antibodies, as antitoxins or agglutinins, obtained by inoculation of animals and used for injection into other animals to provide immunity to a specific disease. [ANTI- + SERUM]

an·ti·slav·er·y (an′tē slā′və rē, -slāv′rē, an′tī-), *n.* **1.** opposition to slavery, esp. Negro slavery. —*adj.* **2.** of or pertaining to antislavery. [ANTI- + SLAVERY]

an·ti·so·cial (an′tē sō′shəl, an′tī-), *adj.* **1.** unwilling or unable to associate normally with other people: *He's not antisocial, just shy.* **2.** antagonistic, hostile, or unfriendly toward others; menacing; threatening. **3.** opposed to social order or the principles on which society is constituted: *antisocial behavior.* Also, **an′ti·so′cial·is′tic.** [ANTI- + SOCIAL] —**an·ti·so·ci·al·i·ty** (an′tē sō′shē al′i tē, an′tī-), *n.* —**an′ti·so′cial·ly,** *adv.*

an·ti·so·lar (an′tē sō′lər, an′tī-), *adj.* *Astron.* (on the celestial sphere) opposite the sun. [ANTI- + SOLAR]

an·ti·spas·mod·ic (an′tē spaz mod′ik, an′tī-), *adj.* **1.** relieving or preventing spasms. —*n.* **2.** an antispasmodic agent. [ANTI- + SPASMODIC]

An·tis·the·nes (an tis′thə nēz′), *n.* 444?–365? B.C., Greek philosopher: founder of the Cynic school.

an·tis·tro·phe (an tis′trə fē), *n.* **1.** the part of an ancient Greek choral ode answering a previous strophe, sung by the chorus when returning from left to right. **2.** the movement performed by the chorus while singing an antistrophe. **3.** *Pros.* the second of two metrically corresponding systems in a poem. Cf. **strophe** (def. 2). [< Gk: a turning about. See ANTI-, STROPHE] —**an·ti·stroph·ic** (an′ti strof′ik, -strō′fik), **an·tis′tro·phal,** *adj.* —**an′ti·stroph′i·cal·ly,** *adv.*

an·ti·su·dor·if·ic (an′tē so͞o′də rif′ik, an′tī-), *Med.* —*n.* **1.** an antiperspirant. —*adj.* **2.** inhibiting perspiration. [ANTI- + SUDORIFIC]

an·ti·sym·met·ric (an′tē si me′trik, an′tī-), *adj.* *Math.* noting a relation in which one element's dependence on a second implies that the second element is not dependent on the first, as the relation "greater than." [ANTI- + SYMMETRIC] —**an′ti·sym·met′ri·cal,** *adj.*

an·ti·syph·i·lit·ic (an′tē sif′ə lit′ik, an′tī-), *Med.* —*adj.* **1.** curing or preventing syphilis. —*n.* **2.** an antisyphilitic agent. [ANTI- + SYPHILITIC]

an·ti·tank (an′tē taŋk′, an′tī-), *adj.* *Mil.* designed for use against tanks or other armored vehicles: *antitank gun.* [ANTI- + TANK]

an·tith·e·sis (an tith′i sis), *n., pl.* **-ses** (-sēz′). **1.** opposition; contrast: *the antithesis of right and wrong.* **2.** the direct opposite (usually fol. by *of* or *to*). **3.** *Rhet.* **a.** the placing of a sentence or one of its parts against another to which it is opposed, as in "Give me liberty or give me death." **b.** the second sentence or part thus set in opposition, as "or give me death." **4.** *Philos.* See under **Hegelian dialectic.** [< L < Gk: opposition, equiv. to *anti(ti)thé(nai)* (to) oppose + *-sis* -SIS. See ANTI-, THESIS]

an·ti·thet·ic (an′tə thet′ik), *adj.* **1.** of the nature of or involving antithesis. **2.** directly opposed or contrasted. Also, **an′ti·thet′i·cal.** [< Gk *antithetik(ós),* equiv. to *anti(ti)thé(nai)* (to) set in opposition + *-tikos* -TIC] —**an′ti·thet′i·cal·ly,** *adv.*

an·ti·torque′ ro′tor (an′tē tôrk′, an′tī-), *Aeron.* (on certain helicopters) a small rotor on the tail, turning in the vertical plane and providing a thrust that generates a torque which opposes and compensates for the torque of the main rotor. [ANTI- + TORQUE]

an·ti·tox·ic (an′ti tok′sik, an′tē-), *adj.* **1.** counteracting toxic influences. **2.** of or serving as an antitoxin. [ANTI- + TOXIC]

an·ti·tox·in (an′ti tok′sin, an′tē-), *n.* **1.** a substance formed in the body, which counteracts a specific toxin. **2.** the antibody formed in immunization with a given toxin, used in treating certain infectious diseases or in immunizing against them. Also, **an·ti·tox·ine** (an′ti tok′sin, -sēn, an′tē-). [ANTI- + TOXIN]

an·ti·trade (an′ti trād′), *n.* **1. antitrades,** westerly winds lying above the trade winds in the tropics. —*adj.* **2.** noting or pertaining to such a wind. [ANTI- + TRADE]

an·tit·ra·gus (an ti′trə gəs), *n., pl.* **-gi** (-jī′). *Anat.* a process of the external ear. See diag. under **ear.** [< NL < Gk *antítragos.* See ANTI-, TRAGUS]

an·ti·trust (an′tē trust′, an′tī-), *adj.* opposing or intended to restrain trusts or large combinations of business and capital, esp. with a view to promoting competition: *antitrust legislation.* [ANTI- + TRUST]

an·ti·twi′light arch′ (an′tē twī′līt, an′tī-), a narrow band, pink or with a purple cast, which sometimes appears at twilight just above the horizon opposite the sun. Also called **anticrepuscular arch.** [ANTI- + TWILIGHT]

an·ti·type (an′ti tīp′), *n.* that which is foreshadowed by a type or symbol, as a New Testament event prefigured in the Old Testament. [< ML *antityp(us)* < LGk *antítypos* (impression) answering to a die. See

an′ti·po·et′ic, *adj.*
an′ti·po·et′i·cal, *adj.;* **-ly,** *adv.*
an′ti·po′lar, *adj.*
an′ti-Pol′ish, *n., adj.*
an′ti·po·lit′i·cal, *adj.;* **-ly,** *adv.*
an′ti·pol′i·tics, *adj.*
an′ti·pol·lu′tion, *adj.*
an′ti·pop′er·y, *n.*
an′ti·pop′u·lar·i·za′tion, *adj., n.*
an′ti·pop′u·lism, *n.*
an′ti-Pop′u·list, *n., adj.*
an′ti·prag·mat′ic, *adj.*
an′ti·prag·mat′i·cal, *adj.;* **-ly,** *adv.*
an′ti·prag·mat′i·cism, *n.*
an′ti·prag′ma·tism, *n.*
an′ti·prag′ma·tist, *n., adj.*
an′ti·prel′a·tism, *n.*
an′ti·prel′a·tist, *n., adj.*
an′ti·priest′, *adj.*
an′ti·priest′hood, *adj.*
an′ti·pro·duc′tive, *adj.;* **-ly,** *adv.;* **-ness,** *n.*
an′ti·pro′duc·tiv′i·ty, *adj., n.*
an′ti·pro′hi·bi′tion, *adj., n.*
an′ti·pro′hi·bi′tion·ist, *n., adj.*
an′ti-Prot′es·tant, *n., adj.*
an′ti-Prot′es·tant·ism, *n.*
an′ti·psalm′ist, *n., adj.*
an′ti·Pu′ri·tan, *n., adj.*
an′ti-Pu′ri·tan, *n., adj.*
an′ti-Pu′ri·tan·ism, *n.*
an′ti·ra′cial, *adj.;* **-ly,** *adv.*
an′ti·rac′ing, *n., adj.*
an′ti·ra′di·ant, *adj.*
an′ti·ra′di·at′ing, *adj.*
an′ti·ra′di·a′tion, *adj.*
an′ti·rad′i·cal, *n., adj.;* **-ly,** *adv.*
an′ti·rad′i·cal·ism, *n.*
an′ti·ra′tion·al, *adj.;* **-ly,** *adv.*
an′ti·ra′tion·al·ism, *n.*
an′ti·ra′tion·al·ist, *n., adj.*
an′ti·ra′tion·al·is′tic, *adj.*
an′ti·ra′tion·al′i·ty, *n., adj.*
an′ti·re·act′ing, *adj.*
an′ti·re·ac′tion, *n., adj.*
an′ti·re·ac′tion·ar′y, *n., pl.* **-ar·ies,** *adj.*
an′ti·re·ac′tive, *adj.*
an′ti·re′al·ism, *n.*
an′ti·re′al·ist, *n., adj.*
an′ti·re′al·is′tic, *adj.*
an′ti·re′al·is′ti·cal·ly, *adv.*
an′ti·re·al′i·ty, *adj.*
an′ti·red′, *adj., n.*
an′ti·re·duc′er, *n.*
an′ti·re·duc′ing, *adj., n.*
an′ti·re·duc′tion, *adj.*
an′ti·re·duc′tive, *adj.*
an′ti·re·form′, *adj.*
an′ti·re·form′er, *n.*
an′ti·re·form′ing, *adj., n.*
an′ti·re·form′ist, *n., adj.*
an′ti·re·li′gion, *adj.*
an′ti·re·li′gion·ist, *n., adj.*
an′ti·re·li′gi·os′i·ty, *n.*
an′ti·re·li′gious, *adj.;* **-ly,** *adv.*
an′ti·re·pub′li·can, *adj., n.*
an′ti·re·pub′li·can·ism, *n.*
an′ti·res′to·ra′tion, *adj.*
an′ti·re·vi′sion·ist, *n., adj.*
an′ti·rev′o·lu′tion, *adj.*
an′ti·rev′o·lu′tion·ar′y, *n., pl.* **-ar·ies,** *adj.*
an′ti·rev′o·lu′tion·ist, *n.*
an′ti·rit′u·al, *adj.*
an′ti·rit′u·al·ism, *n.*
an′ti·rit′u·al·ist, *n., adj.*
an′ti·rit′u·al·is′tic, *adj.*
an′ti-Ro′man, *adj., n.*
an′ti·ro·mance′, *adj.*
an′ti·ro·man′tic, *adj., n.*
an′ti·ro·man′ti·cism, *n.*
an′ti·ro·man′ti·cist, *n., adj.*
an′ti-Ro′man·ist, *n., adj.*
an′ti·roy′al, *adj.*
an′ti·roy′al·ism, *n.*
an′ti·roy′al·ist, *n., adj.*
an′ti-Rus′sia, *adj.*
an′ti-Rus′sian, *adj., n.*
an′ti-Scan′di·na′vi·a, *adj.*
an′ti·scep′tic, *n.*
an′ti·scep′ti·cal, *adj.*
an′ti·scep′ti·cism, *n.*
an′ti·scho·las′tic, *adj., n.*
an′ti·scho·las′ti·cal·ly, *adv.*
an′ti·scho·las′ti·cism, *n.*
an′ti·school′, *adj.*
an′ti·sci′ence, *adj.*
an′ti·sci′en·tif′ic, *adj.*
an′ti·sci′en·tif′i·cal·ly, *adv.*
an′ti·scrip′tur·al, *adj.*
an′ti-Scrip′ture, *adj.*
an′ti-Scrip′tur·ist, *n., adj.*
an′ti·sen′si·tiv′i·ty, *n., adj.*
an′ti·sen′si·tiz′er, *n.*
an′ti·sen′si·tiz′ing, *adj.*
an′ti·sen′su·al′i·ty, *n., adj.*
an′ti·sen′su·ous, *adj.;* **-ly,** *adv.;* **-ness,** *n.*
an′ti-Serb′, *adj., n.*
an′ti·sic′ca·tive, *adj.*
an′ti·skep′tic, *n.*
an′ti·skep′ti·cal, *adj.*
an′ti·skep′ti·cism, *n.*
an′ti·skid′, *adj.*
an′ti·skid′ding, *adj.*
an′ti-Slav′, *n.*
an′ti-Slav′ic, *adj., n.*
an′ti·slip′, *adj.*
an′ti·smok′ing, *adj., n.*
an′ti-Soc′ra·tes, *adj.*
an′ti-So·crat′ic, *adj.*
an′ti·soph′ism, *n.*
an′ti·soph′ist, *n., adj.*
an′ti·so·phis′tic, *adj.*
an′ti·so·phis′ti·ca′tion, *n.*
an′ti·soph′ist·ry, *n.*
an′ti·sop′o·rif′ic, *adj., n.*
an′ti-So′vi·et, *n.*
an′ti-Spain′, *adj.*
an′ti-Span′ish, *adj.*
an′ti·spir′it·u·al, *adj.;* **-ly,** *adv.*
an′ti·spir′it·u·al·ism, *n.*
an′ti·spir′it·u·al·ist, *n., adj.*
an′ti·spir′it·u·al·is′tic, *adj.*
an′ti·split′ting, *adj., n.*
an′ti·spread′er, *n.*
an′ti·spread′ing, *adj., n.*
an′ti·stall′ing, *adj.*
an′ti·state′, *adj.*
an′ti·stat′er, *n.*
an′ti·stat′ism, *n.*
an′ti·stat′ist, *n., adj.*
an′ti·stim′u·lant, *adj., n.*
an′ti·stim′u·la′tion, *n.*
an′ti·strike′, *adj.*
an′ti·strik′er, *n.*
an′ti·sub′ma·rine′, *adj.*
an′ti·suf′frage, *adj.*
an′ti·suf′fra·gist, *n., adj.*
an′ti·su′per·nat′ur·al, *adj., n.*
an′ti·su′per·nat′ur·al·ism, *n.*
an′ti·su′per·nat′ur·al·ist, *n., adj.*
an′ti·su′per·nat′ur·al·is′tic, *adj.*
an′ti-Swe′den, *adj.*
an′ti-Swe′dish, *adj.*
an′ti·sym′me·try, *adj., n.*
an′ti·syn′di·cal·ism, *n.*
an′ti·syn′di·cal·ist, *n., adj.*
an′ti·syn′di·ca′tion, *adj.*
an′ti·syn′od, *adj.*
an′ti·tar′nish, *adj.*
an′ti·tar′nish·ing, *adj.*
an′ti·tar·tar′ic, *adj.*
an′ti·tax′, *adj.*
an′ti·tax·a′tion, *adj.*
an′ti·tem′per·ance, *adj.*
an′ti-Teu′ton, *adj., n.*
an′ti-Teu·ton′ic, *adj.*
an′ti·the′o·lo′gian, *n., adj.*
an′ti·the′o·log′i·cal, *adj.*
an′ti·the·ol′o·giz′ing, *adj., n.*
an′ti·the·ol′o·gy, *adj.*
an′ti·ton′ic, *adj., n.*
an′ti·tra·di′tion, *adj.*
an′ti·tra·di′tion·al, *adj.;* **-ly,** *adv.*
an′ti·tra·di′tion·al·ist, *n., adj.*
an′ti-Trin′i·tar′i·an, *adj., n.*
an′ti-Trin′i·tar′i·an·ism, *n.*
an′ti·tu·ber′cu·lous, *adj.*
an′ti-Turk′ish, *adj.*

ANTI-, TYPE] —**an·ti·typ·ic** (an′ti tip′ik), **an′ti·typ′i·cal,** *adj.* —**an′ti·typ′i·cal·ly,** *adv.*

an·ti·un·ion (an′tē yo͞on′yən, an′tī-), *adj. U.S.* opposed to trade unions or unionism. [ANTI- + UNION] —**an′ti·un′ion·ist,** *n.*

an·ti·ven·in (an′tē ven′in, an′tī-), *n.* **1.** an antitoxin present in the blood of an animal following repeated injections of venom. **2.** the antitoxic serum obtained from such blood. [*antiven(ene)* (ANTI- + *venene* < L *venēnum* love-potion, poison; see VENUS) + -IN²]

an·ti·world (an′tē wûrld′, an′tī-), *n.* Often, **anti-worlds.** *Physics.* a hypothetical world composed of antimatter. [ANTI- + WORLD]

an′ti·xe·roph·thal′mic vi′tamin (an′tē zēr′of thal′mik, an′-tī-, an′tē-, an′tī-), *Biochem.* See **vitamin A.** [ANTI- + XEROPHTHALM(IA) + -IC]

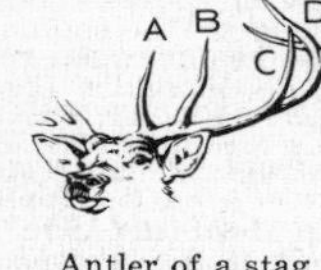

Antler of a stag
A, Brow antler
B, Bay antler
C, Royal antler
D, Crown antler

ant·ler (ant′lər), *n.* one of the solid deciduous horns, usually branched, of an animal of the deer family. [late ME *aunteler* < MF *antoillier* < VL **anteoculār(em)* (*rāmum*), acc. sing of **anteoculāris* (*rāmus*) anteocular branch of a stag's horn. See ANTE-, OCULAR] —**ant′ler·less,** *adj.*

ant·lered (ant′lərd), *adj.* **1.** having antlers. **2.** decorated with antlers. [ANTLER + -ED³]

Ant·li·a (ant′lē ə), *n., gen.* **-li·ae** (-lē ē′) for 1, *pl.* **-li·ae** (-lē ē′) for 2. **1.** *Astron.* the Air Pump, a small southern constellation between Vela and Hydra. **2.** (*l.c.*) *Entomol.* the proboscis of a lepidopterous insect. [< L *antlia* pump, machine for drawing water < Gk *antlía* bilge-water, a ship's hold, equiv. to *ántl(os)* the hold (of a ship), bilge-water + *-ia* -IA] —**ant·li·ate** (ant′lē āt′), *adj.*

ant·li·on (ant′lī′ən), *n.* any of several neuropterous insects of the family *Myrmeleontidae*, the larva of which digs a pit in sand where it lies in wait for ants or other insects. [ANT + LION]

an·to·don·tal·gic (an′tō don tal′jik), *adj., n. Dentistry.* antiodontalgic.

An·to·fa·gas·ta (än′tō fə gä′stə; *Sp.* än′tô fä gäs′tä), *n.* a seaport in N Chile. 89,114 (1960).

An·toine (äN twAN′), *n.* **1. An·dré** (äN drā′), 1858–1943, French theatrical director, manager, and critic. **2. Père** (per) (*Francisco Ildefonso Mareno*), 1748–1829, Roman Catholic priest in Louisiana, tried to establish Inquisition.

An·toi·nette (an′twə net′; *Fr.* äN twA net′), *n.* **1. Marie** (mə rē′; *Fr.* mA rē′), 1755–93, queen of France 1774–93: wife of Louis XVI. **2.** a girl's given name.

An·ton (an′tən, -ton), *n.* a boy's given name, form of **Anthony.**

An·tone (an tōn′), *n.* a boy's given name, form of **Anthony.**

An·to·nel·lo da Mes·si·na (än′tō nel′lō dä mes sē′nä), (*Antonello di Giovanni degli Antonj*) 1430?–79, Sicilian painter.

An·to·net (an′tō net′, -tə-), *n.* a girl's given name, form of **Antoinette.**

An·to·ni·a (an tō′nē ə, -tōn′yə), *n.* a girl's given name.

an·to·nin·i·a·nus (an′tə nin′ē ā′nəs), *n., pl.* **-ni** (-nī). a Roman coin of the 3rd century A.D., originally of silver but later debased. [< LL: lit., pertaining to ANTONINUS (who introduced the coin) + *-iānus* -IAN]

An·to·ni·nus (an′tə nī′nəs), *n.* **Marcus Aurelius.** See **Marcus Aurelius.**

Antoni′nus Pi′us (pī′əs), A.D. 86–161, emperor of Rome 138–161.

An·to·ni·us (an tō′nē əs), *n.* **Marcus.** See **Antony, Mark.**

an·to·no·ma·sia (an′tə nə mā′zhə), *n.* **1.** *Rhet.* the identification of a person by an epithet or appellative that is not his name, as *his lordship.* **2.** the use of the name of a person who was distinguished by a particular characteristic, as Don Juan, Annie Oakley, etc., to designate a person or group of persons having the same characteristic. [< L < Gk *antonomasía* (var. s. of *antonomázein* to name anew, equiv. to *ant-* ANT- + *onomázein* to name deriv. of *ónoma* name) + *-ia* -IA] —**an·to·no·mas·tic** (an′tə nō mas′tik), **an′to·no·mas′ti·cal,** *adj.* —**an′to·no·mas′ti·cal·ly,** *adv.*

An·to·ny (an′tə nē), *n.* **1. Mark** (*Marcus Antonius*), 83?–30 B.C., Roman general: friend of Caesar; member of the second triumvirate and rival of Octavian. **2.** a boy's given name. Also, **Anthony.**

An′tony and Cleopa′tra, a tragedy (1606–7?) by Shakespeare.

an·to·nym (an′tə nim), *n.* a word opposite in meaning to another. "*Fast*" is the antonym of "*slow.*" Cf. **synonym** (def. 1). [back formation from Gk *antōnym(ía)* (to) have an opposite denomination. See ANT-, SYNONYM] —**an·ton·y·mous** (an ton′ə məs), *adj.*

ant-pip·it (ant′pip′it), *n.* gnateater.

an·tre (an′tər), *n. Chiefly Poetic.* a cavern; cave. [< MF < L *antr(um).* See ANTRUM]

An·trim (an′trim), *n.* a county in NE Northern Ireland. 243,800 (est. 1956); 1098 sq. mi. *Co. seat:* Belfast.

an·trorse (an trôrs′), *adj. Bot., Zool.* bent or directed forward or upward. [< NL *antrors(us),* equiv. to *antr-* (var. of *antero-* ANTERO-) + *-orsus* abstracted from L *introrsus* INTRORSE, etc.] —**an·trorse′ly,** *adv.*

an·trum (an′trəm), *n., pl.* **-tra** (-trə). *Anat.* a cavity in a bone, esp. that in the maxilla. [< L < Gk *ántron* cave] —**an′tral,** *adj.*

ant·shrike (ant′shrīk′), *n.* any of several antbirds, esp. of the genus *Thamnophilus,* superficially resembling the shrike. [ANT(BIRD) + SHRIKE]

Ant·si·ra·ne (änt′sə rä′nā), *n.* Diego-Suarez.

ant-thrush (ant′thrush′), *n.* any of several antbirds, esp. of the genus *Formicarius.*

ANTU (an′to͞o), *n. Trademark.* a gray, water-insoluble, poisonous powder, $C_{10}H_7NHCSNH_2$, used for killing rodents; alpha-naphthylthiorea.

An·tung (an′to͝ong′; *Chin.* än′do͝ong′), *n.* **1.** a seaport in S Manchuria, in NE China, at the mouth of the Yalu. 360,000 (1953). **2.** a former province of China, in Manchuria.

Ant·werp (an′twərp), *n.* **1.** a seaport in N Belgium, on the Scheldt. 259,658 (est. 1959). **2.** a province in N Belgium. 1,416,000 (est. 1959); 1104 sq. mi. French, **Anvers.** Flemish, **Ant·wer·pen** (änt′ver pən).

Ant′werp blue′, *Chem.* any of several iron-blue pigments usually containing a considerable amount of extender.

Ant′werp hol′lyhock, an herb, *Althaea ficifolia,* of Europe, having showy, lemon-yellow or orange flowers in double or single terminal spikes.

A·nu (ä′no͞o), *n.* the Akkadian god of heaven: the counterpart of the Sumerian An.

A·nu·bis (ə no͞o′bis, ə nyo͞o′-), *n. Egyptian Religion.* a deity, the god of tombs and embalming and weigher of the hearts of the dead: represented as having the head of a jackal.

Anubis

a·nu·cle·ate (ā no͞o′klē it, ā nyo͞o′-), *adj. Biol.* having no nucleus. Also, **a·nu·cle·at·ed** (ā no͞o′klē ā′tid, ā nyo͞o′-). [A-⁶ + NUCLEATE]

-anum, a suffix occurring in scientific words of Latin origin: *laudanum.* [< L, neut. of *-ānus* -AN]

A number 1. See **A one** (def. 2).

A·nun·na·ki (ä no͝on′nä kē), *n.* (*construed as pl.*) various unnamed Sumerian deities who constituted the divine assembly presided over by An and Enlil and of whom seven were judges in the afterworld.

A·nu·ra·dha·pu·ra (ə no͝or′ə də po͝or′ə, un′o͝o rä′də-), *n.* a city in central Ceylon: ruins of ancient Buddhist temples. 18,390 (1953).

an·u·ran (ə no͝or′ən, ə nyo͝or′-), *n.* **1.** any amphibian of the order *Anura,* comprising the frogs and toads. —*adj.* **2.** belonging or pertaining to the *Anura.* [AN-¹ + UR(O)-² + -AN]

an·u·ri·a (ə no͝or′ē ə, ə nyo͝or′-), *n. Med.* the absence or suppression of urine. [< NL; see AN-¹, UR(O)-¹, -IA] —**an·u′ric, an·u·ret·ic** (an′yə ret′ik), *adj.*

an·u·rous (an′yər əs, ə no͝or′əs, ə nyo͝or′-), *adj. Zool.* having no tail. Also, **anourous.** [AN-¹ + UR(O)² + -OUS]

a·nus (ā′nəs), *n., pl.* **a·nus·es.** *Anat.* the opening at the lower end of the alimentary canal, through which the solid refuse of digestion is excreted. See diag. under **intestine.** [< L *ānus* ring, anus]

-anus, a suffix occurring in scientific words of Latin origin: *Platanus.* [< L; see -AN]

An·vers (äN ver′), *n.* French name of **Antwerp.**

an·vil (an′vil), *n.* **1.** a heavy iron block with a smooth face, frequently of steel, on which metals, usually heated until soft, are hammered into desired shapes. **2.** anything on which blows are struck. **3.** the fixed jaw in certain measuring instruments. **4.** incus. **5.** a musical percussion instrument having steel bars that are struck with a wooden or metal beater. [ME *anvelt, anfelt* < OE *anfilt(e), anfealt;* c. MD *anvilte,* OHG *anafalz.* See ON, FELT²]

Anvil (def. 1)

anx·i·e·ty (aŋ zī′i tē), *n., pl.* **-ties. 1.** distress or uneasiness of mind caused by apprehension of danger or misfortune: *He felt anxiety about his loss of income.* **2.** solicitous desire; eagerness: *his keen anxiety about his promotion.* **3.** *Psychiatry.* a state of apprehension and psychic tension found in most forms of mental disorder. [< L *anxietāt-* (s. of *anxietās*), equiv. to *anxi(us)* ANXIOUS + *-etāt-,* var. of *-itāt-* -ITY]
—**Syn. 1.** fear, foreboding; worry, distress, disquiet. See **apprehension.** —**Ant. 1.** certainty.

anx·ious (aŋk′shəs, aŋ′-), *adj.* **1.** full of mental distress or uneasiness because of apprehension of danger or misfortune; greatly worried; solicitous: *Her parents were very anxious about her poor health.* **2.** earnestly desirous; eager (usually fol. by an infinitive or *for*): *anxious to please; anxious for our happiness.* **3.** attended with or showing solicitude or uneasiness: *anxious forebodings.* [< L *anxius* troubled in mind; akin to ANGER] —**anx′ious·ly,** *adv.* —**anx′ious·ness,** *n.*
—**Syn. 1.** concerned, disturbed, apprehensive, fearful, uneasy. —**Ant. 1.** calm, confident.

anx′ious seat′, *U.S.* a seat reserved at a revival meeting for those troubled by conscience and eager for spiritual assistance. Also called **anx′ious bench′.**

an·y (en′ē), *adj.* **1.** one, a, an, or some; one or more without specification or identification: *If you have any witnesses, produce them. Pick out any six you like.* **2.** whatever or whichever it may be: *at any price.* **3.** in whatever quantity or number, great or small; some: *Have you any butter?* **4.** every; all: *Any schoolboy would know that. Read any books you find on the subject.* **5.** (following a negative) at all: *She can't endure any criticism.* —*pron.* **6.** any unspecified person or persons; anybody; anyone: *He does better than any before him.* **7.** any single one or any ones; any unspecified thing or things; any quantity or number: *We don't have any left.* —*adv.* **8.** in whatever degree; to some extent; at all: *Do you feel any better?* [ME *eni, ani,* OE *ǣnig* (OE′ *ān* ONE + *-ig* -Y¹)]
—**Syn. 3.** See **some.**
—**Usage.** See **anyone.**

an·y·bod·y (en′ē bod′ē, -bud′ē), *pron., n., pl.* **-bod·ies.** —*pron.* **1.** any person. —*n.* **2.** a person of some importance. [ANY + BODY]

an·y·how (en′ē hou′), *adv.* **1.** in any way whatever. **2.** in any case; at all events. **3.** in a careless manner; haphazardly. [ANY + HOW]

an·y·one (en′ē wun′, -wən), *pron.* any person at all; anybody. [ANY + ONE]
—**Usage.** ANYONE, SOMEONE, and EVERYONE are accepted as either one-word or two-word forms. A convenient distinction is often made so that the one-word form means "any person" (*Is anyone home?*) while the two-word form means "any specific or single person" (*Can any one of the boys play the flute?*).

an·y·place (en′ē plās′), *adv. Informal.* anywhere. [ANY + PLACE]
—**Usage.** ANYPLACE (or, occasionally, ANY PLACE), when adverbial, is usually regarded as suitable only in informal usage: *We couldn't find the book anyplace.* Precise speakers or writers prefer ANYWHERE. The two-word form, when PLACE is a noun, is acceptable in formal usage as well: *I will go to any place you order me.* Similarly, EVERYWHERE is preferred to EVERYPLACE, NOWHERE to NOPLACE, and SOMEWHERE to SOMEPLACE.

an′y road′, *Brit. Slang.* anyway; anyhow.

an·y·thing (en′ē thiŋ′), *pron.* **1.** any thing whatever; something, no matter what. —*n.* **2.** a thing of any kind. —*adv.* **3.** in any degree; to any extent. **4. anything but,** in no degree or respect; not in the least: *The plans were anything but definite.* [ANY + THING¹]

an·y·time (en′ē tīm′), *adv.* **1.** at any time; regardless of hour, date, etc.; whenever. **2.** invariably; without doubt or exception; always: *I can do better than that anytime.* [ANY + TIME]

an·y·way (en′ē wā′), *adv.* **1.** in any way or manner. **2.** in any case; anyhow. **3.** carelessly; haphazardly: *Don't do the job just anyway.* [ANY + WAY]
—**Usage.** See **anyways.**

an·y·ways (en′ē wāz′), *adv. Chiefly Dial.* anyway. [ANYWAY + -S¹]
—**Usage.** ANYWAYS is generally not found in formal usage and only rarely in informal usage; it is a dialectal form: *Is he going to sing anyways?* It is more desirable to use ANYWAY.

an·y·where (en′ē hwâr′, -wâr′), *adv.* **1.** in, at, or to any place. **2.** to any extent; to some degree: *Does my answer come anywhere near the correct one?* **3. get anywhere,** *Informal.* to achieve success: *You'll never get anywhere with that attitude!* [ANY + WHERE]
—**Usage.** See **anyplace, anywheres.**

an·y·wheres (en′ē hwârz′, -wârz′), *adv. Chiefly Dial.* anywhere. [ANYWHERE + -S¹]
—**Usage.** ANYWHERES is a dialect form rarely found in formal or informal usage. ANYWHERE is preferred.

an·y·wise (en′ē wīz′), *adv.* in any way or respect. [ANY + -WISE²]

An·zac (an′zak), *n.* **1.** a member of the Australian and New Zealand Army Corps during World War I. **2.** a soldier from Australia or New Zealand. **3.** any Australian or New Zealander.

An·zen·gru·ber (än′tsən gro͞o′bər), *n.* **Lud·wig** (lo͞ot′viKH, lo͞od′-), 1839–89, Austrian playwright and novelist.

An·zhe·ro-Sud·zhensk (än zhe′ro so͝od zhensk′), *n.* a city in the S RSFSR, in the central Soviet Union in Asia. 116,000 (1959).

ANZUS (an′zəs), *n.* Australia, New Zealand, and the United States, esp. as associated in the mutual defense treaty (**ANZUS Pact** or **ANZUS Treaty**) of 1952.

A/O, account of. Also, **a/o**

A·oe·de (ā ē′dē), *n. Class. Myth.* one of the original three Muses; the Muse of song. Also, **A·oi·de** (ā oi′dē).

a·oi′ tsu′ba (ä oi′), a tsuba having four heart-shaped lobes, used esp. in the 12th century. [< Jap]

A-O.K. (ā′ō kā′), *adj.* O.K.; perfect: *an A-O.K. rocket launching.*

A·o·ki (ä ô′kē), *n.* **Shu·zo** (sho͞o′zô), 1844–1914, first Japanese ambassador to U.S., 1905–09.

A·o·mo·ri (ä′ô mô′rē), *n.* a seaport on N Honshu, in N Japan. 183,747 (1955).

A one (ā′ wun′), **1.** noting a vessel regarded by a shipping-classification society as being equipped to the highest standard and with equipment maintained in first-class condition. **2.** Also, **A number 1.** *Informal.* first-class; excellent; superior: *The meals there are A one.* Also, **A-one, A 1, A-1**

A·o·ran·gi (ä′ō räŋ′gē), *n.* See **Cook, Mount.**

a·o·rist (ā′ə rist), *Gram.* —*n.* **1.** a verb tense, as in Classical Greek, expressing action or, in the indicative mood, past action, without further limitation or implication. —*adj.* **2.** of or in this tense. [< Gk *aórist(os)* unlimited, equiv. to *a-* A-⁶ + *horistós* limited (*horis-* (var. s. of *horízein* to bound, limit; see HORIZON) + *-tos* ptp. suffix)]

a·o·ris·tic (ā′ə ris′tik), *adj.* **1.** *Gram.* pertaining to the aorist. **2.** indefinite; indeterminate. [AORIST + -IC] —**a′o·ris′ti·cal·ly,** *adv.*

A·or·nis (ā ôr′nis), *n. Class. Myth.* one of the five tributaries of the river Styx.

A·or·num (ā ôr′nəm), *n. Class. Myth.* the entrance through which Orpheus descended to Hades to find Eurydice.

a·or·ta (ā ôr′tə), *n., pl.* **-tas, -tae** (-tē). *Anat.* the main trunk of the arterial system, conveying blood from the left ventricle of the heart to all of the body expect the lungs. See diag. under **heart.** [< ML < Gk *aortḗ* the great artery, lit. something hung, carried; akin to *aeírein* to lift, raise, bear, carry] —**a·or′tic, a·or′tal,** *adj.*

aor′tic arch′, *Embryol.* one member of a series of paired curved blood vessels that arise in the embryo from the ventral aorta, pass around the pharynx through the branchial arches, and join with the dorsal aorta.

aor′tic insuffi′ciency, *Pathol.* abnormal closure of the aortic valve resulting in regurgitation of blood to the left ventricle. Also called **aor′tic incom′petence.**

aor′tic steno′sis, *Pathol.* abnormal narrowing of the aorta, esp. of its orifice, usually as a result of rheumatic fever or other diseases.

aor′tic valve′, *Anat.* a semilunar valve between the aorta and the left ventricle of the heart that prevents the blood from flowing back into the left ventricle.

a·or·ti·tis (ā′ôr tī′tis), *n. Pathol.* inflammation of the aorta. [< NL; see AORTA, -ITIS]

a·or·to·cla·sia (ā ôr′tə klā′zhə, -zhē ə), *n. Pathol.* rupture of the aorta. [AORT(A) + -O- + *-clasia* < Gk *klás(is),* equiv. to *klá(n)* (to) break + *-sis* -SIS + -IA]

a·or·tog·ra·phy (ā′ôr tog′rə fē), *n., pl.* **-phies.** x-ray examination of the aorta following injection of radiopaque dye. [AORT(A) + -O- + -GRAPHY]

A.O.U., American Ornithologists' Union.

a·ou·dad (ä′o͝o dad′), *n.* a wild sheep, *Ammotragus lervia,* of northern Africa, having a long fringe of hairs on the throat, chest, and forelegs. Also called **Barbary sheep.** [< F < Berber *audad*]

à ou·trance (A o͞o träNs′), *French.* to the utmost.

AP, 1. Associated Press. **2.** See **Air Police.** Also, **A.P.**

ap-¹, var. of **ad-** before *p: appear.*

an′ti·u·til′i·tar′i·an, *adj., n.* **an′ti·u·til′i·tar′i·an·ism,** *n.* **an′ti·vac′ci·na′tion,** *adj.* **an′ti·vac′ci·na′tion·ist** *n.* **an′ti·vac′cin·ist,** *n.* **an′ti·vi′ral,** *adj.* **an′ti·vi′rus,** *adj.* **an′ti·war′,** *adj.* **an′ti-Zi′on·ism,** *n.* **an′ti-Zi′on·ist,** *n., adj.*

ap-², var. of **apo-** before a vowel or *h: aphelion.*

Ap., 1. Apostle. **2.** Apothecaries'. **3.** April.

A/P, 1. account paid. **2.** accounts payable. **3.** authority to pay or purchase. Also, **a/p**

a.p., 1. additional premium. **2.** author's proof.

a·pa (ə pä′), *n.* a tree, *Eperua falcata,* of tropical America, having reddish-brown wood used in the construction of houses. [< Tupi]

APA, 1. American Psychological Association. **2.** American Psychiatric Association.

A.P.A., 1. American Philological Association. **2.** American Protestant Association. **3.** American Protestant Association. **4.** American Psychological Association. **5.** American Psychiatric Association. **6.** Associate in Public Administration.

a·pace (ə pās′), *adv.* with speed; quickly; swiftly. [ME *a pas(e)* at a (good) pace. See A-¹, PACE]

a·pache (ə päsh′, ə pash′; *Fr.* A PASH′), *n., pl.* **a·pach·es** (ə pä′shiz, ə pash′iz; *Fr.* A PASH′). a Parisian gangster or ruffian. [< F: *Apache*]

A·pach·e (ə pach′ē), *n., pl.* **A·pach·es,** (*esp. collectively*) **A·pach·e. 1.** a member of an Athapaskan people of the southwestern U.S. **2.** any of the several Athapaskan languages of Arizona and the Rio Grande basin. [< Sp, perh. < Zuñi *Apachu,* lit., enemy]

apache′ dance′, a violent dance for two people, originated by the Parisian apaches.

Ap′a·lach′ee Bay′ (ap′ə lach′ē, ap′-), a bay of the Gulf of Mexico, on the coast of NW Florida. ab. 30 mi. wide.

Ap·a·lach·i·co·la (ap′ə lach′ə kō′lə), *n.* a river flowing S from NW Florida into the Gulf of Mexico. 90 mi. long.

ap·a·nage (ap′ə nij), *n.* appanage.

a·pa·ra·vid·ya (ə pu′rä vid′yä), *n. Hinduism.* intellectual knowledge. Cf. **paravidya.** [< Skt]

a·pa·re·jo (ap′ə rā′ō, -rä′hō, ä′pə-; *Sp.* ä′pä RE′hō), *n., pl.* **-jos** (-ōz, -hōz; *Sp.* -hōs). *Spanish.* a Mexican packsaddle formed of stuffed leather cushions. [lit., preparation (i.e., equipment)]

A·par·ri (ä pär′Rē), *n.* a seaport on N Luzon, in the N Philippines. 26,409 (est. 1955).

a·part (ə pärt′), *adv.* **1.** into pieces or parts; to pieces: *to take a watch apart; falling apart from decay.* **2.** separately in place, time, motion, etc.: *New York and Tokyo are thousands of miles apart. Our birthdays are three days apart.* **3.** to or at one side, with respect to place, purpose, or function: *to put money apart for education; to keep apart from the group out of pride.* **4.** separately or individually in consideration: *each viewed apart from the other.* **5.** aside (used with a gerund or noun): *Joking apart, what do you think?* **6. apart from,** aside from; in addition to; besides: *Apart from other considerations, time is a factor.* **7. take apart, a.** to disassemble: *to take a clock apart.* **b.** to criticize; attack: *She was taken apart for her controversial stand.* **c.** to subject to intense examination: *He will take your feeble excuses apart.* —*adj.* **8.** having independent or unique qualities, features, or characteristics (usually used following the noun it modifies): *a class apart.* [ME < OF *a part* to one side. See A-⁵, PART] —**a·part′ness,** *n.*

a·part·heid (ə pärt′hāt, -hīt), *n.* (in the Republic of South Africa) racial segregation and discrimination against Negroes and others of colored descent. [< SAfrD, equiv. to *apart* APART + *-heid* -HOOD]

a·part·ment (ə pärt′mənt), *n.* **1.** a room or a combination of rooms, among similar sets in one building, designed for use as a dwelling. **2.** a building containing or made up of such rooms. **3.** any room in a house or other dwelling: *We heard cries from an apartment at the back of the house.* **4. apartments,** *Brit.* a set of rooms used as a dwelling by one person or one family. [syncopated var. of *appartiment* < ML *appartiment(um),* equiv. to *appartī(re)* (to) divide (see AP-¹, PART) + *-mentum* -MENT] —**a·part·men·tal** (ə pärt men′tᵊl), *adj.*

—**Syn. 1.** APARTMENT, COMPARTMENT agree in denoting a space enclosed by partitions or walls. APARTMENT, however, emphasizes the idea of separateness or privacy: *one's own apartment.* COMPARTMENT suggests a section of a larger space: *compartments in a ship's hold, in an orange crate.*

apart′ment hotel′, a hotel which rents furnished apartments or suites suitable for housekeeping, on a weekly or more permanent basis, and usually supplies all hotel services.

apart′ment house′, *U.S.* a building divided into a number of apartments. Also called **apart′ment build′ing.**

ap·as·tron (ə pas′trən, -tron), *n., pl.* **-tra** (-trə). *Astron.* the point at which the stars of a binary system are farthest apart (opposed to *periastron*). [< NL < Gk *ap-* AP-² + *ástron* star, constellation]

ap·a·tet·ic (ap′ə tet′ik), *adj. Zool.* assuming colors and forms which effect deceptive camouflage. [< Gk *apatētik(ós)* fallacious, equiv. to *apatē-* (var. s. of *apateúein* to deceive) + *-tikos* -TIC]

ap·a·thet·ic (ap′ə thet′ik), *adj.* **1.** having or exhibiting little or no emotion: *apathetic behavior; an apathetic face.* **2.** not interested or concerned; indifferent or unresponsive: *an apathetic audience.* Also, **ap′a·thet′i·cal.** [APATH(Y) + (PATH)ETIC] —**ap′a·thet′i·cal·ly,** *adv.*

—**Syn. 1.** unfeeling, impassive, cool. **2.** uninterested, unconcerned. —**Ant. 1.** emotional. **2.** concerned.

ap·a·thy (ap′ə thē), *n., pl.* **-thies. 1.** absence or suppression of passion, emotion, or excitement. **2.** lack of interest in or concern for things which others find moving or exciting. **3.** Also, **ap·a·thei·a, ap·a·thi·a** (ap′ə thē′ə). *Stoicism.* freedom from emotion of any kind. [< L *apathīa* < Gk *apátheia* insensibility to suffering, equiv. to *apathe-* (s. of *apathḗs*) unfeeling (*a-* A-⁶ + *pathe-* (s. of *páthos*) suffering) + *-ia* -IA]

—**Syn. 1.** coolness. **2.** indifference. —**Ant. 1.** ardor, fervor.

ap·a·tite (ap′ə tīt′), *n.* a common mineral, calcium fluophosphate, $Ca_5FP_3O_{12}$, occurring crystallized and massive, and varying in color, used in the manufacture of phosphate fertilizers. [< Gk *apát(ē)* trickery, fraud, deceit + -ITE¹]

Ap·a·tu·ri·a (ap′ə to͝or′ē ə, -tyo͝or′-), *n.* **1.** (*sometimes construed as pl.*) an annual religious festival in ancient Greece giving occasion for reunion for the members of phratries. **2.** an epithet of Athena, meaning "deceitful."

APC, 1. *Pharm.* a compound consisting of aspirin, phenacetin, and caffeine, used to relieve the pain of headache or neuralgia and the symptoms of a cold. **2.** *Facetious.* all-purpose cure. Also, **A.P.C.**

ape (āp), *n., v.,* **aped, ap·ing.** —*n.* **1.** a tailless monkey or a monkey with a very short tail. **2.** any monkey. **3.** See **anthropoid ape. 4.** an imitator; a mimic. —*v.t.* **5.** to imitate; mimic: *to ape another's style of writing.* **6. go ape over** or **for,** *U.S. Slang.* to be extremely enthusiastic over: *She goes ape over Frankie.* [ME; OE *apa;* c. OS *apo,* Icel *api,* OHG *affo* (> G *Affe*)] —**ape′like′,** *adj.*

a·peak (ə pēk′), *Naut.* —*adj.* **1.** more or less vertical. **2.** (of a dropped anchor) as nearly vertical as possible without being free of the bottom. **3.** (of an anchored vessel) having the anchor cable as nearly vertical as possible without freeing the anchor. —*adv.* **4.** vertically. Also, **a·peek′.** [A-¹ + PEAK¹]

a·pei·ron (ə pī′ron, ə pā′ron), *n.* the infinite or indeterminate matter out of which differentiated objects come into being, as in the philosophy of Anaximander. [< Gk *ápeiron* (neut. of *ápeiros* (adj.) infinite), equiv. to *a-* A-⁶ + *-peiron* deriv. of *peirat-* (s. of *peîrar* end)]

A·pel·doorn (ä′pəl dōrn′, -dôrn′), *n.* a city in the central Netherlands. 103,126 (est. 1960).

A·pel·les (ə pel′ēz), *n.* 360?–315? B.C., Greek painter.

ape·man (āp′man′), *n., pl.* **-men. 1.** a primate representing a transitional point between true man and the higher anthropoid apes. Cf. **missing link** (def. 1). **2.** a human assumed to have been reared by apes.

A·pe·mi·us (ə pē′mē əs), *n. Class. Myth.* an epithet of Zeus, meaning "averter of ills."

Ap·e·mos·y·ne (ap′ə mos′ə nē), *n. Class. Myth.* a daughter of Catreus, ravished by Hermes and unjustly killed by her brother, Althaemenes, who considered her immoral.

Ap′en·nine Moun′tains (ap′ə nīn′), **1.** a mountain range in the northern hemisphere of the face of the moon extending into the second and first quadrants, and forming the SE border of the Mare Imbrium: about 600 miles long having peaks as high as 18,500 feet. **2.** Apennines.

Ap·en·nines (ap′ə nīnz′), *n.* (*construed as pl.*) a mountain range in Italy, extending across the length of the entire peninsula from NW to SW. Highest peak, Monte Corno, 9585 ft.

A·pe·pi (ä pe′pē), *n. Egyptian Myth.* Apophis. [Egypt]

a·per·çu (A PER SY′), *n., pl.* **-çus** (-SY′). *French.* **1.** a hasty glance; a glimpse. **2.** an immediate estimate or judgment; understanding; insight. **3.** an outline or summary. [lit., perceived]

a·pe·ri·ent (ə pēr′ē ənt), *Med.* —*adj.* **1.** purgative; laxative. —*n.* **2.** a medicine or food that acts as a mild laxative. [< L *aperient-* (s. of *aperiēns* opening, prp. of *aperīre* to make open), equiv. to *a-* A-⁴ + *peri-* (var. of *pari-,* s. of *parere* to make) + *-ent-* -ENT]

a·pe·ri·od·ic (ā′pēr ē od′ik), *adj.* **1.** not periodic; irregular. **2.** *Physics.* of or pertaining to vibrations with irregular periods. [A-⁶ + PERIODIC] —**a′pe·ri·od′i·cal·ly,** *adv.* —**a·pe·ri·o·dic·i·ty** (ā pēr′ē ə dis′i tē), *n.*

a·pé·ri·tif (ä per′i tēf′, ə per′-; *Fr.* A PĀ RĒ TĒF′), *n., pl.* **-tifs** (-tēfs′; *Fr.* -TĒF′). a small drink of alcoholic liquor taken to stimulate the appetite before a meal. [< F: lit., for opening; see APERITIVE]

a·per·i·tive (ə per′i tiv), *adj., n.* aperient. [< ML *aperitīv(us),* var. of *apertīvus* < L *apert-* (see APERTURE) + *-īvus* -IVE]

ap·er·tom·e·ter (ap′ər tom′i tər), *n. Optics.* an instrument for measuring the angular and numerical aperture of the objective lens of a microscope. [APERT(URE) + -O- + -METER]

ap·er·ture (ap′ər chər), *n.* **1.** an opening, as a hole, slit, crack, gap, etc. **2.** Also called **ap′erture stop′.** *Optics.* an opening, usually circular, that limits the quantity of light that can enter an optical instrument. [< L *apertūr(a)* an opening, equiv. to *apert(us)* opened (ptp. of *aperīre*) (*a-* A-⁴ + *per-* (var. of *par-,* base of *parere* to make) + *-tus* ptp. suffix) + *-ūra* -URE] —**ap·er·tur·al** (ap′ər cho͝or′əl), *adj.* —**ap′er·tured,** *adj.*

ap′erture ra′tio, *Optics.* See **relative aperture.**

ap·er·y (ā′pə rē), *n., pl.* **-er·ies. 1.** apish behavior; mimicry. **2.** a silly trick. [APE + -ERY]

a·pet·al·ous (ā pet′ᵊləs), *adj. Bot.* having no petals. [< NL *apetalus.* See A-⁶, PETALOUS] —**a·pet′al·ous·ness, a·pet′a·ly,** *n.*

a·pex (ā′peks), *n., pl.* **a·pex·es, a·pi·ces** (ap′i sēz′, ā′pi-). **1.** the tip, point, or vertex; the summit. **2.** climax; acme: *His election to the presidency was the apex of his career.* **3.** *Astron.* See **solar apex.** [< L: conical cap; tip, point, summit]

a′pex of the sun′s′ way′, *Astron.* See **solar apex.**

aph., aphetic.

a·phaer·e·sis (ə fer′i sis), *n.* apheresis. —**aph·ae·ret·ic** (af′ə ret′ik), *adj.*

a·pha·ki·a (ə fā′kē ə), *n. Ophthalm.* absence of the crystalline lens. Also, **a·pha·cia** (ə fā′shə, -shē ə, -sē ə). [< NL < *a-* A-⁶ + Gk *phak(ós)* lentil + -IA] —**a·pha′kic, a·pha′ki·al, a·pha·cic** (ə fā′sik), **a·pha·cial** (ə fā′shəl), *adj.*

aph·a·nite (af′ə nīt′), *n. Petrog.* a fine-grained igneous rock having such compact texture that the constituent minerals cannot be detected with the naked eye. [< Gk *aphan(ḗs)* unseen, hidden, invisible (*a-* A-⁶ + *phan-,* s. of *phainein* to bring to light, disclose) + -ITE¹] —**aph·a·nit·ic** (af′ə nit′ik), *adj.* —**aph′a·nit′ism,** *n.*

Aph·a·reus (af′ə ro͞os′), *n. Class. Myth.* the grandson of Perseus.

a·pha·sia (ə fā′zhə), *n. Pathol.* impairment or loss of the faculty of using or understanding spoken or written language. [< Gk: speechlessness, equiv. to *a-* A-⁶ + *phas-* (var. s. of *phánai* to speak) + *-ia* -IA]

a·pha·si·ac (ə fā′zē ak′), *n. Pathol.* one affected with aphasia. [APHASI(A) + -AC]

a·pha·sic (ə fā′zik, -sik), *Pathol.* —*adj.* **1.** pertaining to or affected with aphasia. —*n.* **2.** an aphasiac. [APHAS(IA) + -IC]

a·phe·li·on (ə fē′lē ən, ə fēl′yən, ap hē′lē ən), *n., pl.* **a·phe·li·a** (ə fē′lē ə, ə fēl′yə, ap hē′lē ə). the point in the orbit of a planet or a comet at which it is furthest from the sun. Cf. **perihelion.** [Hellenized form of NL *aphēlium* < Gk **aphḗlion* (*diástēma*) off-sun (distance), neut. of **aphḗlios* (adj.), equiv. to *ap-* AP-² + *hḗli(os)* sun + *-os* adj. suffix. See APOGEE] —**a·phe′li·an,** *adj.*

Sun
Aphelion
Perihelion

Aphelion and perihelion

a·phe·li·o·trop·ic (ə fē′lē ə trop′ik, ap hē′-), *adj. Bot.* turning or growing away from the sun. [AP-² + HELIOTROPIC] —**a·phe′li·o·trop′i·cal·ly,** *adv.*

a·phe·li·ot·ro·pism (ə fē′lē o′trə piz′əm, ap hē′lē-), *n.* apheliotropic tendency or type of growth. [APHELIOTROP(IC) + -ISM]

a·phe·mi·a (ə fē′mē ə), *n. Med.* a type of aphasia characterized by the inability to express ideas in spoken words. [< NL < Gk *a-* A-⁶ + *phḗm(ē)* speech + *-ia* -IA]

a·pher·e·sis (ə fer′i sis), *n.* the loss or omission of one or more letters or sounds at the beginning of a word, as in *squire* for *esquire,* or *count* for *account.* Also, **aphaeresis.** [< L *aphaeresis* < Gk *aphaíresis* a taking away, equiv to *aphairé(ein)* (to) take away (*ap-* AP-² + *hairéein* to snatch) + *-sis* -SIS] —**aph·e·ret·ic** (af′ə ret′ik), *adj.*

aph·e·sis (af′i sis), *n. Historical Ling.* the disappearance or loss of an unstressed initial vowel or syllable. [< Gk *áphesis* a letting go, equiv. to *aphe-* (var. s. of *aphiénai* to let go, set free: *ap-* AP-² + *hiénai* to send) + *-sis* -SIS]

A·phe·si·us (ə fē′shē əs, -shəs), *n. Class. Myth.* an epithet of Zeus, meaning "releaser," referring to the time he released all of Greece from a prolonged drought.

a·phet·ic (ə fet′ik), *adj.* pertaining to or due to aphesis. [< Gk *áphet(os)* freed, discharged (*aphe-* (see APHESIS) + *-tos* ptp. suffix) + -IC] —**a·phet′i·cal·ly,** *adv.*

a·phid (ā′fid, af′id), *n.* any of numerous soft-bodied homopterous insects of the family *Aphididae* that suck the sap from the stems and leaves of various plants. Also called **plant louse.** [back formation from APHIDES, pl. of APHIS] —**a·phid·i·an** (ə fid′ē ən), *adj., n.* —**a·phid′i·ous,** *adj.*

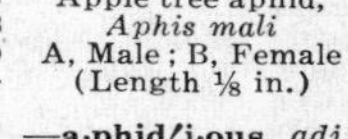

Apple tree aphid, *Aphis mali* A, Male; B, Female (Length ⅛ in.)

A·phi·das (ə fī′dəs), *n. Class. Myth.* a son of Arcas who ruled Tegea: the father of Aleus.

a·phid·li·on (ā′fid lī′ən, af′id-), *n.* the larva of a lacewing, usually predaceous on aphids. Also, **a′phid li′on, a′phid·li′on, a·phis·li·on** (ā′fis lī′ən, af′is-), **a′phis li′on, a′phis·li′on.** [APHID + LION]

a·phis (ā′fis, af′is), *n., pl.* **aph·i·des** (af′i dēz′). an aphid. [< NL; coined by Linnaeus]

a·phlas·ton (ə flas′ton), *n. Naut.* aplustre. [< Homeric Gk]

a·pho·ni·a (ā fō′nē ə), *n. Pathol.* loss of voice due to an organic or functional disturbance of the vocal organs. [< NL < Gk: speechlessness. See A-⁶, PHON-, -IA]

a·phon·ic (ā fon′ik), *adj.* **1.** mouthed but not spoken; noiseless; silent. **2.** *Phonet.* **a.** lacking phonation; unvoiced. **b.** without voice; voiceless **3.** *Pathol.* affected with aphonia. —*n.* **4.** *Pathol.* one affected with aphonia. [< Gk *áphōn(os)* voiceless (see APHONIA) + -IC]

aph·o·rise (af′ə rīz′), *v.i.,* **-rised, -ris·ing.** *Chiefly Brit.* aphorize. —**aph′o·ris′er,** *n.*

aph·o·rism (af′ə riz′əm), *n.* a terse saying embodying a general truth, as "Art is long, and life is short." [< ML *aphorism(us)* < Gk *aphorismós* definition, equiv. to *aphor(ízein)* (to) define (see APHORIZE) + *-ismos* -ISM] —**aph′o·ris′mic, aph·o·ris·mat·ic** (af′ə riz mat′ik), *adj.*

aph·o·rist (af′ə rist), *n.* one who makes or uses aphorisms. [APHOR(IZE) + -IST]

aph·o·ris·tic (af′ə ris′tik), *adj.* **1.** of, like, or containing aphorisms: *His sermons were richly aphoristic.* **2.** given to making or quoting aphorisms. [< Gk *aphoristik(ós).* See APHORIST, -IC] —**aph′o·ris′ti·cal·ly,** *adv.*

aph·o·rize (af′ə rīz′), *v.i.,* **-rized, -riz·ing.** to utter aphorisms; write or speak in aphorisms. Also, *esp. Brit.,* **aphorise.** [< Gk *aphoríz(ein)* (to) mark off, define, determine, equiv. to *ap-* AP-² + *horízein* to limit, define; see HORIZON] —**aph′o·riz′er,** *n.*

a·pho·tic (ā fō′tik), *adj.* lightless; dark. [A-⁶ + PHOTIC]

aph·ro·di·sia (af′rə dizh′ə, -diz′ē ə), *n.* sexual desire. [< NL < Gk, neut. pl. of *aphrodísios* of Aphrodite. See APHRODISIAC]

aph·ro·dis·i·ac (af′rə diz′ē ak′), *adj.* **1.** arousing sexual desire. —*n.* **2.** an aphrodisiac agent, as a drug. [< Gk *aphrodisiak(ós)* relating to love or desire, equiv. to *aphrodísi(os)* of Aphrodite + *-akos* -AC]

Aph·ro·di·te (af′rə dī′tē), *n.* the ancient Greek goddess of love and beauty, identified by the Romans with Venus. Also called **Anadyomene, Cytherea.**

Aphrodi′te of Me′los. See **Venus de Milo.**

Aph·ro·ge·nei·a (af′rō jə nī′ə), *n. Class. Myth.* an epithet of Aphrodite, meaning "foam-born."

aph′thous fe′ver (af′thəs, ap′thəs). See **foot-and-mouth disease.** [< medical L *apth(æ)* thrush (< Gk *áphthai,* pl. of *áphtha* spot, speck) + -OUS]

a·phyl·lous (ā fil′əs), *adj. Bot.* naturally leafless. [< NL *aphyllus* < Gk *áphyllos* leafless. See A-⁶, -PHYLLOUS] —**a′phyl·ly,** *n.*

API, American Petroleum Institute. Also, **A.P.I.**

A·pi·a (ä pē′ä, ä′pē ä′), *n.* a seaport in and the capital of Western Samoa, on N Upolu. 16,000 (est. 1955).

a·pi·a·ceous (ā′pē ā′shəs), *adj.* pertaining to the umbelliferous plants of the genus *Apium,* as parsley, celery, etc. [< NL *Api(ācíae)* plant family name (L *api(um)* celery + *-āceae* -ACEAE) + -ACEOUS]

a·pi·an (ā′pē ən), *adj.* of or pertaining to bees. [< L *apiān(us)* equiv. to *api(s)* a bee + *-ānus* -AN]

Ap·i·a·nus (ap′ē ā′nəs, -ä′nəs), *n.* a crater in the fourth quadrant of the face of the moon: about 39 miles in diameter.

a·pi·ar·i·an (ā′pē âr′ē ən), *adj.* relating to bees or to the breeding and care of bees. [APIARY + -AN]

a·pi·a·rist (ā′pē ə rist), *n.* one who keeps an apiary. [APIAR(Y) + -IST]

a·pi·ar·y (ā′pē er′ē), *n., pl.* **-ar·ies.** a place in which a colony or colonies of bees are kept; a stand or shed for beehives; a bee house containing a number of beehives. [< L *apiārium* a beehive, equiv. to *api(s)* a bee + *-ārium* -ARY]

ap·i·cad (ap′ə kad′), *adv. Rare.* toward the apex. [< L *apic-* (s. of *apex*) APEX + *ad* to, toward]

ap·i·cal (ap′i kəl, ā′pi-), *adj.* **1.** of, at, or forming the apex. **2.** *Phonet.* (of a speech sound) articulated principally with the aid of the tip of the tongue, as *t, d,* etc. —*n.* **3.** *Phonet.* an apical sound. [< L *apic-* (s. of *apex*) APEX + -AL[1]] —**ap′i·cal·ly,** *adv.*

ap′ical mer′istem, meristem at the apex of a root or shoot.

ap·i·ces (ap′i sēz′, ā′pi-), *n.* a pl. of **apex.**

a·pic·u·late (ə pik′yə lit, -lāt′), *adj. Bot.* tipped with a short, abrupt point, as a leaf. [< NL *apiculāt(us).* See APICULUS, -ATE[1]]

a·pi·cul·ture (ā′pə kul′chər), *n.* beekeeping, esp. on a commercial scale for the sale of honey. [< L *api(s)* bee + CULTURE] —**a′pi·cul′tur·al,** *adj.* —**a′pi·cul′tur·ist,** *n.*

a·pic·u·lus (ə pik′yə ləs, ā pik′-), *n., pl.* **-li** (-lī′). *Bot.* a small point or tip. [< L, equiv. to *apic-* (s. of *apex*) APEX + *-ulus* -ULE]

a·piece (ə pēs′), *adv.* for each piece, thing, or person; for each one; each: *We ate an orange apiece. The cakes cost a dollar apiece.* [ME *a pece.* See A[2], PIECE]

à pied (A pyā′), *French.* afoot; walking; on foot.

a·pi·ol·o·gy (ā′pē ol′ə jē), *n.* the scientific study of bees, esp. honeybees. [< L *api(s)* bee + -O- + -LOGY] —**a′pi·ol′o·gist,** *n.*

A·pis (ā′pis), *n.* **1.** Also called **Hapi, Hap.** *Egyptian Religion.* a sacred bull worshiped at Memphis: identified originally with Ptah and later assimilated with Osiris to form the Ptolemaic Serapis. **2.** *Class. Myth.* **a.** a son of Phoroneus. **b.** a son of Apollo who drove all the serpents out of Argos.

ap·ish (ā′pish), *adj.* **1.** having the qualities, appearance, or ways of an ape. **2.** slavishly imitative. **3.** foolishly affected. [APE + -ISH[1]] —**ap′ish·ly,** *adv.* —**ap′ish·ness,** *n.*

a·piv·or·ous (ā piv′ər əs), *adj. Zool.* feeding on bees, as certain birds. [< L *api(s)* bee + -VOROUS]

Apl., April.

a·pla·cen·tal (ā′plə sen′tᵊl, ap′lə-), *adj. Zool.* not placental; having or forming no placenta, as the lowest mammals. [A-[6] + PLACENTAL]

ap·la·nat·ic (ap′lə nat′ik), *adj. Optics.* free from spherical aberration and coma. [A-[6] + Gk *planá(ein)* (to) wander + -TIC. See PLANET] —**ap′la·nat′i·cal·ly,** *adv.*

a·plan·o·gam·ete (ā plan′ə gə mēt′, ā plan′ə gə mēt′, ā′plan ə gam′ēt), *n. Bot., Zool.* a nonmotile gamete. [< Gk *aplan(ḗs)* unmoving (see A-[6], PLANET) + -O- + GAMETE]

a·plan·o·spore (ā plan′ə spôr′, -spōr′), *n.* (in certain algae and fungi) a nonmotile, asexual spore formed within a cell, the wall of which is distinct from that of the parent cell. Cf. **akinete.** [*aplano-* (see APLANOGAMETE) + SPORE]

a·pla·sia (ə plā′zhə), *n. Pathol.* defective development or congenital absence of an organ or tissue. [A-[6] + -PLASIA] —**a·plas·tic** (ā plas′tik), *adj.*

aplas′tic ane′mia, *Pathol.* severe anemia due to destruction or depressed functioning of the bone marrow, with no regenerative hyperplasia. [A-[6] + -PLASTIC]

a·plen·ty (ə plen′tē), *Informal.* —*adj.* **1.** in sufficient quantity; in generous amounts (usually used following the noun it modifies): *He had troubles aplenty.* —*adv.* **2.** sufficiently; enough; more than sparingly: *He howled aplenty when hurt.* Also, **a-plen′ty.** [A-[1] + PLENTY]

ap·lite (ap′līt), *n.* a fine-grained granite composed essentially of feldspar and quartz. Also, **haplite.** [*apl-* (var. of HAPLO-) + ITE[1]] —**ap·lit·ic** (ap lit′ik), *adj.*

a·plomb (ə plom′, ə plum′), *n.* **1.** imperturbable self-possession, poise, or assurance. **2.** the perpendicular, or vertical, position. [< F *à plomb* according to the plummet, i.e., straight up and down, vertical position]

a·plus·tre (ə plus′trē), *n. Naut.* an ornamental termination for the stern of any of various ancient Mediterranean vessels. Also called **aphlaston.** Cf. **acroterium** (def. 2). [< L, prob. < Etruscan < Gk *áphlaston*]

ap·ne·a (ap nē′ə, ap′nē ə), *n. Pathol.* **1.** temporary suspension of respiration. **2.** asphyxia. Also, **ap·noe′a.** [< NL *apnoea* < Gk *ápnoia,* equiv. to *ápno(os)* breathless (*a-* A-[6] + *pno-,* var. s. of *pneîn* to breathe + *-os* adj. suffix) + *-ia* -IA] —**ap·ne′al, ap·ne′ic, ap·noe′al, ap·noe′ic,** *adj.*

ap·neus·tic (ap nōō′stik, -nyōō′-), *adj. Entomol.* having no open spiracles, as the tracheal systems of certain aquatic insect larvae. [A-[6] + Gk *pneustik(ós)* pertaining to breathing, equiv. to **pneust(os)* (verbid of *pneîn* to breathe) + *-ikos* -IC]

A·po (ä′pô), *n.* an active volcano in the S Philippines, on S Mindanao: highest peak in the Philippines. 9690 ft.

apo-, a learned borrowing from Greek, occurring in direct loan words where the meaning is usually no longer clear (*apodosis*) and with the meaning "away," "different from," as an element in the formation of compound words (*apomorphine; apogeotropism*). Also, *esp. before a vowel,* **ap-**[2]. [< Gk, comb. form of *apó;* akin to Skt *apa,* L *ab,* OFF]

A.P.O., Army Post Office. Also, **APO**

Apoc., **1.** Apocalypse. **2.** Apocrypha. **3.** Apocryphal.

a·poc·a·lypse (ə pok′ə lips), *n.* **1.** See **Revelation of St. John the Divine. 2.** any of a class of Jewish or Christian writings that appeared from about 200 B.C. to A.D. 350 and were assumed to make revelations of the ultimate divine purpose. **3.** revelation; discovery; disclosure. [ME < LL *apocalyps(is)* < Gk *apokálypsis* revelation, equiv. to *apokalýp(tein)* to uncover, reveal (*apo-* APO- + *kalýptein* to cover, conceal) + *-sis* -SIS]

a·poc·a·lyp·tic (ə pok′ə lip′tik), *adj.* **1.** of or like an apocalypse; affording a revelation or prophecy. **2.** pertaining to the Apocalypse or biblical book of Revelations. **3.** presaging imminent disaster and total or universal destruction: *the apocalyptic vision of some contemporary writers.* Also, **a·poc′a·lyp′ti·cal.** [< LGk *apokalyptik(ós),* equiv. to *apokalýpt(ein)* (to) uncover, disclose (see APOCALYPSE) + *-ikos* -IC] —**a·poc′a·lyp′ti·cal·ly,** *adv.*

a·poc·a·lyp·ti·cism (ə pok′ə lip′ti siz′əm), *n. Theol.* **1.** any doctrine concerning the end of the temporal world, esp. one that is based on the supposed prophetic passages in the Revelations of St. John the Divine. **2.** the millennial doctrine of the Second Advent and personal reign of Jesus Christ on earth. [APOCALYPTIC + -ISM]

ap·o·carp (ap′ə kärp′), *n. Bot.* a gynoecium having separate carpels. [APO- + -CARP]

ap·o·car·pous (ap′ə kär′pəs), *adj. Bot.* having the carpels separate. [APO- + -CARPOUS] —**ap′o·car′py,** *n.*

Apocarpous
C, Carpels

ap·o·ca·tas·ta·sis (ap′ō kə tas′tə sis), *n.* **1.** state of being restored or reestablished; restitution. **2.** the doctrine that Satan and all sinners will ultimately be restored to God. Also, **apokatastasis.** Cf. **universalism** (def. 3). [< L < Gk: a setting up again. See APO-, CATASTASIS] —**ap·o·cat·a·stat·ic** (ap′ə kat′ə stat′ik), *adj.*

ap·o·cen·ter (ap′ə sen′tər), *n. Astron.* the point in the orbit of a heavenly body furthest from a primary other than the earth or the sun. Cf. **pericenter.** [APO- + CENTER] —**ap′o·cen′tric,** *adj.* —**ap·o·cen·tric·i·ty** (ap′ə sen tris′i tē), *n.*

ap·o·chro·mat·ic (ap′ə krō mat′ik, -ō krə-), *adj. Optics.* corrected for spherical aberration at two wave lengths or colors and for chromatic aberration at three wave lengths. [APO- + CHROMATIC] —**ap·o·chro·ma·tism** (ap′ə krō′mə tiz′əm), *n.*

a·poc·o·pate (ə pok′ə pāt′), *v.t.,* **-pat·ed, -pat·ing.** to shorten by apocope. [v. use of *apocopate* (adj.) curtailed, docked. See APOCOPE, -ATE[1]] —**a·poc′o·pa′tion,** *n.*

a·poc·o·pe (ə pok′ə pē), *n.* loss or omission of the last letter, syllable, or part of a word. [< LL < Gk *apokopḗ* a cutting off, equiv. to *apokóp(tein)* (to) cut off (*apo-* APO- + *kóptein* to cut) + *-ē* n. suffix] —**ap·o·cop·ic** (ap′ə kop′ik), *adj.*

a·poc·ry·pha (ə pok′rə fə), *n.* (*often construed as sing.*) **1.** (*cap.*) a group of 14 books, not considered canonical, included in the Septuagint and the Vulgate as part of the Old Testament, but usually omitted from Protestant editions of the Bible. **2.** various religious writings of uncertain origin regarded by some as inspired, but rejected by most authorities. **3.** works of doubtful authorship or authenticity. Cf. **canon**[1] (defs. 6, 7, 9). [ME < LL < Gk, neut. pl. of *apókryphos* hidden, unknown, spurious, equiv. to *apokryph-* (var. s. of *apokrýptein* to hide away; see APO-, CRYPT) + *-os* adj. suffix]

a·poc·ry·phal (ə pok′rə fəl), *adj.* **1.** of doubtful authorship or authenticity. **2.** *Eccles.* **a.** (*cap.*) of or pertaining to the Apocrypha. **b.** of doubtful sanction; uncanonical. **3.** false; spurious: *He told an apocryphal story about the sword, but the truth was later revealed.* [APOCRYPH(A) + -AL[1]] —**a·poc′ry·phal·ly,** *adv.* —**a·poc′ry·phal·ness,** *n.*

a·poc·y·na·ceous (ə pos′ə nā′shəs), *adj.* belonging to the *Apocynaceae,* or dogbane family, which includes the dogbane, periwinkle, oleander, and various other plants, mostly tropical, some having medicinal and industrial uses. [< NL *Apocyn(um)* genus name (< Gk *apókynon* dogbane: *apo-* APO- + *kyn-* (s. of *kýōn*) dog, + *-on* n. suffix) + -ACEOUS]

ap·o·dal (ap′ə dᵊl), *adj. Zool.* **1.** having no distinct feet or footlike members. **2.** belonging or pertaining to the orders *Apoda* and *Apodes,* comprising various groups of animals without limbs. Also, **apodous.** [< Gk *apod-,* s. of *ápous* footless (see A-[6], -POD) + -AL[1]]

a·po·deip·non (ä pô ᵺēp′nôn; *Eng.* ap′ə dīp′non), *n., pl.* **-deip·na** (-ᵺēp′nä; *Eng.* -dīp′nə). *Gk. Orth. Ch.* complin. [< MGk; Gk *apo-* APO- + *deîpnon* meal]

a·pod·e·ma (ə pod′ə mə), *n., pl.* **a·pod·e·mas, ap·o·dem·a·ta** (ap′ə dem′ə tə) apodeme.

ap·o·deme (ap′ə dēm′), *n.* a ridgelike ingrowth of the exoskeleton of an arthropod which forms the endoskeleton and provides the attachment points for the muscles. [< NL *apodema,* equiv. to *apo-* APO- + *-dema* < Gk *dêma(s)* body] —**a·pod·e·mal** (ə pod′ə məl), **ap·o·dem·a·tal** (ap′ə dem′ə tᵊl), *adj.*

ap·o·dic·tic (ap′ə dik′tik), *adj.* **1.** incontestable because demonstrated or demonstrable. **2.** *Logic.* (of a proposition) necessarily true or logically certain. Also, **ap·o·deic·tic** (ap′ə dīk′tik), **ap′o·dic′ti·cal.** [< L *apodīctic(us)* < Gk *apodeiktikós* proving fully. See APO-, DEICTIC] —**ap′o·dic′ti·cal·ly, ap′o·deic′ti·cal·ly,** *adv.*

a·pod·o·sis (ə pod′ə sis), *n., pl.* **-ses** (-sēz′). the clause expressing the consequence in a conditional sentence, often beginning with *then,* as "then I will" in "If you go, then I will." Cf. **protasis** (def. 1). [< LL < Gk: a returning, answering clause, equiv. to *apo(di)dó(nai)* to give back (*apo-* APO- + *didónai* to give) + *-sis* -SIS]

ap·o·dous (ap′ə dəs), *adj.* apodal. [APOD(AL) + -OUS]

ap·o·en·zyme (ap′ō en′zīm), *n. Biochem.* the protein component that with a coenzyme forms a complete enzyme. [APO- + ENZYME]

ap·o·fer·ri·tin (ap′ō fer′i tin), *n. Biochem.* a homogeneous protein, found esp. in the intestinal mucosa and the liver, that interacts with a ferric hydroxide-ferric phosphate complex to form ferritin. [APO- + FERRITIN]

a·pog·a·my (ə pog′ə mē), *n. Bot.* the development of a sporophyte from a cell or cells of the gametophyte other than the egg. [APO- + -GAMY] —**ap·o·gam·ic** (ap′ə gam′ik), **a·pog′a·mous,** *adj.* —**ap′o·gam′i·cal·ly, a·pog′a·mous·ly,** *adv.*

ap·o·gee (ap′ə jē′), *n.* **1.** *Astron.* the point in the orbit of a heavenly body, esp. the moon, or of a man-made satellite at which it is furthest from the earth. Cf. **perigee. 2.** the highest or most distant point; climax. [alter. (after F *apogée*) of earlier *apogaeum* < L < Gk *apógaion* (*diástema*) off-earth (distance), neut. of *apógaios* adj., equiv. to *apo-* APO- + *gâios* of the earth, deriv. of *gaîa,* var. of *gê* the earth] —**ap′o·ge′al, ap′o·ge′an, ap′o·ge′ic,** *adj.*

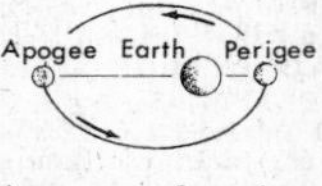

Apogee and perigee

ap·o·ge·ot·ro·pism (ap′ə jē o′trə piz′əm), *n. Bot.* growth or orientation away from the earth; negative geotropism. [APO- + GEOTROPISM] —**ap·o·ge·o·trop·ic** (ap′ə jē′ə trop′ik), *adj.* —**ap′o·ge′o·trop′i·cal·ly,** *adv.*

ap·o·graph (ap′ə graf′, -gräf′), *n.* transcript (defs. 1, 2). [< L *apograph(on)* < Gk *apógraphon,* n. use of neut. of *apógraph(os)* (adj.) copied. See APO-, -GRAPH] —**ap·o·graph·ic** (ap′ə graf′ik), **ap′o·graph′i·cal,** *adj.*

à point (A pwaN′), *French.* **1.** just in time. **2.** (of cooking) to a turn; perfectly.

ap·o·ka·tas·ta·sis (ap′ō kə tas′tə sis), *n.* apocatastasis. —**ap·o·kat·a·stat·ic** (ap′ə kat′ə stat′ik), *adj.*

A-pole (ā′pōl′), *n.* a wooden A-frame.

a·po·lit·i·cal (ā′pə lit′i kəl), *adj.* **1.** unconcerned with or uninterested in politics or political problems. **2.** lacking political influence or effect. [A-[6] + POLITICAL] —**a′po·lit′i·cal·ly,** *adv.*

A·pol·li·naire (A pô lē ner′), *n.* **Guil·laume** (gē yōm′), (*Wilhelm Apollinaris de Kostrowitzki*), 1880–1918, French poet, novelist, and dramatist.

A·pol·lo (ə pol′ō), *n., pl.* **-los** for 2, 3. **1.** the ancient Greek and Roman god of light, healing, music, poetry, prophecy, and manly beauty; the son of Leto and brother of Artemis. **2.** a very handsome young man. **3.** *U.S.* a three-man spacecraft designed to travel to and land on the moon. **4.** a town in central Pennsylvania. 2694 (1960).

Apollo

Apol′lo Belvedere′, a Roman marble statue, possibly a copy of a Greek original of the 4th–1st centuries B.C.

Ap·ol·lo·ni·an (ap′ə lō′nē ən), *adj.* **1.** pertaining to the cult of Apollo. **2.** (*l.c.*) serene, calm, or well-balanced; poised and disciplined. **3.** (*l.c.*) having the properties of or preferring classic beauty. **4.** *Anthropol.* orderly, sober, and conservative in character: *the Apollonian social order found among some American Indian peoples.* Cf. **Dionysian.** [< Gk *apollṓni(os)* of APOLLO + -AN]

Ap·ol·lo·ni·us (ap′ə lō′nē əs), *n.* a crater in the first quadrant of the face of the moon: about 30 miles in diameter.

A·pol·lyon (ə pol′yən), *n.* the destroyer; the angel of the bottomless pit; Abaddon. Rev. 9:11. [< Gk *apollýōn* (prp. of *apollýnai* to utterly destroy), equiv. to *ap-* AP-[2] + *olly-* destroy + *-ōn* prp. suffix]

a·pol·o·gete (ə pol′ə jēt′), *n.* apologist (def. 2a). [back formation from APOLOGETIC]

a·pol·o·get·ic (ə pol′ə jet′ik), *adj.* **1.** containing an apology or excuse for a fault, failure, insult, injury, etc.: *An apologetic letter to his creditors explained the delay.* **2.** defending by speech or writing. **3.** willing or eager to apologize. **4.** sorry; regretful. Also, **a·pol′o·get′i·cal.** [< L *apologētic(us)* < Gk *apologētikós* fit for defense, equiv. to *apologē-* (verbid s. of *apologeîsthai* to speak in defense; see APOLOGIA) + *-tikos* -TIC] —**a·pol′o·get′i·cal·ly,** *adv.*

a·pol·o·get·ics (ə pol′ə jet′iks), *n.* (*construed as sing.*) the branch of theology concerned with the defense or proof of Christianity. [see APOLOGETIC, -ICS]

ap·o·lo·gi·a (ap′ə lō′jē ə), *n.* **1.** an apology, as in defense or justification. **2.** *Literature.* a work written as an explanation or justification of one's motives, convictions, or acts. [< LL < Gk: a speaking in defense. See APO-, LOG-, -IA]

Ap·o·lo·gi·a pro Vi·ta Su·a (ap′ə lō′jē ə prō vī′tə sōō′ə), a religious autobiography (1864) of Cardinal John Henry Newman.

A·pol′o·gie for Po′e·trie (ə pol′ə jē; pō′i trē), an essay (1580?) by Sir Philip Sidney, published in 1595. Also called **Defence of Poesie.**

a·pol·o·gise (ə pol′ə jīz′), *v.i.,* **-gised, -gis·ing.** *Chiefly Brit.* apologize. —**a·pol′o·gis′er,** *n.*

a·pol·o·gist (ə pol′ə jist), *n.* **1.** one who makes an apology or defense in speech or writing. **2.** *Eccles.* **a.** Also, **apologete.** one skilled in apologetics. **b.** one of the authors of the early Christian apologies in defense of the faith. [APOLOG(Y) + -IST]

a·pol·o·gize (ə pol′ə jīz′), *v.i.,* **-gized, -giz·ing. 1.** to offer an apology or excuse for some fault, insult, failure, or injury: *He apologized for accusing her falsely.* **2.** to make a formal defense in speech or writing. Also, *esp. Brit.,* **apologise.** [APOLOG(Y) + -IZE] —**a·pol′o·giz′er,** *n.*

ap·o·logue (ap′ə lôg′, -log′), *n.* **1.** a didactic narrative; a moral fable. **2.** an allegory. [< L *apolog(us)* < Gk *apólogos* fable. See APO-, -LOGUE] —**ap′o·log′al,** *adj.*

a·pol·o·gy (ə pol′ə jē), *n., pl.* **-gies. 1.** a written or spoken expression of one's regret, remorse, or sorrow for having insulted, failed, injured, or wronged another. **2.** a defense, excuse, or justification in speech or writing, as for a cause or doctrine. **3.** (*cap., italics.*) a dialogue by Plato, centering on Socrates' defense before the tribunal which condemned him to death. **4.** a poor specimen or substitute; makeshift: *The tramp wore a sad apology for a hat.* [earlier *apologie* < LL *apologia* < Gk; see APOLOGIA]
—**Syn. 1.** plea. **2.** vindication, defense. See **excuse.**

ap·o·lune (ap′ə lōōn′), *n.* the point in a lunar orbit that is farthest from the moon. [APO- + *lune* < L *lūna* moon]

ap·o·mict (ap′ə mikt), *n.* an organism produced by apomixis. [back formation from APOMICT(IC)]

ap·o·mic·tic (ap′ə mik′tik), *adj.* of or pertaining to an apomict or to apomixis. Also, **ap′o·mic′ti·cal.** [APO- + Gk *mikt(ós)* mixed + -IC] —**ap′o·mic′ti·cal·ly,** *adv.*

ap·o·mix·is (ap′ə mik′sis), *n., pl.* **-mix·es** (-mik′sēz). any of several types of asexual reproduction, as apogamy or parthenogenesis. [< NL < Gk *apo-* APO- + *mixis* a mixing, equiv. to *mig(nýnai)* to mix + *-sis* -SIS]

ap·o·mor·phine (ap′ə môr′fēn, -fin), *n. Pharm.* a crystalline alkaloid, $C_{17}H_{17}NO_2$, derived from morphine: used, usually in the form of its hydrochloride, as an emetic and expectorant. Also, **ap·o·mor·phin** (ap′ə-môr′fin). [APO- + MORPHINE]

Ap·o·my·i·us (ap′ə mī′ē əs), *n. Class. Myth.* an epithet of Zeus, meaning "averter of flies," in reference to his freeing Elis from the pestilence brought on by flies.

ap·o·neu·ro·sis (ap′ə nŏŏ rō′sis, -nyŏŏ-), *n., pl.* **-ses** (-sēz). *Anat.* a whitish, fibrous membrane formed by the expansion of a tendon. [< Gk *aponeúrōsis* the part of a muscle becoming a tendon, equiv. to *aponeur(oein)* to change to tendon (see APO-, NEURO-) + *-ōsis* -OSIS] —**ap·o·neu·rot·ic** (ap′ə nŏŏ rot′ik, -nyŏŏ-), *adj.*

ap·o·pemp·tic (ap′ə pemp′tik), *adj.* **1.** pertaining to leave-taking or departing; valedictory. —*n.* **2.** *Obs.* a farewell address; valedictory. [< Gk *apopemptik(ós)* of, pertaining to sending away, equiv. to *apopémp(ein)* to send away, dismiss (*apo-* APO- + *pémpein* to send, dispatch) + *-tikos* -TIC]

a·poph·a·sis (ə pof′ə sis), *n. Rhet.* denial of one's intention to speak of a subject which is at the same time named or insinuated, as "I shall not mention Caesar's avarice, nor his cunning, nor his morality." [< LL < Gk: a denial, equiv. to *apóphanai* to say no, deny (*apo-* APO- + *phánai* to say) + *-sis* -SIS]

A·po·phis (ə pō′fis), *n. Egyptian Myth.* a demon serpent of darkness whom Ra, as sun god, destroys every morning at dawn. Also, **Apepi.**

a·poph·o·ny (ə pof′ə nē), *n., pl.* **-nies.** ablaut. [APO- + -PHONY] —**ap·o·phon·ic** (ap′ə fon′ik), *adj.*

ap·o·phthegm (ap′ə them′), *n.* apothegm. —**ap·o·phtheg·mat·ic** (ap′ə theg mat′ik), **ap′o·phtheg·mat′i·cal,** *adj.*

a·poph·y·ge (ə pof′i jē′), *n. Archit.* **1.** a small, concave, outward curve joining the shaft of a column, esp. a classical column, to its base. **2.** Also called **hypophyge.** a similar curve joining the shaft of a column to its capital. Also, **apophysis.** [< Gk: escape, apophyge, equiv. to *aphophyg-* (var. s. of *apopheúgein* to flee away: *apo-* APO- + *pheúgein* to flee; akin to -FUGE) + *-ē* n. suffix]

a·poph·yl·lite (ə pof′ə līt′, ap′ə fil′īt), *n.* a hydrous potassium and calcium silicate mineral occurring in white crystals. [APO- + -PHYLL + -ITE¹]

a·poph·y·sis (ə pof′i sis), *n., pl.* **-ses** (-sēz′). **1.** *Anat., Bot.* an outgrowth; process; projection or protuberance. **2.** *Archit.* apophyge. [< NL < Gk: offshoot, equiv. to *apo-* APO- + *phýsis* growth: *phý(ein)* to bring forth + *-sis* -SIS] —**a·poph·y·sate** (ə pof′i sit, -sāt′), *adj.* —**ap·o·phys·e·al, ap·o·phys·i·al** (ap′ə fiz′ē əl), **a·poph·y·sar·y** (ə pof′i ser′ē), *adj.*

ap·o·plec·tic (ap′ə plek′tik), *adj.* Also, **ap′o·plec′ti·cal. 1.** of or pertaining to apoplexy. **2.** having or inclined to apoplexy. —*n.* **3.** a person having or predisposed to apoplexy. [< LL *apoplēctic(us)* < Gk *apoplēktikós* pertaining to a (paralytic) stroke, equiv. to *apóplēkt(os)* struck down (verbal of *apoplḗssein;* see APOPLEXY) + *-ikos* -IC] —**ap′o·plec′ti·cal·ly,** *adv.*

ap·o·plex·y (ap′ə plek′sē), *n. Pathol.* **1.** a sudden, usually marked loss of bodily function due to rupture or occlusion of a blood vessel. **2.** hemorrhage into the tissue of any organ, esp. the brain. [ME *apoplexia* < LL < Gk, equiv. to *apoplēk-* (var. s. of *apoplḗssein* to strike down) + *-s(is)* -SIS + *-ia* -Y³] —**ap·o·plec·ti·form** (ap′ə plek′tə fôrm′), **ap′o·plec′toid,** *adj.*

ap·o·pyle (ap′ə pīl′), *n. Zool.* (in sponges) a pore in each of the saclike chambers formed by the evagination of the body wall, through which water passes into the excurrent canals. Cf. **prosopyle.** [APO- + Gk *pýlē* gate, entrance; see PYLON]

a·po·ri·a (ə pôr′ē ə, ə pōr′-), *n., pl.* **a·po·ri·as, a·po·ri·ae** (ə pôr′ē ē′, ə pōr′-). **1.** *Rhet.* the expression of a simulated or real doubt, as about where to begin or what to do or say. **2.** *Logic, Philos.* a difficulty encountered in establishing the theoretical truth of a proposition, created by the presence of evidence both for and against it. [< LL < Gk: state of being at a loss, equiv. to *ápor(os)* impassable (see A-⁶, PORE²) + *-ia* -IA]

a·port (ə pôrt′, ə pōrt′), *adv. Naut.* upon or toward the port side. [A-¹ + PORT²]

a·port·last (ə pôrt′ləst, ə pōrt′-), *adv. Naut. Obs.* at anchor with the lower yards lowered to the bulwarks, as in heavy weather; aportoise. [(*down*) a portlast < ?]

a·port·oise (ə pôr′tiz, ə pōr′-), *adv. Naut. Obs.* aportlast.

ap·o·se·mat·ic (ap′ə sə mat′ik), *adj. Zool.* colored or constructed so as to indicate special capabilities for defense. [APO- + SEMATIC] —**ap′o·se·mat′i·cal·ly,** *adv.*

ap·o·si·o·pe·sis (ap′ə sī′ə pē′sis), *n., pl.* **-ses** (-sēz). *Rhet.* a sudden breaking off in the midst of a sentence, as if from inability or unwillingness to proceed. [< LL < Gk: lit., a full silence, equiv. to *aposiōpē-* (var. s. of *aposiōpâein* to be fully silent: *apo-* APO- + *siōpâein* to be silent) + *-sis* -SIS] —**ap·o·si·o·pet·ic** (ap′ə sī′ə pet′ik), *adj.*

ap·o·spor·y (ap′ə spôr′ē, -spōr′ē, ə pos′pə rē), *n. Bot.* the development of a gametophyte from a sporophyte without meiosis. [APO- + SPOR- + -Y³] —**ap·o·spor·ic** (ap′ə spôr′ik, -spōr′-), **a·pos·por·ous** (ə pos′pər əs, ap′ə spôr′əs, -spōr′-), *adj.*

a·pos·ta·sy (ə pos′tə sē), *n., pl.* **-sies.** a total desertion of or departure from one's religion, principles, party, cause, etc. [ME *apostasye* < LL *apostasia* < Gk: a standing away, withdrawing, equiv. to *apóstas(is)* (*apo-* APO- + *sta-* stand + *-sis* -SIS) + *-ia* -IA]

a·pos·tate (ə pos′tāt, -tit), *n.* **1.** one who forsakes his religion, cause, party, etc. —*adj.* **2.** of or characterized by apostasy. [ME < LL *apostat(a)* < Gk *apostátēs,* equiv. to *aposta-* (see APOSTASY) + *-t-* verbid suffix + *-ēs* n. suffix] —**a·pos·tat·i·cal·ly** (ap′ə stat′ik lē), *adv.*

a·pos·ta·tise (ə pos′tə tīz′), *v.i.,* **-tised, -tis·ing.** *Chiefly Brit.* apostatize.

a·pos·ta·tize (ə pos′tə tīz′), *v.i.,* **-tized, -tiz·ing.** to commit apostasy. [< LL *apostatizāre.* See APOSTATE, -IZE] —**a·pos·ta·tism** (ə pos′tə tiz′əm), *n.*

a pos·te·ri·o·ri (ā′ po stēr′ē ôr′ī, -ōr′ī, -ôr′ē, -ōr′ē), **1.** from effect to cause; based upon actual observation or upon experimental data: *an a posteriori argument that derives the theory from the evidence.* Cf. **a priori** (def. 1). **2.** not existing in the mind prior to or independent of experience. Cf. **a priori** (def. 2). [< L: lit., from the one behind. See A-⁴, POSTERIOR]

a·pos·til (ə pos′til), *n.* a marginal annotation or note. Also, **a·pos′tille.** [< F *apostille* < *(l)a postille* < ML *postilla* < L *post* after + *illa* those things]

a·pos·tle (ə pos′əl), *n.* **1.** one of the 12 disciples sent forth by Christ to preach the gospel. **2.** the first or the best-known Christian missionary in any region or country. **3.** *Eastern Ch.* one of the 70 disciples of Jesus. **4.** the title of the highest ecclesiastical official in certain Protestant sects. **5.** (among the Jews of the Christian epoch) a title borne by persons sent on foreign missions. **6.** one of the 12 administrative officials of the Mormon Church. **7.** a pioneer of any great moral reform. **8.** *Naut.* a knighthead, esp. one having its top projecting and used as a bitt or bollard. [ME, var. of *apostel,* OE *apostol* < LL apostol(us) < Gk *apóstolos,* lit., one who is sent out; akin to *apostéllein* to send off; see APO-] —**a·pos′tle·hood′, a·pos′tle·ship′,** *n.*

Apos′tle pitch′er, a stoneware pitcher decorated in relief with figures of the apostles.

Apos′tles' Creed′, a creed, dating back to about A.D. 500, traditionally ascribed to Christ's apostles and having widespread acceptance in the Christian church. It begins "I believe in God the Father Almighty."

Apos′tle spoon′, (in the 15th and 16th centuries) a spoon having at the end of the handle the figure of one of the 12 apostles, given as a christening present.

a·pos·to·late (ə pos′tᵊlit, -tᵊlāt′), *n.* **1.** the dignity or office of an apostle. **2.** *Rom. Cath. Ch.* **a.** the dignity and office of the pope as head of the Apostolic See. **b.** the mission of bishops in their dioceses. **c.** an organization of the laity devoted to the mission of the Church. Cf. **Catholic Action.** [< LL *apostolāt(us)* the office of an apostle, equiv. to LL *apostol(us)* APOSTLE + *-ātus* -ATE¹]

ap·os·tol·ic (ap′ə stol′ik), *adj.* **1.** of or characteristic of an apostle. **2.** pertaining to or characteristic of the 12 apostles. **3.** derived from the apostles in regular succession. **4.** of or pertaining to the pope; papal. Also, **ap′os·tol′i·cal.** [< LL *apostolic(us)* < Gk *apostolikós,* equiv. to *apóstol(os)* APOSTLE + *-ikos* -IC] —**ap′os·tol′i·cal·ly,** *adv.* —**ap·os·tol·i·cism** (ap′ə stol′i siz′əm), *n.* —**a·pos·to·lic·i·ty** (ə pos′tᵊlis′i tē), **ap′os·tol′i·cal·ness,** *n.*

ap′ostol′ic age′, the earliest period of Christianity, lasting through the death of the last apostle.

Ap′ostol′ic Church′, 1. the Christian church as founded by the apostles. **2.** See **Apostolic See** (def. 2).

ap′ostol′ic del′egate, a representative of the pope in a country that has no regular diplomatic relations with the Vatican. Cf. **nuncio.**

Ap′ostol′ic Fa′thers, 1. the fathers of the early Christian church whose lives overlapped those of any of the apostles. **2.** the collection of works attributed to them.

Ap′ostol′ic See′, 1. the Church of Rome, traditionally founded by St. Peter. **2.** Also called **Apostolic Church.** a church founded by an apostle. [APOSTOLIC + SEE²]

apostol′ic succes′sion, *Rom. Cath. Ch., Orth. Ch., Anglican Ch.* the unbroken line of succession beginning with the apostles and perpetuated through bishops, considered essential for orders and sacraments to be valid.

ap′ostol′ic vic′ar. See **vicar apostolic.**

A·pos·to·los (ä pôs′tô lôs; *Eng.* ə pos′tᵊlos′), *n. Gk. Orth. Ch.* **1.** a book containing parts of the Epistles and parts of the Acts of the Apostles. **2.** a reading from this book. [< LGk < Gk: APOSTLE]

a·pos·tro·phe¹ (ə pos′trə fē), *n.* the sign ('), as used: to indicate the omission of one or more letters in a word, whether unpronounced, as in *o'er* for *over,* or pronounced, as in *gov't* for *government;* to indicate the possessive case, as in *man's;* or to indicate plurals of abbreviations and symbols, as in *several M.D.'s, 3's.* [alter. (by confusion with APOSTROPHE²) of earlier *apostrophus* < LL < Gk *apóstrophos* (*prosōidía*) eliding (mark), lit., (mark) of turning away, verbid of *apostréphein* to turn away, equiv. to *apo-* APO- + *stréphein* to turn; see STROPHE] —**ap·os·troph·ic** (ap′ə strof′ik), *adj.*

a·pos·tro·phe² (ə pos′trə fē), *n. Rhet.* a digression in the form of an address to someone not present, or to a personified object or idea. [< LL < Gk: a turning away, equiv. to *apostroph-* (var. s. of *apostréphein;* see APOSTROPHE¹) + *-ē* n. suffix] —**ap·os·troph·ic** (ap′ə strof′ik), *adj.*

A·pos·tro·phi·a (ə pos′trō fī′ə, ap′ə strō′fē ə), *n. Class. Myth.* an epithet of Aphrodite, meaning "rejecter of sinful passions."

a·pos·tro·phise (ə pos′trə fīz′), *v.t., v.i.,* **-phised, -phis·ing.** *Chiefly Brit.* apostrophize.

a·pos·tro·phize (ə pos′trə fīz′), *v.,* **-phized, -phiz·ing.** *Rhet.* —*v.t.* **1.** to address by apostrophe. —*v.i.* **2.** to utter an apostrophe. [APOSTROPH(E)² + -IZE]

apoth′ecaries' meas′ure, a system of units used chiefly in compounding and dispensing liquid drugs. In the U.S. 60 minims (♏) = 1 fluid dram (f ʒ); 8 fluid drams = 1 fluid ounce (f ℥); 16 fluid ounces = 1 pint (O.); 8 pints = 1 gallon (C.) (231 cubic inches). In Great Britain 20 minims = 1 fluid scruple; 3 fluid scruples = 1 fluid dram; 8 fluid drams = 1 fluid ounce; 20 fluid ounces = 1 pint; 8 pints = 1 imperial gallon (277.42 cubic inches).

apoth′ecaries' weight′, a system of weights used chiefly in compounding and dispensing drugs: 20 grains = 1 scruple (℈); 3 scruples = 1 dram (ʒ); 8 drams = 1 ounce (℥); 12 ounces = 1 pound. The grain, ounce, and pound are the same as in troy weight, the grain alone being the same as in avoirdupois weight.

a·poth·e·car·y (ə poth′ə ker′ē), *n., pl.* **-car·ies. 1.** a druggist; a pharmacist. **2.** a pharmacy or drug store. **3.** (esp. in England and Ireland) a druggist licensed to prescribe medicine. [ME < ML *apothēcāri(us)* shopkeeper, equiv. to *apothēc(a)* shop, storehouse (< Gk *apothḗkē;* see APO-, THECA) + *-ārius* -ARY]

apoth′ecary jar′, a small, covered jar, formerly used by druggists to hold pharmaceuticals, now chiefly in household use to hold spices, candies, cosmetics, etc., or, if decorative, as a lamp base, flower vase, etc.

ap·o·the·ci·um (ap′ə thē′shē əm, -sē-), *n., pl.* **-ci·a** (-shē ə, -sē ə). *Bot.* the fruit of certain lichens and fungi: usually an open, saucer-shaped or cup-shaped body, the inner surface of which is covered with a layer which bears asci. [<NL < Gk *apo-* APO- + *thḗkion,* equiv. to *thḗkē* case (see THECA) + *-ion* dim. suffix] —**ap·o·the·cial** (ap′ə thē′shəl), *adj.*

ap·o·thegm (ap′ə them′), *n.* a short, pithy, instructive saying; a terse remark or aphorism. Also, **apophthegm.** [earlier *apothegm(a)* < Gk *apóphthegma,* equiv. to *apophtheg-* (var. s. of *apophthéng(esthai)* (to) speak out: *apo-* APO- + *phthéngesthai* to speak) + *-ma* n. suffix] —**ap·o·theg·mat·ic** (ap′ə theg mat′ik), **ap′o·theg·mat′i·cal,** *adj.* —**ap′o·theg·mat′i·cal·ly,** *adv.*

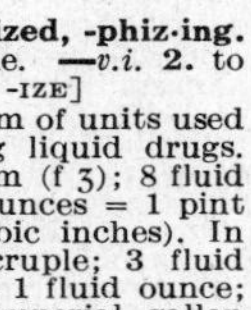

ap·o·them (ap′ə them′), *n. Geom.* a perpendicular from the center of a regular polygon to one of its sides. [< Gk *apo(ti)thé(nai)* (to) set off + *-m(a)* n. suffix. See APO-, THEME]

A
90°
B

AB, Apothem

a·poth·e·o·sis (ə poth′ē ō′sis, ap′ə thē′ə sis), *n., pl.* **-ses** (-sēz, -sēz′). **1.** the elevation or exaltation of a person to the rank of a god. **2.** the glorification of a person as an ideal: *The movie star was the apotheosis of courage to his fans.* **3.** a deified or glorified ideal: *His brave act was the apotheosis of daring.* [< LL < Gk. See APO-, THEO-, -OSIS]

a·poth·e·o·sise (ə poth′ē ə sīz′, ap′ə thē′ə sīz′), *v.t.,* **-sised, -sis·ing.** *Chiefly Brit.* apotheosize.

a·poth·e·o·size (ə poth′ē ə sīz′, ap′ə thē′ə sīz′), *v.t.,* **-sized, -siz·ing.** to deify; glorify. [APOTHEOS(IS) + -IZE]

ap·o·tro·pa·ic (ap′ə trə pā′ik), *adj.* intended to ward off evil. [< Gk *apotrópai(on)* something that averts evil (neut. of *apotrópaios* off-turning; see APO-, TROPE) + -IC]

ap·o·tro·pa·ism (ap′ə trə pā′iz əm), *n.* the use of magic and ritualistic ceremony to anticipate and prevent evil. [< Gk *apotrópai(on)* object that averts evil (see APOTROPAIC) + -ISM]

app., 1. apparatus. **2.** apparent. **3.** appendix. **4.** applied. **5.** appointed. **6.** approved. **7.** approximate.

ap·pal (ə pôl′), *v.t.,* **-palled, -pal·ling.** appall.

Ap·pa·la·chi·a (ap′ə lā′chē ə, -chə, -lach′ē ə, -lach′ə), *n.* **1.** *Geol.* a Paleozoic land mass, the erosion of which provided the sediments to form the rocks of the Appalachian Mountains. **2.** a region in the E United States, in the area of the S Appalachian Mountains, usually including NE Alabama, NW Georgia, NW South Carolina, E Tennessee, W Virginia, E Kentucky, West Virginia, and SW Pennsylvania. [from APPALACHIAN]

Ap·pa·la·chi·an (ap′ə lā′chē ən, -chən, -lach′ē ən, lach′ən), *adj.* **1.** of or pertaining to the Appalachian Mountains. **2.** *Geol.* of or pertaining to the orogeny and accompanying intrusion that occurred during the Pennsylvanian and Permian periods. [perh. < *Apalachee* tribal name + -AN]

Ap′pala′chian Moun′tains, a mountain range in E North America, extending from S Quebec province to N Alabama. Highest peak, Mt. Mitchell, 6684 ft. Also called **Ap′pa·la′chi·ans.**

Ap′pala′chian tea′, 1. the leaves of any of certain plants of the genus *Ilex* of the Eastern U.S., as the shrub or small tree *I. vomitoria,* sometimes used as a tea. **2.** a plant yielding such leaves.

Ap′pala′chian trail′, a hiking trail extending through the Appalachian Mountains from central Maine to N Georgia. 2050 mi. long.

ap·pall (ə pôl′), *v.t.* to fill or overcome with horror, consternation, or fear; dismay: *He was appalled by the damage from the fire. I am appalled at your mistakes.* Also, **appal.** [ME < MF *ap(p)all(ir)* (to) grow or make pale, equiv. to *a-* A-⁵ + *pal(l)ir* in same sense; see PALE¹] —**Syn.** horrify, daunt. See **frighten.**

ap·pall·ing (ə pô′ling), *adj.* causing dismay or horror: *an appalling accident.* [APPALL + -ING²] —**ap·pall′ing·ly,** *adv.*

Ap·pa·loo·sa (ap′ə lo͞o′sə), *n.* one of a hardy breed of riding horses, developed in the American West, having a mottled hide, vertically striped hoofs, and eyes that show a relatively large proportion of white. [prob. alter. of *Palouse,* name of an Indian tribe]

ap·pa·nage (ap′ə nij), *n.* **1.** land or some other source of revenue assigned for the maintenance of a member of the family of a ruling house. **2.** whatever belongs rightfully or appropriately to one's rank or station in life. **3.** a natural or necessary accompaniment; adjunct. Also, **apanage.** [< MF < ML *appānāg(ium),* equiv. to *appān(āre)* (to) endow with a maintenance (< L *ap-* AP-¹ + *pān-* bread + *-ā-* thematic vowel + *-re* inf. suffix) + *-āgium* -AGE]

appar., 1. apparent. **2.** apparently.

ap·pa·rat·chik (ä′pä rä′chik; *Eng.* ä′pə rä′chik), *n., pl.* **-chi·ki** (-chi ki); *Eng.* **-chiks.** *Russian.* a highly disciplined bureaucrat of any official communist organization. [< Russ *apparat* lit., apparatus + *-chik* agent suffix]

ap·pa·rat·us (ap′ə rat′əs, -rā′təs), *n., pl.* **-tus, -tus·es. 1.** a group or aggregate of instruments, machinery, tools, materials, etc., having a particular function or intended for a specific use. **2.** any complex instrument or machine for a particular purpose. **3.** any system or systematic organization of activities, functions, processes, etc., directed toward a specific goal: *the apparatus of government; espionage apparatus.* **4.** *Physiol.* a group of structurally different organs working together in the performance of a particular function: *the digestive apparatus.* [< L *apparātus* (ptp. of *apparāre*) provided, equiv. to *ap-* AP-¹ + *par-* prepare + *-ātus* -ATE¹]

ap·pa·ra·tus crit·i·cus (äp′pä rä′to͝os krit′i ko͝os′; *Eng.* ap′ə rat′əs krit′ə kəs, -rā′təs), *Latin.* supplementary information, as variant readings, added to a text to provide material for study or criticism.

ap·par·el (ə par′əl), *n., v.,* **-eled, -el·ing** or (*esp. Brit.*) **-elled, -el·ling.** —*n.* **1.** a person's clothing; garments; attire; raiment. **2.** anything that decorates or covers. **3.** superficial appearance; aspect; guise. **4.** *Naut.* the masts, sails, anchor, etc., used to equip a vessel. **5.** *Eccles.* a piece of embroidery, usually oblong, on certain vestments, esp. on the alb or amice. —*v.t.* **6.** to dress or clothe. **7.** to adorn; ornament. **8.** *Naut.* to equip a vessel with its apparel. [ME *appareill(en)* < OF *apareillier(r)* (to) make fit, fit out < VL **appariculāre,* equiv. to *ap-* AP-¹ + **paricul(us)* a fit (see PAR, -CULE) + *-ā-* thematic vowel + *-re* inf. suffix] —**Syn. 1.** clothes, dress, garb, costume, habiliments, vesture. **2.** garb, attire. **6.** outfit; array, deck out.

ap·par·ent (ə par′ənt, ə pâr′-), *adj.* **1.** exposed to sight; open to view; visible: *The crack in the wall was readily apparent.* **2.** capable of being easily perceived or understood; plain or clear; obvious: *The solution to the problem was apparent to all.* **3.** according to appearances, initial evidence, incomplete results, etc.; ostensible rather than actual: *He was the apparent winner of the election.* **4.** absolutely entitled to an inherited throne, title, or other estate, by right of birth. Cf. **heir apparent, heir presumptive.** [< L *apparēnt-* (s. of *apparēns* appearing; see APPEAR, -ENT); r. ME *aparant* < MF] —**ap·par′ent·ly,** *adv.* —**ap·par′ent·ness,** *n.* —**Syn. 1.** discernible. **2.** open, conspicuous, manifest, unmistakable. APPARENT, EVIDENT, OBVIOUS, PATENT all refer to something easily perceived. APPARENT applies to that which can readily be seen or perceived: *an apparent effort.* EVIDENT applies to that which facts or circumstances make plain: *His innocence was evident.* OBVIOUS applies to that which is unquestionable, because completely manifest or noticeable: *an obvious change of method.* PATENT, a more formal word, applies to that which is open to view or understanding by all: *a patent error.* —**Ant. 2.** concealed, obscure.

appar′ent can′dle·pow·er (kan′dᵊl pou′ər), *Optics.* a measure of the luminous intensity of an extended source of light in terms of the candlepower of a point source of light that has an equivalent luminous intensity when placed at the same distance as the extended source.

ap·pa·rente·ment (A PA RÄNTᵊ MÄN′), *n., pl.* **-ments** (-MÄN′). *Fr. Govt.* a coalition formed between political parties during an election.

appar′ent hori′zon, horizon (def. 1).

appar′ent mag′nitude, *Astron.* the magnitude of

a star as it appears to an observer on the earth. Cf. **absolute magnitude.**

appar′ent time′, local time measured by the hour angle of the sun. Cf. **mean solar time.**

appar′ent wind′ (wind), the velocity of air as measured from a moving object, as a ship.

ap·pa·ri·tion (ap′ə rish′ən), *n.* **1.** a ghostly appearance; a specter or phantom; wraith: *a ghostly apparition at midnight.* **2.** anything that appears, esp. something remarkable or startling: *the surprising apparition of cowboys in New York City.* **3.** act of appearing; manifestation. **4.** *Astron.* the appearance or time when a comet, esp. a periodic one, is visible: *the 1910 apparition of Halley's comet.* [late ME < L *appāritiōn-* (s. of *appāritiō*) attendance, equiv. to *appārit(us)* appeared in public (ptp. of *appārēre;* see APPEAR, -ITE[2]) + *-iōn-* -ION] —**ap′pa·ri′tion·al,** *adj.*

—**Syn 1.** ghost, spirit, shade. APPARITION, PHANTASM, PHANTOM are terms for a supernatural appearance. An APPARITION of a person or thing is an immaterial appearance which seems real, and is generally sudden or startling in its manifestation: *an apparition of a headless horseman.* Both PHANTOM and PHANTASM denote an illusory appearance, as in a dream; the former may be pleasant, while the latter is usually frightening: *a phantom of a garden; a monstrous phantasm.*

ap·par·i·tor (ə par′i tər), *n.* (in ancient Rome) a subordinate official of a magistrate or of the court. [< L: servant, esp. an official's attendant in public < *appārit(us)* (ptp.; see APPARITION) + *-or* -OR[2]]

ap·pas·sio·na·to (ə pä′sē ə nä′tō; *It.* äp päs′syô nä′tô), *adj. Music.* impassioned; with passion or strong feeling. [< It; see AP-, PASSION, -ATE[1]]

ap·pau·mé (ap′ō mā′), *adj. Heraldry.* showing the palm: *a dexter hand appaumé.* [< F, equiv. to *ap-* AP-[1] + *paume* PALM[1] + *-é* (< L *-ātus* -ATE[1])]

appd., approved.

ap·peal (ə pēl′), *n.* **1.** an earnest request for aid, support, mercy, etc.; entreaty; petition; plea. **2.** a request or reference to some person or authority for a decision, corroboration, judgment, etc. **3.** *Law.* **a.** an application or proceeding for review by a higher tribunal. **b.** (in a legislative body or assembly) a formal question as to the correctness of a ruling by a presiding officer. **c.** *Obs.* a formal charge or accusation. **4.** the power or ability to attract, interest, amuse, or stimulate the mind or emotions: *The game has lost its appeal.* **5.** *Obs.* a summons or challenge. —*v.i.* **6.** to ask for aid, mercy, sympathy, or the like; make an earnest entreaty. **7.** *Law.* to apply for review of a case or particular issue to a higher tribunal. **8.** to have need of or ask for proof, a decision, corroboration, etc. **9.** to offer a special attraction, interest, enjoyment, etc.: *The red hat appeals to me.* —*v.t.* **10.** *Law.* **a.** to apply for review of (a case) to a higher tribunal. **b.** *Obs.* to charge with a crime before a tribunal. **11. appeal to the country,** *Brit.* country (def. 10). [ME *a(p)pel(en)* < MF *a(p)pele(r)* < L *appellāre* to speak to, appeal to (lit., approach), equiv. to *ap-* AP-[1] + *pell-* move, go + *-ā-* thematic vowel + *-re* inf. suffix] —**ap·peal′a·bil′i·ty,** *n.* —**ap·peal′a·ble,** *adj.* —**ap·peal′er,** *n.*

—**Syn. 1.** prayer, supplication, invocation. **2.** suit, solicitation. **4.** attraction. **6.** request, ask. APPEAL, ENTREAT, PETITION, SUPPLICATE mean to ask for something wished for or needed. APPEAL and PETITION may concern groups and formal or public requests. ENTREAT and SUPPLICATE are usually more personal and emotional. To APPEAL is to ask earnestly for help or support, on grounds of reason, justice, common humanity, etc.: *to appeal for contributions to a cause.* To PETITION is to ask by written request, by prayer, or the like, that something be granted: *to petition for more playgrounds.* ENTREAT suggests pleading: *The child entreated his father not to punish him.* To SUPPLICATE is to beg humbly, usually from a superior, powerful, or stern (official) person: *to supplicate that the lives of prisoners be spared.*

ap·peal·ing (ə pē′ling), *adj.* that appeals; attractive. [APPEAL + -ING[2]] —**ap·peal′ing·ly,** *adv.* —**ap·peal′ing·ness,** *n.*

ap·pear (ə pēr′), *v.i.* **1.** to come into sight; become visible: *A man appeared in the doorway.* **2.** to have the appearance of; seem; look: *to appear wise.* **3.** to be obvious or easily perceived; be clear or made clear by evidence: *It appears to me that you are right.* **4.** to come or be placed before the public: *His biography appeared last year.* **5.** to perform publicly, as in a play, dance, etc.: *He appeared as the king in the play.* **6.** to attend or be present, esp. to arrive late or stay but a short time: *He appeared at the party but left quickly.* **7.** to come into being; be created, invented, or developed: *Speech appears in the child's first or second year.* **8.** *Law.* to come formally before a tribunal, authority, etc., as defendant, plaintiff, counsel, etc. [ME *a(p)pere* < OF *aper-* (tonic s. of *apareir*) < L *appār(ēre)* (to) appear, attend, attend in public, equiv. to *ap-* + AP-[1] + *pārēre* to appear]

—**Syn. 1.** emerge, arise. **2.** See **seem.**

ap·pear·ance (ə pēr′əns), *n.* **1.** the act or fact of appearing, as to the eye, the mind, the public, etc.: *the unannounced appearance of dinner guests; the last appearance of Caruso in Aïda; his first appearance at a stockholders' meeting.* **2.** the state, condition, manner, or style in which a person or object appears: *a table of antique appearance; a man of noble appearance.* **3.** outward show or seeming; semblance: *to avoid the appearance of coveting an honor.* **4.** *Law.* the coming into court of either party to a suit or action. **5. appearances,** outward impressions, indications, or circumstances: *By all appearances, he enjoyed himself.* **6.** an apparition. **7.** *Philos.* the sensory, or phenomenal, aspect of existence to an observer. **8. keep up appearances,** to maintain a public impression of decorum, prosperity, etc., despite reverses, unfavorable conditions, etc.: *They tried to keep up appearances after losing all their money.* **9. make an appearance,** to come; arrive: *He didn't make an appearance until after midnight.* **10. put in an appearance,** to attend (a social gathering, meeting, etc.), esp. for a very short time: *The author put in an appearance at the cocktail party on his way to dinner.* [APPEAR + -ANCE; r. ME *aparance* < MF, deriv. of *apar(eir)* (to) APPEAR]

—**Syn. 1.** arrival, coming, advent. **2.** demeanor, presence. APPEARANCE, ASPECT, GUISE refer to the way in which something outwardly presents itself to view. APPEARANCE refers to the outward look: *the shabby appearance of his car.* ASPECT refers to the appearance at some particular time or in special circumstances; it often has emotional implications, either ascribed to the object itself or felt by the beholder: *In the dusk the forest had a terrifying aspect.* GUISE suggests a misleading appearance, assumed for an occasion or a purpose: *under the guise of friendship.* **3.** face, pretense.

ap·pease (ə pēz′), *v.t.,* **-peased, -peas·ing. 1.** to bring to a state of peace, quiet, ease, or contentment; pacify; soothe: *to appease an angry king.* **2.** to satisfy, allay, or relieve; assuage: *The fruit appeased his hunger.* **3.** to yield or concede to the belligerent demands of (a nation, group, person, etc.) in a conciliatory effort, sometimes at the expense of justice or other principles. [ME *apese* < OF *apais(i)er,* equiv. to *a-* A-[5] + *paisi-* PEACE + *-er* inf. suffix] —**ap·peas′a·ble,** *adj.* —**ap·peas′a·ble·ness,** *n.* —**ap·peas′a·bly,** *adv.* —**ap·pease′ment,** *n.* —**ap·peas′er,** *n.* —**ap·peas′ing·ly,** *adv.*

—**Syn. 1.** calm, placate. **3.** APPEASE, CONCILIATE, PROPITIATE imply trying to preserve or obtain peace. To APPEASE is to make anxious overtures and often undue concessions to satisfy the demands of someone with a greed for power, territory, etc.: *Chamberlain tried to appease Hitler at Munich.* To CONCILIATE is to win an enemy or opponent over by displaying a willingness to be just and fair: *When mutual grievances are recognized, conciliation is possible.* To PROPITIATE is to admit a fault, and, by trying to make amends, to allay hostile feeling: *to propitiate an offended neighbor.* —**Ant. 1.** enrage. **2.** sharpen. **3.** defy.

ap·pel (ə pel′, a pel′; *Fr.* A pel′), *n., pl.* **ap·pels** (ə pelz′, a pelz′; *Fr.* A pel′). *Fencing.* **1.** a tap or stamp of the foot, formerly serving as a warning of one's intent to attack. **2.** a smart stroke with the blade used for the purpose of procuring an opening. [< F; see APPEAL]

ap·pe·la·tion con·trô·lée (A pe lA syôN′ kôN trō lā′), (of a French wine) having use of its name or designation controlled by the government with respect to the region of production, the variety of grapes used, and the level of quality maintained. [< F: lit., controlled appellation]

ap·pel·lant (ə pel′ənt), *n.* **1.** one who appeals. **2.** *Law.* the party that appeals to a higher tribunal. [late ME *appellaunt* < AF < OF *apelant,* prp. of *apeler* to APPEAL; see -ANT]

ap·pel·late (ə pel′it), *adj. Law.* **1.** pertaining to appeals. **2.** having the power or authority to review and decide appeals, as a court. [< L *appellāt(us)* called upon, named, appealed to (ptp. of *appellāre*), equiv. to *ap-* AP-[1] + *pell-* move, go + *-ātus* -ATE[1]]

appel′late divi′sion, *Law.* the section of a court that hears appeals, sometimes existing as an intermediate court between a trial court and a court of last resort.

ap·pel·la·tion (ap′ə lā′shən), *n.* **1.** a name, title, or designation. **2.** act of naming. [< L *appellātiōn-* (s. of *appellātiō*) a naming, equiv. to *appellāt(us)* (see APPELLATE) + *-iōn-* -ION]

ap·pel·la·tive (ə pel′ə tiv), *n.* **1.** a common noun. **2.** a descriptive name or designation, as *Simple* in *Simple Simon.* —*adj.* **3.** pertaining to a common noun. **4.** designative; descriptive. **5.** tending toward or serving for the assigning of names: *the appellative function of some primitive rites.* [< LL *appellātīv(us).* See APPELLATE, -IVE] —**ap·pel′la·tive·ly,** *adv.* —**ap·pel′la·tive·ness,** *n.*

ap·pel·lee (ap′ə lē′), *n. Law.* the defendant or respondent in an appellate proceeding. [< AF *appelle* < OF *apele,* ptp. of *apeler* to APPEAL; see -EE]

ap·pel·lor (ə pel′ôr, ap′ə lôr′), *n. Brit. Law.* **1.** a person who prosecutes in an appellate proceeding. **2.** *Obs.* a person who accuses another in a criminal appeal. [late ME *apelour* < AF, equiv. to OF *apeleor* < L *appellātor* appellant. See APPELLATE, -OR[2]]

ap·pend (ə pend′), *v.t.* **1.** to add as a supplement, accessory or appendix; subjoin: *to append a note to a letter.* **2.** to attach or suspend as a pendant. **3.** to sign a document with; affix: *to append one's signature.* [< LL *append(ere)* (to) make hang to. See AP-[1], PEND]

ap·pend·age (ə pen′dij), *n.* **1.** a subordinate part attached to something; an auxiliary part; addition. **2.** *Biol.* any member of the body diverging from the axial trunk. **3.** *Bot.* any subsidiary part superadded to another part. **4.** a person in a subordinate or dependent position, esp. a servile or parasitic follower. [APPEND + -AGE] —**ap·pend′aged,** *adj.*

ap·pend·ant (ə pen′dənt), *adj.* **1.** attached or suspended; annexed. **2.** associated as an accompaniment or consequence: *the salary appendant to a position.* **3.** *Law.* pertaining to a legal appendant. —*n.* **4.** a person or thing attached or added. **5.** *Law.* any subordinate possession or right historically annexed to or dependent on a greater one and automatically passing with it, as by sale or inheritance. Also, **ap·pend′ent.** [ME < MF: belonging to (prp. of *appendre* to APPEND). See AP-[1], PENDANT] —**ap·pend′ance, ap·pend′an·cy, ap·pend′ence, ap·pend′en·cy,** *n.*

ap·pen·dec·to·my (ap′ən dek′tə mē), *n., pl.* **-mies.** *Surg.* excision of the vermiform appendix. Also, **appendicectomy.** [APPEND(IX) + -ECTOMY]

ap·pen·di·ceal (ap′ən dish′əl, ə pen′di sē′əl), *adj.* of or pertaining to the vermiform appendix. Also, **ap·pen·di·cal** (ə pen′di kəl), **ap·pen·di·cial** (ap′ən dish′əl). [< L *appendic-* (see APPENDIX) + *-eal,* var. of -IAL]

ap·pen·di·cec·to·my (ə pen′di sek′tə mē), *n., pl.* **-mies.** appendectomy.

ap·pen·di·ci·tis (ə pen′di sī′tis), *n. Pathol.* inflammation of the vermiform appendix. [< NL < L *appendic-* (s. of *appendix*) APPENDIX + *-ītis* -ITIS]

ap·pen·di·cle (ə pen′di kəl), *n.* a small appendage. [< L *appendicul(a)* small appendage, equiv. to *appendic-* (see APPENDIX) + *-ula* -ULE]

ap·pen·dic·u·lar (ap′ən dik′yə lər), *adj.* **1.** of or pertaining to an appendage or limb. **2.** *Anat.* appendiceal. [< L *appendicul(a)* APPENDICLE + -AR[1]]

ap·pen·dic·u·late (ap′ən dik′yə lit, -lāt′), *adj. Bot., Zool.* **1.** having appendages. **2.** forming an appendage or appendicle. [< L *appendicul(a)* APPENDICLE + -ATE[1]]

ap·pen·dix (ə pen′diks), *n., pl.* **-dix·es, -di·ces** (-di sēz′). **1.** supplementary material at the end of a book, article, or other text, usually of an explanatory, statistical, or bibliographic nature. **2.** an appendage. **3.** *Anat.* **a.** a process or projection. **b.** See **vermiform appendix. 4.** *Aeron.* the short tube at the bottom of a balloon bag, by which the intake and release of buoyant gas is controlled. [< L: appendage, equiv. to *append(ere)* (to) APPEND + *-ix* (equiv. to *-ic-* n. suffix + *-s* nom. sing. ending)]

—**Syn. 1.** addendum, adjunct. APPENDIX, SUPPLEMENT both mean material added after the end of a book. An APPENDIX gives useful additional information, but even without it the rest of the book is complete: *In the appendix are forty detailed charts.* A SUPPLEMENT, bound in the book or published separately, is given for comparison, as an enhancement, to provide corrections, to present later information, and the like: *A yearly supplement is issued.*

ap·pen·tice (ə pen′tis, a pen′-), *n.* penthouse (def. 3). [< F *appentis* << OF *apentis,* deriv. of *apend(re)* (to) APPEND]

ap·pen·zell (ap′ən zel′; *Ger.* ä′pən tsel′), *n.* (*sometimes cap.*) a type of embroidery, used chiefly on fine handkerchiefs. [named after APPENZELL, town where it is made]

Ap·pen·zell (ap′ən zel′; *Ger.* ä′pən tsel′), *n.* **1.** a canton in NE Switzerland, divided into two independent areas. Cf. **Appenzell Ausser Rhoden, Appenzell Inner Rhoden. 2.** a town in and the capital of Appenzell Inner Rhoden. 5000 (est. 1961).

Ap·pen·zell Aus·ser Rho·den (*Ger.* ä′pən tsel′ ou′sər rōd′ən), a demicanton in NE Switzerland: Protestant. 48,920 (1960); 94 sq. mi. *Cap.:* Herisau.

Ap·pen·zell In·ner Rho·den (*Ger.* ä′pən tsel′ in′ər rōd′ən), a demicanton in NE Switzerland: Catholic 12,943 (1960); 66 sq. mi. *Cap.:* Appenzell.

ap·per·ceive (ap′ər sēv′), *v.t.,* **-ceived, -ceiv·ing.** *Psychol.* **1.** to be conscious of perceiving; comprehend. **2.** to comprehend (a new idea) by assimilation with the sum of one's previous knowledge and experience. [ME < OF *aperceiv(re).* See AP-[1], PERCEIVE]

ap·per·cep·tion (ap′ər sep′shən), *n. Psychol.* **1.** conscious perception. **2.** the act or process of apperceiving. [< NL *apperceptiōn-,* s. of *apperceptiō.* See AP-[1], PERCEPTION] —**ap′per·cep′tive,** *adj.* —**ap′per·cep′tive·ly,** *adv.*

ap·per·son·a·tion (a pûr′sə nā′shən, ə pûr′-), *n. Psychiatry.* the unconscious assumption of the personality characteristics of another, usually well known, person. Also, **ap·per·son·i·fi·ca·tion** (ap′ər son′ə fə kā′shən). [AP-[1] + PERSONATION, modeled on G *Appersonierung*]

ap·per·tain (ap′ər tān′), *v.i.* to belong as a part, right, possession, attribute, etc.; pertain or relate (usually fol. by *to*): *privileges which appertain to members of the royal family.* [ME *a(p)perte(y)ne* < OF *aperten(ir).* See AP-[1], PERTAIN]

ap·pe·tence (ap′i təns), *n.* **1.** intense desire; strong natural craving; appetite. **2.** instinctive inclination or natural tendency. **3.** material or chemical attraction or affinity. Also, **appetency.** [*appete* (obs.) to seek for, long for (< L *appete(re),* equiv. to *ap-* AP-[1] + *petere* to seek) + -ENCE]

ap·pe·ten·cy (ap′i tən sē), *n., pl.* **-cies.** appetence. [< L *appetentia* a craving for, equiv. to *appetent-* (s. of *appetēns,* prp. of *appetere;* see APPETENCE) + *-ia* -IA; see -ENCY]

ap·pe·tite (ap′i tīt′), *n.* **1.** a desire for food or drink: *to work up an appetite for lunch.* **2.** a desire to satisfy any bodily need or craving. **3.** a desire or liking for something; fondness; taste: *an appetite for power; an appetite for pleasure.* [ME *appetit* < L *appetīt(us)* a craving, deriv. of *appetītus* craved (ptp. of *appetere*). See APPETENCE, -ITE[2]]

—**Syn. 1–3.** longing, hunger. **1, 3.** thirst. **2.** inclination, wish. **3.** relish, gusto, zest. —**Ant. 1–3.** satiety.

ap·pe·ti·tive (ap′i tī′tiv), *adj.* pertaining to appetite. [APPETITE + -IVE]

ap·pe·tiz·er (ap′i tī′zər), *n.* **1.** a small portion of a food or drink served before or at the beginning of a meal to stimulate the desire to eat. **2.** any small portion that stimulates a desire for more or that indicates more is to follow: *The first game was an appetizer to a great football season.* [APPETIZ(ING) + -ER[1]]

ap·pe·tiz·ing (ap′i tī′zing), *adj.* **1.** appealing to or stimulating the appetite; savory. **2.** appealing; tempting. [APPET(ITE) + -IZE + -ING[2], modeled on F *appétissant*] —**ap′pe·tiz′ing·ly,** *adv.*

Ap·pia (*Fr.* A pyA′), *n.* **A·dolphe** (*Fr.* A dôlf′), 1862–1928, Swiss stage designer and theatrical producer.

Ap′pi·an Way′ (ap′ē ən), an ancient Roman highway extending from Rome to Brundisium (now Brindisi): begun 312 B.C. by Appius Claudius Caecus. ab. 350 mi. long.

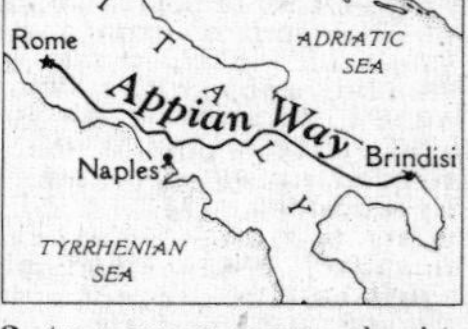

ap·plaud (ə plôd′), *v.i.* **1.** to clap the hands as an expression of approval, appreciation, acclamation, etc.: *They applauded wildly at the end of the opera.* **2.** to express approval; give praise; acclaim. —*v.t.* **3.** to clap the hands so as to show approval, appreciation, etc., of: *to applaud an actor; to applaud a speech.* **4.** to praise or express approval of: *to applaud his ambition.* [< L *applaud(ere),* equiv. to *ap-* AP-[1] + *plaudere* to clap the hands] —**ap·plaud′a·ble,** *adj.* —**ap·plaud′a·bly,** *adv.* —**ap·plaud′er,** *n.* —**ap·plaud′ing·ly,** *adv.*

ap·plause (ə plôz′), *n.* **1.** hand clapping as a demonstration of approval, appreciation, acclamation, etc. **2.** any positive expression of appreciation or approval; acclamation. [< L *applaus(us)* struck upon, applauded (ptp. of *applaudere*) < *ap-* AP-[1] + *plaud-* clap + *-tus* ptp. suffix] —**ap·plau·sive** (ə plô′siv, -ziv), *adj.*

—**Syn. 2.** acclaim, plaudit.

ap·ple (ap′əl), *n.* **1.** the usually round, red or yellow, edible fruit of a rosaceous tree, *Malus pumila* (**Pyrus Malus**). **2.** the tree, cultivated in most temperate regions. **3.** the fruit of any of certain other species of tree of the same genus. **4.** any of these trees. **5.** any of various other similar fruits, or fruitlike products or plants, as the custard apple, love apple, May apple, oak apple. **6.** anything resembling an apple in size and shape, as a ball, esp. a baseball. **7.** *Bowling Slang.* an ineffectively bowled ball. [ME < OE *æppel;* c. OS *appel,* Icel *apal(l),* OHG *apful* (> G *Apfel*)]

ap′ple blos′som, the flower of the apple tree: the State flower of Arkansas and Michigan.

ap′ple bran′dy, applejack (def. 1).

ap′ple but′ter, apples stewed to a paste, sweetened, spiced, and served as a spread or condiment.

ap·ple·cart (ap′əl kärt′), *n.* **1.** a pushcart used by a vendor of apples. **2. upset the** or **one's applecart,** to ruin plans or arrangements; spoil something: *He tattled to the teacher and upset our applecart.* [APPLE + CART]

ap′ple green′, a clear, light green.

ap·ple·jack (ap′əl jak′), *n. U.S.* **1.** a brandy distilled from fermented cider; apple brandy. **2.** See **hard cider.** [APPLE + JACK[1]]

ap′ple mint′. See **horse mint** (def. 1).

ap′ple of dis′cord, *Class. Myth.* a golden apple inscribed "For the fairest," thrown by Eris, goddess of discord, among the gods. Its award by Paris to Aphrodite caused events which led to the Trojan War. Cf. **Helen, Paris.**

ap′ple of one's eye′, something very precious or dear: *Her son is the apple of her eye.*

ap′ple pandow′dy, pandowdy.

ap′ple-pie′ bed′ (ap′əl pī′), a bed that has been short-sheeted as a joke.

ap′ple-pie or′der, *Informal.* excellent or perfect order: *Her desk is always in apple-pie order.*

ap·ple-pol·ish (ap′əl pol′ish), *v.i. Informal.* to curry favor with someone, esp. in an obsequious or flattering manner. **—ap′ple pol′isher. —ap′ple-pol′ish·er,** *n.*

ap′ples and pears′, *Chiefly Brit. Slang.* **1.** stairs. **2.** arranged in a stairlike manner, as of fruit displayed in a stall. [rhyming slang]

ap·ple·sauce (ap′əl sôs′), *n.* **1.** apples stewed to a soft pulp and sweetened. **2.** *Slang.* nonsense; bunk. [APPLE + SAUCE]

Ap·ple·seed (ap′əl sēd′), *n.* **Johnny** (*John Chapman*), 1774–1845, American pioneer and orchardist: prototype for character in American folklore.

Ap′ples of the Hesper′ides, *Class. Myth.* the golden apples given to Hera as a wedding gift. They were in the safekeeping of the Hesperides and of the dragon Ladon.

Ap·ple·ton (ap′əl tən), *n.* **1. Sir Edward Victor,** 1892–1965, British physicist: Nobel prize 1947. **2.** a city in E Wisconsin. 48,411 (1960).

Ap′pleton lay′er. See **F₂ layer.** [named after Sir E. V. APPLETON]

ap′ple tree′ bor′er, **1.** Also called **flatheaded apple tree borer.** the larva of a metallic wood-boring beetle, *Chrysobothris femorata,* that bores into the wood of apple and other fruit trees. **2.** Also called **roundheaded apple tree borer.** the larva of a long-horned beetle, *Saperda candida,* that bores into the wood of apple and other fruit trees.

ap·pli·ance (ə plī′əns), *n.* **1.** an instrument, apparatus, or device for a particular purpose or use. **2.** a piece of equipment, usually operated electrically, esp. for use in the home or for performance of domestic chores, as a refrigerator, washing machine, toaster, etc. **3.** act of applying; application. **4.** *Archaic.* a measure; stratagem. **5.** *Obs.* compliance. [APPLY + -ANCE]

ap·pli·ca·ble (ap′lə kə bəl, ə plik′ə-), *adj.* applying or capable of being applied; relevant; suitable; appropriate: *an applicable rule; a solution that is applicable to the problem.* [< L *applic(āre)* (to) APPLY + -ABLE] **—ap′pli·ca·bil′i·ty, ap′pli·ca·ble·ness,** *n.* **—ap′pli·ca·bly,** *adv.*
—Syn. fitting, proper, germane, pertinent.

ap·pli·cant (ap′lə kənt), *n.* a person who applies for or requests something; a candidate: *an applicant for a position.* [< L *applicant-* (s. of *applicāns* applying, prp. of *applicāre*). See APPLY, -ANT]

ap·pli·ca·tion (ap′lə kā′shən), *n.* **1.** the act of putting to a special use or purpose: *the application of common sense to a problem.* **2.** the quality of being usable for a particular purpose or in a special way; relevance: *This has no application to the case.* **3.** the act of laying on or bringing into contact with: *the application of salve to a wound.* **4.** a salve, or healing agent. **5.** act of requesting. **6.** a written or spoken request or appeal: *to file an application for admission to a university.* **7.** close attention; persistent effort: *Application to one's studies is necessary.* [late ME < L *applicātiōn-* (s. of *applicātiō*), equiv. to *applicāt(us)* applied (ptp. of *applicāre* to APPLY) + *-iōn-* -ION]
—Syn. 1. utilization. **2.** aptitude, suitability, pertinence. **6.** solicitation, petition. **7.** assiduity, industry, persistence, perseverance. See **effort.**

ap·pli·ca·tive (ap′lə kā′tiv, ə plik′ə-), *adj.* usable or capable of being used; practical; applicatory. [*applicate* (now obs.) to apply (see APPLICATION) + -IVE] **—ap′pli·ca′tive·ly,** *adv.*

ap·pli·ca·tor (ap′lə kā′tər), *n.* a simple device, as a rod, spatula, or the like, for applying medication, glue, or any other substance not usually touched with the fingers. [*applicate* (see APPLICATIVE) + -OR[2]]

ap·pli·ca·to·ry (ap′lə kə tōr′ē, -tôr′ē), *adj.* fitted for application or use; practical. [*applicate* (see APPLICATIVE) + -ORY[1]] **—ap′pli·ca·to′ri·ly,** *adv.*

ap·plied (ə plīd′), *adj.* **1.** having a practical purpose: *applied psychology.* **2.** derived from or involved with actual phenomena (distinguished from *theoretical,* opposed to *pure*): *applied mathematics; applied science.* **3.** of or pertaining to those arts or crafts that have a primarily utilitarian function, or to the designs and decorations used in these arts. [APPLY + -ED[2]]

applied′ kinemat′ics, kinematics (def. 2).

applied′ linguis′tics, **1.** linguistic theory as applied to such fields as lexicography, psychology, the teaching of reading, the creation of orthographies, and esp. language teaching. **2.** the study of practical applications of linguistics, as to telephone engineering, data processing, and data retrieval.

ap·pli·qué (ap′lə kā′), *adj., n., v.,* **-quéd, -qué·ing.** **—adj. 1.** ornamented by a different material or a piece of the same type, sewn on or otherwise applied. **—n. 2.** the ornamentation so used or to be so used. **3.** work so formed. **4.** a decorative feature, as a sconce, applied to a surface. **—v.t. 5.** to apply as appliqué to. [< F: applied, fastened to, ptp. of *appliquer* to APPLY]

ap·ply (ə plī′), *v.,* **-plied, -ply·ing.** **—v.t. 1.** to make use of as relevant, suitable, or pertinent: *to apply a theory to a problem.* **2.** to put to use, esp. for a particular purpose: *to apply pressure to open the door.* **3.** to bring into action; use; employ: *They know where to apply their workers. He applied the brakes and skidded to a stop.* **4.** to use for or assign to a specific purpose: *He applied a portion of his salary each week to savings.* **5.** to put into effect: *They applied the rules to new members only.* **6.** to place in contact with; lay or spread on: *to apply paint to a wall; to apply a bandage to a wound.* **7.** to bring into physical contact with or close proximity to: *to apply a match to gunpowder.* **8.** to devote or employ diligently or with close attention: *to apply one's mind to a problem; to apply oneself to a task.* **9.** to credit to, as an account: *to apply $10 to his account at the store.* **—v.i. 10.** to be pertinent, suitable, or relevant: *The argument applies to the case. The theory doesn't apply.* **11.** to make an application or request; ask: *to apply for a job; to apply for a raise.* **12.** to lay or spread on: *The plastic coating is easy to apply on any surface.* **13.** to be placed or remain in contact: *This paint doesn't apply very easily.* [ME *applie* < MF *aplie(r)* < L *applicāre,* equiv. to *ap-* AP-[1] + *plicāre* to fold; see PLY[2]] **—ap·pli′a·ble,** *adj.* **—ap·pli′a·ble·ness,** *n.* **—ap·pli′a·bly,** *adv.* **—ap·pli′er,** *n.*
—Syn. 3. utilize. **4.** appropriate, allot, assign, dedicate. **11.** petition, sue, entreat.

Written Played

A

B

Appoggiatura
A, Short; B, Long

appmt., appointment.

ap·pog·gia·tu·ra (ə poj′ə to͝or′ə, -tyo͝or′ə; *It.* äp pôd′jä to͞o′rä), *n., pl.* **-tu·ras,** *It.* **-tu·re** (-to͞o′re). *Music.* a short or long note of embellishment preceding another note and taking a portion of its time. [< It: a propping, equiv. to *appoggiat(o),* ptp. of *appoggiare* to support (see AP-[1], PODI(UM), -ATE[1]) + *-ura* -URE]

ap·point (ə point′), *v.t.* **1.** to name or assign to a position, an office, or the like; designate: *to appoint a new secretary; to appoint a judge to the bench.* **2.** to determine by authority or agreement; fix; set: *to appoint a time for the meeting.* **3.** *Law.* to designate (a person) to take the benefit of an estate created by a deed or will. **4.** *Archaic.* to order or establish by decree or command; ordain; constitute: *laws appointed by God.* **5.** *Obs.* to provide with what is necessary; equip; furnish: *They appointed the house with all the latest devices.* **6.** *Obs.* to point at by way of censure. **—v.i. 7.** *Obs.* to ordain; resolve; determine. [ME *apoint(en)* < MF *apointe(r),* equiv. to *a-* A-[5] + *pointer* to POINT] **—ap·point′a·ble,** *adj.* **—ap·point′er,** *n.*
—Syn. 1. name, select. **2.** prescribe, establish. **—Ant. 1.** dismiss.

ap·point·ed (ə poin′tid), *adj.* **1.** by, through, or as a result of an appointment (often in contrast with *elected*): *an appointed official.* **2.** predetermined; arranged; set: *They met at the appointed time in the appointed place.* **3.** provided with what is necessary; equipped; furnished: *a beautifully appointed office.* [APPOINT + -ED[2]]

ap·point·ee (ə poin tē′, ap′oin tē′), *n.* **1.** a person who is appointed. **2.** a beneficiary under a legal appointment. [APPOINT + -EE, modeled on F *appointé*]

ap·poin·tive (ə poin′tiv), *adj.* **1.** pertaining to or filled by appointment: *an appointive office.* **2.** having the ability or authority to appoint: *appointive powers.* [APPOINT + -IVE]

ap·point·ment (ə point′mənt), *n.* **1.** the act of appointing, designating, or placing in office: *to fill a vacancy by appointment.* **2.** an office, position, or the like to which a person is appointed: *He received his appointment after a short delay.* **3.** a fixed mutual agreement for a meeting or the meeting itself; engagement: *I have an appointment to meet him at six o'clock. He kept the appointment.* **4.** Usually, **appointments.** equipment, furnishings, or accouterments. **5. appointments,** accouterments for a soldier or a horse. **6.** *Manège.* a horse-show class in which the contestant need not be a member of a hunt but must wear regulation hunt livery. Cf. **Corinthian** (def. 8). **7.** *Archaic.* decree; ordinance. [late ME *apoynt(e)ment* < MF *ap(p)ointement.* See APPOINT, -MENT]
—Syn. 2. APPOINTMENT, OFFICE, POST, STATION mean a place of duty or employment. APPOINTMENT refers to a position for which special qualifications are required. OFFICE often suggests a position of trust or authority. POST in the U.S. is usually restricted to military or other public positions; in England it may be used of any position. STATION means a sphere of duty or occupation; it emphasizes the location of work to be done. See **position. 3.** assignation, rendezvous, tryst, date. **4.** furnishing(s).

Appoint′ment in Samar′ra, a novel (1934) by John O'Hara.

ap·poin·tor (ə poin′tər; ə poin tôr′, ap′oin-), *n. Law.* one who exercises a power of appointment of property. [APPOINT + -OR[2]]

Ap·po·mat·tox (ap′ə mat′əks), *n.* **1.** a town in central Virginia where Lee surrendered to Grant on April 9, 1865, ending the Civil War. **2.** a river flowing E from E central Virginia to the James River. 137 mi. long.

ap·por·tion (ə pōr′shən, ə pôr′-), *v.t.* to distribute or allocate proportionally; divide and assign according to some rule of proportional distribution: *to apportion expenses among the three men.* [< MF *apportionn(er),* equiv. to *ap-* AP-[1] + *portionner* to PORTION] **—ap·por′tion·a·ble,** *adj.* **—ap·por′tion·er,** *n.*

ap·por·tion·ment (ə pōr′shən mənt, ə pôr′-), *n.* **1.** act of apportioning. **2.** *U.S.* **a.** the determination of the number of members of the U.S. House of Representatives according to the proportion of the population of each State to the total population of the U.S. **b.** the apportioning of members of any other legislative body. [APPORTION + -MENT]

ap·pose (ə pōz′), *v.t.,* **-posed, -pos·ing.** **1.** to place side by side, as two things; place next to; juxtapose. **2.** to put or apply (one thing) to or near to another. [< MF *a(p)pose(r)* (to) set before, beside, or upon, equiv. to *a-* A-[5] + *poser* to POSE[1]] **—ap·pos′a·bil′i·ty,** *n.* **—ap·pos′a·ble,** *adj.* **—ap·pos′er,** *n.*

ap·po·site (ap′ə zit, ə poz′it), *adj.* suitable; well-adapted; pertinent; relevant; apt: *an apposite answer.* [< L *apposit(us)* applied to, added to, put near (ptp. of *appōnere*), equiv. to *ap-* AP-[1] + *positus* placed (*posi-* place + *-tus* ptp. suffix)] **—ap′po·site·ly,** *adv.* **—ap′po·site·ness,** *n.*

ap·po·si·tion (ap′ə zish′ən), *n.* **1.** the act of placing together or bringing into proximity; juxtaposition. **2.** the addition or application to one thing of another thing. **3.** *Gram.* a syntactic relation between expressions, usually consecutive, which have the same function and the same relation to other elements in the sentence, the second expression identifying or supplementing the first. In *Washington, our first President,* the phrase *our first President* is in apposition with *Washington.* **4.** *Biol.* growth of a cell wall by the deposition of new particles in layers on the wall. Cf. **intussusception** (def. 2). [< LL *appositiōn-* (s. of *appositiō*) < L *apposit(us)* (see APPOSITE) + *-iōn-* -ION] **—ap′po·si′tion·al,** *adj.* **—ap′po·si′tion·al·ly,** *adv.*

ap·pos·i·tive (ə poz′i tiv), *Gram.* **—n. 1.** a word or phrase in apposition. **—adj. 2.** placed in apposition. **3.** (of an adjective or adjectival phrase) directly following the noun it modifies. [APPOSIT(ION) + -IVE] **—ap·pos′i·tive·ly,** *adv.*

ap·prais·al (ə prā′zəl), *n.* **1.** the act of estimating the value of an asset or assets, goods, etc. **2.** an estimate of value, as for sale, assessment, or taxation; valuation. **3.** the act of estimating the nature, quality, importance, etc., of: *an expert appraisal of pop art; an incorrect appraisal of public opinion.* Also, **ap·praise′ment.** [APPRAISE + -AL[2]]

ap·praise (ə prāz′), *v.t.,* **-praised, -prais·ing.** **1.** to estimate as to quality, size, weight, etc. **2.** to estimate the monetary value of; determine the worth of; assess: *We had an expert appraise the house before we bought it.* **3.** to estimate the nature, quality, importance, etc., of: *He tried to appraise the poetry of John Updike.* [AP-(PRIZE) + PRAISE (in obs. sense to PRIZE[2])] **—ap·prais′a·ble,** *adj.* **—ap·prais′er,** *n.* **—ap·prais′ing·ly,** *adv.* **—ap·prais′ive,** *adj.*

ap·pre·ci·a·ble (ə prē′shē ə bəl, -shə bəl), *adj.* capable of being readily perceived or estimated; considerable: *There is an appreciable difference between socialism and communism.* [APPRECI(ATE) + -ABLE] **—ap·pre′ci·a·bly,** *adv.*

ap·pre·ci·ate (ə prē′shē āt′), *v.,* **-at·ed, -at·ing.** **—v.t. 1.** to value or regard highly; place a high estimate on: *His great ability was fully appreciated by his friends.* **2.** to be fully conscious of; be aware of; detect: *to appreciate the dangers of a situation.* **3.** to be grateful for: *They appreciated his thoughtfulness.* **4.** to raise in value. **—v.i. 5.** to increase in value: *Property values appreciated yearly.* [< ML *appreciāt(us)* valued, appraised < LL *appretiātus* (ptp. of *appretiāre*) appraised < L *ap-* AP-[1] + *preti(um)* PRICE + *-ātus* -ATE[1]] **—ap·pre′ci·at′ing·ly,** *adv.* **—ap·pre′ci·a′tor,** *n.*
—Syn. 1. APPRECIATE, ESTEEM, PRIZE, VALUE imply holding something in high regard. To APPRECIATE is to exercise wise judgment, delicate perception, and keen insight in realizing the worth of something. To ESTEEM is to feel respect combined with a warm, kindly feeling. To VALUE is to attach importance to a thing because of its worth (material or otherwise). To PRIZE is to value highly and cherish.

ap·pre·ci·a·tion (ə prē′shē ā′shən), *n.* **1.** the act of estimating the qualities of things and giving them their proper value. **2.** clear perception or recognition, esp. of aesthetic quality. **3.** gratitude: *They showed their appreciation by giving him a gold watch.* **4.** an increase in the value of property, goods, etc. **5.** critical notice; evaluation; opinion, as of a situation, person, etc. **6.** a critique or written evaluation, esp. when favorable. [earlier *appretiation* < LL *appretiāt(us)* (see APPRECIATE) + -ION] **—ap·pre′ci·a′tion·al,** *adj.*

ap·pre·cia·tive (ə prē′shə tiv, -shē ā′-), *adj.* capable of appreciating; feeling or manifesting appreciation: *an appreciative audience at the concert.* [APPRECIATE + -IVE] **—ap·pre′cia·tive·ly,** *adv.* **—ap·pre′cia·tive·ness,** *n.*

ap·pre·ci·a·to·ry (ə prē′shē ə tōr′ē, -tôr′ē, -shə-), *adj.* appreciative. [APPRECIATE + -ORY[1]] **—ap·pre′ci·a·to′ri·ly,** *adv.*

ap·pre·hend (ap′ri hend′), *v.t.* **1.** to take into custody; arrest by legal warrant or authority: *The sheriff apprehended the bandits thirty miles away.* **2.** to grasp the meaning of; understand, esp. intuitively; perceive. **3.** to expect with anxiety, suspicion, or fear; anticipate: *I apprehend no violence.* **—v.i. 4.** to understand. **5.** to be apprehensive, suspicious, or fearful; fear. [ME *apprehend(en)* < L *apprehende(re)* (to) grasp, equiv. to *ap-* AP-[1] + *prehendere* to seize (*pre-* PRE- + *-hendere,* akin to GET)] **—ap′pre·hend′er,** *n.*

ap·pre·hen·si·ble (ap′ri hen′sə bəl), *adj.* capable of being understood. [< LL *apprehensibil(is)* < L *apprehens(us)* grasped (ptp. of *apprehendere*), equiv. to *apprehend-* (see APPREHEND) + *-t(us)* ptp. suffix + *-ibilis* -IBLE] **—ap′pre·hen′si·bil′i·ty,** *n.* **—ap′pre·hen′si·bly,** *adv.*

ap·pre·hen·sion (ap′ri hen′shən), *n.* **1.** anticipation of adversity; dread or fear of coming evil. **2.** the faculty or act of apprehending, esp. intuitive understanding; perception on a direct and immediate level. **3.** acceptance of or receptivity to information without passing judgment on its validity, often without complete comprehension. **4.** a view, opinion, or idea on any subject. **5.** the act of arresting; seizure. [ME < LL *apprehensiōn-* (s. of *apprehensiō*), equiv. to *apprehens-* (see APPREHENSIBLE) + *-iōn-* -ION]
—Syn. 1. alarm, worry, uneasiness; suspicion. APPREHENSION, ANXIETY, MISGIVING imply an unsettled and uneasy state of mind. APPREHENSION is an active state of fear, usually of some danger or misfortune: *apprehension before opening a telegram.* ANXIETY is a somewhat prolonged state of apprehensive worry: *anxiety because of a reduced income.* MISGIVING implies a dubious uncertainty or suspicion, as well as uneasiness: *to have misgivings about the investment.* **5.** capture. **—Ant. 1.** composure. **5.** release.

ap·pre·hen·sive (ap′ri hen′siv), *adj.* **1.** uneasy or fearful about something that might happen: *apprehensive of one's safety.* **2.** quick to learn or understand. **3.** perceptive; discerning (usually fol. by *of*). [< ML *apprehensīv(us).* See APPREHENSIBLE, -IVE] **—ap′pre·hen′sive·ly,** *adv.* **—ap′pre·hen′sive·ness,** *n.*

ap·pren·tice (ə pren′tis), *n., v.,* **-ticed, -tic·ing.** **—n. 1.** a person who works for another in order to learn a trade: *an apprentice to a plumber.* **2.** *Hist.* a person legally bound through indenture to a master craftsman in order to learn a trade. **3.** a learner; novice; tyro. **4.** *U.S. Navy.* an enlisted man receiving specialized training. **5.** a jockey with less than one year's experience who has won fewer than 40 races. **—v.t. 6.** to bind to or place with an employer, master craftsman, or the like, for instruction in a trade. [ME *aprentis* < MF, equiv. to *aprentif* for **aprendif* (*aprend-* < L *apprend-* APPREHEND + *-if* < L *-īvus* -IVE) + *-s* nom. suffix] **—ap·pren′tice·ship′;** *Archaic.* **ap·pren′tice·ment;** *Obs.* **ap·pren′tice·hood′,** *n.*

ap·pressed (ə prest′), *adj.* pressed closely against or fitting closely to something. [< L *appress(us)* pressed to (ptp. of *apprimere*), equiv. to *ap-* AP-[1] + *pressus* (see PRESS[1]) + -ED[2]]

ap·prise[1] (ə prīz′), *v.t.*, **-prised, -pris·ing.** to give notice to; inform; advise (often fol. by *of*): *to be apprised of the situation by a friend.* Also, **apprize.** [< F *appris(e)* taught, informed, ptp. of *apprendre;* see APPREHEND]

ap·prise[2] (ə prīz′), *v.t.*, **-prised, -pris·ing.** *Obs.* appraise.

ap·prize[1] (ə prīz′), *v.t.*, **-prized, -priz·ing.** *Obs.* appraise. [ME *aprise* < MF *apris(i)er*, equiv. to *a-* A-[5] + *prisier* to PRIZE[2]] —**ap·priz′er,** *n.*

ap·prize[2] (ə prīz′), *v.t.*, **-prized, -priz·ing.** apprise[1].

ap·proach (ə prōch′), *v.t.* **1.** to come near or nearer to: *to approach the city.* **2.** to come near to in quality, character, time, or condition; to come within range for comparison: *As a poet he hardly approaches Keats.* **3.** to present, offer, or make a proposal to: *to approach the president with a suggestion.* **4.** to begin work on; set about: *to approach a problem.* **5.** to make a tentative sexual advance: *He approached her at the party, but she refused him.* **6.** *Rare.* to bring near to something. —*v.i.* **7.** to come nearer; draw near: *A storm is approaching.* **8.** to come near in character, time, amount, etc.; approximate. —*n.* **9.** the act of drawing near: *the approach of a horseman.* **10.** nearness or close approximation: *a fair approach to accuracy.* **11.** any means of access, as a road, ramp, etc.: *the approaches to a city.* **12.** the method used or steps taken in setting about a task, problem, etc.: *His approach to all problems was to prepare an outline.* **13.** the course to be followed by an aircraft in approaching for a landing or in joining a traffic pattern: *The plane's approach to the airport was hazardous.* **14.** a tentative sexual advance. **15.** Sometimes, **approaches.** a presentation, offer, or proposal. **16. approaches,** *Mil.* works for protecting forces in an advance against a fortified position. **17.** *Golf.* a stroke made after teeing off, by which a player attempts to get the ball onto the putting green. **18.** *Bowling.* **a.** the steps taken and the manner employed in delivering the ball: *He favors a four-step approach.* **b.** the area behind the foul line, from which the ball is delivered. [ME *a(p)proche(n)* < MF *a(p)proch(i)e(r)* < LL *adpropiāre* < L *ad-* AD- + *propi(us)* nearer (comp. of *prope* near) + *-ā-* thematic vowel + *-re* inf. suffix] —**ap·proach′er,** *n.* —**ap·proach′less,** *adj.*
—**Syn. 1.** near, close with. **3.** sound out. —**Ant. 1.** withdraw.

ap·proach·a·ble (ə prō′chə bəl), *adj.* **1.** capable of being approached; accessible. **2.** (of a person) easy to meet, know, talk with, etc. [APPROACH + -ABLE] —**ap·proach′a·bil′i·ty, ap·proach′a·ble·ness,** *n.*

ap·pro·bate (ap′rə bāt′), *v.t.*, **-bat·ed, -bat·ing.** *Chiefly U.S.* to approve officially. [late ME < L *approbāt(us)* approved (ptp. of *approbāre*), equiv. to *ap-* AP-[1] + *probātus* proved; see PROBATE] —**ap′pro·ba′tor,** *n.*

ap·pro·ba·tion (ap′rə bā′shən), *n.* **1.** approval; commendation. **2.** sanction. **3.** *Obs.* conclusive proof. [ME < L *approbātiōn-* (s. of *approbātiō*). See APPROBATE, -ION]

ap·pro·ba·tive (ap′rə bā′tiv, ə prō′bə-), *adj.* approving; expressing approbation. Also, **ap·pro·ba·to·ry** (ə prō′bə tôr′ē, -tōr′ē). [< ML *approbātīv(us).* See APPROBATE, -IVE] —**ap′pro·ba′tive·ness,** *n.*

ap·pro·pri·a·ble (ə prō′prē ə bəl), *adj.* capable of being or liable to be appropriated. [APPROPRI(ATE) + -ABLE]

ap·pro·pri·ate (*adj.* ə prō′prē it; *v.* ə prō′prē āt′), *adj.*, *v.*, **-at·ed, -at·ing.** —*adj.* **1.** suitable or fitting for a particular purpose, person, occasion, etc.: *an appropriate example; an appropriate dress.* **2.** belonging to or peculiar to a person; proper: *Each played his appropriate part.* —*v.t.* **3.** to set apart, authorize, or legislate for some specific purpose or use: *The legislature appropriated funds for the university.* **4.** to take to or for oneself; take possession of. **5.** to take without consent; seize; expropriate: *He appropriated the trust funds for himself.* **6.** to steal, esp. to commit petty theft. [< LL *appropriāt(us)* made one's own (ptp. of *appropriāre*) < L *ap-* AP-[1] + *propri-(us)* one's own + *-ātus* -ATE[1]] —**ap·pro′pri·ate·ly,** *adv.* —**ap·pro′pri·ate·ness,** *n.* —**ap·pro·pri·a·tive** (ə prō′prē ā′tiv, -ə tiv), *adj.* —**ap·pro′pri·a′tive·ness,** *n.* —**ap·pro′pri·a′tor,** *n.*
—**Syn. 1.** befitting, apt, meet, felicitous, suited, proper, due, becoming, pertinent. **2.** individual, separate. **3.** apportion, allocate, assign. —**Ant. 1.** unsuitable, inept.

ap·pro·pri·a·tion (ə prō′prē ā′shən), *n.* **1.** the act of appropriating. **2.** anything appropriated for a special purpose, esp. money. **3.** an act of a legislature authorizing money to be paid from the treasury for a special use. **4.** the money thus authorized: *a large appropriation for aid to libraries.* [ME < LL *appropriātiōn-* (s. of *appropriātiō*). See APPROPRIATE, -ION]

ap·prov·al (ə prōō′vəl), *n.* **1.** act of approving; approbation. **2.** formal permission or sanction. **3. on approval,** without obligation to buy unless satisfactory to the customer upon trial or examination (and, otherwise, returnable): *We ship merchandise on approval.* [APPROVE + -AL[2]]

ap·prove (ə prōōv′), *v.*, **-proved, -prov·ing.** —*v.t.* **1.** to speak or think favorably of; pronounce or consider agreeable or good; judge favorably: *to approve the policies of the administration.* **2.** to confirm or sanction formally; ratify: *The Senate promptly approved the bill.* **3.** *Obs.* **a.** to demonstrate; show. **b.** to make good; attest. **c.** to prove by trial. **d.** to convict. —*v.i.* **4.** to speak or consider favorably (sometimes fol. by *of*): *Mother didn't approve of him. The boss wouldn't approve of the plan. He said that he approved.* [ME *a(p)prove* < OF *aprove(r)* < L *approbāre*, equiv. to *ap-* AP-[1] + *probāre* to PROVE] —**ap·prov′a·bil′i·ty,** *n.* —**ap·prov′a·ble,** *adj.* —**ap·prov′a·bly,** *adv.* —**ap·prov′ed·ly,** *adv.* —**ap·prov′ed·ness,** *n.* —**ap·prov′ing·ly,** *adv.*
—**Syn. 1.** appreciate, esteem. APPROVE, COMMEND, PRAISE mean to have, and usually to express, a favorable opinion. To APPROVE is to have a very good opinion, expressed or not, of someone or something: *He approved the new plan.* To COMMEND is to speak or write approvingly, often formally and publicly, to congratulate or honor for something done: *to commend a fireman for a heroic act.* To PRAISE is to speak or write, often in glowing and emotional terms, to or about one or more persons: *to praise the Boy Scouts.* **2.** authorize, endorse, validate. —**Ant. 2.** reject.

approved′ school′, (in Britain) a government school for delinquent boys or girls.

ap·prov·er (ə prōō′vər), *n.* **1.** a person who approves. **2.** *Old Eng. Law.* an accomplice to a felony who confesses his guilt and gives king's evidence against his confederates. [ME; see APPROVE, -ER[1]]

approx., approximately.

ap·prox·i·mal (ə prok′sə məl), *adj.* *Anat.* near or adjacent, as surfaces of teeth. [AP-[1] + PROXIMAL]

ap·prox·i·mate (*adj.* ə prok′sə mit; *v.* ə prok′sə māt′), *adj.*, *v.*, **-mat·ed, -mat·ing.** —*adj.* **1.** near or approaching a certain state, condition, goal, or standard. **2.** nearly exact; not perfectly accurate or correct: *The approximate time is 10 o'clock.* **3.** near; close together. **4.** very similar; almost equal: *an approximate situation.* —*v.t.* **5.** to come near to; approach closely to: *to approximate a solution to a problem.* **6.** to estimate: *We approximated the distance at three miles.* **7.** to simulate; imitate closely: *The motions of the stars can be approximated in a planetarium.* **8.** to bring near. —*v.i.* **9.** to come near in position, character, amount, etc. [< LL *approximāt(us)* drawn near to, approached (ptp. of *approximāre*). See AP-[1], PROXIMATE] —**ap·prox′i·mate·ly,** *adv.*

ap·prox·i·ma·tion (ə prok′sə mā′shən), *n.* **1.** a guess or estimate: *About 93,000,000 miles is an approximation of the distance of the earth from the sun.* **2.** nearness in space, position, degree, or relation; proximity; closeness. **3.** *Math., Physics.* a result that is not necessarily exact, but is within the limits of accuracy required for a given purpose. [APPROXIMATE + -ION]

ap·pulse (ə puls′), *n.* **1.** energetic motion toward a point. **2.** the act of striking against something. **3.** *Astron.* the approach or occurrence of conjunction between two celestial bodies. [< L *appuls(us)* driven to, landed (ptp. of *appellere*), equiv. to *ap-* AP-[1] + *pul-* (past s. of *pellere* to drive, push) + *-sus*, var. of *-tus* ptp. suffix] —**ap·pul′sive,** *adj.* —**ap·pul′sive·ly,** *adv.*

ap·pur·te·nance (ə pûr′tənəns), *n.* **1.** something subordinate to another, more important thing: an adjunct; accessory. **2.** *Law.* a right, privilege, or improvement belonging to and passing with a principal property. **3. appurtenances,** apparatus; instruments. [ME < AF, equiv. to *ap-* AP-[1] + *-purtenance* a belonging; see PURTENANCE]

ap·pur·te·nant (ə pûr′tənənt), *adj.* **1.** appertaining or belonging; pertaining. —*n.* **2.** an appurtenance. [ME (see APPURTEN(ANCE), -ANT); r. ME *apertinent* < LL *appertinent-* (s. of *appertinēns*, prp. of *appertinēre*). See AP-[1], PERTINENT]

Apr., April.

APRA (ä′prä), *n.* the political party in Peru that advocates sweeping social reforms, drawing its chief support from rural and labor groups. [< Sp *A(lianza) P(opular) R(evolucionaria) A(mericana)* Popular American Revolutionary League]

a·prax·i·a (ə prak′sē ə, ā prak′-), *n.* *Pathol.* a disorder of the nervous system, characterized by an inability to perform purposeful movements, but not accompanied by a loss of sensory function or paralysis. [< NL; see A-[6], PRAX(IS), -IA] —**a·prax′ic,** *adj.*

A·près-mi·di d'un Faune, L' (*Fr.* lᴀ pre mē dē′ dœɴ fōn′). See **L'Après-midi d'un Faune.**

a·près moi le dé·luge (ᴀ pre mwᴀ′ lə dā lʏzh′), *French.* after me, the deluge (attributed to Louis XV).

A·pres·o·line (ə pres′ə lēn′), *n.* *Pharm., Trademark.* hydralazine.

ap·ri·cot (ap′rə kot′, ā′prə-), *n.* **1.** the downy, yellow, sometimes rosy fruit, somewhat resembling a small peach, of the tree *Prunus Armeniaca.* **2.** the tree. **3.** a pinkish yellow or yellowish pink. [alter. (by mishearing) of earlier *apricock*, var. (with *p* < LL *praecoquum* apricot) of *abrecock* < Pg *albricoque* << Ar *al* the + *birqūq* << LL *praecoquum*, var. of *praecox*, short for *persicum praecox* early-ripening peach; see PRECOCIOUS]

A·pril (ā′prəl), *n.* **1.** the fourth month of the year, containing 30 days. **2.** a girl's given name. [ME < OE *Aprīl(is)* < L; r. ME *averil* < OF *avrill* < L *Aprīl(is)*]

A′pril fool′, **1.** the victim of a joke or jokes on April Fools' Day. **2.** a joke played on that day.

A′pril Fools′ Day′, April 1, a day when jokes are played on unsuspecting people. Also called **All Fools' Day.**

a pri·o·ri (ā′ prī ôr′ī, -ōr′ī, ā′ prē ôr′ē, -ōr′ē, ä′ prē-ôr′ē, -ōr′ē), **1.** from cause to effect; from a general law to a particular instance; valid independently of observation. Cf. **a posteriori** (def. 1). **2.** existing in the mind prior to and independent of experience, as a faculty or character trait. Cf. **a posteriori** (def. 2). **3.** not based on prior study or examination; nonanalytic: *an a priori judgment.* [< L: lit., from the one before. See A-[4], PRIOR] —**a·pri·or·i·ty** (ā′prī ôr′i tē, -or′-), *n.*

a·pri·o·rism (ā′prī ôr′iz əm, -ōr′-, ā′prē-, ä′prē-), *n.* *Philos.* belief in, or reliance upon, a priori reasoning, arguments, or principles. [prob. trans. of D *apriorisme.* See A PRIORI, -ISM] —**a′pri·or′ist,** *n.* —**a·pri·o·ris·tic** (ā prī′ə ris′tik), *adj.* —**a·pri′o·ris′ti·cal·ly,** *adv.*

a·pron (ā′prən), *n.* **1.** an article of apparel covering part of the front of the body and tied at the waist, for protecting the wearer's clothing. **2.** *Anglican Ch.* a similar garment extending to the knees, worn by bishops, deans, and archdeans. **3.** a metal plate or cover, usually vertical, for a machine, mechanism, artillery piece, etc., for protecting those who operate it. **4.** a continuous conveyor belt for bulk materials, consisting of a chain of steel plates. **5.** (in a lathe) a part of the carriage holding the clutches and gears moving the toolholder. **6.** a paved or hard-packed area abutting an airfield's buildings and hangars, where planes are parked, loaded, or the like. **7.** *Civ. Eng.* **a.** any device for protecting a surface of earth, such as a river bank, from the action of moving water. **b.** a platform to receive the water falling over a dam. **8.** the part of a stage floor in front of the curtain line. **9.** *Furniture.* skirt (def. 6). **10.** the outer border of a green of a golf course. **11.** the part of the floor of a boxing ring that extends outside of the ropes. **12.** Also called **skirt.** a flat, broad piece of interior window trim immediately beneath the sill. **13.** a strip of metal set into masonry and bent down to cover the upper edge of flashing; counterflashing. **14.** the open part of a pier for loading and unloading vessels. **15.** *Naut.* (in a wooden vessel) a piece reinforcing the stem on the after side and leading down to the deadwood. **16.** *Geol.* a deposit of gravel and sand extending forward from a moraine. **17.** the frill of long hairs on the throat and chest of certain long-haired dogs, as the collie. **18. tied to someone's apron strings,** completely dependent on or dominated by someone, esp. one's mother or wife: *He's forty years old, but he won't leave home because he's tied to his mother's apron strings.* —*v.t.* **19.** to put an apron on; furnish with an apron. [ME *napron* (later *a napron* > *an apron;* see ADDER) < MF *naperon* < *nape* tablecloth (< L *mappa* napkin) + *-ron* dim. suffix] —**a′pron·like′,** *adj.*

a′pron piece′, (in a staircase) a header receiving the ends of rough strings, carriage pieces, and the joists of landings. Also called **pitching piece.**

ap·ro·pos (ap′rə pō′), *adv.* **1.** to the purpose; opportunely. **2.** with reference or regard; in respect (usually fol. by *of*): *apropos of the preceding statement.* **3.** *Obs.* by the way. —*adj.* **4.** opportune; pertinent: *apropos remarks.* [< F *à propos*, lit., to purpose < L *ad prōpositum.* See AD-, PROPOSITION]

à pro·pos de rien (ᴀ prô pō də ʀyaɴ′), *French.* apropos of nothing; with reference to nothing in particular.

a·pros·ex·i·a (ā′pro sek′sē ə), *n.* *Psychiatry.* inability to maintain attentiveness. [< Gk: heedlessness, equiv. to *a-* A-[6] + *prósex(is)* heedfulness (*prosek-* (var. s. of *prosēchein* to heed, equiv. to *pros-* before + *échein* to hold) + *-s(is)* -SIS) + *-ia* -IA]

a·prowl (ə proul′), *adj.* moving about in stealthy search; covertly stalking or hunting; prowling (usually used predicatively): *The sudden silence in the jungle gave warning that some huge carnivore was aprowl.* [A-[1] + PROWL]

A.P.S., **1.** American Peace Society. **2.** American Philatelic Society. **3.** American Philosophical Society. **4.** American Physical Society. **5.** American Protestant Society.

A.P.S.A., American Political Science Association.

Ap·sa·ras (up′sər əs), *n.*, *pl.* **-sa·ras·es** (-sər ə siz). **1.** *Hindu Myth.* a supernatural female being, either the mistress of a soul in paradise or a succubus. **2.** a representation of such a being. [< Hindi]

apse (aps), *n.* **1.** *Archit.* a vaulted semicircular or polygonal recess in a building, esp. at the end of the choir of a church. See diag. under **basilica. 2.** *Astron.* an apsis. [var. of APSIS] —**ap·si·dal** (ap′si dəl), *adj.* —**ap′si·dal·ly,** *adv.*

apse′ line′, *Astron.* See **line of apsides.**

ap·sid·i·ole (ap sid′ē ōl′), *n.* a small apse, esp. one attached to a larger apse or a transept. [< F *absidiole* < *abside* APSIS (< ML *absid-*, s. of *absis*) + *-i-* -I- + *-ole* (< L *-ola* dim. suffix)]

ap·sis (ap′sis), *n.*, *pl.* **-si·des** (-si dēz′). **1.** *Astron.* either of two points in an eccentric orbit, one **(higher apsis)** furthest from the center of attraction, the other **(lower apsis)** nearest to the center of attraction. **2.** *Archit.* an apse. [< L < Gk *hapsís* (felloe of) a wheel, arch, vault, orig., fastening, equiv. to *háp(tein)* (to) fasten + *-sis* -SIS]

Ap·su (äp′sōō), *n.* an Akkadian god: the consort of Tiamat and the father of the gods.

Ap·syr·tus (ap sûr′təs), *n.* *Class. Myth.* a son of Aeëtes, killed by his sister Medea, who, while fleeing with Jason, threw pieces of her brother's body into the sea so that her father Aeëtes, in pursuing her, might be delayed while picking them up. Also, **Absyrtus.**

apt (apt), *adj.* **1.** inclined; disposed; given; prone: *too apt to slander others.* **2.** likely: *Am I apt to find him at home?* **3.** unusually intelligent; able to learn quickly and easily: *an apt pupil.* **4.** suited to the purpose or occasion: *an apt metaphor; a few apt remarks on world peace.* **5.** *Archaic.* prepared; ready; willing. [ME < L *apt(us)* fastened, fitted, fitting, appropriate, equiv. to *ap-* fasten, attach + *-tus* ptp. suffix] —**apt′ly,** *adv.* —**apt′ness,** *n.*
—**Syn. 1.** liable. **2.** See **likely. 3.** clever, bright; adaptable; handy, adroit, dexterous, skillful. **4.** appropriate, fitting, meet, germane, felicitous. APT, PERTINENT, RELEVANT all refer to something suitable or fitting. APT means to the point and particularly appropriate: *an apt comment.* PERTINENT means pertaining to the matter in hand: *a pertinent remark.* RELEVANT means directly related to and important to the subject: *a relevant opinion.*

apt., *pl.* **apts.** apartment.

ap·ter·al (ap′tər əl), *adj.* **1.** *Archit.* (of a classical temple) not having a surrounding colonnade; not peripteral. **2.** (of a church) having no aisles. **3.** (of a church façade) revealing no aisles. [< Gk *ápter(os)* wingless (*a-* A-[6] + *-pteros* -PTEROUS) + -AL[1]]

ap·te·ri·um (ap tēr′ē əm), *n.*, *pl.* **-te·ri·a** (-tēr′ē ə). *Ornith.* one of the featherless portions of the skin of a bird. Cf. **pteryla.** [< NL; see A-[6], PTER-, -IUM] —**ap·te′ri·al,** *adj.*

ap·ter·ous (ap′tər əs), *adj.* **1.** *Zool.* wingless, as some insects. **2.** *Bot.* without membranous expansions, as a stem. [< Gk *ápteros* wingless. See A-[6], -PTEROUS]

ap·ter·yg·i·al (ap′tə rij′ē əl), *adj.* *Zool.* having no wings, fins, or limbs, as snakes and eels. [A-[6] + Gk *pteryg-* (s. of *ptéryx* wing) + -IAL]

ap·ter·y·gote (ap ter′ə gōt′, ap′tər-), *adj.* belonging or pertaining to the *Apterygota*, a subclass of primitive wingless insects that undergo little or no metamorphosis. Also, **ap·ter·y·go·tous** (ap ter′ə gō′təs). [< NL *Apterygot(a)* name of the subclass, equiv. to *a-* A-[6] + *Pterygota* < Gk neut. pl. of *pterygōt(ós)* winged, deriv. of *pteryg-* (s. of *ptéryx*) wing]

ap·ter·yx (ap′tə riks), *n.* kiwi (def. 1). [A-[6] + Gk *ptéryx* wing]

ap·ti·tude (ap′ti tōōd′, -tyōōd′), *n.* **1.** capability; ability; innate or acquired capacity for something; talent: *He has a special aptitude for mathematics.* **2.** readiness in learning; intelligence: *He was placed in honors classes because of his general aptitude.* **3.** state or quality of being apt; special fitness. [late ME < LL *aptitūdō.* See APT, -I-, -TUDE] —**ap′ti·tu′di·nal,** *adj.* —**ap′ti·tu′di·nal·ly,** *adv.*
—**Syn. 1.** predilection, proclivity, bent, gift, faculty.

ap′titude test′, a special test given to find out what sort of work or skills a person has the ability to learn, such as clerical work, mechanical work, etc.

Ap·u·le·ius (ap′yə lē′əs), *n.* **Lucius,** born A.D. 125?, Roman philosopher and satirist.

A·pu·lia (ə pyōōl′yə), *n.* a department in SE Italy. 3,220,485 (1951); 7442 sq. mi. *Cap.:* Bari. Italian, **Puglia.** —**A·pu′lian,** *adj.*

a pun·ta d'ar·co (ä pōōn′tə där′kō; *It.* ä pōōn′tä där′kō), *Music.* (of performance of a musical passage for a stringed instrument) with the point of the bow. [< It; see AD-, POINT, ARC]

A·pu·re (ä pōō′ʀe), *n.* a river flowing E from W Venezuela to the Orinoco. ab. 500 mi. long.

A·pu·rí·mac (ä′po͞o rē′mäk), *n.* a river flowing NW from S Peru to the Ucayali River. ab. 550 mi. long.

A·pus (ā′pəs), *n., gen.* **Ap·o·dis** (ap′ə dis). *Astron.* the Bird of Paradise, a southern constellation between Octans and Triangulum Australe. [< NL < Gk *ápous* footless, equiv. to *a-* A-[6] + *poús* FOOT]

apx., appendix.

a·py·ret·ic (ā′pī ret′ik), *adj. Pathol.* free from fever. [A-[6] + PYRETIC]

AQ, *Psychol.* See **achievement quotient.**

Aq., water. Also, **aq.** [< L *aqua*]

A·qa·ba (ä′kä bä′), *n.* **1.** a seaport in SW Jordan, at the N end of the Gulf of Aqaba. 2835 (1950). **2. Gulf of,** an arm of the Red Sea, between Saudi Arabia and the United Arab Republic. 100 mi. long.

aq. bull., (in prescriptions) boiling water. [< L *aqua bullīens*]

aq. comm., (in prescriptions) common water. [< L *aqua commūnis*]

aq. dest., (in prescriptions) distilled water. [< L *aqua dēstillāta*]

aq. ferv., (in prescriptions) hot water. [< L *aqua fervēns*]

aq·ua (ak′wə, ä′kwə), *n., pl.* **aq·uae** (ak′wē, ä′kwē), **aq·uas,** *adj.* —*n.* **1.** *Chiefly Pharm.* **a.** water. **b.** a liquid. **c.** a solution, esp. in water. **2.** a light greenish-blue color. —*adj.* **3.** having the color aqua. [< L: water]

aq′ua am·mo′ni·ae (ə mō′nē ē′), ammonia (def. 2). Also, **aq′ua ammo′nia.** [< NL: lit., water of ammonia]

aq·ua·cade (ak′wə kād′, ä′kwə-; ak′wə kād′, ä′kwə-), *n.* an elaborate aquatic exhibition consisting of swimming, diving, etc., usually accompanied by music [AQUA + (CAVAL)CADE]

aq·uae·ma·na·le (ak′wē mə nā′lē, ä′kwē-), *n., pl.* **-na·li·a** (-nā′lē ə). aquamanile.

aq′ua for′tis, *Chem.* See **nitric acid.** [< L: lit., strong water]

aq·ua·lung (ak′wə lung′, ä′kwə-), *n.* a device consisting of a cylinder of compressed air, usually strapped onto the back, with a tube or tubes leading through an automatic pressure regulator to a mouthpiece, enabling a swimmer or skin-diver to breathe under water and to move about freely. Cf. **scuba.** [AQUA + LUNG]

aq·ua·ma·na·le (ak′wə mə nā′lē, ä′kwə-), *n., pl.* **-na·li·a** (-nā′lē ə). aquamanile.

aq·ua·ma·ni·le (ak′wə mə nī′lē, ä′kwə mə nē′lā), *n., pl.* **-ni·les** (-nī′lēz, -nē′lās), **-nil·i·a** (-nil′ē ə). **1.** a medieval ewer, often made in grotesque animal forms. **2.** *Eccles.* a basin used by a celebrant for washing his hands during the saying of the Mass. Also, **aquaemanale, aquamanale.** [< L *aquaemanāl(is),* orig. adj.: pertaining to water for the hands, equiv. to *aquae* (dat. of *aqua* water) + *man(us)* hand + *-ālis* -AL[1]]

aq·ua·ma·rine (ak′wə mə rēn′, ä′kwə-), *n.* **1.** a transparent, light-blue or greenish-blue variety of beryl, used as a gem. **2.** light blue-green or greenish blue. [< L *aqua marīna* sea water (named from its color). See AQUA, MARINE]

aq·ua·naut (ak′wə nôt′, -not′, ä′kwə-), *n.* a skin-diver. [AQUA + (AERO)NAUT]

aq·ua·plane (ak′wə plān′, ä′kwə-), *n., v.,* **-planed, -plan·ing.** —*n.* **1.** a board which skims over water when towed at high speed by a motorboat, used to carry a rider in aquatic sports. —*v.i.* **2.** to ride an aquaplane. [AQUA + (AIR)PLANE] —**aq′ua·plan′er,** *n.*

aq′ua pu′ra (pyo͝or′ə), pure water. [< L]

aq′ua re′gi·a (rē′jē ə), *Chem.* a yellow, fuming liquid composed of one part of nitric acid and three to four parts of hydrochloric acid: used chiefly to dissolve metals as gold, platinum, or the like. Also called **nitrohydrochloric acid.** [< NL: lit., royal water]

aq·ua·relle (ak′wə rel′, ä′kwə-; *Fr.* A KWA REL′), *n., pl.* **-relles** (-relz′; *Fr.* -REL′). **1.** (*italics.*) *French.* See **water color. 2.** *Print.* a printed picture which has been colored manually by applying water color through stencils, each color requiring a different stencil. [< F < It *acquarella* (now obs.) water color, equiv. to *acqua* water + *-rella* -REL] —**aq′ua·rel′list,** *n.*

a·quar·ist (ə kwâr′ist, ə kwer′-), *n.* a curator, collector, or ichthyologist associated with an aquarium. [AQUAR(IUM) + -IST]

a·quar·i·um (ə kwâr′ē əm), *n., pl.* **a·quar·i·ums, a·quar·i·a** (ə kwâr′ē ə). **1.** a pond, tank, bowl, or the like, in which living aquatic animals or plants are kept, as for exhibition. **2.** a building or institution in which aquatic animals or plants are kept for exhibit, study, etc. [< L: watering place for cattle, n. use of neut. of *aquārius* of water, equiv. to *aqu(a)* water + *-ārius* -ARY] —**a·quar′i·an, a·quar′i·al,** *adj.*

A·quar·i·us (ə kwâr′ē əs), *n., gen.* **A·quar·i·i** (ə kwâr′ē ī′) for 1. **1.** *Astron.* the Water Bearer, a zodiacal constellation between Pisces and Capricornus. **2.** *Astrol.* the eleventh sign of the zodiac. See diag. under **zodiac.**

a·quat·ic (ə kwat′ik, ə kwot′-), *adj.* **1.** of, in, or pertaining to water. **2.** living or growing in water: *aquatic plant life.* **3.** practiced on or in water: *aquatic sports.* —*n.* **4. aquatics,** sports practiced on or in water. [< L *aquātic(us),* equiv. to *aqu(a)* water + *-āticus* (see -ATE[1], -IC); r. late ME *aquatyque* < MF < L] —**a·quat′i·cal·ly,** *adv.*

aq·ua·tint (ak′wə tint′, ä′kwə-), *n.* **1.** a process imitating the broad flat tints of ink or wash drawings by etching a microscopic crackle on the copperplate intended for printing. **2.** an etching made by this process. —*v.t., v.i.* **3.** to etch in aquatint. [var. of *aqua-tinta* < It *acqua tinta,* lit., tinted water. See AQUA, TINT] —**aq′ua·tint′er,** *n.*

aq·ua·tone (ak′wə tōn′, ä′kwə-), *n.* **1.** a lithographic process for printing by offset from a metal plate coated with photosensitized gelatine. **2.** a print so produced. [AQUA + TONE]

aq·ua·vit (ä′kwə vēt′, ak′wə-), *n.* akvavit.

aq′ua vi′tae (vī′tē), **1.** alcohol. **2.** spirituous liquor, as brandy or whiskey. [< L: water of life]

aq·ue·duct (ak′wi dukt′), *n.* **1.** *Civ. Eng.* **a.** a conduit or artificial channel for conducting water from a distance, usually by means of gravity. **b.** a structure which carries a conduit or canal across a valley or over a river. **2.** *Anat.* a canal or passage through which liquids pass. [< ML *aquēduct(us)* < L *aquae ductus* a drawing off of water. See AQUA, DUCT]

aq′ueduct of Syl′vi·us (sil′vē əs), *Anat.* a canal in the midbrain, connecting the third and fourth ventricles of the brain. [named after *Sylvius,* Latinized name of Jacques Dubois (d. 1555), French anatomist]

a·que·ous (ā′kwē əs, ak′wē-), *adj.* **1.** of, like, or containing water; watery: *an aqueous solution.* **2.** (of rocks) formed by matter deposited in or by water. [AQU(A) + -EOUS] —**a′que·ous·ly,** *adv.* —**a′que·ous·ness,** *n.*

a′queous ammo′nia, ammonia (def. 2).

a′queous hu′mor, *Anat.* the limpid watery fluid which fills the space between the cornea and the crystalline lens in the eye.

A·que·us (ā′kwē əs), *n. Class. Myth.* an epithet of Zeus, meaning "watery," referring to the time when ancient priestesses interpreted the murmur of the water of a sacred spring as the voice of Zeus.

aq·ui·clude (ak′wə klo͞od′), *n.* any geological formation which may contain considerable quantities of water but which does not transmit it at a sufficient rate to supply springs, wells, etc. [< L *aqui-* (comb. form of *aqua* water) + *clude(re),* var. of *claudere* to CLOSE]

aq·ui·cul·ture (ak′wə kul′chər), *n.* hydroponics. [< L *aqui-* (comb. form of *aqua* water) + (AGRI)CULTURE] —**aq′ui·cul′tur·al,** *adj.* —**aq′ui·cul′tur·ist,** *n.*

aq·ui·fer (ak′wə fər), *n.* any geological formation containing water, esp. one which supplies the water for wells, springs, etc. [< L *aqui-* (comb. form of *aqua* water) + -FER]

Aq·ui·la (ak′wə lə), *n., gen.* **-lae** (-lē′). the Eagle, a northern constellation south of Cygnus, containing the bright star Altair.

Aq·ui·la (ak′wə lə; *It.* ä′kwē lä), *n.* a city in central Italy. 58,202 (1959). Also called **L'Aquila, Aq·ui·la de·gli A·bruz·zi** (ä′kwē lä de′lyē ä broo͞t′tsē).

aq·ui·le·gi·a (ak′wə lē′jē ə, ā′kwə-), *n.* any plant of the genus *Aquilegia,* comprising the columbines. [< NL < ML, var. of *aquileia* columbine]

A·qui·le·ia (ä′kwē le′yä), *n.* an ancient Roman city at the northern end of the Adriatic: founded in 181 B.C.; destroyed by Attila in A.D. 452.

aq·ui·line (ak′wə līn′, -lin), *adj.* **1.** of or like the eagle. **2.** (of the nose) shaped like an eagle's beak; hooked. [< L *aquilin(us).* See AQUILA, -INE[1]]

Aq·ui·lo (ak′wə lō′), *n.* the ancient Roman personification of the north wind. Cf. **Boreas.**

A·qui·nas (ə kwī′nəs), *n.* **Saint Thomas** ("*the Angelic Doctor*"), 1225?–74, Italian scholastic philosopher: a major theologian of the Roman Catholic Church. —**A·qui′nist,** *n.*

a·quí se ha·bla es·pa·ñol (ä kē′ se ä′blä es′pä-nyôl′), *Spanish.* Spanish is spoken here.

Aq·ui·taine (ak′wi tān′; *Fr.* A kē ten′), *n.* a lowland region in SW France, formerly an ancient Roman province and medieval duchy. Latin, **Aq·ui·ta·ni·a** (ak′wi tā′nē ə).

a·quiv·er (ə kwiv′ər), *adj.* in a state of trepidation or vibrant agitation; trembling; quivering (usually used predicatively): *The bamboo thicket was aquiver with small birds and insects. The exciting news set her aquiver.* [A-[1] + QUIVER[1]]

a quo (ä kwō′; *Eng.* ā kwō′), *Latin.* from which; following from: used as a point of departure, as for an idea, plan, etc.

Ar, *Chem.* **1.** argon. **2.** aryl.

ar-, var. of **ad-** before *r: arrear.*

-ar[1], a formal element meaning "pertaining to," appearing in adjectives borrowed from Latin: *regular; singular.* [< L *-ār(is)* (used instead of *-ālis* when the preceding syllable had an *l*); r. ME *-er* < AF, OF]

-ar[2], a noun suffix meaning "pertaining to," "having the character of," borrowed from Latin: *vicar.* Also, **-er**[2]. [< L *-ār(ius),* or *-ār(is)* one connected with]

-ar[3], var. of **-er**[1] on the model of **-ar**[2], used in the formation of nouns of agency: *liar; beggar.*

AR, 1. annual return. **2.** Army Regulation; Army Regulations. Also, **A.R.**

Ar., 1. Also, **Ar** Arabic. **2.** Aramaic. **3.** argentum.

ar., 1. arrival. **2.** arrive; arrives.

a.r., 1. *Insurance.* all risks. **2.** analytical reagent.

A·ra (ā′rə, âr′ə), *n., gen.* **A·rae** (ā′rē, âr′ē). *Astron.* the Altar, a southern constellation between Triangulum Australe and Scorpius. [< L: altar]

ARA, Agricultural Research Administration.

A.R.A., 1. American Railway Association. **2.** Associate of the Royal Academy.

Ar·ab (ar′əb), *n.* **1.** a member of a Semitic people inhabiting Arabia and parts of northern Africa. **2.** See **Arabian horse. 3.** See **street Arab. 4.** a town in NE Alabama. 2989 (1960). —*adj.* **5.** Arabian. [back formation from L *Arabs* (taken as pl.) < Gk *Áraps* Arabian, an Arabian or Arab]

Arab., 1. Arabia. **2.** Arabian. **3.** Arabic.

ar·a·ban (ar′ə ban′), *n. Biochem.* a pentosan, found chiefly in vegetable gums, that yields arabinose upon hydrolysis. [ARAB(INOSE) + *-an;* see -ANE]

Ar·a·bel (ar′ə bel′), *n.* a girl's given name.

ar·a·besque (ar′ə besk′), *n.* **1.** any ornament or ornamental object, as a rug, mosaic, etc., in which flowers, foliage, fruits, vases, animals, and figures (in strict Islamic use, no animate objects) are represented in a fancifully combined pattern. **2.** *Fine Arts.* a sinuous, spiraling, undulating, or serpentine line or linear motif. **3.** a pose in ballet in which the dancer stands on one leg with one arm extended in front and the other leg and arm extended behind. **4.** a short, fanciful musical piece, typically for piano. —*adj.* **5.** decorated with or characterized by arabesques: *arabesque design.* [< F: Arabian < It *arabesc(o),* equiv. to *Arab(o)* Arab + *-esco* -ISH[1]] —**ar′a·besque′ly,** *adv.*

A·ra·bi·a (ə rā′bē ə), *n.* a peninsula in SW Asia, including Saudi Arabia, Yemen, Oman, and Aden: divided in ancient times into Arabia Deserta, Arabia Petraea, and Arabia Felix. 12,638,000 (est. 1950–55); ab. 1,000,000 sq. mi.

Ara′bia De·ser′ta (di zûr′tə), an ancient division of Arabia, in the N part between Syria and Mesopotamia.

Ara′bia Fe′lix (fē′liks), an ancient division of Arabia, in the S part: sometimes restricted to Yemen.

A·ra·bi·an (ə rā′bē ən), *adj.* **1.** of or pertaining to Arabia or the Arabs. —*n.* **2.** an Arab. [ARABI(A) + -AN]

Ara′bian cam′el, the dromedary.

Ara′bian Des′ert, 1. a desert in the United Arab Republic between the Nile valley and the Red Sea. ab. 80,000 sq. mi. **2.** the desert region in the N part of the Arabian peninsula.

Ara′bian horse′, one of a breed of horses, raised originally in Arabia and adjacent countries, noted for their intelligence, grace, and speed. Also called **Arab.**

Ara′bian jas′mine, a climbing shrub, *Jasminum Sambac,* of India, having hairy branches and very fragrant, white flowers which turn purple with age, used in making jasmine tea. Also called **zambac.**

Ara′bian Nights′ Entertain′ments, The, a collection of Eastern folk tales derived in part from Indian and Persian sources and dating from the 10th century A.D. Also called **The Thousand and One Nights.**

Ara′bian prim′rose, an annual, bushy primrose, *Arnebia cornuta,* of the Orient, having black-spotted orange flowers.

Ara′bian Sea′, the NW arm of the Indian Ocean between India and Arabia.

Ara′bia Pe·trae′a (pi trē′ə), an ancient division of Arabia, in the NW part.

Ar·a·bic (ar′ə bik), *adj.* **1.** of, belonging to, or derived from, Arabia or the Arabs. **2.** noting, pertaining to, or in the alphabetical script used for the writing of Arabic probably since about the fourth century A.D., and adopted with modifications by Persian, Urdu, and many other languages. A distinguishing feature of this script is the fact that etymologically short vowels are not normally represented. —*n.* **3.** any of the Semitic languages that developed out of the language of the Arabians of the time of Muhammad, spoken in North Africa, Egypt, Arabia, Palestine, Syria, and Iraq. **4.** the standard literary and classical language as established by the Koran. [ME *arabik* < L *arībic(us),* equiv. to *Arab(ia)* + *-icus* -IC]

Ar′abic nu′merals, the characters 0, 1, 2, 3, 4, 5, 6, 7, 8, 9, in general European use since the 12th century. Also, **Ar′abic fig′ures.**

a·rab·i·nose (ə rab′ə nōs′, ar′ə bə-), *n. Chem.* a white, crystalline, water-soluble solid, $C_5H_{10}O_5$, obtained from plant gums or made synthetically from glucose, used chiefly as a culture medium in bacteriology. Also called **pectin sugar, pectinose.** [*arabin* the soluble essence of certain gums ((GUM) ARAB(IC) + -IN[2]) + -OSE[2]] —**a·rab·i·nos·ic** (ə rab′ə nos′ik, ar′ə bə-), *adj.*

Ar·ab·ist (ar′ə bist), *n.* an expert or authority on Arabia and the Arabs or on the Arabic language and literature. [ARAB + -IST]

ar·a·ble (ar′ə bəl), *adj.* **1.** capable of producing crops; suitable for farming; suited to the plow and for tillage: *arable land; arable soil.* —*n.* **2.** land that can be or is cultivated. [< L *arābil(is),* equiv. to *arā(re)* (to) plow + *-bilis* -BLE; r. late ME *erable,* equiv. to *er(en)* (to) plow (OE *erian*) + *-able* -ABLE] —**ar′a·bil′i·ty,** *n.*

Ar′ab League′, a confederation formed in 1945 by Egypt, Iraq, Lebanon, Saudi Arabia, Syria, and Jordan and later joined by Libya, Sudan, Morocco, Tunisia, and Kuwait.

Ar′ab Pal′estine. See under **Palestine** (def. 2).

Ar·a·by (ar′ə bē), *n. Archaic.* Arabia. [ME *Arabye* < OF *Arabie* < L *Arabia*]

A·ra·ca·ju (ä′rə kä′zho͞o), *n.* a seaport in E Brazil. 98,677 (est. 1958).

A·ra·ça·tu·ba (ä′rə sə to͞o′bə), *n.* a city in SE Brazil. 26,862 (1950).

a·ra·ceous (ə rā′shəs), *adj. Bot.* belonging to the *Araceae,* or arum family of plants, which includes the arums, skunk cabbage, sweet flag, calla lily, taro, etc. [AR(UM) + -ACEOUS]

ar·a·chid·ic (ar′ə kid′ik), *adj. Chem.* of or derived from arachidic acid. Also, **a·rach·ic** (ə rak′ik). [< NL *Arachid-* (s. of *Arachis* genus name < Gk *arakís* kind of plant) + -IC]

ar′achid′ic ac′id, *Chem.* a white, crystalline, water-insoluble solid, $CH_3(CH_2)_{18}COOH$, obtained from peanut oil: used chiefly in the manufacture of lubricants, plastics, and waxes.

ar′a·chis oil′ (ar′ə kis). See **peanut oil.** [< Gk *arakís* kind of plant]

A·rach·ne (ə rak′nē), *n. Class. Myth.* a Lydian woman who challenged Athena to a weaving contest and was changed into a spider for her presumption.

a·rach·nid (ə rak′nid), *n.* any arthropod of the class *Arachnida,* comprising the spiders, scorpions, mites, ticks, etc. [< NL *Arachnid(a)* < Gk *aráchn(ē)* spider, spider's web + NL *-ida* -ID[2]] —**a·rach·ni·dan** (ə rak′ni dən), *adj., n.*

A·rach·ni·da (ə rak′ni də), *n.* the class comprising the arachnids. [< NL; see ARACHNID]

a·rach·noid (ə rak′noid), *adj.* **1.** resembling a spider's web. **2.** of or belonging to the arachnids. **3.** *Anat.* of or pertaining to the arachnoid membrane. **4.** *Bot.* formed of or covered with long, delicate hairs or fibers. —*n.* **5.** an arachnid. **6.** *Anat.* the serous membrane forming the middle of the three coverings of the brain and spinal cord. Cf. **dura mater, pia mater.** [< NL *arachnoīdes* < Gk *arachnoeidḗs* cobweb-like. See ARACHNID, -OID]

A·rad (ä räd′, är′äd), *n.* a city in W Rumania, on the Mures River. 106,460 (1956).

a·rae·o·style (ə rē′ə stīl′), *adj. Archit.* having an intercolumniation of four diameters. See illus. under **intercolumniation.** Also, **areostyle.** [< L *araeostȳl(us)* < Gk *araióstȳlos* with few columns, equiv. to *araió(s)* thin, few + *stŷl(os)* a column, pillar + *-os* adj. suffix]

a·rae·o·sys·tyle (ə rē′ə sis′tīl), *adj. Archit.* having an intercolumniation alternately of two and four diameters. Also, **areosystyle.** [AERO(STYLE) + SYSTYLE]

CONCISE PRONUNCIATION KEY: *act, āble, dâre, ärt; ebb, ēqual; if, īce; hot, ōver, ôrder, oil, bo͝ok, o͞oze, out; up, ûrge; chief; sing; shoe; thin, that;* zh *as in measure.* ə = *a* as in *alone, e* as in *system, i* as in *easily, o* as in *gallop, u* as in *circus;* ə as in *button* (but′ən), *fire* (fīər), *cradle* (krād′əl). See the full key inside the front cover.

Ar·a·fat (ar′ə fat′), *n.* **Ya·sir** (yä′sər), born 1929, Palestinian political leader.

A′ra·fu′ra Sea′ (är′ə fo͝or′ə, är′ə-), a part of the Pacific between N Australia and SW New Guinea.

Ar·a·gats (ar′ə gats′), *n.* **Mount,** an extinct volcano in NW Armenia, in the S Soviet Union in Europe. 13,435 ft. Also called **Mount Alagez.** Turkish, **Alagöz.**

Ar·a·go (ar′ə gō′), *n.* a crater in the first quadrant of the face of the moon: about 18 miles in diameter.

Ar·a·gon (ᴀ ʀᴀ gôɴ′ *for 1;* ar′ə gon′ *for 2*), *n.* **1. Louis** (lwē), born 1891, French novelist, poet, and journalist. **2.** Spanish, **A·ra·gón** (ä′ʀä gôn′), a region in NE Spain: formerly a kingdom; later a province. 18,181 sq. mi.

Ar·a·go·nese (ar′ə gə nēz′, -nēs′), *adj., n., pl.* **-nese.** —*adj.* **1.** of Aragon. —*n.* **2.** a native or inhabitant of Aragon. **3.** the dialect of Spanish spoken in Aragon. [Aʀᴀɢᴏɴ (the province) + -ᴇsᴇ]

a·rag·o·nite (ə rag′ə nīt′, ar′ə gə-), *n.* a mineral, orthorhombic calcium carbonate, $CaCO_3$, chemically identical with calcite but differing in crystallization and in having a higher specific gravity and less marked cleavage. [named after Aʀᴀɢᴏɴ (the province, where first found) + -ɪᴛᴇ[1]]

A·ra·gua·rí (ä′ʀə gwə ʀē′), *n.* a city in central Brazil. 36,653 (1960).

A·ra·gua·ya (ä′ʀə gwä′yä), *n.* a river flowing N from central Brazil to the Tocantins River. ab. 1100 mi. long.

ar·ak (ar′ik, -ak), *n.* arrack.

A′ra·kan′ Moun′tains (ä′rä kän′, ä′rä-, ar′ə kan′, ar′-), a mountain range in W Burma. Highest peak, Mount Victoria, 10,016 ft.

a·ra·li·a·ceous (ə rā′lē ā′shəs), *adj. Bot.* belonging to the *Araliaceae,* a large family of plants including the American spikenard, ginseng, etc. [< NL *Arali(a)* genus name (< ?) + -ᴀᴄᴇᴏᴜs]

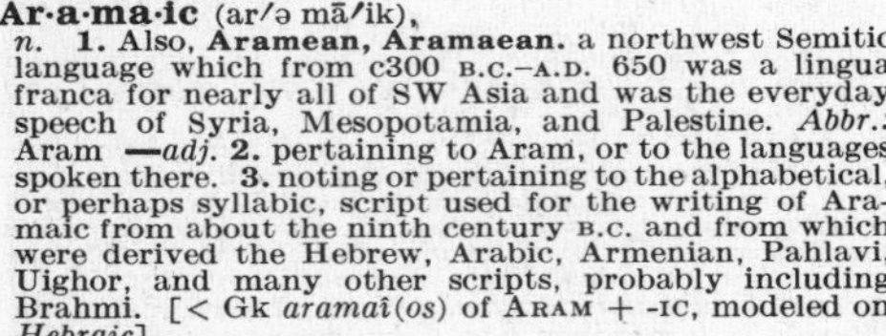

A·ral·lu (ä rä′lo͞o), *n.* the ancient Babylonian world of the dead. Also, **A·ra′lu.**

Ar′al Sea′ (ar′əl), an inland sea in the SW Soviet Union in Asia, E of the Caspian Sea. 26,166 sq. mi. Also called **Lake Aral.**

A·ram (ā′ram, âr′əm), *n.* Biblical name of ancient Syria. See map under **Philistia.**

Aram, Aramaic (def. 1).

Aram., Aramaic.

Ar·a·ma·ic (ar′ə mā′ik), *n.* **1.** Also, **Aramean, Aramaean.** a northwest Semitic language which from c300 ʙ.ᴄ.–ᴀ.ᴅ. 650 was a lingua franca for nearly all of SW Asia and was the everyday speech of Syria, Mesopotamia, and Palestine. *Abbr.:* Aram —*adj.* **2.** pertaining to Aram, or to the languages spoken there. **3.** noting or pertaining to the alphabetical, or perhaps syllabic, script used for the writing of Aramaic from about the ninth century ʙ.ᴄ. and from which were derived the Hebrew, Arabic, Armenian, Pahlavi, Uighur, and many other scripts, probably including Brahmi. [< Gk *aramaî(os)* of Aʀᴀᴍ + -ɪᴄ, modeled on *Hebraic*]

A·ram·bu·ru (ä′räm bo͞o′ʀo͞o), *n.* **Pe·dro E·u·ge·nio** (pe′thʀô e′o͞o he′nyô), born 1903, president of Argentina 1955–58.

Ar·a·me·an (ar′ə mē′ən), *n.* **1.** a Semite of the division associated with Aram. **2.** Aramaic (def. 1). Also, **Ar′a·mae′an.** [< L *Aramae(us)* (< Gk *aramaîos* of Aʀᴀᴍ) + -ᴀɴ]

A·ran·da (ə ran′də, ə rän′-), *n., pl.* **-das,** (*esp. collectively*) **-da.** Arunta.

ar·a·ne·i·form (ar′ə nē′ə fôrm′), *adj.* shaped like a spider; spiderlike. [< L *arāne(a)* a spider, spider's web, cobweb (akin to Gk *aráchnē*) + -ɪ- + -ꜰᴏʀᴍ]

a·ra·ne·ose (ə rā′nē ōs′), *adj.* arachnoid, esp. as a plant. Also, **a·ra·ne·ous** (ə rā′nē əs). [< L *araneōs(us)* pertaining to a spider, equiv. to *arāne(a)* spider + *-ōsus* -ᴏsᴇ[1]]

A·ra·nha (ä rä′nyä), *n.* **Os·wal·do** (ôs wäl′dô), 1894–1960, Brazilian politician.

A·ran·ya·ka (ä run′yə kə), *n. Hinduism.* one of a class of the Vedic texts that, together with the Upanishads, make up the closing portions of the Brahmanas. [< Skt: a forest book]

A·rap·a·ho (ə rap′ə hō′), *n., pl.* **-hos,** (*esp. collectively*) **-ho. 1.** a member of a tribe of North American Indians of Algonquian speech stock, once dwelling in the Colorado plains and now in Oklahoma and Wyoming. **2.** an Algonquian language, the language of the Arapaho.

A·rap·a·hoe (ə rap′ə hō′), *n., pl.* **-hoes,** (*esp. collectively*) **-hoe.** Arapaho.

ar·a·pai·ma (ar′ə pī′mə), *n.* a large, fresh-water fish, *Arapaima gigas,* found in Brazil and Guiana reputed to reach a length of 15 feet and a weight of 500 pounds. [< Pg < Tupi]

A·ra·pesh (ä′rə pesh′), *n., pl.* **-pesh·es,** (*esp. collectively*) **-pesh. 1.** a Papuan people of New Guinea. **2.** a member of this people.

Ar·a·rat (ar′ə rat′), *n.* a mountain in E Turkey, near the borders of Iran and Armenia: traditionally considered the landing place of Noah's Ark. 16,945 ft. Also called **Mount Ararat.**

a·ra·ro·ba (ar′ə rō′bə), *n.* the wood of a Brazilian, leguminous tree, *Andira araroba,* from which Goa powder is derived. **2.** *Pharm.* See **Goa powder.** [< Pg < Tupi, perh. var. of *araribá*]

A·ras (ä räs′ *for 1;* ar′əs *for 2*), *n.* **1.** Ancient, **Araxes.** a river in SW Asia, flowing from E Turkey along part of the boundary between NW Iran and Armenia and Azerbaijan into the Kura River. ab. 600 mi. long. **2.** *Class. Myth.* the first king of Phliasia.

A·ra·tus (ə rā′təs, ə rä′-), *n.* a crater in the first quadrant of the face of the moon: about 6 miles in diameter.

A·ra·tus of Sic·y·on (ə rā′təs əv sish′ē on′, sis′-), 271–213 ʙ.ᴄ., Greek general, leader of the Achaean League.

A·rau·can (ə rô′kən), *n., pl.* **-cans,** (*esp. collectively*) **-can,** *adj.* Araucanian. [< Sp *araucano,* equiv. to *Arauc(o)* province in central Chile + *-ano* -ᴀɴ]

Ar·au·ca·ni·a (ar′ô kā′nē ə; *Sp.* ä′ʀou kä′nyä), *n.* a region in central Chile.

Ar·au·ca·ni·an (ar′ô kā′nē ən), *n.* **1.** a member of an Indian people of central Chile. **2.** the language of the Araucanians, spoken in central Chile and northern Argentina. —*adj.* **3.** pertaining to the Araucanians or to their language. [Aʀᴀᴜᴄᴀɴɪ(ᴀ) + -ᴀɴ]

ar·au·car·i·a (ar′ô kâr′ē ə), *n.* any pinaceous tree of the genus *Araucaria* of South America, Australia, and Polynesia. [< NL, named after *Arauc(o)* province in central Chile; see -ᴀʀɪᴀ] —**ar′au·car′i·an,** *adj.*

Ar·a·wak (ar′ə wäk′, -wak′), *n., pl.* **-waks,** (*esp. collectively*) **-wak. 1.** a member of an Indian people once widespread in the Antilles but now confined to northeastern South America. **2.** the language of the Arawaks.

Ar·a·wak·an (ar′ə wä′kən, -wak′ən), *n.* **1.** a family of numerous and widely scattered languages spoken formerly from Florida to Chile but now only in South America. —*adj.* **2.** of or belonging to Arawakan or to the Arawak. [Aʀᴀᴡᴀᴋ + -ᴀɴ]

Ar·awn (äʀ′oun), *n. Welsh Myth.* the lord of Annfwn.

A·ra·xá (ä′ʀə shä′), *n.* a city in E Brazil. 24,041 (1960).

A·rax·es (ə rak′sēz), *n.* ancient name of **Aras.**

ar·ba kan·foth (äʀ bä′ kän fôt′), *Hebrew.* a rectangular piece of cotton, wool, or other cloth with fringes, or zizith, at the four corners and a hole in the center for the head, worn under the clothes by Orthodox Jewish males. Also called **tallith katan.** [lit., four corners]

ar·ba·lest (är′bə list), *n.* a powerful medieval crossbow. Also, **ar′ba·list.** [var. of *arbalist, arblast* (late OE *arblast*) < OF *arbaleste* < LL *arcuballista.* See ᴀʀᴄ, ʙᴀʟʟɪsᴛᴀ] —**ar·ba·lest·er, ar·ba·list·er** (är′bə lis′tər), *n.*

Ar·be·la (är bē′lə), *n.* an ancient city of Assyria, E of the Tigris, on the site of modern Erbil: headquarters of Darius III before his defeat by Alexander the Great at Gaugamela 331 ʙ.ᴄ.

Ar·bil (ir′bil), *n.* Erbil.

ar·bi·ter (är′bi tər), *n.* **1.** a person empowered to decide matters at issue; judge; umpire. **2.** a person who has the sole or absolute power of judging or determining. [late ME < L: judge in equity, umpire; r. late ME *arbitre* < MF < L *arbiter*]

ar·bi·ter e·le·gan·ti·ae (äʀ′bi teʀ′ ā′le gän′tē ī′; *Eng.* är′bi tər el′ə gan′shē ē′), *Latin.* a judge of elegance or matters of taste. Also, **ar·bi·ter e·le·gan·ti·a·rum** (äʀ′bi ter′ ā′le gän′tē ä′ʀo͞om; *Eng.* är′bi tər el′ə gan′shē âr′əm).

ar·bi·tra·ble (är′bi trə bəl), *adj.* capable of arbitration; subject to the decision of an arbiter or arbitrator: *an arbitrable dispute.* [< L *arbitrā(rī)* (to) decide (see ᴀʀʙɪᴛʀᴀᴛᴇ) + -ʙʟᴇ]

ar·bi·trage (är′bi träzh′ *for 1;* är′bi trij *for 2*), *n.* **1.** *Finance.* the simultaneous purchase and sale of the same securities, commodities, or foreign exchange in different markets to profit from unequal prices. **2.** *Archaic.* arbitration. [< F, equiv. to *arbitr(er)* (to) arbitrate, regulate (< L *arbitrārī;* see ᴀʀʙɪᴛʀᴀᴛᴇ) + *-age* -ᴀɢᴇ]

ar·bi·trag·er (är′bi trä′zhər), *n.* a person who engages in arbitrage. Also, **ar·bi·tra·geur** (är′bi trä zhûr′). [< F *arbitrageur,* equiv. to *arbitrage* ᴀʀʙɪᴛʀᴀɢᴇ + *-eur* -ᴇʀ[1]]

ar·bi·tral (är′bi trəl), *adj.* pertaining to an arbiter or to arbitration. [< LL *arbitrāl(is).* See ᴀʀʙɪᴛᴇʀ, -ᴀʟ[1]]

ar·bit·ra·ment (är bi′trə mənt), *n.* **1.** arbitration. **2.** the decision or sentence pronounced by an arbiter. **3.** the power of absolute and final decision. Also, **arbitrement.** [late ME < ML *arbitrāment(um)* < L *arbitrā(rī)* (to) ᴀʀʙɪᴛʀᴀᴛᴇ + *-mentum* -ᴍᴇɴᴛ]

ar·bi·trar·y (är′bi trer′ē), *adj., n., pl.* **-trar·ies.** —*adj.* **1.** subject to individual will or judgment without restriction; contingent solely upon one's discretion: *an arbitrary choice.* **2.** decided by a judge or arbiter rather than by a law or statute. **3.** using or abusing unlimited power; uncontrolled or unrestricted by law; despotic; tyrannical: *an arbitrary government.* **4.** capricious; unreasonable; unsupported: *an arbitrary demand.* **5.** *Math.* undetermined; not assigned a specific value: *an arbitrary constant.* —*n.* **6. arbitraries,** *Brit. Print.* peculiar (def. 8). [late ME < L *arbitrāri(us)* uncertain (i.e., depending on an arbiter's decision). See ᴀʀʙɪᴛᴇʀ, -ᴀʀʏ] —**ar·bi·trar·i·ly** (är′bi trer′ə lē, är′bi trâr′-), *adv.* —**ar′bi·trar′i·ness,** *n.*

ar·bi·trate (är′bi trāt′), *v.,* **-trat·ed, -trat·ing.** —*v.t.* **1.** to decide as arbiter or arbitrator; determine. **2.** to submit to arbitration; settle by arbitration: *to arbitrate a dispute.* —*v.i.* **3.** to act as arbiter; decide between opposing or contending parties or sides. **4.** to submit a matter to arbitration. [< L *arbitrāt(us)* decided, judged (ptp. of *arbitrārī*), equiv. to *arbit(e)r* ᴀʀʙɪᴛᴇʀ + *-ātus* -ᴀᴛᴇ[1]] —**ar′bi·tra′tive,** *adj.*

ar·bi·tra·tion (är′bi trā′shən), *n.* **1.** the hearing and determining of a dispute between parties by a person or persons chosen or agreed to by them. **2.** *Internat. Law.* the application of judicial methods to the settlement of international disputes. [ME < L *arbitrātiōn-* (s. of *arbitrātiō*), equiv. to *arbitrāt(us)* (see ᴀʀʙɪᴛʀᴀᴛᴇ) + *-iōn-* -ɪᴏɴ] —**ar′bi·tra′tion·al,** *adj.* —**ar′bi·tra′tion·ist,** *n.* —**Syn. 1.** See **mediation.**

Arbitration, The, a comedy (c300 ʙ.ᴄ.) by Menander, extant only as a fragment.

arbitra′tion bar′, *Metall.* a bar of cast iron used as a sample for the batch to which it belongs.

ar·bi·tra·tor (är′bi trā′tər), *n.* a person chosen to decide a dispute, esp. one formally empowered to examine the facts and decide the issue. [< LL; see ᴀʀʙɪᴛʀᴀᴛᴇ, -ᴏʀ[2]]

ar·bit·re·ment (är bi′trə mənt), *n.* arbitrament.

ar·bi·trer (är′bi trər), *n. Obs.* arbitrator. [ME *arbitrour* < OF *arbitreor* < LL *arbitrātōr-;* see ᴀʀʙɪᴛʀᴀᴛᴏʀ]

ar·bi·tress (är′bi tris), *n.* a female arbiter. [ME < MF *arbitresse,* equiv. to *arbitre* ᴀʀʙɪᴛ(ᴇ)ʀ + *-esse* -ᴇss]

Ar·blay, d′ (där′blā; *Fr.* dᴀʀ blā′), **Madame Frances.** See **Burney, Frances.**

ar·bor[1] (är′bər), *n.* **1.** a leafy, shady recess formed by tree branches, shrubs, or vines, often intertwined on a latticework; a bower. **2.** *Obs.* a grass plot; lawn; garden; orchard. Also, *esp. Brit.,* **arbour.** [ME *(h)erber* < AF, OF *(h)erbier* ʜᴇʀʙᴀʀɪᴜᴍ]

ar·bor[2] (är′bər), *n.* **1.** *Mach.* **a.** a bar, shaft, or axis which holds, turns, or supports rotating cutting tools, often having a tapered shank fitting tightly into the spindle of a machine tool. Cf. **mandrel. b.** *Obs.* a beam, shaft, axle, or spindle. **2.** *Foundry.* a reinforcing member of a core or mold. [< L: beam, pole, gallows; r. earlier *arber, arbre* < F]

ar·bor[3] (är′bər), *n., pl.* **ar·bo·res** (är′bə rēz′). *Bot.* a tree. [< NL, L: tree, beam, etc.] —**ar′bo·resque′,** *adj.*

Ar′bor Day′, a day, varying in date but always in the spring, observed in certain States of the U.S. by the planting of trees.

ar·bo·re·al (är bōr′ē əl, -bôr′-), *adj.* **1.** of or pertaining to trees; treelike. **2.** Also, **arboreous.** living in or among trees. **3.** *Zool.* adapted for living and moving about in trees, as the limbs and skeleton of opossums, squirrels, monkeys, and apes. [< L *arbore(us)* of trees (*arbor* tree + *-eus* adj. suffix) + -ᴀʟ[1]] —**ar·bo′re·al·ly,** *adv.*

ar·bored (är′bərd), *adj.* furnished with an arbor; shaded; lined with trees. Also, *esp. Brit.,* **ar′boured.** [ᴀʀʙᴏʀ[1] + -ᴇᴅ[3]]

ar·bo·re·ous (är bōr′ē əs, -bôr′-), *adj.* **1.** abounding in trees; wooded. **2.** arboreal (def. 2). **3.** arborescent. [< L *arboreus* of trees, equiv. to *arbor* tree + *-eus* -ᴇᴏᴜs]

ar·bo·res·cent (är′bə res′ənt), *adj.* treelike in size and form. [< L *arborēscent-* (s. of *arborēscēns*), prp. of *arborēscere* to grow into a tree. See ᴀʀʙᴏʀ[3], -ᴇsᴄᴇɴᴛ] —**ar′bo·res′cence,** *n.* —**ar′bo·res′cent·ly,** *adv.*

ar·bo·re·tum (är′bə rē′təm), *n., pl.* **-tums, -ta** (-tə). a plot of land where different trees or shrubs are grown for study or display. [< L: a place grown with trees, equiv. to *arbor* tree + *-ētum* suffix denoting place]

ar·bor·i·cul·ture (är′bər ə kul′chər), *n.* the cultivation of trees and shrubs. [< L *arbori-* (s. of *arbor* tree) + ᴄᴜʟᴛᴜʀᴇ, modeled on *agriculture*] —**ar′bor·i·cul′tur·al,** *adj.* —**ar′bor·i·cul′tur·ist,** *n.*

ar·bor·i·za·tion (är′bər i zā′shən), *n.* a treelike appearance, as in certain minerals or fossils. [ᴀʀʙᴏʀ[3] + -ɪᴢᴀᴛɪᴏɴ]

ar·bor·ous (är′bər əs), *adj.* of or pertaining to trees. [ᴀʀʙᴏʀ[3] + -ᴏᴜs]

ar·bor vi·tae (är′bər vī′tē), *Anat.* a treelike appearance in a vertical section of the cerebellum, due to the arrangement of the white and gray nerve tissues. [< L: tree of life]

ar·bor·vi·tae (är′bər vī′tē), *n.* **1.** any of several pinaceous trees of the genus *Thuja,* of North America and eastern Asia. **2.** *Anat.* See **arbor vitae.** [< L: tree of life]

ar·bour (är′bər), *n. Chiefly Brit.* arbor[1].

arbtrn., arbitration.

Ar·buth·not (är buth′nət, är′bəth not′), *n.* **John,** 1667–1735, Scottish satirist and physician: friend of Alexander Pope and Jonathan Swift.

ar·bu·tus (är byo͞o′təs), *n., pl.* **-tus·es. 1.** any of the evergreen ericaceous shrubs or trees of the genus *Arbutus,* esp. *A. unedo,* of southern Europe, with scarlet berries, cultivated for ornament and food. **2.** Also called **trailing arbutus.** a creeping, ericaceous herb, *Epigaea repens,* of eastern North America, having fragrant white or pink flowers: the State flower of Massachusetts. [< L: the wild strawberry tree]

arc (ärk), *n., v.,* **arced** (ärkt) or **arcked, arc·ing** (är′king) or **arck·ing.** —*n.* **1.** *Geom.* any unbroken part of the circumference of a circle or other curved line. **2.** Also called **electric arc.** *Elect.* a luminous bridge formed in a gap between two conductors or terminals when they are separated. Cf. **spark**[1] (def. 2). **3.** *Astron.* the part of a circle representing the apparent course of a heavenly body. **4.** anything bow-shaped. —*v.i.* **5.** to form an electric arc. **6.** to move in a curve suggestive of an arc. [ME *ark* < L *arc(us)* bow, arch, curve]

ARC, American Red Cross. Also, **A.R.C.**

ar·ca (är′kə), *n., pl.* **-cae** (-sē). a chest for valuables, used in medieval Spain and Italy. [< L: chest, box. See ᴀʀᴋ]

ar·cade (är kād′), *n., v.,* **-cad·ed, -cad·ing.** —*n.* **1.** *Archit.* **a.** a series of arches supported on piers or columns. **b.** an arched, roofed-in gallery. **2.** an arched or covered passageway, usually with shops on each side. **3.** an ornamental carving, as on a piece of furniture, in the form of a row of arches. —*v.t.* **4.** to provide with or form as an arcade or arcades. [< F < It *arcata* arch (c. ML *arcāta*), equiv. to *arc(o)* arch (see ᴀʀᴄ) + *-āta* -ᴀᴅᴇ[1]]

Ar·ca·di·a (är kā′dē ə), *n.* **1.** a city in SW California, E of Los Angeles. 41,005 (1960). **2.** a town in NW Louisiana. 2547 (1960). **3.** a mountainous region of ancient Greece, traditionally known for the contented pastoral innocence of its people.

Ar·ca·di·an (är kā′dē ən), *adj.* **1.** of Arcadia. **2.** pastoral; rustic; simple; innocent. —*n.* **3.** a native of Arcadia. [Aʀᴄᴀᴅɪ(ᴀ) (def. 3; see Aʀᴄᴀᴅʏ) + -ᴀɴ] —**Ar·ca′di·an·ism,** *n.* —**Ar·ca′di·an·ly,** *adv.*

Arca′dian stag′, *Class. Myth.* See **Cerynian stag.** Also called **Arca′dian hind′.**

Ar·ca·dy (är′kə dē), *n. Poetic.* Arcadia. [earlier *Arcadie* < L *Arcadia* < Gk *Arkadía*]

ar·cane (är kān′), *adj.* mysterious; secret; obscure: *Poor writing can make even the most familiar things seem arcane.* [< L *arcān(us),* equiv. to *arc(ēre)* (to) shut up, keep (deriv. of *arca* a chest, box) + *-ānus* -ᴀɴᴇ]

ar·can·ist (är kā′nist), *n.* a person professing special secret knowledge concerning ceramics, esp. concerning the making of porcelain. [ᴀʀᴄᴀɴ(ᴜᴍ) + -ɪsᴛ]

ar·ca·num (är kā′nəm), *n., pl.* **-na** (-nə). **1.** Often, **arcana.** a secret; a mystery. **2.** a supposed great secret of nature which the alchemists sought to discover. **3.** a secret and powerful remedy. [< L, neut. (used as n.) of *arcānus* ᴀʀᴄᴀɴᴇ]

ar·ca·num ar·ca·no·rum (äʀ kä′no͝om äʀ′kä nō′ʀo͝om; *Eng.* är kā′nəm är′kə nōr′əm, -nôr′-), *Latin.* secret of secrets.

Ar·ca·ro (är kâr′ō), *n.* **Edward** (*Eddie*), born 1916, U.S. jockey.

Ar·cas (är′kəs), *n. Class. Myth.* a son of Zeus and Callisto, the ancestor of the Arcadians who was set among the stars by Zeus.

Ar·ca·ta (är kā′tə), *n.* a town in NW California. 5235 (1960).

ar·ca·ture (är′kə chər), *n. Archit.* **1.** an arcade of small dimensions. **2.** a blind arcade, as a series of arches superimposed on the walls of a building for decoration. [< ML *arcāt(a)* an arch (see ARCADE) + -URE]

arc-back (ärk′bak′), *n. Electronics.* an undesirable phenomenon, occurring in rectifier tubes, in which current flows in the reverse direction, from anode to cathode, as a result of arcing, limiting the usable voltage of the tube. Also called **backfire.**

arc-bou·tant (AR bo͞o täN′), *n., pl.* **arcs-bou·tants** (AR bo͞o täN′). *French.* See **flying buttress.** [lit., thrusting arch]

arc′ cose′cant, *Trig.* the angle, measured in radians, that has a cosecant equal to a given number. *Symbol:* arc csc, csc^{-1}. Also called **inverse cosecant.**

arc′ co′sine, *Trig.* the angle, measured in radians, that has a cosine equal to a given number. *Symbol:* arc cos, cos^{-1}. Also called **inverse cosine.**

arc′ cotan′gent, *Trig.* the angle, measured in radians, that has a cotangent equal to a given number. *Symbol:* arc cot, cot^{-1}. Also called **inverse cotangent.**

Arc, d′ (DARK), **Jeanne** (zhän). See **Joan of Arc.**

Arc de Tri·omphe (ARK də tRē ôNf′), the arch, located in Paris, begun in 1806 by Napoleon in honor of his victorious armies and completed in 1836. The unknown soldier of France and the eternal flame were placed beneath the arch after World War I. Also, **Arc de Tri·omphe′ de l′É·toile′** (də lā twAl′). [< F: arch of triumph]

Ar·ce (är′sē), *n. Class. Myth.* a daughter of Thaumas and the sister of Iris and the Harpies. Zeus took away her wings when she aided the Titans in their war against him.

Ar·cel·la (är sel′ə), *n.* a genus of fresh-water protozoans that secrete a hard, umbrellalike shell having a single opening through which the pseudopodia extend. [NL, equiv. to L *arc(a)* a chest, box + *-ella* dim. suffix]

Ar·ces·i·la·us (är ses′ə lā′əs), *n.* 316–241 B.C., Greek philosopher.

Ar·ces·i·us (är ses′ē əs), *n. Class. Myth.* a son of Zeus and Euryodia, father of Laertes, and grandfather of Odysseus.

arc·form (ärk′fôrm′), *adj.* noting a type of cargo-ship construction in which the sides have the form of arcs so drawn that the greatest breadth is at load waterline, the purpose being to promote the flow of water to the propeller with an easy bilge and without loss of capacity. [ARC + -FORM]

arc′ fur′nace, a furnace in which heat is generated by an electric arc.

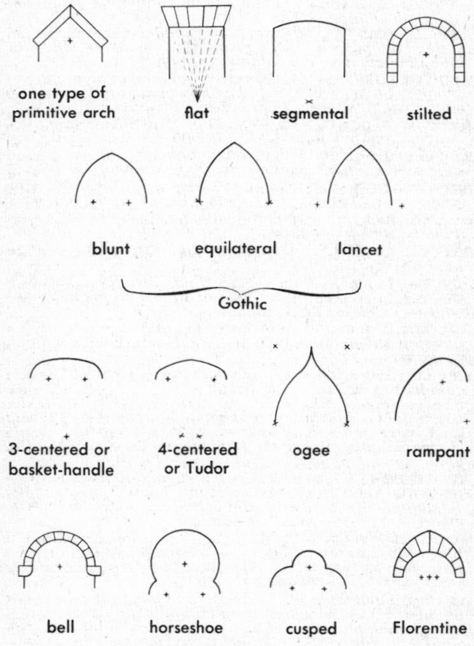

one type of primitive arch · flat · segmental · stilted

blunt · equilateral · lancet

Gothic

3-centered or basket-handle · 4-centered or Tudor · ogee · rampant

bell · horseshoe · cusped · Florentine

Arches

arch[1] (ärch), *n.* **1.** *Archit.* **a.** a curved masonry construction for spanning an opening, consisting of a number of wedgelike stones, bricks, or the like, set with the narrower side toward the opening in such a way that forces on the arch are transmitted as vertical or oblique stresses on either side of the opening. **b.** an upwardly curved construction, as of steel or timber functioning in the manner of a masonry arch. **c.** a doorway, gateway, etc., having a curved head; an archway. **d.** the curved head of an opening, as a doorway. **2.** any curvature in the form of an arch: *the arch of the heavens.* **3.** something bowed or curved; any bowlike part: *the arch of the foot.* **4.** a device inserted in or built into shoes for supporting the arch of the foot. **5.** a dam construction having the form of a barrel vault running vertically with its convex face toward the impounded water. **6.** *Glassmaking.* **a.** a chamber or opening in a glassmaking furnace. **b.** See **pot arch.** —*v.t.* **7.** to cover with a vault, or span with an arch: *the rude bridge that arched the flood.* **8.** to throw or make into the shape of an arch or vault; curve: *A horse arches its neck.* —*v.i.* **9.** to form an arch: *elms arching over the road.* **10.** *Naut.* hog (def. 16). [ME *arch(e)* < OF *arche* < VL **arca,* fem. var. of L *arcus* ARC]

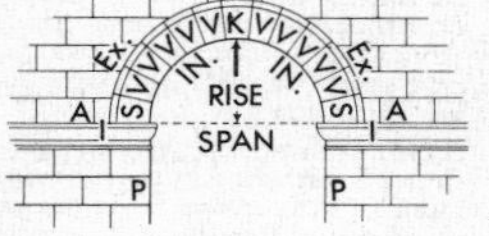

Ex · K · V · In · RISE · S · A · SPAN · P

Arch
A, Abutment; S, Springer; V, Voussoir; K, Keystone; Ex., Extrados; P, Pier; I, Impost; In., Intrados

arch[2] (ärch), *adj.* **1.** chief; most important; principal: *the arch rebel.* **2.** cunning; sly; roguish; mischievous: *an arch smile.* —*n.* **3.** *Obs.* a person who is preeminent; a chief. [see ARCH-] —**arch′ly,** *adv.* —**arch′ness,** *n.*

arch-, a learned borrowing from Greek meaning "chief," used in the formation of compound words: *archbishop; archfiend.* Also, **-arch, archi-, -archy.** [ME; OE *arce-, erce-* < L *arch(e)-, archi-* < Gk *arch-* (s. of *archḗ*)]

-arch, var. of **arch-** as final element of a compound word: *monarch; heresiarch.* [late ME *-arch(a)* < L < Gk *-archēs,* equiv. to *árch(ein)* (to) be first, rule + *-ēs* n. suffix]

Arch., Archbishop.

arch., **1.** archaic. **2.** archaism. **3.** archery. **4.** archipelago. **5.** architect. **6.** architectural. **7.** architecture. **8.** archive; archives.

Ar·chae·an (är kē′ən), *adj., n.* Archean.

archaeo-, var. of **archeo-:** *Archaeozoic; archaeopteryx.*

Ar·chae·o·cy·a·thid (är′kē ō sī′ə thid, är kē′ə-), *n.* one of the marine invertebrates of the extinct phylum *Archaeocyatha,* widely distributed during the Cambrian period, having a limy, typically conical or cylindrical skeleton composed of sievelike inner and outer walls. [< NL *Archaeocyath(us)* genus name (*archaeo-* ARCHAEO- + L *cyathus* ladle < Gk *kýathos*) + -ID[2]]

arch·ae·o·cyte (är′kē ə sīt′), *n.* archeocyte.

archaeol., **1.** archaeological. **2.** archaeology.

ar·chae·o·log·i·cal (är′kē ə loj′i kəl), *adj.* of or pertaining to archaeology. Also, **ar′chae·o·log′ic, archeological, archeologic.** [< Gk *archaiologik(ós)* (see ARCHAEOLOGY, -IC) + -AL[1]] —**ar′chae·o·log′i·cal·ly,** *adv.*

ar·chae·ol·o·gy (är′kē ol′ə jē), *n.* **1.** the scientific study of historic or prehistoric peoples and their cultures by analysis of their artifacts, inscriptions, monuments, and other such remains, esp. those that have been excavated. **2.** *Rare.* ancient history; the study of antiquity. Also, **archeology.** [< Gk *archaiología* the discussion of antiquities. See ARCHAEO-, -LOGY] —**ar′chae·ol′o·gist,** *n.*

Archaeopteryx

ar·chae·op·ter·yx (är′kē op′tə riks), *n.* a fossil bird of the genus *Archaeopteryx,* from the late Jurassic period, having teeth and a long, feathered, vertebrate tail: the oldest known avian type. [ARCHAEO- + Gk *ptéryx* wing]

ar·chae·or·nis (är′kē ôr′nis), *n.* an extinct bird of the genus *Archaeornis,* from the late Jurassic period, similar to the archaeopteryx. [< NL, equiv. to *archae(o)-* ARCHAEO- + Gk *órnis* bird]

Ar·chae·o·zo·ic (är′kē ə zō′ik), *adj., n.* Archeozoic.

ar·cha·ic (är kā′ik), *adj.* **1.** marked by the characteristics of an earlier period; antiquated: *an archaic manner; an archaic notion.* **2.** (of a linguistic form) current of an earlier time but rare in present-day usage. **3.** forming the earliest stage; prior to full development: *the archaic period of psychoanalytic research.* **4.** (*cap.*) pertaining to or designating the style of the fine arts, esp. painting and sculpture, developed in Greece from the middle 7th to the early 5th century B.C., chiefly characterized by an increased emphasis on the human figure in action, naturalistic proportions and anatomical structure, simplicity of volumes, forms, or design, and the evolution of a definitive style for the narrative treatment of subject matter. Cf. **classical** (def. 2), **Hellenistic** (def. 5). **5.** primitive; ancient; old: *an archaic form of animal life.* [< Gk *archaïk(ós)* antiquated, old-fashioned, equiv. to *archaî(os)* old + *-ikos* -IC] —**ar·cha′i·cal·ly,** *adv.*

archa′ic smile′, *Fine Arts.* a conventional representation of the mouth characterized by slightly upturned corners of the lips, found esp. on Greek sculpture produced prior to the 5th century B.C.

ar·cha·ise (är′kē īz′, -kā-), *v.t., v.i.,* **-ised, -is·ing.** *Chiefly Brit.* archaize. —**ar′cha·is′er,** *n.*

ar·cha·ism (är′kē iz′əm, -kā-), *n.* **1.** something archaic, as a word or expression. **2.** the use of what is archaic, as in literature or art: *The archaism of his style provided charm, nostalgia, and a degree of obscurity.* **3.** the survival or presence of something from the past: *an elderly lady whose gentility was a delightful archaism.* Also, **ar·cha·i·cism** (är kā′i siz′əm). [earlier *archaism(us)* < L < Gk *archaïsmós.* See ARCHAIZE, -ISM] —**ar′cha·ist,** *n.* —**ar′cha·is′tic,** *adj.*

ar·cha·ize (är′kē īz′, -kā-), *v.,* **-ized, -iz·ing.** —*v.t.* **1.** to give an archaic appearance or quality to. —*v.i.* **2.** to use archaisms. Also, *esp. Brit.* **archaise.** [< Gk *archaïz(ein)* (to) imitate the language of ancient authors. See ARCHAEO-, -IZE] —**ar′cha·iz′er,** *n.*

arch·an·gel (ärk′ān′jəl), *n.* **1.** *Theol.* a chief or principal angel; in medieval angelology one of the nine orders of celestial attendants on God. Cf. **angel** (def. 1). **2.** angelica (def. 1). [early ME < L *archangel(us)* < Gk *archángelos.* See ARCH-, ANGEL] —**arch·an·gel·ic** (ärk′an jel′ik), **arch′an·gel′i·cal,** *adj.*

Arch·an·gel (ärk′ān′jəl), *n.* **1.** Russian, **Arkhangelsk.** a seaport in the NW Soviet Union in Europe, on Dvina Bay. 256,000 (1959). **2. Gulf of.** See **Dvina Bay.**

Arch·bald (ärch′bôld), *n.* a town in NE Pennsylvania. 5471 (1960).

arch·banc (*Fr.* ARSH bäN′), *n., pl.* **-bancs** (-bäN′). archebanc.

arch′ beam′, a crowned metal beam, as of the deck of a ship.

arch·bish·op (ärch′bish′əp), *n.* a bishop of the highest rank who presides over an archbishopric or archdiocese. [ME, OE *arcebiscop* (*arce-* ARCH- + *biscop* BISHOP), modeled on L *archiepiscopus* < Gk *archiepískopos;* r. OE *hēahbiscop* (see HIGH)]

arch·bish·op·ric (ärch′bish′əp rik), *n.* the see, diocese, or office of an archbishop. [ME *archebischopric,* OE *arcebiscoprīce,* equiv. to *arcebiscop* ARCHBISHOP + *rīce* region, realm; c. Icel *rīki,* Goth *reiki,* OHG *rīhki* (> G *Reich*)]

arch′ board′, *Naut.* a feature at the stern of a vessel, curving upward at the center and giving the name and port of the vessel within a carved and painted frame; escutcheon.

arch′ brace′, *Carpentry.* a curved brace, esp. one of a pair used to give the effect of an arch in a roof frame.

arch·con·fra·ter·ni·ty (ärch′kon frə tûr′ni tē), *n., pl.* **-ties.** *Rom. Cath. Ch.* a confraternity having the right to associate itself with confraternities that are similar to it, and to impart to them its privileges and indulgences. [< It *arciconfraternità.* See ARCH-, CONFRATERNITY]

archd., **1.** archdeacon. **2.** archduke. Also, **Archd.**

arch′ dam′, a dam resisting the pressure of impounded water by an arch principle, esp. a dam having in plan the form of a single arch abutted by natural rock formations.

arch·dea·con (ärch′dē′kən), *n.* **1.** an ecclesiastic, ranking next below a bishop and having charge of the temporal and external administration of a diocese, with jurisdiction delegated from the bishop. **2.** *Rom. Cath. Ch.* a title of honor conferred only on a member of a cathedral chapter. [ME *archideken,* OE *arcediacon* < LL *archidiācon(us)* < Gk *archidiákonos.* See ARCH-, DEACON] —**arch′dea′con·ate, arch′dea′con·ship′,** *n.*

arch·dea·con·ry (ärch′dē′kən rē), *n., pl.* **-ries.** the jurisdiction, residence, or office of an archdeacon. [ARCHDEACON + -RY]

arch·di·o·cese (ärch′dī′ə sēs′, -sis), *n.* the diocese of an archbishop. [ARCH- + DIOCESE] —**arch·di·oc·e·san** (ärch′dī os′i sən), *adj.*

arch·du·cal (ärch′do͞o′kəl, -dyo͞o′-), *adj.* of or pertaining to an archduke or an archduchy. [earlier *archiducal* < F. See ARCHI-, DUCAL]

arch·duch·ess (ärch′duch′is), *n.* **1.** the wife of an archduke. **2.** a princess of the Austrian imperial family. [ARCH- + DUCHESS, modeled on F *archiduchesse*]

arch·duch·y (ärch′duch′ē), *n., pl.* **-duch·ies.** the domain of an archduke or an archduchess. [ARCH- + DUCHY, modeled on F *archeduché* (now *archiduché*)]

arch·duke (ärch′do͞ok′, -dyo͞ok′), *n.* a title of the sovereign princes of the former ruling house of Austria. [earlier *archeduke* < F *archeduc* (now *archiduc*). See ARCH-, DUKE]

arche-[1], var. of **archi-:** *archespore.*

arche-[2], var. of **archeo-** before a vowel.

Arch. E., Architectural Engineer.

Ar·che·an (är kē′ən), *Geol. Obs.* —*adj.* **1.** noting or pertaining to the Precambrian era, esp. the oldest part; Archeozoic. —*n.* **2.** the Archeozoic period. Also, **Archaean.** [ARCHE-[2] + -AN]

arche·banc (ARSH bäN′), *n., pl.* **-bancs** (-bäN′). *Fr. Furniture.* a bench or settle of the medieval and Renaissance periods, wide enough for several persons and having a seat with a chest beneath, arms at the ends, and a high back. Also, **archbanc.** [< F; see ARCH[1], ARCA, BANK[3]]

arched (ärcht), *adj.* **1.** made, covered, or spanned with an arch or arches. **2.** having the form of an arch. **3.** *Heraldry.* noting an ordinary or partition line formed as a slight curve; enarched. [ARCH[1] + -ED[3]]

arched′ truss′, a truss having an archlike form but unlike a true arch in that it is free to move horizontally at its base, as in expanding or contracting because of temperature changes. Cf. **braced arch.**

Ar·che·ge·tes (är kej′i tēz′), *n. Class. Myth.* an epithet of Apollo, meaning "founder," referring to an altar established in his honor by the first Greek colonists of Sicily.

ar·che·go·ni·um (är′kə gō′nē əm), *n., pl.* **-ni·a** (-nē ə). *Bot.* the female reproductive organ in ferns, mosses, etc. [< NL, equiv. to *archegon-* (< Gk *archégon(os)* first of a race; see ARCHE-[1], GONO-) + *-ium* < Gk *-ion* dim. suffix] —**ar′che·go′ni·al, ar·che·go·ni·ate** (är′kə gō′nē it, -āt′), *adj.*

Ar·che·la·us (är′kə lā′əs), *n. Class. Myth.* a son of Temenus and a descendant of Hercules: founder of the royal house of Macedonia.

Ar·chel·o·chus (är kel′ə kəs), *n.* (in the *Iliad*) a son of Antenor and Theano who joined Aeneas in skirmishes against the Greeks and was killed by Telamonian Ajax.

Ar·chem·o·rus (är kem′ər əs), *n. Class. Myth.* Opheltes.

arch·en·e·my (ärch′en′ə mē), *n., pl.* **-mies.** **1.** a chief enemy. **2.** Satan; the Devil. [ARCH- + ENEMY]

ar·chen·ter·on (är ken′tə ron′), *n. Embryol.* the primitive enteron or digestive cavity of a gastrula. [ARCH(EO)- + ENTERON] —**ar·chen·ter·ic** (är′kən ter′ik), *adj.*

archeo-, a learned borrowing from Greek meaning "primitive," used in the formation of compound words: *Archeozoic.* Also, **archaeo-;** *esp. before a vowel,* **arche-.** [earlier *archaio-* < Gk *archaîo(s)* old]

arch·e·o·cyte (är′kē ə sīt′), *n. Zool.* (in sponges) a type of amoebocyte capable of developing into other types of cells, esp. reproductive cells. Also, **archaeocyte.** [ARCHEO- + -CYTE]

ar·che·ol·o·gy (är′kē ol′ə jē), *n.* archaeology. —**ar·che·o·log·i·cal** (är′kē ə loj′i kəl), **ar′che·o·log′ic,** *adj.* —**ar′che·o·log′i·cal·ly,** *adv.* —**ar′che·ol′o·gist,** *n.*

Ar·che·o·zo·ic (är′kē ə zō′ik), *Geol.* —*adj.* **1.** noting or pertaining to a period of the Precambrian era, occurring from about 1,000,000,000 to perhaps 3,000,000,000 years ago, during which the earliest datable rocks were formed and the earliest known life, algae and fungi, came into being. See table under **era.** —*n.* **2.** the Archeozoic period or rock system. Also, **Archaeozoic.** [ARCHEO- + Gk *zō(ḗ)* life + -IC]

Ar·chep·tol·e·mus (är′kep tol′ə məs), *n.* (in the *Iliad*) the son of Iphitus who served as a charioteer for Hector.

arch·er (är′chər), *n.* **1.** one who shoots with a bow and arrow; a bowman. **2.** (*cap.*) *Astron., Astrol.* the constellation or sign of Sagittarius. **3.** an archerfish. [ME < AF; OF *archier* < L *arcār(ius),* equiv. to *arc(us)* bow (see ARC) + *-ārius* -ARY]

Ar·cher (är′chər), *n.* **1. William,** 1856–1924, Scottish playwright, drama critic, and translator. **2.** a boy's given name.

ar·cher·fish (är′chər fish′), *n., pl.* (*esp. collectively*) **-fish,** (*esp. referring to two or more kinds or species*) **-fish·es.** **1.** a percoid fish, *Toxotes jaculatrix,* found off the East Indies, which forcibly ejects drops of water from its mouth at insects to knock them into the water, where it feeds upon them. 2. any of several closely related fishes of the family *Toxotidae*. [ARCHER + FISH]

ar·cher·y (är′chə rē), *n.* 1. the art, practice, or skill of an archer. 2. archers collectively. 3. the equipment of an archer, as bows, arrows, etc. [ME *archerye* < MF *archerie*, equiv. to *arch(i)er* ARCHER + *-ie* -Y^{3}]

ar·che·spore (är′ki spōr′, -spôr′), *n.* *Bot.* the primitive cell, or group of cells, which give rise to the cells from which spores are derived. [ARCHE-^{1} + SPORE] —**ar′che·spo′ri·al,** *adj.*

ar·che·spo·ri·um (är′ki spōr′ē əm, -spôr′-), *n., pl.* **-spo·ri·a** (-spōr′ē ə, -spôr′-). *Bot.* archespore. [< NL]

ar·chet·to (är ket′ō), *n., pl.* **-tos.** *Ceram.* a tool, consisting of a bow strung with wire, for trimming excess material from a piece being modeled. [< It, equiv. to *arc(o)* bow (see ARC) + *-etto* -ET]

ar·che·type (är′ki tīp′), *n.* 1. the original pattern or model after which a thing is made; a model or first form; prototype. 2. (in Jungian psychology) an unconscious idea, pattern of thought, image, etc., inherited from the ancestors of the race and universally present in individual psyches. [< L *archetyp(um)* an original < Gk *archétypon* a model, pattern (neut. of *archétypos* of the first mold, equiv. to *arche-* ARCHE-^{1} + *týp(os)* mold, TYPE + *-os* adj. suffix)] —**ar·che·typ·al** (är′ki tī′pəl), **ar·che·typ·i·cal** (är′ki tip′i kəl), **ar′che·typ′ic,** *adj.* —**ar′che·typ′al·ly, ar′che·typ′i·cal·ly,** *adv.*

arch·fiend (ärch′fēnd′), *n.* 1. a chief fiend. 2. Satan. [ARCH- + FIEND]

arch′ head′, *Mach.* a vertical, arc-shaped member fixed to the end of a walking beam, for supporting a chain from which a pump rod or the like is suspended in such a way as to let it rise and fall vertically.

archi-, 1. var. of **arch-:** *archiepiscopal.* 2. var. of **archeo-:** *archiplasm.* [< L < Gk: foremost, early, old; akin to *árchein* to begin, lead]

Ar·chi·as (är′kē əs), *n.* *Class. Myth.* a descendant of Hercules who was the founder of the city of Syracuse in Sicily.

Ar·chi·bald (är′chə bôld′, -bəld), *n.* a boy's given name.

ar·chi·blast (är′kə blast′), *n.* *Biol.* the formative part of the egg, as distinguished from the part that nourishes the embryo. [ARCHI- + -BLAST]

ar·chi·blas·tic (är′kə blas′tik), *adj.* of, pertaining to, or derived from an archiblast. [ARCHIBLAST + -IC]

ar·chi·carp (är′kə kärp′), *n.* *Bot.* the female sex organ in various ascomycetous fungi, commonly a pluricellular coiled hypha differentiated into a terminal trichogyne and the ascogonium. [ARCHI- + -CARP]

ar·chi·di·ac·o·nal (är′ki dī ak′ə nəl), *adj.* of or pertaining to an archdeacon or his office. [< LL *archidiācon(us)* ARCHDEACON + -AL^{1}]

Ar·chie (är′chē), *n.* a boy's given name, form of **Archibald.** Also, **Archy.**

ar·chi·e·pis·co·pa·cy (är′kē i pis′kə pə sē), *n.* a form of church government in which power is vested in archbishops. [< LL *archiepiscop(us)* ARCHBISHOP + -ACY]

ar·chi·e·pis·co·pal (är′kē i pis′kə pəl), *adj.* of or pertaining to an archbishop or his office. [< ML *archiepiscopāl(is),* equiv. to LL *archiepiscop(us)* ARCHBISHOP + *-ālis* -AL^{1}] —**ar′chi·e·pis′co·pal′i·ty;** *Obs.* **ar·chi·e·pis·co·pate** (är′kē ə pis′kə pit, -pāt′), *n.* —**ar′chi·e·pis′co·pal·ly,** *adv.*

ar′chiepis′copal cross′. See **patriarchal cross.**

ar·chil (är′kil), *n.* orchil.

Ar·chil·o·chus (är kil′ə kəs), *n.* fl. c650 B.C., Greek poet.

ar·chi·mage (är′kə māj′), *n.* a great magician. [ARCHI- + MAGE]

ar·chi·man·drite (är′kə man′drīt), *n.* *Eastern Ch.* 1. the head of a monastery; an abbot. 2. a superior abbot, having charge of several monasteries. 3. a title given to distinguished celibate priests. [< ML *archimandrīt(a)* < LGk *archimandrítēs* abbot, equiv. to Gk *archi-* ARCHI- + LGk *mándr(a)* monastery (orig., fold, enclosure) + *-ítēs* -ITE^{1}]

Ar·chi·me·de·an (är′kə mē′dē ən, -mi dē′ən), *adj.* 1. of, pertaining to, or discovered by Archimedes. 2. *Math.* of or pertaining to any ordered field, as the field of real numbers, having the property that, for any two unequal positive elements there is an integral multiple of the smaller which is greater than the larger. [ARCHIMEDE(S) + -AN]

Ar·chi·me·des (är′kə mē′dēz), *n.* 1. 287?–212 B.C., Greek mathematician, physicist, and inventor. He discovered the principles of specific gravity and of the lever. 2. a walled plain in the second quadrant of the face of the moon: about 50 miles in diameter.

Ar′chime′des′ prin′ciple, *Physics.* the law that a body immersed in a fluid is buoyed up by a force **(buoyant force)** equal to the weight of the fluid displaced by the body.

Ar′chime′des′ screw′, a device consisting essentially of a spiral passage within an inclined cylinder for raising water to a height when rotated. Also, **Ar′chime′dean screw′.** Also called **water snail.**

ar·chine (är shēn′), *n.* arshin. [< F]

arch·ing (är′ching), *n.* arched work or formation. [ARCH^{1} + -ING^{1}]

ar·chi·pel·a·go (är′kə pel′ə gō′), *n., pl.* **-gos, -goes.** 1. any large body of water with many islands. 2. an island group. 3. **the Archipelago,** the Aegean Sea. [< It *arcipelago,* equiv. to *arci-* ARCHI- + *pelago* < L *pelag(us)* < Gk *pélagos* sea] —**ar·chi·pe·lag·ic** (är′kə pə laj′ik), **ar·chi·pe·la·gi·an** (är′kə pə lā′jē ən, -jən), *adj.*

Ar·chi·pen·ko (är′kə peng′kō; *Russ.* är kē′pen kō), *n.* **A·le·ksan·der Por·fir·ie·vich** (al′ig zan′dər pər fēr′ə vich, -zän′-; *Russ.* ä′le ksän′dər por fēr′yə vich), 1889–1964, U.S. sculptor born in Russia.

ar·chi·pho·neme (är′kə fō′nēm, är′kə fō′nēm), *n.* *Ling.* 1. an abstract phonological unit consisting of the distinctive features common to two phonemes that differ only in that one has a distinctive feature lacking in the other. The archiphoneme is said to be realized when in a certain position an otherwise phonemic opposition is neutralized; thus, in German, while *p* and *b* are separate phonemes differing only in the distinctive feature of voicing, in final position the voicing or unvoicing of the labial stop is nondistinctive, and the *p*-sound of *leib* "life" may be called the realization of the archiphoneme. 2. such a unit occurring in a position where the contrast between two or more phonemes is neutralized. [ARCHI- + PHONEME]

Ar·chi·pié·la·go de Co·lón (är′chē pye′lä gō′ t͟he kō lōn′), Spanish name of **Galápagos Islands.**

ar·chi·plasm (är′kə plaz′əm), *n.* 1. the most basic or primitive living substance; protoplasm. 2. *Cytology.* (in cell division) the substance surrounding the centrosome. Also, **archoplasm.** [ARCHI- + -PLASM, modeled on G *Archiplasma*] —**ar′chi·plas′mic,** *adj.*

archit., architecture.

ar·chi·tect (är′ki tekt′), *n.* 1. a person who engages in the profession of architecture. 2. a person professionally engaged in the design of certain large constructions other than buildings and the like: *landscape architect; naval architect.* 3. the deviser, maker, or creator of anything: *the architects of the Constitution.* —*v.t.* 4. to plan, organize, or structure as an architect: *The house has been architected to harmonize with the landscape.* [< L *architect(us)* < Gk *architéktōn,* equiv. to Gk *archi-* ARCHI- + *-tektōn* worker]

ar·chi·tec·ton·ic (är′ki tek ton′ik), *adj.* 1. of or pertaining to the principles of architecture. 2. resembling architecture, esp. in its highly organized manner or technique of structure: *the architectonic perfection of his new novel.* [< L *architectonic(us)* < Gk *architektonikós* of, belonging to architecture. See ARCHI-, TECTONIC] —**ar′chi·tec·ton′i·cal·ly,** *adv.*

ar·chi·tec·ton·ics (är′ki tek ton′iks), *n.* the science of planning and constructing buildings. [see ARCHITECTONIC, -ICS]

ar′chitect's ta′ble. See **drawing table.**

ar·chi·tec·tur·al (är′ki tek′chər əl), *adj.* 1. of or pertaining to architecture: *architectural metals.* 2. conforming to the basic principles of architecture. 3. having the qualities of architecture; characteristic of architecture; structural; architectonic. [ARCHITECTURE + -AL^{1}] —**ar′chi·tec′tur·al·ly,** *adv.*

architec′tural bronze′, a brass alloy of about 57 percent copper, 41 percent zinc, and 2 percent lead.

ar·chi·tec·ture (är′ki tek′chər), *n.* 1. the profession of designing buildings, open areas, communities, and other artificial constructions and environments, usually with some regard to aesthetic effect. The professional services of an architect often include design or selection of furnishings and decorations, supervision of construction work, and the examination, restoration, or remodeling of existing buildings. 2. the character or style of building: *the architecture of Paris; Romanesque architecture.* 3. the action or process of building; construction. 4. the result or product of architectural work, as a building. 5. buildings collectively. 6. the structure of anything: *the architecture of a novel.* [< L *architectūr(a).* See ARCHITECT, -URE]

ar·chi·trave (är′ki trāv′), *n.* *Archit.* 1. the lowermost member of a classical entablature, resting originally upon columns. 2. a molded or decorated band framing a panel or an opening, esp. a rectangular one, as of a door or window. [< It; see ARCHI-, TRAVE] —**ar′chi·tra′val,** *adj.* —**ar′chi·traved′,** *adj.*

ar·chi·val (är kī′vəl), *adj.* of or pertaining to archives or valuable records; contained in or comprising such archives or records. [ARCHIVE + -AL^{1}]

ar·chive (är′kīv), *n.* 1. Usually, **archives.** documents or records relating to the activities, rights, claims, treaties, constitutions, etc., of a family, corporation, community, nation or historical figure. 2. **archives,** a place where public records or other historical documents are kept. 3. any extensive record or collection of data: *The Bible is an archive of man's spiritual growth. The experience was sealed in the archive of his memory.* [< LL *archī(v)(um)* < Gk *archeîon* government building (where records were kept), equiv. to *arche-* (s. of *archḗ*) government, rule + *-ion* suffix of place]

ar·chi·vist (är′kə vist), *n.* a custodian of archives. [< ML *archivist(a).* See ARCHIVE, -IST]

ar·chi·volt (är′kə vōlt′), *n.* *Archit.* a molded or decorated band following the extrados of an arch or forming an archlike frame for an opening. [< It *archivolt(o)* < ML *archivolt(um).* See ARCHI-, VAULT^{1}]

arch·lute (ärch′lo͞ot′), *n.* a lute with two pegboxes, one for the stopped strings and the other for the bass strings, which run outside the fingerboard. [ARCH- + LUTE, modeled on It *arciliuto*]

Arch′ of Tri′umph. See **Arc de Triomphe.**

ar·chon (är′kon), *n.* 1. a higher magistrate in ancient Athens. 2. any ruler. [< Gk *árchōn* magistrate, ruler (n. use of prp. of *árchein* to be first, rule), equiv. to *arch-* (see -ARCH) + *-ōn* prp. suffix] —**ar′chon·ship′,** *n.*

ar·cho·plasm (är′kə plaz′əm), *n.* archiplasm. —**ar′cho·plas′mic,** *adj.*

arch·priest (ärch′prēst′), *n.* 1. a priest holding first rank, as among the members of a cathedral chapter or among the clergy of a district outside the episcopal city. 2. *Rom. Cath. Ch.* a priest acting as superior of the Roman Catholic secular clergy in England, first appointed in 1598 and superseded by a vicar apostolic in 1623. [late ME *archeprest* (modeled on LL *archipresbyter* < Gk *archipresbýter(os)*). See ARCH-, PRIEST] —**arch′priest′hood,** *n.* —**arch′priest′ship,** *n.*

arch·see (ärch′sē′), *n.* archbishopric. [ARCH- + SEE^{2}]

arch′ support′, an insert placed inside a shoe to relieve, or reduce strain on, the muscles forming the arch of the foot.

archt., architect.

arch·way (ärch′wā′), *n.* *Archit.* 1. an entrance or passage under an arch. 2. a covering or enclosing arch. [ARCH^{1} + WAY]

Ar·chy (är′chē), *n.* a boy's given name, form of **Archibald.** Also, **Archie.**

-archy, a word element meaning "rule," "government," used in the formation of abstract nouns from stems in **-arch:** *monarchy.* [ME *-archie* < L *-archia* < Gk, equiv. to *arch-* (see -ARCH) + *-ia* -Y^{3}]

Ar·chy·tas (är kī′təs), *n.* a crater in the first quadrant of the face of the moon: about 21 miles in diameter.

ar·ci·fin·i·ous (är′sə fin′ē əs), *adj.* having a frontier that forms a natural boundary, esp. as a defense against incursion. [< L *arcifinius,* equiv. to *arci-* (s. of *arx* stronghold, protection) + *fīni(s)* boundary + *-us* -OUS]

ar·ci·form (är′sə fôrm′), *adj.* resembling an arch in appearance. [< L *arci-* (comb. form of *arcus* bow; see ARC) + -FORM]

Ar·cim·bol·di (är′chim bōl′dē; *It.* är′chēm bôl′dē), *n.* **Giu·sep·pe** (jo͞o zep′pe), 1527–93, Italian painter.

Ar·ci·nie·gas (är sē nye′gäs), *n.* **Ger·mán** (her män′), born 1900, Colombian author, editor, and diplomat.

arc′ light′, 1. Also, **arc′ lamp′.** a lamp in which the light source of high intensity is an electric arc, usually between carbon rods. 2. the light produced.

ar·co (är′kō), *adv.* *Music.* (of the performance of a passage for stringed instruments) with the bow. [< It: bow < L *arc(us).* See ARC]

Arc′ of Lo′witz (lō′vits), *Meteorol.* a halo or arc of light, occurring infrequently, which extends diagonally downward from a 22° parhelion. Also, **Lowitz arc.** Also called **lateral tangent arc, vertical arc of the 22° parhelion.**

arc·o·graph (är′kə graf′, -gräf′), *n.* *Geom.* an instrument for drawing arcs, having a flexible arc-shaped part adjusted by an extensible straight bar connecting its sides. Also called **cyclograph.** [ARC + -O- + -GRAPH]

ar·co·so·li·um (är′kə sō′lē əm), *n., pl.* **-li·a** (-lē ə). (in Roman catacombs) an arched recess for a sarcophagus. [< NL, equiv. to L *arc(us)* ARC + -o- -O- + *solium* sarcophagus]

A.R.C.S., 1. Associate of the Royal College of Science. 2. Associate of the Royal College of Surgeons.

arc′ se′cant, *Trig.* the angle, measured in radians, that has a secant equal to a given number. *Symbol:* arc sec, sec^{-1}. Also called **inverse secant.**

arc′ sine′, *Trig.* the angle, measured in radians, of which a given number is the sine. *Symbol:* arc sin, sin^{-1}. Also, **inverse sine.**

arc′ spec′trum, *Physics.* a spectrum formed from the light produced by an electric arc, characteristic of the gas or vapor through which the arc passes.

arc′ tan′gent, *Trig.* the angle, measured in radians, that has a tangent equal to a given number. *Symbol:* arc tan, tan^{-1}. Also called **inverse tangent.**

arc·tic (ärk′tik *or, esp. for* 8, är′tik), *adj.* 1. *(often cap.)* of, at, or near the North Pole: *the arctic region.* 2. coming from the North Pole or the arctic region: *an arctic wind; an arctic blast.* 3. characteristic of the weather at the North Pole or in the arctic region; frigid; bleak: *an arctic winter.* 4. used, or resembling that which is used, in the arctic: *arctic boots.* 5. extremely cold in manner, atmosphere, etc.: *an arctic reception.* 6. *Astron. Rare.* of, near, or lying under the Great and the Little Bear. —*n.* 7. *(often cap.)* the region lying north of the Arctic Circle or of the northernmost limit of tree growth; the polar area north of the timber line. 8. **arctics,** warm, waterproof overshoes. [< L *arctic(us)* < Gk *arktikós* northern, lit., of the Bear, equiv. to *árkt(os)* bear (see URSA MAJOR) + *-ikos* -IC; r. ME *artik* < MF *artique* < L *ar(c)ticus*] —**arc′ti·cal·ly,** *adv.*

Arc′tic Cir′cle, an imaginary line drawn parallel to the equator, at 23°28′ S of the North Pole: between the North Frigid Zone and the North Temperate Zone. See diag. under **zone.**

Arc′tic dai′sy, a daisy, *Chrysanthemum arcticum,* of the arctic regions, having asterlike heads of white or lilac flowers. Also called **aster daisy.**

arc′tic fox′, a thickly furred, foxlike canine, *Alopex lagopus,* of the arctic regions, brownish gray in summer and white in winter. Also called **white fox.**

Arc′tic O′cean, an ocean N of North America, Asia, and the Arctic Circle. ab. 5,540,000 sq. mi.

arc·ti·col·o·gist (ärk′tə kol′ə jist, är′-), *n.* a person who specializes in arcticology. [ARCTICOLOG(Y) + -IST]

arc·ti·col·o·gy (ärk′tə kol′ə jē, är′-), *n.* the scientific study of the Polar Regions. [ARCTIC + -O- + -LOGY]

arc′tic seal′, rabbit fur that has been sheared and dyed to simulate sealskin.

arc′tic smoke′. See **steam fog.** Also called **arc′tic sea′ smoke′.**

Arc′tic tern′, a tern, *Sterna paradisaea,* resembling the common tern, that breeds in arctic regions and winters in antarctic regions.

Arc′tic Zone′, the section of the earth's surface lying between the Arctic Circle and the North Pole. See diag. under **zone.**

Arc·to·gae·a (ärk′tə jē′ə), *n.* a biogeographical division comprising the Holarctic and Paleotropical regions. Also, **Arc′to·ge′a.** [NL, equiv. to *arcto-* (< L < Gk *arkto-* comb. form of *árktos;* see ARCTIC) + *gaea* (< Gk *gaîa* land, earth)] —**Arc′to·gae′an, Arc′to·ge′an, Arc′to·gae′al, Arc′to·ge′al, Arc′to·gae′ic, Arc′to·ge′ic,** *adj.*

Arc·tu·rus (ärk to͝or′əs, -tyo͝or′-), *n.* *Astron.* a first-magnitude star in the constellation Boötes. [< L < Gk *Arktoûros,* equiv. to *árkt(os)* bear + *-oûros* keeper; r. ME *arture* < MF] —**Arc·tu′ri·an,** *adj.*

ar·cu·ate (är′kyo͞o it, -āt′), *adj.* bent or curved like a bow. Also, **ar′cu·at′ed.** [< L *arcuāt(us)* bent like a bow, curved (ptp. of *arcuāre*), equiv. to *arcu(s)* a bow + *-ātus* -ATE^{1}] —**ar′cu·ate·ly,** *adv.*

ar·cu·a·tion (är′kyo͞o ā′shən), *n.* 1. state of being bent or curved. 2. the use of arches in building. 3. a system or grouping of arches. [< LL *arcuātiōn-* (s. of *arcuātiō*) a curving, equiv. to L *arcuāt(us)* curved (see ARCUATE) + *-iōn-* -ION]

ar·cus (är′kəs), *n., pl.* **-cus.** a dense cloud, horizontal and roll-shaped, sometimes occurring at the lower front portion of a cumulonimbus. Also called **roll cloud.** [< L: bow, arch]

arc′wise connect′ed set′ (ärk′wīz′), *Math.* a set in which every two points can be connected by an arc completely contained in the set. Cf. **connected** (def. 3).

Ard (ärd), *n.* a boy's given name, form of **Arden, Ardmore.**

-ard, a noun suffix, orig. intensive but now pejorative or without special force: *coward; drunkard; wizard.* Also, **-art.** [ME < OF < OLG *-hard* (c. OE *-heard*) in men's names, as *Bernhard* Bernard); cf. OHG *-(h)ard, -(h)art* hardy]

ar·deb (är′deb), *n.* a unit of capacity used for dry measure in Egypt and neighboring countries, officially equivalent in Egypt to 5.62 U.S. bushels, but varying greatly in different localities. [< Ar *ardabb* < Gk *artábē* < OPers *artaba*]

Ar·dèche (ar desh′), *n.* a department in SE France. 248,516 (1962); 2145 sq. mi. *Cap.:* Privas.

Ar·deen (är dēn′), *n.* a girl's given name. Also, **Ardene.**

ar·de·id (är′dē id), *adj.* belonging or pertaining to the family *Ardeidae,* comprising the herons and bitterns. [< NL *Ardeid(ae)* name of the family, equiv. to *Arde(a)* name of the genus < L *ardea* heron + *-idae* -ID^{2}]

Ar·del·la (är del′ə), *n.* a girl's given name. Also, **Ar·delle** (är del′).

Ar·den (är′dən), *n.* **1. Forest of,** a forest district in central England, in N Warwickshire: scene of Shakespeare's *As You Like It.* **2. Elizabeth,** 1891–1966, U.S. cosmetician, born in Canada. **3.** Also, **Ardin.** a boy's given name.

ar·den·cy (är′dən sē), *n.* **1.** passion; ardor; fervor; intensity. **2.** *Naut.* the tendency of a sailing vessel to head into the wind, esp. when the wind is abeam or on the quarter. [ARD(ENT) + -ENCY]

Ar·dene (är dēn′), *n.* a girl's given name. Also, **Ar·deen.**

Ar·dennes (AR den′), *n.* **1. Forest of,** a wooded plateau region in W Europe, in NE France, SE Belgium, and Luxemburg: World War I battle 1914; World War II battles 1944–45. **2.** a department in NE France. 300,247 (1962); 2028 sq. mi. *Cap.:* Mézières.

ar·dent (är′dənt), *adj.* **1.** having, expressive of, or characterized by intense feeling, emotion, or devotion; passionate; fervent; zealous: *an ardent patriot; an ardent vow.* **2.** vehement; fierce: *They were terrified by his ardent, burning eyes.* **3.** *Naut.* (of a vessel) characterized by marked or excessive ardency. **4.** *Obs.* burning, fiery, or hot. [< L *ārdent-* (s. of *ārdēns,* prp. of *ārdēre* to burn), equiv. to *ārd-* burn + *-ent-* -ENT; r. ME *ardant* < MF] —**ar′dent·ly,** *adv.* —**ar′dent·ness,** *n.*
—**Syn. 1.** fervid, eager, enthusiastic; vehement.

ar′dent spir′its, strong alcoholic liquors made by distillation, as brandy, whiskey, or gin.

Ar·din (är′dən), *n.* a boy's given name. Also, **Arden.**

Ar·dis (är′dis), *n.* a girl's given name.

ar·dish (är′dish), *n.* (in Indian architecture) tracery carved from plaster containing pieces of glass. [< Hindi]

Ard·more (ärd′mōr, -môr), *n.* **1.** a city in S Oklahoma. 20,184 (1960). **2.** a boy's given name.

ar·dor (är′dər), *n.* **1.** great warmth of feeling; fervor; zeal; passion: *He spoke persuasively and with ardor.* **2.** *Obs.* burning heat. Also, *esp. Brit.,* **ar′dour.** [< L, equiv. to *ārd(ēre)* (to) burn + *-or* -OR²; r. ME *ardure* < OF *ardur* < L; 17th century *ardour* < AF < L]
—**Syn. 1.** fervency, passion.

Ards·ley (ärdz′lē), *n.* a town in SE New York. 3991 (1960).

ar·du·ous (är′jo͞o əs *or, esp. Brit.,* är′dyo͞o-), *adj.* **1.** requiring great exertion; laborious; difficult: *an arduous undertaking.* **2.** energetic; vigorous; strenuous: *making an arduous effort.* **3.** hard to climb; steep: *an arduous path.* **4.** hard to endure; full of hardships; severe: *an arduous winter.* [< L *arduus* erect, steep, laborious; see -OUS] —**ar′du·ous·ly,** *adv.* —**ar′du·ous·ness,** *n.*
—**Syn. 1.** hard, toilsome, onerous, wearisome, burdensome, exhausting. —**Ant. 1.** easy.

are[1] (är; *unstressed* ər), *v.* pres. indic. pl. and 2nd pers. sing. of **be.** [ME, OE (Northumbrian) *aron;* c. Icel *eru,* 3rd pers. pl. See ART²]

are[2] (âr, är), *n.* *Metric System.* a surface measure equal to 100 square meters, or 119.6 square yards; 1/100 of a hectare. *Abbr.:* a [< F < L *āre(a).* See AREA]

A.R.E., Associate in Religious Education.

ar·e·a (âr′ē ə), *n.* **1.** any particular extent of surface; geographical region; tract: *the settled area; the Chicago area.* **2.** any section reserved for a specific function: *the business area of a town; the dining area of a house.* **3.** extent, range, or scope: *inquiries that embrace the whole area of science.* **4.** field of study, or a branch of a field of study: *Related areas of inquiry often reflect borrowed notions.* **5.** a piece of unoccupied ground; an open space. **6.** the space or site on which a building stands; the yard attached to or surrounding a house. **7.** *Brit.* areaway (def. 1). **8.** the quantitative measure of a plane or curved surface; two-dimensional extent. **9.** *Anat.* **a.** a limited space or surface. **b.** a zone of the cerebral cortex having a specific function. [< L *ārea* vacant piece of level ground, open space in a town, courtyard, playground, orig. dry place, suitable for games, etc.; akin to *ārēre* to be dry. See ARID] —**ar′e·al,** *adj.*

ar′ea bomb′ing, aerial bombing in which bombs are dropped over the general area of a target. Cf. **pattern bombing, precision bombing.**

ar′ea code′, a three-digit code which identifies one of the telephone areas into which the U.S. is divided and which precedes the local telephone number when dialing a call between areas. Area codes also exist for some parts of Canada and Mexico.

ar′ea o·pa′ca (ō pā′kə), *Embryol., Zool.* the opaque area of the blastoderm surrounding the area pellucida. [< NL]

ar′ea pel·lu′ci·da (pə lo͞o′si də), *Embryol., Zool.* the translucent, central area of the blastoderm of birds and reptiles, within which the body of the embryo develops. [< NL]

ar′ea stud′y, anthropological or sociological research intended to gather and relate data on various aspects of a geographical region and its inhabitants, as natural resources, history, language, institutions, cultural and economic characteristics, etc.; a field investigation into human ecology.

ar′ea vas·cu·lo′sa (vas′kyə lō′sə), *Embryol., Zool.* that part of the area opaca in which the blood cells and vessels are formed. [< NL; see AREA, VASCULUM, -OSE¹]

ar′ea vit·el·li′na (vit′əl ī′nə), *Embryol., Zool.* the nonvascular part of the area opaca surrounding the area vasculosa. [< NL: vitelline area]

ar·e·a·way (âr′ē ə wā′), *n.* **1.** a sunken area leading to a cellar or basement entrance, or in front of basement or cellar windows. **2.** *U.S.* a passageway. [AREA + WAY]

ar·e·ca (ar′ə kə, ə rē′-), *n.* **1.** any palm of the genus *Areca,* of tropical Asia and the Malay Archipelago, esp. *A. Catechu,* the betel palm, which bears a nut. **2.** Also called **ar′eca nut′.** the nut itself. **3.** any of various palms formerly referred to the genus *Areca.* Also called **ar′eca palm′** (for defs. 1, 3). [< Pg < Malayalam *aḍekka, aṭekka*]

A·re·ci·bo (är′i sē′bō; *Sp.* ä′re sē′bō), *n.* a seaport in N Puerto Rico. 28,828 (1960).

Ar·e·ïth·o·üs (ar′ē ith′ō əs), *n.* (in the *Iliad*) the father of Menesthius, who used an iron mace in battle. He was killed by Lycurgus.

A·rei·us (ə rē′əs), *n.* *Class. Myth.* Areus.

A.Rel., Associate in Religion.

A·re·li·a (ə rēl′yə), *n.* a girl's given name.

a·re·na (ə rē′nə), *n.* **1.** the oval space in a Roman amphitheater for combats or other performances. **2.** a platform, ring, area, or the like, used for sports or other forms of entertainment, surrounded by seats for spectators: *a boxing arena; a circus arena.* **3.** a building housing an arena. **4.** a field of conflict, activity, or endeavor: *the arena of politics.* [< L *(h)arēna* sand, sandy place, area sanded for combat]

ar·e·na·ceous (ar′ə nā′shəs), *adj.* **1.** sandlike; sandy. **2.** (of plants) having a sandy habitat. [< L *(h)arēnaceus.* See ARENA, -ACEOUS]

Are′na Chap′el, a private chapel in Padua containing a fresco cycle painted (1305–6) by Giotto. Also called **Scrovegni Chapel.**

are′na the′ater, a theater with seats arranged on at least three sides around a central stage. Also called **theater-in-the-round.**

Ar·endt (âr′ənt, är′-), *n.* **Hannah,** born 1906, U.S. author, political scientist, and teacher; born in Germany.

A·re·ne (ə rē′nē), *n.* *Class. Myth.* the mother of Lynceus and Idas.

ar·e·nic·o·lous (ar′ə nik′ə ləs), *adj.* inhabiting sand. [< NL: lit., living in sand. See ARENA, -I-, -COLOUS]

ar·e·nose (ar′ə nōs′), *adj.* sandy; gritty. Also, **ar·e·nous** (ar′ə nəs), **a·ren·u·lous** (ə ren′yə ləs). [< L *(h)arēnōs(us)* sandy. See ARENA, -OSE¹] —**ar·e·nos·i·ty** (ar′ə nos′i tē), *n.*

A·ren·sky (ə ren′skē; *Russ.* ä REN′ski), *n.* **An·ton Ste·pa·no·vich** (än tôn′ sti pä′no vich), 1861–1906, Russian composer.

aren't (ärnt, är′ənt), **1.** contraction of *are not.* **2.** contraction of *am not.*
—**Usage.** AREN'T, in the sense of "am not" in such questions as *I'm doing well, aren't I?,* is generally acceptable in preference to AIN'T. It is questioned by precise grammarians; it is regarded as cute or affected by many users of English.

areo-, a learned borrowing from Greek meaning "the planet Mars," used in the formation of compound words: *areocentric.* [< Gk *Áreo(s),* gen. of *Árēs* ARES]

ar·e·o·cen·tric (âr′ē ō sen′trik), *adj.* *Astron.* having the planet Mars as center. [AREO- + CENTRIC]

a·re·o·la (ə rē′ə lə), *n., pl.* **-lae** (-lē′), **-las.** *Biol.* **1.** a ring of color, as around a pustule or the human nipple. **2.** a small interstice, as between the fibers of connective tissue. [< L, equiv. to *āre(a)* AREA + *-ola* dim. suffix] —**a·re′o·lar,** *adj.* —**a·re·o·late** (ə rē′ə lit, -lāt′), **a·re·o·lat·ed** (ə rē′ə lā′tid), *adj.* —**ar·e·o·la·tion** (âr′ē ə lā′shən), *n.*

ar·e·ole (âr′ē ōl′), *n.* *Biol.* an areola. [< F *aréole* < L *āreola* a small open space. See AREOLA]

ar·e·ol·o·gy (âr′ē ol′ə jē), *n.* *Astron.* the observation and study of the planet Mars. [AREO- + -LOGY] —**ar·e·o·log·ic** (âr′ē ə loj′ik), **ar′e·o·log′i·cal,** *adj.* —**ar′e·o·log′i·cal·ly,** *adv.* —**ar′e·ol′o·gist,** *n.*

Ar·e·op·a·gite (ar′ē op′ə jīt′, -gīt′), *n.* *Gk. Hist.* a member of the council of the Areopagus. [< L *Areopagīt(ēs)* < Gk *Areiopagītēs* a member of the AREOPAGUS; see -ITE¹] —**Ar·e·op·a·git·ic** (ar′ē op′ə jit′ik), *adj.*

Ar·e·op·a·git·i·ca (ar′ē op′ə jit′ə kə), *n.* a pamphlet (1644) by Milton, advocating freedom of the press.

Ar·e·op·a·gus (ar′ē op′ə gəs), *n.* **1.** a hill in Athens, Greece, W of the Acropolis. **2.** *Gk. Hist.* the council which met on this hill, originally having wide public functions but later becoming a purely judicial body. **3.** any high tribunal. [< L < Gk *Áreio(s) págos* hill of Ares]

a·re·o·style (ə rē′ə stīl′, ar′ē ō-), *adj.* araeostyle.

a·re·o·sys·tyle (ə rē′ə sis′tīl, ar′ē ō-), *adj.* araeosystyle.

Ar·e·qui·pa (ar′ə kē′pə; *Sp.* ä′re kē′pä), *n.* a city in S Peru. 117,208 (est. 1957).

Ar·es (âr′ēz), *n.* the ancient Greek god of war, a son of Zeus and Hera, identified by the Romans with Mars.

a·rête (ə rāt′), *n.* *Phys. Geog.* a sharp rugged ridge on a mountain. [< F; OF *areste* sharp ridge < L *arist(a)* awn, ear of wheat, spine of fish]

A·re·te (ə rē′tē), *n.* *Class. Myth.* **1.** the wife of Alcinous, who had much influence over her husband. **2.** the personification of courage.

ar·e·thu·sa (ar′ə tho͞o′zə), *n.* **1.** any of several plants of the genus *Arethusa,* esp. *A. bulbosa,* of North America, a small bog orchid having a pink or white flower. **2.** (*cap.*) *Class Myth.* a nymph who was changed into a spring to save her from the river god Alpheus, who was pursuing her.

A·re·ti·no (är′i tē′nō; *It.* ä′RE tē′nô), *n.* **Pie·tro** (pye′trô), 1492–1556, Italian satirist and dramatist.

A·re·tus (ə rē′təs), *n.* (in the *Iliad*) one of the 50 sons of Priam. He was killed by Automedon while trying to seize the immortal horses of Achilles.

A·re·us (ə rē′əs), *n.* *Class. Myth.* **1.** a son of Bias and Pero who, with his brothers, Leodocus and Talaus, became an Argonaut. **2.** an epithet of Zeus, meaning "warlike." Also, **Areius.**

A·ré·va·lo Mar·tí·nez (ä RE′vä lô mär tē′nes), **Ra·fa·el** (RÄ′fä el′), born 1884, Guatemalan novelist and short-story writer.

A·rez·zo (ə ret′sō; *It.* ä Ret′tsô), *n.* a city in central Italy. 74,245 (1961).

arf·ved·son·ite (är′vid sə nīt′), *n.* a mineral, a sodium-rich amphibole, occurring in green to black crystals in alkali rocks. [named after J. A. *Arfvedson* (d. 1841), Swedish chemist; see -ITE¹]

Arg., Argentina.

arg., argentum.

Ar·ga·des (är′gə dēz′), *n.* *Class. Myth.* one of the four sons of Ion.

ar·gal[1] (är′gəl), *n.* argol.

ar·gal[2] (är′gəl), *n.* argali.

ar·ga·li (är′gə lē), *n., pl.* **-li.** a wild sheep, *Ovis ammon,* of Asia, having long, thick, spirally curved horns. Also, **argal.** [< Mongolian]

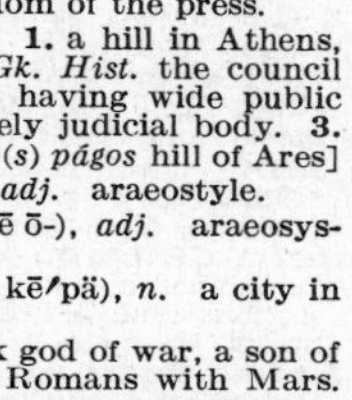

Argali (4 ft. high at shoulder; horns 20 in.)

Ar·gall (är′gôl, -gəl), *n.* **Sir Sam·uel,** 1572–1639, explorer, colonial governor in America, 1617–19.

Ar′gand burn′er (är′gand, -gänd, -gənd), a type of oil or gas burner in which air is fed directly into the flame through a metal tube inside a cylindrical wick. [named after Aimé *Argand* (1750–1803), Swiss scientist]

Ar′gand di′agram, *Math.* a Cartesian coordinate system consisting of two perpendicular axes for graphing complex numbers, the real part of a number being plotted along the horizontal axis and the imaginary part along the vertical axis. Also called **Ar′gand plane′, Gauss plane.** Cf. **imaginary axis, real axis.** [named after Jean-Robert *Argand* (1768–1822), Swiss mathematician]

Ar′gand lamp′, an oil lamp with a chimney, having a tubular wick that permits air to reach the center of the flame. [named after A. *Argand.* See ARGAND BURNER]

ar·ga·sid (är′gə sid), *n.* **1.** any of numerous ticks of the family *Argasidae,* comprising the soft ticks. —*adj.* **2.** belonging or pertaining to the family *Argasidae.* [< NL *Argasid(ae)* name of the family, equiv. to *Argas* name of the genus, perh. irreg. < Gk *a-* A-⁶ + *ergos* (deriv. of *érgon* work) + *-idae* -ID²]

Ar·gei·phon·tes (är′jī fon′tēz), *n.* *Class. Myth.* an epithet of Hermes, meaning "slayer of Argus." Also, **Argiphontes.**

Ar·ge·lan·der (äR′gə län′dəR *for 1;* är′gə lan′dər, -län′- *for 2*), *n.* **1. Frie·drich Wil·helm Au·gust** (fRē′-dRiKH vil′helm ou′go͝ost), 1799–1875, German astronomer. **2.** a crater in the fourth quadrant of the face of the moon: about 20 miles in diameter.

ar·gent (är′jənt), *n.* **1.** *Heraldry.* the tincture or metal silver. **2.** *Archaic.* **a.** silver. **b.** something silvery or white. **3.** *Obs.* money. —*adj.* **4.** like silver; silvery-white. **5.** *Heraldry.* of the tincture or metal silver: *a lion argent.* [late ME *argent(um)* < L: silver, money]

argent-, var. of **argento-,** esp. before a vowel. Also, **argenti-.**

ar·gen·tal (är jen′təl), *adj.* of, pertaining to, containing, or resembling silver. [ARGENT- + -AL¹]

ar·gen·te·ous (är jen′tē əs), *adj.* silvery. Also, **ar·gen·tate** (är′jən tāt′). [< L *argenteus.* See ARGENT-, -EOUS]

Ar·gen·teuil (AR zhän tœ′yə), *n.* a city in N France, on the Seine near Paris. 82,458 (1962).

ar·gen·tic (är jen′tik), *adj.* *Chem.* of or containing silver and having a valence greater than the corresponding argentous compound. [ARGENT- + -IC]

ar·gen·tif·er·ous (är′jən tif′ər əs), *adj.* silver-bearing. [< L *argent(um)* silver + -I- + -FEROUS]

Ar·gen·ti·na (är′jən tē′nə; *Sp.* äR′hen tē′nä), *n.* a republic in S South America. 22,252,000 (est. 1965); 1,084,120 sq. mi. *Cap.:* Buenos Aires. Also called **the Argentine.** Official name, **Ar′gentine Repub′lic.**

ar·gen·tine[1] (är′jən tin, -tīn′), *adj.* **1.** pertaining to or resembling silver. —*n.* **2.** a silvery substance obtained from fish scales, used in making imitation pearls. [late ME < L *argentin(us)* silvery. See ARGENTINE²]

ar·gen·tine[2] (är′jən tin, -tīn′), *n.* any of various silvery marine fishes, esp. those of the genus *Argentina.* [< NL *Argentin(a)* genus name, L, fem. of *argentīnus* silvery. See ARGENT, -INE¹]

Ar·gen·tine (är′jən tēn′, -tīn′), *n.* **1.** a native or inhabitant of Argentina. **2.** Argentina (usually prec. by *the*): *They vacationed in the Argentine.* —*adj.* **3.** of or pertaining to Argentina. Also, **Ar·gen·tin·e·an** (är′jən-tin′ē ən).

Ar′gentine ant′, a brown ant, *Iridomyrmex humilis,* introduced into the southern U.S. from South America, commonly found as a household pest. [so called because native to Argentina]

Ar′gentine cloth′, a glazed cotton fabric, similar to tarlatan, used for curtains and to protect dresses from dust.

ar·gen·tite (är′jən tīt′), *n.* a dark lead-gray sectile mineral, silver sulfide, Ag_2S, occurring in crystals and massive: an important ore of silver. [ARGENT- + -ITE¹]

argento-, a learned borrowing from Latin meaning "silver," used in the formation of compound words: *argento-cuprous sulfide.* Also, **argenti-;** *esp. before a vowel,* **argent-.** [< L *argent(um)* + -o-]

ar·gen′to-cu′prous sul′fide (är jen′tō ko͞o′prəs), stromeyrite.

ar·gen·tous (är jen′təs), *adj.* *Chem.* containing univalent silver, as argentous chloride, AgCl. [ARGENT- + -OUS]

ar·gen·tum (är jen′təm), *n.* *Chem.* silver. [< L]

Ar·ges (är′jēz), *n.* *Class. Myth.* one of the Cyclopes.

ar·ghool (är go͞ol′), *n.* an Arabian wind instrument of the oboe family, consisting of two pipes, one of which is a drone. [< Ar *arghūl*]

Ar·gi·a (är jī′ə), *n.* *Class. Myth.* **1.** a daughter of Oceanus and Tethys. **2.** the wife of Polybus and the mother of Argus, builder of the *Argo.* **3.** Aegia. **4.** the mother of Eurysthenes and Procles.

ar·gil (är′jil), *n.* *Obs.* clay, esp. potter's clay. [ME *argill(a)* < L < Gk *árgill(os),* equiv. to *arg(ós)* white + *-il(l)os* n. suffix]

ar·gil·la·ceous (är′jə lā′shəs), *adj.* **1.** of the nature of or resembling clay; clayey. **2.** containing a considerable amount of clayey matter. [< L *argillāceus* clayish. See ARGIL, -ACEOUS]

ar·gil·lif·er·ous (är′jə lif′ər əs), *adj.* *Mineral.* composed mainly or wholly of clay. [< L *argill(a)* ARGIL + -I- + -FEROUS]

ar·gil·lite (är′jə līt′), *n.* any compact sedimentary rock composed mainly of clay materials; clay stone. [< L *argill(a)* ARGIL + -ITE¹] —**ar·gil·lit·ic** (är′jə-lit′ik), *adj.*

ar·gi·nine (är′jə nīn′), *n.* *Biochem.* one of the essential amino acids, $C_6H_{14}O_2N_4$, that make up plant and animal proteins, present in the sperm of salmon and herring. [< Gk *argin(óeis)* bright-shining + -INE²]

Ar·gi·o·pe (är jī′ə pē′), *n.* *Class. Myth.* **1.** the wife of Agenor and the mother of Cadmus and Europa. **2.** a nymph. **3.** a daughter of Teuthras.

Ar·gi·phon·tes (är′jī fon′tēz), *n.* *Class. Myth.* Argeiphontes.

Ar·give (är′jīv, -gīv), *adj.* **1.** of or pertaining to Argos. **2.** Greek. —*n.* **3.** a native of Argos. **4.** any Greek. [< L *Argīv(us)* < **Argīv(us)* (see ARCHIVE), var. of *Argeus* < Gk *Argeîos* of Argos]

ar·gle-bar·gle (är′gəl bär′gəl; *Scot.* äR′gəl bäR′gəl), *n., v.,* **-bar·gled, -bar·gling.** *Scot.* —*n.* **1.** haggling. —*v.i.* **2.** to argue; haggle. Also, **argy-bargy.** [redupl. of *argle,* var. of ARGUE]

Ar·go (är′gō), *n., gen.* **Ar·gus** (är′gəs) for 1. **1.** *Astron.* a very large southern constellation, now divided into four separate constellations, lying largely south of Canis Major. 2. *Class. Myth.* the ship in which Jason sailed in quest of the Golden Fleece. [constellation named after ship] —**Ar·go′an,** *adj.*

ar·gol (är′gəl), *n.* a crude tartar, produced as a by-product in casks by the fermentation of wine grapes, used as a mordant in dyeing, in the manufacture of tartaric acid, and in fertilizers. Also, **argal.** [ME *argul, argoile* (c. AF *argoil*) < ?]

Ar·go·lis (är′gə lis), *n.* 1. an ancient district in SE Greece. 2. **Gulf of,** a gulf of the Aegean, in SE Greece. ab. 30 mi. long. —**Ar·gol·ic** (är gol′ik), **Ar·go·li·an** (är gō′lē ən), **Ar′go·lid,** *adj.*

ar·gon (är′gon), *n.* *Chem.* a colorless, odorless, chemically inactive, monatomic, gaseous element that, because of its inertness, is used for filling fluorescent and incandescent lamps and radio vacuum tubes. *Symbol:* A, Ar; *at. no.:* 18; *at. wt.:* 39.948. [< Gk, neut. of *argós* not working, idle, equiv. to *a-* A-[6] + (*é*)*rg*(*on*) work + *-os* adj. suffix]

Ar·go·naut (är′gə nôt′), *n.* 1. *Class. Myth.* a member of the band that sailed to Colchis with Jason in the ship Argo in search of the Golden Fleece. 2. (*sometimes l.c.*) one in search of something, esp. of something dangerous and rewarding; an adventurer. 3. a person who emigrated to California during the gold rush 1848–49. 4. (*l.c.*) See **paper nautilus.** [< L *Argonaut*(*a*) < Gk *Argonaút*(*ēs*) crewman of the ship ARGO; see NAUTICAL] —**Ar′go·nau′tic,** *adj.*

Ar′gonne For′est (är′gon; *Fr.* AR gôn′), a wooded region in NE France: battles, World War I, 1918; World War II, 1944. Also called **Argonne** (AR gôn′).

ar′gon potas′sium dat′ing. See **potassium argon dating.**

Ar·gos (är′gos, -gəs), *n.* an ancient city in SE Greece, on the Gulf of Argolis: a powerful rival of Sparta, Athens, and Corinth.

ar·go·sy (är′gə sē), *n., pl.* **-sies.** 1. a large merchant ship, esp. one with a rich cargo. 2. a fleet of such ships. 3. an opulent supply. [earlier *ragusy* < It *Ragusea* (ship) of *Ragusa*]

ar·got (är′gō, -gət), *n.* 1. an idiomatic vocabulary peculiar to a particular class or group of people, esp. that of an underworld group, as thieves, devised for private communication and identification: The Beggar's Opera *is rich in thieves' argot.* 2. the special vocabulary and idiom of a particular profession or social group: *sociologists' argot.* [< F < ?] —**ar·got·ic** (är got′ik), *adj.*

ar·gue (är′gyōō), *v.,* **-gued, -gu·ing.** —*v.i.* 1. to present reasons for or against a thing: *He argued for an allowance and received one.* 2. to contend in argument; dispute: *He argued with his parents about his allowance.* —*v.t.* 3. to state the reasons for or against: *The lawyers argued the case.* 4. to maintain in reasoning: *to argue that something must be so.* 5. to persuade, drive, etc., by reasoning: *to argue one out of a plan.* 6. to show; prove; imply; indicate: *His clothes argue poverty.* [ME < L *argue*(*re*) (to) make clear, prove, declare, accuse, etc.] —**ar′gu·a·ble,** *adj.* —**ar′gu·er,** *n.*

—**Syn.** 1. ARGUE, DEBATE, DISCUSS imply using reasons or proofs to support or refute an assertion, proposition, or principle. ARGUE implies reasoning or trying to understand; it does not necessarily imply opposition: *to argue with oneself.* To DISCUSS is to present varied opinions and views: *to discuss ways and means.* To DEBATE is to interchange formal (usually opposing) arguments, esp. on public questions: *to debate a proposed amendment.*

Ar·güe·das (äR gwe′thäs), *n.* **Al·ci·des** (äl sē′thes), 1879–1946, Bolivian author, sociologist, and statesman.

ar·gu·fy (är′gyə fī′), *v.t., v.i.,* **-fied, -fy·ing.** to argue or wrangle, esp. obstinately over something insignificant. [ARGUE + -FY] —**ar′gu·fi′er,** *n.*

ar·gu·ment (är′gyə mənt), *n.* 1. a discussion involving differing points of view; debate: *They were deeply involved in the argument.* 2. disagreement; verbal opposition; contention; altercation: *a violent argument.* 3. a process of reasoning; series of reasons: *I did not follow his argument.* 4. a statement or fact for or against a point: *This is a strong argument in favor of the theory.* 5. an address or composition intended to convince or persuade; persuasive discourse. 6. subject matter; theme: *The central argument of his paper was presented with clarity.* 7. an abstract or summary of the major points in a work of prose or poetry, or of sections of such a work. 8. *Math.* a. an independent variable of a function. b. Also called **amplitude.** the angle made by a given vector with the reference axis. c. the angle corresponding to a point representing a given complex number in polar coordinates. Cf. **principal argument.** 9. *Obs.* a. evidence or proof. b. a matter of contention. [ME < L *argūment*(*um*). See ARGUE, -MENT]

—**Syn.** 1. ARGUMENT, CONTROVERSY, DISPUTE imply the expression of opinions for and against some idea. An ARGUMENT usually arises from a disagreement between two persons, each of whom advances facts supporting his own point of view. A CONTROVERSY or a DISPUTE may involve two or more persons. A DISPUTE is an oral contention, usually brief, and often of a heated, angry, or undignified character: *a violent dispute over a purchase.* A CONTROVERSY is an oral or written expression of contrary opinions, and may be dignified and of some duration: *a political controversy.*

ar·gu·men·ta·tion (är′gyə men tā′shən), *n.* 1. the process of developing an argument; reasoning. 2. discussion; debate; disputation: *The lengthy argumentation tired many participants.* 3. a discussion dealing with a controversial point. 4. the setting forth of reasons together with the conclusion drawn from them. 5. the premises and conclusion so set forth. 6. argument (def. 5). [late ME < L *argūmentātiōn-* (s. of *argūmentātiō*). See ARGUMENT, -ATION] —**ar′gu·men·ta′tious,** *adj.*

ar·gu·men·ta·tive (är′gyə men′tə tiv), *adj.* 1. fond of or given to argument and dispute; disputatious; contentious: *The law students were an argumentative group.* 2. controversial. 3. *Law.* (of a pleading) containing conclusions in the statement of the facts. [ARGUMENT + -ATIVE] —**ar′gu·men′ta·tive·ly,** *adv.* —**ar′gu·men′ta·tive·ness,** *n.*

ar′gument from design′, *Philos.* See **teleological argument.**

ar′gument prin′ciple, *Math.* the theorem that the change in the argument of an analytic function of a complex variable along a closed curve is equal to 2π times the difference between the number of zeros and the number of poles of the function.

ar·gu·men·tum (äR′gōō men′tōōm; *Eng.* är′gyə men′təm), *n., pl.* **-ta** (-tä; *Eng.* -tə). *Latin.* argument.

argumen′tum ad ho′minem. See **ad hominem.**

argumen′tum ad rem′. See **ad rem.**

argumen′tum a fortio′ri, an argument based on the assumption that if something previously conceded is true, what is maintained at present is true for even stronger reasons.

Ar·gus (är′gəs), *n.* 1. *Class. Myth.* a giant with 100 eyes, set to guard the heifer Io: his eyes were transferred after his death to the peacock's tail. 2. a son of Phrixus and builder of the Argo. 3. any observant or vigilant person; a guardian. 4. (*l.c.*) Also, **ar′gus pheas′ant.** any of several brilliantly marked Malayan pheasants of the *Argusianus* or *Rheinardia* genera. 5. a boy's given name. [< L < Gk *Árgos,* deriv of *argós* bright, shining]

Ar·gus-eyed (är′gəs īd′), *adj.* keen-eyed; vigilant.

ar·gy-bar·gy (är′gē bär′gē; *Scot.* äR′gē bäR′gē), *n., pl.* **-gies,** *v.i.* **-gied, -gy·ing.** *Scot.* argle-bargle.

ar·gyle (är′gīl), *n.* (*sometimes cap*). a gravy vessel having a chamber for hot water between an inner and outer wall. [named after a Duke of *Argyle*]

Ar·gyle (är′gīl), (*sometimes l.c.*) *adj.* 1. (of knitted articles) having a diamond-shaped pattern in two or more colors. —*n.* 2. a diamond-shaped pattern of two or more colors, used in knitting socks, sweaters, etc. 3. a sock having this pattern. [var. of ARGYLL; so called because patterned after tartan of this clan]

Ar·gyll (är gīl′), *n.* a county in W Scotland. 57,839 (est. 1956); 3110 sq. mi. *Co. seat:* Inveraray. Also called **Ar·gyll·shire** (är gīl′shēr, -shər).

Ar·gy·ra (är′jər ə), *n.* *Class. Myth.* the nymph of the spring of Argyra, whose love for the handsome Selemnus waned when his youth faded.

ar·gyr·o·dite (är jēr′ə dīt′), *n.* a steel-gray mineral, Ag_8GeS_6, containing silver, germanium, and sulfur. [< Gk *argyrōd*(*es*) rich in silver (*árgyr*(*os*) silver + *-ōdes* -ODE[1]) + -ITE[1]]

Ar·gy·rol (är′jə rōl′, -rôl′, -rol′), *n.* *Pharm., Trademark.* See **mild silver protein.**

Ar·gy·ro·tox·us (är′gə rō tok′səs), *n.* *Class. Myth.* an epithet of Apollo, meaning "lord of the silver bow," referring to the bow and arrows made for him by Hephaestus.

Ar·hat (äR′hət), *n.* a Buddhist who has attained Nirvana. Cf. **Bodhisattva.** [< Skt: meriting respect, deriv. of *arhati* he merits] —**Ar′hat·ship′,** *n.*

År·hus (ôR′hōōs), *n.* a seaport in E Jutland, in Denmark. 177,234 (1960). Also, **Aarhus.**

a·rhyth·mi·a (ə riṯẖ′mē ə, ə riṯẖ′-), *n.* *Pathol.* arrhythmia. —**a·rhyth·mic** (ə riṯẖ′mik, ə riṯẖ′-), **a·rhyth′mi·cal,** *adj.* —**a·rhyth·mi·cal·ly,** *adv.*

a·ri·a (är′ē ə, âr′ē ə), *n.* 1. an air or melody. 2. an elaborate melody for a single voice, with accompaniment, in an opera, oratorio, etc. [< It; see AIR[1]]

A·ri·a (är′ē ə, ə rī′ə), *n.* *Class. Myth.* a nymph, the mother of Miletus, by Apollo.

-aria, a suffix occurring in scientific terms of Latin origin, esp. in names of biological genera and groups: *filaria.* [< L: neut. pl. of *-ārius* -ARY]

a·ri·a da ca·po (är′ē ə də kä′pō), *pl.* **arias da capo.** an operatic aria in three sections, with the first and third sections alike and the middle section contrasting. [< It: lit., air from the head, i.e. beginning]

Ar·i·ad·ae·us (ar′ē ad′ē əs), *n.* a crater in the first quadrant of the face of the moon: about 9 miles in diameter.

Ar·i·ad·ne (ar′ē ad′nē), *n.* 1. *Class. Myth.* a daughter of Minos and Pasiphaë who gave Theseus the thread by which he escaped from the labyrinth: deserted by Theseus on Naxos, she became the bride of Dionysus. 2. Also, **Ar·i·ad·na** (ar′ē ad′nə). a girl's given name.

A·ri·ad·ne auf Nax·os (*Ger.* ä Rē äd′nə ouf näk′sôs), an opera (1912) by Richard Strauss.

Ar·i·an (âr′ē ən, ar′-), *adj.* 1. of or pertaining to Arius or Arianism. —*n.* 2. an adherent of Arianism. [< LL *Ariān*(*us*) of, pertaining to ARIUS; see -AN]

Ar·i·an (âr′ē ən, ar′-), *adj., n.* Aryan.

-arian, 1. a combination of **-aria** and **-an,** used in the formation of adjectives from stems in **-aria:** *filarian.* 2. a combination of **-ary** and **-an,** used in the formation of personal nouns from stems in **-ary:** *librarian.* 3. a suffix, modeled on def. 2, used in the formation of personal nouns from stems other than **-ary:** *vegetarian.* 4. a formal element resulting from the combination of **-an** with stems in "-ari-": *riparian.* [< L *-āri*(*us*) -ARY + -AN]

Ar·i·ane (ar′ē an′; *Fr.* A RYAN′), *n.* a girl's given name, French form of **Ariadne.**

Ar·i·an·ism (âr′ē ə niz′əm, ar′-), *n.* *Theol.* the doctrine, taught by Arius, that Christ the Son was not consubstantial with God the Father. [ARIAN + -ISM] —**Ar′i·an·is′tic, Ar′i·an·is′ti·cal,** *adj.*

Ar·ian·rhod (äR yän′rôd), *n.* *Welsh Legend.* a beautiful goddess, the sister and mistress of Gwydion and the mother of Llew Llaw Gyffes, whom she cursed and forbade ever to have a name, weapons, or a wife.

A·ri·ca (ə rē′kə; *Sp.* ä Rē′kä), *n.* 1. a seaport in N Chile. 46,542 (1960). 2. See **Tacna-Arica.**

ar·id (ar′id), *adj.* 1. without moisture; extremely dry; parched: *arid land; an arid plain.* 2. barren from lack of moisture; unproductive: *arid farmland.* 3. unimaginative; unsuggestive; sterile; jejune: *an arid treatment of a topic.* 4. uninteresting; dull; lifeless: *an arid subject.* [< L *ārid*(*us*), equiv. to *ār*(*ēre*) (to) be dry + *-idus* -ID[4]] —**a·rid·i·ty** (ə rid′i tē), **ar′id·ness,** *n.* —**ar′id·ly,** *adv.*
—**Syn.** 1. See **dry.**

A·riege (A Ryezh′), *n.* a department in S France. 137,192 (1962); 1893 sq. mi. *Cap.:* Foix.

ar·i·el (âr′ē əl), *n.* an Arabian gazelle, *Gazella arabica.* Also, **ar′iel gazelle′.** [< Ar *aryal*]

Ar·i·el (âr′ē əl), *n.* 1. (in Shakespeare's *Tempest*) a spirit of the air who is required to use his magic to help Prospero. 2. *Astron.* one of the five satellites of Uranus. 3. Also, **Ar·i·elle** (ar′ē el′, âr′-). a girl's given name. 4. a boy's given name.

Ar·ies (âr′ēz, -ē ēz′), *n., gen.* **A·ri·e·tis** (ə rī′i tis). 1. *Astron.* the Ram, a zodiacal constellation between Pisces and Taurus. 2. *Astrol.* the first sign of the zodiac. See illus. under **zodiac.** [< L: ram]

ar·i·et·ta (ar′ē et′ə; *It.* ä′Rē et′tä), *n., pl.* **-et·tas, -et·te** (-et′ə; *It.* -et′te). *Music.* a short aria. Also, **ar·i·ette** (ar′ē et′). [< It, equiv. to *ari*(*a*) ARIA + *-etta* -ETTE]

a·right (ə rīt′), *adv.* rightly; correctly; properly: *I want to set things aright.* [ME; OE *ariht.* See A-[1], RIGHT]

a·ri·ki (ä rē′kē), *n., pl.* **-ki.** (in Polynesia) a chieftain or king. [Maori]

ar·il (ar′il), *n.* *Bot.* an accessory covering or appendage of certain seeds, esp. one arising from the placenta, funicle, or hilum. [short for *arillus* < NL, ML *arill*(*ī*) dried grapes] —**ar′il·loid′,** *adj.*

ar·il·late (ar′ə lāt′, -lit), *adj.* *Bot.* having an aril. [< NL *arill*(*us*) ARIL + -ATE[1]]

ar·il·lode (ar′ə lōd′), *n.* *Bot.* a false aril; an aril which originates from the micropyle instead of at or below the hilum, as in the nutmeg. [< NL *arill*(*us*) ARIL + -ODE[1]]

Ar·i·mas·pi·ans (ar′ə mas′pē ənz), *n.pl.* *Class. Myth.* a one-eyed people of Scythia.

Ar·i·ma·thae·a (ar′ə mə thē′ə), *n.* a town in ancient Palestine. Matt. 27:57. Also, **Ar′i·ma·the′a.** —**Ar′i·ma·thae′an, Ar′i·ma·the′an,** *adj.*

A·rim·i·num (ə rim′ə nəm), *n.* ancient name of **Rimini.**

A·ri·on (ə rī′ən), *n.* 1. fl. 7th century B.C., Greek poet: inventor of the dithyramb. 2. *Class. Myth.* a winged horse often believed to be the offspring of Poseidon and Demeter.

ar·i·ose (ar′ē ōs′, ar′ē ōs′), *adj.* characterized by melody; songlike. [Anglicized var. of ARIOSO]

a·rio·so (är′ē ō′sō, ar′-; *It.* ä Ryô′sô), *adj., adv., n., pl.* **-sos.** *Music.* —*adj., adv.* 1. in the manner of an air or melody. —*n.* 2. an arioso composition or section. [< It: lit., songlike. See ARIA, -OSE[1]]

A·ri·os·to (är′ē os′tō, -ō′stō, ar′-; *It.* ä′Rē ôs′tô), *n.* **Lu·do·vi·co** (lōō′dô vē′ko), 1474–1533, Italian poet; author of *Orlando Furioso.*

-arious, 1. a combination of **-aria** and **-ous,** used in the formation of adjectives from stems in **-aria:** *urticarious.* 2. a formal element resulting from the combination of **-ous** with stems in "-ari-": *precarious.*

Ar·i·o·vis·tus (ar′ē ō vis′təs), *n.* fl. c71–58 B.C., Germanic leader of the Suevi.

-aris, an element occurring in scientific terms in Latin: *polaris.* [< L *-āris;* see -AR[1]]

A·ris·be (ə ris′bē), *n.* *Class. Myth.* 1. the wife of Priam and then of Hyrtacus, to whom she was given by Priam. 2. the daughter of Teucer and the wife of Dardanus.

a·rise (ə rīz′), *v.i.,* **a·rose, a·ris·en** (ə riz′ən), **a·ris·ing.** 1. to come into being, action, or notice; originate; appear; spring up: *New problems arise daily.* 2. to result or proceed; spring or issue (sometimes fol. by *from*): *It is difficult to foresee the consequences that may arise from this action. After such destruction many problems in resettlement often arise.* 3. to move upward; mount; ascend. 4. to get up from sitting, lying, or kneeling; rise. [ME *arise*(*n*), OE *ārīsan,* equiv. to *ā-* up + *rīsan* to RISE]
—**Syn.** 1. emerge, spring, flow. 3. climb.

a·ris·ta (ə ris′tə), *n., pl.* **-tae** (-tē). 1. *Bot.* a bristlelike appendage of grain, etc.; an awn. 2. *Entomol.* a prominent bristle on the antenna of some dipterous insects. [< L: awn, beard or ear of grain]

A·ris·ta (ä Rēs′tä), *n.* **Ma·ri·a·no** (mä Ryä′nô), 1802–55, Mexican general: president of Mexico 1851–53.

Ar·is·tae·us (ar′i stē′əs), *n.* *Class. Myth.* a son of Apollo and Cyrene who was worshiped in various regions and colonies of Greece as the god of beekeeping, winemaking, and other forms of husbandry: responsible for the death of Eurydice.

ar·is·tarch (ar′i stärk′), *n.* *Rare.* a severe critic. [after ARISTARCHUS] —**Ar′i·star′chi·an,** *adj.*

Ar·is·tar·chus (ar′i stär′kəs), *n.* 1. **of Samos.** late 3rd century B.C., Greek astronomer. 2. an extremely bright crater in the second quadrant of the face of the moon: about 29 miles in diameter from crest to crest.

ar·is·tarch·y (ar′i stär′kē), *n.* rule by the best people in the country. [< LGk *aristarchía,* equiv. to *aristarch-* (*os*) best-ruling (*árist*(*os*) best + *árch*(*ein*) to rule + *-os* adj. suffix) + *-ia* -Y[3]]

a·ris·tate (ə ris′tāt), *adj.* 1. *Bot.* having aristae; awned. 2. *Zool.* tipped with a thin spine. [< LL *aristāt*(*us*) awned. See ARISTA, -ATE[1]]

Ar·is·ti·des (ar′i stī′dēz), *n.* ("*the Just*") 530?–468? B.C., Athenian statesman and general.

Ar·i·stil·lus (ar′i stil′əs), *n.* a crater in the first quadrant of the face of the moon: about 35 miles in diameter.

Ar·is·tip·pus (ar′i stip′əs), *n.* 435?–356? B.C., Greek philosopher: founder of the Cyrenaic school of philosophy.

aristo-, a learned borrowing from Greek meaning "best," occurring either in direct loans (*aristocratic*), or in the formation of compound words: *aristotype.* [< Gk, comb. form of *áristos*]

ar·is·toc·ra·cy (ar′i stok′rə sē), *n., pl.* **-cies.** 1. a class of persons holding exceptional rank and privileges, esp. the hereditary nobility. 2. a government or state ruled by an aristocracy, elite, or privileged upper class. 3. government by the best or most able men in the state. 4. a governing body composed of the best or most able men in the state. 5. any class or group considered to be superior. [< ML *aristocracia* (var. of *-tia*) < Gk *aristokratía* rule of the best. See ARISTO-, -CRACY]

a·ris·to·crat (ə ris′tə krat′, ar′i stə-), *n.* 1. a member of an aristocracy, esp. a nobleman. 2. a person who has the tastes, manners, etc., characteristic of members of an aristocracy. 3. an advocate of an aristocratic form of government. [back formation from ARISTOCRATIC, modeled on F *aristocrate*]
—**Syn.** 1. noble, peer, lord.

a·ris·to·crat·ic (ə ris′tə krat′ik, ar′i stə-), *adj.* 1. of or pertaining to government by an aristocracy. 2. belonging to or favoring the aristocracy. 3. characteristic of an aristocrat; having the manners, values, or qualities associated with the aristocracy: *aristocratic behavior; aristocratic bearing; aristocratic snobbishness.* Also, **a·ris′to·crat′i·cal.** [< Gk *aristokratik*(*ós*) pertaining to ARISTOCRACY; see -IC] —**a·ris′to·crat′i·cal·ly,** *adv.* —**a·ris′to·crat′i·cal·ness, a·ris′to·crat′ic·ness,** *n.*

a·ris·to·de·moc·ra·cy (ə ris′tō di mok′rə sē), *n., pl.* **-cies.** *Rare.* a form of government in which power is vested in the nobility and the common people. [ARISTO(CRACY) + DEMOCRACY]

A·ris·to·de·mus (ə ris′tə dē′məs), *n.* *Class. Myth.* one of the Heraclidae, a son of Aristomachus and father of Eurysthenes and Procles: he was killed by lightning just as he was preparing to invade Peloponnesus.

a·ris·to·lo·chi·a·ceous (ə ris′tᵊlō′kē ā′shəs), *adj.* belonging to the *Aristolochiaceae,* a family of plants including birthwort, Dutchman's-pipe, etc. [< NL *Aristolochi(a)* genus name (< Gk *aristolócheia* birthwort, lit., best child-birth, from the herb's supposed effects; see ARISTO-, LOCHIA) + -ACEOUS]

Ar·is·tom·a·chus (ar′i stom′ə kəs), *n.* *Class. Myth.* one of the Heraclidae, the father of Temenus, Cresphontes, and Aristodemus: he was killed while invading Peloponnesus.

Ar·is·toph·a·nes (ar′i stof′ə nēz′), *n.* 448?–385? B.C., Athenian poet and writer of comedy. —**A·ris·to·phan·ic** (ə ris′tə fan′ik), *adj.*

Ar·is·tot·e·les (ar′i stot′ᵊ lēz′), *n.* a walled plain in the first quadrant of the face of the moon: about 60 miles in diameter.

Ar·is·to·te·lian (ar′i stə tēl′yən, -tē′lē ən, ə ris′tə-) *adj.* **1.** of, pertaining to, based on, or derived from Aristotle or his theories. —*n.* **2.** a follower of Aristotle. [< L *Aristotelī(us)* < Gk *Aristotéleios* of ARISTOTLE + -AN]

Ar·is·to·te·lian·ism (ar′i stə tēl′yə niz′əm, -tē′lē ə-, ə ris′tə-), *n.* **1.** the philosophy of Aristotle. **2.** emphasis upon deduction and upon investigation of concrete and particular things and situations. [ARISTOTELIAN + -ISM]

Ar′istote′lian log′ic, 1. the logic of Aristotle, esp. in the modified form taught in the Middle Ages. **2.** traditional formal logic based on the categorial propositions of the forms: *all S is P; no S is P; some S is P; some S is not P.*

Ar·is·to·tle (ar′i stot′ᵊl), *n.* 384–322 B.C., Greek philosopher: pupil of Plato; tutor of Alexander the Great.

Ar′istotle Con′templating the Bust′ of Ho′mer, a painting (1653) by Rembrandt.

Ar′istotle's lan′tern, *Zool.* a complex arrangement of muscles and calcareous teeth and plates found in the mouths of most echinoids, functioning in mastication. [so called from a reference by *Aristotle* to a sea urchin resembling in shape certain lanterns]

a·ris·to·type (ə ris′tə tīp′), *n.* **1.** a process of photographic printing in which paper coated with silver chloride in gelatin is used. **2.** a print made by this process. [ARISTO- + -TYPE]

arith., 1. arithmetic. **2.** arithmetical.

ar·ith·man·cy (ar′ith man′sē), *n.* divination by the use of numbers, esp. by the number of letters in names. Also, **arithmomancy.** [< NL *arithmomantia* < Gk *arithmó(s)* number + *manteía* -MANCY]

a·rith·me·tic (*n.* ə rith′mə tik; *adj.* ar′ith met′ik), *n.* **1.** the method or process of computation with figures: the most elementary branch of mathematics. **2.** Also called **higher arithmetic, theoretical arithmetic.** the theory of numbers; the study of the divisibility of whole numbers, the remainders after division, etc. **3.** a book on this subject. —*adj.* **4.** Also, **ar·ith·met′i·cal.** of or pertaining to arithmetic. [< L *arithmētic(a),* neut. pl. of *arithmēticus* < Gk *arithmētikós* of numbers, equiv. to *arithmé(ein)* (to) reckon + *-tikos* -TIC; r. ME *arsmet(r)ike* < OF *arismetique* < LL *arismetica*] —**ar′ith·met′i·cal·ly,** *adv.*

a·rith·me·ti·cian (ə rith′mi tish′ən, ar′ith-), *n.* an expert in arithmetic. [ARITHMETIC + -IAN, modeled on MF *arithmeticien*]

ar′ithmet′ic mean′, *Math.* the mean obtained by adding several quantities together and dividing the sum by the number of quantities: the arithmetic mean of 1, 5, 2, 8 is 4.

arithmet′ic progres′sion, a sequence in which each term is obtained by the addition of a constant number to the preceding term, as 1, 4, 7, 10, 13, and 6, 1, -4, -9, -14. Also called **ar′ithmet′ic se′ries.**

a·rith·mo·man·cy (ə rith′mə man′sē, ar′ith-), *n.* arithmancy.

-arium, var. of **-orium:** *aquarium.*

A·ri·us (ə rī′əs, âr′ē-), *n.* died A.D. 336, Christian priest at Alexandria, founder of Arianism.

-arius, a suffix occurring in scientific words from Latin: *denarius.* [< L: -ARY]

a ri·ve·der·ci (ä′ rē veder′che), *Italian.* arrivederci.

Ariz., Arizona.

Ar·i·zo·na (ar′i zō′nə), *n.* a state in SW United States. 1,302,161 (1960); 113,909 sq. mi. *Cap.:* Phoenix. *Abbr.:* Ariz. —**Ar′i′zo′nan, Ar·i·zo·ni·an** (ar′i zō′nē ən), *adj., n.*

Ar′izo′na cy′press, an evergreen tree, *Cupressus arizonica,* of Arizona, having thick leaves and bluish-green cones, used as a windbreak.

Ar′izo′na ru′by. See **Cape ruby.**

Ar·jun (är′jən; *Skt.* ur′jōōn), *n.* a boy's given name.

Ar·ju·na (är′jə nə; *Skt.* ur′jōō nə), *n.* *Hinduism.* the chief hero of the *Bhagavad-Gita,* befriended by Krishna, who appears as his charioteer and advises him on duty and the immortality of the soul.

ark (ärk), *n.* **1.** *(sometimes cap.)* Also, **Noah's Ark.** the vessel built by Noah for safety during the Flood. Gen. 6–9. **2.** Also called **ark′ of the cov′enant.** a chest or box representing the Deity, carried by the Israelites in their wanderings in the desert after the Exodus: the most sacred object of the tabernacle and the temple in Jerusalem, where it was kept in the holy of holies. **3.** a refuge or place of security. **4.** *(cap.) Judaism.* See **Holy Ark. 5.** a flatboat formerly used on the Mississippi and its tributaries. **6.** *Naut.* See **life car. 7.** *Archaic.* a chest or box. [ME; OE *arc, earc* < L *arca* chest, coffer]

Ark., Arkansas.

Ar·ka·del·phia (är′kə del′fē ə), *n.* a town in central Arkansas. 8069 (1960).

Ar·kan·sas (är′kən sô′; *also for 2* ar kan′zəs), *n.* **1.** state in S central United States. 1,786,272 (1960); 53,103 sq. mi. *Cap.:* Little Rock. *Abbr.:* Ark. **2.** a river flowing E and SE from central Colorado into the Mississippi in SE Arkansas. 1450 mi. long. —**Ar·kan·san** (är kan′zən), **Ar·kan·si·an** (är kan′zē ən), *n., adj.*

Ar·khan·gelsk (äʀ-кнän′gelsk), *n.* Russian name of **Archangel.**

Ar·kie (är′kē), *n.* *Informal.* a migrant worker originally from Arkansas. [ARK(ANSAS) + -IE]

ar·kose (är′kōs), *n.* **1.** a granular sedimentary rock composed of clear quartz and feldspar or mica. **2.** any feldspathic or micaceous sandstone. [< F] —**ar·ko′sic,** *adj.*

ark′ shell′, any marine bivalve of the family *Arcidae,* esp. of the genus *Arca,* characterized by a heavy periostracum with a toothed hinge.

ark·wright (ärk′rīt′), *n.* a maker of arks or chests. [ARK + WRIGHT]

Ark·wright (ärk′rīt′), *n.* **Sir Richard,** 1732–92, English inventor of the spinning jenny.

ark′wright fur′niture, late medieval English furniture of simple construction.

Arl·berg (ärl′berкн′), *n.* **1.** a mountain pass in W Austria. 5946 ft. high. **2.** a tunnel beneath this pass.

Ar·leen (är lēn′), *n.* a girl's given name. Also, **Arlene, Arleyne, Arliene, Arline, Arlyne.**

Ar·len (är′lən), *n.* **1. Harold** *(Hymen Arluck),* born 1905, U.S. composer. **2. Michael** *(Dikran Kouyoumdjian),* 1895–1956, English novelist, born in Bulgaria. **3.** Also, **Arlyn, Ar′lin.** a boy's given name.

Ar·lene (är lēn′), *n.* a girl's given name. Also, **Arleen, Arleyne, Arliene, Arline, Arlyne.**

arles (ärlz), *n.pl.* *Scot. and North Eng.* money paid in advance or as a first installment to bind a commercial transaction, esp. money paid to a newly employed domestic servant as an advance against wages. [ME *erles* < OF *erres* (pl.) < L *arr(h)a(bo)* < Gk *arrabṓn* earnest-money]

Arles (ärlz; *Fr.* arl), *n.* a city in SE France, on the Rhone River: Roman ruins. 42,353 (1962).

Ar·ley (är′lē), *n.* a boy's given name. Also, **Harley.**

Ar·line (är lēn′), *n.* a girl's given name. Also, **Arleen, Arlene, Arleyne′, Ar·liene′, Arlyne.**

Ar·ling·ton (är′ling tən), *n.* **1.** a county in NE Virginia, opposite Washington, D.C.: national cemetery. 163,401 (1960). **2.** a city in E Massachusetts. 49,953 (1960). **3.** a city in N Texas. 44,775 (1960). **4.** a town in SE New York. 8317 (1960).

Ar′lington Heights′, a city in NE Illinois, near Chicago. 27,878 (1960).

Ar′lington Na′tional Cem′etery, a national cemetery located in Arlington, Virginia: site of the Tomb of the Unknown Soldier.

Ar·lis (är′lis), *n.* a boy's given name.

Ar·liss (är′lis), *n.* **George,** 1868–1946, English actor.

Ar·lyn (är′lin), *n.* a boy's given name. Also, **Arlen, Arlin.**

Ar·lyne (är lēn′), *n.* a girl's given name. Also, **Arleen, Arlene, Arleyne, Arliene, Arline.**

arm[1] (ärm), *n.* **1.** the upper limb of the human body, esp. from the shoulder to the wrist. **2.** *Anat.* the upper limb of man from the shoulder to the elbow. **3.** the forelimb of any vertebrate. **4.** some part of an organism like or likened to an arm. **5.** any armlike part or attachment, as of a lever on a machine: *the arm of a record player.* **6.** a covering for the arm, esp. a sleeve of a garment: *the arm of a coat.* **7.** an administrative or operational branch of an organization: *A special arm of the government is to investigate the matter* **8.** *Naut.* any of the curved or bent pieces of an anchor, terminating in the flukes. **9.** Also called **armrest.** a projecting support for the forearm at the side of a chair, sofa, etc. **10.** an inlet or cove: *an arm of the sea.* **11.** *Mil.* a combat branch of the military service, as the infantry, cavalry, field artillery, etc. **12.** power; might; strength; authority: *the long arm of the law.* **13.** *Typography.* either of the extensions to the right of the vertical line of a K or upward from the vertical stem of a Y. **14. arm in arm,** with arms intertwined: *They walked along arm in arm.* **15. at arm's length,** at a distance; not on familiar or friendly terms: *He's the kind of person you pity but want to keep at arm's length.* **16. in the arms of Morpheus,** asleep: *After a strenuous day, he was soon in the arms of Morpheus.* **17. with open arms,** cordially; with warm hospitality: *a country that receives immigrants with open arms.* [ME; OE *arm, earm;* c. Goth *arms,* G *Arm,* L *armus* shoulder, Gk *harmós* joint] —**arm′less,** *adj.* —**arm′like′,** *adj.*

arm[2] (ärm), *n.* **1.** Usually, **arms.** offensive or defensive implements for use in war; weapons. **2. arms,** *Heraldry.* the escutcheon, with its divisions, charges, and tinctures, and the other components forming an achievement which symbolizes and is reserved for a person, family, or corporate body; armorial bearings; coat of arms. **3. bear arms, a.** to carry weapons. **b.** to serve as a member of the military or of contending forces: *His religious convictions kept him from bearing arms, but he served as an ambulance driver with the Red Cross.* **4. take up arms,** to prepare for war; go to war: *to take up arms against the enemy.* **5. To arms!** Prepare to fight! **6. under arms,** ready for battle; trained and equipped: *The number of men under arms is no longer the decisive factor in warfare.* **7. up in arms,** ready to take action; excited; indignant: *There is no need to get up in arms over such a trifle.* —*v.i.* **8.** to enter into a state of hostility or of readiness for war. —*v.t.* **9.** to equip with weapons: *to arm the troops.* **10.** to activate (a fuze) so that it will explode the charge at the time desired. **11.** to cover protectively. **12.** to provide with whatever will add strength, force, or security; support; fortify: *He was armed with statistics and facts.* **13.** to equip or prepare for any specific purpose or effective use; furnish: *The office armed all salesmen with answers to the questions they might expect.* **14.** to prepare for action; make fit; ready. **15.** *Naut.* to fill (a sounding lead) with arming. [ME *arm(en)* < OF *arme(r)* < L *armāre* to arm, deriv. of *arma* (pl.) tools, weapons. See ARMS] —**arm′less,** *adj.*
—**Syn. 13.** ready, outfit. —**Ant. 10.** deactivate, disarm.

Arm., 1. Also, **Arm** Armenian. **2.** Armoric.

Ar.M., Master of Architecture. [< L *Architectūrae Magister*]

Ar·ma·da (är mä′də, -mā′-), *n.* **1.** Also called **Invincible Armada, Spanish Armada.** the fleet sent against England by Philip II of Spain in 1588. It was defeated by the English navy and later dispersed and wrecked by storms. **2.** *(l.c.)* any fleet of warships. **3.** *(l.c.)* a large group or force of vehicles, airplanes, etc.: *an armada of transport trucks.* [< Sp < L *armāta* armed forces, neut. pl. of *armātus* (ptp. of *armāre* to equip with arms). See ARM[2], -ATE[1]]

Arma′da chest′, an iron or iron-bound strongbox of the 17th or 18th century.

ar·ma·dil·lo (är′mə dil′ō), *n., pl.* **-los.** any of several burrowing, chiefly nocturnal, edentate mammals of the family *Dasypodidae,* ranging from the southern U.S. through South America, having strong claws and a jointed protective covering of bony plates: used in certain areas for food. [< Sp, equiv. to *armad(o)* armed (< L *armātus;* see ARM[2], -ATE[1]) + *-illo* < L *-illus* dim. suffix]

Nine-banded armadillo, *Dasypus novemcinctus* (8 in. high at shoulder; total length 2½ ft.; tail 1 ft.)

Ar·ma·ged·don (är′mə ged′ᵊn), *n.* **1.** the place where the final battle will be fought between the forces of good and evil (probably so called in reference to the battlefield of Megiddo. Rev. 16:16). **2.** the last and completely destructive battle: *The arms race can lead to Armageddon.* **3.** any great and crucial conflict.

Ar·magh (är mä′), *n.* a county in S Northern Ireland. 118,600 (est. 1963); 489 sq. mi. *Co. seat:* Armagh.

Ar·mag·nac (är′mən yak′; *Fr.* ar mä nyak′), *n.* a dry brandy distilled in the Gers department in SW France. [< F, after *Armagnac* the district]

ar·ma·ment (är′mə mənt), *n.* **1.** the weapons with which a military unit, esp. a combat airplane, armored vehicle, or warship, is equipped. **2.** a land, sea, or air force equipped for war. **3.** armor (def. 5). **4.** Usually, **armaments.** military strength collectively: *the armaments race; a country without armaments.* **5.** the process of equipping or arming for war. [< L *armāment(a)* fittings, equiv. to *armā(re)* (to) fit out (see ARM[2]) + *-menta* (pl.) -MENT]

Ar·mand (är′mənd; *Fr.* ar män′), *n.* a boy's given name, French form of **Herman.**

ar·mar·i·an (är mâr′ē ən), *n.* *Hist.* a monk in charge of the library and scriptorium in a monastery. [< ML *armāri(us),* equiv. to *armāri(a)* library, orig. neut. pl. < L *armāri(um)* (see ARMARIUM) + -AN]

ar·mar·i·um (är mâr′ē əm), *n., pl.* **-mar·i·a** (-mâr′ē ə). ambry (def. 3). [< L: cupboard, safe, equiv. to *arm(a)* weapons, tools + *-ārium* -ARIUM]

ar·ma·ry (är′mə rē), *n., pl.* **-ries.** *Obs.* ambry (def. 3).

ar·ma·ture (är′mə chər), *n.* **1.** armor. **2.** *Biol.* the protective covering of an animal or plant, or any part serving for defense or offense. **3.** *Elect.* **a.** the part of an electric machine which includes the main current-carrying winding and in which the electromotive force is induced. **b.** the pivoted part of an electric device, as a buzzer or relay, that is activated by a magnetic field. **c.** the iron or steel applied across the poles of a permanent magnet to close it, or across the poles of an electromagnet to transmit a mechanical force. See illus. under **electromagnet. 4.** *Sculpture.* a skeletal framework built as a support on which a clay, wax, or plaster figure is constructed. [< L *armātūr(a)* an outfit, armor, equiv. to *armāt(us)* equipped (see ARM[2], -ATE[1]) + *-ūra* -URE]

ar′mature reac′tion, *Elect.* a change in the magnetic field, often a variance in the flux density, of a dynamo, caused by the magnetic field induced by the current flowing through the armature.

Ar·ma·vir (är′mə vēr′; *Russ.* är mä vēʀ′), *n.* a city in the SW RSFSR, in Europe. 111,000 (1959).

arm·chair (ärm′châr′), *n.* **1.** a chair with sidepieces or arms to support a person's forearms or elbows. —*adj.* **2.** of, pertaining to, or describing one who theorizes without the benefit of practical experience: *an armchair strategist.* [ARM[1] + CHAIR]

armed (ärmd), *adj.* **1.** carrying or bearing arms; having weapons: *a heavily armed patrol; an armed convoy.* **2.** supported or maintained by arms: *armed peace.* **3.** involving the use of weapons: *armed conflict.* **4.** equipped or prepared for any specific purpose: *The students came armed with pencils and notebooks.* **5.** (esp. of an animal) covered protectively, as by a shell. **6.** fortified; made secure: *Armed by an inveterate optimism, he withstood despair.* **7.** (of an artillery shell, bomb, missile, etc.) having the fuze made operative. **8.** *Heraldry.* (of an animal or bird of prey) represented as having the parts used for fighting, as teeth, claws, beak, or talons, of a different tincture from that of the rest of the body: *a lion argent armed gules.* [ARM[2] + -ED[2]]

armed′ bull′head, pogge.

armed′ forc′es, military, naval, and air forces, esp. of a nation or of a number of nations. Also called **armed′ serv′ices.**

armed′ neutral′ity, military preparedness without commitment, esp. as the expressed policy of a neutral nation in wartime; readiness to counter with force an invasion of rights by any belligerent power.

Armen., Armenian.

Ar·me·ni·a (är mē′nē ə, -mēn′yə; *for 3 also Sp.* är me′nyä), *n.* **1.** an ancient country in W Asia: now divided between Armenia, Turkey, and Iran. **2.** Also called **Arme′nian Repub′lic.** a republic in Transcaucasia, S of Georgia and W of Azerbaijan. 3,031,000; ab. 11,500 sq. mi. *Cap.:* Yerevan. **3.** a city in W central Colombia. 135,615.

Ar·me·ni·an (är mē′nē ən, -mēn′yən), *adj.* **1.** of or pertaining to Armenia, its inhabitants, or their language. —*n.* **2.** a native of Armenia. **3.** the language of the Armenians, an Indo-European language written in a distinctive script derived from the Aramaic alphabet. *Abbr.:* Arm [ARMENI(A) + -AN]

Ar·me·noid (är mē′noid, är′mə noid′), *adj.* **1.** of, pertaining to, or constituting a Caucasoid racial type concentrated chiefly in the Middle East. —*n.* **2.** a person belonging to this type. [ARMEN(IA) + -OID]

Ar·men·tières (AR mäN tyeR′), *n.* a city in extreme N France: World War I battles 1914, 1918. 27,254 (1962).

arm·er (är′mər), *n. Obs.* armorer. [ARM[2] + -ER[1]]

armes par·lantes (ARM PAR läNt′), *Heraldry.* See **canting arms.** [< F: speaking arms]

ar·met (är′met), *n. Armor.* a completely enclosed helmet having a visor and hinged cheek pieces fastened under the chin. Cf. **close helmet.** [< MF, equiv. to *arme* ARM[2] + *-et* -ET]

arm·ful (ärm′fo͝ol′), *n., pl.* **-fuls.** the amount that can be held by the arm or both arms; a large quantity. [ARM[1] + -FUL]

arm·guard (ärm′gärd′), *n.* **1.** a band of leather or other material worn about the wrist or lower part of the arm for protection and support. **2.** *Archery.* bracer[2]. [ARM[1] + GUARD]

arm·hole (ärm′hōl′), *n.* an opening in a garment, for the arm. [ARM[1] + HOLE]

ar·mi·ger (är′mi jər), *n.* **1.** one entitled to armorial bearings. **2.** an armorbearer to a knight; a squire. [< ML: squire, L: armorbearer (n.), armorbearing (adj.), equiv. to *armi-* (comb. form of *arma* arms) + *-ger* bearing, deriv. of *gerere* to carry, wear] —**ar·mig·er·al** (är mij′ər əl), *adj.*

ar·mig·er·ous (är mij′ər əs), *adj.* entitled to use a coat of arms; gentle. [ARMIGER + -OUS]

Ar·mil (är′mil), *n.* a girl's given name.

Ar·mil·da (är mil′də), *n.* a girl's given name, form of Armil. Also, **Armilla.**

ar·mill (är′mil), *n.* a garment resembling a stole, worn by a British king at his coronation. Also, **ar′mil, armilla.** [ME *armille* < MF < L *armilla.* See ARMILLARY]

ar·mil·la (är mil′ə), *n., pl.* **-mil·lae** (-mil′ē, -mil′ī), **-mil·las.** armill.

Ar·mil·la (är mil′ə), *n.* a girl's given name, form of Armil. Also, **Armilda.**

ar·mil·lar·y (är′mə ler′ē, är mil′ə rē), *adj.* consisting of hoops or rings. [< L *armill(a)* bracelet, hoop (*arm(us)* shoulder + *-illa* dim. suffix) + -ARY]

ar′millary sphere′, *Astron.* an ancient instrument consisting of an arrangement of rings, all of which are circles of the same sphere, used to show the relative positions of the celestial equator, ecliptic, and other circles on the celestial sphere.

Ar·min (är′min), *n.* a boy's given name, form of **Herman.**

Ar·mi·na (är mē′nə, -mī′nə), *n.* a girl's given name.

arm·ing (är′ming), *n. Naut.* tallow or a similar soft substance placed in a recess of the bottom of a sounding lead to pick up samples of the sand, mud, etc., from the ground under the water in order to show the nature of the bottom. [ARM[2] + -ING[1]]

arm′ing cap′, *Armor.* a padded skullcap worn under a helmet or coif.

arm′ing chest′, a chest for holding armor and weapons.

arm′ing dou′blet, a padded garment worn as a doublet under plate armor.

Ar·min·i·an·ism (är min′ē ə niz′əm), *n. Theol.* the doctrinal teachings of Jacobus Arminius or his followers, esp. the doctrine that Christ died for all men and not only for the elect. Cf. **Calvinism** (def. 1). [J. ARMINI(US) + -AN + -ISM] —**Ar·min′i·an,** *adj., n.*

Ar·min·i·us (är min′ē əs), *n.* **1.** (*Hermann*) 17?B.C.–A.D.21, Germanic hero who defeated Roman army A.D. 9. **2. Ja·co·bus** (jə kō′bəs), (*Jacob Harmensen*), 1560–1609, Dutch Protestant theologian.

ar·mip·o·tent (är mip′ə tənt), *adj.* strong in battle or possessing powerful weapons. [< L *armipotent-* (s. of *armipotēns* potent in arms). See ARM[2], -I-, POTENT] —**ar·mip′o·tence,** *n.*

ar·mi·stice (är′mi stis), *n.* a temporary suspension of hostilities by agreement of the warring parties; a truce: *The armistice ended World War I.* [< NL *armistitium,* equiv. to L *armi-* (comb. form of *arma* ARMS) + *-stitium* a stopping (*stit-* (var. s. of *sistere* to stop; see STAND) + *-ium* n. suffix)]

Ar′mistice Day′, former name of **Veterans Day.**

Ar·mi·tage (är′mi tij), *n.* **Kenneth,** born 1916, English sculptor.

arm·let (ärm′lit), *n.* **1.** *Chiefly Brit.* an ornamental band worn on the arm; a bracelet worn high on the arm, rather than on the wrist. **2.** a little arm: *an armlet of the sea.* [ARM[1] + -LET]

arm·load (ärm′lōd′), *n.* the quantity a person can hold or carry in an arm or both arms: *They emptied the closet by carrying out several armloads of old clothes.* [ARM[1] + LOAD]

ar·moire (ärm wär′), *n.* a large wardrobe or movable cupboard, with doors and shelves. [< MF; OF *ar(maire)* + *(au)moire* AMBRY]

ar·mo·man·cy (är′mə man′sē), *n.* divination by the shoulders of animals. [< ML *armomantia,* equiv. to *armo-* comb. form of *armus* shoulder; see -MANCY]

ar·mor (är′mər), *n.* **1.** any covering worn as a defense against weapons. **2.** a suit of armor. **3.** a metallic sheathing or protective covering, esp. metal plates, used on warships, armored vehicles, airplanes, and fortifications. **4.** mechanized units of military forces, as armored divisions. **5.** Also called **armament.** any protective covering, as on certain animals, insects, or plants. **6.** any quality, characteristic, situation, or thing that serves as protection: *A chilling courtesy was his only armor.* **7.** the outer wrapping of metal, usually fine, braided steel wires, on a cable, primarily for the purpose of mechanical protection. —*v.t.* **8.** to cover with armor or armor plate. Also, *esp. Brit.,* **armour.** [ME *armo(u)r,* var. of *armure* < OF *arm(e)ure* < L *armātūr(a)* ARMATURE]

armor., arms and armor.

ar·mor·bear·er (är′mər bâr′ər), *n.* a retainer bearing the armor or arms of a warrior. Also, *esp. Brit.,* **armourbearer.** [ARMOR + BEARER]

ar·mor-clad (är′mər klad′), *adj.* covered with armor. Also, *esp. Brit.,* **armour-clad** [ARMOR + CLAD]

ar·mored (är′mərd), *adj.* **1.** protected by armor or armor plate. **2.** provided with or using armored equipment, as tanks, armored cars, etc.: *an armored unit; an armored patrol.* Also, *esp., Brit.,* **armoured.** [ARMOR + -ED[3]]

ar′mored ca′ble, *Elect.* a cable covered with a metal wrapping for protection.

ar′mored car′, **1.** a military combat vehicle with wheels, light armor, and usually, machine guns. **2.** an armorplated truck with strong locks and doors, and usually portholes for guards to shoot through, for transporting money and valuables.

ar′mored di′nosaur, ankylosaur.

ar′mored forc′es, military forces composed of tank units and armored infantry, artillery, and other supporting troops. Also called, *esp. Brit.,* **armoured troops.**

Armor (Full plate, 16th century)
A, Helmet; B, Visor; C, Ventail; D, Beaver; E, Gorget; F, Pauldron; G, Rerebrace; H, Couter; I, Vambrace; J, Gauntlet; K, Breastplate; L, Lance rest; M, Fauld; N, Cuisse; O, Poleyn; P, Greave; Q, Sabaton

ar·mor·er (är′mər ər), *n.* **1.** a maker or repairer of arms or armor. **2.** a manufacturer of firearms. **3.** an enlisted man in charge of the upkeep of small arms, machine guns, bicycles, etc. Also, *esp. Brit.,* **armourer.** [late ME; r. ME *armurer* < AF, MF, OF, *armurier.* See ARMOR, -ER[2]]

ar·mo·ri·al (är mōr′ē əl, -môr′-), *adj.* **1.** of or pertaining to heraldry or heraldic bearings. **2.** bearing a coat or coats of arms: *a set of armorial china.* —*n.* **3.** a book containing heraldic bearings and devices. [ARMORY + -AL[1]]

armo′rial bear′ings, a coat, or coats, of arms.

Ar·mor·i·can (är môr′i kən, -mor′-), *adj.* **1.** of or pertaining to Armorica. —*n.* **2.** a native of Armorica. **3.** Breton (def. 2). Also **Ar·mor′ic.** [ARMORIC(A) + -AN]

ar·mor·ist (är′mər ist), *n.* one who is an expert at heraldry. [ARMOR + -IST]

ar·mor-pierc·ing (är′mər pēr′sing), *adj. Mil.* (of bullets, artillery shells, etc.) designed especially for piercing armor. Also, *esp. Brit.,* **armour-piercing.**

ar′mor plate′, a plate or plating of specially hardened steel used to cover warships, tanks, aircraft, fortifications, etc., to protect them from enemy fire. Also, **ar′mor plat′ing.** —**ar′mor-plat′ed,** *adj.*

ar·mor·y (är′mə rē), *n., pl.* **-mor·ies.** **1.** a storage place for weapons and other war equipment. **2.** *U.S. Army.* a building that is the headquarters and drill center of a National Guard unit or of any Army Reserve unit. **3.** *U.S.* a place where arms and armor are made; an armorer's shop; arsenal. **4.** *Heraldry.* the art of blazoning arms. **5.** heraldry. **6.** *Archaic.* heraldic bearings or arms. **7.** *Archaic.* arms or armor collectively. Also, *esp. Brit.,* **armoury** (for defs. 1–4). [ME *armurie,* equiv. to *armure* ARMOR + *-ie* -Y[3]]

ar·mour (är′mər), *n. Chiefly Brit.* armor.

ar·mour·bear·er (är′mər bâr′ər), *n. Chiefly Brit.* armorbearer.

ar·mour-clad (är′mər klad′), *adj. Chiefly Brit.* armor-clad.

ar·moured (är′mərd), *adj. Chiefly Brit.* armored.

ar·moured troops′, *Brit.* See **armored forces.**

ar·mour·er (är′mər ər), *n. Chiefly Brit.* armorer.

ar·mour-pierc·ing (är′mər pēr′sing), *adj. Chiefly Brit.* armor-piercing.

ar·mour·y (är′mə rē), *n., pl.* **-mour·ies.** *Chiefly Brit.* armory (defs. 1, 7).

arm·pad (ärm′pad′), *n.* a small cushion forming part of the arm of a chair or the like. Also called **manchette.**

arm·pit (ärm′pit′), *n. Anat.* the hollow under the arm at the shoulder; axilla. [ARM[1] + PIT[1]]

arm·rest (ärm′rest′), *n.* arm[1] (def. 9). [ARM[1] + REST[1]]

Arms′ and the Man′, a comedy (1898) by G. B. Shaw.

Arm·strong (ärm′strông′), *n.* **1.** (**Daniel**) **Louis** ("*Satchmo*"), born 1900, U.S. jazz trumpeter and band leader. **2. Edwin Howard,** 1890–1954, U.S. electrical engineer and inventor: developed frequency modulation. **3. Neil A.,** born 1930, U.S. astronaut: first man to walk on the moon, July 20, 1969.

Arm·strong-Jones (ärm′strông jōnz′, -strong′-), *n.* **Antony Charles Robert, Earl of Snow·don** (snōd′ən), born 1930, husband of Princess Margaret Rose of England; photographer.

Arm′strong's Pat′ent, *Brit. Naut. Slang.* any piece of machinery, as a windlass, requiring hard physical labor to work.

ar·mure (är′myər), *n.* a woolen or silk fabric woven with a small, raised pattern. [< F. See ARMOR]

ar·my (är′mē), *n., pl.* **-mies.** **1.** the military forces of a nation, exclusive of the navy and in some countries the air force. **2.** (in large military land forces) the second largest unit, consisting of two or more corps. **3.** a large body of men trained and armed for war. **4.** any body of persons organized for any purpose. **5.** a very large number or group of something; a great multitude; a host: *the army of the unemployed.* [ME *armee* < MF < L *armāta.* See ARMADA]

Ar′my Air′ Forc′es, *U.S. Army.* a unit comprising almost all aviation, with its personnel, equipment, etc.: it became part of the Air Force on July 26, 1947.

ar′my ant′, any of the chiefly tropical ants of the suborder *Dorylinae* that travel in vast swarms, preying mainly on arthropods. Also called **driver ant, legionary ant.**

ar′my brat′, *Slang.* the child of an army officer or enlisted man, esp. one who has grown up on an army base or in a military community.

ar′my corps′, corps (def. 1b).

ar′my group′, a military organization for tactical purposes, made up of two or more armies.

ar′my of occupa′tion, an army established in conquered territory to maintain order and to ensure the carrying out of peace or armistice terms.

Ar′my of the Unit′ed States′, the army or armies referred to in the U.S. Constitution, esp. consisting of the Regular Army, National Guard, and Army Reserve. Cf. **United States Army.**

ar·my·worm (är′mē wûrm′), *n.* **1.** the caterpillar of a noctuid moth, *Pseudaletia unipuncta,* that often travels in large numbers over a region, destroying crops of wheat, corn, etc. **2.** any of the larvae of several related moths having similar habits. [ARMY + WORM]

Ar·nae·us (är′nē əs), *n.* (in the *Odyssey*) a beggar who ran errands for the suitors of Penelope. Also called **Irus.**

ar·nat·to (är nat′ō, -nä′tō), *n., pl.* **-tos.** annatto (def. 2).

Arndt (ärnt), *n.* **Ernst Mo·ritz** (eRnst mō′Rits), 1769–1860, German poet and historian.

Arne (ärn *for 1;* är′nē *for 2*), *n.* **1. Thomas Augustine,** 1710–78, English composer of operas and songs. **2.** *Class. Myth.* **a.** the mother of Aeolus and Boeotus. **b.** a princess who was changed into a magpie as a punishment for accepting a bribe.

Ar·nel (är nel′), *n. Trademark.* a man-made fiber of cellulose triacetate.

Arn·hem (ärn′hem), *n.* a city in the central Netherlands, on the Rhine River: World War II battle 1944. 127,955 (1962).

ar·ni·ca (är′nə kə), *n.* **1.** any asteraceous plant of the genus *Arnica,* esp. *A. montana* of Europe. **2.** a tincture of the flowers of *A. montana* and other species of *Arnica,* used as an external application in sprains and bruises. [< NL < ?]

Ar·no (är′nō; *for 2 also It.* äR′nô), *n.* **1. Peter** (*Curtis Arnoux Peters*), 1904–1968, U.S. cartoonist and author. **2.** a river flowing W from central Italy to the Ligurian Sea. 140 mi. long. **3.** a boy's given name.

Ar·nold (är′nəld), *n.* **1. Benedict,** 1741–1801, American general in the Revolutionary War who became a traitor. **2. Sir Edwin,** 1832–1904, English poet and journalist. **3. Henry H.** ("*Hap*"), 1886–1950, U.S. general. **4. Matthew,** 1822–88, English essayist, poet, and literary critic. **5.** his father, **Thomas,** 1795–1842, English clergyman, educator, historian, and writer. **6. Thur·man Wesley** (thûr′mən), born 1891, U.S. lawyer and writer. **7.** a town in central Pennsylvania. 9437 (1960). **8.** a walled plain in the first quadrant of the face of the moon: about 50 miles in diameter. **9.** a boy's given name.

Ar·nold·son (är′nəld sən; *Sw.* äR′no͝old sôn′), *n.* **Klas Pon·tus** (kläs pôn′təs), 1844–1916, Swedish author and politician: Nobel peace prize 1908.

Ar·nol·fi′ni and His Bride′ (är′nôl fē′nē). See **Giovanni Arnolfini and His Bride.**

Ar·nulf (är′no͝olf), *n.* A.D. 850?–899, emperor of the Holy Roman Empire 887–899; crowned 896.

ar·oid (ar′oid, âr′-), *Bot.* —*adj.* **1.** araceous. —*n.* **2.** any araceous plant. [AR(UM) + -OID]

a·roi·de·ous (ə roi′dē əs), *adj.* araceous. [AROID + -EOUS]

a·ro·ma (ə rō′mə), *n.* **1.** an odor arising from spices, plants, etc., esp. an agreeable odor; fragrance. **2.** (of wines and spirits) the odor or bouquet. **3.** a pervasive characteristic or quality. [< L < Gk: spice; r. ME *aromat* < OF < L *arōmat-* (s. of *arōma*)]
—**Syn. 1.** See **perfume.**

ar·o·mat·ic (ar′ə mat′ik), *adj.* **1.** having an aroma; fragrant; sweet-scented; odoriferous. **2.** *Chem.* of or pertaining to an aromatic compound or compounds. —*n.* **3.** a plant, drug, or medicine which yields a fragrant smell, as sage, certain spices and oils, etc. **4.** See **aromatic compound.** [ME *aromatyk* < LL *arōmatic(us)* < Gk *arōmatikós.* See AROMA, -IC] —**ar′o·mat′i·cal·ly,** *adv.* —**ar′o·mat′ic·ness,** *n.*

ar′omat′ic com′pound, *Chem.* any of a class of organic compounds containing an unsaturated ring of carbon atoms, as benzene, naphthalene, anthracene, and their derivatives, and usually having an agreeable odor.

ar·o·ma·tic·i·ty (ar′ə mə tis′i tē, ə rō′mə-), *n.* **1.** quality or state of being aromatic. **2.** *Chem.* the property of being or resembling any of the aromatic compounds. [AROMATIC + -ITY]

ar′omat′ic spir′its of ammo′nia, *Pharm.* a nearly colorless liquid, which yellows on standing, containing ammonia, ammonium carbonate, alcohol, and aromatic oils: used orally as an antacid and carminative and, by inhalation, as a stimulant in the treatment of faintness. Also, **ar′omat′ic spir′it of ammo′nia.**

a·ro·ma·tise (ə rō′mə tīz′), *v.t.,* **-tised, -tis·ing.** *Chiefly Brit.* aromatize. —**a·ro′ma·tis′er,** *n.*

a·ro·ma·ti·za·tion (ə rō′mə ti zā′shən), *n. Chem.* the conversion of aliphatic or alicyclic compounds to aromatic hydrocarbons. Also, *esp. Brit.,* **a·ro′ma·ti·sa′tion.** [< ML *arōmatizātiōn-* (s. of *arōmatizātiō*)]

a·ro·ma·tize (ə rō′mə tīz′), *v.t.,* **-tized, -tiz·ing.** to make aromatic or fragrant. Also, *esp. Brit.,* **aromatise.** [late ME < LL *arōmatizāre* < Gk *arōmatízein* to spice. See AROMA, -IZE] —**a·ro′ma·tiz′er,** *n.*

aro′matized wine′, a wine in which the natural flavor has been altered by the addition of herbs, roots, flowers, and other flavorings.

Ar·on (âr′ən), *n.* a boy's given name. Also, **Aaron.**

A·ron Ko·desh (ä Rôn′ kō′desh), *Hebrew.* See **Holy Ark.**

A·roos·took (ə ro͞os′to͝ok, -tik), *n.* a river flowing NE from N Maine to the St. John River. 140 mi. long.

a·rose (ə rōz′), *v.* pt. of **arise.**

CONCISE ETYMOLOGY KEY: <, descended or derived from; >, whence; b., blend of, blended; c. cognate with; deriv., derivative; equiv., equivalent; imit., imitative; m., modification of; obl., oblique; r., replacing; s., stem; sp., spelling; trans., translation; ?, origin unknown, perhaps; *, hypothetical. See the full key inside the front cover.

a·round (ə round′), *adv.* **1.** in a circle, ring, or the like; so as to surround: *The crowd gathered around.* **2.** on all sides; about: *His land is fenced all around.* **3.** in all directions from a center or point of reference: *He owns the land for miles around.* **4.** in a region about a place: *all the country around.* **5.** in circumference: *The tree was 40 inches around.* **6.** in a circular or rounded course: *to fly around and around.* **7.** through a sequence or series, as of places or persons: *to show someone around.* **8.** through a recurring period, as of time, esp. to the present or a particular time: *when spring rolls around again.* **9.** by a circuitous or roundabout course: *The driveway to the house goes around by the stables.* **10.** to a place or point, as by a circuit or circuitous course: *to get around into the navigable channel.* **11.** with a rotating course or movement: *The wheels turned around.* **12.** in or to another or opposite direction, course, opinion, etc.: *Sit still and don't look around. After our arguments, she finally came around.* **13.** back into consciousness: *The smelling salts brought her around.* **14.** *Chiefly U.S.* in circulation, action, etc.; about: *He hasn't been around lately. She's been around for years. When will she be up and around?* **15.** *U.S. Informal.* somewhere about or near: *to wait around for a person.* **16.** to a specific place: *He came around to see me.* **17. have been around,** *Informal.* to have had much worldly experience; be sophisticated or experienced: *She had been around and had become very bored with life.* —*prep.* **18.** about; on all sides; encircling; encompassing: *a halo around his head.* **19.** so as to encircle, surround, or envelop: *to tie paper around a package.* **20.** on the edge, border, or outer part of: *a skirt with braid around the bottom.* **21.** from place to place in; about: *to get around town.* **22.** in all or various directions from: *to look around one.* **23.** in the vicinity of: *the country around Boston.* **24.** approximately; about: *around five o'clock.* **25.** here and there in: *There are mailboxes all around the city.* **26.** somewhere in or near: *to stay around the house.* **27.** to all or various parts of: *to wander around the country.* **28.** so as to make a circuit about or partial circuit to the other side of: *to go around the lake; to sail around a cape.* **29.** reached by making a turn or partial circuit about: *the church around the corner.* **30.** so as to revolve or rotate about a center or axis: *the earth's motion around its axis.* **31.** personally close to: *Only the few men around the dictator understood his motives.* **32.** so as to get by a difficulty: *They got around the lack of chairs by sitting on the floor.* **33.** so as to have a foundation in: *The novel is built around a strong idea.* [A-¹ + ROUND]

a·round-the-clock (ə round′thə klok′), *adj.* continuing without pause or interruption: *an around-the-clock guard on the prisoner.* Also, **round-the-clock.**

Around′ the World′ in Eight′y Days′, a novel (1873) by Jules Verne.

a·rouse (ə rouz′), *v.*, **a·roused, a·rous·ing.** —*v.t.* **1.** to put in motion; stir to action; awaken: *to arouse one from sleep.* **2.** to provoke; excite: *to arouse a response; to arouse anger.* —*v.i.* **3.** to awake or become aroused. [A-³ + ROUSE¹, modeled on ARISE] —**a·rous′a·ble,** *adj.* —**a·rous·al** (ə rou′zəl), *n.* —**a·rous′er,** *n.*
—**Syn. 1.** animate; inspirit, inspire; incite, excite, provoke, instigate; stimulate, kindle, fire. —**Ant. 1.** calm.

Arp (ärp), *n.* **1. Bill,** pen name of Charles Henry Smith. **2. Hans** (häns) or **Jean** (zhäN), 1888?–1966, French painter and sculptor.

ARP, *British.* Air Raid Precautions.

Ár·pád (är′päd), *n.* died A.D. 907, Hungarian national hero.

ar·peg·gi·a·tion (är pej′ē ā′shən), *n.* the writing or playing of arpeggios: *a page filled with arpeggiation; learning the best fingering for arpeggiation.* [< It *arpeggiat(o),* ptp. of *arpeggiare* (see ARPEGGIO) + -ION]

ar·peg·gi·o (är pej′ē ō′, -pej′ō), *n., pl.* **-gi·os.** *Music.* **1.** the sounding of the notes of a chord in rapid succession instead of simultaneously. **2.** a chord thus sounded. [< It: lit., a harping, equiv. to *arpeggi(are)* (to) play on the harp (< Gmc; cf. OE *hearpi(g)an* to harp) + *-o* n. suffix] —**ar·peg′gi·at′ed,** **ar·peg′gi·oed′,** *adj.*

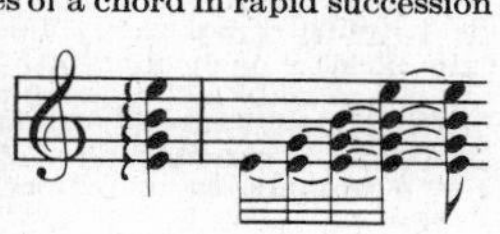

Arpeggio

ar·pent (är′pənt; *Fr.* AR-päN′), *n., pl.* **-pents** (-pənts; *Fr.* -päN′). an old French unit of area equal to about one acre. It is still used in the province of Quebec and in parts of Louisiana. [< MF < LL *arepennis* half-acre < Gaulish; akin to MIr *airchenn* unit of area]

ar·que·bus (är′kwə bəs), *n., pl.* **-bus·es.** harquebus.

ar·que·bus·ier (är′kwə bə sēr′, -kə-), *n.* harquebusier.

arr., 1. arranged. **2.** arrangement. **3.** arrival. **4.** arrive; arrived.

ar·rack (ar′ək), *n.* any of various spirituous liquors distilled in the East Indies and other parts of the East and Middle East from the fermented sap of toddy palms, or from fermented molasses, rice, or other materials. Also, **arak.** [< Ar *'araq* sweat, juice, liquor]

ar·raign (ə rān′), *v.t.* **1.** *Law.* to call or bring before a court to answer to an indictment. **2.** to accuse or charge in general; criticize adversely; censure. —*n.* **3.** arraignment. [ME *araine(n)* < AF *araine(r),* OF *araisnier,* equiv. to *a-* A-⁵ + *raisnier* < VL **ratiōnāre* to talk, reason; see RATIO] —**ar·raign′er,** *n.*

ar·raign·ment (ə rān′mənt), *n.* **1.** *Law.* act of arraigning. **2.** state of being arraigned. **3.** accusation; adverse criticism; a calling into question or a finding fault, esp. with respect to the value or virtue of something; critical examination: *The periodic arraignment of military ethics is generally accompanied by great public interest.* [late ME *arainement* < MF *araisnement.* See ARRAIGN, -MENT]

Ar·ran (ar′ən, ar′ən), *n.* an island in SW Scotland, in the Firth of Clyde. 4300 (est. 1956); 166 sq. mi.

ar·range (ə rānj′), *v.*, **-ranged, -rang·ing.** —*v.t.* **1.** to place in proper, desired, or convenient order; adjust properly: *to arrange books on a shelf.* **2.** to come to an agreement or understanding regarding: *to arrange a divorce.* **3.** to prepare or plan: *to arrange the details of a meeting.* **4.** *Music.* to adapt (a composition) for a particular style of performance by voices or instruments. —*v.i.* **5.** to make preparations: *They arranged for a concert on Wednesday.* **6.** to make a settlement; come to an agreement: *to arrange with the grocer for regular deliveries.* [ME *arraynge(n)* < MF *arangie(r),* equiv. to *a-* A-⁵ + *rangier* to RANGE] —**ar·range′a·ble,** *adj.* —**ar·rang′er,** *n.*
—**Syn. 1.** array; group, sort, dispose; classify; distribute.

ar·range·ment (ə rānj′mənt), *n.* **1.** act of arranging; state of being arranged. **2.** the manner in which things are arranged. **3.** a final settlement; adjustment by agreement. **4.** Usually, **arrangements.** preparatory measures; plans; preparations: *They made arrangements for an early departure.* **5.** something arranged in a particular way: *a floral arrangement.* **6.** *Music.* **a.** the adaptation of a composition to voices or instruments, or to a new purpose. **b.** a piece so adapted. [< F; see ARRANGE, -MENT]

Arrange′ment in Black′ and Gray′. See **Whistler's Mother.**

ar·rant (ar′ənt), *adj.* **1.** downright; thorough; unmitigated; notorious: *an arrant fool.* **2.** *Obs.* wandering; errant. [var. of ERRANT] —**ar′rant·ly,** *adv.*

ar·ras¹ (ar′əs), *n.* **1.** a rich tapestry. **2.** a tapestry weave. **3.** a wall hanging, as a tapestry or similar object. **4.** *Theat.* **a.** a curtain suspended loosely across the stage and used as a backdrop or part of the stage setting. **b.** (in Elizabethan theater) a tapestry curtain, used esp. for concealing the recessed inner stage. [named after ARRAS] —**ar′rased,** *adj.*

ar·ras² (är′äs; *Sp.* är′räs), *n.* (*construed as sing.*) *Law.* a gift presented at marriage by a husband to his wife in consideration of her dowry. [< Sp: lit., earnest money. See ARLES]

Ar·ras (ar′əs; *Fr.* A räs′), *n.* a city in and capital of Pas-de-Calais, in N France: battles in World War I. 45,643 (1962).

Ar·ra·u (är rä′o͞o), *n.* **Clau·dio** (klou′dyô), born 1903, Chilean pianist.

ar·ray (ə rā′), *v.t.* **1.** to place in proper or desired order, as troops for battle; marshal. **2.** to clothe with garments, esp. of an ornamental kind; dress up; deck out. —*n.* **3.** order, as of troops drawn up for battle. **4.** military force, esp. a body of troops. **5.** a large and impressive grouping or organization of things: *He was unable to escape the array of facts.* **6.** regular order or arrangement; series: *an array of figures.* **7.** a large group, number, or quantity of people or things: *an impressive array of scholars; an imposing array of books.* **8.** attire; dress: *in fine array.* **9.** *Math., Statistics.* **a.** an arrangement of a series of terms according to value, as from largest to smallest. **b.** an arrangement of a series of terms in some geometric pattern, as in a matrix. [ME *arraye(n)* < AF *araye(r),* OF *are(y)er* < Gmc; cf. OE *ārǣdan* to prepare, equiv. to *ā-* A-³ + *rǣde* ready]
—**Syn. 1.** arrange, range, place, dispose. **2.** apparel, dress, attire; ornament, adorn, decorate. **3.** disposition, arrangement. **5.** show, exhibit, exhibition. **8.** raiment.

ar·ray·al (ə rā′əl), *n.* **1.** act of arraying; muster; array. **2.** whatever is arrayed. [ARRAY + -AL²]

ar·rear (ə rēr′), *n.* **1.** Usually, **arrears.** state of being behind or late, esp. in the fulfillment of a duty, promise, obligation, or the like. **2.** Often, **arrears.** that which is behind in payment; a debt which, though due, remains unpaid. **3.** *Obs.* the rear. **4. in** or **into arrears,** behind in payment of a debt: *If he falls into arrears, his furniture will be repossessed.* Also, **in arrear.** [n. use of *arrear* (adv., now obs.), ME *arere* behind < MF << L *ad retrō.* See AD-, RETRO-]

ar·rear·age (ə rēr′ij), *n.* **1.** state or condition of being in arrears. **2.** Often, **arrearages.** arrears; amount or amounts overdue. **3.** *Archaic.* a thing or part kept in reserve. [ME *arerage* < OF. See ARREAR, -AGE]

ar·re·not·o·ky (ar′ə not′ə kē), *n.* arrhenotoky. —**ar′re·not′o·kous,** *adj.*

Ar·re·pho·ri·a (är′ə fôr′ē ə, -fōr′-), *n.* (*sometimes construed as pl.*) an annual festival of Athena, celebrated in ancient Athens by the Arrephoroi. Also, **Arrhephoria, Errhephoria.**

Ar·re·pho·ros (är′ə fôr′əs, -fōr′-), *n., pl.* **-pho·roi** (-fôr′oi, -fōr′-). any of four young girls chosen annually to celebrate the Arrephoria: they wove a peplos for Athena and carried baskets with secret contents to her shrine.

ar·rest (ə rest′), *v.t.* **1.** to seize (a person) by legal authority or warrant; take into custody: *The policeman arrested the burglar.* **2.** to catch and hold; attract and fix; engage: *to arrest the attention.* **3.** to check the course of; stop; slow down: *to arrest progress.* **4.** *Med.* to control or stop the active progress of a disease process: *The new drug did not arrest tuberculosis.* **5.** *Archaic.* to capture; seize: *The lion doth arrest his prey.* —*n.* **6.** the taking of a person into legal custody, as by officers of the law: *The police made the arrest at night.* **7.** any seizure or taking by force. **8.** the act of stopping or the state of being stopped. **9.** *Mach.* any device for stopping machinery; stop. **10. under arrest,** in custody of the police or other legal authorities: *They placed the subject under arrest after finding him with incriminating evidence.* [ME *areste(n)* < MF *areste(r),* equiv. to *a-* A-⁵ + *rester* to REST; ME *arest(e)* (n.) < OF (v.)] —**ar·rest′a·ble,** *adj.* —**ar·rest′ment,** *n.*
—**Syn. 1.** apprehend. **2.** secure, rivet, occupy. **3.** stay. See **stop. 6.** detention, apprehension, imprisonment. **8.** stoppage, halt, stay, check. —**Ant. 1–3, 6.** release.

ar·rest·er (ə res′tər), *n.* **1.** one who or that which arrests. **2.** *Elect.* See **lightning arrester. 3.** See **spark arrester.** [ARREST + -ER¹]

ar·rest·ing (ə res′ting), *adj.* that catches the attention; striking; stimulating: *She has a sparkling and arresting personality.* [ARREST + -ING²] —**ar·rest′ing·ly,** *adv.*

arrest′ing gear′, any mechanism or device for slowing something to a stop, as an airplane landing on an aircraft carrier.

ar·res·tive (ə res′tiv), *adj.* tending to arrest or take hold of the attention, interest, etc. [ARREST + -IVE]

arrgt., arrangement.

Ar·rhe·ni·us (är rā′nē o͝os′), *n.* **Svan·te Au·gust** (svän′te ou′go͝ost), 1859–1927, Swedish physicist and chemist: Nobel prize for chemistry 1903.

ar·rhe·not·o·ky (ar′ə not′ə kē), *n.* parthenogenesis in which only males are produced. Also, **arrenotoky.** [< Gk *arrhenotokía,* equiv. to *arrhenotók(os)* bearing male offspring (*arrhēno-* male + *tók(os)* offspring + *-os* adj. suffix) + *-ia* -Y³] —**ar′rhe·not′o·kous,** *adj.*

Ar·rhe·pho·ri·a (är′ə fôr′ē ə, -fōr′-), *n.* Arrephoria.

ar·rhyth·mi·a (ə rith′mē ə, ə rith′-), *n.* *Pathol.* any disturbance in the rhythm of the heartbeat. Also, **arhythmia, arythmia, arrythmia.** [< NL < Gk *arrhythmía.* See A-⁶, RHYTHM, -IA] —**arrhyth·mic** (ə rith′mik, ə rith′-), **ar·rhyth′mi·cal,** *adj.* —**ar·rhyth′mi·cal·ly,** *adv.*

ar·ric·cia·to (är′ē chä′tō; *It.* är′Rēt chä′tô), *n., pl.* **-tos,** *It.* **-ti,** (-tē). arriccio. [< It; see ARRICIO, -ATE¹]

ar·ric·cio (ə rē′chō; *It.* är Rēt′chô), *n., pl.* **-cios,** *It.* **-ci** (-chē). (formerly in fresco painting) a second coat of plaster, somewhat finer than the first coat, applied over the entire surface and on which the drawing for the fresco is done. Also, **arricciato.** Also called **brown coat.** Cf. **intonaco, trullisatio.** [< It, deriv. of *arricci(are)* (to) curl up, make grooves in (*a-* A-⁵ + *riccio* hedgehog < L *erici(us)*)]

ar·ride (ə rīd′), *v.t.*, **-rid·ed, -rid·ing.** *Archaic.* to be agreeable or pleasing to. [< L *arrīd(ēre)* (to) smile upon, please, equiv. to *ar-* (var. of *ad-* AD-) + *rīdēre* to smile, laugh; see RIDICULE]

ar·ri·ère-ban (ar′ē er′ban′; *Fr.* A RYER bäN′), *n., pl.* **-bans** (-banz′; *Fr.* -bäN′). **1.** a group of vassals who owed military service, esp. to French kings. **2.** the message calling on this group for duty. [< F, OF < ML *(h)aribannum* < Gmc; cf. OHG *hari* army, *ban* BAN²]

ar·rière-pen·sée (A RYER päN sā′) *n., pl.* **-pen·sées** (-päN sā′). *French.* a mental reservation; hidden motive. [lit., behind-thought]

ar·rière-vous·sure (ar′ē er′vo͞o so͝or′; *Fr.* A RYER′-vo͞o SYR′), *n., pl.* **-vous·sures** (-vo͞o so͝orz′; *Fr.* -vo͞o-SYR′). a vault or vaultlike formation in the depth of a wall behind an opening that is somewhat lower, made either for decorative purposes or to allow clearance for an arched head on a door or casement opening inward. [< F: behind-vault]

Ar Ri·mal (är′ ri mäl′). See **Rub' al Khali.**

ar·ris (ar′is), *n.* *Archit.* **1.** a sharp ridge, as between adjoining channels of a Doric column. **2.** the line, ridge, or hip formed by the meeting of two surfaces at an exterior angle. Also called **piend.** [< MF *areste*]

ar′ris fil′let, a triangular strip of wood laid on the framing of a roof at the edge or at the junction of the roof with a chimney, parapet, or the like, in order to increase or reduce the pitch of the roofing laid over it; cant strip.

ar′ris gut′ter, a roof gutter having a V-shaped cross section.

ar′ris piece′, *Shipbuilding.* (in a made lower mast) any of several slender, triangular pieces of wood inserted between the adjoining chamfered edges of pairs of the mast timbers to make a cylindrical surface beneath one of the binding hoops.

ar·ris·ways (ar′is wāz′), *adv.* diagonally, as in laying tiles or sawing timbers. Also, **ar·ris·wise** (ar′is wīz′). [ARRIS + -WAYS]

ar·ri·val (ə rī′vəl), *n.* **1.** act of arriving: *His arrival was delayed by traffic.* **2.** the reaching or attainment of any object or condition: *arrival at a conclusion.* **3.** the person or thing that arrives or has arrived: *First arrivals will be the first seated.* [ARRIVE + -AL²; r. ME *arivaille* < MF]
—**Syn. 1.** advent, coming.

ar·rive (ə rīv′), *v.*, **-rived, -riv·ing.** —*v.i.* **1.** to come to a certain point in the course of travel; reach one's destination: *He finally arrived in Rome.* **2.** to come: *The time has arrived.* **3.** to attain a position of success in the world. **4.** *Archaic.* to happen: *It arrived that the master had already departed.* **5.** *Obs.* to come to shore. —*v.t.* **6.** *Obs.* to reach; come to. **7. arrive at, a.** to come to a place after traveling. **b.** to attain the objective in a course or process: *to arrive at a conclusion.* [ME *a(r)rive(n)* < OF *a(r)rive(r)* < VL **arrīpāre* to come to land, equiv. to L *ad rīp(am)* to the river-bank + *-ā-* thematic vowel + *-re* inf. suffix] —**ar·riv′er,** *n.*
—**Syn. 1.** ARRIVE, COME both mean to reach a stopping place. ARRIVE directs the attention to the final point of an activity or state: *The train arrived at noon.* COME rarely refers to the actual moment of arrival but refers instead to the progress toward it. **3.** succeed. —**Ant. 1.** depart.

ar·ri·vé (ar′ē vā′; *Fr.* A Rē vā′), *n., pl.* **-vés** (-vāz′; *Fr.* -vā′). a person who has recently gained wealth, status, or success; upstart, parvenu. [< F: lit., arrived, n. use of ptp. of *arriver* to ARRIVE]

ar·ri·ve·der·ci (äR′ rē ve der′chē), *interj.* *Italian.* until we see each other again; good-by for the present. Also, **a rivederci.**

ar·ri·viste (ar′ē vēst′; *Fr.* A Rē vēst′), *n., pl.* **-vistes** (-vēsts′; *Fr.* -vēst′). a person who has recently acquired status, wealth, or success by questionable or unscrupulous means. [< F; see ARRIVE, -IST]

ar·ro·ba (ə rō′bə; *Sp. and Port.* äR Rô′bä), *n., pl.* **-bas** (-bəz; *Sp. and Port.* -bäs). **1.** a Spanish and Portuguese unit of weight of varying value, equal to 25.37 pounds avoirdupois in Mexico and to 32.38 pounds avoirdupois in Brazil. **2.** a unit of liquid measure of varying value, used esp. in Spain and commonly equal (when used for wine) to 4.26 U.S. gallons. [< Sp < Ar *al rub'* the fourth part, i.e., a quarter of the *qinṭār;* see QUINTAL]

ar·ro·gance (ar′ə gəns), *n.* arrogant quality or nature; offensive exhibition of assumed or real superiority; overbearing pride. Also, **ar′ro·gan·cy.** [ME < MF < L *arrogantia* presumption. See ARROGANT, -ANCE]
—**Syn.** haughtiness, insolence, disdain. —**Ant.** humility.

ar·ro·gant (ar′ə gənt), *adj.* **1.** making unwarrantable claims or pretensions to superior importance or rights; overbearingly assuming; insolently proud: *an arrogant little man.* **2.** characterized by or proceeding from arrogance: *arrogant claims.* [ME < L *arrogant-* (s. of *arrogāns*) presuming, prp. of *arrogāre.* See ARROGATE, -ANT] —**ar′ro·gant·ly,** *adv.*
—**Syn. 1.** presumptuous, haughty, imperious, brazen. See **proud.** —**Ant. 1.** meek. **2.** modest.

ar·ro·gate (ar′ə gāt′), *v.t.*, **-gat·ed, -gat·ing.** **1.** to claim unwarrantably or presumptuously; assume or appropriate to oneself without right: *to arrogate the right to make decisions.* **2.** to attribute or assign to another without just reason. [< L *arrogāt(us)* appropriated, assumed, questioned (ptp. of *arrogāre*), equiv. to *arrog-* (*ar-* var. of *ad-* AD- + *rog(āre)* (to) ask, propose) + *-ātus* -ATE¹] —**ar′ro·gat′ing·ly,** *adv.* —**ar′ro·ga′tion,** *n.* —**ar′ro·ga′tor,** *n.*

ar·ron·disse·ment (ə ron′dis mənt, ar′ən dēs′mənt; *Fr.* A RôN dēs mäN′), *n., pl.* **-ments** (-mənts; *Fr.* -mäN′). **1.** the largest administrative division of a French department, comprising a number of cantons. **2.** an administrative district of certain large cities in France. [< F, equiv. to *arrondiss-* (var. s. of *arrondir* to round out; see A-⁵, ROUND) + *-ment* -MENT]

ar·row (ar′ō), *n.* **1.** a slender, straight, generally pointed missile or weapon made to be shot from a bow and equipped with feathers at the end of the shaft near the nock, for controlling flight. **2.** anything resembling an arrow in form, function, or character. **3.** a linear figure having a wedge-shaped end, used in maps, architectural drawings, etc., to indicate direction or placement. **4.** (*cap.*) *Astron.* the constellation Sagitta. **5.** See **broad arrow.** —*v.t.* **6.** to indicate the proper position of (an insertion) by means of an arrow (often fol. by *in*): *to arrow in a comment between the paragraphs.* [ME *arewe,* OE *arwe;* c. Icel *ör* (pl. *örvar*); akin to L *arcus* bow] —**ar′row·less,** *adj.* —**ar′row·like′,** *adj.*

ar·row·head (ar′ō hed′), *n.* **1.** the head or tip of an arrow, usually separable from the shaft, and conventionally wedge-shaped. **2.** anything resembling or having the conventional shape of an arrowhead. **3.** any plant of the genus *Sagittaria,* usually aquatic, species of which have arrowhead-shaped leaves. **4.** the dartlike form in an egg-and-dart ornament. [late ME; see ARROW + HEAD]

ar·row·root (ar′ō ro͞ot′, -ro͝ot′), *n.* **1.** a tropical American plant, *Maranta arundinacea,* or related species, whose rhizomes yield a nutritious starch. **2.** the starch itself. **3.** a similar starch from other plants, used in light puddings, cookies, etc. [named from use of its root in treatment of wounds made by poisoned arrows]

Ar·row·smith (ar′ō smith′), *n.* a novel (1925) by Sinclair Lewis.

ar·row·wood (ar′ō wo͝od′), *n.* any of several shrubs and small trees, as the wahoo and certain viburnums, with tough, straight shoots, once used for arrows. [named from use in making arrows]

ar·row·worm (ar′ō wûrm′), *n.* any small, elongated, translucent, marine worm of the phylum or class *Chaetognatha,* having lateral and caudal fins. [named from fancied resemblance to arrow]

ar·row·y (ar′ō ē), *adj.* **1.** like an arrow in shape, speed, effect, etc.; swift or piercing. **2.** consisting of arrows. [ARROW + -Y[1]]

ar·roy·o (ə roi′ō), *n., pl.* **-os** (-ōz). (chiefly in southwest U.S.) a small steep-sided watercourse or gulch with a nearly flat floor: usually dry except after heavy rains. [< Sp; akin to L *arrūgia* mine-shaft]

Arroy′o Gran′de, a town in SW California. 3291 (1960).

ar·roz con pol·lo (ä rôth′ kôn pô′lyô, ä rôs′ kôn pô′yô), a Spanish dish of chicken cooked with rice, onions, and saffron, and sometimes with tomatoes, often garnished with pimientos and peas. [lit., rice with pullet]

Ar′ru Is′lands (ä′ro͞o). See **Aru Islands.**

ar·ryth·mi·a (ə rith′mē ə, ə rith′-), *n. Pathol.* arrhythmia. —**ar·ryth·mic** (ə rith′mik, ə rith′-), **ar·ryth′mi·cal,** *adj.* —**ar·ryth′mi·cal·ly,** *adv.*

ars-, a combining form of **arsenic:** *arsonium.*

Ar·sa·ces I (är′sə sēz′, är sā′sēz), founder of the Parthian empire c250 B.C.

Ars A·ma·to·ri·a (ärs′ ä′mä tô′rē ä′; *Eng.* ärz′ am′ə tôr′ē ə, -tōr′-, ärs′). See **Art of Love, The.**

Ars An·ti·qua (ärz′ an tē′kwə, ärs′-), *Music.* the style of composition characteristic of the 13th century, esp. in France. Cf. **Ars Nova.** [< ML: ancient art]

arse (ärs), *n. Slang.* ass[2] (defs. 1, 2).

arsen-, var. of **arseno-,** esp. before a vowel.

ar·se·nal (är′sə nəl), *n.* **1.** a place of storage or a magazine containing arms and military equipment of all kinds for land or naval service. **2.** a building having that incidental purpose but used mainly for the training of troops. **3.** a public establishment where military equipment or munitions are manufactured. **4.** a collection or supply of weapons or munitions. **5.** a collection or supply of anything; storehouse; repertory: *She charmed the visitor with her arsenal of blandishments.* [< It *arsenale* dockyard, alter. of Ar *dār ṣinā'a* workshop (lit., house of hand-work)]

ar·se·nate (är′sə nāt′, -nit), *n. Chem.* a salt or ester of arsenic acid. [ARSEN- + -ATE[2]]

ar·se·nic (*n.* är′sə nik, ärs′nik; *adj.* är sen′ik), *n.* **1.** a grayish-white element having a metallic luster, volatilizing when heated, and forming poisonous compounds. *Symbol:* As; *at. wt.:* 74.92; *at. no.:* 33. **2.** See **arsenic trioxide. 3.** a mineral, the native element, occurring in white or gray masses. —*adj.* **4.** of or containing arsenic, esp. in the pentavalent state. [ME *arsenic(um)* < L < Gk *arsenikón* orpiment, n. use of neut. of *arsenikós* virile (*ársēn* male, strong + *-ikos* -IC), prob. alter. of oriental word (? *arznig, metathetic var. of Syriac *zarnig*) by folk etym.]

arsen′ic ac′id, *Chem.* a white, crystalline, water-soluble powder, $H_3AsO_4 \cdot 1/2H_2O$, used chiefly in the manufacture of arsenates.

ar·sen·i·cal (är sen′i kəl), *adj.* **1.** containing or relating to arsenic. —*n.* **2.** any of a group of pesticides, drugs, or other compounds containing arsenic. [ARSENIC + -AL[1]]

arsen′ical bab′bitt, Babbitt metal containing from 0.1 percent to 3.0 percent arsenic.

arsen′ical py′rite, *Mineral.* arsenopyrite.

ar′senic disul′fide, *Chem.* an orange-red, water-insoluble, poisonous powder, As_4S_4, As_2S_2, or AsS, used chiefly in the manufacture of fireworks. Also called **ar′senic mon·o·sul′fide** (mon′ə sul′fīd).

ar′senic trichlo′ride, *Chem.* a colorless or yellow, oily, poisonous liquid, $AsCl_3$, used chiefly as an intermediate in the manufacture of organic arsenicals. Also called **butter of arsenic.**

ar′senic triox′ide, *Chem.* a white, tasteless, amorphous, slightly water-soluble, poisonous powder, As_2O_3, used chiefly in the manufacture of pigments and glass, as an insecticide, weed-killer, etc.; arsenous acid; arsenic. Also called **arsenous anhydride, arsenous oxide.**

ar·se·nide (är′sə nīd′, -nid), *n. Chem.* a compound containing two elements of which arsenic is the negative one, as silver arsenide, Ag_3As. [ARSEN- + -IDE]

ar·se·ni·ous (är sē′nē əs), *adj. Chem.* arsenous. [ARSEN- + -IOUS]

ar·se·nite (är′sə nīt′), *n. Chem.* a salt or ester of arsenous acid. [ARSEN- + -ITE[1]]

ar·se·niu·ret·ted (är sē′nyə ret′id, -sen′yə-), *adj. Chem.* combined with arsenic so as to form an arsenide. Also, **ar·se′niu·ret′ed.** [ARSENI(C) + -URET + -ED[3]]

arse′niuretted hy′drogen, *Chem.* arsine (def. 1).

ar·se·no (är′sə nō′), *adj. Chem.* containing the arseno group. [see ARSENO-]

arseno-, a combining form of the arseno group, used esp. before a consonant: *arsenoclasite.* Also, *esp. before a vowel,* **arsen-.** [ARSEN(IC) + -O-]

ar′seno group′, *Chem.* the bivalent group, –As=As–. Also called **ar′seno rad′ical.**

ar·sen·o·lite (är sen′əlīt′), *n.* a mineral, arsenic trioxide, As_2O_3, occurring usually as a white incrustation on arsenical ores. [ARSENO- + -LITE]

ar·se·no·py·rite (är′sə nō pī′rīt, är sen′ə-), *n.* a common mineral, iron arsenic sulfide, FeAsS, occurring in silver-white to steel-gray crystals or masses: an ore of arsenic. Also called **arsenical pyrite, mispickel.** [ARSENO- + PYRITE]

ar·se·nous (är′sə nəs), *adj. Chem.* **1.** containing arsenic in the trivalent state, as arsenous chloride, $AsCl_3$. **2.** of or derived from arsenous acid. Also, **arsenious.** [ARSEN- + -OUS]

ar′senous ac′id, *Chem.* **1.** a hypothetical acid, H_3AsO_3 or $HAsO_2$, known only in solution or in the form of its salts. **2.** See **arsenic trioxide.**

ar′senous anhy′dride, *Chem.* See **arsenic trioxide.**

ar′senous ox′ide, *Chem.* See **arsenic trioxide.**

Ar·se·ny (är′sə nē), *n.* a boy's given name.

ars est ce·la·re ar·tem (ärs est ke lä′re är′tem; *Eng.* ärz est si lā′rē är′təm, -lâr′ē, ärs), *Latin.* it is art to conceal art; true art conceals the means by which it is achieved.

ars gra·ti·a ar·tis (ärs′ grä′tē ä′ är′tis; *Eng.* ärz′ grā′shē ə är′tis, ärs), *Latin.* art for art's sake.

ar·shin (är shēn′), *n.* a Russian unit of length equal to 28 inches. Also, **ar·shine′.** [< Russ]

arsin-, var. of **arsino-,** esp. before a vowel.

ar·sine (är sēn′, är′sēn, -sin), *n. Chem.* **1.** Also called **arseniuretted hydrogen.** a colorless, flammable, slightly water-soluble gas, AsH_3, having a fetid, garliclike odor, used in chemical warfare. **2.** any derivative of this compound in which one or more hydrogen atoms are replaced by organic groups. [ARS(ENIC) + -INE[2]]

ar·si·no (är sē′nō), *adj. Chem.* containing the arsino group. [see ARSINO-]

arsino-, a combining form of the arsino group. Also, *esp. before a vowel,* **arsin-.** [ARSINE + -O-]

Ar·sin·o·ë (är sin′ō ē′), *n. Class. Myth.* **1.** the wife of Alcmaeon, who continued to love her husband even though he was unfaithful. **2.** the nurse of Orestes. **3.** a daughter of Leucippus and Philodice.

arsi′no group′, *Chem.* the univalent group, H_2As–. Also called **arsi′no rad′ical.**

Ar·sin·o·us (är sin′ō əs), *n.* (in the *Iliad*) the father of Aecamede.

Ar·sip·pe (är′si pē), *n. Class. Myth.* a daughter of Minyas who was driven mad for mocking Dionysus.

ar·sis (är′sis), *n., pl.* **-ses** (-sēz). **1.** *Music.* the upward stroke in conducting; upbeat. Cf. **thesis** (def. 4). **2.** *Pros.* **a.** the part of a metrical foot that bears the ictus or stress. **b.** (less commonly) a part of a metrical foot that does not bear the ictus. Cf. **thesis** (def. 5). [< L < Gk, equiv. to *ar-* (s. of *aírein* to raise, lift) + *-sis* -SIS]

ars lon·ga, vi·ta bre·vis (ärs lông′gä wē′tä bre′wis; *Eng.* ärz lông′gə vī′tə brē′vis, ärs), *Latin.* art is long, life is short.

Ars No·va (ärz′ nō′və, ärs′), *Music.* the style of composition characteristic of the 14th century in France and Italy. Cf. **Ars Antiqua.**

ar·son (är′sən), *n. Law.* the malicious burning of another's house or property, or in some statutes, the burning of one's own house or property, as to collect insurance. [< AF, OF < LL *ārsiōn-* (s. of *ārsiō*) a burning, equiv. to *ārs-* (L *ārd(ere)* to burn + *-t(us)* ptp. suffix) + *-iōn-* -ION]

ar·son·ist (är′sə nist), *n.* a person who commits arson. [ARSON + -IST]

ars·phen·a·mine (ärs fen′ə mēn′, -min), *n. Pharm.* a yellow, crystalline powder, $C_{12}H_{12}N_2O_2As_2 \cdot 2HCl \cdot 2H_2O$, subject to rapid oxidation, formerly used to treat diseases caused by spirochete organisms, esp. syphilis and trench mouth: first known as "606." [ARS(ENIC) + PHEN(YL) + AMINE]

ars po·e·ti·ca (ärz′ pō et′i kə, ärs′), **1.** the art of poetry or poetics. **2.** (*cap., italics.*) a poem (c20 B.C.) by Horace, setting forth his precepts for the art of poetry.

ar·sy-var·sy (är′sē vär′sē), *Slang.* —*adj.* **1.** wrong end foremost; completely backward: *an arsy-varsy way of doing things.* —*adv.* **2.** in a backward or thoroughly mixed-up fashion: *She filed all the papers arsy-varsy.* Also, **ar·sy-ver·sy** (är′sē vûr′sē). [ARSE + -Y[1] + (RE)VERSE + -Y[1]]

art[1] (ärt), *n.* **1.** the quality, production, or expression, according to aesthetic principles, of what is beautiful, appealing, or of more than ordinary significance. **2.** the class of objects subject to aesthetic criteria; works of art collectively, as paintings, drawings, etc.: *a museum of art; an art collection.* **3.** a field, genre, or category of art: *Dance is an art.* **4.** the fine arts collectively, often excluding architecture: *art and architecture.* **5.** any field using the skills or techniques of art: *advertising art; industrial art.* **6.** *Journalism.* (in newspapers and periodicals) illustrative or decorative material, taken collectively: *Is there any art with this story?* **7.** the principles or methods governing any craft or branch of learning: *the art of baking; the art of sailing.* **8.** the craft or trade using these principles or methods. **9.** exceptional skill in conducting any human activity: *a master at the art of conversation.* **10.** a branch of learning or university study, esp. one of the fine arts or the humanities. **11. arts, a.** (*construed as sing.*) the humanities: *a college of arts and sciences.* **b.** (*construed as pl.*) See **liberal arts. 12.** skilled workmanship, execution, or agency, as distinguished from nature. **13.** trickery; cunning: *glib and oily art.* **14.** studied action; artificiality in behavior. **15.** an artifice or artful device: *the innumerable arts and wiles of politics.* **16.** *Archaic.* science, learning, or scholarship. [ME < OF, acc. of *ars* < L *ars* (nom.), *artem* (acc.)]

art[2] (ärt), *v. Archaic or Poetic.* 2nd pers. sing. pres. indic. of **be.** [ME; OE *eart,* equiv. to *ear-* (see ARE[1]) + *-t* ending of 2nd pers. sing.]

Art (ärt), *n.* a boy's given name, form of **Arthur.**

-art, var. of **-ard:** *braggart.*

art., *pl.* **arts.,** for 1. **1.** article; articles. **2.** artificial. **3.** artillery. **4.** artist.

Ar·ta·ci·a (är tā′shē ə, -shə), *n.* (in the *Odyssey*) the spring in the land of the Laestrygones where the daughter of Antiphates met the companions of Odysseus.

ar·tal (är′täl), *n.* pl. of **rotl.**

Ar·ta·xerx·es I (är′tə zûrk′sēz), ("*Longimanus*"), died 424 B.C., king of Persia 464–24.

Artaxerxes II ("*Mnemon*"), died 359? B.C., king of Persia 404?–359?.

art′ direc′tor, 1. *Motion Pictures, Television.* a person who is responsible for the designing of all visual aspects of a production, including settings, costumes, lighting, etc. **2.** Also called **art′ ed′itor.** a person who is responsible for the selection, execution, production, etc., of graphic art for a publication, advertising agency, or the like. **3.** See **artistic director.**

ar·te·fact (är′tə fakt′), *n.* artifact.

ar·tel (är tel′), *n.* (in the Soviet Union) a peasants' or workers' cooperative; an association of workers or peasants for collective effort. [< Russ; akin to ART]

Ar·te·mas (är′tə məs), *n.* a boy's given name. Also, **Ar′te·mus.**

Ar·te·mis (är′tə mis), *n.* **1.** Also called **Cynthia.** an ancient Greek goddess, the daughter of Leto and the sister of Apollo, characterized as a virgin huntress and associated with the moon: identified by the Romans with Diana. **2.** a girl's given name.

ar·te·mis·i·a (är′tə mizh′ē ə, -mizh′ə, -mish′-), *n.* **1.** any of several composite plants of the genus *Artemisia,* abundant in dry regions, esp. of the Northern Hemisphere. **2.** a North American species, *A. tridentata,* the sagebrush of the western plains. [ME: mugwort < L < Gk, equiv. to *Ártemis* Diana + *-ia* -IA]

Ar·te·mis·i·on (är′tə mis′ē on′, -mish′-), *n.* a building or shrine dedicated to the worship of Artemis. [< Gk *Ártemis* Diana + *-ion* suffix of place]

Ar·te·movsk (är tye′mofsk), *n.* a city in the E Ukraine, in the SW Soviet Union in Europe. 61,000 (1959). Formerly, **Bakhmut.**

ar·te·ri·al (är tēr′ē əl), *adj.* **1.** *Physiol.* pertaining to the blood in the pulmonary vein, the left side of the heart, and in most arteries, which has been oxygenated during its passage through the lungs and which in man is normally bright red. **2.** *Anat.* of, pertaining to, or resembling the arteries. **3.** having a main channel or highway and many branches: *a system of arterial drainage ditches; an arterial system of roads.* [late ME < ML *artēriālis.* See ARTERY, -AL[1]] —**ar·te′ri·al·ly,** *adv.*

ar·te·ri·al·ise (är tēr′ē ə līz′), *v.t.,* **-ised, -is·ing.** *Chiefly Brit.* arterialize. —**ar·te′ri·al·i·sa′tion,** *n.*

ar·te·ri·al·ize (är tēr′ē ə līz′), *v.t.,* **-ized, -iz·ing.** *Physiol.* to convert (venous blood) into arterial blood by the action of oxygen in the lungs. [ARTERIAL + -IZE] —**ar·te′ri·al·i·za′tion,** *n.*

arterio-, a learned borrowing from Greek meaning "artery," used in the formation of compound words: *arteriosclerosis.* [< Gk *artērio-,* comb. form of *artēria* windpipe, ARTERY]

ar·te·ri·ole (är tēr′ē ōl′), *n. Anat.* a small artery. [< NL *artēriola,* equiv. to *artēria* ARTERY + *-ola* dim. suffix]

ar·te·ri·ol·o·gy (är tēr′ē ol′ə jē), *n. Med.* the branch of angiology that deals with the arteries. [ARTERIO- + -LOGY]

ar·te·ri·o·scle·ro·sis (är tēr′ē ō sklə rō′sis), *n. Pathol.* an arterial disease occurring esp. in the elderly, characterized by inelasticity and thickening of the vessel walls, with lessened blood flow. [< NL. See ARTERIO-, SCLEROSIS] —**ar·te·ri·o·scle·rot·ic** (är tēr′ē ō sklə rot′ik), *adj.*

ar·te·ri·ot·o·my (är tēr′ē ot′ə mē), *n., pl.* **-mies.** *Surg.* the incision or opening into the lumen of an artery for the removal of a clot, embolus, or the like, or for bloodletting. [ARTERIO- + -TOMY]

ar·te·ri·o·ve·nous (är tēr′ē ō vē′nəs), *adj. Anat.* of or pertaining to an artery and vein. [ARTERIO- + VENOUS]

ar·te·ri·tis (är′tə rī′tis), *n. Pathol.* inflammation of an artery. [ARTER(IO)- + -ITIS]

ar·ter·y (är′tə rē), *n., pl.* **-ter·ies. 1.** *Anat.* a blood vessel which conveys blood from the heart to any part of the body. **2.** a main channel or highway in any ramifying system of communication or transportation, as in drainage or highways. [ME < L *artēria* < Gk: windpipe, artery. See AORTA]

Ar·te·sia (är tē′zhə), *n.* **1.** a city in SE New Mexico. 12,000 (1960). **2.** a town in S California. 9993 (1960).

ar·te·sian (är tē′zhən), *adj.* noting, pertaining to, or characteristic of an artesian well. [< F *artésien* pertaining to ARTOIS (OF *Arteis* Artois + *-ien* -IAN), after the wells of this kind in the region]

arte′sian well′, a well in which water rises under pressure from a permeable stratum overlayed by impermeable rock.

Artesian well (Cross section) A, Impermeable strata; B, Permeable strata; C, Artesian boring and well

ar·te·so·na·do (är′ti sə nä′dō; *Sp.* är′te sō nä′thō), *n., pl.* **-dos** (-dōz; *Sp.* -thōs). (in Spain) a carved and painted paneled ceiling, introduced by the Moors and continued in use during the Renaissance.

Ar·te·veld (är′tə velt′), *n.* **1. Ja·cob van** (yä′kop vän), 1290?–1345, Flemish statesman. **2.** his son, **Phi·lip van** (fē′lip vän), 1340?–82. Flemish revolutionist and political leader. Also, **Ar·te·vel·de** (är′tə vel′də).

art·ful (ärt′fəl), *adj.* **1.** crafty; cunning; deceitful; tricky: *artful schemes.* **2.** skillful in adapting means to ends; ingenious: *an artful choice of metaphors and similes.* **3.** done with or characterized by art or skill: *artful acting; artful repairs.* **4.** *Archaic.* artificial. [ART[1] + -FUL] —**art′ful·ly,** *adv.* —**art′ful·ness,** *n.*

art′ glass′, 1. (in the late 19th and early 20th centuries) any of the several varieties of glass using combinations of colors, special effects of opaqueness and transparency, etc., to create an aesthetic effect. **2.** any of the objects made of such glass, as lamps, vases, and the like.

Ar·tha (är′thə), *n.* a girl's given name.

ar·thral·gia (är thral′jə), *n. Pathol.* pain in a joint. [ARTHR(O)- + -ALGIA] —**ar·thral′gic,** *adj.*

ar·threc·to·my (är threk′tə mē), *n., pl.* **-mies.** *Surg.* erasion (def. 2b). [ARTHR(O)- + -ECTOMY]

ar·thri·tis (är thrī′tis), *n. Pathol.* inflammation of a joint, as in gout or rheumatism. [< L < Gk: gout. See ARTHRO-, -ITIS] —**ar·thrit·ic** (är thrit′ik), **ar·thrit′i·cal,** *adj.*

arthro-, a learned borrowing from Greek meaning "joint," "jointed," used in the formation of compound words: *arthropod.* [< L < Gk *árthro(n)* a joint]

Ar·thro·bac·ter (är′thrō bak′tər), *n. Bacteriol.* a genus of rod-shaped or spherical bacteria found in the soil. [ARTHRO- + *-bacter;* see BACTERI-]

ar·thro·di·a (är thrō′dē ə), *n., pl.* **-di·ae** (-dē ē′). *Anat.* a joint, as in the carpal articulations, in which the surfaces glide over each other in movement. Also called **gliding joint.** [< Gk *arthrōdía,* equiv. to *arthrōd(ēs)* jointed (*arthr(on)* joint + *-ōdēs* -ODE[1]) + *-ia* -IA] —**ar·thro′di·al, ar·throd·ic** (är throd′ik), *adj.*

ar·thro·dire (är′thrə dīər′), *n.* any of numerous fishes of the extinct order *Arthrodira,* widely distributed during the Devonian period, having the anterior part of the body covered by a shield of bony plates. [< NL *arthrodira* name of group, equiv. to *arthro-* ARTHRO- + *-dira* < Gk *deirḗ* neck, throat] —**ar·thro·di·ran** (är′thrə dīr′ən), **ar′thro·di′rous,** *adj.*

ar·throl·o·gy (är throl′ə jē), *n.* the branch of medicine dealing with the joints. [ARTHRO- + -LOGY]

ar·thro·mere (är′thrə mēr′), *n. Zool.* one of the segments or parts into which the body of articulate animals is divided. [ARTHRO- + -MERE] —**ar·thro·mer·ic** (är′thrə mer′ik), *adj.*

ar·thro·pod (är′thrə pod′), *n.* **1.** any segmented invertebrate of the phylum *Arthropoda,* having jointed legs and including the insects, arachnids, crustaceans, and myriapods. —*adj.* **2.** Also, **ar·throp·o·dal** (är throp′ə dəl), **ar·throp·o·dan** (är throp′ə dən), **ar·throp·o·dous** (är throp′ə dəs). belonging or pertaining to the *Arthropoda.* [back formation < NL *Arthropoda.* See ARTHRO-, -PODA]

Ar·throp·o·da (är throp′ə də), *n.* the phylum comprising the arthropods. [< NL; see ARTHROPOD]

ar·thro·spore (är′thrə spōr′, -spôr′), *n.* **1.** *Bacteriol.* an isolated vegetative cell which has passed into a resting state, occurring in bacteria and not regarded as a true spore. **2.** *Bot.* one of a number of spores of various low fungi and algae, united in the form of a string of beads, formed by fission. [ARTHRO- + SPORE] —**ar′thro·spor′ic, ar′thro·spor′ous,** *adj.*

Ar·thur (är′thər), *n.* **1. Chester Alan,** 1830–86, 21st president of the U.S. 1881–85. **2.** legendary king in ancient Britain: leader of the Knights of the Round Table. **3.** a walled plain in the second quadrant of the face of the moon, in the libration area and near the North Pole: about 60 miles in diameter. **4.** Also, **Artur.** a boy's given name.

Ar·thu·ri·an (är thŏŏr′ē ən), *adj.* of or pertaining to King Arthur, who, with his knights, formed the subject of a large part of medieval romance. [ARTHUR + -IAN]

arti-, a learned borrowing from Latin where it meant "art," used in the formation of compound words: *artifact.* [< L *arti-* (s. of *ars*) + *-i-* -I-]

ar·ti·choke (är′ti chōk′), *n.* **1.** a herbaceous, thistlelike plant, *Cynara Scolymus,* having an edible flower head. **2.** the edible portion, used as a table vegetable. **3.** See **Jerusalem artichoke.** [< It (north) *articiocco,* var. (by dissimilation) of *arciciocco, arcicioffo,* deriv. of **arcarcioffo* < OSp *alcarchofa* < Ar *al kharshūf* the artichoke]

Artichoke, *Cynara Scolymus*

ar·ti·cle (är′ti kəl), *n., v.,* **-cled, -cling.** —*n.* **1.** a written composition in prose, usually nonfiction, on a specific topic, forming an independent part of a book or other publication, as a newspaper, magazine, etc. **2.** an individual thing, member, or portion of a class; an item or particular: *an article of food; articles of clothing.* **3.** something of indefinite character or description: *What is that article?* **4.** *Informal.* a person: *Who's that cute article over there?* **5.** *Gram.* any member of a small class of words, or, as in Swedish or Rumanian, affixes, found in certain languages, as English, French, and Arabic, which are linked to nouns and which typically have a grammatical function identifying the noun as a noun rather than describing it. In English the definite article is *the,* the indefinite article is *a,* or *an,* and their force is generally to impart specificity to the noun or to single out the referent from the class names by the noun. **6.** a clause, item, point, or particular in a contract, treaty, or other formal agreement; a condition or stipulation in a contract or bargain. **7.** a separate clause or provision of a statute. **8.** *Archaic.* a subject or matter of interest, thought, business, etc. **9.** *Obs.* a specific or critical point of time; juncture or moment: *the article of death.* —*v.t.* **10.** to set forth in articles; charge or accuse specifically: *They articled his alleged crimes.* **11.** to bind by articles of covenant or stipulation: *to article an apprentice.* **12.** to bind by articles of agreement. —*v.i.* **13.** to make specific charges. **14.** *Obs.* to agree by articles; stipulate. [ME < eccl. L *articulus* article of faith < L: limb, member, part; lit., little joint, equiv. to *arti-* (comb. form of *artus* joint) + *-culus* -CULE]

Ar′ticles of Confedera′tion, the constitution of the 13 American colonies, adopted in 1781 and replaced in 1789 by the Constitution of the United States.

Ar′ticles of War′, the body of laws and legal procedures of the U.S. Army and Air Force, replaced in 1951 by the Uniform Code of Military Justice.

ar·tic·u·lar (är tik′yə lər), *adj.* of or pertaining to the joints. [late ME < L *articulār(is)* pertaining to the joints. See ARTICLE, -AR[1]] —**ar·tic′u·lar·ly,** *adv.*

ar·tic·u·late (*adj., n.* är tik′yə lit; *v.* är tik′yə lāt′), *adj., v.,* **-lat·ed, -lat·ing,** *n.* —*adj.* **1.** clear; distinct: *Each tiny figure in the pattern was clear and articulate.* **2.** uttered clearly in distinct syllables. **3.** capable of speech; not speechless. **4.** using language easily and fluently; having facility with words: *an articulate person.* **5.** expressed, formulated, or presented with clarity and effectiveness: *an articulate thought.* **6.** made clear, distinct, and precise in relation to other parts: *an articulate form; an articulate shape; an articulate area.* **7.** (of ideas, form, etc.) having a meaningful relation to other parts: *an articulate image.* **8.** having parts or distinct areas organized into a coherent or meaningful whole; unified: *an articulate system of philosophy.* **9.** *Zool.* having joints or articulations; composed of segments. —*v.t.* **10.** to utter clearly and distinctly; pronounce with clarity. **11.** *Phonet.* to make the movements and adjustments of the speech organs necessary to utter (a speech sound). **12.** to give clarity or distinction to: *to articulate a shape; to articulate an idea.* **13.** to bring the various parts of (a work of art, a field of perception, a system of thought, etc.) into a meaningful or coherent relation to one another; unify: *to articulate the areas of a painting.* **14.** *Dentistry.* to subject to articulation. **15.** to unite by a joint or joints. —*v.i.* **16.** to pronounce clearly each of a succession of speech sounds, syllables, or words; enunciate: *to articulate clearly and with precision.* **17.** *Phonet.* to articulate a speech sound. **18.** *Anat., Zool.* to form a joint. **19.** *Obs.* to make terms of agreement. —*n.* **20.** a segmented invertebrate. [< L *articulātus* distinct; lit., jointed (ptp. of *articulāre*). See ARTICLE, -ATE[1]] —**ar·tic′u·la·bil′i·ty,** *n.* —**ar·tic·u·la·ble** (är tik′yə lə bəl), *adj.* —**ar·tic′u·late·ly,** *adv.* —**ar·tic′u·late·ness, ar·tic·u·la·cy** (är tik′yə lə sē), *n.* —**ar·tic′u·la·tive** (är tik′yə lā′tiv, -lə tive), *adj.*

artic′ulated locomo′tive, a steam locomotive having two or three connected sections and two or three independent sets of drivers.

ar·tic·u·la·tion (är tik′yə lā′shən), *n.* **1.** act or process of articulating: *the articulation of a form; the articulation of a new thought.* **2.** *Phonet.* **a.** act or process of articulating speech. **b.** the adjustments and movements of speech organs involved in pronouncing a particular sound, taken as a whole. **c.** any one of these adjustments and movements. **d.** any speech sound, esp. a consonant. **3.** act of jointing. **4.** a jointed state or formation; a joint. **5.** *Bot.* **a.** a joint or place between two parts where separation may take place spontaneously, as at the point of attachment of a leaf. **b.** a node in a stem, or the space between two nodes. **6.** *Anat., Zool.* a joint, as the joining or juncture of bones or of the movable segments of an arthropod. **7.** *Dentistry.* **a.** the positioning of teeth in a denture, usually on an articulator, for correct occlusion. **b.** the bringing of opposing tooth surfaces into contact with each other. **c.** the relations of the upper and lower natural or artificial teeth in occlusion. **8.** a measure of the effectiveness of a telephonic transmission system in reproducing speech comprehensibly, expressed as the percentage of speech units uttered that is correctly understood. [< anatomical L *articulātiōn-,* s. of *articulātiō.* See ARTICULATE, -ION] —**ar·tic·u·la·to·ry** (är tik′yə lə tôr′ē, -tōr′ē), *adj.* —**ar·tic′u·la·to′ri·ly,** *adv.*

ar·tic·u·la·tor (är tik′yə lā′tər), *n.* **1.** one who or that which articulates. **2.** *Phonet.* a movable organ, as the tongue, lips, or uvula, the action of which is involved in the production of intelligible speech sounds. Cf. **point of articulation. 3.** *Dentistry.* a mechanical device, representing the jaws, to which casts may be attached: used in the making of dentures. [ARTICULATE + -OR[2]]

artic′ulatory phonet′ics, the branch of phonetics dealing with the motive processes and anatomy involved in the production of the sounds of speech. Cf. **acoustic phonetics** (def. 1), **physiological phonetics.**

Ar·tie (är′tē), *n.* a boy's given name, form of **Arthur.** Also, **Arty.**

ar·ti·fact (är′tə fakt′), *n.* **1.** any object made by man, esp. with a view to subsequent use. **2.** *Biol.* a substance, structure, or the like, not naturally present in tissue but formed by artificial means, as chemicals. Also, **artefact.** [var. of *artefact* < L phrase *arte factum* something made with skill. See ART, FACT]

ar·ti·fac·ti·tious (är′tə fak tish′əs), *adj.* of, pertaining to, or of the nature of an artifact. [ARTIFACT + -ITIOUS]

ar·ti·fice (är′tə fis), *n.* **1.** a clever trick or stratagem; a cunning, crafty device or expedient; wile. **2.** cunning; ingenuity; inventiveness: *He displayed a great deal of artifice in decorating his new apartment.* **3.** trickery; guile; craftiness. **4.** *Archaic.* a skillful or artful contrivance. **5.** *Obs.* quality of execution; workmanship. [back formation from ARTIFICER]
—**Syn. 1.** subterfuge. See **trick. 3.** deception, deceit, art, duplicity. See **cunning.**

ar·tif·i·cer (är tif′i sər), *n.* **1.** one who is skillful or clever in devising ways of making things; an inventor. **2.** a skillful or artistic worker; craftsman. **3.** *Mil.* a skilled and specialized mechanic in the army or navy. [ME < L *artific-* (s. of *artificium* a work of art; see ART[1], -FIC) + -ER[1]]

ar·ti·fi·cial (är′tə fish′əl), *adj.* **1.** made by human skill; produced by man (opposed to *natural*). **2.** made in imitation or as a substitute; not genuine or real; simulated: *artificial leather; artificial flowers.* **3.** lacking naturalness or spontaneity; forced; contrived; feigned: *an artificial smile.* **4.** full of affectation; affected; stilted: *artificial manners; artificial speech.* **5.** made without regard to the particular needs of a situation, person, etc.; imposed arbitrarily; conventional; unnatural: *artificial rules for dormitory residents.* **6.** *Biol.* based on arbitrary, superficial characteristics rather than natural, organic relationships: *an artificial system of classification.* **7.** *Jewelry.* manufactured to resemble a natural gem, in chemical composition or appearance. Cf. **assembled, imitation** (def. 11), **synthetic** (def. 5). **8.** *Obs.* artful; crafty. [ME < L *artificiāl(is),* equiv. to *artifici(um)* skilled workmanship + *-ālis* -AL[1]] —**ar′ti·fi′cial·ly,** *adv.* —**ar′ti·fi′cial·ness,** *n.*
—**Syn. 1.** synthetic. **2, 3.** counterfeit, factitious. **4.** pretentious. —**Ant. 2.** genuine, real.

ar′tifi′cial aids′, *Manège.* aid (def. 6b).

artifi′cial hori′zon, 1. a level reflector, as a surface of mercury, used in determining the altitudes of stars. **2.** the bubble in a sextant or octant for aerial use. **3.** Also called **flight indicator, gyro horizon.** *Aeron.* an instrument that indicates the banking and pitch of an aircraft with respect to the horizon.

artifi′cial insemina′tion, the injection of semen into the vagina or uterus by means of a syringe or the like rather than by coitus.

artifi′cial intel′ligence, the capacity of a computer to perform operations analogous to learning and decision-making in humans.

ar·ti·fi·ci·al·i·ty (är′tə fish′ē al′i tē), *n., pl.* **-ties. 1.** artificial quality. **2.** an artificial thing or trait: *artificialities of speech.* [ARTIFICIAL + -ITY]

ar′tifi′cial kid′ney, a mechanical device that operates outside of the body and substitutes for the kidney by removing waste products from the blood. Also called **hemodialyzer.**

ar′tifi′cial lan′guage, 1. an invented language, as opposed to a hereditary one, intended for a special use, as in international communication, a secret society, etc. **2.** See **machine language. 3.** code (def. 4).

ar′tifi′cial mag′net, any body that attracts iron, esp. iron or steel that has had an attracting property artificially induced.

ar′tifi′cial per′son, *Law.* See under **person** (def. 11).

artifi′cial radioactiv′ity, *Physics.* radioactivity introduced into a nonradioactive substance by bombarding the substance with charged particles. Also called **induced radioactivity.**

artifi′cial respira′tion, the stimulation of natural respiratory functions in persons whose breathing has failed or in newborn infants by artificially forcing air into and out of the lungs.

artifi′cial selec′tion, a process in the breeding of animals and in the cultivation of plants by which man chooses to perpetuate only those forms having certain desirable inheritable characteristics.

Ar·ti·gas (är tē′gäs), *n.* **1. Jo·sé Ger·va·sio** (hô se′ her vä′syô), 1764–1850, Uruguayan soldier and patriot. **2.** a city in N Uruguay. 18,300 (est. 1954).

ar·til·ler·y (är til′ə rē), *n.* **1.** mounted projectile-firing guns or missile launchers, mobile or stationary, light or heavy, as distinguished from small arms. **2.** the troops or the branch of an army concerned with the service of such weapons. **3.** the science that treats of the use of such weapons. [ME *artellery, artyllery,* equiv. to *arteller, artiller* bowyer < MF *art(e)iller* weapon-maker (*arteil* ARTICLE + *-(i)er* -ER[2]) + *-y* -Y[3]]

ar·til·ler·y·man (är til′ə rē mən), *n., pl.* **-men.** a soldier serving in an artillery unit of the army. Also, **ar·til·ler·ist** (är til′ər ist). [ARTILLERY + MAN[1]]

artil′lery plant′, a spreading, annual herb, *Pilea microphylla,* of tropical America, having small, fleshy leaves and green flowers, grown as a curiosity because the pollen is discharged explosively when dry.

artio-, a learned borrowing from Greek meaning "even number," used in the formation of compound words: *artiodactyl.* [< Gk *ártio(s)* even (in number), perfect; akin to L *ars* art, Skt *arthya* suitable, rich]

ar·ti·o·dac·tyl (är′tē ō dak′til), *adj.* **1.** *Zool.* having an even number of toes or digits on each foot. —*n.* **2.** a hoofed, even-toed mammal of the order *Artiodactyla,* comprising the pigs, hippopotamuses, camels, deer, giraffes, pronghorns, sheep, goats, antelope, and cattle. Cf. **perissodactyl.** [< NL; see ARTIO-, DACTYL] —**ar′ti·o·dac′ty·lous,** *adj.*

Ar·ti·o·dac·ty·la (är′tē ō dak′tə lə), *n.* the order comprising the artiodactyls. [NL; see ARTIODACTYL]

ar·ti·san (är′ti zən), *n.* **1.** one skilled in an applied art; a craftsman. **2.** *Obs.* an artist. [< F < It *artigian(o)* equiv. to L *artīt(us)* trained in arts and crafts (ptp. of *artīre;* see ART[1], -ITE[2]) + It *-iano* (< L *-iānus*) -IAN] —**ar′ti·san·al,** *adj.* —**ar′ti·san·ship′,** *n.* —**Syn. 1.** See **artist.**

art·ist (är′tist), *n.* **1.** one who produces works in any of the arts that are primarily subject to aesthetic criteria. **2.** a person who practices one of the fine arts, esp. a painter or sculptor. **3.** one whose trade or profession requires a knowledge of design, drawing, painting, etc.: *a commercial artist.* **4.** a person who works in one of the performing arts, as an actor, musician, or singer; a public performer: *a mime artist; an artist of the dance.* **5.** one who exhibits exceptional skill in his work. **6.** one who is expert at trickery or deceit: *He's an artist with cards.* **7.** *Obs.* an artisan. [< ML *artist(a)* master of arts. See ART[1], -IST]
—**Syn. 1.** ARTIST, ARTISAN are persons having superior skill or ability, or are capable of a superior kind of workmanship. An ARTIST is a person engaged in some type of fine art. An ARTISAN is engaged in a craft or applied art.

ar·tiste (är tēst′; *Fr.* AR tēst′), *n., pl.* **-tistes** (-tēsts′; *Fr.* -tēst′). an artist, esp. an actor, singer, dancer, or other public performer. [< F; see ARTIST]

ar·tis·tic (är tis′tik), *adj.* **1.** conforming to the standards of art; satisfying aesthetic requirements: *artistic productions.* **2.** showing skill or excellence in execution: *artistic workmanship.* **3.** exhibiting taste, discriminating judgment, or sensitivity: *an artistic arrangement of flowers; artistic handling of a delicate diplomatic situation.* **4.** exhibiting an involvement in or appreciation of art, esp. the fine arts: *He had wide-ranging artistic interests.* **5.** involving only aesthetic considerations, usually taken as excluding moral, practical, religious, political, or similar concerns: *artistic principles.* **6.** of, like, or thought of as characteristic of an artist: *an artistic temperament.* Also, **ar·tis′ti·cal.** [ARTIST + -IC] —**ar·tis′ti·cal·ly,** *adv.*

artis′tic direc′tor, a person who is responsible for the administration of a theater or ballet company, opera house, etc. Also called **artis′tic admin′istrator, art director.**

art·ist·ry (är′ti strē), *n.* **1.** artistic workmanship, effect, or quality. **2.** artistic pursuits. [ARTIST + -RY]

Art′ist's Moth′er, The. See **Whistler's Mother.**

art·less (ärt′lis), *adj.* **1.** free from deceit, cunning, or craftiness; ingenuous: *an artless child.* **2.** not artificial; natural; simple; uncontrived: *artless beauty; artless charm.* **3.** lacking art, knowledge, or skill. **4.** poorly made; inartistic; clumsy; crude: *an artless translation.* [ART[1] + -LESS] —**art′less·ly,** *adv.* —**art′less·ness,** *n.*
—**Syn. 1.** naïve, unsophisticated. **2.** guileless, open, frank, plain, unaffected, candid, sincere. —**Ant.** cunning.

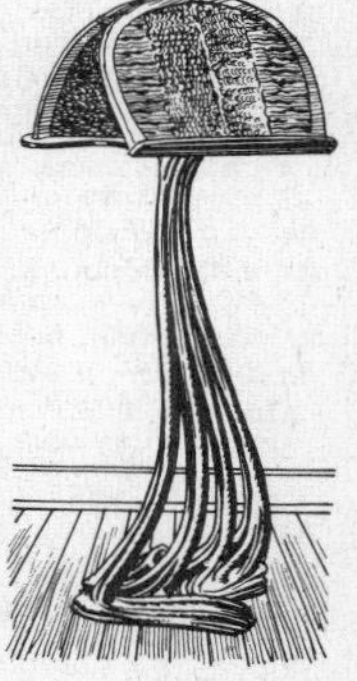
Art Nouveau music stand

art′ lin′ing, *Print.* a system for aligning type in which the baseline is established some distance above the bottom of the body to accommodate letters with unusually long descenders. Cf. **standard lining, title lining.**

Art Nou·veau (är′ nōō vō′, ärt′; *Fr.* AR nōō vō′), (*sometimes l.c.*) *Fine Arts.* a style of fine and applied art current in the late 19th and early 20th centuries, characterized chiefly by curvilinear motifs derived from natural forms. [< F: lit., new art]

Art′ of Love′, The, a series of poems in three books (1? B.C.) by Ovid. Latin, **Ars Amatoria.**

Ar·tois (ar twä′), *n.* a former province in N France: artesian wells. See map under **Agincourt.**

ar·to·pho·ri·on (är′tô fô′rē ôn; *Eng.* är′tə fôr′ē on′, -fôr′-), *n., pl.* **-pho·ri·a** (-fô′rē ä; *Eng.* -fôr′ē ə, -fôr′-). *Gk. Orth. Ch.* pyx (def. 1a). [< MGk, Gk: basket for bread, equiv. to *arto-* (deriv. of *árt(os)* cake, bread) + *-phorion* (akin to *phérein* to bear)]

ar·to·type (är′tə tīp′), *n.* *Print.* collotype. [ART[1] + -O- + TYPE]

arts′ and crafts′, decoration and craftsmanship conceived as a single entity and applied esp. to the production of utilitarian objects, as furniture decorated with floral motifs or boxes having a painted design.

art′ song′, a song intended primarily to be sung in recital, typically set to a poem, and having subtly interdependent voice and piano parts. Cf. **lied.**

art·sy-craft·sy (ärt′sē kraft′sē, -kräft′-), *adj.* **1.** pretending to artistry and craftsmanship or to an interest in arts and crafts, esp. with reference to utilitarian objects produced as a hobby: *an artsy-craftsy chair; an artsy-craftsy person.* **2.** cloyingly charming: *She prefers an artsy-craftsy décor.* Also, **arty-crafty.** [irreg. from *arts and crafts*]

art′ the′ater, a motion-picture theater specializing in the presentation of foreign and experimental films.

Ar·tur (är′tər), *n.* a boy's given name. Also, **Arthur.**

art·work (ärt′wûrk′), *n.* **1.** *Print.* **a.** the elements comprising a mechanical, as type, proofs, illustrations, etc. **b.** a mechanical; paste-up. **2.** the production of artistic or craft objects. **3.** the object so produced. [ART[1] + WORK]

art·y (är′tē), *adj.,* **art·i·er, art·i·est.** *Informal.* characterized by an ostentatious and often affected display of artistic interest, manner, or mannerism. [ART[1] + -Y[1]] —**art′i·ness,** *n.*

Ar·ty (är′tē), *n.* a boy's given name, form of **Arthur.** Also, **Artie.**

Arty., Artillery.

art·y-craft·y (är′tē kraf′tē, -kräf′-), *adj.* artsy-craftsy.

Ar·tzy·ba·sheff (ärt′si bä′shif), *n.* **Bor·is Mi·khai·lo·vich** (bôr′is mi kī′lə vich, bor′-; *Russ.* bo rēs′ mi-khī′lo vich), 1899–1965, U.S. illustrator and writer, born in Russia.

Ar·tzy·ba·shev (är tsi bä′shef), *n.* **Mi·kha·il** (mi-khä ēl′), 1878–1927, Russian writer. Also, **Ar′tsy·ba′·shev.**

A.R.U., American Railway Union.

A·ru·ba (ä ro͞o′bä), *n.* an island in the Netherlands Antilles, in the SE West Indies, off the NW coast of Venezuela. 53,199 (1960); 69 sq. mi.

A′ru Is′lands (är′o͞o), an island group in Indonesia, SW of New Guinea. 3306 sq. mi. Also, **Arru Islands.**

ar·um (âr′əm), *n.* **1.** any plant of the genus *Arum,* having an inflorescence consisting of a spadix enclosed in a large spathe, as the cuckoopint. **2.** any of various allied plants in cultivation, as the calla lily. [< L < Gk *áron* wake-robin] —**ar′um-like′,** *adj.*

Ar·un·del (ar′ən dᵊl; *local* ärn′dᵊl), *n.* a town in S West Sussex, in S England: castle. 2614 (1961).

a·run·di·na·ceous (ə run′də nā′shəs), *adj.* *Bot.* pertaining to or like a reed or cane; reedlike; reedy. [< NL < L *(h)arundin-* (s. of *harundō* reed) + *-āceus* -ACEOUS]

Ar·uns (ar′ənz), *n.* *Rom. Legend.* the Trojan ally who killed Camilla.

A·run·ta (ə run′tə), *n., pl.* **-tas,** *(esp. collectively)* **-ta** for **1. 1.** a member of an aboriginal desert people of north-central Australia. **2.** the language of the Arunta. Also, **Aranda.**

A·ru·ru (ä ro͞o′ro͞o), *n.* the Akkadian goddess personifying earth, who assisted Marduk in the creation of mankind: the counterpart of the Sumerian Ki.

A·ru·sha (ə ro͞o′shə), *n.* a city in N Tanganyika, in Tanzania. 10,038 (1957).

a·rus·pex (ə rus′peks), *n., pl.* **-pi·ces** (-pi sēz′). haruspex.

a·rus·pi·cy (ə rus′pi sē), *n.* haruspicy.

A·ru·wi·mi (ä′ro͞o wē′mē), *n.* a river in the N Republic of the Congo, flowing SW and W into the Congo River. ab. 800 mi. long.

A.R.V., American Revised Version (of the Bible).

Ar·vad·a (är vad′ə), *n.* a city in central Colorado, near Denver. 19,242 (1960).

Ar·val (är′vəl), *n., pl.* **Ar·va·les** (är vā′lēz), *adj.* —*n.* **1.** any of the Arval Brothers. —*adj.* **2.** of or pertaining to the Arval Brothers.

Ar′val Broth′ers, (in ancient Rome) the 12 priests of Dea Dia, who performed sacrifices for the fertility of the fields. They later devoted themselves to the cult of the reigning emperor. Also called **Ar·va·les** (är vā′lēz), **Fratres Arvales.**

Ar·vid (är′vid), *n.* a boy's given name.

Ar·vin (är′vin), *n.* **1.** a town in central California. 5310 (1960). **2.** a boy's given name.

ar·vo (är′vō), *n.* *Australian Slang.* afternoon.

Ar·vol (är′vəl), *n.* a boy's given name.

-ary, a suffix meaning "pertaining to," "connected with," sometimes "a person connected with or engaged in," occurring in loan words from Latin: *honorary; dictionary; functionary; visionary.* [< L *-ārius*]

Ar·y·an (âr′ē ən, âr′yən, ar′-), *n.* **1.** *Ethnol.* a member or descendant of the prehistoric people who spoke Indo-European. **2.** (in Nazi doctrine) a non-Jewish Caucasian, esp. of Nordic stock. **3.** *Archaic.* Indo-European. **4.** *Archaic.* Indo-Iranian. —*adj.* **5.** of or pertaining to an Aryan or the Aryans. **6.** *Archaic.* Indo-European. **7.** *Archaic.* Indo-Iranian. Also, **Arian.** [< Skt *ārya* of high rank (adj.), aristocrat (n.) + -AN]

Ar·y·an·ise (âr′ē ə nīz′, âr′yə-, ar′-), *v.t.,* **-ised, -is·ing.** *Chiefly Brit.* Aryanize.

Ar·y·an·ize (âr′ē ə nīz′, âr′yə-, ar′-), *v.t.,* **-ized, -iz·ing.** (in Nazi doctrine) to remove all non-Aryan persons from (office, business, etc.). [ARYAN + -IZE]

Ar·ya Sa·maj (är′yə sə mäj′), a modern Hindu movement, advocating a return to Vedic doctrines, whose activities include proselytization and extensive social work.

ar·y·bal·los (ar′ə bal′əs), *n., pl.* **-bal·loi** (-bal′oi). *Gk. and Rom. Antiq.* an oil jar, characterized by a spherical body, flat-rimmed mouth, and often a single handle extending from the lip to the shoulder of the jar, used chiefly for fragrant ointments. Cf. **alabastron, askos, lekythos.** [< Gk *arýballos* a draw-purse, equiv. to *arý(ein)* (to) draw + *-ballos,* akin to *ballántion* purse] —**ar′y·bal′loid,** *adj.*

Aryballos

ar·y·bal·lus (ar′ə bal′əs), *n., pl.* **-bal·li** (-bal′ī). aryballos.

ar·y·ep·i·glot·tic (ar′ē ep′ə glot′ik), *adj.* *Anat.* pertaining to or connecting the arytenoid cartilage and the epiglottis. Also, **ar·y·ep·i·glot·tid·e·an** (ar′ē ep′ə glo-tid′ē ən), **arytenoepiglottic.** [< Gk *ary-* (deriv. of *arý(ein)* (to) draw, pull) + EPIGLOTT(IS) + -IC]

ar·yl (ar′il), *adj.* *Chem.* containing an aryl group. [AR(OMATIC) + -YL]

ar·yl·a·mine (ar′il ə mēn′, -am′in), *n.* *Chem.* any of a group of amines in which one or more of the hydrogen atoms of ammonia are replaced by aromatic groups. [ARYL + -AMINE]

ar·yl·ate (ar′ə lāt′), *v.t.,* **-at·ed, -at·ing.** *Chem.* to introduce one or more aryl groups into (a compound). [ARYL + -ATE[1]] —**ar′yl·a′tion,** *n.*

ar′yl group′, *Chem.* any organic group derived from an aromatic hydrocarbon by the removal of a hydrogen atom, as phenyl, C_6H_5–, from benzene, C_6H_6. Also called **ar′yl rad′ical.**

ar·y·te·no·ep·i·glot·tic (ar′i tē′nō ep′ə glot′ik, ə rit′-ᵊnō-), *adj.* *Anat.* aryepiglottic. [ARYTENO(ID) + EPIGLOTT(IS) + -IC]

ar·y·te·noid (ar′i tē′noid, ə rit′ᵊnoid′), *Anat.* —*adj.* **1.** pertaining to either of two small cartilages on top of the cricoid cartilage at the upper, back part of the larynx. **2.** pertaining to the muscles connected with these cartilages. **3.** pertaining to the glands in the aryepiglottic fold of the larynx. —*n.* **4.** an arytenoid cartilage, muscle, or gland. [< NL *arytaenoīd(es)* < Gk *arytainoeid(ḗs),* lit., ladle-shaped, equiv. to *arýtain(a)* ladle, pitcher, funnel + *-oeidēs* -OID] —**ar·y·te·noi·dal** (ar′i tᵊnoid′ᵊl, ə rit′ᵊnoid′-), *adj.*

a·rhyth·mi·a (ə rith′mē ə, ə rith′-), *n.* *Pathol.* arrhythmia. —**a·ryth·mic** (ə rith′mik, ə rith′-), **a·ryth′mi·cal,** *adj.* —**a·ryth′mi·cal·ly,** *adv.*

Ar·za·chel (är′sə chel′, -zə-), *n.* a crater in the third quadrant of the face of the moon: about 60 miles in diameter.

as[1] (az; *unstressed* əz), *adv.* **1.** to such a degree or extent; similarly; equally: *I didn't think the temperature was as high today as it was yesterday.* **2.** for example; for instance: *Some flowers, as the rose, require special care.* **3.** thought to be or considered to be: *the square as distinct from the rectangle; the church as separate from the state.* **4.** in the manner (directed, agreed, promised, etc.): *She sang as promised. He left as agreed.* **5. as well.** See **well**[1] (def. 9). **6. as well as.** See **well**[1] (def. 10). —*conj.* **7.** (used correlatively after an adjective or adverb prec. by an adverbial phrase, the adverbial *as,* or another adverb) to such a degree or extent that: *It came out the same way as it did before. You are as good as you think you are.* **8.** (without antecedent) in the degree, manner, etc., of or that: *She's good as gold. Do as we do.* **9.** at the same time that; while; when: *as you look away.* **10.** since; because: *As you are leaving last, please turn out the lights.* **11.** though: *Questionable as it may be, we will proceed.* **12.** *Informal.* (in independent clauses) that: *I don't know as I do.* **13.** *Brit. Dial.* than. **14. as . . . as,** similar or equal to: *as rich as Croesus.* **15. as for,** with respect to; in reference to: *As for staying away, I wouldn't think of it.* **16. as good as, a.** equivalent to; in effect; practically; *as good as new.* **b.** true to; trustworthy as: *as good as his word.* **17. as if,** as it would be if: *It was as if the world had come to an end.* **18. as is,** *Informal.* in whatever condition something happens to be: *We bought the table as is.* **19. as it were,** in a way; so to speak: *He became, as it were, a man without a country.* **20. as long as,** provided that; since: *As long as you feel that way about it, we'll forget it.* **21. as regards,** with regard or reference to; concerning: *As regards the expense involved, it is of no concern to him.* **22. as such, a.** as being what is indicated; in that capacity: *The officer of the law, as such, is entitled to respect.* **b.** in itself or in themselves: *The position, as such, does not appeal to him, but the salary is a lure.* **23. as yet,** up to the present time; until now: *As yet, no man has set foot on Mars.* —*pron.* **24.** (used relatively) that; who; which (usually prec. by *such* or *the same*): *I have the same trouble as you had.* **25.** a fact that: *She did her job well, as can be proved by the records.* —*prep.* **26.** in the role, function, or status of: *to act as chairman.* [ME *as, als, alse, also* < OE *alswā, ealswā* ALL SO (see ALSO), quite so, quite as, as]

—**Syn. 10.** See **because.**

—**Usage.** As is usually considered less desirable than SINCE or BECAUSE because it seems weaker and less explicit: *Because* (not *As*) *the train was late, we missed the parade.*

Although educated usage now accepts AS . . . AS in both positive and negative comparisons, some people still restrict AS . . . AS to positive comparisons and so . . . AS to negative comparisons: *He is as fat as I am. She is not so smart as her sister.*

AS TO is generally less acceptable than ABOUT, OF, ON, or UPON: *They argued about* (not *as to*) *the price.* When followed by *whether,* it is redundant to use AS TO: *I will notify him whether* (not *as to whether*) *to leave.* There is no objection to AS TO at the beginning of a sentence when it introduces an element that would otherwise have less emphasis: *As to his salary, there is no room for improvement.*

as[2] (as), *n., pl.* **as·ses** (as′iz). **1.** a copper coin and early monetary unit of ancient Rome, originally having a nominal weight of a pound of 12 ounces: discontinued c80 B.C. **2.** a unit of weight: 12 ounces: the pound. equal to 327.4 grams or 5153 grains. [< L: a unit, unity, a copper coin]

As, *Chem.* arsenic (def. 1).

as-, var. of **ad-** before *s: assert.*

AS, Anglo-Saxon. Also, **AS., A.-S., A.S.**

A.S., **1.** Associate in Science. **2.** Anglo-Saxon.

A·sa (ā′sə), *n.* **1.** a king of Judah, 913?–873? B.C. I Kings 15:8–24. **2.** a boy's given name.

A·sa (u′shə), *n.* *Zoroastrianism.* the principle of good. Cf. **Drug.**

ASA, **1.** Acoustical Society of America. **2.** American Standards Association.

As·a·el (as′ā əl, ā′sā-), *n.* a boy's given name.

as·a·fet·i·da (as′ə fet′i də), *n.* *Chem.* a soft, brown, lumpy, somewhat liquid gum resin having a bitter, acrid taste and an obnoxious, alliaceous odor, obtained from the roots of several umbelliferous plants of the genus *Ferula:* a condiment formerly used in medicine as a carminative and antispasmodic. Also, **a′sa·foe′ti·da, assafetida, assafoetida.** Also called **devil's dung, food of the gods.** [< ML *asafoetida,* equiv. to LL *asa* (< Pers *azā* mastic, gum) + L *foetida,* fem. of *foetidus* FETID]

A·sag (ä′säg), *n.* (in Sumerian mythology) a demon living in Kur.

A·sa·hi·ga·wa (ä′sä hē′gä wä), *n.* a city on central Hokkaido, in N Japan. 164,966 (1955). Also, **A·sa·hi·ka·wa** (ä′sä hē′kä wä).

a·sa·na (ä′sə nə), *n.* any of the postures in a Yoga exercise. [< Skt]

A·sar (ä′sär), *n.pl.* Aesir.

A·sa·rah Be·te·bet (ä sä rä′ bə tā′bāt), a Jewish fast day observed on the 10th day of the month of Tebet in memory of the beginning of the siege of Jerusalem in 586 B.C. by the Babylonians under King Nebuchadnezzar. Also, **A·sa·rah Be·te·vet** (ä sôr′ə bə tā′vās).

as·a·ro·tum (as′ə rō′təm), *n., pl.* **-ta** (-tə). (in ancient Roman architecture) a painted pavement. [< L < Gk *asárōton* kind of pavement, n. use of neut. of *asárōtos,* lit., unswept, equiv. to *a-* A-[6] + *sárōtos* (*sarō-* var. s. of *saróein* to sweep clean + *-tos* ptp. suffix)]

as·a·rum (as′ər əm), *n.* *Chem.* the dried rhizom and roots of wild ginger that yield an acrid resin and a volatile, aromatic oil, used chiefly in medicine. [< L < Gk *ásaron* hazelwort, wild spikenard]

A·sat (u′sut), *n.* *Hinduism.* (in Vedic mythology) the realm of nonexistence, populated by demons. Cf. **sat**[2] (def. 1).

asb., asbestos.

As·ben (äs ben′), *n.* Aïr.

as·bes·tos (as bes′təs, az-), *n.* **1.** *Mineral.* **a.** a fibrous amphibole, used for making incombustible or fireproof articles. **b.** the mineral chrysotile, similarly used. **2.** a fabric woven from asbestos fibers, used for theater curtains, firemen's gloves, etc. **3.** *Theat.* a fireproof curtain. Also, **as·bes′tus.** [< L < Gk: lit., unquenched, equiv. to *a-* A-[6] + *sbestós* (*sbes-* var. s. of *sbennýnai* to quench + *-tos* ptp. suffix); r. ME *asbeston,* etc. < MF] —**as·bes·tine** (as bes′tin, az-), **as·bes′tous,** *adj.* —**as·bes′toid, as′bes·toi′dal,** *adj.*

asbes′tos ce·ment′, a compound of asbestos fiber and portland cement, used for various nonstructural building purposes.

as·bes·to·sis (as′be stō′sis, az′-), *n.* *Pathol.* a lung condition caused by the inhalation of asbestos dust. [< NL; see ASBESTOS, -OSIS]

As·björn·sen (äs′byûrn sən), *n.* **Pe·ter Chris·ten** (pā′tər kris′tən), 1812–85, Norwegian naturalist and folklorist.

as·bo·lane (az′bə lān′, as′-), *n.* *Mineral.* a manganese wad containing cobalt oxide. [< Gk *asból(ē)* soot + -ANE]

As·bur·y (az′bə rē), *n.* **Francis,** 1745–1816, English missionary: first bishop of the Methodist Church in America.

As′bur·y Park′ (az′ber′ē, -bə rē), a city in E New Jersey: seashore resort. 17,366 (1960).

As·cal·a·bus (ə skal′ə bəs), *n.* *Class. Myth.* a youth who was changed into a lizard for mocking Demeter for her greed.

As·cal·a·phus (ə skal′ə fəs), *n.* *Class. Myth.* **1.** a gardener in the underworld who, on learning that Persephone could leave Hades provided she had eaten no food there, claimed that he had seen her eat pomegranate seeds. As punishment, he was changed into an owl by Demeter. **2.** a son of Ares who joined the Argonauts and who served as a sentry under Agamemnon in the Trojan War. He was killed by Deïphobus.

As·ca·ni·us (a skā′nē əs), *n.* *Class. Myth.* the son of Aeneas and Creusa, and founder of Alba Longa. Also, **Iulus.** —**As·ca′ni·an,** *adj.*

ASCAP (as′kap), *n.* American Society of Composers, Authors, and Publishers.

as·ca·ri·a·sis (as′kə rī′ə sis), *n.* *Pathol.* infestation with ascarids, esp. *Ascaris lumbricoides.* [< NL; see ASCAR(ID), -IASIS]

as·ca·rid (as′kə rid), *n.* any nematode of the family *Ascaridae,* including the roundworms and pinworms. [< NL *ascarid(ae)* name of the genus < Gk *askarid(es)* threadworms, pinworms (pl. of *askarís*)]

as·car·i·dole (ə skar′i dōl′), *n.* *Chem.* a liquid, $C_{10}H_{16}O_2$, constituting the active principle of chenopodium oil, used chiefly as a catalyst in polymerization reactions. [ASCARID + -OLE]

as·cend (ə send′), *v.i.* **1.** to move, climb, or go upward; mount; rise: *The airplane ascended into the clouds.* **2.** to slant upward. **3.** to rise to a higher point or degree; proceed from an inferior to a superior degree or level. **4.** to go toward the source or beginning; go back in time. **5.** *Music.* to rise in pitch; pass from any tone to a higher one. —*v.t.* **6.** to go or move upward upon or along; climb; mount: *to ascend a lookout tower; to ascend stairs.* **7.** to gain or succeed to; acquire: *to ascend the throne.* [ME *ascende(n)* < L *ascende(re)* (to) climb up, equiv. to *a-* A-[5] + *-scendere,* var. of *scandere* to climb. See SCAN] —**as·cend′a·ble, as·cend′i·ble,** *adj.*

—**Syn. 1.** soar. **3.** tower. **6.** See **climb.** —**Ant. 1, 6.** descend.

as·cend·an·cy (ə sen′dən sē), *n.* state of being in the ascendant; governing or controlling influence; domination. Also, **as·cend′en·cy, as·cend′ance, as·cend′ence.** [ASCEND(ANT) + -ANCY]

—**Syn.** primacy, predomination, command, sovereignty, mastery.

as·cend·ant (ə sen′dənt), *n.* **1.** a position of dominance or controlling influence: possession of power, superiority, or preeminence: *His rivals were in the ascendant, and he lost the commission.* **2.** an ancestor; forebear. **3.** *Astrol.* the point of the ecliptic or the sign of the zodiac rising above the horizon at the time of a birth, etc. **4.** **in the ascendant,** increasing in prosperity, influence, authority, or renown: *His fortunes are in the ascendant.* —*adj.* **5.** ascending; rising. **6.** superior; predominant. **7.** *Bot.* directed or curved upward. Also, **as·cend′ent.** [ME *ascendent* < L *ascendent-* (s. of *ascendēns*) climbing up. See ASCEND, -ENT, -ANT]

as·cend·er (ə sen′dər), *n.* **1.** one who or that which ascends or causes ascension. **2.** *Print.* **a.** the part of a lower-case letter, as b, d, f, h, that rises above x-height. **b.** a letter rising above x-height, as b, d, f, h, etc. [ASCEND + -ER[1]]

as·cend·ing (ə sen′ding), *adj.* **1.** moving upward; rising. **2.** *Bot.* growing or directed upward, esp. obliquely or in a curve from the base. [ASCEND + -ING[2]] —**as·cend′ing·ly,** *adv.*

ascend′ing node′, *Astron.* the node through which an orbiting body passes as it moves to the north (opposed to *descending node*).

As·ce·nez (as′kə nēz′), *n.* *Douay Bible.* Ashkenaz.

as·cen·sion (ə sen′shən), *n.* **1.** act of ascending; ascent. **2.** **the Ascension,** the bodily ascending of Christ from earth to heaven. **3.** (*cap.*) See **Ascension Day.** [ME *ascencion* < L *ascēnsiōn-* (s. of *ascēnsiō*), equiv. to *ascēns(us)* risen up (ptp. of *ascendere*: (*ascend-* climb up (see ASCEND) + *-tus* ptp. suffix) + *-iōn-* -ION] —**as·cen′sion·al,** *adj.*

As·cen·sion (ə sen′shən), *n.* a British island in the S Atlantic Ocean. 210 (est. 1960); 34 sq. mi.

Ascen′sion Day′, the 40th day after Easter, commemorating the Ascension of Christ; Holy Thursday.

as·cen·sive (ə sen′siv), *adj.* ascending; rising. [ASCENS(ION) + -IVE]

as·cent (ə sent′), *n.* **1.** act of ascending; upward movement; a rising movement: *the ascent of smoke.* **2.** movement upward from a lower to a higher state, degree, grade, or status; advancement: *His ascent to the governorship came after a long political career.* **3.** act of climbing or traveling up. **4.** the way or means of ascending; upward slope; acclivity. **5.** a procedure toward a source or beginning. **6.** the degree of inclination; gradient. [deriv. of ASCEND, on the model of DESCENT]

as·cer·tain (as′ər tān′), *v.t.* **1.** to find out definitely; learn with certainty or assurance; determine: *to ascertain the facts.* **2.** *Archaic.* to make certain, clear, or definitely known. [late ME, var. of *assertain, acertain* < MF *acertain* (tonic s. of *acertener* to make certain), equiv. to *a-* A-[5] + *certain* CERTAIN] —**as′cer·tain′a·ble,** *adj.* —**as′cer·tain′a·ble·ness,** *n.* —**as′cer·tain′a·bly,** *adv.* —**as′cer·tain′er,** *n.* —**as′cer·tain′ment,** *n.*
—**Syn. 1.** See **learn.**

as·cet·ic (ə set′ik), *n.* **1.** one who dedicates his life to a pursuit of contemplative ideals and practices extreme self-denial or self-mortification for religious reasons. **2.** any person who leads an austerely simple life, esp. one who abstains from the normal pleasures of life or denies himself material satisfaction. **3.** (in the early Christian church) a monk; hermit. —*adj.* **4.** pertaining to asceticism. **5.** rigorously abstinent; austere: *an ascetic existence.* **6.** exceedingly strict or severe in religious exercises or self-mortification. [< Gk *askētikós* rigorous, hardworking, equiv. to *askē-* (var. s. of *askeîn* to work hard, discipline oneself) + *-tikos* -TIC]
—**Syn. 3.** anchorite, recluse; cenobite. **5.** strict, frugal, plain. **6.** fanatic. —**Ant. 5.** self-indulgent.

as·cet·i·cal (ə set′i kəl), *adj.* pertaining to ascetic discipline or practice. [ASCETIC + -AL[1]] —**as·cet′i·cal·ly,** *adv.*

ascet′ical theol′ogy, the branch of theology dealing with virtue, holiness, and their attainment.

as·cet·i·cism (ə set′i siz′əm), *n.* **1.** the manner of life, practices, or principles of an ascetic. **2.** the doctrine that a person can attain a high spiritual and moral state by practicing self-denial, self-mortification, and the like. **3.** rigorous self-denial; extreme abstinence; austerity. [ASCETIC + -ISM]

Asch (ash), *n.* **Sho·lom** (shô′ləm) or **Sho·lem** (shō′ləm, -lem), 1880–1957, U.S. author, born in Poland.

As·cham (as′kəm), *n.* **Roger,** 1515–68, English scholar and writer: tutor of Queen Elizabeth.

Asch′heim-Zon′dek test′ (äsh′hīm tson′dek, -zon′-), a test for determining the pregnancy of a woman by noting the effect on the ovaries of an immature mouse injected with her urine. Also called **A-Z test.** [named after S. Aschheim (b. 1878) and B. Zondek (b. 1891), German gynecologists]

A′schoff bod′y (ä′shôf), *Pathol.* any of the spindle-shaped nodules found in heart tissue, usually associated with rheumatic fever. Also, **A′schoff nod′ule.** [named after Ludwig *Aschoff* (d. 1942), German pathologist]

as·ci (as′ī), *n.* pl. of **ascus.**

as·cid·i·an (ə sid′ē ən), *Zool.* —*n.* **1.** any solitary or colonial tunicate of the class *Ascidiacea,* exhibiting the vertebrate characteristics of nerve cord and notochord in the larvae only. —*adj.* **2.** belonging or pertaining to the class *Ascidiacea.* [ASCIDI(UM) + -AN]

as·cid·i·um (ə sid′ē əm), *n., pl.* **-cid·i·a** (-sid′ē ə). *Bot.* a baglike or pitcherlike part. [< NL < Gk *askídion* a small bag, equiv. to *ask(ós)* bag + *-idion* -IDIUM]

as·ci·tes (ə sī′tēz), *n.* *Pathol.* accumulation of serous fluid in the peritoneal cavity; dropsy of the peritoneum. [< L < Gk *askítēs* (*hýdrōps*) abdominal (dropsy), equiv. to *ask(ós)* belly + *-ītēs* -ITE[1]] —**as·cit·ic** (ə sit′ik), **as·cit′i·cal,** *adj.*

As·clep·i (as klep′ē), *n.* a crater in the fourth quadrant of the face of the moon: about 22 miles in diameter.

as·cle·pi·a·da·ceous (ə sklē′pē ə dā′shəs), *adj.* belonging to the *Asclepiadaceae,* or milkweed family of plants. [< NL *Asclēpiad-* (s. of *Asclēpias* genus name, L: swallowwort < Gk *asklēpiás,* a plant named after *Asklēpiós* ASCLEPIUS) + -ACEOUS]

As·cle·pi·a·de (as′klə pī′ə dē′), *n.pl.* *Class. Myth.* the descendants of Asclepius.

As·cle·pi·a·de·an (ə sklē′pē ə dē′ən), *Class. Pros.* —*adj.* **1.** noting or pertaining to a verse consisting of a spondee, two or three choriambi, and an iamb. —*n.* **2.** an Asclepiadean verse. [< Gk *Asklēpiádei(os)* pertaining to *Asclepiades,* third-century Greek poet to whom the verse was attributed + -AN]

As·cle·pi·us (ə sklē′pē əs), *n.* a son of Apollo and the ancient Greek god of medicine and healing, identified by the Romans with Aesculapius.

asco-, a learned borrowing from Greek meaning "sac," used in the formation of compound words: *ascomycete.* [< Gk *asko-,* comb. form of *askós* wineskin, bladder, belly]

as·co·carp (as′kə kärp′), *n.* *Bot.* (in ascomycetous fungi) the fructification bearing the asci, as an apothecium, perithecium, etc. [ASCO- + -CARP] —**as′co·carp′ous,** *adj.*

as·cog·e·nous (a skoj′ə nəs), *adj.* *Bot.* of, pertaining to, or producing asci. [ASCO- + -GENOUS]

as·co·go·ni·um (as′kə gō′nē əm), *n., pl.* **-ni·a** (-nē ə). *Bot.* **1.** the female sexual organ in certain ascomycetous fungi. **2.** the portion of the archicarp in certain ascomycetous fungi which receives the antheridial nuclei and puts out the hyphae bearing the asci. [ASCO- + -GONIUM] —**as′co·go′ni·al,** *adj.*

as·co·my·cete (as′kə mī sēt′), *n.* *Bot.* a fungus of the class *Ascomycetes,* including the yeasts, mildews, truffles, etc., characterized by bearing the sexual spores in a sac, the ascus. [ASCO- + -MYCETE(S)]

as·co·my·ce·tous (as′kə mī sē′təs), *adj.* *Bot.* belonging or pertaining to the *Ascomycetes.* [ASCOMYCETE + -OUS]

as·con (as′kon), *n.* *Zool.* a type of sponge having an oval shape and a thin body wall with pores leading directly into the spongocoel. Cf. **leucon, sycon.** [alter. of Gk *askós* skin]

as·co·noid (as′kə noid′), *adj.* pertaining to or resembling an ascon. [ASCON + -OID]

a·scor′bic ac′id (ā skôr′bik, ə skôr′-), *Biochem.* a white, crystalline, water-soluble vitamin, $C_6H_8O_6$, occurring in citrus fruits, green vegetables, etc., usually produced synthetically, essential for normal metabolism: used in the prevention and treatment of scurvy, and in wound-healing and tissue repair. Also called **vitamin C.** [A-[6] + SCORB- (UT)IC]

as·co·spore (as′kə spōr′, -spôr′), *n.* *Bot.* a spore formed within an ascus. [ASCO- + SPORE] —**as·co·spor·ic** (as′kə spôr′ik, -spor′-), **as·cos·po·rous** (as kos′pər əs, as′kə spōr′-, -spôr′-), *adj.*

as·cot (as′kət), *n.* a scarf or necktie with broad ends, tied and arranged so that the ends are laid flat, one across the other. [so called from the fashionable dress worn at the Ascot races]

Ascot

As·cot (as′kət), *n.* a village in SE Berkshire, in S England: annual horse races.

as·cribe (ə skrīb′), *v.t.,* **-cribed, -crib·ing.** **1.** to credit or assign, as to a cause or source; attribute; impute: *The alphabet is usually ascribed to the Phoenicians.* **2.** to attribute or think of as belonging, as a quality or characteristic: *The author ascribed innocence and delicacy to his young ladies of the middle class.* [late ME < L *ascrībe(re),* equiv. to *a-* A-[5] + *scrībere* SCRIBE[2]; r. ME *ascrive* < MF. See SHRIVE] —**a·scrib′a·ble,** *adj.*
—**Syn. 1.** See **attribute.**

as·crip·tion (ə skrip′shən), *n.* **1.** act of ascribing. **2.** a statement ascribing something, esp. praise to the Deity. Also, **adscription.** [< L *ascrīptiōn-* (s. of *ascrīptiō*) a written addition. See A-[5], SCRIPT, -ION]

as·cus (as′kəs), *n., pl.* **as·ci** (as′ī). *Bot.* the sac in ascomycetes in which the sexual spores are formed. [< NL < Gk *askós* bag, sac]

As·cus (as′kəs), *n.* *Class. Myth.* a giant who helped Lycurgus chain Dionysus.

asdic (az′dik), *n.* *Brit.* sonar. [*A(nti-) S(ubmarine) D(etection) I(nvestigation) C(ommittee)*]

-ase, *Chem.* a suffix used in the names of enzymes: *oxidase.* [abstracted from DIASTASE]

a·se·i·ty (ə sē′i tē, ā sē′-), *n.* *Metaphys.* existence originating from and having no source other than itself. [< ML *aseït(ās),* equiv. to L *a se* from oneself (*a* A-[4] + *sē* oneself) + *-itās* -ITY]

a·se·mi·a (ə sē′mē ə), *n.* *Psychiatry.* inability to comprehend or use communicative symbols, as words, gestures, etc. [< Gk *ásēm(os)* signless (*a-* A-[6] + *sēm(a)* sign + *-os* adj. suffix) + *-ia* -IA] —**a·se·mic** (ə sem′ik), *adj.*

As·e·nath (as′ə nath′), *n.* the wife of Joseph and the mother of Manasseh and Ephraim. Gen. 41:45; 46:20. Also, *Douay Bible,* **As·e·neth** (as′ə neth′).

a·sep·sis (ə sep′sis, ā-), *n.* **1.** absence of the microorganisms that produce sepsis or septic disease. **2.** *Med.* methods or treatment, as by surgical operation, characterized by the use of instruments, dressings, etc., that are free from such microorganisms. [A-[6] + SEPSIS]

a·sep·tic (ə sep′tik, ā sep′-), *adj.* free from the living germs of disease, fermentation, or putrefaction. [A-[6] + SEPTIC] —**a·sep′ti·cal·ly,** *adv.* —**a·sep·ti·cism** (ə sep′ti siz′əm, ā sep′-), *n.*

A·ser (ā′sər), *n.* *Douay Bible.* Asher.

a·sex·u·al (ā sek′shōō əl), *adj.* *Biol.* **1.** not sexual. **2.** having no sex or no sexual organs. **3.** independent of sexual processes. [A-[6] + SEXUAL] —**a·sex·u·al·i·ty** (ā sek′shōō al′i tē), *n.* —**a·sex′u·al·ly,** *adv.*

a·sex·u·al·ise (ā sek′shōō ə līz′), *v.t.,* **-ised, -is·ing.** *Chiefly Brit.* asexualize. —**a·sex′u·al·i·sa′tion,** *n.*

a·sex·u·al·ize (ā sek′shōō ə līz′), *v.t.,* **-ized, -iz·ing.** to make incapable of reproduction, as by castrating. [ASEXUAL + -IZE] —**a·sex′u·al·i·za′tion,** *n.*

asex′ual reproduc′tion, *Biol.* reproduction, as budding, fission, spore formation, etc., not involving the union of gametes.

A·se·yev (ä se′yəf), *n.* **Ni·ko·lay Ni·ko·la·e·vich** (ni ko lī′ ni ko lä′yə vich), born 1889, Russian poet.

As·gard (äs′gärd, as′-), *n.* *Scand. Myth.* the home of the Aesir, where Valhalla and the palaces of the individual gods were: connected with the earth by the rainbow bridge, Bifrost. Also, **As·garth** (äs′gärth), **As·gar·dhr** (äs′gär thər). [< Icel *Ásgarthr,* lit., god-courtyard, equiv. to *ās* god (c. OE *ōs*) + *garthr* yard; see GARTH]

Ás·geirs·son (äs′gâr sən), *n.* **As·geir** (äs′gâr), born 1894, Icelandic statesman: president since 1952.

asgmt., assignment.

ash[1] (ash), *n.* **1.** the powdery residue of matter that remains after burning: *Don't drop your cigarette ash. The ashes of the fire are still hot.* **2.** See **sodium carbonate** (def. 1). **3.** *Geol.* finely pulverized lava thrown out by a volcano in eruption. **4.** a light, silvery-gray color. **5.** **ashes, a.** deathlike grayness; extreme pallor suggestive of death. **b.** ruins, esp. the residue of something destroyed; remains; vestiges: *the ashes of their love; the ashes of the past.* **c.** mortal remains, esp. physical or corporeal man as liable to decay. **d.** anything, as an act, gesture, speech, feeling, etc., that is symbolic of penance, regret, remorse, or the like: *He put ashes on his head, apologized profusely, but then went glibly about his business.* **6.** Also, **æsc.** the symbol "æ." [ME *asche,* OE *asce, æsce;* c. Icel *aska,* OHG *asca* (< G *Asche*), Goth *azgō*] —**ash′less,** *adj.*

ash[2] (ash), *n.* **1.** any oleaceous tree of the genus *Fraxinus,* esp. *F. excelsior,* of Europe and Asia, or *F. americana* **(white ash),** of North America. **2.** the wood, tough, straight-grained, and elastic, and valued as timber. [ME *asch,* OE *æsc;* c. OHG *ask* (> G *Esche*), Icel *ask(r);* akin to L *ornus,* Lith *úosis*]

As·hab (äs′häb), *n.pl., sing.* **Sa·hib** (sä′ib, -ēb). *Islam.* those associating with Muhammad at any time in his life. Cf. **Ansar, Muhajirun.**

a·shake (ə shāk′), *adj.* shaking (usually used predicatively): *The very hills were ashake with the violence of the storm.* [A-[1] + SHAKE]

a·shamed (ə shāmd′), *adj.* **1.** feeling shame; distressed or embarrassed by emotions of guilt, foolishness, or disgrace: *He felt ashamed for having spoken insincerely.* **2.** unwilling; restrained by the fear of shame, ridicule, or disapproval: *They were ashamed to show their work.* [orig. ptp. of earlier *ashame* (v.), to be ashamed, OE *ā-scamian,* equiv. to *ā-* A-[3] + *scamian* to SHAME] —**a·sham·ed·ly** (ə shā′mid lē), *adv.* —**a·sham′ed·ness,** *n.*
—**Syn. 1.** ASHAMED, HUMILIATED, MORTIFIED refer to a condition or feeling of discomfort or embarrassment. ASHAMED focuses on the sense of one's own responsibility for an act, whether it is foolish, improper, or immoral: *He was ashamed of his dishonesty. She was ashamed of her mistake.* HUMILIATED stresses a feeling of being humbled or disgraced, without any necessary implication of guilt: *He was humiliated by the king.* Both words are used equally in situations in which one is felt to be responsible for the actions of another: *Robert felt humiliated by his daughter's behavior. Mom was ashamed of the way I looked.* MORTIFIED represents an intensification of the feelings implied by the other two words: *She was mortified by her clumsiness.*

A·shan·ti (ə shan′tē), *n.* **1.** a former native kingdom and British colony in W Africa: now a region of Ghana. 1,108,548 (1960); 9700 sq. mi. *Cap.:* Kumasi. **2.** a native or inhabitant of Ashanti.

Ash·burn (ash′bərn), *n.* a town in central Georgia. 3291 (1960).

Ash·bur·ton (ash′bûr′tən, -bər tən), *n.* **1st Baron** See **Baring, Alexander.**

Ash′bur·y met′al (ash′ber′ē, -bə rē), an alloy of about 80 percent tin, 15 percent antimony, and 5 percent copper, nickel, and zinc. Also, **Ash′ber·ry met′al.**

Ash·by (ash′bē), *n.* a boy's given name.

ash·can (ash′kan′), *n.* **1.** a can or metal receptacle for ashes, garbage, or refuse. **2.** *Informal.* a depth charge. **3.** *Motion Pictures.* an arc light of 1000 watts, enclosed in a reflector. [ASH[1] + CAN[2]]

Ash′can School′, (*sometimes l.c.*) *Fine Arts.* a group of American painters of the early 20th century whose genre paintings were derived from city life.

Ash·che·naz (ash′kə naz′), *n.* Ashkenaz.

ash′ col′or. See **ash gray.**

Ash·croft (ash′krôft, -kroft), *n.* **Dame Peggy** (*Edith Margaret Emily Ashcroft*), born 1907, English actress.

Ash·dod (ash′dod), *n.* a town in W Israel: an important ancient Philistine city; early center of Christianity. 15,600 (1963). Also, **Esdud.** Greek, **Azotos.**

Ash·down (ash′doun′), *n.* a town in SW Arkansas. 2725 (1960).

Ashe·bor·o (ash′bûr ō, -bur ō), *n.* a town in central North Carolina. 9449 (1960).

ash·en[1] (ash′ən), *adj.* **1.** ash-colored; gray. **2.** extremely pale; drained of color; pallid: *His face was ashen.* **3.** consisting of ashes. [ASH[1] + -EN[2]]
—**Syn. 1.** ashy. **2.** pasty, colorless.

ash·en[2] (ash′ən), *adj.* **1.** pertaining to the ash tree or its timber. **2.** made of wood from the ash tree. [OE *æscen* (c. MLG *eschen,* MHG *eschin*), equiv. to *æsc* ASH[2] + *-en* -EN[2]]

Ash·er (ash′ər), *n.* Also, *Douay Bible,* **Aser. 1.** a son of Jacob and Zilpah. Gen. 30:12–13. **2.** one of the 12 tribes of Israel. **3.** Also, **Ashur.** a boy's given name.

A·she·rah (ə shēr′ə), *n., pl.* **A·she·rim** (ə shēr′im), **A·she·rahs** for 2. **1.** an ancient Semitic goddess, sometimes identified with Ashtoreth and Astarte, worshiped by the Phoenicians and Canaanites. **2.** any of various upright wooden objects serving as a sacred symbol of Asherah.

Ash·er·ite (ash′ə rīt′), *n.* a member of the tribe of Asher. [ASHER + -ITE[1]]

Ashe·ville (ash′vil), *n.* a city in W North Carolina. 60,192 (1960).

Ash·ford (ash′fərd), *n.* a boy's given name.

ash′ gray′, pale gray resembling the color of ashes. Also called **ash color.**

A·shi·ka·ga (ä′shē kä′gä), *n.* a member of a powerful family in Japan that ruled as shoguns 1338–1573.

Ash·ke·naz (ash′kə naz′), *n.* **1.** a son of Gomer and grandson of Japheth. Gen 10:1–3; I Chron. 1–6. **2.** an ancient kingdom in eastern Armenia. Also, **Ashchenaz;** *Douay Bible,* **Ascenez.**

Ash·ke·naz·im (äsh′kə nä′zim), *n.pl., sing.* **-naz·i** (-nä′zē). Jews of central and eastern Europe, or their descendants, distinguished from the Sephardim chiefly by their liturgy, religious customs, and pronunciation of Hebrew. [< Heb: pl. of *Ashkenazi,* equiv. to ASHKENAZ + *-i* suffix of membership] —**Ash′ke·naz′ic,** *adj.*

Ash·kha·bad (äsh′kə bäd′; *Russ.* ush khu bät′), *n.* **a city in and the capital of Turkmenistan, in the S part. 312,000. Formerly, Poltoratsk.**

Ash·land (ash′lənd), *n.* **1.** a city in NE Kentucky, on the Ohio River. 31,283 (1960). **2.** a city in N central Ohio. 17,419 (1960). **3.** a town in SW Oregon. 9119 (1960). **4.** a town in central Pennsylvania. 5237 (1960). **5.** a town in central Virginia. 2773 (1960).

ash·lar (ash′lər), *n.* **1.** a squared building stone cut more or less true on all faces adjacent to those of other stones so as to permit very thin mortar joints. **2.** such stones collectively. **3.** masonry made of them. **4.** *Carpentry.* a short stud between joists and sloping rafters, esp. near the eaves. —*v.t.* **5.** to face with ashlars. Also, **ash′ler.** [ME *ascheler* < MF *aissel(i)er* < L *axillār(is),* equiv. to *axill(a)* (*axis* board, plank, AXIS + *-illa* dim. suffix) + *-āris* -AR[2]]

Ashlar
A, Coursed ashlar, rusticated; B, Random ashlar

ash·lar·ing (ash′lər ing), *n.* **1.** *Masonry.* the act of facing a wall with ashlars. **2.** *Building Trades.* ashlars collectively. [ASHLAR + -ING[1]]

ash′lar line′, *Building Trades.* a horizontal line, indicated at a building site with a taut string, through which the exterior surface plane of a masonry wall passes.

Ash·ley (ash′lē), *n.* **1.** a town in central Pennsylvania. 4258 (1960). **2.** a boy's given name.

ash·man (ash′man′), *n., pl.* **-men.** a man who collects and disposes of ashes, garbage, and refuse. [ASH[1] + MAN[1]]

a·shore (ə shōr′, ə shôr′), *adv.* **1.** to the shore; onto the shore: *The schooner was driven ashore.* **2.** on the shore; on land rather than at sea or on the water: *The captain has been ashore for two hours.* [A-[1] + SHORE[1]]

ash·ram (äsh′rəm), *n.* *Hinduism.* a place in which people meet for religious instruction or exercises in common. Also, **asrama.** [< Skt *āśrama* (place) for religious exercise, equiv. to *ā* towards + *śrama* exertion, fatigue]

Ash·ta·bu·la (ash′tə byo͞o′lə), *n.* a port in NE Ohio, on Lake Erie. 24,559 (1960).

Ash·ton (ash′tən), *n.* **1. Sir Frederick** (*William*), born 1906, English dancer and choreographer, born in Ecuador. **2.** a boy's given name.

Ash·ton-un·der-Lyne (ash′tən un′dər līn′), *n.* a city in E Lancashire, in W England, near Manchester. 50,165 (1961).

Ash·to·reth (ash′tə reth′), *n.* an ancient Semitic goddess, the counterpart of the Phoenician Astarte. [< Heb < Phoenician. See ASTARTE]

ash·tray (ash′trā′), *n.* a receptacle for tobacco ashes. [ASH[1] + TRAY]

A·shur (ä′sho͝or for 1; ash′ər for 2), *n.* **1.** Assur. **2.** Also, **Asher.** a boy's given name.

A·shur·ba·ni·pal (ä′sho͝or bä′nē päl′), *n.* died 626? B.C., king of Assyria 668?–616? B.C. Also, **Assurbanipal.**

A·shur·na·sir·pal II (ä′sho͝or nä′zir päl′), ("*the Merciless*") died 859? B.C., warrior king of Assyria 884?–859 B.C. Cf. **Sardanapalus.** Also, **Assurnasirpal II, A·shur-na·sir-a·pal II** (ä′sho͝or nä′zir ä päl′).

Ash′ Wednes′day, 1. the first day of Lent. **2.** (*italics.*) a poem (1930) by T. S. Eliot.

ash·y (ash′ē), *adj.,* **ash·i·er, ash·i·est. 1.** ash-colored; pale; wan: *an ashy complexion.* **2.** of or resembling ashes: *an ashy residue left from a burnt compound.* **3.** sprinkled or covered with ashes. [ASH[1] + -Y[1]]

A·sia (ā′zhə, ā′shə), *n.* a continent bounded by Europe and the Arctic, Pacific, and Indian Oceans. 1,580,229,000 (est. 1961); ab. 16,000,000 sq. mi.

A′sia Mi′nor, a peninsula in W Asia between the Black and Mediterranean seas, including most of Asiatic Turkey. Cf. **Anatolia.**

A·sian (ā′zhən, ā′shən), *adj.* **1.** of, belonging to, or characteristic of Asia or its inhabitants. —*n.* **2.** a native of Asia. [< L *Asiān(us)* < Gk *Asiānós.* See ASIA, -AN]

A′sian chol′era, *Pathol.* cholera (def. 1b).

A′sian flu′, *Pathol.* a form of influenza caused by a virus believed to have been carried from Asia. Also called **A′sian influen′za.**

A·si·an·ic (ā′zhē an′ik, ā′shē-, ā′zē-), *adj.* of or belonging to a group of languages that were spoken in Asia Minor and Mesopotamia, are not generally accepted as related to one another or to any other language, and have been extinct since ancient times. The known Asianic languages are of two distinct kinds: those written in cuneiform and extinct before 500 B.C., as Sumerian and Elamite, and those written in Greek-derived scripts and known only from records dating after 500 B.C., as Carian and Pisidian. [ASIAN + -IC]

A·si·at·ic (ā′zhē at′ik, ā′shē-, ā′zē-), *n., adj.* *Sometimes Offensive.* Asian. [< L *Asiātic(us)* < Gk *Asiātikós.* See ASIA, -ATIC] —**A′si·at′i·cal·ly,** *adv.*

A′siat′ic bee′tle. See **oriental beetle.**

A′siat′ic flu′, *Pathol.* See **Asian flu.** Also called **Asiat′ic influen′za.**

A′siat′ic globe′flower, a hardy, perennial herb, *Trollius asiaticus,* of Siberia, having bronze-green leaves and solitary, orange-colored flowers.

a·side (ə sīd′), *adv.* **1.** on or to one side; to or at a short distance; apart; away from some position or direction: *to turn aside.* **2.** away from one's thoughts or consideration: *to put one's cares aside.* **3.** in reserve; in a separate place, as for safekeeping; apart; away: *to put some money aside.* **4.** away from a present group, esp. for reasons of privacy; off to another part, as of a room; into or to a separate place: *He took him aside and talked business.* **5.** in spite of; put apart; notwithstanding: *all kidding aside; unusual circumstances aside.* **6. aside from,** *U.S. Informal.* **a.** apart from; besides; excluding: *Aside from his salary, he receives money from investments.* **b.** except for: *They had no more food, aside from a few stale rolls.* —*n.* **7.** *Theat.* a part of an actor's lines supposedly not heard by others on the stage and intended only for the audience. **8.** words spoken so as not to be heard by others present. **9.** a temporary departure from a main theme or topic, esp. a parenthetical comment or remark; digression. [A-[1] + SIDE[1]]

a·sid·er·ite (ə sid′ə rīt′), *n.* an iron-free meteorite consisting of friable material. [A-[6] + SIDERITE]

As I Lay Dy′ing, a novel (1930) by William Faulkner.

A·si·ne (a sē′nā), *n.* an ancient town in S Greece, on the Gulf of Argolis.

as·i·nine (as′ə nīn′), *adj.* **1.** stupid; unintelligent, silly: *It is surprising that supposedly intelligent people can make such asinine statements.* **2.** of or like an ass: *equine and asinine features.* [< L *asinīn(us),* equiv. to *asin(us)* ASS[1] + *-īnus* -INE[1]] —**as′i·nine′ly,** *adv.* —**as·i·nin·i·ty** (as′ə nin′i tē), *n.*
—**Syn. 1.** See **foolish.**

A·sir (ä sēr′), *n.* a district in SW Saudi Arabia.

-asis, an element occurring in scientific, esp. medical, words from Greek: *psoriasis.* [< L < Gk *-āsis* state of, act of, result of]

A·si·us (ā′sē əs), *n.* (in the *Iliad*) **1.** the son of Hyrtacus who was slain by Idomeneus. **2.** a son of Dymas and the brother of Hecuba.

ask (ask, äsk), *v.t.* **1.** to put a question to; inquire of: *I asked him.* **2.** to request information about: *to ask the way; to ask a question.* **3.** to try to get by using words; request: *to ask advice; to ask a favor.* **4.** to solicit from; request of (with a personal object, and with or without *for* before the thing desired): *I ask you a great favor. Ask him for advice.* **5.** to demand; expect: *to ask a price for something.* **6.** to call for; require: *This experiment asks patience.* **7.** to invite: *to ask guests to dinner.* **8.** *Archaic.* to publish (banns); publish the banns of (persons). —*v.i.* **9.** to make inquiry; inquire: *to ask about a person.* **10.** to request or petition (usually fol. by *for*): *to ask for leniency; to ask for food.* **11. ask for it,** to persist in an action despite the probability of an unfavorable result: *You couldn't feel sorry for him, because he was asking for it when he continually provoked her.* [ME *ask(en)* *axe(n),* OE *āscian, āxian;* c. OS *ēscon,* OHG *eiscōn* (> G *heischen*), Skt *icch(ati)* seeks] —**ask′er,** *n.*
—**Syn. 1.** question, interrogate. **3, 10.** sue, appeal. **4.** beseech, beg, entreat. **9.** See **inquire.** —**Ant. 1, 9.** answer.

Ask (äsk), *n.* *Scand. Myth.* the first man, made by the gods from an ash tree. Also, **Askr** (äs′kər). Cf. **Embla.** [< Icel; see ASH[2]]

a·skance (ə skans′), *adv.* **1.** with suspicion, mistrust, or disapproval: *He looked askance at my offer.* **2.** with a side glance; sidewise; obliquely. Also, **a·skant** (ə skant′). [ME *asca(u)nce* as if, as much as to say < ?]

as·ka·rel (as′kə rel′), *n.* *Chem.* any of the class of synthetic, nonflammable, liquid dielectrics used chiefly for insulating transformers. [?]

a·skew (ə skyo͞o′), *adv.* **1.** to one side; out of line; in a crooked position; awry: *to wear one's hat askew; to hang a picture askew.* **2.** with disapproval, scorn, contempt, etc., disdainfully: *They looked askew at the dinner.* —*adj.* **3.** crooked; awry: *Your clothes are all askew.* [A-[1] + SKEW]

ask′ing bid′, *Bridge.* a conventional bid by which a bidder asks for specific information about the strength of his partner's hand in a given suit.

ask′ing price′, the price originally demanded by the seller, as before any reduction resulting from bargaining, discount, etc.

Ask·ja (äsk′yä), *n.* a volcano in E central Iceland. 4754 ft.

as·kos (as′kos), *n., pl.* **-koi** (-koi). *Gk. and Rom. Antiq.* an oil or wine jar, characterized by an ellipsoidal body and a short, flanged spout from which a thin handle extends in an arc to join the back of the jar. Cf. **alabastron, aryballos, lekythos.** [< Gk]

a·slant (ə slant′, ə slänt′), *adv.* **1.** at a slant; slantingly; obliquely: *The books have all fallen aslant.* —*adj.* **2.** slanting; oblique. —*prep.* **3.** slantingly across; athwart. [ME *on slont, on slent* on slope, at a SLANT]

a·sleep (ə slēp′), *adv.* **1.** in or into a state of sleep: *He fell asleep quickly.* **2.** into a dormant or inactive state; to a low point; to rest: *Their anxieties were put asleep.* **3.** into the state of death. —*adj.* **4.** sleeping: *He is asleep.* **5.** dormant; inactive. **6.** (of the foot, hand, leg, etc.) numb. **7.** dead. [A-[1] + SLEEP]

a·slope (ə slōp′), *adv.* **1.** at a slope; aslant; slantingly; diagonally. —*adj.* **2.** sloping. [ME; see A-[1], SLOPE]

ASM, air-to-surface missile.

As·ma·ra (äs mär′ə), *n.* a city in and the capital of Eritrea, in N Ethiopia. 123,083 (est. 1956).

As·mo·de·us (az′mə dē′əs, as′-), *n.* *Jewish Demonology.* an evil spirit. [< L *Asmodaeus* < Gk *Asmodaîos* < Heb *Ashmadai*]

As·mo·ne·an (az′mə nē′ən), *n.* Hasmonean. Also, **As′mo·nae′an.**

ASN, Army service number.

As·nières (ä nyer′), *n.* a city in N central France, near Paris. 82,201 (1962).

a·so·cial (ā sō′shəl), *adj.* **1.** withdrawn from society; indifferent to or averse to conforming to conventional standards of behavior. **2.** inconsiderate of others; selfish; egocentric. [A-[6] + SOCIAL]

A·so·ka (ə sō′kə), *n.* died 232 B.C., Buddhist king in India 269?–232? B.C.

a·so·ma·tous (ā sō′mə təs, ə sō′-), *adj.* having no material body; incorporeal. [< LL *asōmatus* < Gk *asṓmatos* bodiless, equiv. to *a-* A-[6] + *sōmat-* (s. of *sôma* SOMA) + *-os* -OUS]

a·so·ni·a (ə sō′nē ə), *n.* *Pathol.* tone deafness. [< NL; see A-[6], -SON(OUS), -IA]

A·so·pus (ə sō′pəs), *n.* *Class. Myth.* a river god whose daughters were ravished by various gods.

A·so·san (ä′sô sän′), *n.* a volcano in SW Japan, in central Kyushu. 5225 ft.; crater 12 mi. across.

asp[1] (asp), *n.* **1.** any of several venomous snakes, esp. the Egyptian cobra or the horned viper. **2.** the common European viper, *Vipera berus.* **3.** *Archaeol.* uraeus. [back formation from ME *aspis* (taken as pl.) < L < Gk] —**asp′ish,** *adj.*

asp[2] (asp), *n., adj.* aspen. [ME *aspe,* OE *æspe;* akin to G *Espe,* Icel *ösp*]

as·par·a·gine (ə spar′ə jēn′, -jin), *n.* *Biochem.* a white, crystalline, water-soluble amino acid, $NH_2COCH_2CH(NH_2)COOH$, obtained from certain plants, esp. legumes, and used chiefly as a nutrient in culture media for certain bacteria, as tubercle bacilli. [< F; see ASPARAG(US), -INE[2]]

as·par′a·gin′ic ac′id (ə spar′ə jin′ik, ə spar′-), *Biochem.* See **aspartic acid.** Also, **as′par·ag′ic ac′id** (as′pə raj′ik, as′-). [ASPARAGINE + -IC]

as·par·a·gus (ə spar′ə gəs), *n.* **1.** any liliaceous plant of the genus *Asparagus,* esp. *A. officinalis,* cultivated for its edible shoots. **2.** the shoots, used as a table vegetable. [< L < Gk *asp(h)áragos;* r. OE *sperage* (< ML) and later *sperage, sparrowgrass,* etc.] —**as·para·gi·nous** (as′pə raj′ə nəs), *adj.*

aspar′agus bean′, a trailing, long-stemmed vine, *Vigna sesquipedalis,* of Asia, having yellow or violet-colored flowers and pods from one to three feet long. Also called **yard-long bean.**

aspar′agus bee′tle, either of two leaf beetles of the genus *Crioceris* that feed on the asparagus plant in both the larval and adult stages.

aspar′agus fern′, a fernlike climbing vine, *Asparagus plumosus,* of South Africa, having very small, whitish flowers and pea-sized, purplish-black berries. Also called **fern asparagus.**

as·par·tame (as′pər tām′, ə spär′tām), *n.* a low-calorie noncarbohydrate sweetener, $C_{14}H_{18}N_2O_5$, synthesized from amino acids. [*aspart(yl phenyl)a(lanine) m(ethyl) e(ster)*]

as·par′tic ac′id (ə spär′tik), *Biochem.* a crystalline amino acid, $HOOCCH(NH_2)CH_2COOH$, produced by the hydrolysis of asparagine and proteins, found chiefly in young sugar cane and sugar-beet molasses, and used in the preparation of culture media and as a dietary supplement. Also called **aminosuccinic acid, asparaginic acid, asparagic acid.** [ASPAR(AGUS) + -TIC]

As·pa·sia (a spā′shə, -zhə), *n.* c470–410 B.C., Athenian courtesan, mistress of Pericles.

A.S.P.C.A., American Society for Prevention of Cruelty to Animals.

as·pect (as′pekt), *n.* **1.** appearance to the eye or mind: *the physical aspect of the country.* **2.** nature; quality; character: *the superficial aspect of the situation.* **3.** a way in which a thing may be viewed or regarded; interpretation; view: *both aspects of a decision.* **4.** part; feature; phase: *That is the aspect of the problem that interests me most.* **5.** facial expression; countenance: *He wore an aspect of gloom. Hers was an aspect of happy optimism.* **6.** bearing; air; mien: *warlike in aspect.* **7.** view commanded; exposure: *The house has a southern aspect.* **8.** the side or surface facing a given direction: *the dorsal aspect of a fish.* **9.** *Gram.* **a.** a category or interrelated set of categories for which the verb is inflected in some languages, typically to indicate the duration, repetition, completion, or quality of the action or state denoted by the verb. **b.** a set of syntactic devices, as in the English perfect with *have* in *I have gone,* with functions similar to such inflections. **c.** any of the members or instances of these categories or sets: *the Latin perfect aspect; the Russian imperfect aspect.* **d.** the meaning of, or meaning typical of, such a category or construction. **e.** such categories or constructions, or their meanings collectively. **10.** *Astrol.* the relative position of planets as determining their influence. **11.** *Archaic.* a look; glance. [ME < L *aspect(us)* sight, look, appearance, n. use of *aspectus* (ptp. of *aspicere*), equiv. to *a-* A-[5] + *spec-* look + *-tus* ptp. suffix]
—**Syn. 1.** See **appearance. 7.** prospect, outlook.

as·pec·tant (ə spek′tənt), *adj.* *Heraldry.* (of birds, fish, and animals other than beasts of prey) face to face; respectant. [< L *aspectant-* (s. of *aspectāns,* prp. of *aspectāre* to gaze at). See ASPECT, -ANT]

as′pect ra′tio, 1. *Aeron.* the ratio of the span of an airfoil to its mean chord. **2.** *Television.* the ratio of the width of an image to its height, usually expressed as 4 to 3. **3.** *Naval Archit.* the ratio of the height of a rudder to its fore-and-aft length. **4.** *Rocketry.* **a.** Also called **fineness ratio, slenderness ratio.** the ratio of the mean diameter of the body of a rocket or missile to its length. **b.** the ratio of the length of the combustion chamber of a rocket motor to its diameter.

as·pec·tu·al (a spek′cho͞o əl), *adj.* *Gram.* **1.** of, pertaining to, or producing a particular aspect or aspects. **2.** used as or like a form inflected for a particular aspect. [< L *aspectu(s)* ASPECT + -AL[1]]

as·pen (as′pən), *n.* **1.** any of several poplars, as *Populus tremula,* of Europe, and *P. tremuloides* **(quaking aspen)** or *P. alba* **(white aspen),** of America, having leaves that tremble in the slightest breeze. —*adj.* **2.** of or pertaining to the aspen. **3.** trembling or quivering, like the leaves of the aspen. [ME *aspen* (adj.), OE *æspen.* See ASP[2], -EN[2]]

As·pen (as′pən), *n.* a village in central Colorado: ski resort. 1101 (1960).

as·per (as′pər), *adj.* *Obs.* harsh; rough. [< L: rough; r. ME *aspre* < MF]

As·per·ges (ə spûr′jēz), *n.* *Rom. Cath. Ch.* **1.** the rite of sprinkling the altar, clergy, and people with holy water before High Mass. **2.** (*italics.*) an anthem sung while the priest performs this rite. [< L: thou shalt sprinkle (2nd pers. sing. fut. of *aspergere*). See A-[5], SPARGE]

as·per·gil·lo·sis (as′pər jə lō′sis), *n., pl.* **-ses** (-sēz). *Vet. Med.* disease in an animal caused by a mold fungus of the genus *Aspergillus.* [< NL; see ASPERGILL(US), -OSIS]

as·per·gil·lum (as′pər jil′əm), *n., pl.* **-gil·la** (-jil′ə), **-gil·lums.** *Rom. Cath. Ch.* a brush or instrument for sprinkling holy water; aspersorium. [< L *asperg(ere)* (to) besprinkle (see A-[5], SPARGE) + *-illum* dim. suffix]

as·per·gil·lus (as′pər jil′əs), *n., pl.* **-gil·li** (-jil′ī). *Bot.* any fungus of the genus *Aspergillus,* family *Aspergillaceae,* whose sporophores are distinguished by a bristly, knoblike top. [< NL: alter. of ASPERGILLUM]

as·per·i·ty (ə sper′i tē), *n., pl.* **-ties** for 4. **1.** roughness or sharpness of tone, temper, or manner; harshness; severity; acrimony: *The cause of her anger did not warrant such asperity.* **2.** hardship; difficulty; rigor. **3.** roughness of surface; unevenness. **4.** something rough or harsh. [< L *asperitāt-* (s. of *asperitās*), equiv. to *asper* rough + *-itāt-* -ITY; r. ME *asprete* < OF < L]
—**Syn. 1.** acerbity, bitterness, astringency.

As′pern Pa′pers, The (as′pərn), a novelette (1888) by Henry James.

as·perse (ə spûrs′), *v.t.,* **-persed, -pers·ing. 1.** to attack with false, malicious, and damaging charges or insinuations; slander. **2.** to sprinkle; bespatter. [late ME < L *aspers(us)* besprinkled (ptp. of *aspergere*), equiv. to *a-* A-[5] + *sper-* (comb. form of *spar-,* var. of *sparg-* SPARGE) + *-sus* var. of *-tus* ptp. suffix] —**as·pers′er,** *n.* —**as·per′sive,** *adj.* —**as·per′sive·ly,** *adv.*
—**Syn. 1.** malign, abuse, traduce.

as·per·sion (ə spûr′zhən, -shən), *n.* **1.** a damaging imputation; a derogatory criticism: *to campaign by casting aspersions on the opponent.* **2.** the act of slandering; vilification; defamation; calumniation; derogation: *Such vehement aspersions cannot be ignored.* **3.** act of aspersing: *to baptize by aspersion.* **4.** *Archaic.* a shower or spray. [< L *aspersiōn-* (s. of *aspersiō*) a sprinkling. See ASPERSE, -ION]
—Syn. 1. reflection, reproach.

as·per·so·ri·um (as′pər sōr′ē əm, -sôr′-), *n., pl.* **-so·ri·a** (-sōr′ē ə, -sôr′-), **-so·ri·ums.** *Rom. Cath. Ch.* **1.** a vessel for holding holy water. See illus. under **stoup. 2.** aspergillum. [< ML; see ASPERSE, -ORIUM]

As·phal·i·us (as fal′ē əs), *n. Class. Myth.* Poseidon: so called because of his power to insure the safety of ships and harbors.

as·phalt (as′fôlt, -falt), *n.* **1.** any of various dark-colored, solid bituminous substances, native in various areas of the earth and composed mainly of hydrocarbon mixtures. **2.** a similar artificial substance, the by-product of petroleum-cracking operations. **3.** a mixture of such substances with gravel, crushed rock, or the like, used for paving. **—*v.t.* 4.** to cover or pave with asphalt. **—*adj.* 5.** of, pertaining to, or containing asphalt: *asphalt tile.* [earlier *asphaltos, -um* < L < Gk *ásphaltos, -on,* ? akin to *asphalizein* to make firm, to secure; r. ME *aspalt(oun)* << Gk *ásphalton*] **—as·phal′tic,** *adj.* **—as′phalt·like′,** *adj.*

as·phal·tene (as fôl′tēn, -fal′-), *n. Chem.* any of the constituents of a bitumen, as asphalt, that are insoluble in pentane, hexane, or naphthalene. Cf. **petrolene.** [ASPHALT + -ENE]

as·phal·tite (as fôl′tīt, -fal′-; as′fôl tīt′, -fôl-), *n.* a natural, solid hydrocarbon having a melting point higher than that of asphalt. [< Gk *asphaltítē(s).* See ASPHALT, -ITE[1]]

as′phalt pa′per, paper treated with asphalt, as to increase toughness, water resistance, etc.

as′phalt rock′, *Geol.* a rock formation, usually of limestone or sandstone, containing large amounts of bitumens.

as·phal·tum (as fôl′təm, -fal′-), *n.* asphalt. [< NL < Gk *ásphalton* ASPHALT]

a·spher·i·cal (ā sfer′i kəl), *adj. Optics.* (of a reflecting surface or lens) deviating slightly from an exactly spherical shape and relatively free from aberrations. Also, **a·spher′ic.** [A-[6] + SPHERICAL]

as·pho·del (as′fə del′), *n.* **1.** any of various liliaceous plants of the genera *Asphodelus* and *Asphodeline,* native to southern Europe, having white, pink, or yellow flowers. **2.** any of various other plants, as the daffodil. [< L *asphodel(us)* < Gk *asphódelos* the asphodel. See DAFFODIL]

As′phodel Fields′, *Class. Myth.* a meadow where the shades of dead heroes wandered sadly.

as·phyx·i·a (as fik′sē ə), *n. Pathol.* the extreme condition caused by lack of oxygen and excess of carbon dioxide in the blood, produced by sufficient interference with respiration, as in choking. [< NL < Gk *asphyxía* a stopping of the pulse, equiv. to *a-* A-[6] + *sphýx(is)* pulse + *-ia* -IA] **—as·phyx′i·al,** *adj.*

as·phyx·i·ant (as fik′sē ənt), *adj.* **1.** asphyxiating or tending to asphyxiate. **—*n.* 2.** an asphyxiating agent or substance. **3.** an asphyxiating condition. [ASPHYXI(ATE) + -ANT]

as·phyx·i·ate (as fik′sē āt′), *v.,* **-at·ed, -at·ing.** **—*v.t.* 1.** to produce asphyxia in. **2.** to cause to die or lose consciousness by impairing normal breathing, as by gas or other noxious agents; choke; suffocate; smother. **—*v.i.* 3.** to become asphyxiated. [ASPHYXI(A) + -ATE[1]] **—as·phyx′i·a′tion,** *n.* **—as·phyx′i·a′tor,** *n.*

as·pic[1] (as′pik), *n.* **1.** a savory jelly usually made with meat or fish stock and gelatin, chilled and used as a garnish and coating for meats, seafoods, eggs, etc. **2.** Also called **tomato aspic.** a similar jelly made with spiced tomato juice and gelatin, chilled and served as a salad. [< F: said to be so called because cold like an asp. See ASPIC[2]]

as·pic[2] (as′pik), *n. Obs.* asp[1]. [< F, perh. equiv. to OF *asp(e)* ASP[1] + *-ic,* modeled after MF *basilique* BASILISK]

as·pic[3] (as′pik), *n.* the great lavender, *Lavandula latifolia,* yielding an oil used in perfumery. [< F; OF *espic* < ML *spīc(us)* spikenard, L *spīcus,* var. of *spīca, spīcum* SPIKE[2]]

as·pi·dis·tra (as′pi dis′trə), *n.* a smooth, stemless, Asian herb, *Aspidistra elatior,* having large evergreen leaves often striped with white, grown as a house plant. [< NL, equiv. to *aspid-* (< Gk: s. of *aspís* shield) + *-istra,* abstracted from *Tupistra* genus of liliaceous plants < Gk *typís* mallet + L *-tra* pl. of *-trum* n. suffix denoting instrument]

As·pin·wall (as′pin wôl′), *n.* a town in SW Pennsylvania. 3727 (1960).

as·pir·ant (ə spīər′ənt, as′pər ənt), *n.* **1.** one who aspires, as one who seeks or desires a career, advancement, status, etc.: *Each of the aspirants for the available grants had yet to prove himself.* **—*adj.* 2.** aspiring. [< L *aspīrant-* (s. of *aspīrāns,* prp. of *aspīrāre*). See ASPIRE, -ANT]

as·pi·ra·ta (as′pə rä′tə), *n., pl.* **-tae** (-tē). *Gk. Grammar.* a strongly fricated voiceless plosive, as ϕ, θ, χ. [NL, equiv. to L *aspīrāt(us)* (see ASPIRATE) + *-a* fem. adj. suffix]

as·pi·rate (*v.* as′pə rāt′; *n., adj.,* as′pər it), *v.,* **-rat·ed, -rat·ing,** *n., adj.* **—*v.t.* 1.** *Phonet.* **a.** to articulate (a speech sound, esp. a stop) so as to produce audible frication, as with the first *t* of *total,* the second *t* being unaspirated. **b.** to articulate (the beginning of a word or syllable) with an *h*-sound, as in *which,* pronounced (hwich), *hitch* as opposed to *witch, itch.* **2.** *Med.* **a.** to remove (a fluid) from a body cavity by use of an aspirator. **b.** to inhale (fluid) into the bronchi and lungs, often after vomiting. **3.** to draw or remove by suction. **—*n.* 4.** *Phonet.* a speech sound having as an obvious concomitant audible frication, as initial stop consonants, initial *h*-sounds, etc. **—*adj.* 5.** *Phonet.* (of a speech sound) pronounced with or accompanied by aspiration; aspirated. [< L *aspīrāt(us)* breathed upon (ptp. of *aspīrāre*). See ASPIRE, -ATE[1]]

as·pi·ra·tion (as′pə rā′shən *for 1-5; Fr.* A spē rä syôN′ *for 6*), *n.* **1.** strong desire, longing, or aim; ambition: *intellectual aspirations.* **2.** the goal or objective desired: *The presidency is the traditional aspiration of young American boys.* **3.** act of aspirating; a breath. **4.** *Phonet.* **a.** articulation accompanied by audible frication, as in the *h*-sound of *how.* or of *when* (hwen), or in the release of initial stops, as in the *k*-sound of *key.* **b.** the use of an aspirate in pronunciation. **5.** *Med.* **a.** the act of removing a fluid, as pus or serum, from a cavity of the body, by a hollow needle or trocar connected with a suction syringe. **b.** the act of inhaling fluid into the bronchi and lungs, often after vomiting. **6.** *Music.* an ornament consisting of a rise in pitch at the end of a held note, used esp. in the music of the 17th and 18th centuries. [< L *aspīrātiōn-* (s. of *aspīrātiō*). See ASPIRATE, -ION]
—Syn. 1. yearning.

as·pi·ra·tor (as′pə rā′tər), *n.* **1.** an apparatus or device employing suction. **2.** a suction pump that operates by the pressure differential created by the high-speed flow of a fluid past an intake orifice. **3.** *Med.* an instrument for removing body fluids by suction. [ASPIRATE + -OR[2]]

as·pir·a·to·ry (ə spīər′ə tōr′ē, -tôr′ē), *adj.* pertaining to or suited for aspiration. [ASPIRATE + -ORY[1]]

as·pire (ə spīər′), *v.i.,* **-pired, -pir·ing. 1.** to long, aim, or seek ambitiously; be eagerly desirous, esp. for something great or of high value (usually fol. by *to, after,* or an infinitive): *to aspire after immortality; to aspire to be a doctor.* **2.** *Archaic.* to rise up; soar; mount; tower. [late ME < L *aspīr(āre)* (to) breathe upon, pant after, equiv. to *a-* A-[5] + *spīrāre* to breathe, blow] **—as·pir′er,** *n.* **—as·pir′ing·ly,** *adv.*
—Syn. 1. yearn. See **ambitious.**

as·pi·rin (as′pə rin, -prin), *n., pl.* **-rin, -rins. 1.** *Pharm.* a white, crystalline derivative of salicylic acid, $C_9H_8O_4$, used to relieve the pain of headache, rheumatism, gout, neuralgia, etc.; acetylsalicylic acid. **2.** an aspirin tablet: *I took four aspirins and went right to bed.* [orig. G trademark, equiv. to *A(cetyl)* ACETYL + *Spir(säure)* salicylic acid (see SPIRAEA) + -IN[2]]

a·sprawl (ə sprôl′), *adv., adj.* being in a sprawling state or posture: *The body lay asprawl among the wreckage.* [A-[1] + SPRAWL]

a·squint (ə skwint′), *adv., adj.* with an oblique glance or squint; askance; slyly; dubiously. [A-[1] + *squint* (< ?); akin to D *schuinte* slope]

As·quith (as′kwith), *n.* **Herbert Henry** (*1st Earl of Oxford and Asquith*), 1852–1928, British statesman: prime minister 1908–16.

Ass, *Equus asinus*
(3½ ft. high at shoulder)

a·sra·ma (ä′shrə mə), *n. Hinduism.* **1.** any of the four phases of the ideally conducted life: education, work, withdrawal from society, or life as a hermit. **2.** ashram. [< Skt]

ass[1] (as), *n.* **1.** a long-eared, slow, patient, sure-footed domesticated mammal, *Equus asinus,* related to the horse, used chiefly as a beast of burden. **2.** any wild species of the genus *Equus,* as the onager. **3.** a fool; a blockhead. [ME *asse,* OE *assa,* prob. hypocoristic form based on OIr *asan* < L *asinus;* akin to Gk *ónos* ass] **—ass′like′,** *adj.*

ass[2] (as), *n.* **1.** *Slang.* the buttocks. **2.** *Slang (vulgar).* rectum. **3.** *Slang (vulgar).* coitus; a woman considered as an object of coitus. [ME *ars, ers,* OE *ærs, ears;* akin to OIcel *ars,* G *Arsch,* Gk *órrhos*]

ass., **1.** assistant. **2.** association. **3.** assorted.

A.S.S., **1.** Associate in Secretarial Science. **2.** Associate in Secretarial Studies.

as·sa·fet·i·da (as′ə fet′i də), *n. Chem.* asafetida. Also, **as′sa·foet′i·da.**

as·sa·gai (as′ə gī′), *n., pl.* **-gais,** *v.t.,* **-gaied, -gai·ing.** assegai.

as·sa·i[1] (ə sä′ē; *It.* äs sä′ē), *adv. Music.* very: *allegro assai* (very quick). [< It: lit., enough << L *ad* (up) to + *satis* enough. See ASSET]

as·sa·i[2] (ə sä′ē), *n.* any of several slender Brazilian palms of the genus *Euterpe,* esp. *E. edulis,* a species bearing a purple fruit from which a beverage is made by infusion. [< Pg < Tupi]

as·sail (ə sāl′), *v.t.* **1.** to set upon with violence; attack; assault. **2.** to attack with arguments, criticism, ridicule, abuse, etc.: *to assail one's opponent with slander.* **3.** to undertake with the purpose of mastering: *He assailed his studies with new determination.* **4.** to impinge upon; make an impact on; beset: *His mind was assailed by conflicting arguments. The light assailed his eyes.* [ME *asayle(n)* < OF *asali(r)* < LL *assalīre,* equiv. to L *as-* AS- + *salīre* to leap, spring] **—as·sail′a·ble,** *adj.* **—as·sail′a·ble·ness,** *n.* **—as·sail′er,** *n.* **—as·sail′ment,** *n.*
—Syn. 1. See **attack. 2.** asperse, malign.

as·sail·ant (ə sā′lənt), *n.* **1.** one who attacks. **—*adj.* 2.** *Archaic.* assailing; attacking; hostile. [< MF *assaillant.* See ASSAIL, -ANT]

As·sam (as sam′), *n.* a state in NE India. 12,209,330 (1961); 85,012 sq. mi. *Cap.:* Shillong.

As·sa·mese (as′ə mēz′, -mēs′), *adj., n., pl.* **-mese.** **—*adj.* 1.** of or pertaining to Assam, its inhabitants, or their language. **—*n.* 2.** a native or inhabitant of Assam. **3.** an Indic language of Assam. [ASSAM + -ESE]

Assam′ States′, a group of former states in NE India, most of which are now part of the present state of Assam.

As·sar·a·cus (ə sar′ə kəs), *n.* (in the *Iliad*) a son of Tros and founder of the royal house to which Anchises and Aeneas belonged.

as·sas·sin (ə sas′in), *n.* **1.** murderer; killer, esp. one who kills for fanatical or monetary reasons: often restricted in usage to the murderer of a prominent person. **2.** (*cap.*) one of an order of Muslim fanatics, active in Persia and Syria from about 1090 to 1272, whose chief object was to assassinate Crusaders. [< ML *assassīnī* (pl.) < Ar *hashshāshīn* eaters of HASHISH]

as·sas·si·nate (ə sas′ə nāt′), *v.t.,* **-nat·ed, -nat·ing.** **1.** to kill suddenly or secretively; murder premeditatedly and treacherously. **2.** to destroy or denigrate treacherously and viciously: *to assassinate a person's character.* [ASSASSIN + -ATE[1]] **—as·sas′si·na′tion,** *n.* **—as·sas′si·na′tive,** *adj.* **—as·sas′si·na′tor,** *n.*
—Syn. 1. murder, slay.

assas′sin bug′, any of numerous hemipterous insects of the family *Reduviidae,* feeding chiefly on other insects but including some forms that are bloodsucking parasites of mammals.

as·sault (ə sôlt′), *n.* **1.** a violent attack; onslaught. **2.** *Mil.* the stage of close combat in an attack. **3.** *Law.* an unlawful physical attack upon another; an attempt or offer to do violence to another, with or without battery, as by holding a stone or club in a threatening manner. **4.** rape[1]. **—*v.t.* 5.** to make an assault upon; attack; assail. [ME *asaut* < OF < LL *assalt(us)* (r. L *assultus*), equiv. to L *as-* AS- + *saltus* a leap, n. use of ptp. of *salīre* (*sal-* leap + *-tus* ptp. suffix)] **—as·sault′a·ble,** *adj.* **—as·sault′er,** *n.*
—Syn. 1. onset, charge; invasion, aggression. **5.** See **attack.**

assault′ and bat′tery, *Law.* an assault with an actual touching or other violence upon another.

assault′ boat′, *Mil.* a portable boat used for landing troops on beaches and for crossing rivers. Also called **storm boat.**

as·say (*v.* ə sā′; *n.* ə sā′, as′ā), *v.t.* **1.** to try or test; put to trial: *to assay one's strength; to assay one's debating abilities.* **2.** *Metall.* to analyze (an ore, alloy, etc.) in order to determine the quantity of gold, silver, or other metal in it. **3.** *Pharm.* to subject (a drug) to an analysis for the determination of its potency. **4.** to examine or analyze: *to assay a situation; to assay an event.* **5.** to judge the quality of; assess; evaluate: *to assay someone's efforts.* **6.** to attempt; endeavor to make or do; try; essay: *to assay a dance.* **—*v.i.* 7.** *U.S.* to contain, as shown by analysis, a certain proportion of usually precious metal. **—*n.* 8.** *Metall.* determination of the amount of metal, esp. gold or silver, in an ore, alloy, etc. **9.** a substance undergoing analysis or trial. **10.** a detailed report of the findings in assaying a substance. **11.** *Obs.* examination; trial; attempt; essay. [ME < MF; var. of ESSAY] **—as·say′a·ble,** *adj.* **—as·say′er,** *n.*

assay′ cup′, a small wine cup for tasting wine to be offered to another person.

assay′ groove′, (in silverwork) a furrow left in a piece by the digging out of metal for assay.

assay′ of′fice, a local testing station for assaying ore, as gold, silver, etc., esp. a government station maintained in connection with registration of mineral claims, purchases of gold, or the like.

assay′ ton′, a unit of weight used in assaying ore, equivalent to 29.167 grams.

as·se·gai (as′ə gī′), *n., pl.* **-gais,** *v.,* **-gaied, -ga·ing.** **—*n.* 1.** the slender javelin or spear of the Bantu-speaking people of southern Africa. **2.** a South African cornaceous tree, *Curtisia faginea,* from whose wood such spears are made. **—*v.t.* 3.** to pierce with an assegai. Also, **assagai.** [earlier *azagaia* < Pg < Ar *az zaghāyah,* equiv. to *al* the + Berber *zaghāyah* assegai]

as·sem·blage (ə sem′blij; *for 3, 4 also Fr.* A säN-blAzh′), *n.* **1.** a number of persons or things assembled; an assembly; collection; aggregate. **2.** act of assembling; state of being assembled. **3.** *Fine Arts.* **a.** a sculptural technique of organizing or composing into a unified whole a group of unrelated and often fragmentary or discarded objects. **b.** a work of art produced by this technique. Cf. **collage, found object, ready-made** (def. 4). **4.** *Archaeol.* the aggregate of artifacts and other remains found on a site, considered as material evidence in support of a theory concerning the culture or cultures inhabiting it. [< F; see ASSEMBLE, -AGE]

as·sem·ble (ə sem′bəl), *v.,* **-bled, -bling.** **—*v.t.* 1.** to bring together; gather into one place, company, body, or whole. **2.** to put or fit together; put together the parts of: *to assemble information for a report; to assemble a toy from a kit.* **3.** *Computer Technol.* compile (def. 4). **—*v.i.* 4.** to come together; gather; meet. [ME < OF *assemble(r)* < VL *assimulāre to bring together, equiv. to L *as-* AS- + *simul* together + *-ā-* thematic vowel + *-re* inf. suffix]
—Syn. 1. convene, convoke. See **gather. 2.** connect. See **manufacture. 4.** congregate, convene. **—Ant. 1, 4.** disperse.

as·sem·blé (*Fr.* A säN blā′), *n., pl.* **-blés** (*Fr.* -blā′). *Ballet.* a jump in which the dancer throws one leg up, springs off the other, and lands with both feet together. [< F, ptp. of *assembler* to ASSEMBLE]

as·sem·bled (ə sem′bəld), *adj.* noting an artificial gem formed of two or more parts, as a doublet or triplet, at least one of which is a true gemstone. [ASSEMBLE + -ED[2]]

as·sem·bler (ə sem′blər), *n.* **1.** one who or that which assembles. **2.** *Computer Technol.* compiler (def. 2). [ASSEMBLE + -ER[1]]

as·sem·bly (ə sem′blē), *n., pl.* **-blies. 1.** a number of persons gathered together, usually for a particular purpose, whether religious, political, educational, or social. **2.** (*cap.*) *Govt.* a legislative body, esp. a lower house of a legislature. **3.** act of assembling; state of being assembled. **4.** *Mil.* **a.** a signal, as by drum or bugle, for troops to fall into ranks or otherwise assemble. **b.** the movement of forces, tanks, soldiers, etc., scattered by battle or battle drill, toward and into a small area. **5.** the putting together of complex machinery, as airplanes, from interchangeable parts of standard dimensions. **6.** a group of machine parts, esp. one forming a self-contained, independently mounted unit. Cf. **subassembly.** [ME *assemblee* < MF, lit., (that which is) assembled, fem. ptp. of *assembler* to ASSEMBLE]
—Syn. 1. assemblage, throng, gathering, mob, congress, meeting. See **convention. 2.** congress, representatives.

assem′bly dis′trict, *U.S. Govt.* one of a fixed number of districts into which a State is divided, each district electing one member to the lower house of the State legislature. Cf. **congressional district, senatorial district.**

assem′bly line′, an arrangement of machines, tools, and workers in which a product is assembled by having each perform a specific, successive operation on an incomplete unit as it passes by in a series of stages organized in a direct line. [ASSEMBLY + LINE[1]]

as·sem·bly·man (ə sem′blē mən), *n., pl.* **-men.** *U.S.* a member of a State legislature, esp. of a lower house. [ASSEMBLY + MAN[1]]

Assem′bly of the No′tables, notable (def. 5).

assem′bly rou·tine′, *Computer Technol.* compiler (def. 2).

as·sent (ə sent′), *v.i.* **1.** to agree or concur; subscribe to (often fol. by *to*): *to assent to a statement.* **2.** to give in; yield; concede: *Assenting to his demands, she did as she was told.* **—*n.* 3.** agreement, as to a proposal; concurrence. **4.** acquiescence; compliance. [ME *asente(n)* <

OF *asente(r)* < L *assentārī*, equiv. to *as-* AS- + *sent-* (see SCENT) + *-t-* freq. suffix + *-ā-* thematic vowel + *-rī* inf. suffix] **—as·sent′ing·ly,** *adv.* **—as·sen′tive,** *adj.* **—as·sen′tive·ness,** *n.*
—Syn. 1. acquiesce. See **agree.**

as·sen·ta·tion (as′en tā′shən), *n.* the practice of assenting readily, esp. obsequiously. [late ME < L *assentātiōn-* (s. of *assentātiō*). See ASSENT, -ATION]

as·sen·tor (ə sen′tər), *n.* **1.** Also, **as·sent′er.** one who assents. **2.** *Brit. Govt.* one of the eight voters who endorse the nomination of a candidate for election to Parliament. [ASSENT + -OR[2]]

As·ser (ä′sər), *n.* **To·bi·as** (tō bī′əs; *Du.* tô bē′äs), 1838–1913, Dutch jurist and statesman: Nobel peace prize 1911.

as·sert (ə sûrt′), *v.t.* **1.** to state with assurance, confidence, or force; state strongly or positively; affirm; aver: *to assert that one is innocent.* **2.** to maintain or defend (claims, rights, etc.). **3.** to put (oneself) forward boldly and insistently. **4.** to state as having existence; affirm; postulate: *to assert a first cause as necessary.* [< L *assert(us)* joined to, defended, claimed (ptp. of *asserere*), equiv. to *as-* AS- + *ser-* (see SERIES) + *-tus* ptp. suffix] **—as·sert′er, as·ser′tor,** *n.* **—as·sert′i·ble,** *adj.*
—Syn. 1. asseverate, avow, maintain. See **declare. 2.** uphold, support. **3.** press. **—Ant. 1.** deny.

as·sert·ed (ə sûr′tid), *adj.* resting on statement or claim unsupported by evidence or proof; alleged: *The asserted value of the property was twice the amount of any offer made by a prospective purchaser.* [ASSERT + -ED[2]] **—as·sert′ed·ly,** *adv.*

as·ser·tion (ə sûr′shən), *n.* **1.** a positive statement or declaration, often without support or reason: *a mere assertion; an unwarranted assertion.* **2.** act of asserting. [late ME *assercion* < L *assertiōn-* (s. of *assertiō*). See ASSERT, -ION] **—as·ser′tion·al,** *adj.*
—Syn. 1. allegation.

as·ser·tive (ə sûr′tiv), *adj.* given to asserting; positive; aggressive; dogmatic: *He is overly assertive in his selling efforts.* [ASSERT + -IVE] **—as·ser′tive·ly,** *adv.* **—as·ser′tive·ness,** *n.*
—Syn. overbearing, forward.

as·ser·to·ry (ə sûr′tə rē), *adj.* stated positively; affirmative: *an assertory proposition.* [< L *assertōri(us).* See ASSERT, -ORY[1]] **—as·ser′to·ri·ly,** *adv.*

as′ses′ bridge′, *Geom.* See **pons asinorum** (Euclid, I 5).

as·sess (ə ses′), *v.t.* **1.** to estimate officially the value of (property, income, etc.) as a basis for taxation. **2.** to fix or determine the amount of (damages, a tax, a fine, etc.). **3.** to impose a tax or other charge on. **4.** to estimate or judge the value, character, etc., of; evaluate: *to assess one's efforts.* [late ME *assesse* < ML *assessā(re)* (to) assess a tax, deriv. of L *assēss(us)* seated beside (a judge) (ptp. of *assidēre*), equiv. to *as-* AS- + *sēd-* (perf. s. of *sedēre* to SIT) + *-tus* ptp. suffix] **—as·sess′a·ble,** *adj.*
—Syn. 2. appraise, adjust.

as·sess·ment (ə ses′mənt), *n.* **1.** act of assessing; appraisal; evaluation. **2.** an amount assessed as payable; an official valuation of taxable property; an assigned value. [ASSESS + -MENT]

as·ses·sor (ə ses′ər), *n.* **1.** one who makes assessments for purposes of taxation. **2.** an advisor or assistant to a judge, esp. one serving as a specialist in some field. **3.** *Archaic.* **a.** one who shares another's position, rank, or dignity. **b.** one sitting beside another in an advisory capacity; an advisory associate. [ME *assessour* < ML *assessor* one who assesses taxes, L: a judge's helper. See ASSESS, -OR[2]] **—as·ses·so·ri·al** (as′i sôr′ē əl, -sōr′-), *adj.* **—as·ses′sor·ship′,** *n.*

as·set (as′et), *n.* **1.** a useful thing or quality: *Organizational ability is an asset.* **2.** a single item of ownership having exchange value. **3. assets, a.** items of ownership convertible into cash; total resources of a person or business, as cash, notes and accounts receivable, securities, inventories, good will, fixtures, machinery, real estate, etc. (opposed to *liabilities*). **b.** *Accounting.* the items detailed on a balance sheet, esp. in relation to liabilities and capital. **c.** all property available for the payment of debts, esp. of a bankrupt or insolvent firm, person, etc. **d.** *Law.* property in the hands of an heir, executor, or administrator, that is sufficient to pay the debts or legacies of a deceased person. [back formation from *assets*, in phrase *have assets*, lit., have enough (to pay obligations) < AF; OF *asez* enough. See ASSAI[1]]

as·sev·er·ate (ə sev′ə rāt′), *v.t.*, **-at·ed, -at·ing.** to declare earnestly or solemnly; affirm positively; aver. [< L *assevērāt(us)* spoken in earnest (ptp. of *assevērāre*), equiv. to *as-* AS- + *sevēr-* (see SEVERE) + *-ātus* -ATE[1]]

as·sev·er·a·tion (ə sev′ə rā′shən), *n.* **1.** act of asseverating. **2.** an emphatic assertion. [< L *assevērātiōn-* (s. of *assevērātiō*). See ASSEVERATE, -ION] **—as·sev·er·a·tive** (ə sev′ə rā′tiv, -ər ə tiv), **as·sev·er·a·to·ry** (ə sev′ər ə tôr′ē, -tōr′ē), *adj.* **—as·sev′er·a′tive·ly,** *adv.*

ass·head (as′hed′), *n.* a stupid, doltish person; blockhead. [ASS[1] + HEAD] **—ass′-head′ed,** *adj.* **—ass′-head′ed·ness,** *n.*

As·shur (ä′shŏŏr), *n.* Assur.

as·sib·i·late (ə sib′ə lāt′), *v.*, **-lat·ed -lat·ing.** *Phonet.* **—***v.t.* **1.** to change into or pronounce with the accompaniment of a sibilant sound or sounds. **—***v.i.* **2.** to change by assibilation. **3.** to become a sibilant or a sound containing a sibilant. [< L *assībilāt(us)* murmured, whispered at, hissed (ptp. of *assībilāre*). See AS-, SIBILATE] **—as·sib′i·la′tion,** *n.*

As·si·de·an (as′i dē′ən), *n.* *Judaism.* a member of a sect, characterized by its religious zeal and piety, which flourished in the 2nd century B.C. during the time of the Maccabees and vigorously resisted the Hellenization of Jewish culture and religion. Also, **As′si·dae′an, Hasidean, Hasidaean.** [< Gk *Assida(ioi)* (pl.) (< Heb *ḥasidhīm* pious ones) + -AN]

as·si·du·i·ty (as′i dōō′i tē, -dyōō′-), *n.*, *pl.* **-ties. 1.** constant or close application; diligence; industry. **2. assiduities,** devoted or solicitous attentions. [< L *assiduitāt-* (s. of *assiduitās*). See ASSIDUOUS, -ITY]

as·sid·u·ous (ə sij′ōō əs), *adj.* **1.** constant; unremitting: *assiduous reading.* **2.** constant in application; working diligently at a task; persevering; industrious; attentive; devoted: *an assiduous student.* [< L *assiduus*, lit., sitting down to, equiv. to *as-* AS- + *sidu-* (var. s. of *sede-* SIT) + *-us* -OUS] **—as·sid′u·ous·ly,** *adv.* **—as·sid′u·ous·ness,** *n.*
—Syn. 1. continuous, tireless, persistent. **2.** studious, diligent, sedulous. **—Ant. 1.** inconstant, lazy.

as·sign (ə sīn′), *v.t.* **1.** to give or allocate; allot: *to assign rooms at a hotel; to assign homework.* **2.** to appoint, as to a post or duty: *to assign one to guard duty.* **3.** to designate; name; specify: *to assign a day for a meeting.* **4.** to ascribe; attribute; bring forward: *to assign a reason.* **5.** *Law.* to transfer: *to assign a contract.* **6.** *Mil.* to place permanently on duty with a unit or under a commander. **—***v.i.* **7.** *Law.* to transfer property, esp. in trust or for the benefit of creditors. **—***n.* **8.** *Law.* a person to whom the property or interest of another is or may be transferred; assignee: *my heirs and assigns.* [ME *assigne(n)* < OF *assigne(r)* < L *assignāre.* See AS-, SIGN] **—as·sign′er;** *Chiefly Law.* **as·sign·or** (ə sī nôr′, as′ə nôr′), *n.*
—Syn. 1. ASSIGN, ALLOCATE, ALLOT mean to apportion or measure out. TO ASSIGN is to distribute available things, designating them to be given to or reserved for specific persons or purposes: *to assign duties.* TO ALLOCATE is to earmark or set aside parts of things available or expected in the future, each for a specific purpose: *to allocate income to various types of expenses.* TO ALLOT implies making restrictions as to amount, size, purpose, etc., and then apportioning or assigning: *to allot spaces for parking.* **3.** fix, determine. **4.** adduce, allege, advance, show, offer.

as·sign·a·ble (ə sī′nə bəl), *adj.* **1.** capable of being specified. **2.** capable of being attributed: *This work is assignable to a 12th-century poet.* **3.** *Law.* capable of being assigned. [ASSIGN + -ABLE] **—as·sign′a·bil′i·ty,** *n.* **—as·sign′a·bly,** *adv.*

as·sig·nat (as′ig nat′; *Fr.* A sē nyA′), *n.*, *pl.* **as·sig·nats** (as′ig nats′; *Fr.* A sē nyA′). *Fr. Hist.* one of the notes issued as paper currency from 1789 to 1796 by the revolutionary government on the security of confiscated lands. [< F < L *assignāt(us)* assigned (ptp. of *assignāre*). See ASSIGN, -ATE[1]]

as·sig·na·tion (as′ig nā′shən), *n.* **1.** an appointment for a meeting, esp. a lover's secret rendezvous; a lover's tryst. **2.** act of assigning; assignment. [late ME *assignacion* < L *assignātiōn-* (s. of *assignātiō*). See ASSIGN, -ATION]

assigned′ coun′sel, *U.S.* any private lawyer designated by a city or county court to represent indigent defendants in criminal cases at public expense. Cf. **public defender.**

assigned′ risk′, *Insurance.* a risk which, under State law, is assigned to an insurer from a pool of insurers who would not otherwise accept it.

as·sign·ee (ə sī nē′, as′ə nē′), *n.* **1.** *Law.* one to whom some right or interest is transferred, either for his own enjoyment or in trust. **2.** *Australian Archaic.* a trusty released from prison and assigned to work under surveillance. [late ME *assigne* < MF, n. use of ptp. of *assigner* to ASSIGN; see -EE]

as·sign·ment (ə sīn′mənt), *n.* **1.** something assigned, as a particular task or duty: *He completed the assignment and went on to other jobs.* **2.** a position of responsibility, post of duty, or the like, to which one is appointed: *He left for his assignment in the Middle East.* **3.** act of assigning. **4.** *Law.* **a.** the transference of a right, interest, or title, or the instrument of transfer. **b.** a transference of property to assignees for the benefit of creditors. [late ME *assignament* < ML *assignāment(um).* See ASSIGN, -MENT]
—Syn. 1. obligation, job.

as·sim·i·la·ble (ə sim′ə lə bəl), *adj.* capable of being assimilated. [< L *assimilābil(is)*, equiv. to *assimilā(re)* (see ASSIMILATE) + *-bilis* -BLE] **—as·sim′i·la·bil′i·ty,** *n.*

as·sim·i·late (ə sim′ə lāt′), *v.*, **-lat·ed, -lat·ing. —***v.t.* **1.** to take in and incorporate as one's own; absorb: *He assimilated many new experiences on his European trip.* **2.** *Physiol.* to convert (food) into a substance suitable for absorption into the system. **3.** to bring into conformity; adapt or adjust (usually fol. by *to* or *with*): *They assimilated their customs and behavior to the new environment.* **4.** to make like; cause to resemble (usually fol. by *to* or *with*). **5.** to compare; liken (usually fol. by *to* or *with*). **6.** *Phonet.* to modify by assimilation. **—***v.i.* **7.** to be or become absorbed. **8.** *Physiol.* (of food) to be converted into the substance of the body; be absorbed into the system. **9.** to become or be like; resemble (usually fol. by *to* or *with*). **10.** to adjust: *The new arrivals assimilated easily and quickly.* **11.** *Phonet.* to become modified by assimilation. [< L *assimilāt(us)* likened to, made like (ptp. of *assimilāre*), equiv. to *as-* AS- + *simil-* (see SIMILAR) + *-ātus* -ATE[1]] **—as·sim′i·la′tor,** *n.*

as·sim·i·la·tion (ə sim′ə lā′shən), *n.* **1.** act or process of assimilating; state or condition of being assimilated. **2.** *Physiol.* the conversion of absorbed food into the substance of the body. **3.** *Bot.* the total process of plant nutrition, including absorption of external foods and photosynthesis. **4.** *Sociol.* the merging of cultural traits from previously distinct cultural groups, not involving biological amalgamation. **5.** *Phonet.* act or process by which a sound becomes identical with or similar to a neighboring sound in one or more defining characteristics, as place of articulation, voice or voicelessness, or manner of articulation, as in (gram′pä) for *grandpa.* Cf. **dissimilation** (def. 2). [< L *assimilātiōn-* (s. of *assimilātiō*). See ASSIMILATE, -ION]

as·sim·i·la·tion·ist (ə sim′ə lā′shə nist), *n.* one who believes in or advocates social assimilation. [ASSIMILATION + -IST]

as·sim·i·la·tive (ə sim′ə lā′tiv, -lə tiv), *adj.* characterized by assimilation; assimilating. Also, **as·sim·i·la·to·ry** (ə sim′ə lə tôr′ē, -tōr′ē). [< ML *assimilātīv(us).* See ASSIMILATE, -IVE] **—as·sim′i·la′tive·ness,** *n.*

As·sin·i·boin (ə sin′ə boin′), *n.*, *pl.* **-boins,** (*esp. collectively*) **-boin. 1.** a member of a Siouan people of northeastern Montana and adjacent parts of Canada. **2.** the dialect of Dakota spoken by the Assiniboin Indians. [appar. < CanF *assiniboi* (< Ojibwa *asini* stone + **bwa* < ?) + -(A)N]

As·sin·i·boine (ə sin′ə boin′), *n.* a river in S Canada, flowing S and E from SE Saskatchewan into the Red River in S Manitoba. 450 mi. long.

As·si·si (ə sē′zē; *It.* äs sē′zē), *n.* a town in E Umbria, in central Italy: birthplace of St. Francis of Assisi. 24,164 (1951).

as·sist (ə sist′), *v.t.* **1.** to give support, aid, or help to: *Please assist him in moving the furniture.* **2.** to be associated with as an assistant. **—***v.i.* **3.** to give aid or help. **4.** to be present, as at a meeting, ceremony, etc. **—***n.* **5.** *Sports.* **a.** *Baseball.* a play that helps to put out a batter or base runner. **b.** *Ice Hockey.* a play that helps a teammate in gaining a goal. **c.** the official credit scored for such plays. **6.** a helpful act: *She finished her homework without an assist from her father.* [< L *assist(ere)* (to) stand by, help, equiv. to *as-* AS- + *sistere* to (cause to) stand (*si-* reduplicative prefix + *-ste-*, var. of *sta-* STAND, + *-re* inf. suffix)] **—as·sist′er;** *Chiefly Law.* **as·sis′tor,** *n.* **—as·sist′ive,** *adj.*
—Syn. 1. sustain, abet, befriend; back, promote. See **help. —Ant.** hinder, frustrate.

as·sis·tance (ə sis′təns), *n.* act of assisting; help; aid; support. [ME *assistence* < ML *assistentia.* See ASSIST, -ENCE, -ANCE]

as·sis·tant (ə sis′tənt), *n.* **1.** one who assists or gives aid and support; a helper. **2.** one subordinate to another in rank, function, etc.; one holding a secondary rank in an office or post: *He served as assistant to the office manager.* **3.** something that aids and is supplementary to another. **4.** a faculty member of a college or university who ranks below instructor and whose responsibilities usually include grading papers, supervising laboratories, and assisting in teaching. **—***adj.* **5.** assisting; helpful. **6.** serving in an immediately subordinate position; having secondary rank: *an assistant manager.* [late ME *assistent* < L *assistent-* (s. of *assistēns*, prp. of *assistere* to ASSIST); see -ENT, -ANT]
—Syn. 2. aide, adjutant.

assis′tant profes′sor, a teacher in a college or university who ranks above an instructor and below an associate professor.

as·sist·ant·ship (ə sis′tənt ship′), *n.* a form of financial aid awarded to a student studying for a graduate degree at a college or university in which he assists a professor, usually in academic or laboratory work. [ASSISTANT + -SHIP]

As·siut (ä syōōt′), *n.* Asyut.

as·size (ə sīz′), *n.* **1.** Usually, **assizes.** a trial session, civil or criminal, held periodically in specific locations in England, usually by a judge of a superior court. **2.** an edict, ordinance, or enactment made at a session of a legislative assembly. **3.** an inquest before jurymen or assessors; a judicial inquiry. **4.** an action, writ, or verdict of an assize. **5.** judgment: *the last assize; the great assize.* **6.** *Rare.* **a.** a course of stonework. **b.** one drum of a column. [ME *asise* < OF: a sitting, n. use of fem. of *asis* seated at (ptp. of *aseeir*), equiv. to *a-* A-[5] + *-sis* < L *sēss(um)* (*sēd-*, perf. s. of *sedēre* to SIT, + *-tus* ptp. suffix)]

assn., association. Also, **Assn.**

assoc., 1. associate. **2.** associated. **3.** association.

as·so·ci·a·ble (ə sō′shē ə bəl, -shə bəl, -sē-), *adj.* capable of being associated. [ASSOCI(ATE) + -ABLE, modeled on *sociable*] **—as·so′ci·a·bil′i·ty, as·so′ci·a·ble·ness,** *n.*

as·so·ci·ate (*v.* ə sō′shē āt′, -sē-; *n.*, *adj.*, ə sō′shē it, -āt′, -sē-), *v.*, **-at·ed, -at·ing,** *n.*, *adj.* **—***v.t.* **1.** to connect or bring into relation, as thought, feeling, memory, etc.: *Many people associate war with death and pestilence.* **2.** to join as a companion, partner, or ally: *to associate oneself with a cause.* **3.** to unite; combine: *coal associated with shale.* **—***v.i.* **4.** to enter into union; unite. **5.** to keep company, as a comrade or intimate: *to associate only with prestigious people.* **—***n.* **6.** one who shares actively in anything as a business, enterprise, or undertaking; partner; colleague; fellow worker: *He consulted with his associates before proceeding further.* **7.** a companion or comrade: *my most intimate associates.* **8.** a confederate; an accomplice; an ally: *criminal associates.* **9.** anything usually accompanying or associated with another; an accompaniment or concomitant. **10.** one who is admitted to a subordinate degree of membership in an association or institution: *an associate of the Royal Academy.* **11.** *Math.* adjoint (def. 2). **—***adj.* **12.** connected, joined, or related, esp. as a companion or colleague; having equal or nearly equal responsibility: *an associate partner.* **13.** having subordinate status; without full rights and privileges: *an associate member.* **14.** allied; concomitant. [< L *associāt(us)* joined to, united with (ptp. of *associāre*), equiv. to *as-* AS- + *soci-* (see SOCIAL) + *-ātus* -ATE[1]]
—Syn. 1. link. **6, 7.** See **acquaintance. —Ant. 1.** dissociate. **6–8.** adversary.

Asso′ciated Press′, a press association, maintained by American newspaper owners, which gathers news throughout the world for exchange and distribution among members and for sale to radio, television, news magazines, and other news media. *Abbr.:* AP, A.P.

asso′ciate profes′sor, a teacher in a college or university who ranks above an assistant professor and below a professor.

as·so·ci·a·tion (ə sō′sē ā′shən, -shē-), *n.* **1.** an organization of people with a common purpose and having a formal structure. **2.** act of associating; state of being associated. **3.** friendship; companionship: *Their close association did not last long.* **4.** connection or combination. **5.** the connection or relation of ideas, feelings, sensations, etc.; correlation of elements of perception, reasoning, or the like. **6.** an idea, image, feeling, etc., suggested by or connected with something other than itself; an accompanying thought, emotion, or the like; an overtone or connotation: *My associations with that painting are of springlike days.* **7.** *Ecol.* a group of plants of one or more species living together under uniform environmental conditions and having a uniform and distinctive aspect. **8.** See **touch football. 9.** *Brit.* soccer. [< ML *associātiōn-* (s. of *associātiō*). See ASSOCIATE, -ION] **—as·so′ci·a′tion·al,** *adj.*
—Syn. 1. alliance, union; society, company; band. **3.** fellowship.

associa′tion cop′y, a copy of a book once owned or annotated by the author, by someone otherwise associated with the book, or by some famous person. Also called **associa′tion book′.**

associa′tion fi′ber, *Anat.* any of several nerve fibers connecting different areas of the cerebral cortex in the same hemisphere.

associa′tion foot′ball, *Brit.* soccer.

as·so·ci·a·tion·ism (ə sō′sē ā′shə niz′əm), *n.* *Psychol.* a systematic theory explicating psychological phenomena in terms of primary mental processes, chiefly association, to which are attributed the simple and complex data and constructs of experience. Cf. **sensationism.** [ASSOCIATION + -ISM] **—as·so′ci·a′tion·ist,** *adj.*, *n.* **—as·so′ci·a′tion·is′tic,** *adj.*

associa′tion of ide′as, *Psychol.* the tendency of an idea, feeling, or perception to recall others linked to it by virtue of being alike or having been experienced simultaneously.

as·so·ci·a·tive (ə sō′shē ā′tiv, -sē-, -shə tiv), *adj.* **1.** pertaining to or resulting from association. **2.** tending to associate or unite. **3.** *Math., Logic.* **a.** (of an operation on a set of elements) giving an equivalent expression when elements are grouped without change of order, as $(a + b) + c = a + (b + c)$. **b.** having reference to this property: *associative law of multiplication.* [ASSOCIATE + -IVE] —**as·so·ci·a·tive·ly** (ə sō′shē ā′tiv lē, -ə tiv-, -sē-), *adv.* —**as·so′ci·a·tive·ness,** *n.*

as·soil (ə soil′), *v.t. Archaic.* **1.** to absolve; acquit; pardon. **2.** to atone for. [ME *asoil(en)* < AF *asoile(r),* OF *asoilier,* var. of *asoldre* < L *absoluere* to ABSOLVE]

as·so·nance (as′ə nəns), *n.* **1.** resemblance of sounds. **2.** *Pros.* rhyme in which the same vowel sounds are used with different consonants in the stressed syllables of the rhyming words, as in *penitent* and *reticence.* **3.** partial agreement or correspondence. [< F, equiv. to *asson(ant)* sounding in answer (see AS-, SONANT) + *-ance* -ANCE] —**as′so·nant,** *adj., n.* —**as·so·nan·tal** (as′ə nan′tᵊl), **as′so·nan′tic,** *adj.*

as·sort (ə sôrt′), *v.t.* **1.** to distribute, place, or arrange according to kind or class; classify; sort: *He spent the evening assorting the photographs and other mementos of past years.* **2.** to furnish with a suitable assortment or variety of goods; make up of articles likely to suit a demand. **3.** *Archaic.* to group with others of the same or similar kind; connect or identify as of a similar class; associate (usually fol. by *with*). —*v.i.* **4.** to agree in sort or kind; be matched or suited. **5.** to associate; consort. [late ME *assorte* < MF *assorte(r).* See AS-, SORT] —**as·sort′a·tive, as·sort′ive,** *adj.* —**as·sort′a·tive·ly,** *adv.* —**as·sort′er,** *n.*

as·sort·ed (ə sôr′tid), *adj.* **1.** consisting of selected kinds; arranged in sorts or varieties: *rows of assorted vegetables.* **2.** consisting of various kinds; miscellaneous: *assorted chocolates.* **3.** matched; suited: *a perfectly assorted pair.* [ASSORT + -ED²]

as·sort·ment (ə sôrt′mənt), *n.* **1.** act of assorting; distribution; classification. **2.** a collection of various kinds of things; a mixed collection. [ASSORT + -MENT]

ASSR, Autonomous Soviet Socialist Republic. Also, **A.S.S.R.**

asst., assistant.

as·suage (ə swāj′), *v.t.,* **-suaged, -suag·ing.** **1.** to make milder or less severe; relieve; ease; mitigate: *to assuage one's grief; to assuage one's pain.* **2.** to appease; satisfy; allay; relieve: *to assuage one's hunger and thirst.* **3.** to mollify; pacify; calm. [ME *aswage(n)* < OF *asouagie(r)* < VL **assuāviāre,* equiv. to L *as-* AS- + *suāvi(s)* SUAVE + *-ā-* thematic vowel + *-re* inf. ending] —**as·suage′ment,** *n.* —**as·suag′er,** *n.*
—**Syn. 1.** alleviate. **2.** relieve.

As·suan (äs wän′), *n.* Aswan. Also, **As·souan′.**

as·sua·sive (ə swā′siv), *adj.* soothing; alleviative. [AS- + (PER)SUASIVE]

As·su·e·rus (as′o͞o er′əs, -ēr′-), *n. Douay Bible.* Ahasuerus.

as·sume (ə so͞om′), *v.t.,* **-sumed, -sum·ing.** **1.** to take for granted or without proof; suppose; postulate; posit: *to assume a principle in reasoning.* **2.** to take upon oneself; undertake: *to assume an obligation.* **3.** to take over the duties or responsibilities of: *to assume office.* **4.** to take on (a particular character, quality, mode of life, etc.); adopt: *He now assumed the style of the aggressive go-getter.* **5.** to take on; be invested or endowed with: *He expected the situation to assume a threatening character.* **6.** to pretend to have or be; feign: *to assume a humble manner.* **7.** to appropriate or arrogate: *to assume a right to oneself.* **8.** to take upon oneself (the debts or obligations of another). **9.** *Archaic.* to take into relation or association; adopt. [< L *assūme(re)* (to) take to, adopt, equiv. to *as-* AS- + *sūmere* to take up (*sub-* SUB- + *-emere* to get)] —**as·sum′a·ble,** *adj.* —**as·sum′a·bly,** *adv.* —**as·sum′er,** *n.*
—**Syn. 1.** presuppose. **6.** See **pretend.**

as·sumed (ə so͞omd′), *adj.* **1.** adopted in order to deceive; fictitious; pretended; feigned: *an assumed name; an assumed air of humility.* **2.** taken for granted; supposed. **3.** usurped. [ASSUME + -ED²] —**as·sum·ed·ly** (ə so͞o′mid lē), *adv.*

assumed′ bond′, a bond issued by one corporation and assumed as an obligation by another.

as·sum·ing (ə so͞o′ming), *adj.* arrogant; presumptuous. [ASSUME + -ING²] —**as·sum′ing·ly,** *adv.*

as·sump·sit (ə sump′sit), *n. Law.* **1.** a legal action for a breach of contract or promise not under seal. **2.** an actionable promise. [< L: he has taken upon himself, he has undertaken]

as·sump·tion (ə sump′shən), *n.* **1.** act of taking for granted or supposing. **2.** something taken for granted; a supposition: *a correct assumption.* **3.** act of taking to or upon oneself. **4.** act of taking possession of something: *the assumption of power.* **5.** arrogance; presumption. **6.** *Eccles.* **a.** (*often cap.*) the bodily taking up into heaven of the Virgin Mary. **b.** (*cap.*) a feast commemorating it, celebrated on August 15. [ME < L *assūmptiōn-* (s. of *assūmptiō*), equiv. to *assūmpt(us)* taken up (ptp. of *assūmere;* see ASSUME) + *-iōn-* -ION]
—**Syn. 1, 2.** supposition, presupposition. **2.** hypothesis, conjecture, guess, postulate, theory. **3.** presumption. **5.** effrontery, forwardness.

As·sump·tion·ist (ə sump′shə nist), *n.* See **Augustinian of the Assumption.** [ASSUMPTION + -IST]

as·sump·tive (ə sump′tiv), *adj.* **1.** taken for granted. **2.** characterized by assumption: *an assumptive statement.* **3.** presumptuous. [< L *assūmptīv(us),* equiv. to *assūmpt(us)* (ptp.) (see ASSUMPTION) + *-īvus* -IVE] —**as·sump′tive·ly,** *adv.*

As·sur (as′ər), *n.* the god of war and supreme national god of Assyria. Also, **Ashur, Asshur, Asur.**

as·sur·ance (ə sho͝or′əns), *n.* **1.** a positive declaration intended to give confidence: *He received assurances of support for the project.* **2.** pledge; guaranty; surety: *He gave his assurance that the job would be done.* **3.** full confidence; freedom from doubt; certainty: *to act in the assurance of success.* **4.** freedom from timidity; self-confidence; self-possession; firmness; courage: *He acted with speed and assurance.* **5.** presumptuous boldness; impudence. **6.** *Brit.* insurance. [ME *ass(e)urau(n)ce* < MF *ass(e)urance.* See ASSURE, -ANCE]
—**Syn. 2.** warranty, oath. **3.** See **trust. 4.** See **confidence. 5.** effrontery, impertinence, nerve, cheek.
—**Ant. 3–5.** uncertainty.

As·sur·ba·ni·pal (ä′so͝or bä′nē päl′), *n.* Ashurbanipal.

as·sure (ə sho͝or′), *v.t.,* **-sured, -sur·ing.** **1.** to declare earnestly to; inform or tell positively; state with confidence to: *He assured us that everything would turn out well.* **2.** to cause to know surely; reassure: *He assured himself that they did as they were told.* **3.** to pledge or promise; give surety of; guarantee: *They were assured a job in the spring.* **4.** to make (a future event) sure; ensure: *This contract assures the company's profit this month.* **5.** to secure or confirm; render safe or stable: *to assure a person's position.* **6.** to give confidence to; encourage. **7.** to insure, as against loss. [ME *as(e)ure, assure* < OF *aseure(r)* < LL *assēcūrāre,* equiv. to L *as-* AS- + *sēcūr-* (see SECURE) + *-ā-* thematic vowel + *-re* inf. suffix] —**as·sur′er, as·sur′or,** *n.*

as·sured (ə sho͝ord′), *adj.* **1.** guaranteed; sure; certain; secure: *an assured income.* **2.** bold; confident; authoritative: *His art was both assured and facile.* **3.** boldly presumptuous. —*n.* **4.** *Insurance.* **a.** the beneficiary under a policy. **b.** the person whose life or property is covered by a policy. [ME; see ASSURE, -ED²] —**as·sur·ed·ly** (ə sho͝or′id lē), *adv.* —**as·sur′ed·ness,** *n.*

as·sur·gent (ə sûr′jənt), *adj. Bot.* curving upward, as leaves; ascending. [< L *assurgent-* (s. of *assurgēns* rising up, prp. of *assurgere*). See AS-, SURGENT] —**as·sur′gen·cy,** *n.*

As·sur·na·sir·pal II (ä′so͝or nä′zir päl′), *n.* See **Ashurnasirpal II.**

Assyr., Assyrian.

As·syr·i·a (ə sir′ē ə), *n.* an ancient empire in SW Asia: greatest extent from ab. 750 to 612 B.C. *Cap.:* Nineveh.

Empire of Assyria
Seventh Century B.C.

As·syr·i·an (ə sir′ē ən), *adj.* **1.** of or pertaining to Assyria, its inhabitants, or their language. —*n.* **2.** a native or an inhabitant of Assyria. **3.** the dialect of Akkadian spoken in Assyria. Cf. **Akkadian** (def. 1). [ASSYRI(A) + -AN]

As·syr·i·ol·o·gy (ə sir′ē ol′ə jē), *n.* the study of the history, language, etc., of the ancient Assyrians. [ASSYRI(A) + -O- + -LOGY] —**As·syr·i·o·log·i·cal** (ə sir′ē ə loj′i kəl), *adj.* —**As·syr′i·ol′o·gist,** *n.*

As·syr·o-Bab·y·lo·ni·an (ə sir′ō bab′ə lō′nē ən), *adj.* **1.** of or pertaining to Assyria and Babylonia. —*n.* **2.** the language of Assyria and Babylonia; Akkadian. [ASSYR(IA) + -O- + BABYLONIAN]

A·staire (ə stâr′), *n.* **Fred,** born 1899, U.S. dancer and actor.

a·star·board (ə stär′bərd), *adv. Naut.* toward or on the starboard side. [A-¹ + STARBOARD]

As·tar·te (a stär′tē), *n.* **1.** an ancient Semitic deity, goddess of fertility and reproduction worshiped by the Phoenicians and Canaanites, corresponding to the Hebrew Ashtoreth and the Babylonian and Assyrian Ishtar, and regarded as a moon goddess by the Greeks and Romans. **2.** (*l.c.*) Also called **chestnut clam.** any of several marine bivalve mollusks of the genus *Astarte,* having a somewhat triangular, chestnut-brown shell.

a·sta·sia (ə stā′zhə, -zhē ə, -zē ə), *n. Med.* inability to stand due to a limitation or absence of muscular coordination. Cf. **abasia.** [< Gk *astasía* instability, equiv. to *ástat(os)* (see ASTATIC) + *-ia* -IA]

a·stat·ic (ā stat′ik), *adj.* **1.** unstable; unsteady. **2.** *Physics.* having no tendency to take a definite position or direction. [< Gk *ástat(os)* not steadfast, unstable (*a-* A-⁶ + *statós* standing) + -IC; see STATIC] —**a·stat′i·cal·ly,** *adv.* —**a·stat·i·cism** (ā stat′i siz′əm), *n.*

astat′ic galvanom′eter, *Elect.* a galvanometer for measuring small currents, which is unaffected by the earth's magnetic field.

as·ta·tine (as′tə tēn′, -tin), *n. Chem.* a rare element of the halogen family. *Symbol:* At; *at. no.:* 85. [< Gk *ástat(os)* not steadfast, unstable (see ASTATIC) + -INE²]

a·stay (ə stā′), *adj., adv. Naut.* in line with or parallel to stays, or to a certain stay, as an anchor cable being heaved in. [A-¹ + STAY³]

as·ter (as′tər), *n.* **1.** any composite plant of the genus *Aster,* having rays varying from white or pink to blue around a yellow disk. **2.** a plant of some allied genus, as the China aster. **3.** *Biol.* a structure formed in a cell during mitosis, composed of astral rays radiating about the centrosome. **4.** *U.S. Furniture.* sunflower (def. 2). [< L < Gk *astḗr* star]

Aster, *Aster novae-angliae*

aster-, var. of **astro-** before a vowel: *asteroid.*

-aster¹, a diminutive or pejorative suffix denoting something that imperfectly resembles or merely apes the true thing: *criticaster; poetaster; oleaster.* [< L]

-aster², *Chiefly Biol.* var. of **astro-** as final element in a compound word: *diaster.* [repr. Gk *astḗr*]

as·ter·a·ceous (as′tə rā′shəs), *adj. Bot.* belonging to the *Asteraceae* or *Carduaceae,* the aster family of plants, usually included in the *Compositae.* [ASTER + -ACEOUS]

as′ter dai′sy. See **Arctic daisy.**

a·ster·e·og·no·sis (ə ster′ē og nō′sis, ā ster′-), *n. Med.* the inability to determine the shape of an object by touching or feeling it. [A-⁶ + STEREO- + -GNOSIS]

A·ste·ri·a (ə stēr′ē ə), *n. Class. Myth.* a Titaness, the daughter of Coeus and Phoebe, sister of Leto, and mother of Hecate: she was transformed into the island of Delos.

as·te·ri·at·ed (a stēr′ē ā′tid), *adj. Crystall.* exhibiting asterism. [< Gk *astéri(os)* starry (see ASTER-) + -ATE¹ + -ED²]

As·te·ri·on (ə stēr′ē ən), *n. Class. Myth.* a son of Cometes who joined the Argonauts. Also, **Asterius.**

as·te·ris·cus (as′tə ris′kəs), *n., pl.* **-cus·es.** *Eastern Ch.* a metal cross bent at the ends, used before the consecration to protect the bread from the covering veil. [< LL; see ASTERISK]

as·ter·isk (as′tə risk), *n.* **1.** the figure of a star (*), used in writing and printing as a reference mark or to indicate omission, doubtful matter, etc. **2.** something in the shape of a star or asterisk. —*v.t.* **3.** to mark with an asterisk: *to asterisk a word that requires a footnote.* [< L *asteriscus* < Gk *asterískos* small star, equiv. to *aster-* ASTER- + *-iskos* dim. suffix]

as·ter·ism (as′tə riz′əm), *n.* **1.** *Astron. Rare.* **a.** a group of stars. **b.** a constellation. **2.** *Crystall.* a property of some crystallized minerals of showing a starlike luminous figure in transmitted light or, in a cabochon-cut stone, by reflected light. **3.** three asterisks (*** or ⁂) printed before a passage to direct attention to it. [< Gk *asterismós* a marking with stars. See ASTER-, -ISM] —**as′ter·is′mal,** *adj.*

As·te·ri·us (ə stēr′ē əs), *n. Class. Myth.* **1.** the king of Crete who married Europa and who named as his heirs her three sons by Zeus. **2.** the giant son of Anax. **3.** the Minotaur born to Pasiphaë and the Cretan Bull. **4.** a son of Hyperasius who joined the Argonauts.

as·ter·ix·is (as′tə rik′sis), *n. Med.* inability to maintain a fixed posture or position, as in the flailing tremors of hepatic coma. [< Gk, equiv. to *a-* A-⁶ + *stḗrixis* fixed position]

a·stern (ə stûrn′), *adv. Naut., Aeron.* **1.** in a backward direction: *The steamer went astern at half speed.* **2.** in a position behind a specified vessel or aircraft: *The cutter was following close astern.* [A-¹ + STERN²]

a·ster·nal (ā stûr′nᵊl), *adj. Anat., Zool.* not reaching to or connected with the sternum. [A-⁶ + STERNAL]

As·te·ro·di·a (as′tə rō dī′ə), *n. Class. Myth.* a Caucasian nymph.

as·ter·oid (as′tə roid′), *n.* **1.** Also called **minor planet.** *Astron.* any of the thousands of small bodies of from 480 miles to less than one mile in diameter that revolve about the sun in orbits lying mostly between those of Mars and Jupiter. **2.** *Zool.* an asteroidean; a starfish. —*adj.* **3.** starlike. [< Gk *asteroeid(ḗs)* starry, starlike. See ASTER-, -O-, -OID] —**as′ter·oi′dal,** *adj.*

As·ter·oi·de·a (as′tə roi′dē ə), *n.* the class comprising the starfishes. [< NL; see ASTEROID]

as·ter·oi·de·an (as′tə roi′dē ən), *n.* **1.** an echinoderm of the class *Asteroidea,* comprising the starfishes. —*adj.* **2.** belonging or pertaining to the *Asteroidea.* [< NL *Aster(ias)* starfish genus (< Gk *asterías* starry; see ASTER-) + -OIDEA]

As·te·ro·pae·us (as′tə rō pē′əs), *n.* (in the *Iliad*) a Trojan ally slain by Achilles.

As·ter·o·pe (a ster′ə pē′), *n. Class. Myth.* Sterope.

as·the·ni·a (as thē′nē ə, as′thə nī′ə), *n. Pathol.* lack or loss of strength; debility. [< NL < Gk *asthéneia* weakness, equiv. to *asthene-,* s. of *asthenḗs* (*a-* A-⁶ + *sthene-,* var. s. of *sthénos* strength) + *-ia* -IA]

as·then·ic (as then′ik), *adj.* **1.** of, pertaining to, or characterized by asthenia; weak. **2.** *Psychol.* (of a physical type) having a slight build or slender body structure. Cf. **athletic** (def. 4), **pyknic** (def. 1). —*n.* **3.** a person of the asthenic type. [< Gk *asthenik(ós),* equiv. to *asthen-* (see ASTHENIA) + *-ikos* -IC]

as·the·nope (as′thə nōp′), *n. Ophthalm.* a person who has asthenopia. [back formation from ASTHENOPIA]

as·the·no·pi·a (as′thə nō′pē ə), *n. Ophthalm.* a fatigue or tiring of the eyes, usually characterized by discomfort, dimness of vision, and headache, caused by overuse of the visual organs, dysfunction of the ocular muscles, and incorrect refraction. [< Gk *asthen(ḗs)* frail (see ASTHENIA) + -OPIA] —**as·the·nop·ic** (as′thə nop′ik), *adj.*

as·then·o·sphere (as then′ə sfēr′), *n. Geol.* the region below the lithosphere, variously estimated as being from fifty to several hundred miles thick, in which the rock is less rigid than that above and below but rigid enough to transmit transverse seismic waves. [< Gk *asthen(ḗs)* frail (see ASTHENIA) + -O- + -SPHERE]

asth·ma (az′mə, as′-), *n.* a paroxysmal, often allergic disorder of respiration, characterized by bronchospasm, wheezing, and difficulty in expiration, often accompanied by coughing and a feeling of constriction in the chest. [< Gk: a panting (akin to *aázein* to breathe hard); r. ME *asma* < ML < Gk *ásthma*]

asth·mat·ic (az mat′ik, as-), *adj.* Also, **asth·mat′i·cal.** **1.** suffering from asthma. **2.** pertaining to asthma: *an asthmatic wheeze.* —*n.* **3.** a person suffering from asthma. [< L *asthmatic(us)* < Gk *asthmatikós,* equiv. to *asthmat-* (s. of *ásthma*) ASTHMA + *-ikos* -IC] —**asth·mat′i·cal·ly,** *adv.*

asth·ma·toid (az′mə toid′), *adj.* **1.** displaying the characteristics of asthma; similar to asthma: *a psychosomatic asthmatoid condition.* **2.** of, pertaining to, or associated with asthma: *an asthmatoid shortness of breath.* [< Gk *asthmat-* (see ASTHMATIC) + -OID]

As·ti (ä′stē), *n.* a city in central Piedmont, in NW Italy. 60,217 (1961).

as·tig·mat·ic (as′tig mat′ik), *Ophthalm.* —*adj.* **1.** pertaining to, exhibiting, or correcting astigmatism. —*n.* **2.** a person who has astigmatism. [A-⁶ + STIGMATIC] —**as′tig·mat′i·cal·ly,** *adv.*

a·stig·ma·tism (ə stig′mə tiz′əm), *n.* **1.** *Ophthalm.* a condition of the eye in which parallel rays of light from an external source converge or diverge unequally in different meridians. **2.** *Optics.* an aberration of a lens or other optical system in which the image of a point is spread out along the axis of the system. Also called **astigmia.** [ASTIGMAT(IC) + -ISM]

a·stig·ma·tiz·er (ə stig′mə tī′zər), *n. Optics.* a cylindrical lens used in a rangefinder to draw out the point image of a point source into a line. [A-⁶ + STIGMATIZER]

as·tig·mat·o·scope (as′tig mat′ə skōp′), *n. Ophthalm.* an instrument for determining the presence and degree of astigmatism. [ASTIGMAT(ISM) + -O- + -SCOPE]

a·stig·ma·tos·co·py (ə stig′mə tos′kə pē), *n., pl.* **-pies.** *Ophthalm.* examination by means of an astigmatoscope. [ASTIGMAT(ISM) + -O- + -SCOPY]

a·stig·mi·a (ə stig′mē ə), *n. Ophthalm.* astigmatism. [< NL; see A-⁶, STIGMA, -IA] —**a·stig′mic,** *adj.*

as·tig·mom·e·ter (as′tig mom′i tər), *n. Ophthalm.* an apparatus for measuring the degree of astigmatism. Also, **a·stig·ma·tom·e·ter** (ə stig′mə tom′i tər). [ASTIGM(ATISM) + -O- + -METER] —**as′tig·mom′e·try, a·stig′ma·tom′e·try,** *n.*

a·stig·mo·scope (ə stig′mə skōp′), *n. Ophthalm.* astigmatoscope.

a·stil·be (ə stil′bē), *n.* any herb of the genus *Astilbe,* having spirelike clusters of small white, pink, or reddish flowers. [< NL, equiv. to *a-* A-⁶ + Gk *stilbḗ,* fem. of *stilbós* glittering]

a·stir (ə stûr′), *adj.* **1.** moving; active; stirring: *The very field was astir with small animals, birds, and insects.* **2.** up and about; out of bed. [A-[1] + STIR[1]]

As·ti spu·man·te (ä′stē spo͞o män′te; *Eng.* as′tē spə-män′tē, spyə-), a sweet, sparkling Italian white wine with a muscat flavor. Also, **As′ti Spuman′te.** [< It lit., effervescent Asti; see SPUME, -ANT]

ASTM, American Society for Testing Materials. Also, **A.S.T.M.**

As·to·lat (as′tō lat′, -tə lat′), *n.* a place in the Arthurian romances, possibly in Surrey.

a·stom·a·tous (ā stom′ə təs, ā stō′mə-), *adj. Zool., Bot.* having no mouth, stoma, or stomata. [A-[6] + STOMATOUS]

As·ton (as′tən), *n.* **Francis William,** 1877–1945, English physicist and chemist: Nobel prize for chemistry 1922.

As′ton dark′ space′, *Physics.* the dark region between the cathode and the cathode glow in a vacuum tube, occurring when the pressure is low. [named after F. W. ASTON]

as·ton·ied (ə ston′ēd), *adj. Archaic.* dazed; bewildered; filled with consternation. [ME, deriv. of *astonyen* to ASTONISH; see -ED[2]]

as·ton·ish (ə ston′ish), *v.t.* to strike with sudden and overpowering wonder; surprise greatly; amaze: *His easy humor and keen intellect astonished me.* [ME *astony(en)* (? OE *āstunian;* see STUN) + -ISH[2]] —**as·ton′ished·ly,** *adv.* —**as·ton′ish·er,** *n.*
—**Syn.** astound, startle, shock. See **surprise.**

as·ton·ish·ing (ə ston′i shing), *adj.* causing astonishment or surprise; amazing: *an astonishing view; an astonishing remark.* [ASTONISH + -ING[2]] —**as·ton′ish·ing·ly,** *adv.* —**as·ton′ish·ing·ness,** *n.*

as·ton·ish·ment (ə ston′ish mənt), *n.* **1.** overpowering wonder or surprise; amazement: *He looked with astonishment at his friends.* **2.** an object or cause of amazement. [ASTONISH + -MENT]

As·tor (as′tər), *n.* **1. John Jacob,** 1763–1848, U.S. capitalist and fur merchant. **2. Nancy (Lang·horne)** (lang′hôrn′, -ərn) **Viscountess,** 1879–1964, first woman Member of Parliament in England.

As·to·ri·a (a stôr′ē ə, a stôr′-), *n.* a seaport in NW Oregon, near the mouth of the Columbia River. 11,239 (1960).

as·tound (ə stound′), *v.t.* **1.** to overwhelm with amazement; astonish greatly; shock with wonder or surprise. —*adj.* **2.** *Archaic.* astonished, astounded. [ME *astoun(e)d,* ptp. of *astonen,* var. of *astonyen* to ASTONISH]
—**Syn. 1.** See **surprise.**

as·tound·ing (ə stoun′ding), *adj.* capable of overwhelming with amazement; stunningly surprising. [ASTOUND + -ING[2]] —**as·tound′ing·ly,** *adv.*

astr., **1.** astronomer. **2.** astronomical. **3.** astronomy.

As·tra (as′trə), *n.* a girl's given name.

As·tra·ba·cus (ə strā′bə kəs), *n. Class. Myth.* a Spartan prince who, with Alopecus, found the wooden image of Artemis that Orestes had hidden in a willow thicket.

as·tra·chan (as′trə kən, -kan′), *n.* **1.** astrakhan. **2.** (*cap.*) *Hort.* **a.** a tart, usually red or yellow variety of apple. **b.** the tree bearing this fruit.

a·strad·dle (ə strad′əl), *adv., adj.* with one leg on each side; in a straddling position; astride: *The boy perched astraddle the fence.* [A-[1] + STRADDLE]

As·trae·a (a strē′ə), *n. Class. Myth.* the goddess of justice and the daughter of Zeus and Themis. She was the last of the immortals to leave mankind at the end of the golden age. Also, **Astrea.** —**As·trae′an,** *adj.*

As·trae·us (a strē′əs), *n. Class. Myth.* a Titan, the consort of Eos and father of the winds and stars.

as·tra·gal (as′trə gəl), *n. Archit., Furniture.* **1.** a small convex molding cut into the form of a string of beads. Cf. **bead and reel. 2.** a plain convex molding; bead. **3.** a molding attached to one or both meeting stiles of a pair of double doors in order to prevent drafts. [< L *astragal(us)* < Gk *astrágalos* a vertebra, the huckle-bone, a molding, a kind of vetch; in pl., dice (i.e., huckle-bones)]

as·trag·a·lo·man·cy (as′trə gə lō man′sē, ə strag′ə-), *n.* divination by means of dice which are marked with letters of the alphabet. [ASTRAGAL + -O- + -MANCY]

a·strag·a·lus (a strag′ə ləs), *n., pl.* **-li** (-lī′). *Zool.* (in higher vertebrates) one of the proximal bones of the tarsus. [< NL; see ASTRAGAL] —**as·trag′a·lar,** *adj.*

as·tra·khan (as′trə kən, -kan′), *n.* **1.** a fur of young lambs, with lustrous, closely curled wool, from Astrakhan. **2.** Also called **as′trakhan cloth′.** a fabric with curled pile resembling astrakhan fur. Also, **astrachan.**

As·tra·khan (as′trə kan′; *Russ.* ä′strä khän′yə), *n.* a city in the S RSFSR, in the SE Soviet Union in Europe, at the mouth of the Volga. 294,000 (1959).

as·tral (as′trəl), *adj.* **1.** pertaining to or proceeding from the stars; consisting of or resembling an aster; star-shaped. **2.** *Biol.* pertaining to or resembling an aster; star-shaped. **3.** *Theosophy.* noting a supersensible substance pervading all space and forming the substance of a second body **(astral body)** belonging to each individual, accompanying him through life and surviving him in death. [< L *astrāl(is),* equiv. to *astr(um)* star (< Gk *ástron*) + *-ālis* -AL[1]] —**as′tral·ly,** *adv.*

as′tral bod′y, **1.** *Astron.* a star, planet, comet, or other heavenly body. **2.** See under **astral** (def. 3).

as′tral crown′, *Heraldry.* a representation of a crown composed of a circlet having above it four stars, three being visible, between pairs of uplifted wings.

as′tral lamp′, an oil lamp designed to avoid the shadow cast upon the table by ordinary lamps.

as′tral ray′, *Biol.* one of the protoplasmic fibers of which an aster is composed.

As·tran·gi·a (ə strān′jē ə), *n.* a genus of corals forming small, encrusting colonies, found in shallow waters off both coasts of the U.S. [< NL < Gk *ástr(on)* star + *angeîa,* pl. of *angeîon* vessel]

as·tra·pho·bi·a (as′trə fō′bē ə), *n. Psychiatry.* an abnormal fear of thunder and lightning. [< NL < Gk *astra(pḗ)* lightning + *-phobia* -PHOBIA]

As·tra·tei·a (as′trə tī′ə), *n. Class. Myth.* Artemis: so called because she stopped an Amazon invasion in Laconia. [< Gk *Astrateía* she that stops an invasion]

a·stray (ə strā′), *adv., adj.* **1.** out of the right way; off the correct or known road, path, or route: *Although they received specific instructions as to how to get there, they nevertheless went astray and were lost all night.* **2.** away from that which is right; into error, confusion, or undesirable action or thought: *They were led astray by the big city and bright lights.* [ME *astraye* < MF *estraie* strayed, ptp. of *estraier* to STRAY]

As·tre·a (a strē′ə), *n.* Astraea.

as·trict (ə strikt′), *v.t.* **1.** to bind fast; confine; constrain or restrict. **2.** to bind morally or legally. [< L *astrict(us)* drawn together, bound, tightened (ptp. of *astringere*), equiv. to *a-* A-[5] + *strīg-* (var. s. of *stringere* to draw) + *-tus* ptp. suffix. See ASTRINGE] —**as·tric′tion,** *n.*

as·tric·tive (ə strik′tiv), *adj., n.* astringent. [ASTRICT + -IVE] —**as·tric′tive·ly,** *adv.* —**as·tric′tive·ness,** *n.*

As·trid (as′trid; *Norw.* äs′trē), *n.* a girl's given name.

a·stride (ə strīd′), *prep.* **1.** with a leg on each side of: *She sat astride the horse.* **2.** on both sides of: *The town lay astride the main road.* **3.** in a dominant position within: *Napoleon stands astride the early 19th century like a giant.* —*adv., adj.* **4.** in a posture of striding or straddling; with legs apart or on either side of something. [A-[1] + STRIDE]

as·tringe (ə strinj′), *v.t.,* **-tringed, -tring·ing.** to compress; bind together; constrict. [< L *astringe(re)* (to) draw together, equiv. to *a-* A-[5] + *stringere* to draw; see STRINGENT]

as·trin·gent (ə strin′jənt), *adj.* **1.** *Med.* contracting; constrictive; styptic. **2.** stern or severe; austere: *His was an astringent style.* —*n.* **3.** *Med.* a substance which contracts the tissues or canals of the body, thereby diminishing discharges, as of mucus or blood. [< L *astringent-* (s. of *astringēns*) prp. of *astringere* to ASTRINGE; see -ENT] —**as·trin′gen·cy,** *n.* —**as·trin′gent·ly,** *adv.*
—**Syn. 2.** sharp, harsh, rigorous. See **acid.**

as·trin·ger (as′trin jər), *n. Falconry.* one who trains and flies short-winged hawks, as the goshawk. Also, **austringer, ostringer.** [ME *ostringer* < MF *ostricier,* deriv. of *ostour* hawk < ML *auceptor,* L *acceptor,* alter. of *accipter* ACCIPTER]

as·tri·on·ics (as′trē on′iks), *n.* (*construed as sing.*) *Rocketry.* the science dealing with the application of electronics to astronautics. [ASTR(O)- + -I- + (ELEC-TR)ONICS]

astro-, a learned borrowing from Greek meaning "star," used in the formation of compound words: *astrophotography.* Also, **aster-, -aster.** [< Gk, comb. form of *ástron* a star, constellation]

as·tro·dome (as′trə dōm′), *n. Aeron.* a transparent dome on top of the fuselage of an aircraft, through which observations are made for celestial navigation. Also called, *Brit.,* **astro hatch.** [ASTRO- + DOME]

as·tro·gate (as′trə gāt′), *v.i., v.t.,* **-gat·ed, -gat·ing.** to navigate in outer space. [ASTRO- + (NAVI)GATE] —**as′tro·ga′tor,** *n.*

as·tro·ga·tion (as′trə gā′shən), *n.* navigation of a spacecraft. [ASTRO- + (NAVI)GATION]

as·tro·ge·ol·o·gy (as′trō jē ol′ə jē), *n.* the science dealing with the structure and composition of planets and other bodies in the solar system. [ASTRO- + GEOLOGY]

as·tro·graph (as′trə graf′, -gräf′), *n.* a navigational device for projecting altitude curves of the stars and planets onto charts or plotting sheets. [ASTRO- + -GRAPH] —**as′tro·graph′ic,** *adj.* —**as·trog·ra·phy** (ə strog′rə fē), *n.*

as′tro hatch′ (as′trō), *Brit.* astrodome.

as·troid (as′troid), *n. Geom.* a hypocycloid with four cusps. [ASTR(O)- + -OID]

as′tro·in·er′tial guid′ance (as′trō i nûr′shəl). See **celestial guidance.**

astrol., **1.** astrologer. **2.** astrological. **3.** astrology.

as·tro·labe (as′trə lāb′), *n.* an astronomical instrument for taking the altitude of the sun or stars and for the solution of other problems in astronomy and navigation, used by Greek astronomers from about 200 B.C. onward and by Arab astronomers during the Middle Ages. [ME, var. of *astrolabie* < ML *astrolabi(um)* < LGk *astrolábion,* Gk *astrolábon* (neut. of *astrolábos,* adj. used as n.), equiv. to *ástro(n)* star + *lab-* (var. s. of *lambánein* to take) + *-on* neut. suffix] —**as·tro·lab·i·cal** (as′trə lab′i kəl, -lā′bi-), *adj.*

as·trol·o·gy (ə strol′ə jē), *n.* **1.** the study which assumes, and professes to interpret the influence of the heavenly bodies on human affairs. **2.** *Obs.* the science of astronomy. [ME < L *astrologia* < Gk. See ASTRO-, -LOGY] —**as·trol′o·ger, as·trol′o·gist,** *n.* —**as·tro·lo·gi·an** (as′trə lō′jē ən), *n., adj.* —**as·tro·log·i·cal** (a′strə loj′i kəl), **as′tro·log′ic, as·trol·o·gous** (ə strol′ə gəs), *adj.* —**as′tro·log′i·cal·ly,** *adv.*

as·tro·man·cy (as′trə man′sē), *n.* divination by means of the stars. [< ML *astromantīa* < Gk *astromanteía.* See ASTRO-, -MANCY] —**as′tro·man′cer,** *n.* —**as′tro·man′tic,** *adj.*

as·trom·e·try (ə strom′i trē), *n.* the branch of astronomy that deals with the measurement of the positions, motions, and distances of the celestial bodies. [ASTRO- + -METRY] —**as·tro·met·ric** (as′trō me′trik), **as′tro·met′ri·cal,** *adj.*

astron., **1.** astronomer. **2.** astronomical. **3.** astronomy.

as·tro·naut (as′trə nôt′), *n.* one who travels outside the earth's atmosphere. [ASTRO- + (AERO)NAUT]

As·tro·nau·ta·rum (as′trō nô tär′əm, -nə-), *n.* **Sinus.** See **Sinus Astronautarum.**

as·tro·nau·tic (as′trə nô′tik), *adj.* of or pertaining to astronautics or astronauts. Also, **as′tro·nau′ti·cal.** [ASTRONAUT + -IC, perh. modeled on F *astronautique*] —**as′tro·nau′ti·cal·ly,** *adv.*

as·tro·nau·tics (as′trə nô′tiks), *n.* (*construed as sing.*) the science or art of travel beyond the earth's atmosphere, including interplanetary and interstellar flights. [see ASTRONAUTIC, -ICS]

As·tro·nauts (as′trə nôts′), *n.* **Gulf of the.** See **Sinus Astronautarum.**

as·tro·nav·i·ga·tion (as′trō nav′ə gā′shən), *n.* See **celestial navigation.** [ASTRO- + NAVIGATION] —**as′tro·nav′i·ga′tor,** *n.*

as·tron·o·mer (ə stron′ə mər), *n.* an expert in astronomy; a scientific observer of the celestial bodies. [earlier *astronomyer.* See ASTRONOMY, -ER[1]]

as·tro·nom·i·cal (as′trə nom′i kəl), *adj.* **1.** of, pertaining to, or connected with astronomy. **2.** extremely large; exceedingly great; enormous: *They spent money on an astronomical scale.* Also, **as′tro·nom′ic.** [< L *astronomic(us)* (< Gk *astronomikós;* see ASTRONOMY, -IC) + -AL[1]] —**as′tro·nom′i·cal·ly,** *adv.*

as′tronom′ical clock′, **1.** a clock indicating or representing the movements of the sun or planets, the phases of the moon, or the sky visible at a given time, used as a means of establishing time or for additional information, as locating celestial bodies or timing their movement. **2.** a clock used for observing the apparent time of the meridian passages of heavenly bodies.

astronom′ical frame′ of ref′erence, *Physics.* a frame of reference in which the sun or center of mass of the universe is fixed and which does not rotate with respect to the fixed stars.

astronom′ical refrac′tion, *Astron.* refraction (def. 3).

as′tronom′ical tel′escope, a telescope having an objective with a long focal length and an eyepiece with a short focal length, usually used for observing celestial bodies. Also called **Kepler telescope.**

as′tronom′ical twi′light, *Astron.* the period after sunset and before sunrise when the center of the sun is less than 18° below the horizon and still visible.

as′tronom′ical u′nit, *Astron.* a unit of length, equal to the mean distance of the earth from the sun: approximately 93 million miles. *Abbr.:* AU

as′tronom′ical year′, year (def. 4b).

as·tron·o·my (ə stron′ə mē), *n.* the science that deals with the material universe beyond the earth's atmosphere. [ME *astronomie* < L *astronomia* < Gk. See ASTRO-, -NOMY]

As′tro·phel and Stel′la (as′trə fel′), a sonnet sequence (1591) by Sir Philip Sidney.

as·tro·pho·tog·ra·phy (as′trō fə tog′rə fē), *n.* the photography of stars and other celestial objects. [ASTRO- + PHOTOGRAPHY] —**as·tro·pho·to·graph·ic** (as′trō fō′tə graf′ik), *adj.*

as·tro·phys·ics (as′trō fiz′iks), *n.* (*construed as sing.*) the branch of astronomy that deals with the physical properties of celestial bodies, and with the interaction between matter and radiation in the interior of celestial bodies and in interstellar space. [ASTRO- + PHYSICS] —**as′tro·phys′i·cal,** *adj.* —**as·tro·phys·i·cist** (as′trō fiz′i sist), *n.*

as·tro·sphere (as′trə sfēr′), *n. Biol.* **1.** the central portion of an aster, in which the centrosome lies. **2.** the whole aster exclusive of the centrosome. [ASTRO- + SPHERE]

as·tu·cious (a sto͞o′shəs, a styo͞o′-), *adj.* astute. [< F *astucieux* crafty, equiv. to *astuci(e)* (< L *astūtia;* see ASTUTE, -IA) + *-eux* -OUS] —**as·tu′cious·ly,** *adv.* —**as·tu·ci·ty** (a sto͞o′si tē, a styo͞o′-), *n.*

As·tu·ri·an (a sto͝or′ē ən, a styo͝or′-), *adj.* **1.** of or pertaining to Asturias, its people, or their language. —*n.* **2.** a native or inhabitant of Asturias. **3.** the dialect of Spanish spoken in Asturias. [< Sp *asturian(o).* See ASTURIAS, -AN]

As·tu·ri·as (a sto͝or′ē əs, a styo͝or′-; *Sp.* äs to͞or′yäs), *n.* a former kingdom and province in NW Spain.

as·tute (ə sto͞ot′, ə styo͞ot′), *adj.* **1.** of keen penetration or discernment; sagacious: *an astute author; an astute businessman.* **2.** clever; cunning; ingenious; shrewd: *an astute merchandising program; an astute manipulation of facts.* [< L *astūt(us)* shrewd, sly, cunning, equiv. to *astū-* (s. of *astus*) cleverness + *-tus* adj. suffix] —**as·tute′ly,** *adv.* —**as·tute′ness,** *n.*
—**Syn. 2.** artful, crafty, wily, sly.

As·ty·a·nax (a stī′ə naks′), *n. Class. Myth.* the young son of Hector and Andromache, thrown from the walls of Troy by the victorious Greeks so that he would not grow up to avenge the Trojan defeat. Also called **Scamandrius.**

As·ty·da·mi·a (as′ti də mī′ə), *n. Class. Myth.* **1.** a daughter of Amyntor who was abducted by Hercules. **2.** the mother of Amphitryon.

a·sty·lar (ā stī′lər), *adj. Archit.* without columns. [< Gk *ástyl(os)* without columns (*a-* A-[6] + *stŷl(os)* pillar + *-os* adj. suffix) + -AR[1]]

ASU, American Students Union.

A·sun·ción (ä′so͞on syôn′, -thyôn′), *n.* a city in and the capital of Paraguay, in the S part. 294,647 (est. 1959).

a·sun·der (ə sun′dər), *adv., adj.* **1.** into separate parts; in or into pieces: *to tear asunder.* **2.** apart or widely separated: *as wide asunder as the poles.* [ME; OE *on sundrum* apart. See A-[1], SUNDRY]

A supply, *Electronics.* a battery or other source of power for heating the filament or cathode heater of an electron tube. Also called **A power supply.** Cf. **B supply, C supply.**

A·sur (as′ər, ä′so͝or), *n.* Assur.

A·su·ra (us′o͝o rə), *n.* (in Vedic mythology) a spirit personifying power, either a god or Aditya, or a demon or Danava. [< Skt: mighty Lord]

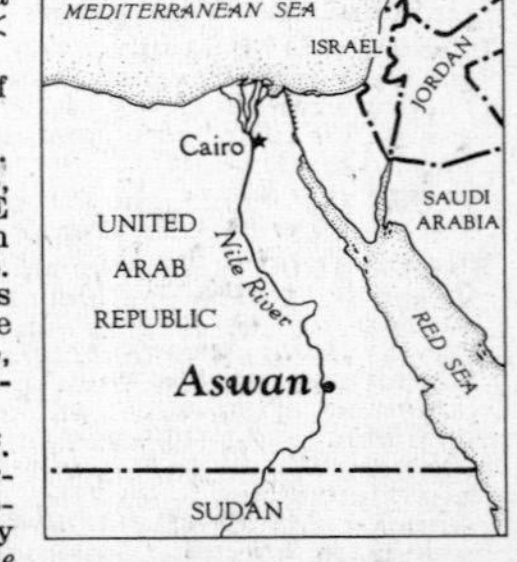

A.S.W., Association of Scientific Workers.

As·wan (as′wän; *Arab.* äs wän′), *n.* **1.** Ancient, **Syene.** a city in the SE United Arab Republic, on the Nile. 28,400 (est. 1957). **2.** a dam near this city, extending across the Nile. 6400 ft. long. Also, **As·wân′, Assuan, Assouan.**

a·swarm (ə swôrm′), *adj.* filled, as by objects, or organisms, etc., esp. in motion; teeming (usually used predicatively): *The garden was aswarm with bees. The air was so clear that the sky seemed aswarm with stars.* [A-[1] + SWARM[1]]

a·syl·lab·ic (ā′si lab′ik), *adj.* not syllabic. [A-[6] + SYLLABIC]

a·sy·lum (ə sī′ləm), *n.* **1.** an institution for the maintenance and care of the blind, the insane, orphans, etc. **2.** an inviolable refuge, as formerly for criminals and debtors; a sanctuary: *He sought asylum in the church.* **3.** *Internat. Law.* a temporary refuge granted political offenders, esp. in a foreign embassy. **4.** any secure retreat. [< L < Gk *ásylon* sanctuary, equiv. to *a-* A-[6] + *sýlon* right of seizure] —**Syn. 1.** See **hospital. 2.** haven, shelter, retreat.

a·sym·met·ric (ā′sə me′trik, as′ə-), *adj.* **1.** not identical on both sides of a central line; unsymmetrical; lacking symmetry: *Most faces are asymmetric.* **2.** (of a logical or mathematical relation) holding true of members of a class in one order but not in the opposite order, as in the relation "being an ancestor of." **3.** *Chem.* **a.** having an unsymmetrical arrangement of atoms in the molecule. **b.** noting a carbon atom bonded to four different atoms or groups. Also, **a′sym·met′ri·cal.** [A-[6] + SYMMETRIC] —**a′sym·met′ri·cal·ly,** *adv.*

a·sym·me·try (ā sim′i trē), *n.* quality or state of being asymmetric. [< Gk *asymmetría* lack of proportion. See A-[6], SYMMETRY]

asym′metry poten′tial, *Physical Chem.* (in hollow electrodes) the property of having a different potential on the inner and outer surfaces.

a·symp·to·mat·ic (ā simp′tə mat′ik), *adj.* showing no evidence of disease. [A-[6] + SYMPTOMATIC] —**a·symp′to·mat′i·cal·ly,** *adv.*

as·ymp·tote (as′im tōt′), *n.* *Math.* a straight line that a given curve approximates as one of the variables, or one of the expressions containing a variable, in the equation of the curve approaches infinity. [< Gk *asýmptōt(os)*, equiv. to *a-* A-[6] + *sýmptōtos* falling together (*sym-* SYM- + *ptōtós* falling, deriv. of *ptō-*, var. s. of *píptein* to fall, + *-tos* verbid suffix)]

as·ymp·tot·ic (as′im tot′ik), *adj.* *Math.* **1.** of or pertaining to an asymptote. **2.** (of a function) approaching a given value as an expression containing a variable tends to infinity. **3.** (of two functions) so defined that their ratio approaches unity as the independent variable approaches a limit or infinity. **4.** (of a formula) becoming increasingly exact as a variable approaches a limit, usually infinity. **5.** coming into consideration as a variable approaches a limit, usually infinity: *asymptotic property; asymptotic behavior.* **6.** using or having to do with asymptotic formulas: *asymptotic methods.* **7.** (of an infinite series of functions, usually divergent) having the property that the sum of the first few terms furnishes an increasingly accurate approximation to the function as the independent variable approaches a limit, usually infinity; semi-convergent. Also, **as′ymp·tot′i·cal.** [ASYMPTOTE + -IC] —**as′ymp·tot′i·cal·ly,** *adv.*

a·syn·chro·nism (ā sin′krə niz′əm, ā sin′-), *n.* want of synchronism, or coincidence in time. [A-[6] + SYNCHRONISM]

a·syn·chro·nous (ā siŋ′krə nəs, ā sin′-), *adj.* **1.** not occurring at the same time. **2.** (of a computer or other electrical machine) having each operation started only after the preceding operation is completed. [A-[6] + SYNCHRONOUS] —**a·syn′chro·nous·ly,** *adv.*

a·syn·de·ton (ə sin′di ton′, -tən), *n.* **1.** *Rhet.* the omission of conjunctions, as in "He has provided the poor with jobs, with opportunity, with self-respect." **2.** *Library Science.* the omission of cross references, esp. from a catalog. [< L < Gk n. use of neut. of *asýndetos* not linked (*a-* A-[6] + *syndé(ein)* (to) link + *-tos* verbid suffix)] —**as·yn·det·ic** (as′in det′ik), *adj.* —**as′yn·det′i·cal·ly,** *adv.*

a·syn·er·gy (ā sin′ər jē), *n.* *Med.* defective coordination between parts, as muscles or limbs, that normally act in unison. Also, **a·sy·ner·gi·a** (ā′si nûr′jə, -jē ə). [A-[6] + SYNERGY]

A·syn·jur (ä′sin yŏŏr′), *n.pl., sing.* **-ja** (-yä′), **-je** (-yā′). (*often l.c.*) *Scand. Myth.* the goddesses of the Aesir, led by Frigg.

a·syn·tac·tic (ā′sin tak′tik), *adj.* *Gram.* (of compounds) consisting of morphemes that are combined differently from their mode of combination as separate words in a phrase, as *bookstore*, which is an asyntactic compound, while the same elements are combined syntactically in *store for books.* [A-[6] + SYNTACTIC]

***As You Like It*,** a comedy (1599?) by Shakespeare.

A·syut (ä syōōt′), *n.* a city in the central United Arab Republic, on the Nile. 104,038 (est. 1957). Also, **A·syût′, Assiut.**

at[1] (at; *unstressed* ət, it), *prep.* **1.** (used to indicate a point or place occupied in space); in, on, or near: *to stand at the door; at the bottom of the barrel.* **2.** (used to indicate a location or position, as in time, on a scale, or in order): *at zero; at noon; at age 65; at the end; at the lowest point.* **3.** (used to indicate presence or location): *at home; at hand.* **4.** (used to indicate amount, degree, or rate): *at great speed; at high altitudes.* **5.** (used to indicate a goal or objective); toward: *Aim at the mark. Look at that.* **6.** (used to indicate occupation or involvement): *at work; at play.* **7.** (used to indicate a state or condition): *at ease;* at *peace.* **8.** (used to indicate a cause): *She was annoyed at his stupidity.* **9.** (used to indicate a method or manner): *He spoke at length.* **10.** (used to indicate relative quality or value): *at one's best; at cost.* [ME; OE *æt*; c. Icel, OS, Goth *at*, OHG *az*, L *ad*] —**Usage.** See **about.**

at[2] (ät, at), *n.* a money of account of Laos, the 100th part of a kip, equal to .000125 of a U.S. dollar. [< Siamese]

at-, var. of **ad-** before *t: attend.*

AT, antitank.

At, ampere-turn.

at., **1.** atmosphere. **2.** atomic. **3.** attorney.

At, *Chem.* astatine.

-ata[1], a plural suffix occurring in loan words from Latin, used esp. in names of zoological groups: *Vertebrata.* [< L, neut. pl. of *-ātus* -ATE[1]]

-ata[2], a plural suffix occurring in loan words from Greek: *stomata.* [< Gk *t*-stems, -*(m)ata* result of, state of, act of; cf. -MENT]

A.T.A., Associate Technical Aide.

at·a·bal (at′ə bal′), *n.* a kind of drum used by the Moors. Also, **attabal.** [< Sp < Ar *aṭ ṭabl* the drum]

A·ta·ba·li·pa (ä′tä bä′lē pä′), *n.* Atahualpa.

At·a·brine (at′ə brin, -brēn′), *n.* *Pharm., Trademark.* quinacrine.

At·a·by·ri·an (at′ə bĭ′rē ən), *n.* *Class. Myth.* Zeus: so called because of his sanctuary on Mount Atabyrium in Rhodes.

A′ta·ca′ma Des′ert (at′ə kam′ə, at′-; *Sp.* ä′tä kä′mä), an arid region in N Chile: rich nitrate deposits. ab. 600 mi. long; ab. 70,000 sq. mi.

at·a·cam·ite (at′ə kam′īt, ə tak′ə mīt′), *n.* a mineral, hydrated chloride of copper, $Cu_2Cl(OH)_3$, occurring in a green, granular form, used as a source of metallic copper. [named after ATACAMA (DESERT); see -ITE[1]]

at·a·ghan (at′ə gan′), *n.* yataghan.

A·ta·hual·pa (ä′tä wäl′pä), *n.* c1500–33, last Incan king of Peru (son of Huayna Capac). Also, **Atabalipa.**

A·tak·a·pa (ə tak′ə pə, -pä′, -pô′), *n., pl.* **-pas,** (*esp. collectively*) **-pa. 1.** a member of an American Indian people living along the coast of Louisiana. **2.** the language of the Atakapa Indians.

At·a·lan·ta (at′ᵊlan′tə), *n.* **1.** Also, **At·a·lan·te** (at′ᵊlan′tē). *Class Myth.* a virgin huntress, the first person to wound the Calydonian boar. She promised to marry the man who could win a foot race against her and finally lost to Hippomenes, who distracted her attention by dropping three golden apples given to him by Aphrodite. Cf. **Melanion. 2.** Also, **Atlanta.** a girl's given name.

at·a·man (at′ə mən), *n., pl.* **-mans.** a chief of Cossacks, elected by the whole group; hetman. [< Russ]

at′a·mas′co lil′y (at′ə mas′kō, at′-), **1.** an amaryllidaceous plant, *Zephyranthes atamasco*, of the southeastern U.S., bearing a single white lilylike flower. **2.** any species of this genus. Also called **at′a·mas′co, fairy lily.** [< AmerInd (Virginia)]

at·ar (at′ər, -är), *n.* attar.

At·a·rax (at′ə raks′), *n.* *Pharm., Trademark.* hydroxyzine.

at·a·rax·i·a (at′ə rak′sē ə), *n.* a state of tranquillity, free from emotional disturbance and anxiety. Also, **at·a·rax·y** (at′ə rak′sē). [< L < Gk: calmness, equiv. to *atarak(tós)* unmoved (*a-* A-[6] + *tarak-*, var. s. of *tarássein* to disturb + *-tos* verbid suffix) + *-s(is)* -SIS + *-ia* -IA] —**at·a·rac·tic** (at′ə rak′tik), **at′a·rax′ic,** *adj., n.*

A·tas·ca·de·ro (ə tas′kə dâr′ō), *n.* a town in SW California. 5983 (1960).

à tâtons (A tä tôN′), *French.* experimentally; gropingly.

A·ta·türk (at′ə tûrk′, ä tä tûrk′), *n.* See **Kemal Atatürk.**

a·tav·ic (ə tav′ik), *adj.* atavistic. [ATAV(ISM) + IC, modeled on F *atavique*]

at·a·vism (at′ə viz′əm), *n.* **1.** *Biol.* the reappearance in an individual of characteristics of some remote ancestor that have been absent in intervening generations. **2.** reversion to an earlier type. [< L *atav(us)* remote ancestor (*at-* father + *avus* grandfather, forefather) + -ISM] —**at′a·vist,** *n.*

at·a·vis·tic (at′ə vis′tik), *adj.* of, pertaining to, or characterized by atavism; reverting to or suggesting the characteristics of a remote ancestor or primitive type: *Hitler's attack on Russia was prompted by the atavistic impulse to go east.* [ATAV(ISM) + -ISTIC] —**at′a·vis′ti·cal·ly,** *adv.*

a·tax·i·a (ə tak′sē ə), *n.* *Pathol.* loss of coordination of the muscles, esp. of the extremities. Also, **a·tax·y** (ə tak′sē, a tak′-). Cf. **locomotor ataxia.** [< NL < Gk, equiv. to *a-* A-[6] + *táx(is)* -TAXIS + *-ia* -IA] —**a·tax′ic,** *adj.*

a·tax·ite (ə tak′sīt, ā tak′-), *n.* *Petrog.* any taxite composed of angular fragments. [ATAX(IA) + -ITE[1]]

At·ba·ra (ät′bä rä′), *n.* **1.** a river in NE Africa, flowing NW from NW Ethiopia to the Nile in E Sudan. ab. 500 mi. long. **2.** a city in NE Sudan. 36,298 (1956).

ATC, 1. Air Traffic Control. **2.** Air Transport Command.

Atch·e·son (ach′i sən), *n.* a boy's given name.

Atch·i·son (ach′i sən), *n.* a city in NE Kansas, on the Missouri River. 12,529 (1960).

ate (āt; *Brit.* et), *v.* a pt. of **eat.**

A·te (ā′tē), *n.* an ancient Greek goddess personifying the fatal blindness or recklessness that produces crime and the divine punishment that follows it. [< Gk, special use of *átē* reckless impulse, ruin, akin to *aáein* to mislead, harm]

-ate[1], a suffix occurring in loan words from Latin, its English distribution paralleling that of Latin. The form originated as a suffix added to *a*-stem verbs to form adjectives (*separate*). The resulting form could also be used independently as a noun (*magistrate; advocate*) and came to be used as a stem on which a verb could be formed (*separate; advocate; agitate*). In English the use as a verbal suffix has been extended to stems of non-Latin origin: *calibrate.* [< L *-ātus* (masc.), *-āta* (fem.), *-ātum* (neut.), equiv. to *-ā-* thematic vowel + *-tus, -ta, -tum* ptp. suffix]

-ate[2], *Chem.* a specialization of **-ate**[1], used to indicate a salt of an acid ending in **-ic,** added to a form of the stem of the element or group: *sulfate.* Cf. **-ite**[3]. [< L *-ātum*, neut. of *-ātus* -ATE[1]]

at·e·brin (at′ə brin, -brēn′), *n.* *Pharm.* quinacrine.

A.Tech., Associate in Technology.

a·tef-crown (ä′tef kroun′), *n.* a symbolic headdress of certain Egyptian gods, as Osiris, and of Egyptian kings, consisting of a tall conical cap flanked by two plumes and bearing representations of the uraeus and the sun. [< Egypt *ātef* father + CROWN]

at·e·lec·ta·sis (at′ᵊlek′tə sis), *n.* *Pathol.* **1.** incomplete expansion of the lungs at birth, as from lack of breathing force. **2.** collapse of the lungs, as from bronchial obstruction. [< NL; see ATELIOSIS, ECTASIS] —**at·e·lec·tat·ic** (at′ᵊlek tat′ik), *adj.*

a·te·lei·o·sis (ə tē′lē ō′sis), *n.* *Pathol.* ateliosis.

a·tel·ic (a tel′ik), *adj.* imperfective. Cf. **telic** (def. 3). [A-[6] + TELIC]

at·el·ier (at′ᵊl yā′; *Fr.* Aᵗᵊ lyā′), *n., pl.* **at·el·iers** (at′ᵊl yāz′; *Fr.* Aᵗᵊ lyā′). a workshop or studio, esp. of an artist, artisan, or craftsman. [< F: lit., pile of chips (hence, workshop); OF *astele* chip (< LL *astella*, dim. of L *astula*, var. of *assula* splinter, equiv. to *ass(is)* plank + *-ula* -ULE) + *-ier* < L *-iārium*; see -ARY]

a·te·li·o·sis (ə tē′lē ō′sis, ə tel′ē-), *n.* *Pathol.* a form of infantilism caused by pituitary malfunction and characterized by a childish face and voice and associated physical underdevelopment, but accompanied by normal intelligence. Also, **ateleiosis.** [< Gk *atélei(a)* imperfection (see A-[6], TELE-[2], -IA) + -OSIS] —**a·tel·i·ot·ic** (ə tel′ē ot′ik), *adj.*

a tem·po (ä tem′pō; *It.* ä tem′pô), *Music.* resuming the speed obtained preceding ritardando or accelerando. [< It: in (the regular) time]

A·ten (ät′ᵊn), *n.* Aton.

a ter·go (ä ter′gō), *Latin.* at or toward the back; from behind; in the rear.

à terre (*Fr.* A teR′), *Ballet.* on the ground. [< F]

A·tes·te (ə tes′tē), *n.* ancient name of **Este.**

Ath·a·bas·can (ath′ə bas′kən), *n., adj.* Athapaskan.

Ath·a·bas·ka (ath′ə bas′kə), *n.* **1. Lake,** a lake in W Canada, in NW Saskatchewan and NE Alberta. ab. 200 mi. long; ab. 3000 sq. mi. **2.** a river in W Canada flowing NE from W Alberta to Lake Athabaska. 765 mi. long.

Ath·a·bas·kan (ath′ə bas′kən), *n., adj.* Athapaskan.

Ath·a·li·ah (ath′ə lī′ə), *n.* a daughter of Ahab and Jezebel and usurper of the throne of Judah, reigned 842–837 B.C. II Kings 11:1–3. Also, *Douay Bible,* **Ath′a·li′a.**

Ath·a·lie (at′ə lē; *Fr.* A tA lē′), *n.* a tragedy (1691) by Racine.

Ath·a·mas (ath′ə mas′), *n.* *Class. Myth.* the husband first of Nephele and later of Ino, and the father of Phrixus, Leucon, Helle, Melicertes, and Learchus.

ath·a·na·sia (ath′ə nā′zhə), *n.* deathlessness; immortality. Also, **a·than·a·sy** (ə than′ə sē). [< Gk, equiv. to *athána(tos)* deathless (*a-* A-[6] + *thánatos* death) + *-sia* (*-s(is)* -SIS + *-ia* -IA)]

Ath·a·na·sian (ath′ə nā′zhən), *adj.* **1.** of or pertaining to Athanasius or to the doctrines ascribed to him. —*n.* **2.** *Theol.* a follower of Athanasius or a believer in the Athanasian Creed. [ATHANASI(US) + -AN]

Athana′sian Creed′, a creed or formulary of Christian faith, of unknown authorship, formerly ascribed to Athanasius.

Ath·a·na·sius (ath′ə nā′shəs), *n.* **Saint,** A.D. 296?–373, bishop of Alexandria: opponent of Arianism.

ath·a·nor (ath′ə nôr′), *n.* *Alchemy.* a digester furnace with a self-feeding fuel supply contained in a towerlike contrivance, ensuring a constant, durable temperature. [late ME << Ar *at tannūr* the furnace]

Ath·a·pas·kan (ath′ə pas′kən), *n.* **1.** a family of languages spoken by American Indians in most of inland northwest Canada and Alaska, in coastal Oregon and California, and in Arizona and the Rio Grande basin, and including esp. Navaho, Chiricahua Apache, San Carlos Apache, Hupa, Mattole, Sarsi, and Chipewyan. Cf. **family** (def. 11). **2.** a member of any of various American Indian peoples speaking Athapaskan. —*adj.* **3.** belonging to or characteristic of the Athapaskans. Also, **Ath′a·pas′can, Athabascan, Athabaskan.** [*Athapask(a)*, name of an aboriginal North American people + -AN]

ath·ar (ath′ər, -är), *n.* attar.

A·thar·va-Ve·da (ə tär′və vā′də, -vē′də), *n.* *Hinduism.* one of the *Samhitas*, a collection of mantras and formulae, some showing pre-Vedic influence. Cf. **Veda.**

a·the·ism (ā′thē iz′əm), *n.* **1.** the doctrine or belief that there is no God. **2.** disbelief in the existence of God or gods. [< Gk *áthe(os)* godless + -ISM]

a·the·ist (ā′thē ist), *n.* one who denies or disbelieves the existence of God or gods. [< Gk *áthe(os)* godless + -IST] —**Syn.** ATHEIST, AGNOSTIC, INFIDEL, SKEPTIC refer to persons not inclined toward religious belief or a particular form of religious belief. An ATHEIST is one who denies the existence of a Deity or of divine beings. An AGNOSTIC is one who believes it impossible to know anything about God or about the creation of the universe and refrains from committing himself to any religious doctrine. INFIDEL means an unbeliever, especially a nonbeliever in Mohammedanism or Christianity. A SKEPTIC doubts and is critical of all accepted doctrines and creeds.

a·the·is·tic (ā′thē is′tik), *adj.* pertaining to or characteristic of atheists; involving, containing, or tending to atheism: *atheistic literature; atheistic people.* Also, **a′the·is′ti·cal.** [ATHEIST + -IC] —**a′the·is′ti·cal·ly,** *adv.* —**a′the·is′tic·ness,** *n.*

Ath·el (ath′əl), *n.* a boy's given name. Also, **Athol.**

ath·el·ing (ath′ə liŋ, ath′-), *n.* *Early Eng. Hist.* a man of royal blood; a prince. [ME; OE *ætheling* (c. OHG *ediling, adalung,* OS *ethiling*), equiv. to *æthel(u)* noble family + *-ing* suffix of appurtenance]

Ath·el·stan (ath′əl stan′), *n.* A.D. 895?–940, king of England 925–940.

ath′el tree′, a tree or large shrub, *Tamarix aphylla*, of the desert regions of western Asia and northern Africa, having small, pink flowers in terminal clusters. Also called **salt tree.** [< Ar *athlah*]

a·the·mat·ic (ā′thē mat′ik), *adj.* inflected without a thematic vowel. [A-[6] + THEMATIC]

A·the·na (ə thē′nə), *n.* **1.** Also, **A·the·ne** (ə thē′nē). Also called **Pallas, Pallas Athena.** the virgin deity of the ancient Greeks worshiped as the goddess of wisdom, fertility, the useful arts, and prudent warfare: identified by the Romans with Minerva. At her birth she sprang forth fully armed from the head of her father, Zeus. **2.** a girl's given name.

Athena

ath·e·nae·um (ath′ə nē′əm), *n.* **1.** an institution for the promotion of literary or scientific learning. **2.** a library or reading room. **3.** (*cap.*) a sanctuary of Athena at Athens, built by the Roman emperor Hadrian, and frequented by poets and men of learning. Also, **ath′e·ne′um.**

Ath·e·nae·us (ath′ə nē′əs), *n.* late 2nd century A.D., Greek philosopher and rhetorician at Naucratis in Egypt.

Athenae′us of At·ta·lei′a (at′ᵊlī′ə), Greek physician in Rome, fl. A.D. c40–65.

Ath·e·nag·o·ras I (ath′ə nag′ər əs; *Gk.* ä thē′nä gô′räs), *n.* (*Aristocles Spyrou*) born 1886, Archbishop Ecumenical of Constantinople and Ecumenical Patriarch of the Greek Orthodox Church since 1948.

A·the·nai (ä thē′ne), *n.* Greek name of **Athens.**

A·the·ni·an (ə thē′nē ən), *adj.* **1.** pertaining to Athens, Greece. **—***n.* **2.** a native or citizen of Athens, Greece. [< L *Athēni(ēnsis)* of Athens + -AN; see -ESE]

A·thé·nienne (ä′tān yen′; *Fr.* A tā nyen′), *n., pl.* **A·thé·niennes** (ä′tān yenz′; *Fr.* A tā nyen′). a small, decorative stand in the form of an antique tripod, used esp. in France in the Louis XVI and Empire periods. [< F, fem. of *Athénien* ATHENIAN]

Ath·ens (ath′inz), *n.* **1.** Greek, **Athenai.** a city in and the capital of Greece, in the SE part. 1,852,709 with suburbs (1961). **2.** a city in N Georgia. 31,355 (1960). **3.** a city in S Ohio. 16,470 (1960). **4.** a town in N Alabama. 9330 (1960). **5.** a town in E Texas. 7086 (1960). **6.** a town in NE Pennsylvania. 4515 (1960). **7.** any city that is compared to Athens, esp. as a cultural center: *the Athens of the Midwest.*

ath·er·ine (ath′ə rīn′, -ər in), *adj.* **1.** belonging or pertaining to the family *Atherinidae*, comprising the silversides. **—***n.* **2.** an atherine fish. [< NL *Atherin(a)* name of the genus < Gk *atherínē* smelt]

ath·er·o·ma (ath′ə rō′mə), *n., pl.* **-mas, -ma·ta** (-mə tə). *Pathol.* **1.** a sebaceous cyst. **2.** a condition characterized by the deposit of fat in the inner linings of the arterial walls. [< L: a tumor filled with matter < Gk *athērōma*, equiv. to *athár(ē)* porridge (*athēr-*, s. of *athēr* chaff) + *-ōma* -OMA]

ath·er·o·scle·ro·sis (ath′ə rō sklə rō′sis, ath′-), *n.* *Pathol.* a form of arteriosclerosis in which fatty substances deposit in and beneath the intima. [< Gk *athēro-* (comb. form of *athēr* chaff) + SCLEROSIS] **—ath·er·o·scle·rot·ic** (ath′ə rō sklə rot′ik, ath′-), *adj.*

Ath·er·ton (ath′ər tən), *n.* **1. Gertrude Franklin** (*Gertrude Franklin Horn*), 1857–1948, U.S. novelist. **2.** a town in W California. 7717 (1960).

ath·e·toid (ath′i toid′), *adj.* **1.** resembling athetosis. **2.** athetosic. [ATHET(OSIS) + -OID]

ath·e·to·sic (ath′i tō′sik), *adj.* of or noting athetosis. Also, **ath·e·tot·ic** (ath′i tot′ik). [ATHETOS(IS) + -IC]

ath·e·to·sis (ath′i tō′sis), *n.* *Pathol.* a condition, chiefly in children, of slow, involuntary, wormlike movements of the fingers, toes, hands, and feet, usually resulting from a brain lesion. [< Gk *áthet(os)* not placed (*a-* A-[6] + *thetós*, equiv. to *the-* s. of *tithénai* to set, put + *-tos* verbid suffix) + -OSIS]

Ath·ie (ath′ē), *n.* a girl's given name, form of **Athalia** or **Athena.**

a·thirst (ə thûrst′), *adj.* **1.** having a keen desire; eager (often fol. by *for*): *She has long been athirst for European travel.* **2.** thirsty. [ME *athurst*, *ofthurst*, OE *ofthyrst*, ptp. of *ofthyrstan.* See A-[2], THIRST]

ath·lete (ath′lēt), *n.* **1.** one trained to compete in contests involving physical agility, stamina, or strength; a trained competitor in a sport, exercise, or game requiring physical skill. **2.** *Brit.* traditionally, one trained for and competing in track-and-field events. [< L *athlēt(a)* < Gk *athlētḗ(s)*, equiv. to *athlē-* (var. s. of *athleîn* to contend for a prize, deriv. of *âthlos* a contest) + *-tēs* suffix of agency]

ath′lete's foot′, *Pathol.* a contagious disease, caused by a fungus that thrives on moist surfaces; ringworm of the feet.

ath′lete's heart′, *Pathol.* enlargement of the heart resulting from excessive exercise. Also, **athlet′ic heart′.**

ath·let·ic (ath let′ik), *adj.* **1.** physically active and strong: *an athletic child.* **2.** of, like, or befitting an athlete. **3.** of or pertaining to athletes; involving the use of physical skills or capabilities, as strength, agility, or stamina: *athletic sports; athletic training.* **4.** *Psychol.* (of a physical type) having a sturdy build or well-proportioned body structure. Cf. **asthenic** (def. 2), **pyknic** (def. 1). [< L *athletic(us)* < Gk *athlētikós.* See ATHLETE, -IC] **—ath·let′i·cal·ly,** *adv.* **—ath·let·i·cism** (ath let′i siz′əm), *n.*

ath·let·ics (ath let′iks), *n.* **1.** (*usually construed as pl.*) athletic sports, as running, rowing, boxing, etc. **2.** *Brit.* traditionally, track-and-field events only. **3.** (*usually construed as sing.*) the practice of athletic exercises; the principles of athletic training. [see ATHLETIC, -ICS]

athlet′ic support′er, jockstrap.

ath·o·dyd (ath′ə did), *n.* a ramjet. [*a(ero)- th(erm)ody-(namic) d(uct)*]

Ath·ol (ath′ôl), *n.* a boy's given name. Also, **Athel.**

at-home (at hōm′), *n.* a reception of visitors at certain hours during which a host or hostess has announced he or she will be "at home." Also, **at home′.**

ath·o·nite (ath′ə nīt′), *adj.* of or relating to Mount Athos. [< L *Athōn* (var. of *Athō, Athōs* < Gk *Athōs* ATHOS) + -ITE[1]]

Ath·os (ath′os, ā′thos; *Gk.* ä′thôs), *n.* **Mount, 1.** the easternmost of three prongs of the peninsula of Chalcidice, in NE Greece: site of an independent republic constituted of 20 monasteries. 2687 (1961). 131 sq. mi.; ab. 35 mi. long. **2.** a headland on this peninsula. 6350 ft. long.

a·thrill (ə thril′), *adj.* affected with a sudden wave of keen emotion or excitement; tingling (usually used predicatively): *After the first shock, he found himself athrill with a sense of discovery.* [A-[1] + THRILL]

ath·ro·cyte (ath′rə sīt′), *n.* *Biol.* a cell that ingests foreign particles and retains them in suspension in the cytoplasm. [< Gk *(h)athró(os)* gathered together + -CYTE] **—ath′ro·cy·to′sis,** *n.*

a·thwart (ə thwôrt′), *adv.* **1.** from side to side; crosswise. **2.** perversely; awry; wrongly. **3.** *Naut.* **a.** at right angles to the fore-and-aft line; across. **b.** broadside to the wind because of equal and opposite pressures of wind and tide: *a ship riding athwart.* **—***prep.* **4.** from side to side of; across. **5.** in opposition to; contrary to. **6.** *Naut.* across the direction or course of. [A-[1] + THWART]

a·thwart·ships (ə thwôrt′ships), *adv.* *Naut.* from one side of a ship to the other. [ATHWART + SHIP + -S[1]]

At·i·la (at′i lə, -əl ə), *n.* a girl's given name. Also, **Attila.**

a·tilt (ə tilt′), *adj., adv.* **1.** a tilt or inclination; tilted: *Hold the bottle slightly atilt.* **2.** in a tilting encounter. [A-[1] + TILT[1]]

a·tin·gle (ə ting′gəl), *adj.* tingling; stimulated. [A-[1] + TINGLE]

-ation, a combination of **-ate**[1] and **-ion,** used to form nouns from stems in **-ate**[1] (*separation*); on this model, used independently to form nouns from stems of other origin: *flirtation.* [< L *-ātiōn-* (s. of *-ātiō*), equiv. to *-āt(us)* -ATE[1] + *-iōn-* -ION; identical with G *-ation*, F *-ation*, etc.]

a·tip·toe (ə tip′tō′), *adv., adj.* **1.** standing or walking on tiptoe (usually used predicatively). **2.** eagerly expectant, as anticipating a desired event or arrival: *waiting atiptoe for the mail.* **3.** moving with caution or stealth, as avoiding calling attention to one's presence: *She walked atiptoe through the sleeping house.* [A-[1] + TIPTOE]

-ative, a combination of **-ate**[1] and **-ive,** used to form adjectives from stems in **-ate**[1] (*regulative*); on this model, used independently to form adjectives from stems of other origin: *explanative.* [< L *-ātiv(us)*, equiv. to *-āt(us)* -ATE[1] + *-īvus* -IVE]

At′ka mack′erel (at′kə), an edible fish, *Pleurogrammus monopterygius*, found in the North Pacific, marked with vertical black bars. [named after *Atka* an island in SW Alaska near the fishing grounds]

At·kins (at′kinz), *n., pl.* **-kins.** See **Tommy Atkins.**

At·kin·son (at′kin sən), *n.* **1. Sir Harry Albert,** 1831–92, New Zealand statesman, born in England: prime minister 1876–77, 1883–84, 1887–91. **2. (Justin) Brooks,** born 1894, U.S. drama critic, journalist, and author.

At·lan·ta (at lan′tə), *n.* **1.** a city in and the capital of Georgia, in the N part. 425,022. **2.** a town in NE Texas. 4076 (1960). **3.** a girl's given name, form of **Atalanta.**

at·lan·tad (at lan′tad), *adv.* *Anat.* toward the atlas. [< NL *atlant-* (s. of *atlas*; see ATLAS) + *-ad* (< L *ad* toward)]

at·lan·tal (at lan′tᵊl), *adj.* *Anat.* of or pertaining to the atlas. [< NL *atlant-* (see ATLANTAD) + -AL[1]]

At·lan·te·an (at′lan tē′ən, -lən-), *adj.* **1.** pertaining to the demigod Atlas. **2.** having the strength of Atlas: *He was of monumental girth and Atlantean power.* **3.** pertaining to Atlantis. [< L *Atlantē(us)* (< Gk *Atlánteios* of ATLAS, equiv. to *Atlant-*, s. of *Átlās*, + *-eios* adj. suffix) + -AN]

at·lan·tes (at lan′tēz), *n.* pl. of **atlas** (def. 9).

At·lan·tic (at lan′tik), *adj.* **1.** of or pertaining to the Atlantic Ocean. **2.** of or pertaining to the Titan Atlas. **—***n.* **3.** a town in SW Iowa. 6890 (1960). **4.** See **Atlantic Ocean. 5.** a steam locomotive having a four-wheeled front truck, four driving wheels, and a two-wheeled rear truck. [< L *Atlantic(um)* (*mare*) the Atlantic (ocean), neut. of *Atlanticus* < Gk *Atlantikós* of (Mount) ATLAS, equiv. to *Atlant-* (s. of *Átlās*) + *-ikos* -IC]

Atlan′tic Char′ter, the joint declaration of President Roosevelt and Prime Minister Churchill (August 14, 1941) resulting from a conference at sea, setting forth the peace aims of their governments for the period following World War II. The declaration was later endorsed by a number of countries.

Atlan′tic Cit′y, a city in SE New Jersey: seashore resort. 59,544 (1960).

Atlan′tic croak′er. See under **croaker** (def. 2).

Atlan′tic High′lands, a town in NE New Jersey. 4119 (1960).

Atlan′tic Intracoast′al Wa′terway. See under **Intracoastal Waterway.**

Atlan′tic O′cean, an ocean bounded by North America and South America in the Western Hemisphere and by Europe and Africa in the Eastern Hemisphere. ab. 31,530,000 sq. mi.; with connecting seas ab. 41,000,000 sq. mi.; greatest known depth, 30,246 ft.

Atlan′tic Pact′. See **North Atlantic Pact.**

Atlan′tic Prov′inces, the Canadian provinces bordering the Atlantic Ocean, comprising New Brunswick, Newfoundland, Nova Scotia, and Prince Edward Island.

Atlan′tic puf′fin. See under **puffin.**

At·lan·tis (at lan′tis), *n.* a mythical island, first mentioned by Plato, said to have existed in the Atlantic Ocean west of Gibraltar and to have sunk finally into the sea.

at·las (at′ləs), *n., pl.* **at·las·es** for 1–3, 5, 7, **at·lan·tes** (at lan′tēz) for 9. **1.** a bound collection of maps. **2.** a bound volume of charts, plates, or tables illustrating any subject. **3.** *Anat.* the first cervical vertebra, which supports the head. **4.** (*cap.*) *Class. Myth.* a Titan, son of Iapetus and brother of Prometheus and Epimetheus, condemned to support the sky on his shoulders: identified by the ancients with the Atlas Mountains. **5.** (*cap.*) one who supports a heavy burden; a mainstay. **6.** a size of drawing or writing paper, 26 × 34 or 33 inches. **7.** (*cap.*) *U.S.* a liquid-propelled intercontinental ballistic missile over 80 feet long and 10 feet in diameter, powered by two booster engines that fire in unison and by one sustainer. **8.** (*cap.*) a crater in the first quadrant of the face of the moon: about 55 miles in diameter. **9.** Also called **telamon.** *Archit.* a figure of a man used as a column. [< L < Gk; akin to *tlênai* to suffer, endure, bear]

At′las ce′dar, a tree, *Cedrus atlantica*, of northern Africa, having rigid, bluish-green leaves and light-brown cones.

At′las Moun′tains, a mountain range in NW Africa, extending through Morocco, Algeria, and Tunisia. Highest peak, Mt. Tizi, 14,764 ft.

At·li (ät′lē), *n.* *Scand. Legend.* Attila, king of the Huns: represented in the *Volsunga Saga* as the brother of Brynhild and the second husband of Gudrun, whose brothers he kills in order to get the Nibelung treasure. With his sons, he is killed by Gudrun. Cf. **Etzel.**

atm., **1.** atmosphere; atmospheres. **2.** atmospheric.

At/m, ampere-turns per meter.

at. m. See **atomic mass.**

at·man (ät′mən), *n.* *Hinduism.* **1.** the breath. **2.** the principle of life. **3.** the individual self, known after enlightenment to be identical with Brahman. **4.** (*cap.*) the World Soul, from which all individual souls derive, and to which they return as the supreme goal of existence. Also, **at·ma** (ät′mə). [< Skt *ātman* breath; akin to ME *ethem*, Gk *atmós*, etc.]

atmo-, a learned borrowing from Greek meaning "air," used in the formation of compound words: *atmosphere.* [< Gk *atmó(s)* vapor, smoke; c. Skt *ātman* breath, soul, OE *ǣthm* breath]

at·mol·y·sis (at mol′i sis), *n., pl.* **-ses** (-sēz′). a process for separating gases or vapors of different molecular weights by transmission through a porous substance. [ATMO- + -LYSIS]

at·mom·e·ter (at mom′i tər), *n.* an instrument for measuring the rate at which water evaporates. Also called **at·mi·dom·e·ter** (at′mi dom′i tər), **evaporation gauge, evaporimeter, evaporometer.** [ATMO- + -METER]

at·mom·e·try (at mom′i trē), *n.* the science of measuring the rate at which water evaporates. [ATMO- + -METRY]

at·mo·phile (at′mə fīl′), *Geol.* **—***adj.* **1.** (of a chemical element in the earth) having an affinity for the atmosphere, as neon, helium, etc. **—***n.* **2.** an atmophile element. [ATMO(SPHERE) + -PHILE]

At·more (at′mōr, -môr), *n.* a town in SW Alabama. 8173 (1960).

At′mos clock′ (at′məs), a self-winding clock utilizing variations of temperature acting on a mercury thermometer to create an imbalance within the winding drum.

at·mos·phere (at′məs fēr′), *n.* **1.** the gaseous envelope surrounding the earth; the air. **2.** this medium at a given place. **3.** *Astron.* the gaseous envelope surrounding a heavenly body. **4.** *Chem.* any gaseous envelope or medium. **5.** a conventional unit of pressure, the normal pressure of the air at sea level, about 14.7 pounds per square inch. *Abbr.:* atm. **6.** a pervading influence; environment: *an atmosphere of peace.* **7.** the dominant mood or emotional tone of a work of art, as of a play or novel. **8.** a distinctive quality, as of a place; character: *The old part of town has lots of atmosphere.* [< NL *atmosphaer(a).* See ATMO-, -SPHERE] **—at′mos·phere′less,** *adj.*

at·mos·pher·ic (at′məs fer′ik), *adj.* **1.** pertaining to, existing in, or consisting of the atmosphere: *atmospheric vapors.* **2.** caused, produced, or operated on by the atmosphere: *atmospheric storms.* **3.** resembling or suggestive of the atmosphere; having muted tones and softened or indistinct outlines; hazy: *atmospheric effects.* **4.** having or producing an emotional atmosphere: *atmospheric quality; atmospheric lighting.* Also, **at′mos·pher′i·cal.** [ATMOSPHERE + -IC] **—at′mos·pher′i·cal·ly,** *adv.*

at′mospher′ic boun′dary lay′er. See **surface boundary layer.**

at′mospher′ic brak′ing, *Rocketry.* a technique of reentry in which the vehicle maneuvers itself in the upper atmosphere so as to lose velocity by utilizing drag, without overheating.

atmospher′ic electric′ity, static electricity produced by charged particles in the atmosphere.

at′mospher′ic en′gine, an early form of single-acting engine in which the power stroke is provided by atmospheric pressure acting upon a piston in an exhausted cylinder.

atmospher′ic perspec′tive. See **aerial perspective.**

at′mospher′ic pres′sure, *Meteorol.* **1.** the pressure exerted by the earth's atmosphere at any given point, being the product of the mass of the atmospheric column of the unit area above the given point and of the gravitational acceleration at the given point. **2.** a value of standard or normal atmospheric pressure, equivalent to the pressure exerted by a column of mercury 760 millimeters (29.12 inches) high, or 1013.2 millibars. Also called **barometric pressure.** Cf. **sea-level pressure.**

at·mos·pher·ics (at′məs fer′iks), *n.* (*construed as pl.*) *Radio.* **1.** noise caused in a radio receiver by natural electromagnetic disturbances in the atmosphere. **2.** natural phenomena causing this interference. Also called **spherics.** [see ATMOSPHERIC, -ICS]

at. no. See **atomic number.**

A·to·ka (ə tō′kə), *n.* a town in SE Oklahoma. 2877 (1960).

at·oll (at′ôl, -ol, -ōl, ə tôl′, ə tol′, ə tōl′), *n.* a ring-shaped coral reef or a string of closely spaced small coral islands, enclosing or nearly enclosing a shallow lagoon. [var. of *atollon*, native name in Maldive Islands]

at·om (at′əm), *n.* **1.** *Physics.* the smallest component of an element having all the properties of the element, consisting of an aggregate of protons, neutrons, and electrons such that the number of protons determines the element. **2.** a hypothetical particle of matter so minute as to admit of no division. **3.** anything extremely small; a minute quantity. [ME *attomos*, *athomus* < L *atomus* < Gk *átomos*, n. use of *átomos* undivided, equiv. to *a-* A-[6] + *tomós* divided, verbid of *témnein* to cut] **—Syn. 3.** iota, jot, whit.

at′om bomb′. See **atomic bomb.**

at·om-bomb (at′əm bom′), *v.t.* **1.** to bomb (a target) with an atomic bomb. **—***v.i.* **2.** to atom-bomb a target.

a·tom·ic (ə tom′ik), *adj.* **1.** of, pertaining to, resulting from, or using atoms, atomic energy, or atomic bombs: *an atomic explosion.* **2.** propelled or driven by atomic energy: *an atomic submarine.* **3.** *Chem.* existing as free, uncombined atoms. **4.** extremely minute. Also, **a·tom′i·cal.** [ATOM + -IC] **—a·tom′i·cal·ly,** *adv.*

atom′ic age′, the period in history initiated by the first use of the atomic bomb and characterized by atomic energy as a military, political, and industrial factor.

atom′ic bomb′, **1.** a bomb whose potency is derived from nuclear fission of atoms of fissionable material with the consequent conversion of part of their mass into energy. **2.** a bomb whose explosive force comes from a chain reaction based on nuclear fission in U-235 or in plutonium. It was first used militarily on Hiroshima, Japan, August 6, 1945. The explosion of such a bomb is extremely violent and is attended by great heat, a brilliant light, and strong gamma-ray radiation. Also, **atom bomb.** Also called **A-bomb, fission bomb.**

atom′ic clock′, *Physics.* an extremely accurate electric clock regulated by the resonance frequency of atoms or molecules of certain substances, as cesium.

atom′ic cock′tail, *Slang.* an oral dose of a radioactive substance used in the treatment or diagnosis of cancer.

atom′ic en′ergy, energy released by rearrangements of atomic nuclei, as in nuclear fission or fusion. Also called **nuclear energy.**

Atom′ic En′ergy Commis′sion, *U.S. Govt.* the board, consisting of five members, charged with instituting and administering all federal programs dealing with nonmilitary uses of atomic energy. *Abbr.:* AEC

at·o·mic·i·ty (at′ə mis′i tē), *n. Chem.* **1.** the number of atoms in the molecule of a gas. **2.** valence. [ATOMIC + -ITY]

atom′ic mass′, *Chem.* the mass of an isotope of an element measured in units formerly based on the weight of one hydrogen atom taken as a unit or on 1/16 the weight of one oxygen atom, but after 1961 based on 1/12 the weight of the carbon-12 atom. *Abbr.:* at. m.

atom′ic mass′ u′nit, *Physics.* **1.** a unit of mass, equal to 1/12 the mass of a carbon (isotope 12) atom and used to express the mass of atomic and subatomic particles. **2.** (formerly) a unit of mass, equal to 1/16 the mass of an oxygen (isotope 16) atom. *Abbr.:* amu

atom′ic num′ber, the number of positive charges or protons in the nucleus of an atom of a given element, and therefore also the number of electrons normally surrounding the nucleus. *Abbr.:* at. no.; *Symbol:* Z

atom′ic pile′, *Physics.* reactor (def. 4).

atom′ic pow′er, power derived from atomic energy.

a·tom·ics (ə tom′iks), *n.* (*construed as sing.*) *Informal.* the branch of physics that deals with atoms, esp. atomic energy. [see ATOMIC, -ICS]

atom′ic struc′ture, *Physics.* the structure of an atom, theoretically consisting of a positively charged nucleus surrounded and neutralized by negatively charged electrons revolving in orbits at varying distances from the nucleus, the constitution of the nucleus and the arrangement of the electrons differing with various chemical elements.

atom′ic the′ory, **1.** *Physics, Chem.* any of several theories describing the structure, behavior, and other properties of the atom and its component parts. **2.** *Philos.* atomism (def. 1).

atom′ic vol′ume, *Chem.* the atomic weight of an element divided by its density. *Abbr.:* at. vol

atom′ic war′fare, warfare employing nuclear weapons.

atom′ic war′head, a warhead containing a fission or fusion bomb. Also called **nuclear warhead.**

atom′ic weight′, *Chem.* the average weight of an atom of an element, formerly based on the weight of one hydrogen atom taken as a unit or on 1/16 the weight of an oxygen atom, but after 1961 based on 1/12 the weight of the carbon-12 atom. *Abbr.:* at. wt.

at·om·ise (at′ə mīz′), *v.t.*, **-ised, -is·ing.** *Chiefly Brit.* atomize. —**at′om·i·sa′tion,** *n.*

at·om·ism (at′ə miz′əm), *n.* **1.** Also called **atomic theory.** *Philos.* the theory that minute, discrete, finite, and indivisible elements are the ultimate constituents of all matter. **2.** *Psychol.* a method or theory that reduces all psychological phenomena to simple elements. [ATOM + -ISM] —**at′om·ist,** *n.* —**at′om·is′tic, at′om·is′ti·cal,** *adj.* —**at′om·is′ti·cal·ly,** *adv.*

at·om·ize (at′ə mīz′), *v.t.*, **-ized, -iz·ing.** **1.** to reduce to atoms. **2.** to reduce to fine particles or spray. **3.** to destroy (a target) by bombing, especially with an atomic bomb. Also, *esp. Brit.*, **atomise.** [ATOM + -IZE] —**at′om·i·za′tion,** *n.*

at·om·iz·er (at′ə mī′zər), *n.* an apparatus for reducing liquids to a fine spray, as for medicinal application. [ATOMIZE + -ER[1]]

at′om smash′er, *Physics.* accelerator (def. 6).

at·o·my[1] (at′ə mē), *n., pl.* **-mies.** *Archaic.* **1.** an atom; mote. **2.** a small creature; pygmy. [< L *atomī*, pl. of *atomus* ATOM used as sing.]

at·o·my[2] (at′ə mē), *n., pl.* **-mies.** *Obs.* a skeleton. [var. of ANATOMY (taken as *an atomy*)]

A·ton (ä′tən), *n. Egyptian Religion.* a solar deity declared by Amenhotep IV to be the only god, represented as a solar disk with rays ending in human hands. Also, **Aten.**

a·ton·al (ā tōn′əl), *adj. Music.* having no key. [A-[6] + TONAL] —**a·ton′al·ism,** *n.* —**a·ton′al·is′tic,** *adj.* —**a·ton′al·ly,** *adv.*

a·to·nal·i·ty (ā′tō nal′i tē), *n. Music.* **1.** the absence of key or tonal center. **2.** an atonal principle or style of composition. [ATONAL + -ITY]

a·tone (ə tōn′), *v.*, **a·toned, a·ton·ing.** —*v.i.* **1.** to make amends or reparation, as for an offense or a crime, or for an offender (usually fol. by *for*): *to atone for one's sins.* **2.** to make up, as for errors or deficiencies (usually fol. by *for*): *to atone for one's failings.* **3.** *Obs.* to become reconciled; agree. —*v.t.* **4.** to make amends for; expiate. **5.** *Obs.* to bring into unity, harmony, concord, etc. [back formation from ATONEMENT] —**a·ton′a·ble, a·tone′a·ble,** *adj.* —**a·ton′er,** *n.* —**a·ton′ing·ly,** *adv.*

a·tone·ment (ə tōn′mənt), *n.* **1.** satisfaction or reparation for a wrong or injury; amends. **2.** (*sometimes cap.*) *Theol.* the doctrine concerning the reconciliation of God and man, esp. as accomplished through the life, suffering, and death of Christ. **3.** *Christian Science.* the state of union with God in which man exemplifies the attributes of God. **4.** *Archaic.* reconciliation; agreement. [from phrase *at onement* at unity (AT[1] + ME *onement*, now obs.); see ONE, -MENT]

a·ton·ic (ə ton′ik, ā ton′-), *adj.* **1.** *Phonet.* **a.** unaccented. **b.** *Obs.* voiceless. **2.** *Pathol.* characterized by atony. —*n.* **3.** *Gram.* an unaccented word, syllable, or sound. [< medical L *atonic(us)*, equiv. to *aton(ia)* ATONY + *-icus* -IC. See A-[6], TONIC]

at·o·nic·i·ty (at′ənis′i tē, ā′tō nis′-), *n. Pathol.* lack of tone; atony. [ATONIC + -ITY]

at·o·ny (at′ənē), *n.* **1.** *Pathol.* lack of tone or energy; muscular weakness, esp. in a contractile organ. **2.** *Phonet.* lack of stress accent. Also, **a·to·ni·a** (ə tō′nē ə, ā tō′-). [< medical L *atonia* < Gk, deriv. of *átonos* unaccented, languid, lit., toneless. See A-[6], TONE]

a·top (ə top′), *adj., adv.* **1.** on or at the top. —*prep.* **2.** on the top of: *atop the flagpole.* [A-[1] + TOP[1]]

-ator, a combination of **-ate**[1] and **-or**[2], used to form agent nouns from stems in **-ate**[1] (*separator*); on this model, used independently to form agent nouns from stems of other origin: *significator.* Cf. **-atrix.** [< L, equiv. to *-āt(us)* -ATE[1] + *-or* -OR[2]]

-atory, a combination of **-ate**[1] and **-ory,** used to form nouns or adjectives from stems in **-ate**[1] (*oratory; migratory*); on this model, used independently to form nouns or adjectives from stems of other origin: *reformatory; explanatory.* [< L *-ātōri(us)*, equiv. to *-ātōr-* (s. of *-ātor* -ATOR) + *-ius* adj. suffix]

ATP, *Biochem.* an ester of adenosine and triphosphoric acid, $C_{10}H_{12}N_5O_3H_4P_3O_9$, formed esp. aerobically by the reaction of ADP and an orthophosphate during oxidation, or by the interaction of ADP and phosphocreatine or certain other substrates, and serving as a source of energy for physiological reactions, esp. muscle contraction. Also called **adenosine triphosphate, adenosinetriphosphoric acid, adenylpyrophosphate, adenylpyrophosphoric acid.**

at·ra·bil·ious (a′trə bil′yəs), *adj.* **1.** sad; gloomy; melancholy; morbid. **2.** irritable; bad-tempered; splenetic. Also, **at′ra·bil′iar.** [< L *ātra bīli(s)* black bile + -OUS] —**at′ra·bil′ious·ness,** *n.*

A·tra·ha·sis (ä′trä hä′sis), *n.* a legendary Akkadian sage who built a boat in which he and his family, servants, and chattels escaped the Deluge. Cf. **Ziusudra.**

A·trax (ā′trəks), *n. Class. Myth.* a son of Peneus.

a·trem·ble (ə trem′bəl), *adv.* in a trembling state. [A-[1] + TREMBLE]

a·tre·sia (ə trē′zhə, -zhē ə, -zē ə, -shə, -sē ə), *n. Med.* the congenital absence, or the pathological closure, of an opening, passage, or cavity. [< NL < Gk *a-* A-[6] + *três(is)* perforation + *-ia* -IA] —**a·tre·sic** (ə trē′zik, -sik), **a·tret·ic** (ə tret′ik), *adj.*

A·tre·us (ā′trē əs, ā′trōōs), *n. Class. Myth.* the father of Plisthenes, Agamemnon, Menelaus, and Anaxibia upon whose house Thyestes pronounced a curse.

a·trich·i·a (ā trik′ē ə, ə trik′-), *n. Med.* congenital absence or loss of hair. Also, **at·ri·cho·sis** (a′trə kō′sis). [< NL; see A-[6], TRICH-, -IA]

A·tri·dae (ə trī′dē), *n. Class. Myth.* a patronymic for Agamemnon and Menelaus, the sons of Atreus. —**A·tri′de·an,** *adj.*

a·tri·o·ven·tric·u·lar (ā′trē ō ven trik′yə lər), *adj. Anat.* of or pertaining to the atria and ventricles of the heart. [< NL *atrio-* (comb. form of *atrium* heart chamber; see ATRIUM) + VENTRICULAR]

a′trioventric′ular bun′dle, *Anat.* a bundle of specialized muscle fibers regulating the heartbeat by conducting impulses from the right atrium to the ventricles. Also called **bundle of His.**

a′trioventric′ular node′, *Anat.* a small mass of muscular fibers at the base of the wall between the atria, conducting impulses received from the sinoatrial node by way of the atrioventricular bundles and, under certain conditions, functioning for the sinoatrial node as pacemaker of the heart.

a·trip (ə trip′), *adj. Naut.* **1.** aweigh **2.** (of a sail) in position and ready for trimming. **3.** (of a yard) hoisted and ready to be fastened in position. **4.** (of an upper mast) unfastened and ready for lowering. [A-[1] + TRIP]

a·tri·um (ā′trē əm), *n., pl.* **a·tri·a** (ā′trē ə). **1.** *Archit.* **a.** Also called **cavaedium.** the main or central room of an ancient Roman house, open to the sky at the center and usually having a pool for the collection of rain water. **b.** a courtyard, flanked or surrounded by porticoes, in front of an early or medieval Christian church. **2.** *Anat.* either of the two upper chambers on each side of the heart that receive blood from the veins and in turn force it into the ventricles. See diag. under **heart.** [< L (anatomical sense in NL)] —**a′tri·al,** *adj.*

-atrix, a suffix used as the feminine form of **-ator:** *aviatrix.* [< L, equiv. to *-āt(o)r* -ATOR + *-īx* fem. suffix]

at·ro·ce·ru·le·ous (a′trō sə rōō′lē əs, -rōōl′yəs), *n.* a deep blue-black color. Also, **at′ro·ce·ru′le·us, at′ro·coe·ru′le·us.** [< L *ātro-* (comb. form of *āter* black) + *caeruleus* azure; see CERULEAN, -OUS]

a·tro·cious (ə trō′shəs), *adj.* **1.** extremely or shockingly wicked, cruel, or brutal: *atrocious behavior; an atrocious crime.* **2.** shockingly bad or lacking in taste; awful; dreadful; abominable; execrable: *She has an atrocious sense of design.* [ATROCI(TY) + -OUS] —**a·tro′cious·ly,** *adv.* —**a·tro′cious·ness,** *n.*
—**Syn. 1.** felonious, diabolical, devilish. **2.** tasteless, detestable.

a·troc·i·ty (ə tros′i tē), *n., pl.* **-ties.** **1.** quality or state of being atrocious. **2.** an atrocious act, thing, or circumstance. [< L *atrōcitāt-* (s. of *atrōcitās*), equiv. to *atrōci-* (s. of *atrōx*) fierce + *-tāt-* -TY[2]]

à trois (A TRWÄ′), *French.* for, among, or composed of three persons collectively (usually used following the word it modifies): *a secret shared* à trois.

At·ro·pa·te·ne (a′trə pə tē′nə), *n.* See **Media Atropatene.**

at·ro·phied (a′trə fēd), *adj.* exhibiting, or affected with, atrophy; wasted; withered; shriveled: *an atrophied arm; an atrophied talent.* [ATROPHY + -ED[3]]

at·ro·phy (a′trə fē), *n., v.,* **-phied, -phy·ing.** —*n.* **1.** Also, **a·tro·phi·a** (ə trō′fē ə). *Pathol.* a wasting away of the body or of an organ or part, as from defective nutrition or other cause. **2.** degeneration; decline; decrease, as from disuse: *He argued that there was a progressive atrophy of freedom and independence of thought.* —*v.t., v.i.* **3.** to affect with or undergo atrophy. [earlier *atrophie* < medical L *atrophia* < Gk, equiv. to *átroph(os)* not fed (see A-[6], TROPHO-) + *-ia* -IA] —**a·troph·ic** (ə trof′ik), *adj.*

at·ro·pine (a′trə pēn′, -pin), *n. Pharm.* a poisonous crystalline alkaloid, $C_{17}H_{23}NO_3$, obtained from belladonna and other solanaceous plants, which prevents the response of various body structures to certain types of nerve stimulation: used chiefly to relieve spasms, to lessen secretions, and, topically, to dilate the pupil of the eye. [< NL *Atrop(a)* belladonna genus (< Gk *átropos*; see ATROPOS) + -INE[2]]

at·ro·pism (a′trə piz′əm), *n. Pathol.* poisoning resulting from atropine or belladonna. Also, **at·ro·pin·ism** (a′trə pi niz′əm). [ATROP(INE) + -ISM]

At·ro·pos (a′trə pos′), *n. Class. Myth.* the Fate who cuts the thread of life. [< Gk: lit., not turning, hence, inflexible. See A-[6], -TROPE]

a·try (ə trī′), *adj. Naut.* lying to under a trysail in heavy weather; trying. [A-[1] + TRY]

ATS, Auxiliary Territorial Service (organized in 1941 for women serving in the British Army; became part of Army in 1949 as WRAC).

A.T.S., **1.** American Temperance Society. **2.** American Tract Society. **3.** American Transport Service.

att., attorney.

at·ta·bal (at′ə bal′), *n.* atabal.

at·ta·boy (at′ə boi′), *interj. Informal.* (used as an expression of enthusiastic approval or admiration.) [reduced form of *that's the boy*]

at·tac·ca (ə tä′kə; *It.* ät täk′kä), *v.* (used as an imperative) *Music.* begin immediately (directing a performer to go without pause to the next section). [< It: impv. of *attaccare* to ATTACK]

attac′ca su′bito, *Music.* attacca.

at·tach (ə tach′), *v.t.* **1.** to fasten or affix; join; connect: *to attach a photograph to application papers with a staple.* **2.** to join in action or function; make part of: *to attach oneself to a group.* **3.** *Mil.* to place on temporary duty with or in assistance to a military unit. **4.** to include as a quality or condition of something: *One proviso is attached to this legacy.* **5.** to assign or attribute: *to attach significance to a gesture.* **6.** to bind by ties of affection or regard: *His mother tried to attach him to herself by various subtle devices.* **7.** *Law.* to take (persons or property) by legal authority. **8.** *Obs.* to lay hold of; seize. —*v.i.* **9.** to adhere; pertain; belong (usually fol. by *to* or *upon*): *No blame attaches to him.* [ME *atache(n)* < AF *atache(r)* (to) seize, OF *atachier* to fasten, equiv. to *a-* A-[5] + *-tachier* to TACK[1]] —**at·tach′a·ble,** *adj.* —**at·tach′er,** *n.*
—**Syn. 1.** subjoin, append, add, annex. —**Ant. 1.** detach.

at·ta·ché (at′ə shā′ *or, esp. Brit.,* ə tash′ā; *Fr.* A TA-SHĀ′), *n., pl.* **at·ta·chés** (at′ə shāz′ *or, esp. Brit.,* ə tash′āz; *Fr.* A TA SHĀ′). **1.** a diplomatic official attached to an embassy or legation, esp. in a technical capacity: *a commercial attaché; a cultural attaché.* **2.** a military officer who is assigned to a diplomatic post to gather military information concerning the country in which he is stationed: *an air attaché; an army attaché; a naval attaché.* [< F: lit., attached, ptp. of *attacher* to ATTACH]

attaché′ case′, a small suitcase for business papers or the like. Also called **dispatch case.**

at·tached (ə tacht′), *adj.* **1.** joined; connected; bound. **2.** having a wall in common with another building (opposed to *detached*): *an attached house.* **3.** *Zool.* permanently fixed to the substratum; sessile. [ATTACH + -ED[2]]

at·tach·ment (ə tach′mənt), *n.* **1.** act of attaching; state of being attached. **2.** a feeling that binds one to a person, thing, cause, ideal, or the like; devotion; regard: *a fond attachment; a profound attachment.* **3.** that which attaches; a fastening or tie: *the attachments of a harness; the attachments of a pair of skis.* **4.** an additional or supplementary device: *attachments for an electric mixer.* **5.** *Law.* seizure of property or person by legal authority, esp. seizure of a defendant's property to prevent its dissipation before trial or to acquire jurisdiction over it. [late ME *attachement* seizure < AF. See ATTACH, -MENT]
—**Syn. 2.** love, devotedness. **3.** junction, connection. **4.** See **addition.**

at·tack (ə tak′), *v.t.* **1.** to set upon forcefully, violently, hostilely, or aggressively with or without a weapon; begin fighting with: *He attacked him with his bare hands.* **2.** to begin hostilities against; start an offensive against: *to attack the enemy.* **3.** to blame or abuse violently or bitterly. **4.** to direct unfavorable criticism against; criticize severely; argue with strongly: *He attacked his opponent's statement.* **5.** to try to destroy, esp. with verbal abuse: *to attack one's reputation.* **6.** to set about (a task) or go to work on (a thing) vigorously: *to attack house-cleaning.* **7.** (of disease, destructive agencies, etc.) to begin to affect. —*v.i.* **8.** to make an attack; begin hostilities. —*n.* **9.** the act of attacking; onslaught; assault. **10.** an offensive military operation with the aim of overcoming the enemy and destroying his armed forces and will to resist. **11.** *Pathol.* seizure by disease or illness: *an attack of indigestion.* **12.** the beginning or initiating of any action; onset. **13.** an aggressive move in a performance or contest. [earlier *atta(c)que* < MF *atta(c)quer* < It *attaccare* to attack, ATTACH] —**at·tack′a·ble,** *adj.* —**at·tack′er,** *n.*
—**Syn. 1.** storm, charge, set upon. ATTACK, ASSAIL, ASSAULT, MOLEST all mean to set upon someone forcibly, with hostile or violent intent. ATTACK is the most general word and applies to a beginning of hostilities, esp. those definitely planned: *to attack from ambush.* ASSAIL implies vehement, sudden, and sometimes repeated attack: *to assail with weapons or with gossip.* ASSAULT almost always implies bodily violence: *to assault with intent to kill.* To MOLEST is to interfere with, to threaten, or to assault: *He was safe, and where no one could molest him.* **4.** criticize, censure; impugn, oppugn, abuse. **9.** onset, encounter. —**Ant. 1.** defend. **9.** defense.

at·tain (ə tān′), *v.t.* **1.** to reach, achieve, or accomplish; gain; obtain: *to attain one's goals.* **2.** to come to or arrive at, esp. after some labor or tedium; reach: *to attain the mountain peak.* —*v.i.* **3.** to arrive at; succeed in reaching or obtaining (usually fol. by *to* or *unto*): *to attain to knowledge.* [ME *atei(g)ne* < OF *ateign-* (s. of *ateindre*) < VL **attange(re)* (var. of L *attingere*), equiv. to L *at-* AT- + *tangere* to touch] —**at·tain′er,** *n.*
—**Syn. 1.** secure. See **gain**[1]. —**Ant. 1, 2.** miss.

at·tain·a·ble (ə tā′nə bəl), *adj.* capable of being attained. [ATTAIN + -ABLE] —**at·tain′a·bil′i·ty, at·tain′a·ble·ness,** *n.*

at·tain·der (ə tān′dər), *n. Obs.* **1.** the legal consequence of judgment of death or outlawry for treason or felony, involving the loss of all civil rights. **2.** dishonor. [late ME, n. use of AF *attaindre* to convict, OF *ataindre* to convict, ATTAIN]

at·tain·ment (ə tān′mənt), *n.* **1.** act of attaining. **2.** something attained; a personal acquirement; achievement. [ME *attenement.* See ATTAIN, -MENT]
—**Syn. 2.** accomplishment.

at·taint (ə tānt′), *v.t.* **1.** *Law.* to condemn by a sentence or a bill or act of attainder. **2.** to disgrace. **3.** *Archaic.* to accuse. **4.** *Obs.* to prove the guilt of. —*n.* **5.** attainder. **6.** a stain; disgrace; taint. **7.** *Obs.* a touch or hit, esp. in tilting. [ME *ataynte*, deriv. of *ataynt* convicted < AF, OF, ptp. of *ataindre* to convict, ATTAIN]

at·tain·ture (ə tān′chər), *n.* **1.** attainder. **2.** imputation. [ATTAINT + -URE, modeled on ML *attinctūra*]

At·tal·la (at′ələ), *n.* a town in NE Alabama. 8257 (1960).

At·ta·lus I (at′ələs), (*Soter*) king of Pergamum 241–197 B.C.

Attalus II, (*Philadelphus*) king of Pergamum c159–138 B.C.

Attalus III, (*Philometor*) king of Pergamum 138–133 B.C.

at·ta·pul·gite (at′ə pul′jīt), *n.* a clay mineral, basic hydrous silicate of magnesium and aluminum, the active ingredient of fuller's earth. [named after *Attapulgus*, town in SW Georgia, U.S., near source of supply; see -ITE[1]]

at·tar (at′ər), *n.* **1.** Also, **atar, athar, ottar, otto.** a perfume or essential oil obtained from flowers or petals. **2.** Also called **at′tar of ros′es.** See **rose oil.** [short for Pers *'atar-gūl* attar of roses, akin to *'atara* to smell sweet, *'itr* fragrance (< Ar)]

at·tem·per (ə tem′pər), *v.t. Archaic.* **1.** to modify or moderate by mixing or blending with something different or opposite. **2.** to regulate or modify the temperature of. **3.** to soothe; mollify; mitigate. **4.** to accommodate; adapt (usually fol. by *to*). [ME *attempre(n)* < L *attemperāre* to adjust (see AT-, TEMPER); r. ME *attempre(n)* < MF *attempre(r)*]

at·tem·per·a·tor (ə tem′pə rā′tər), *n.* any of several apparatuses for keeping the temperature of steam, water, or other fluid at or below a desired maximum. [< L *attemperāt(us)* (ptp. of *attemperāre* to ATTEMPER) + -OR[2]]

at·tempt (ə tempt′), *v.t.* **1.** to make an effort at; try; undertake; seek: *to attempt a debate; to attempt to walk six miles.* **2.** to attack; make an effort against: *to attempt a person's life.* **3.** *Archaic.* to tempt. —*n.* **4.** an effort made to accomplish something: *He made an attempt to finish his studies.* **5.** an attack or assault: *an attempt upon one's life.* [< L *attempt(āre)* (to) test, tamper with. See AT-, TEMPT] —**at·tempt′a·bil′i·ty,** *n.* —**at·tempt′a·ble,** *adj.* —**at·tempt′er,** *n.*
—**Syn. 1.** See **try. 4.** undertaking, endeavor.

at·tend (ə tend′), *v.t.* **1.** to be present at: *to attend a lecture; to attend church.* **2.** to go with as a concomitant or result; accompany: *a cold attended with fever.* **3.** to take care of; minister to; devote one's services to: *The nurse attended the patient daily.* **4.** to wait upon; accompany as a companion or servant: *The retainers attended their lord.* **5.** to take charge of; watch over; look after; tend; guard: *to attend one's health.* **6.** to listen to; give heed to. **7.** *Archaic.* to wait for; expect. —*v.i.* **8.** to take care or charge: *to attend to a sick person.* **9.** to apply oneself: *to attend to one's work; to attend to a taste.* **10.** to pay attention; listen or watch attentively; direct one's thought; pay heed: *to attend to a speaker.* **11.** to be present: *She is a member but does not attend regularly.* **12.** to be present and ready to give service; wait (usually fol. by *on* or *upon*). **13.** to follow; be consequent (usually fol. by *on* or *upon*). **14.** *Obs.* to wait. [ME *atende(n)* < OF *atend(re)* < L *attendere* to bend to, notice. See AT-, TEND[1]] —**at·tend′er,** *n.* —**at·tend′ing·ly,** *adv.*
—**Syn. 4.** See **accompany.**

at·tend·ance (ə ten′dəns), *n.* **1.** act of attending. **2.** the persons or number of persons present. **3.** *Obs.* attendants collectively. **4. dance attendance,** to be obsequious in one's attentions or service; attend constantly: *He was given a larger office and several assistants to dance attendance on him.* [ME < MF. See ATTEND, -ANCE]

attend′ance of′ficer. See **truant officer.**

at·tend·ant (ə ten′dənt), *n.* **1.** one who attends another, as for service or company. **2.** *Chiefly Brit.* an usher or clerk. **3.** that which follows from or accompanies something; a corollary or concomitant thing or quality. **4.** one who is present, as at a meeting. —*adj.* **5.** being present or in attendance; accompanying. **6.** consequent; concomitant; associated; related: *winter holidays and attendant parties; war and its attendant evils; poverty and its attendant hardships.* [ME < MF, prp. of *attendre* to notice, await, etc. See ATTEND, -ANT] —**at·tend′ant·ly,** *adv.*
—**Syn. 1.** escort, companion, comrade; follower, retainer, servant. **3.** accompaniment, consequence.

at·tend·ing (ə ten′ding), *adj.* (of a physician) **1.** having primary responsibility for a specified patient. **2.** holding a staff position in an accredited hospital. [ATTEND + -ING[2]]

at·tent (ə tent′), *adj. Archaic.* attentive; intent. [late ME < L *attent(us)* attentive, intention (ptp. of *attendere*), equiv. to *attend-* (see ATTEND) + *-tus* ptp. suffix] —**at·tent′ly,** *adv.*

at·ten·tion (*n.* ə ten′shən; *interj.* ə ten′shun′), *n.* **1.** act or faculty of attending, esp. by directing the mind to an object. **2.** *Psychol.* **a.** a concentration of the mind on a single object or thought, esp. one preferentially selected from a complex, with a view to limiting or clarifying receptivity by narrowing the range of stimuli. **b.** a state of consciousness characterized by such concentration. **3.** observant care; consideration; notice: *Individual attention is given each child.* **4.** civility or courtesy: *attention to a stranger.* **5. attentions,** acts of courtesy indicating affection, as in courtship. **6.** *Mil.* **a.** (a command to stand or sit in an erect position with eyes to the front, arms to the sides, and heels together.) **b.** state of so standing or sitting: *at attention.* —*interj.* **7.** (used to call one to attention, as in the military services or in school.) [ME *attencioun* < L *attentiōn-* (s. of *attentiō*). See ATTENT, -ION] —**at·ten′tion·al,** *adj.*
—**Syn. 1.** awareness, consciousness, watchfulness, alertness, mindfulness, heed. **4.** deference, politeness, regard; respect, homage. **5.** courtship, address.

at·ten·tion-get·ting (ə ten′shən get′ing), *adj.* drawing attention to something or someone: *an attention-getting device; attention-getting behavior.*

atten′tion span′, the time interval during which the attention is centered on a single object, idea, etc., without shifting.

at·ten·tive (ə ten′tiv), *adj.* **1.** characterized by or giving attention; observant. **2.** thoughtful of others; considerate; polite; courteous. [ATTENT + -IVE] —**at·ten′tive·ly,** *adv.* —**at·ten′tive·ness,** *n.*
—**Syn. 1.** regardful, mindful, aware, alert, awake, watchful.

at·ten·u·ant (ə ten′yo͞o ənt), *adj.* **1.** diluting, as a liquid. —*n.* **2.** a medicine or agent that thins the blood. [< L *attenuant-* (s. of *attenuāns* thinning, prp. of *attenuāre*). See AT-, TENUIS, -ANT]

at·ten·u·ate (*v.* ə ten′yo͞o āt′; *adj.* ə ten′yo͞o it, -āt′), *v.,* **-at·ed, -at·ing,** *adj.* —*v.t.* **1.** to make thin; make slender or fine. **2.** to weaken or reduce in force, intensity, effect, quantity, or value: *attenuated desire; a vaccine of attenuated bacteria.* —*v.i.* **3.** to become thin or fine; lessen. —*adj.* **4.** attenuated; thin. **5.** *Bot.* tapering gradually to a narrow extremity. [< L *attenuāt(us)* (ptp. of *attenuāre* to thin, reduce). See AT-, TENUIS, -ATE[1]]

at·ten·u·a·tion (ə ten′yo͞o ā′shən), *n.* **1.** act of attenuating. **2.** the resulting state. **3.** *Physics.* a decrease in energy per unit area of a wave or beam of particles, occurring as the distance from the source increases and caused by absorption or scattering. [< L *attenuātiōn-* (s. of *attenuātiō*). See ATTENUATE, -ION]

at·ten·u·a·tor (ə ten′yo͞o ā′tər), *n. Elect.* a device for decreasing the amplitude of an electric signal. [ATTENUATE + -OR[2]]

at·test (ə test′), *v.t.* **1.** to bear witness to, certify; declare to be correct, true, or genuine; declare the truth of, in words or writing, esp. affirm in an official capacity: *to attest the truth of a statement.* **2.** to give proof or evidence of; manifest: *His works attest his industry.* —*v.i.* **3.** to testify or bear witness (often fol. by *to*): *to attest to the reliability of an employee.* —*n.* **4.** *Archaic.* witness; testimony; attestation. [< L *attest(ārī)* (to) bear witness to, equiv. to *at-* AT- + *testārī* (*test(is)* a witness + *-ā-* thematic vowel + *-rī* inf. suffix)] —**at·test′a·ble,** *adj.* —**at·test′ant,** *n.* —**at·test′er, at·tes′tor, at·tes·ta·tor** (ə tes′tā tər, at′is tā′-), *n.* —**at·tes′tive,** *adj.*

at·tes·ta·tion (at′e stā′shən), *n.* **1.** act of attesting. **2.** an attesting declaration; testimony; evidence. [< L *attestātiōn-* (s. of *attestātiō*). See ATTEST, -ATION] —**at·tes·ta·tive** (ə tes′tə tiv), *adj.*

Att. Gen., Attorney General.

at·tic (at′ik), *n.* **1.** that part of a building, esp. of a house, directly under a roof; a garret. **2.** a room or rooms in that part. **3.** a low story or decorative wall above an entablature or the main cornice of a building. **4.** *Anat.* the upper part of the tympanic cavity of the ear. [special use of ATTIC]

At·tic (at′ik), *adj.* **1.** of, pertaining to, characteristic of Attica or Athens. **2.** (*often l.c.*) displaying simple elegance, incisive intelligence, and delicate wit. **3.** *Fine Arts.* **a.** designating esp. the style of pottery and vase painting developed in Attica from the late 7th–4th centuries B.C. Cf. **black-figure, red-figure, white-ground. b.** of or pertaining to the sculpture produced in Attica. —*n.* **4.** a native or an inhabitant of Attica; an Athenian. **5.** the dialect of ancient Attica which became the standard language of Classical Greek literature in the 5th and 4th centuries B.C. [< L *Attic(us)* < Gk *Attikós,* equiv. to *Attik(ḗ)* ATTICA + *-os* adj. suffix]

Attica

At·ti·ca (at′ə kə), *n.* **1.** a region in SE Greece, surrounding Athens: under Athenian rule in ancient times. **2.** a town in W Indiana. 4341 (1960). **3.** a town in W New York. 2758 (1960).

At′tic base′, (in classical architecture) a base for a column, consisting of an upper and a lower torus, separated by a scotia between two fillets.

Attic base

At′tic faith′, inviolable faith.

At·ti·cise (at′i sīz′), *v.i., v.t.,* **-cised, -cis·ing.** *Chiefly Brit.* Atticize. Also, **at′ti·cise′.**

At·ti·cism (at′i siz′əm), *n.* **1.** the style or idiom of Attic Greek. **2.** attachment to Athens or to the style, customs, etc. of the Athenians. **3.** concise and elegant expression, diction, or the like. Also, **at′ti·cism.** [< Gk *Attikism(ós)* a siding with Athens, an Attic expression. See ATTIC, -ISM] —**At′ti·cist, at′ti·cist,** *n.*

At·ti·cize (at′i sīz′), *v.,* **-cized, -ciz·ing.** —*v.i.* **1.** to affect Attic style, usages, etc.; intermingle with Attic elements. **2.** to favor or side with the Athenians. —*v.t.* **3.** to make conformable to Attic usage. Also, **at′ti·cize′;** *esp. Brit.,* **Atticise, atticise.** [< Gk *attikíz(ein)* (to) speak Attic, side with Athens. See ATTIC, -IZE]

At′tic salt′, dry, delicate wit. Also called **At′tic wit′.**

At·ti·la (at′ələ, ə til′ə), *n.* **1.** ("*Scourge of God*") A.D. 406?–453, king of the Huns who invaded Europe: defeated by the Romans and Visigoths in 451 at Châlons-sur-Marne in France. **2.** Also, **Atila.** a girl's given name.

at·tin·gent (ə tin′jənt), *adj. Obs.* touching; in contact. [< L *attingent-* (s. of *attingēns* touching, prp. of *attingere*), equiv. to *at-* AT- + *ting-* (comb. form of *tang-* touch) + *-ent-* -ENT] —**at·tin′gence, at·tin′gen·cy,** *n.*

at·tire (ə tīər′), *v.,* **-tired, -tir·ing,** *n.* —*v.t.* **1.** to dress, array, or adorn, esp. for special occasions, ceremonials, etc. —*n.* **2.** clothes or apparel, esp. rich or splendid garments. **3.** the horns of a deer. [ME *atire* < OF *atir(i)e(r),* repr. *a tire* into a row or rank. See A-[3], TIER[1]]

at·tired (ə tīərd′), *adj. Heraldry.* (of a deer or deerlike animal) represented as having antlers of a tincture different from that of the body: *a stag gules attired argent.* [ME; see ATTIRE, -ED[2]]

at·tire·ment (ə tīər′mənt), *n. Obs.* dress; attire. [ATTIRE + -MENT]

At·tis (at′is), *n. Class. Myth.* a Phrygian youth, loved by Cybele. In a jealous rage, she caused him to go mad. He castrated himself and died, and she then begged Jupiter to preserve his body free of decay. Also, **Atys.**

at·ti·tude (at′i to͞od′, -tyo͞od′), *n.* **1.** manner, disposition, feeling, position, etc., with regard to a person or thing; tendency or orientation, esp. of the mind: *a mental attitude; group attitudes.* **2.** position or posture of the body appropriate to or expressive of an action, emotion, etc.: *a threatening attitude; a relaxed attitude.* **3.** *Aeron.* the inclination of the three principal axes of an aircraft relative to the wind, to the ground, etc. **4.** a pose in ballet in which the dancer stands on one leg, the other bent behind. [< F < It *attitud(ine)* < LL *aptitūdini-* (s. of *aptitūdō*) APTITUDE] —**at′ti·tu′di·nal,** *adj.*
—**Syn. 2.** See **position.**

at·ti·tu·di·nar·i·an (at′i to͞od′ənâr′ē ən, -tyo͞od′-), *n.* one who assumes attitudes or poses for effect. [< It *attitudin(e)* ATTITUDE + -ARIAN] —**at′ti·tu′di·nar′i·an·ism,** *n.*

at·ti·tu·di·nise (at′i to͞od′ənīz′, -tyo͞od′-), *v.i.,* **-nised, -nis·ing.** *Chiefly Brit.* attitudinize. —**at′ti·tu′di·nis′er,** *n.*

at·ti·tu·di·nize (at′i to͞od′ənīz′, -tyo͞od′-), *v.i.,* **-nized, -niz·ing.** to assume attitudes; pose for effect. [< It *attitudin(e)* ATTITUDE + -IZE] —**at′ti·tu′di·niz′er,** *n.*

At·ti·us (at′ē əs), *n.* **Lucius.** See **Accius, Lucius.**

At·tle·bor·o (at′əl bûr′ō, -bur′ō), *n.* a city in SE Massachusetts. 27,118 (1960).

Att·lee (at′lē), *n.* **Clement Richard,** 1883–1967, British statesman: prime minister 1945–51.

at·torn (ə tûrn′), *Law.* —*v.i.* **1.** to acknowledge the relation of a tenant to a new landlord. —*v.t.* **2.** to turn over to another; transfer. [late ME *attourne* < AF *attourne(r),* OF *atourner* to turn over to. See AT-, TURN] —**at·torn′ment,** *n.*

at·tor·ney (ə tûr′nē), *n., pl.* **-neys. 1.** a lawyer; attorney-at-law. **2.** an attorney-in-fact; agent. [ME < AF *attourné,* lit., one (who is) turned to, i.e., appointed, ptp. of *attourner* to ATTORN] —**at·tor′ney·ship′,** *n.*

at·tor·ney-at-law (ə tûr′nē ət lô′), *n., pl.* **at·tor·neys-at-law.** *Law.* an officer of the court authorized to appear before it as a representative of a party to a legal controversy.

attor′ney gen′eral, *pl.* **attorneys general, attorney generals. 1.** the chief law officer of a country or State and head of its legal department. **2.** (*caps.*) the head of the U.S. Department of Justice; a member of the president's cabinet.

at·tor·ney-in-fact (ə tûr′nē in fakt′), *n., pl.* **at·tor·neys-in-fact.** *Law.* a person authorized by power of attorney to act on the authorizer's behalf outside a court of law.

at·tract (ə trakt′), *v.t.* **1.** to draw by a physical force causing or tending to cause approach or union; pull (opposed to *repel*): *The gravitational force of the earth attracts smaller bodies to it.* **2.** to draw by other than physical influence; invite or allure; win: *to attract attention; to attract admirers by one's perceptive humor.* —*v.i.* **3.** to possess or exert the power of attraction. [< L *attract(us)* drawn to (ptp. of *attrahere*), equiv. to *at-* AT- + *trac-* (perf. s. of *trahere* to draw) + *-tus* ptp. suffix] —**at·tract′a·ble,** *adj.* —**at·tract′a·ble·ness,** *n.* —**at·tract′ing·ly,** *adv.* —**at·trac′tor, at·tract′er,** *n.*

at·tract·ant (ə trak′tənt), *n.* an attracting agent or substance; a lure: *the sex attractant of the cockroach.* [ATTRACT + -ANT]

at·trac·tion (ə trak′shən), *n.* **1.** act, power, or property of attracting. **2.** attractive quality; magnetic charm; fascination; allurement; enticement: *He found it difficult to escape the subtle attraction of her strange personality.* **3.** one who or that which draws, attracts, allures, or entices: *The main attraction was the after-dinner speaker.* **4.** a characteristic or quality that provides pleasure; an attractive feature: *The chief attractions of the evening were the good drinks and witty conversation.* **5.** *Physics.* the electric or magnetic force that acts between oppositely charged bodies, tending to draw them together. **6.** an entertainment offered to the public. [< ML *attractiōn-* (s. of *attractiō*). See ATTRACT, -ION] —**at·trac′tion·al·ly,** *adv.*
—**Syn. 2.** lure. **6.** show, spectacle.

attrac′tion sphere′, *Biol.* the central portion of an aster in mitosis; centrosphere.

at·trac·tive (ə trak′tiv), *adj.* **1.** appealing to one's sense of beauty; providing pleasure or delight, esp. in appearance or manner; pleasing; charming; alluring: *an attractive woman.* **2.** arousing interest or engaging one's thought, consideration, etc.: *an attractive idea; an attractive price.* **3.** having the quality of attracting. [< LL *attractīv(us)* (medical L) with drawing power. See ATTRACT, -IVE] —**at·trac′tive·ly,** *adv.* —**at·trac′tive·ness,** *n.*

attrac′tive nui′sance, **1.** *Law.* a doctrine of tort law under which a person who creates or permits to exist on his land a dangerous condition attractive to children, as an unfenced swimming pool, is liable for their resulting injuries, even though they are trespassers. **2.** a hazardous condition or object to which this doctrine is applicable.

at·tra·hent (a′trə hənt), *adj.* drawing; attracting. [< L *attrahent-* (s. of *attrahēns* drawing, prp. of *attrahere*), equiv. to *at-* AT- + *trah-* draw + *-ent-* -ENT]

attrib., **1.** attribute. **2.** attributive. **3.** attributively.

at·trib·ute (*v.* ə trib′yo͞ot; *n.* a′trə byo͞ot′), *v.,* **-ut·ed, -ut·ing,** *n.* —*v.t.* **1.** to regard as resulting from; consider as caused by (usually fol. by *to*): *She attributed his bad temper to ill health.* **2.** to consider as belonging, as a quality or characteristic: *He attributed intelligence to his colleagues.* **3.** to consider as made by, esp. with strong evidence but in the absence of conclusive proof: *to attribute a painting to an artist.* **4.** to regard as produced by or originating in or with; credit; assign: *to attribute a work to a particular period; to attribute a discovery to a particular country.* —*n.* **5.** something attributed as belonging; a quality, character, characteristic, or property: *Sensitivity is one of his attributes.* **6.** *Gram.* a word or phrase that is syntactically subordinate to another and serves to limit, identify, particularize, describe, or supplement the meaning of the form with which it is in construction. In *the red house, red* is an attribute of *house.* **7.** *Fine Arts.* an object associated with or symbolic of a character, office, or quality, as the keys of St. Peter or the lion skin of Hercules. **8.** *Philos.* (in the philosophy of Spinoza) any of the essential qualifications of God, thought and extension being the only ones known. Cf. **mode**[1] (def. 3b). **9.** *Logic.* (in a proposition) that which is affirmed or denied concerning the subject. **10.** *Obs.* distinguished character; reputation. [ME < L *attribūt(us)* allotted, assigned, imputed to (ptp. of *attribuere*), equiv. to *at-* AT- + *tribū-* (ptp. s. of *tribuere* to assign (to tribes), classify, ascribe; see TRIBE) + *-tus* ptp. suffix] —**at·trib′ut·a·ble,** *adj.* —**at·trib′ut·er, at·trib′u·tor,** *n.*
—**Syn. 1.** ATTRIBUTE, ASCRIBE, IMPUTE imply definite origin. ATTRIBUTE and ASCRIBE are often used interchangeably, to imply that something originates with a definite person or from a definite cause. ASCRIBE, however, has neutral implications; whereas, possibly because of an association with tribute, ATTRIBUTE is coming to have a complimentary connotation: *to ascribe one's health to outdoor life; to ascribe an accident to carelessness; to attribute one's success to a friend's encouragement.* IMPUTE has gained uncomplimentary connotations, and usually means to accuse or blame someone or something as a cause or origin: *to impute an error to him.* **5.** See **quality.**

at·tri·bu·tion (a′trə byo͞o′shən), *n.* **1.** act of attributing; ascription. **2.** that which is ascribed; an attribute. **3.** *Numis.* a classification for a coin, based on its distinguishing features, as date, design, metal, etc. **4.** *Archaic.* authority or function assigned, as to a ruler, legislative assembly, delegate, or the like. [late ME < L *attribūtiōn-* (s. of *attribūtiō* assignment). See ATTRIBUTE, -ION]

at·trib·u·tive (ə trib′yə tiv), *adj.* **1.** pertaining to or having the character of attribution or an attribute. **2.** *Gram.* expressing an attribute, applied in English esp. to adjectives and adverbs preceding the words which they modify, as *first* in *the first day.* —*n.* **3.** a word expressing an attribute; attributive word, phrase, or clause. [ATTRIBUTE OR ATTRIBUT(ION) + -IVE] —**at·trib′u·tive·ly,** *adv.* —**at·trib′u·tive·ness,** *n.*

at·trite (ə trīt′), *adj., v.,* **-trit·ed, -trit·ing.** —*adj.* **1.** Also, **at·trit′ed.** worn by rubbing or attrition. —*v.t.* **2.** to make smaller by attrition. [< L *attrīt(us)* rubbed against, rubbed away, worn away (ptp. of *atterere*), equiv. to *at-* AT- + *trī-* (perf. s. of *terere* to rub) + *-tus* ptp. suffix] —**at·trite′ness,** *n.*

at·tri·tion (ə trish′ən), *n.* **1.** a rubbing against; friction. **2.** a wearing down or away by friction; abrasion. **3.** a wearing down or weakening of resistance, esp. as a result of continuous pressure or harassment: *The enemy surrounded the town and conducted a war of attrition.* **4.** *Theol.* See **imperfect contrition. 5.** a becoming fewer in number; a decreasing in size: *Many liberal arts colleges have a high rate of attrition because some students decide to specialize in one field.* [< L *attrītiōn-* (s. of *attrītiō*) friction. See ATTRITE, -ION] —**at·tri′tion·al,** *adj.* —**at·tri′tive** (ə trī′tiv), *adj.*

At·tu (at′tōō), *n.* the westernmost of the Aleutian Islands: Japanese occupation 1942–43.

at·tune (ə tōōn′, ə tyōōn′), *v.t.,* **-tuned, -tun·ing. 1.** to adjust; bring into accord, harmony, or sympathetic relationship: *He has attuned himself to living in the quiet country.* **2.** *Archaic.* to tune or bring into harmony, as a musical instrument. [AT- + TUNE]

atty., attorney.

Atty. Gen., Attorney General.

A·tum (ä′təm), *n.* *Egyptian Religion.* a primeval god who by himself begot Shu and Tefnut: the original god of the Ennead.

at. vol. See **atomic volume.**

a·twain (ə twān′), *adv.* *Archaic.* in twain; in two; apart. [ME; see A-[1], TWAIN]

At·wa·ter (at′wô′tər, -wot′ər), *n.* **1.** a town in central California. 7318 (1960). **2.** a boy's given name.

At/Wb, ampere-turns per weber.

at·weel (ə twēl′, at wēl′), *adv.* *Scot.* surely. [aph. var. of phrase (*I*) *wat weel* (I) know well. See WOT, WELL[1]]

a·tween (ə twēn′), *prep., adv.* *Archaic.* between. [A-[1] + *-tween.* See BETWEEN]

a·twit·ter (ə twit′ər), *adj.* excited; nervous; aflutter; twittering: *They were atwitter at the prospect of meeting a Hollywood star.* [A-[1] + TWITTER]

At′wood's machine′ (at′wŏŏdz), *Physics.* a device consisting of two unequal masses connected by a string passed over a pulley, used to illustrate the laws of motion. [named after George *Atwood* (1746–1807), English mathematician who invented it]

at. wt. See **atomic weight.**

A·tym·ni·us (ə tim′nē əs), *n.* (in the *Iliad*) a companion of Sarpedon, slain by Antilochus.

a·typ·i·cal (ā tip′i kəl), *adj.* not typical; not conforming to the type; irregular; abnormal: *a flower atypical of the species.* Also, **a·typ′ic.** [A-[6] + TYPICAL] —**a·typ′i·cal·ly,** *adv.*

A·tys (ā′tis), *n.* Attis.

au (ō), *pl.* **aux** (ō). *French.* to the; at the; with the. Cf. **à la.**

Au, *Chem.* gold. [< L *aurum*]

AU, astronomical unit.

A.U., angstrom unit. Also, **a.u., A.U., Au.**

A.U.A., American Unitarian Association.

au·bade (ō bad′, ō bäd′; *Fr.* ō BAD′), *n., pl.* **au·bades** (ō badz′, ō bädz′; *Fr.* ō BAD′). *Music.* a piece sung or played outdoors at dawn, usually as a compliment to someone. [< F, equiv. to *aube* AUBE + *-ade* -ADE[1], modeled on Sp *albada*]

Au·ba·nel (ō BA nel′), *n.* **Thé·o·dore** (tā ô dôR′), 1829–86, French poet.

Aube (ōb), *n.* **1.** a river in N France, flowing NW to the Seine. 125 mi. long. **2.** a department in NE France. 255,099 (1962); 2327 sq. mi. *Cap.:* Troyes.

Au·ber (ō beR′), *n.* **Da·niel Fran·çois Es·prit** (DA nyel′ fRäN swA′ es pRē′), 1782–1871, French composer.

au·berge (ō berzh′), *n., pl.* **-berges** (-berzh′). *French.* an inn; tavern.

au·ber·gine (ō′bər zhēn′, -jēn′, ō′bər-; ō′bər zhēn′, -jēn′, ō′ber-), *n.* **1.** the deep-purple fruit of the eggplant. **2.** Also, **au′bergine pur′ple.** blackish purple or purplish black. [< F < Catalan *albergínia* < Ar *al- bādhinān* the eggplant]

au·ber·giste (ō beR zhēst′), *n., pl.* **-gistes** (-zhēst′). *French.* an innkeeper.

Au·ber·on (ô′bə ron′), *n.* a boy's given name.

Au·ber·vil·liers (ō beR vē lyā′), *n.* a town in N France, a suburb of Paris. 70,836 (1962).

Au·bin (ô′bin), *n.* a boy's given name. Also, **Aubyn.**

Au·brey (ô′brē), *n.* **1. John,** 1626–97, English antiquary. **2.** a boy's given name.

au·burn (ô′bərn), *n.* **1.** a reddish-brown or golden-brown color. —*adj.* **2.** having auburn color: *auburn hair.* [late ME *abo(u)rne* blond < MF, OF *auborne,* early OF *alborne* < L *alburn(us)* whitish. See ALBURNUM]

Au·burn (ô′bərn), *n.* **1.** a city in central New York: state prison. 35,249 (1960). **2.** a city in SW Maine, on the Androscoggin River. 24,449 (1960). **3.** a city in E Alabama. 16,261 (1960). **4.** a town in NE Indiana. 6350 (1960). **5.** a town in central California. 5586 (1960). **6.** a town in SE Nebraska. 3229 (1960). **7.** a boy's given name.

Au′bus·son rug′ (ō′bə sən, -sôN′; *Fr.* ō bY sôN′), an ornate rug constructed in a flat tapestry weave. [after *Aubusson,* town in central France where made]

Au·byn (ô′bin), *n.* a boy's given name.

A.U.C., **1.** from the founding of the city (of Rome in 753? B.C.). The year 360 A.U.C. would be the 360th year after the founding of Rome. [< L *ab urbe conditā*] **2.** in the year from the founding of the city (of Rome in 753? B.C.). [< L *annō urbis conditae*]

Au·cas·sin and Nic·o·lette (ō′kə san′ ən nik′ə let′), a chante-fable of unknown authorship, dating from the early 13th century. French, **Au·cas·sin et Ni·co·lette** (ō kA saN′ ā nē kô let′).

Auck·land (ôk′lənd), *n.* a seaport on N North Island, in New Zealand. 141,100 (est. 1959).

au con·traire (ō kôN tReR′), *French.* **1.** on the contrary. **2.** on the opposite or adverse side.

au cou·rant (ō kōō RäN′), *French.* up-to-date. [lit., in the current]

auc·tion (ôk′shən), *n.* **1.** a public sale at which property or goods are sold to the highest bidder. **2.** *Cards.* **a.** See **auction bridge. b.** (in bridge or certain other games) the competitive bidding to fix a contract that a player or players undertake to fulfill. —*v.t.* **3.** to sell by auction (often fol. by *off*): *He auctioned off his furniture.* [< L *auctiōn-* (s. of *auctiō*) an increase, esp. in the bidding at a sale, equiv. to *auct(us)* increased, ptp. of *augēre* (*aug-* increase + *-tus* ptp. suffix) + *-iōn-* -ION] —**auc′tion·ar′y,** *adj.*

auc′tion bridge′, a variety of bridge in which odd tricks won in excess of the number named in the contract are scored toward game. Cf. **contract** (def. 6).

auc·tion·eer (ôk′shə nēr′), *n.* **1.** one who conducts sales by auction. —*v.t.* **2.** to auction (something). [AUCTION + -EER]

auc′tion pi′nochle, 1. a variety of pinochle for three to five players in which three active players, having 15 cards each, bid to name the contract and play against the other two active opponents. **2.** pinochle in which players bid to name trump.

auc′tion pitch′, *Cards.* a variety of all fours in which players bid to determine the trump or pitch.

auc·to·ri·al (ôk tōr′ē əl, -tôr′-, ouk′-), *adj.* of, by, or pertaining to an author: *Editors often struggle with auctorial pride and reluctance to change a single comma.* [< L *auctor* + -IAL]

aud., auditor.

au·da·cious (ô dā′shəs), *adj.* **1.** extremely bold or daring; recklessly brave; fearless: *an audacious warrior.* **2.** extremely original; without restriction to prior ideas; highly inventive: *an audacious vision of the future.* **3.** recklessly bold in defiance of convention, propriety, law, or the like; extremely rebellious; impudent; insolent; brazen. **4.** lively; unrestrained; uninhibited: *an audacious interpretation of her role; audacious behavior.* [AUDACI(TY) + -OUS] —**au·da′cious·ly,** *adv.* —**au·da′cious·ness,** *n.*
—**Syn. 1.** venturesome. **3.** unabashed, shameless; impertinent, forward. —**Ant. 1.** cowardly.

au·dac·i·ty (ô das′i tē), *n., pl.* **-ties. 1.** boldness or daring, esp. with confident or arrogant disregard for personal safety, conventional thought, or other restrictions. **2.** effrontery or insolence: *His questioner's audacity shocked the lecturer.* **3.** Usually, **audacities.** audacious acts or statements. [late ME < L *audāci(a)* daring (*aud(ēre)* (to) dare + *-ācia,* equiv. to *-āci-* adj. suffix + *-a* n. suffix) + -TY[2]]
—**Syn. 1.** temerity, foolhardiness.

Aude (ōd), *n.* a department in S France. 269,782 (1962); 2449 sq. mi. *Cap.:* Carcassonne.

Au·den (ôd′ən), *n.* **W(ys·tan) H(ugh)** (wis′tən), born 1907, English poet in the U.S.

Aud·hum·bla (oud′hōōm blä, -lä, -hum-), *n.* *Scand. Myth.* a cow, owned by Ymir and born like him from drops of the melting primeval ice: its licking of a mass of salty ice exposed the first god, Buri. Also, **Aud·hum·la** (oud′hōōm lä, -hum-).

Au·di (ô′dē), *n.* *Archaeol.* any flint artifact found at an Aurignacian site. [?]

au·di·ble (ô′də bəl), *adj.* capable of being heard; loud enough to be heard; actually heard. [< LL *audībil(is),* equiv. to *audī(re)* (to) hear + *-bilis* -BLE] —**au′di·bil′i·ty, au′di·ble·ness,** *n.* —**au′di·bly,** *adv.*

Au·die (ô′dē), *n.* a girl's or boy's given name, form of **Audrey.**

au·di·ence (ô′dē əns), *n.* **1.** the group of spectators at a public event; listeners or viewers collectively, as in attendance at a theater, concert, or the like: *The audience was respectful and appreciative of the speaker's opinion.* **2.** the persons reached by a book, radio broadcast, etc.; public: *Some works of art have a wide and varied audience.* **3.** a regular public that manifests interest, support, enthusiasm, or the like; a following: *Each style or form has its own audience.* **4.** opportunity of being heard; chance to speak to or before a person or group; a hearing. **5.** a formal interview with a sovereign or high officer of government. **6.** act of hearing, or attending to, words or sounds. [ME < MF < L *audientia.* See AUDIENT, -ENCE]

au·di·ence-proof (ô′dē əns prōōf′), *adj.* (of a theatrical production) certain of success.

au′dience room′, a room for holding formal interviews or audiences.

au·di·ent (ô′dē ənt), *adj.* hearing; listening. [< L *audient-* (s. of *audiēns,* prp. of *audīre* to hear), equiv. to *audi-* hear + *-ent-* -ENT]

au·dile (ô′dil, -dīl), *n.* *Psychol.* a person in whose mind auditory images, rather than visual or motor images, are predominant or unusually distinct. [AUD(ITORY) + -ILE]

au·di·o (ô′dē ō′), *adj.* **1.** *Electronics.* designating an electronic apparatus using audio frequencies: *audio amplifier.* **2.** *Television.* pertaining to or employed in the transmission or reception of sound. **3.** of or pertaining to frequencies or signals in the audible range. —*n.* **4.** *Television.* **a.** the audio elements of television, as of a program or script (distinguished from *video*). **b.** the circuits in a receiver for reproducing sound. **5.** auditory. [independent use of AUDIO-]

audio-, a combining form of **audio:** *audiophile.* [comb. form repr. L *audīre* to hear]

au′dio fre′quency, *Acoustics, Electronics.* a frequency between 15 and 20,000 cycles per second, within the range of normally audible sound.

au·di·o·gen·ic (ô′dē ə jen′ik), *adj.* caused by sound. [AUDIO- + GENIC]

au·di·o·gram (ô′dē ō gram′), *n.* *Med.* the graphic record produced by an audiometer. [AUDIO- + GRAM[1]]

au·di·ol·o·gy (ô′dē ol′ə jē), *n.* the science of hearing. [AUDIO- + -LOGY]

au·di·om·e·ter (ô′dē om′i tər), *n.* *Med.* an instrument for gauging and recording the power of hearing. Also called **sonometer.** [AUDIO- + -METER]

au·di·om·e·try (ô′dē om′i trē), *n.* *Med.* the testing of hearing by means of an audiometer. [AUDIO- + -METRY] —**au·di·o·met·ric** (ô′dē ə me′trik), *adj.* —**au′di·o·met′ri·cal·ly,** *adv.*

au·di·on (ô′dē on, -on′), *n.* *Electronics Obs.* a vacuum tube having three electrodes. [formerly trademark]

au·di·o·phile (ô′dē ə fīl′), *n.* a person who is especially interested in high-fidelity sound reproduction, as on radios, phonographs, tape recorders, etc. [AUDIO- + -PHILE]

au·di·o·vis·u·al (ô′dē ō vizh′ōō əl), *adj.* of, pertaining to, involving, or directed at both hearing and sight: *audio-visual facilities; audio-visual techniques.* —**au′di·o·vis′u·al·ly,** *adv.*

au′dio-vis′ual aids′, training or educational materials directed at both the sense of hearing and the sense of sight; films, recordings, photographs, etc., used in classroom instruction, library collections, or the like.

au·di·phone (ô′də fōn′), *n.* *Med.* a kind of diaphragm held against the upper teeth to assist hearing by transmitting sound vibrations to the auditory nerve. [AUDI(O)- + -PHONE, modeled on TELEPHONE]

au·dit (ô′dit), *n.* **1.** an official examination and verification of accounts and records, esp. of financial accounts. **2.** a report or statement reflecting an audit; a final statement of account. **3.** *Archaic.* a judicial hearing. **4.** *Obs.* an audience. —*v.t.* **5.** to make an audit of; examine (accounts, records, etc.) for purposes of verification: *The accountants audited the company's books at the end of the fiscal year.* **6.** *U.S.* to attend (classes, lectures, etc.) as an auditor. —*v.i.* **7.** to examine and verify an account or accounts by reference to vouchers. [late ME *audite* < L *audīt(us)* a hearing, report, n. use of ptp. of *audīre,* equiv. to *audī-* hear + *-tus* ptp. suffix]

au·di·tion (ô dish′ən), *n.* **1.** act, sense, or power of hearing. **2.** a trial hearing given to a musician, actor, speaker, etc., to test voice qualities, performance, stage presence, or the like. **3.** that which is heard. **4.** a reading or other simplified rendering of a theatrical work, performed before a potential backer, producer, etc. —*v.t., v.i.* **5.** to try in an audition: *The producer plans to audition five young people tomorrow.* [< L *audītiōn-* (s. of *audītiō* hearing). See AUDIT, -ION]

au·di·tive (ô′di tiv), *adj.* auditory. [AUDIT(ORY) + -IVE]

au·di·tor (ô′di tər), *n.* **1.** a hearer; listener. **2.** a person appointed and authorized to examine accounts and accounting records, compare the charges with the vouchers, verify balance sheet and income items, and state the result. **3.** *U.S.* a university student registered for a course without credit and without obligation to do work assigned to the class. Also, *referring to a woman,* **auditress.** [< L; see AUDIT, -OR[2]] —**au′di·tor·ship′,** *n.*

au·di·to·ri·um (ô′di tōr′ē əm, -tôr′-), *n., pl.* **-to·ri·ums, -to·ri·a** (-tōr′ē ə, -tôr′-). **1.** the space set apart for the audience in a theater, school, or other public building. **2.** a building for public gatherings; a hall. [< L: lecture hall, n. use of neut. of *audītōrius* AUDITORY]

au·di·to·ry (ô′di tōr′ē, -tôr′ē-), *adj., n., pl.* **-ries.** —*adj.* **1.** *Anat., Physiol.* pertaining to hearing, to the sense of hearing, or to the organs of hearing. **2.** perceived through or resulting from the sense of hearing: *auditory hallucinations.* —*n. Archaic.* **3.** an assembly of hearers; an audience. **4.** an auditorium, esp. the nave of a church. **5.** *Anat.* See **auditory nerve.** [< L *audītōri(us)* relating to hearing. See AUDIT, -ORY[1]] —**au′di·to′ri·ly, au′di·to′ri·al·ly,** *adv.*

au′ditory apha′sia, *Pathol.* aphasia in which there is no comprehension of spoken words; word deafness.

au′ditory nerve′, *Anat.* either one of the eighth pair of cranial nerves, consisting of sensory fibers that conduct impulses from the organs of hearing and from the semicircular canals to the brain. Also called **acoustic nerve.**

au′ditory phonet′ics, the branch of phonetics dealing with the physiological processes involved in the reception of speech. Cf. **acoustic phonetics** (def. 3), **articulatory phonetics, physiological phonetics.**

au′ditory ves′icle, *Embryol.* the vesicle that is formed by the invagination of an ectodermal placode and develops into the internal ear. Also called **otic vesicle, otocyst.**

au·di·tress (ô′di tris), *n.* a female auditor. [AUDIT(O)R + -ESS]

Aud·ley (ôd′lē), *n.* a boy's given name.

Au·drey (ô′drē), *n.* a girl's given name.

Au·du·bon (ô′də bon′, -bən), *n.* **1. John James,** 1785–1851, U.S. naturalist who painted and wrote about the birds of North America. **2.** a town in W Iowa. 2928 (1960).

Au′dubon Soci′ety, a society founded in 1905 for the preservation of wildlife, esp. of birds. [named after J. J. AUDUBON]

Au′dubon's war′bler, a North American wood warbler, *Dendroica auduboni,* resembling the myrtle warbler but having a yellow throat. [named after J. J. AUDUBON]

Au·er (ou′ər), *n.* **Le·o·pold** (lē′ə pōld′; *Hung.* lā′ô pôlt′), 1845–1930, Hungarian violinist.

Au·er·bach (ou′ər bäk′, our′-; *Ger.* ou′əR bäKH′), *n.* **Ber·thold** (beR′tôlt), 1812–82, German novelist.

au fait (ō fe′), *French.* having experience or practical knowledge of a thing; expert; versed. [lit., to the fact]

Auf·klä·rung (ouf′kle′RŏŏNG), *German.* **1.** enlightenment. **2.** *Europ. Hist.* the Enlightenment.

au fond (ō fôN′), *French.* at bottom or to the bottom; thoroughly; in reality; fundamentally.

auf Wie·der·seh·en (ouf vē′dəR zā′ən), *German.* until we meet again; good-by for the present.

Aug., August.

aug., 1. augmentative. **2.** augmented.

Au·ge (ô′jē), *n.* *Class. Myth.* a daughter of King Aleus who became a priestess of Athena to defeat a prophecy that a son of hers would kill her uncles. She was nevertheless assaulted by Hercules and bore him a son, Telephus.

Au·ge·an (ô jē′ən), *adj.* **1.** resembling the Augean stables in filthiness or degradation. **2.** difficult and unpleasant. [< L *augē(us)* of AUGEAS (Gk *Augeí(ās)* + *-us* adj. suffix) + -AN]

Auge′an sta′bles, *Class. Myth.* the stables in which King Augeas kept 3000 oxen, and which had not been cleaned for 30 years. The cleaning of these stables was accomplished by Hercules, who diverted the river Alpheus through them.

Au·ge·as (ô′jē əs, ô jē′əs), *n.* king of the Epeans in Elis and one of the Argonauts. Cf. **Augean stables.**

au·gend (ô′jend, ô jend′), *n.* *Math.* a number to which another is added in forming a sum. Cf. **addend.** [< L *augend(um)* a thing to be increased, n. use of neut. of *augendus* to be increased, ger. of *augēre* to increase]

au·ger (ô′gər), *n.* **1.** *Carpentry.* **a.** a bit, as for a brace. **b.** a boring tool, similar to but larger than a gimlet, consisting of a bit rotated by a transverse handle. **2.** See **earth auger. 3.** a device consisting of a shaft with a broad helical flange rotating within a cylindrical casing to force bulk materials from one end to the other. [ME *nauger* (*a nauger* taken as *an auger*; cf. ADDER, APRON), OE *nafogār* nave-piercer (c. Icel) *nafar(r)*, OHG *nabagēr*) < OE *nafa* NAVE[2] + *gār* spear; see GORE[3]]

au′ger bit′, an auger having a square tang at its upper end and rotated by a brace, used for boring through wood.

Au·ger′ effect′ (ō zhā′), *Physics.* a nonradiative process in which an atom in an excited state undergoes a transition to a lower state by the emission of a bound electron (**Auger′ elec′tron**) rather than by the emission of an x-ray. Also called **autoionization.** [named after Pierre V. *Auger* (b. 1899), French physicist]

aught[1] (ôt), *n.* **1.** anything whatever; any part: *for aught I know.* —*adv.* **2.** in any degree; at all; in any respect. Also, **ought.** [ME *aught, ought,* OE *āht, āwiht, ōwiht,* equiv. to *ā, ō* ever + *wiht* thing, WIGHT[1]]

aught[2] (ôt), *n.* a cipher (0); zero. Also, **ought.** [*a naught,* taken as *an aught* (cf. AUGER). See NAUGHT]

aught[3] (ôKHt), *v.t.* *Scot.* **1.** to own; possess. **2.** to owe (someone or something); be obligated to. —*adj.* **3.** possessed of. —*n.* **4.** *Archaic.* **a.** ownership; possession. **b.** property; a possession. [ME; OE *æht;* c. OHG *ēht,* Goth *aihts;* akin to OWE, OWN]

aught[4] (ôKHt), *adj.* *Scot.* **1.** eight. **2.** eighth. [ME *aghte, aughte,* var. of *eighte;* see EIGHT]

aught·lins (ôKHt′linz), *adv.* *Scot.* oughtlins. [AUGHT + *-lin* (var. of -LING[2]) + -S[1]]

Au·gier (ō zhyā′), *n.* **Guil·laume Vic·tor É·mile** (gē yōm′ vēk tôr′ ā mēl′), 1820–89, French dramatist.

au·gite (ô′jīt), *n.* a mineral, a silicate, chiefly of calcium, magnesium, iron, and aluminum: a dark-green to black variety of monoclinic pyroxene, characteristic of basic rocks. [< L *augītes* < Gk, equiv. to *aug(ē)* + *-ītes* -ITE[1]] —**au·git·ic** (ô jit′ik), *adj.*

aug·ment (*v.* ôg ment′; *n.* ôg′ment), *v.t.* **1.** to make larger; enlarge in size or extent; increase: *His small salary is augmented by a commission.* **2.** *Gram.* to add an augment to. **3.** *Music.* **a.** to raise (the upper note of an interval or chord) by a half step. **b.** to double the note values of (a theme): *In the fugue's development the subject is augmented.* **4.** *Heraldry.* to grant an augmentation to (a coat of arms). —*v.i.* **5.** to become larger. —*n.* **6.** *Gram.* a prefixed vowel or a lengthening of the initial vowel which characterizes certain forms in the non-present inflection of verbs in Greek, Sanskrit, Armenian, and Phrygian. [< LL *augment(āre)* (to) increase, deriv. of *augment(um)* an increase (*aug(ēre)* (to) increase (akin to EKE) + *-mentum* -MENT) + *-ā-* thematic vowel + *-re* inf. ending; r. ME *aument* < MF *aument(er)* <LL, as above] —**aug·ment′a·ble,** *adj.*
—**Syn. 1.** swell. See **increase. 5.** increase.

aug·men·ta·tion (ôg′men tā′shən), *n.* **1.** act of augmenting; state of being augmented. **2.** that by which anything is augmented. **3.** *Music.* modification of a theme by increasing the time value of all its tones. **4.** *Heraldry.* an addition to a coat of arms granted to a person, or to him and his descendants, by a sovereign power in recognition of a notable action. [late ME < L *augmentātiōn-* (s. of *augmentātiō*). See AUGMENT, -ATION; r. late ME *aumentacion* < MF]

aug·ment·a·tive (ôg men′tə tiv), *adj.* **1.** serving to augment. **2.** *Gram.* pertaining to or productive of a form denoting increased size or intensity. In Spanish the augmentative suffix *-ón* is added to a word, as *silla* "chair" to indicate increased size, as in *sillón* "armchair." —*n.* **3.** *Gram.* an augmentative element or formation. [AUGMENT + -ATIVE; r. *augmentatif* < MF] —**aug·men′ta·tive·ly,** *adv.*

augment′ed sixth′, *Music.* **1.** an interval greater than a major sixth by a chromatic half step. **2.** any of various chords having this as the characteristic interval.

aug·ment·er (ôg men′tər), *n.* **1.** one who or that which augments. **2.** *Aeron., Rocketry.* any auxiliary device, as an afterburner, for additional thrust from the exhaust of a jet or rocket engine. Also, **aug·men′tor.** [AUGMENT + -ER[1], -OR[2]]

au grand sé·rieux (ō grän sā ryœ′), *French.* in all seriousness.

au grat·in (ō grät′ən, ō grat′ən; *Fr.* ō gra tan′), *Cookery.* cooked or baked with a topping of either browned crumbs and butter or grated cheese, or with both. [< F: lit., with the scraping, i.e. the burnt part. See SCRATCH]

Augs·burg (ôgz′bûrg; *Ger.* ouks′bŏŏrkh), *n.* a city in Bavaria, in S West Germany. 210,500 (1963).

Augs′burg Confes′sion, the statement of beliefs and doctrines of the Lutherans, formulated by Melanchthon and endorsed by the Lutheran princes, which was presented at the Diet of Augsburg in 1530 and which became the chief creed of the Lutheran Church. Also called **Augustan Confession.**

au·gur (ô′gər), *n.* **1.** one of a body of ancient Roman officials charged with observing and interpreting omens for guidance in public affairs. **2.** any soothsayer; prophet. —*v.t.* **3.** to divine or predict, as from omens; prognosticate. **4.** to afford an omen of; foreshadow; betoken: *mounting sales that augur a profitable year.* —*v.i.* **5.** to conjecture from signs or omens; presage. **6.** to be a sign; bode (usually fol. by *well* or *ill*). [< L *augur* (var. of *auger*) a diviner, soothsayer < ?]

au·gu·ry (ô′gyə rē), *n., pl.* **-ries. 1.** the art or practice of an augur; divination. **2.** the rite or ceremony of an augur. **3.** an omen, token, or indication. [ME < L *auguri(um)* soothsaying, equiv. to *augur* AUGUR + *-ium* n. suffix denoting office] —**au′gu·ral,** *adj.*

au·gust (ô gust′), *adj.* **1.** inspiring reverence or admiration; of supreme dignity or grandeur; majestic: *an august performance of a religious drama.* **2.** venerable; eminent: *an august personage.* [< L *august(us)* sacred, grand, perh. akin to *augēre* to increase. See -EKE] —**au·gust′ly,** *adv.* —**au·gust′ness,** *n.*

Au·gust (ô′gəst), *n.* **1.** the eighth month of the year, containing 31 days. **2.** a boy's given name, form of **Augustus.** [early ME < L *August(us)* (named after AUGUSTUS); r. OE *Agustus* < LL]

Au·gus·ta (ô gus′tə), *n.* **1.** a city in E Georgia, on the Savannah River. 70,626 (1960). **2.** a city in and the capital of Maine, in the SW part, on the Kennebec River. 21,680 (1960). **3.** a town in S Kansas. 6434 (1960). **4.** a girl's given name.

Au·gus·ta·les (ô′gə stā′lēz), *n.pl.* (in ancient Rome) local officials, usually freedmen, appointed in various towns for the worship of deified emperors. [< L, pl. of *Augustālis.* See AUGUSTUS, -AL[1]]

Au·gus·tan (ô gus′tən), *adj.* **1.** of or pertaining to Augustus Caesar or to the age (**Augus′tan Age′**) in which he flourished, which marked the golden age of Latin literature. **2.** of or pertaining to the neoclassic period, esp. of 18th-century English literature. —*n.* **3.** an author in an Augustan age. [< L *Augustān(us).* See AUGUSTUS, -AN]

Augus′tan Confes′sion. See **Augsburg Confession.**

Au·gus·tine (ô′gə stēn′, ô gus′tin), *n.* **1. Saint,** (*Austin*) A.D. 354–430, one of the Latin fathers in the early Christian Church; author; bishop of Hippo in N Africa. **2. Saint,** died A.D. 604, Roman monk: headed group of missionaries who landed in England A.D. 597 and began the conversion of the English to Christianity; first archbishop of Canterbury 601–604. **3.** a boy's given name, form of **Augustus.**

Au·gus·tin·i·an (ô′gə stin′ē ən), *adj.* **1.** pertaining to St. Augustine of Hippo, to his doctrines, or to any religious order following his rule. —*n.* **2.** *Rom. Cath. Ch.* a member of any of several religious orders deriving their name and rule from St. Augustine. **3.** one who adopts the views or doctrines of St. Augustine. [AUGUSTINE + -IAN] —**Au′gus·tin′i·an·ism, Au·gus·tin·ism** (ô gus′tə niz′əm), *n.*

Augustin′ian of the Assump′tion, a member of a Roman Catholic congregation founded in 1847 in France, engaged in missionary and educational work. Also called **Assumptionist.**

Au·gus·tus (ô gus′təs), *n.* Also called **Octavian** (before 27 B.C.) **1.** (*Gaius Julius Caesar Octavianus, Augustus Caesar*), 63 B.C.–A.D. 14, first Roman emperor 27 B.C.–A.D. 14: reformer, patron of arts and literature; heir and successor to Julius Caesar. **2.** a boy's given name. [< L, special use of *augustus* AUGUST]

au jus (ō zhōōs′, ō jōōs′; *Fr.* ō zhy′), (of meat) served in the natural juices that flow from the meat as it cooks. [< F: lit., with the gravy. See JUICE]

auk (ôk), *n.* any of several usually black and white diving birds of the family *Alcidae,* of northern seas, having webbed feet and small wings. Cf. **great auk, razor-billed auk.** [< Scand; cf. Icel *alka*]

Razor-billed auk, *Alca torda* (Length 1½ ft.)

auk·let (ôk′lit), *n.* any of several small auks of the coasts of the North Pacific, as *Aethia cristatella* (**crested auklet**), having a crest of recurved plumes. [AUK + -LET]

au lait (ō lā′; *Fr.* ō le′), *French Cookery.* prepared or served with milk. [< F: lit., with the milk. See LACT-]

Au·lard (ō lar′), *n.* **Fran·çois Vic·tor Al·phonse** (fräN swa′ vēk tôr′ al fôNs′), 1849–1928, French historian.

auld (ôld), *adj.* *Scot. and North Eng.* old.

auld lang syne (ôld′ lang zīn′, sīn′), *Scot. and North Eng.* **1.** old times, esp. times fondly remembered. **2.** old or long friendship. [lit., old long since, i.e. old long-ago (days)]

au·lic (ô′lik), *adj.* pertaining to a royal court. [< L *aulic(us)* < Gk *aulikós* courtly, equiv. to *aul(ē)* hall, court + *-ikos* -IC]

Au′lic Coun′cil, a personal council of the Holy Roman Emperor exercising chiefly judicial powers.

au·lo·phyte (ô′lə fīt′), *n.* a free-living plant growing on or in another plant. [*aulo-* (see AULOS) + -PHYTE]

au·los (ô′läs), *n., pl.* **-loi** (-loi). an ancient Greek double pipe with oboe reeds. [< Gk *aulós* tube, pipe, flute]

AUM, air-to-underwater missile.

Aum (ōm), *n.* *Hinduism.* Om.

aum·bry (am′brē), *n., pl.* **-bries.** ambry.

au·mil·dar (ô′ mil där′, ô′mildär′), *n.* *Anglo-Indian.* **1.** a native manager or agent. **2.** a native collector of revenue [< Hindi]

au na·tu·rel (ō na ty rel′), *French.* **1.** in the natural state; naked. **2.** cooked plainly. **3.** uncooked.

aune (ōn), *n.* an old French unit of measure for fabrics, equivalent to about 47 inches [< F; OF *aulne* < Gmc. See ELL[2]]

aunt (ant, änt), *n.* **1.** the sister of one's father or mother. **2.** the wife of one's uncle. **3.** a benevolent elderly woman. **4.** *Slang.* an aging male homosexual. [ME *aunte* < OF, var. of *ante* < L *amita* father's sister; akin to AMAH] —**aunt′like′,** *adj.*

aunt·ie (an′tē, än′-), *n.* **1.** a familiar or diminutive form of **aunt.** [AUNT + -IE] **2.** *Rocketry Slang.* an antimissile missile. Also, **aunty.** [by shortening and rhyming assoc.]

Aunt′ Sal′ly, *Chiefly Brit.* a scapegoat. [so called from the figure used as a target at fairs]

aunt·y (an′tē, än′-), *n., pl.* **aunt·ies.** auntie.

aur-[1] var. of **auri-**[1]. esp. before a vowel.

aur-[2] var. of **auri-**[2], esp. before a vowel.

au·ra (ôr′ə), *n., pl.* **au·ras** or, for 3, **au·rae** (ôr′ē). **1.** a distinctive and pervasive quality or character; air; atmosphere: *an aura of respectability; an aura of friendliness.* **2.** a subtly pervasive quality or atmosphere seen as emanating from a person, place, or thing: *He had about him an aura of greatness.* **3.** *Pathol.* a sensation, as of a current of cold air, or other sensory experience preceding an attack of epilepsy, hysteria, etc. [< L < Gk: breath (of air)]

Au·ra (ôr′ə), *n.* *Class. Myth.* a companion of Artemis who bore twins to Dionysus. Zeus changed her into a spring because, in a fit of madness, she had killed one of her children.

au·ral[1] (ôr′əl), *adj.* of or pertaining to an aura. [AUR(A) + -AL[1]]

au·ral[2] (ôr′əl), *adj.* of or pertaining to the ear or to the sense of hearing. [< L *aur(is)* the ear + -AL[1]] —**au′ral·ly,** *adv.*

Au·ral (ôr′əl), *n.* a boy's given name.

au·ra·mine (ôr′ə mēn′, -min), *n.* *Chem.* a yellow, crystalline, water-soluble solid, $[(CH_3)_2NC_6H_4]_2C{=}NH{\cdot}HCl$, used chiefly as a dye for paper and leather. [< L *aur(um)* gold + AMINE]

Au·rang·zeb (ôr′əng zeb′), *n.* 1618–1707, Mogul emperor of Hindustan 1658–1707. Also, **Aurungzeb.**

au·rar (oi′rär), *n.* pl. of **eyrir.**

au·re·a me·di·o·cri·tas (ou′rä ä′ me′dē ōk′ri täs′; *Eng.* ôr′ē ə mē′dē ok′ri tas′, -med′ē-), *Latin.* the golden mean.

au·re·ate (ôr′ē it, -āt′), *adj.* **1.** golden. **2.** brilliant; splendid. [late ME *aureat* < LL *aureāt(us)* decorated with gold, equiv. to L *aure(us)* golden, of gold (*aur(um)* gold + *-eus* adj. suffix) + *-ātus* -ATE[1]] —**au′re·ate·ly,** *adv.* —**au′re·ate·ness,** *n.*

au·re·li·a (ô rē′lē ə, ô rēl′yə), *n.* See **moon jellyfish.** [< NL]

Au·rel·ia (ô rēl′yə), *n.* a girl's given name.

au·re·li·an (ô rē′lē ən, ô rēl′yən), *n.* *Brit.* a lepidopterist. [< NL *aureli(a)* chrysalis + -AN]

Au·re·li·an (ô rē′lē ən, ô rēl′yən), *n.* (*Lucius Domitius Aurelianus*) A.D. 212?–275, Roman emperor 270–275.

Au·re·li·us (ô rē′lē əs, ô rēl′yəs), *n.* **Marcus.** See **Marcus Aurelius.**

au′rene glass′ (ôr′ēn), an iridescent American art glass colored gold and blue. [formerly trademark]

au·re·ole (ôr′ē ōl′), *n.* **1.** a radiance surrounding the head or the whole figure in the representation of a sacred personage. **2.** any encircling ring of light or color; a halo. **3.** *Astron.* corona (def. 3). **4.** *Geol.* a zone of altered country rock around an igneous intrusion. Also, **au·re·o·la** (ô rē′ə lə). [ME < L *aureola* (*corona*) golden (crown), equiv. to *aure(us)* golden (see AUREATE) + *-ola,* fem. of *-olus* dim. suffix]

au·re·o·lin (ô rē′ə lin, ə rē′-), *n.* a pigment used in painting, consisting of potassium cobaltinitrite and characterized by its brilliant yellow hue, transparency, and permanence. Also called **cobalt yellow.** [< L *aureol(us)* golden, of gold (see AUREOLE) + -IN[2]] —**au·re·o·line** (ô rē′ə lin, -līn′, ə rē′-), *adj.*

Au·re·o·my·cin (ôr′ē ō mī′sin), *n.* *Pharm., Trademark.* chlortetracycline.

au·re·us (ôr′ē əs), *n., pl.* **au·re·i** (ôr′ē ī′). a gold coin and monetary unit of ancient Rome, from Caesar to Constantine I. [< L: lit., golden]

au re·voir (ō rə vwar′; *Eng.* ō′ rə vwär′), *French.* until we see each other again; good-by for the present.

auri-[1], a combining form meaning "gold": *auriferous.* Also, *esp. before a vowel,* **aur-.** [< L *aur(um)* + -I-]

auri-[2], a combining form meaning "ear," used esp. before a consonant: *auriform.* Also, *esp. before a vowel,* **aur-.** [< L *auri(s)* ear]

au·ric (ôr′ik), *adj.* *Chem.* of or containing gold, esp. in the trivalent state. [< L *aur(um)* gold + -IC]

au·ri·cle (ôr′i kəl), *n.* **1.** *Anat.* **a.** the projecting outer portion of the ear; pinna. See diag. under **ear. b.** Also called **auric′ular append′age.** an ear-shaped appendage projecting from each atrium of the heart. **c.** (loosely) the atrium. **2.** *Bot., Zool.* a part like or likened to an ear. [< L *auricul(a)* the (external) ear, ear lobe. See AURI-[2], -CLE] —**au′ri·cled,** *adj.*

au·ric·u·la (ô rik′yə lə), *n., pl.* **-lae** (-lē′), **-las.** a yellow primrose, *Primula Auricula,* native in the Alps. Also called **bear's-ear.** [< NL, special use of L *auricula* AURICLE]

au·ric·u·lar (ô rik′yə lər), *adj.* **1.** of or pertaining to the ear or to the sense of hearing. **2.** perceived by or addressed to the ear; made in private: *an auricular confession.* **3.** dependent on hearing; understood or known by hearing: *auricular evidence.* **4.** shaped like an ear; auriculate. **5.** *Anat.* pertaining to an auricle of the heart. **6.** *Ornith.* pertaining to certain often modified feathers that cover and protect the opening of a bird's ear. —*n.* **7.** Usually, **auriculars.** *Ornith.* feathers that cover and protect the opening of a bird's ear. [< LL *auriculār(is)* of, pertaining to the ear. See AURICLE, -AR[1]] —**au·ric′u·lar·ly,** *adv.*

au·ric·u·lar·i·a (ô rik′yə lâr′ē ə), *n., pl.* **-lar·i·ae** (-lâr′ē ē′), **-lar·i·as.** the bilaterally symmetrical, ciliated larva of a holothurian. [< NL; see AURICLE, -ARIA]

au·ric·u·late (ô rik′yə lit, -lāt′), *adj.* **1.** having auricles or earlike parts. **2.** shaped like an ear. [< L *auricul-* AURICLE + -ATE[1]] —**au·ric′u·late·ly,** *adv.*

au·ric·u·lo·ven·tric·u·lar (ô rik′yə lō ven trik′yə lər), *adj.* *Anat.* atrioventricular. [*auriculo-* (comb. form of AURICLE) + VENTRICULAR]

au·rif·er·ous (ô rif′ər əs), *adj.* yielding or containing gold. [< L *aurifer* gold-bearing (see AURI-[1], -FER) + -OUS]

au·ri·form (ôr′ə fôrm′), *adj.* shaped like an ear, as the shell of certain mollusks. [AURI-[2] + -FORM]

au·ri·fy (ôr′ə fī′), *v.t.,* **-fied, -fy·ing. 1.** to cause to appear golden; gild: *Dawn came, and sunlight aurified the lead-grey ocean.* **2.** to transmute into gold: *Midas' daughter was aurified by her father's greed.* [AURI-[1] + -FY] —**au·rif·ic** (ô rif′ik), *adj.* —**au′ri·fi·ca′tion,** *n.*

Au·ri·ga (ô rī′gə), *n., gen.* **-gae** (-jē). *Astron.* the Charioteer, a northern constellation between Perseus and Gemini, containing the bright star Capella. [late ME < L: charioteer]

Au·ri·gnac (ô rē nyak′), *n.* a village in S France: many prehistoric artifacts found in area. 1273 (1962).

Au·ri·gna·cian (ôr′in yā′shən), *adj.* of, belonging to, or characteristic of a sequence of related Upper Paleolithic cultures. [AURIGNAC + -IAN]

Au·riol (ôr′ē ōl′, -ôl′; *Fr.* ō ryôl′), *n.* **Vin·cent** (vin′-sənt; *Fr.* van säN′), 1884–1966, French statesman; president 1947–54.

au·ri·scope (ôr′i skōp′), *n.* *Med.* otoscope. [AURI-[2] + -SCOPE] —**au·ri·scop·ic** (ôr′i skop′ik), *adj.* —**au′ri·scop′i·cal·ly,** *adv.*

au·rist (ôr′ist), *n.* a physician specializing in the treatment of ear diseases; otologist. [AUR-[2] + -IST]

au·rochs (ôr′oks), *n., pl.* **-rochs. 1.** a European wild ox, *Bos primigenius,* now extinct. **2.** (not used scientifically) the European bison. [< G, var. (now obs.) of *Auerochs* << OHG *ūrohso,* equiv. to *ūr* (c. OE *ūr* bison) + *ohso* ox]

Aurochs, *Bos primigenius* (6 ft. high at shoulder)

Au·ro·ra (ô rōr′ə, ô rôr′ə, ə rōr′ə, ə rôr′ə), *n.* **1.** the ancient Roman goddess of the dawn, identified by the Greeks with the goddess Eos. **2.** (*l.c.*) the rise or dawn of something. **3.** (*l.c.*) a radiant emission from the upper atmosphere that occurs sporadically over the middle and high latitudes of both hemispheres in the form of luminous bands, streamers, or the like, caused by the bombardment of the atmosphere with charged solar particles that are being guided along the earth's magnetic lines of force. **4.** a city in NE Illinois. 65,715 (1960). **5.** a city in central Colorado, near Denver. 48,548 (1960). **6.** a town in SW Missouri. 4683 (1960). **7.** a town in SE Indiana. 4119 (1960). **8.** a town in NE Ohio. 4049 (1960). **9.** a town in NE Minnesota. 2799 (1960). **10.** a town in central Nebraska. 2576 (1960). **11.** a girl's given name. [late ME < L: dawn, dawn goddess, EAST]

auro′ra aus·tra′lis (ô strā′lis), *Meteorol.* the aurora of the Southern Hemisphere, a phenomenon similar to the aurora borealis. [< NL: southern aurora; see AUSTRAL]

auro′ra bo·re·al′is (bōr′ē al′is, -ā′lis, bôr′-), *Meteorol.* the aurora of the Northern Hemisphere, a luminous meteoric phenomenon appearing at night. Also called **northern lights, auro′ra polar′is.** [< NL: northern aurora; see BOREAL]

au·ro·ral (ô rōr′əl, ô rôr′-), *adj.* **1.** of or like the dawn. **2.** pertaining to a polar aurora. [AUROR(A) + -AL[1]] —**au·ro′ral·ly,** *adv.*

au·ro·re·an (ô rōr′ē ən, ô rôr′-), *adj. Literary.* belonging to the dawn; auroral. [AUROR(A) + -EAN (-E(LOUS) + -AN)]

aur·ous (ôr′əs), *adj.* **1.** *Chem.* of or containing gold in the univalent state. **2.** of or containing gold. [AUR-[1] -OUS]

au·rum (ôr′əm), *n. Chem.* gold. *Symbol:* Au. [< L: gold]

Au·rum (ou′rəm), *n. Trademark.* an orange-flavored liqueur from Italy.

Au·rung·zeb (ôr′ŏŏng zeb′), *n.* Aurangzeb.

Aus., **1.** Austria. **2.** Austrian.

Au·sa·ble (ô sā′bəl), *n.* a river in NE New York, flowing NE through a gorge (**Ausa′ble Chasm′**), into Lake Champlain. 20 mi. long.

Ausch·witz (oush′vits), *n.* a town in SW Poland. 14,400 (est. 1957). Site of Nazi concentration camp during World War II. Polish, **Oswiecim.**

aus·cul·tate (ô′skəl tāt′), *v.t., v.i.,* **-tat·ed, -tat·ing.** *Med.* to examine by auscultation. [back formation from AUSCULTATION] —**aus·cul·ta·tive** (ô′skəl tā′tiv, ô skul′tə-), **aus·cul·ta·to·ry** (ô skul′tə tōr′ē, -tôr′ē), *adj.* —**aus′cul·ta′tor,** *n.*

aus·cul·ta·tion (ô′skəl tā′shən), *n.* **1.** *Med.* the act of listening, either directly or through a stethoscope or other instrument, to sounds within the body, as a method of diagnosis. **2.** act of listening. [< L *auscultātiōn-* (s. of *auscultātiō*) a listening, attending to, equiv. to *auscultāt(us)* listened to (ptp. of *auscultāre; aus-* (var. s. of *auris* ear) + *-cultā-* (< ?) + *-tus* ptp. suffix) + *-iōn-* -ION]

Aus·gleich (ous′glīkh), *n., pl.* **-gleich·e** (-glī′khə). *German.* **1.** an arrangement or compromise between parties. **2.** the agreement made between Austria and Hungary in 1867, regulating the relations between the countries and setting up the Dual Monarchy. [lit., equalization]

Aus·län·der (ous′len′dər; *Eng.* ous′lan′dər, ô′slan′-), *n. German.* a foreigner; an alien or outlander.

Aus·le·se (ous′lā zə), *n.* a wine made in Germany from carefully selected ripe grapes. [< G: lit., selection]

aus·pex (ô′speks), *n., pl.* **aus·pi·ces** (ô′spi sēz′). an augur of ancient Rome. [< L: one who observes birds, soothsayer, diviner, equiv. to *au-* (*avis* bird) + *-spex* watcher (*spec-*, s. of *specere* to look at) + *-s* nom. sing. suffix]

aus·pi·cate (ô′spə kāt′), *v.,* **-cat·ed, -cat·ing.** —*v.t.* **1.** *Rare.* to initiate with ceremonies calculated to ensure good luck; inaugurate. —*v.i.* **2.** *Obs.* to augur; predict with omens. [< L *auspicāt(us)* consecrated by auguries (ptp. of *auspicārī*), equiv. to *auspic-* (s. of AUSPEX) + *-ātus* -ATE[1]]

aus·pice (ô′spis), *n., pl.* **aus·pic·es** (ô′spi siz). **1.** Usually, **auspices,** patronage; support; sponsorship: *under the auspices of the education department.* **2.** Often, **auspices.** a favorable or propitious circumstance. **3.** a divination or prognostication, originally from birds. [< F < L *auspicium* a bird-watching, divination from flight of birds, equiv. to *auspic-* (s. of AUSPEX) + *-ium* n. suffix]

aus·pi·cial (ô spish′əl), *adj.* **1.** of or pertaining to auspices: *auspicial rites.* **2.** auspicious. [< L *auspici(um)* AUSPICE + -AL[1]]

aus·pi·cious (ô spish′əs), *adj.* **1.** promising success; propitious; opportune; favorable: *an auspicious occasion.* **2.** favored by fortune; prosperous; fortunate. [< L *auspici(um)* AUSPICE + -OUS] —**aus·pi′cious·ly,** *adv.* —**aus·pi′cious·ness,** *n.*

Aus·sie (ô′sē), *n. Slang.* an Australian. [AUS(TRALIAN) + -IE]

Aust., **1.** Austria. **2.** Austria-Hungary. **3.** Austrian.

aus·tem·per (ôs′tem′pər), *v.t.* to harden (steel) by heating it to render it austenitic, then maintaining it at a temperature below the critical one for pearlite formation and above that for martensite formation until desired changes have taken place, after which it is cooled. [AUS(TENITE) + TEMPER]

Aus·ten (ô′stən), *n.* **Jane,** 1775–1817, English novelist.

aus·ten·ite (ô′stə nīt′), *n.* **1.** *Metall.* a solid solution of carbon or of carbon and other elements in gamma iron, having a face-centered cubic lattice at all temperatures. **2.** an allotrope of iron, stable between 910°C and 1400°C and having a face-centered cubic lattice; gamma iron. [named after Sir W. C. Roberts-*Austen,* (1843–1902), English metallurgist; see -ITE[1]]

aus·ten·it·ic (ô′stə nit′ik), *adj.* (of an iron alloy) rich in iron and existing in a crystalline form with a face-centered cubic lattice to a greater or lesser degree at a given temperature. [AUSTENITE + -IC]

aus·ten·it·ize (ô′stə ni tīz′), *v.t.,* **-ized, -iz·ing.** *Metall.* to form austenite in (a ferrous alloy) by heating it. [AUSTENITE + -IZE]

Aus·ter (ô′stər), *n. Literary.* the south wind personified. Cf. **Notus.** [< L]

aus·tere (ô stēr′), *adj.* **1.** severe in manner or appearance; stern; uncompromising; strict; forbidding. **2.** rigorously self-disciplined and severely moral; ascetic; abstinent. **3.** grave; sober; solemn; serious: *an austere manner.* **4.** without excess, luxury, or ease; simple; limited; severe: *an austere life.* **5.** severely simple; without ornament: *austere writing.* **6.** lacking softness; hard: *an austere form.* **7.** rough to the taste; sour or harsh in flavor. [ME < L *austēr(us)* < Gk *austērós* harsh, rough, bitter] —**aus·tere′ly,** *adv.* —**aus·tere′ness,** *n.*

aus·ter·i·ty (ô ster′i tē), *n., pl.* **-ties.** **1.** austere quality; severity of manner, life, etc. **2.** Usually, **austerities.** ascetic practices: *austerities of monastery life.* [ME *austerite* < OF *austerite* < L *austēritāt-* (s. of *austēritās*). See AUSTERE, -ITY]
—**Syn. 1.** harshness, strictness, asceticism, rigor.

Aus·ter·litz (ô′stər lits; *Ger.* ous′tər lits), *n.* a town in S Moravia, in the SE Czech Republic: Russian and Austrian armies defeated by Napoleon I 1805. Czech, **Slavkov.**

Aus·tin (ô′stən), *n.* **1. Alfred,** 1835–1913, English poet: poet laureate 1896–1913. **2. John,** 1790–1859, English writer on law. **3. Mary (Hunt·er)** (hun′tər), 1868–1934, U.S. novelist, playwright, and short-story writer. **4. Stephen Fuller,** 1793–1836, American colonizer in Texas. **5. Warren Robinson,** 1877–1962, U.S. diplomat. **6.** See **Augustine, Saint** (def. 1). **7.** a city in and the capital of Texas, in the central part, on the Colorado River. 186,545 (1960). **8.** a city in SE Minnesota. 27,908 (1960). **9.** a town in SE Indiana. 3838 (1960). **10.** a boy's given name, form of **Augustus.**

Aus′tin fri′ar, one of the Hermits of St. Augustine.

Aus′tin Lake′, a town in SW Michigan. 3520 (1960).

aus·tral (ô′strəl), *adj.* **1.** southern. **2.** (*cap.*) Australian. [< L *austrāl(is)* southern, equiv. to *Aust(e)r* AUSTER + *-ālis* -AL[1]]

Austral., **1.** Australasia. **2.** Australia.

Aus·tral·a·sia (ô′strə lā′zhə, -shə), *n.* Australia, New Zealand, and neighboring islands in the S Pacific Ocean. [AUSTRAL(IA) + ASIA] —**Aus′tral·a′sian,** *adj., n.*

Aus·tra·le (ô stral′ē, -strā′lē), *n.* **Mare.** See **Mare Australe** (def. 2).

Aus·tral·ia (ô strāl′yə), *n.* **1.** a continent SE of Asia, between the Indian and the Pacific oceans. 10,157,846 (1961); 2,948,366 sq. mi. **2. Commonwealth of,** a member of the British Commonwealth of Nations, consisting of the federated states and territories of Australia and Tasmania. 10,508,186 (1961); 2,974,581 sq. mi. *Cap.:* Canberra.

Aus·tral·ian (ô strāl′yən), *adj.* **1.** of or pertaining to Australia. **2.** *Zoogeog.* belonging to a geographical division comprising Australia, New Zealand, Tasmania, Celebes, the Moluccas, New Guinea, and adjacent smaller islands. **3.** *Phytogeog.* belonging or pertaining to a geographical division comprising Australia and Tasmania. —*n.* **4.** a native or inhabitant of Australia. **5.** an Australian aborigine. **6.** the speech of the aborigines of Australia, belonging to any of more than a hundred languages. [AUSTRALI(A) + -AN]

Austral′ian Alps′, a mountain range in SE Australia. Highest peak, Mt. Kosciusko, 7328 ft.

Austral′ian bal′lot, a ballot containing the names of all the candidates for public office, handed to the voter at the polling station to be marked in secret: so called because it originated in Australia. Cf. **Indiana ballot, Massachusetts ballot, office-block ballot.**

Austral′ian blue′bell creep′er, an evergreen, twining shrub, *Sollya heterophylla,* of western Australia, having blue flowers in terminal clusters.

Austral′ian Cap′ital Ter′ritory, a federal territory in New South Wales, on the continent of Australia in the SE part: includes Canberra, capital of the Commonwealth of Australia. 59,000 (est. 1961); 939 sq. mi. Formerly, **Federal Capital Territory.**

Austral′ian crawl′, *Swimming.* a crawl in which the swimmer kicks twice with one leg for each stroke of the opposite arm.

Austral′ian fan′ palm′, a fan palm, *Livistona australis,* of Australia, having a slender, reddish-brown trunk, spiny leafstalks, and round fruit.

Austral′ian pea′, a woody vine, *Dolichos lignosus,* of tropical Asia, having white or rose-purple flowers and black seeds.

Austral′ian rye′ grass′. See **Italian rye grass.**

Austral′ian tea′ tree′, a shrubby tree, *Leptospermum laevigatum,* of Australia, having white, bell-shaped flowers.

Aus·tra·loid (ô′strə loid′), *n.* **1.** a member of an ethnic group consisting principally of the Australian aborigines, Papuans, Melanesians, relic dwarf peoples, as Negritos, of the Philippines, Malay Peninsula, and Andaman Islands, and some of the tribes of central and southern India. —*adj.* **2.** pertaining to or having the characteristics of the Australoids. Also, **Aus·tra·li·oid** (ô strā′lē oid′). [var. of *Australioid.* See AUSTRALIA, -OID]

Aus·tra·lo·pith·e·cine (ô strā′lō pith′i sīn, -sin, -pə thē′-), *n.* **1.** a primate of the extinct genus *Australopithecus,* of the Pleistocene epoch, found mainly in southern Africa, having dentition resembling that of man and a braincase resembling that of the apes. —*adj.* **2.** belonging or pertaining to the genus *Australopithecus.* [AUSTRALOPITHEC(US) + -INE[1]]

Aus·tra·lo·pith·e·cus (ô strā′lō pith′ə kəs, -pə thē′kəs), *n.* an extinct genus of primates. Cf. **Australopithecine.** [NL, equiv. to *austral(is)* AUSTRAL + *-o-* -O- + *pithēcus* < Gk *píthēkos* ape]

Aus·tral·orp (ô′strə lôrp′), *n.* one of an Australian breed of chickens. [AUSTRAL(IAN) + ORP(INGTON)]

Aus·tra·sia (ô strā′zhə, -shə), *n.* the E part of the former kingdom of the Franks, comprising parts of what is now NE France, W Germany, and Belgium. *Cap.:* Metz.

Aus·tri·a (ô′strē ə), *n.* a republic in central Europe. 7,060,133 (1961); 32,381 sq. mi. *Cap.:* Vienna. German, **Österreich.** —**Aus′tri·an,** *adj., n.*

Aus·tri·a-Hun·ga·ry (ô′strē ə hung′gə rē), *n.* a monarchy (1867–1918) in central Europe which included the empire of Austria, the kingdom of Hungary, and various crown lands. —**Aus·tro-Hun·gar·i·an** (ô′strō hung gâr′ē ən), *adj., n.*

Aus′trian bri′er, an erect or arching shrub, *Rosa foetida,* of western Asia, having straight prickles and rank-smelling, yellow flowers nearly three inches wide.

aus·trin·ger (ô′strin jər), *n.* astringer.

Austro-, a combining form for Austria: *Austro-Hungarian.*

austro-, a learned borrowing from Latin meaning "south," used in the formation of compound words: *Austronesia.* Also, *esp. before a vowel,* **austr-.** [< L *aust(e)r* the south, the south wind + -o-]

Aus·tro·a·si·at·ic (ô′strō ā′zhē at′ik, -shē-), *n.* **1.** a family of languages spoken in SE Asia and the lands around the Bay of Bengal and consisting principally of Vietnamese, Khmer, Mon, Khasi, Nicobarese, and the Munda languages. —*adj.* **2.** of or pertaining to Austroasiatic. [AUSTRO- + ASIATIC]

Aus·tro·ne·sia (ô′strō nē′zhə, -shə), *n.* the islands of the central and S Pacific. [AUSTRO- + Gk *nês(os)* island + *-ia* -IA]

Aus·tro·ne·sian (ô′strō nē′zhən, -shən), *adj.* **1.** of or pertaining to Austronesia or the Austronesian family of languages. **2.** Malayo-Polynesian. —*n.* **3.** Malayo-Polynesian. [AUSTRONESI(A) + -AN]

Aus′tro-Prus′sian War′ (ô′strō prush′ən), the war (1866) in which Prussia, Italy, and some minor German states opposed Austria, Saxony, Hanover, and the states of southern Germany. Also called **Seven Weeks' War.**

aut-, var. of **auto-**[1] before a vowel: *autacoid.*

au·ta·coid (ô′tə koid′), *n. Physiol.* a substance secreted by one organ into the blood stream or lymph, which controls organic processes elsewhere in the body; hormone. Also, **autocoid.** [AUT- + Gk *ák(os)* remedy + -OID] —**au′ta·coi′dal,** *adj.*

au·tarch (ô′tärk), *n.* an absolute ruler; autocrat; tyrant. [< Gk *aútarch(os)* n. use of *aútarchos* autocratic, equiv. to *aut-* AUT- + *archós* ruler]

au·tar·chy (ô′tär kē), *n., pl.* **-chies.** **1.** absolute sovereignty. **2.** an autocratic government. **3.** autarky. [< Gk *autarchía* self-rule. See AUT-, -ARCHY] —**au·tar′chic, au·tar′chi·cal,** *adj.* —**au·tar′chi·cal·ly,** *adv.* —**au′tar·chist,** *n.*

au·tar·ky (ô′tär kē), *n., pl.* **-kies.** **1.** the condition of self-sufficiency, esp. economic, as applied to a state. **2.** a national policy of economic independence. Also, **autarchy.** [< Gk *autárkeia,* equiv. to *aut-* AUT- + *arké(ein)* (to) suffice + *-ia* -IA] —**au·tar′kic, au·tar′ki·cal,** *adj.* —**au·tar′ki·cal·ly,** *adv.* —**au′tar·kist,** *n.*

aut Cae·sar, aut ni·hil (out kī′sär out ni′hil; *Eng.* ôt sē′zər ôt nī′hil), *Latin.* either Caesar or nothing; all or nothing.

au·te·cism (ô tē′siz əm), *n.* autoecism. —**au·te·cious** (ô tē′shəs), *adj.* —**au·te′cious·ly,** *adv.* —**au·te′cious·ness,** *n.*

aut·e·col·o·gy (ô′tə kol′ə jē), *n.* the branch of ecology dealing with the individual organism and its environment. Cf. **synecology.** [AUT- + ECOLOGY] —**aut·ec·o·log·ic** (ôt′ek ə loj′ik, -ē kə-), **aut′ec·o·log′i·cal,** *adj.* —**aut′ec·o·log′i·cal·ly,** *adv.*

Au·teuil (ō tœ′yə), *n.* an old town, now part of Paris, France: noted for residences of Boileau, Talleyrand, Molière, La Fontaine, and other eminent Frenchmen.

auth., **1.** author. **2.** authorized.

au·then·tic (ô then′tik), *adj.* **1.** entitled to acceptance or belief because of agreement with known facts or experience; reliable; trustworthy: *an authentic portrayal of the past.* **2.** not false or copied; genuine; real: *an authentic antique.* **3.** having the origin supported by unquestionable evidence; authenticated; verified: *an authentic document of the Middle Ages; an authentic work of the old master.* **4.** *Law.* executed with all due formalities: *an authentic deed.* **5.** *Music.* **a.** (of a church mode) having a range extending from the final to the octave above. Cf. **plagal. b.** (of a cadence) consisting of a dominant harmony followed by a tonic. **6.** *Obs.* authoritative. [< LL *authentic(us)* < Gk *authentikós* original, primary, at first hand, equiv. to *authént(ēs)* one who does things himself (*aut-* AUT- + *-hentēs* doer) + *-ikos* -IC; r. ME *autentik* < ML *autentic(us)*] —**au·then′ti·cal·ly,** *adv.*

au·then·ti·cal (ô then′ti kəl), *adj. Archaic.* authentic. [AUTHENTIC + -AL[1]]

au·then·ti·cate (ô then′tə kāt′), *v.t.,* **-cat·ed, cat·ing.** **1.** to make authoritative or valid. **2.** to establish as genuine. **3.** to establish the authorship or origin of conclusively or unquestionably, chiefly by the techniques of scholarship: *to authenticate a painting.* [< ML *authenticāt(us)* made authentic (ptp. of *authenticāre*). See AUTHENTIC, -ATE[1]] —**au·then′ti·ca′tion,** *n.* —**au·then′ti·ca′tor,** *n.*
—**Syn. 1, 2.** confirm, validate, substantiate.

au·then·tic·i·ty (ô′thin tis′i tē, -then-), *n.* quality of being authentic; genuineness. [AUTHENTIC + -ITY]

au·thi·gen·ic (ô′thi jen′ik), *adj. Geol.* (of a constituent of a rock) formed in the rock where it is found. Cf. **allogenic.** [< G *authigen* < Gk *authigen(ḗs)* native to a specific place (*aúthi* there + *genḗs* born) + -IC; see GENIC]

au·thor (ô′thər), *n.* **1.** a person who writes a novel, poem, essay, etc.; the composer of a literary work, as distinguished from a compiler, translator, editor, or copyist. **2.** the literary production or productions of a writer: *to find a passage in an author.* **3.** the maker of anything; creator. —*v.t.* **4.** to write; be the author of: *He authored a history of the Civil War.* **5.** to originate; create a design for: *the French designer who authored a lowering of hemlines.* Also, *referring to a woman,* **auth′or·ess.** [earlier *auct(h)or* < L *auctor* writer, progenitor, deriv. of *auctus* magnified (ptp. of *augēre* to increase; *aug-* augment + *-tus* ptp. suffix) + *-or* -OR[2]; r. ME *auto(u)r* < AF; OF *autor* < L] —**au·tho·ri·al** (ô thōr′ē əl, ô thôr′-), *adj.* —**au′thor·less,** *adj.*

au′thor cat′alog, *Library Science.* a catalog whose entries are listed by author, editor, compiler, or translator.

au·thor·i·sa·tion (ô′thər i zā′shən), *n.* *Chiefly Brit.* authorization.

au·thor·ise (ô′thə rīz′), *v.t.*, **-ised, -is·ing.** *Chiefly Brit.* authorize. —**au′thor·is′a·ble,** *adj.* —**au′thor·is′er,** *n.*

au·thor·ised (ô′thə rīzd′), *adj.* *Chiefly Brit.* authorized.

au·thor·i·tar·i·an (ə thôr′i târ′ē ən, ə thor′-), *adj.* **1.** favoring complete subjection to authority as opposed to individual freedom: *authoritarian principles; authoritarian attitudes.* **2.** exercising complete or almost complete control over the will of another or of others: *an authoritarian parent.* **3.** of or pertaining to a governmental or political system, principle, or practice in which individual freedom is held as completely subordinate to the power or authority of the state, centered either in one person or a small group that is not constitutionally accountable to the people. Cf. **totalitarian** (def. 1). —*n.* **4.** one who favors or acts according to authoritarian principles. [AUTHORIT(Y) + -ARIAN] —**au·thor′i·tar′i·an·ism,** *n.*

au·thor·i·ta·tive (ə thôr′i tā′tiv, ə thor′-), *adj.* **1.** having due authority; having the sanction or weight of authority: *an authoritative opinion.* **2.** substantiated or supported by documentary evidence and accepted by most authorities in a field: *an authoritative edition of Shakespeare; an authoritative treatment of a subject.* **3.** having an air of authority; accustomed to exercising authority; positive; peremptory; dictatorial. [AUTHORIT(Y) + -ATIVE] —**au·thor′i·ta′tive·ly,** *adv.* —**au·thor′i·ta′tive·ness,** *n.*
—**Syn. 1.** official, authentic. **3.** dogmatic, authoritarian.

au·thor·i·ty (ə thôr′i tē, ə thor′-), *n.*, *pl.* **-ties.** **1.** the power to determine, adjudicate, or otherwise settle issues or disputes; jurisdiction; the right to control, command, or determine. **2.** a power or right delegated or given; authorization: *He has the authority to grant permission.* **3.** a person or body of persons in whom authority is vested, as a governmental agency. **4.** Usually, **authorities.** persons having the legal power to make and enforce the law; government. **5.** an accepted source of information, advice, etc. **6.** a quotation or citation from such a source. **7.** an expert on a subject: *He is an authority on baseball.* **8.** persuasive force; conviction: *He spoke with authority.* **9.** a statute, court rule, or judicial decision which establishes a rule or principle of law; a ruling. **10.** right to respect or acceptance of one's word, command, thought, etc.; commanding influence: *the authority of a parent; the authority of a great writer.* **11.** mastery in execution or performance, as of a work of art or literature, a piece of music, etc. **12.** a warrant for action; justification. **13.** testimony; witness. [earlier *auct(h)oritie* < L *auctōritāt-* (s. of *auctōritās*); r. ME *autorite* < OF < L. See AUTHOR, -ITY]
—**Syn. 1.** rule, power, sway. AUTHORITY, CONTROL, INFLUENCE denote a power or right to direct the actions or thoughts of others. AUTHORITY is a power or right, usually because of rank or office, to issue commands and to punish for violations: *to have authority over subordinates.* CONTROL is either power or influence applied to the complete and successful direction or manipulation of persons or things: *to be in control of a project.* INFLUENCE is a personal and unofficial power derived from deference of others to one's character, ability, or station; it may be exerted unconsciously or may operate through persuasion: *to have influence over one's friends.* **3.** sovereign, arbiter.

au·thor·i·za·tion (ô′thər i zā′shən), *n.* act of authorizing; permission or power granted by an authority; sanction. Also, *esp. Brit.,* **authorisation.** [AUTHORIZE + -ATION]

au·thor·ize (ô′thə rīz′), *v.t.*, **-ized, iz·ing.** **1.** to give authority or official power to; empower: *to authorize a detective to make arrests.* **2.** to give authority for; formally sanction (an act or proceeding). **3.** to establish by authority or usage: *authorized by custom.* **4.** to afford a ground for; warrant; justify. Also, *esp. Brit.,* **authorise.** [earlier *auctorize* < ML *auctōriz(āre)*; r. ME *autorise* < MF *autoris(er)* < ML. See AUTHOR, -IZE] —**au′thor·iz′a·ble,** *adj.* —**au′thor·iz′er,** *n.*

au·thor·ized (ô′thə rīzd′), *adj.* **1.** given or endowed with authority: *an authorized agent.* **2.** duly sanctioned. Also, *esp. Brit.,* **authorised.** [AUTHORIZE + -ED²]

au′thorized cap′ital, (of a corporation) the aggregate par value, or in the case of stock without par value, the total subscription price, of all equity shares authorized to be issued under the charter, or under amendments to the charter.

Au′thorized Ver′sion, an English version of the Bible prepared in England under James I and published in 1611. Also called **King James Version.**

au·thors (ô′thərz), *n.* (*construed as sing.*) a card game for two or more persons that is played with a 52-card pack, the object being to take the largest number of tricks consisting of four cards of the same denomination. [pl. of AUTHOR]

au′thor's altera′tion, a correction or change made in typeset copy that is not a correction of an error introduced by the compositor. *Abbr.:* AA, A.A., a.a. Cf. **printer's error.**

au·thor·ship (ô′thər ship′), *n.* **1.** the occupation or career of writing books, articles, etc. **2.** origin, esp. with reference to an author, creator, producer, etc., of a work: *There is difficulty in establishing the authorship of early medieval objects.* [AUTHOR + -SHIP]

Auth. Ver., Authorized Version (of the Bible).

au·tism (ô′tiz əm), *n.* *Psychol.* the tendency to view life in terms of one's own needs and desires, as by daydreams or fantasies, unmindful of objective reality. [AUT- + -ISM] —**au′tist,** *n.* —**au·tis·tic** (ô tis′tik), *adj.*

au·to (ô′tō), *n.*, *pl.* **-tos.** automobile. [by shortening]

auto-¹, a word element meaning "self," "same," used in the formation of compound words: *autograph.* Also, *esp. before a vowel,* **aut-.** [< Gk, comb. form of *autós* self]

auto-², a combining form of **automobile:** *autocade.* [see AUTO]

auto., **1.** automatic. **2.** automobile. **3.** automotive.

au·to·a·larm (ô′tō ə lärm′), *n.* a device for notifying the bridge and radio room of a ship of a radio distress signal when there is no radio operator on watch.

au·to·bahn (ô′tə bän′; *Ger.* ou′tō bän′), *n.*, *pl.* **-bahns, -bahn·en** (-bä′nən). (in Germany) a superhighway. [< G: path for cars]

au·to·bi·o·graph·i·cal (ô′tə bī′ə graf′i kəl), *adj.* marked by or dealing with one's own experiences or life history; of or in the manner of an autobiography: *autobiographical material; an autobiographical novel.* Also, **au′to·bi′o·graph′ic.** [AUTO-¹ + BIOGRAPHICAL] —**au′to·bi′o·graph′i·cal·ly,** *adv.*

au·to·bi·og·ra·phy (ô′tə bī og′rə fē, -bē-), *n.*, *pl.* **-phies.** an account of a person's life written by himself. [AUTO-¹ + BIOGRAPHY] —**au′to·bi·og′ra·pher,** *n.*

Au′tobiog′raphy of Al′ice B. Tok′las (tok′ləs, tō′kləs), a memoir (1933) by Gertrude Stein.

au·to·bus (ô′tə bus′), *n.*, *pl.* **-bus·es, -bus·ses.** bus (def. 1). [AUTO-² + BUS]

au·to·cade (ô′tə kād′), *n.* a procession or parade of automobiles; motorcade. [AUTO-² + (CAVAL)CADE]

Au′to Call′, *Trademark.* a system of electrical bell-like or gonglike sound devices for signaling employees in code, used in department stores, factories, etc.

au·to·ca·tal·y·sis (ô′tō kə tal′i sis), *n.*, *pl.* **-ses** (-sēz′). *Chem., Biochem.* catalysis caused by a catalytic agent formed during a reaction. [AUTO-¹ + CATALYSIS] —**au·to·cat·a·lyt·ic** (ô′tō kat′əlit′ik), *adj.* —**au′to·cat′a·lyt′i·cal·ly,** *adv.*

au·to·ca·thar·sis (ô′tō kə thär′sis), *n.* *Psychiatry.* a therapeutic process designed to free unconscious disturbances by having the patient write about his experiences, impressions, etc. [AUTO-¹ + CATHARSIS]

au·to·ceph·a·lous (ô′tə sef′ə ləs), *adj.* *Eastern Ch.* **1.** (of a church) having its own head or chief bishop, though in communion with other Orthodox churches. **2.** (of a bishop) subordinate to no superior authority; self-governing. [< LGk *autoképhalos* having its own head. See AUTO-¹, -CEPHALOUS]

au·to·ceph·a·ly (ô′tə sef′ə lē), *n.* the state of being autocephalous. [AUTOCEPHAL(OUS) + -Y³]

au·to·chrome (ô′tə krōm′), *n.* *Photog.* an obsolete material for color photography, consisting of a photographic emulsion applied over a multicolored screen of minute starch grains dyed red, green, and blue-violet. [AUTO-¹ + -CHROME] —**au′to·chro′my,** *n.*

au·toch·thon (ô tok′thən), *n.*, *pl.* **-thons, -tho·nes** (-thə nēz′). **1.** an aboriginal inhabitant. **2.** *Ecol.* one of the indigenous animals or plants of a region. **3.** *Geol.* a geological formation formed in the region where found. Cf. **allochthon.** [< Gk *autóchthōn* of the land itself, equiv. to *auto-* AUTO-¹ + *chthṓn* the earth, land, ground]

au·toch·tho·nous (ô tok′thə nəs), *adj.* **1.** pertaining to autochthons; aboriginal; indigenous (opposed to *heterochthonous*). **2.** *Pathol.* **a.** found in the part of the body in which it originates, as a disease. **b.** found in a locality in which it originates, as a disease acquired in a place where the patient is. **3.** *Psychol.* of or pertaining to ideas that arise independently of the individual's own train of thought and seem instead to have some alien or external agency as their source. **4.** *Geol.* (of rocks, minerals, etc.) formed in the region where found. Cf. **allochthonous.** Also, **au·toch′tho·nal, au·toch·thon·ic** (ô′tok thon′ik). [AUTOCHTHON + -OUS] —**au·toch′tho·nism, au·toch′tho·ny,** *n.* —**au·toch′tho·nous·ly,** *adv.* —**au·toch′tho·nous·ness,** *n.*

au·to·clave (ô′tə klāv′), *n.*, *v.*, **-claved, -clav·ing.** —*n.* **1.** a heavy vessel for conducting chemical reactions under high pressure. **2.** See **pressure cooker.** **3.** *Med., Bacteriol.* an apparatus in which steam under pressure effects sterilization. —*v.t.* **4.** to place in an autoclave. [< F, equiv. to *auto-* AUTO-¹ + *clave* < L *clāv-* s. of *clāvis* key and *clāvus* nail]

au·to·coid (ô′tə koid′), *n.* autacoid.

au·to·col·li·ma·tion (ô′tō kol′ə mā′shən), *n.* *Optics.* the process used in an autocollimator. [AUTO-¹ + COLLIMATION]

au·to·col·li·ma·tor (ô′tō kol′ə mā′tər), *n.* *Optics.* an instrument combining the functions of a telescope and collimator, for detecting and measuring very small deviations in a beam of light. [AUTO-¹ + COLLIMATOR]

au·to·cor·re·la·tion (ô′tō kôr′ə lā′shən, -kor′-), *n.* *Statistics.* the correlation of an ordered series of observations with the same series in an altered order. [AUTO-¹ + CORRELATION]

au′to court′, motel.

au·toc·ra·cy (ô tok′rə sē), *n.*, *pl.* **-cies.** **1.** uncontrolled or unlimited authority over others, invested in a single person; the government or power of an absolute monarch. **2.** a nation, state, or community ruled by an autocrat. [< Gk *autokráteia* power over oneself, sole power, equiv. to *autokrat(ḗs)* AUTOCRAT + *-eia* -IA; see -CY]

au·to·crat (ô′tə krat′), *n.* **1.** an absolute ruler; a monarch who holds and exercises the powers of government as by inherent right, not subject to restrictions. **2.** a person invested with, or claiming to exercise, absolute authority. **3.** one who behaves in an authoritarian manner; a domineering person. [< Gk *autokrat(ḗs)* self-ruling, ruling alone, equiv. to *auto-* AUTO-¹ + *krate-* (s. of *krátos* power) + *-ēs* adj. suffix]

au·to·crat·ic (ô′tə krat′ik), *adj.* **1.** pertaining to or of the nature of autocracy or of an autocrat; absolute: *autocratic government.* **2.** like an autocrat; tyrannical; despotic; domineering: *autocratic behavior; an autocratic person.* Also, **au′to·crat′i·cal.** [AUTOCRAT + -IC] —**au′to·crat′i·cal·ly,** *adv.*

au·to-da-fé (ô′tō də fā′), *n.*, *pl.* **au·tos-da-fé.** the public declaration of the judgment passed on persons tried in the courts of the Spanish Inquisition, followed by the execution by the civil authorities of the sentences imposed, esp. of the burning of condemned heretics at the stake. [< Pg: ACT OF THE FAITH]

au·to de fé (ou′tō the fe′), *pl.* **au·tos de fé** (ou′tōs the fe′). *Spanish.* auto-da-fé.

au·to·di·dact (ô′tō dī′dakt, -dī dakt′), *n.* a person who has learned a subject without the benefit of schooling; a self-taught person. [< Gk *autodídaktos* self-taught; see AUTO-, DIDACTIC] —**au′to·di·dact′ic,** *adj.* —**au′to·didact′i·cal·ly,** *adv.*

au·to·dyne (ô′tə dīn′), *n.* *Electronics.* a type of heterodyne circuit containing a vacuum tube or transistor that acts simultaneously as a detector and oscillator. [AUTO-¹ + DYNE]

au·toe·cism (ô tē′siz əm), *n.* *Bot.* the development of the entire life cycle of a parasitic fungus on a single host or group of hosts. Also, **autecism.** [AUT- + *oec-* (< Gk *oik-*, s. of *oîkos* house) + -ISM] —**au·toe·cious** (ô tē′shəs), *adj.* —**au·toe′cious·ly,** *adv.* —**au·toe′cious·ness,** *n.*

au·to·e·rot·ic (ô′tō i rot′ik), *adj.* *Psychoanal.* producing sexual emotion without association with another person. [AUTO-¹ + EROTIC] —**au′to·e·rot′i·cal·ly,** *adv.*

au·to·er·o·tism (ô′tō er′ə tiz′əm), *n.* *Psychoanal.* the arousal and satisfaction of sexual emotion within or by oneself, usually by masturbation. Also, **au·to·e·rot·i·cism** (ô′tō i rot′i siz′əm). [AUTO-¹ + EROTISM]

au·tog·a·my (ô tog′ə mē), *n.* **1.** *Bot.* fecundation of the ovules of a flower by its own pollen; self-fertilization (opposed to *allogamy*). **2.** (in certain protozoans) conjugation by division of the nucleus into two parts that in turn reunite to form a zygote. [AUTO-¹ + -GAMY] —**au·tog′a·mous, au·to·gam·ic** (ô′tō gam′ik), *adj.*

au·to·gen·e·sis (ô′tō jen′i sis), *n.* *Biol.* abiogenesis. Also, **au·tog·e·ny** (ô toj′ə nē). [AUTO-¹ + GENESIS]

au·to·ge·net·ic (ô′tō jə net′ik), *adj.* **1.** self-generated. **2.** *Biol.* of autogenesis. [AUTO-¹ + GENETIC] —**au′to·ge·net′i·cal·ly,** *adv.*

au·tog·e·nous (ô toj′ə nəs), *adj.* **1.** self-produced; self-generated. **2.** *Physiol.* pertaining to substances generated in the body. [< Gk *autogen(ḗs)* self-produced (see AUTO-¹, -GEN) + -OUS] —**au·tog′e·nous·ly,** *adv.*

au·to·gi·ro (ô′tō jī′rō), *n.*, *pl.* **-ros.** an aircraft with unpowered, horizontal revolving wings on a shaft above the fuselage which sustain the machine or allow it to descend slowly and steeply, forward propulsion being secured by a conventional propeller. Also, **autogyro.** Also called **gyroplane.** [formerly trademark]

au·to·graft (ô′tə graft′, -gräft′), *n.* *Surg.* a tissue or organ that is grafted into a new position on the body of the individual from which it was removed. Also called **autoplast, autotransplant.** Cf. **heterograft, homograft.** [AUTO-¹ + GRAFT¹]

au·to·graph (ô′tə graf′, -gräf′), *n.* **1.** a person's own signature. **2.** anything written in one's own hand. **3.** a manuscript in the author's handwriting. —*adj.* **4.** written by a person's own hand: *an autograph letter.* **5.** containing autographs: *an autograph album.* —*v.t.* **6.** to write one's name on or in; to sign: *to autograph a book.* **7.** to write with one's own hand. [< LL *autograph(um)*, n. use of neut. of L *autographus* written with one's own hand < Gk *autógraphos.* See AUTO-¹, -GRAPH] —**au·to·graph·ic** (ô′tə graf′ik), **au′to·graph′i·cal,** *adj.* —**au′to·graph′i·cal·ly,** *adv.*

au·tog·ra·phy (ô tog′rə fē), *n.* the act of writing by hand; the producing of an autograph. [AUTO-¹ + -GRAPHY]

au·to·gy·ro (ô′tə jī′rō), *n.*, *pl.* **-ros.** autogiro.

au·to·harp (ô′tō härp′), *n.* a zither having buttons which, when depressed by the finger, dampen all the strings necessary to the chord desired. [AUTO-¹ + HARP]

au·to·hyp·no·sis (ô′tō hip nō′sis), *n.* self-induced hypnosis or hypnotic state. [AUTO-¹ + HYPNOSIS] —**au·to·hyp·not·ic** (ô′tō hip not′ik), *adj.* —**au′to·hyp·not′i·cal·ly,** *adv.*

au·toi·cous (ô toi′kəs), *adj.* *Bot.* having antheridia and archegonia on the same plant. [AUT- + *oic-* (< Gk *oik-*, s. of *oîkos* house) + -OUS]

au·to·ig·ni·tion (ô′tō ig nish′ən), *n.* **1.** *Auto.* the spontaneous ignition of fuel when introduced into the combustion chamber of an internal-combustion engine, as a result either of glowing carbon in the chamber or of the heat of compression. **2.** See **spontaneous combustion.** [AUTO-¹ + IGNITION]

autoigni′tion point′, *Chem.* the minimum temperature at which a substance will undergo spontaneous combustion.

au·to·in·fec·tion (ô′tō in fek′shən), *n.* *Pathol.* infection from within the body. [AUTO-¹ + INFECTION]

au·to·in·oc·u·la·tion (ô′tō i nok′yə lā′shən), *n.* inoculation of a healthy part with an infective agent from a diseased part of the same body. [AUTO-¹ + INOCULATION] —**au·to·in·oc·u·la·ble** (ô′tō i nok′yə lə bəl), *adj.* —**au′to·in·oc′u·la·bil′i·ty,** *n.*

au·to·in·tox·i·ca·tion (ô′tō in tok′sə kā′shən), *n.* *Pathol.* poisoning with toxic substances formed within the body, as during intestinal digestion. Also called **autotoxemia, autotoxicosis.** [AUTO-¹ + INTOXICATION] —**au·to·tox·ic** (ô′tō tok′sik), *adj.*

au·to·i·on·i·za·tion (ô′tō ī′ə ni zā′shən), *n.* *Physics.* See **Auger effect.** [AUTO-¹ + IONIZATION]

au·to·ist (ô′tō ist), *n.* motorist (def. 1). [AUTO-² + -IST]

au·to·ki·ne·sis (ô′tō ki nē′sis, -kī-), *n.* *Physiol.* spontaneous motion. [AUTO-¹ + KINESIS] —**au·to·ki·net·ic** (ô′tō ki net′ik, -kī-), *adj.*

au′tokinet′ic effect′, *Psychol.* apparent motion of a single point of light or a small object when presented on a dark field and observed continuously. Also called **au′tokinet′ic illu′sion.**

au′to lift′, a device for raising automobiles or the like so that their undersides are accessible for inspection and repairs.

au·to·li·thog·ra·phy (ô′tō li thog′rə fē), *n.* the original and basic lithographic technique by which the artist draws or traces with a brush and pen directly on a stone or plate. [AUTO-¹ + LITHOGRAPHY]

Au·tol·y·cus (ô tol′ə kəs), *n.* **1.** *Class. Myth.* a thief, the son of Hermes and Chione, and the grandfather of Odysseus. He possessed the power of changing the shape of whatever he stole and of making it and himself invisible. **2.** a crater in the first quadrant of the face of the moon: about 24 miles in diameter.

au·to·ly·sin (ô′tᵊlī′sin, ô tol′i-), *n.* any agent producing autolysis. [AUTOLYS(IS) + -IN²]

au·tol·y·sis (ô tol′i sis), *n.* *Biochem.* the breakdown of plant or animal tissue by the action of enzymes contained in the tissue affected; self-digestion. [AUTO-¹ + -LYSIS] —**au·to·lyt·ic** (ôt′ᵊlit′ik), *adj.*

au·to·lyze (ôt′ᵊlīz′), *v.*, **-lyzed, -lyz·ing.** *Biochem.* —*v.t.* **1.** to cause to undergo autolysis. —*v.i.* **2.** to undergo autolysis. [back formation from AUTOLYSIS, modeled on ANALYZE]

au·to·mat (ô′tə mat′), *n.* a restaurant using coin-operated equipment for dispensing articles of food to customers. [short for AUTOMATON]

au·tom·a·ta (ô tom′ə tə), *n.* a pl. of **automaton.**

au·to·mate (ô′tə māt′), *v.*, **-mat·ed, -mat·ing.** —*v.t.* **1.** to apply the principles of automation to (a mechanical process). **2.** to operate or control by automation. —*v.i.* **3.** to install automatic procedures, as for manufacturing, servicing, etc.; follow or utilize the principles of automation: *Many banks have begun to automate.* [back formation from AUTOMATION]

au·to·mat·ic (ô′tə mat′ik), *adj.* **1.** having the power of self-motion; self-moving or self-acting: *an automatic device.* **2.** *Physiol.* occurring independently of volition, as certain muscular actions; involuntary. **3.** (of a firearm, pistol, etc.) utilizing the recoil or part of the force of the explosive to eject the spent cartridge shell, introduce a new cartridge, cock the arm, and fire it repeatedly. **4.** done unconsciously or from force of habit; mechanical. **5.** occurring spontaneously: *automatic enthusiasm.* **—n. 6.** a machine that operates automatically. **7.** See **automatic rifle. 8.** See **automatic pistol.** [< Gk *autómat(os)* self-moving (see AUTOMATON) + -IC] **—au/to·mat/i·cal·ly,** *adv.* **—au·to·ma·tic·i·ty** (ô/tə mə tis/i tē), *n.*

—Syn. 2. AUTOMATIC, INVOLUNTARY both mean not under the control of the will. That which is AUTOMATIC, however, is an invariable reaction to a fixed type of stimulus: *The patella reflex is automatic.* That which is INVOLUNTARY is an unexpected response which varies according to the occasion, circumstances, mood, etc.: *an involuntary cry of pain.*

au/tomat/ic da/ta proc/essing, the processing of information by computers or the like, using techniques which reduce human intervention to a minimum. *Abbr.:* ADP Cf. **integrated data processing.**

au/tomat/ic drive/. See **automatic transmission.**

Au/tomat/ic Ground/ Controlled/ Approach/, *Aeron., Trademark.* a ground controlled approach in which instructions are given on recordings which are selected automatically in response to radar information transmitted electronically. Also, **au/tomat/ic ground/ control/ approach/.**

au/tomat/ic pi/lot, *Aeron.* a control system that automatically maintains an aircraft on a preset heading and attitude. Also called **autopilot, gyropilot, robot.**

au/tomat/ic pis/tol, a pistol having a mechanism that throws out the empty shell, puts in a new one, and prepares the pistol to be fired again. Also called **automatic.**

au/tomat/ic pre/mium loan/, *Insurance.* a provision in a life-insurance policy under which a premium not paid by the end of the grace period is automatically paid by the company, provided there is sufficient cash value.

au/tomat/ic ri/fle, a type of light machine gun capable of firing automatically or in single shots. Also, **machine rifle.**

au/tomat/ic track/ing, *Electronics.* a radar tracking system in which an automatic device uses the echo signal from the tracking object to keep the radar constantly beamed on target and to compute the range of the object.

automat/ic transmis/sion, an automotive transmission requiring either very little or no manual shifting of gears. Also called **automatic drive.**

au·to·ma·tion (ô/tə mā/shən), *n.* **1.** the technique, method, or system of operating or controlling a mechanical or productive process by highly automatic means, as by electronic devices. **2.** act or process of automating; state of being automated. [AUTOM(ATIC OPER)ATION]

au·tom·a·tism (ô tom/ə tiz/əm), *n.* **1.** action or condition of being automatic; mechanical or involuntary action. **2.** *Philos.* the doctrine that all activities of animals, or of men and animals, are entirely controlled by physical or physiological causes in which consciousness takes no part. **3.** *Physiol.* the involuntary functioning of an organic process, esp. muscular, without apparent neural stimulation. **4.** *Psychol.* **a.** performance of acts by an individual without his awareness or conscious volition. **b.** such an act, as sleepwalking. **5.** the act or doctrine, esp. of the Surrealists, of allowing the unconscious mind to find expression through uncontrolled or uncensored images. [< Gk *automatism(ós)* a happening of itself. See AUTOMATON, -ISM] **—au·tom/a·tist,** *n.*

au·to·mat·o·graph (ô/tə mat/ə graf/, -gräf/), *n.* a device for recording involuntary bodily movements. [< Gk *autómato(s)* self-moving (see AUTOMATON) + -GRAPH]

au·tom·a·ton (ô tom/ə ton/, -tən), *n., pl.* **-tons, -ta** (-tə). **1.** a mechanical figure or contrivance constructed to act as if by its own motive power; robot. **2.** a person who acts in a monotonous, routine manner, without active intelligence. **3.** something capable of acting automatically or without an external motive force. [< L: a self-moving machine < Gk, n. use of neut. of *autómatos* self-moving, equiv. to *auto-* AUTO-¹ + *-matos* (*ma-* strive after, move + *-tos* adj. suffix); see MIND] **—au·tom/a·tous,** *adj.*

au·to·mech·an·ism (ô/tō mek/ə niz/əm), *n.* an automatic mechanical system or component, esp. a device which operates automatically under predetermined conditions. [AUTO-¹ + MECHANISM]

Au·tom·e·don (ô tom/i don/), *n.* (in the *Iliad*) the charioteer of Achilles.

au·to·mo·bile (ô/tə mə bēl/, ô/tə mə bēl/, ô/tə mō/bēl, -bil), *n.* **1.** *Chiefly U.S.* a vehicle, esp. one for passengers, carrying its own power-generating and propelling mechanism, for travel on ordinary roads. **—***adj.* **2.** automotive. [< F: lit., self-movable (vehicle). See AUTO-¹, MOBILE] **—au·to·mo·bil·ist** (ô/tə mə bē/list, -mō/bi list), *n.*

automobile/ insur/ance, insurance covering loss or damages arising from the operation or ownership of an automobile.

au·to·mor·phic (ô/tə môr/fik), *adj.* *Petrog.* idiomorphic (def. 1). [AUTO-¹ + -MORPHIC] **—au/to·mor/phi·cal·ly,** *adv.*

au·to·mor·phism (ô/tə môr/fiz əm), *n.* *Math.* an isomorphism from a given set to itself. Cf. **inner automorphism, outer automorphism.** [AUTO- + MORPH- + -ISM]

au·to·mo·tive (ô/tə mō/tiv, ô/tə mō/tiv), *adj.* **1.** pertaining to the design, operation, manufacture, or sale of automobiles. **2.** propelled by a self-contained power plant. [AUTO-¹ + MOTIVE]

Au·ton·o·ë (ô ton/ō ē/), *n.* the daughter of Cadmus and Harmonia, and the mother, by Aristaeus, of Actaeon.

au·to·nom·ic (ô/tə nom/ik), *adj.* **1.** autonomous. **2.** of or pertaining to the autonomic nervous system. **3.** *Bot.* produced by internal forces or causes; spontaneous. Also, **au/to·nom/i·cal.** [AUTONOM(Y) + -IC] **—au/to·nom/i·cal·ly,** *adv.*

au/tonom/ic nerv/ous sys/tem, the system of nerves and ganglia which innervates the blood vessels, heart, smooth muscles, viscera, and glands and controls their involuntary functions, consisting of a sympathetic and parasympathetic division.

au·ton·o·mous (ô ton/ə məs), *adj.* **1.** *Govt.* **a.** self-governing; independent; subject to its own laws only. **b.** pertaining to an autonomy. **2.** *Biol.* existing as an independent organism and not as a form or state of development of an organism. **3.** *Bot.* spontaneous. [< Gk *autónomos* with laws of one's own, independent, equiv. to *auto-* AUTO-¹ + *nóm(os)* law, custom + *-os adj.* suffix] **—au·ton/o·mous·ly,** *adv.*

au·ton·o·my (ô ton/ə mē), *n., pl.* **-mies. 1.** independence or freedom, as of the will, one's actions, etc.: *the autonomy of the individual.* **2.** the condition of being autonomous; self-government, or the right of self-government; independence. **3.** a self-governing community. [< Gk *autonomía* independence, equiv. to *autónom(os)* AUTONOMOUS + *-ia* -Y³] **—au·ton/o·mist,** *n.*

au·to·nym (ô/tə nim), *n.* **1.** one's own name. Cf. **pseudonym. 2.** a book published under the real name of the author. [AUT- + Gk *ónym(a)* name, modeled on SYNONYM, etc.]

au·to·ox·i·da·tion (ô/tō ok/si dā/shən), *n.* *Chem.* autoxidation.

au·to·phyte (ô/tə fīt/), *n.* any plant which produces its own food. [AUTO-¹ + -PHYTE] **—au·to·phyt·ic** (ô/tə fit/ik), *adj.* **—au/to·phyt/i·cal·ly,** *adv.*

au·to·pi·lot (ô/tō pī/lət), *n.* See **automatic pilot.** [AUTO-¹ + PILOT]

au·to·plast (ô/tə plast/), *n.* *Surg.* autograft. [AUTO-¹ + -PLAST]

au·to·plas·ty (ô/tə plas/tē), *n.* *Surg.* the repair of defects with tissue from another part of the patient's body. [AUTO-¹ + -PLASTY] **—au/to·plas/tic,** *adj.*

au·to·pol·y·ploid (ô/tə pol/ə ploid/), *Biol.* **—***adj.* **1.** having more than two haploid sets of chromosomes that are nearly identical and derived from the same species. **—***n.* **2.** an autopolyploid cell or organism. Cf. **allopolyploid.** [AUTO-¹ + POLYPLOID] **—au/to·pol/y·ploi/dy,** *n.*

Au·to·pos·i·tive (ô/tə poz/i tiv), *Trademark.* **—***adj.* **1.** of or pertaining to a photographic process employing certain films, papers, chemicals, etc., to reproduce a positive without an intermediate negative, or vice versa. **—***n.* **2.** a positive or negative made by this process.

au·to·po·tam·ic (ô/tō pə tam/ik), *adj.* (of a plant or animal) living or growing only in flowing fresh-water streams. [AUTO-¹ + POTAMIC]

au·top·sy (ô/top sē, ô/təp-), *n., pl.* **-sies. 1.** inspection and dissection of a body after death, as for determination of the cause of death; post-mortem examination. **2.** an analysis of something after it has been done or made. [< Gk *autopsía* a seeing with one's own eyes, equiv. to *aut-* AUT- + *óps(is)* -OPSIS + *-ia* -Y³] **—au·top/sic, au·top/si·cal,** *adj.* **—au/top·sist,** *n.*

au·to·ra·di·o·graph (ô/tō rā/dē ə graf/, -gräf/), *n.* a picture revealing the presence of radioactive material, the film being laid directly on the object to be tested. Also called **radioautograph.** [AUTO-¹ + RADIOGRAPH]

au·to·ra·di·og·ra·phy (ô/tō rā/dē og/rə fē), *n.* the technique or process of making autoradiographs. Also called **radioautography.** [AUTO-¹ + RADIOGRAPHY]

au·to·re·flec·tion (ô/tō ri flek/shən), *n.* a method of determining the perpendicularity of an optical instrument to a given surface. The instrument used takes a sight on itself by means of a mirror set parallel to the surface and a pierced target (**autoreflec/tion tar/get**) set at the end of the instrument. [AUTO-¹ + REFLECTION]

au·to sa·cra·men·tal (ou/tō sä krä men täl/), *pl.* **au·tos sa·cra·men·ta·les** (ou/tôs sä krä men tä/les). *Spanish.* a medieval allegorical drama dealing with the Mass, usually performed during the feast of Corpus Christi. [lit., sacramental act]

au·to·some (ô/tə sōm/), *n.* *Genetics.* any chromosome other than a sex chromosome. Also called **euchromosome.** [AUTO-¹ + -SOME³]

au·to·sta·bil·i·ty (ô/tō stə bil/i tē), *n.* *Mech.* the ability of a mechanism to maintain a stable performance, due either to the mechanics of its structure or to built-in automatic control devices. [AUTO-¹ + STABILITY]

au·to·stop·er (ô/tō stō/pər), *n.* a stoper held automatically against a rock face. [AUTO-¹ + STOPER]

au·to·sug·ges·tion (ô/tō səg jes/chən, -jesh/-, -sə-), *n.* *Psychol.* suggestion arising from oneself, esp. the repetition of verbal formulas in the hope of changing behavior. [AUTO-¹ + SUGGESTION] **—au·to·sug·gest·i·bil·i·ty** (ô/tō səg jes/tə bil/i tē), *n.* **—au/to·sug·gest/i·ble,** *adj.* **—au/to·sug·ges/tion·ist,** *n.* **—au/to·sug·ges/tive,** *adj.*

au·to·tel·ic (ô/tō tel/ik), *adj.* *Philos.* (of an entity or event) having within itself the purpose of its existence or happening. Cf. **heterotelic.** [AUTO-¹ + TELIC] **—au/to·tel/ism,** *n.*

au·tot·o·mise (ô tot/ə mīz/), *v.t.,* **-mised, -mis·ing.** *Chiefly Brit.* autotomize.

au·tot·o·mize (ô tot/ə mīz/), *v.,* **-mized, -miz·ing.** **—***v.i.* **1.** to undergo autotomy. **—***v.t.* **2.** to effect autotomy of (a part). [AUTOTOM(Y) + -IZE]

au·tot·o·my (ô tot/ə mē), *n., pl.* **-mies. 1.** *Zool.* self-amputation of a damaged or trapped appendage, as tails by lizards, legs by spiders and crabs, etc. **2.** the performance of surgery upon oneself. [AUTO-¹ + -TOMY] **—au·to·tom·ic** (ô/tə tom/ik), *adj.*

au·to·tox·e·mi·a (ô/tō tok sē/mē ə), *n.* *Pathol.* autointoxication. Also, **au/to·tox·ae/mi·a.** [AUTO-¹ + TOXEMIA]

au·to·tox·i·co·sis (ô/tə tok/sə kō/sis), *n.* *Pathol.* autointoxication. [AUTO-¹ + TOXICOSIS]

au·to·tox·in (ô/tə tok/sin), *n.* *Pathol.* a toxin or poisonous principle formed within the body and acting against it. [AUTO-¹ + TOXIN] **—au/to·tox/ic,** *adj.*

au·to·trans·form·er (ô/tō trans fôr/mər), *n.* *Elect.* a transformer having a single coil that serves as both a primary coil and a secondary coil. [AUTO-¹ + TRANSFORMER]

au·to·trans·plant (ô/tə trans/plant/, -plänt/), *n.* *Surg.* autograft. [AUTO-¹ + TRANSPLANT]

au·to·troph (ô/tə trof/, -trôf/), *n.* a microorganism capable of utilizing carbon dioxide for its only source of carbon. Cf. **heterotroph.** [back formation from AUTOTROPHIC]

au·to·troph·ic (ô/tə trof/ik), *adj.* *Biol.* capable of utilizing only inorganic materials as a source of food, as most plants and certain bacteria and protozoans (opposed to *heterotrophic*). [AUTO-¹ + -TROPHIC] **—au/to·troph/i·cal·ly,** *adv.* **—au·tot·ro·phy** (ô to/trə fē), *n.*

au·to·truck (ô/tō truk/), *n.* an automobile truck [AUTO-² + TRUCK]

au·to·type (ô/tə tīp/), *n.* **1.** facsimile (defs. 1, 2). **2.** *Photog.* **a.** a process for producing permanent prints in a carbon pigment. **b.** a print made by this process. [AUTO-¹ + TYPE] **—au·to·typ·ic** (ô/tə tip/ik), *adj.* **—au·to·typ·y** (ô/tə tī/pē), *n.*

au·tox·i·da·tion (ô tok/si dā/shən), *n.* *Chem.* **1.** the oxidation of a compound by exposure to air. **2.** an oxidation reaction in which another substance, in addition to air and the compound being oxidized, must be present. Also, **auto-oxidation.** [AUT- + OXIDATION]

au·tox·i·da·tion-re·duc·tion (ô tok/si dā/shən ri duk/shən), *n.* *Chem.* disproportionation.

au·tres temps, au·tres mœurs (ō trᵊ tän/ ō trᵊ mœr/, mœrs/), *French.* other times, other customs.

au·tumn (ô/təm), *n.* the season between summer and winter; fall: in the Northern Hemisphere, from the September equinox to the December solstice; in the Southern Hemisphere, from the March equinox to the June solstice. [< L *autumn(us)*; r. ME *autumpne* < MF *autompne* < L]

au·tum·nal (ô tum/nᵊl), *adj.* **1.** belonging to or suggestive of autumn; produced or gathered in autumn. **2.** past maturity or middle life. [< L *autumnāl(is).* See AUTUMN, -AL¹] **—au·tum/nal·ly,** *adv.*

autum/nal e/quinox, 1. See under **equinox** (def. 1). **2.** Also called **autum/nal point/.** the position of the sun at the time of the autumnal equinox.

au/tumn cro/cus, any of several liliaceous herbs of the genus *Colchicum,* esp. *C. autumnale,* bearing showy white, pink, or purple flowers in autumn. Also called **meadow saffron.**

Au·tum·ni (ô tum/ nē), *n.* **Mare.** See **Mare Autumni.**

Au/tumn Sea/. See **Mare Autumni.**

au·tun·ite (ôt/ᵊnīt/, ō tun/īt), *n.* a yellow mineral, a hydrous calcium uranium phosphate, $CaU_2P_2O_{12}·8H_2O$, occurring in crystals as nearly square tablets: a minor ore of uranium; lime uranite. [named after *Autun,* city in E France near source of supply; see -ITE¹]

Au·vergne (ō vârn/, ō vûrn/; *Fr.* ō vern/yᵊ), *n.* a former province in central France. See map under **Gascony.**

au vol (ō vol/), *Falconry.* a cry used to encourage a hawk to fly. [< F: to the flight. See VOLLEY]

Au·wers (ou/ wərz, -vərz), *n.* a crater in the first quadrant of the face of the moon: about 12 miles in diameter.

aux (ō), *French.* pl. of **au.**

aux-, var. of **auxo-,** esp. before a vowel: *auxin.*

aux., auxiliary. Also, **auxil.**

aux armes (ō zarm/), *French.* to arms!

Aux Cayes (ō kā/), former name of **Les Cayes.**

aux·e·sis (ôg zē/sis, ôk sē/-), *n.* *Biol.* growth, esp. that resulting from an increase in cell size. Cf. **merisis.** [< Gk: increase, equiv. to *aúx(ein)* (to) increase + *sis* -SIS]

aux·et·ic (ôg zet/ik, ôk set/-), *Biol.* **—***adj.* **1.** pertaining to or promoting auxesis. **—***n.* **2.** an auxetic agent. [< Gk *auxētik(ós)* increasing, equiv. to *auxēt(ós)* increased (deriv. of *aúxein*; see AUXESIS + *-ikos* -IC]

aux·il·ia·ry (ôg zil/yə rē, -zil/ə-), *adj., n., pl.* **-ries.** **—***adj.* **1.** subsidiary; additional; supplementary: *auxiliary troops.* **2.** used as a reserve: *an auxiliary engine.* **3.** giving support; serving as an aid; helpful: *The mind and emotions are auxiliary to each other. Passion is auxiliary to art.* **—***n.* **4.** a person or thing that gives aid of any kind; helper. **5.** an organization allied with, but subsidiary to, a main body of restricted membership, esp. one composed of members' wives, mothers, etc. **6.** See **auxiliary verb. 7. auxiliaries,** foreign troops in the service of a nation at war. **8.** *Navy.* a naval vessel designed for other than combat purposes, as a tug, supply ship, transport, etc. **9.** a sailing vessel carrying an auxiliary propulsion engine or engines. [< L *auxiliāri(us)* assisting, aiding, helping, equiv. to *auxili(um)* aid, help, deriv. of *auxus* increased, augmented (ptp. of *augēre*: *aug-* augment + *-sus,* var. of *-tus* ptp. suffix) + *-ilium* n. suffix + *-ārius* -ARY]

—Syn. 1. abetting. **2.** subordinate, ancillary, secondary. **4.** aide, ally, assistant; help.

auxil/iary equa/tion, *Math.* See **characteristic equation** (def. 2).

auxil/iary lan/guage, a language, as Esperanto, Swahili, or English, used for intercommunication by speakers of various other languages.

auxil/iary raft/er, 1. a rafter reinforcing a principal rafter. **2.** a rafter reinforcing a diagonal member of a queen post truss. Also called **cushion rafter.**

auxil/iary tone/, *Music.* a melodic ornamental tone following a principal tone by a step above or below and returning to the principal tone; embellishment. Also called **auxil/iary note/.**

auxil/iary verb/, a word used in construction with and preceding a certain form of a main verb, as an infinitive or participle, to express distinctions of tense, aspect, mood, etc., as *do* in *I do think, am* in *I am going, have* in *We have spoken, may* in *May we go?, can* in *They can see, shall* in *We shall march.*

aux·i·lyt·ic (ôk/sə lit/ik), *adj.* *Biochem.* promoting lysis or increasing lytic action. [AUX- + -I- + -LYTIC]

aux·i·mone (ôk/sə mōn/), *n.* *Bot., Chem.* a class of substances essential in minute amounts to stimulate growth. [alter. of Gk *aúximon* (on model of PEPTONE), neut. of *aúximos* promoting growth]

aux·in (ôk/sin), *n.* *Bot., Chem.* a class of substances which in minute amounts regulate or modify the growth of plants, esp. root formation, bud growth, fruit and leaf drop, etc. [AUX- + -IN²]

Aux·o (ôk/sō), *n.* *Class. Myth.* one of the Graces worshiped at Athens.

auxo-, a learned borrowing from Greek meaning "growth," "increase," used in the formation of compound words: *auxochrome.* Also, *esp. before a vowel,* **aux-.** [< Gk *aúx(ein)* (to) grow, increase (var. of *auxánein*) + -o-]

aux·o·car·di·a (ôk/sə kär/dē ə), *n.* *Pathol.* enlargement of the heart, as by hypertrophy or dilation. [AUXO- + Gk *kardía* heart]

aux·o·chrome (ôk/sə krōm/), *n.* *Chem.* any group of atoms that intensifies the color of a substance. [AUXO- + CHROME] **—aux/o·chrom/ic,** *adj.*

Au·zout (ō zout/), *n.* a crater in the first quadrant of the face of the moon: about 18 miles in diameter.

Av (ôv; *Heb.* äv), *n.* Ab.

AV, 1. arteriovenous. 2. atrioventricular. 3. auriculoventricular.

av., 1. avenue. 2. average. 3. avoirdupois.

A/V, ad valorem. Also, **a.v.**

A.V., 1. Artillery Volunteers. 2. *Med., Anat.* **a.** arteriovenous. **b.** atrioventricular. **c.** auriculoventricular. 3. Authorized Version (of the Bible).

a·va (ə vä′, ə vô′), *adv. Scot.* of all; at all. Also, **a·va′.**

A·va (ā′və), *n.* a girl's given name.

av·a·da·vat (av′ə də vat′), *n.* a waxbill, *Estrilda amandava,* native to southeastern Asia and often raised as a pet in the U.S. and Europe. The male has scarlet plumage with white dots on the sides and breast. Also, **amadavat.** [bird's name in various languages of India]

a·vail (ə vāl′), *v.t.* 1. to be of use or value to; profit; advantage: *All our efforts availed us little in trying to effect a change.* —*v.i.* 2. to be of use; have force or efficacy; serve; help: *His strength did not avail against the hostile onslaught.* 3. to be of value or profit. 4. **avail oneself of,** to use to one's advantage: *They availed themselves of the opportunity to hear a fine concert free of charge.* —*n.* 5. advantage; use; efficacy; effective use in the achievement of a goal or objective: *of little or no avail.* 6. **avails,** *Archaic.* profits or proceeds. [ME *availe,* equiv. to *a-* A-[2] + *vaile* < OF *vail-* (s. of *valoir*) < L *val(ēre)* (to) be of worth] —**a·vail′ing·ly,** *adv.*

a·vail·a·bil·i·ty (ə vā′lə bil′i tē), *n., pl.* **-ties.** 1. state of being available: *the availability of a candidate.* 2. one who or that which is available. [AVAILA(BLE) + -BILITY]

a·vail·a·ble (ə vā′lə bəl), *adj.* 1. suitable or ready for use; of use or service; at hand: *He used whatever excuse seemed available.* 2. readily obtainable; accessible: *available resources.* 3. having sufficient power or efficacy; valid. 4. *Archaic.* efficacious; profitable; advantageous. [late ME; see AVAIL, -ABLE] —**a·vail′a·ble·ness,** *n.* —**a·vail′a·bly,** *adv.*
—**Syn.** 1. accessible, usable, handy. —**Ant.** 1. unavailable.

avail′able light′, *Photog., Fine Arts.* the natural or usual light on a subject.

av·a·lanche (av′ə lanch′, -länch′), *n., v.,* **-lanched, -lanch·ing.** —*n.* 1. a large mass of snow, ice, etc., detached from a mountain slope and sliding or falling suddenly downward. 2. anything like an avalanche in suddenness and destructiveness: *an avalanche of misfortunes.* 3. Also called **Townsend avalanche.** *Physics, Chem.* a process in which the ions of one generation have collisions that produce a greater number of ions in the succeeding generation. —*v.i.* 4. to come down in, or like, an avalanche. —*v.t.* 5. to overwhelm with an extremely large amount of anything; swamp. [< F < *la valanche* (taken as *l'avalanche*), equiv. to *la* the + *valanche* metathetic var. of dial. *lavantse,* akin to OPr *lavanca* avalanche]

av′alanche wind′ (wind), the wind that is created in front of an avalanche.

A·va·lo·ki·te·sva·ra (uv′ə lō′ki tāsh′vər ə), *n. Buddhism.* a male Bodhisattva, widely revered and identified with various persons and gods. Cf. **Kwan-Yin.**

Av·a·lon (av′ə lon′), *n. Celtic Legend.* an island, represented as an earthly paradise in the western seas, to which King Arthur and other heroes were carried at death. Also, **Av′al·lon′.** [< ML *(insula) avallonis* (island) of Avallon (Geoffrey of Monmouth), lit., apple (island) < OWelsh *aballon* APPLE]

Av·a·lon (av′ə lon′), *n.* a town in SW Pennsylvania. 6859 (1960).

a·vant-garde (ə vänt′gärd′, ə vant′-; *Fr.* A VÄN-GARD′), *n.* 1. the advance group in any field, esp. in the visual, literary, or musical arts, whose works are characterized chiefly by unorthodox and experimental methods. —*adj.* 2. of or pertaining to the experimental treatment of artistic, musical, or literary material. 3. belonging to the avant-garde. [< F: lit., fore-guard. See VANGUARD] —**a·vant′-gard′ist,** *n.*

a·vant-gard·ism (ə vänt′gär′diz əm, ə vant′-), *n.* the attitudes, techniques, etc., of the cultural avant-garde. [AVANT-GARDE + -ISM]

A·var (ä′vär), *n.* a member of a people, probably originating in Asia, who settled in Dacia A.D. c555, later occupied Pannonia, and invaded other parts of central and eastern Europe before their decline in the 9th century.

A·vare, L' (*Fr.* lA VAR′). See **Miser, The.**

av·a·rice (av′ər is), *n.* insatiable greed for riches; inordinate, miserly desire to gain and hoard wealth. [ME < OF < L *avāritia,* equiv. to *avār(us)* greedy + *-itia* -ICE]
—**Syn.** cupidity.

av·a·ri·cious (av′ə rish′əs), *adj.* characterized by avarice; greedy; covetous. [late ME; see AVARICE, -IOUS] —**av′a·ri′cious·ly,** *adv.* —**av′a·ri′cious·ness,** *n.*

a·vast (ə vast′, ə väst′), *interj. Naut.* stop! cease!: *Avast heaving!* [perh. < D *hou(d) vast* HOLD[1] FAST[1]]

av·a·tar (av′ə tär′), *n.* 1. *Hindu Myth.* the descent of a deity to the earth in an incarnate form or some manifest shape; the incarnation of a god. 2. an embodiment or concrete manifestation, as of a principle, attitude, view of life, or the like. [< Skt *avatāra* a passing down, equiv. to *ava* down + *-tāra* a passing over]

a·vaunt (ə vônt′, ə vänt′), *adv. Archaic.* away! go! [ME < MF *avant* to the front < LL *ab ante* before (L: from before). See AB-, ANTE-]

A.V.C., American Veterans' Committee. Also, **AVC**

avdp., avoirdupois.

a·ve (ä′vā, ā′vē), *interj.* 1. hail! welcome! 2. farewell! good-by! —*n.* 3. the salutation "ave." 4. *(cap.)* See **Ave Maria.** 5. *(cap.)* the time for the recitation of the Angelus. [< L: impv. sing. of *avēre* to be well, fare well]

Ave., avenue. Also, **ave.**

a·ve at·que va·le! (ä′we ät′kwe wä′le; *Eng.* ā′vē at′kwē vā′lē, ä′vā ät′kwā vä′lā), *Latin.* hail and farewell!

Ave·bur·y (āv′bə rē), *n.* 1. **Baron.** See **Lubbock, Sir John.** 2. Also, **Abury.** a village in Wiltshire, England: site of a group of prehistoric megaliths.

a·vec plai·sir (A vek′ ple zēr′), *French.* with pleasure.

Av·e·line (av′ə lēn′, -lin′), *n.* a girl's given name. Also, **Av·e·li·na** (av′ə lē′nə, -lī′-).

a·vel·lan (ə vel′ən, av′ə lən), *adj. Heraldry.* (of a cross) having the form of four filberts, in their outer husks, joined in a cruciform arrangement. [< L *Avellān(a) (nux)* (nut) of Avella (a town in S Italy), filbert; see -AN]

A·ve·lla·ne·da (ä ve′yä ne′thä), *n.* a city in E Argentina, near Buenos Aires. 329,626 (1960).

A·ve Ma·ri·a (ä′vā mə rē′ə, ā′vē), 1. *(italics.)* the first two words of the Latin version of a prayer in the Roman Catholic Church, based on the salutation of the angel Gabriel to the Virgin Mary and the words of Elizabeth to her. 2. a recitation of this prayer. 3. the bead or beads on a rosary used to count off each prayer as spoken. Also, **A·ve Mar·y** (ā′vē mâr′ē, ä′vā). Also called **Hail Mary.** [see AVE]

av·e·na·ceous (av′ə nā′shəs), *adj. Bot.* of or like oats; of the oat kind. [< L *avēnāceus,* equiv. to *avēn(a)* oats + *-āceus* -ACEOUS]

Av·e·nal (av′ə nəl), *n.* a town in central California. 3147 (1960).

a·venge (ə venj′), *v.,* **a·venged, a·veng·ing.** —*v.t.* 1. to take vengeance or exact satisfaction for: *to avenge a death.* 2. to take vengeance on behalf of: *to avenge one's brother.* —*v.i.* 3. to take vengeance. [ME *avenge(n)* < OF *avengie(r),* equiv. to *a-* A-[5] + *vengier* < L *vindicāre;* see VINDICATE] —**a·venge′ful,** *adj.* —**a·veng′er,** *n.* —**a·veng′ing·ly,** *adv.*
—**Syn.** 1, 2. vindicate. AVENGE, REVENGE both mean to inflict pain or harm in return for pain or harm inflicted on oneself or those persons or causes to which one feels loyalty. The two words were formerly interchangeable, but have been differentiated until they now convey widely diverse ideas. AVENGE is now restricted to inflicting punishment as an act of retributive justice or as a vindication of propriety: *to avenge a murder by bringing the criminal to trial.* REVENGE implies inflicting pain or harm to retaliate for real or fancied wrongs; a reflexive pronoun is often used with this verb: *Iago wished to revenge himself upon Othello.* —**Ant.** 1, 3. forgive.

av·ens (av′inz), *n., pl.* **-ens.** any perennial, rosaceous herb of the genus *Geum,* having yellow, white, or red flowers. [ME *avence* < OF < ML *avencia* kind of clover]

av·en·tail (av′ən tāl′), *n. Armor.* 1. Also called **camail.** a mail tippet suspended from the lower edges of a 14th-century basinet as a protection for the neck, throat, and shoulders. 2. ventail. [ME, equiv. to *a-* (< ?) + VENTAIL]

Av·en·tine (av′ən tīn′, -tin), *n.* 1. one of the Seven Hills of the city of Rome, Italy. —*adj.* 2. of or pertaining to the Aventine. [< L *Aventīnus (mons)* the Aventine (hill)]

a·ven·tu·rine (ə ven′chə rin), *n.* 1. an opaque, brown glass containing fine, gold-colored particles. 2. any of several varieties of minerals, esp. quartz or feldspar, spangled with bright particles of mica, hematite, or other minerals. Also, **a·ven′tu·rin.** Also called **goldstone.** [< F < It *avventurin(a),* equiv. to *avventur(a)* chance (see ADVENTURE) + *-ina* -INE[2]; so called because rare and found by chance]

av·e·nue (av′ə nyōō′, -nōō′), *n.* 1. a wide street or main thoroughfare. 2. means of access or attainment: *avenues of escape; avenues of success.* 3. a way or means of entering into or approaching a place: *the various avenues to India.* 4. a wide, usually tree-lined road, path, driveway, etc., through grounds to a country house or monumental building. 5. *Brit.* such a roadway only when bordered by trees. [< F, lit., approach, n. use of fem. ptp. of *avenir* < L *advenīre* to come to. See A-[5], VENUE]
—**Syn.** 1. See **street.**

a·ver (ə vûr′), *v.t.,* **a·verred, a·ver·ring.** 1. to affirm with confidence; declare in a positive or peremptory manner. 2. *Law.* to allege as a fact. [ME < MF *aver(er)* < ML *adverāre,* equiv. to *ad-* AD- + *-vēr-* (< L *vērus* true) + *-ā-* thematic vowel + *-re* inf. suffix]

av·er·age (av′ər ij, av′rij), *n., adj., v.,* **-aged, -ag·ing.** —*n.* 1. a typical amount, rate, quality, etc.; norm; mean. 2. *Math.* a quantity intermediate to a set of quantities. 3. See **arithmetic mean.** 4. *Com.* **a.** a small charge paid by the master on account of the ship and cargo, such as pilotage, towage, etc. **b.** an expense, partial loss, or damage to ship or cargo. **c.** the incidence of such an expense or loss on the owners or their insurers. **d.** an equitable apportionment among all the interested parties of such an expense or loss. 5. Often, **averages.** *Stock Exchange.* the mean value of a number of stocks or securities as an indication of current price levels: *Industrial averages were up.* 6. **on the** or **an average,** usually; typically: *She can read 50 pages an hour, on the average.* —*adj.* 7. of or pertaining to an average; estimated by average; forming an average. 8. typical; common; ordinary. —*v.t.* 9. to find an average value for; reduce to a mean. 10. to result in, as an arithmetical mean; amount to, as a mean quantity: *Wheat averages 56 pounds to a bushel.* —*v.i.* 11. *U.S.* to have or show an average: *to average as expected.* 12. **average down,** to purchase more of a security or commodity at a lower price to reduce the average cost of one's holdings. 13. **average out, a.** to come out of a security or commodity transaction with a profit or without a loss. **b.** to reach an average or other figure: *His taxes should average out to about a fifth of his income.* 14. **average up,** to purchase more of a security or commodity at a higher price to take advantage of a contemplated further rise in prices. [late ME *averay* charge on goods shipped, orig. duty (< MF *avarie* < ?) + -AGE] —**av′er·age·ly,** *adv.*

av′erage devia′tion. See **mean deviation.**

av′erage rev′enue, the total receipts from sales divided by the number of units sold, frequently employed in price theory in conjunction with marginal revenue.

A·ve Re·gi·na Coe·lo·rum (ä′vā ri jē′nə che lôr′əm, -lōr′-), a Latin hymn in honor of the Virgin Mary as Queen of Heaven. [lit., Hail, Queen of Heaven]

A·ver·il (ā′vər il), *n.* a boy's given name. Also, **Avril, A′ver·ell.**

a·ver·ment (ə vûr′mənt), *n.* 1. act of averring. 2. a positive statement. [late ME *averrement* < MF. See AVER, -MENT]

A·ver·nus (ə vûr′nəs), *n.* 1. a lake near Naples, Italy, looked upon in ancient times as an entrance to hell, from whose waters vile-smelling vapors arose, supposedly killing birds flying over it. 2. hell. [< L < Gk *áornos* birdless, equiv. to *a-* A-[6] + *órn(is)* bird + *-os* adj. suffix] —**A·ver′nal,** *adj.*

A·ver·ro·ës (ə ver′ō ēz′), *n.* 1126?–98, Arab philosopher in Spain. Also, **A·ver′rho·ës′.**

Av·er·ro·ism (av′ə rō′iz əm, ə ver′ō-), *n.* the philosophy of Averroës, largely based on Aristotelianism and asserting the unity of an active intellect common to all human beings while denying personal immortality. Also, **Av′er·rho′ism.** [AVERRO(ËS) + -ISM] —**Av′er·ro′ist, Av′er·rho′ist,** *n.* —**Av′er·ro·is′tic, Av′er·rho·is′tic,** *adj.*

a·verse (ə vûrs′), *adj.* 1. having a strong feeling of opposition, antipathy, repugnance, etc.; opposed: *He is not averse to a nip now and then.* 2. *Bot.* turned away from the central axis (opposed to *adverse*). [< L *āvers-(us)* turned away, averted (ptp. of *āvertere*), equiv. to *ā-* A-[4] + *vert-* turn + *-tus* ptp. suffix] —**a·verse′ly,** *adv.* —**a·verse′ness,** *n.*
—**Syn.** 1. unwilling, loath. See **reluctant.** —**Ant.** 1. eager.

a·ver·sion (ə vûr′zhən, -shən), *n.* 1. a strong feeling of dislike; repugnance; antipathy (usually fol. by *to*). 2. a cause or object of dislike; person or thing that causes antipathy: *a pet aversion.* 3. *Obs.* act of averting; turning away or preventing. [< L *āversiōn-* (s. of *āversiō*), equiv. to *āvers(us)* turned away (see AVERSE) + *-iōn-* -ION] —**a·ver·sive** (ə vûr′siv, -ziv), *adj.*
—**Syn.** 1. distaste, abhorrence, disgust. AVERSION, ANTIPATHY, LOATHING connote strong dislike or detestation. AVERSION is an unreasoning desire to avoid that which displeases, annoys, or offends: *an aversion to* (or *toward*) *cats.* ANTIPATHY is a distaste, dislike, or disgust toward something: *an antipathy toward* (or *for*) *braggarts.* LOATHING connotes a combination of hatred and disgust, or detestation: *a loathing for* (or *toward*) *venison, a criminal.* —**Ant.** 1. predilection.

a·vert (ə vûrt′), *v.t.* 1. to turn away or aside: *to avert one's eyes.* 2. to ward off; prevent: *to avert evil.* [late ME < MF *avert(ir)* << L *āvertere,* equiv. to *ā-* A-[4] + *vertere* to turn] —**a·vert′ed·ly,** *adv.* —**a·vert′er,** *n.* —**a·vert′i·ble, a·vert′a·ble,** *adj.*

A·ver·tin (ə vûr′tin), *n. Pharm., Trademark.* tribromoethanol.

A·ver·y (ā′və rē), *n.* 1. **Milton,** 1893–1965, U.S. painter. 2. a boy's given name.

Av·er·yl (av′ə ril), *n.* a girl's given name.

A·ves (ā′vēz), *n. (construed as pl.)* the class comprising the birds. [L, pl. of *avis* bird]

A·ves·ta (ə ves′tə), *n.* a collection of sacred Zoroastrian writings, including the *Gathas.*

A·ves·tan (ə ves′tən), *n.* 1. an ancient East Iranian language of the Indo-European family, the language of all the Avesta but the Gathas. Cf. **Gathic** (def. 1). —*adj.* 2. of or pertaining to the Avesta or its language. [AVEST(A) + -AN]

A·vey·ron (A ve RÔN′), *n.* a department in S France. 290,442 (1962); 3387 sq. mi. *Cap.:* Rodez.

avg., average.

avi-, a learned borrowing from Latin meaning "bird," used in the formation of compound words: *aviculture.* [< L, comb. form of *avis*]

a·vi·an (ā′vē ən), *adj.* of or pertaining to birds. [AVI- + -AN]

a′vian diphthe′ria, *Vet. Pathol.* See **fowl pox.**

a′vian leuko′sis, *Vet. Pathol.* leukosis.

a′vian pneu·mo·en·ceph·a·li′tis (nōō′mō en sef′ə lī′tis, nyōō′-), *Vet. Pathol.* See **Newcastle disease.**

a′vian pox′, *Vet. Pathol.* See **fowl pox.**

a′vian pseu′do·plague (sōō′dō plāg′, -də-), *Vet. Pathol.* See **Newcastle disease.**

a′vian spirocheto′sis, *Vet. Pathol.* See **fowl spirochetosis.**

a·vi·ar·y (ā′vē er′ē), *n., pl.* **-ar·ies.** a large cage or a house or enclosure in which birds are kept. [< L *aviāri(um)* a place where birds are kept, n. use of neut. of *aviārius* pertaining to birds. See AVI-, -ARY]

a·vi·ate (ā′vē āt′, av′ē-), *v.i.,* **-at·ed, -at·ing.** to fly in an aircraft. [back formation from AVIATION]

a·vi·a·tion (ā′vē ā′shən, av′ē-), *n.* 1. act, method, or science of flying by mechanical means, esp. with heavier-than-air craft. 2. military aircraft. 3. the design, development, and production of aircraft: *the aviation of the future; advances in American aviation.* [< F; see AVI-, -ATION] —**a·vi·at·ic** (ā′vē at′ik, av′ē-), *adj.*

avia′tion badge′, wings.

avia′tion cadet′, one who trains to become an officer in an air force.

avia′tion med′icine, the branch of medicine dealing with the psychological, physiological, and pathological effects on man of flying in airplanes. Also called **aeromedicine.**

a·vi·a·tor (ā′vē ā′tər, av′ē-), *n.* a pilot of an airplane or other heavier-than-air craft. [AVI- + -ATOR, modeled on F *aviateur*]

a·vi·a·trix (ā′vē ā′triks, av′ē-), *n., pl.* **a·tri·ces** (-ā′tri sēz′, -ə trī′sēz). a female pilot. Also, **a′vi·a′tress.** [AVIAT(OR) + -TRIX]

A·vice (ā′vis), *n.* a girl's given name. Also, **Avis.**

A·vi·ce·brón (ä′vē thə brôn′, -se-), *n.* (*Solomon ben Judah ibn-Gabirol*) 1021?–58, Jewish poet and philosopher in Spain.

Av·i·cen·na (av′i sen′ə), *n.* A.D. 980–1037, Arab physician and philosopher.

a·vic·u·lar·i·um (ə vik′yə lâr′ē əm), *n., pl.* **-lar·i·a** (-lâr′ē ə). *Zool.* a protective zooid of a bryozoan colony, having movable jaws that can be snapped shut. [< NL; see AVI-, -CULE, -ARY] —**a·vic′u·lar′i·an,** *adj.*

a·vi·cul·ture (ā′vi kul′chər), *n.* the rearing or keeping of birds. [AVI- + CULTURE] —**a′vi·cul′tur·ist,** *n.*

av·id (av′id), *adj.* 1. keenly desirous; eager; greedy (often fol. by *for* or *of*): *avid for pleasure; avid of power.* 2. enthusiastic; ardent; dedicated; keen: *an avid moviegoer.* [< L *avid(us),* equiv. to *av(ēre)* (to) crave + *-idus* -ID[4]] —**av′id·ly,** adv.

av·i·din (av′i din, ə vid′in), *n. Biochem.* a protein, found in the white of egg, that prevents the action of biotin, thus injuring the animal that consumes it by producing biotin deficiency in the diet. Cf. **egg-white injury.** [AVID + (BIOT)IN; so named because avid for biotin]

a·vid·i·ty (ə vid′i tē), *n.* eagerness; greediness. [late ME *avidite* < MF < L *aviditāt-* (s. of *aviditās*). See AVID, -ITY]

a·vid·ya (ə vid′yä), *n. Hinduism, Buddhism.* ignorance of the identity of oneself with Brahman, resulting in imprisonment within the cycle of birth and death. Cf. **vidya.** [< Skt *avidyā* ignorance, equiv. to *a-* A-[6] + *vidyā;* see VIDYA]

a·vi·fau·na (ā′və fô′nə), *n.* the birds of a given region, considered as a whole. [AVI- + FAUNA] —**a′vi·fau′nal,** *adj.* —**a′vi·fau′nal·ly,** *adv.*

av·i·ga·tion (av′ə gā′shən), *n.* aerial navigation. [AVI- + (NAVI)GATION] —**av′i·ga′tor,** *n.*

A·vi·gnon (A vē nyôN′), *n.* a city in and the capital of Vaucluse, in SE France, on the Rhone River: papal residence 1309–77. 75,181 (1962).

A·vi·la Ca·ma·cho (ä′vē lä′ kä mä′chô), **Ma·nuel** (mä nwel′), 1897–1955, president of Mexico 1940–46.

A·vil·ion (ə vil′yən), *n.* French name of **Avalon.**

a vin·cu·lo mat·ri·mo·ni·i (ā viŋ′kyŏŏ lō′ ma′tri mō′nē ī′), *Law.* pertaining to or noting a divorce that dissolves the marriage bond and releases husband and wife from all matrimonial obligations: *a divorce a vinculo matrimonii.* [< L: from the bond of marriage]

a·vion (A vyôN′), *n., pl.* **a·vions** (A vyôN′). *French.* airplane.

a·vi·on·ics (ā′vē on′iks, av′ē-), *n.* (*construed as sing.*) the science and technology of the development and use of electrical and electronic devices in aviation. [AVI(ATION ELECTR)ONICS]

a·vir·u·lent (ā vir′yə lənt, ā vir′ə-), *adj.* (of organisms) having no virulence, as a result of age, heat, etc.; nonpathogenic. [A-[6] + VIRULENT] —**a·vir′u·lence,** *n.*

A·vis (ā′vis), *n.* a girl's given name. Also, **Avice.**

a·vi·so (ə vī′zō), *n., pl.* **-sos. 1.** dispatch. **2.** a boat used esp. for carrying dispatches. [< Sp < LL *advīs(um).* See ADVICE]

a·vi·ta·min·o·sis (ā vī′tə mə nō′sis, ā′vi tam′ə nō′sis), *n. Pathol.* any disease caused by a lack of vitamins. [A-[6] + VITAMIN + -OSIS] —**a·vi·ta·min·ot·ic** (ā vī′tə mə not′ik), *adj.*

A·vi·va (ə vē′və), *n.* a girl's given name.

Av·lo·na (äv lô′nä), *n.* Valona.

avn., aviation.

a·vo (ä′vŏŏ), *n., pl.* **a·vos.** a money of account of Macao, the 100th part of a pataca, equivalent to about .0018 of a U.S. dollar. [< Pg]

A·vo (ā′vō), *n.* a girl's given name.

A·vo·ca (ə vō′kə), *n.* a town in NE Pennsylvania. 3562 (1960).

av·o·ca·do (av′ə kä′dō, ä′və-), *n., pl.* **-dos. 1.** Also called **alligator pear.** a tropical American fruit, green to black in color and commonly pear-shaped, borne by the lauraceous tree, *Persea americana,* and its variety *drymifolia,* eaten raw, esp. as a salad fruit. **2.** the tree. [alter. of Sp *abogado,* lit., lawyer (see ADVOCATE), r. AmerSp *aguacate* < Nahuatl *ahuacatl,* lit., testicle. See ALLIGATOR PEAR]

Avocado, *Persea americana*

av·o·ca·tion (av′ə kā′shən), *n.* **1.** a minor or occasional occupation; hobby. **2.** one's regular occupation, calling, or vocation. **3.** *Archaic.* diversion or distraction. **4.** *Obs.* a calling away. [< L *āvocātiōn-* (s. of *āvocātiō*) a calling away. See A-[4], VOCATION]

a·voc·a·to·ry (ə vok′ə tôr′ē, -tōr′ē), *adj.* calling away, off, or back. [< ML *āvocātōri(us)* calling away, equiv. to L *āvocāt(us)* called away (ptp. of *āvocāre; ā-* A-[4] + *vocātus* called, equiv. to *vocā-* v. s. + *-tus* ptp. suffix) + *-ōrius* -ORY[1]]

av·o·cet (av′ə set′), *n.* any of several long-legged, web-footed shore birds of the genus *Recurvirostra,* having a long, slender bill that curves upward. Also, **avoset.** [earlier *avoset* < It *avosett(a)*]

av·o·di·re (av′ə də rā′), *n.* the hard, light-colored wood of a West African, meliaceous tree, *Turraeanthus africana,* used for making furniture. [< F]

A·vo·ga·dro (ä′və gä′drō; *It.* ä′vô gä′drô), *n.* **Count A·ma·de·o** (ä′mä de′ô), 1776–1856, Italian physicist and chemist.

A′voga′dro's law′, *Chem.* the principle that equal volumes of all gases at the same temperature and pressure contain the same number of molecules. [named after Count Amadeo AVOGADRO]

A′voga′dro's num′ber, *Chem.* the constant, 6.02 × 10^{23}, representing the number of atoms in a gram atom or the number of molecules in a gram molecule. Also, **A′voga′dro num′ber.** Also called **A′voga′dro con′stant.** [see AVOGADRO'S LAW]

a·void (ə void′), *v.t.* **1.** to keep away from; keep clear of; shun; evade: *to avoid a person; to avoid danger.* **2.** *Law.* to make void or of no effect; invalidate. **3.** *Obs.* to empty; eject or expel. [ME *avoide* < AF *avoide(r),* equiv. to *a-* A-[4] + *voider* to VOID] —**a·void′a·ble,** *adj.* —**a·void′a·bly,** *adv.* —**a·void′er,** *n.*

—**Syn. 1.** elude. AVOID, ESCAPE mean to come through peril, actual or potential, without suffering serious consequences. To AVOID is to succeed in keeping away from something harmful or undesirable: *to avoid meeting an enemy.* ESCAPE suggests encountering peril but coming through it safely: *to escape drowning.* —**Ant. 1.** confront, face.

a·void·ance (ə void′əns), *n.* **1.** act of keeping away from: *avoidance of scandal.* **2.** *Law.* a making void; annulment. [ME; see AVOID, -ANCE]

avoid′ance play′, *Bridge.* a play by the declarer designed to prevent a particular opponent from taking the lead.

avoir., avoirdupois.

av·oir·du·pois (av′ər də poiz′), *n.* **1.** See **avoirdupois weight. 2.** *Informal.* excess bodily weight: *She's put on a lot of avoirdupois.* [ME *avoir de pois,* lit., property of weight < OF, equiv. to *avoir* (var. of *aveir* < L *habēre*) + *de* (< L *dē*) + *pois* (var. of *peis* < L *pēnsum*)]

avoirdupois′ weight′, the system of weights in British and U.S. use for goods other than gems, precious metals, and drugs: 27 11/32 grains = 1 dram; 16 drams = 1 ounce; 16 ounces = 1 pound; 112 pounds (Brit.) or 100 pounds (U.S.) = 1 hundredweight; 20 hundredweight = 1 ton. The pound contains 7000 grains. *Abbr.:* av.; avdp.; avoir.

a vol (ä vōl′, ä vôl′), *Heraldry.* noting a pair of wings joined with the tips upward (opposed to *in lure*). [< F: in flight. See VOLLEY]

A·von (ā′vən, av′ən), *n.* **1.** a river in central England, flowing SE past Stratford-on-Avon to the Severn. 96 mi. long. **2.** a river in S England, flowing W to the mouth of the Severn. ab. 75 mi. long. **3.** a river in S England, flowing S to the English Channel. ab. 60 mi. long. **4.** a town in central New York. 2772 (1960).

Av·on·dale (av′ən dāl′), *n.* a town in central Arizona. 6151 (1960).

A′von Lake′ (ā′von), a town in N Ohio. 9403 (1960).

A·vonne (ə′von), *n.* a girl's given name.

a·vo·set (av′ə set′), *n.* avocet.

à vo·tre san·té (A vô′trə säN tā′), *French.* to your health.

a·vouch (ə vouch′), *v.t.* **1.** to make frank acknowledgment or affirmation of; declare or assert with positiveness. **2.** to assume responsibility for; guarantee. **3.** to admit; confess. [ME *avouche* < MF *avouchie(r)* < L *advocāre.* See A-[5], VOUCH, ADVOCATE] —**a·vouch′er,** *n.* —**a·vouch′ment,** *n.*

a·vow (ə vou′), *v.t.* to declare frankly or openly; own; acknowledge; confess; admit: *to avow one's principles.* [ME *avowe(n)* < OF *avoue(r)* < L *advocāre.* See ADVOCATE] —**a·vow′a·ble,** *adj.* —**a·vow′er,** *n.*

a·vow·al (ə vou′əl), *n.* an open statement of affirmation; frank acknowledgment or admission. [AVOW + -AL[2]]

a·vowed (ə voud′), *adj.* acknowledged; declared: *an avowed enemy.* [AVOW + -ED[2]] —**a·vow·ed·ly** (ə vou′id lē), *adv.* —**a·vow′ed·ness,** *n.*

a·vow·ry (ə vou′rē), *n., pl.* **-ries.** *Law.* a plea by a defendant in an action of replevin who admits taking the distrained goods and shows just cause for the taking. [ME *avowrie* < OF *avouerie,* equiv. to *avou(er)* (to) AVOW + *-erie* -RY]

Av·ram (āv′rəm, av′rəm), *n.* a boy's given name.

Av·ril (āv′ril) *n.* a boy's given name. Also, **Averil, Averell.**

a·vul·sed (ə vul′sid), *adj. Surg.* (of a wound) having the tissue torn away. [*avulse* tear off (< L *āvuls(us),* ptp. of *āvellere,* equiv. to *ā-* A-[4] + *vul-* pluck (perf. s. of *vellere*) + *-sus,* var. of *-tus* ptp. suffix) + -ED[2]]

a·vul·sion (ə vul′shən), *n.* **1.** a tearing away. **2.** *Law.* the sudden removal of soil by change in a river's course or by a flood, from the land of one owner to that of another. **3.** a part torn off. [< L *āvulsiōn-* (s. of *āvulsiō*), equiv. to *āvuls(us)* torn off (see AVULSED) + *-iōn-* -ION]

a·vun·cu·lar (ə vuŋ′kyə lər), *adj.* **1.** of, pertaining to, or characteristic of an uncle: *avuncular affection.* **2.** *Obs.* of or pertaining to a pawnbroker. [< L *avuncul(us)* a mother's brother, equiv. to *av(us)* a forefather + *-uncul(us)* dim. suffix + -AR[1]]

a·vun·cu·late (ə vuŋ′kyə lit, -lāt′), *n. Anthropol.* a close social relationship between a maternal uncle and his nephew. [< L *avuncul(us)* uncle (see AVUNCULAR) + -ATE[1]]

aw (ô), *interj.* (used as an exclamation expressing protest, disbelief, disgust, or the like.)

AW, Article of War.

a.w., **1.** actual weight. **2.** (in shipping) all water. **3.** atomic weight. Also, **aw**

a·wa (ə wô′, ə wä′), *adv. Scot.* away.

a·wait (ə wāt′), *v.t.* **1.** to wait for; expect; look for. **2.** to be in store for; be ready for. **3.** *Obs.* to lie in wait for. —*v.i.* **4.** to wait, as in expectation. [ME *awaite(n)* < OF (north) *awaitier,* equiv. to *a-* A-[5] + *waitier* to WAIT] —**a·wait′er,** *n.*

—**Syn. 1.** See **expect.**

a·wake (ə wāk′), *v.,* **a·woke** or **a·waked, a·wak·ing,** *adj.* —*v.t., v.i.* **1.** to wake up; rouse from sleep. **2.** to rouse to action; become active: *His flagging interest awoke, and he once again became involved.* **3.** to come or bring to an awareness; become cognizant (often fol. by *to*): *He awoke to the realities of life.* —*adj.* **4.** waking; not sleeping. **5.** vigilant; alert: *He was awake to the danger.* [OE *awacen,* ptp. of *awæcnan*] —**a·wake′a·ble,** *adj.*

a·wak·en (ə wā′kən), *v.t., v.i.* to awake; waken. [ME *awak(e)n(en),* OE *awæcnian* earlier *onwæcnian.* See A-[1], WAKEN] —**a·wak′en·a·ble,** *adj.* —**a·wak′en·er,** *n.*

a·wak·en·ing (ə wā′kə niŋ), *adj.* **1.** rousing; quickening: *an awakening interest.* —*n.* **2.** act of awaking from sleep. **3.** a revival of interest or attention. **4.** a recognition, realization, or coming into awareness of something: *They had a rude awakening to the facts of life.* **5.** a renewal of interest in religion, esp. in a community; a revival. **6.** (*cap., italics.*) a novel (1920) by John Galsworthy. Cf. **Forsyte Saga, The.** [AWAKEN + -ING[2], -ING[1]] —**a·wak′en·ing·ly,** *adv.*

a·ward (ə wôrd′), *v.t.* **1.** to give as due or merited; assign or bestow: *to award prizes.* **2.** to bestow by judicial decree; assign or appoint by deliberate judgment, as in arbitration. —*n.* **3.** something awarded, as a payment or medal. **4.** *Law.* **a.** a decision after consideration; a judicial sentence. **b.** the decision of arbitrators on points submitted to them. [ME *award(en)* < AF *awarde(r),* equiv. to *a-* A-[4] + *warder* << Gmc; cf. OE *weardian* to WARD] —**a·ward′a·ble,** *adv.* —**a·ward′er,** *n.*

a·ware (ə wâr′), *adj.* **1.** having knowledge; conscious; cognizant: *aware of the danger.* **2.** informed; alert; knowledgeable; sophisticated: *He is one of the most politically aware young men around.* [ME, var. of *iwar,* OE *gewær* watchful (c. OHG, OS *giwar,* G *gewahr*), equiv. to *ge-* prefix + *wær* WARE[2]] —**a·ware′ness,** *n.*

—**Syn. 1.** mindful. See **conscious.** —**Ant. 1.** oblivious.

a·wash (ə wosh′, ə wôsh′), *adj., adv.* **1.** *Naut.* **a.** just level or scarcely above the surface of the water, so that waves break over the top. **b.** overflowing with water, as the upper deck of a ship in a heavy sea. **2.** covered with water. **3.** washing about; tossed about by the waves. [A-[1] + WASH]

a·way (ə wā′), *adv.* **1.** from this or that place; off: *to go away.* **2.** far; apart: *away back; away from the subject.* **3.** aside; to another place; in another direction: *to turn your eyes away; to turn away customers.* **4.** out of one's possession or use: *to give money away.* **5.** out of existence or notice; into extinction: *to fade away; to idle away the time of day.* **6.** continuously; repeatedly; on: *He kept on hammering away. She talked away a mile a minute.* **7.** without hesitation: *Fire away.* **8. away with-** **a.** take away: *Away with him!* **b.** go away; leave!: *Away with you!* **9. do away with, a.** to get rid of; abolish; stop. **b.** to kill: *Bluebeard did away with all his wives.* **10. where away?** (of something sighted from a ship) in which direction? where? —*adj.* **11.** absent: *to be away from home.* **12.** distant: *six miles away.* **13.** immediately off and on the way: *The order was given and he was away.* **14.** *Sports.* played in a ball park, arena, or the like, other than the one that is or is assumed to be the center of operations of a team: *winners in their last three away games.* Cf. **home** (def. 14). **15.** *Baseball.* having been put out: *with two away in the top of the seventh.* **16.** *Golf.* **a.** (of a golf ball) lying farthest from the hole. **b.** (of a golfer) having hit such a ball and being required to play first. [ME; OE *aweg,* deriv. of *on weg.* See ON, WAY]

a·way′-go·ing crop′ (ə wā′gō′iŋ), *Law.* a crop planted by a tenant that matures after the expiration of his tenancy and is rightfully his to harvest. Also called **waygoing crop.**

AWB, See **air waybill.**

awe (ô), *n., v.,* **awed, aw·ing.** —*n.* **1.** an overwhelming feeling of reverence, admiration, fear, etc., produced by that which is grand, sublime, extremely powerful, or the like: *in awe of God; in awe of authority.* **2.** *Archaic.* power to inspire fear or reverence. **3.** *Obs.* fear or dread. —*v.t.* **4.** to inspire with awe. **5.** to influence or restrain by awe. [ME *aghe, awe* < Scand; cf. Icel *agi* fear, c. Goth *agis,* OE *ege,* Gk *áchos* pain]

—**Syn. 1.** veneration.

a·weath·er (ə weth′ər), *adv., adj. Naut.* upon or toward the weather side of a vessel; in the direction of the wind (opposed to *alee*). [A-[1] + WEATHER]

awed (ôd), *adj.* filled with or expressing awe. [AWE + -ED[2]] —**awed′ly,** *adv.* —**awed′ness,** *n.*

a·weigh (ə wā′), *adj. Naut.* (of an anchor) just free of the bottom; atrip. [A-[1] + WEIGH[2]]

awe·less (ô′lis), *adj.* awless. [AWE + -LESS] —**awe′less·ness,** *n.*

awe·some (ô′səm), *adj.* **1.** inspiring awe: *an awesome sight.* **2.** characterized by awe. [AWE + -SOME[1]] —**awe′some·ly,** *adv.* —**awe′some·ness,** *n.*

awe-struck (ô′struk′), *adj.* filled with awe. Also, **awe′struck′, awe-strick·en, awe·strick·en** (ô′strik′ən).

aw·ful (ô′fəl), *adj.* **1.** inspiring fear; dreadful; terrible. **2.** extremely bad; unpleasant; ugly. **3.** full of awe; reverential. **4.** solemnly impressive; inspiring awe: *the awful majesty of alpine peaks.* —*adv.* **5.** *Informal.* very; extremely: *He did an awful good job of painting the corncrib.* [ME; see AWE, -FUL; r. OE *egefull* dreadful] —**aw′ful·ness,** *n.*

—**Usage.** In informal use, there is no objection to AWFUL in the sense of "very bad, ugly, mean, etc.," but it has been so overworked that it is ineffective. It is still generally avoided in formal use except in the sense of "awe-inspiring."

aw·ful·ly (ô′fə lē, ôf′lē), *adv.* **1.** very; extremely: *That was awfully nice of you. She's behaving awfully grand these days.* **2.** in a manner provoking censure, disapproval, or the like: *She behaved awfully all evening.* **3.** *Archaic.* **a.** in a manner inspiring awe: *shouting awfully the dreaded curse.* **b.** in a manner expressing awe: *to stare awfully.*

a·while (ə hwīl′, ə wīl′), *adv.* for a short time or period: *Stay awhile.* [A-[2] + WHILE]

—**Usage.** The word AWHILE is an adverb meaning "for a short time" and should not be confused with the article and noun A WHILE, usually in a prepositional phrase: *Stay awhile. Stay for a little while longer.*

a·whirl (ə hwûrl′, ə wûrl′), *adj.* rotating rapidly; spinning; whirling (usually used predicatively): *dancers awhirl to the strains of a lively waltz.* [A-[1] + WHIRL]

awk·ward (ôk′wərd), *adj.* **1.** lacking skill or dexterity; clumsy; inept. **2.** ungraceful; ungainly; uncouth: *awkward gesture.* **3.** ill-adapted for use or handling; unwieldy; unmanageable: *an awkward method; an awkward instrument.* **4.** requiring caution; somewhat hazardous; dangerous: *There's an awkward step there.* **5.** hard to deal with; difficult; unpleasant: *an awkward customer; an awkward situation.* **6.** embarrassing or inconvenient; inopportune: *an awkward moment.* **7.** *Obs.* untoward; perverse. [ME *awk, auk* backhanded (< Scand; cf. Icel *öfug(r)* turned the wrong way) + -WARD] —**awk′ward·ly,** *adv.* —**awk′ward·ness,** *n.*

—**Syn. 1.** unskillful, unhandy, inexpert. —**Ant. 1.** deft, adroit. **2.** graceful.

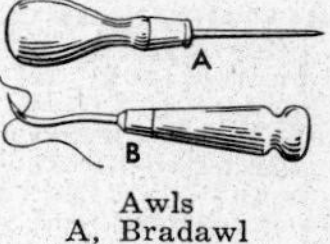

Awls
A, Bradawl
B, Sewing awl

awk′ward age′, early adolescence.

awl (ôl), *n.* a pointed instrument for piercing small holes in leather, wood, etc. [ME *al,* OE *æl;* akin to OHG *āla* (> G *Ahle*), Icel *al(r),* Skt *ārā*]

A.W.L., absent with leave. Also, **a.w.l.**

aw·less (ô′lis), *adj.* without awe; fearless; not to be awed. Also, **aweless.** [AWE + -LESS] —**aw′less·ness,** *n.*

awl·wort (ôl′wûrt′), *n.* a small, stemless, aquatic, cruciferous plant, *Subularia aquatica,* having slender, sharp-pointed leaves. [AWL + WORT[2]]

aw·mous (ô′məs), *n.* (*construed as pl.*) *Scot.* almous.

awn (ôn), *n. Bot.* **1.** a bristlelike appendage of a plant, esp. on the glumes of grasses. **2.** such appendages collectively, as those forming the beard of wheat, barley, etc. **3.** any similar bristle. [ME *awne, agune* < Scand; cf. Icel *ögn* husk, c. Goth *ahana,* OHG *agana, ahana* (> G *Ahne*)] —**awned,** *adj.* —**awn′less,** *adj.*

awn·er (ô′nər), *n.* a machine for cutting the awns from grain. [AWN + -ER[1]]

awn·ing (ô′niŋ), *n.* **1.** a rooflike shelter of canvas or other material extending over a doorway, from the top of a window, over a deck, etc., in order to provide protection, as from the sun. **2.** a shelter. [?] —**aw′ninged,** *adj.*

awn′ing deck′, *Naut.* a weather deck supported on very light scantlings.

awn′ing win′dow, a window frame having one or more sashes hinged at the top and swinging outward.

awn′less brome′ grass′. See **Hungarian brome grass.** [AWN + -LESS]

a·woke (ə wōk′), *v.* a pt. and pp. of **awake.**

A.W.O.L. (*pronounced as initials or, in Mil. slang,* ā′wôl), away from military duties without permission, but without the intention of deserting. Also, **a.w.o.l.** [*A(bsent) W(ith)o(ut) L(eave)*]

A·wo·lo·wo (ä wŏŏ′lō wō′), *n.* **O·ba·fe·mi** (ô bä′fā mē), born 1909, Nigerian lawyer and statesman.

a·wry (ə rī′), *adv., adj.* **1.** with a turn or twist to one side; askew: *to glance or look awry.* **2.** away from the expected or proper direction; amiss; wrong: *Our plans went awry.* [ME *on wry.* See A-[1], WRY]

ax (aks), *n., pl.* **ax·es** (ak′siz), *v.*, **axed, ax·ing.** —*n.* **1.** an instrument with a bladed head on a handle or helve, used for hewing, cleaving, chopping, etc. **2.** *Jazz Slang.* any musical instrument. **3. get the ax,** *Informal.* **a.** to be dismissed from employment. **b.** to be expelled from school. **c.** to be rejected by a lover, friend, etc. **4. have an ax to grind,** *Informal.* to have a personal or selfish motive: *His interest in our venture cannot be sincere, because I know he has an ax to grind.* —*v.t.* **5.** to shape or trim with an ax. **6.** to chop or split with an ax. **7.** *Informal.* to dismiss, restrict, or destroy brutally, as if with an ax: *The main office axed those men in the field who didn't meet their quota. Congress axed the budget. Don't ax the guy's chances just because you're in a huff.* Also, **axe.** [ME; OE *æx;* akin to Goth *aquizi,* OHG *acchus* (> G *Axt*), L *ascia* (< **acsiā*), Gk *axī́nē*] —**ax′like′,** *adj.*

Axes
A, Common ax
B, Hatchet
C, Stonemason's ax

ax-, var. of **axi-,** esp. before a vowel.

ax., axiom.

Ax·a (ak′sə), *n. Douay Bible.* Achsah.

ax·an·thop·si·a (ak′san thop′sē ə), *n. Ophthalm.* a defect of vision in which the retina fails to respond to yellow. [A-[6] + XANTH(O)- + -OPSIA]

Ax·el (ak′səl), *n.* a boy's given name.

a·xen·ic (ā zen′ik), *adj.* uncontaminated; germfree. [A-[6] + XEN- + -IC]

ax·es[1] (ak′sēz), *n.* pl. of **axis**[1].

ax·es[2] (ak′siz), *n.* pl. of **ax.**

axi-, a word element meaning "axis": *axial; axilemma.* Also, **axo-;** *esp. before a vowel,* **ax-.** [comb. form repr. L *axi(s)* axle, wheel; c. Gk *áxōn,* Skt *ákṣas,* Lith *ašìs,* OE *eax*]

ax·i·al (ak′sē əl), *adj.* **1.** of, pertaining to, characterized by, or forming an axis: *an axial relationship.* **2.** situated in an axis or on the axis. Also, **ax·ile** (ak′sil, -sīl). [AXI- + -AL[1]] —**ax′i·al′i·ty,** *n.*

ax·i·al·ly (ak′sē ə lē), *adv.* in the line of the axis. [AXIAL + -LY]

ax′ial pen′cil, *Geom.* the set of all planes that contain a given line.

ax′ial skel′eton, *Anat.* the skeleton of the head and trunk.

ax·il (ak′sil), *n. Bot.* the angle between the upper side of a leaf or stem and the supporting stem or branch. [< L *axil(la)* armpit]

A, Axil

ax·i·lem·ma (ak′sə lem′ə), *n., pl.* **-lem·ma·ta** (-lem′ə tə). *Anat.* the membrane surrounding the axis cylinder of a nerve fiber. [AXI- + LEMMA[2]]

ax·il·la (ak sil′ə), *n., pl.* **ax·il·lae** (ak sil′ē). **1.** *Anat.* the armpit. **2.** *Ornith.* the corresponding region under the wing of a bird. **3.** *Bot.* an axil. [< L]

ax·il·lar (ak′sə lər), *n.* Often, **axillars.** *Ornith.* a number of the feathers growing from the axilla of a bird. [AXILL(A) + -AR[1]]

ax·il·lar·y (ak′sə ler′ē), *adj., n., pl.* **-lar·ies.** —*adj.* **1.** pertaining to the axilla. **2.** *Bot.* pertaining to or growing from the axil. —*n.* **3.** Usually, **axillaries.** *Ornith.* axillars. [AXILL(A) + -ARY]

ax·i·nite (ak′sə nīt′), *n.* a mineral, complex calcium and aluminum borosilicate, usually occurring in thin brown crystals. [< Gk *axín(ē)* an axe + -ITE[1]]

ax·in·o·man·cy (ak′sə nə man′sē, ak sin′ə-), *n.* an ancient method of divination, in which a piece of agate or jet, placed upon a heated ax-head, supposedly moved in the direction of a guilty person. [< L *axinomantia* < Gk *axino-,* comb. form of *axī́nē* ax + *-manteia* -MANCY]

ax′iolog′ical eth′ics, the branch of ethics dealing primarily with the relative goodness or value of the motives and end of any action. Cf. **deontological ethics.** [AXIOLOG(Y) + -ICAL]

ax·i·ol·o·gy (ak′sē ol′ə jē), *n.* the branch of philosophy dealing with values, as those of ethics, aesthetics, or religion. [< Gk *áxio(s)* worthy, estimable + -LOGY] —**ax·i·o·log·i·cal** (ak′sē ə loj′i kəl), *adj.* —**ax′i·o·log′i·cal·ly,** *adv.* —**ax′i·ol′o·gist,** *n.*

ax·i·om (ak′sē əm), *n.* **1.** a self-evident truth. **2.** a universally accepted principle or rule. **3.** *Logic, Math.* a proposition which is assumed without proof for the sake of studying the consequences that follow from it. [late ME < L *axiōm(a)* < Gk: something worthy, equiv. to *axiō̂(ein)* to reckon worthy + *-ma* n. suffix]

ax·i·o·mat·ic (ak′sē ə mat′ik), *adj.* **1.** pertaining to or of the nature of an axiom; self-evident. **2.** aphoristic. Also, **ax′i·o·mat′i·cal.** [< Gk *axiōmatikós,* equiv. to *axiōmat-* (s. of *axíōma* AXIOM) + *-ikos* -IC] —**ax′i·o·mat′i·cal·ly,** *adv.*

ax′iom of choice′, *Math.* the axiom of set theory that given any collection of disjoint sets, a set can be so constructed that it contains one element from each of the given sets. Also called **Zermelo's axiom;** *esp. Brit.,* **multiplicative axiom.**

ax′iom of countabil′ity, *Math.* the property satisfied by a topological space in which the neighborhood system of each point has a base consisting of a countable number of neighborhoods **(first axiom of countability)** or the property satisfied by a topological space that has a base for its topology consisting of a countable number of subsets of the space **(second axiom of countability).**

Ax·i·o·poe·nus (ak′sē ə pē′nəs), *n. Class. Myth.* an epithet of Athena, meaning "just requital."

ax·is[1] (ak′sis), *n., pl.* **ax·es** (ak′sēz). **1.** the line about which a rotating body, such as the earth, turns. **2.** a central line bisecting a body, form, or the like, and in relation to which symmetry is determined. **3.** *Anat.* **a.** a central or principal structure, about which something turns or is arranged: *the skeletal axis.* **b.** the second cervical vertebra. **4.** *Bot.* the longitudinal support on which organs or parts are arranged; the stem and root; the central line of any body. **5.** *Analytic Geom.* any line used as a fixed reference in conjunction with one or more other references for determining the position of a point or of a series of points forming a curve or a surface. Cf. **x-axis, y-axis. 6.** *Aeron.* any one of three lines defining the attitude of an airplane, one being generally determined by the direction of forward motion and the other two at right angles to it and to each other. **7.** *Fine Arts.* an imaginary line, in a given formal structure, about which a form, area, or plane is organized. **8.** the line generated by the midpoints of every section of an arch ring. **9.** an alliance of two or more nations to coordinate their foreign and military policies, and to draw in with them a group of dependent or supporting powers. **10. the Axis,** (in World War II) Germany, Italy, and Japan, often with Bulgaria, Hungary, and Rumania. **11.** a principal line of development, movement, direction, etc. [< L *axis* an axletree, axle, axis. See AXON, AX] —**ax·ised** (ak′sist), *adj.*

ax·is[2] (ak′sis), *n., pl.* **ax·is·es.** a deer, *Axis axis,* of India and Ceylon, having a reddish-brown coat spotted with white. Also, **ax′is deer′.** [< L *axis* a wild animal of India (Pliny)]

ax′is cyl′inder, *Anat.* the central portion of a nerve fiber along which the impulses are conducted.

ax′is cyl′inder proc′ess, *Anat.* an axon.

ax′is of abscis′sas, *Math.* x-axis (def. 1).

ax′is of or′dinates, *Math.* y-axis (def. 1).

ax′is of revolu′tion, *Math.* the axis in the plane, about which an area is revolved to form a solid of revolution.

ax′is of sym′metry, *Math.* a straight line for which every point on a given curve has corresponding to it another point such that the line connecting the two points is bisected by the given line.

ax·le (ak′səl), *n.* **1.** *Mach.* the pin, bar, shaft, or the like, on which or by means of which a wheel or pair of wheels rotates. **2.** the spindle at either end of an axletree. **3.** an axletree. [ME *axel,* OE *eaxl* shoulder, crossbeam (in *eaxle-gespann*); c. OHG *ahsala* shoulder (> G *Achsel*), Icel *öxull,* L *āla* (deriv. of **akslā*)] —**ax′led,** *adj.*

ax·le·tree (ak′səl trē′), *n.* a bar, fixed crosswise under an animal-drawn vehicle, with a rounded spindle at each end upon which a wheel rotates. [ME; see AXLE, TREE]

ax·man (aks′mən), *n., pl.* **-men.** **1.** one who wields an ax. **2.** *Survey.* chainman. [AX + MAN[1]]

Ax′min·ster car′pet (aks′min′stər), a carpet having a stiff jute back and a cut pile of wool. [named after town in SW England where manufactured]

axo-, var. of **axi-,** esp. before a consonant.

ax·o·lotl (ak′sə lot′əl), *n.* any larval salamander of the genus *Ambystoma,* found esp. in lakes and ponds of the southwestern U.S. and Mexico, that is capable of breeding in its larval state. [< Nahuatl]

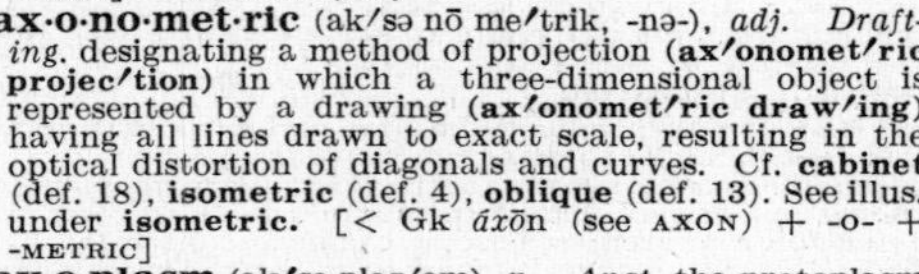

Axolotl,
Ambystoma mexicanus
(Length 6 to 12 in.)

ax·on (ak′son), *n. Anat.* the appendage of the neuron which transmits impulses away from the cell. See diag. under **neuron.** Also, **ax·one** (ak′sōn). Also called **neurite.** [< NL < Gk *áxōn* an axle, axis; c. L *axis*] —**ax′on·al,** *adj.*

ax·o·no·met·ric (ak′sə nō me′trik, -nə-), *adj. Drafting.* designating a method of projection **(ax′onomet′ric projec′tion)** in which a three-dimensional object is represented by a drawing **(ax′onomet′ric draw′ing)** having all lines drawn to exact scale, resulting in the optical distortion of diagonals and curves. Cf. **cabinet** (def. 18), **isometric** (def. 4), **oblique** (def. 13). See illus. under **isometric.** [< Gk *áxōn* (see AXON) + -O- + -METRIC]

ax·o·plasm (ak′sə plaz′əm), *n. Anat.* the protoplasm of an axon. [AXO- + PLASM]

ax·seed (aks′sēd′), *n.* an Old World fabaceous plant, *Coronilla varia,* having pink flowers, naturalized in the U.S. Also called **crown vetch.** [AX + SEED]

Ax·um (äk′sōōm), *n.* Aksum.

ay[1] (ā), *adv. Poetic or Dial.* ever; always. Also, **aye.** [ME *ei, ai* < Scand; cf. Icel *ei,* c. OE *ā* ever]

ay[2] (ā), *interj. Dial.* Ah! Oh!

ay[3] (ī), *adv., n.* aye[1].

A·ya·cu·cho (ä′yä kōō′chô), *n.* a city in SW Peru: decisive victory of Bolívar over Spanish troops 1824. 26,000 (est. 1957).

a·yah (ä′yə), *n.* (in India) a native maid or nurse. [< Hindi *āyā* < Pg *aia* maidservant < L *avia* grandmother, equiv. to *av(us)* grandfather + *-ia* fem. suffix]

a·ya·tol·lah (ä′yə tō′lə), *n.* (among Shiites) a title in the religious hierarchy achieved by scholars who have demonstrated highly advanced knowledge of Islamic law. [< Pers < Ar *āyat* sign or token (of) + ALLAH]

Ay·de·lotte (ād′əl ot′), *n.* **Frank,** 1880–1956, U.S. educator.

aye[1] (ī), *adv.* **1.** yes. —*n.* **2.** an affirmative vote or voter, esp. in British Parliament, corresponding to yea in Congress. Also, **ay.** [earlier *I,* ME *yie,* alter. of *ye,* OE *gī* YEA]

aye[2] (ā), *adv.* ay[1].

aye-aye (ī′ī′), *n.* a nocturnal lemur, *Daubentonia madagascariensis,* of Madagascar, feeding on insects and fruit, and having rodentlike incisors and long fingers. [< F < Malagasy *aiay,* prob. imit. of its cry]

Aye-aye
(Total length 3 ft.; tail 22 in.)

Ayer (âr), *n.* **1. A(lfred) J(ules),** born 1910, English philosopher, teacher, and author. **2.** a town in N Massachusetts. 14,927 (1960).

A·ye·sha (ä′ē shä′), *n.* Aisha.

A.Y.H., American Youth Hostels.

a·yin (ä′yin; *Heb.* ä′yēn), *n.* **1.** the 16th letter of the Hebrew alphabet. **2.** the voiced pharyngeal constrictive consonant represented by this letter and cognate with Arabic 'ain. [< Heb]

Ayles·bur·y (ālz′bə rē, -brē), *n.* one of an English breed of white, domestic ducks. [named after *Aylesbury,* England]

Ay·ma·ra (ī′mä rä′), *n., pl.* **-ras,** (*esp. collectively*) **-ra** for 1. **1.** a member of an Indian people living in the mountainous regions around Lake Titicaca in Bolivia and Peru. **2.** the language of the Aymara people. [< Sp *armarā, aymarā,* of AmerInd orig.] —**Ay′ma·ran′,** *adj.*

Ay·mé (e mā′), *n.* **Mar·cel** (mar sel′), 1902–67, French novelist and short-story writer.

Ayn·tab (in tab′), *n.* Aintab.

a·yous (ā yōōs′), *n.* the wood of the obeche. [< F < an Afr. dial.]

Ayr (âr), *n.* **1.** a seaport in and the county seat of Ayrshire. 43,200 (est. 1956). **2.** Ayrshire (def. 2).

ayre (âr), *Music.* air[1] (def. 7d).

Ayr·shire (âr′shēr, -shər), *n.* **1.** one of a Scottish breed of hardy dairy cattle having long, curving horns. **2.** Also called **Ayr.** a county in SW Scotland. 342,855 (1961); 1132 sq. mi. *Co. seat:* Ayr.

ayr′ stone′, *n.* a fine-grained stone used for polishing marble and as a whetstone. Also called **snakestone.** [named after AYR]

A·yub Khan (ä yōōb′ kän′), **Mohammed,** 1907–74, Pakistani army officer and political leader: president 1958–69.

a·yun·ta·mien·to (ä yōōn′tä myen′tô), *n., pl.* **-tos** (-tôs). *Spanish.* **1.** a municipal government. **2.** a town hall or city hall.

A·yur·ve·da (ä′yər vā′ də), *n.* the ancient Hindu art of medicine and of prolonging life. [< Skt, equiv. to *āyur-* life, vital power + *veda* knowledge] —**A′yur·ve′dic,** *adj.*

A·yu·the·a (ä yōō′thē ä′, -thē ə; *Thai.* ä yōō′tē ä), *n.* a city in central Thailand, on the Menam: former national capital. 30,947 (est. 1957). Also, **A·yudh·ya** (ä yōōd′yä), **A·yut·tha·ya** (ä yōō′tä yä).

az-, var. of **azo-,** esp. before a vowel: *azine.*

a·zal·ea (ə zāl′yə), *n.* any ericaceous plant of a particular group (*Azalea*) of the genus *Rhododendron,* comprising species with handsome various colored flowers, some of which are familiar in cultivation. *Azalea* was once a botanical genus but is now a nursery or horticultural classification. [< NL < Gk *azaléa,* n. use of fem. of *azaléos* dry; so named as growing in dry soil]

a·zan (ä zän′), *n.* (in Islamic countries) the call to prayer proclaimed five times a day by the muezzin. [< Ar *adhān* invitation. See MUEZZIN]

A·zan (ā′zən), *n. Class. Myth.* a son of Arcas and the dryad Erato.

A·za·ña (ä thä′nyä), *n.* **Ma·nuel** (mä nwel′), (*Manuel Azaña y Díez*), 1880–1940, Spanish statesman: prime minister 1931–33, 1936; president 1936–39.

Az·a·ri·ah (az′ə rī′ə), *n.* Uzziah. II Kings 15:1–7.

A·za·zel (ə zā′zəl, az′ə zel′), *n.* **1.** the scapegoat released on the Day of Atonement, or its destination, hell. Lev. 16:8,10,21. **2.** *Islamic Myth.* the jinn who became Shaitan. **3.** one of the fallen angels. [< Heb]

a·zed·a·rach (ə zed′ə rak′), *n.* chinaberry (def. 1). [< F *azédarac* << Pers *āzād dirakht* noble tree]

A·ze·glio (ä ze′lyô), *n.* **Mas·si·mo Ta·pa·rel·li** (mäs′sē mô′ tä′pä rel′lē), **Marchese d',** 1798–1866, Italian statesman and author.

a·ze·o·trope (ə zē′ə trōp′), *n. Physical Chem.* any liquid mixture having constant minimum and maximum boiling points and distilling off without decomposition and in a fixed ratio, as isopropyl alcohol and water. [A-[6] + Gk *zé(ein)* (to) boil + -O- + -TROPE] —**a·ze·o·trop·ic** (ā′zē ə trop′ik), *adj.* —**a·ze·ot·ro·py** (ā′zē o′trə pē), **a′ze·ot′ro·pism,** *n.*

Az·er·bai·jan (ä′zər bī jän′, az′ər bī jan′; *Russ.* u zyir bī jän′), *n.* **1.** Also, **Az′er·bai·dzhan′.** Formerly, **Azerbaijan′ So′viet So′cialist Repub′lic.** a republic in Transcaucasia, N of Iran and W of the Caspian Sea. 7,029,000; 33,430 sq. mi. *Cap.:* Baku. **2.** a region of NW Iran, divided into two provinces in 1938: East Azerbaijan (4,114,084; *Cap.:* Tabriz) and West Azerbaijan (1,971,677; *Cap.:* Orumiyeh).

SOVIET UNION
Azerbaijan
BLACK SEA
CASPIAN SEA
Baku
TURKEY
IRAN

A·zer·bai·ja·ni (ä′zər bī jä′nē, az′ər bī jan′ē), *n., pl.* **-ja·nis,** (*esp. collectively*) **-ja·ni** *for 1, 2.* **1.** a native or inhabitant of Azerbaijan. **2.** a member of an Azerbaijani-speaking people of Azerbaijan and of the Iranian provinces of Azerbaijan. **3.** the Turkic language of the Azerbaijani, written with Cyrillic letters in Azerbaijan and with Arabic letters in Iran. Also, **A′zer·bai·ja′ni·an.** [AZERBAIJAN + *-i* suffix of membership]

az·ide (az′īd, -id, ā′zīd, ā′zid), *n. Chem.* any compound containing the azido group, as sodium azide, NaN_3.

az·i·do (az′i dō′), *adj. Chem.* containing the azido group. [AZIDE + -O-]

az′ido group′, *Chem.* the univalent group, N_3–, derived from hydrazoic acid. Also called **az′ido rad′ical.**

A·zi·ki·we (ä′zē kē′wā), *n.* **Nnam·di** (näm′dē), ("*Zik*"), born 1904, Nigerian statesman: president 1963–66.

A·zil·ian (ə zēl′yən, -ē ən, ə zil′-), *adj.* of, pertaining to, or characteristic of a Mesolithic culture of southern France. [named after Mas d'*Azil,* town in S France, where the culture flourished; see -IAN]

az·i·muth (az′ə məth), *n.* **1.** *Astron., Navig.* the arc of the horizon measured clockwise from the south point, in astronomy, or from the north point, in navigation, to the point where a vertical circle through a given heavenly body intersects the horizon. **2.** *Survey., Gunnery.* the angle of horizontal deviation, measured clockwise, of a bearing from a standard direction, as from north or south. [ME *azimut* < MF << Ar *as sumūt* the ways (i.e., directions)] —**az·i·muth·al** (az′ə muth′əl), *adj.* —**az′i·muth′al·ly,** *adv.*

azimuth′al equidis′tant projec′tion, *Cartog.* a projection in which the shortest distance between any point and a central point is a straight line, such a line representing a great circle through the central point.

azimuth′al quan′tum num′ber, *Physics.* the quantum number that designates the orbital angular momentum of a particular quantum state of an electron in an atom and that assumes integral values from zero to one less than the value of the principal quantum number. Also called **orbital quantum number.**

az′imuth bar′, a device used in measuring azimuths, consisting of a bar with a sighting vane at each end, pivoted at its center, and rotating in a horizontal plane around the center of a compass.

az′imuth cir′cle, a device for measuring azimuths, consisting of a graduated ring equipped with a sighting vane on each side, which fits concentrically over a compass.

az·ine (az′ēn, -in), *n.* *Chem.* any of a group of six-membered heterocyclic compounds containing one or more nitrogen atoms in the ring, the number of nitrogen atoms present being indicated by a prefix, as in diazine, triazine, etc. [AZ- + -INE²]

az′ine dye′, *Chem.* any of various dyes derived from phenazine, used chiefly for dyeing wood, leather, and textiles.

A·zle (ā′zəl), *n.* a town in central Texas. 2969 (1960).

az·lon (az′lon), *n.* *Chem.* any of the class of textile fibers derived from proteins as casein or zein. [AZ- + *-lon,* modeled on NYLON]

az·o (az′ō), *adj.* *Chem.* containing the azo group. [AZO(TE)]

azo-, **1.** a combining form meaning "containing nitrogen." **2.** a combining form of the azo group, used esp. before a consonant: *azomethane.* Also, *esp. before a vowel,* **az-.** [< Gk *ázō(os)* without life, equiv. to *a-* A-⁶ + *zō-* ZO-]

az·o·ben·zene (az′ō ben′zēn, -ben zēn′), *n.* *Chem.* an orange-red, crystalline, water-insoluble powder, $C_6H_5N{=}NC_6H_5$, obtained from nitrobenzene by reduction: used chiefly in the manufacture of dyes and as an insecticide. Also called **benzeneazobenzene.** [AZO- + BENZENE]

az′o dye′, *Chem.* any of a large class of dyes containing one or more azo groups.

A·zof (ä zôf′), *n.* Azov.

az′o group′, *Chem.* the bivalent group, –N=N–, united to two hydrocarbon groups, as in azobenzene, $C_6H_5{-}N{=}N{-}C_6H_5$. Also called **azo radical.**

a·zo·ic¹ (ə zō′ik, ā-), *adj.* *Geol. Obs.* noting or pertaining to the Precambrian era, esp. that part formerly believed to precede the first appearance of life; Archean. Cf. **Eozoic.** [< Gk *ázō(os)* lifeless (see AZO-) + -IC]

a·zo·ic² (a zō′ik), *adj.* of, pertaining to, or characteristic of the azo group. [AZO- + -IC]

azo′ic dye′ (a zō′ik), *Chem.* any of a group of water-insoluble azo dyes used chiefly for dyeing textiles.

az·o·im·ide (az′ō im′īd, -id), *n.* *Chem.* See **hydrazoic acid.** [AZO- + IMIDE]

az·ole (az′ōl, ə zōl′), *n.* *Chem.* any of a group of five-membered heterocyclic compounds containing one or more nitrogen atoms in the ring, the number of nitrogen atoms present being indicated by a prefix, as in diazole. [AZ- + -OLE]

a·zon·al (ā zōn′ᵊl), *adj.* not divided into zones. [A-⁶ + ZONAL]

az′on bomb′ (az′on), a half-ton aerial bomb fitted with radio equipment and a special tail assembly that enables the bombardier to alter the direction of its fall by remote control. [from phrase AZ(IMUTH) ON(LY)]

a·zon·ic (ā zon′ik), *adj.* not confined to any particular zone or region; not local. [< Gk *ázōn(os)* not restricted to a zone (*a-* A-⁶ + *zōn(ē)* belt + *-os* adj. suffix) + -IC]

az·o·phen·yl·ene (az′ō fen′ᵊlēn′, -fēn′-), *n.* *Chem.* phenazine. [AZO- + PHENYLENE]

A·zo·phi (ə zō′fē), *n.* a crater in the fourth quadrant of the face of the moon: about 25 miles in diameter.

az′o rad′ical. See **azo group.**

A·zores (ə zōrz′, ə zôrz′, ā′zōrz, ā′zôrz), *n.* a group of islands in the N Atlantic, W of Portugal: politically part of Portugal. 318,558 (1950); 890 sq. mi. —**A·zo·ri·an** (ə zōr′ē ən, -zôr′-), *adj., n.*

Azores′ high′, *Meteorol.* a subtropcial high centered near the Azores.

A·zo·rín (ä′thô rēn′), *n.* (*José Martínez Ruiz*), 1873–1967, Spanish novelist and critic.

az·ote (az′ōt, ə zōt′), *n.* *Chem.* nitrogen. [< F < Gk *ázōt(os)* ungirt, taken to mean lifeless] —**az·ot·ed** (az′ō tid, ə zō′tid), *adj.*

az·o·te·mi·a (az′ə tē′mē ə), *n.* *Pathol.* accumulation of abnormally large amounts of nitrogenous waste products in the blood, as in uremic poisoning. [AZOTE + -EMIA]

az·oth (az′oth), *n.* *Alchemy.* **1.** mercury, as the assumed first principle of all metals. **2.** the universal remedy of Paracelsus. [late ME *azot* << Ar *az zā'ūq* the quicksilver]

a·zot·ic (ə zot′ik), *adj.* of or pertaining to azote; nitric. [AZOTE + -IC]

az·o·tise (az′ə tīz′), *v.t.*, **-tised, -tis·ing.** *Chiefly Brit.* azotize.

az·o·tize (az′ə tīz′), *v.t.*, **-tized, -tiz·ing.** to nitrogenize. [AZOTE + -IZE]

a·zo·to·bac·ter (a zō′tə bak′tər, ə zō′-), *n.* *Bacteriol.* any of several rod-shaped or spherical, aerobic and heterotrophic bacteria of the genus *Azotobacter,* found as nonsymbiotic nitrogen fixers in the soil. [AZOTE + -O- + BACTER(IUM)]

A·zo·tos (ə zō′tos), *n.* Greek name of **Ashdod.**

A·zov (ä zôf′), *n.* **Sea of,** a bay of the Black Sea in the Soviet Union in Europe, connected with the Black Sea by Kerch Strait. ab. 14,500 sq. mi. Also, **Azof.** See map under **Black Sea.**

Az·ra·el (az′rē əl, -rā-), *n.* (in Jewish and Islamic angelology) the angel who separates the soul from the body at the moment of death.

AZT, *Trademark.* azidothymidine: an antiviral drug used in treating AIDS.

Az·tec (az′tek), *n.* **1.** a member of a Nahuatl people whose complex empire in central Mexico was conquered by Cortés in 1519. **2.** Also called **classical Nahuatl.** an extinct dialect of Nahuatl, formerly the medium of Aztec civilization, written in a chiefly pictographic script. Cf. **Nahuatl** (def. 2). **3.** the Nahuatl language. —**Az′tec·an,** *adj.*

Az′tec mar′igold. See **African marigold.**

A-Z test. See **Aschheim-Zondek test.**

A·zue·la (ä swā′lə; *Sp.* ä swe′lä), *n.* **Ma·ria·no** (mä ryä′nô), 1873–1952, Mexican physician and novelist.

a·zu·le·jo (*Sp.* ä′thōō le′hô; *Port.* ä′zōō le′zhōō), *n., pl.* **-jos** (*Sp.* -hôs; *Port.* -zhōōsh). (in Spanish-speaking and Portuguese-speaking countries) a glazed and painted tile used as a wainscot or facing. [< Sp: blue tile, deriv. of *azul* blue]

az·ure (azh′ər, ā′zhər), *adj.* **1.** of a sky-blue color. **2.** *Heraldry.* of the tincture or color blue. —*n.* **3.** the blue of a clear or unclouded sky. **4.** a light, purplish blue. **5.** *Heraldry.* the tincture or color blue. **6.** the clear, cloudless sky. [ME *asure* < ML *azura* < Ar *(l)azuward(d)* < Pers *lazhuward* lapis lazuli]

az·ur·ite (azh′ə rīt′), *n.* **1.** a blue mineral, a hydrous copper carbonate, $Cu_3(CO_3)_2(OH)_2$; an ore of copper. **2.** a gem of moderate value cut from this mineral. [AZURE + -ITE¹]

az·ur·mal·a·chite (azh′ər mal′ə kīt′), *n.* *Mineral.* a blue-green mixture of azurite and malachite. [AZUR(ITE) + MALACHITE]

A·zu·sa (ə zōō′zə), *n.* *Rocketry.* a missile tracking and guidance system that measures both position and velocity while the missile is in flight.

A·zu·sa (ə zōō′sə), *n.* a city in SW California, near Los Angeles. 20,497 (1960).

a·zy·go·spore (ā zī′gə spōr′, -spôr′), *n.* *Bot.* a reproductive cell formed without the fusion of gametes, as in certain algae and fungi. [AZYGO(US) + -SPORE]

az·y·gous (az′ə gəs), *adj.* *Zool., Bot.* not being one of a pair; single. [< Gk *ázygos,* equiv. to *a-* A-⁶ + *zygós,* deriv. of *zygón* YOKE]

az·yme (az′īm), *n.* *Western Ch.* unleavened bread used in a Eucharistic service. [< LL *azyma* (n.), L *azym(us)* (adj.) unleavened < Gk *ázȳm(os),* equiv. to *a-* A-⁶ + *-zȳmos* (deriv. of *zȳmē* leaven; see ZYME)]

B

B, b (bē), *n., pl.* **B's** or **Bs, b's** or **bs.** **1.** the second letter of the English alphabet, a consonant. **2.** any spoken sound represented by the letter *B* or *b*, as in *bid, bauble, daubed*, etc. **3.** something having the shape of a B. **4.** a written or printed representation of the letter *B* or *b*. **5.** a device, as a printer's type, for reproducing the letter *B* or *b*.

B, **1.** *Chess.* bishop. **2.** black.

B, **1.** the second in order or in a series. **2.** (*sometimes l.c.*) (in some grading systems) a grade or mark, as in school or college, indicating the quality of a student's work as good or better than average. **3.** (*sometimes l.c.*) (in some school systems) a symbol designating the second semester of a school year. **4.** a major blood group or type usually enabling a person whose blood is of this group to donate blood to persons of group B or AB and to receive blood from persons of group O or B. **5.** *Music.* **a.** the seventh tone in the scale of C major or the second tone in the relative minor scale, A minor. **b.** a string, key, or pipe tuned to this tone. **c.** a written or printed note representing this tone. **d.** (in the fixed system of solmization) the seventh tone of the scale of C major, called *ti*. **e.** the tonality having B as the tonic note. **6.** (*sometimes l.c.*) the medieval Roman numeral for 300. Cf. **Roman numerals. 7.** *Chem.* boron. **8.** a proportional shoe width size, narrower than C and wider than A. **9.** a proportional brassiere cup size, smaller than C and larger than A. **10.** (in men's pajama sizes) medium. **11.** *Physics.* See **magnetic induction. 12.** (*sometimes l.c.*) *Elect.* susceptance. **13.** a grade for a mediocre motion picture.

b, **1.** bar; bars. **2.** barn; barns. **3.** black.

B., **1.** bass. **2.** basso. **3.** bay. **4.** Bible. **5.** bolivar. **6.** boliviano. **7.** book. **8.** born. **9.** breadth. **10.** British. **11.** brother. **12.** Brotherhood.

b., **1.** *Baseball.* base; baseman. **2.** bass. **3.** basso. **4.** bay. **5.** blend of; blended. **6.** book. **7.** born. **8.** breadth. **9.** brother. **10.** brotherhood.

B-, *U.S. Mil.* (in designations of aircraft) bomber: *B-29.*

B-1 (bē′wun′), *n., pl.* **B-1s.** **a long-range U.S. bomber, with sweptback wings and a subsonic cruising speed.**

ba (bä), *n. Egyptian Religion.* an aspect of the soul, represented as a human-headed bird. [Egypt]

bā (bä), *n.* the second letter of the Arabic alphabet.

Ba, *Chem.* barium.

B.A., **1.** Bachelor of Arts. [< L *Baccalaureus Artium*] **2.** bastard amber. **3.** British America.

baa (ba, bä), *v.,* **baaed, baa·ing,** *n.* —*v.i.* **1.** to cry as a sheep; bleat. —*n.* **2.** the bleating cry of a sheep. [imit.]

B.A.A., Bachelor of Applied Arts.

baal (bäl), *adv. Australian Slang.* no; not. [< native Austral]

Ba·al (bā′əl, bāl), *n., pl.* **Ba·al·im** (bā′ə lim, bā′lim). **1.** any of numerous local deities among the ancient Semitic peoples, typifying the productive forces of nature and worshiped with much sensuality. **2.** (*sometimes l.c.*) a false god. [< Heb *ba'al* lord]

Baal·bek (bäl′bek, bā′əl-, bäl′-), *n.* a town in E Lebanon: ruins of ancient city; Temple of the Sun. 11,000 (est. 1965). Ancient Greek name, **Heliopolis.**

Ba·al·ish (bā′ə lish, bā′lish), *adj.* **1.** like or pertaining to Baal. **2.** idolatrous. [BAAL + -ISH[1]]

Ba·al·ism (bā′ə liz′əm, bā′liz əm), *n.* **1.** the worship of Baal. **2.** idolatry. [BAAL + -ISM] —**Ba′al·ist, Ba·al·ite** (bā′ə līt′, bā′līt), *n.* —**Ba′al·is′tic, Ba·al·it·i·cal** (bā′ə lit′i kəl, bā lit′-), *adj.*

baal ko·re (bäl kō′rā), *Hebrew.* an official in the synagogue, as a cantor, who reads the weekly portion of the Torah. [lit., reading master]

Ba′al Mer′o·dach (mer′ə dāk′), Marduk.

Baal·shem (bäl shem′, -shäm′), *n. Hebrew.* one who works miracles by calling upon the name of God, esp. one among the German and Polish Jews of the 16th–19th centuries considered to be saintly and to possess magical powers. Also, **Balshem.** [lit., master of the name]

Baal Shem-Tov (bäl′ shem′tōv′, shäm′-), (*Israel ben Eliezer*) ("*BEShT*"), c1700–60, Ukrainian teacher and religious leader: founder of the Hasidic movement of Judaism in Poland. Also, **Baal Shem-Tob** (bäl′ shem′tōb′, shäm′-).

Bab (bäb), *n.* abbreviated form of Bab ed-Din.

Bab., Babylon; Babylonia.

ba·ba (bä′bə; *Fr.* bᴀ bᴀ′), *n., pl.* **-bas** (-bəz; *Fr.* -bᴀ′). a spongelike cake leavened with yeast and often containing raisins, baked in a small mold and usually soaked with a rum syrup. [< F < Pol: kind of cake; lit., old woman]

ba·ba au rhum (bä′bə ō rum′; *Fr.* bᴀ bᴀ ō rôm′), *pl.* **ba·bas au rhum** (bä′bəz ō rum′; *Fr.* bᴀ bᴀ ō rôm′). baba.

Ba·bar (bä′bər), *n.* Baber.

ba·bas·su (bä′bə so͞o′), *n.* a palm, *Orbignya Martiana*, of northeastern Brazil, bearing nuts that yield babassu oil. [< Pg *babaçú* < native Brazilian name]

babassu′ oil′, a yellow oil expressed or extracted from babassu nuts, used chiefly in the manufacture of soaps and cosmetics and as a cooking oil.

Bab·bage (bab′ij), *n.* an elliptical, walled plain in the second quadrant of the face of the moon: about 120 miles long and 80 miles wide.

Bab·bit·ry (bab′i trē), *n.* (*often l.c.*) Babbittry.

bab·bitt (bab′it), *n.* **1.** See **Babbitt metal. 2.** a bearing or lining of Babbitt metal. —*adj.* **3.** pertaining to or made of Babbitt metal. —*v.t.* **4.** to line, face, or furnish with Babbitt metal. [short for BABBITT METAL]

Bab·bitt (bab′it), *n.* **1. Irving,** 1865–1933, U.S. educator and critic. **2.** (*italics*) a novel (1922) by Sinclair Lewis. **3.** (*often l.c.*) a self-satisfied person who conforms readily to conventional, middle-class ideas and ideals, esp. of business and material success: from the main character in the novel. **4.** a town in NE Minnesota. 2587 (1960).

Bab′bitt met′al, *Metall.* **1.** any of various alloys of tin with smaller amounts of antimony and copper, used as an antifriction lining for bearings. **2.** any of various similar alloys. Also, **bab′bitt met′al, bab′bitt.** [named after Isaac *Babbitt* (1799–1862), American inventor]

Bab·bitt·ry (bab′i trē), *n.* (*often l.c.*) the attitude and behavior of a Babbitt. Also, **Babbitry.** [BABBITT + -RY]

bab·ble (bab′əl), *v.,* **-bled, -bling,** *n.* —*v.i.* **1.** to utter sounds or words imperfectly or indistinctly. **2.** to talk idly, irrationally, excessively, or foolishly; chatter or prattle. **3.** to make a continuous, murmuring sound. —*v.t.* **4.** to utter in an incoherent, foolish, or meaningless fashion. **5.** to reveal foolishly or thoughtlessly: *to babble a secret.* —*n.* **6.** inarticulate or imperfect speech. **7.** foolish, meaningless, or incoherent speech; prattle. **8.** a murmuring sound or a confusion of sounds. **9.** babbling (def. 2). **10.** a confused mixture of extraneous sounds in a telephone circuit, resulting from cross talk from other channels. Cf. **cross talk** (def. 1). [ME *babele(n)*; c. Icel *babbla*, D *babbelen*, G *pappelen*]

bab·ble·ment (bab′əl mənt), *n.* babble (defs. 6–8). [BABBLE + -MENT]

bab·bler (bab′lər), *n.* **1.** one who or that which babbles. **2.** any of the birds of the family *Timaliidae*, many of which have a loud, babbling cry. [BABBLE + -ER[1]]

bab·bling (bab′ling), *n.* **1.** foolish or meaningless chatter; prattle: *the constant babbling of idle gossips.* **2.** the random production of meaningless vocal sounds characteristic of infants from about the sixth week. —*adj.* **3.** chattering or prattling aimlessly. [ME; see BABBLE, -ING[1], -ING[2]] —**bab′bling·ly,** *adv.*

babe (bāb), *n.* **1.** a baby or child. **2.** an innocent or inexperienced person. **3.** *Slang.* **a.** a girl or woman, esp. an attractive one. **b.** a term of familiar address to a woman. **4. babe in the woods,** an innocent, unsuspecting person, esp. one likely to be victimized by others: *Some people who are otherwise shrewd are mere babes in the woods where the stock market is concerned.* Also, **babe in the wood.** [ME; early ME *baban*, prob. nursery word in origin]

Babe (bāb), *n.* a girl's or boy's given name.

Bab ed-Din (bäb′ ed dēn′), (*the Bab, Ali Muhammad of Shiraz*), 1819–50, a Persian religious leader: founder of Babism. [< Pers: lit., gate of the faith]

Ba·bel (bā′bəl, bab′əl), *n.* **1.** an ancient city in the land of Shinar in which the building of a tower **(Tower of Babel)** intended to reach heaven was begun and the confusion of the language of the people took place. Gen. 11:4–9. **2.** (*usually l.c.*) a confused mixture of sounds or voices. **3.** (*usually l.c.*) a scene of noise and confusion. [< Heb *Bābel* Babylon] —**Ba·bel·ic** (bā bel′ik, ba-), *adj.*

Ba·bel (bab′əl; *Russ.* bä′bel), *n.* **I·saak Em·ma·nu·i·lo·vich** (ī′zək; *Russ.* i säk′ i mä no͞o ē′lo vich), 1894–1941, Russian author.

Ba·bel·ise (bā′bə līz′, bab′ə-), *v.t.,* **-ised, -is·ing.** (*sometimes l.c.*) *Chiefly Brit.* Babelize. —**Ba′bel·i·sa′tion,** *n.*

Ba·bel·ism (bā′bə liz′əm, bab′ə-), *n.* (*sometimes l.c.*) a confusion, as of ideas, speech, etc. [BABEL + -ISM]

Ba·bel·ize (bā′bə līz′, bab′ə-), *v.t.,* **-ized, -iz·ing.** (*sometimes l.c.*) to make a confusion of (customs, languages, usages, etc.); cause to be mixed or unintelligible; confound. [BABEL + -IZE] —**Ba′bel·i·za′tion,** *n.*

Ba·bel·ized (bā′bə līzd′, bab′ə-), *adj.* (*sometimes l.c.*) reduced to confusion. [BABELIZE + -ED[2]]

Bab el Man·deb (bäb′ el män′deb), a strait between E Africa and SW Arabia, connecting the Red Sea and the Gulf of Aden. 20 mi. wide.

Ba·ber (bä′bər), *n.* (*Zahir ed-Din Mohammed*) 1483–1530, founder of the Mogul Empire. Also, **Babar, Babur.**

ba·be·sia (bə bē′zhə, -zhē ə, -zē ə), *n.* any protozoan of the genus *Babesia*, certain species of which are parasitic and pathogenic for warm-blooded animals. [< NL, named after Victor *Babeş* (1854–1926), Rumanian bacteriologist; see -IA]

ba·be·si·o·sis (bə bē′zē ō′sis), *n. Vet. Pathol.* a disease of cattle, dogs, horses, sheep, and swine, caused by the babesia organism and characterized by fever and languor. Also, **bab·e·si·a·sis** (bab′i sī′ə sis, -zī′-, bā′bə-). Also called **piroplasmosis.** [< NL; see BABESIA, -OSIS]

Ba·bette (ba bet′), *n.* a girl's given name, form of **Barbara.** Also, **Barbette.**

Ba·beuf (bᴀ bœf′), *n.* **Fran·çois No·ël** (fräɴ swᴀ′ nō-el′), (*Gracchus Babeuf*), 1760–97, French revolutionary.

Ba·bi (bä′bē), *n.* **1.** Babism. **2.** a Babist.

ba·biche (bə bēsh′), *n.* (in the Pacific Northwest) thong, thread, or lacings made of rawhide, gut, or sinew, esp. for making snowshoes. [< CanF < Algonquian]

ba·bies′-breath (bā′bēz breth′), *n.* **1.** Also called **gypsum pink.** a tall herb, *Gypsophila paniculata*, of the pink family, having numerous small, fragrant, white or pink flowers. **2.** any of certain other plants, as the grape hyacinth. Also, **baby's-breath.** [so called from its delicate odor and bloom]

Ba·bin′ski's re′flex (bə bin′skēz), a reflex extension of the great toe with flexion of the other toes, normal in children up to one year of age, evoked by stroking the sole of the foot. Its occurrence in older individuals usually denotes brain injury or disease. Also, **Babin′ski re′flex.** Also called **Babin′ski's sign′, Babin′ski sign′.** Cf. **plantar reflex.** [named after J. F. F. *Babinski* (d. 1932), French neurologist]

Babirusa
(2½ ft. high at shoulder; length 3½ ft.)

bab·i·ru·sa (bab′ə ro͞o′sə, bä′bə-), *n.* an East Indian swine, *Babirussa babyrussa*, the male of which has upper canine teeth growing upward through the roof of the mouth and curving toward the eyes, and lower canine teeth growing upward outside the upper jaw. Also, **bab′i·rous′sa, bab′i·rus′sa.** [< Malay *bābi* hog + *rūsa* deer]

CONCISE ETYMOLOGY KEY: <, descended or derived from; >, whence; b., blend of, blended; c., cognate with; deriv., derivative; equiv., equivalent; imit., imitative; m., modification of; obl., oblique; r., replacing; s., stem; sp., spelling; trans., translation; ?, origin unknown, perhaps; *, hypothetical. See the full key inside the front cover.

Bab·ism (bä′biz əm), *n.* an eclectic Persian religion, originated in the 19th century, now supplanted by Bahaism. Also called **Babi.** [BAB + -ISM] —**Bab′ist,** *n., adj.* —**Bab′ite,** *adj.*

bab·ka (bäb′kə), *n.* a sweet, spongy yeast cake with raisins, traditionally made in the form of a high cylinder, either solid or with a hole, often glazed with raspberry-flavored coating, and sometimes flavored with rum. [< Pol, dim. of *baba* BABA]

ba·boo (bä′bo͞o), *n., pl.* **-boos.** babu.

ba·boon (ba bo͞on′ *or, esp. Brit.,* bə-), *n.* **1.** any of various large, terrestrial monkeys of the genus *Papio* and related genera, of Africa and Arabia, having a doglike muzzle, large cheek pouches, and a short tail. **2.** a coarse or brutish person, esp. one of low intelligence. [ME *babewyn* gargoyle, late ME: baboon (equiv. to AL *babevynus*) < MF *babouin* baboon, simpleton] —**ba·boon′ish,** *adj.*

ba·boon·er·y (ba bo͞o′nə rē *or, esp. Brit.,* bə-), *n.* an uncouth, ridiculous, or brutish condition, attitude, or action. [late ME *babwynrie* < *bab(e)wyn* BABOON + *-rie* -ERY]

bab·ra·cot (bab′rə kot′), *n.* a wooden grating used by Indians in South America for roasting and drying food. [? < SAmerInd name]

Babs (babz), *n.* a girl's given name, form of **Barbara.**

Bab·son (bab′sən), *n.* **Roger Ward,** 1875–1967, U.S. statistician and businessman.

ba·bu (bä′bo͞o), *n.* **1.** a Hindu title of address equivalent to Sir, Mr., or Esquire. **2.** a Hindu gentleman. **3.** a native Indian clerk who writes English. **4.** *Usually Disparaging.* any native Indian having a limited knowledge of English. Also, **baboo.** [< Hindi *bābū* father]

ba·bul (bä bo͞ol′, bä′bo͞ol), *n.* **1.** any of several mimosaceous trees of the genus *Acacia* which yield a gum, esp. *A. arabica* of India. **2.** the gum, pods, or bark of such a tree. [< Hindi *babūl* < Pers]

Ba·bur (bä′bər), *n.* Baber.

ba·bush·ka (bə bo͞osh′kə, -bo͞osh′-), *n.* a woman's scarf, often triangular, used as a hood with the ends tied under the chin. [< Russ: grandmother, equiv. to *bab(a)* old woman + *-ushka* dim. suffix]

Ba·bush·kin (bä′bo͞osh kin), *n.* a city in the W RSFSR, in Europe, near Moscow. 112,000 (1959).

Ba·bu·yan′ Is′lands (bä′bo͞o yän′), a group of islands in the Philippines, N of Luzon. 225 sq. mi.

ba·by (bā′bē), *n., pl.* **-bies,** *adj., v.,* **-bied, -by·ing.** —*n.* **1.** an infant; very young child. **2.** a newborn or very young animal. **3.** the youngest member of a family, group, etc. **4.** an immature or childish person. **5.** *Slang.* **a.** a girl or woman, esp. an attractive one. **b.** a girl or woman of whom one is fond; sweetheart. **c.** a man or boy; chap; fellow: *He's a tough baby to have to deal with.* **6.** *Slang.* **a.** an invention, creation, project, etc., that requires special attention or of which one is especially proud. **b.** an object; thing: *Is that car there your baby?* —*adj.* **7.** of or suitable for a baby: *baby carriage.* **8.** of or like a baby; infantile: *baby face.* **9.** *Informal.* small; comparatively little: *a baby car.* —*v.t.* **10.** to treat like a young child; pamper. **11.** to handle or use with special care; treat gently. [ME; see BABE, -Y[2]] —**ba′by·hood′,** *n.* —**ba′by·ish,** *adj.* —**ba′by·ish·ly,** *adv.* —**ba′by·ish·ness,** *n.* —**ba′by·like′,** *adj.*

ba′by beef′, **1.** a young beef animal that has been fattened to be marketed when 12 to 20 months old. **2.** the meat of a baby beef.

ba·by-blue-eyes (bā′bē blo͞o′īz′), *n., pl.* **-eyes.** (*construed as sing. or pl.*) **1.** a plant, *Nemophila insignis,* of the Pacific coast of the U.S., with spotted blue blossoms. **2.** a similar plant, *Nemophila phaceloides,* common in Oklahoma. **3.** a plant, *N. menziesi atomaria,* of the western U.S. [so called from fancied resemblance of its spots to eyes]

ba′by bond′, a bond with a face value of $100 or less.

ba′by boom′, a sudden increase in the birthrate, esp. in the years immediately following WWII. —**ba′by boom′er.**

ba′by car′riage, a small, four-wheeled carriage for a baby. Also called **ba′by bug′gy.**

ba′by face′, **1.** a face having a bland babyish or childish appearance, esp. a plump, small-featured face unmarked by characteristic lines. **2.** a person having such a face. —**ba′by-faced′,** *adj.*

ba′by farm′, *Usually Disparaging.* a place which houses and takes care of babies for a fee. —**ba′by farm′er.** —**ba′by farm′ing.**

ba′by grand′, the smallest form of the grand piano.

Bab·y·lon (bab′ə lən, -lon′), *n.* **1.** an ancient city of SW Asia, on the Euphrates River, famed for its magnificence and culture: the capital of Babylonia and later of the Chaldean empire. **2.** any rich and magnificent city which is believed to be a place of excessive luxury and wickedness. **3.** a city on S Long Island, in SE New York. 11,062 (1960).

Bab·y·lo·ni·a (bab′ə lō′nē ə), *n.* an ancient empire in SW Asia, in the lower Euphrates valley: its greatest period was 2800–1750 B.C. *Cap.:* Babylon.

Bab·y·lo·ni·an (bab′ə lō′nē ən), *adj.* Also, **Babylonish. 1.** of or pertaining to Babylon or Babylonia. **2.** excessively luxurious; wicked; sinful. —*n.* **3.** an inhabitant of ancient Babylonia. **4.** the dialect of Akkadian spoken in Babylonia. Cf. **Akkadian** (def. 1). [BABYLONI(A) + -AN]

Babylo′nian captiv′ity, **1.** the period of the exile of the Jews in Babylonia, 597–538 B.C. **2.** the exile of the popes at Avignon, 1309–77.

Bab·y·lon·ish (bab′ə lon′ish, -lō′nish, bab′ə lō′nish, bab′ə lə nish), *adj.* **1.** Babylonian. **2.** *Obs.* confused in expression; garbled. [BABYLON(IA) + -ISH[1]]

ba′by prim′rose, a tender, perennial herb, *Primula forbesi,* of China and Burma, having white, hairy leaves and rose- and lilac-colored flowers.

ba·by's-breath (bā′bēz breth′), *n.* babies'-breath.

ba·by-sit (bā′bē sit′), *v.i.,* **-sat, -sit·ting.** to take charge of a child or of children while the parents are temporarily away. —**ba′by-sit′ter,** *n.*

ba′by split′, *Bowling Slang.* a split in which the two and seven pins or the three and ten pins remain standing.

ba′by spot′, a small spotlight for illuminating a restricted area from a short distance. Also called **ba′by spot′light.**

ba·by's-slip·pers (bā′bēz slip′ərz), *n., pl.* **-slippers.** (*construed as sing. or pl.*) See **bird's-foot trefoil.**

ba′by step′, (in the game of giant steps) the shortest step permitted a player, executed by placing the heel of one foot against the toe of the other and drawing the back foot up to the front foot. Cf. **umbrella step.**

ba′by talk′, **1.** the speech of children learning to talk, sometimes marked by syntactic distortion and by phonetic modifications like lisping, lalling, omission and substitution of sounds, etc. **2.** a style of speech used by adults in addressing children, pets, or sweethearts, and formed in imitation of the voice and pronunciation of children learning to talk: it is generally characterized in English by the addition of diminutive endings to words, the use of pet names, the systematic distortion of certain words, as *oo* for *you, lickle* for *little,* etc.

ba·by-tears (bā′bē tērz′), *n., pl.* **-tears.** (*construed as sing. or pl.*) a mosslike, urticaceous plant, *Helxine soleiroli,* of Corsica and Sardinia.

ba′by tooth′. See **milk tooth.**

Ba·car·di (bə kär′dē), *n.* **1.** *Trademark.* a dry type of rum of the West Indies. **2.** a cocktail made with Bacardi rum, grenadine, sugar, and lime juice.

Ba·că·u (bə kœ′o͞o), *n.* a city in E Rumania. 65,030 (est. 1964).

B.Acc., Bachelor of Accountancy.

bac·ca (bak′ə), *n., pl.* **bac·cae** (bak′ē). *Bot.* a berry. [< L *bacca, bāca* olive, any round fruit, berry]

bac·ca·lau·re·ate (bak′ə lôr′ē it), *n.* **1.** See **bachelor's degree. 2.** a religious service held at an educational institution, usually on the Sunday before commencement day. **3.** See **baccalaureate sermon.** [< ML *baccalaureāt(us),* equiv. to *baccalaure(us)* advanced student, bachelor (for *baccalārius* (see BACHELOR), alter. by assoc. with L phrase *bacca laureus* laurel berry) + *-ātus* -ATE[1]]

baccalau′reate ser′mon, a farewell sermon addressed to a graduating class in some U.S. colleges and schools.

bac·ca·rat (bä′kə rä′, bak′ə-; bä′kə rä′, bak′ə-; *Fr.* BA KA RA′), *n.* a gambling game at cards played by a banker and two or more punters who bet against him. Also, **bac′ca·ra′.** [var. of *baccara* < F < ?]

bac·cate (bak′āt), *adj. Bot.* **1.** berrylike. **2.** bearing berries. [< L *bāca, bacca,* berry + -ATE[1]]

Bac·chae (bak′ē), *n.pl. Class. Myth.* **1.** the female attendants of Bacchus. **2.** the priestesses of Bacchus. **3.** the women who took part in the Bacchanalia. [< L < Gk *Bákkhai,* pl. of *Bákkhē* maenad]

Bacchae, The, a tragedy (c407 B.C.) by Euripides.

bac·cha·nal (bä′kə näl′, bak′ə nal′, bak′ə nᵊl), *n.* **1.** a follower of Bacchus. **2.** a drunken reveler. **3.** an occasion of drunken revelry; orgy; bacchanalia. —*adj.* **4.** pertaining to Bacchus; bacchanalian. [< L *Bacchānāl(is),* equiv. to *Bacch(us)* + *-ānālis;* see BACCHANALIA]

Bac·cha·na·li·a (bak′ə nā′lē ə, -nāl′yə), *n., pl.* **-li·a, -li·as. 1.** (*sometimes construed as pl.*) a festival in honor of Bacchus. Cf. **Dionysia. 2.** (*l.c.*) a drunken feast; orgy. [< L, equiv. to *Bacch(us)* + *-ān(us)* -AN + *-ālia,* neut. pl. of *-ālis* -AL[1]; prob. modeled on *volcānālia.* See SATURNALIA] —**bac′cha·na′li·an,** *adj.* —**bac′cha·na′li·an·ism,** *n.*

bac·chant (bak′ənt), *n., pl.* **bac·chants, bac·chan·tes** (bə kan′tēz), *adj.* —*n.* **1.** a priest, priestess, or votary of Bacchus; bacchanal. **2.** a drunken reveler. —*adj.* **3.** worshiping Bacchus. **4.** liking alcoholic beverages. [< L *bacchant-* (s. of *bacchāns,* prp. of *bacchārī* to revel). See BACCHUS, -ANT] —**bac·chan·tic** (bə kan′tik), *adj.*

bac·chan·te (bə kan′tē, bə kant′, bak′ənt), *n.* a female bacchant. Also called **maenad, menad, Thyiad.** [back formation from L *bacchante(s),* fem. pl. of *bacchāns* BACCHANT; var. with silent *-e* < F *bacchante,* fem. of *bacchant* bacchant]

Bac·chel·li (bäk kel′lē), *n.* **Ric·car·do** (rēk kär′dô), born 1891, Italian novelist.

Bac·chic (bak′ik), *adj.* **1.** of, pertaining to, or honoring Bacchus. **2.** (*l.c.*) riotously or jovially intoxicated; drunken. [< L *Bacchic(us)* < Gk *Bakkhikós.* See BACCHUS, -IC]

bac·chi·us (bə kī′əs, ba-), *n., pl.* **-chi·i** (-kī′ī). *Pros.* a foot of three syllables that in quantitative meter consists of one short syllable followed by two long ones, and that in accentual meter consists of one unstressed syllable followed by two stressed ones. Cf. **antibacchius.** [< L < Gk *Bakkheios* (*poús*) (foot) of BACCHUS]

Bac·chus (bak′əs), *n. Class. Myth.* the god of wine; Dionysus. [< L < Gk *Bákkhos;* akin to L *bacca* berry. See BAY[4]] —**Bac′chus·like′,** *adj.*

Bac·chyl·i·des (bə kil′i dēz′), *n.* fl. 5th century B.C., Greek poet.

bacci-, a learned borrowing from Latin meaning "berry," used in the formation of compound words: *baccivorous.* [< L, comb. form of *bacca, bāca*]

bac·cif·er·ous (bak sif′ər əs), *adj. Bot.* bearing or producing berries. [< L *baccifer* (see BACCI-, -FER) + -OUS]

bac·ci·form (bak′sə fôrm′), *adj. Bot.* berry-shaped. [BACCI- + -FORM]

bac·cil·lum (bäk kil′lo͞om; *Eng.* bə sil′əm), *n., pl.* **-la** (-lä; *Eng.* -lə). *Latin.* a bougie.

bac·civ·or·ous (bak siv′ər əs), *adj.* feeding on berries. [BACCI- + -VOROUS]

bac·cy (bak′ē), *n., pl.* **-cies.** *Slang.* tobacco. [by aphesis and alter.]

bach (bach), *Informal.* —*v.i.* **1. bach it,** to keep house alone, as a man does whose wife is away. —*n.* **2.** a bachelor. [by apocope]

Bach (bäkh), *n.* **1. Jo·hann Se·bas·ti·an** (yō′hän si bas′chən; *Ger.* yō′hän zä bäs′tē än′), 1685–1750, German organist and composer. **2.** his sons: **Johann Chris·ti·an** (kris′chən; *Ger.* kris′tē än′), 1735–82; **Johann Chris·toph Frie·drich** (kris′tof frē′drik; *Ger.* kris′tôf frē′drikh), 1732–95; **Carl Philipp E·ma·nu·el** (kärl fil′ip i man′yo͞o əl′; *Ger.* kärl fē′lip ā mä′no͞o el′), 1714–88; and **Wil·helm Frie·de·mann** (wil′helm frē′də män′; *Ger.* vil′helm frē′də män′), 1710–84, German organists and composers.

Bach·el·ler (bach′ə lər), *n.* **Irving Addison,** 1859–1950, U.S. novelist and editor.

bach·e·lor (bach′ə lər, bach′lər), *n.* **1.** an unmarried man. **2.** a person who has been awarded a bachelor's degree. **3.** Also called **bachelor-at-arms.** a young knight who followed the banner of another. **4.** a young male fur seal kept from the breeding grounds by the older males. [ME *bacheler* < OF < VL **baccalār(is)* farm hand; akin to LL *baccalāria* piece of land, orig. pl. of **baccalārium* dairy farm, equiv. to **baccāl(is)* of cows (*bacca,* var. of L *vacca* cow + *-ālis* -AL[1]) + *-ārium* place] —**bach′e·lor·dom,** *n.* —**bach′e·lor·hood′,** *n.* —**bach′e·lor·like′,** *adj.* —**bach′e·lor·ly,** *adj.*

bach·e·lor-at-arms (bach′ə lər ət ärmz′, bach′lər-), *n., pl.* **bach·e·lors-at-arms.** bachelor (def. 3).

bach′elor chest′, *Eng. Furniture.* a low chest of drawers of the 18th century, having a top inclining to form a writing surface.

bach′elor girl′, *Informal.* an unmarried girl who lives alone and supports herself.

bach·e·lor·ism (bach′ə lə riz′əm, bach′lə-), *n.* **1.** state of being a bachelor. **2.** a characteristic or peculiarity of a bachelor: *Crustiness had been added to his bachelorisms.* [BACHELOR + -ISM]

Bach′elor of Arts′, **1.** a bachelor's degree in the liberal arts, usually awarded for studies in the social sciences or humanities. **2.** a person having this degree. *Abbr.:* A.B., B.A.

Bach′elor of Sci′ence, **1.** a bachelor's degree, usually awarded for studies in natural science, pure science, or technology. **2.** a person having this degree. *Abbr.:* B.S., B.Sc., S.B., Sc.B.

bach′elor par′ty. See **stag party** (def. 2).

bach·e·lor's (bach′ə lərz, bach′lərz), *n. Informal.* See **bachelor's degree.**

bach·e·lor's-but·ton (bach′ə lərz but′ᵊn, bach′lərz-), *n.* any of various plants with round flower heads, esp. the cornflower, or double-flowered varieties of ranunculus.

bach′elor's degree′, a degree awarded by a college or university to a person who has completed his undergraduate studies. Also called **baccalaureate.**

Bach′ trum′pet, a three-valved trumpet designed especially for playing the high, florid trumpet parts in the works of J. S. Bach and other baroque composers. Cf. **clarino.**

bacill-, a combining form of **bacillus:** *bacillary.*

bac·il·lar·y (bas′ə ler′ē), *adj.* **1.** Also called **ba·cil·li·form** (bə sil′ə fôrm′). of or like a bacillus; rod-shaped. **2.** *Bacteriol.* characterized by bacilli. Also, **ba·cil·lar** (bə sil′ər, bas′ə lər). [BACILL- + -ARY]

bac·il·le·mi·a (bas′ə lē′mē ə), *n. Pathol.* the presence of bacilli in the blood. [BACILL- + -EMIA]

ba·cil·lus (bə sil′əs), *n., pl.* **-cil·li** (-sil′ī). **1.** any of several rod-shaped, aerobic bacteria of the genus *Bacillus,* which produce spores. **2.** any rod-shaped or cylindrical bacterium. **3.** any bacterium. [< LL < L *bacillum* (lictor's) wand < *bac(ulum)* walking-stick + *-illum* dim. suffix]

bacil′lus Cal·mette′-Gué·rin′ (kal met′gā ran′, -ran′), a weakened strain of the tubercle bacillus, *Mycobacterium tuberculosis,* used in the preparation of BCG vaccine. [named after Albert L.C. *Calmette* (1863–1933) and Camille *Guérin* (b. 1872), French bacteriologists]

Ba·cis (bā′sis), *n. Class. Myth.* a Boeotian prophet.

bac·i·tra·cin (bas′i trā′sin), *n. Pharm.* an antibiotic polypeptide derived by the hydrolytic action of *Bacillus subtilis* on protein, used chiefly in the treatment of infections caused by gonococci, meningococci, and Gram-positive bacteria. [BACI(LLUS) + (Margaret) *Trac(y)* (b. 1936), American child whose tissues were found to contain *Bacillus subtilis,* + -IN[2]]

back[1] (bak), *n.* **1.** the rear part of the human body, extending from the neck to the end of the spine. **2.** the part of the body of animals corresponding to the human back. **3.** the rear portion of any part of the body: *the back of the head.* **4.** the whole body, with reference to clothing: *the clothes on his back.* **5.** the part opposite to or farthest from the front; the rear part: *the back of a hall.* **6.** the part which forms the rear of any object or structure: *the back of a chair.* **7.** the part which covers the back: *the back of a coat; the back of a jacket.* **8.** the spine or backbone: *to break his back.* **9.** any rear part of an object serving to support, protect, etc.: *the back of a binder.* **10.** *Naut., Aeron.* the forward side of a propeller blade (opposed to *face*). **11.** the edge of a book formed where its sections are bound together. **12. the backs,** grounds along the River Cam in back of certain colleges at Cambridge University in England: noted for their great beauty. **13.** *Aeron.* the top part or upper surface of an aircraft, esp. of its fuselage. **14.** extrados. **15.** *Carpentry.* **a.** the upper side of a joist, rafter, handrail, etc. **b.** the area of interior wall between a window stool and the floor. **16.** *Mining.* the roof of a stope or drift. **17.** capacity for responsibility, effort, etc. **18.** *Sports.* **a.** a player whose regular position is behind that of players who make initial contact with the opposing team, as behind the forward line in football or nearest his own goal in polo. **b.** the position occupied by this player. **19. behind one's back,** in one's absence; treacherously; secretly: *She's sure to talk about you behind your back.* **20. be (flat, thrown, etc.) on one's back,** to be helpless or beaten: *He's flat on his back after a long succession of failures.* **21. break someone's back,** to cause a person to fail, esp. to cause to become bankrupt: *His family's extravagance is breaking his back.* **22. break the back of something, a.** to complete the principal or hardest part of a project, one's work, etc.: *He finally broke the back of the problem.* **b.** to overcome, defeat, etc., the strength of an argument, system, attack, etc.: *They broke the back of the Establishment.* **23. get off one's back,** to cease to find fault with or to disturb someone: *The fight started when they wouldn't get off my back.* **24. get** or **put one's back up,** to annoy or become annoyed: *She gets her back up whenever her younger brother makes fun of her dates.* **25. have one's back to the wall,** to be in a difficult or hopeless situation. **26. in back of,** *U.S. Informal.* behind: *He hid in back of the billboard. What could be in back of his strange behavior?* Also, **back of. 27. on one's back,** finding fault with or disturbing someone: *She's always on his back if he comes home late.* **28. pat on the back.** See **pat**[1] (defs. 6, 10). **29. stab in the back.** See **stab** (def. 15). **30. turn one's back on, a.** to leave behind, as in anger. **b.** to forsake or neglect: *He was unable to turn his back on any suffering creature.* —*v.t.* **31.** to support, as with authority, influence, help,

or money (often fol. by *up*): *to back a candidate; to back up a theory with facts.* **32.** to bet on: *to back a horse in the race.* **33.** to cause to move backward (often fol. by *up*): *to back a car.* **34.** to furnish with a back: *to back a book.* **35.** to lie at the back of; form a back or background for: *a beach backed by hills.* **36.** to get upon the back of; mount. **37.** to provide with an accompaniment: *a singer backed by piano and bass.* **38.** to write or print on the back of; endorse; countersign. **39.** to attach strips of wood to the upper edge of (a joist or rafter) to bring it to a desired level. **40.** *Naut.* **a.** to alter the position of (a sail) so that the wind will strike the forward face. **b.** to brace (yards) in backing a sail. **c.** to reinforce the hold of (an anchor) by means of a smaller one attached to it and dropped farther away.
—*v.i.* **41.** to go or move backward (often fol. by *up*). **42.** *Naut.* (of wind) to change direction counterclockwise (opposed to *veer*). **43. back and fill, a.** *Naut.* to trim the sails of a boat so that the wind strikes them first on the forward and then on the after side: done against the wind in a narrow channel to maneuver a ship from bank to bank by floating with the current. **b.** *U.S. Informal.* to change one's opinion or position; vacillate. **44. back down,** *Informal.* to abandon an argument, opinion, or claim; withdraw; retreat: *He backed down as soon as a member of the audience challenged his assertion.* **45. back off, a.** to back down: *Now that the time for action had arrived, it was too late to back off.* **b.** *Textiles.* to reverse (the spindle) in mule spinning prior to winding on the newly spun length of yarn. **46. back out** or **out of,** *Informal.* to fail to keep an engagement or promise; withdraw from; abandon: *Two entrants have backed out of competing in the regatta. You can't back out now.* **47. back up, a.** to bring (a stream of traffic) to a standstill: *A stalled car backed up traffic for miles.* **b.** *Printing.* to print a sheet again on its other side. **c.** *Printing.* to fill in (the thin copper shell of an electrotype) with metal in order to strengthen it. **d.** to move backward: *Back up into the garage.* **e.** to support: *We backed up the cardboard with slats so it wouldn't fall down. He backed up my story and they let us go.* **48. back water, a.** *Naut.* to reverse the direction of a vessel. **b.** to retreat from a position; withdraw an opinion: *I predict that the council will back water on the tax issue.* —*adj.* **49.** situated at or in the rear: *at the back door; back fence.* **50.** far away or removed from the front or main area, position, or rank; remote: *back settlements.* **51.** belonging to the past: *back files; back issues.* **52.** in arrears; overdue: *back pay.* **53.** coming or going back; moving backward: *back current.* **54.** *Navig.* reciprocal (def. 5). **55.** *Phonet.* (of a speech sound) produced with the tongue articulating in the back part of the mouth, as in either of the sounds of *go.* [ME *bak* < OE *bæc;* c. OFris *bek,* OS *bak,* Icel *bak*] —**back′less,** *adj.*

—**Syn. 31.** sustain, abet, favor, assist; countenance, endorse. **41.** retire, retreat, withdraw. **49.** BACK, HIND, POSTERIOR, REAR refer to something situated behind something else. BACK means the opposite of front: *back window.* HIND, and the more formal word POSTERIOR, suggest the rearmost of two or more, often similar objects: *hind legs; posterior lobe.* REAR is used of buildings, conveyances, etc., and in military language it is the opposite of fore: *rear end of a truck; rear echelon.* —**Ant. 1, 49.** front.

—**Usage.** The use of BACK OF instead of *in back of* or *behind* is common in informal English and is rapidly gaining general acceptance in standard English: *He hid back of the billboard.* In formal usage, *behind* is usually favored over *in back of: He hid behind the billboard.*

back[2] (bak), *adv.* **1.** at, to, or toward the rear; backward: *to step back.* **2.** in or toward the past: *to look back on one's youth; They met in Chicago back in 1946.* **3.** at or toward the original starting point, place, or condition: *to go back to the old neighborhood.* **4.** in direct payment or return: *to pay back a loan; to answer back.* **5.** in a state of restraint or retention: *to hold back the tears; to hold back salary.* **6. back and forth,** from side to side; to and fro: *The pendulum of the grandfather clock swung back and forth.* **7. go back on,** *Informal.* **a.** to be treacherous or faithless to; betray: *to go back on one's friends.* **b.** to fail to keep; renege on: *to go back on one's promises.* [aph. var. of ABACK]

back[3] (bak), *n.* **1.** a large tub, vat, or cistern used by dyers, brewers, distillers, etc., to contain liquids. **2.** a broad-beamed ferryboat hauled across a body of water by a rope or chain. [< D *bak* tub, trough < LL *bacc(a)* water container; cf. F *bac* ferryboat, punt]

back·ache (bak′āk′), *n.* a pain, esp. in the lumbar region of the back, usually caused by the strain of a muscle or ligament. [BACK[1] + ACHE]

back-al·ley (bak′al′ē), *adj.* dirty, unprepossessing, sordid, or clandestine; having or typical of the unsavory atmosphere or behavior found in a back alley: *back-alley morals; back-alley political schemes.*

back′ an′chor, *Naut.* a small anchor for backing a larger one.

back-and-forth (bak′ən fôrth′, -fōrth′, -ənd-), *adj.* backward and forward; side to side; to-and-fro: *a back-and-forth shuttling of buses to the stadium; the back-and-forth movement of a clock's pendulum.*

back·band (bak′band′), *n.* **1.** *Carpentry.* a piece of millwork surrounding the trim at the top and sides of a door or window. **2.** a broad band passing over the back of a horse, for supporting the shafts of a vehicle. [BACK[1] + BAND[2]]

back′ bar′, *Shipbuilding.* a short length of angle iron fitted over flanges of two angle irons butted together side by side to connect or reinforce them. Also called **backing bar, backing angle.**

Back′ Bay′, a residential area of Boston, Massachusetts.

back′ bench′, *Brit.* any of the rows of seats occupied by the backbenchers. Cf. **front bench.**

back·bench·er (bak′ben′chər, -ben′-), *n.* any of the members of a legislature, esp. of the House of Commons of Great Britain, but not including the leaders of the parties. [BACK BENCH + -ER[1]]

back·bend (bak′bend′), *n.* an acrobatic feat in which a person bends backward from a standing position until his hands touch the floor. [BACK[1] + BEND[1]]

back·bite (bak′bīt′), *v.,* **-bit, -bit·ten** or (*Informal*) **-bit; -bit·ing.** —*v.t.* **1.** to attack the character or reputation of (a person who is not present). —*v.i.* **2.** to speak slanderously of one who is absent. [ME; see BACK[1], BITE] —**back′bit′er,** *n.*

back·blocks (bak′bloks′), *n.* (*construed as pl.*) *Australian.* the outback. [BACK[1] + BLOCK + -S[3]]

back·board (bak′bōrd′, -bôrd′), *n.* **1.** a board placed at or forming the back of anything. **2.** *Med.* a board worn to support or straighten the back. **3.** *Basketball.* a board or other flat surface to which the basket is attached. **4.** *Naut.* a transverse board forming a backrest for those seated in the stern of a boat. —*v.t.* **5.** *Med.* to subject to the wearing of a backboard. [BACK[1] + BOARD]

back·bone (bak′bōn′), *n.* **1.** *Anat.* the spinal or vertebral column; spine. **2.** strength of character; resolution. **3.** something resembling a backbone in appearance, position, or function. **4.** *Bookbinding.* a back or bound edge of a book; spine. **5.** *Naut.* a rope running along the middle of an awning, as a reinforcement and as an object to which a supporting bridle or crowfoot may be attached. **6.** *Naval Archit.* the central fore-and-aft assembly of the keel and keelson, giving longitudinal strength to the bottom of a vessel. [ME *bacbon.* See BACK[1], BONE[1]] —**back′boned′,** *adj.* —**back′bone′less,** *adj.*
—**Syn. 2.** firmness, decision, fortitude.

back·break·ing (bak′brā′king), *adj.* demanding great effort, endurance, etc.; exhausting: *a backbreaking job.* Also, **back′-break′ing.** [BACK[1] + BREAKING] —**back′break′er,** *n.*

back·chat (bak′chat′), *n.* *Informal.* **1.** repartee. **2.** back talk. [BACK[2] + CHAT[1]]

back-check (bak′chek′), *v.i.* *Ice Hockey.* to skate back toward one's defensive zone obstructing or impeding the movement or progress of one or more opponents on attack. Cf. **check** (def. 14), **fore-check.**

back′ clear′ance, runout (def. 2).

back-cloth (bak′klôth′, -kloth′), *n., pl.* **-cloths** (-klôthz′, -klothz′, -klôths′, -kloths′). *Theat. Chiefly Brit.* backdrop (def. 1).

back·court (bak′kōrt′, -kôrt′), *n.* **1.** *Basketball.* the half of a court in which the basket being defended is located. **2.** *Tennis.* the part of a tennis court between the base line and the line, parallel to the net, that marks the in-bounds limit of a service. Cf. **forecourt** (def. 2). [BACK[1] + COURT]

back·cross (bak′krôs′, -kros′), *Genetics.* —*v.t.* **1.** to cross (a hybrid of the first generation) with either of its parents. —*n.* **2.** an instance of such crossing. [BACK[2] + CROSS]

back′ door′, **1.** a door at the rear of a house, building, etc. **2.** a secret, furtive, or illicit method, manner, or means.

back·door (bak′dōr′, -dôr′), *adj.* secret; furtive; illicit; indirect. Also, **back′-door′.** [adj. use of BACK DOOR]

back·down (bak′doun′), *n.* a withdrawal from a previously held position, esp. in the face of superior power or upon further consideration: *The country's resolution to fight was followed by the dramatic backdown of the would-be aggressor.* [n. use of v. phrase *back down*]

back·drop (bak′drop′), *n.* **1.** Also called, *esp. Brit.,* **back-cloth.** *Theat.* the rear curtain of a stage setting. **2.** the background of an event; setting. [BACK[1] + DROP]

backed (bakt), *adj.* **1.** having a back, setting, or support (often used in combination): *a low-backed sofa; a well-backed candidate.* **2.** (of fabric) having an extra set of threads in either the warp or the weft to provide added warmth. Cf. **double cloth.** **3.** *Photog.* (of a film or plate) coated with a substance for absorbing light and thereby reducing halation. [BACK[1] + -ED[3]]

back′ electromo′tive force′, *Elect.* See **counter electromotive force.**

back·er (bak′ər), *n.* one who or that which supports or aids a cause, enterprise, etc. [BACK[1] + -ER[1]]
—**Syn.** supporter, sponsor, guarantor.

back·er-up (bak′ər up′), *n., pl.* **back·ers-up.** *Football.* a linebacker.

back·fall (bak′fôl′), *n.* that which falls back. [BACK[2] + FALL]

back·field (bak′fēld′), *n.* *Football.* **1.** (*construed as pl.*) the members of the team who, on offense, are stationed behind the linemen and, on defense, behind the linebackers. **2.** their positions considered as a unit. **3.** the area where the backs play. [BACK[1] + FIELD]

back·fill (bak′fil′), *n.* **1.** (in construction work) material used for refilling an excavation. —*v.t.* **2.** to refill (an excavation). [BACK[2] + FILL]

back′ fil′let, *Archit.* the return of a slightly projecting member, as a quoin. —**back′-fil′let·ed,** *adj.*

back·fire (bak′fīər′), *v.,* **-fired, -fir·ing,** *n.* —*v.i.* **1.** (of an internal-combustion engine) to have a loud, premature explosion in the intake manifold. **2.** to start a fire deliberately in order to check a forest or prairie fire by creating a barren area in advance of it. **3.** to bring a result opposite to that which was planned or expected: *The plot backfired.* —*n.* **4.** (in an internal-combustion engine) premature ignition of fuel in the intake manifold, from contact with flame from a cylinder. **5.** an explosion coming out of the breech of a firearm. **6.** a fire started intentionally to check the advance of a forest or prairie fire. **7.** *Electronics Rare.* arc-back. [BACK[2] + FIRE]

back′flap hinge′ (bak′flap′), flap (def. 14a).

back·flow (bak′flō′), *n.* a flow of a liquid contrary to the usual or desired direction. [n. use of v. phrase *flow back*]

back′flow valve′. See **backwater valve.**

back′ forma′tion, *Ling.* **1.** the analogical creation of one word from another word that appears to be a derived or inflected form of the first by dropping the apparent affix or by modification. **2.** a word so formed, as *typewrite* from *typewriter.*

back·gam·mon (bak′gam′ən, bak′gam′-), *n.* **1.** a game for two persons played on a board having two tables or parts, with pieces or men moved in accordance with throws of the dice. **2.** a victory at this game, esp. one resulting in a tripled score. —*v.t.* **3.** to defeat at backgammon, esp. to win a triple score over. [BACK[2] + GAMMON[1]]

back′ gear′, (in a lathe) one of several gears for driving the headstock at various speeds. —**back′-geared′,** *adj.*

back·ground (bak′ground′), *n.* **1.** the ground or parts, as of a scene, situated in the rear (opposed to *foreground*). **2.** *Fine Arts.* **a.** the part of a painted or carved surface against which represented objects and forms are perceived or depicted: *a portrait against a purple background.* **b.** the part of an image represented as being at maximum distance from the frontal plane. **3.** the social, historical, and other antecedents which explain an event or condition: *the background of the war.* **4.** a person's origin, education, experience, etc., in relation to his present character, status, etc. **5.** the complex of physical, cultural, and psychological factors that serves as the environment of an event or experience; the set of conditions against which an occurrence is perceived. **6.** *Physics.* the totality of effects that tend to obscure a phenomenon under investigation and above which the phenomenon must be detected. **7.** (in an electronic apparatus for transmitting or receiving signals) the sum of the effects, as noise, random signals, or the like, that a phenomenon must differentiate itself from in character or degree in order to be detected. **8. in** or **into the background,** unobtrusive; inconspicuous; out of sight or notice; in or into obscurity: *He kept his dishonest dealings in the background.* —*adj.* **9.** of, pertaining to, or serving as a background: *background noise.* [BACK[1] + GROUND[1]]

back′ground mu′sic, **1.** music, often recorded, intended to provide a soothing background, usually played over loudspeaker systems in public places, as railway stations, restaurants, etc. **2.** music composed specifically to accompany and heighten the mood of a visual production, as a movie.

back′ground projec′tion, the projection of previously photographed material on a translucent screen, used as background for a television or motion-picture shot. Also called **back projection, rear projection.**

back·hand (bak′hand′), *n.* **1.** a stroke, slap, etc., made with the palm of the hand turned toward the body and the back of the hand turned in the direction of the stroke, slap, etc. **2.** (in tennis, squash, etc.) a stroke made from the side of the body opposite to that of the hand holding the racket, paddle, etc. **3.** writing which slopes toward the left. —*adj.* **4.** backhanded. **5.** (in tennis, squash, etc.) of, pertaining to, or noting a stroke made from the side of the body opposite to that of the hand holding the racket, paddle, etc. Cf. **forehand** (def. 1). —*adv.* **6.** with the back of the hand: *He hit him backhand across the face.* **7.** from across the body; backhanded: *He returned the ball backhand on the first serve.* —*v.t.* **8.** to strike with the back of the hand. **9.** to hit, produce, or accomplish with a backhand. **10.** to catch (a ball or the like) backhanded. [BACK[2] + HAND]

back·hand·ed (bak′han′did), *adj.* **1.** performed with the hand turned backward, crosswise, or in any oblique direction so that the palm of the hand faces in the direction of the body and the back of the hand faces in the direction of forward movement. **2.** sloping in a downward direction from left to right: *backhanded writing.* **3.** oblique or ambiguous in meaning; indirect; insincere; wry: *backhanded methods; a backhanded compliment.* **4.** *Ropemaking.* noting a rope in which the yarns and the strands are laid in the same direction, the rope itself being laid in the opposite direction. —*adv.* **5.** with the hand across the body; backhand: *He caught the ball backhanded.* [BACK[2] + HANDED] —**back′hand′ed·ly,** *adv.* —**back′hand′ed·ness,** *n.*

back·hand·er (bak′han′dər), *n.* *Informal.* a backhanded slap, punch, stroke, or play. [BACKHAND + -ER[1]]

back·haul (bak′hôl′), *n.* the return trip of a vehicle transporting cargo or freight, esp. when carrying goods back over all or part of the same route. [BACK[2] + HAUL]

Back·haus (bäk′hous), *n.* **Wil·helm** (vil′helm), born 1884, German pianist.

back·house (bak′hous′), *n., pl.* **-hous·es** (-hou′ziz). **1.** a building behind the main building. **2.** a privy. [BACK[1] + HOUSE]

back·ing (bak′ing), *n.* **1.** aid or support of any kind. **2.** supporters or backers collectively. **3.** that which forms the back or is placed at or attached to the back of anything to support, strengthen, or protect it. **4.** *Theat.* a curtain or flat placed behind a window, entrance, or other opening in a stage set to conceal the offstage area. **5.** material for backing a joist or rafter. **6.** a bevel given to the outer and upper edge of a hip rafter. **7.** the musical accompaniment for a soloist. [BACK[1] + -ING[1]]

back′ing bar′. See **back bar.** Also called **back′ing an′gle.**

back′ing light′, **1.** Also called **back′ing strip′light, back′ing strip′.** *Theat.* a striplight providing diffused illumination for the background of a stage set. **2.** Also called **backup light.** a light at the rear of a motor vehicle indicating that the vehicle is in reverse gear and lighting the road behind.

back·lash (bak′lash′), *n.* **1.** *Mach.* **a.** the space between the thickness of a gear tooth and the width of the space between teeth in the mating gear, designed to allow for a film of lubricant, binding from heat expansion and eccentricity, or manufacturing inaccuracies. **b.** play or lost motion between loosely fitting machine parts. **2.** *Angling.* a snarled line on a reel, usually caused by a faulty cast. **3.** any sudden and forceful recoil or reaction: *the backlash of Southern conservatives within the party.* —*v.i.* **4.** to make a backlash. [BACK[2] + LASH[1]]

back-light (bak′līt′), *n., v.,* **-light·ed** or **-lit, -light·ing.** —*n.* **1.** the illumination produced by a light behind or at a right angle to an object, person, or scene. —*v.t.* **2.** to illuminate (something) from behind. [BACK[1] + LIGHT[1]]

back·light·ing (bak′lī′ting), *n.* a controlled technique of lighting, used in photography or the theater, in which a light is placed behind or at right angles to an object, person, or scene to produce such effects as depth, separation of subject and background, etc. [BACK[1] + LIGHTING]

back·lins (bak′linz), *adv.* *Scot. and North Eng.* backward; back. Also, **back·lings** (bak′lingz). [ME *bakling* < OE *bæcling* backwards (see BACK[1], -LING[2]) + -S[1]]

back·log (bak′lôg′, -log′), *n., v.,* **-logged, -log·ging.** —*n.* **1.** a reserve or accumulation, as of stock, work, business, etc.: *a backlog of business orders.* **2.** a large log at the back of a hearth to keep up a fire. Cf. **forestick.** —*v.t.* **3.** to hold in reserve, as for future handling, repair, etc. **4.** to enter and acknowledge (an order) for future shipment. [BACK[1] + LOG]

back′ lot′, *Motion Pictures.* land owned by a studio and used as the location for exterior sets and scenes.

back′ mat′ter, *Print.* those parts of a book, excluding the text, that appear at the end, as bibliography, index, appendixes, etc. Also called **end matter.** Cf. **front matter.**

back′ mold′ing, a molding, as a backband, applied to interior window and door trim to conceal the edge of the wall surface.

back′ num′ber, **1.** an out-of-date issue of a serial publication. **2.** anything out-of-date.

back′ o′ beyond′, *Australian Informal.* remote; out-of-the-way; isolated.

back′ or′der, an order to be filled or delivered at some future date.

back·pack (bak′pak′), *n.* **1.** a pack or bundle of supplies to be carried on one's back, often supported on a lightweight metal frame strapped to the body. **2.** a trip or outing requiring such a pack. —*v.i.* **3.** to go on an outing, using a backpack: *to backpack through the mountains.* —*v.t.* **4.** to place or carry in a backpack or on one's back. [BACK[1] + PACK[1]] —**back′pack′er,** *n.*

back′ paint′ing, the act or process of decorating a pane of glass by gluing a print to the back, rendering it transparent, and tinting it.

back·ped·al (bak′ped′ᵊl), *v.i.,* **-aled, -al·ing** or (*esp. Brit.*) **-alled, -al·ling.** **1.** *Boxing Slang.* to retreat from an opponent, esp. by stepping rapidly backward. **2.** to retard the forward motion of a bicycle by pressing backward on the pedal. **3.** to reverse or retreat from one's previous stand on any matter; shift ground: *to back-pedal after severe criticism.*

back′ plas′tering, *Building Trades.* **1.** the introduction of partitions of lath and plaster between the inner and outer surfaces of a stud wall in order to improve the insulating properties of the wall. **2.** parging applied behind the exterior brickwork of a wall in order to exclude moisture and air from the interior of the wall.

back·plate (bak′plāt′), *n.* **1.** *Building Trades.* a wood or metal plate serving as a backing for a structural member. **2.** *Armor.* a piece of plate armor for protecting the back: worn as part of a cuirass. [BACK[1] + PLATE[1]]

back′ press′ure-arm′ lift′ meth′od, a method of artificial respiration in which the patient is placed face downward, pressure then being applied with the hands to the upper part of the back, this movement being alternated with lifting of the arms. Also called **Holger Nielsen method, Holger Nielsen's method, Nielsen method.**

back′ projec′tion. See **background projection.**

back·rest (bak′rest′), *n.* a support used by a person for resting his back. [BACK[1] + REST[1]]

back′ road′, a little used, often unpaved country road.

back·rope (bak′rōp′), *n.* *Naut.* See **martingale backrope.** [BACK[1] + ROPE]

back′ run′, **1.** a period during which a particular process, as the flow of materials in manufacturing, is reversed. **2.** *Australian.* a tract of dry land in the public domain used as an auxiliary pasture by owners of adjacent private property.

back·saw (bak′sô′), *n.* *Carpentry.* a short saw with a reinforced back. [BACK[1] + SAW[1], modeled on *backsword*]

back·scat·ter (bak′skat′ər), *n.* the deflection of nuclear particles or of radiation in a scattering process through an angle greater than 90°. Also, **back′scat′·ter·ing.** [n. use of v. phrase *scatter back*]

back′ score′, *Curling.* a line at each end of the rink parallel to and equidistant from the foot score and the sweeping score.

back′ scratch′er, **1.** a long-handled device for scratching one's own back. **2.** *Informal.* a person who practices back scratching. Also, **back′-scratch′er, back′scratch′er.**

back′ scratch′ing, *Informal.* the practice of exchanging favors or services for mutual advantage.

back′ seat′, **1.** a seat at the rear. **2. take a back seat,** *Informal.* to occupy a secondary or inferior position: *His writing has taken a back seat because of other demands on his time.*

back′-seat driv′er (bak′sēt′), *Usually Disparaging.* **1.** an automobile passenger who offers the driver unsolicited advice, warnings, criticism, etc., esp. from the back seat. **2.** any person who, by means of criticism, unsolicited advice, or the like, interferes in affairs which are neither his concern nor his responsibility.

back·set (bak′set′), *n.* **1.** a setback; relapse; reverse. **2.** an eddy or countercurrent. **3.** (on a lock on a door or the like) the horizontal distance between the face through which the bolt passes and the center line of the knob stem or keyhole. [BACK[2] + SET]

back′ shaft′, a spindle carrying back gears.

back·sheesh (bak′shēsh), *n., v.t., v.i.* baksheesh. Also, **back′shish.**

back·side (bak′sīd′), *n.* **1.** the rear or back part or view of an object, person, scene, etc.; that part which is opposite the front. **2.** the rump. [BACK[1] + SIDE[1]; cf. OE *bæce* backparts]

back·sight (bak′sīt′), *n.* *Survey.* **1.** a sight on a previously occupied instrument station. **2.** (in leveling) the reading on a rod that is held on a point of known elevation, used in computing the elevation of the instrument. [BACK[2] + SIGHT]

back·slap·ping (bak′slap′ing), *n.* *Informal.* the practice of making a loud and effusive display of friendliness, cordiality, etc., as by slapping persons on the back. [BACK[1] + SLAPPING] —**back′slap′per,** *n.*

back·slide (bak′slīd′), *v.,* **-slid, -slid** or **-slid·den, -slid·ing,** *n.* —*v.i.* **1.** to relapse into error or sin. —*n.* **2.** act or instance of backsliding: *a backslide from his early training.* [BACK[2] + SLIDE] —**back′slid′er,** *n.*

back·space (bak′spās′), *v.,* **-spaced, -spac·ing,** *n.* —*v.i.* **1.** to shift the carriage of a typewriter one space backward by depressing a special key. —*n.* **2.** the space made by backspacing. **3.** Also called **back′spac′er, back′space key′.** the key on a typewriter used for backspacing. [BACK[2] + SPACE]

back·spin (bak′spin′), *n.* reverse rotation of a ball causing it to bounce or roll backward or stop short. Also called **underspin.** [BACK[2] + SPIN]

back·splice (bak′splīs′), *n., v.,* **-spliced, -splic·ing.** —*n.* **1.** a knot for finishing a rope end neatly, beginning with a crown and proceeding in a series of tucks, each strand over the first adjoining strand and under the next, the strands being split in half at each tuck. —*v.t.* **2.** to make a backsplice in (a rope end). [BACK[2] + SPLICE]

back·stab (bak′stab′), *v.t.,* **-stabbed, -stab·bing.** to attack or attempt to discredit (a person) by underhanded means, as innuendo, accusation, or the like. [BACK[2] + STAB] —**back′stab′ber,** *n.*

back′ staff′, an obsolete instrument for determining the altitude of the sun by facing away from the sun, sighting upon the horizon, adjusting a cursor until its shadow falls upon the sight through which the horizon appears, and measuring the resulting arc. Also called **Davis's quadrant.**

back·stage (bak′stāj′), *adv.* **1.** behind the curtain in a theater; on the stage, or in the wings or dressing rooms. **2.** toward the rear of the stage; upstage. —*adj.* **3.** located or occurring backstage. —*n.* **4.** *Theat.* a backstage area. [BACK[2] + STAGE]

back′ stairs′, **1.** stairs at the back of a house, as for use by servants. **2.** a means of intrigue.

back·stairs (bak′stârz′), *adj.* indirect; underhand: *backstairs gossip.* Also, **back′stair′.** [adj. use of BACK STAIRS]

back·stay (bak′stā′), *n.* **1.** *Mach.* a supporting or checking piece in a mechanism. **2.** *Naut.* any of various shrouds forming part of a vessel's standing rigging and leading aft from masts above a lower mast to the sides or stern of the vessel in order to reinforce the masts against forward pull. **3.** *Building Trades.* an anchored tension member, as a cable, permanently or temporarily supporting a compression member, as a tower or pole, subject to a pull above its base from the opposite direction. [BACK[1] + STAY[3]]

back·stitch (bak′stich′), *n.* **1.** stitching or a stitch in which the thread doubles back each time on the preceding stitch. —*v.t., v.i.* **2.** to sew by backstitch. [BACK[1] + STITCH[1]]

back·stop (bak′stop′), *n., v.,* **-stopped, -stop·ping.** —*n.* **1.** a wall, wire screen, or the like, serving to prevent a ball from going too far beyond the normal playing area. **2.** *Baseball Informal.* the catcher. **3.** *Informal.* a safeguard, support, or reinforcement, as for a mechanism, methods, principles, etc. —*v.i.* **4.** *Informal.* to act as a backstop. —*v.t.* **5.** (of a person) to provide services useful in connection with those of (another person): *Trained counselors backstop the teaching staff.* [BACK[1] + STOP]

back·strapped (bak′strapt′), *adj.* *Naut.* unable to proceed because of the tide or current. [BACK[2] + STRAPPED]

back′ street′, a street apart from the main or business area of a town. Cf. **side street.**

back·stretch (bak′strech′), *n.* the straight part of a race track opposite the part leading to the finish line. Cf. **homestretch.** [BACK[1] + STRETCH]

back·stroke (bak′strōk′), *n., v.,* **-stroked, -strok·ing.** —*n.* **1.** a backhanded stroke. **2.** a blow or stroke in return; recoil. **3.** *Swimming.* a stroke made while on one's back. —*v.i.* **4.** *Swimming.* to swim the backstroke: *She backstroked across the pool.* [BACK[2] + STROKE[1]]

Backswimmer
Hydrous triangularis
(Length 1½ in.)

back·swept (bak′swept′), *adj.* **1.** slanting backward or away from the front. **2.** *Aeron. Rare.* sweptback. [BACK[2] + SWEPT]

back·swim·mer (bak′swim′ər), *n.* any of numerous aquatic hemipterous insects of the family *Notonectidae* that swim on their backs. Also called **boat bug.** [BACK[1] + SWIMMER]

back·swing (bak′swing′), *n.* *Sports.* the movement of a bat, racket, or the like, toward the back of a player in preparation for the forward movement with which the ball is struck. [BACK[2] + SWING[1]]

back·sword (bak′sōrd′, -sôrd′), *n.* **1.** a sword with only one sharp edge; broadsword. **2.** (formerly) a cudgel having a basket hilt, used in fencing exhibitions. **3.** a backswordman. [BACK[1] + SWORD]

back·sword·man (bak′sōrd′mən, -sôrd′-), *n., pl.* **-men.** a person who uses a backsword. Also, **back·swords·man** (bak′sōrdz′mən, -sôrdz′-). [BACKSWORD + MAN]

back′ talk′, an impudent response; impudent or impertinent replies in general.

back-talk (bak′tôk′), *v.i.* to answer back. [BACK[2] + TALK]

back′ to back′, **1.** adjacent or contiguous but oppositely oriented; having the backs close together or adjoining: *The seats in the day coach are back to back. He held aces back to back.* **2.** (of two similar events) following one immediately after the other; in unbroken sequence: *After losing all day, he picked winners back to back in the last two races.* **3.** *Finance.* (in import-export trade) noting a domestic letter of credit issued to a shipper on the basis of a foreign letter of credit furnished him by a purchaser. —**back′-to-back′,** *adj.*

back·track (bak′trak′), *v.i.* *U.S.* **1.** to return over the same course or route. **2.** to withdraw from an undertaking, position, etc.; reverse a policy. [BACK[2] + TRACK]

back·up (bak′up′), *n.* **1.** one who or that which supports or reinforces another. **2.** an overflow or accumulation due to stoppage, malfunctioning, etc.: *a sewage backup; a backup of cars at the border.* **3.** (in research and development) a program or course of action paralleling another program that is in danger of failing. **4.** *Bowling.* a ball that curves in a direction corresponding to the bowling hand of the bowler. [n. use of v. phrase *back up*]

back′up light′, *Auto.* See **backing light** (def. 2).

back′ vent′, (in plumbing) a vent situated on the sewer side of a trap.

back·ward (bak′wərd), *adv.* Also, **back′wards.** **1.** toward the back or rear. **2.** with the back foremost. **3.** in the reverse of the usual or right way: *counting backward from 100.* **4.** toward the past: *to look backward over one's earlier mistakes.* **5.** toward a less advanced state; retrogressively: *Since the uprising the country has moved steadily backward.* **6. backward and forward,** *Informal.* thoroughly: *He knew his lesson backward and forward.* Also, **backwards and forwards.** —*adj.* **7.** directed toward the back or past. **8.** reversed; returning: *a backward movement; a backward journey.* **9.** behind in time or progress; late; slow: *a backward learner; a backward country.* **10.** bashful or hesitant; shy: *a backward lover.* [ME *bakwarde.* See BACK[1], -WARD] —**back′·ward·ly,** *adv.* —**back′ward·ness,** *n.*
—**Syn. 9.** tardy; retarded, underdeveloped. **10.** disinclined; timid, retiring. —**Ant. 1.** forward.

back·ward·a·tion (bak′wər dā′shən), *n.* (on the London stock exchange) the fee paid by a seller of securities to the buyer for the privilege of deferring delivery of purchased securities. Cf. **contango.** [BACKWARD + -ATION]

back·wash (bak′wosh′, -wôsh′), *n.* **1.** *Naut.* water thrown backward by the motion of oars, propellers, paddle wheels, etc. **2.** *Aeron.* the portion of the wash of an aircraft that flows to the rear, usually created by the power plant. Cf. **wash** (def. 34). **3.** a condition lasting after the event which caused it. —*v.t.* **4.** to affect, as by hitting, rocking, or splashing, with a backwash: *a powerful cutter backwashing the skiers.* [BACK[2] + WASH] —**back′wash′er,** *n.*

back·wa·ter (bak′wô′tər, -wot′ər), *n.* **1.** water held or forced back, as by a dam, flood, tide, etc. **2.** a place or state of stagnant backwardness: *This area of the country is a backwater that continues to resist progress.* **3.** an isolated, peaceful place. [BACK[2] + WATER]

back′water valve′, a valve for preventing flowing liquid, as sewage, from reversing its direction. Also called **backflow valve.**

back·wind (bak′wind′), *v.t.,* **-wind·ed, -wind·ing.** *Naut.* **1.** to divert wind against the lee side of (a sail) from another sail. **2.** to set (a sail) so that the wind is on what would ordinarily be the lee side, as for turning the bow of a boat away from the wind. **3.** to blanket (another sailing vessel) by spilling wind from the sails of one vessel onto the lee side of the sails of the other. [BACK[2] + WIND[1]]

back·woods (bak′wŏŏdz′), *n.pl.* **1.** (*often construed as sing.*) wooded or partially uncleared and unsettled districts. —*adj.* Also, **back′wood′.** **2.** of or pertaining to the backwoods. **3.** unsophisticated; uncouth. [BACK[1] + WOODS]

back·woods·man (bak′wŏŏdz′mən), *n., pl.* **-men.** **1.** one living in or coming from the backwoods. **2.** a person of uncouth manners, rustic behavior or speech, etc. **3.** *Brit.* a peer who never or rarely attends the House of Lords. [BACKWOODS + MAN]

back·yard (bak′yärd′), *n.* **1.** the portion of a lot or building site behind a house, structure, or the like, sometimes fenced, walled, etc. **2.** a familiar or nearby area; stamping ground. [BACK[2] + YARD[2]]

Ba·co (bä′kō), *n.* a crater in the fourth quadrant of the face of the moon: about 40 miles in diameter.

Ba·co·lod (bä kō′lōd), *n.* a seaport on N Negros, in the central Philippines. 140,300 (est. 1965).

ba·con (bā′kən), *n.* **1.** the back and sides of the hog, salted and dried or smoked, usually sliced thin and fried for food. **2. bring home the bacon,** *Slang.* **a.** to provide for material needs; earn a living. **b.** to accomplish a task; be successful or victorious: *The president of the small country went to Washington to appeal for aid and brought home the bacon—$3,000,000.* **3. save one's bacon,** *Slang.* to allow a person to accomplish a desired end; spare a person from injury or loss: *Quick thinking saved our bacon.* [ME *bacoun* < AF, c. OF *bacon* < Gmc **bakōn-*, weak var. of **baka-* BACK[1]; cf. OD *baken* bacon]

Ba·con (bā′kən), *n.* **1. Francis** (*Baron Verulam, Viscount St. Albans*), 1561–1626, English essayist, philosopher, and statesman. **2. Francis,** born 1910, English painter, born in Ireland. **3. Henry,** 1866–1924, U.S. architect. **4. Nathaniel,** 1647–76, American colonist, born in England: leader of a rebellion in Virginia 1676. **5. Roger** ("*The Admirable Doctor*"), 1214?–94?, English philosopher and scientist.

Ba·co·ni·an (bā kō′nē ən), *adj.* **1.** of or pertaining to the philosopher Francis Bacon or his doctrines. —*n.* **2.** an adherent of the Baconian philosophy. [BACON + -IAN] —**Ba·co′ni·an·ism, Ba′co·nism,** *n.*

Baco′nian meth′od, *Logic.* induction (def. 2).

Baco′nian the′ory, the theory attributing the authorship of Shakespeare's plays to Francis Bacon. Cf. **Oxford theory.**

Ba′con's Rebel′lion, an unsuccessful uprising by frontiersmen in Virginia in 1676, led by Nathaniel Bacon against the colonial government in Jamestown.

bact., bacteriology.

bac·te·re·mi·a (bak′tə rē′mē ə), *n.* *Pathol.* the presence of bacteria in the blood. [BACTER- + -EMIA]

bacteri-, a learned borrowing from Greek meaning "bacteria," used in the formation of compound words: *bactericide.* Also, **bacter-, bacterio-.** [< Gk *baktēria* staff, cane; see BACTERIUM]

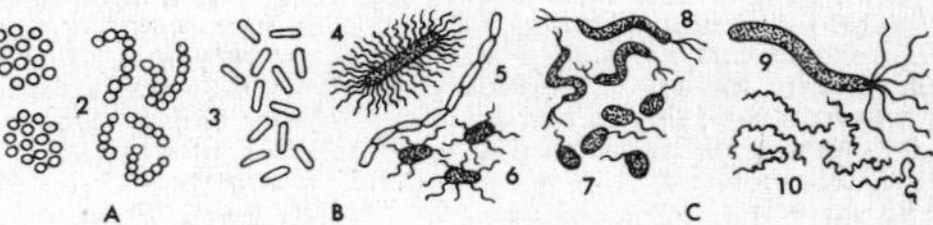

Bacteria (greatly magnified)
A, Cocci (spherical): 1, ***Staphylococcus pyogenes aureus;*** **2,** ***Streptococcus pyogenes.*** **B, Bacilli (rod): 3,** ***Bacillus sporogenes;*** **4,** ***Bacillus proteus;*** **5,** ***Bacillus subtilis;*** **6,** ***Bacillus typhosus.*** **C, Spirilla (spiral): 7,** ***Vibrio cholerae asiaticae;*** **8,** ***Spirillum undulum;*** **9,** ***Theospirillum;*** **10,** ***Spirochaeta***

bac·te·ri·a (bak tēr′ē ə), *n.pl., sing.* **-te·ri·um** (-tēr′ē əm). any of numerous microscopic, spherical, rod-shaped, or spiral organisms of the class *Schizomycetes,* various species of which are concerned in fermentation and putrefaction, the production of disease, the fixing of atmospheric nitrogen, etc.; schizomycete. [< NL < Gk *baktēria,* pl. of *baktērion;* see BACTERIUM] —**bac·te′ri·al,** *adj.* —**bac·te′ri·al·ly,** *adv.*

bacte′rial blight′, *Plant Pathol.* any of several blight diseases of plants caused by bacteria.

bacte′rial can′ker, *Plant Pathol.* a disease of

plants, characterized by cankers and usually by exudation of gum, caused by bacteria, as of the genera *Pseudomonas* or *Corynebacterium.*

bacte′rial vac′cine, *Immunol.* bacterin.

bacte′rial wilt′, *Plant Pathol.* a disease of plants, characterized by wilted leaves and discolored internal tissues, caused by any of several bacteria.

bac·te·ri·cide (bak tēr′i sīd′), *n.* an agent capable of killing bacteria. [BACTERI- + -CIDE] —**bac·te′ri·cid′al,** *adj.*

bac·te·rin (bak′tə rin), *n. Immunol.* a vaccine prepared from bacteria. [BACTER- + -IN[2]]

bac·te·ri·oid (bak tēr′ē oid′), *n.* **1.** bacteroid. —*adj.* **2.** Also, **bac·te′ri·oi′dal.** bacteroid.

bacteriol., bacteriology.

bacteriolog′ical war′fare. See **biological warfare.**

bac·te·ri·ol·o·gy (bak tēr′ē ol′ə jē), *n.* the science that deals with bacteria. [BACTERIO- + -LOGY] —**bac·te·ri·o·log·i·cal** (bak tēr′ē ə loj′i kəl), **bac·te′ri·o·log′ic,** *adj.* —**bac·te′ri·o·log′i·cal·ly,** *adv.* —**bac·te′ri·ol′o·gist,** *n.*

bac·te·ri·ol·y·sis (bak tēr′ē ol′i sis), *n.* disintegration or dissolution of bacteria. [BACTERIO- + -LYSIS] —**bac·te·ri·o·lyt·ic** (bak tēr′ē ə lit′ik), *n., adj.*

bac·te·ri·o·phage (bak tēr′ē ə fāj′), *n.* one of a group of viruses that infect specific bacteria, usually causing their disintegration or dissolution. [BACTERIO- + -PHAGE] —**bac·te·ri·o·phag·ic** (bak tēr′ē ə faj′ik), **bac·te·ri·oph·a·gous** (bak tēr′ē of′ə gəs), *adj.* —**bac·te·ri·oph·a·gy** (bak tēr′ē of′ə jē), *n.*

bac·te·ri·os·co·py (bak tēr′ē os′kə pē), *n.* the examination of bacteria with a microscope. [BACTERIO- + -SCOPY] —**bac·te·ri·o·scop·ic** (bak tēr′ē ə skop′ik), **bac·te′ri·o·scop′i·cal,** *adj.* —**bac·te′ri·o·scop′i·cal·ly,** *adv.* —**bac·te′ri·os′co·pist,** *n.*

bac·te·ri·o·sta·sis (bak tēr′ē ə stā′sis), *n. Bacteriol.* the prevention of the further growth of bacteria. [BACTERIO- + STASIS in sense of stopping growth] —**bac·te·ri·o·stat·ic** (bak tēr′ē ə stat′ik), *adj.* —**bac·te′ri·o·stat′i·cal·ly,** *adv.*

bac·te·ri·o·stat (bak tēr′ ē ə stat′), *n. Bacteriol.* a substance or preparation that inhibits the further growth of bacteria. [BACTERIO- + -STAT]

bac·te·ri·um (bak tēr′ē əm), *n.* **1.** sing. of **bacteria. 2.** (*cap., italics.*) a genus, in certain classifications, of nonsporeforming bacteria now usually classified in other genera. [< NL < Gk *baktḗrion,* dim. of *báktron* walking stick; akin to L *baculum, bacillum*]

bac·ter·ize (bak′tə rīz′), *v.t.,* **-ized, -izing.** to change in composition by means of bacteria. [BACTER- + -IZE] —**bac′ter·i·za′tion,** *n.*

bac·ter·oid (bak′tə roid′), *Bacteriol.* —*n.* **1.** any of the rod-shaped or branched bacteria in the root nodules of nitrogen-fixing plants. —*adj.* **2.** Also, **bac′te·roi′dal.** resembling bacteria. Also, **bacterioid.** [BACTER- + -OID]

bac·te·roi·des (bak′tə roi′dēz), *n., pl.* **-des.** *Bacteriol.* any of several rod-shaped, anaerobic bacteria of the genus *Bacteroides,* certain species of which are pathogenic, that are found in the alimentary and genitourinary tracts of man and animals. [< NL; see BACTER-, -OID]

Bac·tra (bak′trə), *n.* capital of ancient Bactria. Modern, **Balkh.**

Bac·tri·a (bak′trē ə), *n.* an ancient country in W Asia, between the Oxus River and the Hindu Kush Mountains. *Cap.:* Bactra. —**Bac′tri·an,** *adj., n.*

Bactrian camel
(7 ft. high at top of humps; length about 9 ft.)

Bac′trian cam′el, an Asian camel, *Camelus bactrianus,* having two humps on the back.

ba·cu·li·form (bə kyōō′lə fôrm′, bak′yə-), *adj. Biol.* rod-shaped. [< L *bacul(um)* walking stick, staff + -I- + -FORM]

bac·u·line (bak′yə lin, -līn′), *adj.* pertaining to the rod or its use in punishing: *baculine discipline in the classroom.* [< L *bacul(um)* walking stick, staff + -INE[1]]

bac·u·lite (bak′yə līt′), *n.* any ammonite of the genus *Baculites,* of the Cretaceous period, having a straight shell with a spiral tip. [< L *bacul(um)* walking stick, staff + -ITE[1]] —**bac·u·lit·ic** (bak′yə lit′ik), *adj.* —**bac′u·loid′,** *n.*

bad[1] (bad), *adj.,* **worse, worst,** *n., adv.* —*adj.* **1.** not good in any manner or degree. **2.** having or characterized by a wicked or evil character; morally reprehensible: *There is no such thing as a bad boy.* **3.** of poor quality or in bad condition; defective in quality or worth: *a bad diamond; a bad radio tube.* **4.** inadequate or below standard; not satisfactory for use: *bad heating; Living conditions in some slum areas are very bad.* **5.** inaccurate, incorrect, or faulty: *a bad guess.* **6.** invalid, unsound, or false: *a bad insurance claim; bad judgment.* **7.** causing or liable to cause sickness or ill health; injurious or harmful: *Too much candy is bad for your teeth.* **8.** suffering from sickness, ill health, pain, or injury; sick; ill: *He felt bad from eating green apples.* **9.** not healthy or in good physical condition; diseased, decayed, or physically weakened: *Bad eyes kept him out of the army.* **10.** tainted, spoiled, or rotten, esp. to the point of being inedible: *The meat is bad because you left it out of the refrigerator too long.* **11.** having a disastrous or detrimental effect, result, or tendency; unfavorable: *The drought is bad for the farmers. His sloppy appearance made a bad impression.* **12.** causing or characterized by discomfort, inconvenience, uneasiness, or annoyance; disagreeable; unpleasant: *I had a bad trip to Chicago. He had a bad day at the office.* **13.** easily provoked to anger; irascible: *a bad temper.* **14.** cross, irritable, or surly: *If I don't have my morning coffee, I'm in a bad mood all day.* **15.** more uncomfortable, persistent, painful, or dangerous than usual; severe: *a bad attack of asthma.* **16.** causing or resulting in disaster or severe damage or destruction: *a bad flood.* **17.** regretful, contrite, dejected, or upset: *He felt bad about having to leave the children all alone. She felt bad that her cat was ill.* **18.** disobedient, naughty, or misbehaving: *If you're bad at school, you'll go to bed without supper.* **19.** disreputable or dishonorable: *He's getting a bad name from changing jobs so often.* **20.** displaying a lack of skill, talent, proficiency, or judgment: *a bad painting; Bad drivers cause most of the accidents.* **21.** causing distress; unfortunate or unfavorable: *I'm afraid I have bad news for you.* **22.** not suitable or appropriate; disadvantageous or dangerous: *It was a bad place to swim because of the undertow. It was a bad day for fishing.* **23.** inclement; considered too stormy, hot, cold, etc.: *bad weather; We had a bad winter with a lot of snow.* **24.** disagreeable or offensive to the senses: *a bad odor.* **25.** exhibiting a lack of artistic sensitivity: *The room was decorated in bad taste.* **26.** not in keeping with a standard of behavior or conduct; coarse: *bad manners.* **27.** (of a word, speech, or writing) **a.** vulgar, obscene, or blasphemous: *bad language.* **b.** not properly observing rules or customs of grammar, usage, spelling, etc.; incorrect: *He speaks bad English.* **28.** unattractive, esp. because of a lack of pleasing proportions: *She has a bad figure.* **29.** (of the complexion) marred by defects; pockmarked or pimply; blemished. **30.** not profitable or worth the price paid: *The land was a bad buy and he lost thousands when he sold it.* **31.** ill-spent; wasted: *Don't throw good money after bad.* **32.** counterfeit; not genuine: *There was a bad fifty-cent piece in with the change.* **33.** having the character of a villain; villainous: *In the movies the good guys always beat the bad guys.* **34.** (of a return or service in tennis, squash, handball, etc.) failing to land within the in-bounds limits of a court or section of a court. **35.** *Slang.* outstandingly excellent; first-rate: *He's a bad man on drums, and the fans love him.* **36. not bad,** *Informal.* **a.** tolerably good; not without merit: *The dinner wasn't bad, but I've had better.* **b.** not difficult: *Once you know geometry, trigonometry isn't bad.* Also, **not half bad, not so bad, not too bad. 37. too bad,** unfortunate or disappointing: *It's too bad that he didn't go to college.* —*n.* **38.** that which is bad: *You have to take the bad with the good.* **39.** a bad condition, character, or quality: *His health seemed to go from bad to worse.* **40.** (*construed as pl.*) evil persons collectively (usually preceded by *the*): *the bad and the beautiful.* **41. go to the bad,** to deteriorate physically or morally: *She wept at seeing her son go to the bad.* **42. in bad,** *Informal.* **a.** in distress. **b.** in disfavor: *He's in bad with his mother-in-law.* **43. to the bad,** in arrears: *He's $100 to the bad on the deal.* —*adv. Informal.* **44.** badly: *He wanted it bad enough to steal it.* **45. bad off,** in poor or distressed condition or circumstances; destitute: *His family has been pretty bad off since he lost his job.* Also, **badly off.** Cf. **well off.** [ME *badde,* back formation from OE *bǣddel* hermaphrodite, *bǣdling* womanish man] —**bad′ness,** *n.*

—**Syn. 2.** depraved, corrupt, base, sinful, criminal, atrocious. BAD, EVIL, ILL, WICKED are closest in meaning in reference to that which is lacking in moral qualities or is actually vicious and reprehensible. BAD is the broadest and simplest term: *a bad man; bad habits.* EVIL applies to that which violates or leads to the violation of moral law: *evil practices.* ILL now appears mainly in certain fixed expressions, with a milder implication than that in evil: *ill will; ill-natured.* WICKED implies willful and determined doing of what is very wrong: *a wicked plan.* **3.** inferior, poor, deficient. **10.** putrefied. **21.** adverse, unlucky, unhappy. —**Ant.** (except for def. 35) good.

—**Usage.** BAD and BADLY are found with almost equal acceptance in standard English when following *feel,* although *bad* is usually preferred in formal writing: *I feel bad about my mistake. She felt badly about being late.* When preceded by *look, sound, smell,* etc., the usual choice is *bad: It looks bad for our team.*

bad[2] (bad), *v. Archaic.* a pt. of **bid.**

bad′ ac′tor, *Slang.* **1.** a mean, ill-tempered, troublemaking, or evil person. **2.** a vicious animal. **3.** an inveterate criminal.

Ba·da·joz (bä′thä hôth′), *n.* a city in SW Spain. 110,580 (est. 1960).

Ba·dakh·shan (bä däkh shän′), *n.* a former province in NE Afghanistan.

Ba·da·lo·na (bä′thä lô′nä), *n.* a seaport in NE Spain, near Barcelona. 82,845 (1955).

Ba·da·ri·an (bə där′ē ən), *adj.* of, pertaining to, or belonging to the predynastic culture of Upper Egypt, characterized by flint tools, stone axes, and pottery. [named after *Badari,* village in Upper Egypt, where the pottery was discovered, + -AN]

Bad′ Axe′, a town in E Michigan. 2998 (1960).

Badb (bov), *n. Irish Myth.* a spirit who, delighting in war, incited armies to fight and appeared to warriors about to be defeated.

bad′ blood′, unfriendly or hostile relations; enmity; hostility; animosity: *When the territory was being settled there was bad blood between the farmers and the ranchers.*

bad′ check′, a bank check that is returned because it was drawn against funds insufficient to cover it.

bad′ con′duct dis′charge, *U.S. Mil.* **1.** a discharge of a person from military service for an offense less serious than one for which a dishonorable discharge is given. **2.** a certificate of such a discharge.

bad′ debt′, a debt that is uncollectible or unlikely to be paid.

bad·de·ley·ite (bad′əl ē īt′), *n.* a mineral, zirconium oxide, ZrO_2, used as a refractory. [named after Joseph *Baddeley,* Englishman who first brought specimens to Europe (in 19th century) from Asia + -ITE[1]]

bad·der·locks (bad′ər loks′), *n.* (*construed as sing.*) an edible kelp, *Alaria esculenta,* found on the coasts of Europe and the British Isles. [? BALDER + LOCK[2] + -S[3]; cf. *Balder brae* plant name < Icel *Baldro brā* Balder's eyelash]

bad·die (bad′ē), *n. U.S. Slang.* an evil, malicious, or criminal person, esp. as depicted in a film, television show, etc. [BAD + -IE]

bad·dish (bad′ish), *adj.* rather bad; not particularly good. [BAD[1] + -ISH[1]]

bade (bad), *v.* a pt. of **bid.**

bad′ egg′, *Slang.* a person who is bad, dishonest, unreliable, or depraved; a good-for-nothing: *a bad egg who had served several years in prison.*

Ba·den (bäd′ən *for 1, 2;* bād′ən *for 3*), *n.* **1.** a former state in SW West Germany, now incorporated in Baden-Württemberg. **2.** Also, **Ba′den-Ba′den.** a city in W Baden-Württemberg, in SW West Germany. 40,200 (1963). **3.** a town in W Pennsylvania. 6109 (1960).

Ba·den-Pow·ell (bād′ən pō′əl, bad′ən pou′əl), *n.* **Robert Stephenson Smyth** (smith, smīth), **1st Baron,** 1857–1941, British general who founded the Boy Scouts in 1908 and, with his sister Lady Agnes, the Girl Guides in 1910.

Ba·den-Würt·tem·berg (bäd′ən vyrt′əm berkh′), *n.* a state in SW West Germany: formed 1951. 8,066,000 (1963); 13,800 sq. mi. *Cap.:* Stuttgart.

badge (baj), *n., v.,* **badged, badg·ing.** —*n.* **1.** a special or distinctive mark, token, or device worn as a sign of allegiance, membership, authority, achievement, etc.: *a police badge; a merit badge.* **2.** any emblem, token, or distinctive mark: *He considered horn-rimmed glasses to be the scholar's badge.* **3.** an identifying symbol, generally of a simple heraldic design, worn by the servants, retainers, or employees of a person or corporate body and used to mark his or its property. —*v.t.* **4.** to furnish or mark with a badge. [ME *bag(g)e* < ?] —**badge′less,** *adj.*

badg·er (baj′ər), *n.* **1.** any of various burrowing, carnivorous mammals of the family *Mustelidae,* as *Taxidea taxus,* of North America, and *Meles meles,* of Europe and Asia. **2.** the fur of this mammal. **3.** *Australian.* **a.** a wombat. **b.** bandicoot (def. 2). **4.** (*cap.*) a native or inhabitant of Wisconsin (the **Badger State**) (used as a nickname). **5.** a swablike device for cleaning excess mortar from the interiors of newly laid tile drains. —*v.t.* **6.** to harass persistently; pester; nag: *Stop badgering me! I had to badger him into coming with us.* [var. of *badgeard;* BADGE, -ARD, in allusion to white mark or badge on head] —**badg′er·ing·ly,** *adv.* —**badg′er·ly,** *adj.*

American badger,
Taxidea taxus
(Total length 2½ ft.; tail 6 in.)

—**Syn. 6.** vex, bedevil, plague, worry, disturb, bait.

badg′er game′, an extortion scheme in which a woman places a man in a compromising position and then victimizes him by demanding money when her male accomplice, pretending to be an outraged husband or relative, enters and threatens violence, scandal, etc.

badg′er plane′, *Carpentry.* a plane for finishing rabbets or the like.

Badg′er State′, Wisconsin (used as a nickname).

Bad′ Go′desberg (bät), official name of **Godesberg.**

bad′ hat′, *Chiefly Brit. Slang.* a dishonorable or morally objectionable person.

ba·di·geon (bə dij′ən), *n.* a composition for patching surface defects in carpentry or masonry. [< F < ?]

bad·i·nage (bad′ənäzh′, bad′ənij), *n., v.,* **-naged, -nag·ing.** —*n.* **1.** light, playful banter or raillery. —*v.t.* **2.** to banter or tease (someone) playfully. [< F < *badin* jester (whence *badiner* to jest) + *-age* -AGE]

ba·di·ne·rie (ba dē′nə rē; *Fr.* BA dēn° RĒ′), *n.* a short, playful dance form in duple time, sometimes forming part of an 18th-century instrumental suite. [< F < *badin(er)* (to) jest (see BADINAGE) + *-erie* -ERY]

bad-i-sad-o-bist-roz (bä′dē sä′dō bēst′roz′), *n.* Seistan. [< Pers: lit., wind of a hundred days]

bad·lands (bad′landz′), *n.* (*construed as pl.*) a barren area in which soft rock strata are eroded into varied, fantastic forms. [BAD[1] + LAND + -S[3]]

Bad′ Lands′, a barren, severely eroded region in SW South Dakota and NW Nebraska.

bad·ly (bad′lē), *adv.,* **worse, worst,** *adj.* —*adv.* **1.** in a defective or incorrect way: *The car runs badly.* **2.** in an unsatisfactory, inadequate, or unskilled manner: *a vague, badly written letter; He paints badly.* **3.** unfavorably: *His neighbors spoke badly of him. The weather turned out badly for the cruise.* **4.** in a wicked, evil, or morally or legally wrong way. **5.** in a disobedient, naughty, or ethically or socially wrong way: *He treats his parents badly.* **6.** very much; severely; to a great extent or degree: *a house badly in need of repair; to want something badly; to be hurt badly.* **7.** with great distress, resentment, regret, or emotional display: *He took the news of his mother's death badly.* **8. badly off.** See **bad** (def. 45). —*adj. Informal.* **9.** in ill health; sick: *He felt badly.* **10.** sorry; regretful: *I feel badly about your leaving so soon.* **11.** dejected; downcast. [BAD[1] + -LY]

—**Usage.** In the sense of "very much," the word BADLY is now common in standard English, although many users regard it as informal: *I need help badly. He wants that hat badly.* See also **bad.**

bad·man (bad′man′), *n., pl.* **-men.** a bandit, outlaw, desperado, etc., esp. in the early history of the western U.S. [BAD[1] + MAN]

B.Adm.Eng., Bachelor of Administrative Engineering.

bad·min·ton (bad′min tən), *n.* a game played on a rectangular court by two players or two pairs of players equipped with light rackets used to volley a shuttlecock over a high net that divides the court in half. [named after *Badminton,* the country seat of the duke of Beaufort in Gloucestershire, England]

Ba·do·glio (bä dô′lyô), *n.* **Pie·tro** (pye′trô), 1871–1956, Italian general.

bad-tem·pered (bad′tem′pərd), *adj.* cross; cranky; surly; ill-tempered: *a bad-tempered person.*

bad′ time′, a period of great difficulty, distress, or the like: *The prosecutor gave the witness a very bad time.*

BAE, 1. Bureau of Agricultural Economics. **2.** Bureau of American Ethnology.

B.A.E., 1. Bachelor of Aeronautical Engineering. **2.** Bachelor of Agricultural Engineering. **3.** Bachelor of Architectural Engineering. **4.** Bachelor of Art Education. **5.** Bachelor of Arts in Education.

B.A.Ed., Bachelor of Arts in Education.

Bae·da (bē′də), *n.* **Saint.** See **Bede, Saint.**

Bae·de·ker (bā′də kər), *n.* **1.** any of the series of guidebooks for travelers issued by the German publisher

Karl Baedeker, 1801–59, and his successors. **2.** any guidebook, pamphlet, or the like, containing information useful to travelers: *a Baedeker to the restaurants of Europe.*

Baeke·land (bāk′land′; *Flem.* bäk′ə länt′), *n.* **Le·o Hen·drik** (lē′ō hen′drik; *Flem.* lā′ō hen′drik), 1863–1944, U.S. chemist, born in Belgium.

bael (bel, bāl, bīl), *n.* **1.** a spiny, rutaceous tree, *Aegle Marmelos,* of India. **2.** the hard-shelled, greenish-yellow, edible fruit of this tree. Also, **bel.** Also called **Bengal quince.** [< Hindi *bel*]

Baer (bâr), *n.* **1. Karl Ernst von** (kärl ŭrnst fən), 1792–1876, Estonian zoologist and pioneer embryologist. **2. Max,** 1909–59, U.S. boxer: world heavyweight champion 1934.

bae·tyl (bēt′əl), *n.* *Class. Antiq.* a meteorite or stone held sacred or believed to be of divine origin. Also, **bae·tu·lus, bae·ty·lus** (bēt′ələs). [< L *baetul(us)* < Gk *baítylos* meteoric stone] —**bae·tyl·ic** (bē til′ik), *adj.*

Bae·yer (bā′ər; *Ger.* be′yər), *n.* **(Jo·hann Frie·drich Wil·helm) A·dolf von** (yō′hän frē′drik wil′helm ad′olf von, ā′dolf; *Ger.* yō′hän frē′drikh vil′helm ä′dôlf fən), 1835–1917, German chemist: Nobel prize 1905.

Ba·ez (bī ez′, bī′iz), *n.* **Joan,** born 1941, U.S. folk singer.

baff (baf), *Golf.* —*v.i.* **1.** to strike the ground with the club in making a stroke. —*n.* **2.** a baffing stroke, unduly lofting the ball. [? special use of **baff** poor (north dial.), equiv. to Scot *bauch* weak, poor, shaky < Scand; cf. Icel *bāgr* insecure, poor]

Baf·fin (baf′in), *n.* **William,** 1584?–1622, an English navigator who explored arctic North America.

Baf′fin Bay′, a part of the Arctic Ocean between W Greenland and E Baffin Island.

Baf′fin Is′land, a Canadian island in the Arctic Ocean, between Greenland and N Canada. ab. 1000 mi. long; 190,000 sq. mi. Also called **Baf′fin Land′.**

baf·fle (baf′əl), *v.,* **-fled, -fling,** *n.* —*v.t.* **1.** to confuse, bewilder, or perplex: *He was baffled by the technical language of the instructions.* **2.** to frustrate or confound; thwart by creating confusion or bewilderment. **3.** to check or deflect the movement of (sound, light, fluids, etc.). **4.** to equip with a baffle or baffles. **5.** *Obs.* to cheat; trick. —*v.i.* **6.** to struggle ineffectually, as a ship in a gale. —*n.* **7.** something which balks, checks, or deflects; bafflement or perplexity. **8.** an artificial obstruction for checking or deflecting the flow of gases (as in a boiler), sounds (as in the loudspeaker system of a radio or hi-fi set), light (as in a darkroom), etc. **9.** any boxlike enclosure for mounting a loudspeaker. [? < Scot *bauchle* to disgrace, treat with contempt < *bauch* (see BAFF) + -LE] —**baf′fle·ment,** *n.* —**baf′fler,** *n.* —**baf′fling,** *adj.* —**baf′fling·ly,** *adv.* —**baf′fling·ness,** *n.*
—**Syn. 1.** See **thwart.**

baf·fle·plate (baf′əl plāt′), *n.* a plate used as a baffle. [BAFFLE + PLATE¹]

baf′fling wind′ (wind), *Naut.* a light wind changing direction frequently.

baff·y (baf′ē), *n., pl.* **baff·ies.** *Golf.* a short, wooden club with a steep-sloped face, for lofting the ball. Also called **number four wood.** [BAFF + -Y²]

bag (bag), *n., v.,* **bagged, bag·ging,** *interj.* —*n.* **1.** a container or receptacle of leather, cloth, paper, etc., capable of being closed at the mouth; pouch. **2.** something resembling or suggesting such a receptacle. **3.** a suitcase or other portable receptacle for carrying articles, as in traveling. **4.** a purse or moneybag. **5.** any of various measures of capacity. **6.** a sac, as in an animal body. **7.** an udder. **8.** *Hunting.* the amount of game taken, esp. by one hunter in one hunting trip or over a specified period. **9.** something hanging in a loose, pouchlike manner, as skin, cloth, etc.; a baggy part: *He had bags under his eyes from lack of sleep.* **10.** *Baseball.* base¹ (def. 8b). **11.** *Informal.* a style of jazz: *It was hard to tell in what bag their playing belonged.* **12.** *Slang.* an unattractive, often slatternly woman: *a gossipy old bag.* **13.** *Slang.* **a.** a person's avocation, hobby, major interest, or obsession: *Jazz isn't my bag. He's in the opera bag.* **b.** a person's mood or frame of mind: *The boss is in a mean bag today.* **c.** an environment, condition, or situation. **14. bags,** *Brit.* **a.** *Informal.* plenty; much; many (usually fol. by *of*): *bags of time; bags of opportunities.* **b.** *Slang.* trousers. **15. bag and baggage,** *Informal.* **a.** with all one's personal property: *When they went to collect the rent, they found he had left, bag and baggage.* **b.** completely, totally: *The equipment had disappeared, bag and baggage, without a trace.* **16. hold the bag,** *U.S. Informal.* to be forced to bear the entire blame or responsibility that was to have been shared: *His accomplices flew to South America on news of the theft and left him holding the bag.* **17. in the bag,** *Slang.* virtually certain; assured; definite: *His promotion is in the bag. The sale of the house is in the bag.* —*v.i.* **18.** to swell or bulge: *A stiff breeze made the sails bag out.* **19.** to hang loosely like an empty bag: *an oversize coat bagging about him.* —*v.t.* **20.** to cause to swell or bulge; distend: *The wind bagged the curtain.* **21.** to put into a bag. **22.** to kill or catch, as in hunting: *I bagged my first deer when I was a teenager.* **23.** *Theat.* clew (def. 12a). —*interj.* **24. bags!** *Brit. Slang.* (used to lay first claim to something): *Bags it! Bags, I go first!* [ME *bagge* < Scand; cf. Icel *baggi* pack, bundle]
—**Syn. 1.** reticule. BAG, SACK, referring to a pouchlike object, are often used interchangeably, esp. in the Middle West. A BAG, though it may be of any size, is usually small, and made of such materials as paper, leather, etc. A SACK is usually large, oblong, and made of coarse material. **22.** shoot, trap, snare.

B.Ag., Bachelor of Agriculture.

ba·gasse (bə gas′), *n.* **1.** crushed sugar-cane or beet refuse from sugar making. **2.** a kind of paper made from fibers of bagasse. [< F < Sp *bagazo* husks left after pressing of grapes or the like < *bag(age)* refuse (see BAGGAGE) + *-azo* aug. suffix]

bag·a·telle (bag′ə tel′), *n.* **1.** something of little value; a trifle. **2.** a game played on a board having at one end holes into which balls are to be struck with a cue. **3.** pinball. **4.** a short and light musical composition, usually for the piano. [< F < It *bagattella* < *bagatta* small possession < *baga* (< L *bāca* berry, fruit) + *-tt-* dim. suffix (akin to -ETTE) + *-ella* < L *-illa* dim. suffix]

Bag·a·tha (bag′ə thə), *n.* *Douay Bible.* Bigtha.

Bag·dad (bag′dad, bäg däd′), *n.* Baghdad.

B.Ag.E., Bachelor of Agricultural Engineering.

Bage·hot (baj′ət), *n.* **Walter,** 1826–77, English economist, political journalist, and critic.

ba·gel (bā′gəl), *n.* a leavened, doughnut-shaped, hard roll, often eaten with cream cheese and lox. [< Yiddish *beygel,* var. of dial. G *Beugel* < Gmc **baugring* (see BEE²) + *-*il-* n. suffix]

bag·flow·er (bag′flou′ər), *n.* a woody vine, *Clematis thomsonae,* of western Africa, having very showy, branching clusters of flowers with an ivory-white calyx and crimson corolla.

bag·ful (bag′fo͝ol), *n., pl.* **-fuls. 1.** the contents of or amount held by a bag: *three bagfuls of groceries.* **2.** the quantity required to fill a bag; a considerable amount: *a bagful of groceries.* [ME; see BAG, -FUL]

bag·gage (bag′ij), *n.* **1.** trunks, suitcases, etc., used in traveling; luggage. **2.** the portable equipment of an army. **3.** a prostitute. **4.** any immoral, dishonorable, or undignified woman. **5.** *Disparaging.* an old woman. **6.** *Informal.* a pert, playful young woman or girl. [late ME *bagage* < MF < OF *bag(ues)* bundles, packs (? < Scand; see BAG) + *-age* -AGE]

bag′gage car′, a car of a passenger train in which luggage, trunks, etc., are carried.

bag·gage·mas·ter (bag′ij mas′tər), *n.* *U.S.* a person employed, esp. by a railroad, bus company, or steamship line, to take charge of passengers' baggage. [BAGGAGE + MASTER]

bag·ging (bag′ing), *n.* woven material, as of hemp or jute, for bags. [BAG + -ING¹]

bag·gy (bag′ē), *adj.,* **-gi·er, -gi·est.** baglike; hanging loosely. [BAG + -Y¹] —**bag′gi·ly,** *adv.* —**bag′gi·ness,** *n.*

Bagh·dad (bag′dad, bäg däd′), *n.* a city in and the capital of Iraq, in the central part, on the Tigris. 355,958; with suburbs, 730,549 (1957). Also, **Bagdad.**

Bagh′dad Pact′, a treaty (1955) for economic and military cooperation, signed by Great Britain, Iran, Pakistan, Turkey, and Iraq. Iraq withdrew in 1959. Cf. **CENTO.**

Bagh·eer·a (bag ēr′ə), *n.* a crush-resistant velvet made of uncut pile and used in the manufacture of evening wear and wraps.

bagh·la (bug′lä), *n.* an Arabian sailing vessel, having lugsails on two or three masts, a straight, raking stem, and a transom stern. Also, **bag·ga·la** (bug′ə lä′).

bag′ house′, a place in which dust entrained in the combustion gases of a furnace is removed.

ba·gi·o (bä′gē ō′, bäg yō′), *n., pl.* **-gi·os.** baguio.

bag′ la′dy, a homeless woman, usually impoverished and elderly, who carries all her possessions with her in shopping bags and lives on the streets and in public places, as railroad stations. Also called **shopping-bag lady.**

Bag·ley (bag′lē), *n.* **William Chan·dler** (chan′dlər), 1874–1946, U.S. educator and writer.

bag·man (bag′mən), *n., pl.* **-men. 1.** *Brit.* a traveling salesman; drummer. **2.** *Slang.* a racketeer who is assigned by his superiors to collect, carry, or distribute payoff money. **3.** *Australian.* a tramp; swagman. [BAG + MAN]

bagn·io (ban′yō, bän′-), *n., pl.* **-ios. 1.** a brothel. **2.** (esp. in Italy or Turkey) a bath or bathing house. **3.** *Archaic.* a prison for slaves, esp. in the Orient. [< It *bagno* < L *balneum, balineum* < Gk *balaneîon* bathroom, bath]

bag′ of wind′ (wind), windbag.

bag·pipe (bag′pīp′), *n., v.,* **-piped, -pip·ing.** —*n.* **1.** Often, **bagpipes.** a reed instrument consisting of a melody pipe and one or more accompanying drone pipes protruding from a windbag into which the air is blown by the mouth or a bellows. —*v.t.* **2.** *Naut.* to back (a fore-and-aft sail) by hauling the sheet to windward. [late ME *baggepipe.* See BAG, PIPE¹] —**bag′pip′er,** *n.*

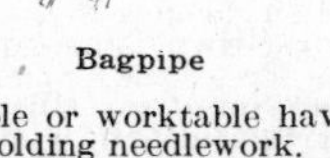

Bagpipe

B.Agr., Bachelor of Agriculture.

Ba·grit·ski (bä grēt′ski), *n.* **E·du·ard** (e do͞o ärt′), *(Eduard Georgievich Dzyubin),* 1895–1935, Russian poet.

B.Ag.Sc., Bachelor of Agricultural Science.

bag′ ta′ble, a sewing table or worktable having a suspended pouch or bag for holding needlework.

ba·guette (ba get′), *n.* **1.** *Jewelry.* **a.** a rectangular cut given to a small gem, esp. a diamond. **b.** a gem having this cut. **2.** *Archit.* a small convex molding, esp. one of semicircular section. Also, **ba·guet′.** [< F < It *bacchetta* little stick < *bacch(io)* stick (< L *baculus*) + *-etta* -ETTE]

ba·gui·o (bä gē ō′, bäg yō′), *n., pl.* **-gui·os.** (in the Philippines) a tropical cyclone. Also, **bagio.** [< Sp < Tagalog *bagyô*]

Ba·gui·o (bä′gē ō′; *Sp.* bä′gyô), *n.* a city on W Luzon, in the N Philippines: summer capital. 36,531 (est. 1960); 4961 ft. high.

bag·wig (bag′wig′), *n.* a wig with the back hair enclosed in a fabric bag, much used in the 18th century. [BAG + WIG] —**bag′wigged′,** *adj.*

bag·wom·an (bag′wo͝om′ən), *n., pl.* **-wom·en.** *Slang.* a female bagman. [BAG + WOMAN]

bag·work (bag′wûrk′), *n.* *Civ. Eng.* a revetment, consisting of heavy material sewn into bags, for protecting embankments against scour. [BAG + WORK]

bag·worm (bag′wûrm′), *n.* the caterpillar of any moth of the family *Psychidae,* which constructs and lives in a bag of silk, leaves, etc. [BAG + WORM]

bah (bä, ba), *interj.* (an exclamation of contempt or annoyance): *Bah! Humbug! There is no Santa Claus!*

ba·ha·dur (bə hô′do͝or, -hä′-), *n.* (*often cap.*) a title of respect commonly affixed to the names of European officers in Indian documents or used in ceremonious mention by Indians: *Jonas Sahib Bahadur.* [< Hindi < Pers]

Ba·há'í (bə hī′), *n., pl.* **-há'ís,** *adj.* —*n.* **1.** an adherent of Bahaism. —*adj.* **2.** of or pertaining to Bahá'ís or Bahaism. [< Pers < Ar < *bahā' (u'llah)* splendor (of God) + *-i* suffix of membership]

Ba·ha·ism (bə hä′iz əm), *n.* a form of Babism, originated in 1863 by Hussain Ali, or Bahaullah, having an oriental, mystical quality and reflecting specifically the attitudes of the Islamic Shiah sect, but with an emphasis on tolerance and a belief in the essential worth of all religions. [BAHAI + -ISM] —**Ba·ha′ist,** *n., adj.*

Ba·ha′ma grass′ (bə hä′mə, -hā′-). See **Bermuda grass.**

Ba·ha·mas (bə hä′məz, -hā′-), *n.* (*construed as pl.*) a group of islands in the British West Indies, SE of Florida: a sovereign member of the British Commonwealth; formerly a colony. 210,000; 4404 sq. mi. *Cap.:* Nassau. Also called **Baha′ma Is′lands.** —**Ba·ha·mi·an** (bə hā′mē ən, -hä′-), *n., adj.*

Ba·ha′sa Indone′sia (bä hä′sə), official name of the Indonesian language.

Ba·ha·ul·lah (bä hä′o͞ol lä′), *n.* *(Hussain Ali)* 1817–92, Persian religious leader; founder of Bahaism. Also, **Bahá′ Ul·lah′.**

Ba·ha·wal·pur (bə hä′wəl po͝or′, bä′wəl-), *n.* **1.** a state in E Pakistan. 3,205,000 (1961); 32,443 sq. mi. **2.** the capital of this state. 41,646 (1951).

Ba·hi·a (bä ē′ə, bə-), *n.* **1.** a coastal state of E Brazil. 5,990,605 (1960); 216,130 sq. mi. *Cap.:* Salvador. **2.** See **São Salvador.**

Ba·hí·a Blan·ca (bä ē′ä bläng′kä), a seaport in E Argentina. 135,800 (est. 1960).

Bahr (bär), *n.* **Her·mann** (her′män), 1863–1934, Austrian playwright and critic.

Bah·rain (bə rīn′, -rān′, bä-), *n.* **1.** an independent state in the W Persian Gulf, consisting of a group of islands: formerly a British protectorate. 300,000; 232 sq. mi. *Cap.:* Manama. **2.** the largest island in this group; oil fields; international banking center. 265,000; 213 sq. mi. Also, **Bah·rein′.**

baht (bät), *n., pl.* **bahts, baht.** a paper money and monetary unit of Thailand, equal to 100 satangs; tical. [< Thai *bāt*]

ba·hut (bä′ho͞ot, -ho͞ot; bə ho͞ot′, -ho͞ot′; *Fr.* ba y′), *n., pl.* **ba·huts** (bä′ho͞ots, -ho͞ots; bə ho͞ots′, -ho͞ots′; *Fr.* ba y′). **1.** a medieval French chest for household goods originally small and portable. **2.** a dwarf parapet or attic wall, esp. one carrying the wall plates of a church roof. [< F]

ba·hu·vri·hi (bä′ho͞o vrē′hē), *n., pl.* **-his.** a compound noun or adjective consisting of two constituents, the first of which is adjectival and describes the person or object denoted by the second, which is nominal: the compound as a whole denotes or describes a person or object having what is denoted by the second element, as *bonehead, heavy-handed, redcoat.* [< Skt: lit., having much rice < *bahu-* much + *vrīhi-* rice; used to name the type of compound word of which it is an example]

bai (bī), *n.* a yellow mist occurring in eastern China and Japan during the spring and fall, caused by dust from the interior of China. Also called **sand mist.**

Ba·iae (bā′yē), *n.* an ancient resort city in SW Italy, near Naples: villas of Caesar, Nero, and Pompey.

bai·dar·ka (bī där′kə), *n.* bidarka.

bai·gneuse (be nyœz′), *n., pl.* **-gneuses** (-nyœz′). *Fr. Furniture.* a day bed of the Empire period, having a back sloping and curving to form a rounded head and foot. [< F: lit., bather (fem.)]

Bai·kal (bī käl′), *n.* **Lake,** a lake in the S Soviet Union in Asia: the deepest lake in the world. 13,200 sq. mi.; 5714 ft. deep.

bail¹ (bāl), *Law.* —*n.* **1.** property given as surety that a person released from custody will return at an appointed time. **2.** the person or persons giving it. **3.** the position or the privilege of being bailed. **4. go** or **stand bail for,** to provide bail for: *He spent the night in jail because no one would stand bail for him.* **5. jump bail,** to abscond while free on bail: *The suspect jumped bail and is now being sought.* **6. on bail,** (of a released suspect in a criminal proceeding) having posted bond: *He was out on bail within 10 hours of his arrest.* —*v.t.* **7.** to grant or obtain the liberty of (a person under arrest) on security given for his appearance when required, as in court for trial. **8.** to deliver possession of (goods) for storage, hire, or other special purpose, without transfer of ownership. [late ME *bayle* < AF *bail* custody, charge < OF, back formation from *baillier* to hand over < L *bāiulāre* to serve as porter < *bāiul(us)* porter]

bail² (bāl), *n.* **1.** the semicircular handle of a kettle or pail. **2.** a hooplike support, as for the canvas cover on a Conestoga wagon. **3.** a metal band or bar equipped with rollers for holding a sheet or sheets of paper against the platen of a printing press, typewriter, etc. Also, **bale.** [late ME *beyl* < Scand; cf. Icel *beyglast* to become bent < *baug(r)* ring (see BEE³) + *-*il* n. suffix + *-ast* middle inf. suffix]

bail[3] (bāl), *v.t.* **1.** to dip (water) out of a boat, as with a bucket. **2.** to clear of water by dipping (usually fol. by *out*): *to bail out a boat.* —*v.i.* **3.** to bail water. **4. bail out, a.** *Informal.* to make a parachute jump from an airplane. **b.** *Slang.* to relieve or assist (a person, company, etc.) in an emergency situation, esp. a financial crisis: *The corporation bailed out its failing subsidiary through a series of refinancing operations.* **c.** *Slang.* to give up or abandon, as to evade a responsibility: *His partner bailed out before the business got on its feet.* —*n.* **5.** Also, **bail′er.** a bucket, dipper, or other container used for bailing. Also, **bale** (for defs. 1–4). [late ME *bayle* < MF *baille* a bucket < VL **bāi(u)la;* akin to L *bāiulus* carrier. See BAIL[1]]

bail[4] (bāl), *n.* **1.** *Cricket.* either of the two small bars or sticks laid across the tops of the stumps which form the wicket. **2.** *Chiefly Brit.* a bar, framework, partition, or the like, for confining or separating cows, horses, etc., in a stable. **3. bails,** *Obs.* the wall of an outer court of a feudal castle. —*v.t.* **4. bail up,** *Australian.* **a.** to confine a cow for milking, as in a bail. **b.** to force (a person) to surrender or identify himself or to state his business. **c.** to waylay or rob (someone). —*interj.* **5. bail up!** *Australian.* (the cry of challenge of a pioneer or person living in the bush.) [ME *baile* < OF < L *bacula,* pl. of *baculum* stick]

bail·a·ble (bā′lə bəl), *adj. Law.* **1.** capable of being set free on bail. **2.** admitting of bail: *a bailable offense.* [BAIL[1] + -ABLE]

bail′ bond′, *Law.* a formal document executed by a prisoner together with one or more sureties that guarantee the presence of the prisoner in court at the appointed time.

Baile Átha Cliath (bäl′yä ä klē′), Gaelic name of **Dublin.**

bail·ee (bā lē′), *n. Law.* one to whom goods are delivered in bailment. [BAIL[1] + -EE]

bai·ley (bā′lē), *n., pl.* **-leys. 1.** the defensive wall surrounding an outer court of a castle. **2.** the courtyard itself. Also, **ballium.** [var. of BAIL[4]]

Bai·ley (bā′lē), *n.* **1. Liberty Hyde,** 1858–1954, U.S. botanist, horticulturist, and writer. **2.** Also, **Bayley, Baily, Baillie.** a boy's given name.

Bai′ley bridge′, a temporary bridge formed of prefabricated, interchangeable, steel truss panels bolted together. [named after Sir Donald *Bailey* (b. 1901), British engineer, its designer]

bail·ie (bā′lē), *n.* (in Scotland) a municipal officer or magistrate, corresponding to an English alderman. [ME *baillie* < OF *bailli,* var. of *baillif* BAILIFF]

bail·iff (bā′lif), *n.* **1.** an officer similar to a sheriff or his deputy, employed to execute writs and processes, make arrests, keep order in the court, etc. **2.** (in Britain) a person charged with local administrative authority, or the chief magistrate in certain towns. **3.** (esp. in Britain) an overseer of a landed estate or farm. [ME *baillif* < OF < *bail* custody (see BAIL[1]) + *-if* -IVE] —**bail′iff·ship′,** *n.*

bail·i·wick (bā′lə wik), *n.* **1.** the district within which a bailie or bailiff has jurisdiction. **2.** a person's area of skill, knowledge, or training: *to confine suggestions to one's own bailiwick.* [late ME < *baili-* BAILIE + *wick* < OE *wīc* << L *vīcus* hamlet]

Bail·laud (bā loud′, -lōd′), *n.* a walled plain in the first quadrant of the face of the moon: about 60 miles in diameter.

Bail·lie (bā′lē), *n.* a boy's given name. Also, **Bailey, Baily, Bayley.**

Bail·ly (bā′lē), *n.* a walled plain in the third quadrant of the face of the moon, in the libration area, near the South Pole: about 183 miles in diameter.

bail·ment (bāl′mənt), *n. Law.* the delivery of personal property returnable to the bailor after being held for some purpose. [earlier *bailement* < AF < OF *baillement.* See BAIL[1], -MENT]

bail·or (bā′lər, bā lôr′), *n.* one who delivers goods or money in bailment. [BAIL[1] + -OR[2]]

bail·out (bāl′out′), *n.* **1.** the act of parachuting from an aircraft, esp. to escape a crash, fire, etc. —*adj.* **2.** of, pertaining to, or consisting of means for relieving an emergency situation: *bailout measures for hard-pressed small businesses.* Also, **bail′-out′.** [n., adj. use of v. phrase *bail out*]

bails·man (bālz′mən), *n., pl.* **-men.** *Law.* a person who acts as bail or surety. [BAIL[1] + -'S[1] + MAN]

Bai·ly (bā′lē), *n.* **1.** a walled plain in the first quadrant of the face of the moon: about 20 miles in diameter. **2.** Also, **Bailey, Bayley, Baillie.** a boy's given name.

Bai′ly's beads′, *Astron.* spots of light that encircle the moon, resembling a string of luminous beads, visible immediately before and after a total eclipse, caused by the sun's light shining between the mountains on the moon's surface. Cf. **diamond ring effect.** [named after Francis *Baily* (1774–1844), English astronomer who first described them]

Bain (bān), *n.* **Alexander,** 1818–1903, Scottish philosopher and psychologist.

Bain·bridge (bān′brij′), *n.* a boy's given name.

bain·ite (bā′nīt), *n.* an aggregate of iron carbide and ferrite, formed from austenite below the temperature at which pearlite forms and above that at which martensite forms, needle-shaped at lower temperatures and having a microstructure with a feathery appearance at high temperatures. Also called **troostite-martensite, troostomartensite.** [named after Edgar C. *Bain* (b. 1891) American physicist and metallurgist + -ITE[1]]

bain-ma·rie (ban′mə rē′; *Fr.* ban ma rē′), *n., pl.* **bains-ma·rie** (ban′mə rē′; *Fr.* ban ma rē′). *Brit.* **1.** (in cooking) a vessel containing hot or boiling water into which other vessels are placed to warm or cook the food in them. **2.** a double boiler. [< F: lit., bath of Mary, i.e., Miriam (sister of Moses), reputed author of a book on alchemy]

Bai·ram (bī räm′, bī′räm), *n.* either of two Islamic festivals, one (**lesser Bairam**) a fast occurring during the first three days of Shawwal, the other (**greater Bairam**) a time of sacrifice beginning on the tenth of Zu'lhijjah and lasting two or three days. [< Turk < Pers]

Baird (bârd), *n.* a boy's given name.

Baird′ Moun′tains, a mountain range in NW Alaska, forming the west range of the Brooks Range.

Baire′ cat′egory the′orem (bâr), *Math.* the theorem that a nonempty, complete pseudometric space cannot be written as the union of a countable number of nowhere-dense sets. Cf. **first category, second category.**

bairn (bârn; *Scot.* barn), *n. Scot. and North Eng.* a child; son or daughter. [ME *berne, barn* < OE *bearn;* c. Icel, OHG, OS, Goth *barn,* OFris *bern,* MD *baren;* akin to BEAR[1]] —**bairn′ish, bairn′ly,** *adj.* —**bairn′ish·ness,** *n.*

Ba. Is., Bahama Islands.

bait (bāt), *n.* **1.** food, or some substitute, used as a lure in angling, trapping, etc. **2.** an allurement; enticement: *Employees were lured with the bait of annual bonuses.* **3.** an object for pulling molten or liquefied material, as glass, from a vat or the like by adhesion. **4.** *Brit. Slang.* food. —*v.t.* **5.** to prepare (a hook or trap) with bait. **6.** to entice by deception or trickery so as to entrap or destroy: *using fake signal lights to bait the ships onto the rocks.* **7.** to lure as with bait; captivate: *baiting a husband with culinary artistry.* **8.** to set dogs upon (an animal) for sport. **9.** to worry; torment; persecute: *a nasty habit of baiting defenseless subordinates.* **10.** to tease: *She loves to bait him about his male vanity.* **11.** to feed and water (a horse or other animal), esp. during a journey. —*v.i. Archaic.* **12.** to stop for food or refreshment during a journey. **13.** (of a horse or other animal) to take food; feed. [ME *baite(n)* < Scand; cf. Icel *beita* to cause to bite (see BATE[3]), *beita* food, akin to BIT[2]] —**bait′er,** *n.*
—**Syn. 9.** badger, heckle, pester.

bait′ cast′ing, *Angling.* the act or technique of casting an artificial or natural lure attached to a silk or nylon line wound on a reel having a revolving spool, the rod used being shorter and less flexible than that used in fly casting.

baith (bāth), *adj., pron. Scot. and North Eng.* both.

baize (bāz), *n., v.,* **baized, baiz·ing.** —*n.* **1.** a soft, usually green, woolen fabric resembling felt, used chiefly for the tops of billiard tables. **2.** an article of this fabric or of a fabric resembling it. —*v.t.* **3.** to line or cover with baize. [earlier *bayes* < F *baies* (n.) < fem. pl. of *bai* (adj.) BAY[5]]

Ba·ja Ca·li·for·nia (bä′hä kä′lē fôr′nyä; *Eng.* bä′hə kal′ə fôr′nyə, -fôr′nē ə), Spanish name of **Lower California.**

ba·ja·da (bə hä′də), *n.* an alluvial plain formed at the base of a mountain by the coalescing of several alluvial fans. [< Sp: slope, swoop, prop. fem. ptp. of *bajar* to descend < VL **bassiāre* < LL *bass(us)* short, low]

Baj·er (bī′ər), *n.* **Fred·rik** (fred′rik; *Dan.* frith′rik), 1837–1922, Danish politician and author: Nobel peace prize 1908.

B.A.Jour., Bachelor of Arts in Journalism.

bake (bāk), *v.,* **baked, bak·ing,** *n.* —*v.t.* **1.** to cook by dry heat in an oven, under coals, or on heated metal or stones. **2.** to harden by heat: *to bake pottery in a kiln.* —*v.i.* **3.** to bake bread, a casserole, etc. **4.** to become baked: *The cake will bake in about half an hour.* —*n.* **5.** *U.S.* a social occasion at which the chief food is baked. **6.** *Scot.* cracker (def. 1). [ME *bake(n)* < OE *bacan;* c. D *bakken,* G *backen,* Icel *baka;* akin to Gk *phōgein* to roast]

baked′ Alas′ka, a dessert consisting of ice cream on a cake base, placed briefly in a hot oven to brown its topping of meringue.

baked′ beans′, beans that have been baked, usually with salt pork, brown sugar or molasses, and seasonings.

baked′ meat′, *Obs.* bakemeat.

bake·house (bāk′hous′), *n., pl.* **-hous·es** (-hou′ziz). a building or room to bake in; bakery. [late ME; see BAKE, HOUSE]

Ba·ke·lite (bā′kə līt′, bāk′līt′), *n. Trademark.* any of a series of thermosetting plastics prepared by heating phenol or cresol with formaldehyde and ammonia under pressure: used for radio cabinets, telephone receivers, electric insulators, and molded plastic ware.

bake·meat (bāk′mēt′), *n. Obs.* **1.** pastry; pie. **2.** cooked food, esp. a meat pie. Also, **baked meat.** [ME *bake mete* < OE *bacen mete* baked food. See BAKE, MEAT]

bake-off (bāk′ôf′, -of′), *n.* a baking contest, esp. among amateur cooks, in which entries must be prepared and baked within a stipulated time.

bak·er (bā′kər), *n.* **1.** a person who bakes, esp. one who makes and sells bread, cake, etc. **2.** a small portable oven. **3.** (a word formerly used in communications to represent the letter *B.*) [ME *baker(e)* < OE *bæcere.* See BAKE, -ER[1]] —**ba′ker-like′,** *adj.*

Bak·er (bā′kər), *n.* **1. Sir Benjamin,** 1840–1907, English engineer. **2. George Pierce,** 1866–1935, U.S. critic, author, and professor of drama. **3. Newton Diehl** (dēl), 1871–1937, U.S. lawyer: Secretary of War 1916–21. **4. Ray Stan·nard** (stan′ərd) ("*David Grayson*"), 1870–1946, U.S. author. **5. Mount,** a mountain in NW Washington, in the Cascade Range: highest peak, 10,750 ft. **6.** a town in NE Oregon. 9986 (1960). **7.** a town in central Louisiana. 4823 (1960).

Bak′er Is′land, an island in the Pacific near the equator, belonging to the U.S. 1 sq. mi.

Ba′ker-Nunn′ cam′era (bā′kər nun′), a large camera for tracking missiles and satellites. Also called **Ba′ker-Nunn′ sat′ellite-track′ing cam′era.**

bak′er's doz′en, a group of 13; a dozen plus one: from the former practice among bakers and other tradesmen of giving 13 items to the dozen as a safeguard against penalties for short weights and measures.

Bak·ers·field (bā′kərz fēld′), *n.* a city in S California. 56,848 (1960).

bak·er·y (bā′kə rē), *n., pl.* **-er·ies. 1.** Also called **bake·shop** (bāk′shop′). a baker's shop. **2.** a place where baked goods are made or sold. [BAKER + -Y[3]; now taken as BAKE + -ERY]

bake·ware (bāk′wâr′), *n.* heat-resistant dishes, as of glass, pottery, etc., in which food may be baked. [BAKE + WARE[1]]

Bakh·mut (bäk′mo͝ot), *n.* former name of **Artemovsk.**

bak·ing (bā′king), *n.* **1.** the act of one who or that which bakes. **2.** the quantity baked at one time; batch. [ME; see BAKE, -ING[1]]

bak′ing pow′der, any of various powders used as a substitute for yeast in baking, composed of sodium bicarbonate mixed with an acid substance capable of setting carbon dioxide free when the mixture is moistened and causing the dough to rise.

bak′ing so′da. See **sodium bicarbonate.**

ba·kla·va (bä′klə vä′, bä′klə vä′), *n.* a Near Eastern pastry made of many layers of paper-thin dough with a filling, usually of honey and ground nuts. Also, **ba·kla·wa** (bä′klə vä′, bä′klə vä′). [< Turk]

bak·sheesh (bak′shēsh), (in India, Turkey, etc.) —*n.* **1.** a tip, present, or gratuity. —*v.t., v.i.* **2.** to give a tip. Also, **bak′shish, backsheesh, bak′shis, backshish.** [< Pers *bakhshīsh* < *bakhshī(dan)* (to) give + *-sh* n. suffix]

Bakst (bäkst), *n.* **Lé·on Ni·ko·la·e·vich** (le ôn′ ni ko lä′yə vich), 1866–1924, Russian painter and designer.

Ba·ku (bu ko͞o′), *n.* a city in and the capital of Azerbaijan, in the E part, on the Caspian Sea. 1,022,000; with suburbs, 1,550,000.

Ba·ku·nin (bä ko͞o′nin), *n.* **Mi·kha·il A·le·ksan·dro·vich** (mi khä ēl′ ä′le ksän′dro vich), 1814–76, Russian anarchist and writer.

bal (bal), *n.* Balmoral (def. 2).

BAL, *Chem.* dimercaprol. [< *B(ritish) A(nti-)L(ewisite)*]

Bal., Baluchistan.

bal., **1.** balance. **2.** balancing.

Ba·la (bā′lə), *n. Douay Bible.* Bilhah.

Ba·laam (bā′ləm), *n.* a Mesopotamian diviner who, when commanded by Balak to curse the Israelites, blessed them and uttered favorable prophecies after having been rebuked by the ass he rode. Num. 22–23. —**Ba·laam·ite** (bā′lə mīt′), *n.* —**Ba·laam·it·i·cal** (bā′lə mit′i kəl), *adj.*

bal·a·cla·va (bal′ə klä′və; *Russ.* bä′lä klä′vä), *n.* a close-fitting, knitted woolen cap that covers the head, neck, and tops of the shoulders, worn esp. by mountain-climbers, soldiers, skiers, etc. Also called **balacla′va hel′met.** [named after BALAKLAVA]

Ba·lak (bā′lak), *n.* a Moabite king who sent for Balaam to come and curse the Israelites. Num. 22–23. Also, *Douay Bible,* **Ba′lac.**

Ba·la·ki·rev (bä′lä kē′ref), *n.* **Mi·li A·le·kse·e·vich** (mē′li ä′le kse′yə vich), 1837?–1910, Russian conductor, pianist, and composer.

Bal·a·kla·va (bal′ə klä′və; *Russ.* bä′lä klä′vä), *n.* a seaport in S Crimea, in the SW Soviet Union, on the Black Sea: scene of English cavalry charge against Russians (1854), celebrated in Tennyson's poem, *Charge of the Light Brigade.*

bal·a·lai·ka (bal′ə lī′kə), *n.* a Russian musical instrument having a triangular body and a neck like that of a guitar. [< Russ]

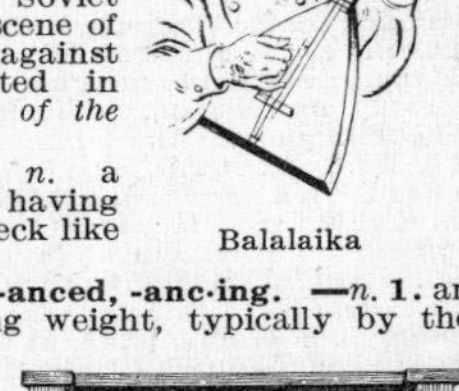

Balalaika

bal·ance (bal′əns), *n., v.,* **-anced, -anc·ing.** —*n.* **1.** an instrument for determining weight, typically by the equilibrium of a bar with a fulcrum at the center, from each end of which is suspended a scale or pan, one holding an object of known weight, and the other holding the object to be weighed. **2.** power to decide as by a balance; authoritative control: *England long held the balance among nations.* **3.** state of equilibrium or equipoise; equal distribution of weight, amount, etc. **4.** mental steadiness or emotional stability; habit of calm behavior, judgment, etc. **5.** *Fine Arts.* composition or placement of elements of design, as figures, forms, or colors, in such a manner as to produce an aesthetically pleasing or harmoniously integrated whole. **6.** something used to produce equilibrium; counterpoise. **7.** act of balancing; comparison as to weight, amount, importance, etc.; estimate. **8.** preponderating weight: *The balance of the blame is on your side.* **9.** *U.S.* the remainder or rest: *He carried what he could and left the balance for his brother to take.* **10.** *Accounting.* **a.** equality between the totals of the two sides of an account. **b.** the difference between the debit total and the credit total of an account. **c.** unpaid difference represented by the excess of debits over credits. **11.** an adjustment of accounts. **12.** *Dance.* a balancing movement. **13.** Also called **balance wheel.** *Horol.* a wheel which oscillates against the tension of a hairspring to regulate the beats of a watch or clock. **14.** (*cap.*) *Astron., Astrol.* the constellation or sign of Libra. **15. in the balance,** at the crisis: *His fate hung in the balance.* —*v.t.* **16.** to weigh in a balance. **17.** to estimate the relative weight or importance of; compare: *to balance all the probabilities of a situation.* **18.** to serve as a counterpoise to; counterbalance; offset: *The advantages more than balance the disadvantages.* **19.** to bring to or hold in equilibrium; poise: *to balance a book on one's head.* **20.** to arrange, adjust, or proportion the parts of symmetrically. **21.** to be equal or proportionate to: *I'm always happy when cash on hand balances expenses. One side of an equation must balance the other.* **22.** *Accounting.* **a.** to add up the two sides of (an account) and determine the difference. **b.** to make the necessary entries in (an account) so that the sums of the two sides will be equal. **c.** to settle by paying what remains due on an account; equalize or adjust. **23.** *Dance.* to move in rhythm to and from: *to balance one's partner.* —*v.i.* **24.** to have an equality or equivalence in weight, parts, etc.; be in equilibrium: *The account doesn't balance. Do these scales balance?* **25.** *Accounting.* to reckon or adjust accounts. **26.** to waver or hesitate: *He would balance and temporize endlessly before reaching a decision.* **27.** *Dance.* to move forward and backward or in opposite directions. [ME *balaunce* < AF; c. OF *balance* < VL **balancia,* var. of **bilancia* < L *bilanc-* (s. of *bilanx* < *bi-* BI-[1] + *lanx* + *-ia* -IA] —**bal′ance·a·ble,** *adj.*

Balance (def. 1)

—**Syn. 4.** poise, composure. **5.** See **symmetry. 9.** See **remainder.**

—**Usage.** Although BALANCE in the sense of "remainder" is now generally acceptable in all varieties of usage, there are still some speakers and writers who regard its use in this sense as colloquial: *The balance of the class was absent.*

bal·anced (bal′ənst), *adj.* **1.** being in harmonious or proper arrangement or adjustment, proportion, etc. **2.** *Football.* pertaining to or noting an offensive line formation having three linemen on each side of the center. Cf. **unbalanced** (def. 5). [BALANCE + -ED²]

bal′anced fund′, *Finance.* a type of open-end investment company that includes bonds and preferred stocks in its portfolio.

bal′anced line′, *Elect.* a transmission line in which the oppositely directed components are symmetrical with respect to each other and to the ground.

bal′anced rud′der, *Naut.* a rudder so designed that the center of the water pressure on the forward face of the rudder, when turned, lies about halfway along its length, minimizing the turning effort required. Also, **balance rudder.** Also called **equipoise rudder.**

bal′anced sen′tence, a sentence consisting of two or more clauses that are parallel in structure.

bal′anced step′, any of a series of staircase winders so planned that they are nearly as wide at the inside of the stair as the adjacent fliers. Also called **dancing step, dancing winder.**

bal′anced tick′et, *U.S. Politics.* a party ticket listing candidates chosen to win support from all major factions of the electorate.

bal′anced valve′, a valve designed so that pressure-induced forces from the fluid being controlled oppose one another so that resistance to opening and closing the valve is negligible. Also called **double-beat valve, double-seated valve.**

bal′ance lug′, *Naut.* a lugsail having a portion of its area forward of the mast and having a long foot, often with a boom. Also called **French lug.**

bal′ance of pay′ments, the difference between a nation's total payments to foreign countries and its total receipts from foreign countries.

bal′ance of pow′er, a distribution and opposition of forces among nations such that no single nation is strong enough to assert its will or dominate all the others.

bal′ance of trade′, the difference between the value of exports and imports of a country, said to be favorable or unfavorable as exports are greater or less than imports.

bal·anc·er (bal′ən sər), *n.* **1.** one who or that which balances. **2.** *Entomol.* halter². **3.** an acrobat, ropedancer, or tumbler. [BALANCE + -ER¹]

bal′ance rud′der. See **balanced rudder.**

bal′ance sheet′, *Accounting.* **1.** a tabular statement of both sides of a set of accounts in which the debit and credit balances add up as equal. **2.** a statement of the financial position of a business on a specified date.

bal′ance spring′, *Horol.* hairspring (def. 1).

bal′ance staff′, *Horol.* a pivoted axle or shaft on which the balance is mounted.

bal′ance wheel′, *Horol.* balance (def. 13).

Bal·an·chine (bal′ən chēn′, bal′ən chēn′), *n.* **George,** 1904–83, U.S. choreographer, born in Russia.

bal·a·noid (bal′ə noid′), *adj.* shaped like an acorn. [< Gk *balanoeid(ēs)* < *bálan(os)* acorn + *-oeidēs* -OID]

ba·lao (bə lou′), *n., pl.* **-laos.** *Ichthyol.* a halfbeak, *Hemiramphus balao,* found in the tropical western Atlantic Ocean. [< AmerSp *balajú* < native name]

Ba·la·ra·ma (bul′ə rä′mə), *n. Hindu Myth.* the elder brother of Krishna and an incarnation of Vishnu.

bal·as (bal′əs, bā′ləs), *n. Mineral.* a rose-red variety of spinel. Also called **bal′as ru′by.** [late ME < ML *balas(ius),* var. of *balascius* < Ar *balakhsh,* back formation from Pers *Badakhshān,* district near Samarkand, where gem is found]

bal·a·ta (bal′ə tə), *n.* **1.** a nonelastic, rubberlike, water-resistant gum that softens in hot water, obtained from the latex of the bully tree, *Mimusops balata:* used chiefly in the manufacture of machinery belts, golf ball covers, and as a substitute for gutta-percha. **2.** See **bully tree.** [< AmerSp < Carib]

Ba·la·ton (bo′lo tôn′), *n.* a lake in W Hungary: the largest lake in central Europe. ab. 50 mi. long; 230 sq. mi. German, **Plattensee.**

ba·laus·tine (bə lôs′tin), *adj.* **1.** of or pertaining to the pomegranate. —*n.* **2.** the dried flowers of the pomegranate used in medicines. [earlier *balaust(y)* pomegranate flower (< L *balausti(um)* < Gk *balaústion* in same sense) + -INE¹]

Bal·bo (bäl′bô), *n.* **I·ta·lo** (ē′tä lô), 1896–1940, Italian aviator, general, and statesman.

Bal·bo·a (bal bō′ə; *Sp.* bäl bō′ä), *n.* **1. Vas·co Nú·ñez de** (bäs′kô nōō′nyeth de), 1475?–1517, Spanish adventurer and explorer who discovered the Pacific Ocean in 1513. **2.** a seaport in the Canal Zone at the Pacific terminus of the Panama Canal. 4162 (1960). **3.** (*l.c.*) a silver coin and monetary unit of Panama, equal to 100 centesimos and equivalent to a U.S. dollar.

bal·brig·gan (bal brig′ən), *n.* a plain-knit cotton fabric, used esp. in hosiery and underwear. [after *Balbriggan,* Ireland, where first made]

Bal·bue·na (bäl bwā′nə; *Sp.* bäl bwe′nä), *n.* **Ber·nar·do de** (bər när′dō də; *Sp.* ber när′thô the), 1568–1627, Mexican poet and priest, born in Spain.

Balch (bôlch), *n.* **Emily Greene,** 1867–1961, U.S. economist, sociologist, and author: Nobel peace prize 1946.

bal·che (bäl chā′), *n.* an alcoholic drink made in Yucatán. Also, **bal·ché′.** [< AmerSp < Mayan]

Balch′ Springs′, a town in NE Texas. 6821 (1960).

bal·co·net (bal′kə net′), *n.* a railing or balustrade before a window, giving the effect of a balcony. Also, **bal′co·nette′.** [BALCON(Y) + -ET]

bal·co·ny (bal′kə nē), *n., pl.* **-nies.** **1.** a balustraded or railed elevated platform projecting from the wall of a building. **2.** a gallery in a theater. [< It *balcone* < *balc(o)* scaffold (< OHG *balcho* beam; see BALK) + *-one* aug. suffix] —**bal′co·nied,** *adj.*

bald (bôld), *adj.* **1.** lacking hair on the scalp: *a bald head; a bald person.* **2.** destitute of some natural growth or covering: *a bald mountain.* **3.** lacking detail or vividness; bare; plain; unadorned: *a bald prose style.* **4.** open; undisguised: *a bald lie.* **5.** *Zool.* having white on the head: *the bald eagle.* —*v.i.* **6.** to become bald. [ME *ball(e)d* < obs. *ball* white spot (cf. Welsh *bāl,* Gk *phaliós* having a white spot) + *-ed* -ED³] —**bald′ish,** *adj.* —**bald′ly,** *adv.* —**bald′ness,** *n.*

bal·da·chin (bal′də kin, bôl′-), *n.* **1.** Also, **baldoquin, baudekin.** *Textiles.* a silk brocade interwoven with gold or silver threads, used chiefly for ceremonial purposes. **2.** *Archit.* a permanent ornamental canopy, as above a freestanding altar or tomb. **3.** a portable canopy carried in religious processions. Also, **bal·dac·chi·no, bal·da·chi·no** (bal′də kē′nō), **bal′da·quin.** [earlier *baldakin* < ML *baldakin(us)* < It *baldacchino* < *Baldacc(o)* Baghdad + *-ino* -INE¹] —**bal′da·chined,** *adj.*

Bal·dad (bal′dad), *n. Douay Bible.* Bildad.

bald′ coot′, *Brit.* the Old World coot, *Fulica atra.*

bald′ cy′press, a tree, *Taxodium distichum,* of the southern U.S., yielding a strong, hard wood used in construction, shipbuilding, etc. Also called **southern cypress.**

bald′ ea′gle, a large eagle, *Haliaetus leucocephalus,* of the U.S. and Canada, having a fully feathered head and, when adult, a white head and tail.

Bald eagle
(Length 2½ ft.;
wingspread to 7½ ft.)

Bal·der (bôl′dər), *n. Scand. Myth.* a god, a son of Odin and Frigg and the twin brother of Hoder, by whom he was killed. Also, **Baldur, Baldr.**

bal·der·dash (bôl′dər dash′), *n.* **1.** a senseless jumble of words; nonsense. **2.** *Obs.* a muddled mixture of liquors. [?]

Bal des Vo·leurs, Le (*Fr.* lə bal dā vô lœr′). See **Thieves' Carnival.**

bald′-faced hor′net (bôld′fāst′). See under **hornet.**

bald·head (bôld′hed′), *n.* **1.** a person who has a bald head. **2.** one of a breed of domestic pigeons. [BALD + HEAD]

bald·head·ed (bôld′hed′id), *adj.* **1.** having a bald head. **2.** *Naut.* (of a schooner rig) having no topmasts. [BALD + -HEADED]

bal·do·quin (bal′də kin, bôl′-), *n.* baldachin (def. 1).

bald·pate (bôld′pāt′), *n.* **1.** baldhead (def. 1). **2.** a brown American widgeon, *Anas americana,* having a gray head with a white crown. [BALD + PATE] —**bald′-pat′ed,** *adj.* —**bald′pat′ed·ness,** *n.*

bal·dric (bôl′drik), *n.* a belt, sometimes richly ornamented, worn diagonally from shoulder to hip, supporting a sword, horn, etc. Also, **bal′drick.** [late ME *bawdrick,* appar. special use of man's name *Baldrīc* (cf. SAM BROWNE BELT); r. ME *baudry* < OF *baudrei* < Frankish *Baldrīc,* lit., bold king] —**bal′dricked,** *adj.*

Bal·dur (bôl′dər), *n.* Balder. Also, **Bal·dr** (bôl′dər; *Icel.* bäl′dər).

Bald·win (bôld′win), *n.* **1. James,** 1924–87, U.S. writer. **2. James Mark,** 1861–1934, U.S. psychologist. **3. Mat·thi·as William** (mə thī′əs), 1795–1866, U.S. inventor, manufacturer, and philanthropist. **4. Stanley** (*1st Earl Baldwin of Bewdley*), 1867–1947, British statesman: prime minister 1923–24, 1924–29, 1935–37. **5.** a variety of red, or red and yellow, winter apple, grown esp. in the northeast U.S. **6.** a town on S Long Island, in SE New York. 30,204 (1960). **7.** a city in W Pennsylvania, near Pittsburgh. 24,489 (1960).

Baldwin I, 1058–1118, king of Jerusalem 1100–18: fought in the first crusade.

Bald′win Park′, a city in SW California, near Los Angeles. 33,951 (1960).

Bald·wins·ville (bôld′winz vil′), *n.* a town in central New York. 5985 (1960).

bale¹ (bāl), *n., v.,* **baled, bal·ing.** —*n.* **1.** a large bundle or package prepared for shipping, storage, or sale, esp. one tightly compressed and secured by wires, hoops, cords, or the like, and sometimes having a wrapping or covering: *a bale of cotton; a bale of hay.* **2.** a group of turtles. —*v.t.* **3.** to make or form into bales: *to bale scrap metal for market.* [ME < Flem < OF < Gmc; cf. OHG *ballā* BALL¹] —**bale′less,** *adj.* —**bal′er,** *n.*

bale² (bāl), *n. Archaic.* **1.** evil; harm; misfortune. **2.** woe; misery; sorrow. [ME < OE *bealu, balu;* c. Icel *böl,* OHG *balo,* Goth *balw-*]

bale³ (bāl), *n.* bail².

bale⁴ (bāl), *v.t., v.i.,* **baled, bal·ing.** bail³ (defs. 1–4).

Bâle (bäl), *n.* French name of **Basel.**

Bal·e·ar′ic Is′lands (bal′ē ar′ik), a group of islands including Ibiza, Mallorca, and Minorca, and constituting a province of Spain in the W Mediterranean Sea. 436,435 (est. 1960); 1936 sq. mi. *Cap.:* Palma. Spanish, **Ba·le·a·res** (bä′le ä′res).

ba·leen (bə lēn′), *n. Zool.* whalebone (def. 1). [late ME *balene* < L *balēna,* var. of *balaena* whale (c. Gk *phálaina*); r. ME *balayn* < MF *balaine* whale(bone) < L]

baleen′ whale′. See **whalebone whale.**

bale·fire (bāl′fīər′), *n.* **1.** a large fire in the open air; bonfire. **2.** a signal fire; beacon. **3.** the fire of a funeral pile. [late ME < *bale* (< Scand; cf. Icel *bāl* funeral pyre) + *fire* FIRE; r. OE *bælfȳr*]

bale·ful (bāl′fəl), *adj.* **1.** full of menacing or malign influences; pernicious. **2.** *Obs.* wretched; miserable. [ME < OE *bealoful.* See BALE², -FUL] —**bale′ful·ly,** *adv.* —**bale′ful·ness,** *n.*

—**Syn. 1.** harmful, malign, injurious, detrimental; evil, wicked; deadly.

Ba·len·ci·a·ga (bə len′sē ä′gə; *Sp.* bä′len thyä′gä), *n.* **Cris·tó·bal** (kri stō′bəl; *Sp.* krē stô′bäl), born 1896?, French fashion designer, born in Spain.

ba·les·tra (bə les′trə), *n. Fencing.* a jump toward the opponent followed immediately by a lunge. [< It: lit., crossbow < LL < L *ballistra,* var. of *ballista* < *ball-* (< Gk *bállein* (to) throw) + *-ista* -IST]

Ba·le·wa (bä′lä wä), *n.* **Sir A·bu·ba·kar Ta·fa·wa** (ä bōō′bä kär′ tä fä′wä), 1912–66, Nigerian statesman: prime minister 1957–66.

Bal·four (bal′fŏŏr), *n.* **Arthur James** (*1st Earl of Balfour*), 1848–1930, British statesman and writer: prime minister 1902–05.

Bal′four Declara′tion, a statement, issued by the British government on November 2, 1917, favoring the establishment in Palestine of a national home for the Jews but without prejudice to the civil and religious rights of existing non-Jewish communities in Palestine.

Bal·fours (bal′fərz, -fŏŏrz), *n.* a town in central North Carolina. 3805 (1960).

Ba·li (bä′lē), *n.* an island in Indonesia, E of Java. 1,775,000. (est. 1961); 2147 sq. mi. *Cap.:* Singaraja.

Ba·lik·pa·pan (bä′lik-pä′pän), *n.* a seaport on E Borneo, in central Indonesia. 88,534 (1961).

ba·line (bə lēn′), *n.* a coarse hemp or jute fabric used to line garments or upholstery and for bagging. [< F < *bal-* BALE¹ + *-ine* -INE¹]

Ba·li·nese (bä′lə nēz′, -nēs′), *adj., n., pl.* **-nese.** —*adj.* **1.** of or pertaining to Bali, its people, or their language. —*n.* **2.** a native or inhabitant of Bali. **3.** the language of Bali, an Indonesian language of the Malayo-Polynesian family. [< D *Balinees* < *Bali* + *-n-* connective + *-ees* -ESE]

Bal·iol (bāl′yəl, bā′lē əl), *n.* **John de,** 1249–1315, king of Scotland 1292–96.

Ba·li·us (bā′lē əs), *n.* (in the *Iliad*) one of the two immortal horses of Achilles.

balk (bôk), *v.i.* **1.** to stop, as at an obstacle, and refuse to proceed or to do something specified (usually fol. by *at*): *He balked at making the speech.* **2.** (of a horse, mule, etc.) to stop short and stubbornly refuse to go on. **3.** *Sports.* to commit a balk. —*v.t.* **4.** to place an obstacle in the way of; hinder; thwart: *a sudden emergency that balked his hopes.* **5.** *Archaic.* to let slip; fail to use: *to balk an opportunity.* —*n.* **6.** a check or hindrance; defeat; disappointment. **7.** a strip of land left unplowed. **8.** a crossbeam in the roof of a house which unites and supports the rafters; tie beam. **9.** any heavy timber used for building purposes. **10.** *Baseball.* an illegal motion by a pitcher while one or more runners are on base, as a pitch in which there is either an insufficient or too long a pause after the windup or stretch, a pretended throw to first or third base or to the batter with one foot on the pitcher's rubber, etc., resulting in a penalty advancing the runner or runners one base. **11.** *Billiards.* any of the eight panels or compartments lying between the cushions of the table and the balklines. **12.** *Obs.* a miss, slip, or failure: *to make a balk.* **13. in balk,** inside any of the spaces in back of the balklines on a billiard table. Also, **baulk.** [ME < OE *balc(a)* bank, ridge; c. Icel *balkr* bar, partition, D *balk,* G *Balken* beam. See BALCONY] —**balk′er,** *n.* —**balk′ing·ly,** *adv.*

—**Syn. 4.** check, retard, obstruct, impede, prevent; frustrate, baffle.

Bal·kan (bôl′kən), *adj.* **1.** pertaining to the Balkan States or their inhabitants. **2.** pertaining to the Balkan Peninsula. **3.** pertaining to the Balkan Mountains. —*n.* **4. the Balkans,** the Balkan States or the land within their borders. —**Bal′kan·ite′,** *n., adj.*

Bal′kan frame′, an overhead frame, fastened to a bed, from which a splinted, fractured limb is suspended and held in traction. [so called because first used in the BALKAN MOUNTAINS]

Bal·kan·ize (bôl′kə nīz′), *v.t.,* **-ized, -iz·ing.** to divide (a country, territory, etc.) into small, quarrelsome, ineffectual states. [BALKAN + -IZE] —**Bal′kan·ism,** *n.*

Bal′kan Moun′tains, a mountain range extending from W Bulgaria to the Black Sea: highest peak, 7794 ft.

Bal′kan Penin′sula, a peninsula in S Europe, S of the Danube River and bordered by the Adriatic, Ionian, Aegean, and Black seas.

Bal′kan States′, the countries in the Balkan Peninsula: Yugoslavia, Bosnia and Herzegovina, Croatia, Macedonia, Slovenia, Rumania, Bulgaria, Albania, Greece, and the European part of Turkey. Also called **the Balkans.**

Bal′kan War′, 1. Also called **First Balkan War.** a war (1912–13) in which Bulgaria, Serbia, and Greece opposed Turkey. **2.** Also called **Second Balkan War.** a war (1913) between Montenegro and Turkey.

Balkh (bälkн), *n.* a town in N Afghanistan: capital of ancient Bactria; center of Zoroastrianism. Ancient, **Bactra.** Also called **Wazirabad.**

Bal·khash (bal kнäsh′), *n.* a salt lake in the SW Soviet Union in Asia, in Kazakstan. ab. 7115 sq. mi.

balk·line (bôk′līn′), *n.* **1.** *Sports.* (in track events) the starting line. **2.** *Billiards.* **a.** a straight line drawn across the table behind which the cue balls are placed in beginning a game. **b.** any of four lines, each near to and parallel with one side of the cushion, which divide the table into a large central panel or section and eight smaller sections or balks lying between these. **c.** a balk lying inside one of these sections. **d.** balk (def. 11). [BALK + LINE¹]

balk·y (bô′kē), *adj.,* **balk·i·er, balk·i·est.** *U.S.* given to balking; stubborn; obstinate: *a balky horse.* [BALK + -Y¹] —**balk′i·ly,** *adv.* —**balk′i·ness,** *n.*

—**Syn.** contrary, perverse.

ball¹ (bôl), *n.* **1.** a spherical or approximately spherical body; sphere. **2.** a round or roundish body, of various sizes and materials, either hollow or solid, for use in games, as baseball, football, tennis, or golf. **3.** a game played with a ball, esp. baseball: *The boys are out playing ball.* **4.** *Baseball.* a pitched ball, not swung at by the batter, that does not pass over home plate between the batter's shoulders and knees. **5.** *Mil.* **a.** a solid, usually spherical projectile for a cannon, rifle, pistol, etc., as distinguished from a shell. **b.** projectiles, esp. bullets, collectively. **6.** any part of a thing, esp. of the human body, that is rounded or protuberant: *the ball of the thumb.* **7.** a round mass of food, as of chopped meat, dough, or candy. **8.** *Slang (vulgar).* a testis. **9.** bolus (def. 1). **10.** *Astron. Rare.* a planetary or celestial body, esp. the earth. **11. carry the ball,** to assume the responsibility; bear the burden: *You can always count on him to carry the ball in an emergency.* **12. have something or a lot on the ball,** *Slang.* to be capable or efficient; have a talent or gift. **13. keep the ball rolling,** to continue or give renewed vigor to an activity already under way: *Interest lagged because there was no conflict to keep the ball rolling.* **14. on the ball,** *Slang.* **a.** alert; vital. **b.** efficient; able; competent: *Her typing is on the ball.* **15. play ball, a.** to begin or continue playing a game. **b.** to start or continue any action. **c.** to work together; cooperate: *union leaders suspected of playing ball with racketeers.* **16. start the ball rolling,** to put something into operation; set an activity going: *The recreation director started the ball rolling by having all the participants introduce themselves.* —*v.t.* **17.** to make into a ball (sometimes fol. by *up*): *The children were balling up snow to make a snowman.* **18.** to wind into balls: *to ball cotton.* —*v.i.* **19.** to form or gather into a ball: *When the spun sugar balls, the candy has cooked sufficiently.* **20. ball the jack,** *Slang.* **a.** to act with speed. **b.** to stake everything on one attempt. **21. ball up,** *Slang.* to make or become hopelessly confused; muddle: *The records had been all balled up by inefficient file clerks.* [ME *bal, balle* < Scand (cf. Icel *böllr,* Sw *bål*); c. G *Ball.* See BALLOCK] —**ball′er,** *n.*

—**Syn. 1.** BALL, GLOBE, SPHERE, ORB agree in referring to a round or rounded object. BALL may be applied to any round or roundish object or part: *a rubber ball.* GLOBE and SPHERE denote something thought of as either exactly or approximately round: *in the form of a globe; a perfect sphere.* ORB is now found only in elevated or scientific use; it is applied esp. to the eye and to the heavenly bodies: *the orb of the full moon.*

ball[2] (bôl), *n.* **1.** a large, usually lavish party featuring social dancing and often given for some particular purpose, as to introduce debutantes, benefit a charitable organization, etc. **2.** *Slang.* a thoroughly good time: *Have a ball on your vacation.* [< F *bal* < *bal(er)* (now *baller*) (to) dance < LL *ballāre* < Gk *ballízein* to dance < *ball-* throw + *-izein* -IZE]

Ball (bôl), *n.* **1. John,** died 1381, English priest: one of the leaders of Wat Tyler's peasants' revolt in 1381. **2.** See **L. F. Ball. 3.** a crater in the third quadrant of the face of the moon: about 25 miles in diameter.

Bal·la (bäl′lä), *n.* **Gia·co·mo** (jä′kô mô), 1871?–1958, Italian painter.

bal·lad (bal′əd), *n.* **1.** a simple, often crude, narrative poem of popular origin, composed in short stanzas, esp. one of romantic character and adapted for singing. **2.** any poem written in similar style. **3.** any light, simple song, esp. one of sentimental or romantic character, having two or more stanzas, all sung to the same melody. **4.** the musical setting for a folk or literary ballad. [earlier *balade* < MF < OPr *balada* dance, dancing-song < *bal(ar)* (to) dance (< LL *ballāre;* see BALL[2]) + *-ada* -ADE[1]] —**bal·lad·ic** (bə lad′ik), *adj.* —**bal′lad·like′,** *adj.*

bal·lade (bə läd′, ba-; *Fr.* bA lAd′), *n., pl.* **-lades** (-lädz′; *Fr.* -lAd′). **1.** a poem consisting commonly of three stanzas having an identical rhyme scheme, followed by an envoy, and having the same last line for each of the stanzas and the envoy. **2.** *Music.* a composition in free style and romantic mood, often for solo piano or for orchestra. [< F, var. of *balade* BALLAD]

bal·lad·eer (bal′ə dēr′), *n.* a person who sings ballads. Also, **bal′lad·ier′.** [BALLAD + -EER]

bal·lad·ise (bal′ə dīz′), *v.t., v.i.,* **-ised, -is·ing.** *Chiefly Brit.* balladize.

bal·lad·ist (bal′ə dist), *n.* a person who writes, composes, or sings ballads. [BALLAD + -IST]

bal·lad·ize (bal′ə dīz′), *v.,* **-ized, -iz·ing.** —*v.t.* **1.** to make (something) into a ballad; write a ballad about. —*v.i.* **2.** to write or compose ballads. [BALLAD + -IZE]

bal·lad·mon·ger (bal′əd mung′gər, -mong′-), *n.* **1.** a seller of ballads. **2.** a bad poet. [BALLAD + MONGER] —**bal′lad·mon′ger·ing,** *n.*

Bal′lad of Read′ing Gaol′, The (red′ing), a poem (1898) by Oscar Wilde.

bal′lad op′era, a theater entertainment of 18th-century England, consisting of popular tunes, folk songs, and dialogue.

bal·lad·ry (bal′ə drē), *n.* ballad poetry. [BALLAD + -RY]

bal′lad stan′za, a stanza often used in ballad poetry, composed of lines of four, three, four, and three stresses, respectively, usually having the rhyme scheme *abcb.*

Bal·lance (bal′əns), *n.* **John,** 1839–93, New Zealand statesman, born in Ireland: prime minister 1891–93.

ball′ and chain′, **1.** a heavy iron ball fastened by a chain to a prisoner's leg. **2.** burdensome restraint: *The steady accumulation of small debts was a ball and chain to his progress.* **3.** *Slang.* a man's wife: *He would leave the ball and chain at home while he went out with the boys.*

ball′-and-claw′ foot′ (bôl′ən klô′), *Furniture.* a foot having the form of a bird's claw grasping a ball. Also called **claw-and-ball foot.**

ball′ and ring′, a simplified bead-and-reel turning, used esp. in English and American furniture of the 17th century.

ball′-and-sock′et joint′ (bôl′ən sok′it), a joint between rods, links, pipes, etc., consisting of a ball-like termination on one part held within a concave, spherical socket on the other. Also called **ball joint.**

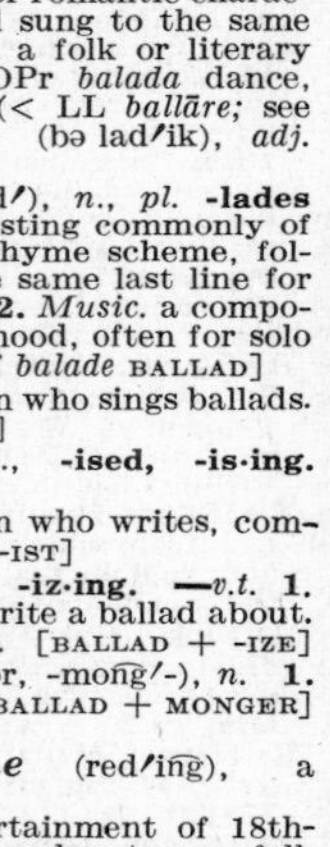

Ball-and-socket joint

Bal·la·rat (bal′ə rat′, bal′ə rat′), *n.* a city in S Victoria, in SE Australia. 53,680 (est. 1959).

Bal·lard (bal′ərd), *n.* a boy's given name.

bal·las (bal′əs), *n.* (*construed as sing.*) *Mineral.* a spherical aggregate of small diamond crystals used for drilling and for various industrial purposes. Also called **shot bort.** [appar. var. of BALAS in phrase *balas ruby* spinel ruby, *balas* being taken to mean spinel]

bal·last (bal′əst), *n.* **1.** *Naut.* any heavy material carried temporarily or permanently in a vessel to provide desired draft and stability. **2.** *Aeron.* something heavy, as bags of sand, placed in the car of a balloon for control of altitude and, less often, of attitude, or placed in an aircraft to control the position of the center of gravity. **3.** anything that gives mental, moral, or political stability or steadiness: *the ballast of a steady income.* **4.** gravel, broken stone, slag, etc., placed between and under the ties of a railroad to give stability, provide drainage, and distribute loads. **5. in ballast,** *Naut.* carrying only ballast; carrying no cargo. —*v.t.* **6.** to furnish with ballast: *to ballast a ship.* **7.** to give steadiness to; keep steady: *responsibilities that ballast a person.* [< MLG < *bal-* bad (see BALE[2]) + *last* load (see LAST[4]); but cf. ODan, OSw *barlast* < *bar* BARE[1] + *last* > *ballast*] —**bal′last·er,** *n.* —**bal·last·ic** (bə las′tik), *adj.*

bal′last line′, *Naut.* the level to which a vessel is immersed when in ballast.

bal·la·ta (bə lä′tə), *n., pl.* **-la·te** (-lä′tā). a 14th-century Italian verse form composed of stanzas beginning and ending with a refrain, often set to music and accompanied by dancing. [< It, OPr *balada* BALLAD]

ball′ bear′ing, *Mach.* **1.** a bearing consisting of a number of hard balls running in grooves in the surfaces of two concentric rings, one of which is mounted on a rotating or oscillating shaft or the like. **2.** any of the balls so used. —**ball′-bear′ing,** adj.

ball′ boy′, a boy employed at a tennis match to supply the players with balls, to clear the court of balls that are out of play, and to retrieve balls that are hit out of bounds.

ball-car·ri·er (bôl′kar′ē ər), *n.* *Football.* the offensive player having the ball and attempting to gain ground.

ball′ club′, **1.** a team of professional players of a ball game, esp. baseball. **2.** a club or similar organization that sponsors and promotes a baseball team.

ball′ cock′, a device for regulating the supply of water in a tank, cistern, or the like, consisting essentially of a valve connected to a hollow floating ball which by its rise or fall shuts or opens the valve.

bal·le·ri·na (bal′ə rē′nə; *It.* bäl′le rē′nä), *n., pl.* **-nas,** *It.* **-ne** (-ne). **1.** a principal female dancer in a ballet company. Cf. **prima ballerina. 2.** (loosely) any female ballet dancer. [< It, fem. of *ballerino* professional dancer < *ball(are)* (to) dance < LL; see BALL[2]]

bal·let (ba lā′, bal′ā; *Fr.* bA lā′), *n., pl.* **bal·lets** (ba lāz′, bal′āz; *Fr.* bA lā′). **1.** a classical dance form demanding grace and precision and employing conventional steps and gestures set in intricate, flowing patterns to create expression through movement. **2.** a theatrical entertainment performed by a company of professional dancers in which dancing and music, often with scenery and costumes, combine to tell a story, establish a particular emotional atmosphere, etc. **3.** a dance interlude in an operatic performance. **4.** a company of professional dancers. **5.** the musical score for a ballet: *the brilliant ballets of Tschaikowsky.* [< F < It *balletto* < *ball(o)* BALL[2] + *-etto* -ET] —**bal·let·ic** (ba let′ik), *adj.* —**bal·let′i·cal·ly,** *adv.*

ballet′ blanc′ (blän), *pl.* **ballets blancs** (blän, blänz). a ballet in which the ballerinas' skirts are white. [< F: lit., white ballet]

ballet′ mas′ter, a man who trains a ballet company. Also called **maître de ballet.**

ballet′ mis′tress, a woman who trains a ballet company.

bal·let·o·mane (ba let′ə mān′, bə-), *n.* a ballet enthusiast. [back formation from *balletomania;* see BALLET, -O-, -MANIA] —**bal·let′o·ma′ni·a,** *n.*

ballet′ slip′per, **1.** a heelless cloth or leather slipper worn by ballet dancers. **2.** a woman's shoe similar in form.

ballet′ suite′, music written for a ballet but suitable or arranged for performance in an orchestral concert.

bal·lett (ba let′), *n.* an early 17th-century dancelike vocal composition similar to the madrigal in style. [? var. of *ballette* BALLAD]

ball′ fern′, a feathery fern, *Davallia bullata,* of southeastern Asia and Japan. Also called **squirrel's-foot fern.**

ball·flow·er (bôl′flou′ər), *n.* *Archit.* a medieval English ornament suggesting a flower of three or four petals enclosing and partly concealing a ball. [BALL[1] + FLOWER]

ball′ foot′, *Furniture.* a ball-like turned foot, used esp. in the 16th and 17th centuries. Cf. **bun foot.**

ball′ game′, any game played with a ball, esp. baseball or softball.

ball′ in′dicator. See **bank indicator.**

Bal·lin·ger (bal′ən jər), *n.* a town in central Texas. 5043 (1960).

Bal·liol (bāl′yəl, bā′lē əl), *n.* a college of Oxford University, founded before 1268.

bal·lism (bal′iz əm), *n.* *Pathol.* **1.** a condition characterized by twisting, shaking, and jerking motions. **2.** See **Parkinson's disease.** Also, **bal·lis·mus** (ba liz′məs). [< NL *ballism(us)* < Gk *ballismós* a jumping around, dancing, < *báll(ein)* (to) throw + *-ismos* -ISM]

bal·lis·ta (bə lis′tə), *n., pl.* **-tae** (-tē). an ancient military engine for throwing stones or other missiles. [< L, prob. < Gk *ballistá(s), dial. var. of *ballistḗs < báll(ein) (to) throw + -istēs -IST]

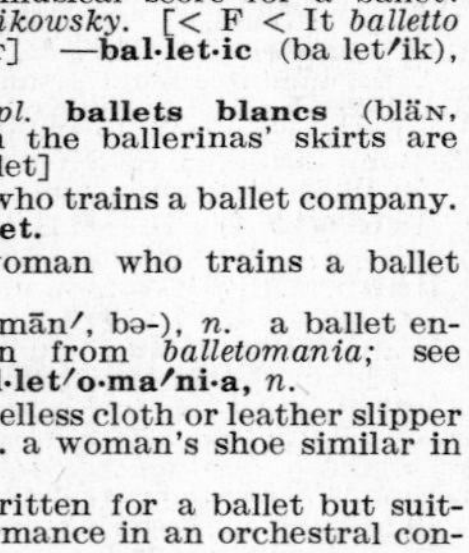

Ballista

bal·lis·tic (bə lis′tik), *adj.* **1.** of or pertaining to ballistics. **2.** having its motion determined or describable by the laws of exterior ballistics: *a ballistic missile.* [BALLIST(A) + -IC] —**bal·lis′ti·cal·ly,** *adv.*

ballis′tic cam′era, a camera for tracking missiles launched at night.

ballis′tic galvanom′eter, *Elect.* a galvanometer used to measure the quantity of electricity in a current of short duration.

ballis′tic mis′sile, *Rocketry.* any missile which, after being launched and possibly guided during takeoff, travels unpowered in a ballistic trajectory.

ballis′tic pen′dulum, *Physics.* a device consisting of a large mass hung from a horizontal bar by two rods, used to measure the velocity of an object, as a bullet, by retaining the object upon impact, its velocity being a function of the displacement of the mass.

bal·lis·tics (bə lis′tiks), *n.* (*usually construed as sing.*) **1.** the science or study of the motion of projectiles, as bullets, shells, or bombs. Cf. **interior ballistics, exterior ballistics. 2.** the art or science of designing projectiles for maximum flight performance. [see BALLISTIC, -ICS] —**bal·lis·ti·cian** (bal′i stish′ən), *n.*

ballis′tic trajec′tory, the path of an unpowered object, as a missile, moving only under the influence of gravity and possibly atmospheric friction and with its surface providing no significant lift to alter the course of flight.

ballis′tic wind′ (wind), a single wind vector that would have the same net effect on the trajectory of a projectile as the varying winds encountered in flight.

bal·lis·tite (bal′i stīt′), *n.* *Chem.* a smokeless powder consisting of nitroglycerine and cellulose nitrate chiefly in a 40 to 60 percent ratio: used as a solid fuel for rockets. [formerly trademark]

bal·lis·to·car·di·o·gram (bə lis′tō kär′dē ə gram′), *n.* *Med.* the graphic record produced by a ballistocardiograph. [BALLIST(IC) + -O- + CARDIOGRAM]

bal·lis·to·car·di·o·graph (bə lis′tō kär′dē ə graf′, -gräf′), *n.* *Med.* a device that determines cardiac output by recording the movements of the body caused by contraction of the heart and ejection of blood into the aorta. [BALLIST(IC) + -O- + CARDIOGRAPH] —**bal·lis·to·car·di·o·graph·ic** (bə lis′tō kär′dē ə graf′ik), *adj.* —**bal·lis·to·car·di·og·ra·phy** (bə lis′tō kär′dē og′rə fē), *n.*

bal·li·um (bal′ē əm), *n.* bailey. [< ML, Latinized var.]

ball-jas·per (bôl′jas′pər), *n.* jasper having concentric bands of red and yellow.

ball′ joint′. See **ball-and-socket joint.**

ball′ light′ning, a rare form of lightning, consisting of a bright, luminous ball that moves rapidly along objects or floats in the air. Also called **globe lightning.**

ball′ mill′, a grinding mill in which the material to be ground is tumbled in a drum with heavy balls of iron, steel, or stone.

bal·locks (bol′əks), *n.pl.* *Vulgar.* testes. [ME *ballokes* (pl.) < OE *beallucas.* See BALL[1]]

Ball′ of Fat′, a short story (1880) by Guy de Maupassant. French, **Boule-de-suif.**

ball′ of fire′, a person capable of or displaying rapid and highly effective thought, action, etc.: *The new manager turned out to be a ball of fire.*

ball′ of wax′, *Informal.* everything, including all details, parts, etc., relating to a particular project, business deal, or the like: *He went out to Chicago and in no time came back with the contract for the whole ball of wax.*

bal·lon (*Fr.* bA lôn′), *n.* *Ballet.* the lightness and grace of movement that make a dancer appear buoyant. Also, **balon.** [< F: lit., BALLOON]

bal·lon d'es·sai (bA lôn de se′), *pl.* **bal·lons d'es·sai** (bA lôn de se′). *French.* See **trial balloon** (def. 1).

bal·lo·net (bal′ə net′), *n.* an air or gasbag compartment in a balloon or airship, used to control buoyancy and maintain shape. [< F < *ballon* BALLOON + *-et* -ET]

bal·lon·né (bal′ə nā′; *Fr.* bA lô nā′), *n., pl.* **-nés** (-nāz′; *Fr.* -nā′). *Ballet.* a broad leap with a battement to the front, side, or back. [< F: lit., ballooned, i.e. done like a balloon]

bal·loon (bə lo͞on′), *n.* **1.** a bag made of a light material, as silk, plastic, etc., filled with a gas lighter than air, designed to rise and float in the atmosphere and often having a car or gondola attached below for carrying passengers or scientific instruments. **2.** an inflatable rubber bag, usually brightly colored, used as a children's plaything. **3.** *Chem. Obs.* a round-bottomed flask. **4.** (in drawings, cartoons, etc.) a balloon-shaped figure enclosing words represented as issuing from the mouth of the speaker. **5.** an ornamental ball at the top of a pillar, pier, or the like. —*v.i.* **6.** to go up or ride in a balloon. **7.** to swell or puff out like a balloon. **8.** to multiply or increase at a rapid rate: *Membership has ballooned beyond all expectations.* —*v.t.* **9.** to fill with air; inflate or distend (something) like a balloon. —*adj.* **10.** puffed out like a balloon: *balloon sleeves.* [< It *ballone* < *ball(a)* BALL[1] + *-one* aug. suffix] —**bal·loon′like′,** *adj.*

balloon′ barrage′, a series of moored balloons, usually strung together and hung with cables, for impeding a low-level attack by enemy aircraft.

bal·loon-ber·ry (bə lo͞on′ber′ē), *n., pl.* **-ber·ries.** See **strawberry raspberry.**

balloon′ chuck′, a lathe chuck having the form of a hollow hemisphere, for enclosing and holding small parts, as balance staffs of watches, so that only their ends are exposed.

balloon′ clock′, a bracket clock of the late 18th century, having a round dial on a short case with concave sides resting on bracket feet.

bal·loon·fish (bə lo͞on′fish′), *n., pl.* **-fish·es,** (*esp. collectively*) **-fish.** a porcupinefish, *Diodon holacanthus,* found in tropical and subtropical waters. [BALLOON + FISH]

balloon′ frame′, a wooden building frame composed of machine-sawed scantlings fastened with nails, having studs rising the full height of the frame with the joists nailed to the studs and supported by sills or by ribbons let into the studs.

balloon′ jib′, *Naut.* a large triangular jib set flying on a racing yacht running free in light wind. Also called **bal·loon′er.**

balloon′ sail′, *Naut.* any light, loose sail, as a jib or spinnaker, used by a yacht in light wind.

balloon′ seat′, *Furniture.* See **bell seat.**

balloon′ tire′, a broad tire filled with air at low

pressure for cushioning the shock of uneven surfaces in the road.

balloon′ train′shed, a trainshed with a vaulted roof.

balloon′ vine′, a tropical, climbing, sapindaceous plant, *Cardiospermum Halicacabum*, bearing big bladder-like pods.

bal·lot (bal′ət), *n.*, *v.*, **-lot·ed, -lot·ing.** —*n.* **1.** a slip or sheet of paper, cardboard, or the like, on which a voter marks his choice or choices. **2.** the whole number of votes cast or recorded: *There was a large ballot.* **3.** the method of secret voting by means of printed or written ballots or by means of voting machines. **4.** voting in general, or a round of voting: *Our candidate was defeated on the third ballot.* **5.** the list of candidates to be voted on: *He demanded his name be placed on the ballot.* **6.** one's right to vote: *to gain the ballot after years of struggle.* **7.** a system or the practice of drawing lots: *The assassin would be chosen by ballot.* **8.** (formerly) a little ball used in voting. —*v.i.* **9.** to vote by ballot. **10.** to draw lots: *to ballot for places.* —*v.t.* **11.** to vote on by ballot (often fol. by *on* or *for*): *Three candidates will be balloted at the convention.* **12.** to canvass or solicit (a group, membership, etc.) for votes: *Members were balloted on the resolution.* **13.** to select, esp. for military service, by ballot: *Certain age-groups will not be balloted at this time.* [< It *ballott(a)* < *ball(a)* BALL[1] + *-otta* dim. suffix] —**bal′lot·er,** *n.*

bal·lo·tade (bal′ə tād′, -täd′), *n.* *Dressage.* a movement similar to a croupade except that the horse draws in its hind legs so that the iron of the shoes is visible. [< F < *ballott(er)* (to) toss (< *ballotte* little ball < It; see BALLOT) + *-ade* -ADE[1]]

bal′lot box′, a receptacle for voters' ballots.

bal·lotte·ment (bə lot′mənt), *n.* *Med.* **1.** a method of diagnosing pregnancy by the rebound of a fetal part displaced from its position by a sudden push of the uterus with the examining finger. **2.** a similar method employed in testing for floating kidney, movable abdominal tumors, etc. [< F: a tossing < *ballotte(r)* (to) toss here and there like a ball (see BALLOTADE) + *-ment* -MENT]

bal·lot·tine (bal′ə tēn′, bal′ə tēn′; *Fr.* bᴀ lô tēn′), *n., pl.* **-tines** (-tēnz′, -tēnz′; *Fr.* -tēn′). a kind of galantine made of meat, poultry, or fish that is stuffed and rolled and usually served hot. [? < F *ballo(tté)* tossed about (see BALLOTTEMENT) + (GALAN)TINE]

ball′ park′, **1.** a tract of land where ball games are played, enclosed by a fence and having seats for spectators: *The local teams played football and baseball in the same ball park.* **2.** a range or approximation: *a proposal in the ball park of $50,000.* —**ball′-park′,** *adj.*

ball′-peen ham′mer (bôl′pēn′), a hammer having a hemispherical peen **(ball′ peen′)** for beating metal.

ball·play·er (bôl′plā′ər), *n.* **1.** a person who plays ball professionally, esp. baseball. **2.** anyone who plays ball. [BALL[1] + PLAYER]

ball′-point pen′ (bôl′point′), a fountain pen in which the point is a fine ball bearing. Also, **ball′ point′ pen′, ball′ pen′, ball′-point′.**

ball·room (bôl′ro͞om′, -ro͝om′), *n.* a large room, as in a hotel, resort, etc., with a polished floor for dancing. [BALL[2] + ROOM]

ball′room dance′, any of a variety of social or recreational dances, by couples or by groups, for performance in a ballroom or the like.

ball′room danc′ing, the practice of performing ballroom dances.

Ball·ston Spa (bôl′stən spä′, spô′), a town in E New York. 4991 (1960).

ball·up (bôl′up′), *n.* *Slang.* a state of confusion; mix-up. Also, *esp. Brit.,* **balls-up** (bôlz′up′). [n. use of v. phrase *ball up*]

ball′ valve′, *Mach.* **1.** a valve controlling flow by means of a ball pierced with an opening in one direction and fixed to rotate on a spindle at right angles to the opening. **2.** any valve that checks flow by the seating of a ball.

Ball valve (Checks motion of fluid in direction shown by arrow)

Ball·win (bôl′win), *n.* a town in E Missouri. 5710 (1960).

bal·ly (bal′ē), *adj., adv.* *Brit. Slang.* damned (euphemism for *bloody*). [by alter.]

bal·ly·hoo (*n.* bal′ē ho͞o′; *v.* bal′ē ho͞o′, bal′ē ho͞o′), *n., pl.* **-hoos,** *v.,* **-hooed, -hoo·ing.** —*n.* **1.** a clamorous attempt to win customers or advance any cause; blatant advertising or publicity. **2.** clamor or outcry. **3.** *Ichthyol.* a halfbeak, *Hemiramphus brasiliensis,* found on both sides of the Atlantic Ocean. —*v.t., v.i.* **4.** to advertise or push by ballyhoo. [?]

bal·ly·rag (bal′ē rag′), *v.t.,* **-ragged, -rag·ging.** bullyrag.

balm (bäm), *n.* **1.** any of various oily, fragrant, resinous substances, often of medicinal value, exuding from certain plants, esp. tropical, burseraceous trees of the genus *Commiphora.* **2.** a plant or tree yielding such a substance. **3.** any aromatic or fragrant ointment. **4.** aromatic fragrance; sweet odor: *a summer breeze redolent with the balm of orange blossoms.* **5.** any of various aromatic, menthaceous plants, esp. of the genus *Melissa,* as *M. officinalis* **(balm′ mint′, garden balm,** or **lemon balm),** having ovate leaves used as a seasoning. **6.** anything which heals, soothes, or mitigates pain: *the balm of friendship in troubled times.* [ME *basme, ba(u)me* < OF *basme* < L *balsam(um)* BALSAM] —**balm′like′,** *adj.*

bal·ma·caan (bal′mə kän′), *n.* a man's short, full-skirted overcoat, often of rough woolen cloth, having raglan sleeves. [after *Balmacaan* near Inverness, Scotland]

Bal′mer se′ries (bäl′mər), *Physics.* a series of lines in the visible spectrum of hydrogen. [named after J. J. *Balmer* (1825–98), Swiss physicist who derived its formula]

balm′ of Gil′ead, **1.** any of several plants of the genus *Commiphora,* esp. *C. opobalsamum* and *C. meccanensis,* which yield a fragrant oleoresin. **2.** Also called **Mecca balsam.** the resin itself, a yellow, green, or brownish-red, turbid, viscid, water-insoluble liquid, used chiefly in perfumery. **3.** a North American poplar, *Populus candicans,* having fragrant buds and foliage.

Bal·mont (bäl′mont), *n.* **Kon·stan·tin Dmi·trey·e·vich** (kon stän tēn′ dmē′tʀi yə vich), 1864–1934, Russian poet.

Bal·mor·al (bal môr′əl, -mor′əl), *n.* **1.** a colored woolen petticoat, formerly worn under a skirt draped so as to reveal portions of it. **2.** (*l.c.*) Also called **bal.** an ankle-high shoe, laced in front. **3.** a brimless Scotch cap with a flat top that projects all around the head. Cf. **tam-o'-shanter.** [after *Balmoral* Castle in Scotland]

Bal·mung (bäl′mo͝ong), *n.* (in the *Nibelungenlied*) a sword seized from the Nibelungs by Siegfried. Also, **Bal·munc** (bäl′mo͝ongk). Cf. **Gram.**

balm·y (bä′mē), *adj.,* **balm·i·er, balm·i·est. 1.** mild and refreshing; soft; soothing: *balmy weather; to enjoy a balmy sleep.* **2.** having the qualities of balm; aromatic; fragrant: *balmy leaves.* **3.** producing balm: *balmy plants; a balmy shrub.* **4.** *Slang.* silly; foolish; eccentric. [BALM + -Y[1]] —**balm′i·ly,** *adv.* —**balm′i·ness,** *n.* —**Syn. 1.** fair, gentle, temperate, clement.

bal·ne·al (bal′nē əl), *adj.* of or pertaining to baths or bathing. [< L *balne(um)* < Gk *balaneîon* bathing-room, bath + -AL[1]]

bal·ne·ol·o·gy (bal′nē ol′ə jē), *n.* *Med.* the science dealing with the therapeutic effects of baths and bathing. [*balne-* (see BALNEAL) + -O- + -LOGY] —**bal·ne·o·log·ic** (bal′nē ə loj′ik), **bal′ne·o·log′i·cal,** *adj.* —**bal′ne·ol′o·gist,** *n.*

Ba·lo·chi (bə lo͞o′chē), *n., pl.* **-chis,** (*esp. collectively*) **-chi.** Baluchi.

ba·lon (*Fr.* bᴀ lôɴ′), *n.* *Ballet.* ballon. [< F]

ba·lo·ney (bə lō′nē), *n.* **1.** *Informal.* bologna. **2.** *Slang.* foolishness; nonsense. Also, **boloney.** [alter. of BOLOGNA (SAUSAGE)]

bal·op·ti·con (ba lop′ti kon′, bə-), *n.* a type of stereopticon for projecting images of objects by reflected light. [formerly trademark]

bal·sa (bôl′sə, bäl′-), *n.* **1.** a bombacaceous tree, *Ochroma Lagopus,* of tropical America, yielding an exceedingly light wood used for life preservers, rafts, toy airplanes, etc. **2.** a raft made of balsa wood. **3.** any life raft. [< Sp: boat]

bal·sam (bôl′səm), *n.* **1.** any of various fragrant exudations from certain trees, esp. burseraceous trees of the genus *Commiphora,* as balm of Gilead. Cf. **balm** (def. 1). **2.** the similar products yielded by the leguminous trees *Myroxylon Pereirae* and *M. Balsamum,* of Central and South America. Cf. **Peru balsam, tolu. 3.** oleoresin (def. 1). **4.** any of certain transparent turpentines, as Canada balsam. **5.** a plant or tree yielding a balsam. **6.** See **balsam fir. 7.** any of several balsaminaceous plants of the genus *Impatiens,* as *I. Balsamina,* a common garden annual. **8.** any aromatic ointment for ceremonial or medicinal use. **9.** any agency that heals, soothes, or restores: *the balsam of understanding and appreciation.* [OE < L *balsam(um)* < Gk *bálsamon.* See BALM] —**bal·sa·ma·ceous** (bôl′sə mā′shəs, bal′-), *adj.* —**bal′sam·y,** *adj.*

bal′sam ap′ple, **1.** a climbing, cucurbitaceous vine, *Momordica Balsamina,* of the Old World tropics. **2.** the orange, ovoid, warty fruit of this plant.

bal′sam ca·pi′vi (kə pē′vē, -pī′-), copaiba.

bal′sam fir′, **1.** a North American fir, *Abies balsamea,* which yields Canada balsam. **2.** the wood of this tree. **3.** any of certain other firs.

bal·sam·ic (bôl sam′ik, bal-), *adj.* of, like, or containing balsam. [BALSAM + -IC] —**bal·sam′i·cal·ly,** *adv.*

bal·sam·if·er·ous (bôl′sə mif′ər əs, bal′-), *adj.* yielding balsam. [BALSAM + -I- + -FEROUS]

bal·sa·mi·na·ceous (bôl′sə mə nā′shəs, bal′-), *adj.* belonging to the *Balsaminaceae,* a family of plants with oddly shaped flowers, including many tropical species and also the balsams of the genus *Impatiens.* [< Gk *balsamín(ē)* garden balsam + -ACEOUS]

bal′sam of fir′. See **Canada balsam.**

bal′sam of Peru′. See **Peru balsam.**

bal′sam of tolu′, tolu.

bal′sam pear′, a tropical, herbaceous vine, *Momordica Charantia,* of the tropical Eastern Hemisphere, having yellow flowers with darker centers and orange-yellow fruit.

bal′sam pop′lar, a poplar, *Populus Tacamahaca,* having broad, heart-shaped leaves, cultivated as a shade tree.

bal′sam spruce′, an evergreen conifer of the genus *Abies.*

Bal·shem (bäl shem′, -shām′), *n.* *Hebrew.* Baalshem.

Balt., Baltic.

Bal·tas·sar (bal tas′ər), *n.* *Douay Bible.* Belteshazzar.

bal·te·us (bal′tē əs, bôl′-), *n., pl.* **-te·i** (-tē ī′). **1.** (on an Ionic capital) the horizontal band connecting the volutes on either side. **2.** (in an ancient Roman amphitheater) a horizontal walk dividing upper and lower tiers. [< L: belt, girdle, ? of Etruscan orig.]

Bal·tha·zar (bal thā′zər, -thaz′ər, bôl-, bäl′thə zär′), *n.* **1.** a wine bottle holding 13 quarts. **2.** a boy's given name.

Bal·tic (bôl′tik), *adj.* **1.** of, near, or on the Baltic Sea. **2.** of or pertaining to the Baltic States. **3.** of or pertaining to a group of languages, as Lettish, Lithuanian, and Old Prussian, that constitute a branch of the Indo-European family. —*n.* **4.** the Baltic branch of the Indo-European family of languages.

Bal′tic Sea′, a sea in N Europe, bounded by Denmark, Sweden, Finland, Estonia, Latvia, Lithuania, Poland, and Germany. ab. 160,000 sq. mi.

Bal′tic States′, Estonia, Latvia, Lithuania, and sometimes Finland.

Bal·ti·more (bôl′tə mōr′, -môr′), *n.* a black nymphalid butterfly, *Melitaea phaeton,* characterized by orange-red, yellow, and white markings, common in those areas of the northeastern U.S. where turtlehead, the food plant of its larvae, is found. [named after Lord *Baltimore;* see BALTIMORE ORIOLE]

Bal·ti·more (bôl′tə mōr′, -môr′), *n.* **1. Lord.** See **Calvert, Sir George. 2.** a seaport in N Maryland, on an estuary near the Chesapeake Bay. 939,024 (1960).

Bal′timore chop′, *Baseball Slang.* a batted ball that takes a high bounce upon hitting the ground on or immediately in front of home plate, often enabling the batter to reach first base safely.

Bal′timore clip′per, a small, fast American sailing vessel of the early 19th century, having a sharp hull form and two masts with a pronounced rake and carrying a brig or schooner rig.

Bal′timore heat′er, a stove for heating a lower and upper room, having its fire door in the lower room.

Bal′timore o′riole, an orange and black oriole, *Icterus galbula,* of North America. [so named because the black and orange of the male were the colors of Lord Baltimore's livery]

Bal·to-Sla·vic (bôl′tō slä′vik, -slav′ik), *n.* a grouping of Indo-European languages comprising the Baltic and Slavic groups. [*Balto-* (comb. form of BALTIC) + SLAVIC]

Ba·lu·chi (bə lo͞o′chē), *n., pl.* **-chis,** (*esp. collectively*) **-chi. 1.** a member of a warlike, aristocratic, nomadic people of Baluchistan who serve as overlords to other, mostly sedentary, peoples. **2.** the language of the Baluchi, an Iranian language of the Indo-European family. Also, **Balochi.** [< Pers]

Ba·lu·chi·stan (bə lo͞o′chi stän′, -stan′), *n.* **1.** an arid mountainous region in S Asia, in SE Iran and NW West Pakistan, bordering on the Arabian Sea. **2.** a former territory of W British India, now incorporated into West Pakistan.

Balu′chistan States′, a group of three former native states in W British India: now incorporated into West Pakistan.

bal·un (bal′ən), *n.* *Elect.* a device for converting a balanced line into an unbalanced line and vice versa. [BAL(ANCE) + UN(BALANCE)]

bal·us·ter (bal′ə stər), *n.* **1.** *Archit.* any of a number of closely spaced supports for a railing. **2. balusters,** a balustrade. **3.** any of various symmetrical supports, as furniture legs, spindles, etc., tending to swell toward the bottom or top. [< F *balustre* < It *balaustro* pillar shaped like calyx-tube of pomegranate flower < *balaust(r)a* < L *balaust(ium)* < Gk *balaústion* flower of pomegranate] —**bal′us·tered,** *adj.*

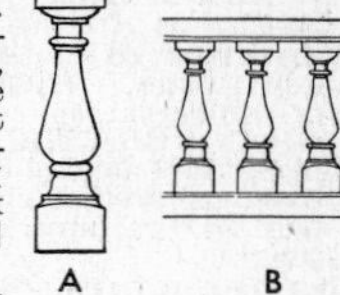

A, Baluster
B, Balustrade

bal′uster meas′ure, an antique liquid measure usually made of pewter, having a concave top on a convex base.

bal′uster stem′, a stem of a drinking glass or the like having a gradual swelling near the top or bottom.

bal·us·trade (bal′ə strād′, bal′ə strād′), *n.* *Archit.* a railing with supporting balusters. [< F *balustre* BALUSTER + *-ade* -ADE[1]; cf. Sp *balaustrada,* It *balaustrata*] —**bal′us·trad′ed,** *adj.*

Bal·zac (bal′zak, bôl′-; *Fr.* bᴀl zᴀk′), *n.* **Ho·no·ré de** (on′ə rā′ də; *Fr.* ô nô ʀā′ də), 1799–1850, French novelist.

B.A.M., 1. Bachelor of Applied Mathematics. **2.** Bachelor of Arts in Music.

Ba·ma·ko (bam′ə kō′; *Fr.* bᴀ mᴀ kō′), *n.* a city in and the capital of Mali: inland port on the Niger River. 100,433 (1954).

Bam·ba·ra (bäm bär′ä), *n.* a Mande language that is used as a trade language in the upper Niger drainage basin in Africa.

Bam·berg (bam′bûrg; *Ger.* bäm′bᴇʀκʜ), *n.* **1.** a city in N Bavaria in south-central West Germany. 73,700 (1963). **2.** a town in central South Carolina. 3081 (1960).

Bam·bi (bam′bē), *n.* a girl's given name.

bam·bi·no (bam bē′nō; *It.* bäm bē′nô), *n., pl.* **-nos,** It., **-ni** (-nē). **1.** a child or baby. **2.** an image of the infant Jesus. [< It < *bamb(o)* childish, simple + *-ino* dim. suffix]

bam·boc·ci·ade (bam′boch ē äd′), *n.* a genre painting dealing with rustic drinking scenes, esp. one treated in an exaggerated or comic manner. Also, **bam·bac·ci·a·ta** (bam boch′ē ä′tə), **bam·boch·ade** (bam′boch äd′). [< F *bambochade* < It *bambocciata* < *bamboccі(o)* little child, simpleton (dim. of *bambo,* childish, simple) + *-ata* -ADE[1]; said to have been a nickname of Pieter van Laer, 17th-century painter of rustic life]

bam·boo (bam bo͞o′), *n., pl.* **-boos. 1.** any of the woody or treelike tropical and semitropical grasses of the genera *Bambusa, Dendrocalamus,* and allied genera. **2.** the hollow, woody stem of such a plant, used as a building material and for making furniture, poles, etc. [sp. var. of earlier *bambu* < Malay; r. *bambus* < D *bamboes;* c. NL *bambūsa*]

Bamboo

bam′boo cur′tain, the barrier of rigid censorship and secrecy in Communist Asia, esp. China. Cf. **iron curtain.**

bamboo′ shoots′, the young shoots produced by the rhizome of a bamboo, cut as soon as they break through the surface of the ground and used as a vegetable.

bamboo′ turn′ing, *Furniture.* turning of spindles and framing members to simulate the jointing of bamboo.

bamboo′ ware′, a dark Wedgwood stoneware of c1770 imitating bamboo.

bam·boo·zle (bam bo͞o′zəl), *v.,* **-zled, -zling.** —*v.t.* **1.** to deceive or get the better of (someone) by trickery, flattery, or the like; humbug; hoodwink (often fol. by *into*): *They bamboozled us into joining the club.* **2.** to perplex; mystify. —*v.i.* **3.** to practice trickery, deception, cozenage, or the like: *to lie, cheat, and bamboozle.* [?] —**bam·boo′zle·ment,** *n.* —**bam·boo′zler,** *n.*

B.A.Mus.Ed., Bachelor of Arts in Music Education.

ban[1] (ban), *v.,* **banned, ban·ning,** *n.* —*v.t.* **1.** to prohibit, forbid, or bar; interdict: *to ban an obscene book; to ban a protest meeting.* **2.** *Archaic.* **a.** to pronounce an ecclesiastical curse upon. **b.** to curse; execrate. —*n.* **3.** act of prohibiting by law; interdiction. **4.** informal denunciation or prohibition, as by public opinion: *society's ban on war.* **5.** *Law.* **a.** a proclamation. **b.** a public condemnation. **6.** *Eccles.* a formal condemnation; excommunication. **7.** a malediction; curse. [ME *banne* < Scand; cf. Icel *banna* to curse, forbid; c. OE *bannan* to summon, proclaim; akin to L *fā(rī)* (to) speak, Skt *bhanati* speaks, etc.] —**Syn. 1.** taboo, outlaw, proscribe. **3.** prohibition, proscription, interdict. **3, 4.** taboo. —**Ant. 1.** allow. **3.** permission.

ban[2] (ban), *n.* **1.** a public proclamation or edict. **2. bans,** *Eccles.* banns. **3.** (in the feudal system) **a.** the summoning of the sovereign's vassals for military service. **b.** the body of vassals summoned. [ME; OE *bannan* to summon, proclaim + *gebann* summons, proclamation + OF *ban* summons < Gmc; cf. G *Bann*]

ban[3] (ban), *n.* **1.** (formerly) the governor of Croatia and Slavonia. **2.** *Hist.* a provincial governor of the southern marches of Hungary. [< Hung < Pers *bān* lord]

ban[4] (bän), *n., pl.* **ba·ni** (bä′nē). a Rumanian coin, the 100th part of a leu, equivalent to about .0008 of a U.S. dollar. [< Rumanian]

Ba′nach space′ (bä′näкн), *Math.* a vector space on which a norm is defined which is complete.

ba·nal (bān′əl, bə nal′, -näl′, ban′əl), *adj.* devoid of freshness or originality; hackneyed; trite: *a banal and sophomoric treatment of an important subject.* [< F (OF *ban* (see BAN[2]) + *-al* -AL[1])] —**ba·nal·i·ty** (bə nal′i tē, bā-), *n.* —**ba′nal·ly,** *adv.* —**Syn.** See **commonplace.**

ba·nan·a (bə nan′ə), *n.* **1.** a tropical plant of the genus *Musa,* certain species of which are cultivated for their nutritious fruit. **2.** the fruit, esp. that of *M. sapientum,* with yellow or red rind. [< Sp < Pg < WAfr native name]

Banana plant (Height 10 to 25 ft.)

Ba·nan·a·land (bə nan′ə land′), *n.* *Australian Archaic.* Queensland.

banan′a oil′, **1.** a sweet-smelling liquid ester, $CH_3COOC_5H_{11}$, a mixture of isomers, esp. of isoamyl acetate, $CH_3COOCH_2CH_2CH(CH_3)_2$, derived from amyl alcohol and having the characteristic odor of bananas: used chiefly as a paint solvent and in artificial fruit flavors; amyl acetate. **2.** *Slang.* insincere talk; nonsense.

ba·nan·a·quit (bə nan′ə kwit′), *n.* any of several tropical American honeycreepers, esp. of the genus *Coereba,* which feed on fruit. [BANANA + *quit* a name prob. imit. of its call]

banan′a repub′lic, *Sometimes Disparaging.* any of the small countries in the tropics, esp. in the Western Hemisphere, whose economies are largely dependent on fruit exports, tourism, and foreign investors.

banan′a shrub′, a tall shrub, *Michelia fuscata,* of China, having light carmine-edged, brownish-yellow flowers and a strong banana odor.

banan′a split′, an elaborate confection, typically consisting of a banana sliced lengthwise, on top of which are placed two or more scoops of ice cream, fruit syrup, and a topping of whipped cream, nuts, and a maraschino cherry.

Ba·na·res (bə när′is), *n.* Benares.

ban·at (ban′it, bä′nit), *n.* a fertile low-lying region extending through Hungary, Rumania, and Yugoslavia. [< Serb or Croat *bānat,* equiv. to *bān* BAN[3] + *-at* suffix akin to -ATE[1]]

ba·naus·ic (bə nô′sik, -zik), *adj.* serving utilitarian purposes only; mechanical; practical: *architecture that was more banausic than inspired.* [< Gk *banausik(ós),* equiv. to *bánaus(os)* artisan + *-ikos* -IC]

Ban·bur·y (ban′ber′ē, -bə rē, bam′-), *n.* a town in N Oxfordshire, in S England. 20,996 (1961).

Ban′bury cake′, a small, oval pastry containing currants, candied peel, honey, and spices, etc., usually with three parallel cuts across the top. Also called **Ban′bury bun′.** [after BANBURY, where it was made]

Ban′bury tart′, a tart filled with a lemon-flavored mixture of currants, raisins, or the like.

banc (bangk), *n.* *Law.* **1.** the seat on which judges sit in court. **2. in banc,** as a full court; with all the judges of a court present: *a hearing in banc.* [ME < OF: bench]

Banchs (bänchs), *n.* **En·ri·que** (en rē′ke), born 1888, Argentine poet.

Ban·croft (ban′krôft, -kroft, bang′-), *n.* **1. George,** 1800–91, U.S. historian and statesman. **2. Hubert Howe,** 1832–1918, U.S. publisher and historian.

band[1] (band), *n.* **1.** a company of persons or, sometimes, animals or things, joined, acting, or functioning together; aggregation; party; troop. **2.** a musical group, usually employing brass, percussion, and often woodwind instruments, that plays esp. for marching or open-air performances. **3.** an orchestra playing popular music, esp. for dancing. **4.** a division of a nomadic tribe; a group of individuals who move and camp together. **5.** a group of persons living outside the law: *a renegade band.* **6. to beat the band,** energetically; abundantly: *It rained all day to beat the band.* —*v.t.* **7.** to unite in a troop, company, or confederacy. —*v.i.* **8.** to unite; confederate (often fol. by *together*): *They banded together to oust the chairman.* [late ME *bande* < MF < OPr *banda* < Goth *bandwa* standard; akin to BAND[2], BAND[3], BEND[1], BOND[1]] —**Syn. 1.** gang, group; body; set; society, association, assembly. See **company.**

band[2] (band), *n.* **1.** a thin, flat strip of some material for binding, confining, trimming, or some other purpose: *a band on each bunch of water cress.* **2.** a fillet, belt, or strap: *a band for the hair; a band for connecting pulleys.* **3.** a stripe, as of color or decorative work. **4.** a strip of paper or other material, esp. one serving as a label: *a cigar band.* **5.** a flat collar commonly worn by men and women in the 17th century in western Europe. **6. bands.** See **Geneva bands.** **7.** (on a phonograph record) one of two or more sets of grooves in which sound has been recorded, separated from an adjacent set or sets by silent grooves. **8.** *Radio.* a set of frequencies that can be tuned in closely together, as by means of a particular set of condensers. **9.** *Computer Technol.* one or more tracks or channels on a magnetic drum. **10.** *Dentistry.* a strip of thin metal encircling a tooth, usually for anchoring an orthodontic apparatus. **11.** *Anat., Zool.* a ribbonlike or cordlike structure encircling, binding, or connecting a part or parts. **12.** (in handbound books) one o several cords of hemp or flax handsewn across the back of the collated signatures of a book to provide added strength. —*v.t.* **13.** to mark, decorate, or furnish with a band or bands. [late ME *bande* < MF; OF *bende* < Gmc; cf. OHG *binta* fillet. See BIND, BAND[1], etc.] —**band′er,** *n.* —**band′less,** *adj.*

band[3] (band), *n.* *Archaic.* **1.** Usually, **bands.** articles for binding the person or the limbs; shackles; manacles; fetters. **2.** an obligation; bond: *the nuptial bands.* [ME < Scand; cf. Icel *band,* OHG *bant*]

Ban·da (ban′də), *n.* **Hastings Ka·mu·zu** (kä mōō′zōō), born 1905, Malawi physician, political leader, and public official: 1st president of Malawi since 1966.

band·age (ban′dij), *n., v.,* **-aged, -ag·ing.** —*n.* **1.** a strip of cloth or other material used to bind up a wound, sore, sprain, etc. **2.** anything used as a band or ligature. —*v.t.* **3.** to bind or cover with a bandage: *to bandage the ankles of a football player to prevent sprains.* —*v.i.* **4.** to put a bandage on a wound, sprain, etc.: *Apply some iodine before you bandage.* [< MF; see BAND[2], -AGE] —**band′ag·er,** *n.*

Band-Aid (band′ād′), *n.* *Trademark.* an adhesive covering with a gauze pad in the center, used for protecting minor abrasions and cuts.

ban·dan·na (ban dan′ə), *n.* **1.** a large, colored handkerchief, usually with white spots or figures on a red or blue background. **2.** any large scarf for the neck or head. Also, **ban·dan′a.** [earlier *bandanno* (second syll. unstressed) < Hindi *bāndhnū* way of dyeing with cloth knotted to keep dye from reaching some parts] —**ban·dan′naed, ban·dan′aed,** *adj.*

Ban·dar Ab·bas (bän där′ ä bäs′), a seaport in S Iran. 14,278 (1956).

Ban·dara·nai·ke (bän′drä nī′kə), *n.* **Si·ri·ma·vo** (sē′rē mä′vô), born 1916, Ceylonese statesman: prime minister of Ceylon since 1960.

Ban′da Sea′ (bän′dä), a sea between Celebes and New Guinea, S of the Moluccas and N of Timor.

band·box (band′boks′), *n.* **1.** a lightweight box of pasteboard, thin wood, etc., for holding a hat or other articles of apparel. **2.** *Informal.* an area or structure that is smaller in dimensions or size than the standard: *Ebbets Field was a bandbox.* [BAND[2] + BOX[1]] —**band′box′i·cal,** *adj.* —**band′box′y,** *adj.*

band′ brake′, a brake using a brake band.

ban·deau (ban dō′, ban′dō), *n., pl.* **-deaux** (-dōz′, -dōz). **1.** a headband, esp. one worn about the forehead. **2.** a narrow brassiere. [< F; OF *bandel,* equiv. to *bande* BAND[2] + *-el* < L *-illus* dim. suffix]

band·ed (ban′did), *adj.* *Archit.* (of a column, door architrave, etc.) having the regular flutings, moldings, etc., interrupted at regular intervals by projecting blocks or drums. [BAND[2] + -ED[2]]

band′ed ant′eater, a nearly extinct Australian marsupial, *Myrmecobius fasciatus,* feeding on termites and having the body marked with whitish transverse bars. Also called **numbat.**

band′ed pur′ple. See under **purple** (def. 7).

band′ed rat′tlesnake. See **timber rattlesnake.**

band′ed rud′derfish, a carangid fish, *Seriola zonata,* found in the western Atlantic Ocean.

ban·de·let (ban′dəlet′, -dəlit, ban′dəlet′), *n.* *Archit.* **1.** a flat molding, broader than a fillet and narrower than a fascia. **2.** annulet (def. 1). Also, **bandlet.** [< F *bandelette,* equiv. to OF *bandele* (fem. of *bandel* BANDEAU) + *-ete* -ETTE]

Ban·del·lo (bän del′lô), *n.* **Mat·te·o** (mät te′ô), 1485–1561, Italian ecclesiastic and author.

ban·de·ril·la (ban′də rē′ə, -rēl′yə; *Sp.* bän′de rē′lyä, -yä), *n., pl.* **-ril·las** (-rē′əz, -rēl′yəz; *Sp.* -rē′lyäs, -yäs). an ornamented dart with barbs used by banderilleros for sticking into the neck or shoulder of the bull. [< Sp, equiv. to *bander(a)* BANNER + *-illa* dim. suffix < L]

ban·de·ril·le·ro (ban′də rē âr′ō, -rēl yâr′-; *Sp.* bän′de rē lye′rô, -ye′-), *n., pl.* **-ril·le·ros** (-rē âr′ōz, -rēl yâr′-; *Sp.* -rē lye′rôs, -ye′-). a matador's assistant who sticks the banderillas into the bull. [< Sp, equiv. to *banderill(a)* BANDERILLA + *-ero* -ARY]

ban·de·role (ban′də rōl′), *n.* **1.** a small flag or streamer fastened to a lance, masthead, etc. **2.** a narrow scroll usually bearing an inscription. **3.** (esp. in Renaissance architecture) a sculptured band, as on a building, adapted to receive an inscription. **4.** a square banner borne at the funeral of a great man and placed over the tomb. Also, **ban′de·rol, bannerol.** [< MF < It *banderuola,* equiv. to *bandier(a)* BANNER + *-uola* < L *-ola* dim. suffix]

ban·der·snatch (ban′dər snach′), *n.* **1.** an imaginary wild animal of fierce disposition. **2.** a person of uncouth or unconventional habits, attitudes, etc., esp. one considered a menace, nuisance, or the like. [coined by Lewis Carroll in *Through the Looking Glass,* 1872]

band·file (band′fīl′), *v.t.,* **-filed, -fil·ing.** to file with a filing band on a band mill or band saw. [BAND[2] + FILE[2]]

ban·di·coot (ban′də kōōt′), *n.* **1.** any of several large, East Indian rats of the genus *Nesokia.* **2.** any of several insectivorous and herbivorous marsupials of the family *Peramelidae,* of Australia and New Guinea. [< Telugu *pandi-kokku* pig-rat]

Bandicoot, *Perameles nasuta* (Total length 2 ft.; tail 8 in.)

Ban·di·nel·li (bän′dē nel′lē), *n.* **Bac·cio** (bät′chô) or **Bar·to·lom·me·o** (bär′tô lôm me′ô), 1493–1560, Italian sculptor.

band·ing (ban′ding), *n.* *Furniture.* decorative inlay, as for bordering or paneling a piece, composed of strips of wood contrasting in grain or color with the principal wood of the surface. [BAND[2] + -ING[1]]

ban·dit (ban′dit), *n., pl.* **ban·dits, ban·dit·ti** (ban dit′ē). **1.** a robber, esp. a member of a marauding band infesting the mountain districts of S Europe and the Middle East; brigand. **2.** an outlaw. [earlier *bandetto,* pl. *banditti* < It *banditi* outlaws, pl. of *bandito* proscribed (ptp. of *bandire,* c. ML *bannīre;* see BAN[1]), equiv. to *bandi-* v. stem + *-to* < L *-tus* ptp. suffix]

ban·dit·ry (ban′di trē), *n.* **1.** the activities or practices of bandits. **2.** bandits collectively; banditti. [BANDIT + -RY]

Ban·djer·ma·sin (ban′jər mä′sin), *n.* Banjermasin. Also, **Ban′djar·ma′sin.**

Band·ke·ram·ik (bänt′kā rä′mik), *n.* a European neolithic pottery having incised parallel lines about the neck. [< G; see BAND[3], CERAMIC]

band·lead·er (band′lē′dər), *n.* the leader of a band, esp. a dance band. [BAND[1] + LEADER]

band·let (band′lit), *n.* **1.** annulet (def. 1). **2.** bandelet.

band·mas·ter (band′mas′tər, -mä′stər), *n.* the conductor of a military band, circus band, etc. [BAND[1] + MASTER]

band′ mill′, a powered machine having two pulleys for a saw band or a file band; band saw.

Ban·doeng (bän′dōōng), *n.* Dutch name of **Bandung.**

ban·dog (ban′dôg′, -dog′), *n.* any dog, as a mastiff or bloodhound, kept tied or chained. [late ME *band-dogge.* See BAND[3], DOG]

ban·do·leer (ban′dəlēr′), *n.* a broad belt worn over the shoulder by soldiers and having a number of small loops or pockets, each containing a cartridge or cartridges. Also, **ban′do·lier′.** [earlier *bandollier* < MF *bandoulliere,* fem. of *bandoullier* (masc.) < Catalan *bandoler* member of a band of men (*bandol* (< Sp *bando* BAND[1]) + *-er* -ER[2])] —**ban′do·leered′, ban′do·liered′,** *adj.*

ban·do·line (ban′dəlēn′, -dəlin), *n.* a mucilaginous preparation made from quince seeds and used for smoothing, glossing, or waving the hair. [< F *bandeau* BANDEAU + L *line(re)* (to) anoint, smear]

ban·dore (ban dōr′, -dôr′, ban′dōr, -dôr), *n.* any of various obsolete musical instruments resembling the lute or the guitar. Also called **pandora, pandore, pandoura, pandure.** [earlier *bandurion* < Sp *bandurria* < L *pandūra* < Gk *pandoûra* three-stringed musical instrument]

band′-pass fil′ter (band′pas′, -päs′), *Elect., Electronics.* a filter that attenuates all frequencies except those of a specific band, which it amplifies.

band′ saw′, *Mach.* a saw consisting of an endless toothed steel band passing over two wheels.

band·saw (band′sô′), *v.t.,* **-sawed, -sawed** or **-sawn, -saw·ing.** to cut with a band saw. [v. use of BANDSAW]

band′ shell′, a concave, acoustically resonant structure in which musicians perform for outdoor concerts.

bands·man (bandz′mən), *n., pl.* **-men.** a musician who plays in a band. [BAND[1] + 's[1] + MAN[1]]

band′ spec′trum, *Physics.* a spectrum consisting of groups of closely spaced lines, always associated with molecules.

band·stand (band′stand′), *n.* **1.** a platform, often roofed, for outdoor band performances. **2.** a raised platform in a nightclub, restaurant, etc., where the members of a band or orchestra sit while performing. [BAND[1] + STAND]

band′-tailed pi′geon (band′tāld′), a wild pigeon, *Columba fasciata,* of western North America, having a gray band on its tail.

Ban·dung (bän′dōōng), *n.* a city in W Java, in Indonesia. 966,359; with suburbs, 1,028,245 (1961). Dutch, **Bandoeng.**

ban·du·ra (ban dōōr′ə), *n.* a Ukrainian stringed instrument of the lute family. [< Russ << L *pandūra* BANDORE]

ban·dur·ria (ban dōōr′yə), *n.* a Spanish musical instrument of the guitar family with six pairs of double strings. [see BANDORE]

band·wag·on (band′wag′ən), *n.* **1.** a wagon, usually large and ornately decorated, for carrying a musical band, as in a circus parade, at the head of a procession. **2. be** or **jump on** or **aboard the bandwagon,** *U.S. Informal.* to support an apparently successful candidate, cause, or movement: *After it became apparent that Jones would win, everyone jumped on the bandwagon.* [BAND[1] + WAGON]

band·width (band′width′, -with′), *n.* *Radio.* a certain range of frequencies within a band. [BAND[2] + WIDTH]

ban·dy (ban′dē), *v.,* **-died, -dy·ing,** *adj., n., pl.* **-dies.** —*v.t.* **1.** to throw or strike to and fro or from side to side, as a ball in tennis. **2.** to pass from one to another or back and forth; give and take; trade; exchange: *to bandy blows; to bandy words.* —*adj.* **3.** (of legs) having a bend or crook outward; bowed: *a new method for correcting bandy legs.* —*n.* **4.** an early form of tennis. **5.** *Chiefly Brit.* (formerly) hockey or shinny. **6.** *Obs.* a hockey or shinny stick. [? < Sp *bande(ar)* (to) conduct, bandy, orig. help, i.e. serve as member of a band of men. See BAND[1]] —**ban′di·ness,** *n.*

ban·dy-leg·ged (ban′dē leg′id, -legd′), *adj.* having crooked legs; bowlegged.

bane (bān), *n.* **1.** one who or that which ruins or spoils: *Gambling was the bane of his existence.* **2.** a deadly poison (often used in combination, as in the names of poisonous plants): *wolfsbane; henbane.* **3.** death; destruction; ruin. **4.** *Obs.* that which causes death or destroys life: *entrapped and drowned beneath the watery bane.* [ME < OE *bana* slayer; c. Icel *bani* death, murderer, OHG *bano* death; akin to Goth *banja* wound, Gk *phónos* slaughter]

bane·ber·ry (bān′ber′ē, -bə rē), *n., pl.* **-ries.** **1.** any ranunculaceous plant of the genus *Actaea,* bearing poisonous, red or white berries. **2.** the berry of such a plant. [BANE + BERRY]

Bane·croft (bān′krôft, -kroft), *n.* a boy's given name.

bane·ful (bān′fəl), *adj.* destructive; pernicious; poisonous: *a baneful superstition; baneful herbs.* [BANE + -FUL] —**bane′ful·ly,** *adv.* —**bane′ful·ness,** *n.* —**Syn.** deadly, mortal; harmful, noxious; venomous.

Ba·ner·jea (bä′nər jē′), *n.* **Sir Su·ren·dra·nath** (sōō rān′drə nät′), 1848–1925, Indian political leader.

Banff (bamf), *n.* **1.** Also called **Banff·shire** (bamf′shēr, -shər). a county in NE Scotland. 46,400 (1961); 630 sq. mi. **2.** a seaport in and the county seat of Banff. 3318 (est. 1964). **3.** a resort town in a national reserve

(**Banff′ Na′tional Park′,** 2585 sq. mi.) in the Rocky Mountains, in SW Alberta, Canada. 2517 (1955).

bang[1] (bang), *n.* **1.** a loud, sudden, explosive noise, as the discharge of a gun. **2.** a resounding stroke or blow: *an awful bang on the head.* **3.** *Informal.* a sudden movement or show of energy: *He started with a bang.* **4.** energy; vitality; spirit: *The bang has gone out of my work.* **5.** *U.S. Slang.* sudden or intense pleasure; thrill; excitement: *a big bang out of seeing movies.* **6.** *Slang (vulgar).* coitus. —*v.t.* **7.** to strike or beat resoundingly; slam: *to bang a door.* **8.** *Slang (vulgar).* to have coitus with (a woman). —*v.i.* **9.** to strike violently or noisily: *to bang on the door.* **10.** to make a loud, sudden, explosive noise like that of a violent blow: *The guns banged all night.* **11.** *Slang (vulgar).* to have coitus. **12. bang up,** to damage the appearance of: *A passing car banged up our fender.* —*adv.* **13.** suddenly and loudly; abruptly or violently: *He fell bang against the wall.* **14.** directly; precisely; right: *He stood bang in the center of the flower bed.* **15. bang off,** *Chiefly Brit. Slang.* immediately; right away. [cf. Icel *banga* to beat, hammer, LG *bangen* to strike, beat]

bang[2] (bang), *n.* **1.** Often, **bangs.** a fringe of hair combed or brushed forward over the forehead. —*v.t.* **2.** to cut (the hair) so as to form a fringe over the forehead. **3.** to dock (the tail of a horse or dog). [short for BANGTAIL]

bang[3] (bang), *n.* bhang.

bang·a·lay (bang′ al′ē), *n.* See **bastard mahogany.**

Ban·ga·lore (bang′gə lōr′, -lôr′), *n.* a city in and the capital of Mysore, in S India. 905,100 (1961).

Ban′galore torpe′do, a metal tube filled with explosives and equipped with a firing mechanism, esp. for destroying barbed-wire entanglements, mine fields, etc.

bang-bang (bang′bang′), *n.* *Rocketry.* a missile-control system which operates on a single command, with variations in motion obtained by repeating the command. [redupl. of BANG[1]]

bang·board (bang′bōrd′, -bôrd′), *n.* (in corn harvesting) a wide board mounted above one side of a wagon, causing ears of corn tossed against it to fall into the wagon. [BANG[1] + BOARD]

bang·er (bang′ər), *n.* *Brit.* **1.** *Slang.* a pork sausage. **2.** *Informal.* a firecracker. [BANG[1] + -ER[1]]

Bang·ka (bang′kə; *Du.* bäng′kä), *n.* an island in Indonesia, E of Sumatra: tin mines. 250,452 (est. 1961); 4611 sq. mi. Also, **Banka.**

Bang·kok (bang′kok), *n.* **1.** a seaport in and the capital of Thailand, in the S central part, on the Menam River. 1,204,894 with suburbs (est. 1957). **2.** (*l.c.*) a kind of Siamese straw. **3.** (*l.c.*) a hat woven of strands of this straw.

Ban·gla·desh (bang′glə desh′, bäng′-), *n.* a republic, E of India on the Bay of Bengal; a member of the British Commonwealth of Nations. 66,000,000 (est. 1972); 54,501 sq. mi. *Cap.:* Dacca. Also, **Ban′gla Desh′.** Formerly (1947–71), **East Pakistan.**

ban·gle (bang′gəl), *n.* **1.** a bracelet in the form of a ring without a clasp. **2.** an ornamental anklet. [< Hindi *banglī*, var. of *bangrī* glass ring, armlet] —**ban′gled,** *adj.*

bang′ on′, *Brit. Slang.* terrific; marvelous; just right: *That hat is absolutely bang on.*

Ban·gor (bang′gôr, -gər), *n.* **1.** a seaport in S Maine, on the Penobscot River. 38,912 (1960). **2.** a town in E Pennsylvania. 5766 (1960).

Bangs (bangz), *n.* **John Ken·drick** (ken′drik), 1862–1922, U.S. humorist.

Bang's′ Disease′ (bangz), *Vet. Pathol.* an infectious disease of cattle caused by a bacterium, *Brucella abortus,* that infects the genital organs and frequently causes abortions. This organism is one of several which causes undulant fever or brucellosis in man. [named after B.L.F. *Bang* (1848–1932), Danish biologist]

bang·tail (bang′tāl′), *n.* *Horse Racing Slang.* a race horse. [*bang* cut (nasal var. of *bag* cut < ?) + TAIL[1]. Cf. PIGTAIL]

Ban·gui (bäɴ gē′), *n.* a city in and the capital of the Central African Republic, in the SW part. 82,555 (est. 1955).

bang-up (bang′up′), *adj.* *Slang.* excellent; extraordinary. [adj. use of v. phrase *bang up*]

Bang·we·u·lu (bang′wē o͞o′lo͞o), *n.* a shallow lake and swamp in NE Zambia. ab. 150 mi. long.

ba·ni (bä′nē), *n.* pl. of **ban**[4].

ban·ia (ban′yə), *n.* banyan (def. 3). Also, **ban·iya** (ban′yə, -ē ə).

ban·ian (ban′yən), *n.* banyan.

ban·ish (ban′ish), *v.t.* **1.** to condemn to exile; expel from or relegate to a country or place by authoritative decree. **2.** to compel to depart; send, drive, or put away: *to banish sorrow.* [ME *banisshe(n)* < MF *baniss-* (long s. of *banir*). See BAN[1], -ISH[2]] —**ban′ish·er,** *n.* —**ban′ish·ment,** *n.*
—**Syn. 1.** exile, expatriate, outlaw; deport.

ban·is·ter (ban′i stər), *n.* **1.** a baluster, esp. a slender one at the edge of a staircase. **2.** Sometimes, **banisters.** the balustrade of a staircase. Also, **bannister.** [var. of BALUSTER]

ban′ister back′, *Furniture.* a back of a chair or the like, usually having semicircular spindles between the top rail and the cross rail or seat.

Ban·jer·ma·sin (bän′jər mä′sin), *n.* a seaport in the S coast of Borneo, in Indonesia. 212,683 (est. 1961). Also, **Bandjermasin.**

ban·jo (ban′jō), *n., pl.* **-jos, -joes.** a musical instrument of the guitar family, having a circular body covered in front with tightly stretched parchment and played with the fingers or a plectrum. [var. of BANDORE] —**ban′jo·ist,** *n.*

Banjo

ban′jo clock′, a clock of the early 19th century in the U.S., having a drumlike case for the dial mounted on a narrow, tapering body, with a boxlike bottom containing the pendulum and its weight. See illus. in next column.

bank[1] (bangk), *n.* **1.** a long pile or heap; mass: *a bank of earth; a bank of clouds.* **2.** a slope or acclivity. **3.** *Phys. Geol.* the slope immediately bordering a stream course along which the water normally runs. **4.** a broad elevation of the sea floor around which the water is relatively shallow: not a hazard to surface navigation. **5.** *Coal Mining.* the surface around the mouth of a shaft. **6.** Also called **cant, superelevation.** the inclination of the bed of a banked road or railroad. **7.** *Aeron.* the lateral inclination of an aircraft, esp. during a turn. **8.** *Billiards, Pool.* the cushion of the table. —*v.t.* **9.** to border with or like a bank; embank: *banking the river with sandbags at flood stage.* **10.** to form into a bank or heap (usually fol. by *up*): *to bank up the snow.* **11.** to slope the bed of (a road or railroad) to compensate for transverse forces, esp. centrifugal forces at curves. **12.** *Aeron.* to tip or incline (an airplane) laterally. **13.** *Billiards, Pool.* **a.** to drive (a ball) to the cushion. **b.** to pocket (the object ball) by driving it against the bank. **14.** to cover up (a fire) with ashes or fuel and close the dampers to make it burn long and slowly. **15.** to suspend the operation of (a furnace). —*v.i.* **16.** to build up in or form banks, as clouds or snow. **17.** *Aeron.* to tip or incline an airplane laterally. **18.** *Horol.* (of a lever or balance) to be halted at either end of its oscillation by striking a pin or the like. [ME *banke* < ODan **banke, bakke;* c. Icel *bakki* elevation, hill, Sw *backe*]
—**Syn. 1.** embankment, mound, ridge, dike. **3.** See **shore.**

Banjo clock

bank[2] (bangk), *n.* **1.** an institution for receiving, lending, exchanging, and safeguarding money and, in some cases, issuing notes and transacting other financial business. **2.** the office or quarters of such an institution. **3.** *Games.* **a.** the stock or fund of pieces from which the players draw. **b.** the fund of the manager or the dealer. **4.** a storage place: *a blood bank.* **5.** a store or reserve. **6.** *Obs.* **a.** a sum of money, esp. as a fund for use in business. **b.** a moneychanger's table, counter, or shop. —*v.i.* **7.** to keep money in or have an account with a bank: *Do you bank across the street?* **8.** to exercise the functions of a bank or banker. **9.** *Games.* to hold the bank. —*v.t.* **10.** to deposit in a bank: *to bank one's paycheck.* **11. bank on** or **upon,** *Informal.* to count on; depend on: *You can bank on him to hand you an outrageous bill for his services.* [< It *banc(a)* table, counter, moneychanger's table < Gmc; cf. OHG *bank* bench]

bank[3] (bangk), *n.* **1.** an arrangement of objects in a line or in tiers: *a bank of seats; a bank of lights.* **2.** *Music.* a row of keys on an organ. **3.** a bench for rowers in a galley. **4.** a row or tier of oars. **5.** the group of rowers occupying one bench or rowing one oar. **6.** *Print.* **a.** a bench on which sheets are placed as printed. **b.** Also called, *esp. Brit.,* **random.** the sloping work surface at the top of the workbench of a compositor. **7.** a table or rack on which type material is stored before being made up in forms. **8.** Also called **deck.** *Journalism.* a part of a headline containing one or more lines of type, esp. a part that appears below the main part. **9.** *Elect.* a number of similar devices connected to act together: *a bank of transformers; a bank of resistors.* —*v.t.* **10.** to arrange in a bank: *to bank the seats; to bank the lights.* [ME *boncke,* OE *-banca* (in *hobanca* bedstead, lit., heel-bench) + OF *banc* bench < Gmc; see BANK[2]]

Ban·ka (bang′kə), *n.* Bangka.

bank·a·ble (bang′kə bəl), *adj.* capable of being received, processed, or acted upon by a bank. [BANK[2] + -ABLE]

bank′ accept′ance, a draft endorsed or otherwise formally acknowledged by a bank on which it is drawn. Also called **banker's acceptance.**

bank′ account′, **1.** an account with a bank. **2.** balance standing to the credit of a depositor at a bank. Also called, *Brit.,* **banking account.**

bank′-and-turn′ in′dicator (bangk′ən tûrn′), *Aeron.* a flight instrument that combines a bank indicator and turn indicator in a single unit. Also called **needle-and-ball indicator, turn-and-bank indicator, turn-and-slip indicator.**

bank′ annu′ity, Usually, **bank annuities.** consol.

bank′ bal′ance, **1.** balance standing to the credit of a depositor at a bank. **2.** *Finance.* the balance that a bank has in the clearing house at a given time.

bank′ bill′, a draft drawn by one bank on another, payable on demand or at a specified future date. Also called **banker's bill.**

bank·book (bangk′bo͝ok′), *n.* a book held by a depositor in which a bank enters a record of his account. [BANK[2] + BOOK]

bank′ check′, **1.** a check that the depositor of a checking account draws on a bank for payment. **2.** See **cashier's check.**

bank′ clerk′, *Brit.* teller (def. 2).

bank′ depos′it, money placed in a bank against which the depositor can withdraw under prescribed conditions.

bank′ depos′it insur′ance, the protection of bank deposits against the insolvency of banks in the U.S., up to $10,000 per account, under special insurance through the Federal Deposit Insurance Corporation.

bank′ dis′count, interest on a loan, deducted in advance from the face value of the note.

bank′ draft′, a draft drawn by one bank on another.

bank·er[1] (bang′kər), *n.* **1.** a person employed by a bank, esp. as an executive or other official. **2.** *Games.* the keeper or holder of the bank. [BANK[2] + -ER[2]]

bank·er[2] (bang′kər), *n.* **1.** a vessel employed in the cod fishery on the banks off Newfoundland. **2.** a fisherman on such a vessel. **3.** *Australian.* a river near flood level, the water being almost bank high. [BANK[1] + -ER[1]]

bank·er[3] (bang′kər), *n.* a bench or table used by masons for dressing stones or bricks. [BANK[3] + -ER[1]]

bank′er's accep′tance. See **bank acceptance.**

bank′er's bill′. See **bank bill.**

bank′er's check′, *Rare.* See **cashier's check.**

ban·ket (bang ket′), *n.* *Mineral.* an auriferous quartz conglomerate found esp. in the Transvaal. [< SAfrD < MD < MF *banquet.* See BANQUET]

bank′ exam′iner, *U.S.* a public official appointed under State or federal laws to inspect and audit the operations and accounts of banks in his jurisdiction.

Bank·head (bangk′hed), *n.* **1. Tal·lu·lah (Brock·man)** (tə lo͞o′lə brok′mən), 1903–68, U.S. actress (daughter of William Brockman Bankhead). **2. Wil·liam Brockman,** 1874–1940, U.S. politician, Speaker of the House 1936–40.

bank′ hol′iday, **1.** a weekday on which banks are closed by law; legal holiday. **2.** *Brit.* a secular day on which banks are closed, obligations then falling due being performable on the secular day next following.

bank′ in′dicator, *Aeron.* a flight instrument that indicates whether or not an aircraft is skidding or slipping. Also called **ball indicator, slip indicator.** Cf. **bank-and-turn indicator.**

bank·ing (bang′king), *n.* **1.** the business carried on by a bank or a banker. **2.** banking as a profession. [BANK[2] + -ING[1]]

bank′ing account′, *Brit.* See **bank account.**

bank′ing pin′, *Horol.* either of two pins for damping or halting the oscillation in either direction of a balance or lever.

bank′ing prin′ciple, the principle that bank notes are a form of credit and should be issued freely in order to maintain an elastic currency. Also called **bank′ing doc′trine.** Cf. **currency principle.**

bank′ let′ter, a pamphlet issued by some large banks periodically, as monthly, devoted chiefly to reporting business conditions in general and often dealing with specific economic problems.

bank′ loan′, an amount of money loaned at interest by a bank to a borrower, usually on collateral security, for a certain period of time.

bank′ night′, *U.S. Informal.* an evening when prizes are awarded to members of the audience at a motion-picture theater.

bank′ note′, a promissory note, payable on demand, issued by a bank and intended to circulate as money.

bank′ of is′sue, a bank, as a Federal Reserve Bank, empowered by a government to issue currency.

bank′ pa′per, **1.** drafts, bills, and acceptances payable by banks. **2.** commercial paper which may be discounted in a bank.

bank′ rate′, **1.** the rate of discount fixed by a bank or banks. **2.** *Brit.* the discount charge set by a central bank, as by the Bank of England.

bank·roll (bangk′rōl′), *U.S.* —*n.* **1.** money in one's possession; monetary resources. —*v.t.* **2.** *Slang.* to finance; provide funds for: *to bankroll a new housing development.* [BANK[2] + ROLL] —**bank′roll′er,** *n.*

bank·rupt (bangk′rupt, -rəpt), *n.* **1.** *Law.* a person who upon his own petition or that of his creditors is adjudged insolvent by a court and whose property is administered for and divided among his creditors under a bankruptcy law. **2.** any insolvent debtor; one unable to satisfy any just claims made upon him. **3.** one who is lacking in a particular thing or quality: *an intellectual bankrupt; a moral bankrupt.* —*adj.* **4.** *Law.* subject to or under legal process because of insolvency; insolvent. **5.** at the end of one's resources; lacking (usually fol. by *of* or *in*): *to be bankrupt of compassion; bankrupt in good manners.* **6.** pertaining to bankrupts or bankruptcy. —*v.t.* **7.** to make bankrupt: *His embezzlement bankrupted the company. Greed had soon bankrupted his convictions.* [< ML *banca rupta* bank broken; r. It *banca rota* and F *banqueroute* in same sense] —**bank′rupt·ly,** *adv.*
—**Syn. 4.** destitute, impoverished.

bank·rupt·cy (bangk′rupt sē, -rəp sē), *n., pl.* **-cies.** **1.** state of being or becoming bankrupt. **2.** utter ruin, failure, depletion, or the like. [BANKRUPT + -CY]

Banks (bangks), *n.* **1. Sir Joseph,** 1734–1820, English naturalist. **2. Nathaniel Pren·tiss** (pren′tis), 1816–94, U.S. army officer and politician: Speaker of the House 1856–57. **3.** a boy's given name.

bank′ shot′, **1.** *Basketball.* a shot into the basket, made by rebounding the ball off the backboard. **2.** *Billiards, Pool.* a shot in which the cue ball or object ball is banked.

bank·si·a (bangk′sē ə), *n.* any Australian shrub or tree of the genus *Banksia,* having leathery leaves and dense cylindrical heads of flowers. [< NL; after Sir Joseph BANKS; see -IA]

Bank·side (bangk′sīd′), *n.* a district in London, England, on the S side of the Thames River.

Banks′′ rose′, a climbing evergreen rose, *Rosa banksiae,* of China, having few hooked prickles and slightly fragrant, thickly clustered, white or yellow flowers. Also called **Lady Banks' rose.** [named after Sir Joseph BANKS]

bank′ state′ment, **1.** a statement required to be published periodically by a bank showing its financial status, as assets, liabilities, etc. **2.** a monthly statement of account mailed by a bank to each of its depositors recording the banking transactions during a period and usually including canceled checks.

bank′ swal′low, a swallow, *Riparia riparia,* of the Northern Hemisphere, which nests in tunnels dug in sand or clay banks.

ban·ner (ban′ər), *n.* **1.** the flag of a country, army, troop, etc. **2.** an ensign or the like bearing some device, motto, or slogan, as one carried in religious processions, political demonstrations, etc. **3.** a flag formerly used as the standard of a sovereign, lord, or knight. **4.** a sign painted on cloth and hung over a street, entrance, etc.: *Banners at the intersection announced the tennis tournament.* **5.** anything regarded or displayed as a symbol of principles. **6.** *Heraldry.* a square flag bearing heraldic devices. **7.** Also called **ban′ner line′, line, screamer, streamer.** *Journalism.* a headline extending across the width of a newspaper page, usually across the top of the front page. **8.** *Chinese Hist.* one of the principal divisions of the Manchu army, each division having a distinguishing banner. **9.** *Bot.* the standard or vexillum of a papilionaceous corolla. —*adj.* **10.** leading or foremost: *a banner year for crops.* [ME *banere* < OF *ban(i)ere* < LL *bann(um)* (var. of *bandum* standard < Goth *bandwa* sign; see BAND[1]) + OF *-iere* < L *-āria* -ARY] —**ban′nered,** *adj.* —**ban′ner·less,** *adj.* —**ban′ner·like′,** *adj.*

ban′ner cloud′, a plume-shaped cloud extending downwind from an isolated mountain peak. Also called **cloud banner.** Cf. **cap cloud** (def. 1).

ban·ner·et[1] (ban′ər it, -ə ret′), *n.* **1.** *Hist.* a knight who could bring a company of followers into the field under his own banner. **2.** a rank of knighthood; knight banneret. [ME *baneret* < OF, equiv. to *baner(e)* BANNER + *-et* < L *-ātus* -ATE[1]]

ban·ner·et[2] (ban′ə ret′), *n.* a small banner. Also, **ban′ner·ette′.** [ME *banerett* < MF *banerete* little banner. See BANNER, -ETTE]

ban·ner·man (ban′ər mən), *n., pl.* **-men. 1.** a person who carries a flag or banner; standard-bearer. **2.** *Chinese Hist.* a member of a banner in the Manchu army. [BANNER + MAN[1]]

ban·ner·ol (ban′ə rōl′), *n.* banderole.

Ban·ning (ban′ing), *n.* a city in S California, near Los Angeles. 10,250 (1960).

ban·nis·ter (ban′i stər), *n.* banister.

Ban·nis·ter (ban′i stər), *n.* **Roger (Gilbert),** born 1929, English athlete.

ban·nock (ban′ək), *n. Scot. and Brit. Cookery.* a flat cake made of oatmeal, barley meal, etc., usually baked on a griddle. [ME *bannok,* OE *bannuc* morsel < OBrit; cf. Gael *bannach*]

Ban·nock·burn (ban′ək bûrn′, ban′ək bûrn′), *n.* a village in central Scotland, in Stirling county: site of the victory (1314) of the Scots under Robert the Bruce over the English, which assured the independence of Scotland.

banns (banz), *n.pl. Eccles.* notice of an intended marriage, given three times in the parish church of each of the betrothed. Also, **bans.** [var. of *bans,* pl. of BAN[2]]

ban·quet (bang′kwit), *n., v.,* **-quet·ed, -quet·ing.** —*n.* **1.** a lavish meal; feast. **2.** a ceremonious public dinner, esp. one honoring a person, benefiting a charity, etc. —*v.t.* **3.** to entertain or regale (a person or oneself) at a banquet: *They banqueted the visiting dignitary in grand style.* —*v.i.* **4.** to have or attend a banquet; feast: *The king banqueted on pheasant and wine.* [< F < It *banchetto* (*banc*(*o*) table (see BANK[2]) + *-etto* -ET); r. *bankett* < It] —**ban′quet·er,** *n.*
—**Syn. 1.** See **feast.**

ban·quette (bang ket′), *n.* **1.** a long bench with an upholstered seat and no arms or back. **2.** an embankment for buttressing the base of a levee and forming a berm. **3.** a bench for passengers on top of a stagecoach. **4.** *Fort.* a platform or step along the inside of a parapet, for soldiers to stand on when firing. **5.** *Southern U.S.* a sidewalk. **6.** a ledge running across the back of a buffet. [< MF < Pr *banqueta,* equiv. to *banc* bench (see BANK[3]) + *-eta* -ETTE]

Ban·quo (bang′kwō, -kō), *n.* (in Shakespeare's *Macbeth*) a murdered thane whose ghost appears to Macbeth.

bans (banz), *n.* (*construed as pl.*) banns.

ban·shee (ban′shē, ban shē′), *n.* (in Irish folklore) a spirit in the form of a wailing woman who appears to or is heard by members of a family as a sign that one of them is about to die. Also, **ban′shie.** [< Ir *bean sídhe* woman of the fairies]

bant (bant), *v.i. Med.* to reduce by Bantingism. [back formation from BANTING]

ban·tam (ban′təm), *n.* **1.** (*often cap.*) a chicken of any of several varieties or breeds characterized by very small size. **2.** a small, quarrelsome person. —*adj.* **3.** diminutive; tiny: *bantam editions of the classics.* **4.** noting a small standard size of vacuum tube. [after BANTAM]

Ban·tam (ban′təm; *Du.* bän täm′), *n.* a village in W Java, in S Indonesia: first Dutch settlement in the East Indies.

ban·tam·weight (ban′təm wāt′), *n.* a boxer or other contestant intermediate in weight between a flyweight and a featherweight, esp. a professional boxer weighing up to 118 pounds. [BANTAM + WEIGHT]

Ban′tam work′. See **Coromandel work.**

ban·ter (ban′tər), *n.* **1.** an exchange of light, playful, teasing remarks; good-natured raillery. —*v.t.* **2.** to address with banter; chaff. —*v.i.* **3.** to use banter. [?] —**ban′ter·er,** *n.* —**ban′ter·ing·ly,** *adv.*
—**Syn. 1.** badinage, joking, jesting, pleasantry, persiflage. **2.** tease, twit; ridicule, deride, mock.

Ban·thine (ban thin′, ban′thēn), *n. Pharm., Trademark.* methantheline.

ban·ting (ban′ting), *n., pl.* **-tings,** (*esp. collectively*) **-ting.** a wild ox, *Bibos banteng,* of southeastern Asia and the Malay Archipelago, resembling the domestic cow. Also, **ban·teng** (ban′teng). [< Malay]

Ban·ting (ban′ting), *n.* **1. Sir Frederick Grant,** 1891–1941, Canadian physician: Nobel prize 1923. **2.** (*often l.c.*) Bantingism.

Ban·ting·ism (ban′ting iz′əm), *n.* (*often l.c.*) *Med.* a method of reducing one's weight, based upon a high protein and low fat and carbohydrate diet. Also, **Banting.** [named after W. *Banting* (19th-century London cabinetmaker); see -ISM]

bant·ling (bant′ling), *n. Disparaging.* a young child; brat. [< G *Bänkling* illegitimate child. See BENCH, -LING[1]]

Ban·tu (ban′tōō), *n., pl.* **-tus,** (*esp. collectively*) **-tu,** *adj.* —*n.* **1.** a member of any of several Negroid peoples forming a linguistically and in some respects culturally interrelated family in central and southern Africa. **2.** a grouping of more than 500 languages of central and southern Africa, as Kikuyu, Swahili, Tswana, and Zulu, all related within a subbranch of the Benue-Congo branch of the Niger-Kordofanian family. —*adj.* **3.** of, pertaining to, or characteristic of Bantu or the Bantu.

Ban·tu·stan (ban′tōō stan′), *n.* any of several semi-autonomous reservations of African Negroes within the boundaries of South Africa.

Ban·ville (bän vēl′), *n.* **Thé·o·dore Faul·lain de** (tā ô dôr′ fō laN′ də), 1823–91, French poet and dramatist.

ban·yan (ban′yən), *n.* **1.** Also called **ban′yan tree′.** an East Indian fig tree, *Ficus benghalensis,* whose branches send out adventitious roots to the ground, sometimes causing the tree to spread over a wide area. **2.** a brightly colored wrapper, sometimes reversible, as that worn by women while doing housework. **3.** Also, **bania, baniya.** (in India) **a.** a loose shirt, jacket, or gown. **b.** a Hindu trader or merchant of a particular caste the rules of which forbid eating flesh. Also, **banian.** [< Pg << Gujarati *vāṇiyān,* pl. of *vāṇiyo* man of trading caste < Skt *vaṇij* merchant, orig. applied to a particular tree of this species near which the traders had built a booth]

Banyan, *Ficus benghalensis* (Height 70 to 100 ft.)

ban·zai (bän zī′, bän′-; *Jap.* bän′zä ē′), *interj.* **1.** (a Japanese patriotic shout or cheer addressed to the emperor and wishing him long life.) **2.** (a shout used, esp. among Japanese combat troops, when attacking or pushing forward.) —*adj.* **3.** reckless; suicidal: *a banzai attack.* [< Jap, equiv. to *ban* ten thousand + *zai* year]

B.A.O., Bachelor of Arts in Oratory.

ba·o·bab (bā′ō bab′, bä′-), *n.* any large, bombacaceous tree having an exceedingly thick trunk of the genus *Adansonia,* esp. *A. digitata,* which is native to tropical Africa and bears a gourdlike fruit. [from a language of equatorial Africa]

Bap., Baptist. Also, **Bapt.**

bap., baptized.

B.A.P.C.T., Bachelor of Arts in Practical Christian Training.

B.App.Arts, Bachelor of Applied Arts.

bap·tise (bap tīz′, bap′tīz), *v.t., v.i.,* **-tised, -tis·ing.** *Chiefly Brit.* baptize.

bap·tism (bap′tiz əm), *n.* **1.** *Eccles.* a ceremonial immersion in water, or application of water, as an initiatory rite or sacrament of the Christian church. **2.** any similar ceremony or action of initiation, dedication, etc. [< LL *baptisma* < Gk (*bapt*(*izein*) (to) BAPTIZE + *-isma* -ISM); r. ME *bapteme* < OF] —**bap·tis·mal** (bap tiz′məl), *adj.* —**bap·tis′mal·ly,** *adv.*

baptis′mal name′. See **Christian name** (def. 1).

baptis′mal regenera′tion, *Theol.* the doctrine that regeneration and sanctification are received in and through baptism.

bap′tism for the dead′, the baptism of a living person in the place of and for the sake of one who has died unbaptized: now practiced chiefly by Mormons.

bap′tism of fire′, 1. spiritual sanctification as a gift of the Holy Ghost. **2.** the first time a soldier faces battle. **3.** any severe ordeal that tests one's endurance.

Bap·tist (bap′tist), *n.* **1.** a member of a Christian denomination that baptizes believers by immersion and that is usually Calvinistic in doctrine. **2.** (*l.c.*) a person who baptizes. **3. the Baptist.** See **John the Baptist.** —*adj.* **4.** Also, **Bap·tis′tic.** of or pertaining to Baptists or their doctrines or practices. [ME *baptiste* < OF < LL *baptista* < Gk *baptistḗs,* equiv. to *bapt*(*izein*) (to) BAPTIZE + *-istēs* -IST]

Bap·tis·ta (bap tis′tə), *n.* a girl's given name.

bap·tis·ter·y (bap′ti stə rē, -ti strē), *n., pl.* **-ter·ies. 1.** a building or a part of a church in which baptism is administered. **2.** (esp. in Baptist churches) a tank for administering baptism by immersion. [< LL *baptistēri*(*um*) < Gk *baptistḗrion* bathing-place (see BAPTIST, -ERY); r. late ME *baptizatory* < ML *baptizātōri*(*um*)]

bap·tist·ry (bap′ti strē), *n., pl.* **-ries.** baptistery.

bap·tize (bap tīz′, bap′tīz), *v.,* **-tized, -tiz·ing.** —*v.t.* **1.** to immerse in water, sprinkle, or pour water on, in the Christian rite of baptism: *They baptized him at the age of six weeks.* **2.** to cleanse spiritually; initiate or dedicate by purifying. **3.** to christen. —*v.i.* **4.** to administer baptism: *a sect that does not baptize.* [ME < LL *baptiz*(*āre*) < Gk *baptízein* to immerse (*bápt*(*ein*) (to) bathe + *-izein* -IZE)] —**bap·tiz′a·ble,** *adj.* —**bap·tize′ment,** *n.* —**bap·tiz′er,** *n.*

bar[1] (bär), *n., v.,* **barred, bar·ring,** *prep.* —*n.* **1.** a relatively long, evenly shaped piece of some solid substance, as metal or wood, used as a guard or obstruction or for some mechanical purpose: *the bars of a cage; the bars of a gate.* **2.** an oblong piece of any solid material: *a bar of soap; a bar of candy.* **3.** the amount of material in a bar. **4.** an ingot, lump, or wedge of gold or silver. **5.** a long ridge of sand, gravel, or other material near or slightly above the surface of the water at or near the mouth of a river or harbor entrance: often an obstruction to navigation. **6.** anything which obstructs, hinders, or impedes; obstacle; barrier: *a bar to legislation.* **7.** a counter or a place where beverages, esp. liquors, or light meals are served to customers; barroom (sometimes used in combination): *a bar and grill; snack bar; milk bar.* **8.** (in a home) a counter, small wagon, or similar piece of furniture for serving food or beverages: *a breakfast bar.* **9.** the legal profession. **10.** the practicing members of the legal profession in a given community. **11.** any tribunal: *the bar of public opinion.* **12.** a band or strip: *a bar of light; a bar of color.* **13.** a railing in a courtroom separating the general public from the part of the room occupied by the judges, jury, attorneys, etc. **14.** crowbar. **15.** *Music.* **a.** Also called **bar line.** the line marking the division between two measures of music. **b.** See **double bar. c.** the unit of music contained between two bar lines; measure. **16.** Also, **barre.** *Ballet.* a handrail placed along a wall at hip height, used by a dancer to maintain balance during practice. **17.** *Law.* **a.** an objection which nullifies an action or claim. **b.** a stoppage or defeat of an alleged right of action. **18.** *Typography.* a horizontal stroke of a type character, as of an A, H, t, and sometimes e. **19.** *Archit.* (in tracery) a relatively long and slender upright of stone treated as a colonette or molded. **20.** *Building Trades.* **a.** an iron or steel shape: *I-bar.* **b.** a muntin. **21.** *Mil.* one of a pair of metal or cloth insignia worn by certain commissioned officers. **22. bars,** the transverse ridges on the roof of the mouth of a horse. **23.** a space between the molar and canine teeth of a horse into which the bit is fitted. **24.** (in a bridle) the mouthpiece connecting the cheeks. **25.** a thread joining across an open space in lace; bride. **26.** *Physics.* **a.** a centimeter-gram-second unit of pressure, equal to 1,000,000 dynes per square centimeter. **b.** (formerly) microbar. *Abbr.:* b **27.** *Heraldry.* a horizontal band, narrower than a fess, that crosses the field of an escutcheon. **28.** *Obs.* a gateway capable of being barred. **29. at bar,** *Law.* **a.** before the court and being tried: *a case at bar.* **b.** before all the judges of a court: *a trial at bar.* —*v.t.* **30.** to equip or fasten with a bar or bars: *They do not bar the windows in an honor prison. Bar the door before retiring for the night.* **31.** to shut in or out by or as by bars: *The police barred the exits in an attempt to prevent the thief's escape.* **32.** to block (a way, passage, etc.), as with a barrier; prevent or hinder, as access: *They barred his entrance to the club.* **33.** to exclude or except: *He was barred from membership because of his reputation.* **34.** to mark with bars, stripes, or bands. —*prep.* **35.** except; omitting; but: *bar none.* [ME *barre* < OF < VL **barra* rod < ?] —**bar′less,** *adj.* —**bar′ra·ble,** *adj.*
—**Syn. 1.** rod, pole. **5.** shoal, reef, bank, sand bar. **6.** deterrent, stop. BAR, BARRIER, BARRICADE mean something put in the way of advance. BAR has the general meaning of hindrance or obstruction: *a bar across the doorway.* BARRIER suggests an impediment to progress, literal or figurative, or a defensive obstruction against attack: *a river barrier.* A BARRICADE is esp. a pile of articles hastily gathered or a rude earthwork for protection in street fighting: *a barricade of wooden boxes.* **7.** saloon, cafe; cocktail lounge. **32.** obstruct, deter, impede, barricade. **33.** eliminate.

A B
Bar[1] (def. 15a, b) A, Single; B, Double

bar[2] (bär), *n. U.S.* See **mosquito net.** [< LaF *bère, baire* < ?]

BAR, See **Browning automatic rifle.**

Bar., *Bible.* Baruch.

bar., 1. barometer. **2.** barrel. **3.** barrister.

B.Ar., Bachelor of Architecture.

Bar·a (bar′ə), *n.* **The·da** (thē′də), (*Theodosia Goodman*), 1890–1955, U.S. actress.

bar·a·bar·a (bär′ə bär′ə), *n.* an Alaskan or north Siberian semisubterranean house built of sod or turf. [< dial. Russ *barabora*]

Bar·ab·bas (bə rab′əs), *n.* a condemned robber or insurrectionist whose release was demanded of Pilate by the mob when they had an opportunity to free Jesus. Mark 15:6–11; John 18:40.

Bar·a·boo (bar′ə bōō′), *n.* a town in central Wisconsin. 6672 (1960).

Ba·rac·a (bə rä′kə), *n.* a former international, interdenominational body of young men organized for Bible study. Cf. **Philathea.** [< Heb *berakah* blessing]

Ba·ra·co·a (bä′rä kô′ä), *n.* a seaport in E Cuba: oldest town in Cuba; settled 1512. 11,459 (1953).

bar·ag·no·sis (bar′ag nō′sis, ba rag′nō-), *n. Med.* loss of the ability to estimate or perceive the weight of an object. Cf. **barognosis.** [BAR(O)- + A-[6] + -GNOSIS]

Bar·ak (bâr′ək), *n.* a military commander who, with Deborah, destroyed the Canaanite army under Sisera. Judges 4. Also, *Douay Bible,* **Bar′ac.**

ba·ra·ka (bə rä′kə), *n.* (in North African Islam) a power popularly believed to be possessed by certain favored persons. [< Ar *barakah;* see BARACA]

bar-and-grill (bär′ən gril′), *n.* a place where alcoholic drinks and food are served to customers; a combined barroom and grillroom.

Ba·ra·nov (bä rä′nof), *n.* **A·le·ksan·dr An·dre·ye·vich** (äle ksän′dər än dre′ye vich), 1747–1819, Russian fur trader in Alaska.

Bá·rány (bä′rän yə), *n.* **Ro·bert** (rō′bert), 1876–1936, Austrian physician: Nobel prize 1914.

ba·rat (bə rät′, bä-), *n.* a strong squall from the northwest occurring on the northern coast of Celebes during December, January, and February. [< native Celebes name]

bar·a·the·a (bar′ə thē′ə), *n.* a closely woven fabric of silk, rayon, cotton, or wool, having a pebbled surface. [formerly a trademark]

barb[1] (bärb), *n.* **1.** a point or pointed part projecting backward from a main point, as of a fishhook, an arrowhead, or the like. **2.** an obviously or openly unpleasant or carping remark. **3.** *Bot., Zool.* a beardlike growth or part. **4.** *Ornith.* one of the processes attached to the rachis of a feather. See illus. under **feather. 5.** one of a breed of domestic pigeons, similar to the carriers or homers, having a short, broad bill. **6.** any of numerous, small, Old World cyprinid fishes of the genera *Barbus* and *Puntius,* often kept in aquariums. **7.** Usually, **barbs.** *Vet. Pathol.* a small protuberance under the tongue in horses and cattle, esp. when inflamed and swollen. **8.** Also, **barbe.** *Clothing.* **a.** a linen covering for the throat and breast, formerly worn by women mourners and now by nuns. **b.** a band or small scarf of lace, worn around the neck by women. **9.** *Obs.* a beard. —*v.t.* **10.** to furnish with a barb or barbs. [ME *barbe* < MF << L *barba* beard or beardlike projection]

barb[2] (bärb), *n.* one of a breed of horses raised originally in Barbary. [< F *barbe* shortened form of It *barbero* Barbary steed, equiv. to *Barber*(*ia*) Barbary + *-o* masc. n. suffix]

bar·ba (bär′bə), *n. Med.* **1.** the beard. **2.** a hair of the head. [< NL, L: beard]

bar′ba am·a·ril′la (am′ə ril′ə), *pl.* **barba amarillas.** fer-de-lance. [< AmerSp: lit., yellow beard]

bar·ba·can (bär′bə kən), *n.* barbican.

Bar·ba·dos (bär bā′dōz, bär′bə dōz′), *n.* an island in the E Lesser Antilles in the E West Indies: a British colony. 231,785 (1960); 161 sq. mi. *Cap.:* Bridgetown. —**Bar·ba·di·an** (bär bā′dē ən), *adj., n.*

Barba′dos al′oe, a tropical aloe, *Aloe vera,* native to northern Africa, having clusters of yellow flowers, grown as an ornamental.

Barba′dos cher′ry, a shrub, *Malpighia glabra,* of tropical America, having rose-pink flowers and red acid fruit the size of a cherry, used as a source of vitamin C.

Barba′dos flow′er fence′. See **Barbados pride** (def. 2).

Barba′dos goose′berry, 1. Also called **lemon vine.** an arborescent cactus, *Pereskia aculeata,* of tropical America, characterized by broad, elliptical leaves and spiny stems bearing a yellow, edible fruit. **2.** the fruit itself. Also called **blade apple.**

Barba′dos nut′. See **physic nut.**

Barba′dos pride′, 1. Also called **bear-tree, flower fence, peacock-flower, red sandalwood.** a tree, *Adenanthera pavonina,* of tropical Africa and Asia, having feathery foliage and seeds which are used for beadwork. **2.** Also called **Barbados flower fence, dwarf poinciana.** a tropical, prickly shrub, *Poinciana pulcherrima,* having orange-yellow flowers with bright red stamens and pods about four inches long.

Barba′dos roy′al palm′, a feather palm, *Roystonea oleracea,* of the West Indies, having drooping leaves from 10 to 15 feet long and hanging clusters of oblong or roundish fruit. Also called **cabbage palm, palmiste.**

Bar·ba·ra (bär′bər ə, -brə), *n. Logic.* a mnemonic for the class of syllogisms of the form "All M is P; all S is M; therefore all S is P." [<ML, part of the mnemonic verses: *Barbara, Celarent, Darii, Ferioque prioris,* etc., the vowels of each word (AAA, etc.) indicating valid moods]

Bar·ba·ra (bär′bər ə, -brə), *n.* a girl's given name.

bar·bar·i·an (bär bâr′ē ən), *n.* **1.** a man in a savage, primitive state; uncivilized person. **2.** a person without culture, refinement, or education; philistine. **3.** (loosely) a foreigner. **4.** (in ancient and medieval periods) **a.** a non-Greek. **b.** a person living outside, esp. north of, the Roman Empire. **c.** a person not living in a Christian country or within a Christian civilization. **5.** (among Italians during the Renaissance) a person of non-Italian origin. —*adj.* **6.** uncivilized; crude; savage. **7.** foreign; alien. [< L *barbari(a)* barbarous country + -AN] —**bar·bar′i·an·ism,** *n.*
—**Syn. 3.** alien. **6.** rude, primitive, wild, rough, coarse, ignorant, uncultivated. BARBARIAN, BARBARIC, BARBAROUS pertain to uncivilized people. BARBARIAN is the general word for anything uncivilized: *a barbarian tribe.* BARBARIC has both unfavorable and mildly favorable connotations, implying crudeness of taste or practice, or conveying an idea of rude magnificence and splendor: *barbaric noise.* BARBAROUS emphasizes the inhumanity and cruelty of barbarian life: *barbarous customs.* —**Ant. 6.** cultivated, civilized.

bar·bar·i·an·ize (bär bâr′ē ə nīz′), *v.t.,* **-ized, -izing.** to make barbarous or barbarian; barbarize. [BARBARIAN + -IZE]

bar·bar·ic (bär bar′ik), *adj.* **1.** without civilizing influences; uncivilized; primitive: *barbaric invaders.* **2.** of, like, or befitting barbarians: *a barbaric empire.* **3.** crudely rich or splendid: *barbaric decorations.* [< L *barbaric(us)* < Gk *barbarikós.* See BARBAROUS, -IC] —**bar·bar′i·cal·ly,** *adv.*
—**Syn. 1.** See **barbarian.**

bar·ba·rise (bär′bə rīz′), *v.t., v.i.,* **-rised, -ris·ing.** *Chiefly Brit.* barbarize. —**bar′ba·ri·sa′tion,** *n.*

bar·ba·rism (bär′bə riz′əm), *n.* **1.** a barbarous or uncivilized state or condition. **2.** a barbarous act; something belonging to or befitting a barbarous condition. **3.** the use in a language of forms or constructions felt by some to be undesirably alien to the established mode or custom of the language. **4.** such a form or construction, as *complected, all the farther.* [< L *barbarism(us)* < Gk *barbarismós* foreign way of speaking. See BARBAROUS, -ISM]

bar·bar·i·ty (bär bar′i tē), *n., pl.* **-ties. 1.** brutal or inhuman conduct; cruelty. **2.** an act or instance of cruelty or inhumanity. **3.** crudity of style, taste, expression, etc. [< L *barbar(us)* (see BARBAROUS) + -ITY]

bar·ba·rize (bär′bə rīz′), *v.,* **-rized, -riz·ing.** —*v.t.* **1.** to make barbarous; brutalize; corrupt: *foreign influences barbarizing the Latin language.* —*v.i.* **2.** to become barbarous; lapse into barbarism. **3.** to use barbarisms in speaking or writing. [partly < Gk *barbarízein,* equiv. to *bárbar(os)* barbarian + *-izein* -ize; partly BARBAR(OUS) + -IZE] —**bar′ba·ri·za′tion,** *n.*

Bar·ba·ros·sa (bär′bə ros′ə), *n.* **Frederick.** See **Frederick I** (def. 1).

bar·ba·rous (bär′bər əs), *adj.* **1.** uncivilized; wild; savage; crude. **2.** savagely cruel or harsh: *to be given barbarous treatment.* **3.** full of harsh sounds; noisy; discordant: *an evening of wild and barbarous music.* **4.** not conforming to classical standards or accepted usage, as language. **5.** foreign; alien. **6.** (among ancient Greeks) designating a person or thing of non-Greek origin. [< L *barbarus* < Gk *bárbaros* non-Greek, foreign, barbarian; akin to Skt *barbara-* stammering, non-Aryan] —**bar′ba·rous·ly,** *adv.* —**bar′ba·rous·ness,** *n.*
—**Syn. 1.** See **barbarian. 2.** ferocious, inhuman, brutal.

Bar·ba·ry (bär′bə rē), *n.* a region in N Africa, extending from W of Egypt to the Atlantic Ocean and including the former Barbary States.

Bar′bary ape′, an ape, *Macaca sylvana,* of northern Africa and Gibraltar.

Bar′bary Coast′, the Mediterranean coastline of the former Barbary States: former pirate refuge.

Bar′bary sheep′, aoudad.

Bar′bary States′, Morocco, Algiers, Tunis, and Tripoli.

bar·bate (bär′bāt), *adj. Zool., Bot.* bearded; tufted or furnished with hairs. [< L *barbāt(us),* equiv. to *barb(a)* beard + *-ātus* -ATE[1]]

barb′ bolt′, a bolt having barbs for resisting pull. Also called **rag bolt.**

barbe (bärb), *n.* barb[1] (def. 8).

bar·be·cue (bär′bə kyōō′), *n., v.,* **-cued, -cu·ing.** —*n.* **1.** *U.S.* a social or political entertainment, usually in the open air, at which meats are roasted over an open hearth or pit. **2.** a framework, as a grill or a spit, on which meat or vegetables are cooked before or over an open fire. **3.** pieces of beef, fowl, fish, or the like, roasted over an open hearth, esp. when basted in a barbecue sauce. **4.** a dressed steer, lamb, or other animal, roasted whole. —*v.t.* **5.** to broil or roast whole or in large pieces before an open fire, on a spit or gridiron, often seasoning with vinegar, spices, salt, and pepper. **6.** to cook (sliced or diced meat or fish) in a highly seasoned sauce. Also, **barbeque.** [< Sp *barbacoa* < WInd (? Taino) *barbacoa,* a raised frame of sticks]

bar′becue sauce′, a piquant sauce often made of vinegar and condiments, used esp. for basting in barbecuing meat.

barbed (bärbd), *adj. Heraldry.* **1.** (of a rose) having sepals displayed: *a rose argent barbed vert.* **2.** (of an arrow) having a head of a tincture different from that of the shaft: *an arrow gules barbed or.* [BARB[1] + -ED[3]]

barbed′ trib′utary, a tributary that joins its mainstream in an upstream direction rather than in the more common downstream direction.

barbed′ wire′, a wire or strand of wires having small pieces of sharply pointed wire twisted around them at short intervals, used chiefly for fencing in livestock, keeping out trespassers, etc. Also called **barbwire.**

bar·bel (bär′bəl), *n.* **1.** a slender, external process on the jaw or other part of the head of certain fishes. **2.** any of various cyprinoid fishes of the genus *Barbus,* esp. *B. barbus,* of Europe. [late ME *barbell* < MF *barbel* (now *barbeau*) < L *barb(us)* bearded fish + *-ellus* dim. suffix]

bar·bell (bär′bel′), *n.* an apparatus used in weight lifting, consisting of a bar with replaceable, disk-shaped weights fastened to the ends. [BAR[1] + BELL[1]]

bar·bel·late (bär′bə lāt′, bär bel′it, -āt), *adj. Bot., Zool.* having short, stiff hairs. [< NL *barbell(a)* (dim. of L *barbula* little beard). See BARBULE]

bar·be·que (bär′bə kyōō′), *n., v.t.,* **-qued, -qu·ing.** barbecue.

bar·ber (bär′bər), *n.* **1.** one whose occupation it is to shave or trim the beard and to cut and dress the hair of customers. **2.** See **frost smoke** (def. 1). —*v.t.* **3.** to trim or dress the beard and hair of. [ME *barbour* < AF; OF *barbeor* < L *barbāt(us)* (see BARBATE) + *-or* -OR[2]]

Bar·ber (bär′bər), *n.* **Samuel,** born 1910, U.S. composer.

Bar·be·ra (bär bâr′ə; *It.* bär be′rä), *n.* **1.** a dry red wine of the Piedmont region of Italy. **2.** an aromatic red wine of California resembling the Italian Barbera.

bar′ber chair′, **1.** a chair used by barbers, adjustable in height and having an adjustable headrest, back, and footrest. **2.** *Eng. Furniture.* a corner chair having a solid splat extending above the toprail to form a headrest. Also, **bar′ber's chair′.**

bar′ber col′lege, a school that teaches barbering.

bar·ber·ite (bär′bə rīt′), *n.* an alloy of about 88 percent copper, 5 percent nickel, 5 percent tin, and 2 percent silicon, resistant to water and sulfuric acid.

Bar′ber of Seville′, a comic opera (1816) by Gioachino Rossini based on a comedy (1775) by Beaumarchais. Italian, **Il Barbiere di Siviglia.**

bar′ber pole′, a pole with red and white spiral stripes symbolizing the barber's trade. Also, **bar′ber's pole′.**

bar·ber·ry (bär′ber′ē, -bə rē), *n., pl.* **-ries. 1.** a shrub of the genus *Berberis,* esp. *B. vulgaris.* **2.** its red, elongated, acid fruit. [late ME *barbere* < ML *bar(baris)* (< Ar) + *-bere* for *berie* BERRY]

bar·ber·shop (bär′bər shop′), *n.* **1.** Also called, *esp. Brit.,* **bar′ber's shop.** the place of business of a barber. —*adj.* **2.** specializing in the part-singing of popular songs in which four voices move in close, highly chromatic harmony: *a barbershop quartet.* **3.** characteristic of such part-singing: *barbershop harmony.* [BARBER + SHOP]

bar′ber's itch′, *Pathol.* ringworm of the bearded areas of the face and neck, caused by any of certain fungi and characterized by reddish patches. Also called **tinea barbae.**

bar·ber-sur·geon (bär′bər sûr′jən), *n.* **1.** (formerly) a barber practicing surgery and dentistry. **2.** an inferior doctor.

Bar·ber·ton (bär′bər tən), *n.* a city in NE Ohio. 33,805 (1960).

bar·bet (bär′bit), *n.* any of several stocky, tropical birds of the family *Capitonidae,* having a stout bill with bristles at the base. [< F << L *barbāt(us);* see BARBATE]

bar·bette (bär bet′), *n.* **1.** (within a fortification) a platform or mound of earth from which guns may be fired over the parapet instead of through embrasures. **2.** *Navy.* an armored cylinder for protecting the lower part of a turret on a warship. [< F; see BARBE, -ETTE; so called because thought to be like a barbe]

Bar·bette (bär bet′), *n.* a girl's given name, form of **Barbara.** Also, **Babette.**

Bar·bi·ca (bär′bə kə), *n.* a girl's given name, form of **Barbara.**

bar·bi·can (bär′bə kən), *n.* **1.** an outwork of a fortified place, as a castle. **2.** a defensive outpost of any sort. Also, **barbacan.** [ME < ML *barbican(a),* var. of *barbacana* < ?. Cf. OF *barbaquenne*]

bar·bi·cel (bär′bi sel′), *n. Ornith.* one of the minute processes fringing the barbules of certain feathers. [< NL *barbicell(a),* equiv. to L *barbi-* (comb. form of *barba* beard) + *-cella* dim. suffix]

Bar·bie·re di Si·vi·glia, Il (*It.* ēl bär bye′re dē sē vē′lyä). See **Barber of Seville.**

bar·bier·ite (bär bēr′īt), *n.* a feldspar, the monoclinic phase of $NaAlSi_3O_8$, found only in crystal solution in orthoclase. [named after Philippe *Barbier,* 20th-century French chemist; see -ITE[1]]

Bar·bi·rol·li (bär′bə rō′lē, -rol′ē), *n.* **Sir John,** born 1899, English conductor.

bar·bi·tal (bär′bi tal′, -tôl′), *n. Pharm.* a barbiturate compound, $CO(NHCO)_2(C_2H_5)_2$, usually used in the form of its sodium salt as a hypnotic. Also called **diethylbarbituric acid, diethylmalonylurea.** [BARBIT(URIC ACID) + (VERONAL)]

bar·bi·tone (bär′bi tōn′), *n. Pharm. Chiefly Brit.* barbital. [BARBIT(URIC) + -ONE]

bar·bi·tu·rate (bär bich′ə rāt′, -ər it; bär′bə tyŏŏr′āt, -it), *n. Chem.* any of a group of barbituric acid derivatives, used in medicine as sedatives and hypnotics. [BARBITUR(IC) + -ATE[2]]

bar·bi·tu·ric (bär′bə tyŏŏr′ik, -tŏŏr′-), *adj. Chem.* of or derived from barbituric acid. [< G *Barbitur(säure)* barbituric acid (< Gk *bárbit(on)* musical instrument which when played was supposed to soothe + *oûr(on)* urine) + -IC]

bar′bitu′ric ac′id, a white, crystalline, slightly water-soluble powder, $CO(NHCO)_2CH_2$, used chiefly in the synthesis of barbiturates. Also called **malonylurea.**

bar·bi·tur·ism (bär bich′ə riz′əm), *n. Med.* chronic poisoning caused by the excessive use of phenobarbital, secobarbital, or other derivatives of barbituric acid. Also, **bar·bi·tal·ism** (bär′bi tal′iz əm), **bar·bi·tu·ism** (bär bich′ōō iz′əm). [BARBITUR(IC) + -ISM]

Bar′bi·zon School′ (bär′bi zon′), a group of French painters of the mid-19th century whose landscapes and genre paintings depicted peasant life and the quality of natural light on objects. [after *Barbizon,* village near Paris, where the painters gathered]

barb·less (bärb′lis), *adj.* not equipped with a barb: *barbless fishhooks.* [BARB[1] + -LESS]

bar·bo·tine (bär′bə tēn′), *n.* a thin clay paste for making ceramic decorations in low relief. [< F, equiv. to *barbot(er)* (to) dabble in mud like a duck + *-ine* -INE[2]]

Bar·bour·ville (bär′bər vil), *n.* a town in SE Kentucky. 3211 (1960).

bar·bu (bär bōō′), *n.* a threadfin, *Polydactylus virginicus,* found along the American coast of the Atlantic Ocean. [< F: lit., bearded < LL **barbū(tus),* for L *barbātus.* See BARBATE]

Bar·bu·da (bär bōō′də), *n.* one of the NE Leeward Islands, in the E West Indies: a dependency of Antigua and a member of the West Indies Associated States; formerly a British colony. 1,145 (1963); 62 sq. mi.

bar·bu·do (bär bōō′dō), *n., pl.* **-dos.** beardfish. [< AmerSp, Sp: bearded]

bar·bule (bär′byōōl), *n.* **1.** a small barb. **2.** one of the small processes fringing the barbs of a feather. [< L *barbul(a).* See BARB[1] + -ULE]

Bar·busse (bar bys′), *n.* **Hen·ri** (äN rē′), 1873?–1935, French journalist and author.

bar·but (bär′bət), *n.* a steel helmet of the 15th century completely enclosing the head and having a T-shaped face slit: similar in form to the ancient Corinthian bronze helmet. Also, **bar′-bute.** [< MF *barbute* < Pr *barbuta,* fem. of *barbut* < LL **barbūt(us),* for L *barbātus* bearded. See BARBATE]

Barbut

barb·wire (bärb′wīər′), *n.* See **barbed wire.**

Bar·ca (bär′kə), *n.* **1.** an ancient Carthaginian family to which Hamilcar, Hasdrubal, and Hannibal belonged. **2.** Cyrenaica. —**Bar′can,** *adj.*

bar·ca·role (bär′kə rōl′), *n.* **1.** a boating song of the Venetian gondoliers. **2.** a piece of music composed in the style of such songs. Also, **bar′ca·rolle′.** [< It *barcarola* boatman's song, fem. of *barcarolo* boatman (*barca* BARK[3] + *-rolo* rower)]

Bar·ce·lon·a (bär′sə lō′nə; *Sp.* bär′the lô′nä), *n.* a seaport in NE Spain, on the Mediterranean. 2,000,000.

B.Arch., Bachelor of Architecture.

bar·chan (bär kän′), *n.* a crescent-shaped sand dune with the convex side in the direction of the wind. [< Russ *barkhan* < Kirghiz]

bar′ chart′. See **bar graph.**

B.Arch.E., Bachelor of Architectural Engineering.

Bar′ches·ter Tow′ers (bär′ches tər, -chi stər), a novel (1857) by Anthony Trollope.

Barc·lay (bärk′lē), *n.* a boy's given name. Also, **Barkleigh, Barkley, Berkeley.**

Bar·clay de Tol·ly (bär klī′ də tô′lyə), **Prince Mi·kha·il** (mi khä ēl′), 1761–1818, Russian field marshal: commander in chief against Napoleon I in 1812.

Bar Coche·ba (bär kôkh′bä, -vä). See **Bar Kokba.** Also, **Bar Coch′ba.**

bar′ code′, a printed code consisting of a set of parallel lines of varying thickness and containing information, as product identification and price, that can be read by an electronic scanner.

bard[1] (bärd), *n.* **1.** one of an ancient Celtic order of poets. **2.** a person who composes and recites epic or heroic poems, often accompanying himself on the harp, lyre, or the like. **3.** (loosely) any poet. [late ME < Celt; cf. Ir, Gael *bard*] —**bard′ic,** *adj.* —**bard′ish, bard′like′,** *adj.* —**bard′ship,** *n.*

bard[2] (bärd), *n.* **1.** *Armor.* any of various pieces of defensive armor for a horse. **2.** *Cookery.* a thin slice of fat or bacon secured to a roast of meat, poultry, or fish to prevent its drying out while cooking. —*v.t.* **3.** *Armor.* to caparison with bards. **4.** *Cookery.* to secure thin slices of fat or bacon to (a roast of meat, poultry, etc.) before cooking. Also, **barde** (for defs. 1, 3). [late ME *barde* < MF < OSp *barda* armor for a horse < Ar *barda'ah* pack-saddle]

barde (bärd), *n., v.,* **bard·ed, bard·ing.** *Armor.* —*n.* **1.** bard[2] (def. 1). —*v.t.* **2.** bard[2] (def. 3).

Bar·deen (bär dēn′), *n.* **John,** born 1908, U.S. physicist: Nobel prize 1956.

bard·ol·a·ter (bär dol′ə tər), *n.* (*sometimes cap.*) a person who idolizes William Shakespeare. [BARD[1] (from the phrase *The Bard of Avon,* frequently applied to Shakespeare) + (ID)OLATER] —**bard·ol·a·try** (bär dol′ə trē), *n.*

Bards·town (bärdz′toun′), *n.* a town in central Kentucky. 4798 (1960).

bard·y (bär′dē), *adj.,* **bard·i·er, bard·i·est.** *Scot.* bold; audacious; defiant. [BARD[1] + -Y[1]] —**bard′i·ly,** *adv.* —**bard′i·ness,** *n.*

bare[1] (bâr), *adj.,* **bar·er, bar·est,** *v.,* **bared, bar·ing.** —*adj.* **1.** without covering or clothing; naked; nude: *bare knees.* **2.** without the usual furnishings, contents, etc.: *bare walls.* **3.** open to view; unconcealed; undisguised: *his bare dislike.* **4.** unadorned; bald; plain: *the bare facts.* **5.** (of cloth) napless or threadbare. **6.** scarcely or just sufficient; mere: *bare necessities.* **7.** *Obs.* with the head uncovered; bareheaded. —*v.t.* **8.** to open to view; reveal; divulge: *to bare one's arms; to bare damaging new facts.* [ME; OE *bær;* c. D *baar,* G *bar,* Icel *berr;* akin to Lith *basas* barefoot] —**bar′ish,** *adj.* —**bare′ness,** *n.*
—**Syn. 1.** undressed. **2.** plain, stark, empty, barren. **6.** See **mere**[1]. **8.** uncover, expose. —**Ant. 1.** covered.

bare[2] (bâr), *v. Archaic.* pt. of **bear.**

Ba·re·a (bə rā′ə; *Sp.* bä re′ä), *n.* **Ar·tu·ro** (är tŏŏr′ō; *Sp.* är tōō′rô), 1897–1957, Spanish author, critic, lecturer, and broadcaster: in England after 1939.

bare·back (bâr′bak′), *adv., adj.* with the back of a horse, burro, etc., bare; without a saddle: *to ride bareback.* Also, **bare′backed′.** [BARE[1] + BACK[1]]

bare·faced (bâr′fāst′), *adj.* **1.** with the face uncovered. **2.** without concealment or disguise; boldly open: *a barefaced approach.* **3.** shameless; impudent; audacious: *a barefaced lie.* [BARE[1] + FACED] —**bare·fac·ed·ly** (bâr′fā′sid lē, -fāst′lē), *adv.* —**bare′fac′ed·ness,** *n.*

bare·fist·ed (bâr′fis′tid), *adj., adv.* with the fists bare: *a fierce, barefisted fight.* [BARE[1] + FISTED]

bare·foot (bâr′fŏŏt′), *adj., adv.* **1.** with the feet bare: *a barefoot boy; to walk barefoot.* **2.** *Carpentry.* (of a post or stud) secured to a sill or the like without mortising. [ME *barfot,* OE *bærfōt.* See BARE[1], FOOT]

Bare′foot Boy′, a poem (1856) by Whittier.

bare·foot·ed (bâr′fŏŏt′id), *adj.* having the feet bare. [BARE[1] + FOOTED]

ba·rege (bə rezh′), *n.* a sheer fabric constructed in a leno weave of silk warp and cotton or worsted filling, often used in the manufacture of veils or dresses. Also, **ba·rège′.** [after *Barèges,* town in southern France]

bare·hand·ed (bâr′han′did), *adj., adv.* **1.** with hands uncovered: *a barehanded boy shivering in the cold; offering to fight barehanded.* **2.** without tools, weapons, or other means: *a useless, barehanded attempt to do the job; foolishly coming barehanded to the city.* [BARE[1] + HANDED]

bare·head·ed (bâr′hed′id), *adj., adv.* with the head uncovered. Also, **bare′head′.** [BARE[1] + -HEADED] —**bare′head′ed·ness,** *n.*

Ba·reil·ly (bə rā′lē), *n.* a city in central Uttar Pradesh, in N India. 254,400 (1961). Also, **Ba·re′li.**

bare·knuck·le (bâr′nuk′əl), *adj.* **1.** (of a prizefight, prizefighter, etc.) without boxing gloves; using the bare fists. **2.** without conventional niceties; rough-and-tumble. —*adv.* **3.** in a rough-and-tumble manner. Also, **bare′knuck′led.** [BARE[1] + KNUCKLE]

bare·leg·ged (bâr′leg′id, -legd′), *adj., adv.* with bare legs. [BARE[1] + LEGGED]

bare·ly (bâr′lē), *adv.* **1.** only; just; no more than: *She is barely 16.* **2.** without disguise or concealment; openly: *They gave the facts to him barely.* **3.** nakedly. **4.** *Archaic.* merely. [ME; OE *bærlīce.* See BARE[1], -LY] —**Syn. 1.** See **hardly.**

Bar·ents (bar′ənts, bär′-; *Du.* bä rents′), *n.* **Wil·lem** (wil′əm), died 1597, Dutch navigator and explorer.

Bar′ents Sea′, a part of the Arctic Ocean between NE Europe and the islands of Spitzbergen, Franz Josef Land, and Novaya Zemlya.

bare·sark (bâr′särk), *n.* **1.** *Scand. Legend.* a berserker. —*adv.* **2.** without armor. [var. of BERSERK, as if BARE[1] + SARK]

bar·es·the·sia (bar′is thē′zhə, -zhē ə, -zē ə), *n.* the sense or perception of pressure. [BAR(O)- + ESTHESIA]

bar·fly (bär′flī′), *n., pl.* **-flies.** *U.S. Slang.* a person who frequents barrooms. [BAR[1] + FLY[2]]

bar′ foot′, *Furniture.* See **runner foot.**

bar·gain (bär′gin), *n.* **1.** an agreement between parties settling what each shall give and take or perform and receive in a transaction. **2.** such an agreement as affecting one of the parties: *a losing bargain.* **3.** that which is acquired by bargaining: *a bargain that required intense haggling.* **4.** an advantageous purchase: *The sale offered bargains galore.* **5.** *Informal.* an agreeable person, esp. one who causes no trouble or difficulty (usually used in negative constructions): *His mother-in-law was no bargain.* **6. in** or **into the bargain,** over and above what has been stipulated; moreover; besides: *The new housekeeper proved to be a fine cook in the bargain.* **7. strike a bargain,** to make a bargain; agree to terms: *They were unable to strike a bargain because the owner's asking price was more than the prospective buyer could afford.* —*v.i.* **8.** to discuss the terms of a bargain; haggle over terms. **9.** to come to an agreement; make a bargain: *We bargained on a three-year term.* —*v.t.* **10.** to arrange by bargain; stipulate: *to bargain a new wage increase.* **11.** to anticipate as likely to occur; expect (usually fol. by a clause): *I'll bargain that he's going to give those company directors plenty of trouble. You can bargain that he'll see a quick return on his investment.* **12. bargain for,** to anticipate or take into account: *The job turned out to be more than he had bargained for.* **13. bargain on,** to count or rely on: *You can't bargain on what he'll do in this situation.* [ME *bargaine* < MF *bargaigne* (n.), *bargaigner* (v.); c. ML *barcāniāre* to trade < ?] —**bar′gain·er,** *n.* —**Syn. 1.** stipulation, arrangement, transaction. See **agreement. 8.** See **trade. 9.** contract, covenant.

bar′gain base′ment, a basement area in some department stores where goods are sold at low prices.

bar·gain-base·ment (bär′gən bās′mənt), *adj.* noticeably lacking in quality; cheap; inferior.

bar′gaining u′nit, a group of employees represented by a union in collective bargaining.

barge (bärj), *n., v.,* **barged, barg·ing.** —*n.* **1.** a capacious, flat-bottomed vessel, usually intended to be pushed or towed, for transporting freight or passengers; lighter. **2.** a vessel of state used in pageants: *elegantly decorated barges on the Grand Canal in Venice.* **3.** *Navy.* a boat reserved for a flag officer. **4.** a boat that is heavier and wider than a shell, often used in racing as a training boat. **5.** *New England.* a large, four-wheel coach with two seats. —*v.t.* **6.** to carry or transport by barge: *Coal and ore had been barged down the Ohio to the Mississippi.* —*v.i.* **7.** to move in the slow, heavy manner of a barge: *a big man who barged along the street dragging his heels.* **8.** *Informal.* to move clumsily; bump into things; collide: *to barge through a crowd.* **9. barge in,** to intrude, esp. rudely: *I hated to barge in without an invitation.* **10. barge into,** *Informal.* **a.** Also, **barge in.** to force oneself upon, esp. rudely; interfere in: *to barge into a conversation.* **b.** to bump into; collide with: *He started to run away and barged into a passer-by.* [ME < MF, equiv. to ML *barga,* ? var. of LL *barca* BARK[3]]

barge·board (bärj′bōrd′, -bôrd′), *n.* a board, often carved, hanging from the projecting end of a sloping roof. Also called **vergeboard.** [?]

barge′ cou′ple, either of the pair of rafters carrying part of a gable roof projecting beyond the gable wall. [?]

barge′ course′, 1. tiling on a gable roof beyond the exterior surface of the gable wall. **2.** the tiles or slates placed on and projecting over the raking edges of a gable roof. **3.** a coping of bricks set on edge, arranged transversely. [?]

bar·gel·lo (bär jel′lō; *Eng.* bär jel′ō), *n., pl.* **-gel·li** (-jel′lē; *Eng.* -jel′ē). *Italian.* a police-headquarters building.

barge·man (bärj′mən), *n., pl.* **-men. 1.** one of the crew of a barge. **2.** a person who owns, manages, or captains a barge or barges. Also called, *esp. Brit.,* **bar·gee** (bär jē′). [BARGE + MAN[1]]

bar′ gem′el, *pl.* **bars gemels.** *Heraldry.* a charge consisting of two barrulets separated by an area the width of a barrulet. Also called **gemel, gemel bar.**

barge′ spike′, a square spike with a chisel point. Also called **boat spike.**

barge·stone (bärj′stōn′), *n.* any of several stones forming the sloping edge of a gable. [?]

bar·ghest (bär′gest), *n.* a doglike goblin appearing as a portent of death or misfortune. [appar. BARR(OW)[2] + *ghest,* OE *gæst,* var. of *gāst* GHOST]

bar′ graph′, a graph using parallel bars of varying lengths, as to illustrate comparative costs, exports, birth rates, etc. Also called **bar chart.**

Bar′ Har′bor, a town on Mount Desert Island, in S Maine: summer resort. 2444 (1960).

bar·hop (bär′hop′), *v.i.,* **-hopped, -hop·ping.** to go to a succession of bars, night clubs, etc., usually with a brief stay at each. [BAR[1] + HOP[1]]

Ba·ri (bär′ē), *n.* a seaport in SE Italy, on the Adriatic. 311,268 (1961). Italian, **Bari delle Puglie.**

bar·ic[1] (bar′ik), *adj.* *Chem.* of or containing barium. [BAR(IUM) + -IC]

bar·ic[2] (bar′ik), *adj.* of or pertaining to weight, esp. that of the atmosphere. [BAR(O)- + -IC]

Ba·ri del·le Pu·glie (bä′rē del′le pōō′lye), Italian name of **Bari.**

ba·rih (bär′ē), *n.* shamal. [< Ar]

ba·ril·la (bə ril′ə), *n.* **1.** either of two European saltworts, *Salsola Kali* or *S. Soda,* whose ashes yield an impure carbonate of soda. **2.** the alkali obtained from the ashes of these and certain other maritime plants. [< Sp *barrilla*]

Ba·ri·nas (bä rē′näs), *n.* a city in W Venezuela. 17,000 (est. 1950).

Bar·ing (bâr′ing), *n.* **1. Alexander** (*1st Baron Ashburton*), 1774–1848, British statesman. **2. Evelyn, 1st Earl of Cromer,** 1841–1917, British statesman and diplomat.

barit., *Music.* baritone.

bar·ite (bâr′īt, bar′-), *n.* a common mineral, barium sulfate, $BaSO_4$, occurring in tabular crystals: the principal ore of barium. Also, **barytes.** Also called **heavy spar.** [BAR(IUM) + -ITE[1]]

bar·i·tone (bar′i tōn′), *Music.* —*n.* **1.** a male voice or voice part intermediate between tenor and bass. **2.** a singer with such a voice. **3.** a large, valved brass instrument shaped like a trumpet or coiled in oval form, used esp. in military bands. —*adj.* **4.** of or pertaining to a baritone; having the compass of a baritone. Also, **barytone.** [< It *baritono* low voice < Gk *barýtonos* deep-sounding. See BARYTONE[2]]

bar′itone clef′, *Music.* an F clef locating F below middle C on the third line of the staff.

bar·i·um (bâr′ē əm, bar′-), *n.* *Chem.* a whitish, malleable, active, divalent, metallic element, occurring in combination chiefly as barite or as witherite. *Symbol:* Ba; *at. wt.:* 137.34; *at. no.:* 56; *sp. gr.:* 3.5 at 20°C. [BAR(YTES) + -IUM]

barium 140, *Chem.* the radioactive isotope of barium having a mass number of 140 and a half life of 12.8 days, used chiefly as a tracer.

bar′ium bro′mate, *Chem.* colorless, slightly water-soluble, poisonous crystals, $Ba(BrO_3)_2{\cdot}H_2O$, used in the preparation of certain bromates.

bar′ium car′bonate, *Chem.* a white, poisonous, water-insoluble powder, $BaCO_3$, used chiefly in the manufacture of rodenticides, paints, and dyes.

bar′ium chlo′ride, *Chem.* a colorless, crystalline, water-soluble, poisonous solid, $BaCl_2{\cdot}2H_2O$, used chiefly in the synthesis of lakes and in the manufacture of rodenticides and pharmaceuticals.

bar′ium hydrox′ide, *Chem.* baryta (def. 2). Also called **bar′ium hy′drate.**

bar′ium ox′ide, *Chem.* baryta (def. 1). Also called **bar′ium monox′ide, bar′ium protox′ide.**

bar′ium perox′ide, *Chem.* a grayish-white, water-insoluble, poisonous powder, BaO_2, used chiefly in the manufacture of hydrogen peroxide and as a bleaching agent for textiles. Also called **bar′ium diox′ide.**

bar′ium ste′arate, *Chem.* a white, crystalline, water-insoluble solid, $Ba(C_{18}H_{35}O_2)_2$, used chiefly as a waterproofing agent and as a lubricant.

bar′ium sul′fate, *Chem.* a white, crystalline, water-insoluble powder, $BaSO_4$, used chiefly in the synthesis of lakes, as a pigment in paints and printing inks, and in medicine, because of its radiopacity, for x-ray diagnosis.

bar′ium sul′fide, *Chem.* a gray or yellowish-green, water-soluble, poisonous powder, BaS, used chiefly as a depilatory, and as an intermediate in the synthesis of pigments, esp. lithopone.

bar′ium thiosul′fate, *Chem.* a white, crystalline, water-insoluble, poisonous solid, $BaS_2O_3{\cdot}H_2O$, used chiefly in the manufacture of explosives, matches, paints, and varnishes.

bar′ joist′, a welded steel joist having an open web consisting of a single bent bar running in a zigzag pattern between horizontal upper and lower chords.

bark[1] (bärk), *n.* **1.** the abrupt, harsh, explosive cry of a dog. **2.** a similar sound made by another animal, as a fox. **3.** a short, explosive sound, as of firearms: *the bark of his revolver.* **4.** a brusque order, reply, etc.: *The foreman's bark sent the idlers back to their machines.* **5.** *Informal.* a cough. —*v.i.* **6.** to utter an abrupt, explosive cry or a series of such cries, as a dog. **7.** to make a similar sound: *The big guns barked.* **8.** to speak or cry out sharply or gruffly: *a man who barks at his children.* **9.** *Chiefly U.S. Informal.* to advertise a theater, side show of a carnival, etc., by standing at the entrance and shouting to attract passers-by. **10.** *Chiefly U.S. Informal.* to cough. —*v.t.* **11.** to utter or give forth with a bark or in a harsh, shouting tone: *barking orders at her subordinates; hucksters barking their wares.* **12. bark at the moon,** to protest in vain: *Telling him that he's misinformed is just barking at the moon.* **13. bark up the wrong tree,** *U.S.* to assail or pursue the wrong person or object; misdirect one's efforts: *If she expects me to get her a job, she's barking up the wrong tree.* [ME *berk(en),* OE *beorcan;* akin to OE *borcian* to bark, Icel *berkja* to bluster, Lith *burgėti* to growl, quarrel] —**bark′less,** *adj.*

bark[2], (bärk), *n.* **1.** *Bot.* the external covering of the woody stems, branches, and roots of plants, as distinct and separable from the wood itself. **2.** *Tanning.* a mixture of oak and hemlock barks. —*v.t.* **3.** to strip the bark from; peel. **4.** to remove a circle of bark from. **5.** to cover, enclose, or encrust with or as with bark. **6.** to treat with a bark infusion; tan. **7.** to rub off the skin of: *to bark one's shins.* [ME < Scand; cf. Icel *bǫrkr,* Dan, Sw *bark*] —**bark′less,** *adj.*

bark[3] (bärk), *n.* **1.** *Naut.* a sailing vessel having three or more masts, square-rigged on all but the aftermost mast, which is fore-and-aft-rigged. **2.** *Poetic.* a boat or sailing vessel. Also, **barque.** [late ME *barke* << LL *barca* < Celt; cf. OIr *barc*]

Bark

bark′ bee′tle, any of numerous beetles of the family *Scolytidae* that nest under the bark of trees.

bar·keep·er (bär′kē′pər), *n.* **1.** a person who owns or manages a bar where alcoholic beverages are sold. **2.** a bartender. Also, **bar′keep′.** [BAR[1] + KEEPER]

bark·en·tine (bär′kən tēn′), *n.* *Naut.* a sailing vessel having three or more masts, square-rigged on the foremast and fore-and-aft-rigged on the other masts. Also, **bark′an·tine′, barquentine, barquantine.** [BARK[3] + (BRIG)ANTINE]

bark·er[1] (bär′kər), *n.* **1.** an animal or person that barks. **2.** *Chiefly U.S. Informal.* a person who stands before a theater, side show of a carnival, etc., calling out to passers-by to enter. [BARK[1] + -ER[1]]

bark·er[2] (bär′kər), *n.* **1.** one who or that which removes bark from trees. **2.** one who or that which prepares bark for tanning. [BARK[2] + -ER[1]]

bark′hau·sen effect′ (bärk′hou′zən, bär′kou′-), *Physics:* the phenomenon of short, sudden changes in the magnetism of a ferromagnetic substance occurring when the intensity of the magnetizing field is continuously altered. [named after H. *Barkhausen* (b. 1881), German physicist]

bark′ing deer′, muntjac.

bark′ing frog′, a robber frog, *Eleutherodactylus latrans,* of Texas, that has a call like a dog's bark.

Bark·la (bärk′lə), *n.* **Charles Glov·er** (gluv′ər), 1877–1944, English physicist: Nobel prize 1917.

Bark·leigh (bärk′lē), *n.* a boy's given name. Also, **Barclay, Barkley, Berkeley.**

Bark·ley (bärk′lē), *n.* **1. Al·ben William** (al′bən), 1877–1956, vice-president of the U.S. 1949–53. **2.** Also, **Barclay, Barkleigh, Berkeley.** a boy's given name.

Bar Kok·ba (bär′ kôkн′bä, -vä), **Simon,** died A.D. 135, Hebrew leader of insurrection against the Romans A.D. 132–135. Also, **Bar Cocheba, Bar Cochba.**

bark·y (bär′kē), *adj.,* **bark·i·er, bark·i·est.** consisting of or containing bark; covered with or resembling bark. [BARK[2] + -Y[1]]

Bar·lach (bär′läk; *Ger.* bär′läкн), *n.* **Ernst Heinrich** (ûrnst hīn′rik; *Ger.* ernst hīn′rікн), 1870–1938, German sculptor and playwright.

bar·ley[1] (bär′lē), *n.* **1.** a widely distributed cereal plant of the genus *Hordeum,* whose awned flowers grow in tightly bunched spikes, with three small additional spikes at each node. **2.** the grain of this plant, used as food and in making beer, ale, and whiskey. —*adj.* **3.** noting a size of anthracite less than 3/16 of an inch and more than 3/64 of an inch in the longest dimension. [ME, OE *bærlic* (adj.), equiv. to *bær-* (var. of *bere* barley; akin to Icel *barr* barley, L *far* spelt) + *-lic* -LY]

bar·ley[2] (bär′lē), *n., pl.* **-leys.** *Scot. and North Eng.* a truce or quarter, esp. in children's games; parley. [? childish var. of PARLEY]

bar·ley-bree (bär′lē brē′), *n.* *Chiefly Scot.* liquor, malt liquor, or the like, esp. whiskey.

bar·ley·corn (bär′lē kôrn′), *n.* **1.** barley, or a grain of barley. **2.** a measure equal to ⅓ of an inch. [BARLEY[1] + CORN[1]]

Bar·ley·corn (bär′lē kôrn′), *n.* **John.** See **John Barleycorn.**

bar′ley stripe′, *Plant Pathol.* a disease of barley, characterized by chlorotic, brown, or frayed stripes on the leaves and blighted heads, caused by a fungus, *Helminthosporium gramineum.*

bar′ley sug′ar, a brittle, amber-colored, transparent candy, formerly boiled in a decoction of barley, consisting of sugar, cream of tartar, and orange or lemon juice, usually twisted into strips or molded into a variety of shapes. Also called **bar′ley can′dy.**

bar·ley-sug·ar (bär′lē shŏŏg′ər), *Brit. Slang.* —*n.* **1.** act of twisting a person's arm, usually behind his back, so as to inflict pain. —*v.t.* **2.** to twist (a person's arm).

bar′ley wa′ter, a decoction of barley, used esp. as a medicament in the treatment of diarrhea in infants.

bar′ line′, *Music.* bar[1] (def. 15a).

Bar·low (bär′lō), *n.* **Joel,** 1754–1812, U.S. poet and diplomat.

barm (bärm), *n.* *Brit. Informal.* yeast formed on malt liquors while fermenting. [ME *berme,* OE *beorma;* c. Fris *berme,* G *Bärme,* Sw *bärme;* akin to FERMENT]

bar′ mag′net, a bar-shaped, usually permanent, magnet.

bar·maid (bär′mād′), *n.* a woman who serves customers in a bar; a female bartender. [BAR[1] + MAID]

bar·man (bär′mən), *n., pl.* **-men.** bartender. [BAR[1] + MAN[1]]

Bar·me·cid·al (bär′mi sīd′əl), *adj.* giving only the illusion of plenty; illusory: *a Barmecidal banquet.* Also, **Barmecide.** [BARMECIDE + -AL[1]]

Bar·me·cide (bär′mi sīd′), *n.* **1.** a member of a

noble Persian family of Baghdad who, according to a tale in *The Arabian Nights' Entertainments*, gave a beggar a pretended feast with empty dishes. —*adj.* **2.** Barmecidal. [Pers. family name, lit., offspring of *Barmek*, with *-ide* -ID² for Pers -ī < Ar]

Bar·men (bär′mən), *n.* Wuppertal.

bar mitz·vah (bär mits′və; *Heb.* bäʀ′ mēts vä′,), (*often caps.*) *Judaism.* **1.** a solemn ceremony held in the synagogue, usually on Saturday morning, to admit as an adult member of the Jewish community a Jewish boy 13 years old who has successfully completed a prescribed course of study in Judaism. **2.** the boy participating in this ceremony. Also, **bar miz′vah.** [< Bibl. Aram *bar* son + Heb *miṣvāh* divine law, commandment]

barm·y (bär′mē), *adj.*, **barm·i·er, barm·i·est.** **1.** containing or resembling barm; frothy. **2.** *Brit. Slang.* balmy (def. 4). [BARM + -Y¹]

barn¹ (bärn), *n.* **1.** a building for storing hay, grain, etc., and often for housing livestock. —*v.t.* **2.** to store (hay, grain, etc.) in a barn. [ME *bern*, OE *berern* (*bere* (see BARLEY¹) + *ern*, *ærn* house, c. Goth *razn* house)] —**barn′like′,** *adj.*

barn² (bärn), *n.* *Physics.* a unit of nuclear cross section, equal to 10^{-24} square centimeter. *Abbr.:* b [special use of BARN¹]

Bar·na·bas (bär′nə bəs), *n.* **1.** the surname of the Cyprian Levite Joseph, a companion of Paul on his first missionary journey. Acts 4:36, 37. **2.** a boy's given name.

Bar·na·by (bär′nə bē), *n.* a boy's given name.

bar·na·cle¹ (bär′nə kəl), *n.* **1.** any marine crustacean of the group *Cirripedia*, usually having a calcareous shell, being either stalked (**goose barnacle**) and found attached to ship bottoms and floating timber, or stalkless (**rock barnacle** or **acorn barnacle**) and found attached to rocks, esp. in the intertidal zone. **2.** a thing or person that clings tenaciously. [dim. of early ME *bernekke* kind of goose, lit., bare neck, alluding to white patches on bird's neck; so called from a medieval belief that barnacles were a larval form of goose] —**bar′na·cled,** *adj.*

Goose barnacle, *Lepas fascicularis*

bar·na·cle² (bär′nə kəl), *n.* **1.** Usually, **barnacles.** an instrument with two hinged branches for pinching the nose of an unruly horse. **2.** **barnacles,** *Brit. Dial.* spectacles. [ME *bernacle* bit, dim. of *bernac* < OF < ?]

bar′nacle goose′, a wild goose, *Branta leucopsis*, of northern Europe and Greenland.

Bar·nard (bär′nərd; *for 1* bär′närd), *n.* **1.** **Chris·tiaan N(eeth·ling)** (kris′tyän nit′liŋ), born 1923, South African surgeon: performed first successful human-heart transplant 1968. **2.** **George Gray,** 1863–1938, U.S. sculptor. **3.** **Henry,** 1811–1900, U.S. educator. **4.** Also, **Bernard.** a boy's given name.

Bar·nar·do (bər när′dō, bär-), *n.* **Thomas John,** 1845–1905, English physician, social reformer, and philanthropist; born in Ireland.

Barnar′do Home′, (in Britain) one of a number of homes for destitute children: founded in 1870 by Dr. Thomas John Barnardo.

Bar·na·ul (bäʀ′nä o͞ol′), *n.* a city in the S RSFSR, on the Ob River. 320,000 (1959).

Barn·burn·er (bärn′bûr′nər), *n.* a member of the progressive faction in the Democratic party in New York State 1845–52. Cf. **Hunker.** [so called with reference to burning down a barn to get rid of rats]

barn′ dance′, **1.** a social gathering typically held in a barn and including square dances, round dances, and hoedown music. **2.** any party featuring country dances, dress, music, etc.

barn·door (bärn′dôr′, -dōr′), *n.* *Photog.* an adjustable, opaque flap on a lamp fixture for cutting off light from a particular area. [BARN¹ + DOOR¹]

barn′-door hang′er (bärn′dôr′, -dōr′), a hanger for an exterior sliding door, having a wheel running in an overhead track.

barn′-door roll′er, a support for a sliding door, consisting of a wheel running in a track on or in a floor.

barn′-door′ skate′, an Atlantic skate, *Raja laevis*, that grows to a length of four feet or more.

barn′-door stay′, a small roller for guiding a sliding door.

Barnes (bärnz), *n.* a town in W Oregon. 5076 (1960).

Barnes·bor·o (bärnz′bûr ō, -bur ō), *n.* a town in central Pennsylvania. 3035 (1960).

Barnes·ville (bärnz′vil), *n.* **1.** a town in central Georgia. 4919 (1960). **2.** a town in E Ohio. 4425 (1960).

Bar·nett (bär net′), *n.* a boy's given name.

Bar·ne·veldt (bäʀ′nə velt′), *n.* **Jan van Ol·den** (yän vän ôl′dᵊn), 1547–1619, Dutch statesman and patriot.

bar·ney (bär′nē), *n.*, *pl.* **-neys.** **1.** *Informal.* **a.** an argument. **b.** prizefight. **c.** a fight or brawl. **d.** a blunder or mistake. **2.** *Australian Informal.* a mob; boisterous crowd. **3.** a small locomotive used in mining and logging. [special uses of BARNEY]

Bar·ney (bär′nē), *n.* a boy's given name, form of **Bernard.**

barn′ grass′. See **barnyard grass.**

barn′ owl′, a yellowish-brown and white owl, *Tyto alba*, often found in barns and other buildings.

barn′ rais′ing, (in rural areas) a party, usually providing food, drink, etc., for the purpose of assisting a neighbor to put up a new barn.

barn′ sash′, a window sash of relatively small size. Also called **utility sash.**

Barns·ley (bärnz′lē), *n.* a city in S Yorkshire, in N England. 74,650 (1961).

Barn·stock (bärn′stok′), *n.* Branstock.

barn·storm (bärn′stôrm′), *v.i.* **1.** to conduct a campaign or speaking tour in rural areas. **2.** *Theat.* to act in plays in small country towns where there are no theaters. **3.** (of a pilot) to give exhibitions of stunt flying, participate in airplane races, etc., in the course of touring country towns and rural areas. **4.** (of a professional athletic team) to tour an area playing exhibition games after the regular season. —*v.t.* **5.** to tour (various places) as a barnstormer. [back formation from *barnstormer* one who storms the barn] —**barn′storm′er,** *n.*

barn′ swal′low, a common swallow, *Hirundo rustica*, which nests in barns and other similar buildings.

Bar·num (bär′nəm), *n.* **P(hineas) T(aylor),** 1810–91, U.S. showman who established a circus in 1871.

Barn·well (bärn′wel), *n.* a town in W South Carolina. 4568 (1960).

barn·yard (bärn′yärd′), *n.* **1.** a yard next to or surrounding a barn. —*adj.* **2.** of, like, or befitting a barnyard. **3.** bucolic; unsophisticated; corny: *barnyard humor.* [BARN¹ + YARD²]

barn′yard grass′, a weedy, annual grass, *Echinochloa crus-galli.* Also called **barn grass.**

baro-, a learned borrowing from Greek meaning "pressure" used in the formation of compound words: *barograph.* [comb. form of Gk *báros* weight; akin to Skt *guru*, L *gravis*, Goth *kaurus* heavy]

Ba·roc·chio (bä ʀôk′kyô), *n.* **Gia·co·mo** (jä′kô mô). See **Vignola, Giacomo da.**

Ba·ro·ci·us (ba rō′sē əs, bə-), *n.* a crater in the fourth quadrant of the face of the moon: about 50 miles in diameter.

bar·o·clin·i·ty (bar′ə klin′i tē), *n.* *Meteorol.* a common state of fluid stratification in which surfaces of constant pressure and others of constant density are not parallel but intersect. Also, **bar·o·cli·nic·i·ty** (bar′ə kli nis′i tē). Cf. **barotropy.** [BARO- + (IN)CLINE + -ITY]

bar·o·cy·clon·om·e·ter (bar′ō sī′klō nom′i tər), *n.* *Meteorol.* an aneroid barometer equipped with an apparatus for determining the location and direction of tropical cyclones. [BARO- + CYCLONE + -O- + -METER]

Ba·ro·da (bə rō′də), *n.* **1.** a former native state in W India. **2.** a city in SE Gujarat state, in W India: former capital of the native state of Baroda. 298,400 (1961).

bar·og·no·sis (bar′og nō′sis, bar′əg-), *n.* the ability to estimate or perceive differences in the weight of an object. Cf. **baragnosis.** [BARO- + -GNOSIS]

bar·o·gram (bar′ə gram′), *n.* *Meteorol.* a record traced by a barograph or similar instrument. [BARO- + -GRAM¹]

bar·o·graph (bar′ə graf′, -gräf′), *n.* any of several automatic recording barometers, of which the most common is the aneroid barograph. [BARO- + -GRAPH] —**bar·o·graph·ic** (bar′ə graf′ik), *adj.*

Ba·ro·ja (bä ʀô′hä), *n.* **Pí·o** (pē′ô), 1872–1956, Spanish novelist.

ba·ro·lo (bə rō′lō; *It.* bä ʀô′lô), *n.* a dry red wine from the Piedmont region of Italy. [after *Barōlo*, locality where it is produced]

ba·rom·e·ter (bə rom′i tər), *n.* **1.** *Meteorol.* any instrument that measures atmospheric pressure. Cf. **aneroid barometer, mercury barometer.** **2.** anything that indicates changes. [BARO- + -METER] —**bar·o·met·ric** (bar′ə me′trik), **bar′o·met′ri·cal,** *adj.* —**bar′o·met′ri·cal·ly,** *adv.*

bar′omet′ric er′ror, *Horol.* error of a timepiece due to the fluctuations in density of the atmosphere through which the balance or pendulum moves.

bar′omet′ric pres′sure. See **atmospheric pressure.**

bar′omet′ric switch′, baroswitch.

bar·o·met·ro·graph (bar′ə me′trə graf′, -gräf′), *n.* barograph. [BAROMET(E)R + -O- + -GRAPH]

ba·rom·e·try (bə rom′i trē), *n.* the process of measuring atmospheric pressure. [BARO- + -METRY]

bar·on (bar′ən), *n.* **1.** a member of the lowest grade of nobility. **2.** (in Britain) **a.** a feudal vassal holding his lands under a direct grant from the king. **b.** a direct descendant of such a vassal or his equal in the nobility. **c.** a member of the House of Lords. **3.** *U.S.* an important financier or industrialist, esp. one with great power in a particular area: *an oil baron.* **4.** a cut of mutton or lamb comprising the two loins, or saddle, and the hind legs. Cf. **baron of beef.** [ME < OF < LL *barōn-* (s. of *barō*) man < Gmc]

Ba·ron (bA ʀôN′), *n.* **Mi·chel** (mē shel′), (*Michel Boyron*), 1653–1729, French actor.

bar·on·age (bar′ə nij), *n.* **1.** the entire British peerage, including all dukes, marquesses, earls, viscounts, and barons. **2.** Also, **barony.** the dignity or rank of a baron. [ME *barunage* (see BARON, -AGE); r. ME *barnage* < OF]

bar·on·ess (bar′ə nis), *n.* **1.** the wife of a baron. **2.** a lady holding a baronial title in her own right. [late ME *baronnesse* < MF (see BARON, -ESS); r. ME *barnesse* < OF]

bar·on·et (bar′ə nit, -net′), *n.* a member of a British hereditary order of honor, ranking below the barons and made up of commoners, designated by *Sir* before the name, and *Baronet*, usually abbreviated *Bart.*, after: *Sir John Smith, Bart.* [late ME; see BARON, -ET] —**bar′o·net′i·cal,** *adj.*

bar·on·et·age (bar′ə nit ij, -net′-), *n.* **1.** baronets collectively. **2.** baronetcy. [BARONET + -AGE]

bar·on·et·cy (bar′ə nit sē, -net′), *n.*, *pl.* **-cies.** the rank or dignity of a baronet. [BARONET + -CY]

ba·ron et femme (bə ron′ et fem′, bar′ən), *Heraldry.* man and wife, when both are armigerous. [< AF]

bar·on·et·ise (bar′ə ni tīz′), *v.t.*, **-ised, -is·ing.** *Chiefly Brit.* baronetize.

bar·on·et·ize (bar′ə ni tīz′), *v.t.*, **-ized, -iz·ing.** to make (someone) a baronet; confer a baronetcy upon. [BARONET + -IZE]

ba·rong (bä rôŋ′, -roŋ′), *n.* a large, broad-bladed knife or cleaver used by the Moros. [appar. Philippine var. of PARANG]

ba·ro·ni·al (bə rō′nē əl), *adj.* **1.** pertaining to a baron, a barony, or to the order of barons. **2.** befitting a baron: *living in baronial splendor.* [BARONY + -AL¹]

bar·on·ize (bar′ə nīz′), *v.t.*, **-ized, -iz·ing.** to make or create (someone) a baron; confer the rank of baron upon. [BARON + -IZE]

bar′on of beef′, *Chiefly Brit.* a joint of beef consisting of the two sirloins joined at the backbone; double sirloin. Cf. **baron** (def. 4).

Bar′ons' War′, a rebellion of English nobles (1263–67) against King Henry III, undertaken in an effort to curtail royal prerogatives and extend the powers of the nobles.

bar·o·ny (bar′ə nē), *n.*, *pl.* **-nies.** **1.** the domain of a baron. **2.** baronage (def. 2). [ME *baronie* < OF. See BARON, -Y³]

ba·roque (bə rōk′; *Fr.* bA ʀôk′), *n.* **1.** (*often cap.*) the baroque style or period. **2.** anything extravagantly ornamented, esp. something so ornate as to be in bad taste. **3.** an irregularly shaped pearl. —*adj.* **4.** (*often cap.*) of or pertaining to a style of art and architecture developed principally in Italy and north of the Alps in middle and western Europe during the 17th and first half of the 18th centuries. **5.** (*sometimes cap.*) of or pertaining to the musical period following the Renaissance, extending roughly from 1600 to 1750. **6.** irregular in shape: *baroque pearls.* [< F < Pg *barroco* rough pearl, masc. of *barroca* stony ground < Ar *burāq*, pl. of *burqah* pebbly ground]

Baroque cupboard c1700

baroque′ or′gan, a pipe organ dating from or built to the specifications of the baroque period at the time of J. S. Bach.

bar·o·scope (bar′ə skōp′), *n.* an instrument showing roughly the variations in atmospheric pressure. [BARO- + -SCOPE] —**bar·o·scop·ic** (bar′ə skop′ik), **bar′o·scop′i·cal,** *adj.*

bar·o·si·nus·i·tis (bar′ə sī′nə-sī′tis), *n.* *Med.* aerosinusitis. [BARO- + SINUSITIS]

bar·o·switch (bar′ə swich′), *n.* a switch actuated by barometric pressure. Also called **barometric switch.** [BARO- + SWITCH]

bar·o·ther·mo·gram (bar′ə thûr′mə gram′), *n.* *Meteorol.* a record made by a barothermograph. [BARO- + THERMO- + -GRAM¹]

bar·o·ther·mo·graph (bar′ə thûr′mə graf′, -gräf′), *n.* *Meteorol.* an automatic instrument for recording pressure and temperature. [BARO- + THERMOGRAPH]

bar·o·ther·mo·hy·gro·gram (bar′ə thûr′mə hī′grə-gram′), *n.* *Meteorol.* a record made by a barothermohygrograph. [BARO- + THERMO- + HYGROGRAM]

bar·o·ther·mo·hy·gro·graph (bar′ə thûr′mə hī′grə graf′, -gräf′), *n.* *Meteorol.* an automatic instrument for recording pressure, temperature, and humidity. [BARO- + THERMO- + HYGROGRAPH]

bar·o·trau·ma (bar′ə trô′mə, -trou′-), *n.*, *pl.* **-ma·ta** (-mə tə), **-mas.** *Pathol.* injury of certain organs, esp. the ear, due to a change in the atmospheric pressure. Cf. **aero-otitis media.** [BARO- + TRAUMA]

bar·o·trop·ic (bar′ə trop′ik), *adj.* (of a fluid) having a density that is a function only of pressure. [BARO- + -TROPIC]

ba·rot·ro·py (bə ro′trə pē), *n.* *Meteorol.* a state of fluid stratification in which surfaces of constant pressure and others of constant density do not intersect but are parallel. Cf. **baroclinity.** [BARO- + -TROPY]

Ba·rot·se·land (bə rot′sə land′), *n.* a province in W Zambia. ab. 366,100 (1963); 44,920 sq. mi.

ba·rouche (bə ro͞osh′), *n.* a four-wheeled carriage with a seat outside for the driver, facing seats inside for two couples, and with a calash top over the back seat. [< dial. G *Barutsche* < It *baroccio* < L *birōtus* two-wheeled, equiv. to *bi-* BI-² + *rot(a)* wheel + *-us* adj. suffix]

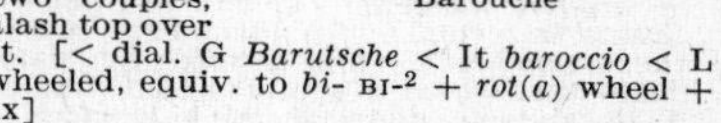

Barouche

Ba·roz·zi (bä ʀôt′tsē), *n.* **Gia·co·mo** (jä′kô mô). See **Vignola, Giacomo da.**

bar′ pin′, a long, slender, decorative pin or brooch.

barque (bärk), *n.* bark³.

bar·quen·tine (bär′kən tēn′), *n.* barkentine. Also, **bar′quan·tine′.**

bar·quette (bär ket′), *n.* a small, boat-shaped pastry shell filled with a savory or sweet mixture and served as an hors d'oeuvre or dessert. [BARQUE + -ETTE]

Bar·qui·si·me·to (bäʀ′kē sē me′tô), *n.* a city in N Venezuela. 235,905 (est. 1965).

barr., barrister.

bar·rack¹ (bar′ək), *n.* Usually, **barracks.** **1.** a building or range of buildings for lodging soldiers, esp. in garrison. **2.** any large, plain building in which many people are lodged. —*v.t.*, *v.i.* **3.** to lodge in barracks. [< F *baraque* < Sp or Catalan *barraca* hut < ?]

bar·rack² (bar′ək), *Australian, Brit.* —*v.i.* **1.** to shout boisterously for or against a player or team; root. —*v.t.* **2.** to shout for or against. [? back formation from *barracking*, var. of *barrakin* gibberish (Cockney) < ?] —**bar′rack·er,** *n.*

Bar′rack-Room Bal′lads (bar′ək ro͞om′, -ro͝om′), a volume of poems (1892) by Rudyard Kipling, including *Gunga Din*, *Danny Deever*, and *Mandalay.*

bar′racks bag′, a bag of heavy cotton, used by military personnel for carrying personal belongings.

bar′racks law′yer, a member of the armed forces who claims to be an authority on military law, regulations, and servicemen's rights, esp. one not formally qualified as an authority.

bar·ra·coon (bar′ə ko͞on′), *n.* (formerly) a place of temporary confinement for slaves or convicts. [< Sp *barracón*, equiv. to *barrac(a)* hut (see BARRACK¹) + *-on* aug. suffix]

Great barracuda, *Sphyraena barracuda* (Length 6 ft.)

bar·ra·cu·da (bar′ə-ko͞o′də), *n.*, *pl.* (*esp. collectively*) **-da,** (*esp. referring to two or more kinds or species*) **-das.** any of several elongated, predaceous, tropical and subtropical marine fishes of the genus *Sphyraena*, certain species of which are used for food. [< AmerSp < ?]

bar·ra·cu·di·na (bar′ə ko͞od′ᵊnə), *n.* any of several slender, large-mouthed, pelagic fishes of the family *Paralepididae.* [< AmerSp, equiv. to *barracud(a)* BARRACUDA + *-ina* dim. suffix]

bar·rage (bə räzh′; *esp. Brit.* bar′äzh *for 1, 2, 4;* bär′ij *for 3*), *n.*, *v.*, **-raged, -rag·ing.** —*n.* **1.** *Mil.* a barrier of artillery fire. **2.** an overwhelming quantity:

a barrage of questions. 3. Civ. Eng. an artificial obstruction in a watercourse to increase the depth of the water, facilitate irrigation, etc. —v.t. 4. to subject to a barrage. [< F; see BAR[1], -AGE]

barrage′ balloon′, a balloon or blimp, usually one of several anchored around a military area, from which wires or nets are hung as a protection against attacks from low-flying aircraft.

bar·ra·mun·da (bar′ə mun′də), n., pl. **-das,** (esp. collectively) **-da.** a lungfish, *Neoceratodus forsteri*, of the rivers of Australia. [< native Austral]

bar·ra·mun·di (bar′ə mun′dē), n., pl. **-dis, -dies,** (esp. collectively) **-di.** barramunda.

bar·ran·ca (bə rang′kə; Sp. bär räng′kä), n., pl. **-cas** (-kəz; Sp. -käs). 1. a steep-walled ravine or gorge. 2. a gully with steep sides; arroyo. [< Sp, var. of *barranco* < ?]

Bar·ran·ca·ber·me·ja (bär rän′kä ver me′hä), n. a city in N Colombia. 25,046 (1950).

Bar·ran·quil·la (bär′rän kē′yä), n. a seaport in N Colombia, on the Magdalena River. 452,140 (est. 1961).

bar·ra·tor (bar′ə tər), n. Law. a person who commits barratry. Also, **bar′ra·ter, barretor.** [ME *barettour* brawler, fighter (*barete, barate* (< Scand; cf. Icel *barātta* contention, fighting, akin to *berja* to fight) + *-our* -OR[2])]

bar·ra·try (bar′ə trē), n. Law. 1. fraud by a master or crew at the expense of the owners of the ship or its cargo. 2. the offense of frequently exciting and stirring up suits and quarrels. 3. the purchase or sale of ecclesiastical preferments or of offices of state. Also, **barretry.** [late ME *barratrie* < MF *baraterie* combat, fighting. See BARRATOR, -Y[3]] —**bar′ra·trous,** adj. —**bar′ra·trous·ly,** adv.

Bar·rault (ba rō′), n. **Jean-Louis** (zhän lwē′), born 1910, French actor and director.

barre (bär), n. Ballet. bar[1] (def. 16).

bar·ré (bä rā′), n. Textiles. 1. a pattern of stripes or bands of color extending across the warp in woven and knitted fabrics. 2. a streak in the filling direction when one or more picks are of a color different from that of adjacent picks. [< F: lit., barred, ptp. of *barrer*, deriv. of *barre* BAR[1]]

Bar·re (bar′ē), n. a city in central Vermont. 10,387 (1960).

barred (bärd), adj. 1. provided with one or more bars: *a barred gate.* 2. striped; streaked: *barred fabrics.* 3. Ornith. (of feathers) marked with transverse bands of distinctive color. [BAR[1] + -ED[3]]

barred′ i′, Phonet. 1. a high central vowel with phonetic quality approximating that of the vowels in *pit, put, putt,* or *pet,* and considered by most phonologists as a phonetic variant of one of these vowels, depending on the context, but by some as an autonomous phoneme in some varieties of English. 2. the phonetic symbol ɨ.

barred′ owl′, a large owl, *Strix varia*, of eastern North America, having its breast barred and abdomen streaked with dark brown.

bar·rel (bar′əl), n., v., **-reled, -rel·ing** or (esp. Brit.) **-relled, -rel·ling.** —n. 1. a cylindrical wooden vessel with slightly bulging sides made of staves hooped together, and with flat, parallel ends. 2. the quantity which such a vessel of some standard size can hold (as 31½ U.S. gallons of liquid, 105 U.S. dry quarts of fruits and vegetables). 3. any large quantity: *a barrel of fun; a barrel of monkeys.* 4. any container, case, or part similar in form. 5. Ordn. the tube of a gun. 6. Mach. the chamber of a pump in which the piston works. 7. a drum turning on a shaft, as in a weight-driven clock. 8. Horol. the cylindrical case in a watch or clock within which the mainspring is coiled. 9. Ornith. Obs. the calamus or quill. 10. the trunk of a quadruped, esp. of a horse, cow, etc. See diag. under **horse.** 11. Naut. the main portion of a capstan, about which the rope winds, between the drumhead at the top and the pawl rim at the bottom. 12. a rotating horizontal cylinder in which manufactured objects are coated or polished by tumbling in a suitable substance. 13. any structure having the form of a barrel vault. 14. **over a barrel,** Slang. in an embarrassing or uncomfortable position; unable to act: *They really had us over a barrel when they foreclosed the mortgage.* —v.t. 15. to put or pack in a barrel or barrels. 16. to finish (metal parts) by tumbling in a barrel. —v.i. 17. Slang. to travel or drive very fast: *to barrel along the speedway.* [ME *barell* < OF *baril,* ? equiv. to *barre* stave (see BAR[1]) + *-il* < L *-īle,* neut. of *-īlis* -ILE]

bar′rel bolt′, a rod-shaped bolt for fastening a door or the like, attached to one side of the door at the edge and sliding into a socket on the frame of the opening. Also called **tower bolt.**

bar′rel chair′, U.S. Furniture. an easy chair having a high, semicircular back forming a single upholstered piece with the wings or arms; tub chair. Also called **bar′rel-back chair′** (bar′əl bak′).

bar·rel-chest·ed (bar′əl ches′tid), adj. having a massive, well-developed chest or thorax.

bar′rel cuff′, a cuff on a sleeve, formed by a band of material, usually fastened by a button. Cf. **French cuff.**

bar′rel distor′tion, Optics. a distortion produced by a lens in which the magnification decreases toward the edge of the field. Cf. **pincushion distortion.**

bar′rel en′gine, an engine having cylinders arranged around and parallel to a shaft, which they rotate by means of the contact of their piston rods with a swash plate or cam on the shaft.

bar·rel·eye (bar′əl ī′), n., pl. **-eyes.** any of the bathypelagic fishes of the family *Opisthoproctidae*, esp. *Macropinna microstoma*, having telescoping eyes. [BARREL + EYE]

bar·rel·fish (bar′əl fish′), n., pl. **-fish·es** (esp. collectively) **-fish.** a blackish stromateid fish, *Palinurichthys perciformis*, found along the coast of New England. Also called **black rudderfish.** [BARREL + FISH]

bar·rel·ful (bar′əl fo͝ol′), n., pl. **-fuls.** 1. all that a barrel can hold; the contents of a barrel. 2. any large quantity: *a barrelful of jokes.* [ME; see BARREL, -FUL]

bar·rel·head (bar′əl hed′), n. either of the round, flat sections which form the top and bottom of a barrel. [BARREL + HEAD]

bar·rel·house (bar′əl hous′), n., pl. **-hous·es** (-hou′ziz) for 1. 1. U.S. Slang. a cheap, disreputable drinking place, esp. one in New Orleans in the early part of the 20th century. 2. a vigorous, unpolished, and loud style of jazz originating in the barrelhouses of New Orleans in the early part of the 20th century. [BARREL + HOUSE]

bar′rel knot′, Angling. a knot for fastening together two strands of gut or nylon, as fishing lines or leaders. Also called **blood knot.**

bar′rel or′gan, a musical instrument in which air from a bellows is admitted to a set of pipes by means of pins inserted into a revolving barrel; hand organ.

bar′rel roll′, Aeron. a maneuver in which an airplane executes a complete roll by revolving once around an axis parallel to the longitudinal axis of the airplane.

bar·rel-roll (bar′əl rōl′), v.i. Aeron. to perform a barrel roll.

bar′rel roof′, 1. a roof or ceiling having a semicylindrical form. 2. See **barrel vault.**

bar′rel vault′, Archit. a vault having the form of a very deep arch, as in a tunnel. Also called **barrel roof, cradle vault, tunnel vault, wagon roof, wagon vault.** See illus. under **vault.** —**bar′rel-vault′ed,** adj.

bar·ren (bar′ən), adj. 1. not producing or incapable of producing offspring; sterile: *a barren woman.* 2. unproductive; unfruitful: *barren land.* 3. without capacity to interest or attract: *a barren period in American architecture.* 4. mentally unproductive; dull; stupid. 5. not producing results; fruitless: *a barren effort.* 6. destitute; bereft; lacking (usually fol. by *of*): *barren of tender feelings.* —n. 7. Usually, **barrens.** level or slightly rolling land, usually with a sandy soil and few trees, and relatively infertile. [ME *barain* < AF; OF *brahain* < ?] —**bar′ren·ly,** adv. —**bar′ren·ness,** n.
—**Syn.** 1. childless, unprolific, infertile. 5. ineffectual, ineffective. —**Ant.** 1–6. fertile.

Bar′ren Grounds′, a sparsely inhabited region of tundras in N Canada, esp. in the area W of Hudson Bay. Also called **Bar′ren Lands′.**

Bar·rès (ba res′), n. **Mau·rice** (mō rēs′), 1862–1923, French novelist, writer on politics, and politician.

bar·ret (bar′it), n. a small cap, akin to the biretta, worn in the Middle Ages by soldiers and ecclesiastics. [< F *barrette* < It *berretta* BERRETTA]

Bar·ret (bar′it), n. a boy's given name. Also, **Bar′rett.**

bar·re·tor (bar′i tər), n. Law. barrator.

bar·re·try (bar′i trē), n. Law. barratry.

Bar·rett (bar′it), n. **Elizabeth.** See **Browning, Elizabeth Barrett.**

bar·rette (bə ret′), n. a clasp for holding a woman's hair. [earlier *barette;* see BAR[1], -ETTE]

bar·ret·ter (bar′et ər, bə ret′-), n. Electronics. a form of detector or control device employing a resistor that varies in proportion to its temperature. [< OF *bareter* to exchange]

Bar′retts of Wim′pole Street′, The (bar′its; wim′pōl), a play (1930) by Rudolf Besier, concerning the courtship of Robert Browning and Elizabeth Barrett.

bar·ri·cade (bar′ə kād′, bar′ə kād′), n., v., **-cad·ed, -cad·ing.** —n. 1. a defensive barrier hastily constructed, as in a street, to stop an enemy. 2. any barrier that obstructs passage: *a barricade of rubbish between the slum buildings.* —v.t. 3. to obstruct or block with a barricade: *barricading the streets to prevent a retreat.* 4. to shut in and defend with or as with a barricade: *The rebels had barricaded themselves within the old city.* [< F; r. BARRICADO] —**bar′ri·cad′er,** n.
—**Syn.** 1. See **bar**[1]. 4. fortify.

bar·ri·ca·do (bar′ə kā′dō), n., pl. **-does, -dos,** v., **-doed, -do·ing.** —n. 1. a barricade. —v.t. 2. to barricade. [< Sp *barricada* (*barric(a)* barrel + *-ada* -ADE[1])]

Bar·rie (bar′ē), n. 1. **Sir James M(atthew),** 1860–1937, Scottish novelist, short-story writer, and playwright. 2. Also, **Barry.** a boy's given name.

bar·ri·er (bar′ē ər), n. 1. anything built or serving to bar passage, as a railing, fence, or the like: *Persons may pass through the barrier only when their train is announced.* 2. any natural bar or obstacle: *a mountain barrier.* 3. anything that restrains or obstructs progress, access, etc.: *a trade barrier.* 4. a limit or boundary of any kind: *the barriers of caste.* 5. Phys. Geog. an antarctic ice shelf or ice front. 6. See **barrier beach.** 7. **barriers,** the palisades or railing surrounding the ground where tourneys and jousts were carried on. 8. Archaic. a fortress or stockade. [< MF *barriere* (*barre* BAR[1] + *-iere* < L *-āria* -ARY); r. ME *barrere* < AF < ML *barrera*]
—**Syn.** 1. palisade, wall. See **bar**[1]. 1–3. obstruction, hindrance, impediment.

bar′rier beach′, a sand ridge that rises slightly above the surface of the sea and runs roughly parallel to the shore from which it is separated by a lagoon.

bar′rier reef′, Oceanog. a reef of coral running roughly parallel to the shore and separated from it by deep water.

Bar′rier Reef′. See **Great Barrier Reef.**

bar′ rig′ging, Naut. See **rod rigging.**

bar·ring (bär′ing), prep. excepting; except for: *Barring accidents, I'll be there.* [BAR[1] + -ING[2]]

Bar·ring·ton (bar′ing tən), n. 1. a town in SW New Jersey. 7943 (1960). 2. a town in NE Illinois. 5434 (1960).

bar·rio (bär′ryô), n., pl. **-rios** (-ryôs). (in Spain and countries colonized by Spain) one of the divisions into which a town or city, together with the contiguous rural territory, is divided. [< Sp < Ar *barrī* of open country (*barr* outside, open country + *-ī* adj. suffix) + *-o* n. suffix]

Bar·rios (bär′ryôs), n. **Jus·to Ru·fi·no** (ho͞o′stô ro͞ofē′nô), 1835–85, Guatemalan statesman: president of Guatemala 1873–85.

bar·ris·ter (bar′i stər), n. Law. 1. (in England) a lawyer who is a member of one of the Inns of Court and who has the privilege of pleading in the higher courts. Cf. **solicitor** (def. 4). 2. U.S. Informal. a lawyer. [*barri-* (comb. form of BAR[1]) + -STER] —**bar·ri·ste·ri·al** (bar′i stēr′ē əl), adj.

bar·room (bär′ro͞om′, -ro͝om′), n. U.S. an establishment or room with a bar for the serving of alcoholic beverages. [BAR[1] + ROOM]

Bar·ros (bär′ro͞osh), **João de** (zhwoun də), ("*the Portuguese Livy*"), 1496–1570, Portuguese historian.

bar·row[1] (bar′ō), n. 1. a flat, rectangular frame used for carrying a load, esp. such a frame with projecting shafts at each end for handles; handbarrow. 2. a wheelbarrow. 3. Brit. a pushcart used by street vendors, esp. by costermongers. [ME *bar(e)we,* OE *bearwe;* akin to BEAR[1]]

bar·row[2] (bar′ō), n. 1. Also called **tumulus.** a burial mound of the prehistoric inhabitants of Great Britain. 2. Chiefly Brit. a hill (sometimes used in combination): *Trentishoe Barrow in North Devon; Whitbarrow in North Lancashire.* [ME *berwe,* OE *beorg* hill, mound; c. D, G *Berg,* Icel *bjarg, berg,* Skt *bṛh-* in *bṛhant* high]

bar·row[3] (bar′ō), n. a castrated male swine. [ME *barow,* OE *bearg;* c. OHG *barug,* Icel *börgr*]

Bar·row (bar′ō), n. 1. Also called **Bar·row-in-Fur·ness** (bar′ō in fûr′nis). a seaport in NW Lancashire, in NW England. 64,824 (1961). 2. **Point,** the N tip of Alaska: the northernmost point of the U.S. 3. a circular area in the first quadrant of the face of the moon, near its north pole: about 45 miles in diameter.

bar·row-boy (bar′ō boi′), n. Brit. a costermonger.

bar·row·man (bar′ō mən, -man′), n., pl. **-men** (-mən, -men′). Brit. a costermonger.

bar·ru·let (bar′ə lit, bar′yə-), n. Heraldry. a diminutive of the bar, narrower than the usual. [*barrul-* (< AF, in *barrulee* barred; see BAR[1], -ULE, -EE) + -ET]

bar·ru·ly (bar′ə lē, bar′yə-), adj. Heraldry. barry of a number in excess of 10: *barruly of 12.* Also, **burele, burelle, burelly.** [*barrul-* (< AF; see BARRULET) + -Y[2]]

bar·ry (bär′ē, bar′ē), adj. Heraldry. (of an escutcheon) divided horizontally into an even number of areas of equal breadth, usually with two alternating tinctures: *barry of six, argent and gules.* [late ME *barri* < MF *barré* barred. See BAR[1], -EE]

Bar·ry (bar′ē), n. 1. **Sir Charles,** 1795–1860, English architect. 2. **John,** 1745–1803, American naval commander in the Revolution. 3. **Philip,** 1896–1949, U.S. playwright. 4. Also, **Barrie.** a boy's given name.

bar·ry-ben·dy (bär′ē ben′dē, bar′-), adj. Heraldry. (of an escutcheon) divided barwise and bendwise to form a lozengy pattern, usually of two alternating tinctures: *barry-bendy argent and azure.* [BARRY + BEND[2] + -Y[1]]

Bar·ry·more (bar′ə mōr′, -môr′), n. 1. **Maurice** (*Herbert Blythe*), 1847–1905, U.S. and English actor, born in India. 2. his children: **Ethel,** 1879–1959, **John,** 1882–1942, and **Lionel,** 1878–1954, U.S. actors.

bar·ry-neb·u·ly (bär′ē neb′yə lē, bar′-), adj. Heraldry. (of an escutcheon) barry with the partition lines nebuly: *barry-nebuly of six, or and gules.* [BARRY + MF *nebulé,* alter. of ML *nebulāt(us)* clouded; see NEBULA, -ATE[1]]

bar·ry-pi·ly (bär′ē pī′lē, bar′-), adj. Heraldry. (of an escutcheon) divided into piles barwise from either side: *barry-pily of eight, or and sable.* [BARRY + PILE[2] + -Y[1]]

bar·ry-wav·y (bär′ē wā′vē, bar′-), adj. Heraldry. (of an escutcheon) barry with the partition lines wavy: *barry-wavy of eight, or and azure.*

Bar·sac (bär′sak), n. 1. a village and wine-growing district in Gironde, in SW France. 2. a sweet, white Sauterne from here.

bar′ sin′ister, 1. an erroneous term for a bend sinister or baton sinister. 2. the proof, condition, or stigma of illegitimate birth.

bar·spoon (bär′spo͞on′), n. a long-handled spoon, usually having the capacity of a teaspoon, used for mixing or measuring ingredients for alcoholic drinks. [BAR[1] + SPOON]

bar·stool (bär′sto͞ol′), n. an individual stool or seat, usually high and having a round, cushioned top, of a type often used for seating customers at a bar. [BAR[1] + STOOL]

Bar·stow (bär′stō), n. a city in S California. 11,644 (1960).

Bart (bärt), n. a boy's given name, form of **Bartholomew, Bartlett,** or **Bartram.**

Bart., Baronet.

bar′ tack′, a close series of stitches crossing a piece of cloth, as in an article of clothing, in order to reinforce it at a point of concentrated strain.

bar·tend (bär′tend′), v.i. to serve or work as a bartender, esp. as an occupation. [back formation from BARTENDER]

bar·tend·er (bär′ten′dər), n. Chiefly U.S. a person who mixes and serves drinks at a bar. [BAR[1] + TENDER[3]]

bar·ter (bär′tər), v.i. 1. to trade by exchange of commodities rather than by the use of money. —v.t. 2. to exchange in trade, as one commodity for another; trade. 3. to bargain away unwisely or dishonorably (usually fol. by *away*): *bartering away his pride for material gain.* —n. 4. act or practice of bartering: *They had varied their diet by barter.* 5. items or an item for bartering: *He arrived with new barter for the natives.* [late ME, of unexplained orig.; cf. MF *barater* to cheat, exchange, deriv. of *barate* confusion, trouble, deceit, appar. < Scand; cf. Icel *barātta* trouble, strife] —**bar′ter·er,** n.
—**Syn.** 1, 2. traffic. See **trade.**

Bar′tered Bride′, The, a comic opera (1866) by Bedřich Smetana.

Barth (bärt), n. **Karl,** born 1886, Swiss theologian.

Barth·i·an (bär′tē ən, -thē-), adj. 1. of or pertaining to Karl Barth or his theology. —n. 2. a supporter or adherent of Karl Barth or his theology. [BARTH + -IAN]

Barth·i·an·ism (bär′tē ə niz′əm, -thē-), n. the theological doctrines and principles of Karl Barth and his followers, esp. in reference to neoorthodoxy. [BARTHIAN + -ISM]

Bar·thol·di (bär thol′dē; Fr. bar tôl dē′), n. **Fré·dé·ric Au·guste** (frā dā rēk′ ō gyst′), 1834–1904, French sculptor who designed the Statue of Liberty.

Bar·thol·o·mew (bär thol′ə myo͞o′), n. 1. one of the 12 apostles. Mark 3:18. 2. a boy's given name.

Bar·thou (bar to͞o′), n. **(Jean) Louis** (zhän lwē), 1862–1934, French statesman and author.

bar·ti·zan (bär′ti zən, bär′ti·zan′), n. Archit. a small overhanging turret on a wall or tower. [alter. of *bertisene,* misspelling of *bretising,* var. of *bratticing.* See BRATTICE] —**bar·ti·zaned** (bär′ti zənd, bär′ti zand′), adj.

Bartizan

Bar·tles·ville (bär′tᵊlz vil), *n.* a city in NE Oklahoma. 27,893 (1960).

Bart·lett (bärt′lit), *n. Hort.* **1.** a large, yellow, juicy variety of pear. **2.** the tree bearing this fruit. Also called **Bart′lett pear′.** [so named by Enoch *Bartlett* of Dorchester, Mass.]

Bart·lett (bärt′lit), *n.* **1. John,** 1820–1905, U.S. publisher and compiler. **2. Josiah,** 1729–95, U.S. physician and statesman. **3. Paul Wayland,** 1865–1925, U.S. sculptor. **4. Robert Abram,** 1875–1946, U.S. arctic explorer, born in Newfoundland. **5. Vernon,** born 1894, English writer. **6.** a boy's given name, form of **Bartholomew.**

Bart·ley (bärt′lē), *n.* a boy's given name, form of **Bartholomew.**

Bar·tók (bär′tok; *Hung.* bôr′tōk), *n.* **Bé·la** (bā′lə; *Hung.* bā′lo), 1881–1945, Hungarian composer.

Bar·to·lom·me·o (bär tol′ə mā′ō; *It.* bär′tô lôm·me′ô), *n.* **Fra** (frä; *It.* frä), (*Baccio della Porta*), 1475–1517, Italian painter.

Bar·to·loz·zi (bär′tô lôt′tsē), *n.* **Fran·ces·co** (frän·ches′kô), 1725?–1815?, Italian engraver.

Bar·ton (bär′tᵊn), *n.* **1. Clara,** 1821–1912, U.S. philanthropist who organized the American Red Cross in 1881. **2. Sir Edmund,** 1849–1920, Australian jurist and statesman: prime minister 1901–03. **3.** a boy's given name.

Bar·ton·ville (bär′tᵊn vil), *n.* a town in central Illinois. 7253 (1960).

Bar·tram (bär′trəm), *n.* **1. John,** 1699–1777, U.S. botanist. **2.** Also, **Bertram.** a boy's given name.

Bar·tra′mi·an sand′piper (bär trā′mē ən). See **upland plover.** [named after John BARTRAM; see -IAN]

Bar·uch (bâr′ək *for 1;* bə ro͞ok′ *for 2, 3*), *n.* **1.** the amanuensis and friend of Jeremiah and nominal author of the book of Baruch in the Apocrypha. Jer. 32:12. **2. Bernard Man·nes** (man′əs), 1870–1965, U.S. statesman and financier. **3.** a boy's given name.

bar·wise (bär′wīz′), *adj. Heraldry.* (of a charge or charges) transversely across an escutcheon, in the manner of a bar. Also, **bar·ways** (bär′wāz′). [BAR¹ + -WISE]

bar·y·cen′tric coor′dinate sys′tem (bar′i sen′trik), *Math.* a coordinate system for an *n*-dimensional Euclidean space in which each point is represented by *n* constants whose sum is 1 and whose product with a given set of linearly independent points equals the point. [< Gk *barý(s)* heavy + CENTRIC]

bar·ye (bar′ē), *n.* microbar. [< F < Gk *barýs* heavy]

Ba·rye (ba rē′), *n.* **An·toine Louis** (äN twaN′ lwē), 1795–1875, French sculptor and painter.

bar·y·on (bar′ē on′), *n. Physics.* a nucleon or a hyperon. [< Gk *barý(s)* heavy + (FERMI)ON]

ba·ry·ta (bə rī′tə), *n. Chem.* **1.** Also called **calcined baryta, barium oxide, barium monoxide, barium protoxide.** a white or yellowish-white poisonous solid, BaO, highly reactive with water: used chiefly as a dehydrating agent and in the manufacture of glass. **2.** Also called **caustic baryta, barium hydroxide, barium hydrate.** the hydroxide, hydrated form of this compound, $Ba(OH)_2{\cdot}8H_2O$, used chiefly in the industrial preparation of beet sugar and for refining animal and vegetable oils. [< NL, equiv. to *bary-* (< Gk *barýs* heavy) + *-ta* (< Gk *-tēs* agent suffix) —**ba·ryt·ic** (bə·rit′ik), *adj.*

bary′ta wa′ter, *Chem.* an aqueous solution of barium hydroxide, used chiefly as a reagent.

ba·ry·tes (bə rī′tēz), *n. Mineral.* barite.

ba·ry·to·cal·cite (bə rī′tə kal′sīt), *n.* a mineral, double carbonate of calcium and barium, $CaCO_3{\cdot}BaCO_3$, usually found in veins of lead minerals. [BARYT(A) + -O- + CALCITE]

bar·y·ton (bar′i ton′; *Fr.* ba rē tôN′), *n., pl.* **-tons** (-tonz′; *Fr.* -tôN′). an 18th-century stringed instrument with six bowed strings and several additional strings vibrating sympathetically. [see BARITONE]

bar·y·tone¹ (bar′i tōn′), *n., adj. Music.* baritone.

bar·y·tone² (bar′i tōn′), *Classical Gk. Gram.* —*adj.* **1.** having the last syllable unaccented. —*n.* **2.** a barytone word. [< Gk *barýton(os),* equiv. to *barý(s)* heavy, deep (of sound) + *tónos* TONE]

B.A.S., 1. Bachelor of Agricultural Science. **2.** Bachelor of Applied Science.

ba·sad (bā′sad), *adv.* toward the base. [BASE¹ + *-ad* < L *ad* to, toward]

ba·sal (bā′səl, -zəl), *adj.* **1.** of, at, or forming the base. **2.** forming a basis; fundamental; basic: *basal characteristics.* **3.** *Physiol.* **a.** indicating a standard low level of activity of an organism as present during total rest. **b.** of an amount required to maintain this level. **4.** *Med.* serving to induce a preliminary or light anesthesia prior to total anesthetization. [BASE¹ + -AL¹] —**ba′sal·ly,** *adv.*

ba′sal conglom′erate, a conglomerate deposited on an erosion surface and comprising the bottom layer of a rock series.

ba′sal gang′lion, *Anat.* any of four masses of gray matter in each cerebral hemisphere.

ba′sal metabol′ic rate′, *Physiol.* the rate of oxygen intake and heat discharge in an organism in a basal state. *Abbr.:* B.M.R.

ba′sal metab′olism, *Physiol.* the energy turnover of the body at a standard low level of activity.

ba′sal ridge′, *Dentistry.* a U-shaped ridge at the base of the posterior surface of the crown of a tooth. Also called **cingulum.**

ba·salt (bə sôlt′, bas′ôlt, bā′sôlt), *n.* the dark, dense igneous rock of a lava flow or minor intrusion, composed essentially of labradorite and pyroxene and often displaying a columnar structure. [< LL *basalt(es),* alter. of L *basanītēs* < Gk *basanī́tēs* (*líthos*) touchstone, prob. of Afr orig.] —**ba·sal′tic, ba·sal·tine** (bə sôl′tin, -tīn), *adj.*

ba·salt·ware (bə sôlt′wâr′, bas′ôlt-, bā′sôlt-), *n.* unglazed stoneware, usually black with a dull gloss, developed by Josiah Wedgwood. Also called **ba·sal·tes** (bə·sôl′tēz). [BASALT + WARE¹]

bas·a·nite (bas′ə nīt′, baz′-), *n. Petrog.* a basaltic rock composed chiefly of plagioclase, olivine, and augite. [< L *basanītē(s);* see BASALT]

bas bleu (bä blœ′), *pl.* **bas bleus** (bä blœ′). *French.* a bluestocking.

B.A.Sc., 1. Bachelor of Agricultural Science. **2.** Bachelor of Applied Science.

bas·cin·et (bas′ə nit, -net′, bas′ə net′), *n. Armor.* basinet.

bas·cule (bas′kyo͞ol), *n. Civ. Eng.* a device operating like a balance or seesaw, esp. an arrangement of a movable bridge (**bas′cule bridge′**) by which the rising floor or section is counterbalanced by a weight. [< F *ba(s)cule,* equiv. to *bas* low, BASE² + *cul* rump (see CULET) + *-e* fem. suffix]

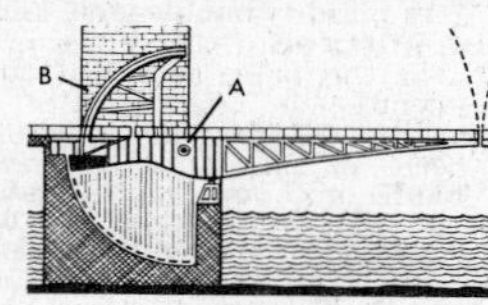

Bascule bridge
A, Pivot about which bridge swings in rising; B, Toothed quadrant engaging with machinery

base¹ (bās), *n., adj., v.,* **based, bas·ing.** —*n.* **1.** the bottom support of anything; that on which a thing stands or rests. **2.** a fundamental principle or groundwork; foundation; basis: *the base of needed reforms.* **3.** the bottom layer or coating, as of make-up or paint. **4.** *Archit.* **a.** the distinctively treated portion of a column or pier below the shaft or shafts. **b.** the distinctively treated lowermost portion of any construction, as a monument, exterior wall, etc. **5.** *Bot., Zool.* **a.** the part of an organ nearest its point of attachment. **b.** the point of attachment. **6.** the principal element or ingredient of anything, considered as its fundamental part: *face cream with a lard base; paint with a lead base.* **7.** that from which a commencement, as of action or reckoning, is made; a starting point or point of departure. **8.** *Baseball.* **a.** any of the four corners of the diamond, esp. first, second, or third base. Cf. **home plate. b.** a square canvas sack containing sawdust or some other light material, for marking first, second, or third base. **9.** a starting line or point for runners, racing cars, etc. **10.** (in hockey and other games) the goal. **11.** *Mil.* **a.** a fortified or more or less protected area or place from which the operations of an army or an air force proceed. **b.** a supply installation for a large military force. **12.** *Geom.* the line or surface forming that part of a figure which is most nearly horizontal or on which it is supposed to stand. **13.** *Math.* **a.** the number that serves as a starting point for a logarithmic or other numerical system. **b.** a collection of subsets of a topological space having the property that every open set in the given topology can be written as the union of sets of the collection. **c.** a collection of neighborhoods of a point such that every neighborhood of the point contains one from the collection. **d.** a collection of sets of a given filter such that every set in the filter is contained in some set in the collection. **14.** Also called **base line.** *Survey.* See under **triangulation** (def. 1). **15.** *Painting.* **a.** vehicle (def. 9). **b.** Also called **carrier.** inert matter. used in the preparation of lakes, onto which a coloring compound is precipitated. **16.** *Chem.* **a.** a compound which reacts with an acid to form a salt, as ammonia, calcium hydroxide, certain nitrogen-containing organic compounds, as the amines and alkaloids, etc. **b.** the hydroxide of a metal or of an electropositive element or group. **c.** a group or molecule which takes up or accepts protons. **d.** a molecule or ion containing an atom with a free pair of electrons that can be donated to an acid; an electron-pair donor. **17.** *Gram.* the part of a complex word, consisting of one or more morphemes, to which derivational or inflectional affixes may be added, as *want* in *unwanted, biolog-* in *biological,* etc. Cf. **root**¹ (def. 11), **stem**¹ (def. 14). **18.** an electrode or terminal on a transistor other than the emitter or collector electrodes or terminals. **19.** *Elect., Electronics.* the part of an incandescent lamp or electron tube that includes the terminals for making electrical connection to a circuit or power supply. **20.** *Heraldry.* the lower part of an escutcheon. **21. bases,** *Armor.* a tonlet formed of two shaped steel plates assembled side by side. **22. get to first base.** See **first base** (def. 2). **23. in base,** *Heraldry.* in the lower part of an escutcheon. **24. off base, a.** *Baseball.* not touching a base: *The pitcher caught him off base and, after a quick throw, he was put out by the second baseman.* **b.** *Informal.* badly mistaken: *The police were way off base when they tried to accuse her of the theft.* **25. on base,** *Baseball.* having reached a base or bases: *Two men are on base.* Also, **on.**
—*adj.* **26.** serving as or forming a base: *The walls will need a base coat and two finishing coats.*
—*v.t.* **27.** to make or form a base or foundation for. **28.** to establish, as a fact or conclusion (usually fol. by *on* or *upon*): *He based his assumption of her guilt on the fact that she had no alibi.* **29.** to place or establish on a base or basis; ground; found; establish: *Our plan is based on a rising economy.* **30.** to station, place, or establish (usually fol. by *at* or *on*): *He is based at Fort Benning. The squadron is based on a carrier.*
—*v.i.* **31.** to have a basis; be based (usually fol. by *on* or *upon*): *Fluctuating prices usually base on a fickle public's demand.* **32.** to have or maintain a base (usually fol. by *on* or *upon*): *I believe they had based on Greenland at one time.* [ME < MF < L *basis* BASIS]
—**Syn. 1.** BASE, BASIS, FOUNDATION refer to anything upon which a structure is built and upon which it rests. BASE usually refers to a literal supporting structure: *the base of a statue.* BASIS more often refers to a figurative support: *the basis of a report.* FOUNDATION implies a solid, secure understructure: *the foundation of a skyscraper or a rumor.*

base² (bās), *adj.,* **bas·er, bas·est,** *n.* —*adj.* **1.** morally low; without dignity of sentiment; mean-spirited; selfish; cowardly. **2.** characteristic of an inferior person or thing: *the base ramblings of a deranged mind.* **3.** of little or no value; worthless: *hastily composed of base materials.* **4.** debased or counterfeit: *base coin; attempting to eliminate the base coinage.* Cf. **base metal. 5.** of illegitimate birth. **6.** *Old Eng. Law.* held by tenure less than freehold in return for a service viewed as somewhat demeaning to the tenant. **7.** not classical or refined: *base language.* **8.** *Archaic.* **a.** of humble origin or station. **b.** of small height. **c.** low in place, position, or degree: *base servitude.* **9.** *Obs.* deep or grave in sound; bass: *the base tones of a piano.* —*n.* **10.** *Music. Obs.* bass¹ (defs. 3, 4). [late ME *bass, bace* < MF *bas* (masc.), *basse* (fem.) < LL *bass(us), -a, -um* low, short, perh. < Gk *bássōn* deeper] —**base′ly,** *adv.* —**base′ness,** *n.*
—**Syn. 1.** despicable, contemptible. See **mean**². **2.** servile, ignoble, abject, slavish, menial. **3.** poor, inferior, cheap, tawdry. **4.** fake, spurious.

base·ball (bās′bôl′), *n.* **1.** a game of ball played by two nine-man teams on a square formed by lines connecting four bases, all of which must be touched by a base runner in order to score a run. **2.** the ball used in this game, being a sphere approximately three inches in diameter with a twine-covered center of cork covered by stitched horsehide. **3.** *Cards.* a variety of five-card or seven-card stud poker in which nines and threes are wild and in which threes and fours dealt face up gain the player either penalties or privileges. [BASE¹ + BALL¹]

base′ball glove′, a padded, leather covering for the hand, having a pocket in the area over the palm, webbing between the sections for the thumb and forefinger, and either separate sections for each finger or sections for more than one finger: used by baseball players in the field for catching batted or thrown balls. Cf. **mitt** (def. 2).

base·board (bās′bōrd′, -bôrd′), *n.* **1.** Also called **mopboard, skirt.** a board forming the foot of an interior wall. **2.** a board forming the base of anything. [BASE¹ + BOARD]

base·born (bās′bôrn′), *adj.* **1.** of humble birth. **2.** born out of wedlock; illegitimate. **3.** having a base nature; mean. [BASE² + BORN]

base′ box′, a unit used in the sale of tin plate, equal to the total area of 112 sheets each measuring 14 inches by 20 inches, or 31,360 square inches.

base′ bul′lion, *Metall.* smelted lead containing impurities, as gold, silver, zinc, etc., which are later removed.

base·burn·er (bās′bûr′nər), *n. U.S.* a stove or furnace with a self-acting fuel hopper over the fire chamber. Also, **base′ burn′er, base′-burn′er.** [BASE¹ + BURNER]

base·coat (bās′kōt′), *n.* **1.** a first coat of a surfacing material, as paint. **2.** any coat of plastering beneath the finish coat. [BASE¹ + COAT]

base′ estate′, *Old Eng. Law.* an estate held from a lord on the condition of performing some service, esp. service of a demeaning nature.

base′ exchange′, *U.S. Air Force.* a department store operated under government supervision at an air base. *Abbr.:* BX

base·heart·ed (bās′här′tid), *adj.* having a base nature or character; mean-spirited. [BASE² + HEARTED]

base′ hit′, *Baseball.* a fair ball enabling the batter to reach first base without the commission of an error in the field or the making of a force-out or fielder's choice on a base runner.

Ba·sel (bä′zəl), *n.* **1.** a city in and the capital of Basel-Stadt, in NW Switzerland, on the Rhine River. 206,746 (1960). **2.** a canton in N Switzerland, divided into two independent areas. Also, **Basle.** French, **Bâle.** Cf. **Basel-Land, Basel-Stadt.**

base·less (bās′lis), *adj.* having no base; without foundation; groundless: *a baseless claim.* [BASE¹ + -LESS]

base′ lev′el, *Phys. Geog.* the lowest level to which running water can erode the land.

base′ line′, 1. *Baseball.* the area between bases within which a base runner must keep when running from one base to another. **2.** *Electronics.* a horizontal or vertical line formed on the face of a cathode ray tube by the sweep of the scanning dot. **3.** *Tennis.* the line at each end of a tennis court, parallel to the net, that marks the in-bounds limit of play. **4.** *Survey.* See under **triangulation** (def. 1). **5.** (in perspective drawing) a horizontal line in the immediate foreground formed by the intersection of the ground plane and the picture plane. **6.** *Naval Archit.* a line on the body plan or sheer plan of a hull, representing a horizontal reference plane for vertical dimensions.

base·line (bās′līn′), *n. Typography.* the imaginary line on which the bottoms of primary letters align. [BASE¹ + LINE¹]

base·lin·er (bās′lī′nər), *n. Tennis.* a player who typically plays near the base line, as distinguished from one who typically goes to the net. [BASE LINE + -ER¹]

Ba·sel-Land (bä′zəl länt′), *n.* a demicanton in N Switzerland. 148,282 (1960); 165 sq. mi. *Cap.:* Liestal.

Ba·sel-Stadt (bä′zəl shtät′), *n.* a demicanton in N Switzerland: virtually coextensive with the city of Basel. 255,588 (1960); 14 sq. mi. *Cap.:* Basel.

base·man (bās′mən), *n., pl.* **-men.** *Baseball.* the first, second, or third baseman. [BASE¹ + MAN¹]

base′ map′, an outline map of an area to which specific information is added for any of various purposes.

base·ment (bās′mənt), *n.* **1.** a story of a building, partly or wholly underground. **2.** (in classical architecture) the portion of a building beneath the principal story, treated as a single compositional unit. **3.** the lowermost portion of a structure. **4.** the substructure of a columnar or arched construction. [BASE¹ + -MENT]

base′ met′al, 1. any metal other than a precious or noble metal, as copper, lead, zinc, tin, etc. Cf. **noble metal, precious metal. 2.** the principal metal of an alloy. **3.** the principal metal of a piece underlying a coating of another metal; core.

Ba·sen·ji (bə sen′jē), *n.* one of an African breed of dogs having a chestnut coat with white points and a curled tail, characterized chiefly by their inability to bark. [pl. of Bantu *mosenji, musenji* native]

base′ on balls′, *pl.* **bases on balls.** *Baseball.* the awarding of first base to a batter to whom four balls have been pitched. Also called **walk, pass.**

base′ pay′, pay received for a given work period, as an hour or week, but not including additional pay, as for overtime work. Also called **base′ sal′ary, base′ wage′.**

base′ pe′riod, a period of time used as a standard of comparison in measuring changes in prices, taxes, income, etc., at other periods of time.

base·plate (bās′plāt′), *n.* **1.** bedplate. **2.** *Dentistry.* **a.** a sheet of plastic material for making trial denture plates. b. the portion of a denture in contact with the jaw. 3. *Metall.* a plate of metal to be clad with another metal. [BASE[1] + PLATE[1]]

base′ price′, 1. a price quoted as a base without including additional charges. 2. a price used as a basis for computing freight charges at a basing point, as for steel.

base′ rate′, the rate of pay per unit of time, as by the hour, or per piece, or for work performed at an established standard rate. Also called **basic rate.**

base′ run′ner, *Baseball.* a player of the team at bat who is on base or is trying to run from one base to another. —**base′ run′ning.**

ba·ses[1] (bā′sēz), *n.* pl. of **basis.**

bas·es[2] (bā′siz), *n.* pl. of **base**[1].

base′ ten′ant, *Old Eng. Law.* a tenant of a base estate.

bash (bash), *Slang.* —*v.t.* 1. to strike with a crushing or smashing blow. —*n.* 2. a crushing blow. 3. a thoroughly enjoyable, lively party; a wildly good time. 4. **have a bash (at),** *Brit.* to attempt; make an attempt. 5. **on the bash,** *Brit.* practicing prostitution. [? alter. of PASH[1]]

Ba·shan (bā′shən), *n.* a region in ancient Palestine, E of the Jordan River.

ba·shaw (bə shô′), *n.* 1. pasha. 2. *Informal.* a person who is important, imperious, or self-important. [< Turk *bāshā,* var. of *pāshā* PASHA]

bash·ful (bash′fəl), *adj.* 1. uncomfortably diffident and easily embarrassed; shy; timid. 2. indicative of, accompanied by, or proceeding from bashfulness. [(A)BASH + -FUL] —**bash′ful·ly,** *adv.* —**bash′ful·ness,** *n.*
—**Syn.** 1. abashed, modest, embarrassed. See **shy**[1].
—**Ant.** arrogant.

bash·i-ba·zouk (bash′ē bə zo͞ok′), *n.* one of a class of irregular mounted troops in the Turkish military service. [< Turk *bashi bozuk,* lit., the head (is) turned]

Bash·kir′ Auton′omous Repub′lic (bäsh kēr′, bash-), an autonomous republic in the Russian Federation in Europe. 3,952,000; 55,430 sq. mi. *Cap.:* Ufa.

Ba·sho (bä shō′), *n.* (*Basho Matsuo*) 1644?–94, Japanese poet.

ba·si·ate (bā′sē āt′), *v.t., v.i.,* **-at·ed, -at·ing.** *Obs.* to kiss. [< L *bāsiāt(us)* (ptp. of *bāsiāre*), equiv. to *bāsi(um)* a kiss + *-ātus* -ATE[1]]
—**ba′si·a′tion,** *n.*

ba·sic (bā′sik), *adj.* 1. of, pertaining to, or forming a base; fundamental: *a basic principle; the basic ingredient.* 2. *Chem.* a. pertaining to, of the nature of, or containing a base. b. not having all of the hydroxyls of the base replaced by the acid group, or having the metal or its equivalent united partly to the acid group and partly to oxygen. c. alkaline. 3. *Metall.* noting, pertaining to, or made by a steelmaking process in which the furnace or converter is lined with a basic or nonsiliceous material, mainly burned magnesite and a small amount of ground basic slag, to aid in sintering. Cf. **acid** (def. 8). 4. *Geol.* (of a rock) having relatively little silica. 5. *Mil.* a. primary: *basic training.* b. of lowest rank: *basic airman.* —*n.* 6. *Mil.* a soldier or airman receiving basic training. [BASE[1] + -IC]

BASIC (bā′sik), *n.* a widely adopted programming language that uses English words, punctuation marks, and algebraic notation to facilitate communication between the operator or lay user and the computer. [*b(eginner's) a(ll-purpose) s(ymbolic) i(nstruction) c(ode)*]

ba′sic air′man. See under **airman** (def. 2).

ba·si·cal·ly (bā′sik lē), *adv.* fundamentally. [BASIC + -AL[1] + -LY]

ba′sic anhy′dride, *Chem.* See under **anhydride** (def. 1).

ba′sic dichro′mate, *Chem.* See **bismuth chromate.**

ba′sic dress′, a simple, usually dark dress that may be worn with various accessories or in a variety of combinations.

Ba′sic Eng′lish, a simplified English with a restricted vocabulary, intended as an international auxiliary language and for use in teaching English. Also called **Bas′ic.**

ba′sic fuch′sin, fuchsin.

ba·sic·i·ty (bā sis′i tē), *n. Chem.* 1. state of being a base. 2. the power of an acid to react with bases, dependent on the number of replaceable hydrogen atoms of the acid. [BASIC + -ITY]

ba′sic lead′ car′bonate (led), *Chem.* ceruse.

ba·sic-lined (bā′sik līnd′), *adj. Metall.* lined with a nonsiliceous material, as a furnace or converter.

ba′sic magen′ta, fuchsin.

ba′sic plum′age, *Ornith.* 1. the plumage assumed by an adult bird at its complete, usually annual, molt. 2. (in birds having more than one plumage in their cycle of molts) usually the duller plumage. Cf. **alternate plumage, supplemental plumage.**

ba′sic proposi′tion, protocol (def. 6).

ba′sic rate′. See **base rate.**

ba′sic sal′ary. See **base pay.**

ba′sic slag′, *Metall.* slag from a basic-lined furnace, used as a furnace or converter lining or as a fertilizer.

ba′sic wage′. See **base pay.**

ba′sic weight′. See **basis weight.** Also called **ba′sic sub′stance weight′.**

ba·sid·i·o·carp (bə sid′ē ō kärp′), *n. Bot.* the fructification of basidiomycetes that produces the basidia. [BASIDI(UM) + -O- + -CARP]

ba·sid·i·o·my·cete (bə sid′ē ō mī sēt′), *n.* a fungus of the class *Basidiomycetes,* characterized by bearing the spores on a basidium, including the smuts, rust, mushrooms, puffballs, etc. [BASIDI(UM) + -O- + -*mycete,* sing. of -MYCETES]

ba·sid·i·o·my·ce·tous (bə sid′ē ō mī sē′təs), *adj.* belonging or pertaining to the class *Basidiomycetes.* [BASIDIOMYCETE + -OUS]

ba·sid·i·o·spore (bə sid′ē ō spōr′, -spôr′), *n. Bot.* a spore that is borne by a basidium. [BASIDI(UM) + -O- + -SPORE]
—**ba·sid·i·os·por·ous** (bə sid′ē os′pər əs, -ē ə spōr′əs, -spôr′-), *adj.*

Basidia
A, Basidium; B, Basidiospore

ba·sid·i·um (bə sid′ē əm), *n., pl.* **-sid·i·a** (-sid′ē ə). *Bot.* a special form of sporophore, characteristic of basidiomycetous fungi, on which the sexual spores are borne, usually at the tips of slender projections. [BAS(IS) + -IDIUM] —**ba·sid′i·al,** *adj.*

Ba·sie (bā′sē), *n.* **William** ("*Count*"), born 1904, U.S. jazz pianist, bandleader, and composer.

ba·si·fixed (bā′sə fikst′), *adj. Bot.* attached at or near the base, as a leaf to a stem. [BASE[1] + -I- + FIXED]

bas·il[1] (baz′əl), *n.* any of several aromatic, labiate herbs of the genus *Ocimum,* as *O. Basilicum* **(sweet basil)** or *O. minimum* **(bush basil),** the leaves of which are used in cooking. [late ME *basile* < MF < LL *basil(icum)* < Gk *basilikón,* neut. of *basilikós* royal. See BASILIC]

bas·il[2] (baz′əl), *n.* bezel (def. 1).

Bas·il (baz′əl, bas′-), *n.* 1. **Saint.** Also **Basilius.** ("*the Great*"), A.D. 329?–379, bishop of Caesarea in Asia Minor (brother of Saint Gregory of Nyssa). 2. a boy's given name.

bas·i·lar (bas′ə lər), *adj.* 1. pertaining to or situated at the base, esp. the base of the skull. 2. basal. Also, **bas·i·lar·y** (bas′ə ler′ē). [< early NL *basilāre,* equiv. to ML *bassil(e)* pelvis + *-āre,* neut. of *-āris* -AR[1]]

bas·i·lard (bas′ə lərd), *n.* a medieval dagger having a tapering blade with straight transverse quillons and a T-shaped pommel. [ME *bas(e)lard,* ML *basalardus, bassilardus.* See BACILLUS, -ARD]

Ba·sil·don (bā′zəl dən), *n.* a town in S Essex, in SE England: designated as a model residential community after World War II. 53,707 (1961).

Ba·sil·i·an (bə zil′ē ən, -zil′yən, -sil′-), *adj.* 1. of or pertaining to St. Basil or to his monastic rule. —*n.* 2. a monk or nun following the rule of St. Basil. [BASIL + -IAN]

ba·sil·ic (bə sil′ik), *adj.* 1. kingly; royal. 2. Also, **ba·sil·i·can** (bə sil′i kən), **ba·sil′i·cal.** of, pertaining to, or like a basilica. [< L *basilic(us)* < Gk *basilikós* royal (*basil(eús)* king + *-ikos* -IC)]

ba·sil·i·ca (bə sil′i kə), *n.* 1. (in ancient Rome) a large oblong building used as a hall of justice and public meeting place. 2. an early Christian or medieval church of the type built esp. in Italy, characterized by a plan including a nave, two or four side aisles, a semicircular apse, a narthex, and often other features, as a short transept, a number of small semicircular apses terminating the aisles, or an atrium. The interior is characterized by strong horizontality, with little or no attempt at rhythmic accents. All spaces are usually covered with timber roofs or ceilings except for the apse or apses, which are vaulted. 3. one of the seven main churches of Rome or another Roman Catholic church accorded the same religious privileges. [< L < Gk *basilikḗ* hall, short for *basilikḗ oikía* royal house. See BASILIC]

Basilica
(Christian)
A, Atrium; B, Nave; C, Aisle; D, Apse; E, High altar; F, Tower

Ba·si·li·ca·ta (bä zē′lē kä′tä), *n.* Italian name of **Lucania.**

basil′ic vein′, *Anat.* a large vein on the inner side of the arm. [< L *vēna basilica* royal vein]

Ba·sil·i·en·sis (bə sil′ē en′sis), *n.* the uncial codex, dating from the 8th century A.D., that contains the Greek text of the Gospels. Cf. **codex** (def. 2). [< ML: of BASEL; see -ESE]

bas·i·lisk (bas′ə lisk, baz′-), *n.* 1. *Class. Myth.* a creature, variously described as a serpent, lizard, or dragon, said to kill by its breath or look. 2. any of several tropical American iguanid lizards of the genus *Basiliscus,* noted for their ability to run across the surface of water on the hind legs. [< L *basilisc(us)* < Gk *basilískos* princeling, basilisk < *basil(eús)* king + *-iskos* dim. suffix] —**bas·i·lis·cine** (bas′ə lis′in, -īn, baz′-), **bas′i·lis′can,** *adj.*

Basilisk
Basiliscus mitratu
(Length 2½ to 3 ft.)

Ba·sil·i·us (bə sil′ē əs, -zil′-), *n.* **Saint.** See **Basil.**

ba·sin (bā′sən), *n.* 1. a circular container with a greater width than depth, contracting toward the bottom, used chiefly to hold water or other liquid, esp. for washing. 2. any container of similar shape, as the pan of a balance. 3. the quantity held by such a container: *We need another basin of water.* 4. a natural or artificial hollow place containing water. 5. a partially enclosed, sheltered area along a shore, often partly manmade or dredged to a greater depth, where boats may be moored: *a boat basin; a yacht basin.* 6. *Geol.* an area in which the strata dip from the margins toward a common center. 7. *Phys. Geog.* a. a hollow or depression in the earth's surface, wholly or partly surrounded by higher land: *ocean basin; lake basin; river basin.* b. the tract of country drained by a river and its tributaries. 8. *Bot.* the depression in the part of an apple, pear, or other pome at the end opposite to that where the stalk connects with the fruit. [ME *bacin* < OF < LL *bacchīn(on)* (*bacc(a)* water vessel + *-inum* -INE[1])] —**ba′sined,** *adj.* —**ba′sin-like′,** *adj.*

bas·i·net (bas′ə nit, -net′, bas′ə net′), *n. Armor.* 1. a globular or pointed helmet of the 14th century, often provided with a visor or aventail: evolved from the cervellière. Cf. **great basinet.** 2. a supplementary cap that is worn underneath a helm, as an arming cap. Also, **bascinet, basnet, bassinet.** [ME *bas(e)net* < MF *bacinet.* See BASIN, -ET]

bas′ing point′, a geographical location from which freight charges are computed by the seller regardless of the point from which the goods are shipped.

ba·si·on (bā′sē on′), *n. Craniom.* a point on the anterior margin of the foramen magnum, in the midsagittal plane of the skull. [< NL < Gk *bás(is)* (see BASIS) + *-ion* n. suffix of uncert. identity]

ba·sip·e·tal (bā sip′i təl), *adj. Bot.* (of a plant structure) developing toward the base during growth. [BASI(S) + *-petal* < L *pet(ere)* (to) seek + -AL[1]; cf. CENTRIPETAL]

ba·sis (bā′sis), *n., pl.* **-ses** (-sēz). 1. the bottom or base of anything; that on which something stands or rests. 2. fundamental principle; groundwork. 3. the principal constituent; a fundamental ingredient. 4. *Math.* a set of linearly independent elements of a given vector space having the property that every element of the space can be written as a linear combination of the elements of the set. Cf. **linear independence.** [< L < Gk *básis;* cf. BASE[1]]
—**Syn.** 1, 2. See **base**[1].

ba′sis weight′, the weight in pounds of a ream of paper of a basic size, usually 25 × 38 inches for book stock, 17 × 22 inches for writing stock, and 20 × 26 inches for cover stock. Also called **basic weight, basic substance weight.**

bask (bask, bäsk), *v.i.* 1. to lie in or be exposed to a pleasant warmth: *to bask in the sunshine.* 2. to enjoy a pleasant situation: *He basked in royal favor.* —*v.t.* 3. *Obs.* to expose to warmth, heat, etc. (usually used reflexively): *to bask ourselves in sunny climes.* [late ME < Scand; cf. Icel *bathask* to bathe oneself, equiv. to *bath-* BATH[1] + *-ask* reflexive suffix]

Bas·ker·ville (bas′kər vil), *n.* 1. **John,** 1706–75, English typographer and manufacturer of lacquered ware. 2. a style of type.

bas·ket (bas′kit, bä′skit), *n.* 1. a receptacle made of twigs, rushes, thin strips of wood, or other flexible material woven together. 2. a container made of pieces of thin veneer, used for packing berries, vegetables, etc. 3. the contents of a basket; a basketful: *to pick a basket of apples.* 4. anything like a basket in shape or use. 5. the car or gondola suspended beneath a balloon, as for carrying passengers or scientific instruments into the atmosphere. 6. *Basketball.* a. an open net suspended from a metal rim attached to the backboard and through which the ball must pass in order for a player to score points. b. a score, counting two for a field goal and one for a free throw. [ME, perh. north OE *bæstet (by dissimilation), equiv. to *bæste (adj.) (c. WS *bæsten* made of BAST) + *-et* n. suffix. Cf. THICKET] —**bas′ket·like′,** *adj.*

bas·ket·ball (bas′kit bôl′, bä′skit-), *n.* 1. a game played by two five-man teams (six, if women) on a rectangular court having a raised basket or goal at each end, points being scored by tossing the ball through the opponent's basket. 2. the round, inflated ball, approximately 30 inches in circumference, used in this game. [BASKET + BALL[1]]

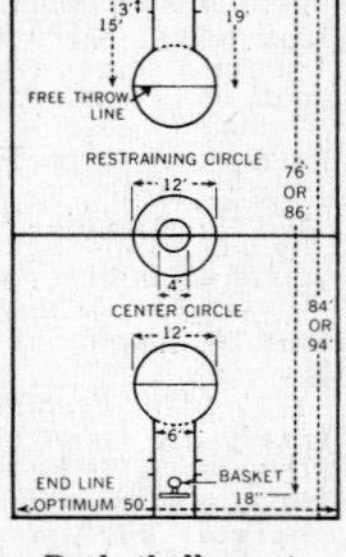

Basketball court

bas′ket case′, *Slang.* a quadruple amputee.

bas′ket chair′, a wicker chair the arms of which are a forward continuation of the back.

bas′ket fern′, a small, compact fern, *Nephrolepis pectinata,* of tropical America, often used in hanging baskets.

bas′ket flow′er, 1. an herb, *Centaurea americana,* found from the central U.S. to Mexico, having heads of tubular flowers surrounded by rose- or flesh-colored ray flowers, grown as an ornamental. 2. a bulbous herb, *Hymenocallis calathina,* of the Andes Mountains in Peru and Bolivia, having tubular flowers nearly 8 in. long.

bas·ket·ful (bas′kit fo͝ol′, bä′skit-), *n., pl.* **-fuls.** 1. a sufficient quantity to fill a basket; the contents of a basket. 2. any considerable quantity: *a basketful of surprises.* [BASKET + -FUL]

bas′ket-han·dle arch′ (bas′kit han′dəl, bä′skit-), *Archit.* an arch having a symmetrical form drawn from an odd number of radii in excess of one, which increase in length from the springing toward the center. See illus. under **arch.**

bas′ket hilt′, the basketlike hilt of a sword, foil, etc., serving to cover and protect the hand. —**bas′ket-hilt′ed,** *adj.*

Bas′ket Mak′er, 1. an American Indian culture of the southwestern U.S. that developed in three phases, immediately preceded the Pueblo culture, and was noted for its basketry, agriculture, use of the bow and arrow, and, in its later stages, the building of semisubterranean houses. 2. an American Indian belonging to the Basket Maker culture.

bas·ket-of-gold (bas′kit əv gōld′, -gōld′, bä′skit-), *n.* gold-dust.

bas·ket·ry (bas′ki trē, bä′ski-), *n.* 1. baskets collectively; basketwork. 2. the art or process of making baskets. [BASKET + -RY]

bas′ket star′, any echinoderm of the class *Ophiuroidea,* esp. of the genus *Gorgonocephalus,* having long, slender, branching arms.

bas′ket weave′, a plain weave with two or more yarns woven together, resembling that of a basket.

bas·ket·work (bas′kit wûrk′, bä′skit-), *n.* objects, textiles, etc., made or woven in the manner of a basket; basketry; wickerwork; interwoven work. [BASKET + WORK]

Bas·kin (bas′kin), *n.* **Leonard,** born 1922, U.S. sculptor and artist.

bask′ing shark′ (bas′king, bä′sking), a large shark, *Cetorhinus maximus,* which frequently comes to the surface to bask in the sun.

Basle (bäl), *n.* Basel.

bas mitz·vah (bäs mits′və), (*often caps.*) *Judaism.* See **bath mitzvah.**

bas·net (bas′nit, -net), *n. Armor.* basinet.

ba·son (bā′sən), *n. Anglican Ch.* a basin.

ba·so·phil (bā′sə fil), *n.* 1. *Biol.* a basophilic cell, tissue, organism, or substance. 2. *Anat.* a leukocyte having a bilobate nucleus and basophilic granules in the cytoplasm. —*adj.* 3. *Biol.* basophilic. Also, **ba·so·phile** (bā′sə fīl′, -fil). [BAS(IC DYE) + -O- + -PHIL]

ba·so·phil·ic (bā′sə fil′ik), *adj. Biol.* having an affinity for basic stains. Also, **ba·soph·i·lous** (bā sof′ə ləs), **basophil, basophile.** [BASOPHIL + -IC]

Ba·sov (bä′səf), *n.* **Ni·ko·lai Gen·ne·di·ye·vich** (nē ko lī′ ge ne dē′yə vich), born 1922, Russian physicist: Nobel prize 1964.

Basque (bask), *n.* **1.** one of a people of unknown origin inhabiting the western Pyrenees regions in France and Spain. **2.** their language, not known to be related to any other language despite attempts to connect it with Iberian, Berber, Etruscan, and the languages of the Caucasus. **3.** (*l.c.*) a close-fitting bodice, sometimes having an extension that covers the hips. **4.** the extension, or that of a doublet. **—*adj.*** **5.** of or pertaining to the Basques or their language.

Basque′ Prov′inces, a region in N Spain, bordering on the Bay of Biscay.

Basque′ shirt′, a knitted pullover shirt having a crew neck, long or short sleeves, and a pattern of horizontal stripes.

Bas·ra (bus′rə, bäs′rä), *n.* a port in SE Iraq, N of the Persian Gulf. 175,678 (est. 1963). Also, **Busra, Busrah.**

bas-re·lief (bä′ri lēf′, bas′-; bä′ri lēf′, bas′-), *n.* relief sculpture in which the figures project slightly from the background. Also called **low relief.** See illus. under **relief**[2]. [< F < It *basso rilievo* low RELIEF. See BASE[1]]

Bas-Rhin (bä′RAN′), *n.* a department in NE France. 782,424 (1962); 1848 sq. mi. *Cap.:* Strasbourg.

bass[1] (bās), *Music.* **—*adj.*** **1.** low in pitch; of the lowest pitch or range: *a bass voice, part, singer, or instrument.* **2.** of or pertaining to the lowest part in harmonic music. **—*n.*** **3.** the bass part. **4.** a bass voice, singer, or instrument. **5.** See **double bass.** [var. of BASE[2] with *ss* of BASSO] **—bass′ly,** *adv.* **—bass′ness,** *n.* **—bass′y,** *adj.*

bass[2] (bas), *n., pl.* (*esp. collectively*) **bass,** (*esp. referring to two or more kinds or species*) **bass·es. 1.** any of numerous edible, spiny-finned, fresh-water or marine fishes of the families *Serranidae* and *Centrarchidae.* **2.** (originally) the European perch, *Perca fluviatilis.* [assimilated var. of OE *bærs;* c. D *baars,* G *Barsch*]

Largemouth bass, *Micropterus salmoides* (Length to 2½ ft.)

bass[3] (bas), *n.* **1.** the basswood or linden. **2.** *Bot.* bast. [var. of BAST]

Bas·sa·no (bə sä′nō; *It.* bäs sä′nô), *n.* **1. Ja·co·po** (yä′kô pô), (*Giacomo da Ponte*), 1510–92, Italian painter. **2.** (his sons) **Fran·ces·co** (fRän ches′kô), 1549–92; **Giam·bat·tis·ta da Pon·te** (jäm′bät tēs′tä dä pôn′te), 1533–?; **Gi·ro·la·mo da Ponte** (jē Rô′lä mô), 1566–1621; **Le·an·dro** (le än′dRô), 1557–1623, Italian painters.

bas·sa·risk (bas′ə risk′), *n.* an animal of the genus *Bassariscus,* esp. the cacomistle. [< NL *Bassarisc(us)* name of genus < Gk *bassár(a)* fox + NL *-iscus* dim. suffix]

bass-bar (bās′bär′), *n.* a strip of wood glued lengthwise inside the belly of instruments of the violin family, used to spread the vibrations over the surface.

bass′ clef′ (bās), *Music.* the symbol placed on the fourth line of a staff to indicate that the fourth line of the staff corresponds to the F next below middle C; F clef. See illus. under **clef.**

bass′ drum′ (bās), a large drum having a cylindrical body and two membrane heads.

basse danse (bäs′ däNs′), *pl.* **basses danses** (bäs′ däNs′). *French.* a ceremonial, Burgundian court dance of the late 15th and early 16th centuries. [lit., low dance]

Basses-Alpes (bäs zALp′), *n.* a department in SE France. 91,843 (1962); 2698 sq. mi. *Cap.:* Digne.

Basses-Py·ré·nées (bäs pē RĀ nā′), *n.* a department in SW France. 466,038 (1962); 2978 sq. mi. *Cap.:* Pau.

bas·set[1] (bas′it), *n.* one of a breed of hounds having short legs, long body and ears, and usually a black, tan, and white coat. Also called **bas′set hound′.** [< F n. use of *basset, -ette* (adj.), of low stature (*bass-* low (see BASE[2]) + *-et* somewhat; see -ET)]

Basset (14 in. high at shoulder)

bas·set[2] (bas′it), *n., v.,* **-set·ed, -set·ing.** *Geol., Mining.* **—*n.*** **1.** an outcrop, as of the edges of strata. **—*v.i.*** **2.** to crop out: *strata of limestone which basset along the riverbank.* [appar. < obs. F *basset* low stool n. use of *basset* (adj.). See BASSET[1]]

bas·set[3] (bas′it), *n.* an 18th-century card game similar to faro. [< F *bassette* < It *bassetta* n. use of fem. of *bassetto, -etta* (adj.) somewhat low. See BASSET[1]]

basse-taille (bäs tī′yᵊ), *adj.* of or pertaining to an enamel piece or enameling technique in which transparent enamels are fused over a background carved in low relief. [< F, equiv. to *basse* low (see BASE[1]) + *taille* cutting (see TAIL[2])]

Basse·terre (bäs târ′), *n.* a seaport in and the capital of St. Kitts island, in the West Indies. 15,742 (1960).

Basse-Terre (bäs târ′; *Fr.* bAs teR′), *n.* a seaport in and the capital of Guadeloupe, in the French West Indies. 15,000 (est. 1960).

bas′set horn′, an alto horn with a soft tone. [< G *Bassetthorn* < It *corno di bassetto* horn of a somewhat low range. See CORN[2], BASSET[1]]

bas′set ta′ble, a card table of the early 18th century in England.

Bas·setts (bas′its), *n.* a town in Virginia. 3148 (1960).

bass′ fid′dle (bās). See **double bass.**

bass′ horn′ (bās), **1.** tuba. **2.** an obsolete wind instrument related to the tuba.

bas·si·net (bas′ə net′, bas′ə net′), *n.* **1.** a basket with a hood over one end, for use as a baby's cradle. **2.** a style of perambulator resembling this. **3.** *Armor.* basinet. [< F: pan; see BASIN, -ET]

bass·ist (bā′sist), *n.* **1.** a singer with a bass voice. **2.** a player of a bass instrument, esp. of the bass viol. [BASS[1] + -IST]

bas·so (bas′ō, bä′sō; *It.* bäs′sô), *n., pl.* **-sos,** *It.* **-si** (-sē). *Music.* one who sings bass; a bass. [< It < LL *bassus.* See BASE[2]]

Bas·so (bas′ō), *n.* **Hamilton,** 1904–64, U.S. journalist and novelist.

bas·so can·tan·te (bas′ō kən tän′tē, bä′sō; *It.* bäs′sô kän tän′te), *pl.* **bas·si can·tan·ti** (bas′ē kən tän′tē, bä′sē; *It.* bäs′sē kän tän′tē). *Music.* a bass voice with an upper range that is more developed than that of the basso profundo. [< It: lit., singing bass]

bas′so contin′uo, *Music.* continuo.

bas·soon (ba sōōn′, bə-), *n.* a large woodwind instrument of low range, with a doubled tube and a curved metal crook to which a double reed is attached. [< F *basson* < It *basson(e)* (*bass(o)* low (see BASE[2]) + *-one* aug. suffix)] **—bas·soon′ist,** *n.*

Bassoon

bas·so pro·fun·do (bas′ō prō fun′dō, bä′sō; *It.* bäs′sô pRô fōōn′dô), *pl.* **bas·si pro·fun·di** (bas′ē prō fun′dē, bä′sē; *It.* bäs′sē pRô fōōn′dē). a singer with a bass voice of the lowest range. [< It: lit., deep bass. See BASSO, PROFOUND]

bas·so-re·lie·vo (bas′ō ri lē′vō), *n., pl.* **-vos.** bas-relief.

bas·so-ri·lie·vo (bäs′sô Rē lye′vô), *n., pl.* **bas·si-ri·lie·vi** (bäs′sē Rē lye′vē). *Italian.* bas-relief.

bass′ re′flex (bās), a loudspeaker equipped with a baffle having openings designed to improve the reproduction of low-frequency sounds.

bass′ response′ (bās), the response of a loudspeaker or other amplifying device to low-frequency sounds.

bass′ sax′ophone (bās), a large saxophone of low range, usually supported on a stand while being played.

bass′ staff′ (bās), *Music.* a staff marked with a bass clef.

Bass′ Strait′ (bas), a strait between Australia and Tasmania. 80–150 mi. wide.

bass′ vi′ol (bās), **1.** viola da gamba. **2.** See **double bass.**

bass·wood (bas′wŏŏd′), *n.* **1.** any tree of the genus *Tilia,* esp. *T. americana,* the American linden. **2.** the wood of a linden. [BASS[3] + WOOD[1]]

bast (bast), *n.* **1.** *Bot.* phloem. **2.** Also called **bast′ fi′ber.** any of several strong, ligneous fibers, as flax, hemp, ramie, or jute, obtained from phloem tissue and used in the manufacture of woven goods and cordage. [ME; OE *bæst;* c. D, G, Icel *bast*]

bas·tard (bas′tərd), *n.* **1.** a person born of unmarried parents; an illegitimate child. **2.** something irregular, inferior, spurious, or unusual. **3.** *Slang.* **a.** a vicious, despicable, or thoroughly disliked person: *They're real bastards.* **b.** one suffering from misfortune: *The poor bastard broke his leg.* **4.** See **bastard culverin. —*adj.*** **5.** illegitimate in birth. **6.** spurious; not genuine; false: *The architecture was bastard Gothic.* **7.** of abnormal or irregular shape or size; of unusual make or proportions: *bastard quartz; bastard mahogany.* **8.** having the appearance of; resembling in some degree: *a bastard Michelangelo; bastard emeralds.* **9.** *Print.* (of a character) not of the font in which it is used or found. [ME < OF, equiv. to *bast* bastardy (lit., pack-saddle, i.e., makeshift bed in phrase *fils de bast* son of an irregular bed) + *-ard* -ARD. Cf. BANTLING]

bas′tard am′ber, a color of gelatin commonly used in stage lighting, similar to light amber but having a pinkish cast.

bas′tard box′, a low, evergreen creeping plant, *Polygala Chamaebuxus,* of central Europe, having boxlike leaves and yellowish-white flowers with a red spot.

bas′tard cul′verin, *Mil.* a 16th-century cannon, smaller than a culverin, firing a shot of between five and eight pounds. Also called **bastard.**

bas′tard eigne′ (ān), *Old Eng. Law.* the first-born illegitimate son of parents whose second son was legitimate. Cf. **mulier puisne.** [*eigne* < AF: elder, akin to OF *aine, aisne* (*ainz* before (< L *ante*) + *ne* born; see NEE)]

bas′tard file′, a file for metal of the commercial grade of coarseness between coarse and second-cut.

bas′tard gun′ter, *Naut.* See **jackass gunter.**

bas′tard in′digo, a bushy shrub, *Amorpha fruticosa,* of the U.S., having clusters of dull purplish or bluish flowers.

bas·tard·ise (bas′tər dīz′), *v.t., v.i.,* **-ised, -is·ing.** *Chiefly Brit.* bastardize. **—bas′tard·i·sa′tion,** *n.*

bas·tard·ize (bas′tər dīz′), *v.,* **-ized, iz·ing. —*v.t.*** **1.** to declare or prove (someone) to be a bastard. **2.** to lower in condition or worth; debase: *hybrid works that neither preserve nor bastardize existing art forms.* **—*v.i.*** **3.** to become debased. [BASTARD + -IZE] **—bas′tard·i·za′tion,** *n.*

bas·tard·ly (bas′tərd lē), *adj.* **1.** bastard; baseborn. **2.** worthless; of no value. **3.** spurious; counterfeit: *a bastardly version of a text.* [BASTARD + -LY]

bas′tard mahog′any, a tree, *Eucalyptus botryoides,* of Australia, having furrowed bark. Also called **bangalay.**

bas′tard point′ing, *Masonry.* an imitation of tuck pointing, having a fillet made from the mortar of the joint. Also called **bas′tard tuck′ point′ing.**

bas·tard-saw (bas′tərd sô′), *v.t.,* **-sawed, -sawed** or **-sawn, -saw·ing.** plain-saw. [BASTARD + SAW[1]]

bas′tard speed′well, a hairy, perennial herb, *Veronica spuria,* of Eurasia, having branched clusters of blue flowers.

bas′tard ti′tle. See **half title** (def. 1).

bas′tard tur′tle, ridley.

bas′tard wing′, *Ornith.* alula (def. 1).

bas·tar·dy (bas′tər dē), *n.* **1.** the state or condition of being a bastard; illegitimacy. **2.** the act of begetting a bastard. [late ME < AF *bastardie,* OF. See BASTARD, -Y[3]]

baste[1] (bāst), *v.t.,* **bast·ed, bast·ing.** to sew with long, loose stitches, as in temporarily tacking together pieces of a garment in the early stages of making it. [late ME *bastin* < MF *basti(r)* (to) build, baste < Gmc; cf. OHG *bestan* to mend, patch for *bastian to bring together with bast thread or string (*bast* BAST + *-i-* v. suffix + *-an* inf. suffix)]

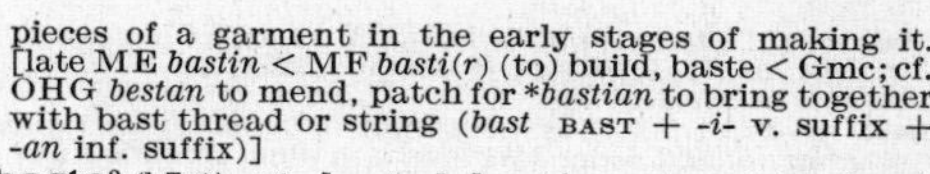

baste[2] (bāst), *v.t.,* **bast·ed, bast·ing.** to moisten (meat or other food) while cooking, with drippings, butter, etc. [?]

baste[3] (bāst), *v.t.,* **bast·ed, bast·ing. 1.** to beat with a stick; thrash; cudgel. **2.** to denounce or scold vigorously: *an editorial basting the candidate for irresponsible statements.* [var. of *baist* < Scand; cf. Icel *beysta* to beat, thrash]

bas′tel house′ (bas′tᵊl, -təl), (on the Anglo-Scottish border) a partly fortified house, usually with a vaulted ground floor. Also, **bastille house, bastle house.** [see BASTILLE]

bast·er[1] (bā′stər), *n. Sewing.* one who or that which bastes. [BASTE[1] + -ER[1]]

bast·er[2] (bā′stər), *n.* **1.** one who bastes meat, chicken, etc. **2.** a large glass, plastic, or metal tube with a rubber bulb at one end and a small opening at the other, to be filled with butter, drippings, etc., for basting meat, chicken, etc., while cooking. [BASTE[2] + -ER[1]]

Bas·ti·a (bä stē′ä), *n.* a seaport on the NE coast of Corsica: the former capital of Corsica. 50,881 (1962).

Ba·sti·an (bäs′tē än′), *n.* **A·dolf** (ä′dôlf), 1826–1905, German anthropologist.

bas·tide (ba stēd′), *n.* **1.** a medieval fortified town, planned as a whole and built at one time, esp. in southern France, for strategic or commercial purposes. **2.** a small country house in southern France. [< MF < Pr *bastida* building n. use of fem. ptp. of *bastir* to build, equiv. to *basti-* (< Gmc; see BASTE[1]) + *-da* < L *-ta* fem. ptp. suffix]

Bas·tien et Bas·tienne (*Fr.* bAs tyaN′ ā bAs tyen′), an opera (1768) by Wolfgang Amadeus Mozart.

bas·tille (ba stēl′; *Fr.* bAs tē′yᵊ), *n., pl.* **bas·tilles** (ba stēlz′; *Fr.* bAs tē′yᵊ). **1.** (*cap.*) a famous fortress in Paris, used as a prison, built in the 14th century and destroyed July 14, 1789. **2.** any prison or jail, esp. one conducted in a tyrannical way. **3.** a fortified tower, as of a castle; a small fortress; citadel. Also, **bas·tile** (ba stēl′). [late ME *bastile* < ML, equiv. to *bast-* build (see BASTE[1]) + L *-ile* n. suffix of place, neut. of *-īlis* -ILE; r. ME *bastel* < OF *bassel*]

Bastille′ Day′, July 14, a national holiday of the French republic, commemorating the fall of the Bastille in 1789.

bastille′ house′. See **bastel house.**

bas·ti·nade (bas′tə nād′), *n., v.t.,* **-nad·ed, -nad·ing.** bastinado.

bas·ti·na·do (bas′tə nā′dō), *n., pl.* **-does,** *v.,* **-doed, -do·ing. —*n.*** **1.** a blow or a beating with a stick, cudgel, etc. **2.** an Oriental mode of punishment, consisting of blows with a stick on the soles of the feet or on the buttocks. **3.** a stick or cudgel. **—*v.t.*** **4.** to beat with a stick, cane, etc., esp. on the soles of the feet or on the buttocks. [earlier *bastanado* < Sp *bastonada* (*bastón* stick + *-ada* -ADE[1])]

bast·ing (bā′sting), *n.* **1.** sewing with long, loose stitches to hold material in place until the final sewing. **2. bastings,** the stitches taken or the threads used. [BASTE[1] + -ING[1]]

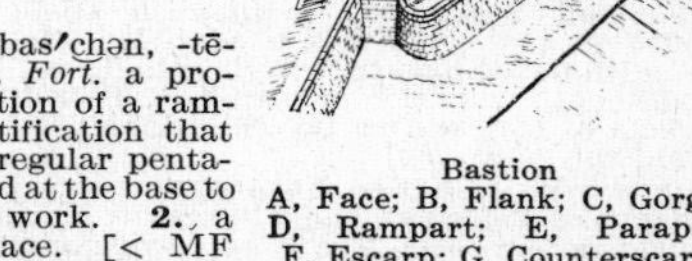

Bastion
A, Face; B, Flank; C, Gorge; D, Rampart; E, Parapet; F, Escarp; G, Counterscarp

bas·tion (bas′chən, -tē ən), *n.* **1.** *Fort.* a projecting portion of a rampart or fortification that forms an irregular pentagon attached at the base to the main work. **2.** a fortified place. [< MF < It *bastion(e),* equiv. to *basti(a)* bastion (see BASTE[1]) + *-one* aug. suffix] **—bas·tion·ar·y** (bas′chə ner′ē), *adj.* **—bas′tioned,** *adj.*

bas·tite (bas′tīt, bä′stīt), *n. Mineral.* See **schiller spar.** [named after *Baste,* a town in Germany; see -ITE[1]]

bas′tle house′ (bas′tᵊl, -təl). See **bastel house.**

Bas·togne (ba stōn′; *Fr.* bA stôn′yᵊ), *n.* a town in SE Belgium: U.S. forces besieged here during German counteroffensive, December, 1944. 6332 (est. 1964).

Bas·trop (bas′trəp), *n.* **1.** a city in N Louisiana. 15,193 (1960). **2.** a town in central Texas. 3001 (1960).

Ba·su·to (bə sōō′tō), *n., pl.* **-tos,** (*esp. collectively*) **-to.** a native or inhabitant of Basutoland.

Ba·su·to·land (bə sōō′tō land′), *n.* former name of **Lesotho.**

bat[1] (bat), *n., v.,* **bat·ted, bat·ting. —*n.*** **1.** *Sports.* **a.** the wooden club used in certain games, as baseball and cricket, to strike the ball. **b.** a racket, esp. one used in badminton or table tennis. **c.** a whip used by a jockey. **d.** act of using a club or racket in a game. **e.** the right or turn to use a club or racket. **2.** a heavy stick, club, or cudgel. **3.** *Informal.* a blow, as with a bat. **4.** any fragment of brick or hardened clay. **5.** *Masonry.* a brick cut transversely so as to leave one end whole. **6.** *Brit. Slang.* speed; rate of motion or progress, esp. the pace of stroke or step of a race. **7.** *Slang.* a spree; binge: *to go on a bat.* **8.** *Ceram.* **a.** a sheet of gelatin or glue used in bat printing. **b.** a slab of moist clay. **c.** a ledge or shelf in a kiln. **d.** a slab of plaster for holding a piece being modeled or for absorbing excess water from slip. **9.** batt. **10. at bat,** *Baseball.* **a.** taking one's turn to bat in a game: *at bat with two men in scoring position.* **b.** an instance at bat officially charged to a batter except when he is hit by a pitch, receives a base on balls, is interfered with by the catcher, or makes a sacrifice hit or sacrifice fly: *two hits in three at bats.* **11. go to bat for,** *Slang.* to intercede for; vouch for; defend: *to go to bat for a friend.* **12. right off the bat,** at once; without delay: *They took us in hand right off the bat.* **—*v.t.*** **13.** to strike or hit with, or as with, a bat or club. **14.** *Baseball.* to have a batting average of; hit: *He batted .325 in spring training.* **—*v.i.*** **15.** *Sports.* **a.** to strike at the ball with the bat. **b.** to take one's turn as a batter. **16.** *Slang.* to rush. **17. bat around,** *Slang.* **a.** to roam; drift. **b.** to ponder; debate: *He batted the idea around in his head.* **18. bat in,** *Baseball.* to cause (a run) to be scored: *He batted in two runs with a double to left.* **19. bat the**

breeze. See **breeze**[1] (def. 5). [ME *batte*, OE *batt*, prob. < Celt; cf. Ir, Gael *bat, bata* staff, cudgel; c. Russ *bat* cudgel. See BATE[2]]

bat[2] (bat), *n.* **1.** any nocturnal or crepuscular flying mammal of the order *Chiroptera*, having modified forelimbs that serve as wings and are covered with a membranous skin extending to the hind limbs. **2. blind as a bat,** nearly blind; having very poor vision: *Anyone can tell that she's blind as a bat, but she won't wear glasses.* **3. have bats in one's belfry,** *Slang.* to have crazy ideas; be very peculiar, erratic, or foolish: *Everyone said the old man had bats in his belfry, but we knew he was just playing it cool.* [appar. < Scand; cf. dial. Sw *natt-batta*, var. of OSw *natt-bakka* night-bat; r. ME *bakke* < Scand; ME *balke* for **blake* < Scand; cf. dial. Sw *natt-blacka*] —**bat′like′,** *adj.*

Bat, *Desmodus rufus* (Length 3½ in.; wingspread 14 in.)

bat[3] (bat), *v.t.*, **bat·ted, bat·ting. 1.** *Informal.* to blink; wink; flutter. **2. not bat an eye,** *Informal.* to show no emotion or surprise; maintain a calm exterior: *She didn't bat an eye when he spilled a drink on her dress.* [var. of BATE[2]]

bat[4] (bät), *n.* **1.** *Anglo-Indian.* the spoken language of India, esp. its slang, idioms, and informal expressions; Hindustani. **2.** *Brit. Slang.* the spoken language of any foreign country, esp. its slang, idioms, and informal expressions. [< Hindi *bāt* speech, word < Skt *vārttā*]

LUZON
SOUTH CHINA SEA
PHILIPPINE SEA
Bataan
Quezon City
CORREGIDOR
MINDORO

bat., 1. battalion. **2.** battery.

Ba·taan (bə tan′, -tän′; *local* bä′tä än′), *n.* a peninsula on W Luzon, in the Philippines: U.S. troops surrendered to Japanese April 9, 1942. Also, **Ba·taán′.**

Ba·tan·gas (bä täng′gäs), *n.* a seaport on SW Luzon, in the N Philippines. 59,582 (1948).

Ba·tan′ Is′lands (bə tän′, bä-), a group of islands in the N Philippines. 13,360 (1960); 76 sq. mi. Also called **Ba·ta·nes** (bä tä′nes).

Bâ·tard-Mon·tra·chet (bä′tär mōn′trä shā′; *Fr.* bä tar′mōn tra she′), *n.* a white wine from Burgundy.

Ba·ta·vi·a (bə tā′vē ə), *n.* **1.** a city in NW New York. 18,210 (1960). **2.** former name of **Djakarta. 3.** a town in NE Illinois. 7496 (1960).

bat′ boy′, *Baseball.* a boy who takes care of the bats and sometimes other equipment of a team.

batch (bach), *n.* **1.** a quantity or number coming at one time or taken together: *a batch of prisoners.* **2.** the quantity of material prepared or required for one operation: *mixing a batch of concrete.* **3.** the quantity of bread, cookies, dough, or the like, made at one baking. **4.** *Glassmaking.* **a.** a quantity of raw materials mixed in proper proportions and prepared for fusion into glass. **b.** the material so mixed. —*v.t., v.i.* **5.** to make by the batch. [late ME *bache*, OE *gebæc*, akin to *bacan* to BAKE; c. G *Gebäck* batch]

bate[1] (bāt), *v.*, **bat·ed, bat·ing.** —*v.t.* **1.** to moderate or restrain: *to bate one's breath; unable to bate our enthusiasm.* **2.** to lessen or diminish; abate: *setbacks that bated his hopes.* —*v.i.* **3.** to diminish or subside; abate. **4. with bated breath,** with breath drawn in or held because of anticipation or suspense: *We watched with bated breath as the runners approached the finish line.* [ME, aph. var. of ABATE]

bate[2] (bāt), *v.*, **bat·ed, bat·ing,** *n.* —*v.t.* **1.** (of a hawk) to flutter its wings and attempt to escape in a fit of anger or fear. —*n.* **2.** a state of violent anger or fear in a hawk. [late ME < MF *(se) bat(re)* << L *battuere* to beat; akin to BATE[1]]

bate[3] (bāt), *v.*, **bat·ed, bat·ing,** *n.* —*v.t., v.i.* **1.** *Tanning.* to soak (leather) after liming in an alkaline solution to soften it and remove the lime. —*n.* **2.** the solution used. [var. of *beat* to pare off turf, OE *bǣt(an)* (to) BAIT; c. Sw *beta* to tan, G *beissen* to macerate]

bat-eared (bat′ērd′), *adj.* (of a dog) having large, erect ears rounded at the top, resembling those of a bat.

ba·teau (ba tō′; *Fr.* ba tō′), *n., pl.* **-teaux** (-tōz′; *Fr.* -tō′). **1.** Also, **batteau.** *Naut.* **a.** a double-ended, flat-bottomed rowboat used on rivers in Canada and the northern United States. **b.** a half-decked, sloop-rigged boat used for fishing on Chesapeake Bay; skipjack. **c.** (in some regions) a scow. **2.** a pontoon of a floating bridge. [< F; OF *batel*, equiv. to *bat* (< OE *bāt* BOAT) + *-el* dim. suffix; cf. ML *batellus* < OF]

Ba·teau I·vre, Le (*Fr.* lə ba tō ē′vrᵊ). See **Le Bateau Ivre.**

bateau′ neck′. See **boat neck.** Also called **bateau′ neck′line.**

ba·te·leur (bat′ᵊlûr′, bat′ᵊlûr′), *n.* a common, African eagle, *Terathopius ecaudatus*, having a very short tail. [< F; OF *basteleur*]

bate′ment light′ (bāt′mənt), a compartment of a window with tracery the bottom of which is formed by the arched head of a compartment or compartments immediately below. [short for ABATEMENT]

Bates (bāts), *n.* **Katherine Lee,** 1859–1929, U.S. educator and author.

Bates·burg (bāts′bûrg), *n.* a town in central South Carolina. 3806 (1960).

Bates·ville (bāts′vil), *n.* **1.** a town in central Arkansas. 6207 (1960). **2.** a town in SE Indiana. 3349 (1960). **3.** a town in NW Mississippi. 3284 (1960).

bat·fish (bat′fish′), *n., pl.* (*esp. collectively*) **-fish,** (*esp. referring to two or more kinds or species*) **-fish·es. 1.** any of the flat-bodied, marine fishes of the family *Ogcocephalidae*, as *Ogcocephalus vespertilio*, common along the southern Atlantic coast of the U.S. **2.** a stingray, *Aetobatis californicus*, found off the coast of California. [BAT[2] + FISH, (n.)]

bat·fowl (bat′foul′), *v.i.* to catch birds at night by dazzling them with a light and then capturing them in a net. [late ME *batfowlyn.* See BAT[2], FOWL (v.)] —**bat′-fowl′er,** *n.*

bath[1] (bath, bäth), *n., pl.* **baths** (bathz, bäthz, baths, bäths), *v.* —*n.* **1.** a washing or immersion of something, esp. the body, in water, steam, etc., as for cleansing, medical treatment, etc.: *I take a bath every day. Give the dog a bath.* **2.** a quantity of water or other agent used for this purpose: *running a bath.* **3.** a container for water or other cleansing liquid, as a bathtub. **4.** a room equipped for bathing; bathroom: *a room and bath.* **5.** a building containing rooms or apartments with equipment for bathing; bathhouse. **6.** Often, **baths.** one of the elaborate bathing establishments of the ancients: *the baths of Caracalla.* **7.** Usually, **baths.** a town or resort visited for medical treatment by bathing or the like; spa. **8.** a preparation, as an acid solution, in which something is immersed. **9.** the container for such a preparation. **10.** a device for controlling the temperature of something by the use of a surrounding medium, as sand, water, oil, etc. **11.** *Metall.* **a.** the depressed hearth of an open-hearth furnace. **b.** the molten metal being made into steel in an open-hearth furnace. **12.** state of being covered by a liquid, as perspiration: *in a bath of sweat.* —*v.t., v.i.* **13.** to wash or soak in a bath. [ME; OE *bæth*; c. G *Bad*, Icel *bath*; akin to G *bähen*, Sw *basa* to warm. See BASK] —**bath′less,** *adj.*

bath[2] (bath), *n.* a Hebrew unit of liquid measure, equal to a quantity varying between 10 and 11 U.S. gallons. [< Heb]

Bath (bath, bäth), *n.* **1.** a city in NE Somerset, in SW England: mineral springs. 80,856 (1961). **2.** a seaport in SW Maine. 10,717 (1960). **3.** a town in S New York. 6166 (1960).

Bath′ brick′, a brick-shaped mass of fine siliceous sand, used for scouring metal.

Bath′ bun′, a round, sweet bun, usually containing raisins, citron, etc.

Bath′ chair′, 1. a wheeled and hooded chair, used esp. by invalids. **2.** any wheelchair. Also, **bath′ chair′.**

bathe (bāth), *v.*, **bathed, bath·ing,** *n.* —*v.t.* **1.** to immerse (all or part of the body) in water or some other liquid, for cleansing, refreshment, etc. **2.** to wet; wash. **3.** to moisten or suffuse with any liquid. **4.** to apply water or other liquid to, with a sponge, cloth, etc.: *to bathe a wound.* **5.** to wash over or against, as by the action of the sea, a river, etc.: *incoming tides bathing the coral reef.* **6.** to cover or surround in the manner of water: *a shaft of sunlight bathing the room; a morning fog bathing the city.* —*v.i.* **7.** to take a bath or sun bath. **8.** to swim for pleasure. **9.** to be covered or surrounded as if with water. —*n.* **10.** *Brit.* act of bathing, esp. in the sea, a lake, or a river; a swimming bath. [ME *bath(i)e(n)*, OE *bathian*, equiv. to *bæth* BATH[1] + *-ian* inf. suffix] —**bath′er,** *n.*

bath·house (bath′hous′, bäth′-), *n., pl.* **-hous·es** (-hou′ziz). **1.** a structure, as at the seaside, containing dressing rooms for bathers. **2.** a building for bathing, sometimes equipped with swimming pools, medical baths, etc. [BATH[1] + HOUSE]

Ba·thil·da (bə thil′də), *n.* a girl's given name. Also, **Batilda.**

Bath·i·nette (bath′ə net′, bä′thə-), *n.* *Trademark.* a folding bathtub for babies, usually of rubberized cloth.

bath′ing beau′ty, a girl or woman in a bathing suit, as an entrant in a beauty contest, an attraction at a pageant, or the like.

bath′ing cap′, a tight-fitting elastic cap, usually of rubber, worn to keep the hair dry while swimming and bathing.

bath·ing-ma·chine (bā′thing mə shēn′), *n.* *Archaic.* a small bathhouse on wheels used as a dressing room in which bathers, esp. women, were also transported from the beach to the water.

bath′ing suit′, a garment worn for swimming. Also called **swimsuit.**

bath′ mat′, a mat or washable rug used to stand on when entering or leaving a bath.

bath mitz·vah (bäs mits′və; *Heb.* bät′ mēts vä′), (*often caps.*) *Judaism.* **1.** a solemn ceremony chiefly among Reform and Conservative Jews that is held in the synagogue, usually on Friday night, to admit formally as an adult member of the Jewish community a girl 12 to 13 years old. **2.** the girl participating in this ceremony. Also, **bas mitzvah.** [< Heb: daughter of the law]

batho-, a learned borrowing from Greek meaning "depth," used in the formation of compound words: *bathometer.* Also, **bathy-.** [comb. form of Gk *báthos*; *bathy-*, s. of *bathýs* deep]

bath·o·lith (bath′ə lith), *n.* *Geol.* a large body of igneous rock, bounded by irregular, cross-cutting surfaces or fault planes, and believed to have crystallized at a considerable depth below the earth's surface. Also, **bath·o·lite** (bath′ə līt′). [BATHO- + -LITH] —**bath′o·lith′ic, bath·o·lit·ic** (bath′ə lit′ik), *adj.*

ba·thom·e·ter (bə thom′i tər), *n.* *Oceanog.* a device for ascertaining the depth of water. [BATHO- + -METER]

ba·thos (bā′thos), *n.* **1.** a ludicrous descent from the exalted or lofty to the commonplace; anticlimax. **2.** triteness or triviality in style. **3.** insincere pathos; sentimentality; mawkishness. [< Gk: depth] —**ba·thet·ic** (bə thet′ik), *adj.*
—**Syn. 2.** insipidity, inanity.

bath·robe (bath′rōb′, bäth′-), *n.* a long, loose, coatlike garment, often tied with a belt of the same material, worn before and after a bath, over sleepwear, or as leisure wear at home. [BATH[1] + ROBE]

bath·room (bath′ro͞om′, -ro͝om′, bäth′-), *n.* **1.** a room equipped for taking a bath. **2.** toilet (def. 2). [BATH[1] + ROOM]

bath′room tis′sue. See **toilet paper.**

bath′ salts′, a preparation used to soften or give a pleasant scent to a bath, as colored, sweet-smelling flakes, crystals, etc.

Bath·she·ba (bath shē′bə, bath′shə-), *n.* **1.** Also, *Douay Bible,* **Bethsabee.** the wife of Uriah and afterward of David: mother of Solomon. II Sam. 11, 12. **2.** a girl's given name.

Bath′ stone′, a cream-colored limestone quarried near Bath, England, for use in building.

bath′ tow′el, a large towel used to dry the body after bathing, usually made of heavy, absorbent material.

bath·tub (bath′tub′, bäth′-), *n.* a tub to bathe in, esp. one forming a permanent fixture in a bathroom. [BATH[1] + TUB]

bath′tub gin′, homemade gin, esp. gin made illegally during Prohibition.

Bath·urst (bath′ərst), *n.* **1.** a port in and the capital of The Gambia. 21,022 (est. 1957). **2.** a town in E New South Wales, in SE Australia. 16,090 (1954).

bathy-, var. of **batho-:** *bathysphere.*

bath·y·al (bath′ē əl), *adj.* of or pertaining to the deeper parts of an ocean, esp. that part between 100 and 1000 fathoms. [BATHY- + -AL[1]]

bath·y·met·ric (bath′ə me′trik), *adj.* **1.** of or pertaining to the measurement of the depths of oceans, seas, or other large bodies of water. **2.** of or pertaining to the contour of the bed of an ocean, sea, or other large body of water. [BATHYMETR(Y) + -IC] —**bath′y·met′ri·cal·ly,** *adv.*

ba·thym·e·try (bə thim′i trē), *n.* **1.** the measurement of the depths of oceans, seas, or other large bodies of water. **2.** the data derived from such measurement. [BATHY- + -METRY] —**ba·thym′e·ter,** *n.*

bath·y·pe·lag·ic (bath′i pə laj′ik), *adj.* pertaining to or living in the bathyal region of an ocean. [BATHY- + PELAGIC]

bath·y·scaphe (bath′i skāf′, -skaf′), *n.* *Oceanog.* a submersible, spherical chamber for exploring the depths of the ocean, having a separate, overhead chamber filled with gasoline for buoyancy and iron or steel weights for ballast. Also, **bath·y·scaph** (bath′i skaf′), **bath·y·scape** (bath′i skāp′). [BATHY- + Gk *skáphē* light boat, skiff]

bath·y·sphere (bath′i sfēr′), *n.* *Oceanog.* a spherical diving apparatus from which to study deep-sea life. [BATHY- + -SPHERE]

bath·y·ther·mo·gram (bath′i thûr′mə gram′), *n.* a record made by a bathythermograph. [BATHY- + THERMO- + -GRAM[1]]

bath·y·ther·mo·graph (bath′i thûr′mə graf′, -gräf′), *n.* an instrument for recording the temperature at various depths in the ocean. [BATHY- + THERMO-GRAPH]

Ba·ti·a (bə tī′ə), *n.* *Class. Myth.* **1.** a nymph. **2.** the mother, by Dardanus, of Erichthonius.

ba·tik (bə tēk′, bat′ik), *n.* **1.** a technique of hand-dyeing fabrics by using wax as a dye repellent to cover parts of a design, dyeing the uncovered fabric with a color or colors, and dissolving the wax in boiling water. **2.** the fabric so decorated. Also, **battik.** [< Javanese: painted]

Ba·til·da (bə til′də), *n.* a girl's given name. Also, **Bathilda.**

bat·ing (bā′ting), *prep.* *Archaic.* with the exception of; excluding. [aph. var. of *abating.* See ABATE]

Ba·tis·ta (bä tēs′tä), *n.* **Ful·gen·cio** (fo͞ol hen′syô), (*Fulgencio Batista y Zaldívar*), born 1901, Cuban military leader: dictator of Cuba 1934–40; president 1940–44, 1952–59.

ba·tiste (bə tēst′, ba-), *n.* a fine, often sheer fabric, constructed in either a plain or figured weave and made of any of various natural or synthetic fibers. [< F; MF *(toile de) ba(p)tiste*, after *Baptiste* of Cambrai, said to have been first maker]

Bat·lle y Or·dó·ñez (bät′ye ē ôr thô′nyes), **Jo·sé** (hô se′), 1856–1929, Uruguayan statesman: president of Uruguay 1903–07, 1911–15.

bat·man (bat′mən), *n., pl.* **-men.** (in the British army) a soldier assigned to an officer as a servant. [short for *bat-horse man*, equiv. to *bat* < F *bât* packsaddle (see BASTARD) + HORSE + MAN[1]]

Bat·na (bat′nə, -na), *n.* a city in NE Algeria. 14,732 (1954).

ba·ton (ba ton′, bə-, bat′ᵊn), *n.* **1.** a staff, club, or truncheon, esp. one serving as a mark of office or authority. **2.** *Music.* the wand used by a conductor. **3.** *Track.* a hollow cylinder of wood, paper, or plastic that is passed in a prescribed area from one member of a relay team to the member next to compete. **4.** *Heraldry.* **a.** a diminutive of the bend sinister, couped at the extremities: used in England as a mark of bastardy. **b.** a similar diminutive of the ordinary bend. [< F *bâton*, OF *baston* < VL **baston-* (s. of **bastō*) stick, club < ?]

Ba·ton (bāt′ᵊn, bā′ton), *n.* *Class. Myth.* the charioteer of Amphiaraus.

Bat·on Rouge (bat′ᵊn ro͞ozh′), the capital of Louisiana, in the SE part: a river port on the Mississippi. 152,419 (1960).

bat′ print′ing, ornamenting of ceramics by means of an adhesive substance, as linseed oil, transferred onto the ceramic surface from a sheet of glue or gelatin, dusted with color, and fired.

ba·tra·chi·an (bə trā′kē ən), *adj.* **1.** belonging or pertaining to the *Batrachia*, a former group comprising the amphibians, and sometimes restricted to the salientians. —*n.* **2.** an amphibian, esp. a salientian. [< NL *Batrach(ia)* (Gk *bátrach(os)* frog + -IAN)]

bat′ ray′, batfish (def. 2). Also called **bat′ sting′-ray.**

bats (bats), *adj.* *Slang.* insane; crazy: *He's gone bats.* [alter. of BATTY]

bats·man (bats′mən), *n., pl.* **-men.** a batter, esp. in cricket. [BAT[1] + 'S[1] + MAN[1]] —**bats′man·ship′,** *n.*

bats·wing (bats′wing′), *n.* a gaslight burner having a long, narrow slit. [BAT[2] + 'S[1] + WING]

batt (bat), *n.* a sheet of matted cotton or wool. Also, **bat.** [special use of BAT[1]]

batt., 1. battalion. **2.** battery.

bat·ta (bat′ə), *n.* *Anglo-Indian.* **1.** a special allowance for subsistence or travel. **2.** (formerly) additional pay granted to British military personnel serving in India. [< Hindi < Skt *bhakta* (something) distributed, allotted, or assigned]

bat·tail·ous (bat′ᵊləs), *adj.* *Archaic.* ready for battle; warlike. [late ME *batailous* < MF *bataillos.* See BATTLE[1], -OUS]

bat·ta·lia (bə tāl′yə, -täl′-), *n.* *Obs.* **1.** order of battle. **2.** an armed or arrayed body of troops. [< It *battaglia* body of troops, BATTLE[1]]

bat·tal·i·on (bə tal′yən), *n.* **1.** *Mil.* a ground force unit composed of a headquarters and two or more companies or similar units. **2.** an army in battle array. **3.** Often, **battalions.** a large number of persons or things; force: *battalions of bureaucrats.* [< F *bataillon* < It *battaglione* large squadron of soldiers, equiv. to *battagli(a)* BATTAGLIA + *-one* aug. suffix]

bat·teau (ba tō′; *Fr.* bA tō′), *n., pl.* **-teaux** (-tōz′; *Fr.* -tō′). bateau (def. 1).

bat·tel (bat′ᵊl), *n., v.,* **-teled, -tel·ing.** *Brit.* —*n.* **1.** an account with or terminal bill from a college of Oxford University for board, kitchen, and buttery expenses. **2. battels,** expenses, bills, and accounts of a student at Oxford, including those for clothing, books, and personal expenses as well as for tuition, lodging, and food. —*v.i.* **3.** to have an account with or to be supplied with food and drink from a college kitchen or buttery at Oxford University. [earlier *battle,* var. of BATTEN[1] (with *-le* for *-en*)] —**bat′tel·er,** *n.*

batte·ment (bat′mənt; *Fr.* batᵊ mäN′), *n., pl.* **-ments** (-mənts; *Fr.* -mäN′). *Ballet.* a movement in which the dancer lifts one leg to the front, side, or back, and returns it to the supporting leg. [< F, equiv. to *batt(re)* (to) beat (see BATE[2]) + *-ment* -MENT]

bat·ten[1] (bat′ᵊn), *v.i.* **1.** to thrive by feeding; grow fat. **2.** to feed gluttonously, as on a particular thing; glut oneself. **3.** to thrive, prosper, or live in luxury, esp. at the expense of others: *robber barons who battened on the poor.* —*v.t.* **4.** to cause to thrive by or as by feeding; fatten. [< Scand; cf. Icel *batna* to improve, c. Goth *(ga)batnan* (*bati* change for the better + *-na* inf. suffix). Cf. OE *bet,* c. Goth *batis,* OHG *baz* better]

bat·ten[2] (bat′ᵊn), *n.* **1.** a small board or strip of wood used for various building purposes, as to cover joints between boards, reinforce certain doors, or supply a foundation for lathing. **2.** a transverse iron or steel strip supporting the flooring strips of a metal fire escape. **3.** *Naut.* **a.** a thin strip of wood inserted in a sail to keep it flat. **b.** a thin, flat length of wood or metal used for various purposes, as to hold the tarpaulin covering a hatch in place. **4.** *Shipbuilding.* a flexible strip of wood used for fairing the lines of a hull on the floor of a mold loft. **5.** *Theat.* **a.** Also called **pipe batten.** a length of metal pipe hung from the gridiron, for suspending scenery or equipment, as drops, flats, or lighting units. **b.** a narrow strip of lumber for constructing, reinforcing, or joining flats. **c.** a similar strip attached to a drop to keep it flat or taut. —*v.t.* **6.** to furnish or bolster with battens. **7.** *Naut.* to cover (a hatch) so as to make it watertight, using several tarpaulins held in place around the coamings with battens and wedges (usually fol. by *down*). **8.** *Mach.* to secure (work) to a table or bed for a machining operation. **9.** *Building Trades.* to join or assemble (a steel column or the like) with batten plates. **10.** *Theat.* **a.** to suspend (scenery, stage lights, etc.) from a batten. **b.** to fasten a batten to (a flat or drop). [var. of BATON] —**bat′ten·er,** *n.*

bat·ten[3] (bat′ᵊn), *n., v.t.* *Textiles.* —*n.* **1.** (in a loom) the swinging frame for holding and positioning the reed. **2.** a part of the lay of a loom. —*v.t.* **3.** to beat (filling yarn) into place with the batten. [alter. of F *battant* hitting, beating. See BATE[2], -ANT]

bat′ten plate′, an iron or steel plate uniting the angles or flanges of a composite girder, column, or strut.

bat·ter[1] (bat′ər), *v.t.* **1.** to beat persistently or hard; pound repeatedly. **2.** to damage by beating or hard usage: *Rough roads had battered the car. High winds were battering the coast.* —*v.i.* **3.** to deal heavy, repeated blows; pound steadily: *continuing to batter at the front door.* —*n.* *Print.* **4.** a damaged area on the face of type or a plate. **5.** the resulting defect in print. [ME *bater(en).* See BAT[1], -ER[6]]
—**Syn. 1.** belabor, smite, pelt. **2.** bruise, wound; smash, shatter, shiver, destroy, ruin.

bat·ter[2] (bat′ər), *n.* a mixture of flour, milk or water, eggs, etc., beaten together for use in cookery. [late ME *bater,* ME *bater(en)* (to) BATTER[1]]

bat·ter[3] (bat′ər), *n.* one who swings a bat or whose turn it is to bat, as in baseball or cricket. [BAT[1] + -ER[1]]

bat·ter[4] (bat′ər), *Archit.* —*v.i.* **1.** (of the face of a wall or the like) to slope backward and upward. —*n.* **2.** a backward and upward slope of the face of a wall or the like. [?]

bat′ter board′, (at a building site) one of a number of boards set horizontally to support strings for outlining the foundation plan of a building.

bat′ter brace′, *Building Trades.* a diagonal brace reinforcing one end of a truss. Also called **bat′ter post′.**

bat′ter bread′. See **spoon bread.**

bat·te·rie (bat′ə rē; *Fr.* batᵊ Rē′), *n., pl.* **bat·te·ries** (bat′ə rēz; *Fr.* batᵊ Rē′). *Ballet.* a beating together of the calves or feet during a leap. [< F; see BATTERY]

bat′tering ram′, an ancient military device with a heavy horizontal ram for battering walls, etc.

bat′ter pile′, *Building Trades.* a pile driven at an angle to the perpendicular.

Bat·ter·sea (bat′ər sē), *n.* **1.** a borough of London, in the SW part, on the Thames. 105,758 (1961). **2.** an enameling technique in which designs are either painted or printed on a white ground fused onto a metal base.

bat′ter stick′, a tapered board held plumb to test the batter of a wall or the like.

bat·ter·y (bat′ə rē), *n., pl.* **-ter·ies.** **1.** *Elect.* **a.** a combination of two or more galvanic cells electrically connected to work together to produce electric energy. **b.** See **galvanic cell.** **2.** a group or series of similar articles, machines, parts, etc. **3.** any large group or series of related things: *a battery of questions.* **4.** *Psychol.* a series of tests yielding a single total score, used for measuring aptitude, intelligence, personality, etc. **5.** *Mil.* **a.** a parapet or fortification equipped with artillery. **b.** two or more pieces of artillery used for combined action. **c.** a tactical unit of artillery, usually consisting of six guns together with the artillerymen, equipment, etc., required to operate them. **6.** *Navy.* **a.** (on a warship) a group of guns having the same caliber or used for the same purpose. **b.** the whole armament of a warship. **7.** *Baseball.* the pitcher and catcher considered as a unit. **8.** act of beating or battering. **9.** *Law.* an unlawful attack upon another person by beating, wounding, or even by touching in an offensive manner. **10.** an instrument used in battering. **11.** *Music.* the instruments comprising the percussion section of an orchestra. [< MF *batterie,* equiv. to *batt(re)* (to) beat (see BATE[2]) + *-erie* -ERY]

Bat·ter·y (bat′ə rē), *n.* **The,** a park at the S end of Manhattan, in New York City. Also called **Bat′tery Park′.**

bat′tery elim′inator, eliminator (def. 2).

bat′tery jar′, a rather large cylindrical container of heavy glass with an open top, used in laboratories.

Bat·ti·ca·lo·a (but′ə kə lō′ə), *n.* a seaport in E Ceylon. 17,439 (1953).

bat·tik (bat′ik), *n.* batik.

bat·ting (bat′ing), *n.* **1.** act or manner of using a bat in a game of ball. **2.** cotton or wool in batts or sheets, used as filling for quilts or bedcovers. [BAT[1] + -ING[1]]

bat′ting av′erage, 1. *Baseball.* a measure of the batting ability of a player, obtained by dividing the number of base hits by the number of official times at bat and carrying out the result to three decimal places. A player with 100 base hits in 300 times at bat has a batting average of .333. **2.** *Informal.* degree of achievement or accomplishment in any activity.

bat′ting eye′, *Baseball.* the batter's visual appraisal of balls pitched toward home plate.

bat·tle[1] (bat′ᵊl), *n., v.,* **-tled, -tling.** —*n.* **1.** a hostile encounter or engagement between opposing military forces. **2.** participation in such hostile encounters or engagements: *wounds received in battle.* **3.** a fight between two persons or animals: *ordering a trial by battle to settle the dispute.* **4.** *Archaic.* a battalion. **5. give** or **do battle,** to enter into conflict with; fight: *He was ready to do battle for his beliefs.* —*v.i.* **6.** to engage in battle: *ready to battle with the enemy.* **7.** to struggle; strive: *to battle for freedom.* —*v.t.* **8.** to fight (a person, army, cause, etc.). **9.** to force or accomplish by fighting, struggling, etc.: *He battled his way to the top of his profession.* [ME *bataile* < OF < LL *battālia* for L *battuālia* (neut. pl.) gladiatorial exercises, equiv. to *battu(ere)* (to) strike (see BATE[2]) + *-ālia* -AL[2]] —**bat′tler,** *n.*
—**Syn. 1.** contest, conflict, war. BATTLE, ACTION, SKIRMISH mean a conflict between organized armed forces. A BATTLE is a prolonged and general conflict pursued to a definite decision: *the Battle of the Bulge in World War II.* An ACTION is part of a spirited military operation, offensive or defensive: *The army was involved in a number of brilliant actions during the battle.* A SKIRMISH is a slight engagement, often preparatory to larger movements: *several minor skirmishes.* **2.** warfare, combat, fighting. **6.** conflict. **8.** contest.

bat·tle[2] (bat′ᵊl), *v.t.,* **-tled, -tling.** *Archaic.* to furnish (a building or wall) with battlements; crenelate. [ME *bataile(n)* < MF *bataill(er)* (to) provide with *batailles.* See BATTLEMENT]

bat·tle-ax (bat′ᵊl aks′), *n.* **1.** an ax for use as a weapon of war. **2.** *Slang.* a domineering, sharp-tempered woman, esp. a wife. Also, **bat′tle-axe′.**

Bat′tle-Ax cul′ture, a Neolithic culture of northern Europe marked esp. by the production of pottery bearing the imprint of cord and by the use of battle-axes as burial accouterments. Also called **Corded culture.**

bat′tle clasp′, clasp (def. 3).

Bat′tle Creek′, a city in S Michigan. 44,169 (1960).

bat′tle cruis′er, a warship of maximum speed and firepower, but with lighter armor than a battleship.

bat′tle cry′, 1. a cry or shout of troops in battle. **2.** the phrase or slogan used in any contest or campaign.

bat·tled (bat′ᵊld), *adj.* *Heraldry.* embattled. [ME *batailed.* See BATTLE[2], -ED[2]]

bat′tled embat′tled, *Heraldry.* **1.** noting a partition line made in a series of crenelations formed by a number of small steps; embattled grady. **2.** (of an ordinary) having an edge or edges so formed; embattled grady.

bat·tle·dore (bat′ᵊl dōr′, -dôr′), *n., v.,* **-dored, -dor·ing.** —*n.* **1.** Also called **bat′tledore and shut′tlecock.** a game from which badminton was developed, played since ancient times in India and other Asian countries. **2.** a light racket for striking the shuttlecock in this game. **3.** a 17th- and 18th-century hornbook of wood or cardboard, used as a child's primer. —*v.t., v.i.* **4.** to toss or fly back and forth: *to battledore the plan among one's colleagues; to battledore between opinions.* [late ME *batyldo(u)re* washing beetle, equiv. to *batyl* to beat (clothes) in washing (freq. of *bat*[1]) + *-dore* dung beetle (BEETLE[1] for BEETLE[2] by way of pun, with allusion to filth on clothes). See DOR[1]]

bat′tle fatigue′, *Psychiatry.* a type of psychoneurosis occurring among soldiers engaged in active warfare, and often making continued service in danger zones impossible. Also called **combat fatigue.** Cf. **shell shock.**

bat·tle·field (bat′ᵊl fēld′), *n.* the field or ground on which a battle is fought. Also called **bat·tle·ground** (bat′ᵊl ground′). [BATTLE[1] + FIELD]

bat·tle·front (bat′ᵊl frunt′), *n.* the extreme forward area of a battlefield, facing the enemy. [BATTLE[1] + FRONT]

bat′tle group′, *U.S. Mil.* a planning or command unit within a division of the army.

bat′tle jack′et, *U.S. Mil.* a waist-length woolen jacket with snugly fitting cuffs and waist, formerly worn as part of the service uniform. Also called **combat jacket.**

bat′tle lan′tern, a portable, battery-operated light for emergency use aboard a warship.

bat′tle line′, the line along which warring troops meet.

bat·tle·ment (bat′ᵊl mənt), *n.* Often, **battlements.** a parapet or cresting, originally defensive but later usually decorative, consisting of a regular alternation of merlons and crenels; crenelation. Also called **embattlement.** [ME *batelment* < MF *bataille* battlement; see -MENT] —**bat·tle·ment·ed** (bat′ᵊl men′tid), *adj.*

Battlement
A, Merlon; B, Crenel; C, Loophole; D, Machicolation

Bat′tle of Brit′ain, (in World War II) the series of aerial combats that took place between British and German aircraft during the autumn of 1940 and that included the severe bombardment of British cities.

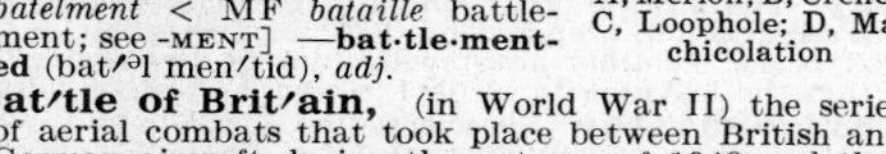

Bat′tle of San′ Ro·ma′no, The (sän rō mä′nō; *It.* Rō mä′nō), a painting (1455?) by Paolo Uccello.

Bat′tle of the Books′, The, a prose satire (1704) by Swift.

bat·tle·plane (bat′ᵊl plān′), *n.* *Obs.* an airplane designed for combat; warplane. [BATTLE[1] + PLANE[1]]

bat′tle roy′al, 1. a fight in which more than two combatants are engaged. **2.** a heated argument: *After a while the discussion turned into a battle royal.*

bat·tle-scarred (bat′ᵊl skärd′), *adj.* **1.** bearing scars or damages received in battle: *a battle-scarred warship.* **2.** showing the effects of hard wear or use: *a sale of battle-scarred desks.*

bat·tle·ship (bat′ᵊl ship′), *n.* **1.** any of a class of warships that are the most heavily armored and are equipped with the most powerful armament. **2.** See **ship of the line.** [BATTLE[1] + SHIP]

bat·tle·some (bat′ᵊl səm), *adj.* argumentative; quarrelsome. [BATTLE[1] + -SOME[1]]

bat′tle star′, *U.S. Mil.* **1.** a small bronze star worn on a campaign ribbon by members of organizations taking part in certain battles or other wartime operations. **2.** a small silver star similarly worn, equivalent to five bronze battle stars.

bat′tle sta′tion, *Mil., Navy.* the place or position that one is assigned to for battle.

bat′tle wag′on, *Informal.* a battleship.

bat·tol·o·gise (bə tol′ə jīz′), *v.t., v.i.,* **-gised, -gis·ing.** *Chiefly Brit.* battologize.

bat·tol·o·gize (bə tol′ə jīz′), *v.,* **-gized, -giz·ing.** —*v.t.* **1.** to repeat (a word, phrase, mannerism, etc.) excessively. —*v.i.* **2.** (of writing or speaking) to repeat words, phrases, etc., to an excessive and tiresome degree. [BATTOLOG(Y) + -IZE]

bat·tol·o·gy (bə tol′ə jē), *n.* excessive and wearisome repetition of words in speaking or writing. [< Gk *battología* (*bátt(os)* stammerer + *-logia* -LOGY)] —**bat·tol′o·gist,** *n.* —**bat·to·log·i·cal** (bat′ᵊloj′i kəl), *adj.*

bat·tue (ba to͞o′, -tyo͞o′; *Fr.* bA tY′), *n., pl.* **-tues** (-to͞oz′, -tyo͞oz′; *Fr.* -tY′). *Chiefly Brit.* **1.** *Hunting.* **a.** the beating or driving of game from cover toward a stationary hunter. **b.** a hunt or hunting party using this method of securing game. **2.** undiscriminating slaughter of defenseless or unresisting crowds. [< F n. use of fem. of *battu,* ptp. of *battre* < L *battuere* to beat. See BATTUTA, BATTLE[1]]

Bat·tus (bat′əs), *n.* *Class. Myth.* **1.** a peasant who saw Hermes steal the cattle of Apollo and who, on breaking his promise not to reveal what he had seen, was turned to stone. **2.** a Libyan ruler who was cured of a speech impediment.

bat·tu·ta (bə to͞o′tə; *It.* bät to͞o′tä), *n., pl.* **-tas,** *It.* **-te** (-te). *Music.* **1.** a beat. **2.** a measure. [< It, fem. ptp. of *battere* to beat < L *battuere*]

bat·tu·to (bə to͞o′tō), *n., pl.* **-tos.** *Italian Cookery.* soffritto. [< It; masc. of BATTUTA]

bat·ty (bat′ē), *adj.,* **-ti·er, -ti·est.** *Slang.* insane; crazy; silly. [BAT[2] + -Y[1]]

Ba·tu Khan (bä′to͞o kän′), d. 1255, Mongol conqueror: leader of the Golden Horde (grandson of Ghenghis Khan).

Ba·tum (bä to͞om′), *n.* a seaport in and the capital of Adzharistan, in SW Georgia, in the SE Soviet Union in Europe, on the Black Sea. 82,000 (1959). Also, **Ba·tu·mi** (bä′to͞o mi).

ba·tu·que (bə to͞o′kə), *n.* a Brazilian round dance of African origin. [< Pg, prob. of Afr orig.]

bat·wing (bat′wing′), *adj.* **1.** formed, shaped, etc., in the manner of a bat's wing or wings. **2.** (of a garment or part of a garment) resembling or conceived of as resembling the wing or wings of a bat, as a loose long sleeve (**bat′wing sleeve′**) having a deep armhole and a tight wrist. [BAT[2] + WING]

B.A.U., British Association unit.

bau·ble (bô′bəl), *n.* **1.** a cheap piece of ornament; trinket; gewgaw. **2.** a jester's staff. [< F *beaubel,* lit., pretty-pretty (cf. BAWCOCK); r. ME *babel* < MF, perh. var. of *beaubel*]

Bau·bo (bô′bō), *n.* *Class. Myth.* an elderly nurse in the house of Celeus at Eleusis.

Bau·cis (bô′sis), *n.* *Class. Myth.* an aged Phrygian peasant woman who, with her husband Philemon, offered their hospitality to the disguised Zeus and Hermes and were rewarded.

baud (bôd), *n.* a unit used in telegraphy to measure the speed of signaling, equal to one pulse or code element per second. Also called **bit.** [named after J. M. E. *Baudot* (1845–1903), French inventor]

bau·de·kin (bô′də kin), *n.* baldachin (def. 1). [ME < MF < ML *baldakin(us)* BALDACHIN]

Bau·de·laire (bōd′ᵊlâr′; *Fr.* bōdᵊleR′), *n.* **Charles Pierre** (sharl pyeR), 1821–67, French poet and critic.

Bau·douin I (bō dwaN′), born 1930, king of the Belgians since 1951.

bau·drons (bô′drənz), *n.* (*construed as sing.*) *Chiefly Scot.* a cat. [late ME *balderonis;* ? akin to ME *badde* cat]

Bau·er (bou′ər; *Ger.* bou′əR), *n.* **Ge·org** (gā ôRk′). See **Agricola, Georgius.**

Baugh (bô), *n.* **Samuel Adrian** ("*Slinging Sammy*"), born 1914, U.S. football player.

Bau·haus (bou′hous′), *n.* **1.** a school of design established in Weimar in 1919 by Walter Gropius, moved to Dessau in 1926, and closed in 1933 as a result of Nazi hostility. —*adj.* **2.** of or pertaining to the concepts, ideas, or styles developed at the Bauhaus, characterized chiefly by an emphasis on functional design in architecture and the applied arts. [< G, equiv. to *Bau-* build, building + *Haus* house]

Ba·ul (bä′o͞ol), *n.* a member of a nonconformist Bengalese sect having gurus but no dogmas, rituals, religious institutions, or scriptures.

baulk (bôk), *v.i., v.t., n.* balk.

Baum (bôm, bäm *for 1;* boum *for 2*), *n.* **1. L(y·man) Frank** (lī′mən), 1856–1919, U.S. journalist, playwright, and author of children's books. **2. Vicki,** 1888–1960, U.S. novelist, born in Austria.

Bau·mé (bō mā′, bō′mā), *adj.* pertaining to, noting, or calibrated according to a Baumé scale.

Bau·meis·ter (bou′mī′stər), *n.* **Wil·li** (vil′ē), 1889–1955, German painter.

Baumé′ scale′, a scale for use with a hydrometer, calibrated in such manner that the specific gravity of a given liquid may be easily computed. [named after A. *Baumé* (1728–1804), French chemist]

baum′ mar′ten (boum), **1.** the European pine marten. **2.** the fur of this animal. [< G *Baum(marder)* tree marten + MARTEN]

Bau·ru (bou ro͞o′), *n.* a city in E Brazil. 85,881 (1960).

bau·son (bô′sən), *n. Archaic.* a badger (applied contemptuously to people). [ME *bausen, bauson* < MF *bausen, bauzan,* var. of *baucent, balcent* BAUSOND]

bau·sond (bô′sənd), *adj. Brit. Dial.* **1.** (of animals) having white spots on a black or bay background; piebald. **2.** (of horses and cattle) having a white patch or streak on the forehead or having one white foot. Also, **baws′nt.** [ME *bausand* < MF *bausant, balcent,* etc. < ?]

Bau·tzen (bout′sən), *n.* a city in E East Germany, on the Spree River: scene of defeat of Prussian and Russian armies by Napoleon I, 1813. 42,008 (1955).

baux·ite (bôk′sīt, bō′zīt), *n.* a rock consisting of hydrous aluminum oxide or hydroxides with various impurities: the principal ore of aluminum. [named after (*Les*) *Baux,* near Arles in southern France; see -ITE[1]]

ba·var·dage (bA vAR-dAzh′), *n. French.* babbling; nonsense.

Ba·var·i·a (bə vâr′ē ə), *n.* a state in S West Germany: formerly a kingdom. 9,799,000 (1963); 27,239 sq. mi. *Cap.:* Munich. German, **Bayern.**

Ba·var·i·an (bə vâr′ē ən), *adj.* **1.** of or pertaining to Bavaria, its inhabitants, or their dialect. —*n.* **2.** a native or an inhabitant of Bavaria. **3.** the High German speech of Bavaria and Austria. Cf. **Alemannic** (def. 1). [BAVARI(A) + -AN]

Bavar′ian cream′, a dessert made with custard, gelatin, and whipped cream.

ba·war·chi (bä′wər chē), *n. Anglo-Indian.* a native male cook. [< Pers *bāwarchī*]

baw·bee (bô bē′, bô′bē), *n.* **1.** an old Scottish bullion coin, originally worth about three halfpence of English coin, later sixpence. **2.** a halfpenny. **3.** *Informal.* anything of little value. [named after A. Orok, 16th-century mintmaster, laird of Sille*bawby*]

baw·cock (bô′kok′), *n. Archaic.* (used familiarly) a fine fellow. [< F *beau coc* fine cock]

bawd (bôd), *n.* **1.** a woman who maintains a brothel; madam. **2.** a prostitute. **3.** *Archaic.* a procuress. [ME *bawde* n. use of MF *baude,* fem. of *baud* gay, dissolute < WGmc; cf. OE *bald* BOLD]

baw·dry (bô′drē), *n.* **1.** *Archaic.* lewdness; obscenity; bawdiness. **2.** *Obs.* **a.** the business of a prostitute. **b.** illicit intercourse; fornication. [late ME *bawdery.* See BAWD, -ERY]

bawd·y (bô′dē), *adj.,* **bawd·i·er, bawd·i·est,** *n.* —*adj.* **1.** obscene; indecent; lewd: *one of Oscar's bawdy stories.* —*n.* **2.** obscene talk or writing; bawdry; bawdiness: *a collection of Elizabethan bawdy.* [BAWD + -Y[1]] —**bawd′i·ly,** *adv.* —**bawd′i·ness,** *n.*

bawd·y·house (bô′dē hous′), *n., pl.* **-hous·es** (-hou′ziz). a brothel. [BAWDY + HOUSE]

bawl (bôl), *v.t.* **1.** to utter or proclaim by outcry; shout out: *to bawl one's dissatisfaction; bawling his senseless ditties to the audience.* **2.** to offer for sale by shouting, as a hawker: *a huckster bawling his wares.* —*v.i.* **3.** to cry or wail lustily. **4. bawl out,** *U.S. Informal.* to scold vociferously; reprimand or scold vigorously: *Your father will bawl you out when he sees this mess.* —*n.* **5.** a loud shout; outcry. **6.** a period or spell of loud crying or weeping: *A good bawl usually makes her feel better.* [late ME < ML *baul(āre)* (to) bark < Gmc; cf. Icel *baula* to low, *baula* cow] —**bawl′er,** *n.*

baw·s'nt (bô′sənt), *adj. Brit. Dial.* bausond.

baw·tie (bô′tē), *n. Scot.* **1.** a dog, esp. a large dog. **2.** *Obs.* a hare. [generic use of *Bawtie* dog's name < MF *baud* kind of dog (n. use of *baud* lively; see BAWD) + -IE]

baw·ty (bô′tē), *n., pl.* **-ties.** *Scot.* bawtie.

Bax (baks), *n.* **Sir Arnold Edward Trevor,** 1883–1953, English composer.

B-axis (bē′ak′sis), *n., pl.* **B-ax·es** (bē′ak′sēz). *Crystall.* the horizontal crystallographic axis that is in a right-left position. Cf. **A-axis, C-axis.**

Bax·ley (baks′lē), *n.* a town in central Georgia. 4268 (1960).

Bax·ter (bak′stər), *n.* **1. Richard,** 1615–91, English Puritan preacher, scholar, and writer. **2.** a boy's given name.

Bax′ter Springs′, a town in SE Kansas. 4498 (1960).

bay[1] (bā), *n.* **1.** a body of water forming an indentation of the shoreline, larger than a cove but smaller than a gulf. **2.** a recess of land, partly surrounded by hills. **3.** *U.S.* an arm of a prairie, extending into woods and partly surrounded by them. [late ME *baye* < MF *baie* < LL *baia*]

bay[2] (bā), *n.* **1.** *Archit.* **a.** any of a number of similar major vertical divisions of a large interior, wall, etc.: *The length of the nave is divided into six bays.* **b.** a division of a window between a mullion and an adjoining mullion or jamb. **c.** See **bay window** (def. 1). **2.** *Aeron.* **a.** any portion of an airplane set off by two successive bulkheads or other bracing members. **b.** a compartment in an aircraft: *a bomb bay; an engine bay.* **3.** a compartment, as in a barn for storing hay. **4.** *Naut.* **a.** the deck space between the anchor windlass and the stem of a vessel. **b.** See **sick bay.** [ME < MF *baee* an opening in a wall, n. use of fem. ptp. of *baer* to stand open, gape < LL *batāre* to stand open, gape (lit., open the mouth)]

bay[3] (bā), *n.* **1.** a deep, prolonged howl, as of a hound on the scent. **2.** the position or stand of an animal or fugitive that is forced to turn and resist pursuers because it is no longer possible to flee (usually prec. by *at* or *to*): *a stag at bay; to bring an escaped convict to bay.* **3.** the situation of a person or thing that is forced actively to oppose or to succumb to some adverse condition (usually prec. by *at* or *to*). **4.** the situation of being actively opposed by an animal, person, etc., so as to be powerless to act fully (often prec. by *at*). —*v.i.* **5.** to howl, esp. with a deep, prolonged sound, as a hound on the scent. —*v.t.* **6.** to assail with deep, prolonged howling: *a troubled hound baying the moon.* **7.** to bring to or to hold at bay: *A dog bays its quarry.* [ME, aph. var. of *abay* < OF *abai* barking, deriv. of *abaier* to bark]

bay[4] (bā), *n.* **1.** Also called **sweet bay.** the European laurel, *Laurus nobilis.* **2.** a West Indian tree, *Pimenta acris,* whose leaves are used in making bay rum. **3.** any of various laurellike trees. **4.** *U.S.* any of several magnolias. **5.** an honorary garland or crown bestowed for victory or excellence. **6. bays,** fame; renown. [ME *bai(e),* OE *beg-* (in *begbēam,* lit., berry tree) + MF *baie* < L *bāca, bacca* berry. See BACCHUS]

bay[5] (bā), *n.* **1.** reddish-brown. **2.** a horse or other animal of reddish-brown color. —*adj.* **3.** (of horses or other animals) having a reddish-brown body. [late ME < MF *bai* < L *badius;* cf. OIr *buide* yellow]

ba·ya (bä′yə, bä yä′), *n.* a common weaverbird, *Ploceus philippinus,* of India. [< Hindi *ba(i)yā*]

ba·ya·dere (bī′ə dēr′, -der′), *n.* a fabric with stripes of brilliant colors horizontal or in the filling direction. [< F < Pg *bailadeira,* fem. of *bailador* dancer (*baila(r)* (to) dance (see BALL[2]) + *-dor* < L *-tor,* as in *actor*)]

ba·ya·mo (bə yä′mō), *n., pl.* **-mos.** a tropical thundersquall of extreme force blowing from the inland mountains on the south coast of Cuba. [< Sp, after *Bayamo,* Cuba, where this type of squall is common]

Ba·ya·mo (bä yä′mô), *n.* a city in S Cuba. 20,178 (1953).

Ba·ya·món (bä′yä môn′), *n.* a city in N Puerto Rico, near San Juan. 15,109 (1960).

bay′ ant′ler, the second prong from the base of a stag's antler. See diag. under **antler.** Also called **bes antler, bez antler.** [*bay* for *bes, bez,* ME *bes* secondary (< MF < L *bis* BIS[1])]

Ba·yar (bä yär′), *n.* **Ce·lâl** (je läl′), born 1884, Turkish statesman: president 1950–60.

Ba·yard (bā′ərd; *for 1 also Fr.* bA yAR′), *n.* **1. Pierre Ter·rail** (pyeR te RA′y[ə]), **Sei·gneur de** (se nyœR′ də), ("*the knight without fear and without reproach*"), 1473–1524, heroic French soldier. **2.** any man of heroic courage and unstained honor. **3.** a boy's given name.

Bay·ard (bā′ərd), *n.* **1.** a magical legendary horse in medieval chivalric romances. **2.** a mock-heroic name for any horse. **3.** (*l.c.*) *Archaic.* a bay horse. [ME < MF; see BAY[5], -ARD]

bay·ber·ry (bā′ber′ē, -bə rē), *n., pl.* **-ries. 1.** any of certain shrubs or trees of the genus *Myrica,* as *M. carolinensis,* a shrub common on seacoasts, or *M. cerifera.* **2.** the berry of such a plant. **3.** Also called **bay rum tree, wild clove.** a West Indian tree, *Pimenta acris,* the leaves of which yield bay oil. [BAY[4] + BERRY]

Bay′ Cit′y, 1. a lake port in E Michigan, near the mouth of the Saginaw River. 53,604 (1960). **2.** a town in SE Texas. 11,656 (1960).

Bay·er (bā′ər), *n.* a crater in the third quadrant of the face of the moon: about 30 miles in diameter.

Bay·ern (bī′əRn), *n.* German name of **Bavaria.**

Ba·yeux′ tap′estry (bā yo͞o′, bä-; *Fr.* bA yœ′), a strip of embroidered linen 231 feet long and 20 inches wide, depicting the Norman conquest of England and dating from c1100.

bay′-head bar′ (bā′hed′), a sand bar at the head of a bay.

Bayle (bāl), *n.* **Pierre** (pyeR), 1647–1706, French philosopher and critic.

bay′ leaf′, the dried leaf of the bay tree, *Pimenta acris,* used in cookery and in making bay rum.

Bay·less (bā′lis), *n.* a boy's given name.

Bay·ley (bā′lē), *n.* a boy's given name. Also, **Bailey, Baillie, Baily.**

bay′ lynx′, bobcat.

Bay′ Mi·nette′ (mə net′), a town in SW Alabama. 5197 (1960).

bay′ oil′, a yellow essential oil distilled from the leaves of the bayberry, *Pimenta acris,* used in the manufacture of perfumes and bay rum.

bay·o·net (bā′ə nit, -net′, bā′ə net′), *n., v.,* **-net·ed** or **-net·ted, -net·ing** or **-net·ting.** —*n.* **1.** a daggerlike steel weapon that is attached to or at the muzzle of a gun and used for stabbing or slashing in hand-to-hand combat. **2.** a pin projecting from the side of an object, as the base of a flashbulb, for securing the object in a bayonet socket. —*v.t.* **3.** to kill or wound with a bayonet. [< F *baïonnette,* after BAYONNE in France (where the weapon was first made or used); see -ET]

Bayonet

bay′onet sock′et, a cylindrical socket having one or more L-shaped slots, the longer side parallel and the shorter side perpendicular to the axis of the socket, along which a knoblike projection on the object slides in such a way that a twist of the object when fully inserted locks it into place.

Ba·yonne (bā yōn′ *for 1;* bA yôn′ *for 2*), *n.* **1.** a seaport in NE New Jersey. 74,215 (1960). **2.** a seaport in SW France, near the Bay of Biscay. 32,575 (1954).

bay·ou (bī′o͞o, bī′ō), *n., pl.* **-ous.** *Southern U.S.* an arm or outlet of a lake, river, etc. [< LaF < Choctaw *bayuk* small stream]

Bay′ou Cane′, a town in SE Louisiana. 3173 (1960).

Bay′ou La Ba′tre (lə ba′trē, lä ba′trə), a town in SW Alabama. 2572 (1960).

bay′ pop′lar, the tupelo, *Nyssa aquatica.*

Bay·port (bā′pôrt′, -pōrt′), *n.* a town in E Minnesota. 3205 (1960).

Bay′ Psalm′ Book′, a translation of the Psalms by John Eliot and others: the first book published (1640) in America.

Bay·reuth (bī′roit; *Ger.* bī roit′), *n.* a city in N Bavaria, in SE West Germany: annual music festivals founded by Richard Wagner. 61,700 (1963).

bay′ rum′, a fragrant liquid used chiefly as an after-shaving lotion, prepared by distilling the leaves of the bayberry, *Pimenta acris,* with rum or by mixing oil from the leaves with alcohol, water, and other oils.

bay′ rum′ tree′, bayberry (def. 3).

bay′ salt′, salt derived by evaporating sea water in the sun.

bay·smelt (bā′smelt′), *n., pl.* **-smelts,** (*esp. collectively*) **-smelt.** topsmelt. [BAY[1] + SMELT[2]]

Bay′ State′, Massachusetts (used as a nickname). —**Bay′ Stat′er.**

Bay St. Lou·is (bā′ sānt′ lo͞o′is), a town in SE Mississippi. 5073 (1960).

Bay·town (bā′toun′), *n.* a city in SE Texas, on Galveston Bay. 28,159 (1960).

bay′ tree′, 1. the European laurel, *Laurus nobilis.* **2.** See **California laurel** (def. 1).

Bay·view-Rose·wood (bā′vyo͞o′ rōz′wo͝od′), *n.* a town in NW California. 2980 (1960).

Bay·ville (bā′vil), *n.* a town on NW Long Island, in SE New York. 3962 (1960).

bay′ win′dow, 1. an alcove of a room, projecting from an outside wall and having its own windows, esp. one having its own foundations. Cf. **bow window, oriel. 2.** *Informal.* a large, protruding belly; paunch.

bay·wood (bā′wo͝od′), *n.* a kind of mahogany, found chiefly near the Gulf of Campeche, in Mexico. [BAY[1] + WOOD[1]]

ba·zaar (bə zär′), *n.* **1.** a market place or shopping quarter, esp. one in the Middle East. **2.** a store in which many kinds of goods are offered for sale; department store. **3.** a sale of miscellaneous articles to benefit some charity, cause, organization, etc. Also, **ba·zar′.** [earlier *bazarro* < It << Pers *bāzār* market]

Ba·zaine (bA zen′), *n.* **Fran·çois A·chille** (fRäN swA′ A shēl′), 1811–88, French general and marshal.

Baz·a·tha (baz′ə thə), *n. Douay Bible.* Biztha.

Ba·zin (bA zaN′), *n.* **Re·né Fran·çois Ni·co·las Ma·rie** (Rə nā′ fRäN swA′ nē kô lä′ mA-Rē′), 1853–1932, French novelist.

Baz·i·o·tes (baz′ē ō′tēz), *n.* **William,** born 1912, U.S. painter.

ba·zoo·ka (bə zo͞o′kə), *n. Mil.* a tube-shaped, portable rocket launcher that fires a rocket capable of penetrating several inches of armor plate, as of a tank or other armored military vehicle. [after musical instrument invented and played by Bob Burns in the late 1930's and 1940's, from a resemblance in appearance]

Bazooka

ba·zoo·ka·man (bə zo͞o′kə mən), *n., pl.* **-men.** a soldier armed with a bazooka. [BAZOOKA + MAN[1]]

BB (bē′bē′), *n.* **1.** a size of shot, .18 inch in diameter, fired from an air rifle or BB gun. **2.** Also called **BB shot.** shot of this size.

bb., *Baseball.* base on balls; bases on balls.

B/B, bottled in bond.

B.B., 1. bail bond. **2.** Blue Book. **3.** B'nai B'rith. **4.** Bureau of the Budget.

b.b., bail bond.

B.B.A., Bachelor of Business Administration.

B battery, *Electronics.* an electric battery for supplying a constant, positive voltage to the plate of a vacuum tube. Cf. **A battery, C battery.**

B.B.C., British Broadcasting Corporation.

bbl., *pl.* **bbls.** barrel.

B/C, bills for collection.

B.C., 1. Bachelor of Chemistry. **2.** Bachelor of Commerce. **3.** bass clarinet. **4.** battery commander. **5.** before Christ (used in reckoning dates). **6.** British Columbia.

BCD, 1. *Mil.* bad conduct discharge. **2.** *Computer Technol.* binary-coded decimal.

B.C.E., 1. Bachelor of Christian Education. **2.** Bachelor of Civil Engineering. **3.** before Common Era.

B.Cer.E., Bachelor of Ceramic Engineering.

BCG vaccine, *Immunol.* a vaccine made from weakened strains of tubercle bacilli, used to produce immunity against tuberculosis. [*B(acillus) C(almette)-G(uérin)*]

bch., *pl.* **bchs.** bunch.

B.Ch., Bachelor of Chemistry.

B.Ch.E., Bachelor of Chemical Engineering.

B.C.L., Bachelor of Civil Law.

B.C.M., Bachelor of Church Music.

B complex. See **vitamin B complex.**

B.Com.Sc., Bachelor of Commercial Science.

B.C.P., Bachelor of City Planning.

B.C.S., Bachelor of Chemical Science.

bd., *pl.* **bds. 1.** board. **2.** bond. **3.** bound. **4.** bundle.

B/D, 1. bank draft. **2.** bills discounted. **3.** *Accounting.* brought down.

B.D., 1. Bachelor of Divinity. **2.** bills discounted.

bde, *Mil.* brigade.

bdel·li·um (del′ē əm, -yəm), *n.* **1.** a fragrant gum resin obtained from certain burseraceous plants, as of the genus *Commiphora.* **2.** a plant yielding it. **3.** a substance mentioned in the Bible. Gen. 2:12; Num. 11:7. [< L < Gk *bdéllion,* prob. from a Sem word akin to Heb *bedhōlah,* name of a fragrant yellowish transparent gum]

B.Des., Bachelor of Design.

bd. ft., board foot; board feet.

bdl., *pl.* **bdls.** bundle.

B.D.S., Bachelor of Dental Surgery.

BDSA, Business and Defense Services Administration.

be (bē; *unstressed* bē, bi), *v.* and *auxiliary v., pres. sing. 1st pers.* **am,** *2nd* **are** or (*Archaic*) **art,** *3rd* **is,** *pres. pl.* **are;** *past sing. 1st pers.* **was,** *2nd* **were** or (*Archaic*) **wast** or **wert,** *3rd* **was,** *past pl.* **were;** *pres. subj.* **be;** *past subj. sing. 1st pers.* **were,** *2nd* **were** or (*Archaic*) **wert,** *3rd* **were;** *past subj. pl.* **were;** *past part.* **been;** *pres. part.* **be·ing.** —*v.i.* **1.** to exist or live: *Churchill, alas, is no more.* **2.** to take place; occur: *The wedding was last week.* **3.** to occupy a place or position: *The book is on the table.* **4.** to continue or remain as before: *Let it be.* **5.** to belong; attend; befall: *May good fortune be with you.* **6.** (used as a copula to connect the subject with its predicate adjective, or predicate nominative, in order to describe, identify, or amplify the subject): *Martha is tall. John is president. This is she.* **7.** (used as a copula to introduce or form interrogative or imperative sentences): *Is that right? Be quiet! Don't be facetious.* —*auxiliary verb.* **8.** (used with the present participle of another verb to form the progressive tense): *I am waiting.* **9.** (used with the present participle or infinitive of the principal verb to indicate future action): *She is visiting there next week. He is to see me today.* **10.**

(used with the past participle of another verb to form the passive voice): *The date was fixed. It must be done.* **11.** (used in archaic or poetic constructions with some intransitive verbs to form the perfect tense): *He is come. Agamemnon to the wars is gone.* [ME *been,* OE *bēon* (*bēo*- (akin to G *bin* (I) am, L *fuī* I have been, Skt *bhavati* he becomes, is) + -*n* inf. suffix). See AM, IS, ARE[1], WAS, WERE]

Be, *Chem.* beryllium.

be-, a native English prefix formerly used in the formation of verbs: *become, besiege, bedaub, befriend.* [ME, OE, unstressed form of *bī* BY]

Bé., Baumé.

B/E, bill of exchange. Also, **b.e.**

B.E., **1.** Bachelor of Education. **2.** Bachelor of Engineering. **3.** Bank of England. **4.** bill of exchange. **5.** Board of Education.

Bea (bē), *n.* a girl's given name, form of **Beatrice.** Also, **Bee.**

beach (bēch), *n.* **1.** an expanse of sand or pebbles along a seashore. **2.** the part of the shore of an ocean, sea, large river, lake, etc., washed by the tide or waves. **3.** the area adjacent to a seashore: *We're vacationing at the beach.* **4. on the beach,** *Slang.* **a.** (of unemployed seamen) not serving on a ship. **b.** out of work. —*v.t., v.i.* **5.** *Naut.* to haul or run onto a beach: *We beached the ship to save her.* [?] —**beach′less,** *adj.*
—**Syn. 2.** coast, seashore, strand, littoral, sands. See **shore**[1]. **5.** ground.

Beach (bēch), *n.* **Rex El·ling·wood** (el′ing wo͝od′), 1877–1949, U.S. novelist and short-story writer.

beach′ as′ter, a seaside herb, *Erigeron glaucus,* of the western coast of the U.S., having solitary, violet- or lilac-colored flowers. Also called **seaside daisy.**

beach′ ball′, a large, light, buoyant ball, used esp. for games at the seashore, at swimming pools, etc.

beach′ boat′, **1.** any of various shallow, flat-bottomed rowboats that can be readily hauled onto a beach. **2.** a small coastal fishing boat of Maine, catrigged with a spritsail.

beach·boy (bēch′boi′), *n.* a male attendant or instructor at a beach. [BEACH + BOY]

beach′ bug′gy, *U.S.* an automobile equipped with oversized tires for traveling on sand beaches.

beach·comb·er (bēch′kō′mər), *n.* **1.** a person who lives by gathering salable articles of jetsam, refuse, etc., from beaches. **2.** a vagrant who lives on the seashore, esp. a white man living in such a way on a South Pacific island. **3.** a long wave rolling in from the ocean onto the beach. [BEACH + COMBER]

beach′ crab′, any of various crabs that live on beaches, as the ghost crab.

beach′ drift′ing, the drifting of sediments, esp. sea sediments, in patterns parallel to the contours of a beach, due to the action of waves and currents.

beach·er (bē′chər), *n.* a long, curling wave of the sea. [BEACH + -ER[1]]

beach′ flea′, any of various small crustaceans, found on beaches, which jump about like fleas.

Beach flea, *Orchestia agilis* (Length ½ in.)

beach′ gold′enrod, an herb, *Solidago sempervirens,* of eastern and southern North America, having a thick stem and large, branched, one-sided, terminal clusters of yellow flowers, growing well on sea beaches or salt marshes. Also called **seaside goldenrod.**

beach′ grass′, any of several erect, strongly rooted grasses, esp. of the genus *Ammophila,* common on exposed sandy shores and dunes.

beach·head (bēch′hed′), *n.* **1.** the area that is the first objective of a military force landing on an enemy shore. **2.** a new advance in any field: *The change marked a beachhead in automotive engineering.* [BEACH + HEAD]

Beach-la-Mar (bēch′lə mär′), *n.* a former name of **Neo-Melanesian.** [alter. of BÊCHE-DE-MER sea-slug, a well-known product of the region where this type of pidgin is spoken]

beach′ pea′, either of two leguminous herbs, *Lathyrus maritimus,* of seashores of the North Temperate Zone, or *L. littoralis,* of the western coast of the U.S.

beach′ plum′, **1.** a shrub, *Prunus maritima,* of the seashores of northeastern North America. **2.** the purple or blackish, edible fruit of this shrub.

beach′ umbrel′la, *U.S.* a large umbrella used to provide shade on sunny beaches, lawns, etc.

beach′ wag′on, *U.S.* See **station wagon.**

beach·wear (bēch′wâr′), *n.* clothing for wear at a beach, swimming pool, or the like. [BEACH + WEAR]

Beach·wood (bēch′wo͝od′), *n.* **1.** a town in N Ohio. 6089 (1960). **2.** a town in E New Jersey. 2765 (1960).

beach·y (bē′chē), *adj. Archaic.* covered with pebbles or sand. [BEACH + -Y[3]]

bea·con (bē′kən), *n.* **1.** a guiding or warning signal, such as a light or fire, esp. one in an elevated position. **2.** a tower or hill used for such purposes. **3.** a lighthouse, signal buoy, etc., on a shore or over dangerous spots at sea to warn and guide vessels. **4.** See **radio beacon.** **5.** a radar device at a fixed location which, upon receiving a radar pulse, transmits a reply pulse that enables the original sender to determine his position relative to the fixed location. **6.** a person, act, or thing that warns or guides. —*v.t.* **7.** to serve as a beacon to; warn or guide. **8.** to furnish or mark with beacons: *a ship assigned to beacon the shoals.* —*v.i.* **9.** to serve or shine as a beacon: *A steady light beaconed from the shore.* [ME *beken,* OE *bēacen* sign, signal; c. OFris *bāken,* OS *bōkan,* OHG *bouhhan*] —**bea′con·less,** *adj.*

bea·con·age (bē′kə nij), *n. Naut.* **1.** a number or system of beacons. **2.** a tax or fee for maintaining beacons. [BEACON + -AGE]

bea′con boat′, a small, untended vessel used as a lightship.

Bea·cons·field (bē′kənz fēld′), *n.* **Earl of.** See **Disraeli, Benjamin.**

bead (bēd), *n.* **1.** a small, usually round object of glass, wood, stone, or the like with a hole through it, often strung with others of its kind in necklaces, rosaries, etc. **2. beads, a.** a necklace of beads: *You don't have your beads on this evening.* **b.** a rosary. **c.** *Obs.* devotions; prayers. **3.** any small, globular or cylindrical body. **4.** a bubble rising through effervescent liquid. **5.** a mass of such bubbles on the surface of a liquid. **6.** a drop of liquid: *beads of sweat.* **7.** the front sight of a gun. **8.** the front sight of a firearm. **9.** *Archit., Furniture.* a small molding having a convex circular section and, usually, a continuous cylindrical surface; astragal. **10.** *Chem.* a globule of borax or some other flux, supported on a platinum wire, in which a small amount of some substance is heated in a flame as a test for its constituents. **11.** *Metall.* the rounded mass of refined metal obtained by cupellation. **12.** *Welding.* a continuous deposit of fused metal, either straight **(stringer bead)** or zigzag **(weave bead).** **13.** a reinforced area of a rubber tire terminating the sidewall and fitting within the rim of a wheel. **14.** *Elect.* a glass, ceramic, or plastic insulator that contains and supports the inner conductor in a coaxial cable. **15. count, say,** or **tell one's beads,** to say one's prayers with rosary beads: *There were a few old women counting their beads in the hushed silence of the chapel.* **16. draw** or **get a bead on,** to take careful aim at: *The marksman drew a bead on his target.* —*v.t.* **17.** to ornament with beads. **18.** to form beads or a bead on. **19.** *Carpentry.* to form a bead on (a piece). —*v.i.* **20.** to form beads; form in beads or drops: *perspiration beading on his forehead.* [ME *bede* prayer, prayer bead, OE (*ge*)*bed* prayer; akin to BID[1], G *gebet,* etc.] —**bead′like′,** *adj.*

bead′ and reel′, *Archit.* a convex molding having the form of elongated beads alternating with disks placed edge-on, or with spherical beads, or with both. Also called **reel and bead.**

Bead and reel

bead·ed (bē′did), *adj.* ornamented with or largely composed of beads: *a beaded handbag.* [BEAD + -ED[3]]

bead·er (bē′dər), *n. Carpentry.* a tool for forming beads on lumber. [BEAD + -ER[1]]

bead·eye (bēd′ī′), *n., pl.* **-eyes.** stonecat. [BEAD(LIKE) + EYE]

bead·flush (bēd′flush′), *adj.* (of paneling) having panels flush with their stiles and rails, and surrounded with a flush bead. [BEAD + FLUSH[2]]

bead·house (bēd′hous′), *n., pl.* **-hous·es** (-hou′ziz). (formerly) an almshouse in which the residents were required to pray for the founder. Also, **bedehouse.** [BEAD + HOUSE]

bead·ing (bē′ding), *n.* **1.** material composed of or adorned with beads. **2.** narrow, lacelike trimming or edging. **3.** narrow openwork trimming through which ribbon may be run. **4.** *Archit., Furniture.* **a.** a bead molding. **b.** all of the bead moldings in a single design. Also, *for defs. 1, 4,* **beadwork.** [BEAD + -ING[1]]

bea·dle (bēd′əl), *n.* **1.** (in British universities) an official who supervises and leads processions; macebearer. **2.** a parish officer having various subordinate duties, as keeping order during services, waiting on the clergyman, etc. **3.** a synagogue officer who has various minor responsibilities during services and other functions. [ME *bedel,* dial. (SE) var. of *bidel,* OE *bydel* apparitor, herald (c. G *Büttel*), equiv. to *bud-* (weak s. of *bēodan* to command) + -*il* n. suffix]

Bea·dle (bēd′əl), *n.* **George Wells,** born 1903, U.S. biologist and educator: Nobel prize for medicine 1958.

bea·dle·dom (bēd′əl dəm), *n.* a stupid or officious display or exercise of authority, as by petty officials. [BEADLE + -DOM]

bead′ mold′ing, *Archit.* **1.** bead (def. 9). **2.** See **pearl molding.**

bead′ plane′, *Carpentry.* a plane for cutting beads.

bead′ plant′, a creeping, perennial herb, *Nertera granadensis,* of New Zealand and South America, having leathery leaves and orange-colored, transparent berries.

bead·roll (bēd′rōl′), *n.* **1.** *Rom. Cath. Ch.* a list of persons to be prayed for. **2.** any list or catalogue: *the long beadroll of Shakespearean annotators.* [BEAD + ROLL]

bead-ru·by (bēd′ro͞o′bē), *n., pl.* **-bies.** the false lily of the valley, *Maianthemum canadense.* Also called **wild lily-of-the-valley.**

beads·man (bēdz′mən), *n., pl.* **-men.** **1.** a person who prays for another as a duty, esp. when paid. **2.** an inmate of a poorhouse; almsman. Also, **bedesman, bedeman.** [*bead's man* man of prayer; r. ME *bedeman.* See BEAD, MAN[1]]

beads·wom·an (bēdz′wo͝om′ən), *n., pl.* **-wom·en.** **1.** a woman who prays for another person as a duty, esp. when paid. **2.** an almswoman.

bead·work (bēd′wûrk′), *n.* beading (defs. 1, 4). [BEAD + WORK]

bead·y (bē′dē), *adj.,* **bead·i·er, bead·i·est.** **1.** beadlike; small, globular, and glittering: *beady eyes.* **2.** covered with or full of beads. [BEAD + -Y[1]] —**bead′i·ly,** *adv.* —**bead′i·ness,** *n.*

bea·gle (bē′gəl), *n.* one of a breed of small hounds having long ears, short legs, and a usually black, tan, and white coat. [ME *begle* < ?]

Beagle (15 in. high at shoulder)

bea·gling (bē′gling), *n. Chiefly Brit.* hunting with beagle hounds. [BEAGLE + -ING[1]]

beak[1] (bēk), *n.* **1.** the bill of a bird; neb. **2.** any similar horny mouthpart in other animals, such as the turtle, duckbill, etc. **3.** *Slang.* a person's nose. **4.** anything beaklike or ending in a point, as the spout of a pitcher. **5.** *Entomol.* proboscis (def. 3). **6.** *Bot.* a narrowed or prolonged tip. **7.** *Naut.* **a.** a metal or metal-sheathed projection from the bows of some obsolete warships, used to ram enemy vessels; ram; rostrum. **b.** See **beak-head.** **8.** *Typography.* a serif on the arm of a character, as of a K. **9.** Also called **bird's beak.** *Archit.* a pendant molding forming a drip, as on the soffit of a cornice. [ME *bec* < OF < L *becc*(*us*) < Gaulish] —**beaked** (bēkt, bē′kid), *adj.* —**beak′less,** *adj.* —**beak′like′,** *adj.* —**beak′y,** *adj.*

Beak

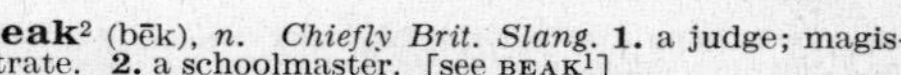

beak[2] (bēk), *n. Chiefly Brit. Slang.* **1.** a judge; magistrate. **2.** a schoolmaster. [see BEAK[1]]

beaked′ sal′mon, sandfish (def. 2).

beaked′ whale′, any of several toothed whales of the family *Ziphiidae,* found in all oceans, having a beaklike snout.

Beaker (def. 3)

beak·er (bē′kər), *n.* **1.** a large drinking cup or glass with a wide mouth. **2.** contents of a beaker: *consuming a beaker of gin at one gulp.* **3.** a flat-bottomed cylindrical vessel, usually with a pouring lip. —*adj.* **4.** (*cap.*) of or pertaining to the Beaker folk. [alter. of ME *biker* < Scand; cf. Icel *bikarr;* c. OS *bikeri,* OHG *behhar* (> G *Becher,* D *beker*)]

Beak′er folk′ (bē′kər), a prehistoric people living in Europe, so called in reference to the bell beakers commonly found buried with their dead in barrows. Also called **Beak′er peo′ple.**

beak-head (bēk′hed′), *n.* a projection on some sailing ships that extends beneath the bowsprit and beyond the bows and that terminates in a point or in a figurehead (discontinued in later years).

beak′ing joint′ (bē′king), *Carpentry.* a straight joint made by several members, as strips of flooring, ending at the same line.

Beal (bel), *n.* a god of the ancient Celts, a personification of the sun.

be-all and end-all (bē′ôl′ ənd end′ôl′), the central and all-important part: *His work was the be-all and end-all of his existence.*

beam (bēm), *n.* **1.** any of various relatively long pieces of metal, wood, stone, etc., manufactured or shaped esp. for use as rigid members or parts of structures or machines. **2.** *Building Trades.* a horizontal bearing member, as a joist or lintel. **3.** *Engineering.* a rigid member or structure supported at each end, subject to bending stresses from a direction perpendicular to its length. **4.** *Naut.* **a.** a horizontal structural member, usually transverse, for supporting the decks and flats of a vessel. **b.** the extreme width of a vessel. **c.** the shank of an anchor. **5.** *Aeron.* the direction perpendicular to the plane of symmetry of an aircraft and outward from the side. **6.** the widest part. **7.** *Slang.* the measure across both hips or buttocks: *broad in the beam.* **8.** *Mach.* **a.** See **walking beam.** **b.** (in a loom) a roller or cylinder on which the warp is wound before weaving. **c.** a similar cylinder on which cloth is wound as it is woven. **9.** the crossbar of a balance, from the ends of which the scales or pans are suspended. **10.** a ray of light: *The sun shed its beams upon the vineyard.* **11.** a group of nearly parallel rays. **12.** *Radio, Aeron.* a signal transmitted along a narrow course, used to guide pilots through darkness, bad weather, etc. **13.** *Electronics.* a narrow stream of electrons, as that emitted from the electron gun of a cathode ray tube. **14.** the angle at which a microphone or loudspeaker functions best. **15.** the cone-shaped range of effective use of a microphone or loudspeaker. **16.** a gleam; suggestion: *a beam of hope.* **17.** the principal stem of the antler of a deer. **18. fly the beam,** *Radio, Aeron.* (of an aircraft) to be guided by a beam. **19. off the beam, a.** not on the course indicated by a radio beam. **b.** *Slang.* wrong; incorrect: *The pollsters were off the beam again for the last presidential election.* **20. on the beam, a.** on the course indicated by a radio beam, as an airplane. **b.** *Naut.* at right angles to the keel. **c.** *Slang.* proceeding well; correct; exact: *The glee club in its last concert was really on the beam.* —*v.t.* **21.** to emit in or as in beams or rays. **22.** *Radio.* to transmit (a signal) on a narrow beam. —*v.i.* **23.** to emit beams, as of light. **24.** to smile radiantly or happily. [ME *beem,* OE *bēam* tree, post, ray of light; c. D *boom,* G *Baum* tree; akin to Goth *bagms,* Icel *bathmr* tree] —**beam′less,** *adj.* —**beam′like′,** *adj.*
—**Syn. 10.** See **gleam.** **21.** See **shine.**

beam′ anten′na, *Radio.* an antenna that transmits its radiation in a particular direction.

beam′ brick′, a face brick for bonding to a concrete lintel poured in place, having a section like a right triangle.

beam′ com′pass, *Drafting.* a compass having adjustable legs, set perpendicular to the paper and sliding along a horizontal bar so as to permit the drawing of large circles.

beam-ends (bēm′endz′), *n.pl.* **1.** *Naut.* the ends of the transverse deck beams of a vessel. **2. on her beam-ends,** *Naut.* heeled so far on one side that the deck is practically vertical: *The schooner was blown over on her beam-ends.* **3. on one's beam-ends,** in desperate straits, esp. financial straits. Also, **on the beam-ends, on the beam's ends.**

beam′ fill′, *Building Trades.* material, as concrete, for filling spaces between beams or joists in or on top of a masonry wall. Also, **beam′ fill′ing.**

beam·ing (bē′ming), *adj.* radiant; bright; cheerful. [BEAM + -ING[2]] —**beam′ing·ly,** *adv.*

beam·ish (bē′mish), *adj. Often Disparaging.* bright, cheerful, and optimistic. [BEAM (n.) + -ISH[1]]

beam′ mill′, *Metalworking.* a rolling mill for roughing a bloom and rolling it into a shape.

beam′-pow′er tube′ (bēm′pou′ər), *Radio.* a vacuum tube in which the stream of electrons flowing to the plate is focused by the action of a set of auxiliary, charged elements, giving an increase in output power.

beam′ reach′, *Naut.* See under **reach** (def. 26).

beam′ sea′, *Naut.* a sea striking the vessel at right angles to its keel.

beam′ wind′ (wind), *Naut.* a wind blowing against a vessel from a direction at right angles to its keel.

beam·y (bē′mē), *adj.,* **beam·i·er, beam·i·est.** **1.** emitting beams of or as of light; radiant. **2.** broad in the beam, as a ship. **3.** *Zool.* having antlers, as a stag. [BEAM + -Y[1]] —**beam′i·ly,** *adv.* —**beam′i·ness,** *n.*

bean (bēn), *n.* **1.** the edible nutritious seed of various species of leguminous plants, esp. of the genus *Phaseolus.* **2.** a plant producing such seeds, used as a snap bean, as a shell bean, or as dry beans. **3.** any of various other beanlike seeds or plants, as the coffee bean. **4.** *Slang.* a person's head. **5.** *Brit. Slang.* a coin, esp. a sovereign or guinea: *I haven't a bean.* **6. beans,** *Informal.* the slightest amount: *He doesn't know beans about navigation.* **7. full of beans,** *Slang.* **a.** energetic; vigorously active; vital: *He is still full of beans at 65.* **b.** stupid; erroneous; misinformed. **8. spill the beans,** *Informal.* to disclose a secret, either accidentally or imprudently, thereby ruining a surprise or plan: *He spilled the beans, and she knew all about the party in advance.* —*v.t.* **9.** *Slang.* to hit on the head, esp. with a baseball. —*interj.* **10. beans,** a mild oath (used to express dissatisfaction, disgust, annoyance, etc.). [ME *bene,* OE *bēan;* c. Icel *baun,* D *boon,* OHG *bona* (G *Bohne*)] —**bean′like′,** *adj.*

bean-bag (bēn′bag′), *n.* a small cloth bag filled with beans, used as a toy.

bean′ ball′, *Baseball Slang.* a ball thrown by a pitcher purposely at or near the head of the batter.

bean′ bee′tle. See **Mexican bean beetle.**

bean′ ca′per, a small tree, *Zygophyllum Fabago,* of the eastern Mediterranean regions, whose flower buds are used as a substitute for capers.

bean·er·y (bē′nə rē), *n., pl.* **-er·ies.** *Slang.* a cheap, usually inferior, restaurant. [BEAN + -ERY]

bean·feast (bēn′fēst′), *n.* *Chiefly Brit. Slang.* **1.** an annual dinner or party given by an employer for employees. **2.** a celebration or festive occasion, esp. when a meal is provided. Also, **bean·fest** (bēn′fest′). [BEAN + FEAST]

bean·ie (bē′nē), *n.* a skullcap, often brightly colored, worn esp. by children. [BEAN + -IE]

bean·o[1] (bē′nō), *n.* bingo. [b. BEAN and KENO]

bean·o[2] (bē′nō), *n., pl.* **bean·os.** *Chiefly Brit. Slang.* beanfeast. [by shortening and alter.]

bean·pole (bēn′pōl′), *n.* **1.** a tall pole for a bean plant to climb on. **2.** *Informal.* a tall, lanky person. [BEAN + POLE[1]]

bean′ pot′, a heavy, covered, crockery or metal pot, suitable for the slow cooking of beans or the like.

bean·shoot·er (bēn′sho͞o′tər), *n.* a child's toy, consisting of a small tube through which dried beans are blown. Cf. **peashooter.** [BEAN + SHOOTER]

bean′ shot′, *Metall.* refined copper having a shotlike form from being thrown into water in a molten state.

bean′ sprouts′, the sprouts of newly germinated beans, esp. of mung beans, used as a vegetable.

bean·stalk (bēn′stôk′), *n.* the stem of a bean plant. [BEAN + STALK[1]]

Bean′ Town′, Boston, Massachusetts (used as a nickname). [so called from phrase *Boston baked beans*]

bean′ tree′, **1.** any of several trees bearing pods resembling those of a bean, as the catalpa and the carob tree. **2.** the laburnum, *Laburnum anagyroides.*

bean′ wee′vil, a seed beetle, *Acanthoscelides obtectus,* the larvae of which live in and feed on growing or stored beans.

bear[1] (bâr), *v.,* **bore** or (*Archaic*) **bare; borne** or **born; bear·ing.** —*v.t.* **1.** to bring forth (young); give birth to: *to bear a child.* **2.** to produce by natural growth: *a tree that bears fruit.* **3.** to hold up; support: *to bear the weight of the roof.* **4.** to hold or remain firm under (a load): *The roof will not bear the strain of his weight.* **5.** to hold up under; be capable of: *His claim doesn't bear close examination.* **6.** to press or push against: *The crowd was borne back by the police.* **7.** to manage (oneself, one's body, one's head, etc.): *to bear oneself erectly.* **8.** to conduct (oneself): *to bear oneself bravely.* **9.** to suffer; endure; undergo: *to bear the blame.* **10.** to sustain without yielding or suffering injury (usually used in negative constructions, unless qualified): *I can't bear your nagging. I can hardly bear to see her.* **11.** to be fit for or worthy of: *It doesn't bear repeating.* **12.** to carry; bring: *to bear gifts.* **13.** to carry in the mind or heart: *to bear love; to bear malice.* **14.** to transmit or spread (gossip, tales, etc.). **15.** to render; afford; give: *to bear witness; to bear testimony.* **16.** to lead; guide; take: *They bore him home.* **17.** to have and be entitled to: *to bear title.* **18.** to exhibit; show: *to bear a resemblance.* **19.** to accept or have, as an obligation: *to bear responsibility; to bear the cost.* **20.** to stand in (a relation or ratio): *the relation that price bears to profit.* **21.** to possess, as a quality, characteristic, etc.; have in or on: *to bear traces; to bear an inscription.* **22.** to have and use; exercise: *to bear authority; to bear sway.* —*v.i.* **23.** to show or use force, strength, influence, or the like: *The Senator is bearing all his resources against the controversial legislation.* **24.** to tend in a course or direction; move; go: *to bear west; to bear left.* **25.** to be located or situated: *The lighthouse bears due north.* **26.** to bring forth young or fruit: *Next year the tree will bear.* **27. bear down, a.** to press or weigh down. **b.** to strive harder; intensify one's efforts: *We can't hope to finish unless everyone bears down.* **c.** *Naut.* to approach from windward, as a ship: *The cutter was bearing down the channel at twelve knots.* **28. bear down on** or **upon, a.** to press or weigh down on. **b.** to strive toward. **c.** to approach something rapidly. **d.** *Naut.* to approach (another vessel) from windward: *The sloop bore down on us, narrowly missing our stern.* **29. bear on** or **upon,** to affect, relate to, or have connection with; be relevant: *This information may bear on the case.* **30. bear out,** to substantiate; confirm: *The facts bear me out.* **31. bear up,** to endure; face hardship bravely: *It is inspiring to see them bearing up so well.* **32. bear with,** to be patient; be forbearing: *Please bear with me until I finish the story.* **33. bring to bear,** to concentrate on with a specific purpose: *Pressure was brought to bear on the congressman to vote against the proposed bill.* [ME *bere(n),* OE *beran;* c. D *baren,* Icel *bera,* Goth *bairan,* G *(ge)bären,* L *fer(re),* Gk *phér(ein),* Skt *bhar(ati)*]

—**Syn. 2.** yield, produce. **3.** uphold, sustain. **6.** thrust, drive, force. **10.** tolerate, brook, abide, suffer. BEAR, STAND, ENDURE refer to supporting the burden of something distressing, irksome, or painful. BEAR is the general word and STAND its colloquial equivalent, but with an implication of stout spirit: *to bear a disappointment well; to stand a loss.* ENDURE implies continued resistance and patience in bearing through a long time: *to endure torture.*

Black bear, *Ursus americanus* (3 ft. high at shoulder; length 5 ft.)

bear[2] (bâr), *n., pl.* **bears,** (*esp. collectively*) **bear,** *adj., v.,* **beared, bear·ing.** —*n.* **1.** any of the plantigrade, carnivorous or omnivorous mammals of the family *Ursidae,* having massive bodies, coarse heavy fur, relatively short limbs, and almost rudimentary tails. **2.** any of various animals resembling the bear, as the ant bear. **3.** a gruff, burly, clumsy, bad-mannered, or rude person. **4.** a person who believes that general business conditions are becoming or will be unfavorable. **5.** one who sells stocks or commodities short in the hope of buying later at a lower price (opposed to *bull*). **6.** *Informal.* one who shows great ability, enthusiasm, interest, etc.: *a bear for physics.* **7.** (*cap.*) *Astron.* either of two constellations, Ursa Major or Ursa Minor. **8.** *Informal.* a player at cards who rarely bluffs. Cf. **bull**[1] (def. 9). **9.** (*cap.*) Russia. **10. be a bear for, a.** to be capable of and eager for (work, strain, etc.). **b.** to display exceptional endurance under strain. —*adj.* **11.** having to do with or marked by declining prices, as of stocks: *bear market.* —*v.t.* **12.** *Stock Exchange.* to attempt to lower the price of; operate in for a decline in price. [ME *bere,* OE *bera;* c. D *beer,* OHG *bero* (G *Bär*); akin to Lith *beras* brown. See BRUIN] —**bear′like′,** *adj.*

bear·a·ble (bâr′ə bəl), *adj.* capable of being borne; endurable. [BEAR[1] + -ABLE] —**bear′a·ble·ness,** *n.* —**bear′a·bly,** *adv.*

bear·bait·ing (bâr′bā′ting), *n.* the former practice of setting dogs to fight a captive bear. [BEAR[2] + BAITING] —**bear′bait′er,** *n.*

bear·ber·ry (bâr′ber′ē, -bə rē), *n., pl.* **-ries.** **1.** a trailing evergreen ericaceous shrub, *Arctostaphylos Uva-ursi,* bearing small bright-red berries and tonic, astringent leaves. **2.** a related species, *A. alpina,* bearing black berries. **3.** any of certain other plants, as *Ilex decidua,* a holly of the southern U.S. **4.** the cranberry, *Oxycoccus macrocarpus.* **5.** cascara. [BEAR[2] + BERRY]

bear·bush (bâr′bo͝osh′), *n.* inkberry (def. 1). [BEAR[2] + BUSH[1]]

bear·cat (bâr′kat′), *n.* **1.** a panda, *Ailurus fulgens.* **2.** binturong. **3.** *Informal.* one who fights or conducts himself with force or fierceness. [BEAR[2] + CAT[1]]

beard (bērd), *n.* **1.** the growth of hair on the face of an adult man, often including the mustache. **2.** *Zool.* a tuft, growth, or part resembling or suggesting a human beard, as the tuft of long hairs on the lower jaw of a goat, the cluster of fine, hairlike feathers at the base of the bill of certain birds, etc. **3.** *Bot.* a tuft or growth of awns or the like, as in wheat, barley, etc. **4.** a barb or catch on an arrow, fishhook, knitting needle, crochet needle, etc. **5.** Also called **neck.** *Print.* **a.** *U.S.* the sloping part of a type which connects the face with the shoulder of the body. **b.** *Brit.* the space on a type between the bottom of the face of an x-high character and the edge of the body, comprising both beard and shoulder. **c.** the cross stroke on the stem of a capital G. See diag. under **type.** —*v.t.* **6.** to seize, pluck, or pull the beard of: *The hoodlums bearded the old man.* **7.** to oppose boldly; defy: *It took courage for the Mayor to beard the pressure groups.* **8.** to supply with a beard. [ME *berd,* OE *beard;* c. G *Bart,* D *baard,* OSlav *brada,* Russ *boroda*] —**beard′less,** *adj.* —**beard′less·ness,** *n.* —**beard′like′,** *adj.*

Beard (bērd), *n.* **1. Charles Austin,** 1874–1948, and his wife **Mary,** 1876–1958, U.S. historians. **2. Daniel Carter,** 1850–1941, U.S. artist and naturalist: organized the Boy Scouts of America in 1910.

beard·ed (bēr′did), *adj.* **1.** having a beard. **2.** having a hairlike growth or tuft, as certain wheats. **3.** having a barb, as a fishhook. [ME *beerdid.* See BEARD, -ED[3]]

beard′ed dar′nel, a darnel, *Lolium temulentum,* the seeds of which yield a narcotic poison.

beard′ed tit′, a small European bird, *Panurus biarmicus,* found in reedy places, the male of which has a tuft of black feathers on each side of the face.

beard′ed vul′ture, lammergeier.

beard·fish (bērd′fish′), *n., pl.* (*esp. collectively*) **-fish,** (*esp. referring to two or more kinds or species*) **-fish·es.** any of several fishes of the family *Polymyxiidae,* found in the deeper waters of the Atlantic and Pacific oceans, having a pair of long barbels under the chin. Also called **barbudo.** [for *bearded fish*]

beard·ing (bēr′ding), *n.* *Shipbuilding.* **1.** the line of intersection of the shell planking with the stem, keel, and sternpost of a wooden vessel. **2.** the line of intersection of the shell plating with the stem or sternpost of a steel or iron vessel. **3.** the taper of an edge or surface of a timber. Also called **beard′ing line′, stepping line** (for defs. 1, 2). [BEARD + -ING[1]]

beard·less (bērd′lis), *adj.* having no beard or one shaved close to the skin. [ME; see BEARD, -LESS] —**beard′less·ness,** *n.*

Beards·ley (bērdz′lē), *n.* **Aubrey Vincent,** 1872–98, English illustrator.

Beards·town (bērdz′toun′), *n.* a town in central Illinois. 6294 (1960).

beard·tongue (bērd′tung′), *n.* any scrophulariaceous plant of the genus *Pentstemon.* [BEARD + TONGUE]

bear·er (bâr′ər), *n.* **1.** a person or thing that carries, upholds, or brings: *Dozens of native bearers aided in the climb of Mt. Everest.* **2.** the person who presents an order for money or goods: *Pay to the bearer.* **3.** a tree or plant that yields fruit or flowers. **4.** the holder of rank or office; incumbent. **5.** pallbearer. **6.** *Anglo-Indian.* a native boy or man employed as a personal or household servant. **7.** *Print.* **a.** furniture (def. 3). **b.** one of several strips of metal fitted at the sides of a plate for support during inking and proving. **8.** a joistlike member supporting the floor boards of a scaffold. **9.** *Furniture.* See **bearing rail.** [ME *berere.* See BEAR[1], -ER[1]]

bear′ gar′den, **1.** a place for keeping or exhibiting bears, esp. for bearbaiting. **2.** a place or scene of tumult: *Registration at the university may seem like a bear garden to an uninitiated freshman.*

bear′ grass′, **1.** any of several American liliaceous plants of the genus *Yucca,* having grasslike foliage. **2.** any of certain similar liliaceous plants, as the camass.

bear′ hug′, **1.** a forcefully tight embrace. **2.** *Wrestling.* a hold in which a contestant locks both arms around his opponent from the front and tries to make him fall on his back.

bear·ing (bâr′ing), *n.* **1.** the manner in which a person conducts or carries himself, including posture, gestures, etc.: *a man of dignified bearing.* **2.** act, capability, or period of producing or bringing forth: *a tree past bearing.* **3.** that which is produced; a crop. **4.** act of enduring or capacity to endure. **5.** reference or relation (usually fol. by *on*): *It has some bearing on the problem.* **6.** *Archit.* **a.** a supporting part of a structure. **b.** the area of contact between a bearing member, as a beam, and a pier, wall, or other underlying support. **7.** *Mach.* the support and guide for a rotating, oscillating, or sliding shaft, pivot, or wheel. **8.** Often, **bearings.** direction or relative position: *The pilot radioed his bearings.* **9.** *Survey.* a horizontal direction expressed in degrees east or west of a true or magnetic north or south direction. **10.** *Heraldry.* any single device on an escutcheon; charge. [ME *beryng.* See BEAR[1], -ING[1]]

—**Syn. 1.** carriage, mien, demeanor, behavior, conduct. See **manner. 5.** connection, dependency; application. **8.** course, aim.

bear′ing bronze′, any of various alloys of copper, tin, and other metals, as lead or zinc, used for bearings.

bear′ing plate′, a heavy metal plate for receiving and distributing concentrated weight, as from a column or one end of a truss.

bear′ing rail′, *Furniture.* a transverse rail carrying a drawer or drawers. Also called **bearer.**

bear′ing rein′, checkrein (def. 1).

bear′ing sword′, a large sword carried for its owner by a squire or servant because of its size.

bear·ish (bâr′ish), *adj.* **1.** like a bear; rough; burly; clumsy; grumpy; bad-mannered; rude. **2.** *Com.* **a.** declining or tending toward a decline in prices. **b.** characterized by unfavorable prospects for the economy or some aspect of it: *bearish economy.* [BEAR[2] + -ISH[1]] —**bear′ish·ly,** *adv.* —**bear′ish·ness,** *n.*

bear′ lead′er, (formerly) a tutor traveling with a wealthy or aristocratic young man. Also, **bear′-lead′er.**

Bé·ar·naise (ber nāz′; *Fr.* bȧ ar nez′), *n.* (*sometimes l.c.*) a sauce of egg yolks, shallots, tarragon, butter, vinegar, and sometimes white wine and chopped chervil. Also called **Béarnaise′ sauce′.** [< F, after *Béarn* district in SW France + *-aise,* fem. of *-ais* -ESE]

bear·paw (bâr′pô′), *n.* *Chiefly Canadian.* **1.** a small, almost round snowshoe used on steep or rocky terrain. **2.** a round horseshoe. [BEAR[2] + PAW]

Bear′ Riv′er, a river in NE Utah, SW Wyoming, and SE Idaho, flowing into the Great Salt Lake. 350 mi. long.

bear's-ear (bârz′ēr′), *n.* auricula.

bear's-foot (bârz′fo͝ot′), *n., pl.* **-foots.** any of various species of hellebore, esp. *Helleborus foetidus.*

bear·skin (bâr′skin′), *n.* **1.** the skin or pelt of a bear. **2.** a tall, black fur cap forming part of the dress uniform of a soldier in some armies. **3.** a coarse, shaggy woolen cloth for overcoats. [BEAR[2] + SKIN]

bear's-paw (bârz′pô′), *n.* a clam of the genus *Hippopus,* having a ridged, white shell with purplish-red spots.

bear-tree (bâr′trē′), *n.* See **Barbados pride** (def. 1).

bear·wood (bâr′wo͝od′), *n.* a buckthorn, *Rhamnus Purshiana.* [BEAR[2] + WOOD[1]]

beast (bēst), *n.* **1.** any animal other than man, esp. a large, four-footed mammal. **2.** the crude animal nature common to humans and nonhumans: *Hunger brought out the beast in him.* **3.** a cruel, coarse, filthy, or otherwise beastlike person. **4.** beasts, or animals, collectively: *What manner of beast is this?* **5. the beast,** the Antichrist. Rev. 13:18. [ME *be(e)ste* < OF *beste* (F *bête*) < L *bestia*] —**beast′like′,** *adj.*

—**Syn. 1.** See **animal.**

beast′ ep′ic, a long verse narrative in which the misadventures of animals satirize human foibles and follies.

beast·ie (bē′stē), *n.* *Chiefly Literary.* a small animal, esp. one toward which affection is felt. [BEAST + -IE]

beast·ings (bē′stingz), *n.* (*construed as sing.*) beestings.

beast·ly (bēst′lē), *adj.,* **-li·er, -li·est,** *adv.* —*adj.* **1.** of or like a beast; bestial. **2.** *Brit. Informal.* nasty; unpleasant; disagreeable. —*adv.* **3.** *Brit. Informal.* very; exceedingly: *It's beastly cold out.* **4.** *Brit. Informal.* disagreeably; outrageously: *beastly rude.* [ME *beasteliche,* later *be(e)stly.* See BEAST, -LY[1]] —**beast′li·ness,** *n.*

beast′ of bur′den, an animal used for carrying heavy loads or pulling heavy equipment, as a donkey, mule, or ox.

beast′ of prey′, a predatory animal.

beat (bēt), *v.,* **beat, beat·en** or **beat, beat·ing,** *n., adj.* —*v.t.* **1.** to strike violently or forcefully and repeatedly. **2.** to dash against: *rain beating the trees.* **3.** to flutter, flap, or rotate in: *beating the air with its wings.* **4.** to sound, as on a drum: *beating a steady rhythm; to beat a tattoo.* **5.** to stir vigorously: *Beat the egg whites well.* **6.** to break, forge, or make by blows: *to beat their swords into plowshares.* **7.** to produce (an attitude, idea, habit, etc.) by repeated efforts: *I'll beat some sense into him.* **8.** to make (a path) by repeated treading. **9.** to thrash (a person) soundly (often fol. by *up*): *He beat up the ruffian.* **10.** *Music.* to mark (time) by strokes, as with the hand or a metronome. **11.** *Hunting.* to scour (the forest, grass, or brush) in order to rouse game. **12.** to overcome in a contest; defeat. **13.** to win over in a race: *We beat the English challenger to Bermuda.* **14.** to be superior to: *Making reservations beats waiting in line.* **15.** to be incomprehensible to; baffle: *It beats me how he got the job.* **16.** to defeat or frustrate (a person), as a problem to be solved: *It beats me how to get her to understand.* **17.** to mitigate or offset the effects of: *beating the hot weather; trying to beat the sudden decrease in land values.* **18.** *U.S. Slang.* to swindle; cheat (often fol. by *out*): *He beat him out of hundreds of dollars on that deal.* **19.** *Textiles.* to strike (the loose pick) into its proper place in the woven cloth by beating the loosely deposited filling yarn with the reed.

—*v.i.* **20.** to strike repeated blows; pound. **21.** to throb or pulsate: *His heart began to beat faster.* **22.** to dash; strike (usually fol. by *against* or *on*): *rain beating against the windows.* **23.** to resound under blows, as a drum. **24.** to achieve victory in a contest; win: *Which team do you think will beat?* **25.** to play, as on a drum. **26.** to scour cover for game. **27.** *Physics.* to make a beat or beats. **28.** to permit beating: *This cream won't beat.* **29.** *Naut.* to tack to windward by sailing close-hauled. **30. beat about, a.** to search through; scour: *After beating about for several hours, he turned up the missing papers.* **b.** *Naut.* to tack into the wind. **31. beat around** or **about the bush.** See **bush**[1] (def. 12). **32. beat a retreat.** See **retreat** (def. 9). **33. beat back,** to force back; compel to withdraw: *to beat back an attacker.* **34. beat down, a.** to bring into subjection; subdue.

b. *Informal.* to persuade a seller to lower his price: *His first price was too high, so we tried to beat him down.* **35. beat it,** *Slang.* to leave; go away: *The only witnesses had beat it by the time the police arrived.* **36. beat off,** to ward off; repulse: *We had to beat off clouds of mosquitoes.* **37. beat out, a.** *Slang.* defeat. **b.** *Carpentry.* to cut (a mortise). **38. beat the air** or **wind,** to make repeated futile attempts. **39. beat the bounds,** *Brit.* to mark off the boundary of a parish by the ritual of marching around it while striking certain points with sticks. **40. beat the rap.** See **rap**[1] (def. 8).
—*n.* **41.** a stroke or blow. **42.** the sound made by one or more such blows: *the beat of drums.* **43.** a throb or pulsation: *a pulse of 60 beats per minute.* **44.** the ticking sound made by a clock or watch escapement. **45.** one's assigned or regular path or habitual round: *a policeman's beat.* **46.** *Music.* **a.** the audible, visual, or mental marking of the metrical divisions of music. **b.** a stroke of the hand, baton, etc., marking time division or accent for music during performance. **47.** *Theat.* a momentary time unit imagined by an actor in timing his actions: *Wait four beats and then cross left.* **48.** *Pros.* the accent stress, or ictus, in a foot or rhythmical unit of poetry. **49.** *Physics.* a pulsation caused by the coincidence of the amplitudes of two oscillations of unequal frequencies, having a frequency equal to the difference between the frequencies of the two oscillations. **50.** *Journalism.* **a.** the reporting of a piece of news in advance, or to the exclusion, of its being reported by a rival or rivals. Cf. **exclusive** (def. 10), **scoop** (def. 8). **b.** Also called **news-beat, run.** the particular news source or activity that a reporter is responsible for covering. **51.** a subdivision of a county, as in Mississippi. **52.** *Informal.* beatnik. **53. off one's beat,** outside of one's routine, general knowledge, or range of experience: *He protested that nonobjective art was off his beat.* **54. on the beat,** in the correct rhythm or tempo: *By the end of the number they were all finally playing on the beat.*
—*adj. Informal.* **55.** exhausted; worn out. **56.** of, or characteristic of members of the beat generation or beatniks. [ME *bete(n),* OE *bēatan;* c. Icel *bauta,* OHG *bōzzan*] —**beat′a·ble,** *adj.*
—**Syn. 1.** belabor, batter, drub, maul, baste, pommel, cudgel, buffet, flog. BEAT, HIT, POUND, STRIKE, THRASH refer to the giving of a blow or blows. BEAT implies the giving of repeated blows: *to beat a rug.* To HIT is usually to give a single blow, definitely directed: *to hit a ball.* To POUND is to give heavy and repeated blows, often with the fist: *to pound a nail, the table.* To STRIKE is to give one or more forceful blows suddenly or swiftly: *to strike a gong.* To THRASH implies inflicting repeated blows as punishment, to show superior strength, and the like: *to thrash a child.* **12.** conquer, subdue, vanquish, overpower. **14.** excel, outdo, surpass. **21.** See **pulsate.**

be·a·ta (bā ä′tə), *n., pl.* **-tae** (-tā), **-tas.** *Rom. Cath. Ch.* a girl or woman who has been beatified. [< L, fem. of *beātus* blessed. See BEATUS]

Be·a·ta Vir·go Ma·ri·a (bā ä′tä vēr′gō mä rē′ä), *Latin.* Blessed Virgin Mary.

beat-beat (bēt′bēt′), *n. Rocketry.* a missile tracking system using Doppler radar. [by redupl.]

beat·en (bēt′ən), *adj.* **1.** formed or shaped by blows; hammered: *a dish of beaten brass.* **2.** much trodden; commonly used: *a beaten path.* **3.** defeated; vanquished; thwarted. **4.** overcome by exhaustion; fatigued by hard work, intense activity, etc. **5.** (of food) whipped up, pounded, pulverized, or the like: *adding three beaten eggs.* **6. off the beaten track** or **path,** novel; uncommon; out of the ordinary: *a tiny shop that was off the beaten track.* [ME *beten,* OE *bēaten,* ptp. of *bēatan* to BEAT]

beat′en bis′cuit, *Southern U.S.* a hard, unleavened biscuit, made to rise by pounding and folding the dough.

beat′en proof′, a proof made by laying paper over type while it is on the composing stone, laying a planer on it, and beating the planer with a mallet.

beat·er (bē′tər), *n.* **1.** a person or thing that beats. **2.** an implement or device for beating something: *a rug beater.* **3.** *Hunting.* a person who rouses or drives game from cover. **4.** *Papermaking.* a machine for beating half-stuff to pulp by separating and shortening the fibers to produce a gelatinous mass. **5.** *Textiles Informal.* the reed. [BEAT + -ER[1]]

beat′ genera′tion, members of the generation that came of age after World War II who, supposedly as a result of disillusionment stemming from the Cold War, espouse mystical detachment and relaxation of social and sexual tensions. [*beat* (var. of BEATEN); popularized by Jack KEROUAC]

be·a·tif·ic (bē′ə tif′ik), *adj.* **1.** bestowing bliss, blessings, happiness, or the like: *beatific peace.* **2.** blissful; saintly: *a beatific smile.* [< LL *beātific(us)* making happy < *beāt(us)* (ptp. of *beāre*) < *be-* bless + *-āt(us)* -ATE[1] + *-i-* -I- + *-ficus* -FIC] —**be′a·tif′i·cal·ly,** *adv.*

be·at·i·fi·ca·tion (bē at′ə fə kā′shən), *n.* **1.** act of beatifying. **2.** state of being beatified. **3.** *Rom. Cath. Ch.* the official act of the pope whereby a deceased person is declared to be enjoying the happiness of heaven, and therefore a proper subject of religious honor and public cult in certain places. [< LL *beātificātiōn-* (s. of *beātificātiō*), equiv. to *beātificāt(us)* (ptp. of *beātificāre* to BEATIFY); see -ATE[1]]

be′atif′ic vi′sion, *Theol.* the vision of God in heaven.

be·at·i·fy (bē at′ə fī′), *v.t.,* **-fied, -fy·ing. 1.** to make blissfully happy. **2.** *Rom. Cath. Ch.* to declare (a deceased person) to be among the blessed and thus entitled to specific religious honor. [< MF *beatifi(er)* < LL *beātificāre.* See BEATIFIC]

beat·ing (bē′ting), *n.* **1.** act of a person or thing that beats, as to punish, clean, mix, etc.: *Give the rug a good beating.* **2.** a defeat. **3.** pulsation; throbbing: *the beating of her heart.* [ME *betynge.* See BEAT, -ING[1]]

beat·ing-up (bē′ting up′), *n.* **1.** *Textiles.* the process by which the loose pick is made an integral part of the woven material. **2.** a severe beating administered for intimidation or revenge.

be·at·i·tude (bē at′ə tōōd′, -tyōōd′), *n.* **1.** supreme blessedness; exalted happiness. **2.** any of the declarations of blessedness pronounced by Jesus in the Sermon on the Mount. [< L *beātitūdō* perfect happiness, equiv. to *beāti-* (see BEATIFIC) + *-tūdō* -TUDE]

beat′ man′. See **district man.**

beat·nik (bēt′nik), *n. Informal.* **1.** a member of the beat generation. **2.** one who rejects or avoids conventional behavior, dress, etc. [BEAT (adj.) (as in BEAT GENERATION) + *-nik* Russ n. suffix designating an agent or one concerned with something, as in *sputnik*]

Bea·ton (bēt′ən), *n.* **Cecil Walter Hardy,** born 1904, English photographer, writer, and stage-set designer.

Be·a·trice (bē′ə tris; *also, for 1, 3, It.* be′ä trē′che), *n.* **1.** (in Dante's *Vita Nuova* and *Divine Comedy*) a symbolic figure developed from the person whom Dante first saw as a child and loved as an ideal of womanhood. **2.** a city in SE Nebraska. 12,132 (1960). **3.** a girl's given name.

Be′atrice and Ben′edict, an opera (1862) by Hector Berlioz.

Beat·tie (bē′tē), *n.* **James,** 1735–1803, Scottish poet.

Beat·ty (bē′tē), *n.* **David** (*1st Earl of the North Sea and of Brooksby*), 1871–1936, British admiral.

beat-up (bēt′up′), *adj.* **1.** *Informal.* dilapidated; in poor condition from use: *a beat-up old jalopy.* —*n.* **2.** the warpwise count of tufts of pile in the warp of carpets. [adj., n. use of v. phrase *beat up*]

be·a·tus (bā ä′təs, -tōōs), *n., pl.* **-ti** (-tē). *Rom. Cath. Ch.* one who has been beatified, esp. a man or boy. [< L, ptp. of *beāre* to make happy, bless]

beau (bō), *n., pl.* **beaus, beaux** (bōz), *v.* —*n.* **1.** a frequent and attentive male companion. **2.** a male escort for a girl or woman. **3.** a dandy; fop. —*v.t.* **4.** to escort (a girl or woman), as to a social gathering: *No one has offered to beau her to the dance.* [ME < F < L *bellus* beautiful] —**beau′ish,** *adj.*

Beau′ Brum′mell (brum′əl), **1.** (*George Bryan Brummell*) 1778–1840, an Englishman who set the fashion in men's clothes. **2.** an extremely or excessively well-dressed man; fop; dandy. **3.** a dressing table for men, having a variety of elaborate arrangements of mirrors, candle brackets, etc. (invented in England in the late 18th century). Also, **Beau′ Brum′mel** (for defs. 2, 3).

Beau·fort (byōō′fərt *for 1;* bō′fərt *for 2, 3*), *n.* **1.** a town in S South Carolina. 6298 (1960). **2.** a town in E North Carolina. 2922 (1960). **3.** a boy's given name.

Beau′fort scale′ (bō′fərt), **1.** a scale of wind forces, described by name and range of velocity, and classified as from force 0 to force 12, or, sometimes, to force 17. **2.** a scale of the states of sea created by winds of these various forces up to and including force 10. [named after Sir Francis *Beaufort* (1774–1857), British admiral who devised it]

BEAUFORT WIND SCALE

Beaufort Force Number	State of Air	Wind Velocity in Knots
0	calm	0–1
1	light airs	1–3
2	slight breeze	4–6
3	gentle breeze	7–10
4	moderate breeze	11–16
5	fresh breeze	17–21
6	strong breeze	22–27
7	moderate gale	28–33
8	fresh gale	34–40
9	strong gale	41–47
10	whole gale	48–55
11	storm	56–65
12	hurricane	above 65

Beau′fort Sea′ (bō′fərt), a part of the Arctic Ocean, NE of Alaska.

beau geste (bō zhest′), *pl.* **beaux gestes** (bō zhest′). *French.* a fine gesture, often only for effect.

beau·greg·o·ry (bō greg′ə rē), *n., pl.* **-ries.** a blue and yellow damselfish, *Eupomacentris leucostictus,* found in the shallow waters off Bermuda, Florida, and the West Indies. [BEAU + *Gregory*]

Beau·har·nais (bō AR ne′), *n.* **1. Eu·gé·nie Hor·tense de** (œ zhā nē′ ôR täNs′ də), 1782–1837, queen of Holland: wife of Louis Bonaparte. **2. Jo·sé·phine de** (zhō zā fēn′ də), 1763–1814, empress of France 1804–09: first wife of Napoleon I.

beau′ ide′al, *pl.* **beaus ideal, beaux ideal** for 1; **beau ideals** for 2. **1.** a conception of perfect beauty. **2.** a model of excellence. [< F *beau idéal,* lit., fine ideal. See BEAU, IDEAL]

Beau·jo·lais (bō′zhə lā′), *n., pl.* **-laises** (-lāz′) for 2. **1.** a wine-growing region in E France, in Rhône department. **2.** a dry, fruity, red Burgundy wine from this region.

Beau·mar·chais (bō MAR she′), *n.* **Pierre Au·gus·tin Ca·ron de** (pyer ō gY stAN′ KA rôN′ də), 1732–99, French dramatist.

beau monde (bō′ mond′; *Fr.* bō mônd′), the fashionable world; high society. [< F: lit., fine world. See BEAU, MONDE]

Beau·mont (bō′mont), *n.* **1. Francis,** 1584–1616, English dramatist who collaborated with John Fletcher. **2. William,** 1785–1853, U.S. surgeon. **3.** a city in SE Texas. 119,175 (1960). **4.** a town in S California. 4288 (1960). **5.** a boy's given name.

Beau·mont (bō′mont), *n.* a walled plain in the fourth quadrant of the face of the moon: about 30 miles in diameter.

Beau·re·gard (bō′rə gärd′; *Fr.* bōʀə GAR′), *n.* **Pierre Gus·tave Tou·tant de** (pyer gY stAv′ tōō täN′ də), 1818–93, Confederate general in the U.S. Civil War.

beaut (byōōt), *n. Informal.* (often ironical) something or someone beautiful, remarkable, or perfect. [by shortening from BEAUTY]

beau·te·ous (byōō′tē əs, -tyəs), *adj. Chiefly Literary.* beautiful. [late ME; see BEAUTY, -OUS] —**beau′te·ous·ly,** *adv.* —**beau′te·ous·ness,** *n.*

beau·ti·cian (byōō tish′ən), *n.* a manager or an employee of a beauty parlor. [BEAUT(Y) + -ICIAN]

beau·ti·ful (byōō′tə fəl), *adj.* **1.** having beauty; delighting the senses or mind: *a beautiful dress; a beautiful speech.* **2.** excellent of its kind: *She served us a beautiful roast of beef; a beautiful putt into the seventh hole.* —**3.** the concept of beauty (usually prec. by *the*). **4.** (*construed as pl.*) beautiful things or people collectively (usually prec. by *the*): *the good and the beautiful.* **5.** the ideal of beauty (usually prec. by *the*): *to strive to attain the beautiful.* [BEAUTY + -FUL] —**beau′ti·ful·ly,** *adv.* —**beau′ti·ful·ness,** *n.*
—**Syn. 1.** comely, seemly, attractive, fair, beauteous. BEAUTIFUL, HANDSOME, LOVELY, PRETTY refer to a pleasing appearance. That is BEAUTIFUL which has perfection of form, color, etc., or noble and spiritual qualities: *a beautiful landscape, girl* (not *man*). HANDSOME often implies stateliness or pleasing proportion and symmetry: *a handsome man.* That which is LOVELY is beautiful but in a warm and endearing way: *a lovely smile.* PRETTY implies a moderate but noticeable beauty, esp. in that which is small or of minor importance: *a pretty child.* —**Ant. 1.** ugly.

beau·ti·fy (byōō′tə fī′), *v.t., v.i.,* **-fied, -fy·ing.** to make or become beautiful. [BEAUTY + -FY] —**beau·ti·fi·ca·tion** (byōō′tə fə kā′shən), *n.* —**beau′ti·fi′er,** *n.*
—**Syn.** adorn, embellish, enhance; bedeck, array.

beau·ty (byōō′tē), *n., pl.* **-ties. 1.** the quality that is present in a thing or person giving intense pleasure or deep satisfaction to the mind. It arises from sensory manifestations (as shape, color, sound, etc.), from a meaningful design or pattern, or from something else (as a personality in which high spiritual qualities are manifest). **2.** an attractive, well-formed girl or woman. **3.** a beautiful thing, as a work of art, building, etc. **4.** Often, **beauties.** that which is beautiful in nature or in some natural or artificial environment. **5.** an individually pleasing or beautiful quality; grace; charm: *a vivid blue area that is the one real beauty of the painting.* **6.** a particular advantage: *One of the beauties of this medicine is the freedom from aftereffects.* **7.** (chiefly in ironical use) something extraordinary: *My hangover next day was a beauty.* **8.** something excellent of its kind: *The yacht was a beauty.* [ME *be(a)ute* < OF *beaute;* r. ME *bealte* < OF, var. of *beltet* < VL **bellitāt-* (s. of **bellitās*) (L *bell(us)* fine + *-itāt-* -ITY)]
—**Syn. 1.** loveliness, pulchritude, comeliness, fairness, attractiveness. **2.** belle. —**Ant. 1.** ugliness.

beau·ty-bush (byōō′tē bōōsh′), *n.* a Chinese shrub, *Kolkwitzia amabilis,* having showy, pinkish flowers.

beau′ty con′test, a competition in which the girls or women with the most beautiful faces and figures are awarded prizes, titles, or the like.

beau′ty par′lor, *U.S.* an establishment for the hair-dressing, manicuring, or other beauty treatment of women. Also called **beau′ty salon′, beau′ty shop′.**

beau′ty sleep′, *Informal.* **1.** sleep before midnight, assumed to be necessary for one's beauty. **2.** any extra sleep.

beau′ty spot′, 1. a tiny patch worn, usually on the face, to set off the fairness of the skin. **2.** a mole or other dark mark on the skin. **3.** any place of exceptional scenic or architectural beauty: *Montserrat is the beauty spot of the islands.*

Beau·vais (bō vā′; *Fr.* bō ve′), *n.* a city in and the capital of Oise, in NW France: 13th century cathedral. 36,533 (1962).

Beau·voir (bōv wär′; *Fr.* bō VWAR′), *n.* **Si·mone de** (sē môn′ də), 1908–86, French playwright, novelist, and essayist.

beaux (bōz; *Fr.* bō), *n.* a pl. of **beau.**

Beaux-Arts (bō zär′; *Fr.* bō ZAR′), *adj.* **1.** noting or pertaining to a style of architecture, popularly associated with the École des Beaux-Arts, in Paris, that prevailed in France in the late 19th century and that was adopted in the U.S. and elsewhere c1900, characterized by the free and eclectic use and adaptation of French architectural features of the 16th–18th centuries, including mansard roofs, heavy rustication, engaged columns, banded columns, quoins, cantons, accentuated jambstones, chenaux, cartouches, and sculpture, combined so as to give a massive, elaborate, and often ostentatious effect, and characterized also by the use of symmetrical plans preferably allowing vast amounts of space for public halls, corridors, etc., as well as for landscaping around buildings. **2.** resembling the architecture, architectural precepts, or teaching methods of the École des Beaux-Arts in Paris: often used in a pejorative sense to designate excessive formalism disregarding considerations of structural truth, advanced aesthetic theory, rational planning, or economy. —*n.* **3.** (*l.c.*) the fine arts, as painting, sculpture, etc.

beaux-es·prits (bō zes prē′), *n. French.* pl. of **bel-esprit.**

Beaux′ Strat′agem, The (bōz), a comedy (1707) by George Farquhar.

beaux yeux (bōz yœ′), *French.* beautiful eyes; good looks (often used ironically): *We didn't hire you for your beaux yeux.*

bea·ver[1] (bē′vər), *n., pl.* **-vers,** (*esp. collectively*) **-ver** for 1. **1.** an amphibious rodent of the genus *Castor,* having sharp incisors, webbed hind feet, and a flattened tail, noted for its ability to dam streams with trees, branches, etc. **2.** the fur of this animal. **3.** a flat, round hat made of beaver fur or a similar fabric. **4.** a tall, cylindrical hat for men, formerly made of beaver and now of a fabric simulating this fur. Cf. **opera hat, silk hat, top hat. 5.** *Informal.* a full beard or a man wearing one. **6.** *Textiles.* **a.** a cotton cloth with a thick nap, used chiefly in the manufacture of work clothes. **b.** (formerly) a heavy, soft, woolen cloth with a thick nap, made to resemble beaver fur. **7.** (*cap.*) a native or inhabitant of Oregon (the **Beaver State**) (used as a nickname). [ME *bever,* OE *beofor, befor;* c. G *Biber,* Lith *bebrùs,* L *fiber,* Skt *babhrús* reddish brown, large ichneumon] —**bea′ver-like′,** *adj.* —**bea′ver·ish,** *adj.*

Beaver, *Castor canadensis* (Total length 3½ ft., tail 1 ft.)

bea·ver[2] (bē′vər), *n. Armor.* **1.** a piece of plate armor for covering the lower part of the face and throat, worn esp. with an open helmet, as a sallet or basinet. Cf. **buffe, wrapper** (def. 7). **2.** a piece of plate armor, pivoted at the sides, forming part of a close helmet below the visor or ventail. Also, **bever, bevor.** [earlier *bever,* orig. short for *bever hat,* hat made of beaver's fur, but also used, by transfer, in sense of face-guard; r. late ME *baviere* < MF, in same sense (OF: bib), equiv. to *bave* slaver + *-iere* < L *-āria*, fem. of *-ārius* -ER[2]]

Bea·ver (bē′vər), *n.* a town in W Pennsylvania. 6160 (1960).

Bea·ver·board (bē′vər bōrd′, -bôrd′), *n. Trademark.* a light, stiff sheeting made of wood fiber and used in building, esp. for partitions, temporary structures, etc.

Bea·ver·brook (bē′vər brŏŏk′), *n.* **William Max·well Aitken, Lord** (*1st Baron*), 1879–1964, English publisher, born in Canada.

bea′ver cloth′, beaver[1] (def. 6).

bea·ver·ette (bē′və ret′), *n.* rabbit fur dyed to resemble beaver. [BEAVER[1] + -ETTE]

Bea′ver Falls′, a city in W Pennsylvania. 16,240 (1960).

bea′ver poi′son, the water hemlock, *Cicuta maculata.*

Bea′ver State′, Oregon (used as a nickname).

Bea·ver·ton (bē′vər tən), *n.* a town in NW Oregon. 5937 (1960).

bea·ver-tree (bē′vər trē′), *n.* See **sweet bay** (def. 2). [BEAVER[1] + TREE]

Be·be (bē′bē), *n.* a girl's given name.

be·bee·rine (bə bēr′ēn, -in, beb′ē ə rēn′), *n. Pharm.* an alkaloid resembling quinine, obtained from the bark of the greenheart and other plants. [< G *Bebeerin*, equiv. to (*Bebeer*(*ubaum*) bebeeru tree + *-in* -INE[2])]

be·bee·ru (bə bēr′ōō), *n.* greenheart (def. 1). [< Sp *bibirú* < Carib]

Be·bel (bā′bəl), *n.* **Fer·di·nand Au·gust** (fûr′dᵊnand′ ô′gəst; *Ger.* feʀ′di nänt′ ou′gŏŏst), 1840–1913, German socialist and writer.

be·bop (bē′bop′), *n. Jazz.* bop[1]. [imit. of staccato beat found in phrasing] —**be′bop′per,** *n.*

Beb·ry·ces (be brī′sēz), *n.pl.* the original inhabitants of Bithynia who lost their land to the Mariandyni.

bec., because.

be·calm (bi käm′), *v.t.* **1.** to deprive (a sailing vessel) of the wind necessary to move it; subject to a calm: *The schooner was becalmed in the horse latitudes for two weeks.* **2.** *Archaic.* to calm; pacify. [BE- + CALM]

be·came (bi kām′), *v.* pt. of **become.**

be·cause (bi kôz′, -koz′, -kuz′), *conj.* **1.** for the reason that; due to the fact that: *The boy was absent because he was ill.* —*adv.* **2.** by reason; on account (usually fol. by *of*): *The game was called because of rain.* [ME *bi cause* BY CAUSE]

—**Syn. 1.** BECAUSE, AS, SINCE, FOR, INASMUCH AS agree in implying a reason for an occurrence or action. BECAUSE introduces a direct reason: *I was sleeping because I was tired.* As and SINCE are so casual as to imply merely circumstances attendant on the main statement: *As* (or *since*) *I was tired, I was sleeping.* The reason, proof, or justification introduced by FOR is like an afterthought or a parenthetical statement: *I was sleeping, for I was tired.* INASMUCH AS implies concession; the main statement is true in view of the circumstances introduced by this conjunction: *Inasmuch as I was tired, it seemed best to sleep.*

—**Usage.** See **reason.**

bec·ca·fi·co (bek′ə fē′kō), *n., pl.* **-cos, -coes.** any of several small, European birds, esp. the garden warbler, *Sylvia hortensis*, esteemed as a delicacy. [< It, equiv. to *becca*(*re*) (to) peck (see BEAK[1]) + *fico* FIG[1]]

bé·cha·mel (bā′shə mel′; *Fr.* bā sha mel′), *n.* a white sauce, sometimes seasoned with onion and nutmeg. Also called **be′chamel sauce′.** [named after Louis, Marquis de *Béchamel* (steward of Louis XIV of France), its originator]

be·chance (bi chans′, -chäns′), *v.i., v.t.* **-chanced, -chanc·ing.** *Archaic.* to befall. [from phrase *by chance*]

be·charm (bi chärm′), *v.t.* to charm; bewitch; captivate. [ME; see BE-, CHARM]

bêche (besh, bāsh), *n.* a grab for retrieving tools used in drilling a well. [< F: spade]

bêche-de-mer (besh′də mâr′), *n., pl.* **bêches-de-mer,** (*esp. collectively*) **bêche-de-mer** for 1. **1.** a trepang. **2.** a former name of **Neo-Melanesian.** [< F: lit., spade of (the) sea, alter. of Pg *biche do mar* worm of the sea, sea-slug]

Bech·u·a·na (bech′ōō ä′nə, bek′yōō-), *n., pl.* **-nas,** (*esp. collectively*) **-na.** Tswana (def. 1).

Bech·u·a·na·land (bech′ōō ä′nə land′, bek′yōō-), *n.* former name of **Botswana.**

beck[1] (bek), *n.* **1.** a beckoning gesture. **2. at someone's beck and call,** ready to do someone's bidding; subject to someone's slightest wish: *He has three secretaries at his beck and call.* **3.** *Chiefly Scot.* a bow or curtsy of greeting. —*v.t., v.i.* **4.** *Archaic.* beckon. [ME *becke*, short var. of *becne*(*n*) (to) BECKON]

beck[2] (bek), *n. Brit. Dial.* a brook, esp. a swiftly running stream with steep banks. [ME *becc* < Scand; cf. Icel *bekkr;* akin to OE *bece*, D *beek*, G *Bach* brook]

beck[3] (bek), *v.t. Metalworking.* to form (a billet or the like) into a tire or hoop by rolling or hammering on a mandrel or anvil. [v. use of *beck* (n.), back formation from *beck-iron*, var. of BICK-IRON]

Beck (bek), *n.* **Dave,** born 1894, U.S. labor leader: president of the International Brotherhood of Teamsters 1952–57.

Beck·er (bek′ər), *n.* **1. Carl Lo·tus** (lō′təs), 1873–1945, U.S. historian. **2. George Ferdinand,** 1847–1919, U.S. scientist and mathematician. **3. Howard Paul,** 1899–1960, U.S. sociologist.

beck·et (bek′it), *n. Naut.* **1.** a short length of rope for securing spars, coils of rope, etc., having an eye at one end and a thick knot or a toggle at the other, which is passed through the eye. **2.** a grommet of rope, as one used as a handle or oarlock. **3.** a grommet or eye on a block to which the standing end of a fall can be secured. **4.** a wooden cleat or hook secured to the shrouds of a sailing vessel to hold tacks and sheets not in use. [?]

Beck·et (bek′it), *n.* **Saint Thomas à,** 1118?–70, archbishop of Canterbury: murdered because of his opposition to Henry II's policies toward the church.

beck′et bend′, *Naut.* See **sheet bend.**

Beck·ett (bek′it), *n.* **Samuel,** born 1906, Irish playwright and novelist, living in France.

Beck·ford (bek′fərd), *n.* **William,** 1759–1844, English writer.

Beck·ley (bek′lē), *n.* a city in SW West Virginia. 18,642 (1960).

Beck·mann (bek′män′), *n.* **Max** (mäks), 1884–1950, German painter.

beck·on (bek′ən), *v.t., v.i.* **1.** to signal, summon, or direct by a gesture of the head or hand. **2.** to lure; entice. —*n.* **3.** a nod, gesture, etc., which beckons, summons, indicates agreement, or the like. [ME *beknen*, OE *gebē*(*a*)*cnian*, deriv. of *bēacen* BEACON] —**beck′on·er,** *n.* —**beck′on·ing·ly,** *adv.*

Beck·y (bek′ē), *n.* a girl's given name, form of **Rebecca.**

be·clasp (bi klasp′, -kläsp′), *v.t.* to clasp all around or on all sides. [BE- + CLASP]

be·cloud (bi kloud′), *v.t.* **1.** to darken or obscure with clouds. **2.** to make confused: *Angry words beclouded the issue.* [BE- + CLOUD]

be·come (bi kum′), *v.,* **be·came, be·come, be·com·ing.** —*v.i.* **1.** to come, change, or grow to be (as specified): *He became tired.* **2.** to come into being. —*v.t.* **3.** to be attractive on; befit in appearance; suit: *That gown becomes you.* **4.** to be suitable or necessary to the dignity, situation, or responsibility of: *conduct that becomes an officer and a gentleman.* **5. become of,** to happen to; be the fate of: *What will become of him?* [ME *becumen*, OE *becuman* to come about, happen; c. D *bekomen*, G *bekommen*, Goth *biqiman*. See BE-, COME]

be·com·ing (bi kum′ing), *adj.* **1.** tending to suit or to give a pleasing effect or attractive appearance, as to a person or thing: *a becoming dress; a becoming hairdo.* **2.** suitable; proper: *a becoming sentiment.* —*n.* **3.** any process of change. **4.** *Aristotelianism.* any change involving realization of potentialities, as a movement from the lower level of potentiality to the higher level of actuality. [BECOME + -ING[1], -ING[2]] —**be·com′ing·ly,** *adv.* —**be·com′ing·ness,** *n.*

—**Syn. 1.** comely. **2.** fitting, meet, appropriate, fit, apt, right, decorous, congruous, seemly.

Béc·quer (be′keʀ), *n.* **Gus·ta·vo A·dol·fo** (gōōs tä′vō ä dôl′fō), 1836–70, Spanish poet.

Bec·que·rel (bek′ə rel′; *Fr.* bekᵊ ʀel′), *n.* **1. A·lex·an·dre Ed·mond** (a lek säN′drᵊ ed môN′), 1820–91, French physicist (son of Antoine César). **2. An·toine Cé·sar** (äN twAN′ sā zAʀ′), 1788–1878, French physicist. **3. An·toine Hen·ri** (äN twAN′ äN ʀē′), 1852–1908, French physicist (son of Alexandre Edmond): Nobel prize 1903.

Becquerel′ effect′, *Physics.* the electromotive force produced by the unequal illumination of two identical electrodes placed in an electrolyte. [named after A. H. BECQUEREL]

Becquerel′ rays′, *Obs.* rays emitted by radioactive substances. [named after A. H. BECQUEREL]

be·crawl (bi krôl′), *v.t.* to crawl toward or over. [BE- + CRAWL]

be·crip·ple (bi krip′əl), *v.t.,* **-pled, -pling.** to make or cause to become crippled. [BE- + CRIPPLE]

bed (bed), *n., v.,* **bed·ded, bed·ding.** —*n.* **1.** a piece of furniture upon which or within which a person sleeps. **2.** the mattress and bedclothes together with the bedstead of a bed. **3.** the bedstead alone. **4.** the act or situation of sleeping: *A cup of cocoa and then bed.* **5.** the use of a bed for the night; lodging: *fifteen shillings for bed and breakfast.* **6.** the marital relationship. **7.** any resting place: *making his bed under a tree.* **8.** something resembling a bed in form or position. **9.** a piece or area of ground in a garden or lawn in which plants are grown. **10.** an area in a greenhouse in which plants are grown. **11.** the plants in such areas. **12.** the bottom of a lake, river, or other body of water. **13.** a piece or part forming a foundation or base. **14.** a layer of rock; a stratum. **15.** a foundation surface of earth or rock supporting a track, pavement, or the like: *a gravel bed for the roadway.* **16.** *Building Trades.* **a.** the underside of a stone, brick, slate, tile, etc., laid in position. **b.** the upper side of a stone laid in position. **c.** the layer of mortar in which a brick, stone, etc., is laid. **d.** the natural stratification of a stone: *a stone laid on bed.* **17.** *Furniture.* skirt (def. 6b). **18.** the flat surface in a printing press on which the form of type is laid. **19.** *Chem.* a compact mass of a substance functioning in a reaction as a catalyst or reactant. **20.** *Sports.* **a.** the canvas surface of a trampoline. **b.** the smooth, wooden floor of a bowling alley. **c.** the slate surface of a billiard table to which the cloth is fastened. **21.** *Zool.* flesh enveloping the base of a claw, esp. the germinative layer beneath the claw. **22.** Also called **mock, mock mold.** *Shipbuilding.* a shaped steel pattern upon which furnaced plates for the hull of a vessel are hammered to shape. **23.** See **bed and board. 24. get up on the wrong side of the bed,** to be irritable or bad-tempered from the start of a day: *Never try to reason with him when he's gotten up on the wrong side of the bed.* **25. in bed, a.** beneath the covers of a bed. **b.** engaged in sexual intercourse. **26. make a bed,** to fit a bed with sheets and blankets. **27. make one's bed,** *Informal.* to be responsible for one's actions and their results: *You've made your bed, now lie in it.* **28. put to bed, a.** to help (someone) go to bed. **b.** *Printing.* to lock up (forms) in a press in preparation for printing. **c.** *Slang.* to work on the preparation of (an edition of a newspaper, periodical, etc.) up to the time of going to press. —*v.t.* **29.** to provide with a bed. **30.** to put to bed. **31.** *Hort.* to plant in or as in a bed. **32.** to lay flat. **33.** to place in a bed or layer: *to bed oysters.* **34.** to embed, as in a substance: *bedding the flagstones in concrete.* **35.** to take or accompany to bed for purposes of sexual intercourse. —*v.i.* **36.** to go to bed: *bedding earlier in winter than in summer.* **37.** to have sleeping accommodations: *wanting to bed in the best hotels.* **38.** *Geol.* to form a compact layer or stratum. **39.** (of a metal structural part) to lie flat or close against another part. **40. bed down, a.** to make a bed for (a person, animal, etc.). **b.** to retire to bed: *They put out the fire and decided to bed down for the night.* [ME; OE *bedd;* c. D *bed*, Icel *bethr*, Goth *badi*, OHG *betti* (G *Bett*); akin to L *fōdere* to dig] —**bed′less,** *adj.* —**bed′like′,** *adj.*

B.Ed., Bachelor of Education.

be·dab·ble (bi dab′əl), *v.t.,* **-bled, -bling.** to dabble all over: *clothes bedabbled with paint.* [BE- + DABBLE]

bed′ and board′, **1.** living quarters and meals: *He paid only $30 a week for his bed and board.* **2.** obligations of marriage; charge of a household: *He said he would not be responsible for her debts after she left his bed and board.*

be·dash (bi dash′), *v.t.* **1.** to dash (something) all over: *to bedash a salad with pepper.* **2.** to dash or strike against: *windows bedashed with rain.* **3.** to demolish or ruin; obliterate: *His dreams of glory were quickly bedashed.* [BE- + DASH]

be·daub (bi dôb′), *v.t.* **1.** to daub all over; besmear; soil. **2.** to ornament gaudily or excessively. [BE- + DAUB]

Be·daux′ sys′tem (bə dō′), a system of payment for work on the basis of the number of points of work done in a given amount of time, each point representing one minute of work on a given job at a normal rate of speed. Also called **Bedaux′ plan′, point system.** [after Charles Eugène *Bedaux* (1887–1944) American industrialist]

be·daz·zle (bi daz′əl), *v.t.,* **-zled, -zling. 1.** to dazzle so as to blind or confuse: *The glare of the searchlights bedazzled him.* **2.** to impress forcefully, esp. so as to make oblivious to faults or shortcomings: *Audiences were bedazzled by her charm.* [BE- + DAZZLE] —**be·daz′zle·ment,** *n.* —**be·daz′zling·ly,** *adv.*

bed′ bolt′, (in a bed) a bolt attaching a side rail to the head or foot.

bed·bug (bed′bug′), *n.* **1.** a flat, wingless, bloodsucking hemipterous insect, *Cimex lectularius*, that infests houses and esp. beds. **2.** any of several other bloodsucking bugs of the family *Cimicidae.* [BED + BUG[1]]

Bedbug (def. 1) (Length 1/8 in.)

bed′ chair′, an adjustable frame for assisting invalids to sit up in bed. Also called **chair bed.**

bed·cham·ber (bed′chām′bər), *n.* bedroom. [ME *bedchaumbre.* See BED, CHAMBER]

bed·clothes (bed′klōz′, -klōthz′), *n.pl.* coverings for a bed, as sheets, blankets, etc.; bedding. [ME; see BED, CLOTHES]

bed·cloth·ing (bed′klō′thing), *n.* bedclothes. [BED + CLOTHING]

bed·cov·er (bed′kuv′ər), *n.* a bedspread. [BED + COVER]

bed·der (bed′ər), *n.* **1.** bedmaker (def. 1). **2.** an ornamental plant that is suitable for planting with other plants in a bed to achieve a certain visual effect. [BED + -ER[1]]

bed·ding (bed′ing), *n.* **1.** blankets, sheets, etc., used on a bed; bedclothes. **2.** litter; straw, etc., as a bed for animals. **3.** *Building Trades.* **a.** a foundation or bottom layer. **b.** a thin layer of putty laid in the rabbet of a window frame or muntin to give a pane of glass an even backing. **4.** *Geol.* arrangement of rocks in strata. [ME, OE; see BED, -ING[1]]

Bed·does (bed′ōz), *n.* **Thomas Lov·ell** (luv′əl), 1803–49, English dramatist and poet.

Bede (bēd), *n.* **Saint** ("*the Venerable Bede*"), A.D. 673?–735, English monk, historian, and theologian: wrote earliest history of England. Also, **Baeda.**

be·deck (bi dek′), *v.t.* to deck out; adorn, esp. in a showy or gaudy manner. [BE- + DECK]

—**Syn.** array, decorate, ornament; beautify, enhance.

bed·e·guar (bed′ə gär′), *n.* a gall on roses, esp. the sweetbrier, produced by a gall wasp. Also, **bed′e·gar′.** [< MF << Pers *bād-āwar*, lit., wind-brought]

bede·house (bēd′hous′), *n., pl.* **-hous·es** (-hou′ziz). beadhouse.

be·del (bēd′əl), *n. Archaic.* beadle. Also, **be′dell.**

bede·man (bēd′mən), *n., pl.* **-men.** beadsman.

bedes·man (bēdz′mən), *n., pl.* **-men.** beadsman.

bedes·wom·an (bēdz′wŏŏm′ən), *n., pl.* **-wom·en.** beadswoman.

be·dev·il (bi dev′əl), *v.t.,* **-iled, -il·ing** or (*esp. Brit.*) **-illed, il·ling. 1.** to torment or harass maliciously or diabolically, as with doubts, distractions, worries, etc. **2.** to possess as with a devil; bewitch. **3.** to cause confusion or doubt in; muddle; confound: *an issue bedeviled by prejudices.* **4.** to beset or hamper continuously: *an office bedeviled by electrical power failures.* [BE- + DEVIL] —**be·dev′il·ment,** *n.*

be·dew (bi dōō′, -dyōō′), *v.t.* to wet with or as with dew. [ME *bydewe.* See BE-, DEW]

bed·fast (bed′fast′, -fäst′), *adj.* confined to bed, as by illness or age. [BED + FAST[1]]

bed·fel·low (bed′fel′ō), *n.* **1.** Also called **bedmate.** a person who shares one's bed. **2.** a collaborator, esp. one who forms a temporary alliance for reasons of expediency: *Politics makes strange bedfellows.* [late ME *bedfelow.* See BED, FELLOW]

Bed·ford (bed′fərd), *n.* **1. John of Lancaster, Duke of,** 1389–1435, English regent of France. **2.** a city in and the county seat of Bedfordshire, in central England. 63,317 (1961). **3.** a city in NE Ohio, near Cleveland. 15,223 (1960). **4.** a town in central Virginia. 5921 (1960). **5.** a town in S Pennsylvania. 3696 (1960). **6.** Bedfordshire. **7.** a boy's given name.

Bed′ford cord′, cotton, worsted, rayon, or silk, distinctively woven with a lengthwise, corded effect.

Bed′ford Heights′, a town in N Ohio. 5275 (1960).

Bed·ford·shire (bed′fərd shēr′, -shər), *n.* a county in central England. 380,704 (1961); 473 sq. mi. *Co. seat:* Bedford. Also called **Bedford, Beds.**

bed·frame (bed′frām′), *n.* the frame of a bed, including the bedrails, headboard, and footboard. [BED + FRAME]

be·dight (bi dīt′), *v.t.,* **-dight, -dight** or **-dight·ed, -dight·ing.** *Archaic.* to deck out; array. [late ME; see BE-, DIGHT]

be·dim (bi dim′), *v.t.,* **-dimmed, -dim·ming.** to make dim. [BE- + DIM]

—**Syn.** darken, obscure, becloud. —**Ant.** illumine, brighten.

Bed·i·vere (bed′ə vēr′), *n.* **Sir,** *Arthurian Legend.* the knight who brought the dying King Arthur to the barge in which the three queens bore him to the Isle of Avalon.

be·di·zen (bi dī′zən, -diz′ən), *v.t.* to dress or adorn in a showy, gaudy, or vulgar manner. [BE- + DIZEN] —**be·di′zen·ment,** *n.*

bed′ jack′et, a short jacket worn over a nightgown or pajamas, esp. while sitting up in bed.

bed·lam (bed′ləm), *n.* **1.** a scene of wild uproar and confusion. **2.** (*cap.*) popular name for the Hospital of St. Mary of Bethlehem, formerly an insane asylum in SE London, England. **3.** any lunatic asylum or madhouse. [ME *bedlem, bethlem,* after *Bethlehem*]

bed·lam·ise (bed′lə mīz′), *v.t.,* **-ised, -is·ing.** *Chiefly Brit.* bedlamize.

bed·lam·ite (bed′lə mīt′), *n.* a lunatic. [BEDLAM + -ITE[1]]

bed·lam·ize (bed′lə mīz′), *v.t.,* **-ized, -iz·ing.** *Archaic.* **1.** to make insane; craze. **2.** to throw into an uproar; cause confusion in. [BEDLAM + -IZE]

bed·lamp (bed′lamp′), *n.* a lamp at the side or head of a bed. [BED + LAMP]

bed·light (bed′līt′), *n.* a bedlamp. [BED + LIGHT[1]]

bed′ lin′en, sheets and pillowcases.

Bedlington terrier (15 in. high at shoulder)

Bed·ling·ton (bed′ling tən), *n.* **1.** Also called **Bed·ling·ton·shire** (bed′ling tən shēr′, -shər). an urban area in E Northumberland, in N England. 29,373 (1961). **2.** See **Bedlington terrier.**

Bed′lington ter′rier, one of an English breed of terriers having a topknot and a thick, fleecy, usually bluish coat, groomed to resemble a lamb. [after BEDLINGTON]

Bed′loe's Is′land (bed′lōz), former name of **Liberty Island.** Also, **Bed′loe Is′land.**

bed·mak·er (bed′mā′kər), *n.* **1.** a person who makes up beds, as a chambermaid. **2.** a person who constructs beds, as a carpenter. [late ME; see BED, MAKER] —**bed′mak′ing,** *n.*

bed·mate (bed′māt′), *n.* **1.** bedfellow (def. 1). **2.** one's husband or wife. [BED + MATE[1]]

bed′ mold′ing, **1.** *Archit.* the molding or group of moldings immediately beneath the corona of a cornice. **2.** any molding under a projection.

bed′ of ros′es, a situation of luxurious ease; a highly agreeable position (often used ironically): *Professional boxing is no bed of roses.*

Bed·ou·in (bed′o͞o in, bed′win), *n., pl.* **-ins,** (*esp. collectively*) **-in,** *adj.* —*n.* **1.** an Arab of the desert, in Asia or Africa; nomadic Arab. **2.** a nomad; wanderer. —*adj.* **3.** of, pertaining to, or characteristic of the Bedouin. Also, **Beduin.** [late ME *Bedoyn* < MF *beduyn* (sing.) < Ar *badawīn,* pl. of *badawīy* desert-dweller (*badw* desert + *-īy* suffix of appurtenance)] —**Bed′ou·in·ism,** *n.*

bed·pad (bed′pad′), *n.* a pad or other protective covering used between the mattress and the bottom sheet of a bed. [BED + PAD[1]]

bed·pan (bed′pan′), *n.* **1.** a shallow toilet pan for use by persons confined to bed. **2.** bedwarmer. [BED + PAN[1]]

bed′ place′, a space housing a bed or bedding, esp. one having the form of a cupboard closed with doors or curtains.

bed·plate (bed′plāt′), *n.* a plate, platform, or frame supporting the lighter parts of a machine. Also called **base plate.** [BED + PLATE[1]]

bed·post (bed′pōst′), *n.* **1.** one of the upright supports of a bedstead. **2.** **bedposts,** *Bowling Slang.* a split in which the seven and ten pins remain standing. [BED + POST[1]]

bed·quilt (bed′kwilt′), *n.* a quilted coverlet. [BED + QUILT]

be·drab·ble (bi drab′əl), *v.t.,* **-bled, -bling.** to drench or muddy. [late ME; see BE-, DRABBLE]

be·drag·gle (bi drag′əl), *v.t.,* **-gled, -gling.** to make limp and soiled, as with rain or dirt. [BE- + DRAGGLE]

bed·rail (bed′rāl′), *n.* a board at the side of a bed connecting the footboard and headboard. [BED + RAIL[1]]

be·drench (bi drench′), *v.t.* to drench thoroughly; soak completely. [late ME; see BE-, DRENCH]

bed′ rest′, a prolonged rest in bed, as in the treatment of an illness.

bed·rid (bed′rid′), *adj.* **1.** bedridden. **2.** worn out; exhausted; decrepit. [ME *bedrede,* OE *bedreda, -rida,* equiv. to *bed* BED + *-rida* rider, akin to RIDE]

bed·rid·den (bed′rid′ən), *adj.* confined to bed. [var. (by confusion with ptp. of RIDE) of BEDRID]

bed·rock (bed′rok′), *n.* **1.** *Geol.* unbroken solid rock, overlaid in most places by soil or rock fragments. **2.** bottom layer; lowest stratum. **3.** any firm foundation or basis: *Technical courses will be founded on a bedrock of sound, general education so as to produce a well-rounded engineer.* **4.** the fundamental principles, as of a teaching, belief, science, etc.: *Let's strip away the cant and get down to bedrock.* —*adj.* **5.** basic; fundamental. [BED + ROCK[1]]

bed·roll (bed′rōl′), *n.* bedding rolled for portability and used esp. for sleeping out-of-doors. [BED + ROLL]

bed·room (bed′ro͞om′, -ro͝om′), *n.* **1.** a room furnished and used for sleeping. —*adj.* **2.** concerned mainly with love affairs or sex: *The movie is a typical bedroom comedy.* **3.** inhabited largely by commuters: *a bedroom community in Connecticut.* [BED + ROOM]

bed′room slip′per, a house slipper, often heelless and backless and with a flexible sole, of leather or any of various fabrics.

bed′room sub′urb. See **dormitory suburb.**

Beds (bedz), *n.* Bedfordshire.

bed·side (bed′sīd′), *n.* **1.** the side of a bed, esp. as the place of one attending the sick. —*adj.* **2.** at or for a bedside: *a bedside table.* [orig. BED + 's[1] + SIDE[1]]

bed′side man′ner, the attitude, approach, and demeanor of a doctor to his patients: *He has a charming bedside manner.*

bed-sit·ter (bed′sit′ər), *n.* *Brit. Informal.* a combination bedroom and sitting room. [BED-SITT(ING ROOM) + -ER[1]]

bed′-sit′ting room′ (bed′sit′ing), *Brit.* bed-sitter. [BED + SITTING ROOM]

bed·sock (bed′sok′), *n.* one of a pair of stockings worn in bed for warmth. [BED + SOCK[1]]

bed·sore (bed′sōr′, -sôr′), *n.* *Pathol.* a sore caused by prolonged contact with bedding, as in a long illness. [BED + SORE]

bed·spread (bed′spred′), *n.* an outer covering, usually decorative, for a bed. [BED + SPREAD]

bed·spring (bed′spring′), *n.* a set of springs for the support of a mattress. [BED + SPRING]

bed·stand (bed′stand′), *n.* a small table next to a bed. Also called **nightstand, night table.** [BED + STAND]

bed·stead (bed′sted′, -stid), *n.* the framework of a bed supporting the springs and a mattress. [late ME *bedstede.* See BED, STEAD]

bed′ stone′, the fixed lower member of a pair of millstones. Cf. **runner** (def. 13).

bed·straw (bed′strô′), *n.* a rubiaceous plant, *Galium verum,* or some allied species, formerly used as straw for stuffing mattresses. [late ME; see BED, STRAW]

bed·tick (bed′tik′), *n.* tick[3]. [BED + TICK[3]]

bed·time (bed′tīm′), *n.* the time at which one goes to bed. [ME; see BED, TIME]

bed′time sto′ry, a story told to a child at bedtime.

Bed·u·in (bed′o͞o in, bed′win), *n., pl.* **-ins** (*esp. collectively*) **-in,** *adj.* Bedouin.

bed′ wag′on, an open framework used in the 18th century to hold a pan of burning charcoal for airing bedding.

bed·ward (bed′wərd), *adv.* to or toward bed. Also, **bedwards.** [late ME; see BED, -WARD]

bed·warm·er (bed′wôr′mər), *n.* a long-handled, covered pan containing hot coals, used for warming beds. Also called **bedpan.** [BED + WARMER]

bed-wet·ting (bed′wet′ing), *n.* urinating in bed, esp. habitually and involuntarily; enuresis.

bee[1] (bē), *n.* **1.** any hymenopterous insect of the superfamily *Apoidea,* including social and solitary species of several families, as the bumblebees, honeybees, etc. **2.** the common honeybee, *Apis mellifera.* **3.** *Chiefly U.S.* a community social gathering in order to perform some task, engage in a contest, etc.: *a sewing bee; a spelling bee.* **4.** **have a bee in one's bonnet, a.** to be obsessed with one idea. **b.** to have eccentric or fanciful ideas or schemes: *The old lady obviously has a bee in her bonnet, but we're very fond of her.* **5.** **put the bee on,** *Informal.* to attempt to obtain money from, as for a loan or donation: *Because he was the richest man in town, the orphanage always put the bee on him at Christmas.* [ME; OE *bīo, bēo;* c. D *bij,* OHG *bīa,* Icel *bý;* akin to G *Biene*] —**bee′like′,** *adj.*

Bee[1] (def. 2)
A, Queen; B, Drone;
C, Worker

bee[2] (bē), *n.* **1.** Also called **bee block.** *Naut.* a piece of hardwood, bolted to the side of the bowsprit, through which to reeve stays. **2.** *Obs.* a metal ring or bracelet. [ME *beh* ring, OE *bēag, bēah;* c. OHG *boug,* Icel *baugr;* akin to BOW[1]]

Bee (bē), *n.* a girl's given name. Also, **Bea.**

B.E.E., Bachelor of Electrical Engineering.

bee′ balm′, a perennial garden or wild flower of the genus *Monarda,* esp. the Oswego tea.

Bee·be (bē′bē), *n.* **(Charles) William,** 1877–1962, U.S. naturalist, explorer, and writer.

bee′ bee′tle, a European beetle, *Trichodes apiarius,* which sometimes infests beehives.

bee′ bird′, any of several birds, as the bee-eaters, that feed on bees.

bee′ block′, *Naut.* bee[2] (def. 1).

bee·bread (bē′bred′), *n.* a mixture of pollen and honey stored by bees and fed to their young. [BEE[1] + BREAD]

beech (bēch), *n.* **1.** any tree of the genus *Fagus,* of temperate regions, having a smooth gray bark, and bearing small, edible, triangular nuts. **2.** Also called **beech·wood** (bēch′wo͝od′). the wood of such a tree. [ME *beche,* OE *bēce* < Gmc **bōkjōn-.* See BOOK] —**beech′en,** *adj.* —**beech′y,** *adj.*

Bee·cham (bē′chəm), *n.* **Sir Thomas,** 1879–1961, English conductor and impresario.

beech·drops (bēch′drops′), *n.* (*construed as sing. or pl.*) **1.** a low annual plant, *Epifagus virginiana,* without green foliage, parasitic upon the roots of the beech. **2.** the squawroot. [BEECH + DROP + -S[3]]

Bee·cher (bē′chər), *n.* **1.** **Henry Ward,** 1813–87, U.S. preacher and writer. **2.** his father **Ly·man** (lī′mən), 1775–1863, U.S. preacher and theologian.

beech′ fern′, a fern, *Dryopteris Phegopteris,* of northern temperate regions.

beech′ mar′ten. See **stone marten.**

beech′ mast′, the edible nuts of the beech, esp. when lying on the ground.

beech·nut (bēch′nut′), *n.* the small, triangular, edible nut of the beech. [BEECH + NUT]

bee·di (bē′dē), *n.* bidi.

bee-eat·er (bē′ē′tər), *n.* any of several colorful, insectivorous birds of the family *Meropidae,* of the Old World tropics, which feed chiefly on bees.

beef (bēf), *n., pl.* **beeves** (bēvz) for 2; **beefs** for 4, *v.* —*n.* **1.** the flesh of a cow, steer, or bull raised and killed for its meat. **2.** an adult cow, steer, or bull raised for its meat. **3.** *Informal.* **a.** brawn; muscular strength. **b.** strength; power. **c.** weight, as of a person. **d.** human flesh. **4.** *U.S. Slang.* a complaint. —*v.i.* **5.** *U.S. Slang.* to complain; grumble. **6.** **beef up,** *Informal.* to strengthen; add strength, men, force, etc., to: *During the riots, the police department was beefed up by volunteers.* [ME < OF *boef* < L *bov-* (s. of *bōs*) ox, cow; akin to COW[1]] —**beef′less,** *adj.*

beef′ bouil′lon. See **beef tea.**

beef·burg·er (bēf′bûr′gər), *n.* hamburger. [BEEF + (HAM)BURGER]

beef·cake (bēf′kāk′), *n.* *Slang.* photographs of scantily clad young men in magazines or the like, posed to display their muscles. [BEEF + CAKE, modeled on *cheesecake*]

beef′ cat′tle, cattle, as Hereford, raised for its edible meat.

beef·eat·er (bēf′ē′tər), *n.* **1.** a yeoman of the English royal guard or a warder of the Tower of London. **2.** *Slang.* an Englishman. **3.** a person who eats beef. **4.** a well-fed person. [BEEF + EATER]

beef′ ex′tract, a soluble paste of beef or beef blood extracts.

bee′ fly′, any of numerous dipterous insects of the family *Bombyliidae,* some of which resemble bees.

beef·steak (bēf′stāk′), *n.* a slice of beef for broiling, pan-frying, etc. [BEEF + STEAK]

beef′steak bego′nia, an herb, *Begonia feasti,* having nearly round, thick, fleshy leaves that are red on the underside and light-pink flowers.

beef′ tea′, a broth made either by straining water in which bits of lean beef have been cooked or by dissolving beef extract in hot water. Also called **beef bouillon.**

beef-wit·ted (bēf′wit′id), *adj.* thick-witted; stupid. —**beef′-wit′ted·ly,** *adv.* —**beef′-wit′ted·ness,** *n.*

beef·wood (bēf′wo͝od′), *n.* **1.** Also called **horsetail tree.** any of several, chiefly Australian trees of the genus *Casuarina,* having feathery branches that lack true foliage leaves. **2.** the hard, reddish wood of any of these trees, used for making furniture. [BEEF + WOOD[1]]

beef·y (bē′fē), *adj.,* **beef·i·er, beef·i·est.** **1.** of or like beef. **2.** brawny; thickset; heavy. **3.** obese. [BEEF + -Y[1]] —**beef′i·ly,** *adv.* —**beef′i·ness,** *n.*

bee′ glue′, propolis.

bee′ gum′, *Southern and Western U.S.* **1.** a gum tree, hollowed as by decay, in which bees live or from which hives are made. **2.** a beehive.

bee·hive (bē′hīv′), *n.* **1.** a hive or receptacle, conventionally dome-shaped, constructed as a habitation for bees. **2.** a natural habitation for bees, as in a hollowed-out tree or the like. **3.** a crowded, busy place. **4.** something resembling an artificial beehive in appearance, as a hut, a hairdo, etc. **5.** Also called **bee′hive ov′en.** an oven for making coke, characterized by its dome-shaped roof. [BEE[1] + HIVE]

Bee′hive State′, Utah (used as a nickname).

beek (bēk), *Scot. and North Eng.* —*v.t., v.i.* **1.** to bask or warm in the sunshine or before a fireplace, stove, or bonfire. **2.** (of wood) to season by exposure to heat. —*n.* **3.** *Obs.* the act of basking or warming by a fire. [ME *beke;* ? akin to BAKE]

bee·keep·er (bē′kē′pər), *n.* a person who raises bees. [BEE[1] + KEEPER]

bee·keep·ing (bē′kē′ping), *n.* the rearing and breeding of honeybees. [BEE[1] + KEEPING]

bee′ kil′ler. See **robber fly.**

bee′ lark′spur. See **candle larkspur.**

bee·line (bē′līn′), *n.* a direct line or route: *The minute he arrived at the party he made a beeline for the kitchen.* [BEE[1] + LINE[1]]

Be·el·ze·bub (bē el′zə bub′), *n.* **1.** the chief devil; Satan. **2.** a devil. **3.** (in Milton's *Paradise Lost*) one of the fallen angels, second only to Satan.

bee′ mar′tin, *U.S. Dial.* the kingbird, *Tyrannus tyrannus.*

bee′ moth′, a brownish pyralid moth, *Galleria mellonella,* the larvae of which feed on the honeycombs in beehives. Also called **wax moth.**

been (bin), *v.* pp. of **be.**

beep (bēp), *n.* **1.** a short, relatively high-pitched tone produced by a horn or other device as a signal, warning, or the like. **2.** one of the periodic signals sounded by a beeper. —*v.i.* **3.** to make or emit a beeping sound. —*v.t.* **4.** to sound (a horn, warning signal, etc.): *impatient drivers beeping their horns.* **5.** to announce or make known by beeping: *impatient drivers beeping their annoyance.* [imit.]

beep·er (bē′pər), *n.* **1.** a device that connects into a telephone circuit and transmits a periodic signal as an indication that the conversation over the circuit is being recorded. **2.** *Informal.* a device emitting signals for radio control of a pilotless aircraft. **3.** *Slang.* a person who directs the flight of a pilotless aircraft. [BEEP + -ER[1]]

bee′ plant′, any plant frequently used by bees as a source of nectar, esp. the cleome, *Cleome surrelata,* or figwort.

beer (bēr), *n.* **1.** an alcoholic beverage made by brewing and fermentation from cereals, usually malted barley, and flavored with hops and the like for a slightly bitter taste. **2.** any of various beverages, whether alcoholic or not, made from roots, molasses or sugar, yeast, etc.: *root beer; ginger beer.* **3.** an individual serving of beer; a glass or bottle of beer. [ME *bere,* OE *bēor;* c. D, G *Bier* (Icel *bjórr,* prob. < OE)]

Beer (bēr), *n.* **Thomas,** 1889–1940, U.S. author.

Beer (bēr; *Ger.* bār), *n.* a crater in the second quadrant of the face of the moon: about 8 miles in diameter.

beer′ and skit′tles, *Brit.* amusement; pleasure; fun, with or without beer or other drinks.

Beer·bohm (bēr′bōm), *n.* **Sir Max,** 1872–1956, English essayist, critic, and caricaturist.

beer′ en′gine, *Brit.* See **beer pump.**

beer′ gar′den, an outdoor tavern, usually resembling a garden, where beer and other alcoholic beverages are served.

beer′ hall′, a bar, cabaret, or the like, chiefly serving beer and usually offering music, dancing, etc.

beer·house (bēr′hous′), *n., pl.* **-hous·es** (-hou′ziz). *Brit.* an establishment licensed to serve only liquors fermented from malt, as beer, ale, or the like. [BEER + HOUSE]

Beer·naert (*Fr.* ber NART′; *Eng.* bâr′närt), *n.* **Auguste Ma·rie Fran·çois** (*Fr.* ō gyst′ MA RĒ′ FRÄN SWA′), 1829–1912, Belgian statesman: Nobel peace prize 1909.

beer·pull (bēr′po͝ol′), *n.* **1.** the handle of a beer pump. **2.** the pump itself. [BEER + PULL]

beer′ pump′, a pump for drawing beer directly from a keg or cask.

Beers (bērz), *n.* **Clifford Whit·ting·ham** (hwit′ing əm, wit′-), 1876–1943, U.S. pioneer in mental hygiene.

Beer·she·ba (bēr shē′bə, bēr′shə-), *n.* **1.** a city in Israel, near the northern limits of the Negev desert: the southernmost city of ancient Palestine. 43,158 (1960). **2.** **from Dan to Beersheba.** See **Dan** (def. 4).

beer·y (bēr′ē), *adj.*, **beer·i·er, beer·i·est.** **1.** of, like, or abounding in beer. **2.** affected by or suggestive of beer: *beery exuberance; a beery breath.* [BEER + -Y[1]] —**beer′i·ness,** *n.*

bee′ sage′. See **crimson sage.**

bees′ and hon′ey, *Chiefly Brit. Slang.* money. [rhyming slang]

beest·ings (bē′stingz), *n.* (*construed as sing.*) the first milk or colostrum of a mammal, esp. a cow, after giving birth. Also, **beastings, biestings.** [late ME *bestynge,* OE *bȳsting,* equiv. to *bēost* beestings (c. OHG *biost* > G *Biest*) + *-ing* -ING[1]]

bees·wax (bēz′waks′), *n.* **1.** wax[1] (def. 1). —*v.t.* **2.** to rub or treat with beeswax. [BEE[1] + 's[1] + WAX[1]]

bees·wing (bēz′wing′), *n.* a light flaky deposit found in port and some other bottle-aged wines. [BEE[1] + 's[1] + WING]

beet[1] (bēt), *n.* **1.** any of various biennial chenopodiaceous plants of the genus *Beta,* esp. *B. vulgaris,* having a fleshy red or white root. Cf. **sugar beet. 2.** the edible root of such a plant. **3.** the leaves served as a salad or cooked vegetable. [late ME *bete,* OE *bēte* < L *bēta*] —**beet′like′,** *adj.*

beet[2] (bēt), *v.t. Brit. Dial.* **1.** to correct, repent of, or atone for one's sins or faults. **2.** to mend, repair, or improve something. **3.** to relieve thirst, hunger, or any form of want; to supply another's needs. **4.** to kindle or mend a fire. Also, **bete.** [ME *bēte(n),* OE *bētan* to amend < Gmc **bōtjan* (**bōt-* BOOT[2] + *-jan* inf. suffix)]

Bee·tho·ven (bā′tō vən; *Ger.* bāt′hō fən), *n.* **Lud·wig van** (lud′wig van, lōōd′-; *Ger.* lōōt′viKH fän, lōōd′-), 1770–1827, German composer. —**Bee·tho·vi·an** (bā tō′vē ən), **Bee·tho·ve·ni·an** (bā′tō vē′nē ən, -vēn′yən), *adj.*

bee·tle[1] (bēt′ᵊl), *n., v.,* **-tled, -tling.** —*n.* **1.** any of numerous insects of the order *Coleoptera,* characterized by hard, horny forewings that cover and protect the membranous flight wings. **2.** (loosely) any of various insects resembling this insect, as a cockroach. —*v.i.* **3.** *Brit.* to move about like a beetle; scurry: *He beetled off to catch the train.* [ME *bētylle, bityl,* OE *bitela* (*bitel-* biting (*bit-* BITE + *-el* adj. suffix) + *-a* n. suffix)]

Beetle[1] (def. 1), *Pantomorus godmani* (Length ⅓ in.)

bee·tle[2] (bēt′ᵊl), *n., v.,* **-tled, -tling.** —*n.* **1.** a heavy hammering or ramming instrument, usually of wood, used to drive wedges, force down paving stones, compress loose earth, etc. **2.** any of various wooden instruments for beating linen, mashing potatoes, etc. —*v.t.* **3.** to use a beetle on; drive, ram, beat, or crush with a beetle. **4.** to finish (cloth) by means of a beetling machine. [late ME *betel,* OE *bētl, bȳtel* hammer (c. MLG *bētel* chisel), equiv. to *bēat-* BEAT + *-il* n. suffix] —**bee′tler,** *n.*

bee·tle[3] (bēt′ᵊl), *adj., v.,* **-tled, -tling.** —*adj.* **1.** projecting; overhanging: *beetle brows.* —*v.i.* **2.** to project; jut out; overhang: *a cliff that beetles over the sea.* **3.** to hang or tower over in a threatening or menacing manner: *The prospect of bankruptcy beetled over him.* [back formation from BEETLE-BROWED]

beet′ leaf′hop·per, a leafhopper, *Circulifer tenellus,* of the western U.S., a vector of curly top, esp. in beets.

bee·tle-browed (bēt′ᵊl broud′), *adj.* **1.** having heavy projecting eyebrows. **2.** scowling; sullen; reproachful. [ME *bitel-browed.* See BEETLE[1], BROW, -ED[3]]

bee·tle-crush·er (bēt′ᵊl krush′ər), *n. Brit.* **1.** a large boot. **2.** a large foot, esp. if flat. **3.** *Slang.* a policeman. [BEETLE[1] + CRUSHER]

bee·tle·head (bēt′ᵊl hed′), *n.* a stupid person; blockhead. [BEETLE[2] + HEAD] —**bee′tle·head′ed,** *adj.*

bee′ tree′, a hollow tree used by wild bees as a hive, esp. the basswood or American linden.

beet′ root′, *Chiefly Brit.* beet[1] (def. 2).

beet′ sug′ar, sugar from the roots of the sugar beet.

beeves (bēvz), *n.* a pl. of **beef.**

bee′ wolf′, a larva of the bee beetle.

bef., before.

B.E.F., British Expeditionary Force; British Expeditionary Forces.

be·fall (bi fôl′), *v.,* **-fell, -fall·en, -fall·ing.** —*v.i.* **1.** to happen or occur. **2.** *Archaic.* to come, as by right. —*v.t.* **3.** to happen to. [ME *befall(en),* OE *befeallan.* See BE-, FALL (V.)]

be·fit (bi fit′), *v.t.,* **-fit·ted, -fit·ting.** to be fitting or appropriate for; be suited or becoming to: *His clothes befit the occasion.* [late ME; see BE-, FIT[1]]

be·fit·ting (bi fit′ing), *adj.* fitting; suitable; proper; becoming: *planned with a befitting sense of majesty.* [BEFIT + -ING[2]] —**be·fit′ting·ly,** *adv.* —**be·fit′ting·ness,** *n.*
—**Syn.** appropriate, apt, seemly. —**Ant.** improper.

be·flag (bi flag′), *v.t.,* **-flagged, -flag·ging.** to cover or deck with flags. [BE- + FLAG[1]]

be·fog (bi fog′, -fôg′), *v.t.,* **-fogged, -fog·ging. 1.** to envelop in fog or obscurity; becloud: *Low-hanging clouds befogged the city.* **2.** to render unclear, as a problem or complex matter by irrelevancies or distractions: *Petty differences befogged the legislators' task.* [BE- + FOG[1]]

be·fool (bi fōōl′), *v.t.* **1.** to fool; deceive; dupe: *innocents befooled by confidence men.* **2.** *Obs.* to treat as a fool; call (someone) a fool. [late ME *befole(n).* See BE-, FOOL[1]]

be·fore (bi fōr′, -fôr′), *adv.* **1.** in front; in advance; ahead: *The king entered with macebearers walking before.* **2.** in time preceding; previously: *If we'd known before, we'd have let you know.* **3.** earlier or sooner: *Begin at noon, not before.* —*prep.* **4.** in front of; ahead of; in advance of: *a lawn before a house; one's shadow advancing before him.* **5.** previous to; earlier than: *life before the war.* **6.** ahead of; in the future of; awaiting: *The golden age is before us.* **7.** in preference to; rather than: *They would die before surrendering.* **8.** in precedence of, as in order or rank: *We put freedom before fame.* **9.** in the presence or sight of: *to appear before an audience.* **10.** under the jurisdiction or consideration of: *He was summoned before a magistrate.* **11.** confronted by; in the face of: *Before such wild accusations, he was too stunned to reply.* **12.** in the regard of: *a crime before man and God.* **13.** under the overwhelming influence of: *bending before the storm.* **14.** without reckoning: *income before deductions.* —*conj.* **15.** previously to the time when: *before we go.* **16.** sooner than; rather than: *I will die before I submit.* [ME *before(n),* OE *beforan,* equiv. to *be* BY + *foran* before (*fore* FORE[1] + *-an* adv. suffix)]
—**Ant. 1.** behind. **2.** afterward. **3.** later.

be·fore·hand (bi fōr′hand′, -fôr′-), *adv., adj.* in anticipation; in advance; ahead of time: *We should have known that beforehand. I hope to be beforehand with my report.* [ME *bifor-hand.* See BEFORE, HAND]

be·fore·time (bi fōr′tīm′, -fôr′-), *adv. Archaic.* formerly. [ME *bifor time.* See BEFORE, TIME]

be·foul (bi foul′), *v.t.* to make foul; defile; sully: *a bird that befouls its own nest.* [ME *bi-foulen.* See BE-, FOUL] —**be·foul′er,** *n.* —**be·foul′ment,** *n.*

be·friend (bi frend′), *v.t.* to make friends or become friendly with; act as a friend to; aid: *to befriend the poor and the weak.* [BE- + FRIEND]

be·fud·dle (bi fud′ᵊl), *v.t.,* **-dled, -dling. 1.** to make stupidly drunk. **2.** to confuse, as with glib statements or arguments: *Stop befuddling the public with campaign promises.* [BE- + FUDDLE] —**be·fud′dler,** *n.* —**be·fud′dle·ment,** *n.*

beg (beg), *v.,* **begged, beg·ging.** —*v.t.* **1.** to ask for as a gift, as charity, or as a favor: *to beg alms; to beg forgiveness.* **2.** to ask to give one something or to do something; implore: *He begged me for alms. Sit down, I beg you.* **3.** to take for granted without basis or justification: *a statement that begs the very point we're disputing.* **4.** to fail or refuse to come to grips with; avoid; evade: *a report that consistently begs the whole problem.* —*v.i.* **5.** to ask alms or charity; live by asking alms. **6.** to ask humbly or earnestly: *begging for help; begging to differ.* **7.** (of a dog) to sit up, as trained, in a posture of entreaty. **8. beg off, a.** to entreat (someone) for release from (an obligation, promise, etc.). **b.** to obtain release from: *He had promised to drive us to the recital but begged off at the last minute.* **9. beg the question,** to assume the truth of the very point raised in a question. **10. go begging,** to remain open or available, as a position which is unfilled, an unsold item, etc.: *The job went begging for lack of qualified applicants.* [ME *begg(en),* by assimilation, OE **bedician,* syncopated var. of *bedecian* to beg; cf. Goth *bidagwa* beggar. See BEAD]
—**Syn. 2.** entreat, pray, crave, beseech, petition. BEG and REQUEST are used in certain conventional formulas, in the sense of *ask.* BEG, once a part of many formal expressions used in letter writing, debate, etc., is now used chiefly in such courteous formulas as *I beg your pardon; The Committee begs to report,* etc. REQUEST, more impersonal and now more formal, is used in giving courteous orders (*You are requested to report*) and in commercial formulas like *to request payment.*

beg (bāg; *Eng.* beg), *n. Turkish.* bey.

beg., **1.** begin. **2.** beginning.

be·ga·bled (bi gā′bəld), *adj.* abounding in or covered with gables. [BE- + GABLED]

be·gan (bi gan′), *v.* pt. of **begin.**

be·gar (bā′gär), *n. Anglo-Indian.* compulsory labor, as for the repair of bridges, roads, etc. [< Hindi *begār*]

be·gat (bi gat′), *v. Archaic.* pt. of **beget.**

be·gats (bi gats′), *n.pl. Slang.* genealogical lists, esp. those in the Old Testament books of the Bible. [n. pl. use of BEGAT]

be·gem (bi jem′), *v.t.,* **-gemmed, -gem·ming.** to cover with gems. [BE- + GEM]

be·get (bi get′), *v.t.,* **be·got** or (*Archaic*) **be·gat; be·got·ten** or **be·got; be·get·ting. 1.** (esp. of a male parent) to procreate or generate (offspring). **2.** to cause; produce as an effect: *the belief that power begets power.* [ME *beget(en)* (see BE-, GET); r. ME *biyete(n),* OE *begetan;* c. Goth *bigitan,* OHG *bigezzan*] —**be·get′ter,** *adv.*

beg·gar (beg′ər), *n.* **1.** one who begs alms, or lives by begging. **2.** a penniless person. **3.** a wretched fellow; rogue: *the surly beggar who collects the rents.* **4.** *Chiefly Brit.* a child or youngster (usually prec. by *little*): *a sudden urge to throttle the little beggar.* —*v.t.* **5.** to reduce to beggary; impoverish: *The family had been beggared by the war.* **6.** to cause one's resources of or ability for (description, comparison, etc.) to seem poor or inadequate. [ME *beggare, -ere.* See BEG[1] -ER[1]] —**beg′gar·hood′,** *n.*

beg·gar·dom (beg′ər dəm), *n.* beggary (def. 2). [BEGGAR + -DOM]

beg·gar·ly (beg′ər lē), *adj.* **1.** like or befitting a beggar. **2.** meanly inadequate: *I'm supposed to take all that responsibility for a beggarly $2500 a year.* [BEGGAR + -LY] —**beg′gar·li·ness,** *n.*

beg·gar's-lice (beg′ərz līs′), *n.* **1.** (*construed as pl.*) seeds or fruits which stick to clothing. **2.** (*construed as sing. or pl.*) any plant producing them. Also, **beg·gar-lice** (beg′ər līs′).

Beg′gar's Op′era, The, a ballad opera (1728) with text by John Gay and music arranged by John Pepusch.

beg·gar's-tick (beg′ərs tik′), *n.* **1.** one of the prickly awns or achenes of *Bidens frondosa* or similar plants. **2. beggar's-ticks,** (*construed as sing. or pl.*) the plant itself. **3.** See **bush trefoil.**

beg·gar-tick (beg′ər tik′), *n.* **1.** beggar's-tick. **2.** beggar's-lice.

beg·gar·weed (beg′ər wēd′), *n.* **1.** any of various tick trefoils, esp. *Desmodium purpureum,* grown for forage in subtropical regions. **2.** *Chiefly Brit.* any weed that impoverishes soil. [BEGGAR + WEED[1]]

beg·gar·y (beg′ə rē), *n., pl.* **-gar·ies** for 3. **1.** state or condition of utter poverty. **2.** beggars collectively. **3.** a place lived in or frequented by beggars. [late ME *beggerie.* See BEGGAR, Y[3]]

Beg·giat·o·a (bə jat′ō ə, bej′ə tō′ə), *n.* a genus of segmented, filamentous bacteria often occurring in masses in fresh and salt water containing compounds of sulfur. [< NL; named after F. S. *Beggiato,* 19th-century Italian botanist]

Beg·hard (beg′ərd, bi gärd′), *n.* a member of a former lay brotherhood, founded in Flanders in the 13th century, living after the manner of the Beguines. [< ML *beghard(us),* equiv. to *beg-* (see BEGUINE) + *-hardus* -ARD]

be·gin (bi gin′), *v.,* **be·gan, be·gun, be·gin·ning.** —*v.i.* **1.** to proceed to perform the first or earliest part of some action; commence; start: *Where shall I begin?* **2.** to come into existence; arise; originate: *The custom began during the Civil War.* —*v.t.* **3.** to proceed to perform the first or earliest part of (some action): *Begin the job tomorrow.* **4.** to originate; be the originator of: *civic leaders who began the reform movement.* [ME *beginn(en),* OE *beginnan,* equiv. to *be-* BE- + *-ginnan* to begin, perh. orig. to open, akin to YAWN] —**be·gin′ner,** *n.*
—**Syn. 3.** BEGIN, COMMENCE, INITIATE, START (when followed by noun or gerund) refer to setting into motion or progress something which continues for some time. BEGIN is the common term: *to begin knitting a sweater.* COMMENCE is a more formal word, often suggesting a more prolonged or elaborate beginning: *to commence proceedings in court.* INITIATE implies an active and often ingenious first act in a new field: *to initiate a new procedure.* START means to make a first move or to set out on a course of action: *to start paving a street.* **4.** institute, inaugurate, initiate. —**Ant. 1.** end.

Be·gin (bā′gin), *n.* **Me·na·hem** (mə nä′ khəm), born 1913, Israeli statesman, born in Poland: premier 1977–83; Nobel peace prize 1978.

begin′ner's luck′, the initial good fortune or success commonly supposed to accrue to a person who has recently taken up a new pursuit, as a sport, game, etc.: *Making a grand slam the first time you play bridge is simply beginner's luck.*

be·gin·ning (bi gin′ing), *n.* **1.** act or circumstance of entering upon an action or state. **2.** the point of time or space at which anything begins: *the beginning of the Christian era.* **3.** Often, **beginnings.** the first part or initial stage of anything: *the beginning of a book; the beginnings of science.* **4.** origin; source; first cause: *A misunderstanding was the beginning of their quarrel.* [ME *beginnung, -ing.* See BEGIN, -ING[1]]
—**Syn. 1.** initiation, inauguration, inception. **2.** start, commencement, outset, onset, arising, emergence. —**Ant. 1.** ending. **2.** end.

be·gird (bi gûrd′), *v.t.,* **-girt** or **-gird·ed, -gird·ing.** to gird about; encompass; surround. [ME *begird(en),* OE *begierdan.* See BE-, GIRD[1]]

be·gone (bi gôn′, -gon′), *v.i.* to go away; depart (usually used in the imperative). [ME; see BE (impv.), GONE]

be·gon·ia (bi gōn′yə, -gō′nē ə), *n.* any tropical plant of the genus *Begonia,* including species cultivated for the handsome, succulent, often varicolored leaves and waxy flowers. [< NL, named after Michel *Bégon* (1638–1710), French patron of science; see -IA; name coined by Plumier, French botanist]

be·gor·ra (bi gôr′ə, -gor′ə, bē-), *interj. Irish Eng.* euphemism for *by God: Begorra, it's a fine day.* Also, **be·gor′ah, be·gor′rah.**

be·got (bi got′), *v.* pt. and a pp. of **beget.**

be·got·ten (bi got′ᵊn), *v.* a pp. of **beget.**

be·grime (bi grīm′), *v.t.,* **-grimed, -grim·ing.** to make grimy. [BE- + GRIME]

be·grudge (bi gruj′), *v.t.,* **-grudged, -grudg·ing. 1.** to envy or resent the pleasure or good fortune of (someone): *She begrudged her friend the award.* **2.** to be reluctant to give, grant, or allow: *She did not begrudge the money spent on her children's education.* [late ME *bigrucche(n).* See BE-, GRUDGE] —**be·grudg′ing·ly,** *adv.*
—**Syn. 1.** See **envy.**

be·guile (bi gīl′), *v.t.,* **-guiled, -guil·ing. 1.** to influence by guile; mislead; delude. **2.** to take away from by cheating or deceiving (usually fol. by *of*): *to be beguiled of money.* **3.** to charm or divert: *a multitude of attractions to beguile the tourist.* **4.** to pass (time) pleasantly: *beguiling the long afternoon with a good book.* [ME *bigile(n).* See BE-, GUILE] —**be·guile′ment,** *n.* —**be·guil′er,** *n.*
—**Syn. 1.** deceive, cheat. **3.** amuse, entertain.

Beg·uin (beg′in; *Fr.* be gaN′), *n.* a Beghard. [back formation from BEGUINE]

be·guine (bi gēn′), *n.* **1.** a South American dance in bolero rhythm. **2.** a modern social dance based on the beguine. **3.** music for either of these dances. [< F (West Indies) *béguine,* equiv. to *béguin* BIGGIN[1], trifling love affair + *-e* fem. n. suffix]

Beg·uine (beg′ēn), *n. Rom. Cath. Ch.* a member of a lay sisterhood, founded in Liège in the 12th century, in which private property is retained and members may leave the sisterhood at any time. [late ME *begyne* < MF *beguine,* after Lambert *Begue* (i.e., stammerer), founder of the order, + *-ine* -INE[1]]

be·gum[1] (bē′gəm), *n.* (in India) a high-ranking Muslim lady, often a widow. [< Urdu *begam* << Turkic *bigim* (*big* prince + *-im* fem. suffix). See BEY]

be·gum[2] (bi gum′), *v.t.,* **-gummed, -gum·ming.** to smear, soil, clog, etc., with or as with gum or a gummy substance. [BE- + GUM[1]]

be·gun (bi gun′), *v.* pp. of **begin.**

Be·haim (bā′hīm), *n.* a crater in the fourth quadrant of the face of the moon: about 35 miles in diameter.

be·half (bi haf′, -häf′), *n.* **1. in** or **on behalf of,** as a representative of or a proxy for: *On behalf of my colleagues, I address you tonight.* **2. in** or **on one's behalf,** in the interest or aid of: *He interceded in my behalf.* [ME *behalve* beside, OE *be healfe* (*him*) by (his) side. See BE-, HALF]

Be·han (bē′ən), *n.* **Bren·dan (Francis)** (bren′dən), 1923–64, Irish playwright.

Be·har (bi här′, bə-), *n.* Bihar.

be·have (bi hāv′), *v.,* **-haved, -hav·ing.** —*v.i.* **1.** to act in a particular way; conduct or comport oneself or itself: *The ship behaves well.* **2.** to act properly: *Did the child behave?* —*v.t.* **3.** to comport (oneself) in a proper manner: *Sit up, blow your nose, and behave yourself.* [ME *behave(n)* (reflexive). See BE-, HAVE]
—**Syn. 1.** perform, acquit oneself, deport oneself.

be·hav·ior (bi hāv′yər), *n.* **1.** manner of behaving or acting. **2.** *Psychol.* **a.** the aggregate of observable responses of the organism in their interrelationships. **b.** any activity of the organism taken as the subject matter of psychology. **3.** the action or reaction of any material under given circumstances: *the behavior of tin under heat.* Also, *esp. Brit.,* **be·hav′iour.** [BEHAVE + *-ior* (on model of *havior,* var. of *havor* < MF *(h)avoir* << L *habēre* to have); r. earlier *behavoure, behaver.* See BEHAVE, -OR[1]] —**be·hav′ior·al,** *adj.* —**be·hav′ior·al·ly,** *adv.*
—**Syn. 1.** demeanor, manners, bearing, carriage. BEHAVIOR, CONDUCT, DEPORTMENT, COMPORTMENT refer to one's actions before or toward others, esp. on a particular occasion: *His behavior at the party was childish.* CONDUCT refers to actions viewed collectively, esp. as measured by an ideal standard: *Conduct is judged according to principles of ethics.* DEPORTMENT is behavior related to a code or to an arbitrary standard: *Deportment is guided by rules of etiquette. The teacher gave Susan a mark of B in deportment.* COMPORTMENT is behavior

as viewed from the standpoint of one's management of one's own actions: *His comportment was marked by a quiet assurance.*

behav′ioral sci′ence, a science or branch of learning, as psychology, sociology, etc., deriving its concepts from observation of the behavior of living organisms.

be·hav·ior·ism (bi hāv′yə riz′əm), *n.* *Psychol.* the theory or doctrine that regards objective and accessible facts of behavior or activity of man and animals as the only proper subject for psychological study. [BEHAVIOR + -ISM] —**be·hav′ior·ist,** *n., adj.* —**be·hav′ior·is′tic,** *adj.* —**be·hav′ior·is′ti·cal·ly,** *adv.*

behav′ior pat′tern, *Sociol.* a recurrent way of acting by an individual or group toward a given object or in a given situation.

be·head (bi hed′), *v.t.* **1.** to cut off the head of; kill or execute by decapitation. **2.** *Geol.* (of a pirate stream) to divert the headwaters of (a river, stream, etc.). [ME *behe(f)d(en), beheved(en),* OE *behēafdian.* See BE-, HEAD] —**be·head′al,** *n.* —**be·head′er,** *n.*

be·held (bi held′), *v.* pt. and pp. of **behold.**

be·he·moth (bi hē′məth, bē′ə-), *n.* **1.** an animal, perhaps the hippopotamus, mentioned in Job 40:15–24. **2.** *U.S. Informal.* any monstrous or grotesque creature or thing. [< Heb *b'hēmōth* (expressing dignity, greatness), pl. of *b'hēmāh* beast; r. ME *bemoth*]

be·hen·ic (bə hen′ik, -hē′nik), *adj.* *Chem.* of or derived from behenic acid; docosanoic. [*behen,* var. of BEN² + -IC]

behen′ic ac′id, *Chem.* a saturated fatty acid, $C_{21}H_{43}COOH$, obtained from plant sources, used chiefly in the manufacture of cosmetics, waxes, and plasticizers.

be·hest (bi hest′), *n.* **1.** a command or directive. **2.** an earnest or strongly worded request. [ME, OE *behǣs* promise. See BE-, HEST]

be·hind (bi hīnd′), *prep.* **1.** at or toward the rear of: *Look behind the house.* **2.** after; later than: *You are behind the appointed time.* **3.** in the state of making less progress than: *We can't afford to fall behind our competitors.* **4.** on the farther side of; beyond: *behind the mountain.* **5.** supporting; promoting: *He is behind the plan.* **6.** hidden or unrevealed by: *Malice lay behind her smile.* **7.** at the controls of: *behind the wheel of a car.* —*adv.* **8.** at or toward the rear; rearwards: *to lag behind.* **9.** in a place, state, or stage already passed. **10.** in arrears; behindhand: *to be behind in one's rent.* **11.** slow, as a watch or clock: *more than 20 minutes behind.* **12.** as a cause or often latent feature of: *Behind their harassment lay the traditional fear of foreigners.* **13.** *Archaic.* in reserve; to come: *Greater support is yet behind.* —*adj.* **14.** following: *the man behind.* —*n.* **15.** *Slang.* the buttocks. [ME *behinde(n),* OE *behindan.* See BE-, HIND¹]
—**Syn. 1, 2.** BEHIND, AFTER both refer to a position following something else. BEHIND applies primarily to position in space, and suggests that one person or thing is at the back of another; it may also refer to (a fixed) time: *He stood behind the chair. The train is behind schedule.* AFTER applies primarily to time; when it denotes position in space, it is not used with precision, and refers usually to bodies in motion: *Rest after a hard day's work. They entered the room, one after another.*
—**Usage.** See **back.**

be·hind·hand (bi hīnd′hand′), *adv., adj.* **1.** late; tardy. **2.** behind in progress; backward: *She was never behindhand in following artistic fads.* **3.** in debt or arrears. [BEHIND + HAND]

Be·his·tun (bā′hi stōōn′), *n.* a ruined town in W Iran: site of a cliff which bears on its face a cuneiform inscription in Old Persian, Elamite, and Babylonian that provided a key for the decipherment of cuneiform in other languages. Also, **Bisitun, Bisutun.**

Beh·men (bā′mən), *n.* **Ja·kob** (jä′kəb). See **Böhme, Jakob.**

Beh·men·ism (bā′mə niz′əm), *n.* Boehmenism.

Beh·men·ist (bā′mə nist), *n.* Boehmenist. Also, **Beh·men·ite** (bā′mə nīt′).

be·hold (bi hōld′), *v.,* **be·held, be·hold·ing,** *interj.* —*v.t.* **1.** to observe; look at; see. —*interj.* **2.** look; see: *And, behold, three sentries of the King did appear.* [ME *behold(en),* OE *behaldan* to keep. See BE-, HOLD¹] —**be·hold′a·ble,** *adj.* —**be·hold′er,** *n.*
—**Syn. 1.** regard, gaze upon, view; watch; discern.

be·hold·en (bi hōl′dən), *adj.* obligated; indebted: *a man beholden to no one.* [ME, adj. use of *beholden,* old ptp. of BEHOLD]

be·hoof (bi hōōf′), *n., pl.* **-hooves** (-hōōvz′). use; advantage; benefit: *The money was spent for his own behoof.* [ME *behove,* OE *behōf* profit, need; c. D *behoef,* G *Behuf*]

be·hoove (bi hōōv′), *v.,* **-hooved, -hoov·ing.** (*chiefly in impersonal use*) —*v.t.* **1.** to be necessary or proper for, as for moral or ethical considerations; be incumbent on: *It behooves the court to weigh evidence impartially.* **2.** to be worthwhile, as for personal profit or advantage: *It would behoove you to be nicer to her because she could do a lot for you.* —*v.i.* **3.** to be needful, proper, or due: *It behooves that I be silent.* [ME *behove(n),* OE *behōfian* to need (*behōf* BEHOOF + *-ian* inf. suffix)]

Beh·rens (bâr′ənz; *Ger.* bā′Rəns), *n.* **Pe·ter** (pē′tər; *Ger.* pā′tər), 1868–1940, German architect.

Beh·ring (bā′Ring), *n.* **1. E·mil von** (ā′mēl fən), 1854–1917, German physician and bacteriologist: Nobel prize in medicine 1901. **2. Vi·tus** (vē′tōōs). See **Bering, Vitus.**

Behr·man (bâr′mən), *n.* **S(amuel) N(athan),** 1893–1973, U.S. playwright and author.

Bei·der·becke (bī′dər bek′), *n.* **Leon Bismarck** (*"Bix"*), 1903–31, U.S. jazz cornetist and composer.

beige (bāzh), *n.* **1.** very light brown, as of undyed wool; light gray with brownish tinge. —*adj.* **2.** of the color beige. [< F < ?]

Bei·jing (bā′jing′), *n.* Pinyin spelling of **Peking.**

Bei·lan′ Pass′ (bā län′), a mountain pass in SE Turkey near Syria. 2395 ft.

be·ing (bē′ing), *n.* **1.** the fact of existing; existence (as opposed to nonexistence). **2.** conscious, mortal existence; life: *Our being is as an instantaneous flash of light in the midst of eternal night.* **3.** substance or nature: *of such a being as to arouse fear.* **4.** something that exists: *inanimate beings.* **5.** a living thing: *strange, exotic beings that live in the depths of the sea.* **6.** a human being; person: *the most beautiful being you could imagine.* **7.** (*cap.*) God. **8.** *Philos.* **a.** that which has actuality either materially or in idea. **b.** absolute existence in a complete or perfect state, lacking no essential characteristic; essence. [ME; see BE, -ING¹]
—**Usage.** The expressions BEING AS and BEING THAT (*Being as it's midnight, let's go home*) are not generally accepted in standard English as substitutes for SINCE, AS, or BECAUSE (*Since it's midnight, let's go home*).

Bei·ra (bā′rə), *n.* a seaport in central Mozambique. 57,072 (est. 1955).

Bei·rut (bā rōōt′, bā′rōōt), *n.* a seaport in and the capital of Lebanon. 400,000 (est. 1953). Also, **Beyrouth.**

bej·el (bej′əl), *n.* *Pathol.* a nonvenereal treponematosis that occurs chiefly among Arab children, thought to be due to the spirochete *Treponema pallidum.* [< Ar]

be·jew·el (bi jōō′əl), *v.t.,* **-eled, -el·ing** or (*esp. Brit.*) **-elled, -el·ling.** to adorn with or as with jewels. [BE- + JEWEL]

bel¹ (bel), *n.* *Physics.* a unit of power ratio, equal to 10 decibels. [named after A. G. BELL]

bel² (bel), *n.* bael.

Bel (bāl, bel), *n.* a deity of the Babylonians and Assyrians, god of the earth. [< L *Bēl(us)* < Gk *Bêlos* BAAL]

Bel (bel), *n.* a girl's given name. Also, **Bell, Bella, Belle.**

Bel., **1.** Belgian. **2.** Belgic. **3.** Belgium.

Be·la (bā′lə, bel′ə; *Hung.* bā′lo), *n.* a boy's given name.

be·la·bor (bi lā′bər), *v.t.* **1.** to assail persistently, as with scorn or ridicule: *a book that belabors the provincialism of his contemporaries.* **2.** to work away at (something) for an unreasonable amount of time; worry: *He kept belaboring the point long after we had agreed.* **3.** *Archaic.* to beat vigorously; ply with heavy blows. **4.** *Obs.* to labor at. Also, *Brit.,* **be·la′bour.** [BE- + LABOR]

Bel·a·fon·te (bel′ə fon′tē, -tā), *n.* **Harry,** born 1926, U.S. singer and actor.

Bel Air (bel âr′), a town in NE Maryland. 4300 (1960).

Bel-a-mi (bel A mē′), *n.* a novel (1885) by Guy de Maupassant.

Bel′ and the Drag′on, a book of the Apocrypha which is included as chapter 14 of Daniel in the Douay Bible.

Be·las·co (bi las′kō), *n.* **David,** 1854–1931, U.S. playwright, actor, and producer.

be·lat (bə lät′), *n.* a strong northwesterly wind that blows seaward on the southeast coast of Arabia, esp. during the winter and early spring, accompanied by dust and sand carried from the interior. [< Ar]

be·lat·ed (bi lā′tid), *adj.* **1.** coming or being after the customary, useful, or expected time: *belated birthday greetings.* **2.** made late; delayed or detained: *We started the meeting without the belated representative.* **3.** obsolete; old-fashioned; out-of-date: *a belated view of world politics.* **4.** *Archaic.* overtaken by darkness or night. [*belate* to delay (BE- + LATE) + -ED²] —**be·lat′ed·ly,** *adv.* —**be·lat′ed·ness,** *n.*

Bel·a·trix (be lā′triks), *n.* a star of the second magnitude in the constellation Orion. [< L: warrior (fem.)]

be·laud (bi lôd′), *v.t.* to praise (someone or something) excessively, esp. with sarcasm or implied ridicule. [BE- + LAUD] —**be·laud′er,** *n.*

Be·la·ún·de (be′lä ōōn′de), *n.* **Fer·nan·do** (feR nän′dō), (*Fernando Belaúnde Terry*), born 1913?, Peruvian architect and statesman: president 1963–68, 1980–.

be·lay (bi lā′), *v.,* **-layed, -lay·ing,** *n.* —*v.t.* **1.** *Naut.* to fasten (a rope) by winding around a pin or short rod inserted in a holder so that both ends of the rod are clear. **2.** *Mountain Climbing.* **a.** to secure (a person) by attaching to one end of a rope. **b.** to secure (a rope) by attaching to a person or to an object offering stable support. **3.** (used chiefly in the imperative) to cease (an action). —*v.i.* **4.** to belay a rope: *Belay on that cleat over there.* —*n.* **5.** *Mountain Climbing.* a rock, bush, or other object sturdy enough for a running rope to be passed around it to secure a hold. [ME *belegge(n),* OE *belecgan.* See BE-, LAY¹]

belay′ing cleat′, cleat (def. 2).

belay′ing pin′, *Naut.* a short, round bar of metal or wood, inserted in a fife rail or pin rail, to which a rope is belayed.

Belaying pins

bel can·to (bel′ kan′tō; *It.* bel kän′tō), *Music.* a smooth, cantabile style of singing. [< It: lit., fine singing, equiv. to *bel* (c. BEAU) + *canto* (see CANTO)]

belch (belch), *v.i.* **1.** to eject gas spasmodically and noisily from the stomach through the mouth; eruct. **2.** to emit contents violently, as a gun, geyser, or volcano. **3.** to issue spasmodically; gush forth. —*v.t.* **4.** to eject (gas or the like) spasmodically or violently; give forth: *an air shaft belching fire and smoke.* —*n.* **5.** an instance of belching; eructation. **6.** a violent emittance of flame, smoke, gas, etc. [ME *belche(n),* OE *bealcan;* c. D *balken* to bray] —**belch′er,** *n.*

beld (beld), *adj.* *Scot.* bald; hairless.

bel·dam (bel′dəm), *n.* **1.** an old woman, esp. an ugly one; hag. **2.** *Obs.* grandmother. Also, **bel·dame** (bel′dəm, -dām′). [late ME, equiv. to *bel-* grand- (< MF *bel, belle* fine; see BEAU, BELLE) + *dam* mother (see DAM²)]

Bel·ding (bel′ding), *n.* a town in central Michigan. 4887 (1960).

be·lea·guer (bi lē′gər), *v.t.* **1.** to surround with an army. **2.** to surround with annoyances or troubles. [BE- + LEAGUER¹] —**be·lea′guer·er,** *n.*

be·lec·tion (bi lek′shən), *n.* *Archit., Furniture.* bolection.

Be·lém (bə lem′; *Port.* be leNM′), *n.* a seaport in N Brazil on the Pará River. 380,667 (1960). Also called **Pará.**

bel·em·nite (bel′əm nīt′), *n.* *Paleontol.* a conical fossil, several inches long, consisting of the internal calcareous rod of an extinct animal allied to the cuttlefish; a thunderstone. [< Gk *bélemn(on)* a dart (akin to *bállein* to throw) + -ITE¹]

Be·len (bə len′), *n.* a town in central New Mexico. 5031 (1960).

bel-es·prit (bel es prē′), *n., pl.* **beaux-es·prits** (bō zes prē′). *French.* a person of great wit or intellect.

Bel·fast (bel′fast, -fäst, bel fast′, -fäst′), *n.* **1.** a seaport in and capital of Northern Ireland, on the E coast. 440,100 (est. 1958). **2.** a town in S Maine. 6140 (1960).

Bel·fort (bel fôR′), *n.* **1.** a fortress city in E France, strategically located on a mountain pass between the Vosges and Jura mountains: siege 1870–71; battle 1944. 51,280 (1962). **2. Ter·ri·toire de** (te Rē twar′ də), a department in E France. 113,027 (1962); 235 sq. mi. *Cap.:* Belfort.

bel·fry (bel′frē), *n., pl.* **-fries.** **1.** a bell tower, either attached to a church or other building or standing apart. **2.** the part of a steeple or other structure in which a bell is hung. **3.** a frame of timberwork which sustains a bell. **4.** *Slang.* head; mind: *a belfry full of curious notions.* [late ME *belfray,* appar. b. earlier *berfray* (< MF < Gmc) + ML *belfredus,* dissimilated var. of *berefredus* < Gmc; cf. MHG *ber(c)frit,* equiv. to *berc* defense, protection, refuge (c. OE *gebeorg;* see HARBOR) + *frit* peace, (place of) safety (c. OE *frith*)]

Belg., **1.** Belgian. **2.** Belgium.

bel·ga (bel′gə), *n.* the Belgian currency unit in foreign exchange, introduced 1926, equal to five Belgian francs. [< F, Flem < L *Belga,* sing. of BELGAE]

Bel·gae (bel′jē), *n.* (*construed as pl.*) an ancient people, chiefly Celtic, that lived in northern Gaul.

Bel·gaum (bel goum′), *n.* a city in S Maharashtra, in W India. 85,988 (1951).

Bel·gian (bel′jən, -jē ən), *n.* **1.** a native or an inhabitant of Belgium. **2.** one of a breed of large, strong, draft horses, raised originally in Belgium. —*adj.* **3.** of or pertaining to Belgium. [BELGI(UM) + -AN]

Bel′gian Con′go, a former name of **Zaire.**

Bel′gian grif′fon, one of a variety of the Brussels griffon having a black or reddish-brown and black coat.

Bel′gian hare′, one of a breed of domestic rabbits.

Bel′gian sheep′dog, one of a breed of dogs raised originally in Belgium for herding sheep. Cf. **Groenendael.**

Bel′gian truss′, a truss, used esp. in sloping roofs, having parallel struts and an unequal number of panel points along the slope and the tie rod. See illus. under **truss.**

Bel·gic (bel′jik), *adj.* **1.** of or pertaining to the Belgae. **2.** Belgian. [< L *belgic(us).* See BELGAE, -IC]

Bel·gium (bel′jəm, -jē əm), *n.* a kingdom in W Europe, bordering the North Sea, N of France. 9,229,000 (est. 1961); 11,779 sq. mi. *Cap.:* Brussels. French, **Bel·gique** (bel zhēk′).

Bel·go·rod-Dnes·trov·ski (byel′go rôt′dnye strôf′ski), *n.* a seaport in SE Moldavia, in the SW Soviet Union in Europe, on the Black Sea. 38,600 (1959). Rumanian, **Cetatea Alba.** Formerly, **Akkerman.**

Bel·grade (bel′grād, -gräd, -grad, bel grād′, -gräd′, -grad′), *n.* a city in and the capital of Yugoslavia and the republic of Serbia, at the confluence of the Danube and Sava rivers. 1,209,360. Serbo-Croatian, **Beograd.**

Bel·gra·no (bel grä′nō; *Sp.* bel grä′nō), *n.* **Ma·nuel** (mä nwel′), 1770–1820, Argentine general.

Bel·gra·vi·a (bel grā′vē ə), *n.* **1.** a fashionable district in London, England, adjoining Hyde Park. **2.** *Brit.* the newly rich, upper middle class.

Bel·gra·vi·an (bel grā′vē ən), *adj.* *Brit.* **1.** of or from Belgravia. **2.** fashionable in the style of the upper middle class. [BELGRAVI(A) + -AN]

Be·li·al (bē′lē əl, bēl′yəl), *n.* **1.** *Theol.* the spirit of evil personified; the devil; Satan. **2.** (in Milton's *Paradise Lost*) one of the fallen angels. [< Heb, equiv. to *b'li* negative + *ya'al* use, profit]

be·lie (bi lī′), *v.t.,* **-lied, -ly·ing.** **1.** to misrepresent: *The newspaper belied the facts.* **2.** to show to be false; contradict: *His trembling hands belied his calm voice.* **3.** to act unworthily according to the standards of (a tradition. one's ancestry, etc.). **4.** *Archaic.* to lie about; slander. —**be·li′er,** *n.*

be·lief (bi lēf′), *n.* **1.** something believed; an opinion or conviction: *the belief that the earth is flat.* **2.** confidence in the truth or existence of something not immediately susceptible to rigorous proof: *a statement unworthy of belief.* **3.** confidence; faith; trust: *a child's belief in his parents.* **4.** a religious tenet or tenets: *the Christian belief.* [earlier *bile(e)ve* (n. use of v.); r. ME *bileave,* equiv. to *bi-* BE- + *leave,* OE *(ge)lēafa;* c. D *geloof,* G *Glaube;* akin to Goth *galaubeins*]
—**Syn. 1.** view, tenet, persuasion. **2.** assurance BELIEF, CERTAINTY, CONVICTION refer to acceptance of, or confidence in, an alleged fact or body of facts as true or right without positive knowledge or proof. BELIEF is such acceptance in general: *belief in astrology.* CERTAINTY indicates unquestioning belief and positiveness in one's own mind that something is true: *I know this for a certainty.* CONVICTION is settled, profound, or earnest belief that something is right: *a conviction that a decision is just.* **4.** doctrine, dogma.

be·lieve (bi lēv′), *v.,* **-lieved, -liev·ing.** —*v.i.* **1.** to have confidence in the truth, the existence, or the reliability of something, although without absolute proof that one is right in doing so: *Only if one believes in something can he act purposefully.* —*v.t.* **2.** to have confidence or faith in the truth of (a positive assertion, story, etc.). **3.** to have confidence in the assertions of (a person). **4.** to have a conviction that (a person or thing) is, has been, or will be engaged in a given action or involved in a given situation: *The fugitive is believed to be headed for the Mexican border.* **5.** to be more or less confident; suppose (usually fol. by a noun clause): *I believe that he has left town.* **6. believe in, a.** to be persuaded of the truth or existence of: *to believe in Zoroastrianism; to believe in ghosts.* **b.** to have faith in the reliability, honesty, benevolence, etc., of: *I can help only if you believe in me.* [ME *bileve(n),* equiv. to *bi-* BE- + *leven,* OE (Anglian) *(ge)lēfan;* c. D *gelooven,* G *glauben,* Goth *galaubjan*] —**be·liev′a·bil′i·ty, be·liev′a·ble·ness,** *n.* —**be·liev′a·ble,** *adj.* —**be·liev′a·bly,** *adv.* —**be·liev′er,** *n.* —**be·liev′ing·ly,** *adv.*

be·like (bi līk′), *adv.* *Archaic.* very likely; perhaps; probably. [BE- + LIKE¹]

Be·lin·da (bə lin′də), *n.* a girl's given name.

Bel·i·sar·i·us (bel′i sâr′ē əs), *n.* A.D. 505?–565, general of the Eastern Roman Empire.

Be·li·tong (be lē′tong), *n.* Billiton. Also, **Be·li·toeng, Be·li·tung** (be lē′tōōng).

be·lit·tle (bi lit′əl), *v.t.*, **-tled, -tling.** to regard, consider, or portray (something) as less impressive or important than it apparently is; depreciate; disparage. [BE- + LITTLE] —**be·lit′tle·ment,** *n.* —**be·lit′tler,** *n.* —**Syn.** minimize, decry.

be·live (bi līv′), *adv. Scot.* before long; soon. [ME *bi live* BY LIFE, i.e., with liveliness]

Be·lize (be lēz′), *n.* **1.** a republic in N Central America: formerly a British colony; independent since 1981; member of the British Commonwealth of Nations. 151,607; 8867 sq. mi. *Cap.:* Belmopan. Formerly **British Honduras. 2.** a port in and the largest city in Belize. 45,000.

bell[1] (bel), *n.* **1.** a hollow instrument of cast metal, typically cup-shaped with a flaring mouth, suspended from the vertex and rung by the strokes of a clapper, hammer, or the like. **2.** the stroke or sound of such an instrument: *We rose at the bell.* **3.** anything in the form of a bell. **4.** the large end of a funnel, or the end of a pipe, tube, or any musical wind instrument, when its edge is turned out and enlarged. **5.** *Archit.* the underlying part of a foliated capital. **6.** *Naut.* **a.** any of the half-hour units of nautical time rung on the bell of a ship. **b.** each individual ring of the bell, counted with others to reckon the time: *It is now four bells.* **c.** a signal on the telegraph of a large power vessel, made between the navigating officers and the engineer. **7.** *Zool.* umbrella (def. 2). **8.** the bell-shaped corolla of a flower. **9. ring a bell,** to strike a response; remind one of something: *His name rings a bell.* **10. ring the bell,** to provide what is desired; be satisfactory or successful: *This new book rings the bell with teen-agers.* **11. saved by the bell, a.** (of a boxer) saved from a knockout by the ringing of a gong signaling the end of a round. **b.** (of any person) spared from anticipated trouble by some extraneous event. **12. with bells on,** *Informal.* eagerly; ready to enjoy oneself: *I'll come to your party with bells on.* —*v.t.* **13.** to cause to swell or expand like a bell (often fol. by *out*): *Belling out the tubes will permit a freer passage of air.* **14.** to put a bell on. —*v.i.* **15.** to take or have the form of a bell. **16.** *Bot.* to produce bells; be in bell (said of hops when the seed vessels are forming). **17. bell the cat.** See **cat**[1] (def. 14). [ME, OE *belle;* c. D *bel;* akin to BELL[2]] —**bell′-less′,** *adj.*

bell[2] (bel), *v.i., v.t.* **1.** to bellow like a deer in rutting time. **2.** *Obs.* to bellow; roar. —*n.* **3.** the cry of a rutting deer. [ME *bell(en),* OE *bellan* to roar; c. OHG *bellan* (G *bellen* to bark), Icel *belja.* See BELLOW]

Bell (bel), *n.* **1. Ac·ton** (ak′tən), pen name of Anne Brontë. **2. Alexander Graham,** 1847–1922, U.S. scientist, born in Scotland: inventor of the telephone. **3. (Arthur) Clive (Howard),** 1881–1964, English critic of literature and art. **4. Cur·rer** (kûr′ər), pen name of Charlotte Brontë. **5. Ellis,** pen name of Emily Brontë. **6. John,** 1797–1869, U.S. political leader: Speaker of the House 1834–35. **7.** a city in SW California, near Los Angeles. 19,450 (1960).

Bel·la (bel′ə), *n.* a girl's given name. Also, **Bel, Belle.**

bel·la·don·na (bel′ə don′ə), *n.* **1.** Also called **deadly nightshade.** a poisonous, solanaceous herb, *Atropa Belladonna,* having purplish-red flowers and black berries. **2.** *Pharm.* a drug from the leaves and root of this plant, containing atropine and related alkaloids: used in medicine to check secretions and spasms, to relieve pain, and as a cardiac and respiratory stimulant. [< It *bella donna,* lit., fair lady (so called because it was believed to have been used by women to dilate the pupils of the eyes and to create an artificial pallor). See BELLE, DONNA]

bel′ladon′na lil′y, amaryllis (def. 1).

Bel·laire (bə lâr′, bel âr′), *n.* a city in SE Texas, within the city limits of Houston. 19,872 (1960).

Bel·la·my (bel′ə mē), *n.* **Edward,** 1850–98, U.S. author.

bell′ arch′, a round arch resting on prominent corbels. See illus. under **arch.**

bel·lar·mine (bel′är mēn′, bel′är mēn′, -ər-), *n.* a fat, narrow-necked stoneware bottle of the 16th and 17th centuries, ornamented with a bearded mask. Also called **greybeard, longbeard.** [after Cardinal *Bellarmino* (1542–1621), Italian churchman, the object of the caricature on the bottle]

Bel·lay (be lā′), *n.* **Jo·a·chim du** (zhô A kēm′ dʏ), c1525–60, French poet.

bell′ beak′er, *Archaeol.* a bell-shaped beaker, esp. one associated with the Beaker folk.

bell·bird (bel′bûrd′), *n.* any of several birds whose notes resemble the sound of a bell, esp. certain South American cotingas of the genus *Procnias.* [BELL[1] + BIRD]

bell′ book′, *Naut.* a book in which all orders affecting the main engines of a ship are recorded. [so called from the special use of bells on a ship]

bell-bot·tom (bel′bot′əm), *adj.* **1.** Also, **bell′-bot′tomed.** (of trousers) wide and flaring at the bottoms of the legs. —*n.* **2. bell-bottoms,** (*construed as pl.*) bell-bottom trousers, esp. as worn by sailors.

bell·boy (bel′boi′), *n. U.S.* a man who is employed to carry luggage, run errands, etc., at a hotel, club, etc. Also called **bellhop, bellman.** [BELL[1] + BOY]

bell′ bu′oy, *Naut.* a buoy having a bell that is rung by the motion of the buoy.

bell′ cap′tain, a hotel employee who supervises the work of bellboys.

bell′ cote′, a small shelter for bells, having a gable or shed roof. Also, **bell′ cot′.**

bell′ crank′, *Mach.* a lever or rocker having two arms meeting at a pivot at a right angle, used for transmitting motion between two parts meeting at an angle. —**bell′-cranked′,** *adj.*

bell′ deck′, a weatherproof floor in an open belfry.

belle (bel), *n.* a woman or girl admired for her beauty and charm, esp. the most beautiful among a number of rivals: *the belle of the ball.* [< F; OF *bele* < L *bella,* fem. of *bellus* fine, good-looking. See BEAU]

Belle (bel), *n.* a girl's given name. Also, **Bel, Bella.**

Bel′leau Wood′ (bel′ō; *Fr.* be lō′), a forest in N France, NW of Château-Thierry: a memorial to the U.S. Marines who won a battle there 1918.

Belle Dame Sans Mer·ci, La (*Fr.* lA bel dAm sän mer sē′). See **La Belle Dame Sans Merci.**

Bel·leek (bə lēk′), *n.* a fragile Irish porcelain with a bright luster. Also called **Belleek′ ware′.** [after *Belleek,* town in Northern Ireland where it is made]

Belle É·poque, La (lA bel ā pôk′), *French.* the period (1871–1914) between the end of the Franco-Prussian War and the outbreak of World War I, characterized by relative peacefulness in Western Europe and by marked advances and productivity in the arts, literature, technology, etc. [lit.: the beautiful epoch]

Belle·fonte (bel′font), *n.* a town in central Pennsylvania. 6088 (1960).

Belle′ Fourche′ (fo͞osh; *spelling pron.* fo͞orsh), a town in W South Dakota. 4087 (1960).

Belle′ Isle′, Strait of, a strait between Newfoundland and Labrador, Canada. 10–15 mi. wide.

Belle′ Meade′ (mēd), a town in central Tennessee. 3082 (1960).

Belle′ Plaine′ (plān), a town in E Iowa. 2923 (1960).

Bel·ler·o·phon (bə ler′ə fon′), *n. Class. Myth.* a Corinthian hero who, mounted on Pegasus, killed the Chimera. Also, **Bel·ler·o·phon·tes** (bə ler′ə fon′tēz). Cf. **Antia.** —**Bel′ler·o·phon′tic,** *adj.*

Bel′lerophon′tic let′ter, any communication containing material prejudicial to the bearer. [< Gk *Bellerophónt(ēs)* BELLEROPHON + -IC]

belles-let·tres (bel le′trᵊ), *n.pl.* **1.** light and elegant literature, esp. that which is excessively refined, characterized by aestheticism, and concerned chiefly with trivia. **2.** literature regarded as a fine art, esp. as having a purely aesthetic function. [< F: lit., fine letters. See BELLE, LETTER[1]] —**bel·let·rist** (bel le′trist), *n.* —**bel·let·ris·tic** (bel′li tris′tik), *adj.* —**Syn. 1.** See **literature.**

Belle·ville (bel′vil), *n.* **1.** a city in SW Illinois. 37,264 (1960). **2.** a city in NE New Jersey. 35,005 (1960). **3.** a town in N Kansas. 2940 (1960).

Belle′ville spring′, *Mach.* a spring having the form of a washer or dished disk with an open center, used for cushioning heavy loads with short motion.

Belle·vue (bel′vyo͞o), *n.* **1.** a town in N Kentucky. 9336 (1960). **2.** a town in E Nebraska. 8831 (1960). **3.** a town in N Ohio. 8286 (1960).

bell·flow·er (bel′flou′ər), *n.* a campanula. [BELL[1] + FLOWER]

Bell·flow·er (bel′flou′ər), *n.* a city in SW California, near Los Angeles. 44,846 (1960).

bell′ frog′, any of several tree frogs having a bell-like call.

bell′ ga′ble, an extension of a gable, serving as a bell cote.

Bell′ Gar′dens, a town in SW California, near Los Angeles. 26,467 (1960).

bell′ glass′. See **bell jar.**

bell′-hang·er's bit′ (bel′hang′ərz), *Carpentry.* a bit for drilling small holes through studs or the like.

bell′ heath′er, a European heath, *Erica tetralix,* having prostrate branches with terminal clusters of red flowers. Also called **heather bell.**

bell·hop (bel′hop′), *n.* bellboy. [lit., one who hops when the bell rings]

bel·li·cose (bel′ə kōs′), *adj.* inclined or eager to fight; aggressively hostile; belligerent; pugnacious. [< L *bellicōs(us),* equiv. to *belli-,* s. of *bellum* war + *-icus* -IC + *-ōsus* -OSE[1]] —**bel′li·cose′ly,** *adv.* —**bel·li·cos·i·ty** (bel′ə kos′i tē), **bel′li·cose′ness,** *n.*

bel·lied (bel′ēd), *adj.* having a belly, esp. one of a specified kind, size, shape, condition, etc. (usually used in combination): *big-bellied.* [BELLY + -ED[3]]

bel·lig·er·ence (bə lij′ər əns), *n.* **1.** warlike nature. **2.** act of carrying on war; warfare. [BELLIGER(ENT) + -ENCE]

bel·lig·er·en·cy (bə lij′ər ən sē), *n.* position or status as a belligerent; state of being actually engaged in war. [BELLIGER(ENT) + -ENCY]

bel·lig·er·ent (bə lij′ər ənt), *adj.* **1.** warlike; given to waging war. **2.** of warlike character; aggressively hostile; bellicose: *a belligerent tone.* **3.** waging war; engaged in war: *a peace treaty between belligerent powers.* **4.** pertaining to war or to those engaged in war: *belligerent rights.* —*n.* **5.** a state or nation at war. **6.** a member of the military forces of such a state. [< L *belliger* waging war (*belli-,* comb. form of *bellum* war + *-ger-,* root of *gerere* to conduct) + -ENT; r. *belligerant* < L *belligerant-* (s. of *belligerāns,* prp. of *belligerāre* to wage war); see -ANT] —**bel·lig′er·ent·ly,** *adv.*

Bel·ling·ham (bel′ing ham′), *n.* a seaport in NW Washington. 34,688 (1960).

Bel·li·ni (bə lē′nē; *It.* bel lē′nē), *n.* **1. Gen·ti·le** (jen tē′le), 1427?–1507, Venetian painter (son of Jacopo): teacher of Giorgione and Titian. **2. Gio·van·ni** (jô vän′nē), 1430?–1516, Venetian painter (son of Jacopo). **3. Ja·co·po** (yä′kô pô), 1400?–70, Venetian painter. **4. Vin·cen·zo** (vēn chen′dzô), 1801?–35, Italian composer of opera.

Bel·lin·zo·na (bel′in zō′nə; *It.* bel′lēn tsô′nä), *n.* a town in and the capital of Ticino, in S Switzerland. 13,435 (1960).

bell′ jar′, a bell-shaped glass vessel or cover, as for protecting delicate instruments, bric-a-brac, or the like, or for holding gases, a vacuum, etc., in chemical experiments. Also called **bell glass.**

bell·man (bel′mən), *n., pl.* **-men. 1.** a person who carries or rings a bell, esp. a town crier or watchman. **2.** bellhop. [BELL[1] + MAN[1]]

Bell·mead (bel′mēd), *n.* a town in central Texas. 5127 (1960).

bell′ met′al, an alloy of about 80 percent copper and 20 percent tin, sometimes with small amounts of lead and zinc, having low damping qualities and used esp. for bells.

Be·llo (be′yô), *n.* **An·drés** (än dres′), 1781–1865, Venezuelan poet, philologist, and educator.

Bel·loc (bel′ək, -ok), *n.* **Hi·laire** (hi lâr′), 1870–1953, English essayist, poet, and satirist; born in France.

Be·lo Ho·ri·zon·te (*Port.* be′lô rē zônn′ti). See **Belo Horizonte.**

Bel·lo·na (bə lō′nə), *n.* the ancient Roman goddess of war, variously described as the wife or sister of Mars, identified by the Greeks with the goddess Enyo. —**Bel·lo·ni·an** (bə lō′nē ən), *adj.*

Bel·lot·to (bə lot′ō; *It.* bel lôt′tô), *n.* **Ber·nar·do** (bər när′dō; *It.* ber när′dô), (*Canaletto*), 1720–80, Italian painter.

bel·low (bel′ō), *v.i.* **1.** to emit a hollow, loud, animal cry, as a bull or cow. **2.** to roar; bawl: *bellowing with rage.* —*v.t.* **3.** to utter in a loud deep voice: *He bellowed his answer across the room.* —*n.* **4.** act or sound of bellowing. [ME *belwe(n),* OE *bylgan* to roar; akin to BELL[2]] —**bel′low·er,** *n.* —**Syn. 2.** See **cry.**

Bel·low (bel′ō), *n.* **Saul,** born 1915, U.S. novelist, born in Canada: Nobel prize 1976.

bel·lows (bel′ōz, -əs), *n.* (*construed as sing. or pl.*) **1.** an instrument or machine for producing a strong current of air, as for a draft for a fire or sounding a musical instrument, consisting essentially of an air chamber which can be expanded to draw in air through a valve and contracted to expel the air through a tube or tubes. **2.** anything resembling or suggesting bellows in form, as the collapsible part of a camera or enlarger. **3.** the lungs. [ME *belwes* (pl.), OE *belg,* short for *blǣst belg* blast-bag. See BELLY] —**bel′lows·like′,** *adj.*

Bel·lows (bel′ōz), *n.* **George Wesley,** 1882–1925, U.S. painter and lithographer.

Bel′lows Falls′, a town in SE Vermont. 3831 (1960).

bel′lows fish′, snipefish.

bell′ pep′per. See **sweet pepper.**

bell·pull (bel′po͝ol′), *n.* a handle, cord, or strip of cloth pulled to ring a doorbell, servant's bell, etc. [BELL[1] + PULL]

Bell′ pur′chase, a tackle consisting of two standing single blocks, two running single blocks, a fall, and a runner, so arranged that the fall is rove through one running block, to which one end of the runner is attached, is then rove through one standing block, and is finally attached to the other running block, which supports the load and to which the other end of the runner is attached after being rove through both it and the other standing block: gives a mechanical advantage of six, neglecting friction. Also, **Bell's′ pur′chase.**

Bell purchase

bell′ salt′, an English bell-shaped container of c1600, usually of silver, having a pepper caster mounted on two salt cellars, each detachable from the others.

bell′ seat′, (on some 18th-century chairs) a seat having an outline resembling that of a bell. Also called **balloon seat.**

Bells′ for John′ White′side's Daugh′ter (hwīt′sīdz′, wīt′-), an elegiac poem (1924) by John Crowe Ransom.

bells′ of Ire′land, a branching herb, *Molucella laevis,* of western Asia, having round or heart-shaped leaves and fragrant white or pinkish flowers with a prickly calyx in which the nutlets grow. Also called **Molucca balm, shellflower.** [so called from the green calyx in the form of a bell]

bell′ toad′. See **tailed frog.**

bell·weth·er (bel′weth′ər), *n.* **1.** a wether or other male sheep which leads the flock, usually bearing a bell. **2.** one who or that which assumes the leadership or forefront, as of a profession, industry, etc.: *Paris remains the bellwether of the fashion industry.* **3.** one who leads a mob, mutiny, conspiracy, or the like; a ringleader. [BELL[1] + WETHER]

bell′ whis′tle, a steam or air whistle in which the jet is forced up against a bell-like casting mounted on a central spindle. Also called **dome whistle.**

Bell·wood (bel′wo͝od′), *n.* a city in NE Illinois, near Chicago. 20,729 (1960).

bell·wort (bel′wûrt′), *n.* **1.** any campanulaceous plant. **2.** a liliaceous plant of the genus *Uvularia,* having a delicate, slenderly bell-shaped, yellow flower. [BELL[1] + WORT[2]]

bel·ly (bel′ē), *n., pl.* **-lies,** *v.,* **-lied, -ly·ing.** —*n.* **1.** the front or under part of a vertebrate body from the breastbone to the pelvis, containing the abdominal viscera; the abdomen. **2.** the stomach with its adjuncts. **3.** appetite or capacity for food; gluttony. **4.** the womb. **5.** the inside or interior of anything: *The hold of a ship may be referred to as its belly.* **6.** a protuberant or bulging surface of anything: *the belly of a flask.* **7.** *Anat.* the fleshy part of a muscle. **8.** the front, inner, or under surface or part, as distinguished from the back. **9.** *Music.* the front surface of a violin or similar instrument. **10.** a bulge on a vertical surface of fresh concrete. **11.** *Aeron.* the underpart of the fuselage of an airplane. —*v.t., v.i.* **12.** to swell out. [ME *bely,* OE *belig, belg* bag, skin; c. G *Balg,* Goth *balg(s),* Icel *belgr,* MIr *bolg* sack] —**bel′ly·like′,** *adj.*

bel·ly·ache (bel′ē āk′), *n., v.,* **-ached, -ach·ing.** —*n.* **1.** *Informal.* a pain in the abdomen or bowels. —*v.i.* **2.** *Slang.* to complain; grumble. [BELLY + ACHE] —**bel′ly·ach′er,** *n.*

bel·ly·band (bel′ē band′), *n.* **1.** a band worn about the belly, as of a harnessed horse. See illus. under **harness. 2.** *Naut.* a thickness of canvas sewn to a sail as a reinforcement for the reef points. [BELLY + BAND[2]]

bel·ly·but·ton (bel′ē but′ᵊn), *n. Informal.* the navel. Also, **bel′ly but′ton.** [BELLY + BUTTON]

bel′ly dance′, 1. an Oriental solo dance, performed by a woman, emphasizing exaggerated movements of the abdominal muscles. **2.** a similar, provocative solo dance performed by a nude or nearly nude woman. Also called **danse du ventre.** —**bel′ly danc′er.** —**bel′ly danc′ing.**

bel′ly flop′, a dive in which the abdomen bears the brunt of the impact with the water. Also, **bel′ly flop′per.** Also called **belly whop, belly whopper.**

bel·ly-flop (bel′ē flop′), *v.i.,* **-flopped, -flop·ping.** to do a belly flop; belly-whop.

bel·ly·ful (bel′ē fo͝ol′), *n., pl.* **-fuls.** *Slang.* all that one can tolerate: *He's got a bellyful of her coy ways.* [BELLY + -FUL]

bel·ly-helve (bel′ē helv′), *n. Brit. Metalworking.* a triphammer in which the cams act at a point along the helve, partway between the fulcrum and the head.

bel·ly-land (bel′ē land′), *Aeron.* —*v.t.* **1.** (of an aviator) to land (an aircraft) directly on the fuselage, without using the landing gear. —*v.i.* **2.** (of an aircraft) to land directly on the fuselage, without using the landing gear. —**bel′ly-land′ing,** *n.*

bel′ly laugh′, *Informal.* a deep, loud, hearty laugh.

bel·ly-wash (bel′ē wosh′, -wôsh′), *n. U.S. Slang.* any drinkable liquid or beverage, as soda, beer, coffee, soup, etc.

bel′ly whop′. See **belly flop.** Also, **bel′ly whop′-per.**

bel·ly-whop (bel′ē hwop′, -wop′), *v.i.*, **-whopped, -whop·ping.** belly-flop.

Bel·mar (bel′mär), *n.* a town in E New Jersey. 5190 (1960).

Bel·mond (bel′mond), *n.* a town in N Iowa. 2506 (1960).

Bel·mont (bel′mont), *n.* **1.** a town in E Massachusetts near Boston. 28,715 (1960). **2.** a city in W California, near San Francisco. 15,996 (1960). **3.** a town in S North Carolina. 5007 (1960).

Bel·mon·te (bel môn′te), *n.* **Juan** (hwän), 1893–1962, Spanish matador.

Be·lo Ho·ri·zon·te (be′lô rē zônn′ti), a city in SE Brazil. 663,215 (1960). Also, **Bello Horizonte.**

be·loid (bē′loid), *adj.* (of a human skull) narrow in the frontal region and broad in the occipital region, when seen from above. [< Gk *bél(os)* missile, arrow (akin to *bállein* to throw) + -OID]

Be·loit (bə loit′), *n.* **1.** a city in S Wisconsin. 32,846 (1960). **2.** a town in N Kansas. 3837 (1960).

bel·o·man·cy (bel′ə man′sē), *n.* divination using arrows drawn at random from a quiver or other holder. [< Gk *bélo(s)* arrow, dart + -MANCY]

be·long (bi lông′, -long′), *v.i.* **1.** to be in the relation of a member, adherent, inhabitant, etc. (usually fol. by *to*): *He belongs to the Plain Grove Grange. I belong to Glasgow.* **2.** to have the proper qualifications, esp. social qualifications, to be a member of a group: *You don't belong in this club.* **3.** to be proper or due; be properly or appropriately placed, situated, etc.: *One belongs in every home. This belongs on the shelf. He is a statesman who belongs among the great.* **4. belong to, a.** to be the property of: *The book belongs to him.* **b.** to be a part or adjunct of: *That cover belongs to this jar.* **c.** to be a quality, function, or concern of: *Your objection does not belong to this discussion.* [ME *belong(en)*, equiv. to *be-* BE- + *longen* to belong, v. use of *long* (adj.) belonging, OE *gelang* ALONG[1]]

be·long·ing (bi lông′ing, -long′-), *n.* **1.** something that belongs. **2. belongings,** possessions; goods; personal effects. [BELONG + -ING[1]]

bel·o·noid (bel′ə noid′), *adj.* needlelike; styloid. [< Gk *belonoeid(ēs)*, equiv. to *belón(ē)* needle (akin to *bélos*; see BELOID) + *-oeidēs* -OID]

Be·lo·rus·sia (byel′ə rush′ə, bel′ə-), *n.* Byelorussia. —**Be′lo·rus′sian,** *adj., n.*

Be·los·tok (bye lə stôk′), *n.* Białystok.

be·love (bi luv′), *v.t.*, **-loved.** to love (usually used passively and fol. by *of* or *by*): *Mary is beloved of John.* [ME *beluve(n)*. See BE-, LOVE (v.)]

be·lov·ed (bi luv′id, -luvd′), *adj.* **1.** greatly loved; dear to the heart. —*n.* **2.** a person who is greatly loved. [BELOVE + -ED[2]]

Be·lo·vo (be′lo vo), *n.* a city in the SW RSFSR, in the S Soviet Union in Asia. 107,000 (1959).

be·low (bi lō′), *adv.* **1.** in or toward a lower place: *Look out below!* **2.** on, in, or toward a lower level, as a lower deck of a ship: *The captain turned over the command of the ship and went below.* **3.** on earth: *the fate of creatures here below.* **4.** in hell or the infernal regions. **5.** at a later point on a page or in a text: *See the statistics below.* Cf. **above** (def. 4). **6.** in a lower rank or grade: *He was demoted to the class below.* **7.** *Theat.* downstage; downstage of. Cf. **above** (def. 7). **8.** *Zool.* on the lower or ventral side. —*prep.* **9.** lower down than: *below the knee.* **10.** lower in rank, degree, amount, rate, etc., than: *below cost; below freezing.* **11.** too low or undignified to be worthy of; beneath: *He considered such an action below his notice.* [ME *bilooghe*, equiv. to *bi-* by (see BE-) + *looghe* LOW[1]]

—**Syn. 9.** BELOW, UNDER, BENEATH indicate position in some way lower than something else. BELOW implies being in a lower plane: *below the horizon, the water line.* UNDER implies being lower in a perpendicular line: *The plaything is under a chair.* BENEATH may have a meaning similar to BELOW, but more usually denotes being under so as to be covered, overhung, or overtopped: *the pool beneath the falls.*

be·low·decks (bi lō′deks′), *adv.* within the hull of a vessel: *Fire raged belowdecks.* [BELOW + DECK + -S[3]]

be·low·ground (bi lō′ground′), *adj.* **1.** situated beneath the surface of the earth; subterranean. **2.** no longer living; buried, as in a cemetery (usually used predicatively): *The truth cannot properly be published until all those whose reputations would be affected are belowground.* [BELOW + GROUND[1]]

below′ stairs′, *Chiefly Brit.* **1.** downstairs; the first floor of a house. **2.** (formerly) the first-floor or basement rooms usually used by servants, as servants' quarters, the kitchen, laundry room, etc.

below′ the line′, *Bridge.* See under **line**[1] (def. 31).

bel pa·e·se (bel′ pä ā′zē; *It.* bel′ pä e′ze), a semi-soft, mild Italian cheese. [formerly trademark]

Bel·pre (bel′prē), *n.* a town in SE Ohio. 5418 (1960).

Bel-Ridge (bel′rij′), *n.* a town in E Missouri. 4395 (1960).

Bel·sen (bel′zən), *n.* locality in NE West Germany: site of Nazi concentration camp during World War II. Also called **Bergen-Belsen.**

Bel·shaz·zar (bel shaz′ər), *n.* a prince of Babylon, son of Nabonidus and co-regent with him, referred to in the Bible as a king of Babylon and son of Nebuchadnezzar. Dan. 5. [< Heb < Babylonian *Bēl-sharra-uzur* may Bel guard the king]

belt (belt), *n.* **1.** a band of flexible material, as leather, cord, etc., for encircling the waist. **2.** any encircling or transverse band, strip, or stripe. **3.** an elongated region having distinctive properties or characteristics: *a belt of cotton plantations.* **4.** *Mach.* an endless flexible band passing about two or more pulleys, used to transmit motion from one pulley to the other or others or to convey materials and objects. **5.** *Navy.* a series of armor plates forming part of the hull of a warship. **6.** *Mil.* **a.** a cloth strip with loops or a series of metal links with grips, for holding cartridges fed into an automatic gun. **b.** a band of leather or webbing, worn around the waist and used as a support for weapons, ammunition, etc. **7.** a broad, flexible strip of rubber, canvas, wood, etc., moved along the surface of a fresh concrete pavement to put a finish on it after it has been floated. **8.** a road, railroad, or the like, encircling an urban center to handle peripheral traffic. **9. below the belt,** contrary to rules or to principles of fairness: *criticism that hit below the belt.* **10. tighten one's belt, a.** to undergo hardship patiently. **b.** to curtail one's expenditures; be more frugal: *They were urged to tighten their belts for the war effort.* **11. under one's belt,** *Informal.* **a.** in one's stomach, as food and drink: *With a few Scotches under his belt, he's everyone's friend.* **b.** considered as a matter of past experience: *He already had a few hand-to-hand fights under his belt when he was sent to the front.* —*v.t.* **12.** to gird or furnish with a belt. **13.** to surround or mark as if with a belt or band: *Garbage cans should be belted with orange paint.* **14.** to fasten on (a sword, gun, etc.) by means of a belt. **15.** to beat with a belt, strap, etc. **16.** *Slang.* to give a hard blow to. [ME; OE < L *balte(us)*] —**belt′less,** *adj.*

—**Syn. 3.** BELT and ZONE agree in their original meaning of a girdle or band. BELT is more used in popular or journalistic writing: *the corn or wheat belt.* ZONE tends to be used in technical language: *the Torrid Zone; a parcel-post zone.* **12.** girdle, encircle. **14.** gird (on). **15.** flog, lash.

Bel·tane (bel′tān), *n.* an ancient Celtic festival observed on May Day in Scotland and Ireland. [late ME (Scot) < Gael *bealltainn* < OIr *beltene*]

belt′ course′, *Archit.* stringcourse.

belt·ed (bel′tid), *adj.* **1.** girded with or wearing a belt, esp. as a mark of distinction: *the belted lords and emissaries.* **2.** marked with a band of color different from that of the rest of the body: *a belted cow.* [BELT + -ED[2]]

belt′ed king′fisher, a grayish-blue, North American kingfisher, *Megaceryle alcyon*, having a white breast marked with a grayish-blue band.

belt′ed sand′fish, a sea bass, *Serranellus subligarius*, found in shallow warm waters of the western Atlantic Ocean.

Bel·te·shaz·zar (bel′ti shaz′ər), *n.* the Babylonian name given to Daniel. Dan. 1:7. Also, *Douay Bible,* **Baltassar.**

belt·ing (bel′ting), *n.* **1.** material for belts. **2.** belts collectively. **3.** *Obs.* belt. **4.** a beating or thrashing. [BELT + -ING[1]]

belt′ line′, a transportation system partially or wholly surrounding a city, terminal, district, or port.

belt·line (belt′līn′), *n.* the waistline. [BELT + LINE[1]]

belt·man (belt′mən), *n., pl.* **-men. 1.** a worker responsible for the inspection, maintenance, and repair of machine belts. **2.** *Australian.* lifeguard. [BELT + MAN[1]]

Belt′ Moun′tains. See **Big Belt Mountains, Little Belt Mountains.**

Bel·ton (bel′tᵊn), *n.* **1.** a town in central Texas. 8163 (1960). **2.** a town in NW South Carolina. 5106 (1960). **3.** a town in W Missouri. 4897 (1960).

Bel·tra·mi (bel trä′mē; *It.* bel trä′mē), *n.* **E·u·ge·nio** (e′o͞o je′nyô), 1835–1900, Italian mathematician.

be·lu·ga (bə lo͞o′gə), *n.* **1.** Also called **hausen.** a white sturgeon, *Acipenser huso*, found in the Black and Caspian seas, valued as a source of caviar and isinglass. **2.** Also called **white whale.** a cetacean, *Delphinapterus leucas*, of northern seas, that has a rounded head and is white when adult. [< Russ *byeluga*, akin to *byelyi* white]

Be·lus (bē′ləs), *n. Class. Myth.* **1.** the twin of Agenor who became king of Chemmis. **2.** the father of Dido.

bel·ve·dere (bel′vi dēr′, bel′vi dēr′; *for 3 also It.* bel′ve de′re), *n.* **1.** a building, or architectural feature of a building, designed and situated to look out upon a pleasing scene. **2.** a cigar, shorter and with thinner ends than a corona. **3.** (*cap.*) a palace in the Vatican City, Rome, used as an art gallery. [< It: fine view < L *bel(lus)* fine + *vidēre* to see]

Bel·vi·dere (bel′vi dēr′), *n.* a town in NW New Jersey. 2636 (1960).

Be·ly (be′lē), *n.* **An·drei** (än drā′), (*Boris Nikolayevich Bugayev*), 1880–1934, Russian writer.

Bel·zo·ni (bel tsô′nē), *n.* **1. Gio·van·ni Bat·tis·ta** (jô vän′nē bät tē′stä), 1778–1823, Italian explorer and a specialist in the study of Egyptian antiquities. **2.** a town in W Mississippi. 4142 (1960).

B.E.M., Bachelor of Engineering of Mines.

be·ma (bē′mə), *n., pl.* **-ma·ta** (-mə tə). **1.** *Eastern Ch.* the enclosed space surrounding the altar; the sanctuary or chancel. **2.** (in a Christian basilica) an open space between the end of the nave arcade and the apse. **3.** bimah. **4.** a platform for public speaking. [< LL < Gk *bêma* step, platform (*bē-* (s. of *ébē* he went and alternative s. of *baínein* to step, go) + *-ma* n. suffix)]

be·maul (bi môl′), *v.t.* to maul severely. [BE- + MAUL]

be·mazed (bi māzd′), *adj. Archaic.* muddled; confused; dazed. [ME *bemaze(n)*. See BE-, MAZE, -ED[2]]

Bem·ba (bem′bə), *n., pl.* **-bas,** (*esp. collectively*) **-ba.** a member of a numerous agricultural people of Northern Rhodesia.

Bem·berg (bem′bûrg), *n. Trademark.* a regenerated rayon thread or yarn produced by dissolving cellulose in a cuprammonium solution.

be·mean (bi mēn′), *v.t.*, **-meaned, -mean·ing.** to make mean; demean; debase (usually used reflexively): *He would never bemean himself by bickering.* [BE- + MEAN[2]]

Be·mel·mans (bē′məl mənz, bem′əl-), *n.* **Lud·wig** (lud′wig, lo͞od′-), 1898–1962, U.S. humorous satirist and painter: author and illustrator of children's books, born in Austria.

Be·midj·i (bə mij′ē), *n.* a town in central Minnesota. 9958 (1960).

be·mire (bi mīᵊr′), *v.t.*, **-mired, -mir·ing. 1.** to soil with mire: *A tramp through the woods had bemired his clothing.* **2.** to cause (an object or person) to sink in mire: *The muddy road bemired the wagon.* [BE- + MIRE] —**be·mire′ment,** *n.*

Be·mis (bē′mis), *n.* **1. Samuel Flagg,** born 1891, U.S. historian, educator, and author. **2.** a town in W Tennessee. 3127 (1960).

be·moan (bi mōn′), *v.t.* **1.** to moan over; bewail; lament: *to bemoan one's fate.* **2.** to express pity for. —*v.i.* **3.** to lament; mourn. [BE- + MOAN; r. *bemene*, ME *bimene(n)*, OE *bimǣnan* (*bi-* BE- + *mǣnan* to moan)] —**be·moan′ing·ly,** *adv.*

be·mock (bi mok′), *v.t.* to mock or jeer at (something or someone); mislead in a mocking manner: *to bemock a trusting heart.* [BE- + MOCK]

be·mud·dle (bi mud′ᵊl), *v.t.*, **-dled, -dling.** to muddle or completely confuse (someone). [BE- + MUDDLE]

be·muse (bi myo͞oz′), *v.t.*, **-mused, -mus·ing.** to confuse, muddle, or stupefy (someone). [BE- + MUSE] —**be·muse′ment,** *n.*

be·mused (bi myo͞ozd′), *adj.* **1.** confused; muddled; stupefied. **2.** lost in thought; preoccupied. [BEMUSE + -ED[2]] —**be·mus·ed·ly** (bi myo͞o′zid lē), *adv.*

ben[1] (ben), *Scot.* —*n.* **1.** the inner or back room of a two-room cottage, esp. when used as a combined parlor and bedroom. —*adv., prep.* **2.** within; inside. —*adj.* **3.** inside; inner. [late ME, north var. of *bin*, ME *binne*, OE *binna(n)* (c. G *binnen*), equiv. to *bi-* BE- + *innan* within]

ben[2] (ben), *n.* **1.** a tree, *Moringa oleifera*, of Arabia, India, and elsewhere, bearing a winged seed which yields an oil **(oil of ben),** used in extracting flower perfumes, lubricating delicate machinery, etc. **2.** the seed of such a tree. [< Ar *bān*]

ben[3] (ben), *n. Scot., Irish.* a mountain peak; a high hill. [< Gael *beann* peak]

ben[4] (ben), *n.* (*often cap.*) son of (used esp. in Hebrew and Arabic names): *Moses ben Maimon.*

Ben (ben), *n.* a boy's given name, form of **Benjamin.**

Ben·a·dryl (ben′ə dril), *n. Pharm., Trademark.* diphenhydramine.

be·name (bi nām′), *v.t.*, **-named; -named, -nempt,** or **-nempt·ed; -nam·ing.** *Obs.* to name; call by name. [ME; see BE-, NAME; r. OE *benemnan;* akin to G *benennen*, Sw *benämna*]

Be·nar·es (bə när′is, -ēz), *n.* a city in SE Uttar Pradesh, in NE India, on the Ganges River: Hindu holy city. 471,300 (1961). Also called **Banares, Varanasi.**

Be·na·ven·te y Mar·ti·nez (be′nä ven′te ē mär-tē′neth), *n.* **Ja·cin·to** (hä thēn′tô), (*Jacinto Benavente y Martinez*), 1866–1954, Spanish dramatist: Nobel prize 1922.

Ben Av·on (ben av′ən), a town in SW Pennsylvania. 2553 (1960).

Ben Bel·la (ben bel′lä, bel′ə), **Ahmed,** born 1919, Algerian statesman: premier 1962–65; president 1963–65.

Ben·bow (ben′bō′), *n.* **John,** 1653–1702, English admiral.

Ben·brook (ben′bro͝ok′), *n.* a town in N Texas. 3254 (1960).

bench (bench), *n.* **1.** a long seat for several persons. **2.** a seat occupied by an official or officials, esp. judges. **3.** such a seat as a symbol of the office and dignity of a judge, of an individual judge, or of judges as a group. **4.** the office or dignity of various other officials, or the officials themselves. **5.** *Sports.* **a.** the seat on which the players of a team sit during a game while not in action. **b.** the quality and number of the players of a team who are usually used as substitutes: *A weak bench hurt their chances for the championship.* **6.** Also called **workbench.** the strong work table of a carpenter or other mechanic. **7.** a platform on which animals are placed for exhibition, esp. at a dog show. **8.** a contest or exhibition of dogs; dog show. **9.** *Phys. Geog.* a shelf-like area of rock with steep slopes above and below. **10.** *Mining.* a step or working elevation in a mine. **11.** berm (def. 3). **12. on the bench, a.** serving as a judge in a court of law; presiding. **b.** *Sports.* (of a player) not participating in play, either for part or all of a game. —*v.t.* **13.** to furnish with benches. **14.** to seat on a bench or on the bench: *an election that benched him in the district court.* **15.** to place in exhibition: *to bench a dog.* **16.** to cut away the working faces of (a mine or quarry) in benches. **17.** *Sports.* to remove from a game or keep from participating in a game: *benched because of poor hitting.* [ME, OE *benc;* c. D, G *bank* BANK[3]] —**bench′less,** *adj.*

bench′ dog′, a dog on exhibit at a dog show before and after competition in the show ring.

bench·er (ben′chər), *n.* **1.** (in England) a senior member of an Inn of Court. **2.** a person who handles an oar; boatman. [BENCH + -ER[1]]

bench′ hook′, *Carpentry.* a device with a hook-like part fitting over the front edge of a workbench as a means of preventing an object from moving toward the rear of the bench.

bench′ing i′ron, *Survey.* a triangular, pronged plate driven into the ground to provide a temporary bench mark or turning point.

bench′ jock′ey, *Chiefly Baseball Slang.* a player, coach, or manager who makes a specialty of baiting or harassing the umpires or opposing players, usually from the bench.

Bench·ley (bench′lē), *n.* **Robert (Charles),** 1889–1945, U.S. humorist, drama critic, and actor.

bench-made (bench′mād′), *adj.* (of articles made of leather, wood, etc.) individually produced and finished, as on a craftsman's bench; custom-made.

bench′ mark′, *Survey.* a marked point of known or assumed elevation from which other elevations may be established.

bench′ screw′, *Carpentry.* a wooden or metal screw rotated by a handle fixed to one end within a threaded block fixed to a workbench: used with various jaws to form a vise.

bench′ show′, a dog show in which the animals of each breed are judged and awarded prizes on the basis of meeting certain standards established for that breed.

bench′ stop′, *Carpentry.* a metal device set flush with the top of a workbench and having a portion able to be raised to stop longitudinal movement of an object placed against it.

bench′ ta′ble, *Archit.* a course of masonry forming a bench at the foot of a wall.

bench·warm·er (bench′wôr′mər), *n. Sports.* a substitute who rarely plays in a game. Also, **bench′ warm′er, bench′-warm′er.** [BENCH + WARMER]

bench′ war′rant, *Law.* a warrant issued or ordered by a judge or court for the apprehension of an offender.

bend[1] (bend), *v.,* **bent** or (*Archaic*) **bend·ed; bend·ing,** *n.* —*v.t.* **1.** to force (an object, esp. a long or thin one) from a straight form into a curved or angular one, or from a curved or angular form into some different form:

to bend an iron rod into a hoop; to bend a crooked thing straight. 2. to cause to submit: *to bend someone to one's will.* 3. to turn in a particular direction: *to bend one's steps homeward.* 4. to incline mentally (usually fol. by *to* or *toward*): *bending his thoughts back toward his childhood.* 5. to pull back the string of (a bow or the like) in preparation for shooting. 6. *Naut.* to fasten. 7. *Archaic.* to strain or brace tensely (often fol. by *up*). —*v.i.* 8. to become curved, crooked, or bent: *a bow that bends easily.* 9. to assume a bent posture; stoop (often fol. by *over*): *to bend as one walks; to bend over and pick up something.* 10. to bow in submission or reverence; yield; submit: *bending to one's monarch.* 11. to turn or incline in a particular direction; be directed: *The road bent toward the south.* 12. to direct one's energies: *We bent to our work as the bell sounded.* 13. **bend over backward(s),** to exert oneself to the utmost; make a serious effort: *She bent over backward to make sure that he was always pleased.* Also, **bend over backwards.** —*n.* 14. the act of bending; state of being bent. 15. a bent thing or part; curve; crook: *a bend in the curtain rod; bends in the road.* 16. *Naut.* any of various loops or knots for joining the ends of two ropes or the like, or for joining the end of a rope or the like to some other object. 17. **bends, a.** *Naut.* thick planking immediately below the waterways of a wooden vessel. **b.** *Naut.* the wales of a vessel. **c.** *Informal.* See **caisson disease. d.** *Informal.* aeroembolism (usually prec. by *the*). 18. **round the bend,** *Brit. Slang.* insane; crazy: *These interruptions will send me round the bend!* [ME *bend(en),* OE *bendan* to bind, bend (a bow); c. Icel *benda* to bend; akin to OE *bend* band, chain. See BAND[3]] —**bend′a·ble,** *adj.*

—**Syn. 1.** curve, crook, flex, bow. **2.** mold, subdue, influence. **3, 4.** direct, incline. **4.** dispose, bias. **9.** BEND, BOW, STOOP imply taking a bent posture. BEND and BOW are used of the head and upper body; STOOP is used of the body only. **10.** acquiesce, agree. **15.** bow.

bend[2] (bend), *n.* 1. *Heraldry.* a diagonal band extending from the dexter chief of an escutcheon to the sinister base. Cf. **bend sinister.** 2. *Tanning.* half of a trimmed butt or hide. 3. **in bend,** *Heraldry.* (of a charge or charges) set diagonally or in a diagonal row. 4. **per bend,** *Heraldry.* in the direction of a bend; bendwise: *party per bend.* [ME: coalescence of OE *bend* band (see BEND[1]) and MF *bende* BAND[2]]

Bend (bend), *n.* a city in central Oregon. 11,936 (1960).

Ben·da (ben′də; *Fr.* băN dA′), *n.* **Ju·lien** (jo͞ol′yən; *Fr.* zhY lyaN′), 1867–1956, French philosopher.

Ben Da·vis (ben dā′vis), 1. a variety of red apple that ripens in early winter. 2. the tree bearing this fruit.

Ben′ Day′ proc′ess (ben′ dā′), *Photoengraving.* a technique for producing shading, texture, or tone in line drawings and photographs by overlaying a fine screen or a pattern of dots on the original artwork, on a negative of it, or on the plate before etching. Also, **Ben′day′ proc′ess.** [named after *Ben(jamin) Day* (1838–1916), American printer]

bend′ dex′ter, *Heraldry.* the ordinary bend, extending from the dexter chief to the sinister base.

bend·ed (ben′did), *v. Archaic.* pp. of **bend.**

bend·er (ben′dər), *n.* 1. one who or that which bends, as a pair of pliers, a powered machine, etc. 2. *U.S. Slang.* a drinking spree. 3. *Baseball Slang.* curve (def. 5a). 4. *Brit. Slang.* a sixpence; a sixpenny bit. [BEND[1] + -ER[1]]

Bend′er Gestalt′ test′ (ben′dər), *Psychol.* a test used in the determination of personality disturbance, in which the subject is required to reproduce graphically nine simple designs. [named after L. *Bender* (b. 1897), American psychiatrist]

Ben·di·geid Vran (ben dig′īd vrän′), *Welsh Legend.* Blessed Bran: an epithet of Bran when regarded as a Christian saint.

Ben·di·go (ben′də gō′), *n.* a city in central Victoria in SE Australia: gold mining. 41,140 (est. 1959).

bend′ing mo′ment, *Physics.* the algebraic sum of the moments about the neutral axis of any cross section of a beam.

bend·let (bend′lit), *n. Heraldry.* a narrow diminutive of a bend. [BEND[2] + -LET]

bend′ sin′ister, *n. Heraldry.* a diagonal band extending from the sinister chief of an escutcheon to the dexter base: a supposed mark of bastardy.

bend·wise (bend′wīz′), *adj. Heraldry.* in the direction or manner of a bend. Also, **bend·ways** (bend′wāz′). [BEND[2] + -WISE]

Bend sinister

bend·y[1] (ben′dē), *n., pl.* **bend·ies.** a tropical, malvaceous tree, *Thespesia populnea,* having cordate leaves and showy, yellow or purple, bell-shaped flowers. Also called **ben′dy tree′.** [< Hindi *bindhī*]

bend·y[2] (ben′dē), *adj. Heraldry.* divided bendwise into several areas of equal width, usually having two alternating tinctures: *bendy of six, argent and gules.* [ME; see BEND[2], -Y[1]]

bene[1] (bēn), *n. Obs.* a prayer or petition, esp. one to God. [ME, OE *bēn;* c. Icel *bōn* BOON[1]]

be·ne[2] (ben′ā; *Latin.* be′ne), *adv.* well. [< L]

bene-, an element occurring in loan words from Latin where it meant "well": *benediction.* [comb. form of *bene* (adv.) BENE[2]]

be·neaped (bi nēpt′), *adj. Naut.* neaped. [BE- + NEAPED]

be·neath (bi nēth′, -nēth′), *adv.* 1. below; in or to a lower place, position, state, or the like: *We could hear the trains rumbling beneath.* 2. underneath: *heaven above and the earth beneath.* —*prep.* 3. below; under: *beneath the same roof.* 4. further down than; underneath; lower in place than: *The first drawer beneath the top one.* 5. lower down on a slope than: *beneath the crest of a hill.* 6. inferior or less important, as in position, rank, power, etc.: *A captain is beneath a major.* 7. unworthy of; below the level or dignity of: *beneath contempt.* [ME *benethe,* OE *beneothan,* equiv. to *be-* BE- + *neothan* below, akin to OHG *nidana,* Icel *nithan.* See NETHER]
—**Syn. 3.** See **below.** —**Ant. 1.** above.

Ben·e·dic·i·te (ben′i dis′i tē), *n.* 1. *Eccles.* the canticle beginning in Latin *Benedicite, omnia opera Domini,* and in English "O all ye works of the Lord." 2. a musical setting for it. 3. (*l.c.*) an invocation for a blessing. —*interj.* 4. (*l.c.*) bless you! [< L, impv. 2nd person pl. of *benedīcere* (*bene* BENE- + *dīcere* to speak)]

Ben·e·dick (ben′i dik), *n.* 1. (in Shakespeare's *Much Ado About Nothing*) the confident bachelor who courts and finally marries Beatrice. 2. (*l.c.*) benedict.

ben·e·dict (ben′i dikt), *n.* 1. a newly married man, esp. one who has been long a bachelor. 2. a married man. [var. of BENEDICK]

Ben·e·dict (ben′i dikt), *n.* 1. **Ruth (Fulton),** 1887–1948, U.S. writer and anthropologist. 2. **Saint,** A.D. 480?–543?, Italian monk: founded Benedictine order. 3. **Stanley Ros·si·ter** (ros′i tər), 1884–1936, U.S. biochemist. 4. a boy's given name.

Benedict I, died A.D. 579, pope 575–579.

Benedict II, Saint, died A.D. 685, pope 684–685.

Benedict III, died A.D. 858, pope 855–858.

Benedict IV, died A.D. 903, pope 900–903.

Benedict V, died A.D. 966, pope 964.

Benedict VI, died A.D. 974, pope 973–974.

Benedict VII, died A.D. 983, pope 974–983.

Benedict VIII, died 1024, pope 1012–24.

Benedict IX, died 1056?, pope 1032–44; 1045; 1047–48.

Benedict XI, (*Niccolò Boccasini*) 1240–1304, Italian ecclesiastic: pope 1303–04.

Benedict XII, (*Jacques Fournier*) died 1342, French ecclesiastic: pope 1334–42.

Benedict XIII, (*Pietro Francesco Orsini*) 1649–1730, Italian ecclesiastic: pope 1724–30.

Benedict XIV, (*Prospero Lambertini*) 1675–1758, Italian pope 1740–58, scholar and patron of the arts.

Benedict XV, (*Giacomo della Chiesa*) 1854–1922, Italian pope 1914–22.

Ben·e·dic·ta (ben′i dik′tə), *n.* a girl's given name.

Ben·e·dic·tine (ben′i dik′tin, -tēn, -tīn *for 1;* ben′i-dik′tēn *for 2, 3*), *n.* 1. *Rom. Cath. Ch.* **a.** a member of an order of monks founded at Monte Cassino by St. Benedict about A.D. 530. **b.** a member of any congregation of nuns following the rule of St. Benedict. 2. a French liqueur originally made by Benedictine monks. —*adj.* 3. of or pertaining to St. Benedict or the Benedictines. [St. BENEDICT + -INE[1]]

ben·e·dic·tion (ben′i dik′shən), *n. Eccles.* 1. act of uttering a blessing. 2. the form of blessing pronounced by an officiating minister, as at the close of divine service. 3. a ceremony by which things are set aside for sacred uses, as a church, vestments, bells, etc. 4. (*usually cap.*) Also called **Benedic′tion of the Bless′ed Sac′rament.** *Rom. Cath. Ch.* a service consisting of prayers, at least one prescribed hymn, censing of the congregation and the Host, and a blessing of the congregation by moving in the form of a cross the ciborium or monstrance containing the Host. 5. the advantage conferred by blessing; a mercy or benefit. [late ME < L *benedictiōn-* (s. of *benedictiō*). See BENEDICTUS, -ION] —**ben·e·dic·to·ry** (ben′i dik′tə rē), *adj.*

ben·e·dic·tion·al (ben′i dik′shə nəl), *adj.* 1. of or pertaining to benediction. —*n.* 2. Also, **ben·e·dic·tion·a·le** (ben′i dik′shə nā′lē). a book of benedictions. [BENEDICTION + -AL[1]]

Ben′edict's test′, *Biochem.* a test for determining the presence of reducing sugars, as glucose or the like, in a liquid, as urine, by heating the liquid and an alkaline copper sulfate solution together, the presence of reducing sugars being indicated by the formation of a colored precipitate. [named after S. R. BENEDICT]

Ben·e·dic·tus (ben′i dik′təs), *n. Eccles.* 1. the short canticle or hymn beginning in Latin *Benedictus qui venit in nomine Domini,* and in English "Blessed is He that cometh in the name of the Lord." 2. the canticle or hymn beginning in Latin *Benedictus Dominus Deus Israel,* and in English "Blessed be the Lord God of Israel." 3. a musical setting of either of these canticles. [< L: blessed (ptp. of *benedīcere* to commend, bless). See BENE-, DICTUM]

ben·e·fac·tion (ben′ə fak′shən, ben′ə fak′-), *n.* 1. act of conferring a benefit; the doing of good; a good deed: *He is known throughout the region for his many benefactions.* 2. the benefit conferred; charitable donation: *to solicit benefactions for earthquake victims.* [< LL *benefactiōn-* (s. of *benefactiō*), equiv. to *bene* BENE- + *fact-* (*us*) done (see FACT) + *-iōn-* -ION]

ben·e·fac·tor (ben′ə fak′tər, ben′ə fak′-), *n.* 1. one who confers a benefit; kindly helper. 2. one who makes a bequest or endowment, as to an institution. Also, *referring to a woman,* **ben·e·fac·tress** (ben′ə fak′tris, ben′ə fak′-). [< LL, equiv. to *benefact-* (see BENEFACTION) + *-or* -OR[2]]

be·nef·ic (bə nef′ik), *adj.* doing or promoting good; beneficent: *a benefic truce; a benefic confluence of planets.* [< L *benefic(us).* See BENE-, -FIC]

ben·e·fice (ben′ə fis), *n., v.,* **-ficed, -fic·ing.** —*n.* 1. a position or post granted to an ecclesiastic which guarantees a fixed amount of property or income. 2. the revenue itself. —*v.t.* 3. to invest with a benefice or ecclesiastical living. [ME < MF < L *benefic(ium)* (*benefic(us)* BENEFIC + *-ium* n. suffix)] —**ben′e·fice·less,** *adj.*

be·nef·i·cence (bə nef′i səns), *n.* 1. the doing of good; active goodness or kindness; charity. 2. a beneficent act or gift; benefaction. [< L *beneficentia* < *benefic(us)* BENEFIC + *-entia* -ENCE]

be·nef·i·cent (bə nef′i sənt), *adj.* doing good or causing good to be done; conferring benefits; kindly in action or purpose. [BENEFI(CENCE) + -ENT] —**be·nef′i·cent·ly,** *adv.*

ben·e·fi·cial (ben′ə fish′əl), *adj.* 1. conferring benefit; advantageous; helpful: *the beneficial effect of sunshine.* 2. *Law.* **a.** helpful in the meeting of needs: *a beneficial association.* **b.** involving the personal enjoyment of proceeds: *a beneficial owner.* [< L *beneficiāl(is),* equiv. to *benefici(um)* kindness (see BENEFICE) + *-ālis* -AL[1]] —**ben′e·fi′cial·ly,** *adv.* —**ben′e·fi′cial·ness,** *n.*
—**Syn. 1.** salutary, wholesome, serviceable, useful, favorable, profitable. —**Ant. 1.** harmful.

ben·e·fi·ci·ar·y (ben′ə fish′ē er′ē, -fish′ə rē), *n., pl.* **-ar·ies.** 1. one who receives benefits, profits, or advantages. 2. a person designated as the recipient of funds or other property under a trust, insurance policy, etc. 3. *Eccles.* the holder of a benefice. [< L *beneficiāri-* (*us*), equiv. to *benefici(um)* BENEFICE + *-ārius* -ARY]

ben·e·fi·ci·ate (ben′ə fish′ē āt′), *v.t.,* **-at·ed, -at·ing.** *Metall.* to treat (ore) for smelting. [< Sp *benefici(ar)* (to) benefit, profit from (especially mining or farming) (< *beneficio* << L *beneficium;* see BENEFICE) + -ATE[1]]

ben·e·fit (ben′ə fit), *n., v.,* **-fit·ed, -fit·ing.** —*n.* 1. anything that is advantageous or for the good of a person or thing: *He explained the benefits of public ownership. We have a pension plan, free insurance, and other benefits. Was he doing that for my benefit?* 2. a theatrical performance or other public entertainment to raise money for a charitable organization or cause. 3. a payment or other assistance given by an insurance company, mutual benefit society, or public agency. 4. *Archaic.* an act of kindness; good deed; benefaction. 5. **for one's benefit,** so as to produce a calculated effect in one's mind: *He wasn't really angry; that was just an act for his girl friend's benefit.* —*v.t.* 6. to do good to; be of service to: *a health program to benefit all mankind.* —*v.i.* 7. to derive benefit or advantage; profit; make improvement: *someone who has never benefited from experience.* [late ME *benefytt, -fett* (see BENE-); r. ME *b(i)enfet, -fait* < AF *benfet,* MF *bienfait* < L *benefact(um)* good deed; see FACT] —**ben′e·fit·er,** *n.*
—**Syn. 1.** favor, service. See **advantage.**

ben′efit of cler′gy, 1. the rites or sanctions of a church. 2. the formality of a civil or ecclesiastical marriage ceremony: *living together without benefit of clergy.* 3. the privilege claimed by church authorities to try and punish, by an ecclesiastical court, any clergyman accused of a serious crime. The privilege was abolished in the U.S. in 1790 and in England in 1827.

ben′efit soci′ety, *Insurance.* an association of persons to create a fund, either by dues or assessments, for the assistance of members and their families in case of sickness, death, etc. Also called **ben′efit associa′tion.**

Ben·e·lux (ben′əluks′), *n.* 1. a customs union comprising Belgium, the Netherlands, and Luxembourg, begun January 1, 1948. 2. Belgium, the Netherlands, and Luxembourg considered together.

Ben·e·mid (ben′ə mid), *n. Pharm., Trademark.* probenecid.

be·nempt (bi nempt′), *v. Obs.* a pp. of **bename.** Also, **be·nempt′ed.**

Beneš (ben′esh), *n.* **Ed·u·ard** (e′do͝o ärt′), 1884–1948, Czech patriot and statesman: president of Czechoslovakia, 1935–1938 and 1945–1948.

Be·nét (bi nā′), *n.* 1. **Stephen Vincent,** 1898–1943, U.S. poet and novelist. 2. his brother **William Rose,** 1886–1950, U.S. poet and critic.

Be·net·ta (bə net′ə), *n.* a girl's given name, form of **Benedicta.**

be·ne va·le (be′ne wä′le; *Eng.* ben′ē vā′lē), *Latin.* farewell.

Be·ne·ven·to (ben′ə ven′tō; *It.* be′ne ven′tô), *n.* a city in N Campania, in S Italy: monumental arch erected by Trajan. 54,744 (1961).

be·nev·o·lence (bə nev′ə ləns), *n.* 1. desire to do good to others; good will; charitableness: *to be filled with benevolence toward one's fellow man.* 2. an act of kindness; charitable gift. 3. *Eng. Hist.* a forced contribution to the sovereign. [ME < L *benevolentia.* See BENEVOLENT, -IA, -ENCE]
—**Ant. 1.** malevolence.

be·nev·o·lent (bə nev′ə lənt), *adj.* 1. desiring to do good to others: *gifts from several benevolent alumni.* 2. intended for benefits rather than profit: *a benevolent institution.* 3. characterized by or expressing good will or kindly feelings: *a benevolent attitude; her benevolent smile.* [< L *benevolent-* (s. of *benevolēns*) kindhearted (*bene-* BENE- + *vol-* wish (akin to WILL[1]) + *-ent-* -ENT)] —**be·nev′o·lent·ly,** *adv.* —**be·nev′o·lent·ness,** *n.*
—**Syn. 1.** good, kind, humane, generous, liberal, benign, charitable, philanthropic, altruistic. —**Ant.** cruel.

Beng., 1. Bengal. **2.** Bengali.

Ben·gal (ben gôl′, beng-; ben′gəl, beng′-), *n.* 1. a former province in NE India: now divided between India and Pakistan. Cf. **East Bengal, West Bengal. 2. Bay of,** a part of the Indian Ocean between India and Burma. 3. *Textiles.* **a.** a raw silk from Bengal. **b.** a fabric, esp. one made of silk and hair. **c.** a fabric, similar to muslin, with printed stripes.

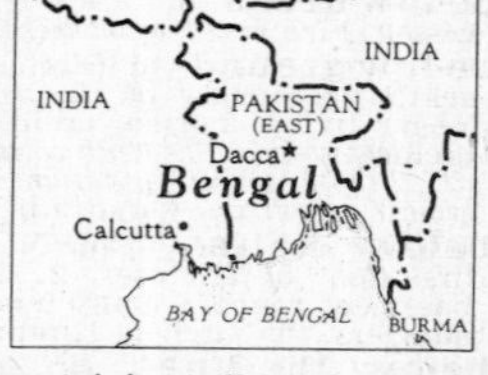

Ben′gal cat′echu, catechu.

Ben·ga·lese (ben′gə lēz′, -lēs′, beng′-), *adj., n., pl.* **-lese.** —*adj.* 1. of or pertaining to Bengal. —*n.* 2. a native or inhabitant of Bengal. [BENGAL + -ESE]

Ben·ga·li (ben gô′lē, beng-), *n.* 1. a native or an inhabitant of Bengal. 2. the modern language of Bengal, a language of the Indic subbranch of Indo-European. See diag. under **language.** —*adj.* 3. of or pertaining to Bengal, its inhabitants, or their language; Bengalese.

ben·ga·line (beng′gə lēn′, beng′gə lēn′), *n.* a poplin-like fabric having a crosswise corded effect, woven with coarse yarn in the filling direction. [< F; see BENGAL, -INE[2]]

Ben′gal light′, a vivid, sustained, blue light used in signaling, fireworks, etc.

Ben′gal quince′, bael.

Ben′gal rose′. See **China rose** (def. 1).

Ben·gha·zi (ben gä′zē), *n.* a seaport in N Libya. 69,718 (1954). Also, **Ben·ga′si.**

Ben·gue′la Cur′rent (ben gā′lə), a cold ocean current flowing N along the W coast of southern Africa.

Ben-Gu·ri·on (ben′go͝o ryôn′, ben go͝or′ē ən), *n.* **David,** born 1886, Israeli statesman, born in Poland: prime minister of Israel 1948–53, 1955–63.

Ben Hur (ben′ hûr′), a historical novel (1880) by Lew Wallace.

Be·ni (be′nē), *n.* a river flowing NE from W Bolivia to the Madeira River. ab. 600 mi. long.

Be·ni·cia (bə nē′shə), *n.* a town in W California. 6070 (1960).

be·night·ed (bi nī′tid), *adj.* **1.** intellectually or morally ignorant; unenlightened: *benighted ages of barbarism and superstition.* **2.** overtaken by darkness of night. [*benight* (BE- + NIGHT) + -ED²] —**be·night′ed·ness,** *n.*

be·nign (bi nīn′), *adj.* **1.** having a kindly disposition; gracious. **2.** showing or caused by gentleness or kindness: *a benign smile.* **3.** favorable; propitious: *a series of benign omens and configurations in the heavens.* **4.** (of weather) salubrious; healthful; pleasant or beneficial. **5.** *Pathol.* not malignant: *a benign tumor.* [ME *benigne* < MF < L *benigna,* fem. of *benignus* kindly for *benigenus, lit., born good. See BENE-, GENUS] —**be·nign′ly,** *adv.* —**Syn. 1.** good, kindly, benignant, benevolent, tender, humane, gentle, compassionate. —**Ant. 3.** sinister.

be·nig·nant (bi nig′nənt), *adj.* **1.** kind, esp. to inferiors; gracious: *a benignant sovereign.* **2.** exerting a good influence; beneficial: *the benignant authority of the new president.* **3.** *Pathol.* benign. [BENIGN + -ANT, modeled on *malignant*] —**be·nig·nan·cy** (bi nig′nən sē), *n.* —**be·nig′nant·ly,** *adv.*
—**Syn. 1.** benevolent, benign, generous, open, charitable.

be·nig·ni·ty (bi nig′ni tē), *n., pl.* **-ties. 1.** quality of being benign; kindness. **2.** *Archaic.* a good deed or favor; an instance of kindness: *benignities born of selfless devotion.* [ME *benignite* < MF < L *benignitāt-* (s. of *benignitās*). See BENIGN, -ITY]

Be·ni Ha·san (ben′ē hä′sän), a village in the central United Arab Republic, on the Nile, N of Asyut: ancient cliff tombs.

Be·nin (be nēn′), *n.* **1.** Formerly, **Dahomey.** a republic in W Africa; formerly part of French West Africa; gained independence in 1960. 4,142,000; 44,290 sq. mi. *Cap.:* Porto Novo. **2.** a former native kingdom in W Africa: now incorporated into Nigeria. **3.** a river in S Nigeria, flowing into the Bight of Benin.

ben·i·son (ben′i zən, -sən), *n.* *Archaic.* benediction. [ME < MF *beneison* < L *benedictiōn-* BENEDICTION]

Be·ni·ta (bə nē′tə), *n.* a girl's given name, form of **Benedicta.**

Be·ni·to Ce·re·no (bā nē′tō sä rā′nō, bə nē′tō sə rā′nō), a short story (1855) by Herman Melville.

be·ni·to·ite (bə nē′tō īt′), *n.* a rare mineral, barium titanium silicate, occurring in blue hexagonal crystals exhibiting dichroism. [named after San *Benito,* Cal. county; see -ITE¹]

ben·ja·min (ben′jə mən), *n.* benzoin¹ (def. 1). [var. [(by analogy with *Benjamin*) of *benjoin* BENZOIN]

Ben·ja·min (ben′jə mən), *n.* **1.** the youngest son of Jacob and Rachel, and the brother of Joseph. Gen. 35:18. **2.** one of the 12 tribes of ancient Israel. **3. Ash·er** (ash′ər), 1773–1845, U.S. architect and writer. **4. Judah Philip,** 1811–84, Confederate statesman. **5.** a boy's given name.

ben·ja·min-bush (ben′jə mən bo͝osh′), *n.* spicebush.

Ben·ja·min-Con·stant (bän zhä män′kôn stän′), *n.* **Jean Jo·seph** (zhän zhō zef′). See **Constant, Jean Joseph Benjamin.**

Ben·ja·min·ite (ben′jə mə nīt′), *n.* a member of the tribe of Benjamin. Also, **Ben·ja·mite** (ben′jə mīt′). [BENJAMIN + -ITE¹]

Ben·jy (ben′jē), *n.* a boy's given name, form of **Benjamin.**

Ben Lo·mond (ben lō′mənd), a mountain in central Scotland, in Stirlingshire, on the E shore of Loch Lomond. 3192 ft.

ben·most (ben′mōst′, -məst), *adj.* *Scot., Irish.* innermost; inmost. [BEN¹ + -MOST]

Benn (ben), *n.* **Gott·fried** (gôt′frēd), 1886–1956, German physician, critic, poet, and essayist.

ben·ne (ben′ē), *n.* sesame (defs. 1, 2). [< Malay *bene* < ?]

ben·net (ben′it), *n.* **1.** either of two American avens, *Geum virginianum,* or *G. canadense.* **2.** See **herb bennet.** [ME *(herbe) beneit* < OF *(herbe) beneite,* trans. of L *(herba) benedicta* blessed (herb). See BENEDICTUS]

Ben·nett (ben′it), *n.* **1. (Enoch) Arnold,** 1867–1931, English novelist. **2. Floyd,** 1890–1928, U.S. aviator. **3. James Gordon,** 1795–1872, U.S. journalist. **4. Richard Bedford,** 1870–1947, Canadian statesman: prime minister 1930–35. **5. Robert Russell,** born 1894, U.S. composer and conductor. **6.** Also, **Ben′net.** a boy's given name, form of **Benedict.**

Ben Ne·vis (ben nē′vis, nev′is), a mountain in NW Scotland, in the Grampians: highest peak in Great Britain. 4406 ft.

Ben·nie (ben′ē), *n.* **1.** a boy's given name, form of **Benjamin. 2.** a girl's given name. Also, **Ben′ny.**

Ben·ning·ton (ben′ing tən), *n.* a town in SW Vermont: defeat of British by the Green Mountain Boys 1777. 8023 (1960).

Ben·nu (ben′o͞o), *n.* Benu.

ben·ny (ben′ē), *n., pl.* **-nies.** *Slang.* **1.** Benzedrine, esp. in tablet form. **2.** any amphetamine tablet. [by alter. and shortening of BENZEDRINE; see -Y²]

Be·noît (bə nwä′), *n.* **Pierre** (pyer) (or **Peter**) **Lé·o·nard Lé·o·pold** (lā ô när′ lā ô pôld′), 1834–1901, Belgian composer.

Be·noît de Sainte-Maure (be nwä′ də saNt-môr′), fl. 12th cent., French trouvère.

Be·no·ni (bə nō′nī), *n.* a city in the NE of the Republic of South Africa, near Johannesburg: gold mines. 122,052 (1960).

Ben·sen·ville (ben′sən vil′), *n.* a town in NE Illinois. 9141 (1960).

Ben·son (ben′sən), *n.* **1.** a town in W Minnesota. 3678 (1960). **2.** a boy's given name.

bent¹ (bent), *adj.* **1.** curved; crooked: *a bent bow; a bent stick.* **2.** determined; set; resolved (usually fol. by *on*): *to be bent on buying a new car.* —*n.* **3.** direction taken, as by one's interests; inclination; leaning; bias: *a bent for painting.* **4.** capacity or endurance: *to work to the top of one's bent.* **5.** *Civ. Eng.* a transverse frame of a bridge or a building, designed to support either vertical or horizontal loads. **6.** *Archaic.* bent state or form; curvature. [ptp. of BEND¹]
—**Syn. 1.** bowed, flexed. **2.** fixed. **3.** tendency, propensity, proclivity, predilection, disposition, penchant, partiality.

bent² (bent), *n.* **1.** See **bent grass. 2.** a stalk of bent grass. **3.** *Scot., Northern Eng.* (formerly) any stiff grass or sedge. **4.** *Brit. Dial.* a moor; heath; a tract of uncultivated, grassy land, used as a pasture or hunting preserve. [ME; OE *bionot-, beonot-;* c. OHG *binuz* (cf. G *Binse*) rush]

bent′ grass′, any grass of the genus *Agrostis,* esp. the redtop.

Ben·tham (ben′thəm, -təm), *n.* **Jeremy,** 1748–1832, English jurist and philosopher.

Ben·tham·ism (ben′thə miz′əm, -tə-), *n.* the utilitarianism of Bentham, characterized esp. by moral and ethical evaluation of actions as good if tending to produce pleasure and as bad if tending to produce pain. [BENTHAM + -ISM] —**Ben·tham·ic** (ben tham′ik, -tam′-), *adj.* —**Ben·tham·ite** (ben′thə mīt′, -tə-), *n.*

ben·thos (ben′thos), *n.* the aggregate of organisms living on or at the bottom of a body of water. [< Gk *bénthos* depth (of the sea); akin to BATHOS, BATHY-] —**ben′thic, ben′thal, ben·thon·ic** (ben thon′ik), *adj.*

Ben·tinck (ben′tingk), *n.* **William Henry Cavendish, Duke of Portland,** 1738–1809, British statesman: prime minister 1783; 1807–09.

Bent·ley (bent′lē), *n.* **1. Eric (Russell),** born 1916, U.S. critic, editor, and translator; born in England. **2. Phyllis,** born 1894, English novelist. **3. Richard,** 1662–1742, English scholar and critic. **4.** a boy's given name.

Bent·ley·ville (bent′lē vil′), *n.* a town in SW Pennsylvania. 3160 (1960).

Ben·ton (ben′tᵊn), *n.* **1. Thomas Hart** (*"Old Bullion"*), 1782–1858, U.S. political leader. **2.** his grandnephew **Thomas Hart,** born 1889, U.S. painter and lithographer. **3.** a town in S Illinois. 7023 (1960). **4.** a town in SW Kentucky. 3074 (1960). **5.** a boy's given name.

Ben′ton Har′bor, a city in SW Michigan, on Lake Michigan. 19,136 (1960).

Ben′ton Heights′, a town in SW Michigan. 6112 (1960).

ben·ton·ite (ben′tᵊnīt′), *n.* *Mineral.* a clay formed by the decomposition of volcanic ash, having the ability to absorb large quantities of water and to expand to several times its normal volume. [named after Fort *Benton,* Montana; see -ITE¹]

Ben·ton·ville (ben′tᵊn vil′), *n.* a town in NW Arkansas. 3649 (1960).

ben tro·va·to (ben′ trô vä′tô), *Italian.* well conceived; ingenious.

ben·tu de so·li (ben′to͞o de sô′lē), *n.* an east wind on the coast of Sardinia. [< Sardinian: lit., wind of the sun]

bent·wood (bent′wo͝od′), *n.* **1.** wood steamed and bent for use in furniture. —*adj.* **2.** noting or pertaining to furniture made principally of pieces of wood of circular or oval section, steamed, bent, and screwed together. [BENT¹ + WOOD¹]

Bentwood chair

Ben·u (ben′o͞o), *n.* the sacred bird of ancient Egypt, corresponding to the phoenix. Also, **Bennu.** [< Egypt]

Be·nue (bā′nwā), *n.* a river in W Africa, flowing W from Cameroon to the Niger River in Nigeria. 870 mi.

Be·nue-Con·go (bā′nwā kong′gō), *n.* a branch of Niger-Congo that comprises a large number of languages, as Efik, Tiv, and the Bantu languages, spoken in central and southern Africa.

be·numb (bi num′), *v.t.* **1.** to make numb; deprive of sensation: *benumbed by cold.* **2.** to render inactive; stupefy. [back formation from ME *benomen,* ptp. of *benimen* to take away, OE *beniman;* c. D *benemen,* G *benehmen,* Goth *biniman.* See BE-, NIMBLE, NUMB] —**be·numbed·ness** (bi numd′nis, -num′id-), *n.* —**be·numb′ing·ly,** *adv.* —**be·numb′ment,** *n.*

Ben·ve·nu·to Cel·li·ni (ben′və no͞o′tō chə lē′nē, -nyo͞o′-; *It.* ben′ve no͞o′tô chel lē′nē), an opera (1838) by Hector Berlioz.

Ben·wood (ben′wo͝od′), *n.* a town in NW West Virginia. 2850 (1960).

Ben Ye·hu·dah (ben′ ye ho͞o′dä), **El·i·ez·er** (el′ē-ez′ər), 1858–1922, Jewish scholar, born in Lithuania.

benz-, var. of **benzo-** before a vowel: *benzaldehyde.*

ben·zal (ben′zal), *adj.* *Chem.* containing the benzal group; benzylidene. [BENZ- + -AL³]

ben·zal·ac·e·tone (ben′zal as′i tōn′), *n.* *Chem.* See **benzylidene acetone.** [BENZAL + ACETONE]

ben′zal chlo′ride, *Chem.* a colorless, oily liquid, $C_6H_5CHCl_2$, used chiefly in the synthesis of benzaldehyde, and in the manufacture of dyes. Also called **benzyl dichloride, benzylidene chloride.**

benz·al·de·hyde (ben zal′də hīd′), *n.* *Chem.* a colorless or yellowish, water-soluble, volatile oil, C_6H_5CHO, having a bitter, almondlike odor, used chiefly in the organic synthesis of dyes, perfumes, and flavors, and as a solvent; artificial oil of bitter almond. Also called **benzoic aldehyde.** [BENZ- + ALDEHYDE]

ben′zal group′, *Chem.* the bivalent group, C_6H_5CH–, derived from benzaldehyde. Also called **ben′zal rad′ical.**

ben·zal·ko·ni·um chlo·ride (ben′zal kō′nē əm), *Chem.* a white or yellowish-white, water-soluble mixture of ammonium chloride derivatives having the structure, $[C_6H_5CH_2N(CH_3)R]Cl$, where R is a mixture of radicals ranging from C_8H_{17}– to $C_{18}H_{37}$–, that occurs as an amorphous powder or in gelatinous lumps: used chiefly as an antiseptic and a disinfectant. [BENZ- + ALK(YL) + (AMM)ONIUM]

ben·za·mine (ben′zə mēn′), *n.* *Pharm.* eucaine. [BENZ- + AMINE]

Ben·ze·drex Inhaler (ben′zi dreks′), *n.* *Trademark.* a nasal inhaler containing propylhexedrine and aromatic substances for the treatment of nasal congestion.

Ben·ze·drine (ben′zi drēn′, -drin), *n.* *Pharm., Trademark.* amphetamine.

ben·zene (ben′zēn, ben zēn′), *n.* *Chem.* a colorless, volatile, flammable, toxic, slightly water-soluble, liquid, aromatic compound, C_6H_6, obtained chiefly from coal tar: used in the manufacture of commercial and medicinal chemicals, dyes, and as a solvent for resins, fats, or the like. Also called **benzol, cyclohexatriene.** [BENZ- + -ENE]

ben·zene·az·o·ben·zene (ben′zēn az′ō ben′zēn, ben zēn′az ō ben zēn′), *n.* *Chem.* azobenzene. [BENZENE + AZOBENZENE]

ben′zene·car·box·yl′ic ac′id (ben′zēn kär′bok-sil′ik, ben zēn′kär-), *Chem.* See **benzoic acid.** [BENZENE + CARBOXYLIC]

ben′zene hexachlo′ride, *Chem.* a white to yellowish, crystalline, water-soluble, poisonous solid, $C_6H_6Cl_6$, used chiefly as an insecticide.

ben′zene ring′, *Chem.* the graphic representation of the structure of benzene as a hexagon with a carbon atom at each of its points. Each carbon atom is united with an atom of hydrogen, one or more of which may be replaced to form benzene derivatives. Also called **ben′zene nu′cleus.** Cf. **cyclohexane, Kekulé's formula, meta², ortho, para³.**

Benzene ring
(Kekulé's formula)
X, Graphic representation; **Y,** Positions numbered for replacement of one or more hydrogen atoms, leading to benzene derivatives; **Z,** used when cyclohexane is not indicated. Double bonds are assumed

ben′zene·sul·fon′ic ac′id (ben′zēn sul fon′ik, ben-zēn′-), *Chem.* a fine, needlelike substance, $C_6H_5SO_3H$, used chiefly as a catalyst and in the synthesis of phenol, resorcinol, and other organic products. [BENZENE + SULFONIC ACID]

ben·ze·tho′ni·um chlo′ride (ben′zə thō′nē əm), *Chem.* a colorless, water-soluble, crystalline solid, ammonium chloride derivative, $(C_{27}H_{42}O_2N)Cl{\cdot}H_2O$, used chiefly as an antiseptic. [BENZ(YL + M)ETH(YL + AMM)ONIUM]

ben·zi·dine (ben′zi dēn′, -din), *n.* *Chem.* a grayish, crystalline, slightly water-soluble, basic compound, $NH_2(C_6H_4)_2NH_2$, usually derived from nitrobenzene: used chiefly in the synthesis of certain azo dyes, esp. Congo red. [BENZ- + -ID³ + -INE²]

ben·zine (ben′zēn, ben zēn′), *n.* a colorless, volatile, flammable, liquid mixture of various hydrocarbons, obtained in the distillation of petroleum, and used in cleaning, dyeing, etc. Also, **ben·zin** (ben′zin). [BENZ- + -INE²]

benzo-, a combining form indicating benzene, benzoic acid, or the presence of one or more phenyl groups in a substance: *benzocaine.* Also, *esp. before a vowel,* **benz-.** [comb. form of BENZOIN]

ben·zo·ate (ben′zō āt′, -it), *n.* *Chem.* a salt or ester of benzoic acid. [BENZO- + -ATE²]

ben′zoate of so′da, *Chem.* See **sodium benzoate.**

ben·zo·caine (ben′zō kān′), *n.* *Pharm.* ethyl aminobenzoate; a white, crystalline powder, $H_2N{\cdot}C_6H_4CO{\cdot}OC_2H_5$, used as a local anesthetic, usually in ointment form. [BENZO- + (CO)CAINE]

ben·zo·fu·ran (ben′zō fyo͝or′an, -fyə ran′), *n.* *Chem.* coumarone. [BENZO- + FURAN]

ben·zo·ic (ben zō′ik), *adj.* *Chem.* of or derived from benzoin or benzoic acid. [BENZO- + -IC]

benzo′ic ac′id, *Chem., Pharm.* a white, crystalline, slightly water-soluble powder, C_6H_5COOH, usually derived from benzoin or other balsams, or synthesized from phthalic acid or toluene: used chiefly as a preservative, in the synthesis of dyes, and in medicine as a germicide. Also called **benzenecarboxylic acid, phenylformic acid.**

benzo′ic al′dehyde, *Chem.* benzaldehyde.

ben·zo·in¹ (ben′zō in, -zoin, ben zō′in), *n.* **1.** Also called **benjamin, gum benjamin, gum benzoin.** a reddish-brown, aromatic, water-insoluble balsamic resin occurring in almondlike fragments and having a vanillalike odor, obtained from trees of the genus *Styrax,* esp. *S. Benzoin,* of Java, Sumatra, etc.: used in the manufacture of perfume and cosmetics and in medicine internally as an expectorant and externally as an antiseptic. **2.** any lauraceous plant of the genus *Lindera (Benzoin)* which includes the spicebush and other aromatic plants. [earlier *benjoin* < MF < Pg *beijoim* + Sp *benjuí* (c. It *benzoi*) < Ar *(lu)bān jāwī* frankincense of Java; *z* of *benzoin* < It]

ben·zo·in² (ben′zō in, -zoin, ben zō′in), *n.* *Chem.* a white, slightly water-soluble powder, $C_6H_5CHOHCOC_6H_5$, derived by the condensation of benzaldehyde in the presence of potassium cyanide, and used in organic synthesis. [BENZO- + -IN²]

ben·zol (ben′zōl, -zôl, -zol), *n.* **1.** *Chem.* benzene. **2.** an impure form of this, used for industrial purposes. [BENZ- + -OL¹]

ben·zon·i·trile (ben zon′i tril), *n.* *Chem.* a clear, colorless, viscous, poisonous liquid, C_6H_5CN, used chiefly as an intermediate in organic synthesis. [BENZO- + NITRILE]

ben·zo·phe·none (ben′zō fi nōn′), *n.* *Chem.* a crystalline, water-insoluble ketone, $C_6H_5COC_6H_5$, used in organic synthesis. Also called **diphenyl ketone.** [BENZO- + PHEN- + -ONE]

ben·zo·sul·fi·mide (ben′zō sul′fə mīd′), *n.* *Chem.* saccharin. [BENZO- + SULF- + IMIDE]

ben·zo·tri·chlo·ride (ben′zō trī klōr′īd, -id, -klôr′-), *n.* *Chem.* a colorless or yellowish liquid, $C_6H_5CCl_3$, used chiefly in the manufacture of dyes. Also called **toluene trichloride.** [BENZO- + TRICHLORIDE]

ben·zo·tri·flu·o·ride (ben′zō trī flo͞o′ə rīd′, -flōr′id, -flōr′-, -flôr′-), *n.* *Chem.* a colorless, flammable liquid, $C_6H_5CF_3$, used chiefly as an intermediate in the manufacture of dyes and pharmaceuticals, and as a solvent. Also called **toluene trifluoride.** [BENZO- + TRI- + FLUORIDE]

benzoxy-, a combining form of the benzoyl group, used esp. before a vowel: *benzoxyacetanilide.* [BENZ- + OXY-²]

ben·zo·yl (ben′zō il), *adj.* *Chem.* containing the benzoyl group. [BENZO- + -YL]

ben·zo·yl·ate (ben′zō ə lāt′, ben zō′-), *v.t.,* **-at·ed, -at·ing.** *Chem.* to introduce the benzoyl group into (an organic compound). [BENZOYL + -ATE²] —**ben′zo·yl·a′tion,** *n.*

ben′zoyl group′, *Chem.* the univalent group, C_6H_5CO–, derived from benzoic acid. Also called **ben′zoyl rad′ical.**

CONCISE PRONUNCIATION KEY: *act, āble, dâre, ärt; ebb, ēqual; if, īce; hot, ōver, ôrder, oil, bo͝ok, o͞oze, out; up, ûrge; chief; sing; shoe; thin, that; zh as in measure.* ə = *a* as in *alone, e* as in *system, i* as in *easily, o* as in *gallop, u* as in *circus;* ᵊ as in *button* (butᵊn), *fire* (fīᵊr), *cradle* (krādᵊl). See the full key inside the front cover.

ben′zoyl perox′ide, *Chem.* a white, crystalline, water-insoluble, explosive solid, $(C_6H_5CO)_2O_2$, used chiefly as a bleaching agent for flour, fats, oils, and waxes, and as a catalyst in polymerization reactions.

Ben-Zvi (ben tsvē′), *n.* **Itz·hak** (yits′hok), 1884?–1963, Israeli statesman, born in Russia: president of Israel 1952–63.

ben·zyl (ben′zil), *adj.* *Chem.* containing the benzyl group. [BENZ- + -YL] —**ben·zyl′ic,** *adj.*

ben′zyl ac′etate, *Chem.* a colorless liquid, $CH_3COOCH_2C_6H_5$, having a flowerlike odor: used chiefly for flavoring tobacco and in soaps and cosmetics.

ben′zyl al′cohol, *Chem.* a colorless, faintly aromatic, slightly water-soluble liquid, $C_6H_5CH_2OH$, used chiefly as a solvent in the manufacture of perfumes and flavorings, and as an intermediate in the synthesis of benzyl esters and ethers. Also called **phenylcarbinol.**

ben′zyl ben′zoate, *Chem.* a colorless, faintly aromatic liquid, $C_6H_5COOCH_2C_6H_5$, used chiefly as a fixative and solvent in the manufacture of flavorings and perfume and in medicine in the treatment of certain skin conditions.

ben′zyl bu′tyrate, *Chem.* a liquid, $C_3H_7COOCH_2C_6H_5$, having a fruitlike odor, used as a plasticizer and in flavoring.

ben′zyl chlo′ride, *Chem.* a colorless, corrosive liquid, $C_6H_5CH_2Cl$, used chiefly as an intermediate in the synthesis of benzyl compounds.

ben′zyl dichlo′ride, *Chem.* See **benzal chloride.**

ben′zyl flu′oride, *Chem.* a colorless liquid, $C_6H_5CH_2F$, used in organic synthesis.

ben′zyl group′, *Chem.* the univalent group, $C_6H_5CH_2-$, derived from toluene. Also called **ben′zyl rad′ical.**

ben·zyl·i·dene (ben zil′i dēn′), *adj.* benzal. [BENZYL + -ID[3] + -ENE]

benzyl′idene ac′etone, *Chem.* a colorless, crystalline, water-insoluble solid, $C_6H_5CH{-}CHCOCH_3$, having a vanillalike odor, used chiefly as a scent in the manufacture of perfume. Also called **benzalacetone, methyl styryl ketone.**

benzyl′idene chlo′ride, *Chem.* See **benzal chloride.**

ben′zyl isoam′yl e′ther, *Chem.* See **isoamyl benzyl ether.**

benzyloxy-, a combining form of the benzyl group, used esp. before a vowel: *benzyloxyamine.* [BENZYL + OXY-[2]]

ben′zyl thiocy′anate, *Chem.* a colorless, crystalline, water-insoluble solid, $C_6H_5CH_2CNS$, used as an insecticide.

Be·o·grad (be ô′gräd), *n.* Serbian name of **Belgrade.**

Be·o·wulf (bā′ə wo͝olf′), *n.* an English alliterative epic poem of the early 8th century A.D.

B.E.P., Bachelor of Engineering Physics.

be·paint (bi pānt′), *v.t.* **1.** to cover with paint. **2.** to color or tint: *a face bepainted with excessive make-up.* [BE- + PAINT]

Be′ Prepared′, the motto of the Girl Scouts of America and of the Boy Scouts of America.

be·queath (bi kwēth′, -kwēth′), *v.t.* **1.** *Law.* to dispose of (personal property, esp. money) by last will. **2.** to hand down; pass on. **3.** *Obs.* to commit; entrust. [ME *bequethe(n),* OE *becwethan* (*be-* BE- + *cwethan* to say, c. OHG *quedan,* Goth *qithan*)] —**be·queath′a·ble,** *adj.* —**be·queath·al** (bi kwē′thəl, -thəl), **be·queath′ment,** *n.* —**be·queath′er,** *n.*

be·quest (bi kwest′), *n.* **1.** *Law.* a disposition in a will concerning personal property, esp. money. **2.** a legacy: *A small bequest allowed her to live independently.* [ME *biqueste;* akin to BEQUEATH]

Bé·ran·ger (bā rän zhā′), *n.* **Pierre Jean de** (pyer zhän də), 1780–1857, French poet.

Be·rar (bā rär′), *n.* a former division of the Central Provinces and Berar, in central India; now part of Maharashtra state.

be·ras·cal (bi ras′kəl), *v.t.* to call (someone) a rascal. [BE- + RASCAL]

be·rate (bi rāt′), *v.t.,* **-rat·ed, -rat·ing.** to scold; rebuke: *She berated him in public.* [BE- + RATE[2]] —**Syn.** abuse, vilify, vituperate, objurgate.

Ber·ber (bûr′bər), *n.* **1.** a member of a group of North African tribes living in Barbary and the Sahara. **2.** a subfamily of Afro-Asiatic, consisting of the languages of the Berbers, including Tuareg and Kabyle. —*adj.* **3.** of or pertaining to the Berbers or their language. [< Ar, var. of *Barbar.* See BARB[2]]

Ber·ber·a (bûr′bər ə), *n.* a seaport in Somalia, on the Gulf of Aden: former capital of British Somaliland. 9080 (1951).

ber·be·ri·da·ceous (bûr′bər i dā′shəs), *adj.* belonging to the *Berberidaceae,* a family of plants including the barberry, May apple, blue cohosh, etc. [< ML *berberid-* (s. of *berberis*) BARBERRY + -ACEOUS]

ber·ber·ine (bûr′bə rēn′), *n.* *Pharm.* a white or yellow, crystalline, water-soluble alkaloid, $C_{20}H_{19}NO_5$, derived from barberry or goldenseal, and usually prepared in the form of its sulfate or hydrochloride: used as an antiperiodic, tonic, and stomachic. [< ML *berber-* (var. s. of *berberis*) BARBERRY + -INE[1]]

ber·ceuse (*Fr.* ber sœz′), *n., pl.* **-ceuses** (*Fr.* -sœz′). *Music.* a cradlesong; lullaby. [< F, equiv. to *berc(er)* (to) rock + *-euse,* fem. suffix of agency]

Berch·ta (*Ger.* berkh′tä), *n.* Perchta.

Berch·tes·ga·den (berkh′təs gäd′ən), *n.* a town in the SE extremity of Bavaria, in SE West Germany: site of the fortified mountain chalet of Adolf Hitler. 5736 (1950).

Ber·cy (bâr sē′; *Fr.* ber sē′), *n.* a sauce consisting of shallots, white wine, butter, parsley, and tarragon in a base of thin brown gravy. Also called **Bercy′ sauce′.** [after a ward or borough of Paris, France]

ber·dache (bər dash′), *n.* (in some American Indian tribes) a man who adopts the dress and social role of a woman. [< F *bardache* < Sp *bardajo* < Ar *bardaj* slave]

Ber·di·chev (ber dē′chef), *n.* a city in the central Ukraine, in the SW Soviet Union. 70,000 (est. 1956).

Ber·dya·ev (ber dyä′yef), *n.* **Ni·ko·lai A·le·ksan·dro·vich** (ni ko lī′ ä le ksän′dro vich), 1874–1948, Russian theologian and philosopher: in France after 1922.

Be·re·a (bə rē′ə), *n.* **1.** a city in NE Ohio, near Cleveland. 16,592 (1960). **2.** a town in central Kentucky. 4302 (1960). —**Be·re′an,** *n.*

be·reave (bi rēv′), *v.t.,* **-reaved** or **-reft, -reav·ing.** **1.** to deprive ruthlessly or by force (usually fol. by *of*): *The war bereaved them of their home.* **2.** to deprive or make desolate, esp. by death (usually fol. by *of*): *Illness bereaved them of their mother.* **3.** *Obs.* to take away by violence. [ME *bereve(n),* OE *berēafian;* c. D *berooven,* G *berauben,* Goth *biraubōn.* See BE-, REAVE[1]] —**be·reave′ment,** *n.* —**be·reav′er,** *n.*

Ber·e·cyn·ti·a (ber′i sin′tē ə), *n.* Cybele.

be·reft (bi reft′), *v.* **1.** a pt. and pp. of **bereave.** —*adj.* **2.** deprived: *They are bereft of their senses. He is bereft of all happiness.* [BE- + REFT]

Ber·e·ni·ce (ber′ə nī′sē), *n.* a boy's given name.

Bé·ré·nice (*Fr.* bā rā nēs′), *n.* a tragedy (1670) by Racine.

Bereni′ce's Hair′, *Astron.* the constellation Coma Berenices.

Ber·en·son (ber′ən sən), *n.* **Bernard** or **Bernhard,** 1865–1959, U.S. art critic, born in Lithuania.

Ber·es·ford (ber′iz fərd, -is-), *n.* **Lord Charles William de la Poer** (po͝or), 1846–1919, English admiral, explorer, and author.

be·ret (bə rā′, ber′ā; *Fr.* be re′), *n., pl.* **be·rets** (bə-rāz′, ber′āz; *Fr.* be re′). a soft, visorless cap with a close-fitting headband and a wide, round top often with a tab at its center. [< F < Béarnaise *berret(o).* See BIRETTA]

ber·et·ta (bə ret′ə), *n.* biretta.

Be·re·zi·na (*Pol.* be′re zē′nä; *Russ.* be′re zi nä′), *n.* a river in the W Soviet Union in Europe, flowing SE into the Dnieper River: crossed by Napoleon 1812. 350 mi. long.

Be·rez·ni·ki (bi rez′ni ki), *n.* a city in the RSFSR, in the E Soviet Union in Europe, near the Ural Mountains. 106,000 (1959).

berg (bûrg), *n.* *Oceanog.* iceberg. [by shortening]

Berg (berg; *Ger.* berkh), *n.* **Al·ban** (äl bän′, äl′bän), 1885–1935, Austrian composer: student of Schönberg.

ber·gall (bûr′gôl), *n.* cunner. [< Scand; cf. dial. Norw *berggalt* kind of fish, equiv. to *berg* (see ICEBERG) + *galt* swine]

Ber·ga·ma (ber gä′mə, bər-, bûr′gə mə), *n.* **1.** a town in W Turkey in Asia. 16,351 (1956). Ancient, **Pergamum.** **2.** Bergamo.

ber·ga·mas·ca (*It.* ber′gä mäs′kä), *n., pl.* **-che** (-ke). **1.** a fast dance similar to the tarantella. **2.** the music for this dance. [< It, n. use of fem. of *Bergamasco* of Bergamo]

Ber·ga·mo (ber′gə mō′, bûr′-), *n., pl.* **-mos.** a Turkish rug characterized by a long pile, floral or geometric patterns, and red-orange hues. Also, **Bergama, Ber·ga·mee** (bûr′gə mē′), **Ber·ga·mot** (bûr′gə mot′, -mət). [after BERGAMA]

Ber·ga·mo (ber′gä mô), *n.* a city in central Lombardy, in N Italy. 113,512 (1961).

ber·ga·mot (bûr′gə mot′), *n.* **1.** a small citrus tree, *Citrus Bergamia,* having fruit whose rind yields a fragrant essential oil. **2.** Also called **essence of bergamot.** the oil or essence itself. **3.** any of various plants of the mint family, as *Monarda fistulosa,* yielding an oil resembling essence of bergamot. **4.** *Hort.* **a.** a variety of pear. **b.** the tree bearing this fruit. [< F *bergamote,* variety of pear, hence sweet lemon < It *bergamotta* < Turkic **beg-armutu* lord-pear, akin to Turk *bey* BEY + *armudu* pear]

ber′gamot mint′, a European, perennial herb, *Mentha citrata,* naturalized in North America, having underground, rooting stems and small, purple, pink, or white flowers.

Ber·gen (bûr′gən; *for 2 also Nor.* ber′gən), *n.* **1.** a city in SW Norway, on the Atlantic Ocean. 112,981 (est. 1959). **2.** Also, **Bergin.** a boy's given name.

Ber·gen-Bel·sen (ber′gən bel′zən; *Eng.* bûr′gən bel′sən), *n.* Belsen.

Ber·gen·field (bûr′gən fēld′), *n.* a city in NE New Jersey. 27,203 (1960).

Ber·ge·rac (ber zhə rak′), *n.* **Sa·vi·nien Cy·ra·no de** (sa vē nyan′ sē ra nō′ də), 1619–55, French soldier, swordsman, and writer: hero of play by Rostand.

ber·gère (bər zhâr′; *Fr.* ber zher′), *n., pl.* **-gères** (-zhârz′; *Fr.* -zher′). a chair of the 18th century, having arms with closed spaces between them and the seat. [< F: lit., shepherdess, fem. of *berger* shepherd]

Ber·gin (bûr′gin), *n.* a boy's given name. Also, **Bergen.**

Ber·gi·us (ber′gē o͞os′), *n.* **Frie·drich** (frē′drikh), 1884–1949, German chemist: Nobel prize 1931.

Berg·man (bûrg′mən; *Swed.* bar′yᵊ män′), *n.* **Ingmar** (ing′mär; *Swed.* ing′mär), born 1918, Swedish motion picture director and writer.

berg·schrund (berk′shro͝ont), *n.* a crevasse, or series of crevasses, at the upper end of a mountain glacier. [< G (*Berg* mountain + *Schrund(e)* crevice)]

Bergs·ma (bûrgz′mə), *n.* **William,** born 1921, U.S. composer.

Berg·son (bûrg′sən, berg′-; *Fr.* berg sôn′), *n.* **Hen·ri** (än rē′), 1859–1941, French philosopher and writer: Nobel prize for literature 1927. —**Berg·so·ni·an** (bûrg sō′nē ən, berg-), *adj., n.*

Berg·son·ism (bûrg′sə niz′əm, berg′-), *n.* the philosophy of Bergson, emphasizing duration as the central fact of experience, and asserting the existence of the élan vital as an original life force essentially governing all organic processes. [BERGSON + -ISM]

berg′ wind′ (wind), a foehn blowing coastward from the interior plateau of South Africa.

berg′y bit′ (bûr′gē), a small iceberg, somewhat larger than a growler. [BERG + -Y[2]]

be·rhyme (bi rīm′), *v.t.,* **-rhymed, -rhym·ing.** to celebrate in verse. Also, **berime.** [BE- + RHYME]

Be·ri·a (ber′ē ə), *n.* **La·vren·ti Pa·vlo·vich** (lä vren′-ti pä vlô′vich), 1899–1953, Soviet official: executed for treason.

be·rib·boned (bi rib′ənd), *adj.* adorned with ribbons. [*beribbon* (BE- + RIBBON) + -ED[2]]

ber·i·ber·i (ber′ē ber′ē), *n.* *Pathol.* a disease of the peripheral nerves caused by a deficiency of vitamin B_1, characterized by pain in and paralysis of the extremities, and severe emaciation or swelling of the body. It is common in China, Japan, and the Philippines. [< Singhalese redupl. of *beri* weakness] —**ber′i·ber′ic,** *adj.*

be·rime (bi rīm′), *v.t.,* **-rimed, -rim·ing.** berhyme. [BE- + RIME[1]]

Ber·ing (bēr′ing, ber′-, bâr′-; *Dan.* bā′ring), *n.* **Vi·tus** (vē′to͞os), 1680–1741, Danish navigator: explorer of the N Pacific. Also, **Behring.**

Ber′ing Sea′, a part of the N Pacific, N of the Aleutian Islands. 878,000 sq. mi.

Ber′ing Strait′, a strait between Alaska and the Soviet Union in Asia, connecting the Bering Sea and the Arctic Ocean. 36 mi. wide.

Ber′ing time′. See under **standard time.**

Ber·io·so·va (ber yô′sô-vä′), *n.* **Svet·la·na** (svet lä′nä), born 1932, English ballet dancer, born in Lithuania.

Ber. Is., Bermuda Islands.

Be·rith (bə rēt′; *Eng.* bris), *n.* *Hebrew.* the Jewish rite of circumcising a male child eight days after his birth. Also, **Be·rit′, Brith, Brit.** Cf. **Berith Milah.** [lit., covenant]

Be·rith Mi·lah (bə rēt′ mē lä′), *Hebrew.* the covenant between God and Abraham with respect to circumcision. Gen. 17:10–14. Cf. **Berith.** [lit., covenant of circumcision]

Berke·le·ian (bûrk lē′ən, bûrk′lē-; *Brit.* bärk lē′ən, bärk′lē-), *adj.* **1.** pertaining or relating to George Berkeley or his philosophy. —*n.* **2.** an advocate of the philosophy of George Berkeley, esp. its denial of the existence of a material world. [BERKELEY + -AN] —**Berke·le′ian·ism,** *n.*

Berke·ley (bûrk′lē; *for 1, 2, 6 also Brit.* bärk′lē), *n.* **1. George,** 1685?–1753, Irish bishop and philosopher. **2. Sir William,** 1610–77, British colonial governor of Virginia 1642–76. **3.** a city in W California, on San Francisco Bay. 111,268 (1960). **4.** a city in E Missouri, near St. Louis. 18,676 (1960). **5.** a town in NE Illinois. 5792 (1960). **6.** Also **Barclay, Barkleigh, Barkley.** a boy's given name.

ber·ke·li·um (bər kē′lē əm), *n.* *Chem.* a synthetic, radioactive, metallic element. *Symbol:* Bk; *at. no.:* 97. [named after BERKEL(EY), California, where it was discovered; see -IUM]

Berk·ley (bûrk′lē), *n.* a city in SE Michigan, near Detroit. 23,275 (1960).

Berk·shire (bûrk′shēr, -shər; *Brit.* bärk′shēr, -shər), *n.* **1.** Also called **Berks** (bûrks; *Brit.* bärks). a county in S England. 503,357 (1961); 725 sq. mi. *Co. seat:* Reading. **2.** one of an English breed of black hogs, having white markings on the feet, face, and tail.

Berk′shire Hills′ (bûrk′shēr, -shər), a range of low mountains in W Massachusetts: resort region. Highest peak, Mt. Greylock, 3505 ft. Also called **Berk′shires.**

Berl (bûrl), *n.* a boy's given name.

Ber·len (bûr len′, bûr′lin), *n.* a boy's given name. Also, **Berlin, Berlyne.**

ber·ley (bûr′lē), *n.* *Australian.* chum[2] (defs. 1, 2). [?]

ber·lin (bər lin′, bûr′lin), *n.* **1.** a large, four-wheeled, closed carriage hung between two perches and having two interior seats. **2.** *Auto. Obs.* a limousine with a movable glass partition behind the driver's seat. **3.** (*sometimes cap.*) See **Berlin wool.** Also, **ber·line** (bər-lin′; *Fr.* ber lēn′) (for defs. 1, 2). [< F *berline;* after *Berlin,* Germany, where it was first made]

Berlin

Ber·lin (bər lin′ *for 1, 2;* bûr′lin *for 3, 4; for 2 also Ger.* ber lēn′), *n.* **1. Irving,** born 1888, U.S. songwriter. **2.** the capital of Germany, in the NE part: constitutes a state. 3,121,000; 341 sq. mi. Formerly (1948–90) divided into a western zone **(West Berlin),** a part of West Germany; and an eastern zone **(East Berlin),** the capital of East Germany. **3.** a town in central Connecticut. 15,121. **4.** a city in N New Hampshire. 13,084.

Ber·li·ner (bûr′lə nər), *n.* **Emile,** 1851–1928, U.S. inventor, born in Germany.

Ber·lin·er (bûr lin′ər), *n.* a native or resident of Berlin, esp. Berlin, Germany. [BERLIN + -ER[1]]

Ber′lin Wall′, a guarded concrete wall 28 mi. long, with minefields and controlled checkpoints, erected across Berlin by East Germany in 1961.

Berlin′ wool′, a soft woolen yarn for embroidery or knitting. Also called **berlin.**

Ber·li·oz (ber′lē ōz′; *Fr.* ber lyôz′), *n.* **Louis Hec·tor** (lwē ek tôr′), 1803–69, French composer.

Ber·lon (bûr′lən), *n.* a boy's given name.

Ber·lyne (bûr lin′), *n.* a boy's given name.

berm (bûrm), *n.* **1.** *U.S.* an edge or shoulder running alongside a road, canal, etc. **2.** Also, **berme.** *Fort.* a horizontal surface between the exterior slope of a rampart and the moat. **3.** Also called **bench.** any level strip of ground at the summit or sides, or along the base, of a slope. **4.** a nearly flat back portion of a beach, formed of material deposited by the action of the waves. [< D (whence F *berme*); akin to BRIM[1]]

Ber·man (bûr′mən, bär′-; *Fr.* ber män′), *n.* **Eu·gène** (yo͞o jēn′; *Fr.* œ zhen′), born 1899, U.S. painter and set designer, born in Russia.

Ber·me·jo (ber me′hô), *n.* a river in N Argentina, flowing SE to the Paraguay River. 1000 mi. long.

Ber·mu·da (bər myo͞o′də), *n.* a group of islands in the Atlantic, 580 miles E of North Carolina: a British colony; resort. 56,056 (1960); 19 sq. mi. *Cap.:* Hamilton. Also called **Ber·mu′das.** —**Ber·mu′dan, Ber·mu·di·an** (bər myo͞o′dē ən), *adj., n.*

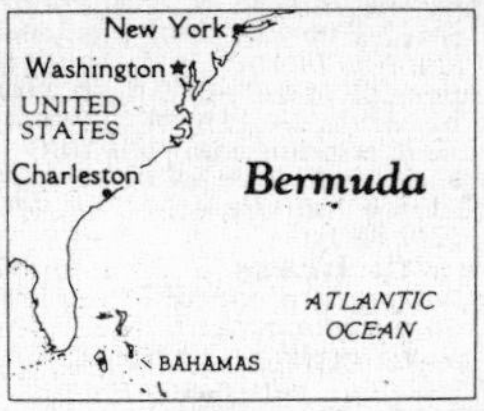

Bermu′da but′ter·cup, a bulbous herb, *Oxalis cernua,* of South Africa, having nodding, yellow flowers.

Bermu′da cut′ter, *Naut.* a Marconi-rigged cutter.

Bermu′da grass′, a perennial, creeping grass, *Cynodon Dactylon,* of southern Europe, grown in the southern U.S. and Bermuda for lawns and pastures. Also called **Bahama grass, devil grass, scutch grass.**

Bermu′da high′, *Meteorol.* a subtropical high centered near Bermuda.

Bermu′da lil′y, a lily, *Lilium longiflorum eximium,* having white, funnel-shaped flowers.

Bermu′da on′ion, any of several mild, flat varieties of onion, grown in Texas and, to some extent, in other parts of the southern U.S. and in Bermuda.

Bermu′da palmet′to, a palm, *Sabal blackburniana,* of Bermuda, having leaves that are checkered beneath and small, roundish, black fruit.

Bermu′da rig′. See **Marconi rig.** Also, **Bermu′dan rig′, Bermu′dian rig′.**

Bermu′da shorts′, shorts reaching just above the knee, worn by men and women for informal dress.

Bermu′da Tri′angle, the triangular area in the Atlantic Ocean bounded by lines drawn between Bermuda, Puerto Rico, and a point west of Florida, in which a number of ships and aircraft are alleged to have disappeared mysteriously esp. since 1945.

Bern (bûrn; *for 1, 2 also Fr.* bern), *n.* **1.** a city in and the capital of Switzerland, in the W part: capital of Bern canton. 163,172 (1960). **2.** a canton in W Switzerland. 889,523 (1960); 2658 sq. mi. *Cap.:* Bern. **3.** a boy's given name. Also, **Berne** (for defs. 1, 2).

Ber·na (bûr′nə), *n.* a girl's given name, form of **Bernadette** or **Bernadine.**

Ber·na·dette (bûr′nə det′; *Fr.* ber na det′), *n.* **1. Saint.** Also called **Bernadette′ of Lourdes′.** (*Marie Bernarde Soubirous* or *Soubiroux*), 1844–79, French nun. **2.** a girl's given name.

Ber·na·dine (bûr′nə dēn′), *n.* a girl's given name. Also, **Bernardine.**

Ber·na·dotte (bûr′nə dot′; *Fr.* ber na dôt′), *n.* **Jean Bap·tiste Jules** (zhäN ba tēst′ zhyl), 1764–1844, French marshal under Napoleon; as Charles XIV, king of Sweden and Norway 1818–44.

Ber·na·lil·lo (bûr′nə lē′yō), *n.* a town in central New Mexico. 2574 (1960).

Ber·na·nos (ber na nôs′), *n.* **Georges** (zhôrzh), 1888–1948, French novelist and pamphleteer.

Ber·nard (ber nar′ *for 1;* bûr′nərd, bûr närd′ *for 2*), *n.* **1. Claude** (klōd), 1813–78, French physiologist. **2.** Also, **Barnard.** a boy's given name.

Ber·nar·din de Saint-Pierre (ber nar daN′ də saN pyer′), **Jacques Hen·ri** (zhäk äN rē′), 1737–1814, French writer.

Ber·nard·ine (bûr′nər din, -dēn′), *adj.* **1.** of or pertaining to St. Bernard of Clairvaux. **2.** of or pertaining to the Cistercians. —*n.* **3.** a Cistercian. **4.** Also, **Bernadine.** a girl's given name.

Ber·nard of Clair·vaux (bûr närd′ əv klâr vō′), **Saint** ("*the Mellifluous Doctor*"), 1090–1153, French monk, preacher, and mystical writer.

Ber·nards·ville (bûr′nərdz vil), *n.* a town in central New Jersey. 5515 (1960).

Berne (bûrn), *n.* **1.** a town in E Indiana. 2644 (1960). **2.** Bern (defs. 1, 2).

Ber·nese (bûr′nēz, -nēs, bûr nēz′, -nēs′), *adj., n., pl.* **-nese.** —*adj.* **1.** of or pertaining to Bern, its inhabitants, or their language. —*n.* **2.** an inhabitant or native of Bern. [Bern + -ese]

Ber′nese Alps′, a mountain range in SW Switzerland, part of the Alps: highest peak, 14,026 ft.

Ber′nese moun′tain dog′, one of a Swiss breed of large, long-haired dogs having a black coat with white and russet-brown or deep tan markings.

Ber·nette (bûr net′), *n.* a girl's given name, form of **Bernadette** or **Bernadine.**

Bern·har·di (bern här′dē), *n.* **Frie·drich A. J. von** (frē′drikh fən), 1849–1930, German general.

Bern·hardt (bûrn′härt; *Fr.* ber nar′), *n.* **Sar·ah** (sâr′ə, sar′ə; *Fr.* sa ra′), (*Rosine Bernard*), 1845–1923, French actress.

Ber·nice (bûr nēs′, bûr′nis), *n.* a boy's or girl's given name. Also, **Bern·is′.**

Ber·nie (bûr′nē), *n.* a boy's given name, form of **Bernard.**

Ber·ni·na (bər nē′nə; *It.* ber nē′nä), *n.* **1.** a mountain in SE Switzerland, in the Rhaetian Alps. 13,295 ft. **Berni′na Pass′,** a pass traversing Bernina Mountain, between SE Switzerland and N Italy. 7640 ft. high.

Ber·ni·ni (bər nē′nē; *It.* ber nē′nē), *n.* **Gio·van·ni Lo·ren·zo** (jē′ə vä′nē lə ren′zō; *It.* jô vän′nē lô ren′dzô), 1598–1680, Italian sculptor, architect, and painter. —**Ber·ni·nesque,** (bûr′ni nesk′, ber′-).

Ber·noul·li (bər no͞o′lē), *n.* a crater in the first quadrant of the face of the moon: about 25 miles in diameter.

Ber·noul·li (bər no͞o′lē; *Ger.* ber no͞o′lē; *Fr.* ber no͞o-yē′), *n.* **1. Dan·iel** (dan′yəl; *Ger.* dä′nē el′; *Fr.* da-nyel′), 1700–82, Swiss physicist and mathematician born in the Netherlands (son of Johann Bernoulli). **2. Ja·kob** (*Ger.* yä′kôp) or **Jacques** (*Fr.* zhäk), 1654–1705, Swiss mathematician and physicist. **3. Jo·hann** (*Ger.* yō′hän) or **Jean** (*Fr.* zhäN), 1667–1748, Swiss mathematician (brother of Jakob Bernoulli). Also, **Ber·nouil′li.** —**Ber·noul′li·an,** *adj.*

Bernoul′li distribu′tion, *Statistics.* See **binomial distribution.** [named after Jakob Bernoulli]

Bernoul′li effect′, *Hydraulics.* the decrease in pressure as the velocity of a fluid increases. [named after Jakob Bernoulli]

Bernoul′li equa′tion, *Math.* a differential equation of the form $\frac{dy}{dx} + f(x)y = g(x)y^n$, where n is any number other than 0 or 1. [named after Daniel Bernoulli]

Bernoul′li's lemnis′cate, lemniscate. [named after Jakob Bernoulli]

Bernoul′li's the′orem, 1. See **law of averages. 2.** *Hydrodynamics.* an expression of the conservation of energy in streamline, fluid flow, stating that the sum of the ratio of the pressure to the mass density, the product of the gravitational constant and the vertical height, and the square of the velocity divided by 2, are constant. [named after Jakob Bernoulli]

Bernoul′li tri′als, *Math.* repeated independent experiments having two possible outcomes for each experiment with the probability for each outcome remaining constant throughout the experiments, as tossing a coin several times. [named after Jakob Bernoulli]

Bern·stein (bûrn′stīn, -stēn), *n.* **Leonard,** born 1918, U.S. conductor, composer, and pianist.

Bern·storff (bern′shtôrf), *n.* **Count Jo·hann-Hein·rich** (yō′hän hīn′rikh), 1862–1939, German diplomat.

Ber·o·ë (ber′ō ē′), *n.* *Class. Myth.* **1.** the nurse of Semele. **2.** a daughter of Adonis and Aphrodite.

Be·ro·sus (bə rō′sis), *n.* a walled plain in the first quadrant of the face of the moon: about 38 miles in diameter.

ber·ret·ta (bə ret′ə), *n.* *Rom. Cath. Ch.* biretta.

ber·ried (ber′ēd), *adj.* **1.** covered with or yielding berries. **2.** of or like a berry; baccate. **3.** (of lobsters, crayfish, etc.) having eggs. [berry + -ed[3]]

ber·ry (ber′ē), *n., pl.* **-ries,** *v.,* **-ried, -ry·ing.** —*n.* **1.** any small, usually stoneless, juicy fruit, irrespective of botanical structure, as the gooseberry, strawberry, hackberry, etc. **2.** the hip of the rose. **3.** a dry seed or kernel, as of wheat. **4.** *Bot.* a simple fruit having a pulpy pericarp in which the seeds are embedded, as the grape, gooseberry, currant, tomato, etc. **5.** one of the eggs of a lobster, crayfish, etc. —*v.i.* **6.** to bear or produce berries: *These bushes should be ready to berry next year.* **7.** to gather or pick berries: *We were berrying all morning.* [ME *berie,* OE; c. OHG *beri* (G *Beere*), Icel *ber;* akin to D *besie,* Goth *-basi*] —**ber′ry·less,** *adj.* —**ber′ry·like′,** *adj.*

Ber·ry (ber′ē; *Fr.* be rē′), *n.* a former province in central France. Also, **Ber′ri.**

Ber·ry·man (ber′ē mən), *n.* **John,** 1914–72, U.S. poet and critic.

ber′ry spoon′, a small spoon of the late 18th century having a perforated bowl. Also called **ber′ry la′dle, sugar sifter.**

ber·sa·glie·re (ber′səl yâr′ē; *It.* ber′sä lye′re), *n., pl.* **-sa·glie·ri** (-səl yâr′ē; *It.* -sä lye′rē). one of a class of riflemen or sharpshooters in the Italian army. [< It: lit., marksman (*bersagli(o)* target + *-iere* -ary)]

ber·seem (bər sēm′), *n.* a clover, *Trifolium alexandrinum,* of Egypt and Syria, grown for forage in the southwestern U.S. Also called **Egyptian clover.** [< Ar *barsīm* < Coptic *bersim*]

ber·serk (bər sûrk′, -zûrk′), *adj.* **1.** violently and destructively frenzied. —*adv.* **2.** into a frenzied, violent rage: *to go berserk.* —*n.* **3.** a berserker. [see berserker]

ber·serk·er (bər sûr′kər, -zûr′-), *n.* *Scand. Legend.* any ancient Norse warrior of great strength and courage who fought with frenzied rage in battle; baresark. [< Icel *berserkr,* equiv. to *ber-* meaning and orig. uncert. + *serkr* sark]

Bert (bûrt), *n.* a boy's given name, form of **Albert, Bertram, Herbert, Hubert, Robert,** etc.

Ber·ta (bûr′tə), *n.* a girl's given name, form of **Bertha.**

Ber·taud (bûr toud′), *n.* the larger of two adjoining craters in the third quadrant of the face of the moon, the other being Sirsalis: about 22 miles in diameter.

berth (bûrth), *n.* **1.** a shelflike sleeping space for one person, as on a ship, airplane, railroad car, etc. **2.** *Naut.* **a.** the cabin of a ship's officer. **b.** the distance maintained between a vessel and the shore, another vessel, or any object. **c.** the space allotted to a vessel at anchor or at a wharf. **d.** the position or rank of a ship's officer. **3.** *Chiefly Brit.* a job; position. **4. give a wide berth to,** to shun; remain discreetly away from: *Since his riding accident, he has given a wide berth to skittish horses.* **5. on the berth,** *Naut.* moored and ready to receive cargo. —*v.t.* **6.** *Naut.* to allot to (a vessel) a certain space at which to anchor or tie up. —*v.i.* **7.** *Naut.* to come to a dock, anchorage, or moorage. [? bear[1] + -th[1]]

ber·tha (bûr′thə), *n.* a collar or trimming, as of lace, worn about the shoulders by women, as over a low-necked waist or dress. [named after *Bertha* (d. a.d. 783), wife of Frankish king Pepin the Short; she was famed for her modesty]

Ber·tha (bûr′thə), *n.* a girl's given name.

berth·age (bûr′thij), *n.* *Naut.* **1.** a place assigned to a vessel for anchoring or tying up. **2.** a charge made for the occupancy of such a place. [berth + -age]

Bert·ie (bûr′tē), *n.* **1.** a boy's given name, form of **Albert, Bertram, Herbert, Hubert, Robert,** etc. **2.** a girl's given name, form of **Alberta, Roberta,** etc.

Ber·til·lon (bûr′tᵊlon′; *Fr.* ber tē yôN′), *n.* **Al·phonse** (al′fons, -fonz; *Fr.* al fôNs′), 1853–1914, French anthropologist.

Ber′tillon sys′tem, a system of identifying persons, esp. criminals, by a record of individual physical measurements and peculiarities. [named after A. Bertillon]

Ber·ti·na (bûr tē′nə), *n.* a girl's given name, form of **Bertha.**

Ber·to (ber′tô), *n.* **Giu·sep·pe** (jo͞o zep′pe), born 1914, Italian novelist.

Ber·toi·a (bər toi′ə), *n.* **Harry,** born 1915, U.S. sculptor, born in Italy.

Ber·told (bûr′tōld; *Ger.* ber′tôld), *n.* a boy's given name.

Ber·ton (bûr′tᵊn), *n.* a boy's given name, form of **Bertram.**

Ber·tram (bûr′trəm), *n.* a boy's given name. Also, **Bartram.**

Ber·trand (bûr′trənd; *Fr.* ber träN′), *n.* a boy's given name.

Ber·trant (bûr′trənt), *n.* a boy's given name, form of **Bertram.**

Ber·wick (ber′ik), *n.* **1.** Also called **Ber·wick·shire** (ber′ik shēr′, -shər), a county in SE Scotland. 23,200 (est. 1960); 457 sq. mi. *Co. seat:* Duns. **2.** Berwick-upon-Tweed. **3.** a town in S Louisiana. 3880 (1960).

Ber·wick-up·on-Tweed (ber′ik ə pon′twēd′), *n.* a town in N Northumberland, in N England, on the North Sea at the mouth of the Tweed. 12,166 (1961). Also called **Berwick.**

Ber·wyn (bûr′win), *n.* a city in NE Illinois, near Chicago. 54,224 (1960).

ber·yl (ber′əl), *n.* a mineral, beryllium aluminum silicate, $Be_3Al_2Si_6O_{18}$, usually green, but also blue, rose, white, and golden, and both opaque and transparent, the latter variety including the gems emerald and aquamarine: the principal ore of beryllium. [ME *beril* < ML *bērill(us),* L *bēryllus* < Gk *bḗryllos*] —**ber·yl·ine** (ber′ə lin, -līn′), *adj.*

Ber·yl (ber′il), *n.* a girl's given name.

be·ryl·li·um (bi ril′ē əm), *n.* *Chem.* a steel-gray, bivalent, hard, light, metallic element, the salts of which are sweet: used chiefly in copper alloys for better fatigue endurance, in springs, and in contacts. *Symbol:* Be; *at. wt.:* 9.0122; *at. no.:* 4; *sp. gr.:* 1.8 at 20° C. Also called **glucinium, glucinum.** [< L *bēryll(us)* beryl + -ium]

beryl′lium cop′per, a copper alloy containing a small amount of beryllium and often some nickel or cobalt, having high strength, hardness, and electrical conductivity.

be·ryl·lon·ite (bi ril′ə nīt′), *n.* a mineral, sodium beryllium phosphate, $NaBePO_4$, occurring in colorless or light yellow crystals, sometimes used as a gemstone. [< Gk *bḗryll(i)on* (*bḗryll(os)* beryl + *-ion* dim. suffix) + -ite[1]]

Ber·ze·li·us (bər zē′lē əs; *Swed.* ber sā′lē o͝os′), *n.* **Jöns Ja·kob** (yœns yä′kôp), **Baron,** 1779–1848, Swedish chemist.

Ber·ze·li·us (bər zā′lē əs, -zē′-, -zāl′yəs, -zēl′-), *n.* a crater in the first quadrant of the face of the moon: about 24 miles in diameter.

Bes (bes), *n.* *Egyptian Religion.* the patron deity of music, dancing, and children, represented as a hairy dwarf having a tail and wearing a lion's skin.

B.E.S., Bachelor of Engineering Science.

bes·a·gue (bes′ə gyo͞o′), *n.* *Armor.* a plate protecting an open area, as at the elbow or armpit. Also called **moton.** [< MF]

Be·san·çon (bə zäN sôN′), *n.* a city in and the capital of Doubs, in E France: Roman ruins. 101,729 (1962).

be·sant (bez′ənt, bə zant′), *n.* bezant (defs. 1, 2).

Bes·ant (bez′ənt *for 1;* bə zant′, *older* bez′ənt *for 2*), *n.* **1. Annie (Wood),** 1847–1933, English theosophist. **2. Sir Walter,** 1836–1901, English novelist.

bes′ ant′ler (bes, bās). See **bay antler.**

be·screen (bi skrēn′), *v.t.* screen (def. 16). [be- + screen]

be·scrib·ble (bi skrib′əl), *v.t.,* **-bled, -bling.** to scribble all over (something). [be- + scribble[1]]

be·seech (bi sēch′), *v.,* **-sought, -seech·ing.** —*v.t.* **1.** to implore urgently: *They beseeched him to go at once.* **2.** to beg eagerly for; solicit. —*v.i.* **3.** to make urgent appeal: *Earnestly did I beseech, but to no avail.* [ME *biseche(n),* OE *besēcan.* See be-, seek] —**be·seech′er,** *n.* —**be·seech′ing·ly,** *adv.* —**be·seech′ing·ness,** *n.*
—**Syn. 1.** pray, petition, supplicate, adjure. **1, 2.** entreat, importune.

be·seem (bi sēm′), *v.t.* **1.** to be fit for or worthy of; become: *conduct that beseems a gentleman.* —*v.i.* **2.** to be suitable or fitting. [ME *bisem(en).* See be-, seem]

Be·sel·e·el (bi sel′ē əl), *n.* *Douay Bible.* Bezaleel.

be·set (bi set′), *v.t.,* **-set, -set·ting. 1.** to attack on all sides; assail; harass: *to be beset by enemies; beset by difficulties.* **2.** to surround; hem in: *a dense forest that beset the village.* **3.** to set or place upon; bestud: *beset with jewels.* **4.** *Naut.* to surround (a vessel) by ice, so that control of the helm is lost. [ME *besett(en),* OE *besettan.* See be-, set] —**be·set′ment,** *n.* —**be·set′ter,** *n.*
—**Syn. 2.** encircle, enclose, besiege, beleaguer. **3.** stud, decorate, ornament.

be·set·ting (bi set′ing), *adj.* constantly assailing or obsessing, as with temptation: *a besetting sin.* [beset + -ing[2]]

be·show (bi shō′), *n.* a sablefish. [< AmerInd (Nootka)]

be·shrew (bi shro͞o′), *v.t.* *Archaic.* to curse; invoke evil upon. [ME *beshrew(en).* See be-, shrew[1]]

BeShT (besht), *n.* See **Baal Shem-tov.**

be·side (bi sīd′), *prep.* **1.** by or at the side of; near: *Sit down beside me.* **2.** compared with: *Beside him other writers see amateurish.* **3.** apart from; not connected with: *beside the point; beside the question.* **4.** besides (def. 4). **5. beside oneself,** almost out of one's senses from a strong emotion, as from joy, delight, anger, fear, grief, etc.: *He was beside himself with rage when the train left without him.* —*adv.* **6.** along the side of something: *The ladies rode in the carriage, and I ran along beside.* **7.** *Rare.* in addition; besides. [ME, OE *be sīdan* by side]
—**Usage.** Beside, besides may both be used as prepositions, although with different meanings. Beside is almost exclusively used as a preposition meaning by the side of: *beside the house, the stream.* Besides is used as a preposition meaning in addition to or over and above: *Besides these honors he received a sum of money.*

be·sides (bi sīdz′), *adv.* **1.** moreover: *Besides, I promised her we would come.* **2.** in addition: *There are three elm trees and two maples besides.* **3.** otherwise; else: *They had a roof over their heads but not much besides.* —*prep.* **4.** over and above; in addition to: *Besides a mother he has a sister to support.* **5.** other than; except: *There's no one here besides Bill and me.* [beside + -s[1]]
—**Syn. 1.** furthermore, further. Besides, moreover both indicate something additional to what has already been stated. Besides often suggests that the addition is in the nature of an afterthought: *The bill cannot be paid as yet; besides, the work is not completed.* Moreover is more formal and implies that the addition is something particular, emphatic, or important: *I did not like the house; moreover, it was too high-priced.*
—**Usage.** See **beside.**

be·siege (bi sēj′), *v.t.,* **-sieged, -sieg·ing. 1.** to lay siege to. **2.** to crowd around; crowd in upon; surround: *vacationers besieging the travel offices.* **3.** to assail or ply, as with requests, demands, etc. [ME *bysege(n).* See be-, siege] —**be·siege′ment,** *n.* —**be·sieg′er,** *n.* —**be·sieg′ing·ly,** *adv.*

Bes·ier (bes′yər), *n.* **Rudolf,** 1878–1942, English dramatist.

be·slob·ber (bi slob′ər), *v.t.* to slobber all over (something): *The child thoroughly beslobbered his bib.* [BE- + SLOBBER]

be·smear (bi smēr′), *v.t.* **1.** to smear all over; bedaub. **2.** to sully; defile; soil: *to besmear someone's reputation.* [ME *bismer(en),* OE *besmerian.* See BE-, SMEAR] —**be·smear′er,** *n.*

be·smirch (bi smûrch′), *v.t.* **1.** to soil; tarnish; discolor. **2.** to detract from the honor or luster of: *to besmirch someone's good name.* [BE- + SMIRCH] —**be·smirch′er,** *n.*

be·som (bē′zəm), *n.* **1.** a broom, esp. one of brush or twigs. **2.** broom (def. 2). [ME *besem,* OE *bes(e)ma;* c. D *bezem,* G *Besen*]

be·sot (bi sot′), *v.t.,* **-sot·ted, -sot·ting.** **1.** to stupefy with drink; make intoxicated. **2.** to make stupid or foolish: *a mind besotted with fear and superstition.* **3.** to infatuate; obsess: *He is besotted by her youth and beauty.* [BE- + SOT] —**be·sot′ted·ly,** *adv.* —**be·sot′ted·ness,** *n.* —**be·sot′ting·ly,** *adv.*

be·sought (bi sôt′), *v.* pt. and pp. of **beseech.**

be·spake (bi spāk′), *v. Archaic.* pt. of **bespeak.**

be·span·gle (bi spang′gəl), *v.t.,* **-gled, -gling.** to cover or adorn with, or as with, spangles; make sparkle brilliantly: *grass bespangled with dewdrops; poetry bespangled with vivid imagery.* [BE- + SPANGLE]

be·spat·ter (bi spat′ər), *v.t.* **1.** to soil by spattering; splash with water, dirt, etc. **2.** to slander: *a reputation bespattered by malicious gossip.* [BE- + SPATTER]

be·speak (bi spēk′), *v.t.,* **-spoke** or (*Archaic*) **-spake; -spo·ken** or **-spoke; -speak·ing.** **1.** to ask for in advance: *to bespeak the reader's patience.* **2.** *Brit.* to reserve beforehand; engage in advance; make arrangements for: *to bespeak a seat in a theater.* **3.** *Poetic.* to speak to; address. **4.** to show; indicate: *This bespeaks a kindly heart.* **5.** *Obs.* to foretell; forebode. [ME *bespek(en),* OE *besprecan.* See BE-, SPEAK]

be·spec·ta·cled (bi spek′tə kəld), *adj.* wearing eyeglasses. [BE- + SPECTACLED]

be·spoke (bi spōk′), *v.* **1.** a pt. and pp. of **bespeak.** —*adj.* **2.** *Brit.* **a.** (of clothes) made to individual order; custom-made. **b.** making or selling such clothes: *a bespoke tailor.* **3.** spoken for; engaged to be married.

be·spo·ken (bi spō′kən), *v.* **1.** a pp. of **bespeak.** —*adj.* **2.** bespoke.

be·spread (bi spred′), *v.t.,* **-spread, -spread·ing.** to spread over (a surface); cover (usually fol. by *with*): *to bespread a table with fine linens.* [ME *bespred(en).* See BE-, SPREAD]

be·sprent (bi sprent′), *adj. Archaic.* besprinkled; bestrewn. [ME *bespre(y)nt,* ptp. of *besprengen,* OE *besprengan,* equiv. to *be-* BE- + *sprengan* to sprinkle, akin to SPRING]

be·sprin·kle (bi spring′kəl), *v.t.,* **-kled, -kling.** to sprinkle (something) all over, as with water, flour, seasoning, etc.: *He was furiously besprinkling his food with salt.* [BE- + SPRINKLE]

Bess (bes), *n.* a girl's given name, form of **Elizabeth.** Also, **Bessie, Bessy, Bessye.**

Bes·sa·ra·bi·a (bes′ə rā′bē ə), *n.* a region in Moldavia, in the SW Soviet Union in Europe, on the W shore of the Black Sea. —**Bes′sa·ra′bi·an,** *adj., n.*

Bes·sar·i·on (bə sâr′ē ən), *n.* a crater in the second quadrant of the face of the moon: about 6 miles in diameter.

Bes·sel (bes′əl), *n.* **1. Frie·drich Wil·helm** (frē′drik wil′helm; *Ger.* frē′drikh vil′helm), 1784–1846, German astronomer. **2.** a crater in the first quadrant of the face of the moon, on the Mare Serenitatis: about 12 miles in diameter.

Bes′sel func′tion, *Math.* one of several transcendental functions, usually represented as power series, that are solutions to the differential equation (**Bes′sel equa′tion**), $x^2\frac{d^2y}{dx^2} + x\frac{dy}{dx} + (x^2-a^2)y = 0$, where a is an arbitrary constant. [named after F. W. BESSEL]

Bes′sel meth′od, a method of ascertaining position by the use of a map showing prominent features of the terrain and enabling one to sight through them to obtain a fix. [named after F. W. BESSEL]

Bes·se·mer (bes′ə mər), *n.* **1. Sir Henry,** 1813–98, English engineer: inventor of the Bessemer process. **2.** a city in central Alabama. 33,054 (1960). **3.** a town in NW Michigan, in the Upper Peninsula. 3304 (1960).

Bes′semer Cit′y, a town in SW North Carolina. 4017 (1960).

Bes′semer convert′er, the refractory-lined metal container in which steel is produced by the Bessemer process.

Bes′semer pro′cess, *Metall.* a process of producing steel, in which impurities are removed by forcing a blast of air through molten iron.

Bes′semer steel′, steel made by the Bessemer process.

Bes·sie (bes′ē), *n.* a girl's given name, form of **Elizabeth.** Also, **Bes′sy, Bes′sye.**

best (best), *adj., superl. of* **good** *with* **better** *as compar.* **1.** of the highest quality, excellence, or standing: *the best work; the best students.* **2.** most advantageous, suitable, or desirable: *the best way.* **3.** largest; most: *the best part of a day.* —*adv., superl. of* **well** *with* **better** *as compar.* **4.** most excellently or suitably; with most advantage or success: *a hairdo that best suits her features.* **5.** in or to the highest degree; most fully (usually used in combination): *best-suited; best-known; best-loved.* **6. as best one can,** in the best way possible under the circumstances: *We tried to smooth over the difficulties as best we could.* **7. had best,** would be wisest or most reasonable to; ought to: *You had best phone your mother to tell her where you are going.* —*n.* **8.** that which is best, as a part, state, circumstance, etc.: *You haven't heard the best. They always demand and get the best. The best of us can make mistakes.* **9.** one's finest clothing: *It's important that you wear your best.* **10.** one's most agreeable or desirable emotional state (often prec. by *at*). **11.** one's highest degree of competence, inspiration, etc. (often prec. by *at*). **12.** the highest quality to be found in a given activity or category of things (often prec. by *at*): *cabinetmaking at its best.* **13.** the best effort that a person, group, or thing can make: *The State Department is doing its best.* **14.** one's best wishes or kindest regards: *Please give my best to your father.* **15. all for the best,** for the good as the final result; to an ultimate advantage: *It was at the time hard to realize how it could be all for the best.* Also, **for the best. 16. at best,** under the most favorable circumstances: *You may expect to be treated civilly, at best.* **17. get** or **have the best of, a.** to gain the advantage over. **b.** to defeat; subdue: *His arthritis gets the best of him from time to time.* **18. make the best of,** to manage as well as one can under unfavorable or adverse circumstances: *After the husband's retirement the couple had a smaller income, but they made the best of it and were happy.* **19. with the best,** on a par with the most capable: *He can play bridge with the best.* —*v.t.* **20.** to defeat; get the better of; beat: *He easily bested his opponent in hand-to-hand combat. He bested me in the argument.* [ME *beste,* OE *betst, best;* c. D *best,* OHG *bezzist* (G *best*), Icel *bezt,* Goth *batists.* See BETTER[1], -EST]

best′-ball′ four′some (best′bôl′), *Golf.* a match, scored by holes, between two pairs of players, in which the score of the lower scoring member of each pair is taken as their score for the hole.

best′-ball′ match′, *Golf.* a match, scored by holes, in which one player competing against two or more others must score lower than his lowest scoring opponent to win a hole.

best′ bow′er (bou′ər), *Naut.* the heavier of two bower anchors carried by a vessel. Cf. **small bower.**

be·stead (bi sted′), *v.,* **-stead·ed, -stead·ed** or **-stead, -stead·ing,** *adj.* —*v.t.* **1.** to help; assist; serve; avail: *His threadbare coat did little to bestead him against the chill north wind.* [BE- + STEAD] —*adj.* **2.** *Archaic.* placed or situated, often unfavorably or in difficulty. [ME *bestedd,* equiv. to *be-* BE- + *stedd,* var. of *stadd* placed < Scand; cf. Icel *staddr,* ptp. of *stethja* to place, deriv. of *stathr* place]

bes·tial (bes′chəl, best′yəl), *adj.* **1.** of, pertaining to, or having the form of a beast: *the belief that a man could assume bestial form after death; the bestial signs of the zodiac.* **2.** brutal; inhuman; without reason or intelligence: *bestial treatment of prisoners.* **3.** beastlike in gratifying one's sensual desires; carnal; debased. [late ME < L *bēstiāl(is)* (L *bēsti(a)* BEAST + *-ālis* -AL[1])] —**bes′tial·ly,** *adv.*

bes·tial·ise (bes′chə līz′, best′yə-), *v.t.,* **-ised, -is·ing.** *Chiefly Brit.* bestialize.

bes·ti·al·i·ty (bes′chē al′i tē, -tē al′-), *n., pl.* **-ties.** **1.** brutish or beastly character or behavior; beastliness. **2.** indulgence in beastlike appetites, instincts, impulses, etc. **3.** an instance of bestial character or behavior. **4.** sexual relations between a person and an animal; sodomy. [late ME *bestialite* < ML *bēstiālitāt-* (s. of *bēstiālitās*). See BESTIAL, -ITY]

bes·tial·ize (bes′chə līz′, best′yə-), *v.t.,* **-ized, -iz·ing.** to make bestial or beastlike: *War bestializes its participants.* Also, *esp. Brit.,* **bestialise.** [BESTIAL + -IZE]

bes·ti·ar·y (bes′chē er′ē, -tē-), *n., pl.* **-ar·ies.** a collection of moralized fables about actual or mythical animals, of a class widely known in the Middle Ages. [< ML *bēstiāri(um),* neut. of L *bēstiārius.* See BEAST, -ARY] —**bes·ti·a·rist** (bes′chē ər ist, -tē ər-, -chər-), *n.*

be·stir (bi stûr′), *v.t.,* **-stirred, -stir·ring.** to stir up; rouse to action (often used reflexively): *She bestirred herself at the first light of morning.* [ME *bestire(n),* OE *bestyrian* to heap up. See BE-, STIR[1]]

best′ man′, the chief attendant of the bridegroom at a wedding.

be·stow (bi stō′), *v.t.* **1.** to present as a gift; give; confer (usually fol. by *on* or *upon*): *The trophy was bestowed upon the winner.* **2.** to put to some use; apply: *Time spent in study is time well bestowed.* **3.** *Archaic.* **a.** to house; provide quarters for. **b.** to put; stow; deposit; store. [ME *bestowe(n).* See BE-, STOW[1]] —**be·stow′al, be·stow′ment,** *n.* —**Syn. 1.** grant, vouchsafe.

be·strad·dle (bi strad′əl), *v.t.,* **-dled, -dling.** to bestride. [BE- + STRADDLE]

be·strew (bi strōō′), *v.t.,* **-strewed, -strewed** or **-strewn, -strew·ing.** **1.** to strew or cover (a surface). **2.** to strew or scatter about. **3.** to lie scattered over. [ME *bistrewe(n),* OE *bestrēowian.* See BE-, STREW]

be·stride (bi strīd′), *v.t.,* **-strode** or **-strid, -strid·den** or **-strid, -strid·ing.** **1.** to get or be astride of; spread the legs on both sides of. **2.** to step over or across with long strides. **3.** to stand or tower over; dominate: *a literary colossus that bestrides two centuries.* [ME *bestride(n),* OE *bestrīdan.* See BE-, STRIDE]

be·strow (bi strō′), *v.t.,* **-strowed, -strown** or **-strowed, -strow·ing.** *Archaic.* bestrew.

best′ sell′er, **1.** a book that is among those having the largest sales during a given period. **2.** the author of such a book. **3.** any product that among those of its kind is selling particularly well at a given time: *This dress is a best seller in the South.* —**best′sell′er·dom,** *n.* —**best′-sell′ing,** *adj.*

be·stud (bi stud′), *v.t.,* **-stud·ded, -stud·ding.** to set with or as with studs distributed over a surface; dot: *an evening sky bestudded with stars.* [BE- + STUD]

bet (bet), *v.,* **bet** or **bet·ted, bet·ting,** *n.* —*v.t.* **1.** to pledge (something) as a forfeit if one's forecast of a future event is wrong, usually in return for a similar pledge by another if the forecast is right. —*v.i.* **2.** to lay a wager: *Do you want to bet?* **3. you bet!** *Informal.* of course! surely!: *You bet I'd like to be there!* —*n.* **4.** a pledge of something to be forfeited, in case one is wrong, to another who has an opposite or differing opinion: *Where do we place our bets?* **5.** that which is pledged: *a two-dollar bet.* **6.** a competitor, possible happening, or other thing not absolutely predictable, considered as something to bet on: *That horse looks like a good bet.* **7.** an act or instance of betting: *It's a bet, then?* **8.** a person, plan of action, etc., considered as being good or bad with relation to a number of alternatives: *Your best bet is to sell your stocks now.* [? special use of *bet* better, in phrase *the bet* the advantage, i.e., the odds]

bet., between.

be·ta (bā′tə, bē′-), *n.* **1.** the second letter of the Greek alphabet (β, B). **2.** the consonant sound represented by this letter. **3.** (*cap.*) *Astron.* a star that is usually the second brightest of a constellation: *The second brightest star in Taurus is Beta Tauri.* **4.** *Chem.* **a.** one of the possible positions of an atom or group in a compound. **b.** one of two or more isomeric compounds. **5.** *Chiefly Brit.* a grade showing that a student is in the middle or second of three scholastic sections in his class. Cf. **alpha** (def. 6), **gamma** (def. 9). [< L < Gk *bêta* < Sem; cf. Heb *bēth* BETH]

be′ta brass′, an alloy of copper and zinc having a body-centered cubic lattice and containing from 45 to 50 percent zinc.

be·ta·caine (bā′tə kān′, bē′-), *n. Pharm.* eucaine. [BETA + (EU)CAINE]

Be′ta Cru′cis, a star of the first magnitude in the constellation Southern Cross.

be′ta decay′, *Physics.* a radioactive process in which a beta particle is emitted from the nucleus of an atom, raising the atomic number of the atom by one if the particle is negatively charged, lowering it by one if positively charged.

be·ta-eu·caine (bā′tə yōō′kān, bē′tə-), *n. Pharm.* eucaine.

bet·a·fite (bet′ə fīt′), *n.* a rare radioactive material, hydrous columbate and titanate of uranium. [named after *Betafo,* Madagascar, one of its localities; see -ITE[1]]

be′ta func′tion, *Math.* a function of two variables, usually expressed as an improper integral and equal to the quotient of the product of the values of the gamma function at each variable divided by the value of the gamma function at the sum of the variables.

be′ta-in·dole·a·ce′tic ac′id (bā′tə in′dōl ə sē′tik, -ə set′ik, bē′-), *Biochem.* See **indoleacetic acid.**

be·ta·ine (bē′tə ēn′, -in; bi tā′ēn, -in), *n. Chem., Pharm.* a colorless, crystalline, water-soluble, sweet-tasting alkaloid, $(CH_3)_3NCH_2COO$, usually obtained from sugar beets or synthesized from glycine, used chiefly in medicine in the form of its hydrochloride. Also, **be·ta·in** (bē′tə in, bi tā′-). Also called **lycine, oxyneurine, trimethylglycine.** [< L *bēta* beet + -INE[2]]

be′ta i′ron, *Metall.* an allotrope of iron, stable between 768°C and 910°C, similar to alpha iron except in being nonmagnetic.

be·take (bi tāk′), *v.t.,* **-took, -tak·en, -tak·ing.** **1.** to cause to go (usually used reflexively): *She betook herself to town.* **2.** *Archaic.* to resort or have recourse (usually used reflexively). [ME *bitake(n).* See BE-, TAKE]

be·ta-naph·thol (bā′tə naf′thōl, -thôl, -thol, -nap′-, bē′tə-), *n. Chem.* naphthol (def. 2). [BETA + NAPHTHOL]

be′ta-naph′thyl group′ (bā′tə naf′thil, -nap′-, bē′-, bā′-, bē′-), *Chem.* See **naphthyl group** (def. 2). Also called **be′ta-naph′thyl rad′ical.**

Bet·an·court (bet′ən kôôr′, -kôrt′; *Sp.* bet′än kôrt′), *n.* **Ró·mu·lo** (rom′yə lō′; *Sp.* rō′mōō lô′), born 1908, Venezuelan journalist and political leader: president of Venezuela 1945–48, and 1959–63.

be·ta-naph·thyl·am·ine (bā′tə naf′thə lə mēn′, -nap′-), *n. Chem.* a white to reddish, crystalline, water-soluble, extremely toxic solid, $C_{10}H_7NH_2$, used chiefly in the manufacture of azo dyes. [BETA + NAPHTHYL + AMINE]

be′ta par′ticle, *Physics.* a charged particle equivalent to an electron if negative or a positron if positive, emitted from a nucleus in radioactive decay or fission.

be′ta ray′, *Physics.* a stream of beta particles.

be′ta test′, *Psychol.* a set of mental tests designed to measure the general intelligence of individuals unable to read and write adequately or at all, used by the U.S. Army in World War I. Cf. **alpha test.**

be·ta·tron (bā′tə tron′, bē′-), *n. Physics.* an accelerator in which electrons are accelerated to high energies by an electric field produced by a changing magnetic field. [BETA (see BETA PARTICLE) + -TRON]

bete (bēt), *v.t. Brit. Dial.* beet[2].

be·tel (bēt′əl), *n.* an East Indian pepper plant, *Piper Betle.* Also, **be′tel pep′per.** [< Pg *betele,* var. of *vitele* < Tamil *veṭṭilei*]

Be·tel·geuse (bēt′əl jōōz′, bet′əl jœz′), *n. Astron.* a first magnitude red giant star in the constellation Orion. Also, **Be′tel·geux′.** [< F < Ar *bīt al jauzā′* shoulder of the giant (i.e., of Orion)]

be′tel nut′, the areca nut, chewed with limes by East Indian natives.

be′tel palm′, a tall, graceful, Asiatic palm, *Areca Catechu,* that bears the areca nut or betel nut, so named from its association in native usage with the betel plant.

bête noire (bet NWAR′; *Eng.* bāt′ nwär′), *pl.* **bêtes noires** (bet NWAR′; *Eng.* bāt′ nwärz′). *French.* something that one especially dislikes or dreads, either a person, task, or object; bugbear. [lit., black beast]

beth (bet), *n.* **1.** the second letter of the Hebrew alphabet. **2.** either of the consonant sounds represented by this letter. [< Heb *bēth* house, from an earlier form of the letter; see BETA]

Beth (beth), *n.* a girl's given name, form of **Elizabeth.**

Beth·al·to (bə thal′tō), *n.* a town in SW Illinois. 3235 (1960).

Beth·a·ny (beth′ə nē), *n.* **1.** a village in W Jordan, near Jerusalem, at the foot of the Mount of Olives: Biblical home of Lazarus and his sisters, Martha and Mary. John 11:1. **2.** a town in NW Missouri. 2771 (1960).

Beth Din (bāt′ dēn′), *Hebrew.* a Jewish court of law. [lit., house of law]

Be·the (bā′tə), *n.* **Hans Al·brecht** (hanz ôl′brekt, häns; *Ger.* häns äl′brekht), born 1906, U.S. physicist, born in Alsace-Lorraine.

beth·el (beth′əl), *n.* **1.** a sacred area or sanctuary. Gen. 28:19. **2.** a church or hostel for sailors. **3.** *Brit.* a dissenters' chapel or meeting house. [< Heb *bēth 'ēl* house of God]

Beth·el (beth′əl; *for 1 also* beth′el, beth′el′), *n.* **1.** a village in NW Jordan, near Jerusalem: dream of Jacob, Gen. 28:19. **2.** a city in W Pennsylvania, near Pittsburgh. 23,650 (1960). **3.** a town in SW Connecticut. 5624 (1960). **4.** a boy's or girl's given name.

Be·thes·da (bə thez′də), *n.* **1.** a pool in biblical Jerusalem, believed to have healing powers. John 5:2–4. **2.** a city in central Maryland; residential suburb of Washington, D.C. 56,527 (1960). **3.** (*l.c.*) a chapel.

Beth Hil·lel (bāt′ hē lāl′), *Hebrew.* the school of Jewish philosophy and hermeneutics founded in Jerusalem in the 1st century B.C. by the Jewish spiritual leader Hillel and characterized by an interpretation of and approach to Jewish law and tradition chiefly in terms of the welfare of man, his nature, and his needs. Cf. **Beth Shammai.** [lit., house of Hillel]

be·think (bi thiŋgk′), *v.*, **-thought, -think·ing.** —*v.t.* **1.** to think; consider (used reflexively): *He bethought himself a moment.* **2.** to remind (oneself): *to bethink oneself of family obligations.* **3.** to remember; recall (used reflexively): *She lives in the past now, bethinking herself of happier days.* **4.** to determine; resolve: *Under the circumstances I could not otherwise bethink me.* **5.** *Archaic.* to bear in mind; remember. —*v.i.* **6.** *Archaic.* to consider; meditate. [ME *bethenk(en)*, OE *bethencan.* See BE-, THINK¹]

Beth·le·hem (beth′lē əm, -li hem′), *n.* **1.** a town in NW Jordan, near Jerusalem: birthplace of Jesus and David. 30,000 (est. 1962). **2.** a city in E Pennsylvania. 75,408 (1960).

Beth′lehem sage′, a low, perennial herb, *Pulmonaria Saccharata*, of Europe, having mottled, white leaves and white or reddish-purple flowers in clusters.

Beth·mann-Holl·weg (bāt′män hôl′väKH), *n.* **Theo·bald von** (tā′ō bält′ fən), 1856–1921, German statesman: chancellor 1909–17.

Beth′nal Green′ (beth′nəl), a borough of London, England, N of the Thames. 47,018 (1961).

be·thought (bi thôt′), *v.* pt. and pp. of **bethink.**

beth·root (beth′ro͞ot′, -ro͝ot′), *n.* birthroot (def. 1).

Beth·sa·be·e (beth sā′bē ē′), *n.* *Douay Bible.* Bathsheba.

Beth·sa·i·da (beth sā′i də), *n.* an ancient town in N Israel, near the N shore of the Sea of Galilee.

Beth Sham·mai (bāt′ shä mī′), *Hebrew.* the school of Jewish philosophy and hermeneutics founded in Jerusalem in the 1st century B.C. by the Jewish teacher Shammai and characterized by an interpretation of and approach to Jewish law and tradition chiefly in terms of the written word and the facts. Cf. **Beth Hillel.** [lit., house of Shammai]

be·tide (bi tīd′), *v.*, **-tid·ed, -tid·ing.** —*v.t.* **1.** to happen; befall; come to: *Woe betide the villain!* —*v.i.* **2.** to come to pass: *Whatever betides, maintain your courage.* [ME *betide(n).* See BE-, TIDE²]

be·times (bi tīmz′), *adv.* **1.** early; in good time: *He was up betimes doing his lessons.* **2.** within a short time; soon: *We hope to repay your visit betimes.* [ME *bitimes*, equiv. to *bitime* (from phrase *bi time* by time) + *-s* -s¹]

bê·tise (be tēz′), *n.* **1.** lack of understanding, perception, or the like; stupidity. **2.** a stupid or foolish act or remark. **3.** something inconsequential or without merit; absurdity; trifle. [< F: lit., foolishness, equiv. to *bête* foolish (see BEAST) + *-ise* -ICE]

Bet·je·man (bech′ə mən), *n.* **John,** born 1906, English poet.

be·to·ken (bi tō′kən), *v.t.* **1.** to give evidence of; indicate: *to betoken one's fidelity with a vow; a kiss that betokens one's affection.* **2.** to be or give a token or sign of; portend: *a thunderclap that betokens foul weather; an angry word that betokens hostility.* [ME *bitocnen, bitacnen.* See BE-, TOKEN]

bé·ton (*Fr.* bā tôɴ′), *n.* *Obs.* a type of concrete composed of a mixture of cement, sand, and gravel. [< F << Pr *betun* < L *bitūmen* BITUMEN]

bé·ton brut (bā tôɴ bʀʏt′), *French.* See **brut concrete.** [lit., rough concrete]

bet·o·ny (bet′ənē), *n., pl.* **-nies. 1.** a plant, *Stachys* (formerly *Betonica*) *officinalis*, of the mint family, formerly used in medicine and dyeing. **2.** any of various similar plants, esp. of the genus *Pedicularis.* [late ME, appar. short for OE *betonice* < L *betonica*, var. of *vettonica (herba)* Vettonic (herb) (*Vetton(es)* an Iberian tribe + *-ica*, fem. of *-icus* -IC); r. ME *beteine*, c. OF *betoine* < VL **betonia*]

be·took (bi to͝ok′), *v.* pt. of **betake.**

be·tray (bi trā′), *v.t.* **1.** to deliver or expose to an enemy by treachery or disloyalty: *Do not betray us!* **2.** to be unfaithful in guarding or maintaining: *to betray a trust.* **3.** to be disloyal to; disappoint the hopes or expectations of: *to betray one's confidence.* **4.** to reveal or disclose in violation of confidence: *to betray a secret.* **5.** to reveal unconsciously (something one would preferably conceal): *Her mannerisms betray her insecurity.* **6.** to show or exhibit; reveal; disclose: *an unfeeling remark that betrays his lack of concern.* **7.** to deceive; mislead: *a young woman betrayed by social ambitions into irreparable folly.* **8.** to seduce and desert (a woman). [ME *bitrai*, equiv. to *bi-* BE- + *trai* < OF *trai(r)* < L *trādere* to betray. See TRAITOR] —**be·tray′al,** *n.* —**be·tray′er,** *n.*
—**Syn. 6.** display, manifest, expose, uncover.

be·troth (bi trōth′, -trôth′), *v.t.* **1.** to arrange for the marriage of; affiance (usually used in passive constructions): *The couple was betrothed with the family's approval.* **2.** *Archaic.* to promise to marry. [ME *betrouthe*, var. of *betreuthe* (*be-* BE- + *treuthe* TRUTH; see TROTH)]

be·troth·al (bi trō′thəl, -trô′thəl), *n.* act or fact of being betrothed; engagement. Also, **be·troth′ment.** [BETROTH + -AL²]

be·trothed (bi trōthd′, -trôtht′), *adj.* **1.** engaged to be married: *She is betrothed to that young lieutenant.* —*n.* **2.** the person to whom one is engaged: *He introduced us to his betrothed.* [BETROTH + -ED²]

Bet·sy (bet′sē), *n.* a girl's given name, form of **Elizabeth.** Also, **Bet′sey, Bet′si.**

Bett (bet), *n.* a girl's given name, form of **Elizabeth.** Also, **Bet·ta** (bet′ə), **Bet·te** (bet′ē), **Betty.**

bet·ta (bet′ə), *n.* See **fighting fish.** [< NL < ?]

bet·ted (bet′id), *v.* a pt. and pp. of **bet.**

bet·ter¹ (bet′ər), *adj., compar. of* **good** *with* **best** *as superl.* **1.** of superior quality or excellence: *a better coat; a better speech.* **2.** morally superior; more virtuous: *She's no better than a strumpet.* **3.** of superior value, use, fitness, desirability, acceptableness, etc.: *a better time for action.* **4.** larger; greater: *the better part of a lifetime.* **5.** improved in health; healthier. **6. no better than one should be,** *Contemptuous.* morally inferior; immoral or amoral. —*adv., compar. of* **well** *with* **best** *as superl.* **7.** in a more excellent way or manner: *to behave better.* **8.** to a greater degree; more completely or thoroughly: *He knows the way better than we do. I probably know him better than anyone else.* **9.** more: *I walked better than a mile to town.* **10. better off, a.** in better circumstances. **b.** more fortunate; happier: *Because of his asthma, he would be better off in a different climate.* **11. go (someone) one better,** to exceed another's effort; be superior to: *The neighbors went us one better by buying two new cars.* **12. had better,** would be wiser or more reasonable to; ought to: *We had better stay indoors today.* **13. think better of,** to reconsider and decide more favorably or wisely: *She was tempted to make a sarcastic retort, but thought better of it.* —*v.t.* **14.** to make better; improve; increase the good qualities of: *to better the lot of the suburban commuter.* **15.** to improve upon; surpass; exceed: *We have bettered last year's production record.* **16.** *Cards.* to raise (a previous bid). **17. better oneself,** to improve one's social standing, financial position, or education: *He is going to night school to get a college degree because he wants to better himself.* —*n.* **18.** that which has greater excellence: *the better of two choices.* **19.** Usually, **betters.** those superior to one in wisdom, wealth, etc. **20. for the better,** in a way that is an improvement: *His health changed for the better.* **21. get the better of, a.** to get an advantage over. **b.** to prevail against. [ME *bettre*, OE *betera;* c. OHG *bezziro* (G *besser*), Goth *batiza*, equiv. to *bat-* (akin to BOOT²) + *-iza* comp. suffix]
—**Syn. 14.** amend; advance, promote; reform, correct, rectify. See **improve.**

bet·ter² (bet′ər), *n.* bettor. [BET + -ER¹]

Bet′ter Busi′ness Bu′reau, any of a nation-wide system of local organizations, supported by businessmen, whose function is to receive and investigate customer complaints of dishonest business practices.

bet′ter days′, a time when one was younger, happier, or more prosperous: *She has seen better days.*

bet′ter half′, *Slang. Facetious.* **1.** one's wife. **2.** (less frequently) one's husband.

bet·ter·ment (bet′ər mənt), *n.* **1.** that which is made or becomes better; an improvement. **2.** *Law.* an improvement of property other than by mere repairs. [BETTER¹ + -MENT]

bet′terment tax′, a tax on real property, for use by a government for the improvement of public property.

Bet·ter·ton (bet′ər tən), *n.* **Thomas,** 1635?–1710, English actor and dramatist.

Bet·ti (bet′tē), *n.* **U·go** (o͞o′gô), 1892–1953, Italian poet and dramatist.

Bet·ti·na (be tē′nə; *It.* bet tē′nä), *n.* a girl's given name, form of **Elizabeth.**

bet′ting shop′, *Brit.* a licensed bookmaking establishment that takes off-the-track bets on horse races; the shop or office of a legalized bookmaker.

Bet·ti·nus (bet′ənəs), *n.* a crater in the third quadrant of the face of the moon: about 60 miles in diameter.

bet·tor (bet′ər), *n.* one who bets. [BET + -OR²]

bet·ty (bet′ē), *n., pl.* **-ties.** a baked dessert consisting of layers of fruit, buttered crumbs, sugar, and spices. [back formation from BROWN BETTY]

Bet·ty (bet′ē), *n.* a girl's given name, form of **Elizabeth.** Also, **Bett, Betta, Bette.**

bet·u·la·ceous (bech′o͝o lā′shəs), *adj.* belonging to the *Betulaceae*, a family of trees and shrubs including the birch, alder, etc. [< L *betul(a)* birch + -ACEOUS]

bet′u·la oil′ (bech′ə lə). See **methyl salicylate.**

be·tween (bi twēn′), *prep.* **1.** in the space separating (two points, objects, etc.): *between New York and Chicago.* **2.** intermediate to, in time, quantity, or degree: *between 12 and 1 o'clock; between pink and red.* **3.** linking; connecting: *air service between cities.* **4.** in portions for two; shared by two equally: *Adam and Eve were responsible for the sin between them.* **5.** in portions for more than two; among: *The villagers divided the food between themselves.* **6.** distinguishing one from the other: *He couldn't see the difference between good and bad.* **7.** in comparing: *no preference between the two wines.* **8.** existing confidentially for: *We'll keep this matter between the two of us.* **9.** involving; concerning: *war between nations; choice between things.* **10.** by joint action or possession of: *Between them they own most of this company.* **11.** *Heraldry.* in the midst of, so as to make a symmetrical composition: *a cross argent between four bezants.* **12. between ourselves,** confidentially; in trust. Also, **between you and me, between you, me, and the post (lamppost, gatepost, etc.).** —*adv.* **13.** in the intervening space or time; in an intermediate position or relation: *two windows with a door between; visits that were far between.* **14. in between, a.** situated between two points, things, etc.: *two houses and a yard in between.* **b.** in the way: *I reached for the leash, but the dog got in between.* [ME *betwene*, OE *betwēonan, betwēonum*, equiv. to *be-* BE- + *twēon-* (c. Goth *tweihn(ai)* two each) + *-um* dat. pl. suffix] —**be·tween′ness,** *n.*
—**Syn.** See **among.**
—**Usage.** BETWEEN YOU AND I, occasionally heard in the usage of educated persons, is a case of being over "correct": *Between you and I, he's been stealing stamps.* Since the pronouns are objects of the preposition BETWEEN, the usual form is *between you and me.* See also **among.**

be·tween·brain (bi twēn′brān′), *n.* the diencephalon. [BETWEEN + BRAIN]

be·tween-deck (bi twēn′dek′), *n.* See **'tween deck.**

be·tween-maid (bi twēn′mād′), *n.* *Brit.* tweeny.

be·tween·times (bi twēn′tīmz′), *adv.* between periods of work, activity, etc.: *a part-time teacher who studied law betweentimes.* [BETWEEN + TIME + -S¹]

be·tween·whiles (bi twēn′hwīlz′, -wīlz′), *adv.* betweentimes. [BETWEEN + WHILES]

be·twixt (bi twikst′), *prep., adv.* **1.** *Archaic.* between. **2. betwixt and between,** neither the one nor the other; in a middle position: *The child of Anglo-Indian parents, he felt somehow betwixt and between.* [ME *betwix*, OE *betwix, betweox*, equiv. to *be-* BE- + *tweox*, c. OHG *zwisk(i)* two each; akin to G *zwischen* between (prep.)]

Beu·lah (byo͞o′lə), *n.* **1.** a name applied to the land of Israel or Jerusalem, possibly as denoting their future prosperity. Isa. 62:4. Cf. **Hephzibah** (def. 2). **2.** See **Land of Beulah. 3.** a girl's given name. [< Heb: married woman]

beurre fondu (bûr′ fon do͞o′; *Fr.* bœʀ fôɴ dʏ′), *Cookery.* melted butter. [< F]

beurre ma·nié (bûr män yā′; *Fr.* bœʀ′ ᴍᴀ nyā′), *Cookery.* a smooth paste of flour and butter, used esp. in binding sauces. [< F: lit., kneaded butter]

beurre noir (bûr′ nwär′; *Fr.* bœʀ ɴᴡᴀʀ′), a sauce of darkly browned butter, sometimes flavored with herbs, vinegar, etc. [< F: lit., black butter]

Beu·then (boit′ən), *n.* German name of **Bytom.**

BEV (bev), *Physics.* billion electron-volts. Also, **Bev, bev**

Bev·an (bev′ən), *n.* **1. A·neu·rin** (ə nī′rən), 1897–1960, British political leader: Minister of Health, 1945–50. **2.** a boy's given name.

bev·a·tron (bev′ə tron′), *n.* *Physics.* an accelerator in which protons are raised to energies of several billion electron-volts by modulating the frequency of the accelerating voltage. [BEV + *-a-* connective + -TRON]

bev·el (bev′əl), *n., v.,* **-eled, -el·ing** or (*esp. Brit.*) **-elled, -el·ling,** *adj.* —*n.* **1.** the inclination that one line or surface makes with another when not at right angles. **2.** (of a lock bolt) the oblique end that hits the strike plate. **3.** (of a lock with a beveled bolt) the side facing in the same direction as the bevel at the end of the bolt. Cf. **regular bevel, reverse bevel. 4.** See **bevel square. 5.** an adjustable instrument for drawing angles or adjusting the surface of work to a particular inclination. **6.** *Print.* beard (def. 5). **7.** bezel (def. 1). —*v.t., v.i.* **8.** to cut or slant at a bevel: *to bevel an edge to prevent splintering.* —*adj.* **9.** Also, **beveled;** *esp. Brit.,* **bevelled.** oblique; sloping; slanted. [< MF **bevel* (whence F *béveau*) < ?] —**bev′el·er;** *esp. Brit.,* **bev′el·ler,** *n.*

bev′el-faced ham′mer (bev′əl fāst′), a riveting hammer having an oblique face.

bev′el gear′, *Mach.* a gear having teeth cut into a conical surface, usually meshing with a similar gear set at right angles. Cf. **hypoid gear.**

Bevel gears

bev′el joint′, *Carpentry.* a miter joint, esp. one in which two pieces meet at other than a right angle.

bev′el sid′ing, *Carpentry.* siding composed of tapered pieces, as clapboards, laid with the thicker lower edge of any piece overlapping the thinner upper edge of the piece below it.

bev′el square′, an adjustable tool used by woodworkers for laying out angles and for testing the accuracy of surfaces worked to a slope.

Bevel square

bev·er¹ (bev′ər, bē′vər, bā′-), *v.i.* *Brit. Dial.* to shake or tremble, esp. to quiver due to cold. [ME *biv(en)*, OE *beofian* + -ER⁶]

be·ver² (bē′vər), *n.* *Armor.* beaver².

be·ver³ (bē′vər, bā′-), *n.* *Brit.* **1.** *Dial.* a light lunch or snack. **2.** *Archaic.* a time for drinking, esp. a short respite from work in order to have a drink. **3.** *Obs.* a drink; liquor. [late ME < MF *beivre* < L *bibere* to drink. See BIB]

bev·er·age (bev′ər ij, bev′rij), *n.* a drink of any kind other than water, as tea, coffee, beer, milk, etc.: *The price of the meal includes a beverage.* [ME < MF *bevrage*, equiv. to *bevr* BEVER³ + *-age* -AGE]

bev′erage room′, *Canadian.* a tavern or bar, esp. one in a hotel, in which only beer, ale, and other malt liquors are sold.

Bev·er·idge (bev′ər ij, bev′rij), *n.* **1. Albert Jeremiah,** 1862–1927, U.S. senator and historian. **2. Sir William Henry,** 1879–1963, English economist.

Bev′eridge plan′, the plan for comprehensive social insurance, proposed by Sir William Beveridge in Great Britain in 1941.

Bev·er·ley (bev′ər lē), *n.* a boy's or girl's given name. Also, **Beverly.**

Bev·er·ly (bev′ər lē), *n.* **1.** a city in NE Massachusetts. 36,108 (1960). **2.** a town in W New Jersey. 3400 (1960). **3.** Also, **Beverley.** a boy's or girl's given name.

Bev′erly Hills′, 1. a city in SW California, near Los Angeles. 30,817 (1960). **2.** a town in SE Michigan. 8633 (1960).

bev·illed (bev′əld), *adj.* *Heraldry.* **1.** noting a zigzag partition line having two offset, overlapping parts connected by a diagonal line. **2.** (of an ordinary) having an edge or edges so formed. [var. of *bevelled;* see BEVEL]

Bev·in (bev′in), *n.* **Ernest,** 1881–1951, British labor leader: foreign minister 1941–51.

bev·or (bē′vər), *n.* *Armor.* beaver².

bev·y (bev′ē), *n., pl.* **bev·ies. 1.** a flock of birds, esp. larks or quails. **2.** a group, esp. of girls or women. **3.** a group of roebucks. [late ME *bevey* < ?]
—**Syn. 1.** covey, flight; brood. **2.** assembly, company.

BEW, Board of Economic Warfare.

be·wail (bi wāl′), *v.t.* **1.** to express deep sorrow for; lament: *a vain woman bewailing her vanished youth.* —*v.i.* **2.** to express grief. [BE- + WAIL] —**be·wail′ing·ly,** *adv.* —**be·wail′ment,** *n.*
—**Syn. 1.** bemoan, mourn.

be·ware (bi wâr′), *v.,* **-wared, -war·ing.** —*v.t.* **1.** to be wary, cautious, or careful of (usually used imperatively): *Beware such inconsistency. Beware his waspish wit.* —*v.i.* **2.** to be cautious or careful: *Beware of the dog.* [from phrase of warning *be ware.* See BE, WARE²]

be·weep (bi wēp′), *v.t.,* **-wept, -weep·ing.** to weep over (something): *to beweep one's foolish mistakes.* [ME *bewep(en)*, OE *bewēpan.* See BE-, WEEP¹]

be·whisk·ered (bi hwis′kərd, -wis′-), *adj.* **1.** having whiskers; bearded. **2.** ancient, as a witticism, expression, etc.; trite; passé: *a bewhiskered catchword of a bygone era.* [BE- + WHISKERED]

Bew·ick (byo͞o′ik), *n.* **Thomas,** 1753–1828, English wood engraver.

be·wigged (bi wigd′), *adj.* wearing a wig. [BE- + WIG + -ED²]

be·wil·der (bi wil′dər), *v.t.* to confuse or puzzle completely; perplex: *These shifting attitudes bewilder me.* [BE- + WILDER (v.)] —**be·wil′dered·ly,** *adv.* —**be·wil′der·ing·ly,** *adv.*
—**Syn.** mystify, nonplus, confuse, daze, confound, stagger, muddle.

be·wil·der·ment (bi wil′dər mənt), *n.* **1.** bewildered state. **2.** a confusing maze or tangle, as of objects, conditions, etc.: *We entered into a bewilderment of smoke, noise, and crowding people.* [BEWILDER + -MENT]

be·witch (bi wich′), *v.t.* **1.** to affect by witchcraft or magic; cast a spell over. **2.** to enchant; charm; fascinate. [ME *biwicche(n).* See BE-, WITCH] —**be·witch′er,**

n. **—be·witch′er·y,** *n.* **—be·witch′ing·ly,** *adv.* **—be·witch′ing·ness,** *n.* **—be·witch′ment,** *n.*
—Syn. 2. captivate, enrapture, transport.

be·wray (bi rā′), *v.t. Obs.* **1.** to reveal or expose. **2.** to betray. [ME *bewraie(n),* equiv. to *be-* BE- + *wraien,* OE *wrēgan* to accuse, c. OHG *ruogen* (G *rügen*), Goth *wrohjan*] **—be·wray′er,** *n.*

bey (bā), *n., pl.* **beys. 1.** a provincial governor in the Ottoman Empire. **2.** (formerly) a title of respect for Turkish dignitaries. **3.** (formerly) the title of the native ruler of Tunis or Tunisia. Turkish, **beg.** [< Turk: lord, prince]

Beyle (bāl), *n.* **Ma·rie Hen·ri** (MA RĒ′ ÄN RĒ′), real name of **Stendhal.**

Bey·lic (bā′lik), *n.* the power or jurisdiction of a bey. [< Turk, equiv. to *bey* BEY + *-lik* -Y³]

Bey·og·lu (bā′ə lo͞o′; *Turk.* bā′ōKH lo͞o′), *n.* Pera.

be·yond (bē ond′, bi yond′), *prep.* **1.** on or to the farther side of: *Beyond those trees you'll find his house.* **2.** farther on than; more distant than: *beyond the horizon; beyond the confines of earth.* **3.** outside the understanding, limits, or reach of; past: *beyond human comprehension; beyond endurance; injured beyond help.* **4.** superior to; surpassing; above: *wise beyond all others.* **5.** more than; in excess of; over and above: *They soon realized they were staying beyond their welcome.* **—adv. 6.** farther on or away: *as far as the house and beyond.* **7. the beyond, a.** that which is at a great distance. **b.** Also, **the great beyond.** the life after the present one; after death. [ME *beyonde(n),* OE *begeondan.* See BE-, YOND (adv.)] **—be·yond′ness,** *n.*

Beyond′ Good′ and E′vil, a philosophical work (1886) by Friedrich Nietzsche. German, **Jenseits von Gute und Böse.**

Bey·routh (bā′ro͞ot, bā ro͞ot′), *n.* Beirut.

Be·zae (bē′zē), *n.* the uncial codex, dating from the 5th or 6th century A.D., that contains the Gospels and the Acts of the Apostles in Greek and Latin, on facing pages. Cf. **codex.** [< NL: of *Beza,* Latinized form of *Bèze* (Théodore de) 1519–1605, owner of the ms]

Be·zal·e·el (bi zal′ē əl), *n.* the chief architect of the tabernacle. Ex. 31:1–11. Also, *Douay Bible,* **Beseleel.** **—Be·zal·e·el·i·an** (bi zal′ē el′ē ən, bez′ə lē′lē-), *adj.*

bez·ant (bez′ənt, bi zant′), *n.* **1.** Also, **bezzant.** the gold solidus of the Byzantine Empire; widely circulated throughout Europe in the Middle Ages. **2.** Also, **byzant.** (in Romanesque architecture) any of a number of disklike ornaments, similar in form to the classical patera, used esp. on the faces of archivolts. **3.** *Heraldry.* a roundel or. Also, **besant** (for defs. 1, 2). [ME *besant* < OF < L *byzant(ius)* (*nummus*) Byzantine (coin), equiv. to *Byzanti(um)* + *-us* adj. suffix]

bez′ ant′ler (bez, bāz). See **bay antler.**

be·zan·ty (bə zan′tē), *adj. Heraldry.* semé of bezants. [< F *besanté.* See BEZANT, -Y¹]

bez·el (bez′əl), *n.* **1.** the diagonal face at the end of the blade of a chisel, or the like, leading to the edge. **2.** *Jewelry.* **a.** that part of a ring, bracelet, etc., to which gems are attached. **b.** crown (def. 29). **3.** the grooved ring or rim holding a gem or watch crystal in its setting. [akin to F *biseau* bevel, chamfer. See BEVEL]

Bé·ziers (bā zyā′), *n.* a city in S France, SW of Montpellier. 75,541 (1962).

be·zique (bə zēk′), *n. Cards.* a game resembling pinochle, played with 64 cards. [alter. of F *bésigue* < ?]

be·zoar (bē′zōr, -zôr), *n.* **1.** a calculus or concretion found in the stomach or intestines of certain animals, esp. ruminants, formerly reputed to be an effective remedy for poison. **2.** *Obs.* a counterpoison or antidote. [late ME *bezear* < ML *bezahar* < Ar *bā(di)zahr* < Pers *bādzahr,* var. of *pād-zahr* counter-poison; *-o-* < NL]

be·zo·ni·an (bi zō′nē ən), *n. Archaic.* an indigent rascal; scoundrel. [obs. *besoni(o)* raw recruit (< It *bisogno* need, needy soldier < ?) + -AN]

bez·zant (bez′ənt, bi zant′), *n.* bezant (def. 1).

bf., *Legal.* brief.

B/F, *Accounting.* brought forward.

B.F., 1. Bachelor of Finance. **2.** Bachelor of Forestry.

b.f., *Printing.* boldface. Also, **bf**

B.F.A., Bachelor of Fine Arts.

B.F.A.Mus., Bachelor of Fine Arts in Music.

BFDC, Bureau of Foreign and Domestic Commerce.

B.F.S., Bachelor of Foreign Service.

B.F.T., Bachelor of Foreign Trade.

bg., bag.

B.G., 1. Birmingham gauge. **2.** Brigadier General.

B.G.E., Bachelor of Geological Engineering.

B.Gen.Ed., Bachelor of General Education.

B-girl (bē′gûrl′), *n.* a woman employed by a bar, nightclub, etc., to act as a companion to male customers and induce them to buy expensive drinks, usually paid a percentage of what they spend. [prob. B(AR)¹ + GIRL]

Bglr., bugler.

Bha·bha (bä′bä), *n.* **Ho·mi J(e·han·gir)** (hō′mē jə hän gēr′), 1909–1966, Indian physicist and government official.

Bhad·gaon (bud′goun), *n.* a city in central Nepal, near Katmandu. ab. 100,000. Also, **Bhatgaon.**

Bha·ga·vad-Gi·ta (bug′ə vəd gē′tä), *n. Hinduism.* a portion of the Mahabharata, having the form of dialogue between the hero Arjuna and his charioteer, the avatar Krishna, in which a doctrine combining Brahmanical and other elements is evolved. [< Skt: Song of the Blessed One]

bha·jan (buj′ən), *n. Hinduism.* a religious song of praise. [< Skt]

bhak·ta (buk′tə), *n.* one who practices bhakti. [< Skt: devoted; akin to BHAKTI]

bhak·ti (buk′tē), *n. Hinduism.* **1.** selfless devotion as a means of reaching Brahman. Cf. **jnana, karma.** (def. 1). **2.** (*cap.*) a popular religious movement centered around the personal worship of gods, esp. Vishnu and Shiva. Cf. **Saiva, Vaishnava.** [< Skt: share, portion, devotion; akin to BHAKTA]

bhak·ti-mar·ga (buk′ti mär′gə), *n. Hinduism.* See under **marga.**

bhang (bang), *n.* **1.** the Indian hemp plant. **2.** a preparation of its leaves and tops used in India as an intoxicant and narcotic. Also, **bang.** [< Hindi *bhāṅg* < Skt *bhaṅgā* hemp]

bhan·gi (buŋ′gē), *n. Anglo-Indian.* a Hindu scavenger who belongs to one of the untouchable castes. Also, **bhungi.** [< Hindi *bhaṅgī:* lit., user of BHANG]

bhar·al (bûr′əl), *n.* a wild sheep, *Pseudois nahoor,* of Tibet and adjacent mountainous regions, having goatlike horns that curve backward. Also, **burrhel.** Also called **blue sheep.** [< Hindi *bharal*]

Bha·rat (bu′rut), *n.* Hindi name of the republic of **India.**

Bhat·gaon (bud′goun), *n.* Bhadgaon.

Bhau·na·gar (bou nug′ər), *n.* a seaport in S Gujarat, in W India. 176,000 (1961). Also, **Bhav·na·gar** (bäv-nug′ər).

Bha·va·bhu·ti (bä′və bo͞o′tē), *n.* fl. 8th century, Indian dramatist.

Bha·ve (bä′vā), *n.* **Vi·no·ba** (vē nō′bə), born 1895, Indian religious leader and mystic.

bhees·ty (bē′stē), *n., pl.* **-ties.** (in India) water carrier. Also, **bhees′tie.** [< Urdu *bhīstī* < Pers *bihishtī,* equiv. to *bihisht* paradise + *-ī* suffix of membership]

Bhik·ku (bik′o͞o, -o͝o), *n. Buddhism.* **1.** a monk. **2.** any of the original disciples of Buddha. Sanskrit, **Bhikshu.** [< Pali < Skt *bhikshu*]

Bhik·ku·ni (bik′o͞o nē), *n. Buddhism.* a female Bhikku; nun. [< Pali; fem. of BHIKKU]

Bhik·shu (bik′sho͞o), *n. Sanskrit.* Bhikku.

Bhil (bēl), *n.* a people inhabiting the hills of west central India.

Bhi·li (bē′lē), *n.* an Indic language of west central India, the language of the Bhils.

B.H.L., 1. Bachelor of Hebrew Letters. **2.** Bachelor of Hebrew Literature.

Bhoo·dan (bo͞o dän′), *n.* (in India) a socio-agricultural movement, started by Vinoba Bhave in 1951, in which village landowners are persuaded to give land to the landless. Also, **Bhu·dan′.**

Bho·pal (bō päl′), *n.* **1.** a former state in central India: now part of Madhya Pradesh state. **2.** a city in and the capital of Madhya Pradesh state, in central India. 185,400 (1961).

B horizon, *Geol.* the subsoil in a soil profile. Cf. **A horizon, C horizon.**

bhp, See **brake horsepower.** Also, **BHP, B.H.P., b.hp., b.h.p.**

Bhu·mi·bol A·dul·ya·dej (po͞o mē pôn′ ä do͞ol-yä′de). See **Rama IX.**

bhun·gi (buŋ′gē), *n.* bhangi.

bhut (bo͞ot), *n.* See **dust devil.** Also, **bhoot** (bo͞ot). [< Hindi < Skt *bhūta* (*bhū* BE + *-ta* v. suffix)]

Bhu·tan (bo͞o tän′), *n.* a principality in the Himalayas, NE of India: partly controlled by India. 700,000 (est. 1963); ab. 19,300 sq. mi. *Cap.:* Thimbu.

Bhu·tan·ese (bo͞ot′ənēz′, -ənēs′), *n., pl.* **-ese,** *adj.* **—n. 1.** a native or inhabitant of Bhutan. **2.** the Tibetan language as spoken in Bhutan. **—adj. 3.** of, pertaining to, or characteristic of Bhutan, its inhabitants, or their language. [BHUTAN + -ESE]

Bhu·ta·ta·tha·ta (bo͞o′tə tə tə tä′), *n. Buddhism.* Tathata. [< Skt; see BHUT, TATHATA]

Bi, *Chem.* bismuth.

bi-¹, a learned borrowing from Latin meaning "twice," "two," used in the formation of compound words: *bifacial; bifarious.* Cf. **bin-.** [< L, comb. form of *bis* TWICE]

bi-², var. of **bio-,** esp. before a vowel: *biopsy.*

B.I., British India.

Bi·a (bī′ə), *n.* the ancient Greek personification of force, the daughter of Pallas and Styx, and sister of Cratus, Nike, and Zelos.

bi·a·ce·tyl (bī′ə sēt′əl, -set′-, bī as′i təl), *n. Chem.* a yellow, water-soluble liquid, $CH_3COCOCH_3$, occurring in butter and in certain essential oils, as bay, and also synthesized: used chiefly to augment the flavor and odor of vinegar, coffee, and other foods. Also, **diacetyl.** [BI-¹ + ACETYL]

Bi·a·di·ce (bē′ə dī′sē), *n. Class. Myth.* the wife of Cretheus.

Bi·a·fra (bē ä′frə), *n.* **1.** a former secessionist state (1967–70) in SE Nigeria, in W Africa. 12,348,646 (1963); 29,484 sq. mi. *Cap.:* Enugu. **2. Bight of,** a wide bay in the E part of the Gulf of Guinea, off the W coast of Africa. **—Bi·a′fran,** *adj., n.*

Bi·ak (bē yäk′), *n.* an island N of West Irian, in Indonesia. 21,382 (est. 1950); 948 sq. mi. Also, **Wiak.**

Bia·lik (byä′lik), *n.* **Cha·im Nach·man** (KHī ēm′ näKH män′; *Eng.* KHī′im näKH′mən), 1873–1934, Hebrew poet, born in Russia.

bi·a·ly (bē ä′lē), *n.* a small, flat, circular, onion-flavored roll made of white flour, having a depression at the center and a crusty bottom. Also, **bia·ly** (byä′wi). Also called **bia′lystok roll′.** [after BIALYSTOK]

Bia·ly·stok (byä′wi stôk), *n.* a city in E Poland. 130,000 (est. 1963). Also, **Belostok.** Russian, **Byelostok.**

Bian·ca (byäng′kä), *n.* a girl's given name.

Bian·chini (byän kē′nē, byäng kē′-), *n.* a crater in the second quadrant of the face of the moon: about 25 miles in diameter.

Bian·co (byäng′kô), *n.* **Mon·te** (môn′te), Italian name of **Mont Blanc.**

bi·an·gu·lar (bī ang′gyə lər), *adj.* having two angles or corners. [BI-¹ + ANGULAR]

bi·an·nu·al (bī an′yo͞o əl), *adj.* **1.** occurring twice a year; semiannual. **2.** (loosely) occurring every two years; biennial. [BI-¹ + ANNUAL] **—bi·an′nu·al·ly,** *adv.*

bi·an·nu·late (bī an′yə lit, -lāt′), *adj. Zool.* having two ringlike bands, as of color. [BI-¹ + ANNULATE]

Biar·ritz (bē′ə rits′; *Fr.* bya RĒTS′), *n.* a city in SW France, on the Bay of Biscay: resort. 25,514 (1962).

bi·ar·tic·u·late (bī′är tik′yə lit, -lāt′), *adj. Zool.* having two joints, as the antennae of certain insects. Also, **bi′ar·tic′u·lat′ed.** [BI-¹ + ARTICULATE]

bi·as (bī′əs), *n., adj., adv., v.,* **bi·ased, bi·as·ing** or (*esp. Brit.*) **bi·assed, bi·as·sing. —n. 1.** an oblique or diagonal line of direction, esp. across a woven fabric. **2.** a particular tendency or inclination, esp. one which prevents unprejudiced consideration of a question. **3.** *Statistics.* a systematic, as opposed to a random distortion of a statistic as a result of sampling procedure. **4.** *Lawn Bowling.* **a.** a slight bulge or greater weight on one side of the ball or bowl. **b.** the curved course made by such a ball when rolled. **5.** *Electronics.* a steady voltage inserted in series with an element of an electronic device, as of a vacuum tube or transistor. **6. on the bias, a.** in the diagonal direction of the cloth. **b.** out of line; slanting. **—adj. 7.** cut, set, folded, etc., diagonally: *This material requires a bias cut.* **—adv. 8.** in a diagonal manner; obliquely; slantingly: *to cut material bias.* **—v.t. 9.** to cause prejudice in (a person); influence, esp. unfairly: *a tearful plea designed to bias the jury.* [< MF *biais* oblique < OPr, prob. << Gk *epikársios* oblique, equiv. to *epi-* EPI- + *-karsios* oblique]
—Syn. 2. predisposition, preconception, predilection, partiality, proclivity; bent, leaning. BIAS, PREJUDICE mean a strong inclination of the mind or a preconceived opinion about something or someone. A BIAS may be favorable or unfavorable: *bias in favor of or against an idea.* PREJUDICE implies a preformed judgment even more unreasoning than BIAS, and usually implies an unfavorable opinion: *prejudice against a race.* **9.** predispose, bend, incline, dispose. **—Ant. 2.** impartiality.

Bi·as (bī′əs), *n.* **1.** fl. 570 B.C., Greek philosopher born in Ionia. **2.** *Class. Myth.* a son of Amythaon and Idomene, who, with the help of his brother Melampus, secured the cattle of Phylacus and wed Pero.

bi·ased (bī′əst), *adj.* having or showing bias or prejudice: *They gave us a biased report on the situation.* Also, *esp. Brit.,* **bi′assed.** [BIAS + -ED²] **—bi′ased·ly;** *esp. Brit.,* **bi′assed·ly,** *adv.*

bi·ath·lon (bī ath′lon), *n.* a contest in which cross-country skiers, carrying rifles, make four stops to shoot at targets set up along a 12.5-mile course. [BI-¹ + Gk *âthlon* contest; modeled on DECATHLON]

bi·au·ric·u·lar (bī′ô rik′yə lər), *adj. Anat.* **1.** having two auricles. **2.** pertaining to both ears. [BI-¹ + AURICULAR]

bi·au·ric·u·late (bī′ô rik′yə lit, -lāt′), *adj. Biol.* having two auricles or earlike parts. [BI-¹ + AURICULATE]

bi·ax·i·al (bī ak′sē əl), *adj.* **1.** having two axes. **2.** (of a crystal) having two optical axes along which double refraction does not occur. [BI-¹ + AXIAL] **—bi·ax′i·al′i·ty,** *n.* **—bi·ax′i·al·ly,** *adv.*

bib (bib), *n., v.,* **bibbed, bib·bing. —n. 1.** a cloth for tying under the chin of a child to protect the clothing while the child is eating or being fed. **2.** the upper part of an apron. **3.** *Fencing.* a piece of canvas attached to the base of the mask, for protecting the throat. **4.** bibcock. **—v.t., v.i. 5.** *Archaic.* to tipple; drink. [ME *bibb(en)* < L *bibe(re)* (to) drink] **—bib′less,** *adj.* **—bib′like′,** *adj.*

Bib., 1. Bible. **2.** Biblical.

bib., (in prescriptions) drink. [< L *bibe*]

bib′ and tuck′er, *Informal.* clothes: *to dress in one's best bib and tucker.*

bi·ba·sic (bī bā′sik), *adj. Chem.* dibasic. [BI-¹ + BASIC]

bibb (bib), *n.* **1.** *Naut.* any of several brackets or timbers bolted to the hounds of a mast to give additional support to the trestletrees. **2.** bibcock. [alter. of BIB]

bib·ber (bib′ər), *n.* a steady drinker; tippler (usually used in combination): *winebibber.* [BIB + -ER¹]

bib·cock (bib′kok′), *n. Plumbing.* a faucet having a nozzle bent downward. Also, **bib, bibb.** [BIB + COCK¹]

bi·be·lot (bib′lō; *Fr.* bēbə lō′), *n., pl.* **-lots** (-lōz; *Fr.* -lō′). a small object of curiosity, beauty, or rarity. [< F, equiv. to *bibel-* (? alter. of *belbel;* see BAUBLE) + *-ot* n. suffix]

Bi·bie·na (bē bye′nä), *n.* **1. Fer·di·nan·do Gal·lo da** (feR′di nän′dô gäl′lô dä), 1657–1743, Italian stage designer and architect. **2.** his sons: **A·les·san·dro** (ä′les sän′dRô), 1687–1769, **An·to·nio** (än tô′nyô), 1700–44, **Giu·sep·pe** (jo͞o zep′pe), 1696–1756, Italian stage designers, architects, and artists. Also, **Bib·bie·na** (bēb bye′nä).

bi·bi·va·lent (bī′bī vā′lənt, bī biv′ə-), *adj. Chem.* noting an electrolytic compound which splits into two ions, each with a valence of two. [BI-¹ + BIVALENT]

bibl., 1. biblical. **2.** bibliographical. **3.** bibliography.

Bibl., 1. Biblical. **2.** bibliographical.

Bi·ble (bī′bəl), *n.* **1.** the collection of sacred writings of the Christian religion, comprising the Old and New Testaments. **2.** the collection of sacred writings of the Jewish religion, comprising the Old Testament only. **3.** (*often l.c.*) the sacred writings of any religion. **4.** (*l.c.*) any book, reference work, periodical, etc., accepted as authoritative, informative, or reliable: *The old sea captain regarded his Bowditch as his bible.* [ME, OE *bibli-* (var. of *biblio-*) in *biblithēca* < LL *bibliothēca* Bible. See BIBLIOTHECA]

Bi′ble Belt′, an area of the U.S., esp. in the south-central Midwest noted for its religious fundamentalism.

Bi′ble class′, a class or course of study devoted to the Bible or Biblical subjects, as in a Sunday School.

Bi′ble pa′per, a very thin, strong, opaque rag paper often used for Bibles, prayer books, dictionaries, and the like. Also called **India paper.**

Bi′ble school′, a school or organized study program primarily devoted to Biblical or religious teaching, as a Sunday School, church study group, etc.

Bi′ble Soci′ety, a Christian organization devoted to the printing and distribution of the Bible.

BiblHeb, Biblical Hebrew.

Bi·bli·a Pau·pe·rum (bib′lē ä pou′pə ro͝om′, pô′-pər əm), any of the picture books illustrating Biblical events and usually containing a short text, used chiefly in the Middle Ages for purposes of religious instruction. [< NL: lit., Bible of poor men]

Bib·li·cal (bib′li kəl), *adj.* **1.** of or in the Bible: *a Biblical name.* **2.** in accord with the Bible. Also, **bib′li·cal.** [< ML *biblic(us)* (*bibl(ia)* Bible + *-icus* -IC) + -AL¹] **—Bib′li·cal·ly, bib′li·cal·ly,** *adv.*

Bib′lical He′brew, the Hebrew language used in the Old Testament. *Abbr.:* BiblHeb

Bib′lical Lat′in, the form of Latin used in the translation of the Bible and which became current in western Europe at the beginning of the Middle Ages.

Bib·li·cism (bib′li siz′əm), *n.* literal interpretation of the Bible. [BIBLIC(AL) + -ISM]

Bib·li·cist (bib′li sist), *n.* **1.** a person who interprets the Bible literally. **2.** a Biblical scholar. [< ML *biblic(us)* (see BIBLICAL) + -IST] **—Bib′li·cis′tic,** *adj.*

biblio-, a prefix occurring in loan words from Greek (*bibliography*); on this model, used in the formation of compound words with the meaning "book" (*bibliophile*), and sometimes with the meaning "Bible" (*bibliolatry*, on the model of *idolatry*). [< L < Gk, comb. form of *biblíon* book, var. of *byblíon*, equiv. to *býbl(os)* book, paper (*Býblos* city in Phoenicia noted for export trade in paper) + *-ion* dim. suffix]

bib·li·o·clast (bib′lē ə klast′), *n.* one who mutilates or destroys books. [BIBLIO- + *-clast*, modeled on *iconoclast*] —**bib′li·o·clasm,** *n.*

bib·li·o·film (bib′lē ə film′), *n.* a microfilm used esp. in libraries to photograph the pages of valuable or much-used books. [BIBLIO- + FILM]

bibliog., 1. bibliographer. 2. bibliography.

bib·li·og·o·ny (bib′lē og′ə nē), *n.* the art of producing and publishing books. Also called **bib·li·o·gen·e·sis** (bib′lē ō jen′i sis). [BIBLIO- + -GONY]

bib·li·og·ra·pher (bib′lē og′rə fər), *n.* an expert in bibliography. [< Gk *bibliográph(os)* book-writer (see BIBLIO-, -GRAPH) + -ER[1]]

bib·li·og·ra·phy (bib′lē og′rə fē), *n., pl.* **-phies.** 1. a complete or selective list of readings on a particular subject. 2. a list of works by a particular author. 3. a list of source materials which are used or consulted in the preparation of a work or which are referred to in the text. 4. a branch of library science dealing with the history, physical description, comparison, and classification of books and other written or printed works. [< Gk *bibliographía*. See BIBLIO-, -GRAPHY] —**bib·li·o·graph·ic** (bib′lē ə graf′ik), **bib′li·o·graph′i·cal,** *adj.* —**bib′li·o·graph′i·cal·ly,** *adv.*

bib·li·o·klept (bib′lē ə klept′), *n.* a person who steals books. [BIBLIO- + Gk *klépt(ēs)* thief; see KLEPTOMANIA]

bib·li·ol·a·try (bib′lē ol′ə trē), *n.* 1. excessive reverence for the Bible as literally interpreted. 2. extravagant devotion to or dependence upon books. [BIBLIO- + -LATRY] —**bib′li·ol′a·ter, bib′li·ol′a·trist,** *n.* —**bib′li·ol′a·trous,** *adj.*

bib·li·ol·o·gy (bib′lē ol′ə jē), *n., pl.* **-gies.** bibliography (def. 4). [BIBLIO- + -LOGY] —**bib·li·o·log·i·cal** (bib′lē ə loj′i kəl), *adj.* —**bib′li·ol′o·gist,** *n.*

bib·li·o·man·cy (bib′lē ō man′sē), *n.* divination by means of a book, esp. the Bible, opened at random to some verse or passage, which is then interpreted. [BIBLIO- + -MANCY]

bib·li·o·ma·ni·a (bib′lē ō mā′nē ə, -mān′yə), *n.* excessive fondness for acquiring and possessing books. [BIBLIO- + -MANIA; r. *bibliomanie* < F] —**bib·li·o·ma·ni·ac** (bib′lē ō mā′nē ak′), *n.* —**bib·li·o·ma·ni·a·cal** (bib′lē ō mə nī′ə kəl), *adj.*

bib·li·op·e·gy (bib′lē op′ə jē), *n.* the art of binding books. [BIBLIO- + Gk *pēg-* (s. of *pēgnýnai* to fasten) + -Y[3]] —**bib·li·o·peg·ic** (bib′lē ə pej′ik, -pē′jik), *adj.* —**bib′li·op′e·gist,** *n.* —**bib′li·op′e·gis′tic, bib′li·op′e·gis′ti·cal,** *adj.*

bib·li·o·phage (bib′lē ə fāj′), *n.* an ardent reader; a bookworm. [BIBLIO- + -PHAGE] —**bib·li·oph·a·gous** (bib′lē of′ə gəs), **bib·li·o·phag·ic** (bib′lē ə faj′ik), *adj.*

bib·li·o·phile (bib′lē ə fīl′, -fil), *n.* one who loves or collects books. Also, **bib·li·oph·i·list** (bib′lē of′ə list). [BIBLIO- + -PHILE] —**bib′li·oph′i·lism, bib′li·oph′i·ly,** *n.* —**bib′li·oph′i·lis′tic, bib·li·o·phil·ic** (bib′lē ō fil′ik), *adj.*

bib·li·o·phobe (bib′lē ə fōb′), *n.* one who hates, fears, or distrusts books. [BIBLIO- + -PHOBE] —**bib′li·o·pho′bi·a,** *n.*

bib·li·o·pole (bib′lē ə pōl′), *n.* a bookseller, esp. a dealer in rare or second-hand books. Also, **bib·li·op·o·list** (bib′lē op′ə list). [< L *bibliopōl(a)* < Gk *bibliopṓlēs* (*biblio-* BIBLIO- + *pōl-* (s. of *pōleîsthai* to sell) + *-ēs* agentive suffix)] —**bib·li·o·pol·ic** (bib′lē ə pol′ik), **bib′li·o·pol′i·cal, bib′li·o·po′lar,** *adj.* —**bib′li·o·pol′i·cal·ly,** *adv.* —**bib·li·op·o·lism** (bib′lē op′ə liz′əm), **bib′li·op′o·ly,** *n.* —**bib′li·op′o·lis′tic,** *adj.*

bib·li·o·taph (bib′lē ə taf′, -täf′), *n.* one who caches or hoards books. Also, **bib′li·o·taphe′.** [BIBLIO- + Gk *táph(os)* burial; see EPITAPH] —**bib′li·o·taph′ic,** *adj.*

bib·li·o·the·ca (bib′lē ə thē′kə), *n., pl.* **-cas, -cae** (-kē). 1. a collection of books; a library. 2. a list of books, esp. a bookseller's catalogue. 3. *Obs.* the Bible. [< L: library, collection of books (ML: bible; cf. OE *bibliothēce* bible) < Gk *bibliothḗkē*. See BIBLIO-, THECA] —**bib′li·o·the′cal,** *adj.*

bib·li·o·ther·a·py (bib′lē ō ther′ə pē), *n.* *Psychiatry.* the use of reading as an ameliorative adjunct to therapy. [BIBLIO- + THERAPY] —**bib·li·o·ther·a·peu·tic** (bib′lē ō ther′ə pyōō′tik), *adj.* —**bib′li·o·ther′a·pist,** *n.*

bib·li·ot·ics (bib′lē ot′iks), *n.* (*construed as sing. or pl.*) the analysis of handwriting and documents, esp. for authentication of authorship. [BIBLIO- + *-t-* (connective) + *-iks*, var. of -ICS] —**bib′li·ot′ic,** *adj.* —**bib·li·o·tist** (bib′lē ə tist), *n.*

Bib·list (bib′list, bī′blist), *n.* 1. one who regards the Bible as the only rule of faith. 2. Biblicist. [BIBLE + -IST] —**Bib′lism,** *n.*

bib·u·lous (bib′yə ləs), *adj.* 1. addicted to alcoholic drinking. 2. absorbent; spongy. [< L *bibulus* (*bib(ere)* (to) drink (c. Skt *pibati* he drinks) + *-ulus* -ULOUS)] —**bib′u·lous·ly,** *adv.* —**bib′u·lous·ness, bib·u·los·i·ty** (bib′yə los′i tē), *n.*

bi·cam·er·al (bī kam′ər əl), *adj.* *Govt.* having two branches, chambers, or houses, as a legislative body. [BI-[1] + LL *camer(a)* CHAMBER + -AL[1]] —**bi·cam′er·al·ism,** *n.* —**bi·cam′er·al·ist,** *n.*

bi·cap·su·lar (bī kap′sə lər), *adj.* *Bot.* divided into two capsules; having a two-celled capsule. [BI-[1] + CAPSULAR]

bi·carb (bī kärb′), *n.* *Informal.* See **sodium bicarbonate.** [by shortening]

bicarb., 1. bicarbonate. 2. bicarbonate of soda.

bi·car·bo·nate (bī kär′bə nit, -nāt′), *n.* *Chem.* a salt of carbonic acid, containing the HCO_3^- group; an acid carbonate, as sodium bicarbonate, $NaHCO_3$. [BI-[1] + CARBONATE]

bicar′bonate of so′da. *Chem.* See **sodium bicarbonate.**

bice (bīs), *n.* blue or green as prepared from carbonates of copper. [ME *bis* dark grey < MF; c. with Pr *bis*, It *bigio*]

bi·cen·te·nar·y (bī sen′tᵊner′ē, bī′sen ten′ə rē), *adj., n., pl.* **-nar·ies.** *Chiefly Brit.* bicentennial. [BI-[1] + CENTENARY]

bi·cen·ten·ni·al (bī′sen ten′ē əl), *adj.* 1. pertaining to or in honor of a 200th anniversary: *bicentennial celebration; a bicentennial exposition.* 2. consisting of or lasting 200 years: *a bicentennial period.* 3. occurring every 200 years: *the bicentennial return of a comet.* —*n.* 4. a 200th anniversary: *The town will have its bicentennial next year.* 5. a celebration of such an anniversary: *The bicentennial lost a great deal of money.* Also, *esp. Brit.*, **bicentenary.** [BI-[1] + CENTENNIAL] —**bi′cen·ten′ni·al·ly,** *adv.*

bi·cen·tric (bī sen′trik), *adj.* *Biol.* 1. (of a taxon) having two centers of evolution. 2. (of a plant or animal) having two centers of distribution. [BI-[1] + CENTRIC] —**bi·cen′tri·cal·ly,** *adv.*

bi·ceph·a·lous (bī sef′ə ləs), *adj.* *Bot., Zool.* having two heads. [BI-[1] + -CEPHALOUS]

bi·ceps (bī′seps), *n., pl.* **-ceps·es** (-sep siz), **-ceps.** *Anat.* 1. a muscle on the front of the arm, the action of which bends the elbow. 2. the hamstring muscle on the back of the thigh, the action of which assists in bending the knee and extending the hip joint. [< L, equiv. to *bi-* BI-[1] + *-ceps* (s., *-cipit-*), comb. form of *caput* head]

Bi·chat (bē shA′), *n.* **Ma·rie Fran·çois Xa·vier** (mA rē′ frän swA′ gzA vyā′), 1771–1802, French physician.

bi·chlo·ride (bī klōr′īd, -id, -klôr′-), *n.* *Chem.* 1. a compound in which two atoms of chlorine are combined with another element or group. 2. See **mercuric chloride.** [BI-[1] + CHLORIDE]

bichlo′ride of mer′cury, *Chem.* See **mercuric chloride.**

bi·chro·mate (bī krō′māt), *n.* *Chem.* 1. dichromate. 2. See **potassium dichromate.** [BI-[1] + CHROMATE]

bi·cip·i·tal (bī sip′i tᵊl), *adj.* 1. having two heads; two-headed. 2. *Anat.* pertaining to the biceps. [< L *bicipit-* (s. of *biceps*) BICEPS + -AL[1]]

bick·er[1] (bik′ər), *v.i.* 1. to engage in petulant or peevish argument; wrangle: *The couple had bickered for years as a matter of habit.* 2. to run rapidly; move quickly; rush; hurry: *The raging stream bickered down the valley.* 3. to quiver; flicker; glitter: *The afternoon sun bickered through the trees.* —*n.* 4. an angry dispute; quarrel; contention. [ME *biker(en)* < ?] —**bick′er·er,** *n.*

bick·er[2] (bik′ər), *n.* *Scot.* 1. any wooden dish or bowl, esp. a wooden porridge bowl. 2. *Obs.* a wooden drinking cup. [ME *biker* BEAKER]

bick·er·ing (bik′ər ing), *n.* peevish or ill-natured quarreling, disputing, etc., esp. when frequent, prolonged, or habitual: *constant bickerings between brothers.* [ME; see BICKER[1], -ING[1]]

bick·i·ron (bik′ī′ərn, bik′ərn), *n.* the tapered end of an anvil. [alter. (by assoc. with IRON) of earlier *bickern* for *bycorne* two-horned anvil < L *bicorn(is)* two-horned (see BICORN); meaning perh. influenced by MF *bigorne* in same sense]

Bick·nell (bik′nᵊl), *n.* a town in SW Indiana. 3878 (1960).

Bi·col (bē kōl′), *n., pl.* **-cols,** (*esp. collectively*) **-col.** Bikol.

bi·col·lat·er·al (bī′kə lat′ər əl), *adj.* *Bot.* (of a bundle) having the xylem lined with phloem on both its inner and outer faces. [BI-[1] + COLLATERAL] —**bi′col·lat′er·al′i·ty,** *n.*

bi·col·or (bī′kul′ər), *adj.* having two colors: *a bicolor flower.* Also, **bi′col′ored;** *esp. Brit.*, **bi′col′our, bi′col′oured.** [< L; see BI-, COLOR]

bi·com·pact (bī′kəm pakt′), *adj.* *Math.* compact[1] (def. 7). [BI-[1] + COMPACT[1]]

bi·con·cave (bī kon′kāv, bī′kon kāv′), *adj.* concave on both sides, as a lens. See illus. under **lens** [BI-[1] + CONCAVE] —**bi·con·cav·i·ty** (bī′kᵊn kav′i tē), *n.*

bi·cone (bī′kōn′), *n.* an object shaped like two cones with their bases together. [BI-[1] + CONE] —**bi·con·i·cal** (bī kon′i kəl), *adj.* —**bi·con′i·cal·ly,** *adv.*

bi·con·vex (bī kon′veks, bī′kon veks′), *adj.* convex on both sides, as a lens. See illus. under **lens.** [BI-[1] + CONVEX]

bi·corn (bī′kôrn), *adj.* Also, **bi·cor·nate** (bī kôr′nit, -nāt), **bi·cor·nu·ate** (bī kôr′nōō it, -āt′, -nyōō-), **bi·cor′nu·ous.** 1. *Bot., Zool.* having two horns or hornlike parts. 2. shaped like a crescent. —*n.* 3. bicorne. [< L *bicorn(is)*, equiv. to *bi-* BI-[1] + *corn(u)* horn]

Bi·corn (bī′kôrn), *n.* (in early French and English literature) a mythical animal, usually depicted as a grotesquely fat beast, that existed solely by devouring virtuous husbands. Cf. **Chichivache.** [late ME *Bycorne* < MF < L *bicornis*]

bi·corne (bī′kôrn), *n.* 1. a two-cornered cocked hat worn esp. in the 18th and early 19th centuries. 2. *Rare.* a two-horned animal. Also, **bicorn.** [< F < L *bicornis* BICORN]

bi·cor·po·ral (bī kôr′pər əl), *adj.* having two bodies, main divisions, symbols, etc. Also, **bi·cor·po·re·al** (bī′kôr pôr′ē əl, -pōr′-). [< L *bicorpor* (*bi-* BI-[1] + *corpor-*, s. of *corpus* body) + -AL[1]]

bi·cron (bī′kron, bik′ron), *n.* *Physics.* one billionth of a meter. [BI(LLION) + *-cron*, as in *micron*]

bi·cus·pid (bī kus′pid), *adj.* 1. Also, **bi·cus′pi·date′.** having or terminating in two cusps or points, as certain teeth. —*n.* 2. premolar (def. 4). [BI-[1] + CUSPID]

bicus′pid valve′. See **mitral valve.**

bi·cy·cle (bī′si kəl, -sik′əl), *n., v.,* **-cled, -cling.** —*n.* 1. a vehicle with two wheels in tandem, usually propelled by pedals and having handlebars for steering and a saddlelike seat. 2. Also called **safety bicycle.** a similar vehicle, sometimes equipped with a motor, in which the seat is mounted between tandem wheels of equal or nearly equal size, the rear wheel being connected to the pedals by a chain. —*v.i.* 3. to ride a bicycle. [< F; see BI-[1], CYCLE] —**bi′cy·clist, bi′cy·cler,** *n.*

bi′cycle race′, *Sports.* cycling (def. 2). Also, **bi′cycle rac′ing.**

bi·cy·clic (bī sī′klik, -sik′lik), *adj.* 1. consisting of or having two cycles or circles. 2. *Bot.* in two whorls, as the stamens of a flower. 3. pertaining to or resembling a bicycle. Also, **bi·cy′cli·cal.** [BI[1]- + CYCLIC]

bicy′clic ter′pene, *Chem.* See under **terpene** (def. 2).

bid[1] (bid), *v.,* **bade** or **bad** for 1, 2, 5, 7 or **bid** for 3, 4, 6, 8–11; **bid·den** or **bid** for 1, 2, 5, 7 or **bid** for 3, 4, 6, 8–11; **bid·ding;** *n.* —*v.t.* 1. to command; order; direct: *Bid them depart.* 2. to say as a greeting, benediction, or wish: *to bid farewell to the visiting prime minister.* 3. *Com.* to make an offer of (a price at an auction or as terms in a competition) to secure a contract: *They bid $25,000 and got the contract.* 4. *Cards.* to enter a bid of a given quantity or suit: *to bid two no-trump; to bid spades.* 5. to summon by invitation; invite. 6. **bid defiance,** to refuse to yield; offer resistance. —*v.i.* 7. to command; order; direct: *I will do as you bid.* 8. to make an offer to purchase at a price: *She bid frantically for the old chair.* 9. **bid fair.** See **fair**[1] (def. 21). 10. **bid in,** *Com.* to overbid all offers for (property) at an auction in order to retain ownership. 11. **bid up,** *Com.* to increase (the market price) by increasing bids. —*n.* 12. act or instance of bidding: *My bid was rejected in favor of his.* 13. *Cards.* a. an offer to make a specified number of points or to take a specified number of tricks. b. the amount of such an offer. c. the turn of a person to bid. 14. *Informal.* an invitation: *a bid to join the club.* 15. an attempt to attain some goal or purpose: *a bid for election.* [ME *bidd(en)*, OE *biddan* to beg, ask, pray, require, demand; c. G *bitten*, Icel *bithja*, Goth *bidjan*] —**bid′der,** *n.*
—**Syn.** 1. charge; require, enjoin. 3. offer, tender, proffer. 12. offer, proposal; proffer.

bid[2] (bid), *v.* *Archaic.* pp. of **bide.**

B.I.D., Bachelor of Industrial Design.

b.i.d., (in prescriptions) twice a day. [< L *bis in diē*]

bi·dar·ka (bī där′kə), *n.* the sealskin boat of the Alaskan Eskimo. Also, **bi·dar·kee** (bī där′kē), **baidarka.** [< Russ *baidarka* (*baidar(a)* coracle + *-ka* dim. suffix)]

Bi·dault (bē dō′), *n.* **Georges** (zhôrzh), 1899–1983, French statesman.

bid·da·ble (bid′ə bəl), *adj.* 1. willing to do what is asked; obedient; docile: *a very biddable little maid.* 2. *Cards.* adequate to bid upon: *a biddable suit at bridge.* [BID[1] + -ABLE] —**bid′da·bil′i·ty, bid′da·ble·ness,** *n.* —**bid′da·bly,** *adv.*

Bid·de·ford (bid′ə fərd), *n.* a city in SW Maine. 19,255 (1960).

bid·den (bid′ᵊn), *v.* 1. a pp. of **bid.** —*adj.* 2. invited.

bid·ding (bid′ing), *n.* 1. command; summons; invitation: *I went there at his bidding.* 2. a bid. 3. bids collectively, or a period during which bids are made or received: *The bidding began furiously. The bidding has been postponed until tomorrow.* 4. **at someone's bidding,** subordinate to one; performing one's orders: *He seemed to have the whole world at his bidding.* 5. **do someone's bidding,** to submit to one's orders; perform services for one: *She was terribly spoiled and expected people to do her bidding as a matter of course.* [BID[1] + -ING[1]]

bid′ding prayer′, 1. the formal petitionary prayer, said esp. in the Anglican Church immediately before the sermon. 2. an intercessory prayer for persons living and dead, said in English churches up to about the middle of the 16th century.

Bid·dle (bid′ᵊl), *n.* 1. **Francis,** 1886–1968, U.S. attorney general, 1941–45. 2. **John,** 1615–62, English theologian: founder of English Unitarianism. 3. **Nicholas,** 1786–1844, U.S. financier.

bid·dy[1] (bid′ē), *n., pl.* **-dies.** a chicken; fowl. [?]

bid·dy[2] (bid′ē), *n., pl.* **-dies.** a fussbudget, esp. a fussy old woman. [special use of BIDDY]

Bid·dy (bid′ē), *n.* a girl's given name, form of **Bridget.**

bide (bīd), *v.,* **bid·ed** or **bode; bid·ed** or (*Archaic*) **bid; bid·ing.** —*v.t.* 1. *Archaic.* to endure; bear. 2. *Obs.* to encounter. —*v.i.* 3. *Archaic.* to dwell; abide; wait; remain; continue. 4. **bide one's time,** to wait for a favorable opportunity: *He wanted to ask for a raise but bided his time until the right moment.* [ME *bide(n)*, OE *bīdan*; c. OHG *bītan*, Icel *bītha*, Goth *beidan*] —**bid′er,** *n.*

bi·den·tate (bī den′tāt), *adj.* *Biol.* having two teeth or toothlike parts or processes. [< L *bident-* (s. of *bidēns*, equiv. to *bi-* BI-[1] + *dēns* tooth) + -ATE[1]]

bi·den·tic·u·late (bī′den tik′yə lit, -lāt′), *adj.* *Zool.* having two small teeth or toothlike processes. [BI-[1] + DENTICULATE]

bi·det (bē dā′, bi det′), *n.* 1. a low, basinlike bath, used esp. in France, for bathing one's private parts. 2. a small saddle horse. [< MF: pony; akin to OF *bider* to trot]

bi·di (bē′dē), *n.* (in India) an inexpensive cigarette, usually produced usually from cut tobacco rolled in leaf. Also, **beedi, biri.** [alter. of Hindi *bīṛī* < Skt *vīṭikā* a preparation rolled in betel leaf]

bi·di·rec·tion·al (bī′di rek′shə nᵊl, -dī-), *adj.* (of an antenna, microphone, etc.) capable of reacting or functioning in two, usually opposite, directions. [BI-[1] + DIRECTIONAL]

B.I.E., Bachelor of Industrial Engineering.

Biedermeier cabinet

Bie·der·mei·er (bē′dər mī′ər), *adj.* noting or pertaining to a style of furnishing common in German-speaking areas in the early and middle 19th century, generally existing as a simplification of the French Empire style, usually executed in fruitwood with much use of matched veneers, with accents of ebony inlay or black paint, and often displaying architectural motifs. [after Gottlieb *Biedermeier*, imaginary unsophisticated author of poems actually composed by various writers and published in German magazine *Fliegende Blätter* from 1855 on]

Biel (bēl), *n.* **Lake.** See **Bienne, Lake of.**

Bie·la (bē′lä, -lə), *n.* a crater in the fourth quadrant of the face of the moon: about 46 miles in diameter.

bield (bēld), *n.* *Scot.* a shelter; refuge. [ME *beild*, *beeld* courage, confidence, means of help, OE *bieldo* boldness; akin to Goth *balthei* confidence. See BOLD]

Bie·le·feld (bē′lə felt′), *n.* a city in N West Germany. 172,800 (1963).

Bie·ler·see (bē′lər zā′), *n.* German for **Bienne.**

bien en·ten·du (byaN nän tän dʏ′), *French.* naturally; of course. [lit., well understood]

Bienne (byen), *n.* **Lake of,** a lake in NW Switzerland: traces of prehistoric lake dwellings. 16 sq. mi. Also called **Lake Biel.** German, **Bielersee.**

bi·en·ni·al (bī en′ē əl), *adj.* **1.** happening every two years: *biennial games.* **2.** lasting or enduring for two years: *to grow or function on a biennial cycle.* **3.** *Bot.* completing its normal term of life in two years, flowering and fruiting the second year, as beets or winter wheat. —*n.* **4.** any event occurring once in two years. **5.** *Bot.* a biennial plant. Also, **biyearly** (for defs. 1, 2). [BIENNI(UM) + -AL[1]] —**bi·en′ni·al·ly,** *adv.*

bi·en·ni·um (bī en′ē əm), *n., pl.* **-en·ni·ums, -en·ni·a** (-en′ē ə). a period of two years. [< L, equiv. to *bi-* BI-[1] + *enn-* (var. s. of *annus* year) + *-ium* n. suffix]

bien·ve·nu (byaN və ny′), *adj.* *French.* welcome. [lit., well arrived]

bien·ve·nue (byaN və ny′), *French.* —*adj.* **1.** welcome (used when addressing or referring to a woman). —*n.* **2.** a welcome; kindly greeting or reception.

Bien·ville (byaN vēl′), *n.* **Jean Bap·tiste Le Moyne** (zhäN bA tēst′ lə mwAN′), **Sieur de** (syœr də), 1680–1768, French governor of Louisiana.

bier (bēr), *n.* a frame or stand on which a corpse or the coffin containing it is laid before burial. [ME *bere*, OE *bēr, bǣr;* c. OHG *bāra* (G *Bahre*); akin to BEAR[1]]

Bierce (bērs), *n.* **Ambrose (Gwin·nett)** (gwi net′), 1842–1914?, U.S. journalist and short-story writer.

bier·stu·be (bēr′shtōō bə), *n., pl.* **-bes, -ben** (-bən). a tavern or café offering German or German-style atmosphere, décor, food, beer, etc. [< G: beer room]

biest·ings (bē′stingz), *n.* (*construed as sing.*) beestings.

bi·fa·cial (bī fā′shəl), *adj.* **1.** having two faces or fronts. **2.** having the opposite surfaces alike. **3.** *Bot.* having the opposite surfaces unlike, as a leaf. [BI-[1] + FACIAL]

bi·far·i·ous (bī fâr′ē əs), *adj.* *Bot.* in two vertical rows. [< L *bifārius* twofold, double (*bi-* BI-[1] + *f(acere)* (to) make, do + *-ārius* -ARIOUS)] —**bi·far′i·ous·ly,** *adv.*

biff (bif), *U.S. Slang.* —*n.* **1.** a blow; punch. —*v.t.* **2.** to hit; punch. [? imit.]

bif·fin (bif′in), *n.* **1.** a deep red cooking apple native to Britain. **2.** *Brit.* a baked apple, esp. when flattened into a cake and sprinkled with sugar or cinnamon. [var. of *beefing* (so called from color of beef); see -ING[1]]

bi·fid (bī′fid), *adj.* separated or cleft into two equal parts or lobes. [< L *bifid(us)*, equiv. to *bi-* BI-[1] + *fid-* (var. s. of *findere* to split; akin to BITE) + *-us* adj. suffix] —**bi·fid′i·ty,** *n.* —**bi′fid·ly,** *adv.*

bi·fi·lar (bī fī′lər), *adj.* furnished or fitted with two filaments or threads. [BI-[1] + L *fīl(um)* (see FILE[1]) + -AR[1]] —**bi·fi′lar·ly,** *adv.*

bi·flag·el·late (bī flaj′ə lāt′, -lit), *adj.* *Zool.* having two whiplike flagella. [BI-[1] + FLAGELLATE]

bi·flex (bī′fleks), *adj.* bent at two places. [BI-[1] + *-flex* < L *flex(us)*; see FLEX]

bi·fluor·ide (bī flōō′ə rīd′, -flōōr′id, -flôr′-, -flōr′-), *n.* *Chem.* an acid salt of hydrofluoric acid containing the group HF_2–, as ammonium bifluoride, NH_4HF_2. [BI-[1] + FLUORIDE]

bi·fo·cal (bī fō′kəl, bī′fō-), *adj.* **1.** *Chiefly Optics.* having two foci. **2.** (of an eyeglass lens) having two portions, one for near and one for far vision. —*n.* **3. bifocals,** eyeglasses with bifocal lenses. [BI-[1] + FOCAL]

bi·fo·li·ate (bī fō′lē it, -āt′), *adj.* having two leaves. [BI-[1] + FOLIATE]

bi·fo·li·o·late (bī fō′lē ə lāt′, -lit), *adj.* *Bot.* having two leaflets. [BI-[1] + FOLIOLATE]

bi·fo·rate (bī fōr′āt, -fôr′-, bī′fə rāt′, bif′ə-), *adj.* *Biol.* having two pores or perforations. [< NL **biforāt(us)* (*bi-* BI-[1] + L *forātus* perforated) ptp. of *forāre* to bore -ATE[1]]

bi·forked (bī′fôrkt′), *adj.* bifurcate. [BI-[1] + FORKED]

bi·form (bī′fôrm′), *adj.* having or combining two forms, as a centaur, mermaid, etc. Also, **bi′formed′.** [< L *biform(is)*, equiv. to *bi-* BI-[1] + *form(a)* FORM + *-is* adj. suffix] —**bi·for′mi·ty,** *n.*

Bif·rost (biv′rost), *n.* *Scand. Myth.* the rainbow bridge of the gods from Asgard to earth. [< Icel *Bifröst* < *bif-* (root of *bifa*, c. OE *bifian* to shake) + *röst*, c. OHG *rasta* stretch of road]

bi·func·tion·al (bī fungk′shə nəl), *adj.* *Chem.* having or involving two functional groups. [BI-[1] + FUNCTIONAL]

bi·fur·cate (*v., adj.* bī′fər kāt′, bī fûr′kāt; *adj. also* bī′fər kit, bī fûr′-), *v.,* **-cat·ed, -cat·ing,** *adj.* —*v.t., v.i.* **1.** to divide or fork into two branches. —*adj.* **2.** divided into two branches. [< ML *bifurcāt(us)*, ptp. of *bifurcāre* (*bi-* BI-[1] + *furc(a)* fork + *-ātus* -ATE[1])] —**bi·fur·cate·ly** (bī′fər kāt′lē, bī fûr′kāt lē, -kit-), *adv.* —**bi′fur·ca′tion,** *n.*

big[1] (big), *adj.,* **big·ger, big·gest,** *adv.* —*adj.* **1.** large, as in size, height, width, amount, etc.: *a big house.* **2.** filled; brimming: *eyes big with tears.* **3.** important, as in influence, standing, wealth, etc.: *the big man of his town.* **4.** boastful; pretentious; haughty: *a big talker.* **5.** magnanimous; generous; kindly: *A big person forgives others. He certainly has a big heart.* **6.** loud; orotund: *a big voice.* **7.** near the full term of pregnancy (usually fol. by *with*): *big with child.* **8.** of major concern, importance, gravity, or the like: *a big problem.* **9.** outstanding for a specified quality: *He's a big liar. The movie was a big gyp.* **10.** *Obs.* very strong; powerful. —*adv.* **11.** *Informal.* boastfully; pretentiously: *to act big; to talk big.* **12.** *Slang.* successfully; with great success: *to go over big.* [ME *big(ge)* < ?] —**big′gish,** *adj.* —**big′ly,** *adv.* —**big′ness,** *n.*
—**Syn. 1.** large, huge, immense; bulky, massive; capacious, voluminous; extensive. See **great. 2.** overflowing. **3.** consequential. —**Ant. 1.** little.

big[2] (big), *v.t.,* **bigged, big·ging.** *Brit. Dial.* to build. Also, **bigg.** [ME *bigg(en)* < Scand; cf. Icel *byggja* to inhabit, c. OE *bū(i)an*, G *bauen*]

big[3] (big), *n.* *Scot. and North Eng.* bigg[1].

bi·ga (bē′gä, -gə, bī′-), *n., pl.* **-gae** (-gē, -jē, -gī). *Class. Antiq.* a two-wheeled chariot drawn by two horses harnessed abreast. Cf. **quadriga, triga.** [< L *bi(iu)ga* (*bi-* BI-[1] + *iug(um)* YOKE + *-a* fem. nom. sing. ending)]

big·a·mist (big′ə mist), *n.* one who commits bigamy. [BIGAM(Y) + -IST] —**big′a·mis′tic,** *adj.* —**big′a·mis′ti·cal·ly,** *adv.*

big·a·mous (big′ə məs), *adj.* **1.** having two wives or husbands at the same time; guilty of bigamy. **2.** involving bigamy. [< LL *bigamus*, equiv. to *bi-* BI-[1] + Gk *-gamos* -GAMOUS] —**big′a·mous·ly,** *adv.*

big·a·my (big′ə mē), *n., pl.* **-mies. 1.** *Law.* the crime of marrying while one has a wife or husband still living, from whom no valid divorce has been effected. **2.** *Eccles.* any violation of canon law concerning marital status, which would disqualify a person from receiving holy orders or from retaining or surpassing his ecclesiastical rank. [ME *bigamie* < ML *bigamia* (LL *bigam(us)* BIGAMOUS + L *-ia* -Y[3])]

Big′ Ap′ple, the, *Slang.* **1.** New York City. **2.** any large city.

big·ar·reau (big′ə rō′, big′ə rō′), *n.* **1.** a large, heart-shaped variety of sweet cherry, having firm flesh. **2.** the tree bearing this fruit. [< F, equiv. to *bigarr(é)* variegated + *-eau* n. suffix (earlier *-el* < L *-ellus*)]

big′ band′, a jazz or dance band that is the size of an orchestra. Cf. **combo.**

big′-bang′ the′ory (big′bang′), *Astron.* the theory that the universe was created from the explosion of a mass of hydrogen atoms, is still expanding, and will eventually contract into one mass to explode again to complete the cycle, the complete cycle to take 80 billion years. Cf. **steady-state theory.**

Big′ Belt′ Moun′tains, a range of the Rocky Mountains, in W Montana.

Big′ Ben′, the bell in the clock tower of the Houses of Parliament in London, England.

Big′ Bend′ Na′tional Park′, a national park in W Texas, on the Rio Grande. 1080 sq. mi.

Big′ Ber′tha, *Informal.* a large German gun or cannon used during World War I.

Big′ Board′, (*sometimes l.c.*) *Informal.* the New York Stock Exchange.

big-boned (big′bōnd′), *adj.* having a bone structure that is massive in contrast with the surrounding flesh.

big′ broth′er, 1. an elder brother. **2.** (*sometimes cap.*) a man who individually or as a member of an organized group undertakes to sponsor or assist a boy in need of help, guidance, or the like, as an orphan, juvenile delinquent, etc. **3.** (*usually cap.*) the head or public spokesman of a totalitarian regime. **4.** (*usually cap.*) the aggregate of powerful individuals and policy makers of a totalitarian state.

big′ busi′ness, 1. *Often Derogatory.* **a.** monopoly or monopolies of financial or business resources, esp. when conceived as having excessive control over an economy or society. **b.** any large organization of a noncommercial nature resembling this. **2.** any large business enterprise.

big′ casi′no, *Casino.* the ten of diamonds.

big′ cheese′, *Slang.* an influential or important person: *Who's the big cheese around here?*

big′-cone pine′ (big′kōn′). See **Coulter pine.**

Big′ Di′omede. See under **Diomede Islands.**

Big′ Dip′per, *Astron.* Dipper (def. 3a).

big′ end′, *Mach.* the end of a connecting rod or piston rod that is attached to a crankpin.

bi·gen·er (bī′jē nər, -jə-), *n.* a bigeneric hybrid, as a mule. [< L (*bi-* BI-[1] + *gener-* (s. of *genus*) GENUS)]

bi·ge·ner·ic (bī′jə ner′ik), *adj.* of, pertaining to, or involving two genera. [BI-[1] + GENERIC]

big·eye (big′ī′), *n., pl.* (*esp. collectively*) **-eye,** (*esp. referring to two or more kinds or species*) **-eyes.** any of several silver and red fishes of the family *Priacanthidae*, found in the warm waters of the Pacific Ocean and in the West Indies, having a short, flattened body and large eyes. [BIG[1] + EYE]

big′eye scad′, a carangid fish, *Selar crumenophthalmus*, found in tropical seas and along the Atlantic coast of the U.S., having prominent eyes. Also called **goggle-eye.**

Big′ Five′, 1. the United States, Great Britain, France, Italy, and Japan during World War I and at the Paris Peace Conference in 1919. **2.** (after World War II) the United States, Great Britain, the Soviet Union, China, and France.

bigg[1] (big), *n.* *Scot. and North Eng.* four-rowed barley, a hardier but inferior variety of the common six-rowed or winter barley. Also, **big.** [ME *big, bigge* < Scand; cf. Icel *bygg* barley, c. OE *bēow*]

bigg[2] (big), *v.t.* big[2].

big′ game′, 1. large wild animals, esp. when hunted for sport. **2.** large fish, as tuna and marlin, when sought by deep-sea anglers.

big·gie (big′ē), *n.* *Slang.* See **big shot.** [BIG[1] + -IE]

big·gin[1] (big′in), *n.* **1.** a close-fitting cap worn esp. by children. **2.** *Brit. Archaic.* a soft cap worn while sleeping; nightcap. [< MF *beguin* kind of hood or cap, orig. one worn by a BEGUINE]

big·gin[2] (big′in), *n.* a coffee pot, usually silver, having a separate container in which the coffee is immersed while being boiled. [after proper name *Biggin*, its early 19th-century inventor]

big·ging (big′in), *n.* *Scot. and North Eng.* a building; home. [ME *biging.* See BIG[2], -ING[1]]

Biggs (bigz), *n.* **E(dward George) Pow·er** (pou′ər), 1906–77, English organist, in the U.S.

big′ gun′, *Slang.* an influential or important person or thing: *He became a big gun in scientific circles.*

big·gy (big′ē), *n., pl.* **-gies.** *Slang.* See **big shot.** [BIG[1] + -Y[2]]

big·head (big′hed′), *n.* **1.** *Vet. Path.* an inflammatory swelling of the tissues of the head of sheep, caused by the anaerobic bacillus, *Clostridium novyi.* **2.** *Informal.* an excessive estimate of one's importance; conceit. [BIG[1] + HEAD] —**big′head′ed,** *adj.*

big-heart·ed (big′här′tid), *adj.* generous; kind. —**big′heart′ed·ly,** *adv*

big′ hook′, *Railroad Slang.* See **wrecking crane.**

big·horn (big′hôrn′), *n., pl.* **-horns,** (*esp. collectively*) **-horn.** a wild sheep, *Ovis canadensis*, of the Rocky Mountains, with large, curving horns. Also called **Rocky Mountain bighorn, Rocky Mountain sheep.** [BIG[1] + HORN]

Bighorn
(3½ ft. high at shoulder; horns to 3½ ft.; length to 5½ ft.)

Big·horn (big′hôrn′), *n.* a river flowing from central Wyoming to the Yellowstone River in S Montana. 336 mi. long.

Big′ Horn′ Moun′tains, a mountain range in N Wyoming, part of the Rocky Mountains. Highest peak, Cloud Peak, 13,165 ft. Also called **Big′ Horns′.**

big′ house′, *Slang.* a penitentiary (usually prec. by *the*).

bight (bīt), *n.* **1.** the middle part of a rope, as distinguished from the ends. **2.** the loop or bent part of a rope, as distinguished from the ends. **3.** a bend or curve in the shore of a sea or river. **4.** a body of water bounded by such a bend. **5.** a bay or gulf. —*v.t.* **6.** to fasten with a bight of rope. [ME *byght*, OE *byht* bend, bay; c. D *bocht*, G *Bucht;* akin to BOW[1]]

big′ ide′a, *Slang.* **1.** an unsolicited or objectionable plan or proposal: *You're always coming around here with your big ideas.* **2.** purpose; intention; aim: *What's the big idea of shouting at me?*

Big′ Lake′, a town in W Texas. 2668 (1960).

big′ league′, *Sports Informal.* See **major league.** —**big′-league′,** *adj.*

big-lea·guer (big′lē′gər), *n.* *Baseball Informal.* **1.** a player in a major league. **2.** a skilled player; one who behaves or plays as if he belonged in a major league.

big′-leaved magno′lia (big′lēvd′). See **evergreen magnolia.**

big′ lie′, a false statement of outrageous magnitude employed as a propaganda measure in the belief that a lesser falsehood would not be credible.

Big′low Pa′pers (big′lō), a collection of satirical writings by James Russell Lowell, published in two series, the first (1846–48) on the Mexican War, and the second (1867) on the Confederacy. [named after Hosea *Biglow*, pseudonym of James Russell Lowell]

big′ mar′igold. See **African marigold.**

Big′ Mon′ey, The, a novel (1936) by John Dos Passos. Cf. **U.S.A.**

big·mouth (big′mouth′), *n., pl.* **-mouths** (-mouthz′) for 1; (*esp. collectively*) **-mouth,** (*esp. referring to two or more kinds or species*) **-mouths** for 2. **1.** *Slang.* a loud, talkative person, esp. one who lacks discretion. **2.** any of several fishes having an unusually large mouth.

big′mouth buf′falofish, a buffalofish, *Ictiobus cyprinellus*, found in central North America, characterized by a large mouth.

Big′ Mud′dy, a nickname of the Mississippi River

Big′ Mud′dy Riv′er, a river in SW Illinois, flowing SW into the Mississippi. ab. 120 mi. long.

big′ name′, one who has a preeminent public reputation in a specified field; a famous or widely acclaimed person: *He's a big name in education.*

big-name (big′nām′), *adj.* **1.** having a widespread public reputation as a leader in a specified field; famous: *a big-name doctor; a big-name actress.* **2.** of, pertaining to, or composed of a big-name person or persons.

big·no·ni·a (big nō′nē ə), *n.* any chiefly tropical American climbing shrub of the genus *Bignonia*, cultivated for the showy, trumpet-shaped flowers. [< NL, after Abbé *Bignon* (librarian of Louis XIV of France); see -IA]

big·no·ni·a·ceous (big nō′nē ā′shəs), *adj.* belonging or pertaining to the *Bignoniaceae*, a family of plants including trumpet creeper, catalpa, etc. [BIGNONI(A) + -ACEOUS]

big·ot (big′ət), *n.* a person who is utterly intolerant of any creed, belief, or opinion that differs from his own. [from proper name *Bigot* < ?]

big·ot·ed (big′ə tid), *adj.* utterly intolerant of any creed, belief, or opinion that differs from one's own. [BIGOT + -ED[2]] —**big′ot·ed·ly,** *adv.*
—**Syn.** See **intolerant.**

big·ot·ry (big′ə trē), *n., pl.* **-ries. 1.** stubborn and complete intolerance of any creed, belief, or opinion that differs from one's own. **2.** actions, beliefs, prejudices, etc., of a bigot. [BIGOT + -RY, formation parallel to F *bigoterie*]

Big′ Rap′ids, a town in central Michigan. 8686 (1960).

big′ shot′, *Slang.* an important or influential person.

big′ sis′ter, 1. an elder sister. **2.** (*sometimes cap.*) a woman who individually or as a member of an organized group undertakes to sponsor or assist a girl in need of help, guidance, or the like, as an orphan, juvenile delinquent, etc. **3.** (*sometimes cap.*) a girl in the junior or senior class in college who advises a girl in the freshman class on studies, social activities, etc., often as a part of a sorority program.

big′ skate′. See under **skate**[2].

Big′ Spring′, a city in W Texas. 31,230 (1960).

big′ stick′, force, esp. political or military, as a means of influence.

Big′ Stone′ Gap′, a town in SW Virginia. 4688 (1960).

big′ talk′, *Slang.* exaggeration; bragging.

Big·tha (big′thə), *n.* one of the seven eunuchs who served in the court of King Ahasuerus. Esther 1:10. Also, *Douay Bible,* **Bagatha.**

big′ time′, 1. *Slang.* the highest or most important level in any profession or occupation. **2.** *Slang.* a very good time. **3.** *Theat.* (in vaudeville) any highly successful circuit of theaters that produces two performances daily. —**big′-time′,** *adj.* —**big′-tim′er,** *n.*

big′ toe′, the first, innermost, largest digit of the foot.

big′ top′, *Informal.* **1.** the largest or main tent of a circus. **2.** a circus.

big′ tree′, a large coniferous tree, *Sequoiadendron giganteum* (formerly *Sequoia gigantea*), of California, often reaching 300 feet in height. Also called **giant sequoia.** Cf. **sequoia.**

big′ wheel′, *Slang.* an influential or important person: *He wanted to become a big wheel in business.*

big·wig (big′wig′), *n.* *Informal.* an important person, esp. an official: *senators and other political bigwigs.* [rhyming compound from phrase *big wig*, i.e., person important enough to wear such a wig] —**big′wigged′,** *adj.* —**big′wig′ged·ness** (big′wig′id nis), *n.*

Bi·har (bē här′), *n.* **1.** a state in NE India. 46,455,610 (1961); 67,164 sq. mi. *Cap.:* Patna. **2.** a city in central Bihar. 78,600 (1961). Also, **Behar.**

Bihar′ and O·ris′sa (ō ris′ə, ô ris′ə), a former province of NE India: now divided into the states of Bihar and Orissa.

Bi·ha·ri (bē här′ē), *n.* an Indic language, the language of Bihar.

bi·hour·ly (bī our′lē, -ou′ər-), *adj.* occurring every two hours. [BI-[1] + HOURLY]

Bih·zad (bē′zäd), *n.* **Ka·mal ad-Din** (kä′mäl äd dēn′), c1440–c1527, Persian painter and calligrapher.

Bi·isk (bē′isk), *n.* Bisk.

bi·jec·tion (bī jek′shən), *n.* *Math.* a map or function that is one-to-one and onto. [BI-[1] + *-jection,* as in *projection*]

bi·jou (bē′zho͞o, bē zho͞o′), *n., pl.* **-joux** (-zho͞oz, -zho͞oz′). **1.** a jewel. **2.** something small, delicate, and exquisitely wrought. [< F < Breton *bizou,* earlier *besou* jeweled ring; c. Cornish *bisou* finger-ring, deriv. of *bis* finger]

bi·jou·te·rie (bē zho͞o′tə rē), *n.* jewelry. [< F, equiv. to *bijou* BIJOU + *-t-* (hiatus-filler) + *-erie* -ERY]

bi·ju·gate (bī′jo͝o gāt′, bī jo͞o′gāt, -git), *adj.* *Bot.* (of leaves) having two pairs of leaflets or pinnae. Also, **bi·ju·gous** (bī′jo͝o gəs). [BI-[1] + JUGATE]

Bi·ka·ner (bē′kə nēr′), *n.* **1.** a former native state of NW India: now incorporated into Rajasthan state. **2.** a city in NW Rajasthan. 150,494 (1961).

bike[1] (bīk), *n., v.,* **biked, bik·ing.** —*n.* **1.** *Informal.* a bicycle. **2.** *Harness Racing.* a sulky with tires like those of a bicycle. —*v.i.* **3.** *Informal.* to bicycle. [*bi(cy)c(le)*]

bike[2] (bīk), *n.* *Scot. and North Eng.* **1.** a colony, nest, or swarm of wild bees, wasps, or hornets. **2.** a teeming crowd; swarm of people. [ME, equiv. to **bi* bee (< Scand; cf. Icel *bȳ* BEE[1]) + **yeke,* OE *gēoc* help, safety]

bi·ki·ni (bi kē′nē), *n.* a very brief two-piece bathing suit. [named after BIKINI]

Bi·ki·ni (bē kē′nē), *n.* an atoll in the N Pacific, in the Marshall Islands: atomic bomb tests 1946. 3 sq. mi.

Bi·kol (bē kōl′), *n., pl.* **-kols,** (*esp. collectively*) **-kol.** a member of a Malayan people in SE Luzon and the nearby Philippines: converted to Christianity early in the Spanish conquest. Also, **Bicol.**

bi·la·bi·al (bī lā′bē əl), *Phonet.* —*adj.* **1.** produced with the lips close together or touching: the lips touch at one phase of the production of the bilabial consonants *p, b,* and *m;* they do not for the bilabial *w.* —*n.* **2.** a bilabial speech sound. [BI-[1] + LABIAL]

bi·la·bi·ate (bī lā′bē āt′, -it), *adj.* *Bot.* two-lipped, as a corolla. [BI-[1] + LABIATE]

Bi·lac (bē läk′), *n.* **O·la·vo** (ə lä′vō), 1865–1918, Brazilian poet.

bil·an·der (bil′ən dər, bī′lən-), *n.* *Naut.* a small merchant vessel with two masts, used on canals and along the coast of Holland. [< D *bijlander,* equiv. to *bij* BY + *land* LAND + *-er* -ER[1]]

bi·lat·er·al (bī lat′ər əl), *adj.* **1.** *Bot., Zool.* pertaining to the right and left sides of a structure, plane, etc. **2.** pertaining to or affecting two or both sides, factions, parties, or the like: *bilateral agreement; bilateral sponsorship.* **3.** located on opposite sides of an axis; two-sided, esp. when of equal size, value, etc. **4.** *Chiefly Law.* (of a contract) binding the parties to reciprocal obligations. **5.** through both parents equally: *bilateral affiliation.* Cf. **unilateral** (def. 9). [BI-[1] + LATERAL] —**bi·lat′er·al·ism, bi·lat′er·al·ness,** *n.* —**bi·lat′er·al·ly,** *adv.*

Bil·ba·o (bēl bä′ō), *n.* **1.** a seaport in N Spain, near the Bay of Biscay. 267,293 (est. 1960). **2.** *U.S. Furniture.* a mirror of the late 18th century, originally imported from Spain, having a frame partly or wholly of marble and a gilt openwork cresting.

bil·ber·ry (bil′ber′ē, -bə rē), *n., pl.* **-ries.** the fruit of several shrubby species of the genus *Vaccinium.* [*obs. bil* (< Scand; cf. Dan *bölle* bilberry) + BERRY]

bil·bo[1] (bil′bō), *n., pl.* **-boes.** Usually, **bilboes.** a long iron bar or bolt with sliding shackles and a lock, formerly used to confine the feet of prisoners. [earlier *bilbow* < ?]

bil·bo[2] (bil′bō), *n., pl.* **-boes.** *Archaic.* a finely tempered sword. [short for *Bilboa blade* sword made in *Bilboa* (var. of BILBAO)]

Bilbo[1]

bil·by (bil′bē), *n., pl.* **-bies.** See **rabbit bandicoot.** Also, **bil′bi.** [< native Austral]

Bil·dad (bil′dad), *n.* a friend of Job. Job 2:11. Also, *Douay Bible,* **Baldad.**

bile (bīl), *n.* **1.** *Physiol.* a bitter, alkaline, yellow or greenish liquid, secreted by the liver, which aids esp. in the absorption and digestion of fats. **2.** ill temper; peevishness. [< F < L *bīl(is)*]

bi·lec·tion (bī lek′shən), *n.* bolection.

bile·stone (bīl′stōn′), *n.* gallstone. [BILE + STONE]

bilge (bilj), *n., v.,* **bilged, bilg·ing.** —*n.* **1.** *Naut.* **a.** either of the rounded areas that form the transition between the bottom and the sides on the exterior of a hull. **b.** Also, **bilges.** (in a hull with a double bottom) an enclosed area between frames at each side of the floors, where seepage collects. **c.** Also, **bilge well.** a well into which seepage drains to be pumped away. **d.** Also, **bilge water.** seepage accumulated in bilges. **2.** *Slang.* foolish, offensive, or worthless talk or ideas. **3.** the widest circumference or belly of a cask. —*v.i.* **4.** *Naut.* **a.** to leak in the bilge. **b.** (of white paint) to turn yellow. **5.** to bulge or swell out. —*v.t.* **6.** *Naut.* to damage the lower part of (a hull) so as to open it to the sea. [perh. var. of BULGE]

bilge′ block′, *Naut.* a wedge-shaped block supporting part of the bilge of a vessel in drydock.

bilge′ board′, *Naut.* either of two boards able to be lowered from the bilges of a sailing vessel at an angle to the perpendicular so that when the board on the lee side of the vessel is lowered, it offers a vertical fore-and-aft surface to resist the pressure of the wind when the vessel heels.

bilge-hoop (bilj′ho͞op′), *n.* the hoop of a barrel or cask nearest the bilge.

bilge′ keel′, *Naut.* either of two keellike projections extending lengthwise along a ship's bilge, one on each side, to retard rolling. Also called **bilge′ piece′, rolling chock.**

bilge′ rail′, *Naut.* a rail fitted on the bilge of a lifeboat to permit persons in the water to hold onto the boat if it is overturned. Also called **keel rail.**

bilge′ wa′ter, 1. *Naut.* bilge (def. 1d). **2.** *Slang.* nonsense; rubbish.

bilge·way (bilj′wā′), *n.* any of the longitudinal timbers placed under the bilge of a ship on the ways. [BILGE + WAY]

bilge′ well′, *Naut.* bilge (def. 1c).

bilg·y (bil′jē), *adj.,* **bilg·i·er, bilg·i·est.** *Naut.* smelling like bilge water. [BILGE + -Y[1]]

Bil·hah (bil′hə), *n.* the mother of Dan and Naphtali. Gen. 30:1–8. Also, *Douay Bible,* **Bala.**

bil·har·zi·a·sis (bil′här zī′ə sis), *n.* *Pathol.* schistosomiasis. Also, **bil·har·zi·o·sis** (bil här′zē ō′sis). [named after Theodor *Bilharz* (d.1862), German physician; see -IASIS]

bil·i·ar·y (bil′ē er′ē), *adj.* **1.** *Physiol.* **a.** of bile. **b.** conveying bile: *a biliary duct.* **2.** *Archaic.* bilious. [< NL *biliāri(s),* equiv. to L *bīli(s)* BILE + *-āris* -ARY]

bil′iary cal′culus, *Pathol.* gallstone.

bi·lin·e·ar (bī lin′ē ər), *adj.* *Math.* **1.** of, pertaining to, or having reference to two lines: *bilinear coordinates.* **2.** of the first degree in each of two variables, as an equation. [BI-[1] + LINEAR]

bilin′ear form′, *Math.* a function or functional of two variables which is linear with respect to each variable when the other variable is held fixed.

bilin′ear transforma′tion, *Math.* See **Möbius transformation.**

bi·lin·e·ate (bī lin′ē āt′, -it), *adj.* *Zool.* marked with two usually parallel lines. Also, **bi·lin′e·at′ed.** [BI-[1] + LINEATE]

bi·lin·gual (bī liŋ′gwəl), *adj.* **1.** able to speak one's native language and another with approximately equal facility. **2.** spoken or written in two different languages: *Public notices at the embassy are bilingual.* —*n.* **3.** bilinguist. [< L *bilingu(is)* (*bi-* BI-[1] + *lingu-,* s. of *lingua* tongue + *-is* adj. suffix) + -AL[1]] —**bi·lin′gual·ly,** *adv.*

bi·lin·gual·ism (bī liŋ′gwə liz′əm), *n.* **1.** habitual use of two languages. **2.** fluent command or ability in two languages. Also, **bi·lin·gual·i·ty** (bī′liŋ gwal′i tē). [BILINGUAL + -ISM]

bi·lin·guist (bī liŋ′gwist), *n.* a person who is fluent in two languages. [BI-[1] + LINGUIST]

bil·ious (bil′yəs), *adj.* **1.** *Physiol., Pathol.* pertaining to bile or to an excess secretion of bile. **2.** *Pathol.* suffering from, caused by, or attended by trouble with the bile or liver. **3.** peevish; irritable; cranky. **4.** extremely unpleasant or distasteful: *a long scarf of bright, bilious green.* [< L *bīliōs(us).* See BILE, -OUS] —**bil′ious·ly,** *adv.* —**bil′ious·ness,** *n.*

bil′ious chol′era, *Pathol.* a form of cholera characterized by bilious feces. Cf. **cholera** (def. 1).

bi·lit·er·al (bī lit′ər əl), *adj.* **1.** using or consisting of two letters. **2.** (of Semitic roots) having a shape consisting of two consonants. [BI-[1] + LITERAL] —**bi·lit′er·al·ism,** *n.*

bi·lith (bī′lith), *n.* a prehistoric structure consisting of a horizontal stone slab supported by an upright stone. Also, **bi·lith·on** (bī lith′on). [BI-[1] + -LITH]

-bility, a suffix used to form nouns from adjectives with stems in **-ble:** *nobility; credibility.* Also, **-ability, -ibility.** [ME *-bilite* < MF < L *-bilitāt-* (s. of *-bilitās*). See -BLE, -ITY]

bilk (bilk), *v.t.* **1.** to evade payment of (a debt). **2.** to defraud; cheat: *He tried to bilk the government out of his back taxes.* **3.** to frustrate: *She bilked his efforts to divorce her.* **4.** to escape from; elude: *He bilked his creditors and got out of the country.* —*n.* **5.** a cheat; swindler. **6.** *Obs.* a trick; fraud; deceit. [?] —**bilk′er,** *n.*

bill[1] (bil), *n.* **1.** a statement of money owed for goods or services supplied. **2.** See **bill of exchange. 3.** a piece of paper money worth a specified amount: *a ten-dollar bill; a five-dollar bill.* **4.** *Slang.* one hundred dollars. **5.** *Govt.* a form or draft of a proposed statute presented to a legislature, but not yet enacted or passed and made law. **6.** a written or printed public notice or advertisement: *Post no bills.* **7.** any written paper containing a statement of particulars: *a bill of charges; a bill of expenditures.* **8.** *Law.* a written statement, usually of complaint, presented to a court. **9.** playbill. **10.** entertainment scheduled for presentation; program: *a good bill at the movies.* **11.** *Obs.* **a.** a promissory note. **b.** a written and sealed document. **c.** a written, formal petition. **12. fill the bill,** *Informal.* to fulfill all requirements: *As a sprightly situation comedy this show fills the bill.* —*v.t.* **13.** to enter (charges) in a bill; make a bill or list of: *to bill goods.* **14.** to charge for by bill; send a bill to: *The store will bill me.* **15.** to advertise by bill or public notice: *A new actor was billed for this week.* **16.** to schedule on a program: *The management billed the play for two weeks.* [ME *bille* < AL *billa* for LL *bulla* BULL[2]] —**bill′er,** *n.*
—**Syn. 1.** reckoning, invoice, statement. **6.** bulletin, handbill, notice, advertisement, poster, placard, announcement, circular, throw-away, flyer, broadside.

bill[2] (bil), *n.* **1.** the parts of a bird's jaws that are covered with a horny or leathery sheath; beak. **2.** *Geol.* a beaklike promontory or headland. —*v.i.* **3.** to join bills or beaks, as doves. **4. bill and coo,** to whisper endearments, as lovers: *My sister and her boyfriend were billing and cooing on the front porch.* [ME *bile, bille,* OE *bile* beak, trunk; akin to BILL[3]]

bill[3] (bil), *n.* **1.** a medieval shafted weapon having at its head a hooklike cutting blade with a beak at the back. **2.** Also called **billman.** a person armed with a bill. **3.** Also called **billhook.** a sharp, hooked instrument used for pruning, cutting, etc. **4.** Also called **pea.** *Naut.* the extremity of a fluke of an anchor. [ME *bil,* OE *bill* sword; c. OHG *bil* pickax]

Bill[3] (def. 3)

bill[4] (bil), *n.* *Brit. Dial.* the cry of the bittern. [akin to BELL[2], BELLOW]

Bill (bil), *n.* a boy's given name, form of **William.**

bill·a·ble (bil′ə bəl), *adj.* that may or should be billed. [BILL[1] + -ABLE]

bil·la·bong (bil′ə boŋ′), *n.* *Australian.* **1.** a branch of a river flowing away from the main stream but leading to no other body of water; a blind or dead-end channel. **2.** a creek bed holding water only in the rainy season; a dried-up watercourse. **3.** a stagnant backwater or slough formed by receding flood waters. [< native Austral]

bill·board[1] (bil′bōrd′, -bôrd′), *n.* **1.** *U.S.* a flat surface or board, usually outdoors, on which advertisements or notices are posted. **2.** *Radio and Television.* an announcement for eliciting the interest of the audience, usually made at the beginning and end of a broadcast and containing a list of cast members, entertainers, or features of the program, as well as identification of the sponsor. [BILL[1] + BOARD]

bill·board[2] (bil′bōrd′, -bôrd′), *n.* *Naut.* See **anchor bed.** [BILL[3] + BOARD]

bill-brok·er (bil′brō′kər), *n.* a money dealer who buys, sells, discounts, or negotiates bills of exchange or promissory notes.

bill·bug (bil′bug′), *n.* any of several weevils, esp. of the genera *Calendra* and *Sitophilus,* that feed on various grasses. [BILL[2] + BUG[1]]

bil·let[1] (bil′it), *n., v.,* **-let·ed, -let·ing.** —*n.* **1.** lodging for a soldier, esp. lodging in private or nonmilitary public buildings. **2.** *Mil.* an official order, written or verbal, directing the person to whom it is addressed to provide such lodging. **3.** a place assigned, as a bunk, berth, or the like, to a member of a ship's crew. **4.** job; appointment. **5.** *Obs.* a written note, short letter, or the like. —*v.t.* **6.** *Mil.* to direct (a soldier) by ticket, note, or verbal order, where to lodge. **7.** to provide lodging for; quarter: *We arranged with the townspeople to billet the students.* —*v.i.* **8.** to obtain lodging; stay: *They billeted in youth hostels.* [late ME *bylet, billett* < AL *billetta* (*bill(a)* BILL[1] + *-etta* dim. suffix)] —**bil′let·er,** *n.*

bil·let[2] (bil′it), *n.* **1.** a small chunk of wood; a short section of a log, esp. one cut for fuel. **2.** *Metalworking.* a comparatively narrow, generally square, bar of steel, esp. one rolled or forged from an ingot; a narrow bloom. **3.** an iron or steel slab upon concrete, serving as a footing to a column. **4.** *Archit.* any of a series of closely spaced cylindrical objects, often in several rows, used as ornaments in a hollow molding or cornice. **5.** a strap that passes through a buckle, as to connect the ends of a girth. **6.** a pocket or loop for securing the end of a strap that has been buckled. **7.** thumbpiece. **8.** *Heraldry.* a small, rectangular figure with the longer sides generally vertical, said to represent a block of wood. [late ME *bylet, bel(l)et* < MF *billette,* equiv. to *bille* log, tree-trunk (? < Gmc; see BILL[2]) + *-ette* -ETTE]

Billets[2] (def. 4)

bil′let car′, a low-sided railroad car for transporting billets and other heavy materials.

bil·let-doux (bil′ē do͞o′, bil′ā-; *Fr.* bē yā do͞o′), *n., pl.* **bil·lets-doux** (bil′ē do͞oz′, bil′ā-; *Fr.* bē yā do͞o′). a love letter. [< F: lit., sweet little letter. See BILLET[1], DOUCE]

bil·let·head (bil′it hed′), *n.* *Naut.* a carved ornamental scroll or volute terminating a stem or cutwater at its upper end in place of a figurehead. Also called **scrollhead.** [BILLET[2] + HEAD]

bil·let·y (bil′i tē), *adj.* *Heraldry.* semé of billets: *azure, billety or.* [< F *billeté;* see BILLET[2]]

bill·fish (bil′fish′), *n., pl.* (*esp. collectively*) **-fish,** (*esp. referring to two or more kinds or species*) **-fish·es.** any of various fishes having a long, sharp bill or snout, as a gar, needlefish, or saury. [BILL[2] + FISH]

bill·fold (bil′fōld′), *n.* *U.S.* a folding leather case for carrying paper money, personal cards, etc. Also called, *esp. Brit.,* **notecase.** [BILL[1] + FOLD[1]]

bill·head (bil′hed′), *n.* **1.** a printed heading, usually giving one's name and address, on a sheet of paper on which a statement of money due is rendered. **2.** a sheet of paper with this heading. **3.** a printed form for itemized statements. [BILL[1] + HEAD]

bill·hook (bil′ho͝ok′), *n.* bill[3] (def. 3). [BILL[3] + HOOK]

bil·liard (bil′yərd), *adj.* **1.** of or used in billiards. —*n.* **2.** *U.S. Informal.* carom (def. 1). [< F *billard* cue, equiv. to *bille* stick (see BILLET[2]) + *-ard* -ARD]

bil′liard ball′, one of the balls used in the game of billiards.

bil′liard par′lor, poolroom (def. 1).

bil′liard room′, a room in a house, club, etc., where billiards is played.

bil·liards (bil′yərdz), *n.* (*construed as sing.*) any of several games played with hard balls of ivory or of a similar material that are driven with a cue on a cloth-covered table enclosed by a raised rim of rubber, esp. a game played with a cue ball and two object balls on a table without pockets. Cf. **pool**[2] (def. 8). [pl. of BILLIARD] —**bil′liard·ist,** *n.*

bil′liard ta′ble, an oblong table with a slate surface covered by a cloth and enclosed by a raised rim of vulcanized rubber, for use in playing billiards.

Bil·lie (bil′ē), *n.* **1.** a boy's given name, form of **William. 2.** a girl's given name, often a form of **Beverly.** Also, **Billy, Billye.**

bill·ing (bil′iŋ), *n.* **1.** the relative position in which a performer or act is listed on handbills, posters, etc.: *A star usually receives billing above the title of the play.* **2.** advertising; publicity: *The show was a sell-out weeks ahead of the opening because of advance billing.* **3.** the amount of business done by a firm, esp. an advertising agency, within a specified period of time. [BILL[1] + -ING[1]]

bill′ing machine′, an automatic or semiautomatic business machine used to itemize and total customer accounts, produce bills, post account records, etc.

Bil·lings (bil′iŋz), *n.* **1. Josh,** pen name of Henry Wheeler Shaw. **2.** a city in S Montana. 52,851 (1960).

bil·lings·gate (bil′iŋz gāt′, *or, esp. Brit.,* -git), *n.* coarsely or vulgarly abusive language. [orig. the kind of speech often heard at *Billingsgate,* a London fishmarket at the *gate* named after a certain *Billing*]
—**Syn.** vituperation, vilification, invective, scurrility, vulgarity.

bil·lion (bil′yən), *n., pl.* **-lions,** (*as after a numeral*) **-lion,** *adj.* —*n.* **1.** *U.S.* a thousand millions. **2.** *Brit.* a million millions. —*adj.* **3.** equal in number to a billion. [< F; see BI-[1], MILLION] —**bil′lionth,** *adj., n.*

bil·lion·aire (bil′yə nâr′), *n.* a person who has assets worth a billion dollars, francs, pounds, or the like. [BILLION + *-aire,* modeled after *millionare*]

Bil·li·ton (bē′lē ton′, bē lē′ton), *n.* an island in Indonesia, between Borneo and Sumatra. ab. 73,500; 1866 sq. mi. Also, **Belitong, Belitoeng, Belitung.**

bill·man (bil′mən), *n., pl.* **-men.** bill[3] (def. 2). [BILL[2] + MAN[1]]

bill′ of attain′der, *Hist.* an act of legislature finding a person guilty of treason or felony.

bill′ of en′try, an account of imported or exported goods kept at a custom house.

bill′ of exchange′, a written authorization or order to pay a specified sum of money to a specified person.

bill′ of fare′, a list of foods that are served; menu.

bill′ of goods′, **1.** a quantity of saleable items, as an order, shipment, etc. **2.** *U.S. Slang.* merchandise, a business deal, story, argument, etc., esp. something unwanted, undesirable, or unbelievable: *He tried to sell me a bill of goods, but I wouldn't listen to him.*

bill′ of health′, **1.** a certificate, carried by a ship, attesting to the prevailing state of health in a port from which it has come. **2. clean bill of health,** *Informal.* an attestation of fitness or qualification; a commendation: *The investigation committee gave him a clean bill of health.*

bill′ of lad′ing, a written receipt given by a carrier for goods accepted for transportation. *Abbr.:* b.l., B.L., b/l, B/L

bill′ of partic′ulars, *Law.* **1.** a formal statement prepared by a plaintiff or a defendant itemizing his claim or counterclaim in a suit. **2.** an itemized statement prepared by the prosecution and informing the accused of the charges in a criminal case.

Bill′ of Rights′, **1.** (*l.c.*) a formal statement of the fundamental rights of the people of a nation. **2.** such a statement incorporated in the Constitution of the United States as Amendments 1–10, and in all State constitutions. **3.** an English statute of 1689 confirming, with minor changes, the Declaration of Rights, declaring the rights and liberties of the subjects and settling the succession in William III and Mary II.

bill′ of sale′, a document transferring title in personal property from seller to buyer. *Abbr.:* b.s., B.S., b/s, B/S

bil·lon (bil′ən), *n.* **1.** an alloy used in coinage, consisting of gold or silver with a larger amount of base metal. **2.** an alloy of silver with copper or the like, used for coins of small denomination. **3.** any coin struck from such an alloy. [< F: debased metal, orig. ingot, equiv. to MF *bille* log (see BILLET[2]) + *-on* n. suffix]

bil·low (bil′ō), *n.* **1.** a great wave or surge of the sea. **2.** any surging mass: *billows of smoke.* —*v.i.* **3.** to rise or roll in or like billows; surge. **4.** to swell out, puff up, etc., as by the action of wind: *flags billowing in the breeze.* —*v.t.* **5.** to make rise, surge, swell, or the like: *A sudden wind billowed the tent alarmingly.* [< Scand; cf. Icel *bylgja* a wave, c. MLG *bulge;* akin to OE *gebylgan* to anger, provoke]

bil′low cloud′, a cloud consisting of broad, parallel bands oriented perpendicularly to the wind.

Bil·lows (bil′ōz), *n.* **Bay of.** See **Sinus Aestuum.**

bil·low·y (bil′ō ē), *adj.,* **-low·i·er, -low·i·est.** characterized by or full of billows; surging: *a rough, billowy sea.* [BILLOW + -Y[1]] —**bil′low·i·ness,** *n.*

bill·post·er (bil′pō′stər), *n.* one who posts bills and advertisements. Also called **bill·stick·er** (bil′stik′ər). [BILL[1] + POSTER] —**bill′post′ing, bill′stick′ing,** *n.*

Bill·roth (bil′rōt), *n.* **Al·bert Chris·ti·an The·o·dor** (äl′bert kris′tē än′ tā′ō dōr′), 1829–94, Austrian surgeon.

bil·ly (bil′ē), *n., pl.* **-lies.** **1.** *Informal.* a policeman's club or baton. Also called **billy club.** **2.** a heavy wooden stick used as a weapon; cudgel. **3.** *Scot Dial.* comrade. **4.** Also called **bil·ly·can** (bil′ē kan′). *Australian.* any container in which water may be carried and boiled over a campfire, ranging from a makeshift tin can to a special earthenware kettle; any pot or kettle in which tea is boiled over a campfire. **5.** *Textiles Brit.* a roving machine. [BILL[3] + -Y[2]]

Bil·ly (bil′ē), *n.* **1.** a boy's given name, form of **William.** **2.** a girl's given name, usually a form of **Beverly.** Also, **Billie, Bil′lye.**

Bil·ly (bil′ē), *n.* a crater in the third quadrant of the face of the moon: about 31 miles in diameter.

bil·ly·boy (bil′ē boi′), *n. Brit.* a sea-going or river barge having a flat bottom and a bluff bow, often rigged as a sloop or ketch, and sometimes having leeboards. [*Billy* (the name) + BOY]

Bil′ly Budd′ (bud), a short novel by Herman Melville, written shortly before his death: first published in 1924.

bil′ly club′, billy (def. 1).

bil·ly·cock (bil′ē kok′), *n. Chiefly Brit.* **1.** a round, low-crowned, soft felt hat. **2.** a derby hat. Also called **bil′lycock hat′.** [alter. of *bullycocked* (*hat*); see BULLY[1], COCKED]

bil′ly goat′, a male goat.

Bil′ly the Kid′, **1.** (*William H. Bonney*) 1859–81, U. S. outlaw. **2.** (*italics*) a ballet (1938) by Aaron Copland.

bi·lo·bate (bī lō′bāt), *adj.* consisting of or divided into two lobes. Also, **bi·lo′bat·ed, bi·lobed** (bī′lōbd′). [BI-[1] + LOBATE]

bi·lo·ca·tion (bī′lō kā′shən), *n.* the state of being or the ability to be in two places at the same time. [BI-[1] + LOCATION]

bi·loc·u·lar (bī lok′yə lər), *adj. Biol.* divided into two chambers or cells, or containing two cells internally. Also, **bi·loc·u·late** (bī lok′yə lit, -lāt′). [BI-[1] + LOCULAR]

Bi·lox·i (bi lok′sē, -luk′-), *n.* a city in SE Mississippi, on the Gulf of Mexico. 44,053 (1960).

bil·sted (bil′sted), *n.* the liquidambar tree. [?]

bil·tong (bil′tông′), *n.* (in South Africa) strips of lean meat dried in the open air. [< SAfrD, equiv. to *bil* rump + *tong* TONGUE]

Bim (bim), *n.* a boy's given name.

bi·mac·u·late (bī mak′yə lit), *adj. Zool.* marked with two spots. Also, **bi·mac·u·lat·ed** (bī mak′yə lā′tid). [BI-[1] + MACULATE]

bi·mah (bē mä′, bē′mə, bim′ə), *n.* a platform in a synagogue holding the reading table used in chanting or reading the designated portions of the Torah and the Prophets on the days prescribed. Also, **bema, bi′ma.** Also called **almemar.** [< Yiddish *bime* < Russ *bima* < LGk, Gk *bēma;* see BEMA]

bi·mane (bī′mān), *n.* a bimanous animal. [BI-[1] + *mane* (< L *manus* hand)]

bim·a·nous (bim′ə nəs, bī mā′-), *adj. Zool.* having two hands, usually unlike the feet, as primates. [< NL *biman(a)* (*animalia*) two-handed (animals) + -OUS. See BIMANE]

bi·man·u·al (bī man′yo͞o əl), *adj.* involving or requiring the use of both hands. [BI-[1] + MANUAL] —**bi·man′u·al·ly,** *adv.*

bim·bo (bim′bō), *n., pl.* **-bos, -boes.** **1.** *Slang.* a man or fellow, often a disreputable one. **2.** a morally loose woman; tramp. [?]

bi·men·sal (bī men′səl), *adj. Obs.* occurring once in two months; bimonthly. [BI-[1] + MENSAL[1]]

bi·mes·ter (bī mes′tər, bī′mes-), *n.* a two-month period. [< L *bimēstr(is),* equiv. to *bi-* BI-[1] + *mē(n)s-* (s. of *mēnsis*) month + *-tris* adj. suffix]

bi·mes·tri·al (bī mes′trē əl), *adj.* **1.** occurring every two months; bimonthly. **2.** lasting two months. [< L *bimestri(s)* BIMESTER + -AL[1]]

bi·me·tal·lic (bī′mə tal′ik), *adj.* **1.** made or consisting of two metals. **2.** pertaining to bimetallism. **3.** *Engraving.* (of an offset plate) consisting of a face layer of chromium, stainless steel, or chemically prepared aluminum over a layer of copper. [< F *bimétallique.* See BI-[1], METALLIC]

bi′metal′lic bal′ance, *Horol.* See **compensating balance.**

bi·met·al·lism (bī met′əliz′əm), *n.* **1.** the use of two metals, ordinarily gold and silver, at a fixed relative value, as the monetary standard. **2.** the doctrine or policies supporting such a standard. [BI-[1] + METAL + -ISM] —**bi·met′al·list,** *n.* —**bi·met′al·lis′tic,** *adj.*

bi·meth·yl (bī meth′əl), *n. Chem.* ethane. [BI-[1] + METHYL]

bi·mil·len·ni·um (bī′mi len′ē əm), *n., pl.* **-len·ni·ums, -len·ni·a** (-len′ē ə). **1.** two thousand years. **2.** a two thousandth anniversary. [BI-[1] + MILLENNIUM]

Bim′i·ni Is′lands (bim′ə nē), a group of islands in the W Bahamas: resort center; supposed site of the Fountain of Youth for which Ponce de León searched. 1222 (est. 1955); 9 sq. mi. Also called **Bim′i·nis.**

bi·mod·al (bī mōd′əl), *adj. Statistics.* (of a distribution) having two modes. [BI-[1] + MODAL] —**bi′mo·dal′i·ty,** *n.*

bi·mod·ule (bī′moj′o͞ol), *n. Math.* a module with a ring of right operators and a ring of left operators. [BI-[1] + MODULE]

bi·mo·lec·u·lar (bī′mə lek′yə lər), *adj. Chem.* having or involving two molecules. [BI-[1] + MOLECULAR] —**bi′mo·lec′u·lar·ly,** *adv.*

bi·month·ly (bī munth′lē), *adj., n., pl.* **-lies,** *adv.* —*adj.* **1.** occurring every two months. **2.** (loosely) occurring twice a month; semimonthly. —*n.* **3.** a bimonthly publication. —*adv.* **4.** every two months: *Next year we plan six field trips to take place bimonthly.* **5.** (loosely) twice a month; semimonthly. [BI-[1] + MONTHLY]

—**Usage.** Since it is not always clear which meaning of BIMONTHLY is intended—"twice a month" or "every two months"—the use of SEMIMONTHLY for "twice a month" is preferable because it is unambiguous. Since there is no single, unambiguous term for "every two months," this phrase itself is the least confusing to use.

bi·mo·tor (bī′mō′tər), *n.* an airplane that has two engines. [BI-[1] + MOTOR]

bi·mo·tored (bī mō′tərd), *adj. Aeron.* having two engines. [BI-[1] + MOTORED]

bin (bin), *n., v.,* **binned, bin·ning.** —*n.* **1.** a box or enclosed place for storing grain, coal, or the like. —*v.t.* **2.** to store in a bin. [ME *binne,* OE *binn(e)* crib, perh. < Celt; cf. Welsh *benn* cart]

bin-, a learned borrowing from Latin meaning "two," "two at a time," used in the formation of compound words: *binary; binocular.* Cf. **bi-**[1]. [comb. form of L *bīnī* two by two]

bi·nal (bīn′əl), *adj.* **1.** double; twofold. **2.** *Phonet.* (of a syllable) having two pitch peaks. [< NL *bīnāl(is)* twin, double. See BIN-, -AL[1]]

bi·na·ry (bī′nə rē), *adj., n., pl.* **-ries.** —*adj.* **1.** consisting of, indicating, or involving two. **2.** of or pertaining to a system of numerical notation to the base 2, in which each place of a number, expressed as 0 or 1, corresponds to a power of 2. The decimal number 58 appears as 111010 in binary notation, since $58 = 1 \times 2^5 + 1 \times 2^4 + 1 \times 2^3 + 0 \times 2^2 + 1 \times 2^1 + 0 \times 2^0$. **3.** of or pertaining to the digits or numbers used in binary notation. **4.** *Math.* **a.** of or pertaining to a binary system. **b.** (of an operation) assigning a third quantity to two given quantities, as in the addition of two numbers. **5.** *Chem.* noting a compound containing only two elements or groups, as sodium chloride, methyl bromide, or methyl hydroxide. **6.** *Metall.* (of an alloy) having two principal constituents. —*n.* **7.** a whole composed of two. **8.** *Astron.* See **binary star.** **9.** Also called **bi′nary num′ber.** a number of a binary system. [< LL *bīnāri(us),* equiv. to *bīn(ī)* (see BIN-) + *-ārius* -ARY]

bi′nary cell′, *Computer Technol.* an electronic element that can assume either of two stable states and is capable of storing a binary digit.

bi′nary code′, *Computer Technol.* a system of representing letters, numbers, or other characters, using binary notation.

bi′na·ry-cod·ed dec′imal sys′tem (bī′nə rē-kō′did), a numerical system in which each decimal digit is represented by a unique collection of binary digits, not necessarily the same as those used in binary notation. *Abbr.:* BCD

bi′nary fis′sion, *Biol.* fission into two organisms approximately equal in size. Cf. **multiple fission.**

bi′nary form′, a basic musical form having two closely related sections.

bi′nary opposi′tion, *Ling.* a relation between the members of a pair of linguistic items, as a pair of distinctive features, such that one is the absence of the other, as voicelessness and voice, or that one is at the opposite pole from the other, as stridency and mellowness.

bi′nary star′, *Astron.* a system of two stars that revolve round their common center of gravity.

bi′nary sys′tem, **1.** a system involving only two elements, as 0 and 1 or yes and no. **2.** a system of counting or measurement whose units are powers of two. Cf. **binary** (def. 2). Also called **dyadic system.**

bi·nate (bī′nāt), *adj. Bot.* double; produced or borne in pairs. [< NL *bīnāt(us),* appar. abstracted from LL *combīnātus* yoked together. See BIN-, -ATE[1]] —**bi′nate·ly,** *adv.*

Binate leaf

bi·na·tion (bī nā′shən), *n.* celebration of Mass twice on the same day by the same priest. [< NL *bīnātiōn-* (s. of *bīnātiō*), equiv. to L *bīn(ī)* BIN- + *-ātiōn-* -ATION]

bin·au·ral (bī nôr′əl, bin ôr′əl), *adj.* **1.** of, with, or for both ears: *binaural hearing; a binaural stethoscope.* **2.** having two ears. [BIN- + AURAL[2]]

binau′ral broad′casting, a system of radio broadcasting in which a microphone in one part of a studio broadcasts via FM and one in another part via AM. FM and AM receivers similarly placed provide a stereophonic effect.

Bin·chois (*Fr.* baN shwa′), *n.* **Gil·les** (*Du.* KHil′əs; *Fr.* zhēl) or **E·gid·i·us** (*Du.* ā KHē′dē o͞os′), c1400–60, Flemish composer.

bind (bīnd), *v.,* **bound, bind·ing,** *n.* —*v.t.* **1.** to fasten or secure with a band or bond. **2.** to encircle with a band or ligature: *She bound her hair with a ribbon.* **3.** to swathe or bandage (often fol. by *up*): *to bind up one's wounds.* **4.** to fasten around; fix in place by girding: *They bound his hands behind him.* **5.** to tie up anything, esp. sheaves of grain. **6.** to cause to cohere: *Ice bound the soil.* **7.** to unite by any legal or moral tie: *to be bound by the ties of matrimony.* **8.** to hold to a particular state, place, employment, etc.: *Business kept him bound to the city.* **9.** to place under obligation or compulsion (usually used passively): *We are bound by good sense to obey the country's laws.* **10.** *Law.* to put under legal obligation, as to keep the peace or appear as a witness (often fol. by *over*): *This action binds them to keep the peace. He was bound over to the grand jury.* **11.** to make compulsory or obligatory: *to bind the order with a deposit.* **12.** to indenture as an apprentice (often fol. by *out*): *In his youth his father bound him out to a coppersmith.* **13.** (of clothing) to chafe or restrict (the wearer): *He wants a shirt that doesn't bind him.* **14.** *Pathol.* to hinder or restrain (the bowels) from their natural operations; constipate. **15.** to fasten or secure within a cover, as a book: *They will bind the new book in morocco.* **16.** to cover the edge of, as for protection or ornament: *Please bind the carpet before cleaning it.* **17.** *Falconry.* (of a hawk) to grasp prey firmly in flight. —*v.i.* **18.** to become compact or solid; cohere. **19.** to be obligatory: *an obligation that binds.* **20.** to chafe or restrict, as poorly fitting garments: *This jacket binds through the shoulders.* **21.** to stick fast, as a drill in a hole. **22. bind off,** *Textiles.* to loop (one stitch) over another in making an edge on knitted fabric. —*n.* **23.** act or process of binding; state or instance of being bound. **24.** something that binds. **25.** *Music.* a tie, slur, or brace. **26.** *Falconry.* the act of binding. **27. in a bind,** *Slang.* in a predicament; under unusual pressure: *This schedule has us in a bind.* [ME *bind(en),* OE *bindan;* c. OHG *bintan,* Icel *binda,* Goth *bindan,* Skt *bandh(ati)*] —**bind′a·ble,** *adj.*
—**Syn. 1.** gird, attach, tie. **2.** confine, restrain. **9.** engage, oblige, obligate. —**Ant. 1.** untie.

B.Ind. Ed., Bachelor of Industrial Education.

bind·er[1] (bīn′dər), *n.* **1.** one who or that which binds. **2.** a detachable cover for loose papers. **3.** one who binds books; a bookbinder. **4.** *Agric.* **a.** an attachment to a harvester or reaper for binding the cut grain. **b.** a machine that cuts and binds grain. **5.** *Insurance.* an agreement by which property or liability coverage is granted pending issuance of a policy. **6.** *Metall.* **a.** a material for holding crushed ore dust together while it is being sintered. **b.** (in powder metallurgy) a substance for holding compacted powder together while it is being sintered. **7.** *Chem.* any substance that causes the components of a mixture to cohere. **8.** *Painting.* a vehicle in which pigment is suspended. **9.** *Building Trades.* **a.** a stone, as a perpend, for bonding masonry together. **b.** a girder supporting the ends of two sets of floor joists. **c.** a material for holding loose material together, as in a macadamized road. [BIND + -ER[1]]

bind·er[2] (bīn′dər), *n. Brit., Australian Slang.* a large quantity, esp. of food. [orig. food that binds, i.e., constipates]

bind·er·y (bīn′də rē, -drē), *n., pl.* **-er·ies.** a place where books are bound. [BIND + -ERY]

bind·heim·ite (bind′hī mīt′), *n.* a mineral, hydrous antimonate of lead, resulting from the alteration of lead antimony ores. [named after J. J. Bindheim (d. 1825), German chemist; see -ITE[1]]

bind·ing (bīn′ding), *n.* **1.** act of fastening, securing, uniting, or the like. **2.** anything that binds. **3.** the covering within which the leaves of a book are bound. **4.** a strip of material that protects or decorates the edge of a tablecloth, rug, etc. —*adj.* **5.** having power to bind or oblige; obligatory: *a binding engagement.* [BIND + -ING[1], -ING[2]] —**bind′ing·ly,** *adv.* —**bind′ing·ness,** *n.*

bind′ing en′ergy, *Physics.* **1.** Also called **separation energy.** the energy required to decompose a molecule, atom, or nucleus into its constituent particles, equal to the energy equivalent of the mass defect. **2.** the energy required to separate a single particle or group of particles from a molecule, atom, or nucleus. Cf. **mass defect.**

bind′ing post′, one of several metal pegs or rods, fitted into a loose-leaf binder, for holding sheets with prepunched holes.

bind′ing raft′er, a timber for supporting rafters between their extremities, as a purlin.

bind′ing strake′, *Shipbuilding.* **1.** the second strake from the sheer strake in a carvel-built wooden open boat, below the landing strake. **2.** an especially strong strake of planking. **3.** Also called **bolt strake.** a thick strake of deck planking on one side of a hatch.

bin·dle (bin′dəl), *n. Slang.* a bundle, usually of bedding, carried by a hobo. [special use of Scot *bindle* binding-rope, ME *bindel,* OE *bindele* bandage]

bin′dle stiff′, *Slang.* a hobo.

bind·weed (bīnd′wēd′), *n.* any of various twining or vinelike plants, esp. certain species of the genus *Convolvulus.* [BIND + WEED[1]]

bine (bīn), *n.* **1.** a twining plant stem, as of the hop. **2.** any bindweed. **3.** woodbine (defs. 1, 2). [var. of BIND]

Bi·net (bi nā′; *Fr.* bē ne′), *n.* **Al·fred** (al′frid; *Fr.* al-fred′), 1857–1911, French psychologist: co-deviser of the Binet-Simon scale.

Bi·net′-Si′mon scale′ (bi nā′sī′mən; *Fr.* bē ne′sē-mōN′), *Psychol.* a test for determining the relative development of the intelligence, esp. of children, consisting of a series of questions and tasks graded with reference to the ability of the normal child to deal with them at successive age levels. Also called **Binet′-Si′mon test′, Binet′ scale′, Binet′ test′.** Cf. **Stanford-Binet test.**

bing[1] (biŋ), *n. Brit. Dial.* a heap or pile. [ME < Scand; cf. OIcel *bingr* bunk (now heap, pile), Dan *bing* bin]

bing[2] (biŋ), *v.i. Obs.* to go. [?]

Bing (biŋ), *n.* **1.** a variety of sweet cherry having a dark red or blackish fruit. **2.** the fruit itself. Also called **Bing′ cher′ry.**

Bing (biŋ), *n.* **1. Rudolf,** born 1902: English opera impresario born in Austria; in the U.S. since 1949. **2.** a boy's given name.

binge (binj), *n. Informal.* a period of excessive indulgence, as in eating, drinking, etc.; spree. [dial. (Lincolnshire) *binge* to soak < ?]

Bing·en (biŋ′ən), *n.* a town in W West Germany, on the Rhine River: whirlpool; tourist center. 20,500 (1963).

Bing·ham (biŋ′əm), *n.* **George Caleb,** 1811–79, U.S. painter.

Bing·ham·ton (biŋ′əm tən), *n.* a city in S New York, on the Susquehanna River. 75,941 (1960).

bing·hi (biŋ′ī), *n.* (*sometimes cap.*) *Australian Slang.* an aborigine. [< native Austral]

bin·gle (biŋ′gəl), *n. Baseball Slang.* See **base hit.** [? B(AT[1] + S)INGLE]

bin·go (biŋ′gō), *n.* (*sometimes cap.*) a form of lotto in which numbered balls are drawn at random and players cover the corresponding numbers printed on their cards, the winner being the first to cover five numbers in any row or diagonal. [appar. alter. of BEANO[1]]

bin·gy (biŋ′ē), *n., pl.* **-gies.** *Australian.* belly. [native Austral]

Binh Dinh (bin′yə din′yə, bin′din′), a city in SE Vietnam. ab. 147,000. Also, **Binh′dinh′.**

bin·na·cle (bin′ə kəl), *n. Naut.* **1.** a stand of wood or nonmagnetic metal for supporting and housing a compass. **2.** *Obs.* a cupboard for holding a compass. [BIN + (*bitt*)-*acle* (late ME *bitakille*) < Pg *bitacol(a)* < L *habitācul(um)* lodge, equiv. to *habitā-* (see INHABIT) + *-culum* -CULE]

Binnacle
A, Opening through which compass is read; B, Quadrantal soft iron sphere; C, Flinders bar; D, Magnet chamber

bin·o·cle[1] (bin′ə kəl), *n.* binocular. [< F < L *bīn(ī)* BIN- + *oculus* eye]

bi·no·cle[2] (bī′nuk əl), *n.* a card game of the bezique family that is played by two persons with a 48-card pack, the lowest card of which is nine. [BI[1] + (PI)NOCHLE]

bin·oc·u·lar (bə nok′yə lər, bī-), *adj.* **1.** involving two eyes: *binocular vision.* —*n.* **2.** Usually, **binoculars.** Also called **pair′ of binoc′ulars, prism binoculars.** an optical device, providing good depth effect, for use with both eyes, consisting of two small telescopes fitted together side by side, each telescope having two prisms between the eyepiece and objective for erecting the image. [BIN- + OCULAR] —**bin·oc′u·lar′i·ty,** *n.* —**bin·oc′u·lar·ly,** *adv.*

binoc′ular fu′sion, *Ophthalm.* fusion (def. 5a).

bi·no·mi·al (bī nō′mē əl), *n.* **1.** *Algebra.* an expression that is a sum or difference of two terms, as $3x + 2y$ and $x^2 - 4x$. **2.** *Zool., Bot.* a taxonomic name consisting of a generic and specific term. —*adj.* **3.** *Algebra.* consisting of or pertaining to two terms or a binomial. **4.** *Zool., Bot.* consisting of or characterized by binomials. [< ML *binōmi(us)* having two names (r. L *binōminis*) + -AL[1]. See BI-[1], NOMINAL] —**bi·no′mi·al·ism,** *n.* —**bi·no′mi·al·ly,** *adv.*

bino′mial coeffi′cient, *Math.* any one of the coefficients of the variables in an expanded binomial series.

bino′mial distribu′tion, *Statistics.* a distribution giving the probability of obtaining a specified number of successes in a finite set of independent trials in which the probability of a success remains the same from trial to trial. Also called **Bernoulli distribution.**

bino′mial no′menclature, *Zool., Bot.* a system of nomenclature in which each organism is given a name that consists of a generic and a specific term.

bino′mial se′ries, *Math.* an infinite series obtained by expanding a binomial raised to a power that is not a positive integer.

bino′mial the′orem, *Math.* the theorem giving the expansion of a binomial raised to a given power expressed as

$$(x + y)^n = x^n + nx^{n-1}y + \frac{n(n-1)}{1\cdot 2}x^{n-2}y^2 + \frac{n(n-1)(n-2)}{1\cdot 2\cdot 3}x^{n-3}y^3 + \ldots + y^n.$$

bi·nor·mal (bī nôr′məl), *n. Geom.* the normal to a curve, lying in the osculating plane at a given point on the curve. [BI-[1] + NORMAL]

bi·nox·a·late (bī nok′sə lāt′, -lit), *n. Chem.* an acid containing the group HC_2O_4-, as ammonium binoxalate, $(NH_4)HC_2O_4$. [BIN- + OXALATE]

bin·tu·rong (bin to͝or′ông), *n.* an arboreal civet, *Arctictis binturong,* of Asia, having a long, prehensile tail. Also called **bearcat.** [< Malay]

bi·nu·cle·ate (bī no͞o′klē āt′, -nyo͞o′-), *adj.* having two nuclei, as certain cells. Also, **bi·nu′cle·ar, bi·nu′cle·at′ed.** [BI-[1] + NUCLEATE]

bio-, a prefix meaning "life" occurring in loan words from Greek (*biography*); on this model, used in the formation of compound words (*bioluminescence*). Also, *esp. before a vowel,* **bi-.** [comb. form of Gk *bíos* life; akin to L *vīvus* living, Skt *jīvás.* See QUICK]

bi·o·as·say (*n.* bī′ō ə sā′, -as′ā; *v.* bī′ō ə sā′), *n., v.,* **-sayed, -say·ing.** —*n.* **1.** determination of the biological activity or potency of a substance, as a vitamin or hormone, by testing its effect on the growth of an organism. —*v.t.* **2.** to subject to a bioassay. [BIO(LOGICAL) + ASSAY]

bi·o·as·tro·nau·tics (bī′ō as′trə nô′tiks), *n.* (*construed as sing.*) the science dealing with the effects of space travel upon life. [BIO- + ASTRONAUTICS]

bi·o·bib·li·og·ra·phy (bī′ō bib′lē og′rə fē), *n., pl.* **-phies.** a bibliography containing biographical sketches of the authors listed. [BIO- + BIBLIOGRAPHY] —**bi′o·bib′li·og′ra·pher,** *n.* —**bi·o·bib·li·o·graph·ic** (bī′ō bib′lē ə graf′ik), **bi′o·bib′li·o·graph′i·cal,** *adj.*

Bí·o-Bí·o (bē′ō bē′ō), *n.* a river in central Chile, flowing NW from the Andes to the Pacific at Concepción. ab. 240 mi. long.

bi·o·cat·a·lyst (bī′ō kat′əlist), *n. Biochem.* an agent, as an enzyme, element, etc., that acts as a biochemical catalyst. [BIO- + CATALYST]

bi·oc·el·late (bī os′ə lāt′, bī′ō sel′it), *adj. Zool., Bot.* marked with two ocelli or eyelike parts. [BI-[1] + OCELLATE]

bi·o·cen·tric (bī′ō sen′trik), *adj.* centered in life; having life as its principal fact. [BIO- + CENTRIC]

biochem′ical ox′ygen demand′, the oxygen required by aerobic organisms, as those in sewage, for metabolism. Also called **biological oxygen demand.**

bi·o·chem·is·try (bī′ō kem′i strē), *n.* **1.** the science dealing with the chemistry of living matter. **2.** the chemistry of living matter. [BIO- + CHEMISTRY] —**bi·o·chem·i·cal** (bī′ō kem′i kəl), *adj., n.* —**bi′o·chem′ic,** *adj.* —**bi′o·chem′i·cal·ly,** *adv.* —**bi′o·chem′ist,** *n.*

bi·o·cli·mat·ic (bī′ō klī mat′ik), *adj.* of or pertaining to the effects of climate on living organisms. [BIO- + CLIMATIC]

bi·o·cli·ma·tol·o·gy (bī′ō klī′mə tol′ə jē), *n.* the study of the effects of climate on the biological processes of plants and animals. [BIO- + CLIMATOLOGY] —**bi·o·cli·ma·to·log·i·cal** (bī′ō klī′mə təloj′i kəl), *adj.* —**bi′o·cli′ma·to·log′i·cal·ly,** *adv.* —**bi′o·cli′ma·tol′o·gist, bi·o·cli·ma·ti·cian** (bī′ō klī′mə tish′ən), *n.*

bi·o·de·grad·a·ble (bī′ō di grā′də bəl), *adj.* capable of decaying and being absorbed by the environment, as paper and kitchen scraps, and as opposed to aluminum cans and many plastics which do not decay but remain garbage forever. [BIO- + DEGRADE + -ABLE]

bi·o·dy·nam·ics (bī′ō dī nam′iks, -di-), *n.* (*construed as sing.*) the branch of biology dealing with energy or the activity of living organisms (opposed to *biostatics*). [BIO- + DYNAMICS] —**bi′o·dy·nam′ic, bi′o·dy·nam′i·cal,** *adj.*

bi·o·e·col·o·gy (bī′ō i kol′ə jē), *n.* the study of the interrelations between plants and animals and their environment. [BIO- + ECOLOGY] —**bi·o·ec·o·log·ic** (bī′ō ek′ə loj′ik), **bi′o·ec′o·log′i·cal,** *adj.* —**bi′o·ec′o·log′i·cal·ly,** *adv.* —**bi′o·e·col′o·gist,** *n.*

bi·o·e·lec·tric (bī′ō i lek′trik), *adj.* of or pertaining to electric phenomena occurring in plants and animals. Also, **bi′o·e·lec′tri·cal.** [BIO- + ELECTRIC] —**bi·o·e·lec·tric·i·ty** (bī′ō i lek tris′i tē, -ē′lek-), *n.*

bi·o·e·lec·tro·gen·e·sis (bī′ō i lek′trō jen′i sis), *n.* the production of electricity by organisms. [BIO- + ELECTRO- + GENESIS] —**bi·o·e·lec·tro·ge·net·ic** (bī′ō-i lek′trō jə net′ik), *adj.* —**bi′o·e·lec′tro·ge·net′i·cal·ly,** *adv.*

bi·o·en·gi·neer·ing (bī′ō en′jə nēr′ing), *n.* the application of engineering principles and techniques to problems in medicine and biology, such as the design and production of artificial limbs and organs. [BIO- + ENGINEERING]

bi·o·feed·back (bī′ō fēd′bak′), *n.* a method of learning to control one's bodily and mental functions with the aid of a visual or auditory display of one's own brain waves, blood pressure, muscle tension, etc.

bi·o·fog (bī′ō fog′), *n. Meteorol.* a fog, resembling steam fog, produced by the contact of very cold air with the warmth and moisture issuing from animal or human bodies. [BIO- + FOG[1]]

biog., 1. biographer. **2.** biographical. **3.** biography.

bi·o·gen (bī′ə jən), *n. Biol., Biochem.* a hypothetical protein molecule, large and unstable, assumed to be basic to fundamental biological processes, as assimilation and dissimilation. [BIO- + -GEN]

bi·o·gen·e·sis (bī′ō jen′i sis), *n.* the production of living organisms from other living organisms. Also, **bi·og·e·ny** (bī oj′ə nē). [BIO- + GENESIS] —**bi·o·ge·net·ic** (bī′ō jə net′ik), **bi′o·ge·net′i·cal, bi·og·e·nous** (bī oj′ə nəs), *adj.* —**bi′o·ge·net′i·cal·ly,** *adv.*

bi·o·gen·ic (bī′ō jen′ik), *adj.* **1.** resulting from the activity of living organisms, as fermentation. **2.** necessary for the life process, as food and water. [BIO- + -GENIC]

bi·o·ge·o·chem·is·try (bī′ō jē′ō kem′i strē), *n.* the science dealing with the relationship between the geochemistry of a given region and its flora and fauna. [BIO- + GEOCHEMISTRY] —**bi·o·ge·o·chem·i·cal** (bī′ō-jē′ō kem′i kəl), *adj.*

bi·o·ge·og·ra·phy (bī′ō jē og′rə fē), *n. Ecol.* the study of the geographical distribution of living things. [BIO- + GEOGRAPHY] —**bi·o·ge·o·graph·ic** (bī′ō jē′ə-graf′ik), **bi′o·ge′o·graph′i·cal,** *adj.* —**bi′o·ge′o·graph′i·cal·ly,** *adv.*

bi·og·ra·phee (bī og′rə fē′), *n.* the subject of a biography; the person whose life is described in a biography. [BIOGRAPH(Y) + -EE]

bi·og·ra·pher (bī og′rə fər, bē-), *n.* a writer of biography. [BIOGRAPH(Y) + -ER[1]]

bi·o·graph·i·cal (bī′ə graf′i kəl), *adj.* **1.** of or pertaining to a person's life: *He's gathering biographical data for his book on Milton.* **2.** pertaining to biography: *a biographical dictionary.* Also, **bi′o·graph′ic.** [BIOGRAPH(Y) + -ICAL] —**bi′o·graph′i·cal·ly,** *adv.*

bi·og·ra·phy (bī og′rə fē, bē-), *n., pl.* **-phies. 1.** a written account of another person's life: *the biography of Byron by Marchand.* **2.** an account in biographical form of an organization, society, theater, animal, etc. **3.** such writings collectively. **4.** the writing of biography as an occupation or field of endeavor. [< Gk *biographía.* See BIO-, -GRAPHY]

biol., 1. biological. **2.** biology.

bi·o·log·i·cal (bī′ə loj′i kəl), *adj.* Also, **bi′o·log′ic. 1.** pertaining to biology. **2.** of or pertaining to the products and operations of applied biology: *a biological test.* —*n.* **3.** *Pharm.* a biochemical product, as a serum, vaccine, antitoxin, or antigen, used in medicine. [BIOLOG(Y) + -ICAL] —**bi′o·log′i·cal·ly,** *adv.*

biolog′ical ox′ygen demand′. See **biochemical oxygen demand.**

biolog′ical sociol′ogy, 1. the study of the evolution of social forms and the development of social behavior in terms analogous to or correlated with the study of vital organisms and biological processes. **2.** the study of social behavior considered as derived from physiological structure. Also called **biosociology.**

biolog′ical war′fare, warfare that makes use of bacteria, viruses, toxins, etc., to disable or destroy man, domestic animals, and food crops. *Abbr.:* B.W.

bi·ol·o·gism (bī ol′ə jiz′əm), *n.* any of various doctrines formulated on the principles of or according to the methods of biological science. [BIOLOG(Y) + -ISM]

bi·ol·o·gist (bī ol′ə jist), *n.* a specialist in biology. [BIOLOGY + -IST]

bi·ol·o·gy (bī ol′ə jē), *n.* **1.** the science of life or living matter in all its forms and phenomena, often esp. with reference to origin, growth, reproduction, structure, etc. **2.** the plant and animal life of a region: *the biology of Pennsylvania.* **3.** the biological phenomena characteristic of an organism or a group of organisms: *the biology of a worm.* [< G *Biologie.* See BIO-, -LOGY]

bi·o·lu·mi·nes·cence (bī′ō lo͞o′mə nes′əns), *n.* the production of light by living organisms. [BIO- + LUMINESCENCE] —**bi′o·lu′mi·nes′cent,** *adj.*

bi·ol·y·sis (bī ol′i sis), *n. Biol.* dissolution of a living organism; death. [< NL; see BIO-, -LYSIS] —**bi·o·lyt·ic** (bī′ə lit′ik), *adj.*

bi·o·mag·net·ism (bī′ō mag′ni tiz′əm), *n.* See **animal magnetism.** [BIO- + MAGNETISM] —**bi·o·mag·net·ic** (bī′ō mag net′ik), *adj.*

bi·o·mass (bī′ō mas′), *n. Ecol.* that part of a given habitat consisting of living matter, expressed either as the weight of organisms per unit area or as the volume of organisms per unit volume of habitat. [BIO- + MASS]

bi·ome (bī′ōm), *n. Ecol.* a complex of communities characterized by a distinctive type of vegetation and maintained under the climatic conditions of the region, as a desert. [BI-[2] + *-ome* -OMA]

bi·o·med·i·cine (bī′ō med′i sən), *n.* clinical medicine dealing with the relationship of body chemistry and function. [BIO- + MEDICINE] —**bi′o·med′i·cal,** *adj.*

bi·om·e·ter (bī om′i tər), *n.* an instrument for measuring the amount of carbon dioxide given off by an organism, tissue, etc. [BIO- + -METER]

bi·o·me·tri·cian (bī′ō mi trish′ən, bī om′i-), *n.* one skilled in biometrics. Also, **bi·o·met·ri·cist** (bī′ō me′-tri sist). [BIOMETRIC(S) + -IAN]

bi·o·met·rics (bī′ō me′triks), *n.* (*construed as sing.*) **1.** *Biol.* the application of mathematical-statistical theory to biology. **2.** biometry (def. 1). [BIOMETR(Y) + -ICS] —**bi′o·met′ric, bi′o·met′ri·cal,** *adj.* —**bi′o·met′ri·cal·ly,** *adv.*

bi·om·e·try (bī om′i trē), *n.* **1.** the calculation of the probable duration of human life. **2.** biometrics (def. 1). [BIO- + -METRY]

bi·o·mor·phic (bī′ō môr′fik), *adj.* (of painted or sculptured shapes) evoking images of biological organisms, esp. without representing any specific organisms. [BIO- + -MORPHIC]

Bi·on (bī′on), *n.* fl. c100 B.C., Greek pastoral poet.

bi·on·ic (bī on′ik), *adj.* **1.** utilizing electronic devices and mechanical parts to assist humans in performing extremely difficult or intricate tasks, as by supplementing or duplicating parts of the body: *The scientist used a bionic arm to examine the radioactive material.* **2.** *Informal.* having superhuman strength or capacity.

bi·on·ics (bī on′iks), *n.* (*construed as sing.*) the study of how man and animals perform certain tasks and solve certain problems, and of the application of the findings to the design of computers and other electronic equipment. [BIO(LOGY + ELECTRO)NICS]

bi·o·nom·ics (bī′ə nom′iks), *n.* (*construed as sing.*) ecology (def. 1). [BIONOM(Y) + -ICS] —**bi′o·nom′ic, bi′o·nom′i·cal,** *adj.* —**bi′o·nom′i·cal·ly,** *adv.* —**bi·on·o·mist** (bī on′ə mist), *n.*

bi·on·o·my (bī on′ə mē), *n.* **1.** physiology. **2.** ecology. [BIO- + -NOMY]

bi·o·phys·ics (bī′ō fiz′iks), *n.* (*construed as sing.*) the branch of biology dealing with the study of biological structures and processes by means of the methods of physics. [BIO- + PHYSICS] —**bi′o·phys′i·cal** (bī′ō-fiz′i kəl), *adj.* —**bi′o·phys′i·cal·ly,** *adv.* —**bi·o·phys·i·cist** (bī′ō fiz′i sist), *n.*

bi·o·plasm (bī′ō plaz′əm), *n. Biol.* living matter; protoplasm. [BIO- + -PLASM] —**bi′o·plas′mic,** *adj.*

bi·op·sy (bī′op sē), *n., pl.* **-sies.** *Med.* the excision for diagnostic study of a piece of tissue from a living body. [BI-[2] + *-opsy* < Gk *-opsia; see* -OPSIS, -IA] —**bi·op·tic** (bī op′tik), *adj.*

bi·o·psy·chic (bī′ō sī′kik), *adj. Psychol.* of, pertaining to, or comprising psychological and biological phenomena. Also, **bi′o·psy′chi·cal.** [BIO- + PSYCHIC]

bi·o·rhythm (bī′ō riŧħ′əm), *n.* an innate rhythm in certain biological processes of organisms that in humans can be charted in long-term (22- to 28-day) cycles of physical, emotional, and intellectual behavior. [BIO- + RHYTHM]

bi·os·co·py (bī os′kə pē), *n., pl.* **-pies.** *Med.* examination of the body to discover whether or not it is alive. [BIO- + -SCOPY] —**bi·o·scop·ic** (bī′ə skop′ik), *adj.*

bi·o·so·cial (bī′ō sō′shəl), *adj.* **1.** of, pertaining to, or entailing the interaction or combination of social and biological factors. **2.** *Sociol.* of, pertaining to, or characteristic of the theories of or phenomena studied in biological sociology. **3.** of or pertaining to social phenomena that are affected by biological factors. Also, **bi·o·so·ci·o·log·i·cal** (bī′ō sō′sē ə loj′i kəl, -shē-). [BIO- + SOCIAL]

bi·o·so·ci·ol·o·gy (bī′ō sō′sē ol′ə jē, -shē-), *n.* See **biological sociology.** [BIO- + SOCIOLOGY]

bi·o·sphere (bī′ə sfēr′), *n.* the part of the earth's crust, waters, and atmosphere where living organisms can subsist. [BIO- + -SPHERE]

bi·o·stat·ics (bī′ō stat′iks), *n.* (*construed as sing.*) the branch of biology dealing with the structure of organisms in relation to their functions (opposed to *biodynamics*). [BIO- + STATICS] —**bi′o·stat′ic, bi′o·stat′i·cal,** *adj.*

bi·o·syn·the·sis (bī′ō sin′thi sis), *n. Biochem.* the formation, by synthesis or degradation, of chemical compounds by a living organism. [BIO- + SYNTHESIS]

bi·o·ta (bī ō′tə), *n. Ecol.* the animal and plant life of a region or period. [< NL < Gk *biotḗ* life]

bi·o·tech·nol·o·gy (bī′ō tek nol′ə jē), *n.* the study of the relationship between human beings and machines, esp. in terms of physiological, psychological, and technological requirements. Cf. **human engineering, psychotechnology.** [BIO- + TECHNOLOGY] —**bi·o·tech·no·log·i·cal** (bī′ō tek′nəloj′i kəl), *adj.* —**bi′o·tech′no·log′i·cal·ly,** *adv.*

bi·ot·ic (bī ot′ik), *adj.* pertaining to life. Also, **bi·ot′i·cal.** [< Gk *biōtikós* of, pertaining to life, equiv. to *biō(nai)* (to) live + *-tikos* -TIC]

biot′ic poten′tial, the capacity of a population of animals or plants to increase in numbers under optimum environmental conditions.

bi·o·tin (bī′ə tin), *n. Biochem.* a crystalline growth vitamin, $C_{10}H_{16}O_3N_2S$, of the vitamin-B complex, widely distributed in plant and animal tissue, and essential in preventing the death of animals from an excess of egg white in the diet; vitamin H. [biot- (< Gk *biotḗ* life) + -IN[2]]

bi·o·tite (bī′ə tīt′), *n.* a very common mineral of the mica group, occurring in dark black, brown, or green sheets and scales: an important constituent of igneous rocks. [named after J. B. *Biot* (1774–1862), French mineralogist and mathematician; see -ITE[1]] —**bi·o·tit·ic** (bī′ə tit′ik), *adj.*

Bi′ot-Sa·vart′ law′ (bē′ō sə vär′, byō′-), *Physics.* the law that the magnetic induction near a long, straight conductor, as wire, varies inversely as the distance from the conductor and directly as the intensity of the current in the conductor. [named after J. B. *Biot* (see BIOTITE) and Felix *Savart* (1791–1841), French physician and physicist]

bi·o·type (bī′ə tīp′), *n. Biol.* a group of organisms having the same hereditary characteristics. [BIO- + -TYPE] —**bi·o·typ·ic** (bī′ə tip′ik), *adj.*

bi·o·typ·ol·o·gy (bī′ə tī pol′ə jē), *n.* the branch of biology dealing with the study of biotypes. [BIOTYPE + -O- + -LOGY]

bi·pack (bī′pak′), *n. Photog.* a film having two superimposed layers, each with an emulsion sensitive to a different color. [BI-[1] + PACK[1]]

bi·pa·ri·e·tal (bī′pə rī′i tᵊl), *adj. Craniom.* of or pertaining to both parietal bones, esp. in their being determinants in measurements of the breadth of the skull. [BI-[1] + PARIETAL]

bip·a·rous (bip′ər əs), *adj.* **1.** *Zool.* bringing forth offspring in pairs. **2.** *Bot.* bearing two branches or axes. [BI-[1] + -PAROUS]

bi·par·ti·san (bī pär′ti zən), *adj.* representing or characterized by two parties: *Government leaders hope to achieve a bipartisan foreign policy.* [BI-[1] + PARTISAN[1]] —**bi·par′ti·san·ism,** *n.* —**bi·par′ti·san·ship′,** *n.*

bi·par·tite (bī pär′tīt), *adj.* **1.** divided into or consisting of two parts. **2.** *Law.* being in two corresponding parts: *a bipartite contract.* **3.** shared by two; joint: *a bipartite pact; bipartite rule.* **4.** *Bot.* divided into two parts nearly to the base, as a leaf. [< L *bipartīt(us)* divided into two parts, bisected (ptp. of *bipartīre*). See BI-[1], PART, -ITE[2]] —**bi·par′tite·ly,** *adv.* —**bi·par·ti·tion** (bī′pär tish′ən), *n.*

bi·par·ty (bī′pär′tē), *adj.* of two distinct parties: *a biparty investigating committee.* [BI-[1] + PARTY]

bi·pec·ti·nate (bī pek′tə nāt′), *adj. Zool., Bot.* having both margins toothed like a comb, as certain antennae. Also, **bi·pec′ti·nat′ed.** [BI-[1] + PECTINATE]

bi·ped (bī′ped), *Zool.* —*n.* **1.** a two-footed animal. —*adj.* **2.** having two feet. [< L *biped-* (s. of *bipēs*) two-footed. See BI-[1], -PED]

bi·pe·dal (bī′ped′ᵊl, bip′i dᵊl), *adj.* biped. [BI-[1] + PEDAL (adj.)]

bi·pet·al·ous (bī pet′ᵊləs), *adj. Bot.* having two petals. [BI-[1] + PETALOUS]

bi·phen·yl (bī fen′ᵊl, -fēn′-), *n. Chem.* a water-insoluble, pleasant-smelling, colorless powder or white scales, $C_6H_5C_6H_5$, composed of two phenyl groups, from which benzidine dyes are derived: used chiefly as a heat-transfer agent and in organic synthesis. Also called **diphenyl, phenylbenzene.** [BI-[1] + PHENYL]

bi·pin·nar·i·a (bī′pi nâr′ē ə), *n., pl.* **-nar·i·ae** (-nâr′ē ē′), **-nar·i·as.** the free-swimming, bilaterally symmetrical larva of certain starfishes. [< NL; see BI-[1], PINNA, -ARIA]

bi·pin·nate (bī pin′āt), *adj. Bot.* pinnate, as a leaf, with the divisions also pinnate. [< NL *bipinnāt(us).* See BI-[1], PINNATE] —**bi·pin′nate·ly,** *adv.*

Bipinnate leaf

bi·plane (bī′plān′), *n.* an airplane with two sets of wings, one above and usually slightly forward of the other. [BI-[1] + (AIR)PLANE]

bi·pod (bī′pod), *n.* a two-legged support, as for an automatic rifle. [BI-[1] + -POD]

bi·po·lar (bī pō′lər), *adj.* **1.** having two poles, as the earth. **2.** pertaining to or found at both poles. [BI-[1] + POLAR] —**bi·po·lar·i·ty** (bī′pō lar′i tē), *n.*

bi·pro·pel·lant (bī′prə pel′ənt), *n. Rocketry.* a missile or rocket propellant, composed of fuel and oxidizer, the components of which are kept in separate compartments prior to combustion. [BI-[1] + PROPELLANT]

bi·pyr·a·mid (bī pir′ə mid), *n.* a crystal form symmetrical about a plane dividing it into two pyramids. Also called **dipyramid.** [BI-[1] + PYRAMID] —**bi·pyr·am·i·dal** (bī′pi ram′i dᵊl), *adj.*

bi·quad·rate (bī kwod′rāt, -rit), *n. Math.* the fourth power. [BI-[1] + QUADRATE]

bi·quad·rat·ic (bī′kwo drat′ik), *adj.* **1.** *Math.* involving the fourth, but no higher, power of the unknown or variable. —*n.* **2.** quartic (def. 2). **3.** biquadrate. [BI-[1] + QUADRATIC]

bi·quar·ter·ly (bī kwôr′tər lē), *adj.* occurring twice in each quarter of a year. [BI-[1] + QUARTERLY]

bi·ra·cial (bī rā′shəl), *adj.* consisting of, representing, or combining two separate races, esp. white and Negro: *a biracial committee on neighborhood problems.* [BI-[1] + RACIAL] —**bi·ra′cial·ism,** *n.*

bi·ra·di·al (bī rā′dē əl), *adj.* having both bilateral and radial symmetry, as ctenophores. [BI-[1] + RADIAL]

bi·ra·mous (bī rā′məs), *adj.* consisting of or divided into two branches: *a biramous appendage.* Also, **bi·ra·mose** (bī rā′mōs, bī′rə mōs′). [BI-[1] + RAMOUS]

birch (bûrch), *n.* **1.** any tree or shrub of the genus *Betula,* comprising species with a smooth, laminated outer bark and close-grained wood. **2.** the wood itself. **3.** a birch rod, or a bundle of birch twigs, used esp. for whipping schoolboys. —*adj.* **4.** birchen. —*v.t.* **5.** to beat or punish with or as with a birch: *The young ruffians were birched soundly by their teacher.* [ME *birche,* OE *birce;* c. OHG *birka* (G *Birke*); akin to Skt *bhūrja* kind of birch]

birch′ beer′, a carbonated or fermented drink containing an extract from the bark of the birch tree. Cf. **root beer.**

birch·en (bûr′chən), *adj.* **1.** of or pertaining to birch. **2.** made or consisting of birch: *birchen furniture.* [late ME; see BIRCH, -EN[2]]

Birch·er (bûr′chər), *n.* a member, advocate, or follower of the John Birch Society and its principles. Also, **Birchite.** [(JOHN) BIRCH (SOCIETY) + -ER[1]]

Birch·es (bûr′chiz), *n.* a poem (1916) by Robert Frost.

Birch·ism (bûr′chiz əm), *n.* the movement, principles, and practices of the John Birch Society. [(JOHN) BIRCH (SOCIETY) + -ISM]

Birch·ite (bûr′chīt), *n.* Bircher. [(JOHN) BIRCH (SOCIETY) + -ITE[1]]

bird (bûrd), *n.* **1.** any warm-blooded vertebrate of the class *Aves,* having a body covered with feathers and forelimbs modified into wings. **2.** *Sports.* **a.** a game bird. **b.** See **clay pigeon.** **c.** a shuttlecock. **3.** *Slang.* a person, esp. one having some peculiarity: *He's a queer bird.* **4.** *Informal.* an airplane. **5.** *Archaic.* the young of any fowl. **6.** **a little bird,** *Informal.* a source of information not to be disclosed: *A little bird told me that today is your birthday.* **7.** **bird in the hand,** a thing possessed in fact as opposed to a thing about which one speculates: *A bird in the hand is worth two in the bush.* Also, **bird in hand.** **8.** **birds of a feather,** people with interests, opinions, or backgrounds in common: *Birds of a feather flock together.* **9.** **eat like a bird,** to eat sparingly: *She couldn't understand why she failed to lose weight when she was, as she said, eating like a bird.* **10.** **for the birds,** *Slang.* regarded with contempt or scorn; not to be taken seriously: *Their opinions on art are for the birds. That sofa is for the birds.* **11.** **kill two birds with one stone,** to achieve two aims with a single effort: *She killed two birds with one stone by shopping and visiting the museum on the same trip.* **12.** **the bird,** *Slang.* **a.** disapproval, as of a performance, by hissing, booing, etc.: *He got the bird when he came out on stage.* **b.** scoffing or ridicule: *He was trying to be serious, but we all gave him the bird.* —*v.i.* **13.** to catch or shoot birds. **14.** to observe birds in their natural habitats. [ME *byrd, bryd,* OE *brid(d)* young bird, chick < ?] —**bird′less,** *adj.*

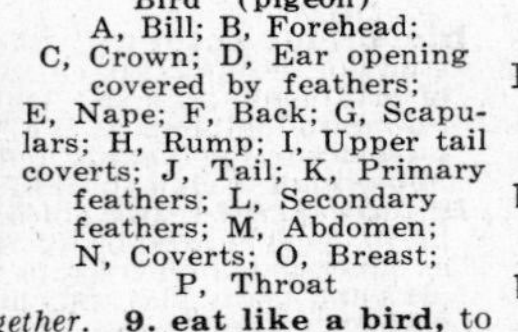

Bird (pigeon)
A, Bill; B, Forehead; C, Crown; D, Ear opening covered by feathers; E, Nape; F, Back; G, Scapulars; H, Rump; I, Upper tail coverts; J, Tail; K, Primary feathers; L, Secondary feathers; M, Abdomen; N, Coverts; O, Breast; P, Throat

Bird (bûrd), *n.* a boy's or girl's given name. Also, **Byrd.**

bird·bath (bûrd′bath′, -bäth′), *n., pl.* **-baths** (-bathz′, -bäthz′). a basin or tublike garden ornament for birds to drink from or bathe in. [BIRD + BATH[1]]

bird·brain (bûrd′brān′), *n. Slang.* a dolt; scatterbrain. [BIRD + BRAIN] —**bird′brained′, bird′-brained′,** *adj.*

bird·cage (bûrd′kāj′), *n.* **1.** a small, usually portable, cage for confining pet birds. **2.** something that resembles a birdcage. [ME; see BIRD, CAGE]

bird′cage clock′. See **lantern clock.**

bird′ call′, **1.** a sound made by a bird. **2.** a sound imitating that of a bird. **3.** a device used to imitate the sound of a bird. Also, **bird′call′.**

bird′ cher′ry, **1.** any of several species of cherry esp. *Prunus padus* **(European bird cherry),** of Europe and Asia, and the pin cherry of the U.S. **2.** the fruit of any such tree, for which birds have a particular liking.

bird′ colo′nel, *U.S. Mil. Slang.* See **chicken colonel.**

bird′ dog′, one of any of various breeds of dogs trained to hunt or retrieve birds.

bird-dog (bûrd′dôg′, -dog′), *v.t., v.i.,* **-dogged, -dog·ging.** *Slang.* to watch carefully or investigate. [v. use of BIRD DOG]

Bir·dell (bər del′), *n.* a boy's given name.

bird·er (bûr′dər), *n.* **1.** one who hunts or raises birds. **2.** See **bird watcher** [BIRD + -ER[1]]

bird-foot (bûrd′fo͝ot′), *n., pl.* **-foots.** bird's-foot.

bird′ grass′, **1.** a grass, *Poa trivialis,* grown in temperate regions of North America largely for lawns and turf. **2.** knotgrass, *Polygonum aviculare.*

bird·house (bûrd′hous′), *n., pl.* **-hous·es** (-hou′ziz). **1.** a box, usually fashioned to resemble a house, for birds to live in. **2.** an aviary. [BIRD + HOUSE]

bird·ie (bûr′dē), *n., v.* **bird·ied, bird·ie·ing.** —*n.* **1.** a small bird. **2.** *Golf.* a score of one stroke under par on a hole. **3.** *Informal.* a shuttlecock. —*v.t.* **4.** *Golf.* to make a birdie on (a hole). [BIRD + -IE]

Bird·ie (bûr′dē), *n.* a boy's or girl's given name.

Bird′ in Space′, a sculptured piece in bronze (1919) by Constantin Brancusi.

bird·like (bûrd′līk′), *adj.* having the appearance or characteristics of a bird, as quickness, lightness, fragility, etc.: *birdlike gestures.* [BIRD + -LIKE]

bird·lime (bûrd′līm′), *n., v.,* **-limed, -lim·ing.** —*n.* **1.** a sticky material prepared from holly, mistletoe, or other plants, and smeared on twigs to catch small birds that light on it. —*v.t.* **2.** to smear or catch with or as with birdlime: *to birdlime the branches of a tree; to be birdlimed by a woman's flattery.* [late ME *bryde-lyme.* See BIRD, LIME[1]]

bird′ louse′. See under **louse** (def. 2).

bird·man (bûrd′man′, -mən), *n., pl.* **-men** (-men′, -mən). **1.** one who keeps or tends birds. **2.** one who hunts birds for food or sport; a fowler. **3.** one who studies birds; an ornithologist. **4.** *Informal.* aviator. [BIRD + MAN[1]]

bird′ of ill′ o′men, one who brings bad news.

bird′ of par′adise, any of several passerine birds of the family *Paradisaeidae,* of New Guinea and adjacent islands, the males of which have ornate, colorful plumage.

Bird′ of Par′adise, *Astron.* the constellation Apus.

bird′-of-par′a·dise bush′ (bûrd′əv par′ə dīs′), a South American shrub or small tree, *Poinciana Gilliesi,* having showy, yellow flowers with red stamens.

bird′-of-par′adise flow′er, a plant, *Strelitzia reginae,* of southern Africa, having showy, orange and purplish flowers resembling a bird in flight.

bird′ of pas′sage, **1.** a bird that migrates seasonally. **2.** a transient or migratory person.

bird′ of peace′, a dove.

bird′ of prey′, any of numerous predacious, flesh-eating birds, as the eagles, hawks, kites, vultures, falcons, owls, etc.

bird′ pep′per, a variety of pepper, *Capsicum frutescens,* with small, elongated berries.

Birds, The, a comedy (414 B.C.) by Aristophanes.

bird's′ beak′, *Archit.* beak[1] (def. 9).

Birds·bor·o (bûrdz′bûr′ō, -bur′ō), *n.* a town in SE Pennsylvania. 3025 (1960).

bird·seed (bûrd′sēd′), *n.* a small seed, esp. that of a grass, *Phalaris canariensis,* used as food for birds. [BIRD + SEED]

bird's-eye (bûrdz′ī′), *adj., n., pl.* **-eyes.** —*adj.* **1.** seen from above, as by a bird in flight; panoramic: *a bird's-eye view of the city.* **2.** lacking in details; hasty; superficial; general: *a bird's-eye view of ancient history.* **3.** having spots or markings resembling birds' eyes: *bird's-eye tweed.* —*n.* **4.** any of various plants having small, round, bright-colored flowers, as a primrose, *Primula farinosa,* or the germander speedwell, *Veronica Chamaedrys.* **5.** *Textiles.* **a.** a woven, allover pattern on fabrics, characterized chiefly by small diamond shapes resembling the eye of a bird. **b.** a fabric having this pattern, esp. a cotton used for diapers or a linen used for toweling. [BIRD + 'S[1] + EYE]

Birds′eye Lamp′ (bûrdz′ī′), *Trademark.* a powerful incandescent lamp with a reflector that eliminates actinic rays, used in motion-picture and television production.

bird's′-eye ma′ple, a cut of sugar maple wood used esp. for veneers, having a wavy grain with many dark, circular markings.

bird's′-eye prim′rose, a hardy, perennial herb, *Primula farinosa,* of alpine regions of Europe and Asia, having small, lilac-colored flowers with yellow throat and eye.

bird's-foot (bûrdz′fo͝ot′), *n., pl.* **-foots.** **1.** any of various plants whose leaves, flowers, or pods resemble or suggest the foot or claw of a bird, esp. leguminous plants of the genus *Ornithopus,* which have clawlike pods. **2.** any similar plant, esp. bird's-foot trefoil or fenugreek. Also, **bird-foot.** [BIRD + 'S[1] + FOOT]

bird's′-foot fern′, **1.** a fern, *Adiantopsis radiata,* of tropical America. **2.** a fern, *Pellaea mucronata,* found in hilly areas of the Pacific coast of the U.S.

bird's′-foot tre′foil, **1.** a fabaceous plant, *Lotus corniculatus,* the legumes of which spread like a crow's foot. **2.** any similar plant of the same genus. Also called **baby's-slippers, bloom-fell, ground honeysuckle.**

bird's′-foot vi′olet, a handsome violet, *Viola pedata,* cultivated for its large light-blue or whitish flowers with yellow eyes: the State flower of Wisconsin.

bird′ shot′, small-sized shot used for shooting birds.

bird's′ mouth′, *Carpentry.* a right-angled notch cut in the underside of a rafter for fitting over a longitudinal member, as a wall plate.

bird's′ nest′, **1.** a nest made by various swiftlets of the genus *Collocalia* from a regurgitated gelatinous substance: used as a food, esp. in oriental cookery. **2.** *Angling Slang.* backlash (def. 2).

bird's′-nest fern′ (bûrdz′nest′), a tropical fern, *Asplenium Nidus,* having fronds arranged in clumps resembling a bird's nest.

bird's′-nest fun′gus, any fungus of the order *Nidulariales,* having fructifications resembling a bird's nest that contains eggs.

bird′-voiced tree′ frog′ (bûrd′voist′), a frog, *Hyla avivoca,* of the southern U.S., having a birdlike, whistling call.

bird-watch (bûrd′woch′), *v.i.* to note and study the appearance, activities, etc., of undomesticated birds, esp. as a hobby.

bird′ watch′er, one who observes and identifies birds in their natural habitats.

bird·wom·an (bûrd′wo͝om′ən), *n., pl.* **-wom·en.** *Informal.* a woman aviator. [BIRD + WOMAN]

bi·rec·tan·gu·lar (bī′rek taŋ′gyə lər), *adj. Geom.* having two right angles. [BI-[1] + RECTANGULAR]

bi·re·frin·gence (bī′ri frin′jəns), *n.* See **double refraction.** [BI-[1] + REFRINGENCE] —**bi′re·frin′gent,** *adj.*

bi·reme (bī′rēm), *n.* a galley having two banks or tiers of oars. [< L *birēm(is)* two-oared, having two banks of oars (*bi-* BI-[1] + *rēm(us)* oar + *-is* adj. suffix)]

bi·ret·ta (bə ret′ə), *n. Rom. Cath. Ch.* a stiff square cap with three or four upright projecting pieces extending from the center of the top to the edge, worn by ecclesiastics. Also, **berretta, birretta.** [< It *berretta* < OPr *berret* < ML *birrett(um)* cap (LL *birr(us)* hooded cape + *-ettum* -ET)]

Biretta

bi·ri (bē′rē), *n.* bidi.

birk (bûrk; *Scot.* birk), *n., adj., v.t. Scot. and North Eng.* birch. [ME *byrk,* OE *birc,* side form of *birce* BIRCH]

Birk·beck (bûrk′bek), *n.* **George,** 1776–1841, English physician and educationist.

birk·en (bûr′kən; *Scot.* bir′kən), *adj. Scot. and North Eng.* birchen; birch. [ME; see BIRK + -EN[2]]

Bir·ken·head (bûr′kən hed′, bûr′kən hed′), *n.* **1.** **Frederick Edwin Smith, 1st Earl of,** 1872–1930, British lawyer, statesman, and writer. **2.** a seaport in NW Cheshire, in W England, on the Mersey River. 141,683 (1961).

Bir·ket Ka·run (bir′kit kə ro͞on′), *n.* a lake in S United Arab Republic. 25 mi. long; ab. 5 mi. wide; 90 sq. mi. Also, **Bir′ket Qâ·run′.**

Birk·hoff (bûr′kôf), *n.* **George David,** 1884–1944, U.S. mathematician.

bir·kie (bûr′kē; *Scot.* bir′kē), *n. Scot.* an aggressive, independent man. [?]

birl (bûrl), *v.t.* **1.** *Lumbering.* to cause (a floating log) to rotate rapidly by treading upon it. **2.** *Brit.* to spin or cause to rotate. —*v.i.* **3.** *Lumbering.* to cause a floating log to rotate rapidly by treading on it. **4.** *Brit.* **a.** to move or rotate rapidly. **b.** *Informal.* to spend money freely. c. *Informal.* to gamble. —*n.* 5. *Brit. Informal.* an attempt; a gamble. [? special use of BIRLE, by assoc. with words of like sound, as WHIRL]

birle (bûrl; *Scot.* biʀl), *v.*, **birled, birl·ing.** *Dial.* —*v.t.* 1. to pour (a drink) or pour a drink for. —*v.i.* 2. to drink deeply; carouse. [ME *birl(en)*, OE *byrelian*, deriv. of *byrele* butler; akin to BEAR[1]]

birl·ing (bûr′ling), *n.* a game played competitively by lumberjacks, in which each tries to keep his balance longest as he stands on a floating log and rotates it with his feet. [ME *birlynge.* See BIRLE, -ING[1]]

Bir·ming·ham (bûr′ming əm *for 1;* bûr′ming ham′ *for 2, 3*), *n.* 1. a city in NW Warwickshire, in central England. 1,105,651 (1961). 2. a city in central Alabama. 340,887 (1960). 3. a city in SE Michigan, near Detroit. 25,525 (1960). 4. a walled plain in the second quadrant of the face of the moon.

bir·ne (bir′nə), *n.* boule[1]. [< G: lit., pear]

Bi·ro·bi·dzhan (bir′ō bi jän′), *n.* **the capital of the Jewish Autonomous Region, in E Siberia, in the SE Russian Federation in Asia, W of Khabarovsk. 82,000. Also, Bi′ro·bi·jan′.**

bi·ro·ta (bi rot′ə), *n.* *Rom. Antiq.* a two-wheeled cart, usually drawn by three mules, used for transporting commercial goods and one or two passengers. [< L, n. use of fem. of *birotus* two-wheeled, equiv. to *bi-* BI-[1] + *rot(a)* wheel + *-us* adj. suffix]

birr (bûr), *n.* 1. force; energy; vigor. 2. emphasis in statement, speech, etc. 3. a whirring sound. —*v.i.* 4. to move with or make a whirring sound. [ME *bire, bur,* OE *byre*strong wind; c. Icel *byrr* favorable wind; akin to BEAR[1]]

Bir·rell (bir′əl), *n.* **Augustine,** 1850–1933, English writer.

bir·ret·ta (bə ret′ə), *n.* biretta.

bir·rus (bir′əs), *n., pl.* **bir·ri** (bir′ī). a hooded cloak of coarse wool much used in ancient Rome. Also, **byrrus.** [< LL: cloak to keep off rain]

birse (bûrs; *Scot.* biʀs), *n.* *Scot.* 1. a bristle; a short hair of the beard or body. 2. anger; rage. [OE *byrst;* c. OHG *borst, burst,* Icel *burst.* See BRISTLE]

Birt (bûrt), *n.* a crater in the third quadrant of the face of the moon: about 15 miles in diameter.

birth (bûrth), *n.* 1. fact of being born: *the day of his birth.* 2. act of bearing or bringing forth offspring; childbirth; parturition: *a difficult birth.* 3. lineage; extraction; descent: *of Grecian birth.* 4. high or noble lineage: *to be foolishly vain about one's birth.* 5. supposedly natural heritage: *a musician by birth.* 6. any coming into existence; origin; beginning: *the birth of Protestantism; the birth of an idea.* 7. *Archaic.* that which is born. 8. **give birth to, a.** to bear (a child). **b.** to initiate; originate: *Her hobby gave birth to a successful business.* [ME *byrth(e)* < Scand; cf. OSw *byrth,* c. OE *gebyrd,* OHG *(gi)burt,* Goth *(ga)baurth(s)*] —**Syn.** 3. parentage, ancestry, line, blood, family, race.

birth′ certif′icate, an official form recording the birth of a baby and containing pertinent data, as name, sex, date, place, parents, etc.

birth′ control′, regulation of the number of one's children through the deliberate control or prevention of conception. Cf. **family planning** (def. 1), **planned parenthood.**

birth′-con·trol pill′ (bûrth′kən trōl′), an oral contraceptive for women that inhibits ovulation, fertilization, or implantation of a fertilized ovum, causing temporary infertility. Also called **the pill.**

birth·day (bûrth′dā′), *n.* 1. the anniversary of one's birth or of the date something originated, was founded, etc. 2. the day of one's birth. 3. a day marking or commemorating the origin, founding, or beginning of something. 4. the festivities or celebration marking such a day or anniversary. [ME; see BIRTH, DAY]

birth′day suit′, *Informal.* bare skin; nakedness: *She was sunbathing in her birthday suit.*

birth·mark (bûrth′märk′), *n.* a minor disfigurement or blemish on a person's skin at birth. [BIRTH + MARK[1]]

birth·night (bûrth′nīt′), *n.* 1. the night of one's birth, esp. a birthday celebration for royalty. 2. the anniversary of such a date. 3. the celebration of a royal birthday. [BIRTH + NIGHT]

Birth′ of Trag′edy, The, (*The Birth of Tragedy from the Spirit of Music*) a philosophical treatise (1872) by Friedrich Nietzsche.

Birth′ of Ve′nus, The, a painting (c1480) by Sandro Botticelli.

birth·place (bûrth′plās′), *n.* place of birth or origin.

birth′ rate′, the proportion of the number of births in a place in a given time to the total population, usually expressed as a quantity per 1000 of population.

birth·right (bûrth′rīt′), *n.* any right or privilege to which a person is entitled by birth: *Democracy maintains that freedom is a birthright.* [BIRTH + RIGHT]

birth·root (bûrth′ro͞ot′, -ro͝ot′), *n.* 1. Also called **bethroot, purple trillium.** a trillium, *Trillium erectum,* the roots of which are used in medicine. 2. any of certain other species of trillium. [BIRTH + ROOT[1]]

birth·stone (bûrth′stōn′), *n.* a precious or semiprecious stone traditionally associated with a particular month or sign of the zodiac and believed to attract good fortune. [BIRTH + STONE]

birth·stool (bûrth′sto͞ol′), *n.* (formerly) a specially shaped seat used in childbirth. [BIRTH + STOOL]

birth′ trau′ma, *Psychoanal.* an emotional shock caused by being born.

birth·wort (bûrth′wûrt′), *n.* 1. a plant, *Aristolochia Clematitis,* native to Europe, reputed to facilitate childbirth. 2. any of certain other species of the same genus. 3. the birthroot. [BIRTH + WORT[2]]

bis[1] (bis), *adv.* 1. twice. 2. a second time. —*interj.* 3. (used, esp. in music, to shout approval and to call for a repetition). [< It < L; OL *duis* TWICE]

bis[2] (bis), *n.* a sheer, often embroidered linen, much used in the manufacture of altar cloths. Also, **bisso.** [ME < L *byss(us)* BYSSUS]

B.I.S., 1. Bank for International Settlements. 2. British Information Service.

Bi·sa·yan (bē sä′yən), *n., pl.* **-yans,** (*esp. collectively*) **-yan.** Visayan.

Bi·sa·yas (bē sä′yäs), *n.pl.* Spanish name of the **Visayan Islands.**

Bis·bee (biz′bē), *n.* a town in SE Arizona. 9914 (1960).

Bis·cay (bis′kā, -kē), *n.* **Bay of,** a bay of the Atlantic between W France and N Spain.

Bis′cayne Bay′ (bis′kān, bis kān′), an inlet of the Atlantic Ocean, on the SE coast of Florida, separating the cities of Miami and Miami Beach.

bis·cuit (bis′kit), *n.* 1. *U.S.* a kind of bread in small, soft cakes, raised with baking powder or soda, sometimes with yeast. 2. *Brit.* **a.** a dry and crisp or hard bread in thin, flat cakes, made without yeast or other raising agent; a cracker. **b.** a cookie. 3. a pale-brown color. 4. Also called **bisque.** *Ceram.* unglazed earthenware or porcelain after firing. 5. Also called **preform.** a piece of plastic or the like, prepared for pressing into a phonograph record. —*adj.* 6. having the color biscuit. [ME *bysquyte* < MF *biscuit* (ML *biscoctus*), var. of *bescuit* seamen's bread, lit., twice cooked, equiv. to *bes* BIS-[1] + *cuit,* ptp. of *cuire* < L *coquere* to COOK[1]] —**bis′cuit·like′,** *adj.*

bis·cuit (bēs kwē′), *n.* *French.* a cooky or cracker.

bis·cuit-fired (bis′kit fīərd′), *adj.* (of a ceramic object) fired to harden the body.

bis′cuit torto′ni, an individual portion of tortoni, frozen and served in a small cup, often topped with minced almonds.

bise (bēz), *n.* a dry, cold north or northeast wind in SE France, Switzerland, and adjoining regions. Also, **bize.** [ME < OF < OHG *bīsa* north wind]

bi·sect (*v.* bī sekt′, bī′sekt; *n.* bī′sekt), *v.t.* 1. to cut or divide into two equal or nearly equal parts. 2. *Geom.* to cut or divide into two equal parts: *to bisect an angle.* 3. to intersect or cross: *the spot where the railroad tracks bisect the highway.* —*v.i.* 4. to split into two, as a road; fork: *There's a charming old inn just before the road bisects.* —*n.* 5. Also called **split.** *Philately.* a portion of a stamp, usually half, used for payment of a proportionate amount of the face value of the whole stamp. [BI-[1] + -SECT] —**bi·sec′tion,** *n.* —**bi·sec′tion·al,** *adj.* —**bi·sec′tion·al·ly,** *adv.*

bi·sec·tor (bī sek′tər, bī′sek-), *n.* *Geom.* a line or plane that bisects an angle or line segment. [BISECT + -OR[2]]

bi·sec·trix (bī sek′triks), *n., pl.* **bi·sec·tri·ces** (bī′sek-trī′sēz). 1. *Crystall.* an imaginary line bisecting either the acute angle **(acute bisectrix)** or the obtuse angle **(obtuse bisectrix)** of the optic axes of a biaxial crystal. 2. *Geom.* a bisector. [BISEC(TOR) + -TRIX]

bi·sel·li·um (bī sel′ē əm), *n., pl.* **-sel·li·a** (-sel′ē ə). an ancient Roman seat of honor for two persons. [< L (*bi-* BI-[1] + *sell(a)* seat (c. SETTLE[2]) + *-ium* n. suffix)]

bi·se·ri·al (bī sēr′ē əl), *adj.* *Statistics.* of or pertaining to the correlation between two sets of measurements, one set of which is limited to one of two values. [BI-[1] + SERIAL] —**bi·se′ri·al·ly,** *adv.*

bi·ser·rate (bī ser′āt, -it), *adj.* *Bot.* doubly serrate; notched like a saw, with the teeth also notched. [BI-[1] + SERRATE]

bi·sex·u·al (bī sek′sho͞o əl), *adj.* 1. *Biol.* **a.** of both sexes. **b.** combining male and female organs in one individual; hermaphroditic. 2. *Psychiatry.* sexually responsive to both sexes. —*n.* 3. *Biol.* one who has the reproductive organs of both sexes. 4. *Psychiatry.* a person sexually responsive to both sexes. [BI-[1] + SEXUAL] —**bi·sex′u·al·ism, bi′sex·u·al′i·ty,** *n.* —**bi·sex′u·al·ly,** *adv.*

Bish·kek (bish kek′), *n.* **the capital of Kirghizia (Kyrgyzstan), in the N part. 616,000. Formerly, Pishpek (until 1926), Frunze (1926–91).**

bish·op (bish′əp), *n., v.,* **-oped, -op·ing.** —*n.* 1. a person who supervises a number of local churches or a diocese, being in the Greek, Roman Catholic, Anglican, and other churches a member of the highest order in the ministry. 2. a spiritual supervisor, overseer, or the like. 3. *Chess.* one of two pieces of the same color which may be moved any unobstructed distance diagonally, one on white squares and the other on black. 4. a hot drink made of port wine, oranges, cloves, etc. 5. Also called **bish′op bird′.** any of several colorful, African weaverbirds of the genus *Euplectes,* often kept as pets. —*v.t.* 6. to appoint to the office of bishop. [ME, OE *bisc(e)op* < VL **(e)biscop(us),* for L *episcopus* < Gk *epískopos* overseer, equiv. to *epi-* EPI- + *skopós* watcher; see SCOPE] —**bish′op·less,** *adj.* —**bish′op·like′,** *adj.*

Bish·op (bish′əp), *n.* 1. **Elizabeth,** 1911–79, U.S. poet. 2. **Hazel** (*Gladys*), born 1906, U.S. chemist and businesswoman. 3. **John Peale,** 1892–1944, U.S. poet and essayist. 4. **Morris** (*Gilbert*), 1893–1973, U.S. humorist, poet, and biographer. 5. a town in S Texas. 3722 (1960). 6. a town in E California. 2875 (1960).

bish·op·ric (bish′əp rik), *n.* the see, diocese, or office of a bishop. [ME *bisshoprike,* OE *biscoprīce,* equiv. to *biscop* BISHOP + *rīce* realm; see RICH]

bish·op's-cap (bish′əps kap′), *n.* miterwort (def. 1).

Bish′op's Hat′field, Hatfield (def. 1).

Bish′op's ring′, *Astron.* a reddish-brown corona occasionally seen around the sun, caused by volcanic dust in the atmosphere.

bish·op's-weed (bish′əps wēd′), *n.* goutweed.

Bish·op·ville (bish′əp vil′), *n.* a town in central South Carolina. 3586 (1960).

bis·hy·drox·y·cou·ma·rin (bis′hī drok′si ko͞o′mə-rin), *n.* *Pharm.* dicoumarin. [BIS[1] + HYDROXY + COUMARIN]

Bi·si·tun (bē′si to͞on′), *n.* Behistun.

bisk (bisk), *n.* bisque[1].

Bisk (bēsk), *n.* a city in the S RSFSR, in the S Soviet Union in Asia, near the Ob River. 146,000 (1959). Also, **Biisk, Biysk.**

Bis·kra (bis′krä), *n.* a town and oasis in NE Algeria, in the Sahara. 52,511 (1954).

bis·ma·nol (bis′mə nōl′, -nôl′), *n.* a highly ferromagnetic alloy of bismuth and manganese, having a high degree of magnetic force. [BIS(MUTH) + MAN(GANESE) + -OL[1]]

Bis·marck (biz′märk; *Ger.* bis′märk), *n.* 1. **Ot·to von** (ot′ō von; *Ger.* ô′tō fən), 1815–98, German statesman: first chancellor of modern German Empire 1871–90. 2. a city in and the capital of N Dakota, in the central part. 27,670 (1960).

Bis′marck Archipel′ago, a group of islands in the SW Pacific NE of New Guinea, including the Admiralty Islands, New Britain, New Ireland, and adjacent islands: under Australian administration. ab. 23,000 sq. mi.

Bis′marck her′ring, salted fillet and roe of herring, pickled in vinegar, white wine, and spices, served cold as an hors d'oeuvre with slices of lemon and raw onion.

Bis·marck·i·an (biz mär′kē ən), *adj.* of, pertaining to, or resembling Otto von Bismarck, esp. in respect to his aggressiveness in politics and diplomacy. [BISMARCK + -IAN] —**Bis·marck′i·an·ism,** *n.*

bis·mil·lah (bis mil′ə), *interj.* *Arabic.* in the name of Allah.

bis·muth (biz′məth), *n.* *Chem.* a brittle, grayish white, red-tinged, metallic element used in the manufacture of fusible alloys and in medicine. *Symbol:* Bi; *at. no.:* 83; *at. wt.:* 208.980. [earlier *bismut(um)* < NL *bisemūtum,* Latinized form of G *Wissmuth* (now *Wismut*) < ?] —**bis′muth·al,** *adj.*

bis′muth chro′mate, *Chem.* an orange-red, amorphous, water-insoluble powder, $Bi_2O_3 \cdot 2CrO_3$, used chiefly as a pigment in paints. Also called **basic dichromate.**

bis·mu·thic (biz myo͞o′thik, -muth′ik), *adj.* *Chem.* of or containing bismuth, esp. in the pentavalent state. [BISMUTH + -IC]

bis·muth·ine (biz′mə thēn′, -thin), *n.* *Chem.* 1. an unstable hydride of bismuth, BiH_3, analogous to arsine and stibine. 2. any derivative of this compound in which the hydrogen atoms are replaced by one or more organic groups. [BISMUTH + -INE[2]]

bis·muth·in·ite (biz muth′ə nīt′, biz′mə thə-), *n.* a mineral, bismuth sulfide, Bi_2S_3, occurring in lead-gray masses: an ore of bismuth. Also called **bis′muth glance′.** [BISMUTHINE + -ITE[1]]

bis·muth·ous (biz′mə thəs), *adj.* *Chem.* containing trivalent bismuth. [BISMUTH + -OUS]

bis′muth oxychlo′ride, *Chem.* a white, crystalline, water-insoluble powder, BiOCl, used chiefly in the manufacture of pigments, face powders, and artificial pearls.

bis·muth·yl (biz′mə thil), *n.* 1. *Chem.* the univalent group, BiO^+, occurring in certain bismuth salts, as bismuth oxychloride, BiOCl. [BISMUTH + -YL]

bis·mut·ite (biz′mə tīt′), *n.* a mineral, bismuth carbonate, resulting from the alteration of bismuth minerals: a minor source of bismuth. [< G *Bismutit,* equiv. to *Bismut* BISMUTH + *-it* -ITE[1]]

bis·na·ga (bis nä′gə), *n.* any of several thorny cacti of the genera *Echinocactus, Ferocactus,* and *Astrophytum* of the southwestern U.S. Also, **biznaga.** [< Sp *biznaga* (prob. by assoc. with *biznaga* parsnip), r. earlier *viznauac* < Nahuatl *huitz-nahuac* thorn-surrounded]

Bison, *Bison bison* (7 ft. high at shoulder; total length to 12 ft.; tail 1½ ft.)

bi·son (bī′sən, -zən), *n., pl.* **-son.** 1. Also called **American bison, American buffalo.** a North American, oxlike ruminant, *Bison bison,* having a large head and high, humped shoulders. 2. Also called **wisent.** a related animal, *Bison bonasus,* of Europe, smaller and less shaggy than the American bison. [ME *bisontes* (pl.) < L (nom. sing. *bison*) < Gmc; cf. OHG *wisunt,* OE *wesend,* Icel *visundr*]

bi·sphe·noid (bī sfē′noid), *n.* a tetrahedral crystal form each edge of which is bisected by the perpendicular bisecting the edge that does not intersect it. Also called **disphenoid.** [BI-[1] + SPHENOID]

bisque[1] (bisk), *n.* 1. a thick soup of puréed shellfish, game, or vegetables, usually in cream. 2. ice cream made with powdered macaroons or nuts. Also, **bisk.** [< F]

bisque[2] (bisk), *n.* *Sports.* a point, extra turn, or the like, as in court tennis or croquet. [< F]

bisque[3] (bisk), *n.* 1. biscuit (def. 4). 2. pinkish-tan. —*adj.* 3. having the color bisque. [short for BISCUIT]

Bis·sau (bi sou′), *n.* a seaport in and the capital of Portuguese Guinea, in the W part. 18,309 (1950). Also, **Bis·são** (bē soun′).

bis·sex·tile (bī seks′til, bi-), *adj.* 1. containing or noting the extra day of leap year: *The years 1960 and 1964 were both bissextile.* —*n.* 2. See **leap year.** [< LL *bi(s)sextil(is)* (*annus*) leap year, equiv. to *bissext(us)* BISSEXTUS + *-ilis* -ILE]

bis·sex·tus (bī seks′təs, bi-), *n.* February twenty-ninth: the extra day added to the Julian calendar every fourth year (except those evenly divisible by 400) to compensate for the approximately six hours a year by which the common year of 365 days falls short of the solar year. [< LL *bissextus* (*diēs*) intercalary (day); see BIS[1], SEXT; so called because the 6th day before the Calends of March (Feb. 24th) appeared twice every leap year]

bis·so (bis′ō), *n.* bis[2].

bis·so·na·ta (bis′ə nä′tə, -nā′-), *n.* a coarse woolen cloth constructed in plain weave and dyed black or brown, used in the manufacture of clerical vestments. [?]

bis·ter (bis′tər), *n.* bistre. —**bis′tered,** *adj.*

bis·tort (bis′tôrt), *n.* 1. Also called **snakeweed.** a European perennial herb, *Polygonum Bistorta,* having a twisted root, which is sometimes used as an astringent. 2. any of several related plants, as *P. virginianum* **(Virginia bistort)** and *P. viviparum* **(alpine bistort).** [< L *bistort(a)* twice twisted. See BIS[1], TORT]

bis·tou·ry (bis′tə rē), *n., pl.* **-ries.** a small, narrow surgical knife. [< F *bistouri,* MF *bistorit* < ?]

bis·tre (bis′tər), *n.* 1. a brown pigment extracted from the soot of wood, much used in pen and wash drawings. 2. a yellowish to dark-brown color. Also, **bister.** [< F] —**bis′tred,** *adj.*

bis·tro (bis′trō; *Fr.* bē strō′), *n., pl.* **bis·tros** (bis′trōz; *Fr.* bē strō′). *Informal.* 1. a small, unpretentious café. 2. a small night club or restaurant. [< F]

bi·sul·cate (bī sul′kāt), *adj.* 1. with two grooves. 2. cloven-hoofed. [< L *bisulc(us)* two-furrowed, cloven (see BI-[1], SULCUS) + -ATE[1]]

bi·sul·fate (bī sul′fāt), *n.* *Chem.* a salt of sulfuric acid, containing the HSO_4^- group; an acid sulfate; a hydrogen sulfate, as sodium bisulfate, $NaHSO_4$. Also, **bi·sul′phate.** [BI-[1] + SULFATE]

bi·sul·fide (bī sul′fīd, -fid), *n.* *Chem.* a disulfide. Also, **bi·sul′phide.** [BI-[1] + SULFIDE]

bi·sul·fite (bī sul′fīt), *n.* *Chem.* a salt of sulfurous acid, containing the HSO_3^- group; an acid sulfite; a hydrogen sulfite, as sodium bisulfite, $NaHSO_3$. Also, **bi·sul′phite.** [BI-[1] + SULFITE]

Bi·su·tun (bē′sə to͞on′), *n.* Behistun.

bi·sym·met·ri·cal (bī′si me′tri kəl), *adj. Bot.* having two planes of symmetry at right angles to each other. Also, **bi′sym·met′ric.** [BI-[1] + SYMMETRICAL] —**bi′sym·met′ri·cal·ly,** *adv.* —**bi·sym·me·try** (bī sim′i trē), *n.*

bit[1] (bit), *n., v.,* **bit·ted, bit·ting.** —*n.* **1.** the mouthpiece of a bridle, having fittings at each end to which the reins are fastened. **2.** anything that curbs or restrains. **3.** *Mach.* **a.** a removable drilling or boring tool for use in a brace, drill press, or the like. **b.** a removable boring head used on certain kinds of drills, as a rock drill. **c.** a device for drilling oil wells or the like, consisting of a horizontally rotating blade or an assembly of rotating toothed wheels. **4.** the blade or iron of a carpenter's plane. **5.** the cutting part of an ax or hatchet. **6.** the wide portion at the end of an ordinary key that moves the bolt. **7. take the bit in** or **between one's teeth,** to cast off control; rebel: *He took the bit in his teeth and acted against his parents' wishes.* —*v.t.* **8.** to put a bit in the mouth of (a horse). **9.** to curb or restrain with, or as with, a bit. **10.** to grind a bit on (a key). [ME *bite,* OE: action of biting; c. G *Biss,* Icel *bit.* See BITE] —**bit′less,** *adj.*

Bits
A, Auger bit;
B, Straight shank drill bit

bit[2] (bit), *n.* **1.** a small piece or quantity of anything: *a bit of string; a bit of one's mind.* **2.** a short time: *Wait a bit.* **3.** *U.S. Slang.* **a.** an amount equivalent to twelve and a half cents (used only in even multiples): *two bits; six bits.* **b.** an act, performance, or routine: *She's doing the Camille bit. He played* Rhapsody in Blue *on the guitar—the whole bit.* **4.** Also, **bit part.** a very small role, as in a play or motion picture, containing few or no lines. Cf. **walk-on** (def. 1). **5.** any small coin: *a threepenny bit.* **6.** a Spanish or Mexican silver real worth 12½ cents, formerly current in parts of the U.S. **7. bit by bit,** by degrees; gradually: *Having saved money bit by bit, they now had enough to buy a piece of land in the West.* **8. do one's bit,** *Informal.* to contribute one's share to an effort: *In an emergency every person should do his bit.* [ME *bite,* OE *bita* bit, morsel; c. G *Bissen,* Icel *biti.* See BITE]
—**Syn. 1.** particle, speck, grain, mite; whit, iota, jot; scrap, fragment.

bit[3] (bit), *n.* **1.** a single, basic unit of information, used in connection with computers and communication theory. **2.** baud. [B(INARY + DIG)IT]

bit[4] (bit), *v.* pt. and a pp. of **bite.**

B.I.T., Bachelor of Industrial Technology.

bi·tar·trate (bī tär′trāt), *n. Chem.* a tartrate in which only one of the two acidic hydrogen atoms of tartaric acid is replaced by a metal or positive group; an acid tartrate; a hydrogen tartrate, as sodium bitartrate, $NaHC_4H_4O_6$. [BI-[1] + TARTRATE]

bitch (bich), *n.* **1.** a female dog. **2.** a female of canines generally. **3.** *Slang.* **a.** a malicious, unpleasant, selfish woman, esp. one who stops at nothing to reach her goal. **b.** a lewd woman. **4.** *Slang.* **a.** a complaint. **b.** anything difficult or unpleasant: *The test was a bitch.* —*v.i.* **5.** *Slang.* to complain; gripe: *He bitched about the service, then bitched about the bill.* —*v.t.* **6.** *Slang.* to spoil; bungle: *He bitched the job completely.* [ME *bicche,* OE *bicce;* c. Icel *bikkja*]

bitch·er·y (bich′ə rē), *n. Slang.* behavior characteristic of a bitch. [BITCH + -ERY]

bitch′ god′dess, *Slang.* worldly or material success personified as a goddess, esp. one requiring sacrifice and being essentially destructive: *He went to New York to worship the bitch goddess.*

bitch·y (bich′ē), *adj.,* **bitch·i·er, bitch·i·est.** *Slang.* pertaining to or characteristic of a bitch. [BITCH + -Y[1]] —**bitch′i·ness,** *n.*

bite (bīt), *v.,* **bit, bit·ten** or **bit, bit·ing,** *n.* —*v.t.* **1.** to cut, wound, or tear with the teeth: *She bit the apple greedily. The lion bit his trainer.* **2.** to grip or hold with the teeth: *Stop biting your thumb!* **3.** to sting, as an insect. **4.** to cause to smart or sting: *an icy wind that bites our faces; a strong tobacco that bites my tongue.* **5.** to sever with the teeth (often fol. by *off*): *Don't bite your nails. The leopard bit off his finger.* **6.** to sink one's teeth into; start to eat (often fol. by *into*): *He bit his attacker on the arm. She bit into her steak.* **7.** to clamp the teeth firmly on or around (often fol. by *on*): *He bit down hard on the stick while they removed the bullet from his leg. The baby bit her teething ring and quieted down.* **8.** to eat into or corrode, as an acid does. **9.** to cut or pierce with, or as with, a weapon: *The sword split his helmet and bit him fatally.* **10.** *Etching.* to etch with acid (a copper or other surface) in such parts as are left bare of a protective coating: *He bit his plates and printed them.* **11.** to take firm hold or act effectively on: *We need a clamp to bite the wood while the glue dries.* **12.** *Slang.* **a.** to take advantage of; cheat; deceive (sometimes used passively): *She bit me for a new fur coat. I got bitten in a mail-order swindle.* **b.** to annoy or upset; anger: *What's biting you, sorehead?* **13.** *Archaic.* to make a decided impression on; affect.
—*v.i.* **14.** to press the teeth into something; attack with the jaws, bill, sting, etc.; snap: *Does your parrot bite?* **15.** *Angling.* (of fish) to take bait: *The fish aren't biting today.* **16.** to accept an offer or suggestion, esp. one intended to trick or deceive: *I knew it was a mistake, but I bit anyway.* **17.** to admit defeat in guessing a riddle or question: *I'll bite, who is it?* **18.** to act effectively; grip; hold: *This wood is so dry the screws don't bite.* **19. bite off more than one can chew,** to attempt something that exceeds one's capacity: *In trying to build a house by himself, he had bitten off more than he could chew.* **20. bite someone's head off,** to respond with anger or impatience to someone's question or comment: *Don't ask for anything because he'll bite your head off.* **21. bite the dust.** See **dust** (def. 14). **22. bite the hand that feeds one,** to repay kindness with malice or injury: *When he berates his boss, he is biting the hand that feeds him.*
—*n.* **23.** act of biting. **24.** a wound made by biting: *a deep bite.* **25.** a cutting, stinging, or nipping effect: *the bite of an icy wind; the bite of strong liquor on the tongue.* **26.** sharpness; incisiveness; effectiveness: *The bite of his story is spoiled by his slovenly style.* **27.** a piece bitten off: *Carefully chew each bite.* **28.** *Slang.* a portion severed from the whole: *the government's weekly bite of my paycheck.* **29.** a morsel of food: *not a bite to eat.* **30.** a small meal: *Let's grab a bite before the theater.* **31.** *Mach.* **a.** the catch or hold that one object or one part of a mechanical apparatus has on another. **b.** a surface brought into contact to obtain a hold or grip, as in a lathe, chuck, or similar device. **32.** the roughness of the surface of a file. **33.** the occlusion of one's teeth: *The dentist said I had a good bite.* **34.** *Metalworking.* the maximum angle, measured from the center of a roll in a rolling mill, between a perpendicular and a line to the point of contact where a given object to be rolled will enter between the rolls. **35. put the bite on,** *Slang.* **a.** to solicit or attempt to borrow money from. **b.** to press (someone) for money, as in extortion: *One of his co-workers found out about his prison record and began to put the bite on him.* [ME *bite(n),* OE *bītan;* c. OHG *bīzan* (G *beissen*), Goth *beitan,* Icel *bīta;* akin to L *findere* to split] —**bit′a·ble, bite′a·ble,** *adj.*
—**Syn. 1.** gnaw, chew, nip. **27.** mouthful, morsel.

bit·er (bī′tər), *n.* **1.** one who or that which bites, esp. viciously, incorrigibly, or the like: *That monkey is a biter.* **2.** *Obs.* a cheat; swindler; fraud. **3. the biter bit,** a situation in which one injures himself while trying to injure or slander another; the tables turned. [ME; see BITE, -ER[1]]

bite·wing (bīt′wing′), *n. Dentistry.* a holder for x-ray film with a projecting fin that is held between the teeth so as to show the crown of the upper and lower teeth in one picture. [BITE + WING]

bit′ gauge′, *Carpentry.* a device for stopping a bit when it has reached a desired depth. Also called **bit stop.**

Bi·thyn·i·a (bi thin′ē ə), *n.* an ancient country in NW Asia Minor. —**Bi·thyn′i·an,** *adj., n.*

bit·ing (bī′ting), *adj.* **1.** nipping; smarting; keen: *biting cold; a biting sensation on the tongue.* **2.** cutting; sarcastic: *a biting remark.* [ME *bitynge.* See BITE, -ING[2]] —**bit′ing·ly,** *adv.* —**bit′ing·ness,** *n.*
—**Syn. 2.** incisive, trenchant; caustic, mordant.

bit′ing house′fly. See **stable fly.**

bit′ing louse′. See under **louse** (def. 2).

bit′ing midge′, punkie.

bit′ key′, a key having a wing bit for moving a leverlike tumbler.

Bi·to·la (bē′tô lä), *n.* a city in S Macedonia. 137,636. Serbo-Croatian, **Bi·tolj** (bē′tôl yə). Turkish, **Monastir.**

Bi·ton (bīt′ən), *n. Class. Myth.* one of the sons of Cydippe. Cf. **Cleobis.**

bi·ton·al (bī tōn′əl), *adj. Music.* marked by or using bitonality. [BI-[1] + TONAL]

bi·to·nal·i·ty (bī′tō nal′i tē), *n., pl.* **-ties.** *Music.* the simultaneous occurrence of two tonalities in a composition. [BI-[1] + TONALITY]

bit′ part′, bit[2] (def. 4).

bit·stock (bit′stok′), *n. Mach.* the stock or handle by which a boring bit is held and rotated; a brace. [BIT[1] + STOCK]

bit′ stop′. See **bit gauge.**

bitt (bit), *Naut.* —*n.* **1.** Also called **bollard.** a strong post of wood or iron projecting, usually in pairs, above the deck of a ship, used for securing cables, lines for towing, etc. —*v.t.* **2.** to wrap (a cable) around a bitt or bitts to secure it. [var. of BIT[1]]

bit·te (bit′ə), *interj. German.* **1.** please. **2.** I beg your pardon. **3.** you're welcome; don't mention it. [short for *ich bitte* I beg]

bit·ten (bit′ən), *v.* a pp. of **bite.**

bit·ter (bit′ər), *adj.* **1.** having a harsh, disagreeably acrid taste, like that of aspirin, quinine, wormwood, or aloes. **2.** hard to admit or accept: *a bitter lesson.* **3.** hard to bear; grievous; distressful: *a bitter sorrow.* **4.** causing pain; piercing; stinging: *a bitter chill.* **5.** characterized by intense antagonism or hostility: *bitter hatred.* **6.** harsh; sarcastic; cutting: *bitter words.* —*n.* **7.** that which is bitter; bitterness. —*v.t.* **8.** to make bitter: *herbs employed to bitter vermouth.* —*adv.* **9.** extremely; very; exceedingly: *a bitter cold night.* [ME, OE *biter;* c. G *bitter,* Icel *bitr,* Goth *baitr(s);* akin to BITE] —**bit′ter·ish,** *adj.* —**bit′ter·ly,** *adv.* —**bit′ter·ness,** *n.*
—**Syn. 1.** acrid, biting, distasteful. **3.** distressing, poignant, painful. **4.** biting, nipping. **5.** fierce, cruel, ruthless, relentless. **6.** acrimonious, caustic, sardonic, scornful.

bit′ter al′mond oil′, *Chem.* See **almond oil** (def. 2).

bit′ter ap′ple, colocynth (defs. 1, 2).

bit′ter cassa′va. See under **cassava** (def. 1).

bit′ter cress′, any cruciferous herb of the genus *Cardamine,* having usually pinnate leaves and clusters of white, pink, or purple flowers.

bit′ter dock′. See under **dock**[4] (def. 1).

bit·ter end (bit′ər end′ *for 1;* bit′ər end′ *for 2*), **1.** the conclusion of a difficult or unpleasant situation; the last or furthest extremity: *Despite the unpleasant scenes in the movie, she insisted on staying until the bitter end.* **2.** *Naut.* **a.** the inboard end of an anchor chain or cable, secured in the chain locker of a vessel. **b.** the end of any chain or cable.

bit·ter·end·er (bit′ər en′dər), *n. Informal.* one who persists until the bitter end without compromising or yielding; diehard.

bit′ter herb′, **1.** an Old World herb, *Centaurium umbellatum,* used dried in medicine as a tonic. **2.** the turtlehead, *Chelone glabra,* used in medicine as a tonic, cathartic, and anthelmintic. **3.** *Judaism.* an herb that tastes bitter, esp. horseradish, traditionally eaten at the Seder, and serving as a reminder of the Israelites' slavery before the Exodus.

bit′ter lake′, a lake containing in solution a high concentration of sulfates and alkaline carbonates.

Bit′ter Lakes′, two lakes in the NE United Arab Republic, forming part of the Suez Canal.

bit′ter lem′on, a beverage made from lemon juice and carbonated quinine water: used in mixing highballs, esp. with gin or vodka.

bit·ter·ling (bit′ər ling), *n.* a cyprinid fish, *Rhodeus sericeus,* found in central and eastern Europe; the female of which has a long ovipositor to deposit eggs in the mantle cavity of mussels. [< G, equiv. to *bitter* BITTER + *-ling* -LING[1]]

American bittern
(Length 2½ ft.; wingspread 3 ft.)

bit·tern[1] (bit′ərn), *n.* **1.** any of several tawny brown herons that inhabit reedy marshes, as *Botaurus lentiginosus* **(American bittern),** of North America and *B. stellaris,* of Europe. **2.** any of several small herons of the genus *Ixobrychus,* as *I. exilis* **(least bittern)** of temperate and tropical North and South America. [earlier *bittorn,* equiv. to ME *bitor* (var. of *botor* < MF *butor*) + *-n* < ?]

bit·tern[2] (bit′ərn), *n. Chem.* a bitter solution remaining in saltmaking after the salt has crystallized out of sea water or brine, used as a source of bromides, iodides, and certain other salts. [var. of *bittering;* see BITTER, -ING[1]]

bit·ter·nut (bit′ər nut′), *n.* a hickory, *Carya cordiformis,* of the eastern and southern U.S., bearing a thin-shelled, bitter seed. [BITTER + NUT]

bit′ter or′ange. See under **orange** (def. 2).

bit′ter prin′ciple, *Chem.* any of several hundred natural compounds, usually of vegetable origin, having a bitter taste, and not admitting of any chemical classification.

bit·ter·root (bit′ər ro͞ot′, -ro͝ot′), *n.* a portulacaceous plant, *Lewisia rediviva,* having fleshy roots and handsome pink flowers: the State flower of Montana. [BITTER + ROOT[1]]

Bit′terroot Range′, a mountain range on the boundary between Idaho and Montana, a part of the Rocky Mountains: highest peak, ab. 10,000 ft. Also, **Bit′ter Root′ Range′.**

bit′ter rot′, *Plant Pathol.* a disease of apples, grapes, and other fruit, characterized by cankers on the branches or twigs and bitter, rotted fruit, caused by any of several fungi.

bit·ters (bit′ərz), *n.* (*construed as pl.*) **1.** a liquid, often an alcoholic liquor, in which bitter herbs or roots have steeped, often used as a flavoring, esp. in mixed drinks, or as a tonic. **2.** *Brit.* a very dry ale having a strong taste of hops. **3.** *Pharm.* **a.** a liquid, usually alcoholic, impregnated with a bitter medicine, as gentian, quassia, etc., used as a stomachic, tonic, or the like. **b.** bitter medicinal substances in general, as quinine, gentian, etc. [BITTER + -S[3]]

bit·ter·sweet (*n.* bit′ər swēt′; *adj.* bit′ər swēt′), *n.* **1.** Also called **woody nightshade.** a climbing or trailing solanaceous plant, *Solanum Dulcamara,* having scarlet berries. **2.** Also called **climbing bittersweet.** any climbing plant of the genus *Celastrus,* bearing orange capsules opening to expose red-coated seeds, esp. *Celastrus scandens.* **3.** pleasure mingled with pain or regret: *the bittersweet of parting.* —*adj.* **4.** both bitter and sweet to the taste: *bittersweet chocolate.* **5.** both pleasant and painful: *a bittersweet memory.* [BITTER + SWEET]

bit·ter·weed (bit′ər wēd′), *n.* **1.** any of various plants containing a bitter principle, as the ragweed. **2.** any sneezeweed of genus *Helenium,* esp. *H. tenuifolium.* [BITTER + WEED[1]]

bit′ter wood′, *Pharm.* quassia (def. 2).

bit·ter·wort (bit′ər wûrt′), *n.* See **yellow gentian.** [BITTER + WORT[2]]

bit·ting (bit′ing), *n.* one of the indentations on the bit of a key. [BIT[1] + -ING[1]]

bit·tock (bit′ək), *n. Chiefly Brit. Dial.* a little bit. [BIT[2] + -OCK]

bi·tu·men (bi to͞o′mən, -tyo͞o′-, bich′o͞o-), *n.* **1.** any of various natural substances, as asphalt, maltha, gilsonite, etc., consisting mainly of hydrocarbons. **2.** (formerly) an asphalt of Asia Minor used as cement and mortar. [late ME *bithumen* < L *bitūmen*] —**bi·tu·mi·noid** (bi to͞o′mə noid′, -tyo͞o′-), *adj.*

bi·tu·mi·nise (bi to͞o′mə nīz′, -tyo͞o′-), *v.t.,* **-nised, -nis·ing.** *Chiefly Brit.* bituminize. —**bi·tu′mi·ni·sa′tion,** *n.*

bi·tu·mi·nize (bi to͞o′mə nīz′, -tyo͞o′-), *v.t.,* **-nized, -niz·ing.** to convert into or treat with bitumen. [< L *bitūmin-* (s. of *bitūmen*) + -IZE] **bi·tu′mi·ni·za′tion,** *n.*

bi·tu·mi·nous (bi to͞o′mə nəs, -tyo͞o′-), *adj.* resembling or containing bitumen: *bituminous shale.* [< L *bitūminōs(us),* equiv. to *bitūmin-* (s. of *bitūmen*) + *-ōsus* -OUS]

bitu′minous coal′, a mineral coal which contains volatile hydrocarbons and tarry matter, and burns with a yellow, smoky flame; soft coal.

bi·u·nique (bī′yo͞o nēk′), *adj. Math.* one-to-one. [BI-[1] + UNIQUE] —**bi′u·nique′ly,** *adv.* —**bi′u·nique′ness,** *n.*

bi·va·lent (bī vā′lənt, biv′ə-), *adj.* **1.** *Chem.* **a.** having a valence of two. **b.** having two valences, as aluminum with valences of two and three. **2.** *Genetics.* pertaining to associations of two similar or identical chromosomes. —*n.* **3.** *Genetics.* a pair of bivalent chromosomes. [BI-[1] + -VALENT] —**bi·va·lence** (bī vā′ləns, biv′ə ləns), **bi·va′len·cy,** *n.*

bi·valve (bī′valv′), *n.* **1.** *Zool.* a mollusk having two shells hinged together, as the oyster, clam, or mussel; a lamellibranch. —*adj.* **2.** *Bot.* having two valves, as a seedcase. **3.** *Zool.* having two shells, usually united by a hinge. [BI-[1] + VALVE] —**bi·val·vu·lar** (bī val′vyə lər), *adj.*

bi·vane (bī′vān′), *n.* a sensitive vane that measures both the horizontal and vertical components of wind direction. [BI-[1] + VANE]

bi·var·i·ate (bī vâr′ē it, -āt′), *adj. Statistics.* of, relating to, or having two variates. [BI-[1] + VARIATE]

bi·vi·nyl (bī vī′nil, -vīn′əl, -vin′il, -vin′əl), *n. Chem.* butadiene. [BI-[1] + VINYL]

bi·vol·tine (bī vōl′tēn, -tən), *adj. Entomol.* producing two broods in one year, as certain silkworm moths. [< F *bivoltin.* See BI-[1], VOLTA, -INE[1]]

biv·ou·ac (biv′o͞o ak′, biv′wak), *n., v.,* **-acked, -ack·ing.** —*n.* **1.** a military encampment made with tents or improvised shelters, usually without shelter or protection from enemy fire. **2.** the place used for such an encampment. **—*v.i.*** **3.** to rest or assemble in such an area. [< F < dial. G *Biwache* night watch (lit. by-watch), equiv. to *bi-* BY- + *Wache* WATCH]

bi·week·ly (bī wēk′lē), *adj.*, *n.*, *pl.* **-lies,** *adv.* **—*adj.*** **1.** occurring every two weeks. **2.** (loosely) occurring twice a week; semiweekly. **—*n.*** **3.** a periodical issued every other week. **—*adv.*** **4.** every two weeks. **5.** (loosely) twice a week. [BI-¹ + WEEKLY]

—Usage. Since it is not always clear which meaning of BIWEEKLY is intended—"twice a week" or "every two weeks"—the use of SEMIWEEKLY for "twice a week" is preferable because it is unambiguous. Since there is no single, unambiguous term for "every two weeks," this phrase itself is the least confusing to use.

bi·year·ly (bī yēr′lē), *adj.* **1.** biennial. **—*adv.*** **2.** biennially; biannually. **3.** (loosely) twice yearly. [BI-¹ + YEARLY]

Bi·ysk (bē′isk), *n.* Bisk.

biz (biz), *n.* *Slang.* business. [by shortening and alter.]

bi·zarre (bi zär′), *adj.* markedly unusual in appearance, style, or general character; whimsically strange; odd: *bizarre clothing and behavior.* [< F Sp *bizarr(o)* brave, perh. < Basque *bizar* beard + *-o* masc. suffix (hence, a he-man)] **—bi·zarre′ly,** *adv.* **—bi·zarre′ness,** *n.*

bize (bēz), *n.* bise.

Bi·zer·te (bi zûr′tə; *Fr.* bē zeʀt′), *n.* a seaport in N Tunisia. 44,681 (1956). Also, **Bi·zer·ta** (bi zûr′tə; *Sp.* bē ᴛʜer′tä, -ser′-). Ancient, **Hippo Zarytus.**

Bi·zet (bē zā′), *n.* **Georges** (zhôʀzh), (*Alexandre César Léopold*), 1838–75, French composer, esp. of opera.

biz·na·ga (bis nä′gə), *n.* bisnaga.

bi·zone (bī′zōn′), *n.* two combined zones. [short for *bizonal territory.* See BI-¹, ZONE, -AL¹] **—bi·zon′al,** *adj.*

Bi·zo·ni·a (bī zō′nē ə, bi-), *n.* both the U.S. and British occupation zones in Germany after World War II.

Biz·tha (biz′thə), *n.* one of the seven eunuchs who served in the court of King Ahasuerus. Esther 1:10. Also, *Douay Bible,* **Bazatha.**

B. J., Bachelor of Journalism.

Bjoer·ling (byœʀ′ling), *n.* **Jus·si** (yŏŏs′ē), 1911–60, Swedish tenor. Also, **Björ′ling.**

Björn·son (byûrn′son; *Norw.* byœʀn′son), *n.* **Björn·stjer·ne** (byœʀn′styeʀ nə), 1832–1910, Norwegian poet, novelist, and playwright: Nobel prize 1903.

Bk, *Chem.* berkelium.

bk., **1.** bank. **2.** book.

bkbndr., bookbinder.

bkcy., *Legal.* bankruptcy.

bkg., banking.

bklr., *Printing.* black letter.

bkpr., bookkeeper.

bks., **1.** banks. **2.** barracks. **3.** books.

bl., **1.** bale; bales. **2.** barrel; barrels. **3.** black. **4.** block. **5.** blue.

b/l, *Com.* See **bill of lading.** Also, **B/L**

B.L., **1.** Bachelor of Laws. **2.** Bachelor of Letters. **3.** See **bill of lading.**

b.l., **1.** See **bill of lading.** **2.** *Ordn.* breech loading.

B.L.A., **1.** Bachelor of Landscape Architecture. **2.** Bachelor of Liberal Arts.

blab (blab), *v.*, **blabbed, blab·bing,** *n.* **—*v.t.*** **1.** to reveal indiscreetly and thoughtlessly: *She blabbed my confidences to every one.* **—*v.i.*** **2.** to talk or chatter indiscreetly and thoughtlessly: *Don't confide in him, because he blabs. She blabbed so much I couldn't hear the concert.* **—*n.*** **3.** idle, indiscreet chattering: *Those stories are false, just so much blab.* **4.** a person who blabs; blabbermouth. [ME *blabbe* (n.), perh. back formation from ME *blaberen* to blabber; c. Icel *blabbra,* G *plappern*] **—blab′ber,** *n.*

blab·ber·mouth (blab′ər mouth′), *n.*, *pl.* **-mouths** (-mouᴛʜz′). a person who talks too much, esp. indiscreetly. [BLABBER + MOUTH]

Bla·cher (blä′ᴋʜər), *n.* **Bo·ris** (bō′ʀis), born 1903, German composer, born in China.

black (blak), *adj.* **1.** lacking hue and brightness; absorbing light without reflecting any of the rays composing it, as the type on this page. **2.** wearing black or dark clothing, armor, etc.: *the black prince.* **3. a.** of, pertaining to, or belonging to an ethnic group characterized by dark skin pigmentation. **b.** pertaining specifically to the dark-skinned peoples of Africa, Oceania, and Australia: the Negroes, Negritos, Papuans, Melanesians, and Australian aborigines. **4.** soiled or stained with dirt: *That shirt was black within an hour.* **5.** characterized by absence of light; involved or enveloped in darkness: *a black night.* **6.** gloomy; pessimistic; dismal: *a black outlook.* **7.** boding ill; sullen; hostile: *black words; black looks.* **8.** deliberate; harmful; inexcusable: *a black lie.* **9.** without any moral light or goodness; evil; wicked: *His black heart has concocted yet another black deed.* **10.** marked by ruin or desolation, as would be indicated in black on a map: *black areas of drought.* **11.** indicating censure, disgrace, or liability to punishment: *a black mark on one's record.* **12.** (of coffee) without milk or cream. **13.** (of steel) unfinished; in the form in which it comes from the rolling mill or forge. **14. black or white,** completely either one way or another, without any intermediate state. **—*n.*** **15.** the color at the extreme end of grays, opposite to white, absorbing all light incident upon it. Cf. **white** (def. 24). **16.** a member of a dark-skinned people; Negro. **17.** black clothing, esp. as a sign of mourning: *He wore black at the funeral.* **18.** *Chess, Checkers.* the dark-colored men or pieces or squares. **19.** black pigment: *lamp black.* **20.** a horse that is entirely black. Cf. **brown** (def. 2). **21. in black and white.** See **black and white. 22. in the black,** operating at a profit or being out of debt (opposed to *in the red*): *New production methods put the company in the black.* **—*v.t.*** **23.** to make black; put black on; blacken. **24.** to polish (shoes, boots, etc.) with blacking. **—*v.i.*** **25.** to become black; take on a black color; blacken. **26. black out, a.** *Mil.* to obscure by concealing all light in defense against air raids. **b.** to lose consciousness: *He blacked out at the sight of blood.* **c.** to forget everything relating to a particular event, person, etc.: *When it came to his war experiences he blacked out completely.* **d.** *Theat.* to extinguish all of the stage lights. **e.** to make or become inoperable: *to black out the radio broadcasts from the U.S.* [ME *blak,* OE *blæc;* c OHG *blah-;* akin to Icel *blakkr* black, *blek* ink] **—black′ish,** *adj.* **—black′ish·ly,** *adv.* **—black′ish·ness,** *n.*

—Syn. 1. dark, dusky; sooty, inky; swart, swarthy; sable, ebony. **4.** dirty, dingy. **6.** sad, depressing, sombre, doleful, mournful, funereal. **7.** disastrous, calamitous. **9.** sinful, inhuman, fiendish, devilish, infernal, monstrous; atrocious, horrible; nefarious, treacherous, traitorous, villainous. **—Ant. 1.** white. **4.** clean. **6.** hopeful, cheerful.

Black (blak), *n.* **1. Hugo Lafayette,** born 1886, U.S. political official: associate justice of the U.S. Supreme Court since 1937. **2. Joseph,** 1728–99, Scottish physician and chemist.

black′ aca′cia, a tall tree, *Acacia melanoxylon,* of Australia, having cream-yellow flowers, and yielding a very light wood. Also called **lightwood.**

black·a·cre (blak′ā′kər), *n.* a fanciful designation for a hypothetical piece of land, esp. as distinguished from whiteacre; formerly used in lawbooks for illustrative purposes. [BLACK + ACRE]

black′ al′der, **1.** Also called **winterberry.** a holly, *Ilex verticillata,* of eastern and midwestern North America. **2.** an alder, *Alnus glutinosa,* of Europe, having a dark-gray bark and sticky foliage.

black·a·moor (blak′ə mŏŏr′), *n.* **1.** a Negro. **2.** any dark-skinned person. [unexplained var. of phrase *black Moor*]

black-and-blue (blak′ən blōō′), *adj.* discolored, as by bruising; exhibiting ecchymosis: *a black-and-blue mark on my knee.*

Black′ and Tan′, **1.** (*l.c.*) a black-and-tan dog. **2.** an armed force of about 6000 men sent by the British government to Ireland in June, 1920, to suppress revolutionary activity: so called from the colors of their uniform. **3.** a member of this force. **4.** (*l.c.*) a drink made of equal parts of ale and stout or porter.

black-and-tan (blak′ən tan′), *adj* **1.** (of a dog) of a black color with tan markings above the eyes and on the muzzle, chest, legs, feet, and breech. **2.** *Slang.* frequented by or catering to Negroes and whites: *a black-and-tan bar.*

black′ and white′, **1.** print or writing: *I want to see that agreement in black and white.* **2.** a monochromatic picture done with black and white only.

black-and-white (blak′ən hwīt′, -wīt′), *adj.* **1.** displaying only black and white tones; without color, as a picture, chart, etc. **2.** of, pertaining to, or constituting a two-valued system, as of logic, morality, etc.; absolute: *To those who think in black-and-white terms, a person must be either entirely good or entirely bad.*

black′ arm′, *Plant Pathol.* a type or phase of bacterial blight of cotton, characterized by black, elongated lesions on the stem and branches, caused by a bacterium, *Xanthomonas malvacearum.*

black′ art′, witchcraft; magic.

black-a-vised (blak′ə vīst′, -vīzd′), *adj.* dark-complexioned. Also, **black-a-viced** (blak′ə vīst′). [Scot *blackaviced,* equiv. to *black a vice* (one) black of face (BLACK + A³ + obs. *vice* < MF *vis;* see VISAGE) + -ED³]

black′-backed gull′ (blak′bakt′), any of several white gulls, as *Larus Marinus* (**great black-backed gull**), having a black back and wings.

black′back floun′der (blak′bak′). See **winter flounder.**

black·ball (blak′bôl′), *n.* **1.** a negative vote, esp. in deciding on an applicant or candidate. **2.** a black ball placed in a ballot box signifying a negative vote. **—*v.t.*** **3.** to vote against (a candidate, applicant, etc.). **4.** to ostracize: *The whole town blackballed them.* **5.** to reject (a candidate) by placing a black ball in the ballot box. [BLACK + BALL¹] **—black′ball′er,** *n.*

black′ bal′sam. See **Peru balsam.**

black′band·ed sun′fish (blak′ban′did), a centrarchid fish, *Enneacanthus chaetodon,* found in streams along the Atlantic coast of the U.S. Also called **chaetodon.** [BLACK + BAND² + -ED²], so called from its markings]

black′ ba·sal′tes (bə sôl′tēz), basaltware.

black′ bass′ (bas), any fresh-water, American game fish of the genus *Micropterus.* Cf. **largemouth bass, smallmouth bass.**

black′ bead′, cat's-claw.

black′ bear′, a North American bear, *Ursus americanus,* having a brown face and dense black fur. See illus. under **bear².**

Black·beard (blak′bērd′), *n.* pseudonym of Edward Teach.

black·bee·tle (blak′bēt′əl), *n.* See **oriental cockroach.** [BLACK + BEETLE¹]

black′-bel·lied plov′er (blak′bel′ēd), a large plover, *Squatarola squatarola,* of both the New and Old Worlds, having black underparts when in nuptial plumage.

black′bel·ly rose′fish (blak′bel′ē), a reddish scorpionfish, *Helicolenus dactylopterus,* found in the deep waters of the western Atlantic Ocean. [BLACK + BELLY]

black belt (blak′ belt′ *for 1, 2;* blak′ belt′ *for 3*), **1.** a preponderantly Negro area in a city or State. **2.** a narrow belt of dark-colored, calcareous soils in central Alabama and Mississippi highly adapted to agriculture, esp. the growing of cotton. **3.** *U.S. Judo.* a belt conferred by a judo association on a player, noting attainment of the fourth of the four ranks of achievement, to be worn on a judo costume. Cf. **brown belt, green belt** (def. 2), **white belt. —black′-belt′,** *adj.*

black·ber·ry (blak′ber′ē, -bə rē), *n.*, *pl.* **-ries. 1.** the fruit, black or very dark purple when ripe, of certain species of the genus *Rubus.* **2.** the plant itself. [ME *blakeberie,* OE *blaceberie.* See BLACK, BERRY] **—black′-ber′ry-like′,** *adj.*

black′berry lil′y, a perennial iridaceous plant, *Belamcanda chinensis,* having red-spotted, orange, lily-like flowers and globose seeds resembling blackberries.

black′ bile′, *Old Physiol.* a humor regarded as causing gloominess.

black′-billed cuck′oo (blak′bild′), a North American cuckoo, *Coccyzus erythrophthalmus,* which has a black bill and which, unlike many cuckoos, constructs its own nest and rears its own young.

black′-billed mag′pie. See under **magpie** (def. 1).

black′ bind′weed, **1.** a twining Old World vine, *Tamus communis,* bearing red berries. **2.** a climbing European herb, *Polygonum Convolvulus,* found in America as a tenacious weed.

black·bird (blak′bûrd′), *n.* **1.** a common European thrush, *Turdus merula,* the male of which is black with a yellow bill. **2.** any of several American birds of the family *Icteridae,* having black plumage. Cf. **crow blackbird, red-winged blackbird, rusty blackbird. 3.** any of several other unrelated birds having black plumage in either or both sexes. **4.** (formerly) a person, esp. a Kanaka, who was kidnaped and sold abroad, usually in Australia, as a slave. **—*v.t.*** **5.** to kidnap (a person), as in blackbirding. **—*v.i.*** **6.** to engage in blackbirding. [late ME *blacke bride.* See BLACK, BIRD]

black·bird·er (blak′bûr′dər), *n.* (formerly) a person or ship illegally engaged in the slave trade, esp. in the Pacific. [BLACKBIRD + -ER¹]

black·bird·ing (blak′bûr′ding), *n.* (formerly) the act or practice of kidnaping persons, esp. Kanakas, and selling them abroad as slaves. [BLACKBIRD + -ING¹]

black′ bliz′zard, *South-Central U.S.* a dust storm.

black·board (blak′bōrd′, -bôrd′), *n.* a sheet of smooth, hard material, esp. dark slate, used in schools, lecture rooms, etc., for writing or drawing on with chalk. Also called **chalkboard.** Cf. **greenboard.** [BLACK + BOARD]

black′ bod′y, *Physics.* a hypothetical body that absorbs without reflection all of the electromagnetic radiation incident on its surface. Also called **perfect radiator.**

black′ book′, **1.** a book of names of people liable to censure or punishment. **2. in (someone's) black books,** in disfavor with someone: *If you continue in this fashion, you will be in my black books.*

black′ bot′tom, a lively American dance, popular in the late 1920's, marked by emphatic, sinuous movements of the hips.

black′ box′, any unit that forms part of an electronic circuit and that has its function, but not its components, specified.

black·boy (blak′boi′), *n.* the grass tree. [BLACK + BOY]

black′ brant′, a small goose, *Branta nigricans,* of western North America, having black underparts.

black′ bread′, a coarse-grained dark bread, often sour and made from whole-grain rye flour.

black′ buck′, a blackish-brown antelope, *Antilope cervicapra,* of India.

Black buck (2½ ft. high at shoulder; horns 2 ft.; length 4 ft.)

black′ buf′falo, a buffalofish, *Ictiobus niger,* of the Great Lakes and Mississippi River drainage systems south to Mexico. Also called **rooter.**

black′ buran′, karaburan.

Black·burn (blak′bərn), *n.* **1.** a city in central Lancashire, in NW England. 106,114 (1961). **2. Mount,** a mountain in SE Alaska, in the Wrangel Mountains. 16,140 ft.

Black·burn′i·an war′bler (blak bûr′nē ən), a black and white North American wood warbler, *Dendroica fusca,* having an orange throat and an orange and black head. [named after Mrs. Hugh *Blackburn,* 18th-century Englishwoman; see -IAN]

black′ but′ter. See **beurre noir.**

black′ cal′la, a perennial herb, *Arum palaestinum,* of Israel and Jordan, having flowers like the calla lily, but blackish purple inside the spathe, grown as an ornamental. Also called **Solomon's lily.**

Black′ Can′yon, a canyon of the Colorado River between Arizona and Nevada: site of Boulder Dam.

black·cap (blak′kap′), *n.*). **1.** any of several birds having the top of the head black, as the chickadee and certain warblers, esp. the Old World blackcap, *Sylvia atricapilla.* **2.** *U.S.* the black raspberry plant or fruit. [BLACK + CAP]

black′-capped chick′adee (blak′kapt′). See under **chickadee.**

black′ car′pet bee′tle. See under **carpet beetle.**

Black′ Cayu′ga, one of an American breed of domestic ducks having black plumage.

black′ chaff′, *Plant Pathol.* a disease of wheat, characterized by dark, elongated stripes on the chaff, caused by a bacterium, *Xanthomonas translucens undulosum.*

black′ cher′ry, **1.** a North American cherry, *Prunus serotina,* bearing a black, sour, edible fruit. **2.** the tree itself. **3.** the hard, reddish-brown wood of this tree, used for making furniture.

black′ choke′berry. See under **chokeberry** (def. 1).

black·coat (blak′kōt′), *n.* *Chiefly Brit.* a clergyman. [BLACK + COAT]

black′-coat′ work′er (blak′kōt′), *Brit.* a sales-clerk in a shop.

black·cock (blak′kok′), *n.* the male of the black grouse. [late ME; see BLACK, COCK¹]

black·cod (blak′kod′), *n.*, *pl.* **-cods,** (*esp. collectively*) **-cod.** sablefish. [BLACK + COD¹]

Black′ Code′, *U.S.* any code of law limiting the rights of Negroes, esp. as passed in some Southern States after the Civil War.

black′ co′hosh, **1.** See under **cohosh. 2.** See **black snakeroot.**

black′ cop′per, *Metall.* a regulus of 95-percent-pure copper, produced in a blast furnace by smelting oxidized copper ores.

black′ cos′mos, a garden plant, *Cosmos diversifolius,* of Mexico, having small, dahlialike tubers and solitary flowerheads with red disk flowers and velvety, dark-red or purplish ray flowers.

Black′ Coun′try, a district in the English Midlands, around Birmingham: so called from the soot and grime produced by the many local industries.

black′ crap′pie. See under **crappie.**

black′crowned night′ her′on, (blak′kround′). See under **night heron.**

black·damp (blak′damp′), *n.* *Mining.* chokedamp. [BLACK + DAMP]

Black′ Death′, a form of bubonic plague which spread over Europe in the 14th century and killed an estimated quarter of the population.

black′ dia′mond, 1. carbonado². 2. **black diamonds,** coal.

black′ disease′, *Vet. Pathol.* an acute, usually fatal disease of sheep caused by general intoxication from *Clostridium novyi,* an anaerobic organism which multiplies in the liver in areas damaged by the common liver fluke.

black′ dog′, *Informal.* melancholy; despondency; the blues: *The black dog is over him.*

black′ duck′, any of several ducks having dusky or black plumage, as *Anas rubripes,* of the northeastern U.S. and Canada.

black′ dur′gon (dûr′gən), a glossy-black triggerfish, *Melichthys buniva,* found in the Indo-Pacific region.

black·en (blak′ən), *v.t.* 1. to make black; darken. 2. to speak evil of; defame: *Don't blacken her reputation.* —*v.i.* 3. to grow or become black. [ME; see BLACK, -EN¹] —**black′en·er,** *n.*

Black′ Eng′lish, a dialect of English associated with some North American blacks, having a vocabulary, grammatical patterns, and pronunciations that diverge in varying degrees from those of Standard English.

Black·ett (blak′et, -it), *n.* **Patrick May·nard Stuart** (mā′nərd, -närd), 1897–1974, English physicist: Nobel prize 1948.

black′ eye′, 1. discoloration of the skin around the eye, resulting from a blow, bruise, etc. 2. *Informal.* **a.** a mark of shame, dishonor, etc.: *These slums are a black eye to our town.* **b.** damaged reputation: *Your behavior will give the family a black eye.*

black′-eyed pea′ (blak′īd′), cowpea.

black′-eyed Su′san, any of a number of plants having flowers with a dark center against a lighter, usually yellow, background, esp. the composite herb, *Rudbeckia hirta:* the State flower of Maryland.

black·face (blak′fās′), *n.* 1. *Theat.* **a.** an entertainer, esp. one in a minstrel show, made up in the role of a Negro. **b.** the make-up, as burnt cork, used in this role: *They performed in blackface.* 2. *Print.* a heavy-faced type. [BLACK + FACE]

black·fel·low (blak′fel′ō), *n.* an aborigine of Australia. [BLACK + FELLOW]

black-fig·ure (blak′fig′yər) *adj.* pertaining to or designating a style of vase painting developed in Greece in the 7th and 6th centuries B.C., chiefly characterized by silhouetted figures painted in black slip on a red clay body, details incised into the design, and a two-dimensional structure of form and space. Also, **black′fig′ured.** Cf. **red-figure.**

black·fin (blak′fin′), *n.* a cisco, *Coregonus nigripinnis,* found in the Great Lakes. Also called **black′fin cis′co.** [BLACK + FIN]

black·fire (blak′fīᵊr′), *n. Plant Pathol.* a disease of tobacco, characterized by angular, dark lesions on the leaves, caused by a bacterium, *Pseudomonas angulata.* [BLACK + FIRE]

black·fish (blak′fish′), *n., pl.* (*esp. collectively*) **-fish,** (*esp. referring to two or more kinds or species*) **-fish·es.** 1. See **black whale.** 2. any of various dark-colored fishes, as the tautog, *Tautoga onitis,* or the sea bass, *Centropristes striatus.* 3. a small, fresh-water food fish, *Dallia pectoralis,* found in Alaska and Siberia, noted for its ability to survive frozen in ice. [BLACK + FISH]

black′ flag′, 1. the pirate flag, usually of black cloth with the white skull and crossbones on it. 2. a flag having two yellow and two black squares, signifying the letter "L" in the International Code of Signals: formerly so called when used, by itself, to indicate the presence of cholera on board a vessel. Also called **blackjack.**

black′ flux′, a reducing flux consisting of finely divided carbon and potassium carbonate, used in metallurgy.

black′ fly′, any of the minute, black gnats of the dipterous family *Simuliidae,* having aquatic larvae. Also called **buffalo gnat.**

black′ fog′, (in Cape Cod, Mass.) a dense fog.

Black·foot (blak′fo͝ot′), *n., pl.* **-feet,** (*esp. collectively*) **-foot,** *adj.* 1. a member of a North American tribe of Indians of Algonquian stock. 2. the Algonquian language of the Blackfeet. —*adj.* 3. of or pertaining to the Blackfeet. [trans. of Blackfoot *Siksika*]

Black·foot (blak′fo͝ot′), *n.* a town in SE Idaho. 7378 (1960).

black′-foot·ed fer′ret (blak′fo͝ot′id), a weasel, *Mustela nigripes,* of prairie regions of the U.S., having a yellowish-brown body with the tip of the tail and legs black.

Black′ For′est, a wooded mountain region in SW West Germany. Highest peak, Feldberg, 4905 ft. German, **Schwarzwald.**

black′ fox′, a red fox in a color phase in which its fur is mostly black.

Black′ Fri′ar, a Dominican friar (so called from the distinctive black mantle worn by the order).

Black′ Fri′day, 1. any Friday on which a misfortune occurs: *Friday, September 24, the day the financial panic of 1869 began, has since been known as Black Friday.* 2. Good Friday: so called because clerical vestments are black on that day.

black′ frost′, intense cold without hoarfrost, causing vegetation to turn black. Cf. **frost** (def. 2).

black′ gang′, *Naut.* the crewmen working in a stokehold.

black′ gold′, petroleum.

black′ gram′. See under **gram²** (def. 2).

black′ grouse′, a large grouse, *Lyrurus tetrix,* of Europe and western Asia, the male of which is black, the female mottled gray and brown.

black·guard (blag′ärd, -ərd), *n.* 1. a low, contemptible person; scoundrel. —*v.t.* 2. to revile in scurrilous language. —*v.i.* 3. to behave like a blackguard. —*adj.* 4. *Obs.* scurrilous; abusive. [BLACK + GUARD] —**black′guard·ism,** *n.*

black·guard·ly (blag′ərd lē), *adj.* 1. of, like, or befitting a blackguard: *to use blackguardly language.* —*adv.* 2. in the manner of a blackguard. [BLACKGUARD + -LY]

black′ guil′lemot. See under **guillemot** (def. 1).

black′ gum′, any of several trees of the genus *Nyssa,* esp. *N. sylvatica,* of E North America. Cf. **tupelo.**

Black′ Hand′, 1. *U.S.* **a.** Italian, **La Mano Nera.** a name loosely applied to criminal gangs or individuals, esp. Italians living in the U.S., practicing blackmail and violence. **b.** any similar group. 2. an anarchistic society in Spain, suppressed in 1883. 3. a nationalistic society in Serbia, suppressed in 1914. —**Black′hand′er,** *n.*

black′ haw′, 1. Also called **stag bush.** a North American shrub or small tree of the honeysuckle family, *Viburnum prunifolium,* having white flowers and black drupes. 2. the sheepberry, *Viburnum Lentago.*

Black′ Hawk′, 1767–1838, American Indian chief of the Sac tribe: leader of Sac and Fox Indians in the Black Hawk War 1830.

black·head (blak′hed′), *n.* 1. a small, wormlike, black-tipped, fatty mass in a skin follicle, esp. of the face; comedo. 2. *Dial.* any of several birds having a black head, as the scaup duck, *Aythya marila.* 3. Also called **enterohepatitis.** *Vet. Pathol.* a malignant, infectious, protozoan disease of turkeys, chickens, and many wild birds, attacking esp. the intestines and liver.

black′-head·ed fire′worm (blak′hed′id). See under **fireworm** (def. 1).

black′-headed gull′, any of several gulls having a dusky or black head, as *Larus ribidundus* of northern Europe and Asia.

black·heart (blak′härt′), *n.* 1. *Plant Pathol.* a disease of plants, as of potatoes and various trees, in which internal plant tissues blacken. 2. *Hort.* **a.** a heart cherry having a dark skin. **b.** the tree bearing this fruit. [BLACK + HEART]

black-heart·ed (blak′här′tid), *adj.* disposed to doing or wishing evil; malevolent; malicious. —**black′-heart′ed·ly,** *adv.* —**black′heart′ed·ness,** *n.*

black′ hel′lebore. See **Christmas rose.**

Black′ Hills′, a group of mountains in W South Dakota and NE Wyoming. Highest peak, Harney Peak, 7242 ft.

black′ hole′, a region or object in space in which the gravitational pull is so great that even light cannot escape: one possible cause is the collapse of a star.

Black′ Hole′, 1. Also called **Black′ Hole′ of Calcut′ta.** a small prison cell in Fort William, Calcutta, in which, in 1756, Indians are said to have imprisoned 146 Europeans, only 23 of whom were alive the following morning. 2. (*l.c.*) any place of imprisonment, esp. a military cell or lockup.

black′ hore′hound, a fetid European weed, *Ballota nigra,* having purple flowers, found in waste land.

black′ huck′leberry, a low shrub, *Gaylussacia baccata,* of eastern North America, having yellowish-green leaves with resinous dots beneath, drooping, clustered, orange-red flowers, and shiny, black, edible fruit. Also called **highbush huckleberry.**

black′ hu′mor, humor that ignores human suffering and looks for the absurdity in any experience, even the most tragic.

black·ing (blak′ing), *n.* any preparation for producing a black coating or finish, as on shoes, stoves, etc.

black′ i′vory, 1. a pigment made from carbonized ivory. 2. Negroes sold in the African slave trade.

black·jack (blak′jak′), *n.* 1. a short, leather-covered club, consisting of a heavy head on a flexible handle, used as a weapon. 2. a large drinking cup or jug for beer, ale, etc., originally made of leather coated externally with tar. Cf. **bombard** (def. 7). 3. See **black flag.** 4. a small oak, *Quercus marilandica,* of the eastern U.S., having a nearly black bark and a wood of little value except for fuel. 5. *Mineral.* a dark, iron-rich variety of sphalerite. 6. caramel or burnt sugar for coloring spirits, vinegar, coffee, etc. 7. *Cards.* **a.** twenty-one (def. 4). **b.** Also called **natural.** (in twenty-one) an ace together with a ten or a face card as the first two cards dealt. **c.** a variety of twenty-one in which any player can become dealer. —*v.t.* 8. to strike or beat with a blackjack. 9. to compel by threat: *He was blackjacked by the gang into keeping his bargain.* [rhyming compound BLACK + JACK¹]

Leather blackjacks (17th century)

black′ kite′, an Old World kite, *Milvus migrans,* having dark brown plumage and a forked tail, and feeding chiefly on carrion.

black′ knot′, *Plant Pathol.* a disease of plants, esp. of plums and cherries, characterized by black knotlike overgrowths on the branches, twigs, etc., caused by a fungus, *Dibotryon morbosa.*

black′ lead′ (led), graphite; plumbago.

black·leg (blak′leg′), *n., v.,* **-legged, -leg·ging.** —*n.* 1. Also called **black quarter, symptomatic anthrax.** *Vet. Pathol.* an infectious, generally fatal disease of cattle and sheep, caused by the soil bacterium *Clostridium chauvoei* and characterized by painful, gaseous swellings in the muscles, usually of the upper parts of the legs. 2. *Plant Pathol.* **a.** a disease of cabbage and other cruciferous plants, characterized by dry, black lesions on the base of the stem, caused by a fungus, *Phoma lingam.* **b.** a disease of potatoes, characterized by wet, black lesions on the base of the stem, caused by a bacterium, *Erwinia atroseptica.* 3. a swindler, esp. in racing or gambling. 4. *Brit. Informal.* a strikebreaker; scab. —*v.t. Brit. Informal.* 5. to replace (a worker) who is on strike. 6. to refuse to support (a union, union workers, or a strike). 7. to betray or deceive (a person or cause). —*v.i.* 8. to return to work before a strike is settled. [BLACK + LEG]

black′ let′ter, *Print.* a heavy-faced type in a style like that of early European handlettering and earliest printed books. Also called **text.** —**black′-let′ter,** *adj.*

This is a sample of black letter

black′-let′ter day′, an unlucky or tragic day: *The day Poland was invaded was a black-letter day for the world.*

black′ light′, invisible infrared or ultraviolet light.

black′ liq′uor, (in making wood pulp for paper) the liquor that remains after digestion. Cf. **white liquor.**

black·list (blak′list′), *n.* 1. a list of persons under suspicion, disfavor, censure, etc.: *His record as an anarchist put him on the government's blacklist.* 2. a list privately exchanged among employers, containing the names of persons to be barred from employment because of untrustworthiness or for holding opinions considered undesirable. 3. a list drawn up by a labor union, containing the names of employers to be boycotted for unfair labor practices. Cf. **white list** (def. 5). —*v.t.* 4. to put (a person) on a blacklist. [BLACK + LIST¹; orig. political]

black′ lo′cust, 1. the locust, *Robinia Pseudo-Acacia.* 2. the honey locust, *Gleditsia triacanthos.* Also called **false acacia, yellow locust.**

black·ly (blak′lē), *adv.* darkly; gloomily; wickedly; angrily: *a plot blackly contrived to wreak vengeance; blackly refusing to yield to reason.* [BLACK + -LY]

black′ mag′ic, magic used for evil purposes; witchcraft; sorcery.

black·mail (blak′māl′), *n.* 1. *Law.* **a.** any payment extorted by intimidation, as by threats of injurious revelations or accusations. **b.** the extortion of such payment: *He confessed rather than suffer the dishonor of blackmail.* 2. a tribute formerly exacted in the north of England and in Scotland by freebooting chiefs for protection from pillage. —*v.t.* 3. to extort money from (a person) by the use of threats. 4. to force or coerce into a particular action, statement, etc.: *The chairman blackmailed him into endorsing the candidate.* [BLACK + *mail,* sp. var. of north ME *mal(e)* tribute, rent, OE *māl* agreement < Scand; cf. Icel *māl* agreement, speech; c. OE *mǣl* speech] —**black′mail′er,** *n.*

black′ ma′ple, a tree, *Acer nigrum,* found from E North America to South Dakota, having furrowed, blackish bark, yellow-green flowers, and smooth fruit.

black′ mar′gate (mär′git), *Ichthyol.* a grayish grunt, *Anisotremus surinamensis,* found in the Atlantic Ocean from Florida to Brazil. Also called **pompon.**

Black′ Ma·ri′a (mə rī′ə), *Informal.* a closed truck used for conveying prisoners to and from jail.

black′ mark′, an indication of failure or censure: *His inefficiency is a black mark against him.*

black′ mar′ket, a market in which there are violations of legal price controls, rationing, etc.

black-mar·ket (blak′mär′kit), *v.i.* 1. to black-marketeer. —*v.t.* 2. to sell (something) in the black market. [v. use of BLACK MARKET]

black′ mar·ke·teer′ (mär′ki tēr′), one who sells articles in the black market.

black-mar·ke·teer (blak′mär′ki tēr′), *v.i.* to sell articles in the black market. [BLACK-MARKET + -EER]

black′ mar′ket·er (mär′ki tər), a black marketeer.

Black′ Mass′, 1. a blasphemous ceremony mocking the Christian Mass, esp. one by an alleged worshiper of the devil. 2. a Requiem Mass. Also, **black′ mass′.**

black′ mea′sles, *Pathol.* a severe form of measles characterized by dark, hemorrhagic eruptions. Also called **hemorrhagic measles.**

black′ med′ic, a medic, *Medicago lupulina,* having small yellow flowers and black pods.

black′ mercu′ric sul′fide. See under **mercuric sulfide.**

black′ mold′. See **bread mold.**

black′ mol′ly, a jet-black molly, a subspecies esp. of *Mollienisia latipinna* or *M. sphenops,* often kept as an aquarium fish.

Black′ Monk′, a Benedictine monk (from the black habit worn by the order). Also, **black′ monk′.** [ME]

Black′ Moun′tains, a mountain range in W North Carolina, part of the Appalachian Mountains. Highest peak, Mount Mitchell, 6684 ft.

black′ mul′berry. See under **mulberry** (def. 2).

Black·mun (blak′mən), *n.* **Harry A(ndrew),** born 1908, U.S. jurist: associate justice of the U.S. Supreme Court since 1970.

Black′ Mus′lim, a member of an organization of Negroes, esp. American Negroes, advocating the religious and ethical teachings of Islam, particularly with regard to temperance in living habits, and the complete separation of races.

black′ mus′tard. See under **mustard** (def. 2).

black·ness (blak′nis), *n.* quality or state of being black. [ME; see BLACK, -NESS]

black′ nick′el ox′ide, *Chem.* See **nickelic oxide.**

black′ night′shade, a common weed, *Solanum nigrum,* having white flowers and black edible berries.

black′ oak′, 1. any of several oak trees, as *Quercus velutina,* characterized by a blackish bark. 2. the hard, durable wood of such a tree, used for making furniture.

black′ o′pal, a dark variety of opal having the characteristic opaline play of color.

black·out (blak′out′), *n.* 1. the extinguishing or concealment of all visible lights in a city, military post, etc., usually as a precaution against air raids. 2. *Theat.* **a.** the extinguishing of all stage lights, as in closing a vaudeville skit or separating the scenes of a play. **b.** Also called **black′out skit′.** a skit ending in a blackout. 3. unconsciousness, esp. in aviation: *He suffered a blackout from the sudden dive.* 4. loss of memory. 5. complete stoppage of a communications medium, as by a strike, catastrophe, electrical storm, etc.: *a newspaper blackout; a radio blackout.* [BLACK + OUT]

Black′ Pan′ther, a member of an American Negro militant organization **(Black′ Pan′ther par′ty)** formed to protect Negro communities and to work for reforms favoring Negroes. Also called **Panther.**

black·patch (blak′pach′), *n. Plant Pathol.* a disease of red and white clover, characterized by brown or blackish lesions on the plant. [BLACK + PATCH]

black′ pa′ternos′ter, an incantation for invoking evil spirits. Cf. **white paternoster.**

black′ pep′per, a hot, sharp condiment prepared from the dried berries of a tropical vine, *Piper nigrum.*

black′ pew′ter, pewter composed of 60 percent tin and 40 percent lead.

black′ pit′, *Plant Pathol.* a disease of lemons, characterized by dark brown, sunken spots on the skin of the fruit, caused by a bacterium, *Xanthomonas syringae.*

Black′ Plague′. See **Great Plague.**

black·plate (blak′plāt′), *n.* 1. *Metalworking.* cold-rolled sheet steel before pickling or cleaning. 2. sheet steel coated with a lacquer or enamel. [BLACK + PLATE¹]

black·poll (blak′pōl′), *n.* a North American warbler, *Dendroica striata*, the adult male of which has the top of the head black. Also called **black′poll war′bler.** [BLACK + POLL[1]]

Black·pool (blak′po͞ol′), *n.* a seaport in W Lancashire, in NW England: resort. 152,133 (1961).

Black′ Pope′, *Disparaging and Offensive.* the head of the Jesuit order (so called from the power he once possessed and from the black habit worn by the order).

black′ pop′lar, 1. a poplar, *Populus nigra*, characterized by spreading branches and a gray bark. **2.** the light, soft wood of this tree, used for making doors, window frames, etc.

black′ pow′der, an explosive powder consisting of saltpeter, sulfur, and charcoal, used chiefly in old guns fired for sport, in fireworks, and for spotting charges in practice bombs.

black′ pow′er, (*sometimes caps.*) a movement among American Negroes to gain political and economic power, esp. as a means of achieving racial equality.

Black′ Prince′. See **Edward,** (def. 1).

black′ pud′ding, 1. See **blood sausage. 2.** a dark dessert pudding made with flour, baking soda, eggs, and molasses.

black′ quar′ter, *Vet. Pathol.* blackleg (def. 1).

black·rag (blak′rag′), *n.* a pelagic, stromateid fish, *Ictius pellucidus.* [BLACK + RAG[1]]

black′ rat′, an Old World rat, *Rattus rattus*, now common in the southern U.S., having a black or brown body with grayish or white underparts.

black′ ring′, *Plant Pathol.* a disease of grasses, characterized by black rings surrounding the stems and blighted seeds, caused by a fungus, *Balansia strangulans.*

Black′ Riv′er Falls′, a town in central Wisconsin. 3195 (1960).

Black′ Rod′, 1. (in England) an official of the Order of the Garter and chief ceremonial usher of the House of Lords: so called from the rod he carries. **2.** a similar official in British colonial and Commonwealth legislatures.

black′ root′ rot′, *Plant Pathol.* a disease of plants, characterized by black lesions on and rotting of the roots, the cessation of growth, and wilting, caused by any of several fungi, as *Thielaviopsis basicola.*

black′ rot′, *Plant Pathol.* any of several diseases of fruits and vegetables, characterized by black discoloration and decay of affected parts, caused by fungi, as *Guignardia bidwellii*, or bacteria, as *Xanthomonas campestris.*

black′ rud′derfish, barrelfish.

black′ ruff′, a large, blackish, pelagic fish, *Centrolophus niger*, found in the Atlantic Ocean, chiefly along the coast of Europe.

Black′ Rus′sian, a cocktail or after-dinner drink made from one part coffee liqueur and two parts vodka, served over ice in an Old Fashioned glass.

black′ rust′, *Plant Pathol.* any of several diseases of plants, characterized by the black teliospores produced by the causal fungus.

black′ sage′, a stiff, perennial herb, *Audibertia stachyoides*, of California, having leaves which are green above and grayish beneath and white or lilac-colored flowers.

Black′ Samp′son. See **hedgehog coneflower.**

black′ sap′, *Plant Pathol.* melaxuma.

Blacks·burg (blaks′bûrg), *n.* a town in SW Virginia.

black′ sco′ter, a European scoter, *Oidemia nigra*, the adult male of which is black.

Black′ Sea′, a sea between Europe and Asia, bordered by Turkey, Rumania, Bulgaria, Ukraine, Georgia, and the Russian Federation. 160,000 sq. mi. Also called **Euxine Sea.** Ancient, **Pontus Euxinus.**

black′ sea′ bass′ (bas), **1.** a small, serranoid food fish, *Centropristes striatus*, found off the coast of eastern North America. **2.** See **giant sea bass.**

black′ sele′nium, *Chem* an allotropic form of selenium occurring as a black, amorphous, water-insoluble, light-sensitive powder: used chiefly in photoelectric cells.

black′ shank′, *Plant Pathol.* a disease of tobacco, characterized by wilting and decayed, blackened roots and stems, caused by a fungus, *Phytophthora parasitica nicotianae.*

black′ sheep′, 1. a sheep with black fleece. **2.** a person who causes shame or embarrassment because of his deviation from the accepted standards of his group.

Black′ Shirt′, *Europ. Hist.* a member of a fascist organization, as the Italian fascist militia or the Nazi Schutzstaffel (so called from the color of the shirt worn as part of their uniform).

black′ skim′mer, a black and white New World skimmer, *Rynchops nigra*, having a bill with a reddish-orange base.

black·smith (blak′smith′), *n.* **1.** a person who makes horseshoes and shoes horses. **2.** one who forges objects of iron. **3.** a blackish damselfish, *Chromis punctipinnis*, found off the coast of southern California. [late ME; see BLACK (in reference to iron or black metal), SMITH[1]; see WHITESMITH]

black·snake (blak′snāk′), *n.* **1.** a blackish racer, *Coluber constrictor* subspecies, of the eastern U.S., that grows to a length of five to six feet. **2.** any of various other snakes of a black or very dark color. **3.** *U.S.* a heavy, tapering, flexible whip of braided cowhide or the like. Also, **black′ snake′.** [BLACK + SNAKE]

black′ snake′root, a tall, perennial herb, *Cimicifuga racemosa*, of eastern North America, having thin, tapering, toothed or deeply cut leaflets and branched clusters of small, white flowers. Also called **black cohosh.**

black′ soap′, *Obs.* a black soap made from lye and fish or whale oil.

black′ spot′, *Plant Pathol.* a disease of plants, characterized by black spots on the fruit and foliage, twig lesions, defoliation, and rotting, caused by any of several fungi, as *Diplocarpon rosae*, or bacteria.

black′ spruce′, 1. a spruce, *Picea mariana*, of North America, having bluish-green leaves and grayish-brown bark. **2.** the light, soft wood of this tree.

black′ squir′rel, a fox squirrel or gray squirrel in that color phase in which the fur is black.

black′ stem′, *Plant Pathol.* a disease of plants, characterized by blackened stems and defoliation, caused by any of several fungi, as *Ascochyta imperfecta* or *Mycosphaerella lethalis.*

black′ stick′, *Slang.* a clarinet.

Black·stone (blak′stōn′, -stən), *n.* **1. Sir William,** 1723–80, English jurist and writer on law. **2.** a town in central Virginia. 3659 (1960). **3.** a river in S Massachusetts, flowing SE across NE Rhode Island to Pawtucket. ab. 40 mi. long.

black′ storm′, karaburan.

black′strap molas′ses (blak′strap′), molasses remaining after maximum extraction of sugar from the raw product, used chiefly as a constituent of cattle feed and as a source of ethyl alcohol. [BLACK + STRAP]

Black′ Stream′. See **Japan Current.**

black′ stud′ies, a program of studies in Negro history and culture offered by a school or college, often including Afro-American history, black literature, and Swahili.

black′ suck′er, a hog sucker, *Hypentelium nigricans*, found in the eastern U.S.

black′ swal′lowtail. See under **swallowtail** (def. 2).

black·tail (blak′tāl′), *n.* an animal having a black tail, esp. a black-tailed deer. [BLACK + TAIL[1]]

black′-tailed deer′ (blak′tāld′), a variety of mule deer, *Odocoileus hemionus columbianus*, found on the western slope of the Rocky Mountains, having a tail that is black above. Also, **black′tail deer′.**

black′ tea′, a tea that has been allowed to wither and ferment in the air for some time before being subjected to a heating process.

black·thorn (blak′thôrn′), *n.* **1.** Also called **sloe.** a much-branched, thorny, Old World shrub *Prunus spinosa*, having white flowers and small plumlike fruits. **2.** a shrub or tree of the genus *Crataegus*, as *C. tomentosa.* **3.** See **pear haw. 4.** a walking stick made of blackthorn. [ME *blak thorn.* See BLACK, THORN]

black′ tie′, 1. a black bow tie, worn with a tuxedo or a dinner jacket. **2.** semiformal evening wear for men (distinguished from *white tie*).

black-tie (blak′tī′), *adj.* requiring that guests wear semiformal attire, esp. that men wear black bow ties with tuxedos or dinner jackets: *a black-tie dance.*

black′ ti′ti. See under titi[2].

black·tongue (blak′tung′), *n.* *Vet. Pathol.* **1.** pellagra in dogs characterized by buccal ulcers, inflammation of the alimentary tract, erythema, and severe nervous symptoms. **2.** a condition of dogs, sometimes considered to be canine leptospirosis. [BLACK + TONGUE]

black·top (blak′top′), *n.* **1.** a bituminous substance, usually asphalt, for paving roads, parking lots, playgrounds, etc. **2.** a road covered with blacktop. —*adj.* **3.** pertaining to or surfaced with blacktop: *a blacktop driveway.* [BLACK + TOP[1]]

black′ turn′stone, a turnstone, *Arenaria melanocephala*, of the Pacific coast of North America, having a black back with a bronzy-green sheen.

black′ vel′vet, a cocktail made with stout and champagne.

Black′ Vol′ta, a river in W Africa, in Ghana: the upper branch of the Volta River. ab. 500 mi. long.

black′ vom′it, *Pathol.* **1.** a dark-colored substance, consisting chiefly of altered blood, vomited in some cases of yellow fever, usually presaging a fatal issue of the disease. **2.** act of throwing up this matter. **3.** any disease characterized by this.

black′ vul′ture, 1. an American vulture, *Coragyps atratus*, having a black, bald head and black plumage. **2.** any of several Old World vultures, esp. *Aegypius monachus*, of S Europe, Asia, and N Africa.

Black′wall frig′ate (blak′wôl′), a full-rigged wooden merchant ship of the early and middle 19th century, built on the model of a frigate with very little sheer, high bulwarks to the main deck, quarter galleries, and staterooms for passengers in the poop. [after *Blackwall*, a London shipyard]

Black′wall hitch′, a hitch made with a rope over a hook so that it holds fast when pulled but is loose otherwise. See illus. under **knot.** [after *Blackwall*, a London shipyard]

black′ wal′nut, 1. a tree, *Juglans nigra*, of North America, which yields a valuable timber. **2.** the nut of this tree. **3.** the wood of this tree.

Black′ Watch′, a famous regiment of Scottish infantry in the British army (so called because of the dark colors in their tartan).

black′wa·ter fe′ver (blak′wô′tər, -wot′ər), *Pathol.* a severe form of malaria characterized by a urine that is dark red or black, found chiefly in the tropics but occasionally in the southern U.S. [BLACK + WATER (urine)]

black′ wat′tle, a variety of the green wattle, *Acacia mollis*, having hairy foliage and ornamental purplish pods.

black·weed (blak′wēd′), *n.* the common ragweed. [BLACK + WEED[1]]

Black·well (blak′wəl, -wel′), *n.* **1. Elizabeth,** 1821–1910, U.S. physician, born in England. **2. Henry Brown,** 1825?–1909, U.S. editor, abolitionist, and suffragist, born in England (husband of Lucy Stone). **3.** a town in N Oklahoma. 9588 (1960).

Black′wells Is′land (blak′welz′, -wəlz), former name of **Welfare Island.**

black′ whale′, any of several black, dolphinlike cetaceans of the genus *Globicephalus.* Also called **blackfish.**

black′ wid′ow, a venomous spider, *Latrodectus mactans*, widely distributed in the U.S., that is jet-black with an hourglass-shaped red mark on the underside of its abdomen.

black′ witch′. See under **witch moth.**

Black·wood (blak′wo͝od′), *n.* **William,** 1776–1834, English publisher.

black·y (blak′ē), *n., pl.* **black·ies.** *Chiefly Brit.* a Negro. [BLACK + -Y[2]]

blad·der (blad′ər), *n.* **1.** *Anat., Zool.* **a.** a membranous sac or organ serving as a receptacle for a fluid or gas. **b.** See **urinary bladder. 2.** *Pathol.* a vesicle, blister, cyst, etc., filled with fluid or air. **3.** *Bot.* an air-filled sac or float, as in certain seaweeds. **4.** something resembling a bladder, as the inflatable lining of a football, basketball, etc. **5.** an air-filled sac, usually made to resemble a club, used for beatings in low comedy, vaudeville, or the like. **6.** anything inflated, empty, or unsound: *to prick the bladder of one's foolish pride; a great, pompous bladder of a man.* [ME, OE *blæddre, blǣdre* bladder, blister, pimple; c. Icel. *blāthra*, Flem *bladder*, G *Blatter;* akin to BLOW[2]] —**blad′der·less,** *adj.* —**blad′der·like′,** *adj.* —**blad′der·y,** *adj.*

blad′der cam′pion, a plant, *Silene latifolia* (*Silene inflata*), having an inflated calyx.

blad′der ket′mi·a (ket′mē ə), a cultivated annual plant, *Hibiscus Trionum*, having a bladdery calyx. [*ketmia* < NL]

blad·der·nose (blad′ər nōz′), *n.* a large seal, *Cystophora cristata*, the male of which has a large, distensible, hoodlike sac on the head. Also called **hooded seal.** [BLADDER + NOSE]

blad·der·nut (blad′ər nut′), *n.* **1.** the bladderlike fruit capsule of any shrub or small tree of the genus *Staphylea*, as *S. trifolia*, of the eastern U.S. **2.** the shrub itself. [BLADDER + NUT]

blad·der·pod (blad′ər pod′), *n.* a perennial herb, *Vesicaria utriculata*, of the Mediterranean region, having yellow flowers. [BLADDER + POD[1], so called from its full shape]

blad′der worm′, *Zool.* the bladderlike, encysted larva of a tapeworm; a cysticercus, coenurus, or hydatid.

blad·der·wort (blad′ər wûrt′), *n.* any of various herbs of the genus *Utricularia*, including aquatic, terrestrial, and epiphytic forms throughout the world. [BLADDER + WORT[2]]

blade (blād), *n.* **1.** the flat cutting part of a sword, knife, etc. **2.** a sword, rapier, or the like. **3.** the leaf of a plant, esp. of a grass or cereal. **4.** *Bot.* the broad part of a leaf, as distinguished from the stalk or petiole. See illus. under **leaf. 5.** the metal part of an ice skate that comes into contact with the ice. **6.** a thin, flat part of something, as of an oar or a bone. **7.** a dashing, swaggering, or jaunty young man: *a gay blade from the nearby city.* **8.** the scapula or shoulder blade. **9.** *Phonet.* the foremost and most readily flexible portion of the tongue, including the tip and implying the upper and lower surfaces and edges. [ME; OE *blæd;* c. D *blad*, Icel *blath*, G *Blatt;* akin to BLOW[3]] —**blade′less,** *adj.*

blade′ ap′ple. See **Barbados gooseberry.**

blade·bone (blād′bōn′), *n.* the scapula. [BLADE + BONE[1]]

Bla·dens·burg (blād′ənz bûrg′), *n.* a town in central Maryland. 3103 (1960).

blae (blā, blē), *adj.* *Scot. and North Eng.* **1.** livid; bluish-black; blue-gray. **2.** bleak; dingy. **3.** (of weather) sunless. [ME *bla* (north) < Scand; cf. Icel *blā* blackish blue; c. G *blau*, whence F *bleu* BLUE]

blae·ber·ry (blā′ber′ē, -bə rē), *n., pl.* **-ries.** *Scot. and North. Eng.* whortleberry. [ME (north dial.) *blaberie.* See BLAE, BERRY]

Blaeu (blou), *n.* **Wil·lem Jans·zoon** (vil′əm yän′sən, -sōn), 1571–1638, Dutch cartographer, geographer, astronomer, and mathematician. Also, **Blaeuw, Blaew.**

Blagg (blag), *n.* a crater in the first quadrant and near the center of the face of the moon: about 2 miles in diameter.

Bla·gon·ra·vov (blä′gon rä′vof), *n.* **A·na·to·li Ar·ka·dye·vich** (ä′nä tô′lē är′kä dye′vich), born 1894, Russian scientist.

Bla·go·ve·shchensk (blä′go ve′shchensk), *n.* a city in the SE RSFSR, in the SE Soviet Union in Asia, on the Amur River. 94,000 (1959).

blah (blä), *U.S. Slang.* —*n.* **1.** nonsense; rubbish: *What they say is blah.* —*adj.* **2.** insipid; dull; uninteresting: *We had a blah evening at that stupid party.* [imit.]

blain (blān), *n.* *Pathol.* an inflammatory swelling or sore. [ME *bleine*, OE *blegen(e).* See CHILBLAIN]

Blaine (blān), *n.* **1. James Gil·les·pie** (gi les′pē), 1830–93, U.S. statesman. **2.** a town in E Minnesota. 7570 (1960).

Blair (blâr), *n.* a town in E Nebraska. 4931 (1960).

Blairs·ville (blârz′vil), *n.* a town in central Pennsylvania. 4930 (1960).

Blaise (blāz; *Fr.* blez), *n.* a boy's given name.

Blake (blāk), *n.* **1. Robert,** 1599–1657, British admiral. **2. William,** 1757–1827, English poet, engraver, and painter. **3.** a boy's given name.

Blake·ly (blāk′lē), *n.* **1.** a town in NE Pennsylvania. 6374 (1960). **2.** a town in SW Georgia. 3580 (1960).

Blake·more (blāk′mōr, -môr), *n.* a boy's given name.

blam·a·ble (blā′mə bəl), *adj.* deserving blame; censurable. Also, **blameable.** [ME; see BLAME, -ABLE] —**blam′a·ble·ness,** *n.* —**blam′a·bly,** *adv.*

blame (blām), *v.,* **blamed, blam·ing,** *n.* —*v.t.* **1.** to place the responsibility for (a fault, error, etc.) on a person: *I blame the accident on him.* **2.** to find fault with; censure: *I don't blame you for leaving him.* **3.** *U.S. Slang and Dial.* to blast (used as a humorous imperative or optative): *Blame my hide if I go!* **4. to blame,** at fault; censurable: *I am to blame for his lateness.* —*n.* **5.** act of attributing fault; censure; reproof: *The judge said he found nothing to justify blame in the accident.* **6.** responsibility for anything deserving of censure: *We must all share the blame for this deplorable condition.* [ME *blame(n)* < OF *blasme(r)* << LL *blasphēmāre* to BLASPHEME] —**blam′er,** *n.*

—**Syn. 1, 2.** reproach, reprove, reprehend, criticize. BLAME, CENSURE, CONDEMN imply finding fault with someone or something. To BLAME is to hold accountable for, and disapprove because of, some error, mistake, omission, neglect, or the like: *Who is to blame for the disaster?* The verb CENSURE differs from the noun in connoting scolding or rebuking even more than adverse criticism: *to censure one for extravagance.* To CONDEMN is to express an adverse (esp. legal) judgment, without recourse: *to condemn conduct, a building, a man to death.* **5.** reprehension, condemnation, stricture, reproach, animadversion. **6.** guilt, culpability, fault, sin.

—**Usage.** Some speakers avoid BLAME ON as informal (*He put the blame on me*), preferring BLAME alone (*He blamed me*) or BLAME FOR (*He blamed me for it*). Since all three forms occur with equal frequency in educated usage, there is no need to regard any one form as less acceptable.

blame·a·ble (blā′mə bəl), *adj.* blamable. —**blame′a·ble·ness,** *n.* —**blame′a·bly,** *adv.*

blamed (blāmd), *U.S. Slang and Dial.* —*adj.* **1.** confounded: *The blamed car won't start.* —*adv.* **2.** confoundedly; excessively. *It's blamed cold out tonight.* [BLAME + -ED²]

blame·ful (blām′fəl), *adj.* **1.** deserving blame; blameworthy: *blameful neglect.* **2.** *Archaic.* imputing blame; accusing. [ME; see BLAME, -FUL] —**blame′ful·ly,** *adv.* —**blame′ful·ness,** *n.*

blame·less (blām′lis), *adj.* free from blame; guiltless: *a blameless child.* [ME; see BLAME, -LESS] —**blame′less·ly,** *adv.* —**blame′less·ness,** *n.*
—**Syn.** irreproachable. See **innocent.** —**Ant.** guilty.

blame·wor·thy (blām′wûr′thē), *adj.* deserving blame; blameful: *a blameworthy administration.* [ME; see BLAME, WORTHY] —**blame′wor′thi·ness,** *n.*

blanc (*Fr.* blän; *for 2, 3 also Eng.* blangk), *n., pl.* **blancs** (*Fr.* blän; *Eng.* blangks) for 2, 3. **1.** (*italics*) *French.* white. **2.** a silver coin of France of the 14th–18th centuries, debased in later years. **3.** an Anglo-Gallic copy of this coin, issued by Henry VI.

Blanc (blän), *n.* **1. Jean Jo·seph Charles Louis** (zhän zhô zef′ sharl lwē), 1811–82, French socialist and historian. **2. Mont.** See **Mont Blanc** (def. 1). **3.** *Astron.* See **Mont Blanc** (def. 2).

Blan·ca·nus (blang kā′nəs, bläng kä′-), *n.* a walled plane in the third quadrant of the face of the moon near the South Pole: about 57 miles in diameter.

Blan′ca Peak′ (blang′kə), a mountain in S Colorado: highest peak in the Sangre de Cristo Range. 14,390 ft.

blanc fixe (blängk′ fēks′; *Fr.* blän fēks′), barium sulfate used as a white pigment in paints. [< F: lit., fixed white. See FIX, BLANK]

blanch¹ (blanch, blänch), *v.t.* **1.** to whiten by removing color; bleach: *Women were blanching linen in the sun.* **2.** *Hort.* to whiten or prevent from becoming green (the stems or leaves of plants, as celery, lettuce, etc.) by excluding light. **3. a.** to scald briefly and then drain, as peaches or almonds to facilitate removal of skins, or as rice or macaroni to separate the grains or strands. **b.** to scald or parboil (meat or vegetables) so as to whiten, remove the odor, prepare for cooking by other means, etc. **4.** *Metall.* to give a white luster to (metals), as by means of acids. **5.** to make pale, as with sickness or fear: *The long illness had blanched her cheeks of their natural color.* —*v.i.* **6.** to become white; turn pale: *The very thought of going made her blanch.* —*adj.* **7.** *Heraldry. Rare.* argent. [ME bla(u)nche < MF blanch(ir) (to) whiten, deriv. of *blanc, blanche* white; see BLANK] —**blanch′er,** *n.*
—**Syn. 1.** See **whiten.**

blanch² (blanch, blänch), *v.t.* to force back or to one side; head off, as a deer or other quarry. [var. of BLENCH¹]

Blan·chard (blan′chərd), *n.* a boy's given name.

Blanche (blanch), *n.* a girl's given name.

Blan·ches·ter (blan′ches′tər, -chi stər), *n.* a town in SW Ohio. 2944 (1960).

blan·chi (blän shē′), *adj.* *French.* blanched.

Blan·chi·nus (blan chē′nəs, -kē′-), *n.* a walled plain in the fourth quadrant of the face of the moon: about 32 miles in diameter.

blanc·mange (blə mänj′, -mänzh′), *n.* **1.** a sweet pudding prepared with almond milk and gelatin and flavored with rum or kirschwasser. **2.** a white, sweet pudding made with milk and cornstarch and flavored with vanilla. [apocopated var. of ME *blancmanger* < MF, lit., white eating. See BLANK, MANGER]

Blan·co-Fom·bo·na (bläng′kô fôm bô′nä), *n.* **Ru·fi·no** (ro͞o fē′nô), 1874–1944, Venezuelan author.

bland (bland), *adj.* **1.** pleasantly gentle or agreeable: *a bland manner in company.* **2.** soothing or balmy, as air. **3.** nonirritating, as food or medicines: *His ulcer necessitated a bland diet.* **4.** nonstimulating, as medicines: *a bland cough syrup.* **5.** lacking in interest, liveliness, individuality, attractiveness, etc.; insipid; dull: *a bland young man who never shouted.* **6.** unemotional, indifferent, or casual: *his bland acknowledgement of guilt.* [< L *bland(us)* of a smooth tongue, pleasant, soothing] —**bland′ly,** *adv.* —**bland′ness,** *n.*
—**Syn. 1.** affable, mild, amiable; suave, urbane. **2, 3.** soft, mild. —**Ant. 1.** cruel; boorish. **2.** harsh. **3.** irritating.

Bland′-Al′li·son Act′ (bland′ al′i sən), *U.S. Hist.* a bill passed by Congress in 1878 requiring the federal government to purchase at the market price from two to four million dollars worth of silver monthly for conversion into silver dollars containing 16 times more silver per coin than gold in dollar coins of gold.

B.Land.Arch., Bachelor of Landscape Architecture.

blan·dish (blan′dish), *v.t.* **1.** to coax or influence by gentle flattery; cajole: *They blandished the guard into letting them through the gate.* —*v.i.* **2.** to use flattery or cajolery. [ME *blandisshe* < MF *blandiss-*, long s. of *blandir* < L *blandīr(ī)* (to) soothe, flatter. See BLAND, -ISH²] —**blan′dish·er,** *n.* —**blan′dish·ing·ly,** *adv.*

blan·dish·ment (blan′dish mənt), *n.* Often, **blandishments.** something, as an action or speech, that tends to flatter, coax, entice, etc.: *Her blandishments left him unmoved. We succumbed to the blandishments of tropical living.* [BLANDISH + -MENT]

blank (blangk), *adj.* **1.** (of paper or other writing surface) having no marks; not written or printed on: *a blank sheet of paper.* **2.** not filled in, as a printed form: *a blank check.* **3.** unrelieved or unbroken by ornament, opening, decoration, etc.: *a blank wall.* **4.** lacking some usual or completing feature: *a blank piece of film.* **5.** void of interest, variety, results, etc.: *She sometimes occupied her blank days with sewing.* **6.** showing no attention, interest, or emotion: *a blank face.* **7.** disconcerted; nonplussed; speechless: *She looked blank when I asked her why she applied for the job.* **8.** complete; utter; unmitigated: *blank stupidity.* **9.** *Archaic.* white; pale; colorless. —*n.* **10.** a place where something is lacking: *a blank in one's memory.* **11.** a space in a printed form to be filled in: *Write your name in the blank.* **12.** a printed form containing such spaces: *Have you filled out one of these blanks?* **13.** a dash put in place of an omitted letter or word, esp. a profane or obscene one. **14.** (used as a substitute for a word which might prove offensive): *I caught my finger in the blank blank door.* **15.** *Mach.* a piece of metal ready to be drawn, pressed, or machined into a finished object. **16.** *Archery.* the bull's-eye. **17.** the object toward which anything is directed; aim; target. **18. draw a blank,** *Informal.* to fail in an attempt; be unsuccessful: *She tried to make him recognize her, but drew a blank.* Also, **draw blank.** —*v.t.* **19.** to cross out or delete, esp. in order to invalidate or void (usually fol. by *out*): *to blank out an entry.* **20.** *Informal.* to keep (an opponent) from scoring in a game. **21.** *Mach.* to stamp or punch out of flat stock, as with a die. [ME < MF *blanc* < Gmc; cf. OE *blanca* white horse, OHG *blanch* bright, white] —**blank′ness,** *n.*
—**Syn. 1–4.** See **empty. 7.** dumfounded, confused, astounded. **8.** pure, simple, unadulterated; perfect, absolute, unqualified. **10.** void, vacancy, emptiness.

blank·book (blangk′bo͝ok′, -bo͝ok′), *n.* **1.** a book containing blank pages, as a notebook, sketchbook, etc. **2.** a book or pad of blank forms, as printed blanks for receipts, reports, etc. [BLANK + BOOK]

blank′ car′tridge, *Ordn.* a cartridge containing powder only, without a bullet.

blank′ check′, 1. a bank check bearing a signature but no stated amount. **2.** unrestricted authority; a free hand: *He was given a blank check in the choice of personnel for the new department.*

blank′ endorse′ment, an endorsement on a check or note naming no payee, and therefore payable to bearer.

blan·ket (blang′kit), *n.* **1.** a large, rectangular piece of soft fabric, often with bound edges, used esp. for warmth as a bed covering. **2.** a covering for a horse, dog, etc. **3.** *U.S. and Canada.* the chief garment worn by some Indians. **4.** any extended covering or layer: *a blanket of snow.* **5.** (in a press for offset printing) the rubber-covered cylinder to which an inked impression is transferred from the plate for transfer directly to the paper. **6.** (in a press for letterpress printing) the resilient covering on the cylinder against which the paper is pressed in printing. **7.** a thick roll or strip of material for thermal insulation. **8. born on the wrong side of the blanket,** born out of wedlock. —*v.t.* **9.** to cover with or as with a blanket: *wild flowers blanketing the hillside.* **10.** to obscure or obstruct; interfere with; overpower (usually fol. by *out*): *An electrical storm blanketed out the radio program.* **11.** to toss (someone) in a blanket, as in fraternity hazing. **12.** *Naut.* (of a vessel) to take wind from the sails of (another vessel) by passing closely to windward of it. —*adj.* **13.** covering or intended to cover a large group or class of things, conditions, situations, etc.: *a blanket proposal; a blanket indictment.* [ME < OF, equiv. to *blanc* white (see BLANK) + *-et* -ET] —**blan′ket·less,** *adj.* —**blan′ket·like′,** *adj.*

blan′ket chest′, *U.S. Furniture.* any chest, with or without drawers, having a rectangular space under a lifting lid or top, used for storing blankets, bedding, or clothing.

blan·ket-flow·er (blang′kit flou′ər), *n.* any composite herb of the genus *Gaillardia,* having showy heads of yellow or purple flowers. [BLANKET + FLOWER]

blan·ket·ing (blang′ki ting), *n.* **1.** blankets: *The blanketing was too warm.* **2.** *Radio.* the effect of a signal from a powerful transmitter which interferes with or prevents the reception of other signals. [BLANKET + -ING¹]

blan′ket roll′, 1. a blanket or sleeping bag rolled into a cylindrical pack for easy carrying and outdoor use by hikers, soldiers, cowboys, etc., often with cooking utensils, food, and personal articles carried inside. **2.** a method of cheating at craps whereby the dice are thrown on a blanket, rug, or other soft surface so that they roll only in a forward direction, making it impossible for the four side numbers to appear face up.

blan′ket sheet′, a newspaper of larger than average size, common in mid-19th-century England.

blan′ket stitch′, a basic sewing stitch in which widely spaced, interlocking loops, or purls, are formed, used for cutwork, as a decorative finish for edges, etc.

blan·ket-stitch (blang′kit stich′), *v.t., v.i.* to sew using a blanket stitch. [v. use of BLANKET STITCH]

blank·e·ty-blank (blang′ki tē blangk′), *adj., adv.* *Informal.* a euphemism for damned, etc., implying an omission of an unprintable or unspeakable word: *The blankety-blank razor is on the blink.* [after the former practice of leaving blank spaces to represent profanity, as *G— d—* for *God damn*]

blank′ flange′, a flange complete except for drilling.

blank·ly (blangk′lē), *adv.* **1.** without expression or understanding: *She stared blankly at her inquisitors.* **2.** totally; fully; in every respect: *He blankly denied ever saying such a thing. The prince had a blankly spurious claim to the throne.* [BLANK + -LY]

blank′ shell′, a shotgun shell containing powder but no shot.

blank′ verse′, unrhymed verse, esp. the unrhymed iambic pentameter most frequently used in English dramatic, epic, and reflective verse.

blank′ wall′, an impassable barricade or obstacle; a situation in which further progress is impossible: *Attempts to get information by questioning the natives ran into a blank wall.*

blan·quette (blän ket′), *n.* a ragout of lamb, veal, or chicken, prepared in a velouté sauce, usually garnished with croutons or small onions and mushrooms. [< F; see BLANK, -ETTE]

blan·qui·llo (bläng kēl′yō; *Sp.* bläng kē′yô), *n., pl.* (*esp. collectively*) **-llo,** (*esp. referring to two or more kinds or species*) **-llos** (-yōz; *Sp.* -yôs). any of several game fishes of the genus *Caulolatilus,* related to the tilefishes. [< Sp, equiv. to *blanc(o)* white (see BLANK) + *-illo* < L *-illus* dim. suffix]

Blan·tyre (blan tīər′), *n.* a city in S Malawi. 30,000 (est. 1956).

blare (blâr), *v.,* **blared, blar·ing,** *n.* —*v.i.* **1.** to emit a loud raucous sound: *The trumpets blared as the procession got under way.* —*v.t.* **2.** to sound loudly; proclaim noisily: *We sat there horrified as the radio blared the awful news.* —*n.* **3.** a loud raucous noise: *The blare of the phonograph made conversation impossible.* **4.** glaring intensity of light or color: *A blare of sunlight flooded the room as she opened the shutters.* **5.** fanfare; flourish; ostentation; flamboyance: *a new breakfast cereal announced with all the blare of a Hollywood spectacle.* [late ME *blere(n)*; akin to MD *blaren,* MLG *blarren,* MHG *blerren* (G *plärren*)]

blar·ney (blär′nē), *n., v.,* **-neyed, -ney·ing.** —*n.* **1.** flattering or wheedling talk; cajolery: *He gets all that blarney from his father's people.* —*v.t., v.i.* **2.** to ply or beguile with blarney; use blarney; wheedle: *He blarneys the girls with the most shameless lies.* [after the hamlet *Blarney,* in Ireland; see BLARNEY STONE]

Blar′ney stone′, a stone in Blarney Castle near Cork, Ireland, said to impart skill in flattery to anyone who kisses it.

Blas·co I·bá·ñez (bläs′kô ē vä′nyeth), **Vi·cen·te** (bē then′te), 1867–1928, Spanish novelist, journalist, and politician.

Blas·dell (blaz′del), *n.* a town in W New York. 3909 (1960).

bla·sé (blä zā′, blä′zā; *Fr.* blä zā′), *adj.* indifferent to or bored with life; unimpressed, as or as if from an excess of worldly pleasures: *He remained blasé throughout the tour.* [< F, ptp. of *blaser* to cloy, sicken from surfeit, perh. < D *blasen* to blow; see BLAST]

blas·pheme (blas fēm′, blas′fēm), *v.,* **-phemed, -phem·ing.** —*v.t.* **1.** to speak impiously or irreverently of (God or sacred things). **2.** to speak evil of; slander; abuse: *He was at first blasphemed and later applauded by the critics.* —*v.i.* **3.** to speak irreverently of God or sacred things; utter impieties. [ME < eccl. L *blasphē-m(āre)* < Gk *blasphēméein* to speak profanely, deriv. of *blásphēm(os)* BLASPHEMOUS] —**blas·phem′er,** *n.*
—**Syn. 1.** See **curse.**

blas·phe·mous (blas′fə məs), *adj.* uttering, containing, or exhibiting blasphemy; irreverent; profane. [< eccl. L *blasphēmus* < Gk *blásphēmos* defaming, speaking evil, equiv. to *blá(p)s(is)* harm, evil (akin to *bláptein* to harm) + *-phēmos* speaking (*phēm(e)* speech + *-os* adj. suffix)] —**blas′phe·mous·ly,** *adv.* —**blas′phe·mous·ness,** *n.*

blas·phe·my (blas′fə mē), *n., pl.* **-mies. 1.** impious utterance or action concerning God or sacred things. **2.** *Judaism.* **a.** act of cursing or reviling God. **b.** pronunciation of the Tetragrammaton in the original, now forbidden manner instead of using a substitute pronunciation. **3.** *Theol.* the crime of assuming to oneself the rights or qualities of God. **4.** irreverent behavior toward anything held sacred, priceless, etc.: *He uttered blasphemes against life itself.* [ME *blasphemie* < eccl. L *blasphēmia* < Gk. See BLASPHEMOUS, -Y³]
—**Syn. 1.** profanity, cursing, swearing; sacrilege.

blast (blast, bläst), *n.* **1.** a sudden and violent gust of wind: *Wintry blasts chilled us to the marrow.* **2.** the blowing of a trumpet, whistle, etc.: *One blast of the siren was enough to clear the street.* **3.** a loud, sudden sound or noise: *The radio let out an awful blast before I could turn it off.* **4.** a forcible stream of air from the mouth, bellows, or the like. **5.** *Mach.* **a.** air forced into a furnace by a blower to increase the rate of combustion. **b.** a jet of steam directed up a smokestack, as of a steam locomotive, to increase draft. **c.** a draft thus increased. **6.** *Slang.* **a.** party, esp. a wild, abandoned one: *Did we have a blast last night!* **7.** *Mining, Civ. Eng.* the charge of dynamite or other explosive used at one firing in blasting operations. **8.** the act of exploding; explosion: *Some say the blast was in the next county.* **9.** a shock wave in areas within the radius of an explosion, due to changes in atmospheric pressure. **10.** any pernicious or destructive influence, esp. on animals or plants; a blight. **11. at full blast,** *Informal.* at maximum capacity; at or with full volume or speed: *The factory is going at full blast.* Also, **full blast.** —*v.t.* **12.** to make a loud noise on; blow (a trumpet, automobile horn, etc.): *He blasted his horn irritably at every car in his way.* **13.** to cause to shrivel or wither; blight. **14.** to affect with any pernicious influence; ruin; destroy: *Failure in the exam blasted his hopes for college. It was an indiscretion that blasted his good reputation.* **15.** to break up or dislodge (rock, a tree stump, etc.): *Their explosives were inadequate to blast the granite.* **16.** to make, form, open up, etc., by blasting: *to blast a tunnel through a mountain.* **17.** to show to be false, unreliable, etc.; discredit: *His facts soundly blasted the new evidence.* **18.** (euphemistically) to curse; damn (usually fol. by *it* or an object): *Blast it, there's the phone again! Blast the time, we've got to finish this work.* **19.** *Slang.* to censure or criticize vigorously; denounce: *In his campaign speech he really blasts the other party.* **20.** *Slang.* to shoot: *The gangster blasted him down.* —*v.i.* **21.** to produce a loud, blaring sound: *The trumpets blasted as the overture began. His voice blasted until the microphone was turned down.* **22.** *Slang.* to shoot: *He whipped out his revolver and started blasting.* **23.** *Slang.* to take narcotics, esp. to smoke marijuana. **24. blast off, a.** (of a rocket) to leave a launch pad under its own power. **b.** (of an astronaut) to travel aloft in a rocket. [ME; OE *blǣst* a blowing; akin to Icel *blāstr,* OHG *blāst* (deriv. of *blāsan;* c. Goth *(uf)blēsan,* Icel *blāsa*). See BLOW²] —**blast′er,** *n.* —**blast′y,** *adj.*
—**Syn. 1.** squall, gale, blow, storm. See **wind**¹. **2.** blare, screech. **8.** discharge, outburst. **14.** annihilate.

-blast, var. of **blasto-** as final element of a compound word: *ectoblast.*

blast·ed (blas′tid, blä′stid), *adj.* **1.** withered; shriveled; blighted; ruined. **2.** damned; confounded (a euphemism): *This blasted pen never did work properly.* [BLAST (v.) + -ED²]

blas·te·ma (bla stē′mə), *n., pl.* **-mas, -ma·ta** (-mə tə). *Embryol.* an aggregation of cells in a young embryo, capable of differentiation into primordia and organs. [< NL < Gk *(blastē-* long s. of *blastē-, ein* to sprout + *-ma* n. suffix)] —**blas·te′mal, blas·te·mat·ic** (blas′tə mat′ik), **blas·tem·ic** (bla stem′ik), *adj.*

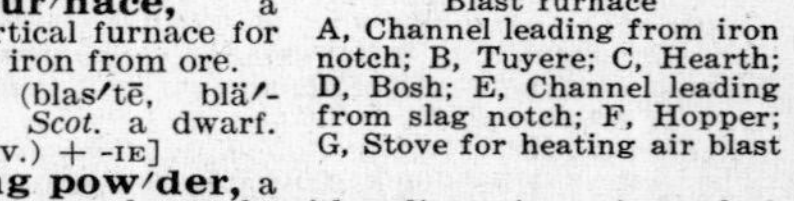

Blast furnace
A, Channel leading from iron notch; B, Tuyere; C, Hearth; D, Bosh; E, Channel leading from slag notch; F, Hopper; G, Stove for heating air blast

blast′ fur′nace, a large vertical furnace for smelting iron from ore.

blas·tie (blas′tē, blä′stē), *n.* *Scot.* a dwarf. [BLAST (v.) + -IE]

blast′ing pow′der, a form of gunpowder made with sodium nitrate instead of saltpeter, used chiefly for blasting rock, ore, etc.

blast′ lamp′, a torch or lamp, as a blowtorch or a lamp for lampworking, in which the flame is fed by an air or oxygen blast.

blast·ment (blast′mənt, bläst′-), *n.* a blasting; a blast or blight. [BLAST + -MENT]

blasto-, a learned borrowing from Greek meaning "embryo," used in the formation of compound words: *blastosphere.* Also, **-blast.** [comb. form of Gk *blastós* a bud, sprout]

blas·to·coel (blas′tə sēl′), *n. Embryol.* the cavity of a blastula, arising in the course of cleavage. Also, **blas′to·coele′.** Also called **segmentation cavity.** [BLASTO- + -COEL] —**blas′to·coel′ic,** *adj.*

blas·to·cyst (blas′tə sist), *n. Embryol.* the blastula of a mammalian embryo. [BLASTO- + -CYST]

blas·to·derm (blas′tə dûrm′), *n. Embryol.* **1.** the primitive layer of cells that results from the segmentation of the ovum. **2.** the layer of cells forming the wall of the blastula, and in most vertebrates enclosing a cavity or a yolk mass. [BLASTO- + -DERM] —**blas′to·der′mic, blas′to·der·mat′ic,** *adj.*

blas·to·disk (blas′tə disk′), *n. Embryol.* the small disk of protoplasm, containing the egg nucleus, which appears on the surface of the yolk mass in the very heavily yolked eggs, as of birds and reptiles. Also, **blas′to·disc′.** [BLASTO- + DISK]

blast-off (blast′ôf′, -of′, bläst′-), *n. Rocketry.* the launching of a rocket or guided missile. [n. use of v. phrase *blast off*]

blas·to·gen·e·sis (blas′tə jen′i sis), *n. Biol.* **1.** reproduction by gemmation or budding. **2.** the theory of the transmission of hereditary characters by germ plasm. **3.** the formation of the blastula of an embryo. [BLASTO- + GENESIS]

blas·to·ma (bla stō′mə), *n., pl.* **-mas, -ma·ta** (-mə tə). *n. Pathol.* a tumor originating from undifferentiated embryonic cells and having little or no connective tissue. [BLAST- + -OMA]

blas·to·mere (blas′tə mēr′), *n. Embryol.* any cell produced during cleavage. [BLASTO- + -MERE] —**blas·to·mer·ic** (blas′tə mer′ik), *adj.*

blas·to·my·co·sis (blas′tō mī kō′sis), *n. Pathol.* any of several diseases caused by certain yeastlike fungi, characterized by suppurating skin nodules and lesions in the viscera and bones. [< NL; see BLASTO-, MYCOSIS] —**blas·to·my·cot·ic** (blas′tō mī kot′ik), *adj.*

blas·to·pore (blas′tə pōr′, -pôr′), *n. Embryol.* the opening of an archenteron. [BLASTO- + *-pore* passage; see PORE²] —**blas·to·por·ic** (blas′tə pôr′ik, -por′-), **blas·to·po·ral** (blas′tə pōr′əl, -pôr′-), *adj.*

blas·to·sphere (blas′tə sfēr′), *n. Embryol.* **1.** a blastula. **2.** a blastocyst. [BLASTO- + -SPHERE]

blas·to·style (blas′tə stīl′), *n. Zool.* the central rodlike portion of a gonangium, upon which buds that develop into medusae are formed. [BLASTO- + STYLE] —**blas′to·sty′lar,** *adj.*

blas·tu·la (blas′cho͝o lə), *n., pl.* **-las, -lae** (-lē′). *Embryol.* the early developmental stage of a metazoan, following the morula stage and consisting of a single, spherical layer of cells that encloses a hollow, central cavity. [< NL < Gk *blast(ós)* bud, sprout + NL *-ula* -ULE] —**blas′tu·lar,** *adj.*

A B
Blastula
A, Exterior view
B, Cross section

blat (blat), *v.,* **blat·ted, blat·ting.** —*v.i.* **1.** to cry out, as a calf or sheep; bleat. —*v.t.* **2.** *Informal.* to utter loudly and indiscreetly; blurt. [back formation from *blattant,* var. of BLATANT]

bla·tant (blāt′ənt), *adj.* **1.** obtrusive; brazenly obvious: *a blatant error in simple addition; the blatant exploitation of a pretty face; a blatant lie.* **2.** offensively noisy or loud; clamorous: *blatant radios.* **3.** tastelessly conspicuous: *the blatant colors of her dress.* **4.** *Poetic.* bleating: *blatant herds.* [coined by Spenser; cf. L *blatīre* to babble, prate; *blaterāre* to talk foolishly, babble] —**bla′tan·cy,** *n.* —**bla′tant·ly,** *adv.*

blate (blāt), *adj. Scot. and North Eng.* **1.** void of feeling or spirit; insensible; spiritless. **2.** bashful; shy. **3.** *Obs.* pale; ghastly. [OE *blāt* livid, pallid; low (said of sound)] —**blate′ly,** *adv.* —**blate′ness,** *n.*

blath·er (blath′ər), *n.* **1.** foolish talk, esp. in great quantity: *His speech was full of the most amazing blather.* —*v.i., v.t.* **2.** to talk or utter foolishly; babble: *The poor thing blathered for hours about the intricacies of his psyche.* Also, **blether.** [ME < Scand; cf. Icel *blathra* to chatter]

blath·er·skite (blath′ər skīt′), *n.* **1.** a person given to voluble, empty talk. **2.** nonsense; blather. [BLATHER + *skite* SKATE³]

blau·bok (blou′bok′), *n., pl.* **-boks,** (*esp. collectively*) **-bok.** an extinct bluish antelope, *Hippotragus leucophaeus,* of southern Africa, having backward curving horns. [< D *blauwbok* blue buck]

Blau·e Rei·ter (blou′ə rī′tər), *German.* (*sometimes l.c.*) a group of artists active in Germany, esp. in or near Munich, during the early 20th century, whose works were characterized by the use of Fauve color and forms distorted for structural or emotive purposes. Also called **Blue Rider.** [< lit., blue rider]

Bla·vat·sky (blə vat′skē), *n.* **Madame** (*Elena Petrovna Blavatskaya, nee Hahn*), 1831–91, Russian theosophist.

blaw (blô), *v.i., v.t. Scot. and North Eng.* blow².

blaze¹ (blāz), *n., v.,* **blazed, blaz·ing.** —*n.* **1.** a bright flame or fire: *the welcome blaze on the hearth.* **2.** a bright, hot gleam or glow: *the blaze of day.* **3.** a sparkling brightness: *a blaze of jewels.* **4.** a sudden, intense outburst, as of fire, passion, fury, etc.: *to unleash a blaze of pent-up emotions; a blaze of glory; a blaze of fury.* **5. blazes,** *Slang.* hell: *Go to blazes!* —*v.i.* **6.** to burn brightly (sometimes fol. by *away, up, forth*): *The bonfire blazed away for hours. The dry wood blazed up at the touch of a match.* **7.** to shine like flame (sometimes fol. by *forth*): *Their faces blazed with enthusiasm. The bird's plumage blazed forth.* **8.** to burn with intense feeling or passion (sometimes fol. by *up*): *He blazed up at the insult.* **9.** to shoot steadily or continuously (usually fol. by *away*): *The contestants blazed away at the clay pigeons.* **10.** *Poetic.* to be meritoriously conspicuous. —*v.t.* **11.** to exhibit vividly: *He didn't hesitate to blaze his extreme anger to everyone present.* [ME, OE *blase* torch, flame; c. MHG *blas* torch] —**blaz′ing·ly,** *adv.*
—**Syn. 1.** See **flame.**

blaze² (blāz), *n., v.,* **blazed, blaz·ing.** —*n.* **1.** a spot or mark made on a tree, as by notching or by chipping away a piece of the bark, to indicate a boundary or a path in a forest. **2.** a white area down the center of the face of a horse, cow, etc. —*v.t.* **3.** to mark with blazes: *to blaze a trail.* **4.** to lead in forming or finding (a new method, course, etc.): *His research in rocketry blazed the way for eventual space travel.* [akin to Icel *blesi,* D *bles,* G *Blässe* white mark on a beast's face, and to G *blass* pale]

blaze³ (blāz), *v.t.,* **blazed, blaz·ing. 1.** to make known; proclaim; publish: *Headlines blazed the shocking news.* **2.** *Obs.* to blow, as from a trumpet. [ME *blase(n)* < MD; c. Icel *blāsa* to blow. See BLAST]

Blaze (blāz), *n.* a boy's or girl's given name.

blaz·er (blā′zər), *n.* **1.** *Informal.* that which blazes or shines brightly. **2.** a lightweight sports jacket, usually having metal buttons and often an insignia on the breast pocket, worn informally, esp. by a member of a club, school, or the like. **3.** a cooking vessel, using as its source of heat a spirit lamp, hot coals, etc., used esp. for preparing food at the table or outdoors. [BLAZE¹ + -ER¹]

blaz′ing star′, 1. any of certain plants with showy flower clusters, as the liliaceous herb *Aletris farinosa* or the composite perennial *Liatris squarrosa.* **2.** a stout, perennial herb, *Mentzelia laevicaulis,* of the western U.S., having light yellow flowers from 2½ to 4 inches wide. **3.** *Archaic.* a person or thing that, because of rare qualities, attracts universal attention.

bla·zon (blā′zən), *v.t.* **1.** to set forth conspicuously or publicly; display; proclaim: *The pickets blazoned their grievances on placards.* **2.** to describe in heraldic terminology. **3.** to depict (heraldic arms or the like) in proper form and color. —*n.* **4.** an escutcheon; coat of arms. **5.** the heraldic description of armorial bearings. **6.** conspicuous display: *The candidate zestfully made a blazon of his opponent's error.* [ME *blaso(u)n* < MF *blason* buckler] —**bla′zon·er,** *n.* —**bla′zon·ment,** *n.*

bla·zon·ry (blā′zən rē), *n.* **1.** brilliant decoration or display: *The wedding had all the blazonry of a coronation.* **2.** *Heraldry.* **a.** the act or technique of describing coats of arms. **b.** a coat, or coats, of arms. [BLAZON + -RY]

bldg., building.

Bldg.E., Building Engineer.

-ble, var. of **-able** (*soluble*); occurring first in words of Latin origin which came into English through French, later in words taken directly from Latin. Also, *esp. after a consonant stem,* **-ible.** [ME < OF < L *-bile(m),* acc. of *-bilis, -bilə* adj. suffix]

B.L.E., Brotherhood of Locomotive Engineers.

bleach (blēch), *v.t., v.i.* **1.** to make or become white: *Why not bleach your shirts as you wash them?* **2.** *Photog.* to convert (the silver image of a negative or print) to a silver halide, either to remove the image or to change its tone. —*n.* **3.** a bleaching agent. **4.** degree of paleness achieved in bleaching. **5.** act of bleaching: *Put the towels back in the machine and give them another bleach.* [ME *bleche(n),* OE *blǣcean,* deriv. of *blāc* pale); c. Icel *bleikja,* OHG *bleichen*] —**bleach′a·bil′i·ty,** *n.* —**bleach′a·ble,** *adj.*
—**Syn. 1.** See **whiten.**

bleach·er (blē′chər), *n.* **1.** one who or that which bleaches. **2.** a container, as a vat, tank, etc., used in bleaching. **3.** Usually, **bleachers.** a section of unreserved seats in tiers, usually unprotected by a roof and inexpensive, for spectators at games. [BLEACH + -ER¹]

bleach·er·y (blē′chə rē), *n., pl.* **-er·ies.** a place or establishment where bleaching is carried on. [BLEACH + -ERY]

bleach′ing pow′der, *Chem.* a white powder having the characteristic odor of gaseous chlorine and regarded, when dry, as a mixed calcium hypochlorite-chloride, Ca(OCl)Cl, that decomposes on contact with water: used as a commercial bleach for wood pulp, textiles, oils, soaps, and in laundering, as a decolorizer, and as a disinfectant. Also called **chloride of lime, chlorinated lime, calcium oxychloride.**

bleak¹ (blēk), *adj.* **1.** bare, desolate, and windswept: *a bleak plain.* **2.** cold and piercing; raw: *a bleak wind.* **3.** without hope or encouragement; depressing; dreary: *a bleak prospect.* [ME *bleke* pale, b. variants *bleche* (OE *blǣc*) + *blake* (OE *blāc*); both c. Icel *bleikr,* G *bleich;* akin to BLEACH] —**bleak′ish,** *adj.* —**bleak′ly,** *adv.* —**bleak′ness,** *n.*

bleak² (blēk), *n.* a European, fresh-water fish, *Alburnus alburnus,* having scales with a silvery pigment that is used in the production of artificial pearls. [late ME *bleke,* n. use of BLEAK¹]

Bleak′ House′, a novel (1852) by Charles Dickens.

blear (blēr), *v.t.* **1.** to make (the eyes or sight) dim, as with tears or inflammation: *a biting wind that bleared the vision.* —*adj.* **2.** (of the eyes) dim from a watery discharge: *His eyes were blear with tears.* **3.** *Rare.* dim; indistinct. —*n.* **4.** a blur; cloudiness; dimness: *He was concerned about the recent blear in his vision.* [ME *bleri, blere* (v.), *blere* (adj.) < ?] —**blear·ed·ness** (blēr′id nis), *n.*

blear-eyed (blēr′īd′), *adj.* **1.** having blear eyes. **2.** dull of perception; short-sighted: *a blear-eyed attitude about life.* Also, **bleary-eyed.** —**blear′-eyed′ness,** *n.*

blear·y (blēr′ē), *adj.,* **blear·i·er, blear·i·est. 1.** (of the eyes or sight) blurred or dimmed, as from sleep or weariness. **2.** indistinct; unclear: *The day begins with a bleary view of one's world.* **3.** fatigued; worn-out. [ME *blery.* See BLEAR (adj.), -Y¹] —**blear′i·ly,** *adv.* —**blear′i·ness,** *n.*

blear·y-eyed (blēr′ē īd′), *adj.* blear-eyed. —**blear′y-eyed′ness,** *n.*

bleat (blēt), *v.i.* **1.** to utter the cry of a sheep, goat, or calf, or a sound resembling such a cry. —*v.t.* **2.** to give forth with or as with a bleat: *He bleated his objections in a helpless rage.* **3.** to babble; prate: *He bleated his gossip from one end of town to the other.* —*n.* **4.** the cry of a sheep, goat, or calf. **5.** any similar sound: *the bleat of distant horns.* **6.** foolish, complaining talk; babble: *I listened to her inane bleat all evening.* [ME *blete(n),* OE *blǣtan;* c. D *blaten,* OHG *blāzen;* akin to L *blēre* to weep] —**bleat′er,** *n.* —**bleat′ing·ly,** *adv.*

ble·aunt (blē′ənt), *n.* a short tunic or blouse, worn in the Middle Ages. [ME *bleaunt, blihand* < AF *bliaunt,* MF, OF *bliaut*]

bleb (bleb), *n. Rare.* **1.** a blister or pustule. **2.** a bubble. [akin to BLOB, BLUBBER] —**bleb′by,** *adj.*

bleed (blēd), *v.,* **bled** (bled), **bleed·ing,** *n., adj.* —*v.i.* **1.** to lose blood from the vascular system, either internally into the body or externally through a natural orifice or break in the skin: *to bleed from the mouth.* **2.** to be severely wounded or die, as in battle: *The soldiers bled for the cause.* **3.** (of blood) to flow out. **4.** (of a plant) to exude sap, resin, etc., from a wound. **5.** (of dye or paint) to run or become diffused: *All the colors bled when the dress was washed. The red first coat bled into the white.* **6.** to feel pity, sorrow, or anguish: *A nation bleeds for its dead heroes.* **7.** *Slang.* to pay money, as when overcharged or threatened with extortion: *As the town was overcrowded, he had to bleed for a hotel room.* **8.** *Print.* (of printed matter) to run off the edges of a page, either by design or through mutilation caused by too close trimming. **9.** *Metall.* (of a cooling ingot or casting) to have molten metal force its way through the solidified exterior because of internal gas pressure. —*v.t.* **10.** to cause to lose blood, esp. surgically: *A doctor no longer bleeds his patient to reduce a fever.* **11.** to lose or emit (blood or sap). **12.** to drain or draw sap, water, electricity, etc., from (something): *to bleed a pipe line of excess air.* **13.** *Slang.* to obtain an excessive amount from; extort money from. **14.** *Print.* **a.** to permit (printed illustrations or ornamentation) to run off the page or sheet. **b.** to trim the margin of (a book or sheet) so closely as to mutilate the text or illustration. **15. bleed white.** See **white** (def. 23). —*n. Print.* **16.** a sheet or page margin trimmed so as to mutilate the text or illustration. **17.** a part thus trimmed off. —*adj.* **18.** *Print.* characterized by bleeding: *a bleed page.* [ME *blede(n),* OE *blēdan,* deriv. of *blōd* BLOOD]

bleed·er (blē′dər), *n.* **1.** a person predisposed to bleeding; hemophiliac. **2.** one who draws blood from a sick person; phlebotomist. **3.** *Slang.* a person who drains another of money, resources, etc.; parasite or usurer. **4.** *Foundry.* an ingot or casting from which some metal has escaped. **5.** Also called **bleed′er resis′tor.** *Elect.* a resistor that is connected across a power supply for voltage regulation and to dissipate the charge remaining in capacitors when the power is discontinued. **6.** *Baseball Slang.* a slow, poorly hit ground ball to the infield that barely enables the batter to reach first base safely. **7.** a valve or opening for draining a tank, tubing, etc. **8.** *Brit. Usually Disparaging.* fellow; man. [BLEED + -ER¹]

bleed′er tile′, a terra-cotta pipe for conveying water from a drainage tile to a sewer or drain. Also called **bleed′er pipe′.**

bleed·ing (blē′ding), *n.* **1.** act, fact, or process of losing blood or having blood flow. **2.** act or process of drawing blood from a person, esp. surgically; bloodletting. **3.** the extension of color beyond an edge or border, esp. so as to combine with a contiguous color or to affect an adjacent area. —*adj.* **4.** sending forth blood: *a bleeding sore* **5.** feeling, expressing, or characterized by extreme or excessive anguish and compassion. **6.** *Brit. Vulgar.* bloody (def. 5). [ME; see BLEED, -ING¹, -ING²]

bleed′ing heart′, 1. any of various plants of the genus *Dicentra,* esp. *D. spetabilis,* a common garden plant having racemes of red, heart-shaped flowers. **2.** *Disparaging.* a person who makes an ostentatious or excessive display of pity or concern for others.

blel·lum (blel′əm), *n. Scot. Obs.* an idle, indiscreet talker; blab. [?]

blem·ish (blem′ish), *v.t.* **1.** to destroy or diminish the perfection of: *The book is blemished by those long descriptions.* —*n.* **2.** a defect or flaw; disfigurement; stain: *a blemish on one's skin; a blemish on his record.* [ME *blemysh* < MF *blemiss-,* long s. of *ble(s)mir* to make livid, perh. < Gmc; see BLAZE²] —**blem′ish·er,** *n.*
—**Syn. 1.** stain, sully, spot, tarnish, taint; injure, mar, damage, impair, deface. **2.** blot, spot, speck, taint, flaw. See **defect.** —**Ant. 1.** purify, repair.

blench¹ (blench), *v.i.* to shrink; flinch; quail: *an unsteady eye that blenched under another's gaze.* [ME *blenche(n),* OE *blencan;* c. Icel *blekkja,* MHG *blenken*] —**blench′er,** *n.* —**blench′ing·ly,** *adv.*

blench² (blench), *v.t., v.i.* to make or become pale or white; blanch. [var. of BLANCH¹]

blend (blend), *v.,* **blend·ed** or **blent, blend·ing,** *n.* —*v.t.* **1.** to mix smoothly and inseparably together: *to blend the ingredients in a recipe.* **2.** to mix (various sorts of grades) in order to obtain a particular kind or quality: *Blend a little red paint with the blue paint.* **3.** to prepare by such mixture: *This tea is blended by mixing camomile with pekoe.* —*v.i.* **4.** to mix or intermingle smoothly and inseparably: *I can't get the eggs and cream to blend.* **5.** to fit or relate harmoniously: *The red sofa did not blend with the purple wall.* **6.** to have no perceptible separation: *Sea and sky seemed to blend.* —*n.* **7.** act or manner of blending: *tea of our own blend.* **8.** a mixture or kind produced by blending: *a special blend of rye and wheat flours.* **9.** *Ling.* a word made by putting together parts of other words, as *dandle,* made from *dance* and *handle.* [ME *blend(en),* OE *blendan* to mix for *blandan;* c. Icel *blanda,* OHG *blantan* to mix]
—**Syn. 1.** compound. See **mix. 1, 4.** mingle, commingle, combine, amalgamate, unite. **4.** coalesce. **7.** combination, amalgamation. —**Ant. 1, 4.** separate.

Blen·da (blen′də), *n.* a girl's given name.

blende (blend), *n.* **1.** sphalerite; zinc sulfide. **2.** any of certain other sulfides. [< G; MHG *blende(n)* (to) make blind, deceive; so called because often deceptively like galena]

blend′ed whis′key, whiskey that is a blend of two or more whiskeys, or of whiskey and neutral spirits, and that contains at least 20 percent of 100-proof straight whiskey by volume after blending.

blend·er (blen′dər), *n.* **1.** one who or that which blends. **2.** a mixing machine consisting of a container with propellerlike blades at the bottom that are whirled by a powerful, high-speed motor to purée foods, grind coffee, mix beverages, etc. **3.** a kitchen utensil having several parallel wires bent in a semicircle and secured by a handle, used esp. for mixing pastry. [BLEND + -ER¹]

blend′ing inher′itance, *Genetics.* inheritance in which contrasting parental characters appear as a blend in the offspring.

Blen·heim (blen′əm), *n.* village in S West Germany, on the Danube: famous victory of the Duke of Marlborough over the French, 1704. German, **Blindheim.**

Blen′heim span′iel, one of a breed of toy spaniels having a short head and long ears. [named after *Blenheim,* country house of Duke of Marlborough in Oxfordshire, England]

blen·ni·oid (blen′ē oid′), *adj.* **1.** *Ichthyol.* resembling a blenny. **2.** pertaining to the blennies. [BLENNY + -OID]

blen·ny (blen′ē), *n., pl.* **-nies.** any of several fishes of the genus *Blennius,* and related genera, having a long, tapering body and small pelvic fins inserted before the pectoral fins. [< L *blenni(us)* a kind of fish < Gk *blénnos* slime, mucus; so called from its slimy coating]

blent (blent), *v.* a pt. and pp. of **blend.**

blephar-, a learned borrowing from Greek meaning "eyelid," used in the formation of compound words: *blepharitis.* Also, *esp. before a consonant,* **blepharo-.** [< Gk *blephar-,* comb. form of *blépharon*]

bleph·a·ri·tis (blef′ə rī′tis), *n. Pathol.* inflammation of the eyelids. [BLEPHAR- + -ITIS] —**bleph·a·rit·ic** (blef′ə rit′ik), *adj.*

bleph·a·ro·spasm (blef′ə rō spaz′əm, -ər ə-), *n. Med.* spasmodic winking. [BLEPHARO- + SPASM]

Blé·riot (blā ryō′), *n.* **Louis** (lwē), 1872–1936, French aviator, pioneer aeronautical engineer, and inventor.

bles·bok (bles′bok′), *n., pl.* **-boks,** (*esp. collectively*) **-bok.** a large antelope, *Damaliscus albifrons,* of southern Africa, having a blaze on the face. Also, **blesbuck.** [< SAfrD, equiv. to D *bles* BLAZE[2] + *bok* BUCK[1]]

bles·buck (bles′buk′), *n., pl.* **-bucks,** (*esp. collectively*) **-buck.** blesbok.

bless (bles), *v.t.,* **blessed** or **blest, bless·sing. 1.** to consecrate or sanctify by a religious rite; make or pronounce holy. **2.** to request of God the bestowal of divine favor on: *Bless this house.* **3.** to bestow good of any kind upon: *a nation blessed with peace.* **4.** to extol as holy; glorify: *Bless the name of the Lord.* **5.** to protect or guard from evil (usually used interjectionally): *Bless you! Bless your innocent little heart!* **6.** to condemn or curse: *I'll be blessed if I can see your reasoning. Bless me if it isn't my old friend!* **7.** to make the sign of the cross over or upon: *The Pope blessed the multitude.* [ME *bless(en),* OE *blētsian, blēdsian* to consecrate, orig. with blood, earlier **blōdisōian* (*blōd* blood + *-isō-* derivational suffix + *-ian* v. suffix)] —**bless′er,** *n.* —**bless′ing·ly,** *adv.*

bless·ed (bles′id, blest), *adj.* Also, **blest. 1.** consecrated; sacred; holy; sanctified: *Blessed be the tie that binds/Our hearts in Christian love.* **2.** worthy of adoration, reverence, or worship: *the Blessed Trinity.* **3.** divinely or supremely favored; fortunate: *to be blessed with a strong, healthy body; blessed with an ability to find friends.* **4.** blissfully happy or contented. **5.** *Rom. Cath. Ch.* beatified. **6.** bringing happiness; pleasurable: *the blessed assurance of a steady income.* **7.** damned (a euphemism): *I'm blessed if I know.* **8.** used for emphasis: *every blessed cent.* —*n.* **9. the blessed,** *Rom. Cath. Ch.* the body of deceased persons who have received beatification: *the blessed in heaven.* [ME; see BLESS, -ED[2]] —**bless′ed·ly,** *adv.* —**bless′ed·ness,** *n.*

Bless′ed Dam′o·zel, The (dam′ə zel′), a poem (1847) by Dante Gabriel Rossetti.

bless′ed event′, *Informal.* the birth of a child.

Bless′ed Sac′rament, *Eccles.* the consecrated Host.

bless′ed this′tle, a pubescent, thistlelike, composite herb, *Cnicus benedictus,* having large heads of yellow flowers.

Bless′ed Trin′ity, Trinity (def. 1).

Bless′ed Vir′gin, the Virgin Mary.

bless·ing (bles′ing), *n.* **1.** act or words of one who blesses. **2.** a special favor, mercy, or benefit: *the blessings of liberty.* **3.** a favor or gift bestowed by God, thereby bringing happiness. **4.** the invoking of God's favor upon a person: *The son was denied his father's blessing.* **5.** praise; devotion; worship, esp. grace said before a meal: *The children took turns reciting the blessing.* **6.** a rebuke, scolding, cursing, or damning (a euphemism): *He got quite a blessing from his superior.* **7.** approval: *a proposed law with the blessing of the governor.* [ME *blessinge, -unge,* OE *bletsung, bledsung.* See BLESS, -ING[1]]

blest (blest), *v.* **1.** a pt. and pp. of **bless.** —*adj.* **2.** blessed.

bleth·er (bleth′ər), *n., v.i., v.t.* blather.

blet·ting (blet′ing), *n.* the ripening of fruit, esp. of fruit stored until the desired degree of decay and softness is attained. [*blet* < F + -ING[1]]

bleu ce·leste (blōō′ si lest′), *Heraldry.* cerulean (def. 2). [< F]

Bleu·ler (bloi′lər), *n.* **Eu·gen** (oi gān′), 1857–1939, Swiss psychiatrist and neurologist.

blew (blōō), *v.* pt. of **blow**[2].

B.L.F.E., Brotherhood of Locomotive Firemen and Enginemen.

B.L.I., Bachelor of Literary Interpretation.

Bli·da (blē′dä), *n.* a city in N Algeria. 61,808 (1954).

Bligh (blī), *n.* **William,** 1754–1817, British naval officer: commander of the mutinied H.M.S. *Bounty,* 1789.

blight (blīt), *n.* **1.** *Plant Pathol.* **a.** the rapid and extensive discoloration, wilting, and death of plant tissues. **b.** a disease so characterized. **2.** any cause of impairment, destruction, ruin, or frustration: *Bankruptcy was the blight of the family.* —*v.t.* **3.** to cause to wither or decay; blast: *Frost blighted the crops.* **4.** to destroy; ruin; frustrate: *Illness blighted his hopes.* —*v.i.* **5.** to suffer blight. [?] —**blight′ing·ly,** *adj.*

blight·er (blī′tər), *n. Brit. Slang.* **1.** a contemptible, worthless man; rascal. **2.** a chap; bloke. [BLIGHT + -ER[1]]

blight·y (blī′tē), *n., pl.* **blight·ies.** *Brit. Slang.* **1.** (*often cap.*) England as one's native land; England as home: *We're sailing for old Blighty tomorrow.* **2.** a wound or furlough permitting a soldier to be sent back to England from the front during World War I. [< Hindi *bilāyatī* the country (i.e., Gt. Britain), var. of *wilāyatī* VILAYET]

bli·mey (blī′mē), *interj. Brit. Slang.* (used to express surprise or amazement): *Blimey, it's the Queen!* Also, **blimy.** [contr. of *blind me*]

blimp (blimp), *n.* **1.** a small, nonrigid airship or dirigible, used chiefly for observation. **2.** *Informal.* any dirigible. **3.** *Slang.* a fat person. **4.** *Motion Pictures.* a soundproof booth for the camera and cameraman, used to prevent the noise of the camera from reaching the microphone. [?]

bli·my (blī′mē), *interj. Brit. Slang.* blimey.

blin (blin), *n., pl.* **bli·ni, bli·ny** (blin′ē), **blin·is.** *Eastern European Cookery.* a pancake usually made with yeast and buckwheat flour, often served with sour cream, caviar, or melted butter. [< Russ]

blind (blīnd), *adj.* **1.** unable to see; lacking the sense of sight: *a blind man.* **2.** unwilling or unable to understand: *He was blind to all arguments.* **3.** not characterized or determined by reason or control: *blind tenacity; blind chance.* **4.** not having or based on reason or intelligence: *She had blind faith in his fidelity.* **5.** lacking all consciousness or awareness: *a blind stupor.* **6.** *Slang.* drunk. **7.** hard to see or understand: *blind reasoning.* **8.** hidden from immediate view, esp. from oncoming motorists: *a blind corner.* **9.** of concealed or undisclosed identity; sponsored anonymously: *a blind ad signed only with a box number.* **10.** having no outlets; closed at one end: *a blind passage; a blind alley; a blind mountain pass.* **11.** *Archit.* (of an archway, arcade, etc.) having no windows, passageways, or the like. **12.** dense enough to form a screen: *a blind hedge of privet.* **13.** done without seeing; by instruments alone: *blind flying.* **14.** made without some prior knowledge: *a blind purchase; a blind lead in a card game.* **15.** of, pertaining to, or for blind persons. **16.** *Bookbinding.* (of a design, title, or the like) impressed into the cover or spine of a book by a die without ink or foil. **17.** *Cookery.* (of pastry shells) baked or fried without the filling. **18.** (of a rivet or other fastener) made so that the end inserted, though inaccessible, can be headed or spread. —*v.t.* **19.** to make blind permanently, temporarily, or momentarily, as by injuring, dazzling, removing, or bandaging the eyes: *The explosion blinded him. We were blinded by the bright lights.* **20.** to make obscure or dark: *The room was blinded by heavy curtains.* **21.** to deprive of discernment, reason, or judgment: *a resentment that blinds his good sense.* **22.** to outshine; eclipse: *a radiance that doth blind the sun.* —*n.* **23.** something that obstructs vision or keeps out light, as a window shade or a blinker for a horse. **24.** a lightly built structure of brush or other growths, esp. one in which hunters conceal themselves. **25.** an activity, organization, or the like, for concealing or masking action or purpose; subterfuge: *The store was just a blind for their gambling operation.* **26.** a decoy. **27.** *Slang.* a bout of excessive drinking; drunken spree. **28.** *Poker.* a compulsory bet made without prior knowledge of one's hand. **29.** (*construed as pl.*) persons who lack the sense of sight (usually preceded by *the*): *The blind often have a more acute sense of hearing than the sighted.* —*adv.* **30.** *Informal.* into a stupor; to the degree at which consciousness is lost: *He drank himself blind.* **31.** without the ability to see; blindly: *They were driving blind through the snowstorm.* **32.** without guidance or forethought: *They were working blind and couldn't anticipate the effects of their actions.* [OE *blind;* c. Goth *blind(s),* Icel *blindr,* G, D *blind,* Lith *blendzas* blind] —**blind′ness,** *n.*

—**Syn. 1.** sightless. BLIND, STONE-BLIND, PURBLIND mean unable to see. BLIND means unable to see with the physical eyes. STONE-BLIND emphasizes complete blindness. PURBLIND refers to weakened vision, literally or figuratively. **4.** irrational, uncritical, rash, thoughtless, unreasoning. **8.** concealed. **23.** blinker, cover. See **curtain. 24.** hiding place, ambush. **25.** ruse, stratagem. —**Ant. 1.** seeing. **2.** receptive. **4.** rational.

blind·age (blīn′dij), *n. Mil.* a screen or other structure, as for protecting men in a trench. [BLIND + -AGE, modeled on F *blindage*]

blind′ al′ley, 1. a road, alley, etc., that is open at only one end. **2.** a position or situation offering no hope of progress or improvement: *That line of reasoning will only lead you up another blind alley.*

blind′ bomb′ing, *Mil.* the bombing of a target that is not visible from the bombing craft.

blind′ cas′ing, (in a box window frame) a rough framework to which the trim is secured.

blind·cat (blīnd′kat′), *n.* any of several catfishes found in subterranean streams, as *Satan eurystomus* **(widemouth blindcat),** of Texas, having rudimentary, functionless eyes and no skin pigmentation. [BLIND + CAT[1]]

blind′ cop′y, a copy of a letter or the like, the original of which bears no evidence that the copy was sent to any other person.

blind′ date′, *Informal.* **1.** a social appointment or date arranged, usually by a third person, between a man and a woman who have never before met. **2.** either of the participants in such an arrangement.

blind′ door′, a door having louvers permitting circulation of air.

blind·er (blīn′dər), *n.* **1.** one who or that which blinds. **2.** *U.S.* a blinker for a horse. [BLIND + -ER[1]]

blind·fish (blīnd′fish′), *n., pl.* **-fish·es,** (*esp. collectively*) **-fish.** a cavefish. [BLIND + FISH]

blind′ flange′, a disk for closing the end of a pipe, having holes for bolting it to a flange.

blind′ floor′, subfloor.

blind·fold (blīnd′fōld′), *v.t.* **1.** to prevent sight by covering (the eyes) with a cloth, bandage, or the like; cover the eyes of. **2.** to impair the awareness or clear thinking of: *Don't let their hospitality blindfold you to the true purpose of your visit.* —*n.* **3.** a cloth or bandage put before the eyes to prevent seeing. —*adj.* **4.** with the eyes covered: *a blindfold test.* **5.** rash; unthinking: *a blindfold denunciation before knowing one's facts.* [BLIND + FOLD[1] to wrap up; r. *blindfell,* lit., a *blind-fall,* OE *blindfellian* to make blind] —**blind′fold′ed·ly,** *adv.* —**blind′fold′ed·ness,** *n.* —**blind′fold′er,** *n.*

blind′ gut′, the cecum.

blind′ head′er, *Masonry.* a brick or stone having the appearance but not the length of a header.

Blind·heim (blint′hīm′), *n.* German name of **Blenheim.**

blind′ hook′ey (hōōk′ē), a gambling game at cards for a banker and any number of players.

blind·ing (blīn′ding), *n.* a layer of sand or fine gravel for filling the gaps in the surfaces of a road or pavement, as one of crushed and compacted stone. [ME; see BLIND, -ING[1]] —**blind′ing·ly,** *adv.*

Blind′ Lead′ing the Blind′, The, a painting (1568) by Pieter Breughel the Elder.

blind·ly (blīnd′lē), *adv.* **1.** in a blind manner: *We felt our way blindly through the black tunnel.* **2.** without understanding, reservation, or objection: *They followed their leaders blindly.* **3.** without continuation: *The passage ended blindly 50 feet away.* [BLIND + -LY]

blind·man's buff (blīnd′manz′ buf′), a game in which a blindfolded player tries to catch and identify one of the others. Also called **blind′man's bluff′.**

blind′ man's′ rule′, a carpenter's rule having large numbers to permit its reading in bad light.

blind′ man's′ watch′, a watch from which the time can be told by touch as well as sight.

blind′ nail′ing, nailing of wooden pieces, as floor boards, in such a way that no nail heads appear in the finished work. Also called **secret nailing, tosh nailing.**

blind′ pig′, *Obs. U.S. Slang.* See **blind tiger.**

blind′ sal′amander, any of several North American salamanders, esp. of the genera *Typhlotriton, Typhlomolge,* and *Haideotriton,* that live in underground streams or deep wells and have little body pigmentation and undeveloped eyes.

blind′ seed′, *Plant Pathol.* a disease of ryegrass, characterized by shriveled, soft seeds, caused by a fungus, *Phialea Temulenta.*

blind′ snake′, 1. any of numerous wormlike, fossorial snakes of the family *Typhlopidae,* found in tropical regions, having the eyes covered by scales. **2.** See **slender blind snake.** Also called **worm snake.**

blind′ spot′, 1. *Anat.* a small area on the retina where the optic nerve leaves the eye and which is insensitive to light. See diag. under **eye. 2.** an area or subject about which one is uninformed, prejudiced, or undiscerning: *She has a blind spot where minority groups are concerned.* **3.** *Radio.* an area in which signals are weak and their reception poor. **4.** Also called **dead spot.** any part of an auditorium, arena, or the like, in which one is unable to see or hear satisfactorily.

blind′ stag′gers, *Vet. Pathol.* stagger (def. 13).

blind-stamp (blīnd′stamp′), *v.t.* to emboss or impress blind.

blind·sto·ry (blīnd′stōr′ē, -stôr′ē), *n., pl.* **-ries.** *Archit.* a story, or major horizontal division of a wall, having no exterior windows or other major openings. [BLIND + STORY[2]]

blind′ ti′ger, *Obs. U.S. Slang.* an illegal liquor saloon. Also called **blind pig.**

blind′ win′dow, (on a façade) a sunken panel treated architecturally as a window.

blind·worm (blīnd′wûrm′), *n.* **1.** a limbless European lizard, *Anguis fragilis,* related to the glass lizards. **2.** a caecilian, *Icthyophis glutinosus,* of the Malay Archipelago, that coils about its eggs. [BLIND + WORM; so called because its eyes are very small]

blink (blingk), *v.i.* **1.** to open and close the eye, esp. involuntarily; wink rapidly and repeatedly: *A tic made his eye blink rapidly.* **2.** to look with winking or half-shut eyes: *I blinked at the harsh morning light.* **3.** to be startled, surprised, or dismayed (usually fol. by *at*): *She blinked at his sudden fury.* **4.** to look evasively or with indifference; ignore (often fol. by *at*): *a person who blinks at responsibility; to blink at another's eccentricities.* **5.** to shine unsteadily, or dimly, or intermittently; twinkle: *The light on the buoy blinked in the distance.* —*v.t.* **6.** to open and close (the eye) rapidly and repeatedly; wink: *She blinked her eyes in an effort to wake up.* **7.** to remove (tears, a foreign body, etc.) from the eyes by blinking. **8.** to cause (something) to blink: *We blinked the light frantically, but there was no response.* **9.** to ignore deliberately; evade; shirk: *There was no blinking the possibility of a scandal.* —*n.* **10.** act of blinking: *The faithful blink of the lighthouse.* **11.** *Chiefly Scot.* a glance or glimpse. **12.** a gleam; glimmer: *There was not a blink of light anywhere.* **13.** *Meteorol.* **a.** iceblink. **b.** snowblink. **14. on the blink,** *Slang.* not in proper working order; in need of repair: *The washing machine is on the blink again.* [ME *blink(en),* var. of *blenken* to BLENCH[1]; c. D, G *blinken*]

—**Syn. 1.** See **wink. 9.** overlook, disregard, avoid, condone. **10.** wink, flicker, twinkle, flutter.

blink·ard (bling′kərd), *n.* **1.** a dull-witted or stupid person. **2.** *Archaic.* one who blinks habitually or who sees imperfectly. [BLINK + -ARD]

blink·er (bling′kər), *n.* **1.** a device for flashing light signals. **2.** a light that flashes intermittently, esp. one that serves as a traffic signal. **3.** either of two leather flaps on a bridle, to prevent a horse from seeing sideways; a blinder. See illus. under **harness. 4. blinkers,** goggle. (def. 1). [BLINK + -ER[1]]

blink·ing (bling′king), *adj.* damned (a euphemism): *Stop that blinking noise! You blinking idiot!* [BLINK + -ING[2]] —**blink′ing·ly,** *adv.*

blintze (blints), *n. Jewish Cookery.* a thin pancake folded or rolled around a filling, as of cheese or fruit, and fried in oil or butter, or baked. Also, **blintz** (blints). [< Yiddish *blintse* < Russ *blinets,* dim. of *blin* pancake]

blip (blip), *n.* **1.** a spot of light on a radar screen indicating the position of a plane, submarine, or other object. **2.** *Slang.* a nickel; five cents. [?]

bliss (blis), *n.* **1.** supreme happiness; utter joy or contentment: *wedded bliss.* **2.** *Theol.* the joy of heaven. **3.** heaven; paradise: *the road to eternal bliss.* **4.** *Archaic.* a cause of great joy or happiness. [ME *blisse,* OE *bliss, bliths,* equiv. to *blīthe* BLITHE + *-s* suffix, c. L *-itia* -ICE] —**bliss′less,** *adj.*

—**Syn. 1.** See **happiness.** —**Ant. 1.** misery.

Bliss (blis), *n.* **1. Tas·ker** (tas′kər) **Howard,** 1853–1930, U.S. general. **2.** a boy's or girl's given name.

Bliss·field (blis′fēld′), *n.* a town in SE Michigan. 2653 (1960).

bliss·ful (blis′fəl), *adj.* full of, abounding in, enjoying, or conferring bliss. [ME; see BLISS, -FUL; r. OE *blissig*] —**bliss′ful·ly,** *adv.* —**bliss′ful·ness,** *n.*

blis·ter (blis′tər), *n.* **1.** a thin vesicle on the skin, containing watery matter or serum, as from a burn or other injury; a bleb. **2.** any similar swelling, as an air bubble in a coat of paint. **3.** a relatively large bubble occurring in glass during blowing. **4.** *Mil.* a transparent bulge or dome on the fuselage of an airplane, usually for mounting a gun. **5.** *Photog.* a bubble of air formed where the emulsion has separated from the base of a film because of defective processing, etc. **6.** the moving bubble in a spirit level. —*v.t.* **7.** to raise a blister or blisters on: *This new shoe has blistered my foot.* **8.** to punish (a child) severely, esp. by whipping or spanking: *Any more of that nonsense and I'll blister you!* **9.** to criticize or rebuke severely; subject to burning shame or disgrace: *The boss blistered his assistant in front of the whole office.* —*v.i.* **10.** to raise in blisters; become blistered. [ME *blister, blester* < Scand; cf. Icel *blǣstri,* dat. of *blāstr* swelling. See BLAST, BLOW[2]] —**blis′ter·ing·ly,** *adv.* —**blis′ter·y,** *adj.*

blis′ter bee′tle, any of various beetles of the family *Meloidae,* many of which produce a secretion capable of blistering the skin.

blis′ter cop′per, *Metall.* a matte of from 96 to 99 percent copper, having a blistered surface after smelting due to the gases generated during solidification.

blis′ter gas′, *Chemical Warfare.* a poison gas that burns or blisters the tissues of the body.

blis′ter rust′, *Plant Pathol.* a disease, esp. of white pines, characterized by cankers and in the spring by blisters on the stems, caused by a rust fungus of the genus *Cronartium.*

blis′ter steel′, *Metall.* steel produced from wrought iron by cementation in covered pots, having a blistered appearance because of the gases generated during the process.

blis·ter·y (blis′tə rē), *adj.* having blisters, as paint or glass. [BLISTER + -Y[1]]

B.Lit., Bachelor of Literature.

blithe (blīth, blīth), *adj.* **1.** joyous, merry, or gay in disposition; glad; cheerful: *Everyone loved her for her blithe heart.* **2.** without thought or regard; carefree; heedless: *a blithe indifference to anyone's feelings.* [ME, OE; c. Icel *blīthr,* OHG *blīdi,* Goth *bleith(s)*] —**blithe′ful,** *adj.* —**blithe′ful·ly,** *adv.* —**blithe′ly,** *adv.* —**blithe′ness,** *n.*
—**Syn. 1.** happy, mirthful, sprightly, light-hearted, buoyant, joyful, blithesome. —**Ant. 1.** joyless.

Blithe (blīth, blīth), *n.* a girl's given name. Also, **Blythe.**

blith·er (blith′ər), *v.i. Informal.* to talk foolishly; blather: *He's blithering about some problem of his.* [var. of BLATHER]

blith·er·ing (blith′ər ing), *adj.* talking nonsensically; jabbering: *He impressed people as a blithering idiot.* [BLITHER + -ING[2]]

blithe·some (blīth′səm, blīth′-), *adj.* light-hearted; merry; cheerful: *a blithesome nature.* [BLITHE + -SOME[1]] —**blithe′some·ly,** *adv.* —**blithe′some·ness,** *n.*

B.Litt., Bachelor of Letters.

blitz (blits), *n.* **1.** *Mil.* war waged by surprise, swiftly and violently, as by the use of aircraft, tanks, etc.: *The German blitz was an instrument of terror.* **2.** any swift, vigorous attack: *a blitz of commercials every few minutes.* **3.** *Football Slang.* act or instance of red-dogging. —*v.t.* **4.** to attack with a blitz: *The town was blitzed mercilessly by enemy planes during the war. The visitors really blitzed the home team.* —*v.i.* **5.** *Football Slang.* red-dog. Also, **blitzkrieg** (for defs. 1, 2, 4). [< G: lightning]

blitz′ can′, *Mil.* See **jerry can** (def. 1).

blitz·krieg (blits′krēg′), *n., v.t.* blitz (defs. 1, 2, 4). [< G: lit., lightning war]

Blitz·stein (blits′stīn), *n.* **Marc,** 1905–64, U.S. composer.

Blix·en (blik′sən), *n.* **Karen.** See **Dinesen, Isak.**

bliz·zard (bliz′ərd), *n.* **1.** a violent windstorm with dry, driving snow and intense cold. **2.** a heavy and prolonged snowstorm covering a wide area. [var. of dial. *blizzer* blaze, flash, blinding flash of lightning; sense widened from lightning to storm; akin to OE *blysa, blyse* torch, *blysian* to burn] —**bliz′zard·y, bliz′zard·ly,** *adj.*

blk., **1.** black. **2.** block. **3.** bulk.

B.LL., Bachelor of Laws.

bloat (blōt), *v.t.* **1.** to expand or distend, as with air, water, etc.; cause to swell: *Their bellies were bloated from overeating.* **2.** to puff up; make vain or conceited: *The promotion has bloated his ego to an alarming degree.* **3.** to cure (fishes) as bloaters. —*v.i.* **4.** to become swollen; be puffed out or dilated. —*n.* **5.** Also called **hoven.** *Vet. Pathol.* (in cattle, sheep, and horses) a distention of the rumen or paunch or of the large colon by gases of fermentation, caused by eating ravenously of green forage, esp. legumes. **6.** one who or that which is bloated. **7.** *Slang.* a drunkard. **8.** bloater (defs. 1 and 2). [*bloat* (adj.), ME *blout* soft, puffy < Scand; cf. Icel *blaut(r)* soft]

bloat·ed (blō′tid), *adj.* **1.** swollen; puffed up; overlarge. **2.** inflated or swollen, as with pride, excessive wealth, etc.: *the bloated rich.* **3.** excessively fat; obese. [BLOAT + -ED[2]] —**bloat′ed·ness,** *n.*

bloat·er (blō′tər), *n.* **1.** a herring cured by being salted and briefly smoked and dried. **2.** a mackerel similarly cured. **3.** a fresh-water cisco, *Coregonus hoyi,* found in the Great Lakes. [*bloat* (adj.) + -ER[1]]

blob (blob), *n., v.,* **blobbed, blob·bing.** —*n.* **1.** a globule of liquid; bubble. **2.** a small lump, drop, splotch, or daub: *A blob of paint marred the surface.* **3.** an object, esp. a large one, having no distinct shape or definition: *There was a blob off to the left that could have been the house.* **4.** a dull, slow-witted, and uninteresting person. **5.** a wrong note, esp. on a wind instrument. —*v.t.* **6.** to mark or splotch with blobs. [? imit.]

bloc (blok), *n.* **1.** (in Europe) a coalition of factions or parties for a particular measure or purpose: *the Axis bloc.* **2.** *U.S.* a group of legislators, usually of both major political parties, who vote together for some particular interest: *the farm bloc.* [< F; see BLOCK]

Bloch (blok; *Ger.* blôKH), *n.* **1. Ernest,** 1880–1959, Swiss composer, in the U.S. after 1916. **2. Felix,** born 1905, Swiss physicist in U.S.: Nobel prize 1952. **3. Konrad E.,** born 1912, U.S. biochemist, born in Germany: Nobel prize in medicine 1964.

block (blok), *n.* **1.** a solid mass of wood, stone, etc., usually with one or more flat or approximately flat faces. **2.** a hollow masonry building unit of cement, terra cotta, etc.: *a wall made of concrete blocks.* **3.** one of a set of cube-shaped pieces of wood, plastic, or the like, used as a child's toy in building. **4.** a mold or piece on which something is shaped or kept in shape: *a hat block.* **5.** a piece of wood used in the arts of making woodcuts or wood engravings. **6.** *Print.* the base on which a plate is mounted to make it type-high. **7.** a projection left on a squared stone to provide a means of lifting it. **8.** a short length of plank serving as a bridging, as between joists. **9.** a stump or wooden structure on which a condemned person is beheaded: *Mary Stuart went bravely to the block.* **10.** a platform from which an auctioneer sells: *one lot of paintings to be put on the block.* **11.** *Mach.* a part enclosing one or more freely rotating, grooved pulleys, about which ropes or chains pass to form a hoisting or hauling tackle. **12.** an obstacle, obstruction, or hindrance: *His stubbornness is a block to all my efforts.* **13.** state or condition of being obstructed; blockage: *The traffic block lasted several hours.* **14.** *Pathol.* an obstruction, as of a nerve. **15.** *Sports.* a hindering of an opponent's actions. **16.** a quantity, portion, or section taken as a unit or dealt with at one time: *a large block of theater tickets.* **17.** *U.S.* **a.** a small section of a city, town, etc., enclosed by neighboring and intersecting streets: *She lives on my block.* **b.** the length of one side of such a section: *We walked two blocks over.* **18.** *Chiefly Brit.* a large building divided into separate apartments, offices, shops, etc. **19.** a large number of bonds or shares of stock sold together as a single unit. **20.** *Computer Technol.* **a.** (on a flow chart) a symbol representing an operation, device, or instruction in a computer program. **b.** a section of storage locations in a computer allocated to a particular set of instructions or data. **c.** a group of consecutive machine words organized as a unit and guiding a particular computer operation, esp. with reference to input and output. **21.** *Railroads.* any of the short lengths into which a track is divided for signaling purposes. **22.** *Philately.* a group of four or more unseparated stamps, not in a strip. **23.** a dull-witted person; blockhead. **24.** *Glassmaking.* a wooden or metal cup for blocking a gather. **25.** *Psychiatry.* a sudden stoppage of speech or thought, usually caused by emotional tension. **26.** *Geol.* an angular mass of solid rock ejected from a volcano. **27.** (in Canada) a wild or remote area of land that has not yet been surveyed: *the Peace River block.* **28.** *Falconry.* a low perch to which a falcon is tethered outdoors.
—*v.t.* **29.** to fit with blocks; mount on a block. **30.** to shape or prepare on or with a block: *to block a hat; to block a sweater.* **31.** to join (the ends of boards or the like) by fastening to a block of wood. **32.** *Theat.* **a.** to plan or work out the movement of performers in a play, pageant, etc.: *Tomorrow we'll block act one.* **b.** to draw a floor plan on (a stage) in order to indicate placement of scenery, stage property, etc.: *He planned to block the stage next morning.* **33.** to obstruct (someone or something) by placing obstacles in the way (sometimes fol. by *up*): *to block one's exit; to block up a passage.* **34.** *Pathol., Physiol.* to stop the passage of impulses in (a nerve). **35.** *Sports.* to hinder or bar the actions or movements of (an opposing player), esp. legitimately. **36.** *Glassmaking.* **a.** to shape (a molten gather) in a wet cup of wood or metal. **b.** to plunge a block of wood into (molten glass) to aid in refining the glass. **37.** *Metalworking.* to give (a forging) a rough form before finishing. **38.** to apply a high negative bias to the grid of (a vacuum tube), for reducing the plate current to zero.
—*v.i.* **39.** to act so as to obstruct an opponent, as in football, boxing, and baseball: *He doesn't get many baskets, but he sure can block.* **40.** *Theat.* to block a play, act, scene, stage, etc.: *The director will block tomorrow.* **41.** *Psychiatry.* to suffer a block. **42. block in** or **out,** to sketch or outline roughly or generally, without details: *She blocked out a color scheme for the interiors.* [ME *blok* log or stump < MD (directly or < MF *bloc* in same sense); perh. akin to BALK]
—**Syn. 12.** impediment, blockade, obstruction, stoppage, jam. **23.** dolt, simpleton, fool, dunce. **30.** mold, form. **33.** close, blockade, impede; hinder, deter, stop. —**Ant. 23.** genius. **33.** encourage, advance.

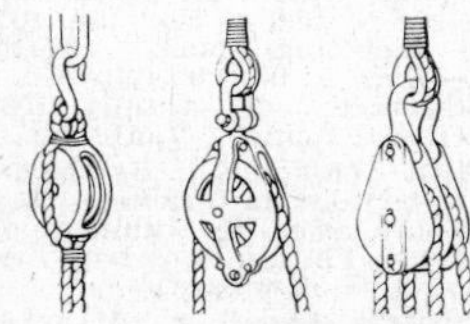

Blocks (def. 11) with single and double sheaves

Block (blok), *n.* **Herbert Lawrence** ("*Herblock*"), born 1909, U.S. cartoonist.

block·ade (blo kād′), *n., v.,* **-ad·ed, -ad·ing.** —*n.* **1.** *Navy, Mil.* the closing or shutting up of a place, esp. a port, harbor, or part of a coast by hostile ships or troops to prevent entrance or exit. **2.** any obstruction of passage or progress: *We had difficulty in getting through the blockade of bodyguards.* —*v.t.* **3.** to subject to a blockade. [BLOCK (v.) + -ADE[1]] —**block·ad′er,** *n.*
—**Syn. 1.** See **siege.**

block·ade-run·ner (blo kād′run′ər), *n.* a ship or person that passes through a blockade. —**block·ade′-run′ning,** *n.*

block·age (blok′ij), *n.* state or instance of being blocked; an obstructed condition or situation: *He suffered from an emotional blockage; the blockage of the streets.* [BLOCK + -AGE]

block′ and tack′le, the ropes or chains and blocks used in a hoisting tackle.

block′ book′ing, a practice among motion-picture distributors of contracting with an exhibitor to show a predetermined series of films.

block·bust·er (blok′bus′tər), *n.* **1.** *Informal.* an aerial bomb containing high explosives and weighing from four to eight tons, used as a large-scale demolition bomb. **2.** something or someone that is forcefully or overwhelmingly impressive, effective, or influential: *The campaign was a blockbuster.* **3.** a real-estate speculator who practices blockbusting. [BLOCK + BUSTER]

block·bust·ing (blok′bus′ting), *adj.* **1.** forcefully or overwhelmingly impressive or effective. —*n.* **2.** the practice of unscrupulous real-estate agents or speculators who profit by reselling or renting homes that they obtain by inducing panic selling at prices below value, esp. by exploiting racial prejudices. [BLOCK + BUST[2] + -ING[2], -ING[1]]

block′ cap′ital, a sans-serif letter with lines of uniform weight. Cf. **block letter.**

block′ coeffi′cient, *Naval Archit.* the ratio of the immersed volume of a vessel to the product of her immersed draft, length, and beam. Also called **coefficient of fineness.**

block′ di′agram, *Geol.* a perspective representation of a land area showing surface contours and generally including two vertical cross sections.

block·er (blok′ər), *n.* **1.** one who or that which blocks. **2.** *Football.* a player whose assignment or special skill is blocking: *The halfback picked up two blockers on the line of scrimmage.* [BLOCK + -ER[1]]

block′ front′, **1.** *U.S. Furniture.* a front of a desk, chest of drawers, etc., of the third quarter of the 18th century, having three vertical divisions of equal width, a sunken one between raised ones, all divided by flat areas to which they are connected by curves; often found with a shell motif forming a rounded termination to each section. **2.** the frontage of a block, esp. in a city or town. —**block′-front′,** *adj.*

Block front, c1790

block′ grant′, a consolidated grant of federal funds, formerly allocated for specific programs, which a state or local government may use at its discretion for such generalized programs as education or urban development.

block·head (blok′hed′), *n.* **1.** a stupid, doltish person; dunce. **2.** *Mining.* a fire block in a mine. [BLOCK + HEAD] —**block′head′ed,** *adj.* —**block′head′ed·ly,** *adv.* —**block′head′ed·ness,** *n.* —**block′head′ism,** *n.*

block·house (blok′hous′), *n., pl.* **-hous·es** (hou′ziz). **1.** *Mil.* a fortified structure with ports or loopholes for gunfire, used against bombs, artillery, and small-arms fire. **2.** (formerly) a building, usually of hewn timber and with a projecting upper story, having loopholes for musketry. **3.** a house built of squared logs. **4.** *Rocketry.* a structure near a launching site for rockets, generally made of heavily reinforced concrete, for housing and protecting personnel, electronic controls, and auxiliary apparatus before and during launching operations. [< MD or Flem *blochuus.* See BLOCK, HOUSE]

block′ in course′ bond′, (in a rowlock arch) a mass of bonded brickwork running through the entire arch ring in the manner of a voussoir.

block·ing (blok′ing), *n. Carpentry.* a number of small pieces of wood for filling interstices, or for spacing, joining, or reinforcing members. [BLOCK + -ING[1]]

block′ing course′, a solid parapet above a cornice.

block·ish (blok′ish), *adj.* like a block; dull; stupid. [BLOCK + -ISH[1]] —**block′ish·ly,** *adv.* —**block′ish·ness,** *n.*

Block′ Is′land, an island off the coast of and a part of Rhode Island, at the E entrance to Long Island Sound.

block′ la′va, *Geol.* lava in the form of angular blocks.

block′ let′ter, *Print.* a sans-serif type face or letter, usually compressed and having tight curves.

This is a sample of block letter

block′ line′, a rope or chain running through the blocks of a tackle.

block′ mast′, *Naut.* a short mast from the head of which a lateen yard is suspended.

block′ mod′el, *Naval Archit.* a half model carved from a single block of wood, either left solid or cut into vertical sections at the principal cross sections.

block′ moun′tain, *Geol.* a mountain caused by the uplift of blocks of the earth's crust.

block′ par′ty, an outdoor festival or carnival, usually held in a closed-off city street and offering refreshments, amusements, etc., often to raise money for a charitable or religious organization.

block′ plane′, *Carpentry.* a small plane for cutting across grain.

block′ print′, *Fine Arts.* a design printed by means of blocks of wood or metal.

block′ sig′nal, a fixed railroad signal governing the movements of trains entering and using a given section of track. —**block′ sig′naling.**

block′ sys′tem, *Railroads.* **1.** a series of consecutive blocks. **2.** a system of blocks and block signals for controlling train movements.

block·y (blok′ē), *adj.,* **block·i·er, block·i·est.** **1.** heavily built; stocky. **2.** marked by blocks or patches of unequally distributed light and shade, as in a photograph. [BLOCK + -Y[1]]

Bloem·fon·tein (blōōm′fon tān′), *n.* a city in and the capital of the Orange Free State, in the central Republic of South Africa. 140,924 with suburbs (1960).

Blois (blwa), *n.* a city in and the capital of Loire-et-Cher, in central France, on the Loire River: historic castle. 36,426 (1962).

Blok (blôk), *n.* **A·le·xan·der A·le·xan·dro·vich** (ä′le ksän′dər ä′le ksän′dro vich), 1880–1921, Russian poet.

bloke (blōk), *n. Chiefly Brit. Slang.* man; fellow. [?]

blond (blond), *adj.* **1.** (of hair, skin, etc.) light-colored: *her soft blond curls.* **2.** (of a person) having light-colored hair and skin. **3.** (of furniture wood) light in tone. —*n.* **4.** a blond person. **5.** silk lace, originally unbleached but now often dyed any of various colors, esp. white or black. Also, *esp. referring to a woman,* **blonde.** [late ME *blounde* light brown < MF *blonde,* fem. of *blond* < Gmc; akin to OE *blondenfeax* grayhaired. See BLEND] —**blond′ness, blonde′ness,** *n.* —**blond′ish,** *adj.*

blood (blud), *n.* **1.** the fluid that circulates in the principal vascular system of man and other vertebrates, in man consisting of plasma in which the cells and platelets are suspended. **2.** the vital principle; life: *The excitement had got into the very blood of the nation.* **3.** a fresh source of energy, vitality, or vigor: *It's time we got some new blood in this company.* **4.** bloodshed; gore; slaughter; murder: *to avenge the blood of his father.* **5.** the juice or sap of plants: *the blood of the grape.* **6.** temperament; state of mind: *a person of hot blood.* **7.** man's fleshly nature: *the frailty of men's blood.* **8.** *Chiefly Brit.* a high-spirited dandy; an adventuresome youth: *the young bloods of Cambridge.* **9.** a profligate or rake. **10.** physical and cultural extraction: *It was a trait that seemed to be in the blood.* **11.** royal extraction: *a prince of the blood.* **12.** descent from a common ancestor; ancestry; lineage: *related by blood.* **13.** *Stockbreeding.* recorded and respected ancestry; purebred breeding. **14. get** or **have one's blood up,** to become or be enraged or impassioned: *Injustice of any sort always gets my blood up.* **15. have someone's blood on one's head** or **hands,** to be to blame for someone's affliction or death: *Though a criminal, he had no blood on his hands.* **16. in cold blood,** deliberately; ruthlessly: *The dictator, in cold blood, ordered the execution of all his enemies.* **17. make one's blood boil,** to inspire resentment, anger, or indignation: *Such carelessness makes his blood boil.* **18. make one's blood run**

cold, to fill with terror; frighten: *The dark, deserted street in that unfamiliar neighborhood made her blood run cold.* **19. sweat blood.** See **sweat** (def. 24). **20. taste blood,** to experience a new sensation, usually a violent or destructive one, and acquire an appetite for it: *Once the team had tasted blood, there was no preventing them from winning by a wide margin.* —*v.t.* **21.** *Hunting.* to give (hounds) a first sight or taste of blood. Cf. **flesh** (def. 16). **22.** *Brit.* (in fox hunting) to perform the ceremony of blooding on (someone). **23.** *Obs.* to stain with blood. [ME *blo(o)d*, OE *blōd*; c. Icel, Goth *blōth*, OHG *bluot* (G *Blut*)] —**blood′like′,** *adj.*

blood′ and thun′der, sensationalism or exaggerated melodrama: *a movie full of blood and thunder.*

blood′ bank′, **1.** a place where blood or blood plasma is collected, processed, stored, and distributed. **2.** such a supply of blood or blood plasma.

blood′ bath′, the ruthless slaughter of great numbers of people; massacre.

blood′ broth′er, **1.** one's brother by birth. **2.** a male person bound to another by ties of great friendship. **3.** something usually associated with or thought to exist inseparably from another thing, quality, circumstance, etc.: *Humility is often the blood brother of incompetence.* **4.** a male established in a close relationship with another male through the performance or a specific ritual, as the commingling of blood.

blood′ cell′, any of the cellular elements of the blood, as erythrocytes or leukocytes. Also called **blood′ cor′puscle.**

blood′ count′, the count of the number of red and white corpuscles and platelets in a specific volume of blood.

blood·cur·dling (blud′kûrd′ling), *adj.* terrifyingly horrible; frightening enough to curdle or congeal one's blood: *a bloodcurdling horror movie.* [BLOOD + CURDLING]

blood·ed (blud′id), *adj.* **1.** having blood (usually used in combination to indicate a specified kind): *warm-blooded animals; a cold-blooded killer.* **2.** (of horses, cattle, etc.) derived from ancestors of good blood; having a good pedigree. [ME; see BLOOD, -ED[3]]

blood·fin (blud′fin′), *n.* a South American characin fish, *Aphyocharax rubropinnis*, having a silvery body and blood-red fins, often kept in aquariums. [BLOOD + FIN]

blood·flow·er (blud′flou′ər), *n.* a showy, perennial milkweed, *Asclepias curassavica*, of tropical America, having brilliant orange-red flowers and smooth fruit. [BLOOD + FLOWER]

blood′ fluke′, a schistosome.

blood′ group′, one of several classes into which human blood can be separated according to its agglutinogens. Also called **blood type.**

blood′ group′ing, determination of the blood group of a sample of blood.

blood·guilt·y (blud′gil′tē), *adj.* guilty of murder or bloodshed. [BLOOD(SHED) + GUILTY] —**blood′guilt′i·ness,** *n.*

blood′ heat′, the normal temperature of human blood, being about 98.6°F or 37°C.

blood·hound (blud′hound′), *n.* one of a breed of medium- to large-sized dogs, usually having a black-and-tan coat, very long ears, loose skin, and an acute sense of smell; used chiefly for following human scents. [ME *blod-hound.* See BLOOD, HOUND[1]]

Bloodhound (26 in. high at shoulder)

blood·ing (blud′ing), *n.* **1.** *Chiefly Brit.* (in fox hunting) an informal initiation ceremony in which the face of a novice is smeared with the blood of the first fox he has seen killed. **2.** *Informal.* an initiation of a youth into any manly pursuit. [BLOOD + -ING[1]]

blood′ knot′, *Angling.* See **barrel knot.**

blood·less (blud′lis), *adj.* **1.** without blood: *bloodless surgery.* **2.** pale: *a bloodless face.* **3.** free from bloodshed: *a bloodless victory.* **4.** spiritless; without vigor, zest, or energy: *a dull, insipid, bloodless young man.* **5.** without emotion or feeling; cold-hearted: *bloodless data.* [ME *blodles*, OE *blōdlēas.* See BLOOD, -LESS] —**blood′less·ly,** *adv.* —**blood′less·ness,** *n.*

blood·let·ting (blud′let′ing), *n.* act or practice of letting blood by opening a vein; phlebotomy. [ME *blod letunge.* See BLOOD, LET[1], -ING[1]] —**blood′let′ter,** *n.*

blood·line (blud′līn′), *n.* (usually of animals) the line of descent; pedigree; strain. [BLOOD + LINE[1]]

blood·mo·bile (blud′mə bēl′), *n.* a small truck with medical equipment for receiving blood donations. [BLOOD + (AUTO)MOBILE]

blood′ mon′ey, **1.** a fee paid to a hired murderer. **2.** compensation paid to the survivors of a slain man. **3.** money paid to an informer, esp. where the criminal's arrest is followed by his execution.

blood·noun (blud′noun′), *n.* *Southern U.S.* a bullfrog, esp. *Rana catesbeiana.* Also, **bloody noun.** [imit.]

blood′ or′ange, any of various sweet oranges having a dark-red pulp.

blood′ plas′ma, the plasma or liquid portion of human blood.

blood′ plate′let, one of numerous, minute, protoplasmic bodies in mammalian blood which aid in coagulation.

blood′ poi′soning, *Pathol.* a condition of the blood caused by the presence of toxic matter or microorganisms, characterized by chills, sweating, fever, and prostration; toxemia; septicemia; pyemia.

blood′ pres′sure, *Physiol.* the pressure of the blood against the inner walls of the blood vessels, varying in different parts of the body during different phases of contraction of the heart and under different conditions of health, exertion, etc.

blood′ pud′ding. See **blood sausage.**

blood′ purge′, the mass execution, esp. by a government, of persons considered guilty of treason or sedition.

blood-red (blud′red′), *adj.* **1.** of the deep-red color of blood: *a fiery, blood-red sunset.* **2.** red with blood: *The blood-red banner symbolized the army's defeat.*

blood′ rela′tion, one related by birth. Also, **blood′ rel′ative.**

blood·root (blud′ro͞ot′, -ro͝ot′), *n.* **1.** a North American papaveraceous plant, *Sanguinaria canadensis*, having a red root and root sap. **2.** an Old World, rosaceous plant, *Potentilla tormentilla*, having a reddish root. [BLOOD + ROOT[1]]

blood′ roy′al, all persons related by birth to a hereditary monarch, taken collectively; the royal kin: *a prince of the blood royal.*

blood′ sau′sage, a dark sausage with a high content of blood, esp. one made with diced pork fat, pork blood, chopped onion, etc., usually stuffed in casings and cooked by broiling, frying, or boiling. Also called **black pudding, blood pudding.**

blood′ se′rum, serum (def. 1).

blood·shed (blud′shed′), *n.* **1.** destruction of life, as in war, murder, etc.; slaughter. **2.** the shedding of blood by injury, wound, etc. Also, **blood′shed′ding.** [n. use of v. phrase to *shed blood*]

blood·shot (blud′shot′), *adj.* (of the eyes) red because of dilated blood vessels. [apocopated var. of *blood-shotten.* See BLOOD, SHOTTEN]

blood′ spav′in, *Vet. Pathol.* See under **spavin** (def. 1).

blood′ sport′, any sport involving killing or the shedding of blood, as bullfighting, hunting, etc.

blood·stain (blud′stān′), *n.* a spot or stain made by blood. [back formation from BLOODSTAINED]

blood·stained (blud′stānd′), *adj.* **1.** stained with blood: *a blood-stained knife.* **2.** guilty of bloodshed; bloodguilty. [BLOOD + *stained*; see STAIN, -ED[2]]

blood·stock (blud′stok′), *n.* race horses of Thoroughbred breeding, taken as a whole. [BLOOD + STOCK]

blood·stone (blud′stōn′), *n.* a greenish variety of chalcedony with small bloodlike spots of red jasper scattered through it. Also called **heliotrope.** [BLOOD + STONE]

blood·stream (blud′strēm′), *n.* the blood flowing through a circulatory system. [ME; see BLOOD, STREAM]

blood·suck·er (blud′suk′ər), *n.* **1.** any animal that sucks blood, esp. a leech. **2.** an extortioner or usurer. **3.** sponger (def. 2). [BLOOD + SUCKER] —**blood′suck′ing,** *adj.*

blood′ sug′ar, **1.** glucose in the blood. **2.** the quantity or percentage of glucose in the blood. **3.** a laboratory measurement of blood glucose.

blood′ test′, a test of a sample of blood to determine blood group, presence of infection, parentage, etc.

blood·thirst·y (blud′thûr′stē), *adj.* **1.** eager to shed blood; murderous: *to capture a bloodthirsty criminal.* **2.** enjoying or encouraging bloodshed or violence, esp. as a spectator or clamorous partisan: *the hypnotic effect of TV on bloodthirsty kids; the bloodthirsty urgings of the fight fans.* [BLOOD + THIRSTY] —**blood′thirst′i·ly,** *adv.* —**blood′thirst′i·ness,** *n.*

blood′ transfu′sion, the injection of blood from one person or animal into the blood stream of another.

blood′ type′. See **blood group.**

blood′ typ′ing, (loosely) blood grouping.

blood′ ves′sel, any of the vessels, as arteries, veins, or capillaries, through which the blood circulates.

Blood′ Wed′ding, a drama (1939) by Federico García Lorca. Spanish, **Bodas de Sangre.**

blood·wort (blud′wûrt′), *n.* **1.** any plant of the *Haemodoracene* having red roots, esp. the redroot, *Gyrotheca tinctoria*, of North America. **2.** any of various plants having red roots, leaves, etc., as the dock or the rattlesnake weed. **3.** bloodroot. [ME *blodwurt.* See BLOOD, WORT[2]]

blood·y (blud′ē), *adj.*, **blood·i·er, blood·i·est,** *v.*, **blood·ied, blood·y·ing,** *adv.* —*adj.* **1.** stained with blood or bleeding: *a bloody handkerchief; a bloody nose.* **2.** characterized by bloodshed: *bloody battle; a bloody rule.* **3.** inclined to bloodshed; bloodthirsty: *a bloody dictator.* **4.** of, pertaining to, or resembling blood; containing or composed of blood: *bloody tissue.* **5.** *Brit. Vulgar.* damned; extraordinary. —*v.t.* **6.** to stain or smear with blood. —*adv.* **7.** *Brit. Vulgar.* damned; very; exceedingly. [ME *blody*, OE *blōdig.* See BLOOD, -Y[1]] —**blood′i·ly,** *adv.* —**blood′i·ness,** *n.*
—**Syn. 1, 2.** sanguinary, ensanguined, gory. **3.** murderous, homicidal; savage, feral, ferocious; cruel, inhuman, ruthless.

blood′y butch′ers. See **red trillium.**

blood′y flux′, dysentery.

Blood′y Mar′y, **1.** a mixed drink made principally with vodka and tomato juice. **2.** See **Mary I.**

blood′y noun′, *Southern U.S.* bloodnoun.

blood′y shirt′, **1.** (formerly) a bloodstained shirt used to incite a mob to vengeance. **2.** any symbol used for this purpose.

bloom[1] (blo͞om), *n.* **1.** the flower of a plant. **2.** flowers collectively: *the bloom of the cherry tree.* **3.** state of having the buds opened: *The gardens are all in bloom.* **4.** a flourishing, healthy condition; the time or period of greatest beauty, artistry, etc: *the bloom of youth; the bloom of Romanticism.* **5.** a glow or flush on the cheek indicative of youth and health: *a serious illness that destroyed her bloom.* **6.** the glossy, healthy appearance of the coat of an animal. **7.** *Bot.* a whitish powdery deposit or coating, as on the surface of certain fruits and leaves: *the bloom of the grape.* **8.** any similar surface coating or appearance: *the bloom of newly minted coins.* **9.** any of certain minerals occurring as powdery coatings on other materials. **10.** Also called **chill.** a clouded or dull area on a varnished or lacquered surface. **11.** the sudden development of conspicuous masses of organisms, as algae or dinoflagellates in bodies of fresh or marine water. —*v.i.* **12.** to produce or yield blossoms. **13.** to flourish: *a recurrent fad that blooms from time to time.* **14.** to be in or achieve a state of healthful beauty and vigor: *a sickly child that bloomed into a beautiful and radiant woman; a poor little talent that somehow bloomed into major artistry.* **15.** to glow with warmth or with a warm color: *A brilliantly decorated Christmas tree bloomed in the front parlor.* —*v.t.* **16.** to cause to yield blossoms. **17.** to make bloom or cause to flourish: *a happiness that blooms the cheek; strength of character that blooms the virtues.* **18.** to invest with luster or beauty: *an industry that blooms one's talents.* **19.** to cause a cloudy area on (something shiny); dampen; chill: *Their breath bloomed the frosty pane.* [ME *blom, blome* < Scand; cf. Icel *blōm, blōmi*; c. Goth *blōma* lily, G *Blume* flower; akin to BLOW[3]] —**bloom′less,** *adj.*
—**Syn. 1.** blossom. **3.** efflorescence. **4.** freshness, glow, flush; vigor, prime. **13.** effloresce.

bloom[2] (blo͞om), *Metalworking.* —*n.* **1.** a piece of steel, square or slightly oblong in section, reduced from an ingot to dimensions suitable for further rolling. **2.** a large lump of iron and slag, of pasty consistency when hot, produced in a puddling furnace or bloomery and hammered into wrought iron. —*v.t.* **3.** to make (an ingot) into a bloom. [OE *blōma* lump of metal]

bloom·er[1] (blo͞o′mər), *n.* **1. bloomers, a.** loose trousers gathered at the knee, formerly worn by women as part of a gymnasium, riding, or other sports outfit. **b.** a woman's undergarment of similar, but less bulky, design. **c.** the trousers of a bloomer (costume). **2.** a costume for women, advocated about 1850 by Mrs. Amelia Jenks Bloomer (1818–94) of New York, consisting of a short skirt, loose trousers gathered and buttoning at the ankle, and often a coat and a wide hat. [named after Mrs. *Bloomer.*]

bloom·er[2] (blo͞o′mər), *n.* **1.** a plant that blooms: *a night bloomer.* **2.** a person, esp. a youth, who develops skills, abilities, interests, etc., commensurate with his capacities: *a quiet, methodical child who became a late bloomer.* [BLOOM[1] + -ER[1]]

Bloo·mer (blo͞o′mər), *n.* a town in central Wisconsin. 2834 (1960).

bloom′er girl′, *Slang.* a daring girl, esp. one of the late 19th or early 20th century, who wore a bloomer costume.

bloom·er·y (blo͞o′mə rē), *n.*, *pl.* **-er·ies.** a hearth for smelting iron in blooms of pasty consistency by means of charcoal. Also called **chafery.** [BLOOM[2] + -ERY]

bloom-fell (blo͞om′fel′), *n.* See **bird's-foot trefoil.**

Bloom·field (blo͞om′fēld′), *n.* **1. Leonard,** 1887–1949, U.S. linguist and educator. **2.** a city in NE New Jersey. 51,867 (1960). **3.** a town in SE Iowa. 2771 (1960).

Bloom·field·i·an (blo͞om fēl′dē ən), *adj.* **1.** *Ling.* influenced by, resembling, or deriving from the linguistic theory and the methods of linguistic analysis advocated by Leonard Bloomfield, characterized esp. by emphasis on the classification of overt formal features. —*n.* **2.** a Bloomfieldian linguist. [BLOOMFIELD + -IAN]

bloom·ing (blo͞o′ming), *adj.* **1.** in bloom; flowering; blossoming. **2.** glowing, as with youthful vigor and freshness: *blooming cheeks.* **3.** flourishing; prospering: *a blooming business.* **4.** *Brit. Informal.* damned (euphemism for *bloody*). [BLOOM[1] + -ING[2]] —**bloom′ing·ly,** *adv.* —**bloom′ing·ness,** *n.*

Bloom·ing·dale (blo͞o′ming dāl′), *n.* a town in N New Jersey. 5293 (1960).

bloom′ing oil′, an oil used as a lubricant in fine sand papering.

Bloom·ing·ton (blo͞o′ming tən), *n.* **1.** a city in SE Minnesota. 50,498 (1960). **2.** a city in central Illinois. 36,271 (1960). **3.** a city in S Indiana. 31,357 (1960).

Blooms·bur·y (blo͞omz′bə rē, -brē), *n.* **1.** a residential and academic district in London, N of the Thames and Charing Cross. Artists, writers, and students living there have given it a reputation as an intellectual center. —*adj.* **2.** noting a group of artistic and literary intellectuals who flourished in the early decades of the 20th century and were associated with the Bloomsbury section of London. **3.** of, pertaining to, following, or imitating the cultural, artistic, literary, and intellectual pursuits, interests, or opinions characteristic of this group: *a Bloomsbury accent.*

bloom·y (blo͞o′mē), *adj.*, **bloom·i·er, bloom·i·est.** **1.** covered with blossoms; in full flower. **2.** *Bot.* having a bloom, as fruit. [BLOOM[1] + -Y[1]]

bloop·er (blo͞o′pər), *n.* **1.** *Slang.* a public blunder, as one spoken over the radio. **2.** *Radio.* a receiving set that generates from its antenna radio-frequency signals that interfere with other nearby receivers. **3.** *Baseball.* **a.** Also called **looper.** a fly ball that carries just beyond the infield. **b.** a pitched ball with backspin, describing a high arc in flight. [*bloop* (imit.) + -ER[1]]

blos·som (blos′əm), *n.* *Bot.* **1.** the flower of a plant, esp. of one producing an edible fruit. **2.** the state of flowering: *The apple tree is in blossom.* —*v.i.* **3.** *Bot.* to produce or yield blossoms. **4.** to flourish; develop (often fol. by *into* or *out*): *a tunesmith who blossomed out into an important composer.* **5.** (of a parachute) to open. [ME *blosme, blossem*, OE *blōs(t)m(a)* flower; c. MD *bloesem*, MLG *blosem, blossem.* See BLOOM[1], BLOW[3]] —**blos′som·less,** *adj.* —**blos′som·y,** *adj.*

Blos·som (blos′əm), *n.* a girl's given name.

blot[1] (blot), *n.*, *v.*, **blot·ted, blot·ting.** —*n.* **1.** a spot or stain, esp. of ink on paper. **2.** a blemish on one's character or reputation: *She had been haunted by a blot on her past.* **3.** *Archaic.* an erasure or obliteration, as in a writing. —*v.t.* **4.** to spot, stain, soil, or the like. **5.** to darken; make dim; obscure or eclipse (usually fol. by *out*): *We watched as the moon blotted the sun.* **6.** to dry with absorbent paper or the like: *to blot the wet pane.* **7.** to remove with absorbent paper or the like. —*v.i.* **8.** to make a blot; spread ink, dye, etc., in a stain: *The more careful I am, the more this pen blots.* **9.** to become blotted or stained: *This paper blots too easily.* **10. blot out, a.** to make indistinguishable; obliterate: *to blot out a name from the record.* **b.** to wipe out completely; destroy: *Whole cities were blotted out by bombs.* [ME *blot(te)*; akin to Icel *blettur* blot, spot, stain] —**blot′less,** *adj.* —**blot′ting·ly,** *adv.* —**blot′ty,** *adj.*
—**Syn. 1.** blotch, inkstain. **2.** stain, taint, dishonor, disgrace, spot. **4.** sully, disfigure. **5.** obliterate, efface, erase, expunge. **7.** absorb.

blot[2] (blot), *n.* **1.** *Backgammon.* an exposed piece liable to be taken or forfeited. **2.** *Archaic.* an exposed or weak point, as in an argument or course of action. [< LG *blat*, akin to *bloot* bare, exposed, unprotected; c. D *bloot*, G *bloss* bare]

blotch (bloch), *n.* **1.** a large, irregular spot or blot. **2.** *Plant Pathol.* **a.** a diseased, discolored spot or area on a plant. **b.** a disease so characterized, usually accompanied by cankers and lesions. **3.** a skin eruption; blemish. —*v.t.* **4.** to mark with blotches; blot, spot, or blur: *The floor of the forest was blotched with cool, dark moss.* —*adj.* **5.** *Textiles.* of or pertaining to blotch printing, or to the colored ground produced by this process. [BL(OT[1] + B)OTCH[2]]

blotch′ print′ing, a fabric-printing method in which the ground color is transferred from the cylinder and the motif retains the original hue of the cloth.

blotch·y (bloch′ē), *adj.,* **blotch·i·er, blotch·i·est.** **1.** having blotches: *a blotchy complexion.* **2.** resembling a blotch. [BLOTCH + -Y[1]]

blot·ter (blot′ər), *n.* **1.** a piece of blotting paper used to absorb excess ink, to protect a desk top, etc. **2.** a book in which transactions or events, as sales, arrests, etc., are recorded as they occur: *a police blotter.* **3.** *Mach.* a soft washer of blotting paper or felt for cushioning a brittle object against shock or pressure, or for increasing the friction or contact area between two surfaces. [BLOT[1] + -ER[1]]

blot′ting pa′per, a soft, absorbent, unsized paper, used esp. to dry the ink on a piece of writing.

blot·to (blot′ō), *adj. Slang.* so drunk as to be unconscious. [BLOT[1] (v.) + *-o* < ?]

blouse (blous, blouz), *n., v.,* **bloused, blous·ing.** —*n.* **1.** a usually lightweight, loose-fitting garment for women and children, covering the body from the neck or shoulders more or less to the waistline, with or without a collar and sleeves, worn inside or outside a skirt, slacks, etc.; waist. **2.** a single-breasted, semifitted jacket worn with the service uniform of the U.S. Army. **3.** a loose outer garment, reaching to the hip or thigh, or below the knee, and sometimes belted, worn esp. by French and Russian peasants and English workmen. Cf. **smock frock.** —*v.i.* **4.** to puff out in a drooping fullness, as a blouse above a fitted waistband. —*v.t.* **5.** to dispose the material of a garment in loose folds, as trouser legs over the tops of boots. [< F] —**blouse′like′,** *adj.*

blous·on (blo͞o zôn′, blo͞o′zôn, blou′son), *n.* **1.** a woman's outer garment having a draw string, belt, or similar closing, at or below the waist, which causes it to blouse. —*adj.* **2.** of or pertaining to such a garment, the style it exemplifies, or something considered to resemble this style, as a hairdo: *a blouson dress; the blouson effect; a blouson bob.* [< F, equiv. to *blouse* BLOUSE + *-on* n. suffix]

blous·y (blou′zē), *adj.,* **blous·i·er, blous·i·est.** blowsy. —**blous′i·ly,** *adv.*

blow[1] (blō), *n.* **1.** a sudden, hard stroke with a hand, fist, or weapon: *a blow to the head.* **2.** a sudden shock, calamity, reversal, etc.: *His wife's death was a terrible blow to him.* **3.** a sudden attack or drastic action: *The invaders struck a blow to the south.* **4. at one blow,** with a single act: *The falling tree damaged two houses at one blow.* Also, **at a blow. 5. come to blows,** to begin to fight, esp. to engage in physical combat: *They came to blows over the referee's ruling.* **6. without striking a blow,** without a battle or contest; effortlessly: *The military coup was accomplished without striking a blow.* [late ME *blaw* (n.), north var. of later *blowe;* akin to OHG *bliuw(an),* Goth *bliggw(an)* (to) beat]

—**Syn. 1.** buffet, thump, thwack, rap, slap, cuff, box, beat, knock. **1, 2.** BLOW, STROKE, HIT, SLAP refer to a sudden or forceful impact, but differ in their literal and figurative uses. BLOW emphasizes the violence of the impact and, figuratively, adverse fortune: *a blow from a hammer; a blow to one's hopes.* STROKE emphasizes movement as well as impact; it indicates precision or, figuratively, either good fortune or sudden or unexpected pain or misfortune: *the stroke of a piston; a stroke of luck, of lightning; a paralytic stroke.* HIT, in its current uses, emphasizes the successful result of a literal or figurative blow, impact, or impression, for example in baseball, social life, the theater: *a two-base hit; to make a hit with someone; a smash hit.* SLAP, a blow with the open hand or with something flat, emphasizes the instrument with which the blow is delivered and, often, the resulting sound; figuratively, it connotes an unfriendly or sarcastic statement, action, or attitude: *Her coldness was like a slap in the face; the slap of a beaver's tail on the water.*

blow[2] (blō), *v.,* **blew, blown, blow·ing,** *n.* —*v.i.* **1.** (of the wind or air) to be in motion. **2.** to move along, carried by or as by the wind: *Dust seemed to blow through every crack in the house.* **3.** to produce or emit a current of air, as with the mouth, a bellows, etc.: *Blow on your hands to warm them.* **4.** *Music.* (of a horn, trumpet, etc.) to give out sound. **5.** to make a blowing sound; whistle: *The siren blew just as we rounded the corner.* **6.** (of horses) to breathe hard or quickly; pant. **7.** *Informal.* to boast; brag: *He kept blowing about his medals.* **8.** *Zool.* (of a whale) to spout. **9.** (of a fuse, light bulb, vacuum tube, tire, etc.) to burst, stop functioning, or be destroyed by exploding, overloading, etc. (often fol. by *out*): *A fuse blew just as we sat down to dinner. The rear tire blew out.* **10.** to burst from internal pressure: *Poorly sealed cans will often blow.* **11.** *Slang.* to leave; depart: *Let's blow.*

—*v.t.* **12.** to drive by means of a current of air: *A sudden breeze blew the smoke from the fire right into the house,* **13.** to spread by report: *Growing panic blew the rumor about.* **14.** to drive a current of air upon. **15.** to clear or empty by forcing air through: *Try blowing your nose.* **16.** to shape (glass, smoke, etc.) with a current of air: *to blow smoke rings.* **17.** to cause to sound, as by a current of air: *Blow your horn at the next crossing.* **18.** *Jazz.* to play (a musical instrument of any kind). **19.** to cause to explode (often fol. by *up, to bits,* etc.): *A mine blew the ship to bits.* **20.** to burst, burn out, or destroy by exploding, overloading, etc. (often fol. by *out*): *to blow a tire, fuse, etc.* **21.** to destroy; demolish: *The storm blew the trees down.* **22.** to put (a horse) out of breath by fatigue. **23.** *Slang.* to damn: *Blow the cost!* **24.** *U.S. Slang.* **a.** to spend money on. **b.** to squander; spend quickly: *He blew a fortune on racing cars.* **25.** *U.S. Slang.* to depart from: *to blow town.* **26.** *Slang.* to botch; bungle: *With one stupid mistake he'll blow the whole project.* **27. blow down,** *Metall.* to suspend working of (a blast furnace) by smelting the existing charge with a diminishing blast. **28. blow hot and cold,** to favor something at first and reject it later on; waver; vacillate. *Her enthusiasm for her job blows hot and cold.* **29. blow in,** *U.S. Slang.* **a.** to arrive at a place, esp. unexpectedly: *My uncle just blew in from Sacramento.* **b.** to spend or squander money: *He blew in his entire savings on a sports car.* **30. blow off, a.** to allow steam to be released. **b.** *Informal.* to reduce or release tension, as by loud talking. **31. blow one's lines,** *Theat.* to forget or make an error in a speaking part or stage directions. **32. blow one's stack.** See **stack** (def. 17). **33. blow one's top.** See **top**[1] (def. 22). **34. blow out, a.** to become extinguished: *The candles blew out at once.* **b.** to lose force or cease: *The storm has blown itself out.* **c.** (of an oil or gas well) to lose oil or gas uncontrollably. **d.** *Metall.* to finish the operation of (a blast furnace) by blowing it down and cleaning it. **35. blow over, a.** to pass away: subside: *The storm blew over in five minutes.* **b.** to be forgotten: *The scandal will eventually blow over.* **36. blow up, a.** to come into being: *A storm blew up.* **b.** to explode: *The ship blew up.* **c.** to cause to explode: *to blow up a bridge.* **d.** to exaggerate; enlarge: *He blew up his own role in his account of the battle.* **e.** *Informal.* to lose one's temper: *When he heard she was going to quit school, he simply blew up.* **f.** *Informal.* to scold or abuse. **g.** to fill with air; inflate: *to blow up a tire.* **h.** *Photog.* to make an enlarged reproduction of. **i.** *Math.* (of a function) to become infinite.

—*n.* **37.** a blast of air or wind: *to clean machinery with a blow.* **38.** a violent windstorm, gale, hurricane, or the like: *one of the worst blows we ever had around here.* **39.** act of producing a blast of air, as in playing a wind instrument: *a few discordant blows by the bugler.* **40.** *Metall.* **a.** a blast of air forced through a converter, as in the production of steel or copper. **b.** the stage of the production process during which this blast is used. **41.** boil (def. 16). [ME *blow(en)* (v.), OE *blāwan;* c. L *flā(re)* (to) blow]

blow[3] (blō), *v.,* **blew, blown, blow·ing,** *n.* —*v.i., v.t.* **1.** *Archaic.* to blossom or cause to blossom. —*n.* **2.** a yield or display of blossoms: *the lilac's violet blows.* **3.** a display of anything bright or brilliant: *a rich, full blow of color.* **4.** state of blossoming; a flowering: *a honeysuckle in full blow.* [ME *blow(en)* (v.), OE *blōwan;* akin to G *blühen* to bloom, L *flōs* flower]

blow·ball (blō′bôl′), *n.* the downy head or pappus of the dandelion, salsify, etc. [BLOW[2] + BALL[1]]

blow-by (blō′bī′), *n., pl.* **-bies.** *Auto.* **1.** leakage of the air-fuel mixture or of combustion gases between a piston and the cylinder wall into the crankcase of an automobile. **2.** a device, fitted to a crankcase, for conducting such gases back to the cylinders for combustion.

blow-by-blow (blō′bī′blō′), *adj.* **1.** (of an oral or written account of a boxing bout, as on the radio or in a newspaper) precisely detailed; describing the manner of execution of each move or blow by the boxers. **2.** detail after detail; action by action: *a blow-by-blow account of the interview.* —*n.* **3.** a blow-by-blow account.

blow-dry (blō′drī′), *v.t.,* **-dried, -dry·ing.** to dry and often style (wet hair) with a blow-dryer. [back formation from BLOW-DRYER]

blow-dry·er (blō′drī′ər), *n.* a hand-held electric appliance for drying hair with a stream of warm air, often combined with a comb for simultaneous styling.

blow·er (blō′ər), *n.* **1.** one who or that which blows. **2.** a machine for supplying air at a moderate pressure, as to supply forced drafts, supercharge and scavenge diesel engines, etc. **3.** *Mining.* a jet of firedamp issuing from a crevice. **4.** *Slang.* a braggart. **5.** the foreman of a crew working a blast furnace. **6.** *Slang.* supercharger. **7.** *Brit. Slang.* a telephone. [BLOW[2] + -ER[1]]

blow·fish (blō′fish′), *n., pl.* (*esp. collectively*) **-fish,** (*esp. referring to two or more kinds or species*) **-fish·es.** puffer (def. 2). [BLOW[2] + FISH]

blow·fly (blō′flī′), *n., pl.* **-flies.** any of numerous dipterous insects of the family *Calliphoridae* that deposit their eggs or larvae on carrion, excrement, etc., or in wounds of living animals. [BLOW[2] + FLY[2]]

blow·gun (blō′gun′), *n.* a pipe or tube through which missiles are blown by the breath. Also called **blowtube.**

blow-hard (blō′härd′), *n. Slang.* an exceptionally boastful and talkative person.

blow·hole (blō′hōl′), *n.* **1.** an air or gas vent, esp. one to carry off fumes from a tunnel, underground passage, etc. **2.** either of two nostrils or spiracles, or a single one, at the top of the head in whales and other cetaceans, through which they breathe. **3.** a hole in the ice to which whales or seals come to breathe. **4.** *Metall.* a defect in a casting or ingot caused by the escape of gas.

blow·ing (blō′ing), *n.* **1.** the sound of any vapor or gas issuing from a vent under pressure. **2.** *Metall.* a disturbance caused by gas or steam blowing through molten metal. **3.** Also called **blow molding.** a method of producing hollowware by injecting air under pressure into a molten mass, as of glass or plastic, and shaping the material within a mold. [BLOW[2] + -ING[1]]

blow·i·ron (blō′ī′ərn), *n.* blowpipe (def. 2).

blow′ mold′, a hinged mold for shaping molten glass during blowing.

blow′ mold′ing, blowing (def. 3).

blown[1] (blōn), *adj.* **1.** inflated; swollen; expanded: *blown stomachs.* **2.** destroyed, misshapen, ruined, or spoiled: *to replace a blown fuse; to dispose of blown canned goods.* **3.** out of breath; fatigued; exhausted: *The horses were blown by the violent exercise.* **4.** flyblown. **5.** formed by blowing: *blown glass.* [ptp. of BLOW[2]]

blown[2] (blōn), *adj. Hort.* fully expanded or opened, as a flower. [ptp. of BLOW[3]]

blown-mold·ed (blōn′mōl′did), *adj.* (of plastic hollowware) made by blowing and shaping in a mold; mold-blown. Also, **blow′-mold′ed, blown′-mold′.**

blown-up (blōn′up′), *adj.* **1.** (of a picture, image, etc.) photographically enlarged. **2.** damaged or destroyed by demolition, explosion, etc.: *blown-up bridges and railheads.* **3.** (of a ball, balloon, etc.) inflated. **4.** overexpanded; unduly large.

blow·off (blō′ôf′, -of′), *n.* **1.** a current of escaping surplus steam, water, etc.: *The safety valve released a violent blowoff from the furnace.* **2.** a device that permits and channels such a current. **3.** *Slang.* one who brags; a blow-hard. [BLOW[2] + OFF]

blow·out (blō′out′), *n.* **1.** a sudden bursting or rupture of an automobile tire. **2.** a sudden or violent escape of air, steam, or the like. **3.** a hollow formed in a region of shifting sands or light soil by the action of the wind. **4.** an uncontrollable escape of oil, gas, or water from a well. **5.** *Aeron.* flameout. **6.** *Slang.* a big, usually lavish, party or entertainment. [BLOW[2] + OUT]

blow·pipe (blō′pīp′), *n.* **1.** a tube through which a stream of air or gas is forced into a flame to concentrate and increase its heating action. **2.** Also called **blow-iron, blowtube.** *Glass Blowing.* a long metal pipe used to gather and blow the molten glass into hollowware. **3.** blowgun. **4.** *Med.* an instrument used to observe or clean a cavity. [BLOW[2] + PIPE[1]]

blows·y (blou′zē), *adj.,* **blows·i·er, blows·i·est.** blowzy. —**blows′i·ly,** *adv.*

blow·torch (blō′tôrch′), *n.* a small portable apparatus that gives an extremely hot gasoline flame intensified by a blast, used esp. in metalworking. [BLOW[2] + TORCH]

Blowtorch

blow·tube (blō′to͞ob′, -tyo͞ob′), *n.* **1.** blowgun. **2.** blowpipe (def. 2). [BLOW[2] + TUBE]

blow·up (blō′up′), *n.* **1.** an explosion. **2.** a violent argument, outburst of temper, or the like, esp. one resulting in estrangement. **3.** Also, **blow′-up′.** *Photog.* an enlargement. [n. use of v. phrase *blow up*]

blow·y (blō′ē), *adj.,* **blow·i·er, blow·i·est. 1.** windy: *a chill, blowy day.* **2.** easily blown about: *flimsy, blowy curtain material.* [BLOW[2] + -Y[1]] —**blow′i·ness,** *n.*

blowzed (blouzd), *adj.* blowzy.

blowz·y (blou′zē), *adj.,* **blowz·i·er, blowz·i·est. 1.** having a coarse, ruddy complexion. **2.** disheveled; unkempt: *blowzy hair.* Also, **blowsy, blowzed, blowsed** (blouzd), **blousy.** [obs. *blowze* wench (< ?) + -Y[1]] —**blowz′i·ly,** *adv.*

BLS, Bureau of Labor Statistics.

bls., **1.** bales. **2.** barrels.

B.L.S., Bachelor of Library Science.

blub (blub), *n.* a swelling of fresh plasterwork. [var. of BLOB]

blub·ber (blub′ər), *n.* **1.** *Zool.* the fat found between the skin and muscle of whales and other cetaceans, from which oil is made. **2.** act of weeping noisily and without restraint. —*v.i.* **3.** to weep noisily and without restraint (usually used contemptuously): *Stop blubbering and tell me what's wrong.* —*v.t.* **4.** to say, esp. incoherently, while weeping: *She seemed to be blubbering something about a lost ring.* **5.** to contort or disfigure (the features) with weeping: *All that crying had really blubbered her face.* —*adj.* **6.** disfigured with blubbering; blubbery: *She dried her blubber eyes.* **7.** fatty; swollen; puffed out (often used in combination): *thick, blubber lips; blubber-faced.* [late ME *bluber* bubble, bubbling water, entrails, whale oil; appar. imit.] —**blub′ber·er,** *n.* —**blub′ber·ing·ly,** *adv.*

blub·ber·head (blub′ər hed′), *n. Slang.* a stupid, inept person; blockhead. [BLUBBER + HEAD]

blub·ber·y (blub′ə rē), *adj.* **1.** abounding in blubber, as a cetacean; resembling blubber; fat. **2.** blubbered; disfigured; swollen: *red, blubbery eyes; blubbery lips.* [BLUBBER + -Y[1]]

blu·cher (blo͞o′kər, -chər), *n.* **1.** a strong, leather half boot. **2.** a shoe with the vamp continued up beneath the top, which laps over it from the sides. [named after Field Marshal von BLÜCHER]

Blü·cher (blo͞o′kər, -chər; *Ger.* blʏ′ᴋʜər), *n.* **Geb·hart Le·be·recht von** (gep′härt lā′bə ʀeᴋʜt′ fən), 1742–1819, Prussian field marshal.

bludge (bluj), *v.,* **bludged, bludg·ing,** *n. Australian.* —*v.t.* **1.** to shirk. **2.** to impose on (someone). —*n.* **3.** an easy task. [false analysis of BLUDGEON (v.) gives phrase *bludge on* to impose on; back formation from BLUDGEON (n.) gives *bludge* (v.) to use a bludgeon, whence *bludger* bully, esp. a harlot's bully, pimp, hence shirker, whence *bludge* (v.) to shirk]

bludg·eon (bluj′ən), *n.* **1.** a short, heavy club with one end weighted, or thicker and heavier than the other. —*v.t.* **2.** to strike or fell with a bludgeon. **3.** to force (someone) into something; coerce; bully: *The boss finally bludgeoned him into accepting responsibility.* [?] —**bludg′eon·er, bludg·eon·eer** (bluj′ə nēr′), *n.*

blue (blo͞o), *n., adj.,* **blu·er, blu·est,** *v.,* **blued, blu·ing** or **blue·ing.** —*n.* **1.** the pure color of a clear sky; azure; the hue between green and violet in the spectrum. **2.** bluing. **3.** something having a blue color: *Place the blue next to the red.* **4.** a person who wears blue or is a member of a group characterized by some blue symbol: *Tomorrow the blues will play the browns.* **5.** a member of the Union army in the American Civil War. Cf. **gray** (def. 11). **6.** bluestocking. **7.** See **blue ribbon** (def. 1). **8.** any of several blue-winged butterflies of the family *Lycaenidae.* **9. out of the blue,** suddenly and unexpectedly: *The inheritance came out of the blue as a stroke of good fortune.* **10. the blue, a.** the sky. **b.** the sea. **c.** the unknown: *to vanish into the blue.* —*adj.* **11.** of the color of blue: *a blue tie.* **12.** (*cap.*) of or pertaining to the Union Army in the United States Civil War. **13.** (of the skin) discolored by cold, contusion, fear, or vascular collapse. **14.** depressed in spirits; dejected; melancholy: *She was blue about not being invited to the dance.* **15.** holding little hope; dismal; bleak: *a blue outlook.* **16.** characterized by or stemming from rigid morals or religion: *blue laws; a town strait-jacketed by statutes that were blue and unrealistic.* **17.** marked by blasphemy: *The air was blue with oaths.* **18.** *Informal.* indecent; risqué: *blue jokes.* **19. blue in the face,** exhausted and speechless, as from excessive anger, physical strain, etc.: *He ran until he was blue in the face. I told him to eat his spinach till I was blue in the face.* —*v.t.* **20.** to make blue; dye a blue color. **21.** to tinge with bluing: *Don't blue your clothes till the second rinse.* [ME *blewe,* OE *blǣwe(n),* contr. of *blǣhǣwe(n),* equiv. to *blǣ* dark blue (see BLAE) + *hǣwe,* light blue, grey + *-en* -EN[2]] —**blue′ly,** *adv.* —**blue′ness,** *n.*

—**Syn. 1.** cerulean, sapphire. **14.** despondent, unhappy, morose, doleful, dispirited, sad, glum, downcast. **15.** gloomy, dispiriting. **16.** righteous, puritanical, moral, severe, prudish. —**Ant. 14.** happy.

blue′ alert′, **1.** (in military or civilian defense) an alert following the first, or yellow, alert, in which air attack seems probable. **2.** an alert sometimes used in connection with hurricane warnings. **3.** the signal or alarm sounded for such alerts. Cf. **red alert, white alert, yellow alert.**

blue′ asbes′tos, *Mineral.* crocidolite.

Blue′ Ash′, a town in SW Ohio. 8341 (1960).

blue′ ba′by, *Pathol.* an infant born with cyanosis resulting from a congenital heart or lung defect.

blue′back salm′on (blo͞o′bak′). See **sockeye salmon.**

Blue·beard (blo͞o′bērd′), *n.* **1.** (in folklore) a nickname of the Chevalier Raoul, whose seventh wife found the bodies of the other six in a room forbidden to her. **2.** any person alleged to have murdered a number of his wives or other women. —**Blue′beard′ism,** *n.*

blue·bell (blo͞o′bel′), *n.* **1.** any of various plants with blue, bell-shaped flowers, as the harebell, a liliaceous plant, *Scilla nonscripta*, of the Old World, or the blue jasmine. **2.** the lungwort, *Mertensia virginica*, of the U.S. **3.** Also called **American abscessroot.** a spreading herb, *Polemonium reptans*, of North America, having light blue flowers in loose clusters. [BLUE + BELL[1]] —**blue′belled′,** *adj.*

blue′ belt′, *Judo.* a blue belt conferred by a judo association on a player, usually in his third year of training, to be worn with his judo costume. Cf. **black belt** (def. 3), **brown belt, green belt** (def. 2), **white belt.** —**blue′-belt′,** *adj.*

blue·ber·ry (blo͞o′ber′ē, -bə rē), *n., pl.* **-ries. 1.** the edible, usually bluish berry of various ericaceous shrubs of the genus *Vaccinium.* **2.** any of these shrubs. [BLUE + BERRY]

blue·bill (blo͞o′bil′), *n. U.S. Dial.* the scaup duck. [BLUE + BILL[2]]

blue·bird (blo͞o′bûrd′), *n.* **1.** any of several small North American songbirds of the genus *Sialia*, having predominantly blue plumage, as the eastern *S. sialis*, having a blue back and a reddish-brown breast. **2.** See **fairy bluebird.** [BLUE + BIRD]

Bluebird, *Sialia sialis* (Length 7 in.)

blue-black (blo͞o′blak′), *adj.* black with bluish highlights. —**blue′-black′ness,** *n.*

blue′ blaz′ing star′, gay-feather (def. 1).

blue′ blood′, 1. alleged superiority by reason of birth; aristocracy: *They boasted a lineage of pure blue blood.* **2.** *Informal.* an aristocrat. [trans. of Sp *sangre azul.* See SANGUINE, AZURE] —**blue′-blood′ed,** *adj.*

blue-blos·som (blo͞o′blos′əm), *n.* a shrub, *Ceanothus thyrsiflorus*, of the western U.S., having clusters of blue flowers. Also called **blue myrtle, California lilac.**

blue·bon·net (blo͞o′bon′it), *n.* **1.** the cornflower, *Centaurea Cyanus.* **2.** a blue-flowered lupine, esp. *Lupinus subcarnosus:* the State flower of Texas. **3.** a broad, flat cap of blue wool, formerly worn in Scotland. **4.** a Scottish soldier who wore such a cap. **5.** any Scot. Also called **blue·cap** (blo͞o′kap′). [BLUE + BONNET]

blue′ book′, 1. *Informal.* a register or directory of socially prominent persons. **2.** *U.S.* a blank book used in taking college examinations, usually with a blue cover. **3.** a British parliamentary or other publication bound in a blue cover. Also, **blue′book′.**

blue·bot·tle (blo͞o′bot′əl), *n.* **1.** cornflower (def. 1). **2.** any of various other plants having blue flowers, esp. of the genera *Campanula* and *Scilla.* **3.** See **bluebottle fly.** [BLUE + BOTTLE[1]]

blue′bottle fly′, any of several iridescent blue blowflies, esp. those of the genus *Calliphora*, some of which are parasitic on domestic animals.

Blue′ Boy′, a painting by Thomas Gainsborough.

blue′-brick univer′sity (blo͞o′brik′), *Brit. Informal.* any university with the highest traditions and prestige, esp. Oxford and Cambridge. Also, **blue′brick univer′sity.** Cf. **red-brick university.**

blue′ bull′, nilgai.

blue′ cheese′, a rich, blue-veined cheese made from cow's milk.

blue′ chip′, 1. *Chiefly Poker.* a blue-colored chip of high value. **2.** a relatively high-priced common stock issue of a leading company that has a record of uninterrupted payment of dividends over a relatively long period. **3.** a secure and valuable item of property held in reserve: *The airfield was a blue chip in the struggle for military supremacy.*

blue-chip (blo͞o′chip′), *adj.* **1.** of, pertaining to, or constituting a blue chip. **2.** having outstanding or exemplary qualities within a specified category; leading: *a group of blue-chip scientists; blue-chip stock.*

blue·coat (blo͞o′kōt′), *n.* **1.** a person who wears a blue coat or uniform. **2.** a policeman. **3.** a soldier in the U.S. Army in earlier times. —**blue′coat′ed,** *adj.*

blue′ co′hosh. See under **cohosh.**

blue-col·lar (blo͞o′kol′ər), *adj.* of or pertaining to wage-earning workers who wear work clothes or other specialized clothing on the job, as mechanics, longshoremen, miners, etc. Cf. **white-collar.**

blue′ comb′, *Vet. Pathol.* a disease resembling Bright's disease in man, affecting domestic fowl and certain other birds, characterized by fever, sunken eyes, and shriveling of the skin of the wattles, shanks, and comb. Also called **x-disease.**

blue′ cop′peras, *Chem.* See **blue vitriol.**

blue′ cor′al, any coral of the genus *Heliopora*, having brown polyps and a blue skeleton, found in the Indo-Pacific region.

blue′ crab′, an edible crab, *Callinectes sapidus*, having a dark green body and bluish legs, found along the Atlantic and Gulf coasts of North America.

blue′ crane′, *Informal.* the great blue heron.

Blue′ Cross′, a nonprofit organization which pays certain hospital expenses incurred by its members, who pay premiums periodically.

blue-curls (blo͞o′kûrlz′), *n., pl.* **-curls. 1.** (*construed as sing. or pl.*) any labiate plant of the genus *Trichostema*, having blue to pink or, rarely, white flowers with long, curved filaments. **2.** selfheal (def. 1). Also, **blue′ curls′.**

blue′ dai′sy, a bushy shrub, *Felicia amelloides*, of South Africa, having solitary, daisylike flowers with yellow disks and blue rays, grown as an ornamental. Also called **blue marguerite.**

blue′ dan′delion, chicory (def. 1).

blue′ dawn′-flow·er (dôn′flou′ər), a perennial vine, *Ipomoea leari*, of tropical America, having showy, white-tubed, blue flowers from four to five inches wide, ultimately turning pink.

blue′ dev′ils, 1. low spirits; depression. **2.** See **delirium tremens.**

blue′ dicks′ (diks), an herb, *Brodiaea capitata*, of the western coast of the U.S., having headlike clusters of blue flowers.

blue′ dog′wood, a shrub or small tree, *Cornus alternifolia*, of eastern North America, having clusters of white flowers and bluish fruit. Also called **pigeonberry.**

Blue′ Earth′, a town in S Minnesota. 4200 (1960).

blue′-eyed grass′ (blo͞o′īd′), any of numerous iridaceous plants of the genus *Sisyrinchium*, having grasslike leaves and small, usually blue, flowers.

blue′-eyed Mar′y, an herb, *Collinsia verna*, of the northern and eastern U.S., having long-stalked flowers with the upper lip white or purple and the lower lip blue. [from the proper name *Mary*]

blue′ false′ in′digo, a perennial herb, *Baptisia australis*, of the U.S., having wedge-shaped leaflets and blue, clustered flowers. Also called **rattle-bush.**

Blue·field (blo͞o′fēld′), *n.* **1.** a city in SW West Virginia. 19,256 (1960). **2.** a town in SW Virginia. 4235 (1960).

Blue·fields (blo͞o′fēldz′), *n.* a seaport in E Nicaragua. 11,248 (est. 1959).

blue′fin tu′na, a large tuna, *Thunnus thynnus*, common in temperate seas, used, canned, as food. [BLUE + FIN]

blue·fish (blo͞o′fish′), *n., pl.* (*esp. collectively*) **-fish,** (*esp. referring to two or more kinds or species*) **-fish·es. 1.** a predaceous, marine, bluish or greenish food fish, *Pomatomus saltatrix*, found along the Atlantic coast of North and South America. **2.** any of various fishes, usually of a bluish color. [BLUE + FISH]

blue′ flag′, any North American plant of the genus *Iris*, esp. *I. prismatica*, or *I. versicolor:* the State flower of Tennessee.

blue′ flash′. See **green flash.**

blue′ fox′, 1. a bluish-gray winter color phase of the arctic fox. **2.** the arctic fox in summer pelage. **3.** the blue fur of this animal. **4.** any white fox fur dyed blue.

blue′ gas′, *Chem.* See **water gas.**

blue·gill (blo͞o′gil′), *n.* a fresh-water sunfish, *Lepomis macrochirus*, found in the Mississippi River valley, used for food. [BLUE + GILL[1]]

blue′ goose′, a bluish-gray wild goose, *Chen caerulescens*, of North America.

blue′ gra′ma. See under **grama grass.**

blue·grass (blo͞o′gras′, -gräs′), *n.* **1.** any grass of the genus *Poa*, as the Kentucky bluegrass, *P. pratensis.* **2.** country music that is polyphonic in character and is played on unamplified stringed instruments, with emphasis esp. on the solo banjo. **3. the Bluegrass.** See **Bluegrass Region.** [BLUE + GRASS]

Blue′grass Re′gion, a region in central Kentucky, famous for its horse farms and fields of bluegrass.

Blue′grass State′, Kentucky (used as a nickname).

blue′-gray gnat′catcher (blo͞o′grā′), a common gnatcatcher, *Polioptila caerulea*, of the U.S., having bluish-gray upper parts and a melodious song.

blue-green (blo͞o′grēn′), *n.* a color about midway between blue and green in the spectrum.

blue′-green al′ga, any unicellular or filamentous alga of the class *Myxophyceae* (*Cyanophycaea*), usually bluish-green owing to the presence of blue pigments in addition to the chlorophyll.

blue′-green flame′. See **green flash.**

blue′ gros′beak, a grosbeak, *Guiraca caerulea*, of the U.S., the male of which is blue with two rusty bars on each wing.

blue′ grouse′, *U.S. Dial.* any of several mottled, slaty gray, North American grouses of the genus *Dendragapus*, esp. the dusky grouse.

blue′ gum′, eucalyptus.

blue·head (blo͞o′hed′), *n.* a wrasse, *Thalassoma bifasciatum*, found in the Atlantic Ocean, the adult male of which has a brilliant purplish-blue head. [BLUE + HEAD]

blue′-head·ed vir′eo (blo͞o′hed′id), a vireo, *Vireo solitarius*, of North and Central America, having the top and sides of the head bluish gray. Also called **solitary vireo.**

blue-hearts (blo͞o′härts′), *n., pl.* **-hearts.** (*construed as sing. or pl.*) a perennial, North American, scrophulariaceous herb, *Buchnera americana*, having deep purple flowers.

blue′ huck′leberry, tangleberry.

blue·ing (blo͞o′ing), *n. Chem.* bluing.

blue·ish (blo͞o′ish), *adj.* bluish.

Blue′ Is′land, a city in NE Illinois, near Chicago 19,618 (1960).

blue·jack (blo͞o′jak′), *n.* a small oak, *Quercus cinerea* or *brevifolia*, of the southern U.S. [BLUE + JACK[1], modeled after BLACKJACK; so called from the bluish look of the leaves]

blue·jack·et (blo͞o′jak′it), *n.* a sailor. [BLUE + JACKET]

blue′ jas′mine, a shrubby vine, *Clematis crispa*, of the southern U.S., having solitary, bell-shaped, blue or bluish-purple to pink flowers and fruit with silky appendages. Also called **curly clematis.**

blue′ jay′, a common, crested jay, *Cyanocitta cristata*, of eastern North America, having a bright blue back and a gray breast.

blue′ jeans′, blue denim trousers having reinforced pockets and seams, worn originally as work pants but now also as leisure attire. Cf. **Levis.**

blue′ laws′, *U.S.* puritanical laws, originating in colonial New England, which forbid certain practices, esp. drinking or working on Sunday, dancing, etc.

blue′ lil′y-turf (lil′ē tûrf′), a perennial herb, *Liriope Muscari*, of Asia, having lilac-purple flowers.

blue′ line′, *Ice Hockey.* either of two lines of the color blue that are parallel to and equidistant from the goal lines and divide the rink into three zones of equal size. Also called **zone line.** Cf. **end zone** (def. 2), **neutral zone.**

blue′ lips′, an herb, *Collinsia grandiflora*, of western central North America, having short-stalked flowers with the upper lip purple or white and the lower lip blue or violet.

blue′ lobel′ia, a perennial herb, *Lobelia siphilitica*, of the eastern U.S., having deep blue or bluish-purple flowers. Also called **great lobelia.**

blue′ lo′tus, 1. See under **Egyptian lotus** (def. 1). **2.** a water lily, *Nymphaea stellata*, of India, having pale blue flowers.

blue′ marguerite′. See **blue daisy.**

blue′ mar′lin, a marlin, *Makaira nigricans*, found in warm seas.

blue′ mass′, *Pharm.* **1.** Also called **mercury mass.** a preparation of metallic mercury with other ingredients, used for making blue pills. **2.** See **blue pill** (def. 1).

blue′ mel′ilot, an annual herb, *Trigonella caerulea*, of Europe, having long-stalked clusters of blue and white flowers.

blue′ mock′ingbird. See under **mockingbird** (def. 2).

blue′ mold′, 1. Also called **green mold.** any fungus of the genus *Penicillium*, which forms a bluish-green, furry coating on foodstuffs inoculated by its spores. **2.** *Plant Pathol.* a disease of plants, characterized by necrosis of leaves or fruit and the growth of bluish or grayish mold on affected parts, caused by any of several fungi, as of the genus *Penicillium* or *Peronospora tabicina.*

blue′ Mon′day, *Informal.* Monday as a depressing workday in contrast to the pleasant relaxation of Sunday.

Blue′ Moun′tains, a range of low mountains in NE Oregon and SE Washington.

blue′ mud′, a deep-sea sediment of fine silt and clay that derives its bluish color from organic material and iron sulfide.

blue′ myr′tle, blue-blossom.

blue·ness (blo͞o′nis), *n.* quality or state of being blue. [BLUE + -NESS]

Blue′ Nile′, a river in E Africa, flowing N NW from Lake Tana in Ethiopia into the Nile at Khartoum: a tributary of the Nile. ab. 950 mi. long. Cf. **Nile.**

blue·nose (blo͞o′nōz′), *n.* **1.** a puritanical person; prude. [BLUE + NOSE] **2.** (*cap.*) a native of the Canadian Maritime Provinces; a Nova Scotian. **3.** *Naut. Slang.* **a.** a sailing vessel of Nova Scotia. **b.** a seaman on such a vessel. [BLUE + NOSE; from the bluish color of the potato grown in Nova Scotia]

blue′ note′, *Jazz.* a flatted note, esp. the third or the seventh degree of the scale, recurring frequently in blues and jazz as a characteristic feature.

blue′ oint′ment, *Pharm.* an ointment containing 10 percent of finely divided mercury, used chiefly in treating pediculosis.

blue′ on′yx. See **German lapis.**

blue-pen·cil (blo͞o′pen′səl), *v.t.,* **-ciled, -cil·ing** or (*esp. Brit.*) **-cilled, -cil·ling.** to alter, abridge, or cancel with or as with a pencil that makes a blue mark, as in editing a manuscript.

blue′ pe′ter, *Naut.* a blue flag with a white square in the center, designating the letter "P" in the International Code of Signals, flown at the head of the foremast of a vessel in port to indicate that the vessel is about to leave.

blue′ phlox′, a perennial herb, *Phlox divaricata*, of eastern North America, having creeping, rooting stems and mauve flowers. Also called **wild sweet william.**

blue′ pick′erel. See **blue pike.**

blue′ pi′geon, *Naut. Slang.* a sounding lead weighing up to 14 pounds.

blue′ pike′, a variety of the walleye, *Strizostedion vitreum glaucum*, found in the Great Lakes. Also called **blue pickerel, blue′ pike′perch, blue walleye.**

blue′ pill′, *Pharm.* **1.** Also called **mercury mass.** a pill of blue mass, used in medicine chiefly as a cathartic. **2.** See **blue mass** (def. 1).

blue′ plate′, 1. a plate, usually decorated with a blue willow pattern, divided by ridges into sections for holding apart several kinds of food. **2.** a main course, as of meat and vegetables, listed as an item on a menu.

blue′ point′, a Siamese cat having a light-colored body and darker, bluish-gray points.

blue·point (blo͞o′point′), *n.* a small oyster, esp. one from the oyster beds near Blue Point, Long Island, usually served raw on the half shell or in a cocktail.

blue′ pow′der, an intimate mixture of finely divided zinc and zinc oxide produced in the early stages of a zinc-refining operation and charged into the furnace again for further refining.

blue·print (blo͞o′print′), *n.* **1.** a process of photographic printing, used chiefly in copying architectural and mechanical drawings, which produces a white line on a blue background. **2.** a print made by this process. **3.** a detailed outline or plan: *a blueprint for the new sales campaign.* —*v.t.* **4.** to make a blueprint of. [BLUE + PRINT] —**blue′print′er,** *n.*

blue′ rac′er, a bluish racer, *Coluber constrictor flaviventris*. found from Ohio to Texas.

blue-red (blo͞o′red′), *n.* a color about midway between blue and red in the spectrum; purplish.

blue′ rib′bon, 1. the highest award or distinction, as the first prize in a contest: *His entry at the state fair won a blue ribbon.* **2.** a blue ribbon worn as a badge of honor, esp. by members of the Order of the Garter of the British knighthood. **3.** (*caps.*) Also, *Brit.,* **Blue′ Rib′band.** a prize awarded to an ocean liner making the fastest recorded trip across the Atlantic Ocean between Ambrose Lightship and Bishop Rock. **4.** a badge used by some temperance organizations to indicate a pledge of abstinence from alcohol.

blue-rib·bon (blo͞o′rib′ən), *adj.* of superior quality; first-rate; specially selected: *The party was a blue-ribbon occasion.* [adj. use of BLUE RIBBON]

blue′-ribbon ju′ry, a jury composed of persons having more than ordinary education and presumably exceptional intelligence and perceptiveness, selected by the court on the motion of plaintiff or defendant to try cases of unusual complexity or importance.

Blue′ Rid′er. See **Blaue Reiter.**

Blue′ Ridge′, a mountain range extending SW from N Virginia to N Georgia: part of the Appalachian Mountains. Also called **Blue′ Ridge′ Moun′tains.**

blue′ rock′fish, a bluish-black rockfish, *Sebastodes mystinus*, found along the Pacific coast of North America. Also called **priestfish.**

blue′ run′ner, a carangid food fish, *Caranx crysos*, of the Atlantic Ocean.

blues[1] (blo͞oz), *n.* **1.** (*construed as pl.*) despondency; melancholy: *This rainy spell is giving me the blues.* **2.** (*often construed as sing.*) *Jazz.* **a.** a song of American Negro origin, that is marked by the frequent occurrence of blue notes, and that takes the basic form, customarily improvised upon in performance, of a 12-bar chorus consisting of a 3-line stanza with the second line repeating the first. **b.** the genre constituting such songs. [BLUE (DEVIL)S]

blues² (blo͞oz), *n.* (*construed as pl.*) any of several blue military uniforms worn by members of the U.S. navy, army, or air force.

Blue′ Scout′, *U.S.* a four-stage sounding probe and small satellite-launch missile.

blue′ shark′, a slender, pelagic shark, *Prionace glauca,* that is indigo blue above, shading to white below. Also called **great blue shark.**

blue′ sheep′, bharal.

Blue′ Shield′, a nonprofit organization which pays certain medical and surgical expenses incurred by its members, who pay premiums periodically.

blue-sky (blo͞o′skī′), *adj.* **1.** (esp. of securities) having dubious value; not financially sound. **2.** for the sake of theory and scientific development rather than for immediate financial profit: *blue-sky thinking.* **3.** fanciful; impractical: *blue-sky ideas.* [so called from the lack of clouds in the sky, i.e. lack of substance]

blue′-sky′ law′, *U.S.* any State law regulating the sale of securities, esp. such a law designed to prevent the promotion of fraudulent stocks.

blue′ spire′a, a grayish, hairy shrub, *Caryopteris incana,* of eastern Asia, having clusters of showy, blue or bluish-purple flowers.

Blue′ Springs′, a town in W Missouri. 2555 (1960).

blue′ spruce′, a spruce, *Picea pungens,* of western North America, having bluish-green leaves, grown as an ornamental: the State tree of Colorado and Utah. Also called **Colorado blue spruce, Colorado spruce.**

blue′ stel′lar ob′ject, *Astron.* any of a class of blue celestial objects, at one time thought to be stars, that do not emit appreciable radio waves. *Abbr.:* **BSO**

blue′ stem′, *Plant Pathol.* a disease of raspberries and blackberries, characterized by blue discoloration of the stem, wilting, and discoloration and decay of the roots, caused by a fungus, *Verticillium albo-atrum.*

blue·stem (blo͞o′stem′), *n.* **1.** any of several prairie grasses of the genus *Andropogon,* having bluish leaf sheaths, now grown in the western U.S. for forage. **2.** See **dwarf palmetto.** [BLUE + STEM¹]

blue·stock·ing (blo͞o′stok′ing), *n.* **1.** a woman with considerable scholarly, literary, or intellectual ability or interest. **2.** a member of a mid-18th century London literary circle: *Lady Montagu was a celebrated bluestocking.* [so called from the informal attire, esp. blue woolen instead of black silk stockings, worn by some women of the group (def. 2)] —**blue′stock′ing·ism,** *n.*

blue′ stone′, *Chem.* See **blue vitriol.**

blue·stone (blo͞o′stōn′), *n.* a bluish, argillaceous sandstone used for building purposes, flagging, etc. [BLUE + STONE]

blue′ streak′, *Informal.* **1.** something moving very fast: *They traveled like a blue streak through Italy.* **2.** something continuous, vehement, or interminable: *She always talks a blue streak.*

blue′ suc′cory, a garden plant, *Catananche caerulea,* of southern Europe, having very hairy leaves and blue flowerheads, used by the ancients as a love potion. Also called **Cupid's-dart.**

blu·et (blo͞o′it), *n.* **1.** any of various plants having blue flowers, as the cornflower. **2.** Often, **bluets.** Also called **innocence, Quaker-ladies.** any of various species of *Houstonia,* esp. *Houstonia caerulea.* [late ME *blewet, blewed,* var. of ME *bloweth, blowed(e)* (see BLUE, BLAE); suffix perh. OE *-et,* as in THICKET]

Blu·et (blo͞o′it), *n.* a girl's given name.

blue′ this′tle, blueweed (def. 1).

blue′throat pike′blenny (blo͞o′thrōt′). See under **pikeblenny.** [BLUE + THROAT]

blue·tick (blo͞o′tik′), *n.* an American hound having a usually black, tan, and white coat flecked or mottled with black, used in hunting foxes and raccoons. [BLUE + TICK¹]

blue′ tit′, an Old World titmouse, *Parus caeruleus,* having a cobalt-blue crown.

blue·tongue (blo͞o′tung′), *n.* *Vet. Pathol.* a disease of sheep and sometimes cattle, transmitted by biting insects and characterized by high fever, excessive salivation, swelling of the lips, tongue, ears, and face, and edema and cyanosis of the tongue. Also called **catarrhal fever.** [BLUE + TONGUE]

blue′ ver′diter. See under **verditer.**

blue′ ver′vain, a hardy, erect, perennial herb, *Verbena hastata,* of eastern North America, having small blue flowers.

blue′ vit′riol, *Chem.* a salt, $CuSO_4·5H_2O$, occurring in large transparent, deep-blue triclinic crystals, appearing in its anhydrous state as a white powder: used chiefly as a mordant, insecticide, fungicide, and in engraving. Also called **blue copperas, blue stone, copper sulfate, cupric sulfate.**

blue′ wall′eye. See **blue pike.**

blue·weed (blo͞o′wēd′), *n.* **1.** Also called **blue thistle.** a bristly, boraginaceous weed, *Echium vulgare,* having showy blue flowers, a native of Europe naturalized in the U.S. **2.** chicory (def. 1). [BLUE + WEED¹]

blue′ whale′, sulphur-bottom.

blue′-winged teal′ (blo͞o′wingd′), a small pond and river duck, *Anas discors,* of North America, having grayish-blue patches on the wings.

blue·wood (blo͞o′wo͝od′), *n.* a rhamnaceous shrub or small tree, *Condalia obovata,* of western Texas and northern Mexico, often forming dense chaparral. [BLUE + WOOD¹]

blue′ wood′ as′ter, a perennial herb, *Aster cordifolius,* of North America, having pale blue flowers.

blue·y (blo͞o′ē), *n.* *Australian.* swag² (def. 2). [BLUE + -Y²; so called because usu. wrapped in a blue blanket]

blue′ ynde′ (ind), *Obs.* blue indigo dye.

bluff¹ (bluf), *adj.* **1.** good-naturedly abrupt or frank; heartily outspoken: *a big, bluff, generous man.* **2.** presenting a bold and nearly perpendicular front, as a coastline: *a bluff, precipitous headland.* **3.** *Naut.* (of the bow of a vessel) having a full, blunt form. —*n.* **4.** a cliff, headland, or hill with a broad, steep face. **5.** *Chiefly Canadian.* a clump or grove of trees on a prairie; copse. [perh. < MLG *blaff* smooth, even, or < MD *blaf* broad, flat (now obs.)] —**bluff′ly,** *adv.* —**bluff′ness,** *n.*
—**Syn. 1.** direct, open, honest; rough, crude. See **blunt. 2.** abrupt, steep. —**Ant. 1.** subtle.

bluff² (bluf), *v.t.* **1.** to mislead by presenting a bold front: *He bluffed me into believing that he was a doctor.* **2.** to gain by bluffing: *He bluffed his way into the job.* **3.** *Poker.* to deceive by a show of confidence in the strength of one's cards. —*v.i.* **4.** to mislead someone by presenting a bold front: *That open face makes it impossible for him to bluff.* —*n.* **5.** act, instance, or practice of bluffing: *Her pathetic story was all a bluff to get money from us. You'll have to get used to his bluff and bluster.* **6.** one who bluffs; bluffer: *That big bluff doesn't have a nickel to his name.* **7. call someone's bluff,** to expose a person's deception; challenge someone to carry out his threat: *He always said he would quit, so we finally called his bluff.* [perh. < LG *bluff(en)* (to) bluster, frighten; akin to MD *bluffen* to make a trick at cards] —**bluff′a·ble,** *adj.* —**bluff′er,** *n.*

Bluff·ton (bluf′tən), *n.* **1.** a town in E Indiana. 6238 (1960). **2.** a town in W Ohio. 2591 (1960).

blu·ing (blo͞o′ing), *n.* *Chem.* a substance, as indigo, used to whiten clothes or give them a bluish tinge. Also, **blueing.** [BLUE + -ING¹]

blu·ish (blo͞o′ish), *adj.* somewhat blue. Also, **blueish.** [BLUE + -ISH¹] —**blu′ish·ness,** *n.*

Blum (blo͞om), *n.* **Lé·on** (lē′on; *Fr.* lā ôN′), 1872–1950, French statesman, journalist, and Socialist Party leader: premier of France 1936–37, 1938, 1946–47.

Blu·ma (blo͞o′mə), *n.* a girl's given name.

blun·der (blun′dər), *n.* **1.** a gross, stupid, or careless mistake: *That's your second blunder this morning.* —*v.i.* **2.** to move or act blindly, stupidly, or without direction or steady guidance: *Without my glasses I blundered into the wrong room.* **3.** to make a gross or stupid mistake, esp. through carelessness or mental confusion: *Just pray that he doesn't blunder again and get the names wrong.* —*v.t.* **4.** to bungle; botch: *Several of the accounts were blundered by that new assistant.* **5.** to utter thoughtlessly; blurt out: *He blundered his surprise at her winning the award.* [ME *blunder(en), blondre(n)* < Scand; cf. dial. Norw *blundra* to behave as if blind, akin to Icel *blunda* to keep the eyes shut. See BLIND] —**blun′der·er,** *n.* —**blun′der·ful,** *adj.* —**blun′der·ing·ly,** *adv.* —**Syn. 1.** error. See **mistake.**

blun·der·buss (blun′dər bus′), *n.* **1.** a short musket of wide bore with expanded muzzle to scatter shot, bullets, or slugs at close range. **2.** a stupid, blundering person. [< D *donderbus* (*donder* thunder + *bus* gun) with *donder* replaced by BLUNDER. See HARQUEBUS]

blunge (blunj), *v.t.,* **blunged, blung·ing.** to mix (clay or the like) with water, forming a liquid suspension. [BL(END + PL)UNGE]

blung·er (blun′jər), *n.* **1.** a large container with rotating arms for mechanical mixing. **2.** one who blunges. [BLUNGE + -ER¹]

blunt (blunt), *adj.* **1.** having an obtuse, thick, or dull edge or point; rounded; not sharp: *a blunt pencil.* **2.** abrupt in address or manner: *a blunt, ill-timed question.* **3.** slow in perception or understanding; dull: *His isolation has made him blunt about the feelings of others.* —*v.t.* **4.** to make blunt: *a knife blunt from use.* **5.** to weaken or impair the force, keenness, or susceptibility of: *Wine first excites, then blunts the imagination.* —*n.* **6.** something blunt, as a small-game arrow, a short sewing needle, or a short, thick cigar. [ME; perh. akin to BLIND] —**blunt′ly,** *adv.* —**blunt′ness,** *n.*
—**Syn. 1.** See **dull. 2.** short, obtuse, gruff, rough, rude, difficult, uncivil, impolite. BLUNT, BLUFF, BRUSQUE, CURT characterize manners and speech. BLUNT suggests lack of polish and of regard for the feelings of others: *blunt and tactless.* BLUFF implies an unintentional roughness together with so much good-natured heartiness that others rarely take offense: *a bluff sea captain.* BRUSQUE connotes sharpness and abruptness of speech or manner: *a brusque denial.* CURT applies esp. to disconcertingly concise language: *a curt reply.* **3.** dimwitted, thick, stolid. **4.** dull. **5.** numb, stupefy.

blur (blûr), *v.,* **blurred, blur·ring,** *n.* —*v.t.* **1.** to obscure or sully (something) as by smearing with ink; stain: *The windows were blurred with soot.* **2.** to obscure by making confused in form or outline; make indistinct: *The fog blurred the outline of the car.* **3.** to dim the perception or susceptibility of; make dull or insensible: *The blow on the head blurred his senses.* —*v.i.* **4.** to become indistinct: *Everything blurred as he ran.* **5.** to make blurs. —*n.* **6.** a smudge or smear which obscures: *a blur of smoke.* **7.** a blurred condition; indistinctness: *They could see nothing in the foggy blur.* **8.** something seen indistinctly: *The ship appeared as a blur against the horizon.* [? akin to BLEAR] —**blur·red·ly** (blûr′id lē, blûrd′-), *adv.* —**blur′red·ness,** *n.* —**blur′ry,** *adj.*

blurb (blûrb), *n.* **1.** a brief advertisement or announcement, esp. a laudatory one: *He wrote a good blurb for his friend's novel.* —*v.t.* **2.** to advertise or praise in the manner of a blurb. [coined by F. G. Burgess (1866–1951), American humorist and artist] —**blurb′ist,** *n.*

blurt (blûrt), *v.t.* **1.** to utter suddenly or inadvertently; divulge unadvisedly (usually fol. by *out*): *He blurted out the hiding place of the spy.* —*n.* **2.** an abrupt utterance. [appar. imit.]

blush (blush), *v.i.* **1.** (of a person) to redden, as from embarrassment or shame: *He blushed when they called him a sissy.* **2.** to feel shame at or for: *Your behavior makes me blush for your poor mother.* **3.** (of the sky, flowers, etc.) to become rosy. **4.** (of new house paint or lacquer) to become cloudy or dull through moisture or excessive evaporation of solvents. —*v.t.* **5.** to make red; flush. **6.** to make known by a blush: *She could not help blushing the truth.* —*n.* **7.** a reddening, as of the face. **8.** rosy or pinkish tinge. **9. at first blush,** without previous knowledge; at first glance: *At first blush, the solution to the problem seemed simple enough.* [ME *blusche(n)* (v.), OE *blyscan* to redden; akin to OE *blysa,* Icel *blys,* MLG *blus* torch, *bloschen* to blaze] —**blush′er,** *n.* —**blush′ful,** *adj.* —**blush′ful·ly,** *adv.* —**blush′ful·ness,** *n.* —**blush′ing·ly,** *adv.* —**blush′less,** *adj.*

blus·ter (blus′tər), *v.i.* **1.** to roar and be tumultuous, as wind. **2.** to be loud, noisy, or swaggering; utter loud, empty menaces or protests: *He blusters but does nothing.* —*v.t.* **3.** to force or accomplish by blustering: *He blustered his way through the crowd.* —*n.* **4.** boisterous noise and violence: *the bluster of the streets.* **5.** noisy, empty menaces or protests; inflated talk: *bluff and bluster.* [perh. < LG *bluster(n), blüstern* to blow violently; cf. Icel *blāstr* blowing, hissing] —**blus′ter·er,** *n.* —**blus′ter·ing·ly,** *adv.* —**blus′ter·y, blus′ter·ous,** *adj.* —**blus′ter·ous·ly,** *adv.*

blvd., boulevard.

-bly, var. of **-ably:** *solubly.* Also, **-ibly.** [-B(LE) + -LY]

blype (blīp), *n.* *Scot.* a thin skin or membrane, esp. a small piece of skin. [?]

Blythe (blīth *or, for 2,* blīth), *n.* **1.** a town in SE California. 6023 (1960). **2.** Also, **Blithe.** a girl's given name.

Blythe·ville (blīth′vil), *n.* a city in NE Arkansas. 20,797 (1960).

BM, *Informal.* bowel movement.

B.M., 1. Bachelor of Medicine. **2.** Bachelor of Music. **3.** British Museum.

B.Mar.E., Bachelor of Marine Engineering.

B.M.E., 1. Bachelor of Mechanical Engineering. **2.** Bachelor of Mining Engineering. **3.** Bachelor of Music Education.

B.M.Ed., Bachelor of Music Education.

B. Met., Bachelor of Metallurgy.

B.Met.E., Bachelor of Metallurgical Engineering.

BMEWS (bē myo͞oz′), *n.* *U.S. Mil.* Ballistic Missile Early Warning System.

B.Mgt.E., Bachelor of Management Engineering.

B.Min.E., Bachelor of Mining Engineering.

B.M.R., basal metabolic rate.

B.M.S., Bachelor of Marine Science.

B.M.T., Bachelor of Medical Technology.

B.Mus., Bachelor of Music.

B.M.V., Blessed Mary the Virgin. [< L *Beāta Maria Virgō*]

Bn., 1. Baron. **2.** Battalion.

bn., battalion.

B.N., Bachelor of Nursing.

B'nai B'rith (bə nā′ brith′), an international Jewish organization, founded in New York City in 1843, which institutes and administers programs designed to promote the social, educational, and cultural betterment of Jews and of the public at large. [< Heb *bĕnē bĕrīth* sons of the covenant]

B.N.S. Bachelor of Naval Science.

B/o, *Accounting.* brought over.

B.O., 1. Board of Ordnance. **2.** *Informal.* body odor. **3.** *Theat.* box office.

b.o., 1. back order. **2.** bad order. **3.** box office. **4.** branch office. **5.** broker's order. **6.** buyer's option.

bo·a (bō′ə), *n., pl.* **bo·as. 1.** any of several nonvenomous, chiefly tropical constrictors of the family *Boidae,* having vestigial hind limbs at the base of the tail. **2.** a stole of feathers, fur, silk, or the like. [< NL, L: water adder]

Bo·ab·dil (bō′äb dil; *Sp.* bō′äb dēl′), *n.* (*abu-Abdallah*) ("*El Chico*"), died 1533?, last Moorish king of Granada 1482–83, 1486–92.

bo′a constric′tor, 1. a boa, *Constrictor constrictor,* of tropical America, noted for its size and ability to crush its prey in its coils. **2.** any large snake of the boa family, such as the python or anaconda.

Boa constrictor (Length 10 ft.)

Bo·ad·i·ce·a (bō′ad i sē′ə), *n.* died A.D. 62, queen of the Iceni: leader of an unsuccessful revolt against the Romans in Britain.

Bo·a·ner·ges (bō′ə nûr′jēz), *n.* **1.** a surname given by Jesus to James and John. Mark 3:17. **2.** (*construed as sing.*) a vociferous preacher or orator. [< LL < Gk << Heb *bĕnē regesh* sons of thunder]

boar (bōr, bôr), *n.* **1.** the uncastrated male of swine. **2.** See **wild boar.** [ME *boor,* OE *bār;* c. D *beer,* G *Bär*]

board (bōrd, bôrd), *n.* **1.** a piece of timber sawed thin, and of considerable length and breadth compared with the thickness. **2.** a flat slab of wood for some specific purpose: *a cutting board.* **3.** a sheet of wood, paper, etc., with or without markings, for some special use: *a board for checkers.* **4. boards, a.** *Theat.* the stage: *The play will go on the boards next week.* **b.** the wooden fence surrounding the playing area of an ice-hockey rink. **c.** a racing course made of wood, used esp. in track meets held indoors: *his first time running on boards.* **5.** stiff cardboard or other material covered with paper, cloth, or the like, to form the covers for a book. **6.** *Building Trades.* composition material made in large sheets, as plasterboard, corkboard, etc. **7.** a table, esp. to serve food on. **8.** daily meals, esp. as provided for pay: *ten dollars a day for room and board.* **9.** an official group of persons who direct or supervise some activity: *a board of directors.* **10.** *Naut.* **a.** the side of a ship. **b.** one leg, or tack, of the course of a ship beating to windward. **11.** *Railroads.* a fixed signal or permanent sign regulating traffic. **12.** a flat surface, as a wall or an object of rectangular shape, on which something is posted, as notices or stock-market quotations: *a bulletin board.* **13.** *Computer Technol.* plugboard (def. 2). **14.** *Informal.* a switchboard. **15.** *Australian.* **a.** the area of a woolshed where shearing is done. **b.** a crew of shearers working in a particular woolshed. **c.** sheep about to be sheared. **16.** *Obs.* the edge, border, or side of anything. **17. across the board,** *Racing.* betting on a horse or dog to finish first, second, or third, so that any result where a selection wins, places, or shows enables the bettor to collect. **18. go by the board, a.** to go over the ship's side. **b.** to be destroyed, neglected, or forgotten: *All his devoted labor went by the board.* **19. on board, a.** on or in a ship, plane, or other vehicle: *There were several movie stars traveling incognito on board the plane.* **b.** *Baseball Slang.* on base: *There were two men on board as the next batter came up.* Also, **aboard. 20. on the boards,** in the theatrical profession: *The family has been on the boards since grandfather's time.* **21. tread the boards.** See **tread** (def. 11). —*v.t.* **22.** to cover or close with boards (often fol. by *up* or *over*): *to board up a house; to board over a well.* **23.** to furnish with meals, or with meals and lodging, esp. for pay: *They boarded him for $20 a week.* **24.** to go on board of or enter (a ship, train, etc.). **25.** to come up alongside of (a ship), as to attack or to go on board: *The pirate ship boarded the clipper.* **26.** *Obs.* to approach; accost. —*v.i.* **27.** to take one's meals, or be supplied with food and lodging at a fixed price: *Several of us board at the same rooming house.* **28.** *Ice Hockey.* to hit an opposing player with sufficient force to throw him against the boards while bodychecking. [ME, OE *bord* board, table, shield; c. D *boord* board, *bord* plate, G *Bort,* Icel *borth,* Goth *-baurd*] —**board′a·ble,** *adj.* —**board′like′,** *adj.*

board′ and bat′ten, *Carpentry.* a siding consisting of wide boards or of sheets of plywood set vertically with butt joints covered by battens. See illus. under **siding.**

board′ chair′man. See **chairman of the board.**

board′ check′, *Ice Hockey.* a body check in which the opponent is thrown against the wooden wall enclosing the rink. Cf. **check** (def. 41).

board·er (bôr′dər, bōr′-), *n.* **1.** a person, esp. a lodger, who is supplied with regular meals. **2.** a person chosen to board an enemy ship. [BOARD + -ER[1]]

board′ foot′, a unit of measure equal to the cubic contents of a piece of lumber one foot square and one inch thick, used in measuring logs and lumber.

board′ game′, a game, such as checkers or chess, played on a board and requiring the moving of pieces from one section of the board to another.

board·ing (bôr′ding, bōr′-), *n.* **1.** wooden boards collectively. **2.** a structure of boards, as in a fence or a floor. **3.** act of one who boards a ship, train, airplane, or the like: *an uneventful boarding.* [BOARD + -ING[1]]

board·ing·house (bôr′ding hous′, bōr′-), *n., pl.* **-hous·es** (-hou′ziz). a house at which board, or board and lodging, may be obtained for payment. Also, **board′ing house′.**

board′ing school′, a school at which board and lodging are furnished for the pupils (distinguished from *day school*).

board′ meas′ure, *Building Trades.* a system of cubic measure in which the unit is the board foot.

board′ of commis′sioners, *U.S.* the administrative body of a county in many States, esp. in the South and the West, having from two to seven elected members. Cf. **board of supervisors.**

board′ of educa′tion, **1.** a board having control over a school system. **2.** *U.S.* an appointive or elective body that directs and administers chiefly the primary and secondary public schools in a town, city, county, or State.

board′ of elec′tions, *U.S. Politics.* a bipartisan board appointed usually by local authorities and charged with control of elections and voting procedure. Also called **election board.**

board′ of es′timate, *U.S.* a special organ of a municipal government, as of New York, composed of the mayor, the president of the city council, and the controller, and charged with approving the city's budget and fiscal matters.

board′ of health′, a government department concerned with public health.

board′ of su′pervisors, *U.S.* the governing body of a county in many States, esp. in the Midwest and the East, consisting of from 15 to 100 members elected from towns, townships, cities, or wards. Cf. **board of commissioners.**

board′ of trade′, **1.** a businessmen's association. **2.** (*cap.*) (in England) the national ministry that supervises and encourages commerce and industry.

board′ room′, **1.** a room in a business office set aside for meetings of the board of directors. **2.** a room in a broker's office where stock-market quotations are listed on a board or by other means.

board′ rule′, a measuring device having scales for finding the cubic contents of a board without calculation.

board′ school′, (in Britain) a school maintained at public expense for the free education of the youth of a district and under the administration of a school board according to the Elementary Education Act of 1870.

board′ side′, the broad side of a piece of lumber.

board·walk (bôrd′wôk′, bōrd′-), *n.* **1.** *U.S.* a promenade made of wooden boards, usually along a beach or shore: *the boardwalk at Atlantic City.* **2.** any walk made of boards or planks. [BOARD + WALK]

boar·fish (bôr′fish′, bōr′-), *n., pl.* (*esp. collectively*) **-fish,** (*esp. referring to two or more kinds or species*) **-fish·es.** any of several fishes having a projecting snout, esp. a small, spiny-rayed, European fish, *Capros aper.* [BOAR + FISH]

boar·hound (bôr′hound′, bōr′-), *n.* any of various large dogs, esp. a Great Dane, used originally for hunting wild boars. [BOAR + HOUND[1]]

boar·ish (bôr′ish, bōr′-), *adj.* swinish; sensual; cruel. [BOAR + -ISH[1]] —**boar′ish·ly,** *adv.* —**boar′ish·ness,** *n.*

boart (bôrt), *n.* bort.

Bo·as (bō′az), *n.* **Franz** (frānts), 1858–1942, U.S. ethnologist, born in Germany.

boast[1] (bōst), *v.i.* **1.** to speak with exaggeration and pride, esp. about oneself. **2.** to speak with pride (usually fol. by *of*): *She boasted of her family's wealth.* —*v.t.* **3.** to speak of with excessive pride or vanity: *He boasts himself a genius.* **4.** to be proud in the possession of: *The town boasts a new school.* —*n.* **5.** a thing boasted of; a cause for pride: *Talent is his boast. It is his boast that he has never betrayed a friend.* **6.** exaggerated or objectionable speech; bragging: *empty boasts and threats.* [ME *bost* (n.), *bosten* (v.) < ?] —**boast′ing·ly,** *adv.* —**boast′less,** *adj.*

—**Syn. 1, 2.** BOAST, BRAG imply vocal self-praise or claims to superiority over others. BOAST usually refers to a particular ability, possession, etc., which may be one of such kind as to justify a good deal of pride: *He boasts of his ability as a singer.* BRAG, a more colloquial term, usually suggests a more ostentatious and exaggerated boasting but less well-founded: *He brags loudly of his marksmanship.* **5.** pride.

boast[2] (bōst), *v.t.* to dress or shape (stone) roughly. [?]

boast·er[1] (bō′stər), *n.* a person who boasts or brags. [BOAST[1] + -ER[1]]

boast·er[2] (bō′stər), *n.* a chisel for boasting stone. [BOAST[2] + -ER[1]]

boast·ful (bōst′fəl), *adj.* given to or characterized by boasting. [ME *bostful.* See BOAST[1], -FUL] —**boast′ful·ly,** *adv.* —**boast′ful·ness,** *n.*

boat (bōt), *n.* **1.** a vessel for transport by water, constructed to provide buoyancy by excluding water and shaped to give stability and permit propulsion. **2.** a small ship, generally for specialized use: *a fishing boat.* **3.** a small vessel carried for use by a large one, as a lifeboat: *They lowered the boats for evacuation.* **4.** a ship. **5.** a serving dish resembling a boat: *a gravy boat.* **6.** *Eccles.* a container for holding incense before it is placed in the censer. **7. in the same boat,** in the same circumstances; faced with the same problems: *The new recruits were all in the same boat.* **8. miss the boat,** *Slang.* **a.** to fail: *He missed the boat when he tried to get into college.* **b.** to miss the point of something; fail to grasp: *I missed the boat on that explanation.* —*v.i.* **9.** to go in a boat: *We boated down the Thames.* —*v.t.* **10.** to transport in a boat: *They boated us across the bay.* **11.** to remove (an oar) from the water and place it athwartships. Cf. **ship** (def. 11). [ME *boot,* OE *bāt;* c. Icel *beit*] —**boat′a·ble,** *adj.* —**boat′less,** *adj.*

boat·age (bō′tij), *n.* *Naut.* **1.** act of hauling by boat. **2.** a charge for such hauling. [BOAT + -AGE]

boat′ bed′. See **sleigh bed.**

boat·bill (bōt′bil′), *n.* a wading bird, *Cochlearius cochlearius,* of tropical America, that is related to the herons and that has a broad bill shaped like an inverted boat. Also called **boat′-billed her′on** (bōt′bild′). [BOAT + BILL[2]]

boat′ bug′, **1.** See **water boatman. 2.** backswimmer.

boat·build·er (bōt′bil′dər), *n.* one who builds boats. [BOAT + BUILDER]

boat′ deck′, *Naut.* a superstructure deck on which most of the lifeboats of a ship are stowed.

boat·el (bō tel′), *n.* *U.S.* a waterside hotel with dock space for persons who travel by private boat. Also, **botel.** [BOAT + (HOT)EL]

boat·er (bō′tər), *n.* **1.** one who boats for pleasure. **2.** a straw hat with a shallow, flat-topped crown, ribbon band, and straight brim. [BOAT + -ER[1]]

boat′ hook′, a hook mounted at the end of a pole, used to pull or push boats toward or away from a landing, to pick up a mooring, etc.

boat·house (bōt′hous′), *n., pl.* **-hous·es** (-hou′ziz). a building or shed, usually built partly over water, for sheltering a boat or boats. [BOAT + HOUSE]

boat·ing (bō′ting), *n.* **1.** the use of boats, esp. for pleasure: *He enjoyed boating and swimming.* —*adj.* **2.** pertaining to boats: *a boating fan.* [BOAT + -ING[1], -ING[2]]

boat·load (bōt′lōd′), *n.* **1.** the cargo that a vessel carries. **2.** the cargo that a vessel is capable of carrying. [BOAT + LOAD]

boat·man (bōt′mən), *n., pl.* **-men. 1.** a person skilled in the use of small craft. **2.** one who sells, rents, or works on boats. Also, **boatsman.** [BOAT + MAN[1]] —**boat′man·ship′,** *n.*

boat′ nail′, a nail with a convex head and a chisel point.

boat′ neck′, a wide, high neckline that follows the curve of the collarbone and ends in points on the shoulder seams. Also called **boat′ neck′line, bateau neck, bateau neckline.**

boat′ patch′, an oval patch for plywood, terminating in a point at each end.

boat′ peo′ple, *Informal.* Indochinese refugees (primarily ethnic Chinese) fleeing esp. from Vietnam in large numbers in the late 1970's, many by small, overcrowded, unseaworthy boats.

boats·man (bōts′mən), *n., pl.* **-men.** boatman.

boat′ spike′. See **barge spike.**

boat·swain (bō′sən; *spelling pron.* bōt′swān′), *n.* a warrant officer on a warship, or a petty officer on a merchant vessel, in charge of rigging, anchors, cables, etc. Also, **bo's'n, bosun.** [late ME *bote-swayn.* See BOAT, SWAIN]

boat′swain bird′, *Naut. Slang.* a tropic bird.

boat′swain's chair′, a seat composed of a plank suspended in a horizontal position from ropes, used by painters and other persons who work on the exteriors of buildings, ships, etc., seated at a considerable height.

boat′swain's pipe′, a high-pitched whistle used by a boatswain for giving signals. Also called **boat′swain's call′.**

boat·tail (bōt′tāl′), *n.* *Rocketry.* a cylindrical section of decreasing diameter at the rear of an aerodynamic missile, for reducing drag. [BOAT + TAIL[1]]

boat′-tailed grack′le (bōt′tāld′), a large grackle, *Cassidix mexicanus,* ranging from the southern U.S. to northern South America.

boat′ train′, a train scheduled to carry passengers to or from a certain dock: *The boat train to Paris was waiting at Cherbourg.*

boat′ truck′, *Theat. Brit.* See **scenery wagon.**

boat·wright (bōt′rīt′), *n.* a craftsman who builds wooden boats. [BOAT + WRIGHT]

boat·yard (bōt′yärd′), *n.* a yard or waterside location at which boats, small craft, and the like, are built, maintained, docked, etc. Cf. **shipyard.** [BOAT + YARD[2]]

Bo·az (bō′az), *n.* **1.** Also, *Douay Bible,* **Booz.** husband of Ruth. Ruth 2–4. **2.** a town in NE Alabama. 4654 (1960).

bob[1] (bob), *n., v.,* **bobbed, bob·bing.** —*n.* **1.** a short, jerky motion: *a bob of the head.* —*v.t.* **2.** to move quickly down and up: *to bob the head.* **3.** to indicate with such a motion: *to bob a greeting.* —*v.i.* **4.** to make a jerky motion with the head or body. **5.** to move about with jerky motions: *The ball bobbed upon the waves.* **6. bob up,** to emerge or appear, esp. unexpectedly: *A familiar face bobbed up in the crowd.* [ME *bob(ben)* (v.) to move like a bob in the wind. See BOB[2]]

bob[2] (bob), *n., v.,* **bobbed, bob·bing.** —*n.* **1.** a style of short haircut for women and children. **2.** a docked horse's tail. **3.** a small, dangling or terminal object, as the weight on a pendulum or a plumb line. **4.** a short, simple line in a verse or song, esp. a short refrain or coda. **5.** *Angling.* **a.** a knot of worms, rags, etc., on a string. **b.** a float for a fishing line. **6.** *Obs.* See **walking beam. 7.** *Scot.* a bunch, cluster, or wad, esp. a small bouquet of flowers. **8.** a bobsled or bob skate. —*v.t.* **9.** to cut short; dock: *They bobbed their hair to be in style.* —*v.i.* **10.** to try to snatch floating or dangling objects with the teeth: *to bob for apples.* **11.** *Angling.* to fish with a bob. [ME *bobbe* (n.) spray, cluster, bunch (of leaves, flowers, fruit, etc.) < ?]

bob[3] (bob), *n., v.,* **bobbed, bob·bing.** —*n.* **1.** a tap; light blow. **2.** a polishing wheel of leather, felt, or the like. —*v.t.* **3.** to tap; strike lightly. [ME *bob(ben)* (v.) (to) strike, beat, perh. imit. See BOP[2]]

bob[4] (bob), *n., pl.* **bob.** *Brit. Informal.* a shilling. [perh. from BOB]

Bob (bob), *n.* a boy's given name, form of **Robert.**

Bo·ba·dil·la (bō′vä dē′lyä, -dē′yä), *n.* **Fran·cis·co de** (frän thēs′kō de, -sēs′-), died 1502, Spanish colonial governor in the West Indies: sent Columbus back to Spain in chains.

bob·ber[1] (bob′ər), *n.* **1.** one who or that which bobs. **2.** a fishing bob. [BOB[1] + -ER[1]]

bob·ber[2] (bob′ər), *n.* a member of a bobsled team. [BOB[2] + -ER[1]]

bob·ber·y (bob′ə rē), *n., pl.* **-ber·ies.** *Informal.* a disturbance; brawl. [< Hindi *bāp re* O father!]

Bob·bie (bob′ē), *n.* **1.** a boy's given name, form of **Robert. 2.** a girl's given name. Also, **Bobby, Bobbye.**

Bob·bie·lee (bob′ē lē′), *n.* a girl's given name.

bob·bin (bob′in), *n.* **1.** a reel, cylinder, or spool upon which yarn or thread is wound, as used in spinning, machine sewing, lace-making, etc. **2.** *Elect.* **a.** a spool-like form around which a coil of insulated wire is wound to provide an inductance. **b.** the coil itself. [< MF *bobine* hank of thread, perh. BOB[2] + MF *-ine* -INE[2]]

bob′bin and fly′ frame′, a roving machine used in the final stages of converting spun cotton fiber into yarn.

Bob′bin and Joan′, the European arum, *Arum maculatum.*

bob·bi·net (bob′ə net′), *n.* a net of hexagonal mesh, made on a lace machine. [BOBBIN + NET[1]]

bob·bing (bob′ing), *n.* *Radar.* the effect on a radarscope of the fluctuation of a radar echo because of alternating interference and reinforcement of the reflected waves. [BOB[1] + -ING[1]]

bob′bin lace′, lace made by hand with bobbins of thread, the thread being twisted around pins stuck into a pattern placed on a pillow or pad. Also called **pillow lace.**

bob·ble (bob′əl), *n., v.,* **-bled, -bling.** —*n.* **1.** a repeated, jerky movement; bob. **2.** *Informal.* a momentary fumbling or juggling of a batted or thrown baseball. **3.** *U.S. Informal.* an error; mistake. —*v.t.* **4.** *Informal.* to juggle or fumble (a batted or thrown baseball) momentarily, usually resulting in an error. [BOB[1] + -LE]

bob·by (bob′ē), *n., pl.* **-bies.** *Brit. Informal.* a policeman. [special use of *Bobby,* for Sir *Robert* PEEL, who set up the Metropolitan Police system of London in 1828]

Bob·by (bob′ē), *n.* **1.** a boy's given name, form of **Robert. 2.** a girl's given name. Also, **Bobbie, Bob′bye.**

bob′by calf′, *Brit., Australian.* a calf no more than a week old that is sent to be slaughtered. [*bob* (as in BOB VEAL) + -Y[2]]

bob′by pin′, a flat, springlike metal hairpin having the prongs held close together by tension.

bob·by·socks (bob′ē soks′), *n.pl.* *Informal.* anklets, esp. as worn by teen-age girls. [*bobby* (for *bobbed,* altered by assoc. with BOBBY PIN) + SOCKS[1]]

bob·by·sox·er (bob′ē sok′sər), *n.* *Informal.* an adolescent girl, esp. during the 1940's, following youthful fads and fashions. Also, **bob′by sox′er.** [BOBBY-SOCKS + -ER[1]]

bob·cat (bob′kat′), *n., pl.* **-cats** (*esp. collectively*) **-cat.** an American wildcat, *Lynx rufus,* having a brownish coat with black spots. Also called **bay lynx.** [BOB(TAIL) + CAT[1]]

bo·bêche (bō besh′), *n.* a slightly cupped ring placed over the socket of a candleholder to catch the drippings of a candle. [< F]

Bo·bette (bo bet′), *n.* a girl's given name.

Bo·bo (bō′bō), *n.* a boy's or girl's given name.

Bo·bo-Diou·las·so (bō′bō dyōō-las′ō), *n.* a city in W Upper Volta. ab. 45,000.

bob·o·link (bob′ə lingk′), *n.* a common North American passerine songbird, *Dolichonyx oryzivorus,* which winters in South America. [short for *Bob o' Lincoln,* the bird's call as heard by speakers of English]

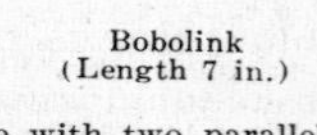

Bobolink
(Length 7 in.)

bob′ skate′, a type of ice skate with two parallel blades. [BOB(SLED) + SKATE[1]]

bob·sled (bob′sled′), *n., v.,* **-sled·ded, -sled·ding.** —*n.* **1.** a sled having two pairs of runners, a brake, and a steering wheel or other mechanism that enables the front rider to direct the sled down a steeply banked run or chute. **2.** a sled formed of two short sleds coupled one behind the other. **3.** either of the sleds thus coupled. —*v.i.* **4.** to ride on a bobsled. [BOB[2] + SLED] —**bob′sled′der,** *n.*

bob·sled·ding (bob′sled′ing), *n.* the act or sport of coasting or competing in races on a bobsled. [BOBSLED + -ING[1]]

bob·sleigh (bob′slā′), *n., v.i.* *Rare.* bobsled.

bob·stay (bob′stā′), *n.* *Naut.* a rope, chain, or rod from the outer end of the bowsprit to the cutwater. [BOB[1] + STAY[3]]

Bob's′ your un′cle, *Chiefly Brit.* a phrase used in a statement for emphasis, esp. when an unstated part is obvious: *If the boss sees you come in late, Bob's your uncle. Bob's your uncle when our team leads at the half.*

bob·tail (bob′tāl′), *n.* **1.** a short or docked tail. **2.** an animal with such a tail. —*adj.* **3.** docked; cut short. —*v.t.* **4.** to cut short the tail of; dock, often by cutting a muscle in a horse's tail to make it stand erect. [BOB[2] + TAIL[1]]

bob′ veal′, the flesh of an unborn or newborn calf, used for food. [dial. (Cornwall) *bob* young calf (from its uncertain, staggering movements; see BOB[1])]

bob·white (bob′hwīt′, -wīt′), *n.* a common North American quail, *Colinus virginianus,* having mottled reddish-brown, black, and white plumage. [from its cry, as heard by speakers of English]

bob′ wire′. See **barbed wire.** [by folk etymology]

bo·cac·cio (bō kä′chō), *n., pl.* **-cios.** a large, brown, big-mouthed rockfish, *Sebastodes paucispinis,* found in California. [< It *boccaccio* ugly mouth, equiv. to *bocc(a)* mouth (< L *bucca*) + *-accio* pejorative suffix, appar. r. an AmerSp fish-name of like formation; cf. Sp *bocacha* big mouth]

bo·cage (bō käzh′), *n.* *Fine Arts.* a decorative motif of trees, branches, or foliage, as in a tapestry or a ceramic figure group. [< F; OF *boscage* BOSCAGE]

Boc·cac·ci·o (bō kä′chē ō′, -chō, bə-; *It.* bôk kät′chō), *n.* **Gio·van·ni** (jē′ə vä′nē; *It.* jō vän′nē), 1313–75, Italian writer and poet.

Boc·che·ri·ni (bok′ə rē′nē; *It.* bôk′ke rē′nē), *n.* **Lu·i·gi** (lo͞o ē′jē), 1743–1805, Italian composer and cellist.

boc·cie (boch′ē), *n.* an Italian variety of lawn bowling played on a court that is shorter and narrower than the rink of a bowling green. Also, **boc·ci** (boch′ē; *It.* bôt′chē), **boc·ce** (boch′ē; *It.* bôt′che), **boc·cia** (boch′ə; *It.* bôt′chä). [< It *bocce* bowls, pl. of *boccia* ball]

Boc·cio·ni (bo chō′nē; *It.* bôt chô′nē), *n.* **Um·ber·to** (o͞om ber′tô), 1882–1916, Italian painter and sculptor.

Boche (bosh, bôsh), *n.* *Disparaging.* a German, esp. a German soldier in World War I. Also, **boche.** [< F, aph. var. of *Alboche* German, equiv. to *Al(lemand)* German + *(ca)boche* blockhead, head of a nail]

Bo·chum (bō′ kho͞om), *n.* a city in central North Rhine-Westphalia, in W West Germany. 361,000 (1963).

bock′ beer′ (bok), a strong, dark beer commonly brewed in the fall and aged through the winter for consumption the following spring. Also called **bock.** [< G *Bockbier,* lit., buck beer, nickname of *Eimbecker Bier* beer of Eimbeck in Lower Saxony, Germany]

bod[1] (bod), *n.* bott[2].

bod[2] (bod), *n.* *Brit. Slang.* a person: *We need a few more bods on the staff.* [short for BODY]

B.O.D., biochemical oxygen demand.

bo·da·cious (bō dā′shəs), *adj.* *South Midland and Southern U.S.* **1.** thorough; blatant; unmistakable: *a bodacious gossip.* **2.** remarkable; outstanding: *a bodacious story.* **3.** audacious; bold or brazen.

Bo·danz·ky (bō dänts′kē), *n.* **Ar·tur** (är′to͝or), 1877–1939, Austrian opera director and orchestra conductor: in the U.S. after 1915.

Bo·das de San·gre (*Sp.* bô′thäs de säng′gre). See **Blood Wedding.**

bode[1] (bōd), *v.,* **bod·ed, bod·ing.** —*v.t.* **1.** to be an omen of; portend: *The news bodes evil days for him.* **2.** *Archaic.* to announce beforehand; predict. —*v.i.* **3.** to portend: *The news bodes well for him.* [ME *bode,* OE *bodian* to announce, foretell (c. Icel *botha*), deriv. of *boda* messenger, c. G *Bote,* Icel *bothi*] —**bode′ment,** *n.*

bode[2] (bōd), *v.* a pt. of **bide.**

Bode (bōd), *n.* a ring formation in the second quadrant of the face of the moon: about 11 miles in diameter.

bo·de·ga (bō thē′gä; *Eng.* bō dē′gə), *n., pl.* **-gas** (-gäs; *Eng.* -gəz). *Spanish.* **1.** (esp. among Spanish-speaking Americans) a grocery store. **2.** a wineshop. **3.** a warehouse for wine.

bo·de·gón (bō′the gôn′; *Eng.* bō′də gōn′), *n., pl.* **-go·nes** (-gō′nes; *Eng.* gō′nēz). *Spanish.* a genre or still-life painting of a domestic subject.

Bo·den·heim (bōd′ən hīm′), *n.* **Maxwell,** 1892–1954, U.S. poet and novelist.

Bo·den See (bōd′ən zā′), German name of **Lake Constance.** Also, **Bo′den·see′.**

bodg·ie (boj′ē), *n.* *Australian.* a juvenile delinquent; youthful troublemaker. [dial. (York) *bodge* clumsy worker (see BOTCH) + -IE]

Bod·go Ge·gen (bod′gō gā′gän), a former Buddhist leader of the Mongols.

bo·dhi (bō′dē), *n.* *Buddhism.* supreme knowledge or enlightenment. [< Skt: he awakens]

Bo·dhi·dhar·ma (bō′di dur′mə), *n.* died A.D. c530, Indian Buddhist philospher and missionary: founder of Ch'an in China, which was later called Zen in Japan.

Bo·dhi·satt·va (bō′di sat′wa), *n.* *Buddhism.* one who has attained prajna, or enlightenment, but who postpones Nirvana in order to help others to attain enlightenment: individual Bodhisattvas are the subjects of devotion in certain sects and are often represented in painting and sculpture. Cf. **Arhat.** [< Skt, equiv. to *bodhi* illumination + *sattva* existence; see SOOTH]

bo′dhi tree′. See **bo tree.**

bod·ice (bod′is), *n.* **1.** a woman's cross-laced outer garment covering the waist and bust, common in peasant dress. **2.** the part of a woman's dress covering the body between the neck or shoulders and the waist. Cf. **waist** (def. 4). **3.** a woman's fitted vest or waist; that part of a dress extending from the waistline to the neckline, excluding sleeves and ornaments. **4.** *Obs.* stays or a corset.

Bodice

bod·i·less (bod′ē lis), *adj.* having no body or material form; incorporeal. [ME *bodiles.* See BODY, -LESS] —**bod′i·less·ness,** *n.*

bod·i·ly (bod′əlē), *adj.* **1.** of or pertaining to the body. **2.** corporeal or material, as contrasted to spiritual or mental. —*adv.* **3.** as a physical entity; as a complete physical unit: *The tornado picked him up bodily and threw him against the wall.* [ME *bodylich.* See BODY, -LY]

bod·ing (bō′ding), *n.* **1.** a foreboding; omen. —*adj.* **2.** foreboding; ominous. —**bod′ing·ly,** *adv.*

bod·kin (bod′kin), *n.* **1.** a small, pointed instrument for making holes in cloth, leather, etc. **2.** a long pin-shaped instrument used by women to fasten up the hair. **3.** a blunt, needlelike instrument for drawing tape, cord, etc., through a loop, hem, or the like. **4.** *Obs.* a small dagger; stiletto.

Bod·lei·an (bod lē′ən, bod′lē-), *n.* **1.** the library of Oxford University, reestablished by Sir Thomas Bodley, 1545–1613, English diplomat and scholar. —*adj.* **2.** of, pertaining to, or belonging to this library. [after Sir Thomas *Bodley;* see -AN]

Bod·ley (bod′lē), *n.* **George Frederick,** 1827–1907, English architect.

Bod·ö (bo͞o′dœ), *n.* a seaport in W Norway.

Bo·do·ni (bə dō′nē; *for 1 also It.* bô dô′nē), *n.* **1. Giam·bat·tis·ta** (jäm′bät tēs′tä), 1740–1813, Italian painter and printer. **2.** *Print.* a style of type based on a design by G. Bodoni.

bod·y (bod′ē), *n., pl.* **bod·ies,** *v.,* **bod·ied, bod·y·ing,** *adj.* —*n.* **1.** the physical structure and material substance of an animal or plant, living or dead. **2.** a corpse; carcass. **3.** the trunk or main mass of a thing: *the body of a tree.* **4.** *Zool., Anat.* the physical structure of man or an animal not including the head, limbs, and tail; trunk. **5.** *Archit.* the principal mass of a building. **6.** the boxlike shell of a vehicle, minus wheels and other appendages, in or on which passengers or the load is carried. **7.** *Naut.* the hull of a ship. **8.** *Aeron.* the fuselage of a plane. **9.** *Print.* the shank of a type, supporting the face. See diag. under **type. 10.** *Geom.* a figure having the three dimensions of length, breadth, and thickness; a solid. **11.** *Physics.* a mass, esp. one considered as a totality. **12.** the major portion of an army, population, etc.: *The body of the American people favors the president's policy.* **13.** the principal part of a speech or document, minus introduction, conclusion, indexes, etc. **14.** *Informal.* a person: *She's a quiet sort of body.* **15.** *Law.* the physical person of an individual. **16.** a collective group, or an artificial person: *student body; corporate body.* **17.** an object in space, as a planet or star. **18.** a separate physical mass or quantity, esp. as distinguished from other masses or quantities. **19.** consistency or density; richness; substance: *This wine has good body. Wool has more body than rayon.* **20.** that part of a dress which covers the trunk, or the trunk above the waist. **21.** *Ceram.* the basic material of which a ceramic article is made. **22. in a body,** as a group; together; collectively: *We left the party in a body.* **23. keep body and soul together,** to support oneself; maintain life: *Few writers can make enough to keep body and soul together without another occupation.* —*v.t.* **24.** to invest with or as with a body. **25.** to represent in bodily form (usually fol. by *forth*). —*adj.* **26.** of or pertaining to the body; bodily. **27.** of or pertaining to the main reading matter of a book, article, etc., as opposed to headings, illustrations, or the like. [ME; OE *bodig;* akin to OHG *botah*]

—**Syn. 1, 2.** BODY, CARCASS, CORPSE, CADAVER agree in referring to a physical organism, usually human or animal. BODY refers to the material organism of an individual man or animal, either living or dead: *the muscles in a horse's body; the body of a victim (man or animal).* CARCASS refers only to the dead body of an animal, unless applied humorously or contemptuously to the human body: *a sheep's carcass; Save your carcass.* CORPSE refers only to the dead body of a human being: *preparing a corpse for burial.* CADAVER refers to a dead body, usually a corpse, particularly one used for scientific study: *dissection of cadavers in anatomy classes.* **3.** substance, bulk.

bod′y blow′, *Boxing.* a blow driven to the opponent's body between the breastbone and the navel.

bod′y Brus′sels. See under **Brussels carpet.**

bod′y cav′ity, *Zool., Anat.* the space or cavity in the body of man or animals containing the viscera.

bod·y-cen·tered (bod′ē sen′tərd), *adj.* *Crystall.* (of a crystal structure) having lattice points at the centers of the unit cells. Cf. **face-centered.**

bod′y check′, *Ice Hockey.* an obstructing or impeding with the body of the movement or progress of an opponent. Cf. **check** (def. 41).

bod·y·check (bod′ē chek′), *v.t., v.i.* to give (an opponent) a body check. [v. use of BODY CHECK]

bod′y cor′porate, *Law.* a person, association, or group of persons legally incorporated; corporation.

bod′y Eng′lish, *Sports.* a twisting of the body by a player as if to help a ball already hit, rolled, or kicked to travel in the desired direction.

bod·y·guard (bod′ē gärd′), *n.* **1.** one employed to guard an individual, as a high official, from bodily harm. **2.** a retinue; escort. [BODY + GUARD]

bod′y louse′. See under **louse** (def. 2).

Bod′y of Christ′, 1. the community of believers of which Christ is the head. I Cor. 12:27. **2.** the consecrated bread of the Eucharist.

bod′y plan′, *Naval Archit.* a diagrammatic elevation of a hull, consisting of an end view of the bow on one side of the center line and an end view of the stern on the other side of the center line, marked with water lines, diagonals, bow or buttock lines, stations, and sometimes details of the hull. Cf. **half-breadth plan, sheer plan.**

bod′y pol′itic, *Political Science.* a people as forming a political body under an organized government.

bod′y post′, *Naut.* sternpost.

bod′y shop′, a factory or machine shop in which bodies for vehicles, as automobiles, trucks, or the like, are manufactured, repaired, etc.

bod′y slam′, *Wrestling.* a throw in which an opponent is lifted and hurled to the mat, landing on his back.

bod′y snatch′ing, the act of robbing a grave to obtain a subject for dissection. —**bod′y snatch′er.**

bod′y track′, the tracks of a railroad yard used for switching or sorting cars.

bod′y type′, *Print.* type used in the main text of printed matter, generally less than 14 points. Cf. **display type.**

bod·y·work (bod′ē wûrk′), *n.* **1.** the work involved in making or repairing vehicle bodies. **2.** the body of a vehicle, esp. with regard to the details or the quality of its construction. [BODY + WORK]

Bo·ece (bō ēs′), *n.* Boethius.

Bo·ë·dro·mi·us (bō′i drō′mē əs), *n.* *Class. Myth.* an epithet of Apollo, meaning "rescuer."

Boeh·me (*Ger.* bœ′mə), *n.* **Ja·kob** (*Ger.* yä′kōp). See **Böhme, Jakob.**

Boeh·men·ism (bā′mə niz′əm), *n.* the mystical doctrines or conceptions of Jakob Böhme. Also, **Behmenism.** [J. BÖHME + *-n* (as in BEHMEN) + -ISM]

Boeh·men·ist (bā′mə nist), *n.* a supporter or adherent of Boehmenism. Also, **Behmenist, Boeh′men·ite′, Behmenite, Boeh′mist.** [J. BÖHME + *-n* (as in BEHMEN) + -IST]

Boehm·i·an (bā′mē ən), *adj.* of or pertaining to Boehmenism. [J. BÖHME + -IAN]

Boehm·ite (bā′mit, bō′-), *n.* a mineral, hydrous aluminum oxide, AlO(OH), a major component of bauxite. [< G *Böhmit,* named after J. *Böhm,* 20th-century German scientist; see -ITE[1]]

Boehm′ sys′tem (bām, bōm), a system of improved fingering and keying for the flute and clarinet, invented by the German musician Theobald Boehm (1794–1881).

Boe·o·tia (bē ō′shə), *n.* a district in ancient Greece, NW of Athens. *Cap.:* Thebes.

Boe·o·tian (bē ō′shən), *adj.* **1.** of or pertaining to Boeotia or its inhabitants. **2.** dull; obtuse; without cultural refinement. —*n.* **3.** a native or inhabitant of Boeotia. **4.** a dull, obtuse person; Philistine. [BOEOTI(A) + -AN]

Boe·o·tus (bē ō′təs), *n.* *Class. Myth.* a son of Arne and Poseidon.

Boer (bōr, bôr; *Du.* bo͞or), *n.* **1.** a South African of Dutch extraction. —*adj.* **2.** of or pertaining to the Boers. [< D: peasant, countryman. See BOOR]

Boer′ War′, 1. a war in which Great Britain fought against the Transvaal and Orange Free State, 1899–1902. **2.** a war between Great Britain and the Transvaal, 1880–81.

Bo·e·thi·us (bō ē′thē əs), *n.* **A·ni·ci·us Man·li·us Sev·e·ri·nus** (ə nish′ē əs man′lē əs sev′ə rī′nəs), A.D. 475?–525?, Roman philosopher and statesman. Also, **Bo·e·tius** (bō ē′shəs). Also called **Boece.** —**Bo·e′thi·an,** *adj.*

boff (bof), *n.* **1.** *Slang.* a loud hearty laugh; belly laugh. **2.** *Theat.* **a.** a humorous line producing hearty laughter. **b.** a box-office hit. Also, **boffo, boffola.** [? *b(elly l)augh*]

bof·fin (bof′in), *n.* *Brit. Slang.* a scientist or technical expert. [?]

bof·fo (bof′ō), *n., pl.* **-fos.** *Slang.* boff. Also, **bof·fo·la** (bo fō′lə).

Bo′fors gun′ (bō′fôrz, -fôrs), **1.** a 40-millimeter automatic gun used chiefly as an antiaircraft weapon. **2.** two such guns mounted and fired together as one unit. [named after *Bofors,* Sweden, where first made]

bog (bog, bôg), *n., v.,* **bogged, bog·ging.** —*n.* **1.** wet, spongy ground, with soil composed mainly of decayed vegetable matter. **2.** an area or stretch of such ground. **3.** Usually, **bogs.** *Brit. Slang.* a privy; outhouse. —*v.t., v.i.* **4.** to sink in or as in a bog (often fol. by *down*): *We were bogged down by overwork.* [< Ir or Gael *bog(ach)* soft ground (*bog* soft + *-ach* n. suffix)] —**bog′gi·ness,** *n.* —**bog′gish, bog′gy,** *adj.*

Bo·ga·lu·sa (bō′gə lo͞o′sə), *n.* a city in SE Louisiana. 21,423 (1960).

Bo·gan (bō′gən), *n.* **Louise,** born 1897, U.S. poet.

Bo·gart (bō′gärt), *n.* **Humphrey (DeForest)** ("*Bogey*"), 1900–57, U.S. motion picture actor.

bog′ as′phodel, either of two liliaceous plants, *Narthecium ossifragum* of Europe, and *N. americanum* of the U.S., growing in boggy places.

bog·bean (bog′bēn′, bôg′-), *n.* See **buck bean.** [BOG + BEAN]

bo·gey (bō′gē), *n., pl.* **-geys,** *v.,* **-geyed, -gey·ing.** —*n.* **1.** bogy. **2.** *Golf.* **a.** a score of one stroke over par on a hole. **b.** par (def. 4). **3.** *Australian.* a swim. —*v.t.* **4.** *Golf.* to make a bogey on (a hole): *Arnold Palmer bogeyed the 18th hole.* [sp. var. of BOGY]

bo·gey-hole (bō′gē hōl′), *n.* *Australian.* a swimming hole.

bog·gle[1] (bog′əl), *v.,* **-gled, -gling,** *n.* —*v.i.* **1.** to take alarm; start with fright. **2.** to hesitate or scruple; waver; shrink. **3.** to dissemble; equivocate. **4.** to be awkward; bungle. —*v.t.* **5.** to astound; shock; stagger: *The distance of a light-year boggles the imagination.* —*n.* **6.** the act of shying or taking alarm. **7.** a scruple; demur; hesitation. **8.** bungle; botch. [? from BOGGLE[2]] —**bog′gler,** *n.* —**bog′gling·ly,** *adv.*

bog·gle[2] (bog′əl), *n.* bogle.

Bo·ghaz·köy (bō′gäz kœ′ē, -koi′), *n.* a village in N central Turkey: site of the ancient Hittite city of Hattusas. Also, **Bo·ghaz·keu·i** (bō′gäz kœ′ē).

bog′head coal′ (bog′hed′), compact bituminous coal that burns brightly and yields large quantities of tar and oil upon distillation. [named after *Boghead,* Scotland]

bo·gie (bō′gē), *n.* **1.** bogy. **2.** *Auto.* (on a truck) a rear wheel assembly composed of four wheels on two axles, either or both driving axles, so mounted as to support the rear of the truck body jointly. **3.** *Chiefly Brit.* a trunk under a locomotive or railroad car, sliding from side to side or rotating about a central pivot. **4.** *Brit. Informal.* **a.** any low, strong, four-wheeled cart or truck, as one used by masons to move stones. **b.** truck[1] (def. 4). [?]

bog′-i·ron ore′ (bog′ī′ərn), limonite.

bo·gle (bō′gəl, bog′əl), *n.* a bogy; specter. Also, **boggle.** [*bog* (var. of BUG bugbear) + -LE]

bog′ myr′tle. See **sweet gale.**

bog′ oak′, oak or other wood preserved in peat bogs.

Bog·o·mil (bog′ə mil), *n.* a member of a dualistic sect, flourishing chiefly in Bulgaria in the Middle Ages, which rejected most of the Old Testament and which was strongly anticlerical in polity. Also, **Bog·o·mile** (bog′ə mīl′). [< Russ; named after *Bogomilu,* 10th-century Bulgarian priest who founded the sect] —**Bog′o·mil′i·an,** *adj.* —**Bog′o·mil·ism,** *n.*

Bo·gor (bō′gôr), *n.* a city on W Java, in Indonesia. 146,907 (est. 1961). Former Dutch name, **Buitenzorg.**

Bo·go·ta (bə gō′tə), *n.* a town in NE New Jersey, 7965 (1960).

Bo·go·tá (bō′gə tä′; *Sp.* bô′gô tä′), *n.* a city in and the capital of Colombia, in the central part. 1,256,640 (est. 1961).

bog′ spav′in, *Vet. Pathol.* See under **spavin** (def. 1).

bog·trot·ter (bog′trot′ər, bôg′-), *n.* **1.** one who lives among bogs. **2.** *Disparaging.* a rural Irishman. [BOG + TROTTER]

bogue (bōg), *v.i.,* **bogued, bogu·ing.** *Naut.* (of a sailing vessel) to tend to fall off from the wind. [? akin to dial. *bog* to move off]

bo·gus (bō′gəs), *adj.* **1.** *U.S.* counterfeit; spurious; sham. —*n.* **2.** *Print., Journ.* matter set, by union requirement, by a compositor and later discarded, duplicating the text of an advertisement for which a plate has been supplied or type set by another publisher. [orig. an apparatus for coining false money; ? akin to BOGIE]

Bo·gu·slaw·sky (bō′gə släf′skē), *n.* a walled plain in the fourth quadrant of the face of the moon: about 60 miles in diameter.

bog′ vi′olet, an herb, *Pinguicula vulgaris,* of the Northern Hemisphere, having violet-blue flowers. Also called **sheepweed.**

bo·gy (bō′gē), *n., pl.* **-gies. 1.** a hobgoblin; evil spirit. **2.** anything that haunts, frightens, annoys or harasses. **3.** *Mil. Slang.* an unidentified or unrecognized aircraft. Also, **bogey, bogie.** [*bog,* var. of BUG (n.) + -Y[2]]

Bo·hea (bō hē′), *n.* an inferior grade of black tea. [< dial. Chin (Fukien) *Bu-i* for Mandarin *Wu-i* hilly district where this tea was grown]

Bo·hème, La (*Fr.* LA bô em′). See **La Bohème.**

Bo·he·mi·a (bō hē′mē ə, -hēm′yə), *n.* **1.** Czech, **Čechy.** a region in W Czechoslovakia: formerly in Austria; a part of Bohemia-Moravia 1939–45. 6,072,744 (est. 1963); 20,101 sq. mi. 2. a district inhabited by persons whose behavior is characterized by a disregard for conventional rules. 3. the social circles where such behavior is prevalent.

Bo·he·mi·a-Mo·ra·vi·a (bō hē′mē ə mō rā′vē ə, -mô-, bō hēm′yə-), *n.* a former German protectorate including Bohemia and Moravia, 1939–45.

Bo·he·mi·an (bō hē′mē ən, -hēm′yən), *n.* **1.** a native or inhabitant of Bohemia. **2.** *Archaic.* the Czech language. **3.** (*often l.c.*) a person with real or pretended artistic or intellectual aspirations who lives and acts with disregard for conventional rules of behavior. **4.** a Gypsy. **—***adj.* **5.** of or pertaining to Bohemia, its people, or their language. **6.** (*often l.c.*) pertaining to or characteristic of persons with real or pretended artistic or intellectual aspirations who live and act with disregard for conventional rules of behavior. **7.** living a wandering or vagabond life, as a Gypsy. [BOHEMI(A) + -AN] **—Bo·he′mi·an·ism,** *n.*

Bohe′mian Breth′ren, a Christian denomination formed in Bohemia in 1467 from various Hussite groups, reorganized in 1722 as the Moravian Church.

Bohe′mian For′est, a wooded mountain range in central Europe, on the boundary between the SW Czech Republic and SE Germany. Highest peak, Arber, 4780 ft. German, Böhmerwald.

Bohe′mian ru′by, *Jewelry.* a variety of rose quartz used as a gem: not a true ruby.

Bohe′mian wax′wing. See under **waxwing.**

Boh·len (bō′lin), *n.* **Charles Eus·tis** (yōō′stis), born 1904, U.S. diplomat.

Böhm (bœm), *n.* **1. Do·mi·ni·kus** (dō mē′nē kōōs′), born 1880, German architect. **2. Karl,** born 1894, Austrian opera conductor. **3. Ja·kop** (yä′kōp). See **Böhme, Jakop.**

Böh·me (bœ′mə), *n.* **Ja·kob** (yä′kōp), 1575–1624, German theosophist and mystic. Also, **Behmen, Boehme, Böhm.**

Böh·mer·wald (bœ′mər vält′), *n.* German name of **Bohemian Forest.**

Boh·nen·ber·ger (bō′nən bûr′gər), *n.* a walled plain in the fourth quadrant of the face of the moon: about 22 miles in diameter.

Bo·hol (bō hôl′), *n.* an island in the central Philippines. 680,870 (est. 1960); 1492 sq. mi.

bo·hor·ok (bō hôr′ok), *n.* (in northern Sumatra) a dry, warm wind blowing from May to September. [< Malay]

Bohr (bōr, bôr), *n.* **Niels Hen·rik Dav·id** (nēls hen′rēk dav′id), 1885–1962, Danish physicist: Nobel prize 1922.

Bohr′ at′om, *Physics.* a model of the hydrogen atom, proposed by Niels Bohr, in which a nucleus containing a single proton has one electron moving about it. Cf. **Bohr theory.**

Bohr′ mag′neton, *Physics.* a unit that is used to indicate the magnetic moment of the electron structure in an atom, equal to 9.27×10^{-21} erg/gauss. Also called **electronic Bohr magneton.** [named after N. BOHR]

Bohr′ the′ory, *Physics.* a theory of atomic structure derived from observations of the emission by the hydrogen atom of electromagnetic radiation and generalized to atoms of other elements from the hypotheses that the hydrogen atom consists of a nucleus containing a single proton with a single electron moving in a nearly circular orbit about it, that the possible energy states in which the atom may appear are quantized, and that radiation is emitted when the atom moves from one energy state to a lower energy state. [named after N. BOHR]

bo·hunk (bō′hungk′), *n.* *Disparaging.* an unskilled or semiskilled foreign-born laborer, esp. from east central or southeastern Europe. Cf. **hunky**[2]. [Bo(HEMIAN) + HUNG(ARIAN), with devoicing of the *-g-*]

Bo·iar·do (boi är′dō; *It.* bô yär′dô), *n.* **Mat·te·o Ma·ri·a** (mä tā′ō mə rē′ə; *It.* mät te′ô mä rē′ä), 1434–94, Italian poet. Also, **Bojardo.**

Boi·el·dieu (bwa el dyœ′), *n.* **Fran·çois A·dri·en** (frän swa′ a drē an′), 1775–1834, French composer.

boil[1] (boil), *v.i.* **1.** to change from a liquid to a gaseous state, producing bubbles of gas that rise to the surface of the liquid, agitating it as they rise. **2.** to reach or be brought to the boiling point: *When the water boils, add the meat and cabbage.* **3.** to be in a similarly agitated state: *The sea boiled in the storm.* **4.** to be agitated by angry feeling: *She was boiling when he arrived late.* **5.** to contain, or be contained in, a liquid that boils: *The kettle is boiling. The vegetables are boiling.* **—***v.t.* **6.** to cause to boil or to bring to the boiling point: *Boil two cups of water.* **7.** to cook (something) in boiling water: *to boil eggs.* **8.** to separate (sugar, salt, etc.) from a solution containing it by boiling off the liquid. **9.** *Metall.* to oxidize and remove the impurities from (molten tin) by stirring it with poles of green wood so that it seethes. **10. boil down, a.** to reduce the quantity of something by boiling off some of its liquid. **b.** to shorten; abridge. **c.** to point; indicate, esp. as a final judgment or analysis: *It all boils down to a clear case of murder.* **11. boil off,** *Textiles.* **a.** to degum (silk). **b.** to remove (the size and impurities) from a fabric by subjecting it to a hot scouring solution. **12. boil over, a.** to overflow while boiling or as if while boiling; burst forth; erupt. **b.** to be unable to repress excitement, anger, etc.: *Any mention of the incident makes her boil over.* **—***n.* **13.** the act or an instance of boiling. **14.** the state or condition of boiling: *She brought a cup of water to a boil.* **15.** an area of agitated, swirling, bubbling water, as part of a rapids. **16.** Also called **blow.** an unwanted flow of water and solid matter into an excavation, due to excessive outside water pressure. [ME *boill(en)* < OF *boill(ir)* < L *bullire,* equiv. to *bull(a)* bubble + *-ī-* thematic vowel + *-re* inf. suffix] **—boil′a·ble,** *adj.* **—boil′ing·ly,** *adv.*

—Syn. 3. foam, churn, froth. **4.** rage. BOIL, SEETHE, SIMMER, STEW are used figuratively to refer to agitated states of emotion. To BOIL suggests the state of being very hot with anger or rage: *Rage made his blood boil.* To SEETHE is to be deeply stirred, violently agitated, or greatly excited: *A mind seething with conflicting ideas.* To SIMMER means to be on the point of bursting out or boiling over: *to simmer with curiosity, with anger.* To STEW is informal for to worry, to be in a restless state of anxiety and excitement: *to stew about (or over) one's troubles.*

boil[2] (boil), *n.* *Pathol.* a painful, suppurating, inflammatory sore forming a central core, caused by microbic infection. Also called **furuncle.** [ME *bile, bule,* OE *byle;* c. G *Beule* boil, hump, akin to Icel *beyla* hump, swelling]

Boi·leau-Des·pré·aux (bwa lō′dā prā ō′), *n.* **Ni·co·las** (nē kô lä′), 1636–1711, French critic and poet.

boiled (boild), *adj.* *Slang.* drunk. [BOIL[1] + -ED[2]]

boiled′ din′ner, a meal of meat and vegetables, as of corned beef, cabbage, and potatoes, prepared by boiling. Also called **New England boiled dinner.**

boiled′ dress′ing, a cooked dressing thickened with egg yolks and often containing mustard, served with various kinds of salads.

boiled′ oil′, *Chem.* any oil, as linseed oil, heated together with driers to improve its drying properties.

boiled′ shirt′, *Slang.* a man's formal or semiformal dress shirt with a starched front.

boiled′ sweet′, *Brit.* a hard candy.

boil·er (boi′lər), *n.* **1.** a closed vessel or arrangement of vessels and tubes, together with a furnace or other heat source, in which steam or other vapor is generated from water to drive turbines or engines, supply heat, process certain materials, etc. Cf. **fire-tube boiler, water-tube boiler. 2.** a vessel, as a kettle, for boiling or heating. **3.** *Brit.* a large tub in which laundry is boiled or sterilized. **4.** a tank in which water is heated and stored, as for supplying hot water. [BOIL[1] + -ER[1]] **—boil′er·less,** *adj.*

boil′er horse′power, a unit of measurement of the ability of a boiler to evaporate water, usually given as the ability to evaporate 34½ lbs. of water an hour, into dry saturated steam from and at 212° F.

boil·er·mak·er (boi′lər mā′kər), *n.* **1.** a person employed to make and repair boilers or other heavy metal items. **2.** whiskey with beer as a chaser. [BOILER + MAKER]

boil′er plate′, 1. plating of iron or steel for making the shells of boilers, covering the hulls of ships, etc. **2.** *Journalism.* syndicated copy in the form of stereotype plates, used esp. by weekly newspapers.

boil′er room′, 1. a room in a building, ship, etc., that houses one or more steam boilers. **2.** *Slang.* a place where illicit brokers engage in high-pressure peddling, over the telephone, of securities of a highly speculative nature or of dubious value.

boil′ing point′, *Physical Chem.* the temperature at which the vapor pressure of a liquid is equal to the pressure of the atmosphere on the liquid, equal to 212°F or 100°C for water at sea level.

boil′ing stone′, a small object, as a stone, marble, or porcelain chip, placed in boiling liquids to prevent bumping. Also called **boil′ing chip′.**

boil-off (boil′ôf′, -of′), *n.* **1.** *Rocketry Slang.* any vapor loss from the oxidizer or fuel in a rocket during countdown. **2.** *Textiles.* the process of degumming silk. [n. use of v. phrase *boil off*]

bois brû·lé (*Fr.* bwä bry lā′), *pl.* **bois brû·lés** (bwä bry lā′). *Canadian.* an offspring or descendant of an Indian and a white Canadian, esp. a French-Canadian. [< F: lit., burnt wood]

Bois de Bou·logne (bwä′ də bōō lōn′; *Fr.* bwäd bōō lôn′yə), a park W of Paris, France. 2095 acres.

bois de vache (bwä′ də vash′), *Hist.* dried buffalo dung, used as fuel by Canadian and U.S. fur trappers in the 18th and 19th centuries. [< CanF: cow's wood]

Boi·se (boi′zē, -sē), *n.* a city in and the capital of Idaho, in the SW part: built on the site of an army post on the Oregon Trail. 34,481 (1960).

bois·e·rie (bwä zə rē′), *n.* sculptured paneling, esp. that of French architecture in the 18th century. [< F: wainscot, equiv. to *bois* wood + *-erie* -ERY]

Bois-le-Duc (bwä lə dyk′), *n.* French name of **s'Hertogenbosch.**

bois·ter·ous (boi′stər əs, -strəs), *adj.* **1.** rough and noisy; noisily jolly or rowdy; clamorous; unrestrained. **2.** (of waves, weather, wind, etc.) rough and stormy. **3.** *Obs.* rough and massive. [late ME *boistre(ou)s,* var. of ME *boistous* crude, strong, fierce, gross; by some said to be < MF *boisteux* lame] **—bois′ter·ous·ly,** *adv.* **—bois′ter·ous·ness,** *n.*

—Syn. 1. uproarious, obstreperous, roistering, loud, vociferous, impetuous. **1, 2.** tempestuous, tumultuous, turbulent, violent, wild. **—Ant. 1, 2.** calm, serene.

boîte (bwat), *n., pl.* **boîtes** (bwat). *French.* a nightclub; cabaret. Also called **boîte de nuit** (bwat də nwē′).

Bo·i·to (bô′ē tō′; *It.* bô′ē tô), *n.* **Ar·ri·go** (ə rē′gō; *It.* är rē′gô), 1842–1918, Italian opera composer, poet, and novelist.

Bo·jar·do (boi är′dō; *It.* bô yär′dô), *n.* **Mat·te·o Ma·ri·a** (mä tā′ō mə rē′ə; *It.* mät te′ô mä rē′ä). See **Boiardo, Matteo Maria.**

Boj·er (boi′ər), *n.* **Jo·han** (yō′hän; *Nor.* yō hän′), 1872–1959, Norwegian novelist and playwright.

Bok (bok), *n.* **Edward William,** 1863–1930, U.S. editor and writer, born in the Netherlands.

Bo·kha·ra (bō kär′ə; *Russ.* bōō khä′rä), *n.* Bukhara. **—Bo·kha′ran,** *adj.*

Bokha′ra clo′ver. See **white melilot.**

Bok·mål (bōōk′môl′), *n.* one of the two official norms for writing Norwegian, being the one derived from the Danish writing of urban Norwegians. Also called **Dano-Norwegian, Riksmål.** Cf. **Nynorsk.** [< Norw: book language]

bo·ko (bō′kō), *n., pl.* **-kos.** *Brit. Slang.* the nose. [?]

Bo·ko Gun·to (bô′kô gōōn′tô), Japanese name of the **Pescadores.** Also called **Bo·ko·to** (bô′kô tô′).

Bol., Bolivia.

bol., (in prescriptions) bolus.

bo·la (bō′lə), *n., pl.* **-las** (-ləz). a weapon consisting of two or more heavy balls secured to the ends of one or more strong cords, hurled by the Indians and Gauchos of southern South America to entangle the legs of cattle and other animals. Also, **bolas.** [< Sp: ball < L *bulla* bubble, ball; see BOIL[1]]

Bo·lan′ Pass′ (bō län′), a mountain pass in W West Pakistan. ab. 60 mi. long.

bo·lar (bō′lər), *adj.* of or pertaining to bole or clay. [BOLE[2] + -AR[1]]

bo·las (bō′ləs), *n., pl.* **bo·las** (bō′ləz), **bo·las·es** (bō′lə-siz). (*construed as sing.*) bola.

bold (bōld), *adj.* **1.** not hesitating in the face of actual or possible danger or rebuff; courageous and daring: *a bold hero.* **2.** not hesitating to breach the rules of propriety; forward; immodest: *He apologized for being so bold as to speak to the emperor.* **3.** necessitating courage and daring; challenging: *a bold adventure.* **4.** imaginative; beyond the usual limits of conventional thought or action: *Einstein was a bold mathematician. A difficult problem needs a bold answer.* **5.** conspicuous to the eye; flashy; showy: *a bold pattern.* **6.** steep; abrupt: *a bold promontory.* **7.** *Naut.* deep enough to be navigable close to the shore: *bold waters.* **8.** *Print.* typeset in boldface. **9.** *Obs.* trusting; assured. **10. make bold,** to venture; dare: *I made bold to offer my suggestion.* [ME *bald, bold,* OE *b(e)ald;* c. OS, OHG *bald,* D *boud* bold, OIcel *ballr* dire] **—bold′ly,** *adv.* **—bold′ness,** *n.*

—Syn. 1. fearless, courageous, brave, valiant, intrepid, daring, dauntless. **2.** BOLD, BRAZEN, FORWARD, PRESUMPTUOUS may refer to manners in a derogatory sense. BOLD suggests impudence, shamelessness, and immodesty (esp. in women): *a bold stare.* BRAZEN suggests the same, together with a defiant manner: *a brazen hussy.* FORWARD implies making oneself unduly prominent or bringing oneself to notice with too much assurance. PRESUMPTUOUS implies overconfidence, effrontery, taking too much for granted. **—Ant. 2.** modest.

bold·face (bōld′fās′), *n., adj., v.,* **-faced, -fac·ing.** *Print.* **—***n.* **1.** type that has thick, heavy lines, used for emphasis, headings, etc. **—***adj.* **2.** typeset in boldface. **—***v.t.* **3.** to mark (copy) to be set in boldface. Cf. **lightface.** [BOLD + FACE]

This is a sample of boldface

bold-faced (bōld′fāst′), *adj.* **1.** impudent; brazen: *He had the bold-faced effrontery to call her his sweetheart.* **2.** *Print.* (of type) having thick, heavy lines. **—bold-fac·ed·ly** (bōld′fā′sid lē, -fāst′-), *adv.* **—bold′-fac′ed·ness,** *n.*

bold·heart·ed (bōld′här′tid), *adj.* daring; intrepid. [BOLD + HEARTED] **—bold′heart′ed·ly,** *adv.* **—bold′-heart′ed·ness,** *n.*

bol·do (bol′dō), *n., pl.* **-dos.** a Chilean evergreen tree, *Peumus Boldus,* cultivated in California for its aromatic foliage. [< AmerSp < Araucanian *boldu*]

bole[1] (bōl), *n.* *Bot.* the stem or trunk of a tree. [ME < Scand; cf. Icel *bolr* trunk (of a tree), torso, c. G *Bohle* thick plank; see BULWARK]

bole[2] (bōl), *n.* **1.** any of a variety of soft, unctuous clays of various colors, used as pigments. **2.** a medium reddish-brown color made from such clay. Also, **bolus.** [ME *bol* < LL *bōl(us)* lump; see BOLUS]

bo·lec·tion (bō lek′shən), *n.* *Archit., Furniture.* a raised molding, esp. one having flat edges and a raised center, for framing a panel, doorway, fireplace, etc. Also, **bilection.** [?] **—bo·lec′tioned,** *adj.*

bo·le·ro (bə lâr′ō, bō-; *Sp.* bô le′rô), *n., pl.* **-le·ros** (-lâr′-ōz; *Sp.* -le′rôs). **1.** a lively Spanish dance in triple meter. **2.** the music for this dance. **3.** a jacket ending above or at the waistline, with or without collar, lapel, and sleeves, worn open in front. [< Sp]

bo·le′tic ac′id (bō lē′tik), *Chem.* See **fumaric acid.** [BOLET(US) + -IC]

bo·le·tus (bō lē′təs), *n., pl.* **-tus·es, -ti** (-tī). any mushroomlike fungus of the genus *Boletus,* having an easily separable layer of tubes on the underside of the cap or pileus. [< L < Gk *bōlítēs* a kind of mushroom, perh. equiv. to *bōl(os)* (see BOLUS) + *-ītēs* -ITE[1]]

Bol·eyn (bŏŏl′in, bŏŏ lin′), *n.* **Anne,** 1507–36, second wife of Henry VIII of England: mother of Queen Elizabeth I.

Bol·ger (bōl′jər), *n.* **Ray(mond Wallace),** born 1904, U.S. actor and dancer.

bo·lide (bō′līd, -lid), *n.* *Astron.* a large, brilliant meteor, esp. one that explodes; fireball. [< F < Gk *bolid-* (s. of *bolís*) missile]

Bol·ing·broke (bol′ing brŏŏk′; *older* bŏŏl′-), *n.* **Henry St. John** (sin′jən), **1st Viscount,** 1678–1751, British statesman, writer, and orator.

bo·li·var (bol′ə vər; *Sp.* bô lē′vär), *n., pl.* **bol·i·vars,** *Sp.* **bo·li·va·res** (bô′lē vä′res). a silver coin and monetary unit of Venezuela, equal to 100 centimos and equivalent to about .22 of a U.S. dollar. *Abbr.:* B. [< AmerSp, after Simón BOLÍVAR]

Bol·i·var (bol′ə vər), *n.* **1.** a town in central Missouri. 3512 (1960). **2.** a town in SW Tennessee. 3338 (1960).

Bol·i·var (bol′ə vər; *Sp.* bô lē′vär), *n.* **Si·món** (sī′mən; *Sp.* sē mōn′), ("*El Libertador*"), 1783–1830, Venezuelan statesman: leader of revolt of South American colonies against Spanish rule.

Bo·liv·i·a (bō liv′ē ə, bə-; *Sp.* bô lē′vyä), *n.* **1.** a republic in W South America. 3,653,000 (est. 1964); 404,388 sq. mi. *Caps.:* La Paz and Sucre. **2.** (*often l.c.*) a twill fabric made of cut pile with lines either in the warp direction or on the bias. **—Bo·liv′i·an,** *adj., n.*

bo·li·via·no (bō liv′ē ä′nō, bə-; *Sp.* bô′lē vyä′nô), *n., pl.* **-nos** (-nōz; *Sp.* -nôs). a paper money and monetary unit of Bolivia, equal to 100 centavos and equivalent to about .084 of a U.S. dollar. *Abbr.:* B. [< Sp; see BOLIVIA, -AN]

boll (bōl), *n.* *Bot.* a rounded seed vessel or pod of a plant, as of flax or cotton. [earlier sp. of BOWL[1]]

Bol·land (bol′ənd), *n.* **Jean de** (*Fr.* zhäN də) or **Jo·hann van** (*Flemish.* yō hän′ vän) or **John,** 1596–1665, Belgian Jesuit hagiographer. Also, **Bol·lan·dus** (bō lan′-dəs).

Bol·land·ist (bol′ən dist), *n.* any of the editors of the *Acta Sanctorum.* [after Jean de BOLLAND; see -IST]

bol·lard (bol′ərd), *n.* **1.** *Naut.* **a.** a thick, low post, usually of iron or steel, mounted on a wharf or the like, to which mooring lines from vessels are attached. **b.** a small post to which lines are attached. **c.** bitt. **2.** *Brit.* one of a series of short posts for excluding or diverting motor vehicles from a road, lawn, or the like. [? BOLE[1] + -ARD]

bol·lix (bol′iks), *v.t.* *Informal.* to do (something) badly; bungle (often fol. by *up*): *His interference bollixed up the whole deal.* Also, **bol′lox.** [var. of BALLOCKS]

bol·lock (bol′ək), *n.* *Naut.* a block, at the head of a topmast, through which the tye of a topsail yard is rove. [by shortening and alter. of *bullock block*]

boll′ wee′vil, a snout beetle, *Anthonomus grandis*, that attacks the bolls of cotton.

boll·worm (bōl′wûrm′), *n.* **1.** See **pink bollworm. 2.** See **corn earworm.** [BOLL + WORM]

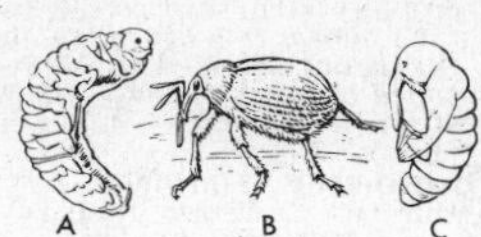

Boll weevil
A, Larva; B, Adult; C, Pupa

bo·lo[1] (bō′lō), *n., pl.* **-los.** a large, heavy, single-edged knife or machete for hacking, used in the Philippines and by the U.S. Army. [< Philippine Sp < native dial.]

bo·lo[2] (bō′lō), *n., pl.* **-los,** *v.,* **-loed, -lo·ing.** *U.S. Mil. Slang.* —*n.* **1.** a soldier who does not meet the minimum standards of marksmanship. —*v.i.* **2.** to fail to meet the minimum standards of marksmanship. [after *Bolo Pascha* (d. 1918), German agent in France during World War I]

bo·lo·gna (bə lō′nē, -nə, -lōn′yə), *n.* a large seasoned sausage made of finely ground meat, usually beef and pork, that has been cooked and smoked. Also called **bolo′gna sau′sage.** [after BOLOGNA, Italy]

Bo·lo·gna (bə lōn′yə; *It.* bô lô′nyä), *n.* **1. Gio·van·ni da** (jə̄′ə vä′nē; *It.* jô vän′nē), *(Jean de Boulogne, Giambologna)*, c1525–1608, Italian sculptor, born in France. **2.** a city in N Italy. 441,143 (1961).

Bo·lo·gnese (bō′lə nēz′, -nēs′, -lən yēz′, -yēs′), *adj., n., pl.* **-gnese.** —*adj.* **1.** of or pertaining to Bologna or its inhabitants. **2.** *Fine Arts.* noting a style or manner of painting developed in Bologna during the late 16th century by the Carracci, characterized chiefly by forms and colors derived from the Roman High Renaissance and from the Venetians. —*n.* **3.** a native or inhabitant of Bologna. [< It; see BOLOGNA, -ESE]

bo·lo·graph (bō′lə graf′, -gräf′), *n.* *Physics.* (no longer current) the record produced by the action of a bolometer. [< Gk *bol(ḗ)* ray + -o- + -GRAPH] —**bo·lo·graph·ic** (bō′lə graf′ik), *adj.* —**bo′lo·graph′i·cal·ly,** *adv.* —**bo·log·ra·phy** (bə log′rə fē), *n.*

bo·lom·e·ter (bō lom′i tər, bə-), *n.* *Physics.* a device for measuring minute amounts of radiant energy by determining the changes of resistance in an electric conductor caused by changes in its temperature. [< Gk *bol(ḗ)* ray + -o- + -METER] —**bo·lo·met·ric** (bō′lə-me′trik), *adj.* —**bo′lo·met′ri·cal·ly,** *adv.*

bo·lo·ney (bə lō′nē), *n.* baloney.

Bol·she·vik (bōl′shə vik, bol′-; *Russ.* bôl′shə vēk′), *n., pl.* **-viks, -vik·i** (-vik′ē, -vē′kē; *Russ.* -vi kē′). **1.** (in Russia) **a.** a member of the more radical majority of the Social Democratic party, 1903–17, advocating immediate and forceful seizure of power by the proletariat. **b.** (since 1918) a member of the Russian Communist party. **2.** (loosely) a member of the Communist party, esp. outside of the Soviet Union. **3.** *Derogatory.* an extreme political radical; revolutionary or anarchist. Also, **bol′she·vik.** [back formation from Russ *Bolsheviki* (pl.) Radical Socialists (now Communists), equiv. to *bolshe* greater (amount of socialization), comp. of *bolshoi* big, + *-vik* n. suffix + *-i* pl. suffix]

Bol·she·vism (bōl′shə viz′əm, bol′-), *n.* **1.** the doctrines, methods, or procedure of the Bolsheviks. **2.** *(sometimes l.c.)* the principles or practices of ultraradical socialists or political ultraradicals generally. Also, **bol′she·vism, Bol·she·vik·ism, bol·she·vik·ism** (bōl′shə vi kiz′əm, bol′-). [BOLSHEV(IK) + -ISM]

Bol·she·vist (bōl′shə vist, bol′-), *n.* **1.** a follower or advocate of the doctrines or methods of the Bolsheviks. **2.** *(sometimes l.c.)* an ultraradical socialist; any political ultraradical. —*adj.* **3.** Bolshevistic. [BOLSHEV(IK) + -IST]

Bol·she·vis·tic (bōl′shə vis′tik, bol′-), *adj.* of, pertaining to, or characteristic of Bolshevists or Bolshevism. Also, **bol′she·vis′tic.** [BOLSHEVIST + -IC] —**Bol′she·vis′ti·cal·ly, bol′she·vis′ti·cal·ly,** *adv.*

Bol·she·vize (bōl′shə vīz′, bol′-), *v.,* **-vized, -viz·ing.** —*v.t.* **1.** to bring under the influence or domination of Bolshevists; render Bolshevik or Bolshevistic. —*v.i.* **2.** to become Bolshevik or Bolshevistic; act like a Bolshevik. Also, **bol′she·vize′.** [BOLSHEV(IST) + -IZE] —**Bol′she·vi·za′tion,** *n.*

Bol·shie (bōl′shē, bol′-), *n.* *Slang.* Bolshevik. [by shortening and alter.; see -IE]

Bol·shy (bōl′shē, bol′-), *n., pl.* **-shies.** *Slang.* Bolshevik. [see BOLSHIE, -Y[2]]

bol·són (bōl sōn′; *Sp.* bôl sôn′), *n., pl.* **-sóns** (-sōnz′), *Sp.* **-só·nes** (-sô′nes). a desert valley, the level of which has been raised by aggradation: usually drains into a playa. [< Sp: big purse, equiv. to *bols(a)* purse (< ML *bursa;* see BURSA) + *-ón* aug. suffix]

bol·ster (bōl′stər), *n.* **1.** a long, often cylindrical, cushion or pillow for a bed, sofa, etc. **2.** something resembling this in form or in use as a support. **3.** any pillow, cushion, or pad. **4.** *Naut.* **a.** Also called **bol′ster plate′.** a circular casting on the side of a vessel, through which an anchor chain passes. **b.** a timber used as a temporary support. **c.** a beam for holding lines or rigging without chafing. **d.** a bag filled with buoyant material, fitted into a small boat. **5.** *Metalworking.* an anvillike support for the lower die of a drop forge. **6.** *Masonry.* a timber or the like connecting two ribs of a centering. **7.** *Carpentry.* a horizontal timber on a post for lessening the free span of a beam. **8.** a structural member on which one end of a bridge truss rests. **9.** a chisel with a blade splayed toward the edge, used for cutting bricks. —*v.t.* **10.** to support with or as with a pillow or cushion. **11.** to add to, support, or uphold (a theory, quality, belief, etc.) (sometimes fol. by *up*): *They bolstered their morale by singing. He bolstered his plea with new evidence.* [ME *bolstre,* OE *bolster;* c. Icel *bolstr,* D *bolster,* G *Polster*] —**bol′ster·er,** *n.*
—**Syn. 1.** See **cushion.**

bolt[1] (bōlt), *n.* **1.** a movable bar or rod which when slid into a socket fastens a door, gate, etc. **2.** the part of a lock which is shot from and drawn back into the case, as by the action of the key. **3.** any of several types of strong fastening rods, pins, or screws, usually threaded to receive a nut. **4.** a sudden dash, run, flight, or escape. **5.** a sudden desertion from a meeting, political party, social movement, etc. **6.** a length of woven goods, esp. as it comes on a roll from the loom. **7.** a roll of wallpaper. **8.** *Bookbinding.* the three edges of a folded sheet that must be cut so that the leaves can be opened. **9.** a rod, bar, or plate which closes the breech of a breechloading rifle, esp. a sliding rod or bar which shoves a cartridge into the firing chamber as it closes the breech. **10.** a jet of water, molten glass, etc. **11.** an arrow, esp. a short, heavy one for a crossbow. **12.** a shaft of lightning; thunderbolt. **13.** a length of timber to be cut into smaller pieces. **14.** a slice from a log, as a short, round piece of wood used for a chopping block. **15. bolt from the blue,** a sudden and entirely unforeseen event: *His flunking out of school was a bolt from the blue for his parents for they thought he studied constantly.* **16. shoot one's bolt,** *Slang.* to make a strenuous effort; do all that one can: *The lawyer shot his bolt, but his client received the death penalty.* —*v.t.* **17.** to fasten with or as with a bolt or bolts. **18.** to discontinue support of or participation in; break with: *to bolt a political party.* **19.** to shoot or discharge (a missile), as from a crossbow or catapult. **20.** to utter hastily; say impulsively; blurt out. **21.** to swallow (one's food or drink) hurriedly; eat without chewing: *He bolted his breakfast and ran to school.* **22.** to make (cloth, wallpaper, etc.) into bolts. **23.** *Fox Hunting.* (of hounds) to force (a fox) from an earth, covert, etc., into the open. —*v.i.* **24.** to make a sudden, swift dash, run, flight, or escape; spring away suddenly: *The rabbit bolted into its burrow.* **25.** *U.S.* to break away, as from one's political party. **26.** to eat hurriedly or without chewing. **27.** *Hort.* to produce flowers or seeds prematurely. —*adv.* **28.** suddenly; with sudden meeting or collision. **29. bolt upright,** stiffly upright; rigidly straight: *The announcement caused him to sit bolt upright in his chair.* [ME, OE; c. D *bout,* G *Bolz*] —**bolt′er,** *n.* —**bolt′less,** *adj.* —**bolt′like′,** *adj.*

A
B
C
Bolts (def. 3)
A, Carriage bolt
B, Machine bolt
C, Stove bolt

bolt[2] (bōlt), *v.t.* **1.** to sift through a cloth or sieve. **2.** to examine or search into, as if by sifting. [ME *bult(en)* < OF *bul(e)ter,* metathetic var. of *buteler < Gmc; cf. MHG *biuteln* to sift, deriv. of *biutel,* OHG *būtil* bag, whence G *Beutel* bolting-bag] —**bolt′er,** *n.*

bolt-ac·tion (bōlt′ak′shən), *adj.* (of a rifle) equipped with a manually operated sliding bolt.

bolt′ boat′, a boat suitable for use in rough seas.

bol·tel (bōl′tᵊl), *n.* *Archit.* **1.** Also, **boutel, boutell, bowtel, bowtell.** a convex molding, as a torus or ovolo. **2.** Also, **bottle.** a curved fractable. [late ME *boltell,* equiv. to *bolt* BOLT[1] + *-ell* n. suffix]

bolt·head (bōlt′hed′), *n.* **1.** the head of a bolt. **2.** *Chem.* (formerly) a matrass. [BOLT[1] + HEAD]

bolt′ing cloth′, a sturdy fabric, usually of fine silk or nylon mesh, used chiefly in serigraphy, embroidery, and as a foundation fabric for wigs.

Bol·ton (bōl′tᵊn), *n.* a city in S Lancashire, in NW England. 160,887 (1961).

bol·to·ni·a (bōl tō′nē ə), *n.* any asterlike, perennial herb of the genus *Boltonia,* of the U.S. [< NL; after James Bolton, 18th-century English botanist; see -IA]

bolt·rope (bōlt′rōp′), *n.* **1.** *Naut.* a rope or the cordage sewed on the edges of a sail to strengthen it. **2.** a superior grade of rope. Also, **bolt′ rope′.** [BOLT[1] + ROPE]

bolt′ strake′, *Shipbuilding.* See **binding strake** (def. 3).

Boltz·mann (bôlts′män′; *Eng.* bōlts′mən), *n.* **Lud·wig** (lo͞od′viKH, lo͞ot′-), 1844–1906, Austrian physicist.

Boltz′mann con′stant, *Physics.* the ratio of the universal gas constant to Avogadro's number, equal to 1.3803×10^{-16} erg per degree C. Also, **Boltz′mann's con′stant.** [named after L. BOLTZMANN]

bo·lus (bō′ləs), *n., pl.* **-lus·es. 1.** *Pharm., Vet. Med.* a round mass of medicinal material, larger than an ordinary pill. *Abbr.:* bol. **2.** a soft, roundish mass or lump, esp. of chewed food. **3.** bole[2]. [< LL < Gk *bōlos* clod, lump; see BOLE[2]]

Bo·lyai (bō′lyoi), *n.* **Já·nos** (yä′nōsh), 1802–60, Hungarian mathematician.

Bol·za·no (bōl tsä′nō *for 1;* bôl tsä′nô *for 2*), *n.* **1. Bern·hard** (bern′härt), 1781–1848, Austrian mathematician and theologian. **2.** German, **Bozen.** a city in NE Italy. 83,956 (1959).

Bol·za′no-Wei′er·strass the′orem (bōl zä′nō-vī′ər sträs′, bōlt sä′-), *Math.* the theorem that every bounded set with an infinite number of elements contains at least one accumulation point. [named after B. BOLZANO, and K. *Weierstrass* (1815–97), German mathematician]

Bo·ma (bō′mə), *n.* a city in the W Republic of the Congo, on the Congo River. 31,598 (est. 1958).

Bo·marc (bō′märk), *n.* *U.S.* a winged, surface-to-air interceptor missile. [*Bo(eing)* + *M(ichigan) A(eronautical) R(esearch) C(enter)*]

bomb (bom), *n.* **1.** *Mil.* a projectile, formerly usually spherical, filled with a bursting charge and exploded by means of a fuze, by impact, or otherwise, now generally designed to be dropped from an aircraft. **2.** any similar missile or explosive device used as a weapon, to disperse crowds, etc.: *a smoke bomb; a time bomb.* **3.** *Geol.* a rough spherical or ellipsoidal mass of lava, ejected from a volcano and hardened while falling. **4.** See **aerosol bomb. 5.** *Football Slang.* a long forward pass, esp. one to a teammate who scores a touchdown. **6.** *Slang.* an absolute failure; fiasco. **7.** *Jazz.* a sudden, unexpected accent or rhythmic figure played by a drummer during a performance. **8.** a lead or lead-lined container for transporting and storing radioactive materials. —*v.t.* **9.** to hurl bombs at or drop bombs upon, as from an airplane; bombard: *The enemy planes bombed the city.* **10.** to explode by means of a bomb or explosive. —*v.i.* **11.** to hurl or drop bombs. **12.** to explode a bomb or bombs. **13.** *Slang.* to be or make a complete failure, esp. to fail to please or gain an audience; flop (sometimes fol. by *out*): *His last play bombed on Broadway. The business bombed out with a $25,000 debt.* [earlier *bom(b)e* < Sp *bomba (de fuego)* ball (of fire), akin to *bombo* drum < L *bomb(us)* a booming sound < Gk *bómbos*] —**bomb′a·ble,** *adj.*

bom·ba·ca·ceous (bom′bə kā′shəs), *adj.* belonging to the *Bombacaceae,* a family of woody plants including the silk-cotton trees and the baobab. [< NL *Bombacāce(ae)* name of the family < ML *bombāc-* (s. of *bombāx* cotton, L *bombȳx* silk < Gk) + *-āceae* -ACEAE + -OUS]

bom·bard (*v.* bom bärd′; *n.* bom′bärd), *v.t.* **1.** to attack or batter with artillery fire. **2.** to attack with bombs. **3.** to assail vigorously: *to bombard someone with questions.* **4.** *Physics.* to direct high energy particles or radiations against: *to bombard a nucleus.* —*n.* **5.** the earliest kind of cannon, orig. throwing stone balls. **6.** *Obs.* a bomb ketch. **7.** an English leather tankard of the 18th century and earlier, similar to but larger than a blackjack. **8.** *Obs.* a leather jug. [ME < ML *bombard(a)* stone-throwing engine (L *bomb(us)* booming noise (see BOMB) + *-arda* -ARD)] —**bom·bard′er,** *n.* —**bom·bard′ment,** *n.*

bom·bar·dier (bom′bər dēr′), *n.* **1.** *Mil.* the member of a bombing plane crew who operates the bombsight and bomb-release mechanism. **2.** *Hist.* artilleryman. [< MF; see BOMBARD, -IER]

bom′bardier bee′tle, any ground beetle of the genus *Brachinus* which, when disturbed, ejects a volatile fluid from its abdomen with a popping sound and a puff of smoke.

bom·bar·don (bom′bər dən, bom bär′dᵊn), *n.* **1.** a bass reed stop on a pipe organ. **2.** a large, deep-toned, valved, brass wind instrument resembling a tuba. [< It *bombardon(e)* kind of trumpet, equiv. to *bombard(o)* an oboelike instrument (see BOMBARD) + *-one* aug. suffix]

bom·bast (bom′bast), *n.* **1.** pretentious words; speech too pompous for an occasion. **2.** *Obs.* cotton or other material used to stuff garments; padding. —*adj.* **3.** *Obs.* bombastic. [earlier *bombace* < MF < ML *bombāce(m),* acc. of *bombāx* cotton; see BOMBACACEOUS]

bom·bas·tic (bom bas′tik), *adj.* (of speech, writing, etc.) high-sounding; high-flown; inflated; pretentious. Also, **bom·bas′ti·cal.** [BOMBAST + -IC] —**bom·bas′ti·cal·ly,** *adv.*

Bom·bay (bom bā′), *n.* **1.** a seaport in and the capital of Maharashtra, in W India, on the Arabian Sea. 4,152,180 (1961). **2.** a former state in W India: divided in 1960 into the Gujarat and Maharashtra states.

Bom′bay duck′, 1. a small lizardfish, *Harpadon nehereus,* found in the river mouths and estuaries of Asia. **2.** (in India) the flesh of this fish, impregnated with asafetida, dried, salted, and used as a condiment or relish, esp. with curry. Also called **bummalo.**

bom·ba·zine (bom′bə zēn′, bom′bə zēn′), *n.* a twill fabric constructed of a silk or rayon warp and worsted filling, often dyed black for mourning wear. Also, **bom′ba·sine′, bom′ba·zeen′.** [earlier *bombasin* < MF < ML *bombasin(um),* var. of LL *bombȳcinum,* n. use of neut. of *bombȳcinus* silken (L *bombȳc-* (s. of *bombȳx* silk; see BOMBYCID) + *-inus* -INE[1])]

bomb′ bay′, *Aeron., Mil.* (in the fuselage of a bomber) the compartment in which bombs are carried and from which they are dropped.

bombe (bom, bomb; *Fr.* bôNb), *n., pl.* **bombes** (bomz, bombz; *Fr.* bôNb). a round or melon-shaped frozen mold made from a combination of ice creams, mousses, or ices. [< F: lit., BOMB, i.e., ball, from its shape]

bom·bé (bom bā′; *Fr.* bôN bā′), *adj.* *Furniture.* curving or swelling outward. Also, **bombed.** Cf. **swell front.** [< F: lit., rounded like a bomb (*bombe* BOMB + *-é* adj. suffix < L *-ātus* -ATE[1])]

Bombé desk
(Massachusetts, 1765)

bomb·er (bom′ər), *n.* *Mil.* an airplane equipped to carry and drop bombs. [BOMB + -ER[1]]

bom·bi·lla (bôm bē′yä), *n., pl.* **-llas** (-yäs). *Spanish.* a tube or drinking straw with a strainer at one end, esp. for drinking maté.

bomb′ing run′. See **bomb run.**

bomb′ ketch′, a ketch-rigged vessel of the 17th and 18th centuries, carrying heavy mortars for firing bombs. Also called **mortar ketch.**

bomb′ lance′, a harpoon fitted with an explosive head.

bomb·load (bom′lōd′), *n.* the total load of bombs carried by an airplane, usually expressed in terms of their total weight. [BOMB + LOAD]

bom·bous (bom′bəs), *adj.* *Entomol.* convex; spherical. [BOMB + -OUS]

bomb·proof (bom′pro͞of′), *adj.* **1.** strong enough to resist the impact and explosive force of bombs or shells. —*n.* **2.** a structure of such design and strength as to resist the penetration and the shattering force of shells, usually built, at least in part, beneath the level of the ground. —*v.t.* **3.** to make bombproof. [BOMB + -PROOF]

bomb′ rack′, a device for carrying bombs in an aircraft.

bomb′ run′, the part of a bombing mission between the sighting of the target or its identification by electronic instruments and the release of the bombs. Also, **bombing run.**

bomb·shell (bom′shel′), *n.* **1.** a bomb. **2.** something or someone that has a sudden and sensational effect: *The movie star was a blonde bombshell.* [BOMB + SHELL]

bomb′ shel′ter, a room, area, or small house especially reinforced against the effects of bombs, used as a shelter during an air raid.

bomb·sight (bom′sīt′), *n.* *Mil.* (in an aircraft) an instrument for aiming bombs at a target, esp. a device that can assume complete control of the aircraft during a bombing run, can automatically compensate for speed, winds, etc., and can guide the release of bombs for maximum accuracy in striking the target. [BOMB + SIGHT]

bom·by·cid (bom′bi sid), *n.* **1.** a moth of the family *Bombycidae,* comprising a single species, the Chinese silkworm moth. —*adj.* **2.** belonging or pertaining to the family *Bombycidae.* [back formation from NL *bombȳcidae,* equiv. to L *bombȳc-* (s. of *bombȳx* silkworm < Gk) + *-idae* -IDAE]

Bon (bon), *n.* **Cape,** a cape on the NE coast of Tunisia: surrender of the German Afrika Korps, May 12, 1943. Also called **Ras Addar.**

Bon (bôn), *n.* an annual festival of the Japanese Buddhists, welcoming ancestral spirits to household altars. Also called **Feast of Lanterns.** [< Jap]

Bön (bōn), *n.* a shamanistic Tibetan sect, absorbed by the first Buddhist sects of the 7th century and later.

Bo·na (bō′nə, -nä), *n.* Bône.

bo·na·ci (bō′nə sē′), *n., pl. (esp. collectively)* **-ci,** *(esp. referring to two or more kinds or species)* **-cis.** any of several edible serranid fishes, as *Mycteroperca bonaci.* [< Sp *bonasí* a fish]

Bo·na De·a (bō′nə dē′ə), an ancient Roman goddess of chastity and fertility, worshiped by women and believed to be the wife, sister, or daughter of Faunus. Also called **Fauna.** [< L: lit., (the) Good Goddess]

Bon·a·dox·in (bon′ə dok′sin), *n. Pharm., Trademark.* meclizine.

bo·na fide (bō′nə fīd′, bon′ə; bō′nə fī′dē), in good faith; without fraud. [< L] —**bo·na-fide** (bō′nə fīd′, bon′ə-), *adj.*

bo·na fi·des (bō′nä fē′des; *Eng.* bō′nə fī′dēz), *Latin.* good faith; absence of fraud or deceit; the state of being exactly as claims or appearances indicate: *The* bona fides *of this contract is open to question.* Cf. **mala fides.**

Bon·aire (bô når′), *n.* an island in the E Netherlands Antilles, in the S West Indies. 5614 (1960); 95 sq. mi.

bon a·mi (bôɴ ɴᴀ mē′), *pl.* **bons a·mis** (bôɴ ᴢᴀ mē′). *French.* **1.** a good friend. **2.** a lover.

bo·nan·za (bə nan′zə, bō-), *n. U.S.* **1.** a rich mass of ore, as found in mining. **2.** a source of great and sudden wealth or luck; a spectacular windfall: *The play proved to be a bonanza for its lucky backers.* [< Sp: lit., smooth sea (hence, good luck, rich vein of ore) < nasalized var. of ML *bonacia,* equiv. to L *bon(us)* good + *(mal)acia* calm sea < Gk *malachía* softness *(malach(ós)* soft + *-ia* -ɪᴀ)]

Bo·na·parte (bō′nə pärt′; *Fr.* bô ɴᴀ ᴘᴀʀᴛ′), *n.* **1. Jé·rôme** (jə rōm′; *Fr.* zhā ʀōm′), 1784–1860, king of Westphalia 1807 (brother of Napoleon I). **2. Jo·seph** (jō′zəf; *Fr.* zhô zef′), 1768–1844, king of Naples 1806–08; king of Spain 1808–13 (brother of Napoleon I). **3. Lou·is** (lo͞o′ē; *Fr.* lwē; *Du.* lo͞o ē′), 1778–1846, king of Holland 1806–10 (brother of Napoleon I). **4. Lou·is Na·po·lé·on** (lo͞o′ē nə pō′lē ən; *Fr.* lwē ɴᴀ pô lā ôɴ′). See **Napoleon III. 5. Lu·cien** (lo͞o′shən; *Fr.* lʏ syaɴ′), 1775–1840, Prince of Cannino (brother of Napoleon I). **6. Napoléon.** See **Napoleon I. 7. Napoléon.** See **Napoleon II.** Italian, **Buonaparte.** —**Bo′na·par′te·an,** *adj.*

Bo·na·part·ist (bō′nə pär′tist), *n.* an adherent of the Bonapartes or their policies. [earlier *Buonapartist.* See Bᴏɴᴀᴘᴀʀᴛᴇ, -ɪsᴛ] —**Bo′na·part′ism,** *n.*

bon ap·pé·tit (bô ɴᴀ pā tē′), *French.* (I wish you) a hearty appetite.

Bon·a·ven·tu·ra (bon′ə ven cho͝or′ə; *It.* bô′nä ven-to͞o′ʀä), *n.* a boy's given name.

bon·a·ven·ture (bon′ə ven′chər, bon′ə ven′-), *n.* **1.** See **bonaventure mast. 2.** See **bonaventure mizzen** (def. 1). [< It *buonaventura,* lit., good luck. See ʙᴏɴᴜs, ᴠᴇɴᴛᴜʀᴇ]

Bon·a·ven·ture (bon′ə ven′chər), *n.* **Saint** (*"the Seraphic Doctor"*), 1221–74, Italian scholastic theologian. Also, **Bonaventura.**

bon′aventure mast′, *Naut.* a mast fitted with a lateen sail or lugsail, situated behind the mizzenmast at or near the stern, used in the 16th and early 17th centuries. Also called **bonaventure, bonaventure mizzen.**

bon′aventure miz′zen, *Naut.* **1.** Also called **bonaventure.** a lateen sail set on a bonaventure mast. **2.** See **bonaventure mast.**

bon·a·vist (bon′ə vist), *n.* See **hyacinth bean.** [< It *buonavista* good sight. See ʙᴏᴏɴ[2], ᴠɪsᴛᴀ]

bon·bon (bon′bon′; *Fr.* bôɴ bôɴ′), *n., pl.* **-bons** (-bonz′; *Fr.* -bôɴ′). **1.** a fondant, fruit, or nut center dipped in fondant or chocolate; a chocolate. **2.** a piece of confectionery; candy. [< F: lit., good-good; a repetitive compound, orig. nursery word]

bon·bon·nière (bôɴ bô nyeʀ′), *n., pl.* **-nières** (-nyeʀ′). **1.** a confectioner's store. **2.** *(italics) French.* a box or dish for candies. [< F: lit., candy-holder]

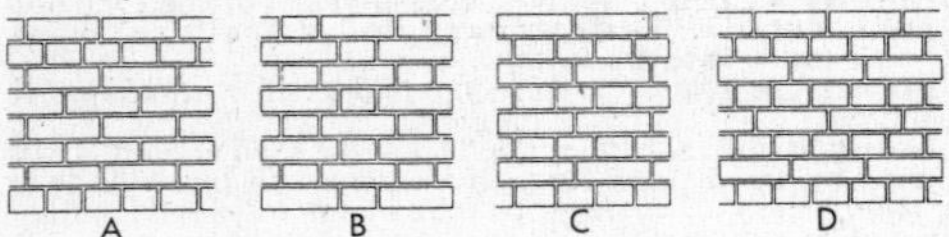

Bonds (def. 17a)
A, American bond; B, Flemish bond; C, English bond; D, English cross bond

bond[1] (bond), *n.* **1.** something that binds, fastens, confines, or holds together. **2.** a cord, rope, band, or ligament. **3.** something that binds a person or persons to a certain line of behavior: *the bond of matrimony.* **4.** something, as an agreement, friendship, etc., that unites individuals or peoples into a group; covenant: *the bond between nations.* **5.** binding security; firm assurance: *My word is my bond.* **6.** a sealed instrument under which a person, corporation, or government guarantees to pay a stated sum of money on or before a specified day. **7.** any written obligation under seal. **8.** *Law.* a written promise of a surety. **9.** *Govt.* the state of dutiable goods on which the duties are unpaid, when stored under a bond in charge of the government: *goods in bond.* **10.** Also called **bonded whiskey.** *U.S.* a whiskey that has been aged at least four years in a bonded warehouse before bottling. **11.** *Finance.* a certificate of ownership of a specified portion of a debt due to be paid by a government or corporation to an individual holder and usually bearing a fixed rate of interest. **12.** *Insurance.* **a.** a surety agreement. **b.** the money deposited, or the promissory arrangement entered into, under any such agreement. **13.** a substance that causes particles to adhere; binder. **14.** adhesion between two substances or objects, as concrete and reinforcing strands. **15.** *Chem.* the attraction between atoms in a molecule. **16.** See **bond paper. 17.** *Masonry.* **a.** any of various arrangements of bricks, stones, etc., having a regular pattern and intended to increase the strength or enhance the appearance of a construction. **b.** the overlap of bricks, stones, etc., in a construction so as to increase its strength. **18.** *Elect.* an electric conductor placed between adjacent metal parts within a structure, as in a railroad track, aircraft, house, etc., to prevent the accumulation of static electricity. **19.** *Obs.* bondsman. —*v.t.* **20.** to put (goods, an employee, official, etc.) on or under bond: *The company refused to bond a former criminal.* **21.** to connect or bind. **22.** *Finance.* to place a bonded debt on or secure a debt by bonds; mortgage. **23.** to join (two materials). **24.** *Masonry.* to lay (bricks, stones, etc.) so as to produce a strong construction. **25.** *Elect.* to provide with a bond: *to bond a railroad track.* —*v.i.* **26.** to hold together or cohere, from or as from being bonded, as bricks in a wall or particles in a mass. [ME; var. of ʙᴀɴᴅ[3]] —**bond′er,** *n.* —**bond′less,** *adj.*

—**Syn. 1.** bonds, chains, fetters. **3.** Bᴏɴᴅ, ʟɪɴᴋ, ᴛɪᴇ agree in referring to a force or influence that unites people. Bᴏɴᴅ, however, usually emphasizes the strong and enduring quality of affection, whereas ᴛɪᴇ may refer more esp. to duty, obligation, or responsibility: *bonds of memory; Blessed be the tie that binds; family ties.* A ʟɪɴᴋ is a definite connection, though a slighter one; it may indicate affection or merely some traceable influence or desultory communication: *a close link between friends.*

bond[2] (bond), *Obs.* —*n.* **1.** a serf or slave. —*adj.* **2.** in serfdom or slavery. [ME *bond(e),* OE *bōnda* < Scand; cf. Icel *bōndi* ʜᴜsʙᴀɴᴅ(ᴍᴀɴ), contr. of **bōunde,* var. of *būande,* c. OE *būend* dweller, equiv. to *bū(an)* (to) dwell (see ʙᴏᴏʀ) + *-end* n. suffix, as in *fiend, friend*]

Bond (bond), *n.* **Car·rie** (kar′ē) (*née* **Jacobs**) (jā′kəbz), 1862–1946, U.S. song writer and author.

Bond, G., a ring formation in the first quadrant of the face of the moon: about 12 miles in diameter.

Bond, W., a walled plain in the first quadrant of the face of the moon: about 100 miles in diameter.

bond·age (bon′dij), *n.* **1.** slavery or involuntary servitude; serfdom. **2.** the state of being bound by or subjected to external control. **3.** *Early Eng. Law.* personal subjection to the control of a superior; villeinage. [ME < AL *bondag(ium).* See ʙᴏɴᴅ[2], -ᴀɢᴇ]

—**Syn. 1.** captivity, restraint; prison. See **slavery. 2.** thraldom, captivity, confinement, imprisonment.

bond′ course′, *Masonry.* a course, as a heading course, for bonding masonry in depth.

bond·ed (bon′did), *adj.* **1.** secured by or consisting of bonds: *bonded debt.* **2.** placed in bond: *bonded goods.* [ʙᴏɴᴅ[1] + -ᴇᴅ[3]]

bond′ed ware′house, a warehouse for goods held in bond by the government.

bond′ed whis′key, bond[1] (def. 10).

bond·hold·er (bond′hōl′dər), *n.* a holder of a bond or bonds issued by a government or corporation. [ʙᴏɴᴅ[1] + ʜᴏʟᴅᴇʀ] —**bond′hold′ing,** *adj., n.*

bond·maid (bond′mād′), *n.* **1.** a female slave. **2.** a female bound to service without wages. [ʙᴏɴᴅ[2] + ᴍᴀɪᴅ]

bond·man (bond′mən), *n., pl.* **-men. 1.** a male slave. **2.** a male bound to service without wages. **3.** *Old Eng. Law.* a villein or other unfree tenant. Also, **bondsman.** [ME *bonde man.* See ʙᴏɴᴅ[2], ᴍᴀɴ[1]]

bond′ pa′per, a superior variety of white paper, esp. used for stationery. Also called **bond.**

bond′ serv′ant, 1. one who serves in bondage; slave. **2.** a person bound to service without wages. Also, **bond′-serv′ant.**

bonds·man[1] (bondz′mən), *n., pl.* **-men.** *Law.* one who is bound or who by bond becomes surety for another. [*bond's man* man of the bond, i.e., its signer; see ʙᴏɴᴅ[1], ᴍᴀɴ[1]]

bonds·man[2] (bondz′mən), *n., pl.* **-men.** bondman. [ME *bondesman.* See ʙᴏɴᴅ[2], ᴍᴀɴ[1]]

bond·stone (bond′stōn′), *n.* a stone, as a perpend, for bonding facing masonry to a masonry backing. [ʙᴏɴᴅ[1] + sᴛᴏɴᴇ]

bonds·wom·an[1] (bondz′wo͝om′ən), *n., pl.* **-wom·en.** *Law.* a woman who is bound or who by bond becomes surety for another. [*bond's woman* woman of the bond, i.e., its signer; see ʙᴏɴᴅsᴍᴀɴ[1]]

bonds·wom·an[2] (bondz′wo͝om′ən), *n., pl.* **-wom·en.** bondwoman. [ʙᴏɴᴅ[2] + ᴡᴏᴍᴀɴ]

bond·wom·an (bond′wo͝om′ən), *n., pl.* **-wom·en.** a female slave. [ME *bonde womman.* See ʙᴏɴᴅ[2], ᴡᴏᴍᴀɴ]

bone[1] (bōn), *n., v.,* **boned, bon·ing.** —*n.* **1.** *Anat., Zool.* **a.** one of the structures composing the skeleton of a vertebrate. **b.** the hard connective tissue forming the substance of the skeleton of most vertebrates. **2.** such a structure from an edible animal, usually with meat adhering to it, as an article of food: *Pea soup should be made with a ham bone.* **3.** any of various similarly hard or structural animal substances, as ivory, whalebone, etc. **4.** something made of or resembling such a substance. **5. bones, a.** the skeleton. **b.** a body: *Let his bones rest in peace.* **c.** *Games Slang.* dice. **d.** *(cap.)* See **Mr. Bones. e.** a simple rhythm instrument consisting of two, sometimes curved, bars or short strips of bone, ivory, wood, or the like, held between the fingers of one hand and clacked together. **6.** a flat strip of whalebone or other material for stiffening corsets, petticoats, etc.; stay. **7.** *Games Slang.* a domino. **8. feel in one's bones,** *U.S.* to think or feel intuitively: *She felt in her bones that it was going to be a momentous day.* **9. have a bone to pick with someone,** to have cause to disagree or argue with somone: *The teacher had a bone to pick with him because his homework paper was identical with his neighbor's.* **10. make no bones about, a.** to deal with in a direct manner; act or speak openly. **b.** to have no fear of or objection to: *He makes no bones about helping his wife with the dishes.* —*v.t.* **11.** to remove the bones from: *to bone a turkey.* **12.** to put whalebone or another stiffener into (clothing). **13.** *Agric.* to put bone meal into, as fertilizer. —*v.i.* **14.** *Slang.* to study intensely; cram (often fol. by *up*): *She's boning up for her finals.* [ME *boon,* OE *bān;* c. D *been* bone, leg, Icel *bein* bone, G *Bein* leg] —**bone′less,** *adj.* —**bone′like′,** *adj.*

bone[2] (bōn), *n. Jazz.* a trombone. [short form]

Bône (bōn), *n.* a seaport in NE Algeria: site of Hippo Regius. 112,010 (1954). Also, **Bona.**

bone′ ash′, the remains of bones calcined in the air, used as a fertilizer and in the making of bone china. Also called **bone′ earth′.**

bone·black (bōn′blak′), *n.* a black, carbonaceous substance obtained by calcining bones in closed vessels, used as a black pigment, a decolorizing agent, etc. Also, **bone′ black′.** [ʙᴏɴᴇ[1] + ʙʟᴀᴄᴋ]

bone′ chi′na, a fine, naturally white china made with bone ash.

bone′ conduc′tion, *Med.* the transmission of sound vibrations to the internal ear through the cranial bones (opposed to *air conduction*).

boned (bōnd), *adj.* **1.** having a particular kind of bone or bony structure (often used in combination): *beautifully boned; raw-boned; small-boned.* **2.** having the bones taken out; cooked or served with the bones removed: *boned chicken; boned veal.* **3.** braced or supported with stays, as a corset. **4.** fertilized with bone: *boned land.* [ʙᴏɴᴇ[1] + -ᴇᴅ[3]]

bone-dry (bōn′drī′), *adj.* **1.** *Informal.* very dry or thirsty. **2.** *Ceram.* (of clay) thoroughly dried.

bone·fish (bōn′fish′), *n., pl.* **-fish·es,** *(esp. collectively)* **-fish.** a marine game fish, *Albula vulpes,* found in shallow tropical waters, having a skeleton composed of numerous small, fine bones. Also called **ladyfish.** [ʙᴏɴᴇ[1] + ꜰɪsʜ]

bone·head (bōn′hed′), *n.* a stupid, obstinate person; blockhead. [ʙᴏɴᴇ[1] + ʜᴇᴀᴅ] —**bone′head′ed,** *adj.* —**bone′head′ed·ness,** *n.*

bone′ meal′, *Agric.* bones ground to a coarse powder, used as fertilizer or feed.

bone′ of conten′tion, the subject or focal point of a dispute: *The terms of the old man's will were a bone of contention to his survivors.*

bone′ oil′, a fetid, tarry liquid obtained in the dry distillation of bone.

bon·er[1] (bō′nər), *n.* one who or that which bones. [ʙᴏɴᴇ[1] + -ᴇʀ[1]]

bon·er[2] (bō′nər), *n. Slang.* a foolish and obvious blunder. [ʙᴏɴᴇ(ʜᴇᴀᴅ) + -ᴇʀ[1]]

bone·set (bōn′set′), *n.* any plant of the genus *Eupatorium,* esp. *E. perfoliatum,* of North America. Also called **thoroughwort.** [ʙᴏɴᴇ[1] + sᴇᴛ (v.), so named (by hyperbole) because supposed to have healing properties]

Boneset, *Eupatorium perfoliatum* (Height 3 to 6 ft.)

bone·set·ter (bōn′set′ər), *n.* one who treats or sets fractures, broken, or dislocated bones, or the like, esp. such a person who is not a regular physician or surgeon; healer. [late ME; see ʙᴏɴᴇ[1], sᴇᴛᴛᴇʀ]

bone′ spav′in, *Vet. Pathol.* See under **spavin** (def. 1).

bone′ tur′quoise, fossil bone or ivory that has been colored naturally or artificially so as to resemble turquoise. Also called **fossil turquoise, odontolite.**

bone·yard (bōn′yärd′), *n.* **1.** Also called **stock.** *Dominoes.* the bank, consisting of the remaining dominoes after each person has made his initial draw. **2.** a place or area where the bones of wild animals accumulate or are collected. **3.** *Informal.* an area where old, useless, or discarded cars, ships, planes, etc., are collected prior to being broken up for scrap or otherwise disposed of. [ʙᴏɴᴇ[1] + ʏᴀʀᴅ[2]]

bon·fire (bon′fīər′), *n.* **1.** a large fire in the open air, for warmth, entertainment, or celebration, to burn leaves, garbage, etc., or as a signal. **2.** any fire built in the open. [late ME *bone fire,* i.e., a fire with bones for fuel]

bon·go[1] (boŋ′gō, bôŋ′gō), *n., pl.* **-gos,** *(esp. collectively)* **-go.** a reddish-brown antelope, *Taurotragus eurycerus,* of the forests of tropical Africa, having white stripes and large, spirally twisted horns. [< an African language]

Bongo (4 ft. high at shoulder)

bon·go[2] (boŋ′gō, bôŋ′gō), *n., pl.* **-gos, -goes.** one of a pair of small tuned drums, played by beating with the fingers. Also called **bon′go drum′.** [< Amer Sp *bongó*]

bon·grace (bon′grās′), *n. Naut.* bowgrace.

bon gré, mal gré (bôɴ′ ɢʀā′ ᴍᴀʟ′ ɢʀā′), *French.* whether willing or not; willy-nilly.

Bon·ham (bon′əm), *n.* a town in NE Texas. 7357 (1960).

Bon·heur (bo nûr′; *Fr.* bô nœʀ′), *n.* **Ro·sa** (rō′zə; *Fr.* ʀôᴢ ᴀ′), *(Maria Rosalie Bonheur),* 1822–99, French painter.

bon·heur-du-jour (bə nûr′do͞o zho͝or′, -dyo͞o-; *Fr.* bô nœʀ dʏ zho͞oʀ′), *n., pl.* **bon·heurs-du-jour** (bə-nûr′do͞o zho͝or′, -dyo͞o-; *Fr.* bô nœʀ dʏ zho͞oʀ′). *French Furniture.* a dainty fall-front desk of the late 18th and early 19th centuries. [< F: lit., happiness of the day, from the favor it found in its time]

bon·ho·mie (bon′ə mē′; *Fr.* bô nô mē′), *n.* frank and simple good-heartedness; a good-natured manner. [< F, equiv. to *bonhomme* good-natured man (see ʙᴏᴏɴ[2], Hᴏᴍᴏ) + *-ie* -ʏ[3]] —**bon·ho·mous** (bon′ə məs), *adj.*

Bon·homme Rich·ard (bon′əm rich′ərd; *Fr.* bô-nôm′ ʀē sʜᴀʀ′), the flagship of John Paul Jones.

Bon·i·face (bon′ə fās′; *for 4 also Fr.* bô nē ꜰᴀs′), *n.* **1. Saint** *(Wynfrith),* ᴀ.ᴅ. 680?–755?, English monk who became a missionary in Germany. **2.** a jovial innkeeper in *The Beaux' Stratagem.* **3.** *(l.c.)* any landlord or innkeeper. **4.** a boy's given name.

Boniface I, Saint, died ᴀ.ᴅ. 422, pope 418–422.

Boniface II, pope ᴀ.ᴅ. 530–532.

Boniface III, pope ᴀ.ᴅ. 607.

Boniface IV, Saint, pope ᴀ.ᴅ. 608–615.

Boniface V, died ᴀ.ᴅ. 625, pope 619–625.

Boniface VI, pope ᴀ.ᴅ. 896.

Boniface VII, antipope ᴀ.ᴅ. 974, 984–985.

Boniface VIII, *(Benedetto Caetani)* c1235–1303, Italian ecclesiastic: pope 1294–1303.

Boniface IX, *(Pietro Tomacelli)* died 1404, Italian ecclesiastic: pope 1389–1404.

Bon·ing·ton (bon′ing tən), *n.* **Richard Parkes** (pärks), 1801–28, English painter.

Bo′nin Is′lands (bō′nin), a group of islands in the N Pacific, SE of Japan: under U.S. administration; uninhabited since World War II. 40 sq. mi. Japanese, **Ogasawara Jima.**

Bo·ni·ta (bə nē′tə, bō-), *n.* a girl's given name.

bo·ni·to (bə nē′tō), *n., pl. (esp. collectively)* **-to,** *(esp. referring to two or more kinds or species)* **-tos. 1.** any mackerellike fish of the genus *Sarda,* as *S. sarda,* found

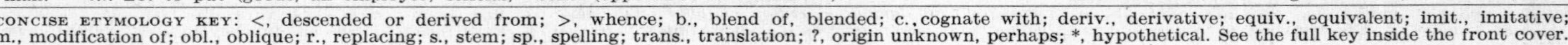

in the Atlantic Ocean. **2.** any of several related species, as the skipjack, *Katsuwonus pelamis.* [< Sp < Ar *bainīth*]

bon·jour (bôN zho͞oʀ′), *interj. French.* good day; hello.

bon·kers (boŋg′kərz), *adj. Brit. Slang.* mad; crazy; mentally unbalanced. [?]

bon mar·ché (bôN maʀ shā′), *pl.* **bons mar·chés** (bôN maʀ shā′). *French.* a bargain. [lit., good market]

bon mot (bôn′ mō′; *Fr.* bôN mō′), *pl.* **bons mots** (bôn′ mōz′; *Fr.* bôN mō′), an especially fitting word or expression; clever saying; witticism. [< F: lit., good word; see BOON², MOTTO]

Bonn (bon; *Ger.* bôn), *n.* a city in and the capital of West Germany, in the west part, on the Rhine River. 143,700 (1963).

Bon·nard (bô naʀ′), *n.* **Pierre** (pyeʀ), 1867–1947, French painter.

Bon·naz (bə naz′), *n.* (*sometimes l.c.*) embroidery made by machine. [named after J. *Bonnaz,* 19th-century French inventor]

bonne (bôn), *n., pl.* **bonnes** (bôn). *French.* **1.** a maidservant. **2.** a child's nurse. [lit., good (fem.)]

bonne a·mie (bô na mē′), *pl.* **bonnes a·mies** (bôn za-mē′). *French.* **1.** a good (female) friend. **2.** a (female) lover.

bonne bouche (bôn bo͞osh′), *pl.* **bonnes bouches** (bôn bo͞osh′). *French.* a tidbit. [lit., good mouth]

bonne foi (bôn fwa′), *French.* sincerity. [lit., good faith]

bonne nuit (bôn nwē′), *French.* good night.

Bon′ner Springs′ (bon′ər), a town in NE Kansas. 3171 (1960).

bon·net (bon′it), *n.* **1.** an outdoor head covering, usually tying under the chin and often framing the face, formerly much worn by women but now worn principally by children or as part of a nun's habit. **2.** *Chiefly Scot.* a man's or boy's cap. **3.** a bonnetlike headdress: *an Indian war bonnet.* **4.** any of various hoods, covers, or protective devices. **5.** a cowl, hood, or wind cap for a fireplace or chimney, to stabilize the draft. **6.** the part of a valve casing through which the stem passes and which forms a guide and seal for the stem. **7.** a chamber at the top of a hot-air furnace from which the leaders emerge. **8.** *Chiefly Brit.* an automobile hood. **9.** *Naut.* a supplementary piece of canvas laced to the foot of a fore-and-aft sail, esp. a jib, in light winds. —*v.t.* **10.** to put a bonnet on. [late ME *bonet* < MF; akin to LL *abonnis* kind of cap < ?] —**bon′net·less,** *adj.* —**bon′net·like′,** *adj.*

Bon·net (bô ne′), *n.* **Georges** (zhôʀzh), born 1889, French statesman.

Bonne Terre (bon târ′), a town in E Missouri. 3219 (1960).

bon′net glass′, monteith (def. 2).

bon·net·head (bon′it hed′), *n.* a hammerhead shark, *Sphyrna tiburo,* found in shallow waters from Brazil to Massachusetts, having a spade-shaped head. Also called **shovelhead.** [BONNET + HEAD]

bonne·tière (bun tyâr′; *Fr.* bôn tyeʀ′), *n., pl.* **-tières** (-tyârz′; *Fr.* -tyeʀ′). *French Furniture.* a tall, narrow wardrobe of the 18th century, found esp. in Normandy and Brittany. [< F: lit., hosier]

bon·net rouge (bô ne ʀo͞ozh′), *pl.* **bon·nets rouges** (bô ne ʀo͞ozh′). *French.* **1.** a red liberty cap, worn by extremists at the time of the French Revolution. **2.** an extremist or radical.

bon′net top′, *U.S. Furniture.* a top to a secretary, highboy, etc., following in outline a broken pediment on the front. Cf. **hooded top.**

Bonnet top of highboy (Newport, 1765)

Bon·ni·belle (bon′ē-bel′), *n.* a girl's given name.

Bon·nie (bon′ē), *n.* a girl's given name. Also, **Bonny.**

bon·ny (bon′ē), *adj.,* **-ni·er, -ni·est,** *adv., n.* —*adj.* **1.** *Chiefly Scot.* pleasing to the eye; handsome; pretty. **2.** *Brit. Dial.* **a.** (of people) healthy, sweet, and lively. **b.** (of places) placid; tranquil. **c.** pleasing; agreeable; good. —*adv.* **3.** *Brit. Dial.* pleasingly; agreeably; very well. —*n.* **4.** *Scot. and North Eng. Archaic.* a pretty girl or young woman. Also, **bon′nie.** [ME *bonie* < OF *bon* good + *-ie* -Y¹, perh. by analogy with *jolie* JOLLY] —**bon′ni·ly,** *adv.* —**bon′ni·ness,** *n.*

Bon·ny (bon′ē), *n.* a girl's given name. Also, **Bonnie.**

bon·ny·clab·ber (bon′ē klab′ər), *n.* sour, thick milk. [< Ir *bainne clabair,* lit., milk of the clapper (i.e., of the churn lid or dasher)]

Bo·non·ci·ni (bô′nôn chē′nē), *n.* **Gio·van·ni Ma·ri·a** (jô vän′nē mä ʀē′ä), 1640–78, and his sons **Giovanni Bat·ti·sta** (bät tē′stä), 1670–1747, and **Marc An·to·nio** (märk än tô′nyô), 1675–1726, Italian composers. Also, **Buononcini.**

Bön·pa (bōn pä′), *n.* a member of the Bön sect.

Bon·pland (bôn pland′, bon-), *n.* a walled plain in the third quadrant of the face of the moon: about 30 miles in diameter.

bon·sai (bōn′sī, bon′-), *n., pl.* **-sai.** **1.** a tree or shrub that is grown in a pot or other container and that has been dwarfed by certain methods, as by pruning the roots and pinching and wiring the shoots and branches to produce a desired shape or effect. **2.** the art or hobby of developing and growing such a plant or plants. [< Jap]

bon·soir (bôN swaʀ′), *interj. French.* good evening; good night.

bon·spiel (bon′spēl, -spəl), *n. Curling.* a match or tournament. [?]

Bontebok (3½ ft. high at shoulder; horns 15 in.; total length 6 ft.; tail 1 ft.)

bon·te·bok (bon′tē bok′), *n., pl.* **-boks,** (*esp. collectively*) **-bok.** a nearly extinct, purplish-red antelope, *Damaliscus pygarus,* of southern Africa, having a white face and rump. [< SAfrD, equiv. to *bont* piebald (< ML *punctus* dotted; see POINT) + *bok* BUCK¹]

bon·te·buck (bon′tē buk′), *n., pl.* **-bucks,** (*esp. collectively*) **-buck.** bontebok.

Bon·tem·pel·li (bôn′tem pel′lē), *n.* **Mas·si·mo** (mäs′-sē mô), 1878–1960, Italian novelist.

Bon·toc (bon tok′), *n., pl.* **-tocs,** (*esp. collectively*) **-toc.** Bontok.

Bon·tok (bon tok′), *n., pl.* **-toks,** (*esp. collectively*) **-tok.** a member of a pagan people inhabiting northern Luzon in the Philippines.

bon ton (bon′ ton′; *Fr.* bôN tôN′), good or elegant form or style; good breeding; fashionable society. [< F: lit., good tone. See BOON², TONE]

bo·nus (bō′nəs), *n., pl.* **-nus·es.** **1.** something given or paid over and above what is due. **2.** a sum of money granted or given to an employee, an agent of a company, a returned soldier, etc., over and above his regular pay, usually in appreciation for work done, length of service, accumulated favors, etc. **3.** something free, as an extra dividend, given by a corporation to a purchaser of its securities. **4.** a premium paid for a loan, contract, etc. **5.** something extra or additional given freely: *Every purchaser of a pound of coffee received a box of cookies as a bonus.* [< L: good]

—**Syn. 1.** reward, honorarium, gift. **2.** BONUS, BOUNTY, PREMIUM refer to something extra beyond a stipulated payment. A BONUS is a gift to reward performance, paid either by a private employer or by a government: *a bonus based on salary; a soldiers' bonus.* A BOUNTY is a public aid or reward offered to stimulate interest in a specific purpose or undertaking and to encourage performance: *a bounty for killing wolves.* A PREMIUM is usually something additional given as an inducement to buy, produce, or the like: *a premium received with a magazine subscription.*

Bo′nus Even′tus, the ancient Roman god of agricultural prosperity, later becoming the god of good luck. Also called **Eventus.**

bon vi·vant (bôN vē väN′), *pl.* **bons vi·vants** (bôN vē väN′). *French.* **1.** a person who lives luxuriously and enjoys good food and drink. **2.** a jovial companion.

bon vo·yage (bon′ voi äzh′; *Fr.* bôN vwa yazh′), pleasant trip. [< F: lit., good journey. See BOON², VOYAGE]

bon·y (bō′nē), *adj.,* **bon·i·er, bon·i·est.** **1.** of or like bone. **2.** full of bones. **3.** having prominent bones; big-boned. [BONE¹ + -Y¹] —**bon′i·ness,** *n.*

bon′y fish′, any fish of the class *Osteichthyes,* characterized by a skeleton composed of bone in addition to cartilage, gill covers, and an air bladder.

bon′y lab′yrinth, *Anat.* See under **labyrinth** (def. 7).

bon·y·tail (bō′nē tāl′), *n.* a fish, *Gila robusta elegans,* found in the Colorado River, having flaring fins and a thin caudal peduncle. [BONY + TAIL¹]

bonze (bonz), *n.* a Buddhist monk, esp. of Japan or China. [appar. back formation from *bonzes* < NL *bonzī* (pl. of *bonzus*) < Jap *bonzi, bonsi* < Chin *fan seng* devout person]

bon·zer (bon′zər), *adj. Australian.* **1.** very big. **2.** remarkable; wonderful. [?]

boo (bo͞o), *interj., n., pl.* **boos,** *v.,* **booed, boo·ing.** —*interj.* **1.** (an exclamation used to express contempt, disapprobation, etc., usually shouted by an audience at a performer.) **2.** (an exclamation used to frighten or startle an individual.) —*n.* **3.** this exclamation. —*v.i.* **4.** to cry "boo." —*v.t.* **5.** to cry "boo" at; show disapproval of by booing. [imit.]

boob (bo͞ob), *U.S. Slang.* —*n.* **1.** a fool; dunce. **2.** a blunder or mistake. —*v.i.* **3.** to commit a blunder. [back formation from BOOBY]

boo-boo (bo͞o′bo͞o′), *n., pl.* **-boos.** *Slang.* **1.** a silly mistake; blunder. **2.** a minor injury. [baby talk]

boo·by (bo͞o′bē), *n., pl.* **-bies.** **1.** a stupid person; dunce. **2.** the worst student, player, etc., of a group. **3.** any of several tropical sea birds of the genus *Sula,* related to the gannets. [earlier *pooby,* appar. b. *poop* to befool (now obs.) and BABY; sense 3. perh. by association with Sp *bobo* < L *balbus* stuttering] —**boo′bi·ly,** *adv.* —**boo′by·ish,** *adj.*

boo′by hatch′, **1.** *Naut.* **a.** a small hatch giving access to a ladder from the weather deck of a vessel to the interior of the hull. **b.** a small companion secured over a deck opening. **c.** a hoodlike hatch cover having a sliding top. **2.** *U.S. Slang.* **a.** an insane asylum. **b.** jail.

boo′by prize′, a prize given in good-natured ridicule to the worst player in a game or contest.

boo′by trap′, **1.** a hidden bomb or mine so placed that it will be set off by an unsuspecting person through such means as moving an apparently harmless object. **2.** any hidden trap set for an unsuspecting person.

boo·by-trap (bo͞o′bē trap′), *v.t.,* **-trapped, -trapping.** to set with or as if with a booby trap; attach a booby trap to or in.

bood (bo͞od), *n. Brit. Dial.* boud.

boo·dle (bo͞od′əl), *n., v.,* **-dled, -dling.** *U.S. Slang.* —*n.* **1.** the lot, pack, or crowd: *Send the whole boodle back to the factory.* **2.** a large quantity of something, esp. money: *He's worth a boodle.* **3.** a bribe or other illicit payment, esp. to or from a politician. **4.** stolen goods; loot; booty; swag. **5. kit and boodle.** See **kit**¹ (def. 7). —*v.i.* **6.** to obtain money dishonestly, as by bribery or swindling. [< D *boedel* stock, lot] —**boo′dler,** *n.*

boo·gey·man (bo͝og′ē man′, bo͞o′gē-), *n., pl.* **-men.** an imaginary evil character of supernatural powers, esp. a mythical hobgoblin supposed to carry off naughty children: *Stop crying or the boogeyman will get you.* [var. of *bogyman.* See BOGY, MAN¹]

boog·ie (bo͝og′ē, bo͞o′gē), *n.* **1.** *Disparaging and Offensive.* a Negro. **2.** boogie-woogie. [? BUGG(ER) + -IE]

boog·ie-woog·ie (bo͝og′ē wo͝og′ē, bo͞o′gē wo͞o′gē), *n. Jazz.* a form of instrumental blues, esp. for piano, using melodic variations over a constantly repeated bass figure. Also called **boogie.** [rhyming compound based on BOOGIE]

boo·hoo (bo͞o′ho͞o′), *v.,* **-hooed, -hoo·ing,** *n., pl.* **-hoos.** —*v.i.* **1.** to weep noisily; blubber. —*n.* **2.** the sound of noisy weeping. **3.** See **frigate mackerel.** [rhyming compound based on BOO]

book (bo͝ok), *n.* **1.** a written or printed work of some length, as a treatise, novel, or other literary composition, esp. on consecutive sheets of paper fastened or bound together in a volume. **2.** a number of sheets of blank or ruled paper bound together for writing, recording commercial transactions, etc. **3.** a division of a literary work, esp. one of the larger divisions. **4. the Book,** the Bible. **5.** *Music.* the text or libretto of an opera, operetta, etc. **6. books.** See **book of account. 7.** *Jazz.* the total repertoire of a band. **8.** *Theat.* a script or story for a play, esp. for a musical. **9.** a record of bets, as on a horse race. **10.** *Cards.* the number of basic tricks or cards which must be taken before any trick or card counts in the score. **11.** a set or packet of tickets, checks, stamps, matches, etc., bound together like a book. **12.** a pile or package of leaves, as of tobacco. **13.** anything that serves for the recording of facts or events: *The petrified tree was a book of Nature.* **14.** *Sports.* a collection of facts and information about the usual playing habits, weaknesses, methods, etc., of an opposing team or player, esp. in baseball: *The White Sox book on Mickey Mantle cautioned pitchers to keep the ball fast and high.* **15.** *Slang.* bookmaker (def. 2). **16. bring to book,** to call to account; bring to justice: *Someday he will be brought to book for his misdeeds.* **17. by the book,** according to the correct form; in the usual manner: *an unimaginative individual who does everything by the book.* **18. close the books,** to balance accounts at the end of an accounting period; settle accounts. **19. in one's bad books,** out of favor; disliked by someone: *He's in the boss's bad books.* **20. in one's book,** in one's personal judgment or opinion: *In my book, he's not to be trusted.* **21. in one's good books,** in favor; liked by someone. Also, **in one's books. 22. like a book,** completely; thoroughly: *He knew the area like a book.* **23. make book, a.** to accept or place the bets of others, as on horse races, esp. as a business. **b.** to wager; bet: *You can make book on it that he won't arrive in time.* **24. one for the book,** a noteworthy incident; something extraordinary: *The daring rescue was one for the book.* **25. on the books,** entered in a list or record: *He claims to have been graduated from Harvard, but his name is not on the books.* **26. the book, a.** a set of rules, conventions, or standards: *The solution was not according to the book but it served the purpose.* **b.** the telephone book: *I've looked him up, but he's not in the book.* **27. throw the book at,** *Slang.* **a.** to sentence (an offender, lawbreaker, etc.) to the maximum penalties for all charges against him. **b.** to punish or chide severely: *Say that again and I'll throw the book at you.* **28. without book, a.** from memory. **b.** without authority: *to punish without book.* —*v.t.* **29.** to enter in a book or list; record; register. **30.** to engage (a place, passage, etc.) beforehand. **31.** to register or list (a person) for a place, passage, appointment, etc. **32.** to engage (a person or company) for a performance or performances. **33.** to enter an official charge against (an arrested suspect) on a police register. **34.** to act as a bookmaker for (a bettor, bet, or sum of money): *The Philadelphia syndicate books 25 million dollars a year on horse racing. If you're only betting two dollars, I'll book you myself.* —*v.i.* **35.** to register one's name. **36.** to engage a place, services, etc. —*adj.* **37.** of or pertaining to a book or books: *the book department downstairs.* **38.** derived from or based on books or their contents: *a book knowledge of sailing.* **39.** shown by a book of account: *The firm's book profit was $53,680.* [ME, OE *bōc;* c. D *boek,* Icel *bōk,* G *Buch;* akin to Goth *boka* letter (of the alphabet)] —**book′less,** *adj.* —**book′like′,** *adj.*

book·bind·er (bo͝ok′bīn′dər), *n.* one whose business or work is the binding of books. [ME; see BOOK, BINDER¹]

book·bind·er·y (bo͝ok′bīn′də rē), *n., pl.* **-er·ies.** an establishment for binding books. [BOOKBINDER + -RY]

book·bind·ing (bo͝ok′bīn′diŋg), *n.* the process or art of binding books. [BOOK + BINDING]

book′ burn′ing, the destruction of writings of which the subject, the view of the author, or the like is considered politically or socially objectionable.

book·case (bo͝ok′kās′), *n.* a set of shelves for books. [BOOK + CASE²]

book′ club′, **1.** a club which lends or sells books to its members, usually at a discount. **2.** a club organized for the discussion and reviewing of books. Also called, *esp. Brit.,* **book society.**

book·craft (bo͝ok′kraft′, -kräft′), *n. Archaic.* literary skill; authorship. [OE *bōccræft.* See BOOK, CRAFT]

book′ end′, a support placed at the end of a row of books to hold them upright, usually used in pairs.

book-flat (bo͝ok′flat′), *n. Theat. Chiefly Brit.* a two-fold.

book′ gill′, the booklike gill of a horseshoe crab, composed of numerous leaflike, membranous structures.

book·ie (bo͝ok′ē), *n. Informal.* bookmaker (def. 2). [BOOK + -IE]

book·ing (bo͝ok′iŋg), *n.* a contract, engagement, or scheduled performance of a professional entertainer. [BOOK + -ING¹]

book′ing clerk′, **1.** one who sells tickets, as for a train, plane, etc. **2.** one who arranges and lists passage for persons, baggage, and goods.

book′ing of′fice, *Brit.* a ticket office, esp. one in a railway station. Also called **book′ing hall′.**

book·ish (bo͝ok′ish), *adj.* **1.** given or devoted to reading or study. **2.** more acquainted with books than with real life. **3.** of or pertaining to books; literary. **4.** stilted; pedantic. [BOOK + -ISH¹] —**book′ish·ly,** *adv.* —**book′ish·ness,** *n.*

book′ jack′et, a detachable paper cover, usually colored and illustrated, for protecting the binding of a book.

book·keep·er (bo͝ok′kē′pər), *n.* one who keeps account books, as for a business. [BOOK + KEEPER]

book·keep·ing (bo͝ok′kē′piŋg), *n.* the work or skill of keeping account books or systematic records of money transactions (distinguished from *accounting*). [BOOK + KEEPING]

book′ learn′ing, **1.** knowledge gained by reading books, as distinguished from that obtained through observation and experience. **2.** formal education: *She thought that common sense was just as important as book learning.* —**book-learn·ed** (bo͝ok′lûr′nid, -lûrnd′), *adj.*

book·let (bo͝ok′lit), *n.* a little book, esp. one with paper covers; pamphlet. [BOOK + -LET]

book′ list′, a list of books, esp. a list of recommended or required readings.

book′ lore′. See **book learning.**

book′ louse′, any of several minute insects of the order *Corrodentia,* often found living among books or papers.

book·lov·er (bŏŏk′luv′ər), *n.* a person who likes books and is fond of reading. [BOOK + LOVER]

book′ lung′, the respiratory organ of a spider or scorpion, composed of thin, membranous structures arranged like the leaves of a book.

book·mak·er (bŏŏk′mā′kər), *n.* **1.** a maker of books. **2.** one who makes a business of accepting the bets of others on the outcome of sport contests, esp. of horse races. [ME *bokmakere.* See BOOK, MAKER] —**book′mak′ing,** *n., adj.*

book·man (bŏŏk′mən, -man′), *n., pl.* **-men** (-mən, -men′). **1.** a studious or learned man; scholar. **2.** *Informal.* one whose occupation is selling or publishing books. [ME *bokeman.* See BOOK, MAN[1]]

book·mark (bŏŏk′märk′), *n.* **1.** a ribbon or the like placed between the pages of a book to mark a place. **2.** a bookplate. [BOOK + MARK[1]]

book′ match′, a match in or from a matchbook.

book·mo·bile (bŏŏk′mə bēl′), *n. U.S.* an automobile, small truck, or trailer constructed to carry books and serve as a traveling library, as for communities where libraries are not accessible. [BOOK + (AUTO)MOBILE]

book′ of account′, **1.** any journal, ledger, and supporting vouchers included in a system of accounts. **2. books of account,** the original records and books used in recording business transactions.

Book′ of Books′, the Bible.

Book′ of Chang′es. See **I Ching.**

Book′ of Com′mon Prayer′. the service book of the Church of England, essentially adopted but changed in details by other churches of the Anglican communion.

book′ of hours′, a book containing the prescribed order of prayers, readings from Scripture, and rites for the canonical hours. Also, **Book′ of Hours′.**

Book′ of Kells′ (kelz), an illuminated manuscript (A.D. c800) in the Hiberno-Saxon style.

Book′ of Mor′mon, a sacred book of the Mormon Church, believed by Mormons to be an abridgment by a prophet **(Mormon)** of a record of certain ancient peoples in America, written on golden plates, and discovered and translated (1827–30) by Joseph Smith.

Book′ of Odes′, a collection of 305 poems compiled in the 6th century B.C. by Confucius. Chinese, **Shih Ching, Shih King.**

book′ of orig′inal en′try, *Bookkeeping.* **1.** a book in which transactions are recorded before being transferred into a ledger. **2.** journal (def. 5a, b).

Book′ of the Dead′, a collection of ancient Egyptian papyrus books, many with elaborate illustrations, each containing prayers, hymns, incantations, and formulas for the behavior of the souls of the dead: such books were buried with the dead during the New Kingdom.

Book′ of the Duch′ess, The, a narrative poem (1369?) by Chaucer.

book·plate (bŏŏk′plāt′), *n.* a label bearing the owner's name and often a design, coat of arms, or the like, for pasting on the front end paper of a book. [BOOK + PLATE[1]]

book·rack (bŏŏk′rak′), *n.* **1.** a support for an open book. **2.** a rack for holding books. [BOOK + RACK[1]]

book·rest (bŏŏk′rest′), *n.* a bookrack for an open book, usually supporting it at a slightly raised angle. [BOOK + REST[1]]

book′ review′, **1.** a critical description, evaluation, or analysis of a book, as by a student or discussion group. **2.** a critical description and evaluation of a newly published book by a critic, journalist, etc., published in a newspaper or magazine. **3.** a section or page of a newspaper or magazine devoted to such descriptions and evaluations. —**book′ review′er.** —**book′ review′ing.**

book′ scor′pion, pseudoscorpion.

book·sel·ler (bŏŏk′sel′ər), *n.* a person whose occupation or business is selling books. [BOOK + SELLER]

book·shelf (bŏŏk′shelf′), *n., pl.* **-shelves.** a shelf for holding books, esp. one of the shelves in a bookcase. [BOOK + SHELF]

book′ soci′ety, *Chiefly Brit.* See **book club.**

book·stack (bŏŏk′stak′), *n.* a set of bookshelves one above another, as in a library; stack. [BOOK + STACK]

book·stall (bŏŏk′stôl′), *n.* **1.** a stall at which books are sold, usually secondhand. **2.** *Brit.* a newsstand. [BOOK + STALL[1]]

book·stand (bŏŏk′stand′), *n.* **1.** a bookrack. **2.** a bookstall. [BOOK + STAND]

book·store (bŏŏk′stōr′, -stôr′), *n.* a store where books are sold. Also called **book·shop** (bŏŏk′shop′). [BOOK + STORE]

book′ tile′, a flat, cellular roofing tile having two parallel edges one of which is convex and the other concave, so that a number may be fit together edge-to-edge between rafters, joists, etc.

book′ val′ue, the value of a business, property, etc., as stated in a book of accounts (distinguished from *market value*).

book·wing (bŏŏk′wing′), *n. Theat. Chiefly Brit.* a two-fold or wing of a stage set.

book·work (bŏŏk′wûrk′), *n.* **1.** work or research that entails studying or reading, as distinguished from laboratory experimentation or the like. **2.** *Print.* work on books or pamphlets, as distinguished from work on newspapers. Also, **book′-work′.** [OE *bōcweorc.* See BOOK, WORK]

book·worm (bŏŏk′wûrm′), *n.* **1.** a person devoted to reading or studying. **2.** any of various insects that feed on books, esp. a book louse. [BOOK + WORM]

Boole (bo͞ol), *n.* **George,** 1815–64, English mathematician and logician.

Bool′e·an al′gebra (bo͞o′lē ən), **1.** *Logic.* a deductive logical system, usually applied to classes, in which, under the operations of intersection and symmetric difference, classes are treated as algebraic quantities. **2.** *Math.* a ring with a multiplicative identity in which every element is an idempotent. [named after G. BOOLE; see -AN]

Bool′ean ring′, *Math.* a nonempty collection of sets having the properties that the union of two sets of the collection is a set in the collection and that the relative complement of each set with respect to any other set is in the collection. Cf. **algebra of sets.** [named after G. BOOLE; see -AN]

Bool′ean sum′. See **symmetric difference.** [named after G. BOOLE; see -AN]

Boole's′ inequal′ity, *Math.* the theorem that the probability of several events occurring is less than or equal to the sum of the probabilities of each event occurring. [named after G. BOOLE]

boom[1] (bo͞om), *v.i.* **1.** to make a deep, prolonged, resonant sound; make a rumbling, humming, or droning noise. **2.** to move with a resounding rush or great impetus. **3.** to progress, grow, or flourish vigorously, as a business, a city, etc. —*v.t.* **4.** to give forth with a booming sound (often fol. by *out*): *The clock boomed out nine.* **5.** to boost or campaign for (a cause, candidate, new product, etc.) vigorously: *His followers are booming George for mayor.* —*n.* **6.** a deep, prolonged, resonant sound. **7.** a roaring, rumbling, or reverberation, as of waves or distant guns. **8.** the cry of the European bittern. **9.** a buzzing, humming, or droning, as of a bee or beetle. **10.** a rapid increase in price, development, numbers, etc. **11.** a period of rapid economic growth, prosperity, high wages and prices, and relatively full employment. **12.** a rise in popularity, as of a political candidate, or efforts to promote such popularity. —*adj.* **13.** *U.S.* caused by or characteristic of a boom: *boom prices.* [late ME *bombon, bummyn* to buzz; c. D *bommen,* G *bummen,* orig. imit.] —**boom′ing·ly,** *adv.*

boom[2] (bo͞om), *n.* **1.** *Naut.* any of various more or less horizontal spars or poles for extending the feet of sails, esp. fore-and-aft sails, for handling cargo, suspending mooring lines alongside a vessel, pushing a vessel away from wharves, etc. **2.** an outrigger used on certain aircraft for connecting the tail surfaces to the fuselage. **3.** a maneuverable and retractable pipe on a tanker aircraft for refueling another aircraft in flight. **4.** a chain, cable, series of connected floating timbers, etc., serving to obstruct navigation, confine floating timber, etc. **5.** the area thus shut off. **6.** *Mach.* a spar or beam projecting from the mast of a derrick for supporting or guiding the weights to be lifted. **7.** chord[1] (def. 4). **8.** (on motion-picture and television stages) a spar or beam on a mobile crane for holding or manipulating a microphone or camera. —*v.t.* **9.** to extend or position, as a sail (usually fol. by *out* or *off*). **10.** to manipulate (an object) by or as by means of a crane or derrick. **11. lower the boom,** *Slang.* to be stern; prohibit; impose discipline; punish: *The government is lowering the boom on monopolies.* [< D: tree, pole, BEAM] —**boom′less,** *adj.*

boom-and-bust (bo͞om′ən bust′), *n. Informal.* a period of extreme economic prosperity followed by a severe depression.

boom·er (bo͞o′mər), *n.* **1.** *Chiefly U.S. Informal.* **a.** one who or that which booms. **b.** a person who settles in areas or towns that are booming. **c.** a wandering or migratory worker; hobo. **2.** *Australian.* a fully grown male kangaroo, esp. a large one. [BOOM[1] + -ER[1]]

boom·er·ang (bo͞o′mə rang′), *n.* **1.** a bent or curved piece of tough wood used by the Australian aborigines as a throwing club, one form of which can be thrown so as to return to the thrower. **2.** a scheme, plan, argument, etc., which recoils upon the user. **3.** *Theat.* **a.** a mobile platform, adjustable to different levels, for painting scenery. **b.** a batten, usually suspended vertically in the wings, for holding lighting units. —*v.i.* **4.** to come back or return, as a boomerang. **5.** (of a scheme, plan, etc.) to cause unexpected harm to the originator. [< native language of New South Wales, Australia]

Boomerangs

Boom′er State′, Oklahoma (used as a nickname).

boom·kin (bo͞om′kin), *n. Naut.* bumpkin[2]. [< Flem *boomken.* See BOOM[2], -KIN]

boom·let (bo͞om′lit), *n.* a small boom or increase in prosperity, development, numbers, size, support, popularity, etc. [BOOM[1] + -LET]

boom′ shot′, *Motion Pictures, Television.* a shot taken by a camera on a boom.

boom′ town′, a town that has grown rapidly as a result of sudden prosperity. Also, **boom′town′.**

boon[1] (bo͞on), *n.* **1.** a benefit enjoyed; a thing to be thankful for; blessing. **2.** *Archaic.* that which is asked; a favor sought. [ME *bone* < Scand; cf. Icel *bōn* prayer; c. OE *bēn*] —**boon′less,** *adj.*

boon[2] (bo͞on), *adj.* **1.** jolly; jovial; convivial: *boon companion.* **2.** *Poetic.* kindly; gracious; bounteous. [ME *bone* < MF < L *bon(us)* good]

boon[3] (bo͞on), *n. Textiles.* the ligneous waste product obtained by braking and scutching flax. Also called **shive, shove.** [ME *bone* (north), OE *bune* reed]

boon·dock·er (bo͞on′dok′ər), *n. Slang.* See **combat boot.** [BOONDOCK(S) + -ER[1]]

boon·docks (bo͞on′doks′), *n.* (*construed as pl.*) *Slang.* **1.** an uninhabited area with thick natural vegetation, as a backwoods or marsh (usually prec. by *the*). **2.** a remote rural area (usually prec. by *the*): *The company moved to a small town out in the boondocks.* [< Tagalog *bundok* mountain + (*the stick*)*s*; see STICK[1]]

boon·dog·gle (bo͞on′dog′əl), *n., v.,* **-gled, -gling.** *U.S.* —*n.* **1.** a belt, knife sheath, ax handle, or other product of simple manual skill. **2.** a cord of plaited leather worn around the neck by Boy Scouts. **3.** *Informal.* work of little or no practical value done merely to keep or look busy. —*v.i.* **4.** *Informal.* to do work of little or no practical value merely to keep or look busy. [said to have been coined by R. H. Link, American scoutmaster, as name for def. 2] —**boon′dog′gler,** *n.*

Boone (bo͞on), *n.* **1. Daniel,** 1734–1820, American pioneer, esp. in Kentucky. **2.** a town in NW North Carolina. 3686 (1960).

Boone·ville (bo͞on′vil), *n.* **1.** a town in NE Mississippi. 3480 (1960). **2.** a town in W Arkansas. 2690 (1960).

boong (bo͞ong, bo′ong), *n. Australian Informal.* **1.** a native of New Guinea. **2.** any aborigine. [< native Austral]

Boon·ton (bo͞on′tən, -tᵊn), *n.* a town in N New Jersey. 7981 (1960).

Boon·ville (bo͞on′vil), *n.* **1.** a town in central Missouri. 7090 (1960). **2.** a town in SW Indiana. 4801 (1960).

boor (bŏŏr), *n.* **1.** a clownish, rude, or unmannerly person. **2.** a rustic; yokel. **3.** an illiterate, dull, or insensitive peasant. **4.** a Dutch or German peasant. **5.** any foreign peasant. **6.** (*cap.*) a Boer. [< D *boer* or LG *būr;* c. G *Bauer* peasant, countryman; see BOND[2]]

boor·ga (bŏŏr′gə), *n.* burga[1].

boor·ish (bŏŏr′ish), *adj.* of or like a boor; rude; rustic. [BOOR + -ISH[1]] —**boor′ish·ly,** *adv.* —**boor′ish·ness,** *n.*

boost (bo͞ost), *U.S.* —*v.t.* **1.** to lift or raise by pushing from behind or below. **2.** to advance or aid by speaking well of; promote: *He always boosts his home town.* **3.** to increase; raise: *to boost prices; He boosted the horsepower of the car by 20 percent.* —*n.* **4.** an upward shove or raise; lift. **5.** an increase; rise: *There's been a tremendous boost in food prices.* **6.** an act, remark, or the like, that helps one's progress, morale, efforts, etc.: *His pep talk was the boost our team needed.* [? Scot dial. *boose* (var. of *pouss* PUSH) + (HOI)ST]

boost·er (bo͞o′stər), *n. U.S.* **1.** one who or that which boosts, esp. an energetic and enthusiastic supporter. **2.** *Elect.* a device connected in series with a current for increasing or decreasing the nominal circuit voltage. **3.** an auxiliary engine for increasing the tractive effort of a locomotive. **4.** *Mil.* an explosive more powerful than a primer, for ensuring the detonation of the main charge of a shell. **5.** *Rocketry.* **a.** a rocket engine used as the principal source of thrust in the take-off of a rocket or missile. **b.** the first stage containing this engine and its fuel supply, which may or may not be detached from the rocket when the fuel has been consumed. **6.** *Med.* Also called **boost′er dose′, boost′er shot′.** a dose of an immunizing substance given to maintain or renew the effect of a previous one. **7.** *Pharm.* a chemical compound, medicinal substance, or the like, that serves as a synergist. **8.** a radio-frequency amplifier for connecting between a radio or television antenna and the receiving set to intensify the received signal. **9.** an auxiliary pump, used in a pipeline or other system, to add to or maintain a prevailing amount of pressure or vacuum. [BOOST + -ER[1]]

boot[1] (bo͞ot), *n.* **1.** a covering of leather, rubber, or the like, for the foot, extending over part or all of the leg. **2.** *Brit.* **a.** any shoe or outer foot covering reaching above the ankle. **b.** a rubber overshoe. **3.** an instrument of torture for the leg, consisting of a kind of vise extending from the knee to the ankle, tightened around the leg by means of screws. **4.** any sheathlike protective covering: *a boot for a weak automobile tire.* **5.** a protective covering for the foot and part of the leg of a horse. **6.** a protecting apron or cover for the driver's seat of a vehicle. **7.** *U.S. Navy, Marines.* a recruit. **8.** the receptacle or place into which the top of a convertible car fits when lowered. **9.** a cloth covering for this receptacle or place. **10.** *Brit.* a compartment or receptacle for baggage in or on a vehicle; an automobile trunk. **11.** *Music.* the box which holds the reed in the reed pipe of an organ. **12.** a kick. **13.** *Slang.* a dismissal; discharge: *They gave him the boot for coming in late.* **14.** *Informal.* enjoyment; delight: *That joke gives me a boot.* **15.** *Baseball Informal.* a fumble of a ball batted on the ground, usually to the infield. **16.** *Theat. Chiefly Brit.* sloat. **17. bet your boots,** to be sure of; be certain: *You can bet your boots that I'll be there!* **18. die with one's boots on,** **a.** to die while actively engaged in one's work, profession, etc. **b.** to die fighting, esp. in battle, or at the hands of another. Also, *esp. Brit.,* **die in one's boots.** **19. lick someone's boots,** to be subservient to; flatter. —*v.t.* **20.** *Slang.* to kick; drive by kicking: *The boy booted a tin can down the street.* **21.** *Football.* to kick. **22.** *Baseball Informal.* to fumble (a ground ball). **23.** to put boots on. **24.** to torture with the boot. **25.** *Slang.* to dismiss; discharge: *They booted him out of school for not studying.* **26.** *Computer Technol.* to load (the operating system or a program) into the memory of a computer. [ME *bote* < MF]

boot[2] (bo͞ot), *n.* **1.** *Archaic.* something given into the bargain. **2.** *Obs.* **a.** advantage. **b.** remedy; relief; help. **3. to boot,** into the bargain; in addition; besides: *We received an extra week's pay to boot.* —*v.i.* **4.** *Archaic.* to be of profit, advantage, or avail: *It boots not to complain.* [ME *bote,* OE *bōt* advantage; c. D *boete,* G *Busse,* Icel *bōt,* Goth *bota;* see BET, BETTER[1]]

boot[3] (bo͞ot), *n. Archaic.* booty; spoil; plunder. [special use of BOOT[2] by assoc. with BOOTY]

boot·black (bo͞ot′blak′), *n.* a person whose occupation is shining shoes, boots, etc. Also called **shoeblack.** [BOOT[1] + BLACK (V.)]

boot′ camp′, *U.S. Mil.* a camp for training recruits.

boot·ed (bo͞o′tid), *adj.* **1.** equipped with boots. **2.** *Ornith.* (of the tarsus of certain birds) covered with a continuous horny, bootlike sheath. [BOOT[1] + -ED[3]]

boot·ee (bo͞o tē′ *or, esp. for 1,* bo͞o′tē), *n.* **1.** a baby's socklike shoe, usually knitted or crocheted, and calf-length or shorter. **2.** any boot having a short leg. [BOOT[1] + *-ee* dim. suffix]

boot·er·y (bo͞o′tə rē), *n., pl.* **-er·ies.** a store selling boots, shoes, etc. [BOOT[1] + -ERY]

Bo·ö·tes (bō ō′tēz), *n., gen.* **-tis** (-tis). *Astron.* the Herdsman, a northern constellation between Ursa Major and Serpens, containing the bright star Arcturus. [< L < Gk: lit., ox-driver; see BOSS[3]]

booth (bo͞oth, bo͞oth), *n., pl.* **booths** (bo͞othz, bo͞oths). **1.** a stall or light structure for the sale of goods or for display purposes, as at a market or fair. **2.** a small compartment, or boxlike room for a specific use by one occupant: *a telephone booth; a motion-picture projection booth.* **3.** a small, temporary structure used by voters at elections. **4.** a partly enclosed compartment or partitioned area, as in a restaurant, music store, etc., equipped for a specific use by one or more persons. **5.** a temporary structure of any material, as boughs, canvas, boards, etc., used esp. for shelter; shed. [ME *bōthe* < Scand; cf. ODan *bōth* booth, c. Icel *būth,* G *Bude,* Pol *buda*]

Booth (bo͞oth; *Brit.* bo͞oth), *n.* **1. Bal·ling·ton** (bal′ing-tən), 1859–1940, founder of the Volunteers of America, 1896 (son of William Booth). **2. Edwin Thomas,** 1833–93, U.S. actor (brother of John Wilkes Booth). **3. Evangeline Co·ry** (kōr′ē, kôr′ē), 1865?–1950, general of the Salvation Army 1934–39 (daughter of William Booth). **4. John Wilkes,** 1838–65, U.S. actor: assassin of Abraham Lincoln (brother of Edwin Thomas

Booth). **5. Junius Brutus,** 1796–1852, English actor (father of Edwin and John Booth). **6. William** ("*General Booth*"), 1829–1912, English religious leader: founder of the Salvation Army 1865. **7. William Bram·well** (bram′wel′, -wəl), 1856–1929, general of the Salvation Army (son of William Booth). **8.** a boy's given name.

Boo·thi·a (bo͞o′thē ə), *n.* **1.** a peninsula in N Canada: the northernmost part of the mainland of North America; former location of the north magnetic pole. **2. Gulf of,** a gulf between this peninsula and Baffin Island.

boot′ hill′, *Western U.S.* a cemetery of a frontier settlement, esp. one in which gunfighters were buried.

boot′ hook′, one of a pair of L-shaped metal hooks fixed to a handle, for drawing on a boot by inserting it through a bootstrap.

boot·jack (bo͞ot′jak′), *n.* **1.** a yokelike device for catching the heel of a boot, as a riding boot, to aid in removing it. **2.** a notch or molding for the same purpose, cut into a piece of furniture. [BOOT[1] + JACK[1]]

boot·lace (bo͞ot′lās′), *n.* **1.** a long, strong lace used to fasten a boot. **2.** *Brit.* a shoelace. [BOOT[1] + LACE]

boot′lace worm′, a brownish-black, ribbonlike nemertean, *Lineus longissimus.*

Boo·tle (bo͞ot′əl), *n.* a city in SW Lancashire, in NW England, on the Mersey estuary. 82,829 (1961).

boot·leg (bo͞ot′leg′), *n., v.,* **-legged, -leg·ging,** *adj. U.S.* **—***n.* **1.** alcoholic liquor unlawfully made, sold, or transported, without registration or payment of taxes. **2.** that part of a boot which covers the leg. **—***v.t.* **3.** to deal in (liquor or other goods) unlawfully. **—***v.i.* **4.** to make, transport, or sell something illegally, esp. liquor. **—***adj.* **5.** made, sold, or transported unlawfully. **6.** illegal or clandestine. **7.** of or pertaining to bootlegging. [BOOT[1] + LEG; secondary senses arose from practice of hiding a liquor bottle in leg of one's boot] **—boot′leg′ger,** *n.*

boot′leg play′, *Football.* a play in which the quarterback pretends to hand the ball to a teammate, hides it by placing it next to his hip, and runs with it.

boot·less (bo͞ot′lis), *adj.* without advantage; unavailing; useless. [ME *bot(e)les,* OE *bōtlēas* unpardonable. See BOOT[2], -LESS] **—boot′less·ly,** *adv.* **—boot′less·ness,** *n.*

boot·lick (bo͞ot′lik′), *Informal.* **—***v.t.* **1.** to seek the favor or good will of (someone) in a servile, degraded way; toady to. **—***v.i.* **2.** to be a toady. [BOOT[1] + LICK] **—boot′lick′er,** *n.*

boots (bo͞ots), *n., pl.* **boots.** *Brit.* a servant, as at a hotel, who blacks or polishes shoes, boots, etc. [pl. of BOOT[1]]

Boots (bo͞ots), *n.* a boy's or girl's given name.

boots′ and sad′dles, *U.S. Army.* (formerly) a cavalry bugle call for mounted drill or formation.

boot·strap (bo͞ot′strap′), *n.* **1.** a loop of leather or cloth sewn at the top rear, or sometimes on each side, of a boot to facilitate pulling it on. **2. pull oneself up by one's (own) bootstraps,** to help oneself without the aid of others; use one's own resources: *I admire him for pulling himself up by his own bootstraps.* [BOOT[1] + STRAP]

boot·top·ping (bo͞ot′top′ing), *n. Naut.* **1.** the area between the water lines of a ship when fully loaded and when unloaded. **2.** a distinctive band of paint covering this area. Also called **boot·top** (bo͞ot′top′). [BOOT[1] + TOPPING]

boot′ tree′, a device of wood, metal, or plastic, inserted in a boot or shoe when it is not being worn, to preserve the shape.

boo·ty (bo͞o′tē), *n., pl.* **-ties. 1.** spoil taken from an enemy in war; plunder; pillage. **2.** that which is seized by violence and robbery. **3.** any prize or gain. [late ME *botye,* var. of *buty* < MLG *bute* booty (orig. a sharing of the spoils), c. Icel *bȳti* exchange, barter; *oo* of BOOT[2]] **—boot′y·less,** *adj.*

Bo·oz (bō′oz), *n. Douay Bible.* Boaz (def. 1).

booze (bo͞oz), *n., v.,* **boozed, booz·ing.** *Informal.* **—***n.* **1.** any alcoholic beverage; whiskey. **2.** a drinking bout or spree. **—***v.t., v.i.* **3.** to drink excessively. [var. of BOUSE[2]] **—booz′er,** *n.*

booz·y (bo͞o′zē), *adj.,* **booz·i·er, booz·i·est.** *Informal.* **1.** drunken; intoxicated. **2.** addicted to liquor. [BOOZE + -Y[1]] **—booz′i·ly,** *adv.* **—booz′i·ness,** *n.*

bop[1] (bop), *n.* the earliest form of modern jazz, developing in the early 1940's with increasingly chromatic and dissonant harmony, subtly complex rhythms, obscured melodic line, and more freedom for and emphasis on the soloist. [(BE)BOP]

bop[2] (bop), *v.,* **bopped, bop·ping,** *n. Slang.* **—***v.t.* **1.** to strike, as with the fist, a stick, etc.; hit. **—***n.* **2.** a blow. [var. of BOB[3]]

Bo-peep (bō pēp′), *n.* peekaboo. [*bo* (var. of BOO) + PEEP[1]]

Bo-Peep (bō pēp′), *n. Chiefly Brit. Slang.* sleep. [rhyming slang]

bop·per (bop′ər), *n.* **1.** a musician who specializes in bop. **2.** a fan of bop. Also called **bop·ster** (bop′stər). [BOP[1] + -ER[1]]

BOQ, *U.S. Mil.* bachelor officers' quarters.

bor-, var. of **boro-** esp. before a vowel.

bor., borough.

bo·ra[1] (bôr′ə, bōr′ə), *n. Meteorol.* (on the Adriatic coasts) a violent, dry, cold wind blowing from the north or northeast. [< dial. It (NE), var. of It *borea* BOREAS]

bo·ra[2] (bôr′ə, bōr′ə), *n. Australian.* an initiation rite of the aborigines in which boys are accepted into the tribe as men. [< Austral aboriginal *bōr, būr* circle]

Bo·ra Bo·ra (bôr′ə bôr′ə; bōr′ə bōr′ə), an island in the Society Islands, in the S Pacific, NW of Tahiti. ab. 1400; 15 sq. mi.

bo·rac·ic (bə ras′ik, bō-, bô-), *adj. Chem.* boric. [*borac-* (s. of BORAX) + -IC]

bo·ra·cite (bôr′ə sīt′, bōr′-), *n.* a strongly pyroelectric mineral, a borate and chloride of magnesium, $Mg_6Cl_2B_{14}O_{26}$, occurring in white or colorless cubic crystals or fine-grained masses. [*borac-* (s. of BORAX) + -ITE[1]]

bor·age (bûr′ij, bôr′-, bor′-), *n.* **1.** a plant, *Borago officinalis,* native of southern Europe, having hairy leaves and stems, used medicinally and in salads. **2.** any of various allied or similar plants of the family *Boraginaceae.* [ME *burage* < MF *bourage* < VL **burrāgō* (LL *burra* hair stuffing + *-gō* n. suffix)]

bo·rag·i·na·ceous (bə raj′ə nā′shəs, bō-, bô-), *adj.* belonging to the *Boraginaceae,* or borage family of plants, including borage, bugloss, heliotrope, forget-me-not, etc. [< NL *Borāginācе(ae)* family name (*Borāgin-,* s. of *Borāgō* genus name; see BORAGE + *-āceae* -ACEAE) + -OUS]

Bo·rah (bōr′ə, bôr′ə), *n.* **William Edgar,** 1865–1940, U.S. senator from Idaho 1906–40.

bor·ak (bôr′ək, bor′-), *n. Australian.* ridicule; a mocking or sarcastic remark. [< native Austral name]

bor·al (bôr′al, -əl, bôr′-), *n. Pharm.* a compound of an aluminum tartrate and borate, used chiefly as an astringent and antiseptic. [BOR(ATE) + AL(UMINUM)]

Bo·rås (bo͞o rôs′), *n.* a city in S Sweden, near Göteborg. 65,648 (1959).

bo·ras·ca (bə ras′kə), *n.* (esp. in the Mediterranean) a squall, usually accompanied by thunder and lightning. Also, **bo·ras·co** (bə ras′kō), **bo·rasque** (bə rask′), **bor·rasca, bourrasque.** [< Sp *borrasca,* equiv. to *borra-* (<< Gk *borrâs,* var. of *boréas* north wind) + *-sca* aug. suffix; r. *borasque* < MF]

bo·rate (*n.* bôr′āt, -it, bôr′-; *v.* bôr′āt, bôr′-), *n., v.,* **-rat·ed, -rat·ing.** *Chem.* **—***n.* **1.** a salt or ester of boric acid. **2.** (loosely) a salt or ester of any acid containing boron. **—***v.t.* **3.** to treat with borate, boric acid, or borax. [BOR- + -ATE[2]]

bo·rax[1] (bôr′aks, -əks, bôr′-), *n., pl.* **bo·rax·es, bo·ra·ces** (bôr′ə sēz′, bôr′-). a white, water-soluble powder or crystals, $Na_2B_4O_7 \cdot 10H_2O$, occurring naturally or obtained from naturally occurring borates: used as a flux, cleansing agent, in the manufacture of glass, porcelain, and enamel, and in tanning; tincal. Also called **sodium borate, sodium pyroborate, sodium tetraborate.** [< ML < Ar *būraq* < Pers *būrah;* r. ME *boras* < MF < ML *borax*]

bo·rax[2] (bôr′aks, -əks, bôr′-), *n. Slang.* cheap, showy, poorly made merchandise, esp. cheaply built furniture of an undistinguished or heterogeneous style. [so called from the premiums for cheap furniture offered by manufacturers of borax soap]

bo′rax pentahy′drate, *Chem.* a white, crystalline, water-soluble solid, $Na_2B_4O_7 \cdot 5H_2O$, used chiefly for killing weeds, as a water softener, and as a disinfectant and deodorizing agent.

bor·bo·ryg·mus (bôr′bə rig′məs), *n., pl.* **-mi** (-mī). *Med.* a rumbling or gurgling sound caused by the movement of gas in the intestines. [< NL < Gk *borborygmós* intestinal rumbling]

bord (bôrd), *n. Brit. Mining.* room (def. 8). [var. of BOARD, so called because orig. floored with boards]

Bor·da (bôr′də), *n.* a walled plain in the fourth quadrant of the face of the moon: about 26 miles in diameter.

bord-and-pil·lar (bôrd′ən pil′ər), *adj. Brit. Mining.* room-and-pillar.

Bor·deaux (bôr dō′), *n.* **1.** a seaport in and the capital of Gironde, in SW France, on the Garonne River. 254,122 (1962). **2.** any of various wines produced in the region surrounding Bordeaux, esp. claret. **3.** See **Bordeaux mixture.**

Bordeaux′ mix′ture, *Hort.* a fungicide consisting of a mixture of copper sulfate, lime, and water. [free trans. of F *bouillie bordelaise.* See BOIL[1], BORDELAISE]

bor·del (bôr′dəl), *n. Archaic.* a brothel. [ME < AF, OF, equiv. to *borde* wooden hut (< Gmc; akin to BOARD) + *-el* < L *-ell(us)* dim. suffix]

Bor·de·lais (bôr′dəlā′; *Fr.* bôʀ də le′), *n.* a wine-growing region in SW France, in Gironde.

Bor·de·laise (bôr′dəlāz′; *Fr.* bôʀ də lez′), *n.* a brown sauce flavored with red wine and shallots, and garnished with poached marrow and parsley. Also called **Bordelaise′ sauce′.** [< F, fem. of *bordelais* of Bordeaux, equiv. to *Bordel-* Bordeaux + *-ais* -ESE]

bor·del·lo (bôr del′ō), *n., pl.* **-los.** a brothel. [< It; see BORDEL]

Bor·den (bôr′dən), *n.* **Sir Robert Laird** (lârd), 1854–1937, Canadian statesman: prime minister 1911–20.

Bor·den·town (bôr′dən toun′), *n.* a town in W New Jersey. 4974 (1960).

bor·der (bôr′dər), *n.* **1.** the part or edge of a surface or area which forms its outer boundary. **2.** the line that separates one country, state, province, etc., from another; frontier line: *He could not cross the French border without a visa.* **3.** the district or region that lies along the boundary line of another. **4.** *U.S.* the frontier of civilization. **5. the border, a.** *U.S.* the border between the U.S. and Mexico, esp. along the Rio Grande. **b.** (in the British Isles) the region along the boundary between England and Scotland. **6.** brink; verge. **7.** an ornamental strip or design around the edge of a printed page, a drawing, etc. **8.** an ornamental design or piece of ornamental trimming around the edge of a fabric, rug, garment, article of furniture, etc. **9.** *Hort.* **a.** a long, narrow bed planted with flowers, shrubs, or trees. **b.** a strip of ground in which plants are grown, enclosing or demarcating an area in a garden or running parallel to a walk or driveway. **c.** the plants growing in such a strip: *The tulips were a border along the path.* **10.** *Theat.* **a.** a narrow curtain or strip of painted canvas hung above the stage, masking the flies and lighting units, and forming the top of the stage set. **b.** See **border light.** **—***v.t.* **11.** to make a border about; adorn with a border. **12.** to form a border or boundary to. **13.** to lie on the border of; adjoin. **14. border on** or **upon,** to approach closely in character; verge on: *The situation borders on tragedy.* [ME *bordure* < AF, OF, equiv. to *bord(er)* (to) border (*bord* ship's side, edge < Gmc; see BOARD) + *-ure* -URE] **—bor′dered,** *adj.* **—bor′der·less,** *adj.*

—Syn 1. rim, periphery, verge. See **edge. 8.** orphrey. **13.** See **adjoining.**

bor·de·reau (bôr′də rō′; *Fr.* bôʀ də ʀō′), *n., pl.* **-reaux** (-rōz′; *Fr.* -ʀō′). a detailed memorandum, esp. one in which documents are listed. [< F, equiv. to *bord* edge (see BORDER) + *-ereau;* see -REL]

bor·der·er (bôr′dər ər), *n.* one who dwells on or near the border of a country, region, etc. [BORDER + -ER[1]]

bor·der·land (bôr′dər land′), *n.* **1.** land forming a border or frontier. **2.** an uncertain, intermediate district, space, or condition. [BORDER + LAND]

bor′der light′, *Theat.* a striplight hung upstage of a border, for lighting the stage. Also, **bor′der·light′.**

bor′der line′, boundary line; frontier.

bor·der·line (bôr′dər līn′), *adj.* **1.** on or near a border or boundary. **2.** uncertain; indeterminate; debatable: *If she's not a psychopath, she's a borderline case.* **3.** approaching bad taste or obscenity: *He made several borderline remarks which offended her.* [BORDER + LINE[1]]

Bor′der Sea′. See **Mare Marginis.**

Bor′der States′, 1. *U.S. Hist.* the slave States inclined to compromise instead of seceding from the Union, comprising Delaware, Maryland, Kentucky, and Missouri, and sometimes extended to include West Virginia and Tennessee. **2.** *U.S.* the states touching the Canadian border. **3.** certain countries of central and northern Europe which border on the Soviet Union and formerly belonged to the Russian Empire: Finland, Poland (prior to 1940); Estonia, Latvia, and Lithuania.

Bor′der ter′rier, one of a British breed of small terriers having a dense, wiry coat ranging in color from red to pale yellow, sometimes being gray and tan, or blue and tan.

Bor·det (bôr dā′; *Fr.* bôʀ de′), *n.* **Jules Jean Baptiste Vin·cent** (zhyl zhäN bA tēst′ vaN säN′), 1870–1961, Belgian physiologist and bacteriologist: Nobel prize for medicine 1919.

bor·dure (bôr′jər), *n. Heraldry.* the area adjacent to the outer edges of an escutcheon, esp. when distinctively treated. [ME; see BORDER]

bore[1] (bōr, bôr), *v.,* **bored, bor·ing,** *n.* **—***v.t.* **1.** to pierce (a solid substance) with some rotary cutting instrument. **2.** to make (a hole) with such an instrument. **3.** to form, make, or construct (a tunnel, mine, well, passage, etc.) by hollowing out, cutting through, or removing a core of material: *to bore a tunnel through the Alps; to bore an oil well 3,000 feet deep.* **4.** *Mach.* to enlarge (a hole) to a precise diameter with a single-edged cutting tool within the hole, by rotating either the tool or the work. **5.** to force or make (a passage); to force (an opening), as through a crowd, by persistent forward thrusting (usually fol. by *through* or *into*). **—***v.i.* **6.** to make a hole in a solid substance with a rotary cutting instrument. **7.** *Mach.* to enlarge a hole to a precise diameter. **8.** (of a substance) to admit of being bored: *Certain types of steel do not bore well.* **—***n.* **9.** a hole made or enlarged by boring. **10.** the inside diameter of a hole, tube, or hollow cylindrical object or device, such as a bushing or bearing, engine cylinder, or the barrel of a gun. [ME *bore(n),* OE *borian;* c. D *boren,* G *bohren,* Icel *bora,* L *for(āre)*] **—bore′a·ble, bor′a·ble,** *adj.*

—Syn. 1. perforate, drill. **10.** caliber.

bore[2] (bōr, bôr), *v.,* **bored, bor·ing,** *n.* **—***v.t.* **1.** to weary by dullness, tedious repetition, unwelcome attentions, etc.: *The game bored me.* **—***n.* **2.** a dull, tiresome, or uncongenial person: *He's a terrible bore.* **3.** a cause of ennui or petty annoyance: *The play was a bore.* [? BORE[1]] **—Syn. 1.** fatigue, tire, annoy. **—Ant. 1.** amuse.

bore[3] (bōr, bôr), *n.* an abrupt rise of tidal water moving rapidly inland from the mouth of an estuary. [ME *bare* < Scand; cf. Icel *bāra* wave]

bore[4] (bōr, bôr), *v.* pt. of **bear**[1].

Bo·re·a·dae (bə rē′ə dē′), *n.pl. Class. Myth.* the descendants of Boreas.

bo·re·al (bôr′ē əl, bôr′-), *adj.* **1.** of or pertaining to the north wind. **2.** of or pertaining to the north. **3.** (*sometimes cap.*) pertaining to Boreas. [late ME *boriall* < LL *boreāl(is)* northern (L *bore(ās)* BOREAS + *-ālis* -AL[1])]

Bo·re·as (bôr′ē əs, bôr′-), *n.* the ancient Greek personification of the north wind. Cf. **Aquilo.**

bore·cole (bôr′kōl′, bôr′-), *n.* kale (def. 1). [< D *boerenkool,* equiv. to *boeren* (see BOOR) + *kool* COLE]

bore·dom (bôr′dəm, bôr′-), *n.* the state or an instance of being bored; tedium; ennui. [BORE[2] + -DOM]

bore·hole (bôr′hōl′, bôr′-), *n. Mining.* a hole drilled in the earth, as for the purpose of extracting a core, releasing gas, oil, or water, etc. [BORE[1] + HOLE]

Bo·rel (bô rel′, bə-; *Fr.* bô ʀel′), *n.* **Fé·lix É·douard É·mile** (fā lēks′ ā dwAʀ′ ā mēl′), 1871–1956, French mathematician.

Bo·rel′-Le·besgue′ the′orem (bô rel′lə beg′), *Math.* See **Heine-Borel theorem.** [named after F.E.E. BOREL and H. LEBESGUE]

bor·er (bôr′ər, bôr′-), *n.* **1.** one who or that which bores or pierces. **2.** *Mach.* a tool used for boring; auger. **3.** *Entomol.* any of several insects that bore into trees, fruits, etc., esp. a beetle that bores into the woody part of plants. **4.** *Zool.* any of various mollusks, worms, etc., that bore into wood, stone, etc. **5.** a marsipobranch fish, as a hagfish, that bores into other fishes to feed on their flesh. [BORE[1] + -ER[1]]

bore·sight (bôr′sīt′, bôr′-), *v.t.* to verify the alignment of the sights and bore of (a firearm). [back formation from *boresighting*]

bore·some (bôr′səm, bôr′-), *adj.* tedious; dull; boring. [BORE[2] + -SOME[1]]

Bo·re·um (bôr′ē əm, bôr′-), *n.* **Mare.** See **Mare Boreum.**

Bor·ger (bôr′gər), *n.* a city in N Texas. 20,911 (1960).

Bor·ger·hout (*Flemish.* bôr′KHər hout′), *n.* a city in N Belgium, near Antwerp. 50,507 (est. 1959).

Bor·ges (bôr′hes), *n.* **Jor·ge Lu·is** (hôr′hā lo͞o ēs′), born 1899, Argentine poet and philosophical essayist.

Bor·ghe·se (bôʀ ge′ze), *n.* a member of a noble Italian family which was originally from Siena and important in Italian politics and society from the 16th to the early 19th century.

Borg·hild (bôrg′hild′), *n.* (in the *Volsunga Saga*) the first wife of Sigmund: she poisons Sinfiotli in revenge for his killing of her brother.

Bor·gia (bôr′jə, -jä; *It.* bôʀ′jä), *n.* **1. Ce·sa·re** (che′zä re), 1476?–1507, Italian cardinal, military leader, and politician. **2. Lu·cre·zia** (lo͞o krē′zhə; *It.* lo͞o kʀe′tsyä), (*Duchess of Ferrara*), 1480–1519, sister and political pawn of Cesare Borgia: patroness of the arts. **3.** their father, **Ro·dri·go Lan·zol** (rô dʀē′gô län zôl′). See **Alexander VI.**

Bor·glum (bôr′gləm), *n.* **John Gut·zon** (gut′sən), 1867–1941, and his brother **Solon Hannibal,** 1868–1922, U.S. sculptors.

bo·ri (bô′rē), *n.* any of various Japanese techniques for carving and engraving ornamental metalwork, as sword mounts. [< Jap]

bo·ric (bôr′ik, bôr′-), *adj. Chem.* of or containing boron; boracic. [BOR- + -IC]

bo′ric ac′id, 1. Also called **orthoboric acid.** *Chem., Pharm.* a white, crystalline acid, H_3BO_3, occurring in nature or prepared from borax: used chiefly in the manufacture of ceramics, cements, glass, enamels, for fireproofing, and in medicine in aqueous solution as a mild antiseptic. **2.** *Chem.* any of a group of acids containing boron.

bo·ride (bôr′īd, bôr′-), *n. Chem.* a compound consisting of two elements of which boron is the more electronegative one. [BOR- + -IDE]

bor·ing (bôr′ing, bôr′-), *n. Mach.* **1.** the act or process of making or enlarging a hole. **2.** the hole so made. **3.** a cylindrical sample of earth strata obtained by boring a vertical hole. **4. borings,** the chips, fragments, or dust produced in boring. [BORE[1] + -ING[1]]

bor′ing bar′, a bar holding a tool for boring a cylinder or the like.

bor′ing machine′, a machine for boring holes in which the cutter is rotated, usually about a horizontal axis.

bor′ing mill′, a machine for boring large holes in heavy work, having a table on which the work rotates while the hole is bored vertically.

Bo·ris (bôr′is, bôr′-), *n.* a boy's given name.

Boris III, 1894–1943, king of Bulgaria 1918–43.

Bo·ris Go·du·nov (bôr′is god′ən nôf′, gŏŏd′-, bôr′-; *Russ.* bo Rēs′ go dŏŏ nôf′), **1.** a play (1825) by Pushkin. **2.** an opera (1874), by Modest Moussorgsky, based on Pushkin's drama. Also, **Bo′ris Go·dou·nov′, Bo′ris Go′du·noff′.**

Bo·ri·slav (bôr′i släv′, bôr′-), *n.* a boy's given name.

born (bôrn), *adj.* **1.** brought forth by birth. **2.** possessing from birth the quality, circumstances, or character stated: *a born musician; a born fool.* **3.** native to the locale stated; immigrated to the present place from the locale stated: *a German-born scientist; a Chicago-born New Yorker.* **4. born yesterday,** naïve; inexperienced: *They wanted to show their associates that they were not born yesterday.* [ME; OE *boren* (ptp. of *beran* to BEAR[1]), equiv. to *bor-* ptp. s. + *-en* -EN[3]]

Born (bôrn), *n.* **Max,** 1882–1970, German physicist: Nobel prize 1954.

born-a·gain (bôrn′ə gen′), *adj. U.S. Informal.* **1.** recommitted to religious faith through an intensely personal experience of salvation through acceptance of Christ: *a born-again Christian.* **2.** enthusiastically committed: *a born-again jogger.*

bor·nan (bôR nän′), *n.* a breeze from southwest Switzerland that blows northward across Lake Geneva. [< SwissF: lit., border wind]

borne[1] (bōrn, bôrn), *v.* a pp. of **bear**[1].

borne[2] (bōrn, bôrn), *n.* a circular sofa having a conical or cylindrical back piece at the center. [< F: pillar; see BOURN[2]]

Borne[2]

Bor·ne·o (bôr′nē ō′), *n.* an island in the Malay Archipelago, including Sabah and Sarawak (formerly British), Brunei, and Indonesian Borneo (formerly Dutch). ab. 4,600,000; ab. 290,000 sq. mi. —**Bor′ne·an,** *adj., n.*

SOUTHEAST ASIA · PHILIPPINES · PACIFIC OCEAN · Borneo · NEW GUINEA · CELEBES · SUMATRA · JAVA · INDIAN OCEAN · AUSTRALIA

bor·ne·ol (bôr′nē ōl′, -ôl′, -ol′), *n. Chem.* a white, translucent, lumpy, very slightly water-soluble, solid terpene alcohol, $C_{10}H_{17}OH$, occurring in various isomeric forms, having a burning, mintlike taste, obtained from the trunk of a tree, *Dryobalanops aromatica,* or by the reduction of camphor: used in the form of its esters in the manufacture of synthetic camphor and in perfumery. Also called **Bor′neo cam′phor, bornyl alcohol, camphol, Malayan camphor, Sumatra camphor.** [BORNE(O) + -OL[1]]

Born·holm (bôRn′hôlm′; *Eng.* bôrn′hōm, -hōlm), *n.* a Danish island in the Baltic Sea, S of Sweden. 48,632 (1955); 227 sq. mi.

Born′holm disease′, *Pathol.* pleurodynia (def. 2). [named after BORNHOLM where it has occurred]

born·ite (bôr′nīt), *n.* a common mineral and important ore of copper, copper iron sulfide, Cu_5FeS_4, occurring in masses, of brownish color when first exposed to the air; peacock ore. [named after I. von *Born* (1742–91), Austrian mineralogist; see -ITE[1]] —**bor·nit·ic** (bôr nit′ik), *adj.*

Bor·nu (bôr nōō′), *n.* a former sultanate in W Africa, S SW of Lake Chad: now largely a province in Nigeria.

bor′nyl ac′etate (bôr′nəl, -nil), *Chem.* a colorless liquid, $C_{10}H_{17}OCOCH_3$, having a piny, camphorlike odor: used chiefly as a scent in the manufacture of perfume, and as a plasticizer. [BORN(EOL) + -YL]

bor′nyl al′cohol, *Chem.* borneol.

bor′nyl for′mate, *Chem.* a colorless liquid, $C_{10}H_{17}OCHO$, having a piny odor, used chiefly as a scent in the manufacture of soaps and disinfectants.

boro-, a combining form of "boron," used esp. before a consonant: *borofluoride.* Also, *esp. before a vowel,* **bor-.**

Bo·ro·din (bôr′ə dēn′; *Russ.* bo Ro dēn′), *n.* **A·le·ksan·dr Por·fir·e·vich** (ä′le ksän′dRə poR fiR ye′vich), 1834–87, Russian composer and chemist.

Bo·ro·di·no (bo Ro dē nô′), *n.* a village in the W Soviet Union, 70 mi. W of Moscow: Napoleon's victory here made possible the capture of Moscow, 1812.

bo·ro·glyc·er·ide (bôr′ə glis′ə rīd′, -ər id, bôr′-), *n. Chem.* any compound containing boric acid and glycerol, used chiefly as an antiseptic. [BORO- + GLYCERIDE]

bo·ro·hy·dride (bôr′ə hī′drīd, -drid, bôr′-), *n. Chem.* any of the class of compounds containing the group BH_4–, as sodium borohydride, used chiefly as reducing agents. [BORO- + HYDRIDE]

bo·ron (bôr′on, bôr′-), *n. Chem.* a nonmetallic element occurring naturally only in combination, as in borax, boric acid, etc., and obtained in either an amorphous or a crystalline form when reduced from its compounds. *Symbol:* B; *at. wt.:* 10.811; *at. no.:* 5. [BOR(AX) + (CARB)ON] —**bo·ron·ic** (bō ron′ik, bô-, bə-), *adj.*

bo′ron car′bide, *Chem.* a black, crystalline, extremely hard, water-insoluble solid, B_4C, used chiefly as a moderator in nuclear reactors, as an abrasive, and as a refractory.

bo·ro·sil·i·cate (bôr′ə sil′ə kit, -kāt′, bôr′-), *n. Chem.* a salt of boric and silicic acids. [BORO- + SILICATE]

bo′ro·si·lic′ic ac′id (bôr′ō si lis′ik, bôr′-, bôr′-, bôr′-), *Chem.* any of several hypothetical acids which form borosilicates. [BORO- + SILICIC ACID]

bor·ough (bûr′ō, bur′ō), *n.* **1.** *U.S.* (in certain States) an incorporated municipality smaller than a city. **2.** one of the five administrative divisions of New York City. **3.** *Brit.* **a.** an urban community incorporated by royal charter, similar to an incorporated city or municipality in the U.S. **b.** a town, area, or constituency represented by a Member of Parliament. **c.** (formerly) a fortified town organized as and having some of the powers of an independent country. [ME *burgh* town, OE *burg* fortified town; c. Icel *borg,* G *Burg* castle, Goth *baurgs* city]

bor·ough-Eng·lish (bûr′ō ing′glish, bur′-), *n.* (in some parts of England) a custom by which the youngest son inherits the entire estate upon the death of his father.

bor·ras·ca (bə ras′kə), *n.* borasca.

bor·rel·i·a (bə rel′ē ə, -rel′yə, -rē′lē ə, -rēl′yə), *n. Bacteriol.* any of several spiral, parasitic bacteria of the genus *Borrelia,* certain species of which are pathogenic for man, other mammals, or birds. [< NL, named after Amédée *Borrel* (d. 1936); see -IA]

Bor·ro·mi·ni (bôr′ō mē′nē; *It.* bôR′Rô mē′nē), *n.* **Fran·ces·co** (frän ches′kō; *It.* fRän ches′kô), 1599–1667, Italian architect and sculptor.

bor·row (bor′ō, bôr′ō), *v.t.* **1.** to take or obtain (something) with the promise to return it or its equivalent: *The neighbors borrowed my lawn mower.* **2.** to use, appropriate, or introduce from another source or from a foreign source: *to borrow an idea from the opposition; to borrow a word from French.* **3.** *Arith.* (in subtraction) to take from one denomination and add to the next lower. —*v.i.* **4.** to borrow something: *Don't borrow unless you expect to repay.* **5.** *Naut.* **a.** to sail close to the wind; luff. **b.** to sail close to the shore. **6.** *Golf.* to putt on other than a direct line from the lie of the ball to the hole, to compensate for the incline or roll of the green. **7. borrow trouble,** to worry prematurely or unnecessarily; be pessimistic: *It was her nature to borrow trouble.* [ME *borow(en),* OE *borgian* to borrow, lend, deriv. of *borg* a pledge; akin to D *borg* a pledge, *borgen* to charge, give credit, G *Borg* credit, *borg(en)* (to) take on credit] —**bor′row·er,** *n.*

Bor·row (bor′ō, bôr′ō), *n.* **George,** 1803–81, English traveler, writer, and student of languages, esp. Romany. —**Bor·ro·vi·an** (bə rō′vē ən), *adj., n.*

bor′rowed time′, an uncertain period of time extending beyond original expectations.

bor′rower's card′. See **library card.**

bor·row·ing (bor′ō ing, bôr′-), *n.* **1.** the act or process of one who borrows. **2.** the result of the process of borrowing; something borrowed, as a word, phrase, etc., taken from a foreign language and used colloquially. [BORROW + -ING[1]]

Bors (bôrs), *n.* **Sir,** *Arthurian Romance.* **1.** Also, **Sir Bors de Gan·is** (də gan′is). a knight of the Round Table, nephew of Lancelot. **2.** a natural son of King Arthur.

borscht (bôrsht), *n.* an eastern European soup containing beets and usually cabbage, served hot or chilled, often with sour cream. Also, **borsch** (bôrsh), **borsht.** [< Russ *borshtsh*]

borscht′ cir′cuit, the nightclubs, hotels, and theaters of the Jewish resort area in the Catskill Mountains. Also called **borscht′ belt′.** [so called, facetiously, from the supposed quantities of beet soup consumed there]

bor·stal (bôr′stəl), *n.* (in England) a school for delinquent boys which provides therapy and vocational training. Also, **bor′stal institu′tion.** [named after *Borstal,* village in Kent, England]

bor′stal boy′, **1.** a boy in an English school for delinquents. **2.** (*caps., italics*) an autobiographical novel (1958) by Brendan Behan.

bort (bôrt), *n.* a quantity of low-quality diamonds and small fragments, valuable only in crushed or powdered form. Also, **boart, bortz** (bôrts). [appar. metathetic var. of **brot* (OE *gebrot* fragment); akin to ME *brotel* brittle, Icel *brot* fragment, etc.] —**bort′y,** *adj.*

bor·zoi (bôr′zoi), *n., pl.* **-zois.** one of a breed of tall, slender dogs having long, silky hair, raised originally in Russia for hunting wolves. Also called **Russian wolfhound.** [< Russ: lit., swift]

Borzoi
(2½ ft. high at shoulder)

Bo·san·quet (bō′zən ket′, -kit), *n.* **Bernard,** 1848–1923, English philosopher and writer.

Bosc (bosk), *n.* **1.** a large, greenish-yellow variety of pear. **2.** the tree bearing this fruit.

bos·cage (bos′kij), *n.* a mass of trees or shrubs; wood, grove, or thicket. Also, **boskage.** [late ME *boskage* < MF *boscage.* See BOSK, -AGE]

Bosch (bosh, bôsh; *for 2 also Du.* bos, bôs), *n.* **1. Carl,** 1874–1940, German chemist: Nobel prize 1931. **2. Hi·e·ro·ny·mus** (hē′ə rō′nə məs), (*Hieronymus van Akeen*), 1450?–1516, Dutch painter.

bosch·bok (bosh′bok′), *n., pl.* **-boks,** (*esp. collectively*) **-bok.** bushbuck.

bosch·vark (bosh′värk′), *n.* See **bush pig.** [< SAfrD: *bosch* wood, BUSH[1] + *vark* pig; see AARDVARK]

Bos·co·bel (bos′kə bel′), *n.* a town in SW Wisconsin. 2608 (1960).

Bos·co·vich (bos′kə vich), *n.* a walled plain in the first quadrant of the face of the moon: about 20 miles in diameter

Bose (bōs), *n.* **Sir Ja·ga·dis Chan·dre** (jə gə dēs′ chun′drə), 1858–1937, Indian physicist and plant physiologist.

Bose′-Ein′stein statis′tics (bōs′in′stīn), *Physics.* quantum statistics for particles not obeying the exclusion principle, based on the assumption that in a given physical system consisting of indistinguishable particles and regions all distinguishable arrangements of the particles have equal probability. [named after S. N. *Bose* (see BOSON) and Albert EINSTEIN]

bosh[1] (bosh), *n. Informal.* nonsense; absurd or foolish talk. [< Turk *boş* empty, useless]

bosh[2] (bosh), *n. Metall.* the section of a blast furnace between the hearth and the stack, having the form of a frustum of an inverted cone. [prob. < G; akin to G *böschen* to slope, *Böschung* slope, scarp]

bosk (bosk), *n. Archaic.* a small wood or thicket, esp. of bushes. [ME *boske,* var. of *busk(e)* < Scand; cf. Icel *buskr* (now obs.), Dan *busk* BUSH[1]]

bos·kage (bos′kij), *n.* boscage.

bos·ker (bos′kər), *adj. Australian Slang.* excellent; very good. [?]

bos·ket (bos′kit), *n.* a grove; thicket. Also, **bosquet.** [earlier *bosquet* < F < It *boschetto,* equiv. to *bosc(o)* wood (see BUSH[1]) + *-etto* -ET]

bosk·y (bos′kē), *adj.,* **bosk·i·er, bosk·i·est. 1.** woody; covered with bushes. **2.** shady. [BOSK + -Y[1]] —**bosk′i·ness,** *n.*

bo′s′n (bō′sən), *n.* boatswain.

Bos·ni·a (boz′nē ə), *n.* a historic region in SE Europe: a former Turkish province; a part of Austria-Hungary (1879–1918) now part of Bosnia and Herzegovina. —**Bos′ni·an,** *adj.*

Bos′nia and Herze·govi′na, a republic in SE Europe: formerly part of Yugoslavia. 3,746,000; 19,909 sq. mi. *Cap.:* Sarajevo.

bos·om (bŏŏz′əm, bōō′zəm), *n.* **1.** the breast of a human being. **2.** that part of a garment which covers the breast. **3.** the breast, conceived of as the center of thought or emotion. **4.** the breasts of a woman. **5.** something likened to the human breast: *the bosom of the earth.* **6.** any warm, comfortable, familiar place: *the bosom of the family.* **7.** *Shipbuilding.* root[1] (def. 15). —*adj.* **8.** of, pertaining to, or worn on or over the bosom. **9.** intimate or confidential: *a bosom friend.* —*v.t.* **10.** to take to the bosom; embrace; cherish. **11.** to hide from view; conceal. [ME; OE *bōs(u)m;* c. D *boesem,* G *Busen*] —**Syn. 3.** heart, affection. **9.** close.

bos′om bar′, *Shipbuilding.* a short piece of angle iron fitted over the interior faces of the flanges of two angle irons butted together edge to edge to join them. Also called **bos′om piece′.**

bos·omed (bŏŏz′əmd, bōō′zəmd), *adj.* **1.** concealed or secreted in the bosom. **2.** having a specified type of bosom (usually used in combination): *a full-bosomed garment; the green-bosomed earth.* [BOSOM + -ED[3]]

bos′om knee′, *Naut.* See **lodging knee.**

bos′om plate′, *Shipbuilding.* a plate connecting the inner faces of the flanges of two angle irons placed edge to edge to produce a compound member similar to a channel iron.

bos·om·y (bŏŏz′ə mē, bōō′zə-), *adj.* (of a woman) having large or prominent breasts. [BOSOM + -Y[1]]

bo·son (bō′son), *n. Physics.* any of several elementary particles, as a photon, having an integral spin and obeying Bose-Einstein statistics. Cf. **fermion.** [named after S. N. *Bose* (b. 1894), Indian physicist; see -(I)ON]

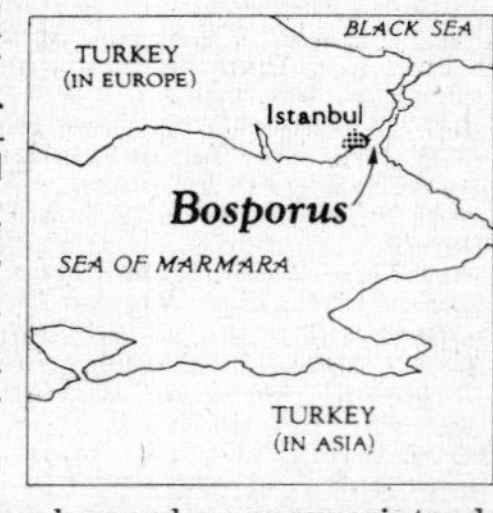

Bos·po·rus (bos′pər əs), *n.* a strait connecting the Black Sea and the Sea of Marmara. 18 mi. long. Also, **Bos·pho·rus** (bos′fər əs). —**Bos′po·ran, Bos·po·ran·ic** (bos′pə ran′ik), **Bos·po·ri·an** (bo spôr′ē ən, -spôr′-), *adj.*

bos·quet (bos′kit), *n.* bosket.

boss[1] (bôs, bos), *n.* **1.** one who employs or superintends workmen; foreman or manager. **2.** *U.S.* a politician who controls his party organization, as in a particular district. **3.** *Informal.* a person who makes decisions, exercises authority, dominates, etc.: *His wife's the boss in his family.* —*v.t.* **4.** to be master of or over; manage; direct; control. —*v.i.* **5.** to be boss. **6.** to be too domineering and authoritative. —*adj.* **7.** chief; master. **8.** *Slang.* first-rate. [< D *baas* master, foreman]

boss[2] (bôs, bos), *n.* **1.** *Bot., Zool.* a protuberance or roundish excrescence on the body or on some organ of an animal or plant. **2.** *Geol.* a knoblike mass of rock, esp. an outcrop of igneous or metamorphic rock. **3.** an ornamental protuberance of metal, ivory, etc.; stud. **4.** *Archit.* **a.** an ornamental, knoblike projection, as a carved keystone at the intersection of ogives. **b.** a stone roughly formed and set in place for later carving. **5.** one of several pieces of brass or other metal inset into the cover of a book to protect the corners or edges or for decoration. **6.** *Mach.* a small projection on a casting or forging. **7.** *Naut.* a projecting part in a ship's hull, or in one frame of a hull, fitting around a propeller shaft. —*v.t.* **8.** to ornament with bosses. **9.** to emboss. **10.** (in plumbing) to hammer sheet metal, as lead, to conform to an irregular surface. [ME *boce* < OF; c. It *bozza* metal projecting part; see BOTCH[2]]

boss[3] (bos, bôs), *n. U.S.* a name for a cow. [var. of dial. *buss* young calf; perh. << L *bōs* ox, cow (see BOVINE)]

boss[4] (bos), *adj. Scot.* hollow; empty. [?]

bos·sage (bô′sij, bos′ij), *n. Masonry.* **1.** stonework blocked out for later carving. **2.** stonework, as rusticated ashlar, having faces projecting beyond the mortar joints. [< F, equiv. to *bosse* BOSS[2] + *-age* -AGE]

bos·sa no·va (bos′ə nō′və), **1.** jazz-influenced music of Brazilian origin, rhythmically related to the samba. **2.** a dance performed to this music. [< Pg: lit., new voice]

boss·eyed (bôs′īd′, bos′-), *adj. Brit. Slang.* injured in one eye or cross-eyed. [perh. BOSS[2] + EYED]

Bos·sier′ Cit′y (bo sēr′), a city in NW Louisiana. 32,776 (1960).

boss·ism (bô′siz əm, bos′iz-), *n.* *U.S.* control by bosses, esp. political bosses. [BOSS[1] + -ISM]

Bos·suet (bô swe′), *n.* **Jacques Bé·ni·gne** (zhäk bā nēn′y), 1627–1704, French bishop, writer, and orator.

boss·y[1] (bô′sē, bos′ē), *adj.*, **boss·i·er, boss·i·est.** *Informal.* domineering; overly authoritative; given to acting like a boss. [BOSS[1] + -Y[1]] —**boss′i·ness,** *n.*

boss·y[2] (bô′sē, bos′ē), *adj.* **boss·i·er, boss·i·est.** studded with bosses. [BOSS[2] + -Y[1]]

bos·sy[3] (bos′ē, bô′sē), *n.*, *pl.* **-sies.** *U.S.* a familiar name for a cow or calf. [BOSS[3] + -Y[2]]

Bos·ton (bô′stən, bos′tən), *n.* **1.** a seaport in and the capital of Massachusetts, in the E part. 562,994. **2.** (*l.c.*) a variety of whist, popular in the early 19th century, played by four persons with two packs of cards. **3.** (*usually l.c.*) a social dance that is a modification of the waltz.

Bos′ton bag′, a two-handled bag for carrying books, papers, etc.

Bos′ton brown′ bread′, a dark-brown steamed bread made of corn meal and rye meal, or graham or wheat flour, sweetened with molasses.

Bos′ton bull′. See **Boston terrier.**

Bos′ton cream′ pie′, a two-layer cake with a thick filling of cream or custard between the layers, often having a chocolate icing on top.

Bos′ton fern′, a variety of sword fern, *Nephrolepis exaltata bostoniensis,* having long, narrow, drooping fronds.

Bos′ton hip′, a covering of a row of shingles, slates, or the like, laid along a roof hip on each of the roof planes so as to overlap.

Bos′ton hook′er. See **Irish boat.**

Bos·to·ni·an (bô stō′nē ən, bo stō′-), *adj.* **1.** of, pertaining to, or typical of Boston, Mass., or its residents: *a Bostonian childhood; Bostonian reserve.* —*n.* **2.** a native or inhabitant of Boston, Mass. [BOSTON + -IAN]

Bostonians, The, a novel (1886) by Henry James.

Bos′ton i′vy, a woody, Oriental, climbing vine, *Parthenocissus tricuspidate,* grown in the U.S. as a wall covering. Also called **Japanese ivy.**

Bos′ton Mas′sacre, *Amer. Hist.* a riot (March 5, 1770) arising from the resentment of Boston colonists toward British troops quartered in the city, in which the troops fired on the mob and killed several persons.

Bos′ton ridge′, a covering of a row of shingles, slates, or the like, laid along a roof ridge on each of the roof planes so as to overlap.

Bos′ton rock′er, a wooden American rocking chair having a solid, curved seat, often painted or grained, a spindle back, narrow rockers, and usually having gilt designs stenciled on the crest rail.

Bos′ton Tea′ Par′ty, *Amer. Hist.* a raid on three British ships in Boston Harbor (December 16, 1773) in which Boston colonists, disguised as Indians, threw the contents of several hundred chests of tea into the harbor as a protest against British taxes on tea and against the monopoly granted the East India Company.

Bos′ton ter′rier, one of an American breed of small, pug-faced, short-haired dogs having erect ears, a short tail, and a brindled or black coat with white markings. Also called **Boston bull.**

Boston terrier (14 in. high at shoulder)

bo·sun (bō′sən), *n.* boatswain.

Bos·well (boz′wel′, -wəl), *n.* **1. James,** 1740–95, Scottish author: biographer of Samuel Johnson. **2.** any devoted biographer of a specific person. —**Bos·well·i·an** (boz wel′ē ən), *adj.*

bos·well·ize (boz′wə līz′), *v.*, **-ized, -iz·ing.** —*v.t.* **1.** to write (an account of) in the manner of Boswell. —*v.i.* **2.** to write in the manner of Boswell. Also, **Bos′well·ize.** [BOSWELL + -IZE] —**bos′well·ism, Bos′well·ism,** *n.*

Bos′worth Field′ (boz′wərth), a battlefield in central England, near Leicester, where Richard III was defeated and slain by the future Henry VII (the first Tudor ruler of England) in 1485.

bot (bot), *n.* the larva of a botfly. Also, **bott.** [?]

bot., **1.** botanical. **2.** botanist. **3.** botany.

B.O.T., Board of Trade.

bo·tan·i·cal (bə tan′i kəl), *adj.* **1.** Also, **bo·tan′ic.** of, pertaining to, made from, or containing plants: *botanical survey; botanical drugs.* —*n.* **2.** *Pharm.* a drug made from part of a plant, as from roots, leaves, bark, etc. [*botanic* (< ML *botanic(us)* < Gk *botanikós* of plants, equiv. to *botán(ē)* herb + *-ikos* -IC) + -AL[1]] —**bo·tan′i·cal·ly,** *adv.*

botan′ical gar′den, a garden for the exhibition and scientific study of collected, growing plants, usually in association with greenhouses, herbariums, laboratories, etc.

bot·a·nise (bot′ənīz′), *v.i., v.t.*, **-nised, -nis·ing.** *Chiefly Brit.* botanize. —**bot′an·is′er,** *n.*

bot·a·nist (bot′ənist), *n.* one skilled in botany. [*botan(ism)* botany (< Gk *botanism(ós),* equiv. to *botán(ē)* plant + *-ismos* -ISM) + -IST]

bot·a·nize (bot′ənīz′), *v.*, **-nized, -niz·ing.** —*v.i.* **1.** to study plants or plant life. **2.** to collect plants for scientific study. —*v.t.* **3.** to explore botanically; study the plant life of. Also, *esp. Brit.,* **botanise.** [< NL *botaniz(āre)* < Gk *botaniz(ein)* (to) gather plants. See BOTANIST, -IZE] —**bot′a·niz′er,** *n.*

bot·an·o·man·cy (bot′ənə man′sē), *n.* divination by means of plants. [< Gk *botano-* (comb. form of *botánē* herb, plant) + -MANCY]

bot·a·ny (bot′ənē), *n.*, *pl.* **-nies.** **1.** the science of plants; the branch of biology that deals with plant life. **2.** the plant life of a region: *the botany of Alaska.* **3.** the biology of a plant or plant group: *the botany of deciduous trees.* **4.** (*sometimes cap.*) See **Botany wool.** [*botan(ic)* (see BOTANICAL) + -Y[3]]

Bot′any Bay′, a bay on the SE coast of Australia, near Sydney.

Bot′any wool′, a fine wool obtained from merino sheep. Also called **botany.**

botch[1] (boch), *v.t.* **1.** to spoil by poor work; bungle: *He botched the job badly.* **2.** to do or say in a bungling manner. **3.** to mend or patch in a clumsy manner. —*n.* **4.** a clumsy or poor piece of work; bungle: *He made a complete botch of his first attempt at baking.* **5.** a clumsily added part or patch. **6.** a disorderly or confused combination; conglomeration. [ME *bocche(n)* < ?] —**botch·ed·ly** (boch′id lē), *adv.* —**botch′er,** *n.* —**botch′er·y,** *n.*

botch[2] (boch), *n.* *Archaic.* **1.** a swelling on the skin; a boil. **2.** an eruptive disease. [ME *bocche* < OF *boche,* dial. var. of *boce* BOSS[2]]

botch·y (boch′ē), *adj.*, **botch·i·er, botch·i·est.** poorly made or done; bungled. [BOTCH[1] + -Y[1]] —**botch′i·ly,** *adv.* —**botch′i·ness,** *n.*

bo·tel (bō tel′), *n.* boatel.

bot·fly (bot′flī′), *n.*, *pl.* **-flies.** any of several dipterous insects of the families *Oestridae* and *Gasterophilidae,* the larvae of which are parasitic in the skin or other parts of animals or man. [BOT + FLY[2]]

both (bōth), *adj.* **1.** one and the other; two together: *He met both girls. Both girls were beautiful.* —*pron.* **2.** the one as well as the other: *Both of us were going to the party.* —*conj.* **3.** alike; equally: *He is both ready and willing.* [ME *bōthe, bāthe* < Scand (cf. Icel *bāthir* both; c. G *beide*); r. ME *bo, ba,* OE *bā;* c. Goth *bai;* akin to L *(am)bō,* Gk *(ám)phō*]

Bo·tha (bō′tə), *n.* **Lou·is** (lo͞o ē′), 1863–1919, South African general and statesman.

Bo·the (bō′tə), *n.* **Wal·ther** (väl′tər), 1891–1957, German physicist: Nobel prize 1954.

both·er (both′ər), *v.t.* **1.** to give trouble to; annoy; pester; worry: *His baby sister bothered him for candy.* **2.** to bewilder; confuse: *His inability to understand her bothered him.* —*v.i.* **3.** to take the trouble; trouble or inconvenience oneself: *Don't bother to call. He has no time to bother with trifles.* —*n.* **4.** something troublesome, burdensome, or annoying: *Doing the laundry every week can be a terrible bother.* **5.** effort, work, or worry: *Gardening takes more bother than it's worth.* **6.** a worried or perplexed state: *Don't get into such a bother about small matters.* **7.** someone who bothers or annoys: *She's a perpetual bother to me.* —*interj.* **8.** *Chiefly Brit.* used to express mild irritation. [? AIr var. of POTHER]
—**Syn. 1.** harass, vex, irritate; molest, disturb. BOTHER, ANNOY, PLAGUE, TEASE imply persistent interference with one's comfort or peace of mind. BOTHER suggests causing trouble or weariness or repeatedly interrupting in the midst of pressing duties. To ANNOY is to vex or irritate by bothering. PLAGUE is a strong word, connoting unremitting annoyance and harassment. To TEASE is to pester, as by long-continued whining and begging.

both·er·a·tion (both′ə rā′shən), *interj.* **1.** an exclamation indicating vexation or annoyance. —*n.* **2.** the act or state of bothering or the state of being bothered. [BOTHER + -ATION]

both·er·some (both′ər səm), *adj.* causing bother; troublesome. [BOTHER + -SOME[1]]

Both·ni·a (both′nē ə), *n.* **Gulf of,** an arm of the Baltic Sea, extending N between Sweden and Finland. ab. 400 mi. long. —**Both′ni·an,** *adj., n.* —**Both′nic,** *adj.*

bo·thrid·i·um (bō thrid′ē əm), *n.*, *pl.* **-thrid·i·a** (-thrid′ē ə), **-thrid·i·ums.** *Zool.* one of several muscular, often hooked projections from the scolex of certain tapeworms. [< NL < Gk *bóthr(os)* pit + *-idion* dim. suffix]

both·ri·um (both′rē əm), *n.*, *pl.* **-ri·a** (-rē ə), **-ri·ums.** *Zool.* one of several slitlike grooves or depressions on the scolex of certain tapeworms. [< NL < Gk *bóthrion,* equiv. to *bóthr(os)* a pit, trench, hole (in the ground) + *-ion* dim. suffix]

Both·well (both′wel′, -wəl, both′-), *n.* **James Hepburn** (hep′bûrn *or, esp. Brit.,* heb′ərn), **Earl of,** 1536?–78, third husband of Mary, Queen of Scots.

both·y (both′ē, both′ē), *n.*, *pl.* **both·ies.** *Scot.* a hut or small cottage, esp. for lodging farm hands or workmen. [perh. ME *both* BOOTH + -Y[2]]

Bot·kin (bot′kin), *n.* **Benjamin Albert,** born 1901, U.S. folklorist, editor, and essayist.

bot·o·née (bot′ənā′, bot′ənā′), *adj.* *Heraldry.* (of a cross) having arms terminating in the form of a trefoil: *cross botonée.* Also, **bot′on·née′, bot·o·ny, bot·on·ny** (bot′ənē). See illus. under **cross.** [< MF: covered with buds, equiv. to *boton* bud, BUTTON + *-ée;* see -EE]

bo′ tree′ (bō), the pipal, or sacred fig tree, *Ficus religiosa,* of India, under which the founder of Buddhism is reputed to have attained the enlightenment which constituted him the Buddha. Also called **bodhi tree.** [< Singhalese *bogaha,* equiv. to *bo* (< Pali *bodhi* < Skt; see BODHISATTVA) + *gaha* tree]

bot·ry·oi·dal (bo′trē oid′əl), *adj.* having the form of a bunch of grapes. Also, **bot′ry·oid′, botryose.** [< Gk *botryoeid(ēs)* shaped like a bunch of grapes (*bótry(s)* bunch of grapes + *-oeidēs* -OID) + -AL[1]] —**bot′ry·oi′dal·ly,** *adv.*

bot·ry·o·my·co·sis (bo′trē ō mī kō′sis), *n.* *Vet. Pathol.* a disease of horses, usually occurring after castration, caused by a staphylococcus and characterized by a tumefaction of the stump of the spermatic cord. [< Gk *botryo-* (comb. form of *bótrys* bunch of grapes) + MYCOSIS] —**bot·ry·o·my·cot·ic** (bo′trē ō mī kot′ik), *adj.*

bot·ry·ose (bo′trē ōs′), *adj.* **1.** botryoidal. **2.** racemose. [< Gk *bótry(s)* bunch of grapes + -OSE[1]]

bo·try·tis (bō trī′tis), *n.* any imperfect fungus of the genus *Botrytis,* having the conidia in grapelike bunches: a major cause of plant disease. [< NL, irreg. < Gk *bótry(s)* bunch of grapes. See -ITIS]

bots (bots), *n.* (*construed as pl.*) *Vet. Pathol.* a disease caused by the attachment of the larvae of botflies to the stomach of a horse. [pl. of BOT]

Bot·sa·res (*Gk.* bô′tsä rēs), *n.* **Mar·kos** (*Gk.* mär′kôs). See **Bozzaris, Marco.**

Bot·swa·na (bot swä′nä), *n.* a republic in S Africa: formerly a British protectorate; gained independence 1966; member of the British Commonwealth. 514,378 (1964); 275,000 sq. mi. *Cap.:* Gaborone. Formerly, **Bechuanaland.**

bott[1] (bot), *n.* bot.

bott[2] (bot), *n.* a conical knob, mounted on a rod, for stopping temporarily the flow of molten metal or slag from a blast furnace or cupola. Also, **bod.** [? special use of dial. *bot* (now obs.) iron tool for marking sheep, itself special use of ME *botte* (var. of BAT[1]) shepherd's crook]

bot·te·ga (bō tā′gə, bə-; *It.* bôt te′gä), *n.*, *pl.* **-te·gas, -te·ghe** (-tā′gē; *It.* -te′ge). the studio of a master artist, in which lesser artists, apprentices, or students may learn by participating in the work. [< It: lit., shop < L *apothēca;* see APOTHECARY]

Bött·ger (bœt′gər), *n.* **Jo·hann Frie·drich** (yō′hän frē′drikh), 1682–1719, German chemist.

Bot·ti·cel·li (bot′i chel′ē; *It.* bôt′tē chel′lē), *n.* **Sandro** (*It.* sän′drô), (*Alessandro di Mariano dei Filipepi*), 1444?–1510, Italian painter. —**Bot′ti·cel′li·an,** *adj.*

Bot·ti·neau (bot′ənō′), *n.* a town in N North Dakota. 2613 (1960).

bot·tle[1] (bot′əl), *n.*, *v.*, **-tled, -tling.** —*n.* **1.** a portable container for holding liquids, characteristically having a neck and mouth and made of glass. **2.** the contents of such a container; as much as such a container contains: *a bottle of wine.* **3.** bottled cow's milk and milk formulas given to infants, as opposed to mother's milk: *raised on the bottle.* **4. hit the bottle,** *Slang.* **a.** to drink to excess often or habitually. **b.** to become intoxicated: *He hits the bottle whenever things become a bit difficult.* **5. the bottle,** intoxicating beverages; liquor: *He became addicted to the bottle.* —*v.t.* **6.** to put into or seal in a bottle: *to bottle grape juice.* **7.** *Brit.* to can or put up fruit or vegetables. **8. bottle up, a.** to repress or restrain: *He kept all of his anger bottled up inside him.* **b.** to enclose or entrap: *Traffic was bottled up in the tunnel.* [ME *botel* < MF, var. of *bo(u)teille* < ML *butticula,* equiv. to LL *butti(s)* BUTT[4] + *-cula* -CULE] —**bot′tle·like′,** *adj.* —**bot′tler,** *n.*

bot·tle[2] (bot′əl), *n.* *Brit. Dial.* **1.** a haystack. **2.** a bale of hay. **3.** a bundle of straw. [ME *botel* < MF, equiv. to *bote* (< MD: bundle) + *-el* -LE]

bot·tle[3] (bot′əl), *n.* *Archit.* boltel (def. 2).

bot′tle ba′by, an infant fed by bottle from birth, as distinguished from one who is breast-fed.

bot′tle cap′, a device for closing or sealing a bottle, esp. a metal cover with a cork gasket fitting tightly over the mouth of a glass or plastic bottle, held in place by crimping the edge of the cap over the lip or flange of the bottle.

bot′tle club′, a club serving drinks to members who have reserved or purchased their own bottles of liquor.

bot′tled gas′, **1.** gas stored in portable cylinders under pressure. **2.** See **liquefied petroleum gas.**

bot′tled in bond′, *U.S.* (of a straight whiskey or brandy) bottled at 100 proof after aging at least four years and being stored untaxed under government supervision until released for sale by the manufacturer.

bot′tle fern′. See **brittle fern.**

bot′tle gen′tian. See **closed gentian.**

bot′tle glass′, (in antique collecting) glass of a deep green or amber color.

bot′tle gourd′. See under **gourd** (def. 1).

bot′tle green′, a deep green. —**bot′tle-green′,** *adj.*

bot′tle imp′. See **Cartesian diver.**

bot·tle·neck (bot′əl nek′), *n.* **1.** a narrow entrance or passageway. **2.** a place or a stage in a process at which progress is impeded. —*v.t.* **3.** to hamper or confine by or as if by a bottleneck. —*v.i.* **4.** to become like a bottleneck; be hindered by or as by a bottleneck. [BOTTLE[1] + NECK]

bot·tle·nose (bot′əl nōz′), *n.* any of various cetaceans having a bottle-shaped nose, as the bottle-nosed dolphin. [BOTTLE[1] + NOSE] —**bot′tle-nosed′,** *adj.*

bot′tle-nosed dol′phin, any of several dolphins of the genus *Tursiops,* common in warm seas, having a bottle-shaped nose. Also, **bot′tlenose dol′phin.**

bot′tle-nosed whale′, a whale of the genus *Hyperoodon,* esp. *H. ampullatus,* having a bottle-shaped snout. Also, **bot′tlenose whale′.**

bot′tle par′ty, a party at which guests supply their own liquor, each usually contributing a bottle.

bot′tle tree′, any of several trees, species of the genus *Sterculia* (*Firmiana*), native to warmer regions, as *S. rupestris* **(narrow-leaved bottle tree)** and *S. trichosiphon* **(broad-leaved bottle tree).**

bot′tle turn′ing, *Furniture.* the turning of the legs of chairs, tables, etc., in manufacturing to give certain sections an ornamental, bottlelike form.

bot·tom (bot′əm), *n.* **1.** the lowest or deepest part of anything, as distinguished from the top: *the bottom of a hill; the bottom of a page.* **2.** the under or lower side; underside: *the bottom of a flatiron.* **3.** the ground under any body of water: *the bottom of the sea.* **4.** Usually, **bot′toms.** Also called **bottom land.** *Phys. Geog.* low alluvial land next to a river. **5.** *Naut.* **a.** the part of a hull between the bilges, including the keel. **b.** the part of a hull that is immersed at all times. **c.** the cargo space in a vessel. **d.** a cargo vessel. **6.** the seat of a chair. **7.** the buttocks; rump. **8.** the fundamental part; basic aspect. **9. bottoms,** (*construed as pl.*) the trousers of a pair of pajamas. **10.** the working part of a plow, comprising the plowshare, landside, and moldboard. **11.** the cause; origin; basis: *Try getting to the bottom of the problem.* **12.** *Chiefly Brit.* **a.** the inmost part or inner end of a recess, bay, lane, etc. **b.** the most remote section of a garden or field. **13.** *Baseball.* **a.** the second half of an inning. **b.** the last three players in the batting order. **14.** lowest limit, esp. of dignity, status, or rank; nadir: *When one sinks that low, he's bound to hit bottom soon.* **15. at bottom,** in reality; fundamentally: *They knew at bottom that they were only deceiving themselves.* Also, **at the bottom. 16. at the bottom of,** really causing; responsible for: *It was thought that Communists were at the bottom of the anti-American demonstrations.* **17. bottoms up!** *Informal.* drink up! **18. on her own bottom,** *Naut.* (of a trading or fishing vessel) free of debt; fully paid for. —*v.t.* **19.** to furnish with a bottom. **20.** to base or found (usually fol. by *on* or *upon*). **21.** to discover the full meaning of (something); fathom. **22.** to bring (a submarine) to rest on the ocean floor: *They had to bottom the sub until the enemy cruisers had passed by.* —*v.i.* **23.** to be based; rest. **24.** to strike against the bottom or end; reach the bottom. —*adj.* **25.** of or pertaining to the bottom or a bottom. **26.** located on or at the bottom: *I want the bottom book in the stack. I'm on the bottom floor.* **27.** lowest: *bottom prices.* **28.** fundamental: *the bottom cause.* **29. bet one's bottom dollar, a.** to wager the last of one's money or resources. **b.** to be positive or assured: *You can bet your bottom dollar that something will prevent us from leaving on time.* [ME *botme,* OE *botm;* akin to Icel *botn,* D *bodem,* G *Boden,* L *fundus,* Gk *pythmḗn,* Skt *budhná*] —**Syn. 1.** base, foot. **8, 11.** foundation, groundwork. **28.** basic.

bot′tom bolt′, a bolt at the bottom of a door or the like, sliding into a socket in a floor or sill and equipped with a device for keeping it raised when the door is not fastened.

bot′tom drawer′ (drôr), *Brit.* any drawer used for a hope chest.

bot′tom gear′, *Brit.* low[1] (def. 47).

bot′tom grass′, any grass that grows on bottoms or lowlands.

bot′tom heat′, *Hort.* heat artificially applied to a container in which plants are grown in order to induce their germination, rooting, or growth.

bot′tom ice′. See **anchor ice.**

bot′tom land′, bottom (def. 4).

bot·tom·less (bot′əm lis), *adj.* **1.** lacking a bottom. **2.** immeasurably deep. **3.** unfathomable; mysterious: *a bottomless problem.* **4.** unlimited; without bounds: *He seems to have a bottomless supply of money.* [ME *bottomles.* See BOTTOM, -LESS] —**bot′tom·less·ly,** *adv.* —**bot′tom·less·ness,** *n.*

bot′tom line′, *Informal.* **1.** the final figure, showing profit or loss, in a financial statement. **2.** the ultimate result or consideration.

bot·tom·most (bot′əm mōst′ *or, esp. Brit,* -məst), *adj.* **1.** of, pertaining to, or situated at the bottom. **2.** (of one of a series) farthest down; lowest. **3.** bottom. [BOTTOM + -MOST]

bot′tom round′, a cut of beef taken from outside the round, which is below the rump and above the upper leg. Cf. **top round.**

bot·tom·ry (bot′əm rē), *n., pl.* **-ries.** *Marine Law.* a contract, of the nature of a mortgage, by which the owner of a ship borrows money to make a voyage, pledging the ship as security. [modeled on D *bodemerij,* equiv. to *bodem* BOTTOM + *-erij* -RY]

bot′tom yeast′, a yeast whose cells, in the manufacture of wine and lager beer, fall to the bottom as a sediment. Also called **sediment yeast.**

Bot·trop (bôt′rôp), *n.* a city in W West Germany, in the Ruhr region. 112,200 (1963).

bot·u·lin (boch′ə lin), *n.* the toxin formed by botulinus and causing botulism. [BOTULIN(US)]

bot·u·li·nus (boch′ə lī′nəs), *n., pl.* **-nus·es.** the bacterium *Clostridium botulinum,* which forms botulin. [< NL, equiv. to L *botul(us)* a sausage + *-inus* -INE[2]]

bot·u·lism (boch′ə liz′əm), *n. Pathol.* a disease of the nervous system caused by botulin developed in spoiled foods eaten by animals and man. [< L *botul(us)* a sausage + -ISM]

Bot·vin·nik (bôt′vē nik), *n.* **Mi·kha·il** (mi кнä ēl′), born 1911, Russian chess master.

Boua·ké (bwä kā′, bwä′kā), *n.* a city in central Ivory Coast. 45,000 (est. 1958).

Bouar (bwär), *n.* a city in the W Central African Republic. 20,700 (1950).

Bou·chard (bo͞o shar′), *n.* **(Louis) Hen·ri** (lwē äɴ-rē′), 1875–1960, French sculptor.

bouche (bo͞osh), *n. Armor.* a curved indentation in an upper corner of a jousting shield, serving as a lance rest: used from the 14th to the 17th century. [< F phrase *à bouche,* lit., with mouth, said of a notched shield. See BOUCHÉE]

Bou·ché (bo͞o shā′), *n.* **Louis,** 1896–1969, U.S. painter.

bou·chée (bo͞o shā′), *n.* a small patty shell of puff pastry, used esp. in serving hot hors d'oeuvres. [< F: lit., a mouthful, equiv. to *bouche* mouth (< L *bucca*) + *-ée* < L *-āta* -ADE[1]]

Bou·cher (bo͞o shā′), *n.* **Fran·çois** (fʀäɴ swa′), 1703–70, French painter.

Bou·cher de Crève·coeur de Perthes (bo͞o-shā′ də kʀev kœʀ′ də peʀt′), **Jacques** (zhäk), 1788–1868, French archaeologist and writer.

Bouches-du-Rhône (bo͞osh dʏ ʀōn′), *n.* a department in SE France. 1,248,355 (1962); 2026 sq. mi. *Cap.:* Marseilles.

bou·chon (bo͞o shon′; *Fr.* bo͞o shôɴ′), *n., pl.* **-chons** (-shonz′; *Fr.* -shôɴ′). **1.** *Horol.* a short length of hard brass tubing inserted into a hole in a plate to provide a pivot hole of proper size. **2.** *Furniture.* a supplementary, baize-covered top set in the center of a bouillotte table. [< F: stopper, plug; OF *bouche* sheaf]

Bou·ci·cault (bo͞o′sē kôlt′, -kō′), *n.* **Di·on** (dī′on, -ən), 1822–90, Irish playwright and actor, in the U.S. after 1853.

bou·clé (bo͞o klā′), *n.* **1.** yarn with loops producing a rough, nubby appearance on woven or knitted fabrics. **2.** a fabric made of this yarn. Also, **bou·cle′.** [< F: lit., curled; see BUCKLE]

boud (bŏd), *n. Brit. Dial.* a weevil, esp. one that breeds in malt. Also, **bood.** [?]

bou·deuse (bo͞o dœz′), *n.* a sofa or settee, usually upholstered, having two seats with a common backrest between them. [< F, n. use of *boudeuse* sulky, sullen (*boud(er)* to sulk, be sullen + *-euse* fem. n. suffix)]

Bou·dic·ca (bo͞o dik′ə), *n.* Boadicea.

bou·doir (bo͞o′dwär, -dwôr), *n.* a lady's bedroom or private sitting room. [< F: lit., a sulking place (*boud(er)* to sulk + *-oir* -ORY[2])]

bouf·fant (bo͞o fänt′; *Fr.* bo͞o fäɴ′), *adj.* **1.** puffed out; full: *a bouffant skirt.* —*n.* **2.** a woman's coiffure in which the hair hangs straight from the top of the head and puffs out over the ears and neck to frame the face. [< F: lit., swelling (*bouff(er)* to swell + *-ant* -ANT)] —**bouf·fan·cy** (bo͞o′fən sē), *n.*

bouffe (bo͞of), *n. Music.* See **opéra bouffe.** [< F < It *buffa,* fem. of *buffo* comic; see BUFFOON]

bou·gain·vil·lae·a (bo͞o′gən vil′ē ə, -vil′yə), *n.* any South American, nyctaginaceous shrub of the genus *Bougainvillaea,* having small flowers, cultivated for ornament. [< NL, named after L. A. de BOUGAINVILLE]

Bou·gain·ville (bo͞o gaɴ vēl′ *for 1;* bo͞o′gən vil′, *Fr.* bo͞o gaɴ vēl′ *for 2*), *n.* **1. Louis An·toine de** (lwē äɴ-twan′ də), 1729–1811, French navigator. **2.** the largest of the Solomon Islands, in the W Pacific Ocean. 53,130 (est. 1959); 4080 sq. mi.

bough (bou), *n.* **1.** a branch of a tree, esp. one of the larger or main branches. **2.** *Archaic.* the gallows. [ME *bogh,* OE *bōg, bōh* shoulder, bough; c. Icel *bōgr,* D *boeg,* G *Bug,* Gk *pâchys,* Skt *bāhus*] —**bough′less,** *adj.* —**Syn. 1.** See **branch.**

bough·pot (bou′pot′; *dial.* bo͞o′pot′), *n.* **1.** a large vase or pot for cut flowers or small branches. **2.** *Brit. Dial.* a bunch of small boughs, ferns, or flowers, used for decorative purposes; bouquet. Also, **bowpot.** [BOUGH + POT[1]]

bought (bôt), *v.* pt. and pp. of **buy.**

bought·en (bôt′ən), *adj. Chiefly Northern U.S. Dial.* bought or purchased, esp. as opposed to homemade. [BOUGHT + -EN]

bou·gie (bo͞o′jē, -zhē, bo͞o zhē′), *n.* **1.** *Med.* **a.** a slender, flexible instrument for introduction into passages of the body for dilating or opening, medicating, etc. **b.** a suppository. **2.** a wax candle. [< F, after *Bougie,* town in Algeria, center of the wax trade]

Bou·guer (bō gâr′, bo͞o-), *n.* a crater in the second quadrant of the face of the moon: about 15 miles in diameter.

Bou·gue·reau (bo͞og[ə] ʀō′), *n.* **A·dolphe Wil·liam** (a dôlf′ vēl yam′), 1825–1905, French painter.

bouil·la·baisse (bo͞ol′yə bās′, bo͞ol′yə bās′; *Fr.* bo͞o-ya bes′), *n.* a soup or stew containing several kinds of fish and shellfish, usually combined with olive oil, tomatoes, and saffron. [< F < Pr *bouiabaisso,* lit., boil (it, then let it simmer) down. See BOIL[1], ABASE]

bouil·li (bo͞o yē′), *adj. French.* boiled.

bouil·lon (bo͝ol′yon, -yən; *Fr.* bo͞ol yôɴ′), *n.* a clear, usually seasoned broth made by straining water in which beef, chicken, etc., has been cooked, or by dissolving a commercially-prepared bouillon cube or cubes in hot water. [< F, equiv. to *bouill(ir)* (to) BOIL[1] + *-on* n. suffix]

bouil′lon cube′, a small cube of dehydrated beef, chicken, or vegetable stock.

bouil′lon cup′, a small, bowl-shaped vessel, with two handles, in which bouillon is served.

bouil′lon spoon′, a spoon with a round bowl, smaller than a soup spoon, used for eating bouillon.

bouil·lotte′ lamp′ (bo͞o yot′), *Fr. Furniture.* a table lamp of the 18th century, having two or three adjustable candle brackets and a common shade sliding on a central shaft. [from its use on a BOUILLOTTE TABLE]

bouillotte′ ta′ble, *Fr. Furniture.* a small round table of the 18th century, having around its top a gallery within which a bouchon could be set for the playing of card games. [< F *bouillotte* card game, equiv. to *bouilli(r)* (to) BOIL[1] + *-otte* n. suffix]

bouk (bo͝ok), *n. Scot and North Eng.* **1.** the trunk of the body. **2.** the carcass of an animal. **3.** the paunch of a man or animal. **4.** bulk; volume; magnitude. [ME; OE *būc* belly; c. D *buik,* G *Bauch* belly, Icel *būkr* torso, belly, body]

Bou·lan·ger (bo͞o läɴ zhā′), *n.* **1. Georges Er·nest Jean Ma·rie** (zhôʀzh eʀ nest′ zhäɴ ma ʀē′), 1837–91, French general and politician. **2. Na·dia (Ju·liette)** (na dya′ zhʏ lyet′), 1887–1979, French musician and teacher.

Bou·lan·gism (bo͞o lan′jiz əm), *n.* the doctrines of militarism and reprisals against Germany, advocated, esp. in the 1880's, by the French general Boulanger. [< F *boulangisme.* See G. E. J. M. BOULANGER, -ISM] —**Bou·lan′gist,** *n.*

boul·der (bōl′dər), *n.* a detached and rounded or worn rock, esp. a large one. Also, **bowlder.** [short for *boulder stone;* ME *bulderston* < Scand; cf. dial. Sw *bullersten* big stone (in a stream), equiv. to *buller* rumbling noise (< OSw *bulder*) + *sten* STONE]

Boul·der (bōl′dər), *n.* a city in N Colorado. 37,718 (1960).

Boul′der Can′yon, a canyon of the Colorado River between Arizona and Nevada, above Boulder Dam.

Boul′der Cit′y, a city in SE Nevada, near Boulder Dam. 4059 (1960).

boul′der clay′, a glacial deposit consisting chiefly of unstratified clay with embedded boulders.

Boul′der Dam′, a dam on the Colorado River, on the boundary between SE Nevada and NW Arizona: the highest dam in the world. 727 ft. high; 1180 ft. long. Official name, **Hoover Dam.**

boul·der·ing (bōl′dər-ing), *n.* pavement made of boulders. Also, **bowldering.** [*boulder* (to) pave with BOULDER(S) + -ING[1]]

boul′der rasp′berry, a perennial, shrubby plant, *Rubus deliciosus,* of Colorado, having white flowers nearly two inches wide and dark reddish-purple fruit. Also called **Rocky Mountain flowering raspberry.**

boule[1] (bo͞ol), *n.* a cylindrical lump of material for synthetic gems, made by the Verneuil process. Also called **birne.** [< F: lit., a ball; see BOWL[2]]

boule[2] (bo͞ol), *n.* (*often cap.*) *Furniture.* buhl. Also, **boulle.** Also called **boule·work** (bo͞ol′wûrk′).

Bou·le (bo͞o′lē), *n.* **1.** the legislative assembly of modern Greece. **2.** (*sometimes l.c.*) a state legislative, advisory, or administrative council in ancient Greece. [< Gk: a council, body of chosen ones]

Boule-de-suif (bo͞ol də swēf′), *n.* See **Ball of Fat.**

bou·leu·te·ri·on (bo͞o′lo͞o tēr′ē on′, bo͞ol′yo͞o-), *n., pl.* **-te·ri·a** (-tēr′ē ə). a council chamber in ancient Greece. [< Gk, n. use of neut. of *bouleutḗrios* council-worthy (*bouleutḗr* (var. of *bouleutḗs* councilor) + *-ios* adj. suffix)]

boul·e·vard (bo͝ol′ə värd′, bo͞o′lə-), *n.* a broad avenue in a city, usually having a parklike appearance, with areas at the sides or center for trees, grass, or flowers. [< F < MD *boliverc;* see BULWARK] —**Syn.** See **street.**

bou·le·var·dier (bo͝ol′ə vär dēr′, bo͞o′lə-; *Fr.* bo͞ol[ə]-var dyā′), *n., pl.* **-diers** (-dērz′; *Fr.* -dyā′). **1.** (in Paris) one who frequents the most fashionable places, esp. a sophisticated male *bon vivant.* **2.** one who roams the streets; idler. [< F; see BOULEVARD, -IER]

bou·le·ver·se·ment (bo͞ol[ə] veʀs mäɴ′), *n. French.* an overturning; upsetting; confusion; turmoil.

bou·lim·i·a (bo͞o lim′ē ə), *n. Med.* bulimia.

Bou·logne (bo͞o lōn′, -loin′, bə-; *Fr.* bo͞o lôn′y[ə]), *n.* a seaport in N France, on the English Channel. 50,036 (1962). Also called **Bou·logne-sur-Mer** (bo͞o lôn′y[ə] sʏʀ-meʀ′).

Bou·logne Bil·lan·court (bo͞o lôn′y[ə] bē yäɴ ko͞oʀ′), a suburb of Paris, in N France. 107,074 (1962). Also called **Bou·logne-sur-Seine** (bo͞o lôn′y[ə] sʏʀ sen′).

Boult (bōlt), *n.* **Sir Adrian Cedric,** born 1889, English conductor.

boul·ter (bōl′tər), *n.* a long, stout fishing line with several hooks attached. [?]

boun (boun, bo͞on), *v.t., v.i. Archaic.* to prepare; make ready. Also, **bown.** [var. of BOUND[4]]

bounce (bouns), *v.,* **bounced, bounc·ing,** *n., adv.* —*v.i.* **1.** (of an object that has fallen, been thrown or dropped, etc.) to spring back from a surface in a lively manner: *The ball bounced off the wall. The ball bounced out of his glove.* **2.** to strike the ground or other surface, and rebound: *The ball bounced once before he caught it.* **3.** to move or walk in a lively, exuberant, or energetic manner: *She bounced into the room.* **4.** to move along in a lively manner, repeatedly striking the surface below, and rebounding: *The box bounced down the stairs.* **5.** to move about or enter or leave noisily or angrily (fol. by *around, about, out, out of, into,* etc.): *She bounced out of the room in a huff.* **6.** *Informal.* (of a check or the like) to fail to be honored by the bank against which it was drawn, due to lack of sufficient funds. —*v.t.* **7.** to cause to bound and rebound: *to bounce a ball; to bounce a child on one's knee.* **8.** *Slang.* to eject, expel, or dismiss summarily or forcibly. **9.** *Brit. Slang.* to obtain (something) or persuade (someone) by bluff or deceptive talk; hustle (someone) out of or into something. **10. bounce back,** *Informal.* to recover quickly, as from a blow, defeat, shock, sickness, etc.: *After losing the first game of the double-header, the Red Sox bounced back to win the second.* —*n.* **11.** a bound or rebound: *to catch a ball on the first bounce.* **12.** a sudden spring or leap: *In one bounce he was at the door.* **13.** *Brit. Slang.* **a.** bluff. **b.** impudence; bluster; swagger. **14.** ability to rebound; resilience: *This tennis ball has no more bounce.* **15.** vitality; energy; liveliness: *There is bounce in his step. This soda water has more bounce to it.* **16.** the fluctuation in magnitude of target echoes on a radarscope. **17.** *Slang.* the fact of being dismissed or ejected; discharge; ejection: *to get the bounce.* —*adv.* **18.** with a bounce; suddenly. [ME *bunci(n), bounse,* var. of *bunkin,* appar. c. D *bonken* to thump, belabor, *bonzen* to knock, bump] —**bounce′a·ble,** *adj.* —**bounce′a·bly,** *adv.*

bounc·er (boun′sər), *n.* **1.** one who or that which bounces. **2.** *Slang.* a man who is employed at a bar, nightclub, etc., to eject disorderly persons. **3.** something large of its kind. **4.** *Brit. Slang.* an impudent, pert person; bounder. [BOUNCE + -ER[1]]

bounc·ing (boun′sing), *adj.* **1.** stout, strong, or vigorous: *a bouncing baby boy.* **2.** exaggerated; big; hearty; noisy. [BOUNCE + -ING[2]] —**bounc′ing·ly,** *adv.*

bounc′ing Bet′ (bet), the soapwort. Also, **bounc′ing Bess′** (bes).

bound[1] (bound), *adj.* **1.** tied; in bonds: *a bound prisoner.* **2.** made fast as if by a band or bond: *She is bound to her family.* **3.** secured within a cover, as a book. **4.** under a legal or moral obligation: *He is bound by the terms of the contract.* **5.** destined; sure; certain: *It is bound to happen.* **6.** determined or resolved: *He is bound to go.* **7.** *Pathol.* constipated; costive. **8.** *Math.* (of a vector) having a specified initial point as well as magnitude and direction. Cf. **free** (def. 31). **9.** held with another element, substance, or material in chemical or physical union. **10.** (of a linguistic form) occurring only in combination with other forms, never alone, as most affixes. **11. bound up in** or **with, a.** inseparably connected with. **b.** devoted or attached to: *She is bound up in her volunteer work.* [ptp. of BIND] —**bound′ness,** *n.*

bound[2] (bound), *v.i.* **1.** to move by leaps; leap; jump; spring: *The colt bounded through the meadow.* **2.** to rebound, as a ball; bounce: *The ball bounded against the wall.* —*n.* **3.** a leap onward or upward; jump. **4.** a rebound; bounce. [< MF *bond* a leap, *bond(ir)* (to) leap, orig. resound << VL **bombitīre* for **bombitāre* to buzz, whiz (L *bomb(us)* (see BOMB) + *-it-* intensive suffix + *-ā-* thematic vowel + *-re* inf. suffix)] —**bound′ing·ly,** *adv.* —**Syn. 1.** See **skip**[1].

bound[3] (bound), *n.* **1.** Usually, **bounds.** limits or boundaries: *the bounds of space and time; within the bounds of his estate; within the bounds of reason.* **2.** that which limits, confines, or restrains. **3. bounds, a.** territories on or near a boundary. **b.** land within boundary lines. **4.** *Math.* a number greater than or equal to, or less than or equal to, all the numbers in a given set. Cf. **greatest lower bound, least upper bound, lower bound, upper bound. 5. out of bounds, a.** beyond the official boundaries, prescribed limits, or restricted area: *The ball bounced out of bounds.* **b.** forbidden; prohibited: *The park is out of bounds to students.* —*v.t.* **6.** to limit by or as by bounds; keep within limits or confines. **7.** to form the boundary or limit of. **8.** to name the boundaries of. —*v.i.* **9.** to abut. [ME *bounde* < AF; OF *bonde,* var. of *bodne* < LL *butina*] —**bound′a·ble,** *adj.* —**Syn. 1.** border, frontier, confine. **7.** demarcate.

bound[4] (bound), *adj.* **1.** going or intending to go; on the way to; destined (usually fol. by *for*): *The train is bound for Denver.* **2.** *Archaic.* prepared; ready. [ME *b(o)un* ready < Scand; cf. Icel *búinn,* ptp. of *búa* to get ready]

-bound[1], a combining form of **bound**[1]: *snowbound.*

-bound[2], a combining form of **bound**[4]: *eastbound.*

bound·a·ry (boun′də rē, -drē), *n., pl.* **-ries. 1.** something that indicates bounds or limits; a limiting or bounding line. **2.** Also called **frontier.** *Math.* the collection of all points of a given set having the property that every neighborhood of each point contains points in the set and in the complement of the set. **3.** *Cricket.* a hit in which the ball reaches or crosses the boundary line of the field on one or more bounces, counting four runs for the batsman. Cf. **six** (def. 5). [BOUND[3] + -ARY]

bound′ary condi′tion, *Math.* a stated restriction, usually in the form of an equation, that limits the possible solutions to a differential equation.

bound′ary lay′er, *Physics.* the portion of a fluid flowing past a body which is in the immediate vicinity of the body and which has a reduced flow due to the forces of adhesion and viscosity.

bound′ary line′, 1. boundary (def. 1). **2.** See **partition line.**

boun′dary rid′er, *n. Australian.* a ranch hand who patrols the boundary of a sheep or cattle station in order to watch the stock, repair fences, etc.

bound′ary val′ue prob′lem, *Math.* any of a series of problems occurring in the solution of a differential equation with boundary conditions.

Bound′ East′ for Car′diff, a play (1916) by Eugene O'Neill. Cf. **Glencairn Cycle.**

bound·ed (boun′did), *adj.* **1.** having bounds or limits **2.** *Math.* **a.** (of a function) having a range with an upper bound and a lower bound. **b.** (of a sequence) having the absolute value of each term less than or equal to some specified positive number. **c.** (of the variation of a function) having the variation less than a positive number. [BOUND[3] + -ED[2]] —**bound′ed·ly,** *adv.* —**bound′ed·ness,** *n.*

bound·en (boun′dən), *adj.* **1.** obliged; under obligation. **2.** obligatory; compulsory: *one's bounden duty.* [var. of BOUND[1]]

bound·er (boun′dər), *n.* *Chiefly Brit. Slang.* an obtrusive, ill-bred person; vulgar upstart. [BOUND[2] + -ER[1]]

bound′ form′, a linguistic form which never occurs by itself but always as part of some larger construction, as *-ed* in *seated.* Cf. **free form** (def. 1).

bound·less (bound′lis), *adj.* without bounds; unlimited: *His boundless energy amazed his friends.* [BOUND[3] + -LESS] —**bound′less·ly,** *adv.* —**bound′less·ness,** *n.*

bound′ var′iable, *Logic.* (in the functional calculus) a variable occurring in a quantifier and in a sentential function within the scope of the quantifier. Cf. **free variable.**

boun·te·ous (boun′tē əs), *adj.* **1.** giving or disposed to give freely; generous; liberal. **2.** freely bestowed; plentiful; abundant. [late ME (*bounte* BOUNTY + *-ous*); r. ME *bountevous* < MF *bontive* (*bonte* BOUNTY + *-ive*, fem. of *-if* -IVE) + -OUS] —**boun′te·ous·ly,** *adv.* —**boun′te·ous·ness,** *n.*

boun·ti·ful (boun′tə fəl), *adj.* **1.** liberal in bestowing gifts, favors, or bounties; munificent; generous. **2.** abundant; ample: *a bountiful supply.* [BOUNTY + -FUL] —**boun′ti·ful·ly,** *adv.* —**boun′ti·ful·ness,** *n.*
—**Syn. 2.** See **plentiful.**

Boun·ti·ful (boun′tə fəl), *n.* a city in N Utah, near Salt Lake City. 17,039 (1960).

boun·ty (boun′tē), *n., pl.* **-ties. 1.** generosity in giving. **2.** whatever is given bounteously; a benevolent, generous gift. **3.** a premium or reward, esp. one offered by a government: *There was a bounty on his head. Some States offer a bounty for dead wolves.* [ME *b(o)unte* < MF *bonte,* OF *bontet* < L *bonitāt-* (s. of *bonitās*) goodness. See BOON[2], -ITY] —**boun′ty·less,** *adj.*
—**Syn. 1.** munificence, liberality, charity, beneficence. **2.** present, benefaction. **3.** See **bonus.**

boun′ty hunt′er, one who hunts criminals, wild animals, etc., for the reward or bounty offered for capturing or killing them.

Bou·pho·ni·a (bo͞o fō′nē ə), *n.* (*sometimes construed as pl.*) Dipolia.

bou·quet (bō kā′, bo͞o- *for 1, 2;* bo͞o kā′ *or, occas.,* bō- *for 3*), *n.* **1.** a bunch of flowers; nosegay. **2.** a compliment: *Critical bouquets greeted her performance.* **3.** the characteristic aroma of wines, liqueurs, etc. [< F: bunch, orig. thicket, grove; OF *bosquet,* equiv. to *bosc* wood (< Gmc; see BOSK, BUSH[1]) + *-et* -ET]

bou·quet gar·ni (bō kā′ gär nē′, bo͞o-; *Fr.* bo͞o ke GAR nē′), *pl.* **bou·quets gar·nis** (bō kāz′ gär nē′, bo͞o-; *Fr.* bo͞o ke GAR nē′). a small bundle of herbs, as thyme, parsley, bay leaf, and the like, often tied in a cheesecloth bag and used for flavoring soups, stews, etc.; fagot. [< F: a garnished bouquet, a tied bunch of herbs]

bouquet′ lark′spur. See **Siberian larkspur.**

Bour·ba·ki (bo͝or′bä kē′; *Fr.* bo͞or BA kē′), *n.* **Ni·co·las** (nē kô lä′), the name under which a series of books in all phases of mathematics has been published since 1935, the books having been written by eminent mathematicians, usually French.

Bour·bon (bo͝or′bən, *Fr.* bo͞or bôN′ *for 1–3;* bûr′bən *for 4, occas. for 3*), *n.* **1.** a member of a French royal family which ruled in France 1589–1792, Spain 1700–1931, and Naples 1735–1806, 1815–60. **2. Charles** (SHARL), ("*Constable de Bourbon*"), 1490–1527, French general. **3.** one who is extremely conservative or reactionary. **4.** (*l.c.*) Also called **bour′bon whis′key.** a straight whiskey distilled from a mash having 51 percent or more corn: originally the corn whiskey produced in Bourbon County, Kentucky.

Bour·bon·ism (bo͝or′bə niz′əm; *occas.* bûr′-), *n.* **1.** adherence to the ideas and system of government practiced by the Bourbons. **2.** extreme conservatism, esp. in politics. [BOURBON + -ISM] —**Bour·bo·ni·an** (bo͝or bō′nē ən), **Bour·bon·ic** (bo͝or bon′ik), *adj.* —**Bour′bon·ist,** *n.*

Bour·bon·nais (bo͝or bō nā′, bər bō′nis), *n.* a town in NE Illinois. 3336 (1960).

bour′bon rose′, a hybrid rose, *Rosa borboniana,* cultivated in many horticultural varieties.

bour·don (bo͝or′dən, bôr′-, bôr′-), *n.* *Music.* **1. a.** the drone pipe of a bagpipe. **b.** the drone string of a stringed instrument. **2.** a low-pitched tone; bass. **3.** a pipe organ stop of very low pitch. **4.** the bell in a carillon having the lowest pitch. [ME < MF; see BURDEN[2]]

Bour′don-tube gauge′ (bo͝or′dən to͞ob′, -tyo͞ob′; *Fr.* bo͞or dôN′), *Chem.* an instrument for measuring the pressure of gases or liquids, consisting of a semicircular or coiled, flexible metal tube attached to a gauge that records the degree to which the tube is straightened by the pressure of the gas or liquid inside. [named after E. *Bourdon,* 19th-century French inventor]

bourg (bo͝org; *Fr.* bo͞or), *n., pl.* **bourgs** (bo͝orgz; *Fr.* bo͞or). **1.** a town. **2.** a French market town. [late ME < MF << LL *burg(us)* < Gmc; see BOROUGH]

bour·geois[1] (bo͝or zhwä′, bo͝or′zhwä; *Fr.* bo͞or ZHWA′), *n., pl.* **-geois,** *adj.* —*n.* **1.** a member of the middle class. **2.** a shopkeeper, merchant, or businessman. **3.** one whose political, economic, and social opinions are believed to be determined mainly by concern for property values: *Communists say all capitalists are bourgeois.* —*adj.* **4.** belonging to, characteristic of, or consisting of the middle class. **5.** conventional; lacking in refinement or elegance; philistine: *bourgeois taste.* **6.** dominated or characterized by materialistic pursuits or concerns. [< F; OF *borgeis* BURGESS]

bour·geois[2] (bər jois′), *n.* *Print.* a size of type approximately 9-point, between brevier and long primer. [? from a printer so named]

Bour·geois (bo͝or zhwä′, bo͝or′zhwä; *Fr.* bo͞or ZHWA′), *n.* **Lé·on Vic·tor Au·guste** (lā ôN′ vēk tôr′ ō gyst′), 1851–1925, French statesman: Nobel peace prize 1920.

bour·geoise (bo͝or′zhwäz, bo͝or zhwäz′; *Fr.* bo͞or-ZHWAZ′), *n., pl.* **-geois·es** (-zhwä ziz, -zhwäz′; *Fr.* -ZHWAZ′). **1.** a female bourgeois. **2.** bourgeoisie (def. 1). [< F; fem. of BOURGEOIS]

Bour·geois Gen·til·homme, Le (lə bo͞or ZHWA′ ZHÄN tē yôm′). See **Le Bourgeois Gentilhomme.**

bour·geoi·sie (bo͝or′zhwä zē′; *Fr.* bo͞or ZHWA zē′), *n.* **1.** the bourgeois class. **2.** (in Marxist theory) the class opposed to the proletariat or wage-earning class. [< F; see BOURGEOIS[1], -Y[3]]

bour·geon (bûr′jən), *n., v.i., v.t.* burgeon.

Bourges (bo͞orzh), *n.* a city in and the capital of Cher, in central France: cathedral. 63,479 (1962).

Bour·get (bo͝or zhā′; *Fr.* bo͞or zhe′), *n.* **Paul** (pôl), 1852–1935, French novelist and critic.

Bour·gogne (bo͞or gôn′yᵊ), *n.* French name of **Burgundy.**

Bour·gui·ba (bo͝or gē′bə), *n.* **Ha·bib ben A·li** (hä′bēb ben ä′lē), born 1903, leader in Tunisian independence movements: president of Tunisia since 1957.

Bour·gui·gnonne′ sauce′ (bo͝or′gēn yun′; *Fr.* bo͞or gē nyôn′), Burgundy (def. 4). [< F, fem. adj. of *Bourguignon* (masc.) of Burgundy]

Bourke-White (bûrk′hwīt′, -wīt′), *n.* **Margaret,** born 1906, U.S. photographer and author.

bour·kha (bo͝or′kə), *n.* burka.

bourn[1] (bōrn, bôrn), *n.* *Scot. and North Eng.* burn[2]. Also, **bourne.**

bourn[2] (bōrn, bôrn, bo͝orn), *n.* **1.** a bound; limit. **2.** destination; goal. **3.** realm; domain. [earlier *borne* < MF; OF *bodne,* etc. BOUND[3]] —**bourn′less,** *adj.*

Bourne·mouth (bo͝orn′məth, bōrn′-, bôrn′-), *n.* a city in SW Hampshire in S England: seashore resort. 153,965 (1961).

bour·non·ite (bōr′nə nīt′, bôr′-, bo͝or′-), *n.* a mineral, a sulfide of lead, antimony, and copper, approximately $PbCuSbS_3$; cogwheel ore; wheel ore. [named after Count J. L. de *Bournon* (d. 1825), French mineralogist; see -ITE[1]]

bour·rasque (bə rask′), *n.* borasca.

bour·rée (bo͞o rā′; *Fr.* bo͞o RĀ′), *n., pl.* **-rées** (-rāz′; *Fr.* -RĀ′). **1.** an old French and Spanish dance, somewhat like a gavotte. **2.** the music for it. [< F: lit., brushwood, equiv. to *bourre* (< VL **burra* body hair, wool, etc.) + *-ée* < L *-āta* -ADE[1]]

Bourse (bo͝ors), *n.* a stock exchange, esp. the Paris stock exchange. [< F: lit., purse; see BURSA]

bour·tree (bo͝or′trē′), *n.* See **European elder.** [late ME *burtre,* equiv. to *bur* (< ?) + *tre* TREE]

bouse[1] (bous, bouz), *v.t.,* **boused, bous·ing.** *Naut.* to haul with tackle. Also, **bowse.** [?]

bouse[2] (bo͞oz, bouz), *n., v.,* **boused, bous·ing.** —*n.* **1.** liquor or drink. **2.** a drinking bout; carouse. —*v.t., v.i.* **3.** to drink, esp. to excess. Also, **bowse.** [ME *bous* strong drink < MD *buse* drinking vessel; see BOOZE]

Bous·sin·gault (bo͞o′sing gält′, bo͞o′sing-), *n.* a walled plain containing two almost concentric ring formations in the fourth quadrant of the face of the moon: about 70 miles in diameter.

bou·stro·phe·don (bo͞o′strə fēd′ən, bou′-), *n.* an ancient method of writing in which the lines run alternately from right to left and from left to right. [< Gk: lit., like ox-turning (in plowing), equiv. to *bou-* (s. of *boûs*) ox + *-strophē-* (see STROPHE) + *-don* adv. suffix]

bous·y (bo͞o′zē, bou′-), *adj.* intoxicated; boozy. [BOUSE[2] + -Y[1]]

bout (bout), *n.* **1.** a contest, as of boxing; trial of strength. **2.** a turn at work or any action. **3.** a going and returning across a field, as in mowing or reaping. **4.** period; session; spell: *a bout of illness.* [var. of obs. *bought* bend, turn, deriv. of *bow* BOW[1]; see BIGHT]

bou·tel (bōt′əl), *n.* boltel (def. 1). Also, **bou′tell.**

bou·tique (bo͞o tēk′), *n.* a small shop, esp. one that sells fashionable clothes and accessories for women. [< F << Gk *apothēkē*; see APOTHECARY, BOTTEGA]

bou·ton·niere (bo͞ot′ənēr′, -ənyâr′), *n.* a flower or small bouquet worn, usually by a man, in the buttonhole of a lapel. [< F *boutonnière* buttonhole (*bouton* BUTTON + *-ière* suffix of appurtenance; see -ARIOUS)]

bou·ton·nière (bo͞o tô nyer′), *n., pl.* **-nières** (-nyer′). *French.* boutonniere.

bouts-ri·més (bo͞o′rē mā′, -māz′; *Fr.* bo͞o rē mā′), *n. pl. Pros.* **1.** words or word endings forming a set of rhymes and used in a given order, as the rhymes of a stanza or poem. **2.** verses using such a set of rhymes. [< F, equiv. to *bouts* ends (see BUTT[2]) + *rimés* rhymed (see RHYME)]

Bou·vard (bo͞o värd′; *Fr.* bo͞o VAR′), *n.* a walled plain in the third quadrant of the face of the moon: about 80 miles in diameter.

bou·var·di·a (bo͞o vär′dē ə), *n.* any tropical, rubiaceous shrub of the genus *Bouvardia,* having cymes of red, yellow, or white tubular flowers. [< NL; named after Charles *Bouvard* (d. 1658), French physician; see -IA]

Bou·vier des Flan·dres (*Fr.* bo͞o vyā′ dā flän′drᵊ), *pl.* **Bou·viers des Flan·dres** (*Fr.* bo͞o vyā′ dā flän′drᵊ). one of a Belgian breed of dogs having eyebrows, a mustache and a beard, and a rough, wiry, tousled coat ranging in color from fawn to pepper-and-salt, gray, brindle, or black. [< F: lit., cowherd of Flanders, from their use with cattle]

bo·va·rism (bō′və riz′əm), *n.* an exaggerated, esp. glamorized, estimate of oneself; conceit. [< F *bovarysme,* after *Madame Bovary,* novel by Flaubert; see -ISM] —**bo′va·rist,** *n.* —**bo′va·ris′tic,** *adj.*

bo·vate (bō′vāt), *n.* an old English unit of land area measurement equivalent to one eighth of a carucate. Also called **oxgang.** [< ML *bovāta,* equiv. to L *bov-* (s. of *bōs*) cow + *-āta* -ATE[1]]

Bo·vet (bō vā′, -vet′), *n.* **Daniel,** born 1907, Italian pharmacologist, born in Switzerland: Nobel prize for medicine 1957.

bo·vid (bō′vid), *adj. Zool.* of or pertaining to the *Bovidae,* or ox family, comprising the hollow-horned ruminants, as oxen, sheep, and goats. [< NL *Bovid(ae)* name of the family (L *bov-* (s. of *bōs*) ox + *-idae* -ID[2])]

bo·vine (bō′vīn, -vin, -vēn), *adj.* **1.** of the ox family, *Bovidae.* **2.** oxlike. **3.** stolid; dull. —*n.* **4.** a bovine animal. [< LL *bovīn(us)* of, pertaining to oxen or cows, equiv. to L *bov-* (s. of *bōs*) ox + *-īnus* -INE[1]] —**bo′vine·ly,** *adv.* —**bo·vin·i·ty** (bō vin′i tē), *n.*

bo′vine trichomoni′asis, *Vet. Pathol.* trichomoniasis (def. 3a).

bow[1] (bou), *v.i.* **1.** to bend the knee or body or incline the head in reverence, submission, salutation, recognition, or acknowledgment. **2.** to yield; submit: *to bow to the inevitable.* **3.** to bend or curve downward; stoop: *the pines bowed low.* —*v.t.* **4.** to bend or incline (the knee, body, or head) in worship, submission, respect, civility, agreement, etc.: *He bowed his head to the crowd.* **5.** to cause to submit; subdue; crush. **6.** to cause to stoop or incline: *Age had bowed his head.* **7.** to express by a bow, or by bowing: *to bow one's thanks.* **8.** to usher (someone) with a bow (usually fol. by *in, out,* etc.): *The page bowed the nobleman in.* **9.** to cause to bend; make curved or crooked. **10. bow and scrape,** to be excessively polite or deferential: *She expects everyone to bow and scrape to her.* —*n.* **11.** an inclination of the head or body in salutation, assent, thanks, reverence, respect, submission, etc. **12. make one's bow,** to appear publicly for the first time, as a performer, politician, etc.: *The young pianist made her bow last night to an appreciative audience.* **13. take a bow,** to step forward or stand up in order to receive recognition, applause, etc.: *The conductor had the soloists take a bow.* [ME *bow(en)* (v.), OE *būgan*; c. D *buigen*; akin to G *biegen,* Goth *biugan,* Icel *buga,* etc.] —**bowed′ness,** *n.* —**bow′ing·ly,** *adv.*
—**Syn. 1.** See **bend**[1].

bow[2] (bō), *n.* **1.** a flexible strip of wood or other material, bent by a string stretched between its ends, for shooting arrows: *He drew the bow and sent the arrow to its target.* **2.** an instrument resembling this, used for various purposes, as rotating a drill or spindle, or loosening entangled or matted fibers. **3.** a bend or curve. **4.** Also, **bowknot.** a looped knot composed of two or more loops and two ends, as for tying together the ends of a ribbon or string. **5.** any separate piece of looped, knotted, or shaped gathering of ribbon, cloth, paper, etc., used as a decoration, as on a package, dress, or the like. **6.** a long rod, originally curved but now nearly straight, with horsehairs stretched from one end to the other, used for playing on a musical instrument of the violin or viol families. **7.** a single movement of such a device over a string or strings of a violin, viol, or the like. **8.** See **bow tie. 9.** something curved or arc-shaped. **10.** a saddlebow. **11.** an archer; bowman: *He is the best bow in the county.* **12.** a frame for a lens in a pair of eyeglasses. **13.** the part of such a frame fitting over the ear. **14.** temple[2] (def. 3). **15.** a U-shaped piece for placing under an animal's neck to hold a yoke. **16.** *Building Trades.* a flexible rod used for laying out large curves. **17.** the part of a key grasped by the fingers. **18.** the loop on the stem of a watch by which the watch is attached to a chain or the like. **19.** a rainbow. —*adj.* **20.** curved; bent like a bow: *bow legs.* **21.** Also, **bowed** (bōd). distorted filling yarn. —*v.t., v.i.* **22.** to bend into the form of a bow; curve. **23.** *Music.* to perform by means of a bow upon a stringed instrument. **24.** *Textiles Obs.* to loosen by passing a vibrating bow among entangled fibers. [ME *bowe* (n.), OE *boga*; c. D *boog,* G *Bogen,* Icel *bogi*; akin to BOW[1]] —**bowed′ness,** *n.* —**bow′less,** *adj.* —**bow′like′,** *adj.*

bow[3] (bou), *n.* **1.** *Naut., Aeron.* **a.** the forward end of a vessel or airship. **b.** either side of this forward end, esp. with reference to the direction of a distant object: *a mooring two points off the port bow.* **2. bows,** *Naut.* the exterior of the forward end of a vessel, esp. one in which the hull slopes back on both sides of the stem. **3.** the foremost oar in rowing a boat. **4.** Also called **bowman, bow oar.** the person who pulls that oar. **5. bows on,** (of a ship) with the bow foremost: *The vessel approached us bows on.* **6. bows under,** (of a ship) shipping water at the bow: *The ship was bows under during most of the storm.* —*adj.* **7.** of or pertaining to the bow of a ship. [< LG *boog* (n.) or D *boeg* or Dan *bov*; see BOUGH]

bow′-and-quar′ter line′ (bō′ən kwôr′tər), *Naut.* See **quarter line.**

bow′ back′ (bō), a chair back formed of a single length of wood bent into a horseshoe form and fitted to a seat or arm rail, with spindles or slats as a filling. Also called **hoop back, loop back.**

Bow′ bells′ (bō), the bells of Bow church, in the East End district of London: traditionally, a true Cockney is born and raised within the sound of Bow bells.

bow′ com′pass (bō), any of several types of compasses having the legs joined by a bow-shaped piece.

Bow·ditch (bou′dich), *n.* **1. Nathaniel,** 1773–1838, U.S. mathematician, astronomer, and navigator. **2.** a handbook of navigation, *American Practical Navigator,* originally prepared by N. Bowditch and published since 1802 in a series of editions.

bow′ divid′er (bō), a bow compass, each leg of which terminates in a needle, used to transfer measurements of a drawing from one area to another.

bowd·ler·ise (boud′lə rīz′), *v.t.,* **-ised, -is·ing.** *Chiefly Brit.* bowdlerize. —**bowd′ler·i·sa′tion,** *n.*

bowd·ler·ize (bōd′lə rīz′, boud′-), *v.t.,* **-ized, -iz·ing.** to expurgate (a play, novel, etc.) by removing or modifying passages prudishly considered immodest. [after Thomas *Bowdler* (1754–1825), English editor of an expurgated edition of Shakespeare] —**bowd′ler·ism,** *n.* —**bowd′ler·i·za′tion,** *n.*

bow·drill (bō′dril′), *n.* a drill rotated by a cord wrapped tightly around it and strung to a bow. [BOW[2] + DRILL[1]]

bow·el (bou′əl, boul), *n., v.,* **-eled, -el·ing** or (*esp. Brit.*) **-elled, -el·ling.** —*n.* **1.** *Anat.* **a.** Usually, **bowels.** the intestine. **b.** a part of the intestine. **2. bowels, a.** the inward or interior parts: *the bowels of the earth.* **b.** *Archaic.* feelings of pity or compassion. —*v.t.* **3.** to disembowel. [ME *b(o)uel* < OF < LL *botell(us)* little sausage (L *bot(ulus)* sausage + *-ellus* dim. suffix)] —**bow′el·less,** *adj.*

Bow·ell (bō′əl), *n.* **Sir Mackenzie,** 1823–1917, Canadian statesman, born in England: prime minister 1894–96.

bow′el move′ment, 1. the evacuation of the bowels; defecation. **2.** excrement from the bowels; feces.

Bow·en (bō′ən), *n.* **1. Catherine (Sho·ber) Drink·er** (shō′bər dring′kər), born 1897, U.S. biographer and essayist. **2. Elizabeth (Dorothea Cole),** born 1899, Anglo-Irish novelist and short-story writer.

bow·en·ite (bō′ə nīt′), *n.* *Mineral.* a compact and dense variety of green serpentine resembling jade. [named after G. T. *Bowen,* 19th-century American geologist; see -ITE[1]]

Bow′en's disease′ (bō′ənz), *Pathol.* a precancerous skin condition characterized by pinkish papules covered with a thick horny layer. [named after John T. *Bowen* (1857–1940), American dermatologist]

bow·er[1] (bou′ər), *n.* **1.** a leafy shelter or recess; arbor. **2.** a rustic dwelling; cottage. **3.** a lady's boudoir in a medieval castle. —*v.t.* **4.** to enclose in or as in a bower; embower. [ME *bour,* OE *būr* chamber; c. Icel *būr* pantry, G *Bauer* bird-cage; akin to NEIGHBOR] —**bow′er·like′,** *adj.*

bow·er² (bou′ər), *n.* an anchor carried at a ship's bow. Also called **bow′er an′chor.** Cf. **best bower, small bower.** [BOW³ + -ER¹]

bow·er³ (bou′ər), *n.* one who or that which bows or bends. [BOW¹ + -ER¹]

bow·er⁴ (bō′ər), *n. Music.* a musician, as a violinist, who performs with a bow on a stringed instrument. [BOW² + -ER¹]

bow·er·bird (bou′ər bûrd′), *n.* any of several oscine birds of the family *Ptilonorhynchidae,* of Australia, New Guinea, and adjacent islands, the males of which build bowerlike structures to attract the females. [BOWER¹ + BIRD]

bow′er plant′ (bou′ər), a woody vine, *Pandorea jasminoides,* of Australia, having white or pinkish flowers.

Bow·ers (bou′ərz), *n.* **Claude Ger·nade** (zhər näd′), 1878–1958, U.S. diplomat and historian.

bow·er·y¹ (bou′ə rē), *adj.* bowerlike; containing bowers; shady: *Trees made the meadow a bowery maze.* [BOWER¹ + -Y¹]

bow·er·y² (bou′ə rē, bou′rē), *n., pl.* **-er·ies. 1.** (among the Dutch settlers of New York) a farm or country seat. **2. the Bowery,** a street and area in New York City, noted for its cheap hotels and saloons and peopled by the destitute and homeless. [< D *bouwerij* farm, equiv. to *bouw* agriculture + *-erij* -ERY]

bow·fin (bō′fin′), *n.* a carnivorous ganoid fish, *Amia calva,* found in sluggish fresh waters of eastern North America. Also called **grindle.** [BOW² + FIN]

bow′ front′ (bō), *Furniture.* See **swell front.**

bow·grace (bou′grās′), *n. Naut.* a fender, pad, or pudding used to protect the bows of a vessel from ice. Also called **bongrace.** [BOW³ + GRACE; perh. by folk etymology < F *bonnegrace* protecting brim on a hat]

bow′ hand′ (bō), **1.** *Archery.* the hand that holds the bow, the left hand for right-handed people. **2.** *Music.* the hand that draws the bow.

bow·head (bō′hed′), *n.* a whalebone whale, *Balaena mysticetus,* of northern seas, having an enormous head and mouth. Also called **Greenland whale.** [BOW² + HEAD]

Bow·ie (bō′ē, bo͞o′ē *for 1, 2;* bo͞o′ē *for 3*), *n.* **1. James,** 1799–1836, U.S. soldier and pioneer. **2. William,** 1872–1940, U.S. geodesist. **3.** a town in N Texas. 4566 (1960).

bow′ie knife′ (bō′ē, bo͞o′ē), a heavy sheath knife having a long, single-edged blade. [named after James BOWIE]

Bowie knife

Bow′ie State′, Arkansas (used as a nickname).

bow·ing (bō′ing), *n.* **1.** the act or art of playing a stringed instrument with a bow. **2.** the individual way in which a musician bows a stringed instrument, including his emotional approach to the music, his articulation of individual notes, and the manner in which he groups together the notes of a passage. [BOW² + -ING¹]

bow·i·ron (bō′ī′ərn), *n.* (on the car of a sidewalk elevator) a metal arch for parting the cellar doors as the elevator rises.

bow·knot (bō′not′), *n.* bow² (def. 4). [BOW² + KNOT¹]

bowl¹ (bōl), *n.* **1.** a rather deep, round dish or basin, used chiefly for holding liquids, food, etc. **2.** the contents of a bowl: *He made some soup and ate a bowl of it.* **3.** a rounded, cuplike, hollow part: *the bowl of a pipe.* **4.** a large drinking cup. **5.** festive drinking; conviviality. **6.** any bowl-shaped depression or formation. **7.** an edifice with tiers of seats forming sides like those of a bowl, having the arena at the bottom; stadium. **8.** Also called **bowl′ game′.** a football game played after the regular season by teams selected by the sponsors of the game, usually as representing the best from a region of the country: *the Rose Bowl.* **9.** *Typography.* a curved or semicircular line of a character, as of a, d, b, etc. —*v.t.* **10.** to give (a floor, as in a theater, auditorium, etc.) a gentle inclination on all sides toward some area, as a stage or platform. [ME *bolle,* OE *bolla;* c. Icel *bolli.* See BOLL] —**bowl′like′,** *adj.*

bowl² (bōl), *n.* **1.** one of the balls, having little or no bias, used in playing ninepins or tenpins. **2.** one of the biased or weighted balls used in lawn bowling. **3. bowls,** (*construed as sing.*) See **lawn bowling. 4.** a cast or delivery of the ball in bowling or lawn bowling. **5.** *Obs.* a rotating cylindrical part in a machine, as one to reduce friction. —*v.i.* **6.** to play with bowls, or at bowling; participate in or have a game or games of bowling: *We bowl every Tuesday night.* **7.** to roll a bowl or ball. **8.** to move along smoothly and rapidly. **9.** *Cricket.* to deliver the ball to be played by the batsman. —*v.t.* **10.** to roll or trundle, as a ball, hoop, etc. **11.** to attain by bowling: *He bowls a good game. She usually bowls a 120 game, but today she bowled 180.* **12.** to knock or strike, as by the ball in bowling (usually fol. by *over* or *down*). **13.** to carry or convey, as in a wheeled vehicle. **14.** *Cricket.* to eliminate (a batsman) by bowling (usually fol. by *out*): *He was bowled for a duck. He was bowled out for a duck.* **15. bowl over,** *Informal.* to surprise greatly; disconcert; upset: *We were bowled over by the news of his death.* [late ME *bowle,* var. of *boule* < MF << L *bulla* bubble, hence, round object]

bowl·der (bōl′dər), *n.* boulder.

bowl·der·ing (bōl′dər ing), *n.* bouldering.

bow·leg (bō′leg′), *n. Pathol.* **1.** outward curvature of the legs causing a separation of the knees when the ankles are close or in contact. **2.** a leg so curved. [BOW² + LEG] —**bow·leg·ged** (bō′leg′id, bō′legd′), *adj.* —**bow·leg·ged·ness** (bō′leg′id nis), *n.*

bowl·er¹ (bō′lər), *n.* **1.** one who bowls, esp. a participant in a bowling game, as candlepins or tenpins. **2.** *Cricket.* the player who throws the ball to be played by the batsman. [BOWL² + -ER¹]

bowl·er² (bō′lər), *n. Chiefly Brit.* derby (def. 4). [BOWL¹ + -ER¹]

Bowles (bōlz), *n.* **1. Chester,** born 1901, U.S. statesman: special adviser on Afro-Asian and Latin-American affairs, ambassador to India 1951–53. **2. Paul (Frederic),** born 1910?, U.S. novelist and composer. **3. Samuel,** 1826–78, U.S. journalist.

bow′ line′ (bou), *Naval Archit.* any of a set of lines on the hull plans of a vessel, formed by the intersection of the forebody of the hull with vertical longitudinal planes at certain distances: they appear as vertical lines on the body plan, as curved or angular forms, lowest amidships, on the sheer plan, and as lines parallel to the center line on the half-breadth plan. Cf. **buttock line** (def. 1).

bow·line (bō′lin, -līn′), *n.* **1.** Also, **bow′line knot′.** a knot used to make a nonslipping loop on the end of a rope. See illus. under **knot. 2.** *Naut.* a rope made fast to the weather leech of a square sail, for keeping the sail as flat as possible when close-hauled. **3. on a bowline,** *Naut.* sailing close-hauled. **4. on an easy bowline,** *Naut.* close-hauled with sails well filled. [ME *bouline,* equiv. to *bou-* (? *boue* BOW³) + *line* LINE¹]

bowl·ing (bō′ling), *n.* **1.** any of several games in which players standing at one end of an alley or green roll balls at standing objects or toward a mark at the other end, esp. a game in which a heavy ball is rolled from one end of a wooden alley at wooden pins set up at the opposite end. Cf. **boccie, candlepin** (def. 2), **duckpin** (def. 2), **lawn bowling, ninepin** (def. 2), **tenpin** (def. 2). **2.** the game of bowls. **3.** the act or an instance of playing or participating in any such game: *Bowling is a pleasant way to exercise.* [BOWL² + -ING¹]

Bowling (Arrangement of pins in tenpins)

bowl′ing al′ley, 1. a long, narrow wooden lane or alley, for the game of tenpins. **2.** a building or enclosed area containing a number of such lanes or alleys.

bowl′ing crease′, *Cricket.* either of two lines, each with a wicket set lengthwise at the center, marking the limit of a bowler's approach in delivering the ball to the opposite wicket.

bowl′ing green′, a level, closely mowed green for lawn bowling.

Bowl′ing Green′, 1. a city in S Kentucky. 28,338 (1960). **2.** a small open area near the S tip of Manhattan in New York City, at the foot of Broadway. **3.** a town in E Missouri. 2650 (1960).

bowl′ing on the green′. See **lawn bowling.**

bow·man¹ (bō′mən), *n., pl.* **-men.** an archer. [BOW² + MAN¹]

bow·man² (bou′mən), *n., pl.* **-men.** *Naut.* bow³ (def. 4). [BOW³ + MAN¹]

Bow′man's cap′sule (bō′mənz), *Anat.* a membranous, double-walled capsule surrounding a glomerulus of a nephron. Cf. **Malpighian corpuscle.** [named after Sir William *Bowman* (1816–1892), English surgeon]

bow′man's root′ (bō′mənz), a perennial herb, *Gillenia trifoliata,* of the eastern U.S., having terminal clusters of white flowers. Also called **false ipecac, Indian hippo.** [by folk etymology from *beaumont root,* deriv. of proper name *Beaumont*]

bown (boun), *v.t., v.i. Archaic.* boun.

bow′ net′ (bō), a clam-shaped net for trapping hawks, set open and baited with a pigeon, and closed upon the hawk by means of a trigger sprung from a blind.

bow′ oar′ (bou), bow³ (def. 4).

bow′ pen′ (bō), *Geom.* a bow compass that has a pen at the end of one leg.

bow·pot (bou′pot′; *dial.* bo͞o′pot′), *n.* boughpot.

bow′ saw′ (bō), a saw having a narrow blade held at both ends by a bowed handle.

bowse¹ (bous, bouz), *v.t.,* **bowsed, bows·ing.** *Naut.* bouse¹.

bowse² (bo͞oz, bouz), *n., v.t., v.i.,* **bowsed, bows·ing.** bouse².

Bows′er boat′ (bou′sər, -zər), *Trademark.* a small boat having gasoline tanks for refueling seaplanes.

bow·shot (bō′shot′), *n.* the distance a bow sends an arrow. [BOW² + SHOT¹]

bow·sprit (bou′sprit, bō′-), *n. Naut.* a spar projecting from the upper end of the bow of a sailing vessel, for holding the tacks of various jibs or stays and often supporting a jib boom. [ME *bouspret* < MLG *bōchspret* (c. D *boegspriet*) (*bōch* BOW³ + *spret* pole, c. OE *sprēot*)]

Bow′ Street′ (bō), a street in London, England: location of metropolitan police court.

bow·string (bō′string′), *n., v.,* **-stringed** or **-strung, -string·ing.** —*n.* **1.** the string of an archer's bow. **2.** (esp. in the Ottoman Empire) a similar string for killing people by strangulation. **3.** a string, typically of horsehair, for the bow of an instrument of the violin and viol families. —*v.t.* **4.** to strangle with a bowstring or any string or band. [BOW² + STRING]

bow′string hemp′, any of various fibrous plants of the genus *Sansevieria,* of Asia and Africa, cultivated in the U.S. for ornament.

bow′string truss′, a structural truss consisting of a curved top chord meeting a bottom chord at each end.

bow·tel (bōt′əl), *n.* boltel (def. 1). Also, **bow′tell.**

bow′ tie′ (bō), **1.** a small necktie tied in a bow at the collar. **2.** a sweet roll having a shape similar to that of a bow tie or butterfly.

bow′ trol′ley (bō). See under **trolley** (def. 4).

bow′ win′dow (bō), a rounded bay window. —**bow′-win′dowed,** *adj.*

bow·wow (bou′wou′, -wou′), *n.* **1.** the bark of a dog. **2.** an imitation of this. **3.** *Chiefly Baby Talk.* a dog. [rhyming compound; imit.]

bow·yang (bō′yang), *n. Brit., Australian Archaic.* a buckled strap or tie, esp. as used to hitch up trousers under the knee. [alter. of dial. *bowy-yanks* leather leggings]

bow·yer (bō′yər), *n.* a maker or seller of bows. [BOW² + *-yer,* var. of -ER¹ after *w*]

box¹ (boks), *n.* **1.** a container, case, or receptacle, usually rectangular, of wood, metal, cardboard, etc., with a lid or removable cover. **2.** the quantity contained in a box: *She ate a box of candy every week.* **3.** a package or case containing presents. **4.** the present or gift itself. **5.** See **post-office box. 6.** a compartment or section in a public place, shut or railed off for the accommodation of a small number of people, esp. in theaters, opera houses, ballrooms, etc. **7.** a small enclosure or area in a courtroom, for witnesses or the jury. **8.** a small shelter: *a sentry's box.* **9.** *Brit.* **a.** a small house, cabin, or cottage, as for use while hunting: *a shooting box.* **b.** a telephone booth. **c.** a wardrobe trunk. **10.** See **box stall. 11.** the driver's seat on a coach. **12.** the section of a wagon in which passengers or parcels are carried. **13.** part of a page of a periodical set off in some manner, as by lines, a border, or white space. **14.** any enclosing, protective case or housing, sometimes including its contents: *a gear box; a fire-alarm box.* **15.** *Baseball.* **a.** either of two marked spaces, one on each side of the plate, in which the batter stands. **b.** either of two marked spaces, one outside of first base and the other outside of third, where the coaches stand. **c.** the pitcher's mound. **d.** the marked space where the catcher stands. **16.** *Agric.* a bowl or pit cut in the side of a tree for collecting sap. **17.** *Jazz.* **a.** a stringed instrument, as a guitar. **b.** a piano. **18.** *Slang.* a phonograph. —*v.t.* **19.** to put into a box: *She boxed the glassware before the movers came.* **20.** to enclose or confine as in a box (often fol. by *in* or *up*). **21.** to furnish with a box. **22.** to form into a box or the shape of a box. **23.** to block so as to keep from passing or achieving better position (often fol. by *in*): *The Lotus was boxed in by two other cars on the 10th lap.* **24.** *Naut.* to boxhaul (often fol. by *off*). **25.** *Building Trades.* to enclose or conceal (a building or structure) as with boarding. **26.** *Agric.* to make a hole or cut in (a tree) for sap to collect. **27.** to mix (paint, varnish, or the like) by pouring from one container to another and back again. **28.** *Meteorol.* to fly around the center of a storm in a boxlike pattern in order to gather meteorological data: *to box a storm.* **29.** *Australian.* **a.** to mix groups of sheep which should be kept separated. **b.** to confuse someone or something. **30. box the compass,** *Naut.* to recite all of the points of the compass in clockwise order. [OE, special use of BOX³; akin to D *bus,* G *Büchse* < LL *buxis* < Gk *pyxís*] —**box′like′,** *adj.*

box² (boks), *n.* **1.** a blow, as with the hand or fist: *He gave the boy a box on his ear.* —*v.t.* **2.** to strike with the hand or fist, esp. on the ear. **3.** to fight against (someone) in a boxing match. —*v.i.* **4.** to fight in a boxing match; spar. **5.** to be a professional prize fighter: *He has boxed since he was 16.* [ME: a buffet < ?]

box³ (boks), *n.* **1.** an evergreen shrub or small tree of the genus *Buxus,* esp. *B. sempervirens,* used for ornamental borders, hedges, etc., and yielding a hard, durable wood. **2.** the wood itself. Cf. **boxwood. 3.** any of various other shrubs or trees, esp. species of eucalyptus. [OE < L *bux(us)* box-tree, boxwood < Gk *pýxos*]

box·ball (boks′bôl′), *n.* a game played between two players on two adjoining squares or sections of a sidewalk or a playground, in which a ball is hit back and forth between the players, each defending a square, the object being to prevent a fair ball from bouncing twice before hitting it back into the opponent's square. [BOX¹ + BALL¹]

box′ beam′, a beam or girder built up from shapes and having a hollow, rectangular cross section. Also called **box girder.**

box′ bed′, 1. a bed completely enclosed so as to resemble a box. **2.** a bed that folds up in the form of a box.

box·ber·ry (boks′ber′ē, -bə rē), *n., pl.* **-ries. 1.** the checkerberry. **2.** the partridgeberry. [BOX³ + BERRY]

box·board (boks′bōrd′, -bôrd′), *n.* cardboard used for making cartons. [BOX¹ + BOARD]

box′ bolt′, a rod-shaped bolt of rectangular section for fastening a door or the like, attached to the inside of the door at the edge and sliding into a socket on the frame.

box′ calf′, a chrome-tanned calfskin with square markings produced by graining.

box′ cam′era, a simple, boxlike camera, without bellows, usually not allowing for adjustment of shutter speed but sometimes of lens opening.

box·car (boks′kär′), *n.* **1.** *Railroads.* a completely enclosed freight car. **2. boxcars,** a pair of sixes on the first throw of the dice in the game of craps. [BOX¹ + CAR¹]

box′ coat′, 1. an outer coat with a straight, unfitted back. **2.** a heavy overcoat worn by coachmen.

box′ col′umn, a hollow wooden column, as for a porch, usually having a rectangular cross section.

box′ cor′nice, *Carpentry.* a hollow cornice of boards and moldings nailed to rafters and lookouts. Also, **boxed′ cor′nice.** Also called **closed cornice.**

box′ el′der, a North American maple, *Acer Negundo,* cultivated as a shade tree, yielding a light, soft wood used in making furniture, woodenware, etc.

box·er (bok′sər), *n.* **1.** a prize fighter; pugilist. **2.** one of a German breed of medium-sized, stocky, short-haired, pug-faced dogs having a brindled or tan coat with white markings. [BOX² + -ER¹]

Box·er (bok′sər), *n.* a member of a Chinese secret society that carried on an unsuccessful uprising in 1900 (**Box′er Rebel′lion**), principally against foreigners, culminating in a siege of foreign legations in Peking which was raised by an international expeditionary force. [rough rendering of Chin *I-hê-t'uan* virtuous harmony fist, a perversion of true name of group, with *t'uan* fist, for orig. *ch'üan* society]

box′er shorts′, men's loose-fitting undershorts with an elastic waistband. Also called **box′ers.**

box·fish (boks′fish′), *n., pl.* **-fish·es,** (*esp. collectively*) **-fish.** trunkfish. [BOX¹ + FISH]

box′ frame′, 1. a monolithic reinforced-concrete structure having walls and floors in the form of slabs. **2.** a window frame with pockets for sash weights.

box·ful (boks′fəl), *n., pl.* **-fuls.** as much as a box can hold: *a boxful of soap.* [BOX¹ + -FUL]

box′ gird′er. See **box beam.**

box′ gut′ter, a gutter set into the slope of a roof above the cornice.

box·haul (boks′hôl′), *v.t. Naut.* to put (a square-rigged sailing vessel) on a new tack by bracing the head yards aback and backing the vessel onto the new heading. [BOX¹ (v.) + HAUL]

box·head (boks′hed′), *n. Print.* a heading, usually at the top of a page, newspaper column, or column of figures, enclosed in a box formed by rules. [BOX¹ + HEAD]

box·hold·er (boks′hōl′dər), *n.* **1.** one who has rented or subscribed for a box, as at a theatrical performance, sporting event, or the like. **2.** one entitled to receive mail in a specific post-office box. [BOX¹ + HOLDER]

box′ huck′leberry, a nearly prostrate evergreen

shrub, *Gaylussacia brachycera*, of the central eastern U.S., having white or pink flowers and blue fruit. Also called **juniper berry.**

box·ing[1] (bok′sing), *n.* **1.** the material used to make boxes or castings. **2.** a boxlike enclosure; casing. **3.** the act or an instance of putting into or furnishing with a box. [BOX[1] + -ING[1]]

box·ing[2] (bok′sing), *n.* the act, technique, or profession of fighting with the fists, with or without boxing gloves. [BOX[2] + -ING[1]]

Box′ing Day′, (in Britain) the first weekday after Christmas, when Christmas gifts or boxes are given to employees, postmen, etc.

box′ing glove′, one of a pair of heavily padded leather mittens laced on the palm side of the wrist and hand, worn by boxers in a match or in training for a match.

box′ing ring′, an enclosed area for a boxing match, usually marked off, in the form of a square, by posts and ropes, and having a padded floor.

box′ i′ron, a flatiron which is heated by inserting live coals or a piece of hot metal in its boxlike holder.

box′ keel′, *Naut.* a keel in the form of a box girder and having internal space for pipes, ballast, etc.

box′ kite′, a tailless kite consisting of two or more light, box-shaped frames joined together, covered except at the ends and around the middle.

box′ loom′, a loom with a number of shuttle boxes on one or both sides of the lay, enabling the weaver to use a variety of colors in the filling direction.

box′ nail′, a nail having a long shank, smooth or barbed, with a sharp point and a flat head.

box′ of′fice, **1.** the office of a theater, stadium, or the like, at which tickets are sold. **2.** *Theat.* **a.** receipts from a play or other entertainment. **b.** entertainment popular enough to attract paying audiences and make a profit: *This show will be good box office.*

box-of·fice (boks′ô′fis, -of′is), *adj.* of or pertaining to the box office or to the business and commercial aspects of the theater: *a box-office window; box-office receipts; box-office attraction.* [adj. use of BOX OFFICE]

box′ pleat′, a double pleat, with the material folded under at each side. Also called **box′ plait′.**

box′ room′, *Brit.* a storage room, esp. one for trunks, suitcases, etc.

box′ scene′, *Theat. Brit.* See **box set.**

box′ score′, *Sports.* a record of the play of a game, esp. a baseball or basketball game, in which, on separate sides of the record, the players on each team are listed in a column by name and position, with additional rows of columns each headed by the abbreviation of the type of information to be given for each player.

box′ seat′, a seat in a box at the theater, opera, etc.

box′ set′, *Theat.* a boxlike stage set consisting of flats that form the back wall, side walls, and often the ceiling, painted to represent the interior of a room. Also called, *esp. Brit.,* **box scene.**

box′ sill′, *Carpentry.* a sill for a building frame, composed of a plate resting on the basement wall and a joist or header at the outer edge of the plate, as well as a soleplate for the studs resting either directly on the joists or on the rough flooring. Cf. **L sill.**

box′ spring′, an upholstered bedspring composed of a number of helical springs, each in a cylindrical cloth pocket.

box′ stair′, a staircase having two closed strings.

box′ stall′, a room-sized stall, usually square, for a horse or other large animal. Cf. **straight stall.**

box′ sta′ple, (on a doorpost) a socket for holding the end of a lock bolt when the door is closed.

box′ stoop′, a high stoop reached by a flight or flights of steps alongside the building front.

box′ stretch′er, *Furniture.* a heavy rectangular stretcher connecting successive legs of a table, chair, etc.

box·thorn (boks′thôrn′), *n.* See **matrimony vine.** [BOX[3] + THORN]

box′ tur′tle, any of several terrestrial turtles of the genus *Terrapene,* of North America, having a hinged shell that can be tightly shut to enclose and protect the body. Also called **box′ tor′toise.**

box′ valve′, a valve having a boxlike chamber.

box·wood (boks′wo͝od′), *n.* **1.** the hard, fine-grained, compact wood of the box shrub or tree, used for wood engravers' blocks, musical and mathematical instruments, etc. **2.** the tree or shrub itself. Cf. **box**[3]. **3.** See **flowering dogwood.** [BOX[3] + WOOD[1]]

box′ wrench′, a wrench having ends that surround the nut or head of a bolt.

boy (boi), *n.* **1.** a male child, from birth to full growth, esp. one less than 18 years of age. **2.** a young man who lacks maturity, judgment, etc. **3.** *Informal.* a grown man, esp. when referred to familiarly: *He liked to play poker with the boys.* **4.** *Offensive.* a man considered by the speaker to be inferior in race, nationality, or occupational status. **5.** a young servant; page. **6.** (in India, China, Japan, etc.) a native male servant, working as a butler, waiter, house boy, etc. **7.** *Naut.* an apprentice seaman or fisherman. **—*interj.*** **8.** an exclamation of wonder, approval, etc., or of displeasure or contempt. [ME *boy(e),* prob. after OE *Bōia* man's name; c. Fris *boi* young man; akin to OE *bōfa,* Icel *bōfi,* OHG *Buobo* man's name (G *Bube* knave, dial. boy, lad)]

bo·yar (bō yär′, boi′ər), *n.* **1.** *Russ. Hist.* a member of the old nobility of Russia, before Peter the Great made rank depend on state service. **2.** a member of a former privileged class in Rumania. Also, **bo·yard** (bō yärd′, boi′ərd). [earlier *boiaren* < Russ *boiarin* lord] **—bo·yar′ism, bo·yard′ism,** *n.*

boy·cott (boi′kot), *v.t.* **1.** to combine in abstaining from, or preventing dealings with, as a means of intimidation or coercion: *to boycott a person; to boycott a store.* **2.** to abstain from buying or using: *to boycott a commercial product.* **—*n.*** **3.** the practice of boycotting. **4.** an instance of boycotting. [after C. C. *Boycott* (1832–97), British army officer, first victim] **—boy′cott·er,** *n.*

Boyd (boid), *n.* **1. Alan S(tephenson),** born 1922, U.S. lawyer and public official: first Secretary of Transportation from 1967. **2.** a boy's given name.

Boy·er·town (boi′ər toun′), *n.* a town in SE Pennsylvania. 4067 (1960).

boy·friend (boi′frend′), *n. Informal.* a frequent or favorite male companion; beau. [BOY + FRIEND]

boy·hood (boi′ho͝od), *n.* **1.** the state or period of being a boy: *Boyhood is a happy time of life.* **2.** boys collectively: *The boyhood of America is strong and healthy.* [BOY + -HOOD]

boy·ish (boi′ish), *adj.* of, like, or befitting a boy. [BOY + -ISH[1]] **—boy′ish·ly,** *adv.* **—boy′ish·ness,** *n.*

boy·la (boi′lə), *n. Australian.* a witch doctor; sorcerer. Also called **koradji.** [< native Austral name]

Boyle (boil), *n.* **1. Kay,** born 1903, U.S. novelist, short-story writer, and poet. **2. Robert,** 1627–91, English chemist and physicist.

Boyle's′ law′, *Thermodynamics.* the principle that, for relatively low pressures, the pressure of an ideal gas kept at constant temperature varies inversely with the volume of the gas. Also called **Mariotte's law.** Cf. **Gay-Lussac's law.** [named after R. BOYLE]

Boyne (boin), *n.* **1.** a river in E Ireland: William III defeated James II near here 1690. 70 mi. long. **2.** a town in NW Michigan. 2797 (1960).

boy·o (boi′ō), *n., pl.* **boy·os.** *Irish Eng., Australian Informal.* boy; lad. Also, **boy′-o.** [BOY + *-o* associative suffix]

boy′ scout′, **1.** a member of an organization of boys (**Boy′ Scouts′**), founded in England in 1908 by Lieut. Gen. Sir Robert S. S. Baden-Powell, to develop in its members manly character, self-reliance, and usefulness to others. **2.** a member of any similar society elsewhere.

boy·sen·ber·ry (boi′zən ber′ē), *n., pl.* **-ries.** a blackberrylike fruit with a flavor similar to that of raspberries, developed by crossing various plants of the genus *Rubus.* [named after R. *Boysen,* 20th-century American botanist, who bred it]

Boz (boz), *n.* pen name of Charles Dickens.

Boz·ca·a·da (bōz′jä ä dä′), *n.* Tenedos.

Boze·man (bōz′mən), *n.* a city in S Montana. 13,361 (1960).

Bo·zen (bō′tsən), *n.* German name of **Bolzano.**

bo·zo (bō′zō), *n., pl.* **-zos.** *Slang.* a fellow, esp. a big, strong, stupid fellow. [rhyming compound based on *bo,* var. sp. of BEAU]

Boz·za·ris (bō zar′is, -zär′-), *n.* **Mar·co** (mär′kō), 1788?–1823, Greek patriot. Also, **Botsares.**

bp., **1.** baptized. **2.** birthplace. **3.** bishop.

B/P, *Com.* bills payable.

B.P., **1.** Bachelor of Pharmacy. **2.** Bachelor of Philosophy. **3.** *Com.* bills payable. **4.** blood pressure.

b.p., **1.** below proof. **2.** *Com.* bills payable. **3.** *Physics, Chem.* boiling point.

B.P.A., Bachelor of Professional Arts.

B.P.D.P.A., Brotherhood of Painters, Decorators, and Paperhangers of America.

B.P.E., Bachelor of Physical Education.

B.Pet.E., Bachelor of Petroleum Engineering.

B.P.H., Bachelor of Public Health.

B.Ph., Bachelor of Philosophy.

B.Pharm., Bachelor of Pharmacy.

B.Phil., Bachelor of Philosophy.

BPI, Bureau of Public Inquiries.

B.P.O.E., Benevolent and Protective Order of Elks.

B power supply. See **B supply.**

Br, *Chem.* bromine.

Br., **1.** Britain. **2.** British.

br., **1.** branch. **2.** brig. **3.** bronze. **4.** brother.

b.r., *Com.* bills receivable. Also, **B.R., B/R**

bra (brä), *n.* brassiere. [by shortening]

Brab·an·çon (brab′ən son′, brə ban′sən), *n.* one of a variety of the Brussels griffon having a short, smooth coat. [< F: lit., a native of BRABANT]

Bra·bant (brə bant′, brä′bənt; *Du.* brä′bänt; *Fr.* BRA BÄN′), *n.* **1.** a former duchy in W Europe: now divided between the Netherlands and Belgium. See map under **Agincourt.** **2.** a province in central Belgium. 1,973,729 (est. 1960); 1268 sq. mi. *Cap.:* Brussels. **3.** a province in the S Netherlands. 1,575,211 (1962); 1894 sq. mi. *Cap.:* s'Hertogenbosch. **—Bra·bant·ine** (brə ban′tin, -tīn), *adj.*

brab·ble (brab′əl), *v.,* **-bled, -bling,** *n. Obs.* **—*v.i.*** **1.** to argue stubbornly about trifles; wrangle. **—*n.*** **2.** noisy, quarrelsome chatter. [< D *brabbelen* to quarrel, jabber] **—brab′ble·ment,** *n.* **—brab′bler,** *n.*

brac·cae (brä′kī, -kē, brak′sē), *n.* (*construed as pl.*) loose, baggy breeches made of hides or coarse wool, worn in ancient Gaul. Also, **bra·cae** (brä′kī, brā′sē). Also called **braies.** [< L *brācae* (pl.) breeches]

brac·cio (brä′chō, -chē ō′), *n., pl.* **brac·cia** (brä′chə, -chē ə). an old Italian unit of length, usually about 26 or 27 inches but varying from 18 and 28 inches. [< It: lit., an arm < L *bracchium;* see BRACE]

brace (brās), *n., v.,* **braced, brac·ing.** **—*n.*** **1.** something that holds parts together or in place, as a clasp or clamp. **2.** anything that imparts rigidity or steadiness. **3.** *Mach.* a device for holding and turning a bit or tools for boring or drilling; bitstock. **4.** *Building Trades.* a piece of timber, metal, etc., for supporting or positioning another piece or portion of a framework. **5.** *Naut.* (on a square-rigged ship) a rope by which a yard is swung about and secured horizontally. **6.** *Music.* leather loops sliding upon the tightening cords of a drum to change their tension and the drum's pitch. **7.** Often, **braces.** *Dentistry.* a round or flat metal wire placed against the surfaces of the teeth for straightening irregularly arranged teeth. **8.** *Med.* an appliance for supporting a weak joint or joints. **9. braces,** *Chiefly Brit.* suspender (def. 1). **10.** a pair; couple: *a brace of grouse.* **11.** *Printing.* **a.** one of two characters { or } used to enclose words or lines to be considered together. **b.** brackets (def. 7). **12.** *Music.* connected staves. **13.** a protective band covering the wrist or lower part of the arm, esp. a bracer. **14.** *Mil.* a position of attention with exaggeratedly stiff posture. [ME < MF: ell < L *brāchia,* pl. of *brāchium,* var. of *bracchium* < Gk *brachīōn* arm] **—*v.t.*** **15.** to furnish, fasten, or strengthen with or as with a brace. **16.** to fix firmly; make steady; secure against pressure or impact: *He braces himself when the ship rolls. Brace yourself for some bad news.* **17.** to make tight; increase the tension of. **18.** to act as a stimulant to. **19.** *Naut.* to swing or turn around (the yards of a ship) by means of the braces. **20.** *Mil.* to order (a subordinate) to assume and maintain a brace. **—*v.i.*** **21.** *Mil.* to assume a brace. **22. brace in,** *Naut.* to brace the yards of (a square-rigged vessel) more nearly athwartships, as for running free. **23. brace up,** *Informal.* to summon up one's courage; become resolute: *She choked back her tears and braced up.* [ME < MF *brac(ier),* deriv. of *brace* (n.)] **—Syn. 1.** vise. **4.** stay, prop, strut. **10.** See **pair.** **15.** support, fortify, prop. **17.** tauten, tense. **18.** fortify.

Brace and bit

brace′ and bit′, a boring tool consisting of an auger rotated by a cranked handle.

braced′ arch′, an arch of steel, timber, etc., having a trusslike framework maintaining rigidity under a variety of eccentric loads: a true arch because it is fixed or tied at both sides of the base. Cf. **arched truss.**

braced′ frame′, *Carpentry.* a building frame employing a heavy, braced framework of solid girts mortised into solid posts the full height of the frame, with studs one story high filling the interstices. Also called **full frame.**

brace′ game′, *Cards.* **1.** *Faro.* a dishonest arrangement between the dealer and the casekeeper. **2.** *Slang.* a dishonest card game.

brace′ jack′, *Theat.* a triangular piece of wood used for propping up scenery from behind.

brace·let (brās′lit), *n.* **1.** an ornamental band or circlet for the wrist or arm. **2. bracelets,** *Slang.* a pair of handcuffs. **3.** *Furniture.* collar (def. 10). [late ME < MF; OF *bracel* (< L *brāchiāle,* n. use of neut. of *brāchiālis* BRACHIAL) + *-et* -ET] **—brace′let·ed,** *adj.*

brace′ mold′ing, *Archit.* keel[1] (def. 6).

brac·er[1] (brā′sər), *n.* **1.** one who or that which braces, binds, or makes firm. **2.** *Informal.* a stimulating drink, esp. one of liquor. [BRACE + -ER[1]]

brac·er[2] (brā′sər), *n. Archery.* a guard or band worn over the wrist of the bow hand to protect it from the snap of the bowstring. [ME < AF; OF *braceure,* equiv. to *brace* arm (see BRACE (n.)) + *-ure* -URE]

bra·ce·ro (brə sâr′ō; *Sp.* brä se′rō), *n., pl.* **-ce·ros** (-sâr′ōz; *Sp.* -se′rōs). a Mexican laborer admitted legally into the U.S. for a short period to perform seasonal, usually agricultural, labor. [< Sp: laborer, lit., one who swings his arms. See BRACE, -ER[2]]

brace′ ta′ble, *Carpentry.* a table giving the lengths of the hypotenuses of right isosceles triangles of varying sizes: used esp. for calculating the lengths of diagonal braces.

brach (brach, brak), *n. Obs.* a hound bitch. [late ME *brach(e),* back formation from *braches* < MF; OF *brachez,* pl. of *bracet,* equiv. to *brac-* (< OHG *bracco* hound that hunts by scent) + *-et* -ET]

brachi-, var. of **brachio-** before a vowel.

bra·chi·al (brā′kē əl, brak′ē-), *Anat., Zool.* **—*adj.*** **1.** belonging to the arm, foreleg, wing, pectoral fin, or other forelimb of a vertebrate. **2.** belonging to the upper part of such a member, from the shoulder to the elbow. **3.** armlike, as an appendage. **—*n.*** **4.** a brachial part or structure. [< L *brāchiāl(is)* of, belonging to the arm. See BRACHI-, -AL[1]]

bra·chi·al·gi·a (brā′kē al′jē ə, -jə, brak′ē-), *n. Pathol.* pain in the nerves of the upper arm. [BRACHI- + -ALGIA]

bra·chi·ate (*adj.* brā′kē it, -āt′, brak′ē-; *v.* brā′kē āt′, brak′ē-), *adj., v.,* **-at·ed, -at·ing.** **—*adj.*** **1.** *Bot.* having widely spreading branches in alternate pairs. **2.** *Zool.* having arms. **—*v.i.*** **3.** to progress by means of brachiation. [< L *brāchiāt(us)* with branches like arms. See BRACHI-, -ATE[1]]

bra·chi·a·tion (brā′kē ā′shən, brak′ē-), *n. Zool.* locomotion accomplished by swinging by the arms from one hold to another. [BRACHIATE + -ION]

bra·chi·a·tor (brā′kē ā′tər, brak′ē-), *n.* an animal that can progress by means of brachiation, as a gibbon. [BRACHIATE + -OR[2]]

brachio-, a learned borrowing from Greek meaning "arm," used in the formation of compound words: *brachiopod.* Also, *esp. before a vowel,* **brachi-.** [comb. form repr. L *brāchium* and Gk *brachīōn*]

bra·chi·o·pod (brā′kē ə pod′, brak′ē-), *n.* **1.** any mollusklike, marine animal of the phylum *Brachiopoda,* having a dorsal and ventral shell; a lamp shell. **—*adj.*** **2.** Also, **brach·i·op·o·dous** (brak′ē op′ə dəs). belonging or pertaining to the *Brachiopoda.* [BRACHIO- + -POD]

bra·chis·to·chrone (brə kis′tə krōn′), *n. Geom.* the curve between two points which is traced in the shortest time by a body moving under an external force without friction; the curve of quickest descent. [< Gk *brāchisto(s)* shortest (superl. of *brachȳs* BRACHY-) + *chrónos* time] **—bra·chis·to·chron·ic** (brə kis′tə kron′ik), **brach·is·toch·ro·nous** (brak′i stok′rə nəs), *adj.*

bra·chi·um (brā′kē əm, brak′ē-), *n., pl.* **bra·chi·a** (brā′kē ə, brak′ē ə). **1.** *Anat.* the part of the arm from the shoulder to the elbow. **2.** the corresponding part of any limb, as in the wing of a bird. **3.** an armlike part or process. [< NL, L, var. of *bracchium* the arm < Gk *brachīōn*]

brachy-, a learned borrowing from Greek meaning "short," used in the formation of compound words: *brachycephalic.* [< Gk, comb. form of *brachȳs;* akin to L *brevis*]

brach·y·car·di·a (brak′i kär′dē ə), *n. Pathol.* bradycardia. [BRACHY- + *cardia;* see CARDIAC]

brach·y·ce·phal·ic (brak′ē sə fal′ik), *adj. Cephalom.* short-headed; having a breadth of head at least four-fifths as great as the length from front to back. Also, **brach·y·ceph·a·lous** (brak′ē sef′ə ləs). Cf. **dolichocephalic** (def. 1). [BRACHY- + -CEPHALIC] **—brach·y·ceph·a·ly** (brak′ē sef′ə lē), **brach′y·ceph′a·lism,** *n.*

bra·chyc·er·ous (brə kis′ər əs), *adj. Entomol.* having short antennae. [BRACHY- + Gk *kér(as)* a horn + -OUS]

brach·y·cra·nic (brak′ē krā′nik), *adj. Craniom.* short-headed; having a breadth of skull at least four-fifths as great as the length from front to back. Cf. **dolichocranic** (def. 1). [BRACHY- + CRAN(IO)- + -IC]

brach·y·dac·tyl·i·a (brak′i dak til′ē ə), *n. Med.* abnormal shortness of the fingers and toes. Also, **brach·y·dac·ty·ly** (brak′ē dak′tᵊlē). [< NL; see BRACHY-, DACTYL, -IA] **—brach′y·dac·tyl′ic, brach·y·dac·ty·lous** (brak′ē dak′tᵊləs), *adj.*

brach·y·dome (brak′i dōm′), *n.* *Crystall.* a dome the faces of which are parallel to the shorter lateral axis. Cf. **macrodome.** [BRACHY- + DOME]

bra·chyl·o·gy (brə kil′ə jē), *n., pl.* **-gies.** brevity of diction; concise or abridged form of expression. [< Gk *brachylogía* brevity in speech. See BRACHY-, -LOGY]

bra·chyp·ter·ous (brə kip′tər əs), *adj.* *Zool., Ornith.* having short wings. [BRACHY- + -PTEROUS]

brach·y·sto·ma·tous (brak′ē stom′ə təs, -stō′mə-), *adj.* having a short proboscis, as certain insects. [BRACHY- + STOMATOUS]

brach·y·ur·an (brak′ē yŏŏr′ən), *adj.* **1.** belonging or pertaining to the suborder *Brachyura*, comprising the true crabs. —*n.* **2.** a brachyuran crustacean. [BRACHYUR(OUS) + -AN]

brach·y·ur·ous (brak′ē yŏŏr′əs), *adj.* *Zool.* short-tailed, as a crab (opposed to *macrurous*). [< NL *Brachyur(a)* name of the group. See BRACHY-, UR-[2], -OUS]

brac·ing (brā′sing), *adj.* **1.** strengthening; invigorating: *This mountain air is bracing.* **2.** of, pertaining to, or serving as a brace. —*n.* **3.** a brace. **4.** braces collectively: *The bracing on this scaffold is weak.* **5.** material, as timber, used for braces. [BRACE (v.) + -ING[1], -ING[2]] —**brac′ing·ly,** *adv.* —**brac′ing·ness,** *n.*

brack·en (brak′ən), *n.* *Brit.* **1.** a large fern or brake, esp. *Pteridium aquilinum.* **2.** a cluster or thicket of such ferns; an area overgrown with ferns and shrubs. [ME *braken* < Scand; cf. Sw *bräken* fern] —**brack′-ened,** *adj.*

Brack·en·ridge (brak′ən rij), *n.* a town in central Pennsylvania. 5697 (1960).

brack·et (brak′it), *n.* **1.** a support, as of metal or wood, projecting from a wall or the like to hold or bear the weight of a shelf, part of a cornice, etc. **2.** a shelf or shelves so supported. **3.** *Archit.* **a.** any horizontally projecting support for an overhanging weight, as a corbel, cantilever, or console. **b.** any of a series of fancifully shaped false consoles beneath an ornamental cornice. **4.** (on a staircase) an ornamental piece filling the angle between a riser and its tread. **5.** *Shipbuilding.* **a.** a flat plate, usually triangular with a flange on one edge, used to unite and reinforce the junction between two flat members or surfaces meeting at an angle. **b.** any member for reinforcing the angle between two members or surfaces. **6.** a projecting fixture for gas or electricity. **7.** one of two marks [or] used in writing or printing to enclose parenthetical matter, interpolations, etc. **8.** *Bot.* the leathery, corky, or woody, shelflike basidiocarp of certain fungi that form on tree trunks, lumber, etc.; conk. **9.** *Math.* **a.** **brackets,** parentheses of various forms indicating that the enclosed quantity is to be treated as a unit. **b.** (loosely) vinculum (def. 2). **10.** a grouping of taxpayers based on the amount of their income: *low-income bracket.* **11.** a class; grouping; classification: *She travels in a different social bracket.* **12.** *Gunnery.* range or elevation producing both shorts and overs on a target. —*v.t.* **13.** to furnish with or support by a bracket or brackets. **14.** to place within brackets; couple with a brace. **15.** to associate, mention, or class together: *The problems seemed easier after they were bracketed into groups.* **16.** *Gunnery.* to place (shots) both over and short of a target. [late ME *braket* kind of nail, prob. < ML *braca* (var. of *broca* projecting part); see -ET]

Brackets (Beneath wooden cornice)

brack′et clock′, a small clock designed to be placed on a bracket or shelf.

brack′eted blen′ny, gunnel.

brack′et foot′, *Furniture.* a corner foot of a chest or the like joining the sides in a concave line.

Bracket feet

brack·et·ing (brak′i ting), *n.* **1.** a series of brackets. **2.** framework for supporting a cove, cornice, plaster ceiling ornament, etc. [BRACKET + -ING[1]]

brack′et saw′, *Carpentry.* a handsaw for cutting curved forms.

Brack′ett se′ries (brak′it), *Physics.* a series of lines in the infrared spectrum of hydrogen.

brack·ish (brak′ish), *adj.* **1.** slightly salt; having a salty or briny flavor. **2.** distasteful; unpleasant. [< D *brak* salty (c. MLG *brach*) + -ISH[1]] —**brack′ish-ness,** *n.*

Brack·nell (brak′nəl), *n.* a town in E Berkshire, in S England. 20,380 (1961).

brac·o·nid (brak′ə nid), *n.* **1.** any of numerous wasps of the family *Braconidae*, the larvae of which are parasitic on aphids and the larvae of moths, butterflies, beetles, etc. —*adj.* **2.** belonging or pertaining to the family *Braconidae*. [< NL *Braconid(ae)* genus (*Bracon* (irreg. < Gk *brachýs* short; see BRACHY-) + *-idae* -ID[2])]

bract (brakt), *n.* *Bot.* a specialized leaf or leaflike part, usually situated at the base of a flower or inflorescence. [earlier *bracte(a)* < L: a thin plate of metal (sp. var. of *brattea*)] —**brac·te·al** (brak′tē əl), *adj.* —**bract′ed,** *adj.* —**bract′less,** *adj.*

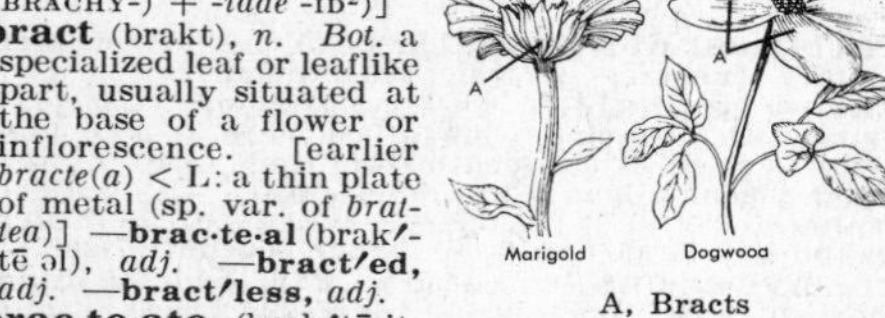

A, Bracts

brac·te·ate (brak′tē it, -āt′), *adj.* **1.** Also, **brac′te·ose′.** *Bot.* having bracts. —*n.* **2.** a thin coin, struck only on one face, the pattern of which shows through on the reverse face. [< L *bracteāt(us)* covered with gold leaf, gilded. See BRACT, -ATE[1]]

brac·te·o·late (brak′tē ə lit, -lāt′), *adj.* *Bot.* having bracteoles. [< NL *bracteolāt(us)*, equiv. to *bracteol(a)* BRACTEOLE + *-ātus* -ATE[1]]

brac·te·ole (brak′tē ōl′), *n.* *Bot.* a small or secondary bract, as on a pedicel. Also, **bract·let** (brakt′lit). [< NL *bracteola*, equiv. to L *bracte(a)* a thin plate of metal, gold leaf + *-ola* dim. suffix]

brad (brad), *n.* **1.** a slender wire nail having either a small, deep head or a projection to one side of the head end. —*v.t.* **2.** to fasten with brads. [late ME *brad*, var. of ME, OE *brod* < Scand; cf. Icel *broddr*, c. OE *brord* spike]

Brad (brad), *n.* a boy's given name.

brad·awl (brad′ôl′), *n.* *Carpentry.* an awl for making small holes in wood for brads. See illus. under **awl.** [BRAD + AWL]

Brad·bur·y (brad′bə rē), *n.* **Ray (Douglas),** born 1920, U.S. science-fiction writer.

Brad·dock (brad′ək), *n.* **1.** **Edward,** 1695–1755, British general in America. **2.** a city in SW Pennsylvania, near Pittsburgh: the site of General Braddock's defeat by the French and Indians 1755. 12,337 (1960).

Bra·den·ton (brād′ən tən), *n.* a city in W Florida. 19,380 (1960).

Bra′denton South′, a town in SW Florida. 3400 (1960).

Brad·ford (brad′fərd), *n.* **1.** **Gamaliel,** 1863–1932, U.S. biographer and novelist. **2.** **Roark** (rōrk, rôrk), 1896–1948, U.S. novelist and short-story writer. **3.** **William,** 1590–1657, Pilgrim settler: second governor of Plymouth Colony 1621–56. **4.** a city in SW Yorkshire, in N England. 295,768 (1961). **5.** a city in N Pennsylvania. 15,061 (1960). **6.** a boy's given name.

Brad′ford spin′ning, a wool-spinning method in which the fibers are oiled prior to combing and subsequently spun into worsted yarn. Also called **Brad′ford sys′tem.** [after BRADFORD, England]

Brad·ley (brad′lē), *n.* **1.** **Francis Herbert,** 1846–1924, English philosopher. **2.** **Omar Nelson,** 1893–1981, U.S. general: Chief of Staff 1948–49; chairman of the Joint Chiefs of Staff 1949–53. **3.** a town in NE Illinois. 8082 (1960). **4.** a boy's given name.

Brad′ley Beach′, a town in E New Jersey. 4204 (1960).

bra·doon (brə do͞on′), *n.* bridoon.

brad·sot (brad′sot), *n.* *Vet. Pathol.* braxy (def. 1). [< Icel; OIcel *brātha-sótt* sudden illness, plague (*brāth* haste + *sótt* illness; c. OE *suht*)]

Brad·street (brad′strēt′), *n.* **1.** **Anne (Dudley),** 1612?–72, American poet. **2.** her husband, **Simon,** 1603–97, governor of the Massachusetts colony 1679–86, 1689–92.

Bra·dy (brā′dē), *n.* **1.** **Mathew B.,** 1823?–96, U.S. photographer, esp. of the Civil War. **2.** a town in central Texas. 5338 (1960). **3.** a boy's given name.

brady-, a learned borrowing from Greek meaning "slow," used in the formation of compound words: *bradykinetic.* [< Gk, comb. form of *bradýs* slow, heavy]

brad·y·aux·e·sis (brad′ē ôg zē′sis, -ôk sē′-), *n.* *Biol.* growth of a part at a slower rate than that of the whole organism. Cf. **isauxesis, tachyauxesis.** [< NL; see BRADY-, AUXESIS] —**brad·y·aux·et·ic** (brad′ē ôg zet′ik, -ok set′-), *adj.* —**brad′y·aux·et′i·cal·ly,** *adv.*

brad·y·car·di·a (brad′i kär′dē ə), *n.* *Med.* a slow heartbeat rate, usually less than 60 beats per minute. [BRADY- + Gk *kardía* heart] —**brad′y·car′dic,** *adj.*

brad·y·ki·net·ic (brad′i ki net′ik, -kī-), *adj.* slow-moving; characterized by slowness in motion. [BRADY- + KINETIC] —**brad·y·ki·ne·sia** (brad′i ki nē′zhə, -kī-), **brad′y·ki·ne′sis,** *n.*

brad·y·tel·ic (brad′i tel′ik), *adj.* *Biol.* of or pertaining to evolution at a rate slower than the standard for a given group of plants or animals. Cf. **horotelic, tachytelic.** [BRADY- + TELIC] —**brad·y·tel·y** (brad′i-tel′ē), *n.*

brae (brā, brē; *Scot.* brā, bre̅), *n.* *Scot. and North Eng.* a slope; declivity; hillside. [ME *brā* < Scand; cf. Icel *brā* eyelash, c. OE *brǣw* eyebrow, eyelid, OHG *brāwa* (G *Braue*)]

brag (brag), *v.,* **bragged, brag·ging,** *n., adj.* —*v.i.* **1.** to use boastful language; boast: *Many conceited people like to brag.* —*v.t.* **2.** to boast of: *He bragged that he had won.* —*n.* **3.** a boast or vaunt. **4.** a thing to boast of. **5.** a boaster. **6.** an old English card game similar to poker. —*adj.* **7.** *Archaic.* unusually fine; first-rate. [ME *brag* (n.), *braggen* (v.) < Scand; cf. Icel *bragga sig* to hearten oneself, dress up] —**brag′ging·ly,** *adv.* —**brag′less,** *adj.*
—**Syn. 1.** See **boast**[1]. —**Ant. 2.** depreciate.

Bra·ga (brä′gə), *n.* a city in N Portugal: an ecclesiastical center. 32,153 (1950).

Brag·don (brag′dən), *n.* **Claude,** 1866–1946, U.S. architect, stage designer, and author.

Bragg (brag), *n.* **1.** **Brax·ton** (brak′stən), 1817–76, Confederate general in the U.S. Civil War. **2.** **Sir William Henry,** 1862–1942, and his son, **Sir William Lawrence,** 1890–1971, English physicists: Nobel prize winners 1915.

brag·ga·do·ci·o (brag′ə dō′shē ō′), *n., pl.* **-os.** **1.** empty boasting; brag. **2.** a boasting person; braggart. [after *Braggadocchio*, boastful character in Spenser's *Faerie Queene*, appar. BRAG + -ADE[1] + It *-occhio* aug. suffix] —**brag′ga·do′ci·an,** *adj.* —**brag′ga·do′ci·an·ism,** *n.*

brag·gart (brag′ərt), *n.* **1.** one given to bragging. —*adj.* **2.** bragging; boastful. [BRAG + -ART] —**brag′-gart·ism,** *n.* —**brag′gart·ly,** *adv.*

brag·ger (brag′ər), *n.* **1.** one who brags. **2.** *Cards.* **a.** (in some forms of brag) the jack of clubs or nine of diamonds. **b.** (in other forms of brag) any jack or nine. **c.** the first bettor in a game of brag. [ME; see BRAG, -ER[1]]

Bragg's′ law′, *Physics.* the law that the intensity of a crystal reflection of an x-ray is a function of the angle (**Bragg′ an′gle**) that is the complement of the angle of incidence of the x-ray, maximum intensity being achieved when the sine of the Bragg angle times twice the distance between layers of atoms in the crystal divided by the wave length of the x-ray equals an integer. [named after Sir W. H. and Sir W. L. BRAGG]

Bra·gi (brä′gē), *n.* *Scand. Myth.* the god of poetry and music, a son and the principal counselor of Odin, and the husband of Idun. Also, **Bra·ge** (brä′gə).

bra·guette (brä get′), *n.* brayette.

Brahe (brä, brä′ē; *Dan.* brä′e), *n.* **Ty·cho** (tē′kō; *Dan.* tY′kō), 1546–1601, Danish astronomer.

Brah·ma (brä′mə, brā′-), *n.* one of a breed of large Asian chickens, having feathered legs and small wings and tail. [short for *Brahmaputra fowl*, so called because brought to England from a town on that river]

Brah·ma (brä′mə, brā′-), *n.* a Brahman bull, steer, or cow. [alter. of BRAHMAN]

Brah·ma (brä′mə), *n.* *Hinduism.* **1.** Brahman (def. 2). **2.** (in later Hinduism) "the Creator," the first member of the Trimurti, with Vishnu the Preserver and Shiva the Destroyer. [< Skt *brahma*, neut. nom. (see def. 1) of *brahman* worship]

Brah·ma·jna·na (brä′mə jə nyä′nə, -gə nyä′-, -jnyä′-, -gnyä′-), *n.* *Hinduism.* jnana. [< Skt; see BRAHMA, JNANA]

Brah·ma·lo·ka (brä′mə lō′kə), *n.* *Hinduism.* the highest part of Kamaloka, where refined souls exist in blissful contemplation of Brahma. [< Skt *Brahma* BRAHMA + *-lōkah* a clearing, c. L *lūcus* sacred grove]

Brah·man (brä′mən), *n., pl.* **-mans.** *Hinduism.* **1.** Also, **Brahmin.** a member of the highest, or priestly, caste among the Hindus. **2.** Also, **Brahma.** the impersonal supreme being, the primal source and ultimate goal of all beings, with which Atman, when enlightened, knows itself to be identical. [< Skt *brāhmaṇa*, deriv. of *brahman* worship] —**Brah·man·ic** (brä man′ik), **Brah·man′i·cal,** *adj.*

Brah·man (brä′mən), *n.* any of several breeds of Indian cattle, esp. a grayish, heat-resistant American breed raised chiefly in the Gulf States. [special use of BRAHMAN priest]

Brah·ma·na (brä′mə nə), *n.* *Hinduism.* one of a class of prose pieces dealing with Vedic rituals and sacrifices. Cf. **Veda.** [< Skt *brāhmaṇa*]

Brah·ma·ni (brä′mə nē), *n., pl.* **-nis.** a woman of the Brahman caste. Also, **Brah′ma·nee.** [< Skt, fem. of *brāhmaṇa* BRAHMAN]

Brah·man·ism (brä′mə niz′əm), *n.* **1.** the religious and social system of the Brahmans and orthodox Hindus, characterized by the caste system and diversified pantheism. **2.** the Hinduism of the Vedas, Brahmanas, and Upanishads. Also, **Brahminism.** [BRAHMAN + -ISM] —**Brah′man·ist,** *n.*

Brah·ma·pu·tra (brä′mə po͞o′trə), *n.* a river in S Asia, flowing from SW Tibet through NE India and joining the Ganges River in E Pakistan. ab. 1700 mi. long.

Brah′ma Sa·maj′. See **Brahmo Samaj.**

Brah′ma Vi·ha′ra, *Buddhism.* vihara (def. 3).

Brah·mi (brä′mē), *n.* a script of India that was probably adapted from the Aramaic alphabet about the 7th century B.C., and from which most of the later Indian scripts developed. [< Skt, equiv. to *brahm-* (see BRAHMAN) + *-ī* as in HINDI, etc.]

Brah·min (brä′min), *n., pl.* **-min, -mins.** **1.** *Hinduism.* Brahman (def. 1). **2.** a person of great culture and intellect, esp. a member of a New England family that is considered aristocratic. **3.** one who is intellectually or socially aloof. [var. of BRAHMAN] —**Brah·min·ic** (brä min′ik), **Brah·min′i·cal,** *adj.*

Brah·min·ism (brä′mə niz′əm), *n.* Brahmanism. —**Brah′min·ist,** *n.*

Brah′mi·ny kite′ (brä′mə nē), a common kite, *Haliastur indus*, of southern Asia and the southwest Pacific islands, having reddish-brown plumage with a white head and breast. [*Brahminy*, deriv. of BRAHMIN, by analogy to such words as *Bengali*]

Brah′mo Sa·maj′ (brä′mō), a modern Hindu movement advocating a monotheistic religion based on the Upanishads, and social and educational reforms according to Western principles. Also, **Brahma Samaj.** [< Bengali *Brahmo Samāj* assembly of Brahma]

Brahms (brämz; *Ger.* bräms), *n.* **Jo·han·nes** (yō hä′nəs), 1833–97, German composer. —**Brahms′i·an,** *adj.* —**Brahms′ite,** *n.*

Bra·hu·i (brä ho͞o′ē), *n.* **1.** a member of a nomadic people of Baluchistan. **2.** the Dravidian language spoken by the Brahui.

braid (brād), *v.t.* **1.** to weave together strips or strands of; plait. **2.** to form by such weaving: *to braid a rope.* **3.** to bind or confine (the hair) with a band, ribbon, etc. **4.** to trim with braid, as a garment. —*n.* **5.** a braided length or plait, esp. of hair. **6.** a hair style formed by interweaving three or more strands of hair. **7.** a narrow, ropelike band formed by plaiting or weaving together several strands of silk, cotton, or other material, used as trimming for garments, drapery, etc. **8.** a band, ribbon, etc., for binding or confining the hair. [ME *braide(n)*, *breide(n)* (v.), OE *bregdan* to move quickly, move to and fro, weave; c. Icel *bregtha*, D *breien*] —**braid′er,** *n.*

braid·ing (brā′ding), *n.* **1.** braids collectively. **2.** braided work. [late ME *breydyng*. See BRAID[1], -ING[1]]

braies (brā), *n.* (*construed as pl.*) **1.** men's loose-fitting breeches worn in the Middle Ages. **2.** braccae. [< F, OF, pl. of *braie* < L *brāca*; see BRACCAE]

brail (brāl), *n.* **1.** *Naut.* any of several horizontal lines fastened to the after leech of a fore-and-aft sail or lateen sail, for gathering the sail in to a mast, yard, or gaff: used esp. with a sail having a standing gaff. **2.** a leather binding for a hawk's wings, to prohibit flight. —*v.t.* **3.** *Naut.* to gather or haul in (a sail) by means of brails (usually fol. by *up*). **4.** *Naut.* to transfer (fish) from a net to the hold of a ship. **5.** to bind (the wings of a bird) in order to prevent it from flying. [late ME, var. of *brayell* < AF *braiel*; OF < LL *brācāle* breech-belt, n. use of neut. of *brācālis*, equiv. to L *brāc(a)* BREECH + *-ālis* -AL[1]]

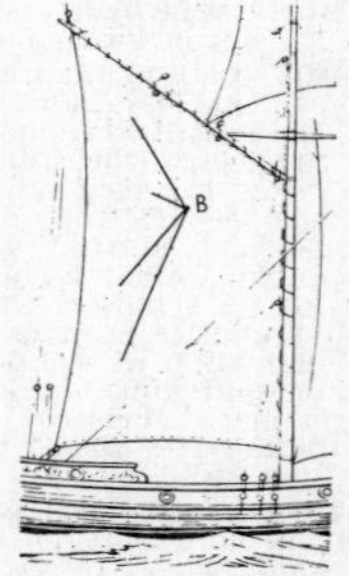

B, Brail

Bră·i·la (brə ē′lä), *n.* a port in E Rumania, on the Danube River. 102,500 (1956).

Braille (brāl), *n., v.,* **Brailled, Brail·ing.** —*n.* **1.** **Louis** (lo͞o′is, lo͞o′ē; *Fr.* lwē), 1809–52, French teacher of the blind. **2.** a system of writing or printing for the blind in which combinations of tangible dots or points are used to represent letters, characters, etc., which are read by touch. —*v.t.* **3.** to write or transliterate in Braille characters. Also, **braille.**

CONCISE ETYMOLOGY KEY: <, descended or derived from; <, whence; b., blend of, blended; c., cognate with; deriv., derivative; equiv., equivalent; imit., imitative; m., modification of; obl., oblique; r., replacing; s., stem; sp., spelling; translation; ?, origin unknown, perhaps; *, hypothetical. See the full key inside the front cover.

Braille·writ·er (brāl′rī′tər), *n.* (*sometimes l.c.*) a machine, similar to a typewriter, for writing texts in Braille. [BRAILLE + WRITER]

Braill·ist (brā′list), *n.* **1.** an expert at writing Braille. **2.** one whose vocation is the writing of Braille. [BRAILLE + -IST]

Brai·low·sky (brī lôf′skē, brā-; *Russ.* brī lôf′ski), *n.* **Alexander,** born 1896, Russian pianist.

brain (brān), *n.* **1.** *Anat., Zool.* the part of the central nervous system enclosed in the cranium of man and other vertebrates, consisting of a soft, convoluted mass of gray and white matter and serving to control and coordinate the mental and physical actions. **2.** *Zool.* (in many invertebrates) a part of the nervous system more or less corresponding to the brain of vertebrates. **3.** Sometimes, **brains.** (*construed as pl.*) understanding; intellectual power; intelligence. **4.** the brain as the center of thought, understanding, etc.; mind; intellect. **5. brains,** *Slang.* an intellectual leader or planner: *The junior partner is the brains of the firm.* **6.** *Informal.* a very intelligent or brilliant person. **7. beat one's brains out,** *Slang.* to try one's utmost, as to understand and work out a problem, remember something, etc.: *She beat her brains out studying, but couldn't keep up with the rest of the class.* **8. have something on the brain,** to have an obsession; be occupied with: *Lately I seem to have food on the brain.* **9. pick someone's brains,** to obtain information by questioning another person rather than by seeking it independently: *He refused to prepare for the exam but counted on being able to pick his roommate's brains.* —*v.t.* **10.** to dash out the brains of; hit or club (someone) on the brain. [ME; OE *brægen, bregen;* c. LG *brägen,* D *brein*] —**brain′like′,** *adj.*
—**Syn. 3.** sense; capacity. See **mind.**

Human brain (cross section) A, Cerebrum; B, Corpus callosum; C, Pineal body; D, Vermis; E, Cerebellum; F, Spinal cord; G, Medulla oblongata; H, Pons; I, Oculomotor nerve; J, Pituitary gland

brain′ cell′, *Anat.* a neuron in the brain.

brain·child (brān′chīld′), *n., pl.* **-chil·dren.** *Informal.* a product of one's creative work or thought. Also, **brain′-child′, brain′ child′.** [BRAIN + CHILD]

brain′ cor′al, any of several reef-building corals of the genus *Meandrina,* having a highly convoluted and furrowed surface.

brain′ drain′, the loss of trained professional personnel, as doctors, engineers, etc., to a competing company or to a foreign country, esp. to a more highly technologically developed country.

Brai′nerd (brā′nərd), *n.* a city in central Minnesota. 12,898 (1960).

brain′ fe′ver. See **cerebrospinal meningitis.**

brain·less (brān′lis), *adj.* mentally weak; witless; stupid. [late ME *braynles.* See BRAIN, -LESS] —**brain′less·ly,** *adv.* —**brain′less·ness,** *n.*

brain·pan (brān′pan′), *n.* the skull or cranium. [ME *brayn panne,* OE *brægenpanne.* See BRAIN, PAN[1]]

brain·pow·er (brān′pou′ər), *n.* **1.** intellectual capacity; mental ability. **2.** people with superior mental abilities: *a conference of all available brainpower.* [BRAIN + POWER]

brain·sick (brān′sik′), *adj.* crazy; mad. [ME *brain-seke,* OE *brægensēoc.* See BRAIN, SICK[1]] —**brain′sick′ly,** *adv.* —**brain′sick′ness,** *n.*

brain·storm (brān′stôrm′), *n.* *Informal.* a sudden inspiration, idea, etc. [BRAIN + STORM]

brain·storm·ing (brān′stôr′ming), *n.* a conference technique of solving specific problems, amassing information, stimulating creative thinking, developing new ideas, etc., by unrestrained and spontaneous participation in discussion. [BRAINSTORM + -ING[1]]

Brains′ Trust′, (*sometimes l.c.*) *Brit.* **1.** See **brain trust. 2.** a panel of experts on radio or television, giving impromptu answers to selected questions from the listening audience.

Brain·tree (brān′trē′), *n.* a town in E Massachusetts, near Boston. 31,969 (1960).

brain′ trust′, a group of experts from various fields who serve as unofficial consultants on matters of policy and strategy. Also, *Brit.,* **Brains Trust.**

brain-trust (brān′trust′), *v.t.* to serve as a brain trust or a brain truster for: *They have brain-trusted many major corporations.*

brain′ trust′er, a member of a brain trust; an important but usually unofficial adviser.

brain·wash (brān′wosh′, -wôsh′), *v.t.* **1.** to cause (someone) to undergo brainwashing. —*n.* **2.** the process of brainwashing: *unprincipled nations employing brainwash in their treatment of prisoners.* **3.** a subjection to brainwashing: *new attitudes after his brainwash.* Also, **brain′-wash′, brain′ wash′.** [back formation from BRAINWASHING] —**brain′wash′er,** *n.*

brain·wash·ing (brān′wosh′ing, -wô′shing), *n.* **1.** a method for systematically changing attitudes or altering beliefs, originated in totalitarian countries, esp. through the use of torture, drugs, or psychological-stress techniques. **2.** any method of controlled systematic indoctrination, esp. one based on repetition or confusion: *brainwashing by TV commercials.* **3.** an instance of subjecting or being subjected to such techniques: *efforts to halt the brainwashing of captive audiences.* Also, **brain′-wash′ing, brain′ wash′ing.** [BRAIN + WASHING]

brain′ wave′, **1.** Usually, **brain waves.** *Med.* electrical potentials or impulses given off by brain tissue. Cf. **electroencephalogram. 2.** *Informal.* a sudden idea or inspiration; brainstorm.

brain·work (brān′wûrk′), *n.* **1.** work or effort consisting principally or largely of mental activity, thought, imagination, etc., as opposed to physical or manual work. **2.** the effort of thought, reasoning, planning, or the like; ordered or directed thinking: *Problem-solving is a form of brainwork.* [BRAIN + WORK]

brain·y (brā′nē), *adj.,* **brain·i·er, brain·i·est.** intelligent; clever; intellectual. [BRAIN + -Y[1]] —**brain′i·ness,** *n.*

braird (brârd), *Chiefly Scot.* *n.* **1.** new growth; the first sprouts or shoots of grass, corn, or other crops. —*v.i.* **2.** (of a crop or a seed) to sprout; appear above the ground. [late ME *breird,* var. of *brerd* a sprout, to sprout, OE *brerd* edge, top; akin to BRAD]

braise (brāz), *v.t.,* **braised, brais·ing.** to cook (meat or vegetables) by sautéeing in fat and then cooking slowly in very little liquid. [< F *braise(r),* deriv. of *braise* live coals < Gmc; akin to Sw *brasa* pyre, fire, whence *brasa* to roast, c. Dan *brase*]

brake[1] (brāk), *n., v.,* **braked, brak·ing.** —*n.* **1.** a device for slowing or stopping a vehicle or other moving mechanism by the absorption or transfer of the energy of momentum, usually by means of friction. **2. brakes,** the drums, shoes, tubes, levers, etc., making up such a device on a vehicle. **3.** Also called **brakeman.** a member of a bobsled team who operates the brake. **4.** Also called **breaker.** a tool or machine for breaking up flax or hemp, to separate the fiber. **5.** Also called **press brake.** a machine for bending sheet metal to a desired shape. **6.** *Obs.* an old instrument of torture. —*v.t.* **7.** to slow or stop (a vehicle or other machine) as by means of a brake. **8.** to furnish with brakes. **9.** to process (flax or hemp) by crushing it in a brake. —*v.i.* **10.** to use or run a brake. **11.** to stop or slow upon being braked. **12.** to run a hoisting machine. [late ME < MD, MLG; akin to BREAK] —**brake′less,** *adj.*

brake[2] (brāk), *n.* a place overgrown with bushes, shrubs, brambles, or cane; thicket. [late ME (in phrase *brake of fern* thicket of fern) < MLG *brake* thicket]

brake[3] (brāk), *n.* any large or coarse fern, esp. *Pteridium aquilinum* or some allied species. [ME *brake,* var. of BRACKEN]

brake[4] (brāk), *v.* *Archaic.* pt. of **break.**

brake·age (brā′kij), *n.* **1.** the action of a brake or set of brakes, as in stopping a vehicle. **2.** brakes collectively. [BRAKE[1] + -AGE]

brake′ band′, a flexible strap, usually of steel, lined with a friction-producing material and tightened against a brake drum to produce a braking action.

brake′ drum′, a narrow metal cylinder, fixed to a rotating shaft or wheel, against which brake shoes or brake bands act.

brake′ horse′power, the horsepower made available by an engine or turbine for driving machinery other than itself, as measured by a dynamometer.

brake′ lin′ing, the material, usually asbestos combined with other materials, used as the friction-producing element of a brake.

brake·man (brāk′mən), *n., pl.* **-men. 1.** a trainman who assists the conductor in the operation of a train. **2.** brake[1] (def. 3). Also, *esp. Brit.,* **brakesman.** [BRAKE[1] + MAN[1]]

brak·er (brā′kər), *n.* **1.** *Shipbuilding.* mask (def. 16). **2.** break (def. 4). [BRAKE[1] + -ER[1]]

brake′ shoe′, a rigid plate, usually of steel in the shape of an arc of a cylinder, coated on the outside of its curved surface with a friction-producing material and tightened against the inside of a brake drum to produce a braking action.

brakes·man (brāks′mən), *n., pl.* **-men.** *Chiefly Brit.* brakeman.

brake′ spring′, *Horol.* an extension of the mainspring, braced against the wall of the barrel to hold the mainspring in a fixed position by friction unless it is overwound, in which case it slips. Also called **bridle, safety spring, slip spring.**

brake-van (brāk′van′), *n.* *Brit.* the caboose of a railway train.

brake′ wheel′, (in a windmill) a bevel gearwheel rotating with the wind shaft.

Brak·pan (brak′pan′), *n.* a city in the E Republic of South Africa, near Johannesburg. 78,778 (1960).

Brale (brāl), *n.* *Trademark.* a conoidal diamond or diamond-pointed tool, having convexly curved sides meeting at an angle of 120°, used as an indenter in testing the hardness of metals.

Bram (bram), *n.* a boy's given name.

Bram·ah (bram′ə, brä′mə), *n.* **Joseph,** 1748–1814, English engineer and inventor.

Bra·man·te (brə män′tā; *It.* brä män′te), *n.* **Do·na·to d'A·gno·lo** (dô nä′tô dä′nyô lô), 1444–1514, Italian architect and painter.

bram·ble (bram′bəl), *n., v.,* **-bled, -bling.** —*n.* **1.** any rosaceous plant of the genus *Rubus.* **2.** *Brit. Dial.* the common blackberry, *R. fruticosus.* **3.** any rough, prickly shrub, as the dog rose. —*v.i.* **4.** *Brit. Dial.* to look for and gather wild blackberries; pick blackberries from the vine. [ME; OE *bræmbel,* var. of *bræmel,* equiv. to *bræm-* (c. D *braam* BROOM) + *-el* -LE]

bram·bling (bram′bling), *n.* an Old World finch, *Fringilla montifringilla,* the male of which is black and white with a reddish-brown breast. [earlier *bramlin* (*bram-* (var. of BROOM) + *-lin* -LING[1]); akin to G *Brämling*]

bram·bly (bram′blē), *adj.,* **-bli·er, -bli·est. 1.** having many brambles. **2.** resembling brambles. [BRAMBLE + -Y[1]]

Bram·well (bram′wəl), *n.* a boy's given name.

bran (bran), *n., v.,* **branned, bran·ning.** —*n.* **1.** the partly ground husk of wheat or other grain, separated from flour meal by bolting. **2.** a by-product of grain processing, used as feed. —*v.t.* **3.** to soak or boil in bran water, as in the tanning of hides. [ME < OF, var. of *bren* < ?] —**bran′ner,** *n.*

Bran (bran), *n.* **1.** *Welsh Legend.* a king of Britain and the brother of Manawyddan and Branwen: his head was buried at London as a magical defense against invasion. He was sometimes regarded as a sea-god or Christian saint. **2.** a boy's given name, form of **Brandon.**

branch (branch, bränch), *n.* **1.** *Bot.* a division or subdivision of the stem or axis of a tree, shrub, or other plant. **2.** a limb, offshoot, or ramification of any main stem: *the branches of a deer's antlers.* **3.** any member or part of a body or system; a section or subdivision: *the various branches of learning.* **4.** a local operating division of a business house, library, or the like. **5.** a line of family descent stemming from a particular ancestor, as distinguished from some other line or lines from the same stock; a division of a family. **6.** a tributary stream or any stream that is not a large river or a bayou. **7.** *Ling.* (in the classification of related languages within a family) a category of a lower order than a subfamily and of a higher order than a subbranch or group, as the Germanic branch of Indo-European. Ca group (def. 5a). **8.** *Computer Technol.* a point in a computer program where the computer selects one of two or more subroutines, according to the conditions of the program. **9.** *Naut.* a warrant or license permitting a pilot (**branch′ pi′lot**) to navigate in certain waters. —*v.i.* **10.** to put forth branches; spread in branches. **11.** to divide into separate parts or subdivisions; diverge: *The main road branches off to the left.* —*v.t.* **12.** to divide as into branches. **13.** to adorn with needlework; decorate with embroidery, as in textile fabrics. **14. branch out,** to expand or extend, as business activities, pursuits, etc.: *He is thinking of branching out by opening another restaurant in the suburbs.* [ME *branch(e)* < OF *branche* < LL *branca* paw] —**branch′less,** *adj.* —**branch′like′,** *adj.*
—**Syn. 1.** offshoot, shoot. BRANCH, BOUGH, LIMB refer to divisions of a tree. BRANCH is general, meaning either a large or a small division. BOUGH refers only to the larger branches: *a bough loaded with apples.* A LIMB is a large primary division of a tree trunk or of a bough: *to climb out on a limb.* **11.** ramify, subdivide.

Branch (branch, bränch), *n.* a boy's given name.

branch′ cut′, *Math.* a method for selecting a single-valued function on a subset of the domain of a multiple-valued function of a complex variable, usually involving Riemann surfaces.

branched′ chain′, *Chem.* an open chain of atoms, usually carbon, with one or more side chains attached to it. Cf. **straight chain.**

branchi-, var. of **branchio-** before a vowel.

bran·chi·a (brang′kē ə), *n., pl.* **-chi·ae** (-kē ē′). *Zool.* a gill. [< Gk: gills, pl. of *bránchion* fin]

bran·chi·al (brang′kē əl), *adj.* of or pertaining to the branchiae or gills or to the homologous, embryonic parts in animals without gills. [BRANCHI- + -AL[1]]

bran′chial arch′, **1.** *Zool.* one of a series of bony or cartilaginous arches on each side of the pharynx that support the gills of fishes and aquatic amphibians; gill bar. **2.** *Embryol.* one of a series of rudimentary, arch-like thickenings of the body wall in the pharyngeal region of the embryo of terrestrial amphibians, reptiles, birds, and mammals. Also called **gill arch.**

bran′chial cleft′, **1.** *Zool.* one of a series of slitlike openings in the walls of the pharynx between the branchial arches of fishes and aquatic amphibians through which water passes from the pharynx to the exterior. **2.** *Embryol.* one of a series of transitory, rudimentary openings from a branchial groove into the pharynx of the embryo of terrestrial amphibians, reptiles, birds, and mammals. Also called **gill cleft, gill slit.**

bran′chial groove′, *Embryol.* one of a series of rudimentary depressions between adjacent branchial arches, homologous to the branchial clefts of gill-breathing ancestral forms.

bran·chi·ate (brang′kē it, -āt′), *adj.* *Zool.* having gills. [BRANCHI- + -ATE[1]]

bran·chi·form (brang′kə fôrm′), *adj.* shaped like a gill. [BRANCHI- + -FORM]

branchio-, a learned borrowing from Greek meaning "gills," used in the formation of compound words: *branchiopod.* Also, *esp. before a vowel,* **branchi-.** [comb. form repr. Gk *bránchia* BRANCHIA]

bran·chi·op·neus·tic (brang′kē op nōō′stik, -nyōō′-), *adj.* *Entomol.* breathing by means of gills, as certain aquatic insect larvae. [BRANCHIO- + Gk *pneustikós,* equiv. to *pneus-* (verbid s. of *pnein* to breathe) + *-tikos* -TIC]

bran·chi·o·pod (brang′kē ə pod′), *n.* **1.** any crustacean of the subclass *Branchiopoda,* having gills on the feet. —*adj.* **2.** Also, **bran·chi·op·o·dous** (brang′kē op′ə dəs). belonging or pertaining to the *Branchiopoda.* [BRANCHIO- + -POD]

bran·chi·os·te·gal (brang′kē os′tə gəl), *Ichthyol.* —*n.* **1.** Also called **branchios′tegal ray′.** one of the long, curved bones just below the operculum, supporting the gill membranes. —*adj.* **2.** of or pertaining to the branchiostegals. [BRANCHIO- + STEG(O)- + -AL[1]]

bran·chi·os·te·gous (brang′kē os′tə gəs), *adj.* *Ichthyol.* **1.** branchiostegal. **2.** having covered gills. [BRANCHIO- + STEG(O)- + -OUS]

branch′ line′, a rail line, directly or indirectly connected with a main line, having its own stations and service.

branch′ point′, **1.** *Elect.* a point in an electric network at which three or more conductors meet. **2.** *Math.* a point such that analytic continuation of a given function of a complex variable in a small neighborhood of the point produces a different functional value at the point.

Bran·chus (brang′kəs), *n.* *Class. Myth.* a son of Apollo, given the power of augury by his father.

branch′ wa′ter, **1.** water in or from a branch, creek, stream, etc. **2.** *U.S.* (in a drink, highball, etc.) ordinary water; plain water as distinguished from soda water, ginger ale, or the like.

branch′ wilt′, *Plant Pathol.* a disease of walnut trees, characterized by sudden wilting, cankers, and discoloration, caused by a fungus, *Hendersonula toruloidea.*

Bran·cu·si (brang kōō′zē; *Rum.* brang kōōsh′), *n.* **Con·stan·tin** (kon′stən tin; *Rum.* kon′stän tēn′), 1876–1957, Rumanian sculptor.

brand (brand), *n.* **1.** kind, grade, or make, as indicated by a stamp, trademark, or the like: *the best brand of coffee.* **2.** a mark made by burning or otherwise, to indicate kind, grade, make, ownership, etc. **3.** a mark formerly put upon criminals with a hot iron. **4.** any mark of infamy; stigma. **5.** an iron for branding. **6.** a burning or partly burned piece of wood. **7.** *Archaic.* a sword. —*v.t.* **8.** to mark with a brand. **9.** to mark with infamy; stigmatize. [ME, OE: burning, a burning piece of wood, torch, sword; c. D *brand,* G *Brand,* Icel *brandr;* akin to BURN[1]] —**brand′er,** *n.* —**brand′less,** *adj.*

Brand (brand), *n.* a boy's given name. Also, **Brant, Brent.**

Bran·deis (bran′dīs), *n.* **Louis Dem·bitz** (dem′bits), 1856–1941, U.S. lawyer and writer: associate justice of the U.S. Supreme Court 1916–39.

Bran·den·burg (bran′dən bûrg′; *Ger.* brän′dən-bōōrk′), *n.* **1.** a former province in E Germany. **2.** a city in central East Germany: former capital of Brandenburg province. 87,700 (est. 1959). —**Bran′den·burg′er,** *n.*

brand·er (bran′dər), *v.t.* **1.** to apply furring to (a surface). —*v.i.* **2.** to apply furring. [ME *brandire,* equiv. to *brand(en)* to BRAND + *ire* IRON]

bran·der·ing (bran′dər iŋ), *n.* furring (def. 4b). [BRANDER + -ING[1]]

Bran·des (brän′des), *n.* **Ge·org Mor·ris** (gē ôrg′ mō′ris), (*Georg Morris Cohen*), 1842–1927, Danish historian and literary critic.

bran·died (bran′dēd), *adj.* flavored, soaked in, or treated with brandy. [BRANDY + -ED[3]]

bran·dish (bran′dish), *v.t.* **1.** to shake or wave, as a weapon; flourish: *Brandishing his sword, he rode into battle.* —*n.* **2.** a flourish or waving, as of a weapon. [ME *bra(u)ndisshe(n)* < MF *brandiss-* (long s. of *brandir*, deriv. of *brand* sword < Gmc). See BRAND, -ISH[2]] —**bran′dish·er,** *n.*

brand·ling (brand′liŋ), *n.* a small, reddish-brown earthworm, *Ersenia foetida*, having yellow markings, found chiefly in manure piles. [BRAND + -LING[1]]

brand-new (brand′no͞o′, -nyo͞o′), *adj.* entirely new. Also, **bran-new.** —**brand′-new′ness,** *n.*

Bran·don (bran′dən), *n.* **1.** a city in SW Manitoba, in S central Canada. 24,796 (1956). **2.** a boy's given name.

bran·dreth (bran′drith), *n.* **1.** a wooden fence around a well. **2.** an iron tripod or trivet placed over a fire. **3.** any similar support or framework. Also, **bran′drith.** [ME < Scand; cf. Icel *brandreith*, equiv. to *brand* BRAND + *reith* vehicle (c. ROAD, RAID); r. OE *brandrād* trivet and *brandrida* fire-grate]

Brandt (brant; *Ger.* bränt), *n.* **Wil·ly** (wil′ē; *Ger.* vil′ē), born 1913, West German political leader: chancellor 1969–74.

bran·dy (bran′dē), *n., pl.* **-dies,** *v.,* **-died, -dy·ing.** —*n.* **1.** a spirit distilled from the fermented juice of grapes or of apples, peaches, plums, etc. —*v.t.* **2.** to mix, flavor, or preserve with brandy: *to brandy peaches.* [short for *brandywine* < D *brandewijn* burnt (i.e., distilled) wine]

bran′dy ball′, *Brit.* a brandy-flavored candy.

bran′dy mint′, peppermint.

Bran·dy·wine (bran′dē wīn′), *n.* a creek in SE Pennsylvania and N Delaware: British defeat of the Americans 1777.

bran·gle (braŋ′gəl), *n., v.,* **-gled, -gling.** *Brit. Archaic.* —*n.* **1.** a squabble. —*v.i.* **2.** to squabble; dispute in a noisy or angry manner. [var. of BRANLE]

Bran·gus (braŋ′gəs), *n., pl.* **-gus·es.** one of an American breed of cattle developed from Brahman and Aberdeen Angus stock, bred to resist the effects of hot climate. [BRA(HMAN + ABERDEEN A)NGUS]

brank·ie (braŋ′kē, bräŋ′-), *adj. Scot. Archaic.* gaudy; showy. Also, **branky.** [late ME *brank* prance (< MD *bronken*; akin to PRANK[2]) + *-ie* -Y[1]]

branks (braŋks), *n.* (*construed as pl.*) a device consisting of a headpiece with a flat, iron bit with which to restrain the tongue, formerly used to punish a shrew or scold. [?]

bran·ky (braŋ′kē, bräŋ′-), *adj.,* **-ki·er, -ki·est.** *Scot. Archaic.* brankie.

bran·le (bran′əl; *Fr.* bräN′lə), *n., pl.* **bran·les** (bran′əlz; *Fr.* bräN′lə). **1.** a lively 16th- and 17th-century round dance originating in France. **2.** the music for this dance. Also, **bransle.** [< MF, deriv. of *branler* to shake, perh. syncopated var. of OF *brandeler* (*brand* BRAND + *-el* dim. suffix); see BRANDISH]

bran-new (bran′no͞o′, -nyo͞o′), *adj.* brand-new.

bran·ni·gan (bran′ə gən), *n.* **1.** a carouse. **2.** a squabble; brawl. [prob. from proper name]

bran·ny (bran′ē), *adj.,* **-ni·er, -ni·est.** of, containing, or like bran. [BRAN + -Y[1]]

Brans (branz), *n.* a boy's given name.

Brans·ford (branz′fərd), *n.* a boy's given name.

brans·le (bran′əl; *Fr.* bräN′lə), *n., pl.* **brans·les** (bran′əlz; *Fr.* bräN′lə). branle.

Bran·stock (brän′stok′), *n.* (in the *Volsunga Saga*) an oak tree in the house of Volsung into which Odin, disguised as a traveler, thrusts the sword Gram, which only Sigmund can withdraw. Also, **Barnstock.**

brant (brant), *n., pl.* **brants,** (*esp. collectively*) **brant.** any of several species of small, dark-colored geese of the genus *Branta*, esp. *B. bernicla*, breeding in high northern latitudes and migrating south in the autumn. Also called **brant′ goose′;** *Brit.,* **brent, brent goose.** [short for *brantgoose, brentgoose;* akin to Icel *brandgās*, G *Brandgans*]

Brant (brant), *n.* **1. Joseph** (native name, *Thayendanegea*), 1742–1807, Mohawk Indian chief who fought on the side of the British in the American Revolution. **2.** Also, **Brand, Brent.** a boy's given name.

Brant·ford (brant′fərd), *n.* a city in S Ontario, in SE Canada, near Lake Erie. 56,000 (1956).

Bran·ting (bran′tiŋ, brän′-), *n.* **Karl Hjal·mar** (kärl yäl′mär), 1860–1925, Swedish statesman: prime minister 1920, 1921–23, 1924–25: Nobel peace prize 1921.

Brants·ford (brants′fərd), *n.* a boy's given name.

Bran·wen (bran′wen), *n.* *Welsh Legend.* a sister of Bran: her son, by Matholwych, was killed by Evnissyen.

Braque (bräk; *Fr.* brak), *n.* **Georges** (jôrj; *Fr.* zhôrzh), 1882–1963, French painter.

brash (brash), *adj.* Also, **brashy. 1.** hasty; rash; impetuous. **2.** impertinent; impudent; tactless. **3.** (used esp. of wood) brittle. [in sense of brittle, deriv. of n.; hasty (by confusion with RASH[1])] —*n.* **4.** a pile or stack of loose fragments or debris, as of rocks, clippings of hedges, etc. **5.** Also called **mush.** *Naut.* small fragments of crushed ice collected by winds or currents near the shore. **6.** *Pathol.* heartburn (def. 1). **7.** *Brit. Dial.* **a.** a sudden shower or burst of rain. **b.** an eructation of fluid; pyrosis. **c.** any sudden, minor sickness or indisposition, esp. of the digestive tract. **8.** *Scot. and Eng. Dial.* an assault; attack. [late ME *brass(c)he* a slap, crash, perh. b. *brok(e)* (OE *broc* breach, fragment, sickness; akin to BREAK) and *dasch* smashing blow; see DASH[1]] —**brash′ly,** *adv.* —**brash′ness,** *n.*

brash·y (brash′ē), *adj.,* **brash·i·er, brash·i·est. 1.** brash. **2.** *Scot.* showery. [BRASH + -Y[1]] —**brash′i·ness,** *n.*

bra·sier (brā′zhər), *n.* brazier.

bra·sil (brə sēl′, -sil′), *n.* brazil.

Bra·sil (*Port.* brə zēl′; *Sp.* brä sēl′), *n.* Portuguese and Spanish name of **Brazil.**

bra·sil·e·in (brə zil′ē in), *n.* *Chem.* brazilein.

Bra·sí·lia (brä sēl′yə), *n.* a city in and the capital of Brazil, on the central plateau. 130,968 (est. 1960).

bras·i·lin (braz′ə lin), *n.* *Chem.* brazilin.

Bra·şov (brä shôv′), *n.* a city in central Rumania. 127,829 (est. 1959). Formerly, **Stalin.** Hungarian, **Brassó.** German, **Kronstadt.**

brasque (brask, bräsk), *n., v.,* **brasqued, brasquing.** *Metall.* —*n.* **1.** a paste of refractory material, as charcoal and clay, used as a lining for furnaces and crucibles. —*v.t.* **2.** to line (a furnace or crucible) with a brasque. [< F < It *brasca* pulverized charcoal, equiv. to *bras-* (see BRAISE) + *-ca* < L *-ica*, fem. of *-icus* -IC]

brass (bras, bräs), *n.* **1.** any of various metal alloys consisting mainly of copper and zinc. **2.** a utensil, ornament, or other article made of such an alloy. **3.** *Mach.* a replaceable semicylindrical shell, usually of bronze, used with another such to line a bearing; a half bushing. **4.** *Music.* **a.** a musical instrument of the trumpet or horn family. **b.** such instruments collectively in a band or orchestra. **5.** *Brit.* **a.** a memorial tablet or plaque incised with an effigy, coat of arms, or the like. **b.** *Slang.* money. **c.** *Slang.* a prostitute. **6.** *Furniture.* any piece of ornamental or functional hardware, as a drawer pull, made of brass. **7.** metallic yellow; lemon, amber, or reddish yellow. **8.** *U.S. Slang.* **a.** high-ranking military officers. **b.** any very important officials. **9.** *Informal.* excessive assurance; impudence; effrontery. —*adj.* **10.** of, made of, or pertaining to brass. **11.** using musical instruments made of brass. **12.** having the color brass. [ME *bras*, OE *bræs;* c. OFris *bres* copper, MLG *bras* metal] —**brass′ish,** *adj.*

brass·age (bras′ij, brä′sij), *n.* a charge to cover the costs of coining money. [< F, equiv. to *brass(er)* (to) stir (OF *bracier*) + *-age* -AGE]

bras·sard (bras′ärd), *n.* **1.** a badge worn around the upper arm. **2.** Also, **brassart** (bras′ärt). a piece of plate armor for protecting the arm. [< F, equiv. to *bras* arm (see BRACE) + *-ard* -ARD]

brass′ band′, *Music.* a band made up principally of brass wind instruments.

brass·bound (bras′bound′, bräs′-), *adj.* **1.** having a frame or reinforcements strengthened or made rigid by brass, bronze, etc., as a trunk, chest, or the like. **2.** rigid; unyielding; inflexible: *a set of brassbound regulations; brassbound mental categories.* **3.** impudent; brazen: *brassbound presumption.* [BRASS + -BOUND[1]]

bras·se·rie (bras′ə rē′; *Fr.* bras^ə rē′), *n., pl.* **-ries** (-rēz′; *Fr.* -rē′). an unpretentious restaurant, tavern, or the like, which serves food, beer, ale, etc. [< F, MF (*brass(er)* (to) brew (see BRASSAGE) + *-erie* -ERY)]

brass·ey (bras′ē, brä′sē), *n., pl.* **-eys.** *Golf.* brassie.

brass′ hat′, *Slang.* a high-ranking army or navy officer.

bras·si·ca (bras′ə kə), *n.* any cruciferous plant of the genus *Brassica*, comprising the cabbages, mustards, cauliflowers, turnips, etc. [< NL, L: cabbage]

bras·si·ca·ceous (bras′ə kā′shəs), *adj.* belonging to the family *Brassicaceae* (or *Cruciferae*), including the common cabbage, watercress, etc. [< NL *Brassicace(ae)* family name (see BRASSICA, -ACEAE) + -OUS]

brass·ie (bras′ē, brä′sē), *n.* *Golf.* a club with a wooden head the brass-plated face of which has more slope than a driver but less than a spoon, for hitting long, low drives on the fairway. Also, **brassy, brassey.** Also called **number two wood.** [BRASS + -IE]

bras·siere (brə zēr′), *n.* a woman's undergarment for supporting the breasts. Also, **bras·sière′.** Also called **bra.** [< F *brassière* (*bras* arm + *-ière* < L *-āria* -ER[2])]

brass′ knuck′les, a band of metal with four finger holes that fits over the root knuckles of the hand, used for increasing the effect of a blow from the fist.

Bras·só (brosh′shô), *n.* Hungarian name of **Braşov.**

brass′ tacks′, *Informal.* the most urgent considerations; essentials; realities: *Let's get the discussion down to brass tacks.*

brass·ware (bras′wâr′, bräs′-), *n.* articles made of brass. [BRASS + WARE[1]]

brass·y[1] (bras′ē, brä′sē), *adj.,* **brass·i·er, brass·i·est. 1.** made of or covered with brass. **2.** resembling brass. **3.** harsh and metallic: *brassy tones.* **4.** brazen; bold; loud: *a brassy salesman.* **5.** noisy; clamorous: *a big, brassy nightclub.* [BRASS + -Y[1]] —**brass′i·ly,** *adv.* —**brass′i·ness,** *n.*

brass·y[2] (bras′ē, brä′sē), *n., pl.* **brass·ies.** *Golf.* brassie.

brat (brat), *n.* a child, esp. an annoying, spoiled, or impolite child (usually used in contempt or irritation). [perh. transferred use of *brat* rag, OE *bratt* cloak < Celt; cf. Ir *brat* outer garment, cloth] —**brat′tish,** *adj.*

bra·ti·na (brə tē′nə, brä′ti nə), *n.* a Russian drinking cup, often covered, used as a loving cup. [appar. < Russ. (*brat* brother + *-ina* -INE[1])]

Bra·ti·sla·va (brat′ə slä′və, brä′tə-; *Czech.* brä′tyi slä vä), *n.* the capital of Slovakia, in the SW part, on the Danube River: a former capital of Hungary. 435,000. Hungarian, **Pozsony.** German, **Pressburg.**

Brat·tain (brat′ən), *n.* **Walter Hou·ser** (hou′zər) born 1902, U.S. physicist: Nobel prize 1956.

brat·tice (brat′is), *n., v.,* **-ticed, -tic·ing.** —*n.* **1.** a partition or lining, as of planks or cloth, forming an air passage in a mine. **2.** Also called **brattishing, bretessé.** (in medieval architecture) any temporary wooden fortification, esp. at the top of a wall. **3.** Also called **brat′tice cloth′.** burlap or other cloth, treated with preservative and used in the brattices of a mine. —*v.t.* **4.** to provide with a brattice; line with planks or cloth. [ME *bretax, bretask, bretice,* etc. < ML *bretescia, bratascia* < OE *brettisc* BRITISH]

brat·tish·ing (brat′i shiŋ), *n.* **1.** Also, **bratticing.** openwork, as a cresting, esp. over a shrine. **2.** brattice (def. 2). [var. of *bratticing.* See BRATTICE, -ING[1]]

brat·tle (brat′əl), *n., v.,* **-tled, -tling.** —*n.* **1.** a clattering noise. —*v.i.* **2.** to scamper noisily. [imit; see RATTLE[1]]

Brat·tle·bor·o (brat′əl bûr′ō, -bur′ō), *n.* a town in SE Vermont. 9315 (1960).

brat·ty (brat′ē), *adj.,* **-ti·er, -ti·est.** characteristic of or resembling a brat; brattish: *bratty remarks; bratty tricks.* [BRAT + -Y[1]]

brat·wurst (brat′wərst, -wo͝orst, brät′-; *Ger.* brät′vo͝orsht′), *n.* sausage made of pork, spices, and herbs, sometimes without a casing. [< G, equiv. to *brat(en)* to roast, bake + *Wurst* sausage]

Brau·haus (brou′hous′), *n., pl.* **-häu·ser** (-hoi′zər). *German.* a tavern or brewery.

Braun (broun; *Ger.* broun), *n.* **1. Karl Fer·di·nand** (kärl fûr′dənand′; *Ger.* kärl fer′dē nänt′), 1850–1918, German physicist and specialist in wireless telegraphy: Nobel prize in physics 1909. **2. Wern·her von** (vâr′nər von, vûr′-, wûr′-; *Ger.* ver′nər fən), 1912–77, German rocket engineer, in U.S. after 1945.

braun·ite (brou′nīt), *n.* a mineral, manganese oxide and silicate, Mn_7SiO_{12}: an ore of manganese. [named after A. E. *Braun* (1809–56), German official; see -ITE[1]]

Braun·schweig (broun′shvīk′), *n.* German name of **Brunswick.**

Braun·schwei·ger (broun′shwī′gər; *Ger.* broun′shvī′gər), *n.* (*sometimes l.c.*) a spiced liver sausage, usually smoked. [< G; see BRAUNSCHWEIG, -ER[1]]

bra·va·do (brə vä′dō), *n., pl.* **-does, -dos.** a pretentious, swaggering display of courage. [< Sp *bravada* (now *bravata* < It), equiv. to *brav(o)* BRAVE + *-ada* -ADE[1]]
—**Syn.** brag, bluster, bombast, braggadocio. See **courage.**

Bra′vais space′ lat′tice (brav′ā, brə vā′), lattice (def. 4). [named after Auguste *Bravais* (d. 1863), French physicist]

brave (brāv), *adj.,* **brav·er, brav·est,** *n., v.,* **braved, brav·ing.** —*adj.* **1.** possessing or exhibiting courage or courageous endurance. **2.** making a fine appearance. **3.** *Archaic.* excellent; fine; admirable. —*n.* **4.** a brave person. **5.** a warrior, esp. among North American Indian tribes. **6.** *Obs.* **a.** a bully. **b.** a boast or challenge. —*v.t.* **7.** to meet or face courageously: *to brave misfortunes.* **8.** to defy; challenge; dare. **9.** *Obs.* to make splendid. —*v.i.* **10.** *Obs.* to boast; brag. [late ME < MF, < It *bravo*, perh. < VL **brabus* for L *barbarus* BARBAROUS] —**brave′ly,** *adv.* —**brave′ness,** *n.*
—**Syn. 1.** bold, intrepid, daring, dauntless, heroic. BRAVE, COURAGEOUS, VALIANT, FEARLESS, GALLANT refer to confident bearing in the face of difficulties or dangers. BRAVE is the most comprehensive: it is especially used of that confident fortitude or daring that actively faces and endures anything threatening. COURAGEOUS implies a higher or nobler kind of bravery, esp. as resulting from an inborn quality of mind or spirit which faces or endures perils or difficulties without fear and even with enthusiasm. VALIANT implies a correspondence between an inner courageousness and external deeds, particularly of physical strength or endurance. FEARLESS implies unflinching spirit and coolness in the face of danger. GALLANT implies chivalrous, impetuous, dashing, or showy bravery. —**Ant. 1.** cowardly.

Brave′ New′ World′, a novel (1932) by Aldous Huxley.

brav·er·y (brā′və rē, brāv′rē), *n., pl.* **-er·ies. 1.** brave spirit or conduct; courage; valor. **2.** showiness; splendor; magnificence. [prob. < It *braveria*, equiv. to *brav(are)* (to) brave + *-eria* -ERY]
—**Syn. 1.** intrepidity, fearlessness, boldness, daring, prowess, heroism, pluck, spirit, audacity, nerve, mettle, spunk. See **courage.** —**Ant. 1.** cowardice.

brave′ west′ winds′, *Naut.* the strong west and west-northwest winds blowing between latitudes 40° S and 60° S.

bra·vis·si·mo (brä vis′ə mō′; *It.* brä vēs′sē mô), *interj.* excellently done! splendid! [< It, superl. of BRAVO]

bra·vo (brä′vō, brä vō′), *interj., n., pl.* **-vos** for 2, 3, **-voes** for 3, *v.,* **-voed, -vo·ing.** —*interj.* **1.** well done! good! —*n.* **2.** a shout of "bravo!" **3.** a daring bandit, assassin, or murderer, esp. one hired to steal or murder for another. **4.** a word used in communications to represent the letter B. —*v.t.* **5.** to shout "bravo!" in approbation of (something). —*v.i.* **6.** to shout "bravo!" [< It; see BRAVE]

bra·vu·ra (brə vyo͝or′ə; *It.* brä vo͞o′rä), *n., pl.* **-ras,** *It.* **-re** (-re) *adj.* —*n.* **1.** *Music.* a florid passage or piece requiring great skill and spirit in the performer. **2.** a display of daring; brilliant performance. —*adj.* **3.** *Music.* spirited; florid; brilliant (applied chiefly to vocal but occasionally to instrumental compositions). [< It: spirit, dash. See BRAVE, -URE]

braw (brô, brä; *Scot.* brô, brä), *adj. Scot. and North Eng.* **1.** fine or fine-looking; excellent. **2.** finely dressed; dressed in a splendid or gaudy fashion. [var. of BRAVE] —**braw′ly, braw′lie, braw·lis, braw·lys** (brô′lis, brä′-), *adv.*

brawl[1] (brôl), *n.* **1.** a noisy quarrel, squabble, or fight. **2.** a bubbling or roaring noise; a clamor. —*v.i.* **3.** to quarrel angrily and noisily; wrangle. **4.** to make a bubbling or roaring noise, as water flowing over a rocky bed. [ME *bral(l), brawl* bully, var. of *broll* brat, wretch contr. of *brothel.* See BROTHEL] —**brawl′er,** *n.*
—**Syn. 1.** wrangle, row, tumult, affray, altercation, rumpus. See **disorder. 3.** squabble, fight, bicker, row.

brawl[2] (brôl), *n.* the branle as danced in England [< MF *bran(s)le* BRANLE]

Braw·ley (brô′lē), *n.* a city in S California. 12,703 (1960).

rawn (brôn), *n.* **1.** well-developed muscles. **2.** muscular strength. **3.** a boar's or swine's flesh, esp. when boiled and pickled. [ME *brawne* < OF *braon* slice of flesh (Pr *bradon*) < Gmc; cf. G *Braten* joint of meat, akin to OE *brǣd* flesh]

brawn·y (brô′nē), *adj.,* **brawn·i·er, brawn·i·est.** muscular; strong. [BRAWN + -Y[1]] —**brawn′i·ly,** *adv.* —**brawn′i·ness,** *n.*

brax·y (brak′sē), *Vet. Pathol.* —*n.* **1.** Also called **bradsot.** an acute bacterial disease of sheep, caused by a bacterium, *Clostridium septicum*, involving inflammation of the bowels. —*adj.* **2.** affected with braxy. [back formation from *braxes* (*brax* for *bracks* (pl. of *brack*, OE *brǣc* rheum; akin to BREAK) + *-es* pl. ending)]

bray[1] (brā), *n.* **1.** a harsh, breathy cry, as of a donkey. **2.** any similar loud, harsh sound. —*v.i.* **3.** to utter a loud and harsh cry, as a donkey. **4.** to make a loud, harsh, disagreeable sound. —*v.t.* **5.** to utter with a loud, harsh sound, like a donkey. [ME *braye(n)* < OF *braire* to cry out (c. ML *bragire* to neigh) < Celt; cf. OIr *braigim* I break wind]

bray² (brā), *v.t.* **1.** to pound or crush fine, as in a mortar. **2.** *Print.* to thin (ink) on a slate before placing it on the ink plate of a press. [ME *braye(n)* < AF, OF *breier* < Gmc; see BREAK]

bray·er (brā′ər), *n.* *Print.* a small roller for inking type by hand, usually for making a proof. [BRAY² + -ER¹]

bra·yer·a (brə yer′ə, brā′ər ə), *n.* *Pharm.* the dried, pistillate flowers of an Ethiopian tree, *Hagenia abyssinica*, used in medicine chiefly for destroying or expelling tapeworms. Also called **cusso, koso, kousso, kusso.** [< NL; named after Dr. *Brayer*, 19th-century French physician]

bray·ette (brā et′), *n.* a piece of plate armor for protecting the groin; a steel codpiece. Also, **braguette.** [< MF, equiv. to *braie* (< L *brāca*, sing. of *brācae* BREECHES) + *-ette* -ETTE]

Bray·ley (brā′lē), *n.* a crater in the second quadrant of the face of the moon: about 10 miles in diameter.

Braz., **1.** Brazil. **2.** Brazilian.

bra·za (brä′thä, -sä), *n., pl.* **-zas** (-thäs, -säs). a unit of length in some Spanish-speaking countries, representing the reach of outspread arms, officially 5.48 U.S. feet in Spain, and 5.68 U.S. feet in Argentina. [< Sp < L *brāchia* the two arms (neut. pl.), taken as fem. sing.; see BRACHIUM]

braze¹ (brāz), *v.t.*, **brazed, braz·ing.** **1.** to make of brass. **2.** to cover or ornament with or as if with brass. **3.** to make brasslike. [ME *brase(n)*, OE *brǣsian*; see BRASS]

braze² (brāz), *v.t.*, **brazed, braz·ing.** *Metall.* to unite (metal objects) by holding them together, usually over a hearth, and joining them with any of various solders that contain copper, zinc, and often other materials and have a high melting point. [< F *brase(r)* (to) solder (MF), burn (OF) < Gmc; cf. Sw *brasa*, Dan *brase* to roast; see BRAISE] —**braz′er,** *n.*

bra·zen (brā′zən), *adj.* **1.** made of brass. **2.** like brass, as in sound, color, strength, etc. **3.** shameless or impudent: *brazen presumption.* —*v.t.* **4.** to make brazen or bold. **5. brazen out** or **through,** to face boldly or shamelessly: *He prefers to brazen it out rather than admit defeat.* [ME *brasen* (adj.), OE *brǣsen* of BRASS] —**bra′zen·ly,** *adv.* —**bra′zen·ness,** *n.*
—**Syn. 2, 3.** brassy. **3.** insolent, defiant. See **bold.** —**Ant. 3.** shy.

bra·zen-faced (brā′zən fāst′), *adj.* openly shameless; impudent. —**bra·zen-fac·ed·ly** (brā′zən fā′sid lē, -fāst′-), *adv.*

bra′zen law′ of wag′es, *Econ.* See **iron law of wages.**

bra·zier¹ (brā′zhər), *n.* a person who makes articles of brass. Also, **brasier.** [ME *brasier*, OE *brǣsi(an)* (to) work in brass + *-er* -ER¹]

bra·zier² (brā′zhər), *n.* **1.** a metal receptacle for holding live coals or other fuel, as for heating a room. **2.** a simple cooking device consisting of a container of live coals covered by a grill or thin metal top upon which the food, usually meat, is placed. Also, **brasier.** [earlier *brasier* < F. See BRAISE, -ER²]

bra·zil (brə zil′), *n.* **1.** a dyewood from various tropical American trees of the genus *Caesalpinia*, esp. *C. echinata*, and allied genera, yielding reds and purples. **2.** the red dye extracted from it. **3.** a hard East Indian dyewood yielding a red color, from the tree *Caesalpinia sappan*. Also, **brasil.** Also called **brazilwood.** [ME *brasile* < ML < It < Sp *brasil*, deriv. of *brasa* live coal (the wood being red in color) < Gmc; see BRAISE]

Bra·zil (brə zil′), *n.* **1.** Official name, **United States of Brazil.** a republic in South America. 66,302,000 (est. 1960); 3,286,170 sq. mi. *Cap.:* Brasília. Portuguese and Spanish, **Brasil.** **2.** a town in W Indiana. 8853 (1960). —**Bra·zil·ian** (brə zil′yən), *adj., n.*

Brazil′ Cur′rent, a warm current in the Atlantic Ocean flowing SE along the E coast of Brazil.

bra·zil·e·in (brə zil′ē in), *n.* *Chem.* a red, crystalline, water-insoluble solid, $C_{16}H_{12}O_5$, obtained by the oxidation of brazilin: used chiefly as a dye for wood and textiles. Also, **brasilein.** [BRAZIL(IN) + *-ein*, var. of -IN²]

Brazil′ian em′erald, a green variety of tourmaline used as a gem: not a true emerald.

Brazil′ian gua′va, a shrub, *Psidium guineese*, of Brazil, having white-fleshed, greenish-yellow fruit.

bra·zil·ian·ite (brə zil′yə nīt′), *n.* a mineral, sodium aluminum phosphate, $Na_2Al_6P_4O_{16}(OH)_8$, occurring in yellow-green crystals with a vitreous luster: used as a gem. [BRAZILIAN (after the place of origin) + -ITE¹]

Brazil′ian morn′ing-glory, a tropical, perennial vine, *Ipomoea setosa*, having purplish, stiff hairs on the stem and rose-purple flowers. [after its place of origin]

Brazil′ian pep′per tree′, a small, evergreen tree or shrub, *Schinus terebinthifolius*, of Brazil, having white flowers and bright red fruit. Also called **Christmasberry tree.**

Brazil′ian per′idot, *Jewelry.* a yellow-green variety of peridot used as a gem: not a true peridot. Also called **Brazil′ian chrys′olite.**

Brazil′ian rhat′any. See under **rhatany** (def. 1).

Brazil′ian rose′wood, **1.** a leguminous tree, *Dalbergia nigra*, of Brazil. **2.** the hard, red, black-streaked wood of this tree, used for making furniture. Also called **palisander.**

Brazil′ian ru′by, **1.** a light-rose spinel used as a gem: not a true ruby. **2.** a rose or pink topaz used as a gem: not a true ruby.

Brazil′ian sap′phire, a blue variety of tourmaline used as a gem: not a true sapphire.

braz·i·lin (braz′ə lin, brə zil′in), *n.* *Chem.* a yellow, water-soluble, needlelike, crystalline solid, $C_{16}H_{14}O_5$, obtained from brazil and sappanwood: used as a dye and an indicator. Also, **brasilin.** [BRAZIL + -IN²]

bra·zil·ite (brə zil′īt, -it), *n.* *Mineral.* baddeleyite. [BRAZIL + -ITE¹]

Brazil′ nut′, the triangular edible seed of the tree *Bertholletia excelsa* and related species, of South America.

bra·zil·wood (brə zil′wo͝od′), *n.* brazil. [BRAZIL + WOOD¹]

braz′ing al′loy. See **hard solder.**

Bra·zos (brä′zōs; *locally* braz′əs, brā′zəs), *n.* a river flowing SE from N Texas to the Gulf of Mexico. 870 mi. long.

Braz·za·ville (braz′ə vil; *Fr.* BRA ZA VĒL′), *n.* a port in and the capital of the Republic of Congo, in the S part, on the Congo River: former capital of French Equatorial Africa. 99,144 (1959).

B.R.C.A., Brotherhood of Railway Carmen of America.

B.R.C.S., British Red Cross Society.

B.R.E., Bachelor of Religious Education.

Bre·a (brē′ə), *n.* a town in S California. 8487 (1960).

breach (brēch), *n.* **1.** the act or a result of breaking; break or rupture. **2.** a gap made in a wall, fortification, line of soldiers, etc.; rift; fissure. **3.** an infraction or violation, as of a law, trust, faith, promise, etc. **4.** a severance of friendly relations. **5.** the leap of a whale above the surface of the water. **6.** *Archaic.* the breaking of waves; the dashing of surf. **7.** *Obs.* wound. —*v.t.* **8.** to make a breach or opening in. **9.** to break or act contrary to (a law, promise, etc.). —*v.i.* **10.** (of a whale) to leap above the surface of the water. [ME *breche*, OE *bræc* breaking; see BREAK] —**breach′er,** *n.*
—**Syn. 1.** fracture. **2.** crack, rent, opening. **4.** alienation, split, rift, schism, separation; dissension.

breach′ of prom′ise, *Law.* a violation of one's promise, esp. of a promise to marry a specific person.

breach′ of the peace′, *Law.* a violation of the public peace, as by a riot, disturbance, etc.

breach′ of trust′, **1.** *Law.* a violation of duty by a trustee. **2.** a violation of duty or responsibility.

bread (bred), *n.* **1.** a kind of food made of flour or meal that has been mixed with milk or water, etc., made into a dough or batter, with or without yeast or the like, and baked. **2.** food or sustenance; livelihood: *to earn one's bread.* **3.** *Eccles.* the wafer or bread used in a Eucharistic service. **4.** *Slang.* money. **5. break bread, a.** to partake of or share food with. **b.** to distribute or participate in Communion. **6. cast one's bread upon the waters,** to act charitably with no thought of personal gain. **7. know on which side one's bread is buttered,** to be aware of those things which are to one's own advantage. **8. take the bread out of (someone's) mouth,** to deprive (someone) of his livelihood. —*v.t.* **9.** *Cookery.* to cover or dress with bread crumbs or meal. [ME *breed*, OE *brēad* fragment, morsel, bread; c. G *Brot*] —**bread′less,** *adj.* —**bread′less·ness,** *n.*

bread′ and but′ter, **1.** bread spread with butter. **2.** *Informal.* source of livelihood; sustenance: *The garment industry is the bread and butter of many New Yorkers.*

bread-and-but·ter (bred′ən but′ər), *adj.* **1.** providing a livelihood; affording a basis for minimum subsistence: *a bread-and-butter item; the agency's bread-and-butter account.* **2.** practical; not speculative; limited to elementary considerations: *bread-and-butter arguments.* **3.** expressing thanks for hospitality, as a letter. **4.** *Archaic.* belonging to or in the stage of childhood or adolescence. [adj. use of n. phrase *bread and butter*]

bread′-and-but′ter mod′el, *Naval Archit.* a wooden hull model carved from a number of horizontal planks glued together to represent the outlines of the various decks.

bread′-and-but′ter pick′le, an unpeeled slice of cucumber marinated in salt water and boiled with vinegar, celery seed, spices, and brown sugar.

bread·bas·ket (bred′bas′kit, -bä′skit), *n.* **1.** a basket or similar container for bread or rolls. **2.** an agricultural area that provides large amounts of food, esp. grain, to other areas. **3.** *Slang.* a person's stomach or abdomen. [BREAD + BASKET]

bread·board (bred′bôrd′, -bōrd′), *n.* **1.** a slab of wood on which dough is kneaded and bread is sliced. **2.** an assembly of experimental electric and electronic circuits, usually mounted on a metal chassis, exposed for easy construction and alteration. [BREAD + BOARD]

bread·fruit (bred′fro͞ot′), *n.* **1.** a large, round, starchy fruit borne by a moraceous tree, *Artocarpus communis* (*A. altilis*), native to the Pacific islands, used, baked or roasted, for food. **2.** the tree bearing this fruit. [BREAD + FRUIT]

Breadfruit
(Fruit, diam. 5 in.)

bread′ knife′, a knife designed or suitable for slicing bread, as one having a wavy or saw-toothed blade.

bread′ line′, a group of persons waiting in line for free food to be distributed, esp. by a government agency.

bread′ mold′, any fungus of the family *Mucoraceae*, esp. *Rhizopus nigricans*, which forms a black, furry coating on foodstuffs. Also called **black mold.**

bread·nut (bred′nut′), *n.* the round, yellow or brown fruit of the ramon, *Brosimum Alicastrum*, used, roasted or boiled, as a substitute for bread in the West Indies. [BREAD + NUT]

bread·root (bred′ro͞ot′, -ro͝ot′), *n.* the edible farinaceous root of *Psoralea esculenta*, a fabaceous plant of central North America. Also called **Indian breadroot, pomme blanche.** [BREAD + ROOT¹]

bread·stuff (bred′stuf′), *n.* **1.** grain, flour, or meal for making bread. **2.** any kind of bread. [BREAD + STUFF]

breadth (bredth, bretth), *n.* **1.** the measure of the second largest dimension of a plane or solid figure. **2.** an extent or piece of something of definite or full width or as measured by its width: *a breadth of cloth.* **3.** freedom from narrowness or restraint; liberality: *breadth of view.* **4.** size in general; extent. **5.** *Art.* a broad or general effect due to subordination of details or nonessentials. [earlier *bredeth*, equiv. to *brede* breadth (ME, OE *brǣdu*, equiv. to *brǣd-*, mutated var. of *brād* BROAD + *-u* n. suffix) + -TH¹; akin to G *Breite*, Goth *braidei*] —**breadth′less,** *adj.*

breadth·ways (bredth′wāz′, bretth′-), *adv.* in the direction of the breadth. Also, **breadth·wise** (bredth′wīz′, bretth′-). [BREADTH + -WAYS]

bread·win·ner (bred′win′ər), *n.* one who earns a livelihood for himself and those dependent upon him. [BREAD + WINNER] —**bread′win′ning,** *n.*

break (brāk), *v.*, **broke** or (*Archaic*) **brake; bro·ken** or (*Archaic*) **broke; break·ing;** *n.* —*v.t.* **1.** to smash, split, or divide into parts violently; reduce to pieces or fragments: *He broke a vase.* **2.** to infringe, ignore, or act contrary to (a law, rule, promise, etc.): *He broke his promise to come straight home.* **3.** to dissolve or annul (often fol. by *off*): *to break off friendly relations with an ally.* **4.** to fracture a bone of (some part of the body): *He broke his leg.* **5.** to lacerate; wound: *to break the skin.* **6.** to destroy or interrupt the regularity, uniformity, continuity, or arrangement of; interrupt: *The bleating of a foghorn broke the silence. The troops broke formation.* **7.** to put an end to; overcome; stop: *His touchdown run broke the tie. She found it hard to break the cigarette habit.* **8.** to discover the system, key, method, etc., for decoding or deciphering (a cryptogram), esp. by the methods of cryptanalysis. **9.** to remove a part from (a set or collection): *He had to break the lot to sell me the two red ones I wanted.* **10.** to exchange for or divide into smaller units or components: *She broke a dollar bill into change. The prism broke the light into all the colors of the rainbow.* **11.** to make a way through; penetrate: *The stone broke the surface of the water.* **12.** *Law.* **a.** to open or force one's way into (a dwelling, store, etc.). **b.** to contest (a will) successfully by judicial action. **13.** to make one's way out of: *to break jail.* **14.** to better (a given score or record): *He never broke 200 in bowling or 80 in golf.* **15.** to disclose or divulge personally in speech or writing: *He broke the good news to her at dinner.* **16.** to solve: *The police needed only a week to break that case.* **17.** to rupture (a blood vessel): *He almost broke a blood vessel from laughing so hard.* **18.** to disable or destroy by or as by shattering or crushing: *to break a watch.* **19.** to cause (a blister, boil, or the like) to burst, as by puncturing: *He broke the blister with a needle.* **20.** to ruin financially; make bankrupt: *He broke the bank at Monte Carlo.* **21.** to overcome or wear down the spirit, strength, or resistance of; to cause to yield, esp. under pressure, torture, or the like: *They broke him by the threat of blackmail.* **22.** to reduce in rank. **23.** to impair or weaken the power, effect, or intensity of: *His arm broke the blow.* **24.** to train to obedience; tame: *to break a horse.* **25.** to train away from a habit or practice (usually fol. by *of*). **26.** *Elect.* to render (a circuit) incomplete; stop the flow of (a current). **27.** *Journalism.* **a.** to release (a story) for publication: *They will break the story tomorrow.* **b.** to continue (a story or article) on another page, esp. when the page is not the following one. **28.** *Pool.* to cause (racked billiard balls) to scatter by striking with the cue ball. **29.** *Sports.* **a.** (of a pitcher, bowler, etc.) to hurl (a ball) in such a way as to cause it to change direction after leaving the hand: *He broke a curve over the plate for a strike.* **b.** (in tennis and other racket games) to score frequently or win against (an opponent's serve). **30.** *Naut.* to unfurl (a flag) suddenly by an easily released knot after hoisting it secured in a furled position. **31.** to prove the falsity or show the lack of logic of: *The FBI broke his alibi by proving he knew how to shoot a pistol.* **32.** to begin or initiate (a plan or campaign), esp. with much publicity: *They were going to break the sales campaign with a parade in April.* **33.** to open the breech or action of (a shotgun, rifle, or revolver), as by snapping open the hinge between the barrel and the butt.
—*v.i.* **34.** to shatter, burst, or become broken; separate into parts or fragments, esp. suddenly and violently: *The glass broke on the floor.* **35.** to become suddenly discontinuous or interrupted; stop abruptly: *He pulled too hard and the string broke.* **36.** to become detached, separated, or disassociated (usually fol. by *away, off, from*, etc.): *The knob broke off in his hand.* **37.** to become inoperative or to malfunction, as through wear or damage: *The television set broke this afternoon.* **38.** to begin suddenly or to change abruptly into something else: *War broke over Europe. The discussion broke out into a fight.* **39.** to begin uttering a sound or series of sounds or to be uttered suddenly: *She broke into song. When they entered, a cheer broke from the audience.* **40.** to express or start to express an emotion or mood: *His face broke into a smile.* **41.** to free oneself or escape suddenly, as from restraint (often fol. by *away*): *He broke away from the arresting officer. She finally broke away from her parents and got an apartment of her own.* **42.** to run or dash toward something suddenly (usually fol. by *for*): *The pass receiver broke for the goal line.* **43.** to force a way (usually fol. by *in, into, through*, etc.): *The hunters broke through the underbrush.* **44.** to burst or rupture: *A blood vessel broke in his arm. The blister broke when he pricked it.* **45.** to interrupt or halt an activity (usually fol. by *in, forth, from*, etc.): *Don't break in on the conversation.* **46.** to appear or arrive suddenly: *A deer broke into the clearing. A rash broke out on his arm.* **47.** to dawn, as the day: *The day broke hot and sultry.* **48.** to begin violently: *The storm broke.* **49.** (of a storm, foul weather, etc.) to cease: *The weather broke after a week, and we were able to sail for home.* **50.** to part the surface of water, as a jumping fish or ascending submarine. **51.** to give way or fail, as health, strength, or spirit: *After years of hardship and worry, his health broke.* **52.** to yield or submit to pressure, torture, or the like: *He broke under questioning.* **53.** (of the heart) to be overwhelmed with sorrow: *Her heart broke when he told her that he no longer loved her.* **54.** (of the voice or a musical instrument) to change suddenly and harshly from one register or pitch to another: *After his voice broke, he could no longer sing soprano parts.* **55.** (of the voice) to cease or change tone abruptly, esp. from emotional strain: *Her voice broke when she mentioned his name.* **56.** (of value or prices) to drop sharply and considerably. **57.** to disperse or collapse by colliding with something: *The waves broke on the shore.* **58.** *Music.* **a.** to change or go from one register to another in a musical way, as a musical instrument or the voice. **b.** to change or be interrupted in a musical way, as a voice or tone. **59.** (of a horse in a harness race) to fail to keep to a trot or pace, as by starting to gallop. **60.** *Bot.* to mutate; sport. **61.** *Ling.* to undergo breaking. **62.** *Billiards, Pool.* to make a break; take the first turn in a game.

63. *Sports.* (of a pitched or bowled ball) to change direction: *The ball broke over the plate.* 64. *Horse Racing, Track.* to leave the starting point: *The horses broke fast from the gate.* 65. *Boxing.* to step back or separate from a clinch: *The fighters fell into a clinch and broke on the referee's order.* 66. to take place; occur. 67. *Journalism.* to become known or published: *The story broke in the morning papers.* 68. *Hort.* to produce flowers or leaves. 69. **break away, a.** to leave or escape, esp. suddenly or hurriedly. **b.** to start prematurely: *The horse broke away from the starting gate.* 70. **break bulk,** *Naut.* to remove a cargo wholly or in part. 71. **break camp,** to pack up tents and equipment and resume a journey or march: *They broke camp at dawn and proceeded toward the mountains.* 72. **break down, a.** to become ineffective. **b.** to lose control; weaken: *She broke down and wept at the sad news.* **c.** to cease to function: *The car broke down.* **d.** *Elect.* (of a circuit, electron, tube, etc.) to fail to function as a result of a spark passing through insulation used to separate electric circuits or electrodes in a vacuum- or gas-filled tube. 73. **break even,** to finish a business transaction, period of gambling, series of games, etc., with no loss or gain in money or prestige: *He played poker all night and broke even.* 74. **break ground, a.** to begin construction, esp. of a building or group of buildings: *to break ground for a new housing development.* **b.** *Naut.* to free an anchor from the bottom; break out. 75. **break in, a.** to enter by force or craft: *Someone broke in and made off with all the furniture.* **b.** to train; accustom; initiate: *The boss is breaking in a new assistant.* **c.** to begin to wear or use: *These shoes haven't been broken in.* **d.** to interrupt: *She broke in with a non sequitur.* **e.** to run (new machinery) initially under reduced load and speed, until any stiffness of motion has departed and all parts are ready to operate under normal service conditions; run in. 76. **break in on** or **upon,** to enter with force upon; intrude upon: *The visitor opened the wrong door and broke in on a private conference.* 77. **break into, a.** to interpose; interrupt: *He broke into the conversation at a crucial moment.* **b.** to begin some activity. **c.** to be admitted into; enter, as a business or profession: *It is difficult to break into the theater.* **d.** to enter by force: *They broke into the store and stole the safe.* 78. **break off, a.** to sever by breaking. **b.** to stop suddenly; discontinue: *We broke off our conversation because it was getting very late.* 79. **break out, a.** to begin abruptly; arise: *An epidemic broke out.* **b.** *Pathol.* (of certain diseases) to appear in eruptions. **c.** (of a person) to manifest a skin eruption. **d.** to prepare for use: *to break out the parachutes.* **e.** to take out of (storage, concealment, etc.) for consumption: *to break out one's best wine.* **f.** *Naut.* to dislodge (the anchor) from the bottom in preparation for weighing it. **g.** to escape; flee: *He spent three years in prison before he broke out.* 80. **break sheer,** *Naut.* (of an anchored vessel) to drift into such a position as to risk fouling the anchors or anchor cables. 81. **break someone's heart,** to overwhelm someone with grief or disappointment, as by scandalous behavior, failure, or rejecting their love: *He broke his mother's heart when he dropped out of school. She broke his heart by dating other men.* 82. **break step.** See **step** (def. 23). 83. **break up, a.** to separate; scatter. **b.** to put an end to; discontinue. **c.** to divide or become divided into pieces. **d.** to dissolve. **e.** to disrupt; upset: *Television commercials during a dramatic presentation break up the continuity of effect.* **f.** (of a personal relationship) to sever or become severed: *to break up a friendship; Their marriage broke up last year.* **g.** to be or cause to be overcome with laughter: *The comedian told several jokes that broke up the audience.* 84. **break with, a.** to sever relations with; separate from: *to break with one's family.* **b.** to depart from; repudiate: *to break with tradition.*
—*n.* 85. an act or instance of breaking; disruption or separation of parts; fracture; rupture: *There was a break in the window.* 86. an opening made by breaking; gap: *The break in the wall had not been repaired.* 87. a rush away from a place; an attempt to escape: *a break for freedom.* 88. a sudden dash or rush, as toward something: *When the rain stopped, I made a break for home.* 89. a suspension of or sudden rupture in friendly relations. 90. an interruption of continuity; suspension; stoppage: *Abstract painters made a break with the traditions of the past.* 91. an abrupt or marked change, as in sound or direction, or a brief pause: *They noticed a curious break in his voice.* 92. *Informal.* an opportunity or stroke of fortune, esp. a lucky one. 93. *Informal.* an indiscreet or inadvertent remark or action; social blunder; faux pas. 94. a brief rest, as from work: *The actors took a ten-minute break from rehearsal.* 95. *Pros.* a pause or caesura. 96. *Jazz.* a solo passage, usually of from 2 to 12 bars, during which the rest of the instruments are silent. 97. *Music.* the point in the scale where the quality of voice of one register changes to that of another, as from chest to head. 98. a sharp and considerable drop in the prices of stock issues. 99. *Elect.* an opening or discontinuity in a circuit. 100. *Print.* **a.** one or more blank lines between two paragraphs. **b. breaks.** See **suspension points.** 101. the place, after a letter, where a word is or may be divided at the end of a line. 102. *Billiards, Pool.* a series of successful strokes; run. 103. *Pool.* the opening play, in which the cue ball is shot to scatter the balls. 104. *Sports.* a change in direction of a pitched or bowled ball. 105. *Horse Racing, Track.* the start of a race. 106. (in harness racing) the act or an instance of a horse's changing from a trot or pace into a gallop or other step. 107. *Bowling.* a failure to knock down all 10 pins after bowling twice. 108. *Boxing.* the act or an instance of stepping back or separating from a clinch: *a clean break.* 109. any of several stages in the grinding of grain in which the bran is separated from the kernel. 110. *Bot.* a sport. 111. *Journalism.* the point at the bottom of a column where a printed story is carried over to another column or page. 112. *Naut.* the place at which a superstructure, deckhouse, or the like, rises from the main deck of a vessel. 113. *Radio, Television.* a brief, scheduled interruption of a program or broadcasting period for the announcement of advertising or station identification. [ME *breke(n)* (v.), OE *brecan;* c. D *breken,* G *brechen,* Goth *brikan;* akin to L *frangere;* see FRAGILE] —**break′a·ble,** *adj.* —**break′a·ble·ness,** *n.* —**break′a·bly,** *adv.* —**break′less,** *adj.*
—**Syn. 1.** fracture, splinter, shiver. BREAK, CRUSH, SHATTER, SMASH mean to reduce to parts, violently or by force. BREAK means to divide by means of a blow, a collision, a pull, or the like: *to break a chair, a leg, a strap.* To CRUSH is to subject to (usually heavy or violent) pressure so as to press out of shape or reduce to shapelessness or to small particles: *to crush a beetle.* To SHATTER is to break in such a way as to cause the pieces to fly in many directions: *to shatter a light globe.* To SMASH is to break noisily and suddenly into many pieces: *to smash a glass.* **2.** disobey, contravene. **6.** disrupt. —**Ant. 1.** repair.

break·age (brā′kij), *n.* **1.** the act or state of breaking; state of being broken. **2.** the amount or quantity of things broken: *There was a great deal of breakage in that shipment of glassware.* **3.** *Com.* an allowance or compensation for the loss or damage of articles broken in transit or in use. **4.** the money accrued by a race track from calculating the pay-off to winning pari-mutuel bettors only in multiples of dimes for each dollar bet. [BREAK + -AGE]

break′ and en′try. See **breaking and entering.**

break·a·way (brāk′ə wā′), *n.* **1.** a separation; a secession: *He made a breakaway from his former life.* **2.** *Chiefly Australian.* **a.** a stampede. **b.** an animal that breaks away from the herd or flock. **3.** *Theat.* a stage property made to be easily shattered or broken. —*adj.* **4.** of, pertaining to, or being that which separates or secedes: *the breakaway faction of the Socialist party.* **5.** (of theatrical scenery or stage properties) constructed of such light-weight material or in such a way as to shatter or come apart easily and to be easily reassembled: *Build a breakaway set for the barroom brawl.* [n., adj. use of v. phrase *break away*]

break′bone fe′ver (brāk′bōn′), *Pathol.* dengue. [BREAK + BONE[1], so called because it makes the bones ache as if breaking at the joints]

break′ danc′ing, an acrobatic form of dancing, often performed by individuals in the street to rap music. —**break′ dance′.** —**break′ danc′er.**

break·down (brāk′doun′), *n.* **1.** a breaking down, wearing out, or sudden loss of health or the ability to function efficiently, as of a machine or of physical or mental capacities; collapse. **2.** *Chem.* **a.** decomposition. **b.** analysis. **3.** an analysis or classification of something; division into parts, categories, processes, etc. **4.** *Elect.* an electric discharge passing through faulty insulation or other material used to separate circuits or passing between electrodes in a vacuum or gas-filled tube. **5.** *U.S.* a noisy, lively folk dance. [n. use of v. phrase *break down*]

break′down lights′. See **not-under-command lights.**

break′down volt′age, *Elect.* the minimum applied voltage that would cause a given insulator or electrode to break down. Cf. **dielectric strength.**

break·er[1] (brā′kər), *n.* **1.** one who or that which breaks. **2.** a wave that breaks or dashes into foam. **3.** Also called **break′er strip′.** *Auto.* a strip of fabric under the tread of a pneumatic tire casing, designed to protect the carcass. **4.** *Textiles.* **a.** brake[1] (def. 4). **b.** a machine that separates the fiber from foreign matter in preparation for the carding process. **5.** Also called **prairie breaker.** a plow with a long, low moldboard for turning virgin land. [ME; see BREAK, -ER[1]] —**Syn. 2.** See **wave.**

break·er[2] (brā′kər), *n.* *Naut.* a small water cask for use in a boat. [said to be alter. of Sp *bareca,* var. of *barrica* small keg]

break′er card′, the first card in the carding process, used to open the raw stock and to convert it into sliver form. Cf. **finisher card, intermediate card.**

break-e·ven (brāk′ē′vən), *adj.* **1.** having income exactly equal to expenditure, thus showing neither profit nor loss. —*n.* **2.** See **break-even point.**

break′-e′ven point′, the point at which the income for a product or service is exactly equal to the invested costs, resulting in neither profit nor loss; the stage at which income equals expenditure.

break·fast (brek′fəst), *n.* **1.** the first meal of the day; morning meal: *A hearty breakfast was served at 7* A.M. **2.** the food eaten at the first meal of the day: *a breakfast of bacon and eggs.* —*v.i.* **3.** to eat breakfast: *He breakfasted on bacon and eggs.* —*v.t.* **4.** to supply with breakfast: *We breakfasted the author in the finest restaurants.* [late ME *brekfast.* See BREAK, FAST[2]] —**break′fast·er,** *n.* —**break′fast·less,** *adj.*

break′fast food′, a cold or hot cereal eaten chiefly for breakfast.

break·front (brāk′frunt′), *adj.* **1.** (of a cabinet, bookcase, etc.) having a central section extending forward from those at either side. —*n.* **2.** a cabinet or the like having such a front. Also, **break′-front′.** [BREAK + FRONT]

break·ing (brā′king), *n.* the change of a pure vowel to a diphthong, esp. in certain environments, as, in Old English, the change of a vowel to a diphthong under the influence of a following consonant or combination of consonants, as the change of *-a-* to *-ea-* and of *-e-* to *-eo-* before preconsonantal *r* or *l* and before *h,* as in *earm* "arm" developed from *arm,* and *eorthe* "earth" from *erthe.* [trans. of G *Brechung*]

break′ing and en′tering, *Crim. Law.* forcible entry into the home or office of another.

break·neck (brāk′nek′), *adj.* dangerous, esp. due to excessive speed; hazardous: *He raced through the streets at breakneck speed.* [BREAK + NECK]

break′ of day′, dawn; daybreak: *At break of day the hikers were already on the trail.*

break·out (brāk′out′), *n.* **1.** an escape, often with the use of force, as from a prison, mental institution, etc. **2.** an appearance or upsurgence, esp. of massive proportions. **3.** the act or process of removing and disassembling equipment which has been used in drilling a well. [n. use of v. phrase *break out*]

break·o·ver (brāk′ō′vər), *n.* jump (def. 58). [n. use of v. phrase *break over*]

break·through (brāk′thro͞o′), *n.* **1.** *Mil.* a movement or advance all the way through and beyond an enemy's defensive system into the unorganized areas in the rear. **2.** an act or action of removing or surpassing an obstruction or restriction: *The president reported breakthroughs in technology, in diplomatic relations, and in prices.* **3.** any significant or sudden advance, development, progress, or increase, as in scientific knowledge, diplomacy, etc., that removes a barrier to progress: *The jet engine was a major breakthrough in air transport.* [n. use of v. phrase *break through*]

break·up (brāk′up′), *n.* **1.** disintegration; disruption; dispersal. **2.** (in Alaska and Canada) **a.** the melting and loosening of ice in rivers and harbors during the early spring. **b.** the first day on which such ice is soft or dispersed enough to permit ships to use the waterways. **3.** a separation, as between friends, a married or engaged couple, etc.: *The breakup between Charles and Vickie was due to an argument.* [n. use of v. phrase *break up*]

break·wa·ter (brāk′wô′tər, -wot′ər), *n.* a barrier which breaks the force of waves, as before a harbor. [BREAK + WATER]

break·weath·er (brāk′weth′ər), *n.* *Australian.* any makeshift shelter. [BREAK + WEATHER]

break·wind (brāk′wind′), *n.* *Australian.* a bark, bough, or thatched hut, used chiefly by aborigines. [BREAK + WIND[1]]

bream[1] (brēm), *n., pl.* (*esp. collectively*) **bream,** (*esp. referring to two or more kinds or species*) **breams. 1.** any of various fresh-water cyprinoid fishes of the genus *Abramis,* as *A. brama,* of Europe, with a compressed, deep body. **2.** any of various related and similar fishes. **3.** any of several porgies, as the sea bream, *Archosargus rhomboidalis.* **4.** any of several fresh-water sunfishes of the genus *Lepomis.* [ME *breme* < MF; OF *bresme* < Gmc; cf. OHG *brahsema,* D *brasem*]

bream[2] (brēm), *v.t.* *Naut.* to clean (a ship's bottom) by applying burning furze, reeds, etc., to soften the pitch and loosen adherent matter. [< MD *brem(e)* furze]

breast (brest), *n.* **1.** *Anat., Zool.* the outer, front part of the thorax, or the front part of the body from the neck to abdomen; chest. **2.** *Zool.* the corresponding part in lower animals. **3.** *Anat., Zool.* either of two projecting, milk-secreting organs on the front of the thorax of a woman or certain female mammals. **4.** either of two flat organs on the front of the thorax of a man, usually having no anatomical function. **5.** that part of a garment which covers the chest. **6.** the bosom conceived of as the center of thought and feeling: *What emotion lay in his breast when he made that speech?* **7.** a projection from a wall, as part of a chimney. **8.** any surface or part resembling or likened to the human breast. **9.** *Mining.* the face or heading at which the work is going on. **10.** *Metall.* **a.** the front of an open-hearth furnace. **b.** the clay surrounding the taphole of a cupola. **11.** *Naut.* **a.** See **breast line. b.** a rounded bow. **12. make a clean breast of,** to confess everything of which one is guilty: *You'll feel better if you make a clean breast of it.* —*v.t.* **13.** to meet or oppose with the breast. **14.** to meet boldly or advance against: *The ship breasted the waves.* **15.** to climb or climb over (a mountain, obstacle, etc.). **16.** to come alongside or abreast of. **17. breast in,** *Naut.* to bind (an object, as a boatswain's chair) securely under a projection, as the flare of a bow. **18. breast off,** *Naut.* **a.** to thrust (a vessel) sideways from a wharf. **b.** to keep (a vessel) away from a wharf by means of timbers. [ME *brest,* OE *brēost;* c. Icel *brjōst;* akin to G *Brust,* Goth *brusts,* D *borst*] —**breast′less,** *adj.*

breast′ beam′, 1. a horizontal bar, located at the front of a loom, over which the woven material is passed on its way to the cloth roll. **2.** breastsummer.

breast-beat·ing (brest′bē′ting), *n.* **1.** a display or episode of highly vocal and self-conscious emotionalism, doubt, remorse, or the like: *The authorities indulged in a great deal of breast-beating about traffic accidents, but failed to pass new driving laws.* —*adj.* **2.** characterized by or involving breast-beating. —**breast′-beat′er,** *n.*

breast·bone (brest′bōn′), *n.* the sternum. [ME *brust-bon,* OE *breostban.* See BREAST, BONE[1]]

breast′ drill′, a geared drill that can be braced against the chest for additional leverage.

Breast·ed (bres′tid), *n.* **James Henry,** 1865–1935, U.S. archaeologist and historian of ancient Egypt.

breast-feed (brest′fēd′), *v.t.,* **-fed, -feed·ing.** to nurse (a baby) at the breast; suckle.

breast-hook (brest′ho͝ok′), *n.* *Naut.* a horizontal knee or gusset reinforcing the bow of a vessel.

breast·ing (bres′ting), *n.* a piece of leather or other material for covering the heel breast of a shoe. [BREAST + -ING[1]]

breast′ line′, *Naut.* a mooring line securing a ship to that part of a pier alongside it. Also called **breast′ fast′.**

breast·pin (brest′pin′), *n.* a pin worn on the breast or at the throat; brooch. [BREAST + PIN]

breast·plate (brest′plāt′), *n.* **1.** a piece of plate armor partially or completely covering the front of the torso: used by itself or as part of a cuirass. **2.** the part of the harness that runs across the chest of a saddle horse. **3.** *Judaism.* **a.** a square, richly embroidered vestment ornamented with 12 precious stones, each inscribed with the name of one of the 12 tribes of Israel, secured to the ephod of the high priest and worn on the chest. Ex. 28:15–28. **b.** a rectangular ornament, typically of silver, suspended by a chain over the front of a scroll of the Torah. [ME *brestplate.* See BREAST, PLATE[1]]

breast·plow (brest′plou′), *n.* *Agric.* a cultivator propelled by a person pressing his chest against a crossbar. Also, *esp. Brit.,* **breast′plough′.** [BREAST + PLOW]

breast·stroke (brest′strōk′), *n.* *Swimming.* a stroke made in the prone position in which both hands move simultaneously forward, outward, and rearward from in front of the chest while the legs move in a frog kick. [BREAST + STROKE[1]]

breast·sum·mer (bres′sum′ər, brest′-, bres′ə mər), *n.* a horizontal beam supporting an exterior wall over an opening, as a shop window. Also, **bressummer, brest summer.** Also called **breast beam.** [BREAST + SUMMER[2]]

breast′ tim′ber, wale (def. 5).

breast′ wall′, a retaining wall or revetment for preventing the ground from collapsing at the edge of an excavation. Also called **face wall.**

breast′ wheel′, a water wheel onto which the propelling water is fed at the height of a horizontal axle.

breast·work (brest′wûrk′), *n. Fort.* a hastily constructed defensive work, usually breast high. [BREAST + WORK]

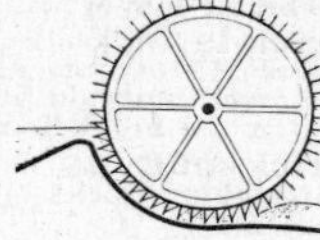
Breast wheel

breath (breth), *n.* **1.** *Physiol.* the air inhaled and exhaled in respiration. **2.** respiration, esp. as necessary to life. **3.** life; vitality. **4.** the ability to breathe easily and normally: *He stopped to regain his breath.* **5.** time to breathe; pause or respite: *Give him a little breath.* **6.** a single inhalation or respiration: *He took a deep breath.* **7.** the brief time required for a single respiration; an instant: *They gave it to her and took it away all in a breath.* **8.** an utterance; whisper: *The breath of slander never touched her.* **9.** a light current of air. **10.** *Phonet.* **a.** the air drawn into or expelled from the lungs to provide the generative source for most speech sounds. **b.** the audible expiration generating voiceless speech sounds, as *p, k, sh,* etc. **11.** moisture emitted in respiration, esp. when condensed and visible. **12.** a trivial circumstance; trifle. **13.** an odorous exhalation, or the air impregnated by it. **14.** *Obs.* odor; vapor. **15. below** or **under one's breath,** in a low voice or whisper; sotto voce: *He protested under his breath because he was afraid to speak up.* **16. catch one's breath,** to pause or rest before continuing an activity or beginning a new one; resume regular breathing: *Let me catch my breath before I begin anything new.* **17. in the same breath,** at once; simultaneously: *She lost her temper and apologized in the same breath.* **18. out of breath,** exhausted or gasping for breath, in consequence of an effort; breathless: *After climbing to the top of the tower, we were so out of breath that we had to sit down.* **19. save one's breath,** to avoid futile discussion: *We were told to save our breath because the matter had already been decided.* **20. take away one's breath,** to make one breathless with astonishment; surprise; stun: *The sheer beauty of the sea took away my breath.* [ME *breth, breeth,* OE *brǣth* smell, exhalation; akin to G *Brodem* vapor, steam]

breathe (brēth), *v.,* **breathed** (brētht), **breath·ing.** —*v.i.* **1.** to take air, oxygen, etc., into the lungs and expel it; inhale and exhale; respire. **2.** (in speech) to control the outgoing breath in producing voice and speech sounds. **3.** to pause, as for breath; take rest: *I can breathe easier now that the work is done.* **4.** to move gently or blow lightly, as air. **5.** to live; exist: *Hardly a man breathes who has not loved a woman.* **6.** to exhale an odor. **7.** to be redolent of. —*v.t.* **8.** to inhale and exhale in respiration. **9.** to allow to rest or recover breath. **10.** to deprive of breath; tire; exhaust. **11.** to give utterance to; whisper. **12.** to express; manifest. **13.** to exhale: *Dragons breathe fire.* **14.** to inject as if by breathing; infuse: *She breathed life into the party.* **15.** to cause to pant; exercise. **16. breathe freely,** to have relief from anxiety or tension: *Now that the crisis was over, he could breathe freely.* Also, **breathe easily, breathe easy. 17. breathe one's last,** to die: *He breathed his last and was buried in the churchyard.* **18. not breathe a word** or **syllable,** to maintain secrecy; keep a matter confidential: *I'll tell you the secret if you promise not to breathe a word of it.* [ME *brethe(n),* deriv. of BREATH] —**breath′a·ble,** *adj.* —**breathe′a·ble·ness,** *n.*

breathed (bretht, brētht), *adj. Phonet.* **1.** not phonated; unvoiced; voiceless. **2.** utilizing the breath exclusively in the production of a speech sound. [ME *brethed.* See BREATH, -ED[3]]

breath·er (brē′thər), *n.* **1.** a pause, as for breath. **2.** vigorous exercise that causes heavy breathing. **3.** one who breathes. **4.** a vent in a container or covering, as in a casing for machinery or in a storage tank, to equalize interior and exterior pressure, permit entry of air, escape of fumes, or the like. **5.** a device for providing air from the atmosphere to submerged or otherwise sealed-off persons, combustion engines, etc.: *the snorkel breather of a submarine.* [ME *brethere.* See BREATHE, -ER[1]]

breath·ing (brē′thing), *n.* **1.** the act of one who or that which breathes; respiration. **2.** a single breath. **3.** the short time required for a single breath. **4.** a pause, as for breath. **5.** utterance or words. **6.** aspiration or longing. **7.** a gentle moving or blowing, as of wind. **8.** *Classical Gk. Gram.* **a.** the manner of articulating the beginning of a word written with an initial vowel sign, with or without aspiration before the vowel. **b.** one of the two symbols used to indicate this. Cf. **rough breathing, smooth breathing.** [ME *brethynge.* See BREATHE, -ING[1]] —**breath′ing·ly,** *adv.*

breath′ing space′, **1.** Also called **breath′ing spell′.** an opportunity to rest or think. **2.** sufficient space in which to move, work, etc.: *The train was so crowded that there was hardly breathing space.*

breath·less (breth′lis), *adj.* **1.** deprived of breath: *The blow left him breathless.* **2.** with the breath held, as in suspense: *breathless listeners of the mystery story.* **3.** causing loss of breath, as excitement, anticipation, tension, etc.: *a breathless ride.* **4.** dead; lifeless. **5.** motionless; still, as air without a breeze: *a breathless summer day.* [ME *brethles.* See BREATH, -LESS] —**breath′less·ly,** *adv.* —**breath′less·ness,** *n.*

breath-tak·ing (breth′tā′king), *adj.* causing extreme pleasure, awe, or excitement: *a breath-taking performance.*

breath·y (breth′ē), *adj.,* **breath·i·er, breath·i·est.** (of the voice) characterized by excessive emission of breath. [BREATH + -Y[1]] —**breath′i·ness,** *n.*

Breaux′ Bridge′ (brō), a town in central Louisiana. 3303 (1960).

B. Rec., bills receivable. Also, **b. rec.**

brec·ci·a (brech′ē ə, bresh′-), *n.* rock composed of angular fragments of older rocks melded together. [< It < Gmc; cf. OHG *brecha* breaking] —**brec′ci·al,** *adj.*

brec·ci·ate (brech′ē āt′, bresh′-), *v.t.,* **-at·ed, -at·ing.** to form as breccia. [BRECCI(A) + -ATE[1]] —**brec·ci·a·tion** (brech′ē ā′shən, bresh′-), *n.*

Brecht (brekt; *Ger.* brekHt), *n.* **Ber·tolt** (ber′tōlt), 1898–1956, German dramatist and poet.

Breck·en·ridge (brek′ən rij′), *n.* **1.** a town in central Texas. 6273 (1960). **2.** a town in W Minnesota. 4335 (1960).

Breck′enridge Hills′, a town in E Missouri. 6299 (1960).

Breck·in·ridge (brek′ən rij′), *n.* **John Cabell,** 1821–75, vice-president of the U.S. 1857–61: Confederate general in the U.S. Civil War.

Breck·noch·shire (brek′nək shēr′, -shər), *n.* a county in S Wales. 55,544 (1961). 733 sq. mi. *Co. seat:* Brecon. Also called **Breck′noch, Brec·on** (brek′ən).

Brecks·ville (breks′vil), *n.* a town in N Ohio. 5435 (1960).

bred (bred), *v.* pt. and pp. of **breed.**

Bre·da (brə dä′), *n.* a city in the S Netherlands. 113,193 (1962).

brede (brēd), *n. Archaic.* a braid.

bree (brē), *n. Scot. and North Eng.* broo. [late ME *bre,* side-form of ME *brī,* OE *brīg,* var. of *brīw* pottage; c. D *brij,* G *Brei*]

breech (*n.* brēch; *v.* brēch, brich), *n.* **1.** the lower, rear part of the trunk of the body; buttocks. **2.** the hinder or lower part of anything. **3.** *Ordn.* the rear part of the bore of a gun, esp. the opening and associated mechanism that permits insertion of a projectile. **4.** *Mach.* the end of a block or pulley farthest from the supporting hook or eye. **5.** *Naut.* the outside angle of a knee in the frame of a ship. —*v.t.* **6.** *Ordn.* to fit or furnish (a gun) with a breech. **7.** to clothe with breeches. [ME *breche,* OE *brēc,* pl. of *brōc,* c. Icel *brōk,* OHG *bruoh;* see BROGUE[2]]

breech′ birth′. See **breech delivery.**

breech·block (brēch′blok′), *n. Ordn.* a movable piece of metal for closing the breech in certain firearms. Also, **breech′-block′.** [BREECH + BLOCK]

breech·cloth (brēch′klôth′, -kloth′), *n., pl.* **-cloths** (-klôthz′, -klothz′, -klôths′, -kloths′). a cloth worn about the breech and loins; loincloth. Also, **breech·clout** (brēch′klout′). [BREECH + CLOTH]

breech′ deliv′ery, *Obstet.* the delivery of an infant with the feet or breech appearing first.

breech·es (brich′iz), *n.* (*construed as pl.*) **1.** Also called **knee breeches.** knee-length trousers, often having ornamental buckles or elaborate decoration at or near the bottoms, commonly worn by men and boys in the 17th, 18th, and early 19th centuries. **2.** See **riding breeches. 3.** *Informal.* trousers: *He wore his new breeches to the dance.* [pl. of BREECH]

Breeches buoy

breech′es buoy′, *Naut.* a rescue device consisting of a life buoy from which is suspended a canvas sling, similar in form to a pair of breeches, in which shipwrecked or disabled persons are hauled from a vessel to the shore or to another vessel by means of a rope and pulley between them.

breech′es part′, *Theat.* a male role played by an actress.

breech·ing (brich′ing, brē′ching), *n.* **1.** the part of a harness that passes around the haunches of a horse. See illus. under **harness. 2.** a smoke pipe connecting one or more boilers with a chimney. **3.** *Navy.* (formerly) a strong rope fastened to a ship's side for securing a gun or checking its recoil. [BREECH (v.) + -ING[1]]

breech·less (brēch′lis), *adj.* **1.** *Ordn.* without a breech. Cf. **muzzleloader. 2.** without breeches or trousers. [ME *breklesse.* See BREECH, -LESS]

breech·load·er (brēch′lō′dər), *n. Ordn.* a firearm, as a rifle, loaded at the breech. [BREECH + LOADER]

breech·load·ing (brēch′lō′ding), *adj. Ordn.* loaded at the breech. [BREECH + LOADING]

breed (brēd), *v.,* **bred, breed·ing,** *n.* —*v.t.* **1.** to produce (offspring); procreate; engender. **2.** to procure by mating; propagate sexually; reproduce: *Ten mice were bred in the laboratory.* **3.** *Hort.* **a.** to cause to reproduce by controlled pollination. **b.** to improve by controlled pollination and selection. **4.** to raise (cattle, sheep, etc.): *He breeds longhorns on the ranch.* **5.** to cause; create; produce: *Dirt breeds disease.* **6.** to be the native place or the source of: *Stagnant water breeds mosquitoes.* **7.** to develop by training or education; to bring up; rear: *He was born and bred a gentleman.* **8.** to impregnate; mate: *Breed a strong mare with a fast stallion and hope for a Derby winner.* —*v.i.* **9.** to produce offspring: *Many animals breed in the spring.* **10.** to be engendered or produced; grow; develop: *Bacteria will not breed in alcohol.* **11.** to procure the birth of young, as in raising stock. **12.** to be pregnant. —*n.* **13.** *Genetics.* a relatively homogenous group of animals within a species, developed and maintained by man. **14.** race; lineage; strain: *She comes from a fine breed of people.* **15.** sort; kind; group: *Scholars are a quiet breed.* **16.** *Offensive.* half-breed (def. 2). [ME *brede(n)* (v.), OE *brēdan* to nourish (c. OHG *bruotan,* G *brüten*)] —**breed′a·ble,** *adj.*
—**Syn. 1, 2.** beget, bear, produce, generate. **7.** raise, nurture. **14.** family, pedigree, line, stock.

breed·er (brē′dər), *n.* **1.** one who or that which produces offspring or reproduces. **2.** one who raises animals or plants primarily for breeding purposes. **3.** Also called **breed′er reac′tor.** *Physics.* a nuclear reactor in which a fissionable element is produced by bombarding a nonfissionable element with neutrons from a radioactive element. [BREED + -ER[1]]

breed·ing (brē′ding), *n.* **1.** the act of one who or that which breeds. **2.** the improvement or development of breeds of livestock, as by selective mating and hybridization. **3.** *Hort.* the production of new forms by selection, crossing, and hybridizing. **4.** training; nurture: *He is a man of good breeding.* **5.** the result of training as shown in behavior and manners; manners, esp. good manners: *You can tell when a girl has breeding.* **6.** *Physics.* the production of fissionable material by the nuclear fission of a second material, in a process in which more fissionable material is produced than consumed, as in the production of an isotope of plutonium by the nuclear fission of U-238. Cf. **conversion** (def. 10). [ME; see BREED, -ING[1]]

breed′ing plum′age. See **nuptial plumage.**

Breed's′ Hill′ (brēdz), a hill adjoining Bunker Hill, where the Battle of Bunker Hill was actually fought.

breeks (brēks, briks; *Scot.* brēks, briks), *n.* (*construed as pl.*) *Scot. and North Eng.* breeches; trousers.

breeze[1] (brēz), *n., v.,* **breezed, breez·ing.** —*n.* **1.** a wind or current of air, esp. a light or moderate one. **2.** a wind of 4–31 miles per hour. **3.** *Chiefly Brit. Informal.* a disturbance or quarrel. **4.** *Informal.* an easy task; something done or carried on without difficulty: *Finding people to join in the adventure was a breeze.* **5. bat** or **shoot the breeze,** *Slang.* **a.** to converse aimlessly; chat. **b.** to talk nonsense or exaggerate the truth: *He likes to shoot the breeze, so don't take everything he says seriously.* —*v.i.* **6.** (of the wind) to blow a breeze (usually used impersonally with *it* as subject): *It breezed from the west all day.* **7.** to move in a carefree, sprightly, or jaunty manner: *She breezed up to the policeman and asked for directions.* **8.** *Informal.* to proceed quickly and easily; skim; move rapidly without intense effort (often fol. by *along, into,* or *through*): *He breezed through the task. The car breezed along the highway.* —*v.t.* **9.** to cause to move in an easy or effortless manner, esp. at less than full speed: *The boy breezed the horse around the track.* **10. breeze in,** *Slang.* **a.** to win effortlessly: *He breezed in with an election plurality of 200,000.* **b.** Also, **breeze into** or **out.** to move or act with a casual or careless attitude: *He breezed out without paying attention to anyone.* [earlier *brize* < OSp *briza* BRISA] —**breeze′less,** *adj.* —**breeze′like′,** *adj.*
—**Syn. 1.** See **wind**[1].

breeze[2] (brēz), *n.* a gadfly. [ME *brese,* OE *breosa*]

breeze[3] (brēz), *n. Brit.* **1.** a pile of cinders; bed of ashes. **2.** dust from coal, coke, or charcoal. **3.** a pile of small particles of or siftings from coal, coke, or charcoal. [var. of dial. *brays* < F *braise* live coals, cinders; see BRAZE[2]]

breeze′ block′, *Brit.* a cinder block.

breeze′ con′crete, concrete having coke cinders as an aggregate.

breeze·way (brēz′wā′), *n.* a porch or roofed passageway with open sides, for connecting two buildings, as a house and a garage. [BREEZE[1] + WAY]

breez·y (brē′zē), *adj.,* **breez·i·er, breez·i·est. 1.** abounding in breezes; windy. **2.** fresh; sprightly: *His breezy manner was half his charm.* [BREEZE[1] + -Y[1]] —**breez′i·ly,** *adv.* —**breez′i·ness,** *n.*

Bre·genz (brā′gents), *n.* a city in W Austria, on the Lake of Constance. 78,729 (1961).

breg·ma (breg′mə), *n., pl.* **-ma·ta** (-mə tə). *Craniom.* the junction point of the sagittal and coronal sutures of the skull. [< Gk: front of the head] —**breg·mat·ic** (breg mat′ik), **breg·mate** (breg′māt), *adj.*

brei (brī), *n. Bacteriol.* a suspension of finely divided tissue in an isotonic medium, used chiefly in virology as a culture for certain viruses. [< G: mush; see BREE]

Breis·lak (brī′slak), *n.* a walled plain in the fourth quadrant of the face of the moon: about 27 miles in diameter.

bre·loque (brə lōk′), *n.* a charm or trinket, esp. one attached to a watch chain. [< F]

Brem·en (brem′ən; *also, for 1, 2, Ger.* brā′mən), *n.* **1.** a state in N West Germany. 721,000 (1963); 156 sq. mi. **2.** a port in and the capital of this state, on the Weser River: formerly a member of the Hanseatic League. 577,900 (1963). **3.** a town in NW Georgia. 3132 (1960). **4.** a town in N Indiana. 3062 (1960).

Brem·er·ha·ven (brem′ər hā′vən; *Ger.* brā′mər hä′fən), *n.* a seaport in N West Germany, at the mouth of the Weser River. 143,200 (1963). Formerly, **Wesermünde.**

Brem·er·ton (brem′ər tᵊn, -tən), *n.* a city in W Washington, on Puget Sound: navy yard. 28,922 (1960).

brems·strah·lung (brem′shträ′ləng), *n. Physics.* radiation in the form of x-rays produced in the collision of an electron with a nucleus having a positive charge. [< G, equiv. to *Brems(e)* brake + *Strahlung* radiation]

Bren·da (bren′də), *n.* a girl's given name.

Bren′ gun′ (bren), a .303 caliber, gas-operated, air-cooled, clip-fed submachine gun. Also, **bren′ gun′.** Also called **Bren, bren.** [named after *Br(no),* Moravia + *En(field),* England, towns of manufacture]

Bren·ham (bren′əm), *n.* a town in central Texas. 7740 (1960).

Bren·nan (bren′ən), *n.* **William Joseph, Jr.,** born 1906, U.S. lawyer and jurist: associate justice of the U.S. Supreme Court since 1956.

Bren′ner Pass′ (bren′ər), a mountain pass in the Alps, on the border between Italy and Austria. 4494 ft. high.

brent (brent), *n. Brit.* brant. Also called **brent′ goose′.**

Brent·wood (brent′wo͝od′), *n.* **1.** a town on central Long Island, in SE New York. 15,387 (1960). **2.** a town in central Maryland. 3693 (1960).

br'er (brûr, brâr; *Sou. dial.* bûr), *n. Chiefly Southern U.S.* brother.

Bres (bres), *n. Irish Legend.* a Fomorian king of Ireland, whose unpopular rule led to the expulsion of the Fomorians by the Tuatha De Danann. Also, **Bress.**

Bre·scia (bre′shä), *n.* a city in central Lombardy, in N Italy. 174,116 (1961). —**Bre·scian** (bresh′ən), *adj.*

Bresh·kov·sky (bresh kôf′skē), *n.* **Catherine,** 1844–1934, Russian revolutionary of noble birth: called "the little grandmother of the Russian Revolution."

Bres·lau (brez′lou; *Ger.* bres′lou), a city on the Oder River in SW Poland: formerly in Germany. 455,200 (est. 1963). Polish, **Wrocław.**

bres·sum·mer (bres′ə mər), *n.* breastsummer.

Brest (brest), *n.* **1.** a seaport in the W extremity of France: German submarine base in World War II; surrendered to Allies September 1944. 142,901 (1962). **2.** Formerly, **Brest Litovsk.** a city in SW Byelorussia, in the W Soviet Union in Europe, on the Bug River: formerly in Poland: German-Russian peace treaty 1918. 73,000 (1959).

Brest Li·tovsk (brest′ li tôfsk′), former name (until 1921) of **Brest.** Polish, **Brześć nad Bugiem.**

brest′ sum′mer (bres, brest), *n.* breastsummer.

Bre·tagne (brə tan′yᵊ), *n.* French name of **Brittany.**

bre·telle (bri tel′), *n.* one of a pair of ornamental suspenderlike shoulder straps that attach to the waistband at the front and back of a garment. [< F, OF < OHG *brittil* BRIDLE]

bre·tes·sé (bret′i sā′, brə tes′ā), *n.* brattice (def. 2). Also, **bre·tèche** (brə tesh′). [< MF: bratticed]

breth·ren (breth′rin), *n.pl.* **1.** fellow members. **2.** *Archaic.* brothers.
—**Syn. 1, 2.** See **brother.**

Breth′ren of the Com′mon Life′, a religious association of clerics and laymen which stressed Christian brotherhood and devotion and founded schools in both Holland and Germany: founded about 1380, principally by Gerhard Groote, and extinct since the middle of the 17th century. Also called **Brothers of the Common Life.**

Bret·on (bret′ᵊn; *Fr.* brə tôN′), *n.* **1.** a native or inhabitant of Brittany. **2.** Also called **Armorican, Armoric.** the Celtic language of Brittany. **3.** (*often l.c.*) a round hat for women, with a flat crown and a turned-up brim. —*adj.* **4.** pertaining to Brittany, the Bretons, or their language. [< F; see BRITON]

Bre·ton (brə tôN′), *n.* **1. An·dré** (äN drā′), 1896–1966, French poet, essayist, and critic. **2. Jules A·dolphe** (zhyl A dôlf′), 1827–1906, French painter.

Bret′on lace′, a net lace with a design embroidered in heavy, often colored, thread.

Brett (bret), *n.* a boy's or girl's given name. Also, **Bret.**

Bret·ta (bret′ə), *n.* a girl's given name.

Bret′ton Woods′ Con′ference (bret′ᵊn), an international conference called at Bretton Woods, N.H., in July, 1944, to deal with international monetary and financial problems: resulted in the creation of the International Monetary Fund and the World Bank.

Breu·er (broi′ər), *n.* **1. Jo·sef** (yō′zef), 1842–1925, Austrian neurologist: pioneer in psychoanalytic techniques. **2. Mar·cel La·jos** (mär sel′ lô′yōsh), 1902–81, Hungarian architect, in the U.S. after 1937.

Breu·ghel (broi′gəl, bro͞o′-; *Flemish.* brœ′gəl), *n.* **1. Pie·ter the Elder** (pē′tər; *Flemish.* pē′tər), ("*Peasant Breughel*"), c1525–69, Flemish genre and landscape painter. **2.** his sons **Jan** (yän), ("*Velvet Breughel*"), 1568–1625, and **Pieter the Younger** ("*Hell Breughel*"), 1564–1637?, Flemish painters. Also, **Breu′gel, Brue·gel, Bruegel.**

brev., **1.** brevet. **2.** brevier.

bre·va (*It.* bre′vä), *n.* a breeze blowing over Lake Como during the day. [< It]

Bre·vard (brə värd′), *n.* a town in SW North Carolina. 4857 (1960).

breve (brēv, brev), *n.* **1.** a mark (˘) over a vowel to show that it is short, or to indicate a specific pronunciation, as ŭ in (kŭt) *cut.* **2.** *Law.* **a.** an initial writ. **b.** a writ, as one issued by a court of law. **3.** *Music.* **a.** the longest modern note, equivalent to two semibreves or whole notes. See illus. under **note. b.** Also, **brevis.** a note in medieval mensural notation equal to one half or one third of a longa. **4.** *Prosody.* a mark (˘) over a syllable to show that it is not stressed. [ME < ML, L *breve*, neut. of *brevis* short; see BRIEF]

bre·vet (brə vet′ *or, esp. Brit.,* brev′it), *n., v.,* **-vet·ted, -vet·ting** *or* **-vet·ed, -vet·ing.** —*n.* **1.** a commission promoting a military officer to a higher rank without increase of pay and with limited exercise of the higher rank, often granted as an honor immediately before retirement. —*v.t.* **2.** to appoint, promote, or honor by brevet. [ME < AF; OF *brievet.* See BRIEF, -ET]

brevi-, a learned borrowing from Latin meaning "short," used in the formation of compound words: *brevirostrate.* [< L, comb. form of *brevis;* akin to Gk *brachýs*]

bre·vi·ar·y (brē′vē er′ē, brev′ē-), *n., pl.* **-ar·ies.** **1.** *Rom. Cath. Ch.* a book containing all daily psalter, hymns, prayers, lessons, etc., necessary to enable a cleric to recite the daily Divine Office. **2.** *Eccles.* a book of daily prayers and readings in some other churches. [< L *breviāri(um)* an abridgment. See BREVI-, -ARY]

bre·vi·ate (brē′vē it), *n.* *Obs.* a brief note. [< L *breviāt(us)* shortened, abridged (ptp. of *breviāre*). See BREVI-, -ATE¹]

brev·i·cau·date (brev′ə kô′dāt), *adj.* *Zool.* having a short tail. [BREVI- + CAUDATE]

bre·vier (brə vēr′), *n.* *Print.* a size of type approximately 8-point, between minion and bourgeois. [< G: lit., BREVIARY; so called from use in printing breviaries]

brev·i·pen·nate (brev′ə pen′āt), *adj.* *Ornith.* having short wings; brachypterous. [BREVI- + PENNATE]

brev·i·ros·trate (brev′ə ros′trāt), *adj.* *Ornith.* having a short beak or bill. [BREVI- + ROSTRATE]

bre·vis (brā′vis, brev′is), *n.* *Music.* breve (def. 3b).

brev·i·ty (brev′i tē), *n.* **1.** shortness of time or duration; briefness: *the brevity of human life.* **2.** conciseness; the quality of expressing much in few words: *Brevity is the soul of wit.* [earlier *brevitie* < L *brevitāt-* (s. of *brevitās*) shortness. See BREVI-, -TY²]
—**Syn. 2.** compactness, succinctness, pithiness. BREVITY, CONCISENESS refer to the use of few words in speaking. BREVITY emphasizes the short duration of speech: *reduced to extreme brevity.* CONCISENESS emphasizes compactness of expression: *clear in spite of great conciseness.* —**Ant. 1, 2.** length.

brew (bro͞o), *v.t.* **1.** to make (beer, ale, etc.) by steeping, boiling, and fermenting malt and hops. **2.** to prepare (a liquid solution or emulsion, esp. a beverage) by mixing, steeping, soaking, or boiling a solid in water. **3.** to concoct, mix, or cook (a beverage or food, esp. one containing unmeasured or unusual ingredients): *She brewed a pot of soup from the leftovers.* **4.** to contrive or bring about: *to brew mischief.* —*v.i.* **5.** to make a fermented alcoholic malt beverage, as beer, ale, etc. **6.** to boil, steep, soak, or cook: *The tea brews and we wait.* **7. be brewing,** to be forming or gathering; be in preparation: *Trouble was brewing.* —*n.* **8.** a quantity brewed in a single process. **9.** a particular brewing or variety of malt liquor. **10.** a hot beverage made by cooking a solid in water, esp. tea or coffee. **11.** any concoction, esp. a liquid produced by a mixture of uncommon ingredients: *a witches' brew.* [ME *brew(en),* OE *brēowan;* akin to D *brouwen,* G *brauen,* Icel *brugga*] —**brew′er,** *n.*

brew·age (bro͞o′ij), *n.* a fermented liquor brewed from malt. [BREW + -AGE; modeled on *beverage*]

Brew·er (bro͞o′ər), *n.* a town in S Maine. 9009 (1960).

Brew′er's black′bird (bro͞o′ərz), a blackbird, *Euphagus cyanocephalus,* of the U.S., the male of which has greenish-black plumage with a purplish-black head. [named after Thomas M. *Brewer* (1814–80), American ornithologist]

Brew′er's mole′. See **hairy-tailed mole.** [see BREWER'S BLACKBIRD]

brew′er's yeast′, a yeast, as of the genus *Saccharomyces,* suitable for use as a ferment in the manufacture of wine and beer.

brew·er·y (bro͞o′ə rē, bro͝or′ē), *n., pl.* **-er·ies.** a building or establishment for brewing beer or other malt liquors, esp. the building where the brewing is done. [BREW + -ERY; r. *brewhouse*]

brew·house (bro͞o′hous′), *n., pl.* **-hous·es** (-hou′ziz). brewery. [ME; see BREW, HOUSE]

brew·ing (bro͞o′ing), *n.* **1.** the act of one who brews. **2.** the process of being brewed. **3.** a quantity or batch brewed in a single process or at one time. [ME; see BREW, -ING¹]

brew·is (bro͞o′is), *n.* *Dial.* **1.** broth. **2.** bread soaked in broth, gravy, etc. [earlier *brewz, brewes,* appar. b. BREE and *browes,* ME *broys* < OF *broez* (nom.) *broet* (acc.), equiv. to *bro* (< OHG *brod* BROTH) + *-et* -ET]

brew·mas·ter (bro͞o′mas′tər, -mä′stər), *n.* the supervisor of the brewing processes in a brewery. [BREW + MASTER]

Brew·ster (bro͞o′stər), *n.* **1. William,** 1560?–1644, Pilgrim settler: leader of the colonists at Plymouth. **2.** a boy's given name.

Brew′ster chair′, a chair of 17th-century New England having heavy turned uprights with vertical turned spindles filling in the back, the space beneath the arms, and the spaces between the legs. Cf. **Carver chair.** [named after W. BREWSTER]

Brew′ster's law′, *Optics.* the law that light will receive maximum polarization from a reflecting surface when it is incident to the surface at an angle (**Brew′ster an′gle, angle of polarization,** or **polarizing angle**) having a tangent equal to the index of refraction of the surface. [named after Sir David *Brewster* (1781–1868), Scottish physicist]

Brew·ton (bro͞ot′ᵊn), *n.* a town in S Alabama. 6309 (1960).

Brezh·nev (brezh′nef; *Russ.* brezh nyôf′), *n.* **Le·o·nid Il·yich** (le o nēt′ il yēch′), 1906–82, Russian engineer and politician: general secretary of the Soviet Communist party 1964–82; president 1977–82.

Bri·an (brī′ən), *n.* a boy's given name. Also, **Bryan, Bryant.**

Bri·an Bo·ru (brī′ən bô ro͞o′, -ro͞o′, brēn′), 926–1014, king of Ireland 1002–14. Also, **Bri·an Bo·ramha, Bri·an Bo·raimhe, Bri·an Bo·roimhe, Bri·an Bo·rumha** (*all pronounced* brī′ən bô ro͞o′, -ro͞o′, brēn′).

Bri·and (brē änd′; *Fr.* brē äN′), *n.* **A·ri·stide** (A rē stēd′), 1862–1932, French statesman: minister of France 11 times; Nobel peace prize 1926.

bri·ar (brī′ər), *n.* brier. —**bri′ar·y,** *adj.*

Bri′ar·cliff Man′or (brī′ər klif′), a town in SE New York. 5105 (1960).

Bri·ard (brē är′), *n.* one of a French breed of dogs having a long, slightly wavy coat, raised originally for herding sheep. [< F; see BRIE, -ARD]

Bri·ar·e·us (brī âr′ē əs), *n.* *Class. Myth.* one of the three Hecatonchires. Also called **Aegaeon.** —**Bri·ar′e·an,** *adj.*

bri·ar·root (brī′ər ro͞ot′, -ro͝ot′), *n.* brierroot.

bri·ar·wood (brī′ər wo͝od′), *n.* brierwood.

bribe (brīb), *n., v.,* **bribed, brib·ing.** —*n.* **1.** any valuable consideration given or promised with a view to corrupting the behavior of a person, esp. in his performance as an athlete, public official, etc.: *The motorist offered the arresting officer a bribe to let him go.* **2.** anything given or serving to persuade or induce: *The children were given candy as a bribe to be good.* —*v.t.* **3.** to give or promise a bribe to: *They bribed the reporter to forget about what he had seen.* **4.** to influence or corrupt by a bribe: *The judge was too honest to be bribed.* —*v.i.* **5.** to give a bribe; practice bribery. [ME < MF: alms (n.), beg (v.)] —**brib′a·bil′i·ty, bribe′a·bil′i·ty,** *n.* —**brib′a·ble, bribe′a·ble,** *adj.* —**brib′er,** *n.*

brib·er·y (brī′bə rē), *n., pl.* **-er·ies.** the act or practice of giving or accepting a bribe: *Bribery of a public official is a felony.* [ME *briberie* theft < MF: begging. See BRIBE, -ERY]

bric-a-brac (brik′ə brak′), *n.* miscellaneous small articles collected, kept, or displayed for their antiquarian, sentimental, decorative, or other interest. Also, **bric′-à-brac′.** [< F, a gradational formation based on *bric* piece; see BRICK, BREAK]

Brice (brīs), *n.* a boy's given name. Also, **Bryce.**

brick (brik), *n.* **1.** a block of clay hardened by drying in the sun or burning in a kiln, and used for building, paving, etc.: traditionally, in the U.S., a rectangle 2¼ × 3¾ × 8 inches, and red, brown, or yellow. **2.** such blocks collectively. **3.** the material of which such blocks are made. **4.** any block or bar having a similar size and shape: *a gold brick; an ice-cream brick.* **5.** the length of a brick as a measure of thickness, as of a wall: *one and a half bricks thick.* **6.** *Informal.* a good or generous person. **7. make bricks without straw, a.** to plan or act on a false premise or unrealistic basis. **b.** to create that which will not last: *To form governments without the consent of the people is to make bricks without straw.* **c.** to perform a task despite the lack of necessary materials. —*v.t.* **8.** to pave, line, wall, fill, or build with brick. —*adj.* **9.** made of, constructed with, or resembling bricks. [late ME *brike* < MD *bricke;* akin to BREAK] —**brick′like′, brick′ish,** *adj.*

Brick (brik), *n.* a boy's given name.

brick·bat (brik′bat′), *n.* **1.** a piece of broken brick, esp. one used as a missile. **2.** any rocklike missile. **3.** *Informal.* an unkind remark; caustic criticism: *The critics greeted the play with brickbats.* [BRICK + BAT¹; an alliterative compound]

brick′ beam′, a beam composed of bricks bound together with iron straps.

brick′ cheese′, a semisoft, sweet-tasting American cheese, made from the whole milk of cows and produced in brick form.

brick·field (brik′fēld′), *n.* *Brit.* brickyard. [BRICK + FIELD]

brick·field·er (brik′fēl′dər), *n.* (in southern Australia) a squally northerly wind. [BRICKFIELD + -ER¹, after the prevalence of high winds blowing across the brickfields near Sydney, Australia]

brick·kiln (brik′kil′, -kiln′), *n.* a kiln or furnace in which bricks are baked or burned. [BRICK + KILN]

brick·lay·ing (brik′lā′ing), *n.* the art or occupation of laying bricks in construction. [BRICK + LAYING] —**brick′lay′er,** *n.*

brick·le (brik′əl), *adj.* *Dial.* easily broken; brittle. [late ME *bryckell,* OE *-brycel* tending to break, equiv. to *bryc-* (mutated ptp. s. of *brecan* to BREAK) + *-el* adj. suffix] —**brick′le·ness,** *n.*

brick·mak·ing (brik′mā′king), *n.* the act or process of making bricks. [BRICK + MAKING] —**brick′mak′er,** *n.*

brick′ red′, yellowish or brownish red. —**brick′-red′,** *adj.*

brick·work (brik′wûrk′), *n.* brick construction, as contrasted with that using other materials. [BRICK + WORK]

brick·y (brik′ē), *adj.,* **brick·i·er, brick·i·est.** constructed of, made of, or resembling bricks. [BRICK + -Y¹]

brick·yard (brik′yärd′), *n.* a place where bricks are made, stored, or sold. [BRICK + YARD²]

bri·cole (bri kōl′, brik′əl), *n.* **1.** *Billiards.* a shot in which the cue ball strikes a cushion after touching the object ball and before hitting the carom ball. **2.** an indirect action or unexpected stroke. [< MF < ML *bricola* catapult; perh. akin to BRICK]

brid·al (brīd′ᵊl), *adj.* **1.** of or pertaining to a bride or a wedding. —*n.* **2.** a wedding. **3.** *Archaic.* a wedding feast. [ME *bridale,* OE *brȳdealu* BRIDE¹ ALE, i.e., wedding feast] —**brid′al·ly,** *adv.*

Brid·al·veil (brīd′ᵊl vāl′), *n.* a waterfall in Yosemite National Park, California. 620 ft. high. Also called **Brid′alveil Fall′.**

brid′al wreath′, **1.** any of several rosaceous shrubs of the genus *Spiraea,* esp. *S. prunifolia,* having sprays of small white flowers. **2.** maiden's-wreath.

bride¹ (brīd), *n.* **1.** a newly married woman or a woman about to be married. **2.** *Brit. Slang.* a teenage girl who consorts with a teenage boy, as with a member of the mods or rocks. [ME; OE *brȳd;* c. D *bruid,* G *Braut,* Icel *brūthr,* Goth *brūths*] —**bride′less,** *adj.* —**bride′like′,** *adj.*

bride² (brīd), *n.* **1.** Also called **tie.** a connection consisting of a thread or a number of threads for joining ornamental details in embroidery or lacemaking. **2.** an ornamental bonnet string. [< F: bonnet-string (ME *bride* bridle < OF did not survive into E) < Gmc; see BRIDLE]

Bride (brīd), *n.* **Saint.** See **Brigid, Saint.**

bride·groom (brīd′gro͞om′, -gro͝om′), *n.* a newly married man or a man about to be married. [BRIDE¹ + GROOM; r. ME *bridegome,* OE *brȳdguma,* equiv. to *brȳd* bride + *guma* man, c. L *homō*]

bride′ price′, (among some primitive peoples) the money or goods given to the family of a bride by the bridegroom or his family.

brides·maid (brīdz′mād′), *n.* a young woman who attends the bride at the wedding ceremony. [BRIDE¹ + 's¹ + MAID]

bride·well (brīd′wel′, -wəl), *n.* *Brit.* **1.** a house of correction for the confinement of vagrants and disorderly persons: so called from a former prison in London at St. Bride's well. **2.** *Informal.* any prison or house of correction.

Brid·ey (brī′dē), *n.* a girl's given name, form of **Bridget.** Also, **Bridie.**

bridge¹ (brij), *n., v.,* **bridged, bridg·ing.** —*n.* **1.** a structure spanning and affording passage over a river, chasm, road, or the like. **2.** a connecting, transitional, or intermediate route or phase between two adjacent elements, activities, conditions, or the like: *Our taking coffee in the den served as a bridge between table talk and serious discussion.* **3.** *Naut.* **a.** a raised transverse platform from which a power vessel is navigated: often includes a pilot house and a chart house. **b.** any of various other raised platforms from which the navigation or docking of a vessel is supervised. **c.** a bridge house or bridge superstructure. **d.** a raised walkway running fore-and-aft. **4.** *Anat.* the ridge or upper line of the nose. **5.** *Dentistry.* an artificial replacement, fixed or removable, of a missing tooth or teeth, supported by natural teeth or roots adjacent to the space. **6.** *Music.* a thin, fixed wedge or support raising the strings of a musical instrument above the sounding board. **7.** a transitional, modulatory passage connecting sections of a musical composition or movement. **8.** (in jazz and popular music) the contrasting third group of eight bars in a thirty-two bar chorus; channel; release. **9.** Also, **bridge passage.** a passage in a literary work or a scene in a play serving as a movement between two other passages or scenes of greater importance. **10.** *Ophthalm.* the part of a pair of eyeglasses that joins the two lenses and rests on the bridge or sides of the nose. **11.** Also called **bridge circuit.** *Elect.* a two-branch network, including a measuring device, such as a galvanometer, in which the unknown resistance, capacitance, inductance, or impedance of one component can be measured by balancing the voltage in each branch and computing the unknown value from the known values of the other components. Cf. **Wheatstone bridge.** **12.** *Railroads.* a gantry over a track or tracks for supporting water spouts, signals, etc. **13.** *Building Trades.* a scaffold built over a sidewalk alongside a construction or demolition site to protect pedestrians and motor traffic from falling materials. **14.** *Metall.* **a.** a ridge or wall-like projection of fire brick or the like, at each end of the hearth in a metallurgical furnace. **b.** any layer of partially fused or densely compacted material preventing the proper gravitational movement of molten material, as in a blast furnace or cupola, or the proper compacting of metal powder in a mold. **15.** (in a twist drill) the conoid area between the flutes at the drilling end. **16.** *Billiards, Pool.* **a.** the arch formed by the hand and fingers to support and guide the striking end of a cue. **b.** a notched piece of wood with a long handle, used to support the striking end of the cue when the hand cannot do so comfortably; rest. **17.** transitional music, commentary, dialogue, or the like, between two parts of a radio or television program. **18.** *Theat.* **a.** a gallery or platform that can be raised or lowered over a stage and is used by technicians, stagehands, etc., for painting scenery **(paint bridge)**, arranging and supporting lights **(light bridge)**, or the like. **b.** *Brit.* a part of the floor of a stage that can be raised or lowered. **19.** (in a clock or watch) a partial plate, supported at both ends, holding bearings on the side opposite the dial. Cf. **cock**[1] (def. 8). **20.** *Chem.* a valence bond illustrating the connection of two parts of a molecule. **21.** a support or prop, usually timber, for the roof of a mine, cave, etc. **22.** any arch or rooflike figure formed by acrobats, dancers, etc., as by joining and raising hands. **23. burn one's bridges (behind one),** to eliminate all possibilities of retreat; make one's decision irrevocable: *She burned her bridges when she married him.* —*v.t.* **24.** to make a bridge or passage over; span: *The road bridged the river. Perseverance bridges the gap between ambition and success.* **25.** to make (a way) by a bridge. —*v.i.* **26.** *Foundry.* (of molten metal) to form layers or areas heterogeneous either in material or in degree of hardness. [ME *brigge,* OE *brycg;* c. D *brug,* G *Brücke;* akin to Icel *bryggja* pier] —**bridge/a·ble,** *adj.* —**bridge/less,** *adj.* —**bridge/like/,** *adj.*

bridge[2] (brij), *n. Cards.* a game derived from whist in which one partnership plays to fulfill a certain declaration against an opposing partnership acting as defenders. Cf. **auction bridge, contract** (def. 6). [appar. alter. of earlier *biritch* < ?]

Bridge (brij), *n.* See **Brücke, Die.**

bridge·board (brij/bōrd/, -bôrd/), *n.* a string or carriage of a stair. [BRIDGE[1] + BOARD]

bridge/ cir/cuit, *Elect.* bridge[1] (def. 11).

bridge/ deck/, *Naut.* **1.** a deck on top of a bridge house; flying bridge. **2.** the first deck in a bridge house. **3.** Also called **navigating bridge deck.** the deck from which a vessel is usually operated; the location of the pilot house.

bridge/ flut/ing, (on the stem of a drinking glass) flutes or facets continuing onto the underside of the bowl.

bridge·head (brij/hed/), *n.* **1.** a position held or to be gained on the enemy side of a river, defile, or other obstacle, to cover the crossing of friendly troops. **2.** a defensive work covering or protecting the end of a bridge toward the enemy. [BRIDGE[1] + HEAD]

bridge/ house/, *Naut.* a deckhouse including a bridge or bridges for navigation.

bridge/ lamp/, a floor lamp, esp. one having the light source on an arm so hinged as to be horizontally adjustable.

bridge·man (brij/mən), *n., pl.* **-men. 1.** one who works on a bridge or on the construction of bridges. **2.** one who manages the loading and unloading of ferries at a landing dock. [BRIDGE[1] + MAN[1]]

Bridge/ of San/ Lu/is Rey/, The (san/ lōō/is rā/, lōō ēs/), a novel (1927) by Thornton Wilder.

Bridge/ of Sighs/, a bridge in Venice across which prisoners were formerly led for trial in the ducal palace. [trans. of It *ponte di sospiri*]

bridge/ pas/sage, bridge (def. 9).

Bridge·port (brij/pōrt/, -pôrt/), *n.* **1.** a seaport in SW Connecticut, on Long Island Sound. 156,748 (1960). **2.** a town in SE Pennsylvania. 5306 (1960). **3.** a town in N West Virginia. 4199 (1960). **4.** a town in E Ohio. 3824 (1960). **5.** a town in N Texas. 3218 (1960). **6.** a town in NE Alabama. 2906 (1960).

Bridg·es (brij/iz), *n.* **1. Calvin Black·man** (blak/mən), 1889–1938, U.S. geneticist. **2. Harry (Alfred Bryant Ren·ton)** (ren/tᵊn), born 1900, U.S. labor leader, born in Australia. **3. Robert (Seymour),** 1844–1930, English poet and essayist: poet laureate 1913–30.

bridge/ sign/, *Naut.* a sign on a pier or quay to show where the bridge of a certain vessel should be when the vessel is moored.

Bridg·et (brij/it), *n.* **1. Saint.** See **Brigid, Saint. 2.** a girl's given name.

bridge/ ta/ble, a square card table with folding legs.

Bridge·ton (brij/tən), *n.* **1.** a city in SW New Jersey. 20,966 (1960). **2.** a town in E Missouri. 7820 (1960).

Bridge·town (brij/toun/), *n.* a seaport on and the capital of Barbados, in the E West Indies. 11,304 (1960).

bridge·tree (brij/trē/), *n.* a beam supporting the shaft on which an upper millstone rotates. [BRIDGE[1] + TREE]

Bridge/ View/, a town in NE Illinois. 7334 (1960).

Bridge·ville (brij/vil), *n.* a town in SW Pennsylvania. 7112 (1960).

bridge·wall (brij/wôl/), *n.* (in a furnace or boiler) a transverse baffle for products of combustion. [BRIDGE[1] + WALL]

Bridge·wa·ter (brij/wô/tər, -wot/ər), *n.* a town in E Massachusetts. 4296 (1960).

bridge·work (brij/wûrk/), *n.* **1.** *Dentistry.* **a.** a dental bridge or dental bridges collectively. **b.** any of several different types of dental bridges. **2.** the art or process of bridge building. [BRIDGE[1] + WORK]

bridg·ing (brij/ing), *n. Building Trades.* a brace or an arrangement of braces fixed between floor or roof joists to keep them in place. [BRIDGE[1] + -ING[1]]

Bridg·man (brij/mən), *n.* **Percy Williams,** 1882–1961, U.S. physicist: Nobel prize 1946.

Brid·ie (brī/dē), *n.* a girl's given name, form of **Bridget.** Also, **Bridey.**

bri·dle (brīd/ᵊl), *n., v.,* **-dled, -dling.** —*n.* **1.** part of the tack or harness of a horse, consisting usually of a headstall, bit, and reins. **2.** anything that restrains or curbs: *His common sense is a bridle to his quick temper.* **3.** *Mach.* a link, flange, or other attachment for limiting the movement of any part of a machine. **4.** *Horol.* See **brake spring. 5.** *Naut.* a rope or chain secured at both ends to an object to be held, lifted, towed, etc., and itself held or lifted by a rope or chain secured at its center. **6.** a raising up of the head, as in disdain. —*v.t.* **7.** to put a bridle on. **8.** to control as with a bridle; restrain; curb. —*v.i.* **9.** to draw up the head and draw in the chin, as in disdain or resentment. [ME *bridel,* OE *bridel* for *brigdels,* equiv. to *brigd-* (var. s. of *bregdan* to BRAID[1]) + *-els* n. suffix; akin to D *breidel,* OHG *brittel*] —**bri/dle·less,** *adj.* —**bri/dler,** *n.*
—**Syn. 2.** governor. **2, 8.** check, control. **8.** govern. **9.** bristle.

bri/dle hand/, (of a horseman) the hand, usually the left hand, that holds both reins or both pairs of reins, leaving the other hand free to manage a whip, crop, lariat, or the like.

bri/dle i/ron, stirrup (def. 4).

bri/dle joint/, *Carpentry.* a heading joint in which the end of one member, notched to form two parallel tenons, is fitted into two gains cut into the edges of a second member.

bri/dle path/, a wide path, barred to automotive traffic, for riding horses.

bri·dle-wise (brīd/ᵊl wīz/), *adj.* (of a horse) obedient to a touch of the reins on the neck, without pressure of the bit on the mouth.

bri·doon (bri dōōn/), *n.* a snaffle when used with a curb on a full bridle. Also, **bradoon.** [< F *bridon,* equiv. to *bride* bridle (see BRIDE[2]) + *-on* n. suffix]

Brie (brē), *n.* a kind of salted, white, soft cheese, ripened with bacterial action, originating in Brie, France. Also called **Brie/ cheese/.**

Brie (brē), *n.* a region in NE France, between the Seine and the Marne.

brief (brēf), *adj.* **1.** of short duration: *a brief stay in the country.* **2.** using few words; concise; succinct: *a brief report on weather conditions.* **3.** abrupt or curt. —*n.* **4.** a short and concise statement or written item. **5.** an outline, the form of which is determined by set rules, of all the possible arguments and information on one side of a controversy: *a debater's brief.* **6.** *Law.* **a.** a writ summoning one to answer to any action. **b.** a memorandum of points of fact or of law for use in conducting a case. **c.** a written argument submitted to a court. **d.** (in England) the material relevant to a case, delivered by a solicitor to the barrister who tries the case. **7.** an outline, summary, or synopsis, as of a book. **8. briefs,** close-fitting, legless underpants. **9.** briefing. **10.** *Rom. Cath. Ch.* a papal letter less formal than a bull, sealed with the pope's signet ring or stamped with the device borne on this ring. **11.** *Theat. Brit.* a free ticket; pass. **12.** *Obs.* a letter. **13. hold a brief for,** to support or defend by argument; endorse. **14. in brief,** in a few words; in short: *The supervisor outlined in brief the duties of those under his charge.* —*v.t.* **15.** to make an abstract or summary of. **16.** to instruct by a brief or briefing: *They brief all the agents before assigning them.* **17.** *Law.* to retain as advocate in a suit. [ME *bref* < OF < L *brev(is)* short; see BREVE] —**brief/ly,** *adv.* —**brief/ness,** *n.*
—**Syn. 1.** short-lived, fleeting, transitory, ephemeral, transient. See **short. 2.** terse, compact, pithy, condensed; curt, abrupt. **4.** outline, précis, epitome, abstract. See **summary. 15.** summarize, outline.

brief/ case/, a flat, rectangular leather case for carrying documents, books, manuscripts, etc.

brief·ing (brē/fing), *n.* **1.** *Mil.* a short, factual oral summary of the details of a current or projected military operation given to the participants or observers. **2.** any set of concise instructions or a summary of events. [BRIEF + -ING[1]]

brief·less (brēf/lis), *adj.* having no brief, as a lawyer without clients. [BRIEF (n.) + -LESS] —**brief/less·ly,** *adv.* —**brief/less·ness,** *n.*

brief/ of ti/tle, an abstract of the legal documents concerning the conferring and transferring of ownership of a given piece of property.

Bri·elle (brē el/), *n.* a town in E New Jersey. 2619 (1960).

bri·er[1] (brī/ər), *n.* **1.** a prickly plant or shrub, esp. the sweetbrier or a greenbrier. **2.** a tangled mass of prickly plants. **3.** a thorny stem or twig. Also, **briar.** [ME *brere,* OE *brēr, brēr;* akin to BRAMBLE] —**bri/er·y,** *adj.*

bri·er[2] (brī/ər), *n.* **1.** the white heath, *Erica arborea,* of France and Corsica, the woody root of which is used for making tobacco pipes. **2.** a pipe made of this woody root. Also, **briar.** [earlier *bruyer* < F *bruyère* < LL *brūcus* heather (< Celt); see -ER[2]]

bri·er·root (brī/ər rōōt/, -rŏŏt/), *n.* **1.** the root wood of the brier. **2.** certain other woods from which tobacco pipes are made. **3.** a pipe made of brierroot. Also, **briarroot.** [BRIER[2] + ROOT[1]]

bri·er·wood (brī/ər wŏŏd/), *n.* brierroot. Also, **briarwood.** [BRIER[2] + WOOD[1]]

Bri·eux (brē œ/), *n.* **Eu·gène** (œ zhen/), 1858–1932, French playwright, journalist, and editor.

brig[1] (brig), *n.* **1.** *Naut.* **a.** a two-masted vessel square-rigged on both masts. Cf. **snow**[2]. **b.** (formerly, in the U.S. Navy) an armed brig-rigged or brigantine-rigged vessel. **c.** the compartment of a ship where prisoners are confined. **2.** *U.S.* a place of confinement or detention, esp. in the U.S. Navy or Marines; guardhouse. [short for BRIGANTINE]

Brig

brig[2] (brig), *n., v.t. Scot. and North Eng.* bridge[1].

Brig., **1.** brigade. **2.** brigadier.

bri·gade (bri gād/), *n., v.,* **-gad·ed, -gad·ing.** —*n.* **1.** a military unit consisting of several regiments, squadrons, groups, or battalions. **2.** a large body of troops. **3.** a group of individuals organized for a particular purpose: *a fire brigade; a rescue brigade.* **4.** See **bucket brigade. 5.** *Hist.* a convoy of canoes, sleds, wagons, or pack animals, esp. as used to supply trappers in the 18th and 19th century Canadian and U.S. fur trade. —*v.t.* **6.** to form into a brigade. **7.** to group together. [< MF < OIt *brigata* troop, band, equiv. to *brig(are)* (to) fight (see BRIGAND) + *-ata* -ADE[1]]

brig·a·dier (brig/ə dēr/), *n.* **1.** *Brit. Army.* a rank between colonel and major general. **2.** *U.S. Army Informal.* a brigadier general. **3.** *Hist.* a noncommissioned rank in the Napoleonic armies. [short for BRIGADIER GENERAL] —**brig/a·dier/ship,** *n.*

brig/adier gen/eral, *pl.* **brigadier generals.** *U.S. Army.* an officer or the rank between colonel and major general. [< F; see BRIGADE, -IER, GENERAL]

brig·and (brig/ənd), *n.* a bandit, esp. one of a gang of robbers in mountain or forest regions. [var. of ME *briga(u)nt* < MF *brigand* < OIt *brigante,* lit., fighting-man, equiv. to *brig(are)* (to) fight (deriv. of *briga* quarreling < ?) + *-ante* -ANT] —**brig/and·ish,** *adj.* —**brig/and·ish·ly,** *adv.*

brig·and·age (brig/ən dij), *n.* the practice of brigands; plundering. Also, **brig/and·ism.** [< MF; see BRIGAND, -AGE]

brig·an·dine (brig/ən dēn/, -dīn/), *n. Armor.* a flexible body armor of overlapping steel plates with an exterior covering of linen, velvet, leather, etc. [late ME *brigandyn* < MF *brigandine.* See BRIGAND, -INE[2]]

brig·an·tine (brig/ən tēn/, -tīn/), *n. Naut.* **1.** a two-masted sailing vessel, square-rigged on the foremast and having a fore-and-aft mainsail with square upper sails. **2.** See **hermaphrodite brig.** [< ML *brigantin(us)* or OIt *brigantino,* orig., fighting-ship (see BRIGAND, -INE[2]); r. *brigandyn* < MF *brigandin*]

Brig·an·tine (brig/ən tēn/), *n.* a town in SE New Jersey. 4201 (1960).

Briggs (brigz), *n.* **1. Henry,** 1561–1630, English mathematician. **2.** a crater in the second quadrant of the face of the moon: about 32 miles in diameter. —**Briggs/i·an,** *adj.*

Briggs/ian log/arithm, *Math.* See **common logarithm.** [named after H. BRIGGS; see -IAN]

Brig·ham (brig/əm), *n.* a boy's given name.

Brig/ham Cit/y, a city in N Utah. 11,728 (1960).

bright (brīt), *adj.* **1.** radiating or reflecting light; luminous; shining: *The bright coins shone in the gloom.* **2.** filled with light: *The room was bright with sunshine.* **3.** vivid or brilliant: *a bright red dress; bright passages of prose.* **4.** clear or translucent, as liquid: *The bright water trickled through his fingers.* **5.** radiant or splendid: *the bright pageantry of court.* **6.** illustrious or glorious, as an era: *the bright days of the Renaissance.* **7.** quick-witted or intelligent: *They gave promotions to bright employees.* **8.** clever or witty, as a remark: *bright comments enlivened the conversation.* **9.** animated; lively; cheerful: *a bright and happy child; a bird's bright song.* **10.** characterized by happiness or gladness: *All the world seems bright and gay.* **11.** favorable or auspicious: *bright prospects for the future.* **12.** having a glossy, glazed, or polished finish. —*n.* **13. brights, a.** the automobile or truck headlights used for driving (opposed to *parking lights* and *signal lights*): *Some people turn on their brights on a dark, rainy day.* **b.** the brighter level of intensity of these lights, usually deflected upward by switching on a bulb in the headlamp that strikes the lens at a different angle. **14.** flue-cured, light-hued tobacco. **15.** an artist's paint brush having short, square-edged bristles. **16.** *Archaic.* brightness; splendor. —*adv.* **17.** in a bright manner; brightly. [ME; OE *briht, beorht;* c. Goth *bairht(s),* OS, OHG *beraht,* Icel *bjartr;* akin to L *flagrāre* to blaze (see FLAGRANT)] —**bright/ish,** *adj.* —**bright/ly,** *adv.*
—**Syn. 1.** refulgent, effulgent, lustrous, lucent, beaming, lambent. BRIGHT, BRILLIANT, RADIANT, SHINING refer to that which gives forth, is filled with, or reflects light. BRIGHT suggests the general idea: *bright flare, stars, mirror.* BRILLIANT implies a strong, unusual, or sparkling brightness, often changeful or varied and too strong to be agreeable: *brilliant sunlight.* RADIANT implies the pouring forth of steady rays of light, esp. as are agreeable to the eyes: *a radiant face.* SHINING implies giving forth or reflecting a strong or steady light: *shining eyes.* **7.** keen, discerning, acute, ingenious, clever. **11.** promising, encouraging. —**Ant. 1.** dull, dim.

Bright (brīt), *n.* **1. John,** 1811–89, British statesman and economist. **2. Richard,** 1789–1858, English physician.

bright·en (brīt/ᵊn), *v.i., v.t.* to become or make bright or brighter. [ME *brightne(n).* See BRIGHT, -EN[1]] —**bright/en·er,** *n.*

bright-field (brīt/fēld/), *adj.* of or pertaining to the illuminated region about the object of a microscope.

bright/line spec/trum (brīt/līn/), *Physical Chem.* the spectrum of an incandescent substance appearing on a spectrogram as one or more bright lines against a dark background. [BRIGHT + LINE[1]]

bright·ness (brīt/nis), *n.* **1.** the quality of being bright. **2.** *Optics.* the luminance of a body, apart from its hue or saturation, that an observer uses to determine the comparative luminance of another body: pure white has the maximum brightness, and pure black the minimum brightness. [ME *brihtnes,* OE *beorhtnes.* See BRIGHT, -NESS]

Bright·on (brīt/ᵊn), *n.* **1.** a city in S Sussex, in SE England: seashore resort. 158,700 (est. 1956). **2.** a city near Melbourne in S Victoria, in SE Australia. 41,302 (1961). **3.** a town in central Colorado. 7055 (1960). **4.** a town in central Alabama. 2884 (1960).

Bright's/ disease/, *Pathol.* a disease characterized by albuminuria and heightened blood pressure. [named after R. BRIGHT]

Bright·wa·ters (brīt/wô/tərz, -wot/ərz), *n.* a town on S Long Island, in SE New York. 3193 (1960).

bright/ wool/, the wool of sheep raised east of the Mississippi River. Cf. **territory wool.** [so called from its shade]

bright·work (brīt/wûrk/), *n.* **1.** polished metal parts, as on a ship or automobile. **2.** *Naut.* all plain or varnished woodwork that is kept scoured on a vessel, excluding all painted woodwork. [BRIGHT + WORK]

Brig·id (brij/id, brē/id), *n.* **1. Saint.** Also, **Bride.** A.D. 453–523, Irish abbess: a patron saint of Ireland. **2.** a girl's given name. Also, **Bridget, Brigit.**

Brig·it (brij′it), *n.* **1.** *Irish Myth.* a goddess of fire, fertility, agriculture, household arts, and wisdom, later associated with St. Brigid. **2. Saint.** See **Brigid, Saint. 3.** Also, **Brigid, Bridget.** a girl's given name.

Bri·gitte (brē zhēt′), *n.* a girl's given name, French form of **Bridget.**

brig-rigged (brig′rigd′), *adj. Naut.* rigged as a brig; square-rigged on two masts.

brig·sail (brig′sāl′; *Naut.* brig′səl), *n. Naut.* a large gaffsail on the mainmast or trysail mast of a brig or snow. [BRIG[1] + SAIL]

brill (bril), *n., pl.* **brills,** (*esp. collectively*) **brill.** a European flatfish, *Scophthalmus rhombus,* closely related to the turbot. [?]

Brill (bril), *n.* **A(braham) A(rden),** 1874–1948, U.S. psychoanalyst and author, born in Austria.

Bril·lat-Sa·va·rin (brē ya′sa va ran′), *n.* **Anthelme** (äN telm′), 1755–1826, French jurist, writer, and gastronome.

bril·liance (bril′yəns), *n.* **1.** great brightness; splendor; luster: *the brilliance of a fine diamond.* **2.** excellence or distinction; conspicuous talent, mental ability, etc. **3.** *Optics.* that luminance of a body consisting of its saturation and brightness. [BRILLI(ANT) + -ANCE]
—Syn. 1. radiance, effulgence, refulgence. **2.** illustriousness, preeminence; genius. **—Ant. 1, 2.** dullness.

bril·lian·cy (bril′yən sē), *n., pl.* **-cies** for 1. **1.** an instance of brilliance: *The brilliancies of Congreve's wit.* **2.** brilliance. [BRILLI(ANT) + -ANCY]

bril·liant (bril′yənt), *adj.* **1.** shining brightly; sparkling; glittering; lustrous. **2.** distinguished; illustrious: *a brilliant example of imaginative functional architecture.* **3.** having or showing great intelligence, talent, quality, etc.: *a brilliant technician.* **—***n.* **4.** *Jewelry.* a gem, esp. a diamond, having any of several varieties of the brilliant cut. **5.** *Print.* a size of type about 3½-point. [< F *brillant* shining (prp. of *briller* < It *brillare* to glitter), equiv. to *brill-* (? akin to BERYL) + *-ant* -ANT] **—bril′liant·ly,** *adv.* **—bril′liant·ness,** *n.*
—Syn. 1. See **bright.**

bril′liant cut′, *Jewelry.* a cut intended to enhance the brilliance of a gem with the least possible sacrifice of weight, characterized by a form resembling two pyramids set base to base, truncated so as to give a broad table and a very small culet, and having from 18 to 104 facets, 58 being typical. **—bril′liant-cut′,** *adj.*

bril·lian·tine (bril′yən tēn′), *n.* **1.** a preparation used to make the hair manageable and lustrous. **2.** a dress fabric resembling alpaca. [< F *brillantine.* See BRILLIANT, -INE[2]] **—bril′lian·tined′,** *adj.*

Brill's′ disease′, *Pathol.* a relatively mild form of typhus. [named after N. E. *Brill* (1859–1925), American physician]

brim[1] (brim), *n., v.,* **brimmed, brim·ming.** **—***n.* **1.** the upper edge of anything hollow; rim; brink: *the brim of a cup.* **2.** a projecting edge: *the brim of a hat.* **3.** *Archaic.* edge or margin. **—***v.i.* **4.** to be full to the brim. **—***v.t.* **5.** to fill to the brim. [ME *brimme* shore, OE *brymm* sea, surf (whence, sea-side); akin to Icel *brim* surf, breakers, OE *bremman* to roar, rage] **—brim′less,** *adj.* **—brim′ming·ly,** *adv.* **—Syn. 1.** See **rim.**

brim[2] (brim), *n., pl.* (*esp. collectively*) **brim,** (*esp. referring to two or more kinds or species*) **brims.** *Southern U.S.* bream[1] (def. 4).

brim·ful (brim′fo͝ol′), *adj.* full to the brim. Also, **brim′full′.** [BRIM[1] + -FUL] **—brim′ful′ly,** *adv.* **—brim′ful′ness, brim′full′ness,** *n.*

brim·mer (brim′ər), *n.* a cup, glass, or bowl full to the brim. [BRIM[1] + -ER[1]]

Bri·mo (brī′mō), *n.* an ancient Greek goddess identified with Demeter, Hecate, or Persephone.

brim·stone (brim′stōn′), *n.* **1.** sulfur. **2.** a virago; shrew. [ME *brinston,* etc., late OE *brynstān.* See BURN[1], STONE] **—brim′ston′y,** *adj.*

Brin·di·si (brēn′dē zē), *n.* an Adriatic seaport in SE Apulia, in SE Italy: important Roman city and naval station. 70,084 (1961). Ancient, **Brundisium.**

brin·dle (brin′dəl), *n.* **1.** a brindled coloring. **2.** a brindled animal. **—***adj.* **3.** brindled. [back formation from BRINDLED]

brin·dled (brin′dəld), *adj.* gray or tawny with darker streaks or spots. Also, **brin·ded** (brin′did). [*brin(ded)* variegated (lit., branded, burnt) + (KIN)DLED; r. late ME *brended,* var. of *branded.* See BRAND, -ED[3]]

brine (brīn), *n., v.,* **brined, brin·ing.** **—***n.* **1.** water saturated or strongly impregnated with salt. **2.** a salt and water solution for pickling. **3.** the sea or ocean. **4.** the water of the sea. **5.** *Chem.* any saline solution. **—***v.t.* **6.** to treat with or steep in brine. [ME; OE *brȳne;* c. D *brijn*] **—brine′less,** *adj.* **—brin′er,** *n.* **—brin′ish,** *adj.* **—brin′ish·ness,** *n.*

Bri·nell′ machine′ (bri nel′), *Metall.* an instrument for calculating the hardness **(Brinell′ hard′ness)** of metal, esp. heat-treated steels, by forcing a hard steel or tungsten carbide ball of standard dimensions into the material being tested, under a fixed pressure. Also called **Brinell′ test′er.** [named after J. A. *Brinell* (1849–1925), Swedish engineer]

Brinell′ num′ber, *Metall.* a numerical expression of Brinell hardness, obtained by dividing the number of kilograms applied by the indenter into the number of square millimeters of surface area of the indention made. Also called **Brinell′ hard′ness num′ber.** *Abbr.:* Bhn [see BRINELL MACHINE]

bring (bring), *v.t.,* **brought, bring·ing.** **1.** to carry, convey, conduct, or cause (someone or something) to come with or to or toward the speaker: *Bring the suitcase to my house. He brought his brother to my office. I'll bring the hamburgers, and you bring the ice cream.* **2.** to cause to come to or toward oneself; attract: *Her scream brought the police. He brought honor to his family by his heroism.* **3.** to cause to recall, to imagine, to appear in the mind: *The letter brought him memories of youth.* **4.** to cause to come about, occur, or come into a particular position or state, as into existence, action, or effect: *to bring the car to a stop.* **5.** to persuade, convince, compel, or induce: *He couldn't bring himself to do it.* **6.** to sell for; fetch: *These cars will bring a good price.* **7.** *Law.* to commence: *to bring an action for damages.* **8. bring about,** to accomplish; cause: *Land reform brought about a great change in the lives of the common people.* **9. bring around** or **round, a.** to convince of a belief or opinion; persuade: *I think we can bring him around to agreeing with the plan.* **b.** to restore to consciousness, as after a faint. **c.** to bring as a visitor: *They brought around a new employee this morning.* **10. bring down, a.** to injure, capture, or kill: *He brought down several ducks on his last hunting trip.* **b.** to lessen; reduce: *I won't buy that lamp unless they bring down the price.* **c.** *Slang.* to cause to be in low spirits; depress. **11. bring forth, a.** to produce; bear: *to bring forth a son.* **b.** to give rise to; introduce: *to bring forth a proposal for reducing costs.* **12. bring forward, a.** to bring to view; show. **b.** to present for consideration; adduce: *to bring forward an opinion.* **13. bring in, a.** to yield, as profits or income: *Her extra job doesn't bring in much, but she enjoys it.* **b.** to present; submit: *The jury brought in its verdict.* **c.** to cause to operate or yield: *They brought in a gusher on his property.* **d.** to introduce; cause to present: *She brought in six new members last month.* **14. bring off,** to accomplish or achieve (something): *He brought off his speech with ease.* **15. bring on, a.** to cause to happen or exist; bring about: *This incident will surely bring on a crisis.* **b.** to introduce; cause to appear: *Bring on the dancing girls.* **16. bring out, a.** to expose; reveal. **b.** to publish, as a book, play, etc. **c.** to introduce officially into society: *to bring out a debutante.* **17. bring to, a.** to bring back to consciousness; revive. **b.** *Naut.* to head (a vessel) close to or into the wind and kill her headway by manipulating helm and sails. **18. bring up, a.** to care for during childhood; rear. **b.** to introduce to notice or consideration. **c.** to vomit. **d.** to stop or cause to stop quickly: *to bring up a car at the curb.* **e.** *Naut.* (of a vessel) to cause to halt, as by lowering an anchor or running aground; fetch up. [ME *bringen,* OE *bringan;* c. D *brengen,* G *bringen,* Goth *briggan*] **—bring′er,** *n.*
—Syn. 1. transport; lead, guide. BRING, FETCH, TAKE imply conveying or conducting in relation to the place where the speaker is. To BRING is simply so to convey or conduct: *Bring it to me. I'm permitted to bring my dog here with me.* It is the opposite of TAKE, which means to convey or conduct away from the place where the speaker is: *Bring it back here. Take it back there.* FETCH means to go, get, and bring back: *Fetch me that bottle.*

bring·ing-up (bring′ing up′), *n.* childhood training or care; up-bringing.

brink (bringk), *n.* **1.** the edge or margin of a steep place or of land bordering water. **2.** any extreme edge; verge. **3.** a crucial or critical situation, esp. a situation or state beyond which success or catastrophe occurs: *We were on the brink of war.* [ME *brink* < Scand or LG; cf. Dan *brink* brink, MLG *brink* edge, hillside, c. Icel *brekka* slope, hill] **—brink′less,** *adj.*

Brink·ley (bringk′lē), *n.* a town in central Arkansas. 4636 (1960).

brink·man·ship (bringk′mən ship′), *n.* the technique or practice of maneuvering a dangerous situation to the limits of tolerance or safety in order to secure the greatest advantage, esp. by creating diplomatic crises. Also, **brinks·man·ship** (bringks′mən ship′). [BRINK + *-manship* (as in *sportsmanship*)]

brin·y[1] (brī′nē), *adj.,* **brin·i·er, brin·i·est.** of or like brine; salty: *a briny taste.* [BRINE + -Y[1]] **—brin′i·ness,** *n.*

brin·y[2] (brī′nē), *n. Informal.* the ocean. [BRINE + -Y[2]]

bri·o (brē′ō), *n. Italian.* vigor; vivacity.

bri·oche (brē′ōsh, -osh; *Fr.* brē ôsh′), *n., pl.* **-och·es** (-ō shiz, -osh iz; *Fr.* -ôsh′). a light, sweet bun or roll made with eggs, yeast, and butter. [< F, MF (Norman dial.), equiv. to *bri(er)* (to) knead (< Gmc; see BREAK) + *-oche* n. suffix]

bri·o·lette (brē′ə let′; *Fr.* brē ô let′), *n., pl.* **-lettes** (-lets′; *Fr.* -let′). any pear-shaped gem having its entire surface cut with triangular facets. [< F, var. of *brillolette,* itself alter. (by assoc. with *brillant* diamond) of *brignolette,* lit., little dried plum (facetious coinage), equiv. to *brignole* (after *Brignoles* in Provence, where the plums are dried) + *-ette* -ETTE]

bri·o·ny (brī′ə nē), *n., pl.* **-nies.** bryony.

bri·quet (bri ket′), *n., v.t.,* **-quet·ted, -quet·ting.** briquette.

bri·quette (bri ket′), *n., v.,* **-quett·ed, -quett·ing.** **—***n.* **1.** a small brick of compressed coal dust or charcoal used for fuel, esp. in barbecuing. **2.** a molded block of any material. **—***v.t.* **3.** to mold into briquettes. [< F; see BRICK, -ETTE]

bri·sa (brē′sä), *n. Spanish.* **1.** (on the northeast coast of South America and in the Caribbean) an easterly or northeasterly trade wind. **2.** (in the Philippines) a northeast monsoon. Also, **briza.**

bri·sance (bri zäns′; *Fr.* brē zäNs′), *n.* the shattering power of high explosives. [< F, equiv. to *bris(er)* (to) break (< Celt; akin to Ir *brisim* I break) + *-ance* -ANCE] **—bri·sant** (bri zänt′; *Fr.* brē zäN′), *adj.*

Bris·bane (briz′bān, -bən), *n.* **1. Arthur,** 1864–1936, U.S. journalist. **2.** a seaport in and the capital of Queensland, in E Australia. 649,500 (est. 1963). **3.** a crater in the fourth quadrant of the face of the moon: about 30 miles in diameter.

bri·sé (brē zā′; *Fr.* brē zā′), *n., pl.* **-sés** (-zāz′; *Fr.* -zā′). *Ballet.* a movement in which the dancer jumps off one foot, beats the legs together, and lands on both feet. [< F: lit., broken, ptp. of *briser* to break; see BRISANCE]

Bri·se·is (brī sē′is), *n.* (in the *Iliad*) the beautiful wife of Mynes, captured by Achilles. She was the cause of the quarrel between Achilles and Agamemnon which resulted in the temporary withdrawal of Achilles from the fighting at Troy.

Bri·se·us (brī′sē əs, -so͞os), *n.* (in the *Iliad*) the father of Briseis: he committed suicide when his daughter was abducted by Achilles.

Bri·sing·a·men (brē′sing ä men′, brē′sēn gä′men), *n. Scand. Myth.* the magic necklace worn by Freya. [< Icel: necklace of the Brisings, akin to OE *Brōsinga mene;* see MANE]

brisk (brisk), *adj.* **1.** quick and active; lively: *a brisk breeze; a brisk walk.* **2.** sharp and stimulating: *brisk weather; brisk wind.* **3.** (of liquors) effervescing vigorously: *brisk cider.* **—***v.t., v.i.* **4.** to make or become brisk; liven (often fol. by *up*). [< Welsh *brysg;* c. Ir *briosc* crisp, quick, akin to *brisim* I break; see BRISANCE] **—brisk′ly,** *adv.* **—brisk′ness,** *n.*
—Syn. 1. spry, energetic, alert. **—Ant. 1.** languid.

bris·ket (bris′kit), *n.* **1.** the breast of an animal, or the part of the breast lying next to the ribs. **2.** *Informal.* the lower part of the chest of a person. [ME *brusket* < Scand; cf. Icel *brjōskit* the gristle, equiv. to *brjōsk* cartilage + *-it* the]

bris·ling (bris′ling), *n.* the sprat. [< Norw; akin to obs. Dan *bretling,* G *Brätling, Breitling*]

bris·tle (bris′əl), *n., v.,* **-tled, -tling.** **—***n.* **1.** one of the short, stiff, coarse hairs of certain animals, esp. hogs, used extensively in making brushes. **2.** anything resembling these hairs. **—***v.i.* **3.** to stand or rise stiffly, like bristles. **4.** to erect the bristles, as an irritated animal (often fol. by *up*): *The hog bristled up.* **5.** to become rigid with anger or irritation: *The man bristled when I asked him to move.* **6.** to be thickly set or filled with something suggestive of bristles: *The plain bristled with bayonets. The enterprise bristled with difficulties.* **7.** to be visibly roused or stirred (usually fol. by *up*). **—***v.t.* **8.** to erect like bristles: *The rooster bristled his crest.* **9.** to furnish with a bristle or bristles. **10.** to make bristly. [ME *bristel,* equiv. to *brist* (OE *byrst* bristle, c. G *Borste,* Icel *burst,* etc.) + *-el* dim. suffix] **—bris′tle·less,** *adj.* **—bris′tle·like′,** *adj.* **—bris′tli·ness,** *n.* **—bris′tly,** *adj.*

bris′tle·cone fir′ (bris′əl kōn′), a California fir, *Abies venusta,* bearing cones having scales tipped with spines. [BRISTLE + CONE]

bris′tlecone pine′, a pine, *Pinus aristata,* of the southwestern U.S., bearing cones having scales tipped with a slender, curved spine. Also called **hickory pine.** [BRISTLE + CONE]

bris·tle·mouth (bris′əl mouth′), *n., pl.* (*esp. collectively*) **-mouth,** (*esp. referring to two or more kinds or species*) **-mouths** (-mouthz′). any of several small, deep-sea fishes of the family *Gonostomatidae,* having numerous sharp, slender teeth covering the jaws. [BRISTLE + MOUTH]

bris·tle·tail (bris′əl tāl′), *n.* any of various wingless insects of the order *Thysanura,* having long, bristlelike, caudal appendages. [BRISTLE + TAIL[1]]

bris′tle-thighed cur′lew (bris′əl thīd′), an Alaskan curlew, *Numenius tahitiensis,* that winters in Polynesia, having bristlelike feathers on its thighs.

bris′tly sarsapari′la, a coarse, perennial herb, *Aralia hispida,* of eastern North America, having small, greenish flowers and black fruit.

Bris·tol (bris′təl), *n.* **1.** a seaport in S Gloucestershire, in SW England, on the Avon River near its confluence with the Severn estuary. 436,440 (1961). **2.** a city in central Connecticut. 45,499 (1960). **3.** a city in NE Tennessee, contiguous with but politically independent of Bristol, Virginia. 17,582 (1960). **4.** a city in SW Virginia. 17,144 (1960). **5.** a town in SE Pennsylvania, on the Delaware River. 12,364 (1960). **6.** Bristol, Tennessee and Bristol, Virginia considered as a unit.

Bris′tol board′, a fine, smooth pasteboard, sometimes glazed.

Bris′tol Chan′nel, an inlet of the Atlantic, between S Wales and SW England, extending to the mouth of the Severn estuary. 85 mi. long.

Bris′tol fash′ion, *Naut.* in a tidy, seamanlike manner: *shipshape and Bristol fashion.* [after BRISTOL, England]

Bris·tow (bris′tō), *n.* **1.** a town in central Oklahoma. 4795 (1960). **2.** Also, **Bristo.** a boy's given name.

bri·sure (bri zho͝or′), *n.* See **cadency mark.** [ME < MF; OF *briseure,* equiv. to *brise(r)* (to) break (see BRISANCE) + *-ure* -URE]

brit (brit), *n.* **1.** the group of small marine animals forming the food of whalebone whales. **2.** the young of herring and sprat. [< Cornish; akin to Welsh *brith* speckled]

Brit (bə rēt′, bə ris′; *Eng.* bris), *n. Hebrew.* Berith.

Brit., 1. Britain. **2.** British.

Brit·ain (brit′ən), *n.* **1.** See **Great Britain. 2.** Britannia (def. 1).

Bri·tan·ni·a (bri tan′ē ə, -tan′yə), *n.* **1.** the ancient Roman name of the island of Great Britain, esp. the S part where the early Roman provinces were. **2.** the British Empire. **3.** *Chiefly Literary.* **a.** Great Britain. **b.** the United Kingdom of Great Britain and Ireland. **4.** the figure of a seated woman with trident and helmet used as a symbolic representation of Great Britain and the British Empire. **5.** See **Britannia metal.**

Britan′nia met′al, a white alloy of tin, antimony, and copper in varying proportions, sometimes with small amounts of zinc, lead, and bismuth, used for tableware and as an antifriction material.

Bri·tan·nic (bri tan′ik), *adj.* **1.** of Britain; British: *His Britannic Majesty.* **2.** Brythonic. **—***n.* **3.** Brythonic. [< L *Britannic(us).* See BRITANNIA, -IC]

Bri·tan·nic·us (bri tan′ə kəs), *n.* a tragedy (1669) by Racine.

britch·es (brich′iz), *n.pl. Informal.* breeches.

Brith (bə rēt′, bə ris′; *Eng.* bris), *n. Hebrew.* Berith.

Brit·i·cism (brit′i siz′əm), *n.* a word, idiom, or phrase characteristic of or restricted to British English, esp. as compared to American English. Also, **Britishism.** [*Britic-* (alter. of BRITISH) + -ISM]

Brit·ish (brit′ish), *adj.* **1.** of or pertaining to Great Britain, the British Commonwealth, or its inhabitants. **2.** of or pertaining to the ancient Britons. **—***n.* **3.** people native to or inhabiting Great Britain or the British Commonwealth, taken collectively. **4.** See **British English. 5.** the Celtic language of the ancient Britons. [ME *Brittische,* OE *Bryttisc,* equiv. to *Brytt(as)* Britons + *-isc* -ISH[1]; see BRITON] **—Brit′ish·ly,** *adv.* **—Brit′ish·ness,** *n.*

Brit′ish Amer′ica. See **British North America.**

Brit′ish Antarc′tic Ter′ritory, a British colony in the S Atlantic, comprising the South Shetland Islands, the South Orkney Islands, and Graham Land: formerly dependencies of the Falkland Islands.

Brit′ish anti-lew′isite, *Chem.* dimercaprol.

Brit′ish Cameroons′. Cameroons (def. 2).

Brit′ish Colum′bia, a province in W Canada on the Pacific coast. 1,629,082 (1961); 366,255 sq. mi. *Cap.:* Victoria. **—Brit′ish Colum′bian.**

Brit′ish Com′monwealth of Na′tions, a group of nations and dependent territories united by a common allegiance to the British crown, including the nations of the United Kingdom of Great Britain and Northern Ireland, Australia, Barbados, Botswana, Canada, Ceylon, Cyprus, The Gambia, Ghana, Guyana, India, Jamaica, Kenya, Lesotho, Malawi, Malaysia, Malta, New Zealand, Nigeria, Pakistan, Rhodesia, Zambia, Sierre Leone, Singapore, Tanzania, Trinidad and Tobago, and Uganda, and their colonies, protectorates, and trusteeships. Also called **Brit′ish Com′monwealth, Commonwealth of Nations;** *esp. Brit.,* **the Commonwealth.**

Brit′ish dol′lar, any of several coins formerly issued by the British Empire for use in certain territories, as the Straits dollar or the Hong Kong dollar.

Brit′ish East′ Af′rica, a comprehensive term for the former British territories of Kenya, Uganda, and Tanzania.

Brit′ish Em′pire, a former collective term for the territories under the leadership or control of the British crown, including those in the British Commonwealth of Nations and their colonies, protectorates, dependencies, and trusteeships.

Brit′ish Eng′lish, the English language as spoken and written in Great Britain, esp. in southern England. Also called **British.**

Brit·ish·er (brit′i shər), *n.* a native or inhabitant of Britain. [BRITISH + -ER[1]]

Brit′ish gal′lon, *Chiefly Brit.* See **Imperial gallon.**

Brit′ish Gui·a′na, former name of **Guyana.**

Brit′ish gum′, dextrin.

Brit′ish Hondu′ras, a former British crown colony in N Central America. See **Belize** (def. 1). —**Brit′ish Hondu′ran.**

Brit′ish In′dia, a part of India, comprising 17 provinces, that prior to 1947 was subject to British law: now divided between India and Pakistan.

Brit′ish In′dian O′cean Ter′ritory, a British colony in the Indian Ocean, constituted of the Seychelles and Chagos Archipelago. 47,059 (est. 1962); 148 sq. mi. *Cap.:* Victoria.

Brit′ish Isles′, a group of islands in W Europe: Great Britain, Ireland, the Isle of Man, and adjacent small islands. 56,811,000 (est. 1963); 120,592 sq. mi.

Brit·ish·ism (brit′i shiz′əm), *n.* **1.** Briticism. **2.** any custom, manner, characteristic, or quality peculiar to or associated with the British people. [BRITISH + -ISM]

Brit′ish Le′gion, (in Britain) a national social club for veterans of the armed forces. Cf. **American Legion.**

Brit′ish Malay′a, a comprehensive term for the former British possessions on the Malay Peninsula and the Malay Archipelago: now part of the federation of Malaysia.

Brit′ish Muse′um, a national depository, library, and museum in London, England, housing some of the world's largest and most important collections related to archeology, art, literature, and natural history.

Brit′ish New′ Guin′ea, former name of the Territory of Papua.

Brit′ish North′ Amer′ica, **1.** Canada. **2.** all parts of the British Commonwealth in or near North America.

Brit′ish North′ Bor′neo, former name of **Sabah.**

Brit′ish Soma′liland, a former British protectorate in E Africa, on the Gulf of Aden: now the N province of the Somali Republic. Former official name, **Somaliland Protectorate.** Cf. **Somali Republic.**

Brit′ish ther′mal u′nit, the amount of heat required to raise the temperature of one pound of water one degree F. *Abbr.:* BTU, B.T.U., B.t.u., B.th.u., Btu

Brit′ish Vir′gin Is′lands, a British colony comprising several small islands in the West Indies, E of Puerto Rico. 7340 (1960); 67 sq. mi. *Cap.:* Road Town.

Brit′ish warm′, *Brit.* a short military overcoat.

Brit′ish West′ Af′rica, a former comprehensive term for Gambia, the Gold Coast, Nigeria, and Sierra Leone.

Brit′ish West′ In′dies, the possessions of Great Britain in the West Indies, including the Bahamas, Barbados, Jamaica, Trinidad and Tobago, and the islands of the Leeward and Windward groups. ab. 12,500 sq. mi. Cf. **West Indies** (def. 2).

Brit·o·mar·tis (brit′ə mär′tis), *n.* *Class. Myth.* a Cretan goddess of fishermen, hunters, and sailors, often identified with Artemis.

Brit·on (brit′ən), *n.* **1.** a native or inhabitant of Great Britain or the British Commonwealth, esp. of England. **2.** one of the Celtic people formerly occupying the southern part of the island of Britain. [< ML *Britōn-* (s. of *Britō*); r. ME *Breton* < OF < LL *Britton(es)* Britons]

brits·ka (brits′kə), *n.* an open carriage with a calash top. Also, **britzka, britzska.** [< G *Britzka*, var. of *Britschka* < Pol *bryczka*, dim. of *bryka* cart, wagon]

Brit·ta·ny (brit′ənē), *n.* a region in NW France, on a peninsula between the English Channel and the Bay of Biscay: a former duchy and province. French, **Bretagne.**

Brit′tany span′iel, one of a French breed of large spaniels developed as a game pointer, and having a reddish-brown and white or orange and white coat.

Brit·ten (brit′ən), *n.* **(Edward) Benjamin,** 1913–76, English composer and pianist.

brit·tle (brit′əl), *adj.* **1.** having hardness and rigidity but little tensile strength; breaking readily with a comparatively smooth fracture, as glass. —*n.* **2.** a confection of melted sugar, usually with nuts, brittle when cooled: *peanut brittle.* [ME *britel*, equiv. to *brit-* (akin to OE *brysten* fragment) + *-el* adj. suffix] —**brit′tle·ness,** *n.*
—**Syn. 1.** fragile. See **frail**[1].

brit·tle·bush (brit′əl bo͝osh′), *n.* any of several plants of the genus *Encelia*, of desert regions of the southwestern U.S. and Mexico. [BRITTLE + BUSH[1], so called from the texture of its leaves]

brit′tle fern′, a fern, *Cystopteris fragilis*, of rocky, wooded areas throughout North America, having grayish-green fronds and brittle stalks. Also called **bottle fern.**

brit′tle star′, any echinoderm of the class *Ophiuroidea*, having the body composed of a central, rounded disk from which radiate long, slender, fragile arms. Also called **serpent star.**

Brit·ton (brit′ən), *n.* **Nathaniel Lord,** 1859–1934, U.S. botanist.

britz·ka (brits′kə; *Pol.* brich′kä), *n.* britska. Also, **britzs′ka.**

Brix (briks), *adj.* **1.** of, noting, or characteristic of a Brix scale. —*n.* **2.** percentage of sugar as determined by a Brix scale.

Brix′ scale′, a graduated scale, used on a hydrometer, that indicates the weight of sugar per volume of solution at a given temperature. [named after A. F. W. *Brix*, 19th-century German inventor]

bri·za (brē′zə), *n.* brisa.

Bri·ze (brī′zē), *n.* *Class. Myth.* a gadfly sent by Hera to annoy Io.

Bri·zo (brī′zō), *n.* an ancient Greek goddess of sailors, noted for prophesying through dreams: she was worshiped mainly by women.

Br·no (bər′nō; *Eng.* bûr′nō), *n.* **a city in S Moravia, in the SE Czech Republic: former capital of Moravia. 390,000. German, Brünn.**

bro., *pl.* **bros.** brother. Also, **Bro.**

broach (brōch), *n.* **1.** *Mach.* an elongated, tapered, serrated cutting tool for shaping and enlarging holes. **2.** a spit for roasting meat. **3.** a gimlet for tapping casks. **4.** Also, **broach′ spire′.** an octagonal spire rising directly from a tower without any intervening feature. **5.** (in a lock) a pin receiving the barrel of a key. **6.** a pointed tool for the rough dressing of stone. —*v.t.* **7.** to enlarge and finish with a broach. **8.** to mention or suggest for the first time: *to broach a subject.* **9.** to draw (beer, liquor, etc.) as by tapping: *to broach beer from a keg.* **10.** to tap or pierce. **11.** to shape or dress (a block of stone). —*v.i.* **12.** *Naut.* (of a sailing vessel) to veer to windward, esp. so as to be broadside to the wind (usually fol. by *to*). **13.** to break the surface of water; rise and extend above the top of the sea, as a fish or a submarine. [ME *broche* < MF < VL **brocca* spike, horn, tap of a cask, etc. (ML *broca*), n. use of fem. of L adj. *brocc(h)us* projecting (said of teeth)] —**broach′er,** *n.*

broach′ post′. See **king post** (def. 1).

broad (brôd), *adj.* **1.** of great breadth: *The river was too broad to swim across.* **2.** measured from side to side: *The desk was three feet broad.* **3.** of great extent; large: *the broad expanse of ocean.* **4.** widely diffused; open; full: *He awoke to broad daylight.* **5.** not limited or narrow; of extensive range or scope: *A modern doctor must have a broad knowledge of medicine.* **6.** liberal; tolerant: *A broad interpretation of the law tempers justice with mercy.* **7.** main or general: *the broad outlines of a subject.* **8.** plain or clear: *Her remark was a broad hint of her feelings.* **9.** bold; plain-spoken. **10.** indelicate; indecent: *He smirked at the broad joke.* **11.** (of conversation) rough; countrified. **12.** unconfined; free; unrestrained: *It was a hilarious evening of broad mirth.* **13.** (of pronunciation) strongly dialectal: *He wore kilts and had a broad Scots accent.* **14.** *Phonet.* (of a transcription) using one basic symbol to represent each phoneme. **15. broad a,** the *a*-sound (ä) when used in lieu of the more common *a*-sound (a) in such words as *half, can't, laugh,* etc. **16. broad on the beam,** *Naut.* bearing 90° to the heading of a vessel. **17. broad on the bow,** *Naut.* bearing 45° to the heading of a vessel. **18. broad on the quarter,** *Naut.* bearing 135° to the heading of a vessel. —*adv.* **19.** fully: *He was broad awake.* —*n.* **20.** the broad part of anything. **21.** a gold coin of England and Scotland, issued by James I and Charles I and equal to 20 shillings. Cf. **carolus, jacobus. 22.** Often, **broads.** *Motion Pictures, Television.* an incandescent or fluorescent lamp used as a general source of light in a studio. **23.** *Slang.* **a.** a woman. **b.** a promiscuous woman. [ME *brood*, OE *brād*; c. D *breed*, G *breit*, Icel *breithr*, Goth *braiths*] —**broad′ish,** *adj.* —**broad′ly,** *adv.*
—**Syn. 1.** See **wide. 3.** extensive, ample, vast. **5.** liberal, open. **6.** open. **10.** gross. —**Ant. 1.** narrow.

Broad (brôd), *n.* **Charlie Dunbar,** 1887–1971, English philosopher.

broad′ ar′row, 1. a mark in the shape of a broad arrowhead, placed upon British government property. **2.** *Archery.* an arrow having an expanded head. **3.** *Heraldry.* pheon.

Broad arrow (def. 1)

broad·ax (brôd′aks′), *n.*, *pl.* **-ax·es** (-ak′siz). **1.** an ax for hewing timber. **2.** an ax with a broad head, used as a battle-ax. Also, **broad′axe′.** [ME *brodax*, OE *brādæx.* See BROAD, AX]

broad·band (brôd′band′), *adj.* *Radio, Electronics.* of, pertaining to, or responsive to a continuous, wide range of frequencies. Cf. **sharp** (def. 22). [BROAD + BAND[2]]

broad′ bean′, a variety of edible bean, *Vicia Faba.* Also called **horse bean.**

broad·bill (brôd′bil′), *n.* **1.** any of several small, often brightly colored passerine birds of the family *Eurylaimidae*, of the Old World tropics, having a broad, flattened bill. **2.** any of various birds with a broad bill, as the scaup duck, shoveler, and spoonbill. **3.** a swordfish. [BROAD + BILL[2]]

broad·brim (brôd′brim′), *n.* **1.** a hat with a broad brim, as that worn by Quakers. **2.** (*cap.*) *Slang.* a Friend; Quaker. [BROAD + BRIM[1]]

broad·cast (brôd′kast′, -käst′), *v.*, **-cast** or **-cast·ed, -cast·ing,** *n.*, *adj.*, *adv.* —*v.t.* **1.** to transmit (programs) from a radio or television station. **2.** to speak, perform, sponsor, or present on a radio or television program: *The President will broadcast his message on all stations tonight.* **3.** to cast or scatter abroad over an area, as seed in sowing. **4.** to spread or disseminate widely: *She broadcast the gossip all over town.* **5.** *Informal.* to divulge or indicate unwittingly to one's opponent (one's next offensive move): *He broadcast his punch and the other man was able to parry it.* —*v.i.* **6.** to transmit programs or signals from a radio or television station. **7.** to scatter or disseminate something widely. **8.** to speak, perform, sponsor, or present all or part of a radio or television program: *The Boston Symphony Orchestra broadcasts every Saturday on our local station.* —*n.* **9.** that which is broadcast. **10.** *Radio.* **a.** the broadcasting of radio messages, speeches, etc. **b.** a radio program. **c.** a single period of broadcasting. **11.** a method of sowing by scattering seed. —*adj.* **12.** (of programs) transmitted from a radio or television station. **13.** of or pertaining to broadcasting. **14.** cast abroad or all over an area, as seed scattered widely. **15.** widely spread or disseminated: *Who are the perpetrators of such broadcast rumors?* —*adv.* **16.** so as to reach the greatest number of people by radio or television: *The vital news was sent broadcast to inform the entire nation.* **17.** so as to be cast abroad over an area: *seed sown broadcast.* [BROAD (adv.) + *cast*, ptp. of CAST[1]]

broad·cast·er (brôd′kas′tər, -kä′stər), *n.* **1.** one who or that which broadcasts. **2.** *Radio and Television.* a person or organization, as a network or station, that broadcasts programs. [BROADCAST + -ER[1]]

broad·cast·ing (brôd′kas′ting, -kä′sting), *n.* **1.** the act of transmitting speech, music, visual images, etc., by radio or television. **2.** radio or television as a business or profession: *She's training for a career in broadcasting.* [BROADCAST + ING[1]]

Broad′ Church′, pertaining or belonging to a party in the Anglican Church emphasizing a liberal interpretation of ritual and favoring such conditions of church membership as will promote wide Christian inclusiveness. Cf. **High Church, Low Church.** —**Broad′-Church′,** *adj.*

Broad′ Church′man, a person belonging to the Broad-Church party in the Anglican Church.

broad·cloth (brôd′klôth′, -kloth′), *n.* *Textiles.* **1.** any fabric woven on a wide loom. **2.** a woolen or worsted dress-goods fabric constructed in a plain or twill weave, having a compact texture and lustrous finish. **3.** a closely woven dress-goods fabric of cotton, rayon, silk, or a mixture of these fibers, having a soft, mercerized finish and resembling poplin. [ME *brode clothe.* See BROAD, CLOTH]

broad·en (brôd′ən), *v.i.*, *v.t.* to become or make broad; widen. [BROAD + -EN[1]]

broad-faced (brôd′fāst′), *adj.* having a broad, wide face.

broad′ gauge′, *Railroads.* See under **gauge** (def. 13). Also, *esp. in technical use,* **broad′ gage′.** —**broad′-gauged′, broad′-gaged′,** *adj.*

broad′ glass′. See **cylinder glass.**

broad′ hatch′et, a hatchet with a broad cutting edge. Also called **hand ax.**

broad·head (brôd′hed′), *n.* **1.** a flat, triangular, steel arrowhead with sharp edges. **2.** an arrow with such an arrowhead. [BROAD + HEAD]

broad′ jump′, *Track.* **1.** a jump for distance, either from a standing position **(standing broad jump)** or with a running start **(running broad jump). 2.** a field event featuring competition in the broad jump. Also called **long jump.**

broad-jump (brôd′jump′), *v.i.* to execute a broad jump.

broad′ jump′er, *Track.* a participant in the broad jump.

broad·leaf (brôd′lēf′), *n.*, *pl.* **-leaves** (-lēvz′). any of several cigar tobaccos having broad leaves. [back formation from *broadleafed.* See BROAD, LEAF, -ED[3]]

broad′-leaved bot′tle tree′ (brôd′lēvd′). See **bottle tree.**

broad′-leaved ma′ple, a maple, *Acer macrophyllum*, of western North America, characterized by dark green, leathery leaves that may reach one foot or more in width.

broad·loom (brôd′lo͞om′), *adj.* **1.** of or pertaining to rugs or carpets woven on a wide loom. —*n.* **2.** See **broadloom carpet.** [BROAD + LOOM[1]]

broad′loom car′pet, any carpet woven on a wide loom and not having seams, esp. one wider than 54 inches.

broad-mind·ed (brôd′mīn′did), *adj.* free from prejudice or bigotry; liberal; tolerant. —**broad′-mind′ed·ly,** *adv.* —**broad′-mind′ed·ness,** *n.*

broad′ reach′, *Naut.* See under **reach** (def. 26).

Broads (brôdz), *n.* (*construed as pl.*) **The,** a low-lying region in E England, in Norfolk and Suffolk: marshy lakes and bogs.

broad′ seal′, the official seal of a country or state.

broad·side (brôd′sīd′), *n.*, *adv.*, *v.*, **-sid·ed, -sid·ing.** —*n.* **1.** *Naut.* the whole side of a ship above the water line, from the bow to the quarter. **2.** *Navy.* **a.** all the guns that can be fired from one side of a warship. **b.** a simultaneous discharge of all the guns on one side of a warship. **3.** any strong or comprehensive attack, as by criticism: *The reviewer leveled a broadside at the bad novel.* **4.** Also called **broad·sheet** (brôd′shēt′). **a.** a sheet of paper printed on one side only, as for distribution or posting. **b.** any printed advertising circular. **5.** any broad surface or side, as of a house. **6.** Also called **broad′side bal′lad.** a song, chiefly in 16th- and 17th-century England, written on a topical subject, printed on broadsides, and sung in public, as on a streetcorner, by a professional balladeer. —*adv.* **7.** with the side, esp. with the broader side facing toward a given point or object: *The truck hit the fence broadside.* —*v.i.* **8.** to proceed or go broadside. **9.** to fire a broadside or broadsides. [BROAD + SIDE[1]]

broad-spec·trum (brôd′spek′trəm), *adj.* *Pharm.* noting an antibiotic effective against a wide range of organisms.

broad·sword (brôd′sôrd′, -sōrd′), *n.* a sword having a straight, broad, flat blade, usually with a basket hilt. [ME *brood swerd*, OE *brād sweord.* See BROAD, SWORD]

broad·tail (brôd′tāl′), *n.* the wavy, moirélike fur or pelt of a young or stillborn karakul lamb. Cf. **caracul** (def. 1), **Persian lamb** (def. 2). [BROAD + TAIL[1]]

Broad·view (brôd′vyo͞o′), *n.* a town in NE Illinois. 8588 (1960).

Broad′view Heights′, a town in N Ohio. 6209 (1960).

Broad·way (brôd′wā′), *n.* **1.** a street in New York City which extends the entire length of Manhattan Island and through The Bronx to the New York City line at Yonkers. **2.** the theater district located on or near this street, esp. as the center of the professional or commercial theater in the U.S. —*adj.* **3.** (of a play, theatrical performance, etc.) pertaining to, suitable for or produced in the commercial theater, esp. on Broadway: *a Broadway show.* **4.** acting or working on Broadway: *a Broadway producer; a Broadway star.* **5.** characteristic of or frequenting the theater district on Broadway. **6.** garish; gaudy; tawdry. —**Broad′way·ite′,** *n.*

Broad′way Boog′ie-Woog′ie, a painting (1942–43) by Piet Mondrian.

broad·wife (brôd′wīf′), *n.*, *pl.* **-wives.** *U.S. Hist.* a female slave whose husband was owned by another master. [BROAD (adv.: far) + WIFE]

broad′-winged hawk′ (brôd′wingd′), an American hawk, *Buteo platypterus,* dark brown above and white barred with rufous below.

brob (brob), *n.* a wedge-shaped spike for securing an end of a timber butting against the side of another. [? alter. of ME *brod* goad < Scand; cf. Icel *broddr* spike]

Brob·ding·nag (brob′ding nag′), *n.* the region in Swift's *Gulliver's Travels* where everything was of enormous size.

Brob·ding·nag·i·an (brob′ding nag′ē ən), *adj.* **1.** of huge size; gigantic; tremendous. —*n.* **2.** an inhabitant of Brobdingnag. **3.** a being of tremendous size; giant. [BROBDINGNAG + -IAN]

Bro·ca (brō′kə; *Fr.* brô ka′), *n.* **Paul** (pôl), 1824–80, French surgeon and anthropologist.

bro·cade (brō kād′), *n., v.,* **-cad·ed, -cad·ing.** —*n.* **1.** fabric woven with an elaborate design, esp. one having a raised overall pattern. —*v.t.* **2.** to weave with a design or figure. [earlier *brocado* < Sp: lit., studded, equiv. to *broc(a)* stud (see BROACH) + *-ado* -ADE[1]]

Bro′ca's ar′ea, *Anat.* a cerebral area, usually in the left inferior frontal gyrus, associated with the movements necessary for speech production. Also called **Bro′ca's gy′rus, Bro′ca's convolu′tion.** [named after P. BROCA]

broc·a·tel (brok′ə tel′), *n.* **1.** a brocade in which the design is woven in high relief. **2.** an ornamental marble with variegated coloring, found esp. in Italy and Spain. Also, **broc′a·telle′.** [< late MF < It *broccatell(o),* equiv. to *broccat(o)* (see BROCADE) + *-ello* dim. suffix]

broc·co·li (brok′ə lē), *n.* **1.** a plant of the mustard family, *Brassica oleracea botrytis,* resembling the cauliflower. **2.** a form of this plant which does not produce a head, the green saps and the stalk of which are a common vegetable. [< It, pl. of *broccolo,* equiv. to *brocc(o)* sprout (see BROACH) + *-olo* dim. suffix]

broch (*Scot.* brokh, brukh), *n.* any of the prehistoric circular stone buildings, having an inner and an outer wall, found on the Orkney Islands, Shetland Islands, the Hebrides, and the mainland of Scotland. [var. of *brough* round tower, a northern form of BOROUGH]

bro·chan·tite (brō shän′tīt), *n.* a mineral, hydrous copper sulfate, $Cu_4(OH)_6SO_4$, occurring in green fibrous masses. [named after A. *Brochant* de Villiers (1773–1840), French mineralogist; see -ITE[1]]

broche (brōsh), *n.* (in weaving tapestries) a device on which the filling yarn is wound, used as a shuttle in passing through the shed of the loom to deposit the yarn. [< F: spindle, a pointed instrument; see BROACH]

bro·ché (brō shā′; *Fr.* brô shā′), *adj., n., pl.* **-chés** (-shāz′; *Fr.* -shā′). —*adj.* **1.** woven with a pattern; brocaded. —*n.* **2.** a pin stripe woven in the warp direction of fabric used in the manufacture of clothing. [< F, ptp. of *brocher* to emboss (linen), weave (cloth) with a figure. See BROACH, BROCADE]

bro·chette (brō shet′; *Fr.* brô shet′), *n., pl.* **-chettes** (-shets′; *Fr.* -shet′). **1.** a skewer, for use in cookery. **2. en brochette** (en, on; *Fr.* äN), on a small spit or skewer. [late ME < MF; OF *brochete.* See BROACH, -ETTE]

bro·chure (brō shŏŏr′), *n.* a pamphlet. [< F, deriv. of *brocher* to stitch (a book). See BROACH, -URE]

brock (brok), *n.* **1.** a European badger. **2.** *Brit.* one who is nasty or contemptible. [ME *brok,* OE *broc* badger < Celt; cf. Ir, Gael *broc,* Welsh *broch*]

brock·age (brok′ij), *n.* *Numis.* a defect or fault imposed on a coin during its minting. [*brock* fragment (ME *brok,* OE *broc;* akin to BREAK) + -AGE]

Brock·en (brok′ən), *n.* a mountain in E West Germany and W East Germany: the highest peak in the Harz Mountains. 3745 ft.

Brock′en bow′ (bō), anticorona.

brock·et (brok′it), *n.* **1.** any of several small, red, South American deer of the genus *Mazama,* having short, unbranched antlers. **2.** the male red deer in the second year, with the first growth of straight horns. [late ME *broket* < AF *broquet,* equiv. to *broque* horn (ML *broca;* see BROACH) + *-et* -ET]

Brock·port (brok′pōrt′, -pôrt′), *n.* a town in W New York. 5256 (1960).

Brock·ton (brok′tən), *n.* a city in E Massachusetts. 72,813 (1960).

Brock·way (brok′wā′), *n.* a town in central Pennsylvania. 2563 (1960).

Bro·cot′ escape′ment (brə kō′, brō′kō), *Horol.* a clock anchor escapement having perpendicular, semicylindrical stones, usually carnelians, as pallets. Also called **pin pallet escapement.** [named after Achille *Brocot* (d. 1878), French horologist]

Brocot′ suspen′sion, *Horol.* a form of pendulum suspension in which the chops are raised or lowered by a gear and screw mechanism operated from the front of the dial in such a way as to alter the virtual length of the pendulum. [see BROCOT ESCAPEMENT]

Brode·hurst (brōd′hûrst), *n.* a boy's given name.

Brod·er·ick (brod′ər ik, brod′rik), *n.* a boy's given name.

bro·die (brō′dē), *n.* (*sometimes cap.*) *Slang.* **1.** a flop; blunder. **2.** a suicidal leap, esp. from a bridge. [after Steve *Brodie,* who said he jumped from Brooklyn Bridge]

Bro·die (brō′dē), *n.* a boy's given name, form of **Broderick.**

broe·boe (brōō′bōō), *n.* *Indonesian.* an easterly foehn in the southwest part of Celebes. Also, **brubu.**

bro·gan (brō′gən), *n.* a coarse, stout shoe, esp. an ankle-high work shoe. Cf. **brogue**[2]. [< Gael: pair of shoes; see BROGUE[2]]

brogh (*Scot.* brokh, brukh), *n.* *Obs.* broch.

Bro·glie (brô glē′), *n.* **1. A·chille Charles Lé·once Vic·tor de** (a shēl′ sharl lā ôns′ vēk tôr′ də), 1785–1870, French statesman. **2.** his grandson **Louis Vic·tor de** (lwē vēk tôr′ də), born 1892, French physicist: Nobel prize 1929. Also, **de Broglie.**

brogue[1] (brōg), *n.* **1.** an Irish accent in the pronunciation of English. **2.** accent (def. 6). [? special use of BROGUE[2]] —**bro′guer·y,** *n.* —**bro′guish,** *adj.*

brogue[2] (brōg), *n.* a durable, comfortable shoe, often having decorative perforations on the vamp and upper. [< Ir *brōg* shoe, OIr *brōce;* c. L *brācae* trousers < Gaulish; see BREECH]

brogue[3] (brōg), *n.* *Scot.* a fraud; trick; prank. [?]

broi·der (broi′dər), *v.t.* *Archaic.* to embroider. [var. of *browder,* ME *broide(n),* *browde(n)* (ptp., taken as inf. of BRAID[1]) + -ER[6]] —**broi′der·er,** *n.* —**broi′der·y,** *n.*

broil[1] (broil), *v.t.* **1.** to cook by direct heat, as on a gridiron or in an oven broiler; grill: *to broil a steak.* **2.** to scorch; make very hot. —*v.i.* **3.** to be subjected to great heat; become broiled. **4.** to burn with impatience, annoyance, etc. —*n.* **5.** the act or state of broiling; state of being broiled. **6.** something broiled: *He ordered a beef broil and salad.* [ME *broille, bruyle* < MF *bruill(ir)* (to) broil, burn, perh. < Gmc; see BROIL[2]] —**broil′ing·ly,** *adv.*

broil[2] (broil), *n.* **1.** an angry quarrel or struggle; disturbance; tumult: *a violent broil over who was at fault.* —*v.i.* **2.** to quarrel; brawl. [late ME *broyle* to bring into confusion < MF *brouill(er)* (to) mix, OF *brooillier* < Gmc; cf. G *brodeln* to bubble (? orig., seethe), equiv. to *brod-* (see BROTH) + *-eln* freq. v. suffix] —**broil′ing·ly,** *adv.*

broil·er (broi′lər), *n.* **1.** any device for broiling meat or fish; a grate, pan, or compartment in a stove for broiling. **2.** a young chicken suitable for broiling. [BROIL[1] + -ER[1]]

bro·kage (brō′kij), *n.* *Archaic.* brokerage. [ME < AF *brocage,* lit., tappage, equiv. to *broc-* tap of a cask (see BROACH) + *-age* -AGE]

broke (brōk), *v.* **1.** a pt. of **break.** **2.** *Nonstandard.* pp. of **break.** **3.** *Archaic.* a pp. of **break.** —*adj.* **4.** *Informal.* without money; penniless; bankrupt. **5. go broke,** *Slang.* **a.** to become destitute of money or possessions. **b.** to go bankrupt: *In that business people are forever going broke.* **6. go for broke,** *Slang.* to exert oneself or employ one's resources to the utmost. —*n.* **7.** *Papermaking.* paper unfit for sale; paper that is to be repulped. **8. brokes,** wool of poor quality taken from the neck and belly of sheep.

bro·ken (brō′kən), *v.* **1.** a pp. of **break.** —*adj.* **2.** reduced to fragments; fragmented. **3.** ruptured; torn; fractured. **4.** *Meteorol.* (of the sky) being more than half, but not totally, covered by clouds. **5.** changing direction abruptly: *The fox ran in a broken line.* **6.** fragmentary or incomplete: *a broken ton of coal weighing 1,500 pounds.* **7.** infringed or violated: *A broken promise is a betrayal of trust.* **8.** interrupted, disrupted, or disconnected: *After the phone call he returned to his broken sleep.* **9.** weakened in strength, spirit, etc.: *His broken health was due to age.* **10.** tamed, trained, or reduced to submission: *The horse was broken to the saddle.* **11.** imperfectly spoken, as language: *Although she has been in America for 50 years, she still speaks broken English.* **12.** spoken in a halting or fragmentary manner, as under emotional strain: *He uttered a few broken words of sorrow.* **13.** not smooth; rough or irregular in texture: *We left the plains and rode through broken country.* **14.** ruined; bankrupt: *the broken fortunes of his family.* **15.** *Papermaking, Print.* a quantity of paper of less than 500 or 1000 sheets. —**bro′ken·ly,** *adv.* —**bro′ken·ness,** *n.*

Bro′ken Ar′row, a town in NE Oklahoma. 5928 (1960).

Bro′ken Bow′ (bō), a town in central Nebraska. 3482 (1960).

bro·ken-check (brō′kən chek′), *n.* *Textiles.* a check pattern in which the rectangular shapes are slightly irregular.

bro′ken col′or, *Painting.* a manner or method of applying colors in short strokes or dots of varying, often contrasting, hue or tone, used esp. in reducing the local color of an area to its component hues. Cf. **impressionism** (def. 1a).

Bro′ken Command′ment, The, a novel (1906) by Tōson Shimazaki. Japanese, **Hakai.**

bro·ken-down (brō′kən doun′), *adj.* shattered or collapsed; having given way with use or age; out of working order: *a broken-down chair.*

bro′ken heart′, despair; disillusionment; devastating sorrow.

bro·ken-heart·ed (brō′kən här′tid), *adj.* burdened with great sorrow, grief, or disappointment. —**bro′ken-heart′ed·ly,** *adv.* —**bro′ken-heart′ed·ness,** *n.*

Bro′ken Hill′, a city in W New South Wales, in SE Australia: mining center. 33,420 (est. 1959).

bro′ken line′, **1.** a discontinuous line or series of line segments, as a series of dashes, or a figure made up of line segments meeting at oblique angles. **2.** a highway marking consisting of a series of disconnected line segments painted between lanes of a roadway, indicating that crossing from one to the other is permissible.

bro′ken lot′. See **odd lot.**

bro′ken ped′iment, a pediment, as over a doorway or window, having its raking cornice interrupted at the crown or apex.

bro′ken wind′ (wind), *Vet. Pathol.* heave (def. 27). —**bro′ken-wind′ed,** *adj.*

bro·ker (brō′kər), *n.* **1.** an agent who buys or sells for a principal on a commission basis without having title to the property. **2.** a middleman or agent. [ME *broco(u)r* << OF *brokeor* (north) < VL **broccātor* tapster. See BROACH, -OR[2]] —**bro′ker·ship′,** *n.*

bro·ker·age (brō′kər ij), *n.* **1.** the business of a broker. **2.** the commission of a broker. [BROKER + -AGE]

bro′ker's loan′, a loan made to a securities broker, with stocks and bonds as collateral.

brol·ly (brol′ē), *n., pl.* **-lies.** *Brit. Slang.* an umbrella. [(UM)BRELL(A) + -Y[2]]

Brom (brom, brum), *n.* a boy's given name.

brom-, var. of **bromo-,** before a vowel.

bro·mal (brō′məl), *n.* *Pharm.* an oily, colorless liquid, CBr_3CHO, used in medicine chiefly as an anodyne and hypnotic. Also called **tribromoacetaldehyde.** [BROM- + -AL[3]]

bro·mate (brō′māt), *n., v.,* **-mat·ed, -mat·ing.** *Chem.* —*n.* **1.** a salt of bromic acid. —*v.t.* **2.** to treat with bromine; brominate. [BROM(IC) + -ATE[2]]

Brom·berg (brom′bûrg; *Ger.* brôm′berkh), *n.* German name of **Bydgoszcz.**

Bro·me (brō′mē), *n.* *Class. Myth.* one of the nymphs who cared for the infant Dionysus.

brome′ grass′ (brōm), any of numerous grasses of the genus *Bromus,* esp. *B. inermis,* a perennial used for hay and pasture. Also called **brome.** [< NL *Brom(us)* genus name (< Gk *brōmos* oats)]

bro·me·li·a·ceous (brō mē′lē ā′shəs), *adj.* belonging to the *Bromeliaceae,* a family of herbaceous, chiefly tropical, American plants, including the pineapple, the Spanish moss, and many ornamentals. [< NL *Bromeli(a)* type genus of family (named after O. *Bromelius* (1639–1705), Swedish botanist) + -ACEOUS]

brom·e·o·sin (brō mē′ə sin), *n.* *Chem.* eosin (def. 1). [BROM- + EOSIN]

Brom·field (brom′fēld′), *n.* **Louis,** 1896–1956, U.S. novelist.

brom·hi·dro·sis (brō′mi drō′sis, brōm′hi-), *n.* *Med.* the secretion of foul-smelling sweat. Also, **bromidrosis.** Also called **osmidrosis.** [BROM- + HIDROSIS]

bro·mic (brō′mik), *adj.* *Chem.* containing pentavalent bromine. [BROM- + -IC]

bro′mic ac′id, *Chem.* an acid, $HBrO_3$, stable only in very dilute solutions, usually produced by the reaction of barium bromate with sulfuric acid: used chiefly as an oxidizing agent in the manufacture of dyes and pharmaceuticals.

bro·mide (brō′mīd, -mid), *n.* **1.** *Chem.* **a.** a salt of hydrobromic acid consisting of two elements one of which is bromine, as sodium bromide, NaBr. **b.** a compound containing bromine, as methyl bromide. **2.** *Informal.* **a.** one who is platitudinous and boring. **b.** a platitude. [BROM- + -IDE; in def. 2 from use of some bromides as sedatives]

bro′mide pa′per, *Photog.* a fast printing paper coated with an emulsion of silver bromide: used mostly for enlargements.

bro·mid·ic (brō mid′ik), *adj.* *Informal.* pertaining or proper to a platitude; being a bromide; trite. [BROMIDE + -IC] —**bro·mid′i·cal·ly,** *adv.*

bro·mi·dro·sis (brō′mi drō′sis), *n.* *Med.* bromhidrosis.

bro·min·ate (brō′mə nāt′), *v.t.,* **-at·ed, -at·ing.** *Chem.* to treat or combine with bromine; bromate. [BROMINE + -ATE[1]] —**bro′mi·na′tion,** *n.*

bro·mine (brō′mēn, -min), *n.* *Chem.* an element that is a dark-reddish, fuming, toxic liquid and a member of the halogen family: obtained from natural brines and ocean water, and used chiefly in the manufacture of gasoline antiknock compounds, pharmaceuticals and dyes. *Symbol:* Br; *at. wt.:* 79.909; *at. no.:* 35; *sp. gr.* (*liquid*): 3.119 at 20°C. [< F *brome* bromine (< Gk *brōmos* stench) + -INE[2]]

bro′mine pentaflu′oride, *Chem.* a colorless, corrosive liquid, BrF_5, used as an oxidizer in liquid rocket propellants.

bro·mise (brō′mīz), *v.t.,* **-mised, -mis·ing.** *Chiefly Brit.* bromize. —**bro′mi·sa′tion,** *n.*

bro·mism (brō′miz əm), *n.* *Pathol.* a condition due to excessive use of bromides, characterized by skin eruptions. Also, **bro·min·ism** (brō′mə niz′əm). [BROM(IDE) + -ISM]

Bro·mi·us (brō′mē əs), *n.* *Class. Myth.* an epithet of Dionysus, meaning "thunder."

bro·mize (brō′mīz), *v.t.,* **-mized, -miz·ing.** *Chem.* to treat or combine with bromine or a bromide. Also, *esp. Brit.* **bromise.** [BROM- + -IZE] —**bro′mi·za′tion,** *n.* —**bro′miz·er,** *n.*

Brom·ley (brom′lē, brum′-), *n.* a boy's given name.

bromo-, a combining form of **bromine,** used esp. before consonants: *bromobenzene.* Also, *esp. before a vowel,* **brom-.**

bro·mo·chlo·ro·meth·ane (brō′mə klôr′ə meth′ān, -klōr′-), *n.* *Chem.* chlorobromomethane. [BROMO- + CHLOROMETHANE]

bro·mo·form (brō′mə fôrm′), *n.* *Chem.* a colorless, heavy liquid, $CHBr_3$, used chiefly as an intermediate in organic synthesis. [BROMO- + -FORM]

bro·moil (brō′moil), *n.* *Photog.* an offset reproduction produced by the bromoil process. [BROM- + OIL]

bro′moil proc′ess, *Photog.* a process for making an offset reproduction by first making a photographic print on paper with a silver bromide emulsion, wetting it, and then using it as a lithographic plate, the lighter parts of the emulsion tending to repel the oil base of the ink while the darker parts tend to hold it.

bro·mo·meth·ane (brō′mə meth′ān), *n.* *Chem.* See **methyl bromide.** [BROMO- + METHANE]

Bromp′ton stock′ (bromp′tən), the stock, *Mathiola incana.* Cf. **stock** (def. 32). [after *Brompton,* a suburb of London, England]

bronch-, var. of **broncho-** before a vowel.

bron·chi (brong′kī), *n.* *Anat.* pl. of **bronchus.**

bron·chi·a (brong′kē ə), *n.* *Anat.* (*construed as pl.*) the ramifications or branches of the bronchi. [< LL < Gk, pl. of *brónchion,* equiv. to *brónch(os)* windpipe + *-ion* dim. suffix]

bron·chi·al (brong′kē əl), *adj.* *Anat.* pertaining to the bronchia or bronchi. [BRONCH- + -IAL] —**bron′chi·al·ly,** *adv.*

bron′chial pneumo′nia, *Pathol.* bronchopneumonia.

bron′chial tube′, a bronchus or any of its ramifications or branches.

bron·chi·ec·ta·sis (brong′kē ek′tə sis), *n.* *Pathol.* a diseased condition in which a bronchus or the bronchi are dilated, characterized by paroxysmal coughing and expectoration of much sputum. [< NL; see BRONCH-, -I-, ECTASIS] —**bron·chi·ec·tat·ic** (brong′kē ek tat′ik), *adj.*

bron·chi·ole (brong′kē ōl′), *n.* *Anat.* a small branch of a bronchus. [< NL *bronchiol(um),* equiv. to *bronchi(a)* BRONCHIA + *-olum* dim. suffix] —**bron·chi·o·lar** (brong′kē ō′lər, brong kī′ə-), *adj.*

bron·chi·tis (brong kī′tis), *n.* *Pathol.* inflammation of the membrane lining of the bronchial tubes. [< NL; see BRONCH-, -ITIS] —**bron·chit·ic** (brong kit′ik), *adj.*

bron·cho (brong′kō), *n., pl.* **-chos.** bronco.

broncho-, a combining form of **bronchus:** *bronchopneumonia.*

bron·cho·bust·er (brong′kō bus′tər), *n.* broncobuster.

bron·cho·cele (brong′kə sēl′), *n.* *Pathol.* **1.** dilatation of a bronchus. **2.** a goiter, esp. a cystic goiter. [< Gk *bronchokḗlē.* See BRONCHO-, -CELE[1]]

bron·cho·pneu·mo·nia (brong′kō nōō mōn′yə, -mō′nē ə, -nyōō-, -nə mōn′-), *n.* *Pathol.* inflammation of the bronchia and lungs; a form of pneumonia. Also called **bronchial pneumonia, catarrhal pneumonia, lobular pneumonia.** [BRONCHO- + PNEUMONIA] —**bron·cho·pneu·mon·ic** (broŋ′kō no͞o mon′ik, -nyo͞o-), *adj.*

bron·chor·rha·gi·a (broŋ′kə rā′jē ə), *n.* *Pathol. Obs.* hemorrhage from the bronchial tubes. [BRONCHO- + -RRHAGIA]

bron·cho·scope (broŋ′kə skōp′), *n.* *Med.* a tubular instrument for examining bronchi and for removing foreign bodies from them. [BRONCHO- + -SCOPE] —**bron·cho·scop·ic** (broŋ′kə skop′ik), *adj.* —**bron′-cho·scop′i·cal·ly,** *adv.* —**bron·chos·co·pist** (broŋ-kos′kə pist), *n.* —**bron·chos′co·py,** *n.*

bron·cho·spasm (broŋ′kə spaz′əm), *n.* spasmodic contraction of the muscular lining of the bronchi, as in asthma, causing difficulty in breathing. [BRONCHO- + SPASM]

bron·chos·to·my (broŋ kos′tə mē), *n., pl.* **-mies.** *Surg.* the operation of forming an opening through the chest wall into a bronchus. [BRONCHO- + -STOMY]

bron·chus (broŋ′kəs), *n., pl.* **-chi** (-kī). *Anat.* either of the two main branches of the trachea. See diag. under **lung.** [< NL < Gk *brónchos* windpipe]

bron·co (broŋ′kō), *n., pl.* **-cos. 1.** a range pony or mustang of the western U.S., esp. one that is not broken, or is only imperfectly broken. **2.** *Canadian Slang.* a Britisher, esp. a recent British immigrant. Also, **bron-cho.** [< MexSp, short for Sp *potro bronco* colt untamed (in MexSp: wild horse, half-tamed horse); appar. nasalized var. of L *broccus* projecting, hence rough; see BROACH]

bron·co·bust·er (broŋ′kō bus′tər), *n.* one who breaks broncos to the saddle. Also, **bronchobuster.** [BRONCO + BUSTER]

Bron·son (bron′sən), *n.* a boy's given name.

Bron·të (bron′tē), *n.* **1. Anne** (*Acton Bell*), 1820–49, English novelist. **2.** her sister, **Charlotte** (*Currer Bell*), 1816–55, English novelist. **3.** her sister, **Emily Jane** (*Ellis Bell*), 1818–48, English novelist.

Bron·tes (bron′tēz), *n.* *Class. Myth.* one of the Cyclopes.

bron·to·saur (bron′tə-sôr′), *n.* an amphibious, herbivorous dinosaur of the genus *Brontosaurus,* from the Jurassic period of North America. [*bronto-* (comb. form of Gk *brontḗ* thunder) + -SAURUS]

Brontosaur, *Apatasaurus excelsus* (Height 12 ft.; length 60 ft.)

Bronx (broŋks), *n.* **The,** a borough of New York City, N of Manhattan. 1,424,815 (1960); 43.4 sq. mi. —**Bronx′ite,** *n.*

Bronx′ cheer′, *U.S.* a vulgar spluttering noise made with the lips and tongue to show contempt or disgust. Also called **raspberry.** Cf. **bird** (def. 12).

Bronx·ville (broŋks′vil), *n.* a town in SE New York. 6744 (1960).

bronze (bronz), *n., v.,* **bronzed, bronz·ing,** *adj.* —*n.* **1.** *Metall.* **a.** any of various alloys consisting essentially of copper and tin, the tin content not exceeding 11 percent. **b.** any of various other alloys having a large copper content. **2.** a metallic brownish color. **3.** a work of art, as a statue, statuette, bust, or medal, composed of bronze, whether cast, hammered, etc. **4.** *Numis.* a coin made of bronze, esp. one from the Roman Empire. —*v.t.* **5.** to give the appearance or color of bronze to. **6.** to make brown, as by exposure to the sun: *The sun bronzed his face.* **7.** *Print.* **a.** to apply a fine metallic powder to (the ink of a printed surface) in order to create a glossy effect. **b.** to apply a fine metallic powder to (areas of a reproduction proof on acetate) in order to increase their opacity. —*adj.* **8.** having the color bronze. [earlier *bronzo* < It, prob. back formation from *bronzino* (adj.) < L (*aes*) *Brundusīnum* (brass) of Brindisi] —**bronz′y, bronze′like′,** *adj.*

Bronze′ Age′, 1. a period in the history of mankind, following the Stone Age and preceding the Iron Age, during which bronze weapons and implements were used. **2.** (*l.c.*) *Class. Myth.* the third of the four ages of man, marked by war and violence: regarded as inferior to the silver age but superior to the following iron age.

bronzed′ grack′le, a subspecies of the purple grackle, *Quiscalus quiscula versicolor,* having bronzy, iridescent plumage.

bronze′ diabe′tes, *Pathol.* hemochromatosis. Also, **bronzed′ diabe′tes.**

Bron·zi·no (brôn dzē′nô), *n.* **A·gno·lo (di Co·si·mo di Ma·ri·a·no)** (ä′nyô lô dē kô′zē mô dē mä rē ä′nô), 1502–72, Italian painter.

bronz·ite (bron′zīt), *n.* *Mineral.* a variety of orthorhombic hydroxene containing from 5 percent to 14 percent ferrous oxide. [BRONZE + -ITE[1]; so called from its sheen]

broo (bro͞o; *Scot.* brœ, bry), *n.* *Scot. and North Eng.* any clear, palatable liquid, as broth, juice, or water. Also, **bree.** [late ME *bro(o),* perh. c. G *Brühe* broth, gravy, juice, Crimean Goth *broe* bread]

brooch (brōch, bro͞och), *n.* a clasp or ornament having a pin at the back for passing through the clothing and a catch for securing the point of the pin. [sp. var. of BROACH]

brood (bro͞od), *n.* **1.** a number of young produced or hatched at one time; a family of offspring or young. **2.** a breed, species, group, or kind: *The museum exhibited a brood of modern paintings.* —*v.t.* **3.** to sit upon (eggs) to hatch, as a bird; incubate. **4.** (of a bird) to warm, protect, or cover (young) with the wings or body. **5.** to think persistently or moodily about; ponder: *He brooded the problem.* —*v.i.* **6.** to sit upon eggs to be hatched, as a bird. **7.** to dwell on a subject or to meditate with morbid persistence. **8. brood above** or **over,** to cover, loom, or seem to fill the atmosphere or scene: *The haunted house on the hill brooded above the village. Hate brooded over the town.* **9. brood over** or **on,** to meditate anxiously on a subject; dwell morbidly upon: *He took to brooding over the death of his brother.* —*adj.* **10.** kept for breeding purposes: *The brood bay foaled a handsome colt.* [ME; OE *brōd;* c. D *broed,* G *Brut.* See BREED] —**brood′less,** *adj.*

—**Syn. 1.** BROOD, LITTER refer to young creatures. BROOD is esp. applied to the young of fowls and birds hatched from eggs at one time and raised under their mother's care: *a brood of young turkeys.* LITTER is applied to a group of young animals brought forth at a birth: *a litter of kittens or pups.* **2.** line, stock, strain.

brood′ bud′, *Bot.* **1.** a bulbil. **2.** a soredium. **3.** a gemma.

brood·er (bro͞o′dər), *n.* **1.** a device or structure for the artificial rearing of young chickens or other birds. **2.** one who or that which broods. [BROOD + -ER[1]]

brood·mare (bro͞od′mâr′), *n.* a mare used for breeding. [BROOD + MARE[1]]

brood′ patch′. See **incubation patch.**

brood·y (bro͞o′dē), *adj.,* **brood·i·er, brood·i·est. 1.** moody; gloomy. **2.** inclined to brood or sit on eggs: *a broody hen.* [BROOD + -Y[1]] —**brood′i·ness,** *n.*

brook[1] (bro͝ok), *n.* a small, natural stream of fresh water. [ME; OE *brōc* stream; c. D *broek,* G *Bruch* marsh] —**brook′less,** *adj.* —**brook′like′,** *adj.* —**Syn.** rivulet, run, burn, branch, rill.

brook[2] (bro͝ok), *v.t.* to bear; suffer; tolerate: *I will brook no interference.* [ME *brouke(n),* OE *brūcen;* c. D *bruiken,* G *brauchen;* akin to Goth *brukjan,* L *fru(ī)* to enjoy] —**brook′a·ble,** *adj.*

Brooke (bro͝ok), *n.* **1. Sir James,** 1803–68, British soldier and adventurer: rajah of Sarawak. **2. Rupert,** 1887–1915, English poet.

Brook′ Farm′, a farm in West Roxbury, Massachusetts where a communistic community was established from 1841 to 1847: it was reorganized as a Fourieristic phalanx during the final two years.

Brook·field (bro͝ok′fēld′), *n.* **1.** a city in NE Illinois, near Chicago. 20,429 (1960). **2.** a city in SE Wisconsin, near Milwaukee. 19,812 (1960). **3.** a town in central Missouri. 5694 (1960).

Brook·ha·ven (bro͝ok hā′vən), *n.* **1.** a town in SW Mississippi. 9885 (1960). **2.** a town in SE Pennsylvania. 5280 (1960).

brook·ie (bro͝ok′ē), *n.* the brook trout of eastern North America. [BROOK[1] + -IE]

Brook·ings (bro͝ok′iŋz), *n.* **1. Robert Som·ers** (sum′ərz), 1850–1932, U.S. merchant and philanthropist. **2.** a city in E South Dakota. 10,558 (1960). **3.** a town in SW Oregon. 2637 (1960).

brook·ite (bro͝ok′īt), *n.* *Mineral.* an allomorph of rutile and anatase. [named after H. J. *Brooke* (1771–1857), English mineralogist; see -ITE[1]]

Brook·lawn (bro͝ok′lôn′), *n.* a town in SW New Jersey. 2504 (1960).

brook·let (bro͝ok′lit), *n.* a small brook. [BROOK[1] + -LET]

brook·lime (bro͝ok′līm′), *n.* any of various speedwells found along brooks, in marshes, etc., as *Veronica americana* **(American brooklime).** [late ME *brokelemke,* equiv. to *broke* BROOK[1] + *lemke,* OE *hleomoce* speedwell, c. MLG *lömeke*]

Brook·line (bro͝ok′līn′), *n.* a town in E Massachusetts, near Boston. 54,044 (1960).

Brook·lyn (bro͝ok′lin), *n.* a borough of New York City, on W Long Island. 2,627,319 (1960); 76.4 sq. mi. —**Brook·lyn·ite** (bro͝ok′lə nīt′), *n.*

Brook′lyn Bridge′, a suspension bridge over the East River, in New York City, connecting Manhattan and Brooklyn: built 1867–84. 5989 ft. long.

Brook′lyn Cen′ter, a city in SE Minnesota, near Minneapolis. 24,356 (1960).

Brook·lyn·ese (bro͝ok′lə nēz′, -nēs′, bro͝ok′lə nēz′, -nēs′), *n.* the pronunciation, vocabulary, etc., thought to be characteristic of a person living in or coming from New York City, esp. the borough of Brooklyn. [BROOKLYN + -ESE]

Brooks (bro͝oks), *n.* **1. Gwendolyn,** born 1917, U.S. poet and novelist. **2. Phillips,** 1835–93, U.S. Protestant Episcopal bishop and pulpit orator. **3. Van Wyck,** 1886–1963, U.S. author and critic. **4.** a boy's given name.

Brooks′ Range′, a mountain range in N Alaska, forming a watershed between the Yukon River and the Arctic Ocean: highest peak, 9239 ft.

Brooks·ville (bro͝oks′vil), *n.* a town in central Florida. 3301 (1960).

brook′ trout′, 1. Also called **speckled trout.** a common trout, *Salvelinus fontinalis,* of eastern North America. **2.** See **brown trout.**

Brook·ville (bro͝ok′vil), *n.* **1.** a town in central Pennsylvania. 4620 (1960). **2.** a town in W Ohio. 3184 (1960). **3.** a town in SE Indiana. 2596 (1960).

brook·weed (bro͝ok′wēd′), *n.* either of two Old World primulaceous plants having small white flowers, *Samolus Valerandi* or *S. floribundus,* the latter naturalized in North America. [BROOK[1] + WEED[1]]

broom (bro͞om, bro͝om), *n.* **1.** an implement for sweeping, consisting of a brush of straw or stiff strands of synthetic material bound tightly to the end of a long handle. **2.** any of the shrubby fabaceous plants of the genus *Cytisus,* esp. *C. scoparius,* common in Western Europe, which grows on uncultivated ground and has long, slender branches having yellow flowers. **3.** *Building Trades.* the crushed and spread part at the head of a wooden pile after driving. —*v.t.* **4.** to sweep: *Broom the porch.* **5.** to splinter or fray mechanically. **6.** to crush and spread the top of (a piling, tent peg, etc.) by pounding or driving with a hammer or the like. —*v.i.* **7.** (of a piling, tent peg, etc.) to be crushed and spread at the top from being driven. [ME *brome,* OE *brōm;* c. D *braam* bramble, G *Bram* broom, *Brombeere* blackberry] —**broom′y,** *adj.*

broom·corn (bro͞om′kôrn′, bro͝om′-), *n.* any of several varieties of sorghum having a long, stiff-branched panicle used in the manufacture of brooms. [BROOM + CORN[1]]

broom·rape (bro͞om′rāp′, bro͝om′-), *n.* any of various parasitic plants, esp. of the genus *Orobanche,* living on the roots of broom and other plants. [half trans., half adoption of ML *rāpum genistae* tuber of the broom plant]

broom·squire (bro͞om′skwīər′, bro͝om′-), *n.* *Brit. Dial.* a Gypsy squatter who earns a living by making brooms out of heather. [BROOM + SQUIRE]

broom·stick (bro͞om′stik′, bro͝om′-), *n.* the long sticklike handle of a broom. [BROOM + STICK[1]]

bros., brothers. Also, **Bros.**

brose (brōz), *n.* *Scot.* a dish made by stirring boiling liquid into oatmeal or other meal. [ME *broys,* etc. < OF *broez;* see BREWIS] —**bros′y,** *adj.*

Brot·e·as (brot′ē əs), *n.* *Class. Myth.* a son of Tantalus made insane for denying the divinity of Artemis.

broth (brôth, broth), *n.* **1.** thin soup of concentrated meat or fish stock. **2.** water that has been boiled with meat, fish, vegetables, or barley. [ME, OE; c. Icel *broth,* OHG *brod;* akin to BREW] —**broth′y,** *adj.*

broth·el (broth′əl, broth′-, brôth′əl, -thəl), *n.* a house or apartment where women work as prostitutes; bordello. [short for *brothel-house* whore-house; ME *brothel* harlot, orig. worthless person, equiv. to *broth-* (ptp. s. of *brethen,* OE *brēothan* to decay, degenerate) + *-el* n. suffix] —**broth′el·like′,** *adj.*

broth·er (bruth′ər *or, for* 7, bruth′ûr′), *n., pl.* **brothers,** (*Archaic*) **brethren;** *interj.;* *v.* —*n.* **1.** a male offspring having both parents in common with another offspring; a male sibling. **2.** Also called **half brother.** a male offspring having only one parent in common with another offspring. **3.** a male numbered among the same kinship group, nationality, profession, etc., as another; an associate; a fellow member, fellow countryman, fellow man, etc.: *a fraternity brother.* **4.** *Eccles.* **a.** (*often cap.*) a male numbered among the lay members of a religious organization which has a priesthood. **b.** a man who devotes himself to the duties of a religious order without taking holy orders, or while preparing for holy orders. **5. brothers,** all members of a particular race, or of the human race in general: *All men are brothers.* **6.** *Slang.* fellow; buddy: *Brother, can you spare a dime?* —*interj.* **7.** *Slang.* (used to express disappointment, disgust, or surprise at another's audacity). —*v.t.* **8.** to treat or address as a brother. [ME; OE *brōthor;* c. D *broeder,* G *Bruder,* Icel *brōthir,* Goth *brothar,* Skt *bhrátr,* Gk *phrā́tēr,* L *frāter*] —**broth′er·less,** *adj.* —**broth′er·like′,** *adj.*

—**Syn. 1.** BROTHERS, BRETHREN are plurals of *brother.* BROTHERS are kinsmen, sons of the same parents: *My mother lives with my brothers.* BRETHREN, now archaic in the foregoing sense, is used of male members of a congregation or of a fraternal organization: *The brethren will meet at the church.*

broth·er·hood (bruth′ər ho͝od′), *n.* **1.** the condition or quality of being a brother or brothers. **2.** the quality of being brotherly; fellowship. **3.** a fraternal or trade organization. **4.** all those engaged in a particular trade or profession or sharing a common interest or quality. **5.** the belief that all men should act brotherly toward one another, regardless of differences in race, creed, nationality, etc. [ME *brithirhod* (see BROTHER, -HOOD); r. early ME *brotherhede;* see -HEAD]

broth·er-in-law (bruth′ər in lô′), *n., pl.* **broth·ers-in-law. 1.** the brother of one's husband or wife. **2.** the husband of one's sister. **3.** (loosely) the husband of one's wife's or husband's sister. [ME]

Broth′er Jon′athan, *Brit. Archaic.* **1.** the government of the United States. **2.** the typical American.

broth·er·ly (bruth′ər lē), *adj.* **1.** of, like, or befitting a brother; fraternal; affectionate and loyal: *brotherly love.* —*adv.* **2.** *Archaic.* as a brother; fraternally. [ME; OE *brōthorlīc.* See BROTHER, -LY] —**broth′er·li·ness,** *n.*

Broth′er of the Chris′tian Schools′, *Rom. Cath. Ch.* **1.** a member of a congregation of brothers, founded in France in 1684 for the education of the poor. **2.** Also, **Irish Christian Brother.** a member of a congregation of teaching brothers, founded in Ireland in 1802. Also called **Christian Brother.**

Broth′ers Kar·a·maz′ov, The (kar′ə maz′ov, -ôv, -ôf, -əv; *Russ.* kä rä mä′zof), a novel (1880) by Dostoevski.

Broth′ers of the Coast′, a group of Caribbean pirates of the 16th and 17th centuries.

Broth′ers of the Com′mon Life′. See **Brethren of the Common Life.**

brot·u·la (broch′ə lə, brot′yə-), *n.* any of several chiefly deep-sea fishes of the family *Brotulidae,* related to the blennies. [< NL *Brotula* genus name < AmerSp *brótula* kind of fish, lit., little bud, equiv. to *brot(ón)* bud + *-ula* -ULE]

brough (*Scot.* brokh, brukh), *n.* *Obs.* broch.

brough·am (bro͞o′əm, bro͞om, brō′əm), *n.* **1.** a four-wheeled, boxlike, closed carriage for two or four persons, having the driver's perch outside. **2.** *Auto. Obs.* **a.** a limousine having an open driver's compartment. **b.** an early type of automobile resembling a coupé, often powered by an electric motor. [named after Lord *Brougham* (1778–1868), English statesman]

Brougham (def. 1)

brought (brôt), *v.* pt. and pp. of **bring.**

brou·ha·ha (bro͞o hä′hä, bro͞o′hä hä′), *n.* **1.** excited public interest, discussion, or the like, as the clamor attending some sensational event: *The brouhaha followed disclosures of graft at City Hall.* **2.** an episode involving excitement, confusion, turmoil, etc., esp. a broil over a minor or ridiculous cause: *A brouhaha by the baseball players resulted in three black eyes.* [< F; imit.]

brouil·lé (bro͞o yā′), *adj.* *French.* scrambled.

Broun (bro͞on), *n.* **(Matthew) Heywood (Campbell),** 1888–1939, U.S. journalist, essayist, and novelist.

Brou·wer (brou′ər; *Flemish, Du.* brou′wər), *n.* **1. A·dri·aen** (ä′drē än′), 1606?–38, Flemish painter. **2. Luit·zen Eg·ber·tus Jan** (loit′sən ekh ber′təs yän), born 1881, Dutch mathematician and philosopher.

Brou′wer fixed′-point′ the′orem (brou′ər fikst′point′), *Math.* the theorem that for any continuous transformation of a circle into itself, including its boundary, there is at least one point that is mapped to itself. [named after L. E. J. BROUWER]

brow (brou), *n.* **1.** *Anat.* the ridge over the eye. **2.** the hair growing on that ridge; eyebrow. **3.** the forehead: *He wore his hat low over his brow.* **4.** a person's countenance or mien. **5.** the edge of a steep place: *She looked down over the brow of the hill.* **6.** *Naut.* **a.** eyebrow (def. 5). **b.** gangplank. [ME *browe,* OE *brū;* akin to Icel *brūn,* Skt *bhrūs*] —**brow′less,** *adj.*

brow′ ant′ler, the first prong from the base of a stag's antler. See diag. under **antler.**

brow·beat (brou′bēt′), *v.t.,* **-beat, -beat·en, -beat·ing.** to intimidate by overbearing looks or words; bully: *She browbeat him into agreeing.* [BROW + BEAT] —**brow′beat′er,** *n.*

brown (broun), *n.* **1.** a dark shade with a yellowish or reddish hue. **2.** a black horse with brown points. **3.** *Brit. Slang.* any copper coin. —*adj.* **4.** of the color brown. **5.** (of animals) having skin, fur, hair, or feathers of that color. **6.** sunburned or tanned. **7.** (of persons) having the skin naturally pigmented a brown color. **8. do it up brown,** *Slang.* to do thoroughly, excellently, or perfectly: *When she gives a dinner party, she always does it up brown.* —*v.t., v.i.* **9.** to make or become brown. **10.** to fry, saute, or scorch slightly in cooking: *She browned the onions and added them to the stew. The potatoes browned in the pan.* **11. browned off,** *Slang.* dissatisfied; angry; fed up: *After months of waiting for new equipment the football team was browned off. He was browned off at his boss because he didn't get a raise.* [ME; OE *brūn;* c. D *bruin,* G *braun,* Icel *brūnn;* akin to Lith *brunas* brown] —**brown′ish, brown′y,** *adj.* —**brown′ness,** *n.*

Brown (broun), *n.* **1. Charles Brock·den** (brok′dən), 1771–1810, U.S. novelist. **2. James Nathaniel** (*Jimmy*), born 1936, U.S. football player. **3. John** (*"Old Brown of Osawatomie"*), 1800–59, U.S. abolitionist: leader of the attack at Harpers Ferry where he was captured, tried for treason, and hanged. **4. Robert,** 1773–1858, Scottish botanist. **5.** a boy's given name.

brown′ al′ga, an alga of the class *Phaeophyceae,* usually brown owing to the presence of brown pigments in addition to the chlorophyll.

brown′ bear′, 1. a variety of the American black bear, having a brownish coat. **2.** a European bear, *Ursus arctos,* having a brownish coat.

brown′ belt′, *Judo.* a brown waistband, to be worn with a judo costume, conferred by a judo association on a player, usually in his fourth year of training. Cf. **black belt** (def. 3), **blue belt, green belt** (def. 2), **white belt.**

brown′ bent′, a perennial grass, *Agrostis canina,* of North America, used for lawns. Also called **dog bent, velvet bent.** [so called from its dark tufts]

brown′ bet′ty, a baked pudding made of apples or other fruit, bread crumbs, sugar, butter, spice, etc.

brown′ bread′, 1. any bread made of flour darker in color than the bolted wheat flour, esp. graham or whole wheat bread. **2.** See **Boston brown bread.**

brown′ bull′head, a fresh-water catfish, *Ictalurus nebulosus,* of eastern North America, having an olive to brown body with dark markings on the sides.

brown′ but′ter. See **beurre noir.**

brown′ can′ker, *Plant Pathol.* a fungous disease of roses, characterized by leaf and flower lesions, stem cankers surrounded by a reddish-purple border, and dieback.

brown′ coal′, lignite.

brown′ coat′, 1. (in plastering) a coat laid over the scratch coat before the finish coat is applied. **2.** arriccio.

brown′ creep′er. See under **creeper** (def. 5).

Browne (broun), *n.* **1. Charles Far·rer** (far′ər), (*"Artemus Ward"*), 1834–67, U.S. humorist. **2. Sir Thomas,** 1605–82, English physician and author.

brown′-eyed Su′san (broun′īd′), a biennial herb, *Rudbeckia triloba,* of the southeastern U.S., having yellow ray flowers with an orange or brown base and brownish-black disk flowers.

brown′ hack′le, *Angling.* an artificial fly having a peacock herl body, golden tag and tail, and brown hackle.

brown′ heart′, *Plant Pathol.* a disease of stored apples, a brown discoloration of the flesh, resulting from high concentrations of carbon dioxide.

brown′ hem′atite, *Mineral.* limonite.

brown′ hye′na, a hyena, *Hyaena brunnea,* of southern Africa, having a blackish-gray coat. Also called **strand wolf.**

Brown′i·an move′ment (brou′nē ən), the irregular motion of small particles suspended in a liquid or a gas, caused by the bombardment of the particles by molecules of the medium: first observed by Robert Brown in 1827. Also called **Brown′ian mo′tion, pedesis.** [BROWN + -IAN]

brown·ie (brou′nē), *n.* **1.** (in folklore) a little brown goblin, esp. one who helps secretly in household work. **2.** *U.S.* a small, chewy, chocolate cake or cooky, often containing nuts. **3.** (*cap.*) a member of the junior division (ages 8–11) of the Girl Scouts or the Girl Guides. [BROWN + -IE]
—**Syn. 1.** See **fairy.**

Brown·ie (brou′nē), *n. Trademark.* an inexpensive camera.

Brown·ing (brou′ning), *n.* **1. Elizabeth Bar·rett** (bar′it), 1806–61, English poet. **2. John Moses,** 1885–1926, U.S. designer of firearms. **3. Robert,** 1812–89, English poet (husband of Elizabeth Barrett Browning).

Brown′ing automat′ic ri′fle, an air-cooled, fully automatic rifle capable of firing 200 to 350 rounds per minute. *Abbr.:* BAR [named after J. M. BROWNING]

brown′ing trow′el, a trowel for rough plastering.

Brown′lee Park′ (broun′lē), a town in S Michigan. 3307 (1960).

brown-nose (broun′nōz′), *v.,* **-nosed, -nos·ing,** *n. Slang.* —*v.i.* **1.** to curry favor; to behave obsequiously. —*v.t.* **2.** to seek favors from (a person) in an obsequious manner; fawn over (a person): *He's always brown-nosing the boss for a raise.* —*n.* **3.** Also, **brown′-nos′er.** a toady; obsequious sycophant. Cf. **apple-polish.**

brown·out (broun′out′), *n.* **1.** the elimination of some or reduction of all electric lights of a city, esp. as a precaution in time of war: *The New York City brownout in World War II prevented ships in the bay from being silhouetted against the skyline at night.* **2.** any curtailment of electric power, as by a severe storm. [BROWN + OUT, modeled on *blackout*]

brown·print (broun′print′), *n.* a process of photographic reproduction using a mixture of iron and silver salts to produce a white image on a sepia ground. [BROWN + PRINT, modeled on *blueprint*]

brown′ rat′. See **Norway rat.**

brown′ rice′, rice from which the bran layers and germs have not been removed by polishing.

brown′ rot′, *Plant Pathol.* a disease, esp. of apples, peaches, plums, and cherries, characterized by browning and decay of tissues, caused by fungi of the genus *Sclerotinia.*

brown′ sauce′, a basic sauce made from reduced meat stock; espagnole. Also called **sauce espagnole.**

Browns·burg (brounz′bûrg), *n.* a town in central Indiana. 4478 (1960).

Brown's′ Descent′, (or *The Willy-Nilly Slide*) a poem (1916) by Robert Frost.

Brown′ Shirt′, 1. a member of the Nazi Sturmabteilung; storm trooper: so called from the color of the shirt worn as part of the uniform. **2.** Also, **brown′-shirt′.** any fascist.

brown′ spot′, *Plant Pathol.* a disease of plants, characterized by irregular, brownish lesions on the fruit and foliage and by stem cankers, caused by any of several fungi, as *Ceratophorum setosum* or *Cephalosporium apii.*

brown′ stem′ rot′, *Plant Pathol.* a disease of soybeans, characterized by brown discoloration and decay of internal tissues of the stem and leaf, caused by a fungus, *Cephalosporium gregatum.*

brown·stone (broun′stōn′), *U.S.* —*n.* **1.** a reddish-brown sandstone, used extensively as a building material. **2.** Also called **brown′stone front′.** a building, esp. a row house, fronted with this stone. —*adj.* **3.** *Archaic.* belonging or pertaining to the well-to-do class. [BROWN + STONE]

brown′ stud′y, deep, serious absorption in thought: *Lost in a brown study, she was oblivious to the noise.*

brown′ sug′ar, unrefined or partially refined sugar.

Browns·ville (brounz′vil), *n.* **1.** a seaport in S Texas, near the mouth of the Rio Grande. 48,040 (1960). **2.** a town in SW Pennsylvania. 6055 (1960). **3.** a town in W Tennessee. 5424 (1960).

Brown′ Swiss′, one of a breed of brownish dairy cattle raised originally in Switzerland.

brown′-tail moth′ (broun′tāl′), a white moth, *Nygmia phaerrhoea,* having a brown tuft at the end of the abdomen, the larvae of which feed on the foliage of shade and fruit trees. Also called **brown′tail′.**

brown′ thrash′er, a common songbird, *Toxostoma rufum,* of the eastern U.S., having reddish-brown plumage. Also called **brown′ thrush′.**

brown′ trout′, a common trout, *Salmo trutta fario,* found in streams of northern Europe.

Brown·wood (broun′wo͝od′), *n.* a city in central Texas. 16,974 (1960).

browse (brouz), *v.,* **browsed, brows·ing,** *n.* —*v.t.* **1.** (of cattle, deer, etc.) to eat; nibble at; eat from. **2.** (of cattle, deer, etc.) to graze; feed on; pasture on. **3.** to look through or glance at casually: *He's browsing the shelves for something to read.* —*v.i.* **4.** (of cattle, deer, etc.) to graze. **5.** to glance at random through a book, magazine, etc. **6.** to look leisurely at goods displayed for sale, as in a booth or store. —*n.* **7.** tender shoots or twigs of shrubs and trees as food for cattle, deer, etc. **8.** the act or an instance of browsing. [late ME *browse(n)* < ?] —**brows′er,** *n.*

Broz (*Serbo-Croatian.* brôz), *n.* **Jo·sip** (yô′sip). See **Tito, Marshal.**

Br. Som., British Somaliland.

B.R.T., Brotherhood of Railroad Trainmen.

Bru·ant (bʀʏ äN′), *n.* **Li·bé·ral** (lē bā räl′), c1635–1697, French architect.

Bru·beck (bro͞o′bek), *n.* **David Warren** (*Dave*), born 1920, U.S. jazz pianist and composer.

bru·bu (bro͞o′bo͞o), *n. Indonesian.* broeboe.

Bruce (bro͞os), *n.* **1. Sir David,** 1855–1931, Australian physician. **2. Robert.** See **Robert I** (def. 1). **3. Stanley Melbourne** (*1st Viscount Bruce of Melbourne*), 1883–1967, Australian statesman: prime minister 1923–29. **4.** a crater in the first quadrant and near the center of the face of the moon: about three miles in diameter. **5.** a boy's given name.

bru·cel·la (bro͞o sel′ə), *n., pl.* **-cel·lae** (-sel′ē), **-cel·las.** *Bacteriol.* any of several rod-shaped, aerobic, parasitic bacteria of the genus *Brucella,* certain species of which, as *B. melitensis,* are pathogenic for man and animals. [< NL; named after Sir David BRUCE + L *-ella* fem. dim. suffix]

bru·cel·lo·sis (bro͞o′sə lō′sis), *n. Pathol.* infection with bacteria of the *Brucella* group, frequently causing abortions in animals and remittent fever in man. Also called **undulant fever, Malta fever, Mediterranean fever, Rock fever.** [BRUCELL(A) + -OSIS]

Bruch (bʀo͝okh), *n.* **Max** (mäks), 1838–1920, German composer and conductor.

bruc·ine (bro͞o′sēn, -sin), *n. Chem.* a white, crystalline, bitter, slightly water-soluble, very poisonous alkaloid, $C_{23}H_{26}N_2O_4$, obtained from the nux vomica tree *Strychnos nux vomica,* and from other species of the same genus, resembling but not as powerful as strychnine in its pharmacological action: used chiefly in the denaturation of alcohol. [named after J. *Bruce* (1730–94), Scottish explorer; see -INE[2]]

bru·cite (bro͞o′sīt), *n.* a mineral, magnesium hydroxide, $Mg(OH)_2$, occurring in tabular, foliated crystals, used in magnesia refractories. [named after A. *Bruce* (1777–1818), American mineralogist; see -ITE[1]]

Brü·cke, Die (dē bʀʏ′kə), *German.* (in fine art) a group of German painters of the early 20th century whose works were characterized by a use of Fauve color and forms distorted for emotive purposes. Also called **Bridge.** Cf. **Expressionism.** [lit., the bridge]

Bruck·ner (bruk′nər; *Ger.* bʀo͝ok′nəʀ), *n.* **An·ton** (an′tən, -ton, -tōn; *Ger.* än′tōn), 1824–96, Austrian composer and organist.

Brue·ghel (broi′gəl, bro͞o′-; *Flemish* bʀœ′gəl), *n.* Breughel. Also, **Brue′gel.**

Bru·ges (bro͞o′jiz, bro͞ozh; *Fr.* bʀʏzh), *n.* a city in NW Belgium: connected by canal with its seaport, Zeebrugge. 52,448 (est. 1964). Flemish, **Brug·ge** (bʀœkh′ə).

brugh (*Scot.* bʀukh), *n. Obs.* broch.

Bruhn (bro͞on), *n.* **Erik** (*Belton Evers*), born 1928, Danish ballet dancer.

bru·in (bro͞o′in), *n.* a bear. [late ME *bruyn* < MD: lit., the brown one, name of the bear in the fable of Reynard the Fox]

bruise (bro͞oz), *v.,* **bruised, bruis·ing,** *n.* —*v.t.* **1.** to injure by striking or pressing, without breaking the skin: *The blow bruised his arm. Her pinching bruised the peaches.* **2.** to injure or hurt superficially, as with an insult or unkind remark: *to bruise a person's feelings.* **3.** to crush (drugs or food) by beating or pounding. **4.** *Metalworking.* to injure the surface of (an ingot or finished object) by collision. —*v.i.* **5.** to develop or bear a discolored spot on the skin as the result of a blow, fall, etc. **6.** to be injured superficially: *His feelings bruise easily.* —*n.* **7.** an injury due to bruising; contusion. [ME *bro(o)sen, bres(s)en, bris(s)en, bruisen,* OE *brȳsan, brēsan,* equiv. to MF *bruisier* to shatter < Celt; cf. Ir *brūigim* I bruise, mash]

bruis·er (bro͞o′zər), *n. Informal.* a strong, tough person: *The boxer was over six feet tall and weighed 250 pounds—a real bruiser.* [BRUISE + -ER[1]]

bruit (bro͞ot), *v.t.* **1.** to voice abroad; rumor (used chiefly in the passive): *The report was bruited through the village.* —*n.* **2.** *Med.* any generally abnormal sound or murmur heard on auscultation. **3.** *Archaic.* rumor; report. **4.** *Archaic.* noise; din; clamor. [late ME < MF < ML *brūgīt(us)* a roar, rumble, equiv. to *brūg-* (< ?) + *-ītus* -ITE[2]] —**bruit′er,** *n.*

bru·ja (bro͞o′hä), *n., pl.* **-jas** (-häs). *Spanish.* a witch; sorceress.

bru·jo (bro͞o′hô), *n., pl.* **-jos** (-hôs). *Spanish.* a wizard or conjurer; sorcerer.

bru·lé (bro͞o lā′; *Fr.* bʀʏ lā′), *n., pl.* **-lés** (-lāz′; *Fr.* -lā′). **1.** (in the Pacific Northwest) an area of forest destroyed by fire. **2.** *Canadian.* land covered with rocks or scrub growth. Also, **bru·lée′.** [< F: burnt, ptp. of *brûler;* see BROIL[1]]

brul·yie (bro͞ol′ē; *Scot.* bʀʏl′yē), *n. Scot. and North Eng.* a disturbance; broil. Also, **brul·zie** (bro͞ol′ē; *Scot.* bʀʏl′yē). [north var. of BROIL[2]] —**brul′yie·ment,** *n.*

Bru·maire (bʀʏ meʀ′), *n.* (in the French Revolutionary calendar) the second month of the year, extending from October 22 to November 20. [< F, equiv. to *brume* BRUME + *-aire* -ARY]

bru·mal (bro͞o′məl), *adj.* wintry. [< L *brūmāl(is)* of, pertaining to winter. See BRUME, -AL[1]]

brum·by (brum′bē), *n., pl.* **-bies.** *Australian.* a wild horse. [native Austral]

brume (bro͞om), *n.* mist; fog. [< F: fog < Pr *bruma* < L: winter, orig. winter solstice, contr. of *brevima (*diēs*) shortest (day); see BREVE] —**bru·mous** (bro͞o′məs), *adj.*

brum·ma·gem (brum′ə jəm), *adj.* **1.** showy but inferior and worthless. —*n.* **2.** a showy but inferior and worthless thing. [an old local var. of BIRMINGHAM, England, by metathesis in first syllable and dissimilative loss of second nasal]

Brum·mell (brum′əl), *n.* **George Bryan II.** See **Beau Brummell.**

brunch (brunch), *n.* **1.** a late-morning meal that serves both as breakfast and lunch. —*v.i.* **2.** to eat brunch: *They brunch at 11:00 on Sunday.* [BR(EAKFAST + L)UNCH]

brunch′ coat′, a knee-length housecoat.

Brun·didge (brun′dij), *n.* a town in SE Alabama. 2523 (1960).

Brun·dis·i·um (brun diz′ē əm), *n.* ancient name of **Brindisi.**

Bru·nei (bro͞o nī′), *n.* **1.** a sultanate under British protection on the NW coast of Borneo: a member of the British Commonwealth of Nations. 83,869 (1960); 2220 sq. mi. **2.** a seaport in and the capital of this sultanate. 9702 (1960).

Bru·nel (bro͞o nel′), *n.* **1. Is·am·bard Kingdom** (iz′əm bärd′), 1806–59, English civil engineer and naval architect. **2.** his father, **Sir Marc Isambard,** 1769–1849, English civil engineer, born in France: chief engineer of New York City 1793–99.

Bru·nel·les·chi (bro͞on′əles′kē; *It.* bro͞o′nel les′kē), *n.* **Fi·lip·po** (fi lip′ō; *It.* fē lēp′pô), 1377?–1446, Italian architect. Also, **Bru·nel·les·co** (bro͞on′əles′kō; *It.* bro͞o′nel les′kō).

bru·net (bro͞o net′), *adj.* **1.** (esp. of a male) brunette. —*n.* **2.** a person, usually a male, with dark hair, eyes, and skin. [< F, equiv. to *brun* BROWN + *-et* -ET] —**bru·net′ness,** *n.*

Bru·ne·tière (bʀʏnᵊ tyeʀ′), *n.* **Fer·di·nand** (feʀ dē näN′), 1849–1906, French literary critic.

bru·nette (bro͞o net′), *adj.* **1.** (of skin, eyes, or hair) dark; brown. **2.** (of a person) having dark or brown hair, eyes, or skin. —*n.* **3.** a person, esp. a female, with dark hair, eyes, and skin. [< F; fem. of BRUNET] —**bru·nette′ness,** *n.*

Brun·hild (bro͝on′hilt, -hild), *n.* (in the *Nibelungenlied*) a queen of Isenland and the bride of Gunther, for whom she was won by Siegfried: corresponds to Brynhild in Scandinavian legends. Also, **Brunhilde, Brünnhilde.**

Brun·hil·da (bro͝on hil′də), *n.* a girl's given name.

Brun·hil·de (bro͝on hil′də), *n.* **1.** Brunhild. **2.** a girl's given name.

Brünn (bʀʏn), *n.* German name of **Brno.**

Brun·ner (bro͝on′ər), *n.* **E·mil** (ā′mēl), 1889–1966, Swiss Protestant theologian.

Brünn·hil·de (bro͝on hil′də; *Ger.* bʀʏn′hil′də), *n.* **1.** the heroine of Wagner's *Ring of the Nibelungs.* Cf. **Siegfried. 2.** Brunhild.

Bru·no (bro͞o′nō; *for 1, 3 also It.* bʀo͞o′nô), *n.* **1. Gior·da·no** (jôʀ dä′nô), 1548?–1600, Italian philosopher. **2. Saint,** c1030–1101, German ecclesiastical writer: founder of the Carthusian order. **3.** a boy's given name.

Bruns·wick (brunz′wik), *n.* **1.** a former state of Germany: now part of Lower Saxony in E West Germany. **2.** a city in Lower Saxony, in E West Germany. 241,300 (1963). **3.** a town in SW Maine. 9444 (1960). **4.** a town in NE Ohio. 6453 (1960). **5.** a town in W Maryland. 3555 (1960). German, **Braunschweig** (for defs. 1, 2).

brunt (brunt), *n.* **1.** the main shock, force, or impact, as of an attack or blow: *His arm took the brunt of the blow. She had to bear the brunt of the criticism.* **2.** *Obs.* a violent attack; assault. [ME; perh. orig. sexual assault, akin to Icel *brundr,* G *Brunft* heat, ruttish state, OE *brunetha* heat, itching; c. OHG *bronado.* See BURN[1]]

Bru·sa (*Turk.* bʀo͞o′sä), *n.* Bursa.

brüs·cha (bro͞osh′chä; *Romansh.* bʀʏsh′chä), *n.* (in Switzerland) a northeasterly wind. [< Romansh; akin to It *brusca,* lit., horse-brush. See BRUSQUE]

brush[1] (brush), *n.* **1.** an implement consisting of bristles, hair, or the like, set in or attached to a handle, used for painting, cleaning, polishing, grooming, etc. **2.** one of a pair of devices consisting of long, thin handles with wire bristles attached, used in jazz or

dance bands for keeping a soft, rhythmic beat on the trap drums or the cymbals. **3.** the act or an instance of brushing; an application of a brush. **4.** the bushy tail of an animal, esp. of a fox. **5.** a brief encounter: *He has already had one brush with the law.* **6.** a quick ride or short race across country. **7.** *Elect.* **a.** a conductor, often made of carbon or copper or a combination of the two, serving to maintain electric contact between stationary and moving parts of a machine, generator, or other apparatus. **b.** See **brush discharge. 8.** any feathery or hairy tuft or tassel, as on the tip of a kernel of grain, worn as an ornament on a man's hat, etc. —*v.t.* **9.** to sweep, paint, clean, polish, etc., with a brush. **10.** to touch lightly in passing; pass lightly over: *His lips brushed her ear.* **11.** to remove by brushing or by lightly passing over: *His hand brushed a speck of lint from his coat.* —*v.i.* **12.** to move or skim with a slight contact. **13.** to move quickly or in haste; rush. **14. brush aside,** to disregard; ignore: *Our complaints were simply brushed aside.* **15. brush off,** *U.S. Slang.* to rebuff; send away: *He had never been brushed off so rudely before.* **16. brush up on,** to revive, review, or resume (studies, a skill, etc.): *She thought of brushing up on her shorthand.* Also, **brush up.** [ME *brusshe* < MF *broisse,* OF *broce* < VL **brustia* < Gmc; cf. MHG *büriste* brush, OE *bryst* BRISTLE] —**brush′a·ble,** *adj.* —**brush′er,** *n.* —**brush′less,** *adj.* —**brush′like′,** **brush′y,** *adj.*
—**Syn. 5.** engagement, action, skirmish. See **struggle.**

brush[2] (brush), *n.* **1.** a dense growth of bushes, shrubs, etc.; scrub; thicket. **2.** a pile or covering of lopped or broken branches; brushwood. **3.** bushes and low trees growing in thick profusion, esp. close to the ground. **4.** land or an area covered with thickly growing bushes and low trees. **5.** *U.S.* backwoods; a sparsely settled wooded region. [late ME *brusshe;* see BRUSH[1]] —**brush′i·ness,** *n.* —**brush′less,** *adj.* —**brush′less·ness,** *n.* —**brush′y,** *adj.*

Brush (brush), *n.* **1. Katharine,** 1902–52, U.S. novelist and short-story writer. **2.** a town in NE Colorado. 3621 (1960).

brush′ cut′, a very short haircut for a man in which the hairs stand up like a brush, similar to a crew cut.

brush′ dis′charge, *Elect.* a type of corona discharge that takes place between two electrodes at atmospheric pressure, characterized by long, branched, luminous streamers of ionized particles.

brush′ fire′, a fire in an area of bushes, shrubs, or brush, as distinct from a forest fire.

brush-fire (brush′fīər′), *adj.* limited in scope, area, or importance, as some labor disputes, battles, etc. Also, **brush′fire′.**

brush′-foot·ed but′terfly (brush′fŏŏt′id), any of several butterflies of the family *Nymphalidae,* including the fritillaries, mourning cloaks, anglewings, commas, etc., characterized by reduced, nonfunctional forelegs. Also called **four-footed butterfly.**

brush-off (brush′ôf′, -of′), *n.* *U.S. Slang.* an abrupt or final dismissal or rebuff. [n. use of v. phrase *brush off*]

brush·pop·per (brush′pop′ər), *n.* *Western U.S.* a cowboy, esp. one who works in the brush. [BRUSH[2] + POPPER]

brush·up (brush′up′), *n.* **1.** the act or process of reviewing a subject, technique, or the like, for the purpose of renewing the memory, skill, etc.: *He gave his Spanish a brushup before his trip to Mexico.* **2.** the act or process of eliminating or repairing minor flaws, removing traces of dust or disorder, etc.: *He gave the collection a final brushup before putting it on display.* [n. use of v. phrase *brush up*]

brush·wood (brush′wŏŏd′), *n.* **1.** the wood of branches which have been cut or broken off or a pile or covering of such branches. **2.** a growth or thicket of densely growing small trees and shrubs. [BRUSH[2] + WOOD[1]]

brush·work (brush′wûrk′), *n.* **1.** the use of a brush as a tool, as in painting. **2.** *Fine Arts.* the surface quality of a painting produced by the distribution of pigment with a brush. **3.** work for which a brush is used, as painting. [BRUSH[1] + WORK]

brusque (brusk; *esp. Brit.* brŏŏsk), *adj.* abrupt in manner; blunt; rough: *A brusque welcome greeted his unexpected return.* [< MF < It *brusco* sour, rough, unripe] —**brusque′ly,** *adv.* —**brusque′ness,** *n.*
—**Syn.** unceremonious, short, curt. See **blunt.**

brus·que·rie (brus′kə rē; *esp. Brit.* brŏŏs′kə rē; *Fr.* bʀys kə ʀē′), *n.* brusqueness. [< F; see BRUSQUE, -ERY]

Brus·sels (brus′əlz), *n.* a city in and the capital of Belgium, in the central part. 170,054 (est. 1960); with suburbs 1,014,000 (est. 1960). Flemish, **Brus·sel** (bʀys′əl); French, **Bruxelles.**

Brus′sels car′pet, a carpet made with three-ply or four-ply worsted yarn drawn up in uncut loops to form a pattern over the entire surface **(body Brussels),** or made of worsted or woolen yarns on which a pattern is printed **(tapestry Brussels).**

Brus′sels grif′fon, one of a Belgian breed of toy dogs having a thick, wiry, reddish-brown coat.

Brus′sels lace′, any fine handmade lace with a floral pattern.

Brus′sels sprout′. Usually, **Brussels sprouts. 1.** a plant, *Brassica oleracea gemmifera,* having small, cabbagelike, edible heads or sprouts along the stalk. **2.** any of the heads or sprouts.

Brussels sprout

brut (brōōt; *Fr.* bʀyt), *adj.* (of wine, esp. champagne) very dry. [< F: raw; see BRUTE[2]]

Brut (brōōt), *n.* any of a number of partly legendary, partly historical chronicles dealing with early English history, written during the Middle Ages and usually beginning with Brutus, the mythic and eponymous ancestor of the country. [< ML *Brutus,* descendant of Aeneas]

bru·tal (brōōt′əl), *adj.* **1.** savage; cruel; inhuman. **2.** crude; coarse; harsh. **3.** irrational; unreasoning. **4.** of or pertaining to lower animals. [late ME < ML *brūtāl(is).* See BRUTE[1], -AL[1]] —**bru′tal·ly,** *adv.*
—**Syn. 1.** ferocious, brutish, barbarous. See **cruel. 2.** gross, rude, rough, uncivil. **4.** bestial, beastly, animal. —**Ant. 1.** kind. **4.** human.

bru·tal·ise (brōōt′əlīz′), *v.t., v.i.,* **-ised, -is·ing.** *Chiefly Brit.* brutalize. —**bru′tal·i·sa′tion,** *n.*

bru·tal·i·tar·i·an (brōō tal′i târ′ē ən), *adj.* practicing or advocating brutality. [BRUTALIT(Y) + -ARIAN] —**bru·tal′i·tar′i·an·ism,** *n.*

bru·tal·i·ty (brōō tal′i tē), *n., pl.* **-ties. 1.** the quality of being brutal. **2.** a brutal act. [BRUTAL + -ITY]

bru·tal·ize (brōōt′əlīz′), *v.t., v.i.,* **-ized, -iz·ing. 1.** to make or become brutal. **2.** to treat (someone) with brutality. Also, *esp. Brit.,* **brutalise.** [BRUTAL + -IZE] —**bru′tal·i·za′tion,** *n.*

brut′ con′crete (brōōt), poured concrete deliberately left unfinished and roughly textured as it comes from the forms.

brute[1] (brōōt), *n.* **1.** a nonhuman creature; beast. **2.** a brutal, insensitive, or crude person. **3.** the animal qualities, desires, etc., of man: *She brought out the brute in him.* —*adj.* **4.** animal; not human. **5.** not characterized by intelligence or reason; irrational. **6.** characteristic of animals; of brutal character or quality. **7.** savage; cruel. **8.** carnal; sensual. [late ME < L *brūt(us)* heavy, stupid, irrational] —**brute′like′,** *adj.* —**brute′ly,** *adv.* —**brute′ness,** *n.*
—**Syn. 1.** See **animal.**

brute[2] (brōōt), *v.t.,* **brut·ed, brut·ing.** to shape (a diamond) by rubbing it with another diamond or a diamond chip. [back formation from *bruting* a rough hewing (of a diamond), half-adoption, half-trans. of F *brutage,* lit., a roughing, equiv. to *brut* rough, raw (see BRUT) + *-age* -AGE]

bru·ti·fy (brōō′tə fī′), *v.t., v.i.,* **-fied, -fy·ing.** to brutalize. [BRUTE[1] + -IFY] —**brut′i·fi·ca′tion,** *n.*

brut·ish (brōō′tish), *adj.* **1.** brutal; cruel. **2.** gross; carnal; bestial. **3.** uncivilized; like an animal. [BRUTE[1] + -ISH[1]] —**brut′ish·ly,** *adv.* —**brut′ish·ness,** *n.*

Bru·tus (brōō′təs), *n.* **Marcus Jun·ius** (jōōn′yəs), 85?–42 B.C., Roman provincial administrator: one of the assassins of Julius Caesar.

Brux·elles (bʀy sel′, bʀyk sel′), *n.* French name of **Brussels.**

brux·ism (bruk′siz əm), *n.* *Med.* habitual, purposeless grinding of the teeth, esp. when occurring during sleep. [< Gk **brŷx(is)* a gnashing of teeth (*brýk(ein)* (to) gnash, bite + *-sis* -SIS) + -ISM]

Bry·an (brī′ən), *n.* **1. William Jen·nings** (jen′ingz), 1860–1925, U.S. political leader. **2.** a city in E Texas. 27,542 (1960). **3.** a town in NW Ohio. 7361 (1960). **4.** Also, **Brian, Bryant.** a boy's given name.

Bry′an-Cha·mor′ro Trea′ty (brī′ən chä môr′ō), a treaty (1914) between the U.S. and Nicaragua by which the U.S. secured exclusive rights to build a canal across Nicaragua, to connect the Atlantic and Pacific.

Bry·ansk (brē änsk′; *Russ.* bʀyänsk), *n.* a city in the W RSFSR, in the W Soviet Union in Europe, SW of Moscow. 206,000 (1959).

Bry·ant (brī′ənt), *n.* **1. Grid·ley** (grid′lē), 1789–1867, U.S. engineer and inventor. **2. William Cullen,** 1794–1878, U.S. poet and journalist. **3.** Also, **Brian, Bryan.** a boy's given name.

Bryce (brīs), *n.* **1. James, 1st Viscount,** 1838–1922, British diplomat, historian, and jurist; born in Ireland. **2.** Also, **Brice.** a boy's given name.

Bryce′ Can′yon Na′tional Park′, a national park in SW Utah: rock formations.

Bryn·hild (brin′hild), *n.* *Scand. Legend.* a Valkyrie and the wife of Gunnar, for whom she was won by Sigurd: corresponds to Brunhild in the *Nibelungenlied.*

Bryn·hildr Sigr·dri·fa (bʀyn′hil dər sig′ər drē′-vä), Sigrdrifa.

bryn·za (brin′zə), *n.* (in Eastern Europe and Asia Minor) a crumbly, sharp cheese made from sheep's milk and cured. Also, **brynd·za** (brind′zə). [< Rumanian]

bry·ol·o·gy (brī ol′ə jē), *n.* the branch of botany dealing with bryophytes. [< Gk *brýo(n)* moss + -LOGY] —**bry·o·log·i·cal** (brī′ə loj′i kəl), *adj.* —**bry·ol′o·gist,** *n.*

bry·o·ny (brī′ə nē), *n., pl.* **-nies.** any Old World, cucurbitaceous vine or climbing plant of the genus *Bryonia,* yielding acrid juice having emetic and purgative properties. Also, **briony.** [OE *bryōnia* < L < Gk: a wild vine]

bry·o·phyte (brī′ə fīt′), *n.* *Bot.* any of the *Bryophyta,* a primary division or group of plants comprising the true mosses and liverworts. [< NL *Bryophyta* name of the group < Gk *brýo(n)* moss + *phytá* pl. of *phytón* -PHYTE] —**bry·o·phyt·ic** (brī′ə fit′ik), *adj.*

Bry·o·zo·a (brī′ə zō′ə), *n.* the phylum comprising the bryozoans. [< NL < Gk *bryō-* (s. of *brýon*) + *-zoa* -ZOA]

bry·o·zo·an (brī′ə zō′ən), *adj.* **1.** belonging or pertaining to the *Bryozoa.* —*n.* **2.** any sessile, marine or fresh-water animal of the phylum *Bryozoa,* forming branching, encrusting, or gelatinous colonies of many small polyps, each having a circular or horseshoe-shaped ridge bearing ciliated tentacles. [BRYOZO(A) + -AN]

Bryth·on (brith′ən), *n.* **1.** a member of the Brythonic-speaking Celts. **2.** a Briton. [< Welsh; see BRITON]

Bry·thon·ic (bri thon′ik), *adj.* **1.** of or belonging to P-Celtic. —*n.* **2.** P-Celtic, esp. that part either spoken in Britain, as Welsh and Cornish, or descended from the P-Celtic speech of Britain, as Breton. Also, **Britannic.** [BRYTHON + -IC]

Brześć nad Bu·giem (bzhesh ch′ näd bŏŏ′gyem), Polish name of **Brest Litovsk.**

B/S, See **bill of sale.**

B/s, **1.** bags. **2.** bales. **3.** See **bill of sale.**

B.S., 1. Bachelor of Science. **2.** Bachelor of Surgery. **3.** See **bill of sale.**

b.s., 1. balance sheet. **2.** See **bill of sale.**

B.S.A., 1. Bachelor of Science in Agriculture. **2.** Bachelor of Scientific Agriculture. **3.** Boy Scouts of America.

B.S.A.A., Bachelor of Science in Applied Arts.

B.S.Adv., Bachelor of Science in Advertising.

B.S.A.E., 1. Bachelor of Science in Aeronautical Engineering. **2.** Bachelor of Science in Agricultural Engineering. **3.** Bachelor of Science in Architectural Engineering.

B.S.Ae.E., Bachelor of Science in Aeronautical Engineering.

B.S.Ag.E., Bachelor of Science in Agricultural Engineering.

B.S.Agr., Bachelor of Science in Agriculture.

B.S.Arch., Bachelor of Science in Architecture.

B.S.Arch.E., Bachelor of Science in Architectural Engineering.

B.S.Arch.Eng., Bachelor of Science in Architectural Engineering.

B.S.Art.Ed., Bachelor of Science in Art Education.

B.S.B.A., Bachelor of Science in Business Administration.

B.S.Bus., Bachelor of Science in Business.

B.S.Bus.Mgt., Bachelor of Science in Business Management.

B.Sc., Bachelor of Science.

B.S.C., Bachelor of Science in Commerce.

B.S.C.E., Bachelor of Science in Civil Engineering.

B.S.Ch., Bachelor of Science in Chemistry.

B.S.Ch.E., Bachelor of Science in Chemical Engineering.

B.Sch.Music, Bachelor of School Music.

B.S.Com., Bachelor of Science in Communications.

B.S.C.P., Brotherhood of Sleeping Car Porters.

B.S.D., Bachelor of Science in Design.

B.S.Des., Bachelor of Science in Design.

B.S.D.Hyg., Bachelor of Science in Dental Hygiene.

B.S.E., 1. Bachelor of Science in Education. **2.** Bachelor of Science in Engineering.

B.S.Ec., Bachelor of Science in Economics.

B.S.Ed., Bachelor of Science in Education.

B.S.E.E., 1. Bachelor of Science in Electrical Engineering. **2.** Bachelor of Science in Elementary Education.

B.S.E.Engr., Bachelor of Science in Electrical Engineering.

B.S.El.E., Bachelor of Science in Electronic Engineering.

B.S.E.M., Bachelor of Science in Engineering of Mines.

B.S.Eng., Bachelor of Science in Engineering.

B.S.E.P., Bachelor of Science in Engineering Physics.

B.S.E.S., Bachelor of Science in Engineering Sciences.

B.S.F., Bachelor of Science in Forestry.

B.S.F.M., Bachelor of Science in Forest Management.

B.S.F.Mgt., Bachelor of Science in Fisheries Management.

B.S.For., Bachelor of Science in Forestry.

B.S.F.S., Bachelor of Science in Foreign Service.

B.S.F.T., Bachelor of Science in Fuel Technology.

B.S.G.E., Bachelor of Science in General Engineering.

B.S.Gen.Ed., Bachelor of Science in General Education.

B.S.Geol.E., Bachelor of Science in Geological Engineering.

B.S.G.Mgt., Bachelor of Science in Game Management.

B.S.Gph., Bachelor of Science in Geophysics.

bsh., bushel; bushels.

B.S.H.A., Bachelor of Science in Hospital Administration.

B.S.H.E., Bachelor of Science in Home Economics.

B.S.H.Ec., Bachelor of Science in Home Economics.

B.S.H.Ed., Bachelor of Science in Health Education.

B.S.Hyg., Bachelor of Science in Hygiene.

B.S.I.E., 1. Bachelor of Science in Industrial Education. **2.** Bachelor of Science in Industrial Engineering.

B.S.Ind.Ed., Bachelor of Science in Industrial Education.

B.S.Ind.Engr., Bachelor of Science in Industrial Engineering.

B.S.Ind.Mgt., Bachelor of Science in Industrial Management.

B.S.I.R., Bachelor of Science in Industrial Relations.

B.S.I.T., Bachelor of Science in Industrial Technology.

B.S.J., Bachelor of Science in Journalism.

bskt., basket.

Bs/L, bills of lading.

B.S.L., 1. Bachelor of Sacred Literature. **2.** Bachelor of Science in Law. **3.** Bachelor of Science in Linguistics.

B.S.L.A. and Nurs., Bachelor of Science in Liberal Arts and Nursing.

B.S.Lab.Rel., Bachelor of Science in Labor Relations.

B.S.L.Arch., Bachelor of Science in Landscape Architecture.

B.S.L.M., Bachelor of Science in Landscape Management.

B.S.L.S., Bachelor of Science in Library Science.

B.S.M., 1. Bachelor of Sacred Music. **2.** Bachelor of Science in Medicine. **3.** Bachelor of Science in Music.

B.S.M.E., 1. Bachelor of Science in Mechanical Engineering. **2.** Bachelor of Science in Mining Engineering. **3.** Bachelor of Science in Music Education.

B.S.Med.Tech., Bachelor of Science in Medical Technology.

B.S.Met., Bachelor of Science in Metallurgy.

B.S.Met.E., Bachelor of Science in Metallurgical Engineering.

B.S.Min., Bachelor of Science in Mineralogy.

B.S.M.T., Bachelor of Science in Medical Technology.

B.S.Mus.Ed., Bachelor of Science in Music Education.

B.S.N., Bachelor of Science in Nursing.

B.S.N.A., Bachelor of Science in Nursing Administration.

B.S.Orn.Hort., Bachelor of Science in Ornamental Horticulture.

B.S.O.T., Bachelor of Science in Occupational Therapy.

B.S.P., Bachelor of Science in Pharmacy.

B.S.P.A., Bachelor of Science in Public Adminstration.

B.S.P.E., Bachelor of Science in Physical Education.

B.S.P.H., Bachelor of Science in Public Health.

B.S.Phar., Bachelor of Science in Pharmacy.

B.S.Pharm., Bachelor of Science in Pharmacy.

B.S.P.H.N., Bachelor of Science in Public Health Nursing.

B.S.Ph.Th., Bachelor of Science in Physical Therapy.

B.S.P.T., Bachelor of Science in Physical Therapy.

B.S.Radio-TV., Bachelor of Science in Radio and Television.

B.S.Rec., Bachelor of Science in Recreation.

B.S.Ret., Bachelor of Science in Retailing.

CONCISE PRONUNCIATION KEY: *act, āble, dâre, ärt; ebb, ēqual; if, īce; hot, ōver, ôrder, oil, bŏŏk, ōōze, out; up, ûrge; chief; sing; shoe; thin, that;* zh *as in measure.* ə = *a* as in *alone, e* as in *system, i* as in *easily, o* as in *gallop, u* as in *circus;* ə as in *button* (but′ən), *fire* (fīər), *cradle* (krād′əl). See the full key inside the front cover.

B.S.R.T., Bachelor of Science in Radiological Technology.

B.S.S., **1.** Bachelor of Secretarial Science. **2.** Bachelor of Social Science.

B.S.S.A., Bachelor of Science in Secretarial Administration.

B.S.S.E., Bachelor of Science in Secondary Education.

B.S.S.S., **1.** Bachelor of Science in Secretarial Studies. **2.** Bachelor of Science in Social Science.

B.S.T.&I.E., Bachelor of Science in Trade and Industrial Education.

B.S.Trans., Bachelor of Science in Transportation.

B supply, *Electronics.* a battery or other source of power for supplying a constant positive voltage to the plate of a vacuum tube. Also called **B power supply.** Cf. **A supply, C supply.**

Bt., Baronet.

bt., **1.** boat. **2.** bought.

B.T., Bachelor of Theology.

B.T.Ch., Bachelor of Textile Chemistry.

B.T.E., Bachelor of Textile Engineering.

B.Th., Bachelor of Theology.

btl., bottle.

btry., battery.

B.T.U., *Physics.* British thermal unit; British thermal units. Also, **BTU, B.t.u., B.th.u., Btu**

bu., **1.** bureau. **2.** bushel; bushels.

bub (bub), *n. Chiefly U.S. Slang.* a term of address, usually condescending; brother; boy; buddy. [perh. < G *Bub*, short for *Bube* boy]

Bub (bub), *n.* a boy's given name.

bu·bal (byo͞o′bəl), *n.* a hartebeest, *Alcelaphus boselaphus*, of northern Africa. Also, **bu·ba·lis** (byo͞o′bə lis). [ME < L *būbal(us)* < Gk *boúbalos* a kind of gazelle or buffalo]

bu·ba·line (byo͞o′bə līn′, -lin), *adj.* **1.** (of antelopes) resembling or like the bubal, as the hartebeests, blesbok, etc. **2.** pertaining to or resembling the true buffaloes. [< L *būbalīn(us)*. See BUBAL, -INE¹]

Bub·ba (bub′ə), *n.* a boy's given name.

bub·ble (bub′əl), *n., v.,* **-bled, -bling.** —*n.* **1.** a nearly spherical body of gas contained in a liquid. **2.** a small globule of gas in a thin liquid envelope. **3.** a globule of air or gas, or a globular vacuum, contained in a solid. **4.** anything that lacks firmness, substance, or permanence; delusion. **5.** an inflated speculation, esp. if fraudulent: *The Florida real-estate bubble ruined many investors.* **6.** the act or sound of bubbling. **7.** a spherical or nearly spherical canopy or shelter; dome: *The bombing plane bristled with machine-gun bubbles. A network of radar bubbles stretches across northern Canada.* —*v.i.* **8.** to form, produce, or release bubbles; effervesce. **9.** to flow or spout with a gurgling noise; gurgle. **10.** to boil: *The tea bubbled in the pot.* **11.** to speak, move, issue forth, or exist in a lively, sparkling manner; exude cheer: *The play bubbled with songs and dances.* **12.** to seethe or stir, as with excitement: *His mind bubbles with plans and schemes.* —*v.t.* **13.** to cause to bubble; make bubbles in. **14.** *Archaic.* to cheat; deceive; swindle. **15. bubble over,** to be overflowing with good spirits, liveliness, etc.: *The last time I saw her she was bubbling over with enthusiasm.* [ME *bobel* (n.); c. MD *bobbel*, MLG *bubbele*, Sw *bubbla*] —**bub′ble·less,** *adj.* —**bub′ble·like′,** *adj.* —**bub′bling·ly,** *adv.*

bub′ble and squeak′, *Brit.* a dish of meat, usually beef, and cabbage fried or boiled together, sometimes with a few potatoes added.

bub′ble bath′, **1.** a crystal, powder, or liquid preparation that foams in, scents, and softens bath water. **2.** a bath with such a preparation added to the water.

bub′ble cham′ber, *Physics.* an apparatus for determining the movements of charged particles, consisting of a chamber containing a superheated transparent liquid that, by boiling and producing bubbles in the path of an ionizing particle, indicates the path of the particle. Cf. **cloud chamber.**

bub′ble dance′, a provocative solo dance performed by a nude or nearly nude woman using one or more balloons for covering. Cf. **fan dance.**

bub′ble danc′er, a female performer, as in a cabaret, who dances nude or nearly nude, using a balloon or balloons for covering. Cf. **fan dancer.**

bub′ble gum′, a variety of chewing gum that can be blown into large bubbles through the lips.

bub′ble nest′, a nest of air bubbles, constructed by certain fishes, in which the eggs are incubated and the young sheltered.

bub·bler (bub′lər), *n.* **1.** a drinking fountain which spouts water directly into the mouth. **2.** *Chem.* any device for bubbling gas through a liquid. [BUBBLE + -ER¹]

bub·bly (bub′lē), *adj.,* **-bli·er, -bli·est,** *n.* —*adj.* **1.** full of, producing, or characterized by bubbles. —*n.* **2.** *Chiefly Brit. Slang.* champagne (def. 1). [BUBBLE + -Y¹]

bub·bly-jock (bub′lē jok′), *n. Scot.* See **turkey cock.** [*bubbly* snotty + *jock* JOCK; perh. from the fancied resemblance of the turkey's comb to a child's running nose]

bub·by (bub′ē, bo͝ob′ē), *n., pl.* **-bies.** *Slang.* a female breast. [? imit. of baby's cry or of sucking sound; see -Y²]

Bu·ber (bo͞o′bər), *n.* **Martin,** 1878–1965, Jewish philosopher, theologian, and scholar of Hasidism: born in Austria, in Israel from 1938.

bu·bing·a (bo͞o bing′ə), *n.* **1.** any of several West African, leguminous trees, esp. *Didelotia africana.* **2.** the hard, reddish wood of any such tree, used for making furniture. [< Bantu]

bu·bo (byo͞o′bō), *n., pl.* **-boes.** *Pathol.* an inflammatory swelling of a lymphatic gland, esp. in the groin or armpit. [< LL < Gk *boubṓn*, lit., groin] —**bu′boed,** *adj.*

Bu·bo·na (byo͞o bō′nə), *n.* an ancient Roman goddess, protectress of cows and oxen.

bu·bon·ic (byo͞o bon′ik, bo͞o-), *adj. Pathol.* **1.** of or pertaining to a bubo. **2.** accompanied by or affected with buboes. [< LL *būbōn-* (s. of *būbō*) BUBO + -IC]

bubon′ic plague′, *Pathol.* a form of plague characterized by buboes. Cf. **plague.**

bu·bon·o·cele (byo͞o bon′ə sēl′, bo͞o-), *n. Pathol.* an inguinal hernia, esp. one in which the protrusion of the intestine is limited to the region of the groin. [< Gk *boubṓ(n)* the groin + -CELE¹]

Bu·ca·ra·man·ga (bo͞o kä′rä mäng′gä), *n.* a city in N Colombia. 208,640 (est. 1961).

buc·cal (buk′əl), *adj. Anat.* **1.** of or pertaining to the cheek. **2.** pertaining to the sides of the mouth or to the mouth; oral. **3.** *Dentistry.* directed toward the cheek. Cf. **distal** (def. 2), **mesial** (def. 2). [BUCC(O)- + -AL¹] —**buc′cal·ly,** *adv.*

buc·ca·neer (buk′ə nēr′), *n.* **1.** a pirate. **2.** one of the piratical adventurers who raided Spanish colonies and ships along the American coast in the second half of the 17th century. [< F *boucanier*, lit., barbecuer, equiv. to *boucan* barbecue (< Tupi, var. of *mukém*) + *-ier* -EER] —**buc′ca·neer′ish,** *adj.*

buc·ca·ro (bo͞o kär′ō), *n.* unglazed pottery. [see BUCCHERO]

buc·che·ro (bo͞ok′ə rō′), *n., pl.* **-ros.** an Etruscan black ceramic ware, often ornamented with incised geometrical patterns or figures carved in relief. [< It < Sp *búcaro* < Pg: clay vessel, earlier *pucaro* << L *pōculum* goblet. See POTION, -CULE]

buc·ci·na·tor (buk′sə nā′tər), *n. Anat.* a thin, flat muscle lining the cheek, the action of which contracts and compresses the cheek. [< L: trumpeter, equiv. to *buccinā(tus)* trumpeted, ptp. of *buccināre*, deriv. of *buccina* horn; see -ATE¹) + *-or* -OR²] —**buc·ci·na·to·ry** (buk′sə nə tōr′ē, -tôr′ē, buk′sə nā′tə rē), *adj.*

bucco-, a learned borrowing from Latin meaning "cheek," "mouth," used in the formation of compound words: *buccolingual.* [comb. form repr. L *bucca*]

buc·co·lin·gual (buk′ə ling′gwəl), *adj. Anat.* of or pertaining to the cheek and tongue. [BUCCO- + LINGUAL]

bu·cen·taur (byo͞o sen′tôr), *n.* the state barge of Venice, from which the doge and other officials performed the ceremonial marriage of the state with the Adriatic, by dropping a ring into the sea on Ascension Day. [alter. of It *bucentero* ?, equiv. to *bu-* (< Gk *bou-*, s. of *boûs* ox) + *centoro* CENTAUR; perh. so called from its figurehead]

Bu·ceph·a·lus (byo͞o sef′ə ləs), *n.* the horse used by Alexander the Great on most of his military campaigns.

Buch (bo͝okн), *n.* a crater in the fourth quadrant of the face of the moon: about 30 miles in diameter.

Buch·an (buk′ən; *Scot.* bukн′ən), *n.* **John** (*Baron Tweedsmuir*), 1875–1940, Scottish novelist and historian: governor general of Canada 1935–40.

Bu·chan·an (byo͞o kan′ən, bə-), *n.* **1. James,** 1791–1868, 15th president of the U.S. 1857–61. **2.** a town in SW Michigan. 5341 (1960). **3.** a boy's given name.

Bu·cha·rest (byo͞o′kə rest′, bo͞o′-), *n.* a city in and the capital of Rumania, in the S part. 1,239,458 (est. 1964). Rumanian, **București.**

Buch·en·wald (bo͝ok′ən wôld′; *Ger.* bo͞okн′ən vält′), *n.* site of a former Nazi concentration camp in SW East Germany, near Weimar.

buch·ite (bo͞o′kīt), *n. Mineral.* a glassy rock formed by the fusion of clay or shale with magma. [named after Baron C. L. von *Buch* (1774–1853), German mineralogist; see -ITE¹]

Buch·man (bo͝ok′mən, buk′-), *n.* **Frank N(athan) D(aniel),** 1879–1961, U.S. religious leader: founder of Moral Re-Armament.

Buch·man·ism (bo͝ok′mə niz′əm), *n.* the principles or the international movement of Moral Re-Armament or of the Oxford Group, or belief in or adherence to them. [F. N. D. BUCHMAN + -ISM] —**Buch·man·ite** (bo͝ok′mə nīt′), *n.*

Buch·ner (bo͝ok′nər; *Ger.* bo͞okн′nər), *n.* **E·du·ard** (ā′do͞o ärt′), 1860–1917, German chemist: Nobel prize 1907.

buck¹ (buk), *n.* **1.** the male of the deer, antelope, rabbit, hare, sheep, or goat. **2.** the male of certain other animals, as the shad. **3.** an impetuous or spirited man or youth. **4.** *Often Disparaging.* a male American Indian or Negro. **5.** *U.S. Slang.* a dollar. **6.** any of various heavy frames, racks, or jigs used to support materials or partially assembled items during manufacture, as in airplane assembly plants. [ME *bukke*, OE *bucca* he-goat, *bucc* male deer; c. D *bok*, G *Bock*, Icel *bukkr*]

buck² (buk), *v.i.* **1.** (of a saddle or pack animal) to leap with arched back and come down with head low and forelegs stiff, in order to dislodge a rider or pack. **2.** *U.S. Informal.* to resist obstinately; object strongly: *The mayor bucked at the school board's suggestion.* **3.** *U.S. Informal.* (of a vehicle) to move by jerks and bounces. —*v.t.* **4.** to throw or attempt to throw (a rider) by bucking. **5.** to force a way through or proceed against (an obstacle): *The plane bucked a strong head wind.* **6.** *U.S.* to strike with the head; butt. **7.** *U.S. Informal.* to resist obstinately; object strongly to. **8.** *Football.* (of a ball-carrier) to charge into (the opponent's line). **9.** to gamble, play, or take a risk against: *He was bucking the odds when he picked up the dice to throw another seven.* **10.** to press a reinforcing device against (the force of a rivet) in order to absorb vibration and increase expansion. **11. buck for,** *Slang.* to strive for a promotion or some other advantage: *to buck for a raise.* **12. buck up,** *Informal.* to make or become more cheerful, vigorous, etc.: *She knew that with a change of scene she would soon buck up.* —*n.* **13.** act of bucking. —*adj.* **14.** *Mil. Slang.* of the lowest of several ranks involving the same principal designation, hence subject to promotion within the rank: *buck private; buck sergeant.* [special use of BUCK¹; in def. 6, alter. of BUTT³]

buck³ (buk), *n.* **1.** a sawhorse. **2.** *Gymnastics.* a cylindrical, leather-covered block mounted in a horizontal position on a single vertical post set in a steel frame, for use chiefly in vaulting. **3.** a doorframe of wood or metal set in a partition, esp. one of light masonry, to support door hinges, hardware, finish work, etc. —*v.t.* **4.** to split or saw (logs, felled trees, etc.). **5. buck in,** *Survey, Optical Tooling.* to set up an instrument in line with two marks. [short for SAWBUCK]

buck⁴ (buk), *n.* **1.** *Poker.* any object in the pot which reminds the winner that he has some privilege or duty when his turn to deal next comes. **2. pass the buck,** *U.S. Informal.* to shift responsibility or blame to another person; evade responsibility: *Never one to admit error, he passed the buck on to his subordinates.* [(def. 1) short for *buckhorn knife*, the object oftenest used]

buck⁵ (buk), *Brit. Dial.* —*n.* **1.** lye used for washing clothes. **2.** clothes washed in lye. —*v.t.* **3.** to wash or bleach (clothes) in lye. [ME *bouken* (v.); cf. MLG *buken, büken* to steep in lye, MHG *būchen, bruchen*]

buck⁶ (buk), *v.i., n. Anglo-Indian.* bukh. [< Hindi *bak* talk]

buck⁷ (buk), *adv. Dial.* completely; stark: *buck naked.* [?]

Buck (buk), *n.* **1. Pearl (Sy·den·strick·er)** (sīd′ən-strik′ər), born 1892, U.S. novelist: Nobel prize 1938. **2.** a boy's given name.

buck′ and wing′, a tap dance derived in style from Negro and Irish clog dances, marked esp. by vigorous hopping, flinging of the legs, and clicking of the heels.

buck·a·roo (buk′ə ro͞o′, buk′ə ro͞o′), *n., pl.* **-roos.** *Western U.S.* a cowboy. Also, **buckayro.** [alter. of Sp *vaquero*, equiv. to *vac(a)* cow (< L *vacca*) + *-ero* -ER²]

buck·ay·ro (bə kâr′ō), *n., pl.* **-ros.** buckaroo.

buck′ bean′, a plant, *Menyanthes trifoliata*, having white or pink flowers, growing in bogs. Also called **bogbean, marsh trefoil.** [earlier *buckes beanes*, for MFlem *bocx boonen*, lit., goat's beans]

Buckboard

buck·board (buk′bōrd′, -bôrd′), *n.* a light, four-wheeled carriage in which a long elastic board or lattice frame is used in place of body and springs. [*buck* body, holder (see BUCKET) + BOARD]

buck·brush (buk′brush′), *n.* wolfberry. [BUCK¹ + BRUSH²]

bucked (bukt), *adj. Brit. Slang.* **1.** tired; exhausted. **2.** happy; elated. [BUCK² + -ED²]

buck·een¹ (bu kēn′), *n. Chiefly Irish Eng.* a poor young man who attempts to copy the habits and dress of wealthy or aristocratic men. [BUCK¹ + *-een* < Ir *-ín* dim. suffix]

buck·een² (bu kēn′), *n. Brit. Informal.* (in British Guiana) a native Indian woman. [< D *bokkin*, fem. of *bok* BUCK¹]

buck·er (buk′ər), *n.* **1.** a horse that bucks. **2.** one who bucks rivets. **3.** a person employed to carry, shovel, lift, or load, as coal, farm produce, etc. [BUCK² + -ER¹]

buck·et (buk′it), *n., v.,* **-et·ed, -et·ing.** —*n.* **1.** a vessel, usually cylindrical, with a flat bottom and a semicircular bail, for collecting, carrying, or holding water, sand, fruit, etc. **2.** anything resembling or suggesting this. **3.** any of the scoops attached to or forming the endless chain in certain types of conveyors or elevators. **4.** a vane or blade of a water wheel, paddle wheel, water turbine, or the like. **5.** (in a dam) a concave surface at the foot of a spillway for deflecting the downward flow of water. **6.** a bucketful: *a bucket of sand.* **7.** *Basketball.* **a.** the part of the keyhole extending from the foul line to the end line. **b.** *Slang.* See **field goal.** **8.** *Bowling.* a leave of the two, four, five, and eight pins, or the three, five, six, and nine pins. See illus. under **bowling.** **9.** the scoop or clamshell of a steam shovel, power shovel, or dredge. **10. drop in the bucket,** a small amount in relation to the whole; an inadequate contribution: *The amount being spent on basic research is a drop in the bucket.* **11. kick the bucket,** *Slang.* to die: *His heirs were greedily waiting for him to kick the bucket.* —*v.t.* **12.** to lift, carry, or handle in a bucket (often fol. by *up* or *out*). **13.** *Chiefly Brit.* to ride (a horse) fast and without concern for tiring it. **14.** to handle (orders, transactions, etc.) in or as if in a bucket shop. —*v.i.* **15.** *Informal.* to move or drive fast; hurry. [ME *buket* < AF < OE *bucc* (var. of *būc* vessel, belly, c. G *Bauch*) + OF *-et* -ET]

buck′et bench′. See **water bench.**

buck′et brigade′, **1.** a line of persons formed to extinguish a fire by passing on buckets of water quickly from a distant source. **2.** a group of persons organized or acting in cooperation to cope with an emergency: *Seeing the two guests of honor bickering, the rest of the group formed a bucket brigade to calm them.*

buck·et·ful (buk′it fo͝ol′), *n., pl.* **-fuls.** as much as a bucket can hold: *a bucketful of water.* [BUCKET + -FUL]

buck′et seat′, an individual seat with a rounded back, as in racing cars, some airplanes, etc., often made to fold forward.

buck′et shop′, *Finance.* a fraudulent brokerage house that speculates on its own account against its customers' interests, failing to execute certain orders placed on margin so that customers' losses are the establishment's gain.

buck·eye (buk′ī′), *n., pl.* **-eyes,** *adj.* —*n.* **1.** any of various trees or shrubs of the genus *Aesculus*, allied to the true horse chestnut, as *A. glabra* **(Ohio buckeye),** the State tree of Ohio. **2.** a butterfly, *Precis lavinia*, having dark brown wings with purple or red eyespots. **3.** (*cap.*) a native or inhabitant of Ohio (the **Buckeye State**) (used as a nickname). **4.** a cheap work of art, esp. a painting, produced rapidly and exclusively for sale, usually thought of as having little or no aesthetic interest. **5.** a poorly designed, ostentatious advertisement. —*adj.* **6.** bold, loud, or shrill, as color, design, sound, etc. [BUCK¹ stag + EYE orig. used to designate def. 1, in allusion to the looks of the seed]

Buck′eye State′, Ohio (used as a nickname).

buck′ fe′ver, **1.** nervous excitement of an inexperienced hunter upon the approach of game. **2.** any nervous excitement preceding a new experience.

Buck·han·non (buk han′ən), *n.* a town in central West Virginia. 6386 (1960).

buck·hound (buk′hound′), *n.* a hound trained to hunt bucks and other game. [BUCK¹ + HOUND¹]

Buck·ing·ham (buk′ing əm, -ham′), *n.* **1. George Villiers, 1st Duke of,** 1592–1628, English courtier, politician, and military leader: lord high admiral 1617. **2.** his son, **George Villiers, 2nd Duke of,** 1628–87, English courtier and writer. **3.** Buckinghamshire.

Buck′ingham Pal′ace, a residence of the British sovereigns since 1837, in London, England: built 1703.

Buck·ing·ham·shire (buk′ing əm shēr′, -shər), *n.* a county in S England. 486,183 (1961); 749 sq. mi. *Co. seat:* Aylesbury. Also called **Buckingham, Bucks.**

buck·ish (buk′ish), *adj.* impetuous; dashing. [BUCK¹ + -ISH¹] —**buck′ish·ly,** *adv.* —**buck′ish·ness,** *n.*

buck·jump (buk′jump′), *v.i.* (of a horse) to buck. [BUCK² + JUMP]

buck·jump·er (buk′jum′pər), *n.* a horse that bucks habitually, esp. such a horse kept for use in rodeos. [BUCKJUMP + -ER[1]]

buck·le (buk′əl), *n., v.,* **-led, -ling.** —*n.* **1.** a clasp consisting of a rectangular or curved rim with one or more movable tongues, fixed to one end of a belt or strap, used for fastening to the other end of the same strap or to another strap. **2.** any similar contrivance used for such purposes. **3.** an ornament of metal, beads, etc., of similar appearance. **4.** a bend, bulge, or kink, as in a board or saw blade. —*v.t.* **5.** to fasten with a buckle or buckles. **6.** to shrivel, by applying heat or pressure; bend; curl. **7.** to prepare (oneself) for action; apply (oneself) vigorously to something. **8.** to bend, warp, or cause to give way suddenly, as with heat or pressure. —*v.i.* **9.** to close or fasten with a buckle: *His boot wouldn't buckle.* **10.** to prepare oneself or apply oneself: *She buckled to the housework.* **11.** to bend, warp, bulge, or collapse: *The bridge buckled in the storm.* **12.** to yield, surrender, or give way to another (often fol. by *under*): *He refused to take the medicine, but buckled under when the doctor told him to.* **13.** to close a buckle (sometimes fol. by *up*): *Buckle up for safety.* **14. buckle down,** to set to work with vigor; concentrate on one's work: *He was by nature a daydreamer and found it hard to buckle down.* [ME *bocle* < MF < L *buccula* beaver (of a helmet), boss (of a shield), equiv. to *bucc(a)* cheek + *-ula* -ULE] —**buck′le·less,** *adj.*

Buck·le (buk′əl), *n.* **Henry Thomas,** 1821–62, English historian.

buck·ler (buk′lər), *n.* **1.** a round shield with a grip for holding and sometimes with straps through which the arm is passed. **2.** any means of defense; protection. —*v.t.* **3.** to be a buckler or shield to; support; defend. [ME *bokeler* < MF *bocler*, equiv. to *bocle* BOSS[2] + *-er* -ER[2]]

Buck·ley (buk′lē), *n.* a town in central Washington. 3538 (1960).

buck′ moth′, a saturniid moth, *Hemileuca maia*, having delicate, grayish wings, each with a band of white.

Buck·ner (buk′nər), *n.* **1. Simon Bol·i·var** (bol′ə vər), 1823–1914, U.S. Confederate general and politician. **2.** his son, **Simon Bolivar, Jr.,** 1886–1945, U.S. general.

buck·o (buk′ō), *n., pl.* **-oes. 1.** *Chiefly Irish Eng.* young fellow; chap; young companion. **2.** *Brit. Slang.* a manly, swaggering sailor. **3.** a bully. [alter. of BUCK[1]]

buck′ pass′er, one who shifts responsibility, blame, etc., to another, esp. unjustly or improperly.

buck·ra (buk′rə), *n.* *Chiefly Southern U.S.* a white man. [< Calabar *mbakara* master]

buck·ram (buk′rəm), *n., v.,* **-ramed, -ram·ing.** —*n.* **1.** a stiff cotton fabric for interlinings, book bindings, etc. **2.** stiffness of manner; extreme preciseness or formality. —*v.t.* **3.** to strengthen with buckram. **4.** *Archaic.* to give a false appearance of importance, value, or strength to. [early ME *bukeram* < MHG *buckeram* or OIt *bucherame*, said to be named after BUKHARA, once noted for textiles]

Bucks (buks), *n.* Buckinghamshire.

buck·saw (buk′sô′), *n.* a saw consisting of a blade set across an upright frame or bow, used with both hands in cutting wood on a sawbuck or sawhorse. [BUCK[3] + SAW[1]]

Bucksaw

buck·shee (buk′shē, buk′shē′), *n.* **1.** *Anglo-Indian, Brit. Mil. Slang.* an extra ration or portion. **2.** an unexpected gift or gratuity. —*adj.* **3.** free of charge; gratuitous. [var. of BAKSHEESH]

buck·shot (buk′shot′), *n.* a large size of lead shot used in shotgun shells for hunting game, as pheasants, ducks, etc. [BUCK[1] + SHOT[1]]

buck·skin (buk′skin′), *n.* **1.** the skin of a buck or deer. **2.** a strong, soft, yellowish or grayish leather, originally prepared from deerskins, now usually from sheepskins. **3. buckskins,** breeches or shoes made of buckskin. **4.** a stiff, firm, starched cotton cloth with a smooth surface and napped back. **5.** a sturdy wool fabric constructed in satin weave, napped and cropped short to provide a smooth finish, and used in the manufacture of outer garments. **6.** a person, esp. a backwoodsman, dressed in buckskin. **7.** a horse the color of buckskin. —*adj.* **8.** having the color of buckskin; yellowish or grayish. **9.** made of buckskin: *buckskin gloves.* [BUCK[1] + SKIN]

buck′ slip′, a piece of paper attached to and showing the destination and source of an interoffice memorandum, file, or the like; routing slip.

buck·stay (buk′stā′), *n.* a beam held by stays to the exterior of a masonry wall, as that of a furnace or boiler, to keep the adjacent areas of the wall from being forced outward. [BUCK[3] + STAY[2]]

buck·tail (buk′tāl′), *n.* *Angling.* an artificial fly made of hairs of or like those of the tail of a deer. [BUCK[1] + TAIL[1]]

buck·thorn (buk′thôrn′), *n.* **1.** any of several, sometimes thorny trees or shrubs of the genus *Rhamnus*, esp. *R. cathartica*, whose berries were formerly used in medicine as a purgative, and *R. frangula*, the bark of which is used in medicine. **2.** a sapotaceous tree or shrub of the genus *Bumelia*, esp. *B. lycioides*, a tree common in the southern and part of the central U.S. [BUCK[1] + THORN, rendering NL *cervi spina*]

buck·tooth (buk′to͞oth′), *n., pl.* **-teeth** (-tēth′). a projecting tooth, esp. an upper front tooth. [BUCK[1] + TOOTH] —**buck′toothed′,** *adj.*

buck·wheat (buk′hwēt′, -wēt′), *n.* **1.** a herbaceous plant, esp. *Fagopyrum esculentum*, cultivated for its triangular seeds, which are used as a feed for animals or made into a flour for human consumption, as in pancakes, cereal, etc. **2.** the seeds. **3.** Also, **buck′wheat flour′,** the flour. —*adj.* *Coal Mining.* **4.** noting a size of anthracite of less than 9/16 of an inch and more than 5/16 of an inch in the longest dimension. **5.** noting any size of anthracite of less than 9/16 of an inch in the longest dimension. [obs. *buck* (OE *bōc* BEECH) + WHEAT; cf. D *boekweit*, G *Buchweizen*; so called because its seeds remind one of beechnuts] —**buck′wheat′like′,** *adj.*

buck′wheat cake′, a pancake made of buckwheat flour.

bu·col·ic (byo͞o kol′ik), *adj.* Also, **bu·col′i·cal. 1.** of or pertaining to shepherds; pastoral. **2.** rustic; rural; unsophisticated: *He yearned for a simple bucolic life.* —*n.* **3.** *Archaic.* a farmer; shepherd; rustic. **4.** a pastoral poem. [< L *būcolic(us)* < Gk *boukolikós* rustic, equiv. to *boukól(os)* herdsman (*bou-*, s. of *boûs* ox. + *-kolos* keeper + *-ikos* -IC] —**bu·col′i·cal·ly,** *adv.* —**Syn. 2, 4.** georgic.

Bu·col·ics (byo͞o kol′iks), *n.* Eclogues.

Bu·col·i·on (byo͞o kol′ē on′), *n.* (in the *Iliad*) a son of Laomedon.

Bu·co·vi·na (bo͞o′kə vē′nə; *Rum.* bo͝o kô vē′nä), *n.* **1.** a region in N Rumania, formerly constituting a province with Northern Bucovina. **2.** See **Northern Bucovina.** Also, **Bukovina.**

bu·cra·ni·um (byo͞o krā′nē əm), *n., pl.* **-ni·a** (-nē ə). (in classical architecture) an ornament, esp. on a frieze, having the form of the skull of an ox. Also, **bu·crane** (byo͞o krān′). [< LL *būcrānium* < Gk *boukrāni(on)* an ox-head, equiv. to Gk *bou-* (s. of *boûs*)ox + *krānion* CRANIUM]

Bu·cu·reş·ti (bo͝o ko͝o resht′), *n.* Rumanian name of **Bucharest.**

bud[1] (bud), *n., v.,* **bud·ded, bud·ding.** —*n.* **1.** *Bot.* **a.** a small axillary or terminal protuberance on a plant, containing rudimentary foliage **(leaf bud),** the rudimentary inflorescence **(flower bud),** or both **(mixed bud). b.** an undeveloped or rudimentary stem or branch of a plant. **2.** *Zool.* (in certain animals of low organization) a prominence which develops into a new individual, sometimes permanently attached to the parent and sometimes becoming detached; gemma. **3.** *Anat.* any small rounded part, as a tactile bud or a gustatory bud. **4.** an immature or undeveloped person or thing. **5. in the bud,** in an immature or undeveloped state: *A child mechanic may be a future physicist in the bud.* Also, **in bud. 6. nip in the bud,** to stop something in the beginning of its development: *The business recession was nipped in the bud.* —*v.i.* **7.** to put forth or produce buds, as a plant. **8.** to begin to grow and develop. **9.** to be in an early stage of development. —*v.t.* **10.** to cause to bud. **11.** *Hort.* to graft by inserting a single bud into the stock. [ME *budde* bud, spray, pod; akin to G (*Hage*)*butte* hip, Icel *budda* purse, dial. Sw *bodd* head, D *buidel* bag, purse, MLG *buddich* swollen] —**bud′der,** *n.* —**bud′less,** *adj.* —**bud′like′,** *adj.*

Leaf buds of the elm

bud[2] (bud), *n.* *Informal.* **1.** brother. **2.** a familiar term of address to a man or boy, usually when his name is not known to the speaker. [back formation from BUDDY]

Bud (bud), *n.* a boy's given name.

Bu·da·pest (bo͞o′də pest′, bo͞o′də pest′; *Hung.* bo͝o′do pesht′), *n.* a city in and the capital of Hungary, in the central part, on the Danube River: formed 1873 from two cities on the W bank of the Danube **(Bu′da** and **Obuda)** and one on the E bank **(Pest).** 1,807,299 (1960).

Budd (bud), *n.* a boy's given name.

Bud·den·brooks (bo͝od′ən bro͝oks′), *n.* a novel (1901) by Thomas Mann.

Bud·dha (bo͝od′ə, bo͞o′də), *n.* **1.** Also called **Butsu, Gautama, Gautama Buddha.** (*Prince Siddhāttha* or *Siddhartha*) 566?–c480 B.C., Indian religious leader: founder of Buddhism. **2.** any of a series of teachers in Buddhism, of whom Gautama was the last, who bring mankind to enlightenment and wisdom. **3.** (*sometimes l.c.*) *Buddhism.* one who has attained full prajna, or enlightenment; Arhat. [< Skt: awakened (*budh-* notice, understand + *-ta* ptp. suffix)]

Buddha

Bud·dha·hood (bo͝od′ə ho͝od′, bo͞o′də-), *n.* the state of existence as a Buddha. [BUDDHA + -HOOD]

Buddh Ga·ya (bo͝od′ gə yä′), a village in central Bihar, in NE India: site of tree under which Siddhartha became the Buddha.

bud·dhi (bo͝od′ē, bo͞o′dē), *n.* *Hinduism, Buddhism.* intellect, seen as an intuitive faculty giving increased spiritual awareness. [< Skt; cf. *bodhati* he awakes]

Bud·dhism (bo͝od′iz əm, bo͞o′diz-), *n.* a religion, originated in India by Buddha (Gautama) and later spreading to China, Burma, Japan, Tibet, and parts of southeast Asia, holding that life is full of suffering caused by desire and that the way to end this suffering is through enlightenment that enables one to halt the endless sequence of births and deaths to which one is otherwise subject. Cf. **Eightfold Path, Four Noble Truths, Hinayana, Mahayana.** [BUDDH(A) + -ISM] —**Bud′dhist,** *n., adj.* —**Bud·dhis′tic, Bud·dhis′ti·cal,** *adj.* —**Bud·dhis′ti·cal·ly,** *adv.*

Bud·dhol·o·gy (bo͞o dol′ə jē, bo͞o-), *n.* the study of Buddha and of the nature and various forms of Buddhahood. [BUDDH(A) + -O- + -LOGY]

Bud·die (bud′ē), *n.* a boy's given name. Also, **Buddy.**

bud·dle (bud′əl, bo͝od′-), *n., v.,* **-dled, -dling.** *Mining.* —*n.* **1.** a shallow trough in which metalliferous ore is separated from gangue by means of running water. —*v.t.* **2.** to wash (ore) in a buddle. [?] —**bud′dler,** *n.*

bud·dle·ia (bud lē′ə, bud′lē ə), *n.* any loganiaceous shrub of the genus *Buddleia*, comprising the butterfly bushes. [named after Adam *Buddle* (d. 1715), English botanist]

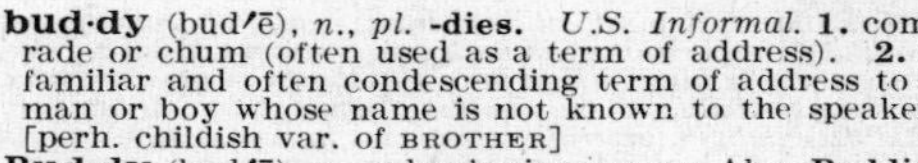

bud·dy (bud′ē), *n., pl.* **-dies.** *U.S. Informal.* **1.** comrade or chum (often used as a term of address). **2.** a familiar and often condescending term of address to a man or boy whose name is not known to the speaker. [perh. childish var. of BROTHER]

Bud·dy (bud′ē), *n.* a boy's given name. Also, **Buddie.**

bud·dy-bud·dy (bud′ē bud′ē), *adj.* *Slang.* very friendly; intimate.

bud′dy sys′tem, (in recreational swimming) the practice of pairing swimmers, each being responsible for the other's safety.

Bu·dën·ny (bo͞o den′ē; *Russ.* bo͞o dyô′nē), *n.* **Se·mën Mi·khai·lo·vich** (se myôn′ mi khī′lo vich), born 1883, Russian general in 1917 revolution and World War II.

budge[1] (buj), *v.,* **budged, budg·ing.** (usually used negatively) —*v.i.* **1.** to move slightly; begin to move: *He pressed the starter and stepped on the gas; the car didn't budge.* **2.** to change one's opinion or stated position; yield: *Once her father had said "no," he wouldn't budge.* —*v.t.* **3.** to cause to move; begin to move: *The three of them couldn't budge the rock.* **4.** to cause (someone) to reconsider or change an opinion, decision, or stated position: *They couldn't budge the lawyer to take the case.* [< MF *boug(er)* (to) stir < VL **bullicāre* to bubble, freq. of L *bullīre* to BOIL[1]] —**budg′er,** *n.*

budge[2] (buj), *n.* **1.** a fur made from lambskin with the wool dressed outward, used esp. as an inexpensive trimming on academic or official gowns. —*adj.* **2.** made from, trimmed, or lined with budge. **3.** *Obs.* pompous; solemn. [ME *bugee*, perh. akin to BUDGET]

Budge (buj), *n.* **(John) Donald,** born 1915, U.S. tennis player.

budg·er·ee (buj′ə rē), *adj.* **1.** *Australian.* good; fine. **2.** pretty. [< native Austral]

budg·er·i·gar (buj′ə rē gär′), an Australian parakeet, *Melopsittacus undulatus*, having greenish plumage with black and yellow markings, bred as a pet in a variety of colors. Also, **budg·er·ee·gah, budg·er·y·gah** (buj′ə rē gä′). Also called **shell parakeet.** [< native Austral]

budg·et (buj′it), *n., v.,* **-et·ed, -et·ing.** —*n.* **1.** an estimate, often itemized, of expected income and expense, or operating results, for a given period in the future. **2.** a plan of operations based on such an estimate. **3.** an itemized allotment of funds for a given period. **4.** the total sum of money set aside or needed for a specific purpose: *The budget for the new factory building was three million dollars.* **5.** a limited stock or supply of something: *His budget of good will was running out.* **6.** *Obs.* a small bag; pouch. —*v.t.* **7.** to plan allotment of (funds, time, etc.). **8.** to deal with (specific funds) in a budget. [late ME *bowgett* < MF *bougette* (*bouge* bag (< L *bulga*; see BULGE) + *-ette* -ETTE)] —**budg·et·ar·y** (buj′i ter′ē), *adj.* —**budg′et·er,** *n.*

budg′et plan′, *U.S.* See **installment plan.**

budg·ie (buj′ē), *n.* *Informal.* budgerigar. [BUDG(ERIGAR) + -IE]

bud′ mu·ta′tion, a variation produced by a genetic change in the bud, such that the seeds produced by the resulting growth perpetuate the change in succeeding generations.

bud′ scale′, scale[1] (def. 3a).

bud′ sport′, a sport resulting from a bud mutation or bud variation.

bud′ stick′, *Hort.* a shoot of a plant from which buds are cut for the propagation of that plant.

bud′ varia′tion, any variation in a bud due to changes in either or both its genetic composition or environment, such that the resulting flower, fruit, or shoot differs from others of the same plant or species.

Bud·weis (*Ger.* bo͝ot′vīs), *n.* a city in W Czechoslovakia, on the Moldau River. 67,944 (1963). Czech, **České Budějovice.**

Bu·ell (byo͞o′əl), *n.* **Don Car·los** (kär′lōs), 1818–98, Union general in the U.S. Civil War.

Bue·na (byo͞o′nə), *n.* a town in S New Jersey. 3243 (1960).

Bue′na Park′ (bwā′nə), a city in SW California. 46,401 (1960).

bue·nas no·ches (bwe′näs nô′ches), *Spanish.* good night.

Bue·na·ven·tu·ra (bwā′nə ven to͝or′ə, -tyo͝or′ə; *Sp.* bwe′nä ven to͞o′rä), *n.* a seaport in W Colombia. 35,087 (1951).

Bue·na Vis·ta (bwe′nä vēs′tä *for 1;* byo͞o′nə vis′tə *for 2*), **1.** a village in NE Mexico, near Saltillo: American victory in battle (1847) during the Mexican War. **2.** a town in W Virginia. 6300 (1960).

bue·no (bwe′nô), *interj.* *Spanish.* good; all right.

Bue·nos Ai·res (bwā′nəs īʳ′iz, bō′nəs âr′ēz; *Sp.* bwe′nôs ī′res), a seaport in and the capital of Argentina, in the E part, on the Rio de la Plata. 3,240,000 (est. 1965).

bue·nos di·as (bwe′nôs dē′äs), *Spanish.* good morning; good day.

buff[1] (buf), *n.* **1.** a kind of thick leather, originally and properly made of buffalo skin but later also of other skins, light yellow with napped surface, used for making belts, pouches, etc. **2.** a buff stick or buff wheel. **3.** a thick, short coat of buffalo leather, worn esp. by soldiers in 17th-century England and by American colonists. **4.** yellowish-brown; medium or dark tan. **5.** *Informal.* the bare skin. **6.** *Informal.* a devotee or well-informed student of some activity or subject: *Civil War buffs avidly read the new biography of Grant. He's always been a trolley-car buff.* **7.** *Informal.* a buffalo. —*adj.* **8.** made of buff leather. **9.** having the color of buff. —*v.t.* **10.** to clean or polish (metal) or give a grainless finish of high luster to (plated surfaces) with or as with a buff stick or buff wheel. **11.** to dye or stain in a buff color. **12.** to polish or shine, esp. with a buffer: *to buff shoes; to buff a waxed floor.* [earlier *buffe* wild ox, back formation from *buffle* < F < LL *būfalus*; see BUFFALO] —**buff′a·bil′i·ty,** *n.* —**buff′a·ble,** *adj.*
—**Syn. 10.** burnish, polish, shine.

buff[2] (buf), *v.t.* **1.** to reduce or deaden the force of; act as a buffer. —*n.* **2.** *Chiefly Dial.* a blow; slap. [late ME *buffe*, back formation from BUFFET[1]]

buf·fa (bo͞o′fə; *It.* bo͞of′fä), *n., pl.* **-fe** (-fā; *It.* -fe). **1.** a woman who sings comic roles in opera. **2.** See **opera buffa.** [< It; fem. of BUFFO]

buf·fa·lo (buf′ə lō′), *n., pl.* **-loes, -los,** (*esp. collectively*) **-lo,** *v.,* **-loed, -lo·ing.** —*n.* **1.** any of several large wild oxen of the family *Bovidae.* Cf. **bison, Cape buffalo, water buffalo. 2.** See **buffalo robe. 3.** a buffalofish. **4.** *Mil. Slang.* a heavily armed and armored amphibious vehicle. **5.** a shuffling tapdance step. —*v.t. U.S. Informal.* **6.** to baffle; confuse; mystify: *He was buffaloed by the complexity of the problem.* **7.** to impress or intimidate by a display of power, importance, etc.: *He didn't let the older boys buffalo him.* [earlier *bufalo* < It < LL *būfalus,* var. of L *būbalus* BUBAL]

Buf·fa·lo (buf′ə lō′), *n.* **1.** a port in W New York, on Lake Erie. 532,759 (1960). **2.** a town in N Wyoming. 2907 (1960).

buf′falo ber′ry, 1. Also called **buf′falo bush′.** either of two North American, elaeagnaceous shrubs, *Shepherdia argentea,* or *S. canadensis,* bearing an edible, yellow or red berry. **2.** the fruit itself.

Buf′falo Bill′. See **Cody, William Frederick.**

buf′falo bird′, a cowbird, *Molothrus ater,* of North America.

buf′falo bug′, the buffalo carpet beetle. See under **carpet beetle.**

buf′falo car′pet bee′tle. See under **carpet beetle.**

buf′falo cloth′, a heavyweight woolen fabric constructed in twill weave and having a shaggy pile.

buf′falo cur′rant, an ornamental shrub, *Ribes odoratum,* of the central U.S., having showy, drooping clusters of fragrant, yellow flowers and edible, black fruit. [so called from its growth in a region where there were buffalo]

buf·fa·lo·fish (buf′ə lō′fish′), *n., pl.* (*esp. collectively*) **-fish,** (*esp. referring to two or more kinds or species*) **-fish·es.** any of several large, carplike, North American, fresh-water fishes of the genus *Ictiobus,* of the sucker family. [BUFFALO + FISH]

buf′falo gnat′. See **black fly.**

buf′falo grass′, 1. a short grass, *Buchloë dactyloides,* very prevalent on the dry plains east of the Rocky Mountains. **2.** any of several short, tufted grasses that do not form continuous sod.

Buf′falo In′dian. See **Plains Indian.**

buf′falo moth′, the buffalo carpet beetle. See under **carpet beetle.**

buf′falo robe′, the prepared skin of an American bison, with the hair left on, used as a lap robe.

buff′ coat′, a defensive coat of the 17th century, worn alone or with a cuirass, made of oiled hide.

buffe (buf), *n. Armor.* a piece of plate armor for the lower part of the face and the throat, used with a burgonet. [var. of *buffie* < It *buff(a)* blow-hole of helmet (see BUFFO) + -IE]

buf·fer[1] (buf′ər), *n.* **1.** an apparatus at the end of a railroad car, railroad track, etc., for absorbing shock during coupling, collision stops, etc. **2.** any device, material, or apparatus used for a shield, cushion, or bumper, esp. on machinery. **3.** any intermediate or intervening shield or device reducing the danger of interaction between two machines, chemicals, electronic components, etc. **4.** See **buffer state. 5.** any reserve moneys, negotiable securities, legal procedures, etc., which protect a person, organization, or country against financial ruin. **6.** one who protects and shields another from petty matters or the brunt of anger or criticism. **7.** *Ecol.* an animal that becomes the prey of a predator that usually feeds on a different species of animal. **8.** *Computer Technol.* an intermediate memory unit for temporarily holding computer data until the proper unit is ready to receive the data, as when the receiving unit has an operating speed lower than that of the unit feeding the data to it. **9.** a circuit with a single output activated by one or more of several inputs. **10.** *Chem.* **a.** any substance or mixture of compounds that, added to a solution, is capable of neutralizing both acids and bases without appreciably changing the original acidity or alkalinity of the solution. **b.** Also, **buff′er solu′tion.** a solution containing such a substance. —*v.t.* **11.** *Chem.* to treat with a buffer. **12.** to cushion, shield, or protect: *The Federal Reserve Bank buffered the economy by its new interest rates.* **13.** to lessen the adverse effect of; ease: *The drug buffered his pain.* [BUFF[2] + -ER[1]]

buff·er[2] (buf′ər), *n.* **1.** a device for polishing or buffing, as a buff stick or buff wheel. **2.** a worker who uses such a device. [BUFF[1] + -ER[1]]

buff·er[3] (buf′ər), *n. Brit. Slang.* **1.** an old-fashioned or incompetent person: *He was a bit of a buffer whenever he tried coping with anything mechanical.* **2.** a fellow; man: *a nice old buffer.* **3.** a chief boatswain's mate in the British navy. [?]

buff′er state′, a small state lying between potentially hostile larger areas.

buf·fet[1] (buf′it), *n., v.,* **-fet·ed, -fet·ing.** —*n.* **1.** a blow, as with the hand or fist. **2.** a violent shock or concussion. —*v.t.* **3.** to strike; as with the hand or fist. **4.** to strike against or push repeatedly: *The wind buffeted the house. The boats were buffeted against one another during the storm.* **5.** to contend against; battle. —*v.i.* **6.** to struggle with blows of hand or fist. **7.** to force one's way by a fight, struggle, etc. [ME < OF *buffe* a blow + *-et* -ET] —**buf′fet·er,** *n.*

buf·fet[2] (bə fā′, bōō-; *Brit.* buf′it; *Fr.* bʏ fe′), *n., pl.* **buf·fets** (bə fāz′, bōō-; *Brit.* buf′its; *Fr.* bʏ fe′), *adj.* —*n.* **1.** a sideboard or cabinet for holding china, table linen, etc. **2.** a counter, bar, or the like, for lunch or refreshments. **3.** a restaurant containing such a counter or bar. **4.** a meal laid out on a table or sideboard so that guests may serve themselves and eat in small, informal groups rather than sitting at a dining table: *Come for cocktails and buffet next Sunday evening.* —*adj.* **5.** consisting of food, refreshments, etc., laid out on tables or buffets from which guests or customers serve themselves: *buffet supper; buffet service.* [< F < ?]

buffet′ car′, *Railroads.* a coach or chair car having facilities for preparing or serving meals.

buff′ing wheel′. See **buff wheel.**

buf·fle·head (buf′əl hed′), *n.* a small North American duck, *Bucephala albeola,* the male of which has bushy head plumage. [*buffle* (see BUFF[1]) + HEAD] —**buf′fle·head′ed,** *adj.*

buf·fo (bōō′fō; *It.* bōōf′fô), *n., pl.* **-fi** (-fē), **-fos.** *Music.* **1.** (in opera) a comedy part, usually bass. **2.** a male opera singer who specializes in comic roles. [< It: ridiculous (adj.), buffoon (n.), akin to *buffa* a jest (orig. a puff of air), *buffare* to puff, blow]

Buf·fon (bʏ fôɴ′), *n.* **Georges Louis Le·clerc** (zhôrzh lwē lə klεʀ′), **Comte de,** 1707–88, French naturalist.

Buf·fon's′ nee′dle prob′lem (bōō fonz′), *Math.* a problem concerned with the probability that a needle of given length tossed onto a sheet with parallel lines spaced evenly at given intervals will land across one of the lines on the sheet.

buf·foon (bə fōōn′), *n.* **1.** one who amuses others by tricks, jokes, odd gestures and postures, etc. **2.** one given to coarse or undignified joking. [earlier *buffon* < F < It *buffone,* equiv. to *buff(o)* BUFFO + *-one* aug. suffix] —**buf·foon·er·y** (bə fōō′nə rē), **buf·foon′ism,** *n.* —**buf·foon′ish,** *adj.* —**buf·foon′ish·ness,** *n.*
—**Syn. 1.** jester, clown, fool. **2.** boor.

buff′ stick′, a small stick covered with leather or the like, used in polishing.

buff′ top′, *Jewelry.* a very low, almost flat, cabochon cut.

buff′ wheel′, a wheel for buffing, consisting of a number of leather or canvas disks. Also, **buff′ing wheel′.**

buf′fy coat′ (buf′ē), *Biochem.* a yellowish-white layer consisting of leukocytes that, upon centrifugation of blood, covers the erythrocytes. [BUFF[1] + -Y[1]]

Bu·ford (byōō′fərd), *n.* **1.** a town in central Georgia. 4168 (1960). **2.** a boy's given name.

bu·fo·ten·ine (byōō′fə ten′ēn, -in), *n. Pharm.* a toxic, crystalline alkaloid, $HOC_8H_5NCH_2CH_2N(CH_3)_2$, obtained from the skin glands of toads, that causes a rise in the blood pressure: used in experimental medicine, chiefly to induce hallucinations. Also, **bu·fo·ten·in** (byōō′fə ten′in). [< L *būfo* toad + *-ten* (< ? Gk *ten(ōn)* sinew, tendon) + -INE[2]]

bug[1] (bug), *n., v.,* **bugged, bug·ging.** —*n.* **1.** Also called **true bug.** a hemipterous insect. **2.** (not used scientifically) any insect or insectlike invertebrate. **3.** *Chiefly Brit.* a bedbug. **4.** *Informal.* any microorganism, esp. a virus: *He was laid up for a week by an intestinal bug.* **5.** *U.S. Informal.* a defect or imperfection, esp. in a mechanical device or a new airplane: *The test flight was to discover the bugs in the new plane.* **6.** *Slang.* **a.** one who has a great enthusiasm for something; fan or hobbyist: *His expensive rig showed he was a hi-fi bug.* **b.** a craze or obsession: *He's got the sport-car bug and goes to all the rallies.* **c.** a hidden microphone. **7.** an asterisk. **8.** *Horse Racing.* the five-pound weight allowance which can be claimed by an apprentice jockey. **9.** a telegraph key that automatically transmits a series of dots when moved to one side and one dash when moved to the other. **10.** *Poker Slang.* a joker that can be used only as an ace or as a wild card to fill a straight or flush. **11.** *Print. Slang.* a label printed on certain matter to indicate that it was produced by a union shop. **12.** any of various fishing plugs resembling an insect. —*v.t. U.S. Slang.* **13.** to install a secret listening device in (a room, building, etc.) or on (a telephone or other device): *The evidence was inadmissible because the phone had been bugged.* **14.** to bother; annoy; pester: *Look, you're bugging me. She's always bugging him to get her into show business.* —*v.i.* **15.** *Slang.* to leave or depart, esp. rapidly (often fol. by *out*). [earlier *bugge* beetle, appar. alter. of ME *budde* (as in *maggot, maddock*), OE *buddha* beetle]

bug[2] (bug), *n. Obs.* a bogy; hobgoblin. [ME *bugge* scarecrow, demon, perh. < Welsh *bwg* ghost]

Bug (bug; *Pol.* bōōg, bŏŏk; *Russ.* bŏŏk), *n.* **1.** a river in E central Europe, forming part of the boundary between E Poland and the W Soviet Union, flowing NW to the Vistula River. 450 mi. long. **2.** a river in the SW Soviet Union in Europe, flowing from the SW Ukraine to the Dnieper estuary. ab. 530 mi. long.

bug·a·boo (bug′ə bōō′), *n., pl.* **-boos.** some imaginary thing that causes fear or worry; bugbear; bogy. [earlier *buggybow.* See BOGY, BOO]

Bu·ga·yev (bōō gä′yəf), *n.* **Bo·ris Ni·ko·la·ye·vich** (bô ʀēs′ nē′ko lä′yə vich). See **Bely, Andrei.**

bug·bane (bug′bān′), *n.* any of several tall, erect, ranunculaceous herbs of the genus *Cimicifuga,* as *C. americana,* of the eastern U.S., having clusters of white flowers which are supposed to repel insects. [BUG[1] + BANE]

bug·bear (bug′bâr′), *n.* **1.** any source, real or imaginary, of needless fright or fear. **2.** *Obs.* a goblin that eats up naughty children. [BUG[2] + BEAR[2]] —**bug′-bear′ish,** *adj.*

bug·eye (bug′ī′), *n., pl.* **-eyes.** *Naut.* a ketch-rigged sailing vessel, formerly sometimes built entirely or partly of logs, having a fore-and-aft rig on two masts of almost equal height raked sharply aft, used on Chesapeake Bay. Also called **Chesapeake bugeye.** [BUG[1] + EYE, after the former practice of painting a large eye on each bow]

bug-eyed (bug′īd′), *adj. Slang.* with bulging eyes, as from surprise; astonished. [BUG[1] + EYED]

bug·ger (bug′ər), *n.* **1.** a sodomite. **2.** a fellow, lad, or child, often used affectionately: *a cute little bugger.* —*v.t.* **3.** to commit sodomy on. —*v.i.* **4. bugger off,** *Brit. Slang.* to depart; leave. [ME *bougre,* var. of *bolgre* < LL *Bulgar(us)* heretic, lit., Bulgarian] —**bug′ger·y,** *n.*

bug·gy[1] (bug′ē), *n., pl.* **-gies. 1.** *U.S.* a light, four-wheeled carriage with a single seat and a transverse spring. **2.** *Brit.* a light, two-wheeled, open carriage. **3.** (in India) a light, two-wheeled carriage with a folding top. **4.** See **baby buggy. 5.** *Slang.* an automobile, esp. an old or dilapidated one. **6.** *Metall.* a car, as for transporting ingots or charges for open-hearth furnaces. **7.** *Mining.* a small car for transporting coal. [?]

Buggy

bug·gy[2] (bug′ē), *adj.,* **-gi·er, -gi·est. 1.** infested with bugs. **2.** *Slang.* crazy; peculiar; silly: *a buggy old lady who continually mutters to herself; a child buggy about dogs.* [BUG[1] + -Y[1]] —**bug′gi·ness,** *n.*

bug·house (bug′hous′), *n., pl.* **-hous·es** (-hou′ziz), *adj. U.S. Slang.* —*n.* **1.** an insane asylum. —*adj.* **2.** insane; crazy. [BUG(S + MAD)HOUSE]

Bug′house Square′, *U.S.* any of several street intersections or park malls in various big cities where political zealots, folk evangelists, etc., congregate to argue and make soap-box speeches, as Union Square in New York City, Pershing Square in Los Angeles, and esp. Washington Square in Chicago.

bug-juice (bug′jōōs′), *n. Slang.* **1.** an alcoholic beverage, esp. of an inferior quality. **2.** an unusual or concocted drink.

bu·gle[1] (byōō′gəl), *n., v.,* **-gled, -gling.** —*n.* **1.** a brass wind instrument resembling a cornet and sometimes having keys or valves, used typically for sounding military signals. —*v.i.* **2.** to sound a bugle. **3.** (of bull elks) to utter a rutting call. —*v.t.* **4.** to call by or with a bugle: *to bugle reveille.* [ME, short for *bugle horn, bugle* < OF < L *būcul(us),* equiv. to *bū-* var. s. of *bōs* ox + *-culus* -CLE] —**bu′gler,** *n.*

Bugle

bu·gle[2] (byōō′gəl), *n.* any menthaceous plant of the genus *Ajuga,* esp. *A. reptans,* a low, blue-flowered herb. [ME < OF < LL *bugul(a)* a kind of plant]

bu·gle[3] (byōō′gəl), *n.* **1.** a tubular glass bead, usually black, used for ornamenting dresses. —*adj.* **2.** Also, **bu′gled.** ornamented with bugles. [?]

bu·gle·weed (byōō′gəl wēd′), *n.* **1.** a menthaceous plant of the genus *Lycopus,* esp. *L. virginicus,* reputed to have medicinal properties. **2.** See **wild indigo. 3.** bugle[2]. [BUGLE[2] + WEED[1]]

bu·gloss (byōō′glos, -glôs), *n.* any of various Old World, boraginaceous herbs, as *Anchusa officinalis,* having rough leaves, used in medicine, and *Lycopsis arvensis,* a bristly, blue-flowered herb. [late ME *buglossa* < L, equiv. to *bū-* ox (see BUGLE[1]) + *glōssa* tongue (< Gk); alter. of Gk *boúglōssos*]

bug·out (bug′out′), *n.* **1.** *Mil. Slang.* a hasty retreat from combat, esp. in defiance of orders. **2.** *Slang.* a person who absents himself from his duties. [n. use of v. phrase *bug out* leave]

bugs (bugz), *adj. Slang.* crazy; insane. [*bug* maniac, mania, perh. deriv. of *bug* adj. (now dial.) self-important, pompous, appar. var. of BIG[1]; cf. BUGGY[2]]

bug·seed (bug′sēd′), *n.* an annual, chenopodiaceous herb, *Corispermum hyssopifolium,* of northern temperate regions: so called from the flat, oval shape of its seeds. [BUG[1] + SEED]

buhl (bōōl), *n.* (*often cap.*) elaborate inlaid work of woods, metals, tortoise shell, ivory, etc. Also, **boule, boulle, buhl·work** (bōōl′wûrk′), **boulework.** [from Germanized form of F *boulle* or *boule,* named after A. C. *Boulle* or *Boule* (1642–1732), French cabinetmaker]

Buhl (byōōl), *n.* a town in S Idaho. 3059 (1960).

buhr (bûr), *n.* **1.** burr[1] (def. 2). **2.** burr[4]. **3.** burstone.

buhr·stone (bûr′stōn′), *n.* burstone.

build (bild), *v.,* **built** or (*Archaic*) **build·ed; build·ing;** *n.* —*v.t.* **1.** to construct (esp. something complex) by assembling and joining parts or materials: *To build a house or an empire requires skill.* **2.** to establish, increase, or strengthen (often fol. by *up*): *to build a business; to build up one's hopes.* **3.** to mold, form, create: *to build boys into men; to build a pile of bricks into a factory.* **4.** to base; found: *Don't build your future on dreams.* **5.** *Games.* **a.** to make (words) from letters. **b.** to assemble (cards) according to number, suit, etc., as in melding. —*v.i.* **6.** to engage in the art, practice, or business of building. **7.** to form or construct a plan, system of thought, etc. (usually fol. by *on* or *upon*): *He built on the philosophies of the past.* **8.** to increase or develop toward a maximum, as of intensity, tempo, magnitude, etc. (often fol. by *up*): *The plot builds steadily toward a final dramatic scene.* **9. build in,** to build or incorporate as part of something else: *to build in bookcases between the windows.* **10. build up, a.** to establish; increase: *to build up a bank account.* **b.** to strengthen. **c.** to prepare in stages. **d.** to fill in with houses; develop into an urban area. **e.** *Slang.* to praise or flatter someone: *His parents built him up to such a degree that he became conceited.* —*n.* **11.** the manner or form of construction: *The house was of modern build. He had a strong build.* **12.** *Masonry.* **a.** a vertical joint. **b.** the vertical dimension of a stone laid on its bed. [ME *bilde(n),* OE *byldan,* deriv. of *bold,* var. of *botl* dwelling, house] —**build′a·ble,** *adj.*

build·er (bil′dər), *n.* **1.** a person who builds. **2.** one who constructs buildings under contract or as a speculation. **3.** a substance, as an abrasive or filler, added to soaps or other cleaning agents to increase their effectiveness. [ME *bildere.* See BUILD, -ER[1]]

build′er's knot′, *Naut.* See **clove hitch.**

build·ing (bil′ding), *n.* **1.** a relatively permanent, essentially boxlike construction having a roof and often windows and enclosing within its walls space, usually on more than one level, for any of a wide variety of activities, as living, entertaining, manufacturing, etc. **2.** anything built or constructed. **3.** the act, business, or practice of constructing houses, office buildings, etc. [ME *byldinge.* See BUILD, -ING[1]] —**build′ing·less,** *adj.*
—**Syn. 1.** BUILDING, EDIFICE, STRUCTURE refer to something built. BUILDING and STRUCTURE may apply to either a finished or an unfinished product of construction, and carry no implications as to size or condition. EDIFICE is not only a more formal word, but narrower in application, referring to a completed structure, and usually a large and imposing one. BUILDING generally connotes a useful purpose (houses, schools, business offices, etc.); STRUCTURE suggests the planning and constructive process.

build′ing and loan′ associa′tion. See **savings and loan association.**

build′ing line′, (on a building lot) a line within, or coinciding with, the property line, beyond which it is illegal to build.

build′ing pa′per, heavy paper used esp. in the construction of frame buildings to block drafts, for insulation, etc.

build′ing trades′, those trades, as carpentry, masonry, or plastering, that are primarily concerned with the construction and finishing of buildings.

build-up (bild′up′), *n.* **1.** a building up, as of military forces in a particular area; increase in amount or number in a particular region; concentration. **2.** a process of growth; strengthening; development: *The build-up of the nation's heavy industry is vital.* **3.** a publicity, public-relations, or advertising campaign designed to enhance a reputation or popularize someone or something: *The studio spent $50,000 on the new star's build-up.* **4.** an accumulation of a particular type of material or form of energy: *The build-up of salt deposits took millions of years. The build-up of heat in the space capsule's outer wall was dangerous.* **5.** a process of preparation or a course of preliminary action undertaken with a view to making possible the achievement of an ultimate objective: *a lengthy build-up to an offer to buy the property for next to nothing; Where women are concerned, never underestimate the value of a build-up.* **6.** a progressive or sequential development: *The build-up of helium atoms from hydrogen occurs in the sun. The build-up of authentic character portrayal from simple words is an actor's duty.* **7.** an increase, as in potential, intensity, pressure, or the like: *The build-up of suspense began halfway through the movie. A build-up of voltage at the grid was caused by a circuit defect.* **8.** encouragement; a psychological lift: *Everytime I need a build-up, I look at her picture.* Also, **build′up′.** [n. use of v. phrase *build up*]

built (bilt), *v.* **1.** pt. and pp. of **build.** —*adj.* **2.** *Naut.* noting any member or part of a vessel assembled from pieces rather than formed as a solid or a single piece: *built frame; built spar.* **3.** *Slang.* having a good figure: *She sure is built!* —*n.* **4.** *Slang.* a good figure or physique: *That's some built on that new secretary!*

built-in (bilt′in′), *adj.* **1.** built so as to be an integral and permanent part of a larger construction: *The wall has a built-in bookcase.* **2.** existing as a natural or characteristic part of something; inherent: *A practical man has a built-in contempt for daydreaming.* —*n.* **3.** a built-in piece of furniture or appliance.

built-up (bilt′up′), *adj.* **1.** built by the fastening together of several parts, or enlarged by the addition of layers: *This shoe has a built-up heel.* **2.** (of an area) filled in with houses or inhabited as an urban region.

built′-up mast′, *Naut.* See **made mast.**

buird·ly (bʏrd′lē), *adj. Scot.* large and strong; well-built; sturdy. [? var. of BURLY]

Buis·son (bwē sôɴ′), *n.* **Fer·di·nand É·douard** (fer-dē näɴ′ ā dwar′), 1841–1932, French educator: Nobel peace prize 1927.

Bui·ten·zorg (boit′ən zôrkʜ′, bœit′-), *n.* the former Dutch name of **Bogor.**

Bu·jum·bu·ra (bo͞o jo͝om bo͝or′ä), *n.* a port in and the capital of Burundi, in the W part, on Lake Tanganyika. 70,000 (est. 1965). Formerly, **Usumbura.**

Bu·ka·vu (bo͞o kä′vo͞o), *n.* a city in the E Republic of the Congo. 33,268 (est. 1958). Formerly, **Costermansville.**

bukh (bo͝ok), *Anglo-Indian.* —*v.i.* **1.** to prate or brag. —*n.* **2.** small talk; prattle; bragging. Also, **buck.** [< Hindi *bak*]

Bu·kha·ra (bo͞o kär′ə; *Russ.* bo͞o kʜä′rä), *n.* **1.** a former state in SW Asia: now incorporated into Uzbekistan, in the SW Soviet Union in Asia. **2.** a city in SE Uzbekistan, in the SW Soviet Union in Asia. 69,000 (1959). Also, **Bokhara.**

Bu·kha·rin (bo͞o kʜä′rin), *n.* **Ni·ko·lai I·va·no·vich** (ni ko lī′ i vä′no vich), 1888–1938, Russian editor, writer, and communist leader.

Bu·ko·vi·na (bo͞o′kə vē′nə; *Rum.* bo͞o kô vē′nä), *n.* Bucovina.

Bul (bo͝ol), *n. Chiefly Biblical.* a month equivalent to Heshvan of the modern Jewish calendar. I Kings 6:38.

bul., bulletin.

Bu·la·wa·yo (bo͞o′lə wä′yō), *n.* a city in SW Rhodesia: mining center. 214,400 (est. 1964).

bulb (bulb), *n.* **1.** *Bot.* **a.** a usually subterranean bud having fleshy leaves, the stem of which is reduced to a flat disk, rooting from the under side, as in the onion, lily, etc. **b.** a plant growing from such a bud. **2.** any round, enlarged part, esp. at the end of a cylindrical object: *the bulb of a thermometer.* **3.** *Elect.* **a.** the glass housing, in which partial vacuum has been established, which contains the filament of an incandescent electric lamp. **b.** an incandescent or fluorescent electric lamp. **4.** See **vacuum tube. 5.** See **medulla oblongata. 6.** *Building Trades.* a rounded thickening at the toe of an angle iron or tee. **7.** *Naut.* a cylindrical or spherical prominence at the forefoot of certain vessels to improve hull characteristics. [< L *bulb(us)* < Gk *bolbós* onion, bulbous plant] —**bulb′less,** *adj.*

Bulb (def. 7)

bulb·ar (bul′bər, -bär), *adj.* of or pertaining to a bulb, esp. to the medulla oblongata. [BULB + -AR[1]]

bulb·if·er·ous (bul bif′ər əs), *adj.* producing bulbs. [< NL *bulbifer* (see BULB, -I-, -FER) + -OUS]

bul·bil (bul′bil), *n. Bot.* **1.** a little bulb. **2.** a small, aerial bulb growing in the axils of leaves, as in the tiger lily, or replacing flower buds, as in the common onion. Also, **bul·bel** (bul′bəl, -bel). [< NL *bulbill(us),* equiv. to L *bulb(us)* BULB + *-illus* dim. suffix]

bulb′ keel′, *Naut.* a narrow keel having a swelling weight of lead or iron at the bottom.

bul·bo·u·re·thral (bul′bō yo͞o rē′thrəl), *adj. Anat., Zool.* of or pertaining to the rounded mass of tissue surrounding the urethra at the root of the penis. [BULB + -O- + URETHRAL]

bul′boure′thral gland′, *Anat., Zool.* See **Cowper's gland.**

bulb·ous (bul′bəs), *adj.* **1.** bulb-shaped; bulging. **2.** having or growing from bulbs. Also, **bul·ba·ceous** (bul-bā′shəs). [< L *bulbōs(us).* See BULB, -OUS]

bulb′ous but′tercup, a European buttercup, *Ranunculus bulbosus,* having yellow flowers: a common weed in the U.S. Also called **bulb′ous crow′foot.**

bul·bul (bo͝ol′bo͝ol), *n.* **1.** a songbird often mentioned in Persian poetry, regarded as being a nightingale. **2.** any of several oscine birds of the family *Pycnonotidae,* of the Old World tropics. [< Pers]

Bul·finch (bo͝ol′finch′), *n.* **1. Charles,** 1763–1844, U.S. architect. **2.** his son, **Thomas,** 1796–1867, U.S. author and mythologist.

Bulg., **1.** Bulgaria. **2.** Bulgarian. Also, **Bulg**

Bul·ga·nin (bo͝ol gä′nin), *n.* **Ni·ko·lai A·le·ksan·dro·vich** (ni ko lī′ ä′le ksän′dro vich), born 1895, Soviet political leader: premier 1955–58.

Bul·gar (bul′gər, bo͝ol′gär), *n.* Bulgarian (def. 1).

Bul·gar·i·a (bul gâr′ē ə, bo͝ol-), *n.* a republic in SE Europe. 8,144,000 (est. 1964); 42,800 sq. mi. *Cap.:* Sofia.

Bul·gar·i·an (bul gâr′ē ən, bo͝ol-), *n.* **1.** Also, **Bulgar.** a native or inhabitant of Bulgaria. **2.** a Slavic language, the language of Bulgaria. *Abbr.:* Bulg —*adj.* **3.** of or pertaining to Bulgaria, its people, or their language. [BULGARI(A) + -AN]

bulge (bulj), *n., v.,* **bulged, bulg·ing.** —*n.* **1.** a rounded projection, bend, or protruding part; protuberance; hump: *a bulge in a wall; a bulge in the rug.* **2.** *Naut. Rare.* bilge (def. 1). **3.** a rising in small waves on the surface of a body of water, caused by the action of a fish or fishes in pursuit of food underwater. **4.** any sudden increase, as of numbers, sales, prices, etc.: *The bulge in profits was due to increased sales effort.* —*v.i.* **5.** to swell or bend outward; be protuberant: *After the huge dinner, his stomach bulged even more.* **6.** to be filled to capacity: *The box bulged with cookies. His mind bulged with ideas.* —*v.t.* **7.** to make protuberant. [ME: bag, hump < OF < L *bulga* bag < Celt; cf. Ir *bolg* bag] —**bulg′i·ness,** *n.* —**bulg′ing·ly,** *adv.* —**bulg′y,** *adj.*

Bulge (bulj), *n.* **Battle of the,** the final major German counteroffensive in World War II, begun December 16, 1944, and thrusting deep into Allied territory in N and E Belgium: repulsed, January, 1945.

bulg·er (bul′jər), *n. Golf.* a wood having a convex face, now rarely used. [BULGE + -ER[1]]

-bulia, *Chiefly Psychiatry.* a learned borrowing from Greek meaning "will," used in the formation of compound words: *abulia.* [< NL < Gk *-boulia,* equiv. to *boul(ḗ)* will + *-ia* -IA]

bu·lim·i·a (byo͞o lim′ē ə), *n. Pathol.* abnormally voracious appetite; a condition characterized by an unnaturally constant hunger. Also, **boulimia.** Also called **hyperphagia.** [< NL < Gk *boulīmía* extreme hunger, equiv. to *bou-* intensive prefix (deriv. of *bou-,* s. of *boûs*) ox + *līm(ós)* hunger + *-ia* -IA] —**bu·lim′ic, bu·lim·i·ac** (byo͞o lim′ē ak′), *adj.*

bulk[1] (bulk), *n.* **1.** magnitude in three dimensions: *a ship of great bulk.* **2.** the greater part; the main mass or body: *The bulk of the debt was paid.* **3.** goods or cargo not in packages, boxes, bags, etc. **4.** food which forms a fibrous residue in digestion, allaying hunger and promoting normal elimination. **5.** (of paper, cardboard, etc.) thickness, esp. in relation to weight. **6.** the body of a living creature. **7. in bulk, a.** unpackaged: *Fresh orange juice is shipped from Florida in bulk by tank car or by ship.* **b.** in large quantities: *The wharves were covered with coffee in bulk.* —*v.i.* **8.** to increase in size; expand; swell. **9.** to be of or give the appearance of great weight, size, or importance: *The problem bulks large in his mind.* **10.** (of paper, cardboard, etc.) to be of a specific thickness, esp. in relation to weight. **11.** to gather, form, or mix into a cohesive or uniform mass. —*v.t.* **12.** to cause to swell, grow, or increase in weight or thickness. **13.** to gather, bring together, or mix. [ME *bolke* heap, cargo, hold < Scand; cf. Icel *búlki* cargo, ship's hold] —**Syn. 1.** See **size**[1].

bulk[2] (bulk), *n.* a structure, as a stall, projecting from the front of a building. [ME: stall; appar. special use of BULK[1]]

bulk·head (bulk′hed′), *n.* **1.** *Naut.* any of various wall-like constructions inside a vessel for forming watertight compartments, subdividing space, strengthening the structure, preventing surge of liquids, etc. **2.** a transverse partition or reinforcing frame in the body of an airplane. **3.** *Civ. Eng.* **a.** a partition built in a subterranean passage to prevent the passage of air, water, or mud. **b.** a retaining structure of timber, steel, or reinforced concrete, used for shore protection and in harbor works. **4.** *Building Trades.* **a.** a horizontal or inclined outside door over a stairway leading to a cellar. **b.** a boxlike structure, as on a roof, covering a stairwell or other opening. [BULK[2] + HEAD] —**bulk′head′ed,** *adj.*

bulk′head deck′, *Naut.* the uppermost continuous deck in the hull of a vessel, forming watertight compartments with the main transverse bulkheads.

bulk·head·ing (bulk′hed′ing), *n.* the construction of bulkheads; bulkheads in general. [BULKHEAD + -ING[1]]

bulk′ mail′, a category of mail established by postal regulations for mailing large numbers of identical printed items to individual addressees at less than first-class rates, as circulars, bulletins, or the like.

bulk′ mod′ulus, *Physics.* a coefficient of elasticity of a substance, expressing the ratio between a pressure that acts to change the volume of the substance and the fractional change in volume produced. Also called **modulus of volume elasticity.**

bulk·y (bul′kē), *adj.,* **bulk·i·er, bulk·i·est.** of relatively great and cumbersome bulk or size. [BULK[1] + -Y[1]] —**bulk′i·ly,** *adv.* —**bulk′i·ness,** *n.*
—**Syn.** massive, ponderous, unwieldy, clumsy, cumbersome. —**Ant.** small.

bull[1] (bo͝ol), *n.* **1.** the male of a bovine animal, esp. of the genus *Bos,* with sexual organs intact and capable of reproduction. **2.** the male of certain other animals: *an elephant bull.* **3.** a large, solidly built person. **4.** a person who believes that general business conditions are or will be favorable. **5.** one who buys, speculates, or operates in stocks or commodities to profit from or cause a rise in prices (opposed to *bear*). **6.** (*cap.*) *Astron., Astrol.* the constellation or sign of Taurus. **7.** a bulldog. **8.** *Slang.* a policeman. **9.** *Poker Informal.* a player who raises frequently without consideration for the cards that he holds. **10. bull in a china shop,** a person lacking the tact, mobility, or comprehension required in a particular situation, esp. a delicate one. **11. take the bull by the horns,** to attack a problem fearlessly. —*adj.* **12.** male. **13.** of, pertaining to, or resembling a bull, as in strength. **14.** having to do with or marked by rising prices, as of stocks: *bull market.* —*v.t.* **15.** *Stock Exchange.* to attempt to raise the price of. **16.** to operate in, for a rise in price. **17.** to force; shove: *to bull a bill through Congress; to bull one's way through a crowd.* **18.** *Naut.* to ram (a buoy). [ME *bule,* OE *bula;* akin to Icel *boli;* see BULLOCK] —**bull′-like′,** *adj.*

bull[2] (bo͝ol), *n.* **1.** a bulla or seal. **2.** *Rom. Cath. Ch.* a formal papal document having a bulla attached. [ME *bulle* < ML *bulla* seal, sealed document; see BULLA]

bull[3] (bo͝ol), *n. Slang.* **1.** exaggerations; lies; nonsense. **2. shoot the bull,** *Slang.* **a.** to talk aimlessly. **b.** to brag or exaggerate: *They have a reputation for shooting the bull.* [< ML *bulla* play, game, jest (whence also Icel *bull* nonsense), perh. special use of L *bulla* bubble; in some expressions, perh. a shortening of slang *bullshit* nonsense]

Bull (bo͝ol), *n.* **John.** See **John Bull.**

Bull (bo͝ol), *n.* **O·le Bor·ne·mann** (ō′lə bôr′nə män′), 1810–80, Norwegian violinist and composer.

bull., bulletin.

bul·la (bo͝ol′ə, bul′ə), *n., pl.* **bul·lae** (bo͝ol′ē, bul′ē). **1.** a seal attached to an official document, as a papal bull. **2.** an ancient Roman pendant, consisting of a rounded box of metal or leather containing an amulet. **3.** *Pathol.* a large vesicle. **4.** *Zool.* a blisterlike or bubblelike prominence of a bone, as that of the tympanic bone in the skull of certain mammals. [< L: bubble, also stud, boss, knob, official decoration (whence ML *bulla* official seal)]

bul·lace (bo͝ol′is), *n.* **1.** the damson. **2.** the muscadine. [ME *bolaz;* akin to ML *bolluca,* F *beloce*]

bul·lar·i·um (bo͞o lâr′ē əm), *n., pl.* **-lar·i·a** (-lâr′ē ə). a collection of papal bulls. [< ML, equiv. to *bul(la)* BULL[2] + *-ārium* -ARY]

bul·la·ry (bo͝ol′ə rē), *n., pl.* **-ries.** bullarium.

bul·late (bo͝ol′āt, -it, bul′-), *adj.* **1.** *Bot., Zool.* having the surface covered with irregular and slight elevations, giving a blistered appearance. **2.** *Anat.* inflated; vaulted. [< L *bullāt(us).* See BULLA, -ATE[1]]

bull·bait·ing (bo͝ol′bā′ting), *n.* the action or sport of setting dogs upon a bull in a pen or arena. [BULL[1] + BAITING]

bull·bat (bo͝ol′bat′), *n. U.S. Dial.* nighthawk (def. 1). [said to be so called from the noise it makes when flying. See BULL[1], BAT[2]]

bull′ bay′, **1.** See **evergreen magnolia. 2.** See **red bay.**

bull′ block′, *Metalworking.* a machine for drawing wire in which the wire is pulled through the dies by a power-operated drum.

bull′ bri′er, a North American, smilacaceous plant, *Smilax pseudo-china,* having tuberous rootstocks.

bull′ chain′, *Lumbering.* a chain for dragging logs to a sawmill. Also called **jack ladder.**

bull′ dike′, *Slang.* the partner in a Lesbian relationship who dresses in masculine clothes and assumes the masculine role.

bull·dog (bo͝ol′dôg′, -dog′), *n., adj., v.,* **-dogged, -dog·ging.** —*n.* **1.** one of an English breed of medium-sized, short-haired, muscular dogs with prominent, undershot jaws, usually having a white and tan or brindled coat, raised originally for bull-baiting. **2.** a short-barreled revolver of large caliber. **3.** Also called **tap cinder, top cinder.** *Metall.* slag from a puddling furnace. **4.** an assistant to the proctor at a British university. —*adj.* **5.** like or characteristic of a bulldog or of a bulldog's jaws: *bulldog obstinacy.* —*v.t.* **6.** to attack in the manner of a bulldog. **7.** *Western U.S.* to throw (a calf, steer, etc.) to the ground by seizing the horns and twisting the head. [BULL[1] + DOG] —**bull′dog′ged·ness,** *n.*

Bulldog (13 in. high at shoulder)

bull′dog edi′tion, the earliest daily edition of a newspaper.

bull·doze (bo͝ol′dōz′), *v.t.,* **-dozed, -doz·ing. 1.** to coerce or intimidate, as with threats. **2.** to clear, level, or reshape the contours of (land) by or as if by using a bulldozer: *to bulldoze a building site.* **3.** to clear away by or as if by using a bulldozer: *to bulldoze trees from a building site.* [BULL[1] + *doze,* Louisiana var. (French pronunciation) of DOSE, taken as v.]

Bulldozer

bull·doz·er (bo͝ol′dō′zər), *n.* **1.** a powerful caterpillar tractor having a vertical blade at the front end for moving earth, tree stumps, rocks, etc. **2.** *Slang.* one who intimidates or coerces. [BULLDOZE + -ER[1]]

Bul·ler (bo͝ol′ər), *n.* **Sir Red·vers Henry** (red′vərz), 1839–1908, British general.

bul·let (bo͝ol′it), *n., v.,* **-let·ed, -let·ing.** —*n.* **1.** a small metal projectile, part of a cartridge, for firing from small arms. See diag. under **cartridge. 2.** a cartridge. **3.** a small ball. **4.** *Print.* a heavy dot for marking paragraphs or otherwise calling attention to particular sections of text, esp. in display advertising. **5.** *Cards Slang.* an ace. —*v.i.* **6.** to move swiftly. [< MF *boullette,* equiv. to *boulle* ball (see BOWL[2]) + *-ette* -ETTE] —**bul′let·less,** *adj.* —**bul′let·like′,** *adj.*

bul·let·head (bo͝ol′it hed′), *n.* **1.** a round head. **2.** a person having such a head. **3.** an obstinate or stupid person. [BULLET + HEAD] —**bul′let·head′ed,** *adj.* —**bul′let·head′ed·ness,** *n.*

bul·le·tin (bo͝ol′i tən, -tin), *n., v.,* **-tined, -tin·ing.** —*n.* **1.** a brief account or statement, as of news or events, issued for the information of the public. **2.** *Journalism.* **a.** a brief, prominently featured newspaper account of an important event or development, based upon information received just before the edition went to press. **b.** a similar brief account broadcast over radio or television pending further information. **3.** a pamphlet or monograph summarizing the past achievements, existing conditions, and future plans of a corporation, educational institution, government agency, etc., esp. one cataloguing the classes taught at a college or university. **4.** a periodical publication, as of a learned society. —*v.t.* **5.** to make known by a bulletin. [< F < It *bullettino,* equiv. to *bullett(a)* (*bulla* BULL[2] + *-etta* -ETTE) + *-ino* -INE[2]]

bul′letin board′, a board for the posting of bulletins, notices, announcements, etc.

bul·let·proof (bo͝ol′it pro͞of′), *adj.* **1.** capable of resisting the impact of a bullet. —*v.t.* **2.** to make (something) bulletproof. [BULLET + -PROOF]

bul′let tree′. See **bully tree.**

bul′let wood′, **1.** the wood of a bully tree. **2.** See **bully tree.**

bull′ fid′dle. *Informal.* See **double bass.**

bull·fight (bo͝ol′fīt′), *n.* a traditional Spanish and Latin American spectacle in which a special breed of fighting bull is tested and tired by banderilleros and mounted picadors, then fought and killed in a prescribed way by a matador using only a cape and sword. [BULL[1] + FIGHT] —**bull′fight′ing,** *n.*

bull·fight·er (bo͝ol′fī′tər), *n.* a person who participates in a bull fight, esp. a matador. [BULL[1] + FIGHTER]

bull·finch[1] (bo͝ol′finch′), *n.* **1.** a European, fringilline bird, *Pyrrhula pyrrhula,* which is often kept as a pet, the male of which has a black, white, and bluish-gray back and a rosy breast. **2.** any of several related or similar birds. [BULL[1] (? bull-necked) + FINCH]

bull·finch[2] (bo͝ol′finch′), *n.* a hedge high enough to impede mounted hunters. [?]

bull′ float′, a machine for giving the finish surface to an area of concrete, as on a road.

bull·frog (bo͝ol′frog′, -frôg′), *n.* a large frog, esp. the North American *Rana catesbeiana,* having a deep voice. [BULL[1] + FROG[1]; so called from its size and voice]

bull′ gear′. See **bull wheel.**

bull′ gun′, a target rifle with a heavy barrel.

bull·head (bo͝ol′hed′), *n.* **1.** any of several North American, fresh-water catfishes of the genus *Ictalurus,* having a rounded or truncate caudal fin. **2.** any of several other fishes, as the fresh-water sculpins of the genus *Cottus,* esp. those species having a hornlike spine on each side of the head. **3.** an obstinate or stupid person. [BULL[1] + HEAD]

bull·head·ed (bo͝ol′hed′id), *adj.* obstinate; blunderingly stubborn; stupid. [BULLHEAD + -ED[3]] —**bull′-head′ed·ly,** *adv.* —**bull′head′ed·ness,** *n.*

bull′ head′er, 1. Also called **bullnose header.** a brick having one of the edges across its width rounded for laying as a header in a sill or the like. **2.** a brick laid on edge as a header, as in a rowlock.

bull′ horn′, a directional, high-powered, electrical loudspeaker or an electrical megaphone. Also, **bull′horn′.** [BULL[1] + HORN]

Bul·lial·dus (bəl yäl′dəs), *n.* a crater in the third quadrant of the face of the moon, on the Mare Nubium: about 39 miles in diameter.

bul·lion (bo͝ol′yən), *n.* **1.** gold or silver considered in mass rather than in value. **2.** gold or silver in the form of bars or ingots. **3.** Also called **bul′lion fringe′.** a thick trimming of cord covered with gold or silver thread, for decorating uniforms. [ME: melted mass of gold or silver < AL *bulliōn-* (s. of *bulliō*) in same sense (whence AF *bullion* mint) < L: a boiling (lit. bubbling), equiv. to *bull(īre)* (to) bubble, BOIL[1] + *-iōn-* -ION] —**bul′lion·less,** *adj.*

bul·lion·ist (bo͝ol′yə nist), *n.* one who advocates a system in which currency is directly convertible to gold or silver. [BULLION + -IST] —**bul′lion·ism,** *n.*

bull·ish (bo͝ol′ish), *adj.* **1.** like a bull. **2.** obstinate or stupid. **3.** *Com.* **a.** rising or tending toward a rise in prices. **b.** characterized by favorable prospects for the economy or some aspect of it. **4.** hopeful; optimistic. [BULL[1] + -ISH[1]] —**bull′ish·ly,** *adv.* —**bull′ish·ness,** *n.*

Bul·litt (bo͝ol′it), *n.* **William C(hristian),** 1891–1967, U.S. diplomat and journalist.

bull·mas·tiff (bo͝ol′mas′tif, -mä′stif), *n.* one of an English breed of dogs having a short, fawn or brindled coat, produced by crossing the bulldog and the mastiff.

Bull′ Moose′, 1. a member of the Progressive party under the leadership of Theodore Roosevelt. **2.** (*l.c.*) a representation of a bull moose as the emblem of this party.

bull-necked (bo͝ol′nekt′), *adj.* having a thick neck. Also, **bull′necked′.**

bull′ nose′, 1. *Vet. Pathol.* a disease of swine caused by bacterial infection of the tissues of the snout causing gross malformation and frequently serious blocking of the nasal passages. **2.** bullnose.

bull·nose (bo͝ol′nōz′), *n.* **1.** Also, **bull's nose.** a rounded or obtuse exterior angle, as the corner made by two walls. **2.** a structural member, as a brick, used in forming such an angle. **3.** Also, **bullnose step.** a step having semicircular or quadrantal ends. [BULL[1] + NOSE]

bull-nosed bow (bo͝ol′nōzd′ bou′), *Naut.* a bow having a bulbous forefoot.

bull′nose head′er. See **bull header** (def. 1).

bull′nose step′, bullnose (def. 3).

bull′nose stretch′er. See **bull stretcher** (def. 1).

bul·lock (bo͝ol′ək), *n.* **1.** a castrated bull; steer. **2.** a young bull. [ME *bullok,* OE *bulluc.* See BULL[1], -OCK]

bul·lock's-heart (bo͝ol′əks härt′), *n.* See **custard apple.** Also, **bul′lock heart′.** [so called from its size, color, and shape]

Bul′lock's o′riole (bo͝ol′əks), an orange and black oriole, *Icterus bullockii,* of western North America. [named after William *Bullock,* 19th-century English naturalist]

bul·lous (bul′əs), *adj.* *Pathol.* pertaining to, similar to, or characterized by bullae. [BULL(A) + -OUS]

bull′ pen′, 1. a pen for a bull or bulls. **2.** *U.S. Informal.* **a.** a place for the temporary confinement of prisoners. **b.** any temporary or crowded quarters, as sleeping quarters in a lumber camp. **3.** *Baseball.* a place where relief pitchers warm up during a game.

bull·pout (bo͝ol′pout′), *n.* See **horned pout.** [BULL(HEAD) + POUT[2]]

Bull·pup (bo͝ol′pup′), *n.* *U.S. Mil.* an air-to-surface guided bomb for air support of troops. [BULL[1] + PUP]

bull·ring (bo͝ol′ring′), *n.* an arena for a bullfight. [BULL[1] + RING[1]]

bull-roar·er (bo͝ol′rōr′ər, -rôr′-), *n.* a wooden slat that produces a roaring sound when whirled around one's head on the end of a string or thong. Also called **thunderstick.**

bull′ rope′, *Naut.* any of various ropes for holding objects to prevent them from rubbing or striking other objects.

Bull′ Run′, a creek in NE Virginia: two important battles of the Civil War were fought near here, both resulting in defeat for the Union forces 1861, 1862. See map under **Antietam.**

bull′ ses′sion, *Slang.* an informal, spontaneous group discussion.

bull's-eye (bo͝olz′ī′), *n., pl.* **-eyes. 1.** the circular spot, usually black or outlined in black, of the center of a target used in target practice. **2.** the center or central area of an actual target, as of a town, factory, or enemy base in a bombing raid. **3.** a missile that strikes the center or central area of a target. **4.** the coordinates or instance of aiming and firing a missile which results in its hitting the center of a target. **5.** *Informal.* **a.** any precise statement or act which is exceptionally to the point or achieves a desired result directly. **b.** that which is decisive or crucial; crux. **6.** a small circular opening or window. **7.** a thick disk or lenslike piece of glass inserted in a roof, ship's deck, etc., to admit light. **8.** *Naut.* an oval or circular wooden block having a groove around it and a hole in the center, through which to reeve a rope. **9.** *Meteorol.* (formerly) **a.** the eye of a storm. **b.** a dark, small cloud having a reddish center, often coming before a storm, and sometimes seen at sea. **c.** Also, **bull's′-eye squall′.** (off the coast of South Africa) a squall having a small, isolated cloud. **10.** a large, round piece of peppermint-flavored hard candy. —**bull's′-eyed′,** *adj.*

bull's′-eye mir′ror, a circular, convex, ornamental mirror.

bull's′-eye rot′, *Plant Pathol.* a disease of apples and pears, characterized by sunken, eyelike spots on the fruit and twig cankers, caused by any of several fungi, esp. of the genus *Neofabraea.*

bull′ shark′, a requiem shark, *Carcharhinus leucas,* found in shallow waters from North Carolina to Brazil. Also called **cub shark.**

bull·shit (bo͝ol′shit′), *n., v.,* **-shit, -shit·ting,** *interj.* *Slang* (*vulgar*). —*n.* **1.** nonsense, lies, or exaggeration. —*v.t.* **2.** to lie or exaggerate to. —*v.i.* **3.** to speak lies or nonsense. —*interj.* **4.** (used to express disbelief, disapproval, or the like.) [BULL[1] + SHIT]

bull·snake (bo͝ol′snāk′), *n.* any of several large, North American constrictors of the genus *Pituophis,* as the gopher snake and pine snake, that feed chiefly upon small rodents. Also, **bull′ snake′.** [BULL[1] + SNAKE]

bull's′ nose′, 1. bullnose (def. 1). **2.** a structural member shaped to or formed by an obtuse or rounded exterior angle, as a corner where two walls meet.

bull′ stretch′er, 1. Also called **bullnose stretcher.** a brick having one of the edges along its length rounded for laying as a stretcher in a sill or the like. **2.** a brick laid on edge as a stretcher. Cf. **bull header.**

bull·ter·ri·er (bo͝ol′ter′ē ər), *n.* one of an English breed of medium-sized, short-haired dogs having a white, brindled, or tan and white coat, produced by crossing the bulldog and the terrier. [BULL(DOG) + TERRIER[1]]

Bullterrier, white variety (18 in. high at shoulder

bull′ this′tle, a tall, biennial thistle, *Cirsium lanceolatum,* having heads of pink to purple flowers.

bull′ tongue′, a plow having a vertical moldboard, used in cultivating cotton.

bull-tongue (bo͝ol′tung′), *v.t., v.i.,* **-tongued, -tonguing.** to plow with a bull tongue.

bull′ wheel′, any large driving gear among smaller gears. Also called **bull gear.**

bull·whip (bo͝ol′hwip′, -wip′), *n.* a rawhide whip having a short handle and a long, plaited lash. Also, **bull′-whip′.** Also called **bull-whack** (bo͝ol′hwak′, -wak′). [so called from its size; see BULL[1], WHIP]

bul·ly[1] (bo͝ol′ē), *n., pl.* **-lies,** *v.,* **-lied, -ly·ing,** *adj., interj.* —*n.* **1.** a blustering, quarrelsome, overbearing person who habitually badgers and intimidates smaller or weaker people. **2.** *Archaic.* a man hired to do violence. **3.** *Obs.* a pimp; procurer. **4.** *Obs.* good friend; good fellow. **5.** *Obs.* sweetheart; darling. —*v.t.* **6.** to act the bully toward; intimidate; domineer. —*v.i.* **7.** to be loudly arrogant and overbearing. —*adj.* **8.** *Informal.* fine; excellent; very good. **9.** dashing; jovial; high-spirited. —*interj.* **10.** *Informal.* good! well done! [< D *boele* (later *boel*) lover] —**bul′ly·a·ble,** *adj.*

bul·ly[2] (bo͝ol′ē), *n.* See **bully beef.** [< F *bouilli,* short for *boeuf bouilli* boiled meat. See BOIL[1], BEEF]

bul′ly beef′, canned or pickled beef.

bul·ly·boy (bo͝ol′ē boi′), *n.* a ruffian, esp. one working for or associated with a political group. [BULLY[1] + BOY]

bul·ly·rag (bo͝ol′ē rag′), *v.t.,* **-ragged, -rag·ging.** to bully; harass; abuse; tease: *to bullyrag fraternity plebs.* Also, **ballyrag.** [earlier *ballarag* < ?] —**bul′ly·rag′ger,** *n.*

bul′ly tree′, any of various tropical American, sapotaceous trees, as *Manilkara bidentata,* of Guiana, which yields the gum balata. [*bully,* alter. of BALATA]

Bü·low (bʏ′lō), *n.* **1. Prince Bern·hard von** (bern′härt fən), 1849–1929, chancellor of Germany 1900–09. **2. Hans (Gu·i·do, Frei·herr) von** (häns go͞o ē′dō, frī′her fən) 1830–94, German pianist and conductor.

bul·rush (bo͝ol′rush′), *n.* **1.** (in Biblical use) the Papyrus, *Cyperus Papyrus.* **2.** any of various rushes of the genera *Scirpus, Juncus,* or *Typha.* [late ME *bulrish* papyrus, prob. BULL[1] + *rish* RUSH[2]]

Bult·mann (bo͝olt′män′), *n.* **Ru·dolf** (ro͞o′dôlf), born 1884, German theologian.

bul·wark (bo͝ol′wərk), *n.* **1.** *Fort.* a wall of earth or other material built for defense; rampart. **2.** any protection against external danger, injury, or annoyance: *The new dam was a bulwark against future floods.* **3.** any person or thing giving strong support or encouragement in time of need, danger, or doubt: *During the crisis, religion was his bulwark. Her career would have failed if her brother hadn't been a bulwark.* **4.** Usually, **bulwarks.** (on a ship) a solid structure extending above the level of a weather or main deck for the protection of persons or objects on deck. —*v.t.* **5.** to fortify or protect with a bulwark; secure by or as if by a fortification. [ME *bulwerk,* prob. < MD, MLG *bolwerk,* equiv. to *bol(l)e* BOLE[1] + *werk* WORK (n.); see BOULEVARD]

Bul·wer (bo͝ol′wər), *n.* **Sir Henry** (*William Henry Lytton Earle Bulwer; Baron Dalling* and *Bulwer*), 1801–1872, British diplomat and author.

Bul·wer-Lyt·ton (bo͝ol′wər lit′ən), *n.* **1st Baron.** See **Lytton, Edward George.**

bum (bum), *n., v.,* **bummed, bum·ming,** *adj.* —*n.* *Informal.* **1.** *U.S.* a shiftless or dissolute person. **2.** *U.S.* a habitual loafer and tramp. **3.** *Chiefly Brit.* the buttocks; rump. **4.** *U.S.* a drunken orgy; debauch. **5. on the bum,** *U.S.* **a.** living the life of a hobo or tramp. **b.** *Slang.* living in any shiftless or disreputable manner. **c.** *Slang.* in a state of disrepair or disorder: *The oven is on the bum again.* —*v.t.* **6.** *U.S. Informal.* to get for nothing; borrow without expectation of returning: *He's always bumming cigarettes from me.* —*v.i.* **7.** *U.S. Informal.* to sponge on others for a living; lead an idle or dissolute life. —*adj.* *U.S. Slang.* **8.** of poor, wretched, or miserable quality; bad. **9.** false; misleading: *a bum steer; He was sent to prison on a bum rap.* [ME *bom* anus < ?] —**bum′mer,** *n.*

—**Syn. 2.** vagabond, vagrant.

bum·bail·iff (bum′bā′lif), *n.* *Brit. Disparaging.* a bailiff or underbailiff employed in serving writs, making arrests, etc. [BUM + BAILIFF, alliterative compound]

bum·ber·shoot (bum′bər sho͞ot′), *n.* *Informal.* an umbrella. [*bumber,* deriv. of *umbr(ella)* + *-shoot,* deriv. of *-chute* as in *parachute*]

bum·ble[1] (bum′bəl), *v.,* **-bled, -bling,** *n.* —*v.i.* **1.** to bungle or blunder; muddle: *He somehow bumbled through two years of college.* **2.** to stumble or stagger. **3.** to mumble; speak in a low, stuttering, halting manner. —*v.t.* **4.** to do (something) clumsily; to botch. —*n.* **5.** a blunder. [? b. BUNGLE and STUMBLE] —**bum′bler,** *n.*

bum·ble[2] (bum′bəl), *v.i.* **-bled, -bling.** to make a buzzing, humming sound, as a bee. [ME *bomblen,* freq. of *bomben* to boom, buzz; imit.]

Bumblebee (queen), *Bombus americanorum* (Length ¾ in.)

bum·ble·bee (bum′bəl bē′), *n.* any of several large, hairy social bees of the family *Apidae.* [BUMBLE[2] + BEE[1]]

bum·ble·bee·fish (bum′bəl bē′fish′), *n., pl.* **-fish·es,** (*esp. collectively*) **-fish.** a goby, *Brachygobius doriae,* found in the Malay Archipelago, having brown and yellow bands on the body that resemble the markings of a bumblebee. [BUMBLEBEE + FISH]

bum·ble·foot (bum′bəl fo͝ot′), *n.* *Vet. Pathol.* a swelling, sometimes purulent, of the ball of the foot in fowl. [BUMBLE[1] + FOOT]

bum·ble·pup·py (bum′bəl pup′ē), *n.* *Cards.* a game of whist played carelessly or contrary to rules and conventions. [BUMBLE[1] + PUPPY]

bum·bling (bum′bling), *adj.* **1.** liable to make blunders: *a bumbling mechanic.* **2.** incompetent or ineffectual: *a bumbling diplomacy.* —*n.* **3.** the practice of making blunders or the act of making blunders: *The bumbling of our salesman cost us the account.* [BUMBLE[1] + -ING[2]] —**bum′bling·ly,** *adv.*

bum·boat (bum′bōt′), *n.* *Naut.* a boat used in peddling provisions and small wares among vessels lying in port or off shore. [BUM + BOAT, allit. compound]

bum·boat·man (bum′bōt′mən), *n., pl.* **-men.** one who sells things from or operates a bumboat. [BUMBOAT + MAN[1]]

bumf (bumf), *n.* *Brit.* **1.** *Slang.* toilet paper. **2.** *Disparaging.* memoranda, official notices, or the like, esp. of a routine or boring nature. [short for *bumfodder.* See BUM, FODDER[1]]

bum·kin (bum′kin), *n.* *Naut.* bumpkin[2].

bum·ma·lo (bum′ə lō′), *n., pl.* **-los.** See **bombay duck.** [earlier *bumbelow* < Mahratti *bombīla,* inflected case-form of *bombīl*]

bump (bump), *v.t.* **1.** to come more or less violently in contact with; collide with; strike: *His car bumped a truck.* **2.** to cause to strike or collide: *The boy bumped the stick against every fence post.* **3.** to dislodge or displace by the force of collision: *The cat bumped the vase off the shelf.* **4.** *Poker Slang.* raise (def. 24). **5.** to take the place of (a person of lower seniority or rank) by requisitioning his job, benefits, or accommodations: *When the general found there was no room on the plane, he bumped a major.* **6.** to dismiss from a job, vote down, or reject: *The voters bumped the senator and elected his rival.* **7.** to force upward; raise: *He bumped the price of corn.* —*v.i.* **8.** to come in contact or collide with (often fol. by *against* or *into*): *She bumped into me.* **9.** to bounce along; proceed in a series of jolts: *The old car bumped down the road.* **10.** to dance by thrusting the pelvis forward abruptly, in a provocative manner, esp. to the accompaniment of an accented musical beat. Cf. **grind** (def. 12). **11.** to boil with violent jolts caused by the sudden eruption of large bubbles through the surface. **12. bump into,** *Informal.* to meet by chance: *Guess who I bumped into on the way to the office.* **13. bump off,** *Slang.* to kill, esp. to murder: *They bumped him off because he knew too much about their illegal activities.* —*n.* **14.** the act or an instance of bumping; collision; blow. **15.** the shock of a blow or collision. **16.** a swelling or contusion from a blow. **17.** a small area raised above the level of the surrounding surface; protuberance: *He tripped over a bump on a road.* **18.** *Slang.* a promotion or demotion; removal to a higher or lower level: *He got a bump to vice-president of the company.* **19.** *Slang.* an increase in amount, esp. of money, as of salary or a wager: *He asked the boss for a 10-dollar bump.* **20.** *Aeron.* a rapidly rising current of air which gives an airplane a severe upward thrust. **21.** a dance movement in which the pelvis is abruptly thrust forward, in a provocative manner, esp. to the accompaniment of an accented musical beat. Cf. **grind** (def. 17). [imit.] —**bump′ing·ly,** *adv.*

bump·er (bum′pər), *n.* **1.** one who or that which bumps. **2.** a metal guard, usually horizontal, for protecting the front or rear of an automobile, truck, etc. **3.** any protective rim, guard, pad, or disk for absorbing shock and preventing damage from bumping, as a rubber-tipped doorstop, an old tire on the side of a boat, etc. **4.** a cup or glass filled to the brim, esp. when drunk as a toast. **5.** *Informal.* something unusually large. **6.** one who molds bricks by hand. **7.** *Foundry.* a machine for ramming sand into a mold. **8.** a carangid fish, *Chlorosombrus chrysurus,* found off the coast of the southern U.S. and Cuba. —*adj.* **9.** unusually abundant: *Bumper crops reaped a big profit for local farmers.* —*v.t.* **10.** to fill to the brim. **11.** to drink a bumper as a toast to. —*v.i.* **12.** to drink toasts. [BUMP + -ER[1]]

bump′er guard′, either of two vertical crosspieces attached to a bumper of a motor vehicle to prevent it from locking bumpers with another vehicle.

bump′er jack′, a jack for lifting a motor vehicle by the bumper.

bump·kin[1] (bump′kin), *n.* an awkward, clumsy yokel. [< MD *bommekijn* little barrel] —**bump′kin·ish, bump′kin·ly,** *adj.*

bump·kin[2] (bump′kin), *n.* *Naut.* a beam or spar projecting outward from the hull of a vessel, for extending a sail, securing blocks, etc. Also, **bumkin, boomkin.** [< D *boomken* little tree. See BEAM, -KIN]

bump·off (bump′ôf′), *n.* *Slang.* murder. [BUMP + OFF]

bump·tious (bump′shəs), *adj.* offensively self-assertive: *He's a bumptious young upstart.* [BUMP + (FRAC)TIOUS] —**bump′tious·ly,** *adv.* —**bump′tious·ness,** *n.*

bump·y (bum′pē), *adj.,* **bump·i·er, bump·i·est. 1.** of uneven surface: *a bumpy sidewalk.* **2.** full of jolts: *a bumpy ride.* **3.** causing jolts: *Bumpy air made the airplane passengers uncomfortable.* [BUMP + -Y[1]] —**bump′i·ly,** *adv.* —**bump′i·ness,** *n.*

bum's′ rush′, *Slang.* **1.** forcible ejection from a place: *When they began to cause a disturbance, they were given the bum's rush.* **2.** any rude or abrupt dismissal: *He gave the job seekers the bum's rush.*

bun[1] (bun), *n.* **1.** any of a wide variety of variously shaped bread rolls, usually leavened and slightly sweetened or plain, sometimes containing spices, dried currants, citron, etc. **2.** hair gathered into a round coil or knot at the nape of the neck or on top of the head in certain coiffures. Also, **bunn.** [ME *bunne* < ?]

bun[2] (bun), *n. Slang.* a drunken condition. [? euphemistic alter. of *bung* drunk, slang use of BUNG[1]]

Bu·na (bo͞o′nə, byo͞o′-), *n. Trademark.* **1.** a synthetic rubber made by copolymerizing butadiene with other material. **2.** Also called **Bu·na-N** (bo͞o′nə en′, byo͞o′-). a synthetic rubber made by copolymerizing butadiene with acrylonitrile. **3.** Also called **Bu·na-S** (bo͞o′nə es′, byo͞o′-). a synthetic rubber made by copolymerizing butadiene with styrene. **4.** a synthetic rubber made by polymerizing butadiene by means of sodium.

Bu·nae·a (byo͞o nē′ə), *n. Class. Myth.* an epithet of Hera, alluding to a temple built for her by Bunus.

bunch (bunch), *n.* **1.** a connected group; cluster: *a bunch of grapes.* **2.** a group of things: *a bunch of papers.* **3.** *Informal.* a group of people: *They're a fine bunch of students.* **4.** a knob; lump; protuberance. —*v.t.* **5.** to group together; make a bunch of. —*v.i.* **6.** to gather into a cluster; gather together. [ME *bunche,* perh. var. of **bunge* < Flem *bondje* bundle, equiv. to *bond* (see BUNDLE) + *-je* dim. suffix; cf. ME *bulche,* var. of BULGE] —**Syn. 1, 2.** lot, batch. See **bundle.**

bunch·ber·ry (bunch′ber′ē, -bə rē), *n., pl.* **-ries.** a dwarf cornel, *Cornus canadensis,* bearing dense clusters of bright-red berries. Also called **crackerberry.** [BUNCH + BERRY]

Bunche (bunch), *n.* **Ralph (Johnson),** born 1904, U.S. diplomat: at the United Nations since 1946; Nobel peace prize 1950.

buncher res′onator, *Electronics.* See under **Klystron.** [BUNCH + -ER[1]]

bunch·flow·er (bunch′flou′ər), *n.* **1.** a liliaceous plant, *Melanthium virginicum,* of the U.S., having grasslike leaves and a panicle of small greenish flowers. **2.** any other plant of the same genus. [BUNCH + FLOWER]

bunch′ grass′, any of various grasses in different regions of the U.S., growing in distinct clumps.

bunch′ light′, a light consisting of a group of small light bulbs mounted in a reflecting box.

bunch′ pink′. See **sweet william.**

bunch·y (bun′chē), *adj.,* **bunch·i·er, bunch·i·est. 1.** having bunches. **2.** bulging or protuberant. [ME; see BUNCH, -Y[1]] —**bunch′i·ly,** *adv.* —**bunch′i·ness,** *n.*

bun·co (buŋ′kō), *n., pl.* **-cos,** *v.,* **-coed, -co·ing.** *U.S. Informal.* bunko.

bun·combe (buŋ′kəm), *n.* bunkum.

bund (bund), *n.* (in India, China, Japan, etc.) an embankment; an embanked quay. [< Hindi *band* < Pers; akin to BIND, BOND[1]]

Bund (bo͝ond; *Ger.* bo͝ont), *n., pl.* **Bün·de** (bo͝on′də; *Ger.* bʏn′də). **1.** a short form of "German-American Volksbund," a Nazi-inspired organization in the U.S. **2.** an alliance or league. [< G: association, league] —**Bund′ist,** *n.*

Bun·del·khand (bun′dəl kund′, -ḵʜund′), *n.* a former group of native states in central India: now part of Madhya Pradesh.

Bun·des·rat (bo͝on′dəs rät′; *Ger.* bo͝on′dəs ʀät′), *n.* **1.** the upper house of the federal legislature of Germany. **2.** the federal council of Switzerland and of Austria. [< G. equiv. to *Bundes,* gen. of *Bund* federation + *Rat* council]

Bun·des·tag (bo͝on′dəs täg′; *Ger.* bo͝on′dəs täk′), *n.* the lower house of the federal legislature of Germany. [< G: federal assembly, equiv. to *Bundes,* gen. of *Bund* federation + *-tag,* deriv. of *tagen* to meet, assemble; see DIET[2]]

bun·dle (bun′dəl), *n., v.,* **-dled, -dling.** —*n.* **1.** several objects or a quantity of material gathered or bound together: *a bundle of personal belongings; a bundle of hay.* **2.** an item, group, or quantity wrapped for carrying; package. **3.** a number of things considered together: *He presented a bundle of ideas to the committee.* **4.** *Bot.* an aggregation of strands of specialized conductive and mechanical tissues. **5.** Also called **bundle of isoglosses.** *Dialect Geog.* a group of close isoglosses running in approximately the same direction, esp. when taken as evidence of an important dialect division. **6.** *Anat., Zool.* an aggregation of fibers, as of nerves or muscles. **7.** *Slang.* a great deal of money. —*v.t.* **8.** to tie together or wrap in a bundle: *Bundle the newspapers for the trash man.* **9.** to send away hurriedly or unceremoniously (usually fol. by *off, out,* etc.): *They bundled her off to the country.* —*v.i.* **10.** to leave hurriedly or unceremoniously (usually fol. by *off, out,* etc.): *They indignantly bundled out of the meeting.* **11.** (esp. of sweethearts in early New England) to sleep or lie in the same bed while fully clothed. **12. bundle up,** to dress warmly or snugly: *A blizzard was raging but we were all bundled up in our woolen mufflers and mittens, parkas, and boots.* [ME *bundel* < MD *bundel, bondel* (cf. G *Bündel*); akin to OE *bindele* bandage] —**bun′dler,** *n.*
—**Syn. 1.** BUNDLE, BUNCH refer to a number of things or an amount of something fastened or bound together. BUNDLE implies a close binding or grouping together, and often refers to a wrapped package: *a bundle of laundry, of dry goods.* A BUNCH is a number of things, usually all of the same kind, fastened together: *a bunch of roses, of keys.* **2.** parcel, pack, packet.

bun′dle of His′ (his), *Anat.* See **atrioventricular bundle.**

bun′dle of i′soglosses, bundle (def. 5).

bun′ foot′, *Furniture.* a foot having the form of a slightly flattened ball. Cf. **ball foot.**

Bun foot

bung[1] (buŋ), *n.* **1.** a stopper for the opening of a cask. **2.** a bunghole. —*v.t.* **3.** to close with or as with a bung; cork; plug (often fol. by *up*). **4.** to beat; bruise; maul (often fol. by *up*). **5.** *Brit. Slang.* to throw (stones). [ME *bunge* < MD *bonghe* stopper]

bung[2] (buŋ), *adj. Australian.* **1.** out of order; broken; unusable. **2.** bankrupt. **3.** *Slang.* dead. [? < native Austral]

bun·ga·loid (buŋ′gə loid′), *adj. Usually Disparaging.* **1.** of, pertaining to, or characteristic of the style or appearance of a bungalow. **2.** (of a town or neighborhood) characterized by having bungalows or bungalow-like structures. [BUNGAL(OW) + -OID]

bun·ga·low (buŋ′gə lō′), *n.* **1.** a cottage. **2.** (in India) a one-storied thatched or tiled house, usually surrounded by a veranda. [< Hindi *banglā,* lit., of Bengal]

bun·gee (bun′jē), *n. Aeron.* any of certain springs or elastic tension devices, as the springs attached to movable controls of aircraft to facilitate their manipulation. [?]

bung·hole (buŋ′hōl′), *n.* a hole or orifice in a cask through which it is filled. [BUNG[1] + HOLE]

bun·gle (buŋ′gəl), *v.,* **-gled, -gling,** *n.* —*v.t.* **1.** to do clumsily and awkwardly; botch: *He bungled the job.* —*v.i.* **2.** to do something awkwardly and clumsily: *He is a fool who bungles consistently.* —*n.* **3.** a bungling performance. **4.** that which has been done clumsily or inadequately. [? < Scand; cf. dial. Sw *bangla* to work ineffectively] —**bun′gler,** *n.* —**bun′gling·ly,** *adv.*

bun·gle·some (buŋ′gəl səm), *adj.* clumsy or awkward. [BUNGLE + -SOME[1]]

bung·start·er (buŋ′stär′tər), *n.* a mallet for loosening or removing the bung of a cask. [BUNG[1] + STARTER]

Bu·nin (bo͞o′nin), *n.* **I·van A·le·kse·e·vich** (i vän′ ä′le kse′yə vich), 1870–1953, Russian poet and novelist: Nobel prize 1933.

bun·ion (bun′yən), *n. Pathol.* a swelling on the foot caused by the inflammation of a synovial bursa, esp. of the great toe. [perh. < older It *bugnone* blain, equiv. to *bugn(a)* projection + *-one* aug. suffix]

bunk[1] (buŋk), *n.* **1.** a built-in platform bed, as on a ship. **2.** *Informal.* any bed. —*v.i.* **3.** *Informal.* to occupy a bunk; sleep, esp. in rough quarters. [back formation from BUNKER]

bunk[2] (buŋk), *n. U.S. Slang.* humbug; nonsense. [short for BUNKUM]

bunk[3] (buŋk), *v.t.* to bump. [by alter.]

bunk[4] (buŋk), *Brit. Slang.* —*v.t.* **1.** to absent oneself from: *to bunk a history class.* —*v.i.* **2.** to run off or away. —*n.* **3. do a bunk,** to leave hastily, esp. under suspicious circumstances; run away. [? special use of BUNK[1]]

bunk′ bed′, a piece of furniture containing two single platformlike beds, one above the other.

bunk·er (buŋ′kər), *n.* **1.** a large bin or receptacle; a fixed chest or box: *a coal bunker; a storage bunker.* **2.** *Golf.* any obstacle, as a sand trap or mound of dirt, constituting a hazard. **3.** a fortification set mostly below the surface of the ground with overhead protection provided by logs and earth or by reinforced concrete and fitted with openings through which guns may be fired. —*v.t.* **4.** *Golf.* to hit (a ball) into a bunker. **5.** *Naut.* **a.** to provide fuel for (a vessel). **b.** to convey (bulk cargo except grain) from a vessel to an adjacent storehouse. [earlier *bonkar* (Scot) box, chest, serving also as a seat < ?]

bunk·er·age (buŋ′kər ij, buŋk′rij), *n.* the act of bunkering a vessel. [BUNKER + -AGE]

Bunk′er Hill′, a hill in Charlestown, Massachusetts: the first major battle of the American Revolution, known as the Battle of Bunker Hill, was fought on adjoining Breed's Hill on June 17, 1775.

bunk·house (buŋk′hous′), *n., pl.* **-hous·es** (-hou′ziz). a rough building used for sleeping quarters, as for construction crews, ranch hands, etc. [BUNK[1] + HOUSE]

bunk·ie (buŋ′kē), *n. Slang.* bunkmate. [BUNK[1] + -IE]

Bun·kie (buŋ′kē), *n.* a town in central Louisiana. 5188 (1960).

bunk·mate (buŋk′māt′), *n.* one who shares sleeping quarters with another or others, esp. one who sleeps in a neighboring bunk or bed. [BUNK[1] + MATE[1]]

bun·ko (buŋ′kō), *n., pl.* **-kos,** *v.,* **-koed, -ko·ing.** *U.S. Informal.* —*n.* **1.** a swindle in which a person is cheated at gambling, persuaded to buy a nonexistent, unsalable, or worthless object, or otherwise victimized. **2.** any swindle or misrepresentation. —*v.t.* **3.** to victimize by a bunko. Also, **bunco.** [shortened form of BUNKUM]

bun′ko steer′er, *U.S. Informal.* a swindler, esp. one who lures another to a gambling game where he will be cheated.

bun·kum (buŋ′kəm), *n.* **1.** insincere speechmaking by a politician intended merely to please local constituents. **2.** insincere talk; claptrap; humbug. Also, **buncombe.** [after speech in 16th Congress, 1819–21, by F. Walker, who said he was bound to speak for *Buncombe* (N.C. county in district he represented)]

Bun·ky (buŋ′kē), *n.* a boy's given name.

bunn (bun), *n.* bun[1].

bun·ny (bun′ē), *n., pl.* **-nies.** *Informal.* **1.** a pet name for a rabbit, esp. a young one. **2.** *Dial.* a squirrel. [dial. *bun* (tail of a) hare or rabbit, in Scot: buttocks (< Gael *bun* bottom) + -Y[2]]

Bun·ny (bun′ē), *n.* a boy's or girl's given name.

bun′ny hug′, a ballroom dance popular in the U.S. in the early 20th century and characterized by a syncopated rhythm.

bu·no·dont (byo͞o′nə dont′), *adj.* having molar teeth with crowns in the form of rounded or conical cusps. Cf. **lophodont.** [< Gk *boun(ós)* hill + -ODONT]

Bun·sen (bun′sən; *Ger.* bo͝on′zən), *n.* **Rob·ert Wil·helm** (rob′ərt wil′helm; *Ger.* rō′beʀt vil′helm), 1811–99, German chemist.

Bun′sen burn′er, a type of gas burner, commonly used in chemical laboratories, with which a very hot, practically nonluminous flame is obtained by allowing air to enter at the base and mix with the gas. [named after R. W. BUNSEN]

bunt[1] (bunt), *v.t.* **1.** (of a goat or calf) to push with the horns or head; butt. **2.** *Baseball.* to bat (a pitched ball) very gently so that it rolls into the infield close to home plate, usually by holding the bat loosely in hands spread apart and allowing the ball to bounce off it. —*v.i.* **3.** to push (something) with the horns or head. **4.** *Baseball.* to bunt a ball. —*n.* **5.** a push with the head or horns; butt. **6.** *Baseball.* **a.** the act of bunting. **b.** a bunted ball. [nasalized var. of BUTT[2]]

bunt[2] (bunt), *n.* **1.** *Naut.* the middle part of a square sail. **2.** the bagging part of a fishing net or bagging middle area of various cloth objects. [?]

Bunsen burner

bunt[3] (bunt), *n. Plant Pathol.* a smut disease of wheat in which the kernels are replaced by the black, foul-smelling spores of fungi of the genus *Tilletia.* Also called **stinking smut.** [?] —**bunt′ed,** *adj.*

bunt·ing[1] (bun′tiŋ), *n.* **1.** a coarse open fabric of worsted or cotton for flags, signals, etc. **2.** patriotic and festive decorations made from such cloth, or from paper, usually in the form of draperies, wide streamers, etc., in the colors of the national flag. **3.** flags, esp. a vessel's flags, collectively. [? orig. cloth for sifting, ME *bont(en)* (to) sift + -ING[1]]

bunt·ing[2] (bun′tiŋ), *n.* any of several small, fringilline birds of the genera *Emberiza, Passerina,* or *Plectrophenax.* Cf. **indigo bunting, reed bunting, snow bunting.** [ME < ?]

bunt·ing[3] (bun′tiŋ), *n.* a hooded sleeping garment for infants. Also called **sleeper.** [special use of BUNTING[1]]

bunt·line (bunt′lin, -līn′), *n. Naut.* one of the ropes attached to the foot of a square sail to haul it up to the yard for furling. [BUNT[2] + LINE[1]]

bun·ton (bun′tən), *n. Mining.* one of a number of struts reinforcing the walls of a shaft and dividing it into vertical compartments. Also called **divider.** [var. of *bunting* crossbeam, equiv. to *bunt* (nasalized var. of *butt* short, thick piece of wood; see BUTT[1]) + -ING[1]]

Bu·nus (byo͞o′nəs), *n. Class. Myth.* the son of Hermes and Aleidamea who raised a temple to Hera in Corinth.

bun·ya-bun·ya (bun′yə bun′yə), *n.* an evergreen tree, *Araucaria bidwilli,* of Australia, having stiff, sharp, glossy needles in distinct rows. [< native Austral]

Bun·yan (bun′yən), *n.* **1. John,** 1628–88, English preacher: author of *Pilgrim's Progress.* **2. Paul.** See **Paul Bunyan.**

Bun·yan·esque (bun′yə nesk′), *adj.* noting, pertaining to, characteristic of, or suggesting the allegorical style of John Bunyan. [BUNYAN + -ESQUE]

Bun·yan·esque (bun′yə nesk′), *adj.* **1.** of, pertaining to, or resembling the legends about Paul Bunyan. **2.** of immense size or stature, as ascribed to Paul Bunyan or to the other characters, exploits, etc., in the legends about him. [BUNYAN + -ESQUE]

bun·yip (bun′yip), *Australian.* —*n.* **1.** an imposter. —*adj.* **2.** counterfeit; phony. [< native Austral]

buo·na not·te (bwô′nä nôt′te), *Italian.* good night.

Buo·na·par·te (*It.* bwô′nä pär′te), *n.* Bonaparte.

Buo·nar·ro·ti (*It.* bwô′när rô′tē), *n.* Michelangelo.

buo·na se·ra (bwô′nä se′rä), *Italian.* good evening.

buon′ fres′co (bwôn), fresco (def. 1). [< It: lit., good fresco]

buon gior·no (bwôn jôr′nô), *Italian.* good morning; good day.

Buo·non·ci·ni (*It.* bwô′nôn chē′nē), *n.* Bononcini.

bu·oy (bo͞o′ē, boi), *n. Naut.* **1.** a distinctively shaped and marked float, sometimes carrying a signal or signals, anchored to mark a channel, anchorage, navigational hazard, etc., or to provide a mooring place away from the shore. **2.** a life buoy. —*v.t.* **3.** to keep afloat or support by or as by a life buoy; keep afloat in a fluid: *The life jacket buoyed her up until help arrived.* **4.** *Naut.* to mark with a buoy or buoys. **5.** to sustain or encourage: *Her courage was buoyed by the doctor's calmness.* —*v.i.* **6.** to float; rise by reason of lightness. **7. buoy up, a.** to keep from sinking. **b.** to support or sustain. **c.** to hearten; cause to rise: *buoyed up spirits.* [late ME *boye* a float < MD << L *boia* a collar, fetter]

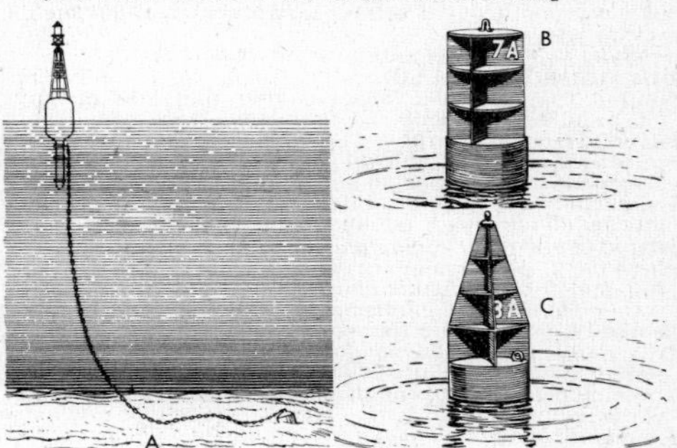

Buoys
A, Light buoy; B, Can buoy; C, Nun buoy

bu·oy·age (bo͞o′ē ij, boi′ij), *n. Naut.* **1.** a system of buoys. **2.** the provision of buoys. **3.** a fee for the use of a mooring buoy. [BUOY + -AGE]

buoy·an·cy (boi′ən sē, bo͞o′yən sē), *n.* **1.** the power to float or rise in a fluid; relative lightness. **2.** the power of supporting a body so that it floats; upward pressure exerted by the fluid in which a body is immersed. **3.** elasticity of spirit; cheerfulness. [BUOY(ANT) + -ANCY]

buoy·ant (boi′ənt, bo͞o′yənt), *adj.* **1.** tending to float or rise in a fluid. **2.** capable of keeping a body afloat, as a liquid. **3.** not easily depressed; cheerful. **4.** cheering or invigorating. [BUOY + -ANT] —**buoy′ant·ly,** *adv.*

buoy′ant force′, *Physics.* See under **Archimedes' principle.** Also called **buoy′ancy force′.**

bu′oy boat′, a boat used in whaling for holding and towing the whales killed during a hunt.

Bu·pha·gus (byōō fā′gəs), *n. Class Myth.* **1.** a son of Iapetus who was killed by Artemis for pursuing her. **2.** an epithet of Hercules, meaning "ox-eater."

Bu·pho·ni·a (byōō fō′nē ə), *n.* (*sometimes construed as pl.*) Dipolia.

bu·pres·tid (byōō pres′tid), *n.* any beetle of the family *Buprestidae*, comprising the metallic wood-boring beetles. [< NL *Buprestid(ae)* name of the family, equiv. to L *būprēst(is)* venomous beetle (< Gk *boúprēstis*, lit., ox-sweller) + *-idae* -ID[2]]

bur[1] (bûr), *n., v.,* **burred, bur·ring.** —*n.* **1.** *Bot.* the rough, prickly case around the seeds of certain plants, as of the chestnut and burdock. **2.** any bur-bearing plant. **3.** something that adheres like a bur. **4.** *Mach.* burr[1] (defs. 1, 2). **5.** *Dentistry.* a rotary cutting tool usually of steel or other hard metal shaped into a shank and a head, for removing carious material from teeth and preparing cavities for filling. **6.** *Surg.* a cutting tool resembling that of a dentist, used for the excavation of bone. —*v.t.* **7.** to extract or remove burs from. [ME *burre* < Scand; cf. Dan *burre* bur]

bur[2] (bûr), *n.* burr[2].

Bur (bōōr), *n. Scand. Myth.* Buri.

Bur., Burma.

bur., bureau.

bu·ran (bōō rän′), *n.* (on the steppes of Russia and Siberia) a violent wind storm, esp. one accompanied by driving snow and intense cold. [< Russ < Turkic]

Bu·raq (bōō räk′), *n. Islam.* a legendary beast, a winged horse with the face of a woman and the tail of a peacock, on which Muhammad is said to have traveled.

Bu·ras-Tri·umph (byōōr′əs trī′əmf), *n.* a town in SE Louisiana. 4908 (1960).

Bur·bage (bûr′bij), *n.* **Richard,** 1567?–1619, English actor: associate of Shakespeare.

Bur·bank (bûr′baŋk), *n.* **1. Luther,** 1849–1926, U.S. horticulturist and plant breeder. **2.** a city in SW California. 90,155 (1960).

Bur·ber·ry (bûr′bə rē, -ber′ē), *n., pl.* **-ries. 1.** a light raincoat made of a waterproof, mercerized cotton fabric. **2.** the fabric itself. **3.** a shaggy cheviot fabric. [back formation from *Burberrys* trademark]

bur·ble (bûr′bəl), *v.,* **-bled, -bling,** *n.* —*v.i.* **1.** to make a bubbling sound; bubble. **2.** to speak with a burble. —*n.* **3.** a bubbling or gentle flow. **4.** a bubbling flow of speech. **5.** *Aeron.* the breakdown of smooth airflow around a wing at a high angle of attack. [ME; perh. var. of BUBBLE] —**bur′bler,** *n.* —**bur′bly,** *adv.*

bur·bot (bûr′bət), *n., pl.* **-bots** (*esp. collectively*) **-bot.** a fresh-water gadid fish, *Lota lota,* found in Europe, Asia, and North America, having an elongated body and a barbel on the chin. [ME < MF *bourbotte,* var. of *bourbete,* deriv. of *bourbeter* to wallow in mud, equiv. to *bourbe* mud + *-t-* freq. suffix + *-er* inf. ending]

Burch·field (bûrch′fēld′), *n.* **Charles Ephraim,** 1893–1967, U.S. painter.

Burck·hardt (bûrk′härt; *Ger.* bōōrk′härt′), *n.* **Jakob** (yä′kôp), 1818–97, Swiss historian.

Burck·hardt (bûrk′härt), *n.* a walled plain in the first quadrant of the face of the moon: about 35 miles in diameter.

bur′ clo′ver, any of several legumes of the genus *Medicago,* as *M. hispida,* having prickly, coiled, black pods.

burd (bûrd), *n. Chiefly Scot.* a lady; maiden. [ME *burde* lady, OE *byrde* well born; akin to BIRTH]

bur·den[1] (bûr′dən), *n.* **1.** that which is carried; load: *a horse's burden of rider and pack.* **2.** that which is borne with difficulty; obligation or trouble: *the burden of leadership.* **3.** *Naut.* **a.** the weight of a ship's cargo. **b.** the carrying capacity of a ship: *a ship of a hundred-tons burden.* **4.** *Mining.* the earth or rock to be moved by a charge of explosives. **5.** *Accounting.* overhead (def. 6). —*v.t.* **6.** to load heavily. **7.** to load oppressively; trouble. [ME, var. of *burthen,* OE *byrthen;* akin to G *Bürde,* Goth *baurthei;* see BEAR[1]] —**bur′den·er,** *n.* —**bur′den·less,** *adj.*
—**Syn. 1.** See **load. 2.** weight, encumbrance, impediment.

bur·den[2] (bûr′dən), *n.* **1.** something often repeated or much dwelt upon; the principal idea. **2.** *Music.* the refrain or recurring chorus of a song. [ME *bordoun* < MF *bourdon* droning sound, instrument making such a sound, etc.]
—**Syn. 1.** substance, core, point, essence.

bur·dened (bûr′dənd), *adj. Navig.* (of a vessel) required to yield to a vessel having the right of way. Cf. **privileged** (def. 5). [BURDEN[1] + -ED[2]]

bur′den of proof′, *Chiefly Law.* **1.** the obligation to offer evidence which the court or jury could reasonably believe, in support of a contention, failing which the case will be lost. **2.** the obligation to establish an alleged fact by convincing a tribunal of its probable truth.

bur·den·some (bûr′dən səm), *adj.* **1.** oppressively heavy. **2.** distressing; troublesome. **3.** *Naut.* having a full hull form, as a merchant vessel built for capacity rather than speed. [BURDEN[1] + -SOME[1]] —**bur′den·some·ly,** *adv.* —**bur′den·some·ness,** *n.*

bur·dock (bûr′dok), *n.* a composite plant of the genus *Arctium,* esp. *A. lappa,* a coarse, broad-leaved weed bearing prickly heads of burs which stick to the clothing. [BUR[1] + DOCK[4]]

Bu·re (bōōr′ə), *n. Scand. Myth.* Buri.

bu·reau (byōōr′ō), *n., pl.* **bu·reaus, bu·reaux** (byōōr′ōz). **1.** *U.S.* a chest of drawers, often with a mirror at the top. **2.** *Chiefly Brit.* a desk or writing table with drawers for papers. **3.** a division of a government department or an independent administrative unit. **4.** an agency or office for collecting or distributing news or information, coordinating the work of related businesses, etc.: *He called a travel bureau for information on winter cruises.* [< F: desk, office, orig., kind of cloth (used to cover desks, etc.), OF *burel,* equiv. to *bur-* (< LL *burra* rough cloth) + *-el* n. suffix]

bu·reauc·ra·cy (byōō rok′rə sē), *n., pl.* **-cies. 1.** government by many bureaus, administrators, and petty officials. **2.** the body of officials and administrators, esp. of a government or government department. **3.** excessive multiplication of, and concentration of power in, administrative bureaus or administrators. **4.** excessive governmental red tape and routine. [BUREAU + -CRACY, modeled on F *bureaucratie*]

bu·reau·crat (byōōr′ə krat′), *n.* **1.** an official of a bureaucracy. **2.** an official who works by fixed routine without exercising intelligent judgment. [< F *bureaucrate.* See BUREAU, -CRAT] —**bu·reau·crat·ism** (byōōr′ə krat iz′əm, byōō rok′rə tiz′-), *n.*

bu·reau·crat·ic (byōōr′ə krat′ik), *adj.* of, pertaining to, or characteristic of a bureaucrat or a bureaucracy. [< F *bureaucratique.* See BUREAUCRAT, -IC] —**bu′reau·crat′i·cal·ly,** *adv.*

bu·reauc·ra·tize (byōō rok′rə tīz′), *v.t.,* **-tized, -tiz·ing. 1.** to divide an administrative agency or office into bureaus. **2.** to increase the number of government or business bureaus. [< F *bureaucratiser.* See BUREAUCRAT, -IZE] —**bu·reauc′ra·ti·za′tion,** *n.*

Bu′reau of Cus′toms, *U.S. Govt.* the division of the Department of the Treasury that collects customs and enforces laws dealing with smuggling.

Bu′reau of Inter′nal Rev′enue, former name of the **Internal Revenue Service.**

Bu′reau of the Bud′get, *U.S. Govt.* the division of the Executive Office of the President that prepares and administers the federal budget.

Bu′reau of the Cen′sus, *U.S. Govt.* the division of the Department of Commerce that gathers, tabulates, and correlates census statistics.

bu·re·lé (bōōr′ə lā′), *n.* **1.** Also, **bu·re·lage** (bōōr′ə läzh′). *Philately.* the netlike pattern of colored lines or dots forming the background design of certain postage stamps. **2.** Also, **bu·rel·ly** (bōōr′ə lē), **bu·rel·le** (bōōr′ə lā). *Heraldry.* barruly. [< F, OF, equiv. to *burel* spoke, ray, bar + *-é* -ATE[1]]

bu·rette (byōō ret′), *n. Chem.* a graduated glass tube, commonly having a stopcock at the bottom, used for accurately measuring or measuring out small quantities of liquid. Also, **bu·ret′.** [< F: cruet, MF, var. of *buirette,* equiv. to *buire* ewer (var. of *buie* < Gmc; cf. OE *būc* pitcher) + *-ette* -ETTE; see BUCKET]

Burette

burg (bûrg), *n.* **1.** *Informal.* a city or town. **2.** *Hist.* a fortified town. [var. of BURGH]

Bürg (bûrg; *Ger.* BYRKH), *n.* a crater in the first quadrant of the face of the moon: about 28 miles in diameter.

bur·ga[1] (bōōr′gə, bûr′-), *n.* (in Alaska) a storm of northeasterly winds with snow. Also, **boorga.** [< Russ *burya*]

bur·ga[2] (bōōr′gə), *n.* burka.

burg·age (bûr′gij), *n. Law.* **1.** (in England) a tenure whereby burgesses or townsmen hold lands or tenements of the king or other lord, usually for a fixed money rent. **2.** (in Scotland) tenure directly from the crown of property in royal burghs in return for the service of watching and warding. [ME *borgage* < ML *burgāg(ium),* equiv. to *burg(us)* burgh, borough + *-āgium* -AGE]

Bur·gas (bōōr gäs′), *n.* a seaport in E Bulgaria, on the Black Sea. 72,526 (1956).

bur·gee (bûr′jē), *n.* a triangular flag or one having a shallow, angular indentation in the fly, forming two tails, used as an identification flag, esp. by yachts. [?]

Bur·gen·land (*Ger.* bōōr′gən länt′), *n.* a province in E Austria, bordering Hungary. 271,001 (1961); 1530 sq. mi. *Cap.:* Eisenstadt.

bur·geon (bûr′jən), *n.* **1.** a bud; sprout. —*v.i.* **2.** to begin to grow, as a bud; to put forth buds, shoots, etc., as a plant (often fol. by *out, forth*). **3.** to grow or develop suddenly: *The town burgeoned into a city. To our surprise, he burgeoned into a fine actor.* —*v.t.* **4.** to put forth as buds. Also, **bourgeon.** [ME *burjon* bud < OF < ?]

burg·er (bûr′gər), *n.* **1.** *Informal.* a hamburger. **2.** (in compounds) a patty or small cake of food, as specified, usually ground or chopped, grilled, and served on a bun: *clamburger; pizza-burger; turkeyburger.* [abstracted from HAMBURGER by false analysis as HAM[1] + *burger*]

Bur·ger (bûr′gər), *n.* **Warren Earl,** born 1907, U.S. jurist: Chief Justice of the U.S. Supreme Court 1969–86.

bur·gess (bûr′jis), *n.* **1.** an inhabitant, esp. a citizen or freeman, of an English borough. **2.** *Hist.* a representative of a borough, corporate town, or university in the British Parliament. **3.** *Amer. Hist.* a representative in the popular branch of the colonial legislature of Virginia or Maryland. [ME *burgeis* < OF, equiv. to *burg* city (< Gmc) + *-eis* -ESE]

Bur·gess (bûr′jis), *n.* **1. (Frank) Ge·lett** (jə let′), 1866–1951, U.S. illustrator and humorist. **2. Thornton Waldo,** 1874–1965, U.S. author, esp. of children's books. **3.** a boy's given name.

burgh (bûrg; *Scot.* bur′ō, bur′ə), *n.* **1.** (in Scotland) an incorporated town having its own charter and some degree of political independence from the surrounding area. **2.** *Archaic.* borough. [var. of BOROUGH] —**burgh·al** (bûr′gəl), *adj.*

burgh·er (bûr′gər), *n.* an inhabitant of a borough; citizen. [< MD < MHG *burger,* equiv. to *burg* BOROUGH + *-er* -ER[1]] —**burgh′er·ship′,** *n.*

bur′ gher′kin, gherkin (def. 2).

Burgh·ley (bûr′lē), *n.* **1st Baron.** See **Cecil, William.** Also, **Burleigh.**

bur·glar (bûr′glər), *n.* one who commits burglary. [< AF *burgler* < AL *burglātor,* appar. equiv. to *burgl-* (< OE *burghal* as in *burghal-penny*) + *-ātor* -OR[2]; OE *burghal,* equiv. to *burg* BOROUGH + *hal* HALL]

bur′glar alarm′, an automatic device for sounding an alarm when a window, door, safe, etc. is opened or tampered with, as by a burglar.

bur·glar·i·ous (bər glâr′ē əs), *adj.* pertaining to or involving burglary. [BURGLAR + -IOUS] —**bur·glar′i·ous·ly,** *adv.*

bur·glar·ize (bûr′glə rīz′), *v.,* **-ized, iz·ing.** —*v.t.* **1.** to break into and steal from (a place): *Thieves burglarized the warehouse.* —*v.i.* **2.** to commit burglary. Also, *esp. Brit.,* **bur′glar·ise′.**

bur·glar·proof (bûr′glər prōōf′), *adj.* safeguarded or secure against burglary. [BURGLAR + -PROOF]

bur·gla·ry (bûr′glə rē), *n., pl.* **-ries.** *Crim. Law.* the felony of breaking into and entering the house of another at night with intent to commit a felony therein, extended by statute to cover the breaking and entering of any of various buildings, by night or day. [< AF *burglarie* < AL *burglaria,* alter. (with *-l-* of *burglātor*) of *burgaria,* var. of *burgeria,* equiv. to *burger-* BURGLER + *-ia* -IA]

bur·gle (bûr′gəl), *v.t., v.i.,* **-gled, -gling.** *Informal.* to burglarize. [back formation from BURGLAR]

bur·go·mas·ter (bûr′gə mas′tər, -mä′stər), *n.* the chief magistrate of a municipal town of Holland, Flanders, Germany, or Austria. [< D *burgemeester,* equiv. to *burg* BOROUGH + *meester* MASTER; akin to G *Bürgermeister* major] —**bur′go·mas′ter·ship′,** *n.*

bur·go·net (bûr′gə net′), *n. Armor.* an open helmet, usually having a peak and hinged cheek pieces, and often accompanied by a buffe. [< ME *burgon* of Burgundy (< MF *Bourgogne* Burgundy) + *-et* -ET, modeled on MF *bourguignotte*]

bur·goo (bûr′gōō, bûr gōō′), *n., pl.* **-goos** for 2b. **1.** a thick oatmeal gruel, esp. as eaten by seamen. **2.** *U.S. Dial.* **a.** a kind of thick, highly seasoned soup or stew, usually made of chicken and several kinds of meats, small game, and vegetables. **b.** a picnic at which such soup or stew is served. [?]

Bur·gos (bōōr′gôs), *n.* a city in N Spain: Gothic cathedral. 89,864 (est. 1960).

Bur·goyne (bər goin′), *n.* **John,** 1722–92, British general and dramatist: surrendered at Saratoga in American Revolutionary War.

bur·grave (bûr′grāv), *n. Ger. Hist.* **1.** the appointed head of a fortress. **2.** the hereditary governor of a castle or town. [< G *Burggraf,* equiv. to *Burg* castle, town + *Graf* count]

Bur·gun·di·an (bər gun′dē ən), *adj.* **1.** of or pertaining to Burgundy or its people. —*n.* **2.** a native or inhabitant of Burgundy. [BURGUNDY + -AN]

Bur·gun·dy (bûr′gən dē), *n., pl.* **-dies,** *adj.* —*n.* **1.** French, **Bourgogne.** a region in SE France: a former kingdom, duchy, and province. **2.** (*often l.c.*) wine, of many varieties, red and white, mostly still, full, and dry, produced in the Burgundy region. **3.** (*often l.c.*) red wine with similar characteristics made elsewhere. **4.** Also called **Bur′gundy sauce′.** a sauce made with red wine and thickened with an espagnole sauce or kneaded butter, served with eggs, meat, fish, or poultry. **5.** (*l.c.*) a grayish red-brown to dark blackish-purple color. —*adj.* **6.** (*l.c.*) having the color burgundy. [< ML *Burgundi(a),* equiv. to L *Burgundi(ōnes),* Latinized form of Germanic tribal name + *-a* territorial suffix]

Bur′gundy tre′foil, alfalfa. [so called from its rich color]

Bu·ri (bōōr′ē), *n. Scand. Myth.* the first of the gods, revealed when the cow Audhumbla licked away the salty ice that covered him. Also, **Bur, Bure.**

bur·i·al (ber′ē əl), *n.* **1.** the act or ceremony of burying. **2.** the place of burying; grave. [BURY + -AL[2]; r. ME *buriel,* back formation from OE *byrgels* burial place, equiv. to *byrg(an)* (to) BURY + *-els* (for *-isl*) n. suffix]

Bur′ial at Or·nans′ (ôr nän′), a painting (1849) by Gustave Courbet.

bur′ial ground′, a tract of land for burial of the dead.

bur′ial mound′, a mound built over a grave. Cf. **barrow**[2] (def. 1).

Bur′ial of Count′ Or·gaz′, The (ôr gäz′), a painting (1586) by El Greco.

Bur·iat (bōōr yät′, bōōr′ē ät′), *n.* one of the Mongolian languages of the Altaic family. Also, **Buryat.**

Buriat′ Auton′omous So′viet So′cialist Repub′lic. See **Buryat Autonomous Soviet Socialist Republic.**

bur·i·er (ber′ē ər), *n.* one who or that which buries. [BURY + -ER[1]]

bu·rin (byōōr′in), *n.* **1.** a tempered steel rod, with a lozenge-shaped point and a rounded handle, used for engraving furrows in metal. **2.** a similar tool used by marble workers. **3.** a prehistoric pointed or chisellike flint tool. [< F < It *burino* (now *bulino*) graving tool, equiv. to *bur-* (? < Gmc; see BORE[1]) + *-ino* -INE[2]]

Burin

bur·ka (bōōr′kə), *n.* a loose garment covering the entire body and having a veiled opening for the eyes, worn by Muslim women. Also, **bourkha, bur′kha, burga.** [< Urdu *burqa′* < Ar]

Burk·bur·nett (bûrk′bər net′), *n.* a town in N Texas. 7621 (1960).

burke (bûrk), *v.t.,* **burked, burk·ing. 1.** to murder, as by suffocation, so as to leave no or few marks of violence. **2.** to suppress or get rid of by some indirect maneuver. [after W. *Burke,* hanged in 1829 in Edinburgh for murders of this kind] —**burk′er, burk·ite** (bûr′kīt), *n.*

Burke (bûrk), *n.* **1. Edmund,** 1729–97, Irish statesman, orator, and writer. **2. Kenneth Du·va** (dōō vā′), born 1897, U.S. literary critic. **3.** a boy's given name.

Bur·ki·na Fa·so (bər kē′nə fä′sō). See **Upper Volta.**

burl (bûrl), *n.* **1.** a small knot or lump in wool, thread, or cloth. **2.** a dome-shaped growth on the trunk of a tree; a wartlike structure sometimes two feet across and a foot or more in height, sliced to make veneer. —*v.t.* **3.** to remove burls from (cloth) in finishing. [late ME *burle* << OF; akin to ML *burla* bunch, sheaf, LL *burra* tuft of wool] —**burl′er,** *n.*

Burl (bûrl), *n.* a boy's given name, form of **Burleigh.**

bur·lap (bûr′lap), *n.* **1.** a plain-woven, coarse fabric of jute, hemp, or the like; gunny. **2.** a lightweight fabric made in imitation of this. [earlier *borelap,* equiv. to *bore(l)* coarse cloth (see BUREAU) + LAP[1]]

bur·le·cue (bûr′lē kyōō′), *n. Slang.* burlesque (def. 3). Also, **bur′ley·cue′.** [by alter.]

Bur·leigh (bûr′lē), *n.* **1. 1st Baron.** See **Cecil, William. 2.** Also, **Burley.** a boy's given name.

bur·lesque (bər lesk′), *n., adj., v.,* **-lesqued, -les·quing.** —*n.* **1.** an artistic composition, esp. literary or dramatic, which, for the sake of laughter, vulgarizes lofty material or treats ordinary material with mock dignity. **2.** any ludicrous parody or grotesque caricature. **3.** Also, **burlesk.** *Theat. U.S.* a humorous and provocative stage show featuring slapstick humor, comic sketches or skits, bawdy songs, striptease acts, suggestive dances, and a scantily clad female chorus. —*adj.* **4.** involving ludicrous or mocking treatment of a solemn subject. **5.** of, pertaining to, or like stage-show burlesque. —*v.t.* **6.** to make ridiculous by mocking representation. —*v.i.* **7.** to use caricature. [< F < It *burlesco,* equiv. to *burl(a)* jest + *-esco* -ESQUE] —**bur·lesque′ly,** *adv.* —**bur·les′quer,** *n.*

—**Syn. 1.** satire, lampoon, farce. BURLESQUE, CARICATURE, PARODY, TRAVESTY refer to the literary or dramatic forms that imitate serious works or subjects to achieve a humorous or satiric purpose. The characteristic device of BURLESQUE is mockery of both high and low through association with their opposites: *a burlesque of high and low life.* CARICATURE, usually associated with visual arts or with visual effects in literary works, implies exaggeration of characteristic details: *The caricature emphasized his nose.* PARODY achieves its humor through application of the manner or technique, usually of a well-known writer, to unaccustomed subjects: *a parody of Swift.* TRAVESTY implies a grotesque form of burlesque: *characters so changed as to produce a travesty.*

bur·let·ta (bər let′ə), *n. Theat.* **1.** (in the 18th century) a musical drama containing rhymed lyrics and resembling comic opera. **2.** (in the 19th century) any three-act play containing at least five songs and resembling burlesque. [< It, equiv. to *burl(a)* jest + *-etta* -ETTE]

bur·ley[1] (bûr′lē), *n., pl.* **-leys.** (*often cap.*) an American tobacco grown esp. in Kentucky and southern Ohio. [appar. from proper name]

bur·ley[2] (bûr′lē), *n., pl.* **-leys.** *U.S. Informal.* a burlesque show. [BURL(ESQUE) + -EY[2]]

Bur·ley (bûr′lē), *n.* **1.** a town in S Idaho. 7508 (1960). **2.** Also, **Burleigh.** a boy's given name.

Bur·lin·game (bûr′lin gām′, -liṅg gām′), *n.* **1. Anson** (an′sən), 1820–70, U.S. diplomat. **2.** a city in W California, S of San Francisco. 24,036 (1960).

Bur·ling·ton (bûr′liṅg tən), *n.* **1.** a city in NW Vermont, on Lake Champlain. 35,531 (1960). **2.** a city in N North Carolina. 33,199 (1960). **3.** a city in SE Iowa, on the Mississippi River. 32,430 (1960). **4.** a town in SE Wisconsin. 5856 (1960). **5.** a town in NW Washington. 2968 (1960).

bur·ly (bûr′lē), *adj.,* **-li·er, -li·est. 1.** great in bodily size; stout; sturdy. **2.** bluff; brusque. [ME *borli, burli,* OE *borlīce* excellent(ly), equiv. to *bor(a)* ruler (lit., high-born one; see BEAR[1]) + *-līce* -LY] —**bur′li·ly,** *adv.* —**bur′li·ness,** *n.*

Bur·ma (bûr′mə), *n.* an independent republic in SE Asia: a British dependency until 1948; traditionally divided into the coastal region W of Thailand **(Lower Burma),** the inland area **(Upper Burma),** and the Shan States. 20,662,000 (est. 1960); 261,789 sq. mi. *Cap.:* Rangoon. Official name, **Un′ion of Bur′ma.** Cf. **Shan States.**

Bur·man (bûr′mən), *n., pl.* **-mans,** *adj.* Burmese (defs. 1, 3). [BURM(A) + -AN]

bur′ mar′igold, any of various composite herbs of the genus *Bidens,* esp. those having conspicuous yellow flowers.

Bur′ma Road′, a road extending from Lashio, Burma to Chungking, China: used during World War II to supply Allied military forces in China.

Bur·mese (bər mēz′, -mēs′), *n., pl.* **-mese,** *adj.* —*n.* **1.** a native or inhabitant of Burma. **2.** the principal language of Burma, a Sino-Tibetan language. —*adj.* **3.** of or pertaining to Burma, its people, or their language. Also, **Burman** (for defs. 1, 3). [BURM(A) + -ESE]

Bur′mese glass′, an American art glass of the late 19th century, ranging from greenish-yellow to pink.

Bur′mese jade′, *Jewelry.* jadeite of the finest quality: a true jade. Also, **Bur′ma jade′.**

bur·mite (bûr′mīt), *n. Mineral.* a variety of amber found in Burma. [BURM(A) + -ITE[1]]

burn[1] (bûrn), *v.* **burned** or **burnt, burn·ing,** *n.* —*v.i.* **1.** to undergo rapid combustion or consume fuel in such a way as to give off heat, gases, and usually, light; be on fire: *The house burned and we ran for our lives. The fire burned in the grate.* **2.** (of a fireplace, furnace, etc.) to contain a fire. **3.** to feel heat or a physiologically identical sensation; feel pain from or as if from a fire: *His face burned in the wind. The wound burned and throbbed.* **4.** to give off light or to glow brightly: *The lights in the house burned all night.* **5.** to give off heat or be hot: *The pavement burned in the noon sun.* **6.** to produce pain or a stinging sensation similar to that of fire; to cause to smart: *The whiskey burned in his throat.* **7.** *Games.* to be extremely close to finding a concealed object or guessing an answer. **8.** to feel extreme anger: *When she said I was rude, I really burned.* **9.** to feel strong emotion or passion: *He burned with the desire to become a doctor.* **10.** *Chem.* **a.** to undergo combustion, either fast or slow; oxidize. **b.** to undergo fission or fusion. **11.** to become charred or overcooked by heat: *The steak burned around the edges.* **12.** to become reddened or discolored by heat or other rays: *She burned too easily to stay out in the sun for long.* **13.** to be damned: *You may burn for that sin.* **14.** *Slang.* to be electrocuted in an electric chair: *The murderer was sentenced to burn.* —*v.t.* **15.** to cause to undergo combustion or be consumed partly or wholly by fire. **16.** to use as fuel or as a source of light: *He burned coal to heat the house.* **17.** to cause to feel the sensation of heat. **18.** to overcook or char: *She burned the roast again.* **19.** to redden or discolor by heat or other rays. **20.** to injure, endanger, or kill with or as with fire: *Look out, you'll burn yourself!* **21.** to subject to fire or treat with heat as a process of manufacturing. **22.** to produce with or as with fire: *He burned the image of a horse into the wood panel.* **23.** to cause sharp pain or a stinging sensation: *The iodine burned his wound.* **24.** to consume rapidly, esp. to squander: *He burned energy as if he never heard of resting.* **25.** *Informal.* to be badly cheated or disillusioned: *He was burned by that phony stock deal.* **26.** *Chem.* to cause to undergo combustion; oxidize. **27.** to damage through excessive friction, as in grinding or machining; scorch. **28.** *Metall.* to oxidize (a steel ingot), as with a flame. **29.** *Brit.* to scald (a wine, esp. sherry) in an iron container over a fire. **30.** *Cards Slang.* to put (a played or rejected card) face up at the bottom of the pack. **31. burn down,** to burn to the ground: *That barn was struck by lightning and burned down.* **32. burn in,** *Photog.* (in printing) to expose (one part of an image) to more light by masking the other parts. **33. burn off,** (of morning mist) to be dissipated by the warmth of the rising sun. **34. burn on,** to weld lead with lead. **35. burn oneself out,** to expend all one's energy through overwork or intemperance: *They feared that he would burn himself out or break down.* **36. burn out, a.** to cease functioning; become unserviceable: *All of our light bulbs are burned out.* **b.** to deprive of a place to live, work, etc., by reason of fire: *They were burned out and were forced to live with relatives.* **37. burn up, a.** to burn completely or utterly: *The papers burned up in a minute.* **b.** to incite to anger. **c.** to become angry: *He was getting burned up about something.* —*n.* **38.** a burned place or area: *a burn on the hand; a burn where fire had ripped through the forest.* **39.** *Pathol.* an injury caused by heat, abnormal cold, chemicals, poison gas, electricity, or lightning, and characterized by reddening **(first-degree burn),** blistering **(second-degree burn),** or charring **(third-degree burn). 40.** See **slow burn. 41.** the process or an instance of burning or baking, as in brickmaking. **42.** *Australian.* a forest or brush fire. [ME *bernen, brennen,* OE *beornan* (v.i.), (c. Goth, OHG *brinnan*) and OE *bærnan* (v.t.), (c. Goth *brannjan,* OHG *brennen*)] —**burn′a·ble,** *adj.*

—**Syn. 1.** flame. **3.** tingle, glow. **15.** char, toast, brown, tan. BURN, SCORCH, SEAR, SINGE refer to the effect of fire or heat. To BURN is to consume, wholly or in part, by contact with fire or excessive heat: *to burn leaves.* SCORCH implies superficial or slight burning, resulting in a change of color or in injury to the texture because of shriveling or curling: *to scorch a dress while ironing.* SEAR refers esp. to the drying or hardening caused by heat: *to sear a roast of meat.* SINGE applies esp. to a superficial burning that takes off ends or projections: *to singe hair; singe the pinfeathers from a chicken.*

burn[2] (bûrn; *Scot.* bŭrn), *n. Scot. and North Eng.* a brook or rivulet. Also, **bourn, bourne.** [ME *burne, bourne,* OE *burna, brunna* brook; c. Goth *brunna,* D *born, bron,* G *Brunnen,* Icel *brunnr* spring]

burned-out (bûrnd′out′), *adj.* consumed; rendered unserviceable or ineffectual by maximum or excessive use: *a burned-out light bulb; burned-out zeal.* Also, **burnt-out.**

Burne-Jones (bûrn′jōnz′), *n.* **Sir Edward Co·ley** (kō′lē), 1833–98, English painter and designer.

burn·er (bûr′nər), *n.* **1.** one who or that which burns. **2.** that part of a gas fixture, lamp, etc., from which flame issues or in which it is produced. [ME *brenner.* See BURN[1], -ER[1]]

bur·net (bûr′nit), *n.* a rosaceous plant of the genus *Sanguisorba,* esp. *S. minor,* an erect herb having leaves which are used for salads. [ME < MF *burnete,* var. of *brunete* (see BRUNET); so called from its hue]

Bur·net (bər net′, bûr′nit), *n.* **Sir Mac·far·lane** (mək fär′lən), born 1899, Australian physician: Nobel prize 1960.

bur′net rose′. See **Scotch rose.**

Bur·nett (bər net′), *n.* **1. Frances Hodg·son** (hoj′sən), 1849–1924, U.S. novelist, born in England. **2.** a boy's given name.

Bur·ney (bûr′nē), *n.* **1. Charles,** 1726–1814, English organist, composer, and music historian. **2.** his daughter, **Frances** or **Fanny** (*Madame D'Arblay*), 1752–1840, English novelist and diarist.

Burn·ham (bûr′nəm), *n.* **1. Daniel Hudson,** 1846–1912, U.S. architect. **2.** a town in central Pennsylvania. 2755 (1960). **3.** a walled plain in the fourth quadrant of the face of the moon: about 18 miles in diameter.

burn·ing (bûr′niṅg), *adj.* **1.** aflame; on fire. **2.** very hot; simmering: *The water was burning.* **3.** very bright; glowing: *She wore a burning red bathing suit.* **4.** affecting with or as with fire, a burn, or heat: *He had a burning sensation in his throat.* **5.** intense; passionate: *a burning desire.* **6.** urgent or crucial: *a burning question.* —*n.* **7.** the state, process, sensation, or effect of being on fire, burned, or subjected to intense heat. **8.** the baking of ceramic products to develop hardness and other properties. **9.** the heating or the calcining of certain ores and rocks as a preliminary stage in various industrial processes. [ME *brenning* (n., adj.), OE *byrnendum* (adj.). See BURN[1], -ING[1], -ING[2]] —**burn′ing·ly,** *adv.*

burn·ing-bush (bûr′niṅg bŏŏsh′), *n.* **1.** any of various plants, esp. the wahoo, *Euonymus atropurpureus.* **2.** dittany (def. 3). Also, **burn′ing bush′.**

burn′ing glass′, a lens used to produce heat or ignite substances by focusing the sun's rays.

bur·nish (bûr′nish), *v.t.* **1.** to polish (a surface) by friction. **2.** to make smooth and bright. **3.** *Engraving.* to flatten and enlarge the dots of (a halftone) by rubbing with a tool. —*n.* **4.** gloss; brightness; luster: *the burnish of brass andirons.* [ME *burnissh* < MF *bruniss-* (long s. of *brunir* to brown, polish), equiv. to *brun-* BROWN + *-iss-* -ISH[2]] —**bur′nish·a·ble,** *adj.* —**bur′nish·ment,** *n.*

—**Syn. 1.** buff, shine.

bur·nish·er (bûr′ni shər), *n.* **1.** one who burnishes. **2.** a tool, usually with a smooth, slightly convex head, used for polishing, as in dentistry. [late ME *burnesshер.* See BURNISH, -ER[2]]

Burnoose

Burn·ley (bûrn′lē), *n.* a city in E Lancashire, in NW England. 80,588 (1961).

bur·noose (bər no͞os′, bûr′no͞os), *n.* **1.** a hooded mantle or cloak, as that worn by Arabs. **2.** a similar garment worn by women at various periods in Europe and the United States. Also, **bur·nous′.** [< F *burnous* < Ar *burnus*] —**bur·noosed′, bur·noused′,** *adj.*

burn·out (bûrn′out′), *n.* **1.** a fire that is totally destructive of something. **2.** exhaustion. **3.** *Rocketry.* **a.** the termination of effective combustion in a rocket engine, due to exhaustion of propellant. **b.** the end of the powered portion of a rocket's flight. **4.** *Elect.* the breakdown of a lamp, motor, or other electrical device due to the heat created by the current flowing through it. [n. use of v. phrase *burn out*]

Burns (bûrnz), *n.* **1. Robert,** 1759–96, Scottish poet. **2. Tommy** (*Noah Brusso*), 1881–1955, U.S. boxer: world heavyweight champion 1906–08. **3.** a town in central Oregon. 3523 (1960).

Burn·side (bûrn′sīd′), *n.* **Ambrose Everett,** 1824–81, Union general in the U.S. Civil War.

burn·sides (bûrn′sīdz′), *n.pl.* full whiskers and a mustache worn with the chin clean-shaven. [named after Gen. A. E. BURNSIDE]

Burnsides

burnt (bûrnt), *v.* **1.** a pt. and pp. of **burn.** —*adj.* **2.** *Fine Arts.* **a.** of earth pigments that have been calcined and changed to a deeper and warmer color: *burnt ocher; burnt sienna; burnt umber.* **b.** of or pertaining to colors having a deeper or grayer hue than is usually associated with them: *burnt orange; burnt rose.*

burnt′ al′mond. Often, **burnt almonds.** roasted sweet almond.

burnt′ lime′, lime[1] (def. 1).

Burnt′ Nor′ton, a poem (1941) by T. S. Eliot. Cf. **Four Quartets.**

burnt′ of′fering, an offering burnt upon an altar in sacrifice to a deity.

burnt-out (bûrnt′out′), *adj.* burned-out.

bur′ oak′, an oak tree, *Quercus macrocarpa,* of eastern North America, yielding a hard, tough, and durable wood: the State tree of Illinois.

burp (bûrp), *Informal.* —*n.* **1.** a belch; eructation. —*v.i.* **2.** to belch; eruct. —*v.t.* **3.** to cause (a baby) to belch by patting or rubbing its back, esp. to relieve flatulence after feeding. [imit.]

burp′ gun′, *Mil.* See **machine pistol.**

burr[1] (bûr), *n.* **1.** a small, hand-held, power-driven milling cutter, used by machinists, die makers, dentists, etc., for deepening, widening, or undercutting small recesses. **2.** Also, **buhr.** a protruding, ragged metal edge raised on the surface of an object during drilling, shearing, punching, or engraving. **3.** a rough or irregular protuberance on any object, as on a tree. **4.** a lump of brick fused or warped in firing. —*v.t.* **5.** to form a rough point or edge on. **6.** deburr. Also, **bur** (for defs. 1, 2). [var. of BUR[1]]

burr[2] (bûr), *n.* **1.** a washer placed at the head of a rivet. **2.** a blank punched out of a piece of sheet metal. **3.** *Shipbuilding.* roove (def. 1). Also, **bur.** [ME *burrewez* (pl.), *buruhe* circle, var. of *brough* round tower; see BROCH]

burr[3] (bûr), *n.* **1.** a guttural pronunciation of the *r*-sound, as in certain Northern English dialects. **2.** any pronunciation popularly considered rough or nonurban. **3.** a whirring noise or sound. —*v.i.* **4.** to speak with a burr. **5.** to speak roughly, indistinctly, or inarticulately. **6.** to make a whirring noise or sound. —*v.t.* **7.** to pronounce (words, sounds, etc.) with a burr. [appar. both imit. and associative, the sound being thought of as rough like a bur]

burr[4] (bûr), *n.* **1.** burstone. **2.** a mass of harder siliceous rock in soft rock. Also, **buhr.** [ME *burre,* prob. so called from its prickliness]

Burr (bûr), *n.* **Aaron,** 1756–1836, vice-president of the U.S. 1801–05.

burred (bûrd), *adj.* **1.** prickly or rough in texture. **2.** covered by a bur or burs. [BUR[1] + -ED[2]]

bur′ reed′, any plant of the genus *Sparganium,* having ribbonlike leaves and bearing burlike heads of fruit. —**bur′-reed′,** *adj.*

burr·fish (bûr′fish′), *n., pl.* **-fish·es,** (*esp. referring to two or more kinds or species*) **-fish.** any of several porcupinefishes of the genus *Chilomycterus,* covered with short, immovable spines. [so called from its spines; see BURR[1], FISH]

bur·rhel (bûr′əl), *n.* bharal.

bur·ro (bûr′ō, bo͝or′ō, bur′ō), *n., pl.* **-ros. 1.** a small donkey used as a pack animal in the southwestern U.S. **2.** any donkey. [< Sp < Pg, back formation from *burrico* ass < VL **burriccus* for LL *burricus* pony]

Bur·roughs (bûr′ōz, bur′-), *n.* **1. Edgar Rice,** 1875–1950, U.S. novelist and short-story writer: creator of Tarzan. **2. John,** 1837–1921, U.S. naturalist and essayist.

bur·row (bûr′ō, bur′ō), *n.* **1.** a hole or tunnel in the ground made by a rabbit, fox, or similar small animal for habitation and refuge. **2.** a similar place of retreat; shelter or refuge. —*v.i.* **3.** to make a hole or passage in, into, or under something. **4.** to lodge in a burrow. **5.** to hide. —*v.t.* **6.** to put a burrow or burrows into (a hill, mountainside, etc.). **7.** to hide (oneself), as in a burrow. **8.** to make by or as if by burrowing: *The groundhog burrowed a hole in the garden. We burrowed a path through the crowd.* [ME *borow,* earlier *burh,* appar. gradational var. of late ME *beri* burrow, var. of earlier *berg* refuge, OE *gebeorg,* deriv. of *beorgan* to protect; akin to OE *burgen* grave, i.e., place of protection for body; see BURY] —**bur′row·er,** *n.*

bur′rowing blen′ny, graveldiver.

bur′rowing owl′, a long-legged, terrestrial owl, *Speotyto cunicularia,* of North and South America, which digs its nesting burrow in open prairie land.

burr·stone (bûr′stōn′), *n.* burstone.

bur·ry (bûr′ē), *adj.,* **-ri·er, -ri·est.** full of or covered with burs; burlike; prickly. [BUR[1] + -Y[1]]

bur·sa (bûr′sə), *n., pl.* **-sae** (-sē), **-sas. 1.** *Anat., Zool.* a pouch, sac, or vesicle, esp. a sac containing synovia, to facilitate motion, as between a tendon and a bone. **2.** (in the Middle Ages) a dormitory of a university. [< NL, ML: a bag, pouch, purse < Gk *býrsa* a skin, hide] —**bur·sate** (bûr′sāt), *adj.*

Bur·sa (bo͝or′sä), *n.* a city in NW Turkey in Asia: a former capital of the Ottoman Empire. 103,812 (1950). Also, **Brusa.**

bur·sal (bûr′səl), *adj.* of, pertaining to, or acting upon the bursa. [BURS(A) + -AL[1]]

bur·sar (bûr′sər, -sär), *n.* **1.** a treasurer or business officer, esp. of a college or university. **2.** (in the Middle Ages) a university student. **3.** *Chiefly Scot.* a student attending a university on a scholarship. [< ML *bursār(ius)* a purse-keeper, treasurer (see BURSA, -AR[2]); r. late ME *bouser*, var. of *bourser* < AF; OF *borsier*]

bur·sar·i·al (bər sâr′ē əl), *adj.* of, pertaining to, or paid to or by a bursar, or a bursary. [BURSAR + -IAL]

bur·sa·ry (bûr′sə rē), *n., pl.* **-ries. 1.** *Eccles.* the treasury of a monastery. **2.** *Brit.* a college scholarship. [< ML *bursāria* treasurer's room, deriv. of *bursārius* a treasurer. See BURSAR, -Y[3]]

Bur·schen·schaft (bōōr′shən shäft′), *n., pl.* **-schaf·ten** (-shäf′tən). *German.* any of certain associations of students at German universities, formed to promote patriotism, Christian conduct, and liberal ideas, but now primarily social fraternities. [lit., studentship]

burse (bûrs), *n.* **1.** a pouch or case for some special purpose. **2.** (in Scotland) **a.** a fund to provide allowances for students. **b.** an allowance so provided. **3.** *Eccles.* a case or receptacle for a corporal. [ME < AF < ML *bursa* purse; see BURSA]

bur·seed (bûr′sēd′), *n.* a stickseed, *Lappula echinata*, introduced into the U.S. from Europe. [BUR[1] + SEED]

bur·ser·a·ceous (bûr′sə rā′shəs), *adj.* belonging to the family *Burseraceae*, comprising shrubs or trees of warm, often arid, countries, having compound leaves. [< NL *Burserace(ae)* family name (*Bursera* type genus, named after J. Burser (1593–1649), German botanist; see -ACEAE) + -OUS]

bur·si·form (bûr′sə fôrm′), *adj.* *Anat., Zool.* pouch-shaped; saccate. [< NL *bursiform(is).* See BURSA, -I-, -FORM]

bur·si·tis (bər sī′tis), *n.* *Pathol.* inflammation of a bursa. [< NL; see BURSA, -ITIS]

burst (bûrst), *v.,* **burst, burst·ing,** *n.* **—*v.i.*** **1.** to break, break open, or fly apart with sudden violence: *The vase burst when the bullet hit it.* **2.** to issue forth suddenly and forcibly, as from confinement or through an obstacle: *Oil burst to the surface. He burst through the doorway.* **3.** to give sudden expression to or as if to emotion: *She burst into tears. The chorus burst into song.* **4.** to be extremely full, as if ready to break open: *The house was bursting with people.* **5.** to become visible, audible, evident, etc., suddenly and completely: *The sun burst through the clouds.* **—*v.t.*** **6.** to cause to break or break open suddenly and violently: *He burst the balloon with a pin.* **7.** to cause or suffer the rupture of: *He became so excited that he almost burst a blood vessel.* **8.** to separate (the parts of a multi-part stationery form consisting of interleaved paper and carbon paper). **—*n.*** **9.** the act or an instance of bursting. **10.** a sudden display of intense activity, energy, or effort: *The car passed us with a burst of speed. A burst of static interrupted the program.* **11.** a sudden expression or manifestation, as of emotion: *a burst of affection.* **12.** a sudden and violent issuing forth: *a burst of steam from the pipe.* **13.** *Mil.* **a.** the explosion of a projectile, esp. in a specified place: *an air burst.* **b.** a continuous series of shots fired by one pull on the trigger of an automatic weapon: *A burst from the machine gun shattered all the windows.* **14.** the result of bursting; breach; gap: *a burst in the dike.* **15.** a sudden appearance or opening to view. [ME *berste(n), burste(n),* OE *berstan* (pret. pl. *burston*), c. OHG *brestan* (G *berstan*), Icel *bresta*; akin to BREAK]
—Syn. 1. crack, explode. **6.** rend, tear. **10.** spurt. **11, 12.** outbreak.

burst·er (bûr′stər), *n.* **1.** *Australian.* buster (def. 6). **2.** one who or that which bursts. [BURST + -ER[1]]

burst′ing point′, a stage of emotion at which self-control is lost, as with anger or impatience.

burst′ing strength′, 1. the capacity of a thing or substance to resist change when under pressure. **2.** the pressure required to break down the resistance of a substance.

bur·stone (bûr′stōn′), *n.* **1.** *Geol.* any of various siliceous rocks used for millstones. **2.** a millstone of such material. Also, **buhrstone, burrstone.** Also called **buhr, burr.** [BURR[4] + STONE]

Burt (bûrt), *n.* a boy's given name, form of **Albert, Herbert, Bertram, Burton.** Also, **Bert.**

bur·then (bûr′thən), *n., v.t.* *Archaic.* burden[1]. **—bur′then·some,** *adj.*

bur·ton (bûr′tᵊn), *n.* **1.** *Naut.* any of various small tackles for use on shipboard. **2.** See **Spanish burton.** [?]

Bur·ton (bûr′tᵊn), *n.* **1. Harold Hitz** (hits), 1888–1964, associate justice of the U.S. Supreme Court 1945–58. **2. Sir Richard Francis,** 1821–90, English explorer, Orientalist, and writer. **3. Robert** ("*Democritus Junior*"), 1577–1640, English clergyman and author. **4.** a town in central California. 4635 (1960). **5.** a boy's given name.

Bur·ton-on-Trent (bûr′tᵊn on trent′), *n.* a city in E Staffordshire, in central England. 50,766 (1961).

Bu·run·di (bə run′dē, bōō rōōn′dē), *n.* a kingdom in central Africa, E of the Democratic Republic of the Congo: formerly the S part of the Belgian trust territory of Ruanda-Urundi; gained independence 1962. 2,213,480 (1962); 10,747 sq. mi. *Cap.:* Usumbura. See map under **Rwanda.**

Bu·ru·sha·ski (bōōr′ə shä′skē), *n.* a language of NW Kashmir, not known to be related to any other language. [?]

bur·weed (bûr′wēd′), *n.* any of various plants bearing a burlike fruit, as the cocklebur, burdock, etc. [BUR[1] + WEED[1]]

Bur·well (bûr′wəl), *n.* a boy's given name.

bur·y (ber′ē), *v.,* **bur·ied, bur·y·ing,** *n., pl.* **bur·ies.** **—*v.t.*** **1.** to put in the ground and cover with earth: *The pirates buried the chest on the island.* **2.** to put (a corpse) in the ground or a vault, or into the sea, often with ceremony: *They buried the sailor with full military honors.* **3.** to plunge in deeply; cause to sink in: *to bury an arrow in a target.* **4.** to cover in order to conceal from sight: *She buried the card in the deck.* **5.** to immerse (oneself): *He buried himself in his work.* **6.** to put out of one's mind: *to bury an insult.* **7.** to consign to obscurity; cause to appear insignificant by assigning to an unimportant location, position, etc.: *His name was buried in small print at the end of the book.* **8. bury one's head in the sand,** to avoid reality; ignore the facts of a situation: *You cannot continue to bury your head in the sand—you must learn to face facts.* **—*n.*** **9.** *Naut.* housing[1] (def. 8a, b). [ME *berie(n), burye(n),* OE *byrgan* to bury, conceal; akin to OE *beorgan* to hide, protect, preserve; c. D, G *bergen*, Goth *bairgan*, Icel *bjarga*] **—bur′i·er,** *n.*
—Syn. 2. inter, entomb, inhume. **4.** hide, secrete. **—Ant. 2.** disinter, exhume. **4.** uncover.

Bur·yat (bōōr yät′), *adj., n., pl.* **-yats,** (*esp. collectively*) **-yat.** **—*adj.*** **1.** of or pertaining to the Buryat Mongol Republic, its people, or their language. **—*n.*** **2.** a member of any of the Mongol people in the Buryat Republic. **3.** Buriat.

Bur·yat′ Auton′omous Repub′lic, an autonomous republic in the Russian Federation in Asia, E of Lake Baikal. 1,042,000; ab. 135,650 sq. mi. *Cap.:* Ulan Ude. Also, **Buriat Autonomous Republic.**

bur′ying bee′tle, any of various carrion beetles that bury the carcasses of small animals, esp. rodents, in which their eggs have been deposited.

bur′ying ground′, a burial ground.

Bur·y St. Ed·munds (ber′ē sānt ed′məndz), a city in W Suffolk, in E England: medieval shrine. 21,144 (1961).

bus[1] (bus), *n., pl.* **bus·es, bus·ses,** *v.,* **bussed** or **bused, bus·sing** or **bus·ing.** **—*n.*** **1.** Also, **buss.** a motor vehicle with a long body equipped with seats or benches for passengers, usually operating as part of a scheduled service line; omnibus. **2.** a similar horse-drawn vehicle. **3.** *Informal.* a passenger automobile or airplane. **4.** a low, movable filing cabinet. **5.** *Elect.* a rigid conductor in an electric circuit, used to connect three or more circuits, often in the shape of a bar. **6.** (in an electronic computer) a conductor serving to transmit electrical impulses between any of several addresses. **—*v.t.*** **7.** to convey or transport by bus: *to bus the children to another school.* **—*v.i.*** **8.** to travel on or by means of a bus: *We bussed to New York on a theater trip.* [short for OMNIBUS]

bus[2] (bus), *v.i., v.t.,* **bussed** or **bused, bus·sing** or **bus·ing.** *U.S. Informal.* to work or act as a busboy or bus girl: *He bussed for his meals during his student days.* [back formation from BUSBOY]

bus., **1.** business. **2.** bushel; bushels.

bus·boy (bus′boi′), *n.* a waiter's helper in a restaurant or other public dining room, doing the more menial tasks. Also, **bus′ boy′.** [BUS[1] + BOY]

bus·by (buz′bē), *n., pl.* **-bies.** a tall fur hat with a baglike ornament hanging from the top over the right side, worn by hussars, certain guardsmen, etc., in the British army. [from proper name]

Busby

Busch (bōōsh), *n.* **Fritz** (frits), 1890–1951, German conductor.

Busch·ing (bōōsh′ing), *n.* a crater in the fourth quadrant of the face of the moon: about 36 miles in diameter.

bus·girl (bus′gûrl′), *n.* a girl or woman who works as a waiter's helper. Also, **bus′ girl′.** [*Amer.;* BUS(BOY) + GIRL]

bush[1] (bōōsh), *n.* **1.** a plant, esp. a low one with many branches which arise from or near the ground. **2.** *Bot.* a small cluster of shrubs appearing as a single plant. **3.** something resembling or suggesting this, as a thick, shaggy head of hair. **4.** Also called **bush lot.** *Canadian.* a small, wooded lot, esp. a farm lot with trees left standing to provide firewood, fence posts, etc. **5.** the tail of a fox; brush. **6.** *Geog.* a stretch of uncultivated land covered with mixed plant growth, bushy vegetation, trees, etc. **7.** a large uncleared area thickly covered with mixed plant growth, trees, etc., as a jungle. **8.** a large, sparsely populated area most of which is uncleared, as areas of Australia. **9.** a tree branch hung as a sign before a tavern or vintner's shop. **10.** any tavern sign. **11.** *Archaic.* a wineshop. **12. beat around** or **about the bush,** to avoid coming to the point; delay in approaching a subject directly: *She intended to tell him she was leaving, but when the time came she could only beat around the bush.* **13. beat the bushes,** to scout or search for (persons or things) far and wide after having exhausted the more usual sources: *beating the bushes for engineers.* **14. go bush,** *Australian.* **a.** to flee or escape into the bush. **b.** *Slang.* to become wild. **—*v.i.*** **15.** to be or become bushy; branch or spread as or like a bush. **—*v.t.*** **16.** to cover, protect, support, or mark with a bush or bushes. [ME *busshe*, OE *busc* (in place-names); c. D *bos* wood, G *Busch*, Icel *buskr* bush] **—bush′less,** *adj.* **—bush′like′,** *adj.*

bush[2] (bōōsh), *Chiefly Brit.* **—*n.*** **1.** a lining of metal or the like let into an orifice to guard against wearing by friction, erosion, etc. **2.** a bushing. **—*v.t.*** **3.** to furnish with a bush; line with metal. [earlier *busche* < MD *busse* bushing, box; see BOX[1]]

Bush (bōōsh), *n.* **1. George (Herbert Walker),** born 1924, U.S. diplomat and politician: vice-president of the U.S. 1981–89; 41st president of the U.S. since 1989. **2. Van·ne·var** (və nē′vär, -vər), 1890–1974, U.S. electrical engineer: education and research administrator.

bush., bushel; bushels.

bush′ bas′il. See under **basil.**

bush′ bean′, a variety of kidney bean, *Phaseolus vulgaris humilis*, characterized by its bushy growth.

bush·beat·er (bōōsh′bē′tər), *n.* one who searches an area, esp. as a talent scout for actors or athletes. [BUSH[1] + BEATER]

bush′ broom′, an evergreen St.-John's-wort, *Hypericum prolificum*, found from New York to Iowa and southward, having yellow flowers in terminal clusters.

bush·buck (bōōsh′buk′), *n., pl.* **-bucks,** (*esp. collectively*) **-buck.** an African antelope, *Tragelaphus scriptus*, found in wooded and bushy regions, having a reddish body streaked with white. Also, **boschbok.** [trans. of SAfrD *boschbok.* See BUSH[1], BUCK[1]]

bush′ clo′ver, any of several leguminous herbs or shrubs of the genus *Lespedeza*, having pinnately trifoliate leaves and heads of pink, purple, yellow, or white flowers.

bush′ coat′. See **bush jacket.**

bush·craft (bōōsh′kraft′, -kräft′), *n.* *Australian.* skill in anything pertaining to bush country, as in finding one's way, hunting, finding water, or the like. [BUSH[1] + CRAFT]

bush′ cran′berry. See **cranberry tree.**

bushed (bōōsht), *adj.* **1.** overgrown with bushes. **2.** *Informal.* exhausted; tired out: *After all that exercise, I'm bushed.* [BUSH[1] + -ED[2]]

bush·el[1] (bōōsh′əl), *n.* **1.** a unit of dry measure containing 4 pecks, equivalent in the U.S. (and formerly in England) to 2,150.42 cubic inches (**Winchester bushel**), and in Great Britain to 2,219.36 cubic inches (**Imperial bushel**). **2.** a container of this capacity. **3.** a unit of weight equal to the weight of a bushel of a given commodity. [ME *bu(i)sshel* < MF *boissel*, equiv. to *boisse* unit of measure (< Celt; cf. Ir *bos* pl. of *bas* hand, handbreadth) + *-el* n. suffix]

bush·el[2] (bōōsh′əl), *v.t.,* **-eled, -el·ing** or (*esp. Brit.*) **-elled, el·ling.** to alter or repair (a garment). [< G *bosseln* to patch < F *bosseler* to emboss; see BOSS[2]] **—bush′el·er;** *esp. Brit.,* **bush′el·ler,** *n.*

Bush·el (bōōsh′əl), *n.* a boy's given name.

bush·el·bas·ket (bōōsh′əl bas′kət, -bä′skit), *n.* a basket capable of holding one bushel. [BUSHEL[1] + BASKET]

bush′eled i′ron, 1. heterogeneous iron made from scrap iron and steel. **2.** wrought iron of high quality made from selected pieces cut from various muck bars.

bush·el·ful (bōōsh′əl fōōl′), *n., pl.* **-fuls.** an amount equal to the capacity of a bushel. [BUSHEL[1] + -FUL]

bush·el·man (bōōsh′əl man′), *n., pl.* **-men.** a person who alters or repairs garments; busheler. [BUSHEL[2] + MAN[1]]

bush·er (bōōsh′ər), *n.* *Baseball Slang.* See **bush leaguer** (def. 1). [BUSH(LEAGUE) + -ER[1]]

bush·fire (bōōsh′fīər′), *n.* an uncontrolled fire in the trees and bushes of scrubland. [BUSH[1] + FIRE]

bush·ham·mer (bōōsh′ham′ər), *n.* a hammer for dressing stone, having one or two square faces composed of a number of pyramidal points. Also, **bush′ ham′mer.** [< G *Bosshammer*, equiv. to obs. *boss(en)* (to) BEAT + *hammer* HAMMER]

bush′ hon′eysuckle, 1. See **Tartarian honeysuckle. 2.** See **European fly honeysuckle.**

bush′ house′, a one-story frame house with a veranda, as found in Australia and Africa.

bush′ huck′leberry, a shrub, *Gaylussacia dumosa*, of the eastern coast of North America, having sticky, hairy twigs, white or pink flowers, and tasteless but edible black fruit. Also called **gopherberry.**

Bu·shi·do (bōō′shē dō′), *n.* (in feudal Japan) the code of the samurai, stressing unquestioning loyalty and obedience, and valuing honor above life. [< Jap, equiv. to *bushi* (bu military + *shi* man) + *dō* dogma]

bush·i·ness (bōōsh′ē nis), *n.* a bushy state or form. [BUSHY + -NESS]

bush·ing (bōōsh′ing), *n.* **1.** *Elect.* a lining for a hole, intended to insulate and/or protect from abrasion one or more conductors which pass through it. **2.** *Mach.* **a.** a replaceable thin tube or sleeve, usually of bronze, mounted in a case or housing as a bearing. **b.** a replaceable hardened steel tube used as a guide for various tools or parts, as a drill or valve rod. [BUSH[2] + -ING[1]]

Bu·shire (bōō shēr′), *n.* a seaport in SW Iran, on the Persian Gulf. 27,317 (est. 1949).

bush′ jack′et, a belted, hip-length, shirtlike jacket, usually with four patch pockets and a wide collar, adapted from the hunting coat customarily worn in the African bush. Also called **bush coat.**

bush′ league′, *Baseball Slang.* See **minor league.**

bush-league (bōōsh′lēg′), *adj.* inferior or amateurish; mediocre: *a bush-league theatrical performance.*

bush′ lea′guer, 1. Also called **busher.** *Baseball Slang.* **a.** a player in a minor league. **b.** an incompetent player, as one who behaves or plays as if he belonged in a minor league. **2.** *U.S. Slang.* one who performs at an inferior level or in an inferior manner.

bush′ lot′, *Canadian.* bush[1] (def. 4).

bush·man (bōōsh′mən), *n., pl.* **-men. 1.** a woodsman. **2.** *Australian.* a pioneer; dweller in the bush. **3.** (*cap.*) a member of a nomadic, racially distinct, short-statured people of southern Africa. **4.** (*cap.*) any of more than a dozen related Khoisan languages spoken by the Bushmen of southern Africa. [BUSH[1] + MAN[1], modeled on SAfrD *boschjesman*, lit., man of the bush]

bush·mas·ter (bōōsh′mas′tər, -mä′stər), *n.* a pit viper, *Lachesis muta*, of tropical America, that grows to a length of 12 feet. [BUSH[1] + MASTER]

Bush·nell (bōōsh′nᵊl), *n.* a town in W Illinois. 3710 (1960).

bush′ parole′, *Slang.* an escape from prison.

bush′ pea′, a branched, hairy herb, *Thermopsis mollis*, of the southeastern U.S., having yellow, pealike flowers in terminal clusters.

bush′ pig′, a wild swine, *Potamochaerus porcus*, of southern and eastern Africa, having white facial markings. Also called **boschvark.**

bush′ pi′lot, an airplane pilot who flies over unsettled regions, esp. off established routes.

bush′ pop′py, a Californian shrub, *Dendromecon rigidum*, having stiff, leathery leaves and golden-yellow flowers.

bush·rang·er (bōōsh′rān′jər), *n.* **1.** a person who lives in the bush or woods. **2.** *Australian.* **a.** a person who lives by robbing travelers and isolated homesteads in the bush. **b.** a person who drives a hard, and sometimes dishonest, bargain. [BUSH[1] + RANGER] **—bush′rang′ing,** *n.*

bush′ tel′egraph, 1. any system of communication in which the natives of a jungle or bush region transmit news rapidly, as by runners, drum codes, or smoke signals. **2.** *Australian.* **a.** any chain of communications by which criminals, originally bushrangers, are warned of police movements. **b.** *Slang.* rumor; the grapevine.

bush′ tit′, any of several North American titmice of the genus *Psaltriparus*, which construct long, pendent nests.

Bush′ train′shed, a trainshed composed of a continuous row of narrow shelters. [named after Lincoln *Bush*, American engineer]

bush′ tre′foil, a perennial herb, *Desmodium canadense*, of eastern North America, having showy, clustered, purple flowers and pods which stick to the clothing. Also called **beggar's-tick.**

bush·wa (bōōsh′wä, -wô), *n.* *Slang.* rubbishy nonsense; baloney; bull: *You'll hear a lot of boring bushwa about his mechanical skill.* Also, **bush′wah.** [euphemistic for BULLSHIT]

bush·whack (bōōsh′hwak′, -wak′), *U.S.* **—*v.i.*** **1.** to make one's way through woods by cutting at undergrowth, branches, etc. **2.** to travel through woods. **3.** to fight as a bushwhacker. **—*v.t.*** **4.** to fight as a bushwhacker; ambush. [back formation from BUSHWHACKER]

bush·whack·er (bo͝osh′hwak′ər, -wak′ər), *n.* *U.S.* **1.** one who or that which bushwhacks. **2.** *U.S. Hist.* a Confederate guerrilla. **3.** any guerrilla. [BUSH[1] + WHACKER] —**bush′whack′ing,** *n.*

bush·y (bo͝osh′ē), *adj.,* **bush·i·er, bush·i·est.** **1.** resembling a bush. **2.** full of or overgrown with bushes. [ME *busshi.* See BUSH[1], -Y[1]] —**bush′i·ly,** *adv.*

bush·y-beard·ed (bo͝osh′ē bēr′did), *adj.* having a thick or shaggy beard.

bus·i·ly (biz′ə lē), *adv.* in a busy manner; actively. [ME *bisiliche.* See BUSY, -LY]

busi·ness (biz′nis), *n.* **1.** an occupation, profession, or trade: *His business is poultry farming.* **2.** *Econ.* the purchase and sale of goods in an attempt to make a profit. **3.** *Com.* a person, partnership, or corporation engaged in commerce, manufacturing, or a service; profit-seeking enterprise or concern. **4.** volume of trade; patronage: *Most of the store's business comes from women.* **5.** a building or locale where commercial work is carried on, as a factory, store, or office; place of work: *His business is on the corner of Broadway and Elm Street.* **6.** that with which one is principally and seriously concerned: *Words are a writer's business.* **7.** that with which one is rightfully concerned: *What they are doing is none of my business.* **8.** affair; project: *She was exasperated by the whole business.* **9.** an assignment or task; chore: *It's your business to wash the dishes now.* **10.** Also called **stage business.** *Theat.* a movement or gesture, esp. a minor one, used by an actor to give atmosphere to a scene or to help portray a character. **11. business is business,** profit has precedence over personal considerations: *Their creed had always been that business is business.* **12. get down to business,** to apply oneself to serious matters; concentrate on work: *They finally got down to business and signed the contract.* **13. have no business,** to have no right: *You have no business coming into this house.* **14. mean business,** *Informal.* to propose to take action; be serious in intent: *By the fire in his eye we knew that he meant business.* **15. mind one's own business,** to refrain from meddling in the private affairs of others: *If she would only learn to mind her own business, everyone would be much happier.* —*adj.* **16.** of, noting, or pertaining to business, its organization or procedures. **17.** containing, suitable for, or welcoming business or commerce: *There's not much to do there at night, but Houston is a good business town.* [ME; OE *bisignes.* See BUSY, -NESS]
—**Syn. 1.** calling, vocation, employment. See **occupation. 2.** commerce, trade, traffic. **3.** company, firm. **7.** duty, function.

busi′ness a′gent, a paid union official who represents a local and its membership in dealing with an employer.

busi′ness car′, *Railroads.* a railroad car equipped with office, observation, and living quarters for the use of traveling railroad officials.

busi′ness card′, a card on which is printed, typically, a businessman's name, title, firm, business address, and telephone number.

busi′ness col′lege, *U.S.* a school for training students in the clerical aspects of business and commerce, as typing, bookkeeping, etc.

busi′ness cy′cle, a recurrent fluctuation in the total business activity of a country.

busi′ness dou′ble, *Bridge.* a double made to increase the penalty points earned when a player believes the opponents cannot make their bid. Also called **penalty double.** Cf. **informatory double.**

busi′ness educa′tion, **1.** education for general knowledge of business practices. **2.** training in specific skills useful in business, such as typing, shorthand, etc.

busi′ness end′, *Slang.* the front part or end of a tool, weapon, etc., with which the work is done or from which a missile is ejected, as opposed to the handle or butt: *the business end of a revolver; the business end of a screwdriver.*

busi′ness Eng′lish, English in business usage, esp. the styles and forms of business correspondence.

busi·ness·like (biz′nis līk′), *adj.* **1.** conforming to, attending to, or characteristic of business. **2.** efficient, practical, or realistic. [BUSINESS + -LIKE]

busi′ness machine′, a machine for expediting clerical work, as a tabulator or adding machine.

busi·ness·man (biz′nis man′), *n., pl.* **-men.** a man who engages in business or commerce. [BUSINESS + MAN[1]]

busi′nessman's bounce′, *Facetious.* a style of dance-band music marked by simple rhythm, usually two-beat, and a moderately fast, bouncy tempo.

busi′ness reply′ card′, a self-addressed post card enclosed with a business letter or attached to another card to facilitate a requested answer, order, or subscription, and usually bearing a notice that return postage will be paid by the addressee.

busi′ness reply′ en′velope, an envelope, marked like the business reply card, for the enclosure of an answer, order, or subscription.

busi′ness suit′, a man's suit, esp. one of conservative cut and color. Cf. **suit** (def. 2).

busi′ness un′ionism, *U.S.* the practical activities and philosophies of labor unions concentrating on the improvement of wages, hours, working conditions, etc., within and while supporting the general framework of the capitalistic system.

busi·ness·wom·an (biz′nis wo͝om′ən), *n., pl.* **-wom·en.** a woman who engages in business or commerce. [BUSINESS + WOMAN]

Bu·si·ris (byo͞o sī′ris), *n.* *Class. Myth.* a son of Poseidon who was king of Egypt: he attempted to sacrifice Hercules to help avoid a famine but Hercules broke his bonds and killed him.

busk[1] (busk), *v.t.* *Brit. Dial.* to prepare. [ME *busken* < Scand; cf. OIcel *būask* (now *būast*), equiv. to *būa* to prepare, decorate + *-sk* (for *sik* oneself, c. G *sich*) suffix of middle mood]

busk[2] (busk), *n.* **1.** a strip of steel, whalebone, or other stiffening material placed in the front of a corset. **2.** *Dial.* the corset itself. [< MF *busc* < Pr or ML *busca* log, perh. connected with *bustum* BUST[1]] —**busked,** *adj.*

busk[3] (busk), *v.i.* *Brit.* **1.** to entertain by dancing, singing, reciting, or doing tricks on the street or in a pub. **2.** to perform plays in rural areas, esp. with simple theatrical equipment and in makeshift theaters. **3.** to travel to rural areas to swindle the inhabitants, sell defective merchandise, etc. [?] —**busk′er,** *n.*

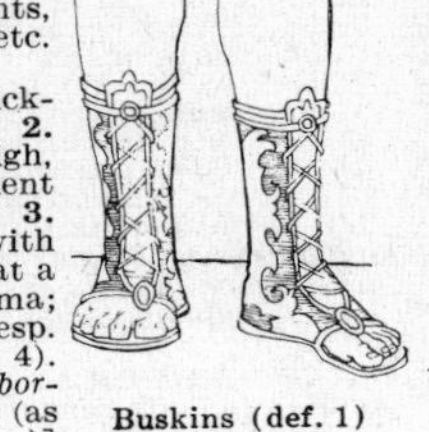

Buskins (def. 1)

bus·kin (bus′kin), *n.* **1.** a thick-soled, laced boot or half boot. **2.** Also called **cothurnus.** the high, thick-soled shoe worn by ancient Greek and Roman actors. **3. buskins,** stockings decorated with gold thread worn by a bishop at a Pontifical Mass. **4.** tragic drama; tragedy. **5.** the art of acting, esp. tragic acting. Cf. **sock**[1] (def. 4). [perh. for earlier **bursakin* < It *borzacchino,* with loss of *r* before *s* (as in *cuss* for *curse, bass* for *barse,* etc.)]

bus·kined (bus′kind), *adj.* **1.** wearing buskins. **2.** resembling or pertaining to tragic drama. [BUSKIN + -ED[3]]

bus′ line′, **1.** the route of a bus or buses. **2.** a company that owns and operates buses.

bus·load (bus′lōd′), *n.* an amount or number as great as a bus can hold. [BUS[1] + LOAD]

bus·man (bus′mən), *n., pl.* **-men.** one who operates a bus. [BUS[1] + MAN[1]]

bus′man's hol′iday, *Informal.* a vacation or day off from work spent in an activity closely resembling one's work, as a bus driver driving his car.

Bu·so·ni (byo͞o sō′nē; *It.* bo͞o zô′nē), *n.* **Fer·ruc·cio (Ben·ve·nu·to)** (fer ro͞ot′chô ben′ve no͞o′tô), 1866–1924, Italian composer and pianist.

Bus·ra (bus′rə), *n.* Basra. Also, **Bus′rah.**

buss[1] (bus), *n., v.t., v.i.* *Informal.* kiss. [? b. obs. *bass* kiss and obs. *cuss* kiss (c. G *Kuss*); r. ME, OE *coss* (c. Icel *koss*)]

buss[2] (bus), *n.* bus[1] (def. 1).

bus·ses (bus′iz), *n.* a plural of **bus**[1].

bust[1] (bust), *n.* **1.** a sculptured, painted, drawn, or engraved representation of the upper part of the human figure, esp. a portrait sculpture showing only the head and shoulders of the subject. **2.** the chest or breast, esp. a woman's bosom. [< F *buste* < It *busto* < ML *bustum* torso, perh. orig. tree-trunk, log; see BUSK[2]]

bust[2] (bust), *Slang.* —*v.i.* **1.** to burst. **2.** to go bankrupt. **3.** to collapse from the strain of making a supreme effort: *He was determined to make a touchdown or bust. Pike's Peak or bust.* —*v.t.* **4.** to burst. **5.** to bankrupt; ruin financially. **6.** (in the Army) to demote in rank or grade: *He was busted from sergeant to private three times.* **7.** to tame; break: *to bust a bronco.* **8.** *Slang.* to arrest: *I was busted on a narcotics charge.* **9.** to hit. **10. bust up,** to break up; separate: *Sam and his wife busted up a year ago.* —*n.* **11.** a failure. **12.** a drinking spree; binge. **13.** a hit; sock; punch: *He got a bust in the nose before he could put up his hands.* **14.** a sudden decline in the economic conditions of a country, marked by an extreme drop in stock-market prices, business activity, and employment; depression. **15.** *Slang.* an arrest. —*adj.* **16.** bankrupt; broke. [dial. or vulgar var. of BURST]

bus·tard (bus′tərd), *n.* any of several large, cursorial, chiefly terrestrial birds of the family *Otididae,* of the Old World and Australia, which are related to the cranes. [late ME, appar. b. MF *bistarde* (OIt *bistarda*) and MF *oustarde,* both < L *avis tarda* slow bird]

bus′tard quail′. See **button quail.**

bus·tee (bus′tē), *n.* *India.* **1.** a small settlement; village. **2.** a slum. Also, **bus′ti.** [< Hindi *bastī,* akin to *basnā* to dwell]

bust·er (bus′tər), *n.* **1.** *U.S. Informal.* one who breaks up something: *crime busters.* **2.** *Slang.* that which is very big or unusual for its kind. **3.** *Slang.* a loud, uproarious reveler. **4.** *Slang.* a frolic; spree. **5.** (*cap.*) *Informal.* a familiar term of address to a man or boy who is an object of the speaker's annoyance or anger: *Look, Buster, you're standing on my hat!* **6.** Also, **burster.** Also called **southerly buster, southerly burster.** *Australian.* a violent, cold, southerly wind. [BUST[2] + -ER[1]]

Bus·ter (bus′tər), *n.* a boy's given name.

Bus′ter Brown′ col′lar, a wide, starched collar with rounded edges, lying flat on the shoulders, worn by women and girls. [after *Buster Brown,* a comic-strip boy drawn by Richard F. Outcault (1863–1928) American cartoonist]

bus·tic (bus′tik), *n.* a tropical American, sapotaceous tree, *Dipholis salicifolia,* yielding a hard, dark brown wood used for making furniture. [?]

bus·tle[1] (bus′əl), *v.,* **-tled, -tling,** *n.* —*v.i.* **1.** to move or act with a great show of energy (often fol. by *about*): *She bustles about cooking breakfast in a most officious manner.* **2.** to abound or teem with something; display an abundance of something (often fol. by *with*): *The office bustled with people and activity.* —*v.t.* **3.** to cause to bustle; hustle. —*n.* **4.** activity with great show of energy; stir; commotion. [ME *bustelen* to hurry aimlessly along, perh. akin to Icel *busla* to splash about, bustle] —**bus′tler,** *n.* —**bus′tling·ly,** *adv.*
—**Syn. 4.** ado.

bus·tle[2] (bus′əl), *n.* **1.** fullness around or below the waist of a dress, as added by a peplum, bows, ruffles, etc. **2.** a pad, cushion, or framework formerly worn under the back of a woman's skirt to expand, support, and display the full cut and drape of a dress. [?] —**bus′tled,** *adj.*

bus′tle pipe′, *Metall.* (in a blast furnace) an annular pipe distributing hot air to the tuyères.

bust-up (bust′up′), *n.* *Informal.* **1.** a separation or dissolution, as of a marriage or a close friendship. **2.** a large party, esp. a noisy one. [n. use of v. phrase *bust up*]

bust·y (bus′tē), *adj.,* **bust·i·er, bust·i·est.** *Informal.* (of a woman) having a large bust. [BUST[1] + -Y[1]]

bus·y (biz′ē), *adj.,* **bus·i·er, bus·i·est,** *v.,* **bus·ied, bus·y·ing.** —*adj.* **1.** actively and attentively engaged in work or a pastime: *busy with his work.* **2.** not at leisure; otherwise engaged: *He couldn't see any visitors because he was busy.* **3.** full of or characterized by activity: *a busy life.* **4.** (of a telephone line) engaged and not immediately available for use. **5.** officious; meddlesome; prying. **6.** ornate; cluttered with small unharmonious details; fussy: *The rug has a busy design.* —*v.t.* **7.** to keep occupied; make or keep busy: *In summer, he busied himself keeping the lawn in order.* [ME *busi, bisi,* OE *bysig, bisig;* c. MLG, MD *besich,* D *bezig*]
—**Syn. 1.** assiduous, hard-working. BUSY, DILIGENT, INDUSTRIOUS imply active or earnest effort to accomplish something, or a habitual attitude of such earnestness. BUSY means actively employed, temporarily or habitually: *a busy official.* DILIGENT suggests earnest and constant effort or application, and usually connotes fondness for, or enjoyment of, what one is doing: *a diligent student.* INDUSTRIOUS often implies a habitual characteristic of steady and zealous application, often with a definite goal: *an industrious clerk working for promotion.* **2.** occupied, employed, working. —**Ant. 1.** indolent. **2.** unoccupied.

bus·y·bod·y (biz′ē bod′ē), *n., pl.* **-bod·ies.** a person who pries into and meddles in the affairs of others. [BUSY + BODY]

bus·y·ness (biz′ē nis), *n.* **1.** the quality or condition of being busy. **2.** lively but meaningless activity. [BUSY + -NESS]

bus·y·work (biz′ē wûrk′), *n.* active but valueless work. [BUSY + WORK]

but[1] (but; *unstressed* bət), *conj.* **1.** on the contrary; yet: *My brother went, but I did not.* **2.** except; save: *She was so overcome with grief she could do nothing but weep.* **3.** unless; if not; except that (fol. by a clause, often with *that* expressed): *Nothing would do but that I should come in. Who knows any man but he be his brother?* **4.** without the circumstance that; except for the fact that; that not: *It never rains but it pours.* **5.** otherwise than: *There is no hope but by prayer.* **6.** that (used esp. after *doubt, deny,* etc., with a negative): *I don't doubt but he will do it.* **7.** who or which not: *No leader worthy of the name ever existed but he was an optimist.* **8.** (used as an intensifier to introduce an exclamatory expression): *But she's beautiful!* —*prep.* **9.** with the exception of; except; save: *No one replied but me.* —*adv.* **10.** only; just: *There is but one God.* **11. but for,** except for; were it not for: *But for the excessive humidity, it might have been a pleasant day.* —*n.* **12.** a restriction or objection: *Do as I tell you, no but about it.* [ME *bute(n),* OE *būtan* for phrase *be ūtan* on the outside, without. See BY, OUT]
—**Syn. 1.** BUT, HOWEVER, NEVERTHELESS, STILL, YET are words implying opposition (with a possible concession). BUT marks an opposition or contrast, though in a casual way: *We are going, but we shall return.* HOWEVER indicates a less marked opposition, but displays a second consideration to be compared with the first: *We are going; however* ("*notice this also*"), *we shall return.* NEVERTHELESS implies a concession, something which should not be forgotten in making a summing up: *We are going; nevertheless* ("*do not forget that*"), *we shall return.* STILL implies that in spite of a preceding concession, something must be considered as possible or even inevitable: *We have to go on foot; still* ("*it is probable and possible that*"), *we'll get there.* YET implies that in spite of a preceding concession, there is still a chance for a different outcome: *We are going; yet* ("*in spite of all, some day*"), *we shall return.* **2.** See **except**[1].
—**Usage.** Some users of English regard BUT WHAT as informal (*I have no doubt but what he'll protest*), preferring BUT THAT (*I have no doubt but that he'll protest*) or THAT alone (*I have no doubt that he'll protest*).

but[2] (but), *n.* *Scot.* **1.** the outer or front room of a house; the outer or front apartment in an apartment house. **2.** the kitchen of a two-room dwelling, esp. of a cottage. [n. use of BUT[1] (adv.) outside or front room]

but[3] (but), butt[5].

bu·ta·caine (byo͞o′tə kān′), *n.* *Pharm.* a compound, $H_2NC_6H_4COO(CH_2)_3N(C_4H_9)_2$, used in the form of its sulfate as a local anesthetic for mucous membranes, esp. the cornea. [BUTA(NE + CO)CAINE]

bu·ta·di·ene (byo͞o′tə dī′ēn, -dī ēn′), *n.* *Chem.* a colorless, flammable, aromatic, water-insoluble gas, $H_2C{-}CHHC{-}CH_2$, usually derived from butane or butene: used chiefly in the manufacture of rubber and paint, and in organic synthesis. Also called **vinylethylene, bivinyl.** [BUTA(NE) + DI-[1] + -ENE]

but-and-ben (but′ən ben′), *n., pl.* **buts-and-bens,** *adv.* *Scot.* —*n.* **1.** a two-room dwelling, esp. a cottage. —*adv.* **2.** to and fro; back and forth, as if from one room of a house to another. **3.** on or at opposite ends. [lit., out and in; see BUT[2], BEN[1]]

bu·tane (byo͞o′tān, byo͞o tān′), *n.* *Chem.* a colorless, flammable gas, C_4H_{10}, a saturated aliphatic existing in two isometric forms: used chiefly in the manufacture of rubber and fuel. [BUT(YL) + -ANE]

bu·ta·nol (byo͞ot′ənōl′, -ənôl′, -ənol′), *n.* *Chem.* See **butyl alcohol.** [BUTANE + -OL[1]]

bu·ta·none (byo͞ot′ənōn′), *n.* *Chem.* See **methyl ethyl ketone.** [BUTANE + -ONE]

butch[1] (bo͝och), *v.t.* *Dial.* **1.** to ruin or spoil; botch. **2.** to butcher; slaughter. [back formation from BUTCHER; meaning influenced by BOTCH[1]]

butch[2] (bo͝och), *n.* **1.** See **butch haircut. 2.** *Slang.* the partner in a Lesbian relationship who assumes the role of the male. [? orig. short-haired one]

Butch (bo͝och), *n.* a boy's given name.

butch·er (bo͝och′ər), *n.* **1.** a retail or wholesale dealer in meat. **2.** one who slaughters certain animals, or who dresses the flesh of animals, fish, or poultry, for food or market. **3.** a person guilty of brutal or indiscriminate slaughter or murder. **4.** a vendor who hawks newspapers, candy, beverages, etc., as on a train, at a stadium, etc. —*v.t.* **5.** to slaughter or dress (animals, fish, or poultry) for market. **6.** to kill indiscriminately or brutally. **7.** to bungle; botch: *to butcher a job.* [ME *bocher* < AF; OF *bo(u)chier,* equiv. to *bo(u)c* he-goat (< Gmc; see BUCK[1]) + *-ier* -ER[2]] —**butch′er·er,** *n.*
—**Syn. 3.** killer, cut-throat. **5, 6.** See **slaughter.**

butch·er·bird (bo͝och′ər bûrd′), *n.* **1.** any of various shrikes of the genus *Lanius,* which impale their prey upon thorns. **2.** any of several large, carnivorous birds of the genus *Cracticus,* of Australia and New Guinea, having shrikelike habits. [BUTCHER + BIRD]

butch′er knife′, a large, very sharp knife for cutting or trimming meat.

butch′er lin′en, a strong, heavy fabric made of rayon or rayon and cotton with a linen finish, constructed in plain weave. Also called **butch′er ray′on.**

butch·er·ly (bo͝och′ər lē), *adj.* like, or characteristic of, a butcher. [BUTCHER + -LY] —**butch′er·li·ness,** *n.*

butch′er pa′per, heavy, moisture-resistant paper, as used for wrapping meat.

butch·er's-broom (bo͝och′ərz bro͞om′, -bro͝om′), *n.* a shrubby, liliaceous evergreen, *Ruscus aculeatus,* of England: used for making brooms.

butch′er shop′, a shop in which meat, poultry, and sometimes fish, are sold.

butch′er's saw′, a type of hacksaw used esp. by butchers for cutting through meat and bones. See illus. under **saw.**

butch·er·y (bo͝och′ə rē), *n., pl.* **-er·ies. 1.** a slaughterhouse. **2.** the trade or business of a butcher. **3.** brutal or wanton slaughter of animals or humans; carnage. [ME *bocherie* < MF *boucherie.* See BUTCHER, -Y[3]]

butch′ hair′cut, *U.S.* **1.** a short haircut for men, similar to a crew cut. **2.** a haircut for women in which the hair is cropped relatively short. Also called **butch.**

Bute (byo͞ot), *n.* **1.** Also, **Buteshire.** a county in SW Scotland, composed of three islands in the Firth of Clyde. 15,129 (1961); 218 sq. mi. *Co. seat:* Rothesay. **2.** an island in the Firth of Clyde, in SW Scotland: part of the county Bute. ab. 12,000; 50 sq. mi.

Bu·te·nandt (bo͞ot′ənänt′), *n.* **A·dolf Frie·drich Jo·hann** (ä′dôlf frē′drĭkh yō′hän), born 1903, German chemist: declined 1939 Nobel prize on the demand of the Nazi government.

bu·tene (byo͞o′tēn), *n.* *Chem.* butylene (def. 1). [BUT(YL) + -ENE]

bu·te·o (byo͞o′tē ō′), *n., pl.* **-os.** any of several buzzards or hawks of the genus *Buteo.* [< L *būteō* a kind of hawk or falcon] —**bu·te·o·nine** (byo͞o′tē ō nīn′, -nin, byo͞otē′-), *adj.*

Bu·tes (byo͞o′tēz), *n.* *Class. Myth.* **1.** a son of Pandion and the brother of Procne, Philomela, and Erechtheus: he was a priest of Athena and of Poseidon. **2.** a son of Boreas who was stricken with madness as punishment for having ravished Coronis. **3.** an Argonaut who, enticed by the song of the Sirens, leaped into the sea and was rescued by Aphrodite.

Bute·shire (byo͞ot′shēr, -shər), *n.* Bute (def. 1).

but·ler (but′lər), *n.* **1.** the chief male servant of a household. **2.** a male servant having charge of the wines and liquors. [ME *buteler* < AF *butuiller,* OF *bouteillier,* equiv. to *bouteille* BOTTLE[1] + *-ier* -ER[2]] —**but′ler-like′,** *adj.* —**but′ler·ship′,** *n.*

But·ler (but′lər), *n.* **1. Benjamin Franklin,** 1818–93, U.S. politician and a Union general in the Civil War. **2. Joseph,** 1692–1752, English bishop, theologian, and author. **3. Nicholas Murray,** 1862–1947, U.S. educator: president of Columbia University 1902–45; Nobel peace prize 1931. **4. Pierce,** 1866–1939, U.S. jurist: associate justice of the U.S. Supreme Court 1923–39. **5. Samuel,** 1612–80, English poet. **6. Samuel,** 1835–1902, English novelist, essayist, and satirist. **7. Smed·ley Dar·ling·ton** (smed′lē där′lĭng tən), 1881–1940, U.S. Marine Corps general. **8.** a city in W Pennsylvania. 20,975 (1960). **9.** a town in N New Jersey. 5414 (1960). **10.** a town in W Missouri. 3791 (1960).

but·ler·age (but′lər ij), *n.* *Old. Eng. Law.* the privilege allowed the king's butler to take a certain quantity of every cask of wine imported by an alien. Cf. **prisage.** [ME *botelerage.* See BUTLER, -AGE]

but′ler's pan′try, a service room between a kitchen and dining room, typically equipped with counters, a sink, and storage space for china and silver.

but′ler's side′board, a sideboard, often with a fall front, having on its top a china cabinet with glazed doors.

but·ler·y (but′lə rē), *n., pl.* **-ler·ies.** a butler's room or pantry; buttery. [ME *botelerie.* See BUTLER, -Y[3]]

Bu·tsu (bo͞ot′so͞o), *n., pl.* **-su** for 1. **1.** a representation of the Buddha. **2.** Buddha (def. 1). [< Jap: BUDDHA]

butt[1] (but), *n.* **1.** the end or extremity of anything, esp. the thicker, larger, or blunt end considered as a bottom, base, support, or handle, as of a log, fishing rod, pistol, pork shoulder, etc. **2.** an end which is not used or consumed; remnant: *a cigar butt.* **3.** *Slang.* the buttocks. **4.** *Slang.* a cigarette. [ME *bott* (thick) end, buttock, OE *butt* tree-stump (in place names); akin to Sw *but* stump, Dan *but* stubby; see BUTTOCK]

butt[2] (but), *n.* **1.** one who or that which is an object of wit, ridicule, sarcasm, contempt, etc. **2.** (on a rifle range) **a.** a wall of earth located behind the targets to prevent bullets from scattering over a large area. **b. butts,** a wall behind which men can safely lower, score, and raise targets during firing practice. **3.** See **butt hinge. 4.** *Obs.* a goal; limit. —*v.i.* **5.** to have an end or projection on; be adjacent to. —*v.t.* **6.** to position or fasten an end (of something). **7.** to place or join the ends (of two things) together; set end-to-end. [ME < MF *but* target, goal < Gmc; see BUTT[1]]

butt[3] (but), *v.t.* **1.** to strike or push with the head or horns. —*v.i.* **2.** to strike or push something or at something with the head or horns. **3.** to project. **4.** (of wheels in a gear train) to strike one another instead of meshing. **5. butt in,** *Slang.* to meddle in the affairs or intrude in the conversation of others; interfere: *It's none of your concern, so please don't butt in.* **6. butt out,** *Slang.* to stop meddling in the affairs or intruding in the conversation of others: *Nobody asked your opinion, so butt out.* —*n.* **7.** a push or blow with the head or horns. [ME *butte(n)* < OF *bo(u)ter* to thrust, strike < Gmc; see BEAT]

butt[4] (but), *n.* **1.** a large cask for wine, beer, or ale. **2.** any cask or barrel. **3.** any of various units of capacity, usually considered equal to two hogsheads. [ME *bote* < MF < OPr *bota* < LL *butta, buttis* < MGk *boûtis* < ?]

butt[5] (but), *n.* any of several flatfishes, esp. the halibut. Also, **but.** [ME *butte;* c. Sw *butta* turbot, G *Butt* brill, turbot, flounder, D *bot* flounder]

but·tals (but′əlz), *n. pl.* *Law.* abuttals.

butt′ chis′el, any woodworking chisel having a blade less than four inches long.

butte (byo͞ot), *n.* *Western U.S., Canadian.* an isolated hill or mountain rising abruptly above the surrounding land. [< F: hillock; MF *bute* mound for target, deriv. of *but* BUTT[2]]

Butte (byo͞ot), *n.* a city in SW Montana: mining center. 27,877 (1960).

but·ter (but′ər), *n.* **1.** the fatty portion of milk, separating as a soft whitish or yellowish solid when milk or cream is agitated or churned. **2.** this substance, processed for cooking and table use. **3.** any of various other soft spreads for bread: *apple butter; peanut butter.* **4.** any of various substances of butterlike consistency, as various metallic chlorides, and certain vegetable oils solid at ordinary temperatures. —*v.t.* **5.** to put butter on or in; spread or grease with butter. **6.** to apply a liquefied bonding material to (a piece or area), as mortar to a course of bricks. **7.** to cover (edges to be welded together) with a preliminary surface of the weld metal. **8. butter up,** *Informal.* to flatter (someone) in order to gain a favor: *He suspected that they were buttering him up when everyone suddenly started being nice to him.* [ME; OE *butere* < L *būtyr(um)* < Gk *boútyron*] —**but′ter·less,** *adj.* —**but′ter·like′,** *adj.*

but′ter-and-egg′ man′ (but′ər ən eg′), *Slang.* a prosperous businessman from a small town or a farmer who spends his money ostentatiously on visits to a big city.

but·ter-and-eggs (but′ər ən egz′), *n., pl.* **but·ter-and-eggs.** (*construed as sing. or pl.*) any of certain plants whose flowers are of two shades of yellow, as the toadflax, *Linaria vulgaris.*

but·ter·ball (but′ər bôl′), *n.* **1.** *U.S. Dial.* the bufflehead. **2.** *Informal.* a chubby person. [BUTTER + BALL[1]]

but′ter bean′, a variety of small-seeded lima bean, *Phaseolus lunatus,* grown in the Southern U.S.

but·ter·bump (but′ər bump′), *n.* *Brit. Dial.* the bittern, *Botaurus stellaris,* of Europe. [BUTTER + BUMP]

but·ter·bur (but′ər bûr′), *n.* an Old World, perennial, composite herb, *Petasites vulgaris,* having large woolly leaves said to have been used to wrap butter. [BUTTER + BUR[1]]

but·ter·bush (but′ər bo͝osh′), *n.* a small tree, *Pittosporum phillyraeoides,* of Australia, having yellow flowers, solitary or in small clusters, and yellow fruit. [BUTTER + BUSH[1]]

but·ter·cup (but′ər kup′), *n.* any of numerous plants of the genus *Ranunculus,* having red, white, or yellow flowers; crowfoot. [BUTTER + CUP, from color and shape of flower]

but·ter·fat (but′ər fat′), *n.* butter; milk fat; a mixture of glycerides, mainly butyrin, olein, and palmitin. [BUTTER + FAT]

but·ter·fin·gers (but′ər fĭng′gərz), *n., pl.* **-gers.** (*construed as sing.*) one who is likely to drop things, as an inept fielder in baseball or a clumsy person. [BUTTER + FINGER + -S[3]] —**but′ter·fin′gered,** *adj.*

but·ter·fish (but′ər fish′), *n., pl.* (*esp. collectively*) **-fish·es,** (*esp. referring to two or more kinds or species*) **-fish. 1.** a small, flattened, marine food fish, *Poronotus triacanthus,* found off the Atlantic coast of the U.S., having very small scales and smooth skin. **2.** the rock gunnel. See under **gunnel**[1]. [BUTTER + FISH]

but·ter·flies (but′ər flīz′), *n.* (*construed as pl.*) *Informal.* a queasy feeling, as from nervousness, excitement, etc. [pl. of BUTTERFLY; so called from the fluttering feeling in the stomach]

but·ter·fly (but′ər flī′), *n., pl.* **-flies,** *v.,* **-flied, -fly·ing,** *adj.* —*n.* **1.** any of numerous diurnal insects of the order *Lepidoptera,* characterized by clubbed antennae, a slender body, and large, broad, often conspicuously marked wings. **2.** a person who flits aimlessly from one interest or group to another: *a social butterfly.* **3.** *Carpentry.* See **butterfly wedge. 4.** *Sculpture.* an X-shaped support attached to an armature. **5.** one of the swinging brackets of a butterfly table. **6.** *Motion Pictures.* a screen of scrim, gauze, or similar material, for diffusing light. —*v.t.* **7.** *Cookery.* to slit open and spread apart to resemble the spread wings of a butterfly. —*adj.* **8.** *Cookery.* split open and spread apart to resemble a butterfly: *butterfly shrimp; butterfly steak.* [ME *boterflye,* OE *buttorflēoge.* See BUTTER, FLY[2]] —**but′ter·fly′like′,** *adj., adv.*

but′terfly bomb′, *Mil.* a small, aerial, antipersonnel bomb with two folding wings that revolve, slowing the rate of descent and arming the fuze.

but′terfly bush′, any tropical, loganiaceous shrub of the genus *Buddleia,* having clusters of showy lilac, white, or yellow flowers.

but′terfly chair′. See **sling chair.**

but′terfly damp′er, a damper, as in a flue, that rotates about a central axis across its face.

but·ter·fly·fish (but′ər flī′fish′), *n., pl.* (*esp. collectively*) **-fish·es,** (*esp. referring to two or more kinds or species*) **-fish. 1.** any tropical marine fish of the family *Chaetodontidae,* having large, broad fins or brilliant coloration, or both. **2.** See **flying gurnard. 3.** a blenny, *Blennius ocellaris,* of Europe. [BUTTERFLY + FISH]

but·ter·fly-flow·er (but′ər flī′flou′ər), *n.* a shrub or small tree, *Bauhinia monandra,* of French Guiana, having clusters of purple-streaked, pink flowers. Also called **Jerusalem date.**

but′terfly net′, a conical net of fine mesh held open by a round rim to which a long handle is attached, used for collecting butterflies and other insects.

but′terfly or′chid, an epiphytic orchid, *Oncidium Papilio,* of Venezuela, having a single, red-mottled leaf and solitary, yellow-spotted, brown flowers nearly 3½ inches wide, blooming in succession.

but·ter·fly-pea (but′ər flī′pē′), *n.* a smooth-stemmed vine, *Clitoria mariana,* of the eastern U.S., having pale blue flowers.

but′terfly roof′, a roof having more than one slope, each descending inward from the eaves.

but′terfly ta′ble, a small occasional table, usually having a round or oval top, with drop leaves supported by swinging brackets pivoted to the stretchers and to the underside of the top.

but′terfly valve′, **1.** a clack valve having two flaps with a common hinge. **2.** a valve, as the throttle valve in a carburetor, that swings about a central axis across its face.

but′terfly wedge′, *Carpentry.* a wooden fastening in the form of a double dovetail for joining two boards at their edges. Also called **butterfly.**

but′terfly weed′, **1.** Also called **orange milkweed.** either of two closely related North American milkweeds, *Asclepias tuberosa* or *A. decumbens,* having orange-colored flowers. **2.** an erect North American herb, *Gaura coccinea,* related to the evening primrose, having wandlike spikes of red flowers.

but′ter knife′, a small knife with a dull blade, for cutting, serving, or spreading butter.

but·ter·milk (but′ər milk′), *n.* the more or less acidulous liquid remaining after the butter has been separated from milk or cream. [BUTTER + MILK]

but′ter mus′lin, *Chiefly Brit.* cheesecloth.

but·ter·nut (but′ər nut′), *n.* **1.** Also called **white walnut.** the edible oily nut of an American tree, *Juglans cinerea,* of the walnut family. **2.** the tree itself. **3.** the light brown wood of this tree, used for making furniture. **4.** See **souari nut. 5.** *U.S. Hist.* a Confederate soldier, whose uniform was dyed with an extract from this tree. [so called from the nut's oiliness]

but′ternut squash′, **1.** a yellowish winter squash having sweet, orange-colored flesh. **2.** the plant bearing this fruit.

but′ter of ar′senic. See **arsenic trichloride.**

but·ter·paste (but′ər pāst′), *n.* a mixture of flour and butter kneaded together, used as a thickening for sauces. Also called **kneaded butter.** [BUTTER + PASTE]

but′ter sauce′, a sauce made of melted butter, often diluted with water, sometimes thickened with flour or egg yolk, or both, and seasoned with lemon juice.

but·ter·scotch (but′ər skoch′), *n.* **1.** a hard, brittle taffy made with butter, brown sugar, etc. **2.** a flavor produced in puddings, frostings, ice cream, etc., by combining brown sugar, vanilla extract, and butter with other ingredients. —*adj.* **3.** having the flavor of butterscotch. [BUTTER + SCOTCH]

but′ter tree′, any of several tropical, sapotaceous trees, as the shea, the seeds of which yield a butterlike oil.

but·ter·weed (but′ər wēd′), *n.* **1.** any wild plant having conspicuously yellow flowers or leaves. **2.** the horseweed. **3.** a ragwort or groundsel, *Senecio glabellus.* [BUTTER + WEED[1]]

but·ter·wort (but′ər wûrt′), *n.* any small herb of the genus *Pinguicula,* having leaves that secrete a viscid substance in which small insects are caught. [BUTTER + WORT[2]]

but·ter·y[1] (but′ə rē), *adj.* **1.** like, containing, or spread with butter. **2.** *Informal.* grossly flattering. [ME *buttry.* See BUTTER, -Y[1]] —**but′ter·i·ness,** *n.*

but·ter·y[2] (but′ə rē, bu′trē), *n., pl.* **-ter·ies. 1.** a room or rooms in which the wines, liquors, and provisions of a household are kept; larder. **2.** a room in colleges, esp. at Oxford and Cambridge Universities, from which certain articles of food and drink are sold or dispensed to the students. [ME *boterie* < MF < LL *botāria,* equiv. to *bot(a)* (for *butta* BUTT[4]) + *-āria* -ERY]

butt′ hinge′, a hinge for a door or the like, secured to the butting surfaces rather than to the adjacent sides of the door and its frame. Cf. **flap** (def. 14).

but·ting (but′ĭng), *n.* a boundary; abuttal; limit. [BUTT[3] + -ING[1]]

butt·in·sky (but in′skē), *n., pl.* **-skies.** *Slang.* one who interferes; meddler. Also, **butt·in′ski.** [*butt in* intrude + *-sky,* abstracted from Slavic surnames]

butt′ joint′, *Building Trades.* a joint formed by two pieces of wood or metal united end to end without overlapping.

but·tle (but′əl), *v.i.,* **-tled, -tling.** to work or serve as a butler. [back formation from BUTLER]

but·tock (but′ək), *n.* **1.** Usually, **buttocks. a.** (in humans) either of the two fleshy protuberances forming the lower and back part of the trunk. **b.** (in animals) the rump. **2.** Sometimes, **buttocks.** *Naut.* the aftermost portion of a hull above the water line and in front of the rudder, merging with the run below the water line. [ME *buttok,* OE *buttuc.* See BUTT[1], -OCK] —**but′tocked,** *adj.*

but′tock line′, *Naval Archit.* **1.** any of a series of lines on the hull plans of a vessel representing the intersection of a series of parallel fore-and-aft vertical planes with the form of the afterbody, usually taken as the inner surface of the shell: such a line appears as a vertical line on the body plan, as a curved or angular form, lowest amidships, on the sheer plan, and as lines parallel to the center line on the half-breadth plan. Cf. **bow line. 2.** (loosely) such a line prolonged into a bow line.

but·ton (but′ən), *n.* **1.** a small disk, knob, or the like, for sewing or otherwise attaching to an article, as of clothing, serving as a fastening when passed through a buttonhole or loop. **2.** anything resembling a button, esp. in being small and round, as any of various candies, ornaments, tags, identification badges, reflectors, markers, etc. **3.** *Bot.* a bud or other protuberant part of a plant. **4.** a young or undeveloped mushroom. **5.** a small knob or disk pressed to operate an electric circuit: *The next war would be fought by pushing buttons.* **6.** Also called **turn button.** a fastener for a door, window, etc., having two arms and rotating on a pivot that is attached to the frame. **7.** *Metall.* (in assaying) a small globule or lump of metal at the bottom of a crucible after fusion. **8.** *Fencing.* the protective knob fixed to the point of a foil. **9.** *Boxing Slang.* the point of the chin. **10.** the hard bonelike structure at the end of the rattles of a rattlesnake. **11.** *Zool.* any of various small parts or structures resembling a button. **12.** *Horol.* crown (def. 26). **13. not have all one's buttons,** *Slang.* to be eccentric or crazy: *Anyone who would do such a thing must not have all his buttons.* —*v.t.* **14.** to fasten with a button or buttons: *He quickly buttoned his jacket.* **15.** to insert (a button) in a buttonhole or loop: *He buttoned the top button of his shirt.* **16.** to provide (something) with a button or buttons. —*v.i.* **17.** to be capable of being buttoned: *This coat buttons, but that one zips.* **18. button up,** *Slang.* **a.** Also, **button one's lip.** to keep silent. **b.** to fasten securely; close up: *Within a short time, everything on the submarine was buttoned up.* **c.** to complete successfully; finish: *The report is all buttoned up.* [ME *boto(u)n* < MF *boton,* equiv. to *boter* to BUTT[3] + *-on* n. suffix] —**but′ton·er,** *n.* —**but′ton·like′,** *adj.*

but·ton·ball (but′ən bôl′), *n.* buttonwood (def. 1). [BUTTON + BALL[1]]

but·ton·bush (but′ən bo͝osh′), *n.* a North American shrub, *Cephalanthus occidentalis,* having globular flower heads. [BUTTON + BUSH[1]]

but·ton-down (but′ən doun′), *adj.* **1.** (of a shirt collar) having buttonholes so it can be buttoned down to the body of the shirt. **2.** (of a shirt) having a button-down collar.

but′ton ear′, a dog's ear that folds forward completely. —**but′ton-eared′,** *adj.*

but′ton head′, snaphead.

but·ton·hole (but′ən hōl′), *n., v.,* **-holed, -hol·ing.** —*n.* **1.** the hole, slit, or loop through which a button is passed and by which it is secured. **2.** *Chiefly Brit.* a boutonniere. **3.** *Surg.* a short straight incision through the wall of a cavity or a canal. —*v.t.* **4.** to sew with a buttonhole stitch. **5.** to make buttonholes in. **6.** to hold by or as by the buttonhole, as to detain (someone) in conversation. [BUTTON + HOLE] —**but′ton·hol′er,** *n.*

but′tonhole stitch′, *Sewing.* a looped stitch used to strengthen the edge of material and keep it from raveling, as around a buttonhole.

but·ton·hook (but′ən ho͝ok′), *n.* a small, usually metal hook for pulling buttons through buttonholes, as on gloves, dresses, breeches, etc. [BUTTON + HOOK]

but·ton·less (but′ən lis), *adj.* having no button or buttons. [BUTTON + -LESS]

but·ton·mold (but′ən mōld′), *n.* a small disk or knob of wood, metal, plastic, etc., to be covered with fabric to form an ornamental button. [BUTTON + MOLD[1]]

but′ton quail′, any of several birds of the family *Turnicidae,* of warmer parts of the Old World, resembling but not related to the true quail. Also called **bustard quail, hemipode.**

but·tons (but′ənz), *n.* (*construed as sing.*) *Chiefly Brit.* a bellboy or page. [so called from the many buttons of his uniform]

but′ton snake′root, 1. any composite herb of the genus *Liatris,* having racemose or spicate heads of handsome rose-purple flowers. **2.** an eryngo, *Eryngium yuccifolium,* of the southeastern U.S., having blue or whitish flowers.

but′ton tree′, 1. a tropical tree or shrub, *Conocarpus erecta,* yielding heavy, hard, compact wood and bearing buttonlike fruits. **2.** buttonwood (def. 1).

but·ton·wood (but′ən wo͝od′), *n.* **1.** Also called **buttonball, button tree.** a tall, North American plane tree, *Platanus occidentalis,* bearing small, pendulous fruit and yielding a useful timber. **2.** See **button tree** (def. 1). [BUTTON + WOOD[1]]

but·ton·y (but′ənē), *adj.* **1.** like a button. **2.** having many buttons. [BUTTON + -Y[1]]

butt′ plate′, a protective plate on the butt end of a gunstock, usually of metal.

but·tress (bu′tris), *n.* **1.** any external prop or support built to steady a structure by opposing its outward thrusts, esp. a projecting support built into or against the outside of a masonry wall. **2.** any prop or support. **3.** a thing shaped like a buttress, as a tree trunk with a widening base. —*v.t.* **4.** to support by a buttress; prop up. **5.** to give encouragement or support to (a person, plan, etc.). [ME *butres* << OF *boterez,* nom. sing. of *boteret* (acc.), equiv. to *boter-* abutment (? < Gmc; see BUTT[3]) + *-et* -ET] —**but′tress·less,** *adj.* —**but′tress·like′,** *adj.*

A, Buttress
B, Flying buttress

butts′ and bounds′, *Law.* the boundary lines of a piece of land, as used in deeds, titles, etc. [*butts* ends (see BUTT[2]); *bounds* sides (see BOUND[3])]

butt′ shaft′, a blunt or barbless arrow.

butt·stock (but′stok′), *n.* the part of the stock located behind the breech mechanism of a firearm. Also, **butt′-stock′.** [BUTT[1] + STOCK]

butt·strap (but′strap′), *n., v.,* **-strapped, -strap·ping.** —*n.* **1.** (in metal construction) a plate which overlaps and fastens two pieces butted together. —*v.t.* **2.** to unite with a buttstrap or buttstraps. [BUTT[1] + STRAP]

butt′ weld′, a weld between two pieces of metal butted together with the abutted ends shortened and thickened and fused together under heat.

bu·tyl (byo͞o′til, byo͞ot′əl), *adj. Chem.* containing a butyl group. [BUT(YRIC) + -YL]

Bu·tyl (byo͞o′til, byo͞ot′əl), *n. Trademark.* a synthetic rubber, prepared by polymerization of butylene containing little butadiene, particularly useful for inner tubes of automobile tires because of its leakproof qualities.

bu′tyl al′cohol, *Chem.* any of four flammable, isomeric, liquid alcohols having the formula C_4H_9OH, esp. $CH_3CH_2CH_2CH_2OH$, used as solvents and in organic synthesis.

bu′tyl al′dehyde, *Chem.* butyraldehyde.

bu·tyl·ene (byo͞ot′əlēn′), *Chem.* —*n.* **1.** Also, **butene.** any of three isomeric, gaseous hydrocarbons having the formula C_4H_8, of the alkene series. —*adj.* **2.** containing the butylene group. [BUTYL + -ENE]

bu′tylene group′, *Chem.* any of four bivalent, isomeric groups having the formula $-C_4H_8-$, esp. $-CH_2CH_2CH_2CH_2-$. Also called **bu′tylene rad′ical.**

bu′tyl group′, *Chem.* any of four univalent, isomeric groups having the formula C_4H_9-, esp. $CH_3(CH_2)_3-$. Also called **bu′tyl rad′ical.**

bu′tyl ox′alate, *Chem.* See **dibutyl oxalate.**

Bu·tyn (byo͞o′tin), *n. Pharm., Trademark.* butacaine.

bu·tyr·a·ceous (byo͞o′tə rā′shəs), *adj.* of the nature of, resembling, or containing butter. [< L *būtyr(um)* BUTTER + -ACEOUS]

bu·tyr·al (byo͞o′tə ral′, -tər əl), *n. Chem.* any acetal of butyraldehyde. [BUTYRAL(DEHYDE)]

bu·tyr·al·de·hyde (byo͞o′tə ral′də hīd′), *n. Chem.* a clear, colorless, flammable liquid, $CH_3(CH_2)_2CHO$, used chiefly as an intermediate in the manufacture of resins and rubber cement. Also called **butyl aldehyde.** [BUTYR(IC) + ALDEHYDE]

bu·tyr·ate (byo͞o′tə rāt′), *n. Chem.* a salt or ester of butyric acid. [BUTYR(IC) + -ATE[2]]

bu·tyr·ic (byo͞o tir′ik), *adj. Chem.* pertaining to or derived from butyric acid. [< L *būtyr(um)* BUTTER + -IC] —**bu·tyr′i·cal·ly,** *adv.*

butyr′ic a′cid, *Chem.* either of two isomeric acids having the formula C_3H_7COOH, esp. a rancid liquid occurring chiefly in spoiled butter, whose esters are used as flavorings.

butyr′ic e′ther, *Chem.* See **ethyl butyrate.**

bu·tyr·in (byo͞o′tər in), *n. Chem.* a colorless, liquid ester present in butter, formed from glycerin and butyric acid. [BUTYR(IC + GLYCER)IN]

bu·tyr·yl (byo͞o′tər il), *adj. Chem.* containing the butyryl group. [BUTYRIC + -YL]

bu′tyryl group′, *Chem.* the univalent group, $CH_3(CH_2)_2CO-$. Also called **bu′tyryl rad′ical.**

bux·om (buk′səm), *adj.* **1.** (of a woman) full-bosomed. **2.** (of a woman) healthy, plump, cheerful, and lively. [ME, earlier *buhsum* pliant, equiv. to OE *būh* (impv. of *būgan* to BOW[1]) + *-sum* -SOME[1]] —**bux′om·ly,** *adv.* —**bux′om·ness,** *n.*

Bux·te·hu·de (bo͝oks′tə ho͞o′də), *n.* **Die·trich** (dē′-trikh), 1637–1707, Danish organist and composer, in Germany after 1668.

buy (bī), *v.,* **bought, buy·ing,** *n.* —*v.t.* **1.** to acquire the possession of, or the right to, by paying or promising to pay an equivalent, esp. in money; purchase. **2.** to obtain or acquire by giving any kind of recompense: *to buy favor with flattery.* **3.** to hire or obtain the services of: *The Yankees bought a new center fielder.* **4.** to bribe: *Most public officials cannot be bought.* **5.** to be the monetary or purchasing equivalent of: *Ten dollars will buy a lot of meat and beans.* **6.** *Chiefly Theol.* to redeem; ransom. **7.** *Cards Slang.* to draw or be dealt (a card): *He bought an ace.* **8.** *Slang.* **a.** to accept or believe: *I don't buy that explanation.* **b.** to be deceived by: *He bought the whole story.* —*v.i.* **9.** to be or become a purchaser. **10. buy in, a.** to buy a supply of; accumulate a stock of. **b.** to buy back one's own possession at an auction. **c.** Also, **buy into.** *Slang.* to gain (a share in a business, membership in an organization, etc.) by paying a sum of money: *They tried to buy into the club but were not accepted.* **11. buy it,** *Brit. Slang.* to get killed; be shot: *He bought it at Dunkirk.* **12. buy off,** to get rid of (a claim, opposition, etc.) by payment; purchase the nonintervention of; bribe: *The corrupt official bought off those who might expose him.* **13. buy out,** to secure all of (an owner or partner's) share or interest in an enterprise: *He bought out an established pharmacist and is doing very well.* **14. buy up,** to buy as much as one can of something, or as much as is offered for sale: *She bought up the last of the strawberries at the fruit market.* —*n.* **15.** the act or an instance of buying. **16.** *U.S.* something bought or to be bought; purchase: *That coat was a sensible buy.* **17.** *U.S. Informal.* a bargain: *The couch was a real buy.* [ME *by(en),* var. of *byggen, buggen,* OE *bycgan;* c. OS *buggjan,* Goth *bugjan* to buy, Icel *byggja* to lend, rent] —**buy′a·ble,** *adj.*

—**Syn. 1.** BUY, PURCHASE imply obtaining or acquiring property or goods for a price. BUY is the common and informal word, applying to any such transaction: *to buy a house, vegetables at the market.* PURCHASE is more formal and may connote buying on a larger scale, in a finer store, and the like: *to purchase a year's supplies.* —**Ant. 1.** sell.

buy′ boat′, *U.S.* a boat sent out by a dealer to purchase the catches of fishing vessels.

buy·er (bī′ər), *n.* **1.** one who buys; purchaser. **2.** a purchasing agent, as for a department or chain store. [ME *beger, bier.* See BUY, -ER[1]]

buy′ers' mar′ket, a market in which goods and services are plentiful and prices relatively low. Cf. **sellers' market.**

buy′ers' strike′, an attempt on the part of consumers to lower price levels by boycotting retailers or certain types of goods.

buy′ing pow′er. See **purchasing power** (def. 1).

Buys-Bal·lot's′ law′ (bīs′bə lots′), *Meteorol.* the law stating that if one stands with one's back to the wind, in the Northern Hemisphere the atmospheric pressure will be lower on one's left and in the Southern Hemisphere it will be lower on one's right: descriptive of the relationship of horizontal winds to atmospheric pressure. [named after C. H. D. *Buys-Ballot* (1817–90), Dutch meteorologist]

buzz[1] (buz), *n.* **1.** a low, vibrating, humming sound, as of bees, machinery, or people talking. **2.** a rumor or report. **3.** *Informal.* a phone call: *When I find out, I'll give you a buzz.* —*v.i.* **4.** to make a low, vibrating, humming sound. **5.** to speak or whisper with such a sound. **6.** to make a murmuring, humming noise, as a group of people talking: *Everyone is buzzing about the scandal.* **7.** to move busily from place to place. **8.** *Chiefly Brit. Slang.* to go; leave (usually fol. by *off* or *along*). —*v.t.* **9.** to make a buzzing sound with: *The fly buzzed its wings.* **10.** to tell or spread (a rumor, gossip, etc.) secretively. **11.** to signal or summon with a buzzer: *He buzzed his secretary.* **12.** *Informal.* to make a phone call to. **13.** *Aeron.* **a.** to fly a plane very low over: *to buzz a field.* **b.** to signal or greet (someone) by flying a plane low and slowing the motor spasmodically. [imit.] —**buzz′ing·ly,** *adv.*

buzz[2] (buz), *n.* **1.** *Brit. Dial.* a bur. **2.** any of various bushy objects, such as a bushy wig, a bushy trout-fishing fly, etc. [?]

buz·zard[1] (buz′ərd), *n.* **1.** any of several broad-winged, soaring hawks of the genus *Buteo,* and allied genera, esp. *B. buteo,* of Europe. **2.** any of several New World vultures of the family *Cathartidae,* esp. the turkey vulture. **3.** *Slang.* **a.** a contemptible or cantankerous man, esp. if old and unkempt (often prec. by *old*): *That old buzzard has lived in the same shack for twenty years.* **b.** a facetious term of address used between males (usually prec. by *old*). —*adj.* **4.** *Obs.* senseless; stupid. [ME *busard* < OF, var. of *buisard,* equiv. to *buis(on)* buzzard (< L *būteōn-,* s. of *būteō* kind of hawk) + *-ard* -ARD] —**buz′zard·like′,** *adj.* —**buz′zard·ly,** *adj., adv.*

buz·zard[2] (buz′ərd), *n. Brit. Dial.* any of various nocturnal buzzing insects, as cockchafers. [BUZZ[1] + -ARD]

Buz′zard's Bay′, an inlet of the Atlantic, in SE Massachusetts. 30 mi. long.

buzz′ bomb′, *Mil.* a type of self-steering aerial bomb, launched from large land-based rocket platforms: used by the Germans in World War II, esp. over England.

buzz·er (buz′ər), *n.* **1.** one who or that which buzzes. **2.** a signaling apparatus similar to an electric bell, but without hammer or gong, producing a buzzing sound by the vibration of an armature. [BUZZ[1] + -ER[1]]

buzz′ saw′, a small, power-operated circular saw, so named because of the noise it makes.

buzz′ track′, *Motion Pictures.* film containing a special sound track used in testing motion-picture reproducing equipment.

buzz·wig (buz′wig′), *n.* **1.** a large, bushy wig. **2.** a person wearing such a wig. **3.** a person of consequence. [*buzze* bur (dial.; ? b. BUR[1] and FUZZ) + WIG]

buzz·word (buz′ wûrd′), *n.* a word or phrase, sometimes sounding technical, that is a popular cliché of a particular group or field.

B.V., 1. Blessed Virgin. [< L *Beāta Virgō*] **2.** farewell. [< L *bene valē*]

b.v., book value.

B.V.A., Bachelor of Vocational Agriculture.

B.V.D., *Trademark.* a suit of men's underwear, esp. a pair of undershorts. Also, **BVDs** Cf. **skivvy.**

B.V.E., Bachelor of Vocational Education.

B.V.M., Blessed Virgin Mary. [< L *Beāta Virgō Maria*]

bvt., 1. brevet. **2.** brevetted.

BW, 1. bacteriological warfare. **2.** biological warfare.

bwa·na (bwä′nə), *n.* (in Africa) master; boss: a term applied by natives to a European. [< Swahili < Ar *abūna* our father]

BWC, Board of War Communications.

B.W.I., British West Indies.

bx, See **base exchange.** Also, **BX**

bx., *pl.* **bxs.** box.

BX cable, *Elect.* a cable consisting of wires contained in a flexible metal tubing, used chiefly in wiring buildings and in supplying electric power to equipment.

by (bī), *prep., adv., adj., n., pl.* **byes.** —*prep.* **1.** near to or next to: *a home by a lake.* **2.** over the surface of, through the medium of, along, or using as a route: *He came by the highway. She arrived by air.* **3.** on, as a means of conveyance: *They arrived by ship.* **4.** to and beyond the vicinity of; past: *He went by the church.* **5.** within the extent or period of, during: *by day; by night.* **6.** not later than, at or before: *I usually finish work by five o'clock.* **7.** to the extent or amount of: *The new tug is larger than the old one by a great deal. He's taller than his sister by three inches.* **8.** according to; from the opinion, evidence, or authority of: *By his own account he was in Chicago at the time. You can't prove it by me.* **9.** in conformity with: *This is a bad movie by any standards. I know him by sight.* **10.** with (something) at stake; on: *to swear by all that is sacred.* **11.** through the agency, efficacy, work, participation, or authority of: *The book was published by Random House.* **12.** from the hand, mind, invention, or creativity of: *Have you read the latest novel by O'Hara? The phonograph was invented by Edison.* **13.** in consequence, as a result, or on the basis of: *We met by chance. We won the game by forfeit.* **14.** accompanied with or in the atmosphere of: *Lovers walk by moonlight.* **15.** on behalf of; in support of: *He did well by his children.* **16.** after; in serial order: *piece by piece; little by little; By the numbers, present arms!* **17.** taken with (a certain number of) times or (of a shape longer than wide) the other dimension: *Multiply 18 by 57. The room was 10 feet by 12 feet.* **18.** using as a divisor; separating into equal parts by the process of division: *Divide 99 by 33.* **19.** according to or involving as a unit of measure: *Apples are sold by the bushel. I'm paid by the week.* **20.** begot or born of: *Eve had two sons by Adam. My brother has one child by his first wife.* **21.** (of quadrupeds) having as a sire: *Equipoise II by Equipoise.* **22.** (as used in the names of the 16 smallest points on the compass) one point toward the east, west, north, or south of N, NE, E, SE, S, SW, W, or NW, respectively: *He sailed N by NE from Pago Pago.* **23.** into, at, or to: *Drop by my office this afternoon.*

—*adv.* **24.** near; in the immediate vicinity; at hand: *The school is close by.* **25.** to and beyond a point near something; past: *The car drove by.* **26.** aside; away: *Put your work by for the moment. Over the years, he laid by enough money to retire.* **27.** over; past: *in times gone by.* **28. by and by,** in a short time; before long; presently: *The clouds will disappear by and by.* **29. by and large,** in general; on the whole: *By and large, there is much to be said for the new system.* **30. by me, a.** (in bridge and other bidding card games) a declaration that the speaker is passing. **b.** (in poker) a declaration that the speaker is checking: *Is my pair of tens still high? By me.*

—*adj.* Also, **bye. 31.** situated to one side: *They came down a by passage.* **32.** secondary, incidental: *It was only a by comment.*

—*n.* **33.** bye. **34. by the by.** See **bye** (def. 5). [ME; OE *bī;* c. D *bij,* OHG *bī* (G *bei*), Goth *bi.* See BE-]

—**Syn. 11.** BY, THROUGH, WITH indicate agency or means of getting something done or accomplished. BY is regularly used to denote the agent (person or force) in passive constructions: *It is done by many; destroyed by fire.* It also indicates means: *Send it by airmail.* WITH denotes the instrument (usually consciously) employed by an agent: *He cut it with the scissors.* THROUGH designates particularly immediate agency or instrumentality or reason or motive: *through outside aid; to yield through fear; wounded through carelessness.*

by-, a combining form of **by:** *byproduct; bystander; byway.* Also, **bye-.**

By·am (bī′əm), *n.* a boy's given name.

by-and-by (bī′ən bī′), *n.* the near future: *in the sweet by-and-by.* [ME *bi and bi* one by one, at once. See BY]

by-bid·der (bī′bid′ər), *n.* a person employed to bid at an auction in order to raise the prices for the auctioneer or seller. [BY- + BIDDER] —**by′-bid′ding,** *n.*

Byb·lis (bib′lis), *n. Class. Myth.* a daughter of Miletus who fell in love with her brother, Caunus, and who pursued him through many lands until she was changed into a fountain.

Byb·los (bib′ləs), *n.* an ancient Phoenician seaport near the modern city of Beirut, Lebanon: chief port for the export of papyrus: site now partially excavated.

by-blow (bī′blō′), *n.* **1.** an incidental or accidental blow. **2.** Also, **bye-blow.** an illegitimate child; bastard. [BY- + BLOW[1]]

by′ crack′y!, *Informal.* (an exclamation used to express surprise or to emphasize a comment): *A fine day, by cracky!*

Byd·goszcz (bid′gôshch), *n.* a city in N Poland. 246,000 (est. 1963). German, **Bromberg.**

bye (bī), *n.* Also, **by. 1.** *Sports.* in a tournament, the position of a player or team not paired with a competitor in an early round and thus automatically advanced to play in the next round: *The top three seeded players received byes in the first round.* **2.** *Golf.* the holes of a stipulated course still unplayed after the match is finished. **3.** *Cricket.* a run made on a ball not struck by the batsman. **4.** something subsidiary, secondary, or out of the way. **5. by the bye,** by the way; incidentally: *By* *the bye, how do you spell your name?* Also, **by the by.** —*adj.* **6.** by. [var. sp. of BY in its n. use]

bye-, var. of **by-:** *bye-election.*

bye-blow (bī′blō′), *n.* by-blow (def. 2).

bye-bye (bī′bī′), *interj.* *Informal.* good-by. [repetitive compound, based on *bye,* short for *bye baby* lulling phrase]

bye·law (bī′lô′), *n.* bylaw.

by-e·lec·tion (bī′i lek′shən), *n.* *Brit.* a special election not held at the time of a general election, to fill a vacancy in Parliament. Also, **bye′-e·lec′tion.** [BY- + ELECTION]

Bye·lo·rus·sia (byel′ō rush′ə, bel′ō-), *n.* **1.** Offical name, **Belarus.** Formerly, **White Russian Soviet Socialist Republic, Byelorus′sian So′viet So′cialist Repub′lic.** a republic in E Europe, N of Ukraine: formerly a part of the Soviet Union. 10,200,000; 80,154 sq. mi. *Cap.:* Minsk. **2.** a region in the W part of former czarist Russia. Also, **Belorussia.** Also called **White Russia.**

Bye·lo·rus·sian (byel′ō rush′ən, bel′ō-), *adj.* **1.** of or pertaining to Byelorussia, its people, or their language. —*n.* **2.** Also called **White Russian.** a native or inhabitant of Byelorussia. **3.** a dialect of Russian, spoken by the population of the Byelorussian S.S.R. and using an alphabet slightly different from the Russian alphabet. Also, **Belorussian.** [BYELORUSSI(A) + -AN]

Bye·lo·stok (bye′lo stôk′, be′-), *n.* Russian name of **Białystok.**

bye-low (bī′lō′), *v.i.* *Baby Talk.* to drift off to sleep. [see BYE-BYE, LOW[1]]

by·gone (bī′gôn′, -gon′), *adj.* **1.** past; gone by; out of date: *The faded photograph brought memories of bygone days.* —*n.* **2.** that which is past: *Let's not talk of bygones.* **3. let bygones be bygones,** to decide to forget past disagreements; become reconciled: *Let's let bygones be bygones and begin again.* [late ME (north) *by-gane* GONE BY]

by·law (bī′lô′), *n.* **1.** a standing rule governing the regulation of a corporation's or society's internal affairs. **2.** a subsidiary law. **3.** *Brit.* an ordinance of a municipality or community. Also, **byelaw.** [BY- + LAW[1]; r. ME *bilawe,* equiv. to *by* town (< Scand; cf. Dan *by*) + *lawe* law]

by-line (bī′līn′), *n.* *Journalism.* a printed line accompanying a news story, article, or the like, giving the author's name. [BY- + LINE[1]]

by·lin·er (bī′lī′nər), *n.* a writer important enough to merit a by-line. [BY-LINE + -ER[1]]

by-name (bī′nām′), *n.* **1.** a secondary name; cognomen; surname. **2.** a nickname. Also, **by′name′.** [ME]

Byng (bing), *n.* **Julian Hed·worth George** (hed′wərth), (*Viscount Byng of Vimy*), 1862–1935, English general: governor general of Canada 1921–26.

by-pass (bī′pas′, -päs′), *n., v.,* **-passed** or (*Rare*) **-past; -passed** or **-past; -pass·ing.** —*n.* **1.** a road enabling motorists to avoid a city or other heavy traffic points or to drive around an obstruction. **2.** a secondary pipe or other channel connected with a main passage, as for conducting a liquid or gas around a fixture, pipe, or appliance. **3.** *Elect.* shunt (def. 9). —*v.t.* **4.** to avoid (an obstruction, city, etc.) by following a by-pass. **5.** to cause (fluid or gas) to follow a secondary pipe or by-pass. **6.** to neglect to consult or to ignore the opinion or decision of (one's superior, a critic, or the like): *He bypassed the foreman and took his grievance straight to the owner.* Also, **by′pass′.** [appar. back formation from *by-passage;* see BY (adj.), PASSAGE[1]] —**by′-pass′er, by′pass′er,** *n.*

by′-pass capac′itor, *Elect.* a capacitor that gives an AC path with relatively low impedance about a specified element in a circuit. Also called **by′-pass condens′er.**

by-past (bī′past′, -päst′), *adj.* bygone; past. [late ME: PASSED BY]

by-path (bī′path′, -päth′), *n., pl.* **-paths** (-pathz′, -päthz′, -paths′, -päths′). a private path or an indirect or secondary course or means; byway. Also, **by′path′.** [ME *bi path.* See BY (adj.), PATH]

by-play (bī′plā′), *n.* an action or speech carried on to the side while the main action proceeds, esp. on the stage. Also, **by′play′.** [BY- + PLAY]

by-plot (bī′plot′), *n.* subplot.

by-prod·uct (bī′prod′əkt), *n.* a secondary or incidental product, as in a process of manufacture. [BY- + PRODUCT]

Byrd (bûrd), *n.* **1. Richard Evelyn,** 1888–1957, rear admiral in U.S. Navy: polar explorer. **2. William,** c1540–1623, English composer and organist. **3.** Also, **Bird.** a boy's given name.

byre (bīər), *n.* *Brit.* a cow barn or shed. [ME, OE: barn, shed, var. of *būr* hut. See BOWER[1]]

byre-man (bīər′mən), *n., pl.* **-men.** *Brit.* a man who raises or tends cows.

Byr·gi·us (bēr′gē əs), *n.* a crater in the third quadrant of the face of the moon: about 40 miles in diameter.

Byrl (bûrl), *n.* a boy's given name.

Byrle (bûrl), *n.* a girl's given name.

Byrne (bûrn), *n.* **Donn** (don). See **Donn-Byrne, Brian Oswald.**

Byrnes (bûrnz), *n.* **1. James Francis,** born 1879, U.S. statesman and jurist: Secretary of State 1945–47. **2. Joseph Wellington,** 1869–1936, U.S. lawyer: Speaker of the House 1935–36.

byr·nie (bûr′nē), *n.* *Armor.* a defensive shirt, usually of mail; hauberk. [ME *byrny,* Scot var. of *brynie, brinie* < Scand; cf. Icel *brynja,* c. OE *byrne* coat of mail, OHG *brunnia*]

by-road (bī′rōd′), *n.* a side road. Also, **by′road′.** [BY- + ROAD]

By·ron (bī′rən), *n.* **1. George Gordon, Lord** (*6th Baron Byron*), 1788–1824, English poet. **2.** a boy's given name.

By·ron·ic (bī ron′ik), *adj.* **1.** of or pertaining to Lord Byron. **2.** possessing the characteristics of Byron or his poetry, esp. melancholy, melodramatic energy, etc. [BYRON + -IC] —**By·ron′i·cal·ly,** *adv.*

byr·rus (bir′əs), *n., pl.* **byr·ri** (bir′ī). birrus.

bys·sus (bis′əs), *n., pl.* **bys·sus·es, bys·si** (bis′ī). **1.** *Zool.* a collection of silky filaments by which certain mollusks attach themselves to rocks. **2.** an ancient cloth, thought to be of linen, cotton, or silk. [< L < Gk *býssos* a fine cotton or linen < Heb *būṣ* or some kindred Sem word] —**bys·sa·ceous** (bi sā′shəs), **bys′soid,** *adj.* —**bys′sal,** *adj.*

by·stand·er (bī′stan′dər), *n.* a person present but not involved; chance spectator. [BY- + STANDER]

by-street (bī′strēt′), *n.* a side street or a private or obscure street; byway. Also, **by′street′.** [BY- + STREET]

by-talk (bī′tôk′), *n.* incidental conversation; small talk; chitchat. [BY- + TALK]

byte (bīt), *n.* *Computer Technol.* a unit of information for processing in certain kinds of electronic computers, equal to one character or eight bits. [arbitrary coinage]

By·tom (bī′tôm), *n.* a city in S Poland: formerly in Germany. 190,000 (est. 1963). German, **Beuthen.**

by·town·ite (bī tou′nīt), *n.* a mineral near the anorthite end of the plagioclase feldspar group. [named after *Bytown* old name of Ottawa, Canada, where it is found; see -ITE[1]]

by·way (bī′wā′), *n.* **1.** a secluded, private, or obscure road. **2.** a subsidiary or obscure field of research, endeavor, etc. [ME *bywey.* See BY (adj.), WAY]

by·wo·ner (bī′vō′nər, bā′-), *n.* (in southern Africa) a farm laborer, esp. a sharecropper. [< SAfrD, equiv. to *by* at (MD *bī*) + *woner* dweller (deriv. of MD *wōnen* to dwell, c. G *wohnen*)]

by·word (bī′wûrd′), *n.* **1.** a word or phrase associated with some person, group, idea, etc.; a characteristic expression, typical formula, or the like, as *hail fellow well met.* **2.** a word or phrase used proverbially; common saying; proverb. **3.** an object of general reproach, derision, scorn, etc. **4.** an epithet, often of scorn. [ME *biworde,* OE *biwyrde.* See BY (adj.), WORD]
—**Syn. 1.** slogan, motto. **2.** maxim, apothegm, aphorism, saw, adage.

by-work (bī′wûrk′), *n.* work done in addition to one's regular work, as in intervals of leisure. [BY- + WORK]

by-your-leave (bī′yər lēv′), *n.* an apology for not having sought permission.

Byz., Byzantine.

byz·ant (biz′ənt, bi zant′), *n.* bezant (def. 2).

Byz·an·tine (biz′ən tēn′, -tīn′, bi zan′tin), *adj.* **1.** of or pertaining to Byzantium. **2.** of or pertaining to the Byzantine Empire. **3.** noting or pertaining to the architecture of the Byzantine Empire and to architecture influenced by or imitating it: characterized by masonry construction, round arches, impost blocks, low domes on pendentives, and by the presence of fine, spiky foliage patterns in low relief on stone capitals and moldings, and by the use of frescoes, mosaics, and revetments of fine stone to cover whole interiors. **4.** *Fine Arts.* pertaining to or designating the style of the fine or decorative arts developed and elaborated in the Byzantine Empire and its provinces, characterized chiefly by an ecclesiastically prescribed iconography, highly formal structure, severe confinement of pictorial space to a shallow depth, and the use of rich, often sumptuous color. **5.** of or pertaining to the Byzantine Church. —*n.* **6.** a native or inhabitant of Byzantium. [< LL *Byzantīn(us)* of BYZANTIUM; see -INE[1]]

Byz′antine chant′, *Music.* liturgical plainsong identified with the Eastern Orthodox Church and dating from the Byzantine Empire.

Byz′antine Church′. See **Orthodox Church** (def. 1).

Byz′antine Em′pire, the Eastern Roman Empire after the fall of the Western Empire in A.D. 476. *Cap.:* Constantinople.

Byz′antine rite′. See **Greek rite.**

By·zan·tin·ism (bi zan′tᵊ niz′əm), *n.* *Eastern Ch.* caesaropapism, esp. before the Great Schism of 1054. [BYZANTINE + -ISM]

By·zan·ti·um (bi zan′shē əm, -tē əm), *n.* an ancient Greek city on the Bosporus and the Sea of Marmara: Constantine I rebuilt it and renamed it Constantinople A.D. 330. Cf. **Istanbul.**

By·zas (bī′zəs), *n.* a son of Poseidon and the eponymous founder of Byzantium.

Bz., benzene.

C

C, c (sē), *n., pl.* **C's** or **Cs, c's** or **cs.** **1.** the third letter of the English alphabet, a consonant. **2.** any spoken sound represented by the letter *C* or *c*, as in *cat, race, circle,* etc. **3.** something having the shape of a C. **4.** a written or printed representation of the letter *C* or *c*. **5.** a device, as a printer's type, for reproducing the letter *C* or *c*.

C, **1.** Calorie. **2.** centigrade. **3.** coulomb.

C, **1.** the third in order or in a series. **2.** (*sometimes l.c.*) (in some grading systems) a grade or mark, as in school or college, indicating the quality of a student's work as fair or average. **3.** *Music.* **a.** the first tone, or keynote, in the scale of C major or the third tone in the relative minor scale, A minor. **b.** a string, key, or pipe tuned to this tone. **c.** a written or printed note representing this tone. **d.** (in the fixed system of solmization) the first tone of the scale of C major, called *do*. **e.** the tonality having C as the tonic note. **f.** a symbol indicating quadruple time and appearing after the clef sign on a musical staff. **4.** (*sometimes l.c.*) the Roman numeral for 100. Cf. **Roman numerals. 5.** *Chem.* carbon. **6.** *Elect.* capacitance. **7.** Also, **C-note.** *U.S. Slang.* a hundred-dollar bill. **8.** a proportional shoe width size, narrower than D and wider than B. **9.** a proportional brassiere cup size, smaller than D and larger than B. **10.** (in men's pajama sizes) large.

c, **1.** calorie. **2.** candle; candles. **3.** about: *c1775*. [< L *circā, circiter, circum*] **4.** cycle; cycles.

c, **1.** *Math.* the cardinal number of the set of all real numbers. **2.** *Optics, Physics.* velocity of light in a vacuum: approximately 186,000 miles per second or 299,793 kilometers per second.

c̄, (in prescriptions) with. [< L *cum*]

C., **1.** Calorie. **2.** Cape. **3.** Catholic. **4.** Celsius (Centigrade). **5.** Celtic. **6.** Centigrade. **7.** College. **8.** (in Costa Rica and El Salvador) colon; colons. **9.** Conservative.

c., **1.** calorie. **2.** candle. **3.** carat. **4.** carbon. **5.** carton. **6.** case. **7.** *Baseball.* catcher. **8.** cathode. **9.** cent; cents. **10.** *Football.* center. **11.** centigrade. **12.** centime. **13.** centimeter. **14.** century. **15.** chairman. **16.** chapter. **17.** chief. **18.** child. **19.** church. **20.** about: *c. 1775.* [< L *circā, circiter, circum*] **21.** cirrus. **22.** city. **23.** cloudy. **24.** cognate. **25.** gallon. [< L *congius*] **26.** copper. **27.** Also, ©. copyright. **28.** corps. **29.** cubic. **30.** (in prescriptions) with. [< L *cum*] **31.** cycle; cycles.

C-, *U.S. Mil.* (in designations of transport aircraft) cargo: *C-54; C-124.*

ca' (kä, kô), *v.t., v.i.* *Scot.* to call, as to call an animal toward one; urge or drive forward by calling.

CA, chronological age.

Ca, *Chem.* calcium.

ca., **1.** cathode. **2.** centiare. **3.** about: *ca.* 476 B.C. [< L *circā*]

C.A., **1.** Central America. **2.** See **chartered accountant. 3.** Coast Artillery.

C/A, **1.** capital account. **2.** cash account. **3.** credit account. **4.** current account.

CAA, Civil Aeronautics Administration. Also, **C.A.A.**

Caa·ba (kä′bə), *n.* Kaaba.

Ca·an·thus (kā an′thəs), *n.* *Class. Myth.* a son of Oceanus who, upon discovering that his sister Melia had been abducted by Apollo, set fire to the god's sacred grove. For this sacrilege, Apollo killed him.

cab[1] (kab), *n., v.,* **cabbed, cab·bing.** —*n.* **1.** a taxicab. **2.** any of various horse-drawn vehicles, as the hansom or brougham, esp. one for public hire. **3.** the covered or enclosed part of a locomotive, truck, crane, etc., where the engineer, driver, or operator sits. —*v.i.* **4.** to ride in a taxicab or horse-drawn cab: *They cabbed to the theater.* [short for CABRIOLET]

cab[2] (kab), *n.* an ancient Hebrew measure equal to about two quarts. Also, **kab.** [< Heb *qabh*]

CAB, Civil Aeronautics Board. Also, **C.A.B.**

Ca·bae·us (kə bē′əs), *n.* a walled plain in the third quadrant of the face of the moon, in the libration area and near the South Pole: about 60 miles in diameter.

ca·bal (kə bal′), *n., v.,* **-balled, -bal·ling.** —*n.* **1.** a small group of secret plotters, as against a government or person in authority. **2.** the plots and schemes of such a group; intrigue. **3.** a clique, as in the artistic, literary, or theatrical fields: *He was a young poet with his own little cabal trailing around after him.* —*v.i.* **4.** to form a cabal; intrigue; conspire; plot. [earlier *cabbal* < ML *cabbal(a).* See CABALA] —**ca·bal′ler,** *n.*
—**Syn. 2.** conspiracy, plot.

cab·a·la (kab′ə lə, kə bä′-), *n.* **1.** a system of esoteric theosophy and theurgy developed by rabbis from about the 7th to the 18th centuries, reaching its peak about the 12th and 13th centuries, and influencing certain medieval and Renaissance Christian thinkers. It was based on a mystical method of interpreting Scripture by which initiates claimed to penetrate sacred mysteries and foretell the future. Among its central doctrines are, all creation is an emanation from the Deity and the soul exists from eternity. **2.** any occult or secret doctrine or science. Also, **cabbala, kabala, kabbala.** [< ML *cab(b)ala* < Heb *qabbālāh* tradition; lit., something received, i.e., handed down]

cab·a·lism (kab′ə liz′əm), *n.* **1.** the principles or doctrines of the cabala. **2.** an interpretation of something according to the doctrines of the cabala. **3.** extreme traditionalism in theological conception or interpretation. **4.** obfuscation or obscurantism, esp. resulting from an excessively recondite vocabulary: *the cabalism of some modern criticism.* [CABAL(A) + -ISM]

cab·a·list[1] (kab′ə list), *n.* **1.** a student of or specialist in the cabala. **2.** a person who is well-versed or highly skilled in difficult, obscure, or esoteric matters. [< ML *cabbalist(a),* equiv. to *cabbala* CABALA + L *-ista* -IST]

cab·a·list[2] (kab′ə list), *n.* *Obs.* a member of a cabal. [? < F *cabaliste.* See CABAL, -IST]

cab·a·lis·tic (kab′ə lis′tik), *adj.* **1.** of or pertaining to the cabala. **2.** mystic; occult. **3.** of or marked by cabalism. Also, **cab′a·lis′ti·cal.** [CABAL + -ISTIC] —**cab′a·lis′ti·cal·ly,** *adv.*

ca·bal·le·ro (kab′əl yâr′ō, kab′ə lâr′ō; *Sp.* kä′vä lye′rô), *n., pl.* **ca·bal·le·ros** (kab′əl yâr′ōz, kab′ə lâr′ōz; *Sp.* kä′vä lye′rôs). **1.** a Spanish gentleman. **2.** *Southwestern U.S.* **a.** a horseman. **b.** an escort; admirer. [< Sp < LL *caballār(ius)* groom; see CAVALIER]

ca·ba·llo (kä vä′lyô, -yô), *n., pl.* **-ba·llos** (-vä′lyôs, -yôs). *Spanish.* horse.

ca·ba·na (kə ban′ə, -ban′yə, bä′nə, -bän′yə), *n.* **1.** a cabin or cottage. **2.** a small cabin or tentlike structure for use as a bathhouse, esp. on a beach or by a swimming pool. Also, **ca·ba·ña** (kä bä′nyä). [< Sp; see CABIN]

Ca·ba·na·tuan (kä′vä nä twän′), *n.* a city on S Luzon, in the N Philippines. 54,668 (1960).

ca·bane (kə ban′), *n.* *Aeron.* a mastlike structure on some early airplanes, for supporting the wing. [< F; see CABIN]

cab·a·ret (kab′ə rā′ *for 1, 3, 4;* kab′ə ret′ *for 2*), *n.* **1.** a large restaurant providing its patrons with food, drink, music, a dance floor, and an elaborate floor show. **2.** a small table, stand, or tray holding a matched set of porcelain or silver dishes and utensils for serving tea, coffee, etc. **3.** *Brit.* the floor show; formal entertainment provided by a night club or restaurant. —*v.i.* **4.** to visit a cabaret, esp. often. [< F: tap-room; orig. disputed]

cabaret′ tax′, a tax levied on entertainment, dancing, floor shows, etc., at places where liquor is served, as at cabarets, night clubs, or the like. Cf. **amusement tax.**

cab·as·set (kab′ə sā′), *n.* a morion of the late 16th and 17th centuries, having a high, domed form with a narrow brim. [< F, dim. of *cabas* < OPr]

cab·bage[1] (kab′ij), *n., v.,* **-baged, -bag·ing.** —*n.* **1.** any of several cultivated varieties of a cruciferous plant, *Brassica oleracea capitata,* having a short stem and leaves formed into a compact, edible head. **2.** the head of a cabbage. **3.** *Slang.* money, esp. paper money. —*v.i.* **4.** (of a plant) to form a head like that of a cabbage. [ME *caboche* < dial. OF (north): head, undetermined deriv. of L *caput* head] —**cab′bage·like′, cab′bag·y,** *adj.*

cab·bage[2] (kab′ij), *n., v.,* **-baged, -bag·ing.** —*n.* **1.** something stolen, esp. pieces of cloth by a tailor when making garments. —*v.t., v.i.* **2.** to steal; pilfer: *He cabbaged whole yards of cloth.* [earlier *carbage* shred, piece of cloth, appar. var. of GARBAGE wheat straw chopped small (obs. sense)]

cab′bage bug′. See **harlequin bug.**

cab′bage but′terfly, any of several white or chiefly white butterflies of the family *Pieridae,* as *Pieris rapae,* the larvae of which feed on the leaves of cabbages and other cruciferous plants.

cab·bage·head (kab′ij hed′), *n.* **1.** cabbage[1] (def. 2). **2.** *Slang.* a dolt. [CABBAGE[1] + HEAD]

cab′bage moth′. See **diamondback moth.**

cab′bage palm′, **1.** any of several palms, as *Sabal Palmetto,* having terminal leaf buds which are eaten like cabbage. **2.** See **Barbados royal palm.**

cab′bage palmet′to, a cabbage palm, *Sabal Palmetto,* of the southeastern U.S.: the State tree of Florida and South Carolina.

cab′bage rose′, an upright rose, *Rosa centifolia,* having fragrant, pink flowers, cultivated in many varieties.

cab′bage tree′, ti[2].

cab′bage-tree hat′ (kab′ij trē′), *Australian.* a broad-brimmed hat made from cabbage-tree leaves.

cab·bage·worm (kab′ij wûrm′), *n.* a caterpillar that feeds on cabbages, esp. of the genus *Pieris.* [CABBAGE[1] + WORM]

cab·ba·la (kab′ə lə, kə bä′-), *n.* cabala. —**cab′ba·lism,** *n.* —**cab′ba·list,** *n.* —**cab′ba·lis′tic, cab′ba·lis′ti·cal,** *adj.* —**cab′ba·lis′ti·cal·ly,** *adv.*

cab·ble (kab′əl), *v.t.,* **-bled, -bling.** *Metall.* to cut up (iron or steel bars) for fagoting. [var. of SCABBLE]

cab·by (kab′ē), *n., pl.* **-bies.** *Informal.* a cabdriver. [CAB[1] + -Y[2]]

cab·driv·er (kab′drī′vər), *n.* a driver of a taxicab or horse-drawn carriage. [CAB[1] + DRIVER]

Cabe (kāb), *n.* a boy's given name, form of **McCabe.**

Ca·bei·ri (kə bī′rī), *n.pl.* Cabiri.

Cab·ell (kab′əl), *n.* **James Branch,** 1879–1958, U.S. novelist, essayist, and critic.

ca·ber (kā′bər), *n.* *Scot.* a pole or beam, esp. one thrown as a trial of strength. [< Gael *cabar* pole]

Ca·ber·net (kab′ər nā′), *n.* a medium-bodied, red table wine.

Ca·bet (kA be′), *n.* **É·tienne** (ā tyen′), 1788–1856, French socialist who established a utopian community in the U.S. called Icaria: became U.S. citizen 1854.

Ca·be·za de Va·ca (kä ve′thä de bä′kä, -ve′sä), **Ál·var Nú·ñez** (äl′vär nōō′nyeth, -nyes), c1490–1557?, Spanish explorer in the Americas.

cab·e·zon (kab′i zon′; *Sp.* kä′ve sôn′), *n., pl.* **-zo·nes** (-zō′nāz; *Sp.* -sô′nes), **-zons.** any of several large-headed fishes, esp. a sculpin, *Scorpaenichthys marmoratus,* found off the Pacific coast of North America. Also, **cab·e·zone** (kab′i zōn′, kab′i zōn′). [< Sp, equiv. to *cabez(a)* head (< VL **capitia* < L *capiti-* (s. of *caput*) head + *-a* n. suffix) + *-on* aug. suffix]

ca·bil·do (kä vēl′thô; *Eng.* kə bil′dō), *n., pl.* **-dos** (thôs; *Eng.* -dōz). *Spanish.* **1.** the chapter house of a cathedral. **2.** a town council. **3.** See **town hall.**

cab·in (kab′in), *n.* **1.** a small house or cottage, usually of simple design and construction: *He was born in a cabin built of rough logs. We rented a cabin near the lake.* **2.** an enclosed space for more or less temporary occupancy, as the living space in a trailer, the passenger space in a cable car, or the like. **3.** an apartment or room in a ship, as for passengers. **4.** See **cabin class. 5.** (in a naval vessel) living accommodations for officers. **6.** *Aeron.* the enclosed space for the pilot, passengers, or cargo in an air or space vehicle. —*adv.* **7.** in cabin-class accommodations, or by cabin-class conveyance: *to travel cabin.* —*v.i.* **8.** to live in a cabin: *They cabin in the woods on holidays.* —*v.t.* **9.** to confine; enclose tightly; cramp. [ME *cabane* < MF < OPr *caban(a)* < LL *capanna*]
—**Syn. 1.** cot, shanty, shack. See **cottage.**

cab′in boy′, a boy employed to wait on the officers and passengers in a merchant vessel.

cab′in class′, the class of accommodations on a passenger ship less costly and luxurious than first class but more so than tourist class. Cf. **second class** (def. 1). —**cab′in-class′,** *adj., adv.*

cab′in court′, a roadside motel having cabins.

cab′in cruis′er, a power-driven pleasure boat having a cabin equipped for living on board ship.

Ca·bin·da (kə bēn′də), *n.* **1.** a Portuguese territory and exclave of Angola, on the W coast of Africa. 50,233 (est. 1950); 2807 sq. mi. **2.** a seaport in and the capital of this territory, on the Congo River. 1554 (1950).

cab′in deck′, *Naut.* (in the bridge house of a ship) the deck above the weather deck.

cab·i·net (kab′ə nit), *n.* **1.** (*often cap.*) a council advising a sovereign, president, etc., esp. the group of ministers or executives responsible for the government of a nation. **2.** *U.S.* an advisory body to the President, consisting of the heads of the eleven executive departments of the federal government. **3.** a piece of furniture with shelves, drawers, etc., for holding or displaying valuable objects, dishes, etc. **4.** a large piece of furniture containing a radio or television set, usually standing on the floor and often having a record player or a place for phonograph records. **5.** an upright box or movable closet for storing goods, materials, equipment, etc.: *a clothes cabinet.* **6.** a wall cupboard used for storage, as of kitchen utensils, toilet articles, etc.: *a kitchen cabinet; a medicine cabinet.* **7.** a small case with compartments for valuables and other small objects. **8.** a small chamber or booth for special use, esp. a shower stall. **9.** a private room. **10.** a room set aside specifically for the exhibition of small works of art or objets d'art. **11.** *Archaic.* a small room. **12.** *Obs.* a small cabin. —*adj.* **13.** pertaining to a political cabinet: *a cabinet meeting.* **14.** pertaining to a private room. **15.** private; confidential; secret. **16.** of suitable value, beauty, or size for a private room, small case, etc.: *a cabinet edition of Milton.* **17.** of, pertaining to, or used by a cabinetmaker or in cabinetmaking. **18.** *Drafting.* designating a method of projection (**cab′inet projec′tion**) in which a three-dimensional object is represented by a drawing (**cab′inet draw′ing**) having all vertical and horizontal lines drawn to exact scale, with oblique lines reduced to about half scale so as to offset the appearance of distortion. Cf. **axonometric, isometric** (def. 4), **oblique** (def. 13). [< MF < It *gabinett(o)* clothes-press; (def. 11) CABIN + -ET]

cab·i·net·mak·er (kab′ə nit mā′kər), *n.* a person who makes fine woodwork, esp. cabinets, chests, shelving, etc. [CABINET + MAKER]

cab·i·net·mak·ing (kab′ə nit mā′king), *n.* **1.** the manufacture of fine woodwork. **2.** the occupation or craft of a cabinetmaker. [CABINET + MAKING]

cab′inet pic′ture, a small easel painting, usually under three feet in width and formerly exhibited in a cabinet or special room.

cab′inet pud′ding, a bread or cake pudding baked in a mold placed in a pan of hot water, usually filled with candied fruit, raisins, and currants, and often served hot with a fruit sauce.

cab·i·net·ry (kab′ə ni trē), *n.* cabinetwork for console model phonographs and the like. [CABINET + -RY]

cab′inet scrap′er, a scraper used in preparing a wood surface for sanding.

cab′inet wine′, high-quality wine from Germany.

cab·i·net·work (kab′ə nit wûrk′), *n.* **1.** fine woodwork, as cabinets, chests, shelves, etc. **2.** cabinetmaking. [CABINET + WORK] —**cab′i·net·work′er,** *n.*

cab′in hook′, a hook and eye for fastening a cabinet door or the like.

Ca·bi·ri (kə bī′rī), *n.pl.* a group of gods, probably of Eastern origin, anciently worshiped in mysteries in various parts of Greece, the cult center being at Samothrace. Also, **Cabeiri, Kabeiri.** —**Cab·i·re·an** (kab′ə rē′ən), **Ca·bir·i·an** (kə bir′ē ən), **Ca·bir·ic** (kə bir′ik), **Cab·i·rit·ic** (kab′ə rit′ik), *adj.*

ca·ble (kā′bəl), *n., v.,* **-bled, -bling.** —*n.* **1.** a heavy, strong rope. **2.** *Naut.* **a.** a rope or chain for mooring a vessel at anchor. **b.** See **cable's length.** **3.** *Elect.* an insulated electrical conductor, often in strands, or a combination of electrical conductors insulated from one another. **4.** cablegram. **5.** *Archit.* one of a number of reedings set into the flutes of a column or pilaster. **6.** cable-stitch. —*v.t.* **7.** to send (a message) by underwater cable. **8.** to send a cablegram to. **9.** to fasten with a cable. **10.** to furnish with a cable or cables. —*v.i.* **11.** to send a message by submarine cable. **12.** cable-stitch. [ME; OE **cæbl* (var. of *cæfl*) < LL *cap(u)lum* halter, equiv. to L *cap(istrum)* halter (< OE *cæbester*) + *-ulum* -ULE] —**ca′ble-like′,** *adj.*

Ca·ble (kā′bəl), *n.* **George Washington,** 1844–1925, U.S. novelist and short-story writer.

ca′ble bu′oy, a buoy marking or supporting part of a submerged cable.

ca′ble car′, an enclosed vehicle used on a cable railway or cableway. Also, **ca′ble-car′.**

ca′ble crane′, cableway.

ca·ble·gram (kā′bəl gram′), *n.* a telegram sent by underwater cable. [CABLE + (TELE)GRAM]

ca·ble·laid (kā′bəl lād′), *adj.* *Ropemaking.* **1.** noting a rope formed of three plain-laid ropes twisted together in a left-handed direction; hawser-laid. **2.** noting a rope formed of three backhanded ropes twisted together in a right-handed direction. [CABLE + LAID]

ca′ble length′. See **cable's length.**

ca′ble mold′ing, a molding in the form of a rope.

ca′ble rail′way, a railway on which the cars are pulled by a moving cable under the roadway.

ca′ble release′, *Photog.* a device consisting of a flexible wire that is pressed at one end to trip a shutter mechanism on a camera.

ca·blese (kā′bə lēz′, -lēs′), *n.* language typical of cablegrams, characterized by the omission, abbreviation, and combination of words. [CABLE + -ESE]

ca′ble ship′, a vessel for laying, maintaining, and repairing underwater telegraph cables.

ca′ble's length′, a nautical unit of length (720 feet in the U.S. Navy; 608 feet in the British Navy). Also, **cable length.**

ca·ble-stitch (kā′bəl stich′), *n.* **1.** a series of stitches used in knitting to produce a cable effect. **2.** the pattern produced by a cable-stitch. —*v.i.* **3.** to produce such a stitch or pattern.

ca·blet (kā′blit), *n.* a small cable, esp. a cablelaid rope under 10 inches in circumference. [CABLE + -ET]

ca′ble tel′evision, a system by which television signals are transmitted to paying subscribers by coaxial cable rather than being broadcast over the air.

ca′ble tram′way, tramway (def. 4).

ca·ble·way (kā′bəl wā′), *n.* a system for hoisting and hauling bulk materials, consisting of a cable or pair of cables suspended between two towers, on which travels a carriage from which a bucket is suspended: used in heavy construction work, in storage plants, etc. Also called **cable crane.** [CABLE + WAY]

ca·bling (kā′bling), *n.* *Archit.* **1.** decoration with cable moldings. **2.** reedings set into the flutes of a column or pilaster. [CABLE + -ING[1]]

cab·man (kab′mən), *n., pl.* **-men.** cabdriver. [CAB[1] + MAN[1]]

ca·bob (kə bob′), *n.* kabob.

ca·boched (kə bosht′), *adj.* caboshed. Also, **ca·bo·ché** (kab′ə shā′).

cab·o·chon (kab′ə shon′; *Fr.* KA bô shôN′), *n., pl.* **-chons** (-shonz′; *Fr.* -shôN′), *adv.* —*n.* **1.** a precious stone of convex hemispherical or oval form, polished but not cut into facets. **2.** an ornamental motif resembling this, used on furniture of the 18th century. —*adv.* **3.** in the form of a cabochon: *en cabochon: a turquoise cut cabochon.* [< MF, equiv. to *caboche* head (see CABBAGE) + *-on* aug. suffix]

ca·bo·clo (kə bō′klo͞o, -klō, -bō′-; *Port.* kə bô′klo͝o), *n., pl.* **-clos** (-klo͞oz, -klōz; *Port.* -klo͝osh). a full-blooded or half-breed Indian of Brazil. [< Pg < Tupi *caboco, caboculo, caboclo*]

ca·boo·dle (kə bo͞od′əl), *n.* **1.** *Informal.* the lot, pack, or crowd: *I have no use for the whole caboodle.* **2. kit and caboodle.** See **kit**[1] (def. 5). [*ca-* (< ?) + BOODLE]

ca·boose (kə bo͞os′), *n.* **1.** *Railroads.* a car on a freight train, used chiefly by the crew and usually attached to the rear of the train. **2.** *Brit.* a kitchen on the deck of a ship; galley. [< MLG *kabūse*]

ca·boshed (kə bosht′), *adj.* *Heraldry.* (of an animal, as a deer) shown facing forward without a neck: *a stag's head caboshed.* Also, **ca·bossed** (kə bost′), **cabched, caboché.** [var. of *caboched,* ptp. of ME *caboche* to behead (a deer) < AF *caboch(er),* deriv. of *caboche* head; see CABBAGE[1]]

Cab·ot (kab′ət), *n.* **1. John** (*Giovanni Caboto*), c1450–98?, Italian navigator in the service of England: discoverer of the North American mainland 1497. **2. Richard Clarke,** 1868–1939, U.S. physician and writer on medical ethics. **3. Sebastian,** 1474?–1557, English navigator and explorer (son of John Cabot). **4.** a boy's given name.

cab·o·tage (kab′ə tij; *Fr.* KA bô tAzh′), *n.* **1.** navigation or trade along the coast. **2.** *Aeron.* the legal restriction to domestic carriers of air transport between points within a country's borders. [< F, deriv. of *caboter* to; see -AGE]

Ca·bral (kə brôl′), *n.* **Pe·dro Ál·va·res** (pe′drо͝o ôl′-və rəsh), c1460–c1520, Portuguese navigator.

Ca·bre·ra (*Sp.* kä vre′rä), *n.* **Ma·nuel Es·tra·da** (*Sp.* mänwel′ es trä′thä). See **Estrada Cabrera, Manuel.**

ca·bret·ta (kə bret′ə), *n.* a leather made from the skins of sheep that grow hair rather than wool, tougher than other sheepskins and used chiefly for gloves and shoes. [< Pg or Sp *cabr(a)* she-goat (< L *capra*) + It *-etta* -ETTE]

ca·bril·la (kə bril′ə), *n.* any of several sea basses, esp. *Epinephelus analogus,* found in the tropical part of the eastern Pacific Ocean. [< Sp: prawn, equiv. to *cabr(a)* she-goat (< L *capra*) + *-illa* dim. suffix]

Ca·bri·ni (kə brē′nē; *It.* kä brē′nē), *n.* **Saint Frances Xavier** (*Mother Cabrini*), 1850–1917, American nun, born in Italy; founder of the Missionary Sisters of the Sacred Heart of Jesus.

cab·ri·ole (kab′rē ōl′; *Fr.* KA brē ôl′), *n., pl.* **-oles** (-ōlz′; *Fr.* -ôl′). **1.** *Furniture.* a curved, tapering leg curving outward at the top and inward farther down so as to end in a round pad, the semblance of an animal's paw, or some other feature; used esp. in the first half of the 18th century. **2.** *Ballet.* a leap in which one leg is raised in the air and the other is brought up to beat against it. [< F: orig. caper; so called because modeled on leg of a capering animal; see CAPRIOLE]

Cabriole

cab·ri·o·let (kab′rē ə lā′), *n.* **1.** a light, two-wheeled, one-horse carriage with a folding top, capable of seating two persons. **2.** *Auto. Obs.* a type of automobile resembling a coupé, with a folding top; a convertible coupé. [< F: lit., little caper; so called from its light movement. See CABRIOLE, -ET]

cab·stand (kab′stand′), *n.* a place where cabs may wait to be hired. [CAB[1] + STAND]

ca·bu·ya (kə bo͞o′yə; *Sp.* kä vo͞o′yä), *n., pl.* **-yas** (-yəz; *Sp.* -yäs). See **giant lily.** [< Sp < Taino]

Cabriolet

C.A.C., Coast Artillery Corps.

Ca·ca (kä′kə), *n.* an ancient Roman goddess of the hearth, often identified with Vesta.

ca·ca·na·pa (kä′kə nä′pə, kak′ə-), *n.* a treelike cactus, *Opuntia lindheimeri,* of the southern U.S. and Mexico, having bluish-green joints, clusters of spines, yellow or red flowers about three inches wide and purple, pear-shaped fruit. [< AmerSp]

ca′can·ny (kä kan′ē, kô-), *n.* *Brit. Slang.* **1.** a trade-union policy of limiting production or the number of workers employed, in order to keep salaries high. **2.** a deliberate reduction of working speed and production by workers, to express their discontent. [lit., drive gently; see CA', CANNY]

ca·ca·o (kə kā′ō, -kä′ō), *n., pl.* **-ca·os.** **1.** a small evergreen sterculiaceous tree, *Theobroma Cacao,* of tropical America, cultivated for its seeds, the source of cocoa, chocolate, etc. **2.** Also, **cocoa.** the fruit and seeds of this tree. [< Sp < Nahuatl *caca-huatl* cacao seeds]

caca′o bean′, cacao (def. 2). Also, **cocoa bean.**

caca′o but′ter, a fatty substance obtained from the seeds of the cacao, used in making soaps, cosmetics, etc. Also, **cocoa butter.**

cac·cia (kä′chə; *It.* kät′chä), *n., pl.* **-ce** (-chā; *It.* -che), **-cias.** a 14th-century Italian vocal form for two voices in canon plus an independent tenor, with a text describing the hunt or the cries and noises of village life. [< It: lit., a hunt; see CATCH, CHASE[1]]

cac·cia·to·re (kä′chə tôr′ē, -tôr′ē), *adj.* *Italian Cookery.* (of casseroles) prepared with or containing tomatoes, mushrooms, herbs, and other seasonings: *chicken cacciatore.* Also, **cac·cia·to·ra** (kä′chə tôr′ə, -tōr′ə). [< It: lit., hunter, equiv. to *cacciat(o)* (ptp. of *cacciare* to hunt; see CATCH, -ATE[1]) + *-ore* -OR[2]]

Cac·ci·ni (kät chē′nē), *n.* **Giu·lio** (jo͞o′lyô), c1546–1618, Italian singer and composer.

cach·a·lot (kash′ə lot′, -lō′), *n.* See **sperm whale.** [< F; of disputed orig.]

cache (kash), *n., v.,* **cached, cach·ing.** —*n.* **1.** a hiding place, esp. one in the ground, for provisions, treasures, etc.: *She hid her jewelry in a little cache in the cellar.* **2.** anything so hidden: *The enemy never found our cache of food.* —*v.t.* **3.** to put in a cache; conceal; hide. [< F, deriv. of *cache(r)* (to) hide < VL **coacticāre* to stow away, orig. to pack together < L *coact(us)* collected (ptp. of *cōgere;* see COACTIVE) + *-icā-* formative v. suffix + *-re* inf. ending]
—**Syn. 3.** secrete.

cache·pot (kash′pot′, -pō′), *n.* an ornamental container, usually of china or tole, for holding and concealing a flowerpot. [< F: lit., hide pot, equiv. to *cache(r)* (to) hide + *pot* POT[1]]

ca·chet (ka shā′, kash′ā; *Fr.* KA she′), *n., pl.* **ca·chets** (ka shāz′, kash′āz; *Fr.* KA she′). **1.** an official seal, as on a letter or document. **2.** a distinguishing mark or feature; stamp: *Courtesy is the cachet of good breeding.* **3.** a sign or expression of approval, esp. from one who has a great deal of prestige. **4.** *Pharm.* a hollow wafer for enclosing an ill-tasting medicine. **5.** *Philately.* a firm name, slogan, or design stamped or printed on an envelope or folded letter. [< MF: lit., something compressed to a small size. See CACHE, -ET]

ca·chex·i·a (kə kek′sē ə), *n.* *Pathol.* general ill health, with emaciation, due to a chronic disease, as cancer. Also, **ca·chex·y** (kə kek′sē) [< LL < Gk, equiv. to *kak(ós)* bad + *héx(is)* condition (*éch(ein)* (to) have + *-sis* -SIS) + *-ia* -IA] —**ca·chec·tic** (kə kek′tik), **ca·chec′ti·cal, ca·chex′ic,** *adj.*

cach·in·nate (kak′ə nāt′), *v.i.,* **-nat·ed, -nat·ing.** to laugh loudly or immoderately. [< L *cachinnāt(us)* laughed aloud, laughed immoderately (ptp. of *cachinnāre*), equiv. to *cachinn-* laugh aloud + *-ātus* -ATE[1]] —**cach′in·na′tion,** *n.* —**cach′in·na′tor,** *n.* —**cach′-in·na′to·ry,** *adj.*

ca·chou (kə sho͞o′, ka-), *n.* **1.** catechu. **2.** a pill or lozenge for sweetening the breath. [< F < Pg *cachu* < Malay; see CATECHU]

ca·chu·cha (kə cho͞o′chə; *Sp.* kä cho͞o′chä), *n., pl.* **-chas** (-chəz; *Sp.* -chäs). **1.** an Andalusian dance resembling the bolero. **2.** the music for this dance. [< Sp: ? lit., fragment; of obscure orig.]

ca·cim·bo (kə sim′bō), *n., pl.* **-bos.** a heavy mist or drizzle that occurs in the Congo basin area, often accompanied by onshore winds. [native name in Portuguese West Africa]

ca·cique (kə sēk′), *n.* **1.** a chief of an Indian clan or tribe in Mexico and the West Indies. **2.** any of several oscine birds of the family *Icteridae,* of the American tropics, which construct long, pendent nests. **3.** (in Spain and Spanish America) a political boss on a local level. **4.** (in the Philippines) a prominent landowner. [< Sp < Taino (Hispaniola), prob. < Arawak]

cack (kak), *n.* a soft-soled, heelless shoe for infants. [?]

cack·le (kak′əl), *v.,* **-led, -ling,** *n.* —*v.i.* **1.** to utter the shrill, broken sound or cry of a hen. **2.** to laugh in a shrill, broken manner. **3.** to chatter noisily; prattle. —*v.t.* **4.** to utter with cackles; express by cackling: *The old women cackled their disapproval of the younger generation.* —*n.* **5.** act or sound of cackling. **6.** idle talk. **7.** *Brit. Slang, Archaic.* the dialogue of a play. [ME *cakel(en);* c. D *kakelen,* LG *kakeln,* Sw *kackla*] —**cack′-ler,** *n.*

caco-, an element meaning "bad," occurring in loan words from Greek (*cacodemon*); on this model, used in the formation of compound words (*cacogenics*). [< Gk *kakó(s)*]

cac·o·de·mon (kak′ə dē′mən), *n.* an evil spirit; devil; demon. Also, **cac′o·dae′mon.** [< Gk *kakodaímōn* having an evil genius, ill-fated. See CACO-, DEMON] —**cac·o·de·mon·ic, cac·o·dae·mon·ic** (kak′ə di mon′ik), **cac·o·de·mo·ni·ac, cac·o·dae·mo·ni·ac** (kak′ə di mō′-nē ak′), *adj.*

cac·o·dyl (kak′ə dil), *Chem.* —*adj.* **1.** containing the cacodyl group. —*n.* **2.** Also called **dicacodyl, tetramethyldiarsine.** an oily, slightly water-soluble, poisonous liquid compound composed of two cacodyl groups, $(CH_3)_2As-As(CH_3)_2$, that has a vile, garliclike odor and that undergoes spontaneous combustion in dry air. [< Gk *kakṓd(es)* ill-smelling (*kak(o)-* CACO- + *-ōd-* smell + *-ēs* adj. suffix) + -YL]

cac·o·dyl·ate (kak′ə dil′āt), *n.* *Chem.* a salt of cacodylic acid. [CACODYL(IC) + -ATE[2]]

cac′odyl group′, *Chem.* the univalent group, $(CH_3)_2As-$, derived from arsine. Also called **cac′odyl rad′ical.**

cac·o·dyl·ic (kak′ə dil′ik), *adj.* of, pertaining to, or characteristic of the cacodyl group. [CACODYL + -IC]

cac′odyl′ic ac′id, *Chem.* a colorless, crystalline, deliquescent, poisonous solid, $(CH_3)_2AsOOH$, used chiefly in the manufacture of dyes and as an herbicide. Also called **alkargen, dimethyl arsinic acid.**

cac·o·ë·thes (kak′ō ē′thēz), *n.* an irresistible urge; mania. [< L < Gk *kakoḗthes,* neut. (used as n.) of *kakoḗthēs* malignant, lit., of bad character; see CACO-, ETHOS] —**cac·o·eth·ic** (kak′ō eth′ik), *adj.*

cac·o·gen·ics (kak′ə jen′iks), *n.* (*construed as sing.*) dysgenics. [CACO- + (EU)GENICS] —**cac′o·gen′ic,** *adj.*

ca·cog·ra·phy (kə kog′rə fē), *n.* **1.** bad handwriting; poor penmanship (opposed to *calligraphy*). **2.** incorrect spelling (opposed to *orthography*). [CACO- + -GRAPHY] —**ca·cog′ra·pher,** *n.* —**cac·o·graph·ic** (kak′ə graf′ik), **cac′o·graph′i·cal,** *adj.*

ca·col·o·gy (kə kol′ə jē, kə-), *n.* defectively produced speech; socially unacceptable diction; nonconforming pronunciation. [CACO- + -LOGY]

cac·o·mis·tle (kak′ə mis′əl), *n.* a carnivorous animal, *Bassariscus astutus,* of Mexico and the southwestern U.S., related to the raccoon but smaller, with a sharper snout and longer tail. Also, **cac·o·mix·le** (kak′ə mis′əl, -mik′səl). Also called **bassarisk, ringtail, ring-tailed cat.** [< MexSp < Nahuatl *tlacomiztli,* equiv. to *tlaco* half + *miztli* cougar]

Cacomistle (Total length 2½ ft.; tail 1½ ft.)

cac·o·phon·ic (kak′ə fon′ik), *adj.* cacophonous. [CACOPHON(Y) + -IC] —**cac′o·phon′i·cal·ly,** *adv.*

ca·coph·o·nous (kə kof′ə nəs), *adj.* having a harsh sound; discordant. [< Gk *kakóphōnos.* See CACO-, -PHONE, -OUS] —**ca·coph′o·nous·ly,** *adv.*

ca·coph·o·ny (kə kof′ə nē), *n., pl.* **-nies.** **1.** harsh discordance of sound; dissonance: *The birds filled the jungle with a cacophony of hoots, cackles, and wails.* **2.** a discordant and meaningless mixture of different sounds: *The cacophony produced by New York traffic at midday is hardly tolerable.* **3.** *Music.* frequent use of discords of a harshness and relationship difficult to understand. [< NL *cacophonia* < Gk *kakophōnía.* See CACO-, -PHONY]

cac·que·teuse (kak′ə to͞oz′; *Fr.* kakᵊ tœz′), *n., pl.* **-teus·es** (-to͞o′ziz; *Fr.* -tœz′). a narrow, upright armchair of 16th-century France, having widely splayed arms and a very narrow back. Also, **caqueteuse, caquetoire.** [< F *caqueteuse,* fem. of *caqueteur* chatterer, equiv. to *caquet(er)* (to) chatter + *-eur* -OR[2]]

cac·ta·ceous (kak tā′shəs), *adj.* belonging to the *Cactaceae,* or cactus family. [< NL *Cactace(ae)* name of the family (see CACTUS, -ACEAE) + -OUS]

cac·tus (kak′təs), *n., pl.* **-tus·es, -ti** (-tī). any of various fleshy-stemmed plants of the family *Cactaceae,* usually leafless and spiny, often producing showy flowers, chiefly native to the hot, dry regions of America. [< L < Gk *káktos* cardoon] —**cac′tus·like′,** **cac′toid,** *adj.*

Cactus (Saguaro), *Carnegiea gigantea* (Height to 50 ft.)

cac′tus dahl′ia, a tuberous-rooted herb, *Dahlia juarezi,* of Mexico and Guatemala, having overlapping flower rays of unequal length.

cac′tus gera′nium, a perennial herb, *Pelargonium echinatum,* of South Africa, having hooked, soft prickles on the stem, toothed leaves, white-felty undersides, and white flowers with one red-spotted petal.

cac′tus wren′, any of several American wrens of the genus *Campylorhynchus,* of arid regions, esp. *C. brunneicapillus,* of the southwestern U.S. and Mexico.

ca·cu·mi·nal (kə kyo͞o′mə nᵊl), *Phonet.* —*adj.* **1.** pronounced with the tip of the tongue curled back so as to touch the roof of the mouth above the gums; retroflex; cerebral. —*n.* **2.** a cacuminal sound. [< L *cacūmin-* (s. of *cacūmen*) top, tip + -AL[1]]

Ca·cus (kā′kəs), *n. Rom. Legend.* a man-eating giant fathered by Vulcan, killed by Hercules.

cad (kad), *n.* **1.** an ill-bred person, esp. one who does not behave in a gentlemanly or responsible way toward women. **2.** *Brit. Oxford Univ. Slang.* a townsman, as opposed to a student. [short for CADDIE (def. 2)]

Cad (kad), *n.* a boy's given name, form of **Cadwallader.**

ca·das·tral (kə das′trəl), *adj.* **1.** *Survey.* (of a map or survey) showing or including boundaries, property lines, etc. **2.** of or pertaining to a cadastre. [< F; see CADASTRE, -AL[1]]

ca·das·tre (kə das′tər), *n.* an official register of the ownership, extent, and value of real property in a given area, used as a basis of taxation. Also, **ca·das′ter.** [< F < Pr *cadastr(o)* < It *catastro,* earlier *catastico* (Venetian) < LGk *katástich(on)* register, deriv. of phrase *katà stíchon* by line; see CATA-, STICH]

ca·dav·er (kə dav′ər, -dā′vər), *n.* a dead body, esp. of a human being; corpse. [< L *cadāver* dead body, corpse, akin to *cadere* to fall, perish] —**ca·dav′er·ic,** *adj.*
—**Syn.** See **body.**

ca·dav·er·ine (kə dav′ə rēn′), *n. Biochem.* a colorless, viscous, toxic, liquid ptomaine, $NH_2(CH_2)_5$, having an offensive odor, formed by the action of bacilli on meat, fish, and other protein: used in polymerization and biological research. Also called **pentamethylenediamine.** [CADAVER + -INE[2]]

ca·dav·er·ous (kə dav′ər əs), *adj.* **1.** of or like a corpse. **2.** pale; wan; ghastly. **3.** haggard and thin. [< L *cadāverōs(us)* like a corpse. See CADAVER, -OUS] —**ca·dav′er·ous·ly,** *adv.* —**ca·dav′er·ous·ness,** *n.*

cad·dice (kad′is, kä′dis), *n.* caddisworm.

cad·die (kad′ē), *n., v.,* **-died, -dy·ing.** —*n.* **1.** *Golf.* a person hired to carry a player's clubs, find the ball, etc. **2.** a person who runs errands, does odd jobs, etc. **3.** See **caddie cart.** —*v.i.* **4.** to work as a caddie. Also, **caddy.** [earlier *cadee,* var. of *cadet* < F; see CADET]

cad′die cart′, a small two-wheeled cart used by golfers to carry their clubs around the course.

cad·dis[1] (kad′is), *n.* **1.** a kind of woolen yarn or braid. **2.** caddisworm. Also, **cad′dice.** [< MF *cadis* < OPr *cadis, cadiz,* perh. so called because imported from Cadiz, Spain; r. ME *cadas* < MF, of obscure orig.] —**cad′dised, cad′diced,** *adj.*

cad·dis[2] (kad′is), *n.* caddisworm. [by shortening]

cad·dis·fly (kad′is flī′), *n., pl.* **-flies.** any of numerous insects of the order *Trichoptera,* having two pairs of membranous, often hairy wings. Also, **cad′dice·fly′.** Cf. **caddisworm.** [see CADDISWORM, FLY[2]]

cad·dish (kad′ish), *adj.* of or like a cad; ill-bred; ungentlemanly: *caddish behavior.* [CAD + -ISH[1]] —**cad′dish·ly,** *adv.* —**cad′dish·ness,** *n.*

cad·dis·worm (kad′is wûrm′), *n.* the aquatic larva of a caddisfly, many of which live in a case built from sand or from plant debris. Also called **caddis, caddice, strawworm.** [*caddis* (perh. < pl., taken as sing., of *caddy,* dim. of *cad* larva, ghost) + WORM]

Caddisfly and larvae A, Caddisfly; B, Larva in case formed of small stones; C, Larva in case formed of grass roots

Cad·do·an (kad′ō ən), *n.* a family of North American Indian languages spoken in the upper Missouri valley in N Dakota, in the Platte valley in Nebraska and SW Arkansas, and in neighboring parts of Oklahoma, Texas, and Louisiana. [< *Caddo* group of American Indian tribes + -AN]

cad·dy[1] (kad′ē), *n., pl.* **-dies.** *Brit.* **1.** a small box, can, or chest for holding or organizing small items: *pencil caddy.* **2.** See **tea caddy.** [var. of CATTY[2]]

cad·dy[2] (kad′ē), *n., pl.* **-dies,** *v.i.,* **-died, -dy·ing.** caddie.

cad′dy spoon′, *Brit.* a small antique spoon used in taking tea from a caddy.

cade[1] (kād), *n.* a juniper, *Juniperus Oxycedrus,* of the Mediterranean area, whose wood on destructive distillation yields an oily liquid (**oil of cade**), used in treating skin diseases. [< MF < OPr; akin to LL *catanus*]

cade[2] (kād), *adj.* (of the young of animals) left by the mother and raised by humans: *a cade lamb.* [late ME < ?]

Cade (kād), *n.* a boy's given name.

-cade, a formal element derived from the analysis of *cavalcade,* used with the meaning "procession" in the formation of compound words: *motorcade.*

ca·delle (kə del′), *n.* a small, blackish beetle, *Tenebroides mauritanicus,* that feeds, as both larva and adult, on stored grain and on other insects. [< F < Pr *cadell(o)* < L *catell(us), catell(a)* puppy < *cat(ulus)* young of an animal + *-ellus, -ella* dim. suffix]

Ca·de·na (kə dē′nə), *n.* a girl's given name, form of **Cadence.**

ca·dence (kād′ᵊns), *n., v.,* **-denced, -denc·ing.** —*n.* Also, **cadency.** **1.** rhythmic flow of a sequence of sounds or words: *the cadence of language.* **2.** (in free verse) a rythmic pattern that is nonmetrically structured. **3.** the beat, rate, or measure of any rhythmic movement: *The chorus line danced in rapid cadence.* **4.** the flow or rhythm of events, esp. the pattern in which something is experienced: *the frenetic cadence of modern life.* **5.** a slight falling in pitch of the voice in speaking or reading, as at the end of a declarative sentence. **6.** the general modulation of the voice. **7.** *Music.* a sequence of notes or chords that indicates the momentary or complete end of a composition, section, phrase, etc. —*v.t.* **8.** to make rhythmical. [ME < MF < It *cadenz(a),* lit., a falling; see CADENZA]

Ca·dence (kād′ᵊns), *n.* a girl's given name.

ca·den·cy (kād′ᵊn sē), *n., pl.* **-cies.** **1.** cadence (defs. 1–7). **2.** *Heraldry.* the relationship to one another and to their common ancestor of the various members and branches of a family, as indicated by the introduction into their various coats of arms of certain charges and marks. [CAD(ENCE) + -ENCY]

ca′dency mark′, *Heraldry.* a charge or minor heraldic difference introduced into the arms of a family to show that it is related by blood to the main branch of the family, which bears the arms as originally granted. Also called **brisure, difference.**

ca·dent (kād′ᵊnt), *adj.* **1.** having cadence. **2.** *Archaic.* falling. [< L *cadent-,* (s. of *cadēns* falling, prp. of *cadere*), equiv. to *cad-* fall + *-ent-* -ENT]

ca·den·tial (kā den′shəl), *adj.* of, pertaining to, or constituting a musical cadence. [see CADENCE, -IAL; modeled on *substance, substantial*]

ca·den·za (kə den′zə), *n. Music.* an elaborate flourish or showy passage introduced near the end of an aria or in a movement of a concerto. [< It < VL **cadentia* a falling, equiv. to L *cad(ere)* to fall + *-entia* -ENCY]

Ca·den·za (kä den′tdzä), *n.* a girl's given name, Italian form of **Cadence.**

ca·det (kə det′), *n.* **1.** a student training for service as an officer in the U.S. Army. Cf. **midshipman.** **2.** a student training to become a merchant marine officer. **3.** a gentleman, usually a younger son, who entered the army to prepare for a subsequent commission. **4.** a trainee in a business or profession. **5.** a younger son or brother. **6.** the youngest son. **7.** Also called **cadet′ blue′.** a grayish to strong blue color. **8.** Also called **cadet′ gray′;** *esp. Brit.,* **cadet′ grey′.** a bluish-gray to purplish-blue color. **9.** *Slang.* a pimp. [< F < Gascon *capdet* little chief, equiv. to *capd* (< L *capit-* head) + *-et* -ET] —**ca·det′ship′, ca·det·cy** (kə det′sē), *n.*

Ca·det (kə det′), *n. Russ. Hist.* a member of the former Constitutional Democratic party. [< Russ *Kadet,* sing. of *Kadeti,* equiv. to *ka* (name of letter *k,* initial of *Konstitutsionalnyie* Constitutional) + *De(mokra)ti* Democrats]

cadet′ cloth′, a heavy woolen cloth of double-cloth construction and bluish-gray color, used for uniforms at military schools.

ca·dette (kə det′), *n. Australian.* a female government employee, esp. a woman appointed to civil service. [CAD(ET) + -ETTE]

cadge[1] (kaj), *v.,* **cadged, cadg·ing.** —*v.t.* **1.** to obtain by imposing on another's generosity or friendship. **2.** to borrow without intent to repay. **3.** *Brit.* to beg or obtain by begging. —*v.i.* **4.** to ask, expect, or encourage another person to pay for or provide one's drinks, meals, etc. **5.** to beg. [ME *cagge(n)* (to) tie, perh. orig. said of hawks; see CADGE[2]] —**cadg′er,** *n.*

cadge[2] (kaj), *n. Falconry.* a frame on which hawks are carried to the field. [appar. var. of CAGE]

cadg·y (kaj′ē), *adj. Scot.* **1.** cheerful; merry. **2.** amorous; wanton. **3.** (of animals) in rut. [?] —**cadg′i·ly,** *adv.* —**cadg′i·ness,** *n.*

ca·di (kä′dē, kā′-), *n., pl.* **-dis.** a judge, in a Muslim community, whose decisions are based on Islamic religious law. Also, **kadi.** [< Ar *qāḍī* judge]

Cad·il·lac (kad′ᵊlak′; *Fr.* ka dē yak′), *n.* **An·toine de la Mothe** (äN twan′ də la mōt′), 1657?–1730, French colonial governor in North America: founder of Detroit.

Ca·diz (kā′diz), *n.* a town in E Ohio. 3259 (1960).

Cá·diz (kā′diz, kə diz′; *Sp.* kä′thēth), *n.* a seaport in SW Spain, on a bay of the Atlantic (**Gulf of Cá′diz**). 122,568 (est. 1963).

Cad·man (kad′mən), *n.* **Charles Wakefield,** 1881–1946, U.S. composer, critic, and organist.

Cad·me·an (kad mē′ən), *adj.* of, pertaining to, or like that of Cadmus. [< L *Cadmē(us)* (< Gk *Kadmeîos* of CADMUS) + -AN]

Cadme′an vic′tory, a victory attained at as great a loss to the victor as to the vanquished.

cad·mi·um (kad′mē əm), *n. Chem.* a white, ductile divalent metallic element resembling tin in appearance: used in plating and in making certain alloys. *Symbol:* Cd; *at. wt.:* 112.41; *at. no.:* 48; *sp. gr.* 8.6 at 20°C. [< NL < L *cadm(ia)* calamine (orig. *Cadmēa terra* < Gk *Kadmeía gê* CADMEAN earth) + -IUM] —**cad′mic,** *adj.*

cad′mium bronze′, an alloy of copper with about 1 percent cadmium.

cad′mium green′, a pigment used in painting, consisting of a mixture of hydrated oxide of chromium with cadmium sulfide, and characterized by its strong green color and slow drying rate.

cad′mium or′ange, a yellow color approaching orange.

cad′mium red′, a pigment used in painting, consisting of cadmium sulfide and cadmium selenide, characterized by its strong red or reddish color, excellent film-forming properties, and slow drying rate.

cad′mium sul′fide, *Chem.* a light yellow or orange, water-insoluble powder, CdS, used chiefly as a pigment in paints, inks, and ceramic glazes.

cad′mium yel′low, a pigment used in painting, consisting of cadmium sulfide and characterized by its strong yellow color and permanence.

Cad·mus (kad′məs), *n.* **Paul,** born 1904, U.S. painter and etcher.

Cad·mus (kad′məs), *n. Class. Myth.* a Phoenician prince who introduced writing to the Greeks and who founded the city of Thebes in the company of five warriors who remained from among a number who had sprung from the dragon's teeth he had planted in the earth. Cf. **Sparti.**

Ca·dog′an tea′pot (kə dug′ən), a lidless teapot that is made from or in imitation of an inverted Chinese wine pot and is filled through the bottom. [perh. named after the 1st Earl of *Cadogan* (d. 1726)]

Ca·dor·na (kə dôr′nə; *It.* kä dôr′nä), *n.* **Count Lu·i·gi** (lo͞o ē′jē), 1850–1928, Italian general: chief of staff 1914–17.

ca·dre (kä′drə; *Mil. usually* kad′rē), *n.* **1.** *Mil.* the key group of officers and enlisted men necessary to establish and train a new military unit. **2.** a group trained or otherwise qualified to form, train, and lead an expanded organization, as a religious or political faction, or a skilled work force: *They hoped to form a cadre of veteran party members. Cadres of construction engineers were sent to underdeveloped countries.* **3.** a member of a cadre; a person qualified to serve in a cadre. **4.** a framework, outline, or scheme: *He gave us the cadre of the project, leaving the details up to us.* [< F: frame < It *quadr(o)* < L *quadr(um)* a square]

Caduceus

ca·du·ce·us (kə do͞o′sē əs, -dyo͞o′-), *n., pl.* **-ce·i** (-sē ī′). **1.** *Class. Myth.* the staff carried by Mercury as messenger of the gods. **2.** a representation of this staff used as an emblem of the medical profession and as the insignia of the U.S. Army Medical Corps. [< L, var. of *cādūceum* < Gk *kārýkeion* (Doric) herald's staff, equiv. to *kâryk-* (s. of *kâryx*) herald + *-eion,* neut. of *-eios* adj. suffix] —**ca·du′ce·an,** *adj.*

ca·du·ci·ty (kə do͞o′si tē, -dyo͞o′-), *n.* **1.** the infirmity or weakness of old age; senility. **2.** frailty; transitoriness: *the caducity of life.* [< F *caducité,* equiv. to *caduc* CADUCOUS + *-ité* -ITY]

ca·du·cous (kə do͞o′kəs, -dyo͞o′-), *adj.* **1.** *Bot.* **a.** tending to fall. **b.** dropping off very early, as leaves; deciduous. **2.** *Zool.* subject to shedding. **3.** transitory; perishable. [< L *cadūcus* destined to fall, perishable, equiv. to *cad(ere)* (to) fall + *-ūcus* adj. suffix]

Cad·wal·la·der (kad wol′ə dər), *n.* a boy's given name.

cae·cil·i·an (sē sil′ē ən), *n.* any wormlike, almost blind, tropical amphibian of the order *Apoda,* certain of which have small scales embedded in the skin. [< L *caecili(a)* a kind of lizard + -AN]

cae·co-, a combining form of **caecum:** *caecotomy.* Also, *esp. before a vowel,* **caec-.**

cae·cum (sē′kəm), *n., pl.* **-ca** (-kə). cecum. —**cae′cal,** *adj.* —**cae′cal·ly,** *adv.*

Cæd·mon (kad′mən), *n.* fl. A.D. c670, Anglo-Saxon religious poet.

Cae·li·an (sē′lē ən), *n.* the southeastern hill of the seven hills of ancient Rome.

Cae·lum (sē′ləm), *n., gen.* **-li** (-lī). *Astron.* the Sculptor's Tool, a small southern constellation between Columba and Eridanus. [< L: engraving tool]

Caen (kän; *Fr.* käN), *n.* a city and the capital of Calvados, in NW France, SW of Le Havre: many Norman buildings destroyed 1944. 95,238 (1962).

Cae·ne·us (sē′nē əs, -no͞os, -nyo͞os), *n. Class. Myth.* an invulnerable Argonaut who was Caenis before Poseidon changed her into a man.

Cae·nis (sē′nis), *n. Class. Myth.* a daughter of Elatus: her request that she become a man was granted by Poseidon after he had violated her. Cf. **Caeneus.**

caeno-, var. of **ceno-**[1]: *Caenozoic.*

cae·no·gen·e·sis (sē′nə jen′i sis, sen′ə-), *n.* cenogenesis. —**cae·no·ge·net·ic** (sē′nō jə net′ik), *adj.* —**cae′no·ge·net′i·cal·ly,** *adv.*

Caen′ stone′, a cream-colored limestone quarried near Caen, France, for use in building.

cae·o·ma (sē ō′mə), *n.* *Bot.* (in fungi) an aecium in which the spores are formed in chains and not enclosed in a peridium. [< Gk *kai(ein)* to burn + -OMA; so named because of its rust color]

Caer·e·mo·ni·a·le E·pis·co·por·um (cher′ə mō′nē ä′lā e pis′kə pôr′ōōm, -pôr′-), *Rom. Cath. Ch.* the liturgical book, used by bishops, containing regulations and prescriptions that are authoritative in matters not covered in the missal or other service books. [L: ceremonial of bishops]

Caer·le·on (kär lē′ən), *n.* a town in S Monmouthshire, in SE Wales: site of ancient Roman fortress, a supposed seat of King Arthur's court. 4184 (1961).

Caer·nar·von (kär när′vən), *n.* **1.** a seaport in and the county seat of Caernarvonshire, in NW Wales, on Menai Strait: 13th-century castle of Edward II. 9225 (1961). **2.** Caernarvonshire. Also, **Carnarvon.**

Caer·nar·von·shire (kär när′vən shēr′, -shər), *n.* a county in NW Wales. 121,194 (1961); 569 sq. mi. *Co. seat:* Caernarvon. Also, **Carnarvonshire.** Also called **Caernarvon, Carnarvon.**

caes·al·pin·i·a·ceous (sez′al pin′ē ā′shəs, ses′-), *adj.* belonging to the *Caesalpiniaceae,* a family of leguminous plants including the honey locust, royal poinciana, Kentucky coffee tree, etc. [< NL *Caesalpini(a)* name of the genus (named after Andrea *Caesalpino* (1519–1603), Italian botanist; see -IA) + -ACEOUS]

Cae·sar (sē′zər), *n.* **1. Ga·ius** (gā′əs) (or **Ca·ius**) (kā′əs) **Julius,** c100–44 B.C., Roman general, statesman, and historian. **2.** a title of the Roman emperors from Augustus to Hadrian, and later of the heirs presumptive. **3.** any emperor. **4.** a tyrant; dictator. **5.** any temporal ruler, in contrast with God; the civil authority. Matt. 22:21. **6.** a boy's given name.

Cae′sar and Cleopa′tra, a comedy (1898) by G. B. Shaw.

Caes·a·re·a (ses′ə rē′ə, sez′-), *n.* **1.** an ancient seaport in NW Israel: Roman capital of Palestine. **2.** ancient name of **Kayseri.**

Cae·sar·e·an (si zâr′ē ən), *adj.* **1.** pertaining to Caesar or the Caesars: *a Caesarean conquest.* —*n.* **2.** (*sometimes l.c.*) See **Caesarean section.** Also, **Cae·sar′i·an, Cesarean, Cesarian.** [< L *Caesare(us)* of CAESAR + -AN]

Caesar′ean sec′tion, (*sometimes l.c.*) an operation by which a fetus is taken from the uterus by cutting through the walls of the abdomen and uterus. Also called **Caesar′ean opera′tion.** [so called because it was supposedly performed at the birth of CAESAR]

Cae·sar·ism (sē′zə riz′əm), *n.* absolute government; imperialism. [CAESAR + -ISM] —**Cae′sar·ist,** *n.*

cae·sa·ro·pap·ism (sē′zə rō pā′piz əm), *n.* **1.** the possession of supreme authority over church and state by one person, often by a secular ruler. **2.** the supremacy of the state over the church in ecclesiastical matters. [CAESAR + -O- + PAPISM] —**cae′sa·ro·pap′ist,** *n., adj.*

cae·si·um (sē′zē əm), *n.* *Chem.* cesium.

caes·pi·tose (ses′pi tōs′), *adj.* cespitose. —**caes′pi·tose′ly,** *adv.*

cae·su·ra (si zhōōr′ə, -zōōr′ə, siz yōōr′ə), *n., pl.* **cae·su·ras, cae·su·rae** (si zhōōr′ē, -zōōr′ē, siz yōōr′ē). **1.** *Pros.* a break, esp. a sense pause, usually near the middle of a verse, and marked in scansion by a double vertical line, as in *know then thyself* ‖ *presume not God to scan.* **2.** *Class. Pros.* a division made by the ending of a word within a foot, or sometimes at the end of a foot, esp. in certain recognized places near the middle of a verse. Also, **cesura.** [< L, equiv. to *caes(us)* cut (ptp. of *caedere*) (*caed-* cut + *-tus* ptp. suffix) + *-ūra* -URE] —**cae·su′ral, cae·su′ric,** *adj.*

C.A.F., 1. cost and freight. **2.** cost, assurance, and freight. Also, **c.a.f.**

ca·fard (KA FAR′), *n.* *French.* profound depression or melancholy.

ca·fé (ka fā′, kə-; *Fr.* KA FĀ′), *n., pl.* **-fés** (-fāz′; *Fr.* -FĀ′). **1.** a restaurant, usually small and unpretentious. **2.** a barroom, cabaret, or night club. **3.** coffee. [< F: lit., COFFEE]

ca·fé au lait (kaf′ā ō lā′, ka fā′; *Fr.* KA FĀ′ ō le′), **1.** hot coffee poured in equal portions with scalded milk. **2.** a light brown color. [< F: lit., coffee with milk]

ca·fé brû·lot (kaf′ā brōō lō′; *Fr.* KA fe′ BRY lō′), *pl.* **ca·fé brû·lots** (kaf′ā brōō lōz′; *Fr.* KA fe′ BRY lō′). an after-dinner drink consisting of black coffee flavored with sugar, lemon and orange rinds, cloves, cinnamon, and brandy, which is ignited and allowed to flame briefly. [< F: burnt brandy coffee]

café′ car′, a railroad car, part of which is used as a diner and part as a lounge, smoker, etc.

ca·fé crème (KA FĀ′ KREM′), *French.* coffee with cream. Also called **ca·fé à la crème** (KA FĀ A LA KREM′).

café′ cur′tain, a short curtain suspended directly downward from a series of rings sliding on a horizontal rod so as to cover the lower and sometimes upper portions of a window.

ca·fé filtre (KA FĀ′ FĒLTRᵊ), *French.* strong, filtered coffee, often flavored with chicory, usually drunk black in a demitasse. Also called **filtre.**

ca·fé noir (KA FĀ′ NWAR′), *French.* black coffee. Also called **ca·fé na·ture** (KA FĀ′ NA TYR′).

ca′fé soci′ety, socialites who regularly frequent fashionable night clubs, resorts, etc.

caf·e·te·ri·a (kaf′i tēr′ē ə), *n.* a restaurant, dining room in a college, etc., in which the patrons wait on themselves, carrying their food to their tables from counters where it is displayed and served. [< AmerSp: coffee shop, equiv. to *café* COFFEE + *-tería* shop]

caf·fa (kaf′ə), *n.* **1.** a silk fabric used in the 16th and 17th centuries. **2.** a painted cotton fabric. [< Ar (dial.) *kaffa, kaffīyah* (Ar *kūfīyah*), after *Al Kufa,* town in Iraq where it was made]

caf·feine (ka fēn′, kaf′ēn, kaf′ē in), *n.* *Chem., Pharm.* a white, crystalline, bitter alkaloid, $C_8H_{10}N_4O_2$, usually derived from coffee or tea: used chiefly in medicine as a stimulant and diuretic. Also, **caf·fei·na** (ka fē′nə). [< F *caféine,* equiv. to *café* COFFEE + *-ine* -INE²] —**caf·fein·ic** (ka fē′nik, kaf′ē in′ik), *adj.* —**caf·fein′ism, caf·fe·ism** (kaf′ē iz′əm), *n.*

caf·tan (kaf′tən, käf tän′), *n.* a long garment having long sleeves and tied at the waist by a girdle, worn under a coat in the Near East. Also, **kaftan.** [< Russ *kaftan* < Turk < Pers *qaftān*] —**caf′taned,** *adj.*

cage (kāj), *n., v.,* **caged, cag·ing.** —*n.* **1.** a boxlike receptacle or enclosure having wires, bars, or the like, for confining and displaying birds or animals. **2.** anything that confines or imprisons; prison. **3.** something like a cage in structure, as for a bank teller. **4.** the car or enclosed platform of an elevator. **5.** *Mining.* an enclosed platform for raising and lowering men and cars in a mine shaft. **6.** any skeleton framework. **7.** *Ordn.* a steel framework for supporting guns. **8.** *Baseball.* a movable backstop for use mainly in batting practice. **9.** a frame with a net attached to it, forming the goal in ice hockey and field hockey. **10.** *Basketball.* the basket. **11.** *Mach.* retainer¹ (def. 3). —*v.t.* **12.** to put or confine in or as in a cage. **13.** *Sports Informal.* to shoot (a puck, basketball, etc.) into the cage so as to score a goal. [ME < OF < L *cavea* birdcage, equiv. to *cav(us)* hollow + *-ea,* fem. of *-eus* adj. suffix] —**cage′less,** *adj.* —**cage′like′,** *adj.*

Cage (kāj), *n.* **John,** born 1912, U.S. composer.

cage·ling (kāj′ling), *n.* a caged bird. [CAGE + -LING¹]

cag·er (kā′jər), *n.* **1.** *Informal.* a basketball player. **2.** *Mining.* a machine for putting cars on or off a cage. [CAGE + -ER¹]

cag·ey (kā′jē), *adj.,* **cag·i·er, cag·i·est.** *Informal.* cautious, wary, or shrewd: *a cagey reply.* Also, **cagy.** [CAGE + -Y¹] —**cag′i·ly,** *adv.* —**cag′i·ness,** *n.*

cage′ zone′ melt′ing, zone melting of a square bar of the material to be purified, done so that the impurities are concentrated at the corners.

Ca·glia·ri (kăl′yə rē; *It.* kä′lyä RĒ′), *n.* **1. Pa·o·lo** (pä′ô lô). See **Veronese, Paolo. 2.** a seaport in S Sardinia. 181,499 (1961).

Ca·glios·tro (kal yō′strō; *It.* kä lyôs′tRô), *n.* **Count A·les·san·dro di** (ä′les sän′dRô dē), (*Giuseppe Balsamo*), 1743–95, Italian adventurer and impostor.

Ca·gou·lard (kag′ōō lär′, kag′ōō lär′; *Fr.* KA gōō lär′), *n., pl.* **-lards** (-lärz′, -lärz′; *Fr.* -lär′). a member of a secret French organization, active from 1932–40, that conspired to overthrow the Third Republic. [< F, equiv. to *cagoule* hood (see COWL) + *-ard* -ARD]

Ca·guas (kä′gwäs), *n.* a city in E central Puerto Rico. 32,015 (1960).

cag·y (kā′jē), *adj.,* **cag·i·er, cag·i·est.** cagey.

ca·hier (ka yā′, kä-; *Fr.* KA yā′), *n., pl.* **-hiers** (-yāz′; *Fr.* -yā′). **1.** *Bookbinding.* a number of sheets of paper or leaves of a book placed together, as for binding. **2.** a report of the proceedings of any body: *A cahier of the committee was presented to the legislature.* **3.** (*italics.*) *French.* **a.** notebook; exercise book; journal. **b.** paperback book. [< F < MF *quaer* gathering (of sheets of a book); see QUIRE]

ca·hill (kā′hil, kā′-), *n.* *Angling.* an artificial fly having a quill body, golden tag, tan-spotted wings and tail, and gray hackle. [? named after its inventor]

ca·hoot (kə hōōt′), *n.* *U.S. Slang.* **1. go cahoots,** to share equally; become partners: *They went cahoots in the establishment of the store.* Also, **go in cahoot with, go in cahoots. 2. in cahoot** or **cahoots, a.** in partnership; in league. **b.** in conspiracy: *in cahoots with the enemy.* [perh. < F *cahute* cabin, hut]

ca·how (kə hou′), *n.* a petrel, *Pterodroma cahow,* of Bermuda, until recently thought to be extinct. [imit.]

Cai·a·phas (kā′ə fəs, kī′-), *n.* a high priest of the Jews from sometime before A.D. 37 who presided at the Sanhedrin that condemned Jesus to death.

Cai′cos Is′lands (kī′kōs). See **Turks and Caicos Islands.**

ca·id (kä ēth′, kīth), *n.* **1.** (in North Africa) a Muslim municipal official or judge. **2.** a Berber chieftain. **3.** an alcaide. Also, **qaid.** [< Sp *caíd* < Ar *qā'id.* See ALCAIDE]

cai·man (kā′mən), *n., pl.* **-mans.** any of several tropical American crocodilians of the genus *Caiman* and allied genera, related to the alligators. Also, **cayman.** [< Sp *caimán* < Carib]

cai′man liz′ard, a crocodilelike lizard, *Dracaena guianensis,* of South America, having powerful jaws for crushing the snails and mussels upon which it feeds.

cain (kān), *n.* **1.** *Scot. and Irish Eng.* rent paid in produce or goods, esp. a percentage of a farm crop. **2.** *Irish Eng. Obs.* a fine; tribute; ransom. [ME *cane* < Celt *cáin* statute, law, rent]

Cain (kān), *n.* **1.** the first son of Adam and Eve, who murdered his brother Abel. Gen. 4. **2.** a murderer. **3. raise Cain,** *Slang.* **a.** become angry or violent. **b.** to behave in a boisterous manner; cause a disturbance. —**Cain′ism,** *n.* —**Cain′ite,** *n.* —**Cain·it·ic** (kā nit′ik), *adj.*

Cain′ and A′bel, *Chiefly Brit. Slang.* table. [rhyming slang]

Caine (kān), *n.* **(Sir Thomas Henry) Hall,** 1853–1931, English novelist.

Cain·gang (kīn′gang′), *n., pl.* **-gangs,** (*esp. collectively*) **-gang. 1.** a member of an Indian people of southern Brazil. **2.** a family of languages spoken by the Caingang. Also, **Kaingang.**

caino-, var. of **ceno-**¹: *Cainozoic.*

Cai·no·zo·ic (kī′nə zō′ik, kā′-), *adj., n.* *Geol.* Cenozoic.

ca·ïque (kä ēk′), *n.* **1.** a long, narrow rowboat used on the Bosporus. **2.** a single-masted sailing vessel used on the eastern Mediterranean Sea, having a sprit mainsail, a square topsail, and two or more other sails. Also, **ca·ique′.** [< F < It *caicc(o)* < Turk *kayık;* r. *caik* < Turk *kayik*]

ça i·ra (SA′ Ē RA′), *French.* it will go on.

caird (kârd; *Scot.* kärd), *n.* *Scot.* **1.** a traveling tinker, esp. a gypsy. **2.** a wandering tramp or vagrant. [< Gael *ceard* tinker; akin to L *cerdo* workman, Gk *kerdō* cunning one]

Caird (kârd), *n.* **Edward,** 1835–1908, Scottish philosopher and theologian.

Caird′ Coast′, a coastal region in Antarctica, E of the Weddell Sea, 23° W and 29° W longitude.

Cai·rene (kī′rēn, kī rēn′), *adj.* **1.** (*sometimes l.c.*) of or pertaining to Cairo, Egypt. —*n.* **2.** a native or resident of Cairo, Egypt. [CAIR(O) + -ENE]

cairn (kârn), *n.* a heap of stones set up as a landmark, monument, tombstone, etc. Also, **carn.** [ME (north) *carn* < Gael: pile of stones; perh. akin to HORN] —**cairn′y,** *adj.*

cairn·gorm (kârn′gôrm′), *n.* *Mineral.* See **smoky quartz.** Also called **Cairn′gorm stone′.** [short for *Cairngorm stone,* i.e., stone from Scottish mountain so named]

Cairns (kârnz), *n.* a seaport in NE Australia. 25,204 (1961).

cairn′ ter′rier, one of a Scottish breed of small, short-legged terriers having a rough coat of any of several solid colors except white. [said to be so called because they frequent areas abounding in cairns]

Cai·ro (kī′rō *for 1;* kâr′ō *for 2, 3*), *n.* **1.** a city in and the capital of the United Arab Republic, in the N part on the E bank of the Nile: wartime conference of Roosevelt, Churchill, and Chiang Kai-shek, November 1943. 3,346,000 (est. 1960). **2.** a city in S Illinois at the confluence of the Mississippi and Ohio rivers. 9348 (1960). **3.** a town in SW Georgia. 7427 (1960).

cais·son (kā′sən, -son), *n.* **1.** a structure used in underwater work, consisting of an airtight chamber, open at the bottom and containing air under sufficient pressure to exclude the water. **2.** a boatlike structure used as a gate for a dock or the like. **3.** *Naut.* **a.** Also called **camel.** a float for raising a sunken vessel, sunk beside the vessel, made fast to it, and then pumped out to make it buoyant. **b.** a watertight structure built against a damaged area of a hull to render the hull watertight; cofferdam. **4.** (formerly) a wooden chest containing bombs or explosives, used as a mine; ammunition chest. **5.** a two-wheeled ammunition wagon, esp. for the artillery. **6.** Also, **cassoon.** *Archit.* coffer (def. 4). [< F, equiv. to *caisse* box (see CASE²) + *-on* aug. suffix] —**cais′soned,** *adj.*

cais′son disease′, *Pathol.* a condition marked by paralysis, pain, etc., developed in coming from an atmosphere of high pressure, as in a caisson, to air of ordinary pressure, and caused by the formation in the blood of bubbles of nitrogen released from solution; bends; nitrogen narcosis.

Caith·ness (kāth′nes, kāth nes′), *n.* a county in NE Scotland. 27,345 (1961); 686 sq. mi. *Co. seat:* Wick.

cai·tiff (kā′tif), *Archaic.* —*n.* **1.** a base, despicable person. —*adj.* **2.** base; despicable. [ME *caitif* < AF < L *captīv(us)* CAPTIVE]

Cait·lin (kāt′lin), *n.* a girl's given name, Irish form of **Cathleen, Kathleen.**

Ca·ius (kā′əs), *n.* **Saint,** died A.D. 296, pope 283–296. Also, **Gaius.**

caj·e·put (kaj′ə pət, -pōōt′), *n.* cajuput.

caj·e·put·ol (kaj′ə pə tōl′, -tôl′, -tol′), *n.* *Chem.* cineole. Also, **caj·e·put·ole** (kaj′ə pə tōl′), **caj′u·put·ol′.** [CAJEPUT + -OL²]

ca·jole (kə jōl′), *v.t., v.i.,* **-joled, -jol·ing.** to persuade by flattery or promises; wheedle; coax. [< F *cajol(er)* (to) cajole or chatter like a jaybird, appar., deriv. of **cajole* birdcage (< LL *caveol(a)* < L *cave(a)* CAGE + *-ola* dim. suffix) + *-er* inf. suffix] —**ca·jole′ment,** *n.* —**ca·jol′er,** *n.* —**ca·jol′ing·ly,** *adv.*

ca·jol·er·y (kə jō′lə rē), *n., pl.* **-er·ies.** persuasion by flattery or promises; wheedling; coaxing. [< F *cajolerie.* See CAJOLE, -ERY]

Ca·jun (kā′jən), *n.* **1.** *Dial.* Acadian. **2.** the French dialect of the Acadians. [aph. var. of ACADIAN; cf. *Injun* for INDIAN]

caj·u·put (kaj′ə pət, -pōōt′), *n.* **1.** an Australian, myrtaceous tree or shrub, *Melaleuca Leucadendron,* having lanceolate, aromatic leaves. **2.** *Pharm.* a green, odorous oil distilled from the leaves of this tree, used for skin conditions, toothaches, and various intestinal disorders. Also, **cajeput, kajeput.** Also called **paper bush, punk tree.** [< Malay *kaju-puteh,* equiv. to *kaju* (sp. var. of *kayu*) wood + *puteh* white]

ca·ju′ rains′ (kə zhōō′), light showers occurring in northeast Brazil during October. [< BrazPg *chuvas de cajú,* lit., showers of cashew, so called because occurring at the time of the blossoming of the cashew tree]

cake (kāk), *n., v.,* **caked, cak·ing.** —*n.* **1.** a sweet, baked, breadlike food, made with or without shortening, and usually containing flour, sugar, baking powder or soda, eggs, and liquid flavoring. **2.** a flat, thin mass of bread, esp. unleavened bread. **3.** pancake; griddle-cake. **4.** a shaped or molded mass of other food: *a fish cake.* **5.** a shaped or compressed mass: *a cake of soap; a cake of ice.* **6. a piece of cake,** something easily done: *He thought his first solo flight a piece of cake.* **7. take the cake,** *Informal.* to surpass all others; be extraordinary or unusual: *His arrogance takes the cake.* —*v.t.* **8.** to form into a crust or compact mass. —*v.i.* **9.** to become formed into a crust or compact mass. [ME < Scand; cf. Icel *kaka;* akin to ME *kechel* little cake, G *Kuchen;* see COOKY]

caked′ breast′, *Pathol.* a painful hardening of one or more lobules of a lactating breast, caused by stagnation of milk in the secreting ducts and accumulation of blood in the expanded veins. Also called **stagnation mastitis.**

cake′ eat′er, *Slang.* an effeminate lover of ease and pleasure.

cake′ flour′, finely ground wheat flour.

cake′ make′-up, pancake (def. 3).

cakes′ and ale′, 1. the good things of life; material pleasures; enjoyment: *Their thoughts were only of cakes and ale.* **2.** (*caps., italics.*) a novel (1930) by W. Somerset Maugham.

cake·walk (kāk′wôk′), *n.* **1.** a promenade or march, of American Negro origin, in which the couples with the most intricate or eccentric steps receive cakes as prizes. **2.** a dance based on this promenade. **3.** music for this dance. —*v.i.* **4.** to walk or dance in or as in a cakewalk. [CAKE + WALK] —**cake′walk′er,** *n.*

cak·ra (chuk′rə), *n.* *Yoga.* any of the six points along the spine supposed to contain certain powers, personified by gods and able to be released through the proper exercises. Also, **chakra.** [< Skt: lit., wheel]

cak·ra·var·tin (chuk′rə vär′tin), *n.* *Indian Philosophy.* an ideal universal, enlightened ruler, under whom the world exists in justice and peace. Also, **chakravartin.** [< Skt, equiv. to *cakera* (see CAKRA) + *vartin* he who turns, deriv. of *vartate* he turns]

Cal (kal), *n.* a boy's given name, form of **Calvin.**

Cal., 1. California. **2.** *Old Physics.* calorie (def. 1b).

cal., 1. caliber. **2.** *Old Physics.* calorie (def. 1a).

Cal·a·bar (kal′ə bär′, kal′ə bär′), *n.* **1.** a river in SE Nigeria. ab. 70 mi. long. **2.** a seaport near the mouth of this river. 46,705 (1953).

Cal′abar bean′, the violently poisonous seed of a fabaceous African climbing plant, *Physostigma venenosum,* the active principle of which is physostigmine. [named after CALABAR, Nigeria]

cal·a·bash (kal′ə bash′), *n.* **1.** any of various gourds, esp. the fruit of the bottle gourd, *Lagenaria Siceraria.* **2.** any of the plants bearing them. **3.** the fruit of a bignoniaceous tree, *Crescentia Cujete,* of tropical America. **4.** Also called **cal′abash tree′.** the tree itself. **5.** the dried, hollow shell of the fruit of the calabash, used as a container or the like. **6.** a bottle, kettle, tobacco-pipe bowl, etc., made from it. **7.** *U.S.* a gourd used as a rattle, drum, etc., esp by Indians. [< MF *calabasse* < Sp *calabaz(a)* < Catalan *carabaça* < Ar *qar'ah yābisah* gourd (that is) dry]

ca·la′ba tree′ (kə lä′bə), an evergreen tree, *Calophyllum antillanum,* of the West Indies, having bright, shiny, leathery leaves and fragrant, white flowers. Also called **Maria tree, Santa Maria tree.** [< Sp < Carib]

cal·a·ba·zil·la (kal′ə bə zē′ə), *n.* a prostrate vine, *Cucurbita foetidissima,* of the south and central U.S., having yellow flowers and smooth, orange-shaped, green and yellow fruit and growing in sandy soil. Also called **Missouri gourd, wild pumpkin.** [< MexSp *calabacilla* < Sp: squirting cucumber, dim. of *calabaza;* see CALABASH]

cal·a·boose (kal′ə bo͞os′, kal′ə bo͞os′), *n.* *U.S. Informal.* jail; lockup. [< Creole F, alter. of Sp *calabozo* dungeon < ?]

cal·a·bra·sel·la (kal′ə brə zel′ə), *n.* a card game for three persons that is played with a 40-card pack made by removing the eights, nines, and tens from a regular 52-card pack. [< It *calabresella,* equiv. to *calabres(e)* (*Calabr(ia)* CALABRIA + *-ese* -ESE) + *-ella* dim. suffix < L]

Ca·la·bri·a (kə lā′brē ə; *It.* kä lä′bʀyä), *n.* **1.** a region in S Italy. 2,045,215 (1961); 5828 sq. mi. *Cap.:* Reggio Calabria. **2.** an ancient district at the extreme SE part of the Italian peninsula. —**Ca·la′bri·an,** *n., adj.*

ca·la·di·um (kə lā′dē əm), *n.* any araceous plant of the genus *Caladium,* mostly herbs of the American tropics, cultivated for their variegated, colorful leaves. [< NL < Malay *kaladi* araceous plant]

Ca·lah (kā′lə), *n.* Biblical name of **Kalakh.**

Ca·lais (kal′ā, kal′is *for 1,* kal′is *for 2; for 1 also Fr.* ka le′), *n.* **1.** a seaport in N France, on the Strait of Dover: the French port nearest England. 70,707 (1962). **2.** a town in E Maine. 4223 (1960).

Ca·lak·mul (kä′läk mo͞ol′), *n.* a ruined Mayan city in SE Mexico.

Ca·la·ma (kä lä′mä), *n.* a city in N Chile. 12,955 (1950).

cal·a·man·co (kal′ə maŋ′kō), *n., pl.* **-cos** for 2. **1.** a glossy woolen fabric checkered or brocaded in the warp so that the pattern shows on one side only, much used in the 18th century. **2.** a garment made from this fabric. Also, **calimanco.** [?]

cal·a·man·der (kal′ə man′dər), *n.* the hard wood of a tree, *Diospyros quaesita,* of Ceylon and India, used for cabinetwork. [metathetic var. of COROMANDEL]

cal·a·mar·y (kal′ə mer′ē, -mə rē), *n., pl.* **-mar** (-mär). a squid, esp. of the genus *Loligo.* [< L *calamāri(us)* pertaining to a writing reed. See CALAMUS, -ARY]

cal·a·mine (kal′ə mīn′, -min), *n.* **1.** a pink, water-insoluble powder consisting of zinc oxide and about 0.5 % ferric oxide, used in ointments, lotions, or the like, for the treatment of inflammatory conditions of the skin. **2.** *Mineral.* hemimorphite. **3.** *Chiefly Brit.* smithsonite (def. 1). [< ML *calamīn(a),* unexplained alter. of L *cadmia* CADMIUM]

cal′amine brass′, an alloy of zinc carbonate and copper, formerly used to imitate gold.

cal·a·mint (kal′ə mint), *n.* any labiate plant of the genus *Satureja,* esp. *S. Calaminthe* and *S. Nepeta.* [m. (by assoc. with MINT²) of ME *calament* < ML *calamentum* < L *calaminth(a)* < Gk *kalaminthē*]

cal·a·mite (kal′ə mīt′), *n.* a Paleozoic fossil plant. [< NL *Calamīte(s)* name of the genus < Gk *kalamītēs* reedlike. See CALAMUS, -ITE¹] —**cal·a·mi·te·an** (kal′ə mī′tē ən), *adj.* —**ca·lam·i·toid** (kə lam′i toid′), *adj.*

ca·lam·i·tous (kə lam′i təs), *adj.* causing or involving calamity; disastrous: *a calamitous defeat.* [CALAMIT(Y) + -OUS] —**ca·lam′i·tous·ly,** *adv.* —**ca·lam′i·tous·ness,** *n.*

ca·lam·i·ty (kə lam′i tē), *n., pl.* **-ties.** **1.** grievous affliction; adversity; misery: *the calamity of war.* **2.** a great misfortune; disaster. [late ME *calamite* < MF < L *calamitāt-* (s. of *calamitās*), perh. akin to *incolumitās* safety]
—**Syn. 1.** distress, trouble, hardship. **2.** reverse, blow, catastrophe, cataclysm; mischance, mishap. See **disaster.**

Calam′ity Jane′, (*Martha Jane Canary Burke*) 1852?–1903, U.S. frontierswoman.

cal·a·mon·din (kal′ə mun′dən), *n.* **1.** a small citrus tree, *Citrus mitis,* of the Philippines. **2.** the small, tart, mandarinlike fruit of this tree. Also called **cal′amondin or′ange.** [< Tagalog *kalamunding*]

cal·a·mus (kal′ə məs), *n., pl.* **-mi** (-mī′). **1.** the sweet flag, *Acorus Calamus.* **2.** its aromatic root. **3.** any palm of the genus *Calamus,* yielding rattan, canes, etc. **4.** the hollow base of a feather; a quill. See illus. under **feather.** [< L < Gk *kálamos* reed, stalk]

Ca·lan·dra (kə lan′drə), *n.* a girl's given name.

Ca·lan·tha (kə lan′thə), *n.* a girl's given name.

Ca·la·pan (kä′lä pän′), *n.* a seaport on NE Mindoro, in the central Philippines. 33,060 (1960).

ca·lash (kə lash′), *n.* **1.** Also, **calèche.** a light, two-horse carriage having four low wheels, inside seats for four passengers, an outside seat for the driver, and, usually, a folding top. **2.** a folding top of a carriage. **3.** calèche (def. 1). **4.** a bonnet that folds back like the top of a calash, worn by women in the 18th century. [< F *calèche* < G *Kalesche* < Czech *kolesa* carriage, lit., something with wheels; see WHEEL]

cal·a·thi·form (kal′ə thə fôrm′, kə lath′ə-), *adj.* cup-shaped; concave. [*calathi-* (comb. form of CALATHUS) + -FORM]

cal·a·thus (kal′ə thəs), *n., pl.* **-thi** (-thī′). kalathos. [< L < Gk *kálathos*]

cal·a·ver·ite (kal′ə vâr′īt), *n.* a silver-white mineral, gold telluride, $AuTe_2$, containing a little silver: an ore of gold. [*Calaver(as),* county in California where first found + -ITE¹]

calc-, 1. a combining form of **calcareous:** *calc-tufa.* **2.** var. of **calci-** before a vowel: *calcic.* [< G *Kalk* lime < L *calc-* (s. of *calx*) lime(stone); see CALX, CHALK]

cal·ca·ne·um (kal kā′nē əm), *n., pl.* **-ne·a** (-nē ə). calcaneus. [short for L (*os*) *calcāneum* (bone) of the heel, equiv. to *calc-* (s. of *calx*) *heel* + *-āneum,* neut. of *-āneus;* see -AN, -EOUS]

cal·ca·ne·us (kal kā′nē əs), *n., pl.* **-ne·i** (-nē ī′). **1.** (in man) the largest tarsal bone, forming the prominence of the heel. **2.** the corresponding bone in other vertebrates. Also, **calcaneum.** [< LL: heel, n. use of *calcāneus* of the heel; see CALCANEUM] —**cal·ca′ne·al, cal·ca′ne·an,** *adj.*

cal·car¹ (kal′kär), *n., pl.* **cal·car·i·a** (kal kâr′ē ə). *Biol.* a spur or spurlike process. [< L: spur, equiv. to *calc-* (s. of *calx*) heel + *-ar* -AR²]

cal·car² (kal′kär), *n., pl.* **cal·car·i·a** (kal kâr′ē ə). *Glassmaking.* a reverberatory furnace for preparing frit. [< It *calcar(a)* < LL *calcāria* lime-kiln < L *calc-* lime (see CHALK) + *-āria* -ARY]

cal·ca·rate (kal′kə rāt′), *adj.* *Biol.* having a calcar or calcaria; spurred. Also, **cal′ca·rat′ed.** [CALCAR¹ + -ATE¹]

Calcarate foot

cal·car·e·ous (kal kâr′ē əs), *adj.* of, containing, or like calcium carbonate; chalky: *calcareous earth.* [var. of *calcarious* < L *calcārius* of lime; see CALX, -ARIOUS] —**cal·car′e·ous·ly,** *adv.* —**cal·car′e·ous·ness,** *n.*

calcar′eous tu′fa, tufa (def. 1).

cal·ca·rif·er·ous (kal′kə rif′ər əs), *adj.* *Biol.* bearing a spur or spurs. [< L *calcar* a spur + -I- + -FEROUS]

calced (kalst), *adj.* wearing shoes; shod (applied chiefly to members of certain religious orders). Cf. **discalced.** [< L *calc(eus)* shoe + -ED³]

cal·ce·i·form (kal′sē ə fôrm′, kal sē′-), *adj.* *Bot.* calceolate. [< L *calce(us)* shoe, half-boot + -I- + -FORM]

cal·ce·o·lar·i·a (kal′sē ə lâr′ē ə), *n.* any plant of the genus *Calceolaria,* often cultivated for its slipperlike flowers. [< L *calceol(us)* small shoe (*calce(us)* shoe + *-olus* dim. suffix) + -ARIA]

cal·ce·o·late (kal′sē ə lāt′), *adj.* *Bot.* having the form of a shoe or slipper, as the labellum of certain orchids. [< L *calceol(us)* a small shoe (*calce(us)* a shoe + *-olus* dim. suffix) -ATE¹]

cal·ces (kal′sēz), *n.* a pl. of **calx.**

Cal·chas (kal′kəs), *n.* *Class. Myth.* the chief soothsayer of the Greeks in the Trojan War.

calci-, a combining form of **calcium,** used with the meaning "calcium salt" or "calcite" in the formation of compound words: *calciferous.* Also, *esp. before a vowel,* **calc-.** [< L *calc-* (s. of *calx* lime; see CHALK) + -I-]

cal·cic (kal′sik), *adj.* pertaining to or containing lime or calcium. [CALC- + -IC]

cal·ci·cole (kal′sə kōl′), *n.* any plant capable of thriving in calcareous soil. Also called **calciphile.** [back formation from *calcicolous* growing in limy earth. See CALCI-, -COLOUS] —**cal·cic·o·lous** (kal sik′ə ləs), *adj.*

cal·cif·er·ol (kal sif′ə rōl′, -rôl′, -rol′), *n.* *Biochem.* a fat-soluble, crystalline, unsaturated alcohol, $C_{28}H_{43}OH$, occurring in milk, fish-liver oils, etc., produced by ultraviolet irradiation of ergosterol, and used as a dietary supplement, as in fortified milk, and medicinally in the prevention and treatment of rickets and other hypocalcemic disorders. Also called **ergocalciferol, vitamin D_2.** [CALCIF(EROUS + ERGOST)EROL]

cal·cif·er·ous (kal sif′ər əs), *adj.* *Chem.* **1.** forming salts of calcium, esp. calcium carbonate. **2.** containing calcium carbonate. [CALCI- + -FEROUS]

cal·cif·ic (kal sif′ik), *adj.* *Zool., Anat.* making or converting into salt of lime or chalk. [CALCI- + -FIC]

cal·ci·fi·ca·tion (kal′sə fə kā′shən), *n.* **1.** a changing into lime. **2.** *Physiol.* the deposition of lime or insoluble salts of calcium and magnesium, as in a tissue. **3.** *Anat., Geol.* a calcified formation. **4.** a soil process in which the surface soil is supplied with calcium in such a way that the soil colloids are always close to saturation. **5.** act of calcifying; state of being calcified: *As the conflict developed there was an increasing calcification of their respective attitudes.* [CALCIFIC + -ATION]

cal·ci·fuge (kal′sə fyo͞oj′), *n.* any plant incapable of thriving in calcareous soil. Also, **calciphobe.** [CALCI- + -FUGE] —**cal·cif·u·gous** (kal sif′yə gəs), *adj.*

cal·ci·fy (kal′sə fī′), *v.t., v.i.,* **-fied, -fy·ing.** **1.** *Physiol.* to make or become calcareous or bony; harden by the deposit of calcium salts. **2.** to make or become rigid, intransigent, unadaptable, or inflexible, as in an intellectual or political position. [CALCI- + -FY]

cal·ci·mine (kal′sə mīn′, -min), *n., v.,* **-mined, -min·ing.** —*n.* **1.** a white or tinted wash for walls, ceilings, etc. —*v.t.* **2.** to wash or cover with calcimine. Also, **kalsomine.** [CALCI- + (KALSO)MINE] —**cal′ci·min′er,** *n.*

cal·cine (kal′sīn, -sin), *v.t., v.i.,* **-cined, -cin·ing.** **1.** to convert or be converted into calx by heat. **2.** to burn to a friable substance; roast. **3.** to oxidize by heating. **4.** to frit. [ME < ML *calcināre* to heat, orig. used by alchemists] —**cal·cin·a·ble** (kal′sə nə bəl), *adj.* —**cal·ci·na·tion** (kal′sə nā′shən), *n.* —**cal·ci·na·tor** (kal′sə nā′tər), *n.* —**cal·cin·a·to·ry** (kal sin′ə tôr′ē, -tōr′ē, kal′sin ə-), *adj., n.*

cal′cined bar′y·ta, *Chem.* baryta (def. 1).

cal·cin·er (kal sī′nər, kal′sī-), *n.* **1.** one who or that which calcines. **2.** an industrial furnace that processes material by calcination. [CALCINE + -ER¹]

cal·ci·phile (kal′sə fīl′), *n.* calcicole. [CALCI- + -PHILE] —**cal·ci·phil·ic** (kal′sə fil′ik), **cal·ciph·i·lous** (kal sif′ə ləs), *adj.*

cal·ci·phobe (kal′sə fōb′), *n.* calcifuge. [CALCI- + -PHOBE] —**cal′ci·pho′bic, cal·ciph·o·bous** (kal sif′ə bəs), *adj.*

cal·cite (kal′sīt), *n.* one of the commonest minerals, calcium carbonate, $CaCO_3$, occurring in a great variety of crystalline forms and a major constituent of limestone, marble, and chalk; calc-spar. [CALC- + -ITE¹] —**cal·cit·ic** (kal sit′ik), *adj.*

cal·ci·um (kal′sē əm), *n.* *Chem.* a silver-white divalent metal, occurring combined in limestone, chalk, gypsum, etc. *Symbol:* Ca; *at. wt.:* 40.08; *at. no.:* 20; *sp. gr.:* 1.52 at 20°C. [CALC- + -IUM]

cal′cium ar′senate, *Chem.* a white, slightly water-soluble, poisonous powder, $Ca_3(AsO_4)_2$, used as an insecticide and as a germicide.

cal′cium car′bide, *Chem.* a grayish-black, lumpy, crystalline powder, CaC_2, usually derived from coke or anthracite by reaction with limestone or quicklime: used chiefly for the generation of acetylene, which it yields upon decomposing in water. Also called **carbide.**

cal′cium car′bonate, *Chem.* a white, crystalline, water-insoluble, tasteless powder, $CaCO_3$, occurring in nature in various forms, as calcite, chalk, and limestone: used chiefly in dentifrices, polishes, and in the manufacture of lime and cement.

cal′cium chlo′ride, *Chem.* a white, lumpy, deliquescent solid, $CaCl_2$, usually derived from calcium carbonate by reaction with hydrochloric acid, or as a by-product of various commercial processes: used chiefly as a drying agent, preservative, and for preventing dust.

cal′cium cyan′amide, *Chem.* a gray-black, often lumpy, powder, CaNCN, unstable in water, obtained by heating calcium carbide and nitrogen: used chiefly as a fertilizer, as an herbicide, and as an intermediate in the synthesis of nitrogen compounds; cyanamide.

cal′cium cyc′la·mate (sik′lə māt′, sī′klə-), *Chem.* a white, crystalline, water-soluble, powder, $(C_6H_{11}NHSO_3)_2Ca{\cdot}2H_2O$, used chiefly as a sweetening agent in soft drinks and in low calorie or diabetic diets when sodium is restricted. Also called **cal′cium cy·clo·hex·yl·sul·fa·mate** (sī′klō hek′səl sul′fə māt′, sī′-). Cf. **sodium cyclamate.**

cal′cium hydrox′ide, *Chem.* See **slaked lime.** Also called **cal′cium hy′drate.**

cal′cium light′, a brilliant white light produced by heating lime to incandescence in an oxyhydrogen or other hot flame; limelight. Also called **oxycalcium light.**

cal′cium ni′trate, *Chem.* a white, deliquescent solid, $Ca(NO_3)_2$, used chiefly in the manufacture of fertilizers, fireworks, matches, and explosives. Also called **Norwegian saltpeter.**

cal′cium ox′ide, *Chem.* lime¹ (def. 1).

cal′cium oxychlo′ride. See **bleaching powder.**

cal′cium perman′ganate, *Chem.* a violet, crystalline deliquescent solid, $Ca(MnO_4)_2{\cdot}4H_2O$, used chiefly as a disinfectant and as a deodorizer. Also called **acerdol.**

cal′cium phos′phate, *Chem.* any of several phosphates of calcium occurring naturally in some rocks and in animal bones, used in medicine, industry, etc.

cal′cium pro′pionate, *Chem.* a white, water-soluble powder, $Ca(CH_3CH_2COO)_2$, used in bakery products to inhibit the growth of fungi.

cal′cium sul′fide, *Chem.* a yellow to light-gray, slightly water-soluble powder, CaS, having the odor of rotten eggs when moist: used chiefly in the preparation of luminous paint, hydrogen sulfide, and as a depilatory in cosmetics. Also called **hepar calcis.**

calc-sin·ter (kalk′sin′tər), *n.* *Mineral.* travertine. [< G *Kalksinter.* See CALC-, SINTER]

calc-spar (kalk′spär′), *n.* calcite. Also, **calc′spar′.** [< Sw *kalk(spat)* calc-spar. See CALC-, SPAR³]

calc-tu·fa (kalk′to͞o′fə), *n.* tufa (def. 1). Also, **calc-tuff** (kalk′tuf′). [CALC- + TUFA]

cal·cu·la·ble (kal′kyə lə bəl), *adj.* **1.** determinable by calculation or computation; ascertainable: *This map was designed so that distances by road are easily calculable.* **2.** capable of being counted on; reliable; dependable. [< L *calculā(re)* (to) reckon + -BLE] —**cal′cu·la·bil′i·ty,** *n.* —**cal′cu·la·bly,** *adv.*

Cal·cu·graph (kal kyo͞o′lə graf′, -gräf′), *n.* *Trademark.* a meter on a telephone switchboard for recording the duration of a telephone call.

cal·cu·late (kal′kyə lāt′), *v.,* **-lat·ed, -lat·ing.** —*v.t.* **1.** to ascertain by mathematical methods; compute: *to calculate the velocity of light.* **2.** to determine by reasoning, common sense, or practical experience; estimate; evaluate; gauge. **3.** to make suitable or fit for a purpose; adapt (usually used passively and with an infinitive): *His remarks were calculated to inspire confidence.* **4.** *Chiefly Northern U.S.* **a.** to think; guess. **b.** to intend; plan. —*v.i.* **5.** to make a computation; form an estimate. **6.** to count or rely (usually fol. by *on* or *upon*): *They calculated on good weather.* [< L *calculāt(us)* reckoned (ptp. of *calculare*), equiv. to *calcul(us)* pebble (see CALCULUS) + *-ātus* -ATE¹]
—**Syn. 1.** count, figure, cast, estimate, weigh.

cal·cu·lat·ed (kal′kyə lā′tid), *adj.* **1.** arrived at by mathematical calculation; ascertained or determined mathematically. **2.** carefully thought out or planned. [CALCULATE + -ED²] —**cal′cu·lat′ed·ly,** *adv.*

cal′culated risk′, a chance of failure, the probability of which is estimated before some action is undertaken.

cal·cu·lat·ing (kal′kyə lā′ting), *adj.* **1.** capable of performing calculations, esp. arithmetical calculations: *a calculating machine.* **2.** shrewd; cautious: *a wise and calculating businessman.* **3.** selfishly scheming: *a cold and calculating woman.* [CALCULATE + -ING²] —**cal′cu·lat′ing·ly,** *adv.*

cal′culating machine′, calculator (def. 2).

cal·cu·la·tion (kal′kyə lā′shən), *n.* **1.** the act or process of calculating; computation. **2.** the result or product of calculating: *His calculations agree with ours.* **3.** an estimate based on the various facts in a case; forecast: *His calculation of the cost of building a new house proved quite accurate.* **4.** forethought; prior or careful planning. **5.** scheming selfishness. [< L *calculātiōn-* (s. of *calculātiō* reckoning). See CALCULATE, -ION] —**cal·cu·la·tive** (kal′kyə lā′tiv, -lə tiv), **cal′cu·la′tion·al, cal′cu·la·to′ry,** *adj.*
—**Syn. 1.** figuring, reckoning, estimation. **4.** circumspection, caution, wariness. See **prudence.**

cal·cu·la·tor (kal′kyə lā′tər), *n.* **1.** a person who calculates or computes. **2.** Also called **calculating machine.** a machine that performs mathematical operations mechanically or electronically. **3.** a person who operates a calculating machine. **4.** a set of tables that facilitates calculation. [< L; see CALCULATE, -OR²]

cal·cu·lous (kal′kyə ləs), *adj.* *Pathol.* characterized by the presence of calculus, or stone. [< L *calculōs(us),* equiv. to *calcul(us)* small stone (see CALCULUS) + *-ōsus* -OUS]

cal·cu·lus (kal′kyə ləs), *n., pl.* **-li** (-lī′), **-lus·es.** **1.** *Math.* a method of calculation, esp. one of several highly systematic methods of treating problems by a special system of algebraic notations, as differential, integral, or infinitesimal calculus. **2.** *Pathol.* a stone, or concretion, found in the gall bladder, kidneys, or other parts of the body. [< L: pebble, small stone (used in reckoning), equiv. to *calc-* (s. of *calx* stone) + *-ulus* -ULE]

cal′culus of fi′nite dif′ferences, *Math.* the branch of mathematics dealing with the application of techniques similar to those of differential and integral calculus to discrete rather than continuous quantities.

cal′culus of pleas′ure. See **hedonic calculus.**

cal′culus of varia′tions, *Math.* the branch of mathematics that deals with the problem of finding a curve or surface that maximizes or minimizes a given expression, usually with several restrictions placed on the desired curve.

Cal·cut·ta (kal kut′ə), *n.* **1.** a seaport in and the capital of West Bengal state, in E India, on the Hooghly River: former capital of British India. 2,927,300 (1961). **2.** Also called **Calcut′ta pool′.** (in golf) a form of pool at club competitions in which gamblers bid for participating golfers in an auction, the proceeds from which are put into a pool for distribution according to a prearranged scale of percentages.

cal·dar·i·um (kal dâr′ē əm), *n., pl.* **-dar·i·a** (-dâr′ē ə). (in an ancient Roman bath) a room having a hot bath. [< L: n. use of neut. of *caldārius* of warming, equiv. to *cal(i)d(us)* warm (*cal(ēre)* (to) be warm + *-idus* -ID[4]) + *-ārius* -ARY]

Cal′de·cott award′ (kôl′də kət), an annual award in the U.S. for an outstanding illustrated juvenile book. [named after Randolph *Caldecott* (1846–86), English illustrator]

Cal·der (kôl′dər), *n.* **Alexander,** 1898–1976, U.S. sculptor: originator of mobiles.

cal·de·ra (kal der′ə; *Sp.* käl de′rä), *n., pl.* **-de·ras** (-der′əz; *Sp.* -de′räs). a large, basinlike depression resulting from the explosion or collapse of the center of a volcano. [< Sp *Caldera,* name of a crater on Canary Islands, lit., cauldron < LL *caldāria,* n. use of fem. of *caldārius* of warming; see CALDARIUM]

Cal·de·rón de la Bar·ca (kal′dər ən del′ə bär′kə; *Sp.* käl′de rôn′ de lä bär′kä), **Pe·dro** (pā′drō, ped′rō; *Sp.* pe′thrō), 1600–81, Spanish dramatist and poet.

Cal·do·ra (kal dōr′ə, -dôr′ə), *n.* a girl's given name.

cal·dron (kôl′drən), *n.* cauldron.

Cald·well (kôld′wel, -wəl), *n.* **1. Erskine,** born 1903, U.S. novelist. **2.** a city in W Idaho. 12,230 (1960). **3.** a town in NE New Jersey. 6942 (1960).

Ca·leb (kā′ləb), *n.* **1.** a Hebrew leader, sent as a spy into the land of Canaan. Num. 13:6. **2.** a boy's given name.

Ca·leb·ite (kā′lə bīt′), *n.* **1.** a member of a tribe descended from Caleb. —*adj.* **2.** of or pertaining to the Calebites. [CALEB + -ITE[1]]

ca·lèche (kA lesh′), *n., pl.* **-lèches** (-lesh′). **1.** Also, **calash.** (in Quebec, Canada) a light, two-wheeled, one-horse vehicle, usually with a folding top, accommodating two passengers and having a seat on the splashboard for a driver. **2.** calash (def. 1). [< F; see CALASH]

Cal·e·do·ni·a (kal′i dō′nē ə), *n.* **1.** *Chiefly Literary.* Scotland. **2.** a town in SE Minnesota. 2563 (1960). **3.** a girl's given name.

Cal·e·do·ni·an (kal′i dō′nē ən), *n.* **1.** a native or inhabitant of Caledonia. —*adj.* **2.** of or pertaining to Caledonia. [CALEDONI(A) + -AN]

Caledo′nian Canal′, a canal in N Scotland, extending NE from the Atlantic to the North Sea. 60½ mi. long.

calef., (in prescriptions) warmed. [< L *calefactus*]

cal·e·fa·cient (kal′ə fā′shənt), *n.* **1.** *Med.* a substance, as mustard, which produces a sensation of heat when applied to the body. —*adj.* **2.** heating; warming. [< L *calefacient-* (s. of *calefaciēns,* prp. of *calefacere* to make warm), equiv. to *cale-* warm (s. of *calēre* to be warm) + *-facient-* -FACIENT]

cal·e·fac·tion (kal′ə fak′shən), *n.* **1.** act of heating. **2.** a heated state. [< L *calefactiōn-* (s. of *calefactiō*) a making warm, equiv. to *cale-* warm (s. of *calēre* to be warm) + *factiōn-* a making; see FACTION] —**cal′e·fac′tive,** *adj.*

cal·e·fac·to·ry (kal′ə fak′tə rē), *adj., n., pl.* **-ries.** —*adj.* **1.** serving to heat. —*n.* **2.** a heated parlor or sitting room in a monastery. [< L *calefactōri(us)* having a warming or heating power, equiv. to *calefact(us)* made warm or hot, heated (ptp. of *calefacere* to make warm) + *-ōrius* -ORY[1]]

cal·en·dar (kal′ən dər), *n.* **1.** any of various systems of reckoning time, esp. with reference to the beginning, length, and divisions of the year: *the Aztec calendar.* Cf. **Gregorian calendar, Julian calendar. 2.** a tabular arrangement of the days of each month and week in a year. **3.** a list or register, esp. one arranged chronologically, as a list of the cases to be tried in a court. **4.** a list, in the order to be considered, of bills, resolutions, etc., brought before a legislative body. **5.** *Obs.* a guide or example. —*v.t.* **6.** to enter in a calendar; register. Also, **kalendar.** [< L *calendār(ium)* account book, equiv. to *Calend(ae)* CALENDS (when debts were due) + *-ārium* -AR[2]; r. ME *calender* < AF] —**ca·len·dri·cal** (kə len′dri kəl), **ca·len′dric, cal·en·dar·i·al** (kal′ən dâr′ē əl), **cal·en·dar·i·an** (kal′ən dâr′ē ən), **cal·en·dar·ic** (kal′ən dar′ik), *adj.*

cal′endar art′, a type of tritely sentimental, picturesque, or vulgar picture commonly used on commercial calendars.

cal′endar clock′, a clock that indicates date of the month, day of the week, etc., as well as the time. It sometimes indicates the phases of the moon and other periodical data.

cal′endar day′, the period from one midnight to the following midnight.

cal′endar month′, month (def. 2).

cal′endar watch′, a watch that indicates date of the month, day of the week, etc., as well as the time.

cal′endar year′. See under **year** (def. 1).

cal·en·der (kal′ən dər), *n.* **1.** a machine in which cloth, paper, or the like, is smoothed, glazed, etc., by pressing between revolving cylinders. **2.** a machine for impregnating fabric with rubber, as in the manufacture of automobile tires. —*v.t.* **3.** to press in a calender. [< ML *calendr(a),* alter. of L *cylindrus* CYLINDER] —**cal′en·der·er,** *n.*

Cal·en·der (kal′ən dər), *n.* (in Islamic countries) one of an order of mendicant dervishes founded in the 14th century. [< Pers *qalandar*]

cal·ends (kal′əndz), *n.* (*usually construed as pl.*) the first day of the month in the ancient Roman calendar, from which the days of the preceding month were counted backward to the ides. Also, **kalends.** [ME *kalendes* < L *kalendae,* equiv. to *cal* (base of *calāre* to proclaim) + *-end-* formative suffix + *-ae* pl. ending; r. OE *calend* beginning of a month < L]

ca·len·du·la (kə len′jə lə), *n.* **1.** any asteraceous plant of the genus *Calendula,* esp. *C. officinalis,* a common marigold. **2.** the dried florets of this plant, used in medicine for healing wounds. [< ML, equiv. to L *calend(ae)* CALENDS + *-ula* -ULE]

cal·en·ture (kal′ən chər, -choor′), *n. Pathol.* a violent fever with delirium, affecting persons in the tropics. [earlier *calentura* < Sp: fever, equiv. to *calent(ar)* (to) heat (< L *calent-,* s. of *calēns,* prp. of *calēre* to be hot) + *-ura* -URE] —**cal′en·tu′ral, cal′en·tu′rish,** *adj.*

ca·le·sa (kä le′sä), *n.* (in the Philippines) a small, two-wheeled calash. [< Sp < F *calèche* CALASH]

ca·les·cent (kə les′ənt), *adj.* growing warm; increasing in heat. [< L *calescent-* (s. of *calescēns* becoming warm, prp. of *calescere*), equiv. to *cal-* (base of *calēre* to be warm) + *-escent-* -ESCENT] —**ca·les′cence,** *n.*

Ca·le·tor (kə lē′tôr), *n.* (in the *Iliad*) a cousin of Hector, slain by Telamonian Ajax.

Ca·lex·i·co (kə lek′sə kō′), *n.* a town in S California. 7992 (1960).

calf[1] (kaf, käf), *n., pl.* **calves** (kavz, kävz). **1.** the young of the domestic cow or of other bovine animals. **2.** the young of certain other mammals, as the elephant, seal, and whale. **3.** calfskin leather. **4.** *Informal.* an awkward, silly boy or man. **5.** a mass of ice detached from a glacier, iceberg, or floe. **6. kill the fatted calf,** to prepare an elaborate welcome. [ME; OE *cealf, calf;* c. OS *kalf,* Icel *kalfr,* OHG *kalb*] —**calf′less,** *adj.* —**calf′-like′,** *adj.*

calf[2] (kaf, käf), *n., pl.* **calves** (kavz, kävz). the fleshy part of the back of the human leg below the knee. [ME < Scand; cf. Icel *kalfi;* akin to CALF[1]]

calf′ love′, temporary infatuation of a boy or girl for a person of the opposite sex. Also called **puppy love.**

calf's-foot jel′ly (kavz′fo͝ot′, kävz′-; kafs′fo͝ot′, käfs′-), jelly made from the stock of boiled calves' feet and flavoring, esp. of wine.

calf·skin (kaf′skin′, käf′-), *n.* **1.** the skin or hide of a calf. **2.** leather made from this skin. [CALF[1] + SKIN]

calf's′ tongue′, *Archit.* a molding having pendant, tonguelike members in relief against a flat or molded surface.

Cal·ga·ry (kal′gə rē), *n.* a city in S Alberta, in SW Canada. 249,641 (1961).

Cal·houn (kal ho͞on′, kəl-), *n.* **1. John Caldwell,** 1782–1850, Vice-President of the U.S. 1825–32. **2.** a town in NW Georgia. 3587 (1960). **3.** a boy's given name.

Calhoun′ Falls′, a town in NW South Carolina. 2525 (1960).

Ca·li (kä′lē), *n.* a city in SW Colombia. 639,900 (est. 1961).

Cal·i·ban (kal′ə ban′), *n.* **1.** the ugly, beastlike slave of Prospero in Shakespeare's *The Tempest.* **2.** a person of uneducable, bestial, and malevolent characteristics, esp. one who is also monstrous or deformed.

cal·i·ber (kal′ə bər), *n.* **1.** the diameter of something of circular section, esp. that of the inside of a tube: *a pipe of three-inch caliber.* **2.** *Ordn.* the diameter of the bore of a gun taken as a unit of measurement. **3.** degree of capacity or competence; ability: *a mathematician of high caliber.* **4.** degree of merit, excellence, or importance; quality: *the high moral caliber of the era.* Also, *esp. Brit.,* **cal′i·bre.** [var. of *calibre* < MF < early It *calibro,* ? alter. of Ar *qālib* mold, last (akin to *qalaba* to turn over, mold, form)] —**cal′i·bered;** *esp. Brit.,* **cal′i·bred,** *adj.*

cal·i·brate (kal′ə brāt′), *v.t.,* **-brat·ed, -brat·ing. 1.** to determine, check, or rectify the graduation of (any instrument giving quantitative measurements). **2.** to divide or mark with gradations, graduations, or other indexes of degree, quantity, etc., as on a thermometer, measuring cup, or the like. **3.** to determine the correct range for (an artillery gun, mortar, etc.) by observing where the fired projectile hits. [CALIBER + -ATE[1]] —**cal′i·bra′tion,** *n.* —**cal′i·bra′tor, cal′i·brat′er,** *n.*

cal·i·ces (kal′i sēz′), *n.* pl. of **calix.**

ca·li·che (kə lē′chē), *n. Geol.* **1.** a surface deposit consisting of sand or clay impregnated with crystalline salts, such as sodium nitrate or sodium chloride. **2.** a zone of calcium or mixed carbonates in soils of semiarid regions. [< Sp: flake of lime, equiv. to *cal* lime (< L *calc-;* see CHALK) + *-iche* n. suffix]

cal·i·cle (kal′i kəl), *n.* **1.** a cuplike depression or formation, as in corals. **2.** *Bot., Zool.* calycle. [< L *calicul(us)* small cup, equiv. to *calic-* (s. of *calix*) cup + *-ulus* -ULE]

cal·i·co (kal′ə kō′), *n., pl.* **-coes, -cos,** *adj.* —*n.* **1.** *U.S.* a plain-woven cotton cloth printed with a figured pattern, usually on one side. **2.** *Brit.* plain white cotton cloth. **3.** *Obs.* a figured cotton cloth imported from India. —*adj.* **4.** made of calico. **5.** resembling printed calico; spotted. [short for *Calico cloth,* var. of *Calicut cloth,* named after city in India which orig. exported it]

cal·i·co·back (kal′ə kō bak′), *n.* See **harlequin bug.**

cal′ico bass′ (bas), the black crappie. See under **crappie.**

cal′ico bug′. See **harlequin bug.**

cal′ico bush′, the mountain laurel, *Kalmia latifolia.* Also called **calico flower, cal′ico tree′.**

cal′ico clam′, any marine bivalve mollusk of the genus *Macrocallista,* esp. *M. nimbosa,* having a smooth, thick, rounded shell marked with violet-brown or lilac spots or streaks.

cal′ico crab′. See **lady crab.**

cal·i·coed (kal′ə kōd′), *adj.* dressed in calico. [CALICO + -ED[3]]

cal′ico flow′er, 1. a slender, tropical vine, *Aristolochia elegans,* of Brazil, having kidney-shaped or heart-shaped leaves and solitary, white-spotted, purple flowers, grown as an ornamental. **2.** See **calico bush.**

ca·lic·u·lus (kə lik′yə ləs), *n., pl.* **-li** (-lī′). calyculus.

Cal·i·cut (kal′ə kut′), *n.* a city in W Kerala, in SW India. 192,500 (1961). Malayalam, **Kozhikode.**

Cal·i·da (kal′i də), *n.* a girl's given name. Also, **Callida.**

cal·i·duct (kal′i dukt′), *n.* a pipe or duct for conveying a heating medium, as hot air, water, or steam. [< L *cali(dus)* warm + DUCT, modeled on *aqueduct*]

ca·lif (kā′lif, kal′if), *n.* caliph.

Calif., California.

cal·if·ate (kal′ə fāt′, -fit, kā′lə-), *n.* caliphate.

Cal·i·for·nia (kal′ə fôr′nyə, -fôr′nē ə), *n.* **1.** a state in the W United States, on the Pacific coast. 15,717,204 (1960); 158,693 sq. mi. *Cap.:* Sacramento. *Abbr.:* Cal., Calif. **2. Gulf of,** an arm of the Pacific, extending NW between the coast of W Mexico and the peninsula of Lower California. ab. 750 mi. long; 62,600 sq. mi. **3.** a town in SW Pennsylvania. 5978 (1960). **4.** a town in central Missouri. 2788 (1960). —**Cal′i·for′nian,** *adj., n.*

Cal′ifor′nia bar′berry, a tall shrub, *Mahonia pinnata,* of the southwestern U.S. and Mexico, having shiny, spiny-toothed leaves, pale-yellow flower clusters, and round, purplish-black fruit.

Califor′nia barracu′da. See **Pacific barracuda.**

Cal′ifor′nia blue′bell, 1. an annual herb, *Phacelia campanularia,* found in the deserts of southern California, having a fleshy stem, hairy leaves, and deep blue, bell-shaped flowers. **2.** a related herb, *P. Whitlavia,* of southern California, having blue or purple, bell-shaped flowers.

Cal′ifor′nia con′dor. See under **condor** (def. 1).

Cal′ifor′nia Cur′rent, a cold current in the Pacific Ocean, flowing SE along the coast of W North America.

Cal′ifor′nia dan′delion, cat's-ear (def. 1).

Cal′ifor′nia fan′ palm′, a tall fan palm, *Washingtonia robusta,* of California, having a trunk shaggy near the top.

Cal′ifor′nia fuch′sia, fuchsia (def. 2).

Califor′nia gold′ fern′, an evergreen fern, *Pityrogramma triangularis,* found from British Columbia to California, having the underside of the leaves covered with a deep yellow, powderlike substance.

Cal′ifor′nia gull′, a large gull, *Larus californicus,* of the western U.S., feeding chiefly on insects.

Cal′ifor′nia job′ case′, *Print.* a job case having sufficient spaces to contain both upper- and lower-case letters and 37 additional characters of foundry type. Cf. **case**[2] (def. 8).

Cal′ifor′nia lau′rel, 1. Also called **bay tree, Oregon myrtle, pepperwood.** a lauraceous tree, *Umbellularia californica,* of the western coast of the U.S., having aromatic leaves and umbels of yellowish-green flowers. **2.** the hard, heavy, light brown wood of this tree, used for making furniture.

Cal′ifor′nia li′lac, blue-blossom.

Califor′nia live′ oak′, an evergreen oak, *Quercus agrifolia,* of the western coast of the U.S., having leathery leaves. Also called **coast live oak.**

Cal′ifor′nia nut′meg, an evergreen tree, *Torreya californica,* of California, having a gray-brown bark and small purple-streaked, light green, egg-shaped fruit.

Cal′ifor′nia pep′per tree′, a pepper tree, *Schinus molle.*

Cal′ifor′nia pop′py, a papaveraceous herb, *Eschscholtzia californica,* having showy, orange-yellow flowers: the State flower of California.

Cal′ifor′nia priv′et, a privet, *Ligustrum ovalifolium,* indigenous to Japan, widely used for hedges in the U.S.

Cal′ifor′nia quail′, a quail, *Lophortyx californica,* of the western coast of the U.S., having grayish-brown plumage with black, white, and chestnut markings.

Califor′nia red′ fir′, a red fir, *Abies magnifica,* of the western U.S., characterized by quadrangular leaves and purplish-brown cones.

Cal′ifor′nia red′wood, redwood[1] (def. 1).

Cal′ifor′nia rose′, a climbing plant, *Convolvulus japonicus,* of eastern Asia, having pink flowers two inches wide.

Cal′ifor′nia rose′bay. See **pink rhododendron.**

Cal′ifor′nia sea′ li′on. See under **sea lion** (def. 1).

cal·i·for·nite (kal′ə fôr′nīt), *n.* See **vesuvianite jade.** [CALIFORN(IA) (where it is found) + -ITE[1]]

cal·i·for·ni·um (kal′ə fôr′nē əm), *n. Chem.* a synthetic, radioactive, metallic element. *Symbol:* Cf. *at. no.:* 98. [CALIFORN(IA) + -IUM; so called because discovered in a laboratory there]

ca·lig·i·nous (kə lij′ə nəs), *adj. Archaic.* misty; dim; dark. [< L *cālīginōs(us)* misty, equiv. to *cālīgin-* (s. of *cālīgō*) mist + *-ōsus* -OUS] —**ca·lig·i·nos·i·ty** (kə lij′ə nos′i tē), **ca·lig′i·nous·ness,** *n.* —**ca·lig′i·nous·ly,** *adv.*

Ca·lig·u·la (kə lig′yə lə), *n.* **Gaius Caesar,** A.D. 12–41, Roman emperor 37–41.

cal·i·man·co (kal′ə maŋ′kō), *n., pl.* **-cos.** calamanco.

ca·li·na (kä lē′nä), *n. Spanish.* a dusty haze occurring in Spain during the summer. [lit., haze]

cal·i·pash (kal′ə pash′, kal′ə pash′), *n.* the part of a turtle next to the upper shield, consisting of a greenish gelatinous substance, considered a delicacy. Also, **callipash.** [?]

Cal·i·pat·ri·a (kal′ə pat′rē ə), *n.* a town in S California. 2548 (1960).

cal·i·pee (kal′ə pē′, kal′ə pē′), *n.* the part of a turtle next to the lower shield, consisting of a yellowish gelatinous substance, considered a delicacy. Cf. **calipash.** [?]

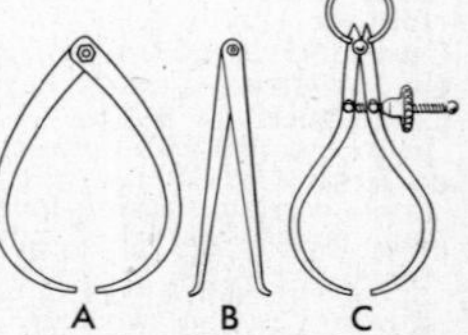

Calipers
A, Outside calipers; B, Inside calipers; C, Spring adjusting calipers

cal·i·per (kal′ə pər), *n.* **1.** Usually, **calipers.** an instrument for measuring thicknesses and internal or external diameters inaccessible to a scale, consisting usually of a pair of pivoted legs adjustable at any distance. **2.** any of various calibrated instruments for measuring thicknesses or distances between surfaces, usually having a screwed or sliding adjustable piece. **3.** thickness or three-dimensional depth, as of paper or a tree. **4.** Usually, **calipers.** the pincers of an earwig. —*v.t.* **5.** to measure with calipers. Also, **calliper.** [var. of CALIBER] —**cal′i·per·er,** *n.*

cal′iper rule′, a caliper with one jaw fixed to or integral with a graduated straight bar on which the other jaw slides.

ca·liph (kā′lif, kal′if), *n.* a title for the religious and civil head of a Muslim state. Also, **calif, kalif, kaliph, khalif.** [ME *caliphe,* etc. < MF < Ar *khalīf(a)* successor (of Muhammad), deriv. of *khalafa* succeed] —**cal·iph·al** (kal′ə fəl, kā′lə-), *adj.*

cal·iph·ate (kal′ə fāt′, -fit, kā′lə-), *n.* the rank, jurisdiction or government of a caliph. Also, **califate, kalifate, khalifate.** [< ML *caliphāt(us).* See CALIPH, -ATE[3]]

Ca·lip·pus (kə lip′əs), *n.* **1.** Callippus. **2.** a walled plain in the first quadrant of the face of the moon: about 19 miles in diameter.

cal·i·sa·ya (kal′i sā′yə), *n.* the medicinal bark of the tree *Cinchona Calisaya.* [< *Calisaya,* name of the Bolivian Indian who told the whites about the medicinal values of cinchona bark]

Ca·lis·ta (kə lis′tə), *n.* a girl's given name.

cal·is·then·ics (kal′is then′iks), *n.* **1.** (*construed as sing.*) the practice or art of calisthenic exercises; the exercise of muscles for the purpose of gaining health, strength, and grace of form and movement. **2.** (*construed as pl.*) light gymnastic exercises designed to develop grace as well as physical health and vigor. Also, **callisthenics.** [*cali-* (var. of CALLI-) + Gk *sthén(os)* strength + -ICS] —**cal′is·then′ic, cal′is·then′i·cal,** *adj.*

ca·lix (kā′liks, kal′iks), *n., pl.* **cal·i·ces** (kal′i sēz′). *Rom. Cath. Ch.* chalice (def. 2a). [< L; see CHALICE]

Ca·lix·tine (kə lik′stin, -stēn), *n.* a member of a body of Hussites in the 15th century holding that the chalice as well as the bread should be received by the laity in the Lord's Supper. Also, **Ca·lix·tin** (kə lik′stin). Also called **Utraquist.** [< eccl. L *Calixtīn(us),* equiv. to *calix* cup + *-tinus* adj. suffix; see VESPERTINE]

Ca·lix·tus I (kə lik′stəs), **Saint,** A.D. c160–222, Italian ecclesiastic: pope 218–222. Also, **Callistus I.**

Calixtus II, died 1124, French ecclesiastic: pope 1119–24. Also, **Callistus II.**

Calixtus III, (*Alfonso de Borja* or *Alfonso Borgia*) 1378–1458, Spanish ecclesiastic: pope 1455–58. Also, **Callistus III.**

calk[1] (kôk), *v.t.* caulk.

calk[2] (kôk), *n.* **1.** Also, **calkin.** a projection on a horseshoe to prevent slipping on ice, pavement, etc. **2.** Also, **calker.** *U.S.* a similar device on the heel or sole of a shoe to prevent slipping. —*v.t.* **3.** to provide with calks. **4.** to injure with a calk. [appar. < L *calc-* (s. of *calx*) spur, heel; cf. OE *calsrond* shod]

calk·er[1] (kô′kər), *n.* caulker.

calk·er[2] (kô′kər), *n.* calk[2] (def. 2). [CALK[2] + -ER[1]]

cal·kin (kô′kin, kal′-), *n.* calk[2] (def. 1). [late ME *kakun* < MD *calcoen* hoof < L *calcāneum* heel; see CALCANEUM]

call (kôl), *v.t.* **1.** to cry out in a loud voice: *He called her name to see if she was home.* **2.** to ask or invite to come: *Will you call the family to dinner? He called him into the office.* **3.** to read over (a roll or a list) in a loud voice. **4.** to attract (someone's attention) to something: *He called the maid's attention to the mess. She tried not to call attention to herself.* **5.** to rouse from sleep, as by a call: *Call me at eight o'clock.* **6.** to telephone to: *Call me when you arrive.* **7.** to command or request to come; summon: *to call a dog; to call a cab; to call a witness.* **8.** to announce authoritatively; proclaim; order: *to call a halt.* **9.** to order into effect; announce the existence of: *The union leader called a strike.* **10.** to summon to an office, duty, etc.: *His country called him to the colors.* **11.** to summon by or as if by divine command: *The Lord called him to the ministry.* **12.** to cause to come; bring: *to call to mind; to call into existence.* **13.** to convoke or convene, as a meeting or assembly: *to call Congress into session.* **14.** to bring under consideration or discussion: *The judge called the case to court.* **15.** to attract or lure (birds or animals) by imitating characteristic sounds. **16.** *Informal.* **a.** to demand of (someone) that he fulfill a promise, furnish evidence for a statement, etc.: *They called him on his story.* **b.** to criticize adversely; express disapproval of; censure: *She called him on his vulgar language.* **17.** *Sports.* (of an official) **a.** to pronounce a judgment on (a shot, pitch, batter, etc.): *The referee called the goal illegal. The umpire called the pitch a strike. He was called out on strikes.* **b.** to put an end to (a contest) because of inclement weather, poor field conditions, etc.: *A sudden downpour forced the umpire to call the game after the third inning.* **18.** to demand payment or fulfillment of (a loan). **19.** to demand presentation of (bonds) for redemption. **20.** to give a name to; name: *His parents named him James, but the boys call him Jim.* **21.** to designate as something specified: *He called me a liar.* **22.** to think of as something specified; consider; estimate: *Now, I call that show a success! I call that a mean remark.* **23.** *Billiards, Pool.* to name (the ball) one intends to drive into a particular pocket. **24.** *Cards.* **a.** to demand (a card). **b.** to demand of (a player) that he show his hand. **c.** *Poker.* to equal (a bet) or equal the bet made by (the preceding bettor) in a round. **d.** *Bridge.* to signal one's partner for a lead of (a certain card or suit). **25.** *Informal.* to forecast correctly: *He certainly can call his shots.* —*v.i.* **26.** to speak loudly, as to attract attention; shout; cry: *She called to the children.* **27.** to make a short visit; stop at a place on some errand or business: *He calls for an hour every Sunday. She called at the store for the package.* **28.** to telephone a person: *He promised to call at noon.* **29.** *Cards.* **a.** to demand a card. **b.** to demand a showing of hands. **c.** *Poker.* to equal a bet. **d.** *Bridge.* to bid or pass. **30.** *Theat.* to issue or post a notice of rehearsal. **31.** (of a bird or animal) to utter its characteristic cry. **32. call away,** to cause to leave or go; summon: *A death in the family called him away.* **33. call back, a.** to summon or bring back; recall: *He called back the messenger.* **b.** to revoke; retract: *to call back an accusation.* **34. call down, a.** to request or pray for; invoke: *to call down the wrath of God.* **b.** to reprimand; scold: *The boss called us down for lateness.* **35. call for, a.** to go or come to get; pick up; fetch. **b.** to request; summon. **c.** to require; demand; need: *The occasion calls for a cool head.* **36. call forth,** to summon into action; bring into existence: *The circumstances of her childhood called forth her courage and resolve.* **37. call in, a.** to call for payment; collect. **b.** to withdraw from circulation: *to call in gold certificates.* **c.** to call upon for consultation; ask for help: *Two specialists were called in to assist in the operation.* **38. call off, a.** to distract; take away: *Please call off your dog.* **b.** *Informal.* to cancel (something) that had been planned for a certain date: *The performance was called off because of rain.* **39. call on** or **upon, a.** to require; appeal to: *They called on him to represent them.* **b.** to visit for a short time: *to call on friends.* **40. call out, a.** to speak in a loud voice; shout. **b.** to summon into service or action: *Call out the militia!* **c.** to bring out; elicit: *The emergency called out his hidden abilities.* **41. call up, a.** to bring forward for consideration or discussion. **b.** to cause to remember; evoke. **c.** to communicate with by telephone. **d.** to summon for action or service: *A large number of reservists were called up.* —*n.* **42.** a cry or shout. **43.** the cry of a bird or other animal. **44.** an instrument for imitating this cry and attracting or luring the animal: *He bought a duck call.* **45.** a summons or signal sounded by a bugle, bell, etc.: *We live so close to the fort that we can hear the bugle calls.* **46.** *Fox Hunting.* any of several cries, or sounds made on a horn by the huntsman to encourage the hounds. **47.** a short visit: *to make a call on someone.* **48.** a summons, invitation or bidding: *The students gathered at the call of the dean.* **49.** *Theat.* **a.** a notice of rehearsal posted by the stage manager. **b.** See **act call. c.** See **curtain call. 50.** a mystic experience of divine appointment to a vocation or service: *He had a call to become a minister.* **51.** the fascination or appeal of a given place, vocation, etc.: *the call of the sea.* **52.** a request or invitation to become pastor of a church, a professor in a university, etc. **53.** a need or occasion: *He had no call to say such things.* **54.** a demand or claim: *to make a call on a person's time.* **55.** a calling of a roll; roll call. **56.** act or instance of telephoning: *She sat near the telephone waiting for his call.* **57.** *Cards.* **a.** a demand for a card or a showing of hands. **b.** *Poker.* an equaling of the preceding bet. **c.** *Bridge.* a bid or pass. **58.** *Sports.* a judgment or decision by an umpire, a referee, or other official of a contest, as on a shot, pitch, or batter: *The umpires were making one bad call after another, or so claimed the fans o the losing team.* **59.** *Finance.* a contract that permits its purchaser to buy a certain amount of stock or commodity at a specified price for a limited period of time. Cf. **put** (def. 45). **60.** a demand for payment of an obligation, esp. where payment is at the option of the creditor. **61. on call, a.** payable or subject to return without advance notice. **b.** readily available for summoning upon short notice. **62. take a call,** to acknowledge the applause of the audience after a performance by appearing for a bow or a curtain call. **63. within call,** within distance or range of being spoken to or summoned: *Please stay within call.* [ME *call(en)* < OE **callian* (Anglian dial.), deriv. of *-calla* herald; c. OE *ceallian* (WS dial.) to shout, MD *kallen* to talk, OHG *kallōn* to shout, Icel *kalla* to call out; akin to Ir *gall* swan, OSlav *glasiti* to call]

—**Syn. 2, 7, 10.** CALL, INVITE, SUMMON imply requesting the presence or attendance of someone at a particular place. CALL is the general word: *to call a meeting.* To INVITE is to ask someone courteously to come as a guest, a participant, etc., leaving him free to refuse: *to invite guests to a concert; to invite them to contribute to a fund.* SUMMON implies sending for someone, using authority or formality in requesting his presence, and (theoretically) not leaving him free to refuse: *to summon a witness, members of a committee,* etc.

cal·la (kal′ə), *n.* **1.** any plant of the genus *Zantedeschia* (or *Richardia*), native to Africa, esp. *Z. aethiopicum* (**cal′la lil′y**), having a large white spathe enclosing a yellow spadix. **2.** an araceous plant, *Calla palustris,* of cold marshes of Europe and North America, having heart-shaped leaves. [< NL, perh. special use of L *calla* a plant]

Cal·la (kal′ə), *n.* a girl's given name.

call·a·ble (kô′lə bəl), *adj.* **1.** capable of being called. **2.** subject to redemption prior to maturity. **3.** subject to payment on demand, as money loaned. [CALL + -ABLE]

Cal·la·ghan (kal′ə hən), *n.* **1. (Leonard) James,** born 1912, British statesman: prime minister since 1976. **2. Morley,** born 1903, Canadian novelist.

cal·lant (kä′lənt), *n.* *Scot. and North Eng.* a lad; boy. Also, **cal·lan** (kä′lən). [< D *kalant* fellow, chap, customer < ONF *caland* customer]

Ca·lla·o (kä yä′ô), *n.* a seaport in W Peru, near Lima. 125,598 (est. 1957).

Cal·las (kal′əs), *n.* **Maria Men·e·ghi·ni** (men′ə gē′nē), 1923–77, U.S. soprano.

call′-back pay′ (kôl′bak′), a guaranteed amount of pay made to an employee who has been called back to his place of employment after he has left for the day.

call-board (kôl′bôrd′, -bōrd′), *n.* a bulletin board, as in a theater, on which notices are posted announcing rehearsals, changes in the cast, etc.

call′ box′, **1.** an outdoor telephone or signal box for calling the police or fire departments. **2.** *Brit.* a public telephone booth.

call·boy (kôl′boi′), *n.* **1.** a boy or man who summons actors just before they go on the stage. **2.** a bellboy. [CALL + BOY]

call·er[1] (kô′lər), *n.* **1.** one who or that which calls. **2.** a person who makes a short visit. [CALL + -ER[1]] —**Syn. 2.** See **visitor.**

cal·ler[2] (kal′ər, kä′lər), *adj.* *Scot. and North. Eng.* **1.** (of fruit, fish, vegetables, etc.) fresh; recently picked or caught. **2.** refreshing. [ME, north. var. of *calver* fresh, alive (said of fish) < ?]

Ca·lles (kä′yes), *n.* **Plu·tar·co E·lí·as** (plōō tär′kô e lē′äs), 1877–1945, Mexican general and statesman: president of Mexico 1924–28.

cal·let (kal′it, kä′lit), *n.* *Brit. Dial.* **1.** a strumpet; a lewd woman. **2.** a cantankerous woman; shrew. [?]

call-fire (kôl′fīər′), *n.* *Mil.* naval artillery support directed against land targets as requested by forces ashore.

call′ girl′, a prostitute with whom an appointment can be arranged by telephone.

call′ house′, **1.** a house or apartment used by prostitutes for arranging or keeping assignations. **2.** a place at which call girls await telephone calls from customers.

calli-, an element meaning "beautiful," occurring in loan words from Greek (*calligraphy*); on this model, used in the formation of compound words (*callisthenics*). [< Gk *kalli-* comb. form of *kállos* beauty, akin to *kalós* beautiful, fair]

Cal·lic·ra·tes (kə lik′rə tēz′), *n.* fl. mid 5th century B.C., Greek architect who together with Ictinus designed the Parthenon.

Cal·li·da (kal′i də), *n.* a girl's given name. Also, **Calida.**

Cal·lid·i·ce (kə lid′i sē′), *n.* *Class. Myth.* a Thesprotian queen whom Odysseus married while on one of his pilgrimages.

Cal·lie (kal′ē), *n.* a girl's given name, form of **Caroline.** Also, **Cally.**

cal·lig·ra·phy (kə lig′rə fē), *n.* **1.** beautiful handwriting; fine penmanship (opposed to *cacography*). **2.** handwriting; penmanship. **3.** fancy penmanship, esp. highly decorative handwriting, as with a great many flourishes: *He appreciated the calligraphy of the 18th century.* **4.** the art of writing beautifully: *He studied calligraphy when he was a young man.* **5.** a script, usually cursive, although sometimes angular, produced chiefly by brush, esp. Chinese, Japanese, or Arabic writing of high aesthetic value. **6.** *Fine Arts.* line or a group of lines that either are derived from or resemble letter forms and are characterized by qualities usually associated with cursive writing, esp. that produced with a brush. [< Gk *kalligraphía* beautiful writing. See CALLI-, -GRAPHY] —**cal·lig′ra·pher, cal·lig′ra·phist,** *n.* —**cal·li·graph·ic** (kal′ə graf′ik), **cal′li·graph′i·cal,** *adj.* —**cal′li·graph′i·cal·ly,** *adv.*

Cal·lim·a·chus (kə lim′ə kəs), *n.* c310–c240 B.C., Greek poet, grammarian, and critic.

call·ing (kô′ling), *n.* **1.** the act of one who or that which calls. **2.** vocation, profession, or trade: *What is your calling?* **3.** a call or summons: *He had a calling to join the church.* **4.** a strong impulse or inclination: *He did it in response to an inner calling.* **5.** a convocation: *the calling of Congress.* [CALL + -ING[1]]

call′ing card′, a small card with the name and often the address of a person or of a couple, for presenting to a host, business firm, etc., when making a visit, for enclosing in presents, etc. Also called **visiting card.**

call′ing crab′. See **fiddler crab.**

call′-in pay′ (kôl′in′), payment made to an employee who reports for work and finds there is no work for him to do. Also called **reporting pay.**

cal·li·o·pe (kə lī′ə pē; *for 1 also* kal′ē ōp′), *n.* **1.** a musical instrument consisting of a set of harsh-sounding steam whistles which are activated by a keyboard. **2.** (*cap.*) *Class. Myth.* the Muse of heroic poetry. [< L < Gk *Kalliópē,* equiv. to *kalli-* CALLI- + *op-* (s. of *óps*) voice + *-ē* fem. ending]

Cal·li·o·pe (kə lī′ə pē), *n.* a girl's given name.

cal·li·o·pe·an (kə lī′ə pē′ən), *adj.* resembling a calliope in sound; piercingly loud: *a calliopean voice.* [CALLIOPE + -AN]

cal·li·op·sis (kal′ē op′sis), *n.* a coreopsis. [CALLI- + -OPSIS]

cal·li·pash (kal′ə pash′, kal′ə pash′), *n.* calipash.

cal·li·per (kal′ə pər), *n., v.t.* caliper. —**cal′li·per·er,** *n.*

Cal·lip·o·lis (kə lip′ə lis), *n.* *Class. Myth.* a son of Alcathous.

Cal·lip′pic cy′cle (ka lip′ik), *Astron.* a period equal to four Metonic cycles less one day, proposed by Callippus to correct the Metonic cycle.

Cal·lip·pus (kə lip′əs), *n.* fl. 4th century B.C., Greek astronomer. Also, **Calippus, Cal·lip′us.**

cal·li·pyg·i·an (kal′ə pij′ē ən), *adj.* having well-shaped buttocks. Also, **cal·li·py·gous** (kal′ə pī′gəs). [< Gk *kallipýg(os)* with beautiful buttocks; referring to a statue of Aphrodite (*kalli-* CALLI- + *pyg(ē)* rump + *-os* adj. suffix) + -IAN]

Cal·lir·rho·ë (kə lēr′ō ē′), *n.* *Class. Myth.* **1.** the mother of Ganymede. **2.** the wife of Alcmaeon who prayed to Zeus that her sons grow to manhood in a day. Cf. **Amphoterus. 3.** a girl whose sacrifice was required in order to end a plague in Calydon.

Cal·lis·te (kə lis′tē), *n.* *Class. Myth.* an epithet of Artemis meaning "fairest."

cal·lis·then·ics (kal′is then′iks), *n.* calisthenics. —**cal′lis·then′ic,** *adj.*

Cal·lis·to (kə lis′tō), *n.* **1.** *Class. Myth.* a nymph attendant on Artemis, punished for a love affair with Zeus by being changed into a bear and slain by Artemis. **2.** *Astron.* one of the 12 satellites of Jupiter: about 3200 miles in diameter and the largest known satellite in the solar system.

Cal·lis·tus I (kə lis′təs). See **Calixtus I.**

Callistus II. See **Calixtus II.**

Callistus III. See **Calixtus III.**

cal·li·thump (kal′ə thump′), *n.* *Northeastern U.S.* a shivaree. [back formation from *callithumpian* rowdy, orig. *gallithumpian,* equiv. to *galli-* scare (var. of *gallow,* akin to OE *āgælwan* alarm) + THUMP + -IAN] —**cal′li·thump′i·an,** *adj., n.*

call′ let′ters, letters or letters in combination with numbers for identifying a radio or television station, an amateur radio transmitting device, or the like. Also called **call sign.**

call′ loan′, a loan repayable on demand. Also called **demand loan.** Cf. **time loan.**

call′ mar′ket, the market for lending call money.

call′ mon′ey, funds available or loaned on call.

call′ num′ber, *Library Science.* a number, frequently accompanied by a classification symbol and an author's designation, indicating the specific location of a book in a library.

Call′ of the Wild′, The, a novel (1903) by Jack London.

cal·lo·sal (ka lō′səl), *adj.* of or pertaining to the corpus callosum. [< NL *callōs(um)* (n. use of L *callōsus* CALLOSE) + -AL[1]]

callo′sal gy′rus, *Anat.* See **cingulate gyrus.** Also called **callo′sal convolu′tion.**

cal·lose (kal′ōs), *adj.* having thickened or hardened spots, as a leaf. [*call-* (< L *call(um)* hard skin) + -OSE[1]; see CALLOUS]

cal·los·i·ty (kə los′i tē), *n., pl.* **-ties. 1.** a callous condition. **2.** *Bot.* a hardened or thickened part of a plant. **3.** *Pathol.* callus (def. 1a). [< LL *callōsitās*, equiv. to *callōs(us)* CALLOUS + *-itās* -ITY]

Cal·lot (KA lō′), *n.* **Jacques** (zhäk), 1592?–1635, French engraver and etcher.

cal·lous (kal′əs), *adj.* **1.** made hard; hardened. **2.** insensitive; indifferent; unsympathetic: *He became callous after many years in the ward. They have a callous attitude toward the sufferings of others.* **3.** having a callus; indurated, as parts of the skin exposed to friction. **—***v.t., v.i.* **4.** to make or become hard or callous. [< L *callōs(us)* hard-skinned, with a hard skin, equiv. to *call(um)* hard, thick skin + *-ōsus* -OUS] **—cal′lous·ly,** *adv.* **—cal′lous·ness,** *n.*
—Syn. 1. hard. **2.** inured, insensible, obtuse. See **hard.**
—Ant. 1. soft. **2.** sensitive.

call′ out′, a letter, number, or other symbol for calling attention to a particular part of an illustration.

cal·low (kal′ō), *adj.* **1.** immature or inexperienced: *a callow youth.* **2.** *Rare.* (of a young bird) featherless; unfledged. **—***n.* **3.** *Entomol.* a recently hatched worker ant. [ME, OE *calu* bald; c. D *kaal*, G *kahl* bald, OSlav *golŭ* bare] **—cal′low·ness,** *n.*

call′ rate′, interest charge on call loans.

call′ sign′. See **call letters.**

call′ slip′, a printed form used by a library patron to request the use of a particular book.

call′ to quar′ters, *U.S. Army.* a bugle call summoning soldiers to their quarters.

call-up (kôl′up′), *n.* **1.** an order to report for active military service. **2.** the number of men drafted during a specific period of time: *The November call-up was set at 15,000.* **3.** arrangement for a customer to visit a prostitute; an assignation. [n. use of v. phrase *call up*]

cal·lus (kal′əs), *n., pl.* **-lus·es,** *v.,* **-lused, -lus·ing.** **—***n.* **1.** *Pathol., Physiol.* **a.** a hardened or thickened part of the skin; a callosity. **b.** a new growth of osseous matter at the ends of a fractured bone, serving to unite them. **2.** *Bot.* **a.** the tissue that forms over the wounds of plants, protecting the inner tissues and causing healing. **b.** a deposit on the perforated area of a sieve tube. **—***v.i.* **3.** to form a callus. **—***v.t.* **4.** to produce a callus or calluses on: *Heavy work callused his hands.* [< L, var. of *callum* hard, thick skin; see CALLOUS]

Cal·ly (kal′ē), *n.* a girl's given name, form of **Caroline.** Also, **Callie.**

calm (käm), *adj.* **1.** without rough motion; still or nearly still: *a calm sea.* **2.** not windy: *a calm day.* **3.** free from excitement or passion; tranquil: *a calm face; a calm manner.* **—***n.* **4.** freedom from motion or disturbance; stillness. **5.** absence of wind on the Beaufort scale; wind speed of less than one mile per hour. **6.** freedom from agitation, excitement, or passion; tranquillity; serenity: *She faced the possibility of death with complete calm.* **—***v.t.* **7.** to make calm: *He calmed the excited dog.* **—***v.i.* **8.** to become calm (usually fol. by *down*). [ME *calme* < MF < early It *calm(a)* < L *cal(ēre)* (to) be hot + LL *(cau)ma* heat < Gk *kaûma* burning heat] **—calm′ing·ly,** *adv.* **—calm′ly,** *adv.* **—calm′ness,** *n.*
—Syn 1. quiet, motionless. **3.** placid, peaceful, serene, self-possessed. CALM, COLLECTED, COMPOSED, COOL imply the absence of agitation. CALM implies an unruffled state, esp. under disturbing conditions: *calm in a crisis.* COLLECTED implies complete inner command of oneself, usually as the result of an effort: *He remained collected in spite of the excitement.* One who is COMPOSED has or has gained dignified self-possession: *pale but composed.* COOL implies clarity of judgment along with apparent absence of strong feeling or excitement, esp. in circumstances of danger or strain: *so cool that he seemed calm.* **7.** still, quiet, tranquilize; allay, assuage, mollify, soothe, soften. **—Ant. 2.** tempestuous. **3.** agitated, excited.

cal·ma·tive (kal′mə tiv, kä′mə-), *Med.* **—***adj.* **1.** having a sedative effect. **—***n.* **2.** a calmative agent. [CALM + -ATIVE]

calm·y (kä′mē), *adj.,* **calm·i·er, calm·i·est.** *Archaic.* calm. [CALM + -Y[1]]

cal·o·mel (kal′ə mel′, -məl), *n.* *Pharm.* a white, tasteless powder, Hg_2Cl_2, used chiefly as a purgative and fungicide. Also called **mercurous chloride.** [? < NL **calomel(as)* < Gk *kalō(s)* fair + *mélas* black]

cal′omel elec′trode, *Physical Chem.* a reference electrode consisting of calomel, mercury, and a solution of potassium chloride.

cal·o·re·cep·tor (kal′ō ri sep′tər), *n.* *Physiol., Biol.* a receptor stimulated by heat. [< L *calor* heat + RECEPTOR]

cal·o·res·cence (kal′ə res′əns), *n.* *Physics.* incandescence caused by absorption by a body of radiation having a frequency below that of visible light. [< L *calor* heat + -ESCENCE] **—cal′o·res′cent,** *adj.*

ca·lor·ic (kə lôr′ik, -lor′-), *adj.* **1.** *Physiol.* of or pertaining to calories: *He was concerned with the caloric content of food.* **2.** of or pertaining to heat. **3.** (of engines) driven by heat. **—***n.* **4.** heat. **5.** *Old Physics.* a hypothetical fluid whose presence in matter determined its thermal state. [< F *calorique*, equiv. to *calor-* (< L *calor* heat) + *-ique* -IC] **—cal·o·ric·i·ty** (kal′ə ris′i tē), *n.*

cal·o·rie (kal′ə rē), *n.* **1.** *Physics.* **a.** Also called **great calorie, kilocalorie, large calorie.** a quantity of heat equal to 1000 gram calories. *Abbr.:* cal **b.** Also called **gram calorie, small calorie.** (formerly) the amount of heat necessary to raise the temperature of one gram of water from 14.5°C to 15.5°C when the water is at atmospheric pressure. *Abbr.:* Cal **2.** *Physiol.* **a.** a unit equal to the large calorie, used to express the heat output of an organism and the fuel or energy value of food. **b.** a quantity of food capable of producing such a unit of energy. Also, **calory.** [< F, equiv. to *calor-* (< L *calor* heat) + *-ie* -Y[3]]

ca·lor·i·fa·cient (kə lôr′ə fā′shənt, -lor′-, kal′ər ə-), *adj.* (of foods) producing heat. [< L *calōri-* (s. of *calor*) heat + -FACIENT]

cal·o·rif·ic (kal′ə rif′ik), *adj.* pertaining to conversion into heat. [< L *calōrific(us)* causing warmth, warming, equiv. to *calōri-* (s. of *calor* heat) + *-ficus* -FIC] **—cal′o·rif′i·cal·ly,** *adv.*

cal·o·rim·e·ter (kal′ə rim′i tər), *n.* *Physics.* an apparatus for measuring quantities of heat. [< L *calōri-* (s. of *calor*) heat + -METER]

cal·o·rim·e·try (kal′ə rim′i trē), *n.* *Physics.* the measurement of heat. [< L *calōri-* (s. of *calor*) heat + -METRY] **—cal·o·ri·met·ric** (kal′ər ə me′trik, kə lôr′-, -lor′-), **cal′o·ri·met′ri·cal,** *adj.* **—cal′o·ri·met′ri·cal·ly,** *adv.*

cal·o·rize (kal′ə rīz′), *v.t.,* **-rized, -riz·ing.** *Metall.* to alloy the surface of (carbon steel or alloy steel) by impregnating it with aluminum. [< L *calor* heat + -IZE] **—cal′o·riz′er,** *n.*

cal·o·ry (kal′ə rē), *n., pl.* **-ries.** calorie.

ca·lotte (kə lot′), *n.* **1.** zucchetto. **2.** skullcap (def. 1). **3.** *Archit.* **a.** small dome. **b.** an upper zone of a dome. **c.** the inner dome of a double dome. **d.** a small semidome. **e.** a metal cap for a spire or cupola. [< MF < It *calott(a)* < Gk *kalýptra* a cover, with loss of *r* by dissimilation; see CALYPTRA]

cal·o·yer (kal′ə yər, kə loi′ər), *n.* a monk of the Eastern Church. [< MF *caloyer* < modGk *kalógēros* venerable, equiv. to *kalô(s)* beautiful + *-gēros* old (*gêr(as)* old age + *-os* adj. suffix)]

cal·pac (kal′pak), *n.* a large black cap of sheepskin or other heavy material, worn by Armenians, Turks, etc. Also, **cal′pack.** [< Turk *kalpak*] **—cal′packed,** *adj.*

Cal·pe (kal′pē), *n.* ancient name of **Gibraltar.**

Cal·pur·ni·a (kal pûr′nē ə), *n.* **1.** fl. 1st century B.C., third wife of Julius Caesar 59–44. Cf. **Cornelia** (def. 2), **Pompeia. 2.** a girl's given name.

calque (kalk), *n.* a loan translation, esp. one resulting from bilingual interference in which the syntactic structure of a borrowed construction is maintained but its morphemes are replaced by those of the native language, as German *halbinsel* for *peninsula.* [< F, deriv. of *calque(r)* (to) copy, base on < It *calcare* to trace over, tread < L: to trample]

Cal·ta·nis·set·ta (kal′tə ni set′ə; *It.* käl′tä nēs set′tä), *n.* a city in central Sicily: cathedral; Norman monastery. 63,011 (1959).

cal·trop (kal′trəp), *n.* **1.** *Bot.* **a.** any of various plants having spiny heads or fruit, esp. of the genera *Tribulus* and *Kallstroemia.* **b.** See **star thistle. c.** an Old World plant, *Tribulus terrestris.* **d.** See **water chestnut. 2.** *Mil.* an iron ball with four projecting spikes so disposed that when the ball is on the ground one of them always points upward: used to obstruct the passage of cavalry, armored vehicles, etc. Also, **cal·throp** (kal′thrəp), **cal′-trap.** [ME *calketrappe*, OE *calca(trippe)* + *(colte)træppe*, equiv. to *calce-* (< L *calci-*, s. of *calx* spur, heel) + *træppe* TRAP[1]]

Caltrop (def. 2)

cal·u·met (kal′yə met′, kal′yə met′), *n.* a long, ornamented tobacco pipe used by North American Indians on ceremonial occasions, esp. in token of peace. Also called **peace pipe.** [< F < VL **calum(us)* reed, pipe (unexplained var. of L *calamus;* see CALAMUS) + *-et* -ET]

Calumet

Cal′u·met Cit′y (kal′yə mit), a city in NE Illinois, near Chicago. 25,000 (1960).

Cal′umet Park′, a town in NE Illinois. 8448 (1960).

ca·lum·ni·ate (kə lum′nē āt′), *v.t.,* **-at·ed, -at·ing.** to make false and malicious statements about; slander: *He took every opportunity to calumniate his political rival.* [< L *calumniāt(us)* accused falsely, tricked (ptp. of *calumniārī*), equiv. to *calumni(a)* CALUMNY + *-ātus* -ATE[1]] **—ca·lum′ni·a′tor,** *n.*

ca·lum·ni·a·tion (kə lum′nē ā′shən), *n.* **1.** the act of calumniating; slander: *He won the election by the calumniation of his opponent.* **2.** a calumny: *He used lies and calumniations in an attempt to increase his own merit in the eyes of others.* [< LL *calumniātiōn-* (s. of *calumniātiō*). See CALUMNIATE, -ION]

ca·lum·ni·ous (kə lum′nē əs), *adj.* of, involving, or using calumny; slanderous; defamatory. Also, **ca·lum·ni·a·to·ry** (kə lum′nē ə tôr′ē, -tōr′ē,). [< L *calumniōs(us)* full of tricks or artifices < L *calumni(a)* CALUMNY + *-ōsus* -OUS] **—ca·lum′ni·ous·ly,** *adv.*

cal·um·ny (kal′əm nē), *n., pl.* **-nies. 1.** a false and malicious statement designed to injure the reputation of someone or something: *The speech was considered a calumny of the administration and its leaders.* **2.** slander; defamation. [< L *calumni(a)*, equiv. to *calv(ī)* (to) deceive + *-mnia* (*-mn-* formative suffix + *-ia* -Y[3])]

cal·u·tron (kal′yə tron′), *n.* *Physics.* a device for separating isotopes by atomic mass, operating in a manner similar to a mass spectrograph. [*Cal(ifornia) U(niversity)* + -TRON]

Cal·va·dos (kal′və dōs′, -dos′, kal′və dōs′, -dos′; *for 1 also Fr.* KAL VA DÔS′), *n.* **1.** a department in NW France. 480,686 (1962). 2198 sq. mi. *Cap.:* Caen. **2.** (*sometimes l.c.*) a dry apple brandy made from apple cider in Normandy.

cal·var·i·a (kal vâr′ē ə), *n.* the dome of the skull. [< L, equiv. to *calv(a)* hairless scalp (*n.* use of fem. of *calvus* bald) + *-āria* -ARY]

Cal·va·ry (kal′və rē), *n., pl.* **-ries** for 2, 3. **1.** Golgotha, the place where Jesus was crucified. Luke 23:33. **2.** (*often l.c.*) a sculptured representation of the Crucifixion, usually erected in the open air. **3.** (*l.c.*) an experience or occasion of extreme suffering, esp. mental suffering. [< LL *Calvāri(a)* Calvary < L *calvāria* a skull, used to translate Gk *kranion* CRANIUM, itself a trans. of the Aramaic name; see GOLGOTHA]

Cal′vary cross′. See **cross of Calvary.**

calve (kav, käv), *v.,* **calved, calv·ing.** **—***v.i.* **1.** to give birth to a calf: *The cow is expected to calve tomorrow.* **2.** (of a glacier, an iceberg, etc.) to break up or splinter so as to produce a detached piece. **—***v.t.* **3.** to give birth to (a calf). **4.** (of a glacier, an iceberg, etc.) to break off or detach (a piece): *The iceberg calved a floe.* [ME *calve(n)*, OE **calfian* (Anglian), deriv. of *calf* CALF[1]; c. OE *cealfian* (WS)]

Cal·vé (KAL vā′), *n.* **Em·ma** (em′ə; *Fr.* em MA′), (*Emma de Roquer Gaspari*), 1863?–1942, French operatic soprano.

Cal·vert (kal′vərt), *n.* **1. Sir George** (*1st Baron Baltimore*), c1580–1632, British statesman: founder of the colony of Maryland. **2.** his son, **Leonard,** 1606–47, first colonial governor of Maryland 1634–47.

calves (kavz, kävz), *n.* pl. of **calf.**

Cal·vin (kal′vin), *n.* **1. John** (*Jean Chauvin* or *Caulvin*), 1509–64, French theologian and reformer in Switzerland: leader in the Protestant Reformation. **2. Melvin,** born 1911, U.S. chemist: Nobel prize 1961. **3.** a boy's given name.

Cal·vi·na (kal vē′nə), *n.* a girl's given name.

Cal·vin·ism (kal′və niz′əm), *n.* *Theol.* **1.** the doctrines and teachings of John Calvin or his followers, emphasizing predestination, the sovereignty of God, the supreme authority of the Scriptures, and the irresistibility of grace. Cf. **Arminianism. 2.** adherence to these doctrines. [CALVIN + -ISM] **—Cal′vin·ist,** *n., adj.* **—Cal′vin·is′tic, Cal′vin·is′ti·cal,** *adj.* **—Cal·vin·is′ti·cal·ly,** *adv.*

cal·vi·ti·es (kal vish′ē ēz′), *n.* state of being calvous; baldness. [< L: baldness, equiv. to *calvi-* (var. s. of *calvus* bald) + *-ti-* -ness + *-ē-* thematic vowel + *-s* nom. sing. suffix]

cal·vous (kal′vəs), *adj.* lacking all or most of the hair on the head; bald. [< L: without hair, hairless]

cal·vus (kal′vəs), *adj.* *Meteorol.* (of a cloud) having its upper portion changing from a rounded, cumuliform shape to a diffuse, whitish, cirriform mass with vertical striations. [< NL < L: CALVUS[1]]

calx (kalks), *n., pl.* **calx·es, cal·ces** (kal′sēz). **1.** the oxide or ashy substance which remains after metals, minerals, etc., have been thoroughly roasted or burned. **2.** lime[1] (def. 1). [< L: lime; r. late ME *cals*, appar. back formation < L *calcis*, etc., obl. cases of *calx*]

Cal·y·ce (kal′i sē′), *n.* *Class. Myth.* a daughter of Aeolus and Enarete and the mother of Endymion.

cal·y·ces (kal′i sēz′, kā′li-), *n.* a pl. of **calyx.**

ca·lyc·i·form (kə lis′ə fôrm′), *adj.* shaped like a calyx. [< L *calyci-* (s. of *calyx* CALYX) + -FORM]

cal·y·cine (kal′i sin, -sīn′), *adj.* pertaining to or resembling a calyx. Also, **ca·lyc·i·nal** (kə lis′ə nəl). [< L *calyc-* (s. of *calyx* CALYX) + -INE[1]]

cal·y·cle (kal′i kəl), *n.* **1.** *Bot.* a set of bracts resembling an outer calyx. **2.** *Zool.* calyculus. [var. of CALYCULUS]

ca·lyc·u·lus (kə lik′yə ləs), *n., pl.* **-li** (-lī′). *Zool.* a structure shaped like a cup. Also, **caliculus.** [< L, equiv. to *calyc-* (s. of *calyx* CALYX) + *-ulus* -ULE]

Cal·y·don (kal′i don′), *n.* an ancient city in W Greece, in Aetolia. **—Cal·y·do·ni·an** (kal′i dō′nē ən, -dōn′yən), *adj.*

Calydo′nian hunt′, *Class. Myth.* the pursuit by Meleager, Atalanta, and others of a savage boar (**Calydo′nian boar′**) sent by Artemis to lay waste to Calydon.

Ca·lyp·so (kə lip′sō), *n., pl.* **-sos. 1.** *Class. Myth.* a nymph who detained Odysseus on Ogygia for seven years. **2.** (*l.c.*) a terrestrial orchid of the genus *Calypso* (*Cytherea*), of the Northern Hemisphere, having a single variegated purple, yellow, and white flower. **3.** (*l.c.*) a musical style of West Indian Negro origin, influenced by jazz, usually having a flexible accent in its topical, often improvised, lyrics. **4.** a girl's given name.

ca·lyp·tra (kə lip′trə), *n.* *Bot.* **1.** the hood which covers the lid of the capsule in mosses. **2.** a hoodlike part connected with the organs of fructification in flowering plants. **3.** a root cap. [< NL < Gk *kalýptra* veil, covering, equiv. to *kalýpt(ein)* (to) veil, cover + *-ra* n. suffix] **—ca·lyp·trate** (kə lip′trāt), *adj.*

ca·lyp·tro·gen (kə lip′trə jən), *n.* *Bot.* the histogen layer that develops into the root cap. [*calyptro-* (comb. form of CALYPTRA) + -GEN]

ca·lyx (kā′liks, kal′iks), *n., pl.* **ca·lyx·es, cal·y·ces** (kal′i sēz′, kā′li-). **1.** *Bot.* the outermost group of floral parts, usually green; the sepals. **2.** *Anat., Zool.* a cuplike part. [< L < Gk *kályx* husk, covering, akin to *kalýptein* to veil, cover] **—cal·y·cate** (kal′i kāt′), *adj.*

Calyxes (def. 1) A, Gamosepalous calyx; B, Bilabiate calyx

cam (kam), *n.* *Mach.* a disk or cylinder having an irregular form such that its motion, usually rotary, gives to a part or parts in contact with it a specific rocking or reciprocating motion or motions. [< D or LG *kam, kamm.* See COMB[1]]

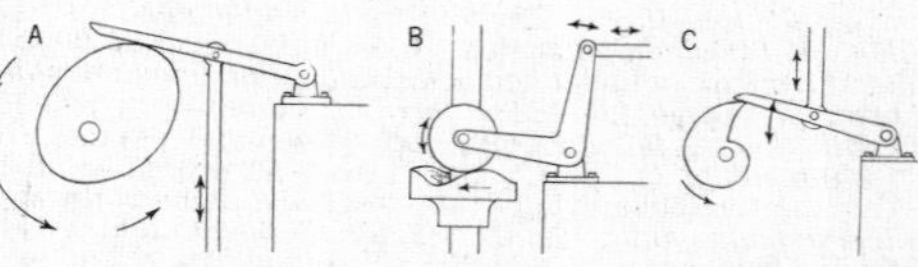

Cams
A, Elliptical cam; B, Crown cam; C, Wiper cam

Cam (kam), *n.* **1.** Also called **Granta.** a river in E England flowing NE by Cambridge, into the Ouse River. 40 mi. long. **2.** a girl's given name, form of **Camilla.**

Cam., Cambridge.

cam·a·ca (kam′ə kə), *n.* a heavy fabric of silk or mixed fibers, much used in the Middle Ages. Also, **cam′a·ka, camoca.** [ME < ML *camoca* < Ar, Pers *kamkha, kimkha*]

Ca·ma·cho (kä mä′chō), *n.* **Ma·nuel Á·vi·la** (mä nwel′ ä′vē lä′). See **Ávila Camacho, Manuel.**

Ca·ma·güey (kam′ə gwā′; *Sp.* kä′mä gwā′), *n.* a city in central Cuba. 132,059 (1953).

ca·mail (kə māl′), *n.* *Armor.* aventail (def. 1). [< F < OPr *capmath*, perh. equiv. to *cap* head (< L *caput*) + *mail* MAIL[2]] **—ca·mailed′,** *adj.*

ca·man·cha·ca (kam′ən chä′kə), *n.* garúa. [< AmerSp]

CONCISE ETYMOLOGY KEY: <, descended or derived from; >, whence; b., blend of, blended; c., cognate with; deriv., derivative; equiv., equivalent; imit., imitative; m., modification of; obl., oblique; r., replacing; s., stem; sp., spelling; trans., translation; ?, origin unknown, perhaps; *, hypothetical. See the full key inside the front cover.

ca·ma·ra·de·rie (kä′mə rä′də rē), *n.* comradeship; good-fellowship. [< F, equiv. to *camarade* COMRADE + *-erie* -ERY]

cam·a·ril·la (kam′ə ril′ə; *Sp.* kä′mä rē′lyä, -yä), *n., pl.* **-ril·las** (-ril′əz; *Sp.* -rē′lyäs, -yäs). a group of unofficial or private advisers to a person of authority, esp. a group much given to intrigues and secret plots; cabal; clique. [< Sp, equiv. to *camar(a)* room (< L; see CAMERA, CHAMBER) + *-illa* dim. suffix < L]

Cam·as (kam′əs), *n.* a town in SW Washington. 5666 (1960).

cam·ass (kam′as), *n.* **1.** any of several liliaceous plants of the genus *Camassia*, esp. *C. quamash*, of western North America, having sweet, edible bulbs. **2.** See **death camass.** Also, **cam′as.** [< Chinook Jargon *kamass* < Nootka *chamas* sweet]

ca·mau·ro (kə mou′rō), *n., pl.* **-ros.** *Rom. Cath. Ch.* a crimson velvet cap trimmed with ermine, worn by the pope on nonliturgical occasions. [< It; cf. ML *camaurum*]

Camb., Cambridge.

cam·ber (kam′bər), *v.t., v.i.* **1.** to arch slightly; bend or curve upward in the middle. —*n.* **2.** a slight arching, upward curve, or convexity, as of the deck of a ship. **3.** a slightly arching piece of timber. **4.** *Aeron.* the rise of the curve of an airfoil, usually expressed as the ratio of the rise to the length of the chord of the airfoil. [< MF (north) *cambre* bent < L *camur* hooked, curved]

cam′ber piece′, a centering for a flat arch, slightly crowned to allow for settling of the arch. Also called **cam′ber slip′.**

Cam·ber·well (kam′bər wel′, -wəl), *n.* a residential borough of S London, England. 174,697 (1961).

Cam′berwell beau′ty. See **mourning cloak.**

cam·bi·at·a (kam′bē ät′ə), *n.* *Music.* a melodic ornamental tone following a principal tone by a skip, usually of a third above or below, and progressing by a step. Also called **changing tone.** Cf. **échappée.** [< It: short for *nota cambiata* changed note; *cambiata*, fem. ptp. of *cambiare* to CHANGE]

C, Cambiatas

cam·bi·on (kam′bē ən), *n.* the offspring of an incubus and a succuba. [appar. connected with LL *cambium* exchange; cf. CHANGELING]

cam·bist (kam′bist), *n.* *Finance.* **1.** a dealer in bills of exchange. **2.** an expert in foreign exchange. **3.** a manual giving the moneys, weights, and measures of different countries, with their equivalents. [< F *cambiste* < It *cambist(a)*. See CAMBIUM, -IST] —**cam′bist·ry,** *n.*

cam·bi·um (kam′bē əm), *n., pl.* **-bi·ums, -bi·a** (-bē ə). *Bot.* a layer of delicate meristematic tissue between the inner bark or phloem and the wood or xylem, which produces new phloem on the outside and new xylem on the inside in stems, roots, etc. It produces all secondary growth in plants and is responsible for the annual rings of wood. [< LL: an exchange, barter; akin to L *cambiāre* to exchange] —**cam′bi·al,** *adj.*

Cam·bo·di·a (kam bō′dē ə), *n.* a republic in SE Asia: formerly part of French Indochina. 5,756,000; 69,866 sq. mi. *Cap.:* Phnom Penh. Official name, **Democratic Kampuchea.**

Cam·bo·di·an (kam bō′dē ən), *adj.* **1.** of, pertaining to, or characteristic of Cambodia, its people, or its culture. —*n.* **2.** a native or inhabitant of Cambodia. **3.** Khmer (def. 2). [CAMBODI(A) + -AN]

cam·bo·gi·a (kam bō′jē ə), *n.* gamboge (def. 1).

Cam·bon (käN bôN′), *n.* **1. Jules Mar·tin** (zhYl MAR taN′), 1845–1935, French diplomat and administrator. **2. Pierre Paul** (pyeR pôl), 1843–1924, French diplomat.

Cam·brai (käN bRe′), *n.* a city in N France: battles 1917, 1918. 35,373 (1962).

cam·brel (kam′brəl), *n.* *Brit. Dial.* gambrel.

Cam·bri·a (kam′brē ə), *n.* medieval name of **Wales.**

Cam·bri·an (kam′brē ən), *adj.* **1.** *Geol.* noting or pertaining to a period of the Paleozoic era, occurring from 500 million to 600 million years ago and characterized by the presence of algae and marine invertebrates. See table under **era. 2.** of or pertaining to Cambria; Welsh. —*n.* **3.** *Geol.* the Cambrian period or system. **4.** a native of Cambria; Welshman. [< ML *Cambri(a)* Wales (var. of *Cumbria* < Welsh *Cymr(y)* Welshman + L *-ia* -IA) + -AN]

cam·bric (kām′brik), *n.* a thin, plain cotton or linen fabric of fine close weave, usually white. [earlier *cameryk* deriv. of *Kameryk*, Flemish name of CAMBRAI]

cam′bric tea′, a mixture of hot water and milk, with sugar and, sometimes, a little tea.

Cam·bridge (kām′brij), *n.* **1.** a city in and the county seat of Cambridgeshire, in E England: famous university founded in 12th century. 95,358 (1961). **2.** a city in E Massachusetts, near Boston. 107,716 (1960). **3.** Cambridgeshire. **4.** a town in E Minnesota. 2728 (1960).

Cam′bridge Cit′y, a town in E Indiana. 2569 (1960).

Cam′bridge Pla′tonist, a member of a group of English idealist philosophers of the 17th century who sought to reconcile religious and scientific thought within a system of principles derived from Platonism and Neoplatonism. —**Cam′bridge Pla′tonism.**

Cam′bridge School′, a group of 20th-century philosophers, influenced esp. by G. E. Moore, who emphasized acceptance of common-sense judgments and the importance of philosophical analysis.

Cam·bridge·shire (kām′brij shēr′, -shər), *n.* a county in E England. 189,913 (1961); 492 sq. mi. *Co. seat:* Cambridge. Also called **Cambridge.**

Cam·by·ses (kam bī′sēz), *n.* died 522 B.C., king of Persia 529–522 (son of Cyrus the Great).

Cam·den (kam′dən), *n.* **1.** a port in SW New Jersey, on the Delaware River opposite Philadelphia. 117,159 (1960). **2.** a city in SW Arkansas. 15,823 (1960). **3.** a town in central South Carolina. 6842 (1960). **4.** a town in S Maine. 3523 (1960). **5.** a town in NW Tennessee. 2774 (1960). **6.** a town in central New York. 2694 (1960).

came[1] (kām), *v.* pt. of **come.**

came[2] (kām), *n.* a slender, grooved bar of lead for holding together the pieces of glass in windows of latticework or stained glass. Also called **ribbon.** See illus. under **quarrel**[2]. [special use of *came* ridge; see KAME, COMB[1]]

cam·el (kam′əl), *n.* **1.** either of two large, humped, ruminant quadrupeds of the genus *Camelus*, of the Old World. Cf. **Bactrian camel, dromedary. 2.** *Naut.* **a.** a float for lifting a deeply laden vessel sufficiently to allow it to cross an area of shallow water. **b.** a float serving as a fender between a vessel and a pier or the like. **c.** caisson (def. 3a). [ME, OE < L *camēl(us)* < Gk *kámēlos* < Sem, as Heb *gāmāl*] —**cam′el·like′,** *adj.*

cam′el back′, a curved back of a chair or the like, having a central rising section between other, lower, rising sections.

cam′el·back truss′ (kam′əl bak′). See **crescent truss.**

cam·el·eer (kam′ə lēr′), *n.* **1.** a camel driver. **2.** a soldier mounted on a camel. [CAMEL + -EER]

cam′el grass′. See **camel hay.**

cam·el·hair (kam′əl hâr′), *n.* **1.** See **camel's hair.** —*adj.* **2.** camel's-hair.

cam′el hay′, a perennial grass, *Cymbopogon Schoenanthus*, of southern Asia and northern Africa, having very fragrant foliage. Also called **camel grass.** [so called from its use as fodder for camels]

ca·mel·lia (kə mēl′yə, -mē′lē ə), *n.* a woody plant, *Camellia* (or *Thea*) *japonica*, native to Asia, having glossy evergreen leaves and white, pink, red, or variegated waxy, roselike flowers. [named after G. J. *Camellus* (1661–1706), Jesuit missionary, who brought it to Europe]

Ca·mel·lia (kə mēl′yə), *n.* a girl's given name.

ca·mel·o·pard (kə mel′ə pärd′), *n.* *Obs.* a giraffe. [ME < ML *camēlopard(us)* < L *camēlopard(ālis)* < Gk *kamēlopárdalis* giraffe, equiv. to *kámēlo(s)* CAMEL + *pardalis* PARD]

Ca·mel·o·par·da·lis (kə mel′ə pär′dᵊlis, kam′ə lō-), *n., gen.* **-lis.** *Astron.* the Giraffe, a northern constellation between Ursa Major and Perseus. [NL < L]

Cam·e·lot (kam′ə lot′), *n.* **1.** the legendary site of King Arthur's palace and court, possibly near Exeter, England. **2.** any idyllic site or period.

cam′el's hair′, 1. the hair of the camel, used for cloth, painters' brushes, certain Oriental rugs, etc. **2.** cloth made of this hair, or of a substitute, usually tan in color. Also, **camelhair.**

cam·el's-hair (kam′əlz hâr′), *adj.* **1.** made of camel's hair. **2.** (of a painter's brush) made from the tail hairs of squirrels.

Cam·em·bert (kam′əm bâr′; *Fr.* KA mäN beR′), *n.* a mellow, soft cheese, the center of which is creamy and of a golden cream color, made from cow's milk. Also called **Cam′embert cheese′.** [after *Camembert*, village in Normandy where it was first marketed]

Ca·me·nae (kə mē′nē), *n.pl., sing.* **-na** (-nə). *Rom. Religion.* four wise and prophetic deities or fountain nymphs: Carmenta, Egeria, Antevorta, and Postvorta; later identified with the Greek Muses.

cam·e·o (kam′ē ō′), *n., pl.* **cam·e·os. 1.** a technique of engraving upon a gem or other stone, as onyx, in such a way that an underlying stone of one color is exposed as a background for a low-relief design of another color. **2.** a gem or other stone so engraved. **3.** a literary sketch, small dramatic scene, or the like, that effectively presents or depicts its subject **4.** Also called **cam′eo role′.** a minor part played by a prominent performer in a single scene of a motion picture or a television play. [< It *cam(m)eo;* cf. ML *cam(m)aeus*]

Cam·e·o (kam′ē ō′), *n.* a girl's given name.

cam′eo encrusta′tion, sulphide (def. 2).

cam′eo glass′, an ornamental glass in which two layers, often blue and opaque white, have been cased, and on which the design has been treated in the manner of a cameo.

cam′eo ware′, jasper[1] (def. 2).

cam·er·a (kam′ər ə, kam′rə), *n., pl.* **-er·as** for 1, 2, **-er·ae** (-ə rē′) for 3. **1.** a boxlike device for holding a film or plate sensitive to light, having an aperture controlled by a shutter which, when opened, admits light enabling an object to be focused, usually by means of a lens, on the film or plate, thereby producing a photographic image. **2.** (in a television transmitting apparatus) the device in which the picture to be televised is formed before it is changed into electric impulses. **3.** a judge's private office. **4. in camera, a.** *Law.* in the privacy of a judge's chambers. **b.** privately. [< L *camera* vaulted room, vault < Gk *kamára* vault; see CHAMBER]

cam·er·al (kam′ər əl), *adj.* **1.** of or pertaining to a judicial or legislative chamber or the privacy of such a chamber. **2.** cameralistic. [< ML *camerāl(is)*, equiv. to *camer(a)* treasury, governmental chamber + *-ālis* -AL[1]; see CHAMBER]

cam·er·a·lism (kam′ər ə liz′əm), *n.* the principles and practices of the cameralists. [CAMERAL + -ISM]

cam·er·a·list (kam′ər ə list), *n.* any of the mercantilist economists or public servants in Europe in the 17th and 18th centuries who held that the economic power of a nation can be enhanced by increasing its monetary wealth, as by the accumulation of bullion. [< G *Kameralist* < NL *cameralist(a)*, equiv. to ML *camerāl(is)* (see CAMERAL) + *-ista* -IST]

cam·er·a·lis·tic (kam′ər ə lis′tik), *adj.* **1.** of or pertaining to public finance. **2.** of or pertaining to cameralism. —*n.* **3. cameralistics,** (*usually construed as sing.*) the science of public finance. [< G *kameralistisch*, equiv. to *Kameralist* CAMERALIST + *-isch* -ISH[1] (replaced by -IC)]

cam′era lu′ci·da (lo͞o′si də), *Optics.* an optical instrument, often attached to the eyepiece of a microscope, by which the image of an external object is projected on a sheet of paper or the like for tracing. [< NL: clear chamber; see CAMERA, LUCID]

cam·er·a·man (kam′ər ə man′, -mən, kam′rə-), *n., pl.* **-men** (-men′, -mən). a man who operates a camera, esp. a motion-picture camera. [CAMERA + MAN[1]]

cam′era ob·scu′ra (ob skyo͝or′ə), a darkened boxlike device in which images of external objects, received through an aperture, as with a convex lens, are exhibited in their natural colors on a surface arranged to receive them: used for sketching, exhibition purposes, etc. [< NL: dark chamber; see CAMERA, OBSCURE]

cam′era tube′, *Television.* a cathode ray tube that converts an optical image into an electric signal by a scanning process, used in television cameras. Also called **image tube.**

cam·er·len·go (kam′ər leng′gō), *n., pl.* **-gos.** *Rom. Cath. Ch.* the cardinal appointed treasurer of the Holy See, who, upon the death of the pope, presides over the conclave that elects the new pope. [< It *camerlingo* < Gmc; akin to OHG *chamarlinc* CHAMBERLAIN]

cam·er·lin·go (kam′ər ling′gō), *n., pl.* **-gos.** *Rom. Cath. Ch.* camerlengo.

Cam·er·on (kam′ər ən), *n.* **1. Richard,** 1648?–80, Scottish Covenanter. **2.** a town in central Texas. 5640 (1960). **3.** a town in NW Missouri. 3674 (1960). —**Cam·er·o·ni·an** (kam′ə rō′nē ən, -rōn′yən), *adj., n.*

Cam·e·roon (kam′ə ro͞on′), *n.* **1.** Also, **Cameroun.** Official name, **Federal Republic of Cameroon.** an independent republic in W Africa: formed 1960 by the French trusteeship of Cameroun; Southern Cameroons incorporated as a self-governing province 1961. 5,103,000 (est. 1964); 183,350 sq. mi. *Cap.:* Yaoundé. **2.** an active volcano in W Cameroon: highest peak on the coast of W Africa. 13,370 ft.

Cam·e·roons (kam′ə ro͞onz′), *n.* (*construed as sing.*) **1.** German, **Kamerun.** a region in W Africa: a German protectorate 1884–1919; divided in 1919 into British and French mandates. **2.** Also called **British Cameroons.** the NW part of this region: a British mandate 1919–46 and trusteeship 1946–61; by a 1961 plebiscite the S part **(Southern Cameroons)** joined the Federal Republic of Cameroon and the N part **(Northern Cameroons)** joined Nigeria.

Came·roun (kam ro͞on′), *n.* **1.** Cameroon (def. 1). **2.** Also called **French Cameroons.** a former French mandate (1919–46) and trusteeship (1946–60) in W Africa: independence 1960: now part of the Federal Republic of Cameroon.

Ca·mil·la (kə mil′ə), *n.* **1.** *Rom. Legend.* a woman warrior who fought on the side of Turnus against Aeneas. **2.** a town in SW Georgia. 4753 (1960). **3.** Also, **Camil′a, Camile, Camille.** a girl's given name.

Ca·mille (kə mēl′), *n.* a girl's given name. Also, **Ca·mile′, Camila, Camilla.**

Ca·mi·lo (kə mē′lō; *Sp.* kä mē′lô), *n.* a boy's given name.

ca·mi·no re·al (kä mē′nô RE äl′), *pl.* **ca·mi·nos re·a·les** (kä mē′nôs RE ä′les). *Spanish.* a main road; highway. [lit., royal road]

cam·i·on (kam′ē ən; *Fr.* KA myôN′), *n., pl.* **cam·i·ons** (kam′ē ənz; *Fr.* KA myôN′). **1.** a strongly built cart or wagon for transporting heavy loads. **2.** a truck, as for military supplies. [< F < ?]

Ca·mi·rus (kə mī′rəs), *n.* *Class. Myth.* a grandson of Helius.

cam·i·sa·do (kam′i sā′dō, -sä′-), *n., pl.* **-dos.** *Archaic.* a military attack made at night. Also, **cam·i·sade** (kam′i sād′, -säd′). [< Sp *camisada* (now obs.), equiv. to *camis(a)* shirt + *-ada* -ADE[1]]

Cam·i·sard (kam′i zärd′, kam′i zärd′; *Fr.* KA mē ZAR′), *n.* any French Protestant, living in the region of the Cévennes Mountains, who carried on a revolt against Louis XIV in the early part of the 18th century. [< F, equiv. to *camis-* (< Pr *camisa* shirt; see CHEMISE) + *-ard* -ARD]

ca·mise (kə mēz′, -mēs′), *n.* a lightweight, loose-fitting shirt or smock with long sleeves. [< Ar *qamīṣ* < LL *camīs(a)*, var. of *camīsia* shirt; see CHEMISE]

cam·i·sole (kam′i sōl′), *n.* **1.** a short garment worn underneath a sheer bodice to conceal the underwear. **2.** a woman's dressing jacket. **3.** a sleeved jacket or jersey once worn by men. **4.** a strait jacket with long sleeves. [< F < Pr *camisol(a)* < LL *camis(a)* shirt (see CHEMISE) + *-ola* -ULE]

cam·la (kam′lə), *n.* a prostrate, perennial herb, *Phlox nivalis*, of the southeastern U.S., having white or pink flowers. Also called **trailing phlox.**

cam·let (kam′lit), *n., v.,* **-let·ted, -let·ting.** —*n.* **1.** a durable, waterproof cloth, esp. for outerwear. **2.** apparel made of this material. **3.** a rich fabric of medieval Asia, believed to have been made of camel's hair or angora wool. —*v.t.* **4.** to decorate (fabric, book edges, etc.) with a colorful, marbled design. [late ME *camelot* < MF < Ar *khamlat* kind of plush fabric, akin to *khaml* nap, pile]

Cam·maerts (kä′märts), *n.* **É·mile** (ā mēl′), 1878–1953, Belgian poet.

cam·o·ca (kam′ə kə), *n.* camaca.

Ca·mo·ëns (kam′ō ens′), *n.* **Lu·is Vaz de** (lo͞o ēsh′ väzh də), 1524?–80, Portuguese poet. Also, **Ca·mões** (kə moiNsh′).

cam·o·mile (kam′ə mīl′), *n.* **1.** any asteraceous plant of the genus *Anthemis*, esp. *A. nobilis*, of Europe, having strongly scented foliage and flowers which are used medicinally. **2.** any of various allied plants, as *Matricaria Chamomilla* **(German camomile).** Also, **chamomile.** [ME *camemille* < ML *c(h)amomill(a)* (sing.) < L *chamaemēla* (pl.) < Gk *chamaímēla* earth-apples, equiv. to *chamaí* on the ground + *mēla*, pl. of *mēlon* apple]

Ca·mor·ra (kə môr′ə, -mor′ə; *It.* kä môR′Rä), *n.* **1.** a secret society of Naples, Italy, first publicly known about 1820, which developed into a powerful political organization and was associated with blackmail, robbery, etc., until its destruction in 1911. **2.** (*l.c.*) any similar society or group. [< It < Sp: dispute, quarrel] —**Ca·mor′rism,** *n.* —**Ca·mor′rist,** *n.*

cam·ou·flage (kam′ə fläzh′), *n., v.,* **-flaged, -flag·ing.** —*n.* **1.** *Mil.* the act, art, means, or result of disguising things to deceive an enemy, as by painting or screening objects so that they are lost to view in the background, or by making up objects that have from a distance the appearance of fortifications, guns, roads, etc. **2.** disguise; deception; pretense. —*v.t.* **3.** to disguise, hide, or deceive by means of camouflage: *to camouflage ships by painting them gray.* **4.** (of a mineral element) to contain a trace of (an element having a similar ionic radius and the same charge as the crystal). [< F, equiv. to *camoufl(er)* (to) disguise (< It *camuffare* to disguise + F *moufler* to cover up) + *-age* -AGE] —**cam′ou·flag′er,** *n.*

ca·mou·flet (kam′ə flā′, kam′ə flā′), *n.* **1.** an underground explosion of a bomb or mine that does not break the surface, but leaves an enclosed cavity of gas and smoke. **2.** the pocket formed by such an explosion. **3.** the bomb or mine so exploded and causing such a pocket. [< F: lit., smoke puffed at one's face]

cam·ou·fleur (kam′ə flûr′; *Fr.* KA mōō flœR′), *n., pl.* **-fleurs** (-flûrz′; *Fr.* -flœR′). *Mil.* one who conceals military objects by camouflage. [< F, equiv. to *camoufl(er)* (to) disguise + *-eur* -OR[2]]

camp[1] (kamp), *n.* **1.** a place where an army or other body of persons is lodged in tents or other temporary means of shelter. **2.** such tents or shelters collectively: *The regiment transported its camp in trucks.* **3.** the persons so sheltered: *The camp slept through the storm.* **4.** the act of camping out: *Camp is far more pleasant in summer than in winter.* **5.** any temporary structure, as a tent or cabin, used on an outing or vacation. **6.** a body of troops, workers, etc., camping and moving together. **7.** army life. **8.** a group of people favoring the same ideals, doctrines, etc.: *Most American voters are divided into two camps, Republicans and Democrats.* **9.** any position in which ideals, doctrines, etc., are strongly entrenched: *After considering each side's argument he changed camps.* **10.** a recreation area in the country, equipped with extensive facilities for sports. **11.** See **day camp. 12.** See **summer camp.** —*v.i.* **13.** to establish or pitch a camp: *The army camped in the valley.* **14.** to live temporarily in or as in a camp (often fol. by *out*): *They camped by the stream for a week.* **15.** to reside or lodge somewhere temporarily or irregularly, esp. in an apartment, room, etc.: *They camped in our apartment whenever they came to town.* **16.** to settle down securely and comfortably; become ensconced: *The kids camped in the living room for the day.* **17.** to take up a position stubbornly: *They camped in front of the president's office.* **18. camp out, a.** to go camping. **b.** to live temporarily or with only the barest essentials in what are normally adequately equipped quarters: *Since we expected to move out again almost immediately, we were camping out in the new apartment.* —*v.t.* **19.** to put or station (troops) in a camp; shelter. [OE: battle(field), field < L *camp(us)* field]

camp[2] (kamp), *n.* **1.** an ironic or amusing quality present in an extravagant gesture, style, or form, esp. when inappropriate or out of proportion to the content that is expressed. When the inappropriate relationship of form and content is used self-consciously or knowledgeably it is considered to be on a high level (**high camp**); however, when used unself-consciously, unknowledgeably, or inadequately it is considered to be on a low level (**low camp**). **2.** delight in artificiality, exaggeration and affectation, esp. when used in conjunction with banality and outlandish trivia. **3.** a person whose actions or works can be judged as possessing these qualities. **4.** an action or object that has this quality. —*v.i. Slang.* **5.** to speak or act so theatrically or affectedly as to parody one's own personality, characteristics, or role in life. **6.** to be so ostentatious, overly decorated, ornate, or outlandish as to gain attention. **7.** to speak or act in a witty or frivolous way: *Stop camping and be serious!* —*v.t.* **8.** *Slang.* to perform or imbue (something) with an ostentatious, affected, or heavily ornate manner (often fol. by *up*): *Gladys really camped up the third act.* **9. camp it up,** *Slang.* **a.** to make an ostentatious or affected display. **b.** to flaunt homosexuality. [? dial. *camp* impetuous, uncouth person (see KEMP[1]); hence, slightly objectionable, effeminate, homosexual; in some senses prob. special use of CAMP[1] brothel, meeting place of male homosexuals]

Camp (kamp), *n.* **Walter Chaun·cey** (chôn′sē, chän′-), 1859–1925, U.S. football coach.

Cam·pa·gna (kam pän′yə, kəm-; *It.* käm pä′nyä), *n., pl.* **-pa·gne** (-pän′yā; *It.* -pä′nye) for 2. **1.** a low plain surrounding the city of Rome, Italy. **2.** (*l.c.*) any flat open plain; champaign. [< It; see CAMPAIGN]

cam·pa·gus (kam′pə gəs), *n., pl.* **-gi** (-jī′). **1.** a shoe, sometimes ornamented, worn by bishops in the Western Church, esp. in the Roman Catholic Church. **2.** *Rom. Antiq.* a low shoe or slipper secured to the ankle with a ribbon or strap extending from the heelpiece. Also called **episcopal sandal.** [< LL]

cam·paign (kam pān′), *n.* **1.** *Mil.* **a.** military operations for a specific objective. **b.** *Obs.* the military operations of an army in the field for one season. **2.** any systematic course of aggressive activities for some special purpose: *a sales campaign.* **3.** the competition by rival political candidates and organizations for public office. **4.** *Metall.* an individual smelting operation of a blast furnace. —*v.i.* **5.** to serve in or go on a campaign: *He planned to campaign for the candidate. He campaigned in France.* [< F *campagne* < It *campagn(a)* < LL *campānia* level district, equiv. to *camp(us)* field + *-ānia* regional suffix] —**cam·paign′er,** *n.*

campaign′ chest′, 1. money collected and set aside for use in a political campaign; a campaign fund. **2.** a low chest of drawers having handles at each side for lifting.

campaign′ fund′, money for the political campaign of a candidate, usually acquired through contributions made by the supporters of a party or candidate.

campaign′ hat′, (formerly in use in the Army and Marine Corps) a felt hat with a broad brim and four dents.

campaign′ med′al, *Mil.* See **service medal.**

campaign′ rib′bon, a distinctively colored ribbon, either on a small, narrow bar or in the form of a strip, representing a military campaign participated in by the wearer.

Cam·pa·nia (kam pā′nē ə; *It.* käm pä′nyä), *n.* a region in SW Italy. 4,756,094 (1961); 5214 sq. mi. *Cap.:* Naples. —**Cam·pa′ni·an,** *adj., n.*

cam·pa·ni·le (kam′pə nē′lē; *It.* käm′pä nē′le), *n., pl.* **-ni·les, -ni·li** (-nē′lē). a bell tower, esp. one somewhat detached from the body of a church. [< It, equiv. to *campan(a)* bell (< LL) + *-ile* locative suffix < L]

Campanile

cam·pa·nol·o·gy (kam′pə nol′ə jē), *n.* **1.** the study of bells. **2.** the principles, science, or art of making bells, bell ringing, etc. [< NL *campānologia* < LL *campān(a)* bell + *-o-* -O- + *-logia* -LOGY] —**cam·pa·no·log·i·cal** (kam′pə nə loj′i kəl), *adj.* —**cam′pa·no·log′i·cal·ly,** *adv.* —**cam′pa·nol′o·gist, cam′pa·nol′o·ger,** *n.*

cam·pan·u·la (kam pan′yə lə), *n.* any plant of the genus *Campanula,* as the harebell or the Canterbury bell; a bellflower. [< NL < LL *campān(a)* bell + L *-ula* -ULE]

cam·pan·u·la·ceous (kam-pan′yə lā′shəs), *adj.* belonging to the *Campanulaceae,* or campanula family of plants. [< NL *Campanulac(ae)* name of the family (see CAMPANULA, -ACEAE) + -OUS]

cam·pan·u·late (kam pan′yə lit, -lāt′), *adj.* bell-shaped, as a corolla. [< NL *campanulāt(us).* See CAMPANULA, -ATE[1]]

Cam·pan·us (kam pan′əs), *n.* a crater in the third quadrant of the face of the moon: about 29 miles in diameter.

camp′ bed′, a light, folding bed.

Camp·bell (kam′bəl, kam′əl), *n.* **1. Alexander,** 1788–1866, U.S. religious leader, born in Ireland: co-founder with his father, Thomas, of the Disciples of Christ Church. **2. Colen** or **Colin,** died 1729, Scottish architect and author. **3. Colin** (*Baron Clyde*), 1792–1863, Scottish general. **4. Sir John,** 1779–1861, English jurist and writer: Lord Chancellor of England 1859–61. **5. Mrs. Patrick** (*Beatrice Stella Tanner*), 1865–1940, English actress. **6. Thomas,** 1763–1854, Irish religious leader, in the U.S. after 1807: co-founder with his son, Alexander, of the Disciples of Christ Church. **7. Thomas,** 1777–1844, Scottish poet and editor.

Camp·bell-Ban·ner·man (kam′bəl ban′ər mən, kam′əl-), *n.* **Sir Henry,** 1836–1908, British statesman, born in Ireland: prime minister 1905–08.

Camp·bell·ism (kam′bə liz′əm), *n.* the practices and principles of the Disciples of Christ. [after Alexander CAMPBELL + -ISM]

Camp·bell·ite (kam′bə līt′, kam′ə-), *n.* *Sometimes Derogatory.* a member of the Disciples of Christ. [after Alexander CAMPBELL + -ITE[1]]

Camp·bells·ville (kam′bəlz vil, kam′əlz-), *n.* a town in central Kentucky. 6966 (1960).

Camp·bel·town (kam′bəl toun′), *n.* a seaport in S Argyll, in W Scotland. 7169 (1951).

camp′ car′, *Railroads.* See **outfit car.**

camp′ ceil′ing, a ceiling having two opposite ends sloping inward with a flat area between them, as a ceiling under a vaulted roof.

camp′ chair′, a light folding chair.

camp·craft (kamp′kraft′, -kräft′), *n.* the art of outdoor camping. [CAMP[1] + CRAFT]

Cam·pe (kam′pē), *n. Class. Myth.* an old woman who was the jailer of Tartarus.

cam·pea′chy wood′ (kam pē′chē), logwood. [alter. of *Campeche,* Mexico, one of its sources]

Cam·pe·che (käm pe′che), *n.* **1.** a state in SE Mexico, on the peninsula of Yucatán. 158,219 (1960); 19,672 sq. mi. **2.** a seaport in and the capital of this state. 43,874 (1960). **3. Gulf of,** the SW part of the Gulf of Mexico.

camp·er (kam′pər), *n.* **1.** a person who camps out for recreation, esp. in the wilderness. **2.** a person who attends a summer camp or day camp. **3.** a compact, portable room, like a trailer without wheels, for mounting on a pickup truck and used for camping or extended motor excursions. [CAMP[1] + -ER[1]]

cam′per·nelle jon′quil (kam′pər nel′, kam′pər-nel′), a narcissus, *Narcissus odorus,* having clusters of two to four fragrant, yellow flowers. [prob. from proper name *Campernelle*]

cam·pe·si·no (käm′pe sē′nô; *Eng.* kam′pi sē′nō), *n., pl.* **-nos** (-nôs; *Eng.* -nōz). *Spanish.* (in Latin America) a peasant, farmer, or rustic.

cam·pes·tral (kam pes′trəl), *adj.* of or pertaining to fields or open country. [< L *campestr-* (s. of *campester* flat, equiv. to *camp(us)* field + *-ester* adj. suffix) + -AL[1]]

camp·fire (kamp′fīᵊr′), *n.* **1.** an outdoor fire for warmth or cooking, as at a camp. **2.** a reunion of soldiers, scouts, etc. [CAMP[1] + FIRE]

camp′fire girl′, a member of an association (**Camp-fire Girls, Inc.**) organized to build good character, health, and citizenship in girls aged 7–18.

camp′ fol′lower, 1. a civilian not officially connected with a military unit, esp. a prostitute, who follows or settles near an army camp. **2.** one who sympathizes with or espouses the aims of a group to which he does not belong without materially contributing to their realization.

camp·ground (kamp′ground′), *n.* a place for a camp or for a camp meeting. [CAMP[1] + GROUND[1]]

cam·phene (kam′fēn, kam fēn′), *n. Chem.* a colorless, crystalline, water-insoluble substance, $C_{10}H_{16}$, occurring in turpentine and many other essential oils, prepared from pinene: used chiefly as an intermediate in the manufacture of synthetic camphor. [< NL *camph(ora)* CAMPHOR + -ENE]

Camp′ Hill′, a town in S Pennsylvania. 8559 (1960).

cam·phol (kam′fəl, -fôl, -fōl), *n. Chem.* borneol. [< NL *camph(ora)* CAMPHOR + -OL[1]]

cam·phor (kam′fər), *n. Chem., Pharm.* **1.** a whitish, translucent, crystalline, pleasant-odored terpene ketone, $C_{10}H_{16}O$, obtained from the camphor tree: used chiefly in the manufacture of celluloid and in medicine as a counterirritant for infections and in the treatment of pain and itching. **2.** any similar substance. [< ML, NL *camphor(a)* < Ar *kāfūr* < Malay *kāpūr*; r. ME *caumfre* < AF] —**cam·phor·ic** (kam fôr′ik, -for′-), *adj.*

cam·pho·rate (kam′fə rāt′), *v.t.,* **-rat·ed, -rat·ing.** to impregnate with camphor. [< ML *camphorāt(us),* equiv. to *camphor(a)* CAMPHOR + *-ātus* -ATE[1]]

cam′phorated oil′, *Pharm.* a solution of one part camphor oil in four parts cottonseed oil, used as a counterirritant. Also called **cam′phor lin′iment.**

cam′phor ball′, a small ball of naphthalene, camphor, etc., used as a moth repellent.

cam′phor ice′, a cosmetic preparation composed of camphor, spermaceti, white beeswax, and a vegetable oil, used chiefly in the treatment of mild skin eruptions.

cam′phor oil′, a colorless liquid obtained from the wood of the camphor tree by distillation and separation from the solid camphor, used in varnish, soaps, shoe polish, and in medicine chiefly as a rubefacient.

cam′phor tree′, 1. a lauraceous tree, *Cinnamomum Camphora,* of Japan, Formosa, China, etc., yielding camphor. **2.** any of various similar trees, as *Dryobalanops aromatica,* of Borneo, Southeast Asia, etc., which yields borneol.

cam·phor·weed (kam′fər wēd′), *n.* vinegarweed. [CAMPHOR + WEED[1]]

Cam·pi·gnian (kam pēn′yən), *adj.* of or pertaining to an early Neolithic culture in France marked by the production of rough-hewn tools, scrapers, and axes, and by a crude style of pottery. [after *Campigny,* French town + -AN]

cam·pim·e·ter (kam pim′i tər), *n. Ophthalm.* an instrument for determining the visual field. [< L *campi-* (comb. form of *campus* field) + -METER] —**cam·pi·met·ri·cal** (kam′pə me′tri kəl), *adj.* —**cam·pim′e·try,** *n.*

Cam·pi·na Gran·de (känm pē′nə grännʹdə), a city in NE Brazil. 126,274 (est. 1960).

Cam·pi·nas (kam pē′nəs; *Port.* känm pē′nəs), *n.* a city in SE Brazil, NNW of São Paulo. 184,529 (1960).

cam·pi·on (kam′pē ən), *n.* any of several caryophyllaceous plants of the genera *Lychnis* or *Silene.* [special use of *campion,* old var. (< AF) of CHAMPION]

Cam·pi·on (kam′pē ən), *n.* **Thomas,** 1567–1620, English songwriter and poet.

camp′ meet′ing, a religious gathering, usually lasting for some days, held in a tent or in the open air.

cam·po (kam′pō, käm′-), *n., pl.* **-pos.** (in South America) an extensive, nearly level, grassy plain. [< Sp < L *camp(us)* field]

Cam·po·bel·lo (kam′pō bel′ō, -pə-), *n.* an island in SE Canada, in New Brunswick province. 1137 (1961).

cam·po·de·an (kam pō′dē ən), *n.* a campodeid. [< Gk *kámp(ē)* caterpillar + *-ōdes* -ODE + -AN]

cam·po·de·id (kam pō′dē id), *n.* **1.** any eyeless, wingless, primitive insect of the family *Campodeidae,* having two long, many-segmented appendages at the rear of its abdomen. —*adj.* **2.** belonging or pertaining to the family *Campodeidae.* [< NL *Campodeid(ae)* name of the family, equiv. to *Campode(a)* name of the genus (< Gk *kámpē* caterpillar + NL *-odea* -ODE[1]) + *-idae* -ID[2]]

cam·po·de·i·form (kam pō′dē ə fôrm′), *adj.* resembling a campodeid in form, as the larvae of certain insects. [CAMPODE(ID) + -I- + -FORM]

Cam·po For·mio (käm′pô fôR′myô), a village in Friuli-Venezia Giulia, in NE Italy, NW of Trieste: treaty between Austria and France 1797. 4261 (1961). Modern, **Cam·po·for·mi·do** (käm′pô fôR′mē dô).

Cam·po Gran·de (känm′pŏŏ grännʹdə), a city in SW Brazil. 31,708 (1950).

cam·pong (käm′pông, -pong, käm pông′, -pong′), *n.* kampong.

cam′po pea′, Pride-of-California.

camp·o·ree (kam′pə rē′), *n.* a small camp gathering of Boy Scouts, usually from a region or district (distinguished from *jamboree*). [CAMP[1] + (JAMB)OREE]

Cam·pos (känm′pŏŏs), *n.* a city in E Brazil, near Rio de Janeiro. 277,459 (est. 1957).

cam·po san·to (käm′pô sän′tô), *pl. It.* **cam·pi san·ti** (käm′pē sän′tē), *Sp.* **cam·pos san·tos** (käm′pôs sän′tôs). *Italian, Spanish.* a cemetery. [lit., holy field]

camp-out (kamp′out′), *n.* a camping out of a group. Also, **camp′out′.** [n. use of v. phrase *camp out*]

camp·shed (kamp′shed′), *v.t.,* **-shed, -shed·ding.** to line (the bank of a river) with campshot. [var. of CAMPSHOT]

camp·shot (kamp′shot′), *n. Brit.* a facing of planks and piles placed along the bank of a river to prevent erosion. Also called **camp′shed′ding, camp′sheet′ing.** [?]

camp·site (kamp′sīt′), *n.* a place used or suitable for camping. Also, **camp′-site′.** [CAMP[1] + SITE]

camp·stool (kamp′stōōl′), *n.* a light folding seat. [CAMP[1] + STOOL]

camp′ stove′, a portable stove used by campers for cooking or heating.

cam·pus (kam′pəs), *n., pl.* **-pus·es.** *U.S.* **1.** the grounds of a college or other school. **2.** a college or university: *The large influx of G.I.'s after the war radically changed many campuses throughout the country.* **3.** the world of higher education as exemplified in the social, intellectual, etc., life of a college or university: *Government and foundation grants have had a marked effect on the character of the American campus.* [< L: flat place, field, plain]

camp·y (kam′pē), *adj.* **camp·i·er, camp·i·est.** *Slang.* **1.** amusingly outlandish, affected, theatrical, or banal: *He had a campy British accent.* **2.** created as artificial or affected; containing extravagant flourishes; mannered. **3.** exhibiting excessive sensibility, elegance, and style. **4.** conspicuously displaying homosexual gestures, speech mannerisms, etc. [CAMP[2] + -Y[1]]

cam·py·lite (kam′pə līt′), *n. Mineral.* a yellow to brown variety of mimetite. Also, **kampylite.** [< Gk *kampýl(os)* curved + -ITE[1]]

cam·py·lot·ro·pous (kam′pə lo′trə pəs), *adj. Bot.* (of an ovule) curved so that the true apex or micropyle is almost at the base. [*campylo-* (< Gk *kampylo-,* deriv. of *kampýl(os)* curved) + -TROPOUS]

cam·shaft (kam′shaft′, -shäft′), *n.* a shaft bearing integral cams. [CAM + SHAFT]

Ca·mus (KA MY′), *n.* **Al·bert** (AL BER′), 1913–60, French novelist, short-story writer, playwright, and essayist: Nobel prize 1957.

can[1] (kan; *unstressed* kən), *auxiliary v.* and *v., pres. sing. 1st pers.* **can,** *2nd* **can** or (*Archaic*) **canst,** *3rd* **can,** *pres. pl.* **can;** *past sing. 1st pers.* **could,** *2nd* **could** or (*Archaic*) **couldst,** *3rd* **could,** *past pl.* **could.** *For auxiliary v.: imperative, infinitive, and participles lacking. For v. (Obs.): imperative* **can;** *infinitive* **can;** *past part.* **could;** *pres. part.* **cun·ning.** —*auxiliary verb.* **1.** to be able to;

CONCISE ETYMOLOGY KEY: <, descended or derived from; >, whence; b., blend of, blended; c., cognate with; deriv., derivative; equiv., equivalent; imit., imitative; m., modification of; obl., oblique; r., replacing; s., stem; sp., spelling; trans., translation; ?, origin unknown, perhaps; *, hypothetical. See the full key inside the front cover.

have the ability, power, or skill to: *She can solve the problem easily, I'm sure.* **2.** to know how to: *He can play chess, although he's not particularly good at it.* **3.** to have the power or means to: *A dictator can impose his will on the people.* **4.** to have the right or qualifications to: *He can change whatever he wishes in the script.* **5.** may; have permission to: *Can I speak to you a moment?* **—*v.t., v.i.*** **6.** *Obs.* to know. [ME, OE, pres. ind. sing. 1st, 3rd pers. of *cunnan* to know, know how; c. G, Icel, Goth *kann;* see KEN, KNOW]

—Syn. 1–5. CAN denotes power or ability to do something: *The child can talk.* MAY refers to probability, possibility, or permission: *Our son may* (possibility or probability) *play football Saturday if the doctor says he may* (permission). The two words are often confused in asking or granting permission; MAY is the preferred usage. On the other hand, CANNOT is often used in nonformal situations to deny permission: *May I go? Yes, you may go* (or, *You may not* or *cannot go*). CANNOT is also used to express either extreme negation of ability or probability: *I cannot work such long hours. I cannot* (possibly) *be mistaken.*

—Usage. CAN BUT, CANNOT BUT are formal expressions suggesting that there is no possible alternative to doing a certain thing. CAN BUT is equivalent to informal CAN ONLY: *We can but do our best* (1. and *must* make the attempt; or 2. and no more than that should be expected of us). CANNOT BUT (do) is equivalent to informal CAN'T HELP (doing): *We cannot but protest against injustice* (we are under moral obligation to do so). CANNOT HELP BUT is common in familiar use, but is frequently frowned upon by careful speakers.

can² (kan), *n., v.,* **canned, can·ning.** **—*n.*** **1.** a container for food, milk, etc., usually of sheet iron coated with tin or other metal. **2.** a receptacle for garbage, ashes, etc. **3.** a bucket, pail, or other container for holding or carrying liquids: *water can.* **4.** a drinking cup; tankard. **5.** *Slang.* toilet; bathroom. **6.** *Slang.* jail: *He's been in the can for a week.* **7.** *Slang.* the buttocks. **8.** *Mil. Slang.* a depth charge. **9. in the can,** (of film) exposed, developed, and edited; ready for distribution or exhibition. **—*v.t.*** **10.** to preserve by sealing in a can, jar, etc. **11.** *Slang.* to dismiss; fire. **12.** *Slang.* to throw (something) away. **13.** *Slang.* to stop (saying, doing, or making something): *Can that noise!* [ME, OE *canne,* c. G *Kanne,* Icel *kanna,* all perh. < WGmc; cf. LL *canna* small vessel < L, c. Gk *kánna* CANE]

Can., **1.** Canada. **2.** Canadian.

can., **1.** canon. **2.** canto.

Ca·na (kā′nə), *n.* an ancient town in N Israel, in Galilee: scene of Jesus' first miracle. John 2:1,11.

Ca·naan (kā′nən), *n.* **1.** the ancient region lying between the Jordan, the Dead Sea, and the Mediterranean: the land promised by God to Abraham. Gen. 12:5–10. **2.** Biblical name of **Palestine.** **3.** any land of promise. **4.** Also, *Douay Bible,* **Chanaan.** a descendant of Ham, the son of Noah. Gen. 10. [< LL *Chanaan* < Gk < Heb *Kena'an*]

Ca·naan·ite (kā′nə nīt′), *n.* **1.** a member of a Semitic people that inhabited parts of ancient Palestine and were conquered by the Israelites and largely absorbed by them. **2.** a group of Semitic languages, including Hebrew and Phoenician, spoken chiefly in ancient Palestine and Syria. **—*adj.*** **3.** of, pertaining to, or characteristic of Canaan, the Canaanites, or the group of Semitic languages known as Canaanite. [ME << Gk *Kananítēs;* see -ITE¹] **—Ca·naan·it·ish** (kā′nə nī′tish), **Ca·naan·it·ic** (kā′nə nit′ik), *adj.*

Can·a·ce (kan′ə sē′), *n.* **1.** *Class. Myth.* a daughter of Aeolus who committed suicide at her father's command because of her incestuous relations with her brother Macareus. **2.** a girl's given name.

Canad., Canadian.

ca·ña·da (kən yä′də, -yad′ə), *n.* *Chiefly Western U.S.* **1.** a dry riverbed. **2.** a small, deep canyon. [< Sp, equiv. to *cañ(a)* CANE + *-ada* n. suffix]

Can·a·da (kan′ə də), *n.* a nation in N North America: a member of the Commonwealth of Nations. 23,110,000. 3,690,410 sq. mi. *Cap.:* Ottawa.

Can′ada bal′sam, a pale yellow or greenish, slightly fluorescent, clear, viscous, bitter-tasting, water-insoluble liquid, having a pleasant aromatic pinelike odor, and solidifying on exposure to air: obtained from the balsam fir, *Abies balsamea,* and used chiefly for mounting objects on microscope slides, in the manufacture of fine lacquers, and as a cement for lenses. Also called **Canada turpentine, balsam of fir.**

Can′ada bar′berry. See **Allegheny barberry.**

Can′ada blue′grass, a European, perennial grass, *Poa compressa,* naturalized in North America, having creeping rootstocks and bluish-green leaves. Also called **wire grass.**

Can′ada crook′neck, a cushaw.

Can′ada goose′, a common wild goose, *Branta canadensis,* of North America. See illus. under **goose.**

Can′ada jay′, a gray jay, *Perisoreus canadensis,* of northern North America, noted for its boldness in stealing food from houses, traps, camps, etc. Also called **whiskey jack.**

Can′ada lil′y. See **meadow lily.**

Can′ada lynx′. See under **lynx.**

Can′ada moon′seed, a vine, *Menispermum canadense,* of eastern North America, having soft, hairy leaves when young and black, grapelike fruit. Also called **yellow perilla.**

Can′ada pota′to. See **Jerusalem artichoke.**

Can′ada this′tle, an Old World herb, *Cirsium arvense,* having small purple or white flower heads, now a troublesome weed in North America.

Can′ada tur′pentine. See **Canada balsam.**

Ca·na·di·an (kə nā′dē ən), *adj.* **1.** of Canada or its people: *the Canadian government.* **—*n.*** **2.** a native or inhabitant of Canada. [CANAD(A) + -IAN; cf. F *canadien*]

Cana′dian ba′con, bacon taken from a boned strip of pork loin.

Cana′dian foot′ball, a game having similarities to football and Rugby that is played on a field 165 × 65 yards by two twelve-man teams. Also called **rouge.**

Cana′dian French′, French spoken as a native language in Canada, esp. in Quebec province, by descendants of the settlers of New France.

Cana′dian hem′lock. See **eastern hemlock.**

Ca·na·di·an·ism (kə nā′dē ə niz′əm), *n.* **1.** devotion to Canada and its institutions. **2.** a custom, trait, or thing peculiar to Canada or its citizens. **3.** an English usage peculiar to the people of Canada. [CANADIAN + -ISM]

Ca·na·di·an·ize (kə nā′dē ə nīz′), *v.t., v.i.,* **-ized, -iz·ing.** to make or become Canadian in character; assimilate to the customs and institutions of Canada. [CANADIAN + -IZE] **—Ca·na′di·an·i·za′tion,** *n.*

Cana′dian Riv′er, a river flowing E from the Rocky Mountains in NE New Mexico to the Arkansas River in E Oklahoma. 906 mi. long.

Cana′dian whis′key, rye¹ (def. 4).

ca·na·fis·tu·la (kän′yə fis′chə lə), *n.* See **pudding-pipe tree.** Also, **ca·na·fis·to·la** (kän′yə fis′tᵊ lə). [< Sp *cañafístula,* equiv. to *caña* CANE + *-fistula;* see FISTULA]

ca·nai·gre (kə nī′grē), *n.* a perennial herb, *Rumex hymenosepalus,* found from Oklahoma to California, having clustered, tuberous roots that yield tannin. [< MexSp]

ca·naille (kə nāl′; *Fr.* KA nä′yᵊ), *n.* riffraff; the rabble. [< F < It *canaglia* pack of dogs, equiv. to *can(e)* dog (< L *canis*) + *-aglia* collective suffix]

Can·a·jo·har·ie (kan′ə jə har′ē), *n.* a town in central New York. 2681 (1960).

can·a·kin (kan′ə kin), *n.* cannikin.

ca·nal¹ (kə nal′), *n., v.,* **-nalled** or **-naled, -nal·ling** or **-nal·ing.** **—*n.*** **1.** an artificial waterway for navigation, irrigation, etc. **2.** a long narrow arm of the sea penetrating far inland. **3.** a tubular passage or cavity for food, air, etc., esp. in an animal or plant; a duct. **4.** Also, **canalis.** (in classical architecture) any groove or channel cut for visual effect. **5.** *Obs.* a channel or watercourse. **—*v.t.*** **6.** to make a canal through. **7.** to furnish with canals. [late ME: waterpipe < L *canāl(i)s,* perh. equiv. to *can(na)* reed, pipe (see CANE) + *-ālis* -AL¹]

ca·nal² (kə nal′), *n.* *Astron.* one of the long, narrow, dark lines on the surface of the planet Mars, as seen telescopically from the earth. [< It *canal(e)* channel < L *canāl(is);* see CANAL¹]

ca·na·la·tu·ra (kan′ᵊlə to͝or′ə, -tyo͝or′ə), *n.* ornamentation on primitive pottery in the form of flutes or channels. [< It; see CANAL², -ATE¹, -URE]

canal′ boat′, a self-propelled or towed barge adapted to service in a canal.

Ca·na·let·to (kan′ᵊlet′ō; *It.* kä′nä let′tô), *n.* **1. An·to·nio** (än tô′nyô), *(Canale),* 1697–1768, Italian painter. **2.** See **Bellotto, Bernardo.**

can·a·lic·u·lus (kan′ᵊlik′yə ləs), *n., pl.* **-li** (-lī′). *Anat., Zool.* a small canal or tubular passage, as in bone. [< L, equiv. to *canāli(s)* CANAL¹ + *-culus* -CULE]—**can′·a·lic′u·lar, can·a·lic·u·late** (kan′ᵊlik′yə lit, -yə lāt′), **can′a·lic′u·lat′ed,** *adj.* **—can·a·lic·u·la·tion** (kan′ᵊlik′yə lā′shən), *n.*

ca·na·lis (kə nal′is, -nä′lis), *n., pl.* **-na·les** (-nal′ēz, -nä′lās). canal¹ (def. 4). [< L]

ca·nal·ise (kə nal′īz, kan′ᵊlīz′), *v.t.,* **-ised, -is·ing.** *Chiefly Brit.* canalize. **—ca·nal′i·sa′tion,** *n.*

ca·nal·ize (kə nal′īz, kan′ᵊlīz′), *v.t.,* **-ized, -iz·ing.** **1.** to make a canal or canals through. **2.** to convert into a canal. **3.** to divide (a stream) into reaches with locks or dams, usually to maintain navigable depths. **4.** to divert into certain channels; give a certain direction to or provide a certain outlet for. [CANAL¹ + -IZE] **—ca·nal′·i·za′tion,** *n.*

ca·nal·ler (kə nal′ər), *n.* a freight boat built for use on canals. [CANAL¹ + -ER¹]

canal′ ray′, *Physics.* a stream of positive ions traveling from a metallic anode to the cathode in a gas-discharge tube. Also called **anode ray, positive ray.**

Canal′ Zone′, a zone in central Panama, crossing the Isthmus of Panama on both sides of the Panama Canal: leased perpetually to and governed by the U.S.; ab. 10 mi. wide; excludes the cities of Panama and Colón. 38,953 (1960); 553 sq. mi.

Can·an·dai·gua (kan′ən dā′gwə), *n.* a town in central New York. 9370 (1960).

Ca·na·ne·a (kan′ə nē′ə, -nā′ə; *Sp.* kä′nä ne′ä), *n.* a city in N Mexico: copper mining and smelting. 17,914 (1950). **—Can′a·ne′an,** *n.*

can·a·pé (kan′ə pē, -pā′; *Fr.* KA NA pā′), *n., pl.* **-pés** (-pēz, -pāz′; *Fr.* -pā′). **1.** a thin piece of bread, toast, etc., spread or topped with cheese, caviar, anchovies, or other appetizing foods. **2.** *Furniture.* a sofa of 18th-century France, made in any of several forms, often with matching chairs. **3.** *Bridge.* a style of bidding in which short suits are bid before long ones. [< F: lit., a covering or netting, orig. for a bed (see CANOPY), by extension for a piece of bread]

Ca·na·ra (kə när′ə, kä′nər ə), *n.* Kanara.

ca·nard (kə närd′; *Fr.* KA NAR′), *n., pl.* **-nards** (-närdz′; *Fr.* -NAR′). **1.** a false story, report, or rumor, usually derogatory; hoax. **2.** *Cookery.* a duck intended or used for food. **3.** *Aeron.* **a.** an airplane that has its horizontal stabilizer and elevators located forward of the wing. **b.** an early airplane having a pusher engine with the rudder and elevator assembly in front of the wings. [< F: lit., duck; OF *quanart* drake, orig. cackler, equiv. to *can(er)* (to) cackle + *-art* -ART]

Ca·na·rese (kä′nə rēz′, -rēs′), *adj., n., pl.* **-rese.** Kanarese.

Canar′ies cur′rent, an ocean current of the North Atlantic flowing southward past Spain and North Africa.

ca·nar·y (kə nâr′ē), *n., pl.* **-nar·ies.** **1.** a finch, *Serinus canarius,* native to the Canary Islands and often kept as a pet, in the wild state greenish with brown streaks above and yellow below, and in the domesticated state usually bright or pale yellow. **2.** Also called **canary yellow.** a light, clear yellow color. **3.** a sweet white wine of the Canary Islands, resembling sherry. **4.** *Slang.* a woman singer, esp. one who sings with a dance band. **5.** *Slang.* a person who, apprehended by the police, informs on his accomplices. Cf. **stool pigeon** (def. 3). **6.** a lively dance of the 16th and 17th centuries, in triple meter. **—*adj.*** **7.** having the color canary. [< Sp (*Gran*) *Canaria* (Grand) Canary < L *Canāria* (*insula*) Dog (Island), equiv. to *can(is)* dog + *-āria,* fem. of *-ārius* -ARY]

ca·nar′y·bird flow′er (kə nâr′ē bûrd′), a nasturtium, *Tropaeolum peregrinum,* of Peru, having pale yellow flowers. Also called **canar′ybird vine′.**

canar′y grass′, any of various grasses of the genus *Phalaris,* as *P. canariensis,* native to the Canary Islands, bearing a seed used as food for cage birds, or *P. arundinacea* (**reed canary grass**), used throughout the Northern Hemisphere as fodder.

Canar′y Is′lands, a group of mountainous islands in the Atlantic Ocean, near the NW coast of Africa: comprising two provinces of Spain. 918,060 (est. 1960); 2894 sq. mi. Also called **Ca·nar′ies.** **—Ca·nar·ian** (kə nâr′ē ən), *adj., n.*

canar′y seed′, birdseed.

canar′y yel′low, canary (def. 2).

ca·nas·ta (kə nas′tə), *n.* *Cards.* a variety of rummy in which the main object is to meld sets of seven or more cards. [< Sp: lit., basket, appar. var. of *canastro* < Gk *kánastron* wicker basket]

Can·a·sto·ta (kan′ə stō′tə), *n.* a town in central New York. 4896 (1960).

Ca·nav·er·al (kə nav′ər əl), *n.* **Cape,** former name of **Cape Kennedy.**

Can·ber·ra (kan′ber ə, -bər ə), *n.* a city in and the capital of Australia, in the SE part, in the Australian Capital Territory. with suburbs, 219,331.

can′ bu′oy, a cylindrical, unlighted buoy used in various ways as a channel marker, esp. on the port side of a channel entering from seaward, painted black and given an odd number. Cf. **nun buoy.** See illus. under **buoy.**

Can·by (kan′bē), *n.* **Henry Sei·del** (sīd′ᵊl), 1878–1961, U.S. author and critic.

canc., **1.** cancel. **2.** cancellation.

can·can (kan′kan′; *Fr.* käN käN′), *n., pl.* **-cans** (-kanz′; *Fr.* -käN′). a dance marked by high kicking, which came into vogue about 1830 in Paris and after 1844 was used as an exhibition dance, esp. on the burlesque and vaudeville stage. [< F, repetitive compound (based on *can*) said to be nursery var. of *canard* duck]

can·cel (kan′səl), *v.,* **-celed, -cel·ing** or (*esp. Brit.*) **-celled, -cel·ling,** *n.* **—*v.t.*** **1.** to make void; revoke; annul: *to cancel a reservation.* **2.** to mark or perforate (a postage stamp, admission ticket, etc.) to render it invalid for reuse. **3.** to neutralize; counterbalance; compensate for: *His sincere apology canceled his sarcastic remark.* **4.** *Accounting.* **a.** to close (an account) by crediting or paying all outstanding charges: *He plans to cancel his account at Macy's.* **b.** to eliminate or offset (a debit, credit, etc.) with an entry for an equal amount on the opposite side of a ledger, as when a payment is received on a debt (often fol. by *out*): *Will you cancel out that charge, please! We will put through a credit memo to cancel the invoice, sir.* **5.** *Math.* to eliminate by striking out a factor common to both the denominator and numerator of a fraction, equivalent terms on opposite sides of an equation, etc. **6.** to cross out (words, letters, etc.) by drawing a line or lines over the item. **7.** *Print.* to omit. **—*v.i.*** **8.** to counterbalance or compensate for one another; become neutralized (often fol. by *out*): *The pros and cons cancel out.* **9.** *Math.* (of factors common to both the denominator and numerator of a fraction, certain terms on opposite sides of an equation, etc.) to be equivalent; to allow cancellation. **—*n.*** **10.** act of canceling. **11.** *Print., Bookbinding.* **a.** omission. **b.** the replacement for an omitted part. [late ME *cancelle* < ML *cancell(āre)* (to) cross out, L: to make like a lattice, deriv. of *cancellī* grating, pl. of *cancellus;* see CANCELLUS] **—can′cel·er;** *esp. Brit.,* **can′cel·ler,** *n.*

—Syn. 1. countermand, rescind. **2, 6.** CANCEL, DELETE, ERASE, OBLITERATE indicate that something is no longer to be considered usable or in force. To CANCEL is to cross something out by stamping a mark over it, drawing lines through it, or the like: *to cancel a stamp, a word.* To DELETE is to cross something out from written matter or from matter to be printed, often in accordance with a printer's or proofreader's symbol indicating the material is to be omitted: *to delete part of a line.* To ERASE is to remove by scraping or rubbing: *to erase a capital letter.* To OBLITERATE is to blot out entirely, so as to remove all sign or trace of: *to obliterate a record.*

can·cel·a·ble (kan′sə lə bəl), *adj.* subject to cancellation, as certain insurance policies. Also, *esp. Brit.,* **can′cel·la·ble.** [CANCEL + -ABLE] **—can′cel·a·bil′i·ty;** *esp. Brit.,* **can′cel·la·bil′i·ty,** *n.*

can′celed type′, a style of type having a horizontal line through each character.

can·cel·late (kan′sə lāt′, -lit), *adj.* **1.** *Anat.* of spongy or porous structure, as bone. **2.** reticulate. Also, **can·cel·lat·ed** (kan′sə lā′tid). [< L *cancell(ātus).* See CANCEL, -ATE¹]

Cancellate bone structure

can·cel·la·tion (kan′sə lā′shən), *n.* **1.** act of canceling. **2.** the marks or perforations made in canceling. **3.** something canceled. [< L *cancellātiōn-* (s. of *cancellātiō*). See CANCELLATE, -ION]

cancella′tion law′, *Math.* a mathematical rule pertaining to certain algebraic structures, as an integral domain or a field, which allows cancellation of a nonzero common factor of two equivalent quantities.

can·cel·lus (kan sel′əs), *n., pl.* **-cel·li** (-sel′ī, -sel′ē). *Archit.* **1.** (in an early Christian basilica) one of a row of bars separating the clergy and sometimes the choir from the congregation. **2.** (in an ancient Roman basilica) one of a row of bars separating the court personnel from the spectators. **3. cancelli,** a screen of such bars. [< L, equiv. to *canc(rī)* grating (var. of *carcer* prison) + *-ellus* dim. suffix]

can·cer (kan′sər), *n., gen.* **Can·cri** (kaŋ′krē) for 3. **1.** *Pathol.* a malignant and invasive growth or tumor, esp. one originating in epithelium, tending to recur after excision and to metastasize to other sites. **2.** any evil condition or thing that spreads destructively; blight. **3.** (*cap.*) *Astron.* the Crab, a zodiacal constellation between Gemini and Leo. **4.** (*cap.*) *Astrol.* the fourth sign of the zodiac. See illus. under **zodiac. 5.** (*cap.*) **tropic of.** See under **tropic** (def. 1a). [ME < L: lit. crab; akin to Gk *karkínos*, Skt *karkaṭa* crab; see CANKER] —**can′cer·ous,** *adj.* —**can′cered,** *adj.* —**can′cer·ous·ly,** *adv.* —**can′cer·ous·ness,** *n.*

can·cer·ate (kan′sə rāt′), *v.i.,* **-at·ed, -at·ing.** to become cancerous; develop into cancer. [< L *cancerāt(us)* cancerous. See CANCER, -ATE[1]]

can·cer·a·tion (kan′sə rā′shən), *n.* the state of becoming cancerous. Also, **can·cer·i·za·tion** (kan′sər i zā′shən). [CANCERATE + -ION]

can′cer stick′, *Slang.* a cigarette.

can·cha (kän′chə), *n.* a court for playing jai alai. Cf. **frontis, rebote** (def. 1). [< Sp < Quechua *camcha*]

can·ción (kän thyôn′, -syôn′), *n., pl.* **-cio·nes** (-thyô′nes, -syô′-). *Spanish.* song.

can·crine (kaŋ′krin), *adj. Pros.* reading the same backwards as forwards: *a cancrine line.* Cf. **palindrome.** [< L *cancr-* (s. of *cancer*) CANCER + -INE[1]]

can·cri·zans (kaŋ′kri zanz′, kan′-), *adj. Music.* having the imitating voice in retrograde motion: *a cancrizans canon.* [< ML, prp. of *cancrizāre* to move backward (L *cancr-* s. of *cancer* CANCER + LL *-izāre* -IZE)]

can·croid (kaŋ′kroid), *adj.* **1.** *Pathol.* resembling a cancer, as certain tumors. **2.** *Zool.* resembling a crab. —*n.* **3.** *Pathol.* a form of cancer of the skin. [< L *cancr-* (s. of *cancer*) CANCER + -OID]

Can·dace (kan′dis, kan′də sē′, kan dā′sē), *n.* a girl's given name. Also, **Candice.**

Can·dee (kan′dē), *n.* a girl's given name, form of **Candace** or **Candida.** Also, **Candie, Candy.**

can·de·la (kan dē′lə), *n. Optics.* a unit of luminous intensity, equal to $^1/_{60}$ of the luminous intensity of a square centimeter of a black body heated to the temperature of the solidification of platinum (1773.5°C): adopted in 1948 as the international standard of luminous intensity. *Abbr.:* cd [< L: candle]

can·de·la·bra (kan′dəlä′brə, -dəlā′-), *n., pl.* **-bras** for 2. **1.** a pl. of **candelabrum. 2.** a candelabrum.

can·de·la·brum (kan′dəlä′brəm, -dəlā′-), *n., pl.* **-bra** (-brə). **-brums.** an ornamental branched holder for more than one candle. [< L: candlestick, equiv. to *candēl(a)* CANDLE + *-ābrum* neut. suffix]

Candelabrum

can·dent (kan′dənt), *adj.* glowing with heat; at a white heat. [< L *candent-* (s. of *candēns*, prp. of *candēre* to be shining white), equiv. to *cand-* bright (see CANDID) + *-ent-* -ENT]

can·des·cent (kan des′ənt), *adj.* glowing; incandescent. [< L *candescent-* (s. of *candescēns*, prp. of *candescere* to become bright), equiv. to *cand-* bright (see CANDID) + *-escent-* -ESCENT] —**can·des′cence,** *n.* —**can·des′cent·ly,** *adv.*

C. & F., *Com.* cost and freight (used by a seller to indicate that the price quoted includes the cost of the merchandise, packing, crating, forwarding, and freight to a specified destination but excludes insurance charges on the shipment). Also, **c. & f., c & f, C & F, C and F**

Can·di·a (kan′dē ə), *n.* **1.** Greek, **Herakleion.** a seaport in N Crete. 63,458 (1961). **2.** Crete (def. 1).

Can·dice (kan′ dis, kan′di sē), *n.* a girl's given name. Also, **Candace.**

can·did (kan′did), *adj.* **1.** frank; outspoken; open and sincere: *a candid reply.* **2.** without reservation, disguise, or subterfuge; straightforward: *a candid opinion.* **3.** informal; unposed: *a candid photo.* **4.** honest; impartial: *a candid mind.* **5.** *Archaic.* white. **6.** *Archaic.* clear; pure. —*n.* **7.** an unposed photograph. [< L *candid(us)* shining white, equiv. to *cand(ēre)* (to) be shining white + *-idus* -ID[4]] —**can′did·ly,** *adv.* —**can′did·ness,** *n.*
—**Syn. 1.** ingenuous, naïve, plain. See **frank.**

Can·di·da (kan′di də), *n.* a girl's given name.

Can·di·da (kan′di də), *n.* a comedy (1898) by G. B. Shaw.

can·di·date (kan′di dāt′, -dit), *n.* **1.** one who seeks an office, honor, etc.: *a candidate for the governorship.* **2.** one who is selected by others as a contestant for an office, honor, etc. **3.** one who is deserving of or seems destined for a certain end or fate: *Such a reckless spender is a candidate for the poorhouse.* **4.** a student studying for a degree: *Candidates for the B.A. will have to meet certain minimum requirements.* [< L *candidāt(us)* clothed in white (adj.), candidate for office (n.: because he wore a white toga). See CANDID, -ATE[1]] —**can·di·da·cy** (kan′di də sē); *Brit.,* **can·di·da·ture** (kan′di də chər), **can′di·date·ship′,** *n.*

can′did cam′era, a small, handy camera, esp. one having a fast lens for unposed or informal pictures.

Can·dide (*Fr.* käɴ dēd′), *n.* a philosophical novel (1759) by Voltaire.

Can·die (kan′dē), *n.* a girl's given name, form of **Candace** or **Candida.** Also, **Candee, Candy.**

can·died (kan′dēd), *adj.* **1.** impregnated or incrusted with or as with sugar: *candied ginger.* **2.** prepared by cooking in sugar or syrup: *candied yams.* **3.** honeyed or sweet; flattering. [CANDY + -ED[3]]

Can·di·ot (kan′dē ot′), *adj.* **1.** of or pertaining to Candia or Crete; Cretan. —*n.* **2.** a Cretan. Also, **Can·di·ote** (kan′dē ōt′). [CANDI(A) + *-ot(e)* < Gk *-ōtēs* suffix of appurtenance]

can·dle (kan′dəl), *n., v.,* **-dled, -dling.** —*n.* **1.** a long, usually slender piece of tallow, wax, etc., with an embedded wick, burned to give light. **2.** something like this in appearance or use. **3.** *Optics.* **a.** candela. **b.** Also called **international candle.** a unit of luminous intensity, defined as a fraction of the luminous intensity of a group of 45 carbon-filament lamps: used from 1909 to 1948 as the international standard. **c.** Also called **standard candle.** a unit of luminous intensity, equal to the luminous intensity of a wax candle of standard specifications: used prior to 1909 as the international standard. *Abbr.:* c. c. **4. burn the candle at both ends,** to overtax one's strength or capacity by undertaking too many activities: *Burning the candle at both ends may have a serious effect on one's health.* **5. not hold a candle to,** to compare unfavorably with: *She's pretty, but she doesn't hold a candle to her sister.* **6. not worth the candle,** not worth the trouble or effort involved: *Trying to win them over to your viewpoint is not worth the candle.* —*v.t.* **7.** to examine (eggs) for freshness by holding them up to a bright light. [ME, OE *candel* < L *candēl(a)*, equiv. to *candē(re)* (to) shine + *-la* fem. suffix; see CANDID] —**can′dler,** *n.*

can·dle·beam (kan′dəl bēm′), *n.* a medieval chandelier formed of crisscrossed timbers. [CANDLE + BEAM]

can·dle·ber·ry (kan′dəl ber′ē), *n., pl.* **-ries. 1.** a wax myrtle of the genus *Myrica.* **2.** its berry. **3.** the candlenut. [CANDLE + BERRY]

can·dle·fish (kan′dəl fish′), *n., pl.* (*esp. collectively*) **-fish,** (*esp. referring to two or more kinds or species*) **-fish·es. 1.** a small, edible, smeltlike fish, *Thaleichthys pacificus,* found off the northwestern coast of North America, being so oily that when dried it can be used as a candle. **2.** sablefish. Also called **eulachon.** [CANDLE + FISH]

can·dle·hold·er (kan′dəl hōl′dər), *n.* a holder for a candle; candlestick. [CANDLE + HOLDER]

can′dle lark′spur, a perennial herb, *Delphinium elatum,* of Eurasia, having long, terminal, spikelike clusters of blue flowers. Also called **bee larkspur.**

can·dle·light (kan′dəl līt′), *n.* **1.** the light of a candle. **2.** a dim artificial light. **3.** twilight; dusk. [ME *candel-liht,* OE *candel-lēoht.* See CANDLE, LIGHT[1]]

can·dle·mak·er (kan′dəl mā′kər), *n.* a person who makes candles. [CANDLE + MAKER]

Can·dle·mas (kan′dəl məs, -mas′), *n.* an ecclesiastical festival, February 2, in honor of the presentation of the infant Jesus in the Temple and the purification of the Virgin Mary: candles are blessed on this day. Also called **Can′dlemas Day′.** [ME *candelmasse,* OE *candelmæsse.* See CANDLE, -MAS]

can·dle·nut (kan′dəl nut′), *n.* **1.** the oily fruit or nut of a euphorbiaceous tree, *Aleurites moluccana,* of the South Sea Islands, Southeast Asia, etc., the kernels of which, when strung together, are used as candles by the natives. **2.** the tree itself. [CANDLE + NUT]

can·dle·pin (kan′dəl pin′), *n.* **1.** a bowling pin that is almost cylindrical and can be set up on either end, used in a game resembling tenpins. **2. candlepins,** (*construed as sing.*) the game played with such pins. [CANDLE + PIN]

can·dle·pow·er (kan′dəl pou′ər), *n. Optics.* **1.** the luminous intensity of a standard candle. **2.** luminous intensity, as of light, or illuminating capacity, as of a lamp, measured in candles. [CANDLE + POWER]

can·dle·stand (kan′dəl stand′), *n.* a tall, slender stand for supporting candlesticks. [CANDLE + STAND]

can·dle·stick (kan′dəl stik′), *n.* a device having a socket or a spike for holding a candle. [ME *candelstikke,* OE *candelsticca.* See CANDLE, STICK[1]]

can·dle·wick (kan′dəl wik′), *n.* **1.** the wick of a candle. **2.** mullein (def. 1). —*adj.* **3.** (of a fabric, usually unbleached muslin) having small, short bunches of wicking tufted to form a design: *a candlewick bedspread.* [CANDLE + WICK[1]]

can·dle·wood (kan′dəl wo͝od′), *n.* **1.** any resinous wood used for torches or as a substitute for candles. **2.** any of various trees or shrubs yielding such wood. [so called because it burns brightly]

Can·dolle (käɴ dôl′), *n.* **Au·gus·tin Py·rame de** (ō gys tan′ pē ram′ də), 1778–1841, Swiss botanist.

can·dor (kan′dər), *n.* **1.** the state or quality of being frank, open, and sincere in speech or expression; candidness: *The candor of the speech impressed the audience.* **2.** freedom from bias; fairness; impartiality: *to consider an issue with candor.* **3.** *Obs.* kindliness. **4.** *Obs.* purity. Also, *esp. Brit.,* **can′dour.** [< L: sincerity, lit., luster; see CANDID, -OR[1]]

c & sc, *Print.* capitals and small capitals.

can·dy (kan′dē), *n., pl.* **-dies,** *v.,* **-died, -dy·ing.** —*n.* **1.** any of a variety of confections made with sugar, syrup, etc., combined with other ingredients. **2.** a single piece of such a confection. **3.** *Slang.* cocaine. —*v.t.* **4.** to cook in sugar or syrup, as sweet potatoes or carrots. **5.** to cook in heavy syrup until transparent, as fruit, fruit peel, or ginger. **6.** to reduce (sugar, syrup, etc.) to a crystalline form, usually by boiling down. **7.** to cover or impregnate with or as if with sugar or sugarlike crystals. **8.** to make sweet, palatable, or agreeable. —*v.i.* **9.** to become covered with sugar. **10.** to crystallize. [short for *sugar candy,* ME *sugre candy* candied sugar < MF *sucre candi; candy* << Ar *qandī* of sugar, equiv. to *qand* sugar (< Pers; perh. orig. piece of sugar cane; if so, akin to Skt *khaṇḍa* piece) + *-ī* suffix of appurtenance] —**can′dy·like′,** *adj.*

Can·dy (kan′dē), *n.* a girl's given name, form of **Candace** or **Candida.** Also, **Candee, Candie.**

can′dy pull′, a social gathering, usually of young people, at which taffy or molasses candy is made.

can·dys (kan′dis), *n.* a robe extending to the ankles, worn in ancient Persia. [< Gk *kándys*]

can′dy store′, a retail shop that sells candy, cigarettes, ice cream, magazines, etc.

can′dy stripe′, a pattern of bright stripes of one color against a plain background, used chiefly in fabrics.

can·dy-striped (kan′dē strīpt′), *adj.* having a design in candy stripe.

can′dy strip′er, *Slang.* a young girl who acts as a volunteer aid to the nurses on a hospital staff.

can·dy·tuft (kan′dē tuft′), *n.* a brassicaceous plant of the genus *Iberis,* esp. *I. umbellata,* a cultivated annual with tufted flowers, originally from the island of Candia. [*Candy* (var. of CANDIA) + TUFT]

cane (kān), *n., v.,* **caned, can·ing.** —*n.* **1.** a stick or short staff used to assist one in walking; walking stick. **2.** a long, hollow or pithy, jointed woody stem, as that of bamboo, rattan, sugar cane, certain palms, etc. **3.** a plant having such a stem. **4.** split rattan, woven or interlaced for chair seats, wickerwork, etc. **5.** any of several tall, bamboolike grasses, esp. of the genus *Arundinaria,* as *A. gigantea* (**cane reed, large cane, giant cane,** or **southern cane**) and *A. tecta* (**small cane** or **switch cane**), of the southern U.S. **6.** the stem of the raspberry or blackberry. **7.** See **sugar cane. 8.** any rod used for flogging. **9.** a slender cylinder or rod, as of sealing wax, glass, etc. **10.** *Glassmaking.* a rod or tube of glass. —*v.t.* **11.** to flog with a cane. **12.** to furnish or make with cane: *to cane chairs.* [ME < MF < L *cann(a)* < Gk *kánna* < Sem.; cf. Ar *qanāh,* Heb *qāneh* reed] —**cane′like′,** *adj.* —**can′y,** *adj.*

Ca·ne·a (kə nē′ə), *n.* a seaport on and the capital of Crete, on the W part. 38,467 (1961). Greek, **Khania.**

cane·brake (kān′brāk′), *n.* a thicket of canes. [CANE + BRAKE[2]]

cane′brake rat′tlesnake, a timber rattlesnake, *Crotalus horridus atricaudatus,* of the southeastern U.S. Also called **cane′brake rat′tler.**

cane′ chair′, a chair, the back and seat of which are made of interlaced strips of cane.

cane′ gall′, *Plant Pathol.* a disease of blackberries, characterized by rough, warty outgrowths on the canes, caused by a bacterium, *Agrobacterium rubi.*

ca·nel·la (kə nel′ə), *n.* the cinnamonlike bark of a West Indian tree, *Canella winterana,* used as a condiment and in medicine. [< ML: cinnamon, equiv. to L *cann(a)* CANE + *-ella* dim. suffix]

Can·ens (kan′enz), *n. Rom. Legend.* a daughter of Janus who cried herself to death over the disappearance of her husband, Picus.

ca·neph·o·ra (kə nef′ər ə), *n., pl.* **-o·rae** (-ə rē′). **1.** (in ancient Greece) one of the maidens who bore upon their heads baskets containing the materials for sacrifice in certain religious festivals. **2.** Also, **can·e·phore** (kan′ə fōr′, -fôr′). *Archit.* a caryatid with a basket on her head. [< L < Gk, n. use of fem. of *kanēphóros* equiv. to *káne(on)* basket + *-phoros* -PHORE]

can·er (kā′nər), *n.* a person who works with cane, esp. one who produces canework for chairs. [CANE + -ER[1]]

cane′ reed′. See under **cane** (def. 5).

ca·nes·cent (kə nes′ənt), *adj.* (of a plant) having a whitish or grayish pubescence. [< L *cānescent-* (s. of *cānescēns,* prp. of *cānescere* to grow grey, equiv. to *cān(us)* grey + *-escent-* ESCENT] —**ca·nes′cence,** *n.*

cane′ sug′ar, sugar obtained from sugar cane, identical with that obtained from the sugar beet. Cf. **sugar** (def. 1).

Ca·nes Ve·nat·i·ci (kā′nēz və nat′i sī′), *gen.* **Ca·num Ve·nat·i·co·rum** (kā′nəm və nat′ə kōr′əm, -kôr′-). *Astron.* the Hunting Dogs, a small northern constellation south of Ursa Major. [< L]

cane·work (kān′wûrk′), *n.* strips of cane that are interlaced and used in cane chairs. [CANE + WORK]

Ca·ney (kā′nē), *n.* a town in SE Kansas. 2682 (1960).

CanF, Canadian French.

can·field (kan′fēld′), *n. Cards.* a game of solitaire often adapted to gambling purposes. [named after R. A. *Canfield* (1855–1914), American gambler, inventor of the game]

Can·field (kan′fēld′), *n.* **1. Dorothy.** See **Fisher, Dorothy Canfield. 2.** a town in E Ohio. 3252 (1960).

can·ful (kan′fo͝ol′), *n., pl.* **-fuls.** the amount that a can will hold. [CAN[2] + -FUL]

cangue (kaŋ), *n.* (in China) a wooden framework, usually several feet square, fastened about the neck of an offender as a portable pillory. [F sp. of *cang* < Pg *cang(o),* var. of *canga* yoke < ?]

ca·nic′o·la fe′ver (kə nik′ə lə), *Pathol.* an acute febrile disease of man and dogs, characterized by inflammation of the stomach and intestines and by jaundice: caused by a spirochete, *Leptospira canicola.* Cf. **canine leptospirosis, leptospirosis.** [< NL *canicola* dog-dweller, equiv. to L *cani(s)* dog + *-cola* dweller; see -COLOUS]

Ca·nic·u·la (kə nik′yə lə), *n. Astron. Rare.* Sirius; the Dog Star. [< L: lit., little dog; see CANINE, -CULE]

ca·nic·u·lar (kə nik′yə lər), *adj. Astron.* pertaining to the rising of the Dog Star or to the star itself; Sothic. [< L *caniculār(is)* of Sirius. See CANICULA, -AR[1]]

can·i·kin (kan′ə kin), *n.* cannikin.

ca·nine (kā′nīn, kə nīn′), *adj.* **1.** of or like a dog; pertaining to or characteristic of dogs. **2.** *Anat., Zool.* of or pertaining to the four pointed teeth, esp. prominent in dogs, situated one on each side of each jaw, next to the incisors. —*n.* **3.** any animal of the *Canidae,* or dog family, including the wolves, jackals, hyenas, coyotes, and foxes. **4.** a dog. **5.** a canine tooth; cuspid. [< L *canīn(us),* equiv. to *can(is)* dog + *-īnus* -INE[1]] —**ca·nin·i·ty** (kā nin′i tē), *n.*

ca′nine distem′per, *Vet. Pathol.* distemper[1] (def. 1a).

ca′nine leptospiro′sis, *Vet. Pathol.* a highly fatal, infectious disease of dogs, caused by the spirochetes *Leptospira canicola* and *L. icterohemorrhagiae,* characterized by weakness, depression, refusal to eat, fever, thirst, loss of weight, and often blood-tinged vomit and diarrhea. Also called **ca′nine ty′phus, Stuttgart disease, Stuttgart's disease.** Cf. **canicola fever, leptospirosis.**

can·ing (kā′niŋ), *n.* **1.** the act of providing chairs or the like with seats made of woven cane. **2.** woven cane for seats of chairs or the like. **3.** a beating with a cane: *The old schoolmaster gave him a severe caning.* [CANE + -ING[1]]

Ca·nis Ma·jor (kā′nis mā′jər), *gen.* **Ca·nis Ma·jo·ris** (kā′nis mə jōr′is, -jôr′-). *Astron.* the Great Dog, a southern constellation between Puppis and Orion, containing Sirius, the Dog Star, the brightest of the stars. [< L: greater dog]

Ca·nis Mi·nor (kā′nis mī′nər), *gen.* **Ca·nis Mi·no·ris** (kā′nis mī nōr′is, -nôr′-). *Astron.* the Little or Lesser Dog, a small southern constellation west of Orion and south of Gemini, containing the bright star Procyon. [< L: lesser dog]

Can·is·te·o (kan′i stē′ō), *n.* a town in S New York. 2731 (1960).

can·is·ter (kan′i stər), *n.* **1.** a small box, usually of metal, for holding tea, coffee, etc. **2.** Also called **can′ister shot′.** See **case shot. 3.** the part of a gas mask containing the neutralizing substances through which poisoned air is filtered. [< L *canistr(um)* wicker basket < Gk *kánastron,* equiv. to *kánn(a)* reed (see CANE) + *-astron* neut. suffix]

can·ker (kaŋ′kər), *n.* **1.** *Pathol.* a gangrenous or ulcerous sore, esp. in the mouth. **2.** *Vet. Pathol.* a disease affecting horses' feet, usually the soles, characterized by a foul-smelling exudate. **3.** *Plant Pathol.* a defined area of diseased tissue, esp. in woody stems. **4.** anything that corrodes, corrupts, destroys, or irritates. **5.** *Dial.* See **dog rose.** —*v.t.* **6.** to infect with canker. **7.** to corrupt; destroy slowly. —*v.i.* **8.** to become infected with or as with canker. [ME; OE *cancer* < L *cancer* crab, gangrene]

can·kered (kang′kərd), *adj.* *Archaic.* **1.** morally corrupt; depraved; debased. **2.** bad-tempered; ill-natured; cranky; spiteful. **3.** (of plants) **a.** destroyed or having portions destroyed by the feeding of a cankerworm. **b.** having a cankerous part; infected with a canker. **4.** ulcerated. [late ME; see CANKER, -ED[3]] —**can′kered·ly,** *adv.* —**can′kered·ness,** *n.*

can′ker let′tuce. See **consumption weed.** [so called because it was believed to cure canker]

can·ker·ous (kang′kər əs), *adj.* **1.** of the nature of or resembling canker. **2.** causing canker. [CANKER + -OUS]

can′ker sore′, *Pathol.* an ulceration of the mucous membrane of the mouth.

can·ker·worm (kang′kər wûrm′), *n.* the striped, green caterpillar of any of several geometrid moths that feed on the foliage of various fruit and shade trees, as *Paleacrita vernata* (**spring cankerworm**). [CANKER + WORM]

can·na (kan′ə), *n.* any tropical plant of the genus *Canna,* of the family *Cannaceae,* cultivated for its large, handsome leaves and showy flowers. [< NL, L: reed; see CANE]

can·na·bin (kan′ə bin), *n.* a poisonous resin extracted from Indian hemp. [< L *cannab(is)* hemp + -IN[2]]

can·na·bis (kan′ə bis), *n.* hashish; the dried pistillate parts of Indian hemp, *Cannabis sativa.* [< L: hemp < Gk *kánnabis;* see HEMP] —**can′na·bic,** *adj.*

Can·nae (kan′ē), *n.* an ancient town in SE Italy: Hannibal defeated the Romans here 216 B.C.

Can·na·nore (kan′ə nōr′, -nôr′), *n.* a port in SW India, on the Arabian Sea. 46,100 (1961). Also, **Kananur.**

canned (kand), *adj.* **1.** preserved in a can or jar: *canned peaches.* **2.** *Slang.* **a.** recorded: *canned music.* **b.** prepared in advance: *canned publicity releases; a canned speech; a canned computer program.* **3.** *Slang.* drunk. [CAN[2] + -ED[2]]

canned′ heat′, fuel provided in small cans for heating, as with chafing dishes or in portable stoves.

can′nel coal′ (kan′əl), an oily, compact coal, burning readily and brightly. Also called **cannel.** [*cannel* from CANDLE (dial. form)]

can·nel·lo·ni (kan′əlō′nē; *It.* kän′nel lô′nē), *n.pl.* tubular or rolled pieces of pasta, usually filled with a mixture of meat or cheese and baked with a cream or tomato sauce. Also, **can·ne·lons** (kan′əlon′). [< It, equiv. to *cannell(o)* tube (deriv. of *canna:* see CANE) + *-one* aug. suffix]

can·ner (kan′ər), *n.* **1.** a person who cans meat, fruit, etc., for preservation. **2.** an animal yielding meat of poor quality, suitable only for canning. [CAN[2] + -ER[1]]

can·ner·y (kan′ə rē), *n., pl.* **-ner·ies.** a place where foodstuffs, as meat, fish, fruit, etc., are canned. [CAN[2] + -ERY]

Cannes (kan, kanz; *Fr.* KAN), *n.* a city in SE France, on the Mediterranean Sea: resort. 59,173 (1962).

can·ne·tille (kan′i tēl′; *Fr.* KAN tē′yə), *n.* a gold or silver thread with a spiral twist, formerly much used in embroidery. [< F < It *canutiglia* < Sp *cañutilla,* dim. of *cañuto* pipe << L *cann(a)* cane]

can·ni·bal (kan′ə bəl), *n.* **1.** a person who eats human flesh. **2.** any animal that eats its own kind. —*adj.* **3.** pertaining to or characteristic of a cannibal or cannibals. **4.** given to cannibalism. [< Sp *Caníbal,* var. of *Caribal,* equiv. to *Canib- Carib-* (< Arawak) + *-al* -AL[1]; the Caribs of the West Indies were thought to eat human flesh] —**can′ni·bal·ly,** *adv.*

can·ni·bal·ism (kan′ə bə liz′əm), *n.* **1.** the practice of eating one's own kind. **2.** savage cruelty; barbarism. **3.** the ceremonial eating of human flesh or parts of the human body for magical or religious purposes, as to acquire the power or skill of a person recently killed. **4.** the act of pecking flesh from a live fowl by a member of the same flock. [CANNIBAL + -ISM] —**can′ni·bal·is′tic,** *adj.* —**can′ni·bal·is′ti·cal·ly,** *adv.*

can·ni·bal·ize (kan′ə bə līz′), *v.,* **-ized, -iz·ing.** —*v.t.* **1.** to subject to cannibalism. **2.** to deprive (something) of parts, materials, or persons in order to repair, strengthen or rehabilitate another of the same kind: *to cannibalize a wrecked airplane for a replacement of parts.* —*v.i.* **3.** to act cannibalistically; practice cannibalism. **4.** to remove parts or people from one thing in order to repair, strengthen, or rehabilitate another of the same kind. [CANNIBAL + -IZE] —**can′ni·bal·i·za′tion,** *n.*

can·ni·kin (kan′ə kin), *n.* **1.** a small can or drinking cup. **2.** a small wooden bucket. Also, **canakin, canikin.** [< MD *cannekin* little can, equiv. to *canne* CAN[2] + *-kin* -KIN]

can·ning (kan′ing), *n.* the act, process, or business of preserving meat, fruits, vegetables, etc., by sealing in cans or jars. [CAN[2] + -ING[1]]

Can·ning (kan′ing), *n.* **1. Charles John, 1st Earl,** 1812–62, British statesman: governor general of India 1856–62. **2.** his father, **George,** 1770–1827, British statesman: prime minister 1827. **3. Sir Stratford.** See **Stratford de Radcliffe, 1st Viscount.**

Can·niz·za·ro (kän′nēd dzär′rō), *n.* **Sta·nis·la·o** (stä′nēz lä′ō), 1826–1910, Italian chemist.

can·non (kan′ən), *n., pl.* **-nons,** (*esp. collectively*) **-non,** *v.* —*n.* **1.** a mounted gun for firing heavy projectiles; a gun, howitzer, or mortar. **2.** *Brit. Mach.* quill (def. 10). **3.** *Armor.* a cylindrical or semicylindrical piece of plate armor for the upper arm or forearm; a vambrace or rerebrace. **4.** Also called **cannon bit, canon bit.** a round bit for a horse. **5.** the part of a bit that is in the horse's mouth. **6.** (on a bell) the metal loop by which a bell is hung. **7.** *Zool.* **a.** See **cannon bone. b.** the part of the leg in which the cannon bone is situated. See diag. under **horse. 8.** *Brit.* a carom in billiards. —*v.i.* **9.** to discharge cannon. **10.** *Brit.* to make a carom in billiards. [earlier *canon* < MF < It *cannon(e),* equiv. to *cann(a)* tube (< L; see CANE) + *-one* aug. suffix]

Can·non (kan′ən), *n.* **Joseph Gur·ney** (gûr′nē), (*"Uncle Joe"*), 1836–1926, U.S. politician and legislator.

can·non·ade (kan′ə nād′), *n., v.,* **-ad·ed, -ad·ing.** —*n.* **1.** a continued discharge of cannon, esp. during an attack. —*v.t., v.i.* **2.** to attack with or discharge cannon. [< F *cannonade* < It *cannonat(a),* equiv. to *cannon(e)* CANNON + *-ata* -ADE[1]]

can·non·ball (kan′ən bôl′), *n.* Also, **can′non ball′. 1.** a missile, usually round and made of iron or steel, designed to be fired from a cannon. **2.** *Tennis.* a served ball that travels with great speed and describes little or no arc in flight. **3.** anything that moves with or is supposed to move with great speed, as an express train. —*adj.* **4.** (in swimming) made from a curled-up position with the arms pressing the knees against one's chest: *a cannonball dive.* **5.** moving at great speed: *the cannonball express.* —*v.i.* **6.** to move like a cannonball, with great rapidity or force: *The fleeing car left the road and cannonballed into a tree.* [CANNON + BALL[1]]

can′non bit′, cannon (def. 4).

can′non bone′, *Zool.* the greatly developed middle metacarpal or metatarsal bone of hoofed quadruped mammals, extending from the hock to the fetlock.

can′non crack′er, a large fire cracker.

can·non·eer (kan′ə nēr′), *n.* an artilleryman. [< MF *canonnier.* See CANNON, -EER] —**can′non·eer′ing,** *n.*

can′non fod′der, soldiers (as the material used up in war).

can·non·ry (kan′ən rē), *n., pl.* **-ries. 1.** a discharge of artillery. **2.** artillery (def. 1). [CANNON + -RY]

can′non shot′, 1. a ball or shot for a cannon. **2.** the shooting of a cannon. **3.** the range of a cannon.

can·not (kan′ot, ka not′, kə-), *v.* a form of **can not.** —**Syn.** See **can**[1].

can·nu·la (kan′yə lə), *n., pl.* **-las, -lae** (-lē′). *Surg.* a metal tube for insertion into the body, used to draw off fluid or to introduce medication. Also, **canula.** [< NL, L: small reed, equiv. to *cann(a)* CANE + *-ula* -ULE] —**can′nu·la′tion,** *n.*

can·nu·lar (kan′yə lər), *adj.* shaped like a cannula; tubular. Also, **can·nu·late** (kan′yə lāt′, -lit), **canular, canulate.** [CANNUL(A) + -AR[1]]

can·ny (kan′ē), *adj.,* **-ni·er, -ni·est,** *adv.* —*adj.* **1.** careful; cautious; prudent: *a canny reply.* **2.** astute; shrewd; knowing; sagacious: *a canny businessman.* **3.** skilled; expert. **4.** *Scot.* **a.** frugal; thrifty. **b.** safe to deal with, invest in, or work at (usually used with a negative). **c.** gentle; careful; steady. **d.** snug; cozy; comfortable. **e.** pleasing; attractive; pretty. **f.** *Archaic.* having supernatural or occult powers. —*adv.* Also, **can′ni·ly. 5.** in a canny manner. **6.** *Scot.* carefully; cautiously. [CAN[1] + -Y[1]] —**can′ni·ness,** *n.*

ca·noe (kə no͞o′), *n., v.,* **-noed, -noe·ing.** —*n.* **1.** any of various slender, open boats propelled by paddles or sails and formed of light framework covered with bark, skins, canvas, etc., or formed from a dug-out or burned-out log or logs. **2.** any of various small, primitive light boats. **3. paddle one's own canoe,** *Informal.* to handle one's own affairs; manage independently: *He's been paddling his own canoe since he was a kid.* —*v.i.* **4.** to paddle a canoe. **5.** to go in a canoe. —*v.t.* **6.** to transport or carry by canoe. [< F < Sp *canoa* < Arawak; r. *canoa* < Sp] —**ca·noe′ist,** *n.*

canoe′ birch′. See **paper birch.**

ca·noe·wood (kə no͞o′wo͝od′), *n.* See **tulip tree.** [CANOE + WOOD[1]]

can·on[1] (kan′ən), *n.* **1.** an ecclesiastical rule or law enacted by a council or other competent authority and, in the Roman Catholic Church, approved by the pope. **2.** the body of ecclesiastical law. **3.** the body of rules, principles, or standards accepted as axiomatic and universally binding in a field of study or art: *the Neoclassical canon.* **4.** a fundamental principle or general rule: *He violated the canons of good behavior.* **5.** a standard; criterion: *He was interested in the canons of taste.* **6.** the books of the Bible recognized by any Christian church as genuine and inspired. **7.** any officially recognized set of sacred books. **8.** any comprehensive list of books within a field. **9.** *Literature.* the works of an author which have been accepted as authentic: *There are 37 plays in the Shakespeare canon.* Cf. **apocrypha** (def. 3). **10.** a catalog or list, as of the saints acknowledged by the Church. **11.** *Liturgy.* that part of the Mass between the Sanctus and the Communion. **12.** *Eastern Ch.* a liturgical sequence sung at matins, usually consisting of nine odes arranged in a fixed pattern, each ode comprising several troparia. **13.** consistent, note-for-note imitation of one melodic line by another, in which the second line starts after the first. **14.** *Print.* a 48-point type. [ME, OE < L < Gk *kanṓn* measuring rod, rule, akin to *kánna* CANE] —**can′on·like′,** *adj.*
—**Syn. 3, 4, 5.** See **principle.**

can·on[2] (kan′ən), *n.* **1.** one of a body of dignitaries or prebendaries attached to a cathedral or a collegiate church; a member of the chapter of a cathedral or a collegiate church. **2.** *Rom. Cath. Ch.* one of the members (**canons regular**) of certain religious orders. [back formation from OE *canōnic* (one) under rule < ML *canōnic(us),* L: of or under rule < Gk *kanōnikós.* See CANON[1], -IC]

ca·ñon (kan′yən), *n.* canyon.

can′on bit′, cannon (def. 4).

Can′on Cit′y (kan′yən), a town in central Colorado. 8973 (1960).

can·on·ess (kan′ə nis), *n.* a member of a Christian community of women living under a rule but not under a vow. [CANON[2] + -ESS]

ca·non·i·cal (kə non′i kəl), *adj.* Also, **ca·non′ic. 1.** pertaining to, established by, or conforming to a canon or canons. **2.** included in the canon of the Bible. **3.** authorized; recognized; accepted: *canonical works.* **4.** *Math.* (of an equation, coordinate, etc.) in simplest or standard form. —*n.* **5. canonicals,** garments prescribed by canon law for clergy when officiating. [late ME < ML *canōnicāl(is),* equiv. to *canōnic(us)* (see CANON[2]) + *-ālis* -AL[1]] —**ca·non′i·cal·ly,** *adv.*

canon′ical age′, *Eccles.* that age, specified by canon law, when a person becomes eligible to participate in a certain rite, hold a certain office, etc.

canon′ical form′, *Ling.* a phonological pattern or one of the patterns evident in and characteristic of the morphs of a given language.

canon′ical hour′, 1. *Eccles.* any of certain periods of the day set apart for prayer and devotion: these are matins (with lauds), prime, tierce, sext, nones, vespers, and complin. **2.** *Brit.* any hour between 8 A.M. and 3 P.M. during which marriage may be legally performed in parish churches.

ca·non·i·cate (kə non′ə kāt′, -kit), *n.* the office or dignity of a canon; a canonry. [ME *canōnicāt(us)* the office of canon. See CANON[2], -ATE[1]]

can·on·ic·i·ty (kan′ə nis′i tē), *n.* the quality of being canonical. [< L *canōnic(us)* according to rule (see CANON[2]) + -ITY]

can·on·ise (kan′ə nīz′), *v.t.,* **-ised, -is·ing.** *Chiefly Brit.* canonize. —**can′on·i·sa′tion,** *n.* —**can′on·is′er,** *n.*

can·on·ist (kan′ə nist), *n.* a person who is expert or versed in canon law. [CANON[1] + -IST] —**can′on·is′tic, can′on·is′ti·cal,** *adj.*

Canonization, The, a poem (1590–1600?) by John Donne, published in 1633.

can·on·ize (kan′ə nīz′), *v.t.,* **-ized, -iz·ing. 1.** *Eccles.* to place in the canon of saints. **2.** to glorify. **3.** to make canonical; place or include within a canon, esp. of scriptural works: *They canonized the Song of Solomon after much controversy.* **4.** to consider or treat as sacrosanct or holy: *They canonized his many verbal foibles and made them gospel.* **5.** to sanction or approve authoritatively, esp. ecclesiastically. **6.** *Archaic.* to deify. Also, *esp. Brit.,* **canonise.** [CANON[1] + -IZE] —**can′on·i·za′tion,** *n.* —**can′on·iz′er,** *n.*

can′on law′, the body of codified ecclesiastical law, esp. of the Roman Catholic Church as promulgated in ecclesiastical councils and by the pope. —**can′on law′yer.**

can·on·ry (kan′ən rē), *n., pl.* **-ries.** the office or benefice of a canon. [CANON[2] + -RY]

can·on·ship (kan′ən ship′), *n.* the position or office of canon; canonry. [CANON[2] + -SHIP]

can′ons reg′ular. See under **canon**[2] (def. 2).

ca·noo·dle (kə no͞od′əl), *v.t., v.i.,* **-dled, -dling.** *Slang.* caress; fondle; pet. [appar. b. CA(RESS) + NOODLE[2]] —**ca·noo′dler,** *n.*

can′ o′pener, a utensil, device, or appliance for opening cans.

Ca·no·pic (kə nō′pik), *adj.* of or pertaining to Canopus. [< L *Canōpic(us)* of CANOPUS; see -IC]

Cano′pic jar′, a jar used in ancient Egypt to hold the entrails of an embalmed body. Also called **Cano′pic vase′.**

Ca·no·pus (kə nō′pəs), *n.* **1.** *Astron.* a first-magnitude star in the constellation Carina: the second brightest star in the heavens. **2.** an ancient seacoast city in Lower Egypt, 15 miles east of Alexandria.

can·o·py (kan′ə pē), *n., pl.* **-pies,** *v.,* **-pied, -py·ing.** —*n.* **1.** a covering, usually of fabric, supported on poles or suspended above a bed, throne, exalted personage, sacred object, etc. **2.** an overhanging projection or covering, as a long canvas awning stretching from the doorway to the curb. **3.** *Archit.* an ornamental, rooflike projection or covering. **4.** the sky. **5.** that part of a parachute that opens up and catches the air, usually made of nylon or silk. **6.** the transparent cover over the cockpit of an airplane. —*v.t.* **7.** to cover with or as with a canopy: *Branches canopied the avenues on his estate.* [ME *canope* < ML *canōpē(um),* var. of L *cōnōpēum* mosquito net < Gk *kōnōpeîon* bed with net to keep gnats off, equiv. to *kṓnōp(s)* gnat + *-eion,* neut. of *-eios* adj. suffix]

ca·no·rous (kə nōr′əs, -nôr′-), *adj.* melodious; musical. [< L *canōrus,* equiv. to *canōr-* (s. of *canor* song, equiv. to *can(ere)* (to) sing + *-or* -OR[1]) + *-us* -OUS] —**ca·no′rous·ly,** *adv.* —**ca·no′rous·ness,** *n.*

Ca·nos·sa (kə nos′ə; *It.* kä nôs′sä), *n.* **1.** a ruined castle in N Italy: scene of the penance of Emperor Henry IV of the Holy Roman Empire before Pope Gregory VII in 1077. **2. go to Canossa,** to humble oneself; apologize; submit: *He will go to Canossa before the day is over.*

ca·no·tier (kan′ə tyā′), *n.* a fabric constructed in a twill weave, used in the manufacture of yachting clothes. [< F: boatman, equiv. to *canot* (*can-* < L *canna* reed, small boat, CANE + F *-ot* dim. suffix) + *-ier* -IER]

Ca·no·va (kə nō′və; *It.* kä nō′vä), *n.* **An·to·nio** (än tô′nyô), 1757–1822, Italian sculptor.

Can·ro·bert (KÄN RÔ BER′), *n.* **Fran·çois Cer·tain** (FRÄN SWA′ SER TAN′), 1809–95, French marshal.

can·so (kan′sō, kän sō′), *n., pl.* **-sos.** a Provençal love song or poem. Also, **canzo.** [< Pr < L *cantiōn-* (s. of *cantiō*) song]

Can·so (kan′sō), *n.* **Cape,** a cape in SE Canada, the NE extremity of Nova Scotia.

canst (kanst), *v.* *Archaic or Poetic.* 2nd pers. sing. pres. of **can.**

cant[1] (kant), *n.* **1.** insincere statements, esp. conventional expressions of enthusiasm for high ideals, goodness, or piety. **2.** the special language or jargon spoken by criminals, gypsies, etc. **3.** the phraseology peculiar to a particular class, party, profession, etc.: *Their self-conscious cant was becoming tiresome.* **4.** whining or singsong speech, esp. of beggars. —*v.i.* **5.** to use cant, esp. to make religious remarks hypocritically; pretend goodness or piety. **6.** to speak in the whining or singsong tone of a beggar; beg. [< L base *cant,* in *cantus* song, *canticus* singsong, etc., whence OE *cantere* singer, *cantic* song; see CHANT] —**cant′ing·ly,** *adv.* —**cant′ing·ness,** *n.* —**cant′ish,** *adj.*

cant[2] (kant), *n.* **1.** a salient angle. **2.** a sudden movement that tilts or overturns a thing. **3.** a slanting or tilted position. **4.** an oblique line or surface, as one formed by cutting off the corner of a square or cube. **5.** an oblique or slanting face of anything. **6.** bank[1] (def. 6). **7.** a sudden pitch or toss. **8.** Also called **flitch.** a partly trimmed log. —*v.t.* **9.** to bevel; to form an oblique surface upon. **10.** to put in an oblique position; tilt; tip. **11.** to throw with a sudden jerk. —*v.i.* **12.** to take or have an inclined position; tilt; turn. [ME: corner, angle, niche, perh., OE *cant(el)* buttress, support < L *cant(h)us* tire of a wheel, corner of the eye < Gk *kanthós* felloe, corner of the eye] —**cant′ic,** *adj.*

cant[3] (känt), *adj.* *Brit. Dial.* hearty; merry. [< LG *kant* merry, bold]

can't (kant, känt), contraction of *cannot.*

Cant., 1. Canterbury. **2.** Canticles.

Cantab., Cantabrigian.

can·ta·bi·le (kän tä′bi lā′, -bē-, kən-; *It.* kän tä′bē le′), *Music.* —*adj.* **1.** songlike and flowing in style. —*n.* **2.** a cantabile style, passage, or piece. [< It < LL *cantābil(is)* worth singing, equiv. to L *cantā(re)* (to) sing (see CANT[1]) + *-bilis* -BLE]

Can·ta·brig·i·an (kan′tə brij′ē ən), *adj.* **1.** of Cambridge, England, or Cambridge University. **2.** of Cambridge, Massachusetts, or Harvard University. —*n.* **3.** a native or inhabitant of Cambridge. **4.** a student at or graduate of Cambridge University or Harvard University. [< ML *Cantabrigi(a)* Cambridge + -AN]

Can·tal (KÄN TAL′), *n.* a department in S central France. 172,977 (1962); 2231 sq. mi. *Cap.:* Aurillac.

can·ta·lev·er (kan′təlev′ər, -təlē′vər), *n.* cantilever. Also, **can·ta·li·ver** (kan′təlē′vər).

can·ta·loupe (kan′tᵊlōp′), n. 1. a variety of melon, *Cucumis Melo cantalupensis,* having a hard, scaly, or warty rind, grown chiefly in Europe. 2. any of several muskmelons resembling the cantaloupe. Also, **can′ta·loup′.** [< F, after *Cantelupo,* former papal estate near Rome where the cultivation of this Armenian melon was begun in Europe]

can·tan·ker·ous (kan taŋ′kər əs), adj. quarrelsome, grouchy, and contentious; peevish; ill-natured; irritable: *a cantankerous old maid.* [perh. var. of earlier *contenkerous; see CONTEN(TIOUS), (RA)NCOROUS] —**can·tan′ker·ous·ly,** adv. —**can·tan′ker·ous·ness,** n.

can·ta·ta (kən tä′tə), n. *Music.* 1. a choral composition, either sacred and resembling a short oratorio, or secular, as a lyric drama set to music but not to be acted. 2. (originally) a metrical narrative set to recitative, or alternate recitative and air, usually for a single voice accompanied by one or more instruments. [< It < *cant(are)* (to) sing (see CHANT) + *-ata* -ADE[1]]

can·ta·tri·ce (*It.* kän′tä trē′che; *Fr.* kän ta trēs′), n., *pl. It.* **-tri·ci** (-trē′chē), *Fr.* **-trices** (-trēs′). *Italian, French.* a professional female singer.

cant′ bod′y, *Naut.* a portion of a vessel at the bow or stern where cant frames are used.

cant′ed col′umn, *Archit.* a column having a faceted rather than a fluted or cylindrical surface.

can·teen (kan tēn′), n. 1. *U.S.* a small container used by soldiers and others for carrying water or other liquids. 2. a place in a military camp, reservation, etc., for the sale of personal necessities and supplies to members of the army. 3. *U.S. Army.* (formerly) post exchange. 4. a place where free entertainment is provided for enlisted men, usually in a town or city near an army camp or post or naval shore station. 5. a box or chest for cutlery and other table utensils. [< F *cantine* < It *cantin(a)* cellar, equiv. to *cant(o)* corner (< L; see CANT[2]) + *-ina* -INE[1]]

can·ter[1] (kan′tər), n. 1. an easy gallop. —v.t., v.i. 2. to go or ride at a canter. [short for *Canterbury* to ride at a pace like that of Canterbury pilgrims]

cant·er[2] (kan′tər), n. a person who is much given to the use of cant. [CANT[1] + -ER[1]]

can·ter·bur·y (kan′tər ber′ē), n., pl. **-buries.** 1. a stand having racks for holding magazines, sheet music, etc., on edge. 2. a supper tray with partitions for cutlery and plates. [after CANTERBURY, England]

Can·ter·bur·y (kan′tər ber′ē, -bə rē, -brē), n. 1. a city in E Kent, in SE England: cathedral; early ecclesiastical center of England. 30,376 (1961). 2. a municipality in E New South Wales, in SE Australia: a part of Sydney. 113,820 (1961). —**Can·ter·bu·ri·an** (kan′tər byŏŏr′ē ən), adj.

Can′terbury bell′, a plant, *Campanula media,* cultivated for its showy violet-blue, pink, or white flowers.

Can′terbury Tales′, The, an uncompleted sequence of tales by Chaucer, for the most part written after 1387.

cant′ frame′, *Naut.* 1. any of several frames bracketed aft of the transom of a vessel and inclined slightly to the fore-and-aft direction. 2. any transverse frame not perpendicular to the fore-and-aft midship line.

can·thar·i·des (kan thar′i dēz′), n.pl., sing. **can·thar·is** (kan thar′is). 1. See **Spanish fly** (def. 1). 2. cantharis. See **Spanish fly** (def. 2). [ME < L, pl. of *cantharis* < Gk *kantharís* blister fly] —**can·thar′i·dal,** adj. —**can·tha·rid·i·an, can·tha·rid·e·an** (kan′thə rid′ē ən), adj.

can·tha·rus (kan′thər əs), n., pl. **-tha·ri** (-thə rī′). kantharos. [< L < Gk *kántharos*]

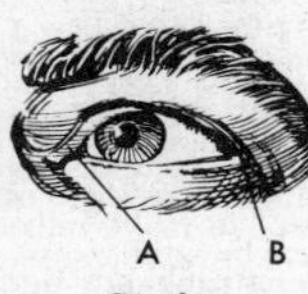
Cant hook

cant′ hook′, a wooden lever with a movable iron hook near the lower end, used chiefly for grasping and canting, or turning over logs. Also called **cant′ dog′.**

can·thus (kan′thəs), n., pl. **-thi** (-thī). *Anat.* the angle or corner on each side of the eye, formed by the junction of the upper and lower lids. [< NL, L; see CANT[2]] —**can′thal,** adj.

A B

Canthus
A, Inner canthus
B, Outer canthus

Can·thus (kan′thəs), n. *Class. Myth.* one of the Argonauts.

can·ti·cle (kan′ti kəl), n. 1. one of the nonmetrical hymns or chants, chiefly from the Bible, used in church services. 2. a song, poem, or hymn, esp. in praise. [< L *canticul(um),* equiv. to *cantic(um)* song (*cant(us),* ptp. of *canere* to sing, + *-icum,* neut. of *-icus* -IC) + *-ulum* -ULE]

Can′ticle of Can′ticles, *Douay Bible.* See **Song of Solomon, The.**

Can·ti·cles (kan′ti kəlz), n. (*construed as sing.*). See **Song of Solomon, The.**

Can·ti·gny (kän tē nyē′), n. a village in N France, S of Amiens: first major battle of U.S. forces in World War I, May 1918.

can·ti·le·na (kan′tᵊlē′nə), n. *Music.* a simple, lyric melody. [< It < L, equiv. to *cantil(āre)* (to) hum, deriv. of *cantus* song]

can·ti·lev·er (kan′tᵊlev′ər, -tᵊlē′vər), n. 1. any rigid structural member projecting from a vertical support, esp. one in which the projection is great with relation to the depth, so that the upper part is in tension and the lower part in compression. 2. *Building Trades, Civ. Eng.* any rigid construction extending horizontally well beyond its vertical support, used as a structural element of a bridge, building foundation, etc. 3. *Aeron.* a form of wing construction in which no external bracing is used. 4. *Archit.* a bracket, low in proportion to its extent, for supporting a balcony, cornice, etc. —*v.i.* 5. to project in the manner of a cantilever. —*v.t.* 6. to construct in the manner of a cantilever. Also, **cantalever, cantaliver.** [? CANT[2] + -I- + LEVER]

can′tilever founda′tion, a building foundation supporting its load partly or wholly upon cantilevers, as to avoid the necessity of deep excavations at a property line.

can·til·late (kan′tᵊlāt′), v.t., **-lat·ed, -lat·ing.** to chant (a liturgical text) in plainsong style; intone. [< LL *cantillāt(us)* sung low, hummed (ptp. of *cantillāre*), equiv. to *cant-* sing (see CANT[1]) + *-ill-* dim. suffix + *-ātus* -ATE[1]]

can·til·la·tion (kan′tᵊlā′shən), n. liturgical intoning; chanting. [CANTILLATE + -ION]

Can·til·lon (kän tē yôN′), n. **Richard,** c1680–1734, French economist, born in Ireland.

can·ti·na (kan tē′nə; *Sp.* kän tē′nä), n., pl. **-nas** (-nəz; *Sp.* -näs). *Southwestern U.S.* a saloon. [< Sp < It; see CANTEEN]

cant′ing arms′, *Heraldry.* a coat of arms the blazon of which contains a punning reference to the family name of the owner, as a heart within a padlock for Lockhart. Also called **armes parlantes.**

can·tle (kan′tᵊl), n. 1. the hind part of a saddle, usually curved upward. See illus. under **saddle.** 2. a corner; piece; portion: *a cantle of land.* [ME *cantel* < ML *cantell(us),* equiv. to L *cant(us)* (see CANT[2]) + *-ellus* dim. suffix]

cant·ling (kant′liŋ), n. a layer of burnt brick lying directly over a clamp of bricks being fired. [CANTLE + -ING[1]]

can·to (kan′tō), n., pl. **-tos.** one of the main or larger divisions of a long poem. [< It < L *cant(us)* song, n. use of *cantus* sung (ptp. of *canere*), equiv. to *can-* sing + *-tus* ptp. suffix]

can·to fer·mo (kän′tō fâr′mō), *Music.* See **cantus firmus.** [< It: lit., firm song]

can·ton (kan′tᵊn, -ton, kan ton′ *for 1–7;* kan ton′, -tōn′ or, *esp. Brit.,* -tōōn′ *for 8*), n. 1. a small territorial district, esp. one of the states of the Swiss confederation. 2. *France.* (in a department) a division of an arrondissement. 3. *Heraldry.* a square area in the dexter chief, or right-hand corner, of an escutcheon, often distinctively treated: a diminutive of the dexter chief quarter. 4. *Archit.* a pilaster or similar feature projecting from the corner of a building. 5. *Obs.* a division, part, or portion of anything. —*v.t.* 6. to divide into parts or portions. 7. to divide into cantons or territorial districts. 8. to allot quarters to (soldiers, troops, etc.). [< MF < It *canton(e),* equiv. to *cant(o)* corner (see CANT[2]) + *-one* aug. suffix] —**can′ton·al,** adj. —**can′ton·al·ism,** n.

Can·ton (kan ton′, kan′ton *for 1;* kan′tᵊn *for 2–7*), n. 1. Chinese, **Kuangchou, Kwangchow.** a seaport in and the capital of Kwangtung province, in SE China, on the Chu-Kiang River. 1,840,000 (est. 1957). 2. a city in NE Ohio: location of the football Hall of Fame. 113,631 (1960). 3. a town in central Mississippi. 9707 (1960). 4. a town in W North Carolina. 5068 (1960). 5. a town in N New York. 5046 (1960). 6. a town in NE Missouri. 2562 (1960). 7. a town in SE South Dakota. 2511 (1960).

Can′ton crepe′, a thin, light, silk or rayon crepe with a finely wrinkled surface, heavier in texture than crepe de chine. [after CANTON, China]

Can·ton·ese (kan′tᵊnēz′, -tᵊnēs′), n., pl. **-ese,** adj. —n. 1. a Chinese language spoken in Canton, the surrounding area of southern China, and Hong Kong. 2. a native or inhabitant of Canton, China. —*adj.* 3. pertaining to Canton, China, its inhabitants, or their language. [CANTON + -ESE]

Can′ton flan′nel, a plain-weave or twill-weave cotton fabric, napped only on the face. Also called **cotton flannel.** [after CANTON, China]

can′ton gin′ger, preserved or crystallized ginger of fine quality. [after CANTON, China]

Can′ton lin′en. See **grass cloth.**

can·ton·ment (kan ton′mənt, -tōn′-; *esp. Brit.* kan-tōōn′mənt), n. 1. a camp, usually of large size, where men are trained for military service. 2. military quarters. 3. the winter quarters of an army. [< F *cantonnement,* equiv. to *cantonne(r)* (to) quarter troops (see CANTON) + *-ment* -MENT]

Can·ton′ Riv′er (kan ton′), Chu-Kiang.

can·tor (kan′tər, -tôr), n. 1. *Eccles.* an officer whose duty is to lead the singing in a cathedral or in a collegiate or parish church; a precentor. 2. *Judaism.* the religious official of a synagogue who conducts the liturgical portion of a service and sings or chants the prayers and parts of prayers designed to be performed as solos. Cf. **rabbi**[1] (def. 1). [< L, equiv. to *cant(us)* sung (ptp. of *canere;* see CANTO) + *-or* -OR[2]] —**can·to·ri·al** (kan tōr′ē əl, -tôr′-), **can′tor·al, can′tor·ous,** adj. —**can′tor·ship′,** n.

Can·tor (kan′tər; *for 2 also Ger.* kän′tôr), n. 1. **Eddie,** 1893–1964, U.S. entertainer. 2. **Ge·org** (gā ôrkh′), 1845–1918, German mathematician, born in Russia.

can·to·ris (kan tōr′is, -tôr′-), adj. of or pertaining to the gospel or liturgical north side of a church (opposed to *decani*). Also, **can·to·ri·al** (kan tōr′ē əl, -tôr′-). [< L, gen. of *cantor* CANTOR]

Can′tor set′, *Math.* the set obtained from the closed interval from 0 to 1 by removing the middle third from the interval, then the middle third from each of the two remaining sets, and continuing the process indefinitely. Also called **Can′tor ter′nary set′.** [named after Georg CANTOR]

Can·tos (kan′tōz), n. a collection of poems by Ezra Pound, as yet uncompleted and published at irregular intervals since 1925.

can·trip (kän′trip), n. *Chiefly Scot.* 1. a charm; spell. 2. mischief; trick. Also, **can·trap, can·traip** (kän′trip). [appar. dissimilated var. of OE *calcatrippe;* see CALTROP]

cant′ strip′, an inclined or beveled strip of wood, for changing the pitch of a roof slope or for rounding out the angle between a flat roof and an adjoining parapet.

can·tus (kan′təs), n., pl. **-tus.** 1. See **cantus firmus.** 2. an ecclesiastical style of music. [< L; see CANTO]

can·tus fir·mus (kan′təs fûr′məs), 1. *Eccles.* the ancient traditional vocal music of the Christian Church, having its form set and its use prescribed by ecclesiastical authority. 2. *Music.* a fixed melody to which other melodic parts are added. [< ML: lit., firm song]

cant·y (kan′tē, kän′-), adj. *Scot. and North Eng.* 1. cheerful. 2. lively; brisk. [< LG *kantig* lively; akin to CANT[3]] —**cant′i·ly,** adv. —**cant′i·ness,** n.

Ca·nuck (kə nuk′), n. *Often Offensive.* a Canadian, esp. a French Canadian. [CAN(ADA) + *-uck* < ?]

ca·nu·la (kan′yə lə), n., pl. **-las, -lae** (-lē′). *Surg.* cannula.

ca·nu·lar (kan′yə lər), adj. cannular. Also, **can·u·late** (kan′yə lāt′, -lit).

Ca·nute (kə nōōt′, -nyōōt′), n. A.D. 994?–1035, Danish king of England, 1017–35; of Denmark, 1018–35; and of Norway, 1028–35. Also, **Cnut, Knut.**

can·vas (kan′vəs), n. 1. a closely woven, heavy cloth of hemp, flax, or cotton, used for tents, sails, etc. 2. a piece of this or similar material on which an oil painting is made. 3. an oil painting on canvas. 4. a tent, or tents collectively. 5. sailcloth. 6. sails collectively. 7. any fabric of linen, cotton, etc., of a coarse loose weave used as a foundation for embroidery stitches, for interlining, etc. 8. **under canvas, a.** *Naut.* with set sails. **b.** *Mil.* in tents; in the field: *to sleep under canvas.* [ME *canevas* < ONF < VL *cannabaceus, equiv. to L *cannab(is)* HEMP + *-aceus* -ACEOUS] —**can′vas·like′,** adj.

can·vas·back (kan′vəs bak′), n., pl. **-backs,** (*esp. collectively*) **-back.** a North American wild duck, *Aythya valisineria,* the male of which has a whitish back and a reddish-brown head and neck. [after the canvaslike color of its back]

can·vass (kan′vəs), v.t. 1. to solicit votes, subscriptions, opinions, etc., from (a district, group of people, etc.). 2. to examine carefully; investigate by inquiry; discuss; debate. 3. *Obs.* to criticize severely. —*v.i.* 4. to solicit votes, opinions, etc. 5. to review election returns. 6. to engage in discussion or debate. —*n.* 7. examination; close inspection; scrutiny. 8. a soliciting of votes, orders, etc. 9. a campaign for election to government office. [var. of CANVAS (n.); orig. meaning of v.: to toss (someone) in a canvas sheet] —**can′vass·er,** n.

can·yon (kan′yən), n. *U.S.* a deep valley with steep sides, often with a stream flowing through it. Also, **cañon.** [< Sp *cañón* a long tube, a hollow, equiv. to *cañ(a)* tube (< L *canna* CANE) + *-on* aug. suffix]

Can·yon (kan′yən), n. a town in N Texas. 5864 (1960).

can′yon wind′ (wind), *Meteorol.* 1. a nocturnal, down-canyon flow of air caused by the cooling of the canyon walls. Cf. **valley wind.** 2. Also called **gorge wind.** a wind modified in direction and speed by being forced to blow through a canyon or gorge.

can·zo (kan′sō, kan sō′), n., pl. **-zos.** canso.

can·zo·na (kän tsō′nä), n., pl. **-zo·ni** (-tsō′nē). canzone.

can·zo·ne (kän tsō′ne), n., pl. **-zo·ni** (-tsō′nē). 1. a variety of lyric poetry in the Italian style, of Provençal origin, which closely resembles the madrigal. 2. any ballad or song. 3. a poem in which each word that appears at the end of a line of the first stanza appears again at the end of one of the lines in each of the following stanzas. Also, **canzona.** [< It < L *cantiōn-* (s. of *cantiō*) song, equiv. to *cant(us)* sung (see CANTO) + *-iōn-* -ION]

can·zo·net (kan′zə net′), n. a short song, esp. a light and gay one. [< It *canzonett(a).* See CANZONE, -ET]

Cao·da·ism (kou dī′iz əm), n. an eclectic religion, originated in Cochin-China in 1926, combining Buddhist, Taoist, and Confucianist elements and affected to some extent by Christianity. [< Vietnamese *Cao Dai,* lit., mighty palace + -ISM]

caou·tchouc (kou′chōōk, kou chōōk′), n. 1. rubber[1] (def. 1). 2. pure rubber. [< F < Sp *cauchuc* (now obs.) < Quechua]

cap[1] (kap), n., v., **capped, cap·ping.** —n. 1. a covering for the head, esp. one fitting closely, made of softer material than a hat and usually having little or no brim. 2. a covering of lace or similar material for a woman's head, usually worn indoors. 3. a headdress denoting rank, occupation, or the like: *a nurse's cap.* 4. mortarboard (def. 2). 5. anything resembling or suggestive of a covering for the head in shape, use, or position: *a cap on a bottle.* 6. summit; top; acme. 7. *Bot.* the pileus of a mushroom. 8. Also called **cap piece, lid.** *Mining.* a short, horizontal piece at the top of a prop for supporting part of a roof. 9. a percussion cap. 10. a noisemaking device for toy pistols, made of a small quantity of explosive wrapped in paper or other thin material. 11. *Naut.* **a.** a fitting of metal placed over the head of a spar, as a mast or bowsprit, and having a collar for securing a further spar, as an upper mast or jib boom, at some distance above its lower end. **b.** a metal band at the end of a spar. **c.** a cover of leather or tarred canvas for the end of a rope. 12. a new tread applied to a worn pneumatic tire. 13. *Archit.* a capital. 14. *Carpentry.* a metal plate placed over the iron of a plane to break the shavings as they rise. 15. *Naut.* a wooden or metal piece at the head of a mast, for supporting and steadying an upper mast, as a topmast or topgallant mast. 16. *Fox Hunting.* See **capping fee.** 17. **cap in hand,** humbly; in supplication: *He went to his father cap in hand and begged his forgiveness.* 18. **set one's cap for,** to attempt to catch as a husband: *Several girls in the class were setting their caps for the new young biology instructor.* —*v.t.* 19. to provide or cover with or as with a cap. 20. to complete. 21. to surpass; follow up with something as good or better: *to cap one joke with another.* 22. to serve as a cap, covering, or top to; overlie. —*v.i.* 23. *Fox Hunting.* to hunt with a hunting club of which one is not a member, on payment of a capping fee. 24. **cap the climax,** to surpass what has been considered the limit; exceed expectations: *This latest prank really caps the climax.* [ME *cappe,* OE *cæppe* < LL *capp(a)* hooded cloak, cap; akin to L *caput* head] —**cap′less,** adj.

cap[2] (kap), n., v., **capped, cap·ping.** —n. 1. a capital letter. 2. Usually, **caps.** upper case: *Please set the underlined in caps.* —*v.t.* 3. to write or print in capital letters, or make an initial letter a capital; capitalize. [by shortening]

CAP, Civil Air Patrol. Also, **C.A.P.**

cap., 1. (in prescriptions) let the patient take. [< L *capiat*] 2. capital. 3. capitalize. 4. capitalized. 5. capital letter. 6. chapter. [< L *capitulum, caput*] 7. foolscap.

ca·pa (kä′pə), n. the red cloak of a bullfighter, for use chiefly in gaining the attention of the bull and guiding the course of its attack. [< Sp < LL *cappa;* see CAPE[1]]

ca·pa·bil·i·ty (kā′pə bil′i tē), n., pl. **-ties.** 1. the quality of being capable; capacity; ability: *His capability was unquestionable.* 2. the ability to undergo or be affected by a given treatment or action: *the capability of glass in resisting heat.* 3. Usually, **capabilities.** qualities, abilities, features, etc., that can be used or developed; potential: *Though dilapidated, the house has great capabilities.* [< LL *capābili(s)* CAPABLE + -TY[2]]

Ca·pa·blan·ca (kap′ə blaŋ′kə; *Sp.* kä′pä vläŋ′kä), n. **Jo·sé Ra·oul** (hō se′ rä ōōl′), 1888–1942, Cuban chess master.

ca·pa·ble (kā′pə bəl), adj. 1. having intelligence and ability; efficient; competent: *a capable instructor.* 2. **capable of, a.** having the ability or capacity for: *a man capable of judging art.* **b.** open to the influence or effect of; susceptible of: *a situation capable of improvement.*

c. predisposed to; inclined to: *capable of murder.* [< LL *capābil(is)* roomy, appar. equiv. to *capā(x)* roomy + *-bilis* -BLE; see CAPACITY] —**ca′pa·ble·ness,** *n.* —**ca′pa·bly,** *adv.*
—**Syn. 1.** skillful, ingenious, accomplished. See **able. 2a.** adapted, suited.

ca·pa·cious (kə pā′shəs), *adj.* capable of holding much; very large: *a capacious storage bin.* [CAPACI(TY) + -OUS] —**ca·pa′cious·ly,** *adv.* —**ca·pa′cious·ness,** *n.*
—**Syn.** spacious, roomy, ample, large. —**Ant.** confining.

ca·pac·i·tance (kə pas′i təns), *n.* *Elect.* **1.** the ratio of an impressed charge on a conductor to the corresponding change in potential. **2.** the ratio of the charge on either conductor of a capacitor to the potential difference between the conductors. **3.** the property of being able to collect a charge of electricity. *Symbol:* C [CAPACIT(Y) + -ANCE]

ca·pac·i·tate (kə pas′i tāt′), *v.t.*, **-tat·ed, -tat·ing.** to make capable; enable. [CAPACIT(Y) + -ATE[1]] —**ca·pac′i·ta′tion,** *n.*

ca·pac·i·tive (kə pas′i tiv), *adj.* *Elect.* pertaining to capacitance. [CAPACIT(Y) + -IVE] —**ca·pac′i·tive·ly,** *adv.*

capac′itive cou′pling, *Elect.* the connection of two or more circuits by means of a capacitor.

capac′itive react′ance, *Elect.* the opposition of capacitance to alternating current, equal to the reciprocal of the product of the angular frequency of the current times the capacitance. *Symbol:* *xc* Cf. **inductive reactance.**

ca·pac·i·tor (kə pas′i tər), *n.* *Elect.* a device for accumulating and holding a charge of electricity, consisting of two equally charged conducting surfaces having opposite signs and separated by a dielectric. Also called **condenser.** [CAPACIT(Y) + -OR[2]]

ca·pac·i·ty (kə pas′i tē), *n., pl.* **-ties. 1.** the power of receiving or containing: *This hotel has a large capacity. The inn is full to capacity.* **2.** cubic contents; volume; that which can be contained: *The gasoline tank has a capacity of 20 gallons.* **3.** power of receiving impressions, knowledge, etc.; mental ability; capability: *That book was written for those with the capacity of scholars.* **4.** actual or potential ability to perform, yield, or withstand: *He has a capacity for hard work. The capacity of the oil well was 150 barrels a day. She has the capacity to go two days without sleep.* **5.** quality or state of being susceptible to a given treatment or action: *Steel has a high capacity to withstand pressure.* **6.** position; function; relation: *He served in the capacity of legal adviser.* **7.** legal qualification. **8.** *Elect.* **a.** capacitance. **b.** maximum possible output. [late ME *capacite* < MF < L *capācitāt-* (s. of *capācitās*), equiv. to *capāci-* (s. of *capāx*) roomy (*cap(ere)* (to) hold + *-āci-* adj. suffix) + *-tāt-* -TY[2]]
—**Syn. 2.** dimensions, amplitude. **4.** aptitude, readiness, adequacy, competence, capability.

cap′ and bells′, a fool's cap hung with bells.

cap′ and gown′, a mortarboard and gown worn as academic costume.

Ca·pa·ne·us (kə pā′nē əs, kap′ə no͞os′, -nyo͞os′), *n.* *Class. Myth.* one of the Seven against Thebes, who was destroyed by Zeus for blasphemy.

cap-a-pie (kap′ə pē′), *adv.* from head to foot. Also, **cap′-à-pie′.** [< MF *de cap a pe* from head to foot < OPr < L *dē capite ad pedem*]

ca·par·i·son (kə par′i sən), *n.* **1.** a decorative covering for a horse or for the tack or harness of a horse; trappings. **2.** rich and sumptuous clothing or equipment. —*v.t.* **3.** to cover with a caparison. **4.** to dress richly; deck. [< MF *caparasson* (now *caparaçon*) < OSp *caparazón*, akin to *capa* CAPE[1]]

ca·pa·taz (kä′pä täth′, -täs′; *Eng.* kap′ə täz′), *n., pl.* **ca·pa·ta·ces** (kä′pä tä′thes, -ses; *Eng.* kap′ə tä′siz). *Spanish.* a foreman or supervisor.

cap′ cloud′, 1. a stationary cloud directly above an isolated mountain peak. Cf. **banner cloud, crest cloud. 2.** pileus (def. 2). Also called **cloud cap.**

cape[1] (kāp), *n.* **1.** a sleeveless garment of various lengths, fastened around the neck and falling loosely from the shoulders, worn separately or attached to a coat or other outer garment. **2.** the capa of a bullfighter. [ME (north); OE *-cāp* (see COPE[2]), reinforced in 16th century by Sp *capa* < LL *cāpa* hooded cloak, COPE[2]] —**caped,** *adj.*

cape[2] (kāp), *n., v.,* **caped, cap·ing,** *adj.* —*n.* **1.** a piece of land jutting into the sea or some other large body of water. **2. the Cape.** See **Cape of Good Hope. 3.** capeskin. —*v.i.* **4.** *Naut.* (of a vessel) to have good steering qualities. —*adj.* **5.** (*cap.*) pertaining to the Cape of Good Hope or to South Africa: *a Cape diamond.* [ME *cap* < MF < OPr < L *cap(ut)* head]

ca·pe·a·dor (kä′pē ə dôr′; *Sp.* kä pe ä ᵺôr′), *n., pl.* **-dors,** *Sp.* **-do·res** (-ᵺō′res). a matador's assistant who waves his red cloak, or capa, before the bull chiefly to harass or confuse it. [< Sp, equiv. to *capead(o)* baited with a cape (ptp. of *capear*; see CAPE[1], -ADE[1]) + *-or* -OR[2]]

Cape′ Bret′on (brit′ən, bret′ən), an island forming the NE part of Nova Scotia, in SE Canada. 169,865 (1961); 3970 sq. mi. Also called **Cape′ Bret′on Is′land.**

Cape′ buf′falo, a large black buffalo, *Syncerus caffer*, of southern Africa, having horns that meet at the base forming a helmetlike structure over the forehead.

Cape′ Cod′, 1. a sandy peninsula in SE Massachusetts between Cape Cod Bay and the Atlantic Ocean. **2.** a style of cottage developed mainly on Cape Cod, Massachusetts, in the 18th and early 19th centuries, typically a one-story wooden cottage covered by a gable roof having a rise equal to the span, without dormers, and having a massive central chimney and a partial basement.

Cape′ Cod′ Bay′, a part of Massachusetts Bay, enclosed by the Cape Cod peninsula.

Cape′ Cod′ Canal′, a canal in SE Massachusetts, connecting Buzzards Bay and Cape Cod Bay. 8 mi. long.

Cape′ Cod′ light′er, a device for lighting a fire, as in a fireplace, consisting of a lump of nonflammable material, on a metal rod, which is soaked in kerosene or the like and lighted with a match.

Cape′ Col′ony, former name of **Cape of Good Hope.**

Cape′ Col′ored, a South African of mixed European and African or Malayan ancestry.

Cape′ cow′slip, any liliaceous herb of the genus *Lachenalia*, of southern Africa, having red or yellow bell-shaped flowers.

cape′ doc′tor, a strong southeast wind in the southern part of South Africa. [so called because thought good for the health]

Cape′ Dutch′, Afrikaans.

Cape′ Fly′away, *Naut. Slang.* an illusion of land on the horizon, caused by a low cloud bank or some other meteorological condition.

Cape′ forget′-me-not, a biennial herb, *Anchusa capensis*, of South Africa, having red buds and blue flowers, grown as an ornamental.

Cape′ Gi·rar·deau′ (jē′rär dō′), a city in SE Missouri, on the Mississippi River. 24,947 (1960).

cape′ goose′berry, a tropical perennial herb, *Physalis peruviana*, having heart-shaped, hairy leaves, purple-throated pale yellow flowers, and edible, yellow berries in a long pointed calyx.

Cape′ Horn′, a headland on a small island at the S extremity of South America: belongs to Chile.

Cape′ Horn′ fe′ver, *Naut. Slang.* illness feigned by malingerers.

Ča·pek (chä′pek), *n.* **Ka·rel** (kär′əl, kar′-, kär′-; *Czech.* kä′rel), 1890–1938, Czech playwright, novelist, and producer.

cap·e·lin (kap′ə lin), *n.* either of two small fishes of the smelt family, *Mallotus villosus*, found off the coast of North America, or *M. catervarius*, found in the North Pacific. Also, **caplin.** [< MF *capelan* < OPr: codfish, lit., CHAPLAIN]

cap·e·line (kap′ə lēn′, -lin), *n.* **1.** *Armor.* an iron skullcap worn by medieval archers. **2.** *Heraldry.* a representation of a hood, sometimes used as a mantling. Also, **cap′el·line′.** [late ME < MF < early It *capellin(a)*, equiv. to *capell(a)* (*capp(a)* CAP[1] + *-ella* dim. suffix) + *-ina* -INE[1]]

Ca·pel·la (kə pel′ə), *n.* **1.** *Astron.* a first-magnitude star in the constellation Auriga. **2.** a walled plain in the fourth quadrant of the face of the moon: about 30 miles in diameter. [< L: lit., she-goat, equiv. to *cap(ra)* she-goat + *-ella* dim. suffix]

Cape of Good Hope

Cape′ May′, a town in S New Jersey. 4477 (1960).

Cape′ May′ war′bler, a North American wood warbler, *Dendroica tigrina*, olive-green striped with black above and yellow striped with black below.

Cape′ of Good′ Hope′, 1. a cape in S Africa, in the SW Republic of South Africa. **2.** Also called **Cape′ Prov′ince.** Formerly, **Cape Colony.** a province in the Republic of South Africa. 5,308,839 (1960); 277,169 sq. mi. *Cap.:* Cape Town.

Cape′ per′iwinkle, a periwinkle, *Vinca rosea*, of Madagascar, having showy pink or white flowers. Also called **Madagascar periwinkle.**

Cape′ pond′weed, an aquatic plant, *Aponogeton distachyus*, of the Cape of Good Hope, having floating leaves and tiny, emersed, fragrant white flowers. Also called **water hawthorn.**

ca·per[1] (kā′pər), *v.i.* **1.** to leap or skip about in a sprightly manner; prance; frisk; gambol. —*n.* **2.** a playful leap or skip. **3.** a prank; capricious action; harebrained escapade. **4.** a frivolous, carefree episode or activity. **5.** *Slang.* a criminal or illegal act, as a burglary, robbery, etc. **6. cut a caper.** See **cut** (def. 39). [fig. use of L *caper* he-goat (c. OE *hæfer*, Icel *hafr*); for the meaning, compare DOG (v.)] —**ca′per·er,** *n.* —**ca′per·ing·ly,** *adv.*

ca·per[2] (kā′pər), *n.* **1.** a shrub, *Capparis spinosa*, of Mediterranean regions. **2.** its flower bud, which is pickled and used for garnish or seasoning. [back formation from *capers* (taken for pl.), ME *caperes* < L *capparis* < Gk *kápparis*]

cap·er·cail·lie (kap′ər kāl′yē), *n.* a large grouse, *Tetrao urogallus*, of Eurasian forests. Also, **cap·er·cail·zie** (kap′ər kāl′yē, -kāl′zē). [< ScotGael *capullcoille* (by dissimilation), lit., horse of the woods; cf. ME *capel* horse, Icel *kapall* nag, akin to *caval-* in CAVALRY]

Ca·per·na·um (kə pûr′nā əm, -nē-), *n.* an ancient town in N Israel, on the Sea of Galilee: center of Jesus' ministry in Galilee.

Cape′ ru′by, a red pyrope garnet, used as a gem: not a true ruby. Also called **Arizona ruby.**

cape·skin (kāp′skin′), *n.* a firm, washable leather used esp. for gloves, originally made from the skin of goats from the Cape of Good Hope, but now from hairy lambskin or sheepskin. [CAPE[2] + SKIN]

Ca·pet (kā′pit, kap′it; *Fr.* ka pe′), *n.* **Hugh** or *Fr.* **Hughes** (yg), A.D. 938?–996, king of France 987–996.

Ca·pe·tian (kə pē′shən), *adj.* **1.** of or pertaining to the French dynasty that ruled France A.D. 987–1328 in the direct line, and in collateral branches, as the Valois and Bourbons, until 1848 (except 1795–1814). —*n.* **2.** a member of this dynasty. [Hugh CAPET + -IAN, modeled on F *capétien*]

Cape′ Town′, a seaport in and the legislative capital of the Republic of South Africa, in the SW part: also capital of Cape of Good Hope province. 718,189 (1960). Also, **Cape′town′.** Afrikaans, **Kaapstad.** —**Cape·to·ni·an** (kāp tō′nē ən), *n.*

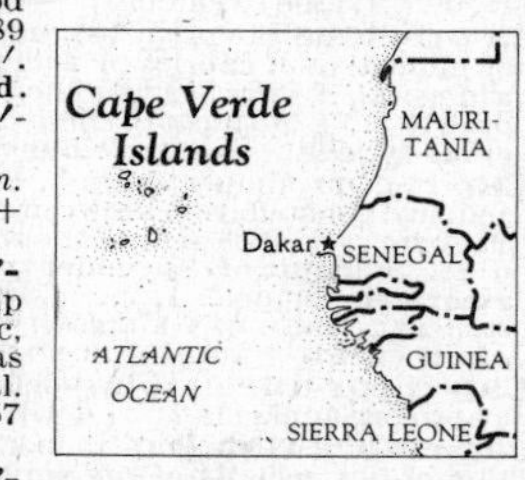

ca·pette (kā pet′), *n.* caponette. [CAP(ON) + -ETTE]

Cape′ Verde′ Is′lands (vûrd), a group of islands in the Atlantic, W of Senegal: an overseas territory of Portugal. 218,000 (est. 1963); 1557 sq. mi. *Cap.:* Praia.

Cape′ York′ Penin′sula, a peninsula in NE Australia, in N Queensland, between the Gulf of Carpentaria and the Coral Sea.

cap·ful (kap′fo͝ol′), *n., pl.* **-fuls.** the amount that a cap will hold. [CAP[1] + -FUL]

cap′ gun′. See **cap pistol.**

caph (käf, kôf), *n.* kaph.

Cap-Ha·i·tien (*Fr.* kap a ē syan′, -tyan′), *n.* a seaport in N Haiti. 26,555 (est. 1957).

Ca·phau·rus (kə fôr′əs), *n.* *Class. Myth.* a son of Amphithemis and the grandson of Apollo.

ca·pi·as (kā′pē əs, kap′ē-), *n.* *Law.* a writ commanding an officer to take a specified person into custody. [late ME < L: lit., you are to take, subj. 2nd sing. of *capere*]

cap·i·ba·ra (kap′ə bär′ə), *n.* capybara.

cap·il·la·ceous (kap′ə lā′shəs), *adj.* **1.** hairlike. **2.** capillary. [< L *capillāceus* hairy, equiv. to *capill(us)* hair + *-āceus* -ACEOUS]

cap·il·lar·i·ty (kap′ə lar′i tē), *n.* **1.** the state of being capillary. **2.** Also called **cap′illary ac′tion.** *Physics.* a manifestation of surface tension by which the portion of the surface of a liquid coming in contact with a solid is elevated or depressed, depending on the adhesive or cohesive properties of the liquid. [CAPILLARY + -TY[2]]

cap·il·lar·y (kap′ə ler′ē), *adj., n., pl.* **-lar·ies.** —*adj.* **1.** pertaining to or occurring in or as in a tube of fine bore. **2.** *Physics.* **a.** pertaining to capillarity. **b.** of or pertaining to the apparent attraction or repulsion between a liquid and a solid, observed in capillarity. **3.** *Bot.* resembling hair in the manner of growth or shape. **4.** *Anat.* pertaining to a capillary or capillaries. —*n.* **5.** *Anat.* one of the minute blood vessels between the terminations of the arteries and the beginnings of the veins. **6.** Also, **cap′illary tube′.** a tube with a small bore. [< L *capillār(is)* of, pertaining to the hair, equiv. to *capill(us)* hair + *-āris* -ARY]

cap·il·la·tus (kap′ə lā′təs), *adj.* *Meteorol.* (of a cloud) having a cirriform upper portion that resembles an anvil or a disorderly mass of hair. [< L *capillātus* having hair]

ca·pi·ta (kap′i tə), *n.* pl. of **caput.**

cap·i·tal[1] (kap′i təl), *n.* **1.** the city or town which is the official seat of government in a county, state, etc.: *What is the capital of Nigeria?* **2.** a capital letter. **3.** the wealth, whether in money or property, owned or employed in business by an individual, firm, corporation, etc. **4.** an accumulated stock of such wealth. **5.** any form of wealth employed or capable of being employed in the production of more wealth. **6.** *Accounting.* **a.** assets remaining after deduction of liabilities; the net worth of a business. **b.** the ownership interest in a business. **7.** any source of profit, advantage, power, etc.: *His indefatigable drive is his greatest capital.* **8.** capitalists as a group or class (distinguished from *labor*): *High taxation has reduced the spending power of capital.* —*adj.* **9.** pertaining to capital: *capital stock.* **10.** principal; highly important: *This guide offers suggestions of capital interest to travelers.* **11.** chief, esp. as being the official seat of government of a country, state, etc. **12.** excellent or first-rate: *a capital hotel; a capital fellow.* **13.** (of an alphabetic letter) of a particular form different from and higher than its corresponding lower-case letter, and occurring as the initial letter of a proper name, of the first word of a sentence, etc., as A, B, Q, R. **14.** involving the loss of life: *capital punishment.* **15.** punishable by death: *a capital crime; a capital offender.* **16.** fatal; serious: *a capital error.* [ME < L *capitāl(is)* of the head (*capit-*, s. of *caput* head, + *-ālis* -AL[1]) + ML *capitāle* wealth, n. use of neut. of *capitālis* (adj.)] —**cap′i·tal·ness,** *n.*
—**Syn. 3.** principal, investment, assets, stock. **10.** prime, primary, first. The adjectives CAPITAL, CHIEF, MAJOR, PRINCIPAL apply to a main or leading representative of a kind. CAPITAL may mean larger or more prominent; it may also suggest preeminence or excellence: *capital letter, idea, virtue,* etc. CHIEF means leading, highest in office or power: *the chief clerk.* MAJOR may refer to greatness of importance, number, or quantity: *a major operation, the major part of a population.* PRINCIPAL refers to most distinguished, influential, or foremost: *principal officer.* —**Ant. 10.** trivial, minor.

cap·i·tal[2] (kap′i təl), *n.* *Archit.* the uppermost portion of a column, pillar, or shaft supporting the entablature. [ME *capitale* head (n. use of neut. of L adj.) for L *capitellum*, equiv. to *capit-* (s. of *caput*) head + *-ellum* dim. suffix]

Capitals[2]
A, Tuscan order
B, Gothic order

cap′ital account′, 1. a business account stating the owner's or shareholder's interest in the assets. **2. capital accounts,** *Accounting.* accounts showing the net worth in a business enterprise, as assets minus liabilities.

cap′ital as′set. See **fixed asset.**

cap′ital bo′nus, *Brit.* dividend (def. 3).

cap′ital bud′get, a statement of proposed financial expenditures, esp. for schools, playgrounds, parks, and other municipal facilities, and often including a plan for financing.

cap′ital expen′diture, *Accounting.* an addition to the value of fixed assets, as by the purchase of a new building.

cap′ital gain′, profit from the sale of assets, such as bonds, real estate, etc.

cap′ital goods′, *Econ.* machines and tools used in the production of other goods (contrasted with *consumer goods*).

cap′ital invest′ment, (in a business) the total funds invested in an enterprise.

cap·i·tal·ise (kap′i təlīz′, kə pit′əlīz′), *v.t.*, **-ised, -is·ing.** *Chiefly Brit.* capitalize. —**cap′i·tal·is′a·ble,** *adj.* —**cap′i·tal·is′er,** *n.*

cap·i·tal·ism (kap′i təliz′əm; *Brit. also* kə pit′əliz′əm), *n.* an economic system in which investment in and ownership of the means of production, distribution, and exchange of wealth is made and maintained chiefly by private individuals or corporations, esp. as contrasted to cooperatively or state-owned means of wealth. [CAPITAL[1] + -ISM]

cap·i·tal·ist (kap′i təlist; *Brit. also* kə pit′əlist), *n.* a person who has capital, esp. extensive capital, invested in business enterprises. [CAPITAL[1] + -IST]

cap·i·tal·is·tic (kap′i təlis′tik; *Brit. also* kə pit′əlis′tik), *adj.* pertaining to capital or capitalists; founded on or believing in capitalism: *capitalistic production; a capitalistic system.* [CAPITALIST + -IC] —**cap′i·tal·is′ti·cal·ly,** *adv.*

cap·i·tal·i·za·tion (kap′i tᵊli zā′shən; *Brit. also* kə pit′ᵊli zā′shən), *n.* **1.** the act of capitalizing. **2.** the authorized or outstanding stocks and bonds of a corporation. **3.** *Accounting.* **a.** the total investment of the owner or owners in a business enterprise. **b.** the total corporate liability. **c.** the total arrived at after addition of liabilities. **4.** conversion into stocks or bonds. **5.** the act of computing the present value of future periodical payments. [CAPITALIZE + -ATION]

cap·i·tal·ize (kap′i tᵊlīz′; *Brit. also* kə pit′ᵊlīz′), *v.t.*, **-ized, -iz·ing.** **1.** to write or print in capital letters or with an initial capital. **2.** to authorize a certain amount of stocks and bonds in the corporate charter: *to capitalize a corporation.* **3.** to issue stock as a dividend, thereby capitalizing retained earnings, or as settlement of an unpaid arrearage of preferred dividends. **4.** *Accounting.* to set up (expenditures) as business assets in the books of account instead of treating as expense. **5.** to supply with capital. **6.** to estimate the value of (a stock or an enterprise). **7.** to take advantage of; turn to one's advantage (often fol. by *on*): *to capitalize on one's opportunities.* Also, *esp. Brit.,* **capitalise.** [CAPITAL[1] + -IZE] **—cap′i·tal·iz′a·ble,** *adj.* **—cap′i·tal·iz′er,** *n.*

cap′ital lev′y, a tax based on capital, as distinguished from a tax on income.

cap′ital loss′, loss from the sale of assets, as of bonds, real estate, etc.

cap·i·tal·ly (kap′i tᵊlē), *adv.* in a capital manner; excellently; very well. [CAPITAL[1] + -LY]

cap′ital pun′ishment, punishment of death for a crime; death penalty.

cap′ital ship′, one of a class of the largest warships; a battleship, battle cruiser, or aircraft carrier.

cap′ital stock′, **1.** the total stock authorized or issued by a corporation. **2.** the book value of the outstanding shares of a corporation, including retained earnings and amounts paid in by stockholders.

cap′ital sum′, *Insurance.* the maximum amount collectable for accidental death or for some major disabling injury, as one resulting in the loss of an eye, leg, or arm. Also called **principal sum.**

cap′ital sur′plus, the surplus of a business, exclusive of its earned surplus.

cap·i·tate (kap′i tāt′), *adj.* **1.** *Bot.* having a globular head; collected in a head. **2.** *Biol.* having an enlarged or swollen, headlike termination. [< L *capitāt(us)* headed, = *capit-* (s. of *caput*) head + *-ātus* -ATE[1]]

cap′itate bone′, *Anat.* the largest and central bone of the carpus, articulating with the second, third, and fourth metacarpal bones.

cap·i·ta·tion (kap′i tā′shən), *n.* **1.** a numbering or assessing by the head. **2.** a poll tax. **3.** a fee or payment of a uniform amount for each person. [< LL *capitātiōn-* (s. of *capitātiō*). See CAPITATE, -ION] **—cap′i·ta′tive,** *adj.*

ca·pi·teux (kᴀ pē tœ′), *adj. French.* (of a wine) heady.

Cap·i·tol (kap′i tᵊl), *n.* **1.** the building in Washington, D.C., used by the Congress of the U.S. for its sessions. **2.** (*often l.c.*) a building occupied by a State legislature; Statehouse. **3.** the ancient temple of Jupiter at Rome, on the Capitoline. **4.** the Capitoline. [< L *capitōl(ium)* temple of Jupiter on Capitoline hill, Rome, = *capit-* (s. of *caput*) head + *-ōlium* < ?; r. ME *capitolie* < ONF]

Cap′itol Hill′, *U.S.* **1.** the small hill in Washington, D.C., on which the Capitol stands. **2.** Congress: *Capitol Hill will adjourn early this year.* Also called **the Hill.**

Cap·i·to·line (kap′i tᵊlīn′), *adj.* **1.** of or pertaining to the Capitoline or to the ancient temple of Jupiter that stood on this hill. **—n. 2.** one of the seven hills on which ancient Rome was built. [< L *Capitōlīn(us).* See CAPITOL, -INE[1]]

ca·pit·u·lar (kə pich′ə lər), *n.* **1.** a member of an ecclesiastical chapter. **2. capitulars,** the laws or statutes of a chapter or of an ecclesiastical council. **—adj. 3.** *Bot.* capitate. **4.** pertaining to an ecclesiastical or other chapter: *a capitular cathedral.* [< ML *capitulār(is),* equiv. to *capitul(um)* chapter (lit., small head; see CAPITULUM) + *-āris* -AR[1]] **—ca·pit′u·lar·ly,** *adv.*

ca·pit·u·lar·y (kə pich′ə ler′ē), *adj., n., pl.* **-lar·ies.** **—adj. 1.** pertaining to a chapter, esp. to an ecclesiastical one. **—n. 2.** a member of a chapter, esp. of an ecclesiastical one. **3.** Often, **capitularies.** an ordinance or law of a Frankish sovereign. [< ML *capitulāri(us),* equiv. to *capitulār(is)* CAPITULAR + *-ius* adj. suffix]

ca·pit·u·late (kə pich′ə lāt′), *v.i.,* **-lat·ed, -lat·ing.** to surrender unconditionally or on stipulated terms. [< ML *capitulāt(us)* drawn up in sections (ptp. of *capitulāre*), equiv. to *capitul(um)* section (lit., small head; see CAPITULUM) + *-ātus* -ATE[1]] **—ca·pit′u·lant,** *n.* **—ca·pit′u·la′tor,** *n.*

ca·pit·u·la·tion (kə pich′ə lā′shən), *n.* **1.** the act of capitulating. **2.** the document containing the terms of a surrender. **3.** a list of the headings or main divisions of a subject; a summary or enumeration. **4.** Often, **capitulations.** a treaty or agreement by which subjects of one country residing or traveling in another are extended extraterritorial rights or special privileges, esp. such a treaty between a European country and the former Ottoman rulers of Turkey. [< ML *capitulātiōn-* (s. of *capitulātiō*). See CAPITULATE, -ION] **—ca·pit·u·la·to·ry** (kə pich′ə lə tôr′ē, -tōr′ē), *adj.*

ca·pit·u·lum (kə pich′ə ləm), *n., pl.* **-la** (-lə). **1.** *Bot.* a close head of sessile flowers; a flower head. **2.** *Anat.* the head of a bone. [< L, equiv. to *capit-* (s. of *caput*) head + *-ulum,* neut. of *-ulus* -ULE]

cap′ jib′, *Naut.* a jib set on a stay to a bowsprit cap.

Cap·let (kap′lit), *n. Trademark.* a medicinal tablet shaped like a capsule and coated for ease in swallowing.

cap·lin (kap′lin), *n.* capelin.

cap. moll., (in prescriptions) soft capsule. [< L *capsula mollis*]

Cap′n (kap′ᵊm), *n.* Captain.

ca·po (kā′pō), *n., pl.* **-pos.** **1.** any of various devices for a guitar, lute, banjo, etc., which when clamped or screwed down across the strings at a given fret will raise each string a corresponding number of half tones. **2.** the nut of a guitar, lute, banjo, etc. Also called **capotasto.** [< It *capotasto* equiv. to *capo* head, top (< L *caput*) + *tasto* touch, key < *tastare* to touch ≪ L *taxāre,* freq. of *tangere*]

cap′ of estate′, *Heraldry.* chapeau (def. 2a). Also called **cap′ of main′tenance.**

ca·pon (kā′pon, -pən), *n.* a rooster castrated to improve the flesh for use as food. [ME; OE *capun* < L *capōn-* (s. of *capō*) castrated cock; akin to Gk *kóptein* to cut, OSlav *skopiti* to castrate]

ca·pon·ette (kā′pə net′), *n.* a capon produced by the administration of a synthetic sex hormone. Also called **capette.** [CAPON + -ETTE]

ca·pon·ise (kā′pə nīz′), *v.t.,* **-ised, -is·ing.** *Chiefly Brit.* caponize. **—ca′pon·i·sa′tion,** *n.* **—ca′pon·is′er,** *n.*

ca·pon·ize (kā′pə nīz′), *v.t.,* **-ized, -iz·ing.** to castrate (a fowl). [CAPON + -IZE] **—ca′pon·i·za′tion,** *n.* **—ca′pon·iz′er,** *n.*

cap·o·ral (kap′ər əl, kap′ə ral′), *n.* a kind of tobacco. [short for F *tabac du caporal* tobacco of the CORPORAL]

Cap·o·ret·to (kap′ə ret′ō; *It.* kä′pô ret′tô), *n.* Italian name of **Kobarid.**

ca·pot (kə pot′, -pō′), *n. Cards.* the taking by one player of all the tricks of a deal, as in piquet. [< F (n. and adj.), designating or describing the player who has no tricks, after *faire capot* (nautical) to capsize]

ca·po·tas·to (kä′pō täs′tō, -pə-), *n., pl.* **ca·po·tas·tos, ca·pi·tas·ti** (kä′pē täs′tē). capo. [< It: master fret, equiv. to *capo* head, chief (< L *caput*) + *tasto* fret (lit., touch), deriv. of *tastare* to touch ≪ L *taxāre,* freq. of *tangere*]

ca·pote (kə pōt′; *Fr.* kᴀ pôt′), *n., pl.* **-potes** (-pōts′; *Fr.* -pôt′). **1.** a long cloak with a hood. **2.** a close-fitting, caplike bonnet worn by women and children in the mid-Victorian period. **3.** a bullfighter's cape; capa. **4.** an adjustable top or hood of a vehicle, as a buggy. [< F, equiv. to *cape* (< Sp *capa* CAPE[1]) + *-ote,* fem. of *-ot* dim. suffix]

Ca·po·te (kə pō′tē), *n.* **Truman,** 1924–84, U.S. novelist, short-story writer, and playwright.

ca·pouch (kə po͞osh′, -po͞och′), *n. Obs.* capuche.

Cap·pa·do·cia (kap′ə dō′shə), *n.* an ancient country in E Asia Minor: it became a Roman province in A.D. 17. **—Cap′pa·do′cian,** *adj., n.*

cap·pa ma·gna (kä′pə mä′nyə, kap′ə mag′nə), *Eccles.* a ceremonial cloak having a long train and a silk or fur-lined hood, worn by cardinals, bishops, and certain other dignitaries. [< ML: great cope]

cap·pa·ri·da·ceous (kap′ə ri dā′shəs), *adj.* belonging to the *Capparidaceae,* or caper family of plants. [< NL *Capparidace(ae)* name of the family (*Capparis* genus name (see CAPER[2]) + *-id-* -ID[2] + *(-aceae* -ACEAE) + -OUS]

capped′ el′bow, *Vet. Pathol.* See **shoe boil.**

capped′ hock′, *Vet. Pathol.* any swelling, inflammatory or otherwise, on the point of the hock of horses.

capped′ pawn′, *Chess.* a pawn that has been singled out or marked by a strong player as the one with which he intends to effect checkmate in giving a weaker opponent odds.

cap·pel·let·ti (kap′ə let′ē; *It.* käp′pel let′tē), *n.* (*construed as sing.*) small pieces of pasta filled with meat or cheese, often served in the stock in which they have boiled, or drained and served with butter and cheese. [< It, pl. of *cappelletto* little hat, dim. of *capell(o)* hat < ML *cappell(us)* cap, dim. of LL *capp(a);* see CAPE[1]]

cap·per (kap′ər), *n.* **1.** one who or that which caps. **2.** *Slang.* an informer, esp. for gamblers. **3.** *Slang.* a by-bidder at an auction. [CAP[1] + -ER[1]]

cap′ piece′, *Mining.* cap[1] (def. 8).

cap·ping (kap′ing), *n. Mining.* overburden (def. 3). [CAP[1] + -ING[1]]

cap′ping fee′, *Fox Hunting.* a fee paid for a day of hunting with an association of hunters of which one is not a member. Also called **cap.**

cap′ pis′tol, a toy gun using caps to imitate the sound of a real pistol. Also called **cap gun.**

Cap·po·tas (kap′ə təs), *n. Class. Myth.* an epithet of Zeus, meaning "reliever."

cap·puc·ci·no (kap′o͝o chē′nō, kä′po͝o-; *It.* käp′po͞ot-chē′nô), *n.* a hot beverage consisting of espresso coffee and steamed milk, often served with powdered cinnamon and topped with whipped cream. [< It; see CAPUCHIN]

cap·re·o·late (kap′rē ə lāt′, kə prē′-), *adj.* **1.** *Bot.* having tendrils. **2.** *Anat.* resembling tendrils. [< L *capreol(ī)* props (pl. of *capreolus* roebuck; see CAPRIOLE) + -ATE[1]]

Ca·pri (kä′prē, kap′rē, kə prē′), *n.* **1.** an island in W Italy, in the Bay of Naples: grottoes; resort. 5½ sq. mi. **2.** a dry white or sometimes red wine of Capri.

capri-, an element meaning "goat," occurring in loan words from Latin (*capricious*); used in the formation of compound words (*caprifoliaceous*). [< L, comb. form of *caper* a goat; see CAPER[1]]

ca·pric·ci·o (kə prē′chē ō′; *It.* kä prēt′chô), *n., pl.* **-ci·os,** *It.* **-ci** (-chē). **1.** a caper; prank. **2.** a caprice. **3.** *Music.* a composition in a free, irregular style. [< It, equiv. to *capr(o)* goat (see CAPER[1]) + *-iccio* < L *-īceus* suffix]

ca·pric·ci·o·so (kə prē′chē ō′sō; *It.* kä′prēt chô′sô), *adj. Music.* capricious; fantastic in style. [< It, equiv. to *capricci(o)* CAPRICE + *-oso* -OUS]

ca·price (kə prēs′), *n.* **1.** a sudden, unpredictable change, as of one's mind, the weather, etc. **2.** a tendency to change one's mind without apparent or adequate motive; whimsicality; capriciousness: *With the caprice of a despotic king, he alternated between kindness and cruelty.* **3.** a work of art, as in literature, painting, etc., that is light and fanciful. **4.** *Music.* capriccio (def. 3). [< F < It; see CAPRICCIO] **—Syn. 1.** vagary, notion.

ca·pri·cious (kə prish′əs), *adj.* **1.** subject to, led by, or indicative of caprice or whim; erratic: *Capricious and whimsical, she lived as her fancy dictated.* **2.** *Obs.* fanciful or witty. [< It *capriccioso* CAPRICCIOSO] **—ca·pri′cious·ly,** *adv.* **—ca·pri′cious·ness,** *n.*

Cap·ri·corn (kap′rə kôrn′), *n.* **1.** *Astron.* the Goat, a zodiacal constellation between Sagittarius and Aquarius. **2.** *Astrol.* the 10th sign of the zodiac. See illus. under **zodiac. 3. tropic of.** See under **tropic** (def. 1a). Also, **Capricornus** (for defs. 1, 2). [ME *Capricorne* < L *Capricorn(us)* (trans. of Gk *aigókerōs* goat-horned), equiv. to *capri-* CAPRI- + *corn(u)* HORN + *-us* adj. suffix]

Cap·ri·cor·nus (kap′rə kôr′nəs), *n., gen.* **-ni** (-nī). Capricorn (defs. 1, 2). [< L]

cap·ri·fi·ca·tion (kap′rə fə kā′shən), *n.* the pollination of figs, usually of the Smyrna variety, by fig wasps attracted by the caprifig fruit hung in the branches of the trees. [< L *caprificātiōn-* (s. of *caprificātiō*), equiv. to *caprificāt(us)* pollinated from the wild fig tree (ptp. of *caprificāre;* see CAPRIFIG) + *-iōn-* -ION] **—cap′ri·fi·ca′tor,** *n.*

cap·ri·fig (kap′rə fig′), *n.* **1.** a fig, *Ficus carica sylvestris,* bearing an inedible fruit used in caprification. **2.** the fruit itself. [< L *caprific(us)* the wild fig tree, lit., the goat-fig, equiv. to *capri-* CAPRI- + *ficus* FIG[1]]

cap·ri·fo·li·a·ceous (kap′rə fō′lē ā′shəs), *adj.* belonging to the *Caprifoliaceae,* a family of plants including the honeysuckle, elder, viburnum, snowberry, etc. [< NL *caprifoliāce(ae)* honeysuckle family (*caprifoli(um)* honeysuckle (genus) < ML, equiv. to L *capri-* CAPRI- + *folium* leaf + NL *-acea* -ACEAE) + -OUS]

cap·ri·ole (kap′rē ōl′), *n., v.,* **-oled, -ol·ing.** **—n. 1.** a caper or leap. **2.** *Dressage.* a movement in which the horse jumps up with its forelegs well drawn in, kicks out with its hind legs in a horizontal position in the air, and then lands again on the same spot. **—v.i. 3.** to execute a capriole. [< MF < OIt *capriol(a),* var. of *capriolo* roebuck < L *capreol(us),* equiv. to *capre(us)* roe (*caper* he-goat (see CAPER[1]) + *-eus* adj. suffix) + *-olus* dim. suffix]

Cap·ri·ote (kap′rē ōt′, -ət), *n.* a native or inhabitant of Capri. [CAPRI + *-ote* < L *-ote(s)* inhabitant]

Capri′ pants′, close-fitting trousers worn by women as informal attire. [after CAPRI]

Ca·pris (kə prēz′), *n.pl.* See **Capri pants.**

cap·ro·ate (kap′rō āt′), *n. Chem.* a salt or ester of caproic acid. [CAPRO(IC) + -ATE[2]]

cap′ rock′, *Geol.* a mass of anhydrite, gypsum, or limestone immediately above the salt of a salt dome.

ca·pro′ic ac′id (kə prō′ik), *Chem.* an oily, colorless or yellow liquid, $CH_3(CH_2)_4COOH$, having a limburger-cheeselike odor, usually obtained from fatty animal tissue or coconut oil, or synthesized: used chiefly in the manufacture of flavoring agents. Also called **hexanoic acid.** [CAPR(I)- + *-oic* (-o- + -IC)]

ca·pryl·ic (kə pril′ik, ka-), *adj.* of or pertaining to an animal odor: *the caprylic odor of a barn.* [CAPR(I)- + -YL + -IC]

caps., **1.** capital letters. **2.** (in prescriptions) a capsule. [< L *capsula*]

cap·sa·i·cin (kap sā′i sin), *n. Chem.* a colorless, crystalline, bitter compound, $C_{18}H_{27}NO_3$, present in capsicum. [earlier *capsicine,* equiv. to CAPSIC(UM) + -INE[2]; refashioned with *capsa* (< L: box) for *caps-* and -IN[2] for -INE[2]]

cap′ screw′, a fastener for machine parts, threaded along the whole length of its shank and held by threads tapped in the hole in which it is screwed. Cf. **machine bolt, machine screw.**

cap·si·cum (kap′sə kəm), *n.* **1.** any solanaceous plant of the genus *Capsicum,* as *C. frutescens,* the common pepper of the garden, occurring in many varieties that range from mild to hot, having pungent seeds, also ranging from mild to hot, enclosed in a podded or bell-shaped pericarp. **2.** the fruit of these plants, or some preparation of it, used as a condiment and once widely used internally and as a local irritant externally. [< NL, equiv. to L *caps(a)* CASE[2] + *-icum,* neut. of *-icus* -IC]

cap·size (kap′sīz, kap sīz′), *v.,* **-sized, -siz·ing.** **—v.i. 1.** to overturn: *The boat capsized.* **—v.t. 2.** to upset: *They capsized the boat.* [?] **—cap′siz·a·ble,** *adj.* **—Syn. 1, 2.** See **upset. —Ant. 2.** right.

cap′sizing mo′ment, *Naval Archit.* See **upsetting moment.**

cap′ spin′ning, a spinning process in which the yarn is twisted and wound onto a revolving bobbin located within a stationary cap, much used in the Bradford spinning process.

Capstan

cap·stan (kap′stən), *n.* any of various windlasses, rotated in a horizontal plane by hand or machinery, for winding in ropes, cables, etc. [ME < OPr *cabestan,* var. of *cabestran* << L *capistrant-* (s. of *capistrāns*), prp. of *capistrāre* to fasten with a halter, deriv. of *capistrum* halter < ?]

cap′stan bar′, a long lever for turning a capstan by hand.

cap′stan lathe′, *Chiefly Brit.* See **turret lathe.**

cap′stan ta′ble. See **drum table.**

cap·stone (kap′stōn′), *n.* a finishing stone of a structure. [CAP[1] + STONE]

cap·su·lar (kap′sə lər), *adj.* of, in, or like a capsule. [< NL *capsulār(is).* See CAPSULE, -AR[1]]

cap·su·late (kap′sə lāt′), *adj.* enclosed in or formed into a capsule. Also, **cap′su·lat′ed.** [< NL *capsulāt(us).* See CAPSULE, -ATE[1]] **—cap′su·la′tion,** *n.*

cap·sule (kap′səl), *n., v.,* **-suled, -sul·ing,** *adj.* **—n. 1.** *Pharm.* a gelatinous case enclosing a dose of medicine. **2.** *Bot.* **a.** a dry dehiscent fruit, composed of two or more carpels. **b.** the sporangium of various cryptogamic plants. **3.** *Anat., Zool.* **a.** a membranous sac or integument. **b.** either of two strata of white matter in the cerebrum. **4.** a small case, envelope, or covering. **5.** *Aeron., Rocketry.* **a.** a small, sealed and pressurized cabin in which a man or animal may ride in flight above the earth's atmosphere or at very high altitudes within the atmosphere. **b.** a similar cabin in a military aircraft, which can be ejected from the aircraft in an emergency. **6.** a thin metal covering for the mouth of a corked bottle. **—v.t. 7.** to furnish with or enclose in or as in a capsule; encapsulate. **8.** to capsulize. **—adj. 9.** small and compact. **10.** short and concise; brief and summarized: *a capsule report.* [< L *capsul(a),* equiv. to *caps(a)* box + *-ula* -ULE]

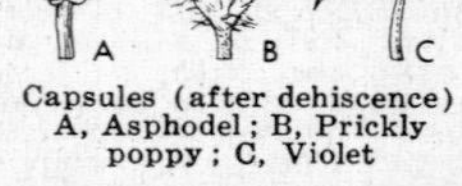

Capsules (after dehiscence) A, Asphodel; B, Prickly poppy; C, Violet

cap·sul·ize (kap′sə līz′), *v.t.,* **-ized, -iz·ing.** to summarize or make very concise; capsule. [CAPSULE + -IZE]

Capt., Captain.

cap·tain (kap′tən, -tin), *n.* **1.** a person who is at the head of or in authority over others; chief; leader. **2.** an officer ranking in most armies above a first lieutenant and below a major. **3.** an officer in the U.S. Navy ranking above a commander and below a rear admiral. **4.** a military leader. **5.** an officer in the police department, ranking above a lieutenant and usually below an inspector. **6.** an officer of the fire department, usually in command of a company, ranking above a lieutenant and below a chief or assistant chief. **7.** the pilot of an airplane. **8.** a local official in a political party responsible for organizing votes on a ward or precinct level. **9.** a person of great power and influence, esp. based on economic wealth. **10.** headwaiter. **11.** See **bell captain.** **12.** the master of a merchant vessel. Cf. **staff captain.** **13.** *Sports.* the field leader of a team. *The captain of the home team elected to receive on the kickoff.* —*v.t.* **14.** to lead or command as a captain. [ME *capitain* < MF *capitaine* < LL *capitān(eus)* chief, equiv. to *capitān(us)* (*capit-* (s. of *caput*) head + *-ānus* -AN) + *-eus* -EOUS]

Cap′tain Car′penter, a poem (1923) by John Crowe Ransom.

Cap′tain Craig′, a narrative poem (1902) by Edwin Arlington Robinson.

cap·tain·cy (kap′tən sē), *n., pl.* **-cies** for 2. **1.** the office or rank of a captain. **2.** a district or area administered by a captain. **3.** the control or skill of a captain; leadership. [CAPTAIN + -CY]

cap′tain glass′, (in the 18th century) a large glass bowl with a stem, set among smaller and similar bowls holding jellies and sweetmeats.

cap′tain of in′dustry, the head of a large business firm, esp. of an industrial complex.

cap′tain's chair′, a chair having a rounded back formed by a heavy rail resting upon vertical spindles and coming forward to form the arms.

Cap′tains Coura′geous, a novel (1897) by Rudyard Kipling.

Cap′tain's Daugh′ter, The, a novel (1836) by Alexander Pushkin.

cap·tain·ship (kap′tən ship′), *n.* **1.** captaincy (def. 1). **2.** the ability of a military captain; leadership or generalship. **3.** captaincy (def. 2). [CAPTAIN + -SHIP]

cap′tain's mast′, a session at which the captain of a naval ship hears and acts on the cases of enlisted men charged with committing offenses.

cap·tion (kap′shən), *n.* **1.** a heading or title, as of a chapter, article, or page. **2.** *Print.* a legend for a picture or illustration, esp. in a magazine. **3.** *Motion Pictures.* the title of a scene, the text of a speech, etc., shown on the screen. **4.** *Law.* the heading of a legal document stating the time, place, etc., of execution or performance. —*v.t.* **5.** to supply a caption or captions for; entitle: *to caption a photograph; to caption an article.* [ME *capcio(u)n* seizure < L *captiōn-* (s. of *captiō*), equiv. to *capt(us)* taken (see CAPTOR) + *-iōn-* -ION] —**cap′tion·less,** *adj.*

cap·tious (kap′shəs), *adj.* **1.** apt to notice and make much of trivial faults or defects; faultfinding; difficult to please: *a captious reviewer of books.* **2.** proceeding from a faultfinding or caviling disposition: *He could never praise without adding a captious remark.* **3.** apt or designed to ensnare or perplex, esp. in argument: *captious questions.* [ME *capcious* < L *captiōs(us)* sophistical, equiv. to *capti(ō)* a taking, hence, sophism (see CAPTION) + *-ōsus* -OUS] —**cap′tious·ly,** *adv.* —**cap′tious·ness,** *n.*

cap·ti·vate (kap′tə vāt′), *v.t.,* **-vat·ed, -vat·ing.** **1.** to enthrall or charm, as by beauty or excellence; enchant: *Her blue eyes and red hair captivated him.* **2.** *Obs.* to capture; subjugate. [< LL *captivāt(us)* taken captive (ptp. of *captivāre*), equiv. to L *captīv(us)* CAPTIVE + *-ātus* -ATE¹] —**cap′ti·vat′ing·ly,** *adv.* —**cap′ti·va′tion,** *n.* —**cap′ti·va′tive,** *adj.* —**cap′ti·va′tor,** *n.*
—**Syn. 1.** fascinate, bewitch, win, catch. **2.** subdue. —**Ant. 1.** repel.

cap·tive (kap′tiv), *n.* **1.** a prisoner. **2.** a person who is captivated or dominated; slave: *He was a captive to her beauty. He is the captive of his own fears.* —*adj.* **3.** made or held prisoner, esp. in war: *captive troops.* **4.** kept in confinement or restraint: *captive animals.* **5.** enslaved by love, beauty, etc.; captivated: *her captive beau.* **6.** of or pertaining to a captive. **7.** managed as an affiliate or subsidiary of a corporation and operated almost exclusively for the use or needs of the parent corporation rather than independently for the general public: *a captive shop; a captive mine.* [ME < L *captīv(us),* equiv. to *capt(us)* taken (see CAPTOR) + *-īvus* -IVE]

cap′tive au′dience, people who have entered into a situation for a particular purpose, as at a restaurant, and are subjected to advertisements, propaganda, solicitations, etc., against their will.

cap′tive balloon′, a balloon held in a particular place by means of a rope or cable, as for observation purposes.

cap′tive bolt′, a gunlike instrument used for slaughtering animals by means of a rod fired to its full length from inside the instrument.

cap′tive test′, *Rocketry.* a missile or space-carrier test in which full engine thrust is developed while the missile or carrier is kept immobile on a test stand.

cap·tiv·i·ty (kap tiv′i tē), *n., pl.* **-ties.** the state or period of being captive. [ME *captivite* < L *captīvitās.* See CAPTIVE, -ITY]
—**Syn.** bondage, servitude, slavery, thralldom, subjection; imprisonment, confinement, incarceration. —**Ant.** freedom.

cap·tor (kap′tər), *n.* a person who has captured a person or thing. [< L, equiv. to *capt(us)* taken (ptp. of *capere*) (*cap-* take + *-tus* ptp. suffix) + *-or* -OR²]

cap·ture (kap′chər), *v.,* **-tured, -tur·ing,** *n.* —*v.t.* **1.** to take by force or stratagem; take prisoner; seize: *The police captured the burglar.* **2.** *Physics.* (of an atomic or nuclear system) to acquire (an additional particle). **3.** *Crystall.* (of a crystal) to contain a trace of (an element having a similar ionic radius but a greater charge, or a smaller ionic radius but the same charge), as a major element of the crystal. —*n.* **4.** the act of capturing. **5.** the thing or person captured. **6.** *Physics.* the process in which an atomic or nuclear system acquires an additional particle. [< MF < L *captūr(a),* equiv. to *capt(us)* taken (see CAPTOR) + *-ūra* -URE] —**cap′tur·a·ble,** *adj.* —**cap′tur·er,** *n.*
—**Syn. 1.** catch, arrest, snare, apprehend, grab, nab. **4.** seizure, arrest, apprehension. —**Ant. 1, 4.** release.

Cap·u·a (kap′yo͞o ə; *It.* kä′pwä), *n.* a town in NW Campania, in S Italy, N of Naples. 18,305 (1961). —**Cap′u·an,** *adj.*

Cap·u·a·nus (kap′o͞o ā′nəs, kap wä′-), *n.* a ring formation in the third quadrant of the face of the moon, having a raised floor: about 35 miles in diameter.

ca·puche (kə po͞osh′, -po͞och′), *n.* a hood or cowl, esp. the long, pointed cowl of the Capuchins. [< MF < It *cappucci(o),* equiv. to *capp(a)* cloak (see CAP¹) + *-uccio* aug. suffix] —**ca·puched′,** *adj.*

cap·u·chin (kap′yo͞o chin, -shin), *n.* **1.** a Central and South American monkey, *Cebus capucinus,* having a prehensile tail and hair on the head resembling a cowl. **2.** any monkey of the genus *Cebus.* **3.** a hooded cloak for women. **4.** (*cap.*) Also called **Friar Minor Capuchin.** *Rom. Cath. Ch.* a friar belonging to the branch of the Franciscan order that observes vows of poverty and austerity. Cf. **Friar Minor, Friar Minor Conventual.** [< MF < It *cappuccin(o),* equiv. to *cappucc(io)* CAPUCHE + *-ino* -INE¹]

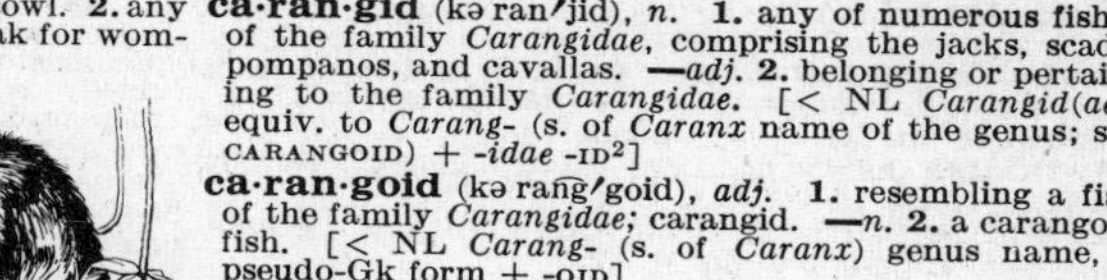

Capuchin, *Cebus capucinus* (Total length 2½ ft.; tail 17 in.)

Cap·u·let (kap′yə let′, -lit), *n.* (in Shakespeare's *Romeo and Juliet*) the family name of Juliet. Cf. **Montague** (def. 1).

ca·put (kā′pət, kap′ət), *n., pl.* **ca·pi·ta** (kap′i tə). *Anat.* any head or headlike expansion on a structure, as on a bone. [< L: head]

ca′put mor′tu·um (môr′cho͞o əm, môr′-), **1.** *Alchemy.* the residue after distillation or sublimation of a substance. **2.** *Chem.* colcothar. [< L: dead head]

cap·y·ba·ra (kap′ə bär′ə), *n.* a South American rodent, *Hydrochoerus capybara,* living along the banks of rivers and lakes, having no tail and partly webbed feet: the largest living rodent. Also, **capibara.** [< NL < Pg *capibara* < Tupi]

Capybara (About 2 ft. high at shoulder; length 3 to 4 ft.)

Ca·pys (kā′pis, kap′is), *n. Class. Myth.* **1.** a Trojan who cautioned his countrymen against bringing the Trojan Horse into the city: he fled Troy with Aeneas and later founded the city of Capua. **2.** the father of Anchises and the grandfather of Aeneas.

caque·teuse (kak′i to͞oz′; *Fr.* kakᵊ tœz′), *n., pl.* **-teuses** (-to͞o′ziz; *Fr.* -tœz′). *Furniture.* cacqueteuse.

caque·toire (kak′i twär′; *Fr.* kakᵊ twȧr′), *n., pl.* **-toires** (-twärz′; *Fr.* -twȧr′). *Furniture.* cacqueteuse. [< F; see CACQUETEUSE, -ORY²]

car¹ (kär), *n.* **1.** an automobile. **2.** a vehicle running on rails, as a streetcar. **3.** *Brit. Dial.* any wheeled vehicle, as a farm cart, wagon, etc. **4.** the part of an elevator, balloon, etc., that carries the passengers, freight, etc. **5.** *Poetic.* a chariot, as of war or triumph. **6.** a perforated box floated in water, for preserving live fish, lobsters, clams, etc. [ME *carre* < AF < LL *carr(a)* (fem. sing.), L *carra,* neut. pl. of *carrum,* var. of *carrus* < Celt.; cf. OIr *carr* wheeled vehicle] —**car′less,** *adj.*

car² (kär), *adj. Chiefly Scot.* **1.** left-handed. **2.** sinister; unnatural. [< ScotGael *cearr*]

Car (kär), *n. Class. Myth.* a son of Phoroneus and Cerdo, sometimes believed to be the founder of Megara.

car., carat; carats.

Car·a (kar′ə), *n.* a girl's given name.

ca·ra·ba·o (kär′ə bä′ō), *n., pl.* **-ba·os.** (in the Philippines) the water buffalo. [< Philippine Sp << Malay *karbau*]

car·a·bin (kar′ə bin), *n.* carbine. Also, **car·a·bine** (kar′ə bīn′). [< MF: carbineer, perh. aph. var. of ONF *escarrabin* corpse-bearer (in epidemics) << L *scarab(aeus)* SCARAB]

car·a·bi·neer (kär′ə bə nēr′), *n.* carbineer. Also, **car′a·bi·nier′.**

ca·ra·bi·ne·ro (kä′rä vē ne′rō; *Eng.* kar′ə bə nâr′ō), *n., pl.* **-ne·ros** (-ne′rōs; *Eng.* -nâr′ōz). *Spanish.* **1.** an officer of the revenue service. **2.** a frontier guard. **3.** carbineer. **4.** (in the Philippines) a coast-guard officer.

ca·ra·bi·nie·re (kä′rä bē nye′re; *Eng.* kar′ə bin yâr′ē), *n., pl.* **-bi·nie·ri** (-bē nye′rē; *Eng.* -bin yâr′ē). *Italian.* **1.** a policeman. **2.** carbineer.

Car·a·cal·la (kar′ə kal′ə), *n.* (*Marcus Aurelius Antoninus Bassianus*) A.D. 188–217, Roman emperor 211–217.

ca·ra·ca·ra (kär′ə kär′ə), *n.* any of certain long-legged hawks of the southern U.S. and Central and South America which feed on carrion. [< Sp or Pg < Tupi; imit. of its cry]

Ca·ra·cas (kə rä′kəs; *Sp.* kä rä′käs), *n.* a city in and the capital of Venezuela, in the N part. 1,500,000 (est. 1962).

car·ack (kar′ək), *n. Naut.* carrack.

car·a·col (kar′ə kol′), *n., v.i.,* **-colled, -col·ling.** caracole. [< Sp] —**car′a·col′ler,** *n.*

car·a·cole (kar′ə kōl′), *n., v.,* **-coled, -col·ing.** —*n.* **1.** a half turn executed by a horseman in riding. **2.** *Rare.* a winding staircase. —*v.i.* **3.** to execute caracoles; wheel. [< F < Sp *caracol* snail, spiral shell or stair, turning movement (of a horse)] —**car′a·col′er,** *n.*

Ca·rac·ta·cus (kə rak′tə kəs), *n.* fl. A.D. c50, British chieftain who opposed the Romans. Also, **Ca·rad·oc** (kə rad′ək).

car·a·cul (kar′ə kəl), *n.* **1.** the skin of the very young of certain Asian or Russian sheep, karakul, dressed as a fur, resembling astrakhan, but with flatter, looser curl. **2.** karakul (def. 1). [after *Kara Kul* Black Lake, in Uzbek Republic, USSR, home of the breed]

ca·rafe (kə raf′, -räf′), *n.* a bottle, usually of glass, for holding water or other beverages. [< F < It *caraff(a)* < Sp *garrafa* < Ar *gharrāfah* dipper, drinking vessel]

ca·ram·bo·la (kar′əm bō′lə), *n.* **1.** an oxalidaceous tree, *Averrhoa Carambola,* of southeastern Asia and the West Indies, bearing a yellowish-brown, smooth-skinned, tart, edible fruit. **2.** the fruit itself. [< Pg < Marathi *karambal*]

car·a·mel (kar′ə məl, -mel′; *Midwest often* kär′məl), *n.* **1.** a liquid made by cooking sugar until it changes color, used for coloring and flavoring food. **2.** a kind of candy, commonly in small blocks, made from sugar, butter, milk, etc. [< F < Sp or Pg *caramel(o)* < LL *calamellus* little reed (by dissimilation), equiv. to *calam(us)* reed (see CALAMUS) + *-ellus* dim. suffix; meaning changed by assoc. with ML *cannamella, canna mellis,* etc., sugar cane, equiv. to L *canna* CANE + *mel* honey (gen. *mellis*)]

car·a·mel·ise (kar′ə mə līz′), *v.t., v.i.,* **-ised, -is·ing.** *Chiefly Brit.* caramelize. —**car′a·mel·i·sa′tion,** *n.*

car·a·mel·ize (kar′ə mə līz′; *Midwest often* kär′mə-līz′), *v.t., v.i.,* **-ized, -iz·ing.** to convert or be converted into caramel. [CARAMEL + -IZE] —**car′a·mel·i·za′tion,** *n.*

Ca·ram·uel (kä′rəm wel), *n.* a ring formation in the second quadrant of the face of the moon, in the libration area: about 105 miles in diameter.

ca·ran·gid (kə ran′jid), *n.* **1.** any of numerous fishes of the family *Carangidae,* comprising the jacks, scads, pompanos, and cavallas. —*adj.* **2.** belonging or pertaining to the family *Carangidae.* [< NL *Carangid(ae),* equiv. to *Carang-* (s. of *Caranx* name of the genus; see CARANGOID) + *-idae* -ID²]

ca·ran·goid (kə raŋ′goid), *adj.* **1.** resembling a fish of the family *Carangidae;* carangid. —*n.* **2.** a carangoid fish. [< NL *Carang-* (s. of *Caranx*) genus name, a pseudo-Gk form + -OID]

ca·ra·pa (kə rap′ə), *n.* **1.** a South American, meliaceous tree, *Carapa guianensis.* **2.** the light, reddish-brown wood of this tree, used for making furniture. [< NL < Carib: oil]

car·a·pace (kar′ə pās′), *n.* a shield, test, or shell covering some or all of the dorsal part of an animal. [< F < Sp *carapach(o)* < ?] —**car′a·paced′,** *adj.* —**car·a·pa·cial** (kar′ə pā′shəl), *adj.*

car·at (kar′ət), *n.* a unit of weight in gem stones, 200 milligrams (about 3 grains of troy or avoirdupois weight). *Abbr.:* c., ct. [< ML *carrat(us)* (used by alchemists) < Ar *qīrāṭ* weight of 4 grains < Gk *kerátion* carob bean, weight of 3⅓ grains, lit., little horn, equiv. to *kerat-* (s. of *kéras*) horn + *-ion* dim. suffix]

Ca·ra·tin·ga (kä′rä teŋ′gə), *n.* a city in E Brazil. 34,742 (1960).

Ca·ra·vag·gio (kar′ə vä′jō; *It.* kä′rä väd′jō), *n.* **Mi·chel·an·ge·lo Me·ri·si da** (mī′kəl an′jə lō′ mə-rē′zē dä, mik′əl-; *It.* mē′kel än′je lō me rē′zē dä), c1565–1609?, Italian painter.

car·a·van (kar′ə van′), *n., v.,* **-vaned** or **-vanned, -van·ing** or **-van·ning.** —*n.* **1.** a group of travelers, as merchants or pilgrims, banded together for safety in journeying through deserts, hostile territory, etc. **2.** any group traveling in or as if in a caravan and using a specific mode of transportation, as pack animals or motor vehicles: *a caravan of trucks; a camel caravan.* **3.** a large covered vehicle, as for conveying passengers, goods, a side show, etc.; van. **4.** a house on wheels; trailer. —*v.i.* **5.** to travel in or as if in a caravan: *They caravaned through Egypt.* [earlier *carovan* < It *carovan(a)* < Pers *kārwān*] —**car′a·van′ist, car′a·van′er,** *n.*

car·a·van·sa·ry (kar′ə van′sə rē), *n., pl.* **-ries.** **1.** (in the Near East) an inn, usually with a large courtyard, for the overnight accommodation of caravans. **2.** any large inn or hotel. Also, **car·a·van·se·rai** (kar′ə van′sə rī′, -rā′). [< Pers *kārwānsarāī,* equiv. to *kārwān* CARAVAN + *sarāī* mansion, inn] —**car·a·van·se·ri·al** (kar′ə van sēr′ē əl), *adj.*

Caravel

car·a·vel (kar′ə vel′), *n.* a small Spanish or Portuguese sailing vessel of the Middle Ages and later, usually lateen-rigged on two or three masts. Also, **carvel.** [< Pg *caravel(a),* equiv. to *cārav(o)* kind of ship (< LL *carabus* < Gk *kárabos* skiff, horned beetle) + *-ela* dim. suffix]

car·a·way (kar′ə wā′), *n.* **1.** an umbelliferous herb, *Carum Carvi.* **2.** Also called **car′away seed′.** the aromatic seedlike fruit of this plant used in cooking and medicine. [ME *car(a)wai,* var. of *carwy* < ML *carui* < Ar *karawiyā* < Gk *kár(on)* caraway]

carb-, var. of **carbo-** before a vowel: *carbazole.*

car·ba·mate (kär′bə māt′, kär bam′āt), *n. Chem.* a salt or ester of carbamic acid. [CARBAM(IC) + -ATE²]

car·bam·ic (kär bam′ik), *adj. Chem.* of or derived from carbamic acid. [CARB- + AM(IDE) + -IC]

carbam′ic ac′id, *Chem.* a hypothetical compound, NH_2COOH, known only in the form of its salts, as ammonium carbamate, or its esters, as urethan.

car·bam·ide (kär bam′īd, -id, kär′bə mīd′, -mid), *n. Chem.* urea. [CARB- + AMIDE]

car·bam·i·dine (kär bam′i dēn′, -din), *n. Chem.* guanidine. [CARB- + AMIDINE]

car·ba·nil (kär′bə nil), *n. Chem.* See **phenyl isocyanate.** [CARB- + ANIL]

car·barn (kär′bärn′), *n.* a depot or garage for streetcars or buses. [CAR¹ + BARN]

car·ba·zole (kär′bə zōl′), *n. Chem.* a white, crystalline, water-insoluble compound, $(C_6H_4)_2NH$, usually found along with anthracene in coal tar, or synthesized: used chiefly in the manufacture of dyes. [CARB- + AZ- + -OLE]

carb′a·zot′ic ac′id (kär′bə zot′ik, -zō′tik, kär′-), *Chem.* See **picric acid.** [CARB- + AZOTIC]

car·bide (kär′bīd, -bid), *n. Chem.* **1.** a compound of carbon with a more electropositive element or group. **2.** See **calcium carbide.** **3.** a very hard mixture of sintered carbides of various metals, esp. tungsten carbide, used for cutting edges and dies. [CARB- + -IDE]

car·bi·mide (kär′bə mīd′, -mid), *n. Chem.* cyanamide (def. 1). [CARB- + IMIDE]

car·bine (kär′bīn, -bēn), *n.* a short rifle (or, formerly musket) carried by combat soldiers and noncommissioned officers who are not equipped with rifles. Also, **carabin, carabine.** [earlier *carabine* < MF: small harquebus, weapon borne by a CARABIN]

car·bi·neer (kär′bə nēr′), *n.* (formerly) a soldier armed with a carbine. Also, **carabineer, carabinier.** [earlier *carabineer,* equiv. to *carabine* CARBINE + -EER]

car·bi·nol (kär′bə nōl′, -nôl′, -nol′), *n. Chem.* **1.** See **methyl alcohol.** **2.** an alcohol derived from methyl alcohol. [< G *Karbinol,* equiv. to *Karbin* methyl (*karb-* CARB- + *-in* -IN²) + *-ol* -OL¹]

carbo-, a combining form of **carbon:** *carbohydrate.*

car′bo·cy′clic com′pound (kär′bə sī′klik, -sik′lik, kär′-), *Chem.* any of a group of organic compounds in which all the atoms composing the ring are carbon atoms, as benzene or cyclopropane. [CARBO- + CYCLIC]

car·bo·hy·drate (kär′bō hī′drāt, -bə-), *n.* any of a class of organic compounds which are polyhydroxy aldehydes or polyhydroxy ketones, or change to such substances on simple chemical transformations, as hydrolysis, oxidation, or reduction, and that form the supporting tissues of plants and are important food for animals and man. [CARBO- + HYDRATE]

car·bo·lat·ed (kär′bə lā′tid), *adj.* containing carbolic acid. [CARBOL(IC) + -ATE² + -ED²]

car·bol·ic (kär bol′ik), *adj. Chem.* of or derived from carbolic acid. [*carbol-* (CARB- + -OL²) + -IC]

carbol′ic ac′id, *Chem.* phenol (def. 1).

car·bo·lise (kär′bə līz′), *v.t.*, **-lised, -lis·ing.** *Chiefly Brit.* carbolize.

car·bo·lize (kär′bə līz′); *v.t.*, **-lized, -liz·ing.** phenolate (def. 2). [CARBOL(IC) + -IZE]

Car·bo·loy (kär′bə loi′), *n. Trademark.* a hard compound of particles of tungsten carbide bonded in a matrix of cobalt, used for dies, cutting tools, and wearing surfaces.

car·bon (kär′bən), *n.* **1.** *Chem.* a widely distributed element which forms organic compounds in combination with hydrogen, oxygen, etc., and which occurs in a pure state as the diamond and as graphite, and in an impure state as charcoal. *Symbol:* C; *at. wt.:* 12.011; *at. no.:* 6; *sp. gr.:* (of diamond) 3.51 at 20°C; (of graphite) 2.26 at 20°C. **2.** *Elect.* **a.** the carbon rod through which current is conducted between the electrode holder and the arc in carbon arc lighting or welding. **b.** the rod or plate, composed in part of carbon, used in batteries. **3.** a sheet of carbon paper. **4.** See **carbon copy.** [< F *carbone*, coinage based on L *carbōn-* (s. of *carbō*) charcoal] —**car′bon·less,** *adj.*

carbon 12, *Chem.* the isotopic carbon atom which comprises 99 percent of naturally-occurring carbon, and which since 1961 has been used as the standard for atomic weight by representing a unit of 12.00000. Also, **car·bon-12** (kär′bən twelv′).

carbon 13, *Chem.* the stable isotope of carbon having an atomic mass number 13, used as a tracer. Also, **carbon-13** (kär′bən thûr tēn′).

carbon 14, *Chem.* radiocarbon (def. 1). Also, **carbon-14** (kär′bən fôr tēn′, -fōr-).

car·bon-14 dating (kär′bən fôr tēn′, -fōr-). See **radiocarbon dating.**

car·bo·na·ceous (kär′bə nā′shəs), *adj.* of, like, or containing carbon. [CARBON + -ACEOUS]

car·bo·na·do¹ (kär′bə nā′dō), *n., pl.* **-does, -dos,** *v.,* **-doed, -do·ing.** —*n.* **1.** a piece of meat, fish, etc., scored and broiled. —*v.t.* **2.** to score and broil. **3.** *Archaic.* to slash; hack. [< Sp *carbonada*, equiv. to *carbón* charcoal (see CARBON) + *-ada* -ADE]

car·bo·na·do² (kär′bə nā′dō), *n., pl.* **-dos, -does.** a massive, black variety of diamond, found chiefly near São Salvador, Brazil, and formerly used for drilling and other cutting purposes. [< Pg: carbonate]

Car·bo·na·ri (kär′bə när′ē; *It.* kär′bô nä′rē), *n.pl., sing.* **-na·ro** (-när′ō; *It.* -nä′rô). *Europ. Hist.* the members of a secret political society in the early part of the 19th century, active in Italy, France, and Spain. [< It, pl. of *carbonaro* charcoal burner < L *carbōnār(ius)*, equiv. to *carbōn-* (s. of *carbō*) charcoal + *-ārius* -ARY] —**Car′bo·na′rism,** *n.* —**Car′bo·na′rist,** *n., adj.*

car·bon·a·ta·tion (kär′bə nə tā′shən), *n. Chem.* saturation or reaction with carbon dioxide.

car·bon·ate (*n.* kär′bə nāt′, -nit; *v.* kär′bə nāt′), *n., v.,* **-at·ed, -at·ing.** —*n.* **1.** *Chem.* a salt or ester of carbonic acid. —*v.t.* **2.** to form into a carbonate. **3.** to charge or impregnate with carbon dioxide. **4.** to make sprightly; enliven. [< NL *carbōnāt(um)* something carbonated. See CARBON, -ATE¹] —**car′bon·a′tor,** *n.*

car·bon·a·tion (kär′bə nā′shən), *n.* **1.** saturation with carbon dioxide, as in making soda water. **2.** reaction with carbon dioxide to remove lime, as in sugar refining. **3.** carbonization. [CARBONATE + -ION]

car′bon bisul′fide, *Chem.* See **carbon disulfide.**

car′bon black′, any of various finely divided forms of amorphous carbon prepared by the partial combustion of hydrocarbons, as of natural gas, or by charring wood, bones, or other plant or animal tissues: used in pigments, as reinforcing agents in the manufacture of rubber products, and as clarifying or filtering agents.

car′bon cop′y, **1.** a duplicate of anything written or typed, made by using carbon paper. **2.** a near or exact duplicate of a given person or thing.

car′bon cy′cle, *Astrophysics.* a cycle of nuclear transformations, with the release of nuclear energy, in the interiors of the stars, by means of which hydrogen is gradually converted into helium.

Car·bon·dale (kär′bən dāl′), *n.* **1.** a city in SW Illinois. 14,670 (1960). **2.** a city in NE Pennsylvania, near Scranton: coal-mining center. 13,595 (1960).

car′bon diox′ide, *Chem.* a colorless, odorless, incombustible gas, CO_2, present in the atmosphere and formed during respiration, usually obtained from coal, coke, or natural gas by combustion, from carbohydrates by fermentation, by reaction of acid with limestone or other carbonates, or naturally from springs; used extensively in industry as dry ice, or carbon dioxide snow, in carbonated beverages, fire extinguishers, etc. Also called **carbonic-acid gas, carbonic anhydride.**

car′bon disul′fide, *Chem.* a clear, colorless or faintly yellow, poisonous, flammable liquid, CS_2, used chiefly in the manufacture of cellophane, viscose rayon, and pesticides and as a solvent for fats, resins, and rubber. Also called **carbon bisulfide.**

car·bon·ic (kär bon′ik), *adj. Chem.* containing tetravalent carbon, as carbonic acid, H_2CO_3. [CARBON + -IC]

carbon′ic ac′id, the acid, H_2CO_3, formed when carbon dioxide dissolves in water, known in the form of its salts and esters, the carbonates.

car·bon′ic-ac′id gas′ (kär bon′ik as′id). See **carbon dioxide.** Also called **carbon′ic anhy′dride.**

Car·bon·if·er·ous (kär′bə nif′ər əs), *Geol.* —*adj.* **1.** noting or pertaining to a period of the Paleozoic era, including the Pennsylvanian, Mississippian, and formerly the Permian periods as epochs: presently regarded as having occurred from 270 million to 350 million years ago. See table under **era.** **2.** (*l.c.*) producing coal. —*n.* **3.** the Carboniferous period or system. [< L *carbōn-* (s. of *carbō*) coal + -I- + -FEROUS]

car·bon·ise (kär′bə nīz′), *v.t.,* **-ised, -is·ing.** *Chiefly Brit.* carbonize. —**car′bon·i·sa′tion,** *n.* —**car′bon·is′a·ble,** *adj.* —**car′bon·is′er,** *n.*

car·bon·i·za·tion (kär′bə ni zā′shən), *n.* **1.** formation of carbon from organic matter. **2.** coal distillation, as in coke ovens. [CARBONIZE + -ATION]

car·bon·ize (kär′bə nīz′), *v.t.,* **-ized, -iz·ing.** **1.** to char, forming carbon. **2.** to coat or enrich with carbon. Also, *esp. Brit.,* **carbonise.** [CARBON + -IZE] —**car′bon·iz′a·ble,** *adj.* —**car′bon·iz′er,** *n.*

car′bon monox′ide, *Chem.* a colorless, odorless, poisonous gas, CO, which burns with a pale-blue flame, produced when carbon burns with insufficient air: used chiefly in organic synthesis, metallurgy, and in the preparation of metal carbonyls, as nickel carbonyl.

car·bon·ous (kär′bə nəs), *adj.* of, containing, or derived from carbon. [CARBON + -OUS]

car′bon oxychlo′ride, *Chem.* phosgene.

car′bon pa′per, **1.** paper faced with a preparation of carbon or other material, used between two sheets of plain paper in order to reproduce on the lower sheet that which is written or typed on the upper. **2.** Also called **carbon tissue.** a paper for making photographs by the carbon process.

car′bon proc′ess, a method of making photographic prints by the use of a pigment, such as carbon, contained in sensitized gelatin.

car′bon star′, *Astron.* a star whose spectrum shows molecular bands in which carbon appears stronger in relation to other elements than in other stars of comparable temperature and luminosity.

car′bon steel′, steel owing its properties principally to its carbon content; ordinary, unalloyed steel.

car′bon tetrachlo′ride, *Chem., Pharm.* a colorless, nonflammable, vaporous, toxic liquid, CCl_4, usually produced by the reaction of chlorine with carbon disulfide, methane, or other carbon-containing compounds: used as a refrigerant, fire extinguisher, cleaning fluid, solvent, insecticide, and in veterinary medicine chiefly as an anthelmintic. Also called **tetrachloromethane, perchloromethane.**

car′bon tis′sue, *Photog.* See **carbon paper** (def. 2).

car·bon·yl (kär′bə nil), *Chem.* —*adj.* **1.** containing the carbonyl group. —*n.* **2.** a compound containing metal combined with carbon monoxide, as nickel carbonyl, $Ni(CO)_4$. [CARBON + -YL]

car·bon·y·late (kär bon′ᵊlāt′), *v.t.,* **-lat·ed, -lat·ing.** *Chem.* to introduce the carbonyl group into (an organic compound). [CARBONYL + -ATE²] —**car·bon′yl·a′tion,** *n.*

car′bonyl chlo′ride, *Chem.* phosgene.

car′bonyl group′, *Chem.* the bivalent group, C=O, occurring in acids, ketones, aldehydes, and their derivatives. Also called **car′bonyl rad′ical.**

car·bon·yl·ic (kär′bə nil′ik), *adj.* of, pertaining to, or characteristic of the carbonyl group. [CARBONYL + -IC]

Car·bo·run·dum (kär′bə run′dəm), *n. Trademark.* any of various abrasives or refractories of silicon carbide, fused alumina, and other materials.

car·box·yl (kär bok′sil), *adj. Chem.* containing the carboxyl group. [CARB- + OX(YGEN) + -YL] —**car′box·yl′ic,** *adj.*

car·box·yl·ase (kär bok′sə lās′), *n. Biochem.* decarboxylase. [CARBOXYL + -ASE]

car·box·yl·ate (kär bok′sə lāt′), *v.,* **-at·ed, -at·ing,** *n. Chem.* —*v.t.* **1.** to introduce the carboxyl group into (an organic compound). —*n.* **2.** a salt or ester of a carboxylic acid. [CARBOXYL + -ATE²]

car·box·yl·a·tion (kär bok′sə lā′shən), *n. Chem.* the process of carboxylating. [CARBOXYL + -ATION]

carbox′yl group′, *Chem.* the univalent group, –COOH, present in and characteristic of organic acids. Also called **carbox′yl rad′ical.**

car′boxyl′ic ac′id, *Chem.* any organic acid containing one or more carboxyl groups. [CARBOXYL + -IC]

car·boy (kär′boi), *n.* a large glass bottle protected by basketwork or a wooden box, used esp. for holding corrosive liquids. [< Pers *qarāba(h)* < Ar *qarrābah* big jug] —**car′boyed,** *adj.*

car′bro proc′ess (kär′brō), *Photog.* a process for making carbon or pigment prints on bromide paper without exposure to light. [CAR(BON) + BRO(MIDE)]

car·bun·cle (kär′bung kəl), *n.* **1.** *Pathol.* a painful circumscribed inflammation of the subcutaneous tissue, resulting in suppuration and sloughing, and having a tendency to spread somewhat like a boil, but more serious in its effects. **2.** a garnet cut in a convex rounded form without facets. **3.** Also called **London brown.** a dark grayish, red-brown color. **4.** *Obs.* any rounded red gem. —*adj.* **5.** having the color carbuncle. [ME < L *carbuncul(us)* red object (stone or tumor), orig. live coal, equiv. to *carbōn-* (s. of *carbō*) burning or burnt wood + *-culus* -CULE]

car·bun·cled (kär′bung kəld), *adj.* **1.** infected with a carbuncle. **2.** having a carbuncle as its stone: *a carbuncled ring.* [CARBUNCLE + -ED³]

car·bun·cu·lar (kär bung′kyə lər), *adj.* of, pertaining to, or resembling a carbuncle, esp. having a carbuncle or a red and inflamed area. [< L *carbuncul(us)* (see CARBUNCLE) + -AR¹]

car·bu·ret (kär′bə rāt′, -byə-, -byə ret′), *v.t.,* **-ret·ed, -ret·ing** or (*esp. Brit.*) **-ret·ted, -ret·ting.** to combine or mix with carbon or hydrocarbons. [CARB- + -URET]

car·bu·ret·ant (kär′bə rāt′ᵊnt, -ret′-, -byə-), *n. Chem.* any substance for carbureting air or a gas. [CARBURET + -ANT]

car·bu·re·tion (kär′bə rā′shən, -byə-, -byə resh′ən), *n.* (in an internal-combustion engine) the process of producing a mixture of air and fuel in the correct proportion for engine combustion. [CARBURET + -ION]

car·bu·re·tor (kär′bə rā′tər, -byə-), *n.* a device for mixing vaporized fuel with air to produce a combustible or explosive mixture, as for an internal-combustion engine. Also, *esp. Brit.,* **car·bu·ret·tor** (kär′byə ret′ər). [CARBURET + -OR²]

car·bu·rise (kär′bə rīz′, -byə-), *v.t.,* **-rised, -ris·ing.** *Chiefly Brit.* carburize. —**car′bu·ri·sa′tion,** *n.* —**car′bu·ris′er,** *n.*

car·bu·rize (kär′bə rīz′, -byə-), *v.t.,* **-rized, -riz·ing.** **1.** to cause to unite with carbon. **2.** to carburet. [CARBUR(ET) + -IZE] —**car′bu·ri·za′tion,** *n.* —**car′bu·riz′er,** *n.*

car·byl·a·mine (kär′bil ə mēn′, -am′in), *n. Chem. Obs.* isocyanide. [CARB- + -YL + AMINE]

car·ca·jou (kär′kə jo͞o′, -zho͞o′), *n.* wolverine (def. 1). [< CanF < Algonquian *karkaju*]

car·ca·net (kär′kə net′, -nit), *n.* **1.** a woman's ornamental circlet for the hair, often of gold decorated with jewels or pearls. **2.** *Archaic.* a jeweled collar or necklace. [*carcan* choker < MF, equiv. to *carc-* throat (< Gmc) + *-an* ring (< L *ānus*) + -ET] —**car′ca·net′ed, car′ca·net′ted,** *adj.*

car′ card′, **1.** a sheet of cardboard bearing an advertising message for display in subway cars, buses, and other public conveyances. **2.** a kind of cardboard coated on one side only.

Car·cas (kär′kəs), *n.* one of the seven eunuchs who served in the court of King Ahasuerus. Esther 1:10. Also, *Douay Bible,* **Charcas.**

car·case (kär′kəs), *n., v.t.,* **-cased, -cas·ing.** carcass.

car·cass (kär′kəs), *n.* **1.** the dead body of an animal. **2.** *Disparaging.* the living or dead body of a human being. **3.** the body of a slaughtered animal after removal of the offal. **4.** anything from which life and power are gone: *The mining town, now a mere carcass, is a reminder of a past era.* **5.** an unfinished framework or skeleton, as of a house or ship. **6.** the body of a balloon tire, resisting by its tensile strength the pressure of the air within the tire, and protected by the tread and other parts. —*v.t.* **7.** to erect the framework for (a building, ship, etc.). Also, **carcase.** [< MF *carcasse* < It *carcass(a)* < ?; r. ME *carkeis, -ois* < AF, answering to ML *carcosium* < ?] —**car′cass·less,** *adj.*
—**Syn. 1.** See **body.**

Car·cas·sonne (KAR KA sôn′), *n.* a city in and the capital of Aude, in S France: medieval fortifications. 43,709 (1962).

Car·chem·ish (kär′kə mish, kär kē′-), *n.* an ancient city in S Turkey, on the upper Euphrates: important city in the Mitanni kingdom; later the capital of the Hittite empire. Also, **Charchemish.**

car·cin·o·gen (kär sin′ə jən), *n. Pathol.* any substance that tends to produce a cancer. [*carcino-* (comb. form of Gk *karkínos* crab, cancer) + -GEN] —**car·cin·o·gen·ic** (kär′sə nō jen′ik), *adj.* —**car·ci·no·ge·nic·i·ty** (kär′sə nō jə nis′i tē), *n.*

car·ci·no·ma (kär′sə nō′mə), *n., pl.* **-mas, -ma·ta** (-mə tə). *Pathol.* a malignant and invasive epithelial tumor that spreads by metastasis and often recurs after excision; cancer. [< L < Gk *karkínōma*, equiv. to *karkín(os)* crab. cancer + *-ōma* -OMA] —**car′ci·no′ma·toid′,** *adj.*

car·ci·no·ma·to·sis (kär′sə nō mə tō′sis), *n. Pathol.* a condition marked by the production of an overwhelming number of carcinomata throughout the body. [< L *carcinōmat-* (s. of *carcinōma*) CARCINOMA + -OSIS]

car·ci·no·sar·co·ma (kär′sə nō sär kō′mə), *n., pl.* **-mas, -ma·ta** (-mə tə). *Pathol.* a malignant tumor composed of both carcinomatous and sarcomatous elements. Also called **sarcocarcinoma.** [< NL; see CARCINO-, SARCOMA]

car′ coat′, a hip-length overcoat for informal wear.

card¹ (kärd), *n.* **1.** a piece of stiff paper or thin pasteboard, usually rectangular, for various uses: *a membership card; a postal card.* **2.** one of a set of small cardboards with spots, figures, etc., used in playing various games. **3. cards,** (*usually construed as sing.*) **a.** a game or games played with such a set. **b.** the playing of such a game: *to win at cards.* **c.** *Casino.* the winning of 27 cards or more. **d.** *Whist.* tricks won in excess of six. **4.** something useful in attaining an objective, as a course of action or position of strength, comparable to a high card held in a game: *If negotiation fails, we still have another card to play.* **5.** a piece of paper or thin cardboard, usually small and rectangular, printed with a message of holiday greeting, congratulations, good wishes, or other sentiment, often with an illustration or decorations, for mailing to a friend or relative on an appropriate occasion. **6.** a program of the events at races, boxing matches, etc. **7.** *Golf.* a paper for recording the score of each hole played. **8.** the circular piece of paper, cardboard, etc., on which the 32 points indicating direction are marked on a compass. **9.** *Informal.* **a.** a person who is amusing or facetious. **b.** any person, esp. one with some indicated characteristic: *a queer card.* **10. in** or **on the cards,** impending; likely; probable: *A reorganization is in the cards.* **11. play one's cards,** to execute one's plans: *We'll succeed if we play our cards right.* **12. put one's cards on the table,** to be completely straightforward and open; conceal nothing: *He always believed in putting his cards on the table.* **13. speak by the card,** to speak accurately or precisely. —*v.t.* **14.** to provide with a card. **15.** to fasten on a card. **16.** to write, list, etc., on cards. [ME *carde*, unexplained var. of CARTE²]

card² (kärd), *n.* **1.** Also called **carding machine.** a machine for combing and paralleling fibers of cotton, flax, wool, etc., prior to spinning to remove short, undesirable fibers and produce a sliver. **2.** a similar implement for raising the nap on cloth. —*v.t.* **3.** to dress (wool or the like) with a card. [ME *carde* < MF: lit., teasel-head < LL *card(us)* thistle, var. of L *carduus*] —**card′er,** *n.*

Card., Cardinal.

car·da·mom (kär′də məm), *n.* **1.** the aromatic seed capsule of various zingiberaceous plants of the genera *Amomum* and *Elettaria*, native to tropical Asia, used as a spice or condiment and in medicine. **2.** any of these plants. Also, **car·da·mon** (kär′də mən), **car′da·mum.** [< L *cardamōm(um)* < Gk *kardámōmon*, equiv. to *kárd(amon)* cress + *ámōmon* a spice plant]

Car′dan joint′ (kär′dan), a universal joint consisting of a crosslike piece, opposite ends of which rotate within the forked end of each of the two shafts connected. [named after G. *Cardano* (1501–1576), Italian mathematician, its inventor]

Car·da·nus (kär′də nəs), *n.* a walled plain in the second quadrant of the face of the moon: about 32 miles in diameter.

card·board (kärd′bôrd′, -bōrd′), *n.* a thin, stiff pasteboard, used for signs, boxes, etc. [CARD¹ + BOARD]

card-car·ry·ing (kärd′kar′ē ing), *adj.* admittedly belonging to a group or party: *a card-carrying Communist.*

card′ case′, a small wallet for one's calling cards.

card·cas·tle (kärd′kas′əl), *n.* See **house of cards.**

card′ cat′alog, a file of cards in alphabetical sequence listing the items in a library collection, each card typically identifying a single item by author, title, or subject.

card′ cloth′ing, a very sturdy fabric with a leather or rubber fillet imbedded with wire teeth for disentangling and cleaning textile fibers, used to cover the rollers or flats of a carding machine.

card-cut (kärd′kut′), *adj.* having a fretwork pattern in low relief, as the woodwork of a Chinese Chippendale piece.

Car·de·a (kär′dē ə), *n.* an ancient Roman goddess of door hinges, protectress of family life.

Cár·de·nas (kär′t͟hə näs′), *n.* **1. Lá·za·ro** (lä′sä rō′), 1895–1970, Mexican general and political reformer: president 1934–40. **2.** a seaport in NW Cuba. 43,750 (1953).

card′ field′, field (def. 22b).

card·hold·er (kärd′hōl′dər), *n.* **1.** a registered member of an organization, esp. of a union or a political party, who has been issued a card in evidence of membership. **2.** a person who has a borrower's card from a library. **3.** (on a typewriter) either of a pair of devices able to be raised to hold stiff objects, as envelopes or cards, in place for typing. [CARD[1] + HOLDER]

card·house (kärd′hous′), *n.* See **house of cards.**

cardi-, var. of **cardio-** before a vowel: *cardialgia.*

car·di·ac (kär′dē ak′), *adj.* **1.** pertaining to the heart. **2.** pertaining to the esophageal portion of the stomach. —*n.* **3.** *Med.* a cardiac remedy. **4.** a person suffering from a heart disease: *A cardiac often requires a special diet.* [< medical L *cardiac(us)* < Gk *kardiakós*, equiv. to *kardí(a)* heart + *-akos* -AC]

car′diac cy′cle, one complete heartbeat: contraction and relaxation of the heart.

car′diac gly′coside, *Pharm.* one of a group of drugs used to stimulate the heart in cases of heart failure, obtained from a number of plants, as the foxglove, squill, or yellow oleander. Also, **car′diac glu′coside.**

car′diac neuro′sis, *Pathol.* a condition characterized after exertion by quick fatigue, short breath, rapid heartbeat, and dizziness, but not caused by disease of the heart. Also called **effort syndrome, irritable heart, neurocirculatory asthenia, soldier's heart.**

car′diac out′put, blood volume in liters pumped by the heart per minute.

car′diac tamponade′, *Pathol.* tamponade (def. 2).

car·di·al·gi·a (kär′dē al′jē ə, -jə), *n.* *Pathol.* **1.** heartburn (def. 1). **2.** cardiodynia. [CARDI- + -ALGIA]

car·di·ec·to·my (kär′dē ek′tə mē), *n.* *Surg.* **1.** excision of the heart. **2.** excision of the cardiac section of the stomach. [CARDI- + -ECTOMY]

Car·diff (kär′dif), *n.* a seaport in and the county seat of Glamorganshire, in SE Wales. 256,270 (1961).

car·di·gan (kär′də gən), *n.* a knitted woolen jacket or sweater, collarless and open in front. Also called **car′digan jack′et, car′digan sweat′er.** [named after J. T. Brudnell, 7th Earl of *Cardigan* (1797–1868), British cavalryman of Crimean War fame]

Car·di·gan (kär′də gən), *n.* **1.** Cardiganshire. **2.** one of a variety of Welsh corgi having a long tail. Cf. **Pembroke** (def. 3). See illus. under **Welsh corgi.**

Car′digan Bay′, an inlet of St. George's Channel, on the W coast of Wales.

Car·di·gan·shire (kär′də gən shēr′, -shər), *n.* a county in W Wales. 53,564 (1961); 692 sq. mi. *Co. seat:* Cardigan. Also called **Cardigan.**

car·di·nal (kär′dᵊnᵊl), *adj.* **1.** of prime importance; chief; principal; fundamental: *of cardinal significance.* **2.** of the color cardinal. —*n.* **3.** *Rom. Cath. Ch.* a high ecclesiastic appointed by the pope to the College of Cardinals and ranking above every other ecclesiastic but the pope. **4.** Also called **cardinal grosbeak.** a crested grosbeak, *Richmondena cardinalis*, of North America, the male of which is bright red. **5.** any of various similar birds. **6.** a deep, rich red color. **7.** See **cardinal number.** [ME < L *cardināl(is)*, equiv. to *cardin-* (s. of *cardō*) hinge, hence, something on which other things hinge + *-ālis* -AL[1]] —**car′di·nal·ly,** *adv.* —**car′di·nal·ship′,** *n.*

Cardinal, *Richmondena cardinalis* (Length 9½ in.)

car·di·nal·ate (kär′dᵊnᵊlāt′), *n.* *Rom. Cath. Ch.* **1.** the body of cardinals. **2.** the office, rank, or dignity of a cardinal. [CARDINAL + -ATE[1]]

car·di·nal-bish·op (kär′dᵊnᵊl bish′əp), *n.* *Rom. Cath. Ch.* the highest-ranking order of cardinals. Cf. **cardinal-deacon, cardinal-priest.**

car·di·nal-dea·con (kär′dᵊnᵊl dē′kən), *n.* *Rom. Cath. Ch.* the third, or lowest-ranking order of cardinals. Cf. **cardinal-bishop, cardinal-priest.**

car·di·nal·fish (kär′dᵊnᵊl fish′), *n., pl.* (*esp. collectively*) **-fish,** (*esp. referring to two or more kinds or species*) **-fish·es.** any of the perchlike fishes of the family *Agonidae*, many species of which are bright red with black markings. [CARDINAL + FISH]

car′dinal flow′er, a North American plant, *Lobelia cardinalis*, with showy red flowers. Also called **scarlet lobelia.** [so called from its color]

car′dinal gros′beak, cardinal (def. 4).

car′dinal num′ber, 1. Also called **car′dinal nu′meral.** any of the numbers that express amount, as *one, two, three,* etc. (distinguished from *ordinal number*). **2.** Also called **potency, power.** *Math.* a number or symbol analogous to the number of elements in a finite set, being identical for two sets which can be placed into one-to-one correspondence: *The cardinal number of the set* $a_1, a_2, \ldots a_n$ *is n.*

car′dinal points′, the four chief directions of the compass; the north, south, east, and west points.

car·di·nal-priest (kär′dᵊnᵊl prēst′), *n.* *Rom. Cath. Ch.* the second-ranking order of cardinals. Cf. **cardinal-bishop, cardinal-deacon.**

car′dinal sys′tem, a system of coding navigational aids by shape, color, and number, according to their positions relative to navigational hazards. Cf. **lateral system.**

car′dinal vir′tues, *Ancient Philos.* justice, prudence, temperance, and fortitude.

car′dinal vow′el, *Phonet.* **1.** any one of eight primary, purportedly invariant, sustained vowel sounds that constitute a reference set for describing the vowel inventory of a language. **2.** any one of the eight or more supplementary or secondary cardinal vowels.

card′ in′dex, an index consisting of entries made on index cards.

card·ing[1] (kär′ding), *n.* *Poker.* a technique for evaluating the playing strength of one's hand. [CARD[1] + -ING[1]]

card·ing[2] (kär′ding), *n.* the process in which fibers, as cotton, worsted, or wool, are manipulated into sliver form prior to spinning. [CARD[2] + -ING[1]]

card′ing machine′, card[2] (defs. 1, 2).

cardio-, a learned borrowing from Greek meaning "heart," used in the formation of compound words: *cardiogram.* Also, *esp. before a vowel,* **cardi-.** [< Gk *kardio-*, comb. form of *kardía*]

car·di·o·dyn·i·a (kär′dē ō din′ē ə), *n.* *Pathol.* pain in the heart region. Also called **cardialgia.** [CARDIO- + Gk *dyn-* (see DYNAMIC) + *-ia* -IA]

car·di·o·gram (kär′dē ə gram′), *n.* electrocardiogram. [CARDIO- + -GRAM[1]]

car·di·o·graph (kär′dē ə graf′, -gräf′), *n.* electrocardiograph. [CARDIO- + -GRAPH] —**car·di·o·graph·ic** (kär′dē ə graf′ik), *adj.* —**car·di·og·ra·phy** (kär′dē og′rə fē), *n.*

Cardioid

car·di·oid (kär′dē oid′), *n.* *Math.* a somewhat heart-shaped curve, being the path of a point on a circle which rolls externally, without slipping, on another equal circle. Equation: $r = a\,(1-\cos A)$. [< Gk *kardioeid(ḗs)* heart-shaped. See CARDI-, -OID]

car·di·ol·o·gy (kär′dē ol′ə jē), *n.* the study of the heart and its functions in health and disease. [CARDIO- + -LOGY] —**car·di·o·log·ic** (kär′dē ə loj′ik), **car′di·o·log′i·cal,** *adj.* —**car′di·ol′o·gist,** *n.*

car·di·o·meg·a·ly (kär′dē ō meg′ə lē), *n.* *Pathol.* abnormal enlargement of the heart. Also, **car·di·o·me·ga·li·a** (kär′dē ō mə gā′lē ə). [CARDIO- + *-megaly* < NL *megalia*; see MEGALO-, -Y[3]]

car·di·o·pul·mo·nar·y (kär′dē ō pul′mə ner′ē, -pŏŏl-), *adj.* of, pertaining to, or affecting the heart and lungs: *cardiopulmonary resuscitation.* [CARDIO- + PULMONARY]

car·di·o·ton·ic (kär′dē ō ton′ik), *Med.* —*adj.* **1.** having a tonic effect on the action of the heart. —*n.* **2.** a cardiotonic substance. [CARDIO- + TONIC]

car·di·o·vas·cu·lar (kär′dē ō vas′kyə lər), *adj.* *Anat.* of, pertaining to, or affecting the heart and blood vessels. [CARDIO- + VASCULAR]

car·di·tis (kär dī′tis), *n.* *Pathol.* inflammation of the pericardium, myocardium, or endocardium, separately or in combination. [< NL; see CARDI-, -ITIS] —**car·dit·ic** (kär dit′ik), *adj.*

car·don (kär don′, kär′don), *n.* a large cactus, *Lemaireocereus weberi*, of Mexico, having clusters of spines and white flowers nearly four inches long. [< AmerSp *cardón* < Sp: teasel < LL *cardōn-* (s. of *cardō*) thistle; see CARDOON]

car·doon (kär dōōn′), *n.* a perennial plant, *Cynara Cardunculus*, of Mediterranean regions, the leaves and leafstalks of which are blanched and eaten like celery. [< MF *cardon* < It *cardon(e)*, equiv. to *card(o)* thistle (< L *cardu(u)s*) + *-one* aug. suffix]

Car·do·zo (kär dō′zō), *n.* **Benjamin Nathan,** 1870–1938, associate justice of U.S. Supreme Court 1932–38.

card·play·er (kärd′plā′ər), *n.* a person who plays cards, esp. one who plays regularly. [CARD[1] + PLAYER]

card′ punch′. See **key punch** (def. 2).

card·room[1] (kärd′rōōm′, -rŏŏm′), *n.* a room equipped for playing cards. [CARD[1] + ROOM]

card·room[2] (kärd′rōōm′, -rŏŏm′), *n.* a room for carding wool. [CARD[2] + ROOM]

cards′ and spades′, a generous handicap given by a competitor as a means of showing his superiority to his opponent.

card·sharp (kärd′shärp′), *n.* a person, esp. a professional gambler, who cheats at card games. Also, **card′sharp′er.** [CARD[1] + SHARP] —**card′sharp′ing,** *n.*

card′ ta′ble, a small, light table for card games.

car·du·a·ceous (kär′jōō ā′shəs), *adj.* belonging to the *Carduaceae* or thistle family of plants, usually regarded as part of the *Compositae*, comprising the goldenrods, asters, boltonias, fleabanes, etc. [< NL *Carduāce(ae)* name of the family (L *cardu-*, s. of *carduus* thistle + *-aceae* -ACEAE) + -OUS]

Car·duc·ci (kär dōōt′chē), *n.* **Gio·suè** (jô swe′), ("*Enotrio Romano*"), 1835–1907, Italian poet and critic: Nobel prize 1906.

car·du·e·line (kär′jōō ē′lin), *adj.* **1.** of or pertaining to the passerine subfamily *Carduelinae*, comprising the goldfinches, siskins, canaries, crossbills, etc. —*n.* **2.** any bird of the subfamily *Carduelinae.* [< L *carduēl(is)* goldfinch (deriv. of *carduus* thistle), + -INE[1]]

car′ dum′per, a device for overturning freight cars to unload dry bulk cargo, as coal, ore, etc.

card′ vote′, *Brit.* a ballot, usually at a trade-union conference, in which each delegate's vote is considered equal to the number of members he represents. —**card′ vot′ing.**

care (kâr), *n., v.,* **cared, car·ing.** —*n.* **1.** worry; anxiety; concern: *Care had aged him.* **2.** a cause of worry, anxiety, distress, etc.: *to be free from care.* **3.** serious attention; solicitude; heed; caution: *He devotes great care to his work.* **4.** protection; charge: *She is under the care of a doctor.* **5.** temporary keeping, as for the benefit of or until claimed by the owner: *He left his valuables in the care of friends. Address my mail in care of the American Embassy.* **6.** an object of concern or attention: *Her child is her greatest care.* **7.** *Obs.* grief; suffering; sorrow. **8. take care,** be alert; be careful: *Take care that you don't fall on the ice!* Also, **have a care. 9. take care of, a.** to watch over; be responsible for: *to take care of an invalid.* **b.** to act on; deal with; attend to: *to take care of paying a bill.* [ME; OE *car(u)* anxiety; c. Goth *kara*, OHG *chara* lament; akin to L *garrire* to chatter] —*v.i.* **10.** to be concerned or solicitous; have thought or regard. **11.** to be concerned or have a special preference (usually used in negative constructions): *I don't care if I do.* **12.** to make provision or look out (usually fol. by *for*): *Will you care for the children while I am away?* **13.** to have an inclination, liking, fondness, or affection (usually fol. by *for*): *I do not care for him very much. She really does care for desserts.* **14.** to wish or be inclined (often fol. by an infinitive): *I don't care to do it today. Would you care to dance?* [ME *care(n)*, OE *c(e)arian* to worry (from n.)] —**car′er,** *n.*

—**Syn. 1.** solicitude, trouble. See **concern. 3.** To take CARE, PAINS, TROUBLE (to do something) implies watchful, conscientious effort to do something exactly right. To take CARE implies the performance of one particular detail: *She took care to close the cover before striking the match.* To take PAINS suggests a sustained carefulness, an effort to see that nothing is overlooked but that every small detail receives attention: *to take pains with fine embroidery.* To take TROUBLE implies an effort which requires a considerable amount of activity and exertion: *to take the trouble to make suitable arrangements.* **6.** burden.

CARE (kâr), *n.* a private organization for the collection of funds, goods, etc., for distribution to the needy in foreign countries. Also, **Care.** [*C(ooperative for) A(merican) R(elief) E(verywhere)*]

ca·reen (kə rēn′), *v.t.* *Naut.* **1.** to cause (a vessel) to lie over on its side, as on a beach, in order to repair, clean, or otherwise work on its bottom; heave down. **2.** to clean or repair (a vessel lying on its side for the purpose). **3.** to cause (a vessel) to heel over or list, as by the force of a beam wind. —*v.i.* **4.** (of a vessel) to heel over or list. **5.** (of a vehicle) to lean, sway, or tip to one side while in motion: *The car careened around the corner.* **6.** *Naut.* to careen a vessel. —*n.* **7.** a careening. **8.** *Naut.* the position of a careened vessel. [< MF *carine* < L *carin(a)* keel, nutshell; akin to Gk *kâryon* nut] —**ca·reen′er,** *n.*

ca·reen·age (kə rē′nij), *n.* **1.** the act or process of careening a vessel. **2.** a place for careening a vessel. [< F *carénage.* See CAREEN, -AGE]

ca·reer (kə rēr′), *n.* **1.** progress or general course of action of a person through life, or through some phase of life, as in some profession or undertaking, some moral or intellectual action, etc.: *His career as a soldier ended with the armistice.* **2.** an occupation or profession, esp. one requiring special training, followed as one's lifework: *He sought a career as a lawyer.* **3.** success in a profession, occupation, etc. **4.** a course, esp. a swift one. **5.** speed, esp. full speed: *The horse stumbled in full career.* **6.** *Obs.* a charge at full speed. —*v.i.* **7.** to run or move rapidly along; go at full speed. —*adj.* **8.** having or following a career; professional: *a career diplomat; a career girl.* [< MF *carriere* < LL *carrāria (via)* vehicular (road), equiv. to L *carr(us)* wagon (see CAR[1]) + *-āria*, fem. of *-ārius* -ARY]

ca·reer·ism (kə rēr′iz əm), *n.* devotion to a successful career, often at the expense of one's personal life, ethics, etc. [CAREER + -ISM]

ca·reer·ist (kə rēr′ist), *n.* **1.** a person who follows a career. **2.** a person who pursues a policy or attitude of careerism. [CAREER + -IST]

care·free (kâr′frē′), *adj.* without anxiety or worry. [CARE + FREE] —**care′free′ness,** *n.*

care·ful (kâr′fəl), *adj.* **1.** cautious in one's actions: *Be careful when you cross the street.* **2.** taking pains in one's work; exact; thorough: *a careful typist.* **3.** (of things) done or performed with accuracy or caution: *careful research.* **4.** solicitously mindful (usually fol. by *of, about,* or *in*): *careful of the rights of others; careful about one's deportment; careful in speech.* **5.** *Archaic.* **a.** troubled. **b.** attended with anxiety. [ME; OE *carful.* See CARE, -FUL] —**care′ful·ly,** *adv.* —**care′ful·ness,** *n.*

—**Syn. 1.** watchful, guarded, chary, circumspect. CAREFUL, CAUTIOUS, DISCREET, WARY imply a watchful guarding against something. CAREFUL implies guarding against mistakes, by paying strict and close attention to details, and, often, trying to use good judgment: *He was careful to distinguish between them.* CAUTIOUS implies a fear of some unfavorable situation and investigation before coming to conclusions: *cautious about investments.* DISCREET implies being prudent in speech and action and being trustworthy as a confidant: *discreet in manner, in keeping secrets.* WARY implies a vigilant lookout for a danger suspected or feared: *wary of polite strangers.* **2.** painstaking, meticulous, discerning. **3.** conscientious. **4.** thoughtful, concerned, solicitous, attentive, heedful, regardful. —**Ant. 1–4.** careless.

care·less (kâr′lis), *adj.* **1.** not paying enough attention to what one does: *a careless typist.* **2.** not exact or thorough: *careless work.* **3.** done or said heedlessly or negligently; unconsidered: *a careless remark.* **4.** not caring or troubling; having no care or concern; unconcerned (usually fol. by *of, about,* or *in*): *careless of the rights o others; careless about one's deportment; careless in speech.* **5.** possessed or caused without effort or art; unstudied: *careless beauty.* **6.** *Archaic.* free from anxiety. [ME; OE *carlēas.* See CARE, -LESS] —**care′less·ly,** *adv.* —**care′less·ness,** *n.*

—**Syn. 1.** inattentive, incautious, unwary, indiscreet, reckless. **2.** inaccurate, negligent. **3.** unthoughtful, unmindful. **4.** thoughtless, forgetful; inconsiderate. —**Ant. 1–4.** careful.

Car·en (kar′ən), *n.* a girl's given name, form of **Carin** or **Catherine.** Also, **Caryn, Karen, Karin, Karyn.**

ca·ress (kə res′), *n.* **1.** an act or gesture expressing affection, as an embrace, pat, kiss, etc. —*v.t.* **2.** to touch or pat gently to show affection. **3.** to touch, stroke, etc., lightly, as if in affection: *The breeze caressed the trees.* **4.** to treat with favor, kindness, etc. [< F *caresse* < It *carezz(a)* < VL **caritia*, equiv. to L *cār(us)* dear + *-itia* -ESS (as in *largess*, etc.)] —**ca·ress′er** *n.* —**ca·ress′ing·ly,** *adv.*

Ca·resse (kə res′), *n.* a girl's given name.

ca·ress·ive (kə res′iv), *adj.* **1.** of the nature of or resembling a caress: *caressive words; a caressive breeze.* **2.** characterized by or given to caresses: *She pestered the child with foolish, caressive attentions.* [CARESS + -IVE] —**ca·ress′ive·ly,** *adv.*

car·et (kar′it), *n.* a mark (∧) made in written or printed matter to show the place where something is to be inserted. [< L *caret* (there) is lacking or wanting, 3rd pers. sing. pres. ind. of *carēre* to be without]

care·tak·er (kâr′tā′kər), *n.* **1.** a person who is in charge of the maintenance of a building, estate, etc.; superintendent. **2.** one who or that which temporarily performs the duties of an office: *a caretaker government.* **3.** *Brit.* a janitor. [CARE + TAKER] —**care′tak′ing,** *n.*

Ca·rew (kə rōō′; *sometimes* kâr′ōō), *n.* **1. Thomas,** 1598?–1639?, English poet. **2.** a boy's given name.

care·worn (kâr′wōrn′, -wôrn′), *adj.* showing signs of care or worry; fatigued by trouble or anxiety; haggard: *a careworn old woman.* [CARE + WORN]

Car·ey (kâr′ē, kar′ē), *n.* **1.** a town in central Ohio. 3722 (1960). **2.** a boy's given name, form of **Carew.** Also, **Carry, Cary. 3.** a girl's given name, form of **Caroline.** Also, **Carie, Carrie, Carry, Cary.**

car·fare (kär′fâr′), *n.* the amount charged for a ride on a streetcar, bus, etc. [CAR[1] + FARE]

car·float (kär′flōt′), *n.* *Railroads.* a barge having tracks for the transportation of rolling stock. Also, **car′ float′.** [CAR[1] + FLOAT]

car·go (kär′gō), *n., pl.* **-goes, -gos. 1.** the lading or freight of a ship, airplane, etc. **2.** load. [< Sp: a load, deriv. of *cargar* to load < LL *carricāre*; see CHARGE] —**Syn. 1.** See **freight. 2.** burden.

car′go clus′ter, a light used during the loading and unloading of cargo from vessels at night, consisting of a number of light-bulb sockets with a common reflector. Also called **car′go reflec′tor.**

Car′go Cult′, a native, religious movement of a millenarian character located in the SW Pacific islands, holding that at the millennium the spirits of the dead will return and bring with them large cargos of modern goods for distribution among its adherents.

car′go mast′, any of a series of rigid masts, erected near the edge of a pier, to which tackles can be attached in loading or unloading vessels.

car·hop (kär′hop′), *n.* a waiter or waitress at a drive-in restaurant who serves patrons in their cars. [CAR[1] + HOP[1]]

Car·i·a (kâr′ē ə), *n.* an ancient district in SW Asia Minor. —**Car′i·an,** *adj., n.*

car·i·am·a (kar′ē am′ə), *n.* seriema. [< NL < Pg]

Car·i·an (kâr′ē ən), *n.* **1.** a native or inhabitant of Caria. **2.** the extinct language of Caria, not known to be related to any other language, written in a script derived from the Greek alphabet. —*adj.* **3.** of or pertaining to Caria. **4.** of or pertaining to the Carians or their language. [CARI(A) + -AN]

Ca·rí·as An·di·no (kä rē′äs än dē′nô), **Ti·bur·cio** (tē vōōr′syô), born 1876, Honduran lawyer, soldier, and statesman: president 1933–49.

Car·ib (kar′ib), *n., pl.* **-ibs,** (*esp. collectively*) **-ib. 1.** a member of an Indian people of NE South America, formerly dominant through the Lesser Antilles. **2.** the language of the Caribs. [< Sp *Carib(e)* < Arawak *Carib*]

Car·ib·be·an (kar′ə bē′ən, kə rib′ē-), *adj.* **1.** pertaining to the Caribs, the Lesser Antilles, or the Caribbean Sea. —*n.* **2.** a Carib. **3.** See **Caribbean Sea.**

Car′ibbe′an cur′rent, an ocean current flowing westward through the Caribbean Sea.

Car′ibbe′an Sea′, a part of the Atlantic Ocean bounded by Central America, the West Indies, and South America. ab. 750,000 sq. mi.; greatest known depth 22,788 ft. Also called **Caribbean.**

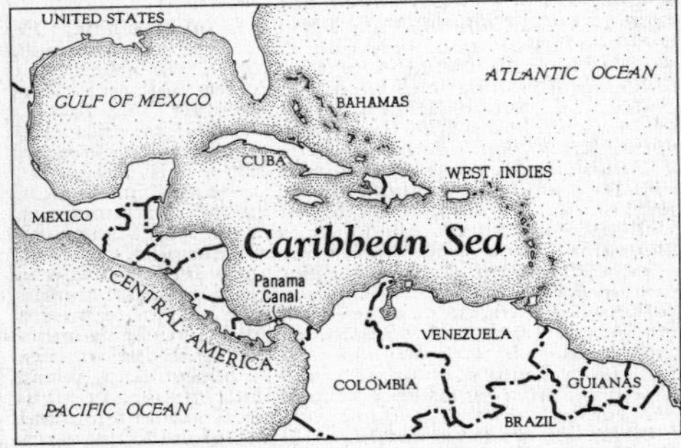

ca·ri·be (kə rē′bē; *Sp.* kä rē′ve), *n., pl.* **-bes** (-bēz; *Sp.* -ves). piranha. [< Sp: cannibal, CARIB]

Car·i·bees (kar′ə bēz′), *n.* See **Lesser Antilles.**

Car′i·boo Moun′tains (kar′ə bōō′), a mountain range in SW Canada, in E central British Columbia, part of the Rocky Mountains: highest peak, ab. 11,750 ft.

car·i·bou (kar′ə bōō′), *n., pl.* **-bous,** (*esp. collectively*) **-bou.** any of several large, North American deer of the genus *Rangifer,* related to the reindeer of the Old World. [< CanF < Algonquian (Micmac) *khalibu,* lit., pawer, scratcher]

Caribou, *Rangifer caribou* (About 4 ft. high at shoulder; length 6 ft.)

Car·i·bou (kar′ə bōō′), *n.* a town in NE Maine. 8305 (1960).

car·i·ca·ture (kar′ə kə chər, -chŏŏr′), *n., v.,* **-tured, -tur·ing.** —*n.* **1.** a picture, description, etc., ludicrously exaggerating the peculiarities or defects of persons or things. **2.** the art or process of producing such pictures, descriptions, etc. **3.** any imitation or copy so inferior as to be ludicrous. —*v.t.* **4.** to make a caricature of; represent in caricature. [earlier *caricatura* < It, equiv. to *caricat(o)* loaded, i.e., distorted (ptp. of *caricare;* see CHARGE) + *-ura* -URE] —**car′i·ca·tur·a·ble,** *adj.* —**car′i·ca·tur·ist,** *n.*
—**Syn. 1.** cartoon. See **burlesque. 3.** travesty.

car′icature plant′, an acanthaceous shrub, *Graptophyllum pictum,* of tropical India, characterized by leaf markings resembling the profile of a human face.

Car·ie (kar′ē), *n.* a girl's given name, form of **Caroline.** Also, **Carey, Carrie, Carry, Cary.**

car·ies (kâr′ēz, -ē ēz′), *n., pl.* **-ies.** decay, as of bone or teeth, or of plant tissue. [< L: decay; akin to Gk *Kēr* goddess of death]

car·il·lon (kar′ə lon′, -lən *or, esp. Brit.,* kə ril′yən; *Fr.* ka rē yôN′), *n., pl.* **car·il·lons** (kar′ə lonz′, -lənz *or, esp. Brit.,* kə ril′yənz; *Fr.* ka rē yôN′), *v.,* **-lonned, -lon·ning.** —*n.* **1.** a set of stationary bells hung in a tower and sounded by manual or pedal action, or by machinery. **2.** a melody played on such bells. **3.** an organ stop which imitates the peal of bells. **4.** a set of horizontal metal plates, struck by hammers, used in the modern orchestra. —*v.i.* **5.** to play a carillon. [< F: set of bells, orig. four; of disputed orig. but based on L *quattuor* four]

car·il·lon·neur (kar′ə lə nûr′ *or, esp. Brit.,* kə ril′yə nər; *Fr.* ka rē yô nœr′), *n., pl.* **car·il·lon·neurs** (kar′ə lə nûrz′ *or, esp. Brit.,* kə ril′yə nərz; *Fr.* ka rē yô nœr′). a person who plays a carillon. [< F: see CARILLON, -OR[2]]

Car·in (kar′in), *n.* a girl's given name. Also, **Caren, Caryn, Karen, Karin, Karyn.**

ca·ri·na (kə rī′nə, -rē′-), *n., pl.* **-nas, -nae** (-nē). *Bot., Zool.* a keellike part or ridge. [< L: keel] —**ca·ri′nal,** *adj.*

Ca·ri·na (kə rī′nə *for 1;* kə rē′nə, -rī′- *for 2*), *n., gen.* **-nae** (-nē) for 1. **1.** *Astron.* the Keel, a southern constellation, containing the bright star, Canopus: one of the subordinate constellations into which Argo is divided. **2.** a girl's given name, form of **Carin.**

car·i·nate (kar′ə nāt′), *adj.* **1.** Also, **car′i·nat′ed.** *Bot., Zool.* formed with a carina; keellike. —*n.* **2.** *Ornith.* a bird having a carinate sternum. [< L *carinātus,* equiv. to *carīn(a)* keel + *-ātus* -ATE[1]] —**car′i·na′tion,** *n.*

Ca·rin·thi·a (kə rin′thē ə), *n.* a province in S Austria. 493,972 (1961); 3681 sq. mi. *Cap.:* Klagenfurt. —**Ca·rin′thi·an,** *adj.*

ca·rin·u·la (kə rin′yə lə), *n. Bot., Zool.* a small carina. Also, **car·i·nule** (kar′ə nōōl′, -nyōōl′). [< NL, equiv. to *carin(a)* CARINA + *-ula* -ULE] —**ca·rin·u·late** (kə rin′yə lāt′, -lit), *adj.*

car·i·o·ca (kar′ē ō′kə), *n.* **1.** a modification of the samba. **2.** the music for this dance. [after CARIOCA]

Car·i·o·ca (kar′ē ō′kə; *Port.* kä′rē ô′kə), *n.* a native of Rio de Janeiro. [< Brazilain Pg < Tupi, equiv. to *cari* white + *oca* house]

car·i·ole (kar′ē ōl′), *n.* **1.** a small, open, two-wheeled vehicle. **2.** a covered cart. Also, **carriole.** [< F *carriole* < OPr *carriol(a),* equiv. to *carri* carriage (see CARRY) + *-ola* -ULE]

car·i·ous (kâr′ē əs), *adj.* having caries, as teeth; decayed. [< L *cariōs(us)* decayed, rotten, equiv. to *cari(ēs)* rot + *-ōsus* -OUS] —**car·i·os·i·ty** (kâr′ē os′i tē), **car′i·ous·ness,** *n.*

Car·is·a (kə ris′ə), *n.* a girl's given name. Also, **Ca·ris′sa.**

car·i·sop·ro·dol (kar′i sop′rə dōl′, -dôl′, -dol′), *n. Pharm.* a crystalline, water-soluble powder, $C_{12}H_{24}N_2O_4$, used chiefly to relieve pain and as a muscle relaxant. Also called **isopropyl meprobamate.** [CAR(BAMATE) + ISOPRO(PYL) + D(I)-[1] + -OL[1]]

Ca·ris·si·mi (kä rēs′sē mē), *n.* **Gia·co·mo** (jä′kô mô), 1605–74, Italian composer of sacred music.

Ca·ri·ta (kə rē′tə), *n.* a girl's given name.

ca·ri·tas (kä′ri täs′; *Eng.* kar′i tas′), *n. Latin.* charity. —**car·i·ta·tive** (kar′i tā′tiv, -tə tiv), *adj.*

car·i·tive (kar′i tiv), *adj.* (in certain inflected languages, esp. of the Caucasian group) abessive. [< L *carit(us)* devoid of, without (ptp. of *carēre* not to have, to want) + -IVE]

Car·i·us (kâr′ē əs), *n. Class. Myth.* an epithet of Zeus, referring to his temple in Caria.

cark (kärk), *n.* **1.** care or worry. —*v.t., v.i.* **2.** *Archaic.* to worry. [ME *cark(en)* (to) be anxious, OE (*be*)*carcian,* appar., deriv. of *car-* (base of *caru* CARE) + *-k-* suffix]

cark·ing (kär′king), *adj.* **1.** anxious; troubled; worried. **2.** distressful. **3.** toiling; moiling. **4.** miserly; stingy; niggardly. [CARK + -ING[2]] —**cark′ing·ly,** *adv.*

car′ knock′er, a person who inspects or repairs railroad cars.

carl (kärl), *n.* **1.** *Scot.* **a.** a strong, robust fellow, esp. a strong manual laborer. **b.** a miser; an extremely thrifty person. **2.** *Archaic.* a churl. **3.** *Obs.* a bondman. Also, **carle.** [ME, OE < Scand; cf. Icel *karl* man; c. OHG *karl;* akin to CHURL] —**carl′ish,** *adj.* —**carl′ish·ness,** *n.*

Carl (kärl), *n.* a boy's given name, form of **Charles.**

Car·la (kär′lə), *n.* a girl's given name, form of **Caroline.** Also, **Karla.**

Car·leen (kär lēn′), *n.* a girl's given name, form of **Caroline.**

Car·le·ta (kär lē′tə), *n.* a girl's given name. Also, **Carlita.**

car·lin[1] (kär′lin), *n. Chiefly Scot.* carline[1].

car·lin[2] (kär′lin), *n. Naut.* carling.

car′ line′. See **trolley line.**

car·line[1] (kär′lin, ker′-), *n. Chiefly Scot.* **1.** an old woman. **2.** a hag; witch. Also, **carlin.** [ME (north) *kerling* < Scand; cf. Icel *kerling* old woman, equiv. to *kerl* (mutated var. of *karl* man) + *-ing* -ING[1]]

car·line[2] (kär′lin), *n. Naut.* carling.

Car·line (kär′lin, -līn), *n.* a girl's given name, form of **Caroline.** Also, **Carlyne.**

car·ling (kär′ling), *n. Naut.* a short fore-and-aft beam running beside a hatchway, mast hole, or other deck opening to support the inner ends of the partial deck beams in way of the opening. Also, **carlin, carline.** [< F *carlingue* < Scand; cf. Icel *kerling* keelson, lit., old woman; see CARLINE]

Car·li·ni (kär lē′nē), *n.* a crater in the second quadrant of the face of the moon: about 5 miles in diameter.

Car·lin·ville (kär′lin vil), *n.* a town in central Illinois. 5440 (1960).

Car·lisle (kär līl′ *for 1;* kär līl′, kär′līl *for 2*), *n.* **1. John Grif·fin** (grif′in), 1835–1910, U.S. politician: Speaker of the House 1883–89. **2.** a city in and the county seat of Cumberland, in NW England. 71,112 (1961). **3.** a city in S Pennsylvania. 16,623 (1960). **4.** *Angling.* a fishhook having a narrow bend.

Car·list (kär′list), *n.* **1.** a supporter of the claims of Don Carlos of Spain or of his successors to the Spanish throne. **2.** a partisan of Charles X of France, and of the elder branch of the Bourbons. [CARL(OS) + -IST] —**Car′lism,** *n.*

Car·li·ta (kär lē′tə), *n.* a girl's given name. Also, **Carleta.**

car·load (kär′lōd′), *n. Chiefly U.S.* **1.** the amount carried by a car, esp. a freight car. **2.** the legal minimum weight entitling a railroad shipper to a rate (**car′load rate′**) lower than that charged for less than this weight. [CAR[1] + LOAD]

car·load·ings (kär′lō′dingz), *n.* Sometimes, **carloading.** carloads of freight in a given period. [CARLOAD + -ING[1] + -S[3]]

car′load lot′, a standard carload shipment of freight which measures up to the legal minimum weight.

Car·los (kär′lōs, -los; *Sp.* kär′lôs), *n.* **Don** (don; *Sp.* dôn), (*Carlos Maria Isidro de Borbón*), 1788–1855, pretender to the Spanish throne.

Car·lo·ta (kär lō′tä *for 1;* kär lot′ə *for 2*), *n.* **1.** 1840–1927, wife of Maximillian: empress of Mexico 1864–67 (daughter of Leopold I of Belgium). English, **Charlotte. 2.** a girl's given name, form of **Charlotte.**

Car·lot·ta (kär lot′ə; *It.* kär lôt′tä), *n.* a girl's given name, form of **Charlotte.** Also, **Carlota.**

Car·lo·vin·gi·an (kär′lə vin′jē ən), *adj., n.* Carolingian.

Car·low (kär′lō), *n.* a county in Leinster, in the SE Republic of Ireland. 33,342 (1961); 346 sq. mi. *Co. seat:* Carlow.

Carls·bad (kärlz′bad), *n.* **1.** German, **Karlsbad.** Czech, **Karlovy Vary.** a city in W Czechoslovakia: mineral springs; Carlsbad Decrees 1819. 43,819 (1963). **2.** a city in SE New Mexico. 25,541 (1960). **3.** a town in S California. 9253 (1960).

Carls′bad Cav′erns, a series of limestone caverns, near Carlsbad, New Mexico; now part of a national park (**Carls′bad Cav′erns Na′tional Park′**). 71 sq. mi.

Carl·son (kärl′sən), *n.* **1. An·ton Julius** (an′tōn, -ton), 1875–1956, U.S. physiologist, born in Sweden. **2. Evans For·dyce** (fôr′dīs, fôr′-), 1896–1947, U.S. Marine Corps general in World War II.

Carl·stadt (kärl′stat), *n.* a town in NE New Jersey. 6042 (1960).

Carl·ton (kärl′tən), *n.* a boy's given name.

Carl′ton ta′ble, an English writing table of c1800, having curved rear corners and a top with drawers surmounted by a U-shaped section of drawers and cabinets, topped by a brass or ormolu gallery surrounding three sides of the central writing area. Also called **Carl′ton House′ desk′, Carl′ton House′ ta′ble.** [named after *Carlton* House, the London mansion it was first made for]

Car·lyle (kär līl′), *n.* **1. Thomas,** 1795–1881, Scottish essayist and historian. **2.** a town in S Illinois. 2903 (1960). **3.** a boy's given name.

Car·lyne (kär′lin, -līn), *n.* a girl's given name, form of **Caroline.** Also, **Carline.**

Car·ma (kär′mə), *n.* a girl's given name. Also, **Karma.**

car·ma·gnole (kär′mən yōl′; *Fr.* kar ma nyôl′), *n., pl.* **-ma·gnoles** (-mən yōlz′; *Fr.* -ma nyôl′). **1.** a dance and song popular during the French Revolution. **2.** a man's loose jacket with wide lapels and metal buttons, worn during the French Revolution. **3.** the costume of the French revolutionists, consisting chiefly of this jacket, black pantaloons, and a red liberty cap. [< F, deriv. of provincial *carmagnola* ceremonial jacket worn by peasants of Dauphiné and Savoy, named after *Carmagnola,* town in Piedmont, Italy]

car·man (kär′mən), *n., pl.* **-men. 1.** one of the crew of a streetcar or the like. **2.** a person who drives a car or cart. [CAR[1] + MAN[1]]

Car·man (kär′mən), *n.* **(William) Bliss,** 1861–1929, Canadian poet and journalist in the U.S.

Car·ma·ni·a (kär mā′nē ə), *n.* a province of the ancient Persian empire, on the Gulf of Oman.

Car·ma·nor (kär mā′nôr), *n. Class. Myth.* the Cretan king who purified Artemis and Apollo after they had killed Python.

Car·mar·then (kär mär′thən), *n.* **1.** a seaport in and the county seat of Carmarthenshire, in S Wales. 12,121 (1961). **2.** Carmarthenshire.

Car·mar·then·shire (kär mär′thən shēr′, -shər), *n.* a county in S Wales. 167,736 (1961); 919 sq. mi. *Co. seat:* Carmarthen. Also called **Carmarthen.**

Car·me (kär′mē), *n. Class. Myth.* the mother, by Zeus, of Britomartis.

car·mel (kär′məl), *n.* a Carmelite monastery or convent. [see CARMELITE]

Car·mel (kär mel′ *for 1;* kär′mel *for 2*), *n.* **1. Mount,** a mountain range in NW Israel, near the Mediterranean coast: highest point, 1818 ft. ab. 14 mi. long. **2.** a girl's given name.

Car·mel·a (kär mel′ə), *n.* a girl's given name, form of **Carmel.** Also, **Carmella.**

Car·mel-by-the-Sea (kär mel′bī thə sē′), *n.* a town in W California. 4580 (1960).

Car·me·li·na (kär′mə lē′nə), *n.* a girl's given name, form of **Carmel.**

Car·me·li·ta (kär′mə lē′tə), *n.* a girl's given name, form of **Carmel.**

Car·mel·ite (kär′mə līt′), *n.* **1.** a mendicant friar belonging to a religious order founded at Mt. Carmel, Palestine, in the 12th century; White Friar. **2.** a nun belonging to this order. —*adj.* **3.** of or pertaining to Carmelites or their order. [late ME < ML *Carmelīt(a),* after CARMEL, first seat of the order; see -ITE[1]]

Car·mel·la (kär mel′ə), *n.* a girl's given name, form of **Carmel.** Also, **Carmela.**

Car·men (*Sp.* kär′men *for 1;* kär′mən *for 2*), *n.* **1.** See **Ciudad del Carmen. 2.** a boy's or girl's given name.

Car·men (kär′mən; *Fr.* kar men′), *n.* an opera (1875) by Georges Bizet.

Car·men·ta (kär men′tə), *n. Rom. Religion.* one of the Camenae, the wife or mother of Evander and the protectress of women during childbirth. Also, **Car·men·tis** (kär men′tis).

Car·mi (kär′mī), *n.* a town in SE Illinois. 6152 (1960).

Car·mi·chael (kär′mī kəl), *n.* **1. Hoag·land Howard** (hōg′lənd), ("*Hoagy*"), born 1899, U.S. songwriter and musician. **2. Stoke·ly** (stōk′lē), born 1941, U.S. civil-rights leader, born in Trinidad: chairman of the Student Nonviolent Coordinating Committee 1966–67. **3.** a town in central California, near Sacramento. 20,455 (1960).

car·min·a·tive (kär min′ə tiv, kär′mə nā′tiv), *n.* **1.** a drug causing expulsion of gas from the stomach or bowel. —*adj.* **2.** expelling gas from the body; relieving flatulence. [< L *carmināt(us)* carded (ptp. of *carmināre*), equiv. to *carmin-* (s. of *carmen*) CARD[2] + *-ātus* -ATE[1] + -IVE]

car·mine (kär′min, -mīn), *n.* **1.** a crimson or purplish red color. **2.** a crimson pigment obtained from cochineal. —*adj.* **3.** crimson-red or purplish-red. [< ML *carminus,* syncopated var. of *carmesīnus,* equiv. to *carmes-* (< Ar *qirmiz* KERMES) + *-īnus* -INE[1]]

car′mine crab′apple, a showy, bushy shrub, *Malus atrosanguinea,* having rose-purple flowers and red fruit.

carn (kärn), *n.* cairn.

Car·nac (kär′nak; *Fr.* kar nak′), *n.* a commune in SW Morbihan, in NW France, SE of Lorient: megalithic monuments. 3641 (1962). —**Car·na·cian** (kär nā′shən), *adj.*

car·nage (kär′nij), *n.* **1.** the slaughter of a great number of men, as in battle; butchery; massacre. **2.** *Archaic.* dead bodies, as of men slain in battle. [<

CONCISE ETYMOLOGY KEY: <, descended or derived from; >, whence; b., blend of, blended; c., cognate with; deriv., derivative; equiv., equivalent; imit., imitative; m., modification of; obl., oblique; r., replacing; s., stem; sp., spelling; trans., translation; ?, origin unknown, perhaps; *, hypothetical. See the full key inside the front cover.

MF < It *carnagg(io)* < LL *carnātic(um)* payment or offering in meat, equiv. to L *carn-* (s. of *caro*) flesh + *-āticum* -AGE]

car·nal (kär′nᵊl), *adj.* **1.** not spiritual; merely human; temporal; worldly: *a man of secular, rather carnal, leanings.* **2.** pertaining to or characterized by the flesh or the body, its passions and appetites; sensual: *carnal pleasures.* [ME < L *carnāl(is),* equiv. to *carn-* (s. of *caro*) flesh + *-ālis* -AL¹] —**car·nal′i·ty, car′nal·ness, car′nal·ism,** *n.* —**car′nal·ly,** *adv.*
—**Syn. 1.** earthly, natural. **2.** fleshly, bodily, animal, lustful, lecherous, lascivious, libidinous, concupiscent.

car′nal abuse′, 1. *Law.* any lascivious contact with the sexual organs of a child by an adult, esp. contact not involving sexual intercourse. **2.** rape, esp. of a young girl.

car′nal knowl′edge, *Chiefly Law.* sexual intercourse.

car·nall·ite (kär′nᵊlīt′), *n.* a hydrous mineral containing potassium, magnesium, and chlorine, $KCl \cdot MgCl_2 \cdot 6H_2O$, used chiefly as a source of potassium. [named after R. von *Carnall* (1804–74), German mining official; see -ITE¹]

Car·nap (kär′nap), *n.* **Rudolf P.,** born 1891, U.S. philosopher, born in Germany.

Car·nar·von (kär när′vən), *n.* **1.** Caernarvon. **2.** Also, **Car·nar′von·shire′.** Caernarvonshire.

Carnar′von arch′, a lintel supported on corbels.

car·nas·si·al (kär nas′ē əl), *Zool.* —*adj.* **1.** (of teeth) adapted for shearing flesh. —*n.* **2.** a carnassial tooth, esp. the last upper premolar or the first lower molar tooth of certain carnivores. [< F *carnassi(er)* flesh-eating, equiv. to *carnass-* carnivore (< L **carnācea;* see CARNAL, -ACEOUS) + *-ier* < L *-ārius* -ARY + -AL¹]

Car·nat·ic (kär nat′ik), *n.* a historically important region on the SE coast of India: now in Madras state.

car·na·tion (kär nā′shən), *n.* **1.** any of numerous cultivated varieties of clove pink, *Dianthus Caryophyllus,* having fragrant flowers of various colors: the State flower of Ohio. **2.** pink; light red. **3.** *Obs.* the color of flesh. —*adj.* **4.** having the color carnation. [< LL *carnātiōn-* (s. of *carnātiō*) fleshlikeness, hence flesh-color, equiv. to L *carn-* (s. of *caro*) flesh + *-ātiōn-* -ATION]

Car·na·tion (kär nā′shən), *n.* a girl's given name.

car·nau·ba (kär nou′bə), *n.* **1.** the Brazilian wax palm, *Copernicia cerifera.* **2.** a yellowish or greenish wax derived from the young leaves of this tree, used as a polish and in phonograph records. [< Brazilian Pg]

Car·ne·a·des (kär nē′ə dēz′), *n.* 214?–129? B.C., Greek philosopher.

Car·ne·gie (kär nā′gē, kär′nə-), *n.* **Andrew,** 1835–1919, U.S. steel manufacturer and philanthropist, born in Scotland.

car·nel·ian (kär nēl′yən), *n.* a red or reddish variety of chalcedony, used in jewelry. Also, **cornelian.** [var. (with *a* of CARNATION) of *cornelian,* ME *cornel(ine)* (< MF, prob. equiv. to OF *cornele* cornel cherry + *-ine* -INE¹, they being alike in color) + -IAN]

car·ne·ous (kär′nē əs), *adj.* fleshlike; flesh-colored. [< LL *carneus,* equiv. to L *carn-* (s. of *caro*) flesh + *-eus* -EOUS]

car·net (kär nā′; *Fr.* KAR ne′), *n., pl.* **-nets** (-nāz′; *Fr.* -ne′). a customs document allowing an automobile to be driven at no cost across international borders. [< F: notebook, book of tickets; MF *quernet* < L *quaterni* group of four]

Car·ne·us (kär nē′əs), *n. Class. Myth.* an epithet of Apollo, alluding to the cornel trees in his sacred grove.

car·ney (kär′nē), *n.* carny. Also, **car′nie.**

car·nif·er·ous (kär nif′ər əs), *adj.* bearing flesh. [< L carni- (comb. form of *caro* flesh) + -ferous]

car·ni·fi·ca·tion (kär′nə fə kā′shən), *n. Pathol.* the conversion into flesh or fleshlike substance of tissue dissimilar in structure, as of lung tissue as a result of pneumonia. [CARNI(FY) + -FICATION]

car·ni·fy (kär′nə fī′), *v.,* **-fied, -fy·ing.** —*v.t.* **1.** to form or turn into flesh. —*v.i.* **2.** *Pathol.* to undergo carnification. [< L *carni-* (comb. form of *caro* flesh) + -FY]

Car·ni·o·la (kär′nē ō′lə, kärn yō′-), *n.* a former duchy and crown land of Austria: now in NW Yugoslavia. —**Car′ni·o′lan,** *adj.*

car·ni·val (kär′nə vəl), *n.* **1.** a traveling amusement show, having side shows, a Ferris wheel, merry-go-rounds, shooting galleries, etc. **2.** any merrymaking, revelry or festival, as a program of sports, entertainment, etc.: *a winter carnival.* **3.** the season immediately preceding Lent, often observed with merrymaking; Shrovetide. [< It *carneval(e),* OIt *carnelevare* taking meat away, equiv. to *carne* (< L *carnem,* acc. of *caro*) + *levare* < L: to lift] —**car′ni·val·esque′, car′ni·val·like′,** *adj.*

Car·niv·o·ra (kär niv′ər ə), *n.* the order comprising the carnivores. [< NL, L, neut. pl. of *carnivor(us);* see CARNIVOROUS]

car·ni·vore (kär′nə vōr′, -vôr′), *n.* **1.** any chiefly flesh-eating mammal of the order *Carnivora,* comprising the dogs, cats, bears, seals, weasels, etc. **2.** an insectivorous plant. [back formation from CARNIVORA or CARNIVOROUS] —**car·niv·o·ral** (kär niv′ər əl), *adj.*

car·niv·o·rous (kär niv′ər əs), *adj.* that eats flesh: *A dog is a carnivorous animal.* [< L *carnivorus,* equiv. to *carni-* (comb. form of *caro* flesh) + *-vorus* -VOROUS] —**car·niv′o·rism,** *n.* —**car·niv′o·rous·ly,** *adv.* —**car·niv′o·rous·ness,** *n.*

car·nose (kär′nōs), *adj.* of or pertaining to flesh; fleshy. Also, **carnous.** [< L *carnōs(us)* fleshy, equiv. to *carn-* (s. of *caro*) flesh + *-ōsus* -OSE¹] —**car·nos·i·ty** (kär nos′i tē), *n.*

car·no·sine (kär′nə sēn′, -sin), *n. Biochem.* a dipeptide, $C_9H_{14}N_4O_3$, found in muscle tissue. [*carnos-* (< L *carnōs(us)* CARNOSE) + -INE²]

Car·not (kär nō′; *Fr.* KAR nō′), *n.* **1. La·zare Ni·co·las Mar·gue·rite** (LA ZAR nē kô lä MAR gə RēT′), 1753–1823, French general and statesman. **2. (Ma·rie Fran·çois) Sa·di** (MA Rē′ fRäN swä′ sad′ē; *Fr.* MA Rē′ fRäN-SWA′ SA dē′), 1837–94, French statesman: president of the Republic 1887–94. **3. Ni·co·las Lé·o·nard Sa·di** (nik′ə ləs len′ərd sad′ē; *Fr.* nē kô lä′ lā ô NAR′ SA dē′), 1796–1832, French physicist: pioneer in the field of thermodynamics.

Carnot′ cy′cle, *Thermodynamics.* an ideal cycle of reversible engine operations in which a substance at one temperature is compressed adiabatically to a second temperature, expanded isothermally at the second temperature, expanded adiabatically from the second temperature to the first temperature, and compressed isothermally at the first temperature. [named after N. L. S. CARNOT]

Carnot′ en′gine, *Thermodynamics.* an engine using a Carnot cycle of operations.

car·no·tite (kär′nə tīt′), *n.* a mineral, a yellow, earthy, hydrous potassium uranium vanadate: an ore of uranium. [named after A. *Carnot* (d. 1920), French mining official; see -ITE¹]

Carnot′ refrig′erator, *Thermodynamics.* a Carnot engine in which the first temperature is higher than the second.

Carnot's′ the′orem, *Thermodynamics.* the principle that no engine operating between two given temperatures can be more efficient than a Carnot engine operating between the same temperatures.

car·nous (kär′nəs), *adj.* carnose.

Car·nov·sky (kär nov′skē, -nôf′-), *n.* **Morris,** born 1897, U.S. actor.

Car·nus (kär′nəs), *n. Class. Myth.* a seer of Apollo who was murdered by one of the Heraclidae invading Peloponnesus.

car·ny (kär′nē), *n., pl.* **-nies.** *Informal.* **1.** a person employed by a carnival. **2.** carnival (def. 1). Also, **carney, carnie.** [CARN(IVAL) + -Y²]

Car·o (kâr′ō), *n.* a town in E Michigan. 3534 (1960).

car·ob (kar′əb), *n.* **1.** the fruit of a caesalpinaceous tree, *Ceratonia Siliqua,* of the Mediterranean regions, a long, dry pod containing hard seeds in a sweet pulp, used for feeding animals and sometimes eaten by man. **2.** the tree. [< MF *carobe* < ML *carrūb(ium)* < Ar *al kharrūbah* bean-pods, carobs]

ca·roche (kə rōch′, -rōsh′), *n.* (in the 17th century) a luxurious or stately coach or carriage. [< MF < It *carrocc(io),* equiv. to *carr(o)* wheeled conveyance (see CAR¹) + *-occio* aug. suffix]

car·ol (kar′əl), *n., v.,* **-oled, -ol·ing** or (*esp. Brit.*) **-olled, -ol·ling.** —*n.* **1.** a song, esp. of joy. **2.** a Christmas song or hymn. **3.** a seat in a bay window or oriel. **4.** a compartment in a cloister, similar to a carrel. **5.** *Obs.* a kind of circular dance. —*v.i.* **6.** to sing, esp. in a lively, joyous manner; warble. —*v.t.* **7.** to sing joyously. **8.** to praise or celebrate in song. [ME *carole* ring, circle (of stones), enclosed place for study (see CARREL), ring-dance with song (hence, song) < OF, appar. < L *coroll(a)* circlet (< *corōna,* CROWN + *-olla* dim. suffix) + Gk *choraúlēs* piper for choral dance < *chor(ós)* chorus + *aul(ós)* pipe + *-ēs* -ER¹] —**car′ol·er;** *esp. Brit.,* **car′ol·ler,** *n.*

Car·ol (kar′əl), *n.* a boy's or girl's given name. Also, **Carrol, Carroll, Caryl.**

Car·ol II (kar′əl; *Rum.* kä′RôL), 1893–1953, king of Rumania 1930–40.

Car·o·la (kar′ə lə), *n.* a girl's given name, form of **Carol.**

Car′ol Cit′y (kar′əl), a town in SE Florida, near Miami. 21,749 (1960).

Car·ole (kar′əl), *n.* a girl's given name. Also, **Carol, Carrol, Carroll, Caryl, Karol.**

Car·o·le·an (kar′ə lē′ən), *adj.* characteristic of the time of Charles I and II: *a Carolean costume.* [< ML *Carolae(us)* (< *Carol(us)* Charles + *-aeus* adj. suffix) + -AN]

Car·o·li·na (kar′ə lī′nə; *for 3 also It., Sp.* kä′Rô lē′nä), *n.* **1.** a former English colony on the Atlantic coast of North America: officially divided into North Carolina and South Carolina in 1729. **2.** Also called **the Car′o·li′nas.** North Carolina and South Carolina. **3.** Also, **Caroline, Karoline.** a girl's given name.

Car′oli′na all′spice, an aromatic shrub, *Calycanthus floridus,* of the southern U.S., having purplish-brown flowers.

Car′oli′na bay′, any of the shallow, usually marshy, oval depressions found in the coastal plains of the eastern U.S. that are heavily forested and have rich soil.

Car′oli′na chick′adee, a chickadee, *Parus carolinensis,* of the southeastern U.S., resembling but smaller than the black-capped chickadee.

Car′oli′na jes′samine, a vine, *Gelsemium sempervirens,* having fragrant, yellow flowers: the State flower of South Carolina. Also, **Car′oli′na jas′mine.** Also called **yellow jasmine.**

Car′oli′na lil′y, a bulbous herb, *Lilium michauxi,* of the southeastern U.S., having bluish-green leaves and nodding, purple-spotted, orange-red flowers from three to five inches long.

Car′oli′na moon′seed, a twining, woody vine, *Cocculus carolinus,* of the southeastern U.S., having greenish flowers and red fruit.

Car′oli′na par′akeet, an extinct, New World parakeet, *Conuropsis carolinensis,* which ranged into the northern U.S., having yellowish-green plumage with an orange-yellow head.

Caroli′na rail′, sora.

Caroli′na rhododen′dron, a showy, evergreen shrub, *Rhododendron carolinianum,* of the mountains of North Carolina, having rusty leaves that are scaly beneath and bell-shaped, pale rose-purple to whitish flowers.

Caroli′na vanil′la, a perennial herb, *Trilisa odoratissima,* of the southeastern U.S., having leaves that are vanilla scented when crushed and rose-purple flower heads. Also called **vanilla leaf.**

Car′oli′na wren′, a large wren, *Thryothorus ludovicianus,* of the U.S., having a musical call.

Car·o·line (kar′ə līn′, -lin), *adj.* of or pertaining to Charles, esp. Charles I and Charles II of England or their times. Also **Carolinian.** [< ML *Carolin(us),* equiv. to *Carol(us)* Charles + *-inus* INE¹]

Car·o·line (kar′ə lin, -līn′), *n.* a girl's given name. Also, **Carolina, Karoline.**

Car′oline Is′lands, a group of over 500 islands in the Pacific, E of the Philippines: formerly a Japanese mandate; now under U.S. administration. 42,627 (1955); 525 sq. mi.

Car·o·lin·gi·an (kar′ə lin′jē ən), *adj.* **1.** of or pertaining to the Frankish dynasty that reigned in France A.D. 751–987 and in Germany until A.D. 911. **2.** pertaining to or designating the arts, script, or culture of the Carolingian period, chiefly characterized by a revival of the forms of classical antiquity modified by ecclesiastical requirements: *Carolingian renaissance.* —*n.* **3.** a member of the Carolingian dynasty. Also, **Carlovingian, Carolinian.** [< F *Carolingien* < ML *Caroling(ī)* (pl.) family of Charles (*Carol(us)* Charles + *-ing-* offspring (< Gmc) + *-i* pl. ending) + F *-ien* -IAN]

Car·o·lin·i·an (kar′ə lin′ē ən), *adj.* **1.** of or pertaining to North Carolina or South Carolina or both. —*n.* **2.** a native or inhabitant of North Carolina or of South Carolina. [CAROLIN(A) + -IAN]

Car·o·lin·i·an (kar′ə lin′ē ən), *adj.* **1.** Carolingian. **2.** Caroline. —*n.* **3.** Carolingian. [< ML *Carolin(us)* CAROLINE + -IAN]

car·o·lus (kar′ə ləs), *n., pl.* **-lus·es, -li** (-lī′). any of various coins issued under monarchs named Charles, esp. the broad of Charles I of England. [< ML: Latinized form of *Charles* or *Karl*]

car·om (kar′əm), *n.* **1.** *Billiards, Pool.* a shot in which the cue ball hits two balls in succession. **2.** any strike and rebound, as a ball striking a wall and glancing off. —*v.i.* **3.** to make a carom. **4.** to strike and rebound. Also, **carrom.** [back formation from *carambole* (taken as *carom ball* by folk etym.) < F < Sp *carambol(a),* special use of fruit name; see CARAMBOLA]

car′om ball′, *Billiards.* the ball struck by the cue ball in rebounding off the object ball. Cf. **object ball** (def. 1).

ca·roon (kə ro͞on′), *n. Brit. Slang, Archaic.* a five-shilling piece. [? alter. of CROWN]

Ca′ro's ac′id (kär′ōz), *Chem.* See **persulfuric acid** (def. 1). [named after Heinrich *Caro* (1834–1910), German chemist]

car·o·tene (kar′ə tēn′), *n. Chem.* any of three isomeric red hydrocarbons having the formula $C_{40}H_{56}$, found in many plants, esp. carrots, and transformed to vitamin A in the liver. Also, **carotin.** [< L *carōt(a)* CARROT + -ENE]

ca·rot·e·noid (kə rot′ᵊnoid′), *Biochem.* —*n.* **1.** any of a group of red and yellow pigments, chemically similar to carotene, contained in animal fat and some plants. —*adj.* **2.** similar to carotene. **3.** pertaining to carotenoids. Also, **ca·rot′i·noid′.** [CAROTENE + -OID]

Ca·roth·ers (kə ruth′ərz), *n.* **Wallace Hume,** 1896–1937, U.S. chemist: associated with the invention of synthetic nylon material.

ca·rot·id (kə rot′id), *Anat.* —*n.* **1.** Also called **carot′id ar′tery.** either of the two large arteries, one on each side of the head, that carry blood to the head and that divide into an external branch supplying the neck, face, and other external parts, and an internal branch supplying the brain, eye, and other internal parts. —*adj.* **2.** pertaining to a carotid artery. [< Gk *karōtíd(es)* neck arteries, equiv. to *karōt(ikós)* soporific (*kár(os)* stupor + *-ōtikos* -OTIC) + *-ides* -ID³; so called by Galen, who found that their compression causes stupor] —**ca·rot′id·al,** *adj.*

carot′id bod′y, *Anat.* a small mass of cells and nerve endings adjacent to the carotid sinus that in response to chemical changes in the blood adjusts the respiratory rate. Also called **carot′id gland′.**

carot′id si′nus, *Anat.* specialized nerve end organs producing a slight dilatation of the carotid artery where it branches into the external and internal carotid arteries, responding to changes in blood pressure by mediating changes in the heartbeat rate.

car·o·tin (kar′ə tin), *n.* carotene.

ca·rous·al (kə rou′zəl), *n.* **1.** a noisy or drunken feast or social gathering; jovial revelry. **2.** carrousel. [CAROUSE + -AL²]

ca·rouse (kə rouz′), *n., v.,* **-roused, -rous·ing.** —*n.* **1.** carousal (def. 1). —*v.i.* **2.** to engage in a drunken revel: *They caroused all night.* **3.** to drink deeply and frequently; drain the cup again and again. [var. of *garouse* < G *gar aus (trinken)* (drink) fully out, i.e. drain the cup; cf. MF *carous* < dial. G *gar ūs*] —**ca·rous′er,** *n.* —**ca·rous′ing·ly,** *adv.*

car·ou·sel (kar′ə sel′, kar′ə zel′), *n.* **1.** merry-go-round (def. 1). **2.** a continuously revolving belt, track or other device on which items are placed for later retrieval: *a baggage carousel at an airport.* [< F: kind of tournament]

carp¹ (kärp), *v.i.* to find fault; cavil; complain unreasonably: *to carp at minor errors.* [ME *carp(en)* (to) speak, prate < Scand; cf. Icel *karpa* to brag, wrangle] —**carp′er,** *n.*

carp² (kärp), *n., pl.* (*esp. collectively*) **carp,** (*esp. referring to two or more kinds or species*) **carps. 1.** a large, freshwater food fish, *Cyprinus carpio.* **2.** any of various other fishes of the family *Cyprinidae.* [ME *carpe* < MF < MD or MLG *karpe;* c. OHG *karpfo*]

-carp, var. of **carpo-¹** as final element in a compound word: *endocarp.*

carp., carpentry.

Car·pac·cio (kär pät′chô), *n.* **Vit·to·re** (vēt tô′Re), c1450–1525, Italian painter.

car·pal (kär′pəl), *Anat.* —*adj.* **1.** pertaining to the carpus: *the carpal joint.* —*n.* **2.** a carpale. [< NL *carpāl(is).* See CARPUS, -AL¹]

car·pa·le (kär pā′lē), *n., pl.* **-li·a** (-lē ə). *Anat.* any of the bones of the wrist. Also, **carpal.** [< NL, neut. of *carpālis* CARPAL]

car′ park′, *Chiefly Brit.* a parking lot.

Car·pa′thi·an Moun′tains (kär pā′thē ən), a mountain range in central Europe, extending from N Slovakia to central Rumania. Highest peak, Gerlachovka, 8737 ft. Also called **Car·pa′thi·ans.**

Car·pa·tho-U·kraine (kär pā′thō yo͞o krān′), *n.* a region in the E Ukraine, in the SW Soviet Union in Europe: ceded by Czechoslovakia in 1945. Cf. **Ruthenia.**

Car·peaux (kär pō′; *Fr.* KAR pō′), *n.* **Jean Bap·tiste** (zhäN bA tēst′), 1827–75, French sculptor.

car·pe di·em (kär′pe dē′em; *Eng.* kär′pē dī′em), **1.** *Latin.* seize the day; get the most out of the day; enjoy the present, as opposed to placing all hope in the future (a maxim of Epicurean philosophy). **2.** *Literature.* a theme or motif, chiefly of lyric poetry, which presents youth as ephemeral and advises or urges the pursuit of pleasure.

car·pel (kär′pəl), *n.* *Bot.* a simple pistil, or a single member of a compound pistil, regarded as a modified leaf. [< NL *carpell(um)*; equiv. to Gk *karp(ós)* fruit + L *-ellum* dim. suffix] —**car·pel·lar·y** (kär′pə ler′ē), *adj.*

car·pel·late (kär′pə lāt′), *adj.* *Bot.* having carpels. [< NL *carpellā-t(us)*. See CARPEL, -ATE¹]

Car·pen·tar·i·a (kär′pən târ′ē ə), *n.* **Gulf of,** a gulf on the coast of N Australia. ab. 480 mi. long; ab. 300 mi. wide.

Carpels
A, Flower with simple pistils
B, Tricarpellary fruit

car·pen·ter (kär′pən tər), *n.* **1.** a person who builds or repairs wooden structures, as buildings, scaffolds, shelving, etc. —*v.i.* **2.** to do carpenter's work. —*v.t.* **3.** to make by carpentry. **4.** to construct (a plot, scene, article, or the like) in a mechanical or unoriginal fashion. [ME < AF < LL *carpentār(ius)* wainwright, equiv. to L *carpent(um)* two-wheeled carriage + *-ārius* -ER²]

Car·pen·ter (kär′pən tər), *n.* **1.** **John Alden,** 1876–1951, U.S. composer. **2.** a walled plain in the second quadrant of the face of the moon: about 39 miles in diameter.

car′penter ant′, a black or brown ant of the genus *Camponotus* that nests in the wood of decaying or dead trees in which it bores tunnels for depositing its eggs.

car′penter bee′, any of several solitary bees of the family *Xylocopidae* that nest in solid wood, boring tunnels in which to deposit their eggs.

car·pen·ter·ing (kär′pən tər ing), *n.* the trade or work of a carpenter. [CARPENTER + -ING¹]

car′penter moth′, a moth, *Prionoxystus robiniae,* the larvae of which bore into the wood of oaks, locusts, and other trees.

Car·pen·ters·ville (kär′pən tərz vil′), *n.* a city in NE Illinois, near Chicago. 17,424 (1960).

car·pen·ter·worm (kär′pən tər wûrm′), *n.* the larva of the carpenter moth. [CARPENTER + WORM]

car·pen·try (kär′pən trē), *n.* **1.** the trade of a carpenter: *He worked at carpentry.* **2.** the work produced by a carpenter: *The carpentry was excellent.* **3.** the way in which something, esp. a work of literature, is structured. [ME *carpentrie* < ONF < L *carpentāria* (*fabrica*) carriage-maker's workshop. See CARPENTER, -Y³]

car·pet (kär′pit), *n.* **1.** a heavy fabric, commonly of wool or nylon, for covering floors. **2.** a covering of this material. **3.** any covering like a carpet: *They walked on the carpet of grass.* **4. on the carpet, a.** under consideration or discussion. **b.** before an authority for a reprimand: *He was called on the carpet again for his carelessness.* **5.** any of a number of airborne electronic devices for jamming radar. **6.** a system of such devices. —*v.t.* **7.** to cover or furnish with or as with a carpet. **8.** to reprimand. [ME *carpete* < ML, LL *carpet(a)* kind of wool fabric, lit., (wool) divided, i.e., carded, equiv. to L *carpe(re)* (to) pluck, separate + *-ta,* fem. of *-tus* ptp. suffix] —**car′pet·less,** *adj.*

car·pet·bag (kär′pit bag′), *n., v.,* **-bagged, -bag·ging.** —*n.* **1.** a bag for traveling, esp. one made of carpeting. —*v.i.* **2.** to journey with little luggage. **3.** to act as a carpetbagger. [CARPET + BAG]

car·pet·bag·ger (kär′pit bag′ər), *n.* **1.** any person, esp. a politician or promoter, who takes up residence in a place in order to seek special advantages for himself. **2.** *U.S. Hist.* a Northerner who went to the South during the Reconstruction period, esp. to seek political office or to take advantage of the disrupted political and social conditions. [CARPETBAG + -ER¹; so called because he came South carrying his belongings in a carpetbag] —**car′pet·bag′ger·y,** *n.*

car′pet bee′tle, any of several small beetles of the family *Dermestidae,* the larvae of which are household pests, feeding on rugs and other woolen fabrics, esp. *Anthrenus scrophulariae* (**buffalo carpet beetle**) and *Attagenus piceus* (**black carpet beetle**). Also called **car′pet bug′.**

car′pet bomb′ing, saturation bombing in which target areas are destroyed successively.

car·pet-cut (kär′pit kut′), *n.* *Theat. Brit.* a cut in the floor of a stage, as a hinged floorboard, for securing an edge, esp. the downstage edge, of a ground cloth.

car·pet·ing (kär′pi ting), *n.* **1.** material for carpets. **2.** carpets in general. [CARPET + -ING¹]

car′pet knight′, *Archaic.* a knight who has spent his time in idleness and luxury. [orig., one knighted on the carpet, i.e. at court, not on the field of battle]

car′pet moth′, a clothes moth, *Trichophaga tapetzella,* the larvae of which infest carpets and other woolen articles. Also called **tapestry moth.**

car′pet shark′, any shark of the family *Orectolobidae,* found in tropical Indo-Pacific waters, having mottled skin and fleshy lobes along the sides of the head.

car′pet slip′per, a house slipper, esp. one for men, made of carpet material.

car′pet sweep′er, an implement for removing dirt, lint, etc., from rugs and carpets, consisting of a metal case enclosing one or more brushes that are rotated by wheeling it by the attached handle.

car′pet tack′, a flat-headed tack used esp. to tack down carpets.

car·pet·weed (kär′pit wēd′), *n.* a North American prostrate weed, *Mollugo verticillata.* [so called because procumbent]

car·phol·o·gy (kär fol′ə jē), *n.* *Pathol.* floccillation. [< NL *carphologia* < LL: fumbling, plucking at straws, blankets < Gk *karphología,* equiv. to *kárpho(s)* twig, straw, piece of wood + *-logia* collection; see -LOGY]

car·pi (kär′pī), *n.* pl. of **carpus.**

-carpic, a combination of **-carp** and **-ic** used in the formation of adjectives from stems in **-carp:** *endocarpic.*

carp·ing (kär′ping), *adj.* **1.** characterized by fussy or petulant faultfinding; querulous or ill-natured: *carping criticism.* —*n.* **2.** act of one who carps. **3.** an instance of carping: *Those carpings of hers have got to stop.* [ME (n.); see CARP¹, -ING², -ING¹] —**carp′ing·ly,** *adv.*

Car·pin·te·ri·a (kär′pin tə rē′ə), *n.* a town in SW California. 4998 (1960).

Car·po (kär′pō), *n.* an ancient Greek goddess of summer fruit, considered by Athenians as one of the Horae.

carpo-¹, a learned borrowing from Greek meaning "fruit," used in the formation of compound words: *carpophore.* Also, **-carp.** [< Gk *karpo-,* comb. form of *karpós* fruit]

carpo-², a learned borrowing from Greek meaning "wrist," used in the formation of compound words: *carpometacarpal.* [< Gk *karpó(s)* wrist]

car·po·go·ni·um (kär′pə gō′nē əm), *n., pl.* **-ni·a** (-nē ə). *Bot.* the one-celled female sex organ of the red algae which, when fertilized, gives rise to the carpospores. [CARPO-¹ + -GONIUM] —**car′po·go′ni·al,** *adj.*

car·pol·o·gy (kär pol′ə jē), *n.* the branch of botany dealing with fruits. [CARPO-¹ + -LOGY] —**car·po·log·i·cal** (kär′pə loj′i kəl), *adj.* —**car′po·log′i·cal·ly,** *adv.* —**car·pol′o·gist,** *n.*

car·po·met·a·car·pal (kär′pə met′ə kär′pəl, -met′ə kär′-), *adj.* **1.** *Anat.* of or pertaining to the carpus and the metacarpus. **2.** *Ornith.* of or pertaining to the carpometacarpus. [CARPO-² + METACARPAL]

car·po·met·a·car·pus (kär′pə met′ə kär′pəs, -met′ə kär′-), *n., pl.* **-pi** (-pī). *Ornith.* **1.** the bone of a bird's wing formed by fusion of the carpal and metacarpal bones. **2.** the part of the wing supported by this bone. [CARPO-² + METACARPUS]

car′ pool′, **1.** an arrangement among owners of automobiles by which each owner in turn drives the others to and from a designated place. **2.** those included in such an arrangement.

car·poph·a·gous (kär pof′ə gəs), *adj.* that eats fruit. [CARPO-¹ + -PHAGOUS]

car·po·phore (kär′pə fōr′, -fôr′), *n.* *Bot.* **1.** a slender prolongation of the floral axis, bearing the carpels of some compound fruits, as in the geranium and in many umbelliferous plants. **2.** the fruit body of the higher fungi. [CARPO-¹ + -PHORE]

A, Carpophore
B, Carpels

Car·poph·o·rus (kär pof′ər əs), *n.* *Class. Myth.* an epithet of both Demeter and her daughter, Persephone, meaning "fruit-bearer".

car·port (kär′pōrt′, -pôrt′), *n.* a roofed, wall-less shed projecting from the side of a building, used as a shelter for an automobile. [CAR¹ + PORT¹]

car·po·spore (kär′pə spōr′, -spôr′), *n.* *Bot.* a nonmotile spore of the red algae. [CARPO-¹ + SPORE] —**car·po·spor·ic** (kär′pə spōr′ik, -spor′-), **car·pos·po·rous** (kär pos′pər əs), *adj.*

car·po·stome (kär′pə stōm′), *n.* *Bot.* the opening in the cystocarp of certain red algae through which the spores are discharged. [CARPO-¹ + -STOME]

-carpous, a combination of **-carp** and **-ous** used in the formation of adjectives from stems in **-carp:** *apocarpous.*

carp·suck·er (kärp′suk′ər), *n.* any of several freshwater suckers of the genus *Carpiodes,* as the quillback and the river carpsucker. [CARP² + SUCKER]

car·pus (kär′pəs), *n., pl.* **-pi** (-pī). *Anat.* **1.** the part of the upper extremity between the hand and the forearm; wrist. **2.** the wrist bones collectively; the group of bones between the bones of the hand and the radius. See diag. under **skeleton.** [< NL < Gk *karpós* wrist]

Car·rac·ci (kə rä′chē; *It.* kär rät′chē), *n.* **1. A·go·sti·no** (ä′gô stē′nô), 1557–1602, and his brother, **An·ni·ba·le** (än nē′bä le), 1560–1609, Italian painters. **2.** their cousin, **Lu·do·vi·co** (lo͞o′dô vē′kô), 1555–1619, Italian painter.

car·rack (kar′ək), *n.* a merchant vessel having various rigs, used esp. by Mediterranean countries in the 15th and 16th centuries; galleon. Also, **carack.** [ME *carrake* < MF *carraque* < OSp *carrac(a),* back formation from Ar *qarāqīr* (pl. of *qurqūr* ship of burden), the *-īr* being taken as pl. ending]

car·ra·geen (kar′ə gēn′), *n.* See **Irish moss.** Also, **car′ra·gheen′.** [named after Carrageen in SE Ireland]

Car·ran·za (kə ran′zə; *Sp.* kär rän′sä), *n.* **Ve·nus·tia·no** (be′no͞os tyä′nô), 1859–1920, Mexican revolutionary and political leader: president 1915–20.

Car·ra·ra (kə rär′ə; *It.* kär rä′rä), *n.* a city in NW Tuscany, in NW Italy: marble quarries. 61,903 (1951). —**Car·ra′ran,** *n., adj.*

car·re·four (kar′ə fo͝or′, kar′ə fo͝or′), *n.* **1.** a crossroads; road junction. **2.** a public square, as a plaza or marketplace, on which streets or roads converge. [< F; MF *quarrefour* < LL *quadrifurc(um),* neut. of *quadrifurc(us)* with four forks, equiv. to *quadri-* QUADRI- + *furc(us) furc(a)* FORK + *-us* adj. suffix)]

car·rel (kar′əl), *n.* a small recess or enclosed area in a library stack, designed for individual study or reading. Also, **car′rell.** Also called **cubicle, stall.** [var. of CAROL enclosure]

Car·rel (kə rel′, kar′əl; *Fr.* KA rel′), *n.* **A·lex·is** (ə lek′sis; *Fr.* A lek sē′), 1873–1944, French surgeon and biologist, in U.S. 1905–39: Nobel prize 1912.

Car·rère (kə râr′), *n.* **John Merven,** 1858–1911, U.S. architect.

car·riage (kar′ij; *also for* 7 kar′ē ij), *n.* **1.** a wheeled vehicle for conveying persons, as one drawn by horses and designed for comfort and elegance. **2.** *Brit.* a railway passenger coach. **3.** a wheeled support, as for a cannon. **4.** a movable part, as of a machine, designed for carrying something. **5.** manner of carrying the head and body; bearing: *the carriage of a soldier.* **6.** Also called **carriage piece, horse.** an inclined beam, as a string, supporting the steps of a stair. **7.** the act of transporting; conveyance: *the expenses of carriage.* **8.** the price or cost of transportation. **9.** (in a typewriter) the moving part carrying the platen and its associated parts, usually set in motion to carry the paper across the point where the type bars strike. **10.** management; administration. [ME *cariage* < ONF, equiv to *cari(er)* (to) CARRY + *-age* -AGE]
—**Syn. 1.** cart, car, wagon. **5.** mien, comportment.

car′riage bolt′, a round-headed bolt for timber, threaded along part of its shank, inserted into holes already drilled. See illus. under **bolt.**

car′riage dog′, Dalmatian (def. 3).

car′riage drive′, *Brit.* **1.** a road through a scenic area. **2.** a private road or drive, as on a large estate.

car′riage for′ward, *Brit.* with delivery charges to be paid on arrival; delivered collect; C.O.D.

car′riage free′, *Brit.* delivered free of charge.

car′riage house′. See **coach house.**

car′riage horse′, a horse trained and groomed to draw carriages.

car′riage paid′, *Brit.* with charges for delivery prepaid.

car′riage piece′, carriage (def. 6).

car′riage trade′, wealthy patrons of a theater, store, etc.

car′riage way′, *Brit.* **1.** a road or lane of a road for use by automobiles, as opposed to a bridle path, truck route, etc. **2.** See **carriage drive.** Also called **car′riage road′.**

car′rick bend′, a knot or bend for joining the ends of two ropes. See illus. under **knot.** [? ME *carryk,* var. of *carrake* CARRACK]

car′rick bitt′, *Naut.* either of a pair of heavy wooden uprights supporting the barrel of a windlass. Also called **windlass bitt.** [see CARRICK BEND]

car′rick head′, *Naut.* the head of a carrick bitt, used for making hawsers fast. [see CARRICK BEND]

Car·rie (kar′ē), *n.* a girl's given name, form of **Caroline.** Also, **Carey, Carie, Carry, Cary.**

car·ri·er (kar′ē ər), *n.* **1.** one who or that which carries. **2.** an employee of the post office who carries mail. **3.** a newsboy who delivers newspapers, magazines, etc., on a particular route. **4.** See **aircraft carrier. 5.** a metallic or wooden frame attached to a vehicle for carrying skis, luggage, etc., as on top of a station wagon. **6.** any person or organization in the business of conveying persons or goods. **7.** *Mach.* a mechanism by which something is carried or moved. **8.** *Immunol.* an individual harboring specific pathogenic organisms who, though often immune to the agent harbored, may transmit the disease to others. **9.** *Chem.* a catalytic agent which brings about a transfer of an element or group of atoms from one compound to another. **10.** *Physical Chem.* a usually inactive substance that acts as a vehicle for an active substance. **11.** Also called **car′rier wave′.** *Radio.* the wave whose amplitude, frequency, or phase is to be varied or modulated to transmit a signal. **12.** See **carrier pigeon. 13.** base¹ (def. 15b). [ME; see CARRY, -ER¹]

Car·rière (KA RYER′), *n.* **Eugène** (œ zhen′), 1849–1906, French painter and lithographer.

car·ri·er-free (kar′ē ər frē′), *adj.* *Chem.* (of a radioactive isotope) capable of functioning as a tracer without the use of a carrier.

car′rier pig′eon, **1.** one of a breed of domestic pigeons having a large wattle around the base of the beak. **2.** a homing pigeon.

Car·ring·ton (kar′ing tən), *n.* a walled plain in the first quadrant of the face of the moon: about 18 miles in diameter.

car·ri·ole (kar′ē ōl′), *n.* cariole.

car·ri·on (kar′ē ən), *n.* **1.** dead and putrefying flesh. **2.** rottenness; anything vile. —*adj.* **3.** feeding on carrion. **4.** of or like carrion. [ME *carion,* var. of *caronye* < ONF *caronie* < VL **caronia,* equiv. to L *carun-* (see CARUNCLE) + *-ia* -Y³]

car′rion bee′tle, any of the beetles of the family *Silphidae* that feed on and deposit their eggs in carrion.

car′rion crow′, **1.** a European crow, *Corvus corone,* that feeds on carrion. **2.** a black vulture, *Coragyps atratus,* of the southern U.S., that feeds on carrion.

car′rion flow′er, **1.** any of several cactuslike, African, asclepiadaceous plants of the genus *Stapelia,* characterized by the putrid odor of their flowers. **2.** a greenbrier, *Smilax herbacea,* with flowers of a similar odor.

car·ritch (kä′RICH), *n.* *Scot.* a catechism. [back formation from *carritches* (taken as pl.), Scot var. of *catechis(e)* (now dial.) < F *catéchèse* < Gk *catēchēs(is)* CATECHESIS; for *t* > *rr,* cf. PORRIDGE]

Car·ri′zo Springs′ (kə rē′zō), a town in SW Texas. 5699 (1960).

Car·rol (kar′əl), *n.* **1.** a boy's given name, form of **Carew.** Also, **Carol, Carroll, Caryl, Karol. 2.** a girl's given name, form of **Carol.** Also, **Carroll, Carole, Caryl, Karol.**

Car·roll (kar′əl), *n.* **1. Charles,** 1737–1832, American patriot and legislator. **2. Lewis,** pen name of Charles Lutwidge Dodgson. **3.** a town in W Iowa. 7682 (1960). **4.** Also, **Carol, Carrol, Caryl, Karol.** a boy's given name. **5.** Also, **Carole, Carrol, Caryl, Karol.** a girl's given name.

car·roll·ite (kar′ə līt′), *n.* a mineral consisting mostly of a sulfide of cobalt with traces of iron, nickel, and copper. [named after *Carroll* Co., Maryland, where found; see -ITE¹]

Car·roll·ton (kar′əl tən), *n.* **1.** a town in central Missouri. 4554 (1960). **2.** a town in N Texas. 4242 (1960). **3.** a town in central Maryland. 3385 (1960). **4.** a town in N Kentucky. 3218 (1960). **5.** a town in E Ohio. 2786 (1960). **6.** a town in W Illinois. 2558 (1960).

car·rom (kar′əm), *n., v.i.* carom.

car·ro·ma·ta (kar′ə mä′tə; *Sp.* kär Rô mä′tä), *n., pl.* **-tas** (-təz; *Sp.* -täs). (in the Philippines) a light, two-wheeled covered vehicle, usually drawn by one horse. [< Sp *carromato* < It *carromatto* cart < L *carru(s)* cart + *-mattus* stupid, drunk, from its motion]

car·ron·ade (kar′ə nād′), *n.* a short piece of muzzle-loading ordnance, formerly in use, esp. in ships. [named after *Carron,* Scotland, where first cast; see -ADE¹]

car′ron oil′ (kar′ən), *Pharm.* a liniment containing limewater and linseed oil, used in medicine chiefly for burns. Also called **lime liniment.** [named after *Carron,* Scotland, where it was used for treatment of ironworks laborers]

car·rot (kar′ət), *n.* **1.** an umbelliferous plant of the genus *Daucus,* esp. *D. carota,* in its wild form a widespread, familiar weed, and in cultivation valued for its yellowish edible root. **2.** the root. —*v.t.* **3.** to treat (furs) with mercuric nitrate preparatory to felting. [< MF *carotte* < L *carōt(a)* < Gk *karōtón,* perh. deriv. of *kárē* head; see -OTIC]

car·rot-top (kar′ət top′), *n.* *Slang.* a person who has red hair.

car·rot·y (kar′ə tē), *adj.* **1.** like a carrot root in color; yellowish red. **2.** having red hair. [CARROT + -Y¹] —**car′rot·i·ness,** *n.*

car·rou·sel (kar′ə sel′, -zel′; kar′ə sel′, -zel′), *n.* **1.** merry-go-round (def. 1). **2.** a tournament in which horsemen executed various formations. Also, **carousel.** [< F: kind of tournament < It *carosell(o)* kind of ball game, var. of dial. (Neapolitan) *carusello* clay ball, lit., little head, equiv. to *carus(o)* shorn head (akin to Gk *kartós* shorn) + *-ello* < L *-ellus* dim. suffix]

car·rus (kär′əs), *n., pl.* **-ri** (-rī). a type of baggage cart used by the Romans, usually drawn by mules or oxen. [< L]

car·ry (kar′ē), *v.,* **-ried, -ry·ing,** *n., pl.* **-ries.** —*v.t.* **1.** to move while supporting; convey; transport: *He carried her for a mile in his arms. This elevator cannot carry more than 10 persons.* **2.** to wear, hold, or have around one: *He carries his change in his pocket. He carries a cane.* **3.** to contain or be capable of containing; hold: *The suitcase will carry enough clothes for a week.* **4.** to serve as an agency or medium for the transmission of: *The wind carried the sound. He carried the message to me.* **5.** to be the means of conveying or transporting (something or someone): *The wind carried the balloon out of sight.* **6.** to be pregnant with: *The woman is carrying twins.* **7.** to put forward or transfer: *to carry a case to a higher court; to carry a footnote to a new page.* **8.** to bear the weight, burden, etc., of; sustain: *These piers once carried an arch.* **9.** *U.S.* to take (a leading or guiding part), as in singing; bear or sustain (a part or melody). **10.** to hold (the body, head, etc.) in a certain manner: *She carries her head high.* **11.** to behave or comport (oneself): *She carries herself with decorum.* **12.** to take the initiative in (a contest): *The Giants carried the game to the Browns.* **13.** to secure the adoption of (a motion or bill). **14.** to get a plurality or majority of electoral votes in (a district). **15.** to extend or continue in a given direction or to a certain point: *to carry the war into enemy territory.* **16.** to bring, impart, hear, transmit, or communicate, as news, a message, etc. **17.** to lead or influence by emotional or intellectual appeal: *The actor carries his audience with him.* **18.** to bear the major burden of (a group, performance, etc.) by superior skill: *The star carried the whole play.* **19.** *Southern U.S.* to lead, escort, or conduct: *to carry a girl to a dance; to carry a mule to a barn.* **20.** to lead or impel; conduct: *This pipe carries water to the house.* **21.** to have as an attribute, property, consequence, etc.: *Violation carries a penalty of five years in prison.* **22.** to support or give validity to (a related claim, argument, etc.): *One decision carries another.* **23.** *Com.* **a.** to keep on hand or in stock. **b.** to keep on one's account books. **24.** to bear as a crop: *This land will not carry corn.* **25.** to support: *Our grain supply will carry the cattle through the winter. This money will carry us for about a week.* **26.** *Golf.* to advance beyond or go by (an object or expanse) with one stroke. **27.** *Ice Hockey.* to cause (a puck) to move forward along the ice and to remain in one's control by a series of light, short taps with the stick. **28.** *Hunting.* to retain and pursue (a scent). **29.** (in addition) to transfer (a number) from one denomination to the succeeding one. **30.** to have as a maximum working pressure: *This boiler carries 190 pounds per square inch.* —*v.i.* **31.** to act as a bearer or conductor. **32.** to have or exert propelling force: *The rifle carries almost a mile.* **33.** to be transmitted, propelled, or sustained: *My voice carries farther than his.* **34.** (of a horse) to bear the head in a particular manner while in action: *The horse carries well.* **35. carry all before one,** to be highly successful: *In his academic and social life he carried all before him* **36. carry a tune,** to sing accurately or on key. **37. carry away, a.** to influence greatly or unreasonably; excite; transport: *The spectators were carried away by the appeal to their patriotism.* **b.** *Naut.* (of the wind or sea) to dislodge or send overboard. **c.** *Naut.* (of a vessel) to lose (an object or objects) through breakage. **d.** *Naut.* (of a rope or chain) to break under strain. **38. carry back,** *Accounting.* to apply (an unused credit or operating loss) to the net income of a prior period in order to reduce the tax for that period. **39. carry forward, a.** to make progress with. **b.** *Bookkeeping.* to transfer (an amount) to the next page, column, or book. **c.** *Accounting.* to apply (an unused credit or operating loss) to the net income of a succeeding period in order to reduce the tax for that period. **40. carry lee helm,** *Naut.* (of a vessel sailing close-hauled) to require constant heading into the wind with the rudder. **41. carry off, a.** to win (a prize, honor, etc.). **b.** to deal with successfully. **c.** to face boldly. **d.** to cause the death of: *The plague in the Middle Ages carried off more than one fourth of the population of Europe.* **42. carry on, a.** to manage; conduct. **b.** *Informal.* to behave in an agitated, foolish, or indiscreet manner. **c.** to continue without stopping; persevere: *Rescue operations were carried on in spite of the storm.* **d.** *Naut.* to proceed under excessive sail for the weather conditions. **43. carry out, a.** to put into operation; execute: *He hasn't the funds to carry out his design.* **b.** to bring to an end; accomplish; complete: *They carried out their plan without incident.* **44. carry over, a.** to hold until a later time; postpone. **b.** to be left; remain. **c.** *Bookkeeping.* to transfer (an amount) to the next page, column, or book. **d.** *Accounting.* to apply (an unused credit or operating loss) to the net income of a succeeding period in order to reduce the tax for that period. **e.** to extend from one activity or time to another: *He does not carry over his business ethics into his personal relationships.* **45. carry (something) too far,** to exceed the limits of good taste, credibility, etc.; go to excess: *She is carrying her crusading too far.* **46. carry the day,** to win the contest; be declared the victor: *The Republicans carried the day.* **47. carry through, a.** to accomplish; complete. **b.** to support or help through a difficult situation. **c.** to continue; persist: *a theme that carried through all his writing.* **48. carry weather helm,** *Naut.* (of a sailing vessel) to require constant heading away from the wind with the rudder; be ardent. —*n.* **49.** range, as of a gun. **50.** *Golf.* the distance a stroked ball travels. **51.** *U.S.* land that separates navigable waters and over which a canoe or boat must be carried; a portage. **52.** a carrying. [ME *cari(en)* < ONF *carie(r)* < LL *carricāre,* appar. var. of **carrucāre,* deriv. of L *carruca* four-wheeled vehicle < Celt; see CAR¹] —**car′ri·a·ble, car′ry·a·ble,** *adj.*

—**Syn. 1.** CARRY, CONVEY, TRANSPORT, TRANSMIT imply taking or sending something from one place to another. CARRY means to take by means of the hands, of a vehicle, etc.: *to carry a book.* CONVEY is a more formal word, suggesting a means of taking, but not any particular method of taking; it is also used figuratively: *to convey wheat to market; to convey one's sympathies.* TRANSPORT means to carry or convey goods, now usually by vehicle or vessel: *to transport milk to customers.* TRANSMIT implies sending or transferring messages or hereditary tendencies: *to transmit a telegram.* **8.** support. **14.** gain, secure.

Car·ry (kar′ē), *n.* **1.** a boy's given name, form of **Carew.** Also, **Carey, Cary. 2.** a girl's given name, form of **Caroline.** Also, **Carey, Carie, Carrie, Cary.**

car·ry·all¹ (kar′ē ôl′), *n.* **1.** a light, four-wheeled, covered carriage having seats for four persons, usually drawn by one horse. **2.** a passenger automobile or bus having two facing benches running the length of the body. [alter. of CARIOLE by folk etymology]

car·ry·all² (kar′ē ôl′), *n.* a large basket, bag, etc. [n. use of v. phrase *carry all*]

car·ry·back (kar′ē bak′), *n.* (in U.S. income-tax law) a special provision allowing part of a net loss or of an unused credit in a given year to be apportioned over one or two preceding years, chiefly in order to ease the tax burden. Cf. **carry-forward** (def. 2). [n. use of v. phrase *carry back*]

car·ry-for·ward (kar′ē fôr′wərd), *n.* **1.** carry-over. **2.** (in U.S. income-tax law) a special provision allowing part of a net loss or of an unused credit in a given year to be apportioned over one or two subsequent years, chiefly in order to ease the tax burden. Cf. **carry-back.** [n. use of v. phrase *carry forward*]

car′rying capac′ity, *Ecol.* the maximum number of organisms that can be supported in a given environment; saturation level.

car′rying charge′, 1. a charge made for carrying an account, usually computed as a percentage of the principal owed. **2.** cost incurred while an asset is unproductive.

car·ry·ing-on (kar′ē ing on′, -ôn′), *n., pl.* **car·ry·ings-on.** *Informal.* excited, foolish, or improper behavior: *His carryings-on were too much.*

car·ry-on (kar′ē on′, -ôn′), *n. Brit. Informal.* carrying-on. [n. use of v. phrase *carry on*]

car·ry-o·ver (kar′ē ō′vər), *n.* **1.** that which is carried over, postponed, or extended, as to a later time, account, etc. **2.** *Bookkeeping.* the total of one page of an account carried forward to the next. **3.** carry-forward (def. 2). [n. use of v. phrase *carry over*]

carse (kärs, KERS), *n. Scot.* fertile alluvial land; bottom land. [ME *cars,* deriv. of *kerss,* equiv. to *ker* marsh (< Scand; cf. Sw *kärr* marsh) + *ss,* north var. of -ISH¹]

car·shops (kär′shops′), *n.pl.* a group of workshops for the repair, maintenance, or construction of railroad rolling stock. [CAR¹ + *shops* (pl. of SHOP)]

car·sick (kär′sik′), *adj.* ill with carsickness. [CAR¹ + SICK¹]

car·sick·ness (kär′sik′nis), *n.* a feeling of nausea and dizziness, sometimes accompanied by vomiting, as a result of the motion of the car in which one is traveling. Cf. **motion sickness.** [CAR¹ + SICKNESS]

Car·son (kär′sən), *n.* **1. Christopher** ("*Kit*"), 1809–68, U.S. frontiersman and scout. **2. Sir Edward Henry** (*Baron Carson*), 1854–1935, Irish public official. **3. Rachel Louise,** 1907–1964, U.S. marine biologist and author. **4.** a boy's or girl's given name.

Car′son Cit′y, a town in and the capital of Nevada, in the W part. 5163 (1960).

Car·stensz (kär′stənz), *n.* **Mount,** a mountain in Netherlands New Guinea: highest mountain in New Guinea. 16,404 ft.

cart (kärt), *n.* **1.** a heavy two-wheeled vehicle, commonly without springs, drawn by mules, oxen, or the like, used for the conveyance of heavy goods. **2.** a light two-wheeled vehicle with springs, drawn by a horse or pony. **3.** any small vehicle moved by hand. **4.** *Obs.* a chariot. **5. on the water cart,** *Brit.* wagon (def. 9). **6. put the cart before the horse,** to do or place things in improper order; be illogical. —*v.t.* **7.** to convey in or as in a cart. —*v.i.* **8.** to drive a cart. [ME *cart(e),* OE *cræt* (by metathesis); c. Icel *kartr* cart] —**cart′a·ble,** *adj.* —**cart′er,** *n.*

cart·age (kär′tij), *n.* the act or cost of carting. [ME; see CART, -AGE]

Car·ta·ge·na (kär′tə jē′nə; *Sp.* kär′tä he′nä), *n.* **1.** a seaport in SE Spain. 118,049 (est. 1955). **2.** a seaport in N Colombia. 179,250 (est. 1961).

carte¹ (kärt; *Fr.* KART), *n. Fencing Rare.* quarte.

carte² (kärt; *Fr.* KART), *n., pl.* **cartes** (kärts; *Fr.* KART). **1.** (*italics*) *French.* menu; bill of fare. Cf. **à la carte. 2.** *Now Rare or Obs.* a playing card. **3.** *Obs.* a map or chart. [ME, OE: writing paper, document, letter < L *charta* in same senses < Gk *chártēs* leaf of paper]

Carte (kärt), *n.* **Richard d'Oy·ly** (doi′lē), 1844–1901, English theatrical producer.

carte blanche (kärt′ blanch′, blänch′; *Fr.* KART BLÄNSH′), *pl.* **cartes blanches** (kärts′ blanch′, blänch′; *Fr.* KART BLÄNSH′). **1.** a sheet of paper that is blank except for a signature and given by the signer to another person to write in what he pleases. **2.** unconditional authority; full discretionary power. **3.** *Cards.* a hand having no face card but with a special scoring value, as in piquet. [< F: lit., blank document; see CARTE², BLANK]

carte de vi·site (KART də vē zēt′), *pl.* **cartes de visite** (KART də vē zēt′). *French.* **1.** See **calling card. 2.** a miniature portrait photograph used as a visiting card.

carte du jour (kärt′ də zhŏŏr′, dōō, dyōō; *Fr.* KART DY ZHŌŌR′), *pl.* **cartes du jour** (kärts′ də zhŏŏr′, dōō, dyōō; *Fr.* KART DY ZHŌŌR′). menu (def. 1). [< F: menu of the day]

car·tel (kär tel′, kär′tᵊl), *n.* **1.** an international syndicate, combine, or trust generally formed to regulate prices and output in some field of business. **2.** a written agreement between belligerents, esp. for the exchange of prisoners. **3.** (*often cap.*) (in French or Belgian politics) a group acting as a unit toward a common goal. **4.** a written challenge to a duel. [< MF < It *cartell(o)* letter of defiance, poster, equiv. to *cart(a)* CARTE² + *-ello* dim. suffix] —**car·tel′ism,** *n.*

—**Syn. 1.** monopoly, merger, combination.

car·tel·ist (kär′tel ist), *n.* **1.** a member of a cartel or an advocate of cartelization. —*adj.* **2.** Also, **car·tel·is·tic** (kär′tᵊlis′tik, -te lis′-). of, pertaining to, or characteristic of a cartel. **3.** characterized by or advocating cartelization. [CARTEL + -IST]

car·tel·ize (kär′tᵊlīz′), *v.i., v.t.,* **-ized, -iz·ing.** to organize into a business cartel. [CARTEL + -IZE] —**car′tel·i·za′tion,** *n.*

Car·ter (kär′tər), *n.* **1. Don(ald James),** born 1926, U.S. bowler. **2. Hod·ding** (hod′ing), 1907–72, U.S. journalist and publisher. **3. Howard,** 1873–1939, English Egyptologist. **4. Jimmy** (*James Earl, Jr.*), born 1924, 39th president of the U.S. 1977–81. **5. Mrs. Leslie** (*Caroline Louise Dudley*), 1862–1937, U.S. actress. **6. Nick,** pen name of authors who wrote detective-story series in which Nick Carter, created by John R. Coryell, is the main character. **7.** a boy's given name.

Car·ter·et (kär′tər it *or, for 2,* kär′tə ret′), *n.* **1. John, Earl of Granville,** 1690–1763, British statesman and orator. **2.** a city in NE New Jersey. 20,502 (1960).

Car·ters·ville (kär′tərz vil′), *n.* a town in NW Georgia. 8668 (1960).

Car·ter·ville (kär′tər vil′), *n.* a town in S Illinois. 2643 (1960).

Car·te·sian (kär tē′zhən), *adj.* **1.** of or pertaining to Descartes, to his mathematical methods, or to his philosophy, esp. with regard to its emphasis on logical analysis, and its mechanistic interpretation of physical nature. —*n.* **2.** one who advocates the philosophy of Descartes. [< NL *Cartesiān(us),* equiv. to *Cartesi(us)* (Latinization of DESCARTES) + *-ānus* -AN] —**Carte′sian·ism,** *n.*

Carte′sian coor′dinates, *Math.* a system of coordinates for locating a point on a plane by its distance from each of two intersecting lines, or in space by its distance from each of three planes intersecting at a point.

Carte′sian div′er, a device used in various physical demonstrations and as a toy, consisting of a vertical glass tube, closed at the bottom and filled with water with an airtight membrane over the top, containing a hollow object that is open at the bottom and has enough air entrapped to allow it to float. Variations in pressure on the membrane affect the relative density of the air in the object, thus affecting its buoyancy and causing it to sink or rise. Also called **Carte′sian dev′il, bottle imp.**

Carte′sian doubt′, *Philos.* willful suspension of all interpretations of experience that are not absolutely certain. Used as a method of deriving, by elimination of such uncertainties, axioms upon which to base theories.

Carte′sian prod′uct, *Math.* the collection of all ordered pairs of two given sets such that the first elements of the pairs are chosen from one set and the second elements from the other set: this procedure generalizes to an infinite number of sets.

Car·thage (kär′thij), *n.* **1.** an ancient city-state in N Africa, near modern Tunis: founded by the Phoenicians in the middle of the 9th century B.C.; destroyed in 146 B.C. in the last of the Punic Wars. **2.** a town in E Texas. 5262 (1960). **3.** a town in N New York. 4216 (1960). **4.** a town in W Illinois. 3325 (1960). —**Car·tha·gin·i·an** (kär′thə jin′ē ən), *adj., n.*

CORSICA
Rome
ITALY
SARDINIA
TYRRHENIAN SEA
MEDITERRANEAN SEA
SICILY
Carthage
AFRICA

Car·thal (kär′thəl), *n.* a boy's given name.

cart′ horse′, a strong horse bred to draw heavy loads.

Car·thu·sian (kär thōō′zhən), *Rom. Cath. Ch.* —*n.* **1.** a member of an austere monastic order founded by St. Bruno in 1086 near Grenoble, France. —*adj.* **2.** of or pertaining to the Carthusians. [< ML *Cartusiān(us)* by metathesis for *Catursiānus,* sing. of *Catursiānī (montēs)* district in Dauphiné where the order was founded; r. ME *charthous*]

Car·tier (KAR tyā′), *n.* **Jacques** (zhäk), 1491–1557, French navigator and explorer of Canada: discovered the St. Lawrence River.

Car·tier-Bres·son (KAR tyā bre sôN′), *n.* **Hen·ri** (äN rē′), born 1908, French photographer.

car·ti·lage (kär′tᵊlij, kärt′lij), *n. Anat., Zool.* **1.** a firm, elastic, flexible type of connective tissue of a translucent whitish or yellowish color; gristle. **2.** a part or structure composed of cartilage. [< L *cartilāg(ō)* gristle; akin to CRATE]

car′tilage bone′, a bone that develops from cartilage. Cf. **membrane bone.**

car·ti·lag·i·nous (kär′tᵊlaj′ə nəs), *adj.* **1.** of or resembling cartilage. **2.** *Zool.* having the skeleton composed mostly of cartilage, as sharks and rays. [< L *cartilāginōs(us),* equiv. to *cartilāgin-* (s. of *cartilāgō*) CARTILAGE + *-ōsus* -OUS]

cartilag′inous quit′tor, *Vet. Pathol.* a purulent infection of horses and other hoofed animals, characterized by chronic inflammation of the lateral cartilage of the foot and formation of fistulas that open above the coronet, usually resulting in lameness.

Car·tist (kär′tist), *n. Rare.* (in Spain and Portugal) a supporter of the constitution. [< Sp *cartist(a),* equiv. to *cart(a)* document + *-ista* -IST]

cart·load (kärt′lōd′), *n.* the amount a cart can hold. [CART + LOAD]

car·to·gram (kär′tə gram′), *n.* a diagrammatic presentation in highly abstracted or simplified form, commonly of statistical data, on a map base or distorted map base. [< F *cartogramme.* See CARTE², -O-, -GRAM¹]

car·tog·ra·phy (kär tog′rə fē), *n.* the production of maps, including construction of projections, design, compilation, drafting, and reproduction. Also, **chartography.** [< L *c(h)art(a)* CARTE² + -O- + -GRAPHY] —**car·to·graph** (kär′tə graf′, -gräf′), *n.* —**car·tog′ra·pher,** *n.* —**car·to·graph·ic** (kär′tə graf′ik), **car′to·graph′i·cal,** *adj.* —**car′to·graph′i·cal·ly,** *adv.*

car·to·man·cy (kär′tə man′sē), *n.* the art of fortune-telling by means of playing cards. [< F *cartomancie,* equiv. to *carte* CARD¹ + *-o-* -O- + *-mancie* -MANCY]

car·ton (kär′tᵊn), *n.* **1.** a large cardboard box. **2.** the contents of a carton. **3.** a small disk within the bull's-eye of a target. **4.** a shot that strikes this disk. **5.** a cardboardlike substance consisting of chewed plant material often mixed with soil, made by certain insects for building nests. [< F < It *carton(e)* pasteboard; see CARTOON]

car·ton·nier (kär′tᵊn yā′; *Fr.* KAR tô nyā′), *n.*, *pl.* **-ton·niers** (-tᵊn yāz′; *Fr.* -tô nyā′). *Fr. Furniture.* an ornamental box for papers, usually for placing on a desk. Also called **serre-papier.** [< F; see CARTON, -ER²]

car·ton-pierre (*Fr.* KAR tôN pyer′), *n.* papier-mâché decorated in imitation of wood, stone, or metal, and chiefly used for ornamental statuary or decorative motifs. [< F: stone cardboard]

car·toon (kär to͞on′), *n.* **1.** a sketch or drawing, usually humorous, as in a newspaper or periodical, symbolizing, satirizing, or caricaturing some action, subject, or person of popular interest. **2.** *Fine Arts.* a full-scale design for a picture, ornamental motif or pattern, or the like, to be transferred to a fresco, tapestry, etc. **3.** See **comic strip. 4.** See **animated cartoon.** —*v.t.* **5.** to represent by a cartoon. —*v.i.* **6.** to draw cartoons. [< It *carton(e)* pasteboard, stout paper, a drawing on such paper, equiv. to *cart(a)* paper (see CARTE²) + *-one* aug. suffix] —**car·toon′ist,** *n.*

car·top·per (kär′top′ər), *n.* a small, open boat that can be carried on the top of an automobile. [CAR¹ + TOP¹ + -ER¹]

car·touche (kär to͞osh′), *n.* **1.** *Archit.* a rounded, convex surface, usually surrounded with carved ornamental scrollwork, for receiving a painted or low-relief decoration, as an escutcheon. **2.** an oval or oblong figure, as on ancient Egyptian monuments, enclosing characters which represent the name of a sovereign. **3.** the case containing the inflammable materials in certain fireworks. **4.** cartridge (def. 1). **5.** a box for cartridges. Also, **car·touch′.** [< MF < It *cartocc(io)*, equiv. to *cart(a)* paper (see CARTE²) + *-occio* aug. suffix]

car·tridge (kär′trij), *n.* **1.** Also called **cartouche.** a cylindrical case of pasteboard, metal, or the like, for holding a complete charge of powder, and often also the bullet or the shot for a rifle, machine gun, or other small arm. **2.** a case containing any explosive charge, as for blasting. **3.** any small container for powder, liquid, or gas, made for ready insertion into some device or mechanism: *an ink cartridge for a pen.* **4.** Also called **cassette, magazine.** *Photog.* a lightproof metal or plastic container for a roll of film, for rapid loading without the necessity of threading the film. **5.** *Radio.* pickup (def. 8). **6.** a flat, compact container measuring 4 x 5¼ inches and enclosing an endless loop of audio tape ¼ inch wide: playable simply by slipping into a slot in a player. [earlier *cartage*, alter. of CARTOUCHE]

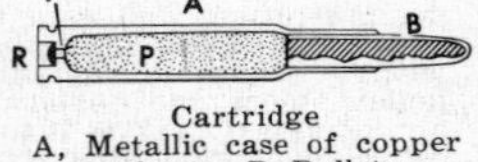

Cartridge
A, Metallic case of copper or brass; B, Bullet; R, Primer; F, Fulminate; P, Powder

car′tridge belt′, *Mil.* a belt of leather or webbing with loops for carrying cartridges or pockets for clips of cartridges.

car′tridge brass′, brass composed of about 70 percent copper and 30 percent zinc.

car′tridge clip′, a metal frame or container holding cartridges for a magazine rifle or automatic pistol. Also called **clip.**

car·tu·lar·y (kär′cho͞o ler′ē), *n.*, *pl.* **-lar·ies.** chartulary.

cart·wheel (kärt′hwēl′, -wēl′), *n.* **1.** the wheel of a cart. **2.** an acrobatic feat in which a person starts from a standing position and revolves the body sideways landing first on the hands and then on the feet and usually repeating this in a series. **3.** *Slang.* any large coin, esp. a U.S. silver dollar. [ME; see CART, WHEEL]

Cart·wright (kärt′rīt′), *n.* **1. Edmund,** 1743–1822, English clergyman: inventor of the power-driven loom. **2.** his brother, **John,** 1740–1824, English parliamentary reformer.

car·u·cate (kar′o͞o kāt′, -yo͞o-), *n.* an old English unit of land-area measurement, varying from 60 to 160 acres. [< ML *carrūcāt(a)*, equiv. to *carrūc(a)* plow (deriv. of *carrus* carriage < Celt) + *-āta* -ATE¹. See CAR¹] —**car′u·cat′ed,** *adj.*

car·un·cle (kar′ung kəl, kə rung′-), *n.* **1.** *Bot.* a protuberance at or surrounding the hilum of a seed. **2.** *Zool.* a fleshy excrescence, as on the head of a bird; a fowl's comb. **3.** *Anat.* a small, fleshy growth. [earlier *caruncula* < L, equiv. to *carun-* (var. of *carn-*, s. of *carō* flesh) + *-cula* -CULE] —**ca·run·cu·lar** (kə rung′kyᵊ lər), **ca·run′cu·lous,** *adj.*

ca·run·cu·late (kə rung′kyə lit, -lāt′), *adj.* having a caruncle. Also, **ca·run′cu·lat′ed.** [< NL *carunculāt(us)*. See CARUNCLE, -ATE¹]

Ca·rú·pa·no (kä ro͞o′pä nô), *n.* a seaport in N Venezuela. 30,684 (1960).

Ca·ru·so (kə ro͞o′sō; *It.* kä ro͞o′zô), *n.* **En·ri·co** (en rē′kō; *It.* en re′kô), 1873–1921, Italian operatic tenor.

Ca·ruth·ers·ville (kə ruth′ərz vil′), *n.* a town in SE Missouri. 8643 (1960).

car·va·crol (kär′və krôl′, -krōl′), *n.* *Chem.* a colorless, thick, oily liquid, $(CH_3)_2CHC_6H_3(CH_3)(OH)$, having a mintlike odor: used chiefly as a disinfectant, as a fungicide, and as a scent in the manufacture of perfume. [< ML *caru(i)* CARAWAY + L *acr-* (s. of *acer* sharp; see ACRID) + -OL¹]

carve (kärv), *v.*, **carved, carv·ing.** —*v.t.* **1.** to cut (a solid material) so as to form something: *to carve stone for a statue.* **2.** to form from a solid material by cutting: *to carve a statue out of stone.* **3.** to make or create for oneself (often fol. by *out*): *He carved out a career in business.* **4.** to cut into slices or pieces, as meat. —*v.i.* **5.** to carve figures, designs, etc. **6.** to cut meat. [ME *kerve(n)*, OE *ceorfan* to cut; c. MLG *kerven*, G *kerben*, Gk *gráph(ein)* (to) mark, write] —**carv′er,** *n.*

car·vel (kär′vəl), *n.* caravel. [late ME *carvile* < D *karveel* CARAVEL]

car·vel-built (kär′vəl bilt′), *adj.* *Shipbuilding.* noting a hull the shell of which is formed of planking (**car′vel plank′ing**) or plating laid close on the frames so as to present a smooth exterior. Cf. **clinker-built** (def. 2).

car′vel work′, *Shipbuilding.* planking or plating on the shell of a carvel-built hull.

carv·en (kär′vən), *adj.* *Poetic.* carved. [CARVE + -EN³; r. ME *corven*, OE *corfen* (ptp.)]

Car·ver (kär′vər), *n.* **1. George Washington,** 1864?–1943, U.S. botanist and chemist. **2. John,** 1575?–1621, Pilgrim leader: first governor of Plymouth Colony 1620–21.

Car′ver chair′, a chair of 17th-century New England, having a frame formed entirely of turned pieces, a back filled with several spindles, and no spindles between the arms and the seat. Cf. **Brewster chair.** [named after John CARVER, who owned one of this kind]

carv·ing (kär′ving), *n.* **1.** act of fashioning or producing by cutting. **2.** carved work; a carved design. [ME; see CARVE, -ING¹]

carv′ing fork′, a fork used in carving meat, commonly having two long tines and, at the base of the handle, a projection on which to rest the forefinger and thumb.

carv′ing knife′, a large, sharp knife for carving meat.

car′ wash′, a place or structure, as at a service station, having special equipment for washing automobiles.

Car·y (kâr′ē, kar′ē), *n.* **1. Alice,** 1820–71, U.S. poet (sister of Phoebe Cary). **2. (Arthur) Joyce (Lu·nel)** (lo͞on′ᵊl), 1888–1957, English novelist. **3. Henry Francis,** 1772–1844, British writer and translator. **4. Phoebe,** 1824–71, U.S. poet (sister of Alice Cary). **5.** a town in central North Carolina. 3356 (1960). **6.** a town in NE Illinois. 2530 (1960). **7.** Also, **Carey, Carry.** a boy's given name, form of **Carew. 8.** Also, **Carey, Carie, Carrie, Carry.** a girl's given name, form of **Caroline.**

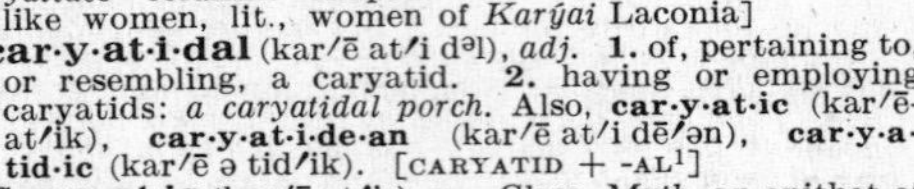
Caryatids

Car·y·a (kar′ē ə), *n.* *Class. Myth.* a Laconian maiden who was changed into a walnut tree by Dionysus.

car·y·at·id (kar′ē at′id), *n.*, *pl.* **-ids, -i·des** (-i dēz′). *Archit.* a sculptured female figure used as a column. Cf. **atlas** (def. 9). [back formation from L *Caryātides* (pl.) < Gk *Karyátides* columns shaped like women, lit., women of *Karýai* Laconia]

car·y·at·i·dal (kar′ē at′i dᵊl), *adj.* **1.** of, pertaining to, or resembling, a caryatid. **2.** having or employing caryatids: *a caryatidal porch.* Also, **car·y·at·ic** (kar′ē at′ik), **car·y·at·i·de·an** (kar′ē at′i dē′ən), **car·y·a·tid·ic** (kar′ē ə tid′ik). [CARYATID + -AL¹]

Car·y·at·is (kar′ē at′is), *n.* *Class. Myth.* an epithet of Artemis, meaning "of the walnut tree."

Car·yn (kar′in), *n.* a girl's given name. Also, **Caren, Carin, Karen, Karin, Karyn.**

caryo-, var. of **karyo-.**

car·y·o·phyl·la·ceous (kar′ē ō fə lā′shəs), *adj.* **1.** belonging to the *Caryophyllaceae* or pink family of plants. **2.** resembling the pink. [< NL *Caryophyllac(eae)* the family (*caryophyll(us)* the genus < Gk *karyóphyll(on)* clove tree; see CARYO-, -PHYLL, -ACEAE) + -OUS]

car·y·op·sis (kar′ē op′sis), *n.*, *pl.* **-ses** (-sēz), **-si·des** (-si dēz′). *Bot.* a small, one-celled, one-seeded, dry indehiscent fruit with the pericarp adherent to the seed coat, as in wheat: the typical fruit of all grasses and grains. [CARY(O)- + -OPSIS]

C.A.S., Certificate of Advanced Studies.

ca·sa (kä′sə, -sä), *n.* *Southwest U.S.* a house. [< Sp < L: hut, cabin]

ca·sa·ba (kə sä′bə), *n.* a kind of winter muskmelon, having a yellow rind and sweet, juicy flesh. Also, **cassaba.** Also called **casa′ba mel′on.** [named after *Kassaba* (now Turgutlu), town near Izmir (Smyrna) in Turkey, which exported it]

Ca·sa·bian·ca (KA ZA byäN KA′), *n.* **Louis de** (lwē də), c1755–98, French naval officer.

Ca·sa·blan·ca (kä′sä bläng′kä, kas′ə blang′kə), *n.* a seaport in NW Morocco: wartime conference of Roosevelt and Churchill January, 1943. 1,550,000 (est. 1972).

Ca·sa de Ber·nar·da Al·ba, La (*Sp.* lä kä′sä the ber när′thä äl′vä). See **House of Bernarda Alba, The.**

Ca·sa·de·sus (kä′sə dā′səs; *Fr.* KA SADᵊ SYS′), *n.* **Ro·bert** (rob′ərt; *Fr.* RÔ BER′), 1899–1972, French pianist and composer, in the U.S.

Ca·sa Gran·de (kä′sä grän′dā, -dē, -sə-), **1.** a national monument in S Arizona, near the Gila River: ruins of a prehistoric culture. **2.** a town in central Arizona. 8311 (1960).

Ca·sals (kə salz′, -sälz′, kä sälz′; *Sp.* kä säls′), *n.* **Pa·blo** (pä′blō; *Sp.* pä′vlô), 1876–1973, Spanish cellist, conductor, and composer; in France after 1936; in Puerto Rico after 1956.

Cas·a·no·va (kaz′ə nō′və, kas′-; *It.* kä′sä nô′vä), *n.* **1. Gio·van·ni Ja·co·po** (jô vän′nē yä′kô pô), 1725–98, Italian adventurer and writer. **2.** a man with a reputation for having many amorous adventures; rake; Don Juan. —**Cas·a·no·van·ic** (kaz′ə nō van′ik, kas′-), *adj.*

ca·saque (KA ZAK′), *n.*, *pl.* **-saques** (-ZAK′). *French.* a loose-fitting blouse for women.

Ca·sa·tus (kə sā′təs), *n.* a walled plain in the third quadrant of the face of the moon: about 70 miles in diameter.

Ca·sau·bon (kə sô′bən; *Fr.* KA ZŌ BÔN′), *n.* **I·saac** (ī′zək; *Fr.* ē ZAK′), 1559–1614, French classical scholar.

Cas·bah (kaz′bə, -bä, käz′-), *n.* Kasbah.

cas·ca·bel (kas′kə bel′), *n.* a knoblike projection at the rear of the breech of a muzzleloading cannon. [< Sp: little round bell, rattle(snake) < OPr *cascavel*, akin to ML *cascabellus*, equiv. to *cascab(us)* pot + *-ellus* dim. suffix]

cas·cade (kas kād′), *n.*, *v.*, **-cad·ed, -cad·ing.** —*n.* **1.** a waterfall descending over a steep, rocky surface. **2.** a series of shallow waterfalls, either natural or artificial. **3.** (in a drain or sewer) a chain of steps for dissipating the momentum of falling water in a steep place in order to maintain a steady rate of flow. **4.** an arrangement of a lightweight fabric in folds falling one over another in random or zigzag fashion. **5.** a type of firework resembling a waterfall in effect. **6.** *Chem.* a series of vessels, from each of which a liquid successively overflows to the next, thus presenting a large absorbing surface, as to a gas. **7.** *Elect.* an arrangement of component devices, as electrolytic cells, each of which feeds into the next in succession. —*v.i.* **8.** to fall in or like a cascade. —*v.t.* **9.** *Elect.* to arrange (components) in a cascade. [< F < It *cascat(a)*, equiv. to *casc(are)* (to) fall (< VL **cāsicāre*, equiv. to *cas(us)* fallen (see CASE¹) + *-icā-* formative v. suffix + *-re* inf. ending) + *-ata* -ADE¹]

Cascade′ Range′, a mountain range extending from N California to W Canada: a part of the Coast Range. Highest peak, Mt. Rainier, 14,408 ft.

Cas·ca·di·a (kas kā′dē ə), *n.* *Geol.* an extensive land mass of the Paleozoic in the Far Western U.S. [after CASCADE (RANGE) + -IA] —**Cas·ca′di·an,** *n.*, *adj.*

cas·car·a (kas kâr′ə), *n.* a buckthorn, *Rhamnus Purshiana*, of the Pacific coast of the U.S., yielding cascara sagrada. Also called **cascar′a buck′thorn, bearberry, chittamwood.** [< Sp *cáscara* bark, perh. akin to *cascar* to crack << VL **quassicāre*, equiv. to L *quass(āre)* (to) shatter (see QUASH) + *-icā-* formative v. suffix + *-re* inf. ending]

cascar′a sa·gra′da (sə grā′də, -grä′-, -grad′ə), the bark of the cascara, used as a cathartic or laxative. [< Sp: lit., sacred bark]

cas·ca·ril·la (kas′kə ril′ə), *n.* **1.** Also called **cascaril′la bark′.** the bitter aromatic bark of a West Indian, euphorbiaceous shrub, *Croton Eluteria*, used as a tonic. **2.** the shrub itself. [< Sp, equiv. to *cascar(a)* bark (see CASCARA) + *-illa* < L *-illa* dim. suffix]

cas·chrom (kas′KHRəm), *n.* *Scot., Irish Archaic.* a farm tool used to cultivate hard ground; a foot plow. [< Gael, equiv. to *cas* foot + *chrom* crooked]

Cas′co Bay′ (kas′kō), a bay in SW Maine.

case¹ (kās), *n.* **1.** an instance of the occurrence, existence, etc., of something: *This is a case of poor judgment.* **2.** the actual state of things: *That is not the case.* **3.** a question or problem of moral conduct: *a case of conscience.* **4.** situation; condition; plight: *Mine is a sad case.* **5.** a person or thing whose plight or situation calls for attention: *This family is a hardship case.* **6.** a state of things requiring discussion, decision, or investigation: *The police studied the case of the missing jewels.* **7.** a statement of facts, reasons, etc., used to support an argument: *He presented a strong case against the proposed law.* **8.** an instance of disease, injury, etc., requiring medical or surgical attention or treatment. **9.** a medical or surgical patient. **10.** *Law.* **a.** a suit or action at law; cause. **b.** a set of facts giving rise to a legal claim, or to a defense to a legal claim. **11.** *Gram.* **a.** a category in the inflection of nouns, pronouns, and adjectives, noting the syntactic relation of these words to other words in the sentence, indicated by the form or the position of the words. **b.** a set of such categories in a particular language. **c.** the meaning of or the meaning typical of such a category. **d.** such categories or their meanings collectively. **12.** *Informal.* a peculiar or unusual person: *He's a case.* **13. in any case,** regardless of circumstances; anyhow: *In any case, there won't be any necessity for you to come along.* **14. in case,** if it should happen that; if: *In case I am late, don't wait to start dinner.* **15. in case of,** in the event of: *In case of an error in judgment, the group leader will be held responsible.* **16. in no case,** under no condition; never: *He should in no case be allowed to get up until he has completely recovered from his illness.* [ME *cas*, OE *cas(us)* case (grammatical term) + OF *cas* event, etc.; both < L *cāsus*; see CASUS] —**case′less,** *adj.* —**case′less·ly,** *adv.*

—**Syn. 1.** CASE, INSTANCE, EXAMPLE, ILLUSTRATION suggest the existence or occurrence of a particular thing representative of its type. CASE and INSTANCE are closely allied in meaning, as are EXAMPLE and ILLUSTRATION. CASE is a general word, meaning a fact, occurrence, or situation typical of a class: *a case of assault and battery.* An INSTANCE is a concrete factual case which is adduced to explain a general idea: *an instance of a brawl in which an assault occurred.* An EXAMPLE is one typical case, from many similar ones, used to make clear or explain the working of a principle (what may be expected of any others of the group): *This boy is an example of the effect of strict discipline.* An ILLUSTRATION exemplifies a theory or principle similarly, except that the choice may be purely hypothetical: *The work of Seeing Eye dogs is an illustration of what is thought to be intelligence in animals.*

case² (kās), *n.*, *v.*, **cased, cas·ing.** —*n.* **1.** a container for receiving and enclosing something, as for carrying, safekeeping, etc.: *a jewel case.* **2.** a sheath or outer covering: *a knife case.* **3.** a box with its contents: *a case of ginger ale.* **4.** the amount contained in a box or other container: *There are a dozen bottles to a case.* **5.** a pair or couple; brace: *a case of pistols.* **6.** a surrounding frame or framework, as of a door. **7.** *Bookbinding.* a completed book cover ready to be fitted to form the binding of a book. **8.** *Print.* a tray of wood, metal, or plastic, divided into compartments for holding types for the use of a compositor and usually arranged in a set of two, the upper (**upper case**) for capital letters and often auxiliary types, the lower (**lower case**) for small letters and often auxiliary types, now generally replaced by the California job case. Cf. **news case. 9.** a cavity in the skull of a sperm whale, containing an oil from which spermaceti is obtained. **10.** Also called **case′ card′.** *Cards.* the last card of a suit or denomination that remains after the other cards have been played: *a case heart; the case jack.* **11.** *Faro.* casebox. **12.** *Metall.* the hard outer part of a piece of casehardened steel. —*v.t.* **13.** to put or enclose in a case; cover with a case. **14.** *U.S. Slang.* to examine or survey (a house, bank, etc.) in planning a crime: *We cased the joint and decided to pull the job on Sunday.* **15.** to fuse a layer of glass onto (glass of a contrasting color or of different properties). **16.** to cover (a surface, as of a wall, well, shaft, etc.) with a facing or lining; revet. **17.** *Bookbinding.* to bind (a book) in a case. **18.** *Cards Slang.* **a.** to arrange (cards or a pack of cards) in a dishonest manner. **b.** to remember the quantity, suit, or denomination of (the cards played). [ME *cas* < ONF *casse* < L *capsa* (book)case, equiv. to *caps-* (old fut. s. of *capere* to take) + *-a* fem. n. suffix] —**cas′er,** *n.*

ca·se·ase (kā′sē ās′), *n.* *Biochem.* a bacterial enzyme that dissolves casein. [CASE(IN) + -ASE]

ca·se·ate (kā′sē āt′), *v.i.*, **-at·ed, -at·ing.** *Pathol.* to undergo caseous degeneration; become like cheese in consistency and appearance. [< L *cāse(us)* CHEESE + -ATE¹]

ca·se·a·tion (kā′sē ā′shən), *n.* **1.** *Pathol.* transformation into a soft cheeselike mass, as of tissue in tuberculosis. **2.** *Biochem.* the formation of cheese from casein during the coagulation of milk. [CASEATE + -ION]

case′ bay′, *Carpentry.* (in a roof or floor) the section between two principals. Cf. **tail bay.**

case·book (kās′bo͝ok′), *n.* a book in which detailed records of a case are kept and from which illustrative material can be taken in the presentation of a thesis, as in a study, lecture, or the like, in law, psychology, medicine, etc. [CASE[1] + BOOK]

case·bound (kās′bound′), *adj. Bookbinding.* **1.** bound in hard covers. **2.** bound by gluing sewn sheets into a cover which has been made separately. [CASE[2] + -BOUND[1]]

case·box (kās′boks′), *n. Faro.* a device, similar to an abacus, for recording the cards as they are drawn from the dealing box. Also called **case.** [CASE[2] + BOX[1]]

ca·se·fy (kā′sə fī′), *v.t., v.i.,* **-fied, -fy·ing.** to make or become like cheese. [< L *cāse(us)* CHEESE + -FY]

case′ glass′, glass composed of two or more layers of glass in different colors, often having the top layer cut or ground away so that the lower layer can serve as background or contrast. Also, **cased′ glass′.** Also called **overlay glass.**

case·hard·en (kās′här′dən), *v.t.* **1.** *Metall.* to make the outside surface of (an alloy having an iron base) hard, leaving the interior tough and ductile by carburizing and heat treatment. **2.** to harden in spirit so as to render insensible to external impressions or influences. [CASE[2] + HARDEN]

case′ his′tory, all the relevant information or material gathered about an individual, family, group, etc., and arranged so as to serve as an organized record and have analytic value for a social worker, student, or the like: used esp. in social work, sociology, psychiatry, and medicine. Also called **case record.**

ca·sein (kā′sēn, -sē in, kā sēn′), *n.* **1.** Also called **paracasein.** *Biochem.* a protein precipitated from milk, as by rennet, and forming the basis of cheese and certain plastics. **2.** *Fine Arts.* **a.** an emulsion made from a solution of this precipitated protein, water, and ammonia carbonate. **b.** a paint in which this emulsion is used as a binder. **c.** a picture produced with this paint and emulsion. [< L *cāse(us)* cheese + -IN[2]]

ca′sein glue′, a glue made from casein, used for plywood, cabinetwork, etc.

ca·sein·o·gen (kā sē′nə jən, kā′sē in′ə-), *n. Biochem.* the principal protein of milk, converted in the presence of rennet into casein. [CASEIN + -O- + -GEN]

case·keep·er (kās′kē′pər), *n. Faro.* the person who records in the casebox a tally of cards as they appear in the box. [CASE[2] + KEEPER]

case′ knife′, **1.** a knife carried or kept in a case. **2.** a table knife.

case′ law′, law established by judicial decisions in particular cases, instead of by legislative action.

case·load (kās′lōd′), *n.* the number of cases handled by a court, an agency, a social worker, etc., either at any given moment or over a stated period. Also, **case′ load′.** [CASE[1] + LOAD]

case·mak·er (kās′mā′kər), *n.* **1.** one who or that which makes cases, esp. for books. **2.** a worker on leather articles who pastes the pieces together for sewing. [CASE[2] + MAKER]

case′mak·ing clothes′ moth′ (kās′mā′king). See under **clothes moth.**

case·mate (kās′māt′), *n.* **1.** an armored enclosure for guns in a warship. **2.** a vault or chamber, esp. in a rampart, with embrasures for artillery. [< MF < OIt *casamatt(a)*, alter. (by folk etymology) of Gk *chásmata* embrasures, lit., openings, pl. of *chásma* CHASM] —**case′mat′ed,** *adj.*

case·ment (kās′mənt), *n.* **1.** a window sash opening on hinges that are generally attached to the upright side of its frame. **2.** Also called **case′ment win′dow.** a window with such a sash or sashes. **3.** *Poetic.* any window. **4.** a casing or covering. [CASE[2] + -MENT] —**case′ment·ed,** *adj.*

Case·ment (kās′mənt), *n.* **(Sir) Roger (David),** 1864–1916, Irish patriot: hanged by the British for treason.

case′ment cloth′, a sheer fabric made of a variety of fibers, used for window curtains and as backing for heavy drapery or decorative fabrics.

case′ment door′. See **French door.**

ca·se·ose (kā′sē ōs′), *n. Biochem.* any of various soluble products formed in the gastric and pancreatic digestion of casein and caseinogen. [CASE(IN) + -OSE[2]]

ca·se·ous (kā′sē əs), *adj.* of or like cheese. [< L *cāse(us)* cheese + -OUS]

case′ rec′ord. See **case history.**

ca·sern (kə sûrn′), *n.* (formerly) a lodging for soldiers in a garrison town: barracks. Also, **ca·serne′.** [< F *caserne*, orig. small room for guardsmen < OPr *cazerna* foursome < L *quaternī* four at a time, equiv. to *quater-* (deriv. of *quattuor* FOUR) + *-nī* distributive suffix]

case′ shot′, a collection of small projectiles in a case, to be fired from a cannon. Also called **canister, canister shot.**

case′ stud′y, **1.** the gathering and organization of all relevant material to enable analysis and explication of individual units, as of a person or family. **2.** See **case history.**

case·work (kās′wûrk′), *n.* **1.** the work of investigation, advice, supervision, etc., by welfare or public assistance agencies, or the like, in cases handled by them. **2.** *Sociol.* a close study of psychological and sociological factors in the history of an individual or family in unfavorable circumstances, with a view to improving personal and family conditions. Also, **case′ work′.** [CASE[1] + WORK]

case·work·er (kās′wûr′kər), *n.* **1.** one who does casework. **2.** an investigator, esp. of a social agency, who aids individuals or families to a satisfactory adjustment chiefly by analysis of their problems and through personal counseling. Also, **case′-work′er, case′ work′er.** [CASE[1] + WORKER]

case·worm (kās′wûrm′), *n.* a caddisworm or other insect larva that constructs a case around its body. [CASE[2] + WORM]

Ca·sey (kā′zē, -sē), *n.* **1.** a town in E Illinois. 2890 (1960). **2.** a boy's given name.

cash[1] (kash), *n.* **1.** money in the form of coin or of negotiable paper, esp. that of a government. **2.** money or an equivalent, as a check, paid at the time of making a purchase. —*v.t.* **3.** to give or obtain cash for (a check, money order, etc.). **4.** *Cards.* **a.** to win (a trick) by leading an assured winner. **b.** to lead (an assured winner) in order to win a trick: *He cashed the aces and then led the queen.* **5. cash in, a.** *U.S. Informal.* to turn in and get cash for (one's chips), as in a gambling casino. **b.** *U.S. Slang.* to end or withdraw from a business agreement; convert one's assets into cash. **c.** *U.S. Slang.* to die: *After her parents cashed in, she lived with her grandmother.* **6. cash in on,** *U.S. Informal.* to profit from; turn to one's advantage: *swindlers who cash in on the credulity of the public.* **7. cash in one's chips,** *U.S. Slang.* to die. Also, *esp. Brit.,* **hand in one's checks.** [appar. back formation from CASHIER[1]] —**cash′a·ble,** *adj.* —**cash′a·ble·ness,** *n.*

cash[2] (kash), *n., pl.* **cash.** any of several low-denomination coins of China, India, and the East Indies, esp. a Chinese copper coin. [< Pg *caixa* < Tamil *kācu* copper coin < Skt *karṣa* a weight (of precious metal)]

cash-and-car·ry (kash′ən kar′ē), *adj.* **1.** sold on a basis of no credit and delivery service. **2.** operated on such a basis: *a cash-and-carry business.*

cash′ au′dit, an audit confined to cash transactions for a prescribed period, for the purpose of determining the amount of cash on hand or on deposit in a bank.

ca·shaw (kə shô′), *n.* cushaw.

cash′ ba′sis, a method of recording income and expenses, in which each item is entered as received or paid. Cf. **accrual basis.**

cash·book (kash′bo͝ok′), *n.* a book in which to record money received and paid out. [CASH[1] + BOOK]

cash·box (kash′boks′), *n.* a box or container for money, esp. one that has separate compartments for coins and bills of different denominations. [CASH[1] + BOX[1]]

cash′ crop′, **1.** any crop that is considered easily marketable, as wheat, cotton, or the like. **2.** a crop for direct sale in a market, as distinguished from a crop for use as livestock feed or for other purposes.

cash′ cus′tomer, a purchaser who pays cash.

cash′ dis′count, **1.** a term of sale by which the purchaser deducts a percentage from the bill if he pays within a stipulated period. **2.** the amount deducted.

cash·drawer (kash′drôr′), *n.* a drawer, as in a cash register, that has separate compartments for coins and bills of different denominations. [CASH[1] + DRAWER]

cash·ew (kash′o͞o, kə sho͞o′), *n.* **1.** an anacardiaceous tree, *Anacardium occidentale,* native to tropical America, whose bark yields a medicinal gum. **2.** Also called **cash′ew nut′.** the small, kidney-shaped, edible nut of this tree. [< Pg *cajú,* aph. var. of *acajú* < Tupi]

cash·ier[1] (ka shēr′), *n.* **1.** an employee, as in a market, department store, restaurant, etc., who collects payments for customer purchases, gives change, etc. **2.** an executive who has charge of money, esp. one who superintends monetary transactions, as in a bank. **3.** an employee of a business establishment who keeps a record of financial transactions. [< MD *kassier* custodian of a money-box < MF *cassier,* equiv. to *casse* money-box (< early It *cassa;* see CASE[2]) + *-ier* -IER]

cash·ier[2] (ka shēr′), *v.t.* **1.** to dismiss from a position of command or trust, esp. with disgrace. **2.** to discard; reject. [< MD *kasseren* < MF *casser* to break, discharge, annul < L *quassāre* to shatter; see QUASH]

cashier's′ check′, a check drawn by a bank on its own funds and signed by its cashier.

cash′ jour′nal, cashbook.

cash′ let′ter, *Banking.* a list or deposit slip mailed usually from one bank to another, and containing items to be credited immediately to the account of the depositing bank.

cash·mere (kazh′mēr, kash′-), *n.* **1.** the fine, downy wool at the roots of the hair of Kashmir goats of India. **2.** a garment made of this wool. **3.** a yarn made from this wool. **4.** a wool or cashmere fabric of plain or twil weave. Also, **kashmir.** [named after CASHMERE]

Cash·mere (kash mēr′), *n.* Kashmir. —**Cash·mer′i·an,** *adj. n.*

cash′ on deliv′ery. See **C.O.D.**

ca·shoo (kə sho͞o′), *n.* catechu. [var. sp. of CACHOU]

cash′ reg′ister, a cashbox with a mechanism for indicating to customers the amounts of individual sales, and with an adding machine for totaling receipts.

cash′ val′ue, *Insurance.* the nonforfeiture value of a life-insurance policy payable to the insured in cash upon its surrender. Also called **cash′ surren′der val′ue, surrender value.**

cas·i·mire (kas′ə mēr′), *n.* cassimere. Also, **cas′i·mere′.**

cas·ing (kā′sing), *n.* **1.** a case or covering. **2.** material for a case or covering. **3.** the framework around a door or window. **4.** *U.S.* the outermost covering of an automobile tire. **5.** any frame or framework. **6.** an iron pipe or tubing, esp. as used in oil and gas wells. **7.** a layer of glass that has been fused to an underlying layer of glass of a different color or of different properties. **8.** the thin, tubular membrane of the intestines of sheep, cattle, or hogs, or a synthetic facsimile, for encasing processed meat, as in making sausages, salamis, etc. **9.** *Naut.* the walls surrounding a fidley or funnel. [CASE[2] + -ING[1]]

cas′ing·head gas′ (kā′sing hed′), natural gas obtained from an oil well. [CASING + HEAD + GAS]

cas′ing knife′, a knife for trimming wallpaper in place.

cas′ing nail′, a nail having a small, conical head, slenderer than a common nail of the same length, used for laying floors, fastening matchboarding, and other work in which the head may remain visible. Cf. **finishing nail.**

ca·si·no (kə sē′nō), *n., pl.* **-nos** for 1–3. **1.** a building or large room used for meetings, entertainment, dancing, etc. **2.** such a place equipped with gambling devices, gambling tables, etc. **3.** (in Italy) a small country house or lodge. **4.** Also, **cassino.** *Cards.* a game in which cards that are face up on the table are taken with eligible cards in the hand. [< It, equiv. to *cas(a)* house + *-ino* dim. suffix]

cask (kask, käsk), *n.* **1.** a container made and shaped like a barrel, esp. one larger and stronger, for holding liquids. **2.** the quantity such a container holds: *wine at 32 guineas a cask.* —*v.t.* **3.** to place or store in a cask. [back formation from CASKET, the *-et* being taken as the dim. suffix] —**cask′like′,** *adj.*

cas·ket (kas′kit, kä′skit), *n.* **1.** *Chiefly U.S.* a coffin. **2.** a small chest or box, as for jewels. —*v.t.* **3.** to put or enclose in a casket. [late ME < ?] —**cas′ket·like′,** *adj.*

Cask′ of Amontilla′do, The, a short story (1846) by Edgar Allan Poe.

Cas·lon (kaz′lən), *n. Print.* an old-style type modeled after the types designed by William Caslon.

Cas·par (kas′pər), *n.* **1.** one of the three Magi. **2.** Also, **Casper.** a boy's given name.

Cas·par′i·an strip′ (kas pâr′ē ən), *Bot.* a thickened strip in the radial walls of some endodermal cells. [named after R. Caspary, 19th-century German botanist; see -AN]

Cas·per (kas′pər), *n.* **1.** a city in central Wyoming. 38,930 (1960). **2.** Also, **Caspar.** a boy's given name.

Cas·pi·an (kas′pē ən), *adj.* **1.** of or pertaining to the Caspian Sea. —*n.* **2.** See **Caspian Sea.**

Cas′pian Sea′, a salt lake between SE Europe and Asia: the largest inland body of water in the world. ab. 169,000 sq. mi.; 85 ft. below sea level.

casque (kask), *n.* **1.** an open, conical helmet with a nose guard, commonly used in the medieval period. **2.** any helmet-shaped head covering. **3.** *Zool.* a process or formation on the head, resembling a helmet. [< MF < Sp *casc(o)* helmet, head, earthen pot; see CASCARA] —**casqued** (kaskt), *adj.*

Cass (kas), *n.* **Lewis,** 1782–1866, U.S. statesman.

cas·sa·ba (kə sä′bə), *n.* casaba.

Cas·san·dra (kə san′drə), *n.* **1.** Also called **Alexandra.** *Class. Myth.* a daughter of Priam and Hecuba, a prophetess cursed by Apollo so that her prophecies, though true, were fated never to be believed. **2.** one who prophesies doom or disaster. **3.** a girl's given name.

Cas·san·der (kə san′dər), *n.* c354–297 B.C., king of Macedonia 301–297 (son of Antipater).

cas·sa·pan·ca (kas′ə pang′kə), *n.* a carved bench of the Italian Renaissance, the seat of which is used as a chest. [< It, equiv. to *cassa* box, chest (see CASE[2]) + *panca,* var. of *banka* bench; see BANK[2]]

cas·sa·reep (kas′ə rēp′), *n.* the juice of bitter cassava root, boiled down to a syrup and used as a flavoring for food, esp. in West Indian cookery. [apocopated var. of *cassarepo* < Carib]

cas·sa·tion (ka sā′shən, kə-), *n.* **1.** annulment; cancellation; reversal. **2.** *Music.* an 18th-century instrumental suite for outdoor performance, similar to the divertimento and the serenade. [ME *cassacio(u)n* < LL *cassātiōn-* (s. of *cassātiō*), equiv. to *cassāt(us)* annulled, ptp. of *cassāre* (*cass-* annul, var. of L *quass-;* see QUASH + *-ātus* -ATE[1]) + *-iōn-* -ION]

Cas·satt (kə sat′), *n.* **Mary,** 1845–1926, U.S. painter.

cas·sa·va (kə sä′və), *n.* **1.** any of several tropical euphorbiaceous plants of the genus *Manihot,* as *M. esculenta* **(bitter cassava)** and *M. dulcis* **(sweet cassava),** cultivated for their tuberous roots, which yield important food products. **2.** a nutritious starch from the roots, the source of tapioca. [< Sp *cazabe* cassava bread or meal < Taino *caçábi*]

Cas′se·grain′i·an tel′escope (kas′ə grā′nē ən, kas′-), *Astron.* a reflecting telescope in which the light, passing through a central opening in the primary mirror, is brought into focus a short distance behind it by a secondary mirror. Also called **Cas′se·grain tel′escope** (kas′ə grān′, kas′ə grān′). [named after N. Cassegrain, 17th-century French scientist, its inventor; see -IAN]

Cas·sel (kas′əl; *Ger.* käs′əl), *n.* Kassel.

Cas′sel brown′, (*sometimes l.c.*) See **Vandyke brown.** Also called **Cas′sel earth′.** [after CASSEL]

Cas′sel yel′low, a lemon-yellow color. [see CASSEL BROWN]

cas·se·role (kas′ə rōl′), *n., v.,* **-roled, -rol·ing.** —*n.* **1.** a baking dish of glass, pottery, etc., usually with a cover. **2.** any food, usually a mixture, cooked in such a dish. **3.** a small dish with a handle, used in chemica laboratories. **4.** *Chiefly Brit.* a stewpan. —*v.t.* **5.** to bake or cook (food) in a casserole. [< F: ladlelike pan, equiv. to *casse* ladle (< OPr *cass(a)* < LL *cattia* < Gk *kyáthia,* neut. pl. (taken as fem. sing.) of *kyáthion,* equiv. to *kýath(os)* cup + *-ion* dim. suffix) + *-(e)role* dim. suffix; see -REL]

cas·sette (kə set′, ka-), *n.* **1.** a compact case measuring 2½ x 4 inches and enclosing a length of audio tape, 1/7 inch wide, that runs between two reels: recordable or playable simply by pushing into a holder in a recorder or player. **2.** a similar compact case of larger size enclosing a length of wider tape for video recording or reproduction. **3.** *Photog.* cartridge (def. 4). [< F, equiv. to *casse* box (see CASE[2]) + *-ette* -ETTE]

cas·sia (kash′ə, kas′ē ə), *n.* **1.** Also called **cas′sia bark′, Chinese cinnamon.** a variety of cinnamon derived from the cassia-bark tree. **2.** any of the caesalpiniaceous herbs, shrubs, and trees of the genus *Cassia,* as *C. Fistula,* an ornamental tropical tree having long pods whose pulp is a mild laxative, and *C. acutifolia* and *C. angustifolia,* which yield senna. **3.** Also called **cas′sia pods′.** the pods of this tree. **4.** Also called **cas′sia pulp′.** the pulp of these pods. [ME, *cas(s)ia,* OE < L < Gk *kas(s)ía* < Sem; cf. Heb *qeṣīʿāh*]

cas′sia-bark tree′ (kash′ə bärk′, kas′ē ə-), a lauraceous tree, *Cinnamomum Cassia,* of eastern Asia.

cas·sie (kas′ē), *n.* huisache. [< F < Pr *caci(o),* for *acacio* ACACIA]

Cas·sie (kas′ē), *n.* a boy's or girl's given name, form of **Cass.**

cas·si·mere (kas′ə mēr′), *n.* a twill-weave, worsted suiting fabric, often with a striped pattern. Also, **casimere, casimire.** [var. of CASHMERE]

Cas·si·ni (kə sē′nē, kä-), *n.* **1. Oleg** (*Oleg Cassini-Loiewski*), born 1913, U.S. fashion designer and businessman, born in France. **2.** a walled plain in the first quadrant of the face of the moon: about 36 miles in diameter. **3.** See **ovals of Cassini.**

cas·si·no (kə sē′nō), *n.* casino (def. 4).

Cas·si·no (kə sē′nō; *It.* käs sē′nô), *n.* a town in SE Latium, in central Italy, NNW of Naples: site of Monte Cassino. 21,105 (1961).

Cas·si·o·do·rus (kas′ē ə dōr′əs, -dôr′-), *n.* **Flavius Magnus Aurelius,** died A.D. 575, Roman statesman and writer.

Cas·si·o·pe (kə sī′ə pē′), *n.* **1.** any evergreen, ericaceous shrub of the genus *Cassiope,* having white or pinkish flowers and scalelike or needlelike leaves. **2.** Cassiopeia. [< NL, L < Gk *Kassiópē* CASSIOPEIA]

Cas·si·o·pe·ia (kas′ē ə pē′ə), *n., gen.* **-pe·iae** (-pē′ē) for 1. **1.** *Astron.* a northern constellation between Cepheus and Perseus. **2.** *Class. Myth.* the wife of Cepheus and mother of Andromeda. Also, **Cas′si·e·pe′a, Cassiope, Cas′si·o·pe′a.** [< L < Gk *Kassiópeia,* var. of *Kassiópē;* see CASSIOPE] —**Cas′si·o·pe′ian, Cas′si·e·pe′an, Cas′si·o·pe′an,** *adj.*

Cas′siope′ia's Chair′, the most conspicuous group of stars in the constellation Cassiopeia, resembling the outline of a chair.

Cas·si·rer (kä sēr′ər, kə-), *n.* **Ernst** (ûrnst, ernst), 1874–1945, German philosopher.

cassis (kä sēs′), *n. French.* a syrup flavored with black currants, used in beverages and desserts. Cf. **crème de cassis, vermouth cassis.**

Cas·site (kas′īt), *n.* Kassite.

cas·sit·er·ite (kə sit′ə rīt′), *n.* a common mineral, tin dioxide, SnO_2; tinstone: the principal ore of tin. [< Gk *kassíter(os)* tin + -ITE[1]]

Cas·sius (kash′əs), *n.* a boy's given name.

Cas′sius Lon·gi′nus (lon jī′nəs), **Ga·ius** (gā′əs), died 42 B.C., Roman general: leader of the conspiracy against Julius Caesar.

cas·sock (kas′ək), *n.* **1.** a long, close-fitting garment worn by clergymen or laymen participating in church services. **2.** a lightweight, double-breasted ecclesiastical coat or jacket, usually of black silk, worn under the Geneva gown. **3.** a clergyman. [< MF *casaque* < early It *casacc(a)* long coat, perh., equiv. to *cas(a)* house + *-acca* n. suffix; for sense, cf. HOUSING[2] and see CHASUBLE]

cas·sol·ette (kas′ə let′), *n.* a container for cooking and serving an individual portion of food, usually made of pottery, silver, or paper, or sometimes of baked dough. [< F < OPr *casolet(a),* equiv. to *casol(a)* (*cass(a)* pan, ladle + *-ola* dim. suffix) + *-eta* -ETTE; see CASSEROLE]

cas·so·ne (kə sō′nē; *It.* käs sô′ne), *n., pl.* **-ni** (-nē). a large Italian chest of the Middle Ages and Renaissance, usually highly ornamented. [< It, equiv. to *cass(a)* box (see CASE[2]) + *-one* aug. suffix]

cas·soon (kə sōōn′), *n.* caisson (def. 6). [< It *casson(e)* CAISSON]

cas·sou·let (kas′ə lā′; *Fr.* KA sōō le′), *n.* a white-bean stew of French origin, often containing pork, mutton, garlic sausage, and preserved goose or duck. [< dial. F: stone dish < Pr, dim. of *cassolo* earthen pan, dish; see CASSOLETTE]

cas·so·war·y (kas′ə wer′ē), *n., pl.* **-war·ies.** any of several large flightless, ratite birds of the genus *Casuarius,* of Australia, New Guinea, and adjacent islands, characterized by a bony casque on the front of the head. [< Malay *kasuārī*]

Cassowary, *Casuarius casuarius* (Height 5 ft.)

cast[1] (kast, käst), *v.,* **cast, cast·ing,** *n., adj.* —*v.t.* **1.** to throw or hurl; fling: *The gambler cast the dice.* **2.** to throw off or away: *He cast the advertisement in the wastebasket.* **3.** to direct (the eye, glance, etc.), esp. in a cursory manner: *She cast her eyes down the page.* **4.** to cause to fall upon something or in a certain direction; send forth: *to cast a soft light; to cast a spell; to cast doubts.* **5.** to draw (lots), as in telling fortunes. **6.** *Angling.* **a.** to throw out (a fishing line, net, bait, etc.): *The fisherman cast his line.* **b.** to fish in (a stream, an area, etc.): *He has often cast this brook.* **7.** to throw down or bring to the ground: *She cast herself on the sofa.* **8.** to part with; lose: *The horse cast a shoe.* **9.** to shed or drop (hair, fruit, etc.): *The snake cast its skin.* **10.** (of an animal) to bring forth (young), esp. abortively. **11.** to send off (a swarm), as bees do. **12.** to throw or set aside; discard or reject; dismiss: *He cast the problem from his mind.* **13.** to throw forth, as from within; emit or eject; vomit. **14.** to throw up (earth, sod, etc.), as with a shovel. **15.** to put or place, esp. hastily or forcibly: *to cast someone in prison.* **16.** to deposit or give (a ballot or vote). **17.** to bestow; confer: *to cast blessings upon someone.* **18.** to arrange; plan out: *He cast his remarks to fit the occasion.* **19.** *Theat.* **a.** to select actors for (a play, motion picture, or the like). **b.** to allot a role to (an actor). **c.** to assign an actor to (a role). **20.** to form (an object) by pouring metal, plaster, etc., in a fluid state into a mold and letting it harden. **21.** to form (metal, plaster, etc.) into a particular shape by pouring it into a mold in a fluid state and letting it harden. **22.** to tap (a blast furnace). **23.** to compute or calculate; add, as a column of figures. **24.** to compute or calculate (a horoscope) astrologically; forecast. **25.** to turn or twist; warp. **26.** *Naut.* to turn the head of (a vessel), esp. away from the wind in getting under way. **27.** *Fox Hunting.* (of a huntsman) to lead or direct (hounds) over ground believed to have been recently traveled by a fox. **28.** *Archaic.* to contrive, devise, or plan. **29.** *Obs.* to ponder: *to cast in one's mind the weaknesses of man.* —*v.i.* **30.** to throw. **31.** to receive form in a mold. **32.** to calculate or add. **33.** to conjecture; forecast. **34.** (of hounds) to search an area for scent: *The setter cast, but found no scent.* **35.** to warp, as timber. **36.** *Naut.* (of a vessel) to turn, esp. to get the head away from the wind; tack. **37.** to select the actors for a play, motion picture, or the like. **38.** *Obs.* **a.** to consider. **b.** to plan or scheme. **39. cast about, a.** to look, as to find something; search; seek: *We cast about for something to do during the approaching summer vacation.* **b.** to scheme; plan: *He cast about how he could avoid work.* **40. cast away, a.** to reject; discard. **b.** to shipwreck. **c.** to throw away; squander: *He will cast away this money just as he has done in the past.* **41. cast back,** to refer to something past; revert to: *The composer casts back to his earlier work.* **42. cast down,** to lower; humble. **43. cast off, a.** to discard; reject. **b.** to let go or let loose, as a vessel from a mooring. **c.** *Print.* to determine the quantity of type or space that a given amount of text will occupy when set. **d.** *Textiles.* to make (the final stitches) in completing a knitted fabric. **e.** to throw (a falcon) off from the fist to pursue game. **44. cast on,** *Textiles.* to set (yarn) on a needle in order to form the initial stitches in knitting. **45. cast out,** to force out; expel; eject: *Anyone who does not come up to the standard will be cast out.* **46. cast up, a.** to add up; compute. **b.** to vomit; eject. **c.** *Chiefly Scot. Rare.* to turn up; appear: *We shall recognize the villain if he casts up in this area again.* —*n.* **47.** act of casting or throwing. **48.** that which is thrown. **49.** the distance to which a thing may be cast or thrown. **50.** *Games.* **a.** a throw of dice. **b.** the number rolled. **51.** *Angling.* **a.** act of throwing a line or net onto the water. **b.** a spot for casting; a fishing place. **52.** *Hunting.* a searching of an area for a scent by hounds. **53.** a stroke of fortune; fortune or lot. **54.** a ride offered on one's way; lift. **55.** the form in which something is made or written; arrangement. **56.** *Theat.* the group of performers to whom parts are assigned. **57.** *Metall.* **a.** act of casting or founding. **b.** the quantity of metal cast at one time. **58.** something formed from a material poured into a mold in a molten or liquid state; casting. **59.** an impression or mold made from something. **60.** *Med.* a rigid surgical dressing, usually made of bandage treated with plaster of Paris. **61.** outward form; appearance. **62.** sort; kind; style. **63.** tendency; inclination. **64.** a permanent twist or turn; *to have a cast in one's eye.* **65.** a warp. **66.** a slight tinge of some color; hue; shade: *A good diamond does not have a yellowish cast.* **67.** a dash or trace; a small amount. **68.** computation; calculation; addition. **69.** a conjecture; forecast. **70.** *Zool.* one of the wormlike coils of sand passed by the lugworm or other worms. **71.** *Ornith.* pellet (def. 6). **72.** *Falconry.* a pair of hawks put in flight together. **73.** *Pathol.* effused plastic matter produced in the hollow parts of various diseased organs. **74.** low-grade, irregular wool. —*adj.* **75.** (of an animal, esp. a horse) lying in such a position that it is unable to return to its feet without assistance. [ME *cast(en)* < Scand; cf. Icel *kasta* to throw] —**cast′a·ble,** *adj.*
—**Syn. 1.** See **throw. 63.** See **turn.**

cast[2] (cäst), *adj. Brit. Obs.* chaste. [ME < L *cast(us).* See CASTE]

Cas·ta·li·a (ka stā′lē ə), *n.* **1.** a spring on Mount Parnassus in Greece, sacred to Apollo and the Muses and regarded as a source of inspiration. **2.** any source of inspiration. —**Cas·ta′li·an,** *adj.*

Cas·tal·i·des (kə stal′i dēz′), *n.pl. Class. Myth.* the Muses.

cas·ta·net (kas′tə net′), *n.* either of a pair of concave pieces of wood held in the palm of the hand and clicked together, usually to accompany dancing. [< Sp *castañet(a),* equiv. to *castañ(a)* chestnut (< L *castanea*) + *-eta* dim. suffix; see -ET, -ETTE]

Castanets

cast·a·way (kast′ə wā′, käst′-), *n.* **1.** a shipwrecked person. **2.** anything cast adrift or thrown away. **3.** an outcast. —*adj.* **4.** cast adrift. **5.** thrown away. [n., adj. use of v. phrase *cast away*]

caste (kast, käst), *n.* **1.** *Sociol.* **a.** an endogamous and hereditary social group limited to persons of the same rank, occupation, economic position, etc., and having mores distinguishing it from other such groups. **b.** any rigid system of social distinctions. **2.** *Hinduism.* any of the four social divisions, the Brahman, Kshatriya, Vaisya, and Sudra, into which Hindu society is rigidly divided, each caste having its own privileges and limitations, transferred by inheritance from one generation to the next. **3.** any class or group of society sharing common cultural features: *low caste; high caste.* **4.** social position conferred upon one by a caste system: *to lose caste.* **5.** *Entomol.* one of the distinct forms among polymorphous social insects, performing a specialized function in the colony, as a queen, worker, soldier, etc. —*adj.* **6.** of, pertaining to, or characterized by caste: *a caste society; a caste system; a caste structure.* [< Pg *cast(a)* race, breed, n. use of *casta,* fem. of *casto* < L *cast(us)* pure, CHASTE] —**caste′less,** *adj.*

Cas·tel Gan·dol·fo (kä stel′ gän dôl′fô), a village in central Italy, 15 mi. SE of Rome: papal palace serving as the summer residence of the Pope.

cas·tel·lan (kas′tᵊlən, ka stel′ən), *n.* the governor of a castle. [< L *castellān(us)* holder of a fort (orig. member of the garrison), n. use of adj., equiv. to *castell(um)* CASTLE + *-ānus* -AN; r. ME *castelain* < ONF] —**cas′tel·lan·ship′,** *n.*

Cas·tel·la·nos (käs′te yä′nôs), *n.* **Ju·lio** (hōō′lyô), 1905–47, Mexican painter.

cas·tel·la·nus (kas′tᵊlā′nəs), *adj. Meteorol.* (of a cloud) having small turrets. [< L *castellānus* CASTELLAN]

cas·tel·la·ny (kas′tᵊlā′nē), *n., pl.* **-nies. 1.** the rank, office, or jurisdiction of a castellan. **2.** the land belonging to a castle. [CASTELLAN + -Y[3]]

cas·tel·lat·ed (kas′tᵊlā′tid), *adj.* **1.** *Archit.* built like a castle, esp. with turrets and battlements. **2.** having many castles. [< ML *castellāt(us)* (see CASTLE, -ATE[1]) + -ED[2]] —**cas′tel·la′tion,** *n.*

cas′tellated beam′, a rolled metal beam the web of which is first divided by a lengthwise zigzag cut, then welded together so as to join the peaks of both halves, thus increasing its depth and strength.

cas′tellated nut′, a tall lock nut having on its outer face radial slits allowing for insertion of a cotter pin or wire through the nut and a hole in its bolt, so as to prevent the nut from coming loose. Also called **castle nut.**

cas·tel·la·tus (kas′tᵊlā′təs), *adj. Meteorol. Obs.* castellanus. [< ML *castellātus* CASTELLATED]

Cas·tel·lón de la Pla·na (käs′te lyôn′ de lä plä′nä), a seaport in E Spain. 57,632 (1955).

cas·tel·lum (ka stel′əm), *n., pl.* **cas·tel·li** (ka stel′ī). *Archaeol.* a small isolated fortress, or one of a series of such fortresses, of the ancient Romans. [< L: stronghold, equiv. to *cast(rum)* stronghold + *-ellum* dim. suffix]

Cas·tel·nuo·vo-Te·des·co (kä′stel nwô′vô te de′skô), *n.* **Ma·rio** (mä′ryô), 1895–1968, U.S. composer, born in Italy.

Cas·te·lo Bran·co (käs te′lōō brȧnn′kōō), **Hum·ber·to de A·len·car** (ōōnm bėr′tōō di ä lenn kär′), 1900–67, Brazilian general and statesman: president 1964–67.

Cas·tel·ve·tro (kas′tᵊl vet′rō; *It.* kä′stel ve′trô), *n.* **Lo·do·vi·co** (lō′də vē′kō; *It.* lô′dô vē′kô), 1505–71, Italian philologist.

caste′ mark′, 1. (in India) a mark, usually on the forehead, symbolizing and identifying caste membership. **2.** a distinctive quality, mannerism, etc., associated with a group or class and marking a person as a member.

cast·er (kas′tər, kä′stər), *n.* **1.** one who or that which casts. **2.** a small wheel on a swivel, set under a piece of furniture, a machine, etc., to facilitate moving it. **3.** a bottle or cruet for holding a condiment. **4.** a stand containing a set of such bottles. **5.** a metal container for sugar, pepper, etc., having a perforated top to permit sprinkling; dredger; muffineer. Also, **castor** (for defs. 2–5). [ME; see CAST[1], -ER[1]] —**cast′er·less,** *adj.*

Cas·ti Con·nu·bi·i (kä′stē kô nōō′bē ē′), *Latin.* Of Chaste Wedlock (opening words and the title of an encyclical of Pope Pius XI issued in 1930 on Christian marriage).

cas·ti·gate (kas′tə gāt′), *v.t.,* **-gat·ed, -gat·ing.** to punish in order to correct; criticize severely. [< L *castīgāt(us)* chastened, lit., driven to be faultless (ptp. of *castīgāre*), equiv. to *cast(us)* pure, CHASTE + *-ig-,* var. s. of *agere* to drive, incite + *-ātus* -ATE[1]] —**cas′ti·ga′tion,** *n.* —**cas′ti·ga′tive, cas·ti·ga·to·ry** (kas′tə gə tōr′ē, -tôr′ē), *adj.* —**cas′ti·ga′tor,** *n.*
—**Syn.** discipline, chastise, chasten; scold, reprove.

Bay of Biscay · France · Navarre · Aragon · Kingdom of Castile · Atlantic Ocean · Portugal · Seville · Granada · Mediterranean Sea · Africa · 1312-1492

Cas·ti·glio·ne (kä′stē lyô′ne), *n.* **Bal·das·sa·re** (bäl′däs sä′re), 1478–1529, Italian diplomat and author.

Cas·tile (ka stēl′), *n.* **1.** Spanish, **Cas·til·la** (käs tē′lyä). a former kingdom comprising most of Spain. **2.** Also called **Castile′ soap′.** a variety of mild soap, made from olive oil and sodium hydroxide. **3.** any hard soap made from fats and oils, often partly from olive oil.

Cas·til·ian (ka stil′yən), *n.* **1.** the accepted standard form of the Spanish language as spoken in Spain. **2.** the dialect of Spanish spoken in Castile. **3.** a native or inhabitant of Castile. —*adj.* **4.** of or pertaining to Castile. [CASTILE + -IAN]

Cas·ti·lla (käs tē′yä), *n.* **Ra·món** (rä môn′), 1797–1867, Peruvian general and statesman: president of Peru 1845–51 and 1855–62.

Cas·ti·lla la Nue·va (käs tē′lyä lä nwe′vä), Spanish name of **New Castile.**

Cas·ti·lla la Vie·ja (käs tē′lyä lä bye′hä), Spanish name of **Old Castile.**

Cas·ti·llo (käs tē′lyô), *n.* **An·to·nio** (än tô′nyô), (*Antonio Cánovas del Castillo del Rey*), born 1908, Spanish fashion designer.

cast·ing (kas′ting, kä′sting), *n.* **1.** the act or process of one who or that which casts. **2.** that which is cast; any article which has been cast in a mold. **3.** the act or process of choosing actors to play the various roles in a theatrical production, motion picture, etc. **4.** the act or skill of throwing a fishing line out over the water by means of a rod and reel: *I'll have to improve my casting if I'm ever going to learn to fish well.* **5.** *Zool.* that which is cast out or off, as a cast. [ME; see CAST[1], -ING[1]]

cast′ing couch′, *Facetious.* a couch in the office of a casting director for him to indulge in amorous dalliance with actresses willing to trade sexual favors for roles in a theatrical production, motion picture, etc.

cast′ing direc′tor, the person responsible for selecting the cast of a theatrical production, motion picture, etc.

cast′ing vote′, the deciding vote of the presiding officer of a deliberative body, made when the other votes are equally divided. Also called **cast′ing voice′.**

cast′ing wheel′, *Foundry.* a wheel having on its circumference molds for receiving molten metal.

cast′ i′ron, an alloy of iron, carbon, and other elements, cast as a soft and strong, or as a hard and brittle iron, depending on the mixture and methods of molding. [*cast* (ptp. of CAST[1]) + IRON]

cast-i·ron (kast′ī′ərn, käst′-), *adj.* **1.** made of cast iron. **2.** inflexible; rigid; unyielding: *a cast-iron regulation.* **3.** strong; hardy: *a cast-iron stomach.*

cast-i·ron-plant (kast′ī′ərn plant′, käst′ī′ərn plänt′), *n.* a hardy foliage plant, *Aspidistra elatior,* of southern China, having long, stiff, leathery leaves and small, bell-shaped, dull brown or purplish-brown flowers.

cas·tle (kas′əl, kä′səl), *n., v.,* **-tled, -tling.** —*n.* **1.** a fortified residence, as of a prince or noble in feudal times. **2.** the chief and strongest part of the fortifications of a medieval city. **3.** a strongly fortified, permanently garrisoned stronghold. **4.** a large and stately residence, esp. one which imitates the forms of a medieval castle. **5.** *Chess.* the rook. —*v.t.* **6.** to place or enclose in or as in a castle. **7.** *Chess.* to move (the king) in castling. —*v.i. Chess.* **8.** to move the king two squares horizontally and bring the appropriate rook to the first square the king has passed over. **9.** (of the king) to be moved in this manner. [ME, OE *castel* < L *castell(um)* stronghold (in LL, also village), equiv. to *cast(rum)* fortress + *-ellum* dim. suffix] —**cas′tle·like′,** *adj.*
—**Syn. 1.** fortress, citadel. **4.** palace, château, mansion.

Castle, The, a novel (1926) by Franz Kafka. German, **Das Schloss.**

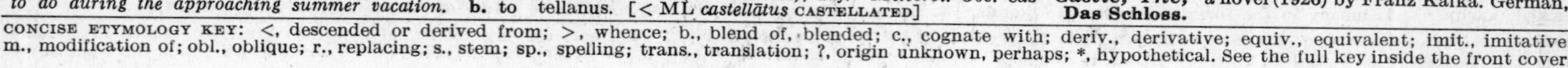

CONCISE ETYMOLOGY KEY: <, descended or derived from; >, whence; b., blend of, blended; c., cognate with; deriv., derivative; equiv., equivalent; imit., imitative; m., modification of; obl., oblique; r., replacing; s., stem; sp., spelling; trans., translation; ?, origin unknown, perhaps; *, hypothetical. See the full key inside the front cover.

cas′tle in the air′, a fanciful or impractical scheme; daydream: *Her estate in the country was only a castle in the air.* Also called **air castle, cas′tle in Spain′.**

cas′tle nut′. See **castellated nut.**

Cas′tle of O·tran′to, The (ə tran′tō), a Gothic novel (1764) by Horace Walpole.

Cas·tle·reagh (kas′əl rā′, kä′səl-), *n.* **Robert Stewart, Viscount** (*2nd Marquess of Londonderry*), 1769–1822, British statesman.

Cas′tle walk′, a popular ballroom dance of the 1920's, performed by couples and consisting of a sedate step to each beat. [named after Vernon and Irene *Castle*, entertainers and dancers of the 1920's]

cast·off (kast′ôf′, -of′, käst′-), *adj.* **1.** thrown away; rejected; discarded: *castoff clothing.* —*n.* **2.** a person or thing that has been cast off. **3.** *Print.* the estimate by a compositor of how many pages copy will occupy when set in type. [adj., n. use of v. phrase *cast off*]

cas·tor[1] (kas′tər, kä′stər), *n.* **1.** Also, **castoreum.** a brownish, unctuous substance with a strong, penetrating odor, secreted by certain glands in the groin of the beaver, used in medicine and perfumery. **2.** a hat made of beaver or rabbit fur. **3.** a heavy woolen cloth used mainly for coats. **4.** a beaver. [< L < Gk *kástōr* beaver]

cas·tor[2] (kas′tər, kä′stər), *n.* caster (defs. 2–4).

Cas·tor (kas′tər, kä′stər), *n.* *Astron.* a star of the second magnitude in the constellation Gemini, the more northerly of the two bright stars in this constellation. [named after *Castor*; see CASTOR AND POLLUX]

Cas′tor and Pol′lux, *Class. Myth.* twin sons of Leda and brothers of Helen, famous for their fraternal affection and regarded as the protectors of persons at sea. Pollux, who was immortal, spent alternate days with the gods and with his brother in Hades.

cas′tor bean′, **1.** the seed of the castor-oil plant. **2.** See **castor-oil plant.** [short for *castor-oil bean*] —**cas′tor-bean′,** *adj.*

Cas·tor·es (ka stôr′ēz), *n.pl.* See **Castor and Pollux.** [< L, pl. of *Castor*]

cas·tor·e·um (ka stôr′ē əm, -stōr′-), *n.* castor[1] (def. 1). [< L < Gk *kastórion*, equiv. to *kastor-* (s. of *kástōr*) beaver + *-ion*, neut. of *-ios* adj. suffix]

cas′tor oil′, a colorless to pale yellow, viscid liquid, usually obtained from the castor bean by a pressing process: used as a lubricant, in the manufacture of certain soaps and creams, and in medicine chiefly as a cathartic. Also called **ricinus oil.** [*castor* (? var. sp. of CASTER) + OIL; perh. so called because of its purgative effect]

cas′tor-oil′ plant′ (kas′tər oil′, kä′stər-), a tall euphorbiaceous plant, *Ricinus communis*, native to India but widely naturalized, bearing a seed that yields castor oil.

cas′tor sug′ar, *Chiefly Brit.* finely ground or powdered sugar.

cas·tra·me·ta·tion (kas′trə mə tā′shən), *n.* the act or process of laying out of military camps. [< ML *castrāmētātiōn-* (s. of *castrāmētātiō*), equiv. to L *castr(a)* camp + *mētāt(us)* laid out (ptp. of *mētārī*; see -ATE[1]) + *-iōn-* -ION]

cas·trate (kas′trāt), *v.t.*, **-trat·ed, -trat·ing.** **1.** to remove the testes of; emasculate. **2.** to remove the ovaries of. **3.** to deprive (a book, text, etc.) of effect or import by deleting certain parts; expurgate. [< L *castrāt(us)* gelded (ptp. of *castrāre*), equiv. to *castr-* geld + *-ātus* -ATE[1]] —**cas·tra′tion,** *n.* —**cas′tra·tor,** *n.*

castra′tion com′plex, *Psychoanal.* an unconscious fear of losing the genital organs, esp. as punishment for oedipal feelings.

cas·tra·to (ka strä′tō, kə-; *It.* kä strä′tô), *n., pl.* **-ti** (-tē). a male singer, esp. in the 18th century, castrated before puberty to prevent his soprano or contralto voice range from changing. [< It < L *castrāt(us)*; see CASTRATE]

Cas·tro (kas′trō; *Sp.* käs′trô), *n.* **Fi·del** (fi del′; *Sp.* fē thel′), (*Fidel Castro Ruz*), born 1927, Cuban lawyer and revolutionary: prime minister since 1959.

Ca·strop-Rau·xel (*Ger.* kä′strôp rouk′səl), *n.* a city in central North Rhine-Westphalia, in W West Germany. 88,500 (1963). Also, **Kastrop-Rauxel.**

Cas′tro Val′ley (kas′trō), a town in W California, near San Francisco Bay. 37,120 (1960).

Cas·tro·ville (kas′trō vil′), *n.* a town in W California. 2838 (1960).

cast′ steel′, any of various steels cast in molds to form objects. —**cast′-steel′,** *adj.*

cas·u·al (kazh′o͞o əl), *adj.* **1.** happening by chance: *a casual meeting.* **2.** without definite or serious intention; offhand: *a casual remark; a casual encounter.* **3.** seeming or tending to be indifferent to what is happening; apathetic; unconcerned: *a casual, nonchalant air.* **4.** (of clothes) appropriate for wearing at home; informal: *casual attire; casual wear.* **5.** irregular; occasional: *a casual criminal; a casual visitor.* **6.** accidental: *a casual mishap.* **7.** *Brit.* pertaining to persons receiving charity or work from a district in which they do not permanently live. **8.** *Obs.* uncertain. —*n.* **9.** a worker employed only irregularly. **10.** *Brit.* one who receives occasional charity from a government agency or church but is not on permanent relief. **11.** a soldier temporarily at a station or other place of duty, and usually en route to another station. [ME < L *cāsuāl(is)*, equiv. to *cāsu(s)* CASE[1] + *-ālis* -AL[1]; r. ME *casuel* < MF] —**cas′u·al·ly,** *adv.* —**cas′u·al·ness,** *n.*
—**Syn. 1.** unexpected, fortuitous, unforeseen. See **accidental. 5.** random. —**Ant. 1.** planned. **2.** deliberate.

cas′ual house′, *Brit.* **1.** a charity ward or home where the impoverished may obtain food and sometimes lodging. **2.** any place from which free food or clothing is dispensed to the poor.

cas·u·al·ism (kazh′o͞o ə liz′əm), *n.* *Philos.* the doctrine that all events happen by chance. [CASUAL + -ISM] —**cas′u·al·ist,** *n.*

cas·u·al·ty (kazh′o͞o əl tē), *n., pl.* **-ties.** **1.** *Mil.* **a.** a member of the armed forces lost to his unit through death, wounds, sickness, capture, or because his whereabouts or condition cannot be determined. **b. casualties,** loss in numerical strength through any cause, as death, wounds, sickness, capture, or desertion. **2.** one who is injured or killed in an accident: *There were no casualties in the traffic accident.* **3.** an unfortunate accident, esp. one involving bodily injury or death; mishap. **4.** any person, group, thing, etc., that is harmed or destroyed as a result of some act or event: *Their house was a casualty of the new road through town.* [CASUAL + -TY[2]; r. ME *casuelte*, equiv. to *casuel* (see CASUAL) + *-te* -TY[2]]

cas′ualty insur′ance, insurance providing coverage against accident and property damages, as automobile, theft, liability, and explosion insurance, but not including life insurance, fire insurance, or marine insurance.

cas′ual ward′, *Brit.* a ward in a workhouse reserved for vagrants in need of temporary public aid.

cas′ual wa′ter, water that has accumulated on a golf course, as after a rain, that is not a set hazard of the course.

cas·u·ist (kazh′o͞o ist), *n.* **1.** one who studies and resolves moral problems of judgments or conduct arising in specific situations. **2.** an oversubtle or disingenuous reasoner, esp. in questions of morality. [< Sp *casuist(a)* < L *cāsu(s)* CASE[1] + *-ista* -IST]

cas·u·is·tic (kazh′o͞o is′tik), *adj.* **1.** pertaining to casuists or casuistry. **2.** oversubtle; intellectually dishonest; sophistical: *casuistic distinctions.* Also, **cas′u·is′ti·cal.** [CASUIST + -IC] —**cas′u·is′ti·cal·ly,** *adv.*

cas·u·ist·ry (kazh′o͞o i strē), *n., pl.* **-ries.** **1.** application of general ethical principles to particular cases of conscience or conduct. **2.** *Disparaging.* fallacious or dishonest application of such principles. **3.** a particular application of such principles. [CASUIST + -RY]

ca·sus (kä′so͞os; *Eng.* kā′səs), *n., pl.* ***ca·sus*** (kä′so͞os; *Eng.* kā′səs). *Latin.* an event or occurrence.

ca·sus bel·li (kä′so͞os bel′lē; *Eng.* kā′səs bel′ī), *pl.* ***ca·sus bel·li*** (kä′so͞os bel′lē; *Eng.* kā′səs bel′ī). *Latin.* an event or political occurrence that brings about a declaration of war.

Cas·well (kas′wəl, kaz′-), *n.* a boy's given name.

cat[1] (kat), *n., v.,* **cat·ted, cat·ting.** —*n.* **1.** a domesticated carnivore, *Felis domestica* or *F. catus*, bred in a number of varieties. **2.** the fur of this animal. **3.** any of several carnivores of the family *Felidae*, as the lion, tiger, leopard, jaguar, etc. **4.** a woman given to spiteful or malicious gossip. **5.** *Slang.* **a.** any person; guy. **b.** a devotee of jazz. **6.** a cat-o'-nine-tails. **7.** *Games.* **a.** *Chiefly Brit.* the tapering piece of wood used in the game of tipcat. **b.** *Chiefly Brit.* the game itself. **c.** See **four old cat, one old cat, three old cat, two old cat. 8.** a catboat. **9.** a catfish. **10.** *Naut.* a tackle used in hoisting an anchor to the cathead. **11.** a double tripod having six legs but resting on only three no matter how it is set down, usually used before or over a fire. **12.** *Navy Informal.* catapult (def. 2). **13.** (in medieval warfare) a movable shelter for providing protection when approaching a fortification. **14. bell the cat,** to attempt something formidable or dangerous. **15. let the cat out of the bag,** to divulge a secret: *She let the cat out of the bag, and the surprise party wasn't a surprise after all.* —*v.t.* **16.** to flog with a cat-o'-nine-tails. **17.** *Naut.* to hoist (an anchor) and secure it to a cathead. —*v.i.* **18.** *Brit. Slang.* to vomit. **19.** *Slang.* to tomcat. [ME *cat, catte*, OE *catt* (masc.), *catte* (fem.); c. Icel *köttr*; perh. < Celt, whence also LL *cattus, catta*; < < ?]

cat[2] (kat), *n.* *Slang.* a caterpillar tractor or other vehicle with a caterpillar tread. [CAT(ERPILLAR)]

CAT, clear-air turbulence: severe turbulence whose presence is not revealed by clouds, precipitation, or other visible meteorological activity.

cat., **1.** catalog; catalogue. **2.** catechism.

cata-, a prefix meaning "down," "against," "back," occurring orig. in loan words from Greek (*cataclysm; catalog; catalepsy*); on this model, used in the formation of other compound words (*catagenesis; cataphyll*). Also, **cat-, cath-, kat-, kata-, kath-.** [< Gk *kata-*, comb. form of *katá* down, through, against, according to, towards, during]

cat·a·bap·tist (kat′ə bap′tist), *n.* *Eccles.* one who is opposed to baptism. [< LGk *katabaptist(ḗs)*. See CATA-, BAPTIST]

ca·tab·a·sis (kə tab′ə sis), *n., pl.* **-ses** (-sēz′). katabasis. —**cat·a·bat·ic** (kat′ə bat′ik), *adj.*

ca·tab·o·lism (kə tab′ə liz′əm), *n.* *Biol., Physiol.* destructive metabolism; the breaking down in living organisms of more complex substances into simpler ones, with the release of energy (opposed to *anabolism*). Also, **katabolism.** [< Gk *katabol(ḗ)* a throwing down (*kata-* CATA- + *bolḗ* a throw; cf. *katabállein* to throw down) + -ISM] —**cat·a·bol·ic** (kat′ə bol′ik), *adj.* —**cat′a·bol′i·cal·ly,** *adv.*

ca·tab·o·lite (kə tab′ə līt′), *n.* *Biol., Physiol.* a product of catabolic action. [CATABOL(ISM) + -ITE[1]]

cat·a·caus·tic (kat′ə kô′stik), *Math., Optics.* —*adj.* **1.** noting a caustic surface or curve formed by the reflection of light. —*n.* **2.** a catacaustic surface or curve. [CATA- + CAUSTIC]

cat·a·chre·sis (kat′ə krē′sis), *n.* **1.** misuse or strained use of words. **2.** the employment of a word under a false form derived through folk etymology: *causeway* and *crawfish* or *crayfish* have their forms by catachresis. [< L < Gk: a misuse (akin to *katachrêsthai* to misuse), equiv. to *kata-* CATA- + *chrêsis* use (*chrê(sthai)* (to) use, need + *-sis* -SIS)] —**cat·a·chres·tic** (kat′ə kres′tik), **cat′a·chres′ti·cal,** *adj.* —**cat′a·chres′ti·cal·ly,** *adv.*

cat·a·cli·nal (kat′ə klīn′əl), *adj.* *Geol.* descending in the same direction as the dip of the surrounding strata. Cf. **anaclinal** [< Gk *kataklin(ḗs)* sloping (*kataklín(ein)* (to) slope down, equiv. to *kata-* CATA- + *klínein* to slope, + *-ēs* adj. suffix) + -AL[1]]

cat·a·clysm (kat′ə kliz′əm), *n.* **1.** any violent upheaval, esp. one of a social or political nature. **2.** *Phys. Geog.* a sudden and violent physical action producing changes in the earth's surface. **3.** an extensive flood; deluge. [< LL *cataclysm(os)* (Vulgate) < Gk *kataklysmós* flood (akin to *kataklýzein* to flood), equiv. to *kata-* CATA- + *klysmós* a washing (*klýz(ein)* (to) wash + *-mos* n. suffix)]
—**Syn. 1.** See **disaster.**

cat·a·clys·mic (kat′ə kliz′mik), *adj.* **1.** of, pertaining to, or resulting from a cataclysm. **2.** of the nature of, or having the effect of, a cataclysm: *cataclysmic changes.* Also, **cat′a·clys′mal.** [CATACLYSM + -IC] —**cat′a·clys′mi·cal·ly,** *adv.*

cat·a·comb (kat′ə kōm′), *n.* **1.** Usually, **catacombs.** an underground cemetery, esp. one consisting of tunnels and rooms with recesses dug out for coffins and tombs. **2. the Catacombs,** the subterranean burial chambers of the early Christians in and near Rome, Italy. [ME *catacombe*, OE *catacumbe* < LL *Catacumbās* (acc. pl.) < Gk **katakýmbās*, equiv. to *kata-* CATA- + *kýmbās*, acc. pl. of *kýmbē* hollow, cup] —**cat·a·cum·bal** (kat′ə kum′bəl), *adj.*

cat·a·cum·ba (kat′ə kum′bə), *n.* an atrium of an early Christian church. [< LL; see CATACOMB]

cat·a·di·op·tric (kat′ə dī op′trik), *adj.* *Optics.* pertaining to or produced by both reflection and refraction. [CATA- + DIOPTRIC]

ca·tad·ro·mous (kə tad′rə məs), *adj.* (of fish) migrating down a river to the sea to spawn (opposed to *anadromous*). [CATA- + -DROMOUS]

Cat·ae·ba·tes (kat′ə bā′tēz), *n.* *Class. Myth.* an epithet of Zeus, meaning "descender."

cat·a·falque (kat′ə falk′, -fôk′, -fôlk′), *n.* a raised structure on which the body of a deceased person lies or is carried in state. [< F < It *catafalc(o)* < LL **catafalic(um)* scaffolding, equiv. to *cata-* CATA- + *fal(a)* wooden siege tower + *-icum*, neut. of *-icus* -IC]

Catafalque

cat·a·gen·e·sis (kat′ə jen′i sis), *n.* *Biol.* the retrogressive evolution of a species. Cf. **anagenesis** (def. 1). [CATA- + GENESIS] —**cat·a·ge·net·ic** (kat′ə jə net′ik), *adj.*

Cat·a·lan (kat′əlan′, -ələn, kat′əlan′), *adj.* **1.** pertaining to Catalonia, its inhabitants, or their language. —*n.* **2.** a native or inhabitant of Catalonia. **3.** a Romance language spoken in Catalonia and related more closely to Provençal than to Spanish or French. [late ME < Sp]

cat·a·lase (kat′əlās′), *n.* *Biochem.* an enzyme that decomposes hydrogen peroxide into oxygen and water. [CATAL(YSIS) + -ASE]

cat·a·lec·tic (kat′əlek′tik), *Pros.* —*adj.* **1.** (of a line of verse) lacking part of the last foot; metrically incomplete, as the second line of *One more unfortunate,/ Weary of breath.* —*n.* **2.** a catalectic line of verse. Cf. **acatalectic, hypercatalectic.** [< LL *catalēctic(us)* < Gk *katalēktikós* incomplete, equiv. to *katalēd-*, var. s. of *katalḗgein* to leave off (*kata-* CATA- + *lḗgein* to end) + *-tikos* -TIC]

cat·a·lep·sy (kat′əlep′sē), *n.* *Pathol., Psychiatry.* a physical condition characterized by suspension of sensation, muscular rigidity, fixity of posture, and often by loss of contact with environment. Also, **cat′a·lep′sis.** [< ML *catalēpsia*, var. of LL *catalēpsis* < Gk *katálēpsis* seizure (akin to *katalambánein* to hold down), equiv. to *kata-* CATA- + *lêpsis* a grasping (*lēp-*, var. s. of *lambánein* to grasp, + *-sis* -SIS); r. ME *cathalempsia* < ML] —**cat′a·lep′tic,** *adj., n.*

Cat·a·lin (kat′əlin), *n.* *Trademark.* a synthetic resin used esp. for costume jewelry.

Cat·a·li′na Is′land (kat′əlē′nə). See **Santa Catalina.** Also called **Catalina.**

cat·a·lo (kat′əlō′), *n., pl.* **-loes, -los.** cattalo.

cat·a·log (kat′əlôg′, -əlog′), *n.* **1.** *Library Science.* a list of the contents of a library or a group of libraries, arranged according to any of various systems. Cf. **card catalog, union catalog. 2.** a list, usually in alphabetical order, with brief notes on the names, articles, etc., listed. **3.** a book, leaflet, or file containing such a list or record. —*v.t.* **4.** to enter (items) in a catalog; make a catalog of. —*v.i.* **5.** to work on a catalog. [late ME *cataloge* < LL *catalog(us)* < Gk *katálogos* a register (akin to *katalégein* to count up), equiv. to *kata-* CATA- + *-logos* reckoning] —**cat′a·log′er, cat′a·log′ist,** *n.* —**cat·a·log·ic** (kat′əloj′ik), **cat′a·log′i·cal, cat·a·lo·gis·tic** (kat′əlō jis′tik), *adj.*
—**Syn. 1.** roster, register, record. See **list**[1].

cat·a·logue (kat′əlôg′, -əlog′), *n., v.,* **-logued, -logu·ing.** catalog. —**cat′a·logu′er, cat′a·logu′ist,** *n.*

cat·a·logue rai·son·né (kat′əlôg′ rez′ə nā′, -əlog′; *Fr.* KA TA lôg′ RE zô nā′), *pl.* **ca·ta·logues rai·son·nés** (kat′əlôgz′ rez′ə nā′, -əlogz′; *Fr.* KA TA lôg′ RE zô nā′). a catalog with notes or commentary on the items listed; a classified, descriptive catalog. [< F: lit., reasoned catalog]

Cat·a·lo·ni·a (kat′əlō′nē ə, -nyə), *n.* a region in NE Spain, bordering on France and the Mediterranean: formerly a province. Spanish, **Ca·ta·lu·ña** (kä′tä lo͞o′nyä). —**Cat′a·lo′ni·an,** *adj.*

Catalo′nian jas′mine. See **Spanish jasmine.**

ca·tal·pa (kə tal′pə), *n.* any bignoniaceous tree of the genus *Catalpa*, of America and Asia, as *C. speciosa*, of the U.S., having large cordate leaves and bell-shaped white flowers. [< NL; adaptation of Carolina Creek *kutuhlpa* winged head]

cat·a·lu·fa (kat′əlo͞o′fə), *n., pl.* (*esp. collectively*) **-fa,** (*esp. referring to two or more kinds or species*) **-fas.** any of several bigeyes, as *Pristigenys serrula* **(popeye catalufa),** found in the Pacific Ocean. [< Sp < early It *cataluffa* kind of cloth made in Venice]

ca·tal·y·sis (kə tal′i sis), *n., pl.* **-ses** (-sēz′). **1.** *Chem.* the causing or accelerating of a chemical change by the addition of a substance which is not permanently affected by the reaction. **2.** an action between two or more persons or forces, initiated by an agent that itself remains unaffected by the action: *social catalyses occasioned by controversial writings.* Also, **katalysis.** [< NL < Gk *katálysis* dissolution, equiv. to *katalý(ein)* (to) dissolve (*kata-* CATA- + *lýein* to loosen) + *-sis* -SIS] —**cat·a·lyt·ic** (kat′əlit′ik), *adj., n.* —**cat′a·lyt′i·cal,** *adj.* —**cat′a·lyt′i·cal·ly,** *adv.*

cat·a·lyst (kat′əlist), *n.* **1.** *Chem.* a substance that causes catalysis. **2.** that which causes activity between two or more persons or forces without itself being affected. **3.** *Informal.* a person whose talk, enthusiasm, or energy causes others to be more friendly, enthusiastic, or energetic. Also, **katalyst.** [CATALY(SIS) + -IST]

cat·a·lyze (kat′əlīz′), *v.t.*, **-lyzed, -lyz·ing.** *Chem.* to act upon by catalysis. Also, **katalyze.** [CATALY(SIS + -I)ZE] —**cat′a·lyz′er,** *n.*

cat·a·ma·ran (kat′ə mə ran′), *n.* **1.** *Naut.* **a.** a float or sailing raft formed of a number of logs tied side by side some distance apart, used in certain parts of India, South America, etc. **b.** a vessel, usually propelled by sail, formed of two hulls or floats held side by side by a frame above them. Cf. **trimaran.** **2.** *Informal.* a quarrelsome person, esp. a woman. **3.** *Canadian Dial.* a wooden sled. [< Tamil *kaṭṭa-maram* tied wood]

Cat·a·mar·ca (kat′ə mär′kə; *Sp.* kä′tä mär′kä), *n.* a city in N Argentina. 49,291 (1960).

cat·a·me·ni·a (kat′ə mē′nē ə), *n.* (*construed as sing. or pl.*) *Physiol.* menses. [< NL < Gk *katamḗnia*, neut. pl. of Gk *katamḗni(os)* monthly, equiv. to *kata-* CATA- + *mēn* month + *-ios* -IOUS] —**cat′a·me′ni·al,** *adj.*

cat·a·mite (kat′ə mīt′), *n.* a boy kept for pederastic purposes. [< L *Catamīt(us)* < Gk *Ganymḗdēs* GANYMEDE]

Cat·a·mi·tus (kat′ə mī′təs), *n.* ancient Roman name for Ganymede.

cat·am·ne·sis (kat′am nē′sis), *n.*, *pl.* **-ses** (-sēz). a medical history following the onset of an illness. [CATA- + (ANA)MNESIS] —**cat·am·nes·tic** (kat′am nes′tik), *adj.*

cat·a·mount (kat′ə mount′), *n.* **1.** a wild animal of the cat family. **2.** *U.S.* **a.** the cougar. **b.** the lynx. **3.** catamountain. [short for CATAMOUNTAIN]

cat·a·moun·tain (kat′ə moun′tən, -tin), *n.* a wild animal of the cat family, as the European wildcat, the leopard, or panther. Also, **cat-o′-mountain.** [var. of *cat o′ mountain*, ME *cat of (the) mountaine*]

cat-and-dog (kat′ən dôg′, -dog′), *adj.* **1.** continuously or unceasingly vicious and destructive: *a cat-and-dog fight for markets; cat-and-dog competition.* **2.** *Slang.* (of a security) highly speculative and of questionable value.

cat′ and mouse′, **1.** a children's game in which players in a circle raise and lower their clasped hands to keep a player from moving into or out of the circle, and to permit a second player to move into or out of the circle in order to escape the pursuing first player. **2. play cat and mouse with, a.** to toy or trifle with. **b.** to use strategy to overpower or outwit one's opponent, esp. to await one's chance to strike: *The detective played cat and mouse with his quarry.* Also called **cat′ and rat′.**

Ca·ta·nia (kä tä′nyä), *n.* a seaport in E Sicily. 361,466 (1961).

Ca·tan·za·ro (kä′tän dzä′rô), *n.* a city in S Italy. 71,152 (1959).

cat·a·pha·sia (kat′ə fā′zhə, -zhē ə, -zē ə), *n.* *Pathol.* a speech disorder in which a person constantly repeats a word or phrase. [CATA- + -PHASIA]

cat·a·pho·re·sis (kat′ə fə rē′sis), *n.* **1.** *Med.* the causing of medicinal substances to pass through or into living tissues in the direction of flow of a positive electric current. **2.** *Physical Chem.* electrophoresis. [< NL, equiv. to *cata-* CATA- + Gk *phórēsis* a being borne, equiv. to *phorē-* (var. s. of *phorein* to bear, carry) + *-sis* -SIS] —**cat·a·pho·ret·ic** (kat′ə fə ret′ik), *adj.*

cat·a·phract[1] (kat′ə frakt′), *n.* **1.** a heavily armed war galley of ancient Greece. **2.** a suit of ancient Roman scale armor for a man or horse. **3.** *Zool.* the bony plates or scales covering the body of certain fishes or reptiles. [< L *cataphract(us)* fully armored < Gk *katáphraktos* (akin to *kataphrássein* to clothe fully in armor), equiv. to *kata-* CATA- + *phraktós* fenced, protectively clothed (*phrag-* fence + *-tos* ptp. suffix)] —**cat′a·phrac′tic,** *adj.*

cat·a·phract[2] (kat′ə frakt′), *n.* a Roman soldier who dressed in scale armor. [< L *cataphract(ēs)* coat of mail < Gk *kataphráktēs*; see CATAPHRACT[1]]

cat·a·phract·ed (kat′ə frak′tid), *adj.* *Zool.* covered with an armor of horny or bony plates or scales. [CATAPHRACT[1] + -ED[3]]

cat·a·phyll (kat′ə fil), *n.* *Bot.* a simplified leaf form, as a bud scale or a scale on a cotyledon or rhizome. [CATA- + -PHYLL] —**cat′a·phyl′la·ry,** *adj.*

cat·a·plane (kat′ə plān′), *n.* an aircraft designed to be launched by a catapult. [CATA(PULT + AIR)PLANE]

cat·a·pla·sia (kat′ə plā′zhə, -zhē ə, -zē ə), *n.* *Biol.* degeneration of a cell or tissue. Also, **kataplasia.** [CATA- + -PLASIA] —**cat·a·plas·tic** (kat′ə plas′tik), *adj.*

cat·a·plasm (kat′ə plaz′əm), *n.* *Med.* poultice. [< L *cataplasm(a)* < Gk *katáplasma*. See CATA-, -PLASM]

cat·a·pult (kat′ə pult′, -po͝olt′), *n.* **1.** an ancient military engine for hurling stones, arrows, etc. **2.** a device for launching an airplane from the deck of a ship. **3.** *Brit.* a slingshot. —*v.t.* **4.** to hurl as from a catapult. **5.** *Brit.* **a.** to hurl (a missile) from a slingshot. **b.** to hit (an object) with a missile from a slingshot. [< L *catapult(a)* < Gk *katapéltēs*, equiv. to *kata-* CATA- + *péltēs* hurler, akin to *pállein* to hurl] —**cat′a·pul′tic,** *adj.*

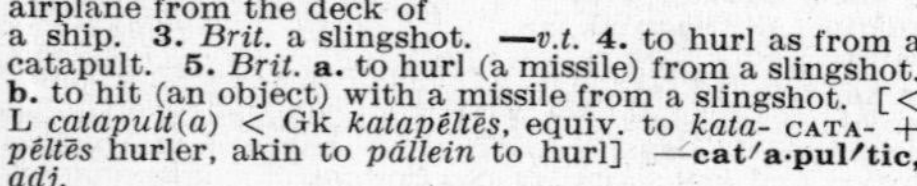
Catapult (def. 1)

cat·a·ract (kat′ə rakt′), *n.* **1.** a descent of water over a steep surface; a waterfall, esp. one of considerable size. **2.** any furious rush or downpour of water; deluge. **3.** *Ophthalm.* **a.** an abnormality of the eye, characterized by opacity of the lens. **b.** the opaque area. [ME *cataracte* < L *catar(r)act(a)* < Gk *katarrák(tēs)* waterfall, floodgate, portcullis (n.), downrushing (adj.), akin to *katarássein* to dash down, equiv. to *kat-* CATA- + *arássein* to smite] —**cat′a·rac′tal, cat′a·rac′tous,** *adj.* —**cat′a·ract′ed,** *adj.*

ca·tarrh (kə tär′), *n.* *Pathol.* inflammation of a mucous membrane, esp. of the respiratory tract, accompanied by excessive secretions. [< medical L *catarrh(us)* < Gk *katárrous*, lit., down-flowing, equiv. to *katarr(ein)* (to) flow down (*kata-* CATA- + *rhein* to flow) + *-ous*, var. of *-oos* adj. suffix] —**ca·tarrh′al, ca·tarrh′ous,** *adj.* —**ca·tarrh′al·ly,** *adv.* —**ca·tarrhed′,** *adj.*

catarrh′al fe′ver, *Vet. Pathol.* bluetongue.

catarrh′al pneumo′nia, *Pathol.* bronchopneumonia.

cat·ar·rhine (kat′ə rīn′), *adj.* **1.** belonging or pertaining to the group *Cattarrhini*, comprising the Old World monkeys, anthropoid apes, and man, having the nostrils close together and opening downward and a nonprehensile, often greatly reduced or vestigial tail. —*n.* **2.** a catarrhine animal. Also, **cat·ar·rhin·i·an** (kat′ə rin′ē ən). [< NL *Catarrhīna* kind of anthropoid < Gk *katarrhīna*, neut. pl. of *katárrhīs* hook-nosed, equiv. to *kata-* CATA- + *rhīs* nose]

Cat·a·sau·qua (kat′ə sô′kwə), *n.* a town in E Pennsylvania. 5062 (1960).

ca·tas·ta·sis (kə tas′tə sis), *n.*, *pl.* **-ses** (-sēz′). the part of a drama, preceding the catastrophe, in which the action is at its height; the climax of a play. Cf. **catastrophe** (def. 4), **epitasis, protasis.** [< Gk *katástasis* stability, akin to *kathistánai* to make stand, settle. See CATA-, STASIS]

ca·tas·tro·phe (kə tas′trə fē), *n.* **1.** a sudden and widespread disaster: *the catastrophe of war.* **2.** a final event or conclusion, usually an unfortunate one; a disastrous end: *the great catastrophe of the old South at Appomattox.* **3.** any misfortune, mishap, or failure; fiasco: *The play was so poor our whole evening was a catastrophe.* **4.** (in a drama) the point at which the circumstances overcome the central motive, introducing the close or conclusion; dénouement. Cf. **catastasis, epitasis, protasis.** **5.** a sudden, violent disturbance, esp. of a part of the surface of the earth; cataclysm. [< Gk *katastrophḗ* an overturning, akin to *katastréphein* to overturn. See CATA-, STROPHE] —**cat·a·stroph·ic** (kat′ə strof′ik), **cat′a·stroph′i·cal, cat′a·stroph′al,** *adj.* —**cat′a·stroph′i·cal·ly,** *adv.*
—**Syn. 1.** misfortune, calamity. **1, 2.** See **disaster.** —**Ant. 1, 2.** triumph.

ca·tas·tro·phism (kə tas′trə fiz′əm), *n.* *Geol.* the doctrine that certain vast geological changes in the earth's history were caused by catastrophes rather than gradual evolutionary processes. [CATASTROPHE + -ISM] —**ca·tas′tro·phist,** *n.*

cat·a·to·ni·a (kat′ə tō′nē ə), *n.* *Psychiatry.* a syndrome seen most frequently in schizophrenia, with muscular rigidity and mental stupor, sometimes alternating with great excitement and confusion. Also, **katatonia.** [< NL < Gk **katatonia*, equiv. to *kata-* CATA- + *-tonia* (*tón(os)* TONE + *-ia* -Y[3])] —**cat′a·to′ni·ac′,** *n.* —**cat·a·ton·ic** (kat′ə ton′ik), *adj.*, *n.*

Ca·taw·ba (kə tô′bə), *n.* **1.** *Hort.* **a.** a reddish variety of grape. **b.** the vine bearing this fruit, grown in the eastern U.S. **2.** a light, dry, white wine made from this grape. **3.** a Siouan language of North and South Carolina. **4.** the portion of the Wateree River in North Carolina. Cf. **Wateree.** [< Choctaw *Kataba*, dial. var. of *Katapa*, lit., (people) apart]

cat·bird (kat′bûrd′), *n.* **1.** a slate-colored North American songbird, *Dumetella carolinensis*, allied to the mockingbird, having a call resembling the mewing of a cat. **2.** *Australian* any of several birds having catlike cries. [CAT[1] + BIRD]

cat′bird seat′, an advantageous situation or condition: *His appointment as acting dean put him in the catbird seat.*

cat′ block′, *Naut.* a block used in catting an anchor.

cat·boat (kat′bōt′), *n.* a boat having one mast set well forward with a single large sail. [CAT[1] + BOAT]

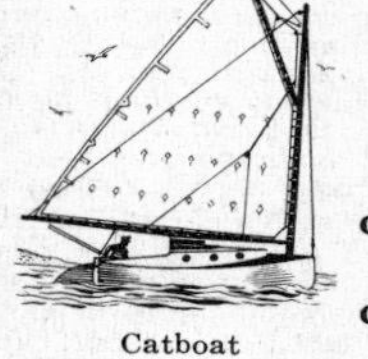
Catboat

cat′ bri′er, any of various species of smilax, as the greenbrier, *Smilax rotundifolia.* [so called because it scratches]

cat-built (kat′bilt′), *adj.* (of a sailing vessel) having a bluff bow and straight stern without a figurehead.

cat′ bur′glar, a burglar who breaks in through upstairs windows; second-story man.

cat·call (kat′kôl′), *n.* **1.** a cry like that of a cat, made by an instrument or by the human voice, used for expressing disapproval at a theater, meeting, etc. **2.** an instrument for producing such a sound. —*v.i.* **3.** to sound catcalls. —*v.t.* **4.** to express disapproval of by catcalls. [CAT[1] + CALL] —**cat′call′er,** *n.*

catch (kach), *v.*, **caught, catch·ing,** *n.*, *adj.* —*v.t.* **1.** to capture, esp. after pursuit: *to catch a criminal; to catch a runaway horse.* **2.** to trap or ensnare: *to catch a fish.* **3.** to deceive: *No one was caught by his sugary words.* **4.** to be in time to get aboard (a train, boat, etc.). **5.** to see or attend: *to catch a show.* **6.** to come upon suddenly; surprise or detect, as in some action: *I caught him doing it.* **7.** to strike; hit: *The blow caught him on the head.* **8.** to intercept and seize; take and hold (something thrown, falling, etc.): *to catch a ball; a barrel to catch rain.* **9.** to check or restrain suddenly (often used reflexively): *She caught her breath in surprise. He caught himself before he said the wrong thing.* **10.** to receive, incur, or contract: *to catch a cold.* **11.** to become inspired by or aware of: *I caught the spirit of the occasion.* **12.** to lay hold of; grasp; clasp: *He caught her arm.* **13.** to grip, hook, or entangle: *The closing door caught his arm.* **14.** to allow (something) to become gripped, hooked, snagged, or entangled: *He caught his coat on a nail.* **15.** to fasten with or as with a catch: *to catch the clasp on a necklace.* **16.** to attract or arrest: *She caught his fancy. His speech caught our attention.* **17.** to attract the attention of; captivate; charm: *She was caught by his smile and good nature.* **18.** to grasp with the intellect; comprehend: *She failed to catch his meaning.* **19.** to hear clearly: *We caught snatches of their conversation.* —*v.i.* **20.** to become gripped, hooked, or entangled: *Her foot caught in the hole.* **21.** to take hold: *The door lock catches.* **22.** to overtake someone or something moving (usually fol. by *up, up with,* or *up to*). **23.** *Baseball.* to play as catcher: *He caught for the entire game.* **24.** to become lighted; take fire; ignite: *The kindling caught instantly.* **25. catch a crab,** (in rowing) to bungle a stroke by failing to get the oar into the water at the beginning or by failing to withdraw it properly at the end. **26. catch as catch can,** in any way at all; without specific plan or order: *They lived catch as catch can.* **27. catch at,** to grasp at eagerly; accept readily: *He caught at the chance to get free tickets.* **28. catch a turn,** *Naut.* to wind a rope around a bitt, capstan, etc., for one full turn. **29. catch it,** *Informal.* to receive a reprimand or punishment: *He'll catch it from his mother for tearing his good trousers again.* **30. catch on,** *Informal.* **a.** to become popular: *That new song is beginning to catch on.* **b.** to grasp mentally; understand: *You'd think he'd catch on that he is boring us.* **31. catch up, a.** to lift or snatch suddenly: *Leaves were caught up in the wind.* **b.** to bring or get up to date (often fol. by *on* or *with*): *to catch up on one's reading.* **c.** to come up to or overtake (something or someone) (usually fol. by *with*): *to catch up with the leader in a race.* **d.** to become involved or entangled with: *caught up in the excitement of the crowd.* **e.** to point out to (a person) minor errors, untruths, etc. (usually fol. by *on*): *We caught the teacher up on a number of factual details.* **f.** *Falconry.* to capture for further training (a hawk that has been flown at hack).
—*n.* **32.** act of catching. **33.** anything that catches, esp. a device for checking motion, as a latch on a door. **34.** a slight, momentary break or crack in the voice. **35.** that which is caught, as a quantity of fish: *The fisherman brought home a large catch.* **36.** a person or thing worth getting, esp. a person regarded as a desirable matrimonial prospect: *Most of the girls think Tommy is quite a catch.* **37.** any tricky or concealed drawback: *It seems so easy that there must be a catch somewhere.* **38.** a fragment: *catches of a song.* **39.** *Music.* a round, esp. one in which the words are so arranged as to produce ludicrous effects. **40.** a game in which a ball is thrown from one person to another: *to play catch; to have a catch.* **41.** *Sports.* the catching and holding of a batted or thrown ball before it touches the ground. **42.** *Rowing.* the first part of the stroke, consisting of the placing of the oar into the water.
—*adj.* **43.** catchy (defs. 1, 2). [ME *cacche(n)* (to) chase, capture < ONF *cachie(r)* < VL **captiāre* (r. L. *captāre* to hunt, seize), equiv. to *capt(us)* taken, ptp. of *capere* (*cap-* take + *-tus* ptp. suffix) + *-iā-* suffix + *-re* inf. ending] —**catch′a·ble,** *adj.*
—**Syn. 1.** apprehend, arrest. **12.** CATCH, CLUTCH, GRASP, SEIZE imply taking hold suddenly of something. To CATCH may be to reach after and get: *He caught my hand.* To CLUTCH is to take firm hold of (often out of fear or nervousness), and retain: *The child clutched his mother's hand.* To GRASP also suggests both getting and keeping hold of, with a connotation of eagerness and alertness, rather than fear (literally or figuratively): *to grasp someone's hand in welcome; to grasp an idea.* To SEIZE implies the use of force or energy in taking hold of suddenly (literally or figuratively): *to seize a criminal; to seize an opportunity.* **17.** enchant, fascinate, win. **32.** capture, apprehension, arrest. **33.** ratchet, bolt. —**Ant. 1, 12, 32.** release.

catch·all (kach′ôl′), *n.* a bag, basket, or other receptacle for odds and ends. [n. use of v. phrase *catch all*]

catch-as-catch-can (kach′əz kach′kan′), *n.* **1.** a style of wrestling in which the contestants are permitted to trip, tackle, and use holds below the waist. Cf. **Greco-Roman** (def. 3). —*adj.* **2.** seizing or taking advantage of any opportunity that comes to hand; using any method that can be applied or that will work, esp. without prior planning or thought: *He was leading a catch-as-catch-can life, working as an itinerant handyman.* —*adv.* **3.** catch (def. 26).

catch′ ba′sin, a receptacle, located where a street gutter opens into a sewer, designed to retain matter that would not readily pass through the sewer.

catch-cord (kach′kôrd′), *n.* *Textiles.* a cord or wire located near a selvage, used to form a loop or deflect the filling yarn not intended to be woven in with the regular selvage.

catch′ crop′, a crop that reaches maturity in a relatively short time, often planted as a substitute for a crop that has failed or at a time when the ground would ordinarily lie fallow, as between the plantings of two staple crops. —**catch′ crop′ping.**

catch·er (kach′ər), *n.* **1.** one who or that which catches. **2.** *Baseball.* the player stationed behind home plate, whose chief duty is to catch pitches not hit by the batter. **3.** *Metalworking.* one who feeds metal rods through a looping mill. [ME; see CATCH, -ER[1]]

Catch′er in the Rye′, The, a novel (1951) by J. D. Salinger.

catch′er res′onator, *Electronics.* See under **Klystron.**

catch·fly (kach′flī′), *n.*, *pl.* **-flies.** any of various plants, esp. of the genus *Silene*, having a viscid secretion on the stem and calyx in which small insects are sometimes caught. [from phrase *catch (the) fly*]

catch·ing (kach′ing), *adj.* **1.** contagious or infectious: *a catching disease; His enthusiasm is catching.* **2.** attractive; fascinating; captivating; alluring: *a catching personality.* [late ME; see CATCH, -ING[2]] —**catch′ing·ly,** *adv.* —**catch′ing·ness,** *n.*

catch·light (kach′līt′), *n.* a highlight reflected from a highly polished or moist surface. [CATCH + LIGHT[1]]

catch·line (kach′līn′), *n.* **1.** a word, phrase, or sentence used esp. in advertising and journalism to arouse interest in or call attention to an item. **2.** a line in which a catchword appears. **3.** a line of lesser importance, set shorter or sometimes in smaller type than the lines above and beneath it. **4.** *Theat.* a line of comic dialogue expected to elicit laughter and gain popularity. **5.** *Journalism.* slug[1] (def. 9a). [CATCH + LINE[1]]

catch·ment (kach′mənt), *n.* **1.** act of catching water. **2.** that which catches water, as a reservoir or basin. **3.** the water that is caught in such a catchment. [CATCH + -MENT]

catch′ment ba′sin, *Phys. Geog., Brit.* a drainage area, esp. of a reservoir or river. Also, **catch′ment ar′ea.**

catch·pen·ny (kach′pen′ē), *adj.*, *n.*, *pl.* **-nies.** —*adj.* **1.** made to sell readily at a low price, regardless of value or use. —*n.* **2.** anything of little value or use, made merely for quick sale. [from phrase *catch (a) penny*]

catch′ phrase′, a phrase that attracts attention. Also, **catch′phrase′.** [CATCH(WORD) + PHRASE]

catch·pole[1] (kach′pōl′), *n.* (formerly) a petty officer of justice, esp. one who arrests persons for debt. Also, **catch′poll′.** [ME *cacchepol*, OE *cæcepol* < ML *cacepoll(us)* tax-gatherer, lit., chase-fowl, equiv. to *cace-* (< ONF; see CATCH) + *pollus* < L *pullus* chick; see PULLET] —**catch′pol′er·y, catch′poll′er·y,** *n.*

catch·pole[2] (kach′pōl′), *n.* a long staff having a spring-operated device for catching and holding fugitives by the neck. [CATCH + POLE[1]]

catch′ stitch′, *Sewing.* a large cross-stitch used in finishing seams and hemming bulky fabrics.
catch-up (kach′up′), *n.* **1.** an accelerated effort to reach or pass a norm, esp. after a period of delay: *After the slowdown there was a catch-up in production.* **2.** an instance of catching up. [n. use of v. phrase *catch up*]
catch·up (kach′əp, kech′-), *n.* ketchup.
catch·weight (kach′wāt′), *n.* *Sports.* the chance or optional weight of a contestant, as contrasted with a weight fixed by agreement or rule. [CATCH + WEIGHT]
catch·word (kach′wûrd′), *n.* **1.** a memorable or effective word or phrase that is repeated so often that it becomes a slogan, as of a political party, in advertising a product, etc. **2.** a word printed at the top of a page in a dictionary or other reference book to indicate the first or last article on that page. **3.** a device, used esp. in old books, to assist the binder in assembling signatures by inserting at the foot of each page the first word of the following page. [CATCH + WORD]
catch·y (kach′ē), *adj.*, **catch·i·er, catch·i·est.** **1.** pleasing and easily remembered: *a catchy tune.* **2.** tricky; deceptive: *a catchy question.* **3.** occurring in snatches; fitful: *a catchy wind.* [CATCH + -Y[1]] —**catch′i·ness,** *n.*
cat′ dav′it, *Naut.* a davit acting as a cathead.
cat′ distem′per, *Vet. Pathol.* distemper[1] (def. 1c).
cate (kāt), *n.* Usually, **cates.** *Archaic.* a choice food; delicacy; dainty. [back formation from late ME *cates*, aph. var. of ME *acates* things bought, pl. of *acat* buying < ONF, deriv. of *acater* to buy < VL **accaptāre*, equiv. to L *ac-* AC- + *captāre* to seize; see CATCH]
cat·e·che·sis (kat′ə kē′sis), *n.*, *pl.* **-ses** (-sēz). oral religious instruction, formerly esp. before baptism or confirmation. [< LL < Gk *katḗchēsis* oral teaching, equiv. to *katēchē-* (var. s. of *katēchein* to teach by word of mouth; see CATECHIST) + *-sis* -SIS]
cat·e·chet·i·cal (kat′ə ket′i kəl), *adj.* pertaining to teaching by question and answer. Also, **cat′e·chet′ic.** [< late ML *catēchētic(us)* (< Gk *katēchētikós*, equiv. to *katēchē-* (see CATECHESIS) + *-tikos* -TIC) + -AL[1]] —**cat′e·chet′i·cal·ly,** *adv.*
catechet′ical school′, (in the early Christian church) a school established for the instruction of catechumens.
cat·e·chin (kat′ə chin, -kin), *n.* *Chem.* an amorphous, yellow compound, $C_{15}H_{14}O_6$, used chiefly in tanning and dyeing. [CATECH(U) + -IN[2]]
cat·e·chise (kat′ə kīz′), *v.t.*, **-chised, -chis·ing.** *Chiefly Brit.* catechize. —**cat′e·chis′a·ble,** *adj.* —**cat′e·chi·sa′tion,** *n.* —**cat′e·chis′er,** *n.*
cat·e·chism (kat′ə kiz′əm), *n.* **1.** *Eccles.* **a.** an elementary book containing a summary of the principles of the Christian religion, esp. as maintained by a particular church, in the form of questions and answers. **b.** the contents of such a book. **2.** a similar book of instruction in other subjects. **3.** *Obs.* **a.** a series of formal questions put to political candidates, etc., to bring out their views. **b.** catechetical instruction. [< LL *catēchism(us)* book of questions and answers, appar., equiv. to *catēch(izāre)* (to) CATECHIZE + *-ismus* -ISM] —**cat′e·chis′mal,** *adj.*
cat·e·chist (kat′ə kist), *n.* **1.** one who catechizes. **2.** *Eccles.* one appointed to instruct catechumens in the principles of religion as a preparation for baptism. [< LL *catēchist(a)* < Gk *katēchistḗs*, equiv. to *katēch(ein)* (to) teach by word of mouth, orig. to din down, i.e. to get results by shouting (*kat-* CATA- + *ēchein* to sound) + *-istēs* -IST] —**cat′e·chis′tic, cat′e·chis′ti·cal,** *adj.* —**cat′e·chis′ti·cal·ly,** *adv.*
cat·e·chize (kat′ə kīz′), *v.t.*, **-chized, -chiz·ing.** **1.** to instruct orally by means of questions and answers, esp. in Christian doctrine. **2.** to question with reference to belief. **3.** to question closely or excessively. Also, *esp. Brit.*, **catechise.** [< LL *catēchiz(āre)* < Gk *katēchiz(ein)* (to) make (someone) learn by teaching (him) orally, equiv. to *katēch(ein)* (to) teach orally (see CATECHIST) + *-izein* -IZE] —**cat′e·chiz′a·ble,** *adj.* —**cat′e·chi·za′tion,** *n.* —**cat′e·chiz′er,** *n.*
—**Syn. 3.** interrogate, quiz, examine, probe.
cat·e·chol (kat′ə chōl′, -chōl′, -kōl′, -kōl′), *n.* *Chem.* a white, crystalline, dihydroxyl derivative of benzene, HOC_6H_4OH, the ortho isomer, used chiefly in photography, for dyeing, and as a reagent; pyrocatechol. [CATECH(U) + -OL[1]]
cat·e·chu (kat′ə cho͞o′, -kyo͞o′), *n.* any of several astringent substances obtained from various tropical plants, esp. from the wood of two East Indian acacias, *Acacia Catechu* and *A. Suma:* used in medicine, dyeing, tanning, etc. Also called **cashoo, cutch.** [< NL < Malay *kachu*]
cat·e·chu·men (kat′ə kyo͞o′mən), *n.* **1.** *Eccles.* one under instruction in the rudiments of Christianity, as in the early church; a neophyte. **2.** a person being taught the elementary facts, principles, etc., of any subject. [< LL *catēchūmen(us)* < Gk *katēchoúmenos* (one who is) being taught by word of mouth, equiv. to *katēch(ein)* (to) teach orally (see CATECHIST) + *-oumenos* prp. suffix; r. ME *cathecumyn* < MF *cathecumine* < LL, as above] —**cat′e·chu′me·nal, cat·e·chu·men·i·cal** (kat′ə kyo͞o men′i kəl), *adj.* —**cat′e·chu·men′i·cal·ly,** *adv.* —**cat·e·chu·me·nate** (kat′ə kyo͞o′mə nāt′, -mə nit), *n.* —**cat′e·chu′men·ism,** *n.*
cat·e·gor·i·cal (kat′ə gôr′i kəl, -gor′-), *adj.* **1.** absolute; unqualified and unconditional: *a categorical denial of an accusation.* **2.** *Logic.* **a.** (of a proposition) analyzable into a subject and an attribute related by a copula, as in the proposition "All men are mortal." **b.** (of a syllogism) having categorical propositions as premises. **3.** of, pertaining to, or in a category. Also, **cat′e·gor′ic.** [< LL *catēgoric(us)* (< Gk *katēgorikós*; see CATEGORY, -IC) + -AL[1]] —**cat′e·gor′i·cal·ly,** *adv.* —**cat′e·gor′i·cal·ness,** *n.*
—**Syn. 1.** positive, flat, downright.
categor′ical imper′ative, **1.** *Ethics.* the rule of Immanual Kant that one must do only what one can will that all others should do under similar circumstances. **2.** the unconditional command of conscience.
cat′egor′ic con′tact, *Social.* behavior toward an individual on the basis of the type or group of people he represents rather than on the basis of his personal make-up. Cf. **sympathetic contact.**
cat·e·go·rise (kat′ə gə rīz′), *v.t.*, **-rised, -ris·ing.** *Chiefly Brit.* categorize. —**cat′e·go·ri·sa′tion,** *n.*
cat·e·go·rize (kat′ə gə rīz′), *v.t.*, **-rized, -riz·ing.** **1.** to arrange in categories or classes; classify. **2.** to describe by labeling or giving a name to; characterize. Also, *esp. Brit.*, **categorise.** [CATEGOR(Y) + -IZE] —**cat·e·go·rist** (kat′ə gôr′ist, -gōr′-), *n.* —**cat′e·go·ri·za′tion,** *n.*
cat·e·go·ry (kat′ə gôr′ē, -gōr′ē), *n.*, *pl.* **-ries.** **1.** a classificatory division in any field of knowledge, as a phylum or any of its subdivisions in biology. **2.** any general or comprehensive division; a class. **3.** *Metaphys.* **a.** (in Aristotelian philosophy) any of the fundamental modes of existence, such as substance, quality, and quantity, as determined by analysis of the different possible kinds of predication. **b.** (in Kantian philosophy) any of the fundamental principles of the understanding, as the principle of causation. **c.** any classification of terms that is ultimate and not susceptible to further analysis. **4.** Also called **Guggenheim. categories,** (*construed as sing.*) a game in which a key word and a list of categories, as dogs, automobiles, or rivers, are selected, and in which each player writes down a word in each category that begins with each of the letters of the key word, the player writing down the most words within a time limit being declared the winner. [< LL *catēgoria* < Gk *katēgoría* accusation (also, kind of predication), equiv. to *katḗgor(os)* accuser, affirmer (*katēgor(eîn)* (to) accuse, affirm, lit., speak publicly against, equiv. to *kata-* CATA- + *-agorein* to speak before the AGORA, + *-os* n. suffix) + *-ia* -Y[3]]
ca·te·na (kə tē′nə), *n.*, *pl.* **-nae** (-nē), a chain or connected series, esp. of extracts from the writings of the fathers of the church. [< L: a chain]
cat·e·nane (kat′ə nān′), *n.* *Chem.* any of the class of compounds containing two or more rings that are interlocked without being bonded chemically. [CATEN(A) + -ANE]
cat·e·nar·y (kat′ə ner′ē; *esp. Brit.* kə tē′nə rē), *n.*, *pl.* **-nar·ies,** *adj.* —*n.* **1.** *Math.* the curve assumed approximately by a heavy uniform cord or chain hanging freely from two points not in the same vertical line. Equation: $y = k\cosh\left(\frac{x}{k}\right)$. **2.** (in electric railroads) the cable, running above the track, from which the trolley wire is suspended. —*adj.* **3.** of, pertaining to, or resembling a catenary **4.** of or pertaining to a chain or linked series. [< L *catēnāri(us)* relating to a chain, equiv. to *catēn(a)* a chain + *-ārius* -ARY]

Catenary
k, Distance from the vertex to the origin at 0

cat′enary fur′nace, *Metalworking.* a continuous furnace for annealing stainless-steel strip which passes through in a hanging strip.
cat·e·nate (kat′ə nāt′), *v.t.*, **-nat·ed, -nat·ing.** to link together; form into a connected series: *catenated cells.* [< L *catēnāt(us)* chained, equiv. to *catēn(a)* a chain + *-ātus* -ATE[1]] —**cat′e·na′tion,** *n.*
cat·e·noid (kat′ə noid′), *n.* *Geom.* the surface generated by rotating a catenary about its axis of symmetry. [< L *catēn(a)* a chain + -OID]
ca·ter (kā′tər), *v.i.* **1.** to provide food, service, etc.: *to cater for a banquet.* **2.** to provide or supply that which amuses, is desired, or gives pleasure, comfort, etc. (usually fol. by *to* or *for*): *to cater to popular demand; to cater for an invalid.* —*v.t.* **3.** to provide food and service for: *to cater a party.* [v. use of obs. *cater*, ME *catour*, aph. var. of *acatour* buyer < AF, equiv. to *acat(er)* (to) buy (see CATE) + *-our* -OR[2]] —**ca′ter·ing·ly,** *adv.*
cat·er·an (kat′ər ən), *n.* a freebooter or marauder of the Scottish Highlands. [< ML *caterān(us)*, Latinized form of ME *catherein* < Gael; see KERN[1]]
cat·er-cor·nered (kat′ə kôr′nərd, kat′ē-, kat′ər-), *adj.* **1.** diagonal. —*adv.* **2.** diagonally. Also, **cat′er-cor′ner, cat′er-cor′ner, catty-corner, catty-cornered, kitty-corner, kitty-cornered.** [dial. *cater* (adv.) diagonally (deriv. of obs. *cater* four < MF *quatre* < L *quattuor*) + CORNERED]
ca·ter-cous·in (kā′tər kuz′ən), *n.* **1.** an intimate friend. **2.** *Obs.* a cousin. [obs. *cater* purveyor, provider (see CATER) + COUSIN]
ca·ter·er (kā′tər ər), *n.* **1.** one whose business is to provide whatever food, supplies, and service are needed at a social gathering. **2.** one who caters. [CATER + -ER[1]]
Cat·e·ri·na (kat′ə rē′nə), *n.* a girl's given name, form of **Catherine.** Also, **Katrina.**
cat·er·pil·lar (kat′ə pil′ər, kat′ər-), *n.* **1.** the wormlike larva of a butterfly or a moth. **2.** (*cap.*) *Trademark.* a tractor having the driving wheels moving inside endless tracks situated on the sides, thus being capable of hauling heavy loads over rough or soft ground. **3.** any device, as a tank or power shovel, moving on such endless tracks. **4.** one who preys on others; extortioner. [late ME tracks situated on the sides, thus being capable of hauling *catyrpel*, equiv. to *catyr* tomcat (< MD *cater*) + *pel*, north var. of *pil* skin, rind (akin to OE *pilian* to PEEL[1]); cf. ONF *catepelose*, equiv. to *cate* cat + *pelose* < L *pilōs(us)* hairy] —**cat′er·pil′lar-like′,** *adj.*
cat′erpillar gate′, (in a dam) a gate, moving on caterpillarlike treads, for controlling the flow of water through a spillway or sluice.
cat′erpillar hunt′er, any ground beetle of the genus *Calosoma*, esp. *C. scrutator*, that preys on caterpillars and other larvae.
cat′erpillar tread′, either of two endless tracks, passing over a number of wheels, on which run tanks, tractors, and other vehicles intended for rough terrain.
cat·er·waul (kat′ər wôl′), *v.i.* **1.** to cry as cats in rutting time. **2.** to utter a similar sound; howl or screech. **3.** to quarrel like cats. —*n.* Also, **cat′er·waul′ing.** **4.** the cry of a cat in rutting time. **5.** any similar sound. [ME *cater(wawen)*, equiv. to *cater* tomcat (< MD) + *wawen* to howl, OE *wāwan* to blow, said of the wind) + *waul*, var. of WAIL] —**cat′er·waul′er,** *n.*
Cates·by (kāts′bē), *n.* a boy's given name.
cat-eyed (kat′īd′), *adj.* **1.** having eyes resembling those of a cat. **2.** capable of seeing in dark places.
cat·face (kat′fās′), *n.* (in plastering) a knob or pit in a finish coat. [after fancied likeness] —**cat′faced′,** *adj.*
cat·fall (kat′fôl′), *n.* *Naut.* the fall of the tackle by which an anchor is hoisted to the cathead; the fall of a cat. [CAT[1] + FALL; cf. HOIST, LIFT]
cat′ fe′ver, *Vet. Pathol.* distemper[1] (def. 1c).
cat·fight (kat′fīt′), *n.* an argument or dispute carried out with intense hostility and bitterness. [CAT[1] + FIGHT]
cat·fish (kat′fish′), *n.*, *pl.* (*esp. collectively*) **-fish,** (*esp. referring to two or more kinds or species*) **-fish·es.** **1.** any of numerous fishes of the order or suborder *Nematognathi* (or *Siluroidei*), characterized by barbels around the mouth and the absence of scales. **2.** a wolffish of the genus *Anarhichas.* **3.** any of various other fishes having a fancied resemblance to a cat. [perh. so called from its spines, likened to a cat's claws]

Channel catfish, *Ictalurus punctatus* (Length to 4 ft.)

cat-foot (kat′fo͝ot′), *v.i.* to move in the soft, stealthy manner of a cat; pussyfoot. [CAT[1] + FOOT]
cat·foot·ed (kat′fo͝ot′id), *adj.* **1.** having feet resembling those of a cat. **2.** catlike in the manner of walking; characterized by noiseless ambulation; stealthy: *cat-footed jewel thief.* [CAT[1] + FOOTED]
cat·gut (kat′gut′), *n.* **1.** a strong cord made by twisting the dried intestines of animals, as sheep, used in stringing musical instruments and tennis rackets, for surgical sutures, etc. **2.** goat's-rue. [? CAT[1] + GUT]
cath-, var. of **cata-** before an aspirate: *cathode.*
Cath., **1.** (*often l.c.*) cathedral. **2.** Catholic.
Cath·ar (kath′är), *n.*, *pl.* **-a·ri** (-ə rī′), **-ars.** (in medieval Europe) a member of any of several rigorously ascetic Christian sects maintaining a dualistic theology. Also called **Cath·a·rist** (kath′ər ist). [< LL *Catharī* (pl.) < LGk *hoi Katharoí* Novatians, lit., the pure; applied in ML to various sects] —**Cath′a·rism,** *n.* —**Cath′a·ris′tic,** *adj.*
Ca·tha·ri·na (kä′tə rē′nə), *n.* a walled plain in the fourth quadrant of the face of the moon: about 55 miles in diameter.
cath′ar·ine wheel′ (kath′rin, -ər in). See **Catherine wheel.**
cat-har·pin (kat′här′pin), *n.* *Naut.* any of a number of short ropes or rods for gathering in shrouds near their tops, to increase tension and to allow the adjacent yard to be braced more sharply. Also, **cat′har′pin.** [var. of *cat-harping*]
ca·thar·sis (kə thär′sis), *n.* **1.** *Med.* purgation. **2.** *Aesthetics.* the effect of certain kinds of art, esp. tragedy and music, in relieving or purging the emotions of an audience. **3.** *Psychiatry.* **a.** psychotherapy that encourages or permits the discharge of pent-up, socially unacceptable, affects. **b.** discharge of pent-up emotions so as to result in the alleviation of symptoms or the permanent relief of the condition. Also, **katharsis.** [< NL < Gk *kátharsis* a cleansing, equiv. to *kathar-* (var. s. of *kathaírein* to cleanse, deriv. of *katharós* pure) + *-sis* -SIS]
Ca·thar·si·us (kə thär′sē əs), *n.* *Class. Myth.* an epithet of Zeus, meaning "purifier."
ca·thar·tic (kə thär′tik), *adj.* **1.** Also, **ca·thar′ti·cal.** evacuating the bowels; purgative. **2.** of or pertaining to catharsis. —*n.* **3.** a purgative. [< LL *catharticus* < Gk *kathartikós* fit for cleansing. See CATHARSIS, -TIC] —**ca·thar′ti·cal·ly,** *adv.* —**ca·thar′ti·cal·ness,** *n.*
—**Syn. 3.** laxative, physic.
Ca·thay (ka thā′), *n.* *Literary.* China. [< ML *Cat(h)aya* < some Turkic dial., as Tatar *Kītai*]
cat·head (kat′hed′), *n.* *Naut.* a projecting timber or metal beam to which an anchor is hoisted and secured. [CAT[1] + HEAD]
ca·the·dra (kə thē′drə, kath′ə-), *n.*, *pl.* **-drae** (-drē, -drē′). **1.** the seat or throne of a bishop in the principal church of his diocese. **2.** an official chair, as of a professor in a university. **3.** an ancient Roman chair used by women, having an inclined, curved back and curved legs flaring outward: the Roman copy of the Greek klismos. [< L < Gk *kathédra* CHAIR]
ca·the·dral (kə thē′drəl), *n.* **1.** the principal church of a diocese, containing the bishop's throne. **2.** (in nonepiscopal denominations) any of various important churches. —*adj.* **3.** pertaining to or containing a bishop's throne. **4.** pertaining to or emanating from a chair of office or authority. [ME < LL *cathedrāl(is)* (*ecclesia*) a cathedral (church). See CATHEDRA, -AL[1]] —**ca·the′dral-like′,** *adj.*
cathe′dral ceil′ing, a ceiling formed by or suggesting an open-timbered roof.
cathe′dral glass′, a semitransparent sheet of rolled glass having a decorative pattern.
ca·thep·sin (kə thep′sin), *n.* *Biochem.* any of a class of intracellular proteolytic enzymes, occurring in animal tissue, esp. the liver, spleen, kidneys, and intestine, that catalyze autolysis in certain pathological conditions and after death. [< Gk *kathéps(ein)* (to) digest (*kath-* CATH- + *hépsein* to boil) + -IN[2]] —**ca·thep·tic** (kə thep′tik), *adj.*
Cath·er (kath′ər or, *often*, kath′-), *n.* **Wil·la (Si·bert)** (wil′ə sē′bərt), 1876–1947, U.S. novelist.
Cath·er·ine (kath′ər in, kath′rin), *n.* a girl's given name. Also, **Catheryn, Katharine, Katherine, Kathryn, Kathrynne.**
Catherine I, (*Marfa Skavronskaya*) 1684?–1727, Lithuanian wife of Peter the Great: empress of Russia 1725–27.
Catherine II, (*Sophia Augusta of Anhalt-Zerbst*) ("*Catherine the Great*") 1729–96, wife of Peter III: empress of Russia 1762–96.
Ca·the·rine de Mé·di·cis (kaᵗʀēn′ də mā dē sēs′), (*Caterina de' Medici*) 1518–89, queen of Henry II of France (mother of Francis II, Charles IX, and Henry III). Also, **Cath·er·ine de' Med·i·ci** (kath′rin də med′i chē, mä′di-, dä, kath′ər in), **Cath′erine de Med′ici.**
Cath′erine How′ard, 1520?–42, fifth queen consort of Henry VIII of England.
Cath′erine of Alexan′dria, **Saint,** A.D. c310, Christian martyr.
Cath′erine of Ar′a·gon (ar′ə gən, -gon′), 1485–1536, first queen consort of Henry VIII of England (mother of Mary I of England).
Cath′erine of Sie′na (sye′nä), **Saint,** 1347–80, Italian ascetic and mystic.
Cath′erine Parr′ (pär), 1512–48, sixth queen consort of Henry VIII of England.
Cath′erine wheel′, **1.** *Heraldry.* a charge representing a spiked wheel used as an instrument of torture. **2.** See **wheel window.** **3.** a kind of firework that is ignited and revolves on a pin, making a wheel of fire or

sparks; pinwheel. Also, **catharine wheel.** [named after St. CATHERINE of Alexandria, from wheel used to torture her]

Cath·er·yn (kath′ər in, kath′rin), *n.* a girl's given name. Also, **Catherine, Katharine, Katherine, Kathryn, Kathrynne.**

cath·e·ter (kath′i tər), *n.* *Med.* a flexible or rigid, hollow tube employed to drain fluids from body cavities or to distend body passages, esp. one for passing into the bladder through the urethra to draw off urine. [< LL < Gk *kathetḗr* kind of tube, lit., something sent or let down, equiv. to *kathe-* (var. s. of *kathiénai*, equiv. to *kat-* CATA- + *hiénai* to send, let go) + *-tēr* instrumental suffix]

cath·e·ter·ise (kath′i tə rīz′), *v.t.*, **-ised, -is·ing.** *Chiefly Brit.* catheterize. —**cath′e·ter·i·sa′tion,** *n.*

cath·e·ter·ize (kath′i tə rīz′), *v.t.*, **-ized, -iz·ing.** to introduce a catheter into. [CATHETER + -IZE] —**cath′e·ter·i·za′tion,** *n.*

cath·e·tus (kath′i təs, kə thē′təs), *n.*, *pl.* **-ti** (-tī′, -tī). (in an Ionic capital) the vertical guide line through the eye of a volute, from which the form of the volute is determined. [< L, (n.) < Gk *káthetos* perpendicular, equiv. to *kathe-* (see CATHETER) + *-tos* adj. suffix]

ca·thex·is (kə thek′sis), *n.*, *pl.* **-thex·es** (-thek′sēz). *Psychoanal.* **1.** the investment of emotional significance in an activity, object, or idea. **2.** the charge of psychic energy so invested. [< NL < Gk *káthexis* a keeping, equiv. to *kathech-* (var. s. of *katéchein* to keep, hold on to, equiv. to *kat(h)-* CATH- + *échein* to have, hold) + *-sis* -SIS; answering to G *Besetzung* a taking possession of (Freud's term)] —**ca·thec·tic** (kə thek′tik), *adj.*

Cath·ie (kath′ē), *n.* a girl's given name, form of **Catherine.** Also, **Cathy.**

ca·this·ma (*Gk.* kä′thēz mä; *Eng.* ka thiz′mə), *n.*, *pl.* **-ma·ta** (*Gk.* -mä tä; *Eng.* -mə tə). kathisma.

Cath·leen (kath lēn′), *n.* a girl's given name, Irish form of **Catherine.** Also, **Kathleen, Kathlene, Kathlyn, Kathlynne.**

cath·ode (kath′ōd), *n.* **1.** the electrode which emits electrons or gives off negative ions and toward which positive ions move or collect in a voltaic cell, electronic or x-ray tube, etc. **2.** the negative pole of a battery or other source of electric current (opposed to *anode*). Also, **kathode.** [< Gk *káthod(os)* a way down, equiv. to *kat-* CATA- + *hodós* way]

cath′ode dark′ space′. See **Crookes dark space.**

cath′ode glow′, *Physics.* a luminous region between the Aston dark space and the Crookes dark space in a vacuum tube, occurring when the pressure is low.

cath′ode ray′, a flow of electrons emanating from a cathode in a vacuum tube and focused into a narrow beam.

cath′ode ray′ tube′, *Electronics.* a vacuum tube that generates a focused beam of electrons which can be deflected by electric fields, magnetic fields, or both. The terminus of the beam is visible as a spot or line of luminescence caused by its impinging on a sensitized screen at one end of the tube. Cathode ray tubes are used to study the shapes of electric waves, to reproduce images in television receivers, as an indicator in radar sets, etc.

cath·od·ic (ka thod′ik, -thō′dik, kə-), *adj.* pertaining to a cathode or phenomena in its vicinity. [CATHODE + -IC] —**ca·thod′i·cal·ly,** *adv.*

cathod′ic protec′tion, protection of ferrous metals against electrolysis by the attachment of sacrificial anodes. Also called **electrolytic protection.**

cath·o·do·lu·mi·nes·cence (kath′ə dō lo͞o′mə nes′əns), *n.* *Physics.* light emitted by a substance undergoing bombardment by cathode rays. [CATHODE + -O- + LUMINESCENCE] —**cath′o·do·lu′mi·nes′cent,** *adj.*

cath·o·lic (kath′ə lik, kath′lik), *adj.* **1.** pertaining to the whole Christian body or church. **2.** universal in extent; involving all; of interest to all. **3.** having sympathies with all; broad-minded; liberal: *to be catholic in one's tastes, interests, etc.* [< L *catholic(us)* < Gk *katholikós* general, equiv. to *kathól(ou)* universally (contr. of phrase *katà hólou* according to the whole; see CATA-, HOLO-) + *-ikos* -IC] —**ca·thol·i·cal·ly, ca·thol·ic·ly** (kə thol′ik lē), *adv.* —**ca·thol′i·cal·ness, cath′o·lic·ness,** *n.*

Cath·o·lic (kath′ə lik, kath′lik), *adj.* **1.** *Theol.* **a.** (among Roman Catholics) claiming to possess exclusively the notes or characteristics of the one, only, true, and universal church having unity, visibility, indefectibility, apostolic succession, universality, and sanctity: used in this sense, with these qualifications, only by the Church of Rome, as applicable only to itself and its adherents and to their faith and organization; often qualified, especially by those not acknowledging these claims, by prefixing the word *Roman.* **b.** (among Anglo-Catholics) noting or pertaining to the conception of the church as the body representing the ancient undivided Christian witness, comprising all the orthodox churches which have kept the apostolic succession of bishops, and including the Anglican Church, the Roman Catholic Church, the Eastern Orthodox Church, Church of Sweden, the Old Catholic Church (in the Netherlands and elsewhere), etc. **2.** pertaining to the Western Church. —*n.* **3.** a member of a Catholic church, esp. of the Roman Catholic Church. [ME; special uses of CATHOLIC]

Cath′olic Ac′tion, *Rom. Cath. Ch.* a movement founded by Pope Pius XI, dedicated to fostering a greater participation of the laity in the apostolate.

ca·thol·i·cate (kə thol′ə kāt′), *n.* the see of a catholicos. [< ML *catholicāt(us)*, equiv. to *catholic(us)* CATHOLICOS + *-ātus* -ATE[1]]

Cath′olic Church′, *Rom. Cath. Ch.* a visible society of baptized Christians professing the same faith under the authority of the invisible head (Christ) and the authority of the visible head (the pope and the bishops in communion with him).

Cath′olic Emancipa′tion Act′, *Eng. Hist.* an act of Parliament (1829) permitting Roman Catholic laymen to hold parliamentary office and repealing other laws that imposed civil disabilities on Catholics.

ca·thol·i·cise (kə thol′i sīz′), *v.t.*, *v.i.*, **-cised, -cis·ing.** *Chiefly Brit.* catholicize. —**ca·thol′i·ci·sa′tion,** *n.* —**ca·thol′i·cis′er,** *n.*

Ca·thol·i·cism (kə thol′i siz′əm), *n.* **1.** the faith, system, and practice of the Catholic Church, esp. the Roman Catholic Church. **2.** (*l.c.*) broad-mindedness; catholicity. [CATHOLIC + -ISM]

cath·o·lic·i·ty (kath′ə lis′i tē), *n.* **1.** the quality of being catholic; universality; broad-mindedness. **2.** (*cap.*) the Roman Catholic Church, or its doctrines and usages. [CATHOLIC + -ITY]

ca·thol·i·cize (kə thol′i sīz′), *v.t.*, *v.i.*, **-cized, -ciz·ing.** **1.** to make or become catholic; universalize. **2.** (*cap.*) to make or become Catholic, esp. Roman Catholic. Also, *esp. Brit.*, **catholicise.** [CATHOLIC + -IZE] —**ca·thol′i·ci·za′tion,** *n.* —**ca·thol′i·ciz′er,** *n.*

ca·thol·i·con (kə thol′ə kən), *n.* a universal remedy; panacea. [late ME < ML < Gk *katholikón* cure-all, neut. of *katholikós* CATHOLIC]

ca·thol·i·cos (kə thol′ə kəs, -kos′), *n.*, *pl.* **-cos·es, -coi** (-koi′). **1.** (*often cap.*) *Eastern Ch.* **a.** any of the heads of certain autocephalous churches. **b.** (in some autocephalous churches) a primate subject to a patriarch and having authority over metropolitans. **2.** (in the early Christian church) the head of a number of monasteries in the same city. Also, **catholicus, Katholikos.** [< LGk *katholikós*, n. use of Gk adj.; see CATHOLIC]

ca·thol·i·cus (kə thol′ə kəs), *n.*, *pl.* **-ci** (-sī′, -kē′). catholicos. [< ML]

Cath·o·my·cin (kath′ō mī′sin), *n.* *Pharm., Trademark.* novobiocin.

cat·house (kat′hous′), *n.*, *pl.* **-hous·es** (-hou′ziz). *Slang.* a brothel. [CAT[1] (in obs. sense of harlot) + HOUSE]

cath·ud (kath′o͝od), *n.* (in Scotland) a stone fireback having a seat behind it. [var. of *catheder* seat; see CATHEDRA]

Cath·y (kath′ē), *n.* a girl's given name, form of **Catherine.** Also, **Cathie.**

cat′ ice′, thin ice originally formed on water which has since receded; shell ice.

Cat·i·li·nar·i·an (kat′ələ nâr′ē ən), *adj.* **1.** pertaining to or resembling Catiline. —*n.* **2.** one who participated in Catiline's conspiracy. **3.** one who resembles or imitates Catiline; conspirator. [< L *Catilinari(us)* (*Catilin(a)* CATILINE + *-ārius*; see -ARY) + -AN]

Cat·i·line (kat′əlīn′), *n.* (*Lucius Sergius Catilina*) 108?–62 B.C., Roman politician and conspirator.

cat·i·on (kat′ī′ən, -on), *n.* *Physical Chem.* **1.** a positively charged ion which is attracted to the cathode in electrolysis. **2.** any positively charged atom or group of atoms (opposed to *anion*). Also, **kation.** [< Gk *katión* going down (neut. of *katión*, prp. of *katiénai*), equiv. to *kat-* CAT- + *-i-* go + *-on*, neut. of prp. suffix] —**cat·i·on·ic** (kat′ī on′ik), *adj.*

cation′ic deter′gent, *Chem.* any of a class of synthetic compounds, as benzalkonium chloride, whose cations are colloidal in solution: used as antiseptics, wetting agents, and emulsifiers. Also called **invert soap.**

ca·tjang (kä′chäng), *n.* a showy, tropical vine, *Vigna Catjang*, having erect pods from three to five inches long. Also called **ca′tjang pea′.** [< D *katjang* < Malay, Sudanese *kachang* bean, pea]

cat·kin (kat′kin), *n.* *Bot.* an ament, as of the willow or birch. [< D *katteken* little cat (now obs.). See CAT[1], -KIN] —**cat·kin·ate** (kat′ki nāt′), *adj.*

cat·lap (kat′lap′), *n.* *Brit. Slang.* any thin or very weak beverage, esp. tea. [so called because the beverage is thought fit only for a cat to lap up]

Cat·letts·burg (kat′lits bûrg′), *n.* a town in NE Kentucky. 3874 (1960).

cat·like (kat′līk′), *adj.* pertaining to or resembling a cat; feline; stealthy: *catlike footsteps.* [CAT[1] + -LIKE]

Cat·lin (kat′lin), *n.* **George,** 1796–1872, U.S. painter.

cat·ling (kat′ling), *n.* **1.** catgut; a catgut string. **2.** a surgical knife. **3.** *Archaic.* a little cat; kitten. [CAT[1] + -LING[1]]

cat·mint (kat′mint′), *n.* catnip. [ME *cattesminte* equiv. to *cattes*, gen. of CAT[1] + *minte* MINT[1]]

cat′ nap′, *U.S.* a short, light nap or doze.

cat·nap (kat′nap′), *v.i.*, **-napped, -nap·ping.** to doze or sleep lightly. [v. use of CAT NAP]

cat·nip (kat′nip), *n.* a plant, *Nepeta Cataria*, of the mint family, having strongly scented leaves of which cats are fond. Also, **catmint.** [CAT[1] + *nip*, var. of ME *nep* catnip, apocopated var. of OE *nepte* < ML *nept(a)*, var. of L *nepeta*]

Ca·to (kā′tō), *n.* **1. Marcus Por·ci·us** (pôr′shē əs, -shəs), ("*the Elder*" or "*the Censor*"), 234–149 B.C., Roman statesman, soldier, and writer. **2.** his great-grandson, **Marcus Porcius** ("*the Younger*"), 95–46 B.C., Roman statesman, soldier, and Stoic philosopher. **3.** a boy's given name.

cat-o'-moun·tain (kat′ə moun′tən, -tin), *n.* catamountain.

Ca·ton (kāt′ən), *n.* a boy's given name.

Cat′ on a Hot′ Tin′ Roof′, a play (1955) by Tennessee Williams.

cat-o'-nine-tails (kat′ə nīn′tālz′), *n.*, *pl.* **-tails.** a whip, usually having nine knotted lines or cords fastened to a handle, used for flogging. [so called in allusion to a cat's scratches]

Ca·tons·ville (kāt′ənz vil′), *n.* a town in central Maryland, near Baltimore. 37,372 (1960).

ca·top·trics (kə top′triks), *n.* (*construed as sing.*) the branch of optics dealing with the formation of images by mirrors. [< Gk *katoptrik(ós)*, equiv. to *kátoptr(on)* mirror (*kat-* CAT- + *op-* see + *-tron* -TRON) + *-ikos* -IC; see -ICS] —**ca·top′tric, ca·top′tri·cal,** *adj.* —**ca·top′tri·cal·ly,** *adv.*

cat′ plague′, *Vet. Pathol.* distemper[1] (def. 1c).

Ca·tre·us (kā′trē əs, -tro͞os), *n.* *Class. Myth.* a king of Crete, a son of Minos and Pasiphaë. Cf. **Althaemenes.**

cat′ rig′, *Naut.* a rig consisting of a single mast with a long boom, set well forward and carrying a single gaff or jib-headed sail: used on catboats. —**cat′-rigged′,** *adj.*

cats′ and dogs′, *Slang.* **1.** highly speculative, low-priced securities. **2.** an odd assortment, esp. of goods on sale. [perh. modeled on *bulls and bears*, indicating a less established order with reference to the proverbial fights between cats and dogs]

CAT′ scan′ner, a specialized X-ray instrument that displays computerized cross-sectional images from within the body. Also, **CT scanner.** [C(OMPUTERIZED) A(XIAL) T(OMOGRAPHY) SCANNER]

cat′ schoon′er, a former fishing schooner of New England, fore-and-aft-rigged on two masts and without headsails.

cat's-claw (kats′klô′), *n.* a spiny shrub or small tree, *Pithecolobium Unguis-cati*, of Central America, having greenish-yellow flowers and red, spirally twisted pods. Also called **black bead, Florida cat's-claw.**

cat's′ cra′dle, a children's game in which two players alternately stretch a looped string over their fingers in such a way as to produce different designs. [fanciful name]

cat′-scratch disease′ (kat′skrach′), *Pathol.* a condition characterized by swelling of the lymph glands, and fever, caused by a viral infection resulting from the scratch or bite of a cat. Also called **cat′-scratch fe′ver.**

cat's-ear (kats′ēr′), *n.* **1.** Also called **California dandelion, gosmore.** a European, composite herb, *Hypochaeris radicata*, common as a weed in North America, having yellow flowers and dandelionlike leaves. **2.** any of several species of pussy's toe.

cat's-eye (kats′ī′), *n.*, *pl.* **-eyes.** any of certain gems having a chatoyant luster, esp. chrysoberyl.

cat's-foot (kats′fo͝ot′), *n.*, *pl.* **-feet.** **1.** See **ground ivy.** **2.** any of several species of pussy's toe, esp. *Antennaria neodioica.*

Cats·kill (kat′skil), *n.* a town in SE New York. 5825 (1960).

Cats′kill Moun′tains, a range of low mountains in E New York. Highest peak, Slide Mountain, 4204 ft. Also called **Cats′kills.**

cat's-paw (kats′pô′), *n.* **1.** a person used by another to serve his purposes; tool. **2.** *Naut.* **a.** a hitch made in the bight of a rope so that two eyes are formed to hold the hook of one block of a tackle. **b.** a light breeze that ruffles the surface of the water over a comparatively small area. **c.** the small area ruffled by such a breeze. Also, **cats′paw′.**

cat's′-tail speed′well (kats′tāl′), a perennial herb, *Veronica spicata*, of Eurasia, having blue flowers in dense clusters.

cat·stick (kat′stik′), *n.* a broomstick or other stick used as a bat, esp. in playing tipcat. [CAT[1] + STICK[1]]

cat·sup (kat′səp, kech′əp, kach′-), *n.* ketchup.

cat's′ whisk′er. See **cat whisker.**

Catt (kat), *n.* **Carrie Chapman Lane,** 1859–1947, U.S. leader in women's suffrage movements.

cat′ tack′le, *Naut.* a tackle for catting an anchor.

cat·tail (kat′tāl′), *n.* **1.** Also called **reed mace.** a tall, reedlike, marsh plant, *Typha latifolia*, having flowers in long, dense, cylindrical spikes. **2.** any of several other plants of the same genus. **3.** *Bot.* an ament or catkin. [late ME *cattestail.* See CAT[1], TAIL[1]]

Cattails, *Typha latifolia*

cat·ta·lo (kat′əlō′), *n.*, *pl.* **-loes, -los.** a hybrid produced by mating the American buffalo with domestic cattle. Also, **catalo.** [CATT(LE) + (BUFF)ALO]

Cat·te·gat (kat′ə gat′), *n.* Kattegat.

Cat·tell (kə tel′), *n.* **James Mc·Keen** (mə kēn′), 1860–1944, U.S. psychologist, educator, and editor.

cat·te·ry (kat′ə rē), *n.*, *pl.* **-ries.** a place where cats are bred. [CAT[1] + -ERY]

cat·tish (kat′ish), *adj.* **1.** catlike; feline. **2.** spiteful; malicious. [CAT[1] + -ISH[1]] —**cat′tish·ly,** *adv.* —**cat′tish·ness,** *n.*

cat·tle (kat′əl), *n.* (*construed as pl.*) **1.** bovine animals, esp. domesticated members of the genus *Bos.* **2.** *Bib.* such animals together with other domesticated quadrupeds, as horses, swine, etc. **3.** *Disparaging.* human beings. [ME *catel* < ONF: (personal) property < ML *cap(i)tāle* wealth; see CAPITAL[1]] —**cat′tle·less,** *adj.*

cat′tle e′gret, an egret, *Ardeola ibis*, cosmopolitan in warmer regions, that feeds on insects on or around grazing animals.

cat·tle·man (kat′əl mən, -man′), *n.*, *pl.* **-men** (-mən, -men′). **1.** a man engaged in the tending or breeding of cattle. **2.** a rancher who rears cattle on a large scale; the owner of a cattle ranch. [CATTLE + MAN[1]]

cat′tle plague′, *Vet. Pathol.* rinderpest.

cat·tle·ship (kat′əl ship′), *n.* a large vessel for the transportation of livestock. [CATTLE + SHIP]

cat·ley·a (kat′lē ə, kat lē′ə, -lā′ə), *n.* any of several tropical American orchids of the genus *Cattleya.* [after William *Cattley* (d. 1832), English botany enthusiast]

Cat·ton (kat′ən), *n.* **(Charles) Bruce,** 1899–1978, U.S. journalist and historian.

cat·ty[1] (kat′ē), *adj.*, **-ti·er, -ti·est.** **1.** catlike; feline. **2.** quietly or slyly malicious; spiteful: *a catty gossip.* [CAT[1] + -Y[1]] —**cat′ti·ly,** *adv.* —**cat′ti·ness,** *n.*

cat·ty[2] (kat′ē), *n.*, *pl.* **-ties.** (in China and southeast Asia) a weight equal to about 1½ pounds avoirdupois. [< Malay *kati*]

cat·ty-cor·nered (kat′ē kôr′nərd), *adj.*, *adv.* catercornered. Also, **cat′ty-cor′ner.**

cat′ ty′phoid, *Vet. Pathol.* distemper[1] (def. 1c).

Ca·tul·lus (kə tul′əs), *n.* **Ga·ius Va·le·ri·us** (gā′əs və lēr′ē əs), 84?–54? B.C., Roman poet. —**Ca·tul·li·an** (kə tul′ē ən), *adj.*

CATV, community antenna television.

cat·walk (kat′wôk′), *n.* any narrow walkway, esp. one high above the surrounding area, used to provide access or allow workers to stand or move, as over the stage in a theater, outside the roadway of a bridge, along the top of a railroad car, etc. [CAT[1] + WALK]

cat′ whisk′er, **1.** *Radio.* a stiff wire forming one contact in a crystal detector and used for probing the crystal. **2.** *Electronics.* any wire for making contact with a semiconductor. Also, **cat's whisker.** Also called **whisker.**

cat′ yawl′, a yawl having the mainmast close to the stem and the after mast on the counter, aft of the rudder.

Cau·ca (kou′kä), *n.* a river in W Colombia: tributary of the Magdalena. 600 mi. long.

Cau·ca·sia (kô kā′zhə, -shə), *n.* a region in the Soviet Union between the Black and Caspian seas: divided by the Caucasus Mountains into Ciscaucasia in Europe and Transcaucasia in Asia. Also, **Caucasus.**

Cau·ca·sian (kô kā′zhən, -shən, -kazh′ən, -kash′-), *adj.* **1.** Caucasoid. **2.** of or pertaining to the Caucasus mountain range. **3.** of or related to the non-Indo-European, non-Turkic languages of the Caucasus region. —*n.* **4.** a person having Caucasoid characteristics; a white person. **5.** a native of the Caucasus. [< L *Caucasi(us)* (< Gk *Kaukásios*, equiv. to *Kaúkas(os)* CAUCASUS + *-ios* adj. suffix) + -AN]

Cau·ca′sian lil′y, a bulbous herb, *Lilium monadelphum,* of Iran, having drooping, golden-yellow flowers nearly five inches wide, with recurved petal tips, and growing nearly six feet high.

Cau·ca·soid (kô′kə soid′), *n.* **1.** a member of a subspecies of mankind including the light-skinned peoples of Europe, North Africa, eastern Asia, and India, and their descendants in other parts of the world. —*adj.* **2.** of or belonging to this subspecies; Caucasian. [CAUCAS(IAN) + -OID]

Cau·ca·sus (kô′kə səs), *n.* **the, 1.** Also called **Cau′casus Moun′tains.** a mountain range in Caucasia, between the Black and Caspian seas, along the border between the Russian Federation, Georgia, and Azerbaijan. Highest peak, Mt. Elbrus, 18,481 ft. **2.** Also, **Caucasia.** a region between the Black and Caspian seas: divided by the Caucasus Mountains into Ciscaucasia in Europe and Transcaucasia in Asia.

Cau·chy (kō shē′ *for 1;* kou′shē *for 2*), *n.* **1. Au·gus·tin Louis** (ō gʏ stan′ lwē′), 1789–1857, French mathematician. **2.** a crater in the first quadrant of the face of the moon: about 8 miles in diameter.

Cau′chy in′tegral for′mula, *Math.* a theorem that gives an expression in terms of an integral for the value of an analytic function at any point inside a simple closed curve of finite length in a domain. [named after A. L. CAUCHY]

Cau′chy in′tegral the′orem, *Math.* the theorem that the integral of an analytic function about a closed curve of finite length in a finite, simply connected domain is zero. [named after A. L. CAUCHY]

Cau′chy-Rie′mann equa′tions (kō′shē rē′män, kō shē′-), *Math.* equations relating the partial derivatives of the real and imaginary parts of an analytic function of a complex variable, as $f(z) = u(x,y) + iv(x,y)$, by $\frac{\partial u}{\partial x} = \frac{\partial v}{\partial y}$ and $\frac{\partial u}{\partial y} = -\frac{\partial v}{\partial x}$. [named after A. L. CAUCHY and G. F. B. RIEMANN]

Cau′chy-Schwarz′ inequal′ity (kō′shē shwôrts′, kō shē′shvärts′), *Math.* **1.** See **Cauchy's inequality. 2.** See **Schwarz inequality.**

Cau′chy se′quence, *Math.* See **fundamental sequence.** [named after A. L. CAUCHY]

Cau′chy's inequal′ity, *Math.* the theorem that for two indexed sets of real numbers with each set having the same number of elements, the square of the sum of the products of corresponding numbers is less than or equal to the sum of the squares of the numbers in one set times the sum of the squares of the numbers in the other set. Also called **Cauchy-Schwarz inequality.** [named after A. L. CAUCHY]

Cau·con (kô′kon), *n. Class. Myth.* a son of either Lycaön or Poseidon who brought the mysteries of Demeter to Messenia.

cau·cus (kô′kəs), *n., pl.* **-cus·es,** *v.* —*n.* **1.** *U.S.* a meeting of the local members of a political party to nominate candidates, elect delegates to a convention, etc., or of the members of a legislative body who belong to the same party to determine upon action in that body. **2.** (in England) a local committee of a political party exercising a certain control over its affairs or actions. —*v.i.* **3.** to hold or meet in a caucus. [prob. < Algonquian; akin to *caucauasu* adviser (Virginia)]

cau·da (kou′də, kô′-), *n., pl.* **cau·dae** (kou′dē, kô′-). *Anat., Zool.* a tail or taillike appendage. [< L: tail]

cau·dad (kô′dad), *adv. Anat., Zool.* toward the tail or posterior end of the body (opposed to *cephalad*). [< L *caud(a)* tail + *ad* to, toward]

cau·da·ite (kô′də īt′), *n.* a small meteorite, generally less than one half millimeter in diameter, containing crystals of more or less pure magnetite. [< L *caud(a)* tail + -ITE[1]]

cau·dal (kôd′əl), *adj.* **1.** *Anat., Zool.* of, at, or near the tail or the posterior end of the body. **2.** *Zool.* taillike: *caudal appendages.* [< NL *caudāl(is),* equiv. to L *caud(a)* tail + *-ālis* -AL[1]] —**cau′dal·ly,** *adv.*

cau′dal anesthe′sia, *Med.* anesthesia below the pelvis, induced by injecting an anesthetic into the sacral portion of the spinal canal.

cau′dal fin′, the terminal vertical fin of a fish. See diag. under **fish.**

cau′dal pedun′cle, the slender posterior portion of the body of a fish, ending in the caudal fin; the part of body between the anal and caudal fins.

cau·date (kô′dāt), *adj. Zool.* having a tail or taillike appendage. Also, **cau′dat·ed.** [< NL *caudāt(us),* equiv. to L *caud(a)* tail + *-ātus* -ATE[1]] —**cau·da′tion,** *n.*

cau·dex (kô′deks), *n., pl.* **-di·ces** (-di sēz′), **-dex·es.** *Bot.* **1.** the axis of a plant, including both stem and root. **2.** a stem bearing the remains or scars of petioles. **3.** the woody or thickened persistent base of a herbaceous perennial. [< L: tree trunk]

cau·dil·lo (kô dēl′yō, -dē′ō; *Sp.* kou thē′lyō, -thē′yō), *n., pl.* **-dil·los** (-dēl′yōz, -dē′ōz; *Sp.* -thē′lyōs, -thē′yōs). (in Spanish-speaking countries) the head of the state; leader. [< Sp < LL *capitellu(m),* equiv. to L *capit-* (s. of *caput*) head + *-ellum* dim. suffix]

Cau′dine Forks′ (kô′dīn), two mountain passes in S Italy, in the Apennines near Benevento.

cau·dle (kôd′əl), *n.* a warm drink for the sick, as of wine or ale mixed with eggs, bread, sugar, spices, etc. [ME *caudel* < ONF < ML *caldell(um),* equiv. to L *calid(um)* warmed watered wine (n. use of neut. of *calidus* warm) + *-ellum* dim. suffix]

cau′dle cup′, a deep drinking cup having two handles and, usually, a cover.

caught (kôt), *v.* pt. and pp. of **catch.**

caul[1] (kôl), *n.* **1.** a part of the amnion sometimes covering the head of a child at birth. **2.** See **greater omentum. 3.** a net lining in the back of a woman's cap or hat. **4.** a cap or hat of net, often elaborately decorated, formerly worn by women. **5.** *Obs.* the net foundation for a wig. [ME *calle* < MF *cale,* prob. back formation from *calotte* kind of cap; see CALOTTE]

caul[2] (kôl), *n.* a form or plate for pressing a veneer or veneers being glued to a backing or to each other. [< F *cale* shim < G *Keil* wedge]

caul-, var. of **caulo-** before a vowel: *caulescent.*

cauld (kôld, käld, kôd), *adj., n. Scot.* cold.

caul·dron (kôl′drən), *n.* a large kettle or boiler. Also, **caldron.** [late ME, m. (by assoc. with L *caldus* warm) of ME *cauderon* < AF, equiv. to *caudere* (< LL *caldāria;* see CALDERA) + *-on* n. suffix]

cau·les·cent (kô les′ənt), *adj. Bot.* having an obvious stem rising above the ground. [CAUL- + -ESCENT]

cauli-, var. of **caulo-:** *cauliform.*

cau·li·cle (kô′li kəl), *n. Bot.* a small or rudimentary stem. [< L *caulicul(us),* equiv. to *cauli(s)* a stalk + *-culus* -CULE]

cau·lic·o·lous (kô lik′ə ləs), *adj. Bot.* growing on the stem of a plant, as certain fungi. [CAULI- + -COLOUS]

cau·lic·u·lus (kô lik′yə ləs), *n., pl.* **-li** (-lī′). *Archit.* (in a Corinthian capital) any of eight fluted sheaths from which pairs of helices issue. Cf. **Corinthian** (def. 4). [< L: little stem; see CAULICLE]

cau·li·flo·rous (kô′lə flôr′əs, -flōr′-), *adj. Bot.* producing flowers or fruit directly from the trunk or branches, as certain trees. [CAULI- + *-florous* (< LL *-flōrus,* equiv. to L *flōr-* (s. of *flōs*) flower)] —**cau·li·flo·ry** (kô′lə flôr′ē, -flōr′ē), *n.*

cau·li·flow·er (kô′lə flou′ər, -lē-, kol′ə-, kol′ē-), *n.* **1.** a cultivated cruciferous plant, *Brassica oleracea botrytis,* whose inflorescence forms a compact, fleshy head. **2.** this head, used as a vegetable. [< L *cauli(s)* COLE + FLOWER; r. *coleflorie* < It *ca(v)olfiore,* equiv. to *cavol* cole + *fiore* < L *flōri-* (s. of *flōs*) flower]

cau′liflower ear′, an ear that has been deformed by repeated injury, resulting in an irregular thickening of scar tissue.

cau·li·form (kô′lə fôrm′), *adj. Bot.* resembling a stem. [CAULI- + -FORM]

cau·line (kô′lin, -līn), *adj. Bot.* of or pertaining to a stem, esp. pertaining to or arising from the upper part of a stem. [< L *caul(is)* a stalk, stem + -INE[1]]

cau·lis (kô′lis), *n., pl.* **-les** (-lēz). *Bot.* the main stalk or stem of a plant, esp. of a herbaceous plant. [< L: stalk, stem; c. Gk *kaulós*]

caulk (kôk), *v.t.* **1.** to fill or close (a seam, joint, etc.), as in a boat. **2.** to make (a vessel) watertight by filling the seams between its planks with oakum or other material driven snug. **3.** to drive the edges of (plating) together to prevent leakage. **4.** to fill or close seams or crevices of (a tank, window, etc.) in order to make watertight, airtight, etc. Also, **calk.** [late ME *caulke* < L *calc(āre)* (to) tramp, equiv. to *calc-* (s. of *calx*) heel + ME *cauken* < OF *cauque(r)* (to) tread < L, as above]

caulk·er (kô′kər), *n.* **1.** one who caulks the seams of boats or the like. **2.** a caulking tool or device. Also, **calker.** [CAULK + -ER[1]]

caulo-, a combining form of **caulis:** *caulocarpous.* Also, **caul-, cauli-.** [< L *caul(is)* stalk, stem + -o-]

cau·lo·car·pous (kô′lə kär′pəs), *adj. Bot.* bearing fruit year after year on the same stems. [CAULO- + -CARPOUS]

cau·lome (kô′lōm), *n. Bot.* the stem structure of a plant, considered as a whole. [CAUL- + *-ome;* see -OMA] —**cau·lom·ic** (kô lom′ik, -lō′mik), *adj.*

Cau·lo·nia (kou lō′nyä), *n.* a town in S Calabria, in S Italy: ruins of ancient Achaean colony. 11,036 (1961).

Cau·nus (kô′nəs), *n. Class. Myth.* the brother of Byblis.

Cau·que·nes (kou ke′nes), *n.* a city in central Chile. 14,849 (1950).

caus., causative.

caus·al (kô′zəl), *adj.* **1.** of, constituting, or implying a cause: *a causal force.* **2.** *Gram.* expressing a cause, as a conjunction. [< L *causāl(is),* equiv. to *caus(a)* CAUSE + *-ālis* -AL[1]] —**caus′al·ly,** *adv.*

cau·sal·gi·a (kô zal′jē ə, -jə), *n.* a neuralgia distinguished by a burning pain along certain nerves, usually of the upper extremities. [< NL, equiv. to Gk *kaûs(is)* a burning + NL *-algia* -ALGIA; see CAUSTIC]

cau·sal·i·ty (kô zal′i tē), *n., pl.* **-ties. 1.** the relation of cause and effect: *The result is the same, however differently the causality is interpreted.* **2.** causal quality or agency. [CAUSAL + -ITY]

cau·sa si·ne qua non (kou′sä si′ne kwä nōn′; *Eng.* kô′zə sī′nē kwā non′), *Latin.* an indispensable condition; requisite. [lit., a cause without which not]

cau·sa·tion (kô zā′shən), *n.* **1.** the action of causing or producing. **2.** the relation of cause to effect. **3.** anything that produces an effect; cause. [< ML *causātiōn-* (s. of *causātiō*), equiv. to *causāt(us)* caused (ptp. of *causāre*) (L *caus(a)* CAUSE + *-ātus* -ATE[1]) + *-iōn-* -ION] —**cau·sa′tion·al,** *adj.*

cau·sa·tion·ism (kô zā′shə niz′əm), *n.* the doctrine or theory that every event is the result of a prior and adequate cause. [CAUSATION + -ISM] —**cau·sa′tion·ist,** *n.*

caus·a·tive (kô′zə tiv), *adj.* **1.** acting as a cause; producing (often fol. by *of*): *a causative agency; an event causative of war.* **2.** *Gram.* noting causation. The causative form of *to fall* is *to fell.* Gothic *-jan* is a causative suffix in *fulljan "to cause to be full; to fill."* —*n.* **3.** *Gram.* a word, esp. a verb, noting causation, as *made* in *He made me eat the apple.* [ME < L *causātīv(us),* equiv. to *causāt(us)* caused (see CAUSATION) + *-īvus* -IVE] —**caus′a·tive·ly,** *adv.* —**caus′a·tive·ness, caus′a·tiv′i·ty,** *n.*

cause (kôz), *n., v.,* **caused, caus·ing.** —*n.* **1.** one who or that which acts, happens, or exists in such a way that some specific thing happens as a result; the producer of an effect: *You have been the cause of much anxiety. What was the cause of the accident?* **2.** the reason or motive for some human action: *This news was a cause for rejoicing.* **3.** good or sufficient reason: *to complain without cause; to be dismissed for cause.* **4.** *Law.* **a.** a ground of legal action; the matter over which a person goes to law. **b.** a case for judicial decision. **5.** any subject of discussion or debate. **6.** the ideal or goal, or the set of these, to which a person or group is dedicated: *the Socialist cause; the cause of better housing.* **7.** the general welfare of a person or group, seen as the subject of concern either to themselves or to others: *liberal support for the cause of the American Negro.* **8.** *Philos.* **a.** the end or purpose for which a thing is done or produced. **b.** *Aristotelianism.* any of the four things necessary for the movement or the coming into being of a thing, namely a material **(material cause),** something to act upon it **(efficient cause),** a form taken by the movement or development **(formal cause),** and a goal or purpose **(final cause). 9. make common cause with,** to unite with in a joint effort; work together with for the same end: *They made common cause with neighboring countries and succeeded in reducing tariffs.* —*v.t.* **10.** to be the cause of; bring about. [ME < L *caus(a)* reason, sake, case] —**caus′a·bil′i·ty,** *n.* —**caus′a·ble,** *adj.* —**cause′less,** *adj.* —**cause′less·ly,** *adv.* —**cause′less·ness,** *n.* —**caus′er,** *n.*

—**Syn. 1.** CAUSE, OCCASION refer to the starting of effects into motion. A CAUSE is an agency, perhaps acting through a long time, or a long-standing situation, which produces an effect: *The cause of the quarrel between the two men was jealousy.* An OCCASION is an event which provides an opportunity for the effect to become evident, or perhaps promotes its becoming evident: *The occasion was the fact that one man's wages were increased.* **3.** See **reason. 10.** effect, make, create, produce.

'cause (kôz, kuz, *unstressed* kəz), *conj., adv. Informal.* because. [aph. var.]

cause-and-ef·fect (kôz′ənd i fekt′), *adj.* noting a relationship between actions or events such that one or more are the result of the other or others.

cause cé·lè·bre (kôz′ sə leb′rə, -leb′; *Fr.* kōz sā leb′[R]), *pl.* **causes cé·lè·bres** (kôz′ sə leb′rəz, -sə lebz′, kô′ziz sə leb′rə, -leb′; *Fr.* kōz sā leb′[R]). any controversy that attracts great public attention, as a celebrated legal case or trial. [< F: lit., famous case]

cau·se·rie (kō′zə rē′; *Fr.* kōz[ə] rē′), *n., pl.* **-ries** (-rēz′; *Fr.* -rē′). **1.** a talk or chat. **2.** a short, informal essay, article, etc. [< F, equiv. to *caus(er)* (to) chat (< L *causārī* to plead at law, deriv. of *causa* case) + *-erie* -ERY]

Cau·se·ries du Lun·di (*Fr.* kōz[ə] rē′ dʏ lœn dē′). See **Monday Conversations.**

cau·seuse (kō zœz′), *n., pl.* **-seuses** (-zœz′). *Fr. Furniture.* an upholstered settee for two persons. [< F, equiv. to *caus(er)* (to) chat (see CAUSERIE) + *-euse,* fem. of *-eur* -OR[2]]

cause·way (kôz′wā′), *n.* **1.** a raised road or path, as across low or wet ground. **2.** a highway or paved way. —*v.t.* **3.** to pave, as a road or street, with cobblestones or pebbles. **4.** to provide with a causeway. [ME; see CAUSEY, WAY]

cau·sey (kô′zē), *n., pl.* **-seys.** *Brit. Dial.* **1.** a causeway. **2.** *Archaic.* an ancient Roman highway, its course, or surviving landmarks, sometimes used as a boundary or path. [ME *cauce* < AF < ONF *caucie,* var. of *cauciee* < LL *(via) calciāta* (road) paved with limestone, equiv. to L *calci-* (s. of *calx*) limestone + *-āta,* fem. of *-ātus* -ATE[1]]

caus·tic (kô′stik), *adj.* **1.** capable of burning, corroding, or destroying living tissue. **2.** severely critical or sarcastic: *a caustic remark.* —*n.* **3.** a caustic substance. **4.** *Optics.* **a.** See **caustic curve. b.** See **caustic surface.** [< L *caustic(us)* < Gk *kaustikós* burning, caustic, equiv. to *kaust(ós)* burnt (*kaus-* (ptp. s. of *kaíein* to burn) + *-tos* ptp. suffix) + *-ikos* -IC] —**caus′ti·cal,** *adj.* —**caus′ti·cal·ly, caus′tic·ly,** *adv.* —**caus·tic·i·ty** (kô stis′i tē), **caus′tic·ness,** *n.*

—**Syn. 2.** biting, mordant, bitter, scathing.

caus′tic al′cohol. See **sodium ethylate.**

caus′tic bary′ta, baryta (def. 2).

caus′tic curve′, *Optics.* a curve formed by a plane section of a caustic surface. Also called **caustic.**

caus′tic lime′, lime[1] (def. 1).

caus′tic pot′ash. See **potassium hydroxide.**

caus′tic so′da. See **sodium hydroxide.**

caus′tic sur′face, *Optics.* the surface to which all light rays emanating from a single point and reflected by a curved surface, as a concave mirror, are tangent. Also called **caustic.**

cau·ter·ant (kô′tər ənt), *Med.* —*n.* **1.** a caustic agent. —*adj.* **2.** cauterizing; caustic. [CAUTER(IZE) + -ANT]

cau·ter·ise (kô′tə rīz′), *v.t.,* **-ised, -is·ing.** *Chiefly Brit.* cauterize. —**cau′ter·i·sa′tion,** *n.*

cau·ter·ize (kô′tə rīz′), *v.t.,* **-ized, -iz·ing.** to burn with a hot iron, fire, or a caustic, esp. for curative purposes; treat with a cautery. [< LL *cautērīz(āre)* (to) brand, equiv. to *cautēr-* (< Gk *kautḗr* branding iron, equiv. to *kau-,* var. s. of *kaíein* to burn, + *-tēr* instrumental suffix) + *-īzāre* -IZE] —**cau′ter·i·za′tion,** *n.*

cau·ter·y (kô′tə rē), *n., pl.* **-ter·ies. 1.** an escharotic substance or a hot iron used to destroy tissue. **2.** the process of destroying tissue with a cautery. [< L *cautēri(um)* < Gk *kautḗrion,* equiv. to *kautḗr* branding iron (see CAUTERIZE) + *-ion* dim. suffix]

cau·tion (kô′shən), *n.* **1.** alertness and prudence in a hazardous situation; care; wariness: *Landslides ahead—proceed with caution.* **2.** a warning against danger or evil; anything serving as a warning: *By way of caution, he told me the difficulties I would face.* **3.** *Informal.* someone or something that astonishes or causes mild apprehension: *She's a caution. The way he challenges your remarks is a caution.* —*v.t.* **4.** to give warning to; advise or urge to take heed. —*v.i.* **5.** to warn or advise: *The newspapers caution against overoptimism.* [ME *caucion* < L *cautiōn-* (s. of *cautiō*) a taking care, equiv. to *caut(us)* guarded against, ptp. of *cavēre* (*cau-* take care + *-tus* ptp. suffix) + *-iōn-* -ION] —**cau′tion·er,** *n.*

—**Syn. 1.** circumspection, discretion, watchfulness, heed, vigilance. **2.** admonition, advice, counsel. **4.** admonish, forewarn. See **warn.** —**Ant. 1.** carelessness.

cau·tion·ar·y (kô′shə ner′ē), *adj.* of the nature of or containing a warning: *cautionary advice; a cautionary tale.* [CAUTION + -ARY]

cau′tion mon′ey, (in British universities) money deposited by a student as security against payment of college bills, fees, etc.

cau·tious (kô′shəs), *adj.* manifesting or characterized by caution: *a cautious man; To be cautious is often to show wisdom.* [CAUTI(ON) + -OUS] —**cau′tious·ly,** *adv.* —**cau′tious·ness,** *n.*

—**Syn.** prudent, guarded, wary, chary, circumspect, watchful, vigilant. See **careful.**

Cau·ver·y (kô′və rē), *n.* a river in S India, flowing SE from the Western Ghats in Mysore state through Madras state to the Bay of Bengal: sacred to the Hindus. 475 mi. long. Also, **Kaveri.**

Cav., cavalry.

cav., **1.** cavalier. **2.** cavalry.

ça va (SA VA′), *French.* all right; fine. [lit., that goes]

ca·vae·di·um (kə vē′dē əm, kä-, kā-), *n., pl.* **-di·a** (-dē ə). atrium (def. 1a). [< L, contr. of *cavum aedium,* lit., hollow of rooms (i.e. house); see CAVE[1], EDIFICE]

Ca·va·fy (kä vä′fē), *n.* **Constantine,** 1868–1933, Greek poet in Egypt. Also, **Kavaphis.**

cav·al·cade (kav′əl kād′, kav′əl kād′), *n.* **1.** a procession of persons riding on horses or in horsedrawn carriages. **2.** any procession. [< MF < early It *cavalcat(a)* horseback raid, equiv. to *cavalc(are)* (to) ride (< LL *caballicāre,* equiv. to *caball(us)* horse (see CAVALIER) + *-icā-* v. suffix + *-re* inf. ending) + *-ata* -ADE[1]]

Cav·a·ler·i·us (kav′ə lâr′ē əs), *n.* a crater in the second quadrant of the face of the moon: about 40 miles in diameter.

cav·a·le·ro (kav′ə lâr′ō, -əl yâr′ō), *n., pl.* **-ros.** **1.** a cavalier. **2.** a caballero.

cav·a·lier (kav′ə lēr′, kav′ə lēr′), *n.* **1.** a horseman, esp. a mounted soldier; knight. **2.** one having the spirit or bearing of a knight; a courtly gentleman; gallant. **3.** a man escorting a woman or acting as her partner in dancing; beau. **4.** (*cap.*) an adherent of Charles I of England in his contest with Parliament. —*adj.* **5.** haughty, disdainful, or supercilious: *an arrogant and cavalier attitude toward others.* **6.** offhand or unceremonious: *The very dignified officials were confused by his cavalier manner.* **7.** (*cap.*) of or pertaining to the Cavaliers. **8.** (*cap.*) of, pertaining to, or characteristic of the Cavalier poets or their work. —*v.i.* **9.** to play the cavalier. **10.** to be haughty or domineering. [< MF: horseman, knight << OPr < LL *caballārī(us)* groom, equiv. to L *caball(us)* nag (< Gk *kabállēs*, perh. < Galatian Celt) + *-ārius* -ARY] —**cav′a·lier′ism, cav′a·lier′ness,** *n.*

Ca·va·lie·ri (kav′əl yâr′ē; *It.* kä′vä lye′rē), *n.* **Fran·ces·co Bo·na·ven·tu·ra** (frän ches′kō bô′nä ven tōō′rä), 1598–1697, Italian mathematician.

cav·a·lier·ly (kav′ə lēr′lē, kav′ə lēr′-), *adv.* **1.** in a cavalier manner. —*adj.* **2.** characteristic of a cavalier; arrogant. [CAVALIER + -LY]

Cav′alier po′ets, a group of English poets, including Herrick, Carew, Lovelace, Suckling, etc., mainly at the court of Charles I, who produced a body of graceful lyric poetry.

ca·va·lier ser·ven·te (kä′vä lyer′ ser ven′te), *pl.* **ca·va·lie·ri ser·ven·ti** (kä′vä lye′rē ser ven′tē). *Italian.* a lover of a married woman; cicisbeo. [lit., serving cavalier]

ca·val·la (kə val′ə), *n., pl.* **-la, -las.** cavally.

Ca·val·le·ri·a Rus·ti·ca·na (kav′ə lə rē′ə rus′tə kan′ə, rōōs′-; *It.* kä′väl le rē′ä rōōs′tē kä′nä), an opera (1890) by Pietro Mascagni.

ca·val·ly (kə val′ē), *n., pl.* **-lies.** **1.** any of several carangoid fishes of the genus *Caranx*, esp. *C. hippos*, a food fish found off both coasts of tropical America. **2.** the cero. Also, **cavalla.** [< Sp *caballa* horse-mackerel, lit., mare (fem. of *caballo* horse); see CAVALIER]

cav·al·ry (kav′əl rē), *n., pl.* **-ries.** **1.** *Mil.* **a.** the part of a military force composed of troops that serve on horseback. **b.** mounted soldiers collectively. **c.** (in armored forces) a unit charged with reconnaissance and with security for larger forces as its principal missions. **2.** horsemen, horses, etc., collectively. **3.** *Obs.* horsemanship, esp. of a knight. [syncopated var. of *cavallery* < It *cavalleria*, equiv. to *cavall(o)* horse (see CAVALIER) + *-eria* -ERY]

cav·al·ry·man (kav′əl rē mən, -man′), *n., pl.* **-men** (-mən, -men′). a member of the cavalry; mounted soldier. [CAVALRY + MAN[1]]

cav′alry twill′, a strong cotton, wool, or worsted fabric constructed in double twill, used in the manufacture of wearing apparel, esp. for the armed forces. Also called **tricotine.**

Cav·an (kav′ən), *n.* **1.** a county in Ulster, in the N Republic of Ireland. 56,594 (1961); 730 sq. mi. **2.** the seat of this county. 3207 (1963).

ca·vate (kā′vāt), *adj.* **1.** hollowed out, as a space excavated from rock. **2.** forming or resembling a cave: *the cavate cliff dwellings of the Indians.* Also, **ca′vat·ed.** [< L *cavāt(us)* made hollow (ptp.), equiv. to *cav(āre)* (to) hollow + *-ātus* -ATE[1]]

cav·a·ti·na (kav′ə tē′nə; *It.* kä′vä tē′nä), *n., pl.* **-ne** (-nā; *It.* -ne). *Music.* a simple song or melody, properly one without a second part and a repeat; an air. [< It, equiv. to *cavat(a)* song (lit., something drawn out, n. use of fem. of *cavata* < L *cavat(us)* hollowed out, hollow; see CAVE[1], -ATE[1]) + *-ina* -INE[1]]

cave[1] (kāv), *n., v.,* **caved, cav·ing.** —*n.* **1.** a hollow in the earth, esp. one opening more or less horizontally into a hill, mountain, etc. **2.** a storage cellar, esp. for wine. **3.** *Eng. Pol.* a secession, or a group of seceders, from a political party on some special question. —*v.t.* **4.** to hollow out. **5.** *Mining.* **a.** to cause (overlying material) to fall into a stope, sublevel, or the like. **b.** to cause (supports, as stulls or sets) to collapse beneath overlying material. **c.** to fill (a stope or the like) with caved-in material: *sub-level caving.* —*v.i.* **6.** *Informal.* to cave in. **7. cave in, a.** to fall in; collapse. **b.** to cause to fall in or collapse. **c.** *Informal.* to yield; submit; surrender: *The opposition caved in before our superior arguments.* [ME < OF < LL *cav(a)* (fem. sing.), L *cava*, neut. pl. of *cavum* hole, n. use of neut. of *cavus* (adj.) hollow] —**cave′like′,** *adj.*

ca·ve[2] (kā′vē), *Brit. Slang.* —*n.* **1.** watch; lookout: *I'm going to keep cave from an upstairs window.* —*interj.* **2.** beware; look out; watch out. [< L, impv. of *cavēre* to be on one's guard, beware; see CAUTION]

ca·ve·a (kā′vē ə, kä′-; *Lat.* kä′wē ä′), *n., pl.* **-ve·ae** (-vē ē′; *Lat.* -wē ī′). the semicircular auditorium of an ancient Roman theater. [< L: hollow place, seats in an amphitheatre. See CAVE[1]]

cave′ art′, the art of the cave man, esp. the art produced during the Paleolithic period and found chiefly in the caves of southwestern Europe.

ca·ve·at (kā′vē at′), *n.* **1.** *Law.* a legal notice to a court or public officer to suspend a certain proceeding until the notifier is given a hearing: *a caveat filed against the probate of a will.* **2.** any warning or caution. [< L: let him beware, 3rd pers. sing. pres. subj. of *cavēre* to take care; see CAUTION]

ca·ve·at emp·tor (kā′vē at′ emp′tôr; *Lat.* kä′we ät′ emp′tôr), the principle that the seller cannot be held responsible for the quality of his product unless guaranteed in a warranty. [< L: lit., let the buyer beware]

ca·ve·a·tor (kā′vē ā′tər), *n.* one who files or enters a caveat. [CAVEAT + -OR[2]]

ca·ve ca·nem (kä′we kä′nem; *Eng.* kā′vē kā′nem), *Latin.* beware of the dog.

cave′ dwell′er, **1.** one whose home is a cave. **2.** a prehistoric man who lived in caves. **3.** *Informal.* one who lives in an apartment building or the like in a large city.

cave·fish (kāv′fish′), *n., pl.* (*esp. collectively*) **-fish,** (*esp. referring to two or more kinds or species*) **-fish·es.** any of several fishes that live in cave waters, as species of the genus *Amblyopsis*, having no body pigment and rudimentary, functionless eyes. [CAVE[1] + FISH]

cave-in (kāv′in′), *n.* a collapse, as of anything hollow: *the worst cave-in in the history of mining.* [n. use of v. phrase *cave in*]

cav·el[1] (kav′əl), *n.* *Naut.* kevel[1].

cav·el[2] (kav′əl), *n.* *Masonry.* kevel[2].

Cav·ell (kav′əl), *n.* **Edith Louisa,** 1865–1915, English nurse: executed by the Germans in World War I.

cave′ man′, **1.** a cave dweller, esp. of the Stone Age. **2.** *Informal.* a man who behaves in a rough, primitive manner, esp. toward women.

cav·en·dish (kav′ən dish), *n.* tobacco that has been softened, sweetened, and pressed into cakes. [presumably named after maker or handler]

Cav·en·dish (kav′ən dish), *n.* **1. Henry,** 1731–1810, English chemist and physicist. **2. William, 4th Duke of Devonshire,** 1720–64, British statesman: prime minister 1756–57. **3.** a walled plain in the third quadrant of the face of the moon: about 32 miles in diameter.

Cav′endish banan′a. See **dwarf banana.**

Cav′endish exper′iment, *Physics.* the experiment, conducted by Henry Cavendish, that determined the constant of gravitation by using a torsion balance and measuring the torsion produced by two masses placed at given distances from the masses on the balance.

cav·er[1] (kā′vər), *n.* one who studies or investigates caves. [CAVE[1] + -ER[1]]

cav·er[2] (kā′vər), *n.* a soft breeze in the Hebrides. Also, **kaver.** [dial. *cave* to toss, push + -ER[1]]

cav·ern (kav′ərn), *n.* **1.** a cave, esp. a large one. **2.** *Pathol.* a cavity that is produced by disease, esp. one produced in the lungs by tuberculosis. [ME *caverne* < L *cavern(a)*, equiv. to *cav(us)* hollow + *-erna*, as in *cisterna* CISTERN]

cav·ern·ous (kav′ər nəs), *adj.* **1.** containing caverns. **2.** deep-set: *cavernous eyes.* **3.** hollow and deep-sounding: *a cavernous voice.* **4.** full of small cavities; porous. **5.** being, resembling, or suggestive of a cavern: *cavernous darkness.* [late ME < L *cavernōs(us).* See CAVERN, -OUS] —**cav′ern·ous·ly,** *adv.*

Caves du Va·ti·can, Les (*Fr.* lā kav dy va tē kän′). See **Lafcadio's Adventures.**

cav·es·son (kav′i sən), *n.* the noseband of a bridle or a halter. [< It *cavezzon(e)* noseband halter, equiv. to *cavezz(a)* halter (< Gmc; cf. OE *cælf* halter, muzzle) + *-one* aug. suffix]

ca·vet·to (kə vet′ō; *It.* kä vet′tô), *n., pl.* **-ti** (-tē), **-tos.** *Archit.* a concave molding the outline of which is a quarter circle. See illus. under **molding.** [< It, equiv. to *cav(o)* (< L *cavus* or *cavum* hollow place; see CAVE[1]) + *-etto* -ET]

cav·i·ar (kav′ē är′, kav′ē är′), *n.* **1.** the roe of sturgeon, esp. the beluga, or other fish, usually served as an hors d'oeuvre or appetizer. **2. caviar to the general,** something beyond the taste or appreciation of the general public: *Art galleries not so long ago were caviar to the general, but today everyone goes to them.* Also, **cav′i·are′.** [appar. back formation from *caviarie* (taken, perh. rightly, as *caviar* + pl. ending, L or It *-i*) < ?; cf. It *caviaro*, Turk *khavyar*]

cav·i·corn (kav′ə kôrn′), *adj.* *Zool.* hollow-horned, as the ruminants with true horns, as distinguished from bony antlers. [< NL *cavicorn(is)* hollow-horned, equiv. to *cavi-* (comb. form of L *cavus* hollow) + *cornis* (L *corn(ū)* horn + *-is* adj. suffix)]

ca·vie (kā′vē), *n.* *Scot.* a hen coop; a cage for fowls. Also, **cavy.** [< D or Flem *kavie* (now obs.) << L *cavea* birdcage, cavity, equiv. to *cav(us)* hollow + *-ea* n. suffix, fem. of *-eus* -EOUS]

cav·il[1] (kav′əl), *v.,* **-iled, -il·ing** or (*esp. Brit.*) **-illed, -il·ling,** *n.* —*v.i.* **1.** to raise irritating and trivial objections; find fault with unnecessarily (usually fol. by *at* or *about*): *Even he could find nothing to cavil about.* —*v.t.* **2.** to oppose by inconsequential, frivolous, or sham objections: *to cavil each item of a proposed agenda.* —*n.* **3.** a trivial and annoying objection: *No one reproached him for the harsh words with which he answered such a cavil.* **4.** the raising of such objections: *He raises captious objections merely for the sake of cavil.* [< L *cavill(ārī)* (to) jeer, scoff, quibble, equiv. to *cavill(a)* scoffing + *-ā-* thematic vowel + *-rī* inf. ending] —**cav′il·er;** *esp. Brit.,* **cav′il·ler,** *n.* —**cav′il·ing·ly;** *esp. Brit.,* **cav′il·ling·ly,** *adv.* —**cav′il·ing·ness;** *esp. Brit.,* **cav′il·ling·ness,** *n.*

—**Syn. 1.** carp, complain, criticize.

cav·il[2] (kav′əl), *n.* *Naut.* kevel[1].

cav·il[3] (kav′əl), *n.* *Masonry.* kevel[2].

cav·i·ta·tion (kav′i tā′shən), *n.* **1.** the rapid formation and collapse of vapor pockets in a flowing liquid in regions of very low pressure, often a frequent cause of structural damage to propellers, pumps, etc. **2.** such a pocket formed in a flowing liquid. [CAVIT(Y) + -ATION]

Ca·vi·te (kä vē′te, kə-), *n.* a seaport on S Luzon, in the N Philippines, on Manila Bay: naval base. 43,759 (est. 1959).

cav·i·ty (kav′i tē), *n., pl.* **-ties.** **1.** any hollow place; hollow: *a cavity in the earth.* **2.** *Anat.* a hollow space within the body, an organ, a bone, etc. **3.** *Dentistry.* the loss of tooth structure, most commonly produced by caries. A cavity may be artificially made to support dental restorations. [< MF *cavite* < LL *cavit(ās)* hollowness, equiv. to L *cav(us)* hollow + *-itās* -ITY] —**cav′i·tied,** *adj.*

—**Syn. 1.** See **hole.**

cav′ity res′onator, *Electronics.* resonator (def. 4a).

ca·vo-re·lie·vo (kä′vō ri lē′vō, kā′-), *n., pl.* **-vos.** *Fine Arts.* **1.** a form of relief sculpture in which the volumes are carved or incised so that the highest points are below or level with the original surface. Cf. **intaglio** (defs. 1–3). **2.** a piece of sculpture in this form. Also called **sunk relief.** [< It *cavo-rilievo* hollow relief. See CAVE[1], RELIEF]

ca·vo-ri·lie·vo (kä′vō ri lē′vō, kā′-; *It.* kä′vô rē lye′vô), *n., pl.* **ca·vi-ri·lie·vi** (kä′vē ri lē′vē, kā′-; *It.* kä′vē rē lye′vē). cavo-relievo.

ca·vort (kə vôrt′), *v.i.* to prance or caper about. [earlier *cavault*, perh. CUR(VET) + VAULT[2]] —**ca·vort′er,** *n.*

Ca·vour (kä vōōr′), *n.* **Ca·mil·lo Ben·so di** (kä mēl′lô ben′sô dē), 1810–61, Italian statesman: leader in the unification of Italy.

CAVU, *Aeron.* ceiling and visibility unlimited. Also, **cavu, c.a.v.u.**

ca·vum (kā′vəm, kā′-), *n., pl.* **-va** (-və). *Anat.* a cavity. [< L: cavity; see CAVE[1]]

ca·vy[1] (kā′vē), *n., pl.* **-vies.** any of several short-tailed or tailless South American rodents of the family *Caviidae*, as the guinea pig, capybara, or agouti. [< NL *Cavi(a)* name of the genus < Carib (Galibi) *cabiai*]

ca·vy[2] (kā′vē), *n., pl.* **-vies.** *Scot.* cavie.

caw (kô), *n.* **1.** the cry of the crow, raven, etc. —*v.i.* **2.** to utter this cry or a similar sound. [imit.]

Cawn·pore (kôn′pōr′, -pôr′), *n.* a city in S Uttar Pradesh, in NE India on the Ganges River. 881,200 (1961). Also, **Cawn·pur** (kôn′pōōr′). Indian, **Kanpur.**

Ca·xi·as (kä shē′əs), *n.* a city in NE Brazil. 19,092 (1960).

Caxi′as do Sul′ (dōō sōōl′), a city in S Brazil. 69,269 (1960).

c-ax·is (sē′ak′sis), *n., pl.* **c-ax·es** (sē′ak′sēz). *Crystall.* the vertical crystallographic axis. Cf. **A-axis, B-axis.**

Cax·ton (kak′stən), *n.* **1. William,** 1422?–91, English printer, translator, and author: established first printing press in England 1476. **2.** *Bibliog.* any one of the books printed by Caxton, all of which are in black letter. **3.** *Print.* a kind of type imitating Caxton's black letter. —**Cax·to·ni·an** (kak stō′nē ən), *adj.*

cay (kā, kē), *n.* a small low island; key. [< Sp *cay(o)*; see KEY[2]]

Cay·ce (kā′sē), *n.* a town in central South Carolina. 8517 (1960).

cay·enne (kī en′, kā-), *n.* a hot, biting condiment composed of the ground pods and seeds of the pepper *Capsicum frutescens longum.* Also called **cayenne′ pep′per.** [short for *cayenne pepper*, formerly *cayan* < Tupi *kyinha* but long assoc. with CAYENNE] —**cay·enned′,** *adj.*

Cay·enne (kī en′, kā-), *n.* **1.** a seaport in and the capital of French Guiana. 18,635 (1961). **2.** (*l.c.*) Also called **cayenne′ whist′.** a variety of whist played with two full packs of 52 cards each.

Cayes (kā), *n.* **Les.** See **Les Cayes.**

Ca·ye·y (kä ye′ē), *n.* a city in central Puerto Rico. 19,738 (1960).

Cay·ley (kā′lē), *n.* **Arthur,** 1821–95, English mathematician. —**Cay′ley·an,** *adj.*

cay·man (kā′mən), *n., pl.* **-mans.** caiman.

Cay·man′ Is′lands (kī män′), three islands in the West Indies, NW of Jamaica: dependencies of Jamaica. 8803 (est. 1960); 104 sq. mi.

Ca·yu·ga (kā yōō′gə, kī-), *n., pl.* **-gas,** (*esp. collectively*) **-ga.** a member of a tribe of North American Indians, the smallest tribe of the Iroquois Confederacy. [< Mohawk *Kweñiōgwen*, lit., place where locusts were taken out]

Cayu′ga Heights′, a town in central New York. 2788 (1960).

Cayu′ga Lake′, a lake in central New York: one of the Finger Lakes. 40 mi. long.

cay·use (kī yōōs′, kī′ōōs), *n.* *Western U.S.* an Indian pony. [named after the *Cayuse* American Indian tribe, now living in Oregon]

Caz·e·no·vi·a (kaz′ə nō′vē ə), *n.* a town in central New York. 2584 (1960).

Cb, *Chem.* columbium.

CB, **1.** See **citizens band.** **2.** *Mil.* construction battalion.

C.B., **1.** Bachelor of Surgery. [< L *Chirurgiae Baccalaureus*] **2.** *Brit.* Companion of the Bath.

C battery, *Electronics.* an electric battery for supplying a constant voltage bias to a control electrode of a vacuum tube. Cf. **A battery, B battery.**

C.B.D., cash before delivery.

C.B.E., Commander of the Order of the British Empire.

C.B.E.L., Cambridge Bibliography of English Literature. Also, **CBEL**

C-bi·as (sē′bī′əs), *n.* *Electronics.* See **grid bias.**

cc., **1.** carbon copy. **2.** chapters. **3.** cubic centimeter. Also, **c.c.**

C.C., **1.** carbon copy. **2.** cashier's check. **3.** chief clerk. **4.** circuit court. **5.** city council. **6.** city councilor. **7.** civil court. **8.** company commander. **9.** county clerk. **10.** county commissioner. **11.** county council. **12.** county court. Also, **c.c.**

C.C.A., **1.** Chief Clerk of the Admiralty. **2.** Circuit Court of Appeals. **3.** County Court of Appeals.

CCC, *U.S.* Civilian Conservation Corps: the former federal agency (1933–1943) that instituted and administered projects for the conservation of natural resources.

C Clefs

C clef, *Music.* a movable clef that, according to its position, locates middle C on the first, third, or fourth line of the staff.

C.Cls., Court of Claims.

ccm., centimeters.

C.C.P., **1.** *Law.* Code of Civil Procedure. **2.** Court of Common Pleas.

CCR, Commission on Civil Rights.

CD, **1.** certificate of deposit. **2.** Civil Defense. **3.** See **compact disk.** Also, **C.D.**

Cd, candela; candelas.

Cd, *Chem.* cadmium.

cd., cord; cords.

C/D, certificate of deposit. Also, **c/d**

c.d., cash discount.

Cdr., Commander. Also, **CDR**

CD-ROM (sē′dē′rom′), *n.* a compact disk that can hold a large quantity of computer data, digitized pictures, etc., for read-only use.

-ce, a multiplicative suffix occurring in *once, twice, thrice.* [ME, OE *-es* adv. suffix, orig. gen. sing. ending; see -S[1]]

Ce, *Chem.* cerium.

C.E., **1.** Civil Engineer. **2.** common era.

c.e., **1.** buyer's risk. [< L *caveat emptor*] **2.** compass error.

CEA, **1.** Commodity Exchange Authority. **2.** See **Council of Economic Advisers.** **3.** County Education Authority.

Ce·a·rá (*Port.* se′ä rä′), *n.* Fortaleza.

cease (sēs), *v.*, **ceased, ceas·ing,** *n.* —*v.i.* **1.** to stop; discontinue: *Not all medieval superstitions have ceased to exist.* **2.** to come to an end: *At last the war has ceased.* **3.** *Obs.* to pass away; die out. —*v.t.* **4.** to put a stop or end to; discontinue: *He begged them to cease their ovation and to resume their seats.* —*n.* **5.** cessation: *The noise of the workmen drilling went on for hours without cease.* [ME *ces(s)e(n)* < OF *cesse(r)* < L *cessāre* to leave off, equiv. to *cess(us)* withdrawn, gone (ptp. of *cēdere*) (*ced-* go + *-tus* ptp. suffix) + *-ā-* thematic vowel + *-re* inf. ending; see CEDE]
—**Syn. 2.** terminate, end, culminate. —**Ant. 1.** begin.

cease′-and-de·sist′ or′der (sēs′ən di zist′, -sist′), an order by a government agency, esp. the FTC, to a person or corporation to terminate a business practice found by the agency to be illegal or unfair.

cease-fire (sēs′fīər′), *n.* **1.** a cessation of hostilities; truce. **2.** *Mil.* an order issued for a cease-fire. [n. use of v. phrase *cease fire*]

cease·less (sēs′lis), *adj.* without stop or pause; unending; incessant: *the ceaseless rain of a tropical summer.* [CEASE + -LESS] —**cease′less·ly,** *adv.* —**cease′less·ness,** *n.*

Ceb·ri·o·nes (sə brī′ə nēz′), *n.* a brother of Hector who served as his charioteer.

Ce·bú (se bo͞o′), *n.* **1.** an island in the central Philippines. 1,402,090 (est. 1960); 1703 sq. mi. **2.** a seaport on this island. 209,111 (est. 1960).

Čech·y (che′ḵhi), *n.* Czech name of **Bohemia.**

Cec·il (ses′əl *or, for 4,* sē′səl), *n.* **1. (Edgar Algernon) Robert** (*1st Viscount Cecil of Chelwood*), 1864–1958, British statesman: Nobel peace prize 1937. **2. William** (*1st Baron Burghley* or *Burleigh*), 1520–98, British statesman: adviser to Elizabeth I. **3. Robert Arthur Talbot Gascoyne-.** See **Gascoyne-Cecil. 4.** a boy's given name.

Ce·cile (si sēl′), *n.* a girl's given name, form of **Cecilia.**

Ce·cil·ia (si sēl′yə), *n.* **1. Saint,** died A.D. 230?, Roman martyr: patron saint of music. **2.** Also, **Ce·cil′lia.** a girl's given name.

Cec·i·ly (ses′ə lē), *n.* a girl's given name, form of **Cecilia.** Also, **Cicely.**

Ce·cro′pi·a moth′ (si krō′pē ə), (*sometimes l.c.*) a large, North American silkworm moth, *Hyalophora cecropia,* the larvae of which feed on the foliage of forest and other trees. Also called **Ce·cro′pi·a.** [< NL *Cecropia* name of the genus, L *Cecropia,* fem. of *Cecropius* pertaining to CECROPS]

Ce·crops (sē′krops), *n.* *Class. Myth.* the founder and first king of Attica, portrayed as half man, half dragon.

ce·cum (sē′kəm), *n., pl.* **-ca** (-kə). *Anat., Zool.* a cul-de-sac, esp. that in which the large intestine begins. Also, **caecum.** [short for L *intestinum caecum* blind gut] —**ce′cal,** *adj.*

Ce·cyle (si sēl′, ses′il), *n.* a girl's given name, form of **Cecilia.**

CED, Committee for Economic Development.

Ce·da·li·on (sə dā′lē ən), *n.* *Class. Myth.* a smith at the forge of Hephaestus who was forced to serve as a guide for the blinded Orion.

ce·dant ar·ma to·gae (kā′dänt är′mä tō′gī; *Eng.* sē′dant är′mə tō′jē). *Latin.* let military power be subject to civil authority: motto of Wyoming. [lit., let arms yield to toga]

ce·dar (sē′dər), *n.* **1.** any of several Old World, coniferous trees of the genus *Cedrus.* Cf. **cedar of Lebanon. 2.** any of various junipers, as the red cedar, *Juniperus virginiana.* **3.** any of various coniferous trees. Cf. **incense cedar, white cedar. 4.** any of several meliaceous trees of the genus *Cedrela,* as the Spanish cedar. **5.** the wood of any of these trees. [ME *cedir,* etc., OE *ceder* < L *cedr(us)* < Gk *kédros;* r. ME *cedre* < OF < L, as above]

ce′dar ap′ple, a brown gall on the branches of the juniper, produced by several rust fungi of the genus *Gymnosporangium.*

Ce·dar·burg (sē′dər bûrg′), *n.* a town in E Wisconsin. 5191 (1960).

Ce′dar Cit′y, a town in SW Utah. 7543 (1960).

Ce′dar Falls′, a city in central Iowa. 21,195 (1960).

Ce′dar Ham′mock, a town in SW Florida. 3089 (1960).

Ce·dar·hurst (sē′dər hûrst′), *n.* a town on W Long Island, in SE New York. 6954 (1960).

Ce′dar Lake′, a town in NW Indiana. 5766 (1960).

ce·darn (sē′dərn), *adj.* **1.** *Literary.* of cedar trees. **2.** made of cedar wood. [CEDAR + -(E)N²]

ce′dar of Leb′anon, a cedar, *Cedrus Libani,* of Asia Minor, having wide, spreading branches.

Ce′dar Rap′ids, a city in E Iowa. 92,035 (1960).

Ce·dar·town (sē′dər toun′), *n.* a town in NW Georgia. 9340 (1960).

ce′dar wax′wing, a North American waxwing, *Bombycilla cedorum,* having light yellowish-brown plumage. Also called **ce′dar bird′.**

Cedar waxwing (Length 7 in.)

cede (sēd), *v.t.,* **ced·ed, ced·ing.** to yield or formally resign and surrender to another; make over, as by treaty: *to cede territory.* [< L *cēde(re)* (to) go, yield] —**ced′er,** *n.*
—**Syn.** relinquish, abandon; grant, transfer, convey. —**Ant.** retain.

ce·dil·la (si dil′ə), *n.* **1.** a mark (¸) placed under a consonant letter, as under *c* in French, Portuguese, and formerly in Spanish, to indicate that it is pronounced (s), under *c* and *s* in Turkish to indicate that they are pronounced, respectively, (ch) and (sh), under *t* and *s* in Rumanian to indicate that they are pronounced, respectively, (ts) and (sh), etc. **2.** this mark used as a diacritic of arbitrary value in transliteration of words from non-Roman into Roman alphabetic characters. [< Sp. var. sp. of *zedilla* little *z,* equiv. to *zed(a)* ZED + *-illa* dim. suffix; the mark was so called from its original form]

Ced·re·a·tis (sed′rē ā′tis), *n.* *Class. Myth.* an epithet of Artemis, meaning "of the cedar tree."

Ced·ric (sed′rik, sē′drik), *n.* a boy's given name.

ced·u·la (sej′ə lə), *n.* **1.** (in Spanish-speaking countries) any of various orders, certificates, or the like. **2.** any of certain securities issued by South American and Central American governments. **3.** (in the Philippines) **a.** a personal registration tax certificate. **b.** the tax itself. Also, **cé·du·la** (sej′ə lə; *Sp.* the′tho͞o lä′, se′-). [< Sp; see SCHEDULE]

C.E.F., Canadian Expeditionary Force.

cei·ba (sā′bə *or, for 2,* sī′-; *Sp.* thā′vä, sā′-), *n., pl.* **-bas** (-bəz; *Sp.* -väs). **1.** the silk-cotton tree, *Ceiba pentandra.* **2.** silk cotton; kapok. [< Sp < Taino *ceyba* or its cognate in another Arawak dial.]

cei·bo (sā′bō; *Sp.* sā′bô), *n., pl.* **-bos** (-bōz; *Sp.* -bôs). a shrub or small tree, *Erythrina Crista-galli,* of Brazil and Argentina, having spiny leaflets and loose clusters of crimson flowers. [< AmerSp; Sp *ceiba*]

ceil (sēl), *v.t.* **1.** to overlay (the interior upper surface of a building or room) with wood, plaster, etc. **2.** to provide with a ceiling. [ME *cele(n)* (to) drape, screen, line < ?]

ceil·er (sē′lər), *n.* *U.S. Shipbuilding.* one who applies ceiling to the frames of a wooden vessel; planker. [CEIL + -ER¹]

cei·lidh (kā′lē), *n.* *Scot.* a party, gathering, or the like, at which singing and storytelling are the usual forms of entertainment. [< IrGael *céilidhe,* ScotGael *cèilidh* < MIr *célide,* deriv. of OIr *céle* companion, husband]

ceil·ing (sē′ling), *n.* **1.** the overhead interior lining of a room. **2.** a lining applied for structural reasons to a framework, esp. in the interior surfaces of a ship or boat. **3.** the top limit imposed by law on the amount of money that can be charged or spent or the quantity of goods that can be produced or sold. **4.** *Aeron.* **a.** the maximum altitude from which the earth can be seen on a particular day, usually equal to the distance between the earth and the base of the lowest cloud bank. **b.** the maximum altitude to which a particular aircraft can rise under specified conditions. **5.** *Meteorol.* the height above the point of observation of the lowest layer of clouds or other obscuring phenomena in the atmosphere; the extent of vertical visibility. **6.** Also called **ceil′ing piece′.** *Theat.* the ceiling or top of an interior set, made of cloth, a flat, or two or more flats hinged together. **7.** act or work of one who ceils. **8.** vaulting, as in a medieval church. **9. hit the ceiling,** *Slang.* to lose control of one's temper; become enraged: *When he saw the amount of the bill, he hit the ceiling.* [CEIL + -ING¹] —**ceil′inged,** *adj.*

ceil′ing light′, a vertically pointing searchlight used in determining, by triangulation, the height of a cloud base.

ceil′ing plate′, *Theat.* a metal plate on the back of a ceiling piece, with a ring for attaching a line from the gridiron.

ceil·om·e·ter (sē lom′i tər, si-), *n.* *Meteorol.* an automatic device for measuring and recording the height of clouds by projecting a modulated beam of light onto a cloud base, receiving the reflection of light through a photoelectric apparatus, and computing the height by triangulation. [CEIL(ING) + -O- + -METER]

Ce·la (the′lä), *n.* **Ca·mi·lo Jo·sé** (kä mē′lô hô se′), born 1916, Spanish writer.

cel·a·don (sel′ə don′, -dən), *n.* **1.** any of several Chinese porcelains having a translucent, pale green glaze. **2.** any porcelain imitating these. **3.** a pale gray-green. —*adj.* **4.** having the color celadon. [after *Céladon,* name of a character in *L'Astrée,* a tale by H. d'Urfé (1568–1625), French writer]

Ce·lae·no (sə lē′nō), *n.* *Class. Myth.* **1.** one of the Pleiades. **2.** (in the *Aeneid*) one of the Harpies.

cel·an·dine (sel′ən dīn′), *n.* **1.** Also called **great′er cel′andine.** a papaveraceous plant, *Chelidonium majus,* having yellow flowers. **2.** Also called **less′er cel′andine.** a ranunculaceous plant, *Ranunculus Ficaria,* having yellow flowers. [late ME *selandyne,* nasalized var. of ME *celydon* < L *chelidon(ia),* n. use of fem. of *chelidonius* < Gk *chelidónios,* equiv. to *chelidoni-* (s. of *chelidṓn*) the swallow + *-os* adj. suffix]

cel′andine pop′py, a papaveraceous plant, *Stylophorum diphyllum,* of the east-central U.S., having yellow flowers.

Cel·a·nese (sel′ə nēz′, sel′ə nēz′), *n.* *Trademark.* an acetate rayon yarn or fabric.

cel·a·ture (sel′ə cho͝or′), *n.* the art of embossing metal. [ME < L *caelātur(a)* art of engraving, equiv. to *caelāt(us)* (ptp. of *caelāre* to engrave) + *-ura* -URE]

-cele¹, a learned borrowing from Greek meaning "tumor," used in the formation of compound words: *varicocele.* [comb. form repr. Gk *kḗlē* a tumor; akin to OE *hēala* hydrocele]

-cele², var. of **-coele:** *blastocele.*

ce·leb (sə leb′), *n.* *Slang.* a celebrity. [by shortening]

Cel·e·bes (sel′ə bēz′; *Du.* se lā′bes), *n.* an island in E Indonesia. 6,571,000 with adjacent islands (est. 1961); 72,986 sq. mi. Indonesian, **Sulawesi.** —**Cel·e·be·sian** (sel′ə bē′zhən), *adj.*

cel·e·brant (sel′ə brənt), *n.* **1.** the officiating priest in the celebration of the Eucharist. **2.** a participant in a public religious rite. **3.** a participant in any celebration. **4.** one who praises or extols a person or thing. [< L *celebrant-* (s. of *celebrāns* solemnizing, prp. of *celebrāre*), equiv. to *celebr-* (see CELEBRATE) + *-ant-* -ANT]

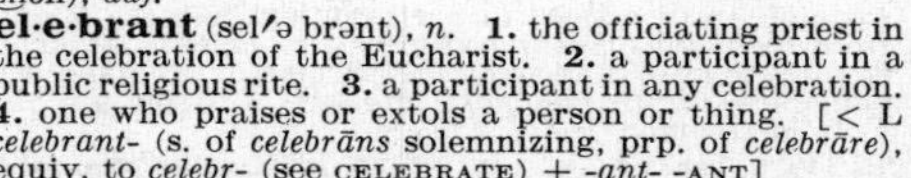

cel·e·brate (sel′ə brāt′), *v.,* **-brat·ed, -brat·ing.** —*v.t.* **1.** to observe (a day) or commemorate (an event) with ceremonies or festivities: *to celebrate Christmas; to celebrate the success of a new play.* **2.** to make known publicly; proclaim: *The newspaper celebrated the end of the war in red headlines.* **3.** to praise widely or to present to widespread and favorable public notice, as through newspapers, novels, etc.: *a man celebrated in the headlines; a novel celebrating the joys of marriage; the countryside celebrated in the novels of Hardy.* **4.** to perform with appropriate rites and ceremonies; solemnize: *to celebrate a marriage.* —*v.i.* **5.** to observe a day or commemorate an event with ceremonies or festivities. **6.** to perform a religious ceremony, esp. Mass or the Lord's Supper. [< L *celebrāt(us)* solemnized, celebrated, honored (ptp. of *celebrāre*), equiv. to *celebr-* (s. of *celeber*) often repeated, famous + *-ātus* -ATE¹] —**cel′e·bra′tive,** *adj.* —**cel′e·bra′tor, cel′e·brat′er,** *n.* —**cel·e·bra·to·ry** (sel′ə brə tōr′ē, -tôr′ē, sə leb′rə-), *adj.*
—**Syn. 1.** commemorate, honor, solemnize. **3.** laud, glorify, applaud, commend.

cel·e·brat·ed (sel′ə brā′tid), *adj.* famous; renowned; well-known. [CELEBRATE + -ED²] —**cel′e·brat′ed·ness,** *n.*
—**Syn.** illustrious. See **famous.**

Cel′ebrated Jump′ing Frog′ of Cal·a·ver′as Coun′ty, The (kal′ə ver′əs), a short story (1865) by Mark Twain.

cel·e·bra·tion (sel′ə brā′shən), *n.* **1.** act of celebrating. **2.** that which is done to celebrate anything. [< L *celebrātiōn-* (s. of *celebrātiō*) big assembly. See CELEBRATE, -ION]

cel·e·bret (sel′ə bret′), *n.* *Rom. Cath. Ch.* a certificate from a bishop or other superior identifying the bearer as a priest authorized to celebrate Mass. [< L: let him celebrate, 3rd pres. sing. subj. of *celebrāre*]

Cel·e·brez·ze (sel′ə brē′zē), *n.* **Anthony J.,** born 1910, U.S. lawyer and government official: Secretary of Health, Education, and Welfare 1962–65.

ce·leb·ri·ty (sə leb′ri tē), *n., pl.* **-ties** for 1. **1.** a famous or well-known person. **2.** fame; renown. [< L *celebritās* multitude, fame, festal celebration, equiv. to *celebr-* (s. of *celeber*) often repeated, famous + *-itās* -ITY]

ce·ler·i·ac (sə ler′ē ak′, -lēr′-), *n.* a variety of celery, *Apium graveolens rapaceum,* having a large, edible, turniplike root. Also called **knob celery, turnip-rooted celery.** [CELERY + -AC]

ce·ler·i·ty (sə ler′i tē), *n.* swiftness; speed. [ME *celerite* < MF < L *celeritāt-* (s. of *celeritās*), equiv. to *celer* swift + *-itāt-* -ITY]
—**Syn.** activity, sprightliness, alacrity, dispatch, briskness, liveliness. See **speed.**

cel·er·y (sel′ə rē), *n.* a plant, *Apium graveolens,* of the parsley family, whose blanched leafstalks are used raw for salad and cooked as a vegetable. [< F *céleri* < It *seleri,* pl. of *selero* << Gk *sélin(on)* parsley]

cel′ery cab′bage. See **Chinese cabbage.**

cel′ery salt′, a seasoning of finely ground celery seed and salt.

ce·les·ta (sə les′tə), *n.* a musical instrument consisting principally of a set of graduated steel plates struck with hammers which are activated by a keyboard. [< F *célest(a),* deriv. of *céleste,* lit., heavenly (see CELESTIAL); the *-a* for *-e* makes the name pseudo-Italian]

Celesta

Ce·leste (sə lest′), *n.* a girl's given name, form of **Celestine.**

ce·les·tial (sə les′chəl), *adj.* **1.** pertaining to the spiritual or invisible heaven; heavenly; divine: *celestial bliss.* **2.** pertaining to the sky or visible heaven. **3.** of or pertaining to celestial navigation: *a celestial fix.* **4.** (*cap.*) of or pertaining to the former Chinese Empire or the Chinese people. —*n.* **5.** an inhabitant of heaven. **6.** (*cap.*) a citizen of the Celestial Empire. [ME < ML *cēlestiāl(is),* equiv. to L *caelesti(s)* heavenly (*cael(um)* heaven, sky + *-estis* adj. suffix) + *-ālis* -AL¹] —**ce·les′tial·ly,** *adv.* —**ce·les′tial·ness, ce·les·ti·al·i·ty** (sə les′chē al′i tē), *n.*

Celes′tial Cit′y, 1. the goal of Christian's journey in Bunyan's *Pilgrim's Progress;* the heavenly Jerusalem. **2.** See **New Jerusalem.**

celes′tial crown′, *Heraldry.* a representation of an eastern crown with a star on the tip of each ray.

Celes′tial Em′pire, the former Chinese Empire.

celes′tial equa′tor, *Astron., Navig.* the great circle of the celestial sphere, lying in the same plane as the earth's equator. Also called **equator, equinoctial, equinoctial line.**

celes′tial globe′. See under **globe** (def. 3).

celes′tial guid′ance, *Rocketry.* a guidance system for a missile or spacecraft by which an automatic device in the vehicle takes periodic fixes on celestial bodies to determine the craft's position and to guide it to its target. Also called **astro-inertial guidance.**

celes′tial hi′erarchy, hierarchy (def. 6).

celes′tial hori′zon, *Astron.* See under **horizon** (def. 2b).

celes′tial lat′itude, *Astron.* the angular distance from the ecliptic of a point on the celestial sphere.

celes′tial lon′gitude, *Astron.* the angular distance of a point on the celestial sphere from the great circle that is perpendicular to the ecliptic at the point of the vernal equinox, measured through 360° eastward parallel to the ecliptic.

celes′tial mechan′ics, the branch of astronomy that deals with the application of the laws of dynamics and Newton's law of gravitation to the motions of heavenly bodies. Cf. **dynamical astronomy.**

celes′tial naviga′tion, navigation by means of observations made of the apparent position of heavenly bodies. Also called **astronavigation, celo-navigation.**

celes′tial pole′, *Astron.* each of the two points in which the extended axis of the earth cuts the celestial sphere and about which the stars seem to revolve. Also called **pole.**

celes′tial sphere′, the imaginary spherical shell formed by the sky, usually represented as an infinite sphere, the center of which is a given observer's position.

Ce·les·ti·na, La (*Sp.* lä the′les tē′nä). See **La Celestina.**

Cel·es·tine (sel′i stīn′, si les′tin, -tīn), *n.* a girl's given name. Also, **Cel·es·ti·na** (sel′i stē′nə).

Celestine I, Saint, died A.D. 432, Italian ecclesiastic: pope 422–432.

Celestine II, (*Guido di Castello*), fl. 12th century, Italian ecclesiastic: pope 1143–44.

Celestine III, (*Giacinto Bobone*), died 1198, Italian ecclesiastic: pope 1191–98.

Celestine IV, (*Godfrey Castiglione*), died 1241, Italian ecclesiastic: pope 1241.

Celestine V, Saint (*Pietro di Murrone* or *Morone*), 1215–96, Italian ascetic: pope 1294.

cel·es·tite (sel′i stīt′), *n.* a white to pale-blue mineral, strontium sulfate, $SrSO_4$, occurring in tabular crystals, the principal ore of strontium. Also, **cel·es·tine** (sel′i stin, -stīn′). [*celest(ine)* celestite (< G *Zölestin* < L *coelest(is)*, var. of *caelestis* CELESTIAL, + G *-in* -IN[2]) + -ITE[1]]

Cel·eu·the·a (sel′yə thē′ə), *n.* *Class. Myth.* an epithet of Athena, meaning "she of the road."

celi-, var. of **coeli-:** *celiac.*

Cel·ia (sēl′yə), *n.* a girl's given name, form of **Cecilia.**

ce·li·ac (sē′lē ak′), *adj.* *Anat.* of, pertaining to, or located in the cavity of the abdomen. Also, **coeliac.** [< L *coeliac(us)* < Gk *koiliakós* of the belly. See CELI-, -AC]

ce′liac disease′, *Pathol.* a chronic disturbance of nutrition in young children, characterized by marked abdominal distention, malnutrition, wasting, and the passage of large, white, frothy, and offensive stools containing large quantities of undigested fat.

ce′liac plex′us, *Anat.* See **solar plexus** (def. 1).

cel·i·ba·cy (sel′ə bə sē; *esp. Brit.* sə lib′ə sē), *n.* **1.** state of being unmarried. **2.** abstention by vow from marriage: *the celibacy of priests.* **3.** abstention from sexual relations. [< L *caelibā(tus)* celibacy (*caelib-,* s. of *caelebs* single, + *-ātus* -ATE[1]) + -CY] —**cel·i·bat·ic** (sel′ə bat′ik), *adj.*

Cé·li·ba·taires, Les (*Fr.* lā sā lē bA teR′). See **Perish in Their Pride.**

cel·i·bate (sel′ə bit, -bāt′), *n.* **1.** one who remains unmarried, esp. for religious reasons. **2.** one who abstains from sexual relations. —*adj.* **3.** unmarried. **4.** observing or pertaining to sexual abstention or a religious vow not to marry. [< L *caelib-* (s. of *caelebs*) single + -ATE[1]]

Ce·li·na (sə lē′nə), *n.* a town in W Ohio. 7659 (1960).

Ce·line (sə lēn′), *n.* a girl's given name, French form of **Celia.**

Cé·line (sā lēn′), *n.* **Louis-Fer·di·nand** (lwē feR dē näN′), (*Louis F. Destouches*), 1894–1961, French physician and novelist.

celio-, var. of **coelio-:** *celiotomy.*

ce·li·o·scope (sē′lē ə skōp′), *n.* *Med.* celoscope. —**ce·li·os·co·py** (sē′lē os′kə pē), *n.*

ce·li·ot·o·my (sē′lē ot′ə mē), *n., pl.* **-mies.** *Surg.* laparotomy (def. 2). [CELIO- + -TOMY]

cell (sel), *n.* **1.** a small room, as in a convent or prison. **2.** any of various small compartments or bounded areas forming part of a whole. **3.** a small group acting as a unit within a larger organization: *a local cell of the Communist Party.* **4.** *Biol.* **a.** a usually microscopic plant or animal structure containing nuclear and cytoplasmic material enclosed by a semipermeable membrane and, in plants, a cell wall; the structural unit of plant and animal life. **b.** a minute cavity or interstice, as in animal or plant tissue. **5.** *Entomol.* one of the areas into which the wing of an insect is divided by the veins. **6.** *Bot.* the pollen sac of an anther. **7.** *Elect.* a device that generates electricity, usually consisting of two different conducting substances placed in an electrolyte. **8.** *Physical Chem.* a device for producing electrolysis, consisting essentially of the electrolyte, its container, and the electrodes **(electrolytic cell). 9.** *Aeron.* the gas container of a balloon. **10.** *Eccles.* a monastery or nunnery, usually small, dependent on a larger religious house. [ME *celle* < ML *cell(a)* monastic cell, L: room; see CELLA] —**cell′-like′,** *adj.*

cel·la (sel′ə), *n., pl.* **cel·lae** (sel′ē). *Archit.* **1.** the principal enclosed chamber of a classical temple. **2.** the whole central structure of a classical temple behind or within the portico or porticos, including both open vestibules and chambers. Also called **naos.** [< L: storeroom, shrine, akin to *cēlāre* to hide]

cel·lar (sel′ər), *n.* **1.** a room, or set of rooms, for the storage of food, fuel, etc., wholly or partly underground and usually beneath a building. **2.** an underground room or story. **3.** See **wine cellar. 4.** *Sports.* the lowest position among a group ranked in order of games won: *The team was in the cellar for most of the season.* —*v.t.* **5.** to place or store in a cellar. [< L *cellār(ium)* pantry, n. use of neut. of *cellārius* pertaining to a storeroom; see CELLA, -ARY; r. ME *celer* < AF < L, as above] —**cel′lar·less,** *adj.*

cel·lar·age (sel′ər ij), *n.* **1.** cellar space. **2.** charges for storage in a cellar. [CELLAR + -AGE]

cel·lar·er (sel′ər ər), *n.* the steward of a monastery. [< LL *cellārār(ius),* equiv. to L *cellār(ium)* CELLAR + *-ārius* -ER[2]; r. ME *celerer* < AF < LL, as above]

cel·lar·et (sel′ə ret′), *n.* a compartment, cabinet, or stand fitted for wine bottles. Also, **cel′lar·ette′.** [CELLAR + -ET]

cel·lar·man (sel′ər mən), *n., pl.* **-men.** one who is in charge of the alcoholic-beverage supply of a hotel or restaurant. [CELLAR + MAN[1]]

cel′lar sash′, a window sash of relatively small size, having two or three lights horizontally arranged.

cell·block (sel′blok′), *n.* a unit of a prison consisting of a number of cells. [CELL + BLOCK]

cell′ divi′sion, *Biol.* the division of a cell in reproduction or growth.

Cel·li·ni (chə lē′nē; *It.* chel lē′nē), *n.* **Ben·ve·nu·to** (ben′və no͞o′tō; *It.* ben′ve no͞o′tô), 1500–71, Italian sculptor, metalsmith, and autobiographer.

Celli′ni's ha′lo, heiligenschein. [named after Benvenuto CELLINI, who described the effect]

cel·list (chel′ist), *n.* one who plays a cello. Also, **'cel′list.** Also called **violoncellist.** [short for VIOLONCELLIST]

cell′ mem′brane, *Biol.* the semipermeable membrane enclosing the protoplasmic material of a cell.

cel·lo (chel′ō), *n., pl.* **-los.** the third largest member of the violin family, rested vertically on the floor between the performer's knees when being played. Also, **'cel′lo, violoncello.** [short for VIOLONCELLO]

Cello

cel·lo·bi·ose (sel′ō bī′ōs), *n.* *Biochem.* a white, crystalline, water-soluble disaccharide, $C_{12}H_{22}O_{11}$, that is obtained by the breakdown of cellulose or lichenin and yields glucose upon hydrolysis: used chiefly in bacteriology as a reagent. [CELL(ULOSE) + -O- + BI-[2] + -OSE[2]]

cel·loi·din (sə loi′din), *n.* *Microscopy.* a concentrated form of pyroxylin used to embed tissues for cutting and microscopic examination. [CELL(ULOSE) + -OID + -IN[2]]

cel·lo·phane (sel′ə fān′), *n.* **1.** a transparent, paperlike product of viscose, impervious to moisture, germs, etc., used to wrap candy, tobacco, etc. —*adj.* **2.** of, made of, or resembling cellophane. [formerly trademark]

cel·lu·lar (sel′yə lər), *adj.* pertaining to or characterized by cellules or cells, esp. minute compartments or cavities. [< NL *cellulār(is),* equiv. to *cellul(a)* live cell (L: little room; see CELLULE) + *-āris* -AR[1]] —**cel·lu·lar·i·ty** (sel′yə lar′i tē), *n.* —**cel′lu·lar·ly,** *adv.*

cel·lu·late (sel′yə lāt′), *adj., v.,* **-lat·ed, -lat·ing.** —*adj.* **1.** cellular. —*v.t.* **2.** to form into cells. [< NL *cellul(a)* (see CELLULAR) + -ATE[1]] —**cel′lu·la′tion,** *n.*

cel·lule (sel′yo͞ol), *n.* a minute cell. [< L *cellul(a)* small room. See CELL, -ULE]

cel·lu·li·tis (sel′yə lī′tis), *n.* *Pathol.* inflammation of cellular tissue. [< NL, equiv. to *cellul(a)* (see CELLULAR) + *-itis* -ITIS]

Cel·lu·loid (sel′yə loid′), *n.* *Trademark.* a substance consisting essentially of soluble guncotton and camphor, usually highly flammable, variously used as a substitute for ivory, vulcanite, etc., and in the manufacture of motion-picture and X-ray film, fountain pens, and numerous other products.

cel·lu·lo·lyt·ic (sel′yə lō lit′ik), *adj.* *Biochem.* (of bacteria or enzymes) capable of hydrolyzing cellulose. [CELLUL(OSE) + -O- + -LYTIC]

cel·lu·lose (sel′yə lōs′), *n.* *Biochem.* an inert carbohydrate, the chief constituent of the cell walls of plants, wood, cotton, hemp, paper, etc. [< NL *cellul(a)* live cell (see CELLULAR) + -OSE[2]] —**cel·lu·los·i·ty** (sel′yə los′i tē), *n.*

cel′lulose ac′etate, *Chem.* any of a group of acetic esters of cellulose, used to make yarns, textiles, nonflammable photographic films, rubber and Celluloid substitutes, etc.

cel′lulose ni′trate, *Chem.* any of a group of nitric esters of cellulose, used in the manufacture of lacquers and explosives. Also called **nitrocellulose.**

cel′lulose triac′etate, *Chem.* a triacetic ester of cellulose characterized by its resistance to most solvents, used chiefly as a coating in the manufacture of textile fibers.

cel·lu·lo·sic (sel′yə lō′sik), *Chem.* —*adj.* **1.** of, containing, or derived from cellulose. —*n.* **2.** any cellulosic compound or substance. [CELLULOSE + -IC]

cel·lu·lous (sel′yə ləs), *adj.* full or consisting of cells. [< NL *cellulōs(us),* equiv. to *cellul(a)* live cell (see CELLULAR) + *-ōsus* -OUS]

cell′ wall′, *Biol.* the definite boundary or wall which is usually part of the structure of a biological cell, esp. a plant cell.

ce·lom (sē′ləm), *n.* coelom.

ce·lo·nav·i·ga·tion (sē′lō nav′ə gā′shən, sel′ō-), *n.* See **celestial navigation.** [CEL(ESTIAL) + -O- + NAVIGATION]

ce·lo·scope (sē′lə skōp′), *n.* *Med.* an instrument for examining a body cavity. Also, **celioscope, coeloscope.** [< Gk *koîlo(s)* hollow or *koîlo(n)* a hollow + -SCOPE]

ce·lot·o·my (sə lot′ə mē), *n., pl.* **-mies.** *Surg.* herniotomy. [< Gk *kēlotomía,* equiv. to *kēle* rupture + *tomia* -TOMY]

Cels., Celsius (centigrade).

Cel·si·us (sel′sē əs, -shē-; *for 1 also Swed.* sel′sē o͝os′), *n.* **1. Anders** (än′dəsh), 1701–44, Swedish astronomer: devised centigrade scale of temperature. **2.** a walled plain in the fourth quadrant of the face of the moon: about 27 miles in diameter. —*adj.* **3.** centigrade (def. 2).

celt (selt), *n.* *Archaeol.* an ax of stone or metal without perforations or grooves, for hafting. [< LL **celt(is)* chisel, found only in the abl. case *celte* (*Vulgate,* Job XIX, 24)]

Celt (selt, kelt), *n.* a member of an Indo-European people now represented chiefly by the Irish, Gaels, Welsh, and Bretons. Also, **Kelt.** [< L *Celt(ae)* (pl.); in Gk *Keltoí* (pl.)]

Celt., Celtic. Also, **Celt**

Cel·tic (sel′tik, kel′-), *n.* **1.** a branch of the Indo-European family of languages including esp. Irish, Scots Gaelic, Welsh, and Breton, which survive now in Ireland, the Scottish Highlands, Wales, and Brittany. —*adj.* **2.** of the Celts or their language. Also, **Keltic.** [< L *Celtic(us),* equiv. to *Celt(ae)* the Celts (see CELT) + *-icus* -IC] —**Cel′ti·cal·ly,** *adv.*

Celt′ic cross′, a cross shaped like a Latin cross and having a ring that intersects each segment of the shaft and crossbar at a point equidistant from their junction. See illus. under **cross.**

Celt·i·cism (sel′ti siz′əm, kel′-), *n.* **1.** a Celtic custom or usage. **2.** a liking for Celtic customs. [CELTIC + -ISM] —**Celt′i·cist, Celt′ist,** *n.*

Celto-, a combining form of **Celt** or **Celtic:** *Celto-Iberian.*

Cel·to-Ger·man·ic (sel′tō jər man′ik, kel′-), *adj.* **1.** having the characteristics of both the Celtic and Germanic peoples. **2.** pertaining to or designating a style of art developed in northern and western Europe from about the 5th–9th centuries A.D., chiefly characterized by the use of recognizable human or animal motifs elaborated into complex interlaced patterns. Also, **Celt′ic-German′ic.**

cel·tuce (sel′tis), *n.* an edible, lettucelike vegetable, *Lactuca sativa asparagina,* used raw in salads or cooked. [CEL(ERY + LET)TUCE]

cel·ure (sel′yər), *n.* an ornamented canopy, as for a bed or dais. [ME, equiv. to *cel(en)* (to) drape (see CEIL) + -URE]

cem·ba·lo (chem′bə lō′), *n., pl.* **-li** (-lē′), **-los.** *Music.* **1.** harpsichord. **2.** dulcimer (def. 1). [< It (*clavi*)*cembalo* < L *cymbalum* CYMBAL] —**cem′ba·list,** *n.*

ce·ment (si ment′), *n.* **1.** any of various soft, sticky substances that dry hard or stonelike, used esp. for making things adhere. **2.** any of various calcined mixtures of clay and limestone, usually combined with an aggregate to form concrete, that are used as a building material. **3.** *Petrog.* the compact groundmass surrounding and binding together the fragments of clastic rocks. **4.** anything that binds or unites: *Time is the cement of friendship.* **5.** *Dentistry.* a hardening, adhesive, plastic substance, used in the repair of teeth for anchoring fillings or inlays, for filling, or for fastening crowns. —*v.t.* **6.** to unite by or as by cement: *to cement stones to form a wall; Time cements friendship.* **7.** to coat or cover with cement: *to cement a floor.* —*v.i.* **8.** to become cemented; join together or unite; cohere. [< L *cēmentum* (um), var. of *caementum* (sing. of *caementa* unprocessed cuttings from the quarry, i.e., rough stone and chips), var. of **caedimentum,* equiv. to *caedi-* (s. of *caedere* to cut) + *-mentum* -MENT; r. ME *cyment* < OF *ciment*] —**ce·ment′er,** *n.* —**ce·ment′less,** *adj.*

ce·men·ta·tion (sē′mən tā′shən, -men-, sem′ən-), *n.* **1.** act, process, or result of cementing. **2.** *Metall.* the heating of two substances in contact in order to effect some change in one of them, esp., the formation of steel by heating iron in powdered charcoal. [CEMENT + -ATION]

ce·ment·ite (si men′tīt), *n.* *Metall.* a carbide, Fe_3C, found as a constituent of steel and cast iron, sometimes having part of its iron replaced by other metals, as manganese. [CEMENT + -ITE[1]]

ce·men·ti·tious (sē′men tish′əs), *adj.* having the properties of a cement. [CEMENT + -ITIOUS]

cement′ steel′, *Metall.* steel produced by the cementation of wrought iron or mild steel. Also called **converted steel.**

ce·men·tum (si men′təm), *n.* *Dentistry.* the bonelike tissue which forms the outer surface of the root of the tooth. See diag. under **tooth.** [< L, var. of *caementum* rough stone; see CEMENT]

cem·e·te·ri·al (sem′i tēr′ē əl), *adj.* of or pertaining to a cemetery or to burial. [CEMETERY + -IAL]

cem·e·ter·y (sem′i ter′ē), *n., pl.* **-ter·ies.** an area set apart for or containing graves or tombs, esp. one which is not a churchyard; burial ground; graveyard. [< LL *coemētēri(um)* < Gk *koimētḗrion* a sleeping place, equiv. to *koimē-* (var. s. of *koimân* to put to sleep) + *-tērion* suffix of locality]

cen., **1.** central. **2.** century.

cen·a·cle (sen′ə kəl), *n.* the room where the Last Supper took place. [< F *cénacle* < LL *cēnacul(um),* dim. of L *cēna* dinner, meal]

Ce·nae·an (sə nē′ən), *n.* *Class. Myth.* Zeus: so called because of a temple in his honor on Cenaeum.

Ce·nae·um (si nē′əm), *n.* (in ancient geography) a NW promontory of Euboea.

Cen·chri·as (seng krī′əs), *n.* *Class. Myth.* a son of Poseidon and Pirene mistakenly killed by Artemis.

Cen·ci (chen′chē), *n.* **Be·a·tri·ce** (be′ä trē′che), 1577–1599, Italian parricide whose life is the subject of various novels and poems.

Cen·ci, The (chen′chē), a verse tragedy (1819) by Shelley.

-cene, var. of **ceno-**[1] as final element of a compound word: *pleistocene.*

ce·nes·the·sia (sē′nis thē′zhə, -zhē ə, -zē ə, sen′is-), *n.* *Psychol.* coenesthesia. Also, **ce·nes·the·sis** (sē′nis thē′sis, sen′is-).

Ce·nis (sə nē′), *n.* **Mont,** a mountain pass between SE France and Italy, in the Alps. 6834 ft. high.

ceno-[1], a learned borrowing from Greek meaning "new," "recent," used in the formation of compound words: *cenogenesis.* [comb. form repr. Gk *kainós*]

ceno-[2], a learned borrowing from Greek meaning "common," used in the formation of compound words: *cenobite.* Also, **coeno-.** [< Gk *koino-,* comb. form of *koinós*]

ce·no·bite (sē′nə bīt′, sen′ə-), *n.* one of a religious order living in a convent or community. Also, **coenobite.** [< LL *coenobīt(a),* equiv. to *coenob-* (< Gk *koinóbios* (adj.) conventual, living together, equiv. to *koino-* CENO-[2] + *bi-* BI-[2] + *-os* adj. suffix) + *-īta* -ITE[1]] —**ce·no·bit·ic** (sē′nə bit′ik, sen′ə-), **ce′no·bit′i·cal, ce·no·bi·an** (si nō′bē ən), *adj.* —**ce′no·bit′i·cal·ly,** *adv.* —**ce·no·bit·ism** (sē′nə bī tiz əm, sen′ə-), *n.*

ce·no·gen·e·sis (sē′nə jen′i sis, sen′ə-), *n.* *Biol.* development of an individual which does not repeat the phylogeny of its race, stock, or group (opposed to *palingenesis*). Also, **caenogenesis, kenogenesis.** [CENO-[1] + GENESIS] —**ce·no·ge·net·ic** (sē′nə jə net′ik, sen′ə-), *adj.* —**ce′no·ge·net′i·cal·ly,** *adv.*

cen·o·taph (sen′ə taf′, -täf′), *n.* a sepulchral monument erected in memory of a deceased person whose body is buried elsewhere. [< L *cenotaph(ium)* < Gk *kenotáphion,* equiv. to *kenó(s)* empty + *-taphion* (*táph(os)* tomb + *-ion* dim. suffix)] —**cen·o·taph·ic** (sen′ə taf′ik), *adj.*

Ce·no·zo·ic (sē′nə zō′ik, sen′ə-), *Geol.* —*adj.* **1.** noting or pertaining to the present era, beginning 70,000,000 years ago and characterized by the appearance of mammals. See table under **era.** —*n.* **2.** the Cenozoic era or group of systems. Also, **Cainozoic.** [CENO-[1] + ZO(Ō)- + -IC]

cense (sens), *v.t.,* **censed, cens·ing.** to burn incense near or in front of; perfume with incense. [aph. var. of INCENSE[1]]

cen·ser (sen′sər), *n.* a container in which incense is burned. [ME < AF, aph. var. of *ensenser* < ML *incensār(ium).* See INCENSE[1], -ER[1]] —**cen′ser·less,** *adj.*

Censer

cen·sor (sen′sər), *n.* **1.** an official who examines books, plays, news reports, motion pictures, radio programs, etc., for the purpose of suppressing parts deemed objectionable on moral, political, military, or other grounds. **2.** any person who supervises the manners or morality of others. **3.** an adverse critic; faultfinder. **4.** (in the ancient Roman republic) either of two officials who kept the register or census of the citizens, let public contracts, and supervised manners and morals. **5.** (in early Freudian dream theory) the force which represses ideas, impulses, and feelings, and prevents them from entering consciousness in their original, undisguised forms. —*v.t.* **6.** to examine and act upon as a censor. **7.** to delete (a word or passage of text) in one's capacity as a censor. [< L, equiv. to *cēns(ēre)* (to) assess, estimate, value, rate + *-or* -OR[2]] —**cen′sor·a·ble,** *adj.* —**cen·so·ri·al** (sen sōr′ē əl, -sôr′-), **cen·so′ri·an,** *adj.*

Cen·sor·i·nus (sen′sō rē′nəs, -sô-), *n.* a crater in the fourth quadrant of the face of the moon: about 3 miles in diameter.

cen·so·ri·ous (sen sôr′ē əs, -sōr′-), *adj.* severely critical; faultfinding; carping. [< L *censōrius* of a censor, hence, rigid, severe, equiv. to *censōr-* (s. of *censor*) CENSOR + *-ius* -IOUS] —**cen·so′ri·ous·ly,** *adv.* —**cen·so′ri·ous·ness,** *n.*

cen·sor·ship (sen′sər ship′), *n.* **1.** act of censoring. **2.** the office or power of a censor. **3.** the time during which a censor holds office. **4.** the inhibiting and distorting activity of the Freudian censor. [CENSOR + -SHIP]

cen·sur·a·ble (sen′shər ə bəl), *adj.* deserving censure. [CENSURE + -ABLE] —**cen′sur·a·ble·ness, cen′sur·a·bil′i·ty,** *n.* —**cen′sur·a·bly,** *adv.*

cen·sure (sen′shər), *n., v.,* **-sured, -sur·ing.** —*n.* **1.** strong or vehement expression of disapproval: *The newspapers were unanimous in their censure of the raising of taxes. He received a Congressional vote of censure.* —*v.t.* **2.** to criticize or reproach in a harsh or vehement manner: *She is more to be pitied than censured.* —*v.i.* **3.** to give censure, adverse criticism, or blame. [< L *censūr(a)* censor's office, hence, judgment, equiv. to *cens(or)* CENSOR + *-ūra* -URE] —**cen′sur·er,** *n.* —**cen′sure·less,** *adj.*
—**Syn. 1.** condemnation, reproof, reproach, reprehension, rebuke, reprimand, stricture, animadversion. See **abuse. 2.** reprove, rebuke, reprimand, chide, blame. See **blame.** —**Ant. 1–3.** praise.

cen·sus (sen′səs), *n., pl.* **-sus·es. 1.** an official enumeration of the population, with details as to age, sex, occupation, etc. **2.** (in ancient Rome) the registration of citizens and their property, for purposes of taxation. [< L: a listing and property assessment of the citizens, n. use of *census* assessed (ptp. of *cēnsēre*)] —**cen·su·al** (sen′shōō əl), *adj.*

cen′sus tak′er, one who gathers information for a census by visiting individual homes.

cen′sus tract′, a standard area in certain large American cities used by the U.S. Bureau of the Census for purposes of population enumeration.

cent (sent), *n.* **1.** a bronze coin of the U.S., the 100th part of a U.S. dollar: made of steel during part of 1943. **2.** the 100th part of the monetary units of various other nations, as Canada, Ceylon, Ethiopia, Hong Kong, Liberia, Malaya, Nationalist China, the Netherlands, Panama, South Africa, and Vietnam. **3.** sen[3]. **4.** *Music.* a 100th of a semitone. [< L *cent(ēsimus)* hundredth (by shortening), equiv. to *cent(um)* 100 + *-ēsimus* ordinal suffix]

cent-, var. of **centi-** before a vowel: *centare.*

cent., **1.** centigrade. **2.** central. **3.** centum. **4.** century.

cen·tal (sen′tᵊl), *n.* *Chiefly Brit.* a hundredweight of 100 pounds. [< L *cent(um* 100 + QUINT)AL]

cen·tare (sen′târ; *Fr.* säN tȧr′), *n., pl.* **-tares** (-târz; *Fr.* -tȧr′). centiare.

cen·tas (sen′täs), *n., pl.* **-tai** (-tī). a former bronze coin of Lithuania, the hundredth part of a litas. [< Lith < E CENT]

cen·taur (sen′tôr), *n.* **1.** *Class. Myth.* one of a race of monsters having the head, trunk, and arms of a man, and the body and legs of a horse. **2.** (*cap.*) *Astron.* the constellation Centaurus. [OE < L *centaur(us)* < Gk *kéntauros*] —**cen·tau′ri·al, cen·tau′ri·an, cen·tau′ric,** *adj.*

Centaur

Cen·tau·rus (sen tôr′əs), *n., gen.* **-tau·ri** (-tôr′ī) for 2. **1.** *Class. Myth.* the son of Ixion and Nephele: father of the centaurs. **2.** *Astron.* the Centaur, a southern constellation between Lupus and Vela, containing the bright stars Alpha Centauri and Beta Centauri. [< L; see CENTAUR]

cen·tau·ry (sen′tô rē), *n., pl.* **-ries. 1.** either of two Old World, gentianaceous herbs, *Chlora perfoliata* or *Centaurium umbellatum* (*Erythraea Centaurium*), having medicinal properties. **2.** any plant of the genus *Centaurium* (*Erythraea*). **3.** any of certain other plants, as those of the gentianaceous genus *Sabatia* (**Amer′ican cen′taury**). [OE *centaurie* < ML *centauria,* appar. < Gk *kentaúria,* neut. pl. (taken in ML as fem. sing.) of *kentaúrion,* n. use of neut. of *kentaúrios* (adj.), equiv. to *kéntaur(os)* centaur + *-ios* adj. suffix]

cen·ta·vo (sen tä′vō; *Sp.* sen tä′vô), *n., pl.* **-vos** (-vōz; *Sp.* -vôs). the 100th part of the monetary units of various nations, as Argentina, Bolivia, Brazil, Colombia, Cuba, the Dominican Republic, Ecuador, El Salvador, Guatemala, Honduras, Mexico, Nicaragua, Peru, the Philippines, Portugal, and various Portuguese territories. [< Sp: the 100th part, equiv. to *cent-* 100 (see CENT) + *-avo* < L *-āvum* as in *octāvum* eighth; see OCTAVO]

cen·te·nar·i·an (sen′tᵊnâr′ē ən), *adj.* **1.** pertaining to or having lived 100 years. —*n.* **2.** one who has reached the age of 100. [< L *centēnāri(us)* (see CENTENARY) + -AN]

cen·te·nar·y (sen′tᵊner′ē; *esp. Brit.* sen ten′ə rē, -tē′nə rē), *adj., n., pl.* **-nar·ies.** —*adj.* **1.** of or pertaining to a period of 100 years. **2.** recurring once in every 100 years: *a centenary celebration.* —*n.* **3.** a centennial. **4.** a period of 100 years; century. [< L *centēnāri(us)* (adj.), equiv. to *centēn(ī)* a hundred each (*cent(um)* 100 + *-ēnī* distributive suffix) + *-ārius* -ARY]

cen·ten·i·o·na·lis (sen ten′ē ō nā′lis), *n., pl.* **-les** (-lēz). a silver coin of ancient Rome, first issued by Diocletian as the 100th part of a solidus, later greatly debased. [< L *centēniōnālis* (*nummus*)]

cen·ten·ni·al (sen ten′ē əl), *adj.* **1.** pertaining to, or marking the completion of, a period of 100 years. **2.** pertaining to a 100th anniversary. **3.** lasting 100 years. **4.** 100 years old. —*n.* **5.** a 100th anniversary; centenary. **6.** its celebration. [< L *cent-* 100 (see CENT) + *-ennial* pertaining to a period of years (abstracted from BIENNIAL)] —**cen·ten′ni·al·ly,** *adv.*

Centen′nial State′, Colorado (used as a nickname).

cen·ter (sen′tər), *n.* **1.** *Geom.* the middle point, as the point within a circle or sphere equally distant from all points of the circumference or surface, or the point within a regular polygon equally distant from the vertices. **2.** a point, pivot, axis, etc., around which anything rotates or revolves: *The sun is the center of the solar system.* **3.** the source of an influence, action, force, etc.: *the center of a problem.* **4.** a point, place, person, etc., upon which interest, emotion, etc., focuses: *Her husband is the center of her life.* **5.** a principal point, place, or object: *a shipping center.* **6.** a person, thing, group, etc., occupying the middle position, esp. a body of troops. **7.** the core or middle of anything: *hard candies with fruit centers.* **8.** See **shopping center. 9.** (*usually cap.*) *Govt.* **a.** the part of a legislative assembly, esp. in continental Europe, that sits in the center of the chamber, a position customarily assigned to members of the legislature who hold political views intermediate between those of the Right and Left. **b.** the members of such an assembly who sit in the Center. **c.** the position of persons who hold moderate political views. **d.** politically moderate persons, taken collectively; Centrists; middle-of-the-roaders: *Unfortunately, his homeland has always lacked a responsible Center.* **10.** *Football.* **a.** a lineman who occupies a position in the middle of the line and who puts the ball into play by tossing it between his legs to a back. **b.** the position played by this lineman. **11.** *Basketball.* **a.** a player who participates in a center jump. **b.** the position of the player in the center of the court, where the center jump takes place at the beginning of play. **12.** *Ice Hockey.* a player who participates in a face-off at the beginning of play. **13.** *Baseball.* See **center field. 14.** *Physiol.* a cluster of nerve cells governing a specific organic process: *the vasomotor center.* **15.** *Math.* **a.** the mean position of a figure or system. **b.** the set of elements of a group which commute with every element of the group. **16.** *Mach.* **a.** a tapered rod, mounted in the headstock spindle (**live center**) or the tailstock spindle (**dead center**) of a lathe, upon which the work to be turned is placed. **b.** one of two similar points on some other machine, as a planing machine, enabling an object to be turned on its axis. **c.** a tapered indentation, in a piece to be turned on a lathe, into which a center is fitted. **17. on center,** from the centerline or midpoint of a structural member, an area of a plan, etc., to that of a similar member, area, etc.: *The studs are set 30 inches on center. Abbr.:* o.c.
—*v.t.* **18.** to place in or on a center: *She centered the clock on the mantelpiece.* **19.** to collect to or around a center; focus: *He centered his novel on the Civil War.* **20.** to determine or mark the center of: *A small brass star centered the tabletop.* **21.** to adjust, shape, or modify (an object, part, etc.) so that its axis or the like is in a central or normal position: *to center the lens of a telescope; to center the work on a lathe.* **22.** *Football.* snap (def. 20). **23.** to pass (a basketball, hockey puck, etc.) from any place along the periphery toward the middle of the playing area.
—*v.i.* **24.** to be at or come to a center. **25. center about, around,** or **on,** *Informal.* to be focused on or at: *The topic today centers about the crisis in the Far East.* Also, *esp. Brit.,* **centre.** [var. of ME *centre* < L *centr(um)* < Gk *kéntron* needle, spur, pivoting point in drawing a circle, equiv. to *kent(eîn)* (to) sting + *-ron* n. suffix] —**cen′ter·a·ble,** *adj.* —**cen′ter·less,** *adj.*
—**Syn. 1.** See **middle.** —**Ant. 1.** edge.

Cen·ter (sen′tər), *n.* a town in E Texas. 4510 (1960).

cen′ter back′, *Volleyball, Water Polo.* the player in the middle of the back line.

cen′ter bit′, *Carpentry.* a bit having a sharp, projecting point for fixing it at the center of the hole to be drilled.

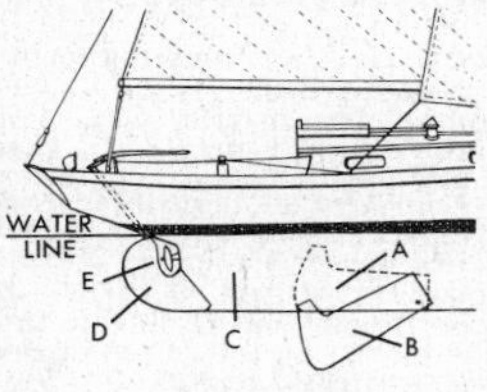

cen·ter·board (sen′tər bōrd′, -bôrd′), *n.* *Naut.* a pivoted fin keel able to be swung upward and aft within a watertight trunk when not in use. Also, *esp. Brit.,* **centreboard.** Also called **drop keel, sliding keel.** Cf. **daggerboard.** [CENTER + BOARD]

Centerboard
(A, Raised; B, Lowered)
C, Keel; D, Rudder;
E, Propeller

cen·tered (sen′tərd), *adj.* **1.** having a central axis: *a centered arc.* **2.** equidistant from all bordering or adjacent areas; situated in the center: *The illustration was centered on the page.* **3.** *Printing.* set above the base line at approximately the level of the hyphen: *centered dot.* [CENTER + -ED[3]]

cen′ter field′, *Baseball.* **1.** the area of the outfield beyond second base and between right field and left field. **2.** the position of the player covering this area.

cen′ter field′er, *Baseball.* the player whose position is center field.

cen·ter-fire (sen′tər fīᵊr′), *adj.* **1.** (of a cartridge) having the primer in the center of the base. Cf. **rimfire** (def. 1). **2.** (of firearms) designed for the use of such cartridges. Also, **central-fire.**

cen′ter half′back, **1.** *Field Hockey.* the player in the middle among the halfbacks. **2.** *Soccer.* the player in the middle of his own half of the field who carries out both offensive and defensive duties.

cen·ter·ing (sen′tər ing), *n.* a temporary framework for supporting a masonry arch during construction until it is able to stand by itself. Also, *esp. Brit.,* **centring.** [CENTER + -ING[1]]

cen′ter jump′, *Basketball.* a jump ball between the centers of the opposing teams, held in the circle at the center of the court, as at the beginning of each period.

cen·ter·line (sen′tər līn′), *n.* **1.** any line that bisects a plane figure: *the centerline of a building plan.* **2.** *Radio.* the perpendicular bisector of the line connecting two radio transmitters. Also, **cen′ter line′.** [CENTER + LINE[1]]

Cen′ter Mo·rich′es (mə rich′ēz), a town on S Long Island, in SE New York. 2521 (1960).

cen′ter of buoy′ancy, *Naval Archit.* a point within a vessel equal to the center of gravity of the volume of water displaced. Also called **center of immersion, center of immersed bulk.**

cen′ter of cur′vature, *Math.* the center of the circle of curvature.

cen′ter of ef′fort, *Naval Archit.* **1.** the point about which the wind pressure on a sail is equal in any pair of opposite directions, so that the wind pressure may be assumed for purposes of calculation to be concentrated upon this point. **2.** the point on a sailing vessel about which the wind pressure upon all the sails is balanced, so that the propulsive force upon the vessel may be assumed for purposes of calculation to be concentrated upon this point. Also called **center of pressure, velic point.**

cen′ter of flota′tion, *Naval Archit.* a perpendicular passing through the center of gravity of a vessel. Also called **tipping center.**

cen′ter of grav′ity, *Mech.* the point through which the resultant of gravitational forces on a body passes and from which the resultant force of attraction of the body on other bodies emanates: coincident with the center of mass in a uniform gravitational field.

cen′ter of immer′sion, *Naval Archit.* See **center of buoyancy.** Also called **cen′ter of immersed′ bulk′.**

cen′ter of lat′eral resist′ance, *Naval Archit.* the point about which the forces resisting lateral movement of the immersed portion of a hull are equal.

cen′ter of mass′, *Mech.* the point at which the entire mass of a body may be considered concentrated, the sum of the moments of inertia of all component particles of the body measured from such a point being zero.

cen′ter of percus′sion, *Mech.* the point on a rigid body, suspended so as to be able to move freely about a fixed axis, at which the body may be struck without changing the position of the axis.

cen′ter of pres′sure. See **center of effort.**

cen′ter of sym′metry, *Crystall.* a given point in a crystal having the property that for every point in the crystal there is a second point such that the line joining the two points is bisected by the given point. Also called **inversion center.** Cf. **symmetry element.**

cen·ter·piece (sen′tər pēs′), *n.* an ornamental object used in a central position, esp. on the center of a dining-room table. Also, *esp. Brit.,* **centrepiece.** [CENTER + PIECE]

Cen·ter·port (sen′tər pōrt′, -pôrt′), *n.* a town on NW Long Island, in SE New York. 3628 (1960).

cen′ter punch′, a punch for making shallow indentations in metal work, as to center drill bits.

cen·ter-punch (sen′tər punch′), *v.t.* to mark with a center punch. [v. use of CENTER PUNCH]

cen′ter spread′, *Journalism.* **1.** the pair of pages facing each other at the center fold of a magazine or newspaper, printed and made up as a single unit. **2.** matter occupying this space, esp. editorial matter. Cf. **double truck** (def. 2).

Cen·ter·ville (sen′tər vil′), *n.* **1.** a town in S Iowa. 6629 (1960). **2.** a town in SW Pennsylvania. 5088 (1960). **3.** a town in W Ohio. 3490 (1960).

Cen′ter·ville-Dub′lin Gulch′ (sen′tər vil dub′lin), a town in SW Montana. 3398 (1960).

cen′ter wheel′, *Horol.* the wheel driving the minute and hour hands of a timepiece.

cen·tes·i·mal (sen tes′ə məl), *adj.* hundredth; pertaining to division into hundredths. [< L *centēsim(us)* hundredth (*cent(um)* 100 + *-ēsimus* ordinal suffix) + -AL[1]] —**cen·tes′i·mal·ly,** *adv.*

cen·tes·i·mo (sen tes′ə mō′; *It.* chen te′zē mô; *Sp.* sen te′sē mô′), *n., pl. It.* **-mi** (-mē), **-mos** (-mōz′; *Sp.* -môs′). **1.** a money of account of Italy, the 100th part of a lira, equivalent to about .000016 of a U.S. dollar. **2.** a cupronickel coin of Uruguay, the 100th part of a peso, equivalent to about .0009 of a U.S. dollar. **3.** a copper coin of Panama, the 100th part of a balboa, equivalent to .01 of a U.S. dollar; cent. [< It, Sp < L *centēsim(us)*; see CENTESIMAL]

cen·te·sis (sen tē′sis), *n., pl.* **-ses** (-sēz). *Surg.* a puncture or perforation. [< NL < Gk, equiv. to *kentē-* (long. s. of *kentéein* to prick) + *-sis* -SIS]

centi-, a learned borrowing from Latin usually meaning "hundredth" but sometimes "hundred," used in the formation of compound words: *centiliter; centimeter; centipede.* Also, *esp. before a vowel,* **cent-.** [< L, comb. form of *centum*]

cen·ti·are (sen′tē âr′; *Fr.* säN tyȧr′), *n., pl.* **-ti·ares** (-tē ârz′; *Fr.* -tyȧr′). a square meter. Also, **centare.** [< F; see CENTI-, ARE[2]]

cen·ti·bar (sen′tə bär′), *n.* a centimeter-gram-second unit of pressure, equal to 1/100 bar or 10,000 dynes per square centimeter. [CENTI- + Gk *bár(os)* weight]

cen·ti·grade (sen′tə grād′), *adj.* **1.** divided into 100 degrees, as a scale. **2.** pertaining to or noting a temperature scale (**Cen′tigrade scale′**) in which 0° represents the ice point and 100° the steam point; Celsius. Celsius is now the preferred term in technical use. *Abbr.:* C See illus. under **thermometer.** [< F; see CENTI-, -GRADE]

cen·ti·gram (sen′tə gram′), *n.* one hundredth of a gram, equivalent to 0.1543 grain. Also, *esp. Brit.,* **cen′ti·gramme′.** [< F *centigramme.* See CENTI-, -GRAM[1]]

cen·ti·li·ter (sen′tᵊlē′tər), *n.* one hundredth of a liter, equivalent to 0.6102 cubic inch, or 0.338 U.S. fluid ounce. Also, *esp. Brit.,* **cen′ti·li′tre.** [< F *centilitre.* See CENTI-, LITER]

cen·til·lion (sen til′yən), *n., pl.* **-lions,** (*as after a numeral*) **-lion,** *adj.* —*n.* **1.** a cardinal number represented in the U.S. and France by one followed by 303 zeros, and, in Great Britain and Germany, by one followed by 600 zeros. —*adj.* **2.** amounting to one centillion in number. [< L *cent(um)* 100 + *-illion* (as in *million, billion,* etc.)] —**cen·til′lionth,** *adj., n.*

Cen·ti·ma·ni (sen′tə mā′nī), *n.* an ancient Roman name for the Hecatonchires.

cen·time (sän′tēm; *Fr.* säN tēm′), *n., pl.* **-times** (-tēmz′; *Fr.* -tēm′). **1.** the 100th part of the francs of various nations and territories, as Algeria, Belgium, France, Lichtenstein, Luxembourg, Martinique, Senegal, Switzerland, and Tahiti. **2.** a money of account of Haiti, the 100th part of a gourde. [< F; OF *centiesme* < L *centēsim(um),* acc. of *centēsimus* hundredth; see CENT]

cen·ti·me·ter (sen′tə mē′tər), *n.* one hundredth of a meter, equivalent to .3937 inch. Also, *esp. Brit.,* **cen′ti·me′tre.** [< F *centimètre.* See CENTI-, METER[1]]

cen·ti·me·ter-gram-sec·ond (sen′tə mē′tər gram′sek′ənd), *adj.* of or pertaining to the system of units in which the centimeter, gram, and second are the principal units of length, mass, and time. *Abbr.:* cgs, c.g.s. Also, *esp. Brit.,* **cen′ti·me′tre-gramme′-sec′ond.**

cén·ti·mo (sen′tə mō′; *Sp.* then′tē mô′, sen′-), *n., pl.*

-mos (-mōz′; *Sp.* -mōs′). the 100th part of the monetary units of various countries, as Costa Rica, Paraguay, Spain, and Venezuela. [< Sp < F *centime.* See CENTIME]

cen·ti·pede (sen′tə pēd′), *n.* any of numerous predaceous, chiefly nocturnal arthropods of the class *Chilopoda,* having an elongated, flattened body composed of from 15 to 173 segments each with a pair of legs, the first pair of which is modified into poison fangs. [< L *centiped(a).* See CENTI-, -PEDE] —**cen·tip·e·dal** (sen tip′i dᵊl, sen′tə pēd′ᵊl), *adj.*

cen′tipede grass′, a grass, *Eremochloa ophiuroides,* introduced into the U.S. from China and used for lawns.

cen′tipede plant′, a polygonaceous shrub, *Muehlenbeckia platyclados,* of the Solomon Islands, having ribbonlike, jointed, green branches that are usually leafless in the flowering stage. Also called **ribbon bush.**

cen·ti·poise (sen′tə poiz′), *n.* a centimeter-gram-second unit of viscosity equal to 1/100 poise. *Abbr.:* cP, cp [CENTI- + POISE^2]

Centipede, *Scutigera coleoptrata* (Body length about 1 in.)

cen·ti·stere (sen′ti stēr′), *n.* one hundredth of a stere. [< F *centistère.* See CENTI-, STERE]

cen·ti·stoke (sen′ti stōk′), *n.* a centimeter-gram-second unit of kinematic viscosity, equal to 1/100 stoke. *Abbr.:* cS, cs [CENTI- + STOKE^2]

cent·ner (sent′nər), *n.* **1.** (in several European countries) a unit of weight of 50 kilograms, equivalent to 110.23 pounds avoirdupois. **2.** a unit of 100 kilograms. [< LG; cf. G *Zentner,* OHG *centenari* < L *centēnārius* of a hundred; see CENTENARY]

cen·to (sen′tō), *n., pl.* **-tos.** **1.** a piece of writing, esp. a poem, composed wholly of quotations from the works of other authors. **2.** anything composed of incongruous parts. **3.** *Obs.* a patchwork. [< L; akin to CENTER] —**cen·ton·i·cal** (sen ton′i kəl), *adj.* —**cen·to·nism** (sen′tᵊniz′əm), **cen·to·ni·za·tion** (sen′tᵊni zā′shən), *n.*

CENTO (sen′tō), *n.* an organization for economic and military cooperation, established in 1959 as successor to the Baghdad Pact, and comprising Great Britain, Iran, Pakistan, and Turkey. The U.S. has affiliate status. [*Cen(tral) T(reaty) O(rganization)*]

centr-, var. of **centri-** before a vowel: *centroid.*

cen·tra (sen′trə), *n.* a pl. of **centrum.**

cen·trad (sen′trad), *adv.* *Anat., Zool.* toward the center. [CENTR- + L *ad* to]

cen·tral^1 (sen′trəl), *adj.* **1.** of or forming the center: *the central hut in the village.* **2.** in, at, or near the center: *a central position.* **3.** constituting that from which other related things proceed or upon which they depend: *a central agency.* **4.** principal; chief; dominant: *the central idea; the central character in a novel.* **5.** *Anat., Zool.* **a.** of or pertaining to the central nervous system. **b.** of or pertaining to the centrum of a vertebra. **6.** *Phonet.* (of a speech sound) produced with the tongue articulating neither expressly forward nor in the back part of the mouth, as any of the sounds of *lull.* **7.** *Physics.* (of a force) directed to or from a fixed point. —*n.* **8.** the office of a telephone system, in which connections are made between different lines. **9.** *Obs.* a telephone operator. [< L *centrāl(is),* equiv. to *centr(um)* CENTER + *-ālis* -AL^1] —**cen′tral·ly,** *adv.*

cen·tral^2 (sen träl′; *Sp.* sen träl′), *n., pl.* **-trals,** *Sp.* **-tra·les** (-trä′les). (in Spanish America and the Philippines) a mill for crushing cane into raw sugar. [< AmerSp, special use of Sp *central* CENTRAL^1]

Cen′tral Af′rican Federa′tion. See **Rhodesia and Nyasaland, Federation of.**

Cen′tral Af′rican Repub′lic, a republic in central Africa: a member of the French Community. 1,177,166 (est. 1960); 238,000 sq. mi. *Cap.:* Bangui. Formerly, **Ubangi-Shari.**

Cen′tral Amer′ica, continental North America, S of Mexico, usually considered to comprise Guatemala, British Honduras, El Salvador, Honduras, Nicaragua, Costa Rica, and Panama. 12,120,000 (est. 1961); 227,933 sq. mi. —**Cen′tral Amer′ican.**

cen′tral an′gle, *Geom.* an angle formed at the center of a circle by two radii.

cen′tral bank′, a bank, as a Federal Reserve Bank, that holds basic banking reserves, issues currency, and acts as lender of last resort and controller of credit.

Cen′tral Bay′. See **Sinus Medii.**

cen′tral cyl′inder, *Bot.* stele (def. 4).

Cen′tral Falls′, a city in NE Rhode Island. 19,858 (1960).

cen·tral-fire (sen′trəl fīᵊr′), *adj.* center-fire.

Cen·tra·lia (sen trāl′yə, -trā′lē ə), *n.* **1.** a city in central Illinois. 13,904 (1960). **2.** a town in SW Washington. 8586 (1960). **3.** a town in central Missouri. 3200 (1960).

Cen′tral In′dia, a former political agency in central India uniting various native states and subordinate agencies: now incorporated into Madhya Pradesh. Also called **Cen′tral In′dian A′gency.**

Cen′tral Intel′ligence A′gency. See **CIA.**

cen·tral·i·sa·tion (sen′trə li zā′shən), *n.* *Chiefly Brit.* centralization.

cen·tral·ise (sen′trə līz′), *v.t.,* **-ised, -is·ing.** *Chiefly Brit.* centralize. —**cen′tral·is′er,** *n.*

cen·tral·ism (sen′trə liz′əm), *n.* a centralizing system; centralization. [CENTRAL^1 + -ISM] —**cen′tral·ist,** *n., adj.* —**cen·tral·is·tic** (sen′trə lis′tik), *adj.*

cen·tral·i·ty (sen tral′i tē), *n., pl.* **-ties.** a central position or state: *the centrality of the sun.* [CENTRAL^1 + -ITY]

cen·tral·i·za·tion (sen′trə li zā′shən), *n.* **1.** act or fact of centralizing; fact of being centralized. **2.** the concentration of administrative power in a central government. **3.** *Chiefly Sociol.* **a.** a process whereby social groups and institutions become increasingly dependent on a central group or institution. **b.** concentration of control or power in a few individuals. Also, *esp. Brit.,* **centralisation.** [CENTRALIZE + -ATION]

cen·tral·ize (sen′trə līz′), *v.,* **-ized, -iz·ing.** —*v.t.* **1.** to draw to or gather about a center or central point. **2.** to bring under one control, esp. in government: *a tendency to centralize administrative authority in a single agency.* —*v.i.* **3.** to come together at or to form a center. Also, *esp. Brit.,* **centralise.** [CENTRAL^1 + -IZE] —**cen′tral·iz′er,** *n.*

cen′tralized school′. See **consolidated school.**

cen′tral mo′ment, *Statistics.* a moment about the center of a distribution, usually the mean.

cen′tral nerv′ous sys′tem, the part of the nervous system comprising the brain and spinal cord.

Cen′tral Park′, **1.** a public park in central Manhattan, New York City. 840 acres. **2.** a town in E Illinois. 2676 (1960).

Cen′tral Pow′ers, (in World War I) Germany and Austria-Hungary, often with their allies Turkey and Bulgaria, as opposed to the Allies.

cen′tral projec′tion, *Geom.* a projection of one plane onto a second plane such that a point on the first plane and its image on the second plane lie on a straight line through a fixed point not on either plane.

Cen′tral Prov′inces and Be·rar′ (bā rär′), a former province in central India: became the state of Madhya Pradesh 1950.

cen′tral sul′cus, *Anat.* the sulcus separating the frontal and parietal lobes of the cerebrum. Also called **fissure of Rolando.**

Cen′tral time′. See under **standard time.**

Cen′tral Trea′ty Organiza′tion. See **CENTO.**

Cen′tral Val′ley, a town in N California. 2854 (1960).

cen·tre (sen′tər), *n., v.,* **-tred, -tring.** *Chiefly Brit.* center. —**cen′tre·less,** *adj.*

cen·tre·board (sen′tər bōrd′, -bôrd′), *n.* *Naut. Chiefly Brit.* centerboard.

cen·tre·piece (sen′tər pēs′), *n.* *Chiefly Brit.* centerpiece.

centri-, a combining form of **center:** *centrifuge.* Also, **centr-, centro-.** [< NL, comb. form of *centrum* CENTER]

cen·tric (sen′trik), *adj.* **1.** pertaining to or situated at the center; central. **2.** *Anat., Physiol.* pertaining to or originating at a nerve center. Also, **cen′tri·cal.** [< Gk *kentrik(ós)* of, pertaining to the center, equiv. to *kéntr(on)* CENTER + *-ikos* -IC] —**cen′tri·cal·ly,** *adv.* —**cen·tric·i·ty** (sen tris′i tē), *n.*

cen·trif·u·gal (sen trif′yə gəl, -ə gəl), *adj.* **1.** moving or directed outward from the center (opposed to *centripetal*). **2.** pertaining to or operated by centrifugal force: *a centrifugal pump.* **3.** *Physiol.* efferent. —*n.* **4.** *Mach.* **a.** a machine for separating different materials by centrifugal force; centrifuge. **b.** a rotating, perforated drum holding the materials to be separated in such a machine. [< NL *centrifug(us)* center-fleeing (*centri-* CENTRI- + *-fugus,* equiv. to L *fug(ere)* (to) flee + *-us* -OUS) + -AL^1] —**cen·trif′u·gal·ly,** *adv.*

centrif′ugal box′, a revolving chamber, used in the spinning of man-made filaments, in which the plastic fibers, subjected to centrifugal force, are slightly twisted and emerge in the form of yarn wound into the shape of a hollow cylinder. Also called **centrif′ugal pot′, spinning box, spinning pot.**

centrif′ugal cast′ing, *Foundry.* casting utilizing centrifugal force within a spinning mold to force the metal against the walls.

centrif′ugal force′, an outward force on a body rotating about an axis, assumed equal and opposite to the centripetal force and postulated to account for the phenomena seen by an observer in the rotating body.

cen·trif·u·gal·ise (sen trif′yə gə līz′, -ə gə-), *v.t.,* **-ised, is·ing.** *Chiefly Brit.* centrifugalize. —**cen·trif′u·gal·i·sa′tion,** *n.*

cen·trif·u·gal·ize (sen trif′yə gə līz′, -ə gə-), *v.t.,* **-ized, -iz·ing.** centrifuge (def. 2). [CENTRIFUGAL + -IZE] —**cen·trif′u·gal·i·za′tion,** *n.*

centrif′ugal spin′ning. See **pot spinning.**

cen·trif·u·gate (sen trif′yə git, -gāt′, -trif′ə-), *n.* the denser of the centrifuged materials. [CENTRIFUG(AL) + -ATE^1]

cen·tri·fuge (sen′trə fyōōj′), *n., v.,* **-fuged, -fug·ing.** —*n.* **1.** an apparatus that rotates at high speed and by centrifugal force separates substances of different densities, as milk and cream. —*v.t.* **2.** Also, **centrifugalize.** to subject to the action of a centrifuge. [< F, n. use of *centrifuge* (adj.) < NL *centrifug(us)* center-fleeing; see CENTRIFUGAL] —**cen·trif·u·ga·tion** (sen trif′yə gā′shən, -trif′ə-), *n.*

cen·tring (sen′tring), *n.* *Chiefly Brit.* centering.

cen·tri·ole (sen′trē ōl′), *n.* *Biol.* a minute body within the centrosome. [CENTRI- + *-ole* < L *-ol(us)* dim. suffix]

cen·trip·e·tal (sen trip′i tᵊl), *adj.* **1.** proceeding or directed toward the center (opposed to *centrifugal*). **2.** operating by centripetal force. **3.** *Physiol.* afferent. [< NL *centripet(us)* center-seeking (*centri-* CENTRI- + *-petus,* equiv. to L *pet(ere)* (to) seek + *-us* -OUS) + -AL^1] —**cen·trip′e·tal·ism,** *n.* —**cen·trip′e·tal·ly,** *adv.*

centrip′etal force′, the force, acting upon a body moving along a curved path, that is directed toward the center of the path and constrains the body to the path.

Cen·trist (sen′trist), *n.* **1.** (*sometimes l.c.*) (esp. in continental Europe) a member of a political party of the Center. —*adj.* **2.** (*sometimes l.c.*) of or pertaining to Centrists, or to their political views. [< F *centriste.* See CENTER, -IST]

centro-, var. of **centri-:** *centrosphere.*

cen·tro·bar·ic (sen′trə bar′ik), *adj.* pertaining to the center of gravity. [CENTRO- + BARIC^2]

cen·tro·cli·nal (sen′trə klīn′ᵊl), *adj.* (of a geological formation) sloping toward a common point or center. [CENTRO- + -CLINAL]

cen·tro·dor·sal (sen′trə dôr′səl), *adj.* central and dorsal, as a plate on the aboral surface of crinoids. [CENTRO- + DORSAL^1] —**cen′tro·dor′sal·ly,** *adv.*

cen·troid (sen′troid), *n.* **1.** *Mech.* the point which may be considered as the center of a one- or two-dimensional figure, the sum of the displacements of all points in the figure from such a point being zero. Cf. **center of mass.** **2.** *Geom.* that point where the medians of a triangle intersect. [CENTR- + -OID] —**cen·troi′dal,** *adj.*

cen·tro·lec·i·thal (sen′trō les′ə thəl), *adj.* *Embryol.* having a centrally located yolk, as certain insect eggs or ova. [CENTRO- + LECITHAL]

cen·tro·lin·e·ad (sen′trō lin′ē ad′, -əd), *n.* a drafting instrument for drawing lines converging on a vanishing point outside the drawing. [CENTRO- + L *line(a)* LINE^1 + *ad* to]

cen·tro·mere (sen′trə mēr′), *n.* *Biol.* (in a chromosome) the specialized region to which a spindle fiber is attached. [CENTRO- + -MERE]

cen·tro·some (sen′trə sōm′), *n.* *Biol.* a minute, protoplasmic body, regarded as the active center of cell division in mitosis. [CENTRO- + -SOME^3] —**cen·tro·som·ic** (sen′trə som′ik), *adj.*

cen·tro·sphere (sen′trə sfēr′), *n.* **1.** *Biol.* the protoplasm around a centrosome; the central portion of an aster, containing the centrosome. **2.** *Geol.* the central or interior portion of the earth. [CENTRO- + -SPHERE]

cen·tro·sym·met·ric (sen′trō si me′trik), *adj.* symmetric in relation to a center. Also, **cen′tro·sym·met′ri·cal.** [CENTRO- + SYMMETRIC] —**cen·tro·sym·met·ry** (sen′trō sim′i trē), *n.*

cen·trum (sen′trəm), *n., pl.* **-trums, -tra** (-trə). **1.** a center. **2.** *Anat., Zool.* the body of a vertebra. [< L; see CENTER]

cen·tum^1 (sen′təm), *n.* one hundred. [< L; see HUNDRED]

cen·tum^2 (ken′təm, -tōōm), *adj.* belonging to or consisting of those branches of the Indo-European family that show distinctive preservation of the Proto-Indo-European labiovelars and that show a historical development of velar articulations, as the sounds (k) or (KH), from Proto-Indo-European palatal phonemes. The centum branches are Germanic, Celtic, Italic, Hellenic Anatolian, and Tocharian. Cf. **satem.** [< L, exemplifying in *c-* the Indo-European velar stop]

cen·tu·ple (sen′tə pəl, -tyə-), *adj., v.,* **-pled, -pling.** —*adj.* **1.** a hundred times as great; hundredfold. —*v.t.* **2.** to increase 100 times. [< MF < LL *centupl(us),* equiv. to L *centu(m)* 100 + *-plus* -FOLD]

cen·tu·pli·cate (*v.* sen tōō′plə kāt′, -tyōō′-; *adj., n.* sen tōō′plə kit, -kāt′, -tyōō′-), *v.,* **-cat·ed, -cat·ing,** *adj., n.* —*v.t.* **1.** to increase 100 times; centuple. —*adj.* **2.** a hundredfold. —*n.* **3.** a number or quantity increased a hundredfold. [< L *centuplic-* (s. of *centuplex*) hundredfold, equiv. to *centu(m)* 100 + *plic-* (base of *plicāre* to fold) + -ATE^1] —**cen·tu′pli·ca′tion,** *n.*

cen·tu·ri·al (sen tŏŏr′ē əl, -tyŏŏr′-), *adj.* pertaining to a century. [< L *centuriāl(is),* equiv. to *centuri(a)* CENTURY + *-ālis* -AL^1]

cen·tu·ried (sen′chə rēd), *adj.* **1.** existing for an indefinite number of centuries. **2.** very old. [CENTURY + -ED^3]

cen·tu·ri·on (sen tŏŏr′ē ən, -tyŏŏr′-), *n.* (in the ancient Roman army) the commander of a century. [ME < L *centuriōn-* (s. of *centuriō*), equiv. to *centur(ia)* CENTURY + *-iōn-* -ION]

cen·tu·ry (sen′chə rē), *n., pl.* **-ries.** **1.** a period of 100 years. **2.** one of the successive periods of 100 years reckoned forward or backward from a recognized chronological epoch, esp. from the assumed date of the birth of Jesus. **3.** any group or collection of 100: *a century of one-act plays.* **4.** (in the ancient Roman army) a company, consisting of approximately 100 men. **5.** one of the voting divisions of the ancient Roman people, each division having one vote. **6.** (*cap.*) *Print.* a style of type. **7.** *Slang.* a hundred-dollar bill; 100 dollars. **8.** *Sports.* a race of 100 yards or meters, as in track or swimming, or of 100 miles, as in bicycle racing. **9.** *Cricket.* a score of at least 100 runs made by one batsman in a single inning. [< L *centuria* unit made up of 100 parts, esp. company of soldiers, equiv. to *cent(um)* 100 + *-uria* unexplained suffix]

cen′tury plant′, a Mexican agave, *Agave americana,* cultivated as an ornamental, erroneously believed to flower only once every century.

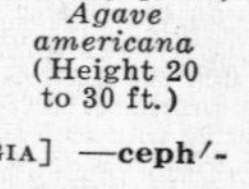

Century plant, *Agave americana* (Height 20 to 30 ft.)

ceorl (che′ôrl), *n.* *Obs.* churl (def. 4). [OE] —**ceorl′ish,** *adj.*

cephal-, var. of **cephalo-** before a vowel: *cephalate.*

ceph·a·lad (sef′ə lad′), *adv.* *Anat., Zool.* toward the head (opposed to *caudad*). [CEPHAL- + L *ad* to, towards]

ceph·a·lal·gia (sef′ə lal′jə, -jē ə), *n.* *Med.* headache (def. 1). [CEPHAL- + -ALGIA] —**ceph′a·lal′gic,** *adj.*

ceph·a·late (sef′ə lit, -lāt′), *adj.* *Zool.* having a head or headlike part. [CEPHAL- + -ATE^1]

ce·phal·ic (sə fal′ik), *adj.* **1.** of or pertaining to the head. **2.** situated or directed toward the head. [< L *cephalic(us)* < Gk *kephalikós* of the head. See CEPHAL-, -IC]

-cephalic, var. of **cephalo-,** as final element of adjectives: *brachycephalic.* [< Gk *-kephal(os)* -CEPHALOUS + -IC]

cephal′ic in′dex, *Cephalom.* the ratio of the greatest breadth of a head to its greatest length from front to back, multiplied by 100.

ceph·a·li·tis (sef′ə lī′tis), *n.* *Pathol.* encephalitis. [CEPHAL- + -ITIS]

ceph·a·li·za·tion (sef′ə li zā′shən), *n.* *Zool.* a tendency in the development of animals to localization of important organs or parts in or near the head. [CEPHAL- + -IZATION]

cephalo-, a learned borrowing from Greek meaning "head," used in the formation of compound words: *cephalometry.* Also, **cephal-, -cephalic, -cephalous, -cephaly.** [< Gk *kephalo-,* comb. form of *kephalḗ* head; akin to GABLE]

ceph·a·lo·chor·date (sef′ə lō kôr′dāt), *adj.* **1.** belonging or pertaining to the *Cephalochordata.* —*n.* **2.** any chordate animal of the subphylum *Cephalochordata,* having fishlike characters but lacking a spinal column, comprising the lancelets. [CEPHALO- + CHORDATE]

ceph·a·lo·di·um (sef′ə lō′dē əm), *n., pl.* **-di·a** (-dē ə). *Bot.* a gall-like outgrowth on the thallus of certain lichens, containing an alga different from that of the lichen. [< NL, equiv. to Gk *kephalṓd(ēs)* like a head (see CEPHAL-, -ODE[1]) + NL *-ium* -IUM]

cephalom., cephalometry.

ceph·a·lom·e·ter (sef′ə lom′i tər), *n.* an instrument for measuring the human head. Cf. **craniometer.** [CEPHALO- + -METER] —**ceph·a·lo·met·ric** (sef′ə lō me′trik), *adj.*

ceph·a·lom·e·try (sef′ə lom′i trē), *n.* the science of measuring the dimensions of the human head. [CEPHALO- + -METRY]

ceph·a·lon (sef′ə lon′, -lən), *n., pl.* **-la** (-lə). *Zool.* the head, esp. of an arthropod. [< NL < Gk **kephalon,* neut. var. of fem. *kephalḗ* head]

Ceph·a·lo·ni·a (sef′ə lō′nē ə, -lōn′yə), *n.* the largest of the Ionian Islands, off the W coast of Greece. 46,314 (1961); 287 sq. mi. Greek, **Kephallenia.**

ceph·a·lo·pod (sef′ə lə pod′), *n.* **1.** any mollusk of the class *Cephalopoda,* having tentacles attached to the head, including the cuttlefish, squid, octopus, etc. —*adj.* **2.** Also, **ceph′a·lop·od′ic, ceph·a·lop·o·dous** (sef′ə lop′ə dəs). belonging or pertaining to the *Cephalopoda.* [CEPHALO- + -POD]

Ceph·a·lop·o·da (sef′ə lop′ə də), *n.* the class comprising the cephalopods. [< NL; see CEPHALOPOD]

ceph·a·lo·tho·rax (sef′ə lō thôr′aks, -thōr′-), *n., pl.* **-tho·rax·es, -tho·ra·ces** (-thôr′ə sēz′, -thōr′-). *Zool.* the anterior part of the body in certain arachnids and crustaceans, consisting of the coalesced head and thorax. [CEPHALO- + THORAX] —**ceph·a·lo·tho·rac·ic** (sef′ə lō thə ras′ik), *adj.*

ceph·a·lous (sef′ə ləs), *adj.* having a head. [CEPHAL- + -OUS]

-cephalous, var. of **cephalo-,** as final element of adjectives: *brachycephalous.* [< Gk *-kephalos,* equiv. to *kephal(ḗ)* head + *-os* -OUS]

Ceph·a·lus (sef′ə ləs), *n.* *Class. Myth.* the husband of Procris.

-cephaly, var. of **cephalo-,** as final element of a compound word: *dolichocephaly.*

Ce′pheid var′iable, *Astron.* a variable star in which changes in brightness are due to alternate contractions and expansions in volume. Also, **ce′pheid var′i·able.** [CEPHE(US) + -ID[1]]

Ce·phe·us (sē′fē əs, -fyōōs), *n., gen.* **-phe·i** (-fē ī′) for 1a. **1.** *Astron.* **a.** a northern circumpolar constellation between Cassiopeia and Draco. **b.** a crater in the first quadrant of the face of the moon: about 28 miles in diameter. **2.** *Class. Myth.* an Ethiopian king, the husband of Cassiopeia and father of Andromeda. —**Ce·phe·id** (sē′fē id), *adj.*

-ceptor, an element occurring in loan words from Latin where it meant "taker," "receiver": *preceptor.* [< L, comb. form of *captor;* see CAPTOR]

cer-, var. of **cero-** before a vowel: *ceraceous.*

ce·ra (sēr′ə), *n.* (in prescriptions) wax. [< L]

ce·ra·ceous (sə rā′shəs), *adj.* waxlike; waxy: *a ceraceous surface.* [< L *cēr(a)* wax (< Gk *kēr(ós)* wax) + -ACEOUS]

Ce·ram (sē ram′; *Port.* se RÄN′; *Du.* sā′ram), *n.* an island of the Moluccas in Indonesia, W of New Guinea. 100,000 (1930); 7191 sq. mi. Also called **Serang.**

ce·ram·al (sə ram′əl), *n.* cermet. [CERAM(IC) + AL(LOY)]

Ce·ram·bus (sə ram′bəs), *n.* *Class. Myth.* a man who was changed into a beetle so that he could fly above a flood sent by Zeus to punish the wicked.

ce·ram·ic (sə ram′ik), *adj.* **1.** of or pertaining to products made from clay and similar materials, as pottery, brick, etc., or to their manufacture: *ceramic art.* —*n.* **2.** ceramic material. Also, **keramic.** [var. of *keramic* < Gk *keramik(ós),* equiv. to *kéram(os)* potters' clay + *-ikos* -IC]

ceram′ic engineer′ing, the branch of engineering concerned with the development and production of ceramics.

ce·ram·ics (sə ram′iks), *n.* **1.** (*construed as sing.*) the art and technology of making objects of clay and similar materials treated by firing. **2.** (*construed as pl.*) articles of earthenware, porcelain, etc. [see CERAMIC, -ICS] —**cer·a·mist** (ser′ə mist), *n.*

ce·rar·gy·rite (sə rär′jə rīt′), *n.* a very soft mineral, silver chloride, AgCl, used as an ore of silver; horn silver. [< Gk *kér(as)* horn + *árgyr(os)* silver + -ITE[1]; cf. F *kérargyre*]

cerat-, a learned borrowing from Greek meaning "horn," used in the formation of compound words: *ceratodus.* [< Gk *kerat-,* comb. form of *kéras;* c. L *cornu,* HORN]

cerat., (in prescriptions) cerate. [< L *cērātum*]

ce·rate (sēr′āt), *n.* **1.** *Pharm.* an unctuous, often medicated, preparation for external application, consisting of lard or oil mixed with wax, rosin, or the like, esp. one which has a firmer consistency than a typical ointment and does not melt when in contact with the skin. —*adj.* **2.** Also, **cerated.** *Ornith.* having a cere. [< L *cērāt(um),* neut. of *cērātus* waxed (ptp. of *cērāre*), equiv. to *cēr(a)* wax + *-ātus* -ATE[1]; cf. Gk *kērōtón* in same sense]

ce·rat·ed (sēr′ā tid), *adj.* **1.** covered with wax. **2.** *Ornith.* cerate (def. 2). [< L *cērāt(us)* waxed (see CERATE) + -ED[2]]

cer·a·tin (ser′ə tin), *n.* keratin.

ce·rat·o·dus (sə rat′ə dəs, ser′ə tō′dəs), *n., pl.* **-dus·es.** a lungfish of either of two genera, *Ceratodus* or *Neoceratodus,* having hornlike ridges on the teeth. Cf. **barramunda.** [< NL, equiv. to *cerat-* CERAT- + *-odus* < Gk *odoús* tooth]

cer·a·toid (ser′ə toid′), *adj.* hornlike; horny. [< Gk *keratoeid(ḗs)* hornlike. See CERAT-, -OID]

cer·a·top·si·an (ser′ə top′sē ən), *n.* any of several herbivorous dinosaurs of the suborder *Ceratopsia,* from the Cretaceous period, having a massive head typically bearing three horns. Also called **horned dinosaur.** [< NL *Ceratopsi(a)* (see CERAT-, -OPSIS, -IA) + -AN]

Cer·ber·us (sûr′bər əs), *n., pl.* **-ber·us·es, -ber·i** (-bə rī′) for 2. **1.** *Class. Myth.* a dog, usually represented as having three heads, which guarded the entrance of the infernal regions. **2.** a watchful and formidable or surly keeper or guard. —**Cer·be·re·an** (sər bēr′ē ən), **Cer′ber·ic,** *adj.*

cer·car·i·a (sər kâr′ē ə), *n., pl.* **-car·i·ae** (-kâr′ē ē′). *Zool.* the disk-shaped larva of flukes of the class *Trematoda,* having a taillike appendage. [< NL, equiv. to *cerc-* (< Gk *kérkos* tail) + *-āria* -ARIA] —**cer·car′i·al,** *adj.* —**cer·car′i·an,** *adj., n.*

cer·ce·lée (sär sel′ē, sûr′sə lā′), *adj.* *Heraldry.* recercelée. Also, **cer·ce′lé.**

Cer·co·pes (sər kō′pēz), *n.pl.* *Class. Myth.* a race of gnomes.

cer·cus (sûr′kəs, ker′-), *n., pl.* **cer·ci** (sûr′sī, ker′kē). one of a pair of appendages at the rear of the abdomen of certain insects and other arthropods, serving as tactile organs. [< NL < Gk *kérkos* tail] —**cer′cal,** *adj.*

Cer·cy·on (sûr′sē ən), *n.* *Class. Myth.* a son of either Hephaestus or Poseidon who became king of Arcadia and who was the father of Alope.

cere[1] (sēr), *n.* *Ornith.* a fleshy, membranous covering of the base of the upper mandible of a bird, esp. a bird of prey or a parrot, through which the nostrils open. [late ME *sere,* sp. var. of **cere* < ML *cēra,* lit., wax < L] —**cered,** *adj.* —**cere′less,** *adj.*

cere[2] (sēr), *v.t.,* **cered, cer·ing. 1.** *Archaic.* to wrap in or as in a cerecloth, esp. a corpse. **2.** *obs.* to wax. [ME *cere(n)* < L *cērā(re)* (to) wax, equiv. to *cēr(a)* wax + *-ā-* thematic vowel + *-re* inf. ending]

Cer.E., Ceramic Engineer.

ce·re·al (sēr′ē əl), *n.* **1.** any gramineous plant yielding an edible farinaceous grain, as wheat, rye, oats, rice, or corn. **2.** the grain itself. **3.** some edible preparation of it, esp. a breakfast food. —*adj.* **4.** of or pertaining to grain or the plants producing it. [< L *Cereāl(is)* of, pertaining to CERES; see -AL[1]]

cer·e·bel·lum (ser′ə bel′əm), *n., pl.* **-bel·lums, -bel·la** (-bel′ə). *Anat., Zool.* a large portion of the brain, serving to coordinate voluntary movements, posture, and balance in man, being in back of and below the cerebrum and consisting of two lateral lobes and a central lobe. [< L, equiv. to *cereb(rum)* brain + *-ellum* dim. suffix] —**cer′e·bel′lar,** *adj.*

cerebr-, var. of **cerebro-** before a vowel: *cerebritis.*

cer·e·bral (ser′ə brəl, sə rē′-), *adj.* **1.** *Anat., Zool.* of or pertaining to the cerebrum or the brain. **2.** betraying or characterized by the use of the intellect rather than intuition or instinct: *His is a cerebral music that leaves many people cold.* **3.** *Phonet.* retroflex (def. 2). —*n.* **4.** *Phonet.* a cerebral sound. [< NL *cerebrāl(is).* See CEREBRUM, -AL[1]] —**cer′e·bral·ly,** *adv.*

cer′ebral pal′sy, *Pathol.* a form of paralysis caused by a prenatal brain defect or by brain injury during birth, most marked in certain motor areas and characterized by involuntary motions and difficulty in control of the voluntary muscles. —**cer′ebral pal′sied.**

cer·e·brate (ser′ə brāt′), *v.i., v.t.,* **-brat·ed, -brat·ing.** to use the mind; think or think about. [back formation from *cerebration.* See CEREBRUM, -ATION] —**cer′e·bra′tion,** *n.* —**cer′e·bra′tion·al,** *adj.*

cer·e·bric (ser′ə brik, sə reb′rik, -rē′brik), *adj.* pertaining to or derived from the brain. [CEREBR(UM) + -IC]

cer·e·bri·tis (ser′ə brī′tis), *n.* *Pathol.* inflammation of the brain, esp. of the cerebrum. [CEREBR- + -ITIS]

cerebro-, a combining form of **cerebrum:** *cerebrospinal.* Also, *esp. before a vowel,* **cerebr-.**

cer·e·broid (ser′ə broid′), *adj.* *Anat.* resembling the cerebrum or the brain. [CEREBR- + -OID]

cer·e·bro·side (ser′ə brə sīd′), *n.* *Biochem.* any of the class of glycolipids, found in brain tissue and the medullary sheaths of nerves, that, upon hydrolysis, yield sphingosine, galactose or certain other sugars, and a fatty acid. [CEREBR- + -OSE[2] + -IDE]

cer·e·bro·spi·nal (ser′ə brō spīn′əl, sə rē′brō-), *adj.* *Anat., Physiol.* **1.** pertaining to or affecting the brain and the spinal cord. **2.** of or pertaining to the central nervous system. [CEREBRO- + SPINAL]

cer′ebrospi′nal flu′id, *Anat.* the fluid in the ventricles of the brain and between the arachnoid and pia mater.

cerebrospi′nal meningi′tis, *Pathol.* an acute inflammation of the meninges of the brain and spinal cord, caused by a specific organism, accompanied by fever and occasionally red spots on the skin. Also called **brain fever, cer′ebrospi′nal fe′ver.**

cer′ebrospi′nal nerv′ous sys′tem, the part of the nervous system comprising the brain and spinal cord together with their cranial and spinal nerves.

cer·e·bro·to·ni·a (ser′ə brə tō′nē ə, sə rē′brə-), *n.* *Psychol.* a personality pattern accompanying the ectomorphic body type and characterized by introversion, sensitivity, and dominant intellectuality. Cf. **somatotonia, viscerotonia.** [< NL, equiv. to *cerebro-* CEREBRO- + *tonia* (L *ton(us)* tension (see TONE) + *-ia* -IA)] —**cer·e·bro·ton·ic** (ser′ə brə ton′ik, sə rē′brə-), *adj., n.*

cer·e·bro·vas·cu·lar (ser′ə brō vas′kyə lər, sə rē′brō-), *adj.* *Anat.* of, pertaining to, or affecting the cerebrum and its associated blood vessels. [CEREBRO- + VASCULAR]

cer·e·bro·vis·cer·al (ser′ə brō vis′ər əl, sə rē′brō-), *adj.* of, pertaining to, or connecting the cerebral and visceral ganglia in mollusks. [CEREBRO- + VISCERAL]

cer·e·brum (ser′ə brəm, sə rē′-), *n., pl.* **-brums, -bra** (-brə). *Anat., Zool.* **1.** the anterior and largest part of the brain, consisting of two halves or hemispheres and serving to control voluntary movements and coordinate mental actions. **2.** the forebrain and the midbrain. [< L: brain]

cere·cloth (sēr′klôth′, -kloth′), *n., pl.* **-cloths** (-klôthz′, -klothz′, -klôths′, -kloths′). **1.** cloth coated or impregnated with wax so as to be waterproof, used for wrapping the dead, for bandages, etc. **2.** a piece of such cloth. [earlier *cered cloth;* see CERE[2]]

cere·ment (sēr′mənt), *n.* Usually, **cerements. 1.** a cerecloth used for wrapping the dead. **2.** any graveclothes. [CERE[2] + -MENT]

cer·e·mo·ni·al (ser′ə mō′nē əl), *adj.* **1.** of, pertaining to, or characterized by ceremony or ceremonies; formal; ritual: *a ceremonial occasion.* **2.** used in or in connection with ceremonies: *ceremonial robes.* —*n.* **3.** a system of ceremonies, rites, or formalities prescribed for or observed on any particular occasion; a rite or ceremony. **4.** *Rom. Cath. Ch.* **a.** the order for rites and ceremonies. **b.** a book containing it. **5.** formal behavior found at, or appropriate to, a certain occasion: *the ceremonial of a state banquet.* [ME < ML *cēremōniāl(is),* LL *caerimōniālis.* See CEREMONY, -AL[1]] —**cer′e·mo′ni·al·ism,** *n.* —**cer′e·mo′ni·al·ist,** *n.* —**cer′e·mo′ni·al·ly,** *adv.*
—**Syn. 1.** solemn, conventional, ceremonious. **3.** ritual, liturgy. —**Ant. 1.** informal.

cer′emo′nial tea′, a Japanese green tea made from choice shade-grown leaves that are cured by a steaming, drying, and powdering process: used in chanoyu.

cer·e·mo·ni·ous (ser′ə mō′nē əs), *adj.* **1.** carefully observant of ceremony; formally or elaborately polite: *He greeted his rival with a ceremonious display of friendship.* **2.** pertaining to, marked by, or consisting of ceremony; formal: *a ceremonious reception.* [CEREMONY + -OUS; cf. MF *cerimonieux* < LL *caerimōniōs(us)*] —**cer′e·mo′ni·ous·ly,** *adv.* —**cer′e·mo′ni·ous·ness,** *n.*
—**Syn. 1.** ceremonial; conventional, punctilious, courteous.

cer·e·mo·ny (ser′ə mō′nē), *n., pl.* **-nies. 1.** the formalities observed on some solemn or important public or state occasion: *The coronation ceremonies continued for weeks.* **2.** a formal religious or sacred observance; a solemn rite: *a marriage ceremony.* **3.** formal observances or gestures collectively; ceremonial observances: *The breathless messenger had no time for ceremony.* **4.** any formal act or observance, esp. a meaningless one: *His low bow was mere ceremony.* **5.** a gesture or act of politeness or civility: *A little girl's curtsy is a charming ceremony.* **6.** strict adherence to conventional forms; formality: *to leave a room without ceremony.* **7. stand on ceremony,** to behave in a formal or ceremonious manner: *There is no need to stand on ceremony with us.* [ME *ceremonie* < ML *cerēmōni(a),* L *caerimōnia* sacred rite; r. ME *cerymonye* < MF *cerimonie* < L, as above]
—**Syn. 1, 2.** CEREMONY, RITE, RITUAL refer to set observances and acts traditional in religious services or on public occasions. CEREMONY applies to more or less formal dignified acts on religious or public occasions: *a marriage ceremony; an inaugural ceremony.* A RITE is an established, prescribed, or customary form of religious or other solemn practice: *the rite of baptism.* RITUAL refers to the form of conducting worship or to a code of ceremonies in general: *Masonic rituals.*

Ce·ren·kov (chə reng′kôf, -kəf, -ren′-; *Russ.* che ren′kof), *n.* **Pa·vel A.** (pä′vel), born 1904, Russian physicist: Nobel prize 1958. Also, **Cherenkov.**

Ceren′kov radia′tion, *Physics.* radiation produced by a particle passing through a medium at a speed greater than that of light through the medium. [named after P. A. CERENKOV]

cer·e·ous (sēr′ē əs), *adj.* *Obs.* waxlike. [< L *cēreus* waxen, equiv. to *cēr(a)* wax + *-eus* -EOUS]

Ce·res (sēr′ēz), *n.* **1.** an ancient Italian goddess of agriculture under whose name the Romans adopted the worship of the Greek goddess Demeter. **2.** *Astron.* the first asteroid to be discovered, being the largest and one of the brightest.

ce·re·us (sēr′ē əs), *n., pl.* **-us·es.** any cactaceous plant of the genus *Cereus,* of tropical America and the western U.S., as *C. Jamacaru,* of northern Brazil, which may grow to a height of 40 feet. [< NL, L *cēreus* wax candle, n. use of *cēreus* CEREOUS]

ce·ri·a (sēr′ē ə), *n.* *Chem.* a white-to-yellow, heavy powder, CeO_2, usually derived from cerium nitrate by decomposition with heat: used chiefly in ceramics, glass polishing, and decolorizing. Also called **cerium dioxide, cerium oxide, ce′ric ox′ide.** [CERI(UM) + *-a* chem. suffix denoting oxide]

ce·ric (sēr′ik, ser′-), *adj.* *Chem.* containing cerium, esp. in the tetravalent state. [CER(IUM) + -IC]

ce·rif·er·ous (si rif′ər əs), *adj.* producing or secreting wax, as a gland. [CER- + -I- + -FEROUS]

Ce·ri·go (che′rē gô), *n.* a Greek island in the Mediterranean, S of Peloponnesus: a temple of Aphrodite located here in antiquity. 6297 (1951); 108 sq. mi. Also called **Cythera.** Greek, **Kythera.**

cer·i·man (ser′ə mən, ser′ə man′, -män′), *n., pl.* **-mans. 1.** a climbing, araceous plant, *Monstera deliciosa,* of tropical America, characterized by cordlike, aerial roots and leaves two to three feet long. **2.** the greenish-yellow, edible, sweet fruit of this tree. Also called **false breadfruit.** [< AmerSp]

ce·rin′ic ac′id (si rin′ik), *Chem.* See **cerotic acid.** [CER- + -IN[2] + -IC]

ce·rise (sə rēs′, -rēz′), *adj., n.* moderate to deep red. [< F; see CHERRY]

ce·rite (sēr′īt), *n.* a rare mineral, hydrous silicate of cerium, occurring in brownish masses: a minor ore of the rare earths. [CER(ES) + -ITE[1]]

ce·ri·um (sēr′ē əm), *n.* *Chem.* a steel-gray, ductile metallic element of the rare-earth group found only in combination. *Symbol:* Ce; *at. wt.:* 140.12; *at. no.:* 58. [CER(ES) + -IUM]

ce′rium diox′ide, *Chem.* ceria. Also called **ce′rium ox′ide.**

ce′rium met′al, *Chem.* any of a subgroup of rare-earth metals of which the terbium and yttrium metals comprise the other two subgroups. Cf. **rare-earth element.**

cer·met (sûr′met), *n.* a durable, heat-resistant alloy formed by compacting and sintering a metal and a ceramic substance, used under conditions of high temperature and stress. Also called **ceramal.** [CER(AMIC) + MET(AL)]

Cer·nă·u·ți (cher′nə ōōts′), *n.* a city in the SW Ukraine, in the SW Soviet Union: formerly in Rumania. 145,000 (1959). German, **Czernowitz.** Russian, **Chernovtsy.**

Cer·nu·da (sər no͞o′də, -nyo͞o′-; *Sp.* ther no͞o′thä), *n.* **Lu·is** (lo͞o ēs′), born 1904, Spanish poet, in England after 1939.

cer·nu·ous (sûr′nyo͞o əs, sûr′no͞o-), *adj. Bot.* drooping or bowing down, as a flower; nodding. [< L *cernuus* falling forwards, face down]

ce·ro (sēr′ō), *n., pl.* (*esp. collectively*) **-ro,** (*esp. referring to two or more kinds or species*) **-ros. 1.** a large, mackerel-like game fish, *Scomberomorus regalis,* found in tropical America. **2.** any of various related fishes. [alter. of SIERRA]

cero-, a learned borrowing from Greek meaning "wax," used in the formation of compound words: *cerotype.* Also, *esp. before a vowel,* **cer-.** [< Gk *kēro-,* comb. form of *kērós* wax]

ce·ro·graph (sēr′ə graf′, -gräf′), *n.* a drawing, design, or text incised into a wax surface. [CERO- + -GRAPH] —**ce·ro·graph·ic** (sēr′ə graf′ik), **ce′ro·graph′i·cal,** *adj.* —**ce·rog·ra·phist** (si rog′rə fist), *n.*

ce·rog·ra·phy (si rog′rə fē), *n.* the process of writing or engraving on wax. [< Gk *kērographí(a).* See CERO-, -GRAPHY]

ce·ro·ma (si rō′mə), *n.* (in an ancient Greek gymnasium or a Roman bath) a room for anointment with oil and wax. [< L *cērōma* ointment, anointing room, etc. < Gk *kḗrōma* that which is made of wax, equiv. to *kēro(un)* (to) wax + *-ma* n. suffix]

ce·ro·plas·tic (sēr′ə plas′tik, ser′ə-), *adj.* **1.** pertaining to modeling in wax. **2.** modeled in wax. [< Gk *kēroplastik(ós).* See CERO-, PLASTIC] —**ce′ro·plas′tics,** *n.*

ce·rot·ic (si rot′ik, -rō′tik), *adj. Chem.* of or derived from cerotic acid. [< L *cērōt(um)* wax salve (< Gk *kērōtón,* n. use of neut. of *kērōtós* waxed, equiv. to *kērō-,* long. s. of *kērós* wax + *-tos* v. suffix) + -IC]

cerot′ic ac′id, *Chem.* a white, crystalline, water-insoluble, odorless wax, $CH_3(CH_2)_{24}COOH$, usually obtained from beeswax or carnauba wax. Also called **cerinic acid, hexacosanoic acid.**

ce·ro·type (sēr′ə tīp′, ser′-), *n.* a process of engraving in which the design or the like is cut on a wax-coated metal plate from which a printing surface is subsequently produced by stereotyping or by electrotyping. [CERO- + -TYPE]

ce·rous (sēr′əs), *adj. Chem.* containing trivalent cerium. [CER(IUM) + -OUS]

Cer·ro de Pas·co (seʀ′ʀō the päs′kō), a town in central Peru: silver-mining district. 27,656 (est. 1957); 14,280 ft. above sea level.

Cer·ro Gor·do (seʀ′ʀō gôʀ′thō), a mountain pass in E Mexico between Veracruz and Jalapa: defeat of Mexican troops by U.S. troops 1847.

cert., **1.** certificate. **2.** certified. **3.** certify.

cer·tain (sûr′tᵊn), *adj.* **1.** free from doubt or reservation; confident; sure: *I am certain he will come. He is certain of their loyalty.* **2.** destined; sure (usually fol. by an infinitive): *He is certain to be there.* **3.** inevitable; bound to come: *They realized then that war was certain.* **4.** established as true or sure; unquestionable; indisputable: *It is certain that he tried.* **5.** fixed; agreed upon; settled: *on a certain day; for a certain amount.* **6.** definite or particular, but not named or specified: *A certain person phoned. He had a certain charm.* **7.** that may be depended on; trustworthy; unfailing; reliable: *His aim was certain.* **8.** some though not much: *a certain reluctance.* **9.** *Obs.* steadfast. **10. for certain,** without a doubt; surely: *I know for certain that I have seen that face before.* [ME < OF < L *cert(us)* sure, settled (*cer-,* base of *cernere* to decide, + *-tus* ptp. suffix) + *-ānus* -AN] —**Syn. 1.** convinced, satisfied. See **sure. 4.** indubitable, incontestable, irrefutable, incontrovertible, obvious, plain, clear. **5.** determined.

cer·tain·ly (sûr′tᵊn lē), *adv.* **1.** with certainty; without doubt; assuredly: *I'll certainly be there.* **2.** yes, of course: *Certainly, you may take the keys.* **3.** surely; to be sure: *She certainly is stupid.* [ME; see CERTAIN, -LY]

cer·tain·ty (sûr′tᵊn tē), *n., pl.* **-ties. 1.** state of being certain. **2.** something certain; an assured fact. **3. for** or **of a certainty,** certainly; without a doubt: *I suspect it, but I don't know it for a certainty.* [ME *certeinte* < AF, equiv. to *certein* CERTAIN + *-te* -TY[2]] —**Syn. 1.** certitude, assurance, confidence. See **belief. 2.** truth.

cer·tes (sûr′tēz), *adv. Archaic.* certainly; in truth. [ME < OF < phrase *a certes* < L **ā certīs,* lit., from sure (things); see A-[4], CERTAIN]

certif., **1.** certificate. **2.** certificated.

cer·ti·fi·a·ble (sûr′tə fī′ə bəl), *adj.* **1.** capable of being certified. **2.** *Brit.* **a.** committable to a mental institution. **b.** *Sometimes facetious.* fit or ready for an insane asylum. **c.** uncontrollable; insane: *a certifiable desire.* [CERTIFY + -ABLE] —**cer′ti·fi′a·ble·ness,** *n.* —**cer′ti·fi′a·bly,** *adv.*

cer·tif·i·cate (*n.* sər tif′ə kit; *v.* sər tif′ə kāt′), *n., v.,* **-cat·ed, -cat·ing.** —*n.* **1.** a document serving as evidence or as written testimony, as of status, qualifications, privileges, the truth of something, etc. **2.** a document attesting to the fact that a person has completed an educational course, issued either by an institution not authorized to grant diplomas, or to a student not qualifying for a diploma. **3.** *Law.* a statement, written and signed, which is by law made evidence of the truth of the facts stated, for all or for certain purposes. **4.** *U.S.* **a.** a paper (**silver certificate**) issued by the federal government for circulation as money equal to and redeemable for silver to a stated value. **b.** a paper (**gold certificate**) similarly issued as the equivalent of a stated amount of gold. —*v.t.* **5.** to attest by a certificate. **6.** to furnish with or authorize by a certificate. [late ME *certificat* < ML *certificāt(um),* n. use of neut. of *certificātus* certified (ptp. of *certificāre*), equiv. to *certific-* (see CERTIFY) + *-ātus* -ATE[1]] —**cer·tif·i·ca·to·ry** (sər tif′ə kə tōr′ē, -tôr′ē), *adj.*

certif′icate of admeas′urement, *Naut.* a certificate issued by a government authority, showing the registered tonnages of a commercial vessel.

certif′icate of depos′it, a written acknowledgment of a bank that it has received from the person named a specified sum of money as a deposit.

certif′icate of enroll′ment, a document issued to a U.S. vessel of 20 tons gross or more, engaged in fishing or in trade along the U.S. coast, on the Great Lakes, or on U.S. inland waters.

certif′icate of incorpora′tion, a statement filed with a State official in forming a corporation, stating its name, purposes, and the nature and distribution of the stock to be issued, and other matters required by law.

certif′icate of indebt′edness, a short-term, negotiable, interest-bearing note representing indebtedness.

certif′icate of or′igin, a document certifying the country of manufacture of a commodity, often required by the customs office before importation.

certif′icate of reg′istry, *Naut.* a document issued to a U.S. vessel engaged in foreign trade, stating its name, nationality, ownership, etc., and claiming for it all privileges pertaining to U.S. nationality.

certif′icate of stock′, a document showing evidence of ownership of one or more shares of stock in a corporation or joint-stock company.

cer·ti·fi·ca·tion (sûr′tə fə kā′shən, sər tif′ə-), *n.* **1.** act of certifying. **2.** state of being certified. **3.** a certified statement. **4.** the writing on the face of a check by which it is certified. **5.** *Law.* a certificate attesting the truth of some statement or event. [late ME *certificacio(u)n* < ML *certificātiōn-* (s. of *certificātiō*). See CERTIFICATE, -ION]

cer·ti·fied (sûr′tə fīd′), *adj.* **1.** having or proved by a certificate: *a certified representative.* **2.** guaranteed; reliably endorsed: *a certified check.* **3.** *Brit.* **a.** legally declared insane. **b.** committed to a mental institution. [CERTIFY + -ED[2]]

cer′tified check′, a check bearing a guarantee of payment by the bank on which the check is drawn.

cer′tified mail′, uninsured first-class mail requiring proof of delivery.

cer′tified milk′, *U.S.* milk, either pasteurized or unpasteurized, that is processed in dairies conforming to official standards of sanitation and procedure.

cer′tified pub′lic account′ant, *U.S.* a person holding an official certificate as an accountant, having fulfilled all the legal requirements. *Abbr.:* C.P.A.

cer·ti·fy (sûr′tə fī′), *v.,* **-fied, -fy·ing.** —*v.t.* **1.** to attest as certain; give reliable information of; confirm: *He certified the truth of his claim by producing proof.* **2.** to testify to or vouch for in writing: *The medical examiner will certify his findings to the court.* **3.** to assure or inform with certainty: *The statement of the witness certified the judge of the plaintiff's just cause.* **4.** to guarantee; endorse reliably: *to certify a document with an official seal.* **5.** (of a bank) to guarantee in writing on (the face of a check) that the account against which it is drawn has sufficient funds to pay it. —*v.i.* **6.** to give assurance; testify; vouch for (usually fol. by *to*). [ME *certifie(n)* < MF *certifie(r)* < LL *certificāre,* equiv. to L *certi-* (comb. form of *certus* decided; see CERTAIN) + *-ficāre* -FY] —**cer′ti·fi′er,** *n.*

cer·ti·o·ra·ri (sûr′shē ə râr′ī), *n. Law.* a writ issuing from a superior court calling up the record of a proceeding in an inferior court for review. [< L: to be informed, certified; lit., made surer (pass. inf. of *certiōrāre* to inform), equiv. to *certiōr-* (s. of *certior* surer, comp. of *certus* sure; see CERTAIN) + *-ā-* thematic vowel + *-rī* pass. inf. ending; the writ is so called because v. form occurred in the Latin original]

cer·ti·tude (sûr′ti to͞od′, -tyo͞od′), *n.* freedom from doubt, esp. in matters of faith or opinion; certainty; confidence. [ME < LL *certitūd(ō),* equiv. to L *certi-* (comb. form of *certus* sure; see CERTAIN) + *-tūdō* -TUDE] —**Syn.** assurance, conviction, belief.

cer·to·si·na (chûr′tə sē′nə; *It.* cher′tô sē′nä), *n.* a technique of inlaying light-colored material, as bone, ivory, metal, or pale wood, in elaborate designs on a dark ground. [< It, fem. of *certosino* Carthusian]

ce·ru·le·an (sə ro͞o′lē ən), *adj., n.* **1.** deep blue; sky blue; azure. **2.** *Heraldry.* a sky-blue tincture, used esp. on the Continent; bleu celeste. [< L *caerule(us)* dark blue, azure (akin to *caelum* sky) + -AN]

ceru′lean blue′, **1.** a light-blue to strong greenish-blue color. **2.** a pigment used in painting consisting mainly of oxides of tin and cobalt, chiefly characterized by its greenish-blue color and permanence.

ceru′lean war′bler, a North American wood warbler, *Dendroica cerulea,* the male of which is blue above and white below.

ce·ru·men (si ro͞o′mən), *n.* a yellowish, waxlike secretion from certain glands in the external auditory canal. Also called **earwax.** [< NL, equiv. to L *cēr(a)* wax + *(alb)umen* ALBUMEN] —**ce·ru′mi·nous,** *adj.*

ce·ruse (sēr′o͞os, si ro͞os′), *n. Chem.* a heavy, white, crystalline, water-insoluble, poisonous powder, $(PbCO_3)_2 \cdot Pb(OH)_2$, used chiefly in oil and water-color paints and in putty; white lead. Also called **basic lead carbonate.** [ME < L *cērussa(a),* equiv. to *cēr(a)* wax + *-ussa* < ?]

ce·rus·site (sēr′ə sīt′, si rus′īt), *n.* a mineral, lead carbonate, $PbCO_3$, found in masses or in white crystals: an important ore of lead. [< L *cēruss(a)* CERUSE + -ITE[1]]

Cer·van·tes (sər van′tēz; *Sp.* ther vän′tes), *n.* **Mi·guel de** (mi gel′ dā; *Sp.* mē gel′ de), (*Miguel de Cervantes Saavedra*), 1547–1616, Spanish novelist and short-story writer.

cer·ve·lat (sûr′və lat′, -lä′, ser′-), *n.* a kind of smoked sausage made of beef or pork, fat, and seasonings. Also, **cer·ve·las** (sur′və lä′, ser′-). [< obs. F; see SAVELOY]

cer·vel·lière (sûr′vəl yâr′), *n. Armor.* a close-fitting cap of mail or plate; coif. Also, **cer′ve·lière′.** [< F, deriv. of *cervelle* brain. See CEREBELLUM]

Cer·ve·ra y To·pe·te (ther ve′rä ē tô pe′te), **Pas·cual** (päs kwäl′), 1839–1909, Spanish admiral.

cervic-, a combining form of **cervix:** *cervicitis.* [< L *cervic-,* s. of *cervix*]

cer·vi·cal (sûr′vi kəl), *adj. Anat.* of or pertaining to the cervix or neck. [< L *cervīc-* (s. of *cervix*) neck + -AL[1]]

cer·vi·ces (sər vī′sēz, sûr′vi sēz′), *n.* a pl. of **cervix.**

cer·vi·ci·tis (sûr′vi sī′tis), *n. Pathol.* inflammation of the cervix. [CERVIC- + -ITIS]

Cer·vin (seʀ vaN′), *n.* **Mont** (môN). French name of the **Matterhorn.**

cer·vine (sûr′vīn, -vin), *adj.* **1.** deerlike. **2.** of or pertaining to the deer family. **3.** of a deep tawny color. [< L *cervīn(us)* of, pertaining to a deer, equiv. to *cerv(us)* deer + *-īnus* -INE[1]]

cer·vix (sûr′viks), *n., pl.* **cer·vix·es, cer·vi·ces** (sər vī′sēz, sûr′vi sēz′). *Anat.* **1.** the neck. **2.** any necklike part, esp. the constricted lower end of the uterus. [< L]

Cer·y·ne·an stag′ (ser′ə nē′ən, ser′-), *Class. Myth.* a stag living in Arcadia, captured by Hercules as one of his labors. Also, **Cer′ynei′an stag′.** Also called **Arcadian hind, Arcadian stag, Cer′yne′an hind′, Cer′ynei′an hind′.**

Ce·ryx (sēr′iks), *n. Class. Myth.* a son of Hermes who served as herald of the gods at the Eleusinian mysteries.

Ce·sar·e·an (si zâr′ē ən), *adj., n.* Caesarean. Also, **Ce·sar′i·an.**

Ce·se·na (che ze′nä), *n.* a city in E central Italy. 79,954 (1961).

ce·si·um (sē′zē əm), *n. Chem.* a rare, highly reactive, soft, metallic element of the alkali metal group, used chiefly in photoelectric cells. *Symbol:* Cs; *at. wt.:* 132.905; *at. no.:* 55; *sp. gr.:* 1.9 at 20°C.; melts at 28.5°C. Also, **caesium.** [< NL, special use of L *caesium,* neut. of *caesius* bluish-grey]

Čes·ké Bu·dě·jo·vi·ce (ches′ke bo͝o′dye yô vi tse), a city in the S Czech Republic, on the Moldau River. 90,415. German, **Budweis.**

ces·pi·tose (ses′pi tōs′), *adj. Bot.* matted together; growing in dense tufts. Also, **caespitose.** [< NL *cespitōs(us),* equiv. to L *cespit-* (s. of *cespes,* var. of *caespes* turf) + *-ōsus* -OSE[1]] —**ces′pi·tose′ly,** *adv.*

cess[1] (ses), *n.* **1.** *Brit.* a tax, assessment, or lien. **2.** (in Scotland) a land tax. **3.** (in Ireland) a military assessment. **4.** (in India) an import or sales tax on a commodity. —*v.t.* **5.** *Brit.* to tax; assess. [aph. var. of obs. *assess* assessment, n. use of ASSESS (v.)]

cess[2] (ses), *n. Irish Eng. Informal.* luck (usually used in the expression *bad cess to*): *Bad cess to them!*

ces·sa·tion (se sā′shən), *n.* a temporary or complete ceasing; discontinuance: *a cessation of hostilities.* [ME *cessacio(u)n* < L *cessātiōn-* (s. of *cessātiō*) delay, inactivity, stoppage, equiv. to *cessāt(us)* delayed, stopped, ptp. of *cessāre* (*cess(us)* yielded, ceded (*ced-* CEDE + *-tus* ptp. suffix) + *-ātus* -ATE[1]) + *-iōn-* -ION]

ces·sa·tive (ses′ə tiv, se sā′-), *adj.* (of a verbal form or aspect) expressing cessation. [< L *cessāt(us)* (ptp. of *cessāre* to delay) + -IVE]

ces·sion (sesh′ən), *n.* **1.** act of ceding, as by treaty. **2.** that which is ceded, as territory. [ME < L *cessiōn-* (s. of *cessiō*) a giving up, equiv. to *cess(us)* yielded, ptp. of *cēdere* (*ced-* perf. s. + *-tus* ptp. suffix) + *-iōn-* -ION]

ces·sion·ar·y (sesh′ə ner′ē), *n., pl.* **-ar·ies.** *Law.* an assignee or grantee. [< ML *cessiōnāri(us),* equiv. to *cessiōn-* CESSION + *-ārius* -ARY]

cess·pipe (ses′pīp′), *n.* a waste pipe, esp. one discharging from a cesspool. [CESS(POOL) + PIPE[1]]

cess·pit (ses′pit′), *n.* a pit for receiving wastes from sinks or water closets. [CESS(POOL) + PIT[1]]

cess·pool (ses′po͞ol′), *n.* **1.** a cistern, well, or pit for retaining the sediment of a drain or for receiving the sewage from the sinks, toilets, etc., of a house. **2.** any filthy receptacle or place. **3.** any place of moral filth, or immorality: *a cesspool of iniquity.* [*cess* (< It *cess(o)* privy < L *recessus* RECESS, place of retirement) + POOL[1]]

ces·ta (ses′tə), *n. Jai Alai.* a narrow, cup-shaped wicker basket fitted on one end to a wooden handle with a glovelike compartment at the base, for catching and throwing the ball. [< Sp: lit., basket < L *cista* CHEST]

c'est-à-dire (se tA dēʀ′), *French.* that is to say; to wit.

c'est au·tre chose (se tō tʀᵊ shōz′), *French.* that is different. [lit., that is another thing]

Ces·ti (ches′tē), *n.* **Marc·an·to·nio** (mäʀ′kän tô′nyô), 1623–69, Italian composer.

c'est la guerre (se lA geʀ′), *French.* such is war; that's war.

c'est la vie (se lA vē′), *French.* such is life; that's life.

Ces·to·da (ses stō′də), *n.* the class comprising the tapeworms. [< NL; see CESTODE]

ces·tode (ses′tōd), *n.* **1.** a parasitic platyhelminth or flatworm of the class *Cestoda,* which comprises the tapeworms. —*adj.* **2.** belonging or pertaining to the *Cestoda.* [< NL *cestōd(ēs).* See CESTUS[1], -ODE[1]]

ces·toid (ses′toid), *adj.* **1.** *Zool.* (of worms) ribbonlike. —*n.* **2.** cestode. [< NL *cestoīd(ēs).* See CESTUS[1], -OID]

c'est plus qu'un crime, c'est une faute (se plY kœN kʀem′, se tYn fōt′), *French.* it is more than a crime, it is a blunder.

Ces·tri·nus (ses trī′nəs), *n. Class. Myth.* a son of Andromache and Helenus.

c'est se·lon (se sə lôN′), *French.* that depends; it all depends. [lit., that's according (to)]

ces·tus[1] (ses′təs), *n., pl.* **-ti** (-tī). **1.** a girdle or belt, esp. as worn by women of ancient Greece. **2.** *Class. Myth.* the girdle of Venus, decorated with every object that could arouse amorous desire. Also, *esp. Brit.,* **ces′tos.** [< L < Gk *kestós* a girdle, lit., (something) stitched, equiv. to *kes-* (var. s. of *kentein* to stitch) + *-tos* v. suffix]

ces·tus[2] (ses′təs), *n., pl.* **-tus·es.** *Rom. Antiq.* a hand covering made of leather strips and often loaded with metal, worn by boxers. [< L, var. of *caestus,* perh. equiv. to *caes(us)* struck, ptp. of *caedere* (*caed-* strike + *-tus* ptp. suffix) + *-tus* ptp. suffix]

ce·su·ra (sə zho͝or′ə, -zo͝or′ə, siz yo͝or′ə), *n., pl.* **ce·su·ras, ce·su·rae** (sə zho͝or′ē, -zo͝or′ē, siz yo͝or′ē). caesura. —**ce·su′ral,** *adj.*

cet-, a learned borrowing from Latin meaning "whale," used in the formation of compound words: *cetane.* [comb. form repr. L *cētus* < Gk *kētos* whale]

Ce·ta·ce·a (si tā′shē ə), *n.* the order comprising the cetacean mammals. [< NL; see CETACEAN]

ce·ta·cean (si tā′shən), *adj.* **1.** belonging to the *Cetacea,* an order of aquatic, chiefly marine mammals, including the whales, dolphins, porpoises, etc. —*n.* **2.** a cetacean mammal. [< NL *Cētāce(a)* name of the order (see CET-, -ACEA) + -AN]

ce·ta·ce·um (si tā′shē əm, -sē əm), *n. Chem.* spermaceti. [< NL, neut. of *cētāceus;* see CETACEAN]

ce·tane (sē′tān), *n. Chem.* a colorless, liquid hydrocarbon of the alkane series, $C_{16}H_{34}$, used as a solvent and in cetane number determinations. [CET(YL) + -ANE]

ce′tane num′ber, *Chem.* a measure of the ignition quality of a diesel engine fuel by comparison with various mixtures in which the alpha form of methylnaphthaline is given a standard value of 0 and cetane is given a standard value of 100. Also called **ce′tane rat′ing.**

Ce·ta·tea Al·bă (che tä′tyä äl′bə), Rumanian name of **Belgorod-Dnestrovski.**

ce·te·ra de·sunt (kā′te rä′ de′so͝ont; *Eng.* set′ər ə dē′sənt), *Latin.* the remaining (parts) are missing.

ce·te·ris pa·ri·bus (kā′te rēs′ pä′ri bo͞os′; *Eng.* set′ər is par′ə bəs), *Latin.* other things being equal.

ce·tin (sēt′ən), *n.* *Biochem.* a white, crystalline, water-insoluble fat, $CH_3(CH_2)_{14}COOCH_2(CH_2)_{14}CH_3$, obtained from spermaceti by extraction with ether: used chiefly as an emulsive agent in the manufacture of pharmaceuticals and cosmetics and as a base in the manufacture of candles and soaps. Also called **cetyl palmitate.** [CET- + -IN²]

Ce·tin·je (tse′ti nye), *n.* a city in S Yugoslavia: former capital of Montenegro. 9109 (1953).

Ce·to (sē′tō), *n.* *Class. Myth.* the mother, by her brother Phorcys, of the Graeae and the Gorgons.

ce·tol·o·gy (sē tol′ə jē), *n.* the branch of zoology dealing with the whales. [CET- + -O- + -LOGY] —**ce·to·log·i·cal** (sēt′əloj′i kəl), *adj.* —**ce·tol′o·gist,** *n.*

Ce·tur·a (si to͝or′ə), *n.* *Douay Bible.* Keturah.

Ce·tus (sē′təs), *n., gen.* **Ce·ti** (sē′tī). *Astron.* the Whale, a constellation lying above the equator, containing the variable star Mira. [< L; see CET-]

ce′tyl al′cohol (sēt′əl), *Chem.* a white, crystalline, water-insoluble solid, $C_{16}H_{33}OH$, used chiefly as an emollient in cosmetics and pharmaceuticals. Also, **ce·tyl′ic al′cohol** (si til′ik). Also called **ethal.** [CET- + -YL (so called because some of its compounds are found in spermaceti)]

cetyl′ic ac′id, *Chem.* See **palmitic acid.** [CETYL + -IC]

ce′tyl pal′mitate, *Biochem.* cetin.

Ceu·ta (syo͞o′tə; *Sp.* the′o͞o tä, se′-), *n.* a seaport and enclave of Spain in N Morocco, on the Strait of Gibraltar. 68,855 (1964).

Cé·vennes (sā ven′), *n.* (*construed as pl.*) a mountain range in S France. Highest peak, Mt. Mézenc, 5753 ft.

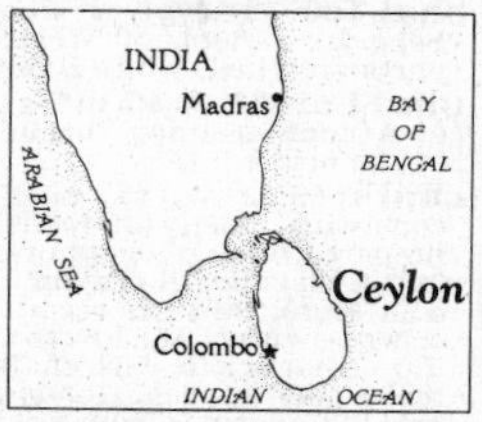

ce′vi·tam′ic ac′id (sē′vī tam′ik, sē′-), *Biochem.* See **ascorbic acid.** [*C vitam(in)* VITAMIN C + -IC]

Cey·lon (si lon′), *n.* **1.** an island republic in the Indian Ocean, S of India: a member of the British Commonwealth. 10,624,507 (1963); 25,332 sq. mi. *Cap.:* Colombo. Formerly, **Serendip.** Official name, **Sri Lanka. 2.** a boy's given name.

Ceylon′ cin′namon. See under **cinnamon** (def. 1).

Cey·lo·nese (sē′lə nēz′, -nēs′), *adj., n., pl.* **-nese.** —*adj.* **1.** of or pertaining to Ceylon, its people, or their language. —*n.* **2.** a native or inhabitant of Ceylon. [CEYLON + -ESE]

Ceylon′ goose′berry, kitambilla.

Ceylon′ morn′ing-glory, a perennial vine, *Ipomoea tuberosa,* of India, having yellow flowers and woody pods.

Ceylon′ moss′, a seaweed, *Gracilaria lichenoides,* of Ceylon and the East Indies: one of the algae from which agar is obtained.

Ce·yx (sē′iks), *n.* *Class. Myth.* the husband of Alcyone.

Cé·zanne (si zan′; *Fr.* sā zan′), *n.* **Paul** (pôl), 1839–1906, French painter.

Cf, *Chem.* californium.

cf., 1. *Bookbinding.* calf. **2.** *Baseball.* center fielder. **3.** compare. [< L *confer*]

c/f, *Bookkeeping.* carried forward.

C.F., cost and freight. Also, **c.f.**

cfd, cubic feet per day.

cfh, cubic feet per hour.

C.F.I., cost, freight, and insurance. Also, **c.f.i.**

cfm., cubic feet per minute. Also, **c.f.m.**

cfs., cubic feet per second. Also, **c.f.s.**

CG, Commanding General.

cg., centigram; centigrams.

C.G., 1. Captain of the Guard. **2.** center of gravity. **3.** Coast Guard. **4.** Commanding General. **5.** Consul General.

c.g., 1. Captain of the Guard. **2.** center of gravity. **3.** Commanding General. **4.** Consul General.

cgm., centigram.

cgs, centimeter-gram-second. Also, **c.g.s., CGS**

ch, *Survey, Civ. Eng.* chain; chains.

Ch., 1. Chaldean. **2.** Chaldee. **3.** chapter. **4.** Château. **5.** *Chess.* check. **6.** China. **7.** Chinese. **8.** church.

ch., 1. chapter. **2.** *Chess.* check. **3.** church.

c.h., 1. candle hours. **2.** clearing house. **3.** courthouse. **4.** custom house.

chab·a·zite (kab′ə zīt′), *n.* a zeolite mineral, essentially a hydrated sodium calcium aluminum silicate, occurring usually in red to colorless rhombohedral crystals. [*chabazie* (< F *chabasie* < LGk *chabázios,* misspelling of *chalázios* hailstonelike (stone), equiv. to *chaláz(a)* hail, hailstone + *-ios* adj. suffix) + -ITE¹; cf. G *Chabasit*]

Chab·lis (shab′lē, shä blē′; *Fr.* sha blē′), *n.* **1.** a very dry, white table wine from the Burgundy region in France. **2.** a similar wine produced elsewhere. [after *Chablis,* town where made]

cha·bouk (chä′bo͝ok), *n.* a horsewhip, often used in the Orient for inflicting corporal punishment. Also, **cha′buk.** [< Urdu *chābuk* < Pers]

Cha·bri·er (shä′brē ā′; *Fr.* sha brē ā′), *n.* **A·lex·is Em·man·u·el** (ə lek′sis i man′yo͞o əl; *Fr.* a lek sē′ e ma ny el′), 1841–94, French composer.

cha-cha (chä′chä′), *n., pl.* **-chas,** *v.,* **-chaed, -cha·ing.** —*n.* **1.** a Latin-American dance similar to the mambo. —*v.i.* **2.** to dance the cha-cha. Also, **cha′-cha′-cha′.** [< AmerSp (Cuban) *cha-cha-cha,* prob. imit. of the musical accompaniment]

cha·cha·la·ca (chä′chə lä′kə; *Sp.* chä′chä lä′kä), *n., pl.* **-kas** (-kəz; *Sp.* -käs). any of several slender guans of the genus *Ortalis,* of Central America, Mexico, and southern Texas, having loud, harsh cries. [< Sp < Nahuatl; imit.]

chack·le (chak′əl), *v.i.,* **chack·led, chack·ling.** *Brit. Dial.* to chatter; jabber. [dialectal variant]

chac·ma (chak′mə), *n.* a large, brownish-gray baboon, *Papio comatus,* of southern Africa. [< Hottentot]

Chacma
(About 2 ft. high at shoulder; total length 4 ft.; tail 1½ ft.)

Cha·co (chä′kō), *n.* **1.** a part of the Gran Chaco region in central South America, in Bolivia, Paraguay, and Argentina. ab. 100,000 sq. mi. **2.** See **Gran Chaco.**

cha·conne (sha kôn′, -kon′, shä-; *Fr.* sha kôn′), *n., pl.* **-connes** (-kônz′, -konz′; *Fr.* -kôn′). **1.** an ancient dance, probably of Spanish origin, in moderate triple meter. **2.** a musical form based on the continuous variation of a series of chords or of a ground bass. [< F < Sp *chacona*]

cha·cun à son goût (sha kœ na sôn go͞o′), *French.* everyone to his own taste.

chad (chad), *n.* *Computer Technol.* the small paper disks formed when holes are punched in a punch card or paper tape. [?]

Chad (chad), *n.* **1. Lake,** a lake in N Africa at the junction of the Chad, Niger, and Nigeria rivers. 10,000 to 20,000 sq. mi. (seasonal variation). **2.** Official name, **Repub′lic of Chad′.** a republic in W central Africa, E of Lake Chad: a member of the French Community; formerly part of French Equatorial Africa. 2,730,000 (est. 1959); 501,000 sq. mi. *Cap.:* Fort-Lamy. **3.** a boy's given name. French, **Tchad** (for defs. 1, 2).

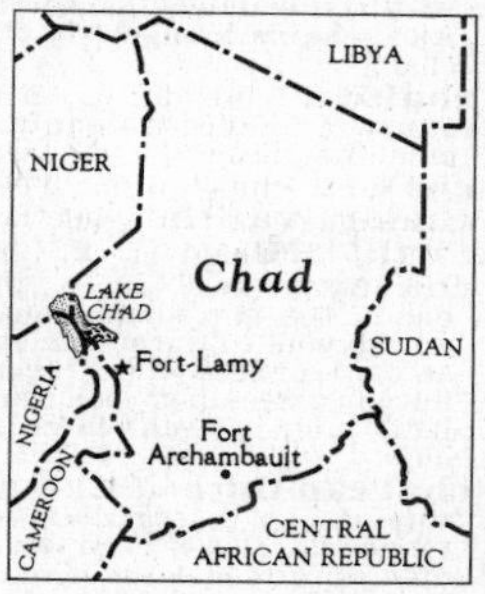

chad·less (chad′lis), *adj.* *Computer Technol.* noting paper tape punched so that the chad remains attached by about one quarter of its circumference to the hole. [CHAD + -LESS]

Chad·ron (shad′rən), *n.* a town in NW Nebraska. 5079 (1960).

Chad·wick (chad′wik), *n.* **1. George Whitefield,** 1854–1931, U.S. composer. **2. James,** 1891–1974, English physicist: discoverer of the neutron; Nobel prize 1935.

Chaer·o·ne·a (ker′ə nē′ə), *n.* an ancient city in E Greece, in Boeotia: victory of Philip of Macedon over the Athenians, Thebans, and their allies, 338 B.C.

chae·ta (kē′tə), *n., pl.* **-tae** (-tē). *Zool.* a bristle or seta, esp. of a chaetopod. [< NL < Gk *chaítē* long hair]

chaeto-, a learned borrowing from Greek meaning "hair," used in the formation of compound words: *chaetophorous.* [comb. form repr. Gk *chaítē;* see CHAETA]

chae·to·don (kē′tə don′), *n.* See **blackbanded sunfish.** [< NL, equiv. to *chaet-* CHAETO- + Gk *odṓn* tooth]

chae·tog·nath (kē′tog nath′, -təg-), *n.* **1.** any animal of the group *Chaetognatha,* comprising the arrowworms. —*adj.* **2.** Also, **chae·tog·na·than** (kē tog′nə thən), **chae·tog′na·thous.** belonging or pertaining to the *Chaetognatha.* [CHAETO- + Gk *gnáth(os)* jaw]

Chae·tog·na·tha (kē tog′nə thə), *n.* the phylum comprising the arrowworms. [< NL; see CHAETOGNATH]

chae·toph·o·rous (ki tof′ər əs), *adj.* *Zool.* bearing bristles; setigerous or setiferous. [CHAETO- + -PHOROUS]

chae·to·pod (kē′tə pod′), *n.* any annelid of the class or group *Chaetopoda,* having the body composed of more or less similar segments with muscular processes bearing setae. [CHAETO- + -POD]

chae·to·tax·y (kē′tə tak′sē), *n.* *Entomol.* the arrangement of bristles on the exoskeleton of an insect. [CHAETO- + -TAXY] —**chae·to·tac·tic** (kē′tə tak′tik), *adj.*

chafe (chāf), *v.,* **chafed, chaf·ing,** *n.* —*v.t.* **1.** to warm by rubbing: *to chafe cold hands.* **2.** to wear or abrade by rubbing: *He chafed his shoes on the rocks.* **3.** to make sore by rubbing: *Her collar chafed her neck.* **4.** to irritate; annoy: *The dripping of the faucet chafed her nerves.* **5.** *Obs.* to heat; make warm. —*v.i.* **6.** to rub; press with friction: *The horse chafed against his stall.* **7.** to become worn or sore from rubbing: *His neck began to chafe from the rough, starched collar.* **8.** to be irritated or annoyed: *He chafed at her constant interruptions.* **9. chafe at the bit,** to become impatient at delay; be eager to progress or proceed: *The work was going very slowly, and he began to chafe at the bit.* —*n.* **10.** irritation; annoyance. **11.** heat, wear, or soreness caused by rubbing. [ME *chaufe(n)* (to) heat, rub, chafe < MF *chaufe(r)* < VL **calfāre,* var. of L *cal(e)facere,* equiv. to *cale-* (s. of *calēre* to be hot) + *facere* to make]

chaf·er (chā′fər), *n.* *Chiefly Brit.* any scarabaeid beetle. [ME *cheaffer, chaver,* OE *ceofor;* akin to G *Käfer*]

chaf·er·y (chā′fə rē), *n., pl.* **-er·ies.** *Metall.* bloomery. [CHAFE + -ERY]

chafe·weed (chāf′wēd′), *n.* See **wood cudweed.** [CHAFE + WEED¹]

chaff¹ (chaf, chäf), *n.* **1.** the husks of grains and grasses which are usually separated during threshing. **2.** straw cut up for fodder. **3.** worthless matter; refuse; rubbish. **4.** the membranous, usually dry, brittle bracts of the flowers of certain plants. **5.** Also called **window.** *Mil.* thin metal strips that are dropped from an aircraft to create confusing signals on radarscopes. [ME *chaf,* OE *ceaf;* c. MLG, D *kaf*] —**chaff′less,** *adj.* —**chaff′like′,** *adj.*

chaff² (chaf, chäf), *v.t., v.i.* **1.** to mock, tease, or jest in a good-natured way; banter: *She chaffed him for working late. They joked and chaffed with each other.* —*n.* **2.** good-natured ridicule or teasing; raillery. [perh. from CHAFF¹] —**chaff′ing·ly,** *adv.*

Chaf·fee (chaf′ē), *n.* a town in SE Missouri. 2862 (1960).

chaf·fer¹ (chaf′ər), *n.* **1.** bargaining; haggling. —*v.i.* **2.** to bargain; haggle: *to chaffer over a price.* **3.** to bandy words; chatter: *to chaffer about nothing in particular.* —*v.t.* **4.** to bandy (words). **5.** *Obs.* to trade or deal in; barter. [ME *chaffare,* deriv. of *chapfare* trading journey, equiv. to OE *cēap* trade (see CHEAP) + *faru* journey; see FARE] —**chaff′er·er,** *n.*

chaf·fer² (chaf′ər), *n.* a person who chaffs or banters.

chaf·finch (chaf′inch), *n.* a common finch, *Fringilla coelebs,* of the Old World, often kept as a pet. [ME *chaffynch,* OE *ceaffinc.* See CHAFF¹, FINCH]

chaff·y (chaf′ē, chä′fē), *adj.,* **chaff·i·er, chaff·i·est.** consisting of, covered with, or resembling chaff. [CHAFF¹ + -Y¹] —**chaff′i·ness,** *n.*

chaf′ing dish′ (chā′fing), **1.** an apparatus consisting of a metal dish with a lamp or heating appliance beneath it, for cooking food or keeping it hot. **2.** a vessel that holds charcoal or the like, for heating anything set over it. [ME *chafing* warming (see CHAFE, -ING¹)]

cha·gal (chä′gəl), *n.* chagul.

Cha·gall (shä gäl′), *n.* **Marc,** born 1887, Russian painter in France and the U.S.

Cha′gas′ disease′ (shä′gəs), *Pathol.* trypanosomiasis, caused by the trypanosome *T. cruzi,* occurring chiefly in tropical America and characterized by irregular fever, palpable lymph nodes, and often heart damage. Also called **American trypanosomiasis.** [named after C. *Chagas* (1879–1934), Brazilian physician, its describer]

Cha·ga·tai (chä′gə tī′, chag′ə-, chä′gə tī′, chag′ə-), *n.* a Turkic literary language of medieval Central Asia. Also, **Jagatai, Jaghatai.**

Cha·gres (chä′gres), *n.* a river in Panama, flowing through Gatun Lake into the Caribbean Sea.

cha·grin (shə grin′), *n., v.,* **-grined** or **-grinned, -grin·ing** or **-grin·ning.** —*n.* **1.** a feeling of vexation, marked by disappointment or humiliation. —*v.t.* **2.** to vex by disappointment or humiliation: *The rejection of his proposal chagrined him deeply.* **3.** *Obs.* shagreen (def. 1). [< F < ?]
—**Syn. 1.** See **shame.**

Chag·rin′ Falls′ (shə grin′, shag′rin), a town in N Ohio. 3458 (1960).

cha·gul (chä′gəl), *n.* a bag made of goatskin: used in the Orient for carrying water. Also, **chagal.** [< Hindi *chāgal* < Skt *chāgala* of a goat]

Cha·har (chä′här′), *n.* a former province of Inner Mongolia in NE China: divided among adjacent provinces 1952. 107,698 sq. mi.

Chai·kov·ski (chī kôf′skē), *n.* **Pëtr Il·ich** (pyô′tər il ēch′). See **Tschaikovsky, Pëtr Ilich.**

chain (chān), *n.* **1.** a series of objects connected one after the other, usually in the form of a series of metal rings passing through one another, used either for various purposes requiring a flexible tie with high tensile strength, as for hauling, supporting, or confining, or in various ornamental and decorative forms. **2.** something that binds or restrains; bond: *the chain of timidity.* **3. chains, a.** bonds or fetters: *to place a prisoner in chains.* **b.** bondage; servitude: *to live one's life in chains.* **c.** *Naut.* (in a sailing vessel) the area outboard at the foot of the shrouds of a mast: the customary position of the leadsman in taking soundings. **d.** See **tire chain. 4.** a series of things connected or following in succession: *a chain of events.* **5.** a range of mountains. **6.** a number of similar establishments, as banks, theaters, or hotels, under one ownership and management. **7.** *Chem.* two or more atoms of the same element, usually carbon, attached as in a chain. Cf. **ring** (def. 19). **8.** *Survey., Civ. Eng.* **a.** a distance-measuring device consisting of a chain of 100 links of equal length, having a total length either of 66 feet **(Gunter's chain** or **surveyor's chain)** or of 100 feet **(engineer's chain). b.** a unit of length equal to either of these. **c.** a graduated steel or invar tape used for distance measurements. *Abbr.:* ch **9.** *Math.* See **totally ordered set. 10.** *Football.* a chain 10 yards in length for determining whether a first down has been earned. **11. in the chains,** *Naut.* standing outboard on the channels or in some similar place to heave the lead to take soundings. —*v.t.* **12.** to fasten or secure with a chain: *to chain a dog to a post.* **13.** to confine or restrain; fetter as with a chain: *His work chained him to his desk.* **14.** *Survey.* to measure (a distance on the ground) with a chain or tape. **15.** to make (a chain stitch or series of chain stitches) in crocheting. —*v.i.* **16.** to form or make a chain. [ME *chayne* < OF *chaeine* < L *catēn(a)* fetter] —**chain′less,** *adj.* —**chain′like′,** *adj.*

Chain (chān), *n.* **Ernst Boris** (ûrnst), born 1906, English biochemist, born in Germany: Nobel prize for medicine 1945.

chain·age (chā′nij), *n.* a length as measured by a surveyor's chain or tape. [CHAIN + -AGE]

chain·break (chān′brāk′), *n.* *Radio and Television.* a brief commercial or announcement run by a network in substitution for a station break. [CHAIN + BREAK]

chain′ cor′al, coral of the extinct genus *Halysites,* from the Ordovician and Silurian periods, consisting of oval, laterally compressed, corallites united to form a chainlike structure.

chain′ drive′, a driving mechanism transmitting power by means of an endless chain.

chain-driv·en (chān′driv′ən), *adj.* driven by a chain drive.

chaî·né (she nā′), *n., pl.* **-nés** (-nāz′; *Fr.* -nā′). *Ballet.* a series of short, usually rapid, turns performed in a straight line across the stage. [< F, n. use of ptp. of *chaîner* to chain]

Chained′ La′dy, *Astron.* the constellation Andromeda.

chain′ gang′, *Chiefly U.S.* a group of convicts chained together, esp. when working outside.

chain′ gear′, a gear assembly in which motion is transmitted by means of a chain.

chain′ing pin′, *Survey.* a pin driven into the ground to mark a measured length. Also called **taping pin, taping arrow, surveyor's arrow.**

chain′ let′ter, a letter sent to a number of people each of whom makes and sends copies to a number of different people who do likewise, often used as a means of spreading a message or raising money.

chain′ light′ning, *U.S.* lightning which seems to move very quickly in wavy or zigzag lines.

chain′ link′ fence′, a mesh fence made of thick steel wire and having a diamond-shaped pattern.

chain′ lock′er, *Naut.* a compartment where the chain or cable of an anchor is stowed when the anchor is raised.

chain′ mail′, *Armor.* mail[2] (def. 1).

chain·man (chān′mən), *n., pl.* **-men.** *Survey.* one who holds and positions a chain in taking measurements. Also called **axman.** [CHAIN + MAN[1]]

chain′ meas′ure, measurement of distance using a chain 66 feet long, of which one link equals 7.92 inches.

chain′ of command′, a series of administrative or military ranks, positions, etc., in which each has direct authority over the one immediately below, as for the purpose of issuing orders, receiving reports or requests, or the like.

chain′ pick′erel. See under **pickerel** (def. 1).

chain′ plate′, *Naut.* any of the metal plates secured to the hull of a sailing vessel or elsewhere to hold shrouds and backstays at their lower ends.

chain′ pump′, a pump consisting of buckets, plates, or the like, rising upon a chain within a cylinder for raising liquids entering the cylinder at the bottom.

chain-re·act·ing (chān′rē ak′ting, -ak′-), *adj. Physics, Chem.* noting or pertaining to a substance undergoing or capable of undergoing a chain reaction.

chain′ reac′tion, 1. *Physics.* a self-sustaining reaction in which the fission of nuclei of one generation of nuclei produces particles which cause the fission of at least an equal number of nuclei of the succeeding generation. 2. *Chem.* a reaction which results in a product necessary for the continuance of the reaction. 3. any series of events in which each event in turn is the result of the one preceding and the cause of the one following.

chain′ reac′tor, reactor (def. 4).

chain′ re′flex, *Psychol.* a sequence of reflex responses in which the stimulus resulting from one response occasions the next response in the series.

chain′ rule′, *Math.* the theorem that defines the method for taking the derivative of a composite function.

chain′ saw′, a power saw, usually portable, having teeth set on an endless chain.

chain′ shot′, *Ordn.* a shot consisting of two balls or half balls connected by a short chain.

chains·man (chānz′mən), *n., pl.* **-men.** *Naut.* one who stands in the chains to take soundings; leadsman. [CHAIN + 'S[1] + MAN[1]]

chain-smoke (chān′smōk′), *v.i., v.t.,* **-smoked, -smoking.** *U.S.* to smoke continually, as by lighting one cigarette, cigar, etc., from the preceding one. —**chain′ smok′er.** —**chain′-smok′er,** *n.*

chain′ stitch′, a kind of ornamental stitching in which each stitch forms a loop through the forward end of which the next stitch is taken.

chain·stitch (chān′stich′), *v.t., v.i.* to sew or crochet using a chain stitch. [v. use of CHAIN STITCH]

chain′ store′, one of a group of retail stores under the same ownership and management.

chain′ wale′, *Naut.* channel[2]. Also, **chain-wale** (chān′wāl′, chan′ᵊl).

chain·work (chān′wûrk′), *n.* any decorative product, handiwork, etc., in which parts are looped or woven together, like the links of a chain. [CHAIN + WORK]

chair (châr), *n.* 1. a seat, esp. for one person, usually having four legs for support and a rest for the back and often having rests for the arms. 2. something that serves as a chair or supports like a chair: *The two men clasped hands to make a chair for their lame companion.* 3. a seat of office or authority. 4. a position of authority, as of a judge, professor, etc. 5. the person occupying a seat of office, esp. the chairman of a meeting: *The speaker addressed the chair.* 6. See **electric chair.** 7. See **sedan chair.** 8. *Railroads Brit.* a metal block for supporting a rail and securing it to a crosstie or the like. 9. (in reinforced-concrete construction) a device for maintaining the position of reinforcing rods or strands during the pouring operation. 10. a glassmaker's bench having extended arms on which a blowpipe is rolled in shaping glass. 11. **take the chair, a.** to begin or open a meeting. **b.** to preside at a meeting; act as chairman. —*v.t.* 12. to place or seat in a chair. 13. to install in office or authority. 14. to preside over; act as chairman of: *to chair a committee.* 15. *Brit.* traditionally, to place (a hero or victor) in a chair and carry aloft in triumph; carry on the shoulders of several members of a triumphant team or crowd. [ME *chaiere* < OF < L *cathedr(a)*; see CATHEDRA] —**chair′less,** *adj.*

chair′ bed′, 1. a chair that can be opened out to form a bed. 2. See **bed chair.**

chair·borne (châr′bōrn′, -bôrn′), *adj.* (of military, esp. Air Force, personnel) having a desk job rather than a field or combat assignment. [b. CHAIR and AIRBORNE]

chair′ car′, *Railroads.* 1. a day coach having two adjustable seats on each side of a central aisle. 2. (not in technical use) See **parlor car.**

chair·la·dy (châr′lā′dē), *n., pl.* **-dies.** chairwoman. [CHAIR + LADY]

chair′ lift′, a series of chairs suspended from an endless cable driven by motors, for conveying skiers up the side of a slope.

chair·man (châr′mən), *n., pl.* **-men,** *v.* **-maned** or **-manned, -man·ing** or **-man·ning.** —*n.* 1. the presiding officer of a meeting, committee, board, etc. 2. a professor who is the administrative head of a department in a college or university. 3. someone employed to carry or wheel a person in a chair. —*v.t.* 4. to act as or be chairman of (a meeting, committee, etc.). [CHAIR + MAN[1]]

chair′man of the board′, the chief executive officer of a business corporation, elected by its board of directors and charged with the supervision and management of the high-level affairs of the company, as making corporate policy, approving actions of the president and vice-presidents, etc. In some instances, a chairman of the board may concurrently hold the post of president. Also called **board chairman.**

chair·man·ship (châr′mən ship′), *n.* the office or rank of chairman. [CHAIRMAN + -SHIP]

Chair′ of Forget′fulness, *Class. Myth.* a stone seat in the underworld which held eternally captive whoever sat in it.

chair·per·son (châr′pûr′sən), *n.* a person who presides over a meeting, committee, etc.: used by some to replace, or in preference to, the title of "chairwoman."

chair′ rail′, a molding on an interior wall for preventing the backs of chairs from rubbing against plaster.

chair-warm·er (châr′wôr′mər), *n. U.S. Slang.* one who lounges for long periods sitting in a chair, as in a hotel lobby; idler.

chair·wom·an (châr′wo͝om′ən), *n., pl.* **-wom·en.** a woman who presides over a meeting, committee, etc. Also called **chairlady.** [CHAIR + WOMAN]

chaise (shāz), *n.* 1. a light, open carriage, usually with a hood, esp. a one-horse, two-wheeled carriage for two persons; shay. 2. See **post chaise.** 3. a chaise longue, esp. a light one used out of doors. 4. Also called **chaise d'or** (shāz dôr′). *Numis.* **a.** a gold coin of France, first issued in the early 14th century, which bears a figure of the king seated on a large throne. **b.** an Anglo-Gallic copy of this coin, issued by Edward III. [< F, var. of *chaire* CHAIR]

Chaise (def. 1)

chaise longue (shāz′ lông′, chāz′; *Fr.* shez lông′), *pl.* **chaise longues,** *Fr.* **chaises longues** (shez lông′). a couch or day bed in the form of a reclining chair with the seat lengthened to make a complete leg rest. Also, **chaise lounge** (shāz′ lounj′, chāz′). [< F: long chair]

chait·ya (chīt′yə), *n.* a Buddhist shrine in India; stupa. [< Skt *caitya*, equiv. to *citā* funeral pyre, deriv. of *cinoti* he piles up]

chak·ra (chuk′rə), *n. Yoga.* cakra.

chak·ra·var·tin (chuk′rə vär′tin), *n.* cakravartin.

Chal., 1. Chaldaic. 2. Chaldean. 3. Chaldee.

cha·la·za (kə lā′zə), *n., pl.* **-zas, -zae** (-zē). 1. *Zool.* one of the two albuminous twisted cords which fasten an egg yolk to the shell membrane. 2. *Bot.* the point of an ovule or seed where the integuments are united to the nucellus. See diag. under **orthotropous.** [< NL < Gk: hail, lump] —**cha·la′zal, cha·la·zi·an** (kə lā′zē ən), *adj.*

chal·can·thite (kal kan′thīt), *n. Chem.* See **blue vitriol.** [< L *chalcanth(um)* (< Gk *chálkanthon* blue vitriol, lit., flower of copper, equiv. to *chalk(ós)* copper + *ánth(os)* flower + *-on* neut. suffix) + -ITE[1]]

Chal·ce·don (kal′si don′, kal sēd′ᵊn), *n.* 1. an ancient city in NW Asia Minor, on the Bosporus, opposite Byzantium. 2. **Council of,** the ecumenical council held here in A.D. 451. —**Chal·ce·do·ni·an** (kal′si dō′nē ən), *adj., n.*

chal·ced·o·ny (kal sed′ᵊnē, kal′sə dō′nē), *n., pl.* **-nies.** a microcrystalline, translucent variety of quartz, often milky or grayish. [ME *calcedonie* < LL *chalcēdōni(us)* (Vulgate, Rev. xix, 19), equiv. to *chalcēdōn-* (< Gk *chalkēdṓn* chalcedony, identified by Saint Jerome with *Chalcedon*, the city) + *-ius* -IOUS] —**chal·ce·don·ic** (kal′si-don′ik), **chal·ced′o·nous,** *adj.*

chal′cid fly′ (kal′sid), any of numerous small, hymenopterous insects of the family *Chalcididae*, often having bright metallic coloration, the larvae of which are chiefly parasitic on various stages of other insects. Also called **chalcid, chal′cid wasp′.** [< Gk *chalk(ós)* copper, brass (with allusion to the coloration) + -ID[2]]

Chal·cid·i·ce (kal sid′i sē), *n.* a peninsula in NE Greece. Greek, **Khalkidike.**

chal·cid·i·cum (kal sid′ə kəm), *n., pl.* **-ca** (-kə). 1. an annex of an ancient Roman basilica. 2. an annex or appendage, esp. a narthex, of an early Christian basilica. [< L, n. use of neut. of *Chalcidicus* < Gk *Chalkidikós*, equiv. to *Chalkid-* (s. of *Chalkís*) CHALCIS + *-ikos* -IC]

Chal·ci·o·pe (kal sī′ə pē′), *n. Class. Myth.* the sister of Medea.

Chal·cis (kal′sis; *Gr.* ᴋʜäl kēs′), *n.* 1. *Class. Myth.* a daughter of Asopus and Metope. 2. a city on Euboea, in SE Greece: important commercial center from ancient times. 24,745 (1961). Also, **Khalkis.**

chalco-, a learned borrowing from Greek meaning "copper," used in the formation of compound words: *chalcolithic.* [< Gk *chalko-*, comb. form of *chalkós* copper]

chal·co·cite (kal′kə sīt′), *n.* a common mineral, cuprous sulfide, Cu_2S: an important ore of copper. [irreg. CHALCO- + (ANTHRA)CITE]

chal·cog·ra·phy (kal kog′rə fē), *n.* the art of engraving on copper or brass. [CHALCO- + -GRAPHY] —**chal·cog′ra·pher, chal·cog′ra·phist,** *n.* —**chal·co·graph·ic** (kal′kə graf′ik), **chal′co·graph′i·cal,** *adj.*

chal·co·lite (kal′kə līt′), *n. Mineral.* torbernite. [CHALCO- + -LITE]

Chal·co·lith·ic (kal′kə lith′ik), *adj.* of, pertaining to, or characteristic of the Copper Age; Aeneolithic. [CHALCO- + -LITHIC]

chal·co·phile (kal′kə fīl′), *Geol.* —*adj.* 1. (of a chemical element in the earth) having an affinity for sulfur. —*n.* 2. a chalcophile element. [CHALCO- + -PHILE]

chal·co·py·rite (kal′kə pī′rīt, -pēr′īt), *n.* a very common mineral, copper iron sulfide, $CuFeS_2$, occurring in brass-yellow crystals or masses: the most important ore of copper; copper pyrites. Also called **yellow copper ore.** [CHALCO- + PYRITE]

chal·co·stib·ite (kal′kə stib′īt), *n.* a mineral, antimony copper sulfide, $CuSbS_2$, occurring in lead-gray crystals. [CHALCO- + STIB(IUM) + -ITE[1]]

Chald., 1. Chaldaic. 2. Chaldean. 3. Chaldee.

Chal·da·ic (kal dā′ik), *adj.* Chaldean (def. 2). [< L *Chaldaic(us)* < Gk *Chaldaïkós*. See CHALDE-AN, -IC]

Chal·de·a (kal dē′ə), *n.* an ancient region in the lower Tigris and Euphrates valley.

Chal·de·an (kal dē′ən), *n.* 1. one of an ancient Semitic people that formed the dominant element in Babylonia. 2. the indigenous Semitic language of the Chaldeans, Aramaic being used as an auxiliary language. 3. an astrologer, soothsayer, or enchanter. Dan. 1:4; 2:2. —*adj.* 4. of or belonging to ancient Chaldea. 5. pertaining to astrology, occult learning, etc. Also, **Chal·dee** (kal dē′, kal′dē). [< L *Chaldae(us)* (< Gk *Chaldaîos* Chaldaea, an astrologer) + -AN]

chal·dron (chôl′drən), *n.* an English dry measure for coal, coke, lime, and the like, varying in different localities from 32 to 36 or more bushels. [earlier *chaudron* < MF *chauderon* CAULDRON]

cha·let (sha lā′, shal′ā; *Fr.* shä le′), *n., pl.* **cha·lets** (sha lāz′, shal′āz; *Fr.* shä le′). 1. a herdsman's hut in the Swiss mountains. 2. a kind of farmhouse, low and with wide eaves, common in Alpine regions. 3. any cottage or villa built in this style. [< F, SwissF, equiv. to **cal(a)* shelter (c. OPr *cala* COVE[1]) + *-et* -ET]

Chalet (def. 3)

Cha·lia·pin (shä lyä′pin), *n.* **Fë·dor I·va·no·vich** (fyô′dor i vä′no vich), 1873–1938, Russian operatic bass.

chal·ice (chal′is), *n.* 1. *Literary.* a drinking cup. 2. *Eccles.* **a.** a cup for the wine of the Eucharist or Mass. **b.** the wine contained in it. 3. a cuplike blossom. [ME < MF < L *calici-* (s. of *calix*) cup; r. ME *caliz, calc,* OE *calic* < L *calici-*, as above] —**chal·iced** (chal′ist), *adj.*

chal′ice vine′, a woody, hairy, climbing plant, *Solandra guttata*, of Mexico, having fragrant, solitary, purple-marked, white flowers that turn yellow.

Cha·li·ni·tis (kal′ə nī′tis), *n. Class. Myth.* an epithet of Athena meaning "bridler," referring to her invention of the bridle.

chalk (chôk), *n.* 1. a soft, white, powdery limestone consisting chiefly of fossil shells of foraminifers. 2. a prepared piece of chalk or chalklike substance for marking; a blackboard crayon. 3. a mark made with chalk. 4. a score, tally, or record of credit. —*v.t.* 5. to mark or write with chalk. 6. to rub over or whiten with chalk. 7. to treat or mix with chalk: *to chalk a billiard cue.* 8. to make pale; blanch: *Terror chalked her face.* —*v.i.* 9. (of paint) to powder from weathering. 10. **chalk up, a.** to score or earn: *They chalked up two runs in the first inning.* **b.** to charge or ascribe to: *It was a poor performance, but may be chalked up to lack of practice.* —*adj.* 11. of, made of, or drawn with chalk. [ME *chalke*, OE *cealc* < L *calc-* (s. of *calx*) lime] —**chalk′like′,** *adj.*

chalk·board (chôk′bōrd′, -bôrd′), *n.* a blackboard. [CHALK + BOARD]

chalk′ line′, *Building Trades.* 1. Also called **snapline.** a chalked string for making a straight line on a large surface, as a wall, by holding the string taut against the surface and snapping it to transfer the chalk. 2. the line so made.

chalk·rail (chôk′rāl′), *n.* a troughlike molding or strip holding chalk, erasers, etc., under a blackboard. [CHALK + RAIL[1]]

chalk·stone (chôk′stōn′), *n. Pathol.* a chalklike concretion in the tissues or small joints of a person with gout. [ME: limestone. See CHALK, STONE] —**chalk′ston′y,** *adj.*

chalk′ stripe′, (on a fabric) a pattern of thin white lines on a dark ground.

chalk′ talk′, a talk or lecture in which the speaker illustrates points that need clarification by drawing on a blackboard: *The coach gave a chalk talk before the big game.*

chalk·y (chô′kē), *adj.,* **chalk·i·er, chalk·i·est.** 1. of or like chalk. 2. of a chalklike consistency: *chalky soil.* 3. without resonance, color, warmth, etc.: *several high tones that were quite chalky.* 4. *Photog.* lacking in detail, due to extreme contrast: *a chalky print.* [late ME; see CHALK, -Y[1]]

chal·lah (ᴋʜä′lə, ᴋʜä lä′), *n., pl.* **chal·lahs,** *Heb.* **chal·loth** (ᴋʜä lôt′). *Jewish Cookery.* a bread leavened with yeast and containing eggs, often made into braided loaves, glazed with egg before baking, prepared esp. for the Jewish Sabbath. Also, **hallah.** [< Heb *khallāh*]

chal·lenge (chal′inj), *n., v.,* **-lenged, -leng·ing.** —*n.* 1. a call or summons to engage in any contest, as of skill, strength, etc. 2. something that by its nature or character serves as a call to battle, contest, etc.: *Communism is a challenge to democracy.* 3. a call to fight, as a battle, a duel, etc. 4. a demand to explain, justify, etc.: *a challenge to the treasurer to itemize expenditures.* 5. *Mil.* the demand of a sentry for identification or a countersign. 6. *Law.* a formal objection to the qualifications of a particular juror, to his serving, or to the legality of an entire jury. Cf. **peremptory challenge.** 7. *U.S.* the assertion that a vote is invalid or that a voter is not legally qualified. 8. difficulty in a job or undertaking that is stimulating to one engaged in it. 9. *Hunting.* the crying of a hound on finding a scent. —*v.t.* 10. to summon to a contest of skill, strength, etc. 11. to demand as something due or rightful. 12. to take exception to; call in question: *to challenge the wisdom of a procedure.* 13. *Mil.* to halt and demand identification or countersign from. 14. *Law.* to take formal exception to (a juror or jury). 15. to have a claim to; invite; arouse; stimulate: *a matter which challenges attention.* 16. *U.S.* **a.** to assert that (a vote) is invalid. **b.** to assert that (a voter) is not qualified to vote. 17. *Archaic.* to lay claim to. —*v.i.* 18. to make or issue a challenge. 19. *Hunting.* (of hounds) to cry or give tongue on picking up the scent. [ME *chalenge* < OF, var. of *chalonge* < L *calumnia* CALUMNY] —**chal′lenge·a·ble,** *adj.*

chal·leng·er (chal′in jər), *n.* 1. one who or that which challenges. 2. *Boxing.* a boxer who fights a champion for his championship title. 3. *Radio.* interrogator (def. 2). [ME; see CHALLENGE, -ER[1]]

chal·leng·ing (chal′in jing), *adj.* 1. stimulating, interesting, and thought-provoking: *a challenging idea.* 2. provocative; intriguing: *a challenging smile.* 3. offering a challenge; that tests one's ability, endurance, etc.: *a challenging course; a challenging game.* [CHALLENGE + -ING[2]] —**chal′leng·ing·ly,** *adv.*

chal·li·ho (chul′ē hō′), *n., pl.* **-hos.** (in India) a strong southerly wind that sometimes lasts about 40 days in the spring. [< Punjabi: lit., pretty one]

chal·lis (shal′ē), *n.* a soft fabric of plain weave in wool, cotton, or rayon, either in a solid color or, more often, a small print. Also, **chal′lie, chal′ly.** [? after *Challis*, the surname]

Chal·lis (chal′is), *n.* a crater in the first quadrant of the face of the moon, in the libration area and near the North Pole: about 35 miles in diameter.

Chal·mers (chä′mərz, chal′-), *n.* **Alexander,** 1759–1834, Scottish biographer, editor, and journalist.

chal·one (kal′ōn), *n. Physiol.* an endocrine secretion that depresses or inhibits physiological activity. [< Gk *chalôn* slackening, loosening, relaxing (prp. of *chalân*), equiv. to *chal-* slack + *-ōn* prp. suffix]

Châ·lons (shä lôɴ′), *n.* **1.** Also called **Châ·lons-sur-Marne** (shä lôɴ/syr marn′). a city in and the capital of Marne, in NE France: defeat of Attila A.D. 451. 45,348 (1962). **2.** Also called **Châ·lons-sur-Saône** (shä lôɴ′-syr sōn′). a city in E France, on the Saône River. 45,993 (1962).

Cha·lu·kya (chä′lə kyə), *n.* a dynasty of central India, ruling A.D. c500–753, and restored A.D. 973–1190. —**Cha′lu·kyan,** *adj.*

chal·u·meau (shal′yə mō′; *Fr.* shä ly mō′), *n., pl.* **-meaux** (-mōz′, *Fr.* -mō′). **1.** *Music.* the low register of the clarinet. **2.** a 17th- or 18th-century woodwind instrument. [< F; OF *chalumel* < VL **calumell(us)*, var. of LL *calamellus*, equiv. to L *calam(us)* reed (see CALAMUS) + *-ellus* dim. suffix]

cha·lutz (ḵä lo͞ots′), *n., pl.* **-lutz·im** (-lo͞o tsēm′). *Hebrew.* halutz.

cha·lyb·e·ate (kə lib′ē it, -āt′), *adj.* **1.** containing or impregnated with salts of iron, as a mineral spring, medicine, etc. —*n.* **2.** a chalybeate water, medicine, or the like. [< NL *chalybeāt(us)*, L *chalybē(ius)* of steel (< Gk *chalybeîos*, equiv. to *chalybe-*, var. s. of *chálybs* iron, + *-is* adj. suffix) + *-ātus* -ATE¹; see CHALYBITE]

chal·y·bite (kal′ə bīt′), *n. Mineral.* siderite (def. 1). [< Gk *chalyb-* (s. of *chálybs*) iron, also iron-worker, member of the Chalybes, a tribe of Asia Minor noted for their blacksmiths + -ITE¹]

cham (kam), *n. Archaic.* khan¹.

cha·made (shə mäd′), *n. Mil. Archaic.* a signal by drum or trumpet inviting an enemy to a parley. [< F < Pg *chamad(a)*, equiv. to *cham(ar)* (to) sound (< L *clamāre* to shout; see CLAIM) + *-ada* -ADE¹]

Cha·mae·le·on (kə mē′lē ən, -mēl′yən), *n., gen.* **-mae·le·on·tis** (-mē′lē on′tis). *Astron.* the Chameleon, a small southern constellation between Musca and Hydrus. [< L]

cham·ber (chām′bər), *n.* **1.** a room, usually private, in a house or apartment, esp. a bedroom: *She retired to her chamber.* **2.** a room in a palace or official residence. **3.** the meeting hall of a legislative or other assembly. **4. chambers,** *Law.* **a.** a place where a judge hears matters not requiring action in open court. **b.** the private office of a judge. **c.** (in England) the quarters or rooms that lawyers use to consult with their clients, esp. in the Inns of Court. **5.** (in early New England) any bedroom above the ground floor, generally named for the ground-floor room beneath it. **6.** the place where the moneys due a government are received and kept; a treasury or chamberlain's office. **7.** a legislative, judicial, or other like body: *the upper or the lower chamber of a legislature.* **8.** a compartment or enclosed space; cavity: *a chamber of the heart.* **9.** (in a canal or the like) the space between any two gates of a lock. **10.** a receptacle for one or more cartridges in a firearm, or for a shell in a gun or other cannon. **11.** (in a gun) the part of the barrel that receives the charge. —*v.t.* **12.** to put or enclose in, or as in, a chamber. **13.** to provide with a chamber. [ME *chambre* < OF < L *camer(a)*, var. of *camara* vaulted room, vault < Gk *kamára* vault]

cham′ber con′cert, a concert of chamber music.

cham′bered nau′tilus, nautilus (def. 1).

cham·ber·er¹ (chām′bər ər), *n. Archaic.* one who frequents ladies' chambers; gallant. [ME: chamberlain < AF; see CHAMBER, -ER²]

cham·ber·er² (chām′bər ər), *n. Obs.* chambermaid. [ME *chamberere* < AF, fem. of *chamberer* chamberlain; see CHAMBERER¹]

cham·ber·lain (chām′bər lin), *n.* **1.** an official charged with the management of a sovereign's or nobleman's living quarters. **2.** an official who receives rents and revenues, as of a municipal corporation; treasurer. **3.** the high steward or factor of a nobleman. **4.** a high official of a royal court. [ME < OF, var. of *chamberlenc* < Frankish **kamerling*, equiv. to *kamer* (< L *camera* room; see CHAMBER) + *-ling* -LING¹]

Cham·ber·lain (chām′bər lin), *n.* **1. (Arthur) Neville,** 1869–1940, British statesman: prime minister 1937–40. **2. Joseph,** 1836–1914, British statesman (father of Sir Austen and Neville Chamberlain). **3. Sir (Joseph) Austen,** 1863–1937, British statesman: Nobel peace prize 1925. **4. Owen,** born 1920, U.S. physicist: Nobel prize 1959. **5. Wilt(on Norman)** ("*Wilt the Stilt*"), born 1936, U.S. basketball player. **6.** a town in S South Dakota. 2598 (1960).

cham·ber·maid (chām′bər mād′), *n.* a maid who makes the beds and cleans and straightens bedrooms and bathrooms. [CHAMBER + MAID]

cham′ber mu′sic, music suited for performance in a room or a small concert hall, esp. for two or more, but usually fewer than ten, solo instruments.

cham′ber of com′merce, an association, primarily of businessmen, to protect and promote the commercial interests of a city, state, country, etc.

cham′ber of hor′rors, 1. a place for the exhibition of gruesome or horrible objects. **2.** a group of such objects, as instruments of torture or murder. **3.** any collection of things or ideas that inspire horror.

cham′ber op′era, an opera written primarily for performance in a small theater and requiring few performers and a small orchestra.

cham′ber pot′, a vessel for urine, used in bedrooms.

Cham·bers (chām′bərz), *n.* **1. Robert,** 1802–1871, Scottish publisher and editor. **2. Robert William,** 1865–1933, U.S. novelist and illustrator.

Cham·bers·burg (chām′bərz bûrg′), *n.* a city in central Pennsylvania. 17,670 (1960).

Cham·ber·tin (shäɴ ber taɴ′), *n.* a dry, red wine from the Burgundy region in France. [named after *Chambertin* in Burgundy, where made]

Cham·bé·ry (shäɴ bā rē′), *n.* **1.** a city in and the capital of Savoie, in SE France. 47,447 (1962). **2.** a dry vermouth from this city.

Cham·blee (cham blē′), *n.* a town in central Georgia. 6635 (1960).

cham·bray (sham′brā), *n.* a fine cloth of cotton, silk, or linen, commonly of plain weave with a colored warp and white weft. [var. of CAMBRIC]

African chameleon, *Chamaeleon chamaeleon* (Length 8 in.)

cha·me·le·on (kə mē′lē ən, -mēl′yən), *n.* **1.** any of numerous Old World agamid lizards of the family *Chamaeleontidae*, characterized by the ability to change the color of their skin, very slow locomotion, and a projectile tongue. **2.** any of several American lizards capable of changing the color of the skin, esp. *Anolis carolinensis* **(American chameleon),** of the southeastern U.S. **3.** an inconstant person. **4.** (*cap.*) *Astron.* the constellation Chamaeleon. [var. of *chamaeleon* < L Gk *chamailéōn*, equiv. to *chamaí* on the ground, dwarf + *léōn* LION; r. ME *camelion* < MF < L, as above] —**cha·me·le·on·ic** (kə mē′lē on′ik), *adj.* —**cha·me′le·on·like′,** *adj.*

cha·metz (ḵä mäts′; *Eng.* ḵō′mits), *n. Hebrew.* hametz.

cham·fer (cham′fər), *n.* an oblique face formed at a corner of a board, post, etc., usually at a 45° angle to the adjacent principal faces; bevel. [back formation from *chamfering* < MF *chamfrein* (taken as *chamfer* + -ING¹) var. of *chanfreint* beveled edge, orig. ptp. of *chanfraindre* to bevel, equiv. to *chant* edge (< L *canthus*; see CANT²) + *fraindre* to break < L *frangere*; see FRANGIBLE] —**cham′fer·er,** *n.*

cham′fer bit′, a bit for beveling the edge of a hole.

cham·fron (cham′frən), *n. Armor.* chanfron.

Cha·mi·nade (shä mē nȧd′), *n.* **Cé·cile Louise Sté·pha·nie** (sā sēl′ lwēz stā fȧ nē′), 1857–1944, French pianist and composer.

cha·mi·so (shə mē′sō, -sə, chə-), *n., pl.* **-sos.** a Californian, rosaceous shrub, *Adenostoma fasciculatum*, that forms a dense thicket. Also, **cha·mise** (shə mēs′, chə-). [< AmerSp, alter. of Sp *chamizo* half-burned tree < Pg *chamiço* stick, deriv. of *chama* flame < L *flamma*]

cham·my (sham′ē), *n., pl.* **-mies,** *v.t.,* **-mied, -my·ing.** chamois (defs. 2–4, 6, 7).

cham·ois (sham′ē; *Fr.* shȧ mwä′), *n., pl.* **cham·ois, cham·oix** (sham′ēz; *Fr.* shȧ mwä′), *v.,* **cham·oised** (sham′ēd), **cham·ois·ing** (sham′ē ing). —*n.* **1.** an agile, goatlike antelope, *Rupicapra rupicapra*, of high mountains of Europe and southwestern Russia. **2.** a soft, pliable leather from any of various skins dressed with oil, esp. fish oil, originally prepared from the skin of the chamois. **3.** a piece of this leather. **4.** a cotton cloth finished to simulate this leather. **5.** a medium to grayish-yellow color. —*v.t.* **6.** to dress (a pelt) with oil in order to produce a chamois. **7.** to rub or buff with a chamois. Also, **chammy, shammy, shamoy** (for defs. 2–4, 6, 7). [< MF < LL *camox* < ?; cf. G *Gemse* < OHG *gamiza* in same sense]

Chamois (About 2½ ft. high at shoulder; horns to 10 in.; length 4 ft.)

cham·o·mile (kam′ə mīl′, -mēl′), *n.* camomile.

Cha·mo·nix (sham′ə nē; *Fr.* shȧ mô nē′), *n.* a mountain valley in E France, N of Mont Blanc. Also, **Chamouni.**

Cha·mor·ro (chə môr′ō; *Sp.* chä môr′rô), *n., pl.* **-mor·ros** (-môr′ōz; *Sp.* -môr′rôs), (*esp. collectively*) **-mor·ro,** *adj.* —*n.* **1.** a people inhabiting the Mariana Islands. **2.** the language of the Chamorro, a Northern Western Indonesian language of the Malayo-Polynesian family. —*adj.* **3.** of, pertaining to, or characteristic of the Chamorro, their people, or their language.

Cha·mos (kā′mos), *n. Douay Bible.* Chemosh. —**Cha·mi·an** (kā′mē ən), *adj.*

cham·o·site (sham′ə zīt′), *n.* a mineral of the chlorite group, hydrous aluminum silicate of iron, occurring in gray or black crystals in oolitic iron ore. [var. of *camoisite*, named after *Chamoison* in the Valais, Switzerland, where found; see -ITE¹]

cha·motte (shə mot′), *n. Foundry.* grog (def. 3). [prob. < F < G *Schamotte*]

Cha·mou·ni (*Fr.* shȧ mo͞o nē′), *n.* Chamonix.

champ¹ (champ), *v.t.* **1.** to bite upon or grind, esp. impatiently: *The horses champed the bit.* **2.** to crush with the teeth and chew vigorously or noisily; munch. **3.** *Scot.* to mash; crush. —*v.i.* **4.** to make vigorous chewing or biting movements with the jaws and teeth. **5. champ at the bit,** to betray impatience, as to begin some action. —*n.* **6.** act of champing. [perh. nasalized var. of CHAP¹; see CHOP¹] —**champ′er,** *n.* —**champ′y,** *adj.*

champ² (champ), *n. Informal.* a champion. [by shortening]

cham·pac (cham′pak, chum′puk), *n.* an East Indian tree, *Michelia Champaca*, of the magnolia family, with fragrant golden flowers and a handsome wood used for making images, furniture, etc. Also, **cham′pak.** [< Hind *campak* < Skt *campaka*]

cham′pa·ca oil′ (cham′pə kə, chum′-), a yellowish oil extracted from the flowers of the champac, used in making perfumes. [see CHAMPAC]

cham·pagne (sham pān′), *n.* **1.** the sparkling, dry, white table wine from the region of Champagne. **2.** a similar sparkling wine produced elsewhere. **3.** (formerly) the nonsparkling, dry, white table wine, produced in the region of Champagne. **4.** a very pale yellow or greenish-yellow color. **5.** any thing considered as the best or as luxurious. —*adj.* **6.** having the color of champagne. **7.** luxurious or expensive: *champagne tastes.*

Cham·pagne (sham pān′; *Fr.* shäɴ pȧɴ′yᵊ), *n.* a region and former province in NE France.

cham·paign (sham pān′), *n.* **1.** level, open country; plain. **2.** *Obs.* a battlefield. —*adj.* **3.** level and open: *champaign fields.* [ME *champai(g)ne* < MF *champa(i)gne* < LL *campānia*; see CAMPAIGN]

Cham·paign (sham pān′), *n.* a city in E Illinois. 49,583 (1960).

cham·per·ty (cham′pər tē), *n. Law.* a sharing in the proceeds of litigation by one who promotes it or carries it on. [ME *champartie*, equiv. to *champart* (< MF: share of the produce, lit., of the field, equiv. to *champ* field (see CAMP¹) + *part* share, see PART) + *-ie* -Y³] —**cham′per·tous,** *adj.*

cham·pi·gnon (sham pin′yən *or, esp. Brit.,* cham-; *Fr.* shäɴ pē nyôɴ′), *n., pl.* **-pi·gnons** (-pin′yənz; *Fr.* -pē nyôɴ′). mushroom (defs. 2, 3). [< MF, appar. << VL **campīn(us)* of the field (see CAMP¹, -INE¹) + L *-iōn-* -ION]

cham·pi·on (cham′pē ən), *n.* **1.** one who has defeated all opponents in a competition or series of competitions, so as to hold first place. **2.** anything that takes first place in competition: *the champion of a cattle show.* **3.** an animal that has won a certain number of points in officially recognized shows: *This dog is a champion.* **4.** one who fights for or defends any person or cause: *a champion of the oppressed.* **5.** a fighter or warrior. —*v.t.* **6.** to act as champion of; defend; support: *to champion a cause.* **7.** *Obs.* to defy. —*adj.* **8.** first among all contestants or competitors. **9.** *Informal.* first-rate. [ME < OF < LL *campiōn-* (s. of *campiō*) < WGmc **kampiōn-*, equiv. to *kamp-* battle (< L *camp(us)* field, battlefield) + *-iōn-* n. suffix; cf. OE *cempa* warrior, etc.] —**cham′pi·on·less,** *adj.* —**cham′pi·on·like′,** *adj.*

—**Syn. 1.** winner, victor. **4.** defender, protector, vindicator. **6.** maintain, fight for, advocate.

Cham′pion of Eng′land, a hereditary official at British coronations, representing the king **(King's Champion)** or the queen **(Queen's Champion)** who is being crowned, and having originally the function of challenging to mortal combat any person disputing the right of the new sovereign to rule.

cham·pi·on·ship (cham′pē ən ship′), *n.* **1.** the distinction or condition of being a champion: *to win a championship; to challenge someone's championship.* **2.** advocacy or defense: *championship of the underdog.* [CHAMPION + -SHIP]

Cham·plain (sham plān′; *for 1 also Fr.* shäɴ plaɴ′), *n.* **1. Sa·mu·el de** (sam′yo͞o əl də; *Fr.* sȧ my el′ də), 1567–1635, French explorer in the Americas: founder of Quebec; 1st colonial governor 1633–35. **2. Lake,** a lake between New York and Vermont. 125 mi. long; ab. 600 sq. mi.

champ·le·vé (shäɴ lə vā′), *adj., n., pl.* **-vés** (-vā′, -vāz′). —*adj.* **1.** of or pertaining to an enamel piece or enameling technique in which enamel is fused onto the incised or hollowed areas of a metal base. —*n.* **2.** an enamel piece made by the champlevé method. **3.** the technique used to produce champlevé enamels. [< F, ptp. of *champlever* to lift (i.e., take out) a field (i.e., a flat part), make hollow places on the ground to be engraved; see CAMP¹, LEVER]

Cham·pol·lion (shäɴ pô lyôɴ′), *n.* **Jean Fran·çois** (zhäɴ fräɴ swȧ′), 1790–1832, French Egyptologist.

Champs É·ly·sées (shäɴ zā lē zā′), a boulevard in Paris, France: cafés, shops, theaters; a tourist center.

Cham·y·ne (kam′ə nē′), *n. Class. Myth.* an epithet of Demeter.

Ch'an (chän), *n. Chinese.* Zen (def. 1).

Chan., 1. Chancellor. **2.** Chancery. Also, **Chanc.**

Cha·naan (kā′nən, -nā ən), *n. Douay Bible.* Canaan (def. 4).

chance (chans, chäns), *n., v.,* **chanced, chanc·ing,** *adj.* —*n.* **1.** the absence of any cause or series of causes of events as they actually happen that can be predicted, understood, or controlled: often personified or treated as a positive agency: *Chance governs all.* **2.** luck or fortune: *a game of chance.* **3.** a possibility or probability of anything happening: *a fifty-percent chance of success.* **4.** an opportunity: *Now is your chance.* **5.** *Baseball.* an opportunity to field the ball and make a put-out or assist. **6.** a risk or hazard: *Take a chance.* **7. chances,** probability: *The chances are that the train hasn't left yet.* **8.** *U.S. Informal.* a quantity or number (usually fol. by *of*). **9.** *Archaic.* an unfortunate event; mishap. **10. by chance,** without plan or intent; accidentally: *I met her again by chance in a department store in Paris.* **11. on the chance,** in the mild hope or against the possibility: *I'll wait on the chance that she'll come. Take an umbrella on the chance it might rain.* **12. on the off chance,** in the very slight hope or against the very slight possibility. —*v.i.* **13.** to happen or occur by chance: *It chanced that our arrivals coincided.* —*v.t.* **14.** *Informal.* to take the chances or risks of; risk (often fol. by impersonal *it*): *I'll have to chance it, whatever the outcome.* **15. chance on** or **upon,** to come upon by chance; meet unexpectedly: *She chanced on a rare kind of mushroom on her walk through the woods.* —*adj.* **16.** due to chance: *a chance occurrence.* [ME < OF, var. of *cheance* < VL **cadentia* a befalling, happening; see CADENZA] —**chance′less,** *adj.*

—**Syn. 2.** accident, fortuity. **3.** contingency. **4.** opening. **13.** befall. See **happen. 16.** casual, accidental, fortuitous. —**Ant. 1.** necessity.

chance·ful (chans′fəl, chäns′-), *adj.* **1.** full of chance or chances. **2.** *Archaic.* **a.** dependent on chance. **b.** risky. [CHANCE + -FUL] —**chance′ful·ly,** *adv.* —**chance′ful·ness,** *n.*

chan·cel (chan′səl, chän′-), *n.* the space about the altar of a church, usually enclosed, for the clergy and other officials. [ME < MF < LL *cancell(us)* lattice, railing or screen before the altar of a church, L *cancell(ī)* (pl.) lattice, railing, grating; see CANCEL] —**chan′celed, chan′celled,** *adj.*

chan·cel·ler·y (chan′sə lə rē, -slə rē, chän′-), *n., pl.* **-ler·ies. 1.** the position of a chancellor. **2.** the office or department of a chancellor. **3.** the office attached to an embassy or consulate. **4.** a building or room occupied by a chancellor's department. [ME *chancellerie* < AF, equiv. to *chanceller* CHANCELLOR + *-ie* -Y³]

chan·cel·lor (chan′sə lər, -slər, chän′-), *n.* **1.** the title of various important judges and other high officials. **2.** *U.S.* the judge of a court of equity or chancery. **3.** the chief minister of state, as in West Germany. **4.** a secretary, as to a king or nobleman or of an embassy. **5.** the chief administrative officer in certain American universities. **6.** *Brit.* the honorary, nonresident, titular head of a university. Cf. **vice-chancellor. 7.** the priest in charge of a Roman Catholic chancery. [ME *chanceler* < AF < LL *cancellār(ius)* doorkeeper, lit., man at the barrier (see CHANCEL, -ER²); r. ME *canceler* < OE << LL, as above]

Chan′cellor of the Excheq′uer, the minister of finance in the British government.

chan·cel·lor·ship (chan′sə lər ship′, chän′-), *n.* **1.** the office or rank of chancellor. **2.** a chancellor's term of office. [late ME *chanceler-schepp.* See CHANCELLOR, -SHIP]

Chan·cel·lors·ville (chan′sə lərz vil′, -slərz-, chän′-), *n.* a village in NE Virginia: site of a Confederate victory 1863.

chance-med·ley (chans′med′lē, chäns′-), *n. Law.* a sudden quarrel, with violence. [< AF *chance medlee*]

chan·cer·y (chan′sə rē, chän′-), *n., pl.* **-cer·ies.** **1.** the office or department of a chancellor; chancellery. **2.** an office of public records, esp. those of the Lord Chancellor in England. **3.** (in England) the Lord Chancellor's court, now a division of the High Court of Justice. **4.** *Law.* **a.** Also, **court of chancery.** a court having jurisdiction in equity; court of equity. **b.** equity (defs. 3a, b). **5.** the administrative office of a diocese. **6.** *Rom. Cath. Ch.* a department of the Curia Romana now having the responsibility for issuing bulls to establish new dioceses, benefices, etc. **7. in chancery, a.** *Law.* in litigation in a court of chancery. **b.** *Wrestling.* (of a contestant's head) held under his opponent's arm. **c.** in a helpless or embarrassing position. [ME *chancerie,* var. of *chancelrie,* syncopated var. of *chancellerie* CHANCELLERY]

chan·cre (shang′kər), *n. Pathol.* the initial lesion of syphilis, commonly a more or less distinct ulcer or sore with a hard base. [< MF << L *cancr(um),* acc. of *cancer* CANCER] **—chan′crous,** *adj.*

chan·croid (shang′kroid), *n. Pathol.* an infectious venereal ulcer with a soft base. Also called **simple chancre, soft chancre.** [CHANCRE + -OID] **—chan·croi′dal,** *adj.*

chanc·y (chan′sē, chän′-), *adj.,* **chanc·i·er, chanc·i·est.** **1.** uncertain; risky. **2.** *Chiefly Scot.* lucky. [CHANCE + -Y[1]]

chan·de·lier (shan′dəlēr′), *n.* a light fixture suspended from a ceiling, usually having branched supports for a number of lights. [< F: lit., something that holds candles; see CHANDLER]

chan·delle (shan del′, *Fr.* shäN del′; *v.* shan del′), *n., pl.* **-delles** (-delz′; *Fr.* -del′), *v.* **-delled, -dell·ing.** *Aeron.* **—n. 1.** an abrupt climbing turn in which an aircraft almost stalls while using its momentum to gain a higher rate of climb. **—v.i. 2.** to perform a chandelle. [< F: lit., CANDLE]

Chan·der·na·gor (chun′dər nə gōr′, -gôr′), *n.* a port in S West Bengal, in E India, on the Hooghly River: a former French dependency. 67,100 (1961). Also, **Chan·dar·na·gar** (chun′dər nug′ər).

Chan·di·garh (chun′di gur′), *n.* a city in and the capital of Punjab, in N India: established 1953. 89,300 (1961).

chan·dler (chand′lər, chänd′-), *n.* **1.** a dealer or trader in supplies, provisions, trinkets, etc. **2.** one who makes or sells candles. **3.** a retailer of provisions, groceries, etc. [ME *chandeler* candlestick, maker or seller of candles < AF, OF *chandelier,* lit., someone or something connected with candles, equiv. to *chandelle* CANDLE + *-ier* -IER]

Chan·dler (chand′lər, chänd′-), *n.* **1.** a town in central Arizona. 9531 (1960). **2.** a town in central Oklahoma. 2524 (1960).

chan·dler·y (chand′lə rē, chänd′-), *n.,* pl. **-dler·ies.** **1.** a storeroom for candles. **2.** the warehouse, wares, or business of a chandler. [CHANDLER + -Y[3]]

Chan·dra·gup·ta (chun′drə gōōp′tə), *n.* (*Chandragupta Maurya*) died 286? B.C., king of northern India 322?–298: founder of the Maurya empire. Greek, **Sandrakottos** or **Sandrocottus.**

chan·du·y (chän dōō′ē), *n.* a cool breeze blowing during the dry season in Guayaquil, Ecuador. Also, **chan·du·i′.** [from local native name]

Cha·nel (shə nel′; *Fr.* shA nel′), *n.* **Ga·bri·elle** (gA brē el′), born 1882, French fashion designer.

Cha·ney (chā′nē), *n.* **Lon** (lon), 1883–1930, U.S. motion-picture actor.

chan·fron (chan′frən), *n.* a piece of plate armor for defending a horse's head. Also, **chamfron.** Also called **frontstall, testière.** [late ME *shamfron* < MF *chanfrain* < ?]

chang·a·ble (chān′jə bəl), *adj.* changeable.

Chang·chow·fu (chang′chou′fōō′; *Chin.* chäng′jō′fōō′), *n.* a city in S Fukien, in SE China. 81,200 (est. 1957). Also called **Lungki.**

Chang·chun (chäng′chōōn′), *n.* a city in and the capital of Kirin, in NE China: former capital of Manchuria. 975,000 (est. 1957). Also called **Hsinking.**

Ch'ang Ch'un (chäng′ chōōn′), monastic name of **Ch'iu Ch'u-chi.**

change (chānj), *v.,* **changed, chang·ing,** *n.* **—v.t. 1.** to make the form, nature, content, etc., of (something) different from what it is or from what it would be if left alone: *to change one's name; to change one's opinion; to change the course of history.* **2.** to transform or convert (usually fol. by *into*): *The witch changed the prince into a toad.* **3.** to substitute another or others for; exchange for something else, usually of the same kind: *She changed her hat. He changed seats.* **4.** to give and take reciprocally; interchange: *to change places with someone.* **5.** to give or get smaller money in exchange for: *to change a five-dollar bill.* **6.** to give or get different money in exchange for: *to change dollars into francs.* **7.** to remove and replace the covering or coverings of: *to change a bed; to change a baby.* **—v.i. 8.** to become different: *Overnight the popular mood changed.* **9.** to become altered or modified: *Colors change if they are exposed to the sun.* **10.** to become transformed or converted (usually fol. by *into*): *The toad changed into a prince again.* **11.** to pass gradually into (usually fol. by *to* or *into*): *Summer changed to autumn.* **12.** to make a change or an exchange: *If you cannot see from your seat, I will change with you.* **13.** to change trains or other conveyances: *We can change to an express.* **14.** to change one's clothes: *She changed into a dinner dress.* **15.** (of the moon) to pass from one phase to another. **16.** (of the voice) to become deeper in tone; come to have a lower register: *The boy's voice began to change when he was thirteen.* **17. change front,** *Mil.* to shift a military force in another direction. **18. change hands.** See **hand** (def. 34). **19. change one's mind,** to change one's opinions or intentions. **—n. 20.** act or fact of changing; fact of being changed. **21.** a transformation or modification; alteration: *They noticed the change in his facial expression.* **22.** a variation or deviation: *a change in the daily routine.* **23.** the substitution of one thing for another: *We finally made the change from a coal-burning furnace to an oil-burning furnace.* **24.** variety or novelty: *Let's try a new restaurant for a change.* **25.** the passing from one place, state, form, or phase to another: *a change of seasons; the various changes of the moon.* **26.** *Jazz.* harmonic progression from one tonality to another; modulation. **27.** the supplanting of one thing by another. **28.** that which is or may be substituted for another. **29.** a fresh set of clothing. **30.** money given in exchange for an equivalent of higher denomination. **31.** a balance of money that is returned when the sum tendered in payment is larger than the sum due. **32.** coins of low denomination. **33.** Also, **'change.** *Brit.* exchange (def. 10). **34.** any of the various sequences in which a peal of bells may be rung. **35.** *Obs.* changefulness; caprice. **36. ring the changes, a.** to perform all permutations possible in ringing a set of bells. **b.** to vary the manner of performing an action or of discussing a subject; repeat with variations. [ME *change(n)* < OF *change(r)* < LL *cambiāre,* L *cambīre* to exchange] **—chang·ed·ness** (chān′jid nis, chānjd′-), *n.* **—chang′er,** *n.*

—Syn. 1. transmute, transform; vary, mutate; amend, modify. CHANGE, ALTER both mean to make a difference in the state or condition of a thing or to substitute another state or condition. To CHANGE is to make a material difference so that the thing is distinctly different from what it was: *to change one's opinion.* To ALTER is to make some partial change, as in appearance, but usually to preserve the identity: *to alter a dress* (*to change a dress* would mean to put on a different one). **3.** replace, trade. **4.** trade. **6.** convert. **9.** vary, mutate, amend. **20.** transmutation, mutation, conversion, vicissitude. **23.** exchange. **27, 28.** replacement. **—Ant. 9.** remain. **20.** permanence.

change·a·ble (chān′jə bəl), *adj.* **1.** liable to change or to be changed; variable. **2.** of changing color or appearance: *changeable silk.* Also, **changable.** [ME; see CHANGE, -ABLE] **—change′a·bil′i·ty, change′a·ble·ness,** *n.* **—change′a·bly,** *adv.*

change·ful (chānj′fəl), *adj.* changing; variable; inconstant. [CHANGE + -FUL] **—change′ful·ly,** *adv.* **—change′ful·ness,** *n.*

change′ key′, a key opening only one lock.

change·less (chānj′lis), *adj.* unchanging; constant; steadfast. [CHANGE + -LESS] **—change′less·ly,** *adv.* **—change′less·ness,** *n.*

change·ling (chānj′ling), *n.* **1.** a child surreptitiously or unintentionally substituted for another. **2.** an ugly, stupid, or strange child superstitiously believed to have been left by fairies in place of a pretty, charming child. **3.** *Philately.* a postage stamp which, by accident or intention, has been chemically changed in color. **4.** *Archaic.* **a.** a disloyal person. **b.** an imbecile. [CHANGE + -LING[1]]

change·mak·er (chānj′mā′kər), *n.* a device for supplying coins of specific denominations when a key or lever is moved. [CHANGE + MAKER]

change·ment de pied (*Fr.* shäNzh mäNdᵊ pyā′), *pl.* **change·ments de pied** (*Fr.* shäNzh mäNdᵊ pyā′). *Ballet.* a jump in which the dancer's feet are reversed from the starting position. [< F: lit., change of foot]

change′ of life′, menopause.

change′ of pace′, **1.** a temporary shift or variation in the normal routine or regular pattern of activity, action, interest, or the like: *Reading a mystery novel has been a real change of pace for me.* **2.** *Baseball.* Also called **change-up.** a ball that is thrown by a pitcher with the same motion as for his fast ball but that travels with less speed, making the pitch more difficult for the batter to time.

change′ of ven′ue, *Law.* the removal of a trial to another county.

change·o·ver (chānj′ō′vər), *n.* a conversion or complete change from one thing, condition, or system to another, as in equipment, personnel, methods of production, etc.: *The changeover to modern equipment made the factory more profitable.* [n. use of v. phrase *change over*]

change·pock·et (chānj′pok′it), *n.* a small pocket or compartment of a large pocket for holding coins. [CHANGE + POCKET]

change′ ring′ing, the art of ringing a series of bells of different tones according to any of various orderly sequences.

change-up (chānj′up′), *n. Baseball.* See **change of pace** (def. 2).

Chang Hsueh-liang (jäng′ shYe′lyäng′), born 1898, Chinese Nationalist general against the Japanese.

chang′ing bag′, a light-proof bag with openings made to fit closely around the arms, used in place of a darkroom in some photographic procedures.

chang′ing tone′, cambiata. Also called **chang′ing note′.**

Chang·sha (chäng′shä′), *n.* a city in and the capital of Hunan province, in SE China. 703,000 (est. 1957).

Chang·teh (chäng′du′), *n.* a city in N Hunan, in E China. ab. 300,000.

Chang Tso-lin (jäng′tsō′lin′), 1873–1928, Chinese general: military ruler of Manchuria 1918–28.

chan·nel[1] (chan′əl), *n., v.,* **-neled, -nel·ing** or (*esp. Brit.*) **-nelled, -nel·ling.** **—n. 1.** the bed of a stream or waterway. **2.** *Archit.* **a.** a flute in a column, esp. one having no fillet between it and other flutes. **b.** any of the prominent vertical grooves in a triglyph. **3.** the deeper part of a waterway. **4.** a wide strait, as between a continent and an island. **5.** *Naut.* a navigable route between two bodies of water. **6.** a means of access: *He considers the Senate a channel to the White House.* **7.** a course into which something may be directed: *He hoped to direct the conversation to a new channel.* **8.** a route through which anything passes or progresses: *channels of trade.* **9. channels,** the specific, prescribed, or official course or means of communication: *In an emergency he was able to reach the governor without going through official channels.* **10.** (in jazz or popular music) a bridge. **11.** a frequency band wide enough for one-way communication, its exact width depending upon whether the transmission is for telegraph, telephone, radio, television, or other communication. **12.** *Computer Technol.* **a.** a circuit in a computer for the flow of information. **b.** a line along a paper tape or magnetic tape in which information can be stored. **13.** a tubular passage for liquids or fluids. **14.** a groove or furrow. **15.** *Building Trades.* **a.** any structural member, as one of reinforced concrete, having the form of three sides of a rectangle. **b.** a number of such members: *channel in 100-foot lengths.* **c.** See **channel iron.** **—v.t. 16.** to convey through or as through a channel: *He channeled the information to us.* **17.** to direct toward or into some particular course: *to channel one's interests.* **18.** to excavate as a channel: *The river channeled its course through the valley.* **19.** to form a channel in; groove. **—v.i. 20.** to become marked by a channel or channels: *Soft earth has a tendency to channel during a heavy rain.* [ME *chanel* < OF < L *canāl(is)* waterpipe; see CANAL[1]] **—chan′nel·er;** *esp. Brit.,* **chan′nel·ler,** *n.*

chan·nel[2] (chan′əl), *n. Naut.* a horizontal timber or ledge built outboard from the side of a sailing vessel to spread shrouds and backstays at their feet. Also, **chain wale, chain-wale.** [var. of CHAIN WALE]

chan·nel·ing (chan′əling), *n.* ornamentation with flutes or channels. Also, *esp. Brit.,* **chan′nel·ling.** [CHANNEL[1] + -ING[1]]

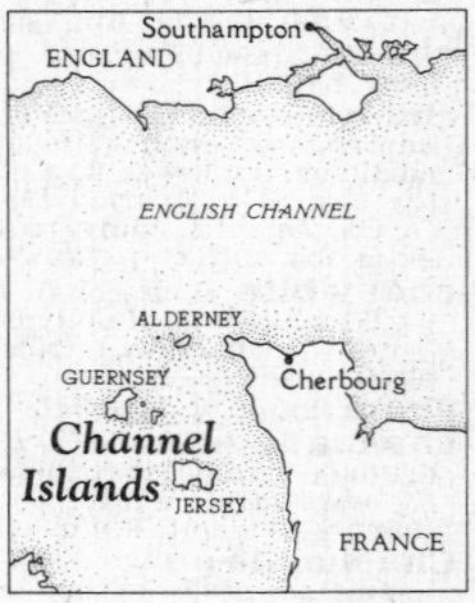

chan′nel i′ron, a rolled steel or iron shape having a U-like cross section with two narrower sides at right angles to a broader one. Also called **chan′nel bar′.**

Chan′nel Is′lands, a British island group in the English Channel, near the coast of France, consisting of Alderney, Guernsey, Jersey, and smaller islands. 104,398 (1961); 75 sq. mi.

chan·nel·ize (chan′əlīz′), *v.t., v.i.,* **-ized, -iz·ing.** to channel [CHANNEL[1] + -IZE] **—chan′nel·i·za′tion,** *n.*

Chan·ning (chan′ing), *n.* **1. Edward,** 1856–1931, U.S. historian. **2. William El·ler·y** (el′ə rē), 1780–1842, U.S. Unitarian clergyman and writer.

cha·no·yu (chä′nô yōō′), *n.* a form of Japanese ceremony at which tea is prepared, served, and taken with great attention to ancient and involved ritual. [< Jap, equiv. to *cha* tea + *no* of + *yu* hot water]

chan·son (shan′sən; *Fr.* shäN sôN′), *n., pl.* **-sons** (-sənz; *Fr.* -sôN′). any of several types of song with French lyrics, occurring from the Middle Ages to the present in a variety of musical styles. [< F < L *cantiōn-* (s. of *cantiō*) song; see CANZONE]

chan·son de geste (shäN sôN də zhest′), *pl.* **chan·sons de geste** (shäN sôN də zhest′). (in medieval French literature) an epic poem written in assonant verse and centering around historical or legendary events or figures. [< F: lit., song of deeds; see CHANSON, GEST]

Chan·son de Ro·land (*Fr.* shäN sôN də rō läN′), a chanson de geste (c1000) relating Roland's brave deeds and his death at Roncesvalles. English, **The Song of Roland.**

chan·son·nier (shan′sən yā′; *Fr.* shäN sô nyā′), *n., pl.* **-son·niers** (-sən yāz′; *Fr.* -sô nyā′). a cabaret performer who specializes in songs that are a combination of melody and rapid spoken patter, typically in French, and are often concerned with topical subjects. [< F; see CHANSON, ER[2]]

chant (chant, chänt), *n.* **1.** a song; singing: *the chant of a bird.* **2.** a short, simple melody, esp. one characterized by single notes to which an indefinite number of syllables are intoned, used in singing the psalms, canticles, etc., in the church service. **3.** a psalm, canticle, or the like, chanted or for chanting. **4.** the singing or intoning of all or portions of a liturgical service. **5.** any monotonous song. **6.** a monotonous intonation of the voice in speaking. **—v.t. 7.** to sing. **8.** to celebrate in song. **9.** to sing to a chant, or in the manner of a chant, esp. in the church service. **—v.i. 10.** to sing. **11.** to sing a chant. [ME *chant(en)* < MF *chante(r)* < L *cantāre,* freq. of *canere* to sing] **—chant′a·ble,** *adj.* **—chant′ing·ly,** *adv.*

chan·tage (shän tAzh′), *n. French.* blackmail.

Chant de guerre pour l'armée du Rhin (*Fr.* shäN də ger′ pōōr lAr mā′ dY RAN′), Marseillaise.

chante-fa·ble (*Fr.* shäNt fä′blə), *n., pl.* **-fa·bles** (-fä′blə). (in medieval French literature) a prose narrative interspersed with verse. [< F; see CHANT, FABLE]

chant·er (chan′tər, chän′-), *n.* **1.** one who chants; singer. **2.** a chorister; precentor. **3.** the chief singer or priest of a chantry. **4.** the pipe of a bagpipe, provided with finger holes for playing the melody. [CHANT + -ER[1]; r. ME *chantour* < AF, var. of OF *chanteor* < L *cantātōr-* (s. of *cantātor*) singer; see -OR[2]] **—chant′er·ship′,** *n.*

chan·te·relle (shan′tə rel′, chan′-), *n.* a mushroom, *Cantharellus cibarius,* a favorite edible species in France. [< F < NL *cantharell(a),* equiv. to L *canthar(us)* tankard (< Gk *kántharos*) + *-ella* dim. suffix]

chan·teuse (shan tōōs′; *Fr.* shäN tœz′), *n., pl.* **-teuses** (-tōō′siz; *Fr.* -tœz′). a female singer, esp. a woman who sings in nightclubs and cabarets. [< F, fem. of *chanteur,* OF *chanteor;* see CHANTER]

chant·ey (shan′tē, chan′-), *n., pl.* **-eys.** a sailors' song, esp. one sung in rhythm to work. Also, **chanty, shantey, shanty.** [alter. of F *chanter* to sing; see CHANT]

chan·ti·cleer (chan′tə klēr′), *n.* a rooster. Also, **chan·te·cler** (chan′tə klär′). [ME *Chauntecler* < OF *Chantecler* n. use of v. phrase *chante cler* sing clear. See CHANT, CLEAR]

Chan·til·ly (shan til′ē; *Fr.* shäN tē yē′), *n.* **1.** a town in N France, N of Paris: lace manufacture. 8324 (1962). **2.** (*sometimes l.c.*) Also called **Chantil′ly lace′.** a delicate silk or linen bobbin lace, in black or white, scalloped along one edge and often having an outlined design of scrolls or vases or baskets of flowers, widely used for bridal gowns and evening gowns. **3.** a dessert topping of whipped cream, sweetening, and flavoring, esp. vanilla. **4.** Also called **Chantilly sauce.** mousseline[2] (def. 1). **—*adj.*** **5.** (of cream) whipped and flavored, esp. with vanilla. **6.** (of food) prepared or served with whipped cream: *strawberries Chantilly.*

chant·ress (chan′tris, chän′-), *n.* a female chanter or singer. [late ME *chanteresse.* See CHANTER, -ESS]

chan·try (chan′trē, chän′-), *n., pl.* **-tries.** *Eccles.* **1.** an endowment for the singing or saying of Mass for the souls of the founders or of persons named by them. **2.** a chapel or the like so endowed. **3.** the priests of a chantry endowment. **4.** a chapel attached to a church, used for minor services. [ME *chanterie* < MF. See CHANT, -ERY]

Chants de Mal·do·ror, Les (lā shäN də mal dō-rôr′). See **Les Chants de Maldoror.**

chant·y (shan′tē, chan′tē), *n., pl.* **chant·ies.** chantey.

Cha·nu·kah (кнä′nŏŏ kä′, -nə kə, hä′-), *n.* *Judaism.* Hanukkah.

Cha·ny (chä′nē, *Russ.* chä′ni), *n.* **Lake,** a salt lake in SW Siberia, in the W Soviet Union in Asia. ab. 1300 sq. mi.

Chao·an (chou′än′), *n.* a city in E Kwangtung, in SE China. ab. 60,000. Also called **Chao·chow·fu** (jou′-jō′fōō′).

Chao K'uang-yin (jou′ kwäng′yin′), 927–976 A.D., Chinese emperor 960–976: founder of the Sung dynasty. Also called **Kao Tsu.**

Cha·on (kā′on), *n.* (in the *Aeneid*) the brother of Helenus.

Chao Phra·ya (chou′ prä yä′), Menam.

cha·o·ri (kä′ə rē), *n.* *Brahminism.* **1.** a large porch in front of a mantapa, used for marriage ceremonies. **2.** mantapa.

cha·os (kā′os), *n.* **1.** state of utter confusion or disorder; a total lack of organization or order. **2.** any confused, disorderly mass: *a chaos of meaningless phrases.* **3.** the infinity of space or formless matter supposed to have preceded the existence of the ordered universe. **4.** (*cap.*) the personification of this in any of several ancient Greek myths. **5.** *Obs.* a chasm or abyss. [ME < L < Gk; akin to CHASM, YAWN]
—Syn. 1. disarray, jumble, turmoil, tumult.

cha·ot·ic (kā ot′ik), *adj.* wholly confused or disordered: *a chaotic mind; a chaotic mass of books and papers.* [CHAO(S) + -TIC] **—cha·ot′i·cal·ly,** *adv.*
—Ant. orderly, systematic.

chap[1] (chap), *v.,* **chapped, chap·ping,** *n.* **—*v.t.*** **1.** (of cold or exposure) to crack, roughen, and redden (the skin): *The windy, cold weather chapped her lips.* **2.** to cause (the ground, wood, etc.) to split, crack, or open in clefts: *The summer heat and drought chapped the river bank.* **—*v.i.*** **3.** to become chapped. **—*n.*** **4.** a fissure or crack, esp. in the skin. **5.** *Scot.* a knock; rap. [ME *chapp(en)*; c. D *kappen* to cut; akin to CHIP[1]]

chap[2] (chap), *n.* **1.** *Informal.* a fellow; man or boy. **2.** *Brit. Dial.* a customer. [short for CHAPMAN]

chap[3] (chop, chap), *n.* chop[3]. [? special use of CHAP[1]]

chap., **1.** Chaplain. **2.** chapter. Also, **Chap.**

cha·pa·ra·jos (shap′ə rā′ōs; *Sp.* chä′pä rä′hōs), *n.pl.* (in Mexico) chaps. Also, **cha·pa·re·jos** (shap′ə rā′ōs; *Sp.* chä′pä re′hōs). [< MexSp, var. of *chaparejos,* equiv. to *chapa(rral)* CHAPARRAL + *aparejos,* pl. of *aparejo* gear; akin to APPAREL]

chap·ar·ral (chap′ə ral′), *n.* *Southwestern U.S.* **1.** a close growth of low, evergreen oaks. **2.** any dense thicket. [< Sp, equiv. to *chaparr(o)* evergreen oak (< Basque *tshapar*) + *-al* collective suffix]

chaparral′ broom′, the coyote-brush.

chaparral′ cock′, roadrunner.

chaparral′ lil′y, a bulbous herb, *Lilium rubescens,* of the western coast of the U.S., having pale lilac-colored flowers which turn rose-purple.

chaparral′ pea′, a spiny, leguminous bush, *Pickeringia montana,* sometimes forming dense thickets in the Pacific coast regions of the U.S.

chaparral′ snap′dragon, an erect or climbing annual herb, *Antirrhinum coulterianum,* of California, having yellow-haired, purple to white flowers.

cha·pa·ti (chə pat′ē, -pä′tē), *n., pl.* **-ti, -tis, -ties.** (in India) a bread made with a stiff dough of flour and water, rolled out like a pancake and baked on a griddle. [< Hindi *capati* < Skt *carpaṭī*]

cha·pat·ti (chə pat′ē, -pä′tē), *n., pl.* **-ti, -tis, -ties.** chapati.

chap·book (chap′bŏŏk′), *n.* a small book or pamphlet of popular tales, ballads, etc., formerly hawked about by chapmen. [*chap* (as in CHAPMAN) + BOOK]

chape (chāp), *n.* the lowermost terminal mount of a scabbard. [ME < MF: (metal) covering < LL *cap(p)a;* see CAP, CAPE[1]] **—chape′less,** *adj.*

cha·peau (sha pō′; *Fr.* sha pō′), *n., pl.* **-peaux** (-pōz′; *Fr.* -pō′), **-peaus. 1.** a hat. **2.** *Heraldry.* **a.** a representation of a low-crowned hat with a turned-up brim, usually of a different tincture, used either as a charge or as part of a crest. **b.** a cap depicted within a representation of a crown or coronet. [< F; OF *chapel* wreath, hat < LL *cappell(us)* hood, hat, equiv. to *capp(a)* (see CAP) + *-ellus* dim. suffix]

chapeau′ bras′ (brä), a small three-cornered hat, formerly in use, which could be folded flat and carried under the arm. [< F: arm hat]

chap·el (chap′əl), *n., v.,* **-eled, -el·ing** or (*esp. Brit.*) **-elled, -el·ling,** *adj.* **—*n.*** **1.** a private or subordinate place of prayer or worship; oratory. **2.** a separately dedicated part of a church, or a small independent churchlike edifice, devoted to special services. **3.** a room or building for worship in an institution, palace, etc. **4.** (in Great Britain) a place of worship for members of various dissenting Protestant churches, as Baptists or Methodists. **5.** a separate place of public worship dependent on the church of a parish. **6.** a religious service in a chapel: *Don't be late for chapel!* **7.** a choir or orchestra of a chapel, court, etc. **8.** a print shop or printing house. **9.** the body of printers belonging to a printing house. **—*v.t.*** **10.** *Naut.* to maneuver (a sailing vessel taken aback) by the helm alone until the wind can be recovered on the original tack. **—*adj.*** **11.** (in England) belonging to any of various dissenting Protestant sects, as the Baptists or Methodists. [ME *chapele* < OF < LL *cappell(a)* hooded cloak, equiv. to *capp(a)* (see CAP) + *-ella* dim. suffix; first applied to the sanctuary where the cloak of St. Martin (4th-century bishop of Tours) was kept as a relic]

cha·pel de fer (sha pel′ də fâr′), *pl.* **cha·pels de fer.** a medieval open helmet, often having a broad brim for deflecting blows from above. Also called **war hat, kettle hat.** [< OF: hat of iron; see CHAPEAU, FERROUS]

Chap′el Hill′, a city in N North Carolina. 12,573 (1960).

chap·er·on (shap′ə rōn′), *n.* **1.** a person, usually a married or elderly woman, who, for propriety, accompanies a young unmarried woman in public or who attends a party of young unmarried men and women. **2.** a round headdress of stuffed cloth with wide cloth streamers that fall from the crown or may be draped around it, worn in the 15th century. **—*v.t.*** **3.** to attend or accompany as chaperon. Also, **chaperone.** [< F: hood, protection, protector, equiv. to *chaper-* (? var. of *chapel* CHAPEAU, with *r* for *l* as in CHAPTER) + *-on* dim. suffix] **—chap·er·on·age** (shap′ə rō′nij), *n.* **—chap′er·on′less,** *adj.*
—Syn. 1, 3. escort.

chap·er·one (shap′ə rōn′), *n., v.t.,* **-oned, -on·ing.** chaperon.

chap·fall·en (chop′fô′lən, chap′-), *adj.* dispirited; chagrined; dejected. Also, **chopfallen.** [CHAP[3] + FALLEN]

chap·i·ter (chap′i tər), *n.* *Archit. Rare.* a capital. [ME; see CHAPTER]

chap·lain (chap′lin), *n.* **1.** an ecclesiastic attached to the chapel of a royal court, college, etc., or to a military unit. **2.** one who says the prayer, invocation, etc., for an organization or at an assembly or gathering. [ME *chapelain* < MF < LL *cappellān(us)* custodian of St. Martin's cloak (see CHAPEL, -AN); r. OE *capellan* < LL] **—chap′lain·cy, chap′lain·ship′, chap′lain·ry,** *n.*

chap·let (chap′lit), *n.* **1.** a wreath or garland for the head. **2.** a string of beads. **3.** *Rom. Cath. Ch.* **a.** a string of beads, one third of the length of a rosary, for counting prayers. **b.** the prayers recited over this. **4.** *Archit.* a small molding carved to resemble a string of beads; astragal. **5.** *Foundry.* an object for separating the core of a mold from a wall, composed of the same metal as the casting and forming an integral part of it. [ME *chapelet* wreath < OF. See CHAPEAU, -ET] **—chap′let·ed,** *adj.*

Chap·lin (chap′lən), *n.* **Sir Charles Spencer** (*Charlie*), 1889–1977, English motion picture actor, mime, producer, and director; in U.S. 1910–52.

chap·man (chap′mən), *n., pl.* **-men. 1.** *Brit.* a hawker or peddler. **2.** *Archaic.* a merchant. [ME; OE *cēapman* (*cēap* buying and selling + *man* MAN[1]); c. D *koopman,* G *Kaufmann;* see CHEAP] **—chap′man·ship′,** *n.*

Chap·man (chap′mən), *n.* **1. Frank Mich·ler** (mik′-lər), 1864–1945, U.S. ornithologist, museum curator, and author. **2. George,** 1559–1634, English poet, dramatist, and translator. **3. John.** See **Appleseed, Johnny.**

chappe (shap), *n.* See **schappe silk.**

chap·pie (chap′ē), *n.* *Brit. Informal.* chap[2] (def. 1). Also, **chap′py.** [CHAP[2] + -IE]

cha·pra·si (chə prä′sē), *n.* *Anglo-Indian.* a native official messenger. Also, **cha·pras′si, chuprassi.** [< Hindi *caprāsī,* deriv. of *caprās* badge]

chaps (chaps, shaps), *n.pl.* *Western U.S.* strong, trouserlike leggings of leather, often widely flared, worn over blue jeans or the like, esp. by cowboys, as protection against burs, rope burns, etc., while on horseback. Also called **chaparajos, chaparejos.** [short for CHAPARAJOS]

chap·tal·i·za·tion (shap′tə li zā′shən), *n.* a method of increasing the alcohol in a wine by adding sugar to the must before or during fermentation. [CHAPTALIZE + -ATION]

chap·tal·ize (shap′tə līz′), *v.t.,* **-ized, -iz·ing.** to subject (wine) to chaptalization. [< F *chaptalise(r),* named after J. A. *Chaptal* (d. 1832), French chemist; see -IZE]

chap·ter (chap′tər), *n.* **1.** a main division of a book, treatise, or the like, usually bearing a number or title. **2.** an important portion or division of anything: *The atomic bomb opened a new chapter in history.* **3.** a branch, usually restricted to a given locality, of a society, organization, fraternity, etc.: *the Connecticut chapter of the American Red Cross.* **4.** *Eccles.* **a.** an assembly of the monks in a monastery, of those in a province, or of the entire order. **b.** a general assembly of the canons of a church. **c.** a meeting of the elected representatives of the provinces or houses of a religious community. **d.** the body of such canons or representatives collectively. **5.** any general assembly. **6.** *Liturgy.* a short Scriptural quotation read at various parts of the office, as after the last psalm in the service of lauds, prime, tierce, etc. **7.** *Horol.* any of the marks or numerals designating the hours on a dial. **—*v.t.*** **8.** to divide into or arrange in chapters. [ME *chapiter,* var. of *chapitre* < OF < L *capitul(um)* little head (*capit-,* s. of *caput* head + *-ulum* -ULE); in LL, also section of a book; in ML: section read at a meeting, hence, the meeting, esp. one of canons, hence, a body of canons] **—chap′ter·al,** *adj.*

chap′ter and verse′, 1. full, cited authority, as for one's action, opinion, etc.: *to give chapter and verse.* **2.** *Slang.* **a.** a set of regulations. **b.** detailed information.

chap′ter head′, printed material appearing before and usually above the text of a chapter, as a title, number, quotation, etc.

chap′ter house′, 1. *Eccles.* a building attached to or a hall forming part of a cathedral or monastery, used as a meeting place for the chapter. **2.** a building used as a meeting place by a chapter of a society, fraternity, etc. [ME *chapitelhus*]

chap′ter ring′, a ringlike band on the dial of a clock which bears the numerals or other symbols of the hours.

chap·trel (chap′trəl), *n.* *Archit.* **1.** a capital, as on a pilaster or vaulting shaft, engaged in masonry on one or more sides. **2.** a small capital. [CHAPTER + *-el* < L *-ell(um)* dim. suffix]

Cha·pul·te·pec (chə pul′tə pek′; *Sp.* chä pōōl′te pek′), *n.* a castle-fortress at the outskirts of Mexico City: captured by U.S. forces (1847) in the Mexican War.

cha·que·ta (chä ke′tä), *n., pl.* **-tas** (-täs). *Spanish.* a heavy jacket, esp. a leather one worn by cowboys.

char[1] (chär), *v.,* **charred, char·ring,** *n.* **—*v.t.*** **1.** to burn or reduce to charcoal: *The fire charred the paper.* **2.** to burn slightly; scorch: *She removed the steak from the grill when the flame had barely charred it.* **—*v.i.*** **3.** to become charred. **—*n.*** **4.** a charred material or surface. **5.** charcoal. [appar. abstraction of *char-* of CHARCOAL; see CHARK]

char[2] (chär), *n., pl.* (*esp. collectively*) **char,** (*esp. referring to two or more kinds or species*) **chars.** any trout of the genus *Salvelinus* (or *Cristovomer*), esp. *S. alpinus,* found in Europe. Also, **charr.** [perh. OE **ceorr(a),* lit., turner, deriv. of *ceorran* to turn, it being thought of as swimming to and fro time and again; see CHAR[3]]

char[3] (chär), *n., v.,* **charred, char·ring.** *Chiefly Brit.* **—*n.*** **1.** a charwoman. **2.** a task, esp. a household chore. **3. chars,** odd jobs, esp. of housework or cleaning, for which one is paid by the hour or day. **—*v.i.*** **4.** to work at housecleaning by the day or hour; rent oneself out as a cleaning woman or handyman who does odd jobs. **—*v.t.*** **5.** to do (housework, odd jobs, or chores); clean, repair, or fix. Also, **chare.** [ME *cherre,* OE *cerr, cierr* turn, time, occasion, affair, deriv. of *cierran* to turn]

char[4] (chär), *n.* *Brit. Slang.* tea. [< AInd < Hind *cā* TEA]

Char (shar), *n.* **Re·né** (rə nā′), born 1907, French poet.

char., **1.** character. **2.** charter.

cha·ra (kar′ə), *n.* any stonewort of the genus *Chara.* [< NL, L: an edible root]

char-à-banc (shar′ə bang′, -bangk′; *Fr.* sha ra bäN′), *n., pl.* **-bancs** (-bangz′, -bangks′; *Fr.* -bäN′). *Brit.* a bus used on sightseeing tours, esp. a sightseeing bus with open sides; any lightweight bus with open sides and no center aisle. Also, **char′a·banc′.** [back formation from F *char-à-bancs,* lit., car with benches, the *-s* being taken as pl. ending of word as a whole]

char·a·cin (kar′ə sin), *n.* any fresh-water fish of the family *Characinidae,* found in Africa and Central and South America. [< NL *Characin(idae)* the family, equiv. to *characin(us)* the genus (*charac-* (< Gk *charak-,* s. of *chárax* a sea-fish) + *-inus* -IN[1]) + *-idae* -IDAE]

char·ac·ter (kar′ik tər), *n.* **1.** the aggregate of features and traits that form the apparent individual nature of some person or thing. **2.** one such feature or trait; characteristic. **3.** moral or ethical quality: *They knew he was a man of fine, honorable character.* **4.** qualities of honesty, courage, or the like; integrity: *It takes character to talk up to bullying like that.* **5.** reputation: *a stain on one's character.* **6.** good repute. **7.** an account of the qualities or peculiarities of a person or thing. **8.** a formal statement from an employer concerning the qualities and habits of a former servant or employee. **9.** status or capacity: *the character of a justice of the peace.* **10.** a person, esp. with reference to behavior or personality: *a suspicious character; a weak character.* **11.** *Informal.* an odd or eccentric person. **12.** a person represented in a drama, story, etc. **13.** *Literature.* (esp. in 17th- and 18th-century England) a formal character sketch or descriptive analysis of a particular human virtue or vice as represented in a person or type. Cf. **character sketch. 14.** a part or role, as in a play, motion picture, or the like. **15.** *Genetics.* any trait, function, structure, or substance of an organism resulting from the effect of one or more genes as modified by the environment. **16.** a significant visual mark or symbol. **17.** a symbol as used in a writing system, as a letter of the alphabet. **18.** the symbols of a writing system collectively. **19.** *Computer Technol.* **a.** any symbol, as a number, letter, punctuation mark, etc., which represents information and which, when encoded, is usable by a machine. **b.** one of a set of basic symbols which singly or in a series of two or more expresses information and, when encoded, is usable in a computer. **c.** a pattern of ones and zeros representing the relationship of positive and negative pulses in a computer. **20.** a style of writing or printing. **21.** *Rom. Cath. Theol.* the ineffaceable imprint received on the soul through the sacraments of baptism, confirmation, and ordination. **22.** *Math.* a homomorphism of a given group, which assigns a complex number to each element of the group. Cf. **character group. 23.** *Obs.* a cipher or cipher message. **24. in character, a.** in harmony with one's personal character or disposition: *Such behavior does not seem in character with what I know of him.* **b.** in accordance with the role or personality assumed in a performance: *an actor in character.* **25. out of character, a.** out of harmony with one's personal character or disposition: *The clothes she wears are out of character.* **b.** away from the role or personality assumed in a performance: *an actor stepping out of character.*
—*adj.* **26.** *Theat.* **a.** (of a part or role) representing or portraying a personality type, esp. by emphasizing distinctive traits, as language, mannerisms, physical makeup, habits, etc. **b.** (of an actor or actress) acting or specializing in such a role or roles.
—*v.t.* *Archaic.* **27.** to portray; describe. **28.** to engrave; inscribe. [< L < Gk *charaktḗr* graving tool, its mark, equiv. to *charak-* (var. s. of *charáttein* to engrave) + *-tēr* instrumental suffix; r. ME *caractere* < MF < L, as above] **—char′ac·ter·less,** *adj.*
—Syn. 1. CHARACTER, INDIVIDUALITY, PERSONALITY refer to the sum of the characteristics possessed by a person. CHARACTER refers esp. to moral qualities, ethical standards, principles, and the like: *a man of sterling character.* INDIVIDUALITY refers to the distinctive qualities which make one recognizable as a person differentiated from others: *a man of strong individuality.* PERSONALITY refers particularly to the combination of outer and inner characteristics that determine the impression which one makes upon others: *a man of vivid or pleasing personality.* **5.** name, repute. See **reputation. 16.** sign.

char·ac·ter·ful (kar′ik tər fəl), *adj.* **1.** highly expressive of character: *a characterful face.* **2.** having remarkable character: *a characterful prose style.* [CHARACTER + -FUL]

char′acter group′, *Math.* the set of all homomorphisms from a given group to the set of complex numbers. Cf. **character** (def. 22).

char·ac·ter·i·sa·tion (kar′ik tər i zā′shən, -tri zā′-), *n.* *Chiefly Brit.* characterization.

char·ac·ter·ise (kar′ik tə rīz′), *v.t.,* **-ised, -is·ing.** *Chiefly Brit.* characterize. **—char′ac·ter·is′a·ble,** *adj.* **—char′ac·ter·is′er,** *n.*

char·ac·ter·is·tic (kar′ik tə ris′tik), *adj.* **1.** Also, **char′ac·ter·is′ti·cal.** pertaining to, constituting, or

indicating the character or peculiar quality of a person or thing; typical; distinctive: *Red and gold are the characteristic colors of autumn.* —*n.* **2.** a distinguishing feature or quality: *Generosity is his chief characteristic.* **3.** *Math.* **a.** the integral part of a common logarithm. Cf. **mantissa. b.** the exponent of 10 in a number expressed in scientific notation. **c.** the smallest positive integer *n* such that each element of a given ring added to itself *n* times results in 0. [< Gk *charaktēristik(ós)*. See CHARACTER, -ISTIC]
—**Syn. 1.** special, peculiar. **2.** attribute, property, trait. See **feature.**

char·ac·ter·is·ti·cal·ly (kar′ik tə ris′tik lē), *adv.* in a characteristic manner; typically. [CHARACTERISTIC + -AL[1] + -LY]

char′acteris′tic equa′tion, 1. the characteristic polynomial of a given matrix, equated to zero. **2.** Also called **auxiliary equation.** an equation with one variable and equated to zero, which is derived from a given linear differential equation and in which the coefficient and power of the variable in each term correspond to the coefficient and order of a derivative in the original equation. **3.** *Physics.* See **equation of state.**

char′acteris′tic func′tion, *Math.* **1.** a function defined on a given set, having value 1 for every element of the set and value 0 for every element not contained in the set. **2.** See **characteristic polynomial.**

characteris′tic polyno′mial, *Math.* an expression obtained from a given matrix by taking the determinant of the difference between the matrix and an arbitrary variable times the identity matrix.

char′acteris′tic root′, *Math.* **1.** a scalar for which there exists a nonzero vector such that the scalar times the vector equals the value of the vector under a given linear transformation on a vector space. **2.** a root of the characteristic equation of a given matrix. Also called **eigenvalue, char′acteris′tic val′ue, proper value.**

char′acteris′tic sub′group, *Math.* a subgroup of a group with operators, whose set of operators is the set of all automorphisms of the group. Cf. **group with operators.**

char′acteris′tic vec′tor, *Math.* a vector for which there exists a scalar such that the value of the vector under a given transformation is equal to the scalar times the vector. Also called **eigenvector.**

char′acteris′tic veloc′ity, *Rocketry.* **1.** a measure of the effectiveness with which the combustion in a rocket engine produces high temperature and pressure, equal to the exhaust velocity divided by the thrust coefficient. **2.** the total of all velocities a space vehicle must develop to complete a given mission. **3.** an expression of the performance of a propellant or propellant system under given operating pressures.

char′acteris′tic x′-ray, *Physics.* an x-ray that is emitted from an atom when an electron is displaced from an inner shell.

char·ac·ter·i·za·tion (kar′ik tər i zā′shən, -tri zā′-), *n.* **1.** portrayal; description. **2.** act of characterizing: *The actor's characterization of a politician was received with enthusiasm.* **3.** the creation and convincing representation of fictitious characters: *Characterization is the chief concern of many novelists.* Also, *esp. Brit.,* **characterisation.** [< ML *charactērizāt(us)* marked (ptp. of *charactērizāre* to CHARACTERIZE; see -ATE[1]) + L *-iōn-* -ION]

char·ac·ter·ize (kar′ik tə rīz′), *v.t.,* **-ized, -iz·ing. 1.** to mark or distinguish as a characteristic; be a characteristic of: *Rich metaphors characterize his poetry.* **2.** to describe the character or individual quality of: *He characterized her in a few well-chosen words.* **3.** to attribute character to: *to characterize someone as a coward.* Also, *esp. Brit.,* **characterise.** [< ML *charactēriz(āre)* < Gk *charaktērízein.* See CHARACTER, -IZE] —**char′ac·ter·iz′a·ble,** *adj.* —**char′ac·ter·iz′er,** *n.*

char′acter piece′, *Music.* a short, simple piece, usually for piano, of a type developed chiefly during the 19th century, often of a descriptive or seemingly improvisatory character.

char′acter sketch′, *Literature.* a short essay in prose or verse describing a person. Cf. **character** (def. 13).

Char′acters of Shake′speare's Plays′, The, a collection of critical essays (1817) by William Hazlitt.

char′acter wit′ness, a person who testifies as to the moral character and reputation of a litigant in a court of law or other legal proceeding.

char·ac·ter·y (kar′ik tə rē, -trē), *n.* **1.** the use of characters or symbols for the expression of meaning. **2.** characters or symbols collectively. [CHARACTER + -Y[3]]

cha·rade (shə rād′; *esp. Brit.* shə räd′), *n.* **1. charades,** (*construed as sing.*) a parlor game in which the players are typically divided into two teams, members of which take turns at acting out in pantomime a word or phrase, often syllable by syllable, which the members of their own team must guess. **2.** a word or phrase acted out in this game. [< F < Pr *charrad(o)* entertainment, equiv. to *charr(a)* (to) chat, chatter + *-ado,* -ADE[1]]

cha·ran·go (chə rang′gō) *n., pl.* **-gos.** a small South American guitar made from the shell of an armadillo or similar animal and having two to five strings. [< Sp, alter. of *charanga* brass band, of imit. orig.]

Char·cas (kär′kəs), *n.* *Douay Bible.* Carcas.

Char·che·mish (kär′kə mish, kär kē′-), *n.* Carchemish.

char·coal (chär′kōl′), *n.* **1.** the carbonaceous material obtained by heating wood or other organic substances in the absence of air. **2.** a drawing pencil of charcoal. **3.** a drawing made with charcoal. —*v.t.* **4.** to blacken, write, or draw with charcoal. [ME *charcole,* perh. orig. live coal, equiv. to OE **cear-* red (< Celt; cf. Gael *cear* blood, *ceara* red) + *col* live coal] —**char′coal′y,** *adj.*

char′coal burn′er, 1. a person employed in the manufacture of charcoal. **2.** a device burning charcoal, as a stove.

char′coal rot′, *Plant Pathol.* a disease of plants, esp. sorghum, corn, etc., characterized by basal stem lesions and a black discoloration and dry rot of the internal tissues at the base of the stem and upper roots, caused by a fungus, *Macrophomina phaseoli.*

Char·cot (shar kō′), *n.* **Jean Mar·tin** (zhäN mar·taN′), 1825–93, French neuropathologist.

char·cu·te·rie (shär koo′tə rē′, shär koo′tə rē; *Fr.* shar kyt[ə] rē′), *n., pl.* **-ries** (-rēz′, -rēz; *Fr.* -rē′). (in France) a pork butcher's shop or delicatessen. [< F; MF *chaircuterie,* equiv. to *chaircut(ier)* CHARCUTIER + *-erie* -ERY]

char·cu·tier (shär koo′tē ā′, shär koo′tē ā′; *Fr.* shar·ky tyā′), *n., pl.* **-tiers** (-tē āz′, -āz′; *Fr.* -tyā′). (in France) a pork butcher. [< F; MF *chaircutier,* equiv. to *chair* flesh (see CHEER) + *cuite* cooked, fem. of *cuit,* ptp. of *cuire* (< L *coquere;* see COOK) + *-ier* -IER]

chard (chärd), *n.* a variety of beet, *Beta vulgaris Cicla,* having large leafstalks and midribs which are used as a vegetable (**Swiss chard**). [appar. < F *chard(on)* thistle; see CARDOON]

Char·din (shar daN′), *n.* **Jean Bap·tiste Si·mé·on** (zhäN ba tēst′ sē mā ôN′), 1699–1779, French painter.

Char·don (shär′dən), *n.* a town in NE Ohio. 3154 (1960).

Char·don·net (shär′dənā′; *Fr.* shar dô ne′), *n.* **Hi·laire Ber·ni·gaud** (ē ler′ ber nē gō′), **Comte de,** 1839–1924, French chemist and inventor.

chare (châr), *n., v.,* **chared, char·ing.** *Chiefly Brit.* char[3].

Cha·rente (sha ränt′), *n.* a department in W France. 327,658 (1962); 2306 sq. mi. *Cap.:* Angoulême.

Cha·rente-Ma·ri·time (sha ränt′ma rē tēm′), *n.* a department in W France. 470,897 (1962); 2792 sq. mi. *Cap.:* La Rochelle.

cha·rette (shə ret′), *n.* charrette.

charg·a·ble (chär′jə bəl), *adj.* chargeable.

charge (chärj), *v.,* **charged, charg·ing,** *n.* —*v.t.* **1.** to fill or furnish (a thing) with the quantity, as of powder or fuel, that it is fitted to receive: *to charge a musket.* **2.** to supply with a quantity of electricity or electrical energy: *to charge a storage battery.* **3.** to suffuse, as with emotion: *The air was charged with excitement.* **4.** *Physics.* to change the net amount of positive or negative electricity of (a particle, body, or system). **5.** to fill (air, water, etc.) with other matter in a state of diffusion or solution: *The air was charged with pollen.* **6.** *Metall.* to insert (materials) into a furnace, converter, etc. **7.** to load or burden (the mind, heart, etc.): *His mind was charged with weighty matters.* **8.** to lay a command or injunction upon: *He charged his secretary with the management of his correspondence.* **9.** to instruct authoritatively, as a judge does a jury. **10.** to impute; ascribe the responsibility for: *He charged the accident to his own carelessness.* **11.** to accuse formally or explicitly (usually fol. by *with*): *They charged him with theft.* **12.** to hold liable for payment; enter a debit against. **13.** to list or record as a debt or obligation; enter as a debit. **14.** to impose or ask as a price: *That store charges $12 for gloves.* **15.** (of a purchaser) to defer payment for (a purchase) until a bill is rendered by the creditor: *The store permitted her to charge the dress.* **16.** to attack by rushing violently against: *The cavalry charged the enemy.* **17.** *Heraldry.* to place charges on (an escutcheon). **18.** to put a load or burden on or in.
—*v.i.* **19.** to make an onset; rush, as to an attack. **20.** to place the price of a thing to one's debit. **21.** to require payment: *to charge for a service.* **22.** to make a debit, as in an account. **23.** (of dogs) to lie down at command. **24. charge off, a.** to write off as an expense or loss. **b.** to attribute to: *I charged off the blunder to inexperience.*
—*n.* **25.** the quantity of anything that an apparatus is fitted to hold, or holds, at one time: *a charge of coal for a furnace.* **26.** a quantity of explosive to be set off at one time. **27.** a duty or responsibility laid upon or entrusted to one. **28.** care, custody, or superintendence: *The child was placed in her nurse's charge.* **29.** anything or anybody committed to one's care or management: *The nurse was careful to let no harm come to her charge.* **30.** *Eccles.* a parish or congregation committed to the spiritual care of a pastor. **31.** a command or injunction; exhortation. **32.** an accusation: *He was arrested on the charge of theft.* **33.** *Law.* an address by a judge to a jury at the close of a trial, instructing them as to the legal points, the weight of evidence, etc., affecting their verdict in the case. **34.** expense or cost: *improvements made at a tenant's own charge.* **35.** a fee or price charged: *a charge of 50 cents for admission.* **36.** a pecuniary burden, encumbrance, tax, or lien; cost; expense; liability to pay: *After his death there were many charges on his estate.* **37.** an entry in an account of something due. **38.** an impetuous onset or attack, as of soldiers. **39.** a signal by bugle, drum, etc., for a military charge. **40.** *Elect.* **a.** Also called **electric charge.** the quantity of electricity or electric energy in or upon an object or substance, noting an excess or deficiency of electrons. **b.** the process of charging a storage battery. **41.** *Heraldry.* any distinctive mark upon an escutcheon, as an ordinary or device, not considered as belonging to the field; bearing. See diag. under **coat of arms. 42.** *Rocketry.* grains of a solid propellant, usually including an inhibitor. **43.** a load or burden. **44.** *Slang.* kick (def. 27a). **45. in charge, a.** in command; having supervisory power. **b.** *Brit.* under arrest; in or into the custody of the police. **46. in charge of, a.** having the care or supervision of: *She is in charge of two libraries.* **b.** under the care or supervision of: *The application should be kept in charge of the personnel office.* [ME *charge(n)* < OF *charg(i)e(r)* < LL *carricāre* to load a wagon, equiv. to *carr(us)* wagon (see CAR[1]) + *-icā-* v. suffix. + *-re* inf. ending] —**charge′less,** *adj.*
—**Syn. 8.** enjoin, exhort, urge, bid, require, order. **11.** indict, arraign, impeach. **16.** assault. **27.** commission, trust. **28.** management. **32.** indictment, imputation, allegation. **35.** See **price. 38.** onslaught, assault. **43.** cargo, freight. —**Ant. 11.** acquit, absolve.

charge·a·ble (chär′jə bəl), *adj.* **1.** that may or should be charged: *chargeable duty on imported goods.* **2.** liable to be accused or held responsible; indictable: *He was held chargeable for the theft.* **3.** liable to become a charge on the public. Also, **chargable.** [ME; see CHARGE, -ABLE] —**charge′a·ble·ness, charge′a·bil′i·ty,** *n.* —**charge′a·bly,** *adv.*

charge′ account′, an account, esp. in retailing, that permits a customer to buy merchandise for which he is billed at a later date.

charge-a-plate (chärj′ə plāt′), *n.* an identification plate, esp. one from which an impression can be taken, issued to a customer and enabling him to make purchases on a credit basis. Also, **charg′a-plate′, charge plate.** [formerly trademark]

charged (chärjd), *adj.* **1.** *Physics.* pertaining to a particle, body, or system possessing a net amount of electricity. **2.** intense; impassioned: *His emotionally charged speech won over the crowd.* **3.** fraught with emotion: *He felt uncomfortable in the charged atmosphere of the room.* **4.** capable of producing violent emotion, arousing controversy, etc.: *He avoided the highly charged issue of birth control.* [ME; see CHARGE, -ED[2]]

char·gé d'af·faires (shär zhā′ də fâr′, shär′zhā; *Fr.* shar zhā da fer′), *pl.* **char·gés d'af·faires** (shär·zhāz′ də fâr′, shär′zhāz; *Fr.* shar zhā da fer′). *Govt.* **1.** Official name, **chargé′ d'affaires′ ad in′terim.** an official placed in charge of diplomatic business during the temporary absence of the ambassador or minister. **2.** an envoy to a state to which a diplomat of higher grade is not sent. Also called **char·gé′.** [< F: lit., one in charge of things]

charge·ful (chärj′fəl), *adj.* *Obs.* costly; expensive. [CHARGE + -FUL]

charge′ of quar′ters, 1. an enlisted man, usually a noncommissioned officer, who remains on duty and handles administrative matters in his unit during the night or on holidays. **2.** the duty of a charge of quarters.

Charge′ of the Light′ Brigade′, The, a narrative poem (1854) by Tennyson, celebrating the 600 men of the British cavalry brigade which attacked the Russian position at Balaklava during the Crimean War.

charge′ plate′, charge-a-plate.

charg·er[1] (chär′jər), *n.* **1.** one who or that which charges. **2.** a horse of a kind suitable to be ridden in battle. **3.** *Elect.* an apparatus which charges storage batteries. [CHARGE + -ER[1]]

charg·er[2] (chär′jər), *n.* *Archaic.* **1.** a platter. **2.** a large, shallow dish for liquids. [ME *chargeour,* lit., load-bearer. See CHARGE, -OR[2]]

Cha·ri (*Fr.* sha rē′), *n.* Shari.

Cha·ric·lo (kə rik′lō), *n.* *Class. Myth.* a beloved companion of Athena. She was the mother, by Everes, of Tiresias.

char·i·ly (châr′ə lē), *adv.* **1.** carefully; warily. **2.** sparingly; frugally. [CHARY + -LY]
—**Syn. 1.** guardedly, cautiously. —**Ant. 1.** boldly. **2.** liberally.

char·i·ness (châr′ē nis), *n.* **1.** the quality of one who or that which is chary. **2.** *Obs.* scrupulous integrity. [CHARY + -NESS]

Char′ing Cross′ (char′ing), a district in central London, England.

char·i·ot (char′ē ət), *n.* **1.** (in ancient Egypt, Greece, Rome, etc.) a light, two-wheeled vehicle for one person, usually drawn by two horses and driven from a standing position, used in warfare, racing, hunting, etc. **2.** a light, four-wheeled pleasure carriage. **3.** any rather stately carriage. —*v.t.* **4.** to convey in a chariot. —*v.i.* **5.** to ride in or drive a chariot. [ME < MF, OF, equiv. to *char* CAR[1] + *-iot* dim. suffix] —**char′i·ot·like′,** *adj.*

Chariot

char·i·ot·eer (char′ē ə tēr′), *n.* **1.** a chariot driver. **2.** (*cap.*) *Astron.* the constellation Auriga. [CHARIOT + -EER; r. ME *charietere* < MF *charetier,* equiv. to OF *charete* cart (*char* CAR[1] + *-ete* -ETTE) + *-ier* -EER]

Cha·ris (kā′ris), *n.* *Class. Myth.* **1.** one of the Graces, married to Hephaestus. **2.** sing. of **Charites.**

Cha·ris (kar′is), *n.* a girl's given name.

cha·ris·ma (kə riz′mə), *n., pl.* **-ma·ta** (-mə tə). **1.** *Theol.* a divinely conferred gift or power. **2.** that special spiritual power or personal quality that gives an individual influence or authority over large numbers of people. **3.** the special virtue of an office, function, position, etc., which confers or is thought to confer on the person holding it an unusual ability for leadership, worthiness of veneration, or the like. Also, **char·ism** (kar′iz əm). [< eccl. L < Gk, equiv. to *char-* (root of *chári̇s* favor and *charízesthai* to favor) + *-isma* -ISM] —**char′is·mat′ic,** *adj.*

char·i·ta·ble (char′i tə bəl), *adj.* **1.** generous in gifts to relieve the needs of indigent or otherwise helpless persons, or of animals: *He wished he had the means to be more charitable.* **2.** kindly or lenient in judging people, acts, etc.: *He is very charitable in his opinions of others.* **3.** pertaining to or concerned with charity: *a charitable institution.* [ME < OF, equiv. to *charit(e)* CHARITY + *-able* -ABLE] —**char′i·ta·ble·ness,** *n.* —**char′i·ta·bly,** *adv.*
—**Syn. 1.** beneficent, liberal, bountiful, benevolent. **2.** broad-minded, considerate, mild. —**Ant. 1.** selfish. **2.** severe, intolerant.

Char·i·tes (kar′i tēz′), *n.pl., sing.* **Cha·ris** (kā′ris). the ancient Greek name for the Graces.

Char·i·ton (shar′i tən), *n.* a town in S Iowa. 5042 (1960).

char·i·ty (char′i tē), *n., pl.* **-ties. 1.** charitable actions, as almsgiving or performing other benevolent actions of any sort for the needy with no expectation of material reward: *to devote one's life to charity.* **2.** something given to a person or persons in need; alms: *She asked for work, not charity.* **3.** a charitable act or work. **4.** a charitable fund, foundation, or institution: *He left his estate to one of his charities.* **5.** benevolent feeling, esp. toward those in need or in disfavor: *She looked so poor that we fed her out of charity.* **6.** Christian love; agape. I Cor. 13. **7.** Jacob's-ladder (def. 1). [ME *charite* < OF < L *cāritāt-* (s. of *cāritās*), equiv. to *cār(us)* dear + *-itāt-* -ITY] —**char′i·ty·less,** *adj.*
—**Syn. 5.** kindliness, consideration, humanity, benignity, sympathy. —**Ant. 5.** malevolence.

Char·i·ty (char′i tē), *n.* a girl's given name.

cha·riv·a·ri (shə riv′ə rē′, shiv′ə rē′, shä′ri vä′rē), *n., pl.* **-ris,** *v.t.,* **-ried, -ri·ing.** shivaree. Also, **chivaree, chivari.** [< F << LL *caribari(a)* headache < Gk *karēbaría,* equiv. to *kárē* head + *-baria* heaviness (*bar(ýs)* heavy + *-ia* -IA)]

chark (chärk), *n.* *Brit. Dial.* **1.** charcoal (def. 1). **2.** coke[1]. —*v.t.* **3.** to char; convert into coke. [back formation from CHARCOAL]

char·kha (chär′kə), *n.* (in India and the East Indies)

a cotton gin or spinning wheel. Also, **char′ka.** [< Urdu < Pers]
char·la·dy (chär′lā′dē), *n., pl.* **-dies.** *Brit.* a charwoman. [CHAR(WOMAN) + LADY]
char·la·tan (shär′lə tᵊn), *n.* one who pretends to more knowledge or skill than he possesses; quack. [< MF < It *ciarlatan(o),* equiv. to *ciarla(tore)* chatterer (deriv. of *ciarlare* to chatter) + *(cerre)tano* hawker, quack, lit., native of *Cerreto,* a village in Umbria, central Italy] —**char·la·tan·ic** (shär′lə tan′ik), **char′la·tan′i·cal, char′la·tan·ish, char′la·tan·is′tic,** *adj.* —**char′la·tan′i·cal·ly,** *adv.*
—**Syn.** impostor, mountebank, fraud, cheat, fake, phony, rogue.
char·la·tan·ism (shär′lə tᵊniz′əm), *n.* **1.** the practice or method of a charlatan. **2.** an instance of this. [CHARLATAN + -ISM]
char·la·tan·ry (shär′lə-tən rē), *n., pl.* **-ries.** charlatanism. [CHARLATAN + -RY]
Char·lee (chär′lē), *n.* a girl's given name.
Char·leen (shär lēn′), *n.* a girl's given name, form of **Caroline.** Also, **Charlene, Charline, Charlyn, Charlyne.**
Char·le·magne (shär′lə mān′; *Fr.* shȧʀ lə-mȧn′yə), *n.* ("*Charles the Great*") A.D. 742–814, king of the Franks 768–814; as Charles I, emperor of the Holy Roman Empire 800–814.

NORTH SEA
ANGLO-SAXONS
London
Paris
SLAVIC PEOPLES
BAY OF BISCAY
Empire of Charlemagne
Rome
MEDIT. SEA
771-814

Char·lene (shär lēn′), *n.* a girl's given name, form of **Caroline.** Also, **Charleen, Charline, Charlyn, Charlyne.**
Char·le·roi (shȧʀ lərwȧ′ *for 1;* shär′lə roi′ *for 2*), *n.* **1.** Also, **Char·le·roy′.** a city in S Belgium. 26,433 (est. 1959). **2.** a town in SW Pennsylvania. 8148 (1960).
Charles (chärlz), *n.* **1.** *(Prince of Edinburgh and of Wales)* born 1948, heir apparent to the throne of Great Britain (son of Elizabeth II). **2. Cape,** a cape in E Virginia, N of the entrance to the Chesapeake Bay. **3.** a river in E Massachusetts, flowing between Boston and Cambridge into the Atlantic. 47 mi. long. **4.** a boy's given name.
Charles I (chärlz; *Fr.* shȧʀl), **1.** Charlemagne. **2.** ("*the Bald*") A.D. 823–877, king of France 840–877; as Charles II, emperor of the Holy Roman Empire 875–877. **3.** 1600–49, king of Great Britain 1625–49 (son of James I). **4.** 1500–58, king of Spain 1516–56; as Charles V, emperor of the Holy Roman Empire 1519–56. **5.** 1887–1922, emperor of Austria 1916–18; as Charles IV, king of Hungary 1916–18.
Charles I Hunting, a portrait (c1635) of King Charles I of England painted by Anthony van Dyck. Also called **Charles I in Hunting Dress.**
Charles II, 1. See **Charles I** (def. 2). **2.** 1630–85, king of Great Britain 1660–85 (son of Charles I of England). **3.** See **Charles III** (def. 1).
Charles III, 1. ("*Charles the Fat*") A.D. 809–888, as Charles II, king of France 884–887; emperor of the Holy Roman Empire 881–887. **2.** See **Charles VI** (def. 2). **3.** 1716–1788, king of Spain 1759–88; as Charles IV, king of Naples 1734–59.
Charles IV, 1. ("*Charles the Fair*") 1294–1328, king of France 1322–28. **2.** See **Charles I** (def. 5). **3.** See **Charles III** (def. 3).
Charles V, 1. ("*Charles the Wise*") 1337–81, king of France 1364–80. **2.** See **Charles I** (def. 4).
Charles VI, 1. ("*Charles the Mad*" or "*Charles the Well-beloved*") 1368–1422, king of France 1380–1422. **2.** 1685–1740, emperor of the Holy Roman Empire 1711–40; as Charles III, king of Hungary 1711–40.
Charles VII, ("*Charles the Victorious*") 1403–61, king of France 1422–61 (son of Charles VI).
Charles IX, 1. 1550–74, king of France 1560–74. **2.** 1550–1611, king of Sweden 1604–11 (son of Gustavus I).
Charles X, 1. (*Charles Gustavus*) 1622–60, king of Sweden 1654–60. **2.** 1757–1836, king of France 1824–30.
Charles XI, 1655–97, king of Sweden 1660–97 (son of Charles X).
Charles XII, 1682–1718, king of Sweden 1697–1718.
Charles XIV. See **Bernadotte, Jean Baptiste Jules.**
Charles′ Cit′y, a town in N Iowa. 9964 (1960).
Charles′ Ed′ward Stu′art. See **Stuart, Charles Edward.**
Charles′′ law′, *Thermodynamics.* See **Gay-Lussac's law.** [named after J. A. C. *Charles* (1746–1823), French physicist, who stated it]
Charles′ Lou′is, (*Karl Ludwig Johann*) 1771–1847, archduke of Austria.
Charles′ Mar·tel′ (mär tel′; *Fr.* mȧʀ tel′), A.D. 690?–741, ruler of the Franks 714–741 (grandfather of Charlemagne).
Charles's Wain (chärl′ziz wān′), *Brit.* dipper (def. 3a). [OE *Carles wægn* Carl's wagon (Carl for Charlemagne); see WAIN]
Charles′ the Great′, Charlemagne.
Charles·ton (chärlz′tən, chärl′stən), *n.* **1.** a city in and the capital of West Virginia, in the W part. 85,796 (1960). **2.** a seaport in SE South Carolina. 65,925 (1960). **3.** a town in SE Missouri. 5911 (1960). **4.** a town in central Mississippi. 2528 (1960).
Charles·ton (chärlz′tən, chärl′stən), *n.* a vigorous, rhythmic ballroom dance popular in the 1920's. [named after CHARLESTON, South Carolina]
Charles′ Town′, a town in E West Virginia. 3329 (1960).
Charles·town (chärlz′toun′), *n.* **1.** a former city in E Massachusetts: since 1874 a part of Boston; navy yard; battle of Bunker Hill June 17, 1775. **2.** a town in SE Indiana. 5726 (1960).
Charle·ton (chärl′tᵊn), *n.* a boy's given name.
Char·le·voix (shär′lə voi′), *n.* a town in NW Michigan. 2751 (1960).
char′ley horse′ (chär′lē), a painful, involuntary contraction of an arm or leg muscle resulting from excessive muscular strain or a blow. [orig. baseball slang]
Char·lie (chär′lē), *n.* **1.** a word used in communications to represent the letter C. **2.** a boy's given name, form of **Charles. 3.** a girl's given name. Also, **Char′ley.**
Char′lie No′ble (nō′bəl), *Naut. Slang.* the smoke pipe of a ship's galley. Also, **Char′ley No′bel.** [prob. after a proper name]
Char·line (shär lēn′), *n.* a girl's given name, form of **Caroline.** Also, **Charleen, Charlene, Charlyn, Charlyne.**
char·lock (chär′lək), *n.* the wild mustard, *Brassica arvensis,* often troublesome as a weed in grainfields. [ME *cherlok,* OE *cerlic* < ?]
Char·lot (shär′lō; *Fr.* shȧʀ lō′), *n.* **Jean** (jēn; *Fr.* zhäɴ), born 1898, U.S. painter, lithographer, and illustrator; born in France.
char·lotte (shär′lət), *n.* a dessert of many varieties, served hot or cold and commonly made by lining a mold with cake or bread and filling it with fruit, whipped cream, custard, or gelatin. [< F, special use of woman's name]
Char·lotte (shär′lət), *n.* **1. Grand Duchess,** born 1896, sovereign of Luxembourg 1919–64. **2.** a city in S North Carolina. 201,564 (1960). **3.** a town in central Michigan. 7657 (1960). **4.** a girl's given name.
Char·lot·te A·ma·li·e (shär lot′ə ä mä′lē ə), a seaport in and the capital of the Virgin Islands, on St. Thomas. 12,880 (1960). Formerly, **St. Thomas.**
Char·lot·ten·burg (shär lot′ᵊn bûrg′; *Ger.* shär lôt′ᵊn bo͝oʀkh′), *n.* a residential neighborhood in West Berlin, Germany.
char′lotte russe′ (ro͞os′), a dessert made by lining a mold with sponge cake or ladyfingers and filling it with Bavarian cream. [< F: lit., Russian charlotte]
Char·lottes·ville (shär′ləts vil′), *n.* a city in central Virginia. 29,427 (1960).
Char·lotte·town (shär′lət toun′), *n.* a seaport on and the capital of Prince Edward Island, in SE Canada. 18,318 (1961).
Char·lye (chär′lē), *n.* a girl's given name.
Char·lyne (shär′lin, shär lēn′), *n.* a girl's given name, form of **Caroline.** Also, **Charleen, Charlene, Charline, Char·lyn** (shär′lin).
charm[1] (chärm), *n.* **1.** a power of pleasing or attracting, as through personality or beauty: *charm of manner; the charm of a mountain lake.* **2.** a trait or feature imparting this power. **3. charms,** attractiveness: *to succumb to feminine charms.* **4.** a trinket to be worn on a chain, bracelet, etc. **5.** something worn for its supposed magical effect; amulet. **6.** any action supposed to have magical power. **7.** the chanting or recitation of a magic verse or formula. **8.** a verse or formula credited with magical power. **9.** *Physics.* a hypothetical quality of an elementary nuclear particle thought to be a fourth quark (**charmed′ quark′**). —*v.t.* **10.** to delight or please greatly by beauty, attractiveness, etc.; enchant: *She charmed us with her graceful manner.* **11.** to act upon (someone or something) with or as with a compelling or magical force: *to charm a bird from a tree.* **12.** to endow with or protect by supernatural powers: *His life seemed to be charmed.* **13.** to gain or influence through personal charm: *He's used to charming his way out of the trouble he causes.* —*v.i.* **14.** to be fascinating or pleasing. **15.** to use charms. **16.** to act as a charm. [ME *charme* < OF < L *carm(en)* song, magical formula, var. of **canmen* (by assimilation), equiv. to *can(ere)* (to) sing + *-men* n. suffix] —**charm·ed·ly** (chär′mid lē), *adv.* —**charm′er,** *n.* —**charm′less,** *adj.* —**charm′less·ly,** *adv.*
—**Syn. 1.** attractiveness, allurement. **4.** bauble. **5.** talisman. **6.** enchantment, spell, sorcery. **8.** spell. **11.** fascinate, captivate, entrance, enrapture, transport, delight, ravish; allure, bewitch. —**Ant. 1.** repulsion.
charm[2] (chärm), *n. Brit. Dial.* blended singing of birds, children, etc. [ME *cherm(e),* OE *cerm, ceorm,* var. of *ci(e)rm* outcry; see CHIRM]
charmed′ cir′cle, a select or privileged group or body: *His extraordinary talent had earned him a place in the charmed circle of concert artists.*
charmed′ life′, a life unusually free of misfortune, as if protected by magic charms.
char·meuse (shär mo͞oz′; *Fr.* shȧʀ mœz′), *n.* a soft, flexible satin, of silk, acetate, nylon, rayon, or other material. [formerly trademark]
Char·mi·an (chär′mē ən), *n.* a girl's given name.
charm·ing (chär′ming), *adj.* **1.** pleasing; delightful. **2.** exercising magic power. [ME; see CHARM[1], -ING[2]] —**charm′ing·ly,** *adv.* —**charm′ing·ness,** *n.*
charm′ school′, a school for teaching proper social behavior and dress.
char·nel (chär′nᵊl), *n.* **1.** a repository for dead bodies. —*adj.* **2.** of, like, or fit for a charnel; deathlike; sepulchral. [ME < MF < LL *carnāl(e),* n. use of neut. of *carnālis* CARNAL]
char′nel house′, a house or place in which the bodies or bones of the dead are deposited.
char·nu (*Fr.* shȧʀ ny′), *adj.* **1.** (of a wine) full-bodied. —*n.* **2.** a full-bodied wine. [< F: lit., fleshed]
Char·on (kâr′ən, kar′-), *n.* **1.** *Class. Myth.* the ferryman who conveyed the souls of the dead across the Styx. **2.** (usually used ironically) any ferryman. —**Cha·ro·ni·an** (kə rō′nē ən), **Cha·ron·ic** (kə ron′ik), *adj.*
Cha·rops (kā′rops), *n. Class. Myth.* an epithet of Hercules, meaning "with bright eyes."
cha·ro·seth (khä rō′set, -ses; *Eng.* khä rō′sis), *n. Hebrew.* haroseth. Also, **cha·ro′set.**
Char·pen·tier (shȧʀ päɴ tyā′), *n.* **1. Gus·tave** (gy-stȧv′), 1860–1956, French composer. **2. Marc An·toine** (mȧʀk äɴ twȧn′), 1634–1704, French composer.
char·poy (chär′poi′), *n.* a light bedstead used in India. Also, **char·pai** (chär′pī′). [< Urdu *chārpāī* < Pers, equiv. to *ch(ah)ār* FOUR + *pāi* FOOT]
char·qui (chär′kē), *n.* jerky[2]. [< Sp < Quechua *ch′arki* dried meat] —**char·quid** (chär′kid), *adj.*
charr (chär), *n., pl.* **charrs,** (*esp. collectively*) **charr.** char[2].
char·rette (shə ret′), *n.* a final, intensive effort to finish a project, esp. an architectural design project, before a deadline. Also, **charette.** [< F: cart, OF, equiv. to *char* chariot, wagon (see CAR[1]) + *-ette* -ETTE, from the idea of speed of wheels]
char·ro (chär′ō; *Sp.* chär′ʀō), *n., pl.* **char·ros** (chär′ōz; *Sp.* chär′ʀōs). (in Mexico) a cowboy. [< MexSp, Sp: coarse, flashy < Basque *txar* poor, weak]
char·ry (chär′ē), *adj.,* **-ri·er, -ri·est.** of, like, or covered with charcoal. [CHAR[1] + -Y[1]]
chart (chärt), *n.* **1.** a sheet exhibiting information in tabulated or methodical form. **2.** a graphic representation, as by curves, of a dependent variable, as temperature, price, etc.; graph. **3.** a map, esp. a hydrographic or marine map. **4.** an outline map showing special conditions or facts: *a weather chart.* **5.** *Jazz.* a musical arrangement. —*v.t.* **6.** to make a chart of. **7.** to plan: *to chart a course of action.* [< MF *charte* < L *c(h)arta;* see CHARTA] —**chart′a·ble,** *adj.* —**chart′less,** *adj.*
—**Syn. 3.** See **map.**
chart., (in prescriptions) a paper. [< L *charta*]
char·ta (kär′tə), *n., pl.* **-tae** (-tē). *Pharm.* **1.** a strip of paper that is impregnated with a medicinal agent, for external application. **2.** Also called **chartula, powder paper.** a paper folded so as to form a packet for a powdered medicament. [< NL, L: sheet of paper, document < Gk *chárt(ēs)* papyrus leaf, sheet of paper, lit., something to make marks on; see CHARACTER]
char·ta·ceous (kär tā′shəs), *adj.* of or like paper; papery. [< L *chartāceus* made of paper. See CHARTA, -ACEOUS]
chart. cerat., (in prescriptions) waxed paper. [< L *charta cērāta*]
char·ter (chär′tər), *n.* **1.** a document, issued by a sovereign or state, outlining the conditions under which a corporation, colony, city, or other corporated body is organized, and defining its rights and privileges. **2.** (*often cap.*) a document defining the formal organization of a corporate body; constitution: *the Charter of the United Nations.* **3.** authorization from a central or parent organization to establish a new branch, chapter, etc. **4.** a grant by a sovereign power creating a corporation, as the royal charters granted to British colonies in America. **5.** Also, **char′ter par′ty.** a contract by which part or all of a ship is leased for a voyage or a stated time. **6.** special privilege or immunity. —*v.t.* **7.** to establish by charter: *to charter a bank.* **8.** to lease or hire: *The company will charter six buses for the picnic.* **9.** to give special favor or privilege to. —*adj.* **10.** done or held in accordance with a charter: *a charter school.* [ME *chartre* < OF < L *chartul(a)* little paper (by assimilation), equiv. to *chart(a)* (see CHARTA) + *-ula* -ULE] —**char′ter·a·ble,** *adj.* —**char′ter·age,** *n.* —**char′ter·er,** *n.* —**char′ter·less,** *adj.*
—**Syn. 8.** See **hire.**
char′ter col′ony, *Amer. Hist.* a colony, as Virginia, Massachusetts, Connecticut, or Rhode Island, chartered to an individual, trading company, etc., by the British crown. Cf. **royal colony** (def. 2).
char′tered account′ant, *Brit.* a member of the institute of accountants granted a royal charter. *Abbr.:* C.A.
Char·ter·house (chär′tər hous′), *n., pl.* **-hous·es** (-hou′ziz). **1.** a Carthusian monastery. **2.** the hospital and charitable institution founded in London, in 1611, on the site of the Carthusian monastery. **3.** the public school into which this hospital was converted. **4.** the modern heir of this school, now located in Surrey. [< AF *chartrouse* (taken as CHARTER + HOUSE), after *Chatrousse,* village in Dauphiné near which the order was founded; see CARTHUSIAN, whence the first *r* of the AF word]
Char′terhouse of Par′ma, The (pär′mə), a novel (1839) by Stendhal. French, **La Char·treuse de Parme** (lȧ shȧʀ trœz′ də pȧʀm′).
char′ter mem′ber, one of the original members or founders of a club, organization, etc.
Char′ter school′, any of the Protestant schools established under English rule in Ireland during the 18th century for the education of poor Roman Catholics.
chart′ house′, *Naut.* a room or deckhouse for storing and working with charts, navigational instruments, etc. Also called **chart room.**
Chart·ism (chär′tiz əm), *n.* the principles or movement of a party of political reformers, chiefly workingmen, in England from 1838 to 1848: so called from the document **(People's Charter** or **National Charter)** which contained a statement of their principles and demands. [CHART charter (now obs.) + -ISM; r. *Charterism;* see CHARTER] —**Chart′ist,** *n., adj.*
char·tist (chär′tist), *n.* **1.** a specialist in the stock market who studies and draws charts of trading actions. **2.** a cartographer. [CHART + -IST]
chart·let (chärt′lit), *n. Navig.* a small chart indicating some special thing, as information relative to a radio navigational aid. [CHART + -LET]
char·tog·ra·phy (kär tog′rə fē), *n.* cartography. —**char·tog′ra·pher,** *n.* —**char·to·graph·ic** (kär′tə-graf′ik), **char′to·graph′i·cal,** *adj.* —**char′to·graph′i·cal·ly,** *adv.*
char·to·phy·la·cium (kär′tō fi lā′shəm), *n., pl.* **-cia** (-shə). (in a medieval church) a place for the keeping of records and documents. [< LGk *chartophylákion,* equiv. to *charto-* (comb. form of *chártēs;* see CHARTA) + *phylákion* a watch; see PHYLACTERY]
char·to·phy·lax (khär′tō fē′läks; *Eng.* kär tof′ə-laks′), *n., pl.* **-lax·es** (-lä kes; *Eng.* -lak′siz). *Gk. Orth. Ch.* an official who serves chiefly as the chancellor and archivist of a diocese. [< LGk, Gk, equiv. to *charto-* (see CHARTOPHYLACIUM) + *phýlax* watcher, guard]
Char·tres (shär′trə, shärt; *Fr.* shȧʀ′trᵊ), *n.* a city in and the capital of Eure-et-Loir, in N France, SW of Paris: cathedral. 33,992 (1962).
char·treuse (shär tro͞oz′; *Fr.* shȧʀ trœz′), *n.* **1.** (*sometimes cap.*) an aromatic liqueur made by the Carthusian monks at Grenoble, France, and, at one time, at Tarragona, Spain. **2.** a clear, light green with a yellowish tinge. —*adj.* **3.** of the color chartreuse. [< F, after La Grande *Chartreuse,* Carthusian monastery near Grenoble, where the liqueur is made]
Char·treuse de Parme, La (*Fr.* lȧ shȧʀ trœz′ də pȧʀm′). See **Charterhouse of Parma, The.**
chart′ room′, *Naut.* See **chart house.**
char·tu·la (kär′chə lə), *n., pl.* **-lae** (-lē′). *Pharm.* charta (def. 2). [< NL, L, equiv. to *chart(a)* piece of paper (see CHARTA) + *-ula* -ULE]
char·tu·lar·y (kär′chə ler′ē), *n., pl.* **-lar·ies. 1.** a register of charters, title deeds, etc. **2.** one who keeps archives. Also, **cartulary.** [< ML *chartulāri(um),* equiv. to L *chartul(a)* CHARTER + *-ārium* -ARY]
Char·va·ka (chär′vä kə, -və-), *n.* Lokayatika.
char·vet (shär′vā, shär vā′), *n.* a soft, lusterless silk or rayon tie fabric, often made with a faint stripe effect. [named after the French firm]

char·wom·an (chär′wo͝om′ən), *n., pl.* **-wom·en.** a woman hired to do household work, esp. heavy cleaning, usually by the day. [CHAR³ + WOMAN]

char·y (châr′ē), *adj.,* **char·i·er, char·i·est. 1.** careful; wary: *He was chary of his reputation.* **2.** shy; timid. **3.** fastidious; choosy: *She is excessively chary about her friends.* **4.** sparing (often fol. by *of*): *chary of his praise.* [ME; OE *cearig* sorrowful (*c(e)ar(u)* CARE + *-ig* -Y¹); c. OS *karag,* OHG *karag* (G *karg* scanty, paltry)] —**Syn. 1.** cautious, circumspect. **4.** frugal. —**Ant. 1.** trustful. **2.** confident. **3.** uncritical. **4.** lavish.

Cha·ryb·dis (kə rib′dis), *n.* **1.** a whirlpool in the Strait of Messina off the NE coast of Sicily. Modern, **Galofalo, Garofalo. 2.** *Class. Myth.* a daughter of Gaea and Poseidon, a monster mentioned in Homer and later identified with the whirlpool Charybdis. Cf. **Scylla** (def. 2). —**Cha·ryb′di·an,** *adj.*

chase¹ (chās), *v.,* **chased, chas·ing,** *n.* —*v.t.* **1.** to pursue in order to seize, overtake, etc.: *The policeman chased the thief.* **2.** to pursue with intent to capture or kill, as game; hunt: *The sportsman chased the buck through the woods.* **3.** to follow or devote one's attention to with the hope of attracting, winning, gaining, etc.: *He chased her for three years, before she consented to marry him.* **4.** to drive by pursuing: *She chased him out of the room.* **5.** to put to flight: *Her look of contempt chased her would-be suitor away.* —*v.i.* **6.** to follow in pursuit: *to chase after someone.* **7.** *Informal.* to run or hasten: *She's always chasing from one store to another.* —*n.* **8.** the act of chasing; pursuit: *The chase lasted a day.* **9.** an object of pursuit; something chased. **10.** *Chiefly Brit.* a private game preserve; a tract of privately owned land reserved for, and sometimes stocked with, animals and birds to be hunted. **11.** *Brit.* the right of keeping game or of hunting on the land of others. **12.** a steeplechase. **13. give chase,** to pursue: *The hunt began and the dogs gave chase.* **14. the chase,** the sport or occupation of hunting. [ME *chace(n)* < MF *chasse(r)* (to) hunt, OF *chacier* < VL **captiāre;* see CATCH] —**chase′a·ble,** *adj.*

chase² (chās), *n.* **1.** a rectangular iron frame in which composed type is secured or locked for printing or platemaking. [< MF *chasse* < L *capsa* CASE²] **2.** a groove, furrow, or trench; a lengthened hollow. **3.** *Ordn.* **a.** the part of a gun in front of the trunnions. **b.** the part containing the bore. [< MF *chas* < LL *capsus* (masc.), *capsum* (neut.) fully or partly enclosed space, var. of *capsa* CASE²]

chase³ (chās), *v.t.,* **chased, chas·ing. 1.** to ornament (metal) by engraving or embossing. **2.** to cut (a screw thread), as with a chaser or machine tool. [aph. var. of ENCHASE]

Chase (chās), *n.* **1. Mary Ellen,** born 1887, U.S. educator, novelist, and essayist. **2. Sal·mon Portland** (sal′mən), 1808–73, U.S. statesman: Chief Justice of the U.S. 1864–73. **3. Samuel,** 1741–1811, U.S. jurist and leader in the American Revolution: associate justice of the U.S. Supreme Court 1796–1811. **4. Stuart,** born 1888, U.S. economist and writer.

Chase′ Cit′y, a town in S Virginia. 3207 (1960).

chase′ mor′tise, a mortise having one inclined narrow side. —**chase′ mor′tised.**

chas·er¹ (chā′sər), *n.* **1.** one who or that which chases or pursues. **2.** *U.S. Informal.* a drink of water, beer, or other mild beverage taken after a drink of liquor. **3.** Also called **chase′ gun′.** (on a vessel) a gun esp. for use when in chase or when being chased. **4.** a hunter. **5.** *Theat.* **a.** *Chiefly Brit.* the final act or musical number of a vaudeville or variety show. **b.** the music played as the audience leaves a theater. [ME; see CHASE¹, -ER¹]

chas·er² (chā′sər), *n.* a tool with multiple teeth for cutting screw threads. [CHASE² + -ER¹]

chas·er³ (chā′sər), *n.* a person who engraves metal. [CHASE³ + -ER¹]

cha·shit·su (chä shēt′so͞o), *n. Japanese.* a building or room in which tea is ceremoniously prepared and drunk.

Cha·sid (hä′sid; *Heb.* ᴋʜä sēd′), *n., pl.* **Cha·sid·im** (hä′si dim, hä sid′im; *Heb.* ᴋʜä sē dēm′). *Judaism.* Hasid. —**Cha·sid·ic** (hä sid′ik, hə-), *adj.* —**Cha′sid·ism,** *n.*

chas·ing (chā′sing), *n.* **1.** a design chased on metal. **2.** an object decorated by chasing. [CHASE³ + -ING¹]

Chas·ka (chas′kə), *n.* a town in central Minnesota. 2501 (1960).

Chasles (shäl), *n.* **Mi·chel** (mē shel′), 1793–1880, French mathematician.

chasm (kaz′əm), *n.* **1.** a yawning fissure or deep cleft in the earth's surface; gorge. **2.** a breach or wide fissure in a wall or other structure. **3.** a marked interruption of continuity; gap: *a chasm in time.* **4.** a sundering breach in relations, as a divergence of opinions, beliefs, etc., between persons or groups. [apocopated var. of *chasma* < L < Gk, equiv. to *cha-* (root of *chaínein* to gape; see YAWN) + *-(a)sma* resultative suffix] —**chas′mal, chas′mic,** *adj.* —**chasmed,** *adj.* —**chasm′y,** *adj.*

chas·mog·a·my (kaz mog′ə mē), *n.* (in flowers that are not self-pollinating) the opening of the perianth at the maturity of the flower, when its stigma is receptive to pollen. [< Gk *chásm(a)* wide opening (see CHASM) + -O- + -GAMY] —**chas·mo·gam·ic** (kaz′mə gam′ik), **chas·mog′a·mous,** *adj.*

chas·mo·phyte (kaz′mə fīt′), *n. Bot.* a plant that grows in the crevices of rocks. [< Gk *chásm(a)* wide opening (see CHASM) + -O- + -PHYTE]

chas·sé (sha sā′; *or, esp. in square dancing,* sa shā′), *n., v.,* **chas·séd, chas·sé·ing.** *Dance.* —*n.* **1.** a kind of gliding step in which one foot is kept in advance of the other. —*v.i.* **2.** to execute a chassé. [< F: lit., chased, followed, ptp. of *chasser* to CHASE¹]

chasse·pot (shas′pō; *Fr.* shᴀs pō′), *n., pl.* **-pots** (-pōz; *Fr.* -pō′). a breechloading rifle, closed with a sliding bolt, introduced into the French army after the war between Austria and Prussia in 1866. [named after A. A. *Chassepot* (1833–1905), French mechanic, who invented it]

chas·seur (sha sûr′; *Fr.* shᴀ sœʀ′), *n., pl.* **-seurs** (-sûrz′; *Fr.* -sœʀ′). **1.** (in the French army) one of a body of troops (cavalry or infantry) equipped and trained for rapid movement. **2.** a uniformed footman or attendant; liveried servant. **3.** one who hunts; hunter. [< F: lit., chaser; see CHASE¹]

chas·sis (shas′ē, -is, chas′ē), *n., pl.* **chas·sis** (shas′ēz, chas′-). **1.** *Auto.* the frame, wheels and machinery of a motor vehicle, on which the body is supported. **2.** *Ordn.* the frame or railway on which a gun carriage moves backward and forward. **3.** the main landing gear of an aircraft; that portion of the landing gear that supports an aircraft. **4.** *Radio and Television.* **a.** the metal base on which the tube sockets, wiring, and other parts of a radio or television set are mounted. **b.** the collection of various sections of a receiving set mounted on a foundation. **5.** a construction forming the sides, top, and bottom of a cabinet, showcase, or the like. [< F *châssis* frame; akin to CHASE²]

chaste (chāst), *adj.,* **chast·er, chast·est. 1.** not having engaged in unlawful sexual intercourse; virtuous. **2.** free from obscenity; decent: *chaste conversation.* **3.** undefiled or stainless: *chaste, white snow.* **4.** pure in style; subdued; simple. **5.** *Obs.* unmarried. [ME < OF < L *cast(us)* clean, pure, chaste] —**chaste′ly,** *adv.* —**chaste′ness,** *n.* —**Syn. 1.** continent. **2.** clean, elevated. **3.** unsullied. **4.** unaffected, unadorned, neat; classic; elegant. —**Ant. 1.** immoral. **2.** coarse. **3.** debased. **4.** ornate.

chas·ten (chā′sən), *v.t.* **1.** to inflict suffering upon for purposes of moral improvement; chastise. **2.** to restrain; subdue: *Age has chastened his violent temper.* **3.** to make chaste in style. [CHASTE + -EN¹; r. chaste (v.), ME *chast(ien)* < OF *chastie(r)* < L *castigāre;* see CASTIGATE] —**chas′ten·er,** *n.* —**chas′ten·ing·ly,** *adv.* —**chas′ten·ment,** *n.* —**Syn. 1.** discipline, punish. **2.** humble. **3.** purify, simplify. —**Ant. 1.** indulge.

chaste′ tree′, a shrub or small tree, *vitex Agnus-castus,* of southern Europe, having pleasant-smelling, hairy foliage and fragrant, pale lilac-blue flowers in dense, showy, terminal spikes. Also called **hemp tree, monk's pepper tree.** [trans. of L *agnus castus,* var. of *agnos castus* (by influence of *agnus* lamb) < Gk *ágnos* kind of willow + L *castus* chaste, reinforcement of the idea thought to be in *ágnos* by confusion with Gk *hagnós* pure]

chas·tise (chas tīz′), *v.t.,* **-tised, -tis·ing. 1.** to discipline, esp. by corporal punishment. **2.** *Archaic.* to restrain; chasten. **3.** *Archaic.* to refine; purify. [ME *chastise(n),* equiv. to *chasti(en)* (to) CHASTEN + *-se(n)* < ?] —**chas·tis′a·ble,** *adj.* —**chas·tise·ment** (chas′tiz mənt, chas tīz′-), *n.* —**chas·tis′er,** *n.* —**Syn. 1.** punish, castigate; whip, beat, flog, lash, spank.

chas·ti·ty (chas′ti tē), *n.* **1.** the state or quality of being chaste. **2.** virginity. [ME *chastite,* var. of *chastete* < OF < L *castitāt-* (s. of *castitās*), equiv. to *cast(us)* CHASTE + *-itāt-* -ITY]

chas′tity belt′, a beltlike device, worn by women esp. in the Middle Ages, designed to prevent sexual intercourse.

chas·u·ble (chaz′yə bəl, -ə bəl, chas′-), *n. Eccles.* a sleeveless outer vestment worn by the celebrant at Mass. [< F < LL *casubla,* unexplained var. of L *casula* little house (see CASA, -ULE); r. ME *chesible* < OF] —**chas′u·bled,** *adj.*

A, Chasuble
B, Maniple

chat¹ (chat), *v.,* **chat·ted, chat·ting,** *n.* —*v.i.* **1.** to converse in a familiar or informal manner. —*n.* **2.** informal conversation: *We had a pleasant chat.* **3.** any of several small, Old World thrushes, esp. of the genus *Saxicola,* having a chattering cry. **4.** See **yellow-breasted chat.** [short for CHATTER] —**chat′ta·ble,** *adj.* —**chat′ting·ly,** *adv.*

chat² (chat), *n.* **1.** an ament, as of a birch. **2.** a samara, as of an ash. **3.** a spike, as of barley. **4.** Usually, **chats.** waste from a zinc mine. [ME *chatte* catkin < MF < L *catta* she-cat; see CAT¹]

Chât., (esp. in Bordeaux wines) Château.

châ·teau (sha tō′; *Fr.* shä tō′), *n., pl.* **-teaus, -teaux** (-tōz′; *Fr.* -tō′). **1.** a castle in a French-speaking country. **2.** a stately residence imitating a distinctively French castle. **3.** a country estate, esp. a fine one, in France and elsewhere on the Continent. **4.** a vineyard estate in the Bordeaux wine region of France. [< F << L *castell(um)* CASTLE]

Châ·teau·bri·and (shä tō brē äN′), *n.* **1. Fran·çois Re·né** (fräN swa′ rə nā′), **Vicomte de,** 1768–1848, French author and statesman. **2.** (*sometimes l.c.*) a thick slice of tenderloin, broiled and served with potatoes and a sauce, often a béarnaise sauce.

châ·teau d'eau (shä tō dō′), *pl.* **châ·teaux d'eau** (shä tō dō′). *French.* an architecturally treated fountain or cistern. [lit: castle of water]

Châ·teau′ d'Y·quem′ (dē kem′), **1.** a sweet white wine of France. **2.** the chateau in the Sauternes district where this wine is produced. Also, **Châ·teau′ Y·quem′.**

Châ·teau·neuf-du-Pape (shä tō nœf dʏ pap′), *n.* a dry red or white wine from the Rhone valley near Avignon. [named after a village, center of its production]

Châ·teau·roux (shä tō ʀo͞o′), *n.* a city in and capital of Indre, in central France. 46,772 (1962).

Châ·teau-Thier·ry (sha tō′tē′ə rē; *Fr.* shä tō tye ʀē′), *n.* a town in N France, on the Marne River: scene of heavy fighting 1918. 10,619 (1962).

châ·teau′ wine′, wine made at a vineyard estate in the Bordeaux region of France.

chat·e·lain (shat′ᵊlān′; *Fr.* shätᵊ lᴀN′), *n., pl.* **chat·e·lains** (shat′ᵊlānz′; *Fr.* shätᵊ lᴀN′). a castellan. [< MF < L *castellān(us)* CASTELLAN]

chat·e·laine (shat′ᵊlān′; *Fr.* shätᵊ len′), *n., pl.* **chat·e·laines** (shat′ᵊlānz′; *Fr.* shätᵊ len′). **1.** the mistress of a castle. **2.** the mistress of an elegant or fashionable household. **3.** a hooklike clasp for suspending keys, trinkets, etc., worn at the waist by women. **4.** a woman's lapel ornament. [< F *châtelaine.* See CHATELAIN]

Chat·ham (chat′əm), *n.* **1. 1st Earl of.** See **Pitt, William, 1st Earl of Chatham. 2.** a city in N Kent, in SE England. 48,989 (1961). **3.** a town in NE New Jersey. 9517 (1960).

Chat′ham Is′lands, a group of islands in the S Pacific, E of and belonging to New Zealand. 372 sq. mi.

cha·ton (shᴀ tôN′), *n., pl.* **-tons** (-tôN′). **1.** Also called **chaton′ foil′.** an imitation gem of paste that has its pavilion backed with metal foil or silver to reflect light. **2.** a bezel in a ring. [< F; OF *chastun* < Gmc]

cha·toy·ant (shə toi′ənt), *adj.* **1.** changing in luster or color: *chatoyant silk.* **2.** *Jewelry.* reflecting a single streak of light when cut in a cabochon. [< F, special use of prp. of *chatoyer* to change luster like a cat's eye, equiv. to *chat* CAT + *-oy-* v. suffix + *-ant* -ANT] —**cha·toy′an·cy,** *n.*

Chat·ta·hoo·chee (chat′ə ho͞o′chē), *n.* **1.** a river flowing S from N Georgia along part of the boundary between Alabama and Georgia into the Apalachicola River. ab. 418 mi. long. **2.** a town in NW Florida. 9699 (1960).

Chat·ta·noo·ga (chat′ᵊno͞o′gə), *n.* a city in SE Tennessee, on the Tennessee River: Civil War battles 1863. 130,009 (1960). —**Chat′ta·noo′gan, Chat·ta·noo·gi·an** (chat′ᵊno͞o′jē ən), *adj., n.*

chat·tel (chat′ᵊl), *n.* **1.** a movable article of property. **2.** any article of tangible property other than land, buildings, and other things annexed to land. **3.** a slave. [ME *chatel* < OF. See CATTLE] —**Syn. 1.** See **property.**

chat′tel mort′gage, *U.S.* a mortgage on household, movable, or other personal property.

chat·ter (chat′ər), *v.i.* **1.** to utter a succession of quick, inarticulate, speechlike sounds, as certain animals, birds, etc.: *The monkey chattered as he swung from branch to branch.* **2.** to talk rapidly and to little purpose; jabber. **3.** to make a rapid clicking noise by striking together, as the teeth from cold. **4.** *Mach.* (of a cutting tool or piece of metal) to vibrate during cutting so as to produce surface flaws on the work. —*v.t.* **5.** to utter rapidly or idly. **6.** to cause to chatter, as the teeth from cold. —*n.* **7.** idle or foolish talk. **8.** a series of waves or ridges on the surface of a piece of metal that has been imperfectly drawn or extruded. **9.** the act or sound of chattering. [ME *chater(en);* imit.] —**chat′ter·ing·ly,** *adv.* —**chat′ter·y,** *adj.*

chat·ter·box (chat′ər boks′), *n.* an excessively talkative person. [i.e., one whose voice box is full of chatter]

chat·ter·er (chat′ər ər), *n.* **1.** one who chatters; a chatterbox. **2.** any of several passerine birds having a chattering cry, as certain waxwings and cotingas. [CHATTER + -ER¹]

chat′ter mark′, 1. a mark left by a tool that has been chattering. **2.** any of a series of irregular gouges made on rock surfaces by the slipping of rock fragments held in the lower portion of a glacier.

Chat·ter·ton (chat′ər tən), *n.* **Thomas,** 1752–70, English poet. —**Chat·ter·to·ni·an** (chat′ər tō′nē ən), *adj., n.*

chat·ty (chat′ē), *adj.,* **-ti·er, -ti·est.** given to or full of chat or familiar talk; conversational: *a chatty letter; a chatty person.* [CHAT¹ + -Y¹] —**chat′ti·ly,** *adv.* —**chat′ti·ness,** *n.*

Chat·wood (chat′wo͝od′), *n.* a town in SE Pennsylvania. 3621 (1960).

Chau·cer (chô′sər), *n.* **Geoffrey,** 1340?–1400, English poet.

Chau·ce·ri·an (chô sēr′ē ən), *adj.* **1.** of, pertaining to, or characteristic of Chaucer's writings: *Chaucerian wit.* —*n.* **2.** a scholar devoted to the study of Chaucer and his writings. [CHAUCER + -IAN]

chaud·froid (*Fr.* shō fʀwä′), *n.* a cooked dish of fowl or game, served cold with aspic, jelly, or a sauce. Also, **chaud-froid′.** [< F: lit., hot-cold, equiv. to *chaud* (< L *cal(i)dus;* see CALDARIUM) + *froid* < L *frigid(us)* FRIGID]

chauf·fer (chô′fər), *n.* a small, portable stove. [ME *chafer* (see CHAFE, -ER¹) + F *chauffoir* heater]

chauf·feur (shō′fər, shō fûr′), *n.* **1.** one employed to drive another's automobile. —*v.t., v.i.* **2.** to drive or work as a chauffeur: *He has chauffeured my car for five years. He chauffeurs for me.* [< F, equiv. to *chauff(er)* (to) heat (see CHAFE) + *-eur* -OR²] —**chauf′feur·ship′,** *n.*

chauf·feuse (shō fœz′), *n., pl.* **-feuses** (-fœz′). *Fr. Furniture.* a fireside chair having a low seat and a high back. [< F, fem. of *chauffeur.* See CHAUFFEUR]

chaul·moo·gra (chôl mo͞o′grə), *n.* an East Indian tree, of the genus *Taraktogenos* (or *Hydnocarpus*), the seeds of which yield chaulmoogra oil. [< Bengali *cāulmugrā* kind of tree]

chaulmoo′gra oil′, a brownish-yellow oil or soft fat expressed from the seeds of a chaulmoogra tree, used formerly in the treatment of leprosy and skin diseases.

Chau·mont (shō môN′), *n.* a city in and the capital of Haute-Marne, in NE France. 23,314 (1962). Also called **Chau·mont-en-Bas·si·gny** (shō môN äN bᴀ sē nyē′).

Chaun·cey (chôn′sē, chän′-), *n.* a boy's given name.

chaunt (chônt, chänt), *n., v.t., v.i. Obs.* chant. —**chaunt′er,** *n.*

chausses (shōs), *n.* (*construed as pl.*) medieval armor of mail for the legs and feet. [late ME *chauces* < MF, pl. of *chauce* << L *calce(us)* shoe, equiv. to *calc-* (s. of *calx*) heel + *-eus* -EOUS]

Chaus·son (shō sôN′), *n.* **Er·nest** (ᴇʀ nest′), 1855–99, French composer.

chaus·sure (shō sʏʀ′), *n., pl.* **-sures** (-sʏʀ′). *French.* footwear; any foot covering, as a shoe, boot, etc.

Chau·tau·qua (shə tô′kwə), *n.* **1. Lake,** a lake in SW New York. 18 mi. long. **2.** a village on this lake: summer educational center. **3.** the annual Chautauqua meeting, providing public lectures, concerts, and dramatic performances during the summer months, usually in an outdoor setting. **4.** (*often l.c.*) any similar assembly, esp. one of a number meeting in a circuit of communities. —*adj.* **5.** of or pertaining to a system of education flourishing in the late 19th and early 20th centuries, originating at Lake Chautauqua, New York. **6.** (*often l.c.*) pertaining to a chautauqua: *a chautauqua program.*

Chau·temps (shō täN′), *n.* **Ca·mille** (kᴀ mē′yᵊ), born 1885, French politician: premier 1930, 1933–34, 1937–38.

chau·vin·ism (shō′və niz′əm), *n.* excessive devotion to any cause, esp. zealous and belligerent patriotism or blind enthusiasm for military glory. [< F *chauvinisme,* equiv. to *chauvin* jingo (named after N. *Chauvin,* a soldier in Napoleon's army noted for loud-mouthed patriotism) + *-isme* -ISM] —**chau′vin·ist,** *n.* —**chau′vin·is′tic,** *adj.* —**chau′vin·is′ti·cal·ly,** *adv.*

Cha·vannes (shᴀ vᴀN′), *n.* **Pu·vis de** (pʏ vē′ də). See **Puvis de Chavannes, Pierre.**

Cha·vez (chä′vez; *Sp.* chä′ves), *n.* **Car·los** (kär′lōs; *Sp.* kär′lōs), born 1899, Mexican composer and conductor.

Cha·vin (chə vēn′), *adj.* of, pertaining to, or characteristic of a Peruvian culture flourishing from the first to the sixth century A.D. [named after *Chavin,* town in Peru]

chaw (chô), *v.t., v.i., n. Dial.* chew. —**chaw′er,** *n.*

chay[1] (shā), *n. Dial.* chaise; shay.

chay[2] (chā, chī), *n.* **1.** the root of an Indian, rubiaceous herb, *Oldenlandia umbellata,* the outer bark of which yields a red dye. **2.** the herb itself. Also, **chay·a** (chā′ə, chī′ə), **choy, choya.** Also called **chay·a·root** (chā′ə rōōt′, -rŏŏt′, chī′-), **choyaroot.** [var. of *chaya* < Tamil, short for *cāya-vēr*]

Chay·ef·sky (chī ef′skē), *n.* **Pad·dy** (pad′ē), born 1923, U.S. playwright.

cha·yo·te (chī ō′tē), *n.* **1.** a cucurbitaceous vine, *Sechium edule,* of tropical America. **2.** the green or white, furrowed, usually pear-shaped, edible fruit of this plant. Also called **mirliton.** [< Sp < Nahuatl *chayotli*]

cha·zan (KHä zän′; *Eng.* KHä′zən), *n., pl.* **cha·zan·im** (KHä zä nēm′; *Eng.* KHä zō′nim, KHä′zənz). *Hebrew.* hazan.

Ch.B., Bachelor of Surgery. [< L *Chirurgiae Baccalaureus*]

Ch.E., Chemical Engineer.

cheap (chēp), *adj.* **1.** of a relatively low price; inexpensive: *a cheap dress.* **2.** costing little labor or trouble: *Words are cheap.* **3.** charging low prices: *a very cheap store.* **4.** of little account; of small value; mean; shoddy: *cheap conduct; cheap workmanship.* **5.** embarrassed; sheepish: *He felt cheap about his mistake.* **6.** obtainable at a low rate of interest: *when money is cheap.* **7.** of decreased value or purchasing power, as currency depreciated due to inflation. **8.** stingy; miserly: *He's so cheap he wouldn't treat his own brother to a cup of coffee.* —*adv.* **9.** at a low price; at small cost: *He is willing to sell cheap.* —*n.* **10. on the cheap,** *Chiefly Brit.* inexpensively; economically: *She's in favor of traveling, provided she can do it on the cheap.* [ME *cheep* (short for phrases, as *good cheep* cheap, lit., good bargain), OE *cēap* bargain, market, trade; c. G *Kauf,* Icel *kaup,* etc.; all < L *caupō* innkeeper, tradesman; see CHAPMAN] —**cheap′ly,** *adv.* —**cheap′ness,** *n.*

—**Syn. 1, 4.** CHEAP, INEXPENSIVE agree in their suggestion of low cost. CHEAP now usually suggests shoddiness, inferiority, showy imitation, complete unworthiness, and the like: *a cheap kind of fur.* INEXPENSIVE emphasizes lowness of price (although more expensive than CHEAP) and suggests that the value is fully equal to the cost: *an inexpensive dress.* It is often used as an evasion for the more specific CHEAP. **4.** paltry, low, poor, inferior, base.

—**Ant. 1.** costly, dear, expensive.

cheap·en (chē′pən), *v.t.* **1.** to make cheap or cheaper. **2.** to belittle; bring into contempt: *Constant swearing cheapened him.* **3.** to decrease the quality or beauty of; make inferior or vulgar: *She cheapened the dress by adding a fringe to it. They cheapened the beer by adding water.* **4.** *Archaic.* to bargain for. —*v.i.* **5.** to become cheap or cheaper. [CHEAP + -EN[1]; r. ME *chepe(n)* (to) price, bargain, OE *cēapian* to bargain, trade, buy; c. Icel *kaupa,* Goth *kaupōn,* G *kaufen*] —**cheap′en·er,** *n.*

cheap-jack (chēp′jak′), *n.* **1.** a hawker or peddler. —*adj.* **2.** of or suitable for a cheap-jack; cheap. Also, **cheap′jack′, cheap-john** (chēp′jon′).

Cheap·side (chēp′sīd′), *n.* a district and thoroughfare in London, England.

cheap·skate (chēp′skāt′), *n. Slang.* one who is stingy and miserly. [CHEAP + SKATE[3]]

cheat (chēt), *n.* **1.** a person who cheats or defrauds: *He is a cheat and a liar.* **2.** a fraud; swindle; deception: *The game was a cheat that cost him $50.* **3.** *Law.* the fraudulent obtaining of another's property by a false pretense or trick. **4.** an impostor: *The man who passed as an earl was a cheat.* **5.** Also called **chess.** an annual, weedy grass, *Bromus secalinus.* —*v.t.* **6.** to defraud; swindle: *He cheated her out of her inheritance.* **7.** to deceive; influence by fraud: *He cheated her into believing him a hero.* **8.** to elude; deprive of something expected: *He cheated the law by suicide.* —*v.i.* **9.** to practice fraud or deceit: *He cheats without regrets.* **10.** to violate rules or regulations: *He cheats at cards.* **11.** *Slang.* to be sexually unfaithful (often fol. by *on*): *He was cheating on his wife. She knew he had been cheating all along.* [ME *chet* (n.) (aph. for *achet,* var. of *eschet* ESCHEAT), *chete(n)* (to) escheat, deriv. of *chet* (n.)] —**cheat′a·ble,** *adj.* —**cheat′ing·ly,** *adv.*

—**Syn. 1.** swindler, trickster, sharper, impostor, dodger, charlatan, fraud, fake, phony, mountebank. **2.** imposture, artifice, trick, hoax. **6.** mislead, dupe, delude; gull, con; hoax, fool. CHEAT, DECEIVE, TRICK, VICTIMIZE refer to the use of fraud or artifice deliberately to hoodwink someone or to obtain an unfair advantage over him. CHEAT implies conducting matters fraudulently esp. for profit to oneself: *to cheat at cards.* DECEIVE suggests deliberately misleading or deluding, to produce misunderstanding or to prevent someone from knowing the truth: *to deceive one's parents.* To TRICK is to deceive by a stratagem, often of a petty, crafty, or dishonorable kind: *to trick someone into signing a note.* To VICTIMIZE is to make a victim of; the emotional connotation makes the cheating, deception, or trickery seem particularly dastardly: *to victimize a blind man.*

cheat·er (chē′tər), *n.* **1.** one who or that which cheats. **2. cheaters,** *Slang.* **a.** eyeglasses; spectacles. **b.** falsies. [ME; see CHEAT, -ER[1]]

Che·bac′co boat′ (shə bak′ō), a fishing vessel, built mainly at Essex, Massachusetts, in the late 18th and early 19th centuries, having a pink-sterned hull with no bowsprit and schooner-rigged on two masts, the foremast being in the eyes of the bow. Cf. **dogbody.** [after *Chebacco,* former name of parish n Essex, Massachusetts]

che·bec (chi bek′), *n.* See **least flycatcher.** [imit.]

che·beck (shi bek′), *n. Naut.* xebec.

Che·bo·ksa·ry (chi bo ksä′ʀi), *n.* a port in and the capital of the Chuvash Autonomous Soviet Socialist Republic, in the W RSFSR, in the central Soviet Union in Europe, on the Volga.

Che·boy·gan (shə boi′gən), *n.* a town in N Michigan. 5859 (1960).

che·cha·ko (chē chä′kō), *n., pl.* **-kos.** (in the Pacific Northwest) cheechako.

Che·chen′-In·gush′ Auton′omous Repub′lic (chə chen′ingōōsh′), an autonomous republic of the Russian Federation, in Caucasia. 1,277,000; 7,350 sq. mi. *Cap.:* Grozny. Also, **Che·chen′o-In·gush′ Auton′omous Republic** (chə chen′ō in gōōsh′).

ché·chia (shāsh′yä), *n.* a close-fitting, cylindrical cap with a tuft or tassel. [< F < Ar dial. (North Africa) *shāshiya,* after *Shāsh,* city in Persia where it was once made]

check (chek), *v.t.* **1.** to stop or arrest the motion of suddenly or forcibly: *He checked the horse at the edge of the cliff.* **2.** to restrain; hold in restraint or control: *They built a high wall to check the tides. The Senate checked the movement begun in the House.* **3.** to cause a reduction, as in rate, intensity, etc.; diminish: *The new measures checked the rapidity with which the epidemic was spreading.* **4.** to investigate or verify as to correctness: *She checked the copy against the original.* **5.** to make an inquiry into, search through, etc.: *We checked the files, but the letter was missing.* **6.** to inspect or test the performance, condition, safety, etc., of (something): *Check a used car thoroughly before buying it.* **7.** to mark (something) so as to indicate examination, correctness, preference, etc. (often fol. by *off*): *Please check the correct answer. She checked off the names of people she wanted to invite.* **8.** to leave in temporary custody: *Check your umbrellas at the door.* **9.** to accept for temporary custody: *We accept responsibility for any article we check here.* **10.** *U.S.* **a.** to send to a destination under the privilege of a passage ticket: *We checked two trunks through to Portland.* **b.** to accept for conveyance, and to convey, under the privilege of a passage ticket: *Check this trunk to Portland.* **11.** to mark with or in a pattern of squares: *to check fabric.* **12.** *Agric.* to plant in checkrows. **13.** *Chess.* to place (an opponent's king) under direct attack. **14.** *Ice Hockey.* to obstruct or impede the movement or progress of (an opponent). Cf. **back-check, fore-check.** —*v.i.* **15.** to prove to be right; correspond accurately: *The reprint checks with the original, item for item.* **16.** *U.S.* to make an inquiry, investigation, etc., as for verification (often fol. by *up, into,* etc.): *He checked to make sure his answer was correct. Check into the matter. I don't know, but I'll check.* **17.** to make a stop; pause: *The horse checked before he jumped, nearly throwing his rider.* **18.** *Chess.* to make a move that puts the opponent's king under direct attack. **19.** to crack or split, usually in small checks: *Painted surfaces may check with age.* **20.** *Poker.* to decline to initiate the betting in a betting round, usually to force another player to make the first bet rather than raise it. **21.** *Hunting.* (of hounds) to stop, esp. because the line of scent has been lost. **22.** *Falconry.* (of a hawk) to forsake the proper prey and follow baser game (fol. by *at*). **23. check in,** to register, as at a hotel; indicate one's arrival or presence at a place, function, etc., usually by signing an appropriate form: *We checked in at the reception desk and then went out to dinner.* **24. check on** or **up on,** to investigate, scrutinize, or inspect something or someone: *Don't forget to check on his work. We have to check up on him.* **25. check out, a.** *U.S.* to leave and pay for one's quarters at a hotel. **b.** *Slang.* to die. **c.** to verify or become verified. **d.** *U.S.* to withdraw (money) from a bank, as by checks: *He checked $100 out.* **e.** to fulfill requirements, as by passing a test: *The engine checked out and we proceeded on our way.* **26. check the helm,** *Naut.* to alter the helm of a turning vessel to keep the bow from swinging too far or too rapidly. —*n.* **27.** a person who or thing that stops, limits, slows, or restrains: *They found that the increase of duty was an effective check on imports. She was a check on his enthusiasm.* **28.** a sudden arrest or stoppage; repulse; rebuff: *Taxation caused a check in the accumulation of vast fortunes.* **29.** a control, test, or inspection that ascertains performance or prevents error: *They ran a check on the dependability of the automobile under stress conditions.* **30.** a criterion, standard, or means to insure against error, fraud, etc.: *This handmade sample is a check that the machine-made samples have to match.* Cf. **checks and balances. 31.** an inquiry, search, or examination: *We made a quick check but found nothing missing.* **32.** See **check mark. 33.** Also, *Brit.,* **cheque.** *Banking.* a written order, usually on a standard printed form, directing a bank to pay money. **34.** a slip or ticket showing the amount owed, esp. a bill for food or beverages consumed: *The waiter brought us separate checks.* **35.** a ticket or token given as a means of identifying the owner of an article left in the temporary custody of another, the purchaser of a ticket, or a person who is to be served next. **36.** a pattern formed of squares, as on a checkerboard. **37.** one of the squares in such a pattern. **38.** a fabric having a check pattern. **39.** *Chess.* the exposure of the king to direct attack: *The king was in check.* **40.** *Ice Hockey.* any of several maneuvers designed to obstruct or impede the forward progress of an opponent. Cf. **board check, body check, cross-check** (def. 5). **hook check, poke check, sweep check. 41.** a counter used in card games, as the chip in poker. **42.** a small crack: *There were several small checks in the paint.* **43.** *Masonry.* a rabbet-shaped cutting on the edge of a stone, by which it is fitted to another stone. **44.** *Hunting.* **a.** the losing of the scent by a dog or pack. **b.** (in fox hunting) a period in a hunt, following the losing of the scent by the hounds, during which the field rests quietly while the hounds cast to regain the scent. **45. in check,** under restraint: *He held his anger in check.* —*adj.* **46.** serving to check, control, verify, etc.: *a check system.* **47.** ornamented with a checkered pattern; checkered: *a check border.* —*interj.* **48.** *Chess.* (used as a call to warn one's opponent that his king is exposed to direct attack, having just one move in which to escape or parry.) [ME *chek* (at chess), etc. < OF *eschec* (by aphesis), var. of *eschac* < Ar *shāh* check (at chess) < Pers: lit., king (an exclamation: i.e., look out, your king is threatened); see SHAH] —**check′a·ble,** *adj.* —**check′less,** *adj.*

—**Syn. 1.** See **stop. 2.** hinder, hamper, obstruct, curtail; chain, bridle, hobble. CHECK, CURB, REPRESS, RESTRAIN refer to putting a control on movement, progress, action, etc. CHECK implies arresting suddenly, halting or causing to halt: *to check a movement toward reform.* CURB implies the use of a means such as a chain, strap, frame, wall, etc., to guide or control or to force to stay within definite limits: *to curb a horse.* REPRESS, formerly meaning to suppress, now implies preventing the action or development which might naturally be expected: *to repress evidence of excitement.* RESTRAIN implies the use of force to put under control, or chiefly, to hold back: *to restrain a person from violent acts.* **6.** examine. **16.** agree. **27.** obstacle, obstruction, hindrance, restriction, restraint, impediment, control, deterrent; bar, barrier; damper; curb, bridle, bit, rein. **34.** receipt, tab, counterfoil. **35.** coupon, tag, stub. —**Ant. 1.** advance.

check·back (chek′bak′), *n.* a check or verification of a process, tabulation, etc., already completed. [n. use of v. phrase *check back*]

check·book (chek′bŏŏk′), *n.* a book containing blank checks or orders on a bank. [CHECK + BOOK]

checked (chekt), *adj.* **1.** having a pattern of squares; checkered: *a checked shirt.* **2.** *Phonet.* (of a vowel) situated in a closed syllable (opposed to *free*). [CHECK + -ED[2]]

check·er[1] (chek′ər), *n.* **1.** a small, usually red or black disk of plastic or wood, used in playing checkers. **2. checkers, a.** Also called, *Brit.,* **draughts.** (*construed as sing.*) a game played by two persons, each with 12 playing pieces, on a checkerboard. **b.** (in a regenerative furnace) loosely stacked brickwork through which furnace gases and incoming air are passed in turn, so that the heat of the exhaust is absorbed and later transferred to the incoming air. **3.** a checkered pattern. **4.** one of the squares of a checkered pattern. **5.** *Bot.* **a.** See **service tree** (def. 1). **b.** the fruit of this tree. —*v.t.* **6.** to mark like a checkerboard. **7.** to diversify in color; variegate. **8.** to diversify in character; subject to alternations: *Sorrow and joy have checkered his life.* Also, *Brit.,* **chequer.** [ME *checker* chessboard < AF *escheker* (by aphesis), equiv. to *eschec* CHECK + *-er* -ER[2]]

check·er[2] (chek′ər), *n.* **1.** one who or that which checks. **2.** one who checks coats, baggage, etc. **3.** a cashier, as in a supermarket or cafeteria. [CHECK + -ER[1]]

check·er·ber·ry (chek′ər ber′ē), *n., pl.* **-ries. 1.** the red fruit of the American wintergreen, *Gaultheria procumbens.* **2.** the plant itself. **3.** the partridgeberry. [perh. so named from its looks]

check·er·bloom (chek′ər blōōm′), *n.* a malvaceous herb, *Sidalcea malvaeflora,* of western North America, having rose-colored flowers. Also called **wild hollyhock.** [CHECKER[1] + BLOOM[1]]

check·er·board (chek′ər bōrd′, -bôrd′), *n.* **1.** a board marked off into sixty-four squares of two alternating colors, arranged in eight vertical and eight horizontal rows, on which checkers or chess is played. —*v.t.* **2.** to arrange in or mark with a checkerboard pattern: *The façade of the building was checkerboarded with black and white tiles.* Also, *Brit.,* **chequerboard.** [CHECKER[1] + BOARD]

check·ered (chek′ərd), *adj.* **1.** marked by wide or frequent alternations; diversified: *a checkered career.* **2.** marked with squares: *a checkered fabric.* **3.** diversified in color; alternately light and shadowed: *the checkered shade beneath trees.* Also, *Brit.,* **chequered.** [CHECKER[1] + -ED[2]]

check′ered lil′y, 1. an herb, *Fritillaria lanceolata,* of western central North America, having dark purple flowers mottled with greenish yellow. **2.** See **toad lily** (def. 2).

check′er plate′, a metal floor plate having a raised pattern of squares or diamonds to improve traction. Also, **check′ered plate′.**

check·er·spot (chek′ər spot′), *n.* any of several butterflies of the genus *Melitaea,* having black wings with yellowish-brown, checkerlike markings. [CHECKER[1] + SPOT]

check′er tree′. See **service tree** (def. 1).

check·er·work (chek′ər wûrk′), *n.* a pile of loosely stacked bricks in the regenerator of a regenerative furnace. [CHECKER[1] + WORK]

check·hook (chek′hŏŏk′), *n.* a hook on the saddle of a harness, for holding the end of the checkrein. [CHECK(REIN) + HOOK]

check-in (chek′in′), *n.* the act or fact of checking in. Cf. **check** (def. 23). [n. use of v. phrase *check in*]

check′ing account′, *U.S.* a bank deposit against which checks can be drawn by the depositor at any time. Cf. **savings account.**

check′ line′, 1. a checkrein. **2.** *Naut.* a line for controlling the progress of a vessel, as along a quay.

check′ list′, *U.S.* items listed together for convenience of comparison or other checking purposes.

check′ mark′, a mark, often indicated by (√), on or appended to something to indicate that an item has been considered, acted upon, or approved. Also called **check.**

check·mate (chek′māt′), *n., v.,* **-mat·ed, -mat·ing,** *interj.* —*n.* **1.** Also called **mate.** *Chess.* **a.** the act or an instance of maneuvering the opponent's king into a check from which it cannot escape, thus bringing the game to a victorious conclusion. **b.** the position of the pieces when a king is checkmated. **2.** a complete check; defeat: *His efforts to escape met with a checkmate.* —*v.t.* **3.** *Chess.* to maneuver (an opponent's king) into a check from which it cannot escape; mate. **4.** to check completely; defeat: *Napoleon was checkmated at Waterloo.* —*interj.* **5.** *Chess.* (used by a player to announce that he has put his opponent's king into inextricable check.) [ME *chek mat(e)* < MF *escec mat* < Ar *shāh māt* < Pers: lit., the king (is) dead]

check·off (chek′ôf′, -of′), *n.* collection of union dues by employers through compulsory deduction from each worker's wages. [n. use of v. phrase *check off*]

check·out (chek′out′), *n.* **1.** the procedure of vacating a hotel room according to regulations. Cf. **check** (def. 25a). **2.** the time before which a hotel room must be vacated if another day's charge is not to be made. **3.** an examination of fitness for performance: *The check-out of the new plane was successful.* **4.** itemization and collection of amounts due for purchases: *to wait for the check-out in a supermarket.* [n. use of v. phrase *check out*]

check·point (chek′point′), *n.* a place along a road, border, etc., where vehicles or travelers are stopped for inspection. [CHECK + POINT]

check′ rail′, (in a window sash) a meeting rail, esp. one closing against the corresponding rail with a diagonal or rabbeted overlap. Also, **check′rail′.** Cf. **plain rail.**

check·rein (chek′rān′), *n.* **1.** a short rein passing from the bit to the saddle of a harness, to prevent the horse from lowering its head. Cf. **overcheck, side check.**

2. a short rein joining the bit of one of a span of horses to the driving rein of the other. [CHECK + REIN]

check·room (chek′ro͞om′, -ro͝om′), *n.* a room where hats, coats, parcels, etc., may be checked. [CHECK + ROOM]

check·row (chek′rō′), *Agric.* —*n.* **1.** one of a number of rows of trees or plants, esp. corn, in which the distance between adjacent trees or plants is equal to that between adjacent rows. —*v.t.* **2.** to plant in checkrows. [CHECK + ROW[1]]

checks′ and bal′ances, limits imposed on each branch of a government by vesting in all branches the right to amend or void those acts of another that fall within their purview.

check·up (chek′up′), *n.* **1.** an examination or close scrutiny for purposes of verification as to accuracy, comparison, etc.: *They gave the motor a checkup.* **2.** a comprehensive physical examination: *He went to the doctor for a checkup.* [n. use of v. phrase *check up*]

check′ valve′, a valve permitting liquids or gases to flow in one direction only.

check·weigh·man (chek′wā′mən), *n., pl.* **-men.** a representative elected by coal miners to check the findings of the mine owner's weighman where miners are paid by the weight of coal mined. Also called **check·weigh·er** (chek′wā′ər). [CHECK + WEIGHMAN]

check·writ·er (chek′rī′tər), *n.* a machine for printing amounts, perforated as in numbers, on checks drawn upon a bank, chiefly to prevent alterations. [CHECK + WRITER]

check·y (chek′ē), *adj.* *Heraldry.* divided into several rows of squares of two alternating tinctures: *a fess checky, or and azure.* Also, **chequy.** [late ME *cheke(e)* < MF *escheque* checked, chequered in pattern, ptp. of *eschequer*, deriv. of *eschec* CHECK]

Che·co·tah (chə kō′tə), *n.* a town in E Oklahoma. 2614 (1960).

Ched·dar (ched′ər), *n.* a hard, smooth-textured, processed cheese, made usually from the whole milk of cows and varying in color from white to deep yellow. Also called **Ched′dar cheese′.** [named after *Cheddar*, village in Somersetshire, England, where it was first made]

ched′dar pink′, a low, mat-forming plant, *Dianthus gratianopolitanus*, of Europe, having showy, solitary, fragrant, rose-colored flowers with fringed petals. [named after *Cheddar*, England; see PINK[1]]

chedd·ite (ched′īt, shed′-), *n.* *Chem.* an explosive for blasting, composed of a chlorate or perchlorate mixed with a fatty substance, as castor oil. [named after *Chedde*, town in Savoy where it was first made; see -ITE[1]]

che·der (KHā′der; *Eng.* KHā′dər), *n., pl.* **cha·da·rim** (KHə dä′rēm), *Eng.* **che·ders.** *Hebrew.* heder.

Che.E., Chemical Engineer.

chee·cha·ko (chē chä′kō), *n., pl.* **-kos.** *Informal.* (in the Pacific Northwest) a tenderfoot; greenhorn; newcomer. Also, **chechako, chee·cha′co.** [< Chinook jargon *chee chalico* < Chinook *t'shi* new + Nootka *chako* to come]

cheek (chēk), *n.* **1.** either side of the face below the eye and above the jaw. **2.** the side wall of the mouth between the upper and lower jaws. **3.** something resembling the side of the human face in form or position, as either of two parts forming corresponding sides of various objects: *the cheeks of a vise.* **4.** *Archit.* **a.** one side of an opening, as a reveal. **b.** either of two similar faces of a projection, as a buttress. **5.** *Carpentry.* **a.** a piece of wood removed from the end of a timber in making a tenon. **b.** a piece of wood on either side of a mortise. **6.** one side of a hammer head. **7.** *Horol.* one of two pieces placed on both sides of the suspension spring of a pendulum to control the amplitude of oscillation or to give the arc of the pendulum a cycloidal form. **8.** one of the two main vertical supports forming the frame of a hand printing press. **9.** *Mach.* either of the sides of a pulley or block. **10.** *Naut.* either of a pair of fore-and-aft members at the lower end of the head of a lower mast, used to support trestletrees which in turn support a top and often the heel of a topmast; one of the hounds of a lower mast. **11.** *Informal.* impudence or effrontery: *He's got a lot of cheek to say that to me!* **12.** *Foundry.* any part of a flask between the cope and the drag. Cf. **false cheek. 13.** *Slang.* a buttock. **14. cheek by jowl,** in close intimacy; side by side: *a row of houses cheek by jowl.* **15. with one's tongue in one's cheek.** See **tongue** (def. 28). [ME *cheke*, OE *cē(a)ce*; akin to D *kaak*, MLG *kake*] —**cheek′less,** *adj.*

cheek′ block′, *Naut.* a blocklike arrangement consisting of a pulley set parallel to a mast, davit, etc., and having a cheek covering its outer surface.

cheek·bone (chēk′bōn′), *n.* the zygomatic bone or the part of that bone below the eye forming the prominence of the cheek. [ME *chekbon*, OE *ceacban*. See CHEEK, BONE[1]]

cheek′ cut′, *Carpentry.* a cut, oblique both to the depth and thickness, made across the upper end of any rafter or across the lower end of a cripple rafter to permit it to butt against a hip rafter, valley rafter, or ridgepole. Also called **side cut.**

cheek·piece (chēk′pēs′), *n.* **1.** either of two vertical bars of a bit, one on each end of the mouthpiece. **2.** See **cheek strap.** [CHEEK + PIECE]

cheek′ pouch′, a bag in the cheek of certain animals, as squirrels, for carrying food.

cheek′ strap′, (of a bridle) one of two straps passing over the cheeks of the horse and connecting the crown piece with the bit or noseband. Also called **cheekpiece.** See illus. under **harness.**

Cheek·to·wa·ga (chēk′tə wä′gə), *n.* a town in NW New York, near Buffalo. 52,362 (1960).

cheek·y (chē′kē), *adj.,* **cheek·i·er, cheek·i·est.** *Informal.* impudent; insolent: *a cheeky fellow; cheeky behavior.* [CHEEK + -Y[1]] —**cheek′i·ly,** *adv.* —**cheek′i·ness,** *n.*

cheep (chēp), *v.i.* **1.** to chirp; peep. —*v.t.* **2.** to express by cheeps. —*n.* **3.** a chirp. [imit.] —**cheep′er,** *n.*

cheer (chēr), *n.* **1.** a shout of encouragement, approval, congratulation, etc.: *The cheers of the audience filled the theater.* **2.** a set or traditional form of shout used by spectators to encourage or show enthusiasm for an athletic team, contestant, etc., as *rah! rah! rah!* **3.** that which gives joy or gladness; encouragement; comfort: *He spoke words of cheer.* **4.** a state of feeling or spirits: *Good cheer overcomes despair.* **5.** gladness, gaiety, or animation: *to make cheer.* **6.** food; provisions: *The tables were loaded with cheer.* **7.** *Archaic.* facial expression. **8. be of good cheer** (used as an exhortation to be cheerful): *Be of good cheer! Things could be much worse.* **9. with good cheer,** cheerfully; willingly: *She accepted her lot with good cheer.* —*interj.* **10. cheers,** *Chiefly Brit.* (used as a salutation or toast.) —*v.t.* **11.** to salute with shouts of approval, congratulation, triumph, etc.: *The team members cheered their captain.* **12.** to gladden or cause joy to; inspire with cheer (often fol. by *up*): *The good news cheered her up.* **13.** to encourage or incite: *She cheered him on when he was about to give up.* —*v.i.* **14.** to utter cheers of approval, encouragement, triumph, etc. **15.** to become more cheerful (often fol. by *up*): *She cheered up as soon as the sun began to shine.* **16.** *Obs.* to be or feel in a particular state of mind or spirits. [ME *chere* face < OF < LL *cara* face, head < Gk *kára* head] —**cheer′er,** *n.* —**cheer′ing·ly,** *adv.*

—**Syn. 3.** solace. **5.** joy, mirth, glee, merriment. **11.** applaud. **12.** CHEER, GLADDEN, ENLIVEN mean to make happy or lively. To CHEER is to comfort, to restore hope and cheerfulness to (now often CHEER UP, when thoroughness, a definite time, or a particular point in the action is referred to): *to cheer a sick person; She soon cheered him up.* (Cf. **eat up, drink up, hurry up.**) To GLADDEN does not imply a state of sadness to begin with, but suggests bringing pleasure or happiness to someone: *to gladden someone's heart with good news.* ENLIVEN suggests bringing vivacity and liveliness: *to enliven a dull evening, a party.* **12.** exhilarate, animate. **13.** inspirit. —**Ant. 12.** discourage. **13.** depress.

cheer·ful (chēr′fəl), *adj.* **1.** full of cheer; in good spirits: *a cheerful person.* **2.** promoting or inducing cheer; pleasant; bright: *cheerful surroundings.* **3.** characterized by or expressive of good spirits or cheerfulness: *cheerful songs.* **4.** hearty or ungrudging: *cheerful giving.* [late ME *cherfull*. See CHEER, -FUL] —**cheer′ful·ly,** *adv.* —**cheer′ful·ness,** *n.*

—**Syn. 1.** cheery, gay, blithe, happy, joyful, joyous, buoyant, sunny, jolly. **4.** generous. —**Ant. 1.** miserable. **4.** grudging.

cheer·i·o (chēr′ē ō′, chēr′ē ō′), *interj., n., pl.* **cheer·i·os.** *Chiefly Brit.* —*interj.* **1.** good-by; good-by and good luck. **2.** (used as a toast to one's drinking companions.) —*n.* **3.** a good-by or farewell. **4.** a toast of "cheerio!" [CHEERY + exclamatory O[2]]

cheer·lead·er (chēr′lē′dər), *n.* a person who leads spectators in traditional or formal cheering, esp. at a pep rally, football game, etc. [CHEER + LEADER]

cheer·lead·ing (chēr′lē′ding), *n.* the action or skill of a cheerleader. [CHEER + LEADING[1]]

cheer·less (chēr′lis), *adj.* without cheer; joyless; gloomy: *drab and cheerless surroundings.* [CHEER + -LESS] —**cheer′less·ly,** *adv.* —**cheer′less·ness,** *n.*

cheer·ly (chēr′lē), *adv.* cheerfully. [CHEER + -LY]

cheer·o (chēr′ō), *interj., n., pl.* **cheer·os.** *Brit.* cheerio.

cheer·y (chēr′ē), *adj.,* **cheer·i·er, cheer·i·est. 1.** in good spirits; blithe; gay. **2.** promoting cheer; enlivening. [CHEER + -Y[1]] —**cheer′i·ly,** *adv.* —**cheer′i·ness,** *n.*

cheese[1] (chēz), *n., v.,* **cheesed, chees·ing.** —*n.* **1.** the curd of milk separated from the whey and prepared in many ways as a food. **2.** a definite mass of this substance, often in the shape of a wheel or cylinder. **3.** something of similar shape or consistency, as a mass of pomace in cider-making. **4.** *Informal.* partly digested milk curds sometimes spit up by infants. **5.** *Metalworking.* **a.** a transverse section cut from an ingot, as for making into a tire. **b.** an ingot or billet made into a convex, circular form by blows at the ends. **6.** a low curtsy. —*v.i.* **7.** *Informal.* (of infants) to spit up partly digested milk curds. —*v.t.* **8.** *Metalworking.* to forge (an ingot or billet) into a cheese. [ME *chese*, OE *cēse* (c. OS *kāsi*, G *Käse*) < L *cāse(us)*]

cheese[2] (chēz), *v.t.,* **cheesed, chees·ing.** *Slang.* **1.** to stop; desist. —*interj.* **2. cheese it, a.** look out! **b.** run away! [? alter. of CEASE]

cheese[3] (chēz), *n.* *Slang.* one who or that which is splendid or important: *He's the big cheese in this outfit.* [? < Urdu *chīz* thing < Pers]

cheese′box seat′ (chēz′boks′), a chair seat, usually of rush, having a rounded form and surrounded with a thin strip of wood. [CHEESE[1] + BOX[1]]

cheese·burg·er (chēz′bûr′gər), *n.* a hamburger cooked with a slice of cheese on top of it. [CHEESE[1] + (HAM)BURGER]

cheese′ cake′, a rich, sweet, rather firm-textured dessert shaped like a cake or pie, made with a thick custardlike preparation containing cottage cheese or cream cheese, or both, sometimes topped with a jamlike fruit mixture.

cheese·cake (chēz′kāk′), *n.* *Slang.* photographs featuring a view of an attractive woman's legs and body: *magazines full of cheesecake.* Also called **leg art.** [? special use of CHEESE CAKE]

cheese·cloth (chēz′klôth′, -kloth′), *n.* a coarse, lightweight cotton fabric of open texture. [so called because first used to wrap cheese]

cheesed (chēzd), *adj.* *Brit. Slang.* disgusted; fed up. Also, **cheesed′ off′.** [CHEESE[2] + -ED[2]]

cheese·par·ing (chēz′pâr′ing), *adj.* **1.** meanly economical; parsimonious. —*n.* **2.** something of little or no value. **3.** niggardly economy. [CHEESE[1] + PARING] —**cheese′par′er,** *n.*

cheese·wood (chēz′wo͝od′), *n.* See **Victorian box.** [CHEESE[1] + WOOD[1]; so called from its yellow cheeselike color]

chees·y (chē′zē), *adj.,* **chees·i·er, chees·i·est. 1.** of or like cheese: *a cheesy aroma; a cheesy taste.* **2.** *U.S. Slang.* of poor quality: *a cheesy party.* [CHEESE[1] + -Y[1]] —**chees′i·ly,** *adv.* —**chees′i·ness,** *n.*

Cheetah (2½ ft. high at shoulder; total length 7½ ft.; tail 2½ ft.)

chee·tah (chē′tə), *n.* a cat, *Acinonyx jubatus*, of southwestern Asia and Africa, resembling a leopard but having certain doglike characteristics, often trained for hunting deer, antelopes, etc. Also, **chetah.** [< Hind *cītā*, appar. shortened < Skt *citrakāya*, equiv. to *citra* mottled + *kāya* body]

cheez·it (chēz′it), *v.* *Slang.* cheese it.

chef (shef), *n.* a cook, esp. a male head cook. [< F; see CHIEF]

chef de cui·sine (shef də kwē zēn′), *pl.* **chefs de cui·sine** (shef də kwē zēn′). *French Cookery.* a head cook. [lit., head of kitchen]

chef-d'oeu·vre (she dœ′vrᵊ), *n., pl.* **chefs-d'oeu·vre** (she dœ′vrᵊ). a masterpiece, esp. in art, literature, or music. [< F]

Che·foo (chē′fo͞o′), *n.* a seaport in NE Shantung, in E China. 227,000 (est. 1950). Also called **Yentai.**

Che·hab (che häb′), *n.* **Fu·ad** (fo͞o äd′), born 1903, Lebanese army officer and statesman: president since 1958. Also, **Shehab.**

Che·ha·lis (chə hā′lis), *n.* a town in SW Washington. 5199 (1960).

chei·li·tis (kī lī′tis), *n.* *Pathol.* inflammation of the lips. [CHEIL(O)- + -ITIS]

cheilo-, var. of **chilo-**[1].

chei·lo·plas·ty (kī′lə plas′tē), *n., pl.* **-ties.** *Surg.* plastic surgery of the lip. Also, **chiloplasty.** [CHEILO- + -PLASTY]

chei·lot·o·my (kī lot′ə mē), *n., pl.* **-mies.** *Surg.* **1.** excision of part of or all of a lip. **2.** excision of an overgrowth at or near the articular end of a long bone. Also, **chilotomy.** [CHEILO- + -TOMY]

cheiro-, var. of **chiro-**: *cheiromancy.*

Chei·ron (kī′ron), *n.* *Class. Myth.* Chiron.

Che·ju (che′jo͞o′), *n.* an island S of and belonging to South Korea. 288,928 (1955); 718 sq. mi. Also called **Quelpart.** Japanese, **Saishuto, Saishu.**

Che·ka (che′kä), *n.* (formerly) the special commission in the U.S.S.R. (1917–22) charged with preventing counterrevolutionary activities. Cf. **G.P.U., MVD, NKVD.** [< Russ, equiv. to *che* + *ka*, names of initial letters of *Chrezvychainaya Kommissiya* Extraordinary Commission] —**Che′kist,** *n.*

Che·khov (chek′ôf, -of; *Russ.* che′KHof), *n.* **An·ton Pa·vlo·vich** (än tôn′ pä vlô′vich), 1860–1904, Russian short-story writer and dramatist. Also, **Tchekhov.**

Che·khov·i·an (chek′ō fē ən, -of ē-, che kō′fē-, -kof′ē-, -kō′vē-), *adj.* of, pertaining to, or characteristic of Anton Chekhov or his writings, esp. as they are evocative of a pervasive mood of introspection, futility, and the complexity of human motivation. [CHEKHOV + -IAN]

Che·kiang (che′kyäng′; *Chin.* ju′gyäng′), *n.* a province in E China, on the East China Sea. 25,280,000 (est. 1957); 39,768 sq. mi. *Cap.:* Hangchow.

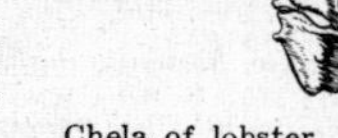

Chela of lobster

che·la[1] (kē′lə), *n., pl.* **-lae** (-lē). the pincerlike organ or claw terminating certain limbs of crustaceans and arachnids. [< NL < Gk *chēlḗ* claw]

che·la[2] (chā′lä), *n.* (in India) a disciple of a religious teacher. [< Hindi *celā* < Skt *ceṭa* slave] —**che′la·ship′,** *n.*

che·late (kē′lāt), *adj., n., v.,* **-lat·ed, -lat·ing.** —*adj.* **1.** *Zool.* having a chela or chelae. **2.** *Chem.* **a.** of or noting a heterocyclic compound having a central metallic ion attached by covalent bonds to two or more nonmetallic atoms in the same molecule. **b.** of or noting a compound having a cyclic structure resulting from the formation of one or more hydrogen bonds in the same molecule. —*n.* **3.** *Chem.* a chelate compound. —*v.i.* *Chem.* **4.** (of a heterocyclic compound) to combine with a metallic ion to form a chelate. **5.** (of a compound) to form a ring by one or more hydrogen bonds. [CHEL(A)[1] + -ATE[1]]

che·la·tion (kē lā′shən), *n.* *Chem.* the process of chelating. [CHELATE + -ION]

cheli-, a learned borrowing from Greek meaning "claws," used, usually with elements of Latin origin, in the formation of compound words: *cheliferous.* [comb. form repr. Gk *chēlḗ* CHELA[1]]

che·lic·er·a (kə lis′ər ə), *n., pl.* **-er·ae** (-ə rē′). one member of the first pair of usually pincerlike appendages of spiders and other arachnids. Cf. **pedipalp.** [CHELI- + CER- + L *-a* neut. pl. ending] —**che·lic′er·al,** *adj.* —**che·lic·er·ate** (kə lis′ə rāt′), *adj.*

Che·li·don (kə lid′ᵊn), *n.* *Class. Myth.* a sister of Aëdon who was raped and then made a slave by her brother-in-law Polytechnus: Artemis changed her into a swallow.

che·lif·er·ous (kə lif′ər əs), *adj.* bearing chelae. [CHELI- + -FEROUS]

che·li·form (kē′lə fôrm′), *adj.* shaped like a chela. [CHELI- + -FORM]

che·li·ped (kē′lə ped′, kel′ə-), *n.* (in decapod crustaceans) either of the pair of appendages bearing a chela. [CHELI- + -PED]

Chel·le·an (shel′ē ən), *adj.* Abbevillian. [< F *chelléen*, after *Chelles*, France, where such tools were unearthed; see -AN]

Chelm·no (KHelm′nô), *n.* a Nazi concentration camp in central Poland.

che·loid (kē′loid), *n.* *Pathol.* keloid.

che·lo·ni·an (ki lō′nē ən), *adj.* **1.** belonging or pertaining to the order *Chelonia*, comprising the turtles. —*n.* **2.** a turtle. [< NL *Chelōni(a)* genus name (*chelōn-* (< Gk *chelṓnē* tortoise) + *-ia* -IA) + -AN]

Chel·sea (chel′sē), *n.* **1.** a borough in SW London, England: many residences of artists and writers. 47,085 (1961). **2.** a city in E Massachusetts, near Boston. 33,749 (1960). **3.** a town in SE Michigan. 3355 (1960).

Chel·ten·ham (chelt′nəm *for 1, 3;* chel′tᵊn ham′ *for 2*), *n.* **1.** a city in N Gloucestershire, in W England: resort. 71,968 (1961). **2.** a town in SE Pennsylvania, near Philadelphia. 35,990 (1960). **3.** *Print.* a style of type. [named after *Cheltenham* in Gloucestershire]

Chel·ya·binsk (chel yä′binsk), *n.* a city in the S RSFSR, in the SW Soviet Union in Asia, near the Ural Mountains. 688,000 (1959).

Chel·yus·kin (chel yo͞os′kin), *n.* **Cape,** a cape in the N Soviet Union in Asia: the northernmost point of the Asia mainland.

chem-, an element derived from the analysis of *chemical, chemistry,* used with elements of Greek origin in the formation of compound words: *chemurgy.* Also, *esp. before a consonant,* **chemo-.** [<< Gk *chēmeía* alloying of metals. See ALCHEMY]

chem., 1. chemical. **2.** chemist. **3.** chemistry.

Chem.E., Chemical Engineer.

chem·ic (kem′ik), *adj.* **1.** of or pertaining to alchemy; alchemic. **2.** of or pertaining to chemistry; chemical. [< Gk *chēm(ía)* alchemy + -IC; r. *chimic* < ML *(al)-chimic(us)*; see ALCHEMY]

chem·i·cal (kem′i kəl), *n.* **1.** a substance produced by or used in a chemical process. —*adj.* **2.** of, used in, produced by, or concerned with the science, operations, or processes of chemistry: *chemical formula; chemical agent.* [CHEMIC + -AL[1]; r. *chimical* chemic] —**chem′i·cal·ly,** *adv.*

chem′ical engineer′ing, the science or profession of applying chemistry to industrial processes. —**chem′ical engineer′.**

Chem′ical Mace′, **1.** *Trademark.* an aerosol container for spraying Mace. **2.** Mace.

chem′ical poten′tial, *Thermodynamics.* a quantity that determines the transport of matter from one phase to another, causing the flow of a component from one phase to another when the potential of the component is greater in the first phase than in the second.

chem′ical sympathec′tomy, *Med.* sympathectomy (def. 2).

chem′ical war′fare, warfare with asphyxiating, poisonous, or corrosive gases, oil flames, etc.

chem·i·cul·ture (kem′i kul′chər), *n.* hydroponics. [CHEM- + -I- + (AGRI)CULTURE]

che·mig·ra·phy (kə mig′rə fē), *n.* any technique for making engravings or etchings using chemicals and without the aid of photography. [CHEM- + -I- + -GRAPHY] —**che·mig′ra·pher,** *n.* —**chem·i·graph·ic** (kem′ə graf′ik), *adj.* —**chem′i·graph′i·cal·ly,** *adv.*

chem·i·lum·i·nes·cence (kem′ə lo͞o′mə nes′əns), *n.* (in chemical reactions) the production of light at low temperatures. [CHEM- + -I- + LUMINESCENCE] —**chem′i·lu′mi·nes′cent,** *adj.*

che·min de fer (shə man′ də fâr′; *Fr.* shə mand[ə]-fer′), *Cards.* a variation of baccarat. [< F: lit., railroad; so called from the speed of the game]

che·mise (shə mēz′), *n.* **1.** a woman's loose-fitting, shirtlike undergarment. **2.** (in women's fashions) a dress designed to hang straight from the shoulders and fit loosely at the waist, sometimes more tightly at the hip. **3.** a revetment for an earth embankment. [ME < OF: shirt < LL *camis(ia),* prob. < Celt; r. ME *kemes,* OE *cemes* < LL *camisia*]

chem·i·sette (shem′i zet′), *n.* a woman's garment of linen, lace, or the like, worn, toward the end of the Victorian era, over a low-cut or open bodice to cover the neck and breast. [< F; see CHEMISE, -ETTE]

chem·ism (kem′iz əm), *n.* chemical action. [CHEM- + -ISM, modeled on F *chimisme,* equiv. to *chim(ie)* chemistry + *-isme* -ISM]

chem·i·sorb (kem′i sôrb′, -zôrb′), *v.t. Chem.* to take up by chemisorption. [CHEM- + -I- + (AD)SORB]

chem·i·sorp·tion (kem′i sôrp′shən, -zôrp′-), *n. Chem.* adsorption involving a chemical linkage between the adsorbent and the adsorbate. [CHEM- + -I- + (AD)SORPTION]

chem·ist (kem′ist), *n.* **1.** one versed in chemistry or professionally engaged in chemical operations. **2.** *Brit.* a pharmacist; druggist. **3.** *Obs.* alchemist. [< Gk *chēm(ía)* alchemy + -IST; r. *chymist* < ML *(al)chimist(a)*]

chem·is·try (kem′i strē), *n., pl.* **-tries.** **1.** the science that deals with or investigates the composition, properties, and changes of properties of substances and various elementary forms of matter. Cf. **organic chemistry, inorganic chemistry, element** (def. 6). **2.** chemical properties, reactions, phenomena, etc.: *the chemistry of carbon.* [CHEMIST + -RY; r. *chymist, chimist* + -RY]

chem·my (shem′ē), *n. Informal.* chemin de fer. [by shortening and alter.]

Chem·nitz (kem′nits), *n.* former name of **Karl-Marx-Stadt.**

chemo-, var. of **chem-,** esp. before a consonant, in imitation of forms of Greek origin: *chemosynthesis; chemotherapy.*

chem·o·ki·ne·sis (kem′ō ki nē′sis, -kī-, kē′mō-), *n.* increased activity of an organism due to a chemical substance. [CHEMO- + KINESIS] —**chem·o·ki·net·ic** (kem′ō ki net′ik, -kī-, kē′mō-), *adj.*

chem·o·nite (kem′ə nīt′, kē′mə-), *n. Chem.* a compound consisting of copper hydroxide, arsenic trioxide, ammonia, acetic acid, and water: used as a wood preservative. [CHEMO- + -N- + -ITE[1]]

chem·o·pal·li·dec·to·my (kem′ō pal′i dek′tə mē, kē′mō-), *n., pl.* **-mies.** *Surg.* an operation for treating Parkinson's disease and certain other diseases characterized by muscular rigidity, consisting of destroying a specific part of the corpus striatum by injecting it with a chemical, usually alcohol. [CHEMO- + NL *pallid(um)* a muscle (n. use of neut. of L *pallidus* pale) + -ECTOMY]

chem·o·pause (kem′ə pôz′, kē′mə-), *n.* the boundary, or transition layer, between the chemosphere and the ionosphere. [CHEMO- + PAUSE]

chem·o·pro·phy·lax·is (kem′ō prō′fə lak′sis, -prof′ə-, kē′mō-), *n. Med.* prophylaxis by means of chemical agents or drugs. [CHEMO- + PROPHYLAXIS]

chem·o·re·cep·tion (kem′ō ri sep′shən, kē′mō-), *n.* the physiological response to chemical stimuli. [CHEMO- + RECEPTION] —**chem·o·re·cep·tive** (kem′ō ri sep′tiv, kē′mō-), *adj.*

chem·o·re·cep·tor (kem′ō ri sep′tər, kē′mō-), *n. Physiol.* a receptor stimulated by chemical means. [CHEMO- + RECEPTOR]

chem·o·re·flex (kem′ə rē′fleks, kē′mə-), *Physiol.* —*n.* **1.** a reflex caused by a chemical stimulus. —*adj.* **2.** of or pertaining to a chemoreflex. [CHEMO- + REFLEX]

Che·mosh (kē′mosh), *n.* a Moabite god. Jer. 48. Also, *Douay Bible,* **Chamos.**

chem·os·mo·sis (kem′oz mō′sis, -os-, kē′moz-, -mos-), *n.* chemical action between substances that occurs through an intervening, semipermeable membrane. [CHEM- + OSMOSIS] —**chem·os·mot·ic** (kem′oz mot′ik, -os-, kē′moz-, -mos-), *adj.*

chem·o·sphere (kem′ə sfēr′, kē′mə-), *n.* the region of the atmosphere most characterized by chemical, esp. photochemical, activity, starting in the stratosphere and including the mesosphere and perhaps part of the thermosphere. [CHEMO- + -SPHERE]

chem·o·sur·ger·y (kem′ō sûr′jə rē, kē′mō-), *n. Surg.* the use of chemical means to obtain a result usually achieved by surgical means, as the removal or destruction of tissue. [CHEMO- + SURGERY]

chem·o·syn·the·sis (kem′ə sin′thi sis, kē′mə-), *n.* *Biol., Biochem.* (of an organism) the synthesis of organic compounds with energy derived from chemical reactions. [CHEMO- + SYNTHESIS] —**chem·o·syn·thet·ic** (kem′ō-sin thet′ik), *adj.* —**chem′o·syn·thet′i·cal·ly,** *adv.*

chem′osynthet′ic bacte′ria, *Bacteriol.* bacteria that synthesize organic compounds, using energy derived from the oxidation of organic or inorganic materials without the aid of light. [CHEMO- + SYNTHETIC]

chem·o·tax·is (kem′ə tak′sis, kē′mə-), *n. Biol.* oriented movement toward or away from a chemical substance. [CHEMO- + -TAXIS] —**chem·o·tac·tic** (kem′ə tak′tik, kē′mə-), *adj.* —**chem′o·tac′ti·cal·ly,** *adv.*

chem·o·ther·a·peu·tics (kem′ō ther′ə pyo͞o′tiks, kē′mō-), *n.* (*construed as sing.*) chemotherapy. [CHEMO- + THERAPEUTICS] —**chem′o·ther′a·peu′tic,** *adj.*

chem·o·ther·a·py (kem′ō ther′ə pē, kē′mə-), *n. Med.* the treatment of disease by means of chemicals which have a specific toxic effect upon the disease-producing microorganisms, or which selectively destroy neoplastic tissue. [CHEMO- + THERAPY] —**chem′o·ther′a·pist,** *n.*

chem·o·troph (kem′ə trof′, -trōf′, -trŏf′, kē′mə-), *n. Bacteriol.* a microorganism, esp. an autotrophic bacterium, requiring an inorganic compound rather than light for its source of energy. [CHEMO- + *-troph* < Gk *trophḗ* food] —**chem·o·troph·ic** (kem′ə trof′ik, kē′-mə-), *adj.*

che·mot·ro·pism (ki mo′trə piz′əm), *n. Biol.* oriented growth or movement in response to a chemical stimulus. [CHEMO- + -TROPISM] —**chem·o·trop·ic** (kem′ə trop′ik, kē′mə-), *adj.* —**chem′o·trop′i·cal·ly,** *adv.*

Che·mul·po (*Korean.* che′mo͞ol pô′), *n.* Inchon.

chem·ur·gy (kem′ûr jē), *n.* a division of applied chemistry concerned with the industrial use of organic substances, esp. from farm produce, as soybeans, peanuts, etc. [CHEM- + -URGY] —**chem·ur′gic, chem·ur′gi·cal,** *adj.*

Che·nab (chi nab′), *n.* a river in S Asia, flowing SW from N India to the Sutlej River in E West Pakistan. ab. 675 mi. long.

che·neau (shā nō′), *n., pl.* **-neaus, -neaux** (-nōz′). *Archit.* **1.** an ornamented cresting on a cornice or coping. **2.** a gutter, esp. an ornamented one, at the eaves of a building. [< F *chêneau,* earlier *chenau;* OF *chenal* < L *canāl(is)* CANAL[1]]

Che·ney (chē′nē), *n.* a town in E Washington. 3173 (1960).

Ch'eng′-Chu′ school′ (cheng′jo͞o′), *Philos.* See **School of Law.**

Cheng·teh (chung′du′), *n.* a city in NE Hopeh, in NE China: former summer residence of the Manchu emperors; capital of the former province of Jehol. 92,900 (est. 1957). Also called **Jehol.**

Cheng·tu (chung′do͞o′), *n.* a city in and the capital of Szechwan, in central China. 1,107,000 (est. 1957).

che·nier (shin′ə rē), *n.* a hummock in a marshy region, with stands of evergreen oaks. Also, **chê′nière.** [< LaF, equiv. to F *chêne* oak + *-ier* -IER]

Ché·nier (shā nyā′), *n.* **An·dré Ma·rie de** (äN drā′ mA rē′ də), 1762–94, French poet.

che·nille (shə nēl′), *n.* **1.** a velvety cord of silk or worsted, for embroidery, fringes, etc. **2.** fabric made with a fringed silken thread used as the weft in combination with wool or cotton. **3.** any fabric with a protruding pile, as in certain rayon bedspreads. **4.** a deep-pile, durable, woolen carpeting with chenille weft: the most expensive power-loomed floor covering. [< F: fuzzy cord, lit., hairy caterpillar < L *canīcul(a)* little dog, equiv. to *cani(s)* dog + *-cula* -CULE]

chenille′ plant′, a plant, *Acalypha hispida,* of the East Indies, having long, drooping, reddish-purple spikes of flowers.

Chen·nault (shə nôlt′), *n.* **Claire Lee** (klâr), 1890–1958, U.S. Air Force general.

che·no·pod (kē′nə pod′, ken′ə-), *n.* any plant of the genus *Chenopodium* or the family *Chenopodiaceae.* [< Gk *chēno-* (comb. form of *chḗn* goose) + -POD; cf. NL *Chenopodium* genus name]

che·no·po·di·a·ceous (kē′nə pō′dē ā′shəs, ken′ə-), *adj.* belonging to the *Chenopodiaceae,* or goosefoot family of plants, including the beet, mangelwurzel, spinach, orach, and many species peculiar to saline, alkaline, or desert regions. [< NL *Chenopodiāce(ae)* family name (*chēnopodi-* CHENOPOD + *-āceae* -ACEAE) + -OUS]

che·no·po′di·um oil′ (kē′nə pō′dē əm, ken′ə-), *Chem.* a colorless or yellowish oil obtained from the seeds and leaves of Mexican tea: used chiefly in medicine as an agent for killing or expelling intestinal worms. Also called **wormseed oil.** [< NL *chēnopodium.* See CHENOPOD, -IUM]

Ch'ên Tu-hsiu (chun′ do͞o′shyo͞o′), 1879–1942, Chinese scholar and political leader.

Che·ops (kē′ops), *n.* king of Egypt c2650–c2630 B.C.: builder of the great pyramid at Giza (brother of Khafre). Also called **Khufu.**

Cheph·ren (kef′rən), *n.* Khafre.

cheque (chek), *n. Brit.* check (def. 33).

cheq·uer (chek′ər), *n. Brit.* checker[1].

cheq·uer·board (chek′ər bôrd′, -bōrd′), *n. Brit.* checkerboard; draughtboard.

cheq·uered (chek′ərd), *adj. Brit.* checkered.

chequ·y (chek′ē), *adj. Heraldry.* checky.

Cher (shâr; *Fr.* sher), *n.* **1.** a river in central France, flowing NW to the Loire River. 220 mi. long. **2.** a department in central France. 293,514 (1962); 2820 sq. mi. *Cap.:* Bourges.

Che·raw (chēr′ō), *n.* a town in NE South Carolina. 5171 (1960).

Cher·bourg (shâr′bo͝org; *Fr.* sher bo͞or′), *n.* a seaport in NW France: taken by U.S. Forces June, 1944. 40,018 (1962).

cher·chez la femme (sher shā′ lA fAm′), *French.* look for the woman: advice offered facetiously in any situation, esp. one of doubt or mystery. Modern usage results from its having become a stereotype in mystery stories, where it suggested that the woman in question was likely to be the cause of the trouble.

che·rem (KHā′rem, -rəm), *n. Hebrew.* herem.

Cher·e·mis (cher′ə mis′, -mēs′, cher′ə mis′, -mēs′), *n.* a Uralic language spoken in scattered communities 300–800 miles E of Moscow by over half a million people. Also, **Cher′e·miss′.**

Che·rem·kho·vo (che rem′KHō vo, che′rem KHô′vo), *n.* a city in the SE RSFSR, in the S Soviet Union in Asia, on the Trans-Siberian Railroad, near Lake Baikal. 113,000 (est. 1965).

Che·ren·kov (chə reng′kôf, -kof, -ren′-; *Russ.* che ren′-kof), *n.* **Pa·vel A.** (pä′vəl). See **Cerenkov, Pavel A.**

cher·gui (sher gē′), *n.* (in northern Morocco) a dry, dusty east or southeast wind blowing from the desert. [< Ar]

Cher·i (sher′ē), *n.* a girl's given name. Also, **Cherie.**

ché·rie (shā rē′), *n., pl.* **-ries** (-rē′). *French.* dear; sweetheart.

Cher·ie (sher′ē), *n.* a girl's given name. Also, **Cheri.**

cher·i·moy·a (cher′ə moi′ə), *n.* **1.** a tropical American tree, *Annona Cherimola.* **2.** the greenish-yellow, smooth-skinned or tuberculate-skinned, edible fruit of this tree. Also, **cher·i·moy·er** (cher′ə moi′ər), **cher·i·mol·la** (cher′ə moi′ə), **chirimoya.** [< Sp *chirimoya* < Quechua]

cher·ish (cher′ish), *v.t.* **1.** to hold or treat as dear: *to cherish one's native land.* **2.** to care for tenderly; nurture: *to cherish a child.* **3.** to cling fondly or inveterately to (hopes, ideas, etc.): *cherishing no resentment.* [ME *cherissh(en)* < MF *cheriss-* (long s. of *cherir*), equiv. to *cher* dear (< L *cārus*) + *-iss* -ISH[2]] —**cher′ish·a·ble,** *adj.* —**cher′ish·er,** *n.* —**cher′ish·ing·ly,** *adv.*

—**Syn. 1.** CHERISH, FOSTER, HARBOR imply giving affection, care, or shelter to something. CHERISH suggests regarding or treating something as an object of affection or as valuable: *to cherish a memory or a friendship.* FOSTER implies sustaining and nourishing something with care, esp. in order to promote, increase, or strengthen it: *to foster a hope; to foster enmity.* HARBOR suggests giving shelter to or entertaining something undesirable, esp. evil thoughts or intentions: *to harbor malice or a grudge.* **2.** nurse, nourish, sustain. **3.** treasure. —**Ant. 2.** neglect. **3.** relinquish.

Cher·kessk′ Auton′omous Re′gion (cher kesk′), an administrative division of the RSFSR, in the S Soviet Union in Europe, in the Caucasus. 277,000 (1959); 1273 sq. mi. *Cap.:* Cherkessk. Official name, **Karachai-Cherkessk Autonomous Region.**

Cher·nov·tsy (cher nôf′tsi), *n.* Russian name of **Cernăuţi.**

cher·no·zem (cher′no zem′), *n.* tschernosem.

Cher·o·kee (cher′ə kē′, cher′ə kē′), *n., pl.* **-kees,** (*esp. collectively*) **-kee** for 1. **1.** a member of an important tribe of North American Indians whose first known center was in the southern Alleghenies and whose present center is Oklahoma. **2.** the Iroquoian language of the Cherokee, written since 1822 in a syllabic script invented for the language by a Cherokee. **3.** a town in NW Iowa. 7724 (1960).

Cher′okee rose′, a smooth-stemmed white rose, *Rosa laevigata,* of Chinese origin, cultivated in the Southern U.S.: the State flower of Georgia.

che·root (shə ro͞ot′), *n.* a cigar having open, untapered ends. [< Tamil *curuṭṭu* roll (of tobacco)]

cher·ry (cher′ē), *n., pl.* **-ries,** *adj.* —*n.* **1.** the fruit of any of various trees of the genus *Prunus,* consisting of a pulpy, globular drupe enclosing a one-seeded smooth stone. **2.** the tree itself. **3.** its wood. **4.** any of various fruits or plants resembling the cherry. **5.** bright red; cerise. **6.** *Slang* (*vulgar*). the hymen or the state of virginity. **7.** *Bowling Slang.* the striking down of only the forward pin or pins in attempting to make a spare. —*adj.* **8.** bright-red; cerise. **9.** (of food and beverages) made with or containing cherries or cherrylike flavoring: *cherry pie; cherry soda.* **10.** (of furniture, woodwork, etc.) made of or covered or decorated with wood from the cherry tree. **11.** being a virgin. [late ME *chery,* var. of *chirie,* back formation from OE *ciris-* (taken for pl.) << VL **ceresium* for **cerasium* (L *cerasum*) < Gk *kerásion* cherry] —**cher′ry·like′,** *adj.*

Cher·ry (cher′ē), *n.* a girl's given name.

cher·ry-bob (cher′ē bob′), *n. Brit.* a pair of cherries joined at the end of their stems. [CHERRY + BOB[2]]

cher′ry bomb′, a red, globe-shaped firecracker with a long fuse and high explosive capability.

cher′ry lau′rel, **1.** Also called **English laurel.** an evergreen shrub or small tree, *Laurocerasus officinalis,* found from southeastern Europe to Iran, having clusters of fragrant, white flowers, and dark purple fruit. **2.** See **laurel cherry.**

Cher′ry Or′chard, The, a play (1904) by Chekhov.

cher′ry pep′per, **1.** a tropical, woody plant, *Capsicum frutescens cerasiforme,* having fruit that is erect or recurved, roundish or heart-shaped, pungent, and either red, yellow, or purplish in color. **2.** the fruit itself.

cher′ry pick′er, any of several types of crane for lifting in a generally vertical direction.

cher′ry pie′, *Bot.* the valerian, *Valeriana officinalis.*

cher·ry·stone (cher′ē stōn′), *n.* **1.** the one-seeded smooth stone of the cherry. **2.** the quahog, *Venus mercenaria,* when larger than a littleneck. [ME *cheriston.* See CHERRY, STONE]

cher′ry toma′to, **1.** a variety of tomato plant, *Lycopersicon esculentum cerasiforme.* **2.** the cherrylike, edible, red or yellow fruit of this plant.

Cher·ry·vale (cher′ē vāl′), *n.* a town in SE Kansas. 2783 (1960).

Cher·ry·ville (cher′ē vil′), *n.* a town in SW North Carolina. 3607 (1960).

cher·so·nese (kûr′sə nēz′, -nēs′), *n.* a peninsula. [< L *chersonēs(us)* < Gk *chersónēsos,* equiv. to *chérs(os)* dry + *nēsos* island]

chert (chûrt), *n.* a compact rock consisting essentially of microcrystalline quartz. [?] —**chert′y,** *adj.*

cher·ub (cher′əb), *n., pl.* **cher·ubs** for 3, 4; **cher·u·bim** (cher′ə bim, -yo͞o bim) for 1, 2. **1.** a celestial being. Gen. 3:24; Ezek. 1,10. **2.** *Theol.* a member of the second order of angels, distinguished by knowledge, often represented as a beautiful, winged child or as a winged head of a child. **3.** a beautiful or innocent person, esp. a child. **4.** a person with a sweet, chubby, innocent face. [ME < L < Gk *cheroúb* < Heb *kerūbh;* r. ME *cherub(in),* OE *c(h)erubin, cerubim* < L *cherūbim* < Gk < Heb *kerūbhīm* (pl.)] —**che·ru·bic** (chə ro͞o′bik), **che·ru′bi·cal,** *adj.* —**che·ru′bi·cal·ly,** *adv.*

cher·ub·fish (cher′əb fish′), *n., pl.* **-fish·es,** (*esp. collectively*) **-fish.** a brilliantly colored butterflyfish, *Centropyge argi,* found in the West Indies: kept in home aquariums. [CHERUB + FISH]

Che·ru·bi·con (*Gk.* ᴋʜe/ʀōō vē kôn/; *Eng.* chi rōō/bi kon/), *n.* *Eastern Ch.* the hymn sung during the Great Entrance by the choir, which represents the cherubim. Also, **Che/ru·bi·kon/.** Also called **Cheru/bic Hymn/.**

Che·ru·bi·ni (ker/ŏŏ bē/nē; *It.* ke/ʀōō bē/nē), *n.* **Ma·ri·a Lu·i·gi Car·lo Ze·no·bio Sal·va·to·re** (mä rē/ä lōō ē/jē kär/lô dze nô/byô säl/vä tô/ʀe), 1760–1842, Italian composer, esp. of opera; in France after 1788.

cher·vil (chûr/vil), *n.* **1.** a herbaceous plant, *Anthriscus Cerefolium*, of the parsley family, having aromatic leaves used to flavor soups, salads, etc. **2.** any of various plants of the same genus or allied genera. [ME *chervelle*, OE *cerfelle* < *caerephyll(a)*, pl. of *caerephyllum* < Gk *chairéphyllon*, equiv. to *chaíre* hail (greeting) + *phýllon* leaf]

cher·vo·nets (cheʀ vô/nits, -nets), *n., pl.* **-von·tsi** (-vônt/sē). a former gold coin and monetary unit of the U.S.S.R., equal to 10 rubles. Also, **tchervonetz.** [< Russ *chervon(yi)* (< Pol *czerwony* red, golden) + *-ets* n. suffix]

Cher·yl (sher/əl), *n.* a girl's given name, form of **Charlotte.**

Cher·y·lene (sher/ə lēn/), *n.* a girl's given name.

Ches·a·ning (ches/ə niṅg), *n.* a town in central Michigan. 2770 (1960).

Ches·a·peake (ches/ə pēk/), *n.* **1.** (*italics.*) a U.S. frigate boarded in 1807 by the British, who removed part of its crew and impressed some members into British service: captured by the British in naval battle near Boston in 1813. **2.** a town in W West Virginia. 2699 (1960).

Ches/apeake and Del/aware Canal/, a canal between N Delaware and NE Maryland, connecting the Chesapeake and Delaware bays. ab. 19 mi. long.

Ches/apeake Bay/, an inlet of the Atlantic, in Maryland and Virginia. 200 mi. long; 4–40 mi. wide.

Ches/apeake Bay/ retriev/er, one of an American breed of retrievers having a short, thick, oily coat ranging in color from brown to a light tan.

Chesh·ire (chesh/ər, -ēr), *n.* **1.** a county in NW England. 1,367,860 (1961); 1015 sq. mi. *Co. seat:* Chester. **2.** a town in central Connecticut. 4072 (1960). **3.** Also called **Chesh/ire cheese/.** a hard cheese, yellowish, orange or white in color, made of cow's milk and similar to cheddar cheese. **4. to grin like a Cheshire cat,** to smile or grin inscrutably, an old saying made popular by the constantly grinning cat in *Alice's Adventures in Wonderland.* Also called **Chester** (for defs. 1, 3).

Chesh·van (hesh/vən, ᴋʜesh/-; *Heb.* ᴋʜesh vän/, ᴋʜesh/vän), *n.* Heshvan.

ches·key (ches/kē), *n., pl.* **-keys.** *Slang.* **1.** a person of Czech extraction. **2.** the Czech language. [appar. var. of *chekski, equiv. to *chek* Czech + *-ski* Slavic suffix]

Ches·na (chez/nə, ches/-), *n.* a girl's given name.

chess[1] (ches), *n.* a game played by two persons, each with sixteen pieces, on a chessboard. [ME < OF *esches*, pl. of *eschec* ᴄʜᴇᴄᴋ]

chess[2] (ches), *n., pl.* **chess, chess·es.** one of the planks forming the roadway of a floating bridge. [late ME *ches* tier, layer < ?]

chess[3] (ches), *n.* cheat (def. 5). [?]

chess·board (ches/bôrd/, -bōrd/), *n.* the board, identical with a checkerboard, used for playing chess. [ᴄʜᴇss[1] + ʙᴏᴀʀᴅ]

chess/ clock/, a double timer for chess players, having a dial for each player on which his accumulated time is recorded and a device for stopping one timer and starting the other at the end of each move.

chess·man (ches/man/, -mən), *n., pl.* **-men** (-men/, -mən). one of the pieces used in the game of chess. [earlier *chesse meyne*, equiv. to *chesse* ᴄʜᴇss[1] + *meyne* household (man, men by folk etymology) < MF *mesniee* < L *mansiōn-* (s. of *mansiō*); see ᴍᴀɴsɪᴏɴ]

chess·tree (ches/trē/), *n.* *Naut.* (in the 17th and 18th centuries) a wooden fastening with one or more sheaves, attached to the topside of a sailing vessel, through which the windward tack of a course was rove. [perh. by folk etymology < F *châssis* frame; see ᴄʜᴀssɪs]

chest (chest), *n.* **1.** the trunk of the body from the neck to the abdomen; thorax. **2.** a box, usually a large, strong one with a lid, for storage, safekeeping of valuables, etc.: *a toy chest; a jewelry chest.* **3.** the place where the funds of a public institution or charitable organization are kept; treasury; coffer. **4.** the funds themselves. **5.** a box in which certain goods, as tea, are packed for transit. **6.** the quantity contained in such a box: *a chest of spices.* **7.** See **chest of drawers. 8. get (something) off one's chest,** *Informal.* to reveal to someone that which is oppressing one's mind or conscience: *He wanted to get his problems off his chest, but there was no one to whom he could talk.* [ME; OE *cest, cist* < L *cist(a)* < Gk *kístē* box]

Ches·ter (ches/tər), *n.* **1.** a city in SE Pennsylvania. 63,658 (1960). **2.** a city in and the county seat of Cheshire, in NW England: only English city with the Roman walls still intact. 59,283 (1961). **3.** Cheshire (defs. 1, 3). **4.** a town in N South Carolina. 6906 (1960). **5.** a town in SW Illinois. 4460 (1960). **6.** a town in N West Virginia. 3787 (1960). **7.** a town in SE Pennsylvania. 3602 (1960). **8.** a boy's given name.

ches·ter·bed (ches/tər bed/), *n.* *Chiefly Canadian.* a sofa or chesterfield that opens into a bed. [ᴄʜᴇsᴛᴇʀ(ғɪᴇʟᴅ) + ʙᴇᴅ]

ches·ter·field (ches/tər fēld/), *n.* **1.** (*sometimes cap.*) a single- or double-breasted topcoat or overcoat with a fly front and a narrow velvet collar. **2.** a large overstuffed sofa or divan with a back and upholstered arms. **3.** *Chiefly Canadian.* any large sofa or couch. [after an Earl of Chesterfield in the 19th century]

Ches·ter·field (ches/tər fēld/), *n.* **1. Philip Dor·mer Stan·hope** (dôr/mər stan/əp), **4th Earl of,** 1694–1773, British statesman and author. **2.** a town in central Indiana. 2588 (1960).

Ches·ter·field·i·an (ches/tər fēl/dē ən), *adj.* of, pertaining to, or like the 4th Earl of Chesterfield or his writings; elegant; urbane; suave. [ᴄʜᴇsᴛᴇʀғɪᴇʟᴅ + -ɪᴀɴ]

Ches·ter·ton (ches/tər tən), *n.* **1. G(ilbert) K(eith),** 1874–1936, English essayist, critic, and novelist. **2.** a town in NW Indiana. 4335 (1960).

Ches·ter·town (ches/tər toun/), *n.* a town in E Maryland. 3602 (1960).

Ches/ter White/, one of an American breed of white hogs, having drooping ears. [named after *Chester*, county in Pennsylvania where first bred]

chest·nut (ches/nut/, -nət), *n.* **1.** the edible nut of trees of the genus *Castanea*, of the beech family. **2.** any of the trees, as *C. sativa* **(European chestnut),** *C. dentata* **(American chestnut),** or *C. crenata* **(Japanese chestnut). 3.** the wood of these trees. **4.** any of various fruits or trees resembling the chestnut, as the horse chestnut. **5.** reddish brown. **6.** *Informal.* an old or stale joke, anecdote, etc. **7.** the callosity on the inner side of the leg of a horse. See diag. under **horse. 8.** a reddish-brown horse having the mane and tail of the same color. Cf. **bay**[5] (def. 2). **9.** Also called **liver chestnut.** a horse of a solid, dark-brown color. **10. pull (someone's) chestnuts out of the fire,** to be pressed into rescuing someone from a difficulty by undertaking the responsibility for remedying it oneself. —*adj.* **11.** reddish-brown. **12.** (of food) containing or made with chestnuts: *chestnut stuffing.* [earlier *chesten nut*, ME *chesten*, OE *cysten* chestnut tree (< L *castanea* < Gk *kastanéa*) + ɴᴜᴛ] —**chest/nut/ty,** *adj.*

American chestnut, *Castanea dentata*
A, Closed bur;
B, Nuts

chest/nut blight/, *Plant Pathol.* a disease of chestnuts, esp. the American chestnut, characterized by bark lesions which girdle and eventually kill the tree, caused by a fungus, *Endothia parasitica.*

chest/nut bot/tle, an American glass bottle or flask of the 19th century, having slightly flattened sides.

chest/nut clam/, Astarte (def. 2). Also called **chest/-nut shell/.**

chest/ of drawers/, *Furniture.* a piece of furniture consisting of a set of drawers in a frame set on short legs, or feet, for holding clothing, household linens, etc.

chest/ of vi/ols, *Music.* a set of several viols, usually played together as an ensemble.

chest-on-chest (chest/on chest/, -ôn-), *n.* a chest of drawers placed upon a slightly wider chest of drawers.

chest/ reg/ister, *Music.* the low register of the human voice.

chest·y (ches/tē), *adj.,* **chest·i·er, chest·i·est. 1.** *Informal.* having a well-developed chest or bosom. **2.** *Slang.* proud; conceited. [ᴄʜᴇsᴛ + -ʏ[1]] —**chest/i·ly,** *adv.* —**chest/i·ness,** *n.*

Ches·wick (chez/wik), *n.* a town in central Pennsylvania. 2734 (1960).

Chet (chet), *n.* a boy's given name, form of **Chester.**

che·tah (chē/tə), *n.* cheetah.

cheth (het, hes; *Heb.* ᴋʜet, ᴋʜes), *n.* **1.** the eighth letter of the Hebrew alphabet. **2.** the consonant sound represented by this letter. [< Heb]

Chet·nik (chet nēk/, chet/nik), *n.* a member of a Serbian nationalist group that fought against the Turks in the early part of the 20th century and carried on guerrilla warfare during World War I and II. [< Serbian, equiv. to *chet(a)* troop + *-nik* agent suffix]

che·val de ba·taille (shə vᴀʟ də bᴀ tä/yᵊ), *pl.* **che·vaux de ba·taille** (shə vōdᵊ bᴀ tä/yᵊ). *French.* **1.** a horse used in battle; charger. **2.** a favorite topic of discussion, argument, etc.

che·val-de-frise (shə val/də frēz/), *n., pl.* **che·vaux-de-frise** (shə vō/də frēz/). Usually, **chevaux-de-frise.** a portable obstacle, usually a sawhorse, covered with projecting spikes or barbed wire, for military use in closing a passage, breaking in a defensive wall, etc. [< F; lit., horse of Frisia, so called because first used by Frisians]

che·val/ glass/ (shə val/), a full-length mirror mounted so that it can be tilted in a frame. [< F *cheval* horse, supporting framework (see ᴄʜᴇᴠᴀʟɪᴇʀ)]

chev·a·lier (shev/ə lēr/), *n.* **1.** a member of certain orders of honor or merit: *a chevalier of the Legion of Honor.* **2.** *Fr. Hist.* the lowest title of rank in the old nobility. **3.** a chivalrous man; cavalier. **4.** *Archaic.* a knight. [< MF; r. late ME *chivaler* < AF. See ᴄᴀᴠᴀʟɪᴇʀ]

Che·va·lier (shə val/yā, -väl/-; *Fr.* shə vᴀ lyā/), *n.* **Mau·rice (Au·guste)** (mô rēs/ ô/gəst; *Fr.* mō ʀēs/ ō gʏst/), 1888–1973, French actor and singer.

Che·va·lier-Mon·tra·chet (shə val/yā mōn/trä shā/, -mon/trə-, -väl/-; *Fr.* shə vᴀ lyā/môɴ ʀᴀ she/), *n.* a white wine from Burgundy.

Che·val·lier (shə väl/yā, -val/-), *n.* a walled plain in the first quadrant of the face of the moon: about 30 miles in diameter.

cheval/ screen/, a fire screen, usually with a cloth panel, having supports at the ends and mounted on legs. [see ᴄʜᴇᴠᴀʟ ɢʟᴀss]

che·vee (shə vā/), *n.* *Jewelry.* **1.** cuvette (def. 2). **2.** a smooth gem with a slightly depressed surface. [< F *chevée*, n. use of fem. of *chevé*, ptp. of *chever* to make a hollow in < L *cavāre*, deriv. of *cavus* hollow; see ᴄᴀᴠᴇ]

cheve·ret (shev/rit, shev ret/), *n.* a small English table of the 18th century, having an oblong top, one or two rows of drawers, and slender legs joined near the bottom by a shelf. Also, **sheveret.** [? alter. of *chevalet* < F: trestle. See ᴄʜᴇᴠᴀʟ ɢʟᴀss, -ᴇᴛ]

Chev·er·ly (shev/ər lē), *n.* a town in central Maryland. 5223 (1960).

Chev·es (chiv/is), *n.* **Lang·don** (laṅg/dən), 1776–1857, U.S. politician: Speaker of the House 1814–15.

che·vet (shə vā/), *n.* an apse, as of a Gothic cathedral. [< F, earlier *chevés*, OF *chevez* << L *capit(ium)* opening or covering for the head. See ᴄᴀᴘᴜᴛ]

che·ville (shə vē/), *n.* *Pros.* a word or expression whose only function is to fill a metrical gap in a verse or to balance a sentence. Cf. **expletive** (def. 2). [< F: plug, peg < L *clāvicul(a)* tendril. See ᴄʟᴀᴠɪᴄʟᴇ]

Chev·i·ot (chev/ē ət, chē/vē-; *commonly* shev/ē ət *for 2*), *n.* **1.** one of a British breed of sheep, noted for its heavy fleece of medium length. **2.** (*l.c.*) a woolen fabric in a coarse twill weave, for coats, suits, etc. [named after the ᴄʜᴇᴠɪᴏᴛ (ʜɪʟʟs)]

Chev/iot Hills/, a range of hills on the boundary between England and Scotland: highest point, 2676 ft.

chev·on (shev/ən), *n.* the flesh of goats, used as food. [*chev-* (< F *chèvre* goat < L *capra* she-goat, fem. of *caper* goat) + *-on*, abstracted from *mutton*]

chev·ret (shə vrā/), *n.* a French cheese made from goat's milk. [< F *chèvre* goat. See ᴄʜᴇᴠᴏɴ]

chev·rette (shəv ret/), *n.* a soft, thin kidskin. [< F: she-kid, equiv. to *chèvre* goat (see ᴄʜᴇᴠᴏɴ) + *-ette* -ᴇᴛᴛᴇ]

chev·ron (shev/rən), *n.* **1.** a badge consisting of stripes meeting at an angle, worn on the sleeve by noncommissioned officers, policemen, etc., as an indication of rank, service, wounds in war, etc. **2.** an ornament in this form, as on a molding. **3.** *Heraldry.* an ordinary in the form of an inverted V. **4. in chevron,** *Heraldry.* (of charges) arranged in the manner of a chevron; chevronwise. **5. per chevron,** *Heraldry.* diagonally upward from either side toward the center: *party per chevron.* [< F: rafter, chevron < VL **capriōn-* (s. of **capriō*), equiv. to *capri-* goat + *-ōn-* n. suffix] —**chev/roned,** *adj.*

Chevrons
A, U.S. Army Sergeant; B, U.S. Air Force Staff Sergeant; C, U.S. Navy Petty Officer Second Class

chev·ron·el (shev/rə nel/), *n.* *Heraldry.* a narrow chevron, one half the usual breadth or less. [ᴄʜᴇᴠʀᴏɴ + *-el* dim. suffix]

chev·ron·ny (shev/rə nē), *adj.* *Heraldry.* (of an escutcheon or charge) divided into an equal number of chevronlike parts: *chevronny of six argent and sable.* Also, **chev/ron·y.** [< F *chevronné*, ptp. of *chevronner* to ornament with chevrons. See ᴄʜᴇᴠʀᴏɴ]

chev·ron·wise (shev/rən wīz/), *adj.* *Heraldry.* in the manner of a chevron in arrangement: *spears chevronwise.* [ᴄʜᴇᴠʀᴏɴ + -ᴡɪsᴇ]

chev·ro·tain (shev/rə tān/, -tin), *n.* any very small, deerlike ruminant of the family *Traguidae*, of Africa, tropical Asia, the Malay Peninsula, etc. Also called **mouse deer.** [< F, equiv. to *chevrot* kid (*chèvre* goat + *-ot* dim. suffix) + *-ain* -ᴀɴ]

chev·y (chev/ē), *v.,* **chev·ied, chev·y·ing,** *n., pl.* **chev·ies.** *Brit.* —*v.t.* **1.** to chase; run after. **2.** to harass; nag; torment. —*v.i.* **3.** to race; scamper. —*n.* **4.** a hunting cry. **5.** a hunt, chase, or pursuit. **6.** the game of prisoner's base. Also, **chivvy, chivy.** [perh. short for ᴄʜᴇᴠʏ ᴄʜᴀsᴇ]

Chev/y Chase/ (chev/ē), a town in central Maryland. 2405 (1960).

Chev/y Chase/, (*The Ballad of Chevy Chase*) a 15th-century English ballad describing the battle of Otterburn between the Percys and the Douglases. Cf. **Otterburn.**

chew (chōō), *v.t.* **1.** to crush or grind with the teeth; masticate. **2.** to crush, damage, injure, etc., as if by chewing (often fol. by *up*): *The faulty lawn mower chewed the grass up.* **3.** to make by or as by chewing: *The puppy chewed a hole in my slipper.* **4.** to meditate on; consider deliberately (often fol. by *over*): *He chewed the problem over in his mind.* —*v.i.* **5.** to perform the act of crushing or grinding with the teeth. **6.** *Informal.* to chew tobacco. **7.** to meditate. **8. chew out,** *Slang.* to scold harshly: *The sergeant chewed out the recruits almost as soon as they arrived.* **9. chew the fat,** *Slang.* to have an informal conversation; chat: *They liked to sit at the sidewalk café in the afternoon, chewing the fat.* **10. chew the rag,** *Slang.* to chew the fat; chat: *It was a quiet night at the station, with the firemen playing cards and chewing the rag.* —*n.* **11.** the act or an instance of chewing. **12.** that which is chewed; a mouthful or portion for chewing, esp. of tobacco. [ME *chew(en)*, OE *cēowan*; c. OHG *kiuwan* (G *kauen*)] —**chew/a·ble,** *adj.* —**chew/er,** *n.*

chew/ing gum/ (chōō/iṅg), a preparation for chewing, usually made of sweetened and flavored chicle.

chew/ing louse/. See under **louse** (def. 2).

Chew/ings fes/cue (chōō/iṅgz), a fine-leaved variety of fescue, *Festuca rubra commutata*, grown in the U.S. and New Zealand. [named after Charles *Chewings* (d. 1937), Australian scientist]

che·wink (chi wiṅk/), *n.* a towhee, *Pipilo erythrophthalmus*, of eastern North America. [imit.]

chew·y (chōō/ē), *adj.,* **chew·i·er, chew·i·est.** (of food) not easily chewed, due to being tough or sticky; requiring much chewing. [ᴄʜᴇᴡ + -ʏ[1]]

Chey·enne (shī en/, -an/), *n., pl.* **-ennes,** (*esp. collectively*) **-enne** for 1. **1.** a member of an American Indian people of the western plains, formerly in central Minnesota and North and South Dakota, and now divided between Montana and Oklahoma. **2.** an Algonquian language, the language of the Cheyenne Indians. **3.** a city in and the capital of Wyoming, in the S part. 43,505 (1960).

Cheyenne/ Riv/er, a river flowing NE from E Wyoming to the Missouri River in South Dakota. ab. 500 mi. long.

Chey·ne (chā/nē, chān), *n.* **Thomas Kel·ly** (kel/ē), 1841–1915, English clergyman and Biblical scholar.

Cheyne/-Stokes/ respira/tion (chān/stōks/, chā/nē-), *Med.* intense and labored respiration alternating with cessation of breath, occurring in certain cerebral, cardiac, and other conditions. Also, **Cheyne/-Stokes/ breath/ing.** [named after J. *Cheyne* (d. 1836), Scottish physician and W. *Stokes* (d. 1878), Irish physician]

chez (shā), *prep.* *French.* at or in the home of; with.

chg., 1. change. **2.** charge.

chi (kī), *n., pl.* **chis. 1.** the 22nd letter of the Greek alphabet (X, χ). **2.** the consonant sound represented by this letter. [< Gk]

chi·ack (chī/ək), *v.t.* *Australian.* to jeer at; tease; deride. Also, **chyack.** [prob. alter. of ᴄʜᴇᴇᴋ]

Chi·an (kī/ən), *adj.* **1.** of or pertaining to Chios or its inhabitants. —*n.* **2.** a native or inhabitant of Chios. [Cʜɪ(ᴏs) + -ᴀɴ]

Chiang Kai-shek (chyäṅg/ kī/shek/, chaṅg/), (*Chang Chung-cheng*) 1886?–1975, Chinese statesman and general: president of the Executive Yuan 1928–45; president of the Republic 1943–50; president of the Republic of China 1950–75. Also, **Chiang Chieh-shih** (chyäṅg/ chye/shœ/).

Chiang·ling (jyäṅg/liṅg/), *n.* Kiangling.

Chiang·mai (chyäṅg/mī/), *n.* a city in NW Thailand. 61,804 (est. 1957). Also, **Chiang/ Mai/, Chiengmai.**

Chiang·rai (chyäng′rī′), *n.* a city in NW Thailand. 25,000 (est. 1960). Also, **Chiang′ Rai′, Chiengrai.**

Chi·an·ti (kē än′tē, -an′-; *It.* kyän′te), *n.* a dry, red, Italian table wine, usually put up in a straw-covered bottle. [after the *Chianti* Mountains in Tuscany]

Chi′an tur′pentine (kī′ən), turpentine (def. 2).

chiao (jyou), *n., pl.* **chiao.** a fractional currency of China, the 10th part of a jên-min-piao, equal to 10 fen and equivalent to about .04 of a U.S. dollar. [< Chin]

Chi·a·pas (chē ä′päs), *n.* a state in S Mexico. 1,215,475 (1960); 28,732 sq. mi. *Cap.:* Tuxtla Gutiérrez.

Chia·ri (chyä′rē), *n.* **Ro·ber·to F(ran·cis·co)** (rô ver′-tô frän sēs′kô), born 1905, Panamanian businessman and politician: president 1960–64.

chi·a·ro·o·scu·ro (kē är′ō ō skyŏŏr′ō), *n., pl.* **-ros.** chiaroscuro. —**chi·a′ro·o·scu′rist,** *n.*

chi·a·ro·scu·ro (kē är′ə skyŏŏr′ō), *n., pl.* **-ros. 1.** the distribution of light and shade in a picture. **2.** *Painting.* the use of deep variations in and subtle gradations of light and shade, esp. to enhance the delineation of character and for general dramatic effect: *Rembrandt is a master of chiaroscuro.* **3.** a woodcut print produced from two or more blocks, each inked with a different tone of the same color and thereby rendering gradations of light and shade. **4.** a sketch in light and shade. Also, **chiaroscuro.** [< It, equiv. to *chiaro* bright (< L *clārus*) + *oscuro* dark (< L *obscūrus*). See CLEAR, OBSCURE]

chi·asm (kī′az əm), *n.* chiasma.

chi·as·ma (kī az′mə), *n., pl.* **-mas, -ma·ta** (-mə tə). **1.** *Genetics.* an exchange of segments between two of the four chromatids of paired chromosomes during late prophase and metaphase. **2.** *Anat.* a crossing or decussation, esp. that of the optic nerves at the base of the brain. [< Gk: crosspiece of wood, cross-bandage, equiv. to *chi* CHI + *-asma* n. suffix] —**chi·as′mal, chi·as′mic,** *adj.*

chi·as·ma·typ·y (kī az′mə tī′pē), *n.* *Genetics.* the process of chiasma formation, which is the basis for crossing over. Cf. **crossing over.** [CHIASMA + -TYPE + -Y³] —**chi·as′ma·type′,** *adj., n.*

chi·as·mus (kī az′məs), *n., pl.* **-mi** (-mī). *Rhet.* a reversal in the order of words in two otherwise parallel phrases, as in "He went to the country, to the town went she." [< Gk *chiasmós,* equiv. to *chi* CHI + *-asmos* masc. n. suffix, akin to *-asma;* see CHIASMA]

chi·as·tic (kī as′tik), *adj.* *Rhet.* characterized by chiasmus. [< Gk *chiast(ós)* diagonally arranged (see CHIASMA) + -IC]

chi·as·to·lite (kī as′tᵊlīt′), *n.* *Mineral.* a variety of andalusite having cruciform carbonaceous inclusions. [alter. of *chiastolith* (see -LITE), equiv. to Gk *chiastó(s)* set crosswise (see CHIASMA) + -LITH]

chiaus (chous, choush), *n., pl.* **chiaus·es.** (in Turkey) a messenger, emissary, etc. [< Turk *çavus* < Pers *chāwush*]

Chi·ba (chē′bä′), *n.* a city on SE Honshu, in central Japan, near Tokyo. 300,631 (est. 1964).

Chib·cha (chib′chə), *n., pl.* **-chas,** (*esp. collectively*) **-cha.** a member of a now extinct tribe of South American Indians, having an advanced culture, who lived on a high plateau of Bogotá, Colombia.

Chib·chan (chib′chən), *n.* a family of languages indigenous to Colombia, Central America, and Ecuador. [CHIBCH(A) + -AN]

chi·bouk (chi bŏŏk′, -bŏŏk′), *n.* a Turkish tobacco pipe with a stiff stem sometimes four or five feet long. Also, **chi·bouque′.** [< Turk *çibuk,* var. of *çubuk* pipe]

chic (shēk, shik), *adj.* **1.** attractive and fashionable in style; stylish: *a chic hat.* —*n.* **2.** style and elegance, esp. in dress: *Paris clothes have such chic.* **3.** stylishness; modishness; fashionableness: *She admired the chic of the first-nighters.* [< F < G *Schick* skill; or, short for CHICANE] —**chic′ly,** *adv.*

Chi·ca·go (shi kä′gō, -kô′-), *n.* **1.** a city in NE Illinois, on Lake Michigan: second largest city in the U.S. 3,005,072. **2.** (*italics*) a poem (1914) by Carl Sandburg. —**Chi·ca′go·an,** *n.*

Chica′go Heights′, a city in NE Illinois, S of Chicago. 34,433 (1960).

Chica′go Ridge′, a town in NE Illinois. 5748 (1960).

Chica′go style′, a style of jazz flourishing in Chicago esp. in the early 1920's, constituting a direct offshoot of New Orleans style, and differing from its predecessor chiefly in the diminished influence of native folk sources, the greater tension of its group improvisation, the increased emphasis on solos, and the regular use of the tenor saxophone as part of the ensemble.

chi·ca·lo·te (chē′kä lō′te), *n.* any of several prickly, papaveraceous plants of arid tropical and subtropical America, as *Argemone mexicana* and *A. platyceras.* [< Sp < Nahuatl *chicalotl*]

chi·cane (shi kān′), *n., v.,* **-caned, -can·ing.** —*n.* **1.** deception; chicanery. —*v.t.* **2.** to trick by chicanery. **3.** to quibble over; cavil at. [< F *chicane* (n.), *chican(er)* (v.), perh. < MLG *schikken* to arrange] —**chi·can′er,** *n.*

chi·can·er·y (shi kā′nə rē), *n., pl.* **-er·ies. 1.** trickery or deception by quibbling or sophistry: *He resorted to the worst flattery and chicanery to win the rich widow.* **2.** a quibble or subterfuge used to trick, deceive, or evade: *Such a chicanery will not bring us any closer to a solution.* [< F *chicanerie.* See CHICANE, -ERY] —**Syn. 1.** fraud, deception, knavery. **2.** evasion.

Chi·ca·no (chi kä′nō, -kā′nō), *n., pl.* **-nos. 1.** an American born of Mexican parents. **2.** a Mexican worker residing in the U.S. —*adj.* **3.** of or pertaining to Mexican-Americans. [MexSp, by shortening and alter. of *Mexicano* Mexican]

chic·co·ry (chik′ə rē), *n., pl.* **-ries.** chicory.

chi·cha (chē′chə), *n.* a beer made from fermented corn in South and Central America. [< Sp < native name current in Hispaniola]

Chi·chén It·zá (chē chen′ ēt sä′, ēt′sə), the ruins of an ancient Mayan city, in central Yucatán state, Mexico.

chi·chi (shē′shē′), *adj.* pretentiously elegant, sophisticated, or stylish. [< F]

Chi·chi·haerh (*Chin.* chē′chē′här′), *n.* Tsitsihar. Also, **Chi′chi′har′.**

chi·chil·i (chē′chi lē), *n.* chili².

Chich·i·vache (chich′ə väsh′), *n.* (in early English literature) a mythical animal, usually depicted as an extremely gaunt cow verging on starvation, that existed solely by devouring virtuous women (opposed to *Bicorn*). [ME < MF (north) *chichefache* thin face, ugly face, monster, hence *vache* cow, by folk etymology, r. *fache*]

chick (chik), *n.* **1.** a young chicken or other bird. **2.** a child. **3.** *Slang.* a girl or young woman: *They took their chicks with them to the game.* [ME *chike,* var. of *chiken* CHICKEN]

Black-capped chickadee, *Parus atricapillus* (Length 5¼ in.)

Chick (chik), *n.* a boy's or girl's given name.

chick·a·dee (chik′ə dē′), *n.* any of several North American titmice of the genus *Parus* (*Penthestes*), esp. *P. atricapillus* (**black-capped chickadee**), having the throat and top of the head black. [imit.]

Chick·a·mau·ga (chik′ə mô′gə), *n.* a creek in NW Georgia: scene of a Confederate victory 1863.

chick·a·ree (chik′ə rē′), *n.* See **red squirrel.** [imit.]

Chick·a·saw (chik′ə sô′), *n., pl.* **-saws,** (*esp. collectively*) **-saw. 1.** a member of a warlike Muskhogean tribe of North American Indians, formerly in northern Mississippi, now in Oklahoma. **2.** a city in SW Alabama. 10,002 (1960).

Chick·a·sha (chik′ə shā′), *n.* a city in central Oklahoma. 14,866 (1960).

chick·en (chik′ən, -in), *n.* **1.** a gallinaceous bird descended from the jungle fowl, *Gallus gallus.* **2.** the young of this bird, esp. when less than a year old. **3.** the flesh of the chicken, esp. of the young bird, used as food. **4.** *Informal.* a young or inexperienced person, esp. a young girl: *She may not be 60 yet, but she's no chicken.* **5.** **count one's chickens before they are hatched,** to rely on a benefit that is still uncertain: *They were already spending in anticipation of their inheritance, counting their chickens before they were hatched.* —*adj.* **6.** (of food) containing, made from, or having the flavor of chicken: *chicken salad; chicken soup.* **7.** *Slang.* cowardly. —*v.i.* **8.** **chicken out,** *Informal.* to refrain from doing something because of fear or cowardice: *I chickened out when I learned that a supply of loaded guns was going along with us.* [ME *chiken,* OE *cicen;* akin to D *kieken, kuiken,* LG *küken*]

chick′en breast′, *Pathol.* a malformation of the chest in which there is abnormal projection of the sternum and the sternal region, often associated with rickets. Also called **pigeon breast.** —**chick′en-breast′ed,** *adj.* —**chick′en-breast′ed·ness,** *n.*

chick′en chol′era, *Vet. Pathol. Rare.* See **fowl cholera.**

chick′en colo′nel, *U.S. Mil. Slang.* a full colonel, as distinguished from a lieutenant colonel. Also called **bird colonel.**

chick′en coop′, 1. a coop for chickens. **2.** *Fox Hunting.* a device for making it easier for a horse to jump wire fences, consisting of two wooden panels set on opposite sides of the fence with the tops of the panels joined at an angle so as to cover the wire.

chick′en feed′, *U.S. Slang.* **1.** a small or insignificant sum of money: *He's so rich that $1000 is just chicken feed to him.* **2.** small change, as pennies and nickels. **3.** misleading information deliberately supplied or leaked by a government to a double agent in its employ or to the spies of another government.

chick′en grape′. See **riverbank grape.**

chick′en hawk′, (not used scientifically) any of various hawks that sometimes prey or are said to prey on poultry. Also called **hen hawk.**

chick·en-heart·ed (chik′ən här′tid, chik′in-), *adj.* *Informal.* timid; cowardly. —**chick′en-heart′ed·ly,** *adv.* —**chick′en-heart′ed·ness,** *n.*

chick′en lad′der, *Building Trades.* an inclined plank with transverse cleats.

chick·en-liv·ered (chik′ən liv′ərd, chik′in-), *adj.* *Informal.* timid; cowardly.

chick′en pox′, *Pathol.* a mild, contagious, eruptive disease, commonly of children. Also called **varicella, water pox.**

chick·en·shit (chik′ən shit′), *Slang* (*vulgar*). —*n.* **1.** boring or annoying details or unimportant tasks. **2.** petty lies or exaggeration. —*adj.* **3.** cowardly. [CHICKEN + SHIT]

chick′en snake′. See **rat snake.**

chicken′ switch′, *Rocketry Slang.* **1.** a device by which an astronaut may eject the capsule in which he rides in the event that a rocket malfunctions. **2.** See **egads button.**

chick′en tet·raz·zi′ni (te′trə zē′nē), diced chicken in a cream sauce, baked in a casserole with noodles and cheese, usually flavored with sherry. [named after Luisa TETRAZZINI]

chick′en tur′tle, an edible, fresh-water turtle, *Deirochelys reticularia,* of the southeastern U.S., characterized by a long neck and by the network of fine, yellow lines marking the dark carapace.

chick′en wire′, a light, wire netting having a large, hexagonal mesh, used esp. as fencing.

chick·pea (chik′pē′), *n.* **1.** Also called **garbanzo.** a leguminous plant, *Cicer arietinum,* bearing edible pealike seeds, used for food esp. in southern Europe and Latin America. **2.** its seed. [alter. of *chich-pea,* equiv. to late ME *chiche* (< MF << L *cicer* chickpea) + PEA]

chick·weed (chik′wēd′), *n.* **1.** any of various caryophyllaceous plants of the genus *Stellaria,* as *S. media,* a common Old World weed whose leaves and seeds are relished by birds. **2.** any of various allied plants. [ME *chiken wede.* See CHICK, WEED¹]

chick′weed win′tergreen, a starflower, *Trientalis borealis.*

Chi·cla·yo (chē klä′yô), *n.* a city in NW Peru. 86,904 (1961).

chic·le (chik′əl), *n.* a gumlike substance obtained from the latex of certain tropical American trees, as the sapodilla, used chiefly in the manufacture of chewing gum. Also called **chic′le gum′.** [< Sp < Nahuatl *chictli*]

chi·co (chē′kō), *n., pl.* **-cos.** greasewood (def. 1). [short for CHICALOTE]

Chi·co (chē′kō), *n.* **1.** a city in central California. 14,757 (1960). **2.** a boy's given name.

Chic·o·pee (chik′ə pē′), *n.* a city in S Massachusetts, on the Connecticut River. 61,553 (1960).

chic·o·ry (chik′ə rē), *n., pl.* **-ries. 1.** Also called **blue dandelion, blueweed, coffeeweed.** a perennial plant, *Cichorium intybus,* having bright-blue flowers, cultivated as a salad plant and for its root, which is used roasted and ground as a substitute or adulterant for coffee. **2.** the root of this plant. **3.** *Brit.* endive (def. 1). Also, **chiccory.** [< MF *chicoree;* r. late ME *cicoree* < MF < L *cichorēa* (pl. of *cichorēum*) < Gk *kichóreia* endive, succory]

Chi′co Ve·ci′no (vi sē′nō), a town in central California. 4688 (1960).

chide (chīd), *v.,* **chid·ed** or **chid; chid·ed** or **chid** or **chid·den; chid·ing.** —*v.i.* **1.** to scold; find fault. —*v.t.* **2.** to harass, nag, impel, or the like by chiding: *She chided him into apologizing.* **3.** to express disapproval of: *She chided the children for their thoughtless pranks.* [ME *chide(n),* OE *cīdan*] —**chid′er,** *n.* —**chid′ing·ly,** *adv.* —**Syn. 1.** fret, fume, chafe. **3.** reprove, rebuke, censure, scold, upbraid, blame. —**Ant. 3.** praise.

chief (chēf), *n.* **1.** the head or leader of an organized body of men; the person highest in authority: *the chief of police.* **2.** the head or ruler of a clan or tribe: *Indian chief.* **3.** (*cap.*) *U.S. Army.* a title of some advisers to the Chief of Staff, who do not, in most instances, command the troop units of their arms or services: *Chief of Engineers; Chief Signal Officer.* **4.** *Slang.* boss or leader: *We'll have to talk to the chief about this.* **5.** *Heraldry.* **a.** the upper area of an escutcheon. **b.** an ordinary occupying this area. **6.** **in chief, a.** in the chief position; highest in rank (used in combination): *editor in chief; commander in chief.* **b.** *Heraldry.* in the upper part of an escutcheon. —*adj.* **7.** highest in rank or authority: *the chief priest; the chief administrator.* **8.** most important; principal: *his chief merit; the chief difficulty.* —*adv.* **9.** *Archaic.* chiefly; principally. [ME < OF < VL **cap(um),* alter. of L *caput* HEAD] —**chief′less,** *adj.* —**Syn. 8.** foremost, essential, leading, prime, paramount, cardinal, vital. See **capital¹.** —**Ant. 7.** subordinate.

chief′ con′stable, *Brit.* chief of police.

chief·dom (chēf′dəm), *n.* **1.** the rank or office of a chief. **2.** the territory or people over which a chief rules. [CHIEF + -DOM]

Chief′ Exec′utive, *U.S.* **1.** the President of the United States. **2.** (*l.c.*) the governor of a State. **3.** (*l.c.*) the head of a government.

chief′ jus′tice, 1. *Law.* the presiding judge of a court having several members. **2.** (*caps.*) official title, **Chief′ Jus′tice of the Unit′ed States′.** the presiding judge of the U.S. Supreme Court. —**chief′ jus′tice·ship′.**

chief·ly (chēf′lē), *adv.* **1.** principally; essentially. **2.** mainly; mostly: *He went along chiefly for the ride.* [ME; see CHIEF, -LY] —**Syn.** See **especially.** —**Ant. 1.** lastly.

chief′ mate′, *Naut.* See **first mate.** Also called **chief′ of′ficer.**

Chief′ of Staff′, *U.S.* **1.** the senior officer of the Army or of the Air Force, a member of the Joint Chiefs of Staff, responsible to the Secretary of his service branch. **2.** (*l.c.*) the senior or principal staff officer in a brigade or division or higher unit in the Army or Marine Corps, in a numbered unit in the Air Force, or in a unit in the Navy commanded by a rear admiral or his superior. **3.** (*l.c.*) the senior officer in command of a general staff, esp. that of the military forces of a nation.

chief′ of state′, the titular head of a nation, as a president, king, etc.

chief′ pet′ty of′ficer, *U.S. Navy and Coast Guard.* a noncommissioned rank above petty officer first class and below senior petty officer. *Abbr.:* CPO, C.P.O.

chief·tain (chēf′tən, -tin), *n.* **1.** a leader of a group, band, etc. **2.** the chief of a clan or a tribe. [ME *cheftayne,* var. of *chevetaine* < OF < LL *capitān(e)-* (us) CAPTAIN] —**chief′tain·cy, chief′tain·ship′,** *n.*

chief′ war′rant of′ficer, *U.S. Mil.* a warrant officer ranking immediately below a second lieutenant or ensign in the armed forces.

chield (chēld), *n.* *Scot.* a young man; fellow. Also, **chiel** (chēl). [var. of CHILD]

Chieng·mai (*Thai.* chyeng′mī′), *n.* Chiangmai.

Chieng·rai (*Thai.* chyeng′rī′), *n.* Chiangrai.

Ch'ien Lung (chyen′ lŏŏng′), (*Kao Tsung*) 1711–99, Chinese emperor of the Ch'ing dynasty 1736–96. Also, **Kien Lung.**

chiff·chaff (chif′chaf′, -chäf′), *n.* a common, gray, Old World warbler, *Phylloscopus collybita.* [gradational compound; imit.]

chif·fon (shi fon′, shif′on), *n.* **1.** a sheer fabric of silk, nylon, or rayon in plain weave. **2.** any bit of feminine finery, as of ribbon or lace. —*adj.* **3.** (of women's dresses, scarves, etc.) resembling or made of chiffon. **4.** (in cooking) having a light, frothy texture, as certain pies and cakes containing beaten egg whites. [< F, equiv. to *chiffe* rag + *-on* n. suffix]

Chiffonier

chif·fo·nade (shif′ə nād′, -näd′), *adj.* a mixture of finely cut vegetables, herbs or the like, for use in soups, salads, etc. [< F; see CHIFFON, -ADE¹]

chif·fo·nier (shif′ə nēr′), *n.* **1.** a high chest of drawers or bureau, often having a mirror. **2.** a low bookcase of the English Regency, with grille doors or doorless. **3.** a shallow, tall, open piece of furniture, of the 18th century, having shelves for the display of china. Also, **chif′fon·nier′.** [< F *chiffonnier.* See CHIFFON, -IER]

chif·fon·nière (shif′ə nēr′; *Fr.* shē fô nyer′), *n., pl.* **-nieres** (-nērz′; *Fr.* -nyer′). *Fr. Furniture.* a work table of the 18th century, having several tiers of shallow drawers. [< F, fem. of *chiffonnier.* See CHIFFONIER]

chif·fo·robe (shif′ə rōb′), *n.* a piece of furniture having both drawers and space for hanging clothes. Also, **chif′fe·robe′, chiff·robe** (shif′rōb). [CHIFFO(NIER + WARD)-ROBE]

Chif·ley (chif′lē), *n.* **Joseph Benedict,** 1885–1951, Australian statesman: prime minister 1945–49.

chig·e·tai (chig′i tī′), *n.* a Mongolian wild ass, *Equus hemionus hemionus,* related to the onager. Also called **dziggetai.** [< Mongolian *tchikhitei,* lit., with long ears, deriv. of *tchikhi* ear]

chig·ger (chig′ər), *n.* **1.** Also called **harvest mite, redbug.** the six-legged larva of a mite of the family *Trombiculidae,* parasitic on man and other vertebrates, sucking blood and causing severe itching and acting as a vector of scrub typhus and other infectious diseases. **2.** chigoe. Also, **jigger.** [var. of CHIGOE]

Chigger, *Eutrombicula alfreddugesi* (Length 1/16 in.)

chi·gnon (shēn′yon, shēn yun′; *Fr.* shē nyôN′), *n., pl.* **chi·gnons** (shēn′yonz, shēn yunz′; *Fr.* shē nyôN′). a large, smooth twist, roll, or knot of hair, worn by women at the nape of the neck or the back of the head. [< F: nape, roll of hair at nape, equiv. to MF *ch(aignon)* (var. of *chainon* link, equiv. to *chaine* CHAIN + *-on* n. suffix) + *(t)ignon* twist of hair (*tigne* (< L *tinea* worm) + *-on* n. suffix)] —**chi·gnoned′,** *adj.*

chig·oe (chig′ō), *n.* a flea, *Tunga penetrans,* of tropical America and Africa, the impregnated female of which imbeds itself in the skin, esp. of the feet, of man and animals and becomes greatly distended with eggs. Also called **chig′oe flea′, chigger, jigger, sand flea.** [< Carib]

Chih·li (chē′lē; *Chin.* ju′lē′), *n.* **1.** former name of **Hopeh. 2. Gulf of,** former name of **Pohai.**

Chi·hua·hua (chi wä′wä, -wə), *n.* **1.** a state in N Mexico. 1,374,358 (est. 1963); 94,831 sq. mi. **2.** the capital of this state. 198,461 (est. 1965). **3.** one of a Mexican or Aztec breed of very small dogs having either short or long hair of any one of a variety of colors.

Chi·ka·mat·su (chē′kä mät′so͞o), *n.* **Mon·za·e·mon** (môn′zä e môn′), 1653–1724, Japanese playwright.

chil·blain (chil′blān′), *n.* Usually, **chilblains.** *Pathol.* an inflammation of the hands and feet caused by exposure to cold and moisture. Also called **pernio.** [CHILL + BLAIN] —**chil′blained′,** *adj.*

Chil·cat (chil′kat), *n., pl.* **-cats,** (*esp. collectively*) **-cat.** Chilkat.

child (chīld), *n., pl.* **chil·dren. 1.** a boy or girl. **2.** a son or daughter: *All my children are married.* **3.** a baby or infant. **4.** a childish person: *He's such a child about money.* **5.** any descendant: *a child of an ancient breed.* **6.** any person or thing regarded as the product or result of particular agencies, influences, etc.: *Abstract art is a child of the 20th century.* **7.** a person regarded as conditioned or marked by a given circumstance, situation, etc.: *a child of poverty; a child of famine.* **8.** *Brit. Dial. Archaic.* a female infant. **9.** *Archaic.* childe. **10. with child,** pregnant: *The woman was obviously with child.* [ME *child,* OE *cild;* akin to Goth *kilthai* womb] —**child′less,** *adj.* —**child′less·ness,** *n.*

child·bear·ing (chīld′bâr′ing), *n.* **1.** the act of producing or bringing forth children. —*adj.* **2.** capable of, suitable for, or relating to the bearing of a child or of children: *the childbearing years.* [ME; see CHILD, BEARING]

child·bed (chīld′bed′), *n.* the condition of a woman giving birth to a child; parturition: *to lie in childbed.* [ME; see CHILD, BED]

child′bed fe′ver, *Pathol.* See **puerperal fever.**

child·birth (chīld′bûrth′), *n.* the act or an instance of bringing forth a child; parturition: *a difficult childbirth.* [CHILD + BIRTH]

childe (chīld), *n.* *Archaic.* a youth of noble birth. [var. of CHILD]

Childe (chīld), *n.* **Vere Gordon** (vēr), 1892–1957, English anthropologist, archaeologist, and writer; born in Australia.

Childe′ Har′old's Pil′grimage, a narrative poem (1812, 1816, 1818) by Byron.

Chil·der·mas (chil′dər məs), *n.* See **Holy Innocents' Day.** [ME *chyldermasse,* equiv. to OE *cildra* (gen. pl. of *cild* CHILD) + *mæsse* MASS]

Childe′ Ro′land to the Dark′ Tow′er Came′, a poem (1855) by Robert Browning.

Chil·ders·burg (chil′dərz bûrg′), *n.* a town in central Alabama. 4884 (1960).

child·hood (chīld′ho͝od), *n.* **1.** the state or period of being a child. **2.** the early stage in the existence of something: *the childhood of the human race; the childhood of science.* [ME *childhode,* OE *cildhād.* See CHILD, -HOOD]

child·ing (chīl′ding), *adj.* bearing children; pregnant. [ME; see CHILD, -ING²]

child·ish (chīl′dish), *adj.* **1.** of, like, or befitting a child: *childish games.* **2.** puerile; weak; silly: *childish fears; an adult with a childish manner.* [ME *childisch,* OE *cildisc.* See CHILD, -ISH¹] —**child′ish·ly,** *adv.* —**child′ish·ness,** *n.*

—**Syn. 1, 2.** CHILDISH, INFANTILE, CHILDLIKE refer to characteristics or qualities of childhood. The ending *-ish* often has unfavorable connotations; CHILDISH therefore refers to characteristics which are undesirable and unpleasant: *childish selfishness, outbursts of temper.* INFANTILE, originally a general word, now often carries an even stronger idea of disapproval or scorn than does CHILDISH: *infantile reasoning, behavior.* The ending *-like* has pleasing or neutral connotations; CHILDLIKE therefore refers to the characteristics which are desirable and admirable: *childlike innocence, trust.* —**Ant. 1, 2.** mature, adult.

child′ la′bor, the employment in gainful occupations of children below a minimum age determined by law or custom: the minimum legal age for ordinary full-time employment is 16 years in the U.S., according to federal law; standards regulating intrastate employment vary from State to State.

child·like (chīld′līk′), *adj.* like a child, as in innocence, frankness, etc.; befitting a child: *childlike candor.* [CHILD + -LIKE] —**child′like′ness,** *n.*

—**Syn.** young, ingenuous, simple, guileless, trusting, innocent. See **childish.** —**Ant.** sophisticated, adult.

child·ly (chīld′lē), *adj.* *Rare.* childlike; childish. [ME *childely,* OE *cildlīc.* See CHILD, -LY]

child·mind·er (chīld′mīn′dər), *n.* *Brit.* a baby-sitter. [CHILD + MIND + -ER¹]

child·ness (chīld′nis), *n.* *Archaic.* the quality of being a child. [CHILD + -NESS]

child·proof (chīld′pro͞of′), *adj.* so designed that children cannot tamper with, esp. to harm themselves: *a childproof cap on an aspirin bottle.* [CHILD + -PROOF]

child′ psychi′atry, psychiatric therapy for children.

child′ psychol′ogy, 1. the study of the mental states and processes of children according to the theories of psychology. **2.** psychological techniques used in the treatment of children.

chil·dren (chil′drən, -drin), *n.* pl. of **child.**

Chil′dren of Her′cules, Heraclidae.

chil′dren of Is′rael, the Hebrews; Jews.

Chil′dren's Crusade′, the ill-fated crusade to recover Jerusalem from the Saracens, undertaken in 1212 by thousands of French and German children who either perished, were sold into slavery, or were turned back.

Chil′dren's Day′, the second Sunday in June, celebrated by Protestant churches with special programs for children, first started in the U.S. in 1868.

Chil′dren's Hour′, The, a play (1934) by Lillian Hellman.

Chil·dress (chil′dris), *n.* a town in N Texas. 6399 (1960).

Child's′ Gar′den of Vers′es, A, a collection of poems (1885) by Robert Louis Stevenson.

child's′ play′, something very easily done: *Passing that course ought to be child's play.*

chil·e (chil′ē), *n.* chili¹.

Chil·e (chil′ē; *Sp.* chē′le), *n.* a republic in SW South America, on the Pacific Coast. 8,515,023 (est. 1964); 286,396 sq. mi. *Cap.:* Santiago. —**Chil′e·an,** *adj., n.*

Chil′ean arborvi′tae, alerce (defs. 1, 2).

Chil′ean bell′flower, a perennial herb, *Nolana atriplicifolia,* of Chile and Peru, having purple-spotted and purple-streaked stems, spoon-shaped, fleshy leaves, and blue flowers with a white and yellow throat.

Chil′ean gua′va, a tropical shrub or small tree, *Myrtus Ugni,* having leathery, oval leaves, rose-pink flowers, and purplish-red, edible fruit.

Chil′ean tar′weed, a coarse, Chilean herb, *Madia sativa,* naturalized in the northwestern U.S., having brownish-yellow flower heads.

chil·e con car·ne (chil′ē kon kär′nē; *Sp.* chē′le kôn kär′ne). See **chili con carne.**

Chil′e saltpe′ter, the naturally occurring form of sodium nitrate, $NaNO_3$, used chiefly as a fertilizer and in the manufacture of sulfuric and nitric acids and potassium nitrate.

chil·i¹ (chil′ē), *n., pl.* **chil·ies. 1.** Also called **chili pepper.** the pod of any species of capsicum, esp. *Capsicum frutescens.* **2.** *U.S.* See **chili con carne.** Also, **chile, chilli.** [< Sp *chile* < Nahuatl *chilli*]

Chil·i² (shil′ē), *n.* (in Tunisia) a hot, dry wind. Also, **chichili.** [of Berber orig.]

chil·i·ad (kil′ē ad′), *n.* **1.** a group of 1000. **2.** a period of 1000 years. [< LL *chiliad-* (s. of *chilias*) < Gk, equiv. to *chíli(oi)* 1000 + *-ad-* -AD¹] —**chil′i·ad′al, chil′i·ad′ic,** *adj.*

chil·i·arch (kil′ē ärk′), *n.* the commander of 1000 men. [< L *chiliarch(ēs)* (or *chiliarch(us)*) < Gk *chiliárch(ēs)* (or *chiliárch(os)*), equiv. to *chíli(oi)* 1000 + *-archēs* (or *-archos*) -ARCH] —**chil′i·arch′y,** *n.*

chil·i·asm (kil′ē az′əm), *n.* *Theol.* the doctrine of Christ's expected return to reign on earth for 1000 years; millennialism. [< Gk *chilíasm(ós),* equiv. to *chíli(oi)* 1000 + *-asmos,* var. of *-ismos* -ISM] —**chil·i·ast** (kil′ē ast′), *n.* —**chil′i·as′tic,** *adj.*

chil·i con car·ne (chil′ē kon kär′nē; *Sp.* chē′le kôn kär′ne), a popular Mexican-style dish made from chilies or chili powder, meat, onion, finely chopped red or green pepper, etc., usually served or mixed with red beans. Also, **chile con carne.** Also called **chile, chili, chilli.** [< Sp: chili with meat. See CARNAL]

chilindre, *n.* *Obs.* See **shepherd's dial.** [ME < ML *chilindr(us)* < L *cylindrus* CYLINDER]

chil′i pep′per, chili¹ (def. 1).

chil·i·pep·per (chil′ē pep′ər), *n.* an edible, crimson rockfish, *Sebastodes goodei,* found off the coast of California. [CHILI + PEPPER]

chil′i pow′der, a powdered mixture of dried chilies, cumin, oregano, garlic, etc., used as a seasoning.

chil′i sauce′, a sauce made of tomatoes simmered with chili peppers and spices.

Chil·kat (chil′kat), *n., pl.* **-kats,** (*esp. collectively*) **-kat.** a member of an Indian people of the Pacific coastal area of southeastern Alaska belonging to the Tlingit group of Indians. Also, **Chilcat.**

Chil′koot Pass′ (chil′ko͞ot), a mountain pass on the boundary between SE Alaska and British Columbia, Canada, in the Coast Range. ab. 3500 ft. high.

chill (chil), *n.* **1.** coldness, esp. a moderate but penetrating coldness: *the chill of evening.* **2.** a sensation of cold, usually with shivering: *She felt a slight chill from the open window.* **3.** sudden coldness of the body, as during the cold stage of an ague: *fevers and chills.* **4.** a depressing influence or sensation: *His entrance cast a chill over everyone in the room.* **5.** *Foundry.* an inserted object or a surface in a mold capable of absorbing large amounts of heat, used to harden the surface of a casting or to increase its rate of solidification at a specific point. **6.** bloom¹ (def. 10). —*adj.* **7.** cold; tending to cause shivering; chilly: *a chill wind.* **8.** shivering with or affected by cold; chilly. **9.** depressing or discouraging: *chill prospects.* **10.** unduly formal; unfriendly; chilly: *a chill reception.* —*v.i.* **11.** to become cold: *The earth chills when the sun sets.* **12.** to be seized with a chill or to shiver from a chill. **13.** *Foundry.* (of a casting) to become hard on the surface by contact with a chill or chills. —*v.t.* **14.** to affect with cold; make chilly: *The rain has chilled me to the bone.* **15.** to make cool: *to chill a dessert; to chill the air.* **16.** to depress; discourage: *The news chilled his hopes.* **17.** *Foundry.* to harden the surface of (a casting) by casting it in a mold having a chill or chills. **18.** bloom¹ (def. 19). [ME *chile,* OE *ci(e)le, cele* coolness; akin to GELID, COOL, COLD] —**chill′ing·ly,** *adv.* —**chill′ness,** *n.*

—**Syn. 7.** See **cold.**

Chi·llán (chē yän′), *n.* a city in central Chile: earthquakes 1835, 1939. 66,717 (est. 1959).

chil·ler (chil′ər), *n.* **1.** one who or that which chills. **2.** *Informal.* a frightening story of murder; melodrama. **3.** a device for cooling or refrigerating. [CHILL + -ER¹]

chil·li (chil′ē), *n., pl.* **-lies.** chili¹.

Chil·li·coth·e (chil′ə koth′ē), *n.* **1.** a city in S Ohio. 24,957 (1960). **2.** a town in central Missouri. 9236 (1960). **3.** a town in central Illinois. 3054 (1960).

Chil·lon (shə lon′, shil′ən; *Fr.* shē yôN′), *n.* an ancient castle in W Switzerland, at the end of Lake Geneva.

chil·ly (chil′ē), *adj.,* **-li·er, -li·est,** *adv.* —*adj.* **1.** mildly cold or producing a sensation of cold; causing shivering; chill: *a chilly breeze.* **2.** feeling cold; sensitive to cold; chill: *Her hands were chilly.* **3.** without warmth of feeling; cool: *He gave her a chilly, haughty glance.* **4.** producing or likely to produce a feeling of fear; frightening: *He told a chilly story of ghosts and murder.* —*adv.* **5.** Also, **chil′li·ly.** in a chill manner: *The wind blew chilly.* [CHILL + -Y¹] —**chil′li·ness,** *n.*

—**Syn. 1.** See **cold.**

chilo-¹, a learned borrowing from Greek meaning "lip," used in the formation of compound words: *chiloplasty.* Also, **cheilo-.** [comb. form of Gk *cheîlos* lip]

chilo-², var. of **kilo-:** *chilopod.*

Chi·lo·e′ Is′land (chil′ō ā′; *Sp.* chē′lô e′), an island off the SW coast of Chile. 4700 sq. mi.

Chi·lom·on·as (kī lom′ə nəs), *n.* a genus of colorless, chiefly saprozoic flagellates, found in fresh waters that have become stagnant. [< NL, equiv. to *chilo-* CHILO- + *-monas,* comb form of MONAD]

Chi·lon (kī′lon), *n.* fl. 556 B.C., Greek sage and ephor at Sparta. Also, **Chi·lo** (kī′lō).

chi·lo·plas·ty (kī′lə plas′tē), *n.* *Surg.* cheiloplasty.

chi·lo·pod (kī′lə pod′), *n.* any arthropod of the class *Chilopoda,* comprising the centipedes. [CHILO- + -POD] —**chi·lop·o·dous** (ki lop′ə dəs), *adj.*

chi·lot·o·my (kī lot′ə mē), *n., pl.* **-mies.** *Surg.* cheilotomy.

Chil·pan·cin·go (chēl′pän sēng′gô), *n.* a city in and the capital of Guerrero, in SW Mexico. 18,022 (1960).

Chil′tern Hun′dreds (chil′tərn), *Brit.* **1.** certain crown lands and manors in Oxfordshire and Buckinghamshire, the stewardship of which is nominally bestowed on a member of the House of Commons to give him an excuse to resign, as members are not allowed to hold titular office from the crown. **2. to apply for the Chiltern Hundreds,** to resign or express a desire to resign from the House of Commons.

Chi·lung (chē′lo͝ong′), *n.* Keelung.

chi·mae·ra (ki mēr′ə, kī-), *n.* **1.** any fish of the family *Chimaeridae,* the male of which has a spiny clasping organ over the mouth. **2.** any similar fish of the group *Holocephali,* which includes this family. **3.** chimera. [< L < Gk *chímaira,* fem. of *chímaros* goat; akin to ON *gymbr* ewe-lamb (of one year), L *hiems* winter]

chim·ar (chim′ər), *n.* chimere.

chimb (chīm), *n.* chime².

Chim·bo·ra·zo (chim′bə rä′zō, -rā′-; *Sp.* chēm′bô-rä′sô), *n.* a volcano in central Ecuador, in the Andes. 20,702 ft.

chime¹ (chīm), *n., v.,* **chimed, chim·ing.** —*n.* **1.** an apparatus for striking a bell or bells so as to produce a musical sound, as one at the front door of a house by which visitors may announce their presence. **2.** Often, **chimes. a.** a set of bells or of slabs of metal, stone, wood, etc., producing musical tones when struck. **b.** a musical instrument consisting of such a set, esp. a glockenspiel. **c.** carillion (def. 2). **3.** carillon (defs. 1, 3). **4.** harmonious sound in general; music; melody. **5.** harmonious relation; accord: *the battling duo, in chime at last.* —*v.i.* **6.** to sound harmoniously or in chimes, as a set of bells: *The bells chimed at noon.* **7.** to produce a musical sound by striking a bell, gong, etc.; ring chimes: *The doorbell chimed.* **8.** to speak in cadence or singsong. **9.** to harmonize; agree: *The scenery chimed perfectly with the eerie mood of the play.* —*v.t.* **10.** to give forth (music, sound, etc.), as a bell or bells. **11.** to strike (a bell, set of bells, etc.) so as to produce musical sound. **12.** to put, bring, indicate, announce, etc., by chiming: *The bells chimed the hour.* **13.** to utter or repeat in cadence or singsong: *The class chimed a greeting to the new teacher.* **14. chime in, a.** to break suddenly and unwelcomely into a conversation, esp. to express agreement. **b.** to harmonize with, as in singing. **c.** to be consistent or compatible; agree: *The new building will not chime in with the surrounding architecture.* [ME *chymbe belle,* var. of **chimbel* (by false analysis), OE *cimbal* CYMBAL] —**chim′er,** *n.*

chime² (chīm), *n.* the edge or brim of a cask, barrel, or the like, formed by the ends of the staves projecting beyond the head or bottom. Also, **chimb, chine.** [ME *chimb(e),* OE *cimb-;* c. MLG, MD *kimme* edge]

chime′ hoop′, a hoop used to secure the chimes of a barrel.

chi·me·ra (ki mēr′ə, kī-), *n., pl.* **-ras. 1.** (*often cap.*) a mythological fire-breathing monster, commonly represented with a lion's head, a goat's body, and a serpent's tail. **2.** any similarly grotesque monster having disparate parts, esp. as depicted in decorative art. **3.** a horrible or unreal creature of the imagination; a vain or idle fancy: *He is far different from the chimera your fears have made of him.* **4.** *Genetics.* an organism composed of two or more genetically distinct tissues, as an organism that is partly male and partly female, or an artificially produced individual having tissues of several species. Also, **chimaera.** [var. of CHIMAERA]

chi·mere (chi mēr′, shi-), *n.* a loose upper robe, esp. of a bishop, to which the lawn sleeves are usually attached. Also, **chimar, chim·er** (chim′ər, shim′-). [ME *chemer, chymere* < AL *chimēra,* special use of CHIMERA]

chi·mer·i·cal (ki mer′i kəl, -mēr′-, kī-), *adj.* **1.** unreal; imaginary; visionary: *a chimerical terrestrial paradise.* **2.** wildly fanciful; highly unrealistic: *a chimerical supposition.* Also, **chi·mer′ic.** [CHIMER(A) + -ICAL] —**chi·mer′i·cal·ly,** *adv.* —**chi·mer′i·cal·ness,** *n.*

—**Syn. 1.** illusory, fantastic. —**Ant. 1.** real.

chime′ whis′tle, a set of steam whistles tuned to sound together harmoniously.

Chim·kent (chim kent′), *n.* a city in S Kazakstan, in the SW Soviet Union in Asia. 153,000 (1959).

chim·ney (chim′nē), *n., pl.* **-neys,** *v.,* **-neyed, -ney·ing.** —*n.* **1.** a structure, usually vertical, containing a passage or flue by which the smoke, gases, etc., of a fire or furnace are carried off and by means of which a draft is created. **2.** that part of such a structure which rises above a roof. **3.** the smokestack or funnel of a locomotive, steamship, etc. **4.** a tube, usually of glass, surrounding the flame of a lamp to promote combustion and keep the flame steady. **5.** anything resembling a chimney, as the vent of a volcano. **6.** *Dial.* fireplace. —*v.i.* **7.** *Metall.* (of the heat and gases in a blast furnace or electric furnace) to concentrate and rise at the center of the furnace as a result of the manner of separation, at various stages of heating, of the material being melted. [ME *chimenai* < MF *cheminee* < L (*camera*) *camīnāta* (room) having a fireplace, equiv. to *camīn*(*us*) (< Gk *kámīnos* furnace) + *-āta* -ATE[1]] —**chim′ney·less,** *adj.* —**chim′ney·like′,** *adj.*

chim′ney cor′ner, 1. the corner or side of a fireplace. **2.** a place near the fire. **3.** fireside; hearth.

chim′ney piece′, 1. *Chiefly Brit.* mantelpiece. **2.** *Obs.* a decoration over a fireplace.

chim′ney pot′, *Chiefly Brit.* an earthenware or metal pipe or deflector, often cylindrical, fitted on the top of a chimney to increase draft and reduce or disperse smoke.

chim′ney-pot hat′ (chim′nē pot′), *Brit.* a high silk hat; top hat.

chim′ney rock′, a column of rock rising above the level of the surrounding area or isolated on the face of a steep slope.

chim′ney swal′low, 1. *Brit.* See **barn swallow. 2.** *U.S.* See **chimney swift.**

chim′ney sweep′, one whose business it is to clean out chimneys. Also, **chim′ney sweep′er.**

chim′ney swift′, an American swift, *Chaetura pelagica,* which often builds its nest in a disused chimney.

chim′ney wheel′, smokejack.

chimp (chimp), *n. Informal.* chimpanzee. [by shortening]

chim·pan·zee (chim′pan zē′, chim pan′zē), *n.* a highly intelligent anthropoid ape, *Pan troglodytes,* of equatorial Africa, smaller, with larger ears, and more arboreal than the gorilla. [< Bantu (northern Angola)]

Chimpanzee
(Height 4 ft.)

Chi·mu (chē mo͞o′), *n., pl.* **-mus,** (*esp. collectively*) **-mu.** —*n.* **1.** a member of an Amerindian people inhabiting the northern coast of Peru and having a highly developed urban culture that lasted until the Chimu were conquered by the Incas. **2.** the language of this people. —*adj.* **3.** of, pertaining to, or characteristic of the Chimu, their language, or their culture.

chin (chin), *n., v.,* **chinned, chin·ning.** —*n.* **1.** the lower extremity of the face, below the mouth. **2.** the prominence of the lower jaw. **3. take it on the chin,** *Slang.* **a.** to suffer defeat; fail completely. **b.** to endure suffering or punishment: *He had to take it on the chin.* —*v.t.* **4.** *Gymnastics.* **a.** to bring one's chin up to (a horizontal bar, from which one is hanging), by bending the elbows. **b.** to bring (oneself) to this position. **5.** *Archaic.* to talk to; chatter with. **6.** *Informal.* to raise or bring up to the chin, as a violin. —*v.i.* **7.** to chin oneself. **8.** *Slang.* to talk; chatter: *A couple of old ladies were chinning on the corner.* [ME; OE *cin*(*n*); c. D *kin,* G *Kinn* chin, Icel *kinn,* Goth *kinnus* cheek, L *gena,* Gk *génu*(*s*) chin, jaw, Skt *hanus* jaw] —**chin′less,** *adj.*

ch'in (chin; *Chin.* chēn), *n.* a Chinese zither consisting of an oblong, slightly curved wooden box over which are stretched strings that are stopped with one hand and plucked with the other. [< Chin]

Ch'in (chin; *Chin.* chēn), *n.* a dynasty in ancient China, 221–206 B.C., marked by the emergence of a unified empire and the construction of much of the Great Wall of China.

Chin., 1. China. **2.** Chinese. Also, **Chin**

chi·na (chī′nə), *n.* **1.** a translucent ceramic material, gloss-fired at a low temperature and biscuit-fired at a high temperature. **2.** any porcelain ware. **3.** plates, cups, saucers, etc., collectively. **4.** figurines made of porcelain or ceramic material, collectively: *She has a beautiful collection of china.* —*adj.* **5.** made of china. **6.** indicating the 20th event of a series, as a wedding anniversary. [< Pers *chīnī* Chinese porcelain]

Chi·na (chī′nə), *n.* **1. People's Republic of.** a country in E Asia: under communist control since 1949. 1,008,175,288 including 13,000,000 in Inner Mongolia and 1,400,000 in Tibet; 3,691,502 sq. mi. *Cap.:* Peking. **2. Republic of.** Also called **Nationalist China.** a republic consisting mainly of the island of Taiwan off the SE coast of mainland China: under Nationalist control since 1948, but claimed by the People's Republic of China. 16,100,000; 13,885 sq. mi. *Cap.:* Taipei.

Chi·na (chī′nə), *n.* (*sometimes l.c.*) *Brit. Slang.* See **China plate.**

Chi′na as′ter, an asterlike plant, *Callistephus chinensis,* cultivated in numerous varieties having white, yellow, blue, red, or purple flowers.

China aster,
Callistephus chinensis

chi′na bark′ (kī′nə, kē′nə), cinchona (def. 1).

chi·na·ber·ry (chī′nə ber′ē), *n., pl.* **-ries. 1.** a tree, *Melia Azedarach,* native to Asia but widely planted elsewhere for its ornamental yellow fruits. **2.** a soapberry, *Sapindus marginatus,* of Mexico, the West Indies, and the southern U.S. Also called **chi′naberry tree′, Chi′na tree′.** [CHINA + BERRY]

chi′na clay′, kaolin.

chi′na clos′et, a cabinet or cupboard, usually glassed, for storing and exhibiting chinaware. Also, **chi′na cab′inet.**

Chi′na grass′ cloth′. See **grass cloth.**

Chi·na·man (chī′nə mən), *n., pl.* **-men. 1.** *Usually Offensive.* a native or inhabitant of China; a Chinese. **2.** (*l.c.*) one who imports or sells china. **3. a Chinaman's chance,** *U.S.* the slightest chance: *He hasn't a Chinaman's chance of getting that job.* [CHINA + MAN[1]]

Chi′na oil′. See **Peru balsam.**

Chi′na plate′, (*sometimes l.c.*) *Chiefly Brit. Slang.* mate; chum; buddy. Also called **China.** [rhyming slang]

chi·nar (chi när′), *n.* the plane tree, *Platanus orientalis.* Also called **chinar′ tree′.** [< Hindi *cinār, canār* < Pers *chanār*]

Chi′na rose′, 1. Also called **Bengal rose.** a rose, *Rosa chinensis,* of China, having slightly fragrant crimson, pink, or white flowers. **2.** Also called **Chinese hibiscus, rose of China, shoeblack plant.** a shrub, *Hibiscus Rosa-sinensis,* of tropical Asia, having showy, usually rose-red flowers.

Chi′na Sea′, the East China Sea and the South China Sea, taken together.

Chi′na silk′, a lightweight silk fabric constructed in plain weave, often used for linings, blouses, slips, etc.

Chi′na stone′, a mineral used for making china, as petuntse.

Chi′na Syn′drome, a theoretical nuclear-reactor disaster in which an uncontrollable melting core burns through the earth to the other side of the globe.

Chi·na·town (chī′nə toun′), *n.* the Chinese quarter of a city. [CHINA + TOWN]

chi·na·ware (chī′nə wâr′), *n.* dishes, ornaments, etc., made of china. [CHINA + WARE[1]; r. *Cheney ware,* equiv. to Pers *chīnī* Chinese + *ware*]

chin·beak (chin′bēk′), *n. Archit.* a molding having a convex upper surface and a concave lower one, with a fillet between them; beak. [CHIN + BEAK[1]]

chin·ca·pin (ching′kə pin), *n.* chinquapin.

chinch (chinch), *n.* **1.** See **chinch bug. 2.** (loosely) a bedbug. [< Sp *chinche* < L *cīmic-* (s. of *cīmex*) bug]

chinch′ bug′, a small lygaeid bug, *Blissus leucopterus,* that feeds on corn, wheat, and other grains.

chin·chil·la (chin chil′ə), *n.* **1.** a small, South American rodent, *Chinchilla laniger,* having a soft, silvery gray fur. **2.** the fur of this animal. **3.** something, as a coat, jacket, etc., made of chinchilla fur: *a floor-length chinchilla.* **4.** a thick, napped, woolen fabric for coats, esp. children's coats. [< Sp, perh., equiv. to *chinche* CHINCH + *-illa* < L *-illa* dim. suffix]

Chinchilla,
Chinchilla laniger
(Total length to 20 in.; tail to 6 in.)

chin-chin (chin′chin′), *n., v.,* **-chinned, -chin·ning,** *interj.* —*n.* **1.** polite and ceremonious speech. **2.** light conversation; chitchat. —*v.i.* **3.** to speak politely and ceremoniously. **4.** to talk casually and lightly; chat. —*interj.* **5.** (used as a greeting or farewell.) **6.** (used as a toast, as in drinking to someone's health.) [< Chin (Peking dial.) *ch'ing-ch'ing* please-please]

chinch·y (chin′chē), *adj.,* **chinch·i·er, chinch·i·est.** *Chiefly Midland and Southern U.S.* stingy; cheap. [ME, deriv. of *chinche* (n. and adj.) < OF *chinche, chiche* < VL **cicc*(*us*) < L *cicc*(*um*) a bagatelle; see -Y[1]]

chin·cough (chin′kôf′, -kof′), *n. Pathol.* See **whooping cough.** [*chink* violent gasp (OE *cinc-* as in *cincung* boisterous laughter) + COUGH]

Chin·dwin (chin′dwin′), *n.* a river in N Burma, flowing S to the Irrawaddy River. 550 mi. long.

chine[1] (chīn), *n. Brit. Dial.* a ravine formed in rock by the action of running water. [ME; OE *cinu* crevice, fissure; c. MD *kene;* cf. OE *cīnan* to gape, crack open]

chine[2] (chīn), *n.* **1.** the backbone or spine, esp. of an animal. **2.** the whole or a piece of the backbone of an animal with adjoining parts, cut for cooking. **3.** a ridge or crest, as of land. **4.** *Naut.* **a.** an angular intersection of the sides and bottom of a vessel. **b.** a longitudinal member running behind this. [ME *eschine* < OF *eschine* < Gmc. See SHIN]

chine[3] (chīn), *n.* chime[2].

chi·né (shē nā′), *adj.* noting or pertaining to a fabric having a variegated pattern produced by warp threads that have been dyed, printed, or painted before weaving. [< F, ptp. of *chin*(*er*), after *Chine* China]

Chin·ese (chī nēz′, -nēs′), *n., pl.* **-nese,** *adj.* —*n.* **1.** the standard language of China, based on the speech of Peiping; Mandarin. **2.** a group of languages of the Sino-Tibetan family, including standard Chinese and most of the other languages of China. **3.** any of the Chinese languages, which vary among themselves to the point of mutual unintelligibility. **4.** a native or descendant of a native of China. —*adj.* **5.** of or pertaining to China, its inhabitants, or one of their languages. **6.** noting or pertaining to the partly logographic, partly phonetic script used for the writing of Chinese, Japanese, and other languages, consisting of thousands of brush-stroke characters written in vertical columns from right to left. [CHIN(A) + -ESE]

Chi′nese an′ise. See **star anise.**

Chi′nese ar′tichoke, an erect, slightly hairy, perennial herb, *Stachys sieboldi,* of China and Japan, having numerous small, white, edible tubers. Also called **chorogi, Japanese artichoke, knotroot.**

Chinese′ banan′a. See **dwarf banana.**

Chi′nese cab′bage, pe-tsai.

Chi′nese cal′endar, the former calendar of China, in which the year consisted of twelve lunar months with an intercalary month added seven times every 19 years to reconcile the lunar year of 354 days with the solar year of 365 days, time being reckoned in 60-year cycles with the first cycle dating from 2637 B.C.

Chi′nese check′ers, a board game for two to six players each of whom has 10 marbles resting in holes and matching the color of his section of a six-pointed star: the object of the game is to move all of the marbles in one section to the opposite side in a manner similar to that of standard checkers.

Chi′nese Chip′pendale, (esp. in furniture) an English rococo style using Chinese or quasi-Chinese motifs.

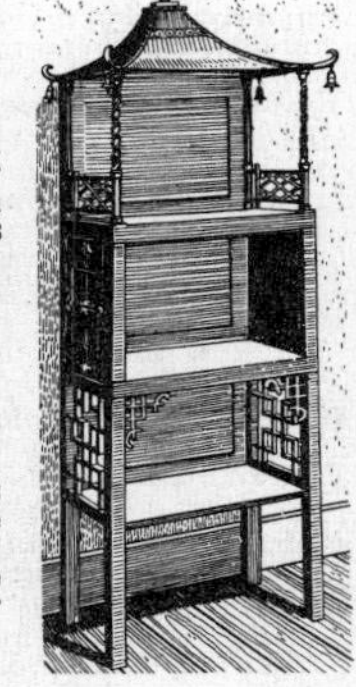

Chinese Chippendale stand

Chi′nese cin′namon, cassia (def. 1).

Chi′nese cres′cent, crescent (def. 7).

Chi′nese Em′pire, China under the rule of various imperial dynasties, usually including China proper, Manchuria, Mongolia, Sinkiang, and Tibet: replaced by a republic in January, 1912.

Chi′nese ev′ergreen, an herb, *Aglaonema simplex,* of tropical Asia and Malaysia, growing well in an aquatic habitat. Also called **Chinese waterplant, Japanese leaf.**

Chi′nese fan′ palm′, a fan palm, *Livistona chinensis,* of central China, having leaves from three to six feet wide and ovalish fruit. Also called **fan palm.**

Chi′nese fleece′-vine. See **silver-lace vine.**

Chi′nese forget′-me-not, an herb, *Cynoglossum amabile,* of eastern Asia, having rough leaves and clustered, showy, blue or pink flowers.

Chi′nese gel′atin, agar (def. 1). Also called **Chi′nese i′singlass.**

Chi′nese glue′, shellac dissolved in alcohol.

Chi′nese hibis′cus. See **China rose** (def. 2).

Chi′nese house′, an herb, *Collinsia bicolor,* of California, having nearly stalkless flowers with the upper lip white and the lower lip rose-purple or violet.

Chi′nese ink′. See **India ink.**

Chi′nese ju′jube, a shrub or small tree, *Zizyphus Jujuba,* of Eurasia, having spines and small, egg-shaped, brownish, edible fruit.

Chi′nese ju′niper, a shrub or tree, *Juniperus chinensis,* of China, Mongolia, and Japan, having scale-like leaves and small, round, purplish-brown fruit.

Chi′nese lan′tern, a collapsible lantern of thin, colored paper, often used for decorative lighting. Also called **Japanese lantern.**

Chi′nese lan′tern plant′. See **winter cherry** (def. 1).

Chi′nese lug′, a lugsail stiffened by battens and kept flat when hoisted: used in Chinese sailing vessels.

Chi′nese pavil′ion, crescent (def. 7).

Chinese′ pista′chio, a tree, *Pistacia chinensis,* of China, having flattened, scarlet fruit that turns purplish, grown as an ornamental.

Chinese′ pota′to. See **Chinese yam.**

Chi′nese prim′rose. See under **primrose** (def. 1).

Chi′nese puz′zle, 1. a very complicated puzzle. **2.** anything very complicated or perplexing: *The American educational system is a Chinese puzzle to most foreigners.*

Chi′nese quince′, a large shrub or small tree, *Chaenomeles sinensis,* of China, having solitary, light-pink flowers.

Chi′nese red′, scarlet; orange red; red chrome.

Chi′nese remain′der the′orem, *Math.* the theorem that given a set of *n* numbers, every pair of which is relatively prime, and a set of *m* integers, it is possible to find integers congruent to each of the *m* integers modulo the various *n* numbers and congruent to each other modulo the product of the *n* numbers.

Chinese′ Revolu′tion, the revolution in China in 1911, resulting in the overthrow of the Manchu dynasty and in the establishment of a republic in 1912.

Chi′nese schol′ar tree′. See **pagoda tree.**

Chi′nese snow′ball, a shrub, *Viburnum macrocephalum,* of China, having scurfy, hairy twigs, hairy leaves, and white flowers in large, showy, globelike clusters.

Chi′nese tag′, a variety of tag in which the tagged player must hold one hand on the part of his body where he was tagged.

Chi′nese trum′pet creep′er, a showy, woody vine, *Campsis grandiflora,* of China, having aerial rootlets and red flowers nearly three inches wide.

Chi′nese Turk′estan. See under **Turkestan.**

Chi′nese vermil′ion, 1. pimento (def. 4). **2.** vermilion (def. 2).

Chi′nese Wall′. See **Great Wall of China.**

Chi′nese wa′termelon. See **wax gourd.**

Chi′nese wa′terplant. See **Chinese evergreen.**

Chi′nese wax′, a white to yellowish-white, gelatinous, water-insoluble substance obtained from the wax secreted by certain insects, esp. a Chinese scale (*Ericerus pela*): used chiefly in the manufacture of polishes, sizes, and candles. Also called **Chi′nese tree′ wax′, insect wax.**

Chi′nese white′, a white pigment made from barium sulfate, largely used in watercolors and for giving opacity to other colors.

Chi′nese wind′lass. See **differential windlass.**

Chinese′ wiste′ria, a high-climbing vine, *Wistaria sinensis,* of China, having fragrant, bluish-violet flowers and velvety pods from five to seven inches long.

Chi′nese wood′ oil′. See **tung oil.**

Chi′nese yam′, a herbaceous vine, *Dioscorea Batatas,* of China, having tubers from two to three feet long and cinnamon-scented flowers. Also called **Chinese potato, cinnamon vine.**

chin·fest (chin′fest), *n. Slang.* gabfest; bull session. [CHIN + -FEST]

Ch'ing (ching), *n.* See under **Manchu** (def. 1). Also called **Ta Ch'ing.**

Ching·hai (ching′hī′), *n.* a province in W China. 2,050,000 (est. 1957); 269,187 sq. mi. *Cap.:* Sining. Also, **Tsinghai.** Also called **Koko Nor.**

Ching-t'u (jing′to͞o′), *n. Chinese.* See **Pure Land.**

chin′ic ac′id (kin′ik, kwin′-), *Chem.* See **quinic acid.**

chink[1] (chingk), *n.* **1.** a crack, cleft, or fissure: *a chink in a wall.* **2.** a narrow opening: *a chink between two buildings.* —*v.t.* **3.** to fill up chinks in. [CHINE[1] + -*k* suffix (see -OCK)]

chink[2] (chingk), *v.t., v.i.* **1.** to make, or cause to make, a short, sharp, ringing sound, as of coins or glasses striking together. —*n.* **2.** a chinking sound: *the chink of ice in a glass.* **3.** *Slang.* coin or ready cash. [imit.]

Chink (chingk), *n. Disparaging and Offensive.* a Chinese. [dial. *chink,* var. of KINK, with reference to the slant of the eye]

chin·ka·pin (ching′kə pin), *n.* chinquapin.

Chin·kiang (chin′kyang′), *n.* a port in S Kiangsu, in E China, on the Yangtze River. 179,000 (est. 1950).

chi·no (chē′nō), *n., pl.* **-nos** for 2, *adj.* **—n. 1.** a tough, twilled cotton cloth used for uniforms, sports clothes, etc. **2.** Usually, **chinos.** a pair of trousers or slacks made of this material. **—adj. 3.** made of chino. [? special use of CHINO-, with reference to yellowish color of cloth]

Chino-, a combining form of **Chinese:** *Chino-Tibetan.*

chi·noi·dine (ki noi′dēn, -din, chi-), *n. Pharm.* quinoidine. Also, **chi·noi·din** (ki noi′din, chi-).

chi·noi·se·rie (shēn woz′ə rē′, -woz′ə rē), *n.* (*sometimes cap.*) **1.** a style of ornamentation current chiefly in the 18th century in Europe, characterized by intricate patterns and an extensive use of motifs identified as Chinese. **2.** an object decorated in this style or an example of this style: *The clock was an interesting chinoiserie.* [< F, equiv. to *chinois* CHINESE + *-erie* -ERY]

chin·o·line (kin′əlēn′, -əlin, chin′-), *n. Chem.* quinoline. Also, **chin·o·leine** (kin′əlēn′, chin′-).

chi·none (kin′ōn, kwin′-), *n. Chem.* quinone.

Chi·nook (shi no͝ok′, -no͞ok′, chi-), *n., pl.* **-nooks,** (*esp. collectively*) **-nook. 1.** a member of a formerly numerous North American Indian people originally inhabiting the northern shore of the mouth of the Columbia River and the adjacent territory. **2.** either of the two languages of the Chinook Indians. Cf. **Lower Chinook, Upper Chinook. 3.** (*l.c.*) a warm, dry wind that blows at intervals down the eastern slopes of the Rocky Mountains. **4.** (*l.c.*) a warm, moist, southwest wind on the coast of Washington and Oregon (**wet chinook**). **5.** (*l.c.*) See **chinook salmon.**

Chi·nook·an (shi no͝ok′ən, -no͞o′kən, chi-), *n.* **1.** a language family comprising only Lower Chinook and Upper Chinook. **—adj. 2.** of or pertaining to the Chinooks or to Chinookan. [CHINOOK + -AN]

Chinook′ Jar′gon, a jargon based on Lower Chinook, now extinct but once widely used as a lingua franca in the Columbia River country.

chinook′ salm′on, a large salmon, *Oncorhynchus tshawytscha,* found in the northern Pacific Ocean. Also called **king salmon, quinnat salmon.** See illus. under **salmon.**

chin·qua·pin (chiŋ′kə pin), *n.* **1.** a shrubby chestnut, *Castanea pumila,* of the U.S., bearing small edible nuts, solitary in the burs. **2.** an evergreen, fagaceous tree, *Castanopsis chrysophylla,* of the Pacific coast, bearing inedible nuts, solitary in the burs. **3.** the nut of either of these trees. Also, **chincapin, chinkapin.** [dissimilated var. of *chincomen,* of Algonquian orig.; cf. Delaware *chinkwa* big, *min* fruit, seed]

chin′ rest′, a device fixed to the top of a violin or viola to permit a firm chin hold by the player.

chinse (chins), *v.t.,* **chinsed, chins·ing.** *Naut.* to fill (the seams of a vessel) with oakum or a similar material. [alter. of dial. *chinch,* var. of CHINK[1]]

chin′ strap′, 1. a strap attached to a hat for passing under the chin of the wearer. **2.** a strap to support the chin in cosmetic facial treatment. **3.** a strap on a bridle or halter that joins the throatlatch and noseband.

chintz (chints), *n.* **1.** a printed cotton fabric, glazed or unglazed, used esp. for draperies. **2.** a painted or stained calico from India. [earlier *chints,* pl. of *chint* < Hindi]

chintz·y (chint′sē), *adj.,* **chintz·i·er, chintz·i·est.** *Informal.* **1.** decorated with chintz. **2.** cheap or gaudy. [CHINTZ + -Y[1]]

chin-up (chin′up′), *n.* the act or an instance of chinning a horizontal bar, rod, or the like.

Chi·o·ne (kī′ō nē′, kī′ə-), *n. Class Myth.* **1.** a daughter of Daedalion who was the mother of twin sons: Philammon, fathered by Apollo, and Autolycus, fathered by Hermes. **2.** a daughter of Boreas and Orithyia.

Chi·os (kī′os, -ōs, kē′-; *Gk.* ᴋʜē′ôs), *n.* **1.** a Greek island in the Aegean, near the W coast of Turkey. 62,223 (1961); 322 sq. mi. **2.** a seaport on and the capital of this island. 24,053 (1961). Greek, **Khios.**

chip[1] (chip), *n., v.,* **chipped, chip·ping. —n. 1.** a small piece, as of wood, separated by chopping, cutting, or breaking. **2.** a very thin slice or small piece of food, candy, etc.: *chocolate chips.* **3. chips,** *Chiefly Brit.* See **French fried potatoes. 4.** a mark or flaw made by the breaking off or gouging out of a small piece: *This glass has a chip.* **5.** any of the small round disks, usually of plastic or ivory, used as tokens for money in certain gambling games, as roulette, poker, etc.; counter. **6.** *Informal.* a small cut or uncut piece of a diamond or crystal. **7.** Also called **microchip.** a tiny piece of semiconducting material, as silicon, containing miniaturized electronic circuitry. **8.** anything trivial or worthless. **9.** something dried up or without flavor. **10.** a piece of dried dung. **11.** wood, straw, etc., in thin strips for weaving into hats, baskets, etc. **12.** *Golf.* See **chip shot. 13.** the strip of material removed by a recording stylus as it cuts the grooves in a record. **14. chip of** or **off the old block,** a person who resembles his parent in appearance, behavior, or both: *It's clear that his son is just a chip off the old block.* **15. chip on one's shoulder,** a disposition to quarrel: *She always has a chip on her shoulder, so nobody wants to be with her.* **16. in the chips,** *Slang.* wealthy; rich. **17. when the chips are down,** in a crucial situation when there is no possibility of compromise, withdrawal, equivocation, etc., without dishonor or betrayal: *When the chips are down he proves to be a loyal friend.* [ME; OE *cipp* log: i.e., piece cut off] **—v.t. 18.** to hew or cut with an ax, chisel, etc. **19.** to cut, break off, or gouge out (bits or fragments): *He chipped a few pieces of ice from the large cube.* **20.** to disfigure by breaking off a fragment: *to chip the edge of a saucer.* **21.** to shape or produce by cutting or flaking away pieces: *to chip a figure out of wood.* **22.** *Brit. Slang.* to jeer or criticize severely; deride; taunt. **23.** *Games.* to bet by means of chips, as in poker. **24.** *Australian.* to hoe; harrow. **—v.i. 25.** to break off in small pieces. **26.** *Golf.* to make a chip shot. **27. chip in,** *Informal.* **a.** to contribute money, as to a fund; participate. **b.** *Games.* to bet a chip or chips, as in poker. **c.** to interrupt a conversation; remark or comment: *We all chipped in with our suggestions for the reunion.* [ME *chipp(en),* OE *-cippian* (in *forcippian* to cut off); akin to MLG, MD *kippen* to chip eggs, hatch] **—chip′pa·ble,** *adj.*

chip[2] (chip), *v.,* **chipped, chip·ping,** *n.* **—v.i. 1.** to utter a short chirping or squeaking sound; cheep. **—n. 2.** a short chirping or squeaking cry. [var. of CHEEP]

chip[3] (chip), *n. Wrestling.* a tricky or special method by which an opponent can be thrown. [n. use of *chip* to trip up; c. G *kippen* to tip over, Icel *kippa* to pull]

chip·board (chip′bōrd′, -bôrd′), *n.* **1.** a low grade of cardboard, used as a backing for pads of paper, a stiffener for photographs in mailing, etc. **2.** a thin, stiff sheet material made from wastepaper. [CHIP[1] + BOARD]

chip′ carv′ing, wood carving, usually executed with a knife and characterized by small incisions and simple geometrical patterns.

Chip·e·wy·an (chip′ə wī′ən), *n.* an Athapaskan language of NW Canada, spoken W of Hudson Bay.

Chip·ley (chip′lē), *n.* a town in NW Florida, 3159 (1960).

chip′ log′, *Naut.* a log for measuring the speed of a vessel, consisting of a log chip streamed at the end of a line divided, after the initial stray line, into lengths of 47 feet 3 inches, the number of such lengths that go overboard in 28 seconds being equal to the number of knots the vessel is making. Also called **hand log.**

Chipmunk, *Tamias striatus* (Total length 10 in.; tail 4 in.)

chip·munk (chip′muŋk), *n.* any of several small, striped, terrestrial squirrels of the genera *Tamias,* of North America, and *Eutamia,* of Asia and North America, esp. *T. striatus,* of eastern North America. [assimilated var. of *chitmunk* < Algonquian; akin to Ojibwa *atchitamon* squirrel, lit., head first, with reference to its way of coming down a tree-trunk]

chipped′ beef′, *U.S.* very thin slices or shavings of dried, smoked beef, usually served in a cream sauce.

Chip·pen·dale (chip′ən dāl′), *n.* **1. Thomas,** 1718?–79, English cabinetmaker and furniture designer. **2.** of or in the style of Thomas Chippendale.

chip·per[1] (chip′ər), *adj. Chiefly U.S. Informal.* lively; cheerful. [var. of dial. *kipper* frisky < ?]

chip·per[2] (chip′ər), *v.i.* **1.** to chirp or twitter: *The birds chippered in the tree.* **2.** to chatter or babble: *The children chippered on their way to school.* [CHIP[2] + -ER[6]]

chip·per[3] (chip′ər), *n.* one who or that which chips or cuts. [CHIP[1] + -ER[1]]

Chip·pe·wa (chip′ə wä′, -wā′, -wə), *n., pl.* **-was,** (*esp. collectively*) **-wa.** Ojibwa.

Chip·pe·way (chip′ə wā′), *n., pl.* **-ways,** (*esp. collectively*) **-way.** Chippewa.

chip·pie (chip′ē), *n. Slang.* chippy[1] (def. 1).

chip′ping spar′row, a small, North American sparrow, *Spizella passerina,* commonly found in urban areas. [CHIP[2] + -ING[2]]

chip-proof (chip′pro͞of′), *adj.* resistant to chipping.

chip·py[1] (chip′ē), *n., pl.* **-pies. 1.** Also, **chippie.** *Slang.* **a.** a flirtatious or promiscuous woman. **b.** *Offensive.* a prostitute. **2.** See **chipping sparrow.** [short for *chipping sparrow*]

chip·py[2] (chip′ē), *n.* a chipmunk. [CHIP(MUNK) + -Y[2]]

chip′ shot′, *Golf.* a shot that is purposely hit fairly high into the air and is meant to roll upon landing, used in approaching the green. Also called **pitch-and-run shot, pitch-and-run.** Cf. **pitch shot.**

Chi·qui·ta (chə kē′tə; *Sp.* chē kē′tä), *n.* a girl's given name.

Chi-Rho (kē′rō′, kī′-), *n., pl.* **-Rhos.** XP. Also called **chrismon.** [< Gk *XP,* first two letters of *Khristós* CHRIST. See CHI, RHO]

Chi·ri·co (kē′rē kō), *n.* **Gior·gio de** (jôr′jō də), 1888–1978, Italian painter.

chir·i·moy·a (chir′ə moi′ə), *n.* cherimoya.

chirk (chûrk), *v.i.* **1.** to make a shrill, chirping noise. **—v.t. 2.** *U.S. Informal.* to cheer, encourage (usually fol. by *up*). **—adj. 3.** *U.S. Informal.* cheerful. [ME *chirk(en)* (v.), OE *circian* to roar]

chirm (chûrm), *v.i.* **1.** to chirp, as a bird; sing; warble. **—n. 2.** the chirping of birds. [ME; OE *cierm* noise]

chi·ro (chēr′ō), *n., pl.* **-ros.** the ladyfish, *Elops saurus.* [?]

chiro-, a learned borrowing from Greek meaning "hand," used in the formation of compound words: *chiromancy.* Also, **cheiro-.** [comb. form of Gk *cheír* hand]

chi·rog·ra·phy (kī rog′rə fē), *n.* handwriting; penmanship. [CHIRO- + -GRAPHY] **—chi·rog′ra·pher,** *n.* **—chi·ro·graph·ic** (kī′rə graf′ik), **chi′ro·graph′i·cal,** *adj.*

chi·ro·gym·nast (kī′rō jim′nast), *n.* an apparatus for strengthening or exercising the fingers for piano-playing, as a set of rings attached by springs to a crossbar. [CHIRO- + GYMNAST]

chi·ro·man·cy (kī′rə man′sē), *n.* the art of divination by analyzing the appearance of the hand; palmistry. [CHIRO- + -MANCY] **—chi′ro·man′cer,** *n.* **—chi′ro·man′tic, chi′ro·man′ti·cal,** *adj.*

Chi·ron (kī′ron), *n. Class Myth.* a wise and beneficent centaur, teacher of Achilles, Asclepius, and others. Also, **Cheiron.**

chi·rop·o·dist (kī rop′ə dist, ki-), *n.* one whose occupation is the practice of chiropody. [CHIRO- + -POD + -IST]

chi·rop·o·dy (kī rop′ə dē, ki-), *n.* the treatment of minor foot ailments, as corns, bunions, etc. [CHIRO- + *-pody;* see -POD, -Y[3]] **—chi·ro·po·di·al** (kī′rə pō′dē əl), **chi·ro·pod·ic** (kī′rə pod′ik), **chi′ro·pod′i·cal,** *adj.*

chi·ro·prac·tic (kī′rə prak′tik), *n.* **1.** a therapeutic system based upon the premise that disease is caused by interference with nerve function, the method being to restore normal condition by adjusting the segments of the spinal column. **2.** a chiropractor. [CHIRO- + *-practic* < Gk *praktikós;* see PRACTICAL]

chi·ro·prac·tor (kī′rə prak′tər), *n.* one whose occupation is the practice of chiropractic. [CHIROPRACT(IC) + -OR[2]]

chi·rop·ter (kī rop′tər), *n.* any mammal of the order *Chiroptera,* comprising the bats. [CHIRO- + -PTER]

Chi·rop·ter·a (kī rop′tər ə), *n.* the order comprising the bats. [< NL; see CHIROPTER]

chi·rop·ter·an (kī rop′tər ən), *n.* **1.** chiropter. **—adj. 2.** of or pertaining to a chiropter. [CHIROPTER + -AN]

chirp (chûrp), *v.i.* **1.** to make a characteristic short, sharp sound, as small birds and certain insects. **2.** to make any similar sound: *The children chirped with amusement.* **—v.t. 3.** to sound or utter in a chirping manner: *The little girl chirped her joy.* **—n. 4.** a chirping sound. [? var. of CHIRK] **—chirp′er,** *n.* **—chirp′ing·ly,** *adv.*

chirp·y (chûr′pē), *adj.,* **chirp·i·er, chirp·i·est.** *Informal.* cheerful; lively; gay. [CHIRP + -Y[1]] **—chirp′i·ly,** *adv.* **—chirp′i·ness,** *n.*

chirr (chûr), *v.i.* **1.** to make a characteristic shrill, trilling sound, as a grasshopper. **2.** to make a similar sound. **—n. 3.** the sound of chirring. Also, **chirre, churr.** [alter. of CHIRP]

chirre (chûr), *v.i.,* **chirred, chirr·ing,** *n.* chirr.

chir·rup (chēr′əp, chûr′-), *v.,* **-ruped, -rup·ing,** *n.* **—v.i. 1.** to chirp. **2.** to make a similar sound: *She chirruped softly to encourage the horse to enter the dark stall.* **—v.t. 3.** to utter with chirps. **4.** to make a chirping sound to. **—n. 5.** the act or sound of chirruping: *a lively chirrup of birds in the trees.* [var. of CHIRP] **—chir′ruper,** *n.*

chir·rup·y (chēr′ə pē, chûr′-), *adj.* chirpy; gay. [CHIRRUP + -Y[1]]

chir·u (chir′o͞o), *n.* a goat antelope, *Pantholops hodgsoni,* of Tibet, the male of which has very long, straight horns. Also called **Tibetan antelope.** [prob. < Tibetan native name]

chi·rur·geon (kī rûr′jən), *n. Archaic.* a surgeon. [< L *chīrūr(gus)* (< Gk *cheirourgós* hand-worker, surgeon; see CHIRO-, DEMIURGE) + (SUR)GEON; r. ME *cirurgian* < OF *cirurgien* surgeon]

chi·rur·ger·y (kī rûr′jə rē), *n. Archaic.* surgery. [CHIRURG(EON) + -ERY; r. late ME *sirurgerie* < MF *cirurgerie* < L *chīrūrg(ia)* (< Gk *cheirourgía;* see CHIRURGEON, -IA + OF *-erie* -ERY] **—chi·rur′gic, chi·rur′gi·cal,** *adj.*

chis·el (chiz′əl), *n., v.,* **-eled, -el·ing** or (*esp. Brit*). **-elled, -el·ling. —n. 1.** a wedgelike tool with a cutting edge at the end of the blade, often made of steel, used for cutting or shaping wood, stone, etc. **—v.t. 2.** to cut, shape, etc., with a chisel: *He chiseled the wood into a statue.* **3.** to form or fashion by carving wood, stone, etc., with a chisel: *He chiseled a statue from the stone.* **4.** *U.S. Slang.* **a.** to cheat or swindle (someone). **b.** to get (something) by cheating or trickery: *He was chiseled out of $1000.* **—v.i. 5.** to work with a chisel. **6.** *U.S. Slang.* to use trickery; cheat. [late ME < AF, var. of OF *cisel* < LL **cīsell(us),* dim. of **cīsus,* akin to L *caesus,* ptp. of *caedere* to cut] **—chis′el·like′,** *adj.*

A B C

Chisels
A, Wood chisel;
B, Bricklayer's chisel;
C, Cold chisel

chis·eled (chiz′əld), *adj.* **1.** cut, shaped, etc., with a chisel: *chiseled stone.* **2.** formed as with a chisel; clear-cut: *She has finely chiseled features.* Also, *esp. Brit.,* **chis′elled.** [CHISEL + -ED[3]]

chis·el·er (chiz′ə lər, chiz′lər), *n.* **1.** *U.S. Slang.* a person who cheats, swindles, or uses unethical practices. **2.** a person who uses a chisel, as a wood carver. Also, *esp. Brit.,* **chis′el·ler,** *n.* [CHISEL + -ER[1]]

chis′el point′, a nail or spike with the point formed by two flat inclined sides meeting at a sharp angle.

Chi·shi·ma (chē′shē mä′), *n.* Japanese name of the **Kurile Islands.**

Chis′holm Trail′ (chiz′əm), a cattle trail leading N from San Antonio, Texas, to Abilene, Kansas: used for about 20 years after the Civil War. [named after Jesse *Chisholm* (1806–68), American scout]

Chi·şi·nă·u (kē′shē nu′o͞o), *n.* Rumanian name of **Kishinev.**

chi-square (kī′skwâr′), *n. Statistics.* a quantity equal to the summation over all variables of the quotient of the square of the difference between the observed and expected values divided by the expected value of the variable.

chi′-square test′, *Statistics.* a test devised by Karl Pearson for testing the mathematical fit of a frequency curve to an observed frequency distribution. Also, **chi′-squared test′.**

chit[1] (chit), *n.* **1.** a voucher of money owed for food, drink, etc. **2.** *U.S. Mil.* any official or semi-official receipt, voucher, or similar document, esp. of an informa nature. **3.** *Chiefly Brit.* a note; a short memorandum. [short for *chitty* < Hindi *chiṭṭī*]

chit[2] (chit), *n.* a child or young person, esp. a pert girl. [late ME; perh. akin to KITTEN or KID]

chit[3] (chit), *n. Hinduism.* cit.

Chi·ta (chi tä′), *n.* a city in the SE RSFSR, in the Soviet Union in Asia. 171,000 (1959).

chi·tar·ro·ne (kē′tə rō′nā; *It.* kē′tär rô′ne), *n., pl.* **-ni** (-nē). an obsolete musical stringed instrument with a long neck and two pegboxes, one above the other. [< It, aug. of *chitarra* < Gk *kithára* lyre]

chit·chat (chit′chat′), *n., v.,* **-chat·ted, -chat·ting. —n. 1.** light conversation; small talk. **2.** idle talk; gossip. **—v.i. 3.** to indulge in chitchat; gossip. [gradative compound based on CHAT[1]] **—chit′chat′ty,** *adj.*

chi·tin (kī′tin), *n.* a characteristic, horny, organic component of the cuticula of arthropods. [< F *chitine* < Gk *chit(ṓn)* tunic + F *-ine* -IN[2]] **—chi′tin·ous,** *adj.* **chi′tin·oid′,** *adj.*

chit·ling (chit′lin, -liŋ), *n.* Usually, **chitlings.** chitterling (def. 1). Also, **chit·lin** (chit′lin).

chi·ton (kīt′ən, kī′ton), *n.* **1.** *Gk. Antiq.* a gown or tunic, with or without sleeves, worn by both sexes, usually next to the skin. **2.** Also called **sea cradle.** a mollusk of the class *Amphineura,* having a mantle covered with calcareous plates, found adhering to rocks. [< Gk *chitṓn* tunic, from a fem. form c. Heb *kuttōneth* tunic]

Chi-tse (jē′dzu′), *n.* See **Ki Tse.** Also, **Chi′-tzu′.**

Chit·ta·gong (chit′ə goŋ′), *n.* a port in SE East Bengal, in E Pakistan, near the Bay of Bengal. 363,000 (est. 1961).

chit·tam·wood (chit′əm wo͝od′), *n.* **1.** See **American smoke tree. 2.** cascara. [*chittam* perh. < Muskhogean + WOOD[1]]

Chit·ten·an·go (chit′ə naŋ′gō), *n.* a town in central New York. 3180 (1960).

chit·ter (chit′ər), *v.i.* **1.** to twitter. **2.** *Brit. Dial.* to shiver or tremble, esp. from cold. [ME *che(a)ter(en), chiter(en),* var. of *chateren* to CHATTER]

chit·ter·ling (chit′ər ling, chit′lin), *n.* **1.** Usually, **chitterlings.** Also, **chitling, chitlin.** a part of the small intestine of swine, usually served fried or in a sauce. **2.** *Obs.* a frill or ruff. [ME *chiterling;* akin to G *Kutteln* in same sense]

Ch'iu Ch'u-chi (chyōō′ chōō′jē′), (*Ch'ang Ch'un*) 1148–1227, Chinese Taoist philosopher and author.

Chiu·si (kyōō′sē), *n.* a town in central Italy, in Tuscany; Etruscan tombs. 8854 (1961). Ancient, **Clusium.**

chiv (shiv), *n.* *Slang.* shiv.

chiv·al·ric (shiv′əl rik, shi val′rik), *adj.* **1.** pertaining to chivalry. **2.** chivalrous. [CHIVALR(Y) + -IC]

chiv·al·rous (shiv′əl rəs), *adj.* **1.** having the qualities of chivalry, as courage, courtesy, and loyalty. **2.** considerate and courteous to women; gallant. **3.** gracious and honorable toward one's enemy, esp. when he is defeated, and toward those who are weak or socially inferior. **4.** chivalric. [ME *chevalrous* < MF *chevalerous,* equiv. to *chevalier* CHEVALIER + *-ous* -OUS] —**chiv′al·rous·ly,** *adv.* —**chiv′al·rous·ness,** *n.*
—**Syn. 1.** fearless, dauntless, valiant; courtly; faithful, true, devoted. —**Ant. 1.** rude, boorish, churlish.

chiv·al·ry (shiv′əl rē), *n., pl.* **-ries** for 6. **1.** the sum of the ideal qualifications of a knight, including courtesy, generosity, valor, and dexterity in arms. **2.** the rules and customs of medieval knighthood. **3.** the medieval system or institution of knighthood. **4.** a group of knights. **5.** gallant warriors or gentlemen: *fair ladies and noble chivalry.* **6.** *Archaic.* a chivalrous act. **7.** *Obs.* the position or rank of a knight. [ME *chivalrie* < AF, c. OF *chevalerie,* equiv. to *chevalier* CHEVALIER + *-ie* -Y[3]]

chiv·a·ree (shiv′ə rē′, shiv′ə rē′), *n., v.t.,* **-reed, -ree·ing.** shivaree. Also, **chiv′a·ri′.**

chive (chīv), *n.* a small bulbous plant, *Allium Schoenoprasum,* related to the leek and onion, having long, slender leaves which are used as a seasoning in cookery. [late ME *chyve* < AF *chive,* equiv. to OF *cive* << L *caepa* onion]

chiv·vy (chiv′ē), *v.t., v.i.,* **-vied, -vy·ing,** *n., pl.* **-vies.** *Brit.* chevy.

chiv·y (chiv′ē), *v.t., v.i.,* **chiv·ied, chiv·y·ing,** *n., pl.* **chiv·ies.** *Brit.* chevy.

Ch. J., Chief Justice.

Chka·lov (chkä′lof), *n.* a city in the E Soviet Union in Europe, on the Ural River. 260,000 (est. 1959). Also called **Orenburg.**

Chlad·ni (chə läd′nē), *n.* a crater in the first quadrant of the face of the moon: about 8 miles in diameter.

chlam·y·date (klam′i dāt′), *adj.* *Zool.* having a mantle or pallium, as a mollusk. [< L *chlamydāt(us),* equiv. to *chlamyd-* (s. of *chlamys*) CHLAMYS + *-ātus* -ATE[1]]

chla·myd·e·ous (klə mid′ē əs), *adj.* *Bot.* pertaining to or having a floral envelope. [< Gk *chlamyd-* (s. of *chlamýs*) CHLAMYS + -EOUS]

chla·myd·o·spore (klə mid′ə spôr′, -spōr′), *n.* *Bot.* a thick-walled, asexual, resting spore of certain fungi and algae. [< Gk *chlamyd-* (s. of *chlamýs*) CHLAMYS + -O- + -SPORE]

chla·mys (klā′mis, klam′is), *n., pl.* **chla·mys·es** (klā′mi siz, klam′i-), **chlam·y·des** (klam′i dēz′). *Gk. Antiq.* a short, fine woolen mantle worn by men. [< L < Gk *chlamýs* type of cloak or mantle]

Chlamys

Chli·da·no·pe (klid′ənō′pē), *n.* *Class. Myth.* a naiad.

chlo·an·thite (klō an′thīt), *n.* a mineral, nickel arsenide, providing a source of nickel. [< Gk *chloanth(ḗs)* (*chlo-* (s. of *chloē;* see CHLOE) + *-anthēs* comb. form, akin to *ánthos* flower) + -ITE[1]]

chlo·as·ma (klō az′mə), *n.* *Pathol.* a condition in which light-brown spots occur on the skin, caused by exposure to sun, by dyspepsia, and by certain specific diseases. [< NL < LGk; greenness, deriv. of Gk *chloázein* to be green, deriv. of *chlóos* green]

Chlod·wig (klōt′vikн), *n.* German name of **Clovis I.**

Chlo·e (klō′ē), *n.* **1.** (in pastoral and other literature) a name for a maiden, esp. one beloved. **2.** Also, **Chlo′ë.** *Class. Myth.* an epithet of Demeter, meaning "green." **3.** a girl's given name. [< Gk, same as *chlóē* young green vegetation, akin to *chlōrós* CHLOR-[1]]

Chlo·ette (klō et′; *Fr.* klō et′), *n.* a girl's given name, form of **Chloe.**

chlor-[1], a learned borrowing from Greek meaning "green," used in the formation of compound words: *chlorine.* Also, *esp. before a consonant,* **chloro-**[1]. [comb. form of Gk *chlōrós* light green, greenish yellow]

chlor-[2], a combining form of **chlorine:** *chloric.* Also, *esp. before a consonant,* **chloro-**[2].

chlo/ra·ce/tic ac/id (klōr′ə sē′tik, -set′ik, klôr′-, klōr′-, klôr′-), *Chem.* See **chloroacetic acid.**

chlo·ral (klōr′əl, klôr′-), *n.* **1.** Also called **trichloroacetaldehyde, trichloracetic acid aldehyde.** *Chem.* a colorless, oily liquid, CCl_3CHO, having a pungent odor, usually derived by the chlorination of ethyl alcohol or of acetaldehyde and which combines with water to form chloral hydrate. **2.** Also called **chlo′ral hy′drate.** *Pharm.* a white, crystalline solid, $CCl_3CH(OH)_2$, formed by combining liquid chloral with water: used as a hypnotic. [CHLOR-[2] + -AL[3]]

chlo·ra·mine (klōr′ə mēn′, klôr′-, klō ram′ēn, klô-), *n.* *Chem.* **1.** an unstable, colorless liquid, NH_2Cl, with a pungent odor, derived from ammonia. **2.** any of a class of compounds obtained by replacing a hydrogen atom of an $=NH$ or $-NH_2$ group with chlorine. [CHLOR-[2] + AMINE]

chlo·ram·phen·i·col (klōr′am fen′ə kōl′, -kôl′, klôr′-), *n.* *Pharm.* a colorless, crystalline, slightly water-soluble antibiotic, $C_{11}H_{12}Cl_2N_2O_5$, obtained from cultures of *Streptomyces venezuelae* or synthesized: used chiefly in the treatment of infections caused by certain bacteria, by rickettsiae, and by certain viruses. [CHLOR-[2] + AM(IDO)- + PHEN- + NI(TR)- + (GLY)COL]

chlo·ran·il (klō ran′əl, klô-, klōr′ə nil, klôr′-), *n.* *Chem.* a yellow, crystalline, water-insoluble solid, $C_6Cl_4O_2$, used chiefly as a fungicide and as an intermediate in the manufacture of dyes. [CHLOR-[2] + ANIL(INE)]

chlor·ar·gyr·ite (klōr′är jēr′īt, klôr′-), *n.* a mineral, silver chloride, AgCl, occurring in cubic crystals associated with native silver. [CHLOR-[2] + Gk *árgyr(os)* silver + -ITE[1]]

chlo·ras·tro·lite (klō ras′trə līt′, klô-), *n.* a green mineral, similar in composition to prehnite, cut and used as a cabochon. [CHLOR-[1] + ASTRO- + -LITE]

chlo·rate (klōr′āt, -it, klôr′-), *n.* *Chem.* a salt of chloric acid. [CHLOR-[2] + -ATE[2]]

chlor·dan (klōr′dan, klôr′-), *n.* *Chem.* a colorless, viscous, water-insoluble, toxic liquid, $C_{10}H_6Cl_8$, used as an insecticide and comprising 60–75 percent of the commercial product, the balance composed of related compounds. Also, **chlor·dane** (klōr′dān, klôr′-). [CHLOR-[2] + *(in)dan(e)* an oily cyclic hydrocarbon, equiv. to IND- + -ANE]

chlor·di·az·e·pox·ide (klōr′dī az′ə pok′sīd, klôr′-), *n.* *Pharm.* a compound, $C_{16}H_{14}ClN_3O$, used in the form of its hydrochloride as a tranquilizer. [CHLOR-[2] + DIAZ(O)- + EPOX(Y) + -IDE]

chlo·rel·la (klə rel′ə), *n.* any fresh-water, unicellular green alga of the genus *Chlorella.* [CHLOR-[1] + L *-ella* dim. suffix] —**chlo·rel·la·ceous** (klōr′ə lā′shəs, klôr′-), *adj.*

chlo·ren·chy·ma (klə reng′kə mə), *n.* *Bot.* parenchyma tissue containing chlorophyll. [CHLOR(OPHYLL) + (PAR)ENCHYMA]

chlor·gua·nide (klōr gwä′nīd, -nid, klôr-), *n.* *Pharm.* chloroguanide.

chlo·ric (klōr′ik, klôr′-), *adj.* *Chem.* of or containing chlorine in the pentavalent state. [CHLOR-[2] + -IC]

chlo/ric ac/id, *Chem.* a hypothetical acid, $HClO_3$, known only in solution or in the form of its salts.

chlo·ride (klōr′īd, -id, klôr′-), *n.* *Chem.* **1.** a salt of hydrochloric acid consisting of two elements, one of which is chlorine, as sodium chloride, NaCl. **2.** a compound containing chlorine, as methyl chloride, CH_3Cl. [CHLOR-[2] + -IDE]

chlo/ride of lime/. See **bleaching powder.** Also called **chlorinated lime.**

chlo/ride pa/per, *Photog.* a relatively slow printing paper coated with an emulsion of silver chloride: used mostly for contact prints.

chlo·ri·dize (klōr′i dīz′, klôr′-), *v.t.,* **-dized, -diz·ing.** *Chem.* to convert (the metal of an ore) into chloride by treating with chlorine or hydrochloric acid. [CHLORIDE + -IZE]

chlo·rin·ate (klōr′ə nāt′, klôr′-), *v.t.,* **-at·ed, -at·ing. 1.** *Chem.* to combine or treat with chlorine. **2.** to disinfect (water) by means of chlorine. **3.** *Metall.* to treat (a gold ore) with chlorine gas in order that the gold may be removed as a soluble chloride. [CHLORINE + -ATE[1]] —**chlo′rin·a′tion,** *n.* —**chlo′rin·a′tor,** *n.*

chlo/rinated lime/, *Chem.* See **bleaching powder.**

chlo·rine (klōr′ēn, -in, klôr′-), *n.* *Chem.* a halogen element, a heavy, greenish-yellow, incombustible, water-soluble, poisonous gas which is highly irritating to the respiratory organs, obtained chiefly by electrolysis of sodium chloride brine: used for water purification, in the making of bleaching powder, and in the manufacture both of chemicals that do not contain chlorine, as ethylene glycol, and of those that do. *Symbol:* Cl; *at. wt.:* 35.453; *at. no.:* 17. [CHLOR-[1] + -INE[2]]

chlorine 36, *Chem.* the radioactive isotope of chlorine having a mass number 36 and a halflife of about 440,000 years, used chiefly as a tracer.

chlo/rine diox/ide, *Chem.* an orange, water-soluble, unstable, extremely explosive gas, ClO_2, used chiefly as a bleaching agent for wood pulp, fats, oils, and flour.

chlo·rin·i·ty (klō rin′i tē, klô-), *n.* *Chem.* the quality, state, or degree of being chlorinous. [CHLORINE + -ITY]

chlo·rin·ous (klōr′ə nəs, klôr′-), *adj.* *Chem.* of, containing, or resembling chlorine. [CHLORINE + -OUS]

Chlor·is (klōr′is), *n.* *Class. Myth.* a daughter of Amphion and Niobe who is sometimes believed to have been spared when her sisters were killed by Artemis in revenge for Niobe's irreverence toward Leto.

chlo·rite[1] (klōr′īt, klôr′-), *n.* a group of minerals, hydrous silicates of aluminum, ferrous iron, and magnesium, occurring in green platelike crystals or scales. [CHLOR-[1] + -ITE[1]] —**chlo·rit·ic** (klō rit′ik, klô-), *adj.*

chlo·rite[2] (klōr′īt, klôr′-), *n.* *Chem.* a salt of chlorous acid, as potassium chlorite, $KClO_2$. [CHLOR-[2] + -ITE[1]]

chloro-[1], var. of **chlor-**[1] before a consonant: *chlorophyll.*

chloro-[2], var. of **chlor-**[2] before a consonant: *chloroform.*

chlo·ro·a·ce·tic (klōr′ō ə sē′tik, -ə set′ik, klôr′-), *adj.* *Chem.* of or derived from chloroacetic acid. [CHLORO-[2] + ACETIC]

chlo/roace/tic ac/id, *Chem.* a colorless, crystalline, deliquescent, water-soluble powder, $CH_2ClCOOH$, usually derived from acetic acid by chlorination: used chiefly in the manufacture of dyes and other organic compounds. Also, **chloracetic acid.** Also called **monochloroacetic acid.**

chlo·ro·ac·e·tone (klōr′ō as′i tōn′, klôr′-), *n.* *Chem.* a colorless, lachrymatory, poisonous liquid, CH_3COCH_2Cl, used chiefly in organic synthesis and in the manufacture of insecticides and perfumes. [CHLORO-[2] + ACETONE]

chlo·ro·ac·e·to·phe·none (klōr′ō as′ə tō fə nōn′, -ə sē′tō-, klôr′-), *n.* *Chem.* a white, crystalline, water-insoluble, poisonous solid, $C_6H_5COCH_2Cl$, used as a tear gas. [CHLORO-[2] + ACETOPHENONE]

chlo·ro·ben·zene (klōr′ə ben′zēn, -ben zēn′, klôr′-), *n.* *Chem.* a colorless, volatile, water-insoluble, flammable liquid, C_6H_5Cl, having an almondlike odor, prepared from benzene by chlorination: used as a solvent for resins, paints, and lacquers, and in the synthesis of benzene derivatives, as DDT and certain drugs and perfumes. [CHLORO-[2] + BENZENE]

chlo·ro·bro/mide pa/per (klōr′ə brō′mīd, -mid, klôr′-), *Photog.* a relatively fast printing paper coated with an emulsion of silver chloride and silver bromide. Also, **chlo·ro·bro/mid pa/per** (klōr′ō brō′mid, klôr′-). [CHLORO-[2] + BROMIDE]

chlo·ro·bro·mo·meth·ane (klōr′ə brō′mə meth′ān, klôr′-), *n.* *Chem.* a clear, colorless, volatile, nonflammable liquid, CH_2ClBr, used chiefly as an extinguishing agent in fire extinguishers and as a solvent in organic synthesis. Also called **bromochloromethane.** [CHLORO-[2] + *bromo-* (comb. form of BROMINE) + METHANE]

chlo·ro·car·bon (klōr′ə kär′bən, klôr′-), *n.* *Chem.* a compound containing carbon and chlorine, as carbon tetrachloride, or containing carbon, chlorine, and hydrogen, as chloroform. [CHLORO-[2] + CARBON]

chlo·ro·eth·ene (klōr′ō eth′ēn, klôr′-), *n.* *Chem.* See **vinyl chloride.** [CHLORO-[2] + ETHENE]

chlo·ro·eth·yl·ene (klōr′ō eth′ə lēn′, klôr′-), *n.* *Chem.* See **vinyl chloride.** [CHLORO-[2] + ETHYLENE]

chlo·ro·form (klōr′ə fôrm′, klôr′-), *n.* **1.** Also called **trichloromethane.** *Chem., Pharm.* a colorless, volatile, nonflammable, slightly water-soluble, pungent, sweet-tasting liquid, $CHCl_3$, usually derived from acetone, acetaldehyde, or ethyl alcohol by the reaction of chloride of lime: used chiefly in medicine as an anesthetic and as a solvent. —*v.t.* **2.** to administer chloroform to. **3.** to put chloroform on (a cloth, object, etc.). [CHLORO-[2] + FORM(YL)] —**chlo′ro·for′mic,** *adj.*

chlo/ro·for·myl chlo/ride (klōr′ə fôr′məl, klôr′-), *Chem.* phosgene. [CHLORO-[2] + FORMYL]

chlo·ro·gua·nide (klōr′ə gwä′nīd, -nid, klôr′-), *n.* *Pharm.* a white, crystalline powder, $ClC_6H_4NHC(NH)NHC(NH)NHCH(CH_3)_2$, used in the form of its hydrochloride chiefly in the treatment of malaria. Also, **chlorguanide.** [CHLORO-[2] + *(bi)guanide* (see BI-[1], GUANIDINE)]

chlo·ro·hy·drin (klōr′ə hī′drin, klôr′-), *n.* *Chem.* any of a class of organic compounds containing a chlorine atom and a hydroxyl group, usually on adjacent carbon atoms. [CHLORO-[2] + HYDR-[2] + -IN[2]]

chlo·ro·hy·dro·qui·none (klōr′ə hī′drō kwi nōn′, klôr′-), *n.* *Chem.* a white to light tan, crystalline, water-soluble solid, $C_6H_3Cl(OH)_2$, used chiefly in organic synthesis and as a developer in photography. [CHLORO-[2] + HYDROQUINONE]

chlo·ro·meth·ane (klōr′ə meth′ān, klôr′-), *n.* *Chem.* See **methyl chloride.** [CHLORO-[2] + METHANE]

Chlo·ro·my·ce·tin (klōr′ō mī sēt′ən, klôr′-), *n.* *Pharm., Trademark.* chloramphenicol.

chlo·ro·naph·tha·lene (klōr′ə naf′thə lēn′, -nap′-, klôr′-), *n.* *Chem.* **1.** either of two isomeric naphthalene compounds containing one chlorine atom. **2.** any of a group of compounds prepared from naphthaline and containing one or more chlorine atoms. [CHLORO-[2] + NAPHTHALENE]

chlo·ro·phae·ite (klōr′ə fē′īt, klôr′-), *n.* *Mineral.* a variety of chlorite found in seams in igneous rocks, green when newly exposed to air but turning brown afterward. [CHLORO-[1] + *phae-* (< Gk *phaiós* dusky) + -ITE[1]]

chlo·ro·phe·nol (klōr′ə fē′nōl, -nôl, -nol, klôr′-), *n.* *Chem.* **1.** any of three isomers having the formula ClC_6H_4OH, derived from chlorine and phenol, used chiefly as intermediates in the manufacture of dyes. **2.** any derivative of phenol of which one or more hydrogen atoms have been replaced by chlorine atoms. Also, **chlorphenol.** [CHLORO-[2] + PHENOL]

chlo/rophe/nol red/, *Chem.* an acid-base indicator, $C_{19}H_{12}Cl_2O_5S$, that changes in color from yellow to red as the acidity of a solution decreases.

chlo·ro·phe·no·thane (klōr′ə fē′nə thān′, klôr′-), *n.* See **DDT.**

chlo·ro·phyll (klōr′ə fil, klôr′-), *n.* *Bot., Biochem.* the green coloring matter of leaves and plants, essential to the production of carbohydrates by photosynthesis, and occurring in a bluish-black form, $C_{55}H_{72}MgN_4O_5$ **(chlorophyll a),** and a dark-green form, $C_{55}H_{70}MgN_4O_6$ **(chlorophyll b),** used as a dye for cosmetics, oils, etc., and as a deodorant. Also, **chlo′ro·phyl.** [CHLORO-[1] + -PHYLL] —**chlo′ro·phyl′loid,** *adj.*

chlo·ro·phyl·lous (klōr′ə fil′əs, klôr′-), *adj.* of or containing chlorophyll. Also, **chlo·ro·phyl·lose** (klōr′ə-fil′ōs, klôr′-). [CHLOROPHYLL + -OUS]

chlo·ro·pic·rin (klōr′ə pik′rin, -pī′krin, klôr′-), *n.* *Chem., Mil.* a colorless, somewhat oily, water-insoluble, poisonous liquid, CCl_3NO_2, which causes lachrymation and headache: used as an insecticide, a fungicide, in organic synthesis, and as a war gas. Also, **chlorpicrin.** Also called **nitrochloroform.** [CHLORO-[2] + PICR(IC ACID) + -IN[2]]

chlo·ro·plast (klōr′ə plast′, klôr′-), *n.* *Bot.* a plastid containing chlorophyll. [CHLORO(PHYLL) + -PLAST] —**chlo′ro·plas′tic,** *adj.*

chlo·ro·pla·tin·ic (klōr′ə plə tin′ik, klôr′-), *adj.* *Chem.* of or derived from chloroplatinic acid. [CHLORO-[2] + PLATINIC]

chlo/roplatin/ic ac/id, *Chem.* a red-brown, crystalline, water-soluble solid, $H_2PtCl_6 \cdot 6H_2O$, used chiefly in platinizing glass, metals, and ceramic ware. Also called **platinic chloride.**

chlo·ro·prene (klōr′ə prēn′, klôr′-), *n.* *Chem.* a colorless, slightly water-soluble liquid, $H_2C{=}CClCH{=}CH_2$, usually produced by the reaction of vinylacetylene with hydrochloric acid, which polymerizes to neoprene. [CHLORO-[2] + (ISO)PRENE]

chlo·ro·sis (klō rō′sis, klô-), *n.* **1.** an abnormally yellow color of plant tissues, resulting from partial failure to develop chlorophyll, caused by a nutrient deficiency or the activities of a pathogen. **2.** Also called **greensickness.** *Pathol.* a benign type of iron-deficiency anemia in adolescent girls, marked by a pale yellow-green complexion. [CHLOR-[1] + -OSIS] —**chlo·rot·ic** (klō rot′ik, klô-), *adj.*

chlo·ro·spi·nel (klōr′ō spi nel′, -spin′əl, klôr′-), *n.* a variety of spinel used as a gem, colored grass-green by the presence of copper. [CHLORO-[1] + SPINEL]

chlo/ro·sul·fon/ic ac/id (klōr′ō sul fon′ik, klôr′-, klōr′-, klôr′-), *Chem.* a colorless or yellowish, highly corrosive, pungent liquid, $HOSO_2Cl$, usually produced by reacting sulfur trioxide with hydrogen chloride: used in organic synthesis to introduce the sulfonyl chloride group, $=SO_2Cl$. [CHLORO-[2] + SULFONIC ACID]

chlo·ro·thi·a·zide (klōr′ə thī′ə zīd′, klôr′-), *n.* *Pharm.* a white, crystalline, slightly water-soluble powder, $C_7H_6ClN_3O_4S_2$, used as a diuretic and in the treatment of hypertension. [CHLORO-[2] + THIAZ(OLE) + -IDE]

chlo·ro·tri·flu·o·ro·eth·yl·ene (klōr′ō trī flōō′ə-rō eth′ə lēn′, -flōr′ō-, -flôr′-, -flōr′-, -flôr′-, klôr′-), *n.* *Chem.* a colorless, flammable gas, $ClFC{-}CF_2$, that polymerizes to form oils, greases, and waxes. [CHLORO-[2] + TRI- + FLUOR-[1] + -O- + ETHYLENE]

chlo·ro·tri·flu·o·ro·meth·ane (klōr′ō trī flōō′ə-rō meth′ān, -flōr′ō-, -flôr′-, -flōr′-, klôr′-), *n.* *Chem.* a colorless gas, $ClCF_3$, used chiefly as a refrigerant, in the hardening of metals, and in pharmaceutical processing.

Also called **trifluorochloromethane.** [CHLORO-[2] + TRI- + FLUOR-[1] + -O- + METHANE]

chlo·rous (klōr′əs, klôr′-), *adj.* *Chem.* **1.** containing trivalent chlorine. **2.** of or derived from chlorous acid. [CHLOR-[2] + -OUS]

chlo′rous ac′id, *Chem.* a hypothetical acid, $HClO_2$, known only in solution or in the form of its salts.

chlor·phe·nir·a·mine (klōr′fə nir′ə mēn′, klôr′-), *n.* *Pharm.* an antihistaminic compound, $C_{20}H_{23}ClN_2O_4$, used chiefly in the form of its maleate in treating the symptoms of allergies. [CHLOR-[2] + PHEN- + (P)YR- + -AMINE]

chlor·phe·nol (klōr fē′nōl, -nôl, -nol, klôr-), *n.* *Chem.* chlorophenol.

chlor·pic·rin (klōr pik′rin, klôr-), *n.* *Chem.* chloropicrin.

chlor·prom·a·zine (klōr prom′ə zēn′, klôr-), *n.* a grayish-white, crystalline powder, $C_{17}H_{19}ClN_2S$, derived from phenothiazine, and used in the form of its hydrochloride chiefly to inhibit nausea and vomiting associated with certain mental disorders. [CHLOR-[2] + PRO- (PYL + A)M(INE) + AZINE]

chlor·pro·phen·py·rid·a·mine (klōr prō′fēn pi-rid′ə mēn′, -min, klôr-), *n.* *Pharm.* chlorpheniramine. [CHLOR-[2] + PRO(PANE) + PHEN(YL) + PYRI(DINE) + D(IMETHYL) + AMINE]

chlor·tet·ra·cy·cline (klōr te′trə sī′klīn, klôr-), *n.* *Pharm.* a yellow, crystalline, antibiotic powder, $C_{22}H_{23}N_2O_8Cl$, biosynthesized by *Streptomyces aureofaciens,* used in the treatment of infections. [CHLOR-[2] + TETRACYCLINE]

Chlor-Tri·me·ton (klōr trī′mi ton′, klôr-), *n.* *Pharm., Trademark.* chlorpheniramine.

chm., **1.** chairman. **2.** checkmate.

chmn., chairman.

cho·a·no·cyte (kō′ə nə sīt′, kō an′ə sīt′), *n.* *Zool.* one of the flagellated cells lining the inner cavity of a sponge, having a collar of protoplasm encircling the base of the flagellum. Also called **collar cell.** [< Gk *choān(ē)* funnel + -O- + -CYTE] —**cho′a·no·cyt′al,** *adj.*

cho·a·no·flag·el·late (kō′ə nō flaj′ə lāt′), *n.* *Zool.* any flagellate of the genera *Monosiga* and *Proterospongia,* having a protoplasmic collar encircling the base of the flagellum. [< NL *Choanoflagellat(a)* name of the order. See CHOANOCYTE, FLAGELLATA]

Choate (chōt), *n.* **1. Joseph Hodges,** 1832–1917, U.S. lawyer and diplomat. **2. Rufus,** 1799–1859, U.S. lawyer, orator, and statesman.

chock (chok), *n.* **1.** a wedge or block of wood, metal, or the like, for filling in a space, holding an object steady, preventing motion, etc. **2.** *Naut.* **a.** any of various heavy metal fittings on a deck or wharf that serve as fairleads for cables or chains. **b.** a shaped support or cradle for a ship's boat, barrel, etc. **c.** a small wooden piece or timber for filling a gap, reinforcing an angle, etc., in a wooden vessel. **3.** *Metalworking.* a bearing supporting the end of a rolling mill. —*v.t.* **4.** to furnish with or secure by a chock or chocks. **5.** *Naut.* to place (a boat) upon chocks. —*adv.* **6.** as close or tight as possible: *chock against the edge.* [?]

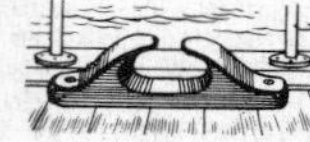
Chock (def. 2a)

chock-a-block (chok′ə blok′), *adv.* **1.** *Naut.* with the blocks drawn close together, as when a tackle is hauled to the utmost; ablock. **2.** in a jammed or crowded condition.

chock-full (chok′fŏŏl′), *adj.* full to the utmost; crammed. Also, **chuck-full, choke-full.** [late ME *chokke-fulle,* equiv. to *chokke* (< ?) + *fulle* FULL[1]]

chock·stone (chok′stōn′), *n.* a rock or mass of rocks wedged in a crevice of a mountain. [CHOCK + STONE]

choc·o·late (chô′kə lit, chok′ə-, chôk′lit, chok′-), *n.* **1.** a preparation of the seeds of cacao, roasted, husked, and ground (without removing any of the fat), often sweetened and flavored, as with vanilla. **2.** a beverage made by dissolving such a preparation in milk or water, served hot or cold: *a cup of hot chocolate.* **3.** any candy made from such a preparation, often in combination with milk and sometimes containing nuts, raisins, etc.: *a piece of chocolate.* **4.** any syrup or flavoring made from this preparation or imitating its flavor by artificial means: *Pour some chocolate on your ice cream.* **5.** a small, individually made piece of candy consisting either of chocolate or of a candy, cream, liquor, or fruit center with a coating of chocolate: *Have another chocolate.* **6.** dark brown. —*adj.* **7.** made, flavored, or covered with chocolate: *chocolate cake; chocolate milk.* **8.** having the color of chocolate; dark-brown. [< F *chocolat* < Sp *chocolate* < Nahuatl *chocolatl*]

choc·o·late-flow·er (chô′kə lit flou′ər, chok′ə-, chôk′lit-, chok′-), *n.* alumroot (def. 3).

choc′olate sol′dier, a nonfighting soldier; a serviceman not assigned to combat duty.

choc′olate tree′, cacao (def. 1).

choc·o·lat·y (chô′kə lə tē, chok′ə-, chôk′lə-, chok′-), *adj.* *Informal.* flavored with or resembling chocolate. [CHOCOLATE + -Y[1]]

Choc·taw (chok′tô), *n., pl.* **-taws,** (*esp. collectively*) **-taw. 1.** a member of a large Muskhogean tribe of North American Indians, formerly living chiefly in southern Mississippi, now in Oklahoma. **2.** the language of the Choctaw and Chickasaw Indians. **3.** *Chiefly Southern U.S.* something unintelligible, as speech, illegible handwriting, or an ineffectual explanation; gibberish: *My best efforts at clarity were Choctaw to him.*

Choc·taw-root (chok′tô rōōt′, -rŏŏt′), *n.* See **Indian hemp.**

Cho·ëph·o·ri (kō ef′ə rī′), *n.* a tragedy (458 B.C.) by Aeschylus. Also called **The Libation-bearers.** Cf. **Oresteia.**

choice (chois), *n., adj.,* **choic·er, choic·est.** —*n.* **1.** the act or an instance of choosing; selection: *Her choice of a red coat was made after she had seen many others.* **2.** power of choosing; option: *The child had no choice about going to school.* **3.** the person or thing chosen or eligible to be chosen: *This book is my choice. He is one of two choices for the Academy Award for best actor.* **4.** an abundance and variety from which to choose: *a wide choice of candidates.* **5.** that which is preferred or preferable to others; the best part of anything: *Mare's Nest is the choice in the sixth race.* **6.** an alternative: *There is another choice.* **7.** a well-chosen supply: *This restaurant has a fine choice of wines.* **8.** *U.S.* (in the grading of beef) **a.** a grade of beef between prime and good. **b.** a cut of beef of this grade. —*adj.* **9.** worthy of being chosen; excellent; superior. **10.** carefully selected: *delivered in choice words.* **11.** *U.S.* (in the grading of beef) rated between prime and good. [ME *chois* < OF, deriv. of *choisir* to perceive, choose < Gmc; see CHOOSE] —**choice′less,** *adj.* —**choice′ly,** *adv.* —**choice′ness,** *n.*

—**Syn. 2.** CHOICE, ALTERNATIVE, OPTION, PREFERENCE all suggest the power of choosing between things. CHOICE implies the opportunity to choose: *a choice of evils.* ALTERNATIVE suggests that one has a choice between only two possibilities. It is often used with a negative to mean that there is no second possibility: *to have no alternative.* OPTION emphasizes free right or privilege of choosing: *to exercise one's option.* PREFERENCE applies to a choice based on liking or partiality: *to state a preference.* **9.** select, rare, uncommon, valuable, precious. See **fine**[1].

choir (kwīər), *n.* **1.** a company of singers, esp. an organized group employed in church service. **2.** any group of musicians or musical instruments; a musical company, or band, or a division of one: *string choir.* **3.** *Archit.* **a.** the part of a church occupied by the singers. **b.** the part of a cruciform church east of the crossing. **4.** (in medieval angelology) one of the orders of angels. —*adj.* **5.** professed to recite or chant the divine office: *a choir monk.* —*v.t., v.i.* **6.** to sing or sound in chorus. [ME *quer* < OF *cuer* < L *chor(us)* CHORUS; r. OE *chor* choir < L] —**choir′like′,** *adj.*

choir·boy (kwīər′boi′), *n.* a boy who sings in a choir, esp. a church choir. [CHOIR + BOY]

choir·girl (kwīər′gûrl′), *n.* a girl who sings in a choir. [CHOIR + GIRL]

choir′ loft′, a gallery in which the choir is stationed, as in certain churches.

choir·mas·ter (kwīər′mas′tər, -mä′stər), *n.* the leader or director of a choir. [CHOIR + MASTER]

choir′ or′gan, 1. an organ of small range, formerly used in churches to accompany the choir. **2.** See **positive organ** (def. 2).

Choi·seul (*Fr.* shwa zœl′), *n.* an island E of New Guinea; one of the British Solomon Islands. 4500 (est. 1951); 1500 sq. mi.

choke (chōk), *v.,* **choked, chok·ing,** *n.* —*v.t.* **1.** to stop the breath of, by squeezing or obstructing the windpipe; strangle; stifle; suffocate. **2.** to stop (the breath, utterance, etc.) by or as by strangling or stifling: *The sudden wind choked his words.* **3.** to check the growth, progress, or action of: *to choke off discussion.* **4.** to stop by filling; obstruct; clog; congest: *Grease choked the drain.* **5.** to suppress (a feeling, emotion, expression of emotion, etc.) (often fol. by *back* or *down*): *She choked back her tears.* **6.** to fill chock-full: *The storeroom was choked with furniture, luggage, and boxes.* **7.** (in an internal-combustion engine) to enrich the fuel mixture of by diminishing the air supply to the carburetor, as when starting a motor. **8.** *Sports.* to grip (a bat, racket, or the like) farther than usual from the end of the handle; shorten one's grip on (often fol. by *up*). —*v.i.* **9.** to suffer from or as from strangling or suffocating: *He choked on a piece of food.* **10.** to become obstructed, clogged, or otherwise stopped: *The words choked in her throat.* **11. choke (someone) up,** to inspire with a deep emotion, as of gratitude or commiseration (often used ironically): *Her complaint that she had to wear last year's mink really choked us up.* **12. choke up, a.** *Informal.* to become speechless, as from the effect of emotion, tension, or stress: *She choked up over the flowers he gave her.* **b.** *Slang.* to become too tense or nervous to perform well: *Our team began to choke up in the last inning.* —*n.* **13.** the act or sound of choking. **14.** (in an internal-combustion engine) a mechanism by which the air supply to a carburetor may be diminished or stopped. **15.** *Mach.* any mechanism which, by blocking a passage, regulates the flow of air, gas, etc. **16.** *Elect.* See **choke coil. 17.** a narrowed part, as in a chokebore. [ME *choke(n), cheken,* var. of *achoken, acheken,* OE *āceocian* to suffocate; akin to Icel *kōk* gullet] —**choke′a·ble,** *adj.*

choke·ber·ry (chōk′ber′ē, -bə rē), *n., pl.* **-ries. 1.** the berrylike fruit of any North American, rosaceous shrub of the genus *Aronia,* as *A. arbutifolia* (**red chokeberry**), *A. melanocarpa* (**black chokeberry**), or *A. prunifolia* (**purple chokeberry**). **2.** the plant which bears this fruit. [CHOKE + BERRY]

choke·bore (chōk′bōr′, -bôr′), *n.* **1.** (in a shotgun) a bore that narrows toward the muzzle to prevent shot from scattering too widely. **2.** a shotgun with such a bore. [CHOKE + BORE[1]]

choke·cher·ry (chōk′cher′ē), *n., pl.* **-ries. 1.** any of several cherries, esp. *Prunus virginiana,* of North America, that bear an astringent fruit. **2.** the fruit itself. [CHOKE + CHERRY]

choke′ coil′, *Elect.* a coil of large inductance which gives relatively large impedance to alternating current. Also called **choke.**

choke′ col′lar, a nooselike collar for restraining powerful dogs.

choke·damp (chōk′damp′), *n.* *Mining.* mine atmosphere so low in oxygen and high in carbon dioxide as to cause choking. Also called **blackdamp.** [CHOKE + DAMP]

choke-full (chōk′fŏŏl′), *adj.* chock-full.

choke′ point′, a bottleneck.

chok·er (chō′kər), *n.* **1.** one who or that which chokes. **2.** *Informal.* **a.** a necklace that fits snugly around the neck. **b.** a neckcloth or high collar. [CHOKE + -ER[1]]

chokes (chōks), *n.* *Informal.* a manifestation of caisson disease that is characterized by dyspnea, coughing, and choking. [see CHOKE]

chok·ey[1] (chō′kē), *adj.,* **chok·i·er, chok·i·est.** choky[1].

chok·ey[2] (chō′kē), *n., pl.* **-eys.** *Brit. Slang.* choky[2].

chok·ing (chō′king), *adj.* **1.** (of the voice) husky and strained because of deep emotion. **2.** causing the feeling of being choked: *a choking cloud of smoke.* [CHOKE + -ING[2]] —**chok′ing·ly,** *adv.*

chok·y[1] (chō′kē), *adj.,* **chok·i·er, chok·i·est.** tending to choke or suffocate: *a choky collar.* Also, **chokey.** [CHOKE + -Y[1]]

chok·y[2] (chō′kē), *n., pl.* **chok·ies.** *Brit. Slang.* **1.** jail; prison. **2.** *Anglo-Indian.* an official station or headquarters, as for levying tolls, for customs, or for the police. Also, **chokey.** [< AInd (by assoc. with CHOKE) < Hindi *chaukī* station, lock-up, dim. of *cauk* market-place < Skt *catuṣka* with four angles, deriv. of *catur* four]

chol-, var. of **chole-** before a vowel: *choline.*

chol·a·gogue (kol′ə gôg′, -gog′, kō′lə-), *Med.* —*adj.* **1.** Also, **chol·a·gog·ic** (kol′ə goj′ik, kō′lə-). promoting the flow of bile. —*n.* **2.** a cholagogue agent. [< F < Gk *cholagōgós.* See CHOL-, -AGOGUE]

chole-, a learned borrowing from Greek meaning "bile," "gall," used in the formation of compound words: *cholesterol.* Also, *esp. before a vowel,* **chol-.** [comb. form of Gk *cholḗ* bile]

cho·le·cal·cif·er·ol (kō′lə kal sif′ə rōl′, -rôl′, -rol′, -käl sif′-), *n.* See **vitamin D.** [CHOLE- + CALCI- + -FER + -OL[1]]

chol·e·cyst (kol′i sist′, kō′li-), *n.* *Anat.* See **gall bladder.** [CHOLE- + -CYST]

chol·e·cys·tec·to·my (kol′i si stek′tə mē, kō′li-), *n., pl.* **-mies.** *Surg.* removal of the gall bladder. [CHOLECYST + -ECTOMY]

cho·le·cys·ti·tis (kol′i si stī′tis, kō′li-), *n.* *Pathol.* inflammation of the gall bladder. [CHOLE- + CYSTITIS]

chol·e·cys·tog·ra·phy (kol′i si stog′rə fē, kō′li-), *n.* *Med.* the production of x-ray photographs of the gall bladder following administration of a radiopaque substance that is secreted by the liver into the gall bladder. [CHOLECYST + -O- + -GRAPHY]

chol·e·cys·tos·to·my (kol′i si stos′tə mē, kō′li-), *n., pl.* **-mies.** *Surg.* a draining of the gall bladder with the organ left in place, usually done to remove gallstones. [CHOLECYST + -O- + -STOMY]

cho·le·cys·tot·o·my (kol′i si stot′ə mē, kō′li-), *n., pl.* **-mies.** *Surg.* incision of the gall bladder. [CHOLE- + CYSTO- + -TOMY]

cho·led·o·chos·to·my (kə led′ə kos′tə mē, kō′lə dō-kos′-, kol′ə-), *n., pl.* **-mies.** *Surg.* formation of a temporary opening through the abdominal wall into the common bile duct, usually to remove stones from it. [< NL *choledoch(us)* (< Gk *cholēdóchos,* equiv. to *cholḗ* CHOLE- + *dóchos* DUCT) + -O- + -STOMY]

cho·led·o·chot·o·my (kə led′ə kot′ə mē, kō′lə dō-kot′-, kol′ə-), *n., pl.* **-mies.** *Surg.* incision of the common bile duct. [< NL *choledoch(us)* (see CHOLEDOCOSTOMY) + -O- + -TOMY]

cho·lee (chō′lē), *n.* choli.

chol·e·lith (kol′ə lith, kō′lə-), *n.* *Pathol.* a gallstone. Also, **chololith.** [CHOLE- + -LITH]

cho·le·li·thi·a·sis (kō′lə li thī′ə sis), *n.* *Pathol.* the presence of gallstones. [CHOLELITH + -IASIS]

cho·lent (chō′lənt, chul′ənt; *Yiddish* chōlnt), *n.* *Jewish Cookery.* a stewed or baked dish, as of meat and vegetables, for the Sabbath, cooked the day before or overnight over a slow fire. [< Yiddish]

chol·er (kol′ər), *n.* **1.** irascibility; anger; wrath; irritability. **2.** *Old Physiol.* See **yellow bile. 3.** *Obs.* biliousness. [ME *coler(a)* < ML; L *cholera* < Gk *cholérā* CHOLERA]

chol·er·a (kol′ər ə), *n.* **1.** Also called **Asian cholera.** *Pathol.* an acute, infectious, often fatal disease, endemic in India and China, and occasionally epidemic elsewhere, characterized by profuse diarrhea, vomiting, cramps, etc. Cf. **bilious cholera, sporadic cholera. 2.** *Vet. Pathol.* any of several diseases characterized by depression, sleepiness, lack of appetite, and diarrhea. Cf. **hog cholera, fowl cholera.** [< L < Gk *cholérā* name of several intestinal diseases] —**chol·e·ra·ic** (kol′ə rā′ik), *adj.*

chol′era in·fan′tum (in fan′təm), *Pathol.* an often fatal form of gastroenteritis occurring in infants, not of the same cause as cholera but having somewhat similar characteristics. [< NL: cholera of infants]

chol′era mor′bus (môr′bəs), *Pathol.* See **sporadic cholera.** Also called **chol′era nos′tras** (nos′trəs). [< NL: disease cholera]

chol·er·ic (kol′ər ik, kə ler′ik), *adj.* **1.** irascible; characterized by anger: *a choleric disposition.* **2.** *Obs.* **a.** bilious. **b.** causing biliousness. [ME *colerik* < ML *coleric(us)* bilious, L *cholericus* < Gk *cholerikós.* See CHOLERA, -IC] —**chol′er·i·cal·ly, chol′er·ic·ly,** *adv.* —**chol′er·ic·ness,** *n.*

—**Syn. 1.** wrathful, testy, irritable, impatient, touchy. —**Ant. 1.** phlegmatic.

cho·les·ter·e·mi·a (kə les′tə rē′mē ə), *n.* *Med.* cholesterolemia.

cho·les·ter·ol (kə les′tə rōl′, -rôl′, -rol′), *n.* **1.** *Biochem.* a sterol, $C_{27}H_{45}OH$, occurring in all animal fats and oils, bile, gallstones, nerve tissue, blood, etc. **2.** the commercial form of this compound, obtained from the spinal cord of cattle, used chiefly as an emulsifying agent in cosmetics and pharmaceuticals, and in the synthesis of vitamin D. Also, **cho·les·ter·in** (kə les′tər in). [< Gk *cholḗ* bile + *ster(eós)* solid + -OL[1]]

cho·les·ter·ol·e·mi·a (kə les′tə rō lē′mē ə, -rô-, -ro-), *n.* *Med.* the presence of an abnormal amount of cholesterol in the blood. Also, **cholesteremia.** [CHOLESTEROL + -EMIA]

Chol Ha·mo·ed (ḵhōl′ hä mō ād′; *Eng.* ḵhōl′ hä mō′ed), *Hebrew.* See **Hol Hamoed.**

cho·li (chō′lē), *n.* a short-sleeved blouse or bodice, often one exposing part of the midriff, worn by Hindu women in India. Also, **cholee.** [< Hindi *colī* < Skt *cola, coda,* prob. of Dravidian orig.]

cho′lic ac′id (kō′lik, kol′ik), **1.** *Biochem.* a hydroxy acid, $C_{24}H_{40}O_5$, related to the sex hormones and cholesterol. **2.** *Chem.* the commercial form of this compound, obtained from beef bile, used chiefly in the manufacture of drugs and in research. [< Gk *cholik(ós)* bilious (*chol(ḗ)* bile + *-ikos* -IC) + ACID]

cho·line (kō′lēn, kol′ēn, -in), *n.* **1.** *Biochem.* a quaternary ammonium base, $C_5H_{15}NO_2$, one of the B-complex vitamins, found in the lecithin of many plants and animals. **2.** the viscous, strongly alkaline commercial form of this compound, usually synthesized, used as a feed supplement, esp. for poultry, and in medicine in certain liver conditions. [CHOL- + -INE[2]]

cho·lin·es·ter·ase (kō′lə nes′tə rās′, kol′ə-), *n.* *Biochem.* an enzyme, found esp. in the heart, brain, and blood, that hydrolyzes acetylcholine to acetic acid and choline. [CHOLINE + ESTERASE]

chol·la (chōl′yä, -yə; *Sp.* chô′yä), *n., pl.* **chol·las** (chōl′yäz, -yəz; *Sp.* chô′yäs). any of several spiny treelike cacti of the genus *Opuntia,* esp. *O. fulgida* of the southwestern U.S. and Mexico. [< MexSp *cholla* head, perh. < OF (dial.) *cholle* ball < Gmc; see KEEL[1]]

Cho·lo (chō′lō; *Sp.* chô′lō), *n., pl.* **-los** (-lōz; *Sp.* -lōs). (in Bolivia and Peru) an Indian of Spanish America.

CONCISE ETYMOLOGY KEY: <, descended or derived from; >, whence; b., blend of, blended; c., cognate with; deriv., derivative; equiv., equivalent; imit., imitative; m., modification of; obl., oblique; r., replacing; s., stem; sp., spelling; trans., translation; ?, origin unknown, perhaps; *, hypothetical. See the full key inside the front cover.

chol·o·lith (kol′ə lith′), *n. Pathol.* cholelith. —**chol′o·lith′ic,** *adj.*

Cho·lon (chə lun′; *Fr.* shô lôɴ′), *n.* a city in S South Vietnam: merged with Saigon to form an urban complex 1932. 481,000 (est. 1953).

Cho·lu·la (chō lo͞o′lä), *n.* a town in S Mexico, SE of Mexico City: ancient Aztec ruins. 12,833 (1960).

chomp (chomp), *v.t., v.i. Dial.* chump².

chon (chon), *n., pl.* **chon.** a money of account of South Korea, the 100th part of a hwan, equivalent to .000077 of a U.S. dollar. [< Korean]

chondr-, var. of **chondrio-** before a vowel.

chon·dral (kon′drəl), *adj. Anat., Zool.* of or pertaining to cartilage or a cartilage. [CHONDR- + -AL¹]

chon·dri·a (kon′drē ə), *n.* a profusely branched red alga, *Chondria tenuissima,* found on the Atlantic and Pacific coasts of North America. [< Gk, pl. of *chondrion,* equiv. to *chondr-* CHONDR- + *-ion* dim. suffix]

Chon·drich·thy·es (kon drik′thē ēz′), *n.* the class comprising the cartilaginous fishes. [< NL, equiv. to *chondr-* CHONDR- + Gk *ichthýes* (pl.) fish]

chondrio-, a learned borrowing from Greek meaning "cartilage," used in the formation of compound words: *chondriosome.* Also, **chondr-, chondro-.** [< Gk *chondrío(n),* dim. of *chóndros* cartilage]

chon·dri·o·cont (kon′drē ō kont′), *n. Biol.* a rodlike or threadlike mitochondrion. [CHONDRIO- + *-cont* < Gk *kont(ós)* rod]

chon·dri·ome (kon′drē ōm′), *n. Biol.* the mitochondria of a cell, considered as a whole. Also, **chon·dri·o·ma** (kon′drē ō′mə). [CHONDRI- + *-ome* (see -OMA)]

chon·dri·o·mite (kon′drē ō mīt′), *n. Biol.* **1.** a chain of granular mitochondria. **2.** a single granular mitochondrion. [CHONDRIO- + Gk *mít(os)* thread]

chon·dri·o·some (kon′drē ō sōm′), *n. Biol.* mitochondrion. [CHONDRIO- + -SOME³] —**chon′dri·o·so′mal,** *adj.*

chon·drite (kon′drīt), *n. Mineral.* a stony meteorite containing chondrules. [CHONDR- + -ITE¹] —**chon·drit·ic** (kon drit′ik), *adj.*

chondro-, var. of **chondrio-:** *chondrosarcoma.*

chon·dro·ma (kon drō′mə), *n., pl.* **-mas, -ma·ta** (-mə tə). *Pathol.* a cartilaginous tumor or growth. [CHONDR- + -OMA] —**chon·dro′ma·tous,** *adj.*

chon·dro·sar·co·ma (kon′drō sär kō′mə), *n., pl.* **-mas, -ma·ta** (-mə tə). *Pathol.* a sarcoma with cartilaginous constituents, or an abnormal growth of the cartilage. Also called **sarcoenchondroma.** [CHONDRO- + SARCOMA] —**chon′dro·sar·co′ma·tous,** *adj.*

chon·drule (kon′dro͞ol), *n. Mineral.* a small round mass of olivine or pyroxene found in stony meteorites. [CHONDR- + -ULE]

chon·drus (kon′drəs), *n., pl.* **-dri** (-drī). *Mineral.* chondrule. [< NL < Gk *chóndros* grain]

Chong·jin (chœng′jin′), *n.* a seaport in W North Korea. 184,301 (1944). Japanese, **Seishin.**

Chon·ju (chœn′jo͞o′), *n.* a city in SW South Korea. 100,624 (1949).

choo-choo (cho͞o′cho͞o′), *n., v.,* **-chooed, -choo·ing.** *Baby Talk.* —*n.* **1.** a train. **2.** the sound of a steam locomotive. —*v.i.* **3.** to make a sound like that made by a steam locomotive. **4.** to travel by train: *We're going to choo-choo far away tomorrow.* [imit.]

chook (cho͝ok, cho͞ok), *Australian.* —*n.* **1.** a hen. —*interj.* **2.** (used as a call for poultry or pigs.) Also, **chook′ie, chooky.** [imit.]

chook·y (cho͝ok′ē, cho͞o′kē), *n., pl.* **chook·ies,** *interj.* chook.

choo·ra (cho͝or′ə), *n.* an Indian dagger having a sharply pointed, single-edged blade. [< Hindi]

choose (cho͞oz), *v.,* **chose; cho·sen** or (*Obs.*) **chose; choos·ing.** —*v.t.* **1.** to select from or in preference to another or other things or persons: *She chose Sunday for her departure.* **2.** to prefer or decide (to do something): *He chose to run for election.* **3.** to want; desire. **4.** (esp. in children's games) to contend with (an opponent) to decide, as by odd or even, who will have first choice of players, playing positions, etc.: *I'll choose you to see who gets to bat first.* —*v.i.* **5.** to make a choice: *He chose carefully.* **6.** to be inclined: *You may stay here if you choose.* **7.** (esp. in children's games) to decide, as by means of odd or even, who will have first choice of players, playing positions, etc.: *Let's choose to see who bats first.* **8. cannot choose but,** cannot do otherwise than; is or are obliged to: *He cannot choose but hear.* **9. choose up** (often with **sides, teams,** etc.), *Informal.* to select players or assemble teams for a contest or game; name opposing players: *The boys chose up sides and then took their positions on the field. Let's choose up to see who goes first.* [ME *chose(n), chēse(n),* OE *cēosan;* c. Goth *kiusan,* OHG *kiosan* (G *kiesen*); akin to Gk *geú(omai)* (to) enjoy, L *gus(tāre)* (to) taste] —**choos′a·ble,** *adj.* —**choos′er,** *n.* —**choos′ing·ly,** *adv.*

—**Syn. 1.** CHOOSE, SELECT, PICK, ELECT, PREFER indicate a decision that one or more possibilities are to be regarded more highly than others. CHOOSE suggests a decision on one of a number of possibilities because of its apparent superiority: *to choose a course of action.* SELECT suggests a choice made for fitness: *to select the proper golf club.* PICK, an informal word, suggests a selection on personal grounds: *to pick a winner.* The formal word ELECT suggests a kind of official action: *to elect a chairman.* PREFER, also formal, emphasizes the desire or liking for one thing more than for another or others: *to prefer coffee to tea.* —**Ant. 1.** reject.

choos·ey (cho͞o′zē), *adj.,* **choos·i·er, choos·i·est.** *Informal.* choosy.

choos·y (cho͞o′zē), *adj.,* **choos·i·er, choos·i·est.** *Informal.* hard to please, particular, fastidious, esp. in making a choice: *She's too choosy about food.* [CHOOSE + -Y¹]

chop¹ (chop), *v.,* **chopped, chop·ping,** *n.* —*v.t.* **1.** to cut or sever with a quick, heavy blow or a series of blows, using an ax, hatchet, etc. (often fol. by *down, off,* etc.): *to chop down a tree.* **2.** to make or prepare for use by so cutting: *to chop logs.* **3.** to cut in pieces; mince (often fol. by *up*): *to chop up an onion; to chop meat.* **4.** (in tennis, cricket, etc.) to hit (a ball) with a chop stroke. **5.** to weed and thin out (growing cotton) with a hoe. **6.** *Fox Hunting.* (of a hound or pack) to attack and kill (a fox that has not begun to run). —*v.i.* **7.** to make a quick, heavy stroke or a series of strokes, as with an ax. **8.** *Boxing.* to throw or deliver a short blow, esp. a downward one while in a clinch. **9.** (in tennis, cricket, etc.) to employ or deliver a chop stroke. **10.** to go, come, or move suddenly or violently. —*n.* **11.** the act or an instance of chopping. **12.** a cutting blow. **13.** *Boxing.* a short blow, esp. a downward one, executed while in a clinch. **14.** a piece chopped off. **15.** an individual cut, thick slice, or portion of mutton, lamb, veal, pork, etc., usually one containing a rib. **16.** a short, irregular, broken motion of waves; choppiness: *There's too much chop for rowing today.* **17.** rough, turbulent water, as of a sea or lake. **18.** See **chop stroke. 19.** *Obs.* a chap; crack; cleft. [var. of CHAP¹]

—**Syn. 1.** See **cut.**

chop² (chop), *v.,* **chopped, chop·ping.** —*v.i.* **1.** to turn, shift, or change suddenly, as the wind: *The wind chopped to the west.* **2.** *Brit. Dial.* to vacillate; change one's mind. **3.** *Obs.* to barter. **4.** *Obs.* to bandy words; argue. **5. chop logic,** to reason or dispute argumentatively; draw unnecessary distinctions: *Instead of deciding the real issue the commentator would chop logic.* [var. of obs. *chap* barter, ME *chap(ien),* OE *cēapian* (deriv. of *cēap* sale, trade; see CHEAP)]

chop³ (chop), *n.* **1.** Usually, **chops.** the jaw. **2. chops,** the oral cavity; mouth. **3.** *Horol.* either of two pieces clasping the end of the suspension spring of a pendulum. **4. lick one's chops,** *Slang.* to await with pleasure; anticipate; relish: *He was already licking his chops over the expected inheritance.* Also, **chap.** [? special use of CHOP¹]

chop⁴ (chop), *n.* **1.** (in India, China, etc.) **a.** an official stamp or seal, or a permit or clearance. **b.** a design, corresponding to a brand or trademark, stamped on goods to indicate their special identity. **2.** *Anglo-Indian Informal.* quality, class, or grade: *first chop.* [< Hindi *chāp* impression, stamp]

cho·pa (chō′pə, chop′ə), *n., pl.* (*esp. collectively*) **-pa,** (*esp. referring to two or more kinds or species*) **-pas.** any of several fishes, esp. of the sea chub family, *Kyphosidae,* and the nibbler family, *Girellidae.* [< Sp < Pg *choupa* < L *clupea;* see CLUPEID]

chop′ chop′, (in pidgin English) quickly! right away! [repetitive compound based on pidgin English *chop* quick]

chop·fall·en (chop′fô′lən), *adj.* chapfallen.

chop·house¹ (chop′hous′), *n., pl.* **-hous·es** (-hou′ziz). a restaurant specializing in chops, steaks, and the like. [CHOP¹ + HOUSE]

chop·house² (chop′hous′), *n., pl.* **-hous·es** (-hou′ziz). *Archaic.* (in China) a custom house. [CHOP⁴ + HOUSE]

chop·in¹ (chop′in), *n.* **1.** an old Scottish unit of liquid measure equivalent to about a quart. **2.** a container holding this amount. [ME < MF *chopine* < MLG *schōpe* SCOOP < MD *schoepe*]

chop·in² (chop′in), *n.* chopine.

Cho·pin (shō′pan; *Fr.* shô paɴ′), *n.* **Fré·dé·ric Fran·çois** (fred′ə rik fran swä′, fred′rik; *Fr.* frā dā rēk′ frän swa′), 1810–49, Polish composer and pianist, in France after 1831.

cho·pine (chō pēn′, chop′in), *n.* a shoe having a thick sole of cork or other material suggesting a short stilt, worn esp. by women in 18th-century Europe after its introduction from Turkey. Also, **chopin.** [< Sp *chapín,* equiv. to *chap(a)* (< MF *chape* CHAPE) + *-in* -IN¹]

chop·log·ic (chop′loj′ik), *n.* **1.** sophistic or overly complicated argumentation. —*adj.* **2.** Also, **chop′log′i·cal.** exhibiting or indulging in choplogic. [CHOP² + LOGIC]

chop·per (chop′ər), *n.* **1.** one who or that which chops. **2.** a short ax with a large blade, used for cutting up meat, fish, etc.; butcher's cleaver. **3.** a device for interrupting an electric current or a beam of light at regular intervals. **4.** *Informal.* a helicopter. **5. choppers,** *Slang.* the teeth. [CHOP¹ + -ER¹]

chop·ping¹ (chop′ing), *adj.* (of the sea, a lake, etc.) choppy (def. 1). [CHOP² + -ING²]

chop·ping² (chop′ing), *adj. Brit. Informal.* large and strong; hardy. [CHOP¹ + -ING²]

chop′ping block′, a thick, often large block of wood on which meat, vegetables, etc., are placed for cutting, trimming, chopping, and the like.

chop·py (chop′ē), *adj.,* **-pi·er, -pi·est. 1.** (of the sea, a lake, etc.) forming short, irregular, broken waves. **2.** (of the wind) shifting or changing suddenly or irregularly; variable. **3.** uneven in style or quality or characterized by poorly related parts: *The book was a choppy first novel.* [CHOP² + -Y¹] —**chop′pi·ly,** *adv.* —**chop′pi·ness,** *n.*

chop·stick (chop′stik′), *n.* one of a pair of thin sticks, usually of wood or ivory, used as eating utensils by the Chinese, Japanese, and other Oriental peoples. [pidgin English *chop* quick + STICK¹]

Chop·sticks (chop′stiks′), *n.* (*construed as sing.*) a harmonically and melodically simple waltz for piano, popularly played with the forefinger of each hand and sometimes having an accompanying part for a second player. [perh. after *chopstick* from the way the fingers are held]

chop′ stroke′, (in tennis, cricket, etc.) a stroke made with a sharp downward movement of the racket, bat, etc., imparting a backspin to the ball. Also called **chop.**

chop′ su′ey (chop′so͞o′ē), *U.S.* a mixed Chinese-style dish consisting of small pieces of meat, chicken, etc., cooked together with onions, bean sprouts, green peppers, mushrooms, or other vegetables and seasoning, in a gravy, often served with rice and soy sauce. Also, **chop′ soo′y.** [< Chin (Cantonese dial.) *shap sui* mixed bits]

cho·ra·gus (kə rā′gəs, kō-, kô-), *n., pl.* **-gi** (-jī), **-gus·es. 1.** (in ancient Greece) **a.** the leader of a dramatic chorus. **b.** a person who undertook the expense of providing for such a chorus. **2.** any conductor of an entertainment or festival. Also, **choregus.** [< L < Gk *chorāgós,* dial. var. of *chorēgós,* equiv. to *chor(ós)* CHORUS + *-ēgos,* comb. form of *ágein* to lead] —**cho·rag·ic** (kə raj′ik, -rā′jik), *adj.*

cho·ral (*adj.* kôr′əl, kôr′-; *n.* kə ral′, kō-, kô-, kôr′əl, kôr′-), *adj.* **1.** of a chorus or a choir. **2.** sung by, adapted for, or containing a chorus or a choir. —*n.* **3.** chorale. [< ML *chorāl(is),* equiv. to *chor(us)* CHORUS + *-ālis* -AL¹] —**cho′ral·ly,** *adv.*

cho·rale (kə ral′, -räl′, kō-, kô-; kôr′əl, kôr′-), *n.* **1.** a choral composition. **2.** a hymn tune. **3.** a simple sacred tune having a plain melody, a strong harmony, and a stately rhythm: *We heard a program of Bach chorales.* **4.** a group of singers specializing in singing such music: *the Robert Shaw chorale.* [< G *Choral,* short for *Choralgesang,* trans. of L *cantus chorālis;* see CHORAL]

cho′rale pre′lude, *Music.* a composition for organ that is based on a chorale or other hymn tune and is typically contrapuntal in style.

cho′ral speak′ing, the recitation of poetry or prose by an ensemble or chorus.

chord¹ (kôrd), *n.* **1.** a feeling or emotion: *His story struck a chord of pity in the listeners.* **2.** *Geom.* the line segment between two points on a given curve. **3.** a principal member of a truss extending from end to end, usually one of a pair of such members, more or less parallel and connected by a web composed of various compression and tension members. **4.** *Aeron.* a straight line joining the trailing and leading edges of an airfoil section. **5.** *Anat.* cord (def. 4). **6.** *Archaic.* a string of a musical instrument. [< L *chord(a)* < Gk *chordḗ* gut, string; r. CORD in senses given] —**chord′ed,** *adj.*

A C B

Chords (Geometrical) AB, AC, chords subtending arcs ACB, AC

chord² (kôrd), *n. Music.* a combination of two or more different tones sounded simultaneously. [earlier *cord,* short for ACCORD; *ch-* of CHORD¹]

chord·al (kôr′dəl), *adj.* **1.** of, pertaining to, or resembling a chord. **2.** of or pertaining to music that is marked principally by vertical harmonic movement rather than by linear polyphony. [CHORD² + -AL¹]

chor·da·mes·o·derm (kôr′də mez′ə dûrm′, -mes′-, -mē′zə-, -sə-), *n. Embryol.* the part of the blastoderm of a young embryo that forms the notochord and related structures. [< NL *chorda* (see CHORD¹) + MESODERM] —**chor′da·mes′o·der′mal, chor′da·mes′o·der′mic,** *adj.*

Chor·da·ta (kôr dā′tə, -dä′-), *n. Zool.* the phylum comprising the chordates. [<NL; see CHORDATE]

chor·date (kôr′dāt), *Zool.* —*adj.* **1.** belonging or pertaining to the phylum *Chordata,* comprising the true vertebrates and those animals having a notochord, as the lancelets and tunicates. —*n.* **2.** a chordate animal. [< NL *chorda* (see CHORD¹) + -ATE¹]

chor·da ten·din·e·a (kôr′də ten din′ē ə), *pl.* **chor·dae ten·din·e·ae** (kôr′dē ten din′ē ē′). *Anat.* any of the tendons of the papillary muscles and the atrioventricular valves that secure the valves and prevent them from moving into the atrium during ventricular contraction. [< NL: tendinous cord]

chord′ chart′, a chart indicating by means of symbols the identity, sequence, and duration of the chords occurring in the accompaniment to a melody.

chor·dee (kôr′dē, -dā, kôr′-), *n. Pathol.* a downward bowing of the penis, of a congenital nature or caused by gonorrhea. [< F *cordée* (fem. ptp.) corded, in the phrase *chaude-pisse cordée* corded gonorrhea]

chord′ of the sixth′, *Music.* See **sixth chord.**

chor·do·phone (kôr′də fōn′), *n.* a stringed instrument of a group including the harps, lutes, lyres, and zithers. [CHORD¹ + -O- + -PHONE]

chord′ or′gan, an electronic organ having a small keyboard for the right hand and for the left a set of buttons each of which produces a full chord when pushed.

chor·do·to·nal (kôr′də tōn′əl), *adj.* (of an insect) responsive to sound vibrations, as certain organs or parts. [CHORD¹ + -O- + TONAL]

chore (chōr, chôr), *n., v.,* **chored, chor·ing.** —*n.* **1.** a small or odd job; a piece of minor domestic work. **2. chores,** routine work around a house or farm. **3.** a hard or unpleasant task: *Solving the problem was quite a chore.* —*v.i.* **4.** to work at chores. [ME *churre,* OE *cyrr,* var. of *cierr, cerr* CHAR³]

—**Syn. 3.** duty, assignment.

cho·re·a (kə rē′ə, kō-, kô-), *n. Pathol.* **1.** any of several diseases of the nervous system characterized by jerky, involuntary movements, chiefly of the face and extremities. **2.** Also called **St. Vitus's dance.** such a disease occurring chiefly in children. **3.** *Vet. Pathol.* a disease of the central nervous system caused by bacterial or organic degeneration, most common in dogs following canine distemper, characterized by irregular, jerky, involuntary muscular movements. [< Gk *choreía* a dance, equiv. to *chor(ós)* CHORUS + *-eia* -Y³] —**cho·re′al, cho·re′ic, cho·re·at·ic** (kôr′ē at′ik, kôr′-), *adj.* —**cho·re·oid** (kôr′ē oid′, kôr′-), *adj.*

chore′ boy′, **1.** a man who is a cook's helper and domestic on a ranch or in a lumber camp. **2.** a person who undertakes responsibility for unpleasant detail.

cho·re·gus (kə rē′gəs, kō-, kô-), *n., pl.* **-gi** (-jī), **-gus·es.** choragus.

chore·man (chōr′mən, -man′, chôr′-), *n., pl.* **-men** (-mən -men′). a menial worker in a factory, logging camp, etc. [CHORE + MAN¹]

cho·re·o·graph (kôr′ē ə graf′, -gräf′, kôr′-), *Dance.* —*v.t.* **1.** to provide the choreography for: *to choreograph a musical comedy.* —*v.i.* **2.** to work as a choreographer. [back formation from CHOREOGRAPHY]

cho·re·og·ra·pher (kôr′ē og′rə fər, kôr′-), *n.* a person who creates dance compositions and plans and arranges dance movements and patterns for stage dances, esp. ballet dances. Also, *esp. Brit.,* **cho·reg·ra·pher** (kə reg′rə fər). [CHOREOGRAPH(Y) + -ER¹]

cho·re·og·ra·phy (kôr′ē og′rə fē, kôr′-), *n.* **1.** the art of composing ballets and other stage dances and planning and arranging the movements, steps, and patterns of stage dancers. **2.** the technique of representing the various movements in dancing by a system of notation. **3.** the art of dancing. Also, *esp. Brit.,* **cho·reg·ra·phy** (kə reg′rə fē, kō-, kô-). [< Gk *chore-* (s. of *choreía* CHOREA) + -O- + -GRAPHY] —**cho·re·o·graph·ic** (kôr′ē ə graf′ik, kôr′-); *esp. Brit.,* **cho·re·graph·ic** (kôr′ə graf′ik, kôr′-), *adj.* —**cho′re·o·graph′i·cal·ly;** *esp. Brit.,* **cho′re·graph′i·cal·ly,** *adv.*

chori-, var. of **chorio.**

cho·ri·amb (kôr′ē amb′, kôr′-), *n. Pros.* a foot of four syllables, two short between two long. [short for CHORIAMBUS] —**cho′ri·am′bic,** *adj.*

cho·ri·am·bus (kôr′ē am′bəs, kôr′-), *n., pl.* **-bi** (-bī), **-bus·es.** choriamb. [< LL < Gk *choríambos,* equiv. to *chor(eîos)* trochaic + *íambos* IAMB]

cho·ric (kôr′ik, kôr′-), *adj.* of, pertaining to, or written for a chorus. [< LL *choricus* < Gk *chorikós,* equiv. to *chor(ós)* CHORUS + *-ikos* -IC]

cho·rine (kôr′in, kôr′ēn), *n. Slang.* a chorus girl. [CHOR(US) + -INE[2]]

chorio-, a learned borrowing from Greek meaning "chorion," "choroid," used in the formation of compound words: *chorioallantois.* Also, **chori-.** [comb. form repr. Gk *chórion*]

cho·ri·o·al·lan·to·ic (kôr′ē ō al′ən tō′ik, kôr′-), *adj. Embryol., Zool.* of or pertaining to the chorioallantois. [CHORIO- + ALLANTOIC]

cho·ri·o·al·lan·to·is (kôr′ē ō ə lan′tō is, -tois, kôr′-), *n. Embryol., Zool.* a vascular, extraembryonic membrane of birds, reptiles, and certain mammals, formed by the fusion of the wall of the chorion with the wall of the allantois. Also called **cho′rioallanto′ic mem′brane.** [CHORIO- + ALLANTOIS]

cho·ri·o·car·ci·no·ma (kôr′ē ō kär′sə nō′mə, kôr′-), *n., pl.* **-mas, -ma·ta** (-mə tə). *Pathol.* a malignant tumor of the chorionic tissue, usually occurring in the uterus or testis. Also, **chorioma.** [CHORIO- + CARCINOMA]

cho·ri·o·ep·i·the·li·o·ma (kôr′ē ō ep′ə thē′lē ō′mə, kôr′-), *n., pl.* **-mas, -ma·ta** (-mə tə). choriocarcinoma.

cho·ri·oid (kôr′ē oid′, kôr′-), *adj., n. Anat.* choroid. [< Gk *chorioeidḗs.* See CHORI-, -OID]

cho·ri·o·ma (kôr′ē ō′mə, kôr′-), *n., pl.* **-mas, -ma·ta** (-mə tə). *Pathol.* choriocarcinoma. [by shortening]

cho·ri·on (kôr′ē on′, kôr′-), *n.* **1.** *Embryol.* the outermost of the extraembryonic membranes of land vertebrates, contributing to the formation of the placenta in the placental mammals. **2.** *Zool.* the membrane around the eggs of certain insects, secreted by cells of the ovary. [< NL < Gk *chórion*] —**cho′ri·on′ic, cho′ri·al,** *adj.*

chorion′ic go·nad·o·tro′pin (gō nad′ə trō′pin), **1.** *Biochem.* a hormone occurring in the urine of pregnant women, produced by the placenta, that stimulates the production of progesterone by the corpus luteum. **2.** *Pharm.* a commercial form of this substance, obtained from the urine of pregnant mares, and used in medicine in the treatment of testicular disorders and functional uterine bleeding, and in veterinary medicine in the treatment of cystic ovaries, esp. in cows and mares Also, **chorion′ic gonadotro′phin.** [GONADOTROP(IC) + -IN[2]]

cho·ri·pet·al·ous (kôr′ə pet′əl əs, kôr′-), *adj. Bot.* having unconnected petals. [< Gk *chōri* apart + PETALOUS]

cho·ri·so (chə rē′sō), *n., pl.* **-sos.** chorizo.

chor·is·ter (kôr′i stər, kor′-), *n.* **1.** a singer in a choir. **2.** a male singer in a church choir; choirboy. **3.** a choir leader. [< ML *chorist(a)* singer in a choir + -ER[1]; r. ME *queristre* < AF, equiv. to *quer* CHOIR + *-istre* -IST]

cho·ri·zo (chə rē′zō), *n., pl.* **-zos.** a Spanish pork sausage highly seasoned with spices and garlic. Also, **choriso.** [< Sp]

C horizon, *Geol.* the layer in a soil profile below the B horizon and immediately above the bedrock, consisting chiefly of weathered, partially decomposed rock. Cf. **A horizon, B horizon.**

cho·rob·a·tes (kō rob′ə tēz′, kō-), *n.* (in ancient Roman surveying) a level using water with a free surface or with two free surfaces at the ends of a trough. [< L < Gk *chōrobátēs,* equiv. to *chṓro(s)* ground, place, space + *-batēs* (*ba-* (s. of *bainein* to walk, step) + *-tēs* suffix forming n. of agent)]

cho·ro·gi (chôr′ō gē′, chôr′-), *n.* See **Chinese artichoke.** [< Jap]

cho·rog·ra·phy (kə rog′rə fē, kō-, kô-), *n. Geog.* a systematic, detailed description and analysis of a region or regions. [< L *chorographia* < Gk *chōrographíā,* equiv. to *choro-* (see CHOROBATES) + *-graphiā* -GRAPHY] —**cho·rog′ra·pher,** *n.* —**cho·ro·graph·ic** (kôr′ə graf′ik, kôr′-), **cho′ro·graph′i·cal,** *adj.* —**cho′ro·graph′i·cal·ly,** *adv.*

cho·roid (kôr′oid, kôr′-), *Anat.* —*adj.* **1.** like the chorion; membranous. —*n.* **2.** See **choroid coat.** Also, **chorioid.** [< Gk *choroeid(ḗs)* false reading for *chorioeidḗs* CHORIOID]

cho′roid coat′, *Anat.* a delicate, highly vascular layer of the eye that is continuous with the iris and lies between the sclera and the retina. Also called **choroid, cho′roid mem′brane.** See diag. under **eye.**

cho·roid·i·tis (kôr′oi dī′tis, kôr′-), *n. Ophthalm.* inflammation of the choroid coat. [< NL; see CHOROID, -ITIS]

chor·ten (chôr′ten), *n.* (in Tibet) a monument to a distinguished Buddhist, esp. a lama. [< Tibetan, equiv. to *(m)cho(d)* offering + *rten* container]

chor·tle (chôr′təl), *v.,* **-tled, -tling,** *n.* —*v.t., v.i.* **1.** to chuckle or utter with glee. —*n.* **2.** a gleeful chuckle. [b. CHUCKLE and SNORT; coined by Lewis Carroll in *Through the Looking-glass* (1871)] —**chor′tler,** *n.*

cho·rus (kôr′əs, kōr′-), *n., pl.* **-rus·es,** *v.,* **-rused, -rus·ing.** —*n.* **1.** *Music.* **a.** a group of persons singing in unison. **b.** (in an opera, oratorio, etc.) such a company singing choral parts in connection with soloists or individual singers. **c.** a piece of music for singing in unison. **d.** a part of a song, as the refrain, in which others join the principal singer or singers (distinguished from *verse*). **2.** simultaneous utterance in singing, speaking, shouting, etc. **3.** the sounds so uttered: *His proposal was followed by a chorus of jeers.* **4.** (in musical shows) **a.** a company of dancers and singers. **b.** the singing, dancing, or songs performed by such a company. **5.** (in ancient Greece) **a.** a lyric poem, believed to have been in dithyrambic form, that was sung and danced to, originally as a religious rite, by a company of persons. **b.** an ode or series of odes sung by a group of actors in ancient Greek drama. **c.** the group of actors that performed the chorus and served as major participants in, commentators on, or as a supplement to the main action of the drama. **6.** *Theat.* **a.** a group of actors or a single actor having a function similar to that of the Greek chorus, as in Elizabethan drama. **b.** the part of a play performed by such a group or individual. **7. in chorus,** in unison; with all speaking or singing simultaneously: *They shouted in chorus as the ship put out to sea.* —*v.t., v.i.* **8.** to sing or speak in chorus. [< L < Gk *chorós* a dance, band of dancers and singers]

cho′rus boy′, a male singer or dancer of the chorus of a musical comedy, vaudeville show, etc.

cho′rus frog′, any of several small North American frogs of the genus *Pseudacris,* having a loud call commonly heard in the early spring.

cho′rus girl′, a female member of the chorus of a musical comedy, vaudeville show, etc.

Cho·rzów (hô′zhōōf), *n.* a city in S Poland. 143,700 (est. 1957). German, **Königshütte.** Formerly, **Królewska Huta.**

chose[1] (shōz), *v.* **1.** pt. of **choose. 2.** *Obs.* pp. of **choose.**

chose[2] (shōz), *n. Law.* a thing; an article of personal property. [< F < L *causa* case, thing. See CAUSE]

chose ju·gée (shōz zhʏ zhā′), *pl.* **choses ju·gées** (shōz zhʏ zhā′). *French.* a closed case; a settled matter. [lit., a matter judged]

cho·sen (chō′zən), *v.* **1.** a pp. of **choose.** —*adj.* **2.** selected from a number; preferred: *my chosen profession.* **3.** *Theol.* elect (def. 8).

Cho·sen (chō′sen′), *n.* Japanese name of **Korea.**

cho′sen peo′ple, the Israelites. Ex. 19.

chou (shōō), *n., pl.* **choux** (shōōz *for 1;* shōō *for 2*). **1.** a cabbage-shaped decoration, as a rosette or knot, on a woman's dress, hat, etc. **2.** See **cream puff.** [< F: cabbage < L *caul(is)* stem; see CAULIS]

Chou (jō), *n.* a dynasty in China, 1122?–256? B.C., marked by the emergence of great feudal estates and the founding of important philosophical schools, esp. by Confucius and Lao-tse.

Chou En-lai (jō′ en′lī′), 1898–1976, Chinese Communist leader: premier 1949–1976.

chou-fleur (shōō flœr′), *n. French.* cauliflower.

chough (chuf), *n.* any of several crowlike, Old World birds, esp. *Pyrrhocorax pyrrhocorax,* of Europe. [ME *choghe;* akin to OE *cēo,* D *kauw,* Dan *kaa*]

Chou·kou·tien (jō′kō′tyen′), *n.* **1.** a fossil-bearing site near Peking, China, dating from the Middle Pleistocene, in which were found the remains of Peking man and various stone tools. **2.** a stone-tool industry of the Middle Pleistocene, identified with this site.

choul·try (chōl′trē), *n., pl.* **-tries.** (incorrectly) a mantapa. [m. Tamil-Malayalam *cāvaṭi*]

chou′ pas′try. See **cream puff pastry.**

chouse (chous), *v.,* **choused, chous·ing,** *n. Archaic.* —*v.t.* **1.** to swindle; cheat; dupe (often fol. by *of* or *out of*). —*n.* **2.** a swindle. **3.** a swindler. **4.** a dupe. [< Turk *çavuş* messenger] —**chous′er,** *n.*

chow[1] (chou), *n. U.S. Slang.* food. [short for CHOW-CHOW]

chow[2] (chou), (*often cap.*) See **chow chow.** [short form]

Chow (chou), *n. Australian Disparaging.* a Chinese. [special use of CHOW[1]]

Chow·chil·la (chou chil′ə), *n.* a town in central California. 4525 (1960).

chow chow (chou′ chou′), (*Often cap.*) one of a Chinese breed of medium-sized dogs having a thick black, blue, red, or cream coat and a black tongue. Also, **chow.** [< Chin (dial.); akin to Cantonese *kaú* dog]

Chow chow (20 in. high at shoulder)

chow-chow (chou′chou′), *n.* **1.** a Chinese mixed fruit preserve. **2.** (in China, India, etc.) any mixed food, food in general, or a meal. **3.** a relish of mixed pickles in mustard. [pidgin English]

chow·der (chou′dər), *n. U.S.* a kind of soup or stew made of clams, fish, or vegetables, with potatoes, onions, and other ingredients and seasoning. [< F *chaudière* pot, kettle < LL *caldāria* CALDRON]

chow·hound (chou′hound′), *n. Slang.* a person with an extreme fondness for food; glutton. [CHOW[1] + HOUND[1]]

chow′ line′, *Informal.* a line of people waiting for food to be served in an establishment or institution, as in a military camp.

chow mein (chou′ mān′), a steamed, Chinese-style dish of mushrooms, celery, onions, and various Chinese vegetables, topped with shredded chicken, shrimp, etc., and served with fried noodles. [< Chin: fried dough]

choy (choi), *n.* chay[2]. Also, **choy·a** (choi′ə). Also called **choy·a·root** (choi′ə rōōt′, -rŏŏt′).

CHQ, Corps Headquarters.

Chr., Christian.

chrem·sel (krem′zəl; *Yiddish.* KHrem′zəl), *n., pl.* **chremz·lach** (kremz′lək, -läk; *Yiddish* KHremz′ləKH, -läKH). chremzel.

chrem·zel (krem′zəl; *Yiddish.* KHrem′zəl), *n., pl.* **chremz·lach** (kremz′lək, -läk; *Yiddish.* KHremz′ləKH, -läKH). *Jewish Cookery.* a flat cake made from matzo meal, topped or stuffed with a filling, as of ground meat or fruit and nuts. Also, **chremsel.** [< Yiddish]

Chres·tien de Troyes (krā tyan′ də trwä′), c1140–c90, French poet. Also, **Chré·tien′ de Troyes′.**

chres·tom·a·thy (kres tom′ə thē), *n., pl.* **-thies.** a collection of selected literary passages, often by one author and esp. from a foreign language. [< NL *chrestomathia* < Gk *chrēstomátheia,* equiv. to *chrēstó(s)* useful (*chrēs-,* s. of *chrêsthai* to use + *-tos* v. adj. suffix) + *math-* (var. s. of *manthánein* to learn) + *-eia* -Y[3]] —**chres·to·math·ic** (kres′tə math′ik), *adj.*

Chris (kris), *n.* **1.** a boy's given name, form of **Christopher. 2.** a girl's given name, form of **Christine.**

chrism (kriz′əm), *n. Eccles.* **1.** a consecrated oil, usually mixed with balsam or balsam and spices, used by certain churches in various rites, as in baptism, confirmation, and the like. **2.** consecrated oil generally. **3.** a sacramental anointing or a rite which includes such anointing, as the rite of confirmation, esp. in the Greek Church. Also, **chrisom.** [learned respelling of ME *crisme,* OE *crisma* < L *chrisma* < Gk *chrîsma* ungent, unction] —**chris′mal,** *adj.*

Chris·man (kris′mən), *n.* a town in S California. 3923 (1960).

chris·ma·to·ry (kriz′mə tōr′ē, -tôr′ē), *n., pl.* **-ries,** *Eccles.* a receptacle for the chrism. [late ME *crismatorie* < ML *chrīsmatōri(um),* equiv. to *chrīsmat-* (s. of *chrīsma*) CHRISM + *-ōrium* -ORY[2]]

chris·mon (kriz′mon), *n.* Chi-Rho. [< L *Chris(tus)* CHRIST + LL *mon(ogramma)* MONOGRAM]

chris·om (kriz′əm), *n. Eccles.* **1.** chrism. **2.** *Obs.* a white cloth or robe formerly put on a child at baptism, and also at burial if the child died soon after baptism. [var. of CHRISM]

Christ (krīst), *n.* **1.** Jesus of Nazareth, held by Christians to be the fulfillment of a prophecy in the Old Testament regarding the eventual coming of a Messiah. **2.** the Messiah prophesied in the Old Testament (used chiefly in versions of the New Testament). **3.** someone regarded as similar to Jesus of Nazareth. **4.** *Obs.* someone anointed as a ruler. [learned respelling of ME, OE *Crīst* < L *Chrīst(us)* < Gk *chrīstós* anointed, trans. of Heb *māshīah* anointed, Messiah]

Chris·ta·bel (kris′tə bel′), *n.* a girl's given name.

Chris·ta·bel (kris′tə bel′), *n.* a narrative poem (1816) by Samuel Taylor Coleridge.

Christ·church (krīst′chûrch′), *n.* a city on E South Island, in New Zealand. 151,671 (1961).

christ·cross (kris′krôs′, -kros′), *n.* the figure or mark of a cross. [late ME *Crist cross*]

christ·cross-row (kris′krôs′rō′, -kros′-), *n. Archaic.* the alphabet. Also, **criss′cross-row′.**

chris·ten (kris′ən), *v.t.* **1.** to receive into the Christian church by baptism; baptize. **2.** to give a name to at baptism: *They christened her Mary.* **3.** to name and dedicate; give a name to; name: *They christened the farm Stony Brook.* **4.** *Informal.* to make use of for the first time. [ME *cristen(en),* OE *cristnian,* deriv. of *cristen* CHRISTIAN] —**chris′ten·er,** *n.*

Chris·ten·dom (kris′ən dəm), *n.* **1.** Christians collectively. **2.** the Christian world. **3.** *Obs.* Christianity. [ME; OE *cristendōm.* See CHRISTIAN, -DOM]

chris·ten·ing (kris′ə ning, kris′ning), *n.* **1.** the ceremony of baptism, esp. as accompanied by the giving of a name to the infant baptized. **2.** a public ceremony in which a new ship is formally named and launched. **3.** the act or an instance of naming or dedicating something newly completed or acquired. [ME; see CHRISTEN, -ING[1]]

Christ·hood (krīst′hŏŏd), *n.* the condition of being the Christ. [late ME; see CHRIST, -HOOD]

Chris·tian (kris′chən), *adj.* **1.** of, pertaining to, or derived from Jesus Christ or His teachings: *a Christian faith.* **2.** of, pertaining to, believing in, or belonging to the religion based on the teachings of Jesus Christ: *Spain is a Christian country.* **3.** of or pertaining to Christians: *many Christian deaths in the Crusades.* **4.** exhibiting a spirit proper to a follower of Jesus Christ: Christlike: *She displayed true Christian charity.* **5.** *Informal.* **a.** decent; respectable: *They sat down to a good Christian dinner.* **b.** human; not brutal; humane: *Such behavior isn't Christian.* —*n.* **6.** one who believes in Jesus Christ; adherent of Christianity. **7.** one who exemplifies in his life the teachings of Christ: *He died like a true Christian.* **8.** a member of any of certain Protestant churches, as the Disciples of Christ and the Plymouth Brethren. **9.** *Informal.* a decent or presentable person: *Dress like a Christian and not like something the cat dragged in.* **10.** *Chiefly Dial.* a human being as distinguished from an animal: *That little poodle is as smart as a Christian.* **11.** the hero of Bunyan's *Pilgrim's Progress.* **12.** a boy's given name. [< L *Chrīstiān(us)* < Gk *Christiānós,* equiv. to *Christ(ós)* CHRIST + *-iānos* < L *-iānus* -IAN; r. ME *cristen,* OE < L, as above]

Christian IX, 1818–1906, king of Denmark 1863–1906.

Christian X, 1870–1947, king of Denmark 1912–47.

Chris·ti·an·a (kris′tē an′ə), *n.* a girl's given name.

Chris′tian Breth′ren. See **Plymouth Brethren.**

Chris′tian Broth′er. See **Brother of the Christian Schools.**

Chris′tian Endeav′or, an organization of young people of various evangelical Protestant churches, formed in 1881 to promote Christian principles and service.

Chris′tian E′ra, the period, in Christian countries, since the assumed year of Jesus' birth.

Chris′tian existen′tialism, existentialism having as its basis the fundamental beliefs of any of the Christian sects. —**Chris′tian existen′tialist.**

Chris·ti·a·ni·a (kris tyä′nē ä; *also for 2* kris′chē an′ē ə, -tē-), *n.* **1.** former name of **Oslo. 2.** Also called **Christie, Christy.** *Skiing.* any of several turns executed in order to change direction on a downhill run or for decreasing speed or stopping, esp. a turn in which the body is swung around with the skis kept parallel.

Chris·tian·ise (kris′chə nīz′), *v.t., v.i.,* **-ised, -is·ing.** *Chiefly Brit.* Christianize. —**Chris′tian·i·sa′tion,** *n.* —**Chris′tian·is′er,** *n.*

Chris·tian·ism (kris′chə niz′əm), *n.* the beliefs and practices of Christians. [< LL *Chrīstiānism(us)* < Gk *Chrīstiānism(ós)* Christianity, equiv. to *chrīstiān(ós)* CHRISTIAN + *-ismos* -ISM]

Chris·ti·an·i·ty (kris′chē an′i tē), *n., pl.* **-ties. 1.** the Christian religion, including the Catholic, Protestant, and Eastern Orthodox churches. **2.** Christian beliefs or practices; Christian quality or character: *Christianity mixed with pagan elements; the Christianity of Augustine's thought.* **3.** a particular Christian religious system: *She followed fundamentalist Christianity.* **4.** the state of being a Christian. **5.** Christendom. **6.** conformity to the Christian religion or to its beliefs or practices. [ME *cristianite* < L *chrīstiānitāt-* (s. of *chrīstiānitās*), equiv. to *chrīstiān-* CHRISTIAN + *-itāt-* -ITY; r. ME *cristiente* < MF < L, as above]

Chris·tian·ize (kris′chə nīz′), *v.,* **-ized, -iz·ing.** —*v.t.* **1.** to make Christian. **2.** to imbue with Christian principles. —*v.i.* **3.** to become Christian. Also, *esp. Brit.,* **Christianise.** [CHRISTIAN + -IZE] —**Chris′tian·i·za′tion,** *n.* —**Chris′tian·iz′er,** *n.*

Chris·tian·like (kris′chən līk′), *adj.* like or befitting a Christian. [CHRISTIAN + -LIKE]

Chris·tian·ly (kris′chən lē), *adj.* **1.** like a Christian; Christianlike. —*adv.* **2.** in a Christian manner. [CHRISTIAN + -LY]

Chris′tian name′, 1. Also called **baptismal name.** the name given one at baptism, as distinguished from the family name. **2.** a person's given name.

Chris′tian Reformed′, of or pertaining to a Protestant denomination (**Chris′tian Reformed′ Church′**) organized in the U.S. in 1857 by groups which had seceded from the Dutch Reformed Church.

Chris·tian·sand (kris′chən sand′; *Norw.* kris′tyän-sän′), *n.* former name of **Kristiansand.**

Chris·tians·burg (kris′chənz bûrg′), *n.* a town in SW Virginia. 3653 (1960).

Chris′tian Sci′ence, a system of religious teaching, based on the Scriptures, the most notable application of which is the treatment of disease by mental and spiritual means, founded about 1866 by Mary Baker Eddy.

Chris′tian So′cialist, a member of any of certain European political parties advocating a form of social organization based on Christian and socialistic principles. —**Chris′tian So′cialism.**

Chris′tian year′, a year in the ecclesiastical calendar, used esp. in reference to the various feast days and special seasons. Also called **church year.**

Chris·tie (kris′tē), *n. Skiing.* Christiania (def. 2). [by shortening]

Chris·tie (kris′tē), *n.* **1. Agatha,** born 1891, English novelist of detective fiction. **2.** a boy's given name, form of **Christopher. 3.** Also, **Christy.** a girl's given name, form of **Christine.**

Chris·ti·na (kri stē′nə), *n.* **1.** 1626–89, queen of Sweden 1632–54 (daughter of Gustavus Adolphus). **2.** a girl's given name.

Chris·tine (kri stēn′), *n.* a girl's given name. Also, **Christina.**

Christ′ Je′sus, Jesus (def. 1).

Christ·less (krīst′lis), *adj.* **1.** without Christ or the spirit of Christ: *Missionaries brought their faith to Christless people.* **2.** unchristian. [Christ + -less]

Christ·like (krīst′līk′), *adj.* like Christ; showing the spirit of Christ. [Christ + -like]

Christ·ly (krīst′lē), *adj.* **1.** of, like, or resembling that of Christ: *Christly obedience to God's will.* **2.** Christlike. [Christ + -ly] —**Christ′li·ness,** *n.*

Christ·mas (kris′məs), *n.* **1.** the annual festival of the Christian church commemorating the birth of Jesus: celebrated on December 25. **2.** December 25, now generally observed as a legal holiday and an occasion for exchanging gifts, greetings, etc. [ME *cristmasse;* OE *Cristes mæsse* Mass of Christ, see -mas]

Christ·mas·ber·ry (kris′məs ber′ē), *n., pl.* **-ries.** toyon. [Christmas + berry]

Christ′masberry tree′. See **Brazilian pepper tree.**

Christ′mas cac′tus. See **crab cactus.**

Christ′mas card′, a printed and often decorated card for mailing at Christmas to express good wishes.

Christ′mas Car′ol, A, a story (1843) by Dickens.

Christ′mas club′, a plan or system of noninterest-bearing savings accounts designed to provide for the purchase of Christmas gifts, whereby each member makes regular, usually weekly, deposits throughout the year, receiving a check from the bank for the full amount of his savings shortly before Christmas.

Christ′mas disease′, *Pathol.* a hereditary disease characterized by an inability of the blood to clot because of a deficiency of the coagulation factor.

Christ′mas Eve′, the evening preceding Christmas.

Christ′mas fac′tor, *Biochem.* a blood constituent necessary for clotting, the absence of which is characterized by a hemophilialike condition. Also called **plasma thromboplastic component.** Cf. **Christmas disease.**

Christ′mas fern′, an evergreen fern, *Polystichum acrostichoides,* having dense clusters of stiff fronds growing from the crown of the stem.

Christ′mas Is′land, 1. an Australian island in the Indian Ocean, ab. 190 mi. S of Java. 3099 (1961). 62 sq. mi. **2.** one of the Gilbert and Ellice Islands, in the central Pacific: largest atoll in the Pacific; U.S. test center for nuclear warheads. ab. 222 sq. mi.

Christ′mas pan′tomime, pantomime (def. 2).

Christ′mas pud′ding, *Brit.* See **plum pudding.**

Christ′mas rose′, a European hellebore, *Helleborus niger,* having evergreen leaves and white or purplish flowers that bloom in the winter. Also called **black hellebore.**

Christ′mas seal′, *U.S.* a decorative adhesive stamp sold by charitable organizations during the Christmas season to obtain money for the cure and treatment of tuberculosis.

Christ′mas stock′ing, a stocking or stocking-shaped bag, traditionally hung on a mantelpiece or Christmas tree by children on Christmas Eve, for holding Christmas presents, esp. those believed to be brought by Santa Claus.

Christ·mas·tide (kris′məs tīd′), *n.* **1.** the season of Christmas. **2.** the period from Christmas Eve to Epiphany. [Christmas + tide[1]]

Christ′mas tree′, 1. an evergreen tree decorated at Christmas with ornaments and lights, as a tree in a yard or public square or, more commonly, a small, sometimes artificial evergreen displayed in the home. **2.** (at an oil well) an arrangement of pipes and valves on the casing head, for controlling the flow of oil and gas.

Christo-, a combining form of **Christ:** *Christophany.* [< Gk *Christó(s)*]

Chris·to·cen·tric (kris′tə sen′trik), *adj.* having as the focal point the teachings and practices of Jesus Christ or the doctrines derived from Him: *Christocentric theology.* [Christo- + centric[1]] —**Chris′to·cen′trism,** *n.*

Chris·to·gram (kris′tə gram′), *n.* a symbol of Christ, esp. XP. [Christo- + -gram[1]]

Chris·tol·o·gy (kri stol′ə jē), *n., pl.* **-gies** for 2. **1.** the branch of theology dealing with the nature, person, and deeds of Jesus Christ. **2.** an interpretation of the nature, person, and deeds of Christ. [Christo- + -logy] —**Chris·to·log·i·cal** (kris′tᵊloj′i kəl), *adj.* —**Chris·tol′o·gist,** *n.*

Chris·toph·a·ny (kri stof′ə nē), *n., pl.* **-nies.** an appearance of Christ after His Resurrection, esp. as recorded in the New Testament. [Christo- + -phany]

Chris·tophe (krē stôf′), *n.* **Hen·ri** (äN rē′), ("*Henri I*"), 1767–1820, revolutionary general: king of Haiti 1811–20. Also, **Cristophe.**

Chris·to·pher (kris′tə fər), *n.* **1. Saint,** died A.D. c250, Christian martyr: patron saint of travelers. **2.** a town in S Illinois. 2854 (1960). **3.** a boy's given name.

Christ's-thorn (krīsts′thôrn′), *n.* any of certain Old World thorny shrubs or small trees supposed to have been used for Christ's crown of thorns, as the shrub, *Paliurus Spina-Christi,* or the jujube, *Zizyphus Jujuba.* [trans. of L *spīna Christī*]

Christ′ Within′. See **Inner Light.**

Chris·ty (kris′tē), *n., pl.* **-ties.** *Skiing.* Christiania (def. 2). [by shortening]

Chris·ty (kris′tē), *n.* **1. Howard Chan·dler** (chand′lər, chänd′-), 1873–1952, U.S. illustrator and painter. **2.** a boy's given name, form of **Christopher. 3.** Also, **Christie.** a girl's given name, form of **Christine.**

chrom-, 1. a learned borrowing from Greek meaning "color," used in the formation of compound words: *chromic; chromite.* **2.** *Chem.* **a.** a word element referring to chromium: *bichromate.* **b.** a combining form used to distinguish a colored compound from its colorless form. Also, **-chrome;** *esp. before a consonant,* **chromo-.** [def. 1, for Gk *chrôma* color; def. 2, for chromium]

chro·ma (krō′mə), *n.* **1.** the purity of a color, or its freedom from white or gray. **2.** intensity of distinctive hue; saturation of a color. [< Gk *chrôma* color]

chromat-, var. of **chromato-** before a vowel: *chromatid.*

chro·mate (krō′māt), *n. Chem.* a salt of chromic acid, as potassium chromate, K_2CrO_4. [chrom- + -ate[2]]

chro·mat·ic (krō mat′ik, krə-), *adj.* **1.** pertaining to color or colors. **2.** *Music.* **a.** involving a modification of the normal scale by the use of accidentals. **b.** progressing by semitones to a tone having the same letter name, as in C to C sharp. [< Gk *chrōmatik(ós),* equiv. to *chrōmat-* chromat- + *-ikos* -ic] —**chro·mat′i·cal·ly,** *adv.*

chromat′ic aberra′tion, *Optics.* the variation of either the focal length or the magnification of a lens system, with different wavelengths of light, characterized by prismatic coloring at the edges of the optical image and color distortion within it. Also called **chromatism.**

chro·mat·i·cism (krō mat′i siz′əm, krə-), *n. Music.* **1.** the use of chromatic tones. **2.** a style in which chromatic tones predominate. [chromatic + -ism]

chro·ma·tic·i·ty (krō′mə tis′i tē), *n. Optics.* the quality of a color as determined by its dominant wavelength and its purity. [chromatic + -ity]

chro·mat·ics (krō mat′iks, krə-), *n.* (*construed as sing.*) the science of colors. Also called **chromatology.** [chromat- + -ics] —**chro·ma·tist** (krō′mə tist), *n.*

chromat′ic scale′, *Music.* a scale progressing entirely by semitones.

chromat′ic sign′, *Music.* accidental (def. 5).

chro·ma·tid (krō′mə tid), *n. Genetics.* one of two identical chromosomal strands into which a chromosome splits longitudinally preparatory to cell division. [chromat- + -id[3]]

chro·ma·tin (krō′mə tin), *n. Biol.* the readily stainable substance of a cell nucleus, consisting of DNA, RNA, and various proteins, which forms chromosomes during cell division. [chromat- + -in[2]] —**chro′ma·tin′ic,** *adj.* —**chro′ma·toid′,** *adj.*

chro·ma·tism (krō′mə tiz′əm), *n.* **1.** *Optics.* See **chromatic aberration. 2.** the abnormal coloration of leaves or other normally green parts of a plant. [chromat- + -ism]

chromato-, a learned borrowing from Greek meaning "color," used in the formation of compound words in this sense and in the specialized sense of "chromatin": *chromatophore; chromatolysis.* Also, *esp. before a vowel,* **chromat-.** [< Gk *chromat-,* s. of *chrôma* color + -o-]

chro·ma·to·gram (krō′mə tə gram′, krō mat′ə-, krə-), *n. Chem.* the column or paper strip on which some or all of the constituents of a mixture have been adsorbed in chromatographic analysis. [chromato- + -gram[1]]

chro·ma·to·graph (krō′mə tə graf′, -gräf′, krō mat′ə-, krə-), *v.t. Chem.* to separate mixtures by chromatography. [chromato- + -graph]

chro·ma·tog·ra·phy (krō′mə tog′rə fē), *n. Chem.* the separation of mixtures into their constituents by preferential adsorption by a solid, as a column of silica (**column chromatography**) or a strip of filter paper (**paper chromatography**). [chromato- + -graphy] —**chro·ma·to·graph·ic** (krō′mə tə graf′ik, krō mat′ē-, krə-), *adj.* —**chro′ma·to·graph′i·cal·ly,** *adv.*

chro·ma·tol·o·gy (krō′mə tol′ə jē), *n.* **1.** chromatics. **2.** a treatise on colors. [chromato- + -logy]

chro·ma·tol·y·sis (krō′mə tol′i sis), *n. Biol., Pathol.* the dissolution and disintegration of chromatin. [chromato- + -lysis] —**chro·ma·to·lyt·ic** (krō′mə tᵊlit′ik, krō mat′ᵊlit′-, krə-), *adj.*

chro·ma·to·phil (krō′mə tə fil, krō mat′ə-, krə-), *Biol.* —*adj.* **1.** Also, **chro′ma·to·phil′ic, chro·ma·toph·i·lous** (krō′mə tof′ə ləs). chromophil. —*n.* **2.** a chromophil. Also, **chro·ma·to·phile** (krō′mə tə fīl′, -fil, krō mat′ə-, krə-). [chromato- + -phil]

chro·ma·to·phil·i·a (krō′mə tə fil′ē ə, -fēl′yə, krō-mat′ə-, krə-), *n. Biol.* chromophilia. [chromato- + -philia]

chro·ma·to·phore (krō′mə tə fōr′, -fôr′, krō mat′ə-, krə-), *n.* **1.** *Zool.* a cell containing pigment, esp. one which through contraction and expansion produces a temporary color, as in cuttlefishes. **2.** *Bot.* one of the colored plastids in plant cells. [chromato- + -phore] —**chro·ma·to·phor·ic** (krō′mə tə fôr′ik, -for′ik, krō mat′ə-, krə-), **chro·ma·toph·or·ous** (krō′mə tof′ər əs), *adj.*

chrome (krōm), *n., v.,* **chromed, chrom·ing.** —*n.* **1.** chromium, esp. as a source of various pigments, as chrome yellow and chrome green. **2.** (of dyeing) the dichromate of potassium or sodium. **3.** *Informal.* the chromium-plated or other bright-metallic fittings and trimming on an automobile. —*v.t.* **4.** (of dyeing) to subject to a bath of dichromate of potassium or sodium. **5.** to plate (metal) with a compound of chromium. **6.** to treat or tan (a hide or leather) with a chromium compound. [< F < Gk *chrôm(a)* color; see chromium]

-chrome, var. of **chrom-** as the final element of a compound word: *polychrome.*

chrome′ ac′etate, *Chem.* See **chromic acetate.**

chrome′ al′um, *Chem.* **1.** Also called **ammonium chrome alum, chromium ammonium sulfate, ammonium chromic sulfate.** a green, crystalline, water-soluble powder, $CrNH_4(SO_4)_2 \cdot 12H_2O$, used chiefly as a mordant in dyeing. **2.** Also called **potassium chrome alum, chromium potassium sulfate, potassium chromic sulfate.** a violet, crystalline, water-soluble powder, $CrK(SO_4)_2 \cdot 12H_2O$, used chiefly as a mordant in dyeing.

chrome′ green′, the permanent green color made from chromic oxide, or any similar pigment made largely from chromic oxide, used chiefly in printing textiles.

chrome′ i′ron, chromite (def. 2). Also called **chrome′ i′ron ore′.**

Chro·mel (krō′məl), *n. Trademark.* a group of nickel-chromium alloys, some with an iron content, having high electrical resistance: used in heating devices and thermocouples.

chrome′ leath′er, leather tanned with chrome.

chrome·plate (krōm′plāt′), *v.t.,* **-plat·ed, -plat·ing.** to plate with chromium. [chrome + plate[1]]

chrome′ red′, a bright-red pigment consisting of the basic chromate of lead.

chrome′ steel′, any of various steels containing chromium. Also called **chromium steel.**

chrome′ yel′low, any of several yellow pigments in shades from lemon to deep orange, composed chiefly of chromates of lead, barium, or zinc.

chrom·hi·dro·sis (krō′mi drō′sis, krōm′hi-), *n. Med.* the secretion of colored sweat. Also, **chromidrosis.** [chrom- + hidrosis]

chro·mic (krō′mik), *adj. Chem.* **1.** of or containing chromium in the trivalent state, as chromic hydroxide, $Cr(OH)_3$. **2.** of or derived from chromic acid. [chrom- + -ic]

chro′mic ac′etate, *Chem.* a grayish-green, water-soluble powder, $Cr(O_2CCH_3)_3$, used chiefly as a mordant in dyeing and printing textiles. Also called **chrome acetate, chromium acetate.**

chro′mic ac′id, *Chem.* a hypothetical acid, H_2CrO_4, known only in solution or in the form of its salts.

chro′mic chlo′ride, *Chem.* a violet, crystalline compound, $CrCl_3$, occurring in both water-soluble and water-insoluble forms, or a green or violet, water-soluble deliquescent compound, $CrCl_3 \cdot 6H_2O$: used chiefly as a mordant, in chrome-steel plating, and in the synthesis of chromium salts. Also called **chromium chloride.**

chro′mic flu′oride, *Chem.* a green, crystalline, water-insoluble powder, $CrF_3 \cdot 4H_2O$ or $CrF_3 \cdot 9H_2O$: used chiefly in printing and dyeing woolens.

chro·mi·dro·sis (krō′mi drō′sis), *n. Med.* chromhidrosis.

chro·mi·nance (krō′mə nəns), *n. Optics.* the difference in color quality between a color and a reference color that has an equal brightness and a specified chromaticity. [chrom- + (lum)inance]

chro·mite (krō′mīt), *n.* **1.** *Chem.* a salt of chromium in the bivalent state. **2.** Also called **chrome iron.** a cubic mineral, ferrous chromate, $Fe_3Cr_2O_3$, usually having a considerable amount of the ferrous iron and aluminum replaced by magnesium, and some of the chromium by ferric iron: the principal ore of chromium. [chrom- + -ite[1]]

chro·mi·um (krō′mē əm), *n. Chem.* a lustrous, hard, brittle, metallic element used in alloy steels for hardness and corrosion resistance, as in stainless steel, and for plating other metals: chromium salts are used as pigments and mordants. *Symbol:* Cr; *at. wt.:* 51.996; *at. no.:* 24; *sp. gr.:* 7.1. [chrome + -ium]

chromium 51, *Chem.* the radioactive isotope of chromium having a mass number 51 and a halflife of 27.8 days: used as a tracer.

chro′mium ac′etate, *Chem.* See **chromic acetate.**

chro′mium ammo′nium sul′fate, *Chem.* See **chrome alum** (def. 1).

chro′mium chlo′ride, *Chem.* See **chromic chloride.**

chro′mium potas′sium sul′fate, *Chem.* See **chrome alum** (def. 2).

chro′mium steel′. See **chrome steel.**

chro·mo (krō′mō), *n., pl.* **-mos.** chromolithograph. [short form]

chromo-, var. of **chrom-** before a consonant: *chromophore.*

chro·mo·gen (krō′mə jən), *n.* **1.** *Chem.* **a.** any substance found in organic fluids which forms colored compounds when oxidized. **b.** a colored compound which, though not a dye itself, can be converted into a dye. **2.** a chromogenic bacterium. [chromo- + -gen]

chro·mo·gen·ic (krō′mə jen′ik), *adj.* **1.** producing color. **2.** pertaining to chromogen or a chromogen. **3.** (of bacteria) producing some characteristic color or pigment which is useful as a means of identification. [chromogen + -ic]

chro·mo·lith·o·graph (krō′mə lith′ə graf′, -gräf′), *n.* a picture produced by chromolithography. Also called **chromo.** [chromo- + lithograph]

chro·mo·li·thog·ra·phy (krō′mō li thog′rə fē), *n.* the process of lithographing in colors. [chromo- + lithography] —**chro′mo·li·thog′ra·pher,** *n.* —**chro·mo·lith·o·graph·ic** (krō′mō lith′ə graf′ik), *adj.*

chro·mo·mere (krō′mə mēr′), *n.* **1.** *Genetics.* one of the beadlike granules arranged in a linear series in a chromonema. **2.** *Anat.* the central, granular part of a blood platelet. Cf. **hyalomere.** [chromo- + -mere]

chro·mo·ne·ma (krō′mə nē′mə), *n., pl.* **-ma·ta** (-mə-tə). *Genetics.* a chromosome thread that is relatively uncoiled at early prophase, but assumes a spiral form at metaphase. [chromo- + Gk *nêma* thread]

chro·mo·phil (krō′mə fil), *Biol.* —*adj.* **1.** Also, **chro′mo·phil′ic, chro·moph·i·lous** (krō mof′ə ləs), **chromatophilic, chromatophilous.** staining readily. —*n.* **2.** a chromophil cell, tissue, or substance. Also, **chro·mo·phile** (krō′mə fīl′, -fil), **chromatophil, chromatophile.** [chromo- + -phil]

chro·mo·phil·i·a (krō′mə fil′ē ə, -fēl′yə), *n. Biol.* the property of staining readily. Also, **chromatophilia.** [chromo- + -philia]

chro·mo·phobe (krō′mə fōb′), *adj.* **1.** Also, **chro·mo·pho·bic** (krō′mə fō′bik, -fob′ik). *Biol.* not staining readily. —*n.* **2.** *Anat.* a chromophobe cell in the pituitary gland. [chromo- + -phobe]

chro·mo·phore (krō′mə fōr′, -fôr′), *n. Chem.* any chemical group which produces color in a compound, as the azo group –N = N–. [chromo- + -phore] —**chro·mo·phor·ic** (krō′mə fôr′ik, -for′ik), *adj.*

chro·mo·pho·to·graph (krō′mə fō′tə graf′, -gräf′), *n. Photog. Obs.* a color photograph. [chromo- + photograph]

chro·mo·pho·tog·ra·phy (krō′mō fə tog′rə fē), *n. Photog. Obs.* color photography. [chromo- + photography] —**chro·mo·pho·to·graph·ic** (krō′mō fō′tə-graf′ik), *adj.*

chro·mo·plasm (krō′mə plaz′əm), *n. Biol.* chromatin. [chromo- + -plasm] —**chro′mo·plas′mic,** *adj.*

chro·mo·plast (krō′mə plast′), *n. Bot.* a plastid, or specialized mass of protoplasm, containing coloring matter other than chlorophyll. [chromo- + -plast]

chro·mo·some (krō′mə sōm′), *n. Genetics.* any of several threadlike bodies, consisting of chromatin, found in a cell nucleus, that carry the genes in a linear order. [chromo- + -some[3]] —**chro′mo·so′mal,** *adj.* —**chro′mo·so′mal·ly,** *adv.*

chro′mosome num′ber, *Genetics.* the characteristic number of chromosomes in each plant or animal species.

chro·mo·sphere (krō′mə sfēr′), *n. Astron.* **1.** a scarlet, gaseous envelope surrounding the sun outside the photosphere, from which enormous masses of hydrogen and other gases are erupted. **2.** a gaseous envelope surrounding a star. [CHROMO- + -SPHERE] —**chro·mo·spher·ic** (krō′mə sfer′ik), *adj.*

chro·mous (krō′məs), *adj. Chem.* containing chromium in the divalent state, as chromous carbonate, $CrCO_3$. [CHROM- + -OUS]

chro·myl (krō′məl), *adj. Chem.* of or containing chromium in the hexavalent state, as chromyl chloride, CrO_2Cl_2. [CHROM- + -YL]

chron-, var. of **chrono-** before a vowel: *chronaxie.*

Chron., *Bible.* Chronicles.

chron., **1.** chronological. **2.** chronology.

chro·nax·ie (krō′nak sē), *n. Physiol.* the minimum time that a current of twice the threshold strength must flow in order to excite a tissue. Also, **chro′nax·y.** [< F < *chron-* CHRON- + *-axie* < Gk *axía* worth, value]

chron·ic (kron′ik), *adj.* **1.** inveterate; constant; habitual: *a chronic smoker.* **2.** continuing a long time or recurring frequently: *a chronic state of civil war.* **3.** having long had a disease, habit, weakness, or the like: *a chronic invalid.* **4.** (of disease) having long duration (opposed to *acute*). Also, **chron′i·cal.** [< L *chronic(us)* < Gk *chronikós,* equiv. to *chrón(os)* time + *-ikos* -IC] —**chron′i·cal·ly,** *adv.* —**chro·nic·i·ty** (kro nis′i tē), *n.* —**Syn. 1.** habitual, confirmed, hardened.

chron′ic al′coholism, *Pathol.* physical and psychological disturbances resulting from repeated and excessive use of alcohol. Cf. **acute alcoholism.**

chron·i·cle (kron′i kəl), *n., v.,* **-cled, -cling.** —*n.* **1.** a chronological record of events; a history. —*v.t.* **2.** to record in or as in a chronicle. [ME *cronicle* < AF *cronic-* (equiv. to OF *cronique* < ML *cronica* (sing.) < L *chronica* (pl.) < Gk *chroniká* annals, chronology; see CHRONIC) + *-le* -ULE] —**chron′i·cler,** *n.*

chron′icle play′, a drama based on historical material, usually consisting of a series of short episodes or scenes arranged chronologically. Also called **chron′icle his′tory.**

Chron·i·cles (kron′i kəlz), *n.* (*construed as sing.*) either of two books of the Old Testament, I Chronicles or II Chronicles. Also called, *Douay Bible,* **Paralipomenon.**

Chron′icles of Eng′land, Scot′land, and Ire′land, a history in two volumes (1577, enlarged 1587) prepared chiefly by Raphael Holinshed: a major source of ideas and facts for Elizabethan dramatists. Also called **Holinshed's Chronicles.**

chro·nique scan·da·leuse (krô nēk′ skän dȧ lœz′), *pl.* **chro·niques scan·da·leuses** (krô nēk′ skän dȧ lœz′). *French.* a biography, history, or the like, that emphasizes scandalous details and gossip. [lit., scandalous chronicle]

Chro·ni·um (krō′nē əm), *n.* **Mare.** See **Mare Chronium.**

chrono-, a learned borrowing from Greek meaning "time," used in the formation of compound words: *chronometer.* Also, *esp. before a vowel,* **chron-.** [< Gk, comb. form of *chrónos*]

chron·o·gram (kron′ə gram′), *n.* **1.** an inscription in which certain letters, usually conspicuously different from the others, express a date or epoch on being added together by their values as Roman numerals. **2.** a record made by a chronograph. [CHRONO- + -GRAM[1]] —**chron·o·gram·mat·ic** (kron′ō grə mat′ik), **chron′o·gram·mat′i·cal,** *adj.* —**chron′o·gram·mat′i·cal·ly,** *adv.* —**chron′o·gram′ma·tist,** *n.*

chron·o·graph (kron′ə graf′, -gräf′), *n.* **1.** a timepiece fitted with a recording device, as a stylus and rotating drum, used to mark the exact instant of an occurrence, esp. in astronomy. **2.** a timepiece capable of measuring extremely brief intervals of time accurately, as a stop watch capable of measuring ⅕ of a second. [CHRONO- + -GRAPH] —**chro·nog·ra·pher** (krə nog′rə fər), *n.* —**chron·o·graph·ic** (kron′ə graf′ik), *adj.* —**chron′o·graph′i·cal·ly,** *adv.*

chron·o·log·i·cal (kron′ᵊloj′i kəl), *adj.* **1.** arranged in the order of time: *Put the dates in chronological order.* **2.** pertaining to or in accordance with chronology: *a chronological narrative.* Also, **chron′o·log′ic.** [CHRONOLOG(Y) + -ICAL] —**chron′o·log′i·cal·ly,** *adv.*

chro·nol·o·gist (krə nol′ə jist), *n.* one versed in chronology. Also, **chro·nol′o·ger.** [CHRONOLOG(Y) + -IST]

chro·nol·o·gy (krə nol′ə jē), *n., pl.* **-gies. 1.** the sequential order in which past events occur or a particular statement of this order. **2.** the science of arranging time in periods and ascertaining the dates and historical order of past events. **3.** a reference work in the field of history organized according to the dates of past events: *They produced many paper-back chronologies.* [CHRONO- + -LOGY]

chro·nom·e·ter (krə nom′i tər), *n.* a timepiece or timing device with a special mechanism for ensuring and adjusting its accuracy, for use in determining longitude at sea or for any purpose where very exact measurement of time is required. [CHRONO- + -METER] —**chron·o·met·ric** (kron′ə me′trik), **chron′o·met′ri·cal,** *adj.* —**chron′o·met′ri·cal·ly,** *adv.*

chronom′eter escape′ment, *Horol.* a detached deadbeat escapement, used esp. in marine chronometers, in which a pallet on a spring detent locks the escape wheel until the detent is depressed by a pallet oscillating on the balance. Also called **detent escapement.**

chro·nom·e·try (krə nom′i trē), *n.* **1.** the art of measuring time accurately. **2.** measurement of time by periods or divisions. [CHRONO- + -METRY]

chro·non (krō′non), *n.* a hypothetical unit of time, taken as a ratio between the diameter of the electron and the velocity of light, equivalent to approximately 10^{-24} second. [CHRON- + -ON[2]]

chron·o·pher (kron′ə fər, krō′nə-), *n.* an instrument for transmitting time signals, as of the standard clock, to many remote places by means of electricity. [CHRONO- + *-pher,* comb. form of Gk *phérein* to carry]

chron·o·scope (kron′ə skōp′, krō′nə-), *n.* an instrument for measuring accurately very brief intervals of time, as in determining the velocity of projectiles. [CHRONO- + -SCOPE] —**chron·o·scop·ic** (kron′ə skop′ik), *adj.* —**chron′o·scop′i·cal·ly,** *adv.* —**chro·nos·co·py** (krə nos′kə pē), *n.*

Chron·o·tron (kron′ə tron′, krō′nə-), *n. Trademark.* a device for measuring extremely brief time intervals by comparing electric pulses.

chrys-, var. of **chryso-** before a vowel: *chryselephantine.*

chrys·a·lid (kris′ə lid), *Entomol.* —*n.* **1.** a chrysalis. —*adj.* **2.** of a chrysalis. [< *chrysalid-* var. s. of Gk *chrysallís* CHRYSALIS]

chrys·a·lis (kris′ə lis), *n., pl.* **chrys·a·lis·es, chry·sal·i·des** (kri sal′i dēz′). the hard-shelled pupa of a moth or butterfly; an obtect pupa. [< L *chrȳsalis* < Gk *chrȳsallís,* equiv. to *chrȳs-* CHRYS- + *-allis* suffix prob. with dim. value]

Chrysalis of swallowtail butterfly

chry·san·the·mum (kri san′thə məm), *n.* **1.** any of the perennial asteraceous plants of the genus *Chrysanthemum,* as *C. leucanthemum,* the oxeye daisy. **2.** any of many cultivated varieties of the plant *C. morifolium,* a native of China, and of other species of *Chrysanthemum,* notable for the diversity of color and size of their autumnal flowers. **3.** the flower of any such plant. [< L < Gk *chrȳsánthemon,* equiv. to *chrȳs-* CHRYS- + *ánthemon* flower, akin to *ánthos;* see ANTHOLOGY]

Chry·sa·or (krī sā′ôr, kris′ā ôr′), *n. Class. Myth.* a son of Poseidon and Medusa who sprang full grown from his mother's body.

chrys·a·ro·bin (kris′ə rō′bin), *n. Pharm.* a mixture of principles obtained from Goa powder, used in the treatment of psoriasis and other skin conditions. [CHRYS- + (AR)AROB(A) + -IN[2]]

Chry·se·is (krī sē′is), *n. Class. Myth.* the beautiful daughter of Chryses who was captured and given to Agamemnon.

chrys·el·e·phan·tine (kris′el ə fan′tin, -tīn), *adj.* made of or overlaid with gold and ivory, as certain objects made in ancient Greece. [< Gk *chryselephántin(os),* equiv. to *chrȳs-* CHRYS- + *elephántinos* (*elephant-,* s. of *eléphās* ELEPHANT ivory, + *-inos* suffix used for adj. of material)]

Chry·ses (krī′sēz), *n.* (in the *Iliad*) a priest of Apollo.

Chry·sip·pus (krī sip′əs, kri-), *n.* **1.** 280–209? B.C., Greek Stoic philosopher. **2.** *Class. Myth.* a youth who was abducted by King Laius.

Chrys·ler (krīs′lər), *n.* **Walter Percy,** 1875–1940, U.S. automobile manufacturer.

chryso-, a learned borrowing from Greek meaning "gold," used in the formation of compound words: *chrysolite.* Also, *esp. before a vowel,* **chrys-.** [comb. form of Gk *chrȳsós*]

chrys·o·ber·yl (kris′ə ber′əl), *n.* a mineral, beryllium aluminate, $BeAl_2O_4$, occurring in green or yellow crystals, sometimes used as a gem. Also called **cymophane.** [< L *chrysoberyll(us)* < Gk *chrȳsobḗryllos,* equiv. to *chrȳso-* CHRYSO- + *bḗryllos* BERYL]

chrys·o·cale (kris′ə kāl′), *n.* a copper alloy containing zinc and lead. [appar. alter. of L *chrȳsocolla* < Gk *chrȳsókolla,* equiv. to *chrȳsó(s)* gold + *kólla* glue]

chrys·o·car·pous (kris′ə kär′pəs), *adj. Bot.* bearing golden-yellow fruit. [CHRYSO- + -CARPOUS]

chrys·o·col·la (kris′ə kol′ə), *n.* a mineral, hydrous copper silicate, occurring in compact, green or blue masses, sometimes used in ornaments. [< L; see CHRYSOCALE]

chrys·o·graph (kris′ə graf′, -gräf′), *n.* **1.** a manuscript, esp. of the Middle Ages, written in gold or gold and silver ink. —*v.t.* **2.** to write with gold ink. [< Gk *chrysographía.* See CHRYSO-, -GRAPH] —**chry·sog·ra·pher** (kri sog′rə fər), *n.*

chry·sog·ra·phy (kri sog′rə fē), *n.* **1.** the art of writing in ink made of powdered gold suspended in a small amount of glair or gum. **2.** the gold writing produced by this art. [< Gk *chrysographía.* See CHRYSO-, -GRAPHY]

chry·so·i·dine (kri sō′i din, -dēn′), *n. Chem.* a red-brown or greenish-black, crystalline solid, $C_{12}H_{13}N_4Cl$, that yields orange colors in aqueous or alcohol solution: used chiefly in dyeing cotton and silk. [< Gk *chrȳsoeid(ḗs)* like gold (*chrȳs-* CHRYS- + *-oeidēs* -OID) + -INE[2]]

chrys·o·lite (kris′ə līt′), *n. Mineral.* olivine. [< L *chrȳsolith(us)* < Gk *chrȳsólithos,* equiv. to *chrȳso-* CHRYSO- + *líthos* stone; see -LITE] —**chrys·o·lit·ic** (kris′ə lit′ik), *adj.*

chrys·o·mel·id (kris′ə mel′id, -mē′lid), *n.* **1.** a beetle of the family *Chrysomelidae,* comprising the leaf beetles. —*adj.* **2.** belonging or pertaining to the family *Chrysomelidae.* [< NL *Chrysomelid(ae)* name of the family, equiv. to *Chrysomel(a)* name of the genus (m. Gk *chrysómēlon* quince, equiv. to *chryso-* CHRYSO- + *mēlon* apple) + *-idae* -ID[2]]

chry·soph·e·nine (kri sof′ə nēn′, -nin), *n. Chem.* a bright yellow dye derived from stilbene, used chiefly for dyeing leather and textiles. [CHRYSO- + PHEN- + -INE[2]]

chrys·o·prase (kris′ə prāz′), *n. Mineral.* a green variety of chalcedony, sometimes used as a gem. [< L *chrȳsopras(us)* < Gk *chrȳsóprasos,* equiv. to *chrȳso-* CHRYSO- + *prás(on)* leek + *-os* adj. suffix]

Chrys·os·tom (kris′ə stəm, kri sos′təm), *n.* **Saint John,** A.D. 347?–407, ecumenical patriarch of Constantinople.

Chry·sos·to·mus (kri sos′tə məs), *n.* a boy's given name.

Chry·soth·e·mis (kri soth′ə mis), *n. Class. Myth.* a daughter of Agamemnon and Clytemnestra who opposed her sister Electra's plan to avenge the murder of their father.

chrys·o·tile (kris′ə til), *n. Mineral.* a fibrous variety of serpentine; asbestos. [CHRYSO- + Gk *tíl(os)* something plucked]

Chrys·see (kris′ē), *n.* a girl's given name.

Chrys·tal (kris′tᵊl), *n.* a girl's given name. Also, **Crystal.**

chs., chapters.

chtho·ni·an (thō′nē ən), *adj. Class. Myth.* of or pertaining to the deities, spirits, and other beings dwelling under the earth. Also, **chthon·ic** (thon′ik). [< Gk *chthóni(os),* equiv. to *chthṓn* earth + *-ios* adj. suffix + -AN]

Chtho·ni·us (thō′nē əs), *n. Class. Myth.* **1.** one of the Sparti. **2.** an epithet of Zeus, meaning "of the underworld."

Chuan·chow (chwän′jō′), *n.* former name of **Tsinkiang.**

Chuang-tzu (jwäng′dzu′), *n.* **1.** Also, **Chwang-tse** (*Chuang Chow*). fl. 4th century B.C., Chinese mystic and philosopher. **2.** (*italics.*) a fundamental work on Taoism by Chuang-tzu, dating from the 4th century B.C.

chub (chub), *n., pl.* (*esp. collectively*) **chub,** (*esp. referring to two or more kinds or species*) **chubs. 1.** a common, fresh-water fish, *Leuciscus cephalus,* found in Europe, having a thick, fusiform body. **2.** any of various related fishes. **3.** any of several unrelated American fishes, esp. the tautog and whitefishes of the genus *Coregonus,* found in the Great Lakes. [late ME *chubbe* < ?]

chu·bas·co (cho͞o bäs′kō), *n., pl.* **-cos.** a violent thundersquall frequent on the Pacific Coast of Central America during the rainy season. [< Sp < Pg *chuvasco,* equiv. to *chuv(a)* rain (< L *pluvia,* fem of *pluvius* rainy) + *-asco* intensive suffix]

chub·by (chub′ē), *adj.,* **-bi·er, -bi·est.** round and plump: *a chubby child; a chubby face.* [CHUB + -Y[1]] —**chub′bi·ly,** *adv.* —**chub′bi·ness,** *n.*

chub·suck·er (chub′suk′ər), *n.* any of several stout suckers of the genus *Erimyzon,* found in the sluggish streams, backwaters, and lakes of the central and eastern U.S., that exhibit sexual dimorphism. [CHUB + SUCKER]

Chuch·chi (cho͝ok′chē), *n., pl.* **-chis,** (*esp. collectively*) **-chi.** Chukchi.

chuck[1] (chuk), *v.t.* **1.** to pat or tap lightly, as under the chin. **2.** to toss; throw with a quick motion, usually a short distance. **3.** *Chiefly Brit. Slang.* to eject (a person) from a public place; throw out (often fol. by *out*): *They chucked him out of the pub.* **4.** *Informal.* to resign from; relinquish; give up: *He's chucked his job. He's chucked his plans.* **5. chuck it,** *Brit. Slang.* stop it; shut up. —*n.* **6.** a light pat or tap, as under the chin. **7.** *Chiefly Brit.* a toss or pitch; a short throw. [?]

chuck[2] (chuk), *n.* **1.** the cut of beef between the neck and the shoulder blade. **2.** a block or log used as a chock. **3.** *Mach.* **a.** a device for centering and clamping work in a lathe or other machine tool. **b.** a device for holding a drill bit. —*v.t.* **4.** *Mach.* to hold or secure with a chuck. [var. of CHOCK. See CHUNK]

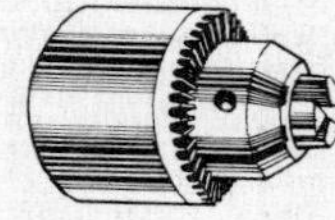
Chuck[2] (def. 3b)

chuck[3] (chuk), *v.t., v.i.* **1.** to cluck. —*n.* **2.** a clucking sound. **3.** *Archaic.* a term of endearment. [ME *chuk* < ?]

chuck[4] (chuk), *n. Western U.S. Slang.* food; provisions. [special use of CHUCK[2]]

Chuck (chuk), *n.* a boy's given name, form of **Charles.**

chuck-a-luck (chuk′ə luk′), *n.* a game played with three dice at which the players bet that a certain number will come up on one die, that the three dice will total a certain number, or that the total will be an odd number, even number, a high number, or a low number. Also called **chuck-luck.**

Chuck·chi (cho͝ok′chē), *n., pl.* **-chis,** (*esp. collectively*) **-chi.** Chukchi.

chuck·er-out (chuk′ər out′), *n., pl.* **chuck·ers-out.** *Brit. Slang.* bouncer (def. 2). [n. use of v. phrase *chuck out*]

chuck-far·thing (chuk′fär′thing), *n.* a former game in which players tossed farthings at a mark, with the person whose coin hit closest to the mark then privileged to pitch all the farthings at a hole and collect those that fell into it. Also called **pitch-farthing.** Cf. **pitch-and-toss.** [CHUCK[1] + FARTHING]

chuck-full (chuk′fo͝ol′), *adj.* chock-full.

chuck·hole (chuk′hōl′), *n.* a hole or depression in a road or street. [CHUCK[1] + HOLE]

chuck·le (chuk′əl), *v.,* **chuck·led, chuck·ling,** *n.* —*v.i.* **1.** to laugh in a soft, amused manner, usually with satisfaction: *They chuckled at the child's efforts to walk.* **2.** to laugh to oneself: *to chuckle while reading.* **3.** to cluck, as a fowl. —*n.* **4.** a soft, amused laugh, usually of satisfaction. **5.** *Obs.* the call of a hen to her young; cluck. [CHUCK[3] + -LE] —**chuck′ler,** *n.* —**chuck′ling·ly,** *adv.*
—**Syn. 4.** See **laugh.**

chuck·le·head (chuk′əl hed′), *n. Slang.* a stupid person; blockhead. [*chuckle* clumsy (CHUCK[2] + -LE) + HEAD] —**chuck′le·head′ed,** *adj.* —**chuck′le·head′ed·ness,** *n.*

chuck-luck (chuk′luk′), *n.* chuck-a-luck.

chuck′ wag′on, *Western U.S.* a wagon carrying cooking facilities and food for serving men working outdoors, as at a ranch or lumber camp.

chuck·wal·la (chuk′wä′lə), *n.* an iguanid lizard, *Sauromelus ohesus,* of arid parts of the southwestern U.S. and Mexico, that feeds on desert plants. [< MexSp *chacahuala,* of native (Shoshonean) orig.]

chuck-will's-wid·ow (chuk′wilz wid′ō), *n.* a goatsucker, *Caprimulgus carolinensis,* of southern U.S., resembling but larger than the whippoorwill. [fanciful imit. of its twitter]

chuck·y (chuk′ē), *n., pl.* **chuck·ies.** *Brit. Dial.* a chicken; fowl. [CHUCK[3] + -Y[2]]

chud·dar (chud′ər), *n.* a kind of fine, plain-colored woolen shawl made in India. Also, **chud·dah** (chud′ə), **chud′der.** [< Hindi < Pers *chaddar*]

Chud·sko·ye O·ze·ro (cho͞ot′sko ye ô′ze ro), Russian name of **Peipus.**

chu·fa (cho͞o′fə), *n.* an African, cyperaceous herb, *Cyperus esculentus,* having a tuberous, edible root. Also called **earth almond.** [< Sp]

chuff[1] (chuf), *n.* **1.** a rustic. **2.** a boor; churl. **3.** a miserly fellow. [late ME *chuffe* < ?]

chuff[2] (chuf, cho͝of), *adj. Brit. Dial.* **1.** chubby; fat. **2.** proud; elated; swollen with pride. [adj. use of obs. *chuff* muzzle, fat cheek]

chuff[3] (chuf), *n.* **1.** a sound of or like the exhaust of a steam engine. —*v.i.* **2.** to emit or proceed with chuffs: *The train chuffed along.* [imit.]

chuff·y (chuf′ē), *adj.,* **chuff·i·er, chuff·i·est.** churlish; surly. [CHUFF[1] + -Y[1]] —**chuff′i·ly,** *adv.* —**chuff′i·ness,** *n.*

chug (chug), *n., v.,* **chugged, chug·ging.** —*n.* **1.** a short, dull, explosive sound: *the steady chug of an engine.* —*v.i.* **2.** to make this sound: *The motor chugged for a* *moment but then stopped.* **3.** to move while making this sound: *The train chugged along.* [imit.]

chug·ger (chug′ər), *n. Angling.* a type of plug that rests on the surface of the water and makes a popping sound when retrieved. Also called **popper.** [Scot *chug* to tug + -ER¹]

Chu Hsi (jo͞o′ shē′), 1130–1200, Chinese philosopher.

chu·kar (chu kär′), *n.* a partridge, *Alectoris chukar,* of Asia and the Near East, introduced into North America as a game bird. Also called **chukar′ par′tridge.** [< Hindi *cakor* < Skt *cakor(a),* prob. of imit. orig.]

Chuk·chee (cho͝ok′chē), *n., pl.* **-chees,** (*esp. collectively*) **-chee.** Chukchi.

Chuk·chi (cho͝ok′chē), *n., pl.* **-chis,** (*esp. collectively*) **-chi. 1.** a member of a Paleo-Asian people of northeastern Siberia. **2.** the Asian language of the Chukchi people, having different pronunciation for men and women. Also, **Chuchchi, Chuckchi, Chukchee.**

Chuk′chi Sea′, a part of the Arctic Ocean, N of the Bering Strait. Also, **Chuckchee Sea.** Russian, **Chukotskoe More.**

Chu-Kiang (cho͞o′jyäng′), *n.* a river in SE China, in S Kwangtung, flowing E and S from Canton and forming an estuary near Hong Kong. ab. 110 mi. long. Also called **Canton River, Pearl River.**

chuk′ka boot′ (chuk′ə), an ankle-high shoe, laced through two pairs of eyelets, often made of suede. Also called **chukka.** Cf. **jodhpur** (def. 2). [so called from its resemblance to a polo boot. See CHUKKER]

chuk·ker (chuk′ər), *n. Polo.* one of the periods of play. Also, **chuk′kar.** [< Hindi *chakkar* < Skt *cakra* WHEEL]

Chu·kot·sko·e Mo·re (cho͝o kôt′sko ye mô′re), Russian name of the **Chukchi Sea.**

Chu·la Vis·ta (cho͞o′lə vis′tə), a city in SW California, near San Diego. 42,034 (1960).

chul·pa (cho͞ol′pə), *n. Archaeol.* a type of prehistoric stone tower, found in Brazil and Peru, having living quarters over a burial chamber. Also, **chull′pa.** [< AmerSp < Aymara *chullpa*]

chum¹ (chum), *n., v.,* **chummed, chum·ming.** —*n.* **1.** an intimate friend or companion: *boyhood chums.* **2.** a roommate, as at college. —*v.i.* **3.** to associate closely. **4.** to share a room or rooms with another. [?]

chum² (chum), *n., v.,* **chummed, chum·ming.** —*n.* **1.** cut or ground bait dumped into the water to attract fish to the area where one is fishing. **2.** fish refuse or scraps discarded by a cannery. —*v.i.* **3.** to fish by attracting fish to one's net or line by dumping cut or ground bait into the water. [?]

Chu·mash (ᴋʜo͞o mäsh′, ᴋʜo͝om′əsh), *n., pl.* **Chu·ma·shim** (ᴋʜo͞o′mä shēm′, ᴋʜo͞o mô′shim). *Hebrew.* Humash.

Chum·ley (chum′lē), *n.* a boy's given name.

chum·my (chum′ē), *adj.,* **-mi·er, -mi·est.** *Informal.* friendly; intimate; sociable. [CHUM¹ + -Y¹] —**chum′mi·ly,** *adv.* —**chum′mi·ness,** *n.*

chump¹ (chump), *n.* **1.** *Informal.* a blockhead or dolt: *Don't be a chump, she's kidding you along.* **2.** a short, thick piece of wood. **3.** the thick, blunt end of anything. **4.** *Slang.* the head. **5. off one's chump,** *Brit. Slang.* crazy; mentally deranged. [? b. CH(UNK and L)UMP] —**chump′ish,** *adj.* —**chump′ish·ness,** *n.*

chump² (chump), *v.t., v.i.* to munch. Also, **chomp.** [var. of CHAMP¹]

chum′ salm′on, a salmonoid food fish, *Oncorhyncus keta,* found in the Pacific Ocean from Alaska to California. Also called **dog salmon.** [perh. < Chinook Jargon *tsum* spots, writing < Chinook]

chung (jo͝ong), *n. Chinese.* (in Confucianism) conscientiousness in one's dealings with others.

Chung·king (cho͝ong′king′; *Chin.* jo͝ong′ging′), *n.* a city in SW China, on the Yangtze River: provisional capital of China 1937–46. 2,121,000 (est. 1957).

chunk (chungk), *n.* **1.** a thick mass or lump of anything: *a chunk of bread.* **2.** *Informal.* a thick-set and strong person. **3.** a strong and stoutly built horse or other animal. **4.** a substantial amount of something: *The circus took a real chunk out of my allowance.* [nasalized var. of CHUCK²]

chunk·y (chung′kē), *adj.,* **chunk·i·er, chunk·i·est. 1.** thick or stout; thick-set; stocky. **2.** in a chunk or chunks. [CHUNK + -Y¹] —**chunk′i·ly,** *adv.* —**chunk′i·ness,** *n.*

chup·pah (ᴋʜo͞o pä′; *Eng.* ᴋʜo͝op′ə), *n., pl.* **chup·poth** (ᴋʜo͞o pōt′), *Eng.* **chup·pahs.** *Hebrew.* huppah.

chu·pras·si (chə prä′sē), *n.* chaprasi.

Chur (ko͝or), *n.* a town in and the capital of Grisons, in E Switzerland. 24,825 (1960).

chu·rad·a (chə rä′də), *n.* (in the Mariana Islands) a violent rain squall occurring esp. in January, February, and March. [native name in the Mariana Islands]

church (chûrch), *n.* **1.** an edifice for public Christian worship. **2.** public worship of God or a religious service in such an edifice: *to attend church regularly.* **3.** the whole body of Christian believers; Christendom. **4.** (*sometimes cap.*) any division of this body professing the same creed and acknowledging the same ecclesiastical authority; a Christian denomination: *the Methodist Church.* **5.** that part of the whole Christian body, or of a particular denomination, belonging to the same city, country, nation, etc. **6.** a body of Christians worshiping in a particular building or constituting one congregation: *She is a member of this church.* **7.** ecclesiastical organization, power, and affairs, as distinguished from the state: *separation of church and state; The missionary went wherever the church sent him.* **8.** the clergy and religious officials of a Christian denomination. **9.** (*cap.*) the Christian Church before the Reformation. **10.** (*cap.*) the Roman Catholic Church. **11.** the clerical profession or calling: *After much study and contemplation, he was prepared to enter the church.* **12.** a place of public worship of a non-Christian religion. **13.** any non-Christian religious society, organization, or congregation: *the Jewish church.* —*v.t.* **14.** to conduct or bring to church, esp. for special services. **15.** *Chiefly Midland U.S.* to subject to church discipline. **16.** to perform a church service of thanksgiving for (a woman after childbirth). [ME *chir(i)che* < OE *cir(i)ce* << Gk *kȳri(a)kón* (*dôma*) the Lord's (house), neut. of *kȳriakós* of the master, equiv. to *kȳri(os)* master (*kȳr(os)* power + *-ios* adj. suffix) + *-akos,* var. of *-ikos* -IC; akin to D *kerk,* G *Kirche,* Icel *kirkja.* See KIRK]

church′ book′, any of various books commonly used by a church, as a service book, a parish register, or the like.

church′ cal′endar. See **ecclesiastical calendar** (def. 2).

church′ coun′cil, (in certain Lutheran churches) a body of lay delegates chosen from the congregation and charged with supporting the pastor in religious instruction, contributions to the church, etc.

church′ fa′ther, father (def. 13).

church·go·er (chûrch′gō′ər), *n.* **1.** one who goes to church, esp. habitually. **2.** *Chiefly Brit.* a member of the Established Church, in contrast to a Nonconformist. [CHURCH + GO + -ER¹] —**church′go′ing,** *n.*

Church·ill (chûr′chil, -chəl), *n.* **1. John, 1st Duke of Marlborough,** ("*Corporal John*"), 1650–1722, British military commander. **2. Lord Randolph (Henry Spencer),** 1849–95, British statesman (father of Winston L. S. Churchill). **3. Winston,** 1871–1947, U.S. novelist. **4. Sir Winston (Leonard Spencer),** 1874–1965, British statesman and author: prime minister 1940–45, 1951–55; Nobel prize for literature 1953. **5.** a river in Canada, flowing NE from E Saskatchewan through Manitoba to Hudson Bay. ab. 1000 mi. long. **6.** a seaport and railway terminus in NE Manitoba, on Hudson Bay at the mouth of this river. 3932 (1961). **7.** a town in SW Pennsylvania. 3428 (1960).

church′ invis′ible, *Theol.* the entire body of Christian believers on earth and in heaven. Cf. **church visible.**

church·less (chûrch′lis), *adj.* **1.** without a church. **2.** not belonging to or attending any church. [CHURCH + -LESS]

church·like (chûrch′līk′), *adj.* resembling or appropriate to a church: *churchlike silence.* [CHURCH + -LIKE]

church·ly (chûrch′lē), *adj.* of or appropriate for the church or a church; ecclesiastical: *churchly vestments.* [OE *ciriclīc,* equiv. to *cirice* CHURCH + *-līc* -LY] —**church′li·ness,** *n.*

church·man (chûrch′mən), *n., pl.* **-men. 1.** an ecclesiastic; clergyman. **2.** an adherent or active supporter of a church. **3.** *Brit.* a member of the Established Church. [CHURCH + MAN] —**church′man·ly,** *adj.* —**church′man·ship′,** *n.*

church′ mil′itant, *Theol.* those Christians on earth who are engaged in a continuous war against evil and the enemies of Christ. Cf. **church triumphant.**

church′ mode′, *Music.* a mode belonging to a codified system of modes in use in Gregorian chant and in other music to c1600. Also called **ecclesiastical mode, Gregorian mode.** Cf. **Aeolian mode, Dorian mode, hypoaeolian mode, hypodorian mode, hypolydian mode, hypomixolydian mode, hypophrygian mode, Lydian mode, mixolydian mode, Phrygian mode.**

Church′ of Christ′, Sci′entist, the official name of the Christian Science Church.

Church′ of Eng′land, the national Church continuous with English history, Catholic in faith and order, but incorporating many emphases of the Protestant Reformation and establishing independence from the papacy.

Church′ of Je′sus Christ′ of Lat′ter-day Saints′, the official name of the Mormon Church.

Church′ of Rome′. See **Roman Catholic Church.**

Church′ of the Breth′ren, the official name of the church of the Dunkers.

Church′ of the New′ Jeru′salem. See **New Jerusalem Church.**

Church′ Point′, a town in S Louisiana. 3606 (1960).

church′ rate′, *Eccles.* (formerly in England and Ireland) a compulsory assessment imposed on the parishioners' holdings of houses or land in order to repair the parish church and maintain its services.

Church′ Slav′ic, a liturgical language used in Eastern Orthodox churches in Slavic countries since the 11th or 12th century, representing a development of Old Church Slavonic through contact with the national Slavic languages.

church′ suf′fering, *Rom. Cath. Ch.* the souls in purgatory.

church′ text′, *Print.* See **Old English** (def. 2).

church′ trium′phant, *Theol.* those Christians in heaven who have triumphed over evil and the enemies of Christ. Cf. **church militant.**

church′ vis′ible, *Theol.* the entire body of Christian believers on earth. Cf. **church invisible.**

church·ward (chûrch′wərd), *adv.* **1.** Also, **church′wards.** toward the church. —*adj.* **2.** directed toward the church: *a churchward summons.* [ME *chircheward.* See CHURCH, -WARD]

church·ward·en (chûrch′wôr′dən), *n.* **1.** *Anglican Ch.* a lay officer who looks after the secular affairs of the church, and who, in England, is the legal representative of the parish. **2.** *Episc. Ch.* a lay church officer who, with other members of the vestry, is in charge of the temporal management of the parish. **3.** a long-stemmed clay pipe for smoking. [late ME *chirche wardeyn*]

church·wom·an (chûrch′wo͝om′ən), *n., pl.* **-wom·en.** a female member, adherent, or active supporter of a church, esp. a member of an Anglican church. [CHURCH + WOMAN]

church·y (chûr′chē), *adj.,* **church·i·er, church·i·est. 1.** adhering strictly to the prescribed form in ecclesiastical matters: *Churchy people are often without the spirit of their faith.* **2.** of, characteristic of, or suggestive of a church: *The stained-glass windows gave the room a churchy look.* [CHURCH + -Y¹] —**church′i·ness,** *n.*

church·yard (chûrch′yärd′), *n.* the yard or ground adjoining a church, often used as a graveyard. [ME *chirche yeard*]

church′ year′. See **Christian year.**

chu·rin·ga (cho͝o ring′gə), *n., pl.* **-ga, -gas.** an object carved from wood or stone by aboriginal tribes in central Australia and held by them to be sacred. [< native Austral word]

churl (chûrl), *n.* **1.** a peasant; rustic. **2.** a rude, boorish, or surly person. **3.** a niggard; miser: *He was a churl in his affections.* **4.** *Eng. Hist.* a freeman of the lowest rank. [ME *cherl* < OE *ceorl* man, freeman; c. D *kerel,* G *Kerl;* akin to CARL, Gk *gérōn* old man]

churl·ish (chûr′lish), *adj.* **1.** of a churl or churls; peasantlike: *The churlish life in olden times was a secure one.* **2.** like a churl or boor; boorish; rude; surly: *churlish behavior.* **3.** niggardly; sordid. **4.** difficult to work or deal with, as soil. [ME *cherlish* < OE *ceorlisc.* See CHURL, -ISH¹] —**churl′ish·ly,** *adv.* —**churl′ish·ness,** *n.*
—**Syn. 2.** coarse, uncouth, vulgar, loutish; ill-natured, uncivil.
—**Ant. 2.** courteous.

churn (chûrn), *n.* **1.** a vessel or machine in which cream or milk is agitated to make butter. **2.** any of various vessels or machines similar in shape or action to a butter churn, as a device for mixing beverages. **3.** *Brit.* a large milk can. —*v.t.* **4.** to stir or agitate in order to make into butter: *to churn cream.* **5.** to make (butter) by the agitation of cream. **6.** to shake or agitate with violence or continued motion: *The storm churned the sea.* —*v.i.* **7.** to operate a churn. **8.** to move in agitation, as a liquid or any loose matter: *The leaves churned along the ground.* [ME *cyrn(a)* (n.) < OE *cyr(i)n;* c. MLG *kerne,* Icel *kjarni, kirna*] —**churn′a·ble,** *adj.* —**churn′a·bil′i·ty,** *n.* —**churn′er,** *n.*

churn·ing (chûr′ning), *n.* **1.** the act of one who or that which churns. **2.** the butter made at any one time. [late ME *chyrnynge.* See CHURN, -ING¹]

churn′ mold′ing, *Rare.* a molding decorated with chevrons.

churr (chûr), *v.i., n.* chirr.

chur·ri·gue·resque (cho͝or′ē gə resk′), *adj.* noting or pertaining to the Baroque architecture of Spain and its colonies in the late 17th and early 18th centuries, characterized by fantastic and lavish detailing. Also, **chur·ri·gue·res·co** (cho͞o rᴇ′ge rᴇs′kō). [< F < Sp *churrigueresc(o),* after José *Churriguera* (1650–1725) baroque architect and sculptor + *-esco* -ESQUE]

chute¹ (sho͞ot), *n., v.,* **chut·ed, chut·ing.** —*n.* **1.** an inclined channel, as a trough, tube, or shaft, for conveying water, grain, coal, etc., to a lower level. **2.** a waterfall or steep descent, as in a river. —*v.t.* **3.** to move or deposit, by or as if by means of a chute: *The dock had facilities for chuting grain directly into the hold of a vessel.* —*v.i.* **4.** to descend by or as if by means of a chute. [< F < OF *cheue* (< VL **caduta*) + *cheoite* (< VL **cadecta*), deriv. of fem. ptps. of *cheoir* < L *cadere* to fall; in some senses, var. spelling of SHOOT]

chute² (sho͞ot), *n.* a steep slope, as for tobogganing. [Frenchified spelling of *shoot, shute* < ME *shote* steep slope; akin to SHOOT]

chute³ (sho͞ot), *n., v.* **chut·ed, chut·ing.** —*n.* **1.** a parachute. —*v.i.* **2.** to descend from the air by or as if by a parachute. —*v.t.* **3.** to drop from an aircraft by means of a parachute: *Supplies were chuted to the snowbound troops.* [by shortening]

Chu Teh (jo͞o′ du′), born 1886, Chinese general and communist leader.

Chute, La (*Fr.* lᴀ shʏt′). See **Fall, The.**

chute′ the chute′, to ride or slide on, or as if on, a chute-the-chute. Also, **chute′ the chutes′.**

chute-the-chute (sho͞ot′thə sho͞ot′), *n.* **1.** a ride or coaster, as at an amusement park or carnival, which provides thrills or excitement by moving passengers down steep dips and around sharp curves, esp. one having a track that ends in water. Cf. **roller coaster. 2.** a steep or curving slide used for purposes of amusement. **3.** any ride, motion, or experience which produces a sensation of or a sensation resembling that of rapid or curving descent: *an emotional chute-the-chute.* Also, **chute′-the-chutes′.** [see CHUTE¹]

chut·ist (sho͞o′tist), *n.* a parachutist. [CHUTE³ + -IST]

chut·ney (chut′nē), *n.* a sauce or relish of East Indian origin compounded of both sweet and sour ingredients, as fruits and herbs, with spices and other seasoning. Also, **chut′nee.** [< Hindi *chatnī*]

chutz·pa (ᴋʜo͝ot′spə), *n. Slang.* unmitigated effrontery or impudence. [< Yiddish]

Chu·vash (cho͞o′väsh), *n., pl.* **Chu·vash·es, Chu·va·shi** (sho͞o vä′shē), (*esp. collectively*) **Chu·vash. 1.** a native or a descendant of a native of the Chuvash Autonomous Soviet Socialist Republic. **2.** the language of the Chuvash, a Turkic language.

Chuvash′ Auton′omous Repub′lic, an autonomous republic in the Russian Federation in Europe. 1,336,000; 7064 sq. mi. *Cap.:* Cheboksary.

Chwang-tse (jwäng′dzu′), *n.* Chuang-tzu (def. 1).

chy·ack (chī′ək), *v.t. Australian.* chiack.

chy·la·ceous (kī lā′shəs), *adj.* of or resembling chyle. [CHYLE + -ACEOUS]

chyle (kīl), *n.* a milky fluid containing emulsified fat and other products of digestion, formed from the chyme in the small intestine and conveyed by the lacteals and the thoracic duct to the veins. [< LL *chȳl(us)* < Gk *chȳlós* juice, akin to *chéin* to pour, L *fundere* to pour] —**chy′lous,** *adj.*

chy·lo·cau·lous (kī′lə kô′ləs), *adj. Bot.* having fleshy stems. [< G *Chylocaul* (see CHYLO-, CAULO-, -OUS)] —**chy′lo·cau′lous·ly,** *adv.*

chy·lo·phyl·lous (kī′lə fil′əs), *adj. Bot.* having fleshy leaves, as certain desert plants. [CHYLE + -O- + -PHYLLOUS] —**chy′lo·phyl′lous·ly,** *adv.*

chyme (kīm), *n.* the semifluid mass into which food is converted by gastric secretion and which passes from the stomach into the small intestine. [< L *chȳmus* < Gk *chȳmós* juice, akin to *chȳlós* CHYLE] —**chy′mous,** *adj.*

chym·is·try (kim′i strē), *n. Archaic.* chemistry. —**chym′ic,** *adj.* —**chym′ist,** *n.*

chy·mo·tryp·sin (kī′mō trip′sin), *n. Biochem.* a proteolytic enzyme, found in pancreatic juice, that catalyzes the hydrolysis of proteins into polypeptides and amino acids. [CHYME + -O- + TRYPSIN]

Ci, curie; curies.

C.I., Channel Islands.

CIA, *U.S.* Central Intelligence Agency: the federal agency that coordinates governmental intelligence activities.

Cia., Company. [< Sp *Compañía*]

Cia·no (chä′nō; *It.* chä′nô), *n.* **Count Ga·le·az·zo** (gä′le ät′tsō), (*Ciano di Cortellazzo*), 1903–44, Italian statesman and Fascist leader: minister of foreign affairs 1936–43.

cia·o (chä′ō; *Eng.* chou), *interj. Italian. Informal.* (used as a word of greeting or parting): hi; so long; see you later.

Ciar·di (chär′dē), *n.* **John,** born 1916, U.S. poet.

cib., (in prescriptions) food. [< L *cibus*]

ci·bar·i·an (si bâr′ē ən), *adj. Obs.* of or pertaining to the structure of the mouth parts of an insect. [< L *cibāri(us)* CIBARIOUS + -AN]

ci·bar·i·ous (si bâr′ē əs), *adj. Archaic.* of or pertaining to food. [< L *cibāri(us)*, equiv. to *cib(us)* food + *-ārius* -ARY, with -OUS for -ary]

ci·bar·i·um (si bâr′ē əm), *n., pl.* **-bar·i·a** (-bâr′ē ə). (of an insect) the preoral space enclosed by the mouth parts, in which food is held or chewed before entering the mouth. [< NL < L *cib(us)* food + *-ārium* -ARY] —**ci·bar′i·al,** *adj.*

Cib·ber (sib′ər), *n.* **Col·ley** (kol′ē), 1671–1757, English actor and dramatist: poet laureate 1730–57.

ci·bo·ri·um (si bōr′ē əm, -bôr′-), *n., pl.* **-bo·ri·a** (-bōr′ē ə, -bôr′-). **1.** a permanent canopy placed over an altar; baldachin. **2.** any vessel designed to contain the consecrated bread or sacred wafers for the Eucharist. **3.** *Archaic.* a severy. [< L: drinking-cup < Gk *kibṓrion* Egyptian lotus, the seed-vessel of which the cup resembles]

Ciborium (def. 2)

C.I.C., 1. Combat Information Center. **2.** Commander in Chief. **3.** Counterintelligence Corps.

ci·ca·da (si kā′də, -kä′-), *n., pl.* **-das, -dae** (-dē). any large homopterous insect of the family *Cicadidae*, the male of which produces a shrill sound by means of vibrating membranes on the underside of the abdomen. [< L]

Cicada, *Magicicada septendecim* (Length about 1 in.)

cica′da kill′er, a black or rust-colored digger wasp, *Sphecius speciosis*, with a yellow-banded abdomen, which preys on cicadas, with which it provisions its nest.

ci·ca·la (si kä′lə; *It.* chē kä′lä), *n., pl.* **-las,** *It.* **-le** (-le). cicada. [< It < L *cicāda* CICADA]

cicatri′cial tis′sue. See **scar tissue.**

cic·a·trise (sik′ə trīz′), *v.t., v.i.,* **-trised, -tris·ing.** *Chiefly Brit.* cicatrize. —**cic′a·tri′sant,** *adj.* —**cic′a·tri·sa′tion,** *n.* —**cic′a·tris′er,** *n.*

cic·a·trix (sik′ə triks, si kā′triks), *n., pl.* **cic·a·tri·ces** (sik′ə trī′sēz). **1.** *Med.* new tissue which forms over a wound and later contracts into a scar: scar. **2.** *Bot.* a scar left by a fallen leaf, seed, etc. Also, **cic·a·trice** (sik′ə tris). [< L: scar] —**cic·a·tri·cial** (sik′ə trish′əl), *adj.* —**ci·cat·ri·cose** (si ka′trə kōs′, sik′ə-), *adj.*

cic·a·trize (sik′ə trīz′), *v.,* **-trized, -triz·ing.** —*v.t.* **1.** to heal by inducing the formation of a cicatrix. —*v.i.* **2.** to become healed by the formation of a cicatrix. Also, *esp. Brit.,* **cicatrise.** [< ML *cicātrīzāre.* See CICATRIX, -IZE] —**cic′a·tri′zant,** *adj.* —**cic′a·tri·za′tion,** *n.* —**cic′a·triz′er,** *n.*

cic·e·ly (sis′ə lē), *n., pl.* **-lies.** a plant, *Myrrhis odorata*, of the parsley family, having a fragrant aroma and sometimes used as a potherb. [< L *seseli* < Gk *séselis, séseli* hartwort, alter. through influence of proper name *Cicely*]

Cic·e·ly (sis′ə lē), *n.* a girl's given name, form of **Cecilia.** Also, **Cecily.**

cic·e·ro (sis′ə rō′), *n., pl.* **-ros.** *Print.* a Continental unit of measurement for type, equal to 12 Didot points, or .178 inches, roughly comparable to a pica. [named after the type cast for a 15th-century edition of Cicero's *De Oratore*]

Cic·e·ro (sis′ə rō′), *n.* **1. Marcus Tul·li·us** (tul′ē əs), ("*Tully*"), 106–43 B.C., Roman statesman, orator, and writer. **2.** a city in NE Illinois, near Chicago. 69,130 (1960).

ci·ce·ro·ne (sis′ə rō′nē, chich′ə-; *It.* chē′che rô′ne), *n., pl.* **-nes,** *It.* **-ni** (-nē). one who shows and explains the antiques, curiosities, history, etc., of a place; guide. [It < L *Cicerōne(m)* acc. of *Cicerō* CICERO, the guide being thought of as having the knowledge and eloquence of Cicero]

Cic·e·ro·ni·an (sis′ə rō′nē ən), *adj.* **1.** of or pertaining to Cicero or his writings: *the Ciceronian orations.* **2.** in the style of Cicero: characterized by melodious language, clarity, and forcefulness of presentation: *Ciceronian invective.* —*n.* **3.** one who is an expert on or specializes in the study of the works of Cicero. **4.** one who admires or imitates the style of Cicero. [< L *Cicerōniān(us)*, equiv. to *Cicerōn-* (s. of *Cicerō*) CICERO + *-iānus* -IAN] —**Cic·e·ron·i·cal·ly,** (sis′ə ron′ik lē), *adv.*

Cic·e·ro·ni·an·ism (sis′ə rō′nē ə niz′əm), *n.* imitation of the style of Cicero, esp. as practiced by certain writers and orators during the Renaissance. [CICERONIAN + -ISM]

cich·lid (sik′lid), *n.* **1.** any of the *Cichlidae*, a family of spiny-rayed, fresh-water fishes of South America, Africa, and southern Asia, superficially resembling the American sunfishes: often kept in home aquariums. —*adj.* **2.** belonging or pertaining to the family *Cichlidae.* [< Gk *kíchlē* thrush, wrasse + -ID²] —**cich·loid** (sik′loid), *n., adj.*

ci·cho·ri·a·ceous (si kōr′ē ā′shəs, -kôr′-), *adj.* belonging to the *Cichoriaceae*, or chicory family of composite plants, as the dandelion, endive, lettuce, salsify, etc. [< L *cichori(um)* < Gk *kichórion* CHICORY + -ACEOUS]

Ci·chus (sē′chəs), *n.* a walled plain in the third quadrant of the face of the moon: about 20 miles in diameter.

ci·cis·be·ism (chē′chiz bā′iz əm), *n.* the social custom of having a *cicisbeo*, as practiced esp. in Italy in the 17th and 18th centuries. [< It *cicisbeismo.* See CICISBEO, -ISM]

ci·cis·be·o (chē′chez be′ô; *Eng.* si sis′bē ō′), *n., pl.* **-be·i** (-be′ē; *Eng.* -bē′). *Italian.* (esp. during the 18th century) an escort or lover of a married woman.

Cic·o·nes (sik′ə nēz′), *n.pl. Class. Myth.* a Thracian people, living on the Aegean coast, whose chief city, Ismarus, was plundered by Odysseus on his return from Troy. Also, **Ci·co·ni·ans** (si kō′nē ənz).

Cid (sid; *Sp.* thēd), *n.* **1. The,** ("*El Cid Campeador*") (*Rodrigo Díaz de Bivar*), c1040–99, Spanish soldier: hero of the wars against the Moors. **2.** See **Le Cid.**

C.I.D., Criminal Investigation Department of Scotland Yard.

-cidal, an element used to form adjectives from stems ending in **-cide:** *homicidal.* [-CIDE + -AL¹]

-cide, a learned borrowing from Latin meaning "killer," used in the formation of compound words: *insecticide.* [late ME < L *-cīda* cutter, killer, equiv. to *-cīd-* (comb. form of *caedere* to cut, kill) + *-a* -ER¹]

ci·der (sī′dər), *n.* the expressed juice of apples (or formerly of some other fruit) used for drinking, either before fermentation (**sweet cider**) or after fermentation (**hard cider**), or for making applejack, vinegar, etc. Also, *Brit.,* **cyder.** [late ME *sidre* < MF < OF *si(s)dre* < LL *sīcera* strong drink < Septuagint Gk *síkera* < Heb *shēkār* (Levit. X, 9); r. ME *sithere* < OF *sidre*] —**ci′der·ish, ci′der·like′,** *adj.*

ci′der gum′, an Australian gum tree, *Eucalyptus Gunnii*, the sap of which is made into a ciderlike beverage.

ci′der press′, a press for crushing apples for cider.

ci′der vin′egar, vinegar produced by fermentation of cider.

ci-de·vant (sēdᵊ väɴ′), *adj. French.* former; late, used esp. in reference to a retired officeholder. [lit., heretofore]

Cid, Le (*Fr.* lə sēd′). See **Le Cid** (defs. 1, 2).

Cid·ney (sid′nē), *n.* a girl's given name.

Cie., company. Also, **cie.** [< F *Compagnie*]

cié·na·ga (syā′nə gə, syen′ə-, sin′-), *n. Southwestern U.S.* a swamp or marsh, esp. one formed and fed by springs. Also, **cie′ne·ga.** [< Sp, deriv. of *cien(o)* mud, slime < L *caen(um)* filth]

Cien·fue·gos (syen fwe′gôs), *n.* a seaport in S Cuba. 70,833 (1953).

cier·zo (thyeʀ′thō, syeʀ′sō; *Eng.* syâr′zō), *n., pl.* **-zos** (-thōs, -sōs; *Eng.* -zōs). *Spanish.* a mistral, esp. one blowing in the lower valley of the Ebro River during autumn and early winter.

C.I.F., cost, insurance, and freight: used by a seller to indicate that the price quoted includes the cost of the merchandise, packing, crating, forwarding, and freight to a specified destination plus insurance charges on the shipment. Also, **CIF, c.i.f.**

ci·gar (si gär′), *n.* a more or less cylindrical roll of tobacco cured for smoking, of any of various lengths, thicknesses, degrees of straightness, etc., usually wrapped in a tobacco leaf. Also, **segar.** [< Sp *cigarr(o)*] —**ci·gar′less,** *adj.*

cig·a·rette (sig′ə ret′, sig′ə ret′), *n.* a cylindrical roll of finely cut tobacco cured for smoking, considerably smaller than most cigars and usually wrapped in thin white paper. Also, **cig′a·ret′.** [< F, equiv. to *cigare* CIGAR + *-ette* -ETTE]

cigarette′ girl′, a woman who sells cigars and packs of cigarettes, usually from a tray displaying various brands, to customers seated at tables in a restaurant or nightclub.

cigarette′ hold′er, a mouthpiece of plastic, ivory, etc., for holding a cigarette while it is being smoked.

ci·gar-flow·er (si gär′flou′ər), *n.* a shrub, *Cuphea platycentra*, of Mexico, having dark-rimmed, red flowers with an ash-white mouth.

cig·a·ril·lo (sig′ə ril′ō), *n., pl.* **-los.** a small, thin cigar. [< Sp, dim. of *cigarro* CIGAR]

cigar′ store′, a retail store specializing in tobacco products, as cigars, cigarettes, etc.

ci·gar′-store In′dian (si gär′stōr′, -stôr′), a wooden statue of an American Indian, formerly displayed as a sign at the entrance of a cigar store.

cil·i·a (sil′ē ə), *n.pl., sing.* **cil·i·um** (sil′ē əm). **1.** the eyelashes. **2.** *Zool.* short, hairlike processes on the surface of protozoans or of metazoan cells, which by their motion accomplish locomotion or produce a current. **3.** *Bot.* minute, hairlike processes. [< L, neut. pl. of *cilium* eyelid, eyelash, possibly a back formation from *supercilium* eyebrow, and possibly akin to *cēlāre* to CONCEAL]

Cilia of a flower

cil·i·ar·y (sil′ē er′ē), *adj.* **1.** noting or pertaining to various anatomical structures in or about the eye. **2.** pertaining to cilia. [CILI(A) + -ARY]

cil′iary bod′y, *Anat.* the part of the tunic of the eye, between the choroid coat and the iris, consisting chiefly of the ciliary muscle and the ciliary processes.

cil′iary mus′cle, *Anat.* the smooth muscle in the ciliary body, the action of which affects the accommodation of the eye. See diag. under **eye.**

cil′iary proc′ess, *Anat.* one of the folds on the ciliary body, connected with the suspensory ligament of the crystalline lens.

Cil·i·a·ta (sil′ē ā′tə), *n.* the class comprising the ciliates. [NL; see CILIATE]

cil·i·ate (sil′ē it, -āt′), *n.* **1.** any protozoan of the class *Ciliata*, having cilia on part or all of the body. —*adj.* **2.** Also, **cil·i·at·ed** (sil′ē ā′tid). *Bot., Zool.* having cilia. **3.** belonging or pertaining to the *Ciliata.* [< NL *ciliāt(us)*, equiv. to *cili(a)* CILIA + *-ātus* -ATE¹] —**cil′i·ate·ly,** *adv.* —**cil′i·a′tion,** *n.*

cil·ice (sil′is), *n.* **1.** a garment of haircloth formerly worn by monks; a hair shirt. **2.** haircloth. [< MF; r. OE *cilic* < L *cilic(ium)* < Gk *kilíkion*, neut. of *kilíkios* Cilician, so called because first made of Cilician goathair]

Ci·li·cia (si lish′ə), *n.* an ancient country in SE Asia Minor: later a Roman province. —**Ci·li′cian,** *adj., n.*

Cili′cian Gates′, a mountain pass in SE Asia Minor, connecting Cappadocia and Cilicia. Turkish, **Gülek Bogaz.**

cil·i·o·late (sil′ē ə lit, -lāt′), *adj.* furnished with minute cilia. [< NL *ciliol(um)*, equiv. to *cili(um)* (see CILIA) + *-olum*, var. of *-ulum* -ULE + -ATE¹]

Ci·lis·sa (sī lis′ə), *n. Class. Myth.* the nurse of Orestes.

cil·i·um (sil′ē əm), *n.* sing. of **cilia.** [< L]

Cil·ix (sil′iks), *n. Class. Myth.* a brother of Europa who went searching for her after she had been abducted by Zeus.

Cil·la (sil′ə), *n. Class. Myth.* a sister of Priam who, with her infant son, was slain by Priam because it had been prophesied that a mother and child of the royal house would cause the destruction of Troy.

Cil·lus (sil′əs), *n. Class. Myth.* the charioteer of Pelops.

Ci·ma·bu·e (chē′mä bōō′e), *n.* **Gio·van·ni** (jō vän′nē), (*Cenni di Pepo*), c1240–1302?, Italian painter and mosaicist.

ci·maise (sē mez′), *n.* cymaise.

Ci·ma·ro·sa (chē′mə rō′zə; *It.* chē′mä rô′sä), *n.* **Do·me·ni·co** (dô me′nē kô), 1749–1801, Italian conductor and composer.

Cim·ar·ron (sim′ə ron′, -rōn′, -ər ən; sim′ə rōn′), *n.* a river flowing E from NE New Mexico to the Arkansas River in Oklahoma. 600 mi. long.

cim·ba·lom (sim′bə ləm), *n.* cymbalom.

Cim·bri (sim′brī, -brē, kim′-), *n.pl.* a Germanic or Celtic people, supposed to have originated in Jutland, who invaded Gaul and northern Italy, and were destroyed by the Romans in 101 B.C. —**Cim′bri·an,** *adj., n.* —**Cim′bric,** *adj.*

ci·me·li·a (si mē′lē ə, -mēl′yə), *n.pl., sing.* **-me·li·um** (-mē′lē əm, -mēl′yəm). treasures, esp. church treasures, as art objects, jeweled vestments, etc. [< ML < Gk *keimḗlion* heirloom, treasure, akin to *keîsthai* to lie, be stored away; see CEMETERY]

ci·me·li·arch (si mē′lē ärk′), *n.* a room for keeping the valuables of a church. [< LL *cīmēliarch(a)* < LGk *kemeliárch(os)* treasury guard. See CIMELIA, -ARCH]

ci·mex (sī′meks), *n., pl.* **cim·i·ces** (sim′i sēz′). a bedbug of the genus *Cimex.* [< L: a bug]

Cim·me·ri·an (si mēr′ē ən), *adj.* **1.** *Class. Myth.* of, pertaining to, or suggestive of a western people believed to dwell in perpetual darkness. **2.** very dark; gloomy: *deep, Cimmerian caverns.* —**Cim·me′ri·an·ism,** *n.*

Cim·mer·i·um (si mēr′ē əm), *n.* **Mare.** See **Mare Cimmerium.**

Ci·mon (sī′mən), *n.* 507–449 B.C., Athenian military leader, naval commander, and statesman (son of Miltiades).

C. in C., Commander in Chief. Also, **C-in-C.**

cinch¹ (sinch), *U.S.* —*n.* **1.** a strong girth used on stock saddles, having a ring at each end to which a strap running from the saddle is secured. **2.** *Informal.* a firm hold or tight grip. **3.** *Slang.* **a.** something sure or easy: *This problem is a cinch.* **b.** a person or thing certain to fulfill an expectation, esp. a team or contestant certain to win a sporting event: *He's a cinch to be boss of this firm someday. The Giants are a cinch to win Sunday's game.* —*v.t.* **4.** to gird with a cinch; gird or bind firmly. **5.** *Slang.* to seize on or make sure of; guarantee: *Ability and hard work cinched his success.* [< Sp *cincha* < L *cingula* girth, equiv. to *cing(ere)* (to) gird + *-ula* -ULE]

cinch² (sinch), *n. Cards.* a variety of the game all fours. [perh. < Sp *cinco* five, a card game]

cin·cho·na (sin kō′nə), *n.* **1.** any of several rubiaceous trees or shrubs of the genus *Cinchona*, as *C. Calisaya*, native to the Andes, cultivated there and in Java and India for their bark, which yields quinine and other alkaloids. **2.** Also called **Peruvian bark.** the medicinal bark of such trees or shrubs. [< NL, named after Countess of *Chinchón* (1576–1639), wife of a Spanish viceroy of Peru; the bark cured her of a fever] —**cin·chon·ic** (sin kon′ik), *adj.*

cin·chon·i·dine (sin kon′i dēn′, -din), *n. Pharm.* a white, crystalline, slightly water-soluble, levorotatory alkaloid, $C_{19}H_{22}ON_2$, stereoisomeric with cinchonine and similarly derived: used chiefly as a quinine substitute. [CINCHON(A) + -ID³ + -INE²]

cin·cho·nine (sin′kə nēn′, -nin), *n. Pharm.* a colorless, crystalline, slightly water-soluble alkaloid, $C_{19}H_{22}ON_2$, a stereoisomer of cinchonidine, obtained from the bark of various species of cinchona: used chiefly as a quinine substitute. [CINCHON(A) + -INE²]

cin·cho·nise (sin′kə nīz′), *v.t.,* **-nised, -nis·ing.** *Chiefly Brit.* cinchonize. —**cin′cho·ni·sa′tion,** *n.*

cin·chon·ism (sin′kə niz′əm), *n. Pathol.* poisoning by any of the cinchona alkaloids, characterized by headache, deafness, and ringing in the ears. [CINCHON(A) + -ISM]

cin·cho·nize (sin′kə nīz′), *v.t.,* **-nized, -niz·ing.** to treat with cinchona or quinine. Also, *esp. Brit.,* **cinchonise.** [CINCHON(A) + -IZE] —**cin′cho·ni·za′tion,** *n.*

Cin·cin·nat·i (sin′sə nat′ē), *n.* **1.** a city in SW Ohio, on the Ohio River. 502,550 (1960). **2.** *Bowling Slang.* a split in which the eight and ten pins remain standing.

Cin·cin·na·tus (sin′sə nā′təs), *n.* **Lucius Quinc·ti·us** (kwingk′tē əs), 519?–439? B.C., Roman general and statesman: dictator 458, 439.

cinc·ture (singk′chər), *n., v.,* **-tured, -tur·ing.** —*n.* **1.** *Archaic, Poetic.* a belt or girdle. **2.** something surrounding or encompassing like a girdle; a surrounding border: *The midnight sky had a cincture of stars.* **3.** (on a classical column) a fillet at either end of a shaft, esp. one at the lower end. Cf. **orle** (def. 3b). **4.** the act of girding or encompassing. —*v.t.* **5.** to gird with or as with a cincture; encircle; encompass. [< L *cinctūr(a)*, equiv. to *cinct(us)* (*cinc-*, var. s. of *cingere* to gird + *-tus* ptp. suffix) + *-ūra* -URE]

cin·der (sin′dər), *n.* **1.** a burned-out or partially burned piece of coal, wood, etc. **2. cinders, a.** any residue of combustion; ashes. **b.** *Geol.* coarse scoriae thrown out of volcanoes. **3.** a live, flameless coal; ember. **4.** *Metall.* **a.** slag (def. 1). **b.** a mixture of ashes and slag. —*v.t.* **5.** *Archaic.* to reduce to cinders. [ME *synder*, OE *sinder* slag; c. G *Sinter*, Icel *sindr; c-* (for *s-*) < F *cendre* ashes] —**cin′der·y, cin′der·ous,** *adj.* —**cin′der·like′,** *adj.*

cin′der block′, a concrete building block made with a cinder aggregate.

cin′der con′crete, concrete having small coal clinkers as an aggregate.

Cin·der·el·la (sin′də rel′ə), *n.* **1.** heroine of a fairy tale or folk tale who is oppressed by a malevolent stepmother but achieves happiness and marries a prince through the benevolent intervention of a fairy godmother. **2.** (*italics*) the fairy tale or folk tale itself, the earliest version of which is in Chinese, dating from the 9th century A.D. **3.** any girl, esp. one of unrecognized beauty, undeservedly forced into a wretched condition. **4.** a girl's given name.

cin′der patch′, *Metall.* a defect on steel caused by the accidental picking up of matter, as from the bottom of a soaking pit.

cin′der track′, a track covered with small cinders, for use in running races.

Cin·die (sin′dē), *n.* a girl's given name, form of **Cynthia.** Also, **Cindy.**

Cin·dy (sin′dē), *n.* a girl's given name, form of **Cynthia.** Also, **Cindie.**

Cin·dy·lou (sin′dē lōō′), *n.* a girl's given name.

cin·e (sin′ē, sin′ā), *n.* **1.** a film; motion picture. **2.** a motion-picture theater. Also, **cin′é.** [short for CINEMA]

cine-, a combining form of **cinema,** used, with the meaning "motion picture," as a prefix in the formation of compound words: *cineradiograph.*

cin·e·aste (sin′ē ast′, sin′ā-), *n.* **1.** a devotee of motion pictures, esp. one interested in the artistic and technical aspects of film production. **2.** one who makes or produces motion pictures. Also, **cin′é·aste′.** [< F *cinéaste,* equiv. to *ciné-* CINE- + *-aste,* as in *gymnast*]

cin·e·ma (sin′ə mə), *n.* **1.** See **motion picture. 2. the cinema,** motion pictures collectively, as an art or form of expression. **3.** a motion-picture theater. [short for CINEMATOGRAPH] **—cin·e·mat·ic** (sin′ə mat′ik), *adj.* **—cin′e·mat′i·cal·ly,** *adv.*

Cin·e·ma·Scope (sin′ə mə skōp′), *n.* *Trademark.* a process of motion-picture reproduction that achieves a realistic effect by using an anamorphic lens camera or projector, an extra-wide curved screen, and a stereophonic arrangement of speakers. **—Cin·e·ma·Scop·ic** (sin′ə mə skop′ik), *adj.*

cin·e·mat·ics (sin′ə mat′iks), *n.* (*construed as sing. or pl.*) the process or art of making motion pictures; cinematography. [CINEMAT(OGRAPH) + -ICS]

cin·e·ma·tize (sin′ə mə tīz′), *v.t., v.i.,* **-tized, -tiz·ing.** *Chiefly Brit.* cinematograph (def. 3). [CINEMA + (DRAMA)TIZE]

cin·e·mat·o·graph (sin′ə mat′ə graf′, -gräf′), *Chiefly Brit.* **—n. 1.** a motion-picture projector. **2.** a motion-picture camera. **—v.t., v.i. 3.** to photograph with a motion-picture camera. Also, **kinematograph.** [< F *cinématographe,* equiv. to *cinémat-* (< Gk *kīnēmat-,* s. of *kī́nēma* motion) + *-o-* -O- + *-graphe* -GRAPH] **—cin·e·ma·tog·ra·pher** (sin′ə mə tog′rə fər), **cin′e·ma·tog′ra·phist,** *n.* **—cin·e·mat·o·graph·ic** (sin′ə mat′ə graf′ik), *adj.* **—cin′e·mat′o·graph′i·cal·ly,** *adv.* **—cin′e·ma·tog′ra·phy,** *n.*

cin·e·ole (sin′ē ōl′), *n.* *Chem., Pharm.* a colorless, oily, slightly water-soluble, liquid terpene ether, $C_{10}H_{18}O$, having a camphorlike odor and pungent, spicy, cooling taste, found in eucalyptus, cajuput, and other essential oils: used in flavoring, perfumery, and in medicine chiefly as an expectorant. Also, **cin·e·ol** (sin′ē ōl′, -ôl′, -ol′). [alter. of NL *oleum cinae,* equiv. to *oleum* OIL + gen. sing. of *cina* wormseed]

cin·e·ra·di·og·ra·phy (sin′ə rā′dē og′rə fē), *n.* the filming of motion pictures through a fluoroscope or x-ray machine. [CINE- + RADIOGRAPHY]

Cin·e·ram·a (sin′ə ram′ə, -rä′mə), *n.* *Trademark.* a motion-picture process designed to produce a three-dimensional effect by using three cameras, set at different angles, to photograph separate, overlapping images of each scene and projecting them on a large, concave screen in conjunction with stereophonic sound.

cin·e·rar·i·a (sin′ə râr′ē ə), *n.* any of several horticultural varieties of an asteraceous herb, *Senecio cruentus,* of the Canary Islands, having heart-shaped leaves and clusters of flowers with white, blue, purple, red, or variegated rays. [< NL, fem. of L *cinerārius* ashen, equiv. to *ciner-* (s. of *cinis* ashes) + *-ārius* -ARY; so named from ash-colored down on leaves]

cin·e·rar·i·um (sin′ə râr′ē əm), *n., pl.* **-rar·i·a** (-râr′ē ə). a place for depositing the ashes of the dead after cremation. [< L, neut. of *cinerārius;* see CINERARIA, -ARIUM]

cin·e·rar·y (sin′ə rer′ē), *adj.* holding or intended for ashes, esp. the ashes of cremated bodies: *a cinerary urn.* [< L *cinerāri(us);* see CINERARIUM]

cin·er·a·tor (sin′ə rā′tər), *n.* an incinerator. [< L *cinerāt(us)* (ptp. of *cinerāre*), equiv. to *ciner-* (s. of *cinis;* see CINERARIA) + *-ātus* -ATE[1] + -OR[2]] **—cin′e·ra′tion,** *n.*

ci·ne·re·ous (si nēr′ē əs), *adj.* **1.** in the state of ashes: *cinereous bodies.* **2.** resembling ashes. **3.** ashen; ash-colored; grayish: *a cinereous bird.* Also, **cin·er·i·tious** (sin′ə rish′əs). [< L *cinereus,* equiv. to *ciner-* (s. of *cinis*) ashes + *-eus* -EOUS]

Cin·ga·lese (sing′gə lēz′, -lēs′), *adj., n., pl.* **-lese.** Singhalese.

cin′gulate gy′rus, *Anat.* a convolution on the medial surface of the cerebrum, above the corpus callosum. Also called **callosal gyrus.** [< NL *cingulāt(us).* See CINGULUM, -ATE[1]]

cin·gu·lec·to·my (sing′gyə lek′tə mē), *n., pl.* **-mies.** *Surg.* excision of part or all of the cingulate gyrus, usually performed in cases of certain mental disorders. [CINGUL(UM) + -ECTOMY]

cin·gu·lum (sing′gyə ləm), *n., pl.* **-la** (-lə). **1.** *Anat., Zool.* a belt, zone, or girdlelike part. **2.** *Anat.* a band of association fibers connecting the cingulate and hippocampal gyri of the cerebrum. **3.** *Dentistry.* See **basal ridge.** [< L: girdle, zone, equiv. to *cing-* (s. of *cingere* to gird; see CINCTURE) + *-ulum* -ULE] **—cin·gu·late** (sing′gyə lit, -lāt′), **cin′gu·lat′ed, cin′gu·lar,** *adj.*

cin·na·bar (sin′ə bär′), *n.* **1.** a mineral, mercuric sulfide, occurring in red crystals or masses: the principal ore of mercury. **2.** red mercuric sulfide, used as a pigment. **3.** bright red; vermilion. [< L *cinnabar(is)* < Gk *kinnábari* < ?; r. ME *cynoper* < ML] **—cin·na·bar·ine** (sin′ə bə rēn′, -bər in, -bär′in, -ēn), **cin·na·bar·ic** (sin′ə bar′ik), *adj.*

cin·na·mene (sin′ə mēn′), *n.* *Chem.* styrene. Also, **cin·na·mol** (sin′ə mōl′, -môl′, -mol′, sin′ə mōl′, -môl′, -mol′). [*cinnam-* (comb. form of L *cinnam(ōmum)* CINNAMON) + -ENE]

cin·nam·ic (si nam′ik, sin′ə mik), *adj.* of or obtained from cinnamon. [CINNAM(ON) + -IC]

cinnam′ic ac′id, *Chem.* a white, crystalline, water-insoluble powder, $C_6H_5CH{=}CHCOOH$, usually obtained from cinnamon or synthesized: used chiefly in the manufacture of perfumes and medicines.

cinnam′ic al′cohol, *Chem.* a white, water-insoluble, crystalline solid, $C_6H_5CH{=}CHCH_2OH$, having a hyacinthine odor, used chiefly as a scent in the manufacture of perfumes.

cinnam′ic al′dehyde, *Chem.* a yellowish oil, $C_6H_5CH{=}CHCHO$, having a cinnamonlike odor, used chiefly as a scent in the manufacture of flavorings and perfumes.

cin·na·mon (sin′ə mən), *n.* **1.** the aromatic inner bark of any of several lauraceous trees of the genus *Cinnamomum,* of the East Indies, Ceylon, etc., esp. the bark of *C. Zeylanicum* **(Ceylon cinnamon),** used as a spice, or that of *C. Loureirii* **(Saigon cinnamon),** used in medicine as a cordial and carminative. **2.** a tree yielding such bark. **3.** any of various allied or similar trees. **4.** a common culinary spice obtained by drying rolled strips of this bark and then usually making them into a powder. **5.** cassia (def. 1). **6.** a yellowish or reddish brown. **—adj. 7.** (of food) containing or flavored with cinnamon: *cinnamon bun.* **8.** reddish-brown or yellowish-brown. [< L < Gk *kínnamon* < Sem, as Heb *qinnāmōn;* r. late ME *cinamome* < MF < L *cinnamōm(um)* < Gk *kinnámōmon*] **—cin′na·moned,** *adj.* **—cin·na·mon·ic** (sin′ə mon′ik), *adj.*

cin′namon bear′, a cinnamon-colored variety of the black bear of North America.

cin′namon fern′, a widely grown coarse fern, *Osmunda cinnamomea,* having rusty-woolly stalks, growing in wet, low woods or thickets.

cin′namon rose′, an erect shrub, *Rosa cinnamomea,* of Eurasia, having short, hooked prickles, leaflets that are densely hairy beneath, and fragrant, solitary, purplish-red flowers.

cin′namon stone′, a light, brown grossularite garnet.

cin′namon teal′, a small, fresh-water, wild duck, *Anas cyanoptera,* of North and South America, having chiefly cinnamon-red plumage.

cin′namon vine′, See **Chinese yam.**

cin·nam·o·yl (si nam′ō il), *adj.* *Chem.* containing the cinnamoyl group. [CINNAMO(N) + -YL]

cinnam′oyl group′, *Chem.* the univalent group, $C_6H_5CH{=}CHCO–$, derived from cinnamic acid. Also called **cinnam′oyl rad′ical.**

cin·nam·yl (si nam′il, sin′ə mil), *adj.* *Chem.* containing the cinnamyl group. [CINNAM(ON) + -YL]

cinnam′yl ac′etate, *Chem.* a colorless liquid, $C_6H_5CH{=}CHCH_2OCOCH_3$, having a piquant, flowerlike odor: used as a fixative in the manufacture of perfumes.

cinnam′yl group′, *Chem.* the univalent group, $C_6H_5CH{=}CHCH_2–$. Also called **cinnam′yl rad′ical.**

cin·quain (sing kān′, sing′kān), *n.* **1.** a group of five. **2.** *Pros.* **a.** a short poem consisting of five, usually unrhymed lines containing respectively two, four, six, eight, and two syllables. **b.** any stanza of five lines. [< F < LL *cinque* (see CINQUE) + F *-ain* collective suffix. See QUATRAIN]

cinque (singk), *n.* the five at dice, cards, etc. [ME *cink* < OF *cinq* < LL *cinque* < L *quinque* five]

cin·que·cen·tist (ching′kwi chen′tist), *n.* an Italian writer or artist of the 16th century. [< It *cinquecentist(a),* equiv. to *cinquecent(o)* (see CINQUECENTO) + *-ista* -IST]

cin·que·cen·to (ching′kwi chen′tō), *n.* (*often cap.*) the 16th century, with reference to Italy, esp. to the Italian art or literature of that period. [< It, short for *mil cinque cento* 1500, used for period A.D. 1500–1599] **—cin′que·cen′tism,** *n.*

cin·que·de·a (ching′kwi dē′ə, -dā′ə), *n.* an Italian short sword of the late 15th and early 16th centuries having a broad, tapering blade, often richly ornamented. [< It, equiv. to *cinque* five (< L *quinque*) + *dea* (dial.) fingers, akin to *dito* finger (< L *digitus;* see DIGIT)]

cinque·foil (singk′foil′), *n.* **1.** any of several rosaceous plants of the genus *Potentilla,* as *P. reptans* **(creeping cinquefoil),** of the Old World, or *P. argentea* **(silvery cinquefoil),** of North America. **2.** Also called **quinquefoil, quintefoil.** *Archit.* a panellike ornament consisting of five lobes, divided by cusps, radiating from a common center. **3.** *Heraldry.* a charge in the form of a five-leaved clover. [ME *sink foil* < MF *cincfoille* < L *quinque folia* five leaves, trans. of Gk *pentáphyllon*]

Cinquefoil (def. 2)

Cinque′ Ports′, an association of maritime towns in SE England, in Sussex and Kent: originally (1278) numbering five (Hastings, Romney, Hythe, Dover, and Sandwich) and receiving special privileges in return for aiding in the naval defense of England. [ME *cink pors* < OF *cink porz.* See CINQUE, PORT[1]]

Cin·y·ras (sin′ər əs), *n.* *Class. Myth.* the king who introduced the worship of Aphrodite on Cyprus: he committed suicide when he discovered that he was guilty of incest with his daughter. Cf. **Myrrha.**

C.I.O., See **Congress of Industrial Organizations.** Also, **CIO**

ci·on (sī′ən), *n.* scion (def. 2).

-cion, var. of **-tion:** *suspicion.* [< L, equiv. to *-c-* final in v. stem + *-iōn-* -ION]

Ci·pan·go (si pang′gō), *n.* *Archaic.* Japan.

ci·pher (sī′fər), *n.* **1.** an arithmetic symbol (0) which denotes naught, or no quantity or magnitude; zero. **2.** any of the Arabic numerals or figures. **3.** Arabic numerical notation collectively. **4.** something of no value or importance. **5.** a person of no influence; nonentity. **6.** a secret method of writing, as by transposition or substitution of letters, specially formed symbols, or the like. Cf. **cryptography. 7.** writing done by such a method; a coded message. **8.** the key to a secret method of writing. **9.** a combination of letters, as the initials of a name, in one design; monogram. **—v.i. 10.** to use figures or numerals arithmetically. **—v.t. 11.** to calculate numerically; figure. **12.** to write in or as in cipher. Also, *esp. Brit.,* **cypher.** [late ME *siphre* < ML *ciphr(a)* < Ar *ṣifr* empty, zero] **—ci′pher·a·ble,** *adj.* **—ci′pher·er,** *n.*

cip·o·lin (sip′ə lin), *n.* an impure variety of marble with alternate white and greenish zones and a layered structure. [< F < It *cipollin(o),* equiv. to *cipoll(a)* onion (< LL *cēpulla,* equiv. to L *cēp(a)* onion + *-ulla* dim. suffix) + *-ino* -INE[1]]

cip·pus (sip′əs), *n., pl.* **cip·pi** (sip′ī). (in classical architecture) a stele. [< L: pillar, gravestone]

Ci·pus (sī′pəs), *n.* **Ge·nu·cius** (jə nōō′shəs, -nyōō′). *Class. Myth.* a praetor who, having heard a prophecy, while away from Rome, that he would be made king when he returned, remained permanently away from the city in order to preserve the republican form of government.

cir., circa. [< L *circa, circiter, circum*]

circ., **1.** circa. **2.** circuit. **3.** circulation. **4.** circumference.

cir·ca (sûr′kə), *prep., adv.* about: used esp. in approximate dates. *Abbr.:* ca, ca., c., c, cir., circ. [< L: around, about, akin to *circus* CIRCUS]

cir·ca·di·an (sûr′kə dē′ən), *adj.* noting or pertaining to rhythmic biological cycles recurring at approximately 24-hour intervals. [< L *circa* about + *di(em)* day + -AN]

Cir·cas·sia (sər kash′ə, -ē ə), *n.* a region in the S Soviet Union in Europe, bordering on the Black Sea.

Cir·cas·sian (sər kash′ən, -ē ən), *n.* **1.** Also called **Adyghe.** a native or inhabitant of Circassia. **2.** a group of North Caucasian languages, including Kabardian. **3.** a literary language based on the western dialects of the Circassian group. **—adj. 4.** of or pertaining to Circassia, its inhabitants, often with respect to their legendary beauty, or their language; Adyghe. [< ML or NL *Circassia* (alter. of Russ *Cherkes*) + -AN]

Cir·ce (sûr′sē), *n.* **1.** Also called **Aeaea.** *Class. Myth.* the enchantress represented by Homer as turning the companions of Odysseus into swine by means of a magic drink. **2.** a dangerously or irresistibly fascinating woman. **—Cir·ce·an, Cir·cae·an** (sər sē′ən), *adj.*

cir·ci·nate (sûr′sə nāt′), *adj.* **1.** made round; ring-shaped. **2.** *Bot.* rolled up on the axis at the apex, as a leaf. [< L *circināt(us)* (ptp. of *circināre*), equiv. to *circin(us)* pair of compasses (akin to CIRCUS) + *-āt(us)* -ATE[1]] **—cir′ci·nate·ly,** *adv.*

Cir·ci·nus (sûr′sə nəs), *n., gen.* **-ni** (-nī′). *Astron.* the Compasses, a small southern constellation between Triangulum and Centaurus. [< L]

Circinate fronds of a young fern

cir·cle (sûr′kəl), *n., v.,* **-cled, -cling.** **—n. 1.** a closed plane curve consisting of all points at a given distance from a point within it called the center. Equation: $x^2 + y^2 = r^2$. **2.** the portion of a plane bounded by such a curve. **3.** any circular or ringlike object, formation, or arrangement: *a circle of dancers.* **4.** a ring, circlet, or crown. **5.** the ring of a circus. **6.** a section of seats in a theater: *dress circle.* **7.** the area within which something acts, exerts influence, etc.; realm; sphere: *A politician has a wide circle of influence.* **8.** a series ending where it began, esp. when perpetually repeated; cycle: *the circle of the year.* **9.** *Logic.* an argument ostensibly proving a conclusion but actually assuming the conclusion or its equivalent as a premise; vicious circle. **10.** a complete series forming a connected whole; cycle: *the circle of the sciences.* **11.** a number of persons bound by a common tie; coterie: *He belongs to a fashionable circle. She told no one outside the family circle.* **12.** *Govt.* an administrative division, esp. of a province. **13.** *Geog.* a parallel of latitude. **14.** *Astron.* **a.** *Rare.* the orbit of a heavenly body. **b.** See **meridian circle. 15.** *Survey.* a glass or metal disk mounted concentrically with the spindle of a theodolite or level and graduated so that the angle at which the alidade is set may be read. **16.** a sphere or orb: *the circle of the earth.* **17.** a ring of light in the sky; halo. **—v.t. 18.** to enclose in a circle; surround; encircle: *Circle the correct answer on the exam paper. The enemy circled the hill.* **19.** to move in a circle or circuit around; rotate or revolve around: *He circled the house cautiously.* **20.** to change course so as to pass by or avoid collision with; bypass; evade: *The ship carefully circled the iceberg. He circled Chicago to save an hour's driving time.* **—v.i. 21.** to move in a circle or circuit: *The plane circled a half hour before landing.* **22.** *Motion Pictures, Television.* to iris (usually fol. by *in* or *out*). [< L *circul(us),* equiv. to *circ(us)* (see CIRCUS) + *-ulus* -ULE; r. ME *cercle* < OF; r. OE *circul* < L] **—cir′cler,** *n.*

Circle r, Radius

—Syn. 11. CIRCLE, CLUB, COTERIE, SET, SOCIETY are terms applied to more or less restricted social groups. A CIRCLE may be a pleasant little group meeting chiefly for conversation; in the plural it often suggests a whole section of society interested in one mode of life, occupation, etc.: *a sewing circle; a language circle; in theatrical circles.* CLUB implies an association with definite requirements for membership, fixed dues, and often a stated time of meeting: *an athletic club.* COTERIE suggests a little group closely and intimately associated because of great congeniality: *a literary coterie.* SET refers to a number of persons of similar background, upbringing, interests, etc., somewhat like a CLIQUE (see RING[1]) but without disapproving connotations; it often implies wealth or interest in social activities: *the country club set.* A SOCIETY is a group associated to further common interests of a cultural or practical kind: *a Humane Society.*

cir·cle-in (sûr′kəl in′), *n.* iris-in.

cir′cle of confu′sion, *Photog.* a circular spot on a film, resulting from the degree to which a pencil of light reflected from the field of view is focused in front of or behind the film, or from aberration of the lens, or from both. The tolerance limits of the size of the spot vary in accordance with the degree of precision required in the finished print, as from $^1/_{250}$ inch for ordinary purposes to $^1/_{1000}$ inch for color reproduction.

cir′cle of conver′gence. See **interval of convergence.**

cir′cle of cur′vature, *Math.* the circle with its center on the normal to the concave side of a curve at a given point on the curve and with its radius equal to the radius of curvature at the point. Also called **osculating circle.**

cir′cle of least′ confu′sion, *Optics.* the smallest cross section in a beam of paraxial rays, lying in the plane of least spherical aberration.

cir·cle-out (sûr′kəl out′), *n.* iris-out.

cir·clet (sûr′klit), *n.* **1.** a small circle. **2.** a ring. **3.** a ring-shaped ornament, esp. for the head. [CIRCLE + -ET; r. late ME *serclett* < MF]

cir′cling disease′, *Vet. Pathol.* a fatal disease of cattle and sheep, caused by the bacterium *Listeria monocytogenes,* which damages the nervous system and often causes the affected animal to walk in circles.

cir·cuit (sûr′kit), *n.* **1.** the act or an instance of going or moving around. **2.** a circular journey or one beginning and ending at the same place; a round. **3.** a roundabout journey or course. **4.** a periodical journey from place to place, to perform certain duties, as by judges to hold court, ministers to preach, or salesmen covering a route. **5.** the persons making such a journey. **6.** the route followed, places visited, or district covered by such a journey. **7.** the line going around or bounding any area or object; the distance about an area or object: *The mountains formed a long circuit about the valley.* **8.** the space within a bounding line; district: *Colorful wild flowers filled the circuit of the valley.* **9.** a number of theaters, night clubs, etc., controlled by one owner or manager or visited in turn by the same entertainers or acting companies. **10.** *Elect.* **a.** the complete path of an electric current, including the generating apparatus, intervening resistors, capacitors, etc. **b.** any well-defined segment of a complete circuit. **11.** a league or association: *He used to play baseball for the Texas circuit.* —*v.t.* **12.** to go or move around; make the circuit of. —*v.i.* **13.** to go or move in a circuit. [late ME < L *circuit(us),* var. of *circumitus,* equiv. to *circ(um)* (see CIRCUM-) + *-itus* (ptp. of *īre* to go), equiv. to *i-* perf. s. + *-tus* ptp. suffix] —**cir′cuit·al,** *adj.*
—**Syn. 2.** tour, revolution, orbit. **7.** circumference, perimeter, periphery, boundary, compass. **8.** region, compass, area, range, field. **9.** chain.

cir′cuit an′alyzer, *Elect.* multimeter.

cir′cuit bind′ing, a bookbinding having soft edges that project beyond and fold over the edges of the pages to protect them. Also called **divinity circuit, yapp, yapp binding.**

cir′cuit break′er, *Elect.* a device for interrupting an electric circuit to prevent excessive current, as that caused by a short circuit, from damaging the apparatus in the circuit or from causing a fire.

cir′cuit court′, **1.** a court holding sessions at various intervals in different sections of a judicial district. **2.** (*caps.*) *U.S.* the court of general jurisdiction in a number of States.

cir′cuit court′ of appeals′, any of the courts of appeals in the U.S. federal judicial system before 1948.

cir′cuit edg′es, the soft edges of a circuit binding.

cir·cuit·er (sûr′ki tər), *n.* one who travels a circuit: *This judge is a circuiter.* [CIRCUIT + -ER[1]]

cir′cuit judge′, a judge of a circuit court.

cir·cu·i·tous (sər kyōō′i təs), *adj.* roundabout; not direct: *a circuitous route; a circuitous argument.* [< ML *circuitōs(us),* equiv. to *circuit(us)* CIRCUIT + *-ōsus* -OUS] —**cir·cu′i·tous·ly,** *adv.* —**cir·cu′i·tous·ness,** *n.*

cir′cuit rid′er, a minister, esp a Methodist one, who rides from place to place to preach along a circuit.

cir·cuit·ry (sûr′ki trē), *n.* **1.** a detailed plan of an electric network or circuit. **2.** the components of an electric circuit or network. [CIRCUIT + -RY]

cir·cu·i·ty (sər kyōō′i tē), *n., pl.* **-ties.** circuitous quality or roundabout character. [CIRCUIT + -Y[3]]

cir·cu·lar (sûr′kyə lər), *adj.* **1.** of or pertaining to a circle: *a circular plane.* **2.** having the form of a circle; round: *a circular tower.* **3.** moving in or forming a circle or a circuit: *the circular rotation of the earth.* **4.** moving or occurring in a cycle or round: *the circular succession of the seasons.* **5.** circuitous; roundabout; indirect: *a circular argument.* **6.** pertaining to a circle or set of persons. **7.** (of a letter, memorandum, etc.) addressed to a number of persons or intended for general circulation. —*n.* **8.** a letter, advertisement, notice, or statement for circulation among the general public for business or other purposes. [< LL *circulār(is)* < *circul(us)* CIRCLE + *-āris* -AR[1]] —**cir·cu·lar·i·ty** (sûr′kyə lar′i tē), **cir′cu·lar·ness,** *n.* —**cir′cu·lar·ly,** *adv.*

cir′cular er′ror, **1.** *Horol.* loss of isochronism in a pendulum moving through circular arcs of different sizes: sometimes avoided by causing the pendulum to move through cycloidal arcs. **2.** *Mil.* error measured as the distance from the center of a target to the point of impact of a bomb or shell, or to the ground zero of an aerial burst.

cir′cular er′ror prob′able, *Mil.* a measure of the inaccuracy of artillery or missiles at a certain range, equal to the radius of a circle about the target center such that the probability that the point of impact, or ground zero, will fall within the circle is exactly one-half. Also called **circular probable error.**

cir′cular func′tion, *Math.* See **trigonometric function** (def. 1).

cir·cu·lar·ise (sûr′kyə lə rīz′), *v.t.,* **-ised, -is·ing.** *Chiefly Brit.* circularize. —**cir′cu·lar·i·sa′tion,** *n.* —**cir′cu·lar·is′er,** *n.*

cir·cu·lar·ize (sûr′kyə lə rīz′), *v.t.,* **-ized, -iz·ing.** **1.** to send circulars to. **2.** to circulate (a letter, memorandum, etc.). **3.** to make circular. [CIRCULAR + -IZE] —**cir′cu·lar·i·za′tion,** *n.* —**cir′cu·lar·iz′er,** *n.*

cir·cu·lar-knit (sûr′kyə lər nit′), *adj.* noting, pertaining to, or made of a fabric made by circular knitting.

cir′cular knit′ting, **1.** a technique of knitting in circular or tubular form with curved or straight needles. **2.** (in machine knitting) a process of knitting tubular and seamless fabrics by using special needles and shaping the fabric by varying the tension or length of the stitches. Cf. **flat knitting.**

cir′cular light′, *Optics.* light that is circularly polarized.

cir′cular meas′ure, a measurement system for circles: 1 circle = 360 degrees (4 quadrants); 1 quadrant = 90 degrees; 1 degree = 60 minutes; 1 minute = 60 seconds.

cir′cular mil′, a unit used principally for measuring the cross-sectional area of wires, being the area of a circle having the diameter of one mil.

cir′cular pitch′, *Mach.* See under **pitch**[1] (def. 45a).

cir′cular polariza′tion, *Optics.* polarization in which the vector representing the instantaneous intensity of the electric field describes a circular helix in the direction of propagation. Cf. **elliptical polarization.**

cir′cular prob′able er′ror. See **circular error probable.**

cir′cular sail′ing. See **spherical sailing.**

cir′cular saw′, a power saw consisting of a circular disk, usually with a toothed edge. See illus. under **saw.**

cir′cular tri′angle, a triangle that has arcs of circles as sides.

cir′cular veloc′ity, the velocity at which a body must move in order to maintain an orbit at the outer edge of the earth's atmosphere. Cf. **orbital velocity.**

cir·cu·late (sûr′kyə lāt′), *v.,* **-lat·ed, -lat·ing.** —*v.i.* **1.** to move in a circle or circuit; move or pass through a circuit back to the starting point, as the blood in the body. **2.** to pass from place to place, from person to person, etc.: *She circulated among her guests.* **3.** to be distributed or sold, esp. over a wide area. —*v.t.* **4.** to cause to pass from place to place, person to person, etc.; disseminate; distribute: *to circulate a rumor.* [< L *circulāt(us)* (ptp. of *circulārī* to gather round one, LL *circulāre* to encircle), equiv. to *circul(us)* CIRCLE + *-ātus* -ATE[1]] —**cir·cu·la·tive** (sûr′kyə lā′tiv, -lə tiv), *adj.* —**cir·cu·la·to·ry** (sûr′kyə lə tôr′ē, -tōr′ē), *adj.*

cir′culating cap′ital, the portion of capital goods which consists of goods in process, inventories of finished goods, and raw materials. Also called **cir′culating cap′ital goods′.** Cf. **fixed capital.**

cir′culating dec′imal, a decimal in which a series of digits is repeated ad infinitum, as 0.147232323 . . . Also called **recurring decimal, repeater, repeating decimal.**

cir′culating li′brary, **1.** a library whose books circulate among its members or subscribers. **2.** See **lending library.**

cir′culating me′dium, **1.** any coin or note passing, without endorsement, as a medium of exchange. **2.** such coins or notes collectively.

cir·cu·la·tion (sûr′kyə lā′shən), *n.* **1.** the act or an instance of circulating, moving in a circle or circuit, or flowing. **2.** the continuous movement of blood through the heart and blood vessels, which is maintained chiefly by the action of the heart, and by which food, oxygen, and internal secretions are carried to and wastes are carried from the body tissues. **3.** any similar circuit, passage, or flow, as of the sap in plants or air currents in a room. **4.** the transmission or passage of anything from place to place or person to person: *the circulation of a rumor; the circulation of money.* **5.** the distribution of copies of a periodical among readers. **6.** the number of copies of each issue of a newspaper, magazine, etc., distributed. **7.** coins, notes, bills, etc., in use as money; currency. **8.** *Mech.* a quantity analogous to work and equal to the line integral of the component of fluid velocity about a closed contour. **9. in circulation,** participating actively in social or business life: *After a month in the hospital, he's back in circulation.* [< L *circulātiōn-* (s. of *circulātiō*), equiv. to *circulāt(us)* (see CIRCULATE) + *-iōn-* -ION] —**cir·cu·la·ble** (sûr′kyə lə bəl), *adj.*

cir·cu·la·tor (sûr′kyə lā′tər), *n.* **1.** one who travels or moves from place to place. **2.** one who circulates money, news, information, etc. **3.** a talebearer or scandalmonger. **4.** any of various devices for circulating fluids. **5.** *Obs.* a mountebank. [< L *circulātor* a quack, peddler. See CIRCULATE, -OR[2]]

cir′culatory sys′tem, *Anat., Zool.* the system of organs and tissues, including the heart, blood, blood vessels, lymph, lymphatic vessels, and lymph glands, involved in circulating blood and lymph through the body.

cir·cu·lus (sûr′kyə ləs), *n., pl.* **-li** (-lī′). any of the concentric circles on each scale of a fish, each of which indicates the annual growth of that scale. [< L: CIRCLE]

circum-, an element occurring in loan words from Latin (*circumstance*); used, with the meaning "around," "about," in the formation of compound words (*circumnutate*). [< L, prefix akin to CIRCUS, CIRCA]

cir·cum·am·bi·ent (sûr′kəm am′bē ənt), *adj.* surrounding; encompassing: *circumambient gloom.* [< LL *circumambient-* (s. of *circumambiēns*). See CIRCUM-, AMBIENT] —**cir′cum·am′bi·ence, cir′cum·am′bi·en·cy,** *n.*

cir·cum·am·bu·late (sûr′kəm am′byə lāt′), *v.t., v.i.,* **-lat·ed, -lat·ing.** to walk or go about or around. [< LL *circumambulāt(us)* (ptp. of *circumambulāre*). See CIRCUM-, AMBULATE] —**cir′cum·am′bu·la′tion,** *n.* —**cir′cum·am′bu·la′tor,** *n.* —**cir′cum·am′bu·la·to′ry,** *adj.*

cir·cum·ba·sal (sûr′kəm bā′səl), *adj.* surrounding the base: *circumbasal decorations.* [CIRCUM- + BASAL]

cir·cum·bend·i·bus (sûr′kəm ben′də bəs), *n., pl.* **-bus·es.** *Informal.* a roundabout way; circumlocution. [CIRCUM- + BEND[1] + L *-ibus* abl. pl. ending]

cir·cum·cen·ter (sûr′kəm sen′tər), *n.* *Geom.* the center of a circumscribed circle; that point where any two perpendicular bisectors of the sides of a polygon inscribed in the circle intersect. [CIRCUM- + CENTER]

cir·cum·cise (sûr′kəm sīz′), *v.t.,* **-cised, -cis·ing.** **1.** to remove the prepuce of (a male), esp. as a religious rite. **2.** to perform an analogous operation on (a female). **3.** to purify spiritually. [ME *circumcise(n)* < L *circumcīs(us)* (ptp. of *circumcīdere* to cut around), equiv. to *circum-* CIRCUM- + *-cīsus* (*cīd-* cut + *-tus* ptp. suffix)] —**cir′cum·cis′er,** *n.*

cir·cum·ci·sion (sûr′kəm sizh′ən), *n.* **1.** the act, an instance, or the rite of circumcising. **2.** spiritual purification. **3. the circumcision, a.** (*usually cap.*) the Jews, as the circumcised people of the Bible. **b.** those spiritually purified. **4.** (*cap.*) a church festival in honor of the circumcision of Jesus, observed on January 1. [ME < LL *circumcīsiōn-* (s. of *circumcīsiō*), equiv. to L *circumcīs(us)* (see CIRCUMCISE) + *-iōn-* -ION]

cir·cum·col·um·nar (sûr′kəm kə lum′nər), *adj.* *Archit.* surrounding a column. [CIRCUM- + COLUMNAR]

cir·cum·fer·ence (sər kum′fər əns), *n.* **1.** the outer boundary, esp. of a circular area; perimeter: *the circumference of a circle.* **2.** the length of such a boundary: *a one-mile circumference.* **3.** the area within a bounding line: *the large circumference of his mind.* [late ME < LL *circumferentia,* equiv. to *circum-* CIRCUM- + *fer-* (s. of *ferre* to carry) + *-entia* -ENCE]
—**Syn. 1.** periphery, circuit.

cir·cum·fer·en·tial (sər kum′fə ren′shəl), *adj.* **1.** of, at, or near the circumference; surrounding; lying along the outskirts. **2.** lying within the circumference. **3.** circuitous; indirect: *a circumferential manner of speech.* [< L *circumferenti(a)* CIRCUMFERENCE + -AL[1]]

cir·cum·fer·en·tor (sûr′kəm fə ren′tər), *n.* an alidade equipped with a compass. Also called **Dutch circle.** [< L *circumferent(ia)* CIRCUMFERENCE + -OR[2]]

cir·cum·flex (sûr′kəm fleks′), *adj.* **1.** consisting of, indicated by, or bearing the mark ˆ, ˜, or ˉ, placed over a vowel symbol in some languages to show that the vowel or the syllable containing it is pronounced in a certain way, as, in French, that the vowel so marked is of a certain quality and long, in Albanian, that the vowel is nasalized and stressed, or, in Classical Greek, that the syllable bears the word accent and is pronounced, according to the ancient grammarians, with a rise and fall in pitch. **2.** pronounced with or characterized by the quality, quantity, stress, or pitch indicated by such a mark. **3.** bending or winding around. —*n.* **4.** a circumflex mark or accent. —*v.t.* **5.** to bend around. [< L *circumflex(us),* equiv. to *circum-* CIRCUM- + *flexus,* ptp. of *flectere* to bend; see FLEX]

cir·cum·flu·ent (sər kum′flōō ənt), *adj.* flowing around; encompassing: *two circumfluent rivers.* [< L *circumfluent-* (s. of *circumfluēns,* prp. of *circumfluere* to flow around). See CIRCUM-, FLUENT] —**cir·cum′flu·ence,** *n.*

cir·cum·flu·ous (sər kum′flōō əs), *adj.* **1.** circumfluent. **2.** surrounded by water: *Ireland is a circumfluous country.* [< L *circumfluus,* equiv. to *circum-* CIRCUM- + *flu-* (s. of *fluere* to flow) + *-us* -OUS]

cir·cum·fuse (sûr′kəm fyōōz′), *v.t.,* **-fused, -fus·ing.** **1.** to pour around; diffuse. **2.** to surround as with a fluid; suffuse: *An atmosphere of joy circumfused the celebration.* [< L *circumfūs(us)* (ptp. of *circumfundere* to pour around). See CIRCUM-, FUSE[2]] —**cir·cum·fu·sion** (sûr′kəm fyōō′zhən), *n.*

cir·cum·gy·ra·tion (sûr′kəm jī rā′shən), *n.* a revolution or circular movement. [< LL *circumgȳrāt(us)* (see CIRCUM-, GYRATE) + -ION] —**cir·cum·gy·ra·to·ry** (sûr′kəm jī′rə tôr′ē, -tōr′ē), *adj.*

cir·cum·in·ces·sion (sûr′kəm in sesh′ən), *n.* *Theol.* the reciprocal existence in one another of the three persons of the Trinity. Also, **cir′cum·in·ses′sion.** [< ML *circumincessiōn-* (s. of *circumcessiō*), equiv. to L *circum-* CIRCUM + ML *incessiōn-* < L *incess(us)* (ptp. of *incedere* to give in, to, go along with, equiv. to *in-* IN-[2] + *cēdere* to go); see CEDE, CESSION]

cir·cum·ja·cent (sûr′kəm jā′sənt), *adj.* lying around; surrounding: *the circumjacent parishes.* [< L *circumjacent-* (s. of *circumjacēns,* prp. of *circumjacēre* to lie around), equiv. to *circum-* CIRCUM- + *jac-* lie + *-ent-* -ENT] —**cir′cum·ja′cence, cir′cum·ja′cen·cy,** *n.*

cir·cum·lo·cu·tion (sûr′kəm lō kyōō′shən), *n.* **1.** a roundabout or indirect way of speaking; the use of more words than necessary to express an idea. **2.** a roundabout expression. [< L *circumlocūtiōn-* (s. of *circumlocūtiō*). See CIRCUM-, LOCUTION] —**cir·cum·loc·u·to·ry** (sûr′kəm lok′yə tôr′ē, -tōr′ē), **cir′cum·lo·cu′tion·al, cir′cum·lo·cu′tion·ar′y,** *adj.* —**cir′cum·lo·cu′tion·ist,** *n.*

cir·cum·lu·nar (sûr′kəm lōō′nər), *adj.* rotating about or surrounding the moon. [CIRCUM- + LUNAR]

cir·cum·nav·i·gate (sûr′kəm nav′ə gāt′), *v.t.,* **-gat·ed, -gat·ing.** to sail around; make the circuit of by navigation: *It took three years for the small ship to circumnavigate the earth.* [< L *circumnāvigāt(us)* (ptp. of *circumnāvigāre*), equiv. to *circum-* CIRCUM- + *nāvigātus;* see NAVIGATE] —**cir·cum·nav·i·ga·ble** (sûr′kəm nav′ə gə bəl), *adj.* —**cir′cum·nav′i·ga′tion,** *n.* —**cir′cum·nav′i·ga′tor,** *n.* —**cir·cum·nav·i·ga·to·ry** (sûr′kəm nav′ə gə tôr′ē, -tōr′ē), *adj.*

cir·cum·nu·tate (sûr′kəm nōō′tāt, -nyōō′-), *v.i.,* **-tat·ed, -tat·ing.** (of the apex of a stem or other growing part of a plant) to bend or move around in an irregular circular or elliptical path. [CIRCUM- + *nutate* < L *nūtāt(us)* (ptp. of *nūtāre* to sway, totter), equiv. to *nū-* (s. of *-nuere* to nod) + *-tā-* freq. suffix + *-tus* ptp. suffix] —**cir′cum·nu·ta′tion,** *n.* —**cir·cum·nu·ta·to·ry** (sûr′kəm nōō′tə tôr′ē, -tōr′ē, -nyōō′-), *adj.*

cir·cum·oc·u·lar (sûr′kəm ok′yə lər), *adj.* *Ophthalm.* surrounding the eye. [CIRCUM- + OCULAR]

cir·cum·po·lar (sûr′kəm pō′lər), *adj.* around one of the poles of the earth or of the heavens. [CIRCUM- + POLAR]

cir·cum·ra·di·us (sûr′kəm rā′dē əs), *n., pl.* **-di·i** (-dē ī′), **-di·us·es.** *Geom.* the radius of the circle circumscribed around a triangle. [CIRCUM- + RADIUS]

cir·cum·ro·tate (sûr′kəm rō′tāt), *v.i.,* **-tat·ed, -tat·ing.** to rotate like a wheel. [< L *circumrotāt(us)* (ptp. of *circumrotāre*), equiv. to *circum-* CIRCUM- + *rotātus;* see ROTATE] —**cir′cum·ro·ta′tion,** *n.* —**cir·cum·ro·ta·to·ry** (sûr′kəm rō′tə tôr′ē, -tōr′ē), *adj.*

cir·cum·scis·sile (sûr′kəm sis′il), *adj.* *Bot.* opening along a transverse circular line, as a seed vessel. [CIRCUM- + SCISSILE]

Circumscissile pod of plantain, genus *Plantago*

cir·cum·scribe (sûr′kəm skrīb′, sûr′kəm skrīb′), *v.t.,* **-scribed, -scrib·ing.** **1.** to draw a line around; encircle; surround: *to circumscribe a city on a map.* **2.** to enclose within bounds; limit or confine, esp. narrowly: *He circumscribed the social activities of his daughter.* **3.** to mark off; define; delimit: *to circumscribe the area of a science.* **4.** *Geom.* **a.** to draw (a figure) around another figure so as to touch as many points as possible. **b.** (of a figure) to enclose (another figure) in this manner. [< L *circumscrīb(ere),* equiv. to *circum-* CIRCUM- + *scrībere* to write] —**cir′cum·scrib′a·ble,** *adj.* —**cir′cum·scrib′er,** *n.*
—**Syn. 1.** circle. **2.** restrict, restrain, check, hamper, hinder.

cir·cum·scrip·tion (sûr′kəm skrip′shən), *n.* **1.** the act or an instance of circumscribing. **2.** circumscribed state; limitation. **3.** anything that circumscribes, surrounds, or encloses; boundary. **4.** periphery; outline. **5.** a circumscribed area. **6.** a circular inscription on a coin, seal, etc. **7.** *Archaic.* limitation of a meaning; definition. [< L *circumscrīptiōn-* (s. of *circumscrīptiō*), equiv. to *circumscrīpt(us)* (ptp. of *circumscrībere* to CIRCUMSCRIBE; see CIRCUM-, SCRIPT) + *-iōn-* -ION] —**cir′cum·scrip′tive,** *adj.* —**cir′cum·scrip′tive·ly,** *adv.*

cir·cum·so·lar (sûr′kəm sō′lər), *adj.* around the sun: *the earth's circumsolar course.* [CIRCUM- + SOLAR]

cir·cum·spect (sûr′kəm spekt′), *adj.* **1.** watchful and discreet; cautious; prudent: *circumspect behavior.* **2.** well-considered: *circumspect ambition.* [< L *circumspect(us)* (ptp. of *circumspicere* to look around), equiv. to *circum-* CIRCUM- + *spec(ere)* to look + *-tus* ptp. suffix] —**cir′cum·spect′ly,** *adv.* —**cir′cum·spect′ness,** *n.*
—**Syn. 1.** careful, vigilant, guarded. —**Ant. 1.** careless, indiscreet.

cir·cum·spec·tion (sûr′kəm spek′shən), *n.* circumspect observation or action; caution; prudence: *Not knowing who might be his friends, he approached everyone with circumspection.* [< L *circumspectiōn-* (s. of *circumspectiō*), equiv. to *circumspect(us)* CIRCUMSPECT + *-iōn-* -ION]

cir·cum·spec·tive (sûr′kəm spek′tiv), *adj.* given to or marked by circumspection; watchful; cautious: *As he was fearful by nature, his behavior was characteristically circumspective.* [CIRCUMSPECT + -IVE] —**cir′cum·spec′tive·ly,** *adv.*

cir·cum·stance (sûr′kəm stans′ *or, esp. Brit.,* -stəns), *n., v.,* **-stanced, -stanc·ing.** —*n.* **1.** a condition, detail, part, or attribute, with respect to time, place, manner, agent, etc., which accompanies, determines, or modifies a fact or event; a modifying or influencing factor: *Do not judge the act without considering all the circumstances.* **2.** Usually, **circumstances.** the existing conditions or state of affairs surrounding and affecting an agent: *Weather and other circumstances permitting, we sail on Monday.* **3.** an unessential accompaniment of any fact or event; secondary or accessory matter; minor detail: *The author dwells on circumstances rather than essentials.* **4. circumstances,** the condition or state of a person with respect to income and material welfare: *a family in reduced circumstances.* **5.** an incident or occurrence: *His arrival was a fortunate circumstance.* **6.** detailed or circuitous narration; specification of particulars: *The speaker expatiated with great circumstance upon his theme.* **7.** ceremonious accompaniment or display: *with great pomp and circumstance.* **8. under no circumstances,** regardless of events or conditions; never: *Under no circumstances should you see them again.* **9. under the circumstances,** because of the conditions; as the case stands: *Under the circumstances, there is little hope for an early settlement.* Also, **in the circumstances.** —*v.t.* **10.** to place in particular circumstances or relations: *He was favorably circumstanced by the rise in tariffs.* **11.** *Obs.* **a.** to furnish with details. **b.** to control or guide by circumstances. [ME < L *circumstantia* (*circumstant-,* s. of *circumstāns,* prp. of *circumstāre* to stand round), equiv. to *circum-* CIRCUM- + *stā-* stand + *-nt* prp. suffix + *-ia* n. suffix]

cir·cum·stanced (sûr′kəm stanst′ *or, esp. Brit.,* -stənst), *v.* **1.** pt. and pp. of **circumstance.** —*adj.* **2.** being in a condition, or state, esp. with respect to income and material welfare, as specified: *They were far better circumstanced than their neighbors.* [CIRCUMSTANCE + -ED[3]]

cir·cum·stan·tial (sûr′kəm stan′shəl), *adj.* **1.** of pertaining to, or derived from circumstances: *a circumstantial result.* **2.** of the nature of a circumstance, or unessential accompaniment; secondary; incidental: *of circumstantial importance.* **3.** dealing with or giving circumstances or details; detailed; particular: *a circumstantial report of a business conference.* **4.** pertaining to conditions of material welfare. [< L *circumstanti(a)* CIRCUMSTANCE + -AL[1]] —**cir′cum·stan′tial·ly,** *adv.*
—**Syn. 3.** minute, thorough, exact, precise, exhaustive, full.

cir′cumstan′tial ev′idence, proof of facts offered as evidence from which other facts are to be inferred (contrasted with *direct evidence*).

cir·cum·stan·ti·al·i·ty (sûr′kəm stan′shē al′i tē), *n., pl.* **-ties** for 2. **1.** quality of being circumstantial; minuteness; fullness of detail. **2.** a circumstance; a particular detail. [CIRCUMSTANTIAL + -ITY]

cir·cum·stan·ti·ate (sûr′kəm stan′shē āt′), *v.t.,* **-at·ed, -at·ing. 1.** to set forth or support with circumstances or particulars: *He produced documents to circumstantiate his evidence.* **2.** to describe fully or minutely: *He circumstantiated the accident.* [< L *circumstanti(a)* CIRCUMSTANCE + -ATE[1]] —**cir′cum·stan′ti·a′tion,** *n.*

cir·cum·val·late (sûr′kəm val′āt), *adj., v.,* **-lat·ed, -lat·ing.** —*adj.* **1.** surrounded by or as by a rampart. —*v.t.* **2.** to surround with or as with a rampart. [< L *circumvallāt(us)* (ptp. of *circumvallāre*), equiv. to *circum-* CIRCUM- + *vall(um)* rampart, wall + *-āt(us)* -ATE[1]] —**cir′cum·val·la′tion,** *n.*

cir·cum·vas·cu·lar (sûr′kəm vas′kyə lər), *adj. Bot., Zool.* around a vessel or duct. [CIRCUM- + VASCULAR]

cir·cum·vent (sûr′kəm vent′, sûr′kəm vent′), *v.t.* **1.** to surround or encompass, as by stratagem; entrap: *to circumvent a body of enemy troops.* **2.** to go around or bypass: *to circumvent the lake; The politician carefully circumvented the real issues.* **3.** to avoid (defeat, failure, unpleasantness, etc.) by artfulness or deception; avoid by anticipating or outwitting: *He circumvented their objection to the plan by having one of their own members propose it.* [< L *circumvent(us)* (ptp. of *circumvenīre* to come around, surround, oppress, defraud), equiv. to *circum-* CIRCUM- + *ven(īre)* (to) come + *-tus* ptp. suffix] —**cir′cum·vent′er, cir′cum·ven′tor,** *n.* —**cir′cum·ven′tion,** *n.* —**cir′cum·ven′tive,** *adj.*
—**Syn. 1.** encircle; ensnare.

cir·cum·vo·lu·tion (sûr′kəm və lo͞o′shən), *n.* **1.** the act of rolling or turning around: *planetary circumvolution.* **2.** a single complete turn or cycle. **3.** a winding or folding about something: *the circumvolutions of a boa.* **4.** a fold so wound: *the circumvolution of a snail shell.* **5.** a winding in a sinuous course; a sinuosity: *the circumvolutions of the river.* **6.** a roundabout course or procedure, or an instance of such: *The speaker's circumvolutions bored the audience to tears.* [< ML *circumvolūtiōn-* (s. of *circumvolūtiō*), equiv. to L *circumvolūt(us)* (ptp. of *circumvolvere* to CIRCUMVOLVE) *circum-* CIRCUM- + *volū-* ptp. s. of *volvere* to roll + *-tus* ptp. suffix) + *-iōn-* -ION] —**cir·cum·vo·lu·to·ry** (sur′kəm və lo͞o′tə rē), *adj.*

cir·cum·volve (sûr′kəm volv′), *v.t., v.i.,* **-volved, -volv·ing.** to revolve or wind about. [< L *circumvolv(ere),* equiv. to *circum-* CIRCUM- + *volvere* to roll]

cir·cus (sûr′kəs), *n., pl.* **-cus·es. 1.** a large public entertainment, typically presented in one or more very large tents, featuring exhibitions of pageantry, feats of skill and daring, performing animals, etc., interspersed throughout with the slapstick antics of clowns. Cf. **big top. 2.** a troupe of performers, esp. a traveling troupe, that presents such entertainments, together with officials, other employees, and the company's performing animals, traveling wagons, tents, cages, and equipment. **3.** a circular arena surrounded by tiers of seats, in which public entertainments are held; arena. **4.** (in ancient Rome) **a.** a large, usually oblong or oval, roofless enclosure, surrounded by tiers of seats rising one above another, for chariot races, public games, etc. **b.** an entertainment given in this Roman arena, as a chariot race, public game, etc.: *The Caesars appeased the public with bread and circuses.* **5.** anything resembling the Roman circus, or arena, as a natural amphitheater, a circular range of houses, etc. **6.** See **flying circus. 7.** *Brit.* an open circle, square, or plaza where several streets converge: *Piccadilly Circus.* **8.** uproar; a display of rowdy sport. **9.** *Obs.* a circlet or ring. [< L: ring, circle]

cir′cus make′-up, *Journalism.* a style of make-up for a newspaper page in which numerous assorted cuts, boxes, and type fonts are used to create startling, attention-getting effects.

Cir′cus Max′i·mus (mak′sə məs), the great ancient Roman circus between the Palatine and Aventine hills.

ci·ré (si rā′), *n.* **1.** a brilliant, highly glazed surface produced on fabrics by subjecting them to a wax, heat, and calendering treatment. **2.** a double fabric having such a finish. [< F < L *cērāt(us)* waxed, equiv. to *cēr(a)* wax + *-ātus* -ATE[1]]

Cir·e·na·i·ca (sir′ə nā′ə kə, sī′rə-; *It.* chē re nä′ē kä), *n.* Cyrenaica.

cire per·due (sēr′ per do͞o′, -dyo͞o′; *Fr.* sēr per-dy′), *Foundry.* See **lost-wax process.** [short for F *moulage à cire perdue* mold on lost wax]

cirque (sûrk), *n.* **1.** a circular space, esp. a natural amphitheater, as in mountains. **2.** *Literary.* a circle or ring of any kind. **3.** a circus. [< F < L *circ(us)* circle < Gk *kírkos* ring]

cir·rate (sir′āt), *adj. Bot., Zool.* having cirri. [< L *cirrāt(us),* equiv. to *cirr(us)* a curl + *-ātus* -ATE[1]]

cir·rho·sis (si rō′sis), *n. Pathol.* a disease of the liver characterized by increase of connective tissue and alteration in gross and microscopic make-up. [< Gk *kirrh(ós)* orange-tawny + -OSIS] —**cir·rhot·ic** (si rot′ik), *adj.* —**cir·rhosed′,** *adj.*

cirri-, var. of **cirro-.**

cir·ri·form (sir′ə fôrm′), *adj.* having the appearance or character of cirrus clouds. [CIRRI- + -FORM]

cir·ri·ped (sir′ə ped′), *n.* **1.** any crustacean of the order or group *Cirripedia,* typically having slender legs bearing bristles used in gathering food. —*adj.* **2.** having legs like cirri. **3.** belonging or pertaining to the *Cirripedia.* [CIRRI- + -PED]

cirro-, a combining form of **cirrus:** *cirro-stratus.* Also, **cirri-.**

cir·ro·cu·mu·lus (sir′ō kyo͞o′myə ləs), *n., pl.* **-lus.** *Meteorol.* a cloud of a class characterized by thin, white patches, each of which is composed of very small granules or ripples: of high altitude, about 20,000–40,000 feet. [CIRRO- + CUMULUS] —**cir′ro·cu′mu·lar, cir·ro·cu·mu·la·tive** (sir′ō kyo͞o′myə lā′tiv), **cir′ro·cu′mu·lous,** *adj.*

cirrocu′mulus castella′nus, *pl.* **cirrocumulus castellanus.** *Meteorol.* a cirrocumulus cloud having its summit shaped like a crenelated tower. Also, **cirrocumulus castellatus.**

cirrocu′mulus castella′tus, *pl.* **cirrocumulus castellatus.** *Meteorol.* See **cirrocumulus castellanus.**

cir′rocu′mulus floc′cus, *pl.* **cirrocumulus floccus.** *Meteorol.* a cirrocumulus cloud having its summit in the shape of small cumuliform tufts or masses.

cirrocu′mulus lenticular′is, *pl.* **cirrocumulus lenticularis.** *Meteorol.* a cirrocumulus cloud having sharply outlined lenticular shapes and sometimes showing irisation.

cirrocu′mulus stratifor′mis, *pl.* **cirrocumulus stratiformis.** *Meteorol.* a cirrocumulus cloud that is disposed in one or more long, horizontal layers that may be discontinuous.

cir·rose (sēr′ōs, si rōs′), *adj.* **1.** *Bot., Zool.* **a.** having a cirrus or cirri. **b.** resembling cirri. **2.** *Meteorol.* of the nature of cirrus clouds. Also, **cir·rous** (sir′əs). [< NL *cirrōs(us).* See CIRRO-, -OSE[1]] —**cir′rose·ly,** *adv.*

cir·ro·stra·tus (sir′ō strā′təs, -strat′əs), *n., pl.* **-tus.** *Meteorol.* a cloud of a class characterized by a composition of ice crystals and often by the production of halo phenomena and appearing as a whitish and usually somewhat fibrous veil, often covering the whole sky and sometimes so thin as to be hardly discernible: of high altitude, about 20,000–40,000 feet. [CIRRO- + STRATUS] —**cir′ro·stra′tive,** *adj.*

cir′rostra′tus fibra′tus, *pl.* **cirrostratus fibratus.** *Meteorol.* a cirrostratus cloud having a thin, striated or fibrous appearance. Also called **cirrostratus filosus.**

cir′rostra′tus filo′sus, *pl.* **cirrostratus filosus.** *Meteorol.* See **cirrostratus fibratus.**

cir′rostra′tus nebulo′sus, *pl.* **cirrostratus nebulosus.** *Meteorol.* a cirrostratus cloud having hazy and indistinct details.

cir·rus (sir′əs), *n., pl.* **cir·ri** (sir′ī) for 1, 2, **cir·rus** for 3. **1.** *Bot.* a tendril. **2.** *Zool.* a filament or slender appendage serving as a barbel, tentacle, foot, arm, etc. **3.** *Meteorol.* a cloud of a class characterized by thin white filaments or narrow bands and a composition of ice crystals: of high altitude, about 20,000–40,000 feet. [< L: a curl, tuft, plant filament like a tuft of hair]

cir′rus castella′nus, *pl.* **cirrus castellanus.** *Meteorol.* a cirrus cloud having its summit shaped like a crenelated tower. Also, **cirrus castellatus.**

cir′rus castella′tus, *pl.* **cirrus castellatus.** *Meteorol.* See **cirrus castellanus.**

cir′rus den′sus, *pl.* **cirrus densus.** *Meteorol.* See **cirrus spissatus.**

cir′rus fibra′tus, *pl.* **cirrus fibratus.** *Meteorol.* a cirrus cloud that is hairlike or striated in composition.

cir′rus floc′cus, *pl.* **cirrus floccus.** *Meteorol.* a cirrus cloud having its summit in the shape of small cumuliform tufts or masses.

cir′rus intor′tus, *pl.* **cirrus intortus.** *Meteorol.* a cirrus cloud whose filaments are very irregular and appear entangled.

cir′rus no′thus, *pl.* **cirrus nothus.** *Meteorol.* See **cirrus spissatus.**

cir′rus spissa′tus, *pl.* **cirrus spissatus.** *Meteorol.* a cirrus cloud characterized chiefly by density or opacity, formed from the top of a cumulonimbus cloud. Also called **cirrus densus, cirrus nothus, false cirrus, thunderstorm cirrus.**

cir′rus unci′nus, *pl.* **cirrus uncinus.** *Meteorol.* a cirrus cloud having hook-shaped elements.

cir·sec·to·my (sûr sek′tə mē), *n., pl.* **-mies.** *Surg.* excision of a section of a varix. [< Gk *kirsó(s)* (see CIRSOID) + -ECTOMY]

cir·soid (sûr′soid), *adj. Pathol.* varixlike; varicose. [< Gk *kirsoeid(ēs),* equiv. to *kirs(ós)* enlargement of a vein + *-oeidēs* -OID]

cis-, 1. an element occurring in loan words from Latin meaning "on the near side of" (*cisalpine*); on this model, used in the formation of compound words (*cisatlantic*). **2.** *Chem.* a specialization of this denoting a geometric isomer having a pair of identical atoms or groups attached on the same side of two atoms linked by a double bond. Cf. **trans-** (def. 2). [< L; akin to HERE]

cis·al·pine (sis al′pīn, -pin), *adj.* on this (the Roman or south) side of the Alps. [< L *Cisalpin(us),* equiv. to *cis-* CIS- + *Alpinus* ALPINE]

Cisal′pine Gaul′. See under **Gaul** (def. 1).

cis·at·lan·tic (sis′ət lan′tik), *adj.* on this (the speaker's or writer's) side of the Atlantic. [CIS- + ATLANTIC]

Cis·cau·ca·sia (sis′kô kā′zhə, -shə), *n.* the part of Caucasia north of the Caucasus Mountains. [CIS- + CAUCASIA]

cis·co (sis′kō), *n., pl.* **-coes, -cos.** any of several whitefishes of the genus *Coregonus,* found in the Great Lakes and smaller lakes of eastern North America. [< CanF *cisco(ette)* SISCOWET]

Cis·co (sis′kō), *n.* a town in central Texas. 4499 (1960).

ci·seaux (sē zō′), *n., pl.* **-seaux** (-zōz; -zō′). *Ballet.* a jump in which the dancer's legs are opened wide in the air and closed on landing. [< F: lit., scissors]

ci·se·lé (sē′zə lā′; *Fr.* sēzᵊ lā′), *adj.* noting or pertaining to velvet having a chiseled or embossed pattern produced by contrasting cut and uncut pile. [< F: chiseled (ptp. of *cisel(er)*; see CHISEL)]

ci·se·leur (sēzᵊ lœr′), *n., pl.* **-leurs** (-lœr′). *French.* a maker of metal ornaments for furniture. [lit., chiseler]

ci·se·lure (sēzᵊ lyr′), *n., pl.* **-lures** (-lyr′). *French.* **1.** the art or technique of chasing metal. **2.** a chased metal object.

cis·lu·nar (sis lo͞o′nər), *adj. Astron.* of or pertaining to the space between the earth and the orbit of the moon. [CIS- + LUNAR]

cis·mon·tane (sis mon′tān), *adj.* on this, esp. the north, side of the mountains. [< L *cismontān(us),* equiv. to *cis-* CIS- + *montānus* MONTANE]

cis·pa·dane (sis′pə dān′, sis pā′dān), *adj.* on this (the Roman or south) side of the Po River. [CIS- + LL *Padān(us),* equiv. to L *Pad(us)* the Po + *-ānus* -AN]

Cis·sae·a (si sē′ə), *n. Class. Myth.* an epithet of Athena, meaning "ivy goddess."

cis·sing (sis′ing), *n. Obs.* a preparatory operation in the graining of wood. [?]

$\theta = \pi/2$ $\theta = 0$

Cissoid (def. 1)

cis·soid (sis′oid), *Geom.* —*n.* **1.** a curve having a cusp at the origin and a point of inflection at infinity. Equation: $r = 2a\sin\theta\tan\theta$. —*adj.* **2.** *Rare.* included between the concave sides of two intersecting curves (opposed to *sistroid*): *a cissoid angle.* [< Gk *kissoeid(ēs),* equiv. to *kiss(ós)* ivy + *-oeid(ēs)* -OID] —**cis·soi′dal,** *adj.*

Cis·sy (sis′ē), *n.* a girl's given name, form of **Cecilia.** Also, **Sissie.**

cist[1] (sist), *n. Class. Antiq.* a box or chest, esp. for sacred utensils. [< L *cist(a)* < Gk *kístē* CHEST]

cist[2] (sist, kist), *n.* a prehistoric sepulchral tomb or casket. Also, **kist.** [< Welsh < L *cista.* See CIST[1]] —**cist′ed,** *adj.* —**cis′tic,** *adj.*

cis·ta·ceous (si stā′shəs), *adj.* belonging to the *Cistaceae,* or rockrose family of plants. [< Gk *kíst(os),* var. of *kísthos* rockrose + -ACEOUS]

Cis·ter·cian (si stûr′shən), *n.* **1.** a member of an order of monks and nuns founded in 1098 at Citeaux, near Dijon, France, under the rule of St. Benedict. —*adj.* **2.** of or pertaining to the Cistercians. [< ML *Cisterciān(us)* < L *Cisterci(um)* place name (now *Citeaux*) + *-ānus* -AN] —**Cis·ter′cian·ism,** *n.*

cis·tern (sis′tərn), *n.* **1.** a reservoir, tank, or vessel for storing or holding water or other liquid. **2.** *Anat.* a reservoir or receptacle of some natural fluid of the body. [ME *cistern(e)* < L *cistern(a),* equiv. to *cist(a)* (see CIST[1]) + *-erna* n. suffix]

cis·ter·na (si stûr′nə), *n., pl.* **-nae** (-nē). *Anat.* cistern (def. 2). [< NL < L] —**cis·ter′nal,** *adj.*

cis′tern barom′eter, a mercury barometer having the lower mercury surface of greater area than the upper. Also called **cup barometer.** Cf. **mercury barometer.**

cis·toph·o·rus (si stof′ər əs), *n., pl.* **-o·ri** (-ə rī′). a silver coin of western Asia Minor, first issued in the 2nd century B.C. as equal to three or four drachmas: under the Roman Empire, it became the monetary unit of western Asia Minor, equal to three denarii. [< L < Gk *kistophóros* < *kíst(ē)* chest + *-o-* -o- + *-phoros* -PHOROUS, after the basket engraved on it. See CIST[1]] —**cis·to·phor·ic** (sis′tə fôr′ik, -for′-), *adj.*

cist·vaen (kist′vīn, -vān), *n.* cist[2].

cit (chit), *n. Hinduism.* pure consciousness. Also, **chit.** Cf. **Sat-cit-ananda.**

cit., 1. citation. **2.** cited. **3.** citizen. **4.** citrate.

cit·a·del (sit′ə dᵊl, -ə del′), *n.* **1.** a fortress located in or near a city and intended to keep the inhabitants in subjection or to form a final point of defense during a siege. **2.** any strongly fortified place; stronghold. **3.** (formerly) a heavily armored structure on a warship, for protecting the engines, magazines, etc. [< MF *citadelle* < OIt *cittadell(a),* equiv. to *cittad(e)* CITY + *-ella* dim. suffix]

ci·ta·tion (sī tā′shən), *n.* **1.** the act of citing or quoting. **2.** the quoting of a passage, book, author, etc.; a reference to an authority or a precedent. **3.** a passage cited; quotation. **4.** mention or enumeration. **5.** a call or summons, esp. to appear in court. **6.** a document containing such a summons. **7.** *Mil.* mention of a soldier or a unit in orders, usually for gallantry: *Presidential citation.* **8.** any award or commendation, as for outstanding service, hard work, devotion to duty, etc., esp. a formal letter or statement recounting a person's achievements: *The firemen who had taken part in the rescue received a citation from the mayor.* [ME *citacio(u)n* < L *citātiōn-* (s. of *citātiō*), equiv. to *citāt(us)* (*citā-* CITE + *-tus* ptp. suffix) + *-iōn-* -ION] —**ci·ta·to·ry** (sī′tə tôr′ē, -tôr′ē), *adj.*

cite[1] (sīt), *v.t.,* **cit·ed, cit·ing. 1.** to quote (a passage, book, author, etc.), esp. as an authority: *He cited the Constitution in his defense.* **2.** to mention in support, proof, or confirmation; refer to as an example: *He cited* *many instances of abuse of power.* **3.** to summon officially or authoritatively to appear in court. **4.** to call to mind; recall: *citing my gratitude to him.* **5.** *Mil.* to mention (a soldier, unit, etc.) in orders, as for gallantry. **6.** to commend, as for outstanding service, hard work, devotion to duty, etc. **7.** to summon or call; rouse to action: *The king cited the warrior to the field of battle.* [late ME < eccl. L *cit(āre)* (to) summon before a church court; in L, to hurry, deriv. of *cit(us)* quick] —**cit′a·ble, cite′a·ble,** *adj.* —**cit′er,** *n.*

cite² (sīt), *n.* *Informal.* citation (def. 3). [by shortening]

Ci·thae·ron (si thēr′ən), *n.* *Class. Myth.* a savage murderer who threw himself and his brother, Helicon, over a precipice: both were changed into mountains.

Cith·aer·o·ni·an (sith′ə rō′nē ən), *n.* *Class. Myth.* Zeus: so called because Mount Cithaeron was sacred to him.

cith·a·ra (sith′ər ə), *n.* kithara. —**cith′a·rist,** *n.*

cith·er (sith′ər), *n.* cittern. Also, **cith·ern** (sith′ərn). [< L *cithar(a)* < Gk *kithára*]

cit·ied (sit′ēd), *adj.* **1.** occupied by a city or cities. **2.** formed into or like a city. [CITY + -ED³]

cit·i·fied (sit′i fīd′), *adj.* *Sometimes Disparaging.* having city habits, fashions, etc. Also, **cityfied.** [CITIFY + -ED²]

cit·i·fy (sit′i fī′), *v.t.,* **-fied, -fy·ing.** to cause to conform to city habits, fashions, etc. [CITY + -FY] —**cit′i·fi·ca′tion,** *n.*

cit·i·zen (sit′i zən, -sən), *n.* **1.** a native or naturalized member of a state or nation who owes allegiance to its government and is entitled to its protection (distinguished from *alien*). **2.** an inhabitant of a city or town, esp. one entitled to its privileges or franchises. **3.** an inhabitant, or denizen: *The deer is a citizen of our woods.* **4.** a civilian, as distinguished from a soldier, police officer, etc. Also, *referring to a woman,* **cit·i·zen·ess** (sit′i zə nis, -sə-). [ME *citesein* < AF *citesein,* OF *citeain* (with hiatus-filling *-s-*), equiv. to *cite* CITY + *-ain* -AN] —**cit′i·zen·ly,** *adj.*

cit·i·zen·ry (sit′i zən rē, -sən-), *n., pl.* **-ries.** citizens collectively. [CITIZEN + -RY]

cit′izens band′, federally designated frequencies for short-distance two-way radio communication between licensed individuals with mobile or base stations.

cit·i·zen·ship (sit′i zən ship′, -sən-), *n.* **1.** the state of being vested with the rights, privileges, and duties of a citizen. **2.** the character of an individual viewed as a member of society; behavior in terms of the duties, obligations, and functions of a citizen: *an award for good citizenship.* [CITIZEN + -SHIP]

cit′izenship pa′pers, *U.S.* the documents conferring citizenship on an alien. Cf. **first papers, second papers.**

Ci·tlal·te·petl (sē′tläl tā′petᵊl), *n.* Orizaba (def. 1).

cito disp., (in prescriptions) let it be dispensed quickly. [< L *cito dispensētur*]

cit·ole (sit′ōl, si tōl′), *n.* cittern. [ME < MF < L *cit(ara)* CITHER + MF *-ole* dim. suffix]

ci·toy·en (sē twa yaN′), *n., pl.* **-toy·ens** (-twa yaN′). *French.* citizen.

cit·ral (si′trəl), *n.* *Chem.* a pale yellow, water-insoluble, liquid aldehyde, $(CH_3)_2C{=}CH(CH_2)_2C(CH_3){=}CHCHO$, having a strong lemonlike odor, consisting in natural form of two isomers (**citral a** or **geranial** and **citral b** or **neral**), usually obtained from the oils of lemon and orange or synthetically: used chiefly in perfumery, flavoring, and the synthesis of vitamin A. [CITR(US) + -AL¹]

cit·range (si′trənj), *n.* **1.** a hybrid citrus tree produced by crossing the trifoliate orange and the sweet orange. **2.** the tart fruit of this tree. [CIT(RUS) + (O)RANGE]

cit·rate (si′trāt, sī′-), *n.* *Chem.* a salt or ester of citric acid. [CITR(IC) + -ATE²]

cit·re·ous (si′trē əs), *adj.* lemon-yellow; greenish-yellow. [< L *citreus* of the citrus tree]

cit·ric (si′trik), *adj.* *Chem.* of or derived from citric acid. [CITR(US) + -IC]

cit′ric ac′id, *Chem.* a white, crystalline, water-soluble powder, $HOOCCH_2(OH)C(COOH)CH_2COOH{\cdot}H_2O$, a tribasic acid having a strong acidic taste, an intermediate in the metabolism of carbohydrates occurring in many fruits, esp. limes and lemons, obtained by fermentation: used chiefly in the flavoring of beverages, confections, and pharmaceuticals.

cit·ri·cul·ture (si′trə kul′chər), *n.* the cultivation of citrus fruits. [CITR(US) + -I- + CULTURE] —**cit′ri·cul′tur·ist,** *n.*

cit·rin (si′trin), *n.* *Biochem.* See **vitamin P.** [CITR(US) + -IN²]

cit·rine (si′trēn, -trīn, -trin), *adj.* **1.** pale-yellow; lemon-colored. —*n.* **2.** a translucent, yellow variety of quartz, often sold as topaz; false topaz; topaz quartz. [CITR(US) + -INE¹]

cit·ron (si′trən), *n.* **1.** a pale-yellow fruit resembling the lemon but larger and with thicker rind, borne by a small tree or large bush, *Citrus medica,* allied to the lemon and lime. **2.** the tree itself. **3.** the rind of the fruit, candied and preserved. **4.** a grayish-green yellow color. —*adj.* **5.** having the color citron. [< MF < It *citron(e)* < L *citr(us)* + It *-one* aug. suffix]

cit·ro·na·lis (si′trə nā′lis), *n.* See **lemon verbena.** [< NL; see CITRON, -AL¹]

cit·ron·el·la (si′trə nel′ə), *n.* **1.** a fragrant grass, *Cymbopogon Nardus,* of southern Asia, cultivated as the source of citronella oil. **2.** See **citronella oil.** [< NL < F *citronelle,* equiv. to *citron* CITRON + *-elle* dim. suffix]

citronel′la cir′cuit, (*sometimes caps.*) a circuit of summer theaters; a strawhat circuit. [so called from the use of citronella oil to repel insects]

cit·ron·el·lal (si′trə nel′al), *n.* *Chem.* a colorless, slightly water-soluble liquid mixture of isometric aldehydes having the formula $C_9H_{17}CHO$, with a strong lemonlike odor, occurring in many essential oils, usually derived from lemon, citronella oil, and other oils: used chiefly as a flavoring agent and in the manufacture of perfume. [CITRONELL(A) + -AL³]

citronel′la oil′, a light-yellowish, pungent oil, distilled from citronella, used in the manufacture of liniment, perfume, and soap, and as an insect repellant. Also called **citronella.**

cit·ro·nel·lol (si′trə nel′ōl, -ôl, -ol), *n.* *Chem.* a clear, colorless liquid mixture of isomeric alcohols having the formula $C_9H_{17}CH_2OH$, usually obtained from an essential oil, as citronella oil, and having a roselike odor: used chiefly as a scent in the manufacture of perfume. [CITRONELL(A) + -OL¹]

cit′ron mel′on, *U.S.* a round, hard-fleshed watermelon, *Citrullus vulgaris citroides,* used for preserving.

cit′ron wood′, **1.** the wood of the citron. **2.** the wood of the sandarac.

ci·trov′o·rum fac′tor (si trov′ər əm), *Biochem.* See **folinic acid.** [< NL, equiv. to *citr(us)* CITRUS + *-o-* + *-vorum,* neut. sing. of L *-vorus* -VOROUS + FACTOR]

cit·rus (si′trəs), *n., pl.* **-rus·es** **1.** any rutaceous tree or shrub of the genus *Citrus,* which includes the citron, lemon, lime, orange, grapefruit, etc. —*adj.* **2.** Also, **cit′rous.** of or pertaining to such trees or shrubs. [< L: citrus tree, citron tree]

cit′rus fruit′, **1.** a fruit of any tree or shrub of the genus *Citrus,* as of the lemon or orange tree. **2.** such fruit collectively.

Cit·tà del Va·ti·ca·no (chēt-tä′ del vä′tē kä′nô), Italian name of **Vatican City.**

cit·tern (sit′ərn), *n.* an old musical instrument related to the guitar, having a flat, pear-shaped soundbox and wire strings. Also, **cither, cithern, citole, gittern, zittern.** [b. CITH(ER and GITT)ERN]

Cittern

cit·y (sit′ē), *n., pl.* **cit·ies.** **1.** a large or important town. **2.** *U.S.* an incorporated municipality, usually governed by a mayor and a board of aldermen or councilmen. **3.** the inhabitants of a city collectively: *The entire city is mourning his death.* **4.** *Canadian.* a municipality of high rank, usually based on population. **5.** *Brit.* a borough, usually the seat of a bishop, upon which the dignity of the title has been conferred by the Crown. **6. the City,** the commercial and financial area of London, England. **7.** city-state. [ME *cite* < OF *cite(t)* < L *cīvitāt-* (s. of *cīvitās*) citizenry, town, equiv. to *cīvi(s)* citizen + *-tāt-* -TY²] —**cit′y·less,** *adj.* —**cit′y·like′,** *adj.*
—**Syn. 1.** See **community.**

cit·y-born (sit′ē bôrn′), *adj.* born in a city.

cit·y-bred (sit′ē bred′), *adj.* reared in a city.

cit′y chick′en, breaded pieces of veal, pork, or other meat, usually braised and served on a skewer. Also called **mock chicken.**

cit′y coun′cil, a municipal body having legislative and administrative powers, such as passing ordinances, appropriating funds, etc.

cit′y desk′, a newspaper department responsible for editing local news.

Cit′y Diony′sia. See **Greater Dionysia.**

cit′y edi′tion, an early edition of a daily newspaper that is distributed for sale locally, usually following, or sometimes including, the edition mailed to out-of-town subscribers and distributors.

cit′y ed′itor, **1.** *U.S.* a newspaper editor in charge of local news and assignments to reporters. **2.** *Brit.* a newspaper or magazine editor in charge of the financial and commercial news.

cit′y fa′ther, one of the officials and prominent citizens of a city.

cit·y·fied (sit′i fīd′), *adj.* citified.

cit′y hall′, the administration building of a city government.

cit′y man′, *Brit.* a financier, esp. one employed in the banking firms of the City. Also, **Cit′y man′.**

cit′y man′ager, a person not publicly elected but appointed by a city council to manage a city.

Cit′y of Broth′erly Love′, Philadelphia, Pa. (used as a nickname.)

Cit′y of Da′vid, **1.** Jerusalem. II Sam. 5:6–7. **2.** Bethlehem. Luke 2:4.

Cit′y of God′, the New Jerusalem; heaven.

Cit′y of God′, The, a work in 22 books (A.D. 413–26) by St. Augustine of Hippo, expounding an early Christian view of society and history. Latin, **De Civitate Dei.**

Cit′y of Light′, Paris, France (used as a nickname).

Cit′y of Sev′en Hills′, Rome, Italy (used as a nickname).

cit′y plan′ning, the activity or profession of determining the future physical arrangement and condition of a community, involving an appraisal of the present condition, a forecast of future requirements, a plan for the fulfillment of these requirements, and proposals for a series of constructional, legal, and financial programs and provisions to implement the plan. Also called **town planning, urbanism.**

cit′y room′, **1.** the room in which local news is handled for a newspaper, a radio or television station, or for another journalistic agency. **2.** the editorial staff of this room.

cit·y·scape (sit′ē skāp′), *n.* **1.** a view of a city, esp. a large urban center: *The cityscape is impressive as one approaches New York from the sea.* **2.** a picture representing such a view or containing elements suggestive of such a view, as rectangular shapes of various proportions resembling the forms of buildings. [CITY + *-scape,* as in *landscape*]

cit′y slick′er, *Often Disparaging.* (in rural areas) a worldly, nattily dressed city dweller.

cit·y-state (sit′ē stāt′), *n.* a sovereign state consisting of an autonomous city with its dependencies.

cit·y·ward (sit′ē wərd), *adv.* to, toward, or in the direction of the city. Also, **cit′y·wards′.** [ME; see CITY, -WARD]

Ciu·dad Bo·lí·var (syōō thäth′ bô lē′vär), a port in E Venezuela, on the Orinoco River. 40,111 (est. 1955).

Ciu·dad del Car·men (syōō thäth′ thel kär′men), a city in SE Mexico, on the Gulf of Campeche. 21,154 (1960). Also called **Carmen.**

Ciu·dad Juá·rez (syōō thäth′ hwä′res), a city in N Mexico, across the Rio Grande from El Paso, Texas. 220,000 (est. 1958).

Ciu·dad O·bre·gón (syōō thäth′ ô vre gôn′), a city in W Mexico. 67,956 (1960).

Ciu·dad Tru·jil·lo (syōō thäth′ trōō hē′yô), the former name of the capital of the Dominican Republic: used from 1936 until 1961, when the original name, Santo Domingo, was restored.

Ciu·dad Vic·to·ria (syōō thäth′ bēk tô′ryä), a city in NE Mexico. 50,797 (1960).

Civ., **1.** civil. **2.** civilian.

civ·et (siv′it), *n.* **1.** a yellowish, unctuous substance with a strong musklike odor, obtained from a pouch in the genital region of civets and used in perfumery. **2.** any catlike, carnivorous mammal of the subfamily *Viverrinae,* of southern Asia and Africa, having glands in the genital region that secrete civet. **3.** any of various related or similar animals, as the palm civet. Also called **Civ′et cat′** (for defs. 2, 3). [< MF *civette* < It *zibett(o)* < Ar *zubād* civet perfume] —**civ′et·like′,** *adj.*

African civet, *Civettictis civetta* (Total length 4 ft.; tail 1½ ft.)

Civ·i·a (siv′ē ə), *n.* a girl's given name.

civ·ic (siv′ik), *adj.* **1.** of or pertaining to a city; municipal: *civic problems.* **2.** of or pertaining to citizenship; civil: *civic duties.* **3.** of citizens: *civic pride.* [< L *cīvic(us),* equiv. to *cīv(is)* citizen + *-icus* -IC] —**civ′i·cal·ly,** *adv.*

civ·ic-mind·ed (siv′ik mīn′did), *adj.* concerned with the well-being of the community. —**civ′ic-mind′ed·ly,** *adv.* —**civ′ic-mind′ed·ness,** *n.*

civ·ics (siv′iks), *n.* (*construed as sing.*) the science of civic affairs. [see CIVIC, -ICS]

civ·ies (siv′ēz), *n.pl.* *U.S. Informal.* civilian clothes, as distinguished from a military uniform. Also, **civvies.** [short for CIVI(LIAN CLOTH)ES]

civ·il (siv′əl), *adj.* **1.** of, pertaining to, or consisting of citizens: *civil life; civil society.* **2.** of the commonwealth or state: *civil affairs.* **3.** of citizens in their ordinary capacity, or of the ordinary life and affairs of citizens, as distinguished from military and ecclesiastical life and affairs. **4.** of the citizen as an individual: *civil liberty.* **5.** befitting a citizen: *a civil duty.* **6.** of, or in a condition of, social order or organized government; civilized: *civil peoples.* **7.** adhering to the norms of polite social intercourse; not deficient in common courtesy: *After their disagreement, their relations were civil rather than cordial. A lady is civil to everyone she meets.* **8.** marked by benevolence: *He was a very civil sort, and we liked him immediately.* **9.** (of divisions of time) legally recognized in the ordinary affairs of life: *the civil year.* **10.** *Law.* **a.** of or in agreement with Roman civil law. **b.** of the civil law, as the medieval and modern law derived from the Roman system. **c.** pertaining to the private rights of individuals and to legal proceedings connected with these (distinguished from *criminal*). [< L *cīvil(is),* equiv. to *cīv(is)* citizen + *-ilis* -IL] —**civ′il·ness,** *n.*
—**Syn. 7, 8.** respectful, deferential, gracious, complaisant, suave, affable, urbane, courtly. CIVIL, AFFABLE, COURTEOUS, POLITE all imply avoidance of rudeness toward others. CIVIL suggests a minimum of observance of social requirements. AFFABLE suggests ease of approach, often with a touch of condescension. COURTEOUS implies positive, dignified, sincere, and thoughtful consideration for others. POLITE implies habitual courtesy, arising from a consciousness of one's training and the demands of good manners. —**Ant. 7, 8.** boorish, churlish.

civ′il affairs′, civilian activities of a government subordinate to the occupation forces of a foreign power; governmental affairs pertaining to the civilian population of an area occupied by and under the control of the military forces of a foreign country: *the civil affairs branch of the army.*

civ′il day′, *Astron.* day (def. 3c).

civ′il death′, *Law.* loss or deprivation of civil rights, sometimes consequent of conviction of some grave crime or sentence of life imprisonment.

civ′il defense′, plans or activities organized by civilians and civilian authorities for the protection of civilian population and property in times of such disasters or emergencies as floods, war, etc.

civ′il disobe′dience, **1.** the refusal to obey certain governmental laws or demands for the purpose of influencing legislation or government policy, characterized by the employment of such nonviolent techniques as boycotting, picketing, and nonpayment of taxes. Cf. **noncooperation** (def. 2), **passive resistance.** **2.** (*caps., italics*) an essay (1848) by Thoreau.

civ′il engineer′, a person who designs public works, as roads, bridges, canals, dams, harbors, etc., or supervises their construction or maintenance.

civ′il engineer′ing, the work or profession of a civil engineer.

ci·vil·ian (si vil′yən), *n.* **1.** a person engaged in civil pursuits, as distinguished from a soldier, sailor, etc. **2.** a person versed in or studying Roman or civil law. —*adj.* **3.** of, pertaining to, formed by, or administered by a civilian or civilians. [late ME < L (*jūs*) *cīvīle* civil (law) + -IAN]

Civil′ian Conserva′tion Corps′. See CCC

civ·i·li·sa·tion (siv′ə li zā′shən), *n.* *Chiefly Brit.* civilization. —**civ′i·li·sa′tion·al,** *adj.*

civ·i·lise (siv′ə līz′), *v.t.,* **-lised, -lis·ing.** *Chiefly Brit.* civilize. —**civ′i·lis′a·ble,** *adj.* —**civ·i·lis·a·to·ry** (siv′ə lī′zə tôr′ē, -tōr′ē), *adj.* —**civ′i·lis′er,** *n.*

civ·i·lised (siv′ə līzd′), *adj.* *Chiefly Brit.* civilized. —**civ·i·lis·ed·ness** (siv′ə lī′zid nis, -līzd′-), *n.*

ci·vil·i·ty (si vil′i tē), *n., pl.* **-ties.** **1.** courtesy; politeness. **2.** a polite attention or expression: *an exchange of civilities.* **3.** *Archaic.* civilization; culture; good breeding. [late ME *civilite* < MF < L *cīvīlitāt-* (s. of *cīvīlitās*) courtesy. See CIVIL, -ITY]

civ·i·li·za·tion (siv′ə li zā′shən), *n.* **1.** an advanced state of human society, in which a high level of culture, science, industry, and government has been reached. **2.** those people or nations that have reached such a state. **3.** the type of culture, society, etc., of a specific place, time, or group: *Greek civilization.* **4.** the act or process of civilizing or being civilized: *Rome's civilization of barbaric tribes was admirable.* **5.** cultural refinement; refinement of thought and cultural appreciation: *The letters of Madame de Sévigné reveal her wit and civilization.* **6.** cities or populated areas in general, as opposed to unpopulated or wilderness areas: *The plane crashed in* *the jungle, hundreds of miles from civilization.* 7. modern comforts and conveniences, as made possible by science and technology: *After a week in the woods, without television or even running water, the campers looked forward to civilization again.* Also, *esp. Brit.,* **civilisation.** [CIVILIZE + -ATION] —**civ′i·li·za′tion·al,** *adj.*

civ·i·lize (siv′ə līz′), *v.t.,* **-lized, -liz·ing.** to make civil; bring out of a savage, uneducated, or rude state; elevate in social and private life; enlighten; refine: *Rome civilized the barbarians. His years in Paris civilized him.* Also, *esp. Brit.,* **civilise.** [CIVIL + -IZE] —**civ′i·liz′a·ble,** *adj.* —**civ·i·liz·a·to·ry** (siv′ə lī′zə tôr′ē, -tōr′ē), *adj.* —**civ′i·liz′er,** *n.*

civ·i·lized (siv′ə līzd′), *adj.* **1.** having an advanced culture, society, etc. **2.** polite; well-bred; refined. **3.** of or pertaining to civilized people: *The civilized world must fight ignorance.* Also, *esp. Brit.,* **civilised.** [CIVILIZE + -ED[2]] —**civ·i·liz·ed·ness** (siv′ə lī′zid nis, -līzd′-), *n.*

civ′il law′, 1. the body of laws of a state or nation regulating ordinary private matters, as distinct from laws regulating criminal, political, or military matters. **2.** *Rom. Hist.* the body of law proper to the city or state of Rome, as distinct from that common to all nations. Cf. **jus civile. 3.** the system of law derived from Roman law, as distinct from common law and canon or ecclesiastical law. —**civ′il-law′,** *adj.*

civ′il lib′erty, the liberty of an individual freely to exercise those rights guaranteed by the laws of a country.

civ′il list′, *Brit.* **1.** the annual list of moneys appropriated by Parliament to pay the expenses of the sovereign and the royal household. **2.** the annual list of moneys appropriated to pay the salaries of all members of the civil government; the payroll budget of the civil government.

civ·il·ly (siv′ə lē), *adv.* **1.** in accordance with civil law. **2.** politely; courteously. [CIVIL + -LY]

civ′il mar′riage, a marriage performed by a government official rather than a clergyman.

civ′il rights′, *(Often caps.) U.S.* **1.** rights to personal liberty established by the 13th and 14th Amendments to the U.S. Constitution and certain Congressional Acts, esp. as applied to an individual or a minority group. **2.** the rights to full legal, social, and economic equality extended to Negroes. —**civ·il-rights** (siv′əl rīts′), *adj.*

civ′il serv′ant, *Chiefly Brit.* a civil-service employee.

civ′il serv′ice, 1. those branches of public service concerned with all governmental functions outside the armed services. **2.** the body of persons employed in these branches. **3.** a system or method of appointing government employees on the basis of competitive examinations, rather than by political patronage.

civ′il war′, a war between political factions or regions within the same country. Cf. **American Civil War, English Civil War, Spanish Civil War.**

civ·ism (siv′iz əm), *n.* good citizenship. [< F *civisme* < L *cīv(is)* citizen + F *-isme* -ISM]

civ·vies (siv′ēz), *n.pl.* civies.

CJ, Chief Justice.

ck., 1. cask. **2.** check.

ckw., clockwise.

Cl, *Chem.* chlorine.

cl., 1. carload. **2.** Also, **cl** centiliter; centiliters. **3.** claim. **4.** class. **5.** classification. **6.** clause. **7.** clearance. **8.** clerk. **9.** cloth.

C/L, 1. carload. **2.** carload lot. **3.** cash letter.

c.l., 1. carload. **2.** carload lot. **3.** center line. **4.** civil law.

clab·ber (klab′ər), *n.* **1.** bonnyclabber. —*v.i.* **2.** (of milk) to become thick in souring. [< Ir *clabar* short for *bainne clabair* BONNYCLABBER]

clab·u·lar·i·um (klab′yə lâr′ē əm), *n., pl.* **-lar·i·a** (-lâr′ē ə). a large, sturdy wagon, drawn by eight or ten oxen or horses, used by the ancient Romans for hauling heavy loads. [< LL, neut. of *clabulārius,* equiv. to *clabulār(e)* transport-wagon + *-ius* adj. suffix]

cla·chan (klä′kʜən, klā′-), *n. Scot., Irish.* a small village or hamlet. [< ScotGael, equiv. to *clach* stone + *-an* dim. suffix]

clack (klak), *v.i.* **1.** to make a quick, sharp sound, or a succession of such sounds, as by striking or cracking: *The loom clacked busily under her expert hands.* **2.** to talk rapidly and continually, or with sharpness and abruptness; chatter. **3.** to cluck or cackle. —*v.t.* **4.** to utter by clacking. **5.** to cause to clack: *He clacked the cup against the saucer.* —*n.* **6.** a clacking sound. **7.** something that clacks, as a rattle. **8.** rapid, continual talk; chatter. **9.** *Slang.* the tongue. [ME *clack(en);* imit.] —**clack′er,** *n.*

Clack·man·nan (klak man′ən), *n.* a county in central Scotland. 41,391 (1961); 55 sq. mi. *Co. seat:* Clackmannan. Also called **Clack·man·nan·shire** (klak man′ən shēr′, -shər).

clack′ valve′, a valve having a hinged flap permitting flow only in the direction in which the flap opens. Also called **flap valve.**

Clac·to·ni·an (klak tō′nē ən), *adj.* of, pertaining to, or characteristic of a Lower Paleolithic culture in England marked by the production of tools made from stone flakes. [after *Clacton(-on-Sea),* English town where the tools were first unearthed + -IAN]

clad[1] (klad), *v.* a pt. and pp. of **clothe.** [ME *cladd(e),* OE *clāthod(e)* clothed. See CLOTHE]

clad[2] (klad), *v.t.,* **clad, clad·ding.** to bond a metal to (another metal), esp. to provide with a protective coat. [special use of CLAD[1]]

clad-, var. of **clado-** before a vowel.

cla·dan·thous (klə dan′thəs), *adj. Bot.* pleurocarpous. [CLAD- + -ANTHOUS]

clad·ding (klad′ing), *n.* **1.** the act or process of bonding one metal to another, usually to protect the inner metal from corrosion. **2.** metal bonded to an inner core of another metal. [CLAD[2] + -ING[1]]

clado-, a learned borrowing from Greek meaning "branch," used in the formation of compound words: *cladophyll.* Also, *esp. before a vowel,* **clad-.** [comb. form of Gk *kládos*]

clad·o·car·pous (klad′ə kär′pəs), *adj. Bot.* pleurocarpous. [CLADO- + -CARPOUS]

cla·doc·er·an (klə dos′ər ən), *n.* **1.** any or several small, transparent crustaceans of the order *Cladocera,* having the body covered by a bivalve shell from which the head and antennae extend. —*adj.* **2.** Also, **cla·doc·er·ous** (klə dos′ər əs). belonging or pertaining to the *Cladocera.* [< NL *Cladocer(a).* See CLADO-, CERO-, -AN]

clad·o·phyll (klad′ə fil), *n. Bot.* a leaflike flattened branch. Also called **clad·ode** (klad′ōd). [CLADO- + -PHYLL]

Cladophyll

clad·op·to·sis (klad′op tō′sis), *n. Bot.* the annual shedding of twigs or branches instead of leaves, as in certain cypresses. [CLADO- + PTOSIS]

Clai·borne (klā′bôrn, -bōrn), *n.* a boy's given name. Also, **Clayborn, Clayborne.**

claim (klām), *v.t.* **1.** to demand by or as by virtue of a right; demand as a right or as due: *to claim an estate by inheritance.* **2.** to assert and demand the recognition of (a right, title, possession, etc.); assert one's right to: *to claim payment.* **3.** to assert or maintain as a fact: *She claimed that he was telling the truth.* **4.** to require as due or fitting: *to claim respect.* —*n.* **5.** a demand for something as due; an assertion of a right or an alleged right: *He made unreasonable claims on the doctor's time.* **6.** an assertion of something as a fact: *He made no claims to originality.* **7.** a right to claim or demand; a just title to something: *His claim to the heavyweight title is disputed.* **8.** that which is claimed, esp. a piece of public land for which formal request is made for mining or other purposes. **9.** a payment demanded in accordance with an insurance policy, a workmen's compensation law, etc.: *We filed a claim for compensation from the company.* **10. lay claim to,** to declare oneself entitled to: *I have never laid claim to being an expert in this field.* [ME *claim(en)* < MF *claime(r)* < L *clāmāre* to cry out. See CLAMANT] —**claim′a·ble,** *adj.* —**claim′less,** *adj.*
—**Syn. 1.** See **demand. 5.** request, requisition, call.
—**Ant. 3.** deny.

claim·ant (klā′mənt), *n.* one who makes a claim. [CLAIM + -ANT]

claim·er (klā′mər), *n.* **1.** one who makes a claim; claimant. **2.** *Horse Racing Informal.* **a.** a horse participating in a claiming race. **b.** See **claiming race.** [ME; see CLAIM, -ER[1]]

claim′ing race′, *Horse Racing.* a race in which any horse entered can be purchased at a fixed price by anyone who has made a bid or claim before the start of the race. Cf. **selling race.**

claim-jump·er (clām′jum′pər), *n.* one who seizes another's claim of land. —**claim′-jump′ing,** *n.*

claims·man (klāmz′mən), *n., pl.* **-men.** an insurance adjuster, esp. one dealing with casualty-insurance claims. [*claims* (pl. of CLAIM) + MAN]

Clair (klâr; *Fr.* kleʀ), *n.* **1. Re·né** (rə nā′), born 1898, French motion-picture director and writer. **2.** Also, **Claire, Clare.** a boy's or girl's given name.

Clai·raut (klâ rō′; *Fr.* kle ʀō′), *n.* **1. A·le·xis Claude** (a lek sē′ klōd), 1713–65, French mathematician. **2.** a walled plain in the fourth quadrant of the face of the moon: about 57 miles in diameter.

Clairaut′ equa′tion, *Math.* a differential equation of the form, $y = xy' + f(y')$. [named after A. C. CLAIRAUT]

clair de lune (klâr′ dᵊlōōn′, də lōōn′), **1.** a pale-green color. **2.** a very pale blue color, tinged with lavender, used as a glaze on Chinese porcelain. **3.** porcelain glazed with this color. [< F: light of moon]

Claire (klâr), *n.* **1. Ina,** born 1892, U.S. actress. **2.** Also, **Clare, Clair.** a girl's given name, form of **Clara.**

Clair·seach (*Scot.* klâr′sakʜ, -səkʜ, klär′-), *n.* clarsach. —**clair′seach·er,** *n.*

Clair·ton (klâr′tᵊn), *n.* a city in SW Pennsylvania. 18,389 (1960).

clair·voy·ance (klâr voi′əns), *n.* **1.** the alleged supernatural power of seeing objects or actions removed in space or time from natural viewing. **2.** quick, intuitive knowledge of things and people; sagacity: *He owes his success as a broker to his acumen and clairvoyance.* [< F, equiv. to *clairvoy(ant)* CLAIRVOYANT + *-ance* -ANCE]
—**Syn. 2.** intuition, penetration, discernment, vision.

clair·voy·ant (klâr voi′ənt), *adj.* **1.** having the alleged supernatural power of seeing objects or actions beyond the range of natural vision. **2.** of, by, or pertaining to clairvoyance. —*n.* **3.** a clairvoyant person. [< F, equiv. to *clair* CLEAR + *voyant* seeing (*voi(r)* (to) see < L *vidēre*) + *-ant* -ANT)] —**clair·voy′ant·ly,** *adv.*

clam[1] (klam), *n., v.,* **clammed, clam·ming.** —*n.* **1.** any of various bivalve mollusks, esp. certain edible species. Cf. **quahog, soft-shell clam. 2.** *U.S. Informal.* a secretive or silent person. **3.** clamminess. **4.** *Slang.* a dollar or the sum of a dollar: *I only make 60 clams a week.* —*v.i.* **5.** to gather or dig clams. **6. clam up,** *Slang.* to restrain oneself from talking; withhold information: *The teacher asked who had thrown the eraser, but the class clammed up.* [short for clam-shell, i.e., bivalve with a shell that clamps. See CLAM[2], SHELL] —**clam′like′,** *adj.*

Clam[1] Genus *Anodonta*

clam[2] (klam), *n.* **1.** *Brit.* clamp[1] (defs. 1–3). **2.** *Mach. Rare.* pincers. [ME; OE, deriv. of *clamm* fetter, grasp; c. G *Klamm* fetter; akin to CLAMP[1]]

clam[3] (klam), *n., v.,* **clammed, clam·ming.** *Jazz.* —*n.* **1.** a wrong note or chord. —*v.i.* **2.** to play music inaccurately. [special use of CLAM[1]; so called from the number of wrong notes played at a CLAMBAKE]

cla·mant (klā′mənt), *adj.* **1.** clamorous; noisy. **2.** compelling or pressing; urgent: *a clamant need for reform.* [< L *clāmant-* (s. of *clāmāns,* prp. of *clāmāre* to cry out), equiv. to *clām-* (see CLAIM) + *-ant-* -ANT] —**cla′mant·ly,** *adv.*

clam·a·to·ri·al (klam′ə tôr′ē əl, -tôr′-), *adj.* of or pertaining to the *Clamatores,* a large group of passerine birds with relatively simple vocal organs and little power of song, as the flycatchers. [< NL *clāmātōr(es),* pl. of L *clāmātor* bawler, equiv. to *clāmāt(us)* (ptp. of *clāmāre* to cry out) + *-or* -OR[2] + -IAL]

clam·bake (klam′bāk′), *n. U.S.* **1.** a picnic at the seashore at which the baking of clams, usually on hot stones under seaweed, is a main feature. **2.** *Informal.* any social gathering, esp. a very noisy one. **3.** *Slang.* a bungled rehearsal, esp. of a radio program. **4.** *Jazz.* an informal or, sometimes, an unsuccessful jam session or performance. [CLAM[1] + BAKE]

clam·ber (klam′bər), *v.t., v.i.* **1.** to climb, using both feet and hands; climb with effort or difficulty. —*n.* **2.** the act or an instance of clambering. [late ME *clambre,* equiv. to *clamb-* (akin to CLIMB) + *-re* -ER[6]] —**clam′ber·er,** *n.*

clam·jam·fry (klam jam′frē, kläm jäm′-), *n. Scot. and North Eng.* **1.** the rabble; the mass of undistinguished people. **2.** a mob. **3.** insincere or impertinent talk. Also, **clam·jam′phrie.** [?]

clam·my (klam′ē), *adj.,* **-mi·er, -mi·est. 1.** covered with a cold, sticky moisture; cold and damp: *clammy hands.* **2.** sickly; morbid: *She had a clammy feeling that something was wrong at home.* [perh. < Flem *klammig;* akin to OE *clām* mud, clay; c. MD *klēm*] —**clam′mi·ly,** *adv.* —**clam′mi·ness,** *n.*

clam′my azal′ea. See **swamp azalea.** Also called **clam′my hon′eysuckle.**

clam′my lo′cust, a locust, *Robinia viscosa,* of the southeastern U.S., having glandular twigs and leaf stems.

clam·or[1] (klam′ər), *n.* **1.** a loud uproar, as from a crowd of people: *the clamor of the guests at a party.* **2.** a vehement expression of desire or dissatisfaction: *The clamor of the dissenting members broke up the meeting.* **3.** popular outcry: *The senators could not ignore the clamor against higher taxation.* **4.** any loud and continued noise: *the clamor of traffic; the clamor of birds and animals in the zoo.* —*v.i.* **5.** to make a clamor; raise an outcry. —*v.t.* **6.** to drive, force, put, etc., by clamoring: *The newspapers clamored him out of office.* **7.** to utter noisily: *They clamored their demands at the meeting.* **8.** *Obs.* to disturb with clamor. Also, *esp. Brit.,* **clam′our.** [ME *clamor* < L, equiv. to *clām-* (see CLAIM) + *-or* -OR[1]; ME *clamour* < MF < L *clāmōr-* (s. of *clāmor*)] —**clam′or·er, clam′or·ist;** *esp. Brit.,* **clam′our·er, clam′our·ist,** *n.*
—**Syn. 1.** shouting. **2.** vociferation. **4.** See **noise.**

clam·or[2] (klam′ər), *v.t. Obs.* to silence. [? sp. var. of *clammer,* obs. var. of CLAMBER in sense to clutch, hence reduce to silence]

clam·or·ous (klam′ər əs), *adj.* **1.** full of, marked by, or of the nature of clamor; vociferous; noisy. **2.** vigorous in demands or complaints. [CLAMOR[1] + -OUS] —**clam′or·ous·ly,** *adv.* —**clam′or·ous·ness,** *n.*

clamp[1] (klamp), *n.* **1.** a device, usually of some rigid material, for strengthening or supporting objects or fastening them together. **2.** an appliance with opposite sides or parts that may be adjusted or brought closer together to hold or compress something. **3.** one of a pair of movable pieces, made of lead or other soft material, for covering the jaws of a vise and enabling it to grasp without bruising. **4.** Also called **clamp′ rail′.** *Joinery.* a rail having a groove or a number of mortises for receiving the ends of a number of boards to bind them into a flat piece, as a drawing board or door. **5.** *Naut.* a horizontal timber in a wooden hull, secured to ribs to support deck beams and to provide longitudinal strength. **6.** *Naut.* See **mast clamp.** —*v.t.* **7.** to fasten with or fix in a clamp. **8. clamp down,** *Informal.* to impose or increase controls; become more strict with: *The government is clamping down on tax dodgers.* Also, **clamp down on.** [late ME (n.) < MD *clampe* clamp, cleat; c. MLG *klampe*]

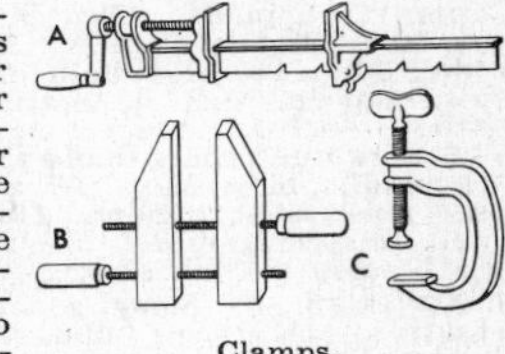

Clamps.
A, Bar clamp ; B, Hand screw clamp ; C, C clamp

clamp[2] (klamp), *v.i.* **1.** to tread heavily; clump. —*n.* **2.** a stack of dried raw bricks ready for burning. [imit.; akin to CLUMP]

clamp·down (klamp′doun′), *n.* crackdown. [n. use of v. phrase *clamp down*]

clamp·er (klam′pər, kläm′-), *n.* **1.** a clamp; pincer. **2.** a spiked metal plate worn on the sole of a shoe to prevent slipping on ice. [CLAMP[1] + -ER[1]]

clamp′ truck′, a vehicle, having parallel arms moving toward each other, for clasping and carrying large, solid objects.

clam·shell (klam′shel′), *n.* **1.** the shell of a clam. **2.** a dredging bucket opening at the bottom, consisting of two similar pieces hinged together at the top. **3.** *Print. Slang.* a platen press. [CLAM[1] + SHELL]

clam′shell door′, Often, **clamshell doors.** a door consisting of two panels that spread open vertically, often located on the underside of a cargo plane.

clam·worm (klam′wûrm′), *n.* any of several burrowing polychaete worms of the genus *Nereis,* used as bait for fishing. [CLAM[1] + WORM]

clan (klan), *n.* **1.** a group of families or households, as among the Scottish Highlanders, the heads of which claim descent from a common ancestor: *a meeting of the clan; the Mackenzie clan.* **2.** a group of people of common descent; family: *Our whole clan got together for Thanksgiving.* **3.** a group of people, as a clique, set, society, or party, esp. as united by some common trait, characteristic, or interest: *a clan of actors and directors.* **4.** *Anthropol.* **a.** the principal social unit of tribal organization, in which descent is reckoned usually in the maternal line. **b.** a group of people regarded as being descended from a common ancestor, real or mythological. [< ScotGael *clann* < OIr *cland* offspring < L *planta* scion, PLANT] —**clan′less,** *adj.*

clan·des·tine (klan des′tin), *adj.* characterized by, done in, or executed with secrecy or concealment, esp. for purposes of subversion or deception; private or surreptitious: *Their clandestine meetings went undiscovered for two years.* [< L *clandestin(us),* equiv. to *clam* secretly + *-des-* (deriv. of *diēs* day) + *-tinus* adj. suffix; see VESPERTINE] —**clan·des′tine·ly,** *adv.* —**clan·des′tine·ness, clan′des·tin′i·ty,** *n.*
—**Syn.** hidden, underhand, confidential, illicit. —**Ant.** open.

clang (klang), *v.i.* **1.** to give out a loud, resonant sound, as that produced by a large bell or two heavy pieces of metal striking together: *The spear clanged against the knight's armor.* **2.** to move with such sounds: *The old truck clanged down the street.* —*v.t.* **3.** to cause to resound or ring loudly. —*n.* **4.** a clanging sound. [< L *clang(ere)* (to) resound, clang]

CONCISE PRONUNCIATION KEY: *act, āble, dâre, ärt; ebb, ēqual; if, īce; hot, ōver, ôrder, oil, bo͝ok, o͞oze, out; up, ûrge; chief; sing; shoe; thin, that;* zh *as in measure.* ə = *a* as in *alone, e* as in *system, i* as in *easily, o* as in *gallop, u* as in *circus;* ᵊ as in *button* (butᵊn), *fire* (fīᵊr), *cradle* (krādᵊl). See the full key inside the front cover.

clang·or (klang′ər, klang′gər), *n.* **1.** a loud, resonant sound; clang. **2.** clamorous noise. —*v.i.* **3.** to make a clangor; clang. Also, *esp. Brit.*, **clang′our.** [< L: loud sound, noise, equiv. to *clang(ere)* (to) CLANG + -OR¹] —**clang′or·ous,** *adj.* —**clang′or·ous·ly,** *adv.*

clank (klangk), *n.* **1.** a sharp, hard, nonresonant sound, like that produced by two pieces of metal striking, one against the other: *the clank of chains; the clank of an iron gate slamming shut.* —*v.i.* **2.** to make such a sound. **3.** to move with such sounds: *The old jalopy clanked up the hill.* —*v.t.* **4.** to cause to make a sharp sound, as metal in collision: *He clanked the shovel against the pail.* [< D *klank* clinking sound] —**clank′ing·ly,** *adv.* —**clank′ing·ness,** *n.* —**clank′less,** *adj.*

clan·nish (klan′ish), *adj.* **1.** of, pertaining to, or characteristic of a clan. **2.** inclined to associate exclusively with the members of one's own group; cliquish. **3.** imbued with or influenced by the sentiments, prejudices, or the like, of a clan. [CLAN + -ISH¹] —**clan′nish·ly,** *adv.* —**clan′nish·ness,** *n.*

clans·man (klanz′mən), *n., pl.* **-men.** a member of a clan. [CLAN + 's¹ + MAN¹] —**clans′man·ship′,** *n.*

clans·wom·an (klanz′wo͝om′ən), *n., pl.* **-wom·en** (-wim′ən). a female clansman. [CLAN + 's + WOMAN]

Clan·ton (klan′tᵊn, -tən), *n.* a town in central Alabama. 5683 (1960).

clap¹ (klap), *v.,* **clapped, clap·ping,** *n.* —*v.t.* **1.** to strike (an object) against something quickly and forcefully, producing an abrupt, sharp sound, or a series of such sounds: *to clap a book on the table.* **2.** to strike the palms of (one's hands) against one another resoundingly, and usually repeatedly, esp. to express approval: *She clapped her hands in appreciation.* **3.** to strike (someone) amicably with a light, open-handed slap, as in greeting, encouragement, or the like: *He clapped his friend on the back.* **4.** to bring together forcefully (facing surfaces of the same object): *She clapped the book shut.* **5.** to applaud (a performance, speech, speaker, etc.) by clapping the hands: *The audience clapped the actors at the end of the act.* **6.** (of a bird) to flap or beat (the wings) so as to strike against one another or to whip noisily through the air. **7.** to put or place quickly or forcefully: *to clap a lid on a jar; She clapped her hand over his mouth. They clapped him in jail.* **8.** *Informal.* to make or arrange hastily (often fol. by *up* or *together*). —*v.i.* **9.** to make an abrupt, sharp sound, as of flat surfaces striking against one another: *The shutters clapped in the wind.* **10.** to move or strike with such a sound: *She clapped across the room in her slippers.* **11.** to clap the hands, as to express approval; applaud: *After the audience stopped clapping, the tenor sang two encores.* **12. clap eyes on.** See **eye** (def. 36). **13. clap hold of,** *Naut.* to take hold of. **14. clap on,** *Naut.* **a.** to attach. **b.** to set (additional sails). —*n.* **15.** the act or an instance of clapping. **16.** the abrupt, sharp sound produced by clapping. **17.** a resounding blow; slap. **18.** a loud and abrupt or explosive noise, as of thunder. **19.** a sudden stroke, blow, or act. **20.** clapper (def. 5). **21.** *Obs.* a sudden mishap. [ME *clapp(en),* OE *clæppan;* c. MLG *kleppen*]

clap² (klap), *n.* *Slang.* gonorrhea (often prec. by *the*). [akin to MF *clapoir* bubu, *clapier* brothel, OPr *clapier* warren]

clap·board (klab′ərd, klap′bōrd′, -bôrd′), *n.* **1.** *U.S.* a long, thin board, thicker along one edge than along the other, used in covering the outer walls of buildings, being laid horizontally, the thick edge of each board overlapping the thin edge of the board below it. **2.** *Brit.* a size of oak board used for making barrel staves and for wainscoting. **3.** *Motion Pictures.* clap-stick. —*adj.* **4.** of or made of clapboard: *a clapboard house.* —*v.t.* **5.** to cover with clapboards. [< MD *klap(holt)* clap-wood (see CLAP¹) + BOARD]

cla·po·tis (klə pō′tis; *Fr.* klA pô tē′), *n.* a standing wave phenomenon caused by the reflection of a wave train from a wall, breakwater, or steep beach. [< F: plashing]

clap·per (klap′ər), *n.* **1.** one who or that which claps. **2.** the tongue of a bell. **3.** *Slang.* the tongue. **4.** Usually, **clappers.** two flat sticks held between the fingers and struck rhythmically against each other to produce abrupt, sharp sounds. **5.** a wooden rattle used in medieval churches on the last three days of Holy Week, when it was customary for the church bells to remain silent. **6.** *Print. Slang.* a platen press. [CLAP¹ + -ER¹]

clap·per·claw (klap′ər klô′), *v.t.* *Archaic.* **1.** to claw or scratch with the hand and nails. **2.** to revile. [CLAPPER + CLAW] —**clap′per·claw′er,** *n.*

clap′per rail′, any of several long-billed rails, as *Rallus longirostris,* that have a harsh, cackling cry and are common on salt marshes of North America.

clap-stick (klap′stik′), *n.* *Motion Pictures.* one of a pair of hinged boards or sticks clapped together in front of the camera at the beginning or end of a scene, to register points for synchronizing the picture and sound track. Also, **clap′stick′.** Also called **clapboard.**

clapt (klapt), *v.* *Archaic.* pt. or pp. of **clap.**

clap·trap (klap′trap′), *n.* **1.** pretentious but insincere or empty language: *His speeches seem erudite, but analysis reveals them to be mere claptrap.* **2.** any artifice or expedient for winning applause or impressing the public: *He built his reputation by intrigue and claptrap.* [CLAP¹ + TRAP¹]

claque (klak), *n.* **1.** a group of persons hired to applaud an act or performer, as in a theater, night club, etc. **2.** any group of persons who bestow praise out of motives of self-interest; a group of sycophants. [< F, deriv. of *claquer* to clap]

cla·queur (kla kûr′; *Fr.* klA kœr′), *n., pl.* **cla·queurs** (kla kûrz′; *Fr.* klA kœr′). a member of a claque. Also, **claqu·er** (klak′ər). [< F, equiv. to *claque* CLAQUE + *-eur* -ER¹]

clar., clarinet.

Clar·a (klâr′ə, klar′ə), *n.* a girl's given name.

clar·a·bel·la (klar′ə bel′ə), *n.* an organ stop which gives soft, sweet tones. [< L, equiv. to *clāra,* fem. sing. of *clārus* clear + *bella,* fem. sing. of *bellus* beautiful]

Clar·a·belle (klâr′ə bel′, klar′-), *n.* a girl's given name.

clar·ain (klâr′ān), *n.* the coal forming the bright layers in banded bituminous coal. Cf. **durain, vitrain.** [< F < L *clār(us)* CLEAR, bright + F *-ain,* as in DURAIN]

Clar·a·mae (klâr′ə mā′, klar′-), *n.* a girl's given name.

Clar′a of As·si′si. See **Clare of Assisi.**

Clare (klâr), *n.* **1.** a county in W Republic of Ireland. 73,702 (1961); 1231 sq. mi. *Co. seat:* Ennis. **2.** Also, **Clair, Claire.** a boy's or girl's given name.

Clare·mont (klâr′mont), *n.* a city in W New Hampshire. 15,563 (1960).

Clare·more (klâr′mōr, -môr), *n.* a town in NE Oklahoma. 6639 (1960).

clar·ence (klar′əns), *n.* a closed, four-wheeled carriage, usually with a glass front, with seats inside for four persons. [named after Duke of *Clarence* (1765–1837), later William IV]

Clar·ence (klar′əns), *n.* a boy's given name.

Clar·en·don (klar′ən dən), *n.* **1. Edward Hyde, 1st Earl of,** 1609–74, British statesman and historian. **2. Council of,** the ecumenical council (1164) occasioned by the opposition of Thomas à Becket to Henry II. **3.** (*l.c.*) *Print.* a condensed form of printing type, like roman in outline but with thicker serifs.

Clar′endon Hills′, a town in NE Illinois. 5885 (1960).

Clare′ of As·si′si, Saint, 1194–1253, Italian nun: founder of the Franciscan order of nuns. Also, **Clara of Assisi.**

clar·et (klar′it), *n.* **1.** the red table wine produced in the Bordeaux region of France: originally it was light-red or yellowish. **2.** a similar wine made elsewhere: *California claret.* **3.** Also called **clar′et red′.** a deep purplish red. **4.** *Slang.* blood. —*adj.* **5.** deep purplish-red. [late ME < MF *(vin) claret* clearish (wine), equiv. to *clar-* CLEAR + *-et* -ISH¹]

clar′et cup′, an iced beverage made of claret and carbonated water with lemon juice, brandy, or other spirits, fruits, sugar, etc.

Cla·re·tian (kla rē′shən, klə-), *n.* *Rom. Cath. Ch.* **1.** a member of the "Congregation of the Missionary Sons of the Immaculate Heart of Mary," founded in Spain in 1849, and devoted chiefly to missionary work. —*adj.* **2.** of or pertaining to the Claretians. [after St. Anthony *Claret* (1807–70), founder of the order; see -IAN]

Clar·i·bel (klâr′ə bel′, klar′-), *n.* a girl's given name. Also, **Clarabelle.**

Clar·ice (klar′is; *Fr.* klA rēs′), *n.* a girl's given name, form of **Clara.**

cla·rif·i·cant (kla rif′ə kənt), *n.* *Chem.* any substance for clarifying a liquid. [< LL *clārificant-* (s. of *clārificāns*), prp. of *clārificāre.* See CLARIFY, -ANT]

clar·i·fy (klar′ə fī′), *v.,* **-fied, -fy·ing.** —*v.t.* **1.** to make (an idea, statement, etc.) clear or intelligible; to free from ambiguity: *After her professor clarified his statement, she understood what he had meant.* **2.** *Chem.* to remove solid matter from (a liquid). **3.** to free (the mind, intelligence, etc.) from confusion; revive: *The cold shower clarified his thoughts.* —*v.i.* **4.** to become clear, pure, or intelligible: *He was certain that the political situation would eventually clarify.* [late ME < MF *clarifi(er)* < LL *clārificāre,* equiv. to L *clār(us)* clear + *-ificāre* -IFY] —**clar′i·fi·ca′tion,** *n.* —**clar′i·fi′er,** *n.*

cla·rin (klə rēn′), *n.* a Mexican wind instrument similar to a trumpet. [< Sp: trumpet, prob. << OF *clarin.* See CLARINET, CLARION]

Cla·rin·da (klə rin′də), *n.* **1.** a town in SW Iowa. 4903 (1960). **2.** a girl's given name, form of **Clara.**

Clarinet

clar·i·net (klar′ə net′), *n.* a woodwind instrument in the form of a cylindrical tube with a single reed attached to its mouthpiece. Also, **clar·i·o·net** (klar′ē ə net′). [< F *clarinette,* equiv. to OF *clarin* clarion + *-ette* -ETTE] —**clar′i·net′ist, clar′i·net′tist,** *n.*

cla·ri·no (klə rē′nō), *n., pl.* **-ni** (-nē), **-nos.** a valveless trumpet used in the 17th and 18th centuries for playing rapid passages in the high register. Cf. **Bach trumpet.** Also called **clarin′ trum′pet.** [< It: trumpet, prob. < Sp *clarin* CLARIN]

clar·i·on (klar′ē ən), *adj.* **1.** clear and shrill: *the clarion call of a battle trumpet.* —*n.* **2.** an ancient trumpet with a curved shape. **3.** the sound of this instrument. **4.** any similar sound. [ME < ML *clāriōn-* (s. of *clāriō*) trumpet, equiv. to *clār-* CLEAR + *-iōn-* -ION]

Clar·i·on (klar′ē ən), *n.* **1.** a town in central Pennsylvania. 4958 (1960). **2.** a town in N Iowa. 3232 (1960).

Cla·ris·sa (klə ris′ə), *n.* a girl's given name, form of **Clara.**

Cla·ris·sa Har·lowe (klə ris′ə här′lō), an epistolary novel (1747–48) by Samuel Richardson.

clar·i·ty (klar′i tē), *n.* **1.** the state or quality of being clear or transparent to the eye; clearness; pellucidity: *the clarity of pure water.* **2.** clearness or lucidity as to perception or understanding; freedom from indistinctness or ambiguity: *a difficult proposition presented with such clarity that everyone understood.* [ME *clarite* < L *clāritās* (see CLEAR, -ITY); r. ME *clarte* < MF]

Clark (klärk), *n.* **1. Champ** (champ), (*James Beauchamp*), 1850–1921, U.S. political leader: Speaker of the House 1911–19. **2. George Rogers,** 1752–1818, U.S. soldier. **3. John Bates** (bāts), 1847–1938, U.S. economist and educator. **4. Mark Wayne,** born 1896, U.S. general. **5. Thomas Campbell** (*Tom*), born 1899, associate justice of the U.S. Supreme Court 1949–67. **6. Walter Van Til·burg** (van til′bərg), born 1909, U.S. author. **7. William,** 1770–1838, U.S. soldier and explorer (brother of George R. Clark). **8.** a boy's given name.

Clarke′ beam′ (klärk), *Carpentry.* a built-up beam composed of two or more planks bolted together one over the other and joined at their edges by smaller boards nailed diagonally edge-to-edge, the direction of those on one side being at right angles to the direction of those on the other.

Clarke's′ gazelle′, dibatag. [perh. after George S. Clarke, Baron Sydenham (1848–1933), English soldier and colonial administrator]

clark·i·a (klär′kē ə), *n.* any onagraceous herb of the genus *Clarkia,* of the western U.S., having narrow leaves and ornamental rose or purple flowers. [named after William CLARK; see -IA]

Clarks·burg (klärks′bûrg), *n.* a city in N West Virginia, on the Monongahela River. 28,112 (1960).

Clarks·dale (klärks′dāl′), *n.* a city in NW Mississippi. 21,105 (1960).

Clark's′ nut′crack·er, a nutcracker, *Nucifraga columbiana,* of western North America, having pale gray plumage and black and white wings and tail. Also, **Clark′ nut′cracker.** Also called **Clark's′ crow′.** [named after William CLARK; see NUTCRACKER]

Clarks′ Sum′mit (klärks), a town in NE Pennsylvania. 3693 (1960).

Clarks·ton (klärk′stən), *n.* a town in SE Washington. 6209 (1960).

Clarks·ville (klärks′vil), *n.* **1.** a city in N Tennessee. 22,021 (1960). **2.** a town in SE Indiana. 8088 (1960). **3.** a town in NW Arkansas. 3919 (1960). **4.** a town in NE Texas. 3851 (1960).

clar·o (klär′ō), *adj., n., pl.* **clar·os.** —*adj.* **1.** (of cigars) light-colored and, usually, mild. —*n.* **2.** such a cigar. [< Sp < L *clārus* CLEAR]

Clar·o·mon·tan·us (klar′ə mon tan′əs, -tā′nəs), *n.* the uncial codex, dating from the 6th century A.D., that contains the Pauline Epistles in Greek and Latin on facing pages. Cf. **codex** (def. 2). [< ML: lit., of *Clermont,* location of monastery which owned the codex]

clar·sach (klâr′saKH, klär′-), *n.* an ancient Irish and Scottish harp. Also, **clairseach, clar·seach** (klâr′saKH, -səKH, klär′-), **clar·sech, clar·seth** (klâr′səKH, klär′-). [< Gael *clairseach* harp, v. late ME (Scot) *clareschaw* < Gael]

clart (klärt), *v.t.* *Scot and North Eng.* to smear or spot with something sticky or dirty. [ME *-clarten* (in *biclarten* besmear) < ?]

clar·y (klâr′ē), *n., pl.* **clar·ies.** any of several plants of the genus *Salvia,* esp. *S. Sclarea,* grown as ornamentals. [late ME *(s)clar(re)y(e),* OE *slarege* < ML *sclareia*]

clash (klash), *v.i.* **1.** to make a loud, harsh noise: *The gears of the old car clashed and grated.* **2.** to collide, esp. noisily: *The cymbals clashed.* **3.** to conflict; disagree: *Their stories of the accident clashed completely.* **4.** (of juxtaposed colors) to be offensive to the eye. **5.** to engage in a physical conflict or contest, as in a game or a battle (often fol. by *with*): *The New York Yankees clash with the Chicago White Sox in the final game of the season. The rival street gangs continually clash.* —*v.t.* **6.** to strike with a resounding or violent collision: *He clashed his fist against the heavy door.* **7.** to produce (sound) by or as by collision: *The tower bell clashed its mournful note.* —*n.* **8.** a loud, harsh noise, as of a collision: *The automobiles collided with a terrible clash.* **9.** a collision, esp. a noisy one. **10.** a conflict; opposition, esp. of views or interests: *The clash between the miners and mine owners led to a strike.* **11.** a battle, fight, or skirmish. [b. CLAP¹ and DASH¹] —**clash′er,** *n.* —**clash′ing·ly,** *adv.*

—**Syn. 1.** clang, crash. **10.** disagreement, altercation, dispute. See **struggle.** —**Ant. 10.** agreement, cooperation.

Clash′ing Rocks′, *Class. Myth.* a pair of cliffs, supposedly at the entrance to the Black Sea, which clashed together whenever a ship tried to pass between them: the Argo successfully navigated the passage, whereupon they became fixed. Also called **Symplegades.**

-clasis, a learned borrowing from Greek meaning "a breaking," used in the formation of compound words: *thromboclasis.* [< NL < Gk *klásis*]

clasp (klasp, kläsp), *n.* **1.** a device, usually of metal, for fastening together two or more things or parts of the same thing: *a clasp for paper money; a clasp on a necklace.* **2.** a firm grasp or grip: *a clasp of hands.* **3.** a tight embrace: *She held the child in a loving clasp.* **4.** a small bar or metal design, as a star, for affixing to the ribbon of a military decoration to indicate that the bearer has been awarded the decoration an additional time. **5.** a tenaculum. —*v.t.* **6.** to fasten with or as with a clasp. **7.** to furnish with a clasp. **8.** to seize, grasp, or grip with the hand: *He clasped the club in his right hand.* **9.** to hold in a tight embrace; hug: *She clasped the child to her breast.* [ME < ?]

—**Syn. 1.** brooch, pin, clip, hook, catch. **3.** hug. **6.** clip, hook, catch. **8.** clutch.

clasp·er (klas′pər), *n.* **1.** one who or that which clasps. **2.** (in insects, fishes, crustaceans, etc.) one of the modified, usually paired organs or parts by which the male clasps the female during copulation. [CLASP + -ER¹]

clasp·ing (klas′ping, kläs′ping), *adj.* (of a leaf) partly or wholly surrounding the stem. [CLASP + -ING²]

clasp′ knife′, a large pocket knife having a blade or blades which may be folded into the handle.

claspt (klaspt, kläspt), *v.* *Archaic.* pt. or pp. of **clasp.**

class (klas, kläs), *n.* **1.** a number of persons or things regarded as forming a group by reason of common attributes, characteristics, qualities, or traits; kind; sort: *A class of objects used in daily living.* **2.** any division of persons or things according to rank or grade: *Do you know anything about second class hotels in France?* **3.** *U.S.* a number of pupils in a school, or of students in a college, pursuing the same studies, ranked together, or graduated in the same year: *He got his degree from Ohio State, class of '59.* **4.** a group of students meeting regularly to study a subject under the guidance of a teacher: *The class had arrived on time for the lecture.* **5.** the period during which a group of students meets for instruction. **6.** a meeting of a group of students for instruction. **7.** a classroom. **8.** *Brit. Univ.* any of three groups into which candidates for honors degrees are divided according to merit on the basis of final examinations. **9.** *Sociol.* a social stratum sharing basic economic, political, or cultural characteristics, and having the same social position: *Mexico has a growing middle class.* **10.** the system of dividing society; caste. **11.** social rank, esp. high rank. **12.** the members of a given group in society, regarded as a single entity. **13.** excellence; exceptional merit: *She's a good performer, but she lacks class.* **14.** *Slang.* elegance of dress and behavior: *His girl friend has real class.* **15.** any of several grades of accommodations available on ships, airplanes, and the like: *We bought tickets for first class.* **16.** drafted or conscripted soldiers, or men available for draft or conscription, all of whom were born in the same year. **17.** *Biol.* the usual major subdivision of a phylum or division in the classification of plants and animals, usually consisting of several orders. **18.** *Gram.* See **form class. 19.** *Eccles.* classis. **20.** (in early Methodism) one of several small companies, each composed of about 12 members under a leader, into which each society or congregation was divided. **21. in a class by itself** or **oneself,** having no peer; like no other; unequaled: *As a cook she was in a class by herself.*

22. the classes, the higher ranks of society, as distinguished from the masses. —*v.t.* **23.** to place or arrange in a class; classify: *to class justice with wisdom.* —*v.i.* **24.** to take or have a place in a particular class: *those who class as believers.* [earlier *classis,* pl. *classes* < L: class, division, fleet, army; sing. *class* back formation from pl.] —**class′a·ble,** *adj.* —**class′er,** *n.*

class., 1. classic. 2. classical. 3. classification 4. classified.

class′ ac′tion, a legal proceeding against a single party filed on behalf of all people having a common complaint. —**class′-ac′tion,** *adj.*

class·book (klas′bo͝ok′, kläs′-), *n. U.S.* **1.** a book kept by a teacher recording student attendance, grades, etc. **2.** a souvenir book produced by a graduating class, containing photographs, articles, etc. [CLASS + BOOK]

class′ con′flict. See **class struggle** (def. 1).

class′ con′sciousness, awareness of one's social or economic rank in society. —**class-con·scious** (klas′kon′shəs, kläs′-), *adj.*

class′ day′, (*sometimes cap.*) a day during the commencement season on which the members of the graduating class in American colleges and schools celebrate the completion of their course with special ceremonies.

clas·sic (klas′ik), *adj.* **1.** of the first or highest class or rank: *a classic piece of work.* **2.** serving as a standard, model, or guide: *the classic method of teaching arithmetic.* **3.** of or pertaining to Greek and Roman antiquity, esp. with reference to literature and art. **4.** modeled upon or imitating the style or thought of ancient Greece and Rome: *The 17th and 18th centuries were obsessed with classic ideals.* **5.** of or adhering to an established set of artistic or scientific standards or methods: *a classic example of mid-Victorian architecture.* **6.** basic; fundamental: *the classic positions of ballet.* **7.** of enduring interest, quality, or style: *a classic design; classic clothes.* **8.** of literary or historical renown: *the classic haunts of famous writers.* **9.** traditional or typical: *a classic comedy routine.* **10.** definitive: *the classic reference work on ornithology.* —*n.* **11.** an author or a literary production of the first rank, esp. in Greek or Latin: *Homer is a classic who is still exciting.* **12. the classics,** the literature of ancient Greece and Rome. **13.** an artist or artistic production considered a standard. **14.** a work that is honored as definitive in its field: *His handbook on mushrooms is a classic.* **15.** something noteworthy of its kind and worth remembering: *His reply was a classic.* **16.** an article, as of clothing, unchanging in style: *Her suit was a simple classic.* **17.** a sports event or contest that is usually held annually and is considered to be the most important of its kind: *The World Series is the fall classic of baseball.* **18.** *Archaic.* a classicist. Also, **classical** (for defs. 1–5, 8, 10). [< L *classicus* belonging to the first or highest class, equiv. to *class(is)* CLASS + *-icus* -IC]

clas·si·cal (klas′i kəl), *adj.* **1.** of, pertaining to, or characteristic of Greek and Roman antiquity: *The classical period.* **2.** (*cap.*) pertaining to or designating the style of the fine arts, esp. painting and sculpture, developed in Greece during the 5th and 4th centuries B.C., chiefly characterized by balanced composition, the separation of figures from an architectural background, and the naturalistic rendering of anatomical details, spatial movement, and distribution of weight in a figure. Cf. **archaic** (def. 3), **Hellenistic** (def. 5). **3.** *Archit.* **a.** noting or pertaining to the architecture of ancient Greece and Rome, esp. the religious and public architecture, characterized by the employment of orders. **b.** noting or pertaining to any of several styles of architecture closely imitating the architecture of ancient Greece or Rome; neoclassic. **c.** noting or pertaining to architectural details or motifs adapted from ancient Greek or Roman models. **d.** (of an architectural design) simple, reposeful, well-proportioned, or symmetrical in a manner suggesting the architecture of ancient Greece and Rome. **4.** conforming to ancient Greek and Roman models in literature or art, or to later systems modeled upon them. **5.** pertaining to or versed in the ancient classics: *a classical scholar.* **6.** marked by classicism: *classical simplicity.* **7.** of or pertaining to a style of literature and art characterized by conformity to established treatments, taste, or critical standards, and by attention to form with the general effect of regularity, simplicity, balance, proportion, and controlled emotion (opposed to *romantic*). **8.** *Music.* **a.** of, pertaining to, or constituting the formally and artistically more sophisticated and enduring types of music, as distinguished from popular and folk music and jazz. Classical music includes symphonies, operas, sonatas, song cycles, and lieder. **b.** of, pertaining to, characterized by, or adhering to the well-ordered, chiefly homophonic musical style of the latter half of the 18th and the early 19th centuries: *Haydn and Mozart are classical composers.* **9.** relating to or teaching academic branches of knowledge, as the humanities, general sciences, etc. (as distinguished from technical subjects). **10.** (of a given field of knowledge) accepted as standard and authoritative, as distinguished from novel or experimental: *classical physics.* **11.** *Eccles.* pertaining to a classis. [CLASSIC + -AL[1]] —**clas′si·cal′i·ty, clas′si·cal·ness,** *n.* —**clas′si·cal·ly,** *adv.*

clas′sical econom′ics, a system of economic thought developed by Adam Smith, Jeremy Bentham, Thomas Malthus, and David Ricardo, advocating minimum governmental intervention, free enterprise, and free trade, considering labor the source of wealth and dealing with problems concerning overpopulation. —**clas′sical econ′omist.**

clas′sical mechan′ics, *Physics.* the branch of mechanics that is based on Newton's laws of motion and that is applicable to systems that are so large that Planck's constant can be regarded as negligibly small (distinguished from *quantum mechanics*).

clas′sical Na′huatl, Aztec (def. 2).

clas′sical San′skrit, Sanskrit of an ancient period earlier than that of the Prakrits and later than Vedic.

clas·si·cism (klas′i siz′əm), *n.* **1.** the principles of classic literature and art. **2.** adherence to such principles. **3.** the classical style in literature and art, or adherence to its principles (contrasted with *romanticism*). Cf. **classical** (def. 7). **4.** a Greek or Latin idiom or form. **5.** classical scholarship or learning. Also, **clas·si·cal·ism** (klas′i kə liz′əm). [CLASSIC + -ISM] —**clas·si·cis·tic** (klas′i sis′tik), *adj.*

clas·si·cist (klas′i sist), *n.* **1.** a person who advocates study of the classics. **2.** an adherent of classicism in literature or art (contrast with *romanticist*). **3.** an authority on the classics; a classical scholar. Also, **clas·si·cal·ist** (klas′i kə list). [CLASSIC + -IST]

clas·si·cize (klas′i sīz′), *v.,* **-cized, -ciz·ing.** —*v.t.* **1.** to make classic. —*v.i.* **2.** to conform to the classic style. Also, *esp. Brit.,* **clas′si·cise′.** [CLASSIC + -IZE]

clas·si·fi·ca·tion (klas′ə fə kā′shən), *n.* **1.** the act of classifying. **2.** the result of classifying or being classified. **3.** one of the groups or classes into which things may be or have been classified. **4.** *Biol.* the assignment of plants and animals to groups within a system of categories distinguished by structure, origin, etc. The usual series of categories is *phylum* (in zoology) or *division* (in botany), *class, order, family, genus, species,* and *variety.* **5.** *U.S. Govt., Mil.* the category assigned to information, a document, etc., based on the degree of protection considered necessary to safeguard it from unauthorized use. **6.** *Library Science.* any of various systems for arranging books and other materials, esp. according to subject or format. [< L *classi(s)* CLASS + -FICATION] —**clas·si·fi·ca·to·ry** (klə sif′ə kə tôr′ē, -tōr′ē, klas′ə fə- *or, esp. Brit.,* klas′ə fə kā′tə rē), *adj.* —**clas′si·fi·ca′tion·al,** *adj.*

clas·si·fied (klas′ə fīd′), *adj.* **1.** arranged or distributed in classes or according to class. **2.** *U.S. Govt., Mil.* (of information, a document, etc.) **a.** bearing the classification *classified.* **b.** limited to persons authorized to use information, documents, etc., so classified. Cf. **classification** (def. 5). **3.** containing classified ads: *the classified section of a newspaper.* —*n.* **4.** See **classified ad.** [CLASSIFY + -ED[2]]

clas′sified ad′, an advertisement, published along with others of the same purpose in a particular section of a newspaper, magazine, etc., typically one column wide, set in small type, brief in text, without illustrations, and with a minimum of white space. Classified ads generally deal with offers of or requests for jobs, houses, apartments, used cars, and the like. Also called **classified, classified advertisement, want ad.**

clas′sified ad′vertising, 1. classified ads collectively. **2.** the business or practice of selling space in one or more publications to buyers of classified ads, including related activities, as writing, classifying into categories for the printer, etc. **3.** the department of a newspaper or other publication that handles classified advertising. **4.** the section of a publication in which classified ads appear; classifieds; want ads.

clas′sified advertise′ment. See **classified ad.**

clas·si·fi·er (klas′ə fī′ər), *n.* **1.** one who or that which classifies. **2.** *Chem.* a device for separating solids of different characteristics by controlled rates of settling. [CLASSIFY + -ER[1]]

clas·si·fy (klas′ə fī′), *v.t.,* **-fied, -fy·ing. 1.** to arrange or organize by classes; order according to class. **2.** *U.S. Govt., Mil.* **a.** to assign a classification to (information, a document, etc.). **b.** to limit the availability of (information, a document, etc.) to authorized persons. Cf. **classification** (def. 5). [< L *classi(s)* CLASS + -FY] —**clas′si·fi′a·ble,** *adj.*

class′ inclu′sion, *Logic.* the relation between two classes in which all members of one class are included in the other, as in the proposition "All men are animals."

clas·sis (klas′is), *n., pl.* **clas·ses** (klas′ēz). (in certain Reformed churches) **1.** the organization of pastors and elders which governs a group of local churches; a presbytery. **2.** the group of churches governed by such an organization. [< L: class]

class·less (klas′lis, kläs′-), *adj.* **1.** of or pertaining to a society in which there are no economic or social distinctions. **2.** (of an individual) not having membership in a social class or group. [CLASS + -LESS]

class·mate (klas′māt′, kläs′-), *n.* a member of the same class at a school or college. [CLASS + MATE[1]]

class′ mean′ing, *Gram.* **1.** the meaning of a grammatical category or a form class, common to all forms showing the category or to all members of the form class, as in the meaning of number common to all Latin nouns or the meaning of singular common to all Latin singular noun and verb forms. **2.** that part of the meaning of a linguistic form which it has by virtue of membership in a particular form class, as the past tense meaning of *ate.*

class′ num′ber, *Library Science.* a classification number on a book indicating its location on the shelves.

class′ rate′, the rate that a common carrier charges for transporting certain categories of goods.

class·room (klas′ro͞om′, -ro͝om′, kläs′-), *n.* a room in a school or college in which classes meet. [CLASS + ROOM]

class′ strug′gle, 1. Also called **class conflict.** conflict between different classes in a community resulting from different social or economic positions and reflecting opposed interests. **2.** Also called **class′ war′, class′ war′fare.** (in Marxist thought) the struggle for political and economic power carried on between capitalists and workers.

class·work (klas′wûrk′, kläs′-), *n.* **1.** the written or oral work done in a classroom by a student (distinguished from *homework*). **2.** the work done in a classroom by the students and teacher jointly. [CLASS + WORK]

class·y (klas′ē), *adj.,* **class·i·er, class·i·est.** *Slang.* of high class, rank, or grade; stylish; admirable. [CLASS + -Y[1]] —**class′i·ly,** *adv.* —**class′i·ness,** *n.*

clas·tic (klas′tik), *adj.* **1.** *Biol.* breaking up into fragments or separate portions; dividing into parts; causing or undergoing disruption or dissolution: *the clastic pole of an ovum; a clastic cell.* **2.** pertaining to an anatomical model made up of detachable pieces. **3.** *Geol.* noting or pertaining to rock or rocks composed of fragments or particles of older rocks or previously existing solid matter; fragmental. [< Gk *klast(ós)* broken in pieces (*klas-* var. s. of *klân* to break + *-tos* verbal adj. suffix) + -IC]

clath·rate (klath′rāt), *adj. Biol.* resembling a lattice; divided or marked like latticework. [< L *clāthrātus* (ptp. of *clāthrāre* to furnish with lattice) < Doric Gk *klâithron* a bar + *-ātus* -ATE[1]]

clat·ter (klat′ər), *v.i.* **1.** to make a loud, rattling sound, as that produced by hard objects striking rapidly one against the other: *The shutters clattered in the wind.* **2.** to move rapidly with such a sound: *The iron-wheeled cart clattered down the street.* **3.** to talk fast and noisily; chatter: *She clattered on and on about her children.* —*v.t.* **4.** to cause to clatter: *The maid clattered the pots and pans in the sink.* —*n.* **5.** a rattling noise or series of rattling noises: *The stagecoach made a terrible clatter going over the wooden bridge.* **6.** noisy disturbance; din; racket: *The clatter of the mob in the streets alarmed us.* **7.** noisy talk; din of voices: *They had to shout over the clatter at the cocktail party.* **8.** idle talk; gossip. [ME *claterin,* OE *clatr-* (in *clatrunge*), c. D *klateren* to rattle] —**clat′ter·er,** *n.* —**clat′ter·ing·ly,** *adv.* —**clat′ter·y,** *adj.*

claucht (klôKHt, kläKHt), *v.* a pt. of **cleek.**

Claude (klôd), *n.* a boy's given name. Also, **Claud.**

Clau·del (klō del′), *n.* **Paul (Louis Charles)** (pôl lwē sharl), 1868–1955, French diplomat, poet, and dramatist.

Clau·dette (klō det′; *Fr.* klō det′), *n.* a girl's given name.

Clau·di·a (klô′dē ə), *n.* a girl's given name.

Clau·di·a Quin·ta (klô′dē ə kwin′tə), *Rom. Legend.* a woman who freed a grounded ship transporting a statue of Cybele: according to soothsayers this feat was proof of chastity.

clau·di·cant (klô′də kənt), *adj. Obs.* limping; lame. [< L *claudicant-,* s. of *claudicāns* (prp. of *claudicāre*), equiv. to *claud(us)* lame, limping + *-ic-* intensive suffix + *-ant-* -ANT]

clau·di·ca·tion (klô′də kā′shən), *n.* a limp. [< L *claudicātiōn-* (s. of *claudicātiō*), equiv. to *claudic(āre)* (to) limp (see CLAUDICANT) + *-ātiōn-* -ATION]

Clau·dine (klō dēn′; *Fr.* klō dēn′), *n.* a girl's given name, form of **Claudia.**

Clau·di·us I (klô′dē əs), 10 B.C.–A.D. 54, Roman emperor A.D. 41–54.

Claudius II, ("*Gothicus*") A.D. 214–270, Roman emperor 268–270.

claught (klôKHt, kläKHt), *v.* a pt. of **cleek.**

clause (klôz), *n.* **1.** *Gram.* a syntactic construction containing a subject and predicate and forming part of a sentence or constituting a whole simple sentence. **2.** part of a written composition containing complete sense in itself, as a sentence or paragraph, now commonly limited to a distinct provision of a law, treaty, will, or other written document. [ME *claus(e)* < ML *clausa,* back formation from L *clausula* CLAUSULA] —**claus′al,** *adj.*

Clau·se·witz (klou′zə vits), *n.* **Karl von** (kärl fən), 1780–1831, German military officer and author of books on military science.

Clau·si·us (klou′zē əs *for defs. 1 and 2;* klô′- *for def. 2*), *n.* **1. Ru·dolf Jul·ius E·man·u·el** (ro͞o′dôlf jo͞ol′yəs i man′yo͞o əl; *Ger.* ro͞o′dôlf yo͞o′lē o͝os′ ā mä′no͞o el′), 1822–88, German mathematical physicist: pioneer in the field of thermodynamics. **2.** a crater in the third quadrant of the face of the moon: about 8 miles in diameter.

Clau′si·us cy′cle (klô′zē əs, klou′-). See **Rankine cycle.**

claus·thal·ite (klous′tə līt′), *n.* a rare mineral, lead selenide, PbSe, occurring in grayish, granular crystals that have a metallic luster. [named after *Clausthal* in Germany; see -ITE[1]]

claus·tral (klô′strəl), *adj.* cloistral; cloisterlike. [< LL *claustrālis,* equiv. to *claustr(um)* bolt barrier (*claus-* perf. s. of *claudere* to shut + *-trum* n. suffix of instrument) + *-ālis* -AL[1]]

claus′tral pri′or, a monk next in rank to an abbot.

claus·tro·phil·i·a (klô′strə fil′ē ə, -fēl′yə), *n. Psychiatry.* a pathological wish to be enclosed in a small space. [< L *claustro-* comb. form of *claustrum* (see CLAUSTRAL) + -PHILIA]

claus·tro·phobe (klô′strə fōb′), *n.* a person who suffers from claustrophobia. [*claustro-* (see CLAUSTROPHILIA) + -PHOBE]

claus·tro·pho·bi·a (klô′strə fō′bē ə), *n. Psychiatry.* an abnormal fear of enclosed or narrow places. [*claustro-* (see CLAUSTROPHILIA) + -PHOBIA] —**claus·tro·pho·bic** (klô′strə fō′bik, -fob′ik), *adj.*

clau·su·la (klô′zhə lə), *n., pl.* **-lae** (-lē′). *Music.* an ornamented cadence found esp. in early Renaissance music. [< L: a closing, conclusion, equiv. to *claus(us)* (ptp. of *claudere* to close) + *-ula* -ULE] —**clau′su·lar,** *adj.*

cla·va (klā′və, klä′-), *n., pl.* **cla·vae** (klā′vē, klä′vī). *Entomol.* the two or more enlarged distal segments that form the bulbous end of a clavate antenna. [< L *clāva* staff, club] —**cla′val,** *adj.*

cla·vate (klā′vāt), *adj.* club-shaped; claviform. [< NL *clāvātus,* equiv. to L *clāv(a)* club + *-ātus* -ATE[1]] —**cla′vate·ly,** *adv.*

clave[1] (klāv), *v. Archaic.* pt. of **cleave.**

cla·ve[2] (klä′vā), *n.* one of a pair of wooden sticks or blocks that are held one in each hand and are struck together to accompany music and dancing. [AmerSp, Sp: keystone < L *clāv(is)* key]

cla·ver (klā′vər, klä′-), *n. Scot. and North Eng.* idle talk; gossip. [?]

clav·i·cem·ba·lo (klav′i chem′bə lō′), *n., pl.* **-li** (-lē′). a harpsichord. [< It < ML *clāvicymbalum,* equiv. to L *clāvi(s)* key + *cymbalum* CYMBAL] —**clav′i·cem′bal·ist,** *n.*

Clavichord

clav·i·chord (klav′ə kôrd′), *n.* an early keyboard instrument producing a soft sound by means of metal blades attached to the inner ends of the keys gently striking the strings. [< ML *clāvichord(ium),* equiv. to L *clāvi(s)* key + *chord(a)* CHORD[2] + *-ium* n. suffix] —**clav′i·chord′ist,** *n.*

clav·i·cle (klav′ə kəl), *n. Anat., Zool.* **1.** a bone of the pectoral arch. **2.** (in man) either of two slender bones, each articulating with the sternum and a scapula and forming the anterior part of a shoulder; collarbone. See diag. under **shoulder.** [< ML *clāvicula* collarbone, in L, tendril, door-bolt, little key, equiv. to *clāvi(s)* key + *-cula* -CULE] —**cla·vic·u·lar** (klə vik′yə lər), *adj.* —**cla·vic·u·late** (klə vik′yə lāt′), *adj.*

clav·i·corn (klav′ə kôrn′), *adj.* **1.** having club-shaped antennae, as many beetles of the group *Clavicornia.* **2.** belonging or pertaining to the group *Clavicornia.* —*n.* **3.** a clavicorn beetle. [< NL *clāvicornis,* equiv. to L *clāv(a)* club + *-i-* + *-cornis,* comb. form of *cornū* horn]

clav·i·cyl·in·der (klav′i sil′in dər), *n.* a keyboard instrument consisting of thin glass rods that are set into vibration by a cylinder rubbing against them. [< G *Klavizylinder,* equiv. to *Klavi-* (< ML *clavi-,* deriv. of L *clāvis* key) + *cylinder* CYLINDER]

clav·i·cy·the·ri·um (klav′i sī thēr′ē əm), *n., pl.* **-the·ri·a** (-thēr′ē ə). upright harpsichord. [*clavi-* (see CLAVICYLINDER) + *cytherium*, deriv. of L *citara* CITHARA]

cla·vier[1] (klə vēr′, klav′ē ər, klā′vē-), *n.* the keyboard of a musical instrument. [< F: keyboard, in OF, key-holder, equiv. to L *clāvi(s)* key + *-ārius* -ARY]

cla·vier[2] (klə vēr′), *n.* any musical instrument having a keyboard, esp. a stringed keyboard instrument, as a harpsichord, clavichord, or piano. Also, **klavier.** [< G *Klavier* < F *clavier* keyboard; see CLAVIER[1]] —**cla·vier′ist,** *n.*

clav·i·form (klav′ə fôrm′), *adj.* club-shaped; clavate. [< L *clāv(a)* club + -I- + -FORM]

Cla·vi·us (klā′vē əs), *n.* a walled plain in the third quadrant of the face of the moon: about 145 miles in diameter.

clav·o·la (klav′ə lə), *n., pl.* **-lae** (-lē′). *Entomol.* **1.** the terminal, enlarged, usually club-shaped portion of a capitate, lamellate, or clavate antenna. **2.** flagellum (def. 3). [< NL, equiv. to L *clāv(a)* club + *-ola*, var. of *-ula* -ULE]

cla·vus (klā′vəs, klä′-), *n., pl.* **-vi** (-vī, -vē). **1.** *Psychiatry.* an intense headache in which the pain is likened to that which would be produced by a sharp object driven into the skull, often a symptom of hysteria. **2.** (in ancient Rome) a vertical stripe or band of purple worn on the tunic by senators and equites. **3.** *Entomol.* clavola. [<L: lit., nail; akin to *clandere* to close]

claw (klô), *n.* **1.** a sharp, usually curved, nail on the foot of an animal, as on a cat, dog, bird, etc. **2.** a similar curved process at the end of the leg of an insect. **3.** the pincerlike extremity of specific limbs of certain arthropods: *lobster claws.* **4.** any part or thing resembling a claw, as the cleft end of the head of a hammer. **5.** *Typography.* the hooklike projection from the right side of an *r* or from the bowl of a *g.* **6.** (in a motion-picture mechanism) a device having one or two teeth that hook into the perforations of a length of film and move it one frame at a time at any given speed. [ME; OE *clawu*, c. OHG *chlō(a)*, akin to D *klauw*, G *Klaue*] —*v.t.* **7.** to tear, scratch, seize, pull, etc., with or as with claws: *The kitten clawed my sweater to shreds.* **8.** to make by or as if by scratching, digging, etc. with hands or claws: *to claw a hole in the earth.* **9.** to proceed by or as by using the hands: *He clawed his way through the narrow tunnel.* —*v.i.* **10.** to scratch, tear, or dig with or as with claws: *The cat clawed and hissed in fear.* **11.** to make fumbling motions: *He clawed at the door. She clawed for the light switch.* **12.** *Scot.* to scratch gently, as to relieve itching. **13. claw off,** *Naut.* to beat to windward to avoid a lee shore or a navigational hazard. [ME *clawen*, OE *claw(i)an*, deriv. of *clawn* (n.); akin to D *klauwen*, G *klauen*] —**claw′er,** *n.* —**claw′less,** *adj.*

claw′-and-ball′ foot′ (klô′ən bôl′), *Furniture.* See **ball-and-claw foot.**

claw′ bar′, a crowbar having a bend at one end with a claw for pulling spikes.

claw′ foot′, **1.** a foot with claws. **2.** a representation of the claws of an animal or bird, esp. on the foot of a piece of furniture. **3.** a pathological distortion of the human foot, consisting chiefly of an abnormally high longitudinal arch.

claw′ ham′mer, **1.** a hammer having a head with one end curved and cleft for pulling out nails. **2.** *Informal.* a dress coat. —**claw′ham′mer,** *adj.*

claw′ hatch′et, a carpenter's hatchet having a claw at its back for pulling out nails.

Clax·ton (klaks′tən), *n.* a town in central Georgia. 2672 (1960).

clay[1] (klā), *n.* **1.** a natural earthy material which is plastic when wet, consisting essentially of hydrated silicates of aluminum: used for making bricks, pottery, etc. **2.** earth; mud. **3.** earth, esp. regarded as the material from which the human body was formed. **4.** the human body, esp. as distinguished from the soul; the flesh. **5.** human character as estimated according to fineness of constitution, endowments, etc.: *The saints and heroes seem of a different clay from most of us.* —*v.t.* **6.** to treat or mix with clay; cover, daub, or fill with clay. **7.** to filter through clay. [ME; OE *clǣg*, c. D, G *Klei*, akin to GLUE] —**clay′ey, clay′ish, clay′like′,** *adj.* —**clay′i·ness,** *n.*

clay[2] (klā), *n.* a lusterless serge having a rough texture. Also, **clay′ wor′sted.** [? short for *clay drab* clay-colored cloth]

Clay (klā), *n.* **1. Bertha M.** (*Charlotte Monica Braeme*), 1836–84, English author, originator of a long series of romantic novels. **2. Cas·sius Mar·cel·lus** (kash′əs mär sel′əs, kash′ē əs, kas′ē-), 1810–1903, U.S. anti-slavery leader and diplomat. **3. Henry,** 1777–1852, U.S. statesman and orator. **4. Lucius Du·Bi·gnon** (dōō′bin yon′; *Fr.* dy bē nyôn′), born 1897, U.S. general. **5.** a boy's given name.

clay·bank (klā′baŋk′), *n.* **1.** a yellow shade; dun; brownish-yellow. **2.** a horse of this color [CLAY[1] + BANK[1]]

Clay·born (klā′bôrn), *n.* a boy's given name. Also, **Claiborne, Clay′borne.**

Clay′ Cen′ter, a town in N Kansas. 4613 (1960).

clay′-col′ored spar′row (klā′kul′ərd), a sparrow, *Spizella pallida*, of western North America, having buff, brown, and white plumage with a pale gray breast.

clay′ court′, an outdoor tennis court having a clay surface. Cf. **grass court, hard court.**

clay′ flour′, *Ceram.* dried and pulverized clay.

clay′ min′eral, any of a group of minerals, hydrous aluminum silicates, that constitute the major portion of most clays.

clay·more (klā′mōr′, -môr′), *n.* **1.** a two-handed sword with a double-edged blade, used by Scottish Highlanders in the 16th century. **2.** (loosely) a Scottish broadsword with a basket hilt. [< ScotGael *claidheamh mōr* great sword]

clay·pan (klā′pan′), *n.* **1.** hardpan (def. 1). **2.** *Australian.* a shallow, normally dry depression in the ground that holds water after a heavy rain. [CLAY[1] + PAN[1]]

clay′ pig′eon, **1.** *Trapshooting, Skeet.* a disk of baked clay or other material hurled into the air from a trap as a target. **2.** *Slang.* a person in a situation where he can be taken advantage of by others.

Clay·pool (klā′pōōl′), *n.* a town in central Arizona. 2505 (1960).

clay′ stone′, *Obs.* **1.** a deeply decomposed igneous rock. **2.** argillite.

Clay·ton (klāt′ən), *n.* **1.** a city in E Missouri, near St. Louis. 15,245 (1960). **2.** a town in SW New Jersey. 4711 (1960). **3.** a town in NE New Mexico. 3314 (1960). **4.** a town in central North Carolina. 3302 (1960). **5.** a boy's given name.

Clay′ton Antitrust′ Act′, an act of Congress in 1914 supplementing the Sherman Antitrust Act and establishing the FTC.

Clay′ton-Bul′wer Trea′ty (klāt′ən bŏŏl′wər), an agreement between the U.S. and Great Britain in 1850 guaranteeing that any canal built to connect the Atlantic and Pacific across Central America would be jointly controlled, open to all nations, and unfortified. Cf. **Hay-Pauncefote Treaty.**

Clay′ton fern′. See **interrupted fern.**

clay·to·ni·a (klā tō′nē ə), *n.* any of the low, succulent, portulacaceous herbs of the genus *Claytonia.* [named after Dr. John *Clayton* (1693–1773), Virginia botanist; -IA]

-cle, var. of **-cule:** *cubicle.* [< L *-culus, -cula, -culum*; in some words, < F *-cle*]

Cle·a (klē′ə), *n.* a girl's given name, form of **Cleopatra.**

clean (klēn), *adj.* **1.** free from dirt; unsoiled; unstained: *She bathed and put on a clean dress.* **2.** free from foreign or extraneous matter: *clean sand.* **3.** *Physics.* **a.** (of a nuclear weapon) producing little or no radioactive fallout. **b.** not radioactive. **4.** free from defect or blemish: *a clean diamond.* **5.** unadulterated; pure: *clean water.* **6.** having few or no corrections; easily readable: *The author demanded clean proofs from the printer.* **7.** free from all writing or marking: *a clean sheet of paper.* **8.** free from encumbrances or obstructions: *a clean harbor.* **9.** characterized by a fresh, wholesome quality: *the clean smell of pine.* **10.** *Naut.* **a.** (of an anchorage, harbor, etc.) free of obstructions or hazards (opposed to *foul*). **b.** (of a hull form) having trim, fast lines. **c.** (of documents carried by a vessel in connection with its activities) free from qualifications or restrictions: *a clean bill of health.* **11.** free from roughness or irregularity: *He made a clean cut with a razor.* **12.** free from defilement; morally pure; innocent; upright; honorable: *He leads a clean life.* **13.** (of the legs of a horse) free from injury or blemish, as capped hocks, splints, scars, or the like. **14.** habitually free of dirt: *Cats are considered clean animals.* **15.** exhibiting regard for the practices of good sportsmanship: *a clean fighter.* **16.** *Chiefly Biblical.* having no physical or moral blemish or carrying no taboo so as to make impure according to the laws, esp. the dietary or ceremonial laws: *a clean animal; clean persons.* **17.** neatly or evenly made or proportioned; shapely; trim: *She has a clean profile.* **18.** not ornate; gracefully spare; forceful and simple: *a clean literary style; the clean lines of the church steeple.* **19.** *Slang.* skillful to a professional degree. **20.** *Slang.* not using narcotics. **21.** dexterously performed; adroit: *a clean serve in tennis.* **22.** (of a jump over an obstacle) made without touching the obstacle. **23.** made without any unanticipated difficulty or interference: *The bank robbers made a clean getaway.* **24.** complete; unqualified: *a clean break with tradition.* **25.** *Slang.* innocent of any crime. **26.** unobjectionable in language or concept; without obscenity: *It was a clean show for the whole family.* **27.** *Slang.* having no concealed weapons: *The cops frisked him, but he was clean.* **28.** *Slang.* without money or funds. **29. with clean hands.** See **clean hands.** —*adv.* **30.** in a clean manner; cleanly: *Nobody wants to box with him because he doesn't fight clean.* **31.** so as to be clean: *This shirt will never wash clean.* **32.** wholly; completely; quite: *The sharp carving knife sliced clean through the roast. In a year, he had gone clean through his inheritance. The thief got clean away.* **33. clean full,** *Naut.* **a.** (of a sail or sails) filled with wind; rap full. **b.** (of a sailing vessel) with all sails full of wind; rap full. **34. come clean,** *Slang.* to tell the truth, esp. to admit one's guilt: *After ten hours of questioning he finally came clean and confessed everything.* —*v.t.* **35.** to make clean: *Clean those dirty shoes.* **36.** *Slang.* to take away or win all or almost all of one's money from: *The cards were marked, and I got cleaned.* **37.** *Foundry.* to remove the seams from (a casting) by filing or grinding. **38.** *Philately.* to delete intentionally the cancellation from (a postage or revenue stamp). —*v.i.* **39.** to perform or undergo a process of cleaning: *This kind of fabric cleans easily. Detergents clean better than most soaps.* **40.** to get rid of dirt, soil, etc. (often fol. by *up*): *to clean for dinner.* **41. clean house,** to wipe out corruption, inefficiency, etc., as in an organization: *It's time for the city government to clean house.* **42. clean out, a.** to empty in order to straighten or clean. **b.** to use up; exhaust: *He had cleaned out his savings.* **c.** *U.S. Slang.* to drive out by force. **d.** *U.S. Informal.* to empty or rid (a place) of occupants, contents, etc.: *Eager customers cleaned out the store on the first day of the sale.* **43. clean up, a.** to wash or tidy up. **b.** to rid of undesirable elements or features: *They cleaned up the local bars.* **c.** to put an end to; finish: *to clean up yesterday's chores.* **d.** *U.S. Informal.* to make a large profit: *They cleaned up in the stock market.* [ME *clene*, OE *clǣne* pure, clear, c. OHG *kleini* (G *klein* small)] —**clean′a·ble,** *adj.* —**clean′ness,** *n.*

—**Syn. 1.** neat, immaculate. CLEAN, CLEAR, PURE refer to freedom from soiling, flaw, stain, or mixture. CLEAN refers esp. to freedom from soiling: *a clean shirt.* CLEAR refers particularly to freedom from flaw or blemish: *a clear pane of glass.* PURE refers esp. to freedom from mixture or stain: *a pure metal; not diluted but pure and full strength.* **4.** unblemished, flawless. **6.** legible. **12.** unsullied, chaste, virtuous. **32.** entirely, thoroughly. **35.** scour, scrub, sweep, brush, wipe, mop, dust, wash, rinse, lave, deterge, purify, clear; decontaminate. CLEAN, CLEANSE refer to removing dirt or impurities. TO CLEAN is the general word with no implication of method or means: *to clean windows, a kitchen, streets.* CLEANSE is esp. used of thorough cleaning by chemical or other technical process; figuratively it applies to moral or spiritual purification: *to cleanse parts of machinery, one's soul of guilt.* —**Ant. 1.** dirty. **3b.** contaminated, radioactive. **12.** impure. **35.** soil.

clean′ bill′ of health′, **1.** a certificate of health attesting the lack of a contagious disease. **2.** *Informal.* an assurance, esp. an official verdict by a committee, that a group or an individual has proved, under investigation, to be morally sound, fit for office, etc.

clean-cut (klēn′kut′), *adj.* **1.** having distinct, regular shape: *a face with clean-cut, almost sharp, features.* **2.** clearly outlined. **3.** firmly established; unmistakable: *The case against him is a clean-cut one.* **4.** neat and wholesome: *a polite, clean-cut lad.*

clean·er (klē′nər), *n.* **1.** a person who cleans, esp. one whose regular occupation is cleaning, as a dry cleaner, building cleaner, etc. **2.** an apparatus or machine for cleaning, as a vacuum cleaner. **3.** a preparation for use in cleaning, as a detergent or chemical bleach. **4.** the owner or operator of a dry-cleaning establishment: *The cleaner said he couldn't get the spot off my coat.* **5.** Usually, **cleaners.** a dry-cleaning establishment: *My suit is at the cleaners.* **6. take to the cleaners.** *Slang.* to cause to lose one's money or personal property: *He was taken to the cleaners in a card game last night.* [CLEAN + -ER[1]]

clean′er tooth′. See **raker tooth.**

clean-faced (klēn′fāst′), *adj.* having a clear, unblemished, or unsoiled face.

clean-hand·ed (klēn′han′did), *adj.* free from wrongdoing; guiltless. —**clean′hand′ed·ness,** *n.*

clean′ hands′, honesty; innocence; guiltlessness: *He came out of the bribery investigation triumphantly when it was proved that he had clean hands.*

clean·ing (klē′niŋ), *n.* **1.** *Slang.* **a.** an overwhelming defeat, esp. in sports (often prec. by *take*): *His team took a cleaning last night, losing by a wide margin.* **b.** an outright or complete financial loss (often prec. by *good*): *Speculators gave the company a good cleaning.* **2.** *Informal.* killing (def. 3). **3. cleanings,** refuse gathered or collected together in making a thing or place clean; sweepings. **4.** the removal of undesirable young trees in a stand. [CLEAN + -ING[1]]

clean′ing wom′an, a woman employed to sweep, mop, or do general cleaning in a house, office, hotel, or the like. Also called **clean′ing la′dy.**

clean-limbed (klēn′limd′), *adj.* having slender, well-proportioned arms and legs: *a clean-limbed athlete.*

clean-liv·ing (klēn′liv′iŋ), *adj.* conducting one's life so as to be beyond moral reproach: *He's a clean-living young fellow.*

clean·ly (*adj.* klen′lē; *adv.* klēn′lē), *adj.,* **-li·er, -li·est,** *adv.* —*adj.* **1.** personally neat; careful to keep or make clean: *The cat is by nature a cleanly animal.* **2.** habitually clean manner. [ME *clenlich(e)*, OE *clǣnlic*, equiv. to *clǣne* CLEAN + *-lic* -LY] —**clean·li·ness** (klen′lē nis), *n.*

clean·out (klēn′out′), *n.* an opening or passage giving access to a place that requires occasional cleaning, as a soil pipe. [n. use of v. phrase *clean out*]

cleanse (klenz), *v.,* **cleansed, cleans·ing.** —*v.t.* **1.** to make clean. **2.** to remove by, or as by, cleaning: *to cleanse sin from the soul.* —*v.i.* **3.** to become clean: *These spoons cleanse without much difficulty.* [ME *clensen*, OE *clǣnsian*, equiv. to *clǣne* CLEAN + *-si* v. suffix + *-an* inf. suffix] —**cleans′a·ble,** *adj.*
—**Syn. 1.** See **clean.**

cleans·er (klen′zər), *n.* **1.** a liquid or powdered preparation for cleansing, esp. for scouring bathtubs, kitchen sinks, etc. **2.** one who or that which cleanses. **3.** a person who cleanses something, esp. as part of a manufacturing process. **4.** *Chiefly Eastern New Eng.* a dry-cleaning establishment. [CLEANSE + -ER[1]]

clean-shav·en (klēn′shā′vən), *adj.* (of men) having the beard and mustache shaved off.

cleans′ing tis′sue, a piece of absorbent paper, used esp. for removing cleansing cream and cosmetics and also serving as a disposable handkerchief.

clean-skin (klēn′skin′), *n.* *Australian.* an unbranded range animal of any age.

Cle·anth (klē′anth), *n.* a boy's given name.

Cle·an·tha (klē an′thə), *n.* a girl's given name.

Cle·an·thes (klē an′thēz), *n.* c300–232? B.C., Greek Stoic philosopher.

clean·up (klēn′up′), *n.* **1.** act or process of cleaning up, esp. of gambling, vice, graft, etc. **2.** *Slang.* a very large profit: *The company made a real cleanup on their new invention.* **3.** *Baseball Slang.* **a.** the fourth position in the batting order: *Mantle is batting cleanup today.* **b.** the player who bats in this position. [n. use of v. phrase *clean up*]

clear (klēr), *adj.* **1.** free from darkness, obscurity, or cloudiness; light: *a clear day.* **2.** bright; shining: *a clear flame.* **3.** transparent; pellucid: *good, clear water.* **4.** of a pure, even color: *a clear yellow.* **5.** without discoloration, defect, or blemish: *a clear complexion; a clear pane of glass.* **6.** easily seen; sharply defined: *a clear outline.* **7.** distinctly perceptible to the ear; easily heard: *a clear sound.* **8.** free from hoarse, harsh, or rasping qualities: *a clear voice; clear as a bell.* **9.** easily understood; without ambiguity: *clear, concise answers.* **10.** entirely comprehensible; completely understood: *The ultimate causes of war may never be clear.* **11.** distinct; evident; plain: *a clear case of misbehavior.* **12.** free from confusion, uncertainty, or doubt: *clear thinking.* **13.** perceiving or discerning distinctly: *a clear mind.* **14.** convinced; certain: *He was not clear on the first point that she made but agreed with the others.* **15.** free from anything that would disturb or blame: *a clear conscience.* **16.** free from suspicion of guilt or complicity: *She was entirely clear of the crime until one of her accomplices turned informer.* **17.** serene; calm; untroubled: *a clear brow.* **18.** free from obstructions or obstacles; open: *a clear view; a clear road.* **19.** free from entanglement or contact; away from: *He kept clear of her after the argument. She managed to keep her dress clear of the mud.* **20.** (of tree trunks or timber) free from branches, knots, or other protruding or rough parts: *The trunk was clear for 20 feet above the ground.* **21.** freed or emptied of contents, cargo, etc. **22.** without limitation or qualification; absolute: *a clear victory.* **23.** free from obligation, liability, or debt: *After twenty years, our house is clear of the mortgage. Municipal bonds return as much as 4 percent, clear of taxes.* **24.** without deduction or diminution: *a clear $1000 after taxes.* **25.** (in cryptography) not coded or enciphered. Cf. **plain text.** **26.** *Phonet.* **a.** (of an *l*-sound) having front-vowel resonance; situated before a vowel in the same syllable. Cf. **dark** (def. 14a). **b.** (of a speech sound) produced without frication or aspiration. **27.** *Obs.* illustrious. —*adv.* **28.** in a clear or distinct manner; clearly. **29.** entirely; completely; clean: *to cut a piece clear off; to climb clear to the top; to run clear off the road.* —*v.t.* **30.** to make clear, transparent, or pellucid; free from cloudiness or impurities: *to clear a liquid by means of a filter.* **31.** to make free of confusion, doubt, or uncertainty: *He spoke to his fiancée to clear his mind about their relationship.* **32.** to make understandable or lucid; free from ambiguity or obscurity: *He rephrased the report in order to clear the essential points.* **33.** to remove people or objects from (usually fol. by *of*): *to clear a courtroom of photographers; to clear the table of dishes.* **34.** to remove (people or objects) (usually fol. by *from*): *to clear the photographers from the courtroom; to clear the dishes from the table.* **35.** (of a commodity) to buy up or sell out the existing supply of: *Bidders quickly cleared the market's wheat stores. The store must clear its winter inventories by April 1st.* **36.** to make (a path, road, etc.) by removing any obstruction: *He had to cut away the underbrush to clear a path.* **37.** to eat all the food on: *to clear one's plate.* **38.** to remove from (the brow) any traces of tension or anxiety, as folds or wrinkles. **39.** to relieve (the throat) of some obstruction, as phlegm, by forcing air through the larynx, usually producing a rasping sound. **40.** to make a similar rasping noise in (the throat), as to express disapproval or to attract attention. **41.** to free of anything defamatory or discrediting: *to clear one's name.* **42.** to free from suspicion, accusation, or imputation of guilt; prove or declare innocent: *The jury cleared the defendant of the charge.* **43.** to pass by or over without contact or entanglement: *The ship cleared the reef. The fisherman cleared his line.* **44.** to pass through or away from: *The ship cleared the tunnel. The bill cleared the Senate.* **45.** to pay (a debt) in full. **46.** to pass (checks or other commercial paper) through a clearing house. **47.** (of mail, telephone calls, etc.) to process, handle, reroute, etc.: *The dispatcher clears hundreds of items each day.* **48.** to free from debt: *Just a few dollars more would clear him. The widow had to borrow money to clear her husband's estate.* **49.** to gain as clear profit: *to clear $1,000 in a transaction.* **50.** to free (a ship, cargo, etc.) from legal detention at a port by satisfying customs and other requirements. **51.** to receive authorization before taking action on: *You must clear your plan with headquarters.* **52.** to give clearance to; authorize: *The chairman must clear our speeches before the meeting.* **53.** *Govt., Mil.* to authorize (a person, agency, etc.) to use classified information, documents, etc.: *He has finally been cleared for highly classified information.* **54.** *U.S.* to try or otherwise dispose of (the cases awaiting court action): *to clear the docket.* **55.** *Bridge.* to establish one or more winning cards in (a given suit) by leading the suit until all the outstanding cards have been drawn: *He cleared the heart suit before attacking spades.* —*v.i.* **56.** to become clear. **57.** to exchange checks and bills, and settle balances, as in a clearing house. **58.** (of a ship) **a.** to comply with customs and other requirements legally imposed on entering or leaving a port (often fol. by *in* or *out*). **b.** to leave port after having complied with such requirements. **59.** to become free from doubt, anxiety, misunderstanding, etc.: *His mind cleared when he heard the truth.* **60.** (of a commodity for sale) to sell out; become bought out: *Wheat cleared rapidly.* **61.** to pass an authority for review, approval, etc.: *The bill must clear through the assembly before it becomes legal.* **62.** to remove dishes, food, etc., from a table following a meal: *Is it my turn to clear?* **63. clear away** or **off, a.** to remove in order to make room. **b.** to leave; escape: *We were warned to clear off before the floods came.* **c.** to disappear; vanish: *When the smoke cleared away, we saw that the house was in ruins.* **64. clear out, a.** to clean; remove. **b.** to go away, esp. quickly or abruptly. **c.** *Informal.* to drive or force out: *The police cleared out the pickets by force.* **65. clear up, a.** to make clear; explain; solve. **b.** to put in order; tidy up. **c.** to become better or brighter, as the weather: *It is beginning to clear up, so we can go out.* —*n.* **66.** a clear or unobstructed space. **67.** See **plain text. 68.** a piece of clear lumber. **69. in the clear, a.** absolved of blame or guilt; free: *He was suspected of the theft, but evidence put him in the clear.* **b.** See **en clair.** [ME *clere* < OF *cler* < L *clārus* clear] —**clear′a·ble,** *adj.*

—**Syn. 1.** fair, cloudless, sunny. **3.** translucent, limpid, crystalline, diaphanous. **5.** See **clean. 9.** intelligible, comprehensible, lucid, plain, perspicuous. **11.** obvious, manifest, apparent, unmistakable. **12.** positive, definite, assured. **18.** unimpeded, unobstructed. **19.** unhampered, unencumbered. **30.** clarify, purify, refine. **42.** exonerate, absolve, vindicate, excuse. —**Ant. 1.** cloudy, dark. **9, 11.** obscure. **12, 14.** uncertain.

clear′-air tur′bulence (klēr′âr′). See **CAT**

clear·ance (klēr′əns), *n.* **1.** the act of clearing. **2.** the distance between two objects; an amount of clear space: *The bridge allowed a clearance of 37 feet at mean high water.* **3.** a clear space; a clearing: *The house stood in a clearance among the trees.* **4.** *Mach.* a space between two moving machine parts, left to avoid clashing or to permit relatively free motion. **5.** the angle between a face of a cutting tool, as a lathe tool, and the work. **6.** Also called **clearance sale.** the disposal of merchandise at reduced prices to make room for new goods: *He bought the coat for half price at a clearance.* **7.** *Banking.* an exchange of checks and other commercial paper drawn on members of a clearing house, usually effected at a daily meeting of the members. **8.** the clearing of a ship at a port. **9.** Also called **clear′ance pa′pers.** the official papers certifying this. **10.** *Govt., Mil.* a formal authorization permitting access to classified information, documents, etc. **11.** *Med.* a test of the excretory function of the kidneys based on the volume of blood which is cleared of a specific substance per minute by renal excretion. [CLEAR + -ANCE]

clear′ance car′, *Railroads.* a car for registering minimum vertical and lateral clearance along a track.

clear′ance sale′, clearance (def. 6).

Cle·ar·chus (klē är′kəs), *n.* died 401 B.C., Spartan general.

clear·cole (klēr′kōl′), *n.* size mixed with white lead, used esp. as a priming in house painting. [< F *claire colle,* equiv. to *claire* fem. of *clair* CLEAR + *colle* << Gk *kólla* glue]

clear-cut (klēr′kut′), *adj.* **1.** cut or formed with clearly defined outlines: *a face with clear-cut features.* **2.** completely evident; definite: *His sale of secrets was a clear-cut example of treachery.* —**clear′-cut′ness,** *n.*
—**Syn. 1.** chiseled, crisp, precise, positive, definite.

clear·er (klēr′ər), *n.* an apparatus on carding and spinning frames, for collecting lint that accumulates in processing cotton fibers. [CLEAR + -ER¹]

clear′er fab′ric, a felt or thickly napped woolen cloth, covering clearers, used for collecting lint from the rollers of a carding or spinning frame.

clear-eye (klēr′ī′), *n., pl.* **-eyes.** the clary, *Salvia Sclarea.* [alter. by folk etymology of CLARY]

clear-eyed (klēr′īd′), *adj.* **1.** having clear, bright eyes. **2.** mentally acute or perceptive; discerning; realistic: *The neutral journalist gave a clear-eyed appraisal of the situation.*

Clear·field (klēr′fēld′), *n.* **1.** a town in central Pennsylvania. 9270 (1960). **2.** a town in N Utah. 8833 (1960).

clear·head·ed (klēr′hed′id), *adj.* having or showing an alert, wide-awake mind. [CLEAR + -HEADED] —**clear′head′ed·ly,** *adv.* —**clear′head′ed·ness,** *n.*

clear·ing (klēr′ing), *n.* **1.** act of one who or that which clears. **2.** a tract of land, as in a forest, that contains no trees or bushes. **3.** the reciprocal exchange between banks of checks and drafts, and the settlement of the differences. **4. clearings,** the total of claims settled at a clearing house. [ME *clering.* See CLEAR, -ING¹]

clear′ing bath′, *Photog.* any solution for removing material from the surface of a photographic image, as silver halide, metallic silver, or a dye or stain.

clear′ing bear′ing, *Navig.* a bearing of a landmark indicating a course upon which a vessel may sail to avoid a navigational hazard.

clear′ing house′, a place or institution where mutual claims and accounts are settled, as between banks.

clear′ing loan′. See **day loan.**

clear′ing mark′, *Navig.* either of a pair of landmarks or marks on a mariner's chart lying upon a line (**clear′ing line′**) along which a vessel can sail to avoid navigational hazards.

clear′ing pole′, *Theat.* a long pole fitted with a crosspiece, for disentangling twisted lines, scenery, etc.

Clear′ Lake′, a town in N Iowa. 6158 (1960).

clear·ly (klēr′lē), *adv.* **1.** in a clear manner: *It is difficult to explain complex matters clearly.* **2.** without equivocation; decidedly: *It is clearly out of the question to drop the case.* [ME *clerli.* See CLEAR, -LY]
—**Syn. 1.** plainly, understandably. CLEARLY, DEFINITELY, DISTINCTLY, EVIDENTLY, imply the way in which something is plainly understood or understandable. CLEARLY suggests without doubt or obscurity: *expressed clearly.* DEFINITELY means explicitly; with precision: *definitely phrased.* DISTINCTLY means without blurring or confusion: *distinctly enunciated.* EVIDENTLY means patently, unquestionably: *evidently an error.*

clear·ness (klēr′nis), *n.* the state or quality of being clear; distinctness. [ME *clernes.* See CLEAR, -NESS]

clear-sight·ed (klēr′sī′tid), *adj.* **1.** having clear eyesight. **2.** having or marked by keen perception or sound judgment: *a clear-sighted, analytical approach.* —**clear′-sight′ed·ly,** *adv.* —**clear′-sight′ed·ness,** *n.*

clear·starch (klēr′stärch′), *v.t., v.i.* to stiffen with clear or transparent boiled starch. [CLEAR + STARCH] —**clear′starch′er,** *n.*

clear·sto·ry (klēr′stôr′ē, -stōr′ē), *n., pl.* **-ries.** clerestory. —**clear′sto′ried,** *adj.*

clear′ text′. See **plain text.**

Clear·wa·ter (klēr′wô′tər, -wot′ər), *n.* a city in W Florida. 34,653 (1960).

Clear′water Moun′tains, a group of mountains in N Idaho.

clear·wing (klēr′wing′), *n.* a moth having wings mostly devoid of scales and transparent, esp. any of the family *Aegeriidae,* many species of which are injurious to plants. Also, **clear′wing moth′.** [CLEAR + WING]

cleat (klēt), *n.* **1.** a wedge-shaped block fastened to a surface to serve as a check or support: *He nailed cleats into the sides of the bookcase to keep the supports from slipping.* **2.** Also called **belaying cleat.** an object of wood or metal having one or two projecting horns to which ropes may be belayed: found esp. on board vessels, as fixed to a deck, bulkhead, stanchion, etc. **3.** a length of wood or the like fixed to a surface, as a ramp, to give a firm foothold or to maintain an object in place. **4.** a strip of wood, metal, etc., fastened across a surface, as of a plank or series of adjacent planks, for strength or support. **5.** one of several strips of metal, wood, or the like, fastened across a ramp or gangway to provide sure footing. **6.** *Shipbuilding.* a hook-shaped piece of metal supporting a small structural member. **7.** an iron plate fastened to the sole or heel of a shoe, to protect against wear. **8.** a conical or rectangular projection, usually of hard rubber, built or screwed into the sole of a shoe to provide greater traction. **9.** a shoe fitted with such projections. **10.** calk² (def. 1). **11.** the cleavage plane of coal as found in a mine. —*v.t.* **12.** to supply or strengthen with cleats; fasten to or with a cleat. [ME *clete* wedge, OE *clēot,* c. OHG *klōz* lump, ball, D *kloot;* akin to CLOT]

Cleat

cleav·a·ble (klē′və bəl), *adj.* that can be cleft or split. [CLEAVE² + -ABLE] —**cleav′a·bil′i·ty,** *n.*

cleav·age (klē′vij), *n.* **1.** the act of cleaving or splitting. **2.** the state of being cleft. **3.** *Biol.* the total or partial division of the egg into smaller cells or blastomeres. **4.** the tendency of crystals, certain minerals and rocks, etc., to break in certain definite directions so as to yield more or less smooth surfaces (**cleav′age planes′**). **5.** *Chem.* the breaking down of a molecule or compound into simpler structures. **6.** the area between a woman's breasts, esp. when revealed by a low-cut neckline. **7.** critical division in opinion, beliefs, interests, etc., as leading to opposition between two groups: *a growing cleavage between the Conservative and Liberal wings of the party.* [CLEAVE² + -AGE]

cleave¹ (klēv), *v.i.,* **cleaved** or (*Archaic*) **clave; cleaved; cleav·ing. 1.** to adhere closely; stick; cling (usually fol. by *to*). **2.** to remain faithful (usually fol. by *to*): *to cleave to one's principles in spite of persecution.* [ME *cleven,* OE *cleofian,* c. OHG *klebēn* (G *kleben*)] —**cleav′ing·ly,** *adv.*

cleave² (klēv), *v.,* **cleft** or **cleaved** or **clove, cleft** or **cleaved** or **clo·ven, cleav·ing.** —*v.t.* **1.** to split or divide by or as by a cutting blow, esp. along a natural line of division, as the grain of wood. **2.** to penetrate or pass through (air, water, etc.): *The bow of the boat cleaved the water cleanly.* **3.** to make by or as by cutting: *to cleave a path through the wilderness.* **4.** to cut off; sever: *to cleave a branch from a tree.* —*v.i.* **5.** to part or split, esp. along a natural line of division. **6.** to penetrate or advance by or as by cutting (usually fol. by *through*). [ME *cleven,* OE *clēofan,* c. OHG *klioban* (G *klieben*), Icel *kljūfa;* akin to Gk *glýphein* to carve, L *glūbere* to peel]

cleav·er (klē′vər), *n.* **1.** one who or that which cleaves. **2.** a heavy knife or long-bladed hatchet, esp. one used by butchers for cutting meat into joints or pieces. [late ME *clevere.* See CLEAVE², -ER¹]

cleav·ers (klē′vərz), *n., pl.* **cleav·ers. 1.** a rubiaceous plant, *Galium Aparine,* having short, hooked bristles by means of which it adheres to clothing, fur, etc. **2.** any of certain related species. Also, **clivers.** Also called **goose grass.** [late ME *clivre,* equiv. to OE *clife* burdock + *-ere* -ER¹]

Cle·burne (klē′bərn), *n.* a city in N Texas, near Fort Worth. 15,381 (1960).

cle·ché (klā shā′, kle-, klesh′ē), *adj.* *Heraldry.* urdy (def. 3). [F < VL **clāvicāt(us),* deriv. of L *clāv(is)* key]

cleek (klēk), *n., v.,* **claught** or **cleeked** or **claucht, cleeked, cleeking.** —*n.* **1.** *Scot. and North Eng.* any large hook, ranging from a large fishing hook to a grappling iron, but esp. a hook fixed to the inside walls of a house to hold clothing, pots, or food. **2.** *Scot.* any gripping disease or seizure, as a cramp in one's leg. **3.** *Golf.* a club with an iron head, a narrow face, and little slope, used for shots from a poor lie on the fairway and sometimes for putting. —*v.t.* **4.** *Scot. and North Eng.* to grasp or seize (something) suddenly and eagerly; snatch. [late ME (Scot) *cleke* hook, deriv. of *cleke* to take hold of, var. of *cleche,* akin to CLUTCH¹]

clef (klef), *n.* *Music.* a symbol placed upon a staff to indicate the name and pitch of the notes corresponding to its lines and spaces. Cf. **bass clef, treble clef, C clef.** [< MF < L *clāvis* key]

A B C

Clefs
A, Treble clef (G clef); B, Bass clef (F clef); C, Alto clef (C clef)

cleft¹ (kleft), *n.* **1.** a space or opening made by cleavage; a split. **2.** a division formed by cleaving. **3.** *Vet. Pathol.* a crack on the bend of the pastern of a horse. [ME *clift,* OE (*ge*)*clyft* split, crack, c. G, Icel *Kluft;* akin to CLEAVE²]
—**Syn. 1.** fissure, crevice, crack, rift, cranny, chasm, crevasse.

cleft² (kleft), *v.* **1.** a pt. and pp. of **cleave**². —*adj.* **2.** cloven; split; divided. **3.** (of a leaf, corolla, lobe, or other expanded plant part) having divisions formed by incisions or narrow sinuses which extend halfway, or more than halfway, to the midrib or the base.

cleft′ lip′, harelip.

cleft′ pal′ate, a congenital defect of the palate in which a longitudinal fissure exists in the roof of the mouth.

cleido-, a learned borrowing from Greek meaning "lock up," used in the formation of compound words: *cleidoic.* [< Gk *kleido-* (s. of *kleidoûn* to lock up), equiv. to *kleid-* (s. of *kleís* bolt, key) + -o- -o-; akin to L *clāvis* key, *claudere* to shut. See CLAVICLE, CLOSE]

clei·do·ic (klī dō′ik), *adj.* *Embryol.* isolated from the environment, as certain eggs enclosed within a shell or membrane. [CLEIDO- + -IC]

Cleis·the·nes (klīs′thə nēz′), *n.* active c515–c495 B.C., Athenian statesman. Also, **Clisthenes.**

cleisto-, a learned borrowing from Greek meaning "closed," "capable of being closed," used in the formation of compound words: *cleistogamy; cleistothecium.* [comb. form repr. Gk *kleistós*]

cleis·to·carp (klī′stə kärp′), *n.* *Bot.* cleistothecium. Also, **clistocarp.** [CLEISTO- + -CARP]

cleis·to·car·pous (klī′stə kär′pəs), *adj.* *Bot.* **1.** (of a fungus) having cleistothecia. **2.** having a closed capsule, as certain mosses. Also, **clistocarpous.** [CLEISTO- + -CARPOUS]

cleis·tog·a·my (klī stog′ə mē), *n.* *Bot.* the condition of having small, inconspicuous flowers, in addition to fully developed ones, that do not open but are pollinated from their own anthers, as in the case of the pansy. [CLEISTO- + -GAMY] —**cleis·tog′a·mous, cleis·to·gam·ic** (klī′stə gam′ik), *adj.* —**cleis·tog′a·mous·ly, cleis′to·gam′i·cal·ly,** *adv.*

cleis·to·the·ci·um (klī′stə thē′shē əm, -sē əm), *n., pl.* **-ci·a** (-shē ə, -sē ə). *Bot.* (in certain ascomycetous fungi) a closed, globose ascocarp from which the ascospores are released only by its rupture or decay. Also, **clistothecium.** [CLEISTO- + THECIUM]

Clel·a (klel′ə), *n.* a girl's given name.

clem (klem), *v.t., v.i.,* **clemmed, clem·ming.** *Brit. Dial.* to starve. [ME *clemmen;* see CLAM²]

Clem (klem), *n.* a boy's given name, form of **Clement.**

clem·a·tis (klem′ə tis), *n.* **1.** any of the flowering vines or erect ranunculaceous shrubs of the genus *Clematis,* as *C. virginiana,* the virgin's-bower of the U.S. **2.** any species of the allied genera *Atragene* or *Viorna.* [< L < Gk *klēmatís* name of several climbing plants]

Cle·men·ceau (klem′ən sō′; *Fr.* kle mäN sō′), *n.* **Georges Eu·gène Ben·ja·min** (jôrj yōō jēn′ ben′jə min, yōō′jēn′; *Fr.* zhôrzh œ zhen′ baN zha maN′), ("*the Tiger*"), 1841–1929, French statesman, journalist, and editor: premier 1906–09, 1917–20.

clem·en·cy (klem′ən sē), *n., pl.* **-cies. 1.** the quality of being clement; disposition to show forbearance, compassion, or forgiveness in judging or punishing; leniency; mercy. **2.** an act or deed showing mercy or leniency. **3.** (of the weather) mildness or temperateness. [< L *clēmentia.* See CLEMENT, -CY]
—**Syn. 1.** forgivingness, gentleness, mercifulness. —**Ant. 1.** harshness. **3.** severity.

Clem·en·cy (klem′ən sē), *n.* a girl's given name.

Clem·ens (klem′ənz), **Samuel Lang·horne** (lang′hôrn, -ərn), ("*Mark Twain*"), 1835–1910, U.S. author and humorist.

clem·ent (klem′ənt), *adj.* **1.** mild or merciful in disposition or character; lenient; compassionate: *A clement judge reduced his sentence.* **2.** (of the weather) mild or temperate; pleasant. [late ME < L *clēment-*, s. of *clēmēns* gentle, merciful] —**clem′ent·ly,** *adv.*

Clem·ent (klem′ənt), *n.* a boy's given name.

Clement I, Saint (*Clement of Rome*), A.D. c30–c100, first of the Apostolic Fathers: pope 88?–97?.

Clement II, (*Suidger*) died 1047, pope 1046–47.

Clement III, (*Paolo Scolari*) died 1191, Italian ecclesiastic: pope 1187–91.

Clement IV, (*Guy Foulques*) died 1268, French ecclesiastic: pope 1265–68.

Clement V, (*Bertrand de Got*) 1264–1314, French ecclesiastic: pope 1305–14.

Clement VI, (*Pierre Roger*) 1291–1352, French ecclesiastic: pope 1342–52.

Clement VII, (*Giulio de' Medici*) 1478–1534, Italian ecclesiastic: pope 1523–34 (nephew of Lorenzo de' Medici).

Clement VIII, (*Ippolito Aldobrandini*) 1536–1605, Italian ecclesiastic: pope 1592–1605.

Clement IX, (*Giulio Rospigliosi*) 1600–69, Italian ecclesiastic: pope 1667–69.

Clement X, (*Emilio Altieri*) 1590–1676, Italian ecclesiastic: pope 1670–76.

Clement XI, (*Giovanni Francesco Albani*) 1649–1721, Italian ecclesiastic: pope 1700–21.

Clement XII, (*Lorenzo Corsini*) 1652–1740, Italian ecclesiastic: pope 1730–40.

Clement XIII, (*Carlo della Torre Rezzonico*) 1693–1769, Italian ecclesiastic: pope 1758–69.

Clement XIV, (*Giovanni Vincenzo Antonio Ganganelli* or *Lorenzo Ganganelli*) 1705–74, Italian ecclesiastic: pope 1769–74.

Cle·men·ti (klə men′tē; *It.* kle men′tē), *n.* **Mu·zio** (mo͞o′tsyô), 1752–1832, Italian pianist and composer in England.

Cle·men·tia (klə men′shə), *n.* a girl's given name. Also, **Clementina, Clementine.**

Clem·en·tine (klem′ən tēn′, -tīn′; *Fr.* kle mäN tēn′), *n.* a girl's given name. Also, **Clementia, Clem·en·ti·na** (klem′ən tē′nə).

Clem′ent of Alexan′dria, A.D. c150–c215, Greek Christian theologian and writer.

Clem·en·ton (klem′ən tən), *n.* a town in SW New Jersey. 3766 (1960).

Clem·mie (klem′ē) *n.* **1.** a boy's given name, form of **Clement. 2.** a girl's given name, form of **Clementine.** Also, **Clem′my.**

Clem·on (klem′ən), *n.* a boy's given name, form of **Clement.**

clench (klench), *v.t.* **1.** to close (the hands, teeth, etc.) tightly. **2.** to grasp firmly; grip. **3.** clinch (def. 3). **4.** clinch (defs. 1, 2, 4). —*v.i.* **5.** to close or knot up tightly: *His hands clenched as he faced his enemy.* —*n.* **6.** act of clenching. **7.** a tight hold; grip. **8.** something that clenches or holds fast. **9.** clinch (defs. 9, 10, 11). [ME *clenchen*, OE *(be)clencan* hold fast]

Cle·o (klē′ō), *n.* a boy's or girl's given name.

Cle·o·bis (klē′ə bis), *n.* *Class. Myth.* a son of Cydippe, known for his affection for his mother; he and his brother Biton died painlessly in their sleep when Cydippe prayed to Hera to give her sons what was best for mortals.

Cle·o·bu·lus (klē′ō byo͞o′ləs, klē′ə-, klē ob′yə ləs), *n.* fl. 560 B.C., Greek sage and lyric poet, a native and tyrant of Lindus, Rhodes.

Cle·o·dae·us (klē′ə dē′is), *n.* *Class. Myth.* the grandson of Hercules and the ancestor of many renowned Spartans.

cle·oid (klē′oid), *n.* *Dentistry.* a claw-shaped dental instrument used to remove carious material from a cavity. [< Gk *kle(ís)* catch, hook (see CLEIDO-) + -OID]

cle·o·me (klē ō′mē), *n.* any of the numerous herbaceous or shrubby plants of the genus *Cleome*, mostly natives of tropical regions, and often bearing showy flowers. [< NL < LL, name of some plant]

Cle·om·e·nes III (klē om′ə nēz′), died c220 B.C., king of Sparta c235–c220.

Cle·on (klē′on), *n.* died 442 B.C., Athenian general and political opponent of Pericles.

Cle·o·ne (klē ō′nē), *n.* *Class. Myth.* a daughter of Asopus.

Cle·o·pa·tra (klē′ə pa′trə, -pä′-, -pā′-), *n.* **1.** 69–30 B.C., queen of Egypt 51–49, 48–30. **2.** a girl's given name.

Cle′opa′tra's Nee′dle, 1. an ancient Egyptian obelisk, now in Central Park, New York City. **2.** an ancient Egyptian obelisk, now on the Thames River embankment, in London.

Cle·o·strat·us (klē′ō strat′əs), *n.* a crater in the second quadrant of the face of the moon: about 35 miles in diameter.

Cle·o·ta (klē ō′tə), *n.* a girl's given name.

Cle·o·the·ra (klē′ə thēr′ə), *n.* *Class. Myth.* a daughter of Pandareus.

clepe (klēp), *v.t.*, **cleped** or **clept** (also **y·cleped** or **y·clept**), **clep·ing.** *Archaic.* to call; name (now chiefly in the pp. as *ycleped* or *yclept*). [ME *clepen*, OE *cleopian*, var. of *clipian*; akin to MLG *kleperen* to rattle]

clep·sy·dra (klep′si drə), *n., pl.* **-dras, -drae** (-drē′). a device for measuring time by the regulated flow of water or mercury through a small aperture. [< L < Gk *klepsýdrā*, equiv. to *kleps-* (var. of *klept-*, s. of *kléptein* to steal) + *hydr-* HYDR-[1] + *-ā* fem. n. suffix]

clept (klept), *v.* a pt. of **clepe.**

clep·to·bi·o·sis (klep′tō bī ō′sis), *n., pl.* **-ses** (-sēz). a mode of living in which one species, as of ants, steals food openly or furtively from another. [< Gk *klépt(ein)* to steal + -o- + -BIOSIS] —**clep·to·bi·ot·ic** (klep′tō bī ot′ik), *adj.*

clep·to·ma·ni·a (klep′tə mā′nē ə, -mān′yə), *n.* *Psychol.* kleptomania. [< Gk *klépt(ein)* to steal + -o- + -MANIA] —**clep′to·ma′ni·ac′,** *n.*

clere·sto·ry (klēr′stôr′ē, -stôr′ē), *n., pl.* **-ries. 1.** *Archit.* a portion of an interior rising above adjacent rooftops and having windows admitting daylight to the interior. **2.** a raised construction, as on the roof of a railroad car, having windows or slits for admitting light or air. Also, **clearstory.** [late ME, equiv. to *clere* CLEAR + STORY[2]] —**clere′sto′ried,** *adj.*

A, Clerestory of early Gothic cathedral; B, Triforium; C, Gallery; D, Ambulatory arcade

cler·gy (klûr′jē), *n., pl.* **-gies.** the group or body of ordained persons in a religion, as distinguished from the laity. [ME *clergie* < OF, equiv. to *clerg-* (var. of *clerc-* CLERK) + *-ie* -Y[3]] —**cler′gy·like′,** *adj.*

cler·gy·man (klûr′jē mən), *n., pl.* **-men. 1.** a member of the clergy. **2.** an ordained Christian minister. [CLERGY + MAN[1]]

cler·ic (kler′ik), *n.* **1.** a member of the clergy. **2.** a member of a clerical party. —*adj.* **3.** pertaining to the clergy; clerical. [< LL *clēricus* priest < Gk *klērikós*, equiv. to *klēr(os)* lot, allotment + *-ikos* -IC]

cler·i·cal (kler′i kəl), *adj.* **1.** of, pertaining to, appropriate for, or assigned to a clerk or clerks: *a clerical job.* **2.** doing the work of a clerk or clerks: *a clerical assistant; a clerical staff.* **3.** of, pertaining to, or characteristic of the clergy or a clergyman. **4.** advocating the power or influence of the clergy in politics, government, etc.: *a clerical party.* —*n.* **5.** a cleric. **6. clericals,** *Informal.* clerical garments. **7.** a person or a party advocating the power or influence of the church in politics, government, etc. **8.** Also called **cler′ical er′ror.** a minor error, as in the keeping of records, the transcribing of documents, or the handling of correspondence. [< LL *clēricālis*, equiv. to *clēric(us)* CLERIC + *-ālis* -AL[1]] —**cler′i·cal′i·ty,** *n.* —**cler′i·cal·ly,** *adv.*

cler′ical col′lar, a stiff, narrow, bandlike white collar fastened at the back of the neck, worn by certain clerics. Also called **reversed collar, Roman collar.**

cler·i·cal·ism (kler′i kə liz′əm), *n.* **1.** clerical principles. **2.** clerical power or influence in government, politics, etc. **3.** support of such power or influence. [CLERICAL + -ISM] —**cler′i·cal·ist,** *n.*

cler·i·hew (kler′i hyo͞o′), *n.* *Pros.* a light verse form, usually consisting of two couplets, with the first line being the full name of a well-known person. [named after E. *Clerihew* Bentley (1875–1956), English writer, its inventor]

cler·i·sy (kler′i sē), *n.* learned men as a class; literati; intelligentsia. [< G *Klerisei* clergy < ML *clēricia*, equiv. to *clēric(us)* CLERIC + *-ia* -IA]

clerk (klûrk; *Brit.* klärk), *n.* **1.** a person employed, as in an office, shop, business, etc., to keep records, accounts, files, handle correspondence, or the like. **2.** *U.S.* a salesclerk. **3.** a person who keeps the records and performs the routine business of a court, legislature, board, etc. **4.** a clergyman; ecclesiastic. **5.** a layman charged with various minor ecclesiastical duties. **6.** *Archaic.* **a.** a person who is able to read, or to read and write. **b.** a scholar. —*v.i.* **7.** to act or serve as a clerk. [ME, OE *clerc*, var. of *cleric* < eccl. L *clēricus* CLERIC] —**clerk′ish,** *adj.* —**clerk′like′,** *adj.*

clerk·ly (klûrk′lē; *Brit.* klärk′lē), *adj.,* **-li·er, -li·est,** *adv.* —*adj.* **1.** of, pertaining to, or characteristic of a clerk or clerks. **2.** *Archaic.* scholarly. —*adv.* **3.** in the manner of a clerk. [CLERK + -LY] —**clerk′li·ness,** *n.*

clerk′ reg′ular, *pl.* **clerks regular.** a member of a Christian monastic order who combines monastic life with the pastoral duties of a secular priest.

clerk·ship (klûrk′ship; *Brit.* klärk′ship), *n.* **1.** the position, office, or function of a clerk. **2.** the phase of undergraduate study in medicine providing for the practical, routine training of a student who works under supervision at specified times in a hospital clinic. **3.** *Archaic.* **a.** scholarship (def. 1). **b.** the clergy. [CLERK + -SHIP]

clerk′ vic′ar. See **lay vicar.**

Cler·mont (kler′mont), *n.* a town in central Florida. 3313 (1960).

Cler·mont-Fer·rand (kler môN′fe räN′), *n.* a city in and the capital of Puy-de-Dôme, in central France. 134,263 (1963).

cle·ro·man·cy (klēr′ə man′sē, kler′-), *n.* the casting of lots as a means of divination. [< ML *clēromantia*, equiv. to Gk *klēro(s)* lot + *manteía* -MANCY]

cle·ruch (klēr′o͝ok, -ək), *n.* (in ancient Greece) a citizen who received land under the system of cleruchy. [< Gk *klēroûch(os)*, equiv. to *klēro(s)* allotment (of land) + *ôchos* tenant, deriv. of *échein* to hold]

cle·ru·chy (klēr′ə kē), *n., pl.* **-chies.** (in ancient Greece) **1.** the system or practice by which citizens were allotted land taken by conquest. **2.** a colony established under this system. [< Gk *klērouchía*. See *klēroûch(os)* CLERUCH, -Y[3]] —**cle·ru′chi·al** (kli ro͞o′kē əl), **cle·ru′chic,** *adj.*

Clete (klēt), *n.* a boy's given name, form of **Cletus.**

Cle·ta (klē′tə), *n.* *Class. Myth.* one of the Graces worshiped at Sparta.

Cle·tus (klē′təs), *n.* **1.** a boy's given name. **2.** See **Anacletus.**

Cle·va (klā′və; *It.* kle′vä), *n.* **Faus·to** (fou′stō; *It.* fou′stô), born 1902, U.S. orchestra conductor, born in Italy.

Cleve (klēv), *n.* a boy's given name.

cleve·ite (klē′vīt, klā′və īt′), *n.* *Mineral.* a variety of uraninite containing up to 10 percent of rare earth oxides. [named after R. T. *Cleve* (1840–1905), Swedish chemist; see -ITE[1]]

Cleve·land (klēv′lənd), *n.* **1. (Stephen) Gro·ver** (grō′vər), 1837–1908, 22nd and 24th president of the U.S. 1885–89, 1893–97. **2.** a port in NE Ohio, on Lake Erie. 876,050 (1960). **3.** a city in SE Tennessee. 16,196 (1960). **4.** a town in E Texas. 5838 (1960). **5.** a town in N Oklahoma. 2519 (1960). **6.** a boy's given name.

Cleve′land Heights′, a city in NE Ohio, near Cleveland. 61,813 (1960).

clev·er (klev′ər), *adj.* **1.** mentally bright; having quick intelligence; able. **2.** superficially skillful, witty, or original in character or construction; facile: *It was an amusing, clever play of no lasting value.* **3.** adroit with the hands or body; dexterous or nimble: *The shortstop made a clever play and ended the inning.* **4.** showing inventiveness or originality; ingenious: *His clever device was the first to solve the problem.* **5.** *Dial.* suitable; convenient; satisfactory. **6.** *Dial.* good-natured. **7.** *Dial.* **a.** handsome. **b.** in good health. [ME *cliver*, akin to OE *clifer* claw, *clife* burdock. See CLEAVERS] —**clev′er·ish,** *adj.* —**clev′er·ish·ly,** *adv.* —**clev′er·ly,** *adv.* —**clev′er·ness,** *n.*

—**Syn. 1.** ingenious, talented, quick-witted; smart, gifted; apt, expert. **3.** skillful, agile, handy. —**Ant. 1.** stupid. **3.** clumsy.

C, Clevis

Cleves (klēvz), *n.* a city in W North Rhine-Westphalia, in W West Germany. 22,100 (1963). German, **Kleve.**

clev·is (klev′is), *n.* a U-shaped yoke at the end of a chain or rod, between the ends of which a lever, hook, etc., can be pinned or bolted. [akin to CLEAVE[2]]

clew (klo͞o), *n.* **1.** a ball or skein of thread, yarn, etc. **2.** *Class. Myth.* the thread by which Theseus found his way out of the labyrinth. **3.** clue (def. 1). **4.** Usually, **clews.** the rigging for a hammock. **5.** *Theat.* a metal device holding scenery lines controlled by one weighted line. **6.** *Naut.* either lower corner of a square sail or the after lower corner of a fore-and-aft sail. **7. from clew to earing,** *Naut.* **a.** from the bottom to the top of a square sail. **b.** thoroughly; completely. **8. spread a large clew,** *Naut.* **a.** to carry a large amount of sail. **b.** to present an impressive appearance. **9. spread a small clew,** *Naut.* **a.** to carry a small amount of sail. **b.** to present an unimpressive appearance. —*v.t.* **10.** to coil into a ball. **11.** clue (def. 3). **12.** *Theat.* **a.** to draw up the bottom edge of (a curtain, drop, etc.) and fold out of view; bag. **b.** to secure (lines) with a clew. **13. clew down,** *Naut.* to secure (a sail) in an unfurled position. **14. clew up,** *Naut.* to haul (the lower corners of a square-rig sail) up to the yard by means of the clew lines. [ME *clewe*, OE *cleowen*, *cliewen*, equiv. to *cliew-* (c. OHG *kliu* ball) + -EN[5]; akin to D *kluwen*]

clew·gar·net (klo͞o′gär′nit), *n.* *Naut.* a tackle for clewing up a course on a square-rigged ship. Also, **clew′ gar′net.** [CLEW + GARNET[2]]

clew′ i′ron, *Naut.* a pierced metal fitting, at each clew of a sail, to which the boltrope, sheet, and clew line or clewgarnet are attached.

Clew·is·ton (klo͞o′i stən), *n.* a town in S Florida. 3114 (1960).

clew′ jig′ger, *Naut.* a small tackle or whip for raising the clews of a course or topsail over their yards.

clew′ line′, *Naut.* a rope or tackle for raising the clews of square sails and certain fore-and-aft sails.

clew′ ring′, *Naut.* a ringlike clew iron.

clew′ rope′, *Naut.* **1.** a rope for raising the clew of a fore-and-aft sail. **2.** a clew line.

cli·ché (klē shā′, kli-; *Fr.* klē shā′), *n., pl.* **-chés** (-shāz′; *Fr.* -shā′), *adj.* —*n.* **1.** a trite, stereotyped expression; a sentence or phrase, usually expressing a popular or common thought or idea, that has lost originality, ingenuity, and impact by long overuse, as *sadder but wiser*, or *strong as an ox.* **2.** (in art, literature, drama, etc.) a trite or hackneyed plot, character development, use of color, musical expression, etc. **3.** *Print. Brit.* **a.** a stereotype or electrotype plate. **b.** a reproduction made in a like manner. —*adj.* **4.** trite; hackneyed; stereotyped; commonplace. [< F, ptp. of *clicher* to stereotype]

—**Syn. 1.** platitude, bromide, stereotype, commonplace.

Cli·chy (klē shē′), *n.* an industrial suburb of Paris, France, on the Seine. 56,495 (1962).

click (klik), *n.* **1.** a slight, sharp sound: *At the click of the latch, the dog barked.* **2.** a small device for preventing backward movement of a mechanism, as a detent or pawl. **3.** *Phonet.* **a.** any one of a variety of ingressive, usually implosive speech sounds, phonemic in some languages, produced by suction occlusion and plosive or affricative release. **b.** any one of a variety of familiar sounds used in calling or urging on horses or other animals, in expressing reprimand or sympathy, or produced in audible kissing. —*v.i.* **4.** to emit or make a slight, sharp sound, or series of such sounds, as by the cocking of a pistol: *The door clicked shut.* **5.** *Informal.* **a.** to succeed; make a hit: *If the play clicks, the producer will be rich.* **b.** to fit together; function well together: *They get along in public, but their personalities don't really click.* **c.** to become intelligible. —*v.t.* **6.** to cause to click. **7.** to strike with a click: *He clicked his heels and saluted.* [? imit., but perh. < D *klick* (n.), *klikken* (v.)] —**click′less,** *adj.*

click′ bee′tle, any of numerous beetles of the family *Elateridae*, having the ability to spring up with a clicking sound when placed on their backs. Also called **skipjack, snapping beetle.**

click·er (klik′ər), *n.* **1.** one who or that which clicks. **2.** *Print.* the foreman of a companionship of printers. [CLICK + -ER[1]]

click·e·ty-clack (klik′i tē klak′), *n.* a rhythmic, swiftly paced succession of alternating clicks and clacks. Also called **click·e·ty-click** (klik′i tē klik′). [alter. of CLICK + CLACK]

Cli·de (klī′dē), *n.* *Class. Myth.* a nymph who lived on the island of Naxos.

cli·ent (klī′ənt), *n.* **1.** a person who applies to a lawyer for advice or commits his cause or legal interests to a lawyer's management. **2.** a person who is receiving the benefits, services, etc., of a social welfare agency, a government bureau, etc. **3.** a customer. **4.** (in ancient Rome) a plebeian who lived under the patronage of a patrician. **5.** anyone under the patronage of another; a dependent. [late ME < L *client-*, s. of *cliēns*, var. of *cluēns*, prp. of *cluēre* to hear; see -ENT] —**cli·en·tal** (klī en′təl, klī′ən təl), *adj.* —**cli′ent·less,** *adj.*

cli·ent·age (klī′ən tij), *n.* a body of clients; clientele. [CLIENT + -AGE]

cli′ent-cen′tered ther′apy (klī′ənt sen′tərd), *Psychol.* a nondirective method of psychotherapy in which treatment consists of helping the patient to use effectively his own latent resources in solving a problem.

cli·en·tele (klī′ən tel′), *n.* **1.** the clients (as of a lawyer or businessman), the customers (as of a shop), or the patients (as of a doctor) considered collectively; a group or body of clients: *This custom designer has a wealthy clientele.* **2.** dependents or followers. [< L *clientēla*, equiv. to *client-* (see CLIENT) + *-ēla* collective n. suffix]

cli′ent's indem′nity, *U.S. Law.* a fund created and administered by the bar associations of some States for the reimbursement of clients who suffered from the defalcations of lawyers.

cliff (klif), *n.* the high steep face of a rocky mass; precipice. [ME *clif*, OE, c. D, LG, Icel *klif*] —**cliff′less,** *adj.*

Cliff (klif), *n.* a boy's given name, form of **Clifford.**

cliff′ brake′, any of several ferns of the genus *Pellaea*, which usually grow on rocks or cliffs.

cliff′ dwell′er, 1. (*usually cap.*) a member of a prehistoric people of the southwestern U.S., who were ancestors of the Pueblo Indians and built houses in caves or on ledges of the cliffs. 2. one who lives in an apartment house, esp. in a large city. —**cliff′ dwell′ing.**

cliff-hang·er (klif′hang′ər), *n.* 1. a melodramatic adventure serial in which each installment ends in suspense in order to interest the reader or viewer in the next installment: *In silent-movie cliff-hangers, each episode ended in imminent disaster.* 2. an event or contest of which the outcome is suspensefully uncertain up to the very last moment: *The race was a cliff-hanger, but the favorite finally won.* Also, **cliff′hang′er.**

cliff-hang·ing (klif′hang′ing), *adj.* of, pertaining to, or characteristic of a cliff-hanger: *a cliff-hanging vote of 20–19.* Also, **cliff′hang′ing.**

Clif·ford (klif′ərd), *n.* 1. **William King·don** (king′dən), 1845–79, English mathematician and philosopher. 2. a boy's or girl's given name.

Cliff′side Park′ (klif′sīd′), a city in NE New Jersey. 17,642 (1960).

cliff′ swal′low, a colonial North American bird, *Petrochelidon pyrrhonota*, which attaches its bottle-shaped nests of mud to cliffs and walls.

cliff·y (klif′ē), *adj.*, **cliff·i·er, cliff·i·est.** abounding in or formed by cliffs: *The steep, cliffy shoreline gave no access to the beach.* [CLIFF + -Y[1]]

clift (klift), *n.* *Chiefly Midland U.S.* cliff. [ME, alter. of CLIFF (by influence of CLEFT[1])]

Clif·ton (klif′tən), *n.* 1. a city in NE New Jersey. 82,084 (1960). 2. a town in SE Arizona. 4191 (1960). 3. a boy's given name.

Clif′ton Forge′, a town in W Virginia. 5268 (1960).

Clif′ton Heights′, a town in SE Pennsylvania. 8005 (1960).

cli·mac·ter·ic (klī mak′tər ik, klī′mak ter′ik), *n.* 1. *Physiol.* a period of decrease of reproductive capacity in men and women, culminating, in women, in the menopause. 2. any critical period. 3. the period of maximum respiration in a fruit, during which it becomes fully ripened. 4. a year in which important changes in health, fortune, etc., are held by some theories to occur, as one's sixty-third year (**grand climacteric**). —*adj.* 5. Also, **cli·mac·ter·i·cal** (klī′mak ter′i kəl). pertaining to a critical period; crucial. [< L *clīmactēricus* < Gk *klīmaktērikós* (*klīmaktḗr* rung of a ladder, critical point in life, equiv. to *klimak-*, s. of *klîmax* (see CLIMAX) + *-tēr* n. suffix) + *-ikos* -IC] —**cli′mac·ter′i·cal·ly,** *adv.*

cli·mac·tic (klī mak′tik), *adj.* pertaining to or coming to a climax: *The tension was climactic, and we knew the crisis was at hand.* Also, **cli·mac′ti·cal.** [from CLIMAX, on model of *syntax, syntactic*] —**cli·mac′ti·cal·ly,** *adv.*

cli·mant (klī′mənt), *adj.* *Heraldry.* rampant, as a goat: *a goat climant.* [modeled on, or partial trans. of, *rampant* (< F, prp. of *ramper* to climb). See CLIMB, -ANT]

climat-, var. of **climato-** before a vowel: *climatic.*

cli·mate (klī′mit), *n.* 1. the composite or generally prevailing weather conditions of a region, as temperature, air pressure, humidity, precipitation, sunshine, cloudiness, and winds, throughout the year, averaged over a series of years. 2. a region or area characterized by a given climate: *Florida is in a warm climate.* 3. the prevailing attitudes, standards, or environmental conditions of a group, period, or place: *In a climate of political unrest, a dictator can often seize power.* [late ME *climat* < L *climat-* (s. of *clima*) < Gk *klimat-*, s. of *klíma* slope, equiv. to *kli-* (akin to *klī́nein* to slope, lean) + *-ma* n. suffix]

cli·mat·ic (klī mat′ik), *adj.* 1. of or pertaining to climate. 2. (of ecological phenomena) due to climate rather than to soil or topography. Also, **cli·mat′i·cal, cli·mat·al** (klī′mi tᵊl). [CLIMAT- + -IC] —**cli·mat′i·cal·ly,** *adv.*

climato-, a combining form of **climate:** *climatology.* Also, *esp. before a vowel:* **climat-.**

cli·ma·tol·o·gy (klī′mə tol′ə jē), *n.* the science that deals with climates or climatic conditions. [CLIMATO- + -LOGY] —**cli·ma·to·log·ic** (klī′mə tᵊloj′ik), **cli′ma·to·log′i·cal,** *adj.* —**cli′ma·to·log′i·cal·ly,** *adv.* —**cli′ma·tol′o·gist,** *n.*

cli·max (klī′maks), *n.* 1. the highest or most intense point in the development or resolution of something; culmination: *His career reached its climax when he was elected president.* 2. (in a dramatic or literary work) a decisive moment that is of maximum intensity or is a major turning point in a plot. 3. *Rhet.* **a.** a figure consisting of a series of related ideas so arranged that each surpasses the preceding in force or intensity. **b.** the last term or member of this figure. 4. an orgasm. 5. *Ecol.* that stage in the ecological succession or evolution of a plant and animal community, which is stable and self-perpetuating. —*v.t., v.i.* 6. to bring to or reach a climax. [< LL < Gk *klîmax* ladder, akin to *klī́nein* to lean] —**Syn.** 1. summit, zenith, acme, apex.

climb (klīm), *v.*, **climbed** or (*Archaic*) **clomb; climbed** or (*Archaic*) **clomb; climb·ing,** *n.* —*v.i.* 1. to mount or ascend, esp. by using both hands and feet: *to climb up a ladder.* 2. to rise slowly or by as by continued effort: *They laboriously climbed to the top of a steep mountain.* 3. to slope upward: *The road climbs steeply up to the house.* 4. to ascend by twining or by means of tendrils, adhesive tissues, etc., as a plant: *The ivy climbed to the roof.* 5. to proceed or move by using the hands and feet; crawl: *to climb along the branch; to climb around on the roof.* 6. to ascend in prominence, fortune, etc.: *From lowly beginnings he climbed to occupy the highest place in the land.* —*v.t.* 7. to ascend, go up, or get to the top of, esp. by the use of hands and feet. 8. **climb down, a.** to descend, esp. by using both hands and feet. **b.** *Informal.* to retreat, as from an indefensible opinion or position: *He was forced to climb down from his untenable position.* —*n.* 9. a climbing; an ascent by climbing: *It was a long climb to the top.* 10. a place to be climbed: *That peak is quite a climb.* [ME *climben*, OE *climban*; c. D, G *klimmen*; akin to CLAMBER] —**climb′a·ble,** *adj.*

—**Syn.** 7. CLIMB, ASCEND, MOUNT, SCALE imply a moving upward. To CLIMB is to make one's way upward with effort: *to climb a mountain.* ASCEND, in its literal meaning (to go up), is general, but it now usually suggests a gradual or stately movement, with or without effort, often to a considerable degree of altitude: *to ascend the Hudson River; to ascend the Himalayas.* MOUNT may be interchangeable with ASCEND, but also suggests climbing on top of or astride of: *to mount a platform, a horse.* SCALE, a more literary word, implies difficult or hazardous climbing up or over something: *to scale a summit.* —**Ant.** 1, 7. descend. 9. descent.

climb-down (klīm′doun′), *n.* *Informal.* a retreat, as from an indefensible opinion or position. [n. use of v. phrase *climb down*]

climb·er (klī′mər), *n.* 1. one who or that which climbs. 2. See **social climber.** 3. a climbing plant. 4. a device to assist in climbing, as a climbing iron or a spiked metal plate fastened to a shoe. [late ME; see CLIMB, -ER[1]]

climb′ in′dicator, *Aeron.* an instrument to show the rate of ascent or descent of an aircraft, operating on a differential pressure principle.

climb′ing bit′tersweet, bittersweet (def. 2).

climb′ing fern′, any of several chiefly tropical, vinelike ferns of the genus *Lygodium*, having climbing or trailing stems.

climb·ing·fish (klī′ming fish′), *n., pl.* **-fish·es,** (*esp. collectively*) **-fish.** See **climbing perch.** [CLIMBING + FISH]

climb′ing fu′mitory, a vine, *Adlumia fungosa*, of eastern North America, climbing by its slender leafstalks. Also called **Allegheny vine, mountain fringe.**

climb′ing hemp′weed (hemp′wēd′), any of several twining herbs of the genus *Mikania*, esp. *M. scandens*, having white or pinkish flowers. [HEMP + WEED[1]]

climb′ing hydran′gea, a woody vine, *Hydrangea petiolaris*, of eastern Asia, having white flower clusters and climbing by aerial rootlets.

climb′ing i′rons, one of a pair of spiked iron frames, strapped to the shoe, leg, or knee, to help in climbing trees, telephone poles, etc.

climb′ing perch′, a brown labyrinth fish, *Anabas testudineus*, of southeastern Asia and the Malay Archipelago, having a specialized breathing apparatus that enables it to leave the water and move about on land.

climb′ing rose′, any of various roses that ascend and cover a trellis, arbor, etc., chiefly by twining about the supports.

climb′ing ylang′-ylang, a woody vine or partly climbing shrub, *Artabotrys odoratissimus*, of tropical Asia, having glossy leaves, a hooked flower stalk, greenish-yellow flowers, and smooth, fragrant, yellow fruit.

climb′ mill′ing, *Mach.* milling of work fed in the direction of the cutter teeth.

clime (klīm), *n.* *Literary.* 1. a tract or region of the earth. 2. climate. [< L *clima*; see CLIMATE]

clin-, *Bot.* a learned borrowing from Greek meaning "bed," used in the formation of compound words: *clinandrium.* [comb. form < Gk *klin-*, s. of *klī́nē* bed]

cli·nah (klī′nə), *n.* *Australian Informal.* a pretty girl; sweetheart. [var. of *cliner* << G *klein* small]

cli·nan·dri·um (kli nan′drē əm), *n., pl.* **-dri·a** (-drē ə). a cavity in the apex of the column in orchids, in which the anthers rest; the androclinium. [< NL; see CLIN-, ANDR-, -IUM]

clinch (klinch), *v.t.* 1. to secure (a nail, screw, etc.) in position by beating down the protruding point: *He drove the nails through the board and clinched the points flat with a hammer.* 2. to fasten (objects) together by nails, screws, etc., secured in this manner. 3. to settle (a matter) decisively: *The salesman clinched the deal and went out to celebrate.* 4. *Naut.* to fasten by a clinch. —*v.i.* 5. *Boxing.* to engage in a clinch: *The exhausted boxers clinched and were separated by the referee.* 6. *Slang.* to embrace and kiss passionately. 7. (of a clinched nail, screw, etc.) to hold fast; be secure. —*n.* 8. act of clinching. 9. *Boxing.* an act or instance of one or both boxers holding the other about the arms or body in order to prevent or hinder the opponent's punches. 10. a clinched nail or fastening. 11. the bent part of a clinched nail, screw, etc. 12. a knot or bend in which a bight or eye is made by making a loop or turn in the rope and seizing the end to the standing part. 13. *Slang.* a passionate embrace and kiss. 14. *Obs.* a pun. Also, **clench** (for defs. 1–4, 9–11). [later var. of CLENCH]

clinch·er (klin′chər), *n.* 1. one who or that which clinches. 2. a nail, screw, etc., for clinching. 3. a statement, argument, fact, situation, or the like, that is decisive or conclusive: *The health value of the proposed anti-smog bill was the clincher. The heat was the clincher that made us decide to leave the city.* 4. *Auto.* a clincher tire. [var. of *clencher* (CLENCH + -ER[1])]

clinch·er-built (klin′chər bilt′), *adj.* clinker-built (def. 2).

clinch′er tire′, *Auto.* an automobile tire having, on each side of its inner circumference, a rubber flange that fits under the turned-over edge of the wheel rim.

clinch′ nail′, a nail designed to be bent over at the point after driving so as to clinch together the objects being fastened.

cline (klīn), *n.* 1. *Biol.* the gradual change in certain characteristics exhibited by members of a series of adjacent populations of organisms of the same species. 2. *Anthropol.* a gradient of the frequency with which a biological characteristic occurs in one area and not in another. [< Gk *klī́nein* to LEAN[1]] —**clin′al,** *adj.* —**clin′al·ly,** *adv.*

cling[1] (kling), *v.*, **clung, cling·ing,** *n.* —*v.i.* 1. to adhere closely; stick to: *The wet paper clings to the smooth side of the glass.* 2. to hold tight, as by grasping or embracing; cleave: *The children clung to each other in the dark.* 3. to be or remain close: *The child clung to her mother's side.* 4. to remain attached, as to an idea, hope, memory, etc.: *Despite the returns, the candidate clung to the belief that he would be elected.* 5. *Obs.* to cohere. —*n.* 6. the act of clinging; adherence; attachment. [ME *clingen*, OE *clingan* to stick together, shrink, wither; akin to CLENCH] —**cling′er,** *n.* —**cling′ing·ly,** *adv.* —**cling′i·ness, cling′ing·ness,** *n.*

cling[2] (kling), *n.* a clingstone. [by shortening from *clingstone*, or special use of CLING[1] (n.)]

Cling·an (kling′gən), *n.* a boy's given name.

cling·fish (kling′fish′), *n., pl.* (*esp. collectively*) **-fish,** (*esp. referring to two or more kinds or species*) **-fish·es.** any fish of the family *Gobiesocidae*, having a sucking disk on the abdomen for clinging to stones, debris, etc. [CLING[1] + FISH]

cling′ing vine′, *Informal.* a woman who behaves in a helpless and dependent manner in her relationships with men.

Cling′mans Dome′ (kling′mənz), a mountain on the border between North Carolina and Tennessee: the highest peak in the Great Smoky Mountains. 6642 ft.

cling·stone (kling′stōn′), *adj.* 1. having a stone to which the pulp adheres closely, as certain peaches. —*n.* 2. a clingstone peach. [CLING[1] + STONE]

cling·y (kling′ē), *adj.*, **cling·i·er, cling·i·est.** apt to cling; adhesive or tenacious: *wet and clingy dirt.* [CLING[1] + -Y[1]]

clin·ic (klin′ik), *n.* 1. a place, as in connection with a medical school or a hospital, for the treatment of nonresident patients. 2. the instruction of medical students by examining or treating patients in their presence or by their examining or treating patients under supervision. 3. a class of students assembled for such instruction. 4. the place for such instruction. 5. any class or group convening for instruction, remedial work, etc., in a special field: *a reading clinic; a speech clinic.* —*adj.* 6. of a clinic; clinical. [< L *clīnic(us)* < Gk *klīnikós* pertaining to a (sick)bed, equiv. to *klī́n(ē)* bed + *-ikos* -IC]

clin·i·cal (klin′i kəl), *adj.* 1. pertaining to a clinic. 2. pertaining to or used in a sickroom: *a clinical bandage.* 3. concerned with or based on actual observation and treatment of disease in patients rather than artificial experimentation or theory. 4. extremely objective and realistic: *She tried to make a clinical examination of her own faults.* 5. *Eccles.* **a.** (of a sacrament) administered on a deathbed or sickbed. **b.** (of a convert or conversion) made on a deathbed or sickbed. [CLINIC + -AL[1]] —**clin′i·cal·ly,** *adv.*

clin′ical pathol′ogy, the branch of pathology dealing with the study of disease and disease processes by means of chemical, microscopic, and serologic examinations.

clin′ical psychol′ogy, the branch of psychology dealing with the diagnosis and treatment of personality and behavioral disorders. —**clin′ical psychol′ogist.**

clin′ical thermom′eter, an instrument used to determine the body temperature.

cli·ni·cian (kli nish′ən), *n.* a physician who studies diseases at the bedside, or is skilled in clinical methods. [CLINIC + -IAN]

clin·id (klin′id), *n.* 1. any of the blennioid fishes of the family *Clinidae*, found in tropical and subtropical seas. —*adj.* 2. belonging or pertaining to the family *Clinidae*. [< NL *Clinid(ae)*, equiv. to *Clin(us)* genus name (< Gk *klīn-*; see CLIN-) + *-idae* -ID[2]]

Cli·nis (klī′nis), *n.* *Class. Myth.* a Mesopotamian man loved by Artemis and Apollo.

clink[1] (klingk), *v.t., v.i.* 1. to make, or cause to make, a light, sharp, ringing sound: *The coins clinked together. He clinked the key against the penknife in his pocket.* 2. *Rare.* to rhyme or jingle. —*n.* 3. a clinking sound. 4. *Metall.* a small crack in a steel ingot resulting from uneven expanding or contracting. 5. a pointed steel bar for breaking up road surfaces. 6. *Brit.* the distinctive cry of certain birds, as the stonechat. 7. *Archaic.* a rhyme; jingle. [ME *clinken* (v.) perh. < MD *clinken*]

clink[2] (klingk), *n.* *Slang.* a prison; jail; lockup. [after *Clink*, name of prison in Southwark, London, perh. < D *klink* door-latch]

clink·er[1] (kling′kər), *n.* 1. a hard brick used esp. for paving. 2. a partially vitrified mass of brick. 3. the scale of oxide formed on iron during forging. 4. a mass of incombustible matter fused together, as in the burning of coal. 5. *Geol.* a mass of vitrified material ejected from a volcano. —*v.i.* 6. to form clinkers in burning, as coal. [< D *klinker* kind of brick]

clink·er[2] (kling′kər), *n.* one who or that which clinks. [CLINK[1] + -ER[1]]

clink·er[3] (kling′kər), *n.* *Slang.* 1. any mistake or error. 2. that which is a failure; a product of inferior quality. 3. *Brit. Slang.* someone or something wonderful or exceedingly well-liked. [special use of CLINKER[2]]

clink·er-built (kling′kər bilt′), *adj.* 1. faced or surfaced with boards, plates, etc., each course of which overlaps that below. 2. Also, **clincher-built.** *Shipbuilding.* noting a hull whose shell is formed of planking (**clink′er plank′ing**) or plating in which each strake overlaps the next one below and is overlapped by the next one above. Cf. **carvel-built.** [*clinker* (var. of CLINCHER) + BUILT]

clink′er plat′ing, *Shipbuilding.* shell or deck plating in which each strake overlaps the next one below or outboard and is overlapped by the next one above or inboard. Also called **clink′er-laid plat′ing** (kling′kər-lād′).

clink′er strake′, *Shipbuilding.* a strake of clinker planking or plating.

clink′er work′, *Shipbuilding.* clinker planking or plating.

clink·stone (klingk′stōn′), *n.* *Petrog.* any of several varieties of phonolite which give out a ringing sound when struck. [CLINK[1] + STONE, modeled on G *Klingstein*]

clino-, a learned borrowing from Latin meaning "slope," used in the formation of compound words: *clinometer.* [< L *-clin(āre)* (c. Gk *klī́n(ein)* (to) cause to lean, Skt *śrayati* he causes to lean) + -O-]

cli·no·graph (klī′nə graf′, -gräf′), *n.* 1. (in mining, construction, etc.) an instrument for measuring the deviation of boreholes or the like from the vertical. 2. *Drafting.* a pair of straightedges hinged together so as to be adjustable to any angle. [CLINO- + -GRAPH] —**cli·no·graph·ic** (klī′nə graf′ik), *adj.*

cli·nom·e·ter (klī nom′i tər, kli-), *n.* an instrument for determining angles of inclination or slope. [CLINO- + -METER] —**cli·nom′e·try,** *n.*

cli·no·met·ric (klī′nə me′trik), *adj.* 1. (of crystals) having oblique angles between one or all axes. 2. pertaining to or determined by a clinometer. Also, **cli′no·met′ri·cal.** [CLINO- + -METRIC]

clin·quant (kling′kənt), *adj.* 1. glittering, esp. with tinsel; decked with garish finery. —*n.* 2. imitation gold leaf; tinsel. 3. *Obs.* tinsel; false glitter. [< MF: clinking, prp. of *clinquer* (< D *klinken* to clink); see -ANT]

Clint (klint), *n.* a boy's given name, form of **Clinton.**

Clin·ton (klin′tᵊn), *n.* **1. De Witt** (də wit′), 1769–1828, U.S. political leader and statesman: governor of New York 1817–21, 1825–28 (son of James Clinton). **2. George,** 1739–1812, governor of New York 1777–95, 1801–04: vice-president of the U.S. 1805–12. **3. Sir Henry,** 1738?–95, commander in chief of the British forces in the American Revolutionary War. **4. James,** 1733—1812, American general in the Revolutionary War (brother of George Clinton). **5.** a city in E Iowa, on the Mississippi River. 33,589 (1960). **6.** a town in W Oklahoma. 9617 (1960). **7.** a town in NW South Carolina. 7937 (1960). **8.** a town in central North Carolina. 7461 (1960). **9.** a town in central Illinois. 7355 (1960). **10.** a town in central Missouri. 6925 (1960). **11.** a town in W Indiana. 5843 (1960). **12.** a town in E Tennessee. 4943 (1960). **13.** a town in W Mississippi. 3438 (1960). **14.** a town in S Connecticut. 2693 (1960). **15.** a boy's given name.

clin·to·ni·a (klin tō′nē ə), *n.* any liliaceous plant of the genus *Clintonia*, comprising stemless, perennial herbs with a few broad, ribbed, basal leaves, and white or greenish-yellow flowers on a short peduncle. [named after De Witt CLINTON; see -IA]

Clin·ton·ville (klin′tᵊn vil′), *n.* a town in central Wisconsin. 4778 (1960).

Cli·o (klī′ō), *n.* **1.** *Class. Myth.* the Muse of history. **2.** a girl's given name. [< L < Gk *Kleiṓ*, equiv. to *klei-* (s. of *kléein* to make famous, celebrate) + *-ō* suffix used for women's names]

clip[1] (klip), *v.*, **clipped, clipped** or **clipt, clip·ping,** *n.* —*v.t.* **1.** to cut, or cut off or out, as with shears: *to clip a rose from a bush.* **2.** to trim by cutting: *to clip a hedge.* **3.** to cut or trim the hair or fleece of; shear: *to clip a poodle.* **4.** to pare the edge of (a coin). Cf. **sweat** (def. 22). **5.** to cut short; curtail: *We clipped our visit by a week to return home earlier.* **6.** to pronounce rapidly, with precise articulation and with omission of certain sounds, as of unstressed vowels: *an annoying habit of clipping his words.* **7.** *Informal.* to hit with a quick, sharp blow: *He clipped him on the jaw with a sudden punch.* **8.** *Slang.* to take or get money from by dishonest means; swindle; rook. —*v.i.* **9.** to clip or cut something. **10.** to cut articles or pictures from a newspaper, magazine, etc. **11.** to move swiftly: *He clipped along route 66 on his motorcycle.* **12.** *Archaic.* to fly rapidly. —*n.* **13.** the act of clipping. **14.** anything clipped off, esp. the wool shorn at a single shearing of sheep. **15.** the amount of wool shorn in one season. **16. clips,** an instrument for clipping; shears. **17.** See **film clip. 18.** *Informal.* clipping (def. 2). **19.** *Informal.* a quick, sharp blow or punch: *a clip on the nose.* **20.** *Informal.* rate; pace: *at a rapid clip.* [ME *clippe(n)* < Scand; cf. Icel *klippa* to cut] —**clip′pa·ble,** *adj.*

clip[2] (klip), *n.*, *v.*, **clipped, clip·ping.** —*n.* **1.** a device that grips and holds tightly. **2.** a metal clasp for holding together papers, letters, etc. **3.** a flange on the upper surface of a horseshoe. **4.** See **cartridge clip. 5.** an article of jewelry or other decoration clipped onto clothing, shoes, hats, etc.: *A diamond clip was pinned to her dress.* **6.** Also called **lug.** *Shipbuilding.* a short length of angle iron connecting and maintaining the angle between two members or surfaces. **7.** *Archaic.* an embrace. —*v.t.*, *v.i.* **8.** to grip tightly; hold together by pressure. **9.** to encircle; encompass. **10.** *Football.* to block by illegally throwing the body across a player's legs from behind. **11.** *Archaic.* to embrace or hug. [ME *clippe(n)*, OE *clyppan* to embrace, surround; c. OFris *kleppa*]

clip·board (klip′bōrd′, -bôrd′), *n.* a stiff, rectangular board having at one end a clip for holding paper, a writing pad, or the like, and serving as a portable writing surface. [CLIP[2] + BOARD]

clip′ bond′, a form of brickwork raking bond for a facing of all stretchers, in which the stretchers are tied in to the backing every few courses by diagonally set bricks that project from the backing into angles made by cutting off the concealed corners of the face brick.

clip-clop (klip′klop′), *n.* clippety-clop.

clip-fed (klip′fed′), *adj.* (of a rifle) loading from a cartridge clip into the magazine. [CLIP[2] + FED]

clip′ joint′, 1. *Slang.* a public place of entertainment that makes a practice of overcharging or cheating customers. **2.** *Masonry.* a mortar joint made higher than usual in order to level the course above.

clip-on (klip′on′, -ôn′), *adj.* fashioned to hold on with a clip. [n. use of v. phrase *clip on*]

clipped (klipt), *adj.* characterized by quick, curt, and clear enunciation: *His clipped way of biting off his words revealed his anger. Can you understand his clipped accent?* [CLIP[1] + -ED[2]]

Clipper (def. 5)

clip·per (klip′ər), *n.* **1.** one who or that which clips or cuts. **2.** Often, **clippers.** a cutting tool, esp. shears: *hedge clippers.* **3.** Usually, **clippers.** a mechanical or electric tool for cutting hair, fingernails, or the like: *He told the barber, "No clippers on the sides, please."* **4.** one who or that which moves along swiftly: *That horse is a real clipper.* **5.** a sailing vessel built and rigged for speed, esp. a type of three-masted ship with a fast hull form and a lofty rig, built in the U.S. from c1845, and in Great Britain from a later date, until c1870, and used in trades in which speed was more important than cargo capacity. **6.** *Electronics.* a device that gives output only for an input above or below a certain critical value. **7.** *Slang.* a first-rate person or thing. [ME; see CLIP[1], -ER[1]]

clip′per bow′ (bou), *Naut.* a bow having a concave stem and a hollow entrance. Also called **fiddle bow.**

Clipper bow

clip·per-built (klip′ər-bilt′), *adj. Naut.* (of a hull) having fast lines, with a high ratio of length to beam and a fine entrance.

clip·pe·ty-clop (klip′i-tē klop′), *n.* the sound struck by the hoofs of a horse trotting on pavement, or any staccato, rhythmic sound resembling it. Also, **clip-clop.** [imit.]

clip·ping (klip′ing), *n.* **1.** the act of one who or that which clips. **2.** a piece clipped off or out, esp. an article, advertisement, etc., clipped from a newspaper or magazine. —*adj.* **3.** that clips. **4.** *Informal.* swift: *a clipping pace.* **5.** *Slang.* first-rate or excellent. [ME (adj.), late ME (n.). See CLIP[1], -ING[2], -ING[1]] —**clip′ping·ly,** *adv.*

clip·sheet (klip′shēt′), *n.* *Journalism.* a sheet of paper printed on one side for convenience in cutting and reprinting, containing news items, features, cartoons, etc., and distributed by public relations firms, publishers, and similar organizations. [CLIP[1] + SHEET[1]]

clipt (klipt), *v.* a pp. of **clip**[1].

clique (klēk, klik), *n.*, *v.*, **cliqued, cli·quing.** —*n.* **1.** a small, exclusive group of people; coterie; set. —*v.i.* **2.** *Informal.* to form, or associate in, a clique. [< F, perh. alter. of *claque* (see CLAQUE) but MF has *clique* clicking sound] —**clique′less,** *adj.* —**cli′quey, cli′quy,** *adj.* —**cli′quism,** *n.*
—**Syn. 1.** circle, crowd. See **ring**[1].

cli·quish (klē′kish, klik′ish), *adj.* **1.** of, pertaining to, or characteristic of a clique: *narrow, cliquish notions about art.* **2.** tending to divide into cliques: *a cliquish neighborhood.* **3.** associating exclusively with the members of one's own clique; clannish. [CLIQUE + -ISH[1]] —**cli′quish·ly,** *adv.* —**cli′quish·ness,** *n.*

clish·ma·cla·ver (klish′mə klā′vər, klēsh′-), *Scot.* —*n.* **1.** gossip; idle or foolish talk. —*v.i.* **2.** to gossip; talk foolishly. [*clish(-clash)* gossip (gradative compound based on CLASH) + *-ma-* (< ?) + CLAVER]

Clis·the·nes (klīs′thə nēz′), *n.* Cleisthenes.

clis·to·carp (klī′stə kärp′), *n.* *Bot.* cleistocarp.

clis·to·car·pous (klī′stə kär′pəs), *adj.* *Bot.* cleistocarpous.

clis·to·the·ci·um (klī′stə thē′shē əm, -sē əm), *n.*, *pl.* **-ci·a** (-shē ə, -sē ə). *Bot.* cleistothecium.

Cli·te (klī′tē), *n.* *Class. Myth.* the wife of Cyzicus, who hanged herself when her husband was mistakenly killed by the Argonauts.

clith·ral (klīth′rəl), *adj.* (of a classical temple) roofed over. Cf. **hypethral.** [< Gk *kleíthr(on)* bar for closing a door (deriv. of *kleíein* to close, shut) + -AL[1]]

clit·o·ris (klit′ər is, klī′tər is), *n.* *Anat.* the erectile organ of the vulva, homologous to the penis of the male. [< Gk *kleitorís*, akin to *kleíein* to shut] —**clit′o·ral, clit·o·rid·e·an** (klit′ə rid′ē ən), *adj.*

Cli·tus (klī′təs), *n.* *Class. Myth.* a son of Mantius who was beloved and abducted by Eos.

Clive (klīv), *n.* **1. Robert** (*Baron Clive of Plassey*), 1725–74, British general and statesman in India. **2.** a boy's given name, form of **Cleve.**

cliv·ers (kliv′ərz), *n.*, *pl.* **cliv·ers.** cleavers.

clk., **1.** clerk. **2.** clock.

clo·a·ca (klō ā′kə), *n.*, *pl.* **-cae** (-sē). **1.** a sewer, esp. an ancient sewer. **2.** a privy. **3.** a place or receptacle of moral filth. **4.** *Zool.* **a.** the common cavity into which the intestinal, urinary, and generative canals open in birds, reptiles, amphibians, many fishes, and certain mammals. **b.** a similar cavity in invertebrates. [< L: sewer, drain; prob. akin to Gk *klýzein* to wash, wash away] —**clo·a′cal,** *adj.*

cloak (klōk), *n.* **1.** a loose outer garment, as a cape or coat. **2.** that which covers or conceals; disguise; pretext: *He conducts his affairs under a cloak of secrecy.* —*v.t.* **3.** to cover with or as with a cloak: *She arrived at the opera cloaked in green velvet.* **4.** to hide; conceal: *The mission was cloaked in mystery.* [ME *cloke* (< OF) < ML *cloca*, var. of *clocca* (bell-shaped) cape, orig. bell; see CLOCK[1]] —**cloak·ed·ly** (klō′kid lē), *adv.* —**cloak′less,** *adj.*
—**Syn. 2.** cover, mask, veil; pretense, dissembling.

cloak-and-dag·ger (klōk′ən dag′ər), *adj.* pertaining to, characteristic of, concerned with, or dealing in intrigue or espionage, esp. of a romantic or dramatic kind: *This is a thrilling cloak-and-dagger story of espionage during the last war.*

cloak-and-suit·er (klōk′ən so͞o′tər), *n.* a manufacturer or seller of clothing, esp. ready-to-wear clothing.

cloak-and-sword (klōk′ən sôrd′), *adj.* (of a drama or work of fiction) dealing with characters who wear cloaks and swords; concerned with the customs and romance of the nobility in times gone by.

cloak·room (klōk′ro͞om′, -ro͝om′), *n.* **1.** a room in which outer garments may be left temporarily, as in a club, restaurant, etc. **2.** *U.S.* a room adjacent to a legislative chamber or legislative room, where legislators may leave their coats, relax, or engage in informal conversation. **3.** *Brit.* **a.** a bathroom; a public restroom. **b.** a baggage room, as at a railway station, where packages and luggage may be left temporarily or checked through to one's destination. [CLOAK + ROOM]

Clo·an·thus (klō an′thəs), *n.* *Rom. Legend.* a companion of Aeneas.

clob·ber[1] (klob′ər), *v.t. Slang.* **1.** to batter severely; strike heavily: *The thieves clobbered the shopkeeper to make him open the safe. He was clobbered on the head by a falling flowerpot.* **2.** to defeat decisively; drub; trounce. [?]

clob·ber[2] (klob′ər), *Brit., Australian Slang.* —*n.* **1.** (*construed as pl.*) clothes. —*v.i.* **2.** to dress, esp. in one's best clothes. [alter. of CLOTHES]

clob·ber[3] (klob′ər), *v.t.* to paint over existing decoration on (a ceramic piece). [obs. *clobber* to mend < ScotGael *clābar* mud]

clob·ber·er (klob′ər ər), *n. Brit.* a person who repairs shoes, mends clothing, etc. [CLOBBER[3] + -ER[1]]

cloche (klōsh, klôsh), *n.* **1.** a bell-shaped glass cover placed over a plant to protect it from frost and to force its growth. **2.** a bell-shaped, close-fitting hat for women. [< F: bell, bell-jar < LL *clocca*. See CLOAK]

clock[1] (klok), *n.* **1.** any of various instruments for measuring and recording time, esp. by mechanical means, usually with hands to indicate the hour and minute. **2.** (*cap.*) *Astron.* the constellation Horologium. **3. around the clock, a.** during all 24 hours; ceaselessly. **b.** without stopping for rest; tirelessly: *working around the clock to stem the epidemic.* —*v.t.* **4.** to time, test, or determine by means of a clock or watch: *The race horse was clocked at two minutes thirty seconds.* —*v.i.* **5. clock in,** to begin work, esp. by punching a time clock: *He didn't clock in until 9:30.* **6. clock out,** to end work, esp. by punching a time clock: *She clocked out early yesterday.* [ME *clok(ke)* < MD *clocke* instrument for measuring time; akin to OHG *glocka* (G *Glocke*), OE *clucge*, OIr *clocc* bell; see CLOAK] —**clock′like′,** *adj.*

clock[2] (klok), *n.* **1.** a short embroidered or woven ornament on each side or on the outer side of a stocking, extending from the ankle upward. **2.** plaiting on a ruff. Cf. **ruff**[1] (def. 1). —*v.t.* **3.** to embroider with such an ornament. [?]

clock·er (klok′ər), *n.* **1.** one who times race horses during tryouts to determine their speed. **2.** an official who times a race. **3.** one who maintains a record of the flow of traffic, as of visitors to a museum. [CLOCK[1] + -ER[1]]

clock′ golf′, a variety of golf, scored by strokes or holes, in which each player in turn putts from twelve equidistant positions marked off on the circumference of a circle into a hole inside the circle.

clock-hour (klok′our′, -ou′ər), *n.* *Educ.* sixty minutes of class instruction. Cf. **hour** (def. 12a).

clock′ jack′, jack[1] (def. 4). [earlier *jack of the clock-(house)*, *jackaclock*; see JACK[1]]

clock·mak·er (klok′mā′kər), *n.* a person who makes or repairs clocks. [CLOCK[1] + MAKER] —**clock′mak′·ing,** *n.*

clock′ watch′, a watch that strikes the hours. Cf. **repeater** (def. 3).

clock′ watch′er, an employee whose lack of interest in his work is exhibited by preoccupation with the time of day and often by undue haste in departing when the workday ends.

clock·wise (klok′wīz′), *adv.* **1.** in the direction of the rotation of the hands of a clock as viewed from the front; circularly to the right from a point taken as the top. —*adj.* **2.** directed clockwise: *a clockwise movement.* [CLOCK[1] + -WISE]

clock·work (klok′wûrk′), *n.* **1.** the mechanism of a clock. **2.** any mechanism similar to that of a clock. **3. like clockwork,** with perfect regularity or precision: *The launching of the missile went off like clockwork.* [CLOCK[1] + WORK]

clod (klod), *n.* **1.** a lump or mass, esp. of earth or clay. **2.** earth; soil. **3.** something of lesser dignity or value, as the body as distinguished from the soul: *this corporeal clod.* **4.** a stupid person; blockhead; dolt. **5.** a part of a shoulder of beef. [late ME *clodde*, OE *clodd-* (in *clodhamer* fieldfare); akin to CLOUD] —**clod′di·ly,** *adv.* —**clod′di·ness,** *n.* —**clod′like′,** *adj.* —**clod′dy,** *adj.*

clod·dish (klod′ish), *adj.* of, pertaining to, or resembling a clod or boor; doltish; stolid. [CLOD + -ISH[1]] —**clod′dish·ly,** *adv.* —**clod′dish·ness,** *n.*

clod·hop·per (klod′hop′ər), *n.* **1.** a clumsy boor; rustic; bumpkin. **2. clodhoppers,** strong, heavy shoes. [CLOD + HOPPER, modeled on GRASSHOPPER]

clod·hop·ping (klod′hop′ing), *adj.* loutish; boorish. [CLODHOPP(ER) + -ING[2]]

clod·poll (klod′pōl′), *n.* a stupid person; blockhead. Also, **clod′pole′, clod·pate** (klod′pāt′). [CLOD + POLL[1]]

Clo·ë (klō′ē), *n.* a girl's given name, form of **Chloe.**

Cloe·li·a (klē′lē ə), *n.* *Rom. Legend.* a girl who escaped from Lars Porsena by swimming across the Tiber.

Cloe·te (klo͞o′tē), *n.* **Stuart,** born 1897, South African novelist, born in France.

clog (klog, klôg), *v.*, **clogged, clog·ging,** *n.* —*v.t.* **1.** to encumber; hamper; hinder. **2.** to hinder or obstruct with thick or sticky matter; choke up: *to clog a drain.* **3.** to crowd excessively; overfill: *Cars clogged the highway.* —*v.i.* **4.** to become clogged, encumbered, or choked up. **5.** to stick; stick together. **6.** to do a clog dance. —*n.* **7.** anything that impedes motion or action; an encumbrance; a hindrance. **8.** a heavy block, as of wood, fastened to a man or beast to impede movement. **9.** a shoe with a thick sole of wood or cork. **10.** a similar but lighter shoe worn in the clog dance. **11.** See **clog dance. 12.** *Brit. Dial.* a thick piece of wood. [late ME *clog(ge)* short log or block of wood < ?] —**clog′gi·ly,** *adv.* —**clog′gi·ness,** *n.* —**clog′gy,** *adj.*
—**Syn. 1.** impede, trammel, fetter.

clog′ al′manac, a block of wood having notches cut in four sides to record the passage of time, formerly used in England and the Scandinavian countries.

clog′ dance′, a dance in which clogs, or heavy shoes, are worn for hammering out the lively rhythm. —**clog′ danc′er.** —**clog′ danc′ing.**

Clo·is (klō′is), *n.* a boy's given name.

cloi·son (kloi′zən), *n.* a thin metal band separating the color areas in cloisonné enamels. [< F: partition < VL *clausiōn- (s. of *clausiō), equiv. to L *claus(us)* (see CLAUSE, CLOSE) + *-iōn* -ION]

cloi·son·né (kloi′zə nā′; *Fr.* klwa zô nā′), *n.* **1.** enamelwork in which colored areas are separated by thin, metal bands fixed edgewise to the ground. —*adj.* **2.** pertaining to, forming, or resembling cloisonné or the pattern of cloisonné. [< F, equiv. to *cloison* (see CLOISON) + *-é* < L *-ātus* -ATE[1]]

Cloi·son·nisme (kloi′zə niz′əm), *n.* Synthetism. [< F *Cloisonnisme*. See CLOISONNÉ, -ISM] —**Cloi·son·nist** (kloi′zə nist), *n.*, *adj.*

clois·ter (kloi′stər), *n.* **1.** *Archit.* **a.** a covered walk, esp. in a religious institution, having an open arcade or colonnade usually opening onto a courtyard. **b.** a courtyard, esp. in a religious institution, bordered with such walks. **2.** a place of religious seclusion, as a monastery or convent. **3.** any quiet, secluded place. **4.** life in a monastery or convent. —*v.t.* **5.** to confine in a

monastery or convent. **6.** to confine in retirement; seclude. **7.** to furnish with a cloister or covered walk. **8.** to convert into a monastery or convent. [ME *cloistre* < OF, equiv. to *cloi(son)* partition, CLOISON + *(clo)stre* < L *claustrum* barrier (LL: enclosed place), equiv. to *claus(us)* (see CLOSE) + *-trum* n. suffix] —**clois′ter·less,** *adj.* —**clois′ter·like′,** *adj.*
—**Syn. 2.** abbey, priory.

Cloister

Clois′ter and the Hearth′, The, a novel (1861) by Charles Reade.

clois·tered (kloi′stərd), *adj.* **1.** secluded from the world; sheltered: *The wealthy recluse led a cloistered life.* **2.** having a cloister or cloisters. [CLOISTER + -ED²]

clois′tered vault′, a vault having the form of a number of intersecting coves. Also, **clois′ter vault′.** Also called **coved vault.**

clois′ter garth′, garth (def. 1).

clois·tral (kloi′strəl), *adj.* **1.** of, pertaining to, or living in a cloister. **2.** cloisterlike. [CLOIST(E)R + -AL¹]

clois·tress (kloi′stris), *n.* *Obs.* a nun. [*cloist(e)rer* monk + -ESS]

cloke (klōk), *n., v.* *Obs.* cloak.

clo·ky (klō′kē), *n., pl.* **-kies,** *adj.* cloque.

clomb (klōm), *v.* *Archaic and Dial.* pt. and pp. of **climb.**

clomp (klomp), *v.i.* clump (def. 6).

clone (klōn), *n.* *Biol.* a group of organisms derived from a single individual by various types of asexual reproduction. Also, **clon** (klon, klōn). [< Gk *klṓn* a slip, twig]

clon·ic (klon′ik, klō′nik), *adj.* *Pathol.* of or relating to clonus. [CLON(US) + -IC] —**clo·nic·i·ty** (klō nis′i tē, klo-), *n.* —**clo′nism,** *n.*

clon′ic spasm′, *Med.* See under **spasm** (def. 1).

clo·nus (klō′nəs), *n., pl.* **-nus·es.** *Pathol.* a rapid succession of flexions and extensions of a group of muscles, usually signifying an affection of the brain or spinal cord. [< NL < Gk *klónos* turmoil]

cloot (klo͞ot; *Scot.* klʏt), *n.* *Scot. and North Eng.* **1.** a cloven hoof; one of the divisions of the cloven hoof of the swine, sheep, etc. **2.** (*usually cap.*) Often, **Cloots.** Satan; the devil. [? akin to D *klauwtje,* equiv. to *klauw* CLAW + *-tje* dim. suffix]

cloot·ie (klo͞o′tē; *Scot.* klʏ′tē), *n.* *Scot. and North Eng.* **1.** cloot (def. 1). **2.** (*usually cap.*) cloot (def. 2). [CLOOT + -IE]

Cloots (klōts), *n.* **Jean Bap·tiste du Val-de-Grâce** (zhäN bA tēst′ dʏ vAl də gräs′), **Baron de** ("*Anacharsis Clootz*"), 1755–94, Prussian leader in French Revolution.

clo·que (klō kā′), *n.* **1.** an embossed or quilted fabric. —*adj.* **2.** having a small, irregular pattern or figured motif woven into a fabric to give a puckered or quilted effect. Cf. **matelassé.** Also, **clo·qué′, cloky.** [< F: *cloque* embossed, blistered, equiv. to dial. F (Picard) *cloque* bell, blister (see CLOAK) + *-é* < L *-ātus* -ATE¹]

Clo·quet (klō kā′), *n.* a town in NE Minnesota. 9013 (1960).

Clo·rin·da (klō rin′də, klō-), *n.* a girl's given name.

Clo·ris (klōr′is, klôr′-), *n.* a boy's given name.

clos (klō), *n., pl.* **clos.** *French.* a walled vineyard. [lit., closed]

Clos de Vou·geot (klō də vo͞o zhō′), a fruity, red wine from Burgundy. [< F: lit., vineyard of Vougeot]

close (*v.* klōz; *adj., adv.* klōs; *n.* klōz *for 59, 60, 63, 64, 66, 67,* klōs *for 61, 62, 65*), *v.,* **closed, clos·ing,** *adj.,* **clos·er, clos·est,** *adv., n.* —*v.t.* **1.** to put (something fashioned for this purpose) in a position to obstruct an entrance, opening, etc.; shut. **2.** to stop or obstruct (a gap, entrance, aperture, etc.): *to close a hole in a wall with plaster.* **3.** to block or hinder passage across or access to: *to close a border to tourists; to close the woods to picnickers.* **4.** to stop or obstruct the entrances, apertures, or gaps in: *He closed the crate and tied it up.* **5.** (of the mind) to make imperceptive or inaccessible: *to close one's mind to the opposite opinion.* **6.** to bring together the parts of; join; unite (often fol. by *up*): *to close the ranks of troops.* **7.** to bring to an end: *to close a debate.* **8.** to arrange the final details of: *to close a sale on a car; to close a deal to everyone's satisfaction.* **9.** to stop rendering the customary services of: *to close a store for the night.* **10.** *Naut.* to come close to: *We closed a schooner on the afternoon of the 19th.* **11.** *Metalworking.* to reduce the internal diameter of (a tube or the like). **12.** *Archaic.* to shut in or surround on all sides; enclose; cover in: *to close a bird in a cage.*
—*v.i.* **13.** to become closed; shut: *The door closed with a bang. This window is stuck and will not close tight.* **14.** to come together; unite: *Her lips closed firmly.* **15.** to come close: *His pursuers closed rapidly.* **16.** to grapple; engage in close encounter (often fol. by *with*): *We closed with the invaders shortly before sundown.* **17.** to come to an end; terminate: *The service closed with a hymn.* **18.** to cease to offer the customary activities or services: *The school closed for the summer.* **19.** (of a theatrical production) to cease to be performed: *The play closed in New York yesterday and will open in Dallas next week.* **20.** *Stock Exchange.* (of a stock, a group of stocks, etc.) to be or to be priced at the end of a trading day or other trading period, as specified: *The market closed low for the fourth straight day.* **21. close down, a.** to terminate the operation of; discontinue: *to close down an air base because of budget cuts.* **b.** to attempt to control or eliminate: *The city must close down on the drug traffic.* **22. close in on** or **upon, a.** to approach so as to capture, attack, arrest, etc.: *The hoodlums closed in on their victim.* **b.** to surround or envelop so as to entrap: *a feeling that the room was closing in upon her.* **23. close out, a.** to reduce the price of (merchandise) for quick sale: *That store is closing out its stock of men's clothing.* **b.** to liquidate or dispose of finally and completely: *They closed out their interests after many years in this city.* [ME *close(n)* < OF *claus-* (< L *claus-,* perfect s. of *claudere* to shut); r. OE *(be)clysan,* deriv. of *clūse* enclosure < LL *clūsa*]
—*adj.* **24.** having the parts or elements near to one another: *a close formation of battleships.* **25.** compact; dense: *a close texture; a close weave.* **26.** being in or having proximity in space or time: *The barn is so close to the house that you can hear the animals. His birthday is in May, close to mine.* **27.** marked by similarity in degree, action, feeling, etc.: *This dark pink is close to red. He left her close to tears.* **28.** near, or near together, in kind or relationship: *a flower close to a rose; a close relative.* **29.** intimate; confidential. **30.** based on a strong uniting feeling of respect, honor, or love: *a close circle of friends.* **31.** fitting tightly: *a close, clinging negligee.* **32.** (of a haircut or shave, the mowing of a lawn, etc.) so executed that the hair, grass, or the like is left flush with the surface or very short. **33.** not deviating from the subject under consideration. **34.** strict; searching; minute: *The matter requires close investigation.* **35.** not deviating from a model or original: *a close, literal translation.* **36.** nearly even or equal: *a close contest.* **37.** strictly logical: *close reasoning.* **38.** shut; shut tight; not open: *a close hatch.* **39.** shut in; enclosed. **40.** completely enclosing or surrounding: *a close siege preventing all escape.* **41.** without opening; with all openings covered or closed. **42.** confined; narrow: *close quarters.* **43.** lacking fresh or freely circulating air: *a hot, close room.* **44.** heavy; oppressive: *a spell of close, sultry weather.* **45.** narrowly confined, as a prisoner. **46.** practicing secrecy; secretive; reticent: *She is so close that you can tell her all your secrets.* **47.** parsimonious; stingy: *He is very close with his money.* **48.** scarce, as money. **49.** not open to public or general admission, competition, etc.: *The entire parish participated in the close communion.* **50.** *Hunting, Angling.* closed (def. 2). **51.** *Phonet.* (of a vowel) articulated with a relatively small opening between the tongue and the roof of the mouth. Cf. **high** (def. 23), **open** (def. 34a). **52.** *Heraldry.* (of a bird) represented as having folded wings: *an eagle close.* **53.** *Rare.* viscous; not volatile.
—*adv.* **54.** in a close manner; closely. **55.** near; close by. **56.** *Heraldry.* immediately behind the ears, so as to show no neck: *a bear's head couped close.* **57. close to the wind,** *Naut.* in a direction nearly opposite to that from which the wind is coming: *to sail close to the wind.* **58. close up,** *Naut.* fully raised; at the top of the halyard: *an answering pennant flown close up.* Cf. **dip** (def. 37). [ME *clos* < MF < L *claus(us)* (ptp. of *claudere* to shut), equiv. to *claud-* + *-tus* ptp. suffix]
—*n.* **59.** act of closing. **60.** the end or conclusion: *at the close of day; the close of the speech.* **61.** an enclosed place or enclosure, esp. one about or beside a cathedral or other building. **62.** any piece of land held as private property. **63.** See **complimentary close. 64.** *Music.* cadence (def. 7). **65.** *Brit. Dial.* **a.** a narrow entry or alley terminating in a dead end. **b.** a courtyard enclosed except for one narrow entrance. **66.** *Archaic.* a junction; union. **67.** *Obs.* a close encounter; a grapple: *The fighters met in a fierce close.* [in some senses, < adj.; in others, < v.] —**clos·a·ble, close·a·ble** (klō′zə bəl), *adj.* —**close·ly** (klōs′lē), *adv.* —**close·ness** (klōs′nis), *n.*
—**Syn. 2.** bar; clog; choke. CLOSE, SHUT mean to cause something not to be open. CLOSE suggests blocking an opening or vacant place: *to close a breach in a wall.* It also connotes more force or more refinement than SHUT. The informal word SHUT refers esp. to blocking or barring openings intended for literal or figurative entering and leaving: *to shut a door, mouth, gate, etc.* **7.** complete, end, conclude, terminate, finish. **8.** settle. **18.** stop; suspend. **25.** firm, solid. **26.** immediate, proximate, nearby. **59.** See **end¹.**

close-at-hand (klōs′ət hand′), *adj.* that lies in the near future or vicinity; nearby or imminent.

close-by (klōs′bī′), *adj.* nearby; adjacent; neighboring.

close′ call′ (klōs), *Informal.* a narrow escape: *We had a close call when our car skidded on the slippery pavement.*

close′ commun′ion (klōs), *Eccles.* a communion service in which only members of the same denomination can participate. Cf. **intercommunion, open communion.** —**close′ commun′ion·ist.**

close′ corpora′tion (klōs). See **closed corporation.**

closed (klōzd), *adj.* **1.** having or forming a boundary or barrier: *He was blocked by a closed door.* **2.** brought to a close; concluded: *It was a closed incident with no repercussions.* **3.** not public; restricted; exclusive. **4.** *Phonet.* (of a syllable) ending with a consonant or a consonant cluster, as *has, hasp.* Cf. **open** (def. 34b). **5.** *Ling.* (of a grammatical construction) not allowing the addition of more elements of the same type. **6.** restricted as to the kind of game that may be legally taken and as to where or when it may be taken: *closed season.* **7.** *Math.* **a.** (of a set and a mathematical operation defined on the set) such that performing the operation on elements of the set results in elements of the set, as multiplication in the set of integers. **b.** (of an interval) containing both of its endpoints. **c.** (of a set) containing all of its accumulation points, as the set of points on and within a circle; having an open set as complement. **d.** (of a map from one topological space to another) having the property that the image of a closed set is a closed set. **e.** (of a curve) not having endpoints; enclosing an area. **f.** (of a surface) enclosing a volume. **g.** (of a function or operator) having as its graph a closed set. [ME; see CLOSE, -ED²]

closed-cap·tioned (klōzd′kap′shənd), *adj.* of or pertaining to a television broadcast containing encoded captions, as for the hearing-impaired, that can be read with the aid of a decoder attached to the receiver.

closed′ chain′, *Chem.* three or more atoms linked together to form a ring or cycle and represented accordingly by its structural formula. Cf. **open chain.**

closed′ cir′cuit, *Elect.* a circuit without interruption, providing a continuous path through which a current can flow. Cf. **open circuit.** —**closed′-cir′cuit,** *adj.*

closed′-cir′cuit tel′evision, a system of televising by wire to designated viewing sets, as within a factory for monitoring production operations, in a theater for viewing a special event taking place elsewhere, etc.

closed′ cor′nice, **1.** a slightly projecting wooden cornice composed of a frieze board and a crown molding without a soffit. **2.** See **box cornice.**

closed′ corpora′tion, an incorporated business the stock of which is owned by a small group. Also, **close corporation.**

closed′ cou′plet, a couplet that concludes with an end-stopped line. Cf. **open couplet.**

closed-door (klōzd′dōr′, -dôr′), *adj.* held in strict privacy; barred to the press and to the public: *a closed-door strategy meeting of company executives.*

closed′-end invest′ment com′pany (klōzd′-end′), an investment company that issues its shares in large blocks at infrequent intervals and is not obligated to redeem or repurchase them. Cf. **open-end investment company.**

closed′ frac′ture. See **simple fracture.**

closed′ gen′tian, a gentian, *Gentiana Andrewsii,* of the eastern and central U.S. Also called **bottle gentian.**

close·down (klōz′doun′), *n.* a termination or suspension of operations; shutdown: *a temporary closedown of a factory.* [n. use of v. phrase *close down*]

closed′ pri′mary, a direct primary in which only persons meeting tests of party membership may vote.

closed′ shell′, *Physics.* **1.** (in atomic structure) a shell that contains the maximum number of electrons permitted by the exclusion principle. **2.** (in nuclear structure) a shell that contains the maximum number of nucleons permitted by the exclusion principle.

closed′ shop′, a shop in which union membership is a condition of hiring as well as of continued employment, or one in which the employer must call on the union to furnish employees.

closed′ sphere′, *Math.* the set of points whose distance from a given point is less than or equal to some specified number. Cf. **open sphere.**

closed′ string′, a staircase string concealing the profile of the steps. Also, **close string.** Also called **curb string.**

closed′ sys′tem, *Physics, Chem.* a region isolated from its surroundings by a boundary that admits no transfer of matter across it. Cf. **open system.**

closed′ trav′erse, *Survey.* a traverse ending at its point of origin.

closed′ un′ion, a labor union in which admission of new members is restricted by rigid requirements. Cf. **open union.**

close-fer·ti·li·za·tion (klōs′fûr′tᵊli zā′shən), *n.* *Bot.* self-fertilization.

close·fist·ed (klōs′fis′tid), *adj.* stingy; miserly. [CLOSE + FISTED] —**close′fist′ed·ly,** *adv.* —**close′fist′ed·ness,** *n.*

close-fit·ting (klōs′fit′ing), *adj.* (of a garment) fitting closely or snugly to the body: *A close-fitting jacket showed off her small waist.* Cf. **loose-fitting.**

close′ gaunt′let (klōz), *Armor.* a gauntlet able to be locked tightly around the handle of a weapon to prevent disarming. Also called **locking gauntlet.**

close-grained (klōs′grānd′), *adj.* (of wood) fine in texture or having inconspicuous annual rings.

close′ har′mony (klōs), *Music.* harmony in which the voices, excluding the bass, occur within an octave or, sometimes, within the interval of a tenth.

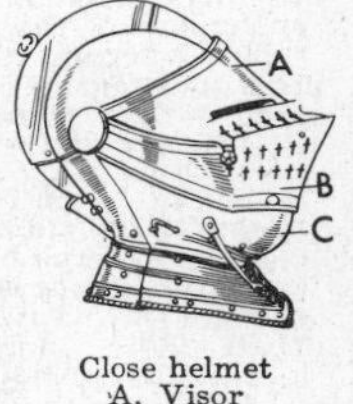

Close helmet
A, Visor
B, Ventail
C, Beaver

close-hauled (klōs′hôld′), *adj., adv.* *Naut.* as close to the wind as a vessel will sail, with sails as flat as possible; full and by.

close′ hel′met (klōz), *Armor.* a completely closed helmet of the late 15th century and after, having a facial defense composed of a visor and beaver or of a visor, ventail, and beaver attached to a pivot on each side.

close-in (klōs′in′), *adj.* **1.** near, as to a common center; adjacent, esp. to a city: *The city is enveloping its close-in suburbs.* **2.** occurring or provided at close quarters: *Fighter planes provided daring close-in air support.*

close′ junc′ture (klōs), *Ling.* absence of juncture. Cf. **open juncture.**

close-knit (klōs′nit′), *adj.* tightly connected or organized.

close-lipped (klōs′lipt′), *adj.* not talking or telling much.

close-mouthed (klōs′mouthd′, -moutht′), *adj.* reticent; uncommunicative.

close′ or′der drill′ (klōs), *U.S. Army.* practice in formation marching and other movements, in the carrying of arms during formal marching, and in the formal handling of arms for ceremonies and guard.

close·out (klōz′out′), *n.* **1.** a sale on all goods in liquidating a business. **2.** a sale on goods of a type that will no longer be carried by the store. [n. use of v. phrase *close out*]

close′ posi′tion (klōs), *Music.* arrangement of a chord so that the voices, excluding the bass, occur within an octave.

close′ quar′ters (klōs), **1.** a small, cramped place or position. **2.** direct and close contact in a fight: *They met at close quarters, exchanging many quick jabs.*

close′ quote′ (klōz), **1.** the quotation mark used to end a quotation, usually an apostrophe or a pair of apostrophes. **2.** an expression used by a speaker to signify that he is ending a quotation. Also, **close′ quotes′.**

clos·er (klō′zər), *n.* **1.** one who or that which closes. **2.** Also, **closure.** *Masonry.* **a.** any of various specially formed or cut bricks for spacing or filling gaps between regular bricks or courses of regular brickwork. Cf. **king closer, queen closer, split** (def. 30). **b.** a quarter-length bat. **c.** a stone laid with ashlar to fill a gap in a course or improve a bond. **3.** a sheet pile of irregular width for completing a wall of a cofferdam. [CLOSE + -ER¹]

close′ reach′ (klōs), *Naut.* See under **reach** (def. 26).

close-reefed (klōs′rēfd′, klōz′-), *adj. Naut.* having most or all of the sail reefs taken in.

close′ shave′ (klōs), *Informal.* a narrow escape: *After having many close shaves during the war, he was killed in a hunting accident.*

close′ shot′ (klōs), *Motion Pictures, Television.* close-up (def. 2).

close-stool (klōz′sto͞ol′, klōs′-), *n.* a stool having a seat with a hole, beneath which a chamber pot is placed. Also called **necessary stool.** [ME]

close′ string′ (klōs). See **closed string.**

clos·et (kloz′it), *n.* **1.** a small room, enclosed recess, or cabinet for storing clothing, food, utensils, etc. **2.** a small private room, esp. one used for prayer, meditation, etc. **3.** See **water closet. 4.** *Heraldry.* a diminutive of the bar, one-half the usual width. —*adj.* **5.** private; secluded. **6.** suited for use or enjoyment in privacy: *closet reflections; closet prayer.* **7.** engaged in private study or speculation; speculative; unpractical: *a closet thinker with no practical experience.* —*v.t.* **8.** to shut up in a private room for a conference, interview, etc. (usually used in the passive voice): *The Secretary of State was closeted with the senator for three hours in a tense session.* [ME < MF, equiv. to *clos* CLOSE (n.) + *-et* -ET]

clos′et dra′ma, 1. drama appropriate for reading rather than for acting. **2.** a play in this form.

close-up (klōs′up′), *n.* **1.** *Photog.* a picture taken at close range or with a long focal-length lens, on a relatively large scale. **2.** Also called **close shot.** *Motion Pictures, Television.* a camera shot taken at a very short distance from the subject, to permit a close and detailed view of an object or action. Cf. **long shot** (def. 2), **medium shot. 3.** an intimate view or presentation of anything. [n. use of adverbial phrase *close up*]

close-wind·ed (klōs′win′did), *adj.* (of a sailing vessel) designed for sailing close to the wind.

clos·ing (klō′zing), *n.* **1.** the end or conclusion, as of a speech. **2.** that which closes; fastening, as of a purse. **3.** See **complimentary close.** [ME; see CLOSE, -ING[1]]

clos′ing er′ror, *Survey.* See **error of closure.**

Clos·ter (klos′tər), *n.* a town in NE New Jersey. 7767 (1960).

clos·trid·i·um (klo strid′ē əm), *n., pl.* **clos·trid·i·a** (klo strid′ē ə). *Bacteriol.* any of several rod-shaped, spore-forming, anaerobic bacteria of the genus *Clostridium,* found in soil and in the intestinal tract of man and animals. [< Gk *klōstr-,* var. s. of *klōster* spindle (*klōs-,* var. s. of *klṓthein* (see CLOTHO) + *-ter* suffix making n. of agent or instrument) + -IDIUM] —**clos·trid′i·al, clos·trid′i·an,** *adj.*

clo·sure (klō′zhər), *n., v.,* **-sured, -sur·ing.** —*n.* **1.** the act or state of closing; the state of being closed. **2.** a bringing to an end; conclusion. **3.** that which closes or shuts. **4.** closer (def. 2). **5.** an architectural screen or parapet, esp. one standing free between columns or piers. **6.** *Phonet.* an occlusion of the vocal tract as an articulatory feature of a particular speech sound. Cf. **constriction** (def. 5). **7.** *Parl. Proc.* a cloture. **8.** *Survey.* completion of a traverse, angle measurement, etc., ideally in such a way as to have calculations consistent with previous data or mathematical laws. **9.** *Math.* **a.** the property of being closed with respect to a particular operation. **b.** the intersection of all closed sets that contain a given set. **10.** *Obs.* that which encloses or shuts in; enclosure. —*v.t., v.i.* **11.** *Parl. Proc.* to cloture. [ME < MF < L *clausūra.* See CLOSE, -URE]

clo′sure rail′, *Railroads.* any rail connecting a switch and a frog or connecting two frogs between the rails of a regular track, as in a switch or turnout.

clot (klot), *n., v.,* **clot·ted, clot·ting.** —*n.* **1.** a mass or lump. **2.** a semisolid mass, as of coagulated blood. **3.** a small compact group of individuals: *a clot of sightseers massed at the entrance.* —*v.i.* **4.** to form into clots; coagulate. —*v.t.* **5.** to cause to clot. **6.** to cover with clots: *Carefully aimed snowballs clotted the house.* **7.** to cause to become blocked or obscured: *to clot the book's narrative with too many characters.* [ME; OE *clott* lump; c. MD *klotte,* G *Klotz* block, log]

cloth (klôth, kloth), *n., pl.* **cloths** (klôt͟hz, klot͟hz, klôths, kloths), *adj.* —*n.* **1.** a fabric formed by weaving, felting, etc., from wool, hair, silk, flax, cotton, or other fiber, used for garments, upholstery, and many other items. **2.** a piece of such a fabric for a particular purpose: *an altar cloth.* **3.** the particular attire of any profession, esp. that of the clergy. Cf. **man of the cloth. 4. the cloth,** the clergy: *men of the cloth.* **5.** *Naut.* **a.** one of the lengths of canvas or duck of standard width sewn side by side to form a sail, awning, or tarpaulin. **b.** any of various pieces of canvas or duck for reinforcing certain areas of a sail. **c.** a number of sails taken as a whole. **6.** *Obs.* a garment; clothing. —*adj.* **7.** of or made of cloth: *She wore a cloth coat trimmed with fur.* [ME *cloth, clath* cloth, garment, OE *clāth;* c. D *kleed,* G *Kleid*] —**cloth′like′,** *adj.*

cloth′ beam′. See **cloth roll.**

cloth·bound (klôth′bound′, kloth′-), *adj.* (of a book) bound with cloth rather than paper, leather, etc. [CLOTH + BOUND[1]]

clothe (klōt͟h), *v.t.,* **clothed** or **clad, cloth·ing. 1.** to dress; attire. **2.** to provide with clothing. **3.** to cover with or as with clothing. [ME *clothe(n),* OE *clāthian,* deriv. of *clāth* CLOTH]

clothes (klōz, klōt͟hz), *n.pl.* **1.** garments for the body; articles of dress; wearing apparel. **2.** bedclothes. [ME; OE *clāthas,* pl. of *clāth,* CLOTH]
—**Syn. 1.** clothing, attire, raiment, costume, garb; vestments, habiliments.

clothes·bas·ket (klōz′bas′kit, -bä′skit, klōt͟hz′-), *n.* a basket for holding and carrying laundry. [CLOTHES + BASKET]

clothes·horse (klōz′hôrs′, klōt͟hz′-), *n.* **1.** a person, esp. a woman, whose chief interest and pleasure is dressing fashionably. **2.** a frame on which to hang wet laundry for drying. [CLOTHES + HORSE]

clothes·line (klōz′līn′, klōt͟hz′-), *n.* a strong, thin rope, cord, wire, etc., usually stretched between two poles or posts, on or from which clean laundry is hung to dry. [CLOTHES + LINE[1]]

clothes′ moth′, any of several small moths of the family *Tineidae,* the larvae of which feed on wool, fur, etc., esp. *Tinea pellionella* (**casemaking clothes moth**).

clothes-peg (klōz′peg′, klōt͟hz′-), *n. Brit.* a clothespin.

clothes·pin (klōz′pin′, klōt͟hz′-), *n.* a device, usually a forked piece of wood or plastic, for fastening articles to a clothesline. [CLOTHES + PIN]

clothes′ pole′, a pole used for supporting a clothesline.

clothes·press (klōz′pres′, klōt͟hz′-), *n.* a receptacle for clothes, as a chest, wardrobe, or closet. [CLOTHES + PRESS[1]]

clothes′ stop′, *Naut.* a short length of cord used to secure a piece of clothing to a clothesline or to tie up a rolled garment being stored, packed, etc.

clothes′ tree′, an upright pole with hooks near the top for hanging coats, hats, etc.

Casemaking clothes moth, *Tinea pellionella* A, Adult; B, Larva

cloth·ier (klōt͟h′yər, -ē ər), *n.* **1.** a retailer of clothing, esp. for men. **2.** a person who makes or sells cloth. [CLOTH + *-ier,* var. of -ER[1]; r. ME *clother*]

cloth·ing (klō′t͟hing), *n.* **1.** garments collectively; clothes; raiment; apparel. **2.** a covering. [ME; see CLOTHE, -ING[1]]

Clo·tho (klō′thō), *n. Class. Myth.* the Fate who spins the thread of life. [< L < Gk *Klōthṓ* lit., the Spinner, equiv. to *klṓth(ein)* (to) spin + *-ō* suffix used in making names of women]

cloth-of-gold (klôth′əv gōld′, kloth′-), *n.* a garden plant, *Crocus susianus,* of the Crimea, having orange-yellow flowers.

cloth′ roll′, a roller, located at the front of the loom, on which woven material is wound after it leaves the breast beam. Also called **cloth beam.**

cloth′ yard′, 36 inches; 3 feet.

Clo·til·da (klō til′də), *n.* a girl's given name. Also, **Clo·til·de** (klō til′də; *Fr.* klō tēld′).

clot·ty (klot′ē), *adj.* **1.** full of clots. **2.** tending to clot. [CLOT + -Y[1]]

clo·ture (klō′chər), *n., v.,* **-tured, -tur·ing.** *U.S. Parl. Proc.* —*n.* **1.** a method of closing a debate and causing an immediate vote to be taken on the question. —*v.t., v.i.* **2.** to close (a debate) by cloture. [< F *clôture,* MF *closture* < VL **clōstūra,* alter. of L *clōstra, claustra,* pl. of *claustrum* barrier. See CLOISTER]

clou (klo͞o), *n.* a major point of interest. [< F: lit., a nail < L *clāvus*]

cloud (kloud), *n.* **1.** a visible collection of particles of water or ice suspended in the air, usually at an elevation above the earth's surface. **2.** any similar mass, esp. of smoke or dust. **3.** a dim or obscure area in something otherwise clear or transparent. **4.** a patch or spot differing in color from the surrounding surface. **5.** anything that obscures or darkens something, or causes gloom, trouble, suspicion, disgrace, etc. **6.** a great number of insects, birds, etc., flying together: *a cloud of locusts obscuring the sun.* **7. in the clouds, a.** in a condition of absent-mindedness; lost in reverie. **b.** impractical: *Her schemes are usually up in the clouds.* **8. on a cloud,** *Slang.* exceedingly happy; in high spirits: *On the night of the prom the seniors were on a cloud.* **9. under a cloud,** in disgrace; under suspicion: *After the fight he left town under a cloud.* —*v.t.* **10.** to overspread or cover with, or as with, a cloud or clouds: *The smoke from the fire clouded the sun from view.* **11.** to overshadow; obscure; darken: *The hardships of war cloud his childhood memories.* **12.** to make gloomy. **13.** (of distress, anxiety, etc.) to reveal itself in (a part of one's face): *Worry clouded his brow.* **14.** to make obscure or indistinct; confuse: *Don't cloud the issue with unnecessary details.* **15.** to place under suspicion, disgrace, etc. **16.** to variegate with patches of another color. —*v.i.* **17.** to grow cloudy; become clouded. **18.** (of a part of one's face) to reveal one's distress, anxiety, etc.: *His brow clouded with anger.* [ME; OE *clūd* rock, hill; see CLOD] —**cloud′like′,** *adj.*
—**Syn. 1.** vapor. CLOUD, FOG, HAZE, MIST differ somewhat in their figurative uses. CLOUD connotes esp. daydreaming: *His mind is in the clouds.* FOG and HAZE connote esp. bewilderment or confusion: *to go around in a fog (haze).* MIST has an emotional connotation and suggests tears: *a mist in one's eyes.* **6.** swarm, horde, multitude, throng, host, crowd, army. —**Ant. 11, 14.** clarify, illuminate.

cloud·age (klou′dij), *n.* See **cloud cover.** [CLOUD + -AGE]

cloud′ ban′ner. See **banner cloud.**

cloud·ber·ry (kloud′ber′ē, -bə rē), *n., pl.* **-ries. 1.** the orange-yellow edible fruit of a raspberry, *Rubus Chamaemorus,* of the Northern Hemisphere. **2.** the plant itself. [CLOUD + BERRY]

cloud·burst (kloud′bûrst′), *n.* a sudden and very heavy rainfall. [CLOUD + BURST]

cloud′ cap′. See **cap cloud.**

cloud-capped (kloud′kapt′), *adj.* surrounded at the top by clouds; having the top obscured by clouds: *immense, cloud-capped mountains.*

cloud′ cham′ber, *Physics.* an apparatus for determining the movements of charged particles, consisting of a chamber containing a supersaturated mixture of gas and vapor, the vapor condensing around ions created by the particle in its passing, thereby revealing the path of the particle. Also called **Wilson cloud chamber.** Cf. **bubble chamber.**

cloud′ cov′er, a covering of clouds over part or all of the sky. Also called **cloudage.**

cloud·ed (klou′did), *adj.* **1.** obscure; beclouded; indistinct: *He presented only a confused and clouded argument.* **2.** confused; muddled; disordered: *a mind clouded by sorrow.* **3.** covered with or as if with clouds. [CLOUD + -ED[2]]

cloud′ed sul′fur. See **common sulfur.**

cloud′ grass′, an annual grass, *Agrostis nebulosa,* of Spain, having clusters of tiny spikelets on slender stalks, used in bouquets.

cloud·land (kloud′land′), *n.* a region of unreality, imagination, etc.; dreamland. [CLOUD + LAND]

cloud·less (kloud′lis), *adj.* having no clouds; clear: *a cloudless sky.* [CLOUD + -LESS] —**cloud′less·ly,** *adv.* —**cloud′less·ness,** *n.*

cloud′less sul′phur, a sulphur butterfly, *Phoebis sennae,* having unmarked yellow wings, the larvae of which feed on the senna plant.

cloud·let (kloud′lit), *n.* a small cloud. [CLOUD + -LET]

cloud′ nine′, *Slang.* a state of perfect happiness or well-being; bliss (usually in the phrase *on cloud nine*): *The newlyweds seemed to be on cloud nine.*

cloud′ phys′ics, the science of the physical properties and processes of clouds.

cloud′ rack′, rack[4] (def. 1).

Clouds (kloudz), *n.* **Sea of.** See **Mare Nubium.**

cloud′ seed′ing, any technique of adding material to a cloud to alter its natural development, usually to increase or obtain precipitation.

Clouds, The, a comedy (423 B.C.) by Aristophanes.

cloud·y (klou′dē), *adj.,* **cloud·i·er, cloud·i·est. 1.** full of or overcast by clouds: *a cloudy sky.* **2.** having little or no sunshine: *a cloudy but rainless day.* **3.** of or like a cloud or clouds; pertaining to clouds. **4.** having cloudlike markings: *cloudy marble.* **5.** not clear or transparent: *He could not see through the cloudy liquid.* **6.** obscure; indistinct. **7.** darkened by gloom, trouble, etc. **8.** under suspicion, disgrace, etc.: *a gambler with a cloudy reputation.* [ME *cloudi,* OE *clūdig* rocky, hilly. See CLOUD, -Y[1]] —**cloud′i·ly,** *adv.* —**cloud′i·ness,** *n.*
—**Syn. 1,** murky, lowering, shadowy, gloomy, depressing. **5.** murky, turbid, muddy, opaque, shadowy. **6.** dim, blurred, shadowy, unclear, befogged, muddled, confused. **7.** gloomy, lowering. **8.** shadowy.

Clou·et (klo͞o e′), *n.* **1. Fran·çois** (fräN swA′), c1510–72, French painter. **2.** his father, **Jean** (zhäN), c 1485–1545, French painter.

clough (kluf, klou), *n. Brit. Dial.* a narrow valley; ravine; glen. [ME *clough, cloge;* c. OHG *klāh-*]

Clough (kluf), *n.* **Arthur Hugh,** 1819–61, English poet.

clout (klout), *n.* **1.** *Informal.* a blow, esp. with the hand; cuff. **2.** *Baseball Slang.* a long hit, esp. an extra-base hit: *A hard clout to deep center field drove in the winning run.* **3.** *Archery.* **a.** the mark or target shot at, esp. in long-distance shooting. **b.** a shot that hits the mark. **4.** Also called **clout′ nail′.** a nail for attaching sheet metal to wood, having a short shank with a broad head. **5.** *Archaic.* **a.** a patch or piece of cloth or other material used to mend something. **b.** any worthless piece of cloth; rag. —*v.t.* **6.** *Informal or Dial.* to strike, esp. with the hand; cuff. **7.** *Archaic or Dial.* **a.** to bandage. **b.** to patch; mend. [ME; OE *clūt* piece of cloth or metal; c. MLG *klūt(e),* Icel *klūt(r)*] —**clout′er,** *n.*

clove[1] (klōv), *n.* **1.** the dried flower bud of a tropical myrtaceous tree, *Eugenia aromatica,* used whole or ground as a spice. **2.** the tree. [ME *clow(e),* short for *clow-gilofre* clove-gillyflower < F *clou de gilofre.* See CLOU, GILLYFLOWER]

clove[2] (klōv), *n. Bot.* one of the small bulbs formed in the axils of the scales of a mother bulb, as in garlic. [ME; OE *clufu* bulb (c. MD *clōve,* D *kloof*); akin to CLEAVE[2]]

clove[3] (klōv), *v.* a pt. of **cleave**[2].

clove[4] (klōv), *n.* a British unit of weight for wool, cheese, etc., usually equivalent to 8 pounds. [< AF *clove,* earlier *clou,* equiv. to AL *clāvus,* L: nail; see CLOVE[1]]

clove′ hitch′, a knot or hitch for fastening a rope to a spar or larger rope, consisting of two half hitches made in opposite directions, the two parts of the rope emerging also in opposite directions. See illus. under **knot.** Also called **builder's knot, heaving-line bend.**

clo·ven (klō′vən), *v.* **1.** a pp. of **cleave**[2] —*adj.* **2.** cleft; split; divided: *Goats have cloven hoofs.*

clo′ven hoof′, the figurative indication of Satan or evil temptation. Also, **clo′ven foot′.**

clo·ven-hoofed (klō′vən ho͝oft′, -ho͞oft′), *adj.* **1.** having split hoofs, once assumed to represent the halves of a single undivided hoof, as in cattle. **2.** devilish; Satanic. Also, **clo′ven-foot′ed.**

clove′ pink′, a pink, *Dianthus Caryophyllus,* having a spicy scent resembling that of cloves. Cf. **carnation** (def. 1).

clo·ver (klō′vər), *n., pl.* **-vers,** (*esp. collectively*) **-ver. 1.** any of various fabaceous herbs of the genus *Trifolium,* having trifoliolate leaves and dense flower heads, many species of which, as *T. pratense,* are cultivated as forage plants. **2.** any of various plants of allied genera, as melilot. **3. in clover,** enjoying luxury or comfort; wealthy or well-off: *They struggled to make their fortune, and now they're in clover.* [ME *clovere,* OE *clāfre;* akin to G *Klee*] —**clo′vered,** *adj.* —**clo′ver·y,** *adj.*

White clover, *Trifolium repens*

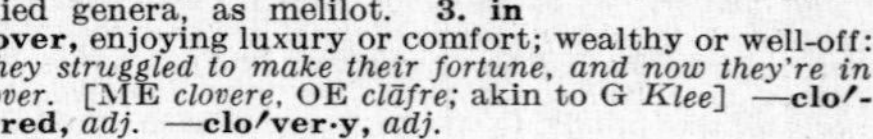

Clo·ver (klō′vər), *n.* **1.** a town in N South Carolina. 3500 (1960). **2.** a girl's given name.

clo′ver broom′, a dome-shaped herb, *Baptisia tinctoria,* of the eastern U.S., having clusters of yellow flowers. Also called **shoofly.**

Clo·ver·dale (klō′vər dāl′), *n.* a town in W California. 2848 (1960).

Cloverleaf (def. 1)

clo·ver·leaf (klō′vər lēf′), *n., pl.* **-leaves,** *adj.* —*n.* **1.** a road arrangement, resembling a four-leaf clover in form, for permitting easy traffic movement between two intersecting high-speed highways. One highway passes over the other, and both are joined by a system of curved feeder roads permitting vehicles to enter and leave the highways. —*adj.* **2.** shaped like or resembling a leaf of clover. [CLOVER + LEAF]

Clo·vis (klō′vis), *n.* **1.** a city in E New Mexico. 23,713 (1960). **2.** a town in central California. 5546 (1960). **3.** a boy's given name.

Clo·vis I (klō′vis; *Fr.* klō vēs′), A.D. c465–511, king of the Franks 481–511. German, **Chlodwig.**

clowd·er (klou′dər), *n.* a group or collection of cats. [alter. of CLUTTER]

clown (kloun), *n.* **1.** a comic performer, as in a circus, theatrical production, or the like, who wears an outlandish costume and make-up and entertains by pantomim-

ing common situations or actions in exaggerated or ridiculous fashion, by juggling or tumbling, etc. 2. a prankster; a practical joker. 3. a coarse, ill-bred person; a boor. 4. a peasant; rustic. —*v.i.* 5. to act like a clown. [akin to Icel *klunni* boor, Dan dial. *klunds,* Sw dial. *klunn* log, etc.] —**clown′ish,** *adj.* —**clown′ish·ly,** *adv.* —**clown′ish·ness,** *n.*
—**Syn.** 3. lout, churl. 4. bumpkin.

clown·er·y (klou′nə rē), *n., pl.* **-er·ies** for 2. 1. clownish behavior. 2. an instance of this. [CLOWN + -ERY]

clown′ white′, *Theat.* white facial make-up used by performers, such as clowns.

cloy (kloi), *v.t.* 1. to weary by an excess of food, sweetness, pleasure, etc.; surfeit; satiate. —*v.i.* 2. to become uninteresting or distasteful through overabundance: *A diet of cake and candy soon cloys.* [aph. var. of ME *acloye(n)* < MF *enclo(y)er* < LL *inclāvāre* to nail in, equiv. to *in-* IN-[2] + *clāv(us)* nail + *-āre* inf. suffix] —**cloy′ed·ness,** *n.* —**cloy′ing·ly,** *adv.* —**cloy′ing·ness,** *n.*
—**Syn.** 1. glut.

cloy·ing (kloi′ing), *adj.* causing or tending to cause disgust or aversion through excess, as food, sentimentality or flattery: *an elfin charm that quickly became cloying.* [CLOY + -ING[2]]

CLU, Civil Liberties Union.

C.L.U., Chartered Life Underwriter.

club (klub), *n., v.,* **clubbed, club·bing,** *adj.* —*n.* 1. a heavy stick, usually thicker at one end than at the other, suitable for use as a weapon; a cudgel. 2. *Sports.* **a.** a stick or bat used to drive a ball in various games, as golf. **b.** See **Indian club.** 3. a group of persons organized for a social, literary, athletic, political, or other purpose. 4. the building or rooms occupied by such a group. 5. an organization that offers its subscribers certain benefits, as discounts, bonuses, or interest, in return for regular purchases or payments: *a book club; a record club; a Christmas club.* 6. a night club or cabaret: *Last night we went to all the clubs in town.* 7. a black trefoil-shaped figure on a playing card. 8. a card bearing such figures. 9. **clubs,** (*construed as sing. or pl.*) the suit so marked: *Clubs is trump. Clubs are trump.* 10. *Naut.* **a.** a short spar attached to the end of a gaff to allow the clew of a gaff topsail to extend beyond the peak of the gaff. **b.** a short spar attached to the truck of a mast to support the upper part of a club topsail. **c.** clubfoot. —*v.t.* 11. to beat with or as with a club. 12. to gather or form into a clublike mass. 13. to unite; combine; join together. 14. to contribute as one's share toward a joint expense; make up by joint contribution (often fol. by *up* or *together*): *They clubbed their dollars together to buy the present.* 15. to defray by proportional shares. 16. to hold (a rifle, shotgun, etc.) by the barrel, so as to use the stock as a club. —*v.i.* 17. to combine or join together, as for a common purpose. 18. to gather into a mass. 19. to contribute to a common fund. 20. *Naut.* to drift in a current with an anchor, usually rigged with a spring, dragging or dangling to reduce speed. —*adj.* 21. of or pertaining to a club. 22. consisting of a combination of foods offered at the price set on the menu: *They allow no substitutions on the club luncheon.* [ME *clubbe* < Scand; cf. Icel *klubba* cudgel; akin to CLUMP]
—**Syn.** 1. bludgeon, billy. 3, 5. association, society. See **circle.** 11. bludgeon, belabor, batter, maul, cudgel.

club·ba·ble (klub′ə bəl), *adj.* fit to be a member of a social club; sociable. Also, **club′a·ble.** [CLUB + -ABLE] —**club′ba·bil′i·ty, club′a·bil′i·ty,** *n.*

club·ber (klub′ər), *n.* 1. one who or that which clubs. 2. a member of a club. [CLUB + -ER[1]]

club·by (klub′ē), *adj.,* **-bi·er, -bi·est.** 1. characteristic of a club: *The room had a warm, clubby atmosphere.* 2. very friendly; intimate; chummy: *He became clubby with the bartender, who slipped him many a free drink.* 3. socially exclusive; cliquish: *a social group that is very clubby and unfriendly.* 4. inclined to join clubs. [CLUB + -Y[1]] —**club′bi·ly,** *adv.*

club′ car′, a railway passenger car equipped with easy chairs, card tables, a buffet, etc.

club′ chair′, a heavily upholstered chair having solid sides and a low back.

club′ coupe′, an automobile equipped with two full-sized rows of seats but having doors only in the front, the seats in the rear being reached by inclining the backs of the front seats forward.

club′ fight′er, *Boxing.* a boxer of limited potential, who fights regularly, usually at the smaller boxing clubs, and is characterized by his ability to punch, willingness to trade punches, and lack or disdain of finesse.

club′ foot′, *Furniture.* a knoblike foot formed from the end of a cabriole leg as a continuation of its lines: less flat than a pad foot but otherwise similar.

club·foot (klub′fo͝ot′), *n., pl.* **-feet** for 1. 1. a deformed or distorted foot. 2. the condition of having such a foot; talipes. 3. Also called **club.** *Naut.* a short boom for fastening to the foot of a jib. [CLUB + FOOT] —**club′foot′ed,** *adj.*

club′ grass′, cattail (def. 1).

club·hand (klub′hand′), *n.* 1. a deformed or distorted hand, similar in nature and causation to a clubfoot. 2. the condition of having such a hand. [CLUB + HAND]

club·haul (klub′hôl′), *v.t.* *Naut.* to cause (a sailing vessel) to come about on a new tack by bending a cable to the lee quarter and to the lee anchor, dropping the anchor as the vessel heads into the wind, and hauling on the cable so as to swing the stern to the lee side: used in emergencies when the vessel is in danger of not coming about by itself. [CLUB + HAUL]

club·house (klub′hous′), *n., pl.* **-hous·es** (-hou′ziz). a building or room occupied by a club. [CLUB + HOUSE]

club·man (klub′mən, -man′), *n., pl.* **-men** (-mən, -men′). a man who belongs to a club, esp. a fashionable club, and is active in club life. [CLUB + MAN[1]]

club′ moss′, any plant of the genus *Lycopodium.*

club·room (klub′ro͞om′, -ro͝om′), *n.* a room used by a club. [CLUB + ROOM]

club·root (klub′ro͞ot′, -ro͝ot′), *n.* *Plant Pathol.* a disease of cabbage and other cruciferous plants, characterized by enlarged, malformed roots, caused by a slime mold, *Plasmodiophora brassicae.* [CLUB + ROOT[1]]

club′ sand′wich, a sandwich of toast, typically three slices, interlaid with pieces of cold chicken or turkey and bacon or ham and containing lettuce, tomato, mayonnaise dressing, etc.

club′ so′da. See **soda water** (def. 1).

club′ so′fa, a heavily upholstered sofa having solid sides and a low back.

club′ steak′, a beefsteak cut from the rib end of the short loin, or sometimes a porterhouse or T-bone steak from which the tenderloin has been trimmed.

club′ top′sail, *Naut.* a triangular gaff topsail having the upper part of the luff raised above the mast truck by a club.

club′ wheat′, a wheat, *Triticum compactum,* characterized by compact, club-shaped spikes, used for making pastry flour and the like.

club·wom·an (klub′wo͝om′ən), *n., pl.* **-wom·en.** a woman who engages in club activities, esp. one prominent in social or civic organizations. [CLUB + WOMAN]

cluck[1] (kluk), *v.i.* 1. to utter the cry of a hen brooding or calling her chicks. 2. to make a similar sound; express concern, approval, etc., by such a sound. —*v.t.* 3. to call or utter by clucking: *The old lady was loudly clucking her sympathy.* —*n.* 4. the sound uttered by a hen when brooding, or in calling her chicks. 5. any clucking sound. [var. of *clock* (now dial. and Scot), ME *clokken,* OE *cloccian* to cluck, c. D *klokken*]

cluck[2] (kluk), *n.* *Slang.* a dull-witted, stupid person; dolt. [special use of CLUCK[1]]

clue (klo͞o), *n., v.,* **clued, clu·ing.** —*n.* 1. anything that serves to guide or direct in the solution of a problem, mystery, etc. 2. clew. —*v.t.* 3. to direct or point out by a clue. 4. clew. [var. of CLEW]

Cluj (klo͞ozh), *n.* a city in NW Rumania. 167,011 (est. 1964). German, **Klausenberg.** Hungarian, **Kolozsvár.**

Clumber spaniel (1½ ft. high at shoulder)

clum′ber span′iel (klum′bər), one of an English breed of short-legged, stocky spaniels having a chiefly white coat, used esp. for retrieving game. [after *Clumber,* estate in Nottinghamshire, England, where dogs were bred]

clump (klump), *n.* 1. a close group or cluster, esp. of trees or other plants. 2. *Immunol.* a cluster of agglutinated bacteria, erythrocytes, etc. 3. a lump or mass. 4. a clumping tread, sound, etc. 5. a thick extra sole on a shoe. —*v.i.* 6. to walk heavily and clumsily. 7. *Immunol.* to gather or be gathered into clumps. —*v.t.* 8. to gather or form into a clump; mass. 9. *Immunol.* to gather or form in clumps. [akin to D *klompe* lump, mass, OE *clympre* lump of metal] —**clump′y, clump′ish, clump′like′,** *adj.*

clump′ block′, *Naut.* a block for use with thick, heavy ropes.

clum·sy (klum′zē), *adj.,* **-si·er, -si·est.** 1. awkward in movement or action; without skill or grace: *He is very clumsy and always breaking things.* 2. awkwardly done or made; unwieldy; ill-contrived: *He made a clumsy, embarrassed apology.* [*clums* benumbed with cold (now obs.) + -Y[1]; akin to ME *clumsen* to be stiff with cold, Sw (Skåne) *klumsig* benumbed, awkward, *klums* numbskull, Icel *klumsa* lock-jawed, etc See CLAM[2]] —**clum′si·ly,** *adv.* —**clum′si·ness,** *n.*
—**Syn.** 1. ungraceful, ungainly, lumbering, lubberly. 2. unhandy, unskillful, maladroit, inexpert, bungling, bumbling, heavy-handed, inept. —**Ant.** 2. adroit, skillful.

clung (klung), *v.* pt. and pp. of **cling.**

Clu·ny (klo͞o′nē; *Fr.* klʏ nē′), *n.* 1. a town in E France, N of Lyons: ruins of a Benedictine abbey. 4412 (1962). 2. a boy's given name.

Clu′ny lace′, 1. ivory-white bobbin lace made of strong linen or cotton thread. 2. a machine lace, usually of cotton, copied from it. [after CLUNY, France]

clu·pe·id (klo͞o′pē id), *n.* 1. any of the *Clupeidae,* a family of chiefly marine, teleostean fishes, including the herrings, sardines, menhaden, and shad. —*adj.* 2. belonging or pertaining to the family *Clupeidae.* [< L *clupe(a)* a type of small river fish + -ID[2]]

clu·pe·oid (klo͞o′pē oid′), *adj.* 1. resembling a fish of the family *Clupeidae;* clupeid. —*n.* 2. a clupeoid fish. [< L *clupe(a)* (see CLUPEID) + -OID]

Clur·man (klûr′mən), *n.* **Harold (Edgar),** born 1901, U.S. theatrical director, author, and critic.

Clu·si·um (klo͞o′sē əm), *n.* ancient name of **Chiusi.**

clus·ter (klus′tər), *n.* 1. a number of things of the same kind, growing or held together; a bunch: *a cluster of grapes.* 2. a group of things or persons close together: *There was a cluster of tourists at the gate.* 3. *U.S. Army.* a small metal design placed on a ribbon representing an awarded medal to indicate that the same medal has been awarded again: *oak-leaf cluster.* 4. *Phonet.* a succession of two or more contiguous consonants in an utterance, as the *str-* cluster of *strap.* —*v.t.* 5. to gather into a cluster or clusters. 6. to furnish or cover with clusters. —*v.i.* 7. to form a cluster or clusters: *The people clustered around to watch.* [ME; OE *cluster, clyster* bunch; c. LG *kluster*] —**clus′ter·ing·ly,** *adv.* —**clus′ter·y,** *adj.*

clus·tered (klus′tərd), *adj.* *Archit.* 1. closely grouped around a central pier, as a number of shafts. 2. (of a pier) so formed as to suggest a number of clustered shafts. [ME; see CLUSTER, -ED[2]]

clus′ter·head pink′ (klus′tər hed′), a perennial herb, *Dianthus carthusianorum,* of central Europe, having numerous, small, purple flowers in a tight cluster from two to three inches wide. [CLUSTER + HEAD]

clus′ter leg′, *Furniture.* a leg having the form of a cluster of columns or shafts.

clus′ter point′, *Math.* 1. a point of a net, having the property that the net is frequently in each neighborhood of the point. 2. See **accumulation point.** 3. a point of a filter having the property that every neighborhood of the point has points in common with every set in the filter.

clutch[1] (kluch), *v.t.* 1. to seize with or as with the hands or claws; snatch: *The bird swooped down and clutched its prey with its claws.* 2. to grip or hold tightly or firmly: *She clutched the child's hand as they crossed the street.* 3. *Slang.* to spellbind; grip a person's emotions, attention, or interest: *Garbo movies really clutch me.* —*v.i.* 4. to try to seize or grasp (usually fol. by *at*): *She clutched at the fleeing child. He clutched at the opportunity.* 5. to operate the clutch in a vehicle. 6. *Slang.* to become tense with fright; panic (sometimes fol. by *up*): *I clutched up on the math exam.* —*n.* 7. the hand, claw, etc., when grasping. 8. Usually, **clutches.** power of disposal or control; mastery: *She fell into the clutches of the enemy.* 9. the act of clutching; a snatch or grasp. 10. a tight grip or hold. 11. a device for gripping something. 12. *Mach.* **a.** a mechanism for readily engaging or disengaging a shaft with or from another shaft or rotating part. Cf. **coupling** (def. 2a). **b.** a control, as a pedal, for operating this mechanism. 13. *Sports.* an extremely important or crucial moment of a game: *He was famous for his coolness in pitching in the clutch.* 14. *Informal.* any critical position or situation; emergency: *She kept complete control in the clutch.* 15. **in the clutches,** *Informal.* under trying or close circumstances or conditions: *The rookie pitcher did very well, especially in the clutches when the hitters bore down.* —*adj.* 16. (of a handbag or purse) without a strap or handle; small and of a shape that may be grasped by the hand. 17. (of a coat) without fasteners; held closed in front by one's hand or arm. [ME *clucchen, clicchen,* OE *clyccan* to clench] —**clutch′ing·ly,** *adv.* —**clutch′y,** *adj.*
—**Syn.** 1. See **catch.**

clutch[2] (kluch), *n.* 1. a hatch of eggs; the number of eggs produced or incubated at one time. 2. a brood of chickens. 3. a number of similar individuals: *a clutch of books; a whole clutch of chorus girls.* —*v.t.* 4. to hatch (chickens). [var. of *cletch* (now dial.); akin to Scot *cleck* to hatch < Scand; cf. Icel *klekja*]

clutch·er (kluch′ər), *n.* *Informal.* a person who habitually takes part in coffee klatsches. [*clutch-* (alter. of KLATSCH) + -ER[1]]

Clute′ Cit′y (klo͞ot), a town in S Texas. 4501 (1960).

clut·ter (klut′ər), *v.t.* 1. to fill or litter with things in a disorderly manner: *Newspapers cluttered the living room.* —*v.i.* 2. *Dial.* to run in disorder; move with bustle and confusion. 3. *Dial.* to make a clatter. 4. to speak so rapidly and inexactly that distortions of sound and phrasing result. —*n.* 5. a disorderly heap or assemblage; litter: *It is impossible to find anything in all this clutter.* 6. a state or condition of confusion; disorderly mess. 7. confused noise; clatter. [var. of *clotter* (now obs.), equiv. to CLOT + -ER[6]]

Clyde (klīd), *n.* 1. a river in S Scotland, flowing NW into the Firth of Clyde. 106 mi. long. 2. **Firth of,** an inlet of the Atlantic, in SW Scotland. 64 mi. long. 3. a town in N Ohio. 4826 (1960). 4. a town in central New York. 2693 (1960). 5. a boy's given name.

Clyde·bank (klīd′bangk′), *n.* a city in SW Scotland, on the Clyde River. 49,654 (1961).

Clydes·dale (klīdz′dāl′), *n.* one of a Scottish breed of strong, hardy draft horses, having a feathering of long hairs along the backs of the legs. [after *Clydesdale,* Scotland]

Clym·e·ne (klim′ə nē′), *n.* *Class. Myth.* 1. a daughter of Catreus who was sold to Nauplius. 2. a daughter of Oceanus, and the mother, by Helios, of Phaëthon and the Heliades. 3. an ocean nymph sometimes believed to be the mother of Prometheus. 4. a daughter of Minyas, and the mother, by Phylacus, of Iphiclus and Alcimede. 5. (in the *Iliad*) an attendant of Helen of Troy.

Cly·me·nus (klī′mə nəs), *n.* *Class. Myth.* 1. an Arcadian who violated his daughter Harpalyce. 2. a Boeotian king who was accidentally injured by a Theban and who ordered his sons to avenge the fatal injury.

clyp·e·ate (klip′ē āt′), *adj.* *Biol.* shaped like a round shield or buckler. Also, **clyp·e·i·form** (klip′ē ə fôrm′). [< L *clypeāt(us).* See CLYPEUS, -ATE[1]]

clyp·e·us (klip′ē əs), *n., pl.* **clyp·e·i** (klip′ē ī′). the area of the facial wall of an insect's head between the labrum and the frons, usually separated from the latter by a groove. [< NL, special use of var. of *clipeus* round shield] —**clyp′e·al,** *adj.*

cly·sis (klī′sis), *n., pl.* **-ses** (-sēz). *Med.* 1. the administration of an enema. 2. intravenous administration of any of a number of solutions to provide nutriment, replace lost body fluid, control blood pressure, or dispel pain. [< NL < Gk *klýsis,* equiv. to *kly-* (var. s. of *klýzein;* see CLYSTER) + *-sis* -SIS]

clys·ter (klis′tər), *n.* *Med.* an enema. [late ME < medical L < Gk *klystḗr,* equiv. to *klys-* (var. s. of *klýzein* to rinse out) + *-ter* n. suffix]

Cly·tem·nes·tra (klī′təm nes′trə), *n.* *Class. Myth.* the daughter of Tyndareus and Leda, the wife of Agamemnon, and the mother of Orestes, Electra, and Iphigenia. She killed Agamemnon and was herself killed, along with her lover, Aegisthus, by Orestes. Also, **Cly′taem·nes′ra.**

Cly·ti·ë (klī′tē ē′, klish′ē ē′), *n.* *Class. Myth.* a water nymph who, having fallen in love with Apollo in his character of sun god, was transformed into the heliotrope. Also, **Clyt·i·a** (klish′ē ə).

Cly·ti·us (klish′ē əs), *n.* *Class. Myth.* 1. (in the *Iliad*) a brother of Priam killed by Hercules. 2. a companion of Jason. 3. one of the Gigantes.

Cm, *Chem.* curium.

cm, centimeter; centimeters. Also, **cm.**

c/m, (of capital stocks) call of more.

c.m., 1. church missionary. 2. common meter. 3. corresponding member. 4. court-martial.

Cmdr., Commander.

C.M.G., Companion of the Order of St. Michael and St. George.

cml., commercial.

CMTC, Citizens' Military Training Camp.

C/N, 1. circular note. 2. credit note.

cne·mis (nē′mis), *n., pl.* **cnem·i·des** (nem′i dēz′). *Anat., Zool.* the tibia or shin. [< Gk *knēmis* greave, akin to *knḗmē* tibia] —**cne′mic, cne′mi·al,** *adj.*

cni·da (nī′də), *n., pl.* **-dae** (-dē). *Zool.* a nematocyst. [< Gk *knídē* nettle]

Cni·di·a (nī′dē ə), *n.* *Class. Myth.* an epithet of Aphrodite referring to the city of Cnidus, where there was a statue of the goddess by Praxiteles.

cnido-, a combining form of **cnida:** *cnidophore.*

cni·do·blast (nī′də blast′), *n.* *Zool.* the cell within which a nematocyst is developed. [CNIDO- + -BLAST]

cni·do·cil (nī′də sil), *n.* *Zool.* a hairlike sensory process projecting from the surface of a cnidoblast, believed to trigger the discharge of the nematocyst. [CNIDO- + *-cil* < L *cilium;* see CILIA]

cni·do·cyst (nī′də sist′), *n.* *Zool.* a nematocyst. [CNIDO- + -CYST]

cni·dog·e·nous (nī doj′ə nəs), *adj.* *Zool.* producing or containing nematocysts. [CNIDO- + -GENOUS]

cni·do·phore (nī′də fōr′, -fôr′), *n.* *Zool.* a part or organ bearing cnidoblasts. [CNIDO- + -PHORE] —**cni·doph·o·rous** (nī dof′ər əs), *adj.*

Cni·dus (nī′dəs), *n.* an ancient city in SW Asia Minor, in Caria: the Athenians defeated the Spartans in a naval battle near here 394 B.C. —**Cni′de·an,** *adj.*

CNO, Chief of Naval Operations.

Cnos·sus (nos′əs), *n.* Knossos. —**Cnos′si·an,** *adj.*

C-note (sē′nōt′), *n.* C (def. 5).

CNS, central nervous system. Also, **cns**

Cnut (kə no͞ot′, -nyo͞ot′), *n.* Canute.

CO, Commanding Officer.

Co, *Chem.* cobalt.

co-, 1. var. of **com-** before a vowel, *h,* and *gn: coadjutor; cohabit; cognate.* 2. *Math., Astron.* a prefix meaning "complement of": *cosine; codeclination.* [< L]

Co., 1. Company. 2. County. Also, **co.**

co., (in prescriptions) a compound; compounded. [< L *compositus*]

C/O, 1. cash order. 2. certificate of origin.

C/o, 1. care of. 2. *Bookkeeping.* carried over.

c/o, 1. care of. 2. *Bookkeeping.* carried over. 3. cash order.

C.O., 1. cash order. 2. Commanding Officer. 3. conscientious objector.

c.o., 1. care of. 2. carried over.

co·ac·er·vate (kō as′ər vit, -vāt′, kō′ə sûr′vit), *n.* *Physical Chem.* a reversible aggregation of emulsoid particles preceding flocculation into liquid rather than solid aggregates. [< L *coacervāt(us)* (ptp. of *coacervāre*), equiv. to *co-* CO- + *acerv(us)* heap, multitude + *-ātus* -ATE[1]]

co·ac·er·va·tion (kō as′ər vā′shən), *n.* *Physical Chem.* the process of becoming a coacervate. [< L *coacervātiōn-* (s. of *coacervātiō*), equiv. to *coacervāt(us)* (see COACERVATE) + *-iōn-* -ION]

coach (kōch), *n.* 1. a large, horse-drawn, four-wheeled carriage, usually enclosed. 2. a type of passenger automobile which is enclosed, has two full-width seats, one behind the other, and usually has one door on each side; a two-door sedan. 3. a public passenger bus. 4. *Railroads.* See **day coach.** 5. *Naut.* an after cabin in a sailing ship, located beneath the poop deck, for use esp. by the commander of the ship. 6. a class of airline travel providing less luxurious accommodations than first class at a lower fare. 7. a person who trains an athlete or a team of athletes: *a football coach.* 8. *Baseball.* a playing or nonplaying member of the team at bat who is stationed in the box outside first or third base to signal instructions to and advise base runners and batters. 9. a private tutor who prepares a student for an examination. 10. a person who instructs an actor or singer. —*v.t.* 11. to give instruction or advice to in the capacity of a coach: *He coached and trained her until she was women's all-State tennis champion.* —*v.i.* 12. to act as a coach. 13. to study with or be instructed by a coach. —*adv.* 14. by coach or in coach-class accommodations: *We flew coach from Denver to New York.* [earlier *coche(e)* < G *Kotsche, Kutsche* < Hung *kocsi,* short for *Kocsi czeker* car of Kocs, place in Hungary] —**coach′a·ble,** *adj.* —**coach′a·bil′i·ty,** *n.*

Coach (def. 1)

coach-and-four (kōch′ən fōr′, -fôr′), *n.* a coach together with the four horses by which it is drawn.

coach′ box′, the seat for the driver of a coach.

coach·build·ing (kōch′bil′ding), *n.* *Brit.* the manufacture of automobile bodies. [COACH + BUILDING] —**coach′build′er,** *n.*

coach′ dog′, Dalmatian (def. 3).

Co·a·chel·la (kō′ə chel′ə), *n.* a town in S California. 4854 (1960).

coach·er (kō′chər), *n.* 1. a person who coaches; a coach. 2. See **coach horse.** 3. *Australian.* a docile bullock used to lead or calm a herd of cattle. [COACH + -ER[1]]

coach′ horse′, a horse, usually strong and heavily built, used or trained for drawing a coach.

coach′ house′, a small building, usually part of an estate or adjacent to a main house, used for housing coaches, carriages, and other vehicles. Also called **carriage house.**

coach′ing glass′, a small drinking glass of c1800 having no foot. Also called **fuddling glass.**

coach·man (kōch′mən), *n., pl.* **-men.** 1. a man employed to drive a coach or carriage. 2. *Angling.* See **royal coachman.** [COACH + MAN[1]] —**coach′man·ship′,** *n.*

coach′ screw′. See **lag screw.**

coach·whip (kōch′hwip′, -wip′), *n.* 1. a whip, usually having a long lash, used in driving a coach horse. 2. Also, **coach′whip snake′.** a long, slender colubrid snake, *Masticophis flagellum,* of the southern U.S. and Mexico, having a thin tail resembling a braided whip. [COACH + WHIP]

coach·work (kōch′wûrk′), *n.* 1. the process or designing of automobile bodies. 2. the craftsmanship involved in the design of an automobile body. [COACH + WORK]

co·act (kō akt′), *v.t., v.i.* to do or act together. [CO- + ACT] —**co·ac′tor,** *n.*

co·ac·tion[1] (kō ak′shən), *n.* force or compulsion, either in restraining or in impelling. [< L *coāctiōn-* (s. of *coāctiō*), equiv. to *coāct(us)* (ptp. of *cōgere;* see COGENT, CO-, ACT) + *-iōn-* -ION]

co·ac·tion[2] (kō ak′shən), *n.* 1. joint action. 2. *Ecol.* any interaction among organisms within a community. [CO- + ACTION]

co·ac·tive[1] (kō ak′tiv), *adj.* compulsory; coercive. [COACT(ION)[1] + -IVE] —**co·ac′tive·ly,** *adv.* —**co′ac·tiv′i·ty,** *n.*

co·ac·tive[2] (kō ak′tiv), *adj.* acting together. [CO- + ACTIVE] —**co·ac′tive·ly,** *adv.* —**co′ac·tiv′i·ty,** *n.*

Coade′ stone′ (kōd), a ceramic imitation of carved stonework popular around 1800 and later. [named after E. *Coade,* 19th-century Englishwoman]

co·ad·ju·tant (kō aj′ə tənt), *adj.* 1. helping reciprocally; cooperating. —*n.* 2. an assistant; aide. [CO- + ADJUTANT]

co·ad·ju·tor (kō aj′ə tər, kō′ə jo͞o′tər), *n.* 1. an assistant. 2. an assistant to a bishop or other ecclesiastic. 3. a bishop who assists another bishop, with the right of succession. [< L, equiv. to *co-* CO- + *adjūtor* helper (see ADJUTANT, -OR[2]); r. late ME *coadjutour* < AF < L]

co·ad·ju·tress (kō aj′ə tris), *n.* a female assistant. [COADJUT(O)R + -ESS]

co·ad·ju·trix (kō aj′ə triks), *n., pl.* **co·ad·ju·tri·ces** (kō aj′ə trī′sēz). coadjutress. [< NL, equiv. to L *co-* CO- + *adjūtrix* female helper; see COADJUTOR, -TRIX]

co·ad·u·nate (kō aj′ə nit, -nāt′), *adj.* *Zool., Bot.* united by growth. [< LL *coadūnāt(us)* (ptp. of *coadūnāre*), equiv. to *co-* CO- + *ad-* AD- + *ūn(us)* one + *-ātus* -ATE[1]] —**co·ad′u·na′tion,** *n.*

co·ad·ven·ture (kō′əd ven′chər), *v.,* **-tured, -tur·ing,** *n.* —*v.i.* 1. to share in an adventure. —*n.* 2. adventure in which two or more share. [CO- + ADVENTURE] —**co′ad·ven′tur·er;** *referring to a woman,* **co·ad·ven·tur·ess** (kō′əd ven′chər is), *n.*

co·ag·u·la·ble (kō ag′yə lə bəl), *adj.* capable of being coagulated. [COAGUL(ATE) + -ABLE] —**co·ag′u·la·bil′i·ty,** *n.*

co·ag·u·lant (kō ag′yə lənt), *n.* a substance that produces coagulation. Also, **co·ag·u·la·tor** (kō ag′yə lā′tər). [< L *coāgulant-* (s. of *coāgulāns,* prp. of *coāgulāre*), equiv. to *coāgul(um)* COAGULUM + *-ant-* -ANT]

co·ag·u·lase (kō ag′yə lās′), *n.* *Biochem.* any of several enzymes, esp. one secreted by certain staphylococci, that cause coagulation of blood or blood plasma. [COAGUL(ATE) + -ASE]

co·ag·u·late (*v.* kō ag′yə lāt′; *adj.* kō ag′yə lit, -lāt′), *v.,* **-lat·ed, -lat·ing,** *adj.* —*v.t., v.i.* 1. to change from a fluid into a thickened mass; curdle; congeal. 2. *Physical Chem.* (of colloidal particles) to flocculate or cause to flocculate by adding an electrolyte to an electrostatic colloid. —*adj.* 3. *Obs.* coagulated. [< L *coāgulāt(us)* (ptp. of *coāgulāre*), equiv. to *coāgul(um)* COAGULUM + *-ātus* -ATE[1]] —**co·ag′u·la′tion,** *n.* —**co·ag·u·la·to·ry** (kō ag′yə lə tōr′ē, -tôr′ē); *Archaic.* **co·ag·u·la·tive** (kō ag′yə lā′tiv, -lə tiv), *adj.*

co·ag·u·lin (kō ag′yə lin), *n.* a precipitin. [COAGUL(ATE) + -IN[2]]

co·ag·u·lum (kō ag′yə ləm), *n., pl.* **-la** (-lə). any coagulated mass; precipitate; clump; clot. [< L: that which binds together or coagulates, rennet, equiv. to *coāg-* (*co-* CO- + *āg-* impel; see AGENT) + *-ulum* n. suffix denoting means or instrument]

Co·a·hui·la (kō′ä wē′lä), *n.* a state in N Mexico. 896,509 (1960); 58,067 sq. mi. *Cap.:* Saltillo.

coak (kōk), *n.* *Carpentry.* 1. (in a scarf joint) a tenon in one member fitting into a corresponding recess of the other. 2. a dowel through overlapping timbers to prevent one from sliding across the other. [? var. of COCK[1] in sense of projection]

coal (kōl), *n.* 1. a black or dark-brown combustible mineral substance consisting of carbonized vegetable matter, used as a fuel. Cf. **anthracite, bituminous coal, lignite.** 2. a piece of glowing, charred, or burned wood or other combustible substance. 3. charcoal (def. 1). 4. **heap coals of fire on someone's head,** to repay evil with good in order to make one's enemy repent. 5. **take, call, rake, haul, or drag over the coals,** to reprimand; scold: *They were raked over the coals for turning out slipshod work.* —*v.t.* 6. to burn to coal or charcoal. 7. to provide with coal. —*v.i.* 8. to take in coal for fuel. [ME *cole,* OE *col;* c. D *kool,* G *Kohle,* Icel *kol*] —**coal′less,** *adj.*

coal′ ball′, a spherical mass of mineral and plant material embedded in coal beds, ranging in size from that of a pea to that of a boulder.

coal·bin (kōl′bin′), *n.* a bin used for holding coal. [COAL + BIN]

coal′ car′, *U.S.* 1. a railway car designed to carry coal. 2. a car for hauling coal in or from a mine.

Coal′ Cit′y, a town in NE Illinois. 2852 (1960).

Coal·dale (kōl′dāl′), *n.* a town in central Pennsylvania. 3949 (1960).

coal·er (kō′lər), *n.* a railroad, ship, etc., used mainly to haul or supply coal. [COAL + -ER[1]]

co·a·lesce (kō′ə les′), *v.,* **-lesced, -lesc·ing.** —*v.i.* 1. to grow together or into one body: *The two lakes coalesced into one.* 2. to unite so as to form one mass, community, etc.: *The various groups coalesced into a crowd.* 3. to blend or come together: *Their ideas coalesced into one theory.* —*v.t.* 4. to cause to unite in one body or mass. [< L *coalēsce(re),* equiv. to *co-* CO- + *al-* (s. of *alere* to nourish, make grow) + *-ēscere* -ESCE] —**co′a·les′cence,** *n.* —**co′a·les′cent,** *adj.*
—**Syn. 1, 2.** unite, combine, join. **2.** amalgamate, fuse, blend, merge.

coal′ field′, an area containing coal deposits.

coal·fish (kōl′fish′), *n., pl.* **-fish·es,** (*esp. collectively*) **-fish.** 1. a sablefish. 2. the pollack, *Pollachius virens.* [COAL + FISH]

coal′ gas′, 1. the gas formed by burning coal. 2. a gas used for illuminating and heating, produced by distilling bituminous coal and consisting chiefly of hydrogen, methane, and carbon monoxide.

Coal′ Grove′, a town in S Ohio. 2961 (1960).

coal′ heav′er, a person who carries or shovels coal.

coal′ hod′, *Chiefly Northern U.S.* a small pail for carrying coal; a coal scuttle.

Co·a·lin·ga (kō′ə ling′gə), *n.* a town in central California. 5965 (1960).

coal′ing sta′tion, a place at which coal is supplied to ships, locomotives, etc.

co·a·li·tion (kō′ə lish′ən), *n.* 1. union into one body or mass; fusion. 2. a combination or alliance, esp. a temporary one between persons, factions, states, etc. [< L *coalitiōn-* (s. of *coalitiō*), equiv. to *coalit(us),* ptp. of *coalēscere* (*co-* CO- + *ali,* ptp. s. of *alere* to feed + *-tus* ptp. suffix) + *-iōn-* -ION; see COALESCE] —**co′a·li′tion·al,** *adj.* —**co′a·li′tion·ist, co′a·li′tion·er,** *n.*
—**Syn. 2.** partnership; league.

coal′ meas′ures, *Geol.* 1. coal-bearing strata. 2. (*caps.*) a portion of the Carboniferous system, characterized by coal deposits.

coal′ mine′, a mine or pit from which coal is obtained. —**coal′ min′er.** —**coal′ min′ing.**

coal′ oil′, *Chiefly Dial.* 1. petroleum obtained by the destructive distillation of bituminous coal. 2. kerosene.

coal′ pit′, 1. a pit where coal is dug. 2. *U.S.* a place where charcoal is made. [ME *colpytte,* OE *collpytt*]

Coal·sack (kōl′sak′), *n.* *Astron.* either of two large dark spaces in the Milky Way, one (**Southern Coalsack**) located in the southern skies near the constellation Crux, the other (**Northern Coalsack**) in the northern skies in the constellation Cygnus. [COAL + SACK[1]]

coal′ scut′tle, a metal bucket, usually with a lip, for holding and carrying coal.

coal′ tar′, a thick, black, viscid liquid formed during the distillation of coal, that upon further distillation yields compounds, as benzene, anthracene, and phenol, from which are derived a large number of dyes, drugs, and other synthetic compounds, and that yields a final residuum (**coal′-tar pitch′**) which is used chiefly in making pavements. —**coal-tar** (kōl′tär′), *adj.*

coal′-tar cre′osote, impure phenol or carbolic acid, distinct from the creosote of wood tar.

coal·y (kō′lē), *adj.,* **coal·i·er, coal·i·est.** of, resembling, or containing coal. [COAL + -Y[1]]

coam·ing (kō′ming), *n.* 1. a raised border around an opening in a deck, roof, or floor, designed to prevent water from running below. 2. *Shipbuilding.* **a.** any of four raised members forming such a border around a deck opening, esp. either of the fore-and-aft members. Cf. **headledge. b.** either of the thickened uppermost and lowermost strakes of plating used to strengthen a metal bulkhead or deckhouse. **c.** a timber sill for a wooden deckhouse. [earlier *coming,* appar., equiv. to COMB (in sense of crest) + -ING[1]]

C, Coaming

Co·an·da (kō än dä′), *n.* **Hen·ri Ma·rie** (äN rē′ ma rē′), born 1885, French engineer and inventor.

co·ap·ta·tion (kō′ap tā′shən), *n.* a joining or adjustment of parts to one another: *the coaptation of a broken bone.* [< LL *coaptātiōn-* (s. of *coaptātiō*), equiv. to *coaptāt(us)* fitted together, ptp. of *coaptāre* (*co-* CO- + *aptātus,* ptp. of *aptāre;* see APT, -ATE[1]) + *-iōn-* -ION]

co·arc·tate (kō ärk′tāt, -tit), *adj.* (of a pupa) having the body enclosed in a hardened shell or puparium. [< L *coarctāt(us),* var. of *coartātus* (ptp. of *coartāre*) pressed together, equiv. to *co-* CO- + *art(us)* tight + *-ātus* -ATE[1]] —**co′arc·ta′tion,** *n.*

Coarctate pupa of fly, *Hylemya cilicrura*

coarse (kōrs, kôrs), *adj.,* **coars·er, coars·est.** 1. of inferior or faulty quality; common; base. 2. composed of relatively large parts or particles: *The beach had rough, coarse sand.* 3. lacking in fineness or delicacy of texture, structure, etc.: *The stiff, coarse fabric irritated her skin.* 4. harsh; grating. 5. lacking delicacy, taste, or refinement; unpolished: *He had coarse manners but an absolutely first-rate mind.* 6. vulgar; obscene: *His coarse language angered the dowager.* 7. (of metals) unrefined. 8. (of a metal file) having the maximum commercial grade of coarseness. [earlier *cowarce* (see COW[1], ARSE), *co(u)rs,* appar. adj. use of abusive vulgarism] —**coarse′ly,** *adv.* —**coarse′ness,** *n.*
—**Syn. 3, 5.** crude, rude, rough. **5.** vulgar, gross, crass. **6.** indecent, indelicate, ribald. —**Ant. 5.** refined, sensitive.

coarse-grained (kōrs′grānd′, kôrs′-), *adj.* 1. having a coarse texture or grain. 2. indelicate; crude; gross: *a coarse-grained person with vulgar tastes and manners.* —**coarse′-grained′ness,** *n.*

coars·en (kōr′sən, kôr′-), *v.t., v.i.* to make or become coarse. [COARSE + -EN[1]]

coars·er (kōr′sər, kôr′-), *adj.* *Math.* of or pertaining to a topology on a topological space whose open sets are included among the open sets of a second specified topology on the space. Cf. **finer.** [COARSE + -ER[4]]

co·ar·tic·u·la·tion (kō′är tik′yə lā′shən), *n.* *Phonet.* 1. concomitance of articulation, as in *fro,* ostensibly a succession of three discrete sounds but physically a single articulation (f-) blending into a coarticulation (-fr-), which blends into an articulation (-r-), which blends into a coarticulation (-ro-), which blends into an articulation (-o). 2. Also called **secondary articulation.** the movement during the articulation of a given sound of one or more articulators not directly involved in producing the sound. [CO- + ARTICULATION]

coast (kōst), *n.* 1. the land next to the sea; seashore: *The seas run high on this coast.* 2. the region adjoining it: *They live on the coast, a few miles from the sea.* 3. a hill or slope down which one may slide on a sled. 4. a slide or ride down a hill or slope, as on a sled. 5. *Obs.* the boundary or border of a country. 6. **the Coast,** *Informal.* (in the U.S.) the region bordering on the Pacific Ocean; the West Coast: *I'm flying out to the Coast next week.* 7. **the coast is clear,** no visible danger or impediment exists; no persons are in the path or vicinity: *The boys waited until the coast was clear before climbing over the wall.* —*v.i.* 8. *U.S.* **a.** to slide on a sled down a snowy or icy hillside or incline. **b.** to descend a hill or the like, as on a bicycle, without using pedals. 9. to sail along, or call at the various ports of, a coast. 10. to continue to move or advance after effort has ceased; keep going on acquired momentum: *We cut off the car engine and coasted for a mile.* 11. to advance or proceed with little or no effort, esp. owing to one's actual or former assets, as wealth, position, or name, or those of another: *He coasted through college. The actor coasted to stardom on his father's name.* 12. *Obs.* to proceed in a roundabout way. —*v.t.* 13. to cause to move along under acquired momentum: *to coast a rocket around the sun.* 14. to proceed along or near the coast of. 15. *Obs.* to keep alongside of (a person moving). 16. *Obs.* to go by the side or border of. [late ME *cost(e)* < MF < L *costa* rib, side, wall]
—**Syn. 1.** strand, seaside, littoral. See **shore**[1].

coast·al (kōs′tᵊl), *adj.* of, relating to, bordering on, or located near a coast: *The coastal regions are inundated at high tide.* [COAST + -AL[1]] —**coast′al·ly,** *adv.*

coast′al plain′, a plain extending along a coast.

coast′ artil′lery, 1. artillery used for defending coastal areas. 2. a military unit manning coast artillery.

Coast′ Artil′lery Corps′, *U.S.* (from 1907 to 1950) a branch and combat arm of the Army, troops of which manned the coast defenses and later the antiaircraft units of the Army. Since 1950 it has been a part of the artillery.

coast·er (kō′stər), *n.* **1.** one who or that which coasts. **2.** a ship engaged in coastwise trade. **3.** a sled for coasting. **4.** See **roller coaster. 5.** a small dish, tray, or mat, esp. for placing under a glass to protect a table from moisture. **6.** a tray, sometimes on wheels, for holding a decanter to be passed around a dining table. [COAST + -ER[1]]

coast′er brake′, a brake on freewheel bicycles, operated by back pressure on the pedals.

Coast′ Guard′, 1. *U.S.* a military service under the Department of Transportation, which in peacetime enforces maritime laws, saves lives and property at sea, and maintains aids to navigation, and which in wartime may be placed under the Navy Department to augment the Navy. **2.** (*l.c.*) any similar organization for aiding navigation, preventing smuggling, etc. **3.** (*l.c.*) Also called **coastguardsman.** a member of any such organization.

coast′-guard cut′ter (kōst′gärd′), a cutter used by the U.S. Coast Guard.

coast·guards·man (kōst′gärdz′mən), *n., pl.* **-men.** See **Coast Guard** (def. 3). [COAST GUARD + 'S[1] + MAN[1]]

coast′ing flight′, *Rocketry.* the portion of the flight of a guided missile or rocket between the burnout of one stage and ignition of the next stage.

coast′ing lead′ (led), *Naut.* a lead used in sounding depths of from 20 to 60 fathoms.

coast′ing trade′, trade between ports along the same coast.

coast′ing wag′on, a toy wagon for children, often used for coasting down hills.

coast·land (kōst′land′), *n.* land along a coast; seacoast. [COAST + LAND]

coast·line (kōst′līn′), *n.* **1.** the outline or contour of a coast; shoreline. **2.** the land and water lying adjacent to a shoreline. [COAST + LINE[1]]

coast′ live′ oak′. See **California live oak.**

coast′ pi′lot, 1. Also called **pilot.** a manual published by a government for mariners, containing descriptions of coastal waters, harbor facilities, etc., for a specific area. **2.** a pilot of coasting vessels.

Coast′ Range′, a series of mountain ranges along the Pacific coast of North America, extending from Lower California to SE Alaska. Also, **Coast′ Moun′tains.**

coast′ red′wood, the redwood, *Sequoia sempervirens.*

coast′ rhododen′dron, a rhododendron, *Rhododendron californicum,* of western North America, having rose-purple flowers spotted with brown: the State flower of Washington.

coast′ tril′lium, a hardy, perennial herb, *Trillium ovatum,* found from British Columbia to California, having erect, narrow-petalled, white flowers that turn rose-colored.

coast·ward (kōst′wərd), *adv.* **1.** Also, **coast′wards.** toward the coast: *We left the sinking ship in lifeboats and rowed coastward as fast as we could.* —*adj.* **2.** directed toward the coast: *Many ambitious young Middle Westerners make coastward migrations.* [COAST + -WARD]

coast·ways (kōst′wāz′), *adv., adj. Archaic.* coastwise.

coast·wise (kōst′wīz′), *adv.* **1.** along the coast: *We sailed coastwise for days before finding a harbor.* —*adj.* **2.** following the coast. [COAST + -WISE]

coat (kōt), *n.* **1.** an outer garment with sleeves, covering at least the upper part of the body. **2.** a natural integument or covering, as the hair, fur, or wool of an animal, the bark of a tree, or the skin of a fruit. **3.** a layer of anything that covers a surface: *A heavy coat of make-up covered her face.* **4.** See **coat of arms. 5.** *Archaic.* a petticoat or skirt. **6.** *Obs.* **a.** a garment indicating profession, class, etc. **b.** the profession, class, etc., so indicated. —*v.t.* **7.** to cover or provide with a coat. **8.** to cover with a layer or coating: *He coated the wall with paint.* **9.** to cover (something) as a layer or coating: *The paint coated the wall.* **10.** to cover thickly, esp. with a viscous fluid or substance: *Heat the mixture until it coats a spoon. The boy was coated with mud from head to foot.* [ME *cote* < OF < Gmc; cf. G *Kotze,* OS *cott* woolen coat] —**coat′less,** *adj.*

coat′ ar′mor, a cloth garment worn over armor, as a surcoat or jupon. [ME *cote armure*]

Coat·bridge (kōt′brij′), *n.* a city in central Scotland, near Glasgow. 53,946 (1961).

coat′ card′. See **face card.**

coat·dress (kōt′dres′), *n.* a tailored dress, usually fitted, having buttons down the front. [COAT + DRESS]

coat·ed (kō′tid), *adj.* **1.** having a coat. **2.** (of paper) having a highly polished coating applied to provide a smooth surface for printing. **3.** (of a fabric) having a coating, as of plastic, paint, or pyroxylin, to make it impervious to moisture. [COAT + -ED[3]]

coat·ee (kō tē′), *n.* a short coat, esp. one with tails [formation modeled on GOATEE]

Coates (kōts), *n.* **1. Eric,** 1886–1957, English violist, composer, and song writer. **2. Joseph Gordon,** 1878–1943, New Zealand statesman: prime minister 1925–28.

Coati, *Nasua narica* (1 ft. high at shoulder; total length 4 ft.; tail to 2½ ft.)

coat′ flow′er. See **saxifrage pink.**

coat′ hang′er, hanger (def. 1).

co·a·ti (kō ä′tē), *n., pl.* **-tis.** any tropical American carnivore of the genus *Nasua,* related to the raccoon, having an elongated body, long, ringed tail, and a slender, flexible snout. Also, **co·a·ti-mon·di, co·a·ti-mun·di** (kō ä′tē mun′dē). [< Pg < Tupi]

coat·ing (kō′ting), *n.* **1.** a layer of any substance spread over a surface. **2.** fabric for making coats. [COAT + -ING[1]]

coat′ of arms′, 1. a surcoat or tabard embroidered with heraldic devices, worn by medieval knights over their armor. **2.** a heraldic achievement of arms. [parallel to F *cotte d'armes*]

Coat of arms
A, Crest; B, Torse; C, Helmet; D, Mantling; E, Shield; F, Bend; G, Charge; H, Scroll; I, Motto

coat′ of mail′, a long defensive garment made of interlinked metal rings; hauberk; byrnie. [parallel to F *cotte de mailles*]

coat′-of-plates′ construc′tion (kōt′əv plāts′), *Armor.* a medieval form of armor construction employing small plates enclosed in cloth or leather.

coat·rack (kōt′rak′), *n.* a rack for the temporary hanging or storing of coats, hats, etc. [COAT + RACK[1]]

coat·room (kōt′ro͞om′, -ro͝om′), *n.* cloakroom (def. 1). [COAT + ROOM]

Coats·worth (kōts′wûrth′), *n.* **Elizabeth,** born 1893, U.S. writer, esp. of children's books.

coat·tail (kōt′tāl′), *n.* **1.** the back of the skirt on a man's coat or jacket. **2.** one of the two back parts of the skirt of a coat, esp. one of the tails on a tail coat. **3. on the coattails of, a.** in the wake of: *His decline in popularity followed on the coattails of the scandal.* **b.** with the aid of: *She became successful on the coattails of her famous father.* Also, **on one's coattails.** [COAT + TAIL[1]]

co·au·thor (kō ô′thər, kō′ô′-), *n.* **1.** one of two or more joint authors, as of a book. —*v.t.* **2.** to write in joint authorship with another: *The two writers decided to coauthor a book.* [CO- + AUTHOR]

coax[1] (kōks), *v.t.* **1.** to attempt to influence by gentle persuasion, flattery, etc.; cajole: *He gently coaxed her to sing, but she refused.* **2.** to obtain by coaxing: *She coaxed the secret from him.* **3.** to manipulate to a desired end by adroit handling or persistent effort: *He coaxed the large chair through the door.* **4.** *Obs.* **a.** to fondle. **b.** to fool; deceive. —*v.i.* **5.** to use gentle persuasion, flattery, etc.: *Though she coaxed and pleaded, he refused to go to the dance.* [v. use of *cokes* fool (now obs.), perh. var. of COX(COMB)] —**coax′er,** *n.* —**coax′ing·ly,** *adv.* —**Syn. 1.** wheedle, cajole, beguile, inveigle, persuade.

co·ax[2] (kō′aks, kō′aks′), *n. Elect.* See **coaxial cable.**

co·ax·i·al (kō ak′sē əl), *adj.* **1.** Also, **co·ax·al** (kō ak′səl). having a common axis or coincident axes. **2.** (of a loudspeaker) having two or more cones with their centers mounted on the same axis. **3.** *Geom.* **a.** (of a set of circles) having the property that each pair of circles has the same radical axis. **b.** (of planes) intersecting in a straight line. [CO- + AXIAL]

coax′ial ca′ble, *Elect.* a cable that consists of an insulated conducting tube through which a central, insulated conductor runs, used for transmitting high-frequency telephone, telegraph, or television signals. Also called **coax.**

cob[1] (kob), *n.* **1.** *U.S.* a corncob. **2.** a male swan. **3.** a short-legged, thick-set horse. **4.** *U.S.* a horse with an unnaturally high gait. **5.** *Brit.* a mixture of clay and straw, used as a building material. **6.** *Brit. Informal.* a spider. **7.** *Brit. Dial.* **a.** a man of importance; leader. **b.** a rounded mass, lump, or heap. [late ME *cob(be)* < Scand; cf. Icel *kubbi* log, lump]

cob[2] (kob), *n. Brit. Dial.* a gull, esp. the great black-backed gull. Cf. **black-backed gull.** Also, **cobb.** [perh. < D *kob* in same sense]

co·balt (kō′bôlt), *n. Chem.* a silver-white metallic element with a faint pinkish tinge, occurring in compounds whose silicates afford important blue coloring substances for ceramics. *Symbol:* Co; *at. wt.:* 58.933; *at. no.:* 27; *sp. gr.:* 8.9 at 20°C. [< G *Kobalt,* var. of *Kobold* goblin]

cobalt 60, *Chem.* the radioactive isotope of cobalt, having a mass number of 60 and a half life of 5.2 years, used chiefly in radiotherapy.

co·balt·am·mine (kō′bôlt am′ēn, -ə mēn′), *n. Chem.* any of the various complex derivatives of cobalt containing one or more molecules of ammonia bonded to the cobalt. [COBALT + AMMINE]

co′balt bloom′, erythrite (def. 1)

co′balt blue′, 1. any of a number of pigments containing an oxide of cobalt. **2.** a deep blue to a strong greenish-blue color. Also called **Thenard's blue.**

co′balt green′, 1. a medium, yellowish-green color. **2.** Also called **zinc green.** a pigment used in painting consisting mainly of oxides of cobalt and zinc, characterized chiefly by its green color, fast drying rate, permanence, and lack of tinting strength.

co′balt hydrox′ide, *Chem.* See **cobaltous hydroxide.**

co·bal·tic (kō bôl′tik), *adj. Chem.* of or containing cobalt, esp. in the trivalent state. [COBALT + -IC]

co·bal·tif′er·ous wad′ (kō′bôl tif′ər əs), *Mineral.* wad containing up to 30 percent cobalt. [COBALT + -I- + -FEROUS]

co·bal·tite (kō bôl′tīt, kō′bôl tīt′), *n.* a mineral, cobalt arsenic sulfide, CoAsS, silver-white with a reddish tinge: an ore of cobalt. Also, **co·balt·ine** (kō′bôl tēn′, -tin). [COBALT + -ITE[1]]

co·bal·tous (kō bôl′təs), *adj. Chem.* containing bivalent cobalt. [COBALT + -OUS]

cobal′tous hydrox′ide, *Chem.* a rose-red, amorphous, water-insoluble powder, $Co(OH)_2$, used chiefly in the preparation of cobalt salts and in the manufacture of paint and varnish driers. Also, **cobalt hydroxide.**

co′balt vi′olet deep′, 1. a medium to strong purple color. **2.** a pigment consisting mainly of phosphate of cobalt, characterized by its violet color, fast drying rate, permanence, and lack of tinting strength.

co′balt vi′olet light′, a pigment used in painting consisting mainly of arsenate of cobalt, characterized chiefly by its violet color, permanence, and poisonous properties.

co′balt yel′low, 1. aureolin. **2.** Also called **co′balt potas′sium ni′trite.** See **potassium cobaltinitrite.**

cobb (kob), *n.* cob[2].

Cobb (kob), *n.* **1. How·ell** (hou′əl), 1815–68, U.S. politician: Speaker of the House 1849–51. **2. Irvin S(hrewsbury),** 1876–1944, U.S. humorist and writer. **3. Ty(rus Raymond)** (tī′rəs), ("*the Georgia Peach*"), 1886–1961, U.S. baseball player.

cob·ber (kob′ər), *n. Australian.* (of men) a close friend; one of a pair; partner; counterpart. [? < Yiddish *chaber* friend]

Cob·bett (kob′it), *n.* **William** ("*Peter Porcupine*"), 1763–1835, English political essayist and journalist in the U.S. and England.

cob·bing (kob′ing), *n. Metall.* old refractory material removed from furnaces. [*cob* (v.) to break up, special use of COB[1] + -ING[1]]

cob·ble[1] (kob′əl), *n., v.,* **-bled, -bling.** —*n.* **1.** a cobblestone. **2. cobbles,** coal in lumps larger than a pebble and smaller than a boulder. **3.** *Metalworking.* **a.** a defect in a rolled piece resulting from loss of control over its movement. **b.** *Slang.* a piece showing bad workmanship. —*v.t.* **4.** to pave with cobblestones. [? COB[1] + -LE]

cob·ble[2] (kob′əl), *v.t.,* **-bled, -bling. 1.** to mend (shoes, boots, etc.); patch. **2.** to put together roughly or clumsily. [? back formation from COBBLER]

cob·bler (kob′lər), *n.* **1.** a person who mends shoes. **2.** *U.S.* a deep-dish fruit pie with a rich biscuit crust, usually only on top. **3.** an iced drink made of wine or liquor, fruits, sugar, etc. **4.** a fabric rejected because of defective dyeing or finishing. **5.** a mummichog. **6.** *Archaic.* a clumsy workman. [ME *cobelere,* equiv. to *cobel* (< ?) + *-ere* -ER[1]]

cob·ble·stone (kob′əl stōn′), *n.* a naturally rounded stone for use in paving. [late ME *cobylstone.* See COBBLE[1], STONE]

cob·bra (kob′rə), *n. Australian.* cobra[2].

cob′ coal′, coal in large round lumps.

Cob·den (kob′dən), *n.* **Richard,** 1804–65, English manufacturer, merchant, economist, and statesman.

co·bel·lig·er·ent (kō′bə lij′ər ənt), *n.* a state or individual that cooperates with, but is not bound by a formal alliance to another in waging war. [CO- + BELLIGERENT]

Cóbh (kōv), *n.* a seaport in S Republic of Ireland: port for Cork. 5266 (1961). Formerly, **Queenstown.**

Cob·ham (kob′əm), *n.* **John Old·cas·tle** (ōld′kas′əl, -kä′səl), **Lord,** 1377–1417, English martyr: leader of a Lollard conspiracy.

co·bi·a (kō′bē ə), *n.* a large, fusiform fish, *Rachycentron canadum,* found off the eastern coast of temperate and tropical America, in the East Indies, and in Japan. [?]

co·ble (kō′bəl, kob′əl), *n. Scot. and North Eng.* a small, flat-bottomed fishing boat with one mast. [ME (Scot), OE (north) *cuople* (dat. sing.) small boat; akin to ML *caupulus* short boat, ? < Celt]

Co·blenz (kō′blents), *n.* a city in W West Germany, at the junction of the Rhine and Moselle rivers. 101,200 (1963). Also, **Koblenz.**

Co·bles·kill (kō′bəl skil, -bəlz kil), *n.* a town in central New York. 3471 (1960).

cob′ mon′ey, silver and gold coinage, issued in Spanish America in the 17th and 18th centuries, having the form of slices from silver bars struck with dies.

cob·nut (kob′nut′), *n.* **1.** the nut of certain cultivated varieties of hazel, *Corylus Avellana grandis.* **2.** a tree bearing such nuts. [late ME *cobylle nutt.* See COBBLE[1], NUT]

COBOL (kō′bôl, -bōl), *n. Computer Technol.* a programming language particularly suited for writing programs to process large files of data, using a vocabulary of common English words, phrases, and sentences. [*co(mmon) b(usiness) o(riented) l(anguage)*]

co·bra[1] (kō′brə), *n.* **1.** any of several highly venomous, Old World elapid snakes of the genus *Naja,* characterized by the ability to flatten the neck into a hoodlike form when disturbed. **2.** any of several similar, related African snakes, as the ringhals. **3.** leather made from the skin of a cobra. [short for COBRA DE CAPELLO]

Indian cobra, *Naja naja* (Length to 6 ft.)

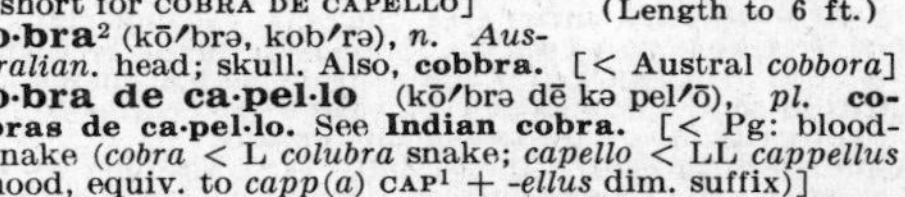

co·bra[2] (kō′brə, kob′rə), *n. Australian.* head; skull. Also, **cobbra.** [< Austral *cobbora*]

co·bra de ca·pel·lo (kō′brə dē kə pel′ō), *pl.* **co·bras de ca·pel·lo.** See **Indian cobra.** [< Pg: blood-snake (*cobra* < L *colubra* snake; *capello* < LL *cappellus* hood, equiv. to *capp(a)* CAP[1] + *-ellus* dim. suffix)]

co·burg (kō′bûrg), *n.* a piece-dyed or printed twill dress fabric or lining cloth. Also, **co·bourg** (kō′bo͝org). [named after Prince ALBERT of Saxe-*Coburg*]

Co·burg (kō′bûrg; *Ger.* kō′bo͝orkh), *n.* a city in N Bavaria, in E West Germany. 43,100 (1963).

cob·web (kob′web′), *n., v.,* **-webbed, -web·bing.** —*n.* **1.** a web spun by a spider to entrap its prey. **2.** a single thread spun by a spider. **3.** something resembling a cobweb; anything finespun, flimsy, or insubstantial. **4.** a network of plot or intrigue; an insidious snare. **5. cobwebs,** confusion, indistinctness, or lack of order: *The new editor will rid the 18th-century text of its cobwebs. She has cobwebs in her head before breakfast.* —*v.t.* **6.** to cover with or as with cobwebs: *Spiders cobwebbed the cellar.* **7.** to confuse or muddle: *Drunkenness cobwebbed his mind.* [ME *coppeweb,* deriv. of OE *-coppe* spider (in *ātorcoppe*); c. MD *koppe;* see WEB]

cob·web·by (kob′web′ē), *adj.* **1.** bearing an accumulation of cobwebs. **2.** having the form, texture, or quality of cobwebs. **3.** long unused or neglected, as something on which spiders have had time to build many webs; dusty: *cobwebby recollections.* [COBWEB + -Y[1]]

cob′web house′leek, a small plant, *Sempervivum arachoideum,* of S Europe, having a dense, globular cluster of cobwebby leaves and red flowers on hairy stalks.

co·ca (kō′kə), *n.* **1.** either of two shrubs, *Erythroxylon Coca* or *E. truxillense,* native to the Andes. **2.** their dried leaves, which are chewed for their stimulant properties and which yield cocaine and other alkaloids. [< Sp < Quechua *kuka*]

co·caine (kō kān′, kō′kān; *tech. often* kō′kə ēn′), *n. Pharm.* a bitter, crystalline alkaloid, $C_{17}H_{21}NO_4$, obtained from coca leaves: used as a local anesthetic. [COCA + -INE[1]]

co·cain·ise (kō kā′nīz, kō′kə nīz′), *v.t.,* **-ised, -is·ing.** *Chiefly Brit.* cocainize. —**co·cain′i·sa′tion,** *n.*

co·cain·ism (kō kā′niz əm, kō′kə niz′əm), *n. Pathol.* an abnormal condition due to excessive or habitual use of cocaine. [COCAINE + -ISM]

co·cain·ize (kō kā′nīz, kō′kə nīz′), *v.t.,* **-ized, -iz·ing.** to treat with or affect by cocaine. Also, *esp. Brit.,* **cocainise.** [COCAINE + -IZE] —**co·cain′i·za′tion,** *n.*

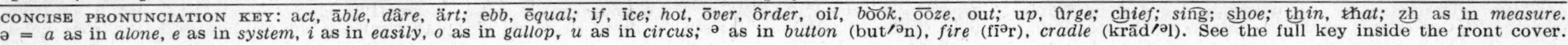

Coc·a·lus (kok′ə ləs), *n. Class. Myth.* a Sicilian king whose daughters saved the fugitive Daedalus from the pursuing King Minos.

-coccal, a combination of **-coccus** and **-al**[1], used to form adjectives from stems in **-coccus:** *streptococcal.*

coc·ci (kok′sī), *n.* pl. of **coccus.**

coc·cid (kok′sid), *n.* any homopterous insect of the superfamily *Coccoidea,* including the scale insects. [cocc(us) + -id[2]]

coc·cid·i·oi′dal granulo′ma (kok sid′ē oid′əl), *Pathol.* chronic coccidioidomycosis, having tuberculosis-like characteristics. [*coccidi(a)* (see coccidiosis) + -oid + -al[1]]

coc·cid·i·oi·do·my·co·sis (kok sid′ē oi′dō mī kō′sis), *n. Pathol.* a disease chiefly of the lungs and skin, caused by infection with the organism *Coccidioides immitis,* characterized by the production of excessive sputum and the development of nodules. [< NL *Coccidioid(es)* name of the genus + -o- + mycosis]

coc·cid·i·o·sis (kok sid′ē ō′sis), *n. Vet. Pathol.* any of a series of specific infectious diseases caused by epithelial protozoan parasites, which usually affect the intestines. The disease is known in birds, cattle, swine, sheep, and dogs; it rarely occurs in man. [< NL *coccidi(a),* pl. of *coccidium* (*cocc(us)* coccus + *-idium* -idium) + -osis]

coc·co·ba·cil·lus (kok′ō bə sil′əs), *n., pl.* **-cil·li** (-sil′ī). *Bacteriol.* a spherelike bacillus. [cocc(us) + -o- + bacillus]

coc·coid (kok′oid), *adj.* **1.** Also, **coc·coi′dal.** resembling a coccus; globular. —*n.* **2.** a coccoid cell or organism. [cocc(us) + -oid]

-coccoid, a combination of **-coccus** and **-oid,** used to form adjectives from stems in **-coccus:** *streptococcoid.*

coc·cus (kok′əs), *n., pl.* **-ci** (-sī). **1.** *Bacteriol.* a spherical bacterium. See diag. under **bacteria. 2.** *Bot.* one of the carpels of a schizocarp. [< NL < Gk *kókkos* grain, seed, berry] —**coc′cal, coc·cic** (kok′sik), *adj.* —**coc′cous,** *adj.*

-coccus, a combining form of **coccus:** *streptococcus.*

Coc·cy·gi·us (kok sī′jē əs), *n. Class. Myth.* an epithet of Zeus meaning "cuckoo," alluding to the story that he took the shape of a cuckoo to win the affection of Hera.

coc·cyx (kok′siks), *n., pl.* **coc·cy·ges** (kok sī′jēz, kok′si jēz′). **1.** a small triangular bone forming the lower extremity of the spinal column in man, consisting of four ankylosed rudimentary vertebrae. See diag. under **spinal column. 2.** a corresponding part in certain animals. [< NL < Gk *kókkyx* cuckoo, from its resemblance to a cuckoo's beak] —**coc·cyg·e·al** (kok sij′ē əl), *adj.*

coch., (in prescriptions) a spoonful. [< L *cochleār*]

Co·cha·bam·ba (kō′chä bäm′bä), *n.* a city in central Bolivia. 99,099 (est. 1959); 8394 ft. above sea level.

co·chair·man (kō châr′mən), *n., pl.* **-men.** one of two or more joint chairmen. [co- + chairman]

coch. amp., (in prescriptions) a tablespoonful. [< L *cochleāre amplum*]

co·chin (kō′chin, koch′in), *n.* one of an Asian breed of chickens, resembling the Brahma but slightly smaller. [short for *Cochin-China fowl*]

Co·chin (kō′chin′), *n.* **1.** a seaport in W Kerala, in the SW extremity of India: first European fort in India built here by Portuguese 1503. 29,881 (1951). **2.** a former state in SW India; merged with Travancore 1949; a part of Kerala state since 1956.

Co·chin-Chi·na (kō′chin chī′nə, koch′in-), *n.* a former state in S French Indochina: now part of South Vietnam. French, **Co·chin·chine** (kô shan shēn′).

coch·i·neal (koch′ə nēl′, koch′ə nēl′), *n.* a red dye prepared from the dried bodies of the females of a scale insect, *Dactylopius coccus,* which lives on cactuses of Mexico, Central America, and other warm regions. [< Sp *cochinilla* < L *coccin(eus)* scarlet-colored (*cocci-,* comb. form of *coccum* scarlet dye, orig. berry (see coccus) + *-neus* adj. suffix) + Sp *-illa* (< L *-illa* dim. suffix)]

coch′ineal cac′tus, a branched cactus, *Nopalea coccinellifera,* of Central and South America, characterized by scarlet flowers and spineless stems bearing edible red berries. Also called, **coch′ineal plant′.**

Co·chise (kō chēs′, -chēz′), *adj.* of, pertaining to, or characteristic of a prehistoric American Indian culture of southeastern Arizona, dating from around 9000 B.C. [named after *Cochise* county, Arizona]

Co·chise (kō chēs′, -chēz′), *n.* c1815–74, a chief of the Chiricahua Apaches.

coch·le·a (kok′lē ə), *n.* **1.** *Anat.* a spiral-shaped cavity forming a division of the internal ear in man and in most other mammals. See diag. under **ear. 2.** Also called **cockle stairs.** a winding staircase. **3.** a tower containing a winding staircase. [< L < Gk *kochlías* snail (with spiral shell), screw, prob. akin to *kónchē* conch] —**coch′le·ar,** *adj.*

coch′lear duct′, *Anat.* a spiral tube enclosed in the bony canal of the cochlea.

coch·le·ate (kok′lē it, -āt′), *adj.* shaped like a snail shell; spiral. Also, **coch′le·at′ed.** [< L *cochleāt(us)* spiral, equiv. to *cochle(a)* cochlea + *-ātus* -ate[1]]

coch. mag., (in prescriptions) a tablespoonful. [< L *cochleāre magnum*]

coch. med., (in prescriptions) a dessertspoonful. [< L *cochleāre medium*]

coch. mod., (in prescriptions) a dessertspoonful. [< L *cochleāre modicum*]

coch. parv., (in prescriptions) a teaspoonful. [< L *cochleāre parvum*]

cock[1] (kok), *n.* **1.** a rooster. **2.** the male of any bird, esp. of the gallinaceous kind. **3.** a weathercock. **4.** a leader; chief person; ruling spirit. **5.** a hand-operated valve or faucet, esp. one opened or closed by rotating a cylindrical or tapered plug having part of the passage pierced through it from side to side. **6.** (in a firearm) **a.** the part of the lock that, by its fall or action, causes the discharge; hammer. See diag. under **flintlock. b.** the position into which the cock, or hammer, is brought by being drawn partly or completely back, preparatory to firing. **7.** *Horol.* a bracketlike plate holding bearings, supported at one end only. Cf. **bridge**[1] (def. 19). **8.** *Curling Rare.* the tee. **9.** *Archaic.* the time of the crowing of the cock; early in the morning; cockcrow. —*v.t.* **10.** to pull back and set the cock, or hammer, of (a firearm) preparatory to firing. —*v.i.* **11.** to cock the firing mechanism of a firearm. [ME *cock,* OE *cocc;* c. Icel *kokkr;* orig. imit.] —**cock′like′,** *adj.*

cock[2] (kok), *v.t.* **1.** to set or turn up or to one side, often in an assertive, jaunty, or significant manner: *He cocked his eyebrow at her in a meaningful way. The dog cocked his ears at the sound of the whistle.* —*v.i.* **2.** to stand or stick up conspicuously. **3.** *Dial.* to strut; swagger; put on airs of importance. **4. cock a snook.** See **snook**[3] (def. 2). —*n.* **5.** the act of turning the head, a hat, etc., up or to one side in a jaunty or significant way. **6.** the position of anything thus placed. [prob. special use of cock[1]]

cock[3] (kok), *n.* **1.** a conical pile of hay, dung, etc. —*v.t.* **2.** to pile (hay, dung, etc.) in cocks. [late ME; c. dial. G *Kocke* heap of hay or dung, Norw *kok* heap, lump; akin to Icel *kökkr* lump]

cock[4] (kok), *n. Obs.* a cockboat. [ME *cokke,* prob. < OF *coque, cogue.* See cog[4]]

cock·ade (ko kād′), *n.* a rosette, knot of ribbon, etc., usually worn on the hat as part of a uniform, as a badge of office, or the like. [alter. of *cocarde* < F, equiv. to *coc* cock[2] + *-arde* -ard] —**cock·ad′ed,** *adj.*

cock-a-doo·dle-doo (kok′ə dōōd′əl dōō′), *interj., n., pl.* **-doos,** *v.,* **-dooed, -doo·ing.** —*interj.* **1.** (used as a conventionalized expression to suggest the crowing of a rooster, as in stories for children.) —*n.* **2.** the loud crow of a cock. **3.** *Baby Talk.* a rooster. —*v.i.* **4.** to crow. [fanciful imit.]

cock-a-hoop (kok′ə hōōp′, -hŏŏp′, kok′ə hōōp′, -hŏŏp′), *adj.* **1.** in a state of unrestrained joy or exultation: *He was cock-a-hoop over his victory.* **2.** askew; out of kilter: *He knocked his hat cock-a-hoop.* [?]

Cock·aigne (ko kān′), *n.* a fabled land of luxury and idleness. Also, **Cockayne.** [ME *cokaygn(e)* < MF (*trouver*) *Cocaigne* (find) an idler's paradise, perh. orig. sugar-cake land < MD *kokenje,* equiv. to *koek* (see cookie) + *-je* dim. suffix]

cock-a-leek·ie (kok′ə lē′kē), *n. Scottish Cookery.* a soup made with chicken broth, chopped leeks, and sometimes a little oatmeal. [var. of *cockie-leekie,* equiv. to cock[1] + -ie + leek + -ie]

cock·a·lo·rum (kok′ə lōr′əm, -lôr′-), *n. Informal.* a self-important, pretentious little man. [< Flem *cockeloeren* to crow (now obs.), altered to make it rhyme with quorum. See cock[1]]

cock′-and-bull′ sto′ry (kok′ən bŏŏl′), an absurd, improbable story presented as the truth: *Don't ask him about his ancestry, unless you want to hear a cock-and-bull story.* [prob. with orig. reference to some fable in which a cock and bull figure]

cock·a·teel (kok′ə tēl′), *n.* a small, crested, long-tailed Australian parrot, *Nymphicus hollandicus,* often kept as a pet. Also, **cock′a·tiel′.** [alter. of D *kaketielje,* itself alter. of Pg *cacatilha,* equiv. to *cacat(ua)* cockatoo + *-ilha* < L *-illa* dim. suffix]

cock·a·too (kok′ə tōō′, kok′ə tōō′), *n., pl.* **-toos. 1.** any of numerous crested parrots of the genera *Cacatua, Callocephalon, Calyptorhynchus,* etc., of the Australasian region, having chiefly white plumage tinged with yellow, pink, or red. **2.** *Australian.* **a.** a person who owns and works a small farm or ranch. **b.** *Slang.* a lookout posted by criminals or the operators of illegal gambling games. [< D *kaketoe* < Malay *kakatua*]

Cockatoo, *Cacatua galerita* (Length 1½ ft.)

cock·a·trice (kok′ə tris), *n.* **1.** a legendary monster with a deadly glance, supposedly hatched by a serpent from the egg of a cock, and commonly represented with the head, legs, and wings of a cock and the body and tail of a serpent. Cf. **basilisk** (def. 1). **2.** a venomous serpent. Isa. 11:8. [late ME *cocatrice* < MF *cocatris* < ML *caucātrīces* (pl.), L **calcātrix* (see -trix), fem. of **calcātor* tracker, equiv. to *calcāt(us),* ptp. of *calcāre* to tread, make tracks (*calc-* heel + *-ātus* -ate[1]) + *-or* -or[2]; rendering Gk *ichneúmon* ichneumon]

Cock·ayne (ko kān′), *n.* Cockaigne.

cock′ bead′, *Joinery.* a bead raised above the adjacent surfaces.

cock·bill (kok′bil′), *v.t. Naut.* to raise one end of (a yard) so that it is at a steep angle, as to permit unloading of a vessel or to show that a ship's company is in mourning. [aph. var. of *acockbill;* see acock, bill[3]]

cock·boat (kok′bōt′), *n.* a small boat, esp. one used as a tender. Also, **cockleboat.** Also called **cockleshell.** [late ME *cokboot,* var. of *cogboot,* equiv. to *cog* boat, ship (akin to Icel *kuggi* small ship; see cock[4]) + *boot* boat]

cock·chaf·er (kok′chā′fər), *n.* any of certain scarabaeid beetles, esp. the European species, *Melolontha melolontha,* which is very destructive to forest trees. [cock[1] (with reference to its size) + chafer]

Cock·croft (kok′krôft, -kroft), *n.* **Sir John Douglas,** 1897–1967, English physicist: Nobel prize 1951.

cock·crow (kok′krō′), *n.* the time at which a cock characteristically crows; daybreak; dawn. Also, **cock′crow′ing.** [cock[1] + crow[2]]

cocked′ hat′, 1. a man's hat, worn esp. in the 18th century, having a wide, stiff brim turned up on two or three sides toward a peaked crown. Cf. **bicorne, tricorne. 2. knock into a cocked hat,** *Slang.* to destroy completely; render unachievable: *The loss of his job knocked his plans into a cocked hat.* [cock[2] + -ed[2]]

Cocked hat

cock·er[1] (kok′ər), *n.* See **cocker spaniel.** [(wood)-cock + -er[1], i.e., woodcock starter]

cock·er[2] (kok′ər), *n.* a person who promotes or patronizes cockfights. [(game)cock + -er[1], i.e., gamecock fancier]

cock·er[3] (kok′ər), *v.t.* to pamper: *to cocker a child.* [? v. use of OE *cocer* sheath, case: sheathe, encase, hence protect, thus cherish too much]

Cocker spaniel (11 in. high at shoulder)

cock·er·el (kok′ər əl, kok′rəl), *n.* a young domestic cock. [late ME *cokerelle.* See cock[1], -rel]

cock′er span′iel, one of a breed of small spaniels having a flat or slightly waved, soft, dense coat of any of several colors.

cock′et cen′tering (kok′it), *Masonry.* an arch centering dispensing with horizontal tie beams at the springing line in order to permit passage of persons, boats, vehicles, etc., with sufficient clearance between the supports.

cock·eye (kok′ī′), *n., pl.* **-eyes.** an eye that squints or is affected with strabismus. [cock[2] (v.) + eye]

cock·eyed (kok′īd′), *adj.* **1.** cross-eyed. **2.** having a squinting eye. **3.** *Slang.* twisted or slanted to one side. **4.** *Slang.* foolish; absurd. **5.** *Slang.* intoxicated; drunk. **6.** *Slang.* completely wrong: *You're cockeyed about thinking she will go.* [cock[2] + eyed]

cock′eyed bob′, *Australian.* a short, violent storm. Also, **cock′eye bob′.** [prob. m. native Australian name]

Cock·eys·ville (kok′ēz vil′), *n.* a town in N Maryland. 2582 (1960).

cock·fight (kok′fīt′), *n.* a fight between gamecocks usually fitted with spurs. [cock[1] + fight] —**cock′fight′ing,** *n., adj.*

cock·horse (kok′hôrs′), *n.* a child's rocking horse or hobbyhorse. [orig. father's leg, on which child rides astride, from cock[1] in sense projection + horse]

cock·ish (kok′ish), *adj. Informal.* cocklike; cocky. [cock[1] + -ish[1]] —**cock′ish·ly,** *adv.* —**cock′ish·ness,** *n.*

cock·le[1] (kok′əl), *n., v.,* **-led, -ling.** —*n.* **1.** any bivalve mollusk of the genus *Cardium,* having somewhat heart-shaped, radially ribbed valves, esp. *C. edule,* the common edible species of Europe. **2.** any of various allied or similar mollusks. **3.** a cockleshell. **4.** a wrinkle; pucker: *a cockle in fabric.* **5.** a small, shallow boat, light in weight. **6.** *U.S.* a small, crisp candy of sugar and flour, bearing a motto. **7. cockles of one's heart,** the depths of one's emotions or feelings: *The happy family scene warmed the cockles of her heart.* —*v.i.* **8.** to contract into wrinkles; pucker: *This paper cockles easily.* **9.** to rise in short, irregular waves; ripple: *The waves cockled along the shore.* —*v.t.* **10.** to cause to wrinkle, pucker, or ripple: *Dampness cockled the pages of the book. The wind cockled the water.* [late ME *cokel,* ME *cock* (OE *-cocc,* in *sæ-cocc* cockle < VL **coccus* for L *concha* conch) + *-el* dim. suffix; r. late ME *cokille* < MF < VL **cocchilia,* L *conchylia,* pl. of *conchȳlium* < Gk *konchȳlion,* equiv. to *konchȳl(e)* mussel + *-ion* dim. suffix]

cock·le[2] (kok′əl), *n.* **1.** a weed, as the darnel *Lolium temulentum,* or rye grass, *L. perenne.* **2.** cowherb. [ME; OE *coccel*]

cock·le·boat (kok′əl bōt′), *n.* cockboat. [cockle[1] + boat]

cock·le·bur (kok′əl bûr′), *n.* **1.** any composite plant of the genus *Zanthium,* comprising coarse weeds with spiny burs. **2.** the burdock, *Arctium Lappa.* [cockle[2] + bur[1]]

cock·le·shell (kok′əl shel′), *n.* **1.** a shell of the cockle. **2.** a shell of some other mollusk, as the scallop. **3.** *Naut.* **a.** cockboat. **b.** any light or frail vessel. [late ME *cokille shell.* See cockle[1], shell]

cock′le stairs′, cochlea (def. 2).

cock·loft (kok′lôft′, -loft′), *n.* **1.** a small loft or attic above the highest finished ceiling of a building. **2.** a completely enclosed space between rafters and a suspended ceiling. [cock[1] + loft]

cock·ney (kok′nē), *n., pl.* **-neys,** *adj.* —*n.* **1.** (*sometimes cap.*) a native of the East End district of London, England, traditionally, one born and reared within the sound of Bow bells. **2.** (*sometimes cap.*) the pronunciation or dialect of cockneys. **3.** *Obs.* **a.** a pampered child. **b.** a squeamish, affected, or effeminate person. —*adj.* **4.** (*sometimes cap.*) of cockneys or their dialect. [ME *cokeney* foolish person, lit., cock's egg (i.e., malformed egg), equiv. to *coken,* gen. pl. of *cok* cock[1] + *ey,* OE *æg* c. G *Ei,* Icel *egg* egg] —**cock′ney·ish,** *adj.* —**cock′ney·ish·ly,** *adv.* —**cock′ney·like′,** *adj.*

cock·ney·dom (kok′nē dəm), *n.* **1.** the region of London, England, inhabited by cockneys. **2.** cockneys collectively. [cockney + -dom]

cock·ney·fy (kok′ni fī′), *v.t.,* **-fied, -fy·ing.** to give a cockney character to: *to cockneyfy the word "horse" by pronouncing it "'orse."* [cockney + -fy] —**cock′ney·fi·ca′tion,** *n.*

cock·ney·ism (kok′nē iz′əm), *n.* **1.** cockney quality or character. **2.** a cockney peculiarity, as of speech. [cockney + -ism]

cock-of-the-rock (kok′əv thə rok′), *n., pl.* **cocks-of-the-rock.** a brilliant orange-red bird of the genus *Rupicola,* of northern South America, having an erect crest that conceals the bill.

Cock of the rock, *Rupicola rupicola* (Length 1 ft.)

cock′ of the walk′, the leader in a group, esp. one with a conceited, domineering manner: *After winning the slalom, he was the cock of the walk at the lodge.*

cock′ of the woods′. See **pileated woodpecker.**

cock·pit (kok′pit′), *n.* **1.** (in some airplanes) an enclosed space containing seats for the pilot and copilot. **2.** a sunken, open area, generally in the after part of a small vessel, as a yacht, providing space for the helmsman, part or all of the crew, or guests. **3.** (in racing or sports cars) the enclosed space, usually open at the top, containing a seat for the driver, and often a seat for a passenger. **4.** (formerly) a space below the water line in a warship, occupied by the quarters of the junior officers and used as a dressing station for the wounded during an action. **5.** a pit or enclosed place for cockfights. **6.** a place where a contest is fought or which has been the scene of many contests or battles: *Belgium is the cockpit of Europe.* [cock[1] + pit[1]]

Cock′rell Hill′ (kok′rəl), a town in N Texas. 3104 (1960).

cock·roach (kok′rōch′), *n.* any of numerous orthopterous insects of the family *Blattidae,* characterized by a flattened body, rapid movements, and nocturnal habits and including several common household pests. Cf. **American cockroach, German cockroach, oriental cockroach.** [< Sp *cucaracha,* deriv. of *cuca* butterfly larva, insect, perh. < Indian language]

German cockroach, *Blatta germanica* (Length ½ in.)

cocks·comb (koks′kōm′), *n.* **1.** the comb or caruncle of a cock. **2.** the cap, resembling a cock's comb, formerly worn by professional fools. **3.** an amaranthaceous garden plant, *Celosia cristata*, with flowers, commonly crimson or purple, in a broad spike somewhat resembling the comb of a cock. **4.** any of several other species of the genus *Celosia*. **5.** a prickleback, *Anoplarchus purpurescens*, living under rocks along the Pacific coast of North America. **6.** a gaslight burner having four or more jets. **7.** coxcomb (def. 1). [for *cock's comb*]

cocks·head (koks′hed′), *n.* an herb of the genus *Onobrychis*, esp. *O. Caputgalli* and *O. sativa*. [for *cock's head*]

cock's′ head′ hinge′, a fancy flap hinge of c1600 having ends with a beaked profile.

cock·shut (kok′shut′), *n.* *Brit. Dial.* the close of the day; evening; twilight. [COCK[1] + SHUT]

cock·shy (kok′shī′), *n., pl.* **-shies.** *Brit.* **1.** the act or sport of throwing missiles at a target. **2.** the target itself. [COCK[1] + SHY[2]]

cock·spur (kok′spûr′), *n.* **1.** a North American thorn, *Crataegus Crus-galli*, cultivated as a small ornamental tree. **2.** a gaslight burner having three jets. [for *cock's spur*]

cock·sure (kok′shŏŏr′), *adj.* **1.** perfectly sure or certain; completely confident in one's own mind: *She was cocksure that she was able to do the job better than anyone else.* **2.** too certain; overconfident: *He was so cocksure he would win the election that he didn't even bother to campaign.* **3.** *Obs.* perfectly secure or safe. [COCK[1] + SURE] —**cock′sure′ly,** *adv.* —**cock′sure′ness,** *n.*
—**Ant. 1.** doubtful. **2.** cautious.

cock·swain (kok′sən; *spelling pron.* kok′swān′), *n.* coxwain.

cock·tail[1] (kok′tāl′), *n.* **1.** any of various short mixed drinks, consisting typically of gin, whiskey, or brandy, with different admixtures, such as vermouth, fruit juices, etc., usually chilled and frequently sweetened. **2.** a portion of food, as sea food served with a sauce, a mixture of fruits, or juice, served as the appetizer course of a meal. —*v.t.* **3.** to give a cocktail party or cocktail parties for (someone): *They lionized and cocktailed the young author.* —*v.i.* **4.** to drink cocktails, esp. at a cocktail party: *They cocktailed before going to the theater.* —*adj.* **5.** (of women's clothing) styled for semiformal wear: *a cocktail dress.* [?]

cock·tail[2] (kok′tāl′), *n.* **1.** a horse with a docked tail. **2.** a horse that is not a thoroughbred. **3.** a person of little breeding who passes for a gentleman. [COCK[2] + TAIL[1]]

cock′tail glass′, a glass for serving cocktails, typically bell-shaped and having a foot and a stem.

cock′tail hour′, the interval before the evening meal during which cocktails and other alcoholic beverages are often served, roughly between 5 and 8 o'clock.

cock′tail lounge′, a public room, as in a hotel or airline terminal, where cocktails and other drinks are served, usually catering to members of both sexes.

cock′tail par′ty, a social gathering, usually held during the cocktail hour, at which cocktails and other alcoholic beverages, hors d'oeuvres, and canapés are served.

Cock′tail Par′ty, The, a play in verse (1950) by T. S. Eliot.

cock′tail sauce′, any of various sauces served with a seafood cocktail, typically one consisting of ketchup, Worcestershire sauce, tabasco sauce, horseradish, and seasonings.

cock′tail ta′ble. See **coffee table.**

cock·up (kok′up′), *n.* **1.** an upward turn or curl at the top of something. **2.** a cap or hat with the front turned up. [COCK[2] + UP]

cock·y[1] (kok′ē), *adj.,* **cock·i·er, cock·i·est.** arrogantly smart; pertly self-assertive; conceited: *He walked in with a cocky air. It's too bad he's such a cocky fellow.* [COCK[1] + -Y[1]] —**cock′i·ly,** *adv.* —**cock′i·ness,** *n.*

cock·y[2] (kok′ē), *n., pl.* **cock·ies.** *Australian.* **1.** cockatoo (defs. 1, 2a). **2.** cockateel. [COCK(ATOO), COCK(ATEEL) + -Y[2]]

cock·y·ol′ly bird′ (kok′ē ol′ē), a pet name for any small bird. Also, **cock′y·ol′y bird′.** [COCK[1] + -Y[2] + (J)OLLY]

Co·cles (kō′klēz), *n.* *Rom. Legend.* Horatius.

co·co (kō′kō), *n., pl.* **-cos.** **1.** See **coconut palm. 2.** coconut (def. 1). [< Pg: grimace; the three holes at the nut's base give this the look of a grinning face]

co·coa[1] (kō′kō), *n.* **1.** the roasted, husked, and ground seeds of the cacao, *Theobroma Cacao*, from which much of the fat has been removed. **2.** cacao (def. 2). **3.** a beverage made from cocoa powder. **4.** brown; yellowish brown; reddish brown. —*adj.* **5.** of or pertaining to cocoa. **6.** of the color of cocoa. [earlier *cocao, cacoa*, var. of CACAO]

co·coa[2] (kō′kō), *n.* coco. [misspelling of coco, by confusion with COCOA[1]]

Co′coa Beach′, a town in central Florida. 3475 (1960).

co′coa bean′. See **cacao bean.**

co′coa but′ter. See **cacao butter.**

Co′coa West′, a town in central Florida. 3975 (1960).

co·co·bo·lo (kō′kə bō′lō), *n.* the hard, durable wood of any of several tropical, leguminous trees of the genus *Dalbergia*, used for making furniture. Also, **co·co·bo·la** (kō′kə bō′lə). [< Sp < Arawak *kakaboli*]

co·co·mat (kō′kō mat′), *n.* **1.** matting made of the fiber from the outer husk of the coconut. **2.** a mat, esp. a door mat, made from this. [COCO(NUT) + MAT[1]]

co·con·scious·ness (kō kon′shəs nis), *n.* *Psychol.* a system of mental processes dissociated from the main stream of consciousness and sometimes capable of influencing it, as by causing slips of the tongue or hallucinations. [CO- + CONSCIOUSNESS] —**co·con′scious,** *adj.* —**co·con′scious·ly,** *adv.*

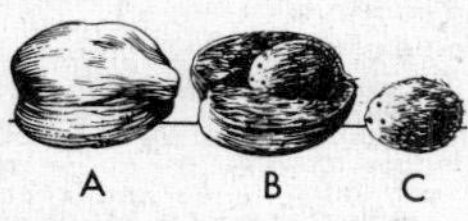

Coconut, *Cocos nucifera*
A, Coconut husk; B, Half opened husk; C, Fruit

co·co·nut (kō′kə nut′, -nət), *n.* **1.** the large, hard-shelled seed of the coconut palm, lined with a white edible meat, and containing a milky liquid. **2.** the meat of the coconut, often shredded and used as a dessert topping. **3.** see **coconut palm.** [COCO + NUT]

co′conut crab′, a large, terrestrial crab, *Birgus latro*, of islands in the South Pacific, that feeds on coconuts. Also called **palm crab, purse crab.**

co′conut cream′, **1.** *East Indian Cookery.* a creamy, white liquid skimmed from the top of coconut milk that has been prepared and allowed to set. **2.** type of custard pie containing shredded or ground coconut.

co′conut oil′, a white, semisolid fat or nearly colorless fatty oil extracted from coconuts, used chiefly in cooking and in the manufacture of soaps, cosmetics, and candles.

co′conut palm′, a tall, tropical palm, *Cocos nucifera*, bearing a large, edible fruit. Also called **co′conut tree′, co′co palm′, coco.**

co·coon (kə ko͞on′), *n.* **1.** the silky envelope spun by the larvae of many insects, as silkworms, serving as a covering while they are in the pupal stage. **2.** any of various similar protective coverings, as the silky case in which certain spiders enclose their eggs. **3.** a protective covering, usually consisting of polyvinyl chloride, sprayed over machinery, large guns on board ships, etc., to provide an airtight seal and prevent rust during long periods of storage. —*v.i.* **4.** to produce a cocoon. —*v.t.* **5.** to wrap or enclose tightly, as if in a cocoon: *The doctor cocooned the patient in blankets.* **6.** to provide (machinery, guns, etc.) with a protective, airtight covering by spraying with polyvinyl chloride or the like. [< F *cocon* < Pr *coucoun* egg-shell, equiv. to *coco* shell (< L *coccum*; see COCHINEAL) + *-on* dim. suffix]

Co′cos Is′lands (kō′kōs), an Australian group of 20 coral islands in the Indian Ocean, SW of Java. 606 (1961); 1½ sq. mi. Also called **Keeling Islands.**

co·cotte[1] (kō kot′, kə-; *Fr.* kô kôt′), *n., pl.* **-cottes** (-kots′; *Fr.* -kôt′). a woman of loose sexual conduct; prostitute. [< F: hen, equiv. to *coq* cock + *-otte* fem. suffix]

co·cotte[2] (kō kot′, kə-; *Fr.* kô kôt′), *n., pl.* **-cottes** (-kots′; *Fr.* -kôt′). a round or oval casserole, usually of earthenware or fireproof porcelain, used especially for cooking an individual portion of meat, fowl, or game. [< F; MF *cocotte, cocasse* pot, alter. of *coquemar(t)* < VL **cucumārium* cooking-pot]

coc·o·zel·le (kok′ə zel′ē), *n.* **1.** a variety of summer squash having a dark-green skin that is usually striped with light green or yellow. **2.** the plant bearing this fruit. [< It dial., equiv. to *cocoz-* (var. of It *cocuzza* squash < ML *cocutia*) + *-elle*, equiv. to It *-ella* < L *-ella* dim. suffix]

Coc·teau (kok tō′; *Fr.* kôk tō′), *n.* **Jean** (zhäN), 1889–1963, French poet, novelist, dramatist, critic, and painter.

Co·cy·tus (kō sī′təs), *n.* *Class. Myth.* a river of Hades connected with the Acheron. [< L < Gk *kōkytós* wailing, equiv. to *kōký(ein)* (to) wail + *-tos* n. suffix] —**Co·cy′te·an,** *adj.*

cod[1] (kod), *n., pl.* (*esp. collectively*) **-cod,** (*esp. referring to two or more kinds or species*) **-cods. 1.** any of several soft-rayed food fishes of the family *Gadidae*, esp. *Gadus callarias*, found in the colder waters of the North Atlantic. **2.** a closely related fish, *Gadus macrocephalus*, found in the North Pacific. **3.** any of several unrelated fishes, as rockfishes of the genus *Sebastodes*. [ME < ?]

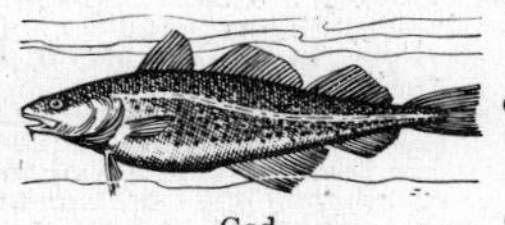
Cod,
Gadus callarias
(Length 6 ft.)

cod[2] (kod), *n.* **1.** a bag or sack. **2.** *Dial.* a pod. [ME; OE *codd*; akin to COD[3]]

cod[3] (kod), *n.* **1.** *Scot. and North Eng.* a pillow; cushion. **2.** one of the bearings of an axle, esp. one of the bolsters on which a church bell swings. [ME *kodde* < Scand; cf. Icel *koddi* pillow]

Cod (kod), *n.* **Cape.** See **Cape Cod.**

COD., codex. Also, **cod.**

C.O.D., *Com.* cash on delivery (payment to be made when delivered to the purchaser). Also, **c.o.d.**

co·da (kō′də), *n.* **1.** *Music.* a more or less independent passage, at the end of a composition, introduced to bring it to a satisfactory close. **2.** *Ballet.* the concluding section of a ballet, esp. the final part of a pas de deux. **3.** a concluding section or part, esp. one of a conventional form and serving as a summation of preceding themes, motifs, etc., as in a work of literature or drama. [< It < L *cauda* tail]

cod·dle (kod′əl), *v.t.,* **-dled, -dling. 1.** to treat tenderly; nurse or tend indulgently; pamper: *to coddle children when they're sick.* **2.** to cook (eggs, fruit, etc.) in water that is just below the boiling point; cook gently. [var. of *caudle*, v. use of CAUDLE] —**cod′dler,** *n.*

code (kōd), *n., v.,* **cod·ed, cod·ing.** —*n.* **1.** any systematic collection of the existing laws of a country, or of those relating to a particular subject: *the Civil Code of France.* **2.** any system or collection of rules and regulations: *a gentleman's code of behavior.* **3.** a system for communication by telegraph, heliograph, etc., in which long and short sounds, light flashes, etc., are used to symbolize the content of a message: *Morse code.* **4.** a system used for brevity or secrecy of communication, in which arbitrarily chosen words, letters, or symbols are assigned definite meanings. **5.** a word, letter, number, or other symbol used in a code system to mark, represent, or identify something: *The code on the label shows the date of manufacture.* **6.** *Computer Technol.* a system of symbols for representing information and the rules for their use. —*v.t.* **7.** to arrange in a code; enter in a code. **8.** to translate (a message) into a code; encode. **9.** *Computer Technol.* to translate (a program) into language which can be communicated to the computer. [ME < F < L *cōdex* CODEX] —**code′less,** *adj.* —**cod′er,** *n.*

code′ book′, a list of code signals with their meanings, usually arranged alphabetically.

co·dec·li·na·tion (kō′dek lə nā′shən), *n.* *Astron.* the complement of declination; the angular distance along a great circle from the celestial pole. [CO- + DECLINATION]

co·de·fend·ant (kō′di fen′dənt), *n.* a joint defendant. [CO- + DEFENDANT]

code′ flag′, *Naut.* **1.** a flag forming part of a signal code. **2.** a flag indicating that a certain signal code is being used. **3.** See **answering pennant.**

co·deine (kō′dēn), *n.* *Pharm.* a white, crystalline, slightly bitter alkaloid, $C_{18}H_{21}NO_3H_2O$, obtained from opium: used in medicine chiefly as an analgesic, sedative, or hypnotic and to inhibit coughing. Also, **co·de·ia** (kō dē′ə), **co·de·i·na** (kō′dē ē′nə). [< Gk *kṓde(ia)* head, poppy-head + -INE[2]]

Code Na·po·lé·on (kôd nȧ pô lā ôN′), **1.** the civil code of France, enacted in 1804 and officially designated the *Code Napoléon* in 1807. **2.** French law as embodied in the five codes enacted between 1804 and 1810.

Code′ of Hammura′bi, a Babylonian legal code of the 20th century B.C., instituted by Hammurabi and dealing with criminal and civil matters.

co·de·pend·ent (kō′di pen′dənt), *adj.* **1.** of or pertaining to a relationship in which one person is physically or psychologically addicted, as to alcohol or gambling, and the other person is psychologically dependent on the first in an unhealthy way. —*n.* **2.** one who is codependent or in a codependent relationship. —**co′de·pend′en·cy, co′de·pend′ence,** *n.*

co·dex (kō′deks), *n., pl.* **co·di·ces** (kō′di sēz′, kod′i-). **1.** a quire of manuscript pages held together by stitching to make the earliest form of a book, replacing the scroll and wax tablets of earlier times. **2.** a manuscript volume, usually of an ancient classic or the Scriptures, as Alexandrinus, Basiliensis, Bezae, Claromontanus, Ephraemi Syri, Koridethianus, Laudianus, Regius, Sangallensis, Sinaiticus, or Vaticanus. **3.** *Archaic.* a code; book of statutes. [< L: tree-trunk, block of wood, writing tablet, book]

Co′dex Ju′ris Ca·no′ni·ci (jŏŏr′is kə non′i sī′), *Rom. Cath. Ch.* an official collection of general church law made effective in 1918.

cod·fish (kod′fish′), *n., pl.* (*esp. collectively*) **-fish,** (*esp. referring to two or more kinds or species*) **-fish·es.** cod[1].

codg·er (koj′ər), *n.* **1.** *Informal.* an odd or eccentric man, esp. one who is old: *a lovable, old codger.* **2.** *Brit. Dial.* a mean, miserly person.

co·di·ces (kō′di sēz′, kod′i-), *n.* pl. of **codex.**

cod·i·cil (kod′i səl), *n.* **1.** a supplement to a will, containing an addition, explanation, modification, etc., of something in the will. **2.** any similar supplement; appendix.

cod·i·cil·la·ry (kod′i sil′ə rē), *adj.* of, pertaining to, or of the nature of a codicil. [CODICIL + -ARY]

cod·i·fi·ca·tion (kod′ə fə kā′shən, kō′də-), *n.* **1.** the act, process, or result of arranging in a systematic form or code. **2.** *Law.* the reducing of unwritten customs or case law to statutory form. [CODE + -I- + -FICATION]

cod·i·fy (kod′ə fī′, kō′də-), *v.t.,* **-fied, -fy·ing. 1.** to reduce (laws, rules, etc.) to a code. **2.** to make a digest of; arrange in a systematic collection. [CODE + -IFY] —**cod′i·fi′er,** *n.*

cod·ing (kō′ding), *n.* *Statistics.* the transforming of a variate into a more convenient variate. [CODE + -ING[1]]

cod·line (kod′līn′), *n.* *Naut.* an 18-thread, untarred cord of hemp or cotton, used for fishing and for various purposes aboard a ship. Also called **whiteline.** [COD[1] + LINE[1]]

cod·ling[1] (kod′ling), *n.* **1.** *Brit.* any of several varieties of elongated apples, used for cooking purposes. **2.** an unripe, half-grown apple. Also, **cod·lin** (kod′lin). [ME *querdling*, equiv. to *querd* (< ?) + *-ling* -LING[1]]

cod·ling[2] (kod′ling), *n.* the young of the cod. [ME; see COD[1], -LING[1]]

cod′ling moth′, a small, olethreutid moth, *Carpocapsa pomonella*, the larvae of which feed on the pulp of apples and other fruits.

cod′-liv·er oil′ (kod′liv′ər), a pale-yellow, fixed oil, extracted from the liver of the common cod or of allied species, used in medicine chiefly as a source of vitamins A and D.

cod·piece (kod′pēs′), *n.* **1.** (in the 15th and 16th centuries) a flap or cover for the crotch in men's hose or tight-fitting breeches, usually matching the costume and often decorated. **2.** *Obs.* penis. [COD[2] + PIECE]

Co·dy (kō′dē), *n.* **1. William Frederick** (*"Buffalo Bill"*), 1846–1917, U.S. Army scout and showman. **2.** a town in NW Wyoming. 4838 (1960).

co·ed (kō′ed′, -ed′), *n.* a female student in a coeducational institution, esp. in a college or university. Also, **co′-ed′.** [short for *coeducational student*]

co·ed·i·tor (kō ed′i tər), *n.* a person who cooperates or collaborates as editor with another. [CO- + EDITOR] —**co·ed′i·tor·ship′,** *n.*

co·ed·u·ca·tion (kō′ej ŏŏ kā′shən), *n.* the joint education of both sexes at the same institution and in the same classes. [CO- + EDUCATION] —**co′ed·u·ca′tion·al,** *adj.* —**co′ed·u·ca′tion·al·ism,** *n.* —**co′ed·u·ca′tion·al·ly,** *adv.*

co·ef·fi·cient (kō′ə fish′ənt), *n.* **1.** *Math.* a number or quantity placed (generally) before and multiplying another quantity, as 3 in the expression $3x$. **2.** *Physics.* a number that is constant for a given substance, body, or process under certain specified conditions, serving as a measure of one of its properties: *coefficient of friction.* —*adj.* **3.** acting in consort; cooperating. [< NL *coefficient-* (s. of *coefficiēns*). See CO-, EFFICIENT] —**co′ef·fi′cient·ly,** *adv.*

coeffi′cient of accelera′tion, *Econ.* See **acceleration coefficient.**

coeffi′cient of elastic′ity, *Physics.* See **modulus of elasticity.**

coeffi′cient of expan′sion, *Physics.* the fractional change in length, area, or volume per unit change in temperature of a solid, liquid, or gas at a given constant pressure. Also called **expansivity.**

coeffi′cient of fine′ness, *Naval Archit.* See **block coefficient.**

coeffi′cient of perform′ance, *Thermodynamics.* a constant that denotes the efficiency of a refrigerator, expressed as the amount of heat removed from a substance being refrigerated divided by the amount of work necessary to remove the heat.

coeffi′cient of restitu′tion, *Physics.* the ratio of the relative velocity after impact to the relative velocity before the impact of two colliding bodies, equal to 1 for an elastic collision and 0 for an inelastic collision.

coeffi′cient of viscos′ity, *Physics.* the measure of the viscosity of a fluid, equal to the force per unit area required to maintain a difference of velocity of one unit distance per unit time between two parallel planes in the fluid that lie in the direction of flow and are separated by one unit distance: usually expressed in poise or centipoise.

coe·horn (kō′hôrn′), *n.* a small mortar for throwing grenades, used in the 18th century. [named after its inventor, Baron Menno van *Coehoorn*, 17th-century Dutch engineer]

coel-, a learned borrowing from Greek meaning "cavity," used in the formation of compound words: *coelenteron.* Also, **-cele, -coele.** [comb. form repr. Gk *koîlos* hollow]

Coelacanth (Length 5 to 6 ft.)

coe·la·canth (sē′lə kanth′), *n.* a crossopterygian fish, *Latimeria chalumnae,* thought to have been extinct since the Cretaceous period, but found in 1938 off the coast of southern Africa. [COEL- + *-acanth* (see ACANTHO-)]

coe·lan·a·glyph·ic (si lan′ə glif′ik), *adj.* (of a carving) executed in cavo-relievo. [COEL- + ANAGLYPHIC]

-coele, var. of **coel-** as final element of a compound word: *enterocoele.* Also, **-cele.**

Coe·len·ter·a·ta (si len′tə rā′tə), *n.* the phylum comprising the coelenterates. [< NL; see COELENTERON, -ATE[1]]

coe·len·ter·ate (si len′tə rāt′, -tər it), *n.* **1.** any invertebrate animal of the phylum *Coelenterata,* having a single internal cavity serving for digestion, excretion, and other functions and having tentacles on the oral end, including the hydras, jellyfishes, sea anemones, corals, etc. —*adj.* **2.** belonging or pertaining to the *Coelenterata.* [COELENTER(ON) + -ATE[1]]

coe·len·ter·on (si len′tə ron′), *n., pl.* **-ter·a** (-tər ə). *Zool.* the body cavity of a coelenterate. [COEL- + ENTERON]

coe·li·ac (sē′lē ak′), *adj.* celiac.

coe·lom (sē′ləm), *n.* *Zool.* the body cavity of higher metazoans, between the body wall and intestine, lined with a mesodermal epithelium. Also, **coe·lome** (sē′lōm), **celom.** [< Gk *koílōma* cavity, equiv. to *koîl(os)* hollow + *-ōma* n. suffix denoting result]

coe·lo·mate (sē′lə māt′, si lō′mit), *adj.* **1.** having a coelom. —*n.* **2.** a coelomate animal. [COELOM + -ATE[1]]

coe·lo·scope (sē′lə skōp′), *n.* *Med.* celoscope. [COEL- + -O- + -SCOPE]

coe·lo·stat (sē′lə stat′), *n.* an apparatus consisting of a stationary telescope and an adjustable mirror, used to follow a celestial body across the heavens and reflect its light into the telescope. Cf. **siderostat.** [*coelo-* (for L *caeli-,* comb. form of *caelum* sky) + -STAT]

co·emp·tion (kō emp′shən), *n.* *Obs.* the buying up of all of a given commodity that is for sale, esp. with a view to controlling its price. [< L *coemptiōn-* (s. of *coemptiō*), equiv. to *coempt(us),* ptp. of *coemere* to buy up (*co-* CO- + *emere* to buy) + *-iōn-* -ION]

coe·nac·u·lum (sē nak′yə ləm), *n., pl.* **-la** (-lə). **1.** (in an ancient Roman house) **a.** a supper room. **b.** an upper room or suite of rooms. **2.** an upper box in an ancient Roman circus. [< L, var. of *cēnāculum* upper room, orig. dining room, equiv. to *cēnā(re)* (to) dine (akin to *cēna* dinner) + *-culum* -CULE]

coe·nes·the·sia (sē′nis thē′zhə, -zhē ə, -zē ə, sen′is-), *n.* *Psychol.* the aggregate of impressions arising from organic sensations that forms the basis of one's awareness of body or bodily state, as the feeling of health, vigor, or lethargy. Also, **coe·nes·the·sis** (sē′nis thē′sis), sen′is-), **cenesthesia, cenesthesis.** [COEN(O)- + ESTHESIA]

coeno-, var. of **ceno-**[2]: *coenocyte.*

coe·no·bite (sē′nə bīt′, sen′ə-), *n.* cenobite. —**coe·no·bit·ic** (sē′nə bit′ik, sen′ə-), **coe′no·bit′i·cal,** *adj.* —**coe·no·bit·ism** (sē′nə bi tiz′əm, sen′ə-), *n.*

coe·no·cyte (sē′nə sīt′, sen′ə-), *n.* *Biol.* an organism made up of a multinucleate, continuous mass of protoplasm enclosed by one cell wall, as in some algae and fungi. [COENO- + -CYTE]

coe·no·sarc (sē′nə särk′, sen′ə-), *n.* *Zool.* the tubular tissue connecting the polyps of a hydroid colony. [COENO- + *-sarc;* see SARC-] —**coe′no·sar′cal, coe′no·sar′cous,** *adj.*

coe·nu·rus (si nŏŏr′əs, -nyŏŏr′-), *n., pl.* **-nu·ri** (-nŏŏr′ī, -nyŏŏr′ī). *Zool.* the larva of a tapeworm of the genus *Multiceps,* consisting of a hollow, fluid-filled, bladderlike structure in which a number of heads or scoleces form. [< NL; see COENO-, URO-[2]]

co·en·zyme (kō en′zīm), *n.* *Biochem.* a biocatalyst required by certain enzymes to produce their reactions. [CO- + ENZYME]

co·e·qual (kō ē′kwəl), *adj.* **1.** equal in rank, ability, etc.: *The two top students were coequal.* —*n.* **2.** a person or thing coequal with another. [CO- + EQUAL] —**co·e·qual·i·ty** (kō′i kwol′i tē), **co·e′qual·ness,** *n.* —**co·e′qual·ly,** *adv.*

co·erce (kō ûrs′), *v.t.,* **-erced, -erc·ing.** **1.** to compel by force, intimidation, or authority, esp. without regard for individual desire or volition: *They coerced him into signing the document.* **2.** to bring about through the use of force or other forms of compulsion: *to coerce obedience.* **3.** to dominate or control, esp. by exploiting fear, anxiety, etc.: *The state is based on successfully coercing the individual.* [< L *coerc(ē)re* (to) hold in, restrain, equiv. to *co-* CO- + *-ercēre,* var. of *arcēre* to keep in, keep away, akin to *arca* ARK] —**co·erc′er,** *n.* —**co·er′ci·ble,** *adj.*

co·er·cion (kō ûr′shən), *n.* **1.** the act of coercing; exercise of force to obtain compliance. **2.** force or the power to use force in gaining compliance. **3.** government by force. [< ML *coerciōn-* (s. of *coerciō*), L *coerctiōn-,* syncopated var. of *coercitiōn-,* equiv. to *coercit(us)* (ptp. of *coercēre* to COERCE) + *-iōn-* -ION; r. late ME *cohercion* < MF] —**co·er′cion·ar·y,** *adj.* —**co·er′cion·ist,** *n.*

co·er·cive (kō ûr′siv), *adj.* serving or tending to coerce: *The government took coercive measures to quell the rioters.* [COERCE + -IVE] —**co·er′cive·ly,** *adv.* —**co·er′cive·ness,** *n.*

coes·ite (kō′sīt′), *n.* a rare mineral, silicon dioxide, a denser polymorph of quartz, originally synthesized from quartz at high temperatures and pressures: later discovered in nature. [named after Loring *Coes,* Jr., 20th-century American who synthesized it; see -ITE[1]]

co·es·sen·tial (kō′i sen′shəl), *adj.* united in essence; having the same essence or nature. [CO- + ESSENTIAL] —**co·es·sen·ti·al·i·ty** (kō′i sen′shē al′i tē), **co′es·sen′tial·ness,** *n.* —**co′es·sen′tial·ly,** *adv.*

co·e·ta·ne·ous (kō′i tā′nē əs), *adj.* of the same age or duration. [< LL *coaetāneus,* equiv. to *co-* CO- + *aet(ās)* age + *-āneus* compound adj. suffix; see -AN, -EOUS] —**co′e·ta′ne·ous·ly,** *adv.* —**co·e·ta·ne·i·ty** (kō′i tə nē′i tē), **co′e·ta′ne·ous·ness,** *n.*

co·e·ter·nal (kō′i tûr′nəl), *adj.* equally eternal; existing with another eternally. [CO- + ETERNAL, prob. influenced by LL *coaeternus,* equiv. to *co-* CO- + *aet(ās)* age + *-ernus* adj. suffix] —**co′e·ter′nal·ly,** *adv.*

co·e·ter·ni·ty (kō′i tûr′ni tē), *n.* coexistence from eternity with another eternal being. [CO- + ETERNITY]

Coeur d'A·lene (kûr′ dəlān′), **1.** a member of an Indian people in N Idaho around Coeur d'Alene Lake. **2.** a Salishan language. **3.** a city in N Idaho. 14,291 (1960).

Coeur de Li·on (kûr′ də lē′ən; *Fr.* kœʀ də lyôɴ′). See **Richard I,** meaning "lionhearted."

Coe·us (sē′əs), *n.* *Class. Myth.* a Titan, son of Uranus and Gaea and father of Leto and Asteria.

co·e·val (kō ē′vəl), *adj.* **1.** of the same age, date, or duration; equally old: *Analysis has proved that this manuscript is coeval with that one.* **2.** contemporary; coincident: *Leonardo da Vinci and Michelangelo were only approximately coeval.* —*n.* **3.** a contemporary: *He is more serious than his coevals.* **4.** a person of the same age as another or others: *Her father treated her as a mature adult and his coeval.* [< LL *coaev(us)* (*co-* CO- + *aev(um)* age + *-us* adj. suffix) + -AL[1]] —**co·e·val·i·ty** (kō′i val′i tē), *n.* —**co·e′val·ly,** *adv.*

co·ex·ec·u·tor (kō′ig zek′yə tər), *n.* a joint executor. [CO- + EXECUTOR]

co·ex·ec·u·trix (kō′ig zek′yə triks), *n., pl.* **-ex·ec·u·tri·ces** (-ig zek′yə trī′sēz). a female coexecutor. [CO- + EXECUTRIX]

co·ex·ist (kō′ig zist′), *v.i.* **1.** to exist together or at the same time. **2.** to exist side by side peaceably: *Although their ideologies differed greatly, the two great powers coexisted for many years.* [CO- + EXIST] —**co′ex·ist′ence, co′ex·ist′en·cy,** *n.* —**co′ex·ist′ent,** *adj.*

co·ex·tend (kō′ik stend′), *v.t., v.i.* to extend equally through the same space or duration. [CO- + EXTEND] —**co·ex·ten·sion** (kō′ik sten′shən), *n.*

co·ex·ten·sive (kō′ik sten′siv), *adj.* equal or coincident in space, time, or scope. [CO- + EXTENSIVE] —**co′ex·ten′sive·ly,** *adv.*

co·fac·tor (kō′fak′tər), *n.* **1.** *Biochem.* any of a number of organic or inorganic substances necessary to the function of an enzyme. **2.** *Math.* **a.** a prefactor or postfactor. **b.** the product of the minor of a given element of a matrix times −1 raised to the power of the sum of the indices of the row and column crossed out in forming the minor. [CO- + FACTOR]

coff (kof), *v.t.,* **coft, coff·ing.** *Scot. Archaic.* to purchase something; buy; acquire; obtain. [back formation from *coft* bought < MD, ptp. of *kōpen,* c. G *kaufen,* akin to CHEAP]

cof·fee (kô′fē, kof′ē), *n.* **1.** a beverage consisting of a decoction or infusion of the roasted ground or crushed seeds (**cof′fee beans′**) of the two-seeded fruit (**cof′fee ber′ry**) of *Coffea arabica* and other species of *Coffea,* rubiaceous trees and shrubs of tropical regions. **2.** the seeds or berries of coffee plants. **3.** the coffee tree or shrub. **4.** a cup of coffee: *We ordered four coffees and three doughnuts.* **5.** a social gathering at which coffee and other refreshments are served: *They had a coffee for the mayoral candidate.* **6.** dark brown. —*adj.* **7.** coffee-colored. [< It *caffè* < Turk *kahve* < Ar *qahwah*]

cof·fee-and (kô′fē and′, kof′ē-), *n.* *Slang.* a snack consisting of coffee along with doughnuts, cake, rolls, or the like: *We're going to Joan's house after the show for coffee-and.*

cof·fee·ber·ry (kô′fē ber′ē, kof′ē-), *n., pl.* **-ries.** an evergreen shrub, *Rhamnus californica,* of the northwestern U.S., having small, greenish flowers and red fruit that turns black, grown as a bee plant. [COFFEE + BERRY]

cof′fee break′, *U.S.* an intermission from work, usually in the middle of the morning or afternoon, for coffee, cake, etc.

cof·fee·cake (kô′fē kāk′, kof′ē-), *n.* a cake or sweetened bread, often flavored with cinnamon and made or topped with nuts, raisins, candied fruit, etc., often served with coffee. [COFFEE + CAKE]

cof·fee-col·ored (kô′fē kul′ərd, kof′ē-), *adj.* having the medium-brown color of coffee mixed with cream or milk; dark brown.

cof′fee cream′, cream for use in coffee; light cream.

cof′fee grind′er, **1.** a device for grinding coffee beans. **2.** *Naut. Slang.* a hand-operated winch for handling running rigging on a racing yacht.

cof·fee·house (kô′fē hous′, kof′ē-), *n., pl.* **-hous·es** (-hou′ziz), *v.,* **-housed, -hous·ing.** —*n.* **1.** a public place that specializes in serving different kinds of coffee and other refreshments and that sometimes provides informal entertainment. **2.** (in 17th and 18th century England) a similar establishment where groups met for a particular purpose, as for informal discussions, card playing, etc. —*v.i.* **3.** *Informal.* to engage in aimless talk or chitchat. [COFFEE + HOUSE]

cof′fee klatsch′ (klach, kläch), a social gathering for informal conversation at which coffee is served. Also, **cof′fee klatch′, kaffee klatsch.** [< G *Kaffeeklatsch,* equiv. to *Kaffee* coffee + *Klatsch* noise. (e.g., of conversation), akin to CLATTER]

cof·fee-klatsch (kô′fē klach′, -kläch′, kof′ē-), *v.i.* to gather socially for informal conversation, usually accompanied by the serving of mild refreshments, as coffee and cake: *The girls coffee-klatsched every Tuesday and Thursday afternoon.*

cof′fee mak′er, **1.** a person or company that blends, roasts, or brews coffee. **2.** an apparatus for brewing coffee; coffeepot.

cof′fee mill′, a small mill for grinding coffee beans.

cof′fee nut′, **1.** the fruit of the Kentucky coffee tree. **2.** the tree bearing this fruit.

cof·fee·pot (kô′fē pot′, kof′ē-), *n.* a container, usually with a handle and a spout or lip, in which coffee is made or served, or both. [COFFEE + POT[1]]

cof′fee ring′, a coffeecake shaped like a ring, plain or fruited, often with a topping of raisins, ground nuts, and icing.

cof′fee shop′, a small restaurant, as in a hotel, where refreshments and light meals are served.

cof′fee spoon′, a small spoon used with demitasse cups.

cof′fee ta′ble, a low table, usually placed in front of a sofa, for holding ash trays, glasses, cups, plates, etc. Also called **cocktail table.**

cof′fee tree′, **1.** any tree, as *Coffea arabica,* yielding coffee beans. **2.** See **Kentucky coffee tree.**

cof·fee·weed (kô′fē wēd′, kof′ē-), *n.* chicory (def. 1). [COFFEE + WEED[1]]

cof·fer (kô′fər, kof′ər), *n.* **1.** a box or chest, esp. one for valuables. **2. coffers,** a treasury; funds: *The coffers of the organization were rapidly filled by the contributions.* **3.** any of various boxlike enclosures, as a cofferdam. **4.** Also called **caisson, lacunar.** *Archit.* one of a number of sunken panels, usually square or octagonal, in a vault, ceiling, or soffit. —*v.t.* **5.** to deposit or lay up in or as in a coffer or chest. **6.** to ornament with coffers or sunken panels. [ME *cofre* < OF << L *cophinus* basket; see COFFIN] —**cof′fer·like′,** *adj.*

Coffers of a ceiling (def 4)

cof·fer·dam (kô′fər dam′, kof′ər-), *n.* **1.** a watertight enclosure placed or constructed in waterlogged soil or under water and pumped dry so that construction or repairs can proceed under normal conditions. **2.** *Naut.* a sealed void between two bulkheads, as for insulation or as an extra barrier to the escape of liquids and vapors. [COFFER + DAM[1]]

cof·fered (kô′fərd, kof′ərd), *adj.* (of a vault, ceiling, or soffit) having coffers. [COFFER + -ED[3]]

Cof·fey·ville (kô′fē vil′, kof′ē-), *n.* a city in SE Kansas. 17,382 (1960).

cof·fin (kô′fin, kof′in), *n.* **1.** the box or case in which a corpse is placed for burial. **2.** the part of a horse's foot containing the coffin bone. **3.** *Print.* **a.** the bed of a platen press. **b.** the wooden frame around the bed of an early wooden press. —*v.t.* **4.** to put or enclose in or as in a coffin. [ME *cofin* < MF < L *cophinus* < Gk *kóphinos* a kind of basket] —**cof′fin·less,** *adj.*

Cof·fin (kô′fin, kof′in), *n.* **Robert P(eter) Tristram,** 1892–1955, U.S. poet, essayist, and biographer.

cof′fin bone′, the terminal phalanx in the foot of the horse and allied animals, enclosed in the hoof.

cof′fin cor′ner, *Football Slang.* a corner of the field inside the 10-yard line, esp. as the target of a punt intended to go out of bounds in this area and so put the receiving team in a position near its goal line.

cof′fin-end spoon′ (kô′fin end′, kof′in-), an American spoon of c1800 having a handle with a coffin-shaped end.

cof·fin·ite (kô′fi nīt, kof′i-), *n.* a mineral, black uranous silicate, $USiO_4$. [COFFIN + -ITE[1]]

cof′fin nail′, *Slang.* a cigarette.

cof·fle (kof′əl), *n.* a train of men, esp. slaves, or of beasts fastened together with chains, ropes, or the like. [< Ar *qāfilah* caravan]

cof·fret (kô′frit, kof′rit), *n.* a small coffer. [late ME < MF. See COFFER, -ET]

Coff's′ Har′bour (kôfs, kofs), a seaport in E Australia. 7188 (1961).

co·fi·nal (kō fīn′əl), *adj.* *Math.* of or pertaining to a subset of a set with a partial order relation, such as "greater than" or "equal to," in which corresponding to each element in the set is an element in the subset which is in relation to the given element. [CO- + FINAL]

C. of S., Chief of Staff.

coft (koft), *v.* *Scot. Archaic.* pt. and pp. of **coff.**

co·func·tion (kō′fungk′shən), *n.* *Trig.* the function of the complement of a given angle or arc: *cos θ is the cofunction of sin θ.* [CO- + FUNCTION]

cog[1] (kog, kôg), *n., v.,* **cogged, cog·ging.** —*n.* **1.** (not in technical use) a gear tooth, formerly esp. one of hardwood or metal, fitted into a slot in a gear wheel of less durable material. **2.** a cogwheel. **3.** *Informal.* a person who plays a minor part in a large organization, activity, etc.: *He's just a small cog in a big wheel.* —*v.i.* **4.** (of an electric motor) to move jerkily. —*v.t.* **5.** to roll or hammer (an ingot) into a bloom or slab. **6. slip a cog,** to make a blunder; err: *One of the clerks must have slipped a cog.* [ME *cogge* < Scand; cf. Sw *kugge,* akin to CUDGEL]

cog[2] (kog, kôg), *v.,* **cogged, cog·ging,** *n.* —*v.t.* **1.** to manipulate or load (dice) unfairly. —*v.i.* **2.** to cheat, esp. at dice. —*n.* **3.** *Obs.* a deception, trick, etc., esp. at dice. [?]

cog[3] (kog, kôg), *n., v.,* **cogged, cog·ging.** *Carpentry.* —*n.* **1.** (in a cogged joint) the tongue in one timber, fitting into a corresponding slot in another. —*v.t., v.i.* **2.** to join with a cog. [special use of COG[1]; r. *cock* in same sense, var. of COCK[1] (in sense of projection); see COAK]

cog[4] (kog, kôg), *n.* **1.** a medieval, single-masted merchant ship of northern Europe. **2.** *Obs.* a small boat, as a cockboat. [ME *cogge* < MD *cogghe* or < OF *coque, coche* small merchant ship; akin to OIt *cocca* < ML *caudica* small ship < L *caudex* tree-trunk; see CODEX]

cog., cognate.

co·gen·cy (kō′jən sē), *n.* the quality or state of being cogent: *The cogency of the argument was irrefutable.* [COG(ENT) + -ENCY]

co·gent (kō′jənt), *adj.* **1.** convincing or believable by virtue of forcible, clear, or incisive presentation; telling. **2.** to the point; relevant; pertinent. [< L *cōgent-* (s. of *cōgēns,* prp. of *cōgere* to drive together, collect, compel), equiv. to *cōg-* (*co-* CO- + *ag-,* root of *agere* to drive) + *-ent-* -ENT] —**co′gent·ly,** *adv.*
—**Syn. 1.** forceful, effective, valid.

cogged′ joint′, *Carpentry.* a joint between two crossing timbers, as beams, in which the supporting beam has gains cut into its upper corners so as to leave a narrow area at the center which fits into a transverse notch cut into the bottom of the crossing timber.

cog·i·ta·ble (koj′i tə bəl), *adj.* able to be considered; thinkable: *The thought of our descendants traveling to the moon has become more cogitable.* [< L *cōgitābil(is)*, equiv. to *cōgitā(re)* (see COGITATE) + *-bilis* -BLE] —**cog′i·ta·bil′i·ty,** *n.*

cog·i·tate (koj′i tāt′), *v.*, **-tat·ed, -tat·ing.** —*v.i.* **1.** to think hard; ponder; meditate: *to cogitate about a problem.* —*v.t.* **2.** to think about; devise: *to cogitate a scheme.* [< L *cōgitāt(us)* (ptp. of *cōgitāre*), equiv. to *co-* CO- + *agitātus;* see AGITATE] —**cog′i·tat′ing·ly,** *adv.* —**cog′i·ta′tor,** *n.*
—**Syn. 1.** deliberate, reflect. **2.** weigh.

cog·i·ta·tion (koj′i tā′shən), *n.* **1.** meditation; contemplation: *After hours of cogitation he came up with a new proposal.* **2.** the faculty of thinking: *She was not a serious student and seemed to lack the power of cogitation.* **3.** a thought; a design or plan: *a pleasant cogitation; to jot down one's cogitations.* [< L *cōgitātiōn-* (s. of *cōgitātiō*), equiv. to *cōgitāt(us)* (see COGITATE) + *-iōn-* -ION; r. ME *cogitaciun* < OF < L]

cog·i·ta·tive (koj′i tā′tiv), *adj.* **1.** meditating; contemplating: *The cogitative faculty distinguishes man from animals.* **2.** given to meditation; thoughtful: *The leaders sat in cogitative silence.* [< ML *cōgitātīv(us)*, equiv. to *cōgitāt(us)* (see COGITATE) + *-īvus* -IVE] —**cog′i·ta′tive·ly,** *adv.* —**cog′i·ta′tive·ness,** *n.*

co·gi·to, er·go sum (kō′gi tō′ ER′gō sŏŏm′; *Eng.* koj′i tō′ ûr′gō sum′), *Latin.* I think, therefore I am (the basic philosophical principle of Descartes).

cog′ locomo′tive. See **rack locomotive.**

co·gnac (kōn′yak, kon′-; *Fr.* kô nyak′), *n.* **1.** (*often cap.*) the brandy distilled in and shipped from the legally delimited area surrounding the town of Cognac, France. **2.** (loosely) any French brandy. **3.** *Informal.* any good brandy. [< F]

co′gnac oil′, *Chem.* See **ethyl oenanthate.**

cog·nate (kog′nāt), *adj.* **1.** related by birth; of the same parentage, descent, etc. **2.** *Ling.* descended or borrowed from the same earlier form: *cognate languages; cognate words.* **3.** allied or similar in nature or quality. —*n.* **4.** a person or thing cognate with another. **5.** a cognate word: *English "cold" is a cognate of German "kalt."* [< L *cognāt(us)*, equiv. to *co-* CO- + *-gnātus* (ptp. of *gnāscī*, var. of *nāscī* to be born)] —**cog′nate·ness,** *n.* —**cog·nat·ic** (kog nat′ik), *adj.*

cog′nate ob′ject, a substantive functioning as the object of a verb, esp. of a verb that is usually intransitive, when both object and verb are derived from the same base. *Speech* in *Speak the speech* is a cognate object.

cog·na·tion (kog nā′shən), *n.* cognate relationship. [< L *cognātiōn-* (s. of *cognātiō*) kinship, equiv. to *cognāt(us)* COGNATE + *-iōn-* -ION]

cog·ni·sa·ble (kog′ni zə bəl, kon′i-, kog nī′-), *adj.* *Chiefly Brit.* cognizable. —**cog′ni·sa·bil′i·ty, cog′ni·sa·ble·ness,** *n.* —**cog′ni·sa·bly,** *adv.*

cog·ni·sance (kog′ni zəns, kon′i-), *n.* *Chiefly Brit.* cognizance.

cog·ni·sant (kog′ni zənt, kon′i-), *adj.* *Chiefly Brit.* cognizant.

cog·nise (kog′nīz), *v.t.*, **-nised, -nis·ing.** *Chiefly Brit.* cognize. —**cog′nis·er,** *n.*

cog·ni·tion (kog nish′ən), *n.* **1.** the act or process of knowing; perception. **2.** the product of such a process; thing thus known, perceived, etc. **3.** *Obs.* knowledge. [< L *cognitiōn-* (s. of *cognitiō*), equiv. to *cognit(us)*, ptp. of *cognōscere* (*co-* CO- + *gni-*, var. s. of *gnōscere, nōscere,* to learn (see KNOW[1]) + *-tus* ptp. suffix) + *-iōn-* -ION] —**cog·ni′tion·al,** *adj.* —**cog·ni·tive** (kog′ni tiv), *adj.* —**cog′ni·tive·ly,** *adv.*

Cog·ni·tum (kog′ni təm), *n.* **Mare.** See **Mare Cognitum.**

cog·ni·za·ble (kog′ni zə bəl, kon′i-, kog nī′-), *adj.* **1.** capable of being perceived or known. **2.** being within the jurisdiction of a court. Also, *esp. Brit.*, **cognisable.** [COGNIZ(ANCE) + -ABLE] —**cog′ni·za·bil′i·ty, cog′ni·za·ble·ness,** *n.* —**cog′ni·za·bly,** *adv.*

cog·ni·zance (kog′ni zəns, kon′i-), *n.* **1.** knowledge; notice; perception: *The guests took cognizance of her snide remark.* **2.** *Law.* **a.** judicial notice as taken by a court in dealing with a cause. **b.** the right of taking jurisdiction, as possessed by a court. **c.** acknowledgment; admission, as a plea admitting the fact alleged in the declaration. **3.** the range or scope of knowledge, observation, etc.: *Such understanding is beyond his cognizance.* **4.** *Heraldry.* a device by which a person, his servants, or his property can be recognized; badge. Also, *esp. Brit.*, **cognisance.** [ME *conisa(u)nce* < MF *con(o)is(s)ance*, equiv. to *conois(tre)* (to) know (< L *cognōscere;* see COGNITION) + *-ance* -ANCE; *-g-* < L]

cog·ni·zant (kog′ni zənt, kon′i-), *adj.* **1.** having cognizance; aware (usually fol. by *of*): *He was cognizant of the difficulty.* **2.** having legal cognizance. Also, *esp. Brit.*, **cognisant.** [COGNIZ(ANCE) + -ANT]
—**Syn. 1.** See **conscious.**

cog·nize (kog′nīz), *v.t.*, **-nized, -niz·ing.** to perceive; become conscious of; know. Also, *esp. Brit.*, **cognise.** [back formation from COGNIZANCE] —**cog′niz·er,** *n.*

cog·no·men (kog nō′mən), *n.*, *pl.* **-no·mens, -nom·i·na** (-nom′ə nə). **1.** a surname. **2.** any name, esp. a nickname. **3.** the third and commonly the last name of a citizen of ancient Rome, indicating his house or family, as "Caesar" in "Gaius Julius Caesar." [< L, equiv. to *co-* CO- + *nōmen* name, with *-g-* after model of *nōscī: cognōscī;* see COGNIZANCE] —**cog·nom·i·nal** (kog nom′ə nəl, -nō′mə-), *adj.* —**cog·nom′i·nal·ly,** *adv.*

co·gno·scen·ti (kon′yə shen′tē, kog′nə-), *n.pl.*, *sing.* **-te** (-tē). those who have or are held to have superior knowledge and understanding of a particular field, esp. in the fine arts, literature, and world of fashion; people with specialized or inside information: *This play will be enjoyed only by the cognoscenti.* Also, **conoscenti.** [< It, Latinized var. of *conoscente* (prp. of *conoscere* to know) < L. See COGNITION, -ENT]

cog·nos·ci·ble (kog nos′ə bəl), *adj.* capable of being known. [< LL *cognōscibil(is)*, equiv. to *cognōsc(ere)* (see COGNIZANCE) + *-ibilis* -IBLE] —**cog·nos′ci·bil′i·ty,** *n.*

cog·nos·ci·tive (kog nos′i tiv), *adj.* having the ability to know or discover: *the cognoscitive powers of man.* [< L *cognōsc(ere)* (to) come to know + -ITIVE] —**cog·nos′ci·tive·ly,** *adv.*

cog·no·vit (kog nō′vit), *n.* *Law.* an acknowledgment or confession by a defendant that the plaintiff's cause, or a part of it, is just, wherefore the defendant, to save expense, permits judgment to be entered without trial. [< L: perf. 3rd pers. sing. of *cognōscere* to recognize; see COGNIZANCE]

co·gon (kō gōn′), *n.* a tall, coarse grass, *Imperata cylindrica*, of the tropics and subtropics, furnishing an excellent material for thatching. [< Sp < Tagalog *kugon*]

cog′ rail′way, a railway having locomotives with a cogged center driving wheel engaging with a cogged rail, to provide sufficient traction for climbing steeper grades than is possible with ordinary wheels. Also called **rack railway.**

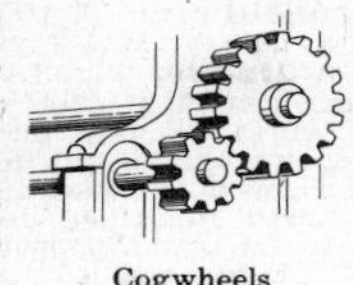
Cogwheels

Cogs′well chair′ (kogz′wel, -wəl), an armchair having a fixed, sloping back, open sides, and cabriole legs. Also, **Coxwell chair.** [from *Cogswell's chair*]

cog·wheel (kog′hwēl′, -wēl′), *n.* (not in technical use) a gear wheel, formerly esp. one having teeth of hardwood or metal inserted into slots. [late ME; see COG[1], WHEEL]

cog′wheel ore′, bournonite.

co·hab·it (kō hab′it), *v.i.* **1.** to live together as man and wife, usually without legal or religious sanction. **2.** *Archaic.* to dwell or reside in company or in the same place. [< LL *cohabit(āre)*, equiv. to *co-* CO- + *habitāre* to have possession, abide (*hab(ēre)* to have + *-itā-* freq. suffix + *-re* inf. ending)] —**co·hab′it·ant, co·hab′it·er,** *n.* —**co·hab′i·ta′tion,** *n.*

Co·han (kō han′, kō′han), *n.* **George M(ichael),** 1878–1942, U.S. actor, playwright, and producer.

Co·has·set (kō has′it), *n.* a town in E Massachusetts. 2748 (1960).

co·heir (kō âr′), *n.* a joint heir. Also, *referring to a woman,* **co·heir·ess** (kō âr′is). [CO- + HEIR] —**co·heir′ship,** *n.*

Co·hen (kō′ən), *n.* **1. Morris Raphael,** 1880–1947, U.S. philosopher and educator, born in Russia. **2. Oc·tav·us Roy** (ok tav′əs), 1891–1959, U.S. short-story writer and novelist.

Co·hen (kō′hān, kō hān′; *Eng.* kō′ən, koin), *n.*, *pl.* **Co·ha·nim** (kō hä′nim, kō hä nēm′), *Eng.* **Co·hens.** *Hebrew.* Kohen.

co·hen·ite (kō′ə nīt′), *n.* a rare microscopic mineral, carbide of iron, nickel, or cobalt, found in some meteorites. [named after E. W. *Cohen,* 19th-century German mineralogist; see -ITE[1]]

co·here (kō hēr′), *v.i.*, **-hered, -her·ing.** **1.** to stick together; be united; hold fast, as parts of the same mass: *The particles of wet flour cohered to form a paste.* **2.** *Physics.* (of two or more similar substances) to be united within a body by the action of molecular forces. **3.** to be naturally or logically connected: *Without sound reasoning no argument will cohere.* **4.** to agree; be congruous: *Her account of the incident cohered with his.* [< L *cohaer(ēre)*, equiv. to *co-* CO- + *haerēre* to stick, cling]
—**Syn. 1.** See **stick**[2]. **3.** follow.

co·her·ence (kō hēr′əns), *n.* **1.** the act or state of cohering; cohesion. **2.** natural or logical connection. **3.** congruity; consistency. Also, **co·her′en·cy.** [COHER(ENT) + -ENCE]
—**Syn. 1, 2.** COHERENCE, COHESION imply a sticking together. COHERENCE is more often applied figuratively, relating to the order and consistency of thought or of statements: *the coherence of an argument; the coherence of a report.* COHESION usually applies to the literal sticking together of material things: *the cohesion of wood and glue in plywood.* **3.** correspondence, harmony, agreement, rationality.

coher′ence the′ory, *Philos.* the theory of truth that every true statement, insofar as it is true, describes its subject in the totality of its relationship with all other things. Cf. **correspondence theory, pragmatic theory.**

co·her·ent (kō hēr′ənt), *adj.* **1.** cohering; sticking together: *a coherent mass of sticky candies.* **2.** having a natural or due agreement of parts; connected: *a coherent design.* **3.** consistent; logical: *a coherent argument.* [< ML *cohērent-*, var. of L *cohaerent-* (s. of *cohaerēns*), prp. of *cohaerēre.* See COHERE, -ENT] —**co·her′ent·ly,** *adv.*

coher′ent light′, *Optics.* light in which the electromagnetic waves maintain a fixed phase relationship over a period of time and in which the phase relationship remains constant for various points that are perpendicular to the direction of propagation.

co·her·er (kō hēr′ər), *n.* **1.** one who or that which coheres. **2.** *Radio.* a device usually used in detecting radio waves, a tube filled with a conducting substance in granular form, whose electrical resistance increases when struck by radio waves. [COHERE + -ER[1]]

co·he·sion (kō hē′zhən), *n.* **1.** the act or state of cohering, uniting, or sticking together. **2.** *Physics.* the molecular force between particles within a body or substance that acts to unite them. Cf. **adhesion** (def. 4). **3.** *Bot.* the congenital union of one part with another. [var. of *cohaesion* < L *cohaes-* (var. s. of *cohaerēre* to COHERE) + *-iōn-* -ION]
—**Syn. 1.** See **coherence.**

co·he·sive (kō hē′siv), *adj.* **1.** characterized by or causing cohesion: *a cohesive agent.* **2.** cohering; tending to cohere: *a cohesive organization.* **3.** *Physics.* of or pertaining to the molecular force within a body, acting to unite its parts. [COHES(ION) + -IVE] —**co·he′sive·ly,** *adv.* —**co·he′sive·ness,** *n.*

Cohn (kōn), *n.* **Fer·di·nand Ju·li·us** (fûr′dᵊnand′ jōōl′yəs; *Ger.* fer′di nänt′ yōō′lē ŏŏs′), 1828–98, German botanist and bacteriologist.

co·ho·bate (kō′hō bāt′), *v.t.*, **-bat·ed, -bat·ing.** *Pharm.* to distill again from the same or a similar substance, as by pouring a distilled liquid back upon the matter remaining in the vessel, or upon another mass of similar matter. [< NL *cohobāt(us)* (ptp. of *cohobāre*), equiv. to *kohob* repetition (Paracelsian term, perh. < dial. Ar *ka'ab* second) + *-ātus* -ATE[1]] —**co′ho·ba′tion,** *n.* —**co′ho·ba′tor,** *n.*

Co·hoes (kō hōz′), *n.* a city in E New York, on the Hudson River. 20,129 (1960).

co·hort (kō′hôrt), *n.* **1.** one of the ten divisions in an ancient Roman legion, numbering from 300 to 600 men. **2.** any group of warriors. **3.** a group or company: *She has a cohort of admirers.* **4.** a companion or associate: *The big-game hunter regaled his cohorts with tales of high adventure.* [< L *cohort-* (s. of *cohors*) yard, military unit, equiv. to *co-* CO- + *hort-* GARTH; r. late ME *cohorte* < MF]

co·hor·ta·tive (kō hôr′tə tiv), *adj.* (of a verbal mood or form) expressing encouragement or exhortation. [< L *cohortāt(us)* urged (ptp. of *cohortāre;* see COHORT) + -IVE]

co·hosh (kō′hosh, kō hosh′), *n.* either of two perennial herbs of the Eastern U.S., the ranunculaceous *Cimicifuga racemosa* (**black cohosh**), or the berberidaceous *Caulophyllum thalictroides* (**blue cohosh**), both used medicinally. [< Algonquian (Mass.): rough]

co·hune (kō hōōn′), *n.* a pinnate-leaved palm, *Orbignya Cohune,* native to Central America, bearing large nuts whose meat yields an oil resembling that of the coconut. Also, **cohune′ palm′.** [< AmerSp < some native Central American dial.]

coif[1] (koif), *n.* **1.** a hood-shaped cap, usually of white cloth and with extended sides, worn beneath a veil, as by nuns. **2.** any of various hoodlike caps, varying through the centuries in shape and purpose, worn by men and women. **3.** a cap similar to a skullcap, worn by a sergeant at law. **4.** *Armor.* a covering for the head and neck, made of leather, padded cloth, or mail. **5.** *Brit.* the rank or position of a sergeant at law. —*v.t.* **6.** to cover or dress with or as with a coif. [ME *coyf(e)* < OF *coiffe* < LL *cofea, cuphia* < OHG **kupfia* cap, akin to COP[2]]

coif[2] (kwäf), *n.* *Informal.* a coiffure. [short form]

coif·feur (kwa fœr′), *n.*, *pl.* **-feurs** (-fœr′). *French.* a hairdresser.

coif·fure (kwä fyŏŏr′; *Fr.* kwa fyr′), *n.*, *pl.* **-fures** (-fyŏŏrz′; *Fr.* -fyr′), *v.*, **-fured** (-fyŏŏrd′), **-fur·ing** (-fyŏŏr′ing). —*n.* **1.** a style of arranging or combing the hair. **2.** a head covering; headdress. —*v.t.* **3.** to provide with a coiffure. [< F, equiv. to *coiff(er)* (to) dress the hair (see COIF[1]) + *-ure* -URE]

coign (koin), *n.*, *v.t.* quoin.

coigne (koin), *n.*, *v.t.*, **coigned, coign·ing.** quoin.

coign′ of van′tage, a favorable position for observation or action: *From my coign of vantage, I could see that the story would have a happy ending.*

coil[1] (koil), *v.t.* **1.** to wind into regularly spaced rings one above the other: *to coil a wire around a pencil.* **2.** to wind on a flat surface into rings one around the other: *He coiled the rope on the deck.* **3.** to gather (rope, wire, etc.) into loops: *She coiled the clothesline and hung it on the hook.* —*v.i.* **4.** to form rings, spirals, etc.; wind: *The snake coiled, ready to strike.* **5.** to move in or follow a winding course: *The river coiled through the valley.* —*n.* **6.** a connected series of spirals or rings into which a rope or the like is wound. **7.** a single such ring. **8.** an arrangement of pipes, coiled or in a series, as in a radiator. **9.** a continuous pipe having inlet and outlet, or flow and return ends. **10.** *Elect.* **a.** a conductor, as a copper wire, wound up in a spiral or other form. **b.** a device composed essentially of such a conductor. **11.** *Philately.* **a.** a stamp issued in a roll, usually of 500 stamps, and usually perforated vertically or horizontally only. **b.** a roll of such stamps. [? var. of CULL[1]]

coil[2] (koil), *n.* **1.** a noisy disturbance; tumult. **2.** trouble; bustle; ado. [?]

coil′ spring′, any spring of wire coiled helically, having a cylindrical or conical outline. See illus. under **spring.**

Co·im·ba·tore (kō im′bä tōr′, -tôr′), *n.* a city in W Madras, in SW India. 286,300 (1961).

Coim·bra (kwēnm′brə), *n.* a city in central Portugal: noted university founded at Lisbon 1290, transferred here 1537. 56,497 (1960).

coin (koin), *n.* **1.** a piece of metal stamped and issued by the authority of the government for use as money. **2.** a number of such pieces. **3.** *Archit.* quoin (defs. 1, 2). **4.** *Obs.* a corner cupboard of the 18th century. **5. pay someone back in his own coin,** to reciprocate in kind; retaliate: *The saleswoman was terribly rude, but I resisted the temptation to pay her back in her own coin.* —*v.t.* **6.** to make (money) by stamping metal: *The mint is coining pennies.* **7.** to convert (metal) into money: *The mint coins copper into pennies.* **8.** to make; invent; fabricate: *to coin words.* —*v.i.* **9.** *Brit. Informal.* to counterfeit, esp. to make counterfeit money. **10.** *Metalworking.* to raise designs on both sides of (a blank) by forcing dies against it. Cf. **emboss** (def. 3). **11. coin money,** *Informal.* to make or gain money rapidly: *Those who bought stock in computers a few years back are now coining money.* [ME *coyn(e), coygne* < MF *coin, cuigne* wedge, corner, die < L *cuneus* wedge] —**coin′a·ble,** *adj.* —**coin′er,** *n.*

coin·age (koi′nij), *n.* **1.** the act, process, or right of making coins. **2.** that which is coined. **3.** coins collectively; currency. **4.** anything made, invented, or fabricated: *"Ecdysiast" is a coinage of H. L. Mencken.* [late ME *coy(g)nage* < MF *coignaige.* See COIN, -AGE]

coin′age bronze′, an alloy of 95 percent copper, 4 percent tin, and 1 percent zinc.

coin′ box′, a locked container or receptacle for holding coins deposited in a pay telephone, pinball machine, or other coin-operated machine.

coin′ chang′er, **1.** a machine that gives change rapidly, as to a customer, typically operated by a manual keyboard and often used in association with a cash register. **2.** a machine that supplies change, as small coins for large or large coins for small, esp. for the use of other coin-operated machines.

co·in·cide (kō′in sīd′), *v.i.*, **-cid·ed, -cid·ing.** **1.** to come to occupy the same place in space, the same point or period in time, or the same relative position: *The centers of concentric circles coincide. Our vacations coincided this year.* **2.** to correspond exactly, as in nature, character, etc.: *His vocation coincides with his avocation.* **3.** to agree or concur, as in thought, opinion, etc.: *Their opinions always coincide.* [< ML *coincide(re)*, equiv. to L *co-* CO- + *incidere* to befall; see INCIDENT]

co·in·ci·dence (kō in′si dᵊns), *n.* **1.** the condition or fact of coinciding. **2.** an instance of this. **3.** a striking occurrence of two or more events at one time apparently by mere chance: *Our meeting in Venice was pure coincidence.* [COINCID(ENT) + -ENCE]

co·in·ci·dent (kō in′si dᵊnt), *adj.* **1.** coinciding; occupying the same place or position. **2.** happening at the same time. **3.** exactly corresponding. **4.** in exact agreement (usually fol. by *with*). [< ML *coincident-* (s. of *coincidēns*) prp. of *coincidere* to COINCIDE; see -ENT]
—**Syn. 2.** simultaneous, synchronous, contemporary.

co·in·ci·den·tal (kō in′si den′tᵊl), *adj.* showing or involving coincidence: *a coincidental meeting.* [COINCIDENT + -AL[1]]

co·in·ci·den·tal·ly (kō in′si den′tᵊlē), *adv.* in a coincidental manner. Also, **co·in·ci·dent·ly** (kō in′si dᵊnt lē). [COINCIDENTAL + -LY]

coin′ glass′, a drinking glass of the 17th and 18th centuries having a coin enclosed in a knop in the stem.

co·in·her·it·ance (kō′in her′i tᵊns), *n.* joint inheritance. [CO- + INHERITANCE]

coin′ of the realm′, *Usually Facetious.* See **legal tender.**

coin′ sil′ver, silver having the standard fineness for coinage purposes.

co·in·stan·ta·ne·ous (kō′in stən tā′nē əs), *adj.* occurring or existing at the same instant; simultaneous. [CO- + INSTANTANEOUS] —**co′in·stan·ta′ne·ous·ly,** *adv.*

co·in·sur·ance (kō′in sho͝or′əns), *n.* **1.** insurance underwritten jointly with another or others. **2.** a form of property insurance in which an insurer assumes liability only for that proportion of a loss which the amount of insurance bears to a specified percentage of the value of the property. [CO- + INSURANCE]

co·in·sure (kō′in sho͝or′), *v.t., v.i.,* **-sured, -sur·ing.** to insure jointly with another or others; insure on the basis of coinsurance. [CO- + INSURE] —**co′in·sur′a·ble,** *adj.*

co·in·sur·er (kō′in sho͝or′ər), *n.* **1.** a person or firm that contracts as an insurer jointly with another or others. **2.** an insured who is liable to bear part of the loss under a coinsurance provision. [CO- + INSURER]

coin·tise (kwan tēz′), *n.* a lappet or mantling, worn beneath the crests of medieval helmets in the late 12th century. [ME < OF, deriv. of *cointe* skillful, well-dressed. See QUAINT]

Coin·treau (kwän′trō; *Fr.* kwan trō′), *n. Trademark.* a colorless, orange-flavored liqueur.

coir (koir), *n.* the prepared fiber of the husk of the coconut fruit, used in making rope, matting, etc. [< Malayalam *kāyar* cord; r. *cairo* < Pg < Tamil *kayiru* rope]

cois·trel (koi′strəl), *n. Archaic.* **1.** a servant in charge of a knight's horses. **2.** a scoundrel; knave. [ME *quystron, custrun, custrell,* appar. b. MF *quistron* (< LL *cocistrōn-,* s. of *cocistrō* taverner) and *coustillier* esquire (lit., dagger man), deriv. of *coustille* dagger]

co′ital exanthe′ma, *Vet. Pathol.* a virus disease affecting horses and cattle, characterized by the appearance on the mucus membranes of the genital organs and neighboring skin of vesicles which later become pustules. It is transmitted by copulation. [< L *coit(us)* (ptp. of *coīre;* see COITION) + -AL¹]

co·i·tion (kō ish′ən), *n.* coitus. [< L *coitiōn-* (s. of *coitiō*) a coming together (*co-* co- + *-itus,* ptp. of *īre* to go, equiv. to *i-* v. stem + *-tus* ptp. suffix) + *-iōn* -ION]

co·i·tus (kō′i təs), *n.* the act of sexual intercourse, esp. between human beings. [< L: a coming together, uniting; see COITION] —**co′i·tal,** *adj.*

co′itus in·ter·rup′tus (in′tə rup′təs), *pl.* **coitus in·ter·rup·ti** (in′tə rup′tī). **1.** coitus that is intentionally interrupted by withdrawal before ejaculation. **2.** an act or instance of this. [< NL: interrupted coitus]

coke¹ (kōk), *n., v.,* **coked, cok·ing.** *Chem.* —*n.* **1.** the solid product resulting from the destructive distillation of coal in an oven or closed chamber or by imperfect combustion, consisting principally of carbon: used chiefly as a fuel in metallurgy to reduce metallic oxides to metals. —*v.t., v.i.* **2.** to convert into or become coke. [var. of *colk* core, ME *colke,* equiv. to OE *col* COAL + *-(o)ca* -OCK] —**coke′like′,** **cok′y,** *adj.*

coke² (kōk), *Slang.* —*n.* **1.** cocaine. —*v.t.* **2.** to affect with a narcotic drug, esp. with cocaine (usually fol. by *up*). [short for COCAINE]

Coke (ko͝ok), *n.* **Sir Edward,** 1552–1634, English jurist and writer on law. Also, **Cooke.**

coke′ ov′en, an oven for the conversion of coal into coke by heating the coal in the absence of air so as to distill the volatile ingredients.

cok·er (kō′kər), *n.* Often, **cokers.** an inhabitant of the mountains of the coal-mining regions of West Virginia and Pennsylvania. [COKE¹ + -ER¹]

co·ker·nut (kō′kər nut′), *n. Chiefly Brit.* coconut.

col (kol; *Fr.* kôl), *n., pl.* **cols** (kolz; *Fr.* kôl). **1.** *Phys. Geog.* a pass or depression in a mountain range or ridge. **2.** *Meteorol.* the region of relatively low pressure between two anticyclones. [< F < L *collum* neck]

col-¹, var. of **com-** before *l:* *collateral.*

col-², var. of **colo-** before a vowel: *colectomy.*

Col., 1. Colombia. **2.** Colonel. **3.** Colorado. **4.** Colossians.

col., 1. (in prescriptions) strain. [< L *colā*] **2.** collected. **3.** collector. **4.** college. **5.** colonial. **6.** colony. **7.** color. **8.** colored. **9.** column.

co·la¹ (kō′lə), *n.* a carbonated soft drink having a syrup base made from the dried leaves of the coca plant and the seeds of kola nuts, together with sweeteners and other flavorings. Also, **kola.** [var. of KOLA]

co·la² (kō′lə), *n.* a pl. of **colon.**

COLA (kō′lə), *n.* an escalator clause, esp. in union contracts, that grants automatic wage increases to cover the rising cost of living due to inflation. [*C(ost) o(f) L(iving) A(djustment)*]

col·a·co·bi·o·sis (kol′ə kō bī ō′sis), *n., pl.* **-ses** (-sēz). (among social insects) life in which one species lives as a parasite in the community of another species. [< Gk *kolak-* (s. of *kólax*) parasite + -o- + -BIOSIS] —**col·a·co·bi·ot·ic** (kol′ə kō bī ot′ik), *adj.*

col·an·der (kul′ən dər, kol′-), *n.* a metal or plastic container with a perforated bottom, for draining and straining foods. Also, **cullender.** [late ME *colyndore,* perh. (with nasalization) < OPr *colador* < ML *cōlātōrium,* equiv. to *cōlāt(us),* ptp. of *cōlāre* to strain (L *cōl(um)* strainer + *-ātus* -ATE¹) + *-ōrium* -ORY²]

co′la nut′. See **kola nut.**

co·la·scio·ne (kō′lä shō′nē, -nā; *It.* kō′lä shô′ne), *n., pl.* **-nes,** *It.* **-ni** (-nē). (esp. during the 16th and 17th centuries) an Italian stringed instrument resembling a lute and having a long neck and two or three strings. [< It]

colat., (in prescriptions) strained. [< L *colātus*]

co·lat·i·tude (kō lat′i to͞od′, -tyo͞od′), *n. Astron., Navig.* the complement of the latitude; the difference between a given latitude and 90°. [CO- + LATITUDE]

Col·bert (kôl bᴇʀ′), *n.* **Jean Bap·tiste** (zhäɴ bᴀ tēst′), 1619–83, French statesman and finance minister under Louis XIV.

Col·by (kōl′bē), *n.* **1.** a town in NW Kansas. 4210 (1960). **2.** a boy's given name.

col·can·non (kəl kan′ən, kōl′kan-), *n.* an Irish dish made of cabbage, kale, or other greens, and potatoes boiled and mashed together. [< Ir *cāl ceannann* white-head cabbage, equiv. to *cāl* (< L *caulis* cabbage) + *ceann* head + *-ann,* weak var. of *fionn* white]

Col·ches·ter (kōl′ches′tər; *Brit.* kōl′chi stər), *n.* a city in NE Essex, in E England. 65,072 (1961).

col·chi·cine (kol′chi sēn′, -sin, kol′ki-), *n. Pharm.* a pale yellow, crystalline alkaloid, $C_{22}H_{25}NO_6$, the active principle of colchicum. [COLCHIC(UM) + -INE²]

col·chi·cum (kol′chə kəm, kol′kə-), *n.* **1.** any Old World liliaceous plant of the genus *Colchicum,* esp. *C. autumnale,* a crocuslike plant. **2.** the dried seeds or corms of this plant. **3.** *Pharm.* a medicine or drug prepared from them, used in medicine chiefly for gout. [< L < Gk *kolchikón* meadow saffron, prob. after *Kolchís* COLCHIS; see -IC]

Col·chis (kol′kis), *n.* an ancient country in Asia, S of the Caucasus and bordering on the Black Sea: the land of the Golden Fleece and of Medea in Greek mythology.

col·co·thar (kol′kə thər), *n. Chem.* the brownish-red oxide of iron which remains after heating ferrous sulfate: used chiefly as a pigment in paints and theatrical rouge, and as a polishing agent. Also called **jewelers' rouge, caput mortuum.** [< ML < OSp *colcotar,* SpAr *qulquṭār* yellow vitriol, perh. < Gk *xálkanthos*]

cold (kōld), *adj.* **1.** having a temperature lower than the normal temperature of the body: *cold hands.* **2.** having a relatively low temperature; having little or no warmth: *cold water; a cold day.* **3.** feeling an uncomfortable lack of warmth; chilled: *The skaters were cold.* **4.** lacking the warmth of life; dead: *When the doctor arrived, the body was already cold.* **5.** *U.S.* unconscious because of a severe blow, shock, etc.: *I knocked him cold with an uppercut.* **6.** lacking in passion, emotion, enthusiasm, ardor, etc.: *cold reason.* **7.** not affectionate, cordial, or friendly; unresponsive: *a cold reply; a cold reception.* **8.** lacking sensual desire; frigid: *She remained cold to his advances.* **9.** failing to excite feeling or interest: *the cold precision of his prose.* **10.** unexcitable; imperturbable: *cold impassivity.* **11.** depressing; dispiriting: *the cold atmosphere of a hospital waiting room.* **12.** faint; weak: *The dogs lost the cold scent.* **13.** (in children's games) distant from the object of search or the correct answer. **14.** *Art.* **a.** having cool colors, esp. muted tones tending toward grayish blue. **b.** being a cool color. **15.** slow to absorb heat, as a soil containing a large amount of clay and hence retentive of moisture. **16.** *Metalworking.* noting or pertaining to any process involving plastic deformation of a metal at a temperature below that at which recrystallization can occur because of the strain: *cold working.* **17. in cold blood.** See **blood** (def. 16). **18. throw cold water on,** to disparage; disapprove of; dampen the enthusiasm of: *There would always be someone to throw cold water on our ambitions.* —*n.* **19.** the relative absence of heat: *Everyone suffered from the intense cold.* **20.** the sensation produced by loss of heat from the body, as by contact with anything having a lower temperature than that of the body: *He felt the cold of the steel against his cheek.* **21.** Also called **common cold.** a respiratory viral infection characterized by catarrh, sneezing, sore throat, coughing, etc. **22.** cold weather: *In three hours the airplane carried them from the cold of winter into the heat of summer.* **23. catch** or **take cold,** to get or suffer from a cold: *We all caught cold during that dreadful winter.* **24. left out in the cold,** neglected; ignored; forgotten: *After the baby came, the young husband felt left out in the cold.* Also, **out in the cold.** —*adv.* **25.** with complete certainty; absolutely: *He learned his lesson cold.* **26.** without preparation or prior notice: *She had to play the lead role cold.* **27.** in an abrupt unceremonious manner: *He quit the job cold.* **28.** *Metalworking.* at a temperature below that at which recrystallization can occur (sometimes used in combination): *The wire was drawn cold; to cold-hammer an iron bar.* [ME; OE *cald, ceald;* c. Goth *kald(s),* Icel *kald(r),* G *kalt,* D *koud;* akin to L *gel-* in *gelidus* GELID] —**cold′ish,** *adj.* —**cold′ly,** *adv.* —**cold′ness,** *n.*

—**Syn. 2.** frigid, gelid, frozen, freezing. COLD, CHILL, CHILLING, CHILLY, COOL refer to various degrees of absence of heat. COLD refers to temperature possibly so low as to cause suffering: *cold water.* CHILL suggests a penetrating cold which causes shivering and numbness: *There was a chill wind blowing.* CHILLING carries a connotation of destructive frost: *a chilling wind.* CHILLY is a weaker word, though it also connotes shivering and discomfort: *a chilly room.* COOL means merely somewhat cold, not warm: *cool and comfortable.* All have figurative uses. **6.** indifferent, uninvolved, cool, unconcerned, imperturbable. **7.** apathetic, unsympathetic, unfeeling, heartless; polite, formal, reserved; unfriendly, inimical, hostile. **9.** uninspiring, dull. **10.** calm, deliberate. —**Ant. 2.** hot. **6.** warm, emotional. **13.** warm.

Cold (kōld), *n.* **Sea of.** See **Mare Frigoris.**

cold-blood·ed (kōld′blud′id), *adj.* **1.** without emotion or feeling; dispassionate; cruel: *a cold-blooded murder.* **2.** sensitive to cold. **3.** designating or pertaining to animals, as fishes and reptiles, whose blood temperature ranges from the freezing point upward, in accordance with the temperature of the surrounding medium. —**cold′-blood′ed·ly,** *adv.* —**cold′-blood′ed·ness,** *n.*

cold′ chis′el, a steel chisel used on cold metal. See illus. under **chisel.**

cold-chis·el (kōld′chiz′əl), *v.t.,* **-eled, -el·ing** or (*esp. Brit.*) **-elled, -el·ling.** to work upon (metal) with a cold chisel.

cold′ col′or, a paint fixed to glass or to a ceramic object without firing.

cold′ com′fort, slight or negligible comfort; almost no consolation: *The theft could have been worse, but that was cold comfort.*

cold′ cream′, a cosmetic, typically of oily and heavy consistency, used to soothe and cleanse the skin, esp. of the face and neck.

cold′ cuts′, various meats and sometimes cheeses, sliced and served cold.

cold′ deck′, *Cards Slang.* a pack with the cards in prearranged order, secretly exchanged for the one in use.

cold-draw (kōld′drô′), *v.t.,* **-drew, -drawn, -drawing.** *Metalworking.* to draw (wire, tubing, etc.) without preheating the metal.

cold′ feet′, *Informal.* a loss or lack of courage or confidence; an onset of uncertainty or fear: *She got cold feet when asked to recite in class.*

cold′ fish′, a person who is very reserved or aloof in manner or lacking in normal cordiality, sympathy, or other feeling: *Shyness made him seem like a cold fish.*

cold′ frame′, a bottomless, boxlike, usually glass-covered structure and the bed of earth that it covers, used to protect plants.

cold′ front′, the zone separating two air masses, of which the cooler, denser mass is advancing and replacing the warmer.

Cold′ Har′bor, a locality in Virginia, NE of Richmond: Civil War battle in 1864.

cold-heart·ed (kōld′här′tid), *adj.* lacking sympathy or feeling; indifferent; unkind. —**cold′-heart′ed·ly,** *adv.* —**cold′-heart′ed·ness,** *n.*

cold′ light′, light emitted by a source that is not incandescent, as from a firefly.

cold′ pack′, 1. a cold towel, ice bag, etc., applied to the body to reduce swelling, relieve pain, etc. **2.** Also called **cold′-pack meth′od, raw-pack method.** a method of canning uncooked food by placing it in hot jars or cans and sterilizing in a bath of boiling water or steam. Cf. **hot pack.**

cold-pack (kōld′pak′), *v.t.* **1.** to place a cold pack on: *to cold-pack a feverish patient.* **2.** to can (food) by the cold-pack method.

cold′ patch′, a patch that may be applied by cement to the tire of an automobile or the like without vulcanization.

cold-patch (kōld′pach′), *v.t.* to apply a cold patch to (a tire tube).

cold′ pole′, the location in the northern or southern hemisphere having the coldest annual mean temperature in that hemisphere. Also called **pole of cold.**

cold-roll (kōld′rōl′), *v.t. Metalworking.* to roll (metal) at a temperature below that at which it recrystallizes.

cold′ rub′ber, *Chem.* a synthetic rubber made at a relatively low temperature (about 40°F) and having greater strength and durability than that made at the usual temperature (about 120°F): used chiefly for re-treading tires.

cold′ short′, *Metalworking.* lack of ductility in a metal, rendering it unfit for cold working.

cold-short (kōld′shôrt′), *adj. Metalworking.* unable to be drawn or worked at the temperature of the surrounding air. [trans. of Sw *kallskör* cold-brittle (see SHORT), equiv. to *kall* COLD + *skör,* akin to SHEAR, SHARD] —**cold′-short′ness,** *n.*

cold′ shoul′der, a show of deliberate indifference or disregard: *We got a cold shoulder from the older, more sophisticated members of the group.*

cold-shoul·der (kōld′shōl′dər), *v.t. Informal.* to snub; show indifference to.

cold′ shut′, 1. *Foundry.* an imperfectly fused junction of two streams of metal in a mold. **2.** *Metalworking.* a part of a forging which has doubled over a surface covered with scale so as to have a poor bond with the body of the forging.

cold·slaw (kōld′slô′, kōl′-), *n.* coleslaw.

cold′ snap′, a sudden onset of a relatively brief period of cold weather. Also called **cold′ spell′.**

cold′ sore′, a vesicular eruption on the face, often accompanying a cold or a febrile condition; herpes simplex.

cold′ steel′, a weapon made of steel, esp. a sword, bayonet, etc.

cold′ stor′age, the storage of food, furs, etc., in any artificially cooled place.

Cold·stream (kōld′strēm′), *n.* a town in SE Berwick, in SE Scotland, on the Tweed River.

Cold′stream Guards′, a guard regiment of the English royal household: formed in Coldstream, Scotland, 1659–60, and instrumental in restoring the English monarchy under Charles II. Also called **Cold·stream·ers** (kōld′strē′mərz).

cold′ sweat′, a chill accompanied by perspiration, caused by fear, nervousness, or the like.

cold′ tur′key, *Slang.* **1.** the sudden and complete withholding of narcotics from an addict, as to effect a cure. **2.** without preparation; impromptu. —**cold-tur·key** (kōld′tûr′kē), *adj.*

cold′ type′, *Print.* type set photographically or by pasting up letters on acetate or paper. Cf. **hot metal.**

cold′ war′, intense economic, political, military, and ideological rivalry between nations just short of military conflict; the application of intense pressure on all levels by hostile nations without becoming engaged in a shooting war.

cold′ wa′ter, *Informal.* deprecation, as of a hope, idea, or plan; speech or actions intended to disparage, disillusion, or discourage: *The executive committee threw cold water on his proposal.*

cold-wa·ter (kōld′wô′tər, -wot′ər), *adj.* **1.** prepared with or requiring cold water: *cold-water paint.* **2.** provided only with cold running water: *a cold-water flat.*

Cold·wa·ter (kōld′wô′tər, -wot′ər), *n.* **1.** a town in S Michigan. 8880 (1960). **2.** a town in W Ohio. 2766 (1960).

cold′ wave′, 1. *Meteorol.* a rapid and considerable fall in temperature, usually affecting a large area. **2.** a permanent wave in the hair set solely by special chemical solutions.

cold-work (kōld′wûrk′), *v.t.* to work (metal) at a temperature below that at which it recrystallizes.

cold-work·ing (kōld′wûr′king), *n.* the process of cold-working metal.

cole (kōl), *n.* any of various plants of the genus *Brassica,* esp. the rape. [ME *col(e),* OE *cāl, cāw(e)l* < L *caulis* stalk, cabbage; cf. Gk *kaulós* stalk]

Cole (kōl), *n.* **1. Thomas,** 1801–48, U.S. painter, born in England. **2. Timothy,** 1852–1931, U.S. wood engraver, born in England. **3.** a boy's given name.

co·lec·to·my (kə lek′tə mē), *n., pl.* **-mies.** *Surg.* the removal of all or part of the colon or large intestine. [COL-² + -ECTOMY]

Cole·man (kōl′mən), *n.* **1.** a town in central Texas. 6371 (1960). **2.** a boy's given name.

cole·man·ite (kōl′mə nīt′), *n.* a mineral, hydrous calcium borate, $Ca_2B_6O_{11}\cdot 5H_2O$, occurring in colorless or milky-white crystals. [named after W. T. *Coleman* of San Francisco in 1884, in whose mine it was found; see -ITE[1]]

colent., (in prescriptions) let them be strained. [< L *colentur*] Also, **colen.**

Co·le·op·ter·a (kō′lē op′tər ə, kol′ē-), *n.* the order comprising the beetles. [< NL < Gk *koleóptera,* neut. pl. of *koleópter(os)* sheath-winged, equiv. to *koleo-* (deriv. of *koleón* sheath) + *-pteros* -PTEROUS]

co·le·op·ter·an (kō′lē op′tər ən, kol′ē-), *adj.* **1.** belonging or pertaining to the order *Coleoptera.* —*n.* **2.** a beetle. [COLEOPTER(A) + -AN]

co·le·op·ter·on (kō′lē op′tə ron′, kol′ē-), *n., pl.* **-ter·a** (-tər ə). a coleopterous insect; a beetle. [< NL < Gk *koleó(n)* sheath, scabbard + *pterón* feather, wing]

co·le·op·ter·ous (kō′lē op′tər əs, kol′ē-), *adj.* belonging or pertaining to the order *Coleoptera,* comprising the beetles. [COLEOPTER(A) + -OUS]

Coleopteron
A, Head; B, Thorax; C, Abdomen; D, Elytron; E, Wing; F, Antenna

co·le·op·tile (kō′lē op′til, kol′ē-), *n. Bot.* (in grasses) the first leaf above the ground, forming a sheath around the stem tip. [< NL *coleoptil(um)* < Gk *koleó(n)* sheath, scabbard + *ptílon* soft feathers, down]

co·le·o·rhi·za (kō′lē ə rī′zə, kol′ē-), *n., pl.* **-zae** (-zē). *Bot.* the sheath which envelops the radicle in certain plants and which is penetrated by the root in germination. [< NL < Gk *koleó(n)* sheath, scabbard + *rhíza* root]

Cole·ridge (kōl′rij), *n.* **Samuel Taylor,** 1772–1834, English poet and critic. —**Cole·ridg′i·an,** *adj.*

Cole·ridge-Tay·lor (kōl′rij tā′lər), *n.* **Samuel,** 1875–1912, English composer.

Coles (kōlz), *n.* a boy's given name.

cole·seed (kōl′sēd′), *n.* **1.** the seed of the rape. **2.** rape[2]. [OE *cawel sæd.* See COLE, SEED]

cole·slaw (kōl′slô′), *n.* a salad of finely sliced or chopped raw cabbage. [< D *koolsla,* equiv. to *kool* cabbage + *sla,* contr. of *salade* salad]

Col·et (kol′it), *n.* **John,** 1467?–1519, English educator and clergyman.

colet., (in prescriptions) let it be strained. [< L *colētur*]

Co·lette (kō let′, ko-; *Fr.* kô let′), *n.* **1.** (*Sidonie Gabrielle Claudine Colette*) 1873–1954, French novelist. **2.** a girl's given name.

co·le·us (kō′lē əs), *n., pl.* **-us·es.** any of several menthaceous plants of the genus *Coleus,* of tropical Asia and Africa, certain species of which are cultivated for their showy, colored foliage and blue flowers. [< NL < Gk *koleós,* var. of *koleón* sheath, scabbard]

cole·wort (kōl′wûrt′), *n.* any plant of the genus *Brassica,* esp. kale and rape. [ME; see COLE, WORT[2]]

Col·fax (kōl′faks), *n.* **1. Schuyler,** 1823–85, U.S. political leader: vice-president of the U.S. 1869–73. **2.** a town in SE Washington. 2860 (1960).

col·ic (kol′ik), *Pathol., Vet. Pathol.* —*n.* **1.** paroxysmal pain in the abdomen or bowels. —*adj.* **2.** pertaining to or affecting the colon or the bowels. [late ME *colike* < L *colica (passiō)* (suffering) of the colon < Gk *kolikós,* equiv. to *kól(on)* COLON[2] + *-ikos* -IC] —**col·ick·y** (kol′ə kē), *adj.*

co·liche·marde (kō′lēsh märd′), *n.* a blade on a small sword, having a triangular section at the forte and tapering abruptly toward the point. [< F, after Count Von *Königsmark* (d. 1688), German soldier and administrator who invented it]

col·ic·root (kol′ik ro͞ot′, -ro͝ot′), *n.* **1.** either of two North American liliaceous herbs, *Aletris farinosa* or *A. aurea,* having small yellow or white flowers in a spikelike raceme and a root reputed to relieve colic. **2.** any of certain other plants reputed to cure colic. **3.** the blazing star, *Liatris squarrosa.* [COLIC + ROOT[1]]

col·ic·weed (kol′ik wēd′), *n. U.S.* **1.** See **squirrel corn. 2.** the Dutchman's-breeches. **3.** any of several plants of the genus *Carydalis,* esp. *C. flavula,* of the eastern U.S. [COLIC + WEED[1]]

col·i·form (kol′ə fôrm′, kō′lə-), *adj.* **1.** of, pertaining to, or resembling a coliform bacillus. —*n.* **2.** See **coliform bacillus.** [< L *cōl(um)* a sieve, strainer + -I- + -FORM]

col′iform bacil′lus, *Bacteriol.* any of several bacilli, esp. of the genera *Escherichia* or *Aerobacter,* found as commensals in the large intestine of man and animals, the presence of which in water indicates fecal pollution. Also, **col′iform bacte′rium.**

Co·li·gny (kô lē nyē′), *n.* **Gas·pard de** (ga spar′ də), 1519–72, French admiral and Huguenot leader. Also, **Co·li·gni′.**

Co·li·ma (kō lē′mä), *n.* **1.** a state in SW Mexico, on the Pacific Coast. 157,339 (1960); 2010 sq. mi. **2.** a city in and the capital of this state, in the E part. 41,007 (1960). **3.** a volcano NW of this city, in Jalisco state.

col·in (kol′in), *n.* any of several American quails, esp. the bobwhite. [< Sp, misprint for Nahuatl *çolin*]

Col·in (kol′in, kō′lin; *Fr.* kô lan′; *Ger.* kō′lin, -lēn), *n.* a boy's given name.

Col·i·nette (kol′ə net′), *n.* a girl's given name.

col·i·se·um (kol′i sē′əm), *n.* **1.** Also, **colosseum.** an amphitheater, stadium, large theater, or the like, for public meetings, sports, exhibitions, etc. **2.** (*cap.*) Colosseum. [< ML *Colisseum;* var. of COLOSSEUM]

col′ise′um i′vy. See **kenilworth ivy.**

co·li·tis (kə lī′tis, kō-), *n. Pathol.* inflammation of the colon. [COL-[2] + -ITIS] —**co·lit·ic** (kō lit′ik), *adj.*

coll., **1.** collect. **2.** collection. **3.** collective. **4.** collector. **5.** college. **6.** collegiate. **7.** colloquial. **8.** (in prescriptions) an eyewash. [< L *collyrium*]

col·la (kōl′yə), *n.* a moderately strong south-to-southwest wind in the Philippines, accompanied by heavy rain and squalls. Also called **colla tempestada.** [< Sp]

collab., **1.** collaboration. **2.** collaborator.

col·lab·o·rate (kə lab′ə rāt′), *v.i.,* **-rat·ed, -rat·ing.** **1.** to work, one with another; cooperate, as on a literary work: *They collaborated on a novel.* **2.** to cooperate, esp. willingly, with an enemy of one's country: *He collaborated with the Nazis before and during World War II.* [< LL *collabōrāt(us)* (ptp. of *collabōrāre*), equiv. to *col-* COL-[1] + *labor* work + *-ātus* -ATE[1]] —**col·lab′o·ra′tor,** *n.*

col·lab·o·ra·tion (kə lab′ə rā′shən), *n.* **1.** the act or process of collaborating. **2.** a product resulting from collaboration: *This dictionary is a collaboration of many minds.* [< F < L *collabōrāt(us)* (see COLLABORATE) + F *-ion* -ION]

col·lab·o·ra·tion·ist (kə lab′ə rā′shə nist), *n.* a person who collaborates with the enemy. [COLLABORATION + -IST] —**col·lab′o·ra′tion·ism,** *n.*

col·lab·o·ra·tive (kə lab′ə rā′tiv, -ər ə tiv), *adj.* characterized or accomplished by collaboration: *collaborative methods; a collaborative report.* [COLLABORATE + -IVE] —**col·lab′o·ra′tive·ly,** *adv.*

col·la·da (kə lä′də; *Sp.* kô yä′thä), *n., pl.* **-das** (-dəz; *Sp.* -thäs). a strong north wind in the Gulf of California. [< Sp: a steady blow]

col·lage (kə läzh′, kō-; *Fr.* kô lazh′), *n., pl.* **-lages** (-lä′zhiz; *Fr.* -lazh′) for 2. **1.** a technique of composing a work of art by pasting on a single surface various materials not normally associated with one another, as newspaper clippings, theater tickets, fragments of an envelope, etc. **2.** a work of art produced by this technique. Cf. **assemblage** (def. 3). [< F, equiv. to *colle* paste, glue (< Gk *kólla*) + *-age* -AGE]

col·la·gen (kol′ə jən), *n. Biochem.* the protein that yields gelatin on boiling, contained in connective tissue and bones. [< Gk *kólla* glue + -GEN]

col·la·gen·ase (kol′ə jə nās′), *n. Biochem.* any of a class of proteolytic enzymes, found esp. in clostridia, that catalyze the hydrolysis of collagen. [COLLAGEN + -ASE]

col·lapse (kə laps′), *v.,* **-lapsed, -laps·ing,** *n.* —*v.i.* **1.** to fall or cave in; crumble suddenly: *The roof collapsed and buried the crowd.* **2.** to be made so that parts can be folded, placed, etc., together: *This bridge table collapses.* **3.** to break down; come to nothing; fail: *Despite all their efforts the project collapsed.* **4.** to lose strength, courage, etc., suddenly: *He had been working much too hard, and one day he just collapsed on the job.* **5.** *Pathol.* **a.** to sink into extreme weakness. **b.** (of lungs) to come into an airless state. —*v.t.* **6.** to cause to collapse: *He collapsed the table easily.* —*n.* **7.** a falling in or together: *Three miners were trapped by the collapse of the tunnel roof.* **8.** a sudden, complete failure; a breakdown: *The investigation brought about the complete collapse of his industrial empire.* [< L *collāps(us)* (ptp. of *collābī* to fall, fall in ruins), equiv. to *col-* COL-[1] + *lāp-,* var. s. of *lābī* to fall + *-sus,* var. of *-tus* ptp. ending] —**col·laps′i·ble, col·laps′a·ble,** *adj.* —**col·laps′i·bil′i·ty, col·laps′a·bil′i·ty,** *n.*

col·lar (kol′ər), *n.* **1.** anything worn or placed around the neck: *The horse wore a collar of flowers after winning the race.* **2.** the part of a shirt, coat, etc., around or near the neck, usually folded over. **3.** *Metall.* **a.** a raised area of metal for reinforcing a weld. **b.** a raised rim at the end of a roll in a rolling mill to check lateral expansion of the metal being rolled. **4.** a leather or metal band or a chain, fastened around the neck of an animal, used esp. as a means of restraint or identification. **5.** the part of the harness that fits across the withers and over the shoulders of a draft animal, designed to distribute the pressure of the load drawn. See diag. under **harness. 6.** an ornamental necklace worn as insignia of an order of knighthood. **7.** a narrow strip of leather or other material stitched around the top of a shoe as reinforcement or trimming. **8.** *Zool.* any of various collarlike markings or structures around the neck; torque. **9.** *Mach.* a short ring formed on or fastened over a rod or shaft as a locating or holding part. **10.** (in iron or steel construction) a rigid frame for maintaining the form of an opening. **11.** the upper rim of a vertical mine shaft, borehole, or shot hole. **12.** Also called **bracelet.** *Furniture.* a horizontal molding at the upper end of a foot. **13.** *Glassmaking.* merese. **14. hot under the collar,** *Slang.* angry; excited; upset: *Don't ask him anything while he's so hot under the collar.* —*v.t.* **15.** to put a collar on; furnish with a collar: *They finally succeeded in collaring the unwilling dog.* **16.** to seize by the collar or neck: *We collared the little fellow and brought him, struggling all the while, into the house.* **17.** to detain (someone anxious to leave) in conversation: *The reporters collared him for an hour.* **18.** *Informal.* to lay hold of, seize, or take. **19.** to roll up and bind (meat, fish, etc.) for cooking. —*v.i.* **20.** *Metalworking.* (of a piece being rolled) to wrap itself around a roller. [< L *collār(e)* neck-band, equiv. to *coll(um)* neck + *-āre* -AR[2]; r. ME *coler* < AF < L] —**col′lar·less,** *adj.*

col′lar beam′, a tie beam bracing a roof truss some distance above its foot. Also called **spanpiece, sparpiece.**

col·lar·bone (kol′ər bōn′), *n.* the clavicle. [COLLAR + BONE[1]]

col′lar but′ton, a button or stud for fastening a detachable collar to the neckband of a shirt or for fastening together the ends of a neckband.

col′lar cell′, choanocyte.

coll' ar·co (kō lär′kō; *It.* kôl är′kô), *adv. Music.* (of performance with a stringed instrument) with the bow. [< It]

col·lard (kol′ərd), *n.* a variety of kale, *Brassica oleracea acephala,* grown in the southern U.S. [var. of COLEWORT, with assimilation of *-wort* to -ARD]

col′lared liz′ard, a long-tailed, iguanid lizard, *Crotaphytus collaris,* of the central and western U.S. and northern Mexico, having a collar of two black bands.

col′lared pec′cary. See under **peccary.**

col·lar·et (kol′ə ret′), *n.* a small collar of fur, lace, or other material, worn by women. Also, **col′lar·ette′.** [COLLAR + -ET, modeled on F *collerette*]

col·la·ri·no (kol′ə rē′nō), *n., pl.* **-nos.** *Archit.* a necking, as on an Ionic, Roman Doric, or Tuscan column. [< It, equiv. to *collar(e)* (< L; see COLLAR) + *-ino* dim. suffix]

col′lar point′, *Heraldry.* See **honor point.**

col′lar rot′, *Plant Pathol.* a disease of plants, characterized by cankers which girdle the stem, caused by any of several fungi, as *Alternaria solani* or *Diplodia theobromae.*

collat., collateral.

col·late (ko lāt′, kə-, kol′āt), *v.t.,* **-lat·ed, -lat·ing.** **1.** to compare (texts, statements, etc.) in order to note points of agreement or disagreement. **2.** (in data processing) to compare, combine, or select from two sequentially ordered stacks of cards to form a new stack or stacks having a similar sequence. **3.** *Bookbinding.* **a.** to verify the arrangement of (the gathered sheets of a book), usually by inspecting the signature at the foot of the first page of each sheet or the mark printed on the back of each sheet or on the spine of each signature. **b.** to gather in their proper order (the sheets of a book, pamphlet, sheaf of papers, etc.). **4.** *Bibliog.* to verify the number and order of the sheets of (a volume) as a means of determining its completeness. **5.** *Eccles.* to present by collation, as to a benefice. [< L *collāt(us)* (ptp. of *conferre* to bring together), equiv. to *col-* COL-[1] + *lā-* (var. s. of *ferre*) + *-tus* ptp. ending] —**col·lat′a·ble,** *adj.*

col′la tem·pes·ta′da (tem′pi stä′də), colla. [< Sp: violent storm]

col·lat·er·al (kə lat′ər əl), *adj.* **1.** situated at the side: *a collateral wing of a house.* **2.** situated or running side by side; parallel: *collateral ridges of mountains.* **3.** *Bot.* standing side by side. **4.** accompanying; attendant; auxiliary: *He received a scholarship and collateral aid.* **5.** additional; confirming: *collateral evidence; collateral security.* **6.** secured by collateral: *a collateral loan.* **7.** aside from the main subject, course, etc.; secondary; indirect: *These accomplishments are merely collateral to his primary goal.* **8.** descended from the same stock, but in a different line; not lineal: *A cousin is a collateral relative.* **9.** pertaining to those so descended. —*n.* **10.** security pledged for the payment of a loan: *He gave the bank some stocks and bonds as collateral for the money he borrowed.* **11.** a collateral kinsman. [< ML *collaterāl(is),* equiv. to *col-* COL-[1] + *laterālis* LATERAL] —**col·lat·er·al·i·ty** (kō lat′ə ral′i tē), **col·lat′er·al·ness,** *n.* —**col·lat′er·al·ly,** *adv.*

collat′eral circula′tion, circulation of blood through a network of minor vessels enlarged and joined with adjacent vessels when a major vein or artery is impaired, as by obstruction.

collat′eral trust′ bond′, a bond secured by securities placed in trust.

col·la·tion (ko lā′shən, kə-, kō-), *n.* **1.** the act of collating. **2.** *Bibliog.* the verification of the number and order of the leaves and signatures of a volume. **3.** the presentation of a clergyman to a benefice, esp. by a bishop who is himself the patron or has acquired the patron's rights. **4.** a light meal that may be permitted on days of general fast. **5.** any light meal. **6.** (in a monastery) the practice of reading and conversing on the lives of the saints or the Scriptures at the close of the day. [ME *collacion,* etc. < ML *collāciōn-, collātiōn-* (s. of *collātiō*), equiv. to L *collāt(us)* (see COLLATE) + *-iōn-* -ION]

col·la·tive (ko lā′tiv, kō-, kol′ā-), *adj.* **1.** marked by collation. **2.** *Eccles.* presented by collation: *collative benefices.* [< L *collātīv(us).* See COLLATE, -IVE]

col·la·tor (ko lā′tər, kol′ā-), *n.* one who or that which collates, as a machine that collects and sometimes binds printed leaves. [< L, equiv. to *collāt(us)* (see COLLATE) + *-or* -OR[2]]

col·league (kol′ēg), *n.* an associate in an office, profession, work, or the like: *He was highly respected by all his colleagues in the English Department.* [< MF *collegue* < L *collēga,* equiv. to *col-* COL-[1] + *lēg-,* perf. s. of *legere* to choose + *-a* n. suffix] —**col′league·ship′,** *n.*

col·lect[1] (kə lekt′), *v.t.* **1.** to gather together; assemble: *The student collected the papers for the professor.* **2.** to accumulate; make a collection of: *to collect stamps.* **3.** to receive or compel payment of: *to collect a bill.* **4.** to regain control of (oneself or one's thoughts, faculties, composure, or the like): *At the news of her escape, Walter took a few minutes to collect himself.* **5.** to call for and take with one: *They collected their mail.* **6.** *Manège.* to bring (a horse) into a collected attitude. **7.** *Archaic.* to infer. —*v.i.* **8.** to gather together; assemble: *The students collected in the assembly hall.* **9.** to accumulate: *Rain water collected in the drainpipe.* **10.** to receive payment (often fol. by *on*): *He collected on the damage to his house.* **11.** to gather or bring together books, stamps, coins, etc., usually as a hobby: *He's been collecting for years.* **12.** *Manège.* (of a horse) to come into a collected attitude. —*adj., adv.* **13.** requiring payment by the recipient: *a collect telephone call.* [< L *collēct(us)* (ptp. of *colligere* to collect), equiv. to *col-* COL-[1] + *lēc-* (ptp. s. of *legere* to gather) + *-tus* ptp. suffix]
—**Syn. 1.** See **gather. 1, 2.** amass, aggregate. —**Ant. 1.** broadcast. **2.** distribute.

col·lect[2] (kol′ekt), *n.* any of certain brief prayers used in Western churches before the epistle in the communion service, and in Anglican churches also used in morning and evening prayers. [ME *collecte,* OE *collecta* < ML, short for *ōrātiō ad collēctam* prayer at collection (see COLLECT[1]), r. *collēctiō* summary (prayer)]

col·lect·a·ble (kə lek′tə bəl), *adj.* **1.** capable of being collected. —*n.* **2.** an object suitable for a collection, originally a work of fine art or an antique, now including also any of a wide variety of items such as bottles, commemorative plates, and memorabilia. Also, **col·lect′i·ble.** [COLLECT + -ABLE] —**col·lect′a·bil′i·ty, col·lect′i·bil′i·ty,** *n.*

col·lec·ta·ne·a (kol′ek tā′nē ə), *n.pl.* collected passages, esp. as arranged in a miscellany or anthology. [< L, neut. pl. of *collectāneus* gathered together, equiv. to *collect(us)* (ptp. of *colligere;* see COLLECT[1]) + *-āneus* adj. suffix]

col·lect·ed (kə lek′tid), *adj.* **1.** having control of one's faculties; self-possessed: *Despite all the furor around him, Bob remained calm, cool, and collected.* **2.** brought or placed together; forming an aggregation from various sources: *the money collected to build an orphanage; the collected essays of Thoreau.* **3.** *Manège.* **a.** (of a moving horse) noting a compact pose in which the legs are well under the body, the head is arched at the poll, the jaw is relaxed, etc. Cf. **extended** (def. 7a). **b.** (of a gait of such a horse) characterized by short, elevated strides. Cf. **extended** (def. 7b). [COLLECT[1] + -ED[2]] —**col·lect′ed·ly,** *adv.* —**col·lect′ed·ness,** *n.*
—**Syn. 1.** See **calm.**

collect′ed edi′tion, an edition of the writings of a particular author, usually comprising all of his extant works.

collect′ing tu′bule, *Anat.* the part of a nephron that collects the urine from the distal convoluted tubule and discharges it into the pelvis of the kidney.

col·lec·tion (kə lek′shən), *n.* **1.** the act of collecting. **2.** that which is collected; a group of objects or an amount of material accumulated in one location, esp. for some purpose or as a result of some process: *a collection of butterflies; a collection of unclaimed hats in the checkroom; a collection of soot in a chimney.* **3.** a sum of money collected, esp. for charity or church use. **4.** *Manège.* act of bringing or coming into a collected attitude. [< L *collēctiōn-* (s. of *collēctiō*), equiv. to *collēct(us)* (ptp. of *colligere;* see COLLECT[1]) + *-iōn-* -ION] —**col·lec′tion·al,** *adj.*
—**Syn. 2.** accumulation, aggregation; mass, heap, pile, hoard, store. **3.** contribution(s), alms.

collec′tion a′gency, a firm that collects unpaid bills from another firm and is usually compensated by receiving a percentage of the amount of the bill collected.

Collec′tion of Ten′ Thou′sand Leaves′, Manyōshū.

col·lec·tive (kə lek′tiv), *adj.* **1.** formed by collection. **2.** forming a whole; combined: *the collective assets of a corporation and its subsidiaries.* **3.** of or characteristic of a group of individuals taken together: *the collective wishes of the membership.* **4.** (of a fruit) formed by the coalescence of the pistils of several flowers, as the mulberry or the pineapple. **5.** organized according to the principles of collectivism: *a collective farm.* —*n.* **6.** See **collective noun. 7.** a collective body; aggregate. **8.** *Govt.* a unit of organization or the organization in a collectivist system. [< L *collēctīv(us),* equiv. to *collēct(us)* (ptp. of *colligere;* see COLLECT[1]) + *-īvus* -IVE] —**col·lec′tive·ly,** *adv.*

collec′tive agree′ment, 1. the contract, written or oral, made between an employer or employers and a union in behalf of all the employees represented by the union. **2.** the schedule of wages, rules, and working conditions agreed upon.

collec′tive bar′gaining, the process by which wages, hours, rules, and working conditions are negotiated and agreed upon by a union with an employer for all the employees collectively whom it represents.

collec′tive behav′ior, *Sociol.* the concerted behavior of individuals acting under the influence of each other.

collec′tive farm′, (esp. in the Soviet Union) a farm, or a number of farms organized as a unit, worked by a community under the supervision of the state.

collec′tive noun′, *Gram.* a noun, as *herd, jury,* or *clergy,* that appears singular in formal shape but denotes a group of persons or objects. When a singular verb is used with such a noun, it is thought of as naming a unit, as *family* in *My family is related to Washington;* when a plural verb is used, it is thought of as referring to individuals, as in *My family are all at home.*

collec′tive secu′rity, a policy or principle in international relations, designed to preserve world peace, according to which all countries collectively guarantee the security of each individual country, as by sanctions or multilateral alliances against an aggressor.

collec′tive uncon′scious, (in Jungian psychology) racially inherited psychic material present in the individual unconscious.

col·lec·tiv·ism (kə lek′tə viz′əm), *n.* the socialist principle of control by the state of all means of production or economic activity. [COLLECTIVE + -ISM] —**col·lec′tiv·ist,** *n., adj.* —**col·lec′tiv·is′tic,** *adj.* —**col·lec′tiv·is′ti·cal·ly,** *adv.*

col·lec·tiv·i·ty (kol′ek tiv′i tē), *n., pl.* **-ties. 1.** collective character. **2.** a collective whole. **3.** the people collectively. [COLLECTIVE + -ITY]

col·lec·ti·vize (kə lek′tə vīz′), *v.t.,* **-vized, -viz·ing.** to organize (a people, industry, economy, etc.) according to the principles of collectivism. [COLLECTIVE + -IZE] —**col·lec′ti·vi·za′tion,** *n.*

collect′ on deliv′ery. See **C.O.D.**

col·lec·tor (kə lek′tər), *n.* **1.** one who or that which collects. **2.** a person employed to collect debts, duties, taxes, etc. **3.** a person who collects books, paintings, stamps, shells, etc., esp. as a hobby. **4.** *Elect.* a device for accumulating current from contact conductors. **5.** *Electronics.* an electrode in a transistor or vacuum tube for collecting electrons, ions, or holes. **6.** *Metall.* promoter (def. 5). [late ME < ML, equiv. to L *collēct(us)* (ptp. of *colligere;* see COLLECT[1]) + *-or* -OR[2]] —**col·lec′tor·ship′, col·lec′tor·ate,** *n.*

collec′tor elec′trode, *Electronics.* See under **Klystron.**

col·leen (kol′ēn, ko lēn′), *n.* **1.** *Irish Eng.* a young girl. **2.** an Irish girl. [< Ir *cailín,* equiv. to *caile* countrywoman + *-īn* dim. suffix]

Col·leen (kol′ēn, ko lēn′), *n.* a girl's given name.

col·lege (kol′ij), *n.* **1.** an institution of higher learning, esp. one providing a general or liberal arts education rather than technical or professional training. Cf. **university. 2.** a constituent unit of a university, furnishing courses of instruction in the liberal arts and sciences, usually leading to a bachelor's degree. **3.** an institution for special or professional instruction, as in medicine, pharmacy, agriculture, or music, often set up as a part of a university. **4.** an endowed, self-governing association of scholars incorporated within a university as at the universities of Oxford and Cambridge in England. **5.** a similar corporation outside a university. **6.** the building or buildings occupied by an institution of higher education. **7.** the administrators, faculty, and students of a college. **8.** (in Britain and Canada) a private secondary school. **9.** an organized association of persons having certain powers and rights, and performing certain duties or engaged in a particular pursuit: *The electoral college formally selects the president.* **10.** a company; assemblage. **11.** Also called **collegium.** a body of clergy living together on a foundation for religious service or similar activity. **12.** *Brit. Slang.* a prison. [late ME < MF < L *collēg(ium),* equiv. to *collēg(a)* COLLEAGUE + *-ium* -Y[3]]

Col′lege Gar′dens, a town in central California. 4132 (1960).

col′lege ice′, *New England.* a sundae.

Col′lege of Arms′. See **Heralds' College.**

Col′lege of Car′dinals, the chief ecclesiastical body of the Roman Catholic Church, electing and advising the pope and comprising all of the cardinals of the church. Official name, **Sacred College of Cardinals.**

Col′lege of Propagan′da. See under **propaganda** (def. 3b).

Col′lege Park′, 1. a city in N Georgia. 23,469 (1960). **2.** a city in central Maryland. 18,482 (1960).

Col′lege Place′, a town in SE Washington. 4031 (1960).

col·lege-pre·par·a·to·ry (kol′ij pri par′ə tōr′ē, -tôr′ē), *adj.* preparing a student for academic work at the college level.

col·leg·er (kol′i jər), *n.* (at Eton College, England) a student supported by funds provided by the college. [COLLEGE + -ER[1]]

col′lege try′, maximum effort for success on behalf of one's team, alma mater, etc. (usually prec. by the phrase *the old*): *We may not make the deadline, but we'll give it the old college try.*

col′lege wid′ow, *U.S. Informal.* an unmarried woman living in a college town who has dated students of several successive classes.

col·le·gian (kə lē′jən, -jē ən), *n.* **1.** a student in, or a graduate of, a college. **2.** a member of a college. [late ME < ML *collēgiān(us),* equiv. to *collēgi(um)* COLLEGE + *-ānus* -AN]

col·le·giate (kə lē′jit, -jē it), *adj.* **1.** of or pertaining to a college: *collegiate life.* **2.** of, characteristic of, or intended for college students: *collegiate clothes; a collegiate dictionary.* **3.** of the nature of or constituted as a college. Also, **col·le·gi·al** (kə lē′jē əl, -jəl). [< LL *collēgiāt(us).* See COLLEGE, -ATE[1]] —**col·le′giate·ly,** *adv.* —**col·le′giate·ness,** *n.*

colle′giate church′, 1. a church which is endowed for a chapter of canons, usually with a dean, and which has no bishop's see. **2.** *Informal.* a chapel connected with a college. **3.** *U.S.* a church or group of churches under the general management of one consistory or session. **4.** a consolidation of formerly distinct churches under one or more pastors. **5.** (in Scotland) a church or congregation the active pastor of which is the colleague and successor of the emeritus pastor.

colle′giate in′stitute, (in Canada) a fully accredited high school teaching academic subjects under the supervision of a provincial government.

col·le·gi·um (kə lē′jē əm), *n., pl.* **-gi·a** (-jē ə). *Eccles.* college (def. 11). [< L]

col·le·gi·um mu·si·cum (kə lē′jē əm myōō′zə kəm; *Lat.* kō leg′ē ōōm′ mōō′si kōōm′), a group of usually amateur musicians, often connected with a university, who meet to study and perform chiefly old or little-known music. [< L: musical society]

col le·gno (kō lān′yō; *It.* kôl le′nyô), *Music.* (of performance with the bow on the strings of a stringed instrument) with the wood. [< It]

col·len·chy·ma (kə leng′kə mə), *n. Bot.* a layer of modified parenchyma consisting of cells which are thickened at the angles and usually elongated. [< NL < Gk *kóll(a)* glue + *énchyma* (*en-* AN-[2] + *chy-,* s. of *chein* to pour + *-ma* n. suffix denoting result of action)] —**col·len·chym·a·tous** (kol′ən kim′ə təs), **col·len·chy·mat·ic** (kə leng′kə mat′ik), *adj.*

Col·les's frac′ture (kol′i sis, -ē ziz), *Med.* a fracture of the lower end of the radius, characterized by a backward and outward displacement of the hand. Also, **Col′les' frac′ture.** [named after A. *Colles* (1773–1843), Irish surgeon]

col·let (kol′it), *n., v.,* **-let·ed, -let·ing.** —*n.* **1.** a collar or enclosing band. **2.** the enclosing rim within which a jewel is set. **3.** a slotted cylindrical clamp inserted tightly into the tapered interior of a sleeve or chuck on a lathe to hold a cylindrical piece of work. **4.** *Horol.* the tiny collar which supports the inner terminal of a hairspring. —*v.t.* **5.** to set (a gem or other stone) in a collet. [< F, equiv. to *col* neck (< L *collum*) + *-et* -ET]

col′let foot′, a round or polygonal base for a small vessel, as a pitcher.

Col·lette (kō let′, kə-), *n.* a girl's given name.

col·lide (kə līd′), *v.i.,* **-lid·ed, -lid·ing. 1.** to strike one another with a forceful impact; come into violent contact; crash: *The two cars collided with an ear-splitting crash.* **2.** to clash; conflict: *Their views on the matter collided.* [< L *collīde(re)* to strike together, equiv. to *col-* COL-[1] + *-līdere,* var. of *laedere* to strike]

col·lie (kol′ē), *n.* one of a breed of dogs having a usually long, black, tan, and white or sable and white coat, raised originally in Scotland for herding sheep. [ME *Colle* dog's name (OE *col* COAL + *-la* suffix used in personal names); see -IE] —**col′lie·like′,** *adj.*

Collie
(2 ft. high at shoulder)

col·lied (kol′ēd), *adj. Brit. Dial.* covered with colly; sooty; grimy. [COLLY + -ED[2]]

col·lier (kol′yər), *n. Chiefly Brit.* **1.** a ship for carrying coal. **2.** a coal miner. **3.** *Obs.* one who carries or sells coal. [ME *koliere,* equiv. to *col-* COAL + *-iere,* var. of *-ere* -ER[1]]

Col·lier (kol′yər), *n.* **Jeremy,** 1650–1726, English clergyman and author.

col·lier·y (kol′yə rē), *n., pl.* **-lier·ies.** *Chiefly Brit.* a coal mine, including all buildings and equipment. [COLLIER + -Y[3]]

col·lie·shang·ie (kol′ē shang′ē), *n. Scot.* a noisy quarrel; a confused fight; row. [? COLLIE + *shangie,* var. of *shangan,* ScotGael *seangan* cleft stick for dog's tail, lit., little bed, equiv. to *seang* bed + *-an* -IE]

col·li·gate (kol′ə gāt′), *v.t.,* **-gat·ed, -gat·ing. 1.** to bind or fasten together. **2.** *Logic.* to bind (facts) together by a general description or by a hypothesis which applies to them all. [< L *colligāt(us)* (ptp. of *colligāre*), equiv. to *col-* COL-[1] + *ligā-* (s. of *ligāre* to bind) + *-tus* ptp. ending] —**col′li·ga′tion,** *n.* —**col′li·ga′tive,** *adj.*

col·li·mate (kol′ə māt′), *v.t.,* **-mat·ed, -mat·ing. 1.** to bring into line; make parallel. **2.** to adjust accurately the line of sight of (a telescope). [< L *collimāt(us),* var. reading for *collineāt(us)* (ptp. of *collineāre* to direct in a straight line), equiv. to *col-* COL-[1] + *linea* line + *-tus* ptp. ending] —**col′li·ma′tion,** *n.*

col·li·ma·tor (kol′ə mā′tər), *n.* **1.** *Optics.* a fixed telescope for use in collimating other instruments. **2.** an optical system that transmits parallel rays of light, as the receiving lens or telescope of a spectroscope. **3.** *Physics.* a device for producing a beam of particles in which the paths of all the particles are parallel. [COLLIMATE + -OR[2]]

col·lin·e·ar (kə lin′ē ər), *adj.* lying in the same straight line. [COL-[1] + LINEAR] —**col·lin·e·ar·i·ty** (kə lin′ē ar′i tē), *n.* —**col·lin′e·ar·ly,** *adv.*

Col·lings·wood (kol′ingz wŏŏd′), *n.* a city in SW New Jersey. 17,370 (1960).

Col·ling·wood (kol′ing wŏŏd′), *n.* a city in SE Australia, near Melbourne. 25,413 (1961).

col·lins (kol′inz), *n.* (*often cap.*) a tall drink made with gin, whiskey, rum, or vodka, and lemon or lime juice, soda water, and sugar. [after the proper name *Collins*]

Col·lins (kol′inz), *n.* **1. Edward Trowbridge** (*Eddie*), 1887–1951, U.S. baseball player. **2. Michael,** 1890–1922, Irish revolutionist and patriot. **3. William,** 1721–59, English poet. **4. (William) Wil·kie** (wil′kē), 1824–89, English novelist.

col·lin·si·a (kə lin′sē ə, -zē ə), *n.* any of the scrophulariaceous herbs of the genus *Collinsia,* bearing whorled, usually parti-colored flowers. [named after Zaccheus *Collins* (1764–1831), American botanist; see -IA]

Col·lins·ville (kol′inz vil′), *n.* a town in NE Oklahoma. 2526 (1960).

col·li·sion (kə lizh′ən), *n.* **1.** the act of colliding; a coming violently into contact; crash: *the collision of two airplanes.* **2.** a clash; conflict: *a collision of ideals.* **3.** *Physics.* the meeting of particles or of bodies in which each exerts a force upon the other, causing the exchange of energy or momentum. [late ME < LL *collīsiōn-* (s. of *collīsiō*), equiv. to *collīs(us)* (ptp. of *collīdere* to COLLIDE) + *-iōn-* -ION] —**col·li′sion·al,** *adj.*

colli′sion course′, a course or path of a vehicle, projectile, etc., which, if unchanged, will lead to a collision with another object.

colli′sion den′sity, *Physics.* the rate at which collisions are occurring per unit volume per unit time, usually pertaining to the collisions of neutrons.

colli′sion diam′eter, *Physics.* the distance between the centers of two colliding molecules when at their closest point of approach.

colli′sion insur′ance, insurance protecting an automobile owner against loss or damage to the automobile resulting from a collision with an object or automobile, or as a result of an upset.

colli′sion mat′, *Naut.* a mat for sealing a hole caused by a collision, set in place by being lowered over the side of the vessel and pressed into the hole by the entering water.

col·lo·blast (kol′ə blast′), *n. Zool.* one of the cells covered with sticky granules on the tentacles of a ctenophore, which aid in capturing prey. Also called **adhesive cell, glue cell.** [< Gk *kóll(a)* glue + *-o-* + -BLAST]

col·lo·cate (kol′ə kāt′), *v.t.,* **-cat·ed, -cat·ing. 1.** to set or place together. **2.** to arrange in proper order: *to collocate events.* [< L *collocāt(us)* (ptp. of *collocāre*), equiv. to *col-* COL-[1] + *loc(us)* place + *-ātus* -ATE[1]]

col·lo·ca·tion (kol′ə kā′shən), *n.* **1.** act of collocating. **2.** state or manner of being collocated. **3.** arrangement, esp. of words in a sentence. [< L *collocātiōn-* (s. of *collocātiō*), equiv. to *collocāt(us)* (see COLLOCATE) + *-iōn-* -ION] —**col′lo·ca′tive,** *adj.*

Col·lo·di (kə lō′dē; *It.* kôl lô′dē), *n.* **Carlo** (kär′lō; *It.* kär′lô), (*Carlo Lorenzini*), 1826–90, Italian writer: creator of Pinocchio.

col·lo·di·on (kə lō′dē ən), *n. Chem.* a yellowish, viscous, highly flammable solution of pyroxylin in ether and alcohol: used in the manufacture of photographic film, in engraving and lithography, and in medicine chiefly for cementing dressings and sealing wounds. [alter. of NL *collōdium* < Gk *kollṓd(ēs)* glutinous (*kóll(a)* glue + *-ōdēs* -ODE[1]) + *-ium* n. suffix]

col·logue (kə lōg′), *v.i.,* **-logued, -lo·guing.** *Dial.* to confer secretly; plot mischief; conspire. [? b. COLLUDE and DIALOGUE]

col·loid (kol′oid), *n.* **1.** *Physical Chem.* a gelatinous substance which when dissolved in a liquid will not diffuse readily through vegetable or animal membranes. Colloidal particles are about 10^{-7} to 5×10^{-5} centimeters in diameter, larger than most inorganic molecules, and remain suspended indefinitely. They are large molecules, as proteins, or groups of molecules, with many properties depending upon their large specific surface. Cf. **crystalloid** (def. 2). **2.** *Med.* a homogeneous, gelatinous substance occurring in some diseased states. —*adj.* **3.** *Physical Chem.* colloidal. [< Gk *kóll(a)* glue + -OID]

col·loi·dal (kə loid′əl), *adj. Physical Chem.* pertaining to or of the nature of a colloid: *colloidal gold and silver.* [COLLOID + -AL[1]] —**col·loi·dal·i·ty** (kol′oi dal′i tē), *n.*

colloi′dal suspen′sion. See under **suspension** (def. 6).

col·lop (kol′əp), *n. Brit. Dial.* **1.** a small slice of meat, esp. a small rasher of bacon. **2.** a small slice, portion, or piece of anything. **3.** a fold or roll of flesh on the body. [ME *colopes* (pl.) (> Sw *kalops*) < ?]

col·lo·phane (kol′ə fān′), *n. Mineral.* a massive, cryptocrystalline variety of apatite, the principal component of phosphate rock and fossil bone. Also, **col·loph·a·nite** (kə lof′ə nīt′, kol′ə fə-). [< Gk *kóll(a)* glue + *-o-* + -PHANE]

col·lo·phore (kol′ə fōr′, -fôr′), *n. Entomol.* a ventral tubelike structure on the abdomen of a springtail. [*collo-* (< Gk *kollo-,* repr. *kólla* glue) + -PHORE]

colloq., 1. colloquial. **2.** colloquialism. **3.** colloquially.

col·lo·qui·al (kə lō′kwē əl), *adj.* **1.** characteristic of or appropriate to ordinary or familiar conversation rather than formal speech or writing. In standard American English, *He hasn't got any* is colloquial, while *He has none* is formal. **2.** conversational. [COLLOQUY + -AL[1]] —**col·lo′qui·al·ly,** *adv.* —**col·lo′qui·al·ness,** *n.*
—**Syn. 1, 2.** COLLOQUIAL, CONVERSATIONAL, INFORMAL refer to types of speech or to usages not on a formal level. COLLOQUIAL is often mistakenly used with a connotation of disapproval, as if it meant "vulgar" or "bad" or "incorrect" usage, whereas it is merely a familiar style used in speaking rather than in writing. CONVERSATIONAL refers to a style used in the oral exchange of ideas, opinions, etc.: *an easy, conversational style.* INFORMAL means without formality, without strict attention to set forms, unceremonious: *an informal manner of speaking;* it describes the ordinary, everyday language of cultivated speakers. —**Ant. 1, 2.** formal.

col·lo·qui·al·ism (kə lō′kwē ə liz′əm), *n.* **1.** a colloquial expression. **2.** colloquial style or usage. [COLLOQUIAL + -ISM] —**col·lo′qui·al·ist,** *n.*

col·lo·qui·um (kə lō′kwē əm), *n., pl.* **-qui·ums, -qui·a** (-kwē ə). an informal conference or group discussion. [< L, equiv. to *colloqu(i)* (*col-* COL-[1] + *loqui* to speak) + *-ium* abstract n. suffix]

col·lo·quy (kol′ə kwē), *n., pl.* **-quies.** **1.** a conversational exchange; dialogue. **2.** a conference. **3.** (in certain Reformed churches) a governing body corresponding to a presbytery. [< L *colloqui(um)* COLLOQUIUM] —**col′lo·quist,** *n.*

col·lo·type (kol′ə tīp′), *n., v.,* **-typed, -typ·ing.** —*n.* Also called **albertype, artotype, heliotype. 1.** any photomechanical process of printing from a plate coated with gelatin. **2.** the plate. **3.** a print made from it. —*v.t.* **4.** to produce (a print) by collotype; albertype; artotype. [< Gk *kóll(a)* glue + *-o-* + -TYPE] —**col·lo·typ·ic** (kol′ə tip′ik), *adj.* —**col·lo·typ·y** (kol′ə tī′pē), *n.*

col·lude (kə lōōd′), *v.i.,* **-lud·ed, -lud·ing. 1.** to act together through a secret understanding. **2.** to conspire in a fraud. [< L *collūde(re)* to play together, equiv. to *col-* COL-[1] + *lūdere*] —**col·lud′er,** *n.*

collun., (in prescriptions) a nose wash. [< L *collūnārium*]

col·lu·nar·i·um (kol′yə nâr′ē əm), *n., pl.* **-nar·i·a** (-nâr′ē ə). *Med.* a solution for application to the nose; nose drops. [< NL, equiv. to L *collu(ere)* to rinse (*col-* COL-[1] + *luere* to wash) + *nār(ēs)* nostrils, nose + *-ium* n. suffix]

col·lu·sion (kə lōō′zhən), *n.* **1.** a secret agreement for fraudulent or treacherous purposes; conspiracy: *Some of his employees were acting in collusion to rob him.* **2.** *Law.* a secret understanding between two or more persons prejudicial to another, or a secret understanding to appear as adversaries though in agreement: *collusion of husband and wife to obtain a divorce.* [< L *collūsiōn-* (s. of *collūsiō*), equiv. to *collūs(us)* (ptp. of *collūdere* to COLLUDE) + *-iōn-* -ION]

col·lu·sive (kə lōō′siv), *adj.* involving collusion; fraudulently contrived by agreement: *a collusive agreement to increase prices.* [COLLUS(ION) + -IVE] —**col·lu′sive·ly,** *adv.* —**col·lu′sive·ness,** *n.*

collut., (in prescriptions) a mouthwash. [< L *collūtōrium*]

col·lu·to·ri·um (kol′ə tōr′ē əm, -tôr′-), *n., pl.* **-to·ri·a** (-tōr′ē ə, -tôr′-). collutory.

col·lu·to·ry (kol′ə tōr′ē, -tôr′ē), *n., pl.* **-to·ries.** *Med.* mouthwash. Also, **collutorium.** [< NL, L *collūtōri(um)*, equiv. to *collūt(us)* (ptp. of *colluere* to rinse) + *-ōrium* -ORY[2]]

col·ly (kol′ē), *v.,* **-lied, -ly·ing,** *n. Brit. Dial.* —*v.t.* **1.** to blacken as with coal dust; begrime. —*n.* **2.** grime; soot. [var. of *collow* (v.), ME *colwen,* deriv. of OE *col* COAL; see -Y[1]]

collyr., (in prescriptions) an eyewash. [< L *collȳrium*]

col·lyr·i·um (kə lēr′ē əm), *n., pl.* **-lyr·i·a** (-lēr′ē ə), **-lyr·i·ums.** *Med.* a solution for application to the eye; an eyewash. [< L < Gk *kollýrion* eye-salve]

col·ly·wob·bles (kol′ē wob′əlz), *n.* (*construed as sing. or pl.*) *Informal and Dial.* intestinal cramps or other intestinal disturbances. [jocular alter. of *chole(ra) morbus*; see CHOLERA]

Col·mar (*Fr.* kôl MAR′; *Ger.* kôl′mär), *n.* a city in and the capital of Haut-Rhin, in NE France. 54,264 (1962).

Cöln (kœln), *n.* former German name of **Cologne.**

colo-, a combining form of **colon**[2]: *colostomy.* Also, *esp. before a vowel,* **col-.**

Colo., Colorado.

col·ob (kol′ob), *n.* guereza. [< NL *colob(us)* < Gk *kolobós* docked, cut off, in reference to its thumbs]

col·o·cynth (kol′ə sinth), *n.* **1.** a cucurbitaceous plant, *Citrullus Colocynthis,* of the warmer parts of Asia, the Mediterranean region, etc., bearing a fruit with a bitter pulp. **2.** the fruit. **3.** *Pharm.* the drug derived from the pulp of the unripe but full-grown fruit of this plant, used in medicine chiefly as a purgative. Also called **bitter apple** (for defs. 1, 2). [< L *colocynth(is)* < Gk *kolokynthís,* var. of *kolókyntha* bitter gourd, bitter cucumber]

co·log (kō′lôg, -log), *n.* cologarithm.

co·log·a·rithm (kō lôg′ə rith′əm, -rith′əm, -log′ə-), *n. Math.* the logarithm of the reciprocal of a number, often used in expressing the logarithm of a fraction: log 7/25 = log 7 + colog 25. *Symbol:* colog [CO- + LOGARITHM]

co·logne (kə lōn′), *n.* a perfumed toilet water; eau de Cologne. Also called **Cologne′ wa′ter.** [short for *Cologne water,* made in COLOGNE since 1709]

Co·logne (kə lōn′), *n.* a city in W West Germany. 832,400 (1963). German, **Köln,** (formerly) **Cöln.**

Cologne′ brown′. See **Vandyke brown.**

Cologne′ spir′its, alcohol (def. 1). Also, **cologne′ spir′its.**

co·lomb (kə lômb′, -lōmb′, -lomb′, kol′əm), *n.* a heraldic representation of a dove. [< MF; OF *colombe* < L *columba* dove]

Co·lomb-Bé·char (kô lôN bā shar′), *n.* a city in W Algeria. 18,090 (1954).

Co·lombes (kô lôNb′), *n.* a city in N France, NW of Paris. 77,090 (1962).

Co·lom·bi·a (kə lum′bē ə; *Sp.* kô lôm′byä), *n.* a republic in NW South America. 14,446,580 (est. 1961); 439,828 sq. mi. *Cap.:* Bogotá. —**Co·lom′bi·an,** *adj., n.*

co·lom·bi·er (kə lum′bē ər), *n. Brit.* columbier.

Co·lom·bo (kə lum′bō), *n.* **1.** a seaport in and the capital of Ceylon, on the W coast. 510,947 (1963). **2.** a walled plain in the fourth quadrant in the face of the moon: about 50 miles in diameter.

Colom′bo a′gent. See **hunter's robe.**

co·lon[1] (kō′lən), *n., pl.* **-lons** for 1, **-la** (-lə) for 2. **1.** the sign (:) used to mark a major division in a sentence, to indicate that what follows is an elaboration, summation, implication, etc., of what precedes, or to separate groups of numbers referring to different things, as hours from minutes in 5:30, or as the members of a proportion in 1 : 2 : : 3 : 6. **2.** *Class. Pros.* one of the members or sections of a rhythmical period, consisting of a sequence of from two to six feet united under a principal ictus or beat. [< L < Gk *kôlon* limb, member, clause]

co·lon[2] (kō′lən), *n., pl.* **-lons, -la** (-lə). *Anat.* the part of the large intestine extending from the cecum to the rectum. See diag. under **intestine.** [< L < Gk *kólon* large intestine]

co·lon[3] (kō lōn′; *Sp.* kô lôn′), *n., pl.* **-lons,** *Sp.* **-lo·nes** (-lô′nes). **1.** the paper monetary unit of El Salvador, equal to 100 centavos and equivalent to about .40 of a U.S. dollar. *Abbr.:* C. **2.** a cupronickel or steel coin and monetary unit of Costa Rica, equal to 100 centimos and equivalent to about .15 of a U.S. dollar. [< AmerSp, after *Colón* Columbus]

co·lon[4] (kō′lon, kə lon′), *n.* a colonial farmer or plantation owner, esp. in Algeria. [< F < L *colōnus* colonist]

Co·lón (kō lon′; *Sp.* kô lôn′), *n.* a seaport in Panama at the Atlantic end of the Panama Canal. 72,889 (1960).

Colón′ Archipel′ago. See **Galápagos Islands.**

co·lo·nate (kə lō′nāt), *n.* the condition of a colonus or serf under Roman and early feudal law. [< L *colōn(us)* farmer + *-atus* -ATE[1]]

colo·nel (kûr′nəl), *n.* an officer ranking in most armies between lieutenant colonel and brigadier general. In England it is an honorary rank. [< MF < It *colon(n)ello,* equiv. to *colonn(a)* COLUMN + *-ello* < L *-ellus* dim. suffix; r. (in writing) *coronel* < MF, metathetic var. of *colonel*]

Colo′nel Blimp′, an elderly, pompous British reactionary, esp. an army officer or government official. [after a character appearing in cartoons by David Low]

colo·nel·cy (kûr′nəl sē), *n.* the rank, position, or status of a colonel. Also, **colo′nel·ship′.** [COLONEL + -CY]

col·o·nette (kol′ə net′), *n.* a small column. [< F *colonnette.* See COLUMN, -ETTE]

Co·lo·nia (kô lô′nyä), *n.* a city in SW Uruguay. 15,000 (est. 1955). Also called **Colo′nia del Sa·cra·men′to** (*th*el sä′krä men′tô).

co·lo·ni·al (kə lō′nē əl), *adj.* **1.** of, concerning or pertaining to a colony or colonies: *the colonial policies of France.* **2.** pertaining to the 13 British colonies which became the United States of America, or to their period. **3.** *Ecol.* forming a colony. **4.** (*cap.*) *Archit., Furniture.* **a.** noting or pertaining to the styles of architecture, ornament, and furnishings of the British colonies in America in the 17th and 18th centuries, mainly adapted to local materials and demands from prevailing English styles. **b.** noting or pertaining to various imitations of the work of American colonial craftsmen. —*n.* **5.** an inhabitant of a colony. [COLONY + -AL[1]] —**co·lo′ni·al·ly,** *adv.*

colo′nial dol′lar, *Australian.* See **holey dollar.**

Colo′nial Heights′, a town in central Virginia. 9587 (1960).

co·lo·ni·al·ise (kə lō′nē ə līz′), *v.t.,* **-ised, -is·ing.** *Chiefly Brit.* colonialize.

co·lo·ni·al·ism (kə lō′nē ə liz′əm), *n.* the policy of a nation seeking to extend or retain its authority over other peoples or territories. [COLONIAL + -ISM] —**co·lo′ni·al·ist,** *n., adj.*

co·lo·ni·al·i·za·tion (kə lō′nē ə li zā′shən), *n.* **1.** the act of bringing into subjection or subjugation by colonialism. **2.** the act of colonializing. **3.** the state or fact of being colonialized. Also, *esp. Brit.,* **co·lo′ni·al·i·sa′tion.** [COLONIAL + -IZATION]

co·lo·ni·al·ize (kə lō′nē ə līz′), *v.t.,* **-ized, -iz·ing.** to make colonial. Also, *esp. Brit.,* **colonialise.** [COLONIAL + -IZE]

colo′nial sid′ing, *Carpentry.* siding composed of boards with parallel faces laid horizontally so that the upper overlaps the one below.

co·lon·ic (kō lon′ik, kə-), *adj. Anat.* of or pertaining to the colon. [COLON[2] + -IC]

Col·o·nie (kol′ə nē), *n.* a town in E New York. 6992 (1960).

col·o·nise (kol′ə nīz′), *v.t.,* **-nised, -nis·ing.** *Chiefly Brit.* colonize. —**col′o·nis′a·bil′i·ty,** *n.* —**col′o·nis′a·ble,** *adj.* —**col′o·ni·sa′tion,** *n.* —**col′o·ni·sa′tion·ist,** *n.* —**col′o·nis′er,** *n.*

col·o·nist (kol′ə nist), *n.* **1.** an inhabitant of a colony. **2.** a member of a colonizing expedition. [COLON(Y) + -IST]

col·o·nize (kol′ə nīz′), *v.,* **-nized, -niz·ing.** —*v.t.* **1.** to plant or establish a colony in; settle: *England colonized Australia.* **2.** to form a colony of: *to colonize laborers in a mining region.* —*v.i.* **3.** to form a colony: *They went out to Australia to colonize.* **4.** to settle in a colony. Also, *esp. Brit.,* **colonise.** [COLON(Y) + -IZE] —**col′o·niz′a·bil′i·ty,** *n.* —**col′o·niz′a·ble,** *adj.* —**col′o·ni·za′tion,** *n.* —**col′o·ni·za′tion·ist,** *n.* —**col′o·niz′er,** *n.*

col·on·nade (kol′ə nād′), *n.* **1.** *Archit.* a series of regularly spaced columns supporting an entablature and usually one side of a roof. **2.** a series of trees planted in a long row, as on each side of a driveway, road, etc. [< F, equiv. to *colonne* COLUMN + *-ade* -ADE[1], modeled on It *colonnato,* equiv. to *colonn(a)* column + *-ato* -ATE[1]] —**col′on·nad′ed,** *adj.*

co·lo·nus (kə lō′nəs), *n., pl.* **-ni** (-nī, -nē). a serf in the latter period of the Roman Empire or in the early feudal period. [< L *colōnus*]

col·o·ny (kol′ə nē), *n., pl.* **-nies. 1.** a group of people who leave their native country to form in a new land a settlement subject to, or connected with, the parent state. **2.** the country or district settled or colonized: *Many nations are former European colonies.* **3.** any people or territory separated from but subject to a ruling power. **4. the Colonies,** those British colonies that formed the original 13 States of the United States: New Hampshire, Massachusetts, Rhode Island, Connecticut, New York, New Jersey, Pennsylvania, Delaware, Maryland, Virginia, North Carolina, South Carolina, and Georgia. **5.** a number of people coming from the same country, or speaking the same language, residing in a foreign country or city, or a particular section of it: *the Polish colony in Israel; the American colony in Paris; the German colony in Yorkville.* **6.** any group of individuals having similar interests, occupations, etc., usually living in a particular locality: *a colony of artists.* **7.** the district, quarter, or dwellings inhabited by any such number or group: *They live in an artists' colony.* **8.** an aggregation of bacteria growing together as the descendants of a single cell. **9.** *Ecol.* a group of animals or plants of the same kind living or growing together in close association. [late ME *colonie* < L *colōnia,* equiv. to *colōn(us)* colonist + *-ia* -Y[3]]

col·o·phon (kol′ə fon′, -fən), *n.* **1.** an inscription at the end of a book or manuscript, used esp. in the 15th and 16th centuries, giving the title or subject of the work, its author, the name of the printer or publisher, and the date and place of publication. **2.** a publisher's distinctive emblem. [< L < Gk *kolophṓn* summit, finishing touch]

Col·o·phon (kol′ə fon′), *n.* an ancient city in Asia Minor: one of the 12 Ionian cities; largely depopulated in 286 B.C.

Col·o·pho·ni·an (kol′ə fō′nē ən), *n.* **1.** a native of Colophon. **2. the,** Antimachus (def. 1). —*adj.* **3.** of or pertaining to Colophon.

col·o·pho·ny (kol′ə fō′nē, kə lof′ə nē), *n.* rosin. [< L *Colophōnia* (*rēsina*) (resin) of Colophon < Gk *Kolophōnía,* fem. of *Kolophṓnios,* equiv. to *Kolophṓn* Colophon + *-ios* adj. suffix; see -Y[3]]

col·o·quin·ti·da (kol′ə kwin′ti də), *n.* colocynth (defs. 1, 2). [< ML < Gk *kolokýnthida,* acc. of *kolokynthís* COLOCYNTH]

col·or (kul′ər), *n.* **1.** the quality of an object or substance with respect to light reflected by the object, usually determined visually by measurement of hue, saturation, and brightness of the reflected light; the property of finite saturation or chroma; hue. **2.** the natural appearance of the skin, esp. of the face; complexion: *She has a lovely color.* **3.** a ruddy complexion: *The wind and sun had given color to the sailor's face.* **4.** racial complexion other than white, esp. Negro: *In certain countries the racial question is clearly not one of color.* **5.** a blush: *His forward remarks brought the color to her face.* **6.** vivid or distinctive quality, as of literary work: *Melville's description of a whaling voyage is full of color.* **7.** details in description, customs, speech, habits, etc., of a place or period, included for the sake of realism: *a novel about the Pilgrims with much local color.* **8.** that which is used for coloring; pigment; paint; tint; dye. **9.** *Painting.* the general effect of all the hues entering into the composition of a picture. **10.** *Print.* the amount of ink used. **11. colors, a.** any distinctive color or combination or pattern of colors, esp. of a badge, ribbon, uniform, or the like, worn or displayed as a symbol of or to identify allegiance to, membership in, or sponsorship by a school, group, or organization. **b.** position; attitude; characteristics; personality: *His behavior in a crisis revealed his true colors.* **c.** a flag, ensign, etc., particularly the national flag, displayed by unmounted troops or a ship. **d.** *U.S. Navy.* the ceremony of hoisting the national flag at 8 A.M. and of lowering it at sunset. **12.** outward appearance or aspect; guise or show: *His dialect lent an informal color to his speech.* **13.** appearance of truth, actuality, etc.; plausibility: *He displayed his scars to lend color to his story of mistreatment by his captors.* **14.** a pretext: *She did it under the color of doing a good deed.* **15.** *Phonet.* timbre. **16.** *Chiefly Law.* an apparent or prima facie right or ground: *to hold possession under color of title.* **17.** *U.S.* a trace or particle of valuable mineral, esp. gold, as shown by washing auriferous gravel. **18.** *Heraldry.* a tincture other than a fur or metal, usually including gules, azure, vert, sable, and purpure. **19. call to the colors,** to summon for service in the armed forces: *Thousands are being called to the colors.* **20. change color, a.** to blush as from embarrassment. **b.** to turn pale, as from fear: *When he saw the size of his opponent, he began to change color.* **21. lose color.** to turn pale; blanch: *As the tiger drew nearer, the hunter trembled and lost color.* **22. serve with the colors,** to be a member of the armed forces: *He was proud to be serving with the colors.* **23. with flying colors.** See **flying colors.** —*v.t.* **24.** to give or apply color to; tinge; paint; dye: *She colored her eyelashes dark blue.* **25.** to cause to appear different from the reality: *In order to influence the jury, he colored his account of what had happened.* **26.** to give a special character or distinguishing quality to: *His personal feelings color his writing.* —*v.i.* **27.** to take on or change color: *The ocean colored at dawn.* **28.** to flush; blush: *She colored when confronted with the evidence.* Also, *esp. Brit.,* **colour.** [ME *col(o)ur* < AF (F *couleur*) < L *colōr-* (s. of *color*) hue] —**col′or·er,** *n.*

color., (in prescriptions) let it be colored. [< L *colōrētur*]

col·or·a·ble (kul′ər ə bəl), *adj.* **1.** capable of being colored. **2.** specious; plausible. **3.** pretended; deceptive. Also, *esp. Brit.,* **colourable.** [late ME; see COLOR, -ABLE] —**col′or·a·bil′i·ty, col′or·a·ble·ness,** *n.* —**col′or·a·bly,** *adv.*

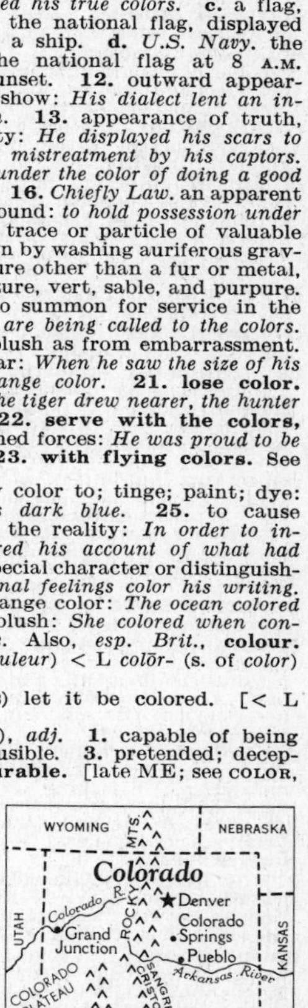

col·o·rad·o (kol′ə rad′ō, -rä′dō), *adj.* (of cigars) of medium color and strength. [< Sp < L *colōrātus* colored. See COLOR, -ATE[1]]

Col·o·rad·o (kol′ə rad′ō, -rä′dō), *n.* **1.** a state in the W United States. 1,753,947 (1960); 104,247 sq. mi. *Cap.:* Denver. *Abbr.:* Colo. **2.** a river flowing SW from N Colorado through Utah and Arizona into the Gulf of California: Grand Canyon; Boulder Dam. 1450 mi. long. **3.** a river flowing SE from W Texas to the Gulf of Mexico. 840 mi. long. —**Col′o·rad′an, Col′o·rad′o·an,** *adj., n.*

Colorad′o bee′tle. See **Colorado potato beetle.**

Colorad′o blue′ spruce′. See **blue spruce.**

Col′orad′o Cit′y, a town in W Texas. 6457 (1960).

Col′orad′o Des′ert, an arid region in SE California, W of the Colorado River. ab. 2500 sq. mi.

col·o·rad·o·ite (kol′ə rad′ō īt′, -rä′dō-), *n.* a mineral, mercury telluride, HgTe, occurring in the form of grayish-black masses. [named after COLORADO; see -ITE[1]]

Colora′do Plateau′, a plateau in the SW United States, in N Arizona, NW New Mexico, S Utah, and SW Colorado: location of the Grand Canyon.

Colora′do pota′to bee′tle, a black and yellow leaf beetle, *Leptinotarsa decemlineata,* originally found in Colorado and neighboring States but now a common pest in all potato-growing regions of the U.S. Also called **Colorado beetle, potato beetle, potato bug.**

Colorad′o red′ ce′dar. See **Rocky Mountain juniper.**

Col′orad′o Springs′, a city in central Colorado: resort; U.S. Air Force Academy. 70,194 (1960).

Col′orad′o spruce′. See **blue spruce.**

col·or·ant (kul′ər ənt), *n.* something used as a coloring matter; pigment; dye. [< F, prp. of *colorer* < L *colōrāre* to color. See COLOR, -ANT]

col·or·a·tion (kul′ə rā′shən), *n.* coloring; appearance as to color: *His coloration is the same as his mother's: both are fair with blue eyes and blond hair.* Also, *esp. Brit.,* **colouration.** [COLOR + -ATION] —**col′or·a′tion·al,** *adj.* —**col′or·a′tion·al·ly,** *adv.*

col·o·ra·tu·ra (kul′ər ə to͝or′ə, -tyo͝or′ə, kol′-, kōl′-), *n.* **1.** runs, trills, and other florid decorations in vocal music. **2.** music marked by this. **3.** a lyric soprano of high range who specializes in such music. —*adj.* **4.** of, pertaining to, or characteristic of coloratura or a coloratura soprano. Also, **col·or·a·ture** (kul′ər ə cho͝or′). [< It < LL: lit., coloring. See COLOR, -ATE[1], -URE]

col′or bar′. See **color line** (def. 1).

col·or·bear·er (kul′ər bâr′ər), *n.* one who carries the colors or standard, esp. of a military body. [COLOR + BEARER]

col·or-blind (kul′ər blīnd′), *adj.* **1.** *Ophthalm.* pertaining to or affected with color blindness. **2.** *Photog.* (of an emulsion) sensitive only to blue, violet, and ultraviolet rays.

col′or blind′ness, defective color perception, independent of the capacity for distinguishing light and shade, and form.

col·or·cast (kul′ər kast′, -käst′), *n., v.,* **-cast, -casting.** —*n.* **1.** a television program broadcast in color. —*v.t., v.i.* **2.** to broadcast or televise in color. [COLOR + (BROAD)CAST]

col·ored (kul′ərd), *adj.* **1.** having color. **2.** (*often cap.*) belonging wholly or in part to a race other than the white, esp. to the Negro race. **3.** pertaining to the Negro race. **4.** specious; deceptive: *The authorities detected a colored quality in her statement.* **5.** influenced or biased: *to overcome one's colored beliefs.* **6.** *Bot.* of some hue other than green. Also, *esp. Brit.,* **coloured.** [ME; see COLOR, -ED[3]]

col′ored stone′, *Jewelry.* any gemstone, colored or colorless, other than a diamond.

col·or·fast (kul′ər fast′, -fäst′), *adj.* maintaining or capable of maintaining its exact color shade despite the effects of cleaning, weather, sunlight, etc.: *colorfast textile.* [COLOR + FAST[1]] —**col′or·fast′ness,** *n.*

col′or fil′ter, *Photog.* a colored filter for modifying the reproduction of the colors in a subject as photographed. Cf. **filter** (def. 4).

col·or·ful (kul′ər fəl), *adj.* **1.** abounding in color: *In their tartans, the Scots guard made a colorful array.* **2.** richly picturesque: *a colorful historical period.* **3.** presenting or suggesting vivid or striking scenes: *a colorful narrative.* Also, *esp. Brit.,* **colourful.** [COLOR + -FUL] —**col′or·ful·ly,** *adv.* —**col′or·ful·ness,** *n.*

col′or guard′, a guard having charge of the colors, as of a regiment.

col·or·if·ic (kul′ə rif′ik), *adj.* **1.** producing or imparting color. **2.** pertaining to color. [COLOR + -I- + -FIC]

col·or·im·e·ter (kul′ə rim′i tər), *n.* a device that analyzes color by measuring a given color in terms of a standard color, a scale of colors, or certain primary colors. [COLOR + -I- + -METER] —**col·or·i·met·ric** (kul′ər ə me′trik), **col′or·i·met′ri·cal,** *adj.* —**col′or·i·met′ri·cal·ly,** *adv.* —**col′or·im′e·trist,** *n.*

col·or·ing (kul′ər ing), *n.* **1.** the act or method of applying color. **2.** appearance as to color: *healthy coloring.* **3.** aspect or tone: *The ethical coloring of the story balanced the rawness of its language.* **4.** specious appearance; show. **5.** a substance used to color something: *food coloring made from vegetable dyes.* Also, *esp. Brit.,* **colouring.** [late ME; see COLOR, -ING[1]]

col′oring book′, a book of outline drawings for coloring in crayons or water colors.

col·or·ist (kul′ər ist), *n.* **1.** a person who uses color skillfully. **2.** a person who colors photographs. **3.** a hairdresser who is skilled in coloring or tinting women's hair. **4.** a painter who emphasizes color relationships in a work of art. Also, *esp. Brit.,* **colourist.** [COLOR + -IST] —**col′or·is′tic,** *adj.*

col·or·less (kul′ər lis), *adj.* **1.** without color: *Pure water is colorless.* **2.** pallid; dull in color: *a colorless complexion.* **3.** lacking vividness or distinctive character; dull; insipid: *a colorless description of the parade.* **4.** unbiased; neutral. Also, *esp. Brit.,* **colourless.** [ME; see COLOR, -LESS] —**col′or·less·ly,** *adv.* —**col′or·less·ness,** *n.*

col′or line′, **1.** Also called **color bar.** social or political distinction based on differences of skin pigmentation, as between white and colored people. **2. draw the color line,** to observe the color line.

col′or phase′, **1.** a genetically controlled variation in the normal color of the skin or pelt of an animal. **2.** an animal exhibiting such variation. **3.** one of two or more color types assumed by an animal, varying with age or season.

col′or point′, *Heraldry.* See **honor point.**

col′or scheme′, an arrangement or pattern of colors or colored objects conceived of as forming an integrated whole: *the color scheme of a living room; the color scheme of a painting.*

col′or ser′geant, a sergeant who has charge of battalion or regimental colors.

col′or wheel′. See under **complementary color** (def. 1a).

Co·los·sae (kə los′ē), *n.* an ancient city in SW Phrygia: seat of an early Christian church to which Paul wrote the Epistle to the Colossians.

co·los·sal (kə los′əl), *adj.* **1.** gigantic; huge; vast. **2.** of or resembling a colossus. [COLOSS(US) + -AL[1]] —**co·los·sal·i·ty** (kol′ə sal′i tē), *n.* —**co·los′sal·ly,** *adv.* —**Syn. 1.** See **gigantic.**

colos′sal or′der, *Archit.* an order having a height much greater than that of any story within the order. Also called **giant order.**

Col·os·se·um (kol′ə sē′əm), *n.* **1.** an ancient amphitheater in Rome, begun A.D. c70 by Vespasian, having the form of an oval 617 by 512 feet. **2.** (*l.c.*) coliseum. [< L, neut. of *colossēus* gigantic, alter. of Gk *kolossiaîos,* equiv. to *koloss(ós)* COLOSSUS + *-iaios* adj. suffix]

Co·los·sian (kə losh′ən), *n.* **1.** a native or inhabitant of Colossae. **2.** one of the Christians of Colossae, to whom Paul addressed one of his Epistles. —*adj.* **3.** of or pertaining to Colossae or its inhabitants. [< L *Coloss(ae)* (< Gk *Kolossaí*) + -IAN]

Co·los·sians (kə losh′ənz), *n.* (*construed as sing.*) a book of the New Testament, written by Paul.

co·los·sus (kə los′əs), *n., pl.* **-los·si** (-los′ī), **-los·sus·es.** **1.** (*cap.*) the legendary bronze statue of Apollo at Rhodes. Cf. **Seven Wonders of the World. 2.** any statue of gigantic size. **3.** anything colossal or gigantic. [< L < Gk *kolossós* gigantic statue]

Colos′sus of Mem′non, an ancient Egyptian stone monument near Thebes, erected by Amenhotep III, that consists of two seated figures 38 feet high. Cf. **Vocal Memnon.**

co·los·to·my (kə los′tə mē), *n., pl.* **-mies.** *Surg.* incision of a temporary or permanent artificial opening into the colon to effect an artificial anus. [COLO- + -STOMY]

co·los·trum (kə los′trəm), *n.* the milk secreted a few days before and after childbirth. [< L, var. of *colustra* beestings] —**co·los′tral,** *adj.*

co·lot·o·my (kə lot′ə mē), *n., pl.* **-mies.** *Surg.* incision or opening of the colon. [COLO- + -TOMY]

col·our (kul′ər), *n., v.t., v.i.* *Chiefly Brit.* color. —**col′our·a′tion,** *n.* —**col′our·a′tion·al,** *adj.* —**col′our·a′tion·al·ly,** *adv.* —**col′oured,** *adj.* —**col′our·er,** *n.* —**col′our·ful,** *adj.* —**col′our·ful·ly,** *adv.* —**col′our·ful·ness,** *n.* —**col′our·ing,** *n.* —**col′our·ist,** *n.* —**col′our·is′tic,** *adj.* —**col′our·less,** *adj.* —**col′our·less·ly,** *adv.* —**col′our·less·ness,** *n.*

col·our·a·ble (kul′ər ə bəl), *adj.* *Chiefly Brit.* colorable. —**col′our·a·bil′i·ty, col′our·a·ble·ness,** *n.* —**col′our·a·bly,** *adv.*

-colous, a learned borrowing from Latin meaning "inhabiting," used in the formation of compound words: *tubicolous.* [< L *-col(a),* comb. form repr. *colere* to inhabit + -OUS]

col·pi·tis (kol pī′tis), *n.* *Pathol.* vaginitis. [< NL < Gk *kólp(os)* bosom, womb; see -ITIS]

Col·po·da (kol pō′də), *n.* a genus of holotrichous ciliates, common in fresh water. [< NL, equiv. to Gk *kolpṓd(es)* embosomed, embayed (*kólp(os)* bosom + *-ōdes* -ODE[1]) + L *-a* neut. pl. ending]

col·por·tage (kol′pōr′tij, -pôr′-; *Fr.* kôl pôr tazh′), *n.* the work of a colporteur. [< F, equiv. to *colport(er)* (to) hawk (lit., carry on the neck; see COL, PORT[5]) + *-age* -AGE]

col·por·teur (kol′pōr′tər, -pôr′-; *Fr.* kôl pôr tœr′), *n., pl.* **-teurs** (-tərz; *Fr.* -tœr′). **1.** a peddler of books. **2.** one employed to travel about distributing Bibles, religious tracts, etc., gratuitously or at a low price. [< F, equiv. to *colport(er)* (see COLPORTAGE) + *-eur* -OR[2]]

col·pot·o·my (kol pot′ə mē), *n., pl.* **-mies.** *Surg.* incision of the vagina. Also called **vaginotomy.** [< NL *colpo-* (< Gk *kólpos* womb, vagina) + -TOMY]

colt (kōlt), *n.* **1.** a young male animal of the horse family. **2.** a male horse of not more than four years of age. **3.** a young or inexperienced person. **4.** *Naut.* (formerly) a knotted end of a rope used as a whip to goad seamen into work. [ME; OE *colt;* cf. dial. Sw *kult* little pig]

Colt (kōlt), *n.* *Trademark.* a revolver.

Colt (kōlt), *n.* **Samuel,** 1814–62, U.S. inventor of the Colt revolver.

colt′ distem′per, *Vet. Pathol.* distemper[1] (def. 1b).

Col·tee (kōl′tē), *n.* a boy's given name.

col·ter (kōl′tər), *n.* a sharp blade or wheel attached to the beam of a plow, used to cut the ground in advance of the plowshare. Also, **coulter.** [ME, OE *culter* < L: knife, plowshare]

colt·ish (kōl′tish), *adj.* **1.** not trained or disciplined; unruly; wild. **2.** playful; frolicsome. **3.** of, pertaining to, or resembling a colt. [COLT + -ISH[1]] —**colt′ish·ly,** *adv.* —**colt′ish·ness,** *n.*

Col·ton (kōl′tən), *n.* a city in SW California, near Los Angeles. 18,666 (1960).

colts·foot (kōlts′fo͝ot′), *n., pl.* **-foots.** a composite perennial, *Tussilago Farfara,* native to the Old World but widespread as a weed, formerly used in medicine. [so called from the shape of the leaves]

col·u·brid (kol′ə brid, -yə-), *n.* **1.** any of numerous cosmopolitan snakes of the family *Colubridae,* including fossorial, arboreal, terrestrial, and aquatic species that comprise about two-thirds of all living snakes. —*adj.* **2.** belonging or pertaining to the *Colubridae.* [< NL *Colubrid(ae)* name of the family, equiv. to *Colubr-* (s. of *Coluber* name of the genus, L *coluber* snake) + *-idae* -ID[2]]

col·u·brine (kol′ə brīn′, -brin, -yə-), *adj.* **1.** of or resembling a snake; snakelike. **2.** belonging or pertaining to the subfamily *Colubrinae,* comprising the typical colubrid snakes. [< L *colubrīn(us),* equiv. to *colubr-* (s. of *coluber*) snake + *-īnus* -INE[1]]

co·lu·go (kə lo͞o′gō), *n., pl.* **-gos.** See **flying lemur.** [< Malayan native name]

Col·um (kol′əm), *n.* **Pa·draic** (pô′drik), born 1881, U.S. poet and dramatist born in Ireland.

Co·lum·ba (kə lum′bə), *n., gen.* **-bae** (-bē) for 2. **1. Saint,** A.D. 521–597, Irish missionary in Scotland. **2.** Also called **Colum′ba No′ae** (nō′ē). *Astron.* the Dove, or Noah's Dove, a southern constellation between Caelum and Canis Major. —**Co·lum′ban,** *adj.*

col·um·bar·i·um (kol′əm bâr′ē əm), *n., pl.* **-bar·i·a** (-bâr′ē ə). **1.** a sepulchral vault or other structure with recesses in the walls to receive the ashes of the dead. **2.** any one of these recesses. **3.** columbary. [< L, equiv. to *columb(a)* dove + *-ārium* -ARY]

col·um·bar·y (kol′əm ber′ē), *n., pl.* **-bar·ies.** a dovecote or pigeon house. Also, **columbarium.** [see COLUMBARIUM]

co·lum·bate (kə lum′bāt, -bit), *n.* *Chem.* niobate. [COLUMB(IUM) + -ATE[2]]

col·um·be·ion (kol′əm bē′yon, -bī′on), *n., pl.* **-be·ia** (-bē′yə, -bī′ə). a fountain in the atrium of a Christian basilica. [< MGk *kolymbeîon* (akin to Gk *kolymbḗthra* place for diving); *-ion* suffix indicating place]

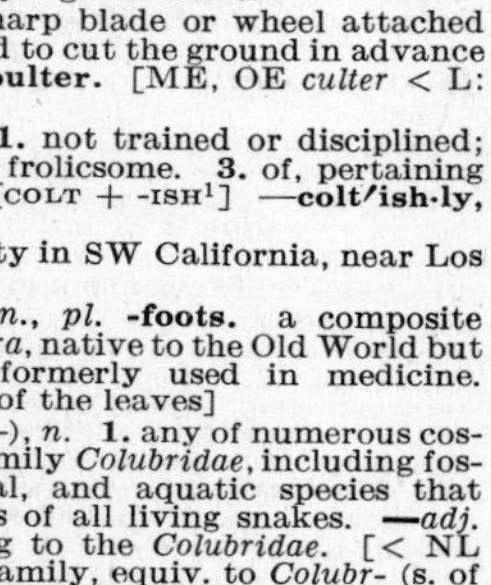

Co·lum·bi·a (kə lum′bē ə), *n.* **1.** a river in SW Canada and the NW United States, flowing S and W from SE British Columbia through Washington along the boundary between Washington and Oregon and into the Pacific. 1214 mi. long. **2.** a city in and the capital of South Carolina, in the central part. 97,433 (1960). **3.** a city in central Missouri. 36,650 (1960). **4.** a city in central Tennessee. 17,624 (1960). **5.** a town in S Mississippi. 7117 (1960). **6.** a town in SW Illinois. 3174 (1960). **7.** *Literary.* the United States of America. **8.** one of an American breed of large sheep, developed by crossbreeding the Lincoln and Rambouillet, noted for its good market lambs and heavy fleece of medium length.

Colum′bia Cit′y, a town in NE Indiana. 4803 (1960).

Colum′bia Heights′, a city in SE Minnesota, near Minneapolis. 17,533 (1960).

Co·lum·bi·an (kə lum′bē ən), *adj.* **1.** pertaining to America or the United States. **2.** pertaining to Christopher Columbus. —*n.* **3.** *Print.* a 16-point type of a size between English and great primer. [COLUMB(IA) and COLUMB(US) + -IAN]

Co·lum·bi·an·a (kə lum′bē an′ə), *n.* a town in E Ohio. 4164 (1960).

co·lum·bic (kə lum′bik), *adj.* *Chem.* niobic. [COLUMB(IUM) + -IC]

co·lum·bi·er (kə lum′bē ər), *n.* *Brit.* a size of drawing or writing paper about 23 ½ × 34 ½ inches. Also, **colombier.** [< F *colombier* dove-cote, a size of paper]

col·um·bine[1] (kol′əm bīn′), *n.* any of several ranunculaceous plants of the genus *Aquilegia,* as *A. caerula,* having bluish-purple flowers: the State flower of Colorado. [ME < ML *columbīn(a)* (*herba*) dovelike (plant), fem. of L *columbīnus* (see COLUMBINE[2]); the inverted flower looks like a group of doves]

col·um·bine[2] (kol′əm bīn′, -bin), *adj.* **1.** of a dove. **2.** dovelike; dove-colored. [ME < L *columbīn(us),* equiv. to *columb(a)* dove + *-īnus* -INE[1]]

Col·um·bine (kol′əm bīn′), *n.* **1.** a female character in comedy, esp. commedia dell'arte and pantomime: sweetheart of Harlequin. **2.** a girl's given name. [< It *Columbina,* lit., dovelike girl; see COLUMBINE[2]]

co·lum·bite (kə lum′bīt), *n.* a black, crystalline mineral, $FeNb_2O_6$, often containing manganese and tantalium: the principal ore of niobium. [COLUMB(IUM) + -ITE[1]]

co·lum·bi·um (kə lum′bē əm), *n.* *Chem.* (formerly) niobium. *Symbol:* Cb [COLUMB(IA) (def. 7) + -IUM]

co·lum·bous (kə lum′bəs), *adj.* *Chem.* niobous. [COLUMB(IUM) + -OUS]

Co·lum·bus (kə lum′bəs), *n.* **1. Christopher** (Sp. *Cristóbal Colón;* It. *Cristoforo Colombo*), 1446?–1506, Italian navigator in Spanish service: discoverer of America 1492. **2.** a city in and the capital of Ohio, in the central part. 471,316 (1960). **3.** a city in W Georgia. 116,779 (1960). **4.** a city in E Mississippi. 24,771 (1960). **5.** a city in central Indiana. 20,778 (1960). **6.** a town in S Texas. 3656 (1960). **7.** a town in central Wisconsin. 3467 (1960). **8.** a town in SE Kansas. 3395 (1960).

Colum′bus Day′, a day, October 12, observed as a holiday in various States of the U.S. in honor of the discovery of the New World by Columbus and his landing in the West Indies on October 12, 1492.

col·u·mel·la (kol′yə mel′ə), *n., pl.* **-mel·lae** (-mel′ē). *Anat., Zool., Bot.* a small columnlike part; an axis. [< L: small column, equiv. to *colum-* (var. of *column-,* s. of *columna* COLUMN) + *-ella* dim. suffix] —**col′u·mel′lar,** *adj.* —**col·u·mel·late** (kol′yə mel′it, -āt), *adj.*

col·u·mel·li·form (kol′yə mel′ə fôrm′), *adj.* like a columella. [COLUMELL(A) + -I- + -FORM]

col·umn (kol′əm), *n.* **1.** *Archit.* **a.** a rigid, relatively slender, upright support, composed of relatively few pieces. **b.** a decorative pillar, composed of stone or resembling stone in proportions or detailing, typically having a cylindrical or polygonal shaft with a capital and usually a base. **2.** any columnlike object, mass, or formation: *a column of smoke.* **3.** a vertical arrangement on a page of horizontal lines of type, usually justified: *There are three columns on this page.* **4.** a vertical row or list: *He arranged the figures in columns.* **5.** a regular department of a newspaper, magazine, or the like, usually having a readily identifiable heading and the by-line of the editor, which reports or comments upon a particular field of interest, as etiquette, politics, or theater, or several related fields, and which may contain contributions from readers, quotations from published works, etc. **6.** a formation of ships in single file. **7.** a long, narrow formation of troops in which there are more members in line in the direction of movement than at right angles to the direction (distinguished from *line*). **8.** *Bot.* a columnlike structure in an orchid flower, composed of the united stamens and style. [late ME *columne* < L *columna,* equiv. to *colum(e)n* peak + *-a* fem. ending; akin to (EX)CEL; r. late ME *colompne* < MF] —**col′umned** (kol′əmd), **col·um·nat·ed** (kol′əm nā′tid), *adj.*

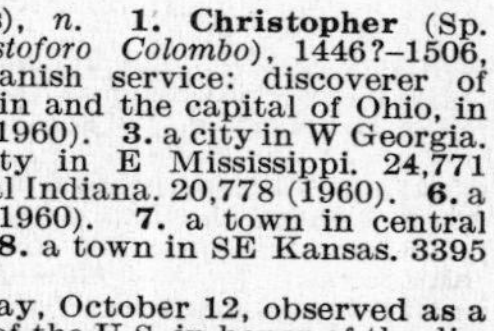

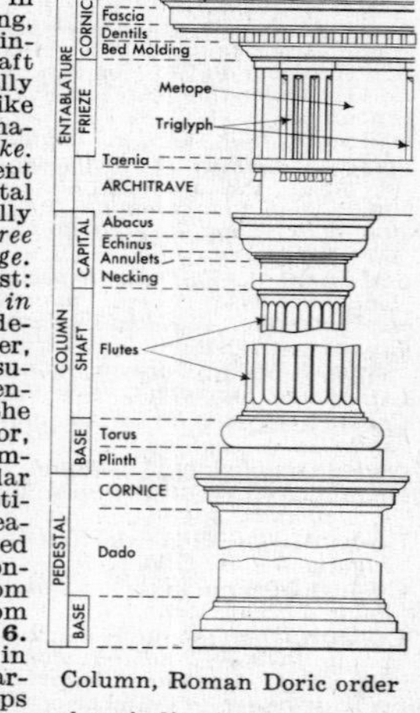

Column, Roman Doric order

—**Syn. 1.** COLUMN, PILLAR refer to upright supports in architectural structures. PILLAR is the general word: *the pillars supporting the roof.* A COLUMN is a particular kind of pillar, esp. one with three identifiable parts: shaft, base, and capital: *columns of the Corinthian style.*

co·lum·na cae·la·ta (kə lum′nə si lā′tə), *pl.* **co·lum·nae cae·la·tae** (kə lum′nē si lā′tē). *Archit.* a column having a shaft decorated with carved ornamentation. [< L: carved column]

co·lum·nar (kə lum′nər), *adj.* **1.** shaped like a column. **2.** characterized by columns: *columnar architecture.* **3.** Also, **co·lum′nal.** printed, arranged, etc., in columns. [< LL *columnār(is),* equiv. to *column(a)* COLUMN + *-āris* -AR[1]] —**co·lum·nar·i·ty** (kol′əm nar′i tē), *n.*

colum′nar epithe′lium, *Biol.* epithelium consisting of one or more layers of elongated cells of cylindrical or prismatic shape.

co·lum·nar·ized (kə lum′nə rīzd′), *adj.* arranged or placed in columns; columnar. [COLUMNAR + -IZE + -ED[2]]

colum′nar joint′ing, (in igneous rocks) a series of generally hexagonal columns formed by vertical joints in the rock.

col′umn chromatog′raphy, *Chem.* See under **chromatography.**

co·lum·ni·a·tion (kə lum′nē ā′shən), *n.* *Archit.* **1.** the employment of columns. **2.** the system of columns in a structure. [abstracted from (INTER)COLUMNIATION]

col′umn inch′, *Print.* type one column wide and one inch deep.

col·umn·ist (kol′əm nist, -ə mist), *n.* the editor of a journalistic column. [COLUMN + -IST]

col′umn kra′ter, kelebe.

col′umn vec′tor, *Math.* a collection of numbers, as the components of a vector, written vertically. Cf. **row vector.**

co·lure (kə lo͝or′, kō-, kō′lo͝or), *n.* *Astron.* either of two great circles of the celestial sphere intersecting each other at the poles, one passing through both equinoxes and the other through both solstices. [< LL *colūr(us)* < Gk *kólour(os)* dock-tailed, equiv. to *kól(os)* docked + *our(á)* tail + *-os* adj. suffix]

Co·lu·sa (kə lo͞o′sə), *n.* a town in central California. 3518 (1960).

Col·ville (kol′vil), *n.* a town in NE Washington. 3806 (1960).

Col·vin (kol′vin), *n.* **Sir Sidney,** 1845–1927, English literary and art critic.

Col·wyn (kol′win), *n.* a town in SE Pennsylvania. 3074 (1960).

co·ly (kō′lē), *n., pl.* **-lies.** any of several slender, fruit-eating, African birds of the family *Coliidae,* having grayish-brown plumage and a long, pointed tail. Also called **mousebird.** [< NL *coli(us)* < Gk *koli(ós)* green woodpecker]

col·za (kol′zə), *n.* rape[2]. [< F < D *koolzaad,* equiv. to *kool* COLE + *zaad* SEED]

col′za oil′. See **rape oil.**

com-, a prefix meaning "with," "together," "in association," and (with intensive force) "completely," occurring in loan words from Latin (*commit*): used in the formation of compound words before *b, p, m*: *combine; compare; commingle.* Also, **co-, con-, col-, cor-.** [< L, var. of prep. *cum* with]

Com., **1.** Commander. **2.** Commission. **3.** Commissioner. **4.** Committee. **5.** Commodore.

com., **1.** comedy. **2.** commerce. **3.** common. **4.** commonly.

co·ma[1] (kō′mə), *n., pl.* **-mas.** a state of prolonged unconsciousness from which it is difficult or impossible to rouse a person, due to disease, injury, poison, etc.; stupor. [< Gk *kôma* deep sleep]

co·ma[2] (kō′mə), *n., pl.* **-mae** (-mē). **1.** *Astron.* the nebulous envelope around the nucleus of a comet. **2.** *Optics.* a monochromatic aberration of a lens or other optical system in which the image from a point source cannot be brought into focus, the image of a point having the shape of a comet. **3.** *Bot.* **a.** a tuft of silky hairs at the end of a seed. **b.** the leafy crown of a tree; cluster of leaves at the end of a stem. **c.** a terminal cluster of bracts, as in the pineapple. [< L: hair < Gk *kómē*]

Coma[2] (def. 3a) on seed of milkweed, *Asclepias syriaca*

Co·ma Ber·e·ni·ces (kō′mə ber′ə nī′sēz), *gen.* **Co·mae Ber·e·ni·ces** (kō′mē ber′ə nī′sēz). *Astron.* Berenice's Hair, a northern constellation situated north of Virgo and between Boötes and Leo. [< L]

Co·mae·tho (kə mē′thō), *n.* *Class. Myth.* **1.** daughter of Pterelaus who, out of love for Amphitryon, betrayed her father by cutting off the lock of golden hair which made him immortal. Despite her love, Amphitryon killed her for her treacherous deed. **2.** a priestess who was sacrificed with her lover, Melanippus, to appease Artemis, in whose sanctuary they had impiously made love.

co·mak·er (kō mā′kər, kō′mā′kər), *n.* *Finance.* one who formally undertakes to discharge the duties of the maker of an instrument, esp. a promissory note, in the event of his default. [CO- + MAKER]

co·mal (kō mäl′; *Sp.* kô mäl′), *n., pl.* **co·mals,** *Sp.* **co·ma·les** (kô mä′les). a griddle made from sandstone or earthenware. [< MexSp < Nahuatl *comalli*]

Co·man·che (kō man′chē, kə-), *n., pl.* **-ches,** (*esp. collectively*) **-che** for 1. **1.** a member of a Shoshonean tribe, the only tribe of the group living entirely on the Plains, formerly ranging from Wyoming to Texas, now in Oklahoma. **2.** their speech, a dialect of Shoshone. [< MexSp < Shoshone]

Co·man·che (kə man′chē), *n.* a town in central Texas. 3415 (1960).

Co·man·che·an (kō man′chē ən, kə), *Geol.* —*adj.* **1.** pertaining to an epoch or series of rocks in parts of North America comprising the early portion of the Cretaceous period or system. —*n.* **2.** an epoch or series of early Cretaceous rocks typically represented in the Gulf of Mexico region. [COMANCHE + -AN]

co·man·dan·te (kom′ən dan′tē; *Sp., It.* kô′män-dän′te), *n., pl.* **-tes** (-tēz; *Sp.* -tes), *It.* **-ti** (-tē). commandant. [< Sp, It]

co·mate[1] (kō māt′), *n.* a mate or companion. [CO- + MATE[1]]

co·mate[2] (kō′māt), *adj.* **1.** *Bot.* having a coma. **2.** hairy; tufted. [< L *comāt(us).* See COMA[2], -ATE[1]]

co·mat·ic (kō mat′ik), *adj.* *Optics.* of, pertaining to, or blurred as a result of a coma. [COMA[2] + -IC; *-t-* irreg. by influence of *comatose*]

com·a·tose (kom′ə tōs′, kō′mə-), *adj.* **1.** affected with or characterized by coma: *The patient was comatose after the stroke.* **2.** lacking alertness or energy; torpid; dull; lethargic: *He was so sleepy that he was almost comatose.* [< Gk *komat-* (s. of *kôma* COMA[1]) + -OSE[1]] —**com′a·tose′ly,** *adv.* —**com′a·tose′ness, com·a·tos·i·ty** (kom′ə tos′i tē), *n.*

co·mat·u·lid (kə mach′ə lid), *n.* a free-swimming, stalkless crinoid; a feather star. [< NL *Comatulidae,* equiv. to *Comatul(a)* genus name (see COMATE[2]) + *-idae* -IDAE]

comb[1] (kōm), *n.* **1.** a toothed strip of bone, metal, plastic, or hard rubber, used for arranging the hair, untangling it, or holding it in place. **2.** a currycomb. **3.** any comblike instrument, object, or formation. **4.** a series of springlike prongs projecting from a spine, usually of plastic, for making a loose-leaf binding. **5.** a machine for separating choice cotton or worsted fibers from noil. **6.** a trowel having a notched edge for applying adhesives in setting tiles or the like. **7.** the fleshy, more or less serrated excrescence or growth on the head of certain gallinaceous birds, esp. the domestic fowl. **8.** something resembling or suggesting this, as the crest of a wave. **9.** *Armor.* a ridge along the top of a helmet, esp. of the morion. **10.** a honeycomb, or any similar group of cells. **11.** a ridge of a roof. **12.** a comblike instrument for imparting a grainlike finish to a painted surface. **13.** ridge (def. 5). **14.** *Masonry.* drag (def. 27). **15.** the upper edge of the buttstock of a rifle or shotgun. —*v.t.* **16.** to arrange or adorn (the hair) with or as with a comb. **17.** to use (something) in the manner of a comb: *She combed her fingers through her hair.* **18.** to remove (anything undesirable) with or as with a comb: *She combed the snarls out of her hair. They combed the cowards from the group.* **19.** to separate (wool fibers) with a comb. **20.** to scrape with or as with a comb. **21.** to sweep across; rake: *High winds combed the seacoast.* **22.** to search everywhere in: *She combed the files for the missing letter.* —*v.i.* **23.** to roll over or break at the crest, as a wave. [ME; OE *comb, camb;* c. OHG *kamb* (G *Kamm*), Icel *kambr,* Gk *gómphos* pin, peg, *gomphíos* molar tooth; see CAM] —**comb′less,** *adj.* —**comb′less·ness,** *n.*

comb[2] (ko͞om, kōm), *n.* combe.

comb., combining.

com·bat (*v.* kəm bat′, kom′bat, kum′-; *n.* kom′bat, kum′-), *v.,* **-bat·ed, -bat·ing** or (*esp. Brit.*) **-bat·ted, -bat·ting,** *n.* —*v.t.* **1.** to fight or contend against; oppose vigorously: *He vowed to combat crime.* —*v.i.* **2.** to fight; battle; contend: *to combat with crippling diseases.* —*n.* **3.** a controversy, struggle, or fight, as between two ideals, men, armies, etc. **4.** *Mil.* active fighting with enemy forces, in contrast to service in supporting activities. [< MF *combatt(re)* < VL **combattere;* equiv. to L *com-* COM- + *battuere* to strike, beat] —**com·bat′a·ble,** *adj.* —**com·bat′er;** *esp. Brit.,* **com·bat′ter,** *n.*

—**Syn. 1, 2.** struggle, contest. **3.** contention, skirmish, battle, brush. See **fight.**

com·bat·ant (kəm bat′ənt, kom′bə tənt, kum′-), *n.* **1.** a person or group that fights. —*adj.* **2.** combating; fighting: *the combatant armies.* **3.** disposed to combat: *a belligerent, combatant little man.* **4.** Also, **com·bat′tant.** *Heraldry.* (of two beasts) represented as rampant and facing each other, as if in the act of fighting. [late ME *combataunt* < MF *combatant.* See COMBAT, -ANT]

com′bat boot′, a heavy leather shoe having a buckled extension above the ankle and a sole and heel of hard rubber.

com′bat ceil′ing, *Aeron.* the altitude under standard air conditions above which a given fighter plane is unable to climb faster than 500 feet per minute, or a given bomber is unable to climb faster than 200 feet per minute. Cf. **service ceiling.**

com′bat du′ty, military duty served in a combat zone.

com′bat fatigue′. See **battle fatigue.**

Com′bat In′fantryman Badge′, *U.S.* a badge awarded to an infantryman in recognition of satisfactory performance of duty in ground combat against the enemy.

com·bat·ive (kəm bat′iv, kom′bə tiv, kum′-), *adj.* ready or inclined to fight; pugnacious: *He displayed a most unpleasant, combative attitude.* [COMBAT + -IVE] —**com·bat′ive·ly,** *adv.* —**com·bat′ive·ness, com·ba·tiv·i·ty** (kom′bə tiv′i tē), *n.*

com′bat jack′et. See **battle jacket.**

com′bat team′, *Mil.* a combination of military units, usually of different types, as infantry and artillery, temporarily under one command while on a special combat mission.

com′bat zone′, *Mil.* an area in a theater of operations where combat forces operate, extending typically from the front line to the communications zone.

comb′ back′, (on a Windsor chair) a back having a section of spindles rising above the top rail to another rail.

combe (ko͞om, kōm), *n.* *England.* a narrow valley or deep hollow, esp. one enclosed on all but one side. Also, **comb, coomb, coombe.** [OE *cumb* valley < Celt; cf. Gaulish *cumba,* Welsh *cwm* valley]

Combe′-Ca·pelle′ man′ (kōm′ ka pel′), a skeleton of the Early Upper Paleolithic Perigordian culture in France. [named after *Combe-Capelle* (near Périgueux, France) where the remains were found]

combed′ ware′, ceramic ware having a finish of several glazes or slips worked on the surface with a comb.

combed′ yarn′, cotton or worsted yarn of fibers laid parallel, superior in smoothness to carded yarn.

comb·er (kō′mər), *n.* **1.** one who or that which combs. **2.** a long, curling wave: *The comber broke against the sea wall.* [COMB[1] + -ER[1]]

comb′er board′, (in weaving) a wooden frame pierced with a series of small holes through which the harness cords are threaded, used to regulate the cords and determine the texture and width of a repeat in a fabric.

comb·fish (kōm′fish′), *n., pl.* (*esp. collectively*) **-fish,** (*esp. referring to two or more kinds or species*) **-fish·es.** any of several rough-skinned fishes of the family *Zaniolepidae,* found off the Pacific coast of North America. [COMB[1] + FISH]

comb′-foot·ed spi′der (kōm′fo͝ot′id), any of numerous spiders of the family *Theridiidae,* having a comblike row of bristles on the tarsi of the hind legs.

com·bi·na·tion (kom′bə nā′shən), *n.* **1.** the act of combining or the state of being combined. **2.** a number of things combined: *a combination of ideas.* **3.** something formed by combining: *A chord is a combination of notes.* **4.** an alliance of persons or parties: *a combination in restraint of trade.* **5.** the set or series of numbers or letters used in setting the mechanism of a combination lock. **6.** the parts of the mechanism operated by this. **7.** a suit of underwear in one piece. **8.** *Math.* **a.** the arrangement of a number of individuals into various groups, as *a, b,* and *c* into *ab, ac,* and *bc.* **b.** a group thus formed. [< LL *combīnātiōn-* (s. of *combīnātiō*), equiv. to *combīnāt(us)* combined (see COMBINE, -ATE[1]) + *-iōn-* -ION] —**com′bi·na′tion·al,** *adj.*

—**Syn. 1.** association, conjunction, union, coalescence, blending. **2.** mixture, amalgamation, amalgam. COMBINATION, COMPOSITE, COMPOUND all mean a union of individual parts. COMBINATION implies a grouping which is close but which may easily be dissolved. A COMPOSITE is a stronger union, in which the parts have become subordinate to a unity. COMPOUND implies a more or less complete merging of individual parts into an organic whole. **4.** association, federation, league, coalition; cartel, combine, monopoly; bloc; cabal, conspiracy.

combina′tion door′, an outside door having a frame into which different types of panels can be inserted, as a screen for summer or storm sash for winter.

combina′tion frame′, *Carpentry.* a cheaper modification of the braced frame, retaining the use of solid sills, posts, and girts and of studs one story high, but employing longer and lighter braces and lighter timbers in general, and dispensing to some extent with mortise and tenon joints in favor of nailing. Also called **half frame.**

combina′tion last′, a shoe last that has a narrower heel or instep than the standard last.

combina′tion lock′, a lock opened by turning one or more specially marked dials a given number of times through a particular set of positions in a prescribed order and direction: used on safes, lockers, etc.

combina′tion plate′, *Engraving.* a plate consisting of both line and halftone. Also called **combina′tion cut′.**

combina′tion prin′ciple, *Physics.* See **Ritz combination principle.**

combina′tion square′, an adjustable device for carpenters, used as a try square, miter square, level, etc.

combina′tion tone′, *Music.* a tone resulting from the simultaneous sounding of two other tones. Also called **resultant tone.**

com·bi·na·tive (kom′bə nā′tiv, kəm bī′nə-), *adj.* **1.** tending or serving to combine. **2.** of, pertaining to, or resulting from combination. [COMBINAT(ION) + -IVE]

com·bi·na·to·ri·al (kəm bī′nə tôr′ē əl, -tōr′-), *adj.* *Math.* of or pertaining to combination, or the modes, properties, etc., of combinations. Also, **com·bi′na·to′ry.** [COMBINATORY + -AL[1]]

combinato′rial anal′ysis, *Math.* the branch of mathematics that deals with permutations and combinations, esp. used in statistics and probability.

combinato′rial topol′ogy, *Math.* the branch of topology which deals with the properties of geometric figures by considering the figures as being comprised of elementary geometric figures, as points or lines.

com·bine (*v.* kəm bīn′; *n.* kom′bīn, kəm bīn′ *for* 6, 7, kom′bīn *for* 8), *v.,* **-bined, -bin·ing,** *n.* —*v.t.* **1.** to bring or join into a close union or whole; unite; associate; coalesce: *She combined the ingredients to make the dough.* **2.** to possess or exhibit in union: *a plan which combines the best features of several other plans.* —*v.i.* **3.** to unite; coalesce: *The clay combined with the water to form a milky suspension.* **4.** to unite for a common purpose; join forces: *After the two armies had combined, they proved invincible.* **5.** to enter into chemical union. —*n.* **6.** a combination. **7.** *U.S. Informal.* a combination of persons or groups for the furtherance of their political, commercial, or other interests. **8.** a machine for cutting and threshing grain in the field. [late ME *combynyn* < LL *combīnāre,* equiv. to *com-* COM- + *bīn-* (s. of *bīnī* two by two) + *-a-* v. suffix + *-re* inf. ending] —**com·bin′a·ble,** *adj.* —**com·bin′a·ble·ness,** *n.* —**com·bin′a·bly,** *adv.* —**com·bin′er,** *n.*

—**Syn. 1.** compound, amalgamate. See **mix. 7.** merger, monopoly, alignment, bloc. —**Ant. 1, 3.** separate.

com·bined (kəm bīnd′), *adj.* **1.** made by combining; joined; united, as in a chemical compound. **2.** taken as a whole; in the aggregate: *outselling all other brands combined.* [late ME; see COMBINE, -ED[2]] —**com·bined·ly** (kəm bīn′lē, -bī′nid-), *adv.* —**com·bined′ness,** *n.*

combined′ opera′tions, war operations carried out by cooperation between two or more allied nations or by coordination of the land, sea, and air forces of one or more nations.

comb·ings (kō′mingz), *n.pl.* hairs removed with a comb or a brush. [COMB[1] + -ING[1] + -S[3]]

combin′ing form′, *Gram.* a linguistic form used only in compound words, never independently, as *hemato-* in *hematology.*

combin′ing weight′, *Chem.* the atomic weight of an atom or radical divided by its valence.

comb′ jel′ly (kōm), ctenophore.

comb′ mo′rion, a type of morion of the late 16th century, having a high, rounded skull, a tall, standing comb, and a broad brim curving upward sharply to peaks at the front and back.

com·bo (kom′bō), *n., pl.* **-bos. 1.** a small jazz or dance band. Cf. **big band. 2.** *Informal.* combination (defs. 2–4). **3.** *Australian Slang.* a white man living with aborigines or having an aborigine wife, usually in a common-law marriage. [alter. and shortening of COMBINATION]

com·bust (kəm bust′), *adj.* *Astrol.* (of a planet) so near the sun as to be obscured by it. [ME < alchemical and astrological L *combūst(us)* burnt up (ptp. of *combūrere,* equiv. to *com-* COM- + *-b-* (< *ambūrere* to char) + *-ūs-* perf. s. + *-tus* ptp. suffix]

com·bus·ti·ble (kəm bus′tə bəl), *adj.* **1.** capable of catching fire and burning; inflammable; flammable: *Gasoline vapor is highly combustible.* **2.** easily excited: *a high-strung, combustible nature.* —*n.* **3.** a combustible substance: *Trucks carrying combustibles will not be allowed to use this tunnel.* [< LL *combūstibil(is).* See COMBUST, -IBLE] —**com·bus′ti·bil′i·ty, com·bus′ti·ble·ness,** *n.* —**com·bus′ti·bly,** *adv.*

com·bus·tion (kəm bus′chən, -bush′-), *n.* **1.** the act or process of burning. **2.** *Chem.* **a.** rapid oxidation accompanied by heat and, usually, light. **b.** chemical combination attended by heat and light. **c.** slow oxidation not accompanied by high temperature and light. **3.** violent excitement; tumult. [< LL *combūstiōn-* (s. of *combūstiō*). See COMBUST, -ION] —**com·bus′tive,** *adj.*

combus′tion cham′ber, *Mach.* a chamber, as in a boiler or engine, where combustion occurs.

combus′tion en′gine, any of various types of engine driven by heat energy produced by combustion.

combus′tion tube′, a tube of hard glass used esp. in a furnace for burning a substance in a current of air or oxygen.

com·bus·tor (kəm bus′tər), *n. Aeron.* the apparatus in a ramjet or other jet engine for initiating and sustaining combustion, consisting of the igniter, fuel-injection system, combustion chamber, and flameholder. [COMBUST(ION) + -OR²]

comdg., commanding.

Comdr., commander. Also, **comdr.**

Comdt., commandant. Also, **comdt.**

come (kum), *v.,* **came, come, com·ing.** —*v.i.* **1.** to move toward a particular person or place: *Come to me. May I come to your house?* **2.** to arrive by movement or in course of progress: *The train from Boston to New York is coming in now.* **3.** to approach or arrive in time, in succession, etc.: *Christmas comes once a year. I'll come to your question next.* **4.** to move into view; appear: *The light comes and goes.* **5.** to extend; reach: *The dress comes to her knees.* **6.** to take place; occur; happen: *Success comes to those who strive.* **7.** to occur at a certain point, position, etc.: *Tuesday comes after Monday. Her aria comes in the third act.* **8.** to be available, produced, offered, etc.: *Toothpaste comes in a tube.* **9.** to occur to the mind: *The idea just came to me.* **10.** to befall: *They promised no harm would come to us.* **11.** to issue; emanate; be derived: *Peaches come from trees. Good results do not come from careless work.* **12.** to arrive or appear as a result: *This comes of carelessness.* **13.** to enter or be brought into a specified state or condition: *to come into popular use.* **14.** to do or manage; fare: *He is coming along well with his work.* **15.** to enter into being or existence; be born: *The baby came at dawn.* **16.** to have been a resident or to be a native of (usually fol. by *from*): *She comes from Florida.* **17.** to become: *His shoes came untied.* **18.** to seem to become: *His fears made the menacing statues come alive. The work will come easy with a little practice.* **19.** (used in the imperative to call attention, express remonstrance, etc.): *Come, that will do!* **20.** to germinate, as grain. **21.** *Slang.* to have an orgasm.
—*v.t.* **22.** *Chiefly Brit.* to do; perform; accomplish. **23.** *Informal.* to play the part of: *to come the grande dame.* **24. come about, a.** to come to pass; happen. **b.** *Naut.* to tack. **25. come across, a.** to find or meet, esp. by chance. **b.** *Slang.* to make good one's promise, as to pay a debt, do what is expected of one, etc.: *to come across with a contribution.* **c.** to be understandable or convincing: *The moral of this story doesn't come across.* **26. come around** or **round, a.** to change one's opinion, decision, etc., esp. to agree with another's. **b.** to recover consciousness; revive. **c.** to cease being angry, hurt, etc. **d.** to visit. **27. come at, a.** to arrive at; attain. **b.** to rush at; attack: *The watchdog came at the intruder.* **28. come back, a.** to return, esp. to one's memory: *It all comes back to me now.* **b.** *Informal.* to return to a former position or state which one had lost. **c.** *Slang.* to talk back; retort: *to come back with a witty remark.* **29. come between,** to estrange; separate: *Love of money came between the brothers.* **30. come by,** to obtain; acquire: *How did he ever come by so much money?* **31. come down, a.** to lose wealth, rank, etc. **b.** to be handed down by tradition or inheritance. **32. come down on** or **upon, a.** to voice one's opposition to: *He came down on the prevailing apathy to the intolerable living conditions of some members of the community.* **b.** to reprimand; scold: *The old woman came down on the children for breaking her window.* **33. come down with,** to become afflicted with (an illness): *Many older people came down with influenza this year.* **34. come forward,** to offer one's services; present oneself; volunteer: *When the chairman called for volunteers, several members of our group came forward.* **35. come home,** *Naut.* **a.** (of an anchor) to begin to drag. **b.** (of an object) to move when hauled upon. **36. come in, a.** to enter. **b.** to take a place among others; arrive. **c.** to come into use or fashion. **d.** to begin to produce or yield: *The oil well finally came in.* **e.** to be among the winners: *His horse came in twice—in the third and fifth races.* **f.** to finish in a race or any competition, as specified: *Orange Slip came in first both times.* **37. come in for,** to receive; get; be subjected to: *This article will no doubt come in for a great deal of criticism.* **38. come into, a.** to acquire; get. **b.** to inherit: *He came into a large fortune at the age of 21.* **39. come off, a.** to happen; occur. **b.** to reach the end; acquit oneself: *to come off with honors.* **c.** to be given or completed; occur; result: *His speech came off satisfactorily.* **40. come off it,** *Slang.* stop being pretentious; come down off that high horse: *Come off it, Ben, we know you married her for money.* **41. come on, a.** Also, **come upon.** to meet or find unexpectedly. **b.** to make progress; develop; flourish. **c.** to appear on stage; make one's entrance. **d.** to begin; appear: *The last showing will be coming on in a few minutes.* **e.** *Informal.* (used chiefly in the imperative) to hurry; begin: *Come on, before it rains!* **f.** *Informal.* (as an entreaty or attempt at persuasion) please: *Come on, go with us to the movies.* **g.** *Slang.* to make an impression; have an effect: *She comes on a bit too strong for my taste.* **42. come out, a.** to be published; appear. **b.** to become known; be revealed. **c.** to make a debut in society, the theater, etc. **d.** to end; terminate; emerge: *The fight came out badly, as both combatants were injured.* **43. come out with, a.** to speak, esp. to confess or reveal something. **b.** to make available to the public; bring out: *The publisher is coming out with a revised edition of the textbook.* **44. come over,** to happen to; affect: *What's come over him?* **45. come round, a.** See **come** (def. 26). **b.** *Naut.* (of a sailing vessel) to head toward the wind; come to. **46. come through,** *U.S. Slang.* **a.** to finish successfully. **b.** to do as expected or hoped; perform: *We knew you'd come through for us.* **c.** to experience religious conversion. **47. come to, a.** to recover consciousness. **b.** to amount to; total. **c.** *Naut.* to take the way off a vessel, as by bringing her head into the wind, anchoring, etc. **48. come to pass,** to happen; occur. **49. come under, a.** to fit into a category or classification: *This play comes under the heading of social criticism.* **b.** to be the province or responsibility of: *This matter comes under the State Department.* **50. come up, a.** to be referred to; arise: *The subject kept coming up in conversation.* **b.** *Brit.* to come into residence at a school or university. **c.** to be presented for action or discussion: *The farm bill comes up for consideration next Monday.* **d.** *Naut.* to slacken the tension on a line. **51. come up to, a.** to approach; near: *A panhandler came up to us in the street.* **b.** to compare with as to quantity, excellence, etc.; equal: *This piece of work does not come up to your usual standard.* **52. come up with, a.** to reach; approach: *I came up with them as they were rounding the corner.* **b.** to produce; supply: *The librarian came up with the missing book.* **c.** to present; propose: *We weren't able to come up with any new suggestions.* [ME *come(n),* OE *cuman;* c. D *komen,* G *kommen,* Goth *qiman,* Icel *koma,* L *ven(īre),* Gk *baín(ein),* Skt *gám(ati)* goes]
—**Syn. 2.** See **arrive.** —**Ant. 2.** leave, depart.

come-at-a·ble (kum at′ə bəl), *adj. Informal.* accessible. Cf. **getatable.**

come·back (kum′bak′), *n.* **1.** *Informal.* a return to a former rank, popularity, position, prosperity, etc.: *The ex-champion kept trying to make a comeback.* **2.** *Slang.* a clever or effective retort; repartee; riposte: *That was a great comeback the comedian made to the hecklers.* **3.** *Slang.* a basis or cause of complaint: *If you insist on buying these pointed shoes, you'll have no comeback when your toes start to hurt.* [n. use of v. phrase *come back*]

co·me·di·an (kə mē′dē ən), *n.* **1.** an actor in comedy. **2.** a writer of comedy. **3.** a professional entertainer who amuses by relating anecdotes, acting out comical situations, engaging in humorous repartee, etc. **4.** any comical or amusing person. [COMEDY + -AN]

co·me·dic (kə mē′dik, -med′ik), *adj.* of, pertaining to, or of the nature of comedy. Also, **co·me′di·cal.** [< L *cōmoedic(us)* < Gk *kōmōidikós,* equiv. to *kōmōid(ía)* COMEDY + *-ikos* -IC] —**co·me′di·cal·ly,** *adv.*

Co·mé·die Fran·çaise (kô mā dē fräɴ sez′), the French national theater, founded in Paris in 1680, famous for its repertoire of classical French drama. Also called **La Maison de Molière, Théâtre-Français.**

Co·mé·die Hu·maine, La (*Fr.* la kô mā dē y men′). See **Human Comedy, The.**

co·me·di·enne (kə mē′dē en′, -mā′-), *n.* **1.** an actress in comedy. **2.** a woman who is a professional comic entertainer. [< F, equiv. to *comédie* COMEDY + *-enne,* fem. of *-en* -AN]

co·me·di·et·ta (kə mē′dē et′ə, -mā′-; *It.* kô′me dyet′tä), *n., pl.* **-tas,** *It.* **-te** (-te). a one-act comedy or farce. [< It, equiv. to *comedi(a)* COMEDY + *-etta* -ETTE]

com·e·dist (kom′i dist), *n.* a writer of comedies. [COMED(Y) + -IST]

com·e·do (kom′i dō′), *n., pl.* **com·e·dos, com·e·do·nes** (kom′i dō′nēz). *Med.* an inspissated secretion plugging a duct of the skin, esp. of a sebaceous gland; blackhead. [< NL, L: glutton, equiv. to *com-* COM- + *ed-* EAT + *-ō* aug. n. suffix]

come·down (kum′doun′), *n. Informal.* an unexpected or humiliating descent from dignity, importance, or prosperity. [n. use of v. phrase *come down*]

com·e·dy (kom′i dē), *n., pl.* **-dies.** **1.** a play, movie, etc., of light and humorous character with a happy or cheerful ending; a dramatic work in which the central motif is the triumph over adverse circumstance, resulting in a successful or happy conclusion. **2.** that branch of the drama which concerns itself with this form of composition. **3.** the comic element of drama, of literature generally, or of life. **4.** any literary composition dealing with a theme suitable for comedy, or employing the methods of comedy. **5.** any comic or humorous incident or series of incidents. [ME *comedye* < ML *cōmēdia,* equiv. to L *cōmoedia* < Gk *kōmōidía,* equiv. to *kōmōid(ós)* comedian (*kômo(s)* merry-making + *aoidós* singer) + *-ia* -Y³] —**co·me·di·al** (kə mē′dē əl), *adj.*

Com′edy of Er′rors, The, an early comedy (1594) by Shakespeare.

com′edy of man′ners, a comedy satirizing the manners and customs of a social class, esp. dealing with the amorous intrigues of fashionable society.

come-hith·er (kum′hith′ər, kə mith′-), *adj.* **1.** inviting or enticing, esp. in a sexually provocative manner: *She gave him a come-hither look.* —*n.* **2.** an alluring or provocative invitation: *Her manner certainly did seem to provide a come-hither to all and sundry.* **3.** any call or coaxing sound made to domestic animals. [adj., n. use of impv. phrase *come hither*]

come·ly (kum′lē), *adj.,* **-li·er, -li·est.** **1.** pleasing in appearance; fair: *a comely face.* **2.** proper; seemly; becoming: *comely behavior.* [ME *cumli,* OE *cȳmlic* lovely, equiv. to *cȳme* exquisite (c. MHG *kūme* weak, tender; akin to G *kaum* with difficulty, OHG *kūmo*) + *-līc* -LY] —**come′li·ly,** *adv.* —**come′li·ness,** *n.*
—**Syn. 1.** pretty, handsome, beautiful, good-looking, personable. —**Ant. 1.** unattractive.

Co·me·ni·us (kə mē′nē əs), *n.* **John Amos** (*Jan Amos Komensky*), 1592–1670, Moravian educational reformer and bishop.

come-on (kum′on′, -ôn′), *n. U.S. Slang.* inducement; lure. [n. use of v. phrase *come on*]

com·er (kum′ər), *n.* **1.** one who or that which comes, or has lately come. **2.** *Informal.* one who or that which is progressing well or is very promising: *He looks like a comer in state politics.* [ME; see COME, -ER¹]

co·mes (kō′mēz), *n., pl.* **com·i·tes** (kom′i tēz′). **1.** *Astron.* companion¹ (def. 6). **2.** *Anat.* a blood vessel accompanying another vessel or a nerve. [< L: fellow-traveler, equiv. to *com-* COM- + *e-* (var. of *i-,* s. of *īre* to go) + *-s* nom. sing. ending]

co·me sta (kô′me stä′), *Italian.* how are you?

co·mes·ti·ble (kə mes′tə bəl), *adj.* **1.** edible; eatable. —*n.* **2.** Usually, **comestibles.** edibles; articles of food: *The table was spread with all kinds of comestibles.* [late ME < LL *comēstibil(is),* equiv. to L *comēst(us),* ptp. of *comēsse* to eat up (*com* -COM- + *-ēs-* *ēss-* (*ēd* perf. s. + *-t-* ptp. suffix) + *-tus* ptp. suffix, added a second time) + *-ibilis* -IBLE; see EAT]

com·et (kom′it), *n. Astron.* a celestial body moving about the sun, usually in a highly eccentric orbit, consisting of a central mass surrounded by a misty envelope which may extend into a stream away from the sun. [< L *comēt(ēs),* *comēt(a)* < Gk *komḗt(ēs)* long-haired, equiv. to *kómē* hair of the head + *-tēs* n. suffix denoting agent] —**com·et·ar·y** (kom′i ter′ē), **co·met·ic** (kə met′ik), **co·met′i·cal,** *adj.* —**com′et·like′,** *adj.*

Co·me·tes (kə mē′tēz), *n. Class. Myth.* the lover of Aegialia.

com·eth (kum′ith), *v. Archaic.* 3rd pers. sing. pres. indic. of **come.**

co·meth·er (kō meth′ər), *adj., n. Brit. Dial.* come-hither.

com′et seek′er, a telescope of low power but with a wide field, used to search for comets. Also called **com′et find′er.**

come·up·pance (kum′up′əns), *n. Informal.* deserved reward or just deserts, usually unpleasant: *He finally got his comeuppance for his misbehavior.* [from phrase *come up* + -ANCE]

com·fit (kum′fit, kom′-), *n.* a dry sweetmeat containing a nut or piece of fruit. [ME *confit* < MF < L *confectum* something prepared. See CONFECT]

com·fort (kum′fərt), *v.t.* **1.** to soothe or console; cheer, as someone grieved: *They comforted him for his loss.* **2.** to make physically comfortable. **3.** *Obs.* to aid; encourage. —*n.* **4.** relief in affliction; consolation; solace: *Her presence was a comfort to him.* **5.** a feeling of relief or consolation: *Her forgiveness afforded him great comfort.* **6.** a person or thing that gives consolation: *She was a great comfort to him.* **7.** a cause or matter of relief or satisfaction: *The patient's recovery was a comfort to the doctor.* **8.** a state of ease and satisfaction of bodily wants, with freedom from pain and anxiety: *He is a man who enjoys his comfort.* **9.** that which promotes such a state: *His wealth allows him to enjoy a high degree of comfort.* **10.** *Chiefly Midland and Southern U.S.* a comforter; bedcover. **11.** *Obs.* strengthening aid; assistance. [ME *comfortie(n),* var. of *confortie(n), conforte(n)* < OF *conforter* < LL *confortāre* to strengthen, equiv. to *con-* CON- + *fort(is)* strong + *-ā* v. suffix + *-re* inf. suffix] —**com′fort·ing·ly,** *adv.* —**com′fort·less,** *adj.* —**com′fort·less·ly,** *adv.* —**com′fort·less·ness,** *n.*
—**Syn. 1.** pacify, calm, solace, gladden. COMFORT, CONSOLE, RELIEVE, SOOTHE imply assuaging sorrow, worry, discomfort, or pain. To COMFORT is to lessen the sadness or sorrow of someone and to strengthen by inspiring with hope and restoring a cheerful outlook: *to comfort a despairing person.* CONSOLE, a more formal word, means to make grief or distress seem lighter, by means of kindness and thoughtful attentions: *to console a bereaved parent.* RELIEVE means to lighten, lessen, or remove pain, trouble, discomfort, or hardship: *to relieve a needy person.* SOOTHE means to pacify or calm: *to soothe a child.* **1, 2, 8.** See **ease.**

Com·fort (kum′fərt), *n.* a girl's given name.

com·fort·a·ble (kumf′tə bəl, kum′fər tə bəl), *adj.* **1.** (of clothing, furniture, etc.) producing physical comfort, support, or ease: *a comfortable chair; comfortable shoes.* **2.** being in a state of physical or mental comfort; contented and undisturbed; at ease: *to be comfortable in new shoes; I don't feel comfortable in the same room with her.* **3.** (of a person, situation, etc.) producing mental comfort or ease; easy to associate with: *She's a comfortable person to be with.* **4.** adequate; sufficient: *a comfortable salary.* **5.** *Obs.* cheerful. —*n.* **6.** *Chiefly Northern U.S.* a quilted bedcover; comforter. [late ME < AF *confortable.* See COMFORT, -ABLE] —**com′fort·a·ble·ness,** *n.* —**com′fort·a·bly,** *adv.*

com·fort·er (kum′fər tər), *n.* **1.** one who or that which comforts. **2.** the Comforter. See **Holy Ghost. 3.** a long, woolen scarf, usually knitted. **4.** *U.S.* a thick, quilted bedcover. **5.** *Brit.* pacifier (def. 2). [ME *confortour* < AF, OF *conforteor* << L **confortātōr-*; see CON-, FORT, -OR²]

com′fort sta′tion, a room or small building with toilet and lavatory facilities for public use, esp. in a public place as in a park, zoo, or the like.

com′fort zone′, the range of atmospheric temperature and humidity considered comfortable for most people.

com·frey (kum′frē), *n., pl.* **-freys.** any boraginaceous plant of the genus *Symphytum,* of Europe and Asia, as *S. officinale,* formerly used as a vulnerary. [ME *cumfirie* < ML *cumfiria,* appar. alter. of L *conferva* CONFERVA]

com·fy (kum′fē), *adj.,* **-fi·er, -fi·est.** *Informal.* comfortable. [by shortening and alter.] —**com′fi·ly,** *adv.* —**com′fi·ness,** *n.*

com·ic (kom′ik), *adj.* **1.** of, pertaining to, or characterized by comedy: *comic opera.* **2.** of or pertaining to one who acts in or writes comedy: *a comic actor; a comic dramatist.* **3.** of, pertaining to, or characteristic of comedy: *comic situations; a comic sense.* **4.** provoking laughter; humorous; funny; laughable: *His behavior was comic.* —*n.* **5.** a comic actor; comedian: *The star is a well-known comic.* **6.** *Informal.* **a.** a comic periodical. **b. comics,** comic strips. **7. the comic,** the element or quality of comedy in literature, art, drama, etc.: *An appreciation of the comic came naturally to her.* [< L *cōmic(us)* < Gk *kōmikós,* equiv. to *kôm(os)* a revel + *-ikos* -IC]

com·i·cal (kom′i kəl), *adj.* **1.** producing laughter; amusing; funny: *a comical fellow.* **2.** *Obs.* pertaining to or of the nature of comedy. [COMIC + -AL¹] —**com′i·cal′i·ty, com′i·cal·ness,** *n.* —**com′i·cal·ly,** *adv.*
—**Syn. 1.** See **amusing.**

com′ic book′, a paper booklet with one or more long comic strips.

com′ic op′era, a diverting opera with spoken dialogue and a happy ending.

com′ic relief′, **1.** an amusing scene, incident, or speech introduced into serious or tragic elements, as in a play, in order to provide temporary relief from tension, or to intensify the dramatic action. **2.** relief from tension caused by the introduction of a comic element.

com′ic strip′, a sequence of drawings, either in color or black and white, relating a comic incident, an adventure or mystery story, etc. often serialized, typically having dialogue printed in balloons, and usually printed as a horizontal strip in daily newspapers and in an uninterrupted block or longer sequence of such strips in Sunday newspapers and in comic books.

COMINCH, *U.S. Navy.* Commander in Chief.

Com. in Chf., Commander in Chief.

Co·mines (kô mēn′), *n.* **Phi·lippe de** (fē lēp′ də), 1445?–1511?, French historian and diplomat. Also, **Commines.**

Com·in·form (kom′in fôrm′), *n.* an organization (1947–56) established by the Communist parties of nine European countries for mutual advice and coordinated activity. [shortening of *Communist Information Bureau*] —**Com′in·form′ist,** *n.*

com·ing (kum′ing), *n.* **1.** approach; arrival; advent: *His coming here was a mistake.* —*adj.* **2.** that comes; approaching: *The coming year will see some changes.* **3.** promising future fame or success: *a coming actor; a coming ideology.* [ME; see COME, -ING[1], -ING[2]]

Com·in·tern (kom′in tûrn′, kom′in tûrn′), *n.* See **Third International.** Also, **Komintern.** [shortening of COMMUNIST INTERNATIONAL]

com·i·ta·tive (kom′i tā′tiv, -tə tiv), *Gram.* —*adj.* **1.** noting a case whose distinctive function is to indicate accompaniment. —*n.* **2.** the comitative case. [< L *comitāt(us)* retinue, escort (*comit-,* s. of *comes* companion (see COUNT[2]) + *-ātus* -ATE[1]) + -IVE]

co·mi·ti·a (kə mish′ē ə), *n. Rom. Antiq.* an assembly of the people convened to pass on laws, nominate magistrates, etc. [< L, pl. of *comitium* assembly, equiv. to *com-* COM- + *-it(us),* ptp. of *īre* to go (*i-* perf. s. + *-tus* ptp. suffix) + *-ium* n. suffix] —**co·mi·tial** (kə mish′əl), *adj.*

com·i·ty (kom′i tē), *n., pl.* **-ties. 1.** mutual courtesy; civility. **2.** *Internat. Law.* courtesy between nations, as in respect shown by one country for the laws, judicial decisions, and institutions of another. [< L *cōmitās,* equiv. to *cōm(is)* affable + *-itās* -ITY]

comm., 1. commander. **2.** commerce. **3.** commission. **4.** committee. **5.** commonwealth.

com·ma (kom′ə), *n.* **1.** the sign (,), a mark of punctuation used for indicating a division in a sentence, as by an interpolated word, phrase, or clause, esp. when such a division is accompanied by a slight pause in speech. It is also used to separate items in a list, to mark off thousands in numerals, to separate types or levels of information in bibliographic and other data, and, in Europe, as a decimal point. **2.** *Class. Pros.* **a.** a fragment or smaller section of a colon. **b.** the part of dactylic hexameter beginning or ending with the caesura. **c.** the caesura itself. **3.** *Music.* the difference in pitch between two enharmonic tones, as G♮ and A♭. **4.** any of several nymphalid butterflies, as *Polygonia comma,* having a comma-shaped silver mark on the underside of each hind wing. [< LL: mark of punctuation, L: division of a period < Gk *kómma,* equiv. to *kop-* (var. s. of *kóptein* to strike, chop) + *-ma* n. suffix denoting result of action]

com′ma bacil′lus, a curved, rod-shaped bacterium, *Vibrio comma,* causing Asiatic cholera.

Com·mack (kō′mak, kom′ak), *n.* a town on central Long Island, in SE New York. 9613 (1960).

com′ma fault′, *Gram.* the use of a comma, rather than a semicolon, colon, or period, to separate related main clauses in the absence of a coordinating conjunction. The comma fault is generally considered to be incorrect or undesirable. Also called **comma splice.**

Com·ma·ger (kom′ə jər), *n.* **Henry Steele,** born 1902, U.S. historian, author, and teacher.

com·mand (kə mand′, -mänd′), *v.t.* **1.** to direct with authority; order: *The captain commanded his men to attack.* **2.** to require with authority; demand: *He commanded silence.* **3.** to have or exercise authority or control over; be master of; have at one's bidding or disposal: *The Pharaoh commanded 10,000 slaves.* **4.** to deserve and receive (respect, sympathy, attention, etc.): *He commands much respect for his attitude.* **5.** to dominate by reason of location; overlook: *The hill commands the sea.* **6.** to have authority over and responsibility for (a military or naval unit or installation). —*v.i.* **7.** to issue an order or orders. **8.** to be in charge; have authority. **9.** to occupy a dominating position; look down upon or over a body of water, region, etc. —*n.* **10.** the act of commanding or ordering. **11.** an order given by one in authority: *The colonel gave the command to attack.* **12.** *Mil.* **a.** an order in prescribed words, usually given in a loud voice to troops at close order drill: *The command was "Right shoulder arms!"* **b.** the order of execution or the second part of any two-part close order drill command, as *face* in *Right face!* **c.** (*cap.*) a principal component of the U.S. Air Force: *Strategic Air Command.* **d.** a body of troops or an area, station, etc., under a commander. **13.** the possession or exercise of controlling authority: *a lieutenant in command of a platoon.* **14.** control; mastery: *He has a command of French, Russian, and German.* **15.** *Brit.* a royal invitation. **16.** power of dominating a region by reason of location; extent of view or outlook: *the command of the valley from the hill.* **17.** *Computer Technol.* **a.** an electric impulse, signal, or set of signals for initiating an operation in a computer. **b.** a character, symbol, or item of information for instructing a computer to perform a specific task. **c.** a single instruction. —*adj.* **18.** of, pertaining to, or for use in the exercise of command: *a command car; command post.* **19.** of or pertaining to a commander: *a command decision.* **20.** ordered by a sovereign, as if by a sovereign, or by the exigencies of a situation: *a command performance; a command investigation into the security leak.* [ME *coma(u)nd(en)* < MF *commande(r)* < ML *commandāre,* equiv. to L *com-* COM- + *mandāre* to entrust, order; see MANDATE] —**command′a·ble,** *adj.* —**com·mand′less,** *adj.*

—**Syn. 1.** bid, demand, charge, instruct, enjoin. See **direct. 3.** govern, control, oversee, manage, lead. See **rule. 4.** exact, compel, require, claim, secure. **10.** direction, bidding, injunction, charge, mandate, instruction. **14.** ascendancy, sway, domination. —**Ant. 1, 7.** obey.

com·man·dant (kom′ən dant′, -dänt′), *n.* **1.** the commanding officer of a place, group, etc.: *the commandant of a naval base.* **2.** the title of the senior officer and head of the U.S. Marine Corps. **3.** *U.S. Army.* a title generally given to the heads of military schools. **4.** a commander. [< F, n. use of prp. of *commander* to COMMAND; see -ANT]

command′ car′, *Mil.* a vehicle, as an armored car designed for this purpose or a jeep, for use on reconnaissance and other missions, by a commander and his staff.

com·man·deer (kom′ən dēr′), *v.t.* **1.** to order or force into active military service. **2.** to seize (private property) for military or other public use: *The police officer commandeered a taxi and took off after the getaway car.* **3.** to seize arbitrarily. [< SAfrD *kommandeer* < F *commander* to COMMAND]

com·mand·er (kə man′dər, -män′-), *n.* **1.** a person who commands. **2.** a person who exercises authority; a leader; chief officer. **3.** the commissioned officer in command of a military unit. **4.** *U.S. Navy.* an officer ranking below a captain and above a lieutenant commander. **5.** a police officer in charge of a precinct or other unit. **6.** the chief officer of a commandery in the medieval orders of Knights Hospitalers, Knights Templars, and others. **7.** a member of one of the higher classes or ranks in certain modern fraternal orders, as in the Knights Templars. [ME < OF *comandere* < *comand-* COMMAND + *-ere* < L *-ātor* -ATOR] —**com·mand′er·ship′,** *n.*

comman′der in chief′, *pl.* **commanders in chief. 1.** Also, **Comman′der in Chief′.** the supreme commander of the armed forces of a nation or, sometimes, of several allied nations: *The President is the Commander in Chief of the Army, Navy, and Air Force.* **2.** an officer in command of a particular portion of an armed force who has been given this title by specific authorization.

com·mand·er·y (kə man′də rē, -män′-), *n., pl.* **-er·ies. 1.** the office or rank of a commander. **2.** the district of a commander. **3.** a district controlled by a commander of certain medieval orders of knights. **4.** a local branch or lodge of certain secret or fraternal orders. [COMMANDER + -Y[3]]

command′ guid′ance, *Electronics.* a guidance system for a missile, in which commands or signals for controlling the flight of the vehicle originate from a source on the ground or in another vehicle (distinguished from *inertial guidance*).

com·mand·ing (kə man′ding, -män′-), *adj.* **1.** having the air, tone, etc., of command; imposing; authoritative: *a man of commanding appearance; a commanding voice.* **2.** dominating by position, usually elevation; overlooking: *a commanding bluff at the mouth of the river.* **3.** (of a view, or prospect) provided by a commanding location and so permitting dominance: *a commanding view of the mouth of the river.* **4.** being in command: *a commanding officer.* —**com·mand′ing·ly,** *adv.* —**com·mand′ing·ness,** *n.* [ME; see COMMAND, -ING[2]]

command′ing of′ficer, *U.S. Army.* a commander of any rank from second lieutenant to colonel.

com·mand·ment (kə mand′mənt, -mänd′-), *n.* **1.** a command or mandate. **2.** any of the Ten Commandments. **3.** the act or power of commanding. [ME *com(m)and(e)ment* < OF *com(m)andement.* See COMMAND, -MENT]

com·man·do (kə man′dō, -män′-), *n., pl.* **-dos, -does. 1.** (in World War II) **a.** any of the specially trained allied military units used for surprise, hit-and-run raids against Axis forces. **b.** *Chiefly U.S.* a member of any of these units. Cf. **ranger** (def. 3). **2.** any military unit organized for operations similar to those of the commandos of World War II. **3.** *South Africa.* an armed force raised for service against marauders. [< SAfrD *kommando* a unit of militia < D *commando* command < Sp *comando,* equiv. to *comand-* COMMAND + *-o* n. ending]

command′ pa′per, a British government document or report submitted to Parliament by a minister on command of the Crown, usually on an important issue or on the work of some department or special committee.

command′ perform′ance, a performance of a play, opera, ballet, or the like, given at the request of a sovereign.

command′ pi′lot, *U.S. Air Force.* the highest aeronautical qualification, awarded to a pilot with at least 15 years of flying experience and 3000 hours of flying time as a pilot or copilot.

command′ post′, *U.S. Army.* the headquarters of the commander of a military unit.

com′ma splice′, *Gram.* See **comma fault.**

com·meas·ur·a·ble (kə mezh′ər ə bəl), *adj.* having the same measure; commensurate. [COM- + MEASURABLE]

com·meas·ure (kə mezh′ər), *v.t.,* **-ured, -ur·ing.** to equal in measure; be coextensive with. [COM- + MEASURE]

comme ci, comme ça (kôm sē′ kôm SA′), *French.* so-so; neither good nor bad. [lit., like this, like that]

com·me·dia dell'ar·te (kə mā′dē ə del är′tē; *It.* kôm me′dyä del lär′te), *pl.* **com·me·di·a dell'ar·tes, com·me·di·as dell'ar·te,** *It.* **com·me·die dell'ar·te** (kôm me′dye del lär′te). Italian popular comedy, developed chiefly during the 16th–18th centuries, in which masked entertainers improvised from a plot outline based on themes associated with stock characters and situations. [< It: lit., comedy of art]

comme il faut (kô mēl fō′; *Eng.* kum′ ēl fō′), *French.* as it should be; proper; fitting; fittingly. [< F]

com·mem·o·rate (kə mem′ə rāt′), *v.t.,* **-rat·ed, -rat·ing. 1.** to serve as a memento or reminder of: *The monument commemorates the signing of the Declaration of Independence.* **2.** to honor the memory of by some observation or celebration: *to commemorate the dead by a moment of silence; to commemorate soldiers killed in the war; to commemorate Bastille Day.* **3.** to make honorable mention of. [< L *commemorāt(us)* (ptp. of *commemorāre*), equiv. to *com-* COM- + *memor* mindful + *-ātus* -ATE[1]] —**com·mem′o·ra·ble,** *adj.* —**com·mem′o·ra′tor,** *n.*

com·mem·o·ra·tion (kə mem′ə rā′shən), *n.* **1.** the act of commemorating. **2.** a service, celebration, etc., in memory of some person or event. **3.** a memorial. **4.** (in many Christian churches) a special service or prayer for commemorating the lesser feast on days on which two feasts of unequal rank are celebrated. [< L *commemorātiōn-* (s. of *commemorātiō*), equiv. to *commemorāt(us)* (see COMMEMORATE) + *-iōn-* -ION] —**com·mem′o·ra′tion·al,** *adj.*

com·mem·o·ra·tive (kə mem′ə rā′tiv, -ər ə tiv), *adj.* **1.** serving to commemorate: *a commemorative monument; a commemorative dinner.* **2.** (of a coin, medal, or postage stamp) issued to commemorate a historical event or to honor the memory of a personage. —*n.* **3.** anything that commemorates. [COMMEMORAT(ION) + -IVE] —**com·mem′o·ra′tive·ly,** *adv.* —**com·mem′o·ra′tive·ness,** *n.*

com·mem·o·ra·to·ry (kə mem′ər ə tôr′ē, -tōr′ē), *adj.* commemorative (def. 1). [COMMEMORATE + -ORY[1]]

com·mence (kə mens′), *v.i., v.t.,* **-menced, -menc·ing.** to begin; start. [ME *comenci, comence* < MF *comenc(er)* < VL **cominitiāre,* equiv. to L *com-* COM- + *initiāre* to begin; see INITIATE] —**com·mence′a·ble,** *adj.* —**com·menc′er,** *n.*

—**Syn.** originate, inaugurate. See **begin.** —**Ant.** finish, end.

com·mence·ment (kə mens′mənt), *n.* **1.** an act or instance of commencing; beginning: *He was there at the commencement of hostilities.* **2.** (in schools, universities, colleges, etc.) the ceremony of conferring degrees or granting diplomas at the end of the academic year. **3.** the day on which this ceremony takes place. [ME < OF. See COMMENCE, -MENT]

com·mend (kə mend′), *v.t.* **1.** to present or mention as worthy of confidence, notice, kindness, etc.; recommend: *to commend a friend to another; to commend an applicant for employment.* **2.** to entrust; give in charge; deliver with confidence: *I commend my child to your care.* **3.** to cite or name with approval or special praise: *to commend a soldier for bravery.* **4.** *Feudal Law.* to place (oneself or one's land) under another's protection so as to become his vassal. **5.** *Archaic.* to recommend (a person) to the kind remembrance of another. [ME *commend(e)* < L *commend(āre),* equiv. to *com-* COM- + *-mendāre,* comb. form of *mandāre;* see MANDATE] —**com·mend′a·ble,** *adj.* —**com·mend′a·ble·ness,** *n.* —**com·mend′a·bly,** *adv.* —**com·mend′er,** *n.* —**com·mend′ing·ly,** *adv.*

—**Syn. 1.** praise, laud, extol, applaud. See **approve.** —**Ant. 1.** censure.

com·men·dam (kə men′dam), *n. Eccles.* **1.** the tenure of a benefice to be held until the appointment of a regular incumbent, the benefice being said to be held *in commendam.* **2.** a benefice so held. [< ML, short for (*dare*) *in commendam* (to give) in trust; *commendam,* acc. sing. of *commenda,* back formation from L *commendāre* to COMMEND]

com·men·da·tion (kom′ən dā′shən), *n.* **1.** the act of commending; recommendation; praise: *to earn commendation for a job well done.* **2.** something that commends: *The soldier received a commendation for bravery.* **3.** *Feudal Law.* the placing of oneself or one's land under the protection of a lord so as to become his vassal. **4. commendations,** *Archaic.* complimentary greeting. [ME *commendaciun* < eccl. L *commendātiōn-* (s. of *commendātiō*) a commending to God, L. See COMMEND, -ATION]

—**Syn. 1.** approval, approbation, applause. **2.** eulogy, encomium, panegyric, laudation. —**Ant. 1, 2.** condemnation.

com·mend·a·to·ry (kə men′də tôr′ē, -tōr′ē), *adj.* **1.** serving to commend; approving; praising. **2.** holding a benefice in commendam. **3.** held in commendam. [< LL *commendātōri(us),* equiv. to *commendāt(us)* (ptp. of *commendāre* to COMMEND; see -ATE[1]) + *-ōrius* -ORY[1]]

com·men·sal (kə men′səl), *adj.* **1.** eating together at the same table. **2.** (of an animal or plant) living with, on, or in another, without injury to either. **3.** *Sociol.* (of a person or group) not competing while residing in or occupying the same area as another individual or group having independent or different values or customs. —*n.* **4.** a companion at table. **5.** a commensal animal or plant. [late ME < ML *commensāl(is).* See COM-, MENSAL[2]] —**com·men′sal·ism,** *n.* —**com·men·sal·i·ty** (kom′en sal′i tē), *n.* —**com·men′sal·ly,** *adv.*

com·men·su·ra·ble (kə men′sər ə bəl, -shər ə-), *adj.* **1.** having a common measure or divisor: *The numbers 6 and 9 are commensurable since they are divisible by 3.* **2.** suitable in measure; proportionate. [< LL *commēnsūrābil(is),* equiv. to L *com-* COM- + *mēnsūrābilis,* equiv. to *mēnsūrā(re)* (see COMMENSURATE) + *-bilis* -BLE)] —**com·men′su·ra·bil′i·ty, com·men′su·ra·ble·ness,** *n.* —**com·men′su·ra·bly,** *adv.*

com·men·su·rate (kə men′sər it, -shər-), *adj.* **1.** having the same measure; of equal extent or duration. **2.** corresponding in amount, magnitude, or degree: *Your paycheck should be commensurate with the amount of time worked.* **3.** proportionate; adequate. **4.** having a common measure; commensurable. [< LL *commēnsūrāt(us),* equiv. to L *com-* COM- + *mēnsūrātus* (ptp. of *mēnsūrāre*), see MEASURE, -ATE[1]] —**com·men′su·rate·ly,** *adv.* —**com·men′su·rate·ness,** *n.* —**com·men·su·ra·tion** (kə men′sə rā′shən, -shə-), *n.*

com·ment (kom′ent), *n.* **1.** a note in explanation, expansion, or criticism of a passage in a book, article, or the like; an annotation. **2.** explanatory or critical matter added to a text. **3.** a remark, observation, or criticism: *a comment about the weather.* **4.** a criticism or interpretation, often by implication or suggestion: *The play is a comment on modern society.* —*v.i.* **5.** to write explanatory or critical notes upon a text. **6.** to make remarks: *He commented humorously about her hat.* —*v.t.* **7.** to make comments or remarks on; furnish with comments. [late ME *coment* < L *comment(um)* invention, contrivance, comment, n. use of neut. of *commentus* (ptp. of *comminīscī* to devise), equiv. to *com-* COM- + *men-* (s. of *mēns, mentis* MIND) + *-tus* ptp. ending] —**com′ment·a·ble,** *adj.* —**com′ment·er,** *n.*

—**Syn. 1.** addendum, commentary. **3.** See **remark. 5.** annotate, elucidate.

com·ment al·lez-vous (kô mäN tA lā vōō′), *French.* how are you?

com·men·tar·y (kom′ən ter′ē), *n., pl.* **-tar·ies. 1.** a series of comments, explanations, or annotations: *a commentary on the Bible.* **2.** an explanatory essay or treatise: *a commentary on a play; Blackstone's commentaries on law.* **3.** anything serving to illustrate a point; comment. **4.** *Usually,* **commentaries.** records of facts or events: *Commentaries written by Roman lawyers give us information on how their courts functioned.* [< L *commentāri(um)* notebook, n. use of neut. of *commentāri(us),* equiv. to *comment(um)* COMMENT + *-ārius* -ARY] —**com·men·tar·i·al** (kom′ən târ′ē əl), *adj.*

com·men·ta·tor (kom′ən tā′tər), *n.* **1.** a person who makes commentaries. **2.** a person who discusses news, sports events, weather, or the like, as on the radio or television. [late ME < LL, equiv. to *commentāt(us)* (ptp. of *commentārī* to study, discuss, write upon), COMMENT, -ATE[1]) + -OR[2]] —**com·men·ta·to·ri·al** (kə men′tə tôr′ē əl, -tōr′-), *adj.* —**com·men′ta·to′ri·al·ly,** *adv.*

com·ment ça va? (kô mäN SA VA′), *French.* how are you? [lit., how goes it?]

com·merce (kom′ərs), *n.* **1.** an interchange of goods or commodities, esp. on a large scale between different countries (**for′eign com′merce**) or between different parts of the same country (**domes′tic com′merce**); trade; business. **2.** social relations, esp. the exchange of views, attitudes, etc. **3.** sexual intercourse. **4.** intellectual or spiritual interchange; communion. [< MF <

L *commerc(ium)*, equiv. to *commerc(ārī)* (to) trade together (*com-* COM- + *mercārī*, deriv. of *merc-*, s. of *merx* goods) + *-ium* n. suffix]
—Syn. 1. See **trade.**

Com·merce (kom′ərs), *n.* **1.** a town in SW California. 9555 (1960). **2.** a town in NE Texas. 5789 (1960). **3.** a town in central Georgia. 3551 (1960).

Com′merce Town′, a town in central Colorado. 8970 (1960).

com·mer·cial (kə mûr′shəl), *adj.* **1.** of, pertaining to, or characteristic of commerce. **2.** engaged in commerce. **3.** prepared, done, or acting with sole or chief emphasis on salability, profit, or success: *a commercial product; His attitude toward theater is very commercial.* **4.** (of an airplane, airline, or flight) **a.** engaged in transporting passengers or goods for profit. **b.** civilian and public, as distinguished from military or private. **5.** not entirely or chemically pure: *commercial soda.* **6.** catering especially to traveling salesmen by offering reduced rates, space for exhibiting products, etc.: *a commercial hotel.* **—*n.* 7.** *Radio and Television.* a brief announcement or visual presentation designed as an advertisement. **8.** *Brit. Informal.* a traveling salesman. [COMMERCE + -IAL] **—com·mer′cial·ly,** *adv.*
—Syn. 1. COMMERCIAL, MERCANTILE refer to the activities of business, industry, and trade. COMMERCIAL is the broader term, covering all the activities and relationships of industry and trade. In a derogatory sense it may mean such a preoccupation with the affairs of commerce as results in indifference to considerations other than wealth: *commercial treaties; a merely commercial viewpoint.* MERCANTILE applies to the purchase and sale of goods, or to the transactions of business: *a mercantile house or class.*

commer′cial a′gency, a concern which investigates for the benefit of its subscribers the financial standing, reputation, and credit rating of individuals, firms, corporations, and others engaged in business.

commer′cial art′, graphic art created specifically for commercial uses, esp. for advertising, illustrations in magazines or books, or the like. Cf. **fine art. —commer′cial art′ist.**

commer′cial attaché′, an attaché in an embassy or legation representing the commercial interests of his country.

commer′cial bank′, a bank specializing in checking accounts and short-term loans.

commer′cial code′, a telegraphic code designed to convey a message with a minimum number of words and thereby reduce toll costs.

commer′cial col′lege, a school that trains people for careers in business.

commer′cial cred′it, credit issued by a bank to a business to finance trading or manufacturing operations.

commer′cial fer′tilizer, fertilizer manufactured chemically, as distinguished from natural fertilizer, as manure.

com·mer·cial·ise (kə mûr′shə līz′), *v.t.*, **-ised, -is·ing.** *Chiefly Brit.* commercialize. **—com·mer′cial·i·sa′tion,** *n.*

com·mer·cial·ism (kə mûr′shə liz′əm), *n.* **1.** the principles, practices, and spirit of commerce. **2.** a commercial attitude in noncommercial affairs; inappropriate or excessive emphasis on profit, success, or immediate results. **3.** a commercial custom or expression. [COMMERCIAL + -ISM] **—com·mer′cial·ist,** *n.* **—com·mer′cial·is′tic,** *adj.*

com·mer·cial·ize (kə mûr′shə līz′), *v.t.*, **-ized, -iz·ing.** **1.** to make commercial in character, methods, or spirit. **2.** to emphasize the profitable aspects of. **3.** to offer for sale; make available as a commodity. Also, *esp. Brit.*, **commercialise.** [COMMERCIAL + -IZE] **—com·mer′cial·i·za′tion,** *n.*

commer′cial law′, the legal regulations governing transactions and related matters in business and trade.

commer′cial pa′per, negotiable paper, as drafts, bills of exchange, etc., given in the course of business.

commer′cial pi′lot, an airplane pilot employed to transport passengers, goods, etc., esp. one who is specially licensed by the government on the basis of competence and experience.

commer′cial trav′eler. See **traveling salesman.**

com·mie[1] (kom′ē), *n.* *Dial.* a playing marble, esp. one that is not used as a shooter. [by shortening and alter.; see COMMON, for common marble]

com·mie[2] (kom′ē), *n., adj.* (*often cap.*) *Informal.* communist. [by shortening and alter.]

com·mi·nate (kom′ə nāt′), *v.t., v.i.*, **-nat·ed, -nat·ing.** **1.** to threaten with divine punishment or vengeance. **2.** to curse; anathematize. [back formation from COMMINATION]

com·mi·na·tion (kom′ə nā′shən), *n.* **1.** a threat of punishment or vengeance. **2.** a denunciation. **3.** (in the Church of England) a penitential office read on Ash Wednesday in which God's anger and judgments are proclaimed against sinners. [< L *comminātiōn-* (s. of *comminātiō*), equiv. to *comminät(us)*, ptp. of *commināri* (*com-* COM- + *min(ae)* threats + *-ātus* -ATE[1]) + *-iōn-* -ION] **—com′mi·na′tor,** *n.* **—com·min·a·to·ry** (kə min′ə tôr′ē, -tōr′ē, kom′in ə-), **com′mi·na′tive,** *adj.*

Com·mines (kô mēn′), *n.* **Phi·lippe de** (fē lēp′ də). See **Comines, Philippe de.**

com·min·gle (kə ming′gəl), *v.t., v.i.*, **-gled, -gling.** to mix or mingle together; combine. [COM- + MINGLE] **—com·min′gler,** *n.*

com·mi·nute (kom′ə no͞ot′, -nyo͞ot′), *v.*, **-nut·ed, -nut·ing,** *adj.* **—*v.t.* 1.** to pulverize; triturate. **—*adj.* 2.** comminuted; divided into small parts. **3.** powdered; pulverized. [< L *comminūt(us)*, ptp. of *comminuere*, equiv. to *com-* COM- + *minuere* to lessen, akin to *minor* MINOR] **—com′mi·nu′tion,** *n.*

com′minuted frac′ture, a fracture of a bone in which the separated parts are splintered or fragmented. See illus. under **fracture.**

com·mis·ce (ko mis′ē), *v.* (in prescriptions) mix together (usually used imperatively). [< L]

com·mis·er·ate (kə miz′ə rāt′), *v.*, **-at·ed, -at·ing.** **—*v.t.* 1.** to feel or express sorrow or sympathy for; pity. **—*v.i.* 2.** to sympathize; condole (usually fol. by *with*): *They commiserated with him over the loss of his wife.* [< L *commiserāt(us)* (ptp. of *commiserārī*), equiv. to *com-* COM- + *miser* pitiable + *-ātus* -ATE[1]] **—com·mis′er·a·ble,** *adj.* **—com·mis′er·a′tion,** *n.* **—com·mis′er·a′tive,** *adj.* **—com·mis′er·a′tive·ly,** *adv.* **—com·mis′er·a′tor,** *n.*

com·mis·sar (kom′i sär′, kom′i sär′), *n.* **1.** the head of any of the major governmental divisions of the U.S.S.R.: called *minister* since 1946. **2.** an official in any communist government whose duties include political indoctrination, detection of political deviation, etc. [< Russ *Kommissar* < G < ML *commissār(ius)* COMMISSARY]

com·mis·sar·i·at (kom′i sâr′ē ət), *n.* **1.** any of the major governmental divisions of the U.S.S.R.: called *ministry* since 1946. **2.** the organized method or manner by which food, equipment, transport, etc., is delivered to armies. **3.** the department of an army charged with supplying provisions. [< NL *commissāriāt(us)*, equiv. to ML *commissāri(us)* COMMISSARY + *-ātus* -ATE[1]]

com·mis·sar·y (kom′i ser′ē), *n., pl.* **-sar·ies.** **1.** a store that supplies food and equipment, esp. in an army, mining camp, or lumber camp. **2.** a dining room or cafeteria, esp. one in a motion-picture studio. **3.** a person to whom some responsibility or role is delegated by a superior power; a deputy. **4.** *Eccles.* an officer who, by delegation from the bishop, exercises spiritual jurisdiction in remote parts of a diocese, or is entrusted with the performance of duties of the bishop in his absence. **5.** commissar. **6.** (in France) a police official, usually just below the police chief and mayor. **7.** *Mil. Obs.* an officer of the commissariat. [late ME *commissarie* < ML *commissāri(us)*, equiv. to L *commiss(us)* (ptp. of *committere* to COMMIT) + *-ārius* -ARY] **—com·mis·sar·i·al** (kom′i sâr′ē əl), *adj.*

com·mis·sion (kə mish′ən), *n.* **1.** the act of committing or giving in charge. **2.** an authoritative order, charge, or direction. **3.** authority granted for a particular action or function. **4.** *U.S.* **a.** a document conferring authority issued by the President of the U.S. to officers in the Army, Navy, and other military services, and by State governments to justices of the peace and others. **b.** the power thus granted. **c.** the position or rank of an officer in any of the armed forces. **5.** a group of persons authoritatively charged with particular functions: *a park commission.* **6.** the condition of being placed under special authoritative responsibility or charge. **7.** a task or matter committed to one's charge: *The designer received a commission to design an office building.* **8.** the act of committing or perpetrating a crime, error, etc.: *The commission of a misdemeanor is punishable by law.* **9.** something that is committed. **10.** authority to act as agent for another or others in commercial transactions. **11.** a sum or percentage allowed to an agent, salesman, etc., for his services: *to work on a twenty percent commission.* **12. in commission, a.** in service. **b.** in operating order: *A great deal of work will be necessary to put this radio in commission again.* **c.** Also, **into commission.** *Navy.* (of a ship) manned and in condition for or ordered to active service. **13. out of commission, a.** not in service. **b.** not in operating order: *The stove is out of commission.* **—*v.t.* 14.** to give a commission to: *to commission a graduate of a military academy.* **15.** to authorize; send on a mission. **16.** to give the order which places a warship, military command, etc., in a state of complete readiness for active duty. **17.** to give a commission or order for: *The owners commissioned a painting for the building's lobby.* [ME < L *commissiōn-* (s. of *commissiō*) a committing. See COM-, MISSION, COMMIT] **—com·mis′sion·al,** *adj.* **—com·mis′sive,** *adj.* **—com·mis′sive·ly,** *adv.*

com·mis·sion·aire (kə mish′ə nâr′), *n.* *Brit.* a person who does small, miscellaneous errands or performs minor services, as a messenger, porter, etc. [< F *commissionnaire*, equiv. to *commission* COMMISSION + *-aire* -ER[2]]

commis′sioned of′ficer, a military or naval officer holding rank by commission (including, in the U.S., second lieutenants, ensigns, and all higher ranks).

com·mis·sion·er (kə mish′ə nər), *n.* **1.** a person commissioned to act officially; a member of a commission. **2.** a government official or representative in charge of a department or district: *the police commissioner; the commissioner of a colony.* **3.** an official chosen by an athletic association to exercise broad administrative or judicial authority: *the baseball commissioner.* **4.** *Slang.* a betting broker. [late ME *comyscioner.* See COMMISSION, -ER[2]] **—com·mis′sion·er·ship′,** *n.*

Commis′sioners Stand′ard Or′dinary Ta′ble, *U.S.* a mortality table used as a minimum standard for reserves and surrender values by most life-insurance companies, based on the combined experience of a large number of insurers for the period 1950–54 and accepted in 1958 after comparison with the experience of a smaller number of insurers for the period 1954–57. *Abbr.:* CSO, C.S.O.

commis′sion house′, a brokerage firm that buys and sells securities on commission for its clients.

commis′sion mer′chant, an agent who receives goods for sale on a commission basis or who buys on this basis and has the goods delivered to a principal.

commis′sion pen′nant, a long pennant flown at the mainmast of a commissioned government ship.

commis′sion plan′, a system of municipal government in which all the legislative and executive powers of the city are concentrated in the hands of a commission.

com·mis·sure (kom′i sho͝or′), *n.* **1.** a joint; seam; suture. **2.** *Bot.* the joint or face by which one carpel coheres with another. **3.** *Anat., Zool.* a connecting band, as of nerve tissue, etc. [late ME < L *commissūr(a)*, equiv. to *commiss-* (see COMMISSARY) + *-ūra* -URE] **—com·mis·su·ral** (kə mish′ər əl, kom′i sho͝or′əl, -so͝or′-), *adj.*

Commissure (def. 2) AB, Line of the commissural faces of the two carpels

com·mis·sur·ot·o·my (kom′i shə rot′ə mē), *n., pl.* **-mies.** *Surg.* the incision of a band of commissures, esp. of mitral fibers. Cf. **valvulotomy.** [COMMISSURE + -o- + -TOMY]

com·mit (kə mit′), *v.t.*, **-mit·ted, -mit·ting.** **1.** to give in trust or charge; consign. **2.** to consign for preservation: *to commit to writing, memory, etc.* **3.** to consign to custody: *to commit a delinquent to a reformatory.* **4.** to send into a battle: *The commander has committed all his troops to the front lines.* **5.** to pledge (oneself) to a position on an issue or question; express (one's intention, feeling, etc.): *Asked if he was a candidate, he refused to commit himself.* **6.** to place in a mental institution or hospital by or as if by legal authority: *He was committed on the certificate of two psychiatrists.* **7.** to bind or obligate, as by pledge or assurance; pledge: *to commit oneself to a promise; to be committed to a course of action.* **8.** to entrust, esp. for safekeeping; commend: *to commit one's soul to God.* **9.** to deliver for treatment, disposal, etc.: *to commit a manuscript to the flames.* **10.** to do; perform; perpetrate: *to commit murder, an error, etc.* **11.** *Parl. Proc.* to refer (a bill or the like) to a committee for consideration. [ME *committe* < L *committe(re)*, equiv. to *com-* COM- + *mittere* to send, give over] **—com·mit′ta·ble,** *adj.* **—com·mit′ter,** *n.*

com·mit·ment (kə mit′mənt), *n.* **1.** the act of committing. **2.** the state of being committed. **3.** *Parl. Proc.* the act of referring or entrusting to a committee for consideration. **4.** consignment, as to prison. **5.** confinement to a mental institution or hospital: *The psychiatrist recommended commitment as the wisest course.* **6.** an order, as by a court, judge, etc., confining a person to a mental institution or hospital: *He was released because his commitment was issued without a hearing.* **7.** *Law.* a written order of a court directing that someone be confined in prison; mittimus. **8.** perpetration or commission, as of a crime. **9.** the act of committing, pledging, or engaging oneself. **10.** a pledge or promise; obligation: *We have made a commitment to pay our bills on time.* **11.** engagement; involvement: *They have a sincere commitment to religion.* **12.** *Stock Exchange.* **a.** an agreement to buy or sell securities. **b.** a sale or purchase of securities. Also, **committal** (for defs. 1, 3–11). [COMMIT + -MENT]

com·mit·tal (kə mit′əl), *n.* an act or instance of committing, as to an institution, a cause, the grave, etc.; commitment: *The committal of large sums of money to the party aided the candidate immensely.* [COMMIT + -AL[2]]

com·mit·tee (kə mit′ē), *n.* **1.** a person or group of persons elected or appointed to perform some service or function, as to investigate, report on, or act upon a particular matter. **2.** See **standing committee.** **3.** *Law.* a person to whom the care of a person or his estate is committed. [late ME < AF, equiv. to *committ* (< E; see COMMIT) + *-ee* -EE] **—com·mit′tee·ism, com·mit′tee·ship′,** *n.*

com·mit·tee·man (kə mit′ē mən, -man′), *n., pl.* **-men** (-mən, -men′). **1.** a member of a committee. **2.** the leader of a political ward or precinct. **3.** See **shop steward.** [COMMITTEE + MAN[1]]

commit′tee of correspond′ence, (during the American Revolutionary period) a committee appointed by a town or colony to communicate or coordinate the measures taken toward redress of grievances.

commit′tee of one′, an individual designated to function alone as a committee.

commit′tee of the whole′, a legislative body consisting of all the members present, sitting in a deliberative rather than a legislative capacity, for informal debate and preliminary consideration of matters awaiting legislative action.

com·mit·tee·wom·an (kə mit′ē wo͝om′ən), *n., pl.* **-wom·en.** a woman serving as a member of a committee. [COMMITTEE + WOMAN]

com·mix (kə miks′), *v.t., v.i.* to mix together; blend. [back formation from earlier *commixt* < L *commixt(us)* (ptp. of *commiscēre*), equiv. to *com-* COM- + *mix-* (var. s. of *miscēre* to mix) + *-tus* ptp. ending]

com·mix·ture (kə miks′chər), *n.* **1.** the act or process of commixing or the condition of being commixed; mixture. **2.** (in a Eucharistic service) the placing of a part of the Host in the chalice. [< L *commixtūr(a)*, equiv. to *commixt(us)* (see COMMIX) + *-ūra* -URE]

Commode

com·mode (kə mōd′), *n.* **1.** a low cabinet or similar piece of furniture, often highly ornamental, containing drawers or shelves. **2.** a stand or cupboard containing a chamber pot or washbasin. **3.** toilet (def. 1). **4.** an elaborate headdress consisting chiefly of a high framework decorated with lace, ribbons, etc., worn by women in the late 17th and early 18th centuries. [< F < L *commod(us)* convenient, equiv. to *com-* COM- + *modus* MODE[1]]

commode′ step′, any of two or more bottom steps of a stair that have curved ends surrounding a newel.

com·mo·di·ous (kə mō′dē əs), *adj.* **1.** spacious and convenient; roomy: *a commodious apartment.* **2.** ample or adequate for the purpose: *a commodious harbor.* [late ME < ML *commodiōs(us)*, equiv. to L *commodi(tās)* convenience (see COMMODITY) + *-ōsus* -OUS] **—com·mo′di·ous·ly,** *adv.* **—com·mo′di·ous·ness,** *n.*

com·mod·i·ty (kə mod′i tē), *n., pl.* **-ties.** **1.** something of use, advantage, or value. **2.** an article of trade or commerce, esp. a product as distinguished from a service. **3.** *Obs.* a quantity of goods. [late ME *commodite* < MF < L *commoditāt-* (s. of *commoditās*), equiv. to *commod(us)* (see COMMODE) + *-itāt-* -ITY]

commod′ity dol′lar, *U.S.* a proposed currency unit whose gold content would vary with fluctuations in an official index of commodity prices.

commod′ity exchange′, an exchange for the buying and selling of commodities (such as butter, coffee, sugar, and grains) for future delivery.

Commod′ity Ex′change Author′ity, *U.S. Govt.* the division of the Department of Agriculture that supervises the trading of futures on commodity exchanges. *Abbr.:* CEA

commod′ity mon′ey, *U.S.* a proposed form of currency using commodity dollars as units.

com·mo·dore (kom′ə dôr′, -dōr′), *n.* **1.** *U.S. Navy.* (not used in peacetime) a grade of flag officer next in rank below a rear admiral. **2.** *Brit. Navy.* an officer in temporary command of a squadron, sometimes over a captain on the same ship. **3.** *Navy.* the senior captain when two or more ships of war are cruising in company. **4.** (in the U.S. Navy and Merchant Marine) the officer in command of a convoy. **5.** the senior captain of a line of merchant vessels. **6.** the president or head of a yacht club or boat club. [var. of *commandore,* equiv. to COMMAND + *-ore,* unexplained var. of -OR[2]]

Com·mo·dus (kom′ə dəs), *n.* **Lucius Ae·li·us Aureli·us** (ē′lē əs), A.D. 161–192, Roman emperor 180–192; son and successor of Marcus Aurelius.

com·mon (kom′ən), *adj.* **1.** belonging equally to, or shared alike by, two or more or all in question: *common property; common interests.* **2.** pertaining or belonging equally to an entire community, nation, or culture; public: *a common language or history; a common water-supply system.* **3.** joint; united: *a common defense.* **4.** widely and unfavorably known; notorious: *a common thief.* **5.** widespread; general; ordinary: *common knowledge.* **6.** of frequent occurrence; usual; familiar: *a common event; a common mistake.* **7.** hackneyed; trite. **8.** of mediocre or inferior quality; mean; low: *a rough-textured suit of the most common fabric.* **9.** coarse; vulgar: *common manners.* **10.** having no rank, station, distinction, etc.; ordinary: *a common soldier; a common person.* **11.** *Anat.* forming or formed by two or more parts or branches: *the common carotid arteries.* **12.** *Pros.* (of a syllable) able to be considered as either long or short. **13.** *Gram.* **a.** not belonging to an inflectional paradigm; fulfilling different functions which in some languages require different inflected forms: *English nouns are in the common case whether used as subject or object.* **b.** constituting one of two genders of a language, esp. a gender comprising nouns that were formerly masculine or feminine: *Swedish nouns are either common or neuter.* **c.** noting a word that may refer to either a male or a female: *French* élève *has common gender. English lacks a common gender pronoun in the third person singular.* **d.** (of a noun) belonging to the common gender. **14.** *Math.* bearing a similar relation to two or more entities. —*n.* **15.** Often, **commons.** a tract of land owned or used jointly by the members of a community, usually a park in a city or town. **16.** *Law.* the right or liberty, in common with other persons, to take profit from the land or waters of another, as by pasturing animals on another's land (**com′mon of pas′turage**) or fishing in another's waters (**com′mon of pis′cary**). **17. commons, a.** the commonalty; the nonruling class. **b.** the body of people not of noble birth or not ennobled, as represented in England by the House of Commons. **c.** (*cap.*) the representatives of this body. **d.** (*cap.*) the elective house of the Parliament of Great Britain and Northern Ireland, Canada, and various other countries in the British Commonwealth of Nations. **e.** *Brit.* food provided at a common table, as in some colleges. **f.** food or provisions for any group. **g.** a large dining room, esp. at a university. **18.** (*sometimes cap.*) *Eccles.* **a.** an office or form of service used on a festival of a particular kind. **b.** the ordinary of the Mass, esp. those parts sung by the choir. **c.** the part of the missal and breviary containing Masses and offices of those saints assigned to them. **19.** *Obs.* **a.** the community or public. **b.** the common people. **20. in common,** in joint possession or use; shared equally: *They have a love of adventure in common.* [ME *comun* < OF < L *commūn(is),* equiv. to *com-* COM- + *mūnis* serviceable, obliging, akin to MEAN[2]] —**com′mon·ness,** *n.*
—**Syn. 1.** See **mutual. 5.** universal, prevalent, popular. See **general. 6.** customary, everyday. **10.** COMMON, VULGAR, ORDINARY refer, often with derogatory connotations of cheapness or inferiority, to what is usual or most often experienced. COMMON applies to what is accustomed, usually experienced, or inferior, to the opposite of what is exclusive or aristocratic: *She is a common person.* VULGAR properly means belonging to the people, or characteristic of common people; it connotes low taste, coarseness, or ill breeding: *the vulgar view of things; vulgar in manners and speech.* ORDINARY means what is to be expected in the usual order of things; or only average, or below average: *That is a high price for something of such ordinary quality.* —**Ant. 1.** individual. **6.** unusual.

com·mon·a·ble (kom′ə nə bəl), *adj.* **1.** held jointly; for general use; public: *commonable lands.* **2.** allowed to be pastured on common land: *common cattle.* [COMMON + -ABLE]

com·mon·age (kom′ə nij), *n.* **1.** the joint use of anything, esp. a pasture. **2.** the right to such use. **3.** the state of being held in common. **4.** something that is so held, as land. **5.** the commonalty. [COMMON + -AGE]

com·mon·al·ty (kom′ə n[ə]l tē), *n., pl.* **-ties. 1.** Also, **com·mon·al·i·ty** (kom′ə nal′i tē). the ordinary people, as distinguished from those with authority, rank, station, etc.; the common people. **2.** an incorporated body or its members. [late ME < MF *comunalte,* equiv. to *comunal-* COMMUNAL + *-te* -TY[2]; r. ME *commuaute* < OF]

com′mon al′um, *Chem.* alum (def. 1).

com′mon bond′, *Masonry.* See **American bond.**

com′mon brad′, a brad having a small tapering head.

com′mon busi′ness or′iented lan′guage, *Computer Technol.* COBOL.

com′mon carot′id, *Anat.* the part of a carotid artery between its origin and its point of division into branches. Also called **com′mon carot′id ar′tery.**

com′mon car′rier, an individual or company, as a railroad or steamship line, engaged in transporting passengers or goods for profit.

com′mon coke′, a grade of hot-dipped tin plate having a coating of 1.10 pounds per base box.

com′mon cold′, cold (def. 21).

com′mon cost′, *Accounting.* costs assignable to two or more products, operations, departments, etc., of a company.

com′mon coun′cil, the local legislative body of a municipal government. —**com′mon coun′cilman.**

com′mon denom′inator, 1. *Math.* a number that is a multiple of all the denominators of a set of fractions. **2.** a trait, characteristic, belief, or the like, common to or shared by all members of a group: *Dedication to the cause of freedom was the common denominator of the American revolutionaries.*

com′mon divi′sor, *Math.* a number that is a submultiple of all the numbers of a given set. Also called **com′mon fac′tor.**

com·mon·er (kom′ə nər), *n.* **1.** one of the commonalty; a common person, as distinguished from one with rank, status, etc. **2.** *Brit.* **a.** any person ranking below a peer; a person without a title of nobility. **b.** a member of the House of Commons. **c.** (at Oxford and some other universities) a student who pays for his commons and other expenses and is not supported by any scholarship or foundation. **3.** a person who has a joint right in common land. [ME *cominer.* See COMMON, -ER[1]]

Com′mon E′ra. See **Christian Era.**

com′mon frac′tion, *Arith.* a fraction represented as a numerator above and a denominator below a horizontal or diagonal line. Also called **vulgar fraction.** Cf. **decimal fraction.**

com′mon ground′, a foundation of common interest or comprehension, as in a social relationship or a discussion: *They had difficulty finding a common ground for beginning negotiations.*

com′mon il′iac ar′tery, *Anat.* See **iliac artery** (def. 1).

com′mon law′, 1. the system of law originating in England, as distinct from the civil or Roman law and the canon or ecclesiastical law. **2.** the unwritten law, esp. of England, based on custom or court decision, as distinct from statute law. **3.** the law administered through the system of courts established for the purpose, as distinct from equity, admiralty, etc. [ME *commune lawe*]

com·mon-law (kom′ən lô′), *adj.* of, pertaining to, or established by common law: *a common-law spouse.*

com′mon-law mar′riage, a marriage without a civil or ecclesiastical marriage ceremony, generally resulting from a couple's living together as man and wife.

com′mon log′arithm, *Math.* a logarithm having 10 as the base. Also called **Briggsian logarithm.** Cf. **natural logarithm.**

com·mon·ly (kom′ən lē), *adv.* **1.** in a common manner. **2.** usually; generally; ordinarily: *George Washington is commonly regarded as the flower of 18th-century colonial gentility.* [ME *communelich.* See COMMON, -LY]

com′mon man′, a man who is not distinguished by birth, station, education, or the like; the average man.

Com′mon Mar′ket, 1. Official name, **European Economic Community.** an economic association established in 1958 and originally composed of Belgium, France, Italy, Luxembourg, the Netherlands, and West Germany, created chiefly to abolish barriers to free trade among member nations and to adopt common import duties on goods from other countries: the United Kingdom, the Republic of Ireland, and Denmark joined in 1973, Greece joined in 1981, and Spain and Portugal joined in 1986. *Abbr.:* CM **2.** (*sometimes l.c.*) any economic association of nations created for a similar purpose.

com′mon meas′ure, 1. Also called **common time.** *Music.* duple or quadruple rhythm. **2.** Also called **hymnal stanza.** *Pros.* a ballad stanza of four iambic lines and strict rhymes, often used in hymns, rhyming *abcb* or *abab.*

com′mon mul′tiple, *Math.* a number that is a multiple of all the numbers of a given set.

com′mon nail′, a cut or wire nail having a slender shaft and a broad flat head: used for framing and other work in which finish is not important.

com′mon peo′ple, those people who do not belong to the aristocracy or who lack social distinction; the masses.

com′mon pitch′er plant′, a pitcher plant, *Sarracenia purpurea,* found east of the Rocky Mountains, having green or dark purple leaves and purplish flowers: the floral emblem of Newfoundland. Also called **Indian pitcher, sidesaddle flower.**

com·mon·place (kom′ən plās′), *adj.* **1.** ordinary; undistinguished or uninteresting; without individuality: *a commonplace person.* **2.** trite; hackneyed; platitudinous: *a commonplace remark.* —*n.* **3.** a well-known, customary, or obvious remark; a trite or uninteresting saying. **4.** anything common, ordinary, or uninteresting. **5.** *Archaic.* a place or passage in a book or writing noted as important for reference or quotation. [trans. of L *locus commūnis,* itself trans. of Gk *koinòs tópos*] —**com′mon·place′ly,** *adv.* —**com′mon·place′ness,** *n.*
—**Syn. 2.** COMMONPLACE, BANAL, HACKNEYED, STEREOTYPED, TRITE describe words, remarks, and styles of expression that are lifeless and uninteresting. COMMONPLACE characterizes thought which is dull, ordinary, and platitudinous: *commonplace and boring.* Something is BANAL which seems inane, insipid, and pointless: *a heavy-handed and banal affirmation of the obvious.* HACKNEYED characterizes that which seems stale and worn out through overuse: *a hackneyed comparison.* STEREOTYPED emphasizes the fact that situations felt to be similar invariably call for the same thought in exactly the same form and the same words: *so stereotyped as to seem automatic.* TRITE describes that which was originally striking and apt, but which has become so well known and been so commonly used that all interest has been worn out of it: *true but trite.* **3.** cliché, bromide, platitude, stereotype.

com′monplace book′, a book in which noteworthy quotations, poems, comments, etc., are written.

com′mon pleas′, 1. *U.S.* any of various courts of civil jurisdiction in several States. **2.** (in England) the chief common-law court of civil jurisdiction, now merged in the King's Bench Division of the High Court.

com′mon pray′er, 1. prayer in which worshipers publicly unite, esp. the liturgy or public form of prayer prescribed by the Church of England for use in all churches and chapels in public worship. **2.** (*caps.*) See **Book of Common Prayer.**

com′mon prop′erty, 1. property belonging to all members of a community. **2.** someone or something regarded as belonging to the public in general: *She enjoyed being a star, but not feeling that she had become common property.* **3.** information that is commonly known; common knowledge: *His jealously guarded secret was soon common property.*

com′mon raft′er, a rafter having no function other than to bear roofing. Cf. **principal rafter.** See diag. under **king post.**

com′mon room′, (in institutions, esp. schools and colleges) a room or lounge for informal use by all.

com′mon rhythm′, *Pros.* See **running rhythm.**

com′mon salt′, salt (def. 1).

com′mon school′, a public school usually including both primary and secondary grades but sometimes primary grades alone.

com′mon scold′, (in early common law) a habitually rude and brawling woman whose conduct was subject to punishment as a public nuisance.

com′mon sen′nit. See **flat sennit.**

com′mon sense′, sound practical judgment that is independent of specialized knowledge, training, or the like; normal native intelligence. [trans. of L *sensus commūnis,* itself trans. of Gk *koinè aísthēsis*] —**com′mon-sense′, com′mon·sense′,** *adj.* —**com′mon·sen′si·cal, com′mon·sen′si·ble,** *adj.* —**com′mon·sen′si·cal·ly, com′mon·sen′si·bly,** *adv.*

Com′mon Sense′, a pamphlet (1776) by Thomas Paine, setting forth arguments for American independence from England.

com′monsense re′alism, *Philos.* See **naïve realism.** —**com′monsense re′alist.**

com′mon snipe′. See under **snipe** (def. 1).

com′mon stock′, stock that ordinarily has no preference in the matter of dividends or assets and represents the residual ownership of a corporate business.

com′mon sul′fur, a sulfur butterfly, *Colias philodice,* having yellow wings with black edges and larvae that feed on clover and other legumes. Also called **clouded sulfur.**

com′mon tan′nin, *Chem.* See under **tannin.**

com′mon tern′. See under **tern**[1].

com′mon time′, *Music.* See **common measure** (def. 1).

com′mon to′paz, topaz (def. 3).

com′mon touch′, the ability to communicate with, appeal to, or inspire ordinary or common people: *a politician with enough of the common touch to make him a success.*

com·mon·weal (kom′ən wēl′), *n.* **1.** the common welfare; the public good. **2.** *Archaic.* the body politic; a commonwealth. Also, **com′mon weal′.**

com·mon·wealth (kom′ən welth′), *n.* **1.** (*cap.*) a group of sovereign states and their dependencies associated by their own choice and linked with common objectives and interests: *the British Commonwealth.* **2.** (*cap.*) a federation of former colonies, esp. as a dominion of the British Commonwealth: *the Commonwealth of Australia.* **3.** (*cap.*) a self-governing territory associated with the U.S.: official designation of Puerto Rico. **4.** (*cap.*) *Eng. Hist.* the English government from the abolition of the monarchy in 1649 until the establishment of the Protectorate in 1653, sometimes extended to include the restoration of Charles II in 1660. **5.** (*cap.*) the official designation (rather than "State") of four States of the U.S.: Kentucky, Massachusetts, Pennsylvania, and Virginia. **6.** any group of persons united by some common interest. **7.** the whole body of people of a nation or state; the body politic. **8.** a state in which the supreme power is held by the people; a republican or democratic state. **9.** *Obs.* the public welfare. [late ME *commen wealthe*]

Com′monwealth Day′, May 24, the anniversary of Queen Victoria's birth, observed in some countries of the British Commonwealth of Nations. Formerly, **Empire Day.**

Com′monwealth of In′dependent States′, an alliance of former Soviet republics formed in December 1991, including: Armenia, Azerbaijan, Belarus, Kazakhstan, Kyrgyzstan, Moldova, Russian Federation, Tajikistan, Turkmenistan, Ukraine, and Uzbekistan. *Abbr.:* C.I.S.

Com′monwealth of Na′tions. See **British Commonwealth of Nations.**

Com′monwealth of the Phil′ippines, former name of the **Philippines.**

com′mon year′, an ordinary year of 365 days; a year having no intercalary period. Cf. **leap year.**

com·mo·ran·cy (kom′ər ən sē), *n., pl.* **-cies.** *Law.* a dwelling in a place; usual or temporary residence in a place. [COMMOR(ANT) + -ANCY]

com·mo·rant (kom′ər ənt), *adj.* *Law.* dwelling; usually or temporarily residing: *now commorant in Boston.* [< L *commorant-* (s. of *commorāns* tarrying, prp. of *commorārī*), equiv. to *com-* COM- + *mor(a)* a delay + *-ant-* -ANT]

com·mo·tion (kə mō′shən), *n.* **1.** violent or tumultuous motion; agitation; noisy disturbance. **2.** political or social disturbance or upheaval; sedition; insurrection. [< L *commōtiōn-* (s. of *commōtiō*), equiv. to *commōt(us)* (ptp. of *commovēre* to COMMOVE) + *-iōn-* -ION] —**com·mo′tion·al,** *adj.* —**com·mo′tive,** *adj.*
—**Syn. 1.** disorder, turmoil, tumult, riot, turbulence, bustle. See **ado.**

com·move (kə mo͞ov′), *v.t.,* **-moved, -mov·ing.** to move violently; agitate; excite. [< L *commov(ēre),* equiv. to *com-* COM- + *movēre* to MOVE; r. ME *commoeve* < MF]

com·mu·nal (kə myo͞on′[ə]l, kom′yə n[ə]l), *adj.* **1.** pertaining to a commune or a community: *communal life.* **2.** of, by, or belonging to the people of a community: *communal ownership; communal land.* **3.** used or shared in common by everyone in a group: *a communal jug of wine.* **4.** engaged in by or involving two or more communities: *communal conflict.* [< F < ML *commūnāl(is),* equiv. to *commūn(a)* COMMUNE[3] + *-ālis* -AL[1]] —**com·mu·nal·i·ty** (kom′yo͝o nal′i tē), *n.* —**com·mu′nal·ly,** *adv.*

com·mu·nal·ise (kə myo͞on′[ə]līz′, kom′yə n[ə]līz′), *v.t.,* **-ised, -is·ing.** *Chiefly Brit.* communalize. —**com·mu′nal·i·sa′tion,** *n.* —**com·mu′nal·is′er,** *n.*

com·mu·nal·ism (kə myo͞on′[ə]liz′əm, kom′yə n[ə]liz′-), *n.* **1.** a theory or system of government according to which each commune is virtually an independent state and the nation is merely a federation of such states. **2.** the principles or practices of communal ownership. **3.** strong allegiance to one's own ethnic group rather than to society as a whole. [COMMUNAL + -ISM] —**com·mu′nal·ist,** *n.* —**com·mu′nal·is′tic,** *adj.*

com·mu·nal·ize (kə myo͞on′[ə]līz′, kom′yə n[ə]līz′), *v.t.,* **-ized, -iz·ing.** to make communal; to make (land, a business, etc.) the property of the community: *The town communalized the estate for a public park.* Also, *esp. Brit.,* **communalise.** [COMMUNAL + -IZE] —**com·mu′nal·i·za′tion,** *n.* —**com·mu′nal·iz′er,** *n.*

commu′nal mar′riage. See **group marriage.**

Com·mu·nard (kom′yə närd′), *n.* (*often l.c.*) *Fr. Hist.* a member or supporter of the Commune of 1871. Cf. **commune**[3] (def. 6b). [< F; see COMMUNE[3], -ARD]

com·mune[1] (*v.* kə myo͞on′; *n.* kom′yo͞on), *v.*, **-muned, -mun·ing,** *n.* —*v.i.* **1.** to converse or talk together, usually with profound intensity, intimacy, etc.; interchange thoughts or feelings. —*n.* **2.** interchange of ideas or sentiments. [ME < MF *comun(er)* (to) share, deriv. of *comun* COMMON] —**com·mun′er,** *n.*

com·mune[2] (kə myo͞on′), *v.i.*, **-muned, -mun·ing.** to partake of the Eucharist. [back formation from COMMUNION]

com·mune[3] (kom′yo͞on), *n.* **1.** the smallest administrative division in France, Italy, Switzerland, etc., governed by a mayor assisted by a municipal council. **2.** a similar division in some other country. **3.** any community organized for the protection and promotion of local interests, and subordinate to the state. **4.** the government or citizens of a commune. **5.** a close-knit community of people who share common interests. **6. the Commune.** Also called **Com′mune of Par′is, Paris Commune. a.** a revolutionary committee that took the place of the municipality of Paris in the revolution of 1789, usurped the authority of the state, and was suppressed by the National Convention in 1794. **b.** a socialistic government of Paris from March 18 to May 27, 1871. [< F < ML *commūn(a)* (fem.), alter. of L *commūne* community, state, orig. neut. of *commūnis* COMMON]

com·mu·ni·ca·ble (kə myo͞o′nə kə bəl), *adj.* **1.** capable of being easily communicated or transmitted: *communicable information; a communicable disease.* **2.** talkative; communicative. [< LL *commūnicābil(is)*, equiv. to *communica(re)* (see COMMUNICATE) + *-bilis* -BLE] —**com·mu′ni·ca·bil′i·ty, com·mu′ni·ca·ble·ness,** *n.* —**com·mu′ni·ca·bly,** *adv.*

com·mu·ni·cant (kə myo͞o′nə kənt), *n.* **1.** a person who partakes or is entitled to partake of the Eucharist; a member of a church. **2.** a person who communicates. —*adj.* **3.** communicating; imparting. [< L *commūnicant-* (s. of *commūnicāns*), equiv. to *communic(āre)* (to) share with (see COMMUNICATE) + *-ant-* -ANT]

com·mu·ni·cate (kə myo͞o′nə kāt′), *v.*, **-cat·ed, -cat·ing.** —*v.t.* **1.** to impart knowledge of; make known: *to communicate information; to communicate one's happiness.* **2.** to give to another; impart; transmit: *to communicate a disease.* **3.** to administer the Eucharist to. **4.** *Archaic.* to share in or partake of. —*v.i.* **5.** to give or interchange thoughts, feelings, information, or the like, by writing, speaking, etc.: *They communicate with each other every day.* **6.** to have or form a connecting passage: *The rooms communicated by means of hallways.* **7.** to partake of the Eucharist. **8.** *Obs.* to take part or participate. [< L *commūnicātus* (ptp. of *commūnicāre* to impart, make common) < *commūn(is)* common + *-ic(us)* -IC + *-ātus* -ATE[1]] —**com·mu′ni·ca′tor,** *n.*
—**Syn. 1.** divulge, announce, disclose, reveal. COMMUNICATE, IMPART denote giving to a person or thing a part or share of something, now usually something immaterial, as knowledge, thoughts, hopes, qualities, or properties. COMMUNICATE, the more common word, implies often an indirect or gradual transmission: *to communicate information by means of letters, telegrams, etc.; to communicate one's wishes to someone else.* IMPART usually implies directness of action: *to impart information.* —**Ant. 1.** withhold, conceal.

com·mu·ni·ca·tion (kə myo͞o′nə kā′shən), *n.* **1.** the act or process of communicating; fact of being communicated. **2.** the imparting or interchange of thoughts, opinions, or information by speech, writing, or signs. **3.** something imparted, interchanged, or transmitted. **4.** a document or message imparting news, views, information, etc. **5.** passage, or an opportunity or means of passage, between places. **6. communications, a.** means of sending messages, orders, etc., including telephone, telegraph, radio, and couriers. **b.** routes and transportation for moving troops and supplies from a base to an area of operations. [< L *commūnicātiōn-* (s. of *commūnicātiō*), equiv. to *commūnicāt(us)* (see COMMUNICATE) + *-iōn-* -ION; r. ME *comynycacioun* < AF]

communica′tions zone′, *Mil.* the part of a theater of operations which adjoins the combat zone and in which communications, supply, and other activities for the support of field forces are established.

com·mu·ni·ca·tive (kə myo͞o′nə kā′tiv, -kə tiv), *adj.* **1.** inclined to communicate or impart: *He has a headache and isn't feeling very communicative today.* **2.** of or pertaining to communication. [< ML *commūnicātīv(us)*, equiv. to *commūnicāt(us)* (see COMMUNICATE) + *-īvus* -IVE] —**com·mu′ni·ca′tive·ly,** *adv.* —**com·mu′ni·ca′tive·ness,** *n.*

com·mu·ni·ca·to·ry (kə myo͞o′nə kə tōr′ē, -tôr′ē), *adj.* inclined to communicate; communicative. [< ML *commūnicātōri(us)*, equiv. to *commūnicāt(us)* (see COMMUNICATE) + *-ōrius* -ORY[1]]

com·mun·ion (kə myo͞on′yən), *n.* **1.** the act of sharing, or holding in common; participation. **2.** the state of things so held. **3.** association; fellowship. **4.** interchange or sharing of thoughts or emotions; intimate communication: *communion with nature.* **5.** a group of persons having a common religious faith; a religious denomination: *Anglican communion.* **6.** (*often cap.*) Also called **Holy Communion.** *Eccles.* **a.** the act of receiving the Eucharistic elements. **b.** the elements of the Eucharist. **c.** the celebration of the Eucharist. **d.** the antiphon sung at a Eucharistic service. [late ME < L *commūniōn-* (s. of *commūniō*) a sharing, equiv. to *commūn(is)* COMMON + *-iōn-* -ION] —**com·mun′ion·a·ble,** *adj.* —**com·mun′ion·al,** *adj.*

commun′ion cloth′, corporal[3].

commun′ion cup′, *Eccles.* **1.** a chalice from which each communicant drinks in turn. **2.** a cup provided for each communicant when a common chalice is not used.

commun′ion hymn′, *Eccles.* a hymn sung immediately before the celebration of communion.

commun′ion in both′ kinds′, *Eccles.* communion in which both the bread and wine are received by the communicants.

commun′ion in one′ kind′, *Eccles.* communion in which the bread only is received by the communicants.

com·mun·ion·ist (kə myo͞on′yə nist), *n.* *Eccles.* **1.** a person with a particular view or interpretation of communion, as specified: **2.** a communicant. [COMMUNION + -IST]

commun′ion of saints′, the spiritual fellowship existing among all faithful Christians, both living and dead.

commun′ion plate′, *Rom. Cath. Ch.* the plate held under the chin of a communicant to catch the Host if it should fall.

commun′ion rail′, *Eccles.* the altar rail where communion is received by the congregation.

Commun′ion Sun′day, *Eccles.* any Sunday on which communion is administered.

commun′ion ta′ble, *Eccles.* the table used in the celebration of communion, or the Lord's Supper; the Lord's table.

com·mu·ni·qué (kə myo͞o′nə kā′, kə myo͞o′nə kā′), *n.* an official bulletin or communication, usually to the press or public. [< F: lit., communicated, ptp. of *communiquer* to communicate]

com·mu·nis (kə myo͞o′nis), *n.* *Ling.* the part that remains identical in two linguistic forms that alternate in the same function. [< L *commūnis* common] .

com·mu·nise (kom′yə nīz′), *v.t.*, **-nised, -nis·ing.** *Chiefly Brit.* communize. —**com′mu·ni·sa′tion,** *n.*

com·mu·nism (kom′yə niz′əm), *n.* **1.** a theory or system of social organization based on the holding of all property in common, actual ownership being ascribed to the community as a whole or to the state. **2.** (*sometimes cap.*) a system of social organization in which all economic and social activity is controlled by a totalitarian state dominated by a single and self-perpetuating political party. **3.** (*cap.*) the principles and practices of the Communist party. **4.** communalism. [< L *commūn(is)* COMMON + -ISM; coined in 1840 by Goodwyn Barmby]

com·mu·nist (kom′yə nist), *n.* **1.** an advocate of communism. **2.** (*cap.*) a member of the Communist party or movement. **3.** (*usually cap.*) a Communard. **4.** a person who is regarded as supporting politically leftist or subversive causes. —*adj.* **5.** pertaining to communists or communism. **6.** (*cap.*) of or pertaining to the Communist party or to Communism. [< L *commūn(is)* COMMON + -IST] —**com′mu·nis′tic, com′mu·nis′ti·cal,** *adj.* —**com′mu·nis′ti·cal·ly,** *adv.*

Com′munist Chi′na. See **China, People's Republic of.**

Com′munist Interna′tional. See **Third International.**

Com′munist Manifes′to, a pamphlet (1848) by Karl Marx and Friedrich Engels: first statement of the principles of modern communism.

Com′munist par′ty, a political party advocating the principles of communism, esp. as developed by Marx and Lenin.

com·mu·ni·tar·i·an (kə myo͞o′ni târ′ē ən), *n.* **1.** a member of a communistic community. **2.** an advocate of such a community. [COMMUNIT(Y) + -ARIAN]

com·mu·ni·ty (kə myo͞o′ni tē), *n.*, *pl.* **-ties. 1.** a social group of any size whose members reside in a specific locality, share government, and have a common cultural and historical heritage. **2.** a social group sharing common characteristics or interests and perceived or perceiving itself as distinct in some respect from the larger society within which it exists (usually prec. by *the*): *the business community; the community of scholars.* **3.** *Eccles.* a group of men or women leading a common life according to a rule. **4.** *Ecol.* an assemblage of plant and animal populations occupying a given area. **5.** joint possession, enjoyment, liability, etc.: *community of property.* **6.** similar character; agreement; identity: *community of interests.* **7. the community,** the public; society: *We must consider the needs of the community.* [< L *commūnitāt-* (s. of *commūnitās*), equiv. to *commūni(s)* COMMON + *-tāt-* -TY[2]; r. ME *comunete* < MF] —**com·mu′ni·tal,** *adj.*
—**Syn. 1.** COMMUNITY, HAMLET, VILLAGE, TOWN, CITY are terms for groups of people living in somewhat close association, and usually under common rules. COMMUNITY is a general term, and TOWN is often loosely applied. A commonly accepted set of connotations envisages HAMLET as a small group, VILLAGE as a somewhat larger one, TOWN still larger, and CITY as very large. Size is, however, not the true basis of differentiation, but properly sets off only HAMLET. Incorporation, or the absence of it, and the type of government determine the classification of the others. **6.** similarity, likeness.

commu′nity cen′ter, (in the U.S. and Canada) a building in which members of a community may gather for social, educational, or cultural activities.

commu′nity chest′, *U.S. and Canada.* a fund for local welfare activities, built up by voluntary contributions.

commu′nity church′, *Chiefly U.S.* an independent or denominational church in a particular community.

commu′nity col′lege, an institution offering courses on a college level, with or without academic credits, to the residents of a community.

commu′nity prop′erty, *U.S. Law.* (in some States) property acquired by a husband, wife, or by both together, that is considered to be jointly owned and equally shared.

commu′nity sing′ing, unrehearsed group singing of well-known songs.

com·mu·nize (kom′yə nīz′), *v.t.*, **-nized, -niz·ing. 1.** to make (something, as land, a house, etc.) the property of the community; to transfer from individual to community ownership. **2.** to make communistic. **3.** (*often cap.*) to impose Communist principles or systems of government on (a country or people). Also, *esp. Brit.*, **communise.** [back formation from *communization*, equiv. to L *commūn(is)* COMMON + -IZATION] —**com′mu·ni·za′tion,** *n.*

com·mut·a·ble (kə myo͞o′tə bəl), *adj.* that may be commuted; exchangeable or interchangeable. [< L *commūtābil(is)*, equiv. to *commūtā(re)* (to) COMMUTE + *-bilis* -BLE] —**com·mut′a·bil′i·ty, com·mut′a·ble·ness,** *n.*

com·mu·tate (kom′yə tāt′), *v.t.*, **-tat·ed, -tat·ing. 1.** to reverse the direction of (a current or currents), as by a commutator. **2.** to convert (alternating current) into direct current by use of a commutator. [back formation from COMMUTATION]

com·mu·ta·tion (kom′yə tā′shən), *n.* **1.** the act of substituting one thing for another; substitution; exchange. **2.** the substitution of one kind of payment for another. **3.** *U.S.* regular travel over some distance between home and work, as from a suburb into a city and back. **4.** the changing of a prison sentence or other penalty to another less severe. **5.** *Elect.* the act or process of commutating. [< L *commūtātiōn-* (s. of *commūtātiō*) change. See COMMUTE, -ATION]

commuta′tion tick′et, *U.S.* a ticket issued at a reduced rate, as by a railroad company, entitling the holder to be carried over a given route during a specific period and usually for a fixed number of times.

com·mu·ta·tive (kə myo͞o′tə tiv, kom′yə tā′tiv), *adj.* **1.** of or pertaining to commutation, exchange, substitution, or interchange. **2.** *Math.* **a.** (of a binary operation) having the property that one term operating on a second is equal to the second operating on the first, as $a \times b = b \times a$. **b.** having reference to this property: *commutative law for multiplication.* [< ML *commūtātīv(us)*, equiv. to L *commūtāt(us)* (ptp. of *commūtāre*; see COMMUTE, -ATE[1]) + *-īvus* -IVE] —**com·mu′ta·tive·ly,** *adv.*

commu′tative law′, *Logic.* a law asserting that the order in which certain logical operations are performed is indifferent.

com·mu·ta·tor (kom′yə tā′tər), *n.* **1.** *Elect.* **a.** a device for reversing the direction of a current. **b.** (in a DC motor or generator) a cylindrical ring or disk assembly of conducting members, individually insulated in a supporting structure with an exposed surface for contact with current-collecting brushes and mounted on the armature shaft, for changing the frequency or direction of the current in the armature windings. **2.** *Math.* the element equal to the product of two given elements in a group multiplied on the right by the product of the inverses of the elements. [COMMUTATE + -OR[2]]

com′mutator group′, *Math.* the subgroup of a given group, which consists of all the commutators in the group.

com·mute (kə myo͞ot′), *v.*, **-mut·ed, -mut·ing.** —*v.t.* **1.** to exchange for another or for something else; give and take reciprocally; interchange. **2.** to change: *to commute iron into silver.* **3.** to change (one kind of payment) into or for another, as by substitution. **4.** to change (a prison sentence or other penalty) to a less severe one: *The death sentence was commuted to life imprisonment.* —*v.i.* **5.** to make substitution. **6.** to serve as a substitute. **7.** to make a collective payment, esp. of a reduced amount, as an equivalent for a number of payments. **8.** *Math.* to give the same result whether operating on the left or on the right. **9.** to travel regularly over some distance between one's home and office, esp. between the suburbs and the city or between one city and another. [< L *commūt(āre)*, equiv. to *com-* COM- + *mūtāre* to change] —**com·mut′er,** *n.*

com·mu·tu·al (kə myo͞o′cho͞o əl), *adj.* *Archaic.* mutual; reciprocal. [COM- + MUTUAL] —**com·mu·tu·al·i·ty** (kə myo͞o′cho͞o al′i tē), *n.*

com·my (kom′ē), *n.*, *pl.* **-mies.** (*often cap.*) *Informal.* communist. [by shortening and alter.]

Com·ne·nus (kom nē′nəs), *n.* a dynasty of Byzantine emperors that ruled at Constantinople, 1057?–1185, and at Trebizond in Asia Minor, 1204–1461?.

Co·mo (kō′mō; *It.* kô′mô), *n.* **1. Lake,** a lake in N Italy, in Lombardy. 35 mi. long; 56 sq. mi. **2.** a city at the SW end of this lake. 82,070 (1961).

Co·mo·do·ro Ri·va·da·via (kô′mô thô′rô rē′vä thä′vyä), a city in E Argentina. 25,651 (1947).

có·mo es·tá (kô′mô es tä′), *Spanish.* how are you?

Com·o·rin (kom′ər in), *n.* **Cape,** a cape on the S tip of India, extending into the Indian Ocean.

Com′o·ro Is′lands (kom′ə rō′), a group of islands between N Madagascar and E Africa. 181,288 (1958); ab. 800 sq. mi. French, **Îles Comores.**

co·mose (kō′mōs), *adj.* hairy; comate. [< L *comōs(us)*, equiv. to *com(a)* (< Gk *kómē* hair, foliage of trees or plants) + *-ōsus* -OSE[1]]

comp[1] (komp), *Informal.* —*n.* **1.** a compositor. **2.** composition. —*v.t.* **3.** to compose (type). [shortened form]

comp[2] (komp), *n.* *Slang.* a complimentary ticket. [shortened form]

comp[3] (komp), *v.i.* *Jazz.* to accompany a soloist with a succession of irregularly spaced chords that punctuate the rhythm. [shortened form of ACCOMPANY]

comp., 1. comparative. **2.** compare. **3.** compensation. **4.** compilation. **5.** compiled. **6.** composition. **7.** compound.

com·pact[1] (*adj., v.* kəm pakt′; *n.* kom′pakt), *adj.* **1.** joined or packed together; closely and firmly united; dense; solid: *compact soil.* **2.** arranged within a relatively small space: *a compact shopping center.* **3.** designed to be small in size and economical in operation: *a compact car.* **4.** solidly or firmly built: *the compact body of a lightweight wrestler.* **5.** expressed concisely; pithy; terse; not diffuse: *a compact review of the week's news.* **6.** composed or made (usually fol. by *of*): *a book compact of form and content.* **7.** *Math.* (of a set) having the property that in any collection of open sets whose union contains the given set there exists a finite number of open sets whose union contains the given set; having the property that every open cover has a finite subcover; bicompact. —*v.t.* **8.** to join or pack closely together; consolidate; condense. **9.** to make firm or stable. **10.** to form or make by close union or conjunction; make up or compose. **11.** *Metall.* to compress (metallic or metallic and nonmetallic powders) in a die to be sintered. —*n.* **12.** a small case containing a mirror, face powder, a puff, and (sometimes) rouge. **13.** a small automobile, esp. one designed for economy of space or operation. **14.** *Metall.* (in powder metallurgy) an object to be sintered formed of metallic or of metallic and nonmetallic powders compressed in a die. [late ME < L *compact(us)* (ptp. of *compingere*), equiv. to *com-* COM- + *pāc-* ptp. s. + *-tus* ptp. ending; akin to PACT, COMPACT[2]] —**com·pact′ed·ly,** *adv.* —**com·pact′ed·ness,** *n.* —**com·pact′i·ble,** *adj.* —**com·pact′ly,** *adv.* —**com·pact′ness,** *n.*
—**Syn. 5.** concise, succinct, brief. **8.** compress.

com·pact[2] (kom′pakt), *n.* a formal agreement between two or more parties, states, etc.; contract: *the proposed economic compact between Germany and France.* [< L *compact(um)*, n. use of neut. of *compactus* (ptp. of *compaciscī* to make an agreement), equiv. to *com-* COM- + *pac-* (s. of *pacīscī* to bargain; akin to PACT, COMPACT[1]) + *-tus* ptp. ending]
—**Syn.** treaty, pact, entente, convention, concordat. See **agreement.**

com′pact disk′, a small grooveless optical disk containing digitized data, as music, that can be decoded and played back by a laser system. *Abbr.:* CD

com·pact·i·fi·ca·tion (kəm pak′tə fə kā′shən), *n.* *Math.* a compact topological space having the property that a given topological space is homeomorphic to a dense subspace of the compact space. [COMPACT[1] + -I- + -FICATION]

com·pac·tion (kəm pak′shən, kom-), *n.* **1.** the act of compacting or the state of being compacted. **2.** *Geol.* the consolidation of sediments resulting from the weight of overlying deposits. [< L *compactiōn-* (s. of *compactiō*) a joining, frame, equiv. to *compact(us)* COMPACT[1] + *-iōn-* -ION]

com·pa·gnie (kôɴ pa nyē′), *n., pl.* **-gnies** (-nyē′). *French.* company.

com·pand·er (kəm pan′dər), *n.* *Electronics.* (in a communications path) a combination of a compressor at one point and an expander at another, the compressor reducing the volume of a signal and the expander restoring it. [COM(PRESS + EX)PAND + -ER[1]]

com·pa·ñe·ro (kom′pən yâr′ō; *Sp.* kôm′pä nye′rô), *n., pl.* **-pa·ñe·ros** (-pən yâr′ōz; *Sp.* -pä nye′rôs). *Southwestern U.S.* companion; friend. [< Sp, equiv. to *compañ(a)* COMPANY + *-ero* -ER[2]]

com·pa·ñi·a (kôm′pä nyē′ä), *n., pl.* **-ñi·as** (-nyē′äs). *Spanish.* company.

com·pan·ion[1] (kəm pan′yən), *n.* **1.** a person who is frequently in the company of, associates with, or accompanies another or others: *my son and his two companions.* **2.** a person employed to accompany, assist, and live with another in the capacity of a helpful friend. **3.** a mate or match for something: *White wine is the usual companion of fish.* **4.** a handbook or guide: *a bird-watcher's companion.* **5.** a member of the lowest rank in an order of knighthood or of a grade in an order. **6.** Also called **companion star, comes.** *Astron.* the fainter of the two stars that constitute a double star. Cf. **primary** (def. 17b). **7.** *Obs.* a fellow. —*v.t.* **8.** to be a companion to; accompany. [< LL *compāniōn-* (s. of *compāniō*) mess-mate, equiv. to *com-* COM- + *pān(is)* bread + *-iōn-* -ION; r. ME *compainoun* < AF, equiv. to OF *compaignon*] —**com·pan′ion·less,** *adj.*
—**Syn. 1.** comrade, partner, mate. See **acquaintance. 2.** nurse, governess.

com·pan·ion[2] (kəm pan′yən), *n.* *Naut.* **1.** a covering or hood over the top of a companionway. **2.** a companionway. [alter. of D *kampanje* quarterdeck < F (*chambre de la*) *compagne* pantry (of a medieval galley)]

com·pan·ion·a·ble (kəm pan′yə nə bəl), *adj.* possessing the qualities of a good companion; pleasant to be with; congenial. [COMPANION[1] + -ABLE] —**com·pan′ion·a·bil′i·ty, com·pan′ion·a·ble·ness,** *n.* —**com·pan′ion·a·bly,** *adv.*

com·pan·ion·ate (kəm pan′yə nit), *adj.* **1.** of, by, or like companions. **2.** tastefully harmonious. [COMPANION[1] + -ATE[1]]

compan′ionate mar′riage, a form of marriage permitting the divorce of a childless couple by mutual consent, leaving neither spouse legally responsible for the financial welfare of the other. Cf. **trial marriage.**

compan′ion cell′, *Bot.* any of a number of cells adjacent to a sieve tube, said to assist it in its functions.

compan′ion lad′der, *Naut.* an inboard ladder or stair, as in a companionway.

compan′ion piece′, a literary or musical work that has a close relationship to another work by the same author or composer.

com·pan·ion·ship (kəm pan′yən ship′), *n.* **1.** association as companions; fellowship. **2.** *Print.* a group of compositors working under a foreman. [COMPANION[1] + -SHIP]

compan′ion star′, *Astron.* companion[1] (def. 6).

com·pan·ion·way (kəm pan′yən wā′), *n.* *Naut.* **1.** a stair or ladder within the hull of a vessel. **2.** the space occupied by this stair or ladder. [COMPANION[2] + WAY]

com·pa·ny (kum′pə nē), *n., pl.* **-nies,** *v.,* **-nied, -ny·ing.** —*n.* **1.** a number of individuals assembled or associated together; group of people: *a large company of mathematicians.* **2.** an assemblage of persons for social purposes. **3.** companionship; fellowship; association: *They invited two people along for company.* **4.** a guest or guests: *We're having company for the weekend.* **5.** society collectively. **6.** a number of persons united or incorporated for joint action, esp. for business: *a publishing company; a company of actors.* **7.** (*cap.*) the member or members of a firm not specifically named in the firm's title: *George Higgins and Company.* **8.** a medieval trade guild. **9.** *Mil.* **a.** a subdivision of a regiment, battle group, or battalion. **b.** any relatively small group of soldiers. **c.** *U.S. Army.* a basic unit with both tactical and administrative functions. **10.** Also called **ship's company.** a ship's crew, including the officers. **11.** a unit of firemen, including their special apparatus: *a hook-and-ladder company.* **12. keep company, a.** to associate with; be a friend of. **b.** *Informal.* to go together, as in courtship: *My sister has been keeping company with a young lawyer.* **13. part company, a.** to cease association or friendship with: *We parted company 20 years ago after the argument.* **b.** to take a different or opposite view; differ: *He parted company with his father on politics.* **c.** to separate: *We parted company at the airport.* —*v.i.* **14.** *Archaic.* to associate. —*v.t.* **15.** *Archaic.* to accompany. [ME, var. of *compaignie* < OF: companionship, equiv. to *compain* (< LL *compāniō*; see COMPANION[1]) + *-ie* -Y[3]] —**com′pa·ny·less,** *adj.*
—**Syn. 1.** group, assemblage, body. COMPANY, BAND, PARTY, TROOP refer to a group of people formally or informally associated. COMPANY is the general word and means any group of people: *a company of motorists.* BAND, used esp. of a band of musicians, suggests a relatively small group pursuing the same purpose or sharing a common fate: *a concert by a band; a band of survivors.* PARTY, except when used of a political group, usually implies an indefinite and temporary assemblage, as for some common pursuit: *a spelunking party.* TROOP, used specifically of a body of cavalry, usually implies a number of individuals organized as a unit: *a troop of cavalry.* **2.** gathering, concourse, crowd. **6.** firm, house, corporation, syndicate, association.

com′pany man′, 1. an employee who identifies completely with the company he works for, rather than with his fellow workers, and who puts his allegiance to the company above his personal beliefs. **2.** an employee whom fellow workers believe to be working against their common interests to the benefit of the employer.

Com′pany of Cap′tain Frans′ Ban′ning Coq′, The (fräns′ bä′ning kôk′). See **Night Watch.**

com′pany of′ficer, *U.S. Army and Marine Corps.* a captain or lieutenant serving in a company.

Com′pany of Je′sus, former name of the Society of Jesus.

com′pany store′, a retail establishment operated by a manufacturer for the convenience of his employees. Also called **industrial store.**

com′pany town′, a town whose inhabitants are mainly dependent on one company for employment, housing, supplies, etc.

com′pany un′ion, *U.S.* **1.** a labor union whose members are dominated by their employer. **2.** a union confined to employees of one business or corporation.

compar., comparative.

com·pa·ra·ble (kom′pər ə bəl), *adj.* **1.** capable of being compared; having sufficient features in common with something else to afford comparison: *He considered the Roman and British empires to be comparable.* **2.** worthy of comparison: *shops comparable to those on Fifth Avenue.* **3.** usable or suitable for comparison: *We have no comparable data on Russian farming.* [late ME < L *comparābil(is)*, equiv. to *comparā(re)* (to) COMPARE + *-bilis* -BLE] —**com′pa·ra·bil′i·ty, com′pa·ra·ble·ness,** *n.* —**com′pa·ra·bly,** *adv.*

com·par·a·tist (kəm par′ə tist), *n.* a specialist in comparative linguistics or comparative literature. [< F *comparatiste* < L *comparāt(us)* (ptp. of *comparāre* to COMPARE) + F *-iste* -IST]

com·par·a·tive (kəm par′ə tiv), *adj.* **1.** of or pertaining to comparison. **2.** proceeding by, founded on, or using comparison as a method of study: *comparative anatomy; comparative literature.* **3.** estimated by comparison; not positive or absolute; relative: *a comparative newcomer in politics; to live in comparative luxury.* **4.** *Gram.* being, noting, or pertaining to the intermediate degree of the comparison of adjectives, as *better* and *more beautiful,* the comparative forms of *good* and *beautiful,* and of adverbs, as *nearer* and *more carefully,* the comparative forms of *near* and *carefully.* Cf. **positive** (def. 20), **superlative** (def. 3). —*n.* *Gram.* **5.** the comparative degree. **6.** a form in the comparative. [< L *comparātīv(us)*, equiv. to *comparāt(us)* (ptp. of *comparāre*; see COMPARE, -ATE[1]) + *-īvus* -IVE] —**com·par′a·tive·ly,** *adv.* —**com·par′a·tive·ness,** *n.*

compar′ative gov′ernment, the systematic study and comparison of the various forms of government in the world.

compar′ative linguis′tics, the study of the correspondences between languages that have a common origin. —**compar′ative lin′guist.**

compar′ative lit′erature, the study of the literatures of two or more national groups differing in cultural background and, usually, in language, concentrating on their relationships to and influences upon each other.

compar′ative meth′od, *Historical Ling.* a body of procedures and criteria used by linguists to determine whether and how two or more languages are related and to reconstruct forms of their hypothetical parent language.

compar′ative musicol′ogy, ethnomusicology.

compar′ative philol′ogy. See **comparative linguistics.**

compar′ative reli′gion, a field of study seeking to derive general principles from a comparison and classification of the growth and influence of various religions.

compar′ative state′ment, a financial statement with figures arranged in two or more parallel columns, each column representing a fiscal year or other period, used to facilitate comparison of performance between periods.

com·pa·ra·tor (kom′pə rā′tər), *n.* **1.** any of various instruments for making comparisons, as of lengths or distances, tints of colors, etc. **2.** *Electronics.* a circuit for comparing two signals, as readings of duplicate information stored in a digital computer, and for giving an indication of agreement or disagreement between them. [< LL *comparātor* a comparer. See COMPARE, -ATE[1], -OR[2]]

com·pare (kəm pâr′), *v.,* **-pared, -par·ing,** *n.* —*v.t.* **1.** to examine (two or more things, ideas, people, etc.) for the purpose of noting similarities and differences: *to compare two pieces of cloth; to compare the governments of two nations.* **2.** to consider or describe as similar; liken: *Shall I compare thee to a summer's day?* **3.** *Gram.* to form or display the degrees of comparison of (an adjective or adverb). —*v.i.* **4.** to bear comparison; be held equal: *Dekker's plays cannot compare with Shakespeare's.* **5.** to appear in a similar standing: *His recital certainly compares with the one he gave last year.* **6.** to differ in quality or accomplishment as specified: *Their gross national product compares poorly with that of neighbor nations.* **7.** to vie: *It is impertinent of her to try to compare with her betters.* **8. compare notes.** See **note** (def. 25). —*n.* **9.** comparison: *Her beauty is beyond compare. Milton's imagery is past compare.* [late ME < L *compar(āre)* (to) match together, equiv. to *compar* a perfect match (see COM-, PAR) + *-ā-* v. suffix + *-re* inf. ending; r. ME *comper* < OF *comperer*] —**com·par′er,** *n.*
—**Syn. 1, 2.** COMPARE, CONTRAST agree in placing together two or more things and examining them to discover characteristics, qualities, etc. To COMPARE means to examine in order to discover like or unlike characteristics. We compare things of the same class *with* each other; things of unlike classes *to* each other: *to compare one story with another, a man to a mountain.* To CONTRAST is to examine with an eye to differences, or to place together so that the differences are striking. We contrast one thing with another: *to contrast living conditions in peace and in war.*

com·par·i·son (kəm par′i sən), *n.* **1.** the act of comparing. **2.** the state of being compared. **3.** a likening; illustration by similitude; comparative estimate or statement. **4.** *Rhet.* the considering of two things with regard to some characteristic that is common to both, as the likening of a hero to a lion in courage. **5.** capability of being compared or likened. **6.** *Gram.* **a.** the function of an adverb or adjective that is used to indicate degrees of superiority or inferiority in quality, quantity, or intensity. **b.** the patterns of formation involved therein. **c.** the degrees of a particular word, displayed in a fixed order, as *mild, milder, mildest, less mild, least mild.* [< L *comparātiōn-* (s. of *comparātiō*). See COMPARE, -ATION]

compar′ison mi′croscope, *Optics.* a microscope having two objective lenses and using a system of prisms to form in one eyepiece adjacent images of two different objects.

compar′ison shop′per, an employee of a retail store hired to visit competing stores in order to gather information regarding styles, quality, prices, etc., of merchandise offered by competitors. —**compar′ison shop′ping.**

compar′ison test′, *Math.* the theorem that a given infinite series converges if the absolute value of each term of the given series is less than or equal to the corresponding term in a known convergent series.

com·par·sa (kəm pär′sə), *n.* a song and folk dance of Cuba. [< AmerSp, Sp: masquerade, group of theatrical supernumeraries < It: supernumerary (fem.), appearance, n. use of fem. of *comparso,* ptp. of *comparire* < L *comparēre* become visible. See COM-, APPEAR]

com·part (kəm pärt′), *v.t.* **1.** to separate or mark out in parts; subdivide. **2.** to distribute and give proportional relationships to the parts of (an architectural design). [< LL *compart(īre)* (to) divide up. See COM-, PART]

com·par·ti·men·to (kôm pär′tē men′tô), *n., pl.* **-ti** (-tē). *Italian.* any of the 18 administrative districts into which Italy is divided.

com·part·ment (kəm pärt′mənt), *n.* **1.** a part or space marked or partitioned off. **2.** a separate room, section, etc.: *a sleeping compartment on a train; a watertight compartment in a ship.* **3.** *U.S. railroads.* a private bedroom with toilet facilities. **4.** a separate aspect, function, or the like: *the compartments of the human mind.* **5.** *Archit.* a distinct major division of a design. **6.** *Heraldry.* a decorative base, as a grassy mound, on which the supporters of an escutcheon stand or rest. —*v.t.* **7.** to divide into compartments. [< MF *compartiment* < It *compartiment(o).* See COMPART, -MENT]
—**Syn. 1.** division, section. **2.** cabin. **3.** roomette. See **apartment.**

com·part·men·tal (kəm pärt men′tᵊl, kom′pärt-), *adj.* divided into compartments: *a compartmental office; a compartmental agency.* [COMPARTMENT + -AL[1]] —**com·part·men′tal·ly,** *adv.*

com·part·men·tal·ize (kəm pärt men′tᵊlīz′, kom′-pärt-), *v.t.,* **-ized, -iz·ing.** to divide into categories or compartments. [COMPARTMENTAL + -IZE] —**com·part·men′tal·i·za′tion,** *n.*

com·part·men·ta·tion (kəm pärt′mən tā′shən), *n.* *Naut.* subdivision of a hull into spaces enclosed by watertight bulkheads and sometimes by watertight decks. [COMPARTMENT + -ATION]

com·pass (kum′pəs), *n.* **1.** an instrument for determining directions, as by means of a freely rotating magnetized needle that indicates magnetic north. **2.** the enclosing line or limits of any area; perimeter: *You can find anything you want downtown within the compass of ten square blocks.* **3.** space within limits; area; extent; range; scope: *the narrow compass of the strait; the broad compass of the novel.* **4.** Also called **range.** the total range of tones of a voice or of a musical instrument. **5.** due or proper limits; moderate bounds: *Her actions stayed within the compass of propriety.* **6.** a passing round; circuit: *the compass of a year.* **7.** Often, **compasses.** an instrument for drawing or describing circles, measuring distances, etc., consisting generally of two movable, rigid legs hinged to each other at one end (usually used with *pair of*): *to spread the legs of a compass and draw a larger circle.* **8.** (*cap.*) *Astron.* **a.** Also called **Mariner's Compass.** the constellation Pyxis. **b. Compasses,** the constellation Circinus. **9.** *Obs.* a circle. —*adj.* **10.** curved; forming a curve or arc: *a compass timber; compass roof.* —*v.t.* **11.** to go or move round; make the circuit of: *It would take a week to compass his property on foot.* **12.** to extend or stretch around; hem in; surround; encircle: *An old stone wall compasses his property.* **13.** to attain or achieve; accomplish; obtain. **14.** to contrive; plot; scheme: *to compass a treacherous plan.* **15.** to make curved or circular. **16.** to comprehend; to grasp, as with the mind: *His mind could not compass the extent of the disaster.* [ME deriv. of *compassen* < OF *compasser* to measure < VL **compassāre, *compassus* equal step (L *com-* COM- + *passus* PACE[1]) whence OF *compas* (*n.*) > ME *compas*] —**com′pass·a·ble,** *adj.* —**com′pass·less,** *adj.*
—**Syn. 3.** See **range.**

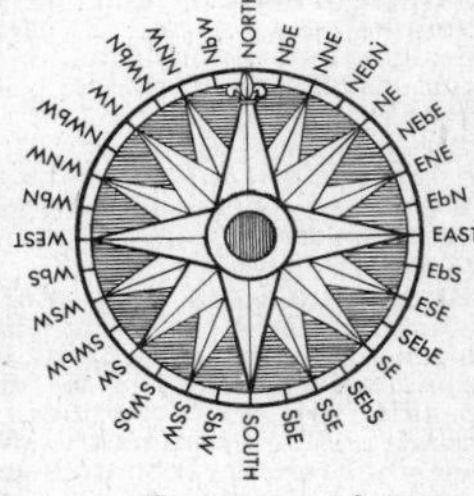

Compass card

com′pass bowl′, a bowl in a ship's compass in which the compass card is mounted.

com′pass card′, *Navig.* a circular card with magnets attached to its underside, the face divided on its rim into points of the compass, degrees clockwise from north, or both, and floating or suspended from a pivot within the bowl of a compass so as to rotate freely.

com′pass course′, *Naut.* a course whose bearing is relative to the meridian as given by the navigator's compass, no compensation being made for variation or deviation. Cf. **true course, magnetic course.**

com′pass devia′tion, deviation (def. 4).

com′pass devia′tion card′, a card, sheet, or the like, with two compass roses printed on it concentrically, for recording, on a given voyage of a given vessel, the amount of deviation for which the navigator must compensate in using the ship's compass to steer a magnetic course.

com·pas·sion (kəm pash′ən), *n.* **1.** a feeling of deep sympathy and sorrow for another who is stricken by suffering or misfortune, accompanied by a strong desire to alleviate the pain or remove its cause. —*v.t.* **2.** *Archaic.* to compassionate. [ME < LL *compassiōn-* (s. of *compassiō*). See COM-, PASSION] —**com·pas′sion·less,** *adj.*
—**Syn. 1.** commiseration, mercy, tenderness, heart, clemency. —**Ant. 1.** mercilessness, indifference.

com·pas·sion·ate (*adj.* kəm pash′ə nit; *v.* kəm pash′ə nāt′), *adj., v.,* **-at·ed, -at·ing.** —*adj.* **1.** having or showing compassion: *a compassionate person; a compassionate letter.* **2.** *Obs.* pitiable. —*v.t.* **3.** to have compassion for; pity. [COMPASSION + -ATE[1]] —**com·pas′sion·ate·ly,** *adv.* —**com·pas′sion·ate·ness,** *n.*
—**Syn. 1.** pitying, sympathizing, sympathetic, tender.

com′pass jel′lyfish, a scyphozoan jellyfish, *Chrysaora hysocella,* marked with radiating, dark streaks on the upper surface of its umbrella.

com′pass north′, *Navig.* magnetic north, as indicated on a particular compass at a given moment. Cf. **deviation** (def. 4).

com′pass plane′, *Carpentry.* a plane for smoothing curved surfaces.

com′pass plant′, any of various plants whose leaves tend to lie in a plane at right angles to the strongest light, hence usually north and south, esp. *Silphium laciniatum.*

com′pass raft′er, a rafter cut to a curve on one or both edges.

com′pass rose′, **1.** *Navig.* a circle divided into 32 points or 360 degrees numbered clockwise from true or magnetic north, printed on a chart or the like as a means of determining the course of a vessel or aircraft. **2.** a similar design, often ornamented, used on maps to indicate the points of the compass.

com′pass saw′, *Carpentry.* a small handsaw with a narrow, tapering blade for cutting curves of small radii.

com′pass tim′ber, *Shipbuilding.* a timber the grain of which is naturally or artificially bent.

com·pa·ter·ni·ty (kom′pə tûr′ni tē), *n.* the relationship between the godparents of a child or between the godparents and the parents of the child. [late ME *compaternite* < ML *compaternitās,* equiv. to *compater* godfather (see COM-, PATER) + *(pater)nitās* PATERNITY]

com·pa·thy (kom′pə thē), *n.* feelings, as happiness, grief, etc., shared with another or others. [COM- + -PATHY]

com·pat·i·ble (kəm pat′ə bəl), *adj.* **1.** capable of existing together in harmony: *the most compatible married couple I know.* **2.** able to exist together with something else: *Prejudice is not compatible with true religion.* **3.** consistent; congruous (often fol. by *with*): *His claims are not compatible with the facts.* **4.** noting a system of television in which color broadcasts can be received on ordinary sets in black and white. [late ME < ML *compatibil(is),* deriv. of LL *compati* (L *com-* COM- + *patī* to suffer). See -BLE] —**com·pat′i·bil′i·ty, com·pat′i·ble·ness,** *n.* —**com·pat′i·bly,** *adv.*

com·pa·tri·ot (kəm pā′trē ət *or, esp. Brit.,* -pa′-), *n.* **1.** a native or inhabitant of one's own country; fellow countryman or countrywoman. —*adj.* **2.** of the same country. [< LL *compatriōt(a).* See COM-, PATRIOT] —**com·pa·tri·ot·ic** (kəm pā′trē ot′ik *or, esp. Brit.,* -pa′-), *adj.* —**com·pa′tri·ot·ism,** *n.*

Comp·a·zine (kom′pə zēn′), *n. Pharm., Trademark.* perchlorperazine.

com·peer (kəm pēr′, kom′pēr), *n.* **1.** an equal in rank, ability, accomplishment, etc.; peer; colleague. **2.** close friend; comrade. —*v.t.* **3.** *Archaic.* to be the equal of; match. [late ME *comper* < MF. See COM-, PEER[1]]

com·pel (kəm pel′), *v.,* **-pelled, -pel·ling.** —*v.t.* **1.** to force or drive, esp. to a course of action: *His flouting of rules compels us to dismiss him.* **2.** to secure or bring about by force. **3.** to force to submit; subdue. **4.** to overpower. **5.** *Archaic.* to drive together; unite by force; herd. —*v.i.* **6.** to use force. **7.** to have a powerful and irresistible effect, influence, etc. [ME *compelle* < L *compelle(re)* (to) crowd, force, equiv. to *com-* COM- + *pellere* to push, drive] —**com·pel′la·ble,** *adj.* —**com·pel′la·bly,** *adv.* —**com·pel′lent,** *adj.* —**com·pel′ler,** *n.* —**com·pel′ling·ly,** *adv.*

—**Syn. 1.** constrain, oblige, coerce. COMPEL, IMPEL agree in the idea of using physical or other force to cause something to be done. COMPEL means to constrain someone, in some way, to yield or to do what one wishes: *to compel a recalcitrant debtor to pay; Fate compels men to face danger and trouble.* IMPEL may mean literally to push forward, but is usually applied figuratively, meaning to provide a strong motive or incentive toward a certain end: *Wind impels a ship. Curiosity impels me to ask.* **3.** overpower, bend.

com·pel·la·tion (kom′pə lā′shən), *n.* **1.** the act of addressing a person. **2.** manner or form of address or designation; appellation. [< L *compellātiōn-* (s. of *compellātiō*) an accosting, a rebuke. See COM-, APPELLATION]

com·pel·ling (kəm pel′ing), *adj.* **1.** tending to compel; driving: *He had to go for unavoidably compelling reasons.* **2.** requiring acute admiration, attention, or respect: *a man of compelling integrity; a drama of compelling power.* [COMPEL + -ING[2]]

com·pen·di·ous (kəm pen′dē əs), *adj.* of or like a compendium; containing the substance of a subject, often an exclusive subject, in a brief form; concise: *a compendious history of the world.* [late ME < L *compendiōs(us).* See COMPENDIUM, -OSE[1]] —**com·pen′di·ous·ly,** *adv.* —**com·pen′di·ous·ness,** *n.*

—**Syn.** summary, comprehensive, succinct, packed.

com·pen·di·um (kəm pen′dē əm), *n., pl.* **-di·ums, -di·a** (-dē ə). **1.** a brief treatment or account of a subject, esp. an extensive subject; concise treatise: *a compendium of modern medicine.* **2.** a summary, epitome, or abridgment. **3.** a full list or inventory: *a compendium of their complaints about working conditions.* Also, **com·pend** (kom′pend). [< L: a shortening (orig. a careful weighing), equiv. to *com-* COM- + *pend-* (s. of *pendere* to cause to hang down, weigh) + *-ium* n. suffix]

—**Syn. 1.** survey, digest, conspectus.

com·pen·sa·ble (kəm pen′sə bəl), *adj.* eligible for or subject to compensation, esp. for a bodily injury. [COMPENS(ATE) + -ABLE]

com·pen·sate (kom′pən sāt′), *v.,* **-sat·ed, -sat·ing.** —*v.t.* **1.** to counterbalance; offset; be equivalent to: *He compensated his homely appearance with great personal charm.* **2.** to recompense for something: *They gave him ten dollars to compensate him for his trouble.* **3.** *Mech.* to counterbalance (a force or the like); adjust or construct so as to offset or counterbalance variations or produce equilibrium. **4.** to change the gold content of (the monetary unit) to counterbalance price fluctuations and thereby stabilize its purchasing power. —*v.i.* **5.** to provide or be an equivalent; make up; make amends (usually fol. by *for*): *His occasional kindness did not compensate for his frequent insults.* [< L *compēnsāt(us)* (ptp. of *compēnsāre* to counterbalance; orig., weigh together). See COM-, PENSIVE, -ATE[1]] —**com′pen·sat′ing·ly,** *adv.* —**com′pen·sa′tor,** *n.*

—**Syn. 1.** counterpoise, countervail. **2.** remunerate, reward, pay. **5.** atone.

com′pensating bal′ance, a balance wheel in a timepiece, designed to compensate for varying degrees of expansion and consequent variations of tension in the hairspring, having its rim composed of two laminated segments of brass and steel, such that the greater coefficient of expansion of the brass bends the segments inward to lessen the virtual diameter of the balance when heat increases and the tension of the hairspring lessens. Also, **com′pensated bal′ance, compensa′tion bal′ance.** Also called **bimetallic balance, split balance.**

com′pensating gear′, *Mach.* See **differential gear.**

com·pen·sa·tion (kom′pən sā′shən), *n.* **1.** the act or state of compensating. **2.** the state of being compensated. **3.** something given or received as an equivalent for services, debt, loss, injury, suffering, lack, etc.; indemnity: *The insurance company paid him $2,000 as compensation for the loss of his car.* **4.** *Biol.* the improvement of any defect by the excessive development or action of another structure or organ of the same structure. **5.** a psychological mechanism by which an individual attempts to compensate for some real or imagined deficiency of personality or behavior by developing or stressing another aspect of his personality or by substituting a different form of behavior. [< L *compēnsātiōn-* (s. of *compēnsātiō*), equiv. to *compēnsāt(us)* (see COMPENSATE) + *-iōn-* -ION] —**com′pen·sa′tion·al,** *adj.*

—**Syn. 3.** recompense, remuneration, payment, amends, reparation; requital, satisfaction, indemnification.

com·pen·sa·to·ry (kəm pen′sə tôr′ē, -tōr′ē), *adj.* serving to compensate, as for loss, lack, injury, etc. Also, **com·pen·sa·tive** (kom′pən sā′tiv, kəm pen′sə-). [COMPENSATE + -ORY[1]]

compen′satory dam′ages, *Law.* damages awarded to a plaintiff as due compensation for his injury. Cf. **exemplary damages.**

com·pete (kəm pēt′), *v.i.,* **-pet·ed, -pet·ing.** to contend with another for acknowledgment, a prize, supremacy, profit, etc.; engage in a contest; vie: *to compete in a race, in business, etc.* [< L *compete(re)* (to) meet, coincide, be fitting, be capable, LL: strive together (for something), equiv. to *com-* COM- + *petere* to seek] —**com·pet′er,** *n.* —**com·pet′ing·ly,** *adv.*

—**Syn.** struggle. COMPETE, CONTEND, CONTEST mean to strive to outdo or excel: they may apply to individuals or groups. COMPETE implies having a sense of rivalry and of striving to do one's best as well as to outdo another: *to compete for a prize.* CONTEND suggests opposition or disputing as well as rivalry: *to contend with an opponent, against obstacles.* CONTEST suggests struggling to gain or hold something, as well as contending or disputing: *to contest a position or ground (in battle); to contest a decision.*

com·pe·tence (kom′pi təns), *n.* **1.** the quality of being competent; adequacy; possession of required skill, knowledge, qualification, or capacity: *He hired her because of her competence as a secretary.* **2.** sufficiency; a sufficient quantity. **3.** an income sufficient to furnish the necessities and modest comforts of life. **4.** *Law.* the quality or state of being legally competent; legal capacity or qualification based on the meeting of certain minimum requirements of age, soundness of mind, citizenship, or the like. **5.** *Embryol.* the sum total of developmental responses of any group of blastemic cells under varied external conditions. [COMPET(ENT) + -ENCE]

com·pe·ten·cy (kom′pi tən sē), *n., pl.* **-cies. 1.** competence (defs. 1–4). **2.** *Law.* (of a witness) eligibility to be sworn and to testify. [< L *competentia* agreement. See COMPETENT, -CY]

com·pe·tent (kom′pi tənt), *adj.* **1.** having suitable or sufficient skill, knowledge, experience, etc., for some purpose; properly qualified: *He is competent to manage the bank branch.* **2.** adequate but not exceptional. **3.** *Law.* (of a witness, a party to a contract, etc.) having legal capacity or qualification. [late ME < L *competent-* (s. of *competēns,* prp. of *competere* to meet, agree). See COMPETE, -ENT] —**com′pe·tent·ly,** *adv.*

—**Syn. 1.** fit, qualified, capable, proficient. See **able.**

com·pe·ti·tion (kom′pi tish′ən), *n.* **1.** the act of competing; struggle or rivalry for supremacy, a prize, etc.: *The competition between the two teams was bitter.* **2.** a contest for some prize, honor, or advantage: *Both girls entered the competition.* **3.** the rivalry offered by a competitor: *The small merchant gets powerful competition from the chain stores.* **4.** a competitor or competitors: *What is your competition offering?* **5.** *Sociol.* rivalry between two or more persons or groups for an object desired in common, usually resulting in a victor and a loser or losers but not necessarily involving the destruction of the latter. **6.** *Ecol.* the struggle among organisms, both of the same and of different species, for food, space, and other requirements for existence. [< LL *competītiōn-* (s. of *competītiō*), equiv. to *competīt(us)* (see COMPETITOR) + *-iōn-* -ION]

—**Syn. 1.** emulation. **2.** struggle.

com·pet·i·tive (kəm pet′i tiv), *adj.* **1.** of, pertaining to, involving, or decided by competition: *competitive sports; a competitive examination.* **2.** able to attain the desired response or results in a competitive situation, as the prices, services, or quality of products of a business organization. Also, **com·pet·i·to·ry** (kəm pet′i tôr′ē, -tōr′ē). [< L *competīt(us)* (see COMPETITOR) + -IVE] —**com·pet′i·tive·ly,** *adv.* —**com·pet′i·tive·ness,** *n.*

com·pet·i·tor (kəm pet′i tər), *n.* a person, team, company, etc., that competes; a rival. [< L, equiv. to *competīt(us),* ptp. of *competere* to COMPETE (*com-* COM- + *petī-* ptp. s. + *-tus* ptp. suffix) + *-or* -OR[2]] —**com·pet′i·tor·ship′,** *n.*

—**Syn.** See **opponent.**

Comp. Gen., Comptroller General.

Com·piègne (kôN pyen′yə), *n.* a city in N France, on the Oise River: nearby were signed the armistices between the Allies and Germany 1918, and between Germany and France 1940. 28,415 (1962).

com·pi·la·tion (kom′pə lā′shən), *n.* **1.** the act of compiling: *the compilation of a technical reference book.* **2.** something compiled, as a book. [< L *compīlātiōn-* (s. of *compīlātiō*). See COMPILE, -ATION] —**com·pil·a·to·ry** (kəm pī′lə tôr′ē, -tōr′ē), *adj.*

com·pile (kəm pīl′), *v.t.,* **-piled, -pil·ing. 1.** to put together (documents, selections, or other materials) in one book or work. **2.** to make (a book, writing, or the like) of materials from various sources: *to compile an anthology of plays; to compile a graph showing changes in profit.* **3.** to gather together: *He compiled all the figures asked for by the tax inspector.* **4.** *Computer Technol.* to translate (a pseudo-code) into another pseudo-code or into machine language; assemble. [late ME < L *compīl(āre)* (to) cram together hastily, equiv. to *com-* COM- + *pīlāre* < ?]

com·pil·er (kəm pī′lər), *n.* **1.** a person who compiles. **2.** Also called **assembler, assembly routine, compiling routine.** *Computer Technol.* a programming routine enabling a computer to translate a program expressed in a pseudo-code into machine language or another pseudo-code for later translation, often involving the assignment of storage locations. [ME *compilour* < AF; OF *compileor* < L *compīlātōr-.* See COMPILATION, -ER[1]]

compil′ing routine′, *Computer Technol.* compiler (def. 2).

com·pla·cen·cy (kəm plā′sən sē), *n., pl.* **-cies. 1. a.** a feeling of quiet pleasure or security, often while unaware of some potential danger, defect, or the like; self-satisfaction or smug satisfaction with an existing situation, condition, etc. **2.** something that gives satisfaction; a cause of pleasure or joy; a comfort. **3.** *Archaic.* **a.** friendly civility. **b.** a civil act. Also, **com·pla·cence** (kəm plā′səns). [< ML *complacentia.* See COMPLACENT, -CY]

com·pla·cent (kəm plā′sənt), *adj.* **1.** pleased, esp. with oneself or one's merits, advantages, situation, etc., often without awareness of some potential danger, defect, or the like; self-satisfied: *She stopped being so complacent after she was demoted.* **2.** pleasant; complaisant. Cf. **complaisant.** [< L *complacent-* (s. of *complacēns,* prp. of *complacēre* to please greatly), equiv. to *com-* COM- + *plac-* PLEASE + *-ent-* -ENT] —**com·pla′cent·ly,** *adv.*

com·plain (kəm plān′), *v.i.* **1.** to express grief, pain, uneasiness, censure, resentment, or dissatisfaction; find fault: *He complained constantly about the noise in the corridor.* **2.** to tell of one's pains, ailments, etc.: *to complain about a pain in one's back.* **3.** to make a formal accusation: *The ambassador complained about the student demonstrations.* [ME *complei(g)ne(n)* < MF *complaign-,* s. of *complaindre* < VL **complangere,* equiv. to L *com-* COM- + *plangere* to lament; see PLAINT] —**com·plain′a·ble,** *adj.* —**com·plain′er,** *n.* —**com·plain′ing·ly,** *adv.* —**com·plain′ing·ness,** *n.*

—**Syn. 1.** COMPLAIN, GRUMBLE, GROWL, MURMUR, WHINE are terms for expressing dissatisfaction or discomfort. TO COMPLAIN is to protest against or lament a condition or cause of wrong: *to complain about high prices.* TO GRUMBLE is to utter surly, ill-natured complaints half to oneself: *to grumble about the service.* GROWL may express more anger than GRUMBLE: *to growl ungraciously in reply to a question.* TO MURMUR is to complain in low or suppressed tones, and may indicate greater dissatisfaction than to GRUMBLE: *to murmur against a government.* TO WHINE is to complain or beg in a mean-spirited, objectionable way, using a nasal tone; whining often connotes persistence in begging or complaining: *to whine like a coward, like a spoiled child.* —**Ant. 1.** rejoice.

com·plain·ant (kəm plā′nənt), *n.* a person, group, or company that makes a complaint, as in a legal action. [late ME < MF *complaignant* (prp. of *complaindre*). See COMPLAIN, -ANT]

com·plaint (kəm plānt′), *n.* **1.** an expression of grief, regret, pain, censure, resentment, or discontent; lament; faultfinding: *his complaint about poor schools.* **2.** a cause of grief, discontent, lamentation, etc. **3.** a cause of bodily pain or ailment; malady: *She suffered from a vast collection of real and imagined complaints.* **4.** *U.S. Law.* the first pleading of the plaintiff in a civil action, stating his cause of action. [ME < MF *complainte* < L *com-* COM- + *plancta* PLAINT]

—**Syn. 3.** sickness, illness, ailment.

com·plai·sance (kəm plā′səns, -zəns, kom′plə zans′), *n.* **1.** the quality of being complaisant. **2.** a complaisant act. [< F; see COMPLAISANT, -ANCE]

com·plai·sant (kəm plā′sənt, -zənt, kom′plə zant′), *adj.* inclined or disposed to please; obliging; agreeable or gracious; compliant: *the most complaisant salesman I've ever met.* Cf. **complacent.** [< F (prp. of *complaire*) < L *complacent-* (s. of *complacēns,* prp. of *complacēre* to please highly). See COM-, PLEASE, -ANT] —**com·plai′sant·ly,** *adv.*

com·pla·nate (kom′plə nāt′), *adj.* made level; put into or on one plane. [< L *complānāt(us)* (ptp. of *complānāre* to make level), equiv. to *com-* COM- + *plān(us)* PLAIN, PLANE[1], PLANE[2] + *-ātus* -ATE[1]] —**com′pla·na′tion,** *n.*

com·pleat (kəm plēt′), *adj., v.t. Archaic.* complete.

Compleat′ An′gler, The, a book on fishing (1653) by Izaak Walton.

com·plect (kəm plekt′), *v.t. Obs.* to interweave; intertwine. [< L *complect(ī)* (to) embrace, enfold, equiv. to *com-* COM- + *plect(ere)* (to) plait, braid + *-ī* pass. inf. ending]

com·plect·ed (kəm plek′tid), *adj.* complexioned: *a light-complected boy.* [*complect-* (irreg. var. s. of COMPLEXION) + -ED[3]]

com·plec·tion (kəm plek′shən), *n.* complexion.

com·ple·ment (*n.* kom′plə mənt; *v.* kom′plə ment′), *n.* **1.** something that completes or makes perfect: *Good brandy is a complement to an evening meal.* **2.** the quantity or amount that completes anything: *We now have a full complement of packers.* **3.** either of two parts or things needed to complete the whole; counterpart. **4.** full quantity or amount; complete allowance. **5.** the full number of officers and crew required to man a ship. **6.** *Gram.* a word or words used to complete a grammatical construction, esp. in the predicate, as an object, *ball* in *He caught the ball,* predicate adjective, as *large* in *The house is large,* or predicate noun, as *John* in *His name is John.* **7.** *Geom.* the quantity by which an angle or an arc falls short of 90° or a quarter of a circle. Cf. **supplement** (def. 4). **8.** Also called **absolute complement.** *Math.* the set of all the elements of a universal set not included in a given set.

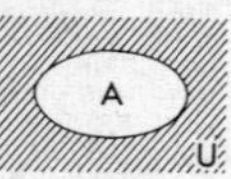

Complement (def. 8)
A, Given set
U, Universal

9. *Music.* the interval that completes an octave when added to a given interval. 10. *Immunol.* a thermolabile substance in blood serum and plasma that in combination with antibodies destroys bacteria, foreign cells, and other antigens. 11. See **complementary color.** —*v.t.* 12. to complete; form a complement to: *This hat complements the dress better than that one.* 13. *Obs.* to compliment. —*v.i.* 14. *Obs.* to compliment. [ME < L *complēment(um)* that which completes, equiv. to *complē(re)* (to) fill up (see COMPLETE) + *-mentum* -MENT] —**com′ple·ment′er,** *n.*

—**Syn. 12.** COMPLEMENT, SUPPLEMENT both mean to make an addition or additions to something. To COMPLEMENT is to provide something felt to be lacking or needed; it is often applied to putting together two things, each of which supplies what is lacking in the other, to make a complete whole: *Two statements from different points of view may complement each other.* To SUPPLEMENT is merely to add to; no definite lack or deficiency is implied nor is there an idea of a definite relationship between parts: *Some additional remarks may supplement either statement or both.*

com·ple·men·tal (kom′plə men′tᵊl), *adj.* **1.** complementary; completing. **2.** *Obs.* **a.** accomplished. **b.** ceremonious. **c.** complimentary. [COMPLEMENT + -AL¹] —**com′ple·men′tal·ly,** *adv.*

com·ple·men·ta·ry (kom′plə men′tə rē, -trē), *adj., n., pl.* **-ries.** —*adj.* **1.** forming a complement; completing. **2.** complementing each other. —*n.* **3.** See **complementary color** (def. 1). [COMPLEMENT + -ARY] —**com′ple·men′ta·ri·ness,** *n.*

com′plemen′tary an′gle, *Math.* either of two angles that added together produce an angle of 90°. Cf. **supplementary angle.**

Complementary angles (Angle BCD, complement of angle ACB; arc BD, complement of arc AB)

complemen′tary cells′, *Bot.* cells fitting closely together in the lenticel.

com′plemen′tary col′or, 1. *Art.* **a.** one of a pair of primary or secondary colors opposed to the other member of the pair on a schematic chart or scale **(color wheel),** as green opposed to red, orange opposed to blue, or violet opposed to yellow. **b.** the relationship of these pairs of colors perceived as completing or enhancing each other. **2.** See **secondary color.**

complemen′tary distribu′tion, *Ling.* a relation such that the members of a pair or set of phones, morphs, or other linguistic units have no environment in common, as aspirated "p" and unaspirated "p," which are in complementary distribution in English, since the first occurs only in positions where the second does not. Also called **complementation.** Cf. **free variation.**

com·ple·men·ta·tion (kom′plə mən tā′shən), *n.* See **complementary distribution.** [COMPLEMENT + -ATION]

com·ple·ment·ed (kom′plə men′tid), *adj.* **1.** having a complement or complements. **2.** *Math.* (of a lattice containing a smallest element and a greatest element) having the property that corresponding to each element of the lattice is a second element such that the greatest lower bound of the two elements is the smallest element of the lattice and the least upper bound of the two elements is the greatest element of the lattice. [COMPLEMENT + -ED³]

com′plement fixa′tion, *Immunol.* the combination of complement with the substance formed by the union of an antigen with its specific antibody. —**com′ple·ment-fix′ing,** *adj.*

com·plete (kəm plēt′), *adj., v.,* **-plet·ed, -plet·ing.** —*adj.* **1.** having all its parts or elements; lacking nothing; whole; entire; full: *a complete set of Mann's novels.* **2.** finished; ended; concluded: *a complete month; a complete orbit.* **3.** having all the required or customary characteristics, skills, or the like; consummate; perfect in kind or quality: *a complete gentleman; a complete scholar.* **4.** thorough; entire; total; undivided, uncompromised, or unmodified: *a complete victory; a complete mess.* **5.** *Gram.* having all modifying or complementary elements included: *The complete subject of "The dappled pony gazed over the fence" is "The dappled pony."* **6.** Also, **completed.** *Football.* (of a forward pass) caught by a receiver. **7.** *Logic.* (of a set of axioms) such that every true proposition able to be formulated in terms of the basic ideas of a given system is deducible from the set. **8.** *Engineering.* noting a determinate truss having the least number of members required to connect the panel points so as to form a system of triangles. Cf. **incomplete** (def. 3), **redundant** (def. 5b). **9.** *Archaic.* (of persons) accomplished; skilled; expert. **10.** *Math.* **a.** of or pertaining to an algebraic system, as a field with an order relation defined on it, in which every set of elements of the system has a least upper bound. **b.** of or pertaining to a set in which every fundamental sequence converges to an element of the set. Cf. **fundamental sequence. c.** (of a lattice) having the property that every subset has a least upper bound and a greatest lower bound. —*v.t.* **11.** to make whole or entire: *I need three more words to complete the puzzle.* **12.** to make perfect: *His parting look of impotent rage completed my revenge.* **13.** to bring to an end; finish: *Has he completed his new novel yet?* **14.** to consummate. **15.** *Football.* to execute (a forward pass) successfully: *He completed 17 passes in 33 attempts.* [ME < L *complēt(us)* (ptp. of *complēre* to fill up, fulfill, equiv. to *com-* COM- + *plē-* fill + *-tus* ptp. suffix] —**com·plet′a·ble,** *adj.* —**com·plet′ed·ness,** *n.* —**com·plete′ly,** *adv.* —**com·plete′ness,** *n.* —**com·plet′er,** *n.* —**com·ple′tive,** *adj.* —**com·ple′tive·ly,** *adv.*

—**Syn. 1.** unbroken, unimpaired, undivided. **3.** developed. **1–3.** COMPLETE, ENTIRE, INTACT, PERFECT imply that there is no lack or defect, nor has any part been removed. COMPLETE implies that a certain unit has all its parts, fully developed or perfected, and may apply to a process or purpose carried to fulfillment: *a complete explanation.* ENTIRE means whole, having unbroken unity: *an entire book.* INTACT implies retaining completeness and original condition: *a package delivered intact.* PERFECT emphasizes not only completeness but also high quality and absence of defects or blemishes: *a perfect diamond.* **11.** conclude, consummate, perfect, accomplish, achieve, terminate. —**Ant. 1.** partial. **3.** defective.

complete′ frac′ture, a bone fracture in which the bone is split completely across.

complete′ly nor′mal space′, *Math.* a normal topological space in which every subspace is normal.

complete′ly reg′ular space′, *Math.* a topological space in which, for every point and a closed set not containing the point, there is a continuous function that has value 0 at the given point and value 1 at each point in the closed set.

complete′ quadrilat′eral, a plane figure composed of four straight lines and their points of intersection.

complet′ing the square′, *Math.* a method, usually of solving quadratic equations, by which a quadratic expression, as $x^2 - 4 + 3$, is written as the sum or difference of a perfect square and a constant, $x^2 - 4x + 4 + 3 - 4 = (x-2)^2 - 1$, by addition and subtraction of appropriate constant terms.

com·ple·tion (kəm plē′shən), *n.* **1.** the act of completing. **2.** the state of being completed. **3.** conclusion; fulfillment: *His last novel represented the completion of his literary achievement.* **4.** *Football.* a forward pass that has been completed. [< L *complētiōn-* (s. of *complētiō*). See COMPLETE, -ION]

com·plex (*adj.* kəm pleks′, kom′pleks; *n.* kom′pleks), *adj.* **1.** composed of interconnected parts; compound; composite: *a complex highway system.* **2.** characterized by a very complicated or involved arrangement of parts, units, etc.: *a complex machine.* **3.** so complicated or intricate as to be hard to understand or deal with: *a complex problem.* **4.** *Gram.* **a.** (of a word) consisting of two parts, at least one of which is a bound form, as *childish,* which consists of the word *child* and the bound form *-ish.* **b.** See **complex sentence. 5.** *Math.* pertaining to a complex number. [< L *complex(us)* ptp. of *complectī* to COMPLECT] —*n.* **6.** an intricate or complicated association or assemblage of related things, parts, units, etc.: *the entire complex of our educational system.* **7.** *Psychol.* a system of interrelated, emotion-charged ideas, feelings, memories, and impulses that is usually repressed and that gives rise to abnormal or pathological behavior. **8.** a fixed idea; an obsessive notion. **9.** *Math.* **a.** an arbitrary set of elements of a group. **b.** a collection of simplexes having specified properties. [< L *complex(us)* an embrace, equiv. to *complex-* (ptp. s. of *complectī* COMPLECT) + *-us* 4th decl. n. suffix] —**com·plex′ly,** *adv.* —**com·plex′ness,** *n.*

—**Syn. 2, 3.** involved, perplexing. **3.** knotty, tangled, labyrinthine. **6.** network, web, tangle, labyrinth. —**Ant. 2, 3.** simple.

com′plex frac′tion, *Math.* a fraction in which the numerator or the denominator or both contain one or more fractions. Also called **compound fraction.**

com·plex·ion (kəm plek′shən), *n.* **1.** the natural color and appearance of the skin, esp. of the face: *a clear, smooth, rosy complexion.* **2.** appearance; aspect; character: *The news of her departure put a different complexion on the situation.* **3.** viewpoint, attitude, or conviction: *The citizens will unite with the mayor regardless of their political complexion.* **4.** *Old Physiol.* constitution or nature of body and mind, regarded as the result of certain combined qualities. **5.** *Obs.* nature; disposition; temperament. Also, **complection.** [ME < medical L *complexiōn-* (s. of *complexiō*) bodily make-up, shape, etc., orig., combination. See COMPLEX, -ION] —**com·plex′ion·al,** *adj.* —**com·plex′ion·al·ly,** *adv.*

com·plex·ioned (kəm plek′shənd), *adj.* having a specified complexion (usually used in combination): *a light-complexioned person.* [late ME; see COMPLEXION, -ED³]

com·plex·ion·less (kəm plek′shən lis), *adj.* devoid of color; pallid; wan. [COMPLEXION + -LESS]

com·plex·i·ty (kəm plek′si tē), *n., pl.* **-ties. 1.** the state or quality of being complex; intricacy: *the complexity of urban life.* **2.** something complex: *the endless complexities of our foreign policy.* [COMPLEX + -ITY]

com′plex machine′, *Mech.* machine (def. 4c).

com′plex num′ber, *Math.* a mathematical expression $(a + bi)$ in which a and b are real numbers and i^2 is defined as -1.

com′plex plane′, *Math.* a plane the points of which are complex numbers. Cf. **Argand diagram.**

com′plex sen′tence, a sentence containing one or more dependent clauses in addition to the main clause, as *When the bell rings* (dependent clause), *walk out* (main clause).

com′plex var′iable, *Math.* a variable to which complex numbers may be assigned as value.

com·pli·a·ble (kəm plī′ə bəl), *adj.* *Obs.* compliant. [COMPLY + -ABLE] —**com·pli′a·ble·ness,** *n.* —**com·pli′a·bly,** *adv.*

com·pli·ance (kəm plī′əns), *n.* **1.** the act of conforming, acquiescing, or yielding. **2.** a tendency to yield readily to others, esp. in a weak and subservient way. **3.** conformity; accordance: *I am writing to the Governor in compliance with your orders.* **4.** cooperation or obedience: *the compliance of all French citizens.* **5.** *Physics.* **a.** the strain of an elastic body expressed as a function of the force producing the strain. **b.** a coefficient expressing the responsiveness of a mechanical system to a periodic force. [COMPLY + -ANCE]

com·pli·an·cy (kəm plī′ən sē), *n., pl.* **-cies.** compliance (defs. 1, 2, 4).

com·pli·ant (kəm plī′ənt), *adj.* complying; obeying, obliging, or yielding, esp. in a submissive way: *a man with a compliant nature.* [COMPLY + -ANT] —**com·pli′ant·ly,** *adv.*

com·pli·ca·cy (kom′plə kə sē), *n., pl.* **-cies. 1.** the state of being complicated; complicatedness. **2.** a complication: *the numerous complicacies of travel in Albania.* [COMPLIC(ATE) + -ACY, modeled on such pairs as *confederacy, confederate*]

com·pli·cate (*v.* kom′plə kāt′; *adj.* kom′plə kit), *v.,* **-cat·ed, -cat·ing,** *adj.* —*v.t.* **1.** to make complex, intricate, involved, or difficult: *Bringing in politics only complicated the argument. His recovery from the operation was complicated by an allergic reaction.* —*adj.* **2.** complex; involved. **3.** *Bot.* folded upon itself: *a complicate embryo.* **4.** *Entomol.* folded longitudinally one or more times, as the wings of certain insects. [< L *complicāt(us)* (ptp. of *complicāre* to fold together), equiv. to *com-* COM- + *plic-* (s. of *plicāre* to fold, akin to *plec-*; see COMPLEX) + *-ātus* -ATE¹]

com·pli·cat·ed (kom′plə kā′tid), *adj.* **1.** composed of elaborately interconnected parts; not simple; complex: *a laboratory of complicated apparatus.* **2.** consisting of many parts not easily separable; difficult to analyze, understand, explain, etc.: *a complicated problem; a complicated person.* [COMPLICATE + -ED²] —**com′pli·cat′ed·ly,** *adv.* —**com′pli·cat′ed·ness,** *n.*
—**Syn. 2.** involved, tangled, knotty.

com·pli·ca·tion (kom′plə kā′shən), *n.* **1.** the act of complicating. **2.** a complicated or involved state or condition. **3.** a complex combination of elements or things. **4.** an element that introduces, usually unexpectedly, some difficulty, problem, change, etc.: *Because of the complications involved in travel to Latvia, we called off the trip.* **5.** *Pathol.* a concurrent disease or a fortuitous condition that aggravates the original disease. **6.** the act of forming a unified idea or impression from a number of sense data, memories, etc. [< LL *complicātiōn-* (s. of *complicātiō*), equiv. to *complicāt(us)* (see COMPLICATE) + *-iōn-* -ION] —**com′pli·ca′tive,** *adj.*

com·plice (kom′plis), *n.* *Archaic.* an accomplice or associate. [late ME < MF < LL *complice(m),* acc. of *complex* confederate (formation modeled on *simplex*), equiv. to *com-* COM- + *-plex* -fold]

com·plic·i·ty (kəm plis′i tē), *n., pl.* **-ties.** the state of being an accomplice; partnership or involvement in wrongdoing: *He was accused of complicity in the crime.* [COMPLICE + -ITY] —**com·plic′i·tous,** *adj.*

com·pli·er (kəm plī′ər), *n.* a person who complies. [COMPLY + -ER¹]

com·pli·ment (*n.* kom′plə mənt; *v.* kom′plə ment′), *n.* **1.** an expression of praise, commendation, or admiration: *A sincere compliment boosts one's morale.* **2.** a formal act or expression of civility, respect, or regard: *He paid her the compliment of escorting her.* **3. compliments,** a courteous greeting; good wishes; regards: *He sends you his compliments.* **4.** *Archaic.* a gift; present. —*v.t.* **5.** to pay a compliment to: *to compliment a child on his good behavior.* **6.** to show kindness or regard for by a gift or other favor: *He complimented us by giving a party in our honor.* **7.** to congratulate; felicitate: *to compliment a prince on the birth of a son.* —*v.i.* **8.** to pay compliments. [< F < It *compliment(o)* < Sp *cumplimiento,* equiv. to *cumpli-* (see COMPLY) + *-miento* -MENT; r. COMPLEMENT in same sense] —**com′pli·ment′a·ble,** *adj.* —**com′pli·ment′er,** *n.* —**com′pli·ment′ing·ly,** *adv.*
—**Syn. 1.** praise, tribute, eulogy, encomium, panegyric. **5.** commend, praise, honor, flatter. —**Ant. 1.** disparagement.

com·pli·men·ta·ry (kom′plə men′tə rē, -trē), *adj.* **1.** of the nature of, conveying, or expressing a compliment, often one that is politely flattering: *complimentary reviews of his novel; a complimentary remark.* **2.** free: *a complimentary ticket; a complimentary copy of a textbook for the teacher.* [COMPLIMENT + -ARY] —**com′pli·men′ta·ri·ly,** *adv.* —**com′pli·men′ta·ri·ness,** *n.*

com′plimen′tary close′ (klōz), the part of a letter that by convention immediately precedes the signature, as "Very truly yours," "Cordially," "Sincerely yours," etc. Also, **com′plimen′tary clos′ing.** Also called **closing, close.**

com·plin (kom′plin), *n.* *Eccles.* the last of the seven canonical hours, or the service for it, originally occurring after the evening meal but now usually following immediately upon vespers. Also, **com·pline** (kom′plin, -plīn). [ME *comp(e)lin,* equiv. to *compli, cump(e)lie* (< OF *complie, cumplie,* < L *complēta* (*hōra*) COMPLETE (hour) + *-in* (of MATIN)]

com·plot (*n.* kom′plot′; *v.* kəm plot′), *n., v.,* **-plot·ted, -plot·ting.** —*n.* **1.** a joint plot; conspiracy. —*v.t., v.i.* **2.** to plot together; conspire. [< MF < ?] —**com·plot′ment,** *n.* —**com·plot′ter,** *n.*

com·plu·vi·um (kəm plo͞o′vē əm, kom-), *n., pl.* **-vi·a** (-vē ə). (in ancient Roman architecture) a central area open to the weather, as in an atrium. [< L, equiv. to *complu(ere)* (to) flow together (*com-* COM- + *pluere* to rain) + *-ium* n. suffix]

com·ply (kəm plī′), *v.i.,* **-plied, -ply·ing. 1.** to act in accordance with wishes, requests, demands, requirements, conditions, etc.; agree (sometimes fol. by *with*): *They asked him to leave and he complied. She has complied with the school's academic requirements.* **2.** *Obs.* to be courteous or conciliatory. [< It *compli(re)* < Sp *cumplir* (see COMPLIMENT) to fulfill, accomplish < L *complēre,* equiv. to *com-* COM- + *plē-* fill + *-re* inf. suffix]
—**Syn. 1.** acquiesce, yield, conform, obey, consent, assent. —**Ant. 1.** refuse, resist.

com·po¹ (kom′pō), *n., pl.* **-pos.** composition material. [by shortening]

com·po² (kom′pō), *n.* *Australian Slang.* See **workmen's compensation insurance.** [COMP(ENSATION) + *-o* suffix of appurtenance]

com·po·nent (kəm pō′nənt), *adj.* **1.** being or serving as an element (in something larger); composing; constituent: *the component parts of a high-fidelity phonograph.* —*n.* **2.** a component part; constituent: *hi-fi components.* **3.** *Physics.* the projection of a vector quantity, as force, velocity, or the like, along an axis. **4.** *Physical Chem.* one of the set of the minimum number of chemical constituents by which every phase of a given system can be described. **5.** *Math.* **a.** a connected subset of a set, not contained in any other connected subset of the set. **b.** a coordinate of a vector. [< L *compōnent-* (s. of *compōnēns,* prp. of *compōnere* to put together), equiv. to *com-* COM- + *pōn(ere)* to put + *-ent-* -ENT] —**com·po·nen·tial** (kom′pə nen′shəl), **com′po·nen′tal,** *adj.* —**com·po′nent·ed,** *adj.*
—**Syn. 2.** See **element.**

com·po·ny (kəm pō′nē), *adj.* *Heraldry.* composed of a single row of squares, metal and color alternating; gobony. Also, **com·po·né** (kəm pō′nē; *Fr.* kôn pô nā′). [< MF *compone,* nasalized var. of *copone,* equiv. to *copon* COUPON + *-e* -EE]

com·port¹ (kəm pōrt′, -pôrt′), *v.t.* **1.** to bear or conduct (oneself); behave: *He comported himself with dignity.* **2.** to be in agreement, harmony, or conformance with: *His remark simply does not comport with his known attitude.* —*n.* **3.** *Obs.* comportment. [< MF *comport(er)* < L *comportāre* to transport, support, equiv. to *com-* COM- + *portāre* to PORT⁵]

com·port² (kom′pōrt, -pôrt), *n.* a large English glass dish of the 18th century used for holding fruit, candy, or the like, and having a wide shallow top supported by heavy stem and foot; compote. [alter. of F *compotier* a dish for COMPOTE]

com·port·ance (kəm pōr′tᵊns, -pôr′-), *n.* *Obs.* comportment. [COMPORT[1] + -ANCE]

com·port·ment (kəm pōrt′mənt, -pôrt′-), *n.* bearing; demeanor; behavior. [< MF *comportement.* See COMPORT[1], -MENT] —**Syn.** See **behavior.**

com·pose (kəm pōz′), *v.,* **-posed, -pos·ing.** —*v.t.* **1.** to make or form by combining things, parts, or elements: *He composed his speech from many research notes.* **2.** to be or constitute a part or element of: *Laws are one of the elements that compose the restraints on human conduct.* **3.** to make up or form the basis of: *Style composes the essence of good writing.* **4.** to put or dispose in proper form or order: *to compose laws into a coherent system.* **5.** *Art.* to organize the parts or elements of (a picture or the like). **6.** to create (a literary, musical, or choreographical work). **7.** to end or settle (a quarrel, dispute, etc.): *Through mediation, the union and management composed their differences.* **8.** to bring (the body, mind, or emotions) to a condition of repose, calmness, etc.; calm; quiet. **9.** *Print.* **a.** to set (type). **b.** to set type for (an article, book, etc.). —*v.i.* **10.** to engage in composition, esp. musical composition. **11.** to enter into composition; fall into an arrangement: *He photographs any scene that composes well.* [late ME < MF *compose(r).* See COM-, POSE[1]] —**com·pos′a·ble,** *adj.*

com·posed (kəm pōzd′), *adj.* calm; tranquil; serene: *His composed face reassured the nervous passengers.* [COMPOSE + -ED[2]] —**com·pos·ed·ly** (kəm pō′zid lē), *adv.* —**com·pos′ed·ness,** *n.* —**Syn.** See **calm.** —**Ant.** agitated, perturbed.

com·pos·er (kəm pō′zər), *n.* **1.** one who or that which composes. **2.** a person who writes music. **3.** an author. [COMPOSE + -ER[1]]

compos′ing room′, a room in which compositors work in a printing establishment.

compos′ing stick′, *Print.* a portable, adjustable, usually metal tray held by the compositor in one hand as he places in it type gathered with the other hand.

Composing stick

com·pos·ite (kəm poz′it), *adj.* **1.** made up of disparate or separate parts or elements; compound: *a composite drawing; a composite philosophy.* **2.** *Bot.* belonging to the *Compositae,* a family of plants, including the daisy, dandelion, aster, etc., in which the florets are borne in a close head surrounded by a common involucre of bracts. The *Compositae* is sometimes divided into several families: *Ambrosiaceae, Carduaceae* or *Asteraceae,* and *Cichoriaceae.* **3.** (*cap.*) *Archit.* noting or pertaining to one of the five classical orders, popular esp. since the beginning of the Renaissance but invented by the ancient Romans, in which the Roman Ionic and Corinthian orders are combined, so that four diagonally set Ionic volutes, variously ornamented, rest upon a bell of Corinthian acanthus leaves. Cf. **Corinthian** (def. 4), **Doric** (def. 3), **Ionic** (def. 1), **Tuscan** (def. 2). See illus. under **order. 4.** *Rocketry.* **a.** (of a rocket or missile) having more than one stage. **b.** (of a solid propellant) composed of a mixture of fuel and oxidizer. **5.** *Naut.* noting a vessel having frames of one material and shells and decking of another, esp. one having iron or steel frames with shells and decks planked; composite-built. **6.** *Math.* of or pertaining to a composite function or a composite number. —*n.* **7.** something composite; a compound. **8.** *Bot.* a composite plant. **9.** a picture, photograph, or the like, that combines several separate pictures. [< L *composit(us)* (ptp. of *compōnere* to put together), equiv. to *com-* COM- + *positus* placed; see POSIT] —**com·pos′ite·ly,** *adv.* —**com·pos′ite·ness,** *n.* —**Syn. 7.** See **combination.**

com·pos·ite-built (kəm poz′it bilt′), *adj.* *Naut.* composite (def. 5).

compos′ite func′tion, *Math.* a function obtained from two given functions, where the range of one function is contained in the domain of the second function, by assigning to an element in the domain of the first function that element in the range of the second function whose inverse image is the image of the element. Also called **compound function.**

compos′ite num′ber, *Math.* a number that is a multiple of at least two other numbers, none of which is equal to 1.

compos′ite pho′tograph, a photograph formed by combining two or more separate photographs.

compos′ite school′, (in Canada) a secondary school that offers courses in academic, commercial, and industrial subjects. Also called **comprehensive school.**

compos′ite shot′. See **split screen.**

com·po·si·tion (kom′pə zish′ən), *n.* **1.** the act of combining parts or elements to form a whole. **2.** the resulting state or product. **3.** manner of being composed; structure: *This painting has an orderly composition.* **4.** make-up; constitution: *His moral composition was impeccable.* **5.** an aggregate material formed from two or more substances: *The metal is a composition and contains copper, lead, tin, and zinc.* **6.** *Fine Arts.* the organization or grouping of the different parts of a work of art so as to achieve a unified whole. **7.** the art of putting words and sentences together in accordance with the rules of grammar and rhetoric. **8.** the act or process of producing a literary work. **9.** an academic course for teaching the techniques of clear, expository writing. **10.** a short essay written as a school exercise. **11.** the art of composing music. **12.** a piece of music. **13.** *Gram.* the formation of compounds: *the composition of "bootblack" consists of "boot" and "black."* **14.** a settlement by mutual agreement. **15.** an agreement or compromise, esp. one by which a creditor or group of creditors accepts partial payment from a debtor. **16.** a sum of money so paid. **17.** the setting up of type for printing. **18.** *Math.* the process of making a composite function of two given functions. [< L *compositiōn-* (s. of *compositiō*), equiv. to *composit(us)* (see COMPOSITE) + *-iōn-* -ION; r. ME *composicioun* < AF] —**com′po·si′tion·al,** *adj.* —**com′po·si′tion·al·ly,** *adv.* —**com·pos·i·tive** (kəm poz′i tiv), *adj.* —**com·pos′i·tive·ly,** *adv.*

composi′tion of forc′es, *Mech.* the union or combination of two or more forces into a single force. Cf. **parallelogram law, parallelogram of forces.**

composi′tion se′ries, *Math.* a normal series of subgroups in which no additional subgroups can be inserted. Also called **principal series.**

com·pos·i·tor (kəm poz′i tər), *n.* a person who sets up type and cuts for printing. [< L, equiv. to *composit-* (see COMPOSITE) + *-or* -OR[2]] —**com·pos·i·to·ri·al** (kəm poz′i tōr′ē əl, -tôr′-), *adj.*

com·pos men·tis (kōm′pōs men′tis; *Eng.* kom′pəs men′tis), *Latin.* sane; mentally sound. [lit., being in full possession of one's mind]

com·pos·si·ble (kom pos′ə bəl, kəm-), *adj.* **1.** compatible; potentially consistent, as with another statement, theory, etc.: *The two theories of political behavior vary, but they are compossible.* **2.** able to exist or happen together. [< ML *compossibil(is).* See COM-, POSSIBLE] —**com·pos′si·bil′i·ty,** *n.*

com·post (kom′pōst), *n.* **1.** a mixture of various decaying organic substances, as dead leaves, manure, etc., used for fertilizing land. **2.** a composition; compound. [late ME < MF < L *compos(i)t(um),* n. use of neut. of *compositus* COMPOSITE; see COMPOTE]

com·po·sure (kəm pō′zhər), *n.* serene state of mind; calmness; tranquillity: *Despite the chaos around him, he retained his composure.* [COMPOSE + -URE] —**Syn.** equability, serenity, quiet, coolness, equanimity, self-possession. —**Ant.** agitation.

com·po·ta·tion (kom′pə tā′shən), *n.* the act or an instance of drinking or tippling together. [< L *compōtātiōn-* (s. of *compōtātiō,* trans. of Gk *sympósion* SYMPOSIUM). See COM-, POTATION]

com·po·ta·tor (kom′pə tā′tər), *n.* a person who drinks or tipples with another. [< LL; see COMPOTATION, -OR[2]] —**com·po·ta·to·ry** (kəm pō′tə tōr′ē, -tôr′ē), *adj.*

com·pote (kom′pōt; *Fr.* kôN pôt′), *n., pl.* **-potes** (-pōts; *Fr.* -pôt′). **1.** fruit stewed or cooked in a syrup, usually served as a dessert. **2.** Also, **compotier.** a dish, usually of glass, china, or silver, having a base, stem, and often a lid, and used for serving fruit, nuts, candy, etc. [< F; MF *composte* < L *composita,* fem. of *compositus* COMPOSITE; see COMPOST]

com·po·tier (kom′pə tēr′; *Fr.* kôN pô tyā′), *n., pl.* **-tiers** (-tērz′; *Fr.* -tyā′). compote (def. 2). [< F; see COMPOTE, -IER]

com·pound[1] (*adj.* kom′pound, kom pound′; *n.* kom′pound; *v.* kəm pound′), *adj.* **1.** composed of two or more parts, elements, or ingredients: *Soap is a compound substance.* **2.** having or involving two or more actions or functions: *The mouth is a compound organ.* **3.** *Gram.* of or pertaining to a compound sentence or compound-complex sentence. **4.** (of a word) consisting of two or more parts that are also bases. **5.** *Bot.* composed of several similar parts that combine to form a whole: *a compound fruit.* **6.** *Zool.* (of an animal) composed of a number of distinct individuals that are connected to form a united whole or colony. **7.** *Music.* of or pertaining to compound time. **8.** *Mach.* noting an engine or turbine expanding the same steam or the like in two successive chambers to do work at two ranges of pressure. —*n.* **9.** something formed by compounding or combining parts, elements, etc. **10.** *Chem.* a pure substance composed of two or more elements whose composition is constant. **11.** a word composed of two or more parts that are also bases, as *housetop, many-sided, playact,* or *upon.* [ME *compouned,* ptp. of *compounen,* as below] —*v.t.* **12.** to put together into a whole; combine: *to compound drugs to form a new medicine.* **13.** to make or form by combining parts, elements, etc.; construct: *to compound a new plan from parts of several former plans.* **14.** to make up or constitute: *all the organs and members that compound a human body.* **15.** to settle or adjust by agreement, esp. for a reduced amount, as a debt. **16.** *Law.* to agree, for a consideration, not to prosecute or punish a wrongdoer: *to compound a crime or felony.* **17.** to pay (interest) on the accrued interest as well as the principal: *My bank compounds interest quarterly.* **18.** to increase or add to: *The misery of his loneliness was now compounded by his poverty.* **19.** *Elect.* to connect a portion of the field turns of (a direct-current dynamo) in series with the armature circuit. —*v.i.* **20.** to make a bargain; come to terms; compromise. **21.** to settle a debt, claim, etc., by compromise. [v. use of adj.; r. ME *compoune(n)* < MF *compon-* (s. of *compondre*) < L *compōnere,* equiv. to *com-* COM- + *pōnere* to put] —**com·pound′a·ble,** *adj.* —**com·pound′ed·ness,** *n.* —**com·pound′er,** *n.* —**Syn. 9.** See **combination.**

com·pound[2] (kom′pound), *n.* **1.** (in the Far East) an enclosure containing residences, business offices, or other establishments of Europeans. **2.** (in Africa) a similar enclosure for native laborers. **3.** any enclosure, esp. for prisoners of war. **4.** any separate cluster of homes, often owned by members of the same family: *the Kennedy compound at Hyannisport.* [< Malay *kampong* cluster of buildings]

com′pound centrif′ugal force′. See **Coriolis effect.**

com′pound-com′plex′ sen′tence (kom′pound-kom′pleks), a compound sentence having one or more dependent clauses, as *The lightning flashed* (independent clause) *and the rain fell* (independent clause) *as he entered the house* (dependent clause).

Compound E, cortisone.

com′pound eye′, an arthropod eye subdivided into many individual, light-receptive elements, each including a lens, a transmitting apparatus, and retinal cells.

Compound F, hydrocortisone.

com′pound flow′er, the flower head of a composite plant.

com′pound frac′tion, *Math.* See **complex fraction.**

com′pound frac′ture, a fracture in which the broken bone is exposed through a wound in the skin.

com′pound func′tion, *Math.* See **composite function.**

com′pound in′terest, interest paid on both the principal and on accrued interest.

com′pound in′terval, *Music.* an interval that is greater than an octave, as a 9th or a 13th.

com′pound leaf′, a leaf composed of a number of leaflets on a common stalk. It may be either digitately or pinnately compound, and the leaflets may be themselves compound.

Compound leaf

com′pound lens′, *Optics.* an optical system consisting of two or more lenses having the same axis.

com′pound mag′net, a magnet consisting of two or more separate magnets placed together with like poles pointing in the same direction.

com′pound mi′croscope, an optical instrument for forming magnified images of small objects, consisting of an objective lens with a very short focal length and an eyepiece with a longer focal length, both lenses mounted in the same tube.

com′pound num′ber, a quantity expressed in more than one denomination or unit, as one foot six inches, one minute twenty seconds, etc.

com′pound o′vary, *Bot.* an ovary composed of more than one carpel.

com′pound pen′dulum, *Physics.* See **physical pendulum.**

com′pound sen′tence, a sentence containing two or more coordinate independent clauses, usually joined by one or more conjunctions, but no dependent clause, as *The lightning flashed* (independent clause) *and* (conjunction) *the rain fell* (independent clause).

com′pound time′, *Music.* metrical time beaten so that three beats are counted as one; time in which each beat is divisible by three.

com·pound-wound (kom′pound wound′), *adj.* *Elect.* noting an electric device in which part of the field circuit is in parallel with the armature circuit and part is in series with it. —**com′pound wind′ing** (wīn′ding).

com·pra·dor (kom′prə dôr′), *n.* (formerly in China) a native agent or factotum, as of a foreign business house. Also, **com′pra·dore′.** [< Pg: buyer, equiv. to *com-* COM- + *prad-* < L *parāt(us)* provision (see PREPARATION) + *-or* -OR[2]]

com·pre·ca·tion (kom′prə kā′shən), *n.* *Archaic.* united or public prayer. [< L *comprecātiōn-* (s. of *comprecātiō*), equiv. to *comprecāt(us)* (ptp. of *comprecārī* to pray to; see COM-, PRAY) + *-iōn-* -ION]

com·preg′nat·ed wood′ (kəm preg′nā tid), veneer impregnated with liquid resin and bonded in layers under pressure. [*compregnate* (b. COMPRESS and IMPREGNATE) + -ED[2]]

com·pre·hend (kom′pri hend′), *v.t.* **1.** to understand the nature or meaning of; grasp with the mind; perceive: *He could not comprehend the significance of the king's remark.* **2.** to take in or embrace; include; comprise: *The course will comprehend all facets of African culture.* [ME *comprehende(n)* < L *comprehende(re),* equiv. to *com-* COM- + *prehendere* to grasp; see PREHENSILE] —**com′pre·hend′er,** *n.* —**com′pre·hend′ing·ly,** *adv.* —**Syn. 1.** See **know. 2.** See **include.**

com·pre·hen·si·ble (kom′pri hen′sə bəl), *adj.* capable of being comprehended, or understood; intelligible. Also, **com·pre·hend·i·ble** (kom′pri hen′də bəl). [< L *comprehensibil(is).* See COMPREHENSION, -IBLE] —**com′pre·hen′si·bil′i·ty, com′pre·hen′si·ble·ness,** *n.* —**com′pre·hen′si·bly,** *adv.*

com·pre·hen·sion (kom′pri hen′shən), *n.* **1.** the act or process of comprehending. **2.** the state of being comprehended. **3.** inclusion. **4.** comprehensiveness. **5.** perception or understanding: *His comprehension of physics is amazing for a young student.* **6.** capacity of the mind to perceive and understand; power to grasp ideas; ability to know. **7.** *Logic.* the connotation of a term. [< L *comprehensiōn-* (s. of *comprehensiō*), equiv. to *comprehens(us)* (ptp. of *comprehendere* to COMPREHEND) + *-iōn-* -ION]

com·pre·hen·sive (kom′pri hen′siv), *adj.* **1.** of large scope; covering or involving much; inclusive: *a comprehensive study of world affairs.* **2.** comprehending mentally; having an extensive mental range or grasp. **3.** *Insurance.* covering or providing broad protection against loss. —*n.* **4.** Often, **comprehensives.** Also called **comprehen′sive examina′tion.** an examination of extensive coverage given to measure a student's general progress, proficiency in his major field of study, or the like: *He hasn't taken the comprehensives for his degree yet.* **5.** the detailed layout of an advertisement, showing placement of photographs, illustrations, copy, etc., as for presentation to a client. Cf. **visual** (def. 3). [< LL *comprehensīv(us).* See COMPREHENSION, -IVE] —**com′pre·hen′sive·ly,** *adv.* —**com′pre·hen′sive·ness,** *n.* —**Syn. 1.** broad, wide, extensive, full.

comprehen′sive school′. See **composite school.**

com·press (*v.* kəm pres′; *n.* kom′pres), *v.t.* **1.** to press together; force into less space. **2.** to cause to become a solid mass: *to compress cotton into bales.* —*n.* **3.** *Med.* a soft, cloth pad held in place by a bandage and used to provide pressure or to supply moisture, cold, heat, or medication. **4.** an apparatus or establishment for compressing cotton bales, etc. [late ME < LL *compress(āre),* freq. of L *comprimere* to squeeze together. See COM-, PRESS[1]] —**com·press′i·ble,** *adj.* —**com·press′i·bly,** *adv.* —**com·press′ing·ly,** *adv.* —**Syn. 1.** condense, squeeze, constrict. See **contract.** —**Ant. 1.** expand, spread.

com·pressed (kəm prest′), *adj.* **1.** pressed into less space; condensed: *compressed gases.* **2.** pressed together: *a stern face with hard eyes and compressed lips.* **3.** flattened by or as by pressure: *compressed wallboard.* **4.** *Bot.* flattened laterally or along the length. **5.** *Zool.* narrow from side to side, and therefore of greater height than width. [ME; see COMPRESS, -ED[2]] —**com·press′ed·ly,** *adv.* —**Ant. 1.** expanded.

compressed′ air′, air compressed, esp. by mechanical means, to a pressure higher than the surrounding atmospheric pressure.

compressed′ petro′leum gas′. See **liquefied petroleum gas.**

com·pres·si·bil·i·ty (kəm pres′ə bil′i tē), *n., pl.* **-ties** for 2. *Physics.* **1.** the quality or state of being compressible; capable of being compressed. **2.** the reciprocal of the bulk modulus, equal to the ratio of the fractional change in volume to the stress applied to a body. [COMPRESSIBLE + -ITY]

compressibil′ity drag′, *Aeron.* a parasite drag acting on an aircraft traveling at very high speed, caused by the excessive compression of the air in front of the aircraft.

com·pres·sion (kəm presh′ən), *n.* **1.** the act of compressing. **2.** the state of being compressed. **3.** the effect, result, or consequence of being compressed. **4.** (in internal-combustion engines) the reduction in volume and increase of pressure of the air or combustible mixture in the cylinder prior to ignition, produced by the motion of the piston toward the cylinder head after intake. Also, **com·pres·sure** (kəm presh′ər) (for defs. 1, 2). [< L *compressiōn-* (s. of *compressiō*), equiv. to *compress(us)*, ptp. of *comprimere* to press together (see COM-, PRESS[1]) + *-iōn-* -ION] —**com·pres′sion·al,** *adj.*

compres′sion igni′tion, ignition of engine fuel by the heat of air compressed in the cylinders into which the fuel is introduced. —**compres′sion-ig·ni′tion,** *adj.*

compres′sion ra′tio, *Auto.* the ratio of the cylinder volume enclosed by the piston at its outermost position to the volume enclosed by it at its innermost position.

compres′sion wave′, a shock wave that compresses the medium through which it is transmitted. Cf. **expansion wave.**

com·pres·sive (kəm pres′iv), *adj.* compressing; tending to compress. [COMPRESS + -IVE] —**com·pres′sive·ly,** *adv.*

com·pres·sor (kəm pres′ər), *n.* **1.** one who or that which compresses. **2.** *Anat.* a muscle that compresses some part of the body. **3.** *Surg.* an instrument for compressing a part of the body. **4.** a pump or other machine for reducing the volume and increasing the pressure of gases in order to condense the gases, drive pneumatically powered machinery, etc. **5.** *Electronics.* a transducer that produces an output with a range of voltages whose ratio is smaller than that of the range of the input signal. Cf. **expander** (def. 2). [< L *compress(us)* (see COMPRESS) + -OR[2]]

com·prise (kəm prīz′), *v.t.*, **-prised, -pris·ing.** **1.** to include or contain: *The Soviet Union comprises several Socialist Republics.* **2.** *Informal.* to consist of; be composed of: *The advisory board comprises six members.* **3.** *Informal.* to form or constitute: *His speeches comprised the day's activities.* [late ME < MF *compris* (ptp. of *comprendre*) < L *comprehensus*; see COMPREHENSION] —**com·pris′a·ble,** *adj.* —**com·pris′al,** *n.*
—**Syn. 1.** See **include.**
—**Usage.** COMPRISE in the sense of *compose* or *constitute* is regarded as poor usage: *Water is composed* (not *comprised*) *of hydrogen and oxygen. The following selections constituted* (not comprised) *the evening's program.*

com·prize (kəm prīz′), *v.t.*, **-prized, -priz·ing.** comprise. —**com·priz′a·ble,** *adj.* —**com·priz′al,** *n.*

com·pro·mis (kom′prə mē′), *n., pl.* **-mises** (-mēz′). *Internat. Law.* a formal document, executed in common by nations submitting a dispute to arbitration, that defines the matter at issue, the rules of procedure and the powers of the arbitral tribunal, and the principles to be followed in determining the award. [< F: lit., compromise]

com·pro·mise (kom′prə mīz′), *n., v.*, **-mised, -mis·ing.** —*n.* **1.** a settlement of differences by mutual concessions; an agreement reached by adjustment of conflicting or opposing claims, principles, etc., by reciprocal modification of demands. **2.** the result of such a settlement. **3.** something intermediate between different things: *The split-level is a compromise between a ranch house and a three-storied house.* **4.** an endangering, esp. of reputation; exposure to danger, suspicion, etc.: *a compromise of one's integrity.* —*v.t.* **5.** to settle by a compromise. **6.** to make liable to danger, suspicion, scandal, etc.; endanger the reputation of. **7.** to involve or affect unfavorably: *Being seen with him compromised my reputation.* **8.** *Obs.* **a.** to bind by bargain or agreement. **b.** to bring to terms. —*v.i.* **9.** to make a compromise: *The conflicting parties agreed to compromise.* **10.** to make a dishonorable or shameful concession: *He is too honorable to compromise with his principles.* [late ME < MF *compromis* < L *comprōmiss(um).* See COM-, PROMISE] —**com′pro·mis′er,** *n.* —**com′pro·mis′ing·ly,** *adv.* —**com·prom·is·sa·ry** (kom prom′i ser′ē), *adj.*

com′promise joint′, *Railroads.* a joint for linking together rails having different sections.

com′promise rail′, *Railroads.* a rail for linking rails having different sections.

Comp·sog·na·thus (komp sog′nə thəs), *n.* a genus of bipedal carnivorous dinosaurs of the late Jurassic period, having a slender body that reached a length of 30 inches. [< NL < Gk *kompsó(s)* elegant + *gnáthos*; see -GNATHOUS]

compt (kount), *v.t., v.i., n. Archaic.* count[1].

compte ren·du (kôNt räN dY′), *pl.* **comptes ren·dus** (kôNt räN dY′). *French.* a report, account, or record, as of a transaction, the proceedings of a meeting, etc. [lit., account rendered]

Comp·tom·e·ter (komp tom′i tər), *n. Trademark.* an office machine for arithmetical calculation.

Comp·ton (komp′tən), *n.* **1. Arthur Hol·ly** (hol′ē), 1892–1962, U.S. physicist: Nobel prize 1927. **2.** his brother, **Karl Taylor** (kärl), 1887–1954, U.S. physicist. **3. Spencer, Earl of Wilmington,** 1673?–1743, British statesman: prime minister 1742–43. **4.** a city in SW California. 71,812 (1960).

Comp′ton effect′, *Physics.* the increase in wavelength of monochromatic, electromagnetic radiation, as a beam of photons or x-rays, when it is scattered by particles whose size is small compared to the wavelength of the radiation. Also called **Comp′ton-De·bye′ effect′** (komp′tən de bī′). [named after Arthur H. COMPTON]

comp·trol·ler (kən trō′lər), *n.* controller (def. 1). [by confusion with COMPT] —**comp·trol′ler·ship′,** *n.*

Comptrol′ler Gen′eral, *pl.* **Comptrollers General.** *U.S.* an official in the federal government whose chief function is to settle claims for and against the U.S. government and to supervise the expenditures of all public agencies.

Comptrol′ler of the Cur′rency, *U.S.* an official of the Department of the Treasury who regulates the national banks and administers the issuance and redemption of Federal Reserve notes.

com·pul·sion (kəm pul′shən), *n.* **1.** the act of compelling; constraint; coercion. **2.** the state or condition of being compelled. **3.** *Psychol.* a strong, usually irresistible impulse to perform an act that is contrary to the will of the subject. [late ME < LL *compulsiōn-* (s. of *compulsiō*), equiv. to L *compuls(us)*, ptp. of *compellere* to COMPEL (*com-* COM- + *pul-* v. s. + *-sus* ptp. suffix) + *-iōn-* -ION]

com·pul·sive (kəm pul′siv), *adj.* **1.** compelling; compulsory. **2.** *Psychol.* **a.** pertaining to, characterized by, or involving compulsion: *a compulsive desire to cry.* **b.** governed by an obsessive need to conform, be scrupulous, etc.: *the compulsive personality.* —*n.* **3.** *Psychol.* a person whose behavior is governed by a compulsion. [obs. *compulse* (< L *compuls(us)*, ptp. of *compellere*; see COMPULSION) + -IVE] —**com·pul′sive·ly,** *adv.* —**com·pul′sive·ness,** *n.*

com·pul·so·ry (kəm pul′sə rē), *adj.* **1.** using compulsion; compelling; constraining: *compulsory measures to control rioting.* **2.** required without exception; mandatory; obligatory: *compulsory examinations; compulsory education.* [< ML *compulsōri(us)*, equiv. to L *compuls(us)* (see COMPULSION) + *-ōrius* -ORY[1]] —**com·pul′so·ri·ly,** *adv.* —**com·pul′so·ri·ness,** *n.*
—**Ant. 1, 2.** voluntary.

com·punc·tion (kəm pungk′shən), *n.* **1.** a feeling of uneasiness or anxiety of the conscience caused by regret for doing wrong or causing pain; contrition; remorse. **2.** any uneasiness or hesitation about the rightness of an action. [< eccl. L *compunctiōn-* (s. of *compunctiō*), equiv. to L *compūnct(us)*, ptp. of *compungere* to prick severely (*com-* COM- + *pūnctus*; see POINT) + *-iōn-* -ION; r. late ME *compunccioun* < AF] —**com·punc′tion·less,** *adj.*

com·punc·tious (kəm pungk′shəs), *adj.* causing or feeling compunction; regretful. [COMPUNCT(ION) + -IOUS] —**com·punc′tious·ly,** *adv.*

com·pur·ga·tion (kom′pər gā′shən), *n.* an early common-law method of trial in which the defendant is acquitted on the sworn endorsement of a specified number of friends or neighbors. [< LL *compurgātiōn-* (s. of *compurgātiō*), equiv. to L *compurgāt(us)* (ptp. of *compurgāre*; see COM-, PURGE) + *-iōn-* -ION] —**com·pur·ga·to·ry** (kəm pûr′gə tôr′ē, -tōr′ē), **com·pur′ga·to′ri·al,** *adj.*

com·pur·ga·tor (kom′pər gā′tər), *n.* a person who vouches for the innocence and truthful testimony of another. [< ML, equiv. to *compurgāt(us)* (see COMPURGATION) + *-or* -OR[2]]

com·pu·ta·tion (kom′pyə tā′shən), *n.* **1.** an act, process, or method of computing; calculation. **2.** a result of computing. **3.** the amount computed. [late ME < L *computātiōn-* (s. of *computātiō*), equiv. to *computāt(us)* (ptp. of *computāre*; see COMPUTE) + *-iōn-* -ION] —**com′pu·ta′tion·al,** *adj.* —**com′pu·ta′tive,** *adj.* —**com′pu·ta′tive·ly,** *adv.*

com·pute (kəm pyōōt′), *v.*, **-put·ed, -put·ing,** *n.* —*v.t.* **1.** to determine by calculation; reckon; calculate: *to compute the period of Jupiter's revolution.* —*v.i.* **2.** to reckon; calculate. —*n.* **3.** computation: *outer space that is vast beyond compute.* [< L *comput(āre)*, equiv. to *com-* COM- + *putāre* to think; see PUTATIVE] —**com·put′a·bil′i·ty,** *n.* —**com·put′a·ble,** *adj.* —**com·put′a·bly,** *adv.* —**com·put·ist** (kəm pyōō′tist, kom′pyə-), *n.*
—**Syn. 1.** estimate, count, figure.

com·put·er (kəm pyōō′tər), *n.* **1.** one who or that which computes. **2.** an electronic apparatus that can receive, process, store, and retrieve data, can carry out mathematical and logical operations at high speed and display the results, and can be programmed. Cf. **analog computer, digital computer.** [COMPUTE + -ER[1]]

com·put·er·ese (kəm pyōō′tə rēz′, -rēs′), *n.* the specialized vocabulary and jargon used by people who work with computers. [COMPUTER + -ESE]

com·put·er·ize (kəm pyōō′tə rīz′), *v.t.*, **-ized, -iz·ing.** to control, perform, process, or store (a system, operation, or information) by means of or in an electronic computer or computers; automate by a computer or computers. [COMPUTER + -IZE] —**com·pu′ter·i·za′tion,** *n.*

com·put·er·ized (kəm pyōō′tə rīzd′), *adj.* utilizing or concerned with electronic computers or their use: *a computerized office.*

compu′ter lan′guage, an artificially devised system of symbols, words, etc., as ALGOL, BASIC, or COBOL, used for programming a computer.

Comr., Commissioner.

com·rade (kom′rad *or, esp. Brit.*, -rid, kum′rid), *n.* **1.** a person who shares closely in one's activities, occupation, interests, etc.; intimate companion, associate, or friend. **2.** a fellow member of a fraternal group, political party, etc. **3.** a member of the Communist party or someone with strongly leftist views. [< MF *camarade* < Sp *camarada* group of soldiers billeted together, equiv. to *cámar(a)* room (< L; see CAMERA) + *-ada* < L *-āta*, fem. of *-ātus* -ATE[1]] —**com′rade·ship′,** *n.*
—**Syn. 1.** crony, fellow, mate.

com′rade in arms′, a fellow soldier.

com·rade·ry (kom′rad rē *or, esp. Brit.*, -rid-, kum′-rid-), *n.* camaraderie.

Com·stock (kum′stok, kom′-), *n.* **Anthony,** 1844–1915, U.S. author and reformer.

com·stock·er·y (kum′stok′ə rē, kom′-), *n.* overzealous moral censorship of the fine arts and literature, often mistaking outspokenly honest works for salacious ones. [after Anthony COMSTOCK; see -ERY]

Com′stock Lode′, the most valuable deposit of silver ore ever recorded, discovered in 1859 by Henry T. P. Comstock near Virginia City, Nevada. Also called **Com′stock Sil′ver Lode′.**

comte (kôNt), *n., pl.* **comtes** (kôNt). *French.* count[2].

Comte (kōnt; *Fr.* kôNt), *n.* **(I·si·dore) Au·guste (Ma·rie Fran·çois)** (ē zē dôr′ ō gYst′ MA Rē′ fRäN swA′), 1798–1857, French founder of the philosophical system of positivism. —**Com·ti·an** (kom′tē ən, kōn′-), *adj.* —**Comt·ism** (kom′tiz əm, kōn′-), *n.* —**Comt′ist,** *n., adj.*

Comte de Mon·te-Cris·to, Le (*Fr.* lə kôNt də mōN tā kRē stō′). See **Count of Monte Cristo, The.**

com·tesse (kôN tes′), *n., pl.* **-tesses** (-tes′). *French.* countess.

Co·mus (kō′məs), *n.* an ancient Roman god of drinking and revelry, represented as a winged young man dressed in white. [< L < Gk *kômos* revel]

Co·mus (kō′məs), *n.* a masque (1634) by John Milton.

Com. Ver., Common Version (of the Bible).

con[1] (kon), *adv.* **1.** against a proposition, opinion, etc.: *I've considered the arguments pro and con.* —*n.* **2.** the argument, position, arguer, or voter against something. Cf. **pro[1].** [short for L *contrā* in opposition, against]

con[2] (kon), *v.t.*, **conned, con·ning.** **1.** to learn; study; peruse or examine carefully. **2.** commit to memory. [var. of CAN[1] in sense become acquainted with, learn to know]

con[3] (kon), *v.*, **conned, con·ning,** *n. Naut.* —*v.t.* **1.** to direct the steering of (a ship). —*n.* **2.** the station of the person who cons. **3.** the act of conning. Also, **conn.** [earlier *cond*, apocopated var. of ME *condie, condue* < MF *cond(u)ire* < L *condūcere* to CONDUCT]

con[4] (kon), *adj., v.*, **conned, con·ning.** *U.S. Slang.* —*adj.* **1.** confidence: *a con game; a con man.* —*v.t.* **2.** to swindle; trick: *That crook conned me out of all my savings.* **3.** to persuade by deception, cajolery, etc. [CON(FIDENCE)]

con[5] (kon), *v.t.*, **conned, con·ning.** *Brit. Dial.* **1.** to strike, hit, or rap (something or someone). **2.** to hammer (a nail or peg). **3.** to beat or thrash a person with the hands or a weapon. [? akin to F *cognée* hatchet, *cogner* to knock in, drive (a nail) home]

con[6] (kon), *n. Slang.* a convict.

con-, var. of **com-** before a consonant (except *b, h, l, p, r, w*) and, by assimilation, before *n*: *convene; condone; connection.* [< L]

Con., **1.** Conformist. **2.** Consul.

con., **1.** concerto. **2.** conclusion. **3.** connection. **4.** consolidated. **5.** consul. **6.** continued. **7.** against. [< L *contrā*]

Co·na·kry (*Fr.* kô nA kRē′), *n.* a seaport in and the capital of Guinea, in NW Africa. 112,491 with suburbs (1960). Also, **Konakri.**

con a·mo·re (*It.* kōn ä mô′Re *for 1;* kon ə mōr′ē, -mōr′ā, -môr′ē, -môr′ā, kōn *for 2*). **1.** (*italics.*) *Italian.* with love, tender enthusiasm, or zeal. **2.** tenderly and lovingly (used as a musical direction).

Co·nant (kō′nənt), *n.* **James Bryant,** born 1893, U.S. chemist and educator: president of Harvard University 1933–53.

co·na·tion (kō nā′shən), *n. Psychol.* the part of mental life having to do with striving, including desire and volition. [< L *cōnātiōn-* (s. of *cōnātiō*) an effort, equiv. to *cōnāt(us)* (ptp. of *cōnārī* to try) + *-iōn-* -ION]

con·a·tive (kon′ə tiv, kō′nə-), *adj.* **1.** *Psychol.* pertaining to or of the nature of conation. **2.** *Gram.* expressing endeavor or effort: *a conative verb.* —*n.* **3.** *Gram.* a conative word, affix, or verbal aspect. [CONAT(ION) + -IVE]

co·na·tus (kō nā′təs), *n., pl.* **-tus.** **1.** an effort or striving. **2.** a force or tendency simulating a human effort. **3.** (in the philosophy of Spinoza) the force in every animate creature toward the preservation of its existence. [< L: exertion, n. use of *cōnātus*, ptp. of *cōnārī* to attempt; see CONATION]

con bri·o (kon brē′ō, kōn; *It.* kôn bRē′ô), with vigor; vivaciously (used as a musical direction). [< It]

conc., **1.** concentrate. **2.** concentrated. **3.** concentration. **4.** concerning.

con·cat·e·nate (kon kat′ənāt′), *v.*, **-nat·ed, -nat·ing,** *adj.* —*v.t.* **1.** to link together; unite in a series or chain. —*adj.* **2.** linked together, as in a chain. [< LL *concatēnāt(us)* (ptp. of *concatēnāre*), equiv. to *con-* CON- + L *catēn(a)* CHAIN + *-ātus* -ATE[1]] —**con·cat′e·na′tor,** *n.*

con·cat·e·na·tion (kon kat′ənā′shən), *n.* **1.** the act of concatenating. **2.** the state of being concatenated; connection, as in a chain. **3.** a series of interconnected or interdependent things or events. [< LL *concatēnātiōn-* (s. of *concatēnātiō*), equiv. to *concatēnāt(us)* CONCATENATE + *-iōn-* -ION]

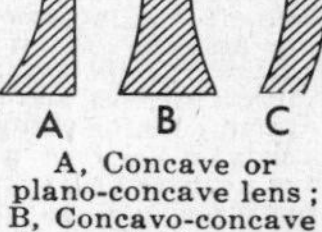

A, Concave or plano-concave lens; B, Concavo-concave lens; C, Concavo-convex lens

con·cave (*adj., v.* kon kāv′, kon′kāv; *n.* kon′kāv), *adj., n., v.*, **-caved, -cav·ing.** —*adj.* **1.** curved like a segment of the interior of a circle or hollow sphere; hollow and curved. Cf. **convex** (def. 1). **2.** *Geom.* (of a polygon) having at least one interior angle greater than 180°. **3.** *Obs.* hollow. —*n.* **4.** a concave surface, part, line, etc. **5.** *Mach.* a concave piece, as one against which a drum rotates. —*v.t.* **6.** to make concave. [< L *concav(us).* See CON-, CAVE[1]] —**con·cave′ly,** *adv.* —**con·cave′ness,** *n.*

con·cav·i·ty (kon kav′i tē), *n., pl.* **-ties.** **1.** the state or quality of being concave. **2.** a concave surface or thing; a hollow; cavity. [late ME *concavite* < LL *concavitāt-* (s. of *concavitās*). See CON-, CAVE[1], -ITY]

con·ca·vo-con·cave (kon kā′vō kon kāv′), *adj.* concave on both sides. [< L *concav(us)* + -o- + CONCAVE]

con·ca·vo-con·vex (kon kā′vō kon veks′), *adj.* **1.** concave on one side and convex on the other. **2.** *Optics.* pertaining to or noting a lens in which the concave face has a greater degree of curvature than the convex face. [< L *concav(us)* + -o- + CONVEX]

con·ceal (kən sēl′), *v.t.* **1.** to hide; withdraw or remove from observation; cover or keep from sight: *He concealed the gun under his coat.* **2.** to keep secret; to prevent or avoid disclosing or divulging: *He concealed the true source of the gold.* [late ME *consele, concele* < AF *concele(r)* < L *concēlāre*, equiv. to *con-* CON- + *cēlāre* to hide; see OCCULT] —**con·ceal′a·ble,** *adj.* —**con·ceal′ed·ly,** *adv.* —**con·ceal′ed·ness,** *n.* —**con·ceal′er,** *n.*
—**Syn. 1.** See **hide[1].**

con·ceal·ment (kən sēl′mənt), *n.* **1.** the act of concealing. **2.** the state of being concealed. **3.** a means or place of hiding. [ME *concelement* < AF. See CONCEAL, -MENT]

con·cede (kən sēd′), *v.*, **-ced·ed, -ced·ing.** —*v.t.* **1.** to acknowledge as true, just, or proper; admit: *He finally conceded that she was right. The Mets finally conceded defeat.* **2.** to acknowledge (an opponent's victory, score, etc.) before it is officially established: *to concede an election before most of the votes are counted.* **3.** to grant as a right or privilege; yield: *to concede a longer vacation for all employees.* —*v.i.* **4.** to make concession; yield; admit: *She was so persistent that I conceded at last.* [< L *concēde(re)*, equiv. to *con-* CON- + *cēdere* to withdraw, yield, CEDE] —**con·ced′ed·ly,** *adv.* —**con·ced′er,** *n.* —**con·ces′si·ble,** *adj.*
—**Syn. 1.** yield, grant. —**Ant. 1.** deny. **3.** refuse.

con·ceit (kən sēt′), *n.* **1.** an exaggerated estimate of one's own ability, importance, wit, etc. **2.** something that is conceived in the mind; a thought; idea: *He jotted down the conceits of his idle hours.* **3.** imagination; fancy. **4.** a fancy; whim; fanciful notion. **5.** an elaborate, fanciful metaphor, esp. of a strained or far-fetched nature. **6.** the use of such metaphors as a literary characteristic, esp. in poetry. **7.** a fancy, purely decorative article. **8.** *Archaic.* **a.** favorable opinion; esteem. **b.** personal opinion or estimation. **9.** *Obs.* the faculty of conceiving; apprehension. **10. out of conceit with,** displeased or dissatisfied with. —*v.t.* **11.** to flatter (esp. oneself). **12.** *Archaic.* to take a fancy to; have a good opinion of. **13.** *Obs.* **a.** to imagine. **b.** to conceive;

apprehend. [ME *conceyte, conceipt,* deriv. of CONCEIVE + L *conceptum* CONCEPT]
—**Syn. 1.** self-esteem, vanity, egotism, complacency. See **pride.** —**Ant. 1.** humility.

con·ceit·ed (kən sē′tid), *adj.* **1.** having an exaggerated opinion of one's own abilities, appearance, importance, etc.: *Many performers become conceited after only modest success.* **2.** *Archaic.* **a.** having an opinion. **b.** fanciful; whimsical. **3.** *Obs.* intelligent; clever. [CONCEIT + -ED[2]] —**con·ceit′ed·ly,** *adv.* —**con·ceit′ed·ness,** *n.*
—**Syn. 1.** vain, proud, egotistical, self-important, self-satisfied.

con·ceiv·a·ble (kən sē′və bəl), *adj.* capable of being conceived; imaginable. [CONCEIVE + -ABLE] —**con·ceiv′a·bil′i·ty, con·ceiv′a·ble·ness,** *n.* —**con·ceiv′a·bly,** *adv.*

con·ceive (kən sēv′), *v.,* **-ceived, -ceiv·ing.** —*v.t.* **1.** to form (a notion, opinion, purpose, etc.): *He conceived the project while he gazed into the distance.* **2.** to form a notion or idea of; imagine. **3.** to hold as an opinion; think; believe: *I conceive that you are entirely right.* **4.** to experience or form (a feeling): *to conceive a great love for music.* **5.** to express, as in words. **6.** to beget. **7.** to become pregnant with. **8.** to begin, originate, or found (something) in a particular way (usually used in the passive): *a new nation conceived in liberty.* **9.** *Archaic.* to understand; comprehend. —*v.i.* **10.** to form an idea; think (usually fol. by *of*). **11.** to become pregnant. [ME < OF *conceiv(re)* < L *concipere* to take fully, take in, equiv. to *con-* CON- + *-cipere,* comb. form of *capere* to take] —**con·ceiv′er,** *n.*
—**Syn. 2, 8.** See **imagine.**

con·cel·e·brate (kon sel′ə brāt′), *v.i.,* **-brat·ed, -brat·ing.** to participate in a concelebration. [< L *concelebrāt(us),* ptp. of *concelebrāre;* see COM-, CELEBRATE]

con·cel·e·bra·tion (kon sel′ə brā′shən), *n.* the celebration of a Mass by two or more clergymen. [CONCELEBRATE + -ION]

con·cent (kən sent′), *n.* *Obs.* concord of sound, voices, etc.; harmony. [< L *concent(us)* harmony, n. use of *concentus harmonized* (ptp. of *concinere*), equiv. to *con-* CON- + *cen-* (var. s. of *-cinere,* comb. form of *canere* to sing) + *-tus* ptp. ending]

con·cen·ter (kon sen′tər), *v.t., v.i.* to bring or converge to a common center; concentrate. Also, *esp. Brit.,* **concentre.** [< MF *concentr(er),* equiv. to *con-* CON- + *centrer* to CENTER]

con·cen·trate (kon′sən trāt′), *v.,* **-trat·ed, -trat·ing,** *n.* —*v.t.* **1.** to bring or draw to a common center or point of union; converge; direct toward one point; focus: *to concentrate one's attention on a problem; to concentrate the rays of the sun with a lens.* **2.** to put or bring into a single place, group, etc.: *The nation's wealth had been concentrated in a few families.* **3.** to intensify; make denser, stronger, or purer by removing or reducing the foreign or inessential: *to concentrate fruit juice; to concentrate a sauce by boiling it down.* **4.** *Mining.* to separate (metal or ore) from rock, sand, etc., so as to improve the quality of the valuable portion. —*v.i.* **5.** to come to or toward a common center; converge; collect: *The bulk of the population concentrates in the cities.* **6.** to bring all efforts, faculties, activities, etc., to bear on one thing or activity (often fol. by *on* or *upon*): *to concentrate on solving a problem; to concentrate on a book.* **7.** to become more intense, stronger, or purer. —*n.* **8.** a concentrated form of something; a product of concentration: *Frozen orange juice is a concentrate.* [back formation from CONCENTRATION] —**con·cen·tra·tive** (kon′sən trā′tiv, kən sen′trə-), *adj.* —**con′cen·tra′tive·ness,** *n.* —**con′cen·tra′tor,** *n.*
—**Syn. 1.** See **contract.** —**Ant. 1.** dissipate, disperse. **5.** diverge.

con·cen·trat·ed (kon′sən trā′tid), *adj.* **1.** applied with all one's attention, energy, etc.: *their concentrated efforts to win the election.* **2.** clustered or gathered together closely: *the concentrated masses in the slums.* **3.** treated to remove what is inessential: *Concentrated orange juice must be diluted with water.* [CONCENTRATE + -ED[2]]

con·cen·tra·tion (kon′sən trā′shən), *n.* **1.** the act of concentrating; the state of being concentrated. **2.** something concentrated: *a concentration of stars.* **3.** exclusive attention to one object; close mental application: *He focused his concentration on the swinging pendulum.* **4.** *Mil.* **a.** the assembling of military or naval forces in a particular area in preparation for further operations. **b.** a specified intensity and duration of artillery fire placed on a small area. **5.** the focusing of a student's academic program on advanced study in a specific subject or field. **6.** *Chem.* (in a solution) a measure of the amount of dissolved substance contained per unit of volume. **7.** Also called **memory.** *Cards.* a game for two or more players in which the pack is spread out face down on the table and each player in turn exposes two cards at a time and replaces them face down if they do not constitute a pair, the object being to take the most pairs by remembering the location of the cards previously exposed. [CON- + L *centr(um)* CENTER + -ATION]

concentra′tion camp′, a guarded compound for the detention or imprisonment of aliens, political opponents, etc., esp. any of the camps established by the Nazis in World War II for the confinement, persecution, and mass execution of prisoners.

concentra′tion cell′, *Physical Chem.* a galvanic cell consisting of two electrodes of the same metal each in different concentrations of a solution of the same salt of that metal.

con·cen·tre (kon sen′tər), *v.t., v.i.,* **-tred, -tring.** *Chiefly Brit.* concenter.

con·cen·tric (kən sen′trik), *adj.* having a common center, as circles or spheres. Also, **con·cen′tri·cal.** [ME *consentrik* < ML *concentric(us).* See CON-, CENTER, -IC] —**con·cen′tri·cal·ly,** *adv.* —**con·cen·tric·i·ty** (kon′sən tris′i tē), *n.*

Con·cep·ción (kôn′sep syôn′), *n.* a city in central Chile, near the mouth of the Bío-Bío River. 167,468 (1960).

con·cept (kon′sept), *n.* **1.** a general notion or idea; conception. **2.** an idea of something formed by mentally combining all its characteristics or particulars; a construct. **3.** a directly conceived or intuited object of thought. [< L *concept(um)* something conceived, orig. neut. of *conceptus* (ptp. of *concipere*), equiv. to *con-* CON- + *cep-* (var. s. of *-cipere,* comb. form of *capere* to seize) + *-tus* ptp. ending]

con·cep·ta·cle (kən sep′tə kəl), *n.* *Biol.* an organ or cavity enclosing reproductive bodies. [< L *conceptāculum,* equiv. to *concept(us)* conceived (see CONCEPT) + *āculum;* see RECEPTACLE] —**con·cep·tac·u·lar** (kon′sep tak′yə lər), *adj.*

con·cep·tion (kən sep′shən), *n.* **1.** the act of conceiving; the state of being conceived. **2.** fertilization; inception of pregnancy. **3.** origination; beginning: *The conception of the United Nations was in 1945.* **4.** something that is conceived: *That machine is the conception of a genius.* **5.** the act or power of forming notions, ideas, or concepts. **6.** a notion; idea; concept: *She has some very odd conceptions about life in general.* **7.** a design; plan: *The architect produced a fine conception for the skyscraper.* **8.** a sketch of something not actually existing: *an artist's conception of a street in ancient Ostia.* [ME *concepcion* < eccl. L *conceptiōn-* (s. of *conceptiō*), equiv. to L *concept-* (see CONCEPT) + *-iōn-* -ION] —**con·cep′tion·al,** *adj.* —**con·cep′tive,** *adj.*
—**Syn. 6.** See **idea.**

con·cep·tu·al (kən sep′cho͞o əl), *adj.* pertaining to concepts or to the forming of concepts. [< ML *conceptuāl(is).* See CONCEPT, -AL[1]] —**con·cep·tu·al·i·ty** (kən sep′cho͞o al′i tē), *n.* —**con·cep′tu·al·ly,** *adv.*

con·cep·tu·al·ise (kən sep′cho͞o ə līz′), *v.t., v.i.,* **-ised, -is·ing.** *Chiefly Brit.* conceptualize. —**con·cep′tu·al·i·sa′tion,** *n.*

con·cep·tu·al·ism (kən sep′cho͞o ə liz′əm), *n.* *Philos.* any of several doctrines existing as a compromise between realism and nominalism and regarding universals as concepts. Cf. **nominalism, realism** (def. 5). [CONCEPTUAL + -ISM] —**con·cep′tu·al·ist,** *n.* —**con·cep′tu·al·is′tic,** *adj.*

con·cep·tu·al·ize (kən sep′cho͞o ə līz′), *v.,* **-ized, -iz·ing.** —*v.t.* **1.** to form into a concept; make a concept of: *the artistry required to conceptualize arbitrary tones into symphonies; men who conceptualized visions into philosophies.* —*v.i.* **2.** to form a concept; think in concepts. Also, *esp. Brit.,* **conceptualise.** [CONCEPTUAL + -IZE] —**con·cep′tu·al·i·za′tion,** *n.*

concep′tual re′alism, *Philos.* the doctrine that universals have real and independent existence. —**con·cep′tual re′alist.**

con·cern (kən sûrn′), *v.t.* **1.** to relate to; be connected with; be of interest or importance to; affect: *The water shortage concerns us all.* **2.** to interest, engage, or involve (used reflexively or in the passive, often fol. by *with* or *in*): *He concerns himself with such trivialities. They are concerned with the project also.* **3.** to trouble, worry, or disquiet: *I am concerned about his health. The problem concerns us deeply.* —*n.* **4.** something that relates or pertains to a person; business; affair: *Revision of the new bill is the chief concern of Congress this week.* **5.** a matter that engages a person's attention, interest, or care, or that affects a person's welfare or happiness: *He made it his concern to make sure that everyone arrived promptly at nine o'clock.* **6.** worry, solicitude, or anxiety: *to show concern for someone in trouble.* **7.** important relation or bearing: *This news is of concern to our understanding of the issue.* **8.** a commercial or manufacturing company or establishment: *the headquarters of an insurance concern.* **9.** *Informal.* any material object or contrivance: *an odd little concern fitted with blinking lights.* [late ME *concerne* < ML: to relate to, distinguish (in LL, to mix for sifting), equiv. to L *con-* CON- + *cernere* to sift]
—**Syn. 1.** touch, involve. **3.** disturb. **5.** burden, responsibility. CONCERN, CARE, WORRY connote an uneasy and burdened state of mind. CONCERN implies an anxious sense of interest in, or responsibility for, something: *concern over a friend's misfortune.* CARE suggests a heaviness of spirit caused by dread, or by the constant pressure of burdensome demands: *Poverty weighs a person down with care.* WORRY is an active state of agitated uneasiness and restless apprehension: *He was distracted by worry over the stock market.* **8.** corporation, house. —**Ant. 6.** indifference.

con·cerned (kən sûrnd′), *adj.* **1.** interested or participating: *all concerned citizens.* **2.** troubled or anxious: *a concerned look.* **3.** having a connection or involvement: *all the students concerned in the riot.* [CONCERN + -ED[2]] —**con·cern′ed·ly,** *adv.* —**con·cern′ed·ness,** *n.*

con·cern·ing (kən sûr′ning), *prep.* relating to; regarding; about: *a discussion concerning foreign aid.* [late ME; see CONCERN, -ING[2]] —**con·cern′ing·ly,** *adv.* —**con·cern′ing·ness,** *n.*

con·cern·ment (kən sûrn′mənt), *n.* *Archaic.* **1.** importance or moment: *a matter of concernment to all voters.* **2.** relation or bearing: *That idea has no concernment to the issue.* **3.** anxiety or solicitude. **4.** a thing in which one is involved or interested: *The letter is none of your concernment.* **5.** interest; participation; involvement. [CONCERN + -MENT]

con·cert (*n., adj.* kon′sûrt, -sərt; *v.* kən sûrt′), *n.* **1.** a public musical performance in which several singers or players, or both, participate. **2.** recital: *The violinist has given concerts all over the world.* **3.** agreement of two or more individuals in a design or plan; combined action; accord or harmony: *His plan was greeted with a concert of abuse and vituperation.* **4.** in **concert,** together; jointly: *The thief and the insured were accused of having acted in concert.* [< F < It *concerto;* see CONCERTO] —*adj.* **5.** designed or intended for concerts: *concert hall.* **6.** performed at concerts: *concert music.* **7.** performing or capable of performing at concerts: *a concert pianist.* —*v.t.* **8.** to contrive or arrange by agreement: *They were able to concert a settlement of their differences.* **9.** to plan; devise: *A program of action was concerted at the meeting.* —*v.i.* **10.** to plan or act together. [< F *concert(er)* < It *concertare* < LL: decide together (in L: contend), equiv. to L *con-* CON- + *certāre* to decide by debate or warfare, deriv. of *certus* settled, certain]

con·cer·tan·te (kon′sər tän′tē; *It.* kôn′ cher tän′te), *adj., n., pl.* **-ti** (-tē). *Music.* —*adj.* **1.** brilliantly virtuosic: *a concertante part for solo violin.* —*n.* **2.** an 18th-century symphonic work with sections for solo instruments. Also, **concertato.** [< It, fem. ptp. of *concertare* to give a concert; see -ANT]

con·cer·ta·to (kon′sər tä′tō; *It.* kôn′cher tä′tô), *adj., n. pl.* **-tos** (-tōz), *It.* **-ti** (-tē). concertante. [< It, ptp. of *concertare* to give a concert; see -ATE[1]]

con·cert·ed (kən sûr′tid), *adj.* **1.** contrived or arranged by agreement; planned or devised together: *a concerted program of defense.* **2.** done or performed together or in cooperation: *a concerted attack on the fortress.* **3.** *Music.* arranged in parts for several voices or instruments. [CONCERT (v.) + -ED[2]] —**con·cert′ed·ly,** *adv.*

con·cert·go·er (kon′sərt gō′ər), *n.* a person who attends concerts frequently. [CONCERT + GOER]

con′cert grand′ pian′o, a grand piano of the largest size, being typically nine feet in length. Also called **con′cert grand′.**

Concertina

con·cer·ti·na (kon′sər tē′nə), *n.* a small musical instrument somewhat resembling an accordion but having buttonlike keys, hexagonal bellows and ends, and more limited range. [CONCERT + *-ina* fem. of L *-inus* -INE[1]] —**con′cer·ti′nist,** *n.*

concerti′na move′ment, a principle of table construction in which hinged sections of the frame, ordinarily folded inward out of sight, can be pulled into line with the parts of the frame ordinarily seen to permit the addition of leaves. Also called **concerti′na ac′tion.**

concerti′na ta′ble, an extensible table having a hinged double top falling onto a hinged frame that unfolds like an accordion when pulled out.

con·cer·ti·no (kon′chər tē′nō; *It.* kôn′cher tē′nô), *n., pl.* **-ni** (-nē). *Music.* **1.** a short concerto. **2.** the group of solo instruments in a concerto grosso. **3.** a section in a concerto grosso played by these instruments. [< It, equiv. to *concert(o)* (see CONCERTO) + *-ino* dim. suffix]

con·cert·ise (kon′sər tīz′), *v.i.,* **-ised, -is·ing.** *Chiefly Brit.* concertize. —**con′cert·is′er,** *n.*

con·cert·ize (kon′sər tīz′), *v.i.,* **-ized, -iz·ing.** to give concerts or recitals professionally, esp. while on tour. [CONCERT + -IZE] —**con′cert·iz′er,** *n.*

con·cert·mas·ter (kon′sərt mas′tər, -mä′stər), *n.* the leader of the first violins in a symphony orchestra, who is usually also the assistant to the conductor. [< G *Konzertmeister.* See CONCERT (n.), MASTER]

con·cer·to (kən cher′tō; *It.* kôn cher′tô), *n., pl.* **-tos,** *It.* **-ti** (-tē). *Music.* a composition for one or more principal instruments, with orchestral accompaniment, now usually in symphonic form. [< It; see CONCERT]

con·cer·to gros·so (kən cher′tō grō′sō; *It.* kôn-cher′tô grôs′sô), *pl.* **con·cer·ti gros·si** (kən cher′tē grō′sē; *It.* kôn cher′tē grôs′sē), **con·cer·to gros·sos.** a musical form, common in the Baroque period, typically comprised of contrasting sections that are played by full orchestra and a group of soloists in alternation. [< It: lit., big concert; see GROSS]

con′cert par′ty, *Brit.* a form of theatrical entertainment popular at seaside resorts, in which specialty acts, songs, dances, etc., are presented.

con′cert pitch′, *Music.* the pitch used in tuning instruments for concert performance; philharmonic pitch or international pitch.

con′cert tour′, a trip, often an extensive one, by a musician or group of musicians to give a series of concerts or recitals.

con·ces·sion (kən sesh′ən), *n.* **1.** the act of conceding or yielding, as a right, a privilege, a point or fact in an argument, etc.: *His concession that he had made a hasty decision was all we wanted to hear.* **2.** the thing or point yielded: *The union won all the concessions they sought.* **3.** something conceded by a government or a controlling authority, as a grant of land, a privilege, or a franchise. **4.** *U.S.* a space or privilege within certain premises for a subsidiary business or service: *the checkroom concession at a restaurant.* [< L *concessiōn-* (s. of *concessiō*), equiv. to *concēs(sus),* (ptp. of *concēdere* to CONCEDE) + *-iōn-* -ION]

con·ces·sion·aire (kən sesh′ə nâr′), *n.* a person, group, or company to whom a concession has been granted, esp. to operate a subsidiary business or service. Also, **con·ces·sion·er** (kən sesh′ə nər). [< F *concessionnaire.* See CONCESSIONARY]

con·ces·sion·ar·y (kən sesh′ə ner′ē), *adj., n., pl.* **-ar·ies.** —*adj.* **1.** pertaining to concession; of the nature of a concession: *concessionary agreements.* —*n.* **2.** a concessionaire. [CONCESSION + -ARY]

con·ces·sive (kən ses′iv), *adj.* **1.** tending or serving to concede. **2.** *Gram.* expressing concession, as the English conjunction *though.* [< LL *concessīv(us).* See CONCESSION, -IVE]

Conch (def. 2) *Strombus alatus* (Length 3 to 4 in.)

conch (kongk, konch), *n., pl.* **conchs** (kongks), **con·ches** (kon′chiz). **1.** the spiral shell of a gastropod, often used as a horn. **2.** any of various marine gastropods. **3.** the fabled shell trumpet of the Tritons. **4.** Also, **concha.** *Archit.* a smooth concave surface consisting of or resembling the interior of a semidome, as the surface of a vault, a trompe, or the head of a niche. [ME < L *concha* < Gk *konchē* mussel, shell] —**conch·ate** (kong′kāt, konch′āt), **conched,** *adj.*

con·cha (kong′kə), *n., pl.* **-chae** (-kē). **1.** *Anat.* **a.** a shell-like structure, esp. the external ear. See diag. under **ear. b.** any turbinate bone, esp. in the nose. **2.** *Archit.* conch (def. 4). [< L: CONCH] —**con′chal,** *adj.*

conch·fish (kongk′fish′, konch′-), *n., pl.* **fish·es,** (*esp. collectively*) **-fish.** a cardinalfish, *Apogon stellatus,* of the Atlantic Ocean. [CONCH + FISH]

con·chie (kon′chē), *n.* conchy.

con·chif·er·ous (kong kif′ər əs), *adj.* having a shell. [CONCH + -I- + -FEROUS]

con·chi·o·lin (kong kī′ə lin), *n.* *Biochem.* an albuminoid, $C_{30}H_{48}O_{11}N_9$, that serves to form a matrix in the shells of mollusks. [CONCH + -I- -ol (< L *-olus* dim. suffix) + -IN[2]]

Con·chi·ta (*Sp.* kôn chē′tä), *n.* a girl's given name.

Con·cho·bar (kong′kō wər, kon′ə hōōr′, kon′ōōr), *n.* *Irish Legend.* a king of Ulster, the uncle of Cuchulainn and the abductor of Deirdre.

$\Theta = \pi/2$ … $\Theta = O$ … O … b

*Conchoid (of Niumedes)

con·choid (kong′koid), *n.* *Geom.* a plane curve such that if a straight line be drawn from a certain fixed point, called the pole of the curve, to the curve, the part of the line intersected between the curve and its asymptote is always equal to a fixed distance. Equation: $r = b \pm a\sec\theta$. [< Gk *konchoeid(ēs)*. See CONCH, -OID]

con·choi·dal (koŋ koid′ᵊl), *adj. Mineral.* noting a shell-like fracture form produced on certain minerals by a blow. [CONCHOID + -AL[1]] —**con·choi′dal·ly,** *adv.*

con·chol·o·gy (koŋ kol′ə jē), *n.* the branch of zoology dealing with the shells of mollusks. [CONCH + -O- + -LOGY] —**con·cho·log·i·cal** (koŋ′kə loj′i kəl), *adj.* —**con′cho·log′i·cal·ly,** *adv.* —**con·chol′o·gist,** *n.*

con·chy (kon′chē), *n., pl.* **-chies.** *Slang.* conscientious objector. Also, **conchie.** [for *consci*, short for CONSCIENTIOUS]

con·cierge (kon′sē ârzh′; *Fr.* kôɴ syerzh′), *n., pl.* **-cierges** (-sē âr′zhiz; *Fr.* -syerzh′). **1.** (esp. in France) a person who has charge of the entrance of a building; a janitor or doorkeeper. **2.** a multilingual official in a hotel who is in charge of welcoming and arranging special services for guests. **3.** *Obs.* a custodian or warden. [< F; OF *cumserges* < L *con-* CON- + *serviēns* prp. of *servīre* to SERVE]

con·cil·i·ar (kən sil′ē ər), *adj.* of, pertaining to, or issued by a council. [< L *concili(um)* COUNCIL + -AR[1]] —**con·cil′i·ar·ly,** *adv.*

con·cil·i·ate (kən sil′ē āt′), *v.t.,* **-at·ed, -at·ing. 1.** to overcome the distrust or hostility of; placate; win over: *to conciliate an enemy.* **2.** to win or gain (regard or favor): *He conciliated the respect of his associates with his cooperativeness.* **3.** to make compatible; reconcile. [< L *conciliāt(us)* (ptp. of *conciliāre* to bring together, unite, equiv. to *concili(um)* COUNCIL + *-ātus* -ATE[1]] —**con·cil·i·a·ble** (kən sil′ē ə bəl), *adj.* —**con·cil′i·at′ing·ly,** *adv.* —**con·cil′i·a′tion,** *n.*
—**Syn. 1.** See **appease.**

con·cil·i·a·tor (kən sil′ē ā′tər), *n.* **1.** a person who conciliates. **2.** arbitrator. [< L *conciliātor*, equiv. to *conciliāt(us)* (see CONCILIATE) + *-or* -OR[2]]

con·cil·i·a·to·ry (kən sil′ē ə tōr′ē, -tôr′ē), *adj.* tending to conciliate: *a conciliatory manner; conciliatory comments.* Also, **con·cil·i·a·tive** (kən sil′ē ā′tiv, -ə tiv, -sil′yə-). [CONCILIATE + -ORY[1]] —**con·cil′i·a·to′ri·ly,** *adv.* —**con·cil′i·a·to′ri·ness,** *n.*

con·cin·nate (kon′sə nāt′), *v.t.,* **-nat·ed, -nat·ing.** to arrange or blend together skillfully, as parts or elements; put or fit together in a harmonious, precisely appropriate, or elegant manner. [< L *concinnāt(us)* (ptp. of *concinnāre* to put together carefully, equiv. to *con-* CON- + *-cinnāre*, equiv. to *cinn(us)* a mixed drink + *-ātus* -ATE[1]]

con·cin·ni·ty (kən sin′i tē), *n., pl.* **-ties. 1.** *Rhet.* **a.** a close harmony of tone as well as logic among the elements of a discourse. **b.** an instance of this harmony. **2.** any harmonious adaptation of parts. [< L *concinnitās*, equiv. to *concinn(us)* CONCINNOUS + *-itās* -ITY]

con·cin·nous (kən sin′əs), *adj.* characterized by concinnity; elegant; harmonious; stylistically congruous. [< L *concinnus* well put together, equiv. to *con-* CON- + *cinnus* a mixed drink] —**con·cin′nous·ly,** *adv.*

con·cise (kən sīs′), *adj.* expressing or covering much in few words; brief in form but comprehensive in scope; succinct; terse: *a quick and concise explanation.* [< L *concīs(us)* cut short (ptp. of *concīdere*), equiv. to *con-* CON- + *-cīd-* (comb. s. of *caedere* to cut) + *-tus* ptp. ending] —**con·cise′ly,** *adv.*
—**Syn.** pithy, compendious, laconic.

con·cise·ness (kən sīs′nis), *n.* the quality of being concise. [CONCISE + -NESS]
—**Syn.** terseness, pithiness. See **brevity.**

con·ci·sion (kən sizh′ən), *n.* **1.** concise quality; brevity; terseness. **2.** *Obs.* a cutting up or off; mutilation. [< L *concīsiōn-* (s. of *concīsiō*), equiv. to *concīs(us)* CONCISE + *-iōn-* -ION]

con·clave (kon′klāv, koŋ′-), *n.* **1.** a private or secret meeting. **2.** the place in which the cardinals of the Roman Catholic Church meet in private for the election of a pope. **3.** the assembly or meeting of the cardinals for the election of a pope. **4.** the body of cardinals; the College of Cardinals. **5.** an assembly or gathering, esp. one that has special authority, power, or influence: *a conclave of political leaders to name the next mayor.* [late ME < ML, L, repr. *(camera) cum clāve* (room) with key. See CON-, CLEF]

con·clav·ist (kon′klā vist, koŋ′-), *n.* either of two persons who attend upon a cardinal at a conclave. [< It *conclavist(a)* < ML *conclāv(e)* CONCLAVE + *-ista* -IST]

con·clude (kən klo͞od′), *v.,* **-clud·ed, -clud·ing.** —*v.t.* **1.** to bring to an end; finish; terminate: *to conclude a speech with a quotation from the Bible.* **2.** to say in conclusion: *At the end of the speech he concluded that we had been a fine audience.* **3.** to bring to a decision or settlement; settle or arrange finally: *to conclude a treaty.* **4.** to determine by reasoning; deduce; infer: *He studied the document and concluded that the author must have been an eyewitness.* **5.** to decide, determine, or resolve: *He concluded that he would go no matter what the weather.* **6.** *Obs.* **a.** to shut up or enclose. **b.** to restrict or confine. —*v.i.* **7.** to come to an end; finish: *He concluded at ten o'clock.* **8.** to arrive at an opinion or judgment; come to a decision; decide: *The jury concluded to set the accused free.* [ME < L *conclūde(re)* to close, to end an argument, equiv. to *con-* CON- + *-clūdere*, var. of *claudere* to close] —**con·clud′a·ble, con·clud′i·ble,** *adj.* —**con·clud′er,** *n.*
—**Syn. 1.** close, complete. —**Ant. 1.** begin.

conclud′ing line′, *Naut.* a small line rove through or hitched to each step or rung of a hanging ladder.

con·clu·sion (kən klo͞o′zhən), *n.* **1.** the end or close; final part. **2.** the last main division of a discourse, usually containing a summing up of the points and a statement of opinion or decisions reached. **3.** a result, issue, or outcome: *One conclusion of the board meeting was that we determined to cut expenses.* **4.** final settlement or arrangement: *The nations decided on a peaceful conclusion of their differences.* **5.** final decision: *The judge has reached his conclusion.* **6.** a reasoned deduction or inference. **7.** *Logic.* a proposition concluded or inferred from the premises of an argument. **8.** *Law.* **a.** the effect of an act by which the person performing the act is bound not to do anything inconsistent therewith; an estoppel. **b.** the end of a pleading or conveyance. **9.** *Gram.* apodosis. **10. in conclusion,** finally: *In conclusion, I would like to thank you for your attention.* **11. try conclusions with,** to engage oneself in a struggle for victory or mastery over, as a person or an impediment. [ME < L *conclūsiōn-* (s. of *conclūsiō*), equiv. to *conclūs(us)* closed, ptp. of *conclūdere* (*con-* CON- + *clūd-* close + *-tus* ptp. suffix) + *-iōn-* -ION] —**con·clu′sion·al,** *adj.* —**con·clu′sion·al·ly,** *adv.*
—**Syn. 1.** ending, termination, completion, finale. See **end. 2.** summation. **6.** judgment, determination.
—**Ant. 1.** beginning.

con·clu·sive (kən klo͞o′siv), *adj.* **1.** serving to settle or decide a question; decisive; convincing: *conclusive evidence; a conclusive argument.* **2.** tending to terminate; closing. [< LL *conclūsīv(us)*, equiv. to L *conclūs(us)* (ptp. of *conclūdere* to CONCLUDE; see CONCLUSION) + *-īvus* -IVE] —**con·clu′sive·ly,** *adv.* —**con·clu′sive·ness,** *n.*
—**Syn.** definitive, final, determining.

con·coct (kon kokt′, kən-), *v.t.* **1.** to prepare or make by combining ingredients, as in cookery: *to concoct a meal from leftovers.* **2.** to devise; make up; contrive: *to concoct an excuse.* [< L *concoct(us)* (ptp. of *concoquere* to cook together), equiv. to *con-* CON- + *coc-*, s. of *coquere* to boil, cook (akin to Gk *péttō*; see PEPSIN, PEPTIC) + *-tus* ptp. ending] —**con·coct′er, con·coc′tor,** *n.* —**con·coc′tive,** *adj.*

con·coc·tion (kon kok′shən, kən-), *n.* **1.** the act or process of concocting. **2.** something concocted: *He served a strange concoction of milk, egg, rum, and lemon flavoring.* [< L *concoctiōn-* (s. of *concoctiō*) digestion, equiv. to *concoct(us)* (see CONCOCT) + *-iōn-* -ION]

con·com·i·tance (kən kom′i təns), *n.* **1.** the quality or relation of being concomitant. **2.** concomitant (def. 2). **3.** *Rom. Cath. Ch.* the coexistence of the body and blood of Christ in the Eucharistic bread. [< ML *concomitantia*. See CONCOMITANT, -ANCE]

con·com·i·tant (kon kom′i tᵊnt, kən-), *adj.* **1.** existing or occurring with something else, often in a lesser way; accompanying; concurrent: *an event and its concomitant circumstances.* —*n.* **2.** a concomitant quality, circumstance, or thing. [< L *concomitant-* (s. of *concomitāns*, prp. of *concomitārī*), equiv. to *con-* CON- + *comit-* (s. of *comes*) COMES + *-ant-* -ANT] —**con·com′i·tant·ly,** *adv.*
—**Syn. 1.** associated.

con·cord (kon′kôrd, koŋ′-), *n.* **1.** agreement between persons; concurrence in attitudes, feelings, etc.; unanimity; accord: *There was complete concord among the delegates.* **2.** agreement between things; mutual fitness; harmony. **3.** *Gram.* agreement (def. 5). **4.** peace; amity. **5.** a treaty; compact; covenant. **6.** *Music.* a stable combination of tones; a chord requiring no resolution. [ME *concorde* < OF < L *concord(ia)*, equiv. to *concord-* (s. of *concors*) harmonious (*con-* CON- + *cord-*, s. of *cors* heart) + *-ia* -IA] —**con·cord′al,** *adj.*

Con·cord (koŋ′kərd *for 1–3, 5; also for 5* kon′kôrd; kon′kôrd, koŋ′- *for 4*), *n.* **1.** a town in E Massachusetts, NW of Boston: second battle of the Revolution fought here April 19, 1775. 3,188 (1960). **2.** a city in and the capital of New Hampshire, in the S part. 28,991 (1960). **3.** a city in W California, near San Francisco. 36,208 (1960). **4.** a city in central North Carolina. 17,799 (1960). **5.** See **Concord grape.**

con·cord·ance (kon kôr′dᵊns, kən-), *n.* **1.** agreement; concord; harmony: *With the concordance of the membership, we will adjourn.* **2.** an alphabetical index of the principal words of a book, as of the Bible, with a reference to the passage in which each occurs and usually some part of the context. **3.** an alphabetical index of subjects or topics. [late ME *concordaunce* < AF, equiv. to MF *concordance* < ML *concordantia*. See CONCORD, -ANCE]

con·cord·ant (kon kôr′dᵊnt, kən-), *adj.* agreeing; harmonious. [late ME *concordaunt* < AF, equiv. to MF *concordant*. See CONCORD, -ANT] —**con·cord′ant·ly,** *adv.*

con·cor·dat (kon kôr′dat), *n.* **1.** an agreement or compact, esp. an official one. **2.** an agreement between the pope and a secular government regarding the regulation of ecclesiastical matters. [< F; r. *concordate* < ML *concordāt(um)* < L, neut. of *concordātus*, ptp. of *concordāre* to be agreed. See CONCORD, -ATE[1]] —**con·cor·da·to·ry** (kon kôr′də tōr′ē, -tôr′ē), *adj.*

Con′cord coach′, *U.S.* a type of stagecoach.

Con·corde (koŋ′kôrd, kon kôrd′, koŋ-), *n. Trademark.* a supersonic, passenger-carrying airplane designed, manufactured, and operated as a joint British-French venture. [< F: concord, harmony]

Con′cord grape′ (koŋ′kərd, kon′kôrd), **1.** a large, dark-blue grape grown for table use. **2.** the vine bearing this fruit, grown in the eastern U.S.

Con·cor·di·a (kon kôr′dē ə), *n.* the ancient Roman goddess of harmony or peace. [< L; see CONCORD]

Con·cor·di·a (kən kôr′dē ə, kəŋ-, kon-), *n.* **1.** a town in N Kansas. 7022 (1960). **2.** a girl's given name.

con·cor·po·rate (kon kôr′pə rāt′), *v.,* **-rat·ed, -rat·ing,** *adj.* —*v.i.* **1.** *Archaic.* to unite in one body, unit, or mass. —*adj.* **2.** *Archaic.* united in one body, unit, or mass. [< L *concorporāt(us)* (ptp. of *concorporāre*). See CON-, CORPORATE] —**con·cor′po·ra′tion,** *n.*

con·course (kon′kōrs, -kôrs, koŋ′-), *n.* **1.** an assemblage; gathering; throng: *a concourse of people.* **2.** a driveway or promenade, esp. in a park. **3.** a boulevard or other broad thoroughfare. **4.** a large open space for accommodating crowds, as in a railroad station. **5.** an area or grounds for racing, athletic sports, etc. **6.** the act or an instance of running or coming together; confluence: *a concourse of events.* [late ME *concours* < MF; r. ME *concurs* < L *concurs(us)* assembly, n. use of *concursus*, ptp. of *concurrere* to run together. See CON-, COURSE]

con·cres·cence (kon kres′əns), *n.* **1.** a growing together, as of parts, cells, etc.; coalescence. **2.** *Embryol.* the moving and growing together of the lips of the blastopore to form the body of the embryo. [< L *concrēscentia*, equiv. to *concrēscent-* (s. of *concrēscēns*, prp. of *concrēscere*; see CON-, CRESCENT) + *-ia* -IA; see -ENCE]

con·crete (kon′krēt, kon krēt′ *for 1–10, 13;* kon krēt′ *for 11, 12*), *adj., n., v.,* **-cret·ed, -cret·ing.** —*adj.* **1.** constituting an actual thing or instance; real: *a concrete proof of his sincerity.* **2.** pertaining to or concerned with realities or actual instances rather than abstractions; particular (opposed to *general*): *concrete ideas.* **3.** representing or applied to an actual substance or thing, as opposed to an abstract quality: *The noun "Man" is concrete, whereas "masculinity" is abstract.* **4.** made of concrete: *a concrete pavement.* **5.** formed by coalescence of separate particles into a mass; united in a coagulated, condensed, or solid mass or state. —*n.* **6.** a concrete idea or term; a word or notion having an actual or existent thing or instance as its referent. **7.** a mass formed by coalescence or concretion of particles of matter. **8.** an artificial, stonelike material used for various structural purposes, made by mixing cement and various aggregates, as sand, pebbles, gravel, shale, etc., with water and allowing the mixture to harden. Cf. **reinforced concrete. 9.** any of various other artificial building or paving materials, as those containing tar. —*v.t.* **10.** to treat or lay with concrete: *to concrete a sidewalk.* **11.** to form into a mass by coalescence of particles; render solid. **12.** to make real, tangible, or particular. —*v.i.* **13.** to coalesce into a mass; become solid; harden. **14.** to use or apply concrete. [< L *concrēt(us)* (ptp. of *concrēscere* to grow together), equiv. to *con-* CON- + *crē-* (s. of *crēscere* to grow, increase) + *-tus* ptp. ending] —**con·crete′ly,** *adv.* —**con·crete′ness,** *n.* —**con·cre′tive,** *adj.* —**con·cre′tive·ly,** *adv.*
—**Ant. 1, 2.** abstract.

con′crete mu′sic. See **musique concrète.**

con′crete noun′, *Gram.* a noun that, because of its grammatical uses, is often thought of as denoting something material and nonabstract. Cf. **abstract noun** (def. 2).

con′crete num′ber, *Arith.* a number that relates to a particular object or thing.

con′crete univer′sal, *Hegelianism.* a logical category having the concrete properties enabling it to enter into dialectical relationship with the absolute idea.

con·cre·tion (kon krē′shən), *n.* **1.** the act, process, or characteristic of concreting or becoming substantial. **2.** the state of being concreted. **3.** a solid mass formed by or as by coalescence or cohesion: *a concretion of candies that had melted and hardened again.* **4.** anything that is made real, tangible, or particular. **5.** *Pathol.* a solid or calcified mass in the body formed by a disease process. **6.** *Geol.* a rounded mass of mineral matter occurring in sandstone, clay, etc., often in concentric layers about a nucleus. [< L *concrētiōn-* (s. of *concrētiō*). See CONCRETE, -ION]

con·cre·tion·ar·y (kon krē′shə ner′ē), *adj.* formed by concretion; consisting of concreted matter or masses. [CONCRETION + -ARY]

con·cre·tize (kon′krə tīz′, koŋ′-; kon krē′tīz, koŋ-, kən-), *v.t.,* **-tized, -tiz·ing.** to make concrete, real, or particular; give tangible or definite form to: *to concretize abstractions.* [CONCRETE + -IZE] —**con·cret′i·za′tion,** *n.*

con·cu·bi·nage (kon kyo͞o′bə nij), *n.* **1.** cohabitation of a man and woman without legal or formal marriage, acceptable in some social systems. **2.** the state of being a concubine. [ME; see CONCUBINE, -AGE]

con·cu·bi·nar·y (kon kyo͞o′bə ner′ē), *adj. n., pl.* **-nar·ies.** —*adj.* **1.** of, pertaining to, or living in concubinage. —*n.* **2.** a person who lives in concubinage. [< ML *concubīnāri(us)*. See CONCUBINE, -ARY]

con·cu·bine (koŋ′kyə bīn′, kon′-), *n.* **1.** a woman who cohabits with a man to whom she is not married. **2.** (among polygamous peoples) a secondary wife. [ME < L *concubīn(a)*, equiv. to *concub-* (var. s. of *concumbere* to lie together; see CON-) + *-ina* fem. suffix]

con·cu·pis·cence (kon kyo͞o′pi səns), *n.* **1.** ardent, usually sensuous longing. **2.** sexual desire; lust. [ME < eccl. L *concupiscentia*. See CONCUPISCENT, -ENCE]

con·cu·pis·cent (kon kyo͞o′pi sənt), *adj.* **1.** lustful or sensual. **2.** eagerly desirous. [< L *concupiscent-* (s. of *concupiscēns*, prp. of *concupiscere* to desire greatly), equiv. to *con-* CON- + *cup-* (s. of *cupere* to desire) + *-iscent-*, var. of *-ēscent-* -ESCENT]

con·cu·pis·ci·ble (kon kyo͞o′pi sə bəl), *adj. Obs.* worthy of being desired; very desirable. [late ME *concupyssible* < MF *concupiscible* < eccl. L *concupiscibil(is)*, equiv. to L *concupisc(ere)* (see CONCUPISCENT) + *-ibilis* -IBLE]

con·cur (kən kûr′), *v.i.,* **-curred, -cur·ring. 1.** to accord in opinion; agree: *Do you concur with his statement?* **2.** to cooperate; work together; combine; be associated: *Members of both parties concurred in urging passage of the bill.* **3.** to coincide; occur simultaneously: *His graduation day concurred with his birthday.* **4.** *Obs.* to run or come together; converge. [late ME < L *concurr(ere)* (to) run together, meet (LL: agree with), equiv. to *con-* -CON- + *currere* to run] —**con·cur′ring·ly,** *adv.*
—**Syn. 1.** See **agree.**

con·cur·rence (kən kûr′əns, -kur′-), *n.* **1.** the act of concurring: *The prime minister announced his decision after the concurrence of his cabinet.* **2.** accordance in opinion; agreement: *With the concurrence of several specialists, our doctor recommended surgery.* **3.** cooperation, as of agents or causes; combined action or effort: *The concurrence of several factions got the bill passed.* **4.** simultaneous occurrence; coincidence: *The concurrence o several unusual events produced a good news story.* **5.** *Geom.* a point that is in three or more lines simultaneously. **6.** *Law.* a power equally held or a claim shared equally. **7.** *Archaic.* competition; rivalry. Also, **con·cur′ren·cy** (for defs. 1–4). [< ML *concurrentia*. See CONCURRENT, -ENCE]

con·cur·rent (kən kûr′ənt, -kur′-), *adj.* **1.** occurring or existing together or side by side: *concurrent attacks by land, sea, and air.* **2.** acting in conjunction; cooperating: *The concurrent efforts of the legislators passed the new law.* **3.** having equal authority or jurisdiction: *two concurrent courts of law.* **4.** accordant or agreeing: *concurrent testimony by three witnesses.* **5.** tending to or intersecting at the same point: *four concurrent lines.* —*n.* **6.** something joint or contributory. **7.** *Archaic.* a rival or competitor. [< L *concurrent-* (s. of *concurrēns*, prp. of *concurrere* to CONCUR); see CON-, CURRENT; r. late ME *concurrant* < MF] —**con·cur′rent·ly,** *adv.*

concur′rent resolu′tion, a resolution adopted by both branches of a legislative assembly which, unlike a joint resolution, does not require the signature of the chief executive.

concur′ring opin′ion, *Law.* (in appellate courts) an opinion filed by a judge that agrees with the conclusion of another opinion on the case but that may base the conclusion on different reasons or state a different view of the case.

con·cus·sion (kən kush′ən), *n.* **1.** the act of shaking or shocking, as by a blow. **2.** shock caused by the impact of a collision, blow, etc. **3.** *Pathol.* jarring of the brain, spinal cord, etc., from a blow, fall, or the like. [late ME < L *concussiōn-* (s. of *concussiō*) a shaking, equiv. to *concuss(us)*, ptp. of *concutere* (*con-* CON- + *cut-*, var. of *quat-*, s. of *quatere* to shake + *-tus* ptp. ending) + *-iōn-* -ION] —**con·cus′sion·al con·cus·sant** (kən kus′ənt), *adj.* —**con·cus′sive,** *adj.*

concus′sion grenade′, a grenade designed to inflict damage by the force of its detonation rather than by the fragmentation of its casing.

con·cy·clic (kən sī′klik, -sik′lik), *adj. Geom.* (of a system of points) lying on the circumference of a circle. [CON- + CYCLIC]

cond., 1. condenser. 2. conditional. 3. conductor.

Con·da·mine (kon′də mēn′), *n.* a crater in the second quadrant of the face of the moon: about 30 miles in diameter. Also, **La Condamine.**

Con·dé (kôN dā′), *n.* **Louis II de Bour·bon** (lwē, də bo͝or bôN′), **Prince de,** (*Duc d'Enghien*) ("*the Great Condé*") 1621–86, French general.

con·demn (kən dem′), *v.t.* **1.** to pronounce an unfavorable or adverse judgment on; express strong disapproval of; censure. **2.** to give grounds or reason for convicting or for censure: *His very looks condemn him.* **3.** to pronounce to be guilty; sentence to punishment: *to condemn a murderer to life imprisonment.* **4.** to judge or pronounce to be unfit for use or service: *The old ship was condemned and sold for scrap.* **5.** to declare incurable. **6.** to force into a specific state or activity: *His amiability condemns him to being a constant listener to others' troubles.* **7.** *U.S. Law.* to acquire ownership of for a public purpose, under the right of eminent domain: *The city condemned the property.* [ME *condempn(en)* < OF *condem(p)ne(r)* < L *condem(p)nāre.* See CON-, DAMN] —**con·dem·na·ble** (kən dem′nə bəl), *adj.* —**con·dem′na·bly,** *adv.* —**con·demn·er** (kən dem′ər), *n.* —**con·demn′ing·ly,** *adv.*
—**Syn. 1.** See **blame.** —**Ant. 3.** exonerate; liberate.

con·dem·na·tion (kon′dem nā′shən, -dəm-), *n.* **1.** the act of condemning. **2.** the state of being condemned. **3.** strong censure; disapprobation; reproof: *They received the condemnation of the neighborhood.* **4.** cause or reason for condemning: *His behavior was all the condemnation they needed.* **5.** *U.S.* the seizure, as of property, for public use. [late ME *condempnacioun* < LL *condemnātiōn-* (s. of *condemnātiō*). See CONDEMN, -ATION]

con·dem·na·to·ry (kən dem′nə tôr′ē, -tōr′ē), *adj.* serving to condemn. [CONDEMNAT(ION) + -ORY[1]]

con·den·sa·ble (kən den′sə bəl), *adj.* capable of being condensed. Also, **condensible.** [CONDENSE + -ABLE] —**con·den′sa·bil′i·ty,** *n.*

con·den·sa·ry (kən den′sə rē), *n., pl.* **-ries.** condensery.

con·den·sate (kən den′sāt), *n.* something formed by condensation, as a liquid reduced from a gas or vapor. [< L *condēnsāt(us)* (ptp. of *condēnsāre* to CONDENSE), equiv. to *condēns(us)* very dense (see CON-, DENSE) + *-ātus* -ATE[1]]

con·den·sa·tion (kon′den sā′shən, -dən-), *n.* **1.** the act of condensing; the state of being condensed. **2.** the result of being made more compact or dense. **3.** a condensed form: *a book in condensation.* **4.** reduction of a book, speech, statement, or the like, to a shorter or terser form; abridgment. **5.** a condensed mass. **6.** the act or process of reducing a gas or vapor to a liquid or solid form. **7.** *Chem.* a reaction between two or more organic molecules leading to the formation of a larger molecule and the elimination of a simple molecule such as water or alcohol. **8.** *Psychoanal.* the representation of two or more ideas, memories, feelings, or impulses by one word or image, as in one's humor, accidental slips, allegories, and dreams. [< LL *condēnsātiōn-* (s. of *condēnsātiō*), equiv. to *condēnsāt(us)* CONDENSATE + *-iōn-* -ION] —**con′den·sa′tion·al,** *adj.* —**con′den·sa′tive,** *adj.*

condensa′tion point′, *Math.* a point of which every neighborhood contains an uncountable number of points of a given set.

condensa′tion polymeriza′tion, *Chem.* See under **polymerization** (def. 2).

condensa′tion trail′, contrail.

con·dense (kən dens′), *v.,* **-densed, -dens·ing.** —*v.t.* **1.** to make more dense or compact; reduce the volume or extent of. **2.** to reduce to a shorter or terser form; abridge: *Condense your answer into a few words.* **3.** to reduce to another and denser form, as a gas or vapor to a liquid or solid state. —*v.i.* **4.** to become denser or more compact or concentrated. **5.** to reduce a book, speech, statement, or the like, to shorter or terser form. **6.** to become liquid or solid, as a gas or vapor: *The steam condensed into water droplets.* [ME *condense(n)* < MF *condense(r)* < L *condēnsāre,* equiv. to *con-* CON- + *dēnsāre* (*dēns(us)* DENSE + *-ā-* v. suffix + *-re* inf. ending)]
—**Syn. 1.** compress, concentrate, consolidate. **2.** digest, epitomize, abstract, abbreviate. See **contract.**
—**Ant. 1.** expand.

con·densed (kən denst′), *adj.* **1.** reduced in volume, area, length, or scope; shortened: *a condensed version of the book.* **2.** made denser, esp. reduced from a gaseous to a liquid state. **3.** thickened by distillation or evaporation; concentrated: *condensed fruit juices.* **4.** *Print.* (of type) narrow in proportion to its height. Cf. **expanded** (def. 3). [CONDENSE + -ED[2]] —**con·densed′ly,** *adv.* —**con·densed′ness,** *n.*

condensed′ milk′, whole milk reduced by evaporation to a thick consistency, with sugar added.

con·dens·er (kən den′sər), *n.* **1.** one who or that which condenses. **2.** an apparatus for condensing. **3.** any device for reducing gases or vapors to liquid or solid form. **4.** *Optics.* a lens or combination of lenses that gather and concentrate light in a specified direction, often used to direct light onto the projection lens in a projection system. **5.** *Elect.* capacitor. [CONDENSE + -ER[1]]

con·den·ser·y (kən den′sə rē), *n., pl.* **-ser·ies.** a factory for the production of condensed or evaporated milk. Also, **condensary.** [CONDENSE + -ERY]

con·den·si·ble (kən den′sə bəl), *adj.* condensable.

con·de·scend (kon′di send′), *v.i.* **1.** to waive dignity or superiority voluntarily and assume equality with an inferior: *He condescended to their intellectual level in order to be understood.* **2.** to stoop or deign to do something: *He condescended to accompany her.* **3.** to behave as if one is conscious of descending from a superior position, rank, or dignity. **4.** *Obs.* **a.** to yield. **b.** to assent. [ME *condescende* < LL *condēscende(re)* (see CON-, DESCEND); r. ME *condescendre* < MF] —**con′des·cend′er, con′des·cend′ent,** *n.*

con·de·scend·ence (kon′di sen′dəns), *n.* **1.** condescension; a stoop. **2.** *Scot.* a list or specification of particulars. [CONDESCEND + -ENCE]

con·de·scend·ing (kon′di sen′ding), *adj.* showing or implying a gracious or patronizing descent from dignity or superiority: *They resented the older neighbors' condescending cordiality.* [CONDESCEND + -ING[2]] —**con′de·scend′ing·ly,** *adv.*

con·de·scen·sion (kon′di sen′shən), *n.* **1.** an act or instance of condescending. **2.** voluntary assumption of equality with an inferior person. **3.** behavior that is obviously patronizing or condescending. [< LL *condēscēnsiōn-* (s. of *condēscēnsiō*). See CON-, DESCENSION] —**con·de·scen·sive** (kon′di sen′siv), *adj.* —**con′de·scen′sive·ly,** *adv.*

con·dign (kən dīn′), *adj.* (chiefly of punishment) well-deserved; fitting; adequate. [late ME *condigne* < MF < L *condign(us),* equiv. to *con-* CON- + *dignus* worthy] —**con·dign′ly,** *adv.*

con·dig·ni·ty (kən dig′ni tē), *n. Scholasticism.* merit earned through good works while in a state of grace, and having a just claim on such rewards as heavenly glory. Cf. **congruity** (def. 4).

Con·dil·lac (kôN dē yak′), *n.* **É·tienne Bon·not de** (ā tyen′ bô nō′ də), 1715–80, French philosopher.

con·di·ment (kon′də mənt), *n.* something used to give a special or additional flavor to food, as a mustard, a salt, or spices. [late ME < MF < L *condīment(um)* spice, equiv. to *condī(re)* (to) season + *-mentum* -MENT] —**con′di·men′tal, con′di·men′ta·ry,** *adj.*

con·dis·ci·ple (kon′di sī′pəl), *n.* a fellow student or disciple. [< L *condiscipul(us)* school-mate. See CON-, DISCIPLE]

Con·dit (kon′dit), *n.* a boy's given name.

con·di·tion (kən dish′ən), *n.* **1.** particular mode of being of a person or thing; situation with respect to circumstances; existing state or case. **2.** state of health: *to be in grave condition.* **3.** fit or requisite state: *to be in no condition to walk alone.* **4.** social position: *in a lowly condition.* **5.** a restricting, limiting, or modifying circumstance: *It can happen only under certain conditions.* **6.** a circumstance indispensable to some result; prerequisite; that on which something else is contingent: *conditions of acceptance.* **7.** something demanded as an essential part of an agreement; provision; stipulation: *He accepted on one condition.* **8.** *Law.* **a.** a stipulation in an agreement or instrument transferring property that provides for a change consequent on the occurrence or nonoccurrence of a stated event. **b.** the event upon which this stipulation depends. **9.** *U.S.* **a.** a requirement imposed on a college student who fails to reach the prescribed standard in a study at the end of the regular period of instruction, permitting credit to be established by later performance. **b.** the study or subject to which the requirement is attached. **10.** *Gram.* protasis. **11.** *Logic.* the antecedent of a conditional proposition. **12. on** or **upon condition that,** with the promise or provision that; provided that; if: *He accepted the position on condition that there would be opportunity for advancement.* —*v.t.* **13.** to put in fit or proper state; prepare: *to condition someone against cold weather.* **14.** air-condition (def. 2). **15.** to form or be a condition of; determine, limit, or restrict as a condition: *Her attitude will condition her success in the job.* **16.** to subject to particular conditions or circumstances: *Her studies conditioned her for her job.* **17.** *U.S.* to impose a condition on (a student). **18.** to test (a commodity) to ascertain its condition. **19.** to make (something) a condition; stipulate. **20.** *Psychol.* to establish a conditioned response in (a subject). **21.** *Textiles.* **a.** to test (fibers or fabrics) for the presence of moisture or other foreign matter. **b.** to replace moisture lost (from fibers or fabrics) in manipulation or manufacture. —*v.i.* **22.** to make conditions. [< L *condition-,* earlier *condiciōn-* (s. of *condiciō*) arrangement, equiv. to *con-* CON- + *dic-* say + *-iōn-* -ION; r. ME *condicioun* < AF] —**con·di′tion·er,** *n.*
—**Syn. 1.** See **state. 7.** requirement, proviso.

con·di·tion·al (kən dish′ə nəl), *adj.* **1.** imposing, containing, subject to, or depending on a condition or conditions; not absolute; made or allowed on certain terms: *conditional acceptance; a conditional sale.* **2.** *Gram.* (of a sentence, clause, mood, or word) involving or expressing a condition, as by the first clause in the sentence *If it rains, he won't go.* **3.** *Logic.* **a.** (of a proposition) asserting that the existence or occurrence of one thing or event depends on the existence or occurrence of another thing or event; hypothetical. **b.** (of a syllogism) containing at least one conditional proposition as a premise. **4.** *Math.* (of an inequality) true for only certain values of the variable, as $x + 3 > 0$ is only true for real numbers greater than –3. Cf. **absolute** (def. 12). —*n.* **5.** *Gram.* (in certain languages) a mood, tense, or other category used in expressing conditions, often corresponding to an English verb preceded by if. Spanish *comería* "he would eat" is in the conditional. [< LL *condiciōnāl(is),* equiv. to *condiciōn-* (s. of *condiciō*) CONDITION + *-ālis* -AL[1]; r. ME *condicionel* < MF] —**con·di′tion·al′i·ty,** *n.* —**con·di′tion·al·ly,** *adv.*
—**Syn. 1.** dependent, contingent, relative.

condi′tional conver′gence, *Math.* the property of an infinite series that converges while the series formed by replacing each term in the given series with its absolute value diverges; the property of an infinite series that converges when the order of the terms is altered. Cf. **absolute convergence** (def. 1).

condi′tional probabil′ity, **1.** *Statistics.* the probability of the occurrence of an event under the condition that only a portion of the cases or alternatives are to be considered. **2.** *Math.* the probability that a result will occur provided that a result of known probability occurs first, equal to the probability that both will occur divided by the probability that the first will occur.

con·di·tioned (kən dish′ənd), *adj.* **1.** existing under or subject to conditions. **2.** characterized by a predictable or consistent pattern of behavior or thought as a result of having been subjected to certain circumstances or conditions. **3.** *Psychol.* proceeding from or dependent on a conditioning of the individual; learned; acquired: *conditioned behavior patterns.* Cf. **unconditioned** (def. 2). **4.** made suitable for a given purpose. **5.** air-conditioned. [late ME; see CONDITION, -ED[2]]
—**Ant. 1.** free, absolute.

condi′tioned response′, *Psychol.* a response that becomes associated with a previously unrelated stimulus through repeated presentation of the stimulus to a subject simultaneously with a stimulus normally yielding the response. Also called **condi′tioned re′flex.**

con·di·tion·er (kən dish′ə nər), *n.* **1.** one who or that which conditions. **2.** something added to another substance to increase its usability, as a water softener. **3.** a trainer of athletes. **4.** an air-conditioner. **5.** *Textiles.* a person who conditions fibers or fabrics. [CONDITION + -ER[1]]

Con·di·tion Hu·maine, La (lȧ kôN dē syôN y men′). See **Man's Fate.**

con·di·tiv·i·um (kon′di tiv′ē əm), *n., pl.* **-tiv·i·a** (-tiv′ē ə). an ancient Roman catacomb for sarcophagi. [< L *conditīvum* tomb, grave, n. use of *conditīvus* (adj.) fit for pickling, equiv. to *condit(us)* (see CONDITORIUM) + *-īvus* -IVE]

con·di·to·ri·um (kon′di tôr′ē əm, -tōr′-), *n., pl.* **-to·ri·a** (-tôr′ē ə, -tōr′-). conditivium. [< L: repository, equiv. to *condit(us)* laid together, ptp. of *condere* (*con-* CON- + *-dere* to put; see DO[1]) + *-ōrium* -ORY][2]

con·do (kon′dō), *n., pl.* **-dos.** *Informal.* condominium (defs. 2, 3).

con·dole (kən dōl′), *v.,* **-doled, -dol·ing.** —*v.i.* **1.** to express sympathy with one who is suffering sorrow, misfortune, or grief; grieve (usually fol. by *with*): *to condole with a friend whose father has died.* —*v.t.* **2.** *Obs.* to grieve with. [< LL *condol(ēre),* equiv. to *con-* CON- + *dolēre* to feel pain; akin to DOLOR] —**con·do·la·to·ry** (kən dō′lə tôr′ē, -tōr′ē), *adj.* —**con·dol′er,** *n.* —**con·dol′ing·ly,** *adv.*

con·do·lence (kən dō′ləns), *n.* expression of sympathy with a person who is suffering sorrow, misfortune, or grief. Also, **con·dole′ment.** [CONDOLE + -ENCE]
—**Syn.** commiseration, comfort, consolation, solace.

con·do·lent (kən dō′lənt), *adj.* feeling or expressing sorrow, sympathy, compassion, or the like. [< LL *condolent-* (s. of *condolēns,* prp. of *condolēre*). See CONDOLE, -ENT]

con do·lo·re (kon′ dəlôr′ā, dəlōr′ā, kōn′; *It.* kôn dō-lō′re), sorrowfully (used as a direction in music). [< It: lit., with sadness; see DOLOR]

con·dom (kon′dəm, kun′-), *n.* a thin sheath, usually of rubber, worn over the penis during sexual intercourse to prevent conception or venereal infection. [named after an 18th-century English physician, said to have devised it]

con·do·min·i·um (kon′də min′ē əm), *n., pl.* **-ums.** **1.** joint or concurrent dominion. **2.** an apartment house or complex the dwelling units of which are individually owned, each owner receiving a recordable deed enabling him to sell, mortgage, exchange, etc., his unit independent of the owners of the others in the building. **3.** a unit in such a building. **4.** *Internat. Law.* joint sovereignty over a territory by several states. [< NL. See CON-, DOMINIUM]

Con·don (kon′dən), *n.* **1. Eddie** (*Albert Edwin Condon*), 1905–73, U.S. jazz guitarist. **2. Edward Uh·ler** (yo͞o′lər) 1902–74, U.S. physicist.

con·do·na·tion (kon′dō nā′shən), *n.* the act of condoning; the overlooking or implied forgiving of an offense. [< NL *condōnātiōn-* (s. of *condōnātiō*), equiv. to *condōnāt(us)* (ptp. of *condonare* to CONDONE) + *-iōn-* -ION. See CON-, DONATION]

con·done (kən dōn′) *v.t.,* **-doned, -don·ing.** **1.** to pardon or forgive (an offense). **2.** to disregard or overlook (something illegal, objectionable, or the like). **3.** to cause the condonation of. **4.** *Law.* to forgive or act so as to imply forgiveness of (a violation of the marriage vow). [< L *condōn(āre)* (to) grant, remit, equiv. to *con-* CON- + *dōnāre* to give; see DONATE] —**con·don′a·ble,** *adj.* —**con·don′er,** *n.*
—**Syn. 1.** excuse, disregard, ignore.

California condor, *Gymnogyps californianus* (Length 4 ft.; wingspread 10 ft.)

con·dor (kon′dər), *n.* **1.** either of two large, New World vultures of the family *Cathartidae, Gymnogyps californianus* **(California condor)** or *Vultur gryphus* **(Andean condor):** the largest flying birds in the Western Hemisphere. **2.** a former coin of Chile equal to 10 pesos. **3.** a former coin of Ecuador equal to 10 sucres. **4.** (*cap.*) *Electronics.* a continuous-wave navigation system that uses one ground source for transmitting signals and that automatically measures range and bearing relative to the ground source. [< Sp < Quechuan *kuntur*]

Con·dor·cet (kôN dôr se′), *n.* **1. Ma·rie Jean An·toine Ni·co·las Ca·ri·tat** (mȧ rē′ zhäN äN twȧn′ nē kô lä′ kȧ rē tȧ′), **Marquis de,** 1743–94, French mathematician and philosopher. **2.** a walled plain in the first quadrant of the face of the moon: about 45 miles in diameter.

con·dot·tie·re (kôn′də tyâr′ā; *It.* kôn′dôt tye′re), *n., pl.* **-tie·ri** (-tyâr′ē; *It.* -tye′rē). **1.** a leader of a private band of mercenary soldiers in Italy, esp. in the 14th and 15th centuries. **2.** a military adventurer; mercenary; soldier of fortune. [< It, equiv. to *condott(o)* (< L *conductus* hireling soldier, lit., led; see CONDUCT) + *-iere* -IER]

con·duce (kən do͞os′, -dyo͞os′), *v.i.,* **-duced, -duc·ing.** to lead or contribute to a result (usually fol. by *to* or *toward*): *A steady seat and quiet hands conduce to good horsemanship.* [< L *condūce(re)* (to) lead, bring together, equiv. to *con-* CON- + *dūcere* to lead, akin to *dux* (see DUKE) and to TOW[1], TUG] —**con·duc′er,** *n.* —**con·duc′i·ble,** *adj.* —**con·duc′i·ble·ness, con·duce′a·bil′i·ty,** *n.* —**con·duc′i·bly,** *adv.* —**con·duc′ing·ly,** *adv.*

con·du·cive (kən do͞o′siv, -dyo͞o′-), *adj.* conducing; contributive; helpful (usually fol. by *to*): *Good eating and sleeping habits are conducive to good health.* [CONDUCE + -IVE] —**con·du′cive·ness,** *n.*

con·duct (*n.* kon′dukt; *v.* kən dukt′), *n.* **1.** personal behavior; way of acting; deportment: *His conduct in society is impeccable.* **2.** direction or management; execution: *the conduct of a business.* **3.** the act of conducting; guidance; escort: *The curator's conduct through the museum was informative.* **4.** *Obs.* a guide; an escort. —*v.t.* **5.** to behave or manage (oneself): *He conducted himself well. The nurse conducts herself obsequiously.* **6.** to direct in action or course; manage; carry on: *to conduct a meeting; to conduct a column on books in a newspaper.* **7.** to direct as leader: *Toscanini conducted the orchestra.* **8.** to lead or guide; escort: *to conduct a tour.* **9.** to serve as a channel or medium for (heat, electricity, sound, etc.): *Copper conducts electricity.* —*v.i.* **10.** to lead. **11.** to act as conductor, esp. of a musical group. [< LL *conduct(us)* escort, n. use of L *conductus* (ptp. of *condūcere* to CONDUCE), equiv. to *con-* CON- + *duc-* lead + *-tus* ptp. suffix; r. ME *conduyt(e)*

CONCISE ETYMOLOGY KEY: <, descended or derived from; >, whence; b., blend of, blended; c., cognate with; deriv., derivative; equiv., equivalent; imit., imitative; m., modification of; obl., oblique; r., replacing; s., stem; sp., spelling; trans., translation; ?, origin unknown, perhaps; *, hypothetical. See the full key inside the front cover.

< OF; see CONDUIT] —**con·duct/i·ble,** *adj.* —**con·duct/i·bil/i·ty,** *n.*
—**Syn. 1.** demeanor, comportment, actions, bearing, manners. See **behavior. 2.** guidance, administration. **5.** deport, bear. **6.** supervise, administer. **8.** See **guide.**

con·duct·ance (kən duk/təns), *n. Elect.* the conducting power, esp. the power to conduct alternating current, of a conductor, equal to the real part of the admittance, and in a circuit with no reactance equal to the reciprocal of the resistance. *Symbol:* G [CONDUCT + -ANCE]

con·duc·tion (kən duk/shən), *n.* **1.** the act of conducting, as of water through a pipe. **2.** *Physics.* **a.** the transfer of heat between two parts of a stationary system, caused by a temperature difference between the parts. **b.** transmission through a conductor. **c.** conductivity. **3.** *Physiol.* the carrying of an impulse by a nerve or other tissue. [< L *conductiōn-* (s. of *conductiō*) a bringing together, a hiring, equiv. to *conduct(us)* (see CONDUCT) + *-iōn-* -ION] —**con·duc/tion·al,** *adj.*

con·duc·tive (kən duk/tiv), *adj.* having the property or capability of conducting. [< L *conduct(us)* (see CONDUCT) + -IVE] —**con·duc/tive·ly,** *adv.*

con·duc·tiv·i·ty (kon/duk tiv/i tē), *n., pl.* **-ties. 1.** *Physics.* the property or power of conducting heat, electricity, or sound. **2.** Also called **specific conductance.** *Elect.* a measure of the ability of a given substance to conduct electric current, equal to the reciprocal of the resistance of the substance. *Symbol:* σ [CONDUCTIVE + -ITY]

con·duc·to·met/ric ti·tra/tion (kən duk/tə me/trik), *Chem.* titration in which the end point is determined by measuring the resistance of the solution to an electric current that is passed through it. [CONDUCT + -O- + -METRIC]

con·duc·tor (kən duk/tər), *n.* **1.** a person who conducts; a leader, guide, director, or manager. **2.** *U.S.* a railroad employee in charge of a train and train crew. **3.** the chief employee on a bus, streetcar, or other public conveyance, usually serving as driver, collector of fares, etc. **4.** a person who directs an orchestra or chorus, communicating to the performers by motions of a baton or the hands his interpretation of the music. **5.** something that conducts. **6.** a substance, body, or device that readily conducts heat, electricity, sound, etc.: *Copper is a good conductor of electricity.* **7.** See **lightning rod.** [< L (see CONDUCT, -OR²); r. late ME *cond(u)itour* < AF, equiv. to MF *conduiteur;* see CONDUIT] —**con·duc·to·ri·al** (kon/duk tōr/ē əl, -tôr/-), *adj.* —**con·duc/tor·less,** *adj.* —**con·duc/tor·ship/,** *n.*

con·duc·tress (kən duk/tris), *n.* a female conductor. [CONDUCT(O)R + -ESS]

con·duc·tus (kən duk/təs), *n., pl.* **-tus.** any of various forms of medieval song with a Latin text. [< ML, n. use of L *conductus* (ptp.); see CONDUCT]

con·duit (kon/dwit, -dōō it, -dyōō it, -dit), *n.* **1.** a pipe, tube, or the like, for conveying water or other fluid. **2.** a similar natural passage. **3.** *Elect.* a structure containing one or more ducts. **4.** *Archaic.* a fountain. [ME < OF, equiv. to ML *conductus* pipe channel, special use of L *conductus* (ptp.) led; see CONDUCT]

con·du·pli·cate (kon dōō/plə kit, -dyōō/-), *adj. Bot.* (of a leaf in the bud) folded lengthwise with the upper face of the blade within. [< L *conduplicāt(us)* (ptp. of *conduplicāre* to double), equiv. to *con-* CON- + *duplicātus* DUPLICATE] —**con·du/pli·ca/tion,** *n.*

con·dy·larth (kon/dᵊ lärth/), *n.* one of the primitive ungulate mammals of the extinct order *Condylarthra,* from the Paleocene and Eocene epochs, having a slender body, low-crowned teeth, and five-toed feet, each toe ending in a small hoof. [< NL *condylarth(ra)* (neut. pl.) < Gk *kóndyl(os)* CONDYLE + *árthra,* pl. of *árthron* joint]

Condylarth, genus *Ectoconus* (1½ ft. high at shoulder; length 3 ft.)

con·dyle (kon/dil, -dᵊl), *n.* **1.** *Anat.* a rounded protuberance on a bone, serving to form an articulation with another bone. **2.** (in arthropods) a similar process formed from the hard integument. [var. of *condyl* < L *condyl(us)* knuckle < Gk *kóndylos*] —**con/dy·lar,** *adj.*

con·dy·loid (kon/dᵊloid/), *adj.* of or like a condyle. [CONDYLE + -OID]

con·dy·lo·ma (kon/dᵊlō/mə), *n., pl.* **-mas, -ma·ta** (-mə tə). *Pathol.* a wartlike excrescence on the skin, usually in the region of the anus or genitals. [< NL < Gk *kondýlōma.* See CONDYLE, -OMA] —**con·dy·lom·a·tous** (kon/dᵊlom/ə təs, -dᵊlō/mə-), *adj.*

cone (kōn), *n., v.,* **coned, con·ing.** —*n.* **1.** *Geom.* a solid whose surface is generated by a line passing through a fixed point and a fixed plane curve not containing the point, consisting of two equal sections joined at a vertex. **2.** a plane surface resembling the cross-section of a solid cone. **3.** *Mach.* a mechanical part having the shape of a cone or conoid. **4.** (in a taper thread screw or bevel gear) an imaginary cone or frustum of a cone concentric to the axis and defining the pitch surface or one of the extremities of the threads or teeth. **5.** *Bot.* **a.** the more or less conical multiple fruit of the pine, fir, etc., consisting of imbricated or valvate scales bearing naked ovules or seeds; a strobile. **b.** a similar fruit, as in cycads, club mosses, etc. **6.** anything shaped like a cone: *sawdust piled up in a great cone.* **7.** See **ice-cream cone. 8.** *Anat.* one of the cone-shaped cells in the retina of the eye, sensitive to color and intensity of light. Cf. **rod** (def. 17). **9.** See **pyrometric cone.** —*v.t.* **10.** to shape like a cone or the segment of a cone. [< L *cōn(us)* < Gk *kônos* pine-cone, cone-shaped figure]

Cone

cone·flow·er (kōn/flou/ər), *n.* **1.** any of several composite herbs of the genus *Rudbeckia,* having flowers usually with yellow rays and a brown or black disk. **2.** any of various allied plants. [CONE + FLOWER]

cone-in-cone (kōn/in kōn/), *n. Geol.* (in a sedimentary rock) a structure, developed under certain pressures, resembling a series of compact, concentric cones.

Con·el·rad (kon/ᵊl rad/), *n. U.S.* an arrangement of the civil defense system whereby the usual radio and television broadcasts cease in the event of an air attack to prevent enemy planes or missiles from homing on radio frequencies, and brief emergency instructions are broadcast to the public over one or two special frequencies. [*con(trol of) el(ectromagnetic) rad(iation)*]

cone/ mill/, *Metalworking.* a mill for seamless tubing, having conical rolls set at an angle so as to force the work, as solid billet, over a mandrel that spreads it into a tube.

cone·nose (kōn/nōz/), *n.* any of several bloodsucking assassin bugs of the genus *Triatoma,* some of which inflict a painful bite and serve as vectors of Chagas' disease. [CONE + NOSE]

cone/ of si/lence, a space, in the shape of an inverted cone, above a radio beacon, in which there is a sharp reduction in the intensity of transmitted signals.

cone/ pep/per, 1. a tropical, woody plant, *Capsicum frutescens conoides,* having cone-shaped or cylindrical, pungent, red, yellow, or purplish fruit. **2.** the fruit itself.

cone/ pul/ley, (on a lathe) a pulley consisting of a conelike arrangement of graduated, concentric pulleys for driving the headstock at different speeds.

cone/ shell/, any of numerous, chiefly tropical, marine gastropods of the genus *Conus,* having a smooth, brightly colored, conical shell with a short, flattened spire. Also called **cone/ snail/.**

Con/es·to/ga wag/on (kon/i stō/gə, kon/-), a large, heavy, broad-wheeled covered wagon, used esp. for transporting persons and goods across North America during the early westward migration. Also called **Con/es·to/ga.** [named after *Conestoga,* Pa., where it was first made]

cone/ wheat/. See **poulard wheat.**

co·ney (kō/nē, kun/ē), *n., pl.* **-neys. 1.** a serranid fish, *Cephalopholis fulva,* found in tropical American waters. **2.** cony.

Co/ney Is/land (kō/nē), an area in S Brooklyn in New York City: amusement park and beach.

conf., 1. (in prescriptions) a confection. [< L *confectiō*] **2.** compare. [< L *confer*] **3.** conference. **4.** confessor.

con·fab (kon/fab), *n., v.,* **-fabbed, -fab·bing.** *Informal.* —*n.* **1.** a confabulation. —*v.i.* **2.** to confabulate: *They spent the morning confabbing over coffee in my office.* [short form]

con·fab·u·late (kən fab/yə lāt/), *v.i.,* **-lat·ed, -lat·ing. 1.** to converse informally; chat. **2.** *Psychiatry.* to engage in confabulation. [< L *confābulāt(us)* (ptp. of *confābulārī* to talk together), equiv. to *con-* CON- + *fābul(a)* (see FABLE) + *-ātus* -ATE¹] —**con·fab/u·la/tor,** *n.*

con·fab·u·la·tion (kən fab/yə lā/shən), *n.* **1.** the act of confabulating; conversation; discussion. **2.** *Psychiatry.* replacement of a gap in memory by a falsification which the subject accepts as correct. [ME < LL *confābulātiōn-* (s. of *confābulātiō*) conversation, equiv. to *confābulāt(us)* (see CONFABULATE) + *-iōn-* -ION] —**con·fab·u·la·to·ry** (kən fab/yōō lə tōr/ē, -tôr/ē), *adj.*

con·far·re·a·tion (kon far/ē ā/shən), *n.* (among the ancient Romans) the highest form of marriage, marked by the offering of a cake made of spelt. [< L *confarreātiōn-* (s. of *confarreātiō*) spelt-wedding, equiv. to *confarreāt(us),* ptp. of *confarreāre* (*con-* CON- + *farre(us)* of spelt + *-ātus* -ATE¹) + *-iōn-* -ION] —**con·far·re·ate** (kən far/ē it, -āt/), **con·far/re·at/ed,** *adj.*

con·fect (*v.* kən fekt/; *n.* kon/fekt), *v.t.* **1.** to make up, compound, or prepare from ingredients or materials: *to confect a home remedy from herbs from the garden.* **2.** to make into a preserve or confection. **3.** to construct, form, or make: *to confect a dress from odds and ends of fabric.* —*n.* **4.** a preserved, candied, or other sweet confection. [< L *confect(us)* (ptp. of *conficere* to produce, effect), equiv. to *con-* CON- + *-fec-* (ptp. s. of *-ficere,* comb. form of *facere* to make) + *-tus* ptp. suffix]

con·fec·tion (kən fek/shən), *n.* **1.** the process of compounding, preparing, or making something. **2.** a sweet preparation of fruit or the like, as a preserve or candy. **3.** a piece of candy; bonbon. **4.** *Med. Obs.* a preparation made with the aid of sugar, honey, syrup, or the like. **5.** a frilly, ready-made garment or accessory for women. —*v.t.* **6.** *Archaic.* to prepare as a confection. [ME < L *confectiōn-* (s. of *confectiō*) completion, equiv. to *confect-* (see CONFECT) + *-iōn-* -ION]

con·fec·tion·ar·y (kən fek/shə ner/ē), *n., pl.* **-ar·ies,** *adj.* —*n.* **1.** a place where confections are kept or made. **2.** a candy; sweetmeat. **3.** a confectioner's shop. —*adj.* **4.** pertaining to or of the nature of confections or their production. [< ML *confectiōnāri(us),* equiv. to *confectiōn-* CONFECTION + *-ārius* -ARY]

con·fec·tion·er (kən fek/shə nər), *n.* a person who makes or sells candies and, sometimes, ice cream, cakes, etc. [CONFECTION + -ER¹]

confec/tioners' sug/ar, an extra-fine variety of powdered sugar, used in icings, confections, etc. *Symbol:* XXXX

con·fec·tion·er·y (kən fek/shə ner/ē), *n., pl.* **-er·ies. 1.** confections or sweetmeats collectively. **2.** the work or business of a confectioner. **3.** confectionary (def. 3). [CONFECTION + -ERY]

con·fed·er·a·cy (kən fed/ər ə sē, -fed/rə sē), *n., pl.* **-cies. 1.** an alliance between persons, parties, states, etc., for some purpose. **2.** a group of persons, parties, states, etc., united by such a confederacy. **3.** a combination of persons for unlawful purposes; conspiracy. **4. the Confederacy.** See **Confederate States of America.** [ME *confederacie,* alter. of LL *confoederātiō* CONFEDERATION; see -ACY]

con·fed·er·ate (*adj., n.* kən fed/ər it, -fed/rit; *v.* kən-fed/ə rāt/), *adj., n., v.,* **-at·ed, -at·ing.** —*adj.* **1.** united in a league, alliance, or conspiracy. **2.** (*cap.*) of or pertaining to the Confederate States of America: *the Confederate army.* —*n.* **3.** a person, group, nation, etc., united with others in a confederacy; an ally. **4.** an accomplice, esp. in a mischievous or criminal act. **5.** (*cap.*) *U.S. Hist.* an adherent of the Confederate States of America. —*v.t., v.i.* **6.** to unite in a league, alliance, or a conspiracy. [ME *confederat* < LL *confoederāt(us)* (ptp. of *confoederāre* to unite in a league), equiv. to *con-* CON- + *foeder-* (s. of *foedus*) treaty + *-ātus* -ATE¹]

Confed/erate Memo/rial Day/, a day set aside in the South to pay tribute to those who served with the Confederate forces during the Civil War. It is observed on April 26 in Alabama, Florida, Georgia, and Mississippi; on May 10 in North Carolina and South Carolina; on May 30 in Virginia; and on June 3 in Kentucky, Louisiana and Tennessee.

Confed/erate rose/, (*sometimes l.c.*) See **cotton rose.**

Confed/erate States/ of Amer/ica, the group of 11 Southern States that seceded from the United States in 1860–61. Also called **the Confederacy.**

Confed/erate vine/, (*sometimes l.c.*) See **coral vine.**

Confed/erate vi/olet, (*sometimes l.c.*) a violet, *Viola priceana,* of the southern U.S., having whitish-blue flowers veined with bluish purple.

con·fed·er·a·tion (kən fed/ə rā/shən), *n.* **1.** the act or state of confederating. **2.** the state of being confederated. **3.** a league or alliance. **4.** a group of confederates, esp. of states more or less permanently united for common purposes. **5. the Confederation,** the union of the 13 original States under the Articles of Confederation 1781–89. [late ME < LL *confoederātiōn-* (s. of *confoederātiō*) an agreement, equiv. to *confoederāt(us)* CONFEDERATE + *-iōn-* -ION] —**con·fed/er/a/tion·ism,** *n.* —**con·fed/er·a/tion·ist, con·fed/er·al·ist,** *n.*
—**Syn. 3.** coalition, federation. See **alliance.**

con·fed·er·a·tive (kən fed/ə rā/tiv, -ər ə tiv), *adj.* pertaining to or characteristic of a confederation. [CONFEDERATE + -IVE]

con·fer (kən fûr/), *v.,* **-ferred, -fer·ring.** —*v.t.* **1.** to bestow upon as a gift, favor, honor, etc.: *to confer a degree on a graduate.* **2.** *Obs.* to compare. —*v.i.* **3.** to consult together; compare opinions; carry on a discussion or deliberation. [< L *confer(re)* (to) bring together, compare, consult with, equiv. to *con-* CON- + *ferre* to bring] —**con·fer/ment,** *n.* —**con·fer/ra·ble,** *adj.* —**con·fer/rer,** *n.*
—**Syn. 1.** See **give. 3.** See **consult.**

con·fer·ee (kon/fə rē/), *n.* **1.** *U.S.* a person, group, etc., that confers or takes part in a conference. **2.** a person on whom something is conferred, esp. the recipient of an academic degree. Also, **con/fer·ree/.** [CONFER + -EE]

con·fer·ence (kon/fər əns, -frəns), *n.* **1.** a meeting for consultation or discussion: *a conference between a student and his adviser.* **2.** the act of conferring or consulting together; consultation, esp. on an important or serious matter. **3.** *Govt.* a meeting, as of various committees, to settle disagreements between the two legislative groups. **4.** *Eccles.* **a.** an official assembly of clergy or of clergy and laymen, customary in many Christian denominations. **b.** a group of churches the representatives of which regularly meet in such an assembly. **5.** an association of athletic teams; league: *an intercollegiate conference.* [< ML *conferentia.* See CONFER, -ENCE] —**con·fer·en·tial** (kon/fə ren/shəl), *adj.*
—**Syn. 1.** interview, parley, colloquy, colloquium. See **convention.**

con·fer·ral (kən fûr/əl), *n.* the act of conferring, or bestowing; conferment: *The high point of the commencement was the conferral of an honorary doctorate on the president.* [CONFER + -AL²]

con·fer·va (kon fûr/və), *n., pl.* **-vae** (-vē), **-vas.** any simple filamentous green alga. [< L: a certain water-plant supposed to heal wounds, akin to *confervēre* to grow together, heal] —**con·fer/val, con·fer·vous** (kən fûr/vəs), *adj.* —**con·fer/va·like/,** *adj.* —**con·fer·void** (kon fûr/void), *adj., n.*

con·fess (kən fes/), *v.t.* **1.** to acknowledge or avow by way of revelation: *She confessed her secret to her friends. He confessed his faults readily enough.* **2.** to own or admit as true: *I must confess that I haven't read it.* **3.** to declare or acknowledge (one's sins), esp. to God or a priest in order to obtain absolution. **4.** (of a priest) to hear the confession of (a person). **5.** to acknowledge one's belief in; declare adherence to: *to confess allegiance to the United States.* **6.** *Archaic.* to reveal by circumstances. —*v.i.* **7.** to make confession; plead guilty; own: *To confess to a crime may be difficult. Are you ready to confess?* **8.** to make confession of sins, esp. to a priest. **9.** (of a priest) to hear confession. [ME *confess(en)* < MF *confesse(r)* < LL *confessāre,* equiv. to L *confess(us),* ptp. of *confitērī* (CON- + *fet-,* var. of *fat-* admit + *-tus* ptp. suffix) + *-āre* inf. suffix] —**con·fess/a·ble,** *adj.* —**con·fess/ingly,** *adv.*
—**Syn. 1.** See **acknowledge. 2.** grant, concede. —**Ant. 1.** conceal. **2.** deny.

con·fess·ed·ly (kən fes/id lē), *adv.* by confession or acknowledgment; admittedly. [CONFESS + -ED² + -LY]

con·fes·sion (kən fesh/ən), *n.* **1.** acknowledgment; avowal; admission: *a confession of negligence.* **2.** acknowledgment or disclosure of sin or sinfulness, esp. to a priest to obtain absolution. **3.** something that is confessed: *His confession was long and detailed.* **4.** Also called **confes/sion of faith/,** a formal profession of belief and acceptance of church doctrines, as before being admitted to church membership. **5.** the tomb of a martyr or confessor or the altar or shrine connected with it. [< L *confessiōn-* (s. of *confessiō*), equiv. to *confess-* (see CONFESS) + *-iōn-* -ION; r. ME *confessioun* < AF]

con·fes·sion·al (kən fesh/ə nᵊl), *adj.* **1.** of, pertaining to, characteristic of, or based on confession: *confessional release.* —*n.* **2.** the place set apart for the hearing of confessions by a priest. **3.** *Fr. Furniture.* a high, upholstered wing chair of the 18th century. [< ML *confessiōnāle,* neut. of *confessiōnālis* (adj.). See CONFESSION, -AL¹]

con·fes·sion·al·ism (kən fesh/ə nᵊliz/əm), *n.* advocacy of the maintenance of a confession of faith. [CONFESSIONAL + -ISM] —**con·fes·sion·a·li·an** (kən-fesh/ə nā/lē ən), *adj., n.*

con·fes·sion·ar·y (kən fesh/ə ner/ē), *adj., n., pl.* **-ar·ies.** —*adj.* **1.** of or pertaining to confession, esp. auricular confession of sins. —*n.* **2.** *Archaic.* a confessional. [< ML *confessiōnāri(us),* equiv. to *confessiōn-* CONFESSION + *-ārius* -ARY]

Confes/sions of an Eng/lish O/pium Eat/er, an autobiographical work (1822) by Thomas De Quincey.

con·fes·sor (kən fes/ər), *n.* **1.** a person who confesses. **2.** a priest authorized to hear confessions. **3.** a person who confesses and adheres to the Christian religion, esp. in spite of persecution and torture but without suffering martyrdom. **4. the,** (*cap.*) See **Edward the Confessor.** Also, **con·fess′er.** [ME, OE (in pl: *confessores*) < LL, equiv. to L *confess(us)* (see CONFESS) + *-or* -OR²]

con·fet·ti (kən fet′ē *for 1; It.* kôn fet′tē *for 2*), *n.pl., sing.* **-fet·to** (*It.* -fet′tô) for 2. **1.** (*construed as sing.*) small bits of paper, usually colored, thrown or dropped from a height to enhance the gaiety of a festive event, as a parade, wedding reception, etc. **2.** confections; bonbons. [< It, pl. of *confetto* COMFIT]

con·fi·dant (kon′fi dant′, -dänt′, kon′fi dant′, -dänt′), *n.* a person to whom secrets are confided or with whom one has private discussion of intimate problems. [< F *confident* < It *confidente,* n. use of adj.; see CONFIDENT]

con·fi·dante (kon′fi dant′, -dänt′, kon′fi dant′, -dänt′), *n.* **1.** a female confidant. **2.** *Furniture.* confidente. [< F *confidente*]

con·fide (kən fīd′), *v.,* **-fid·ed, -fid·ing.** —*v.i.* **1.** to have full trust; have faith: *They confided in their own ability.* **2.** to impart secrets trustfully; discuss intimate problems (usually fol. by *in*): *She confides in no one but her husband.* —*v.t.* **3.** to tell in assurance of secrecy: *He confided all his hopes and dreams to her.* **4.** to entrust; commit to the charge, knowledge, or good faith of another: *Before her trip she confided her jewelry to her sister.* [< L *confīde(re),* equiv. to *con-* CON- + *fīdere* to trust, akin to *foedus;* see CONFEDERATE] —**con·fid′er,** *n.*

con·fi·dence (kon′fi dəns), *n.* **1.** full trust; belief in the trustworthiness or reliability of a person or thing: *The President had confidence in his cabinet. We have every confidence in their ability to succeed.* **2.** (esp. in European politics) the wish to retain an incumbent government in office, as shown by a vote in a particular issue: *The Conservative party's chances to retain its control of the government rest on a vote of confidence.* **3.** self-reliance, assurance, or boldness: *He acted immediately with admirable and justifiable confidence.* **4.** presumption; impudence: *Her disdainful look crushed the confidence of the brash young man.* **5.** certitude; assurance: *He described the situation with such confidence that the audience believed him completely.* **6.** a confidential communication: *to exchange confidences.* **7.** *Archaic.* that which gives confidence; ground of trust. **8. in confidence,** as a secret or private matter, not to be divulged or communicated to others; with belief in a person's sense of discretion: *I told him in confidence.* [late ME < L *confīdenti(a).* See CONFIDE, -ENCE]
—**Syn. 1.** faith, reliance, dependence. See **trust. 3.** courage, intrepidity. CONFIDENCE, ASSURANCE both imply a faith in oneself. CONFIDENCE may imply trust in oneself or arrogant self-conceit. ASSURANCE implies even more sureness of oneself; this may be shown as undisturbed calm or as offensive boastfulness or headstrong conduct. —**Ant. 1.** mistrust.

con′fidence game′, a swindle technique in which the swindler, after gaining the confidence of the victim, robs him by cheating at cards, appropriating funds entrusted for investment, or the like. Also called, *Brit.,* **con′fidence trick′.**

con′fidence lim′its, *Statistics.* a pair of numbers used to estimate a characteristic of a population, such that the numbers can be stated with a specified probability that the population characteristic is included between them.

con′fidence man′, one who practices the confidence game; swindler.

con·fi·dent (kon′fi dənt), *adj.* **1.** having strong belief or full assurance; sure: *confident of fulfillment.* **2.** sure of oneself; having no uncertainty about one's own abilities, correctness, successfulness, etc.; bold: *a confident speaker.* **3.** excessively bold; presumptuous. **4.** *Obs.* trustful or confiding. —*n.* **5.** a confidant. [< L *confīdent-* (s. of *confīdēns*), prp. of *confīdere.* See CONFIDE, -ENT] —**con′fi·dent·ly,** *adv.*
—**Syn. 1.** certain, positive, assured. See **sure. 2.** brave, intrepid. —**Ant. 1.** modest, diffident.

con·fi·dente (kon′fi dant′, -dänt′, kon′fi dant′, -dänt′), *n.* a sofa or settee of the 18th century that has a triangular seat at each end divided from the greater part of the seat by an arm rest and is sometimes composed of a regular sofa with two detachable bergères. Also, **confidante.** [< F, special use of *confidente* female confidant]

con·fi·den·tial (kon′fi den′shəl), *adj.* **1.** spoken, written, acted on, etc., in confidence; secret: *a confidential remark.* **2.** indicating confidence or intimacy; imparting private matters: *a confidential tone of voice.* **3.** having another's confidence; entrusted with secrets or private affairs: *a confidential secretary.* **4.** *U.S. Govt., Mil.* (of information, a document, etc.) **a.** bearing the classification *confidential.* **b.** limited to persons authorized to use information, documents, etc., so classified. Cf. **classification** (def. 5). [< L *confīdenti(a)* CONFIDENCE + -AL¹] —**con′fi·den′ti·al′i·ty, con′fi·den′tial·ness,** *n.* —**con′fi·den′tial·ly,** *adv.*
—**Syn. 1.** restricted, private. **2.** intimate, familiar. **3.** trusted, trustworthy, private. See **familiar.**

confiden′tial communica′tion, *Law.* a confidential statement made to a lawyer, doctor, or pastor, or to one's husband or wife, privileged against disclosure in court if the privilege is claimed by the client, patient, penitent, or spouse. Also called **privileged communication.**

con·fid·ing (kən fī′ding), *adj.* trustful; credulous or unsuspicious: *a confiding nature.* [CONFIDE + -ING²] —**con·fid′ing·ly,** *adv.*

con·fig·u·ra·tion (kən fig′yə rā′shən), *n.* **1.** the relative disposition of the parts or elements of a thing. **2.** external form, as resulting from this; conformation. **3.** *Astron.* **a.** the relative position or aspect of heavenly bodies. **b.** a group of stars. **4.** *Physics, Chem.* the relative position in space of the atoms in a molecule. [< LL *configūrātiōn-* (s. of *configūrātiō*), equiv. to L *configūrāt(us)* shaped like its model, ptp. of *configūrāre* (*con-* CON- + *figūr(a)* FIGURE + *-ātus* -ATE¹) + *-iōn-* -ION] —**con·fig′u·ra′tion·al, con·fig·u·ra·tive** (kən fig′yər ə tiv, -yə rā′tiv), *adj.* —**con·fig′u·ra′tion·al·ly,** *adv.*

con·fig·u·ra·tion·ism (kən fig′yə rā′shə niz′əm), *n.* See **Gestalt psychology.** [CONFIGURATION + -ISM] —**con·fig′u·ra′tion·ist,** *n.*

con·fine (kən fīn′ *for 1, 2, 4, 5b;* kon′fīn *for 3, 5a*), *v.,* **-fined, -fin·ing,** *n.* —*v.t.* **1.** to enclose within bounds; limit or restrict: *She confined her remarks to the subject at hand. Confine your efforts to finishing the book.* **2.** to shut or keep in; prevent from leaving a place because of imprisonment, illness, discipline, etc.: *For that offense he was confined to quarters for thirty days. Until the trial, he confined himself to his apartment. He was confined for a month by pneumonia.* —*n.* **3.** Usually, **confines.** a boundary or bound; border; frontier. **4.** *Archaic.* confinement. **5.** *Obs.* **a.** Often, **confines.** region; territory. **b.** a place of confinement; prison. [< ML *confīn(āre)* (to) border, bound, equiv. to L *confīn(is)* bordering (see CON-, FINE²) + *-āre* inf. suffix] —**con·fin′a·ble, con·fine′a·ble,** *adj.* —**con·fine′less,** *adj.* —**con·fin′er,** *n.*
—**Syn. 1.** circumscribe. —**Ant. 1, 2.** free.

con·fined (kən fīnd′), *adj.* being in childbirth; being in parturition. [CONFINE + -ED²] —**con·fin·ed·ly** (kən fī′nid lē, -fīnd′lē), *adv.* —**con·fin′ed·ness,** *n.*

con·fine·ment (kən fīn′mənt), *n.* **1.** the act of confining. **2.** the state of being confined. **3.** the lying-in of a woman in childbed; accouchement; childbirth. **4.** *Mil.* incarceration in a guardhouse or prison while awaiting trial or as a punishment (distinguished from *arrest*). [CONFINE + -MENT]

con·firm (kən fûrm′), *v.t.* **1.** to establish the truth, accuracy, validity, or genuineness of; corroborate; verify: *This report confirms my suspicions.* **2.** to acknowledge with definite assurance: *to confirm plane reservations.* **3.** to make valid or binding by some formal or legal act; sanction; ratify: *to confirm an agreement, treaty, appointment, etc.* **4.** to make firm or more firm; add strength to; settle or establish firmly: *His support confirmed my determination to run for mayor.* **5.** to strengthen (a person) in habit, resolution, opinion, etc.: *The accident confirmed him in his fear of airplanes.* **6.** *Eccles.* to administer the rite of confirmation to. [< L *confirm(āre)* (see CON-, FIRM¹); r. ME *confermen* < OF] —**con·firm′a·ble,** *adj.* —**con·firm′er;** *Law,* **con·firm·or** (kon′fər môr′, kən fûr′mər), *n.* —**con·firm′ing·ly,** *adv.*
—**Syn. 1.** prove, substantiate, authenticate, validate. **3.** fix. —**Ant. 1.** disprove. **3.** invalidate. **4.** shake.

con·fir·mand (kon′fər mand′, kon′fər mand′), *n. Eccles.* a candidate for confirmation. [< L *confirmand(us)* to be confirmed (ger. of *confirmāre* to CONFIRM), equiv. to *confirmā-* (s. of *confirmāre*) + *-ndus* ger. ending]

con·fir·ma·tion (kon′fər mā′shən), *n.* **1.** the act of confirming. **2.** the state of being confirmed. **3.** something that confirms, as a corroborative statement or piece of evidence: *His broken tooth was confirmation that he had been fighting.* **4.** a rite administered to baptized persons, in some churches as a sacrament for confirming and strengthening the recipient in the Christian faith, in others as a rite without sacramental character by which the recipient is admitted to full communion with the church. **5.** a solemn ceremony among Reform and certain Conservative Jews that is held in the synagogue, usually on Shabuoth, to admit formally as adult members of the Jewish community Jewish boys and girls 14 to 16 years of age who have successfully completed a prescribed period or course of study in Judaism. [ME < L. See CONFIRM, -ATION]

confirma′tion class′, **1.** a class held chiefly to train young people for religious confirmation. **2.** the young people in such a class.

con·firm·a·to·ry (kən fûr′mə tōr′ē, -tôr′ē), *adj.* serving to confirm; corroborative. Also, **con·firm′a·tive.** [< ML *confirmātōri(us)* < L *confirmāt(us)* (ptp. of *confirmāre* to CONFIRM) + *-ōrius* -ORY¹]

con·firmed (kən fûrmd′), *adj.* **1.** made certain as to truth, accuracy, validity, etc.: *confirmed reports of rioting in Cuba.* **2.** settled; ratified. **3.** firmly established in a habit or condition; inveterate: *a confirmed bachelor.* **4.** given additional determination; made resolute. **5.** (of a disease) chronic. [ME *confermyd.* See CONFIRM, -ED²] —**con·firm·ed·ly** (kən fur′mid lē), *adv.* —**con·firm·ed·ness** (kən fûr′mid nis, -fûrmd′-), *n.*

con·fis·ca·ble (kən fis′kə bəl, kon′fi skə bəl), *adj.* liable to be confiscated. [< L *confiscā(re)* (see CONFISCATE) + -BLE]

con·fis·cate (kon′fi skāt′, kən fis′kāt), *v.,* **-cat·ed, -cat·ing,** *adj.* —*v.t.* **1.** to seize as forfeited to the public domain; appropriate, by way of penalty, for public use. **2.** to seize by or as if by authority; appropriate summarily: *The principal confiscated their knives.* —*adj.* **3.** seized. [< L *confiscāt(us)* (ptp. of *confiscāre* to seize for the public treasury), equiv. to *con-* CON- + *fisc(us)* basket, money-bag, public treasury + *-ātus* -ATE¹] —**con′fis·ca′tion,** *n.* —**con′fis·ca′tor,** *n.*

con·fis·ca·to·ry (kən fis′kə tōr′ē, -tôr′ē), *adj.* characterized by, effecting, or resulting in confiscation. [CONFISCATE + -ORY¹]

Con·fit·e·or (kən fit′ē ôr′), *n. Rom. Cath. Ch.* the prayer in the form of a general confession said at the beginning of the Mass and on certain other occasions. [after first word of Latin prayer: I confess]

con·fi·ture (kon′fi cho͝or′), *n.* a confection; a preserve, as of fruit. [ME < MF. See COMFIT, -URE]

con·fla·grant (kən flā′grənt), *adj.* blazing; burning; on fire. [< L *conflagrant-* (s. of *conflagrāns*), prp. of *conflagrāre.* See CONFLAGRATION, -ANT]

con·fla·gra·tion (kon′flə grā′shən), *n.* a destructive fire, usually an extensive one. [< L *conflagrātiōn-* (s. of *conflagrātiō*), equiv. to *conflagrāt(us)* burned up, ptp. of *conflagrāre* (*con-* CON- + *flagr-* (akin to *fulgur* lightning, *flamma* FLAME, Gk *phlóx,* see PHLOX) + *-ātus* -ATE¹) + *-iōn-* -ION] —**con′fla·gra′tive,** *adj.*
—**Syn.** See **flame.**

con·fla·tion (kən flā′shən), *n. Bibliog.* **1.** the combination of two variant texts into a new one. **2.** the text resulting from such a combination. [< L *conflātiōn-* (s. of *conflātiō*) a fusing together, equiv. to *conflāt(us)* (ptp. of *conflāre* (*con-* CON- + *flā-* (akin to BLOW²) + *-tus* ptp. suffix) + *-iōn-* -ION] —**con·flate** (kon′flāt), *adj.*

con·flict (*v.* kən flikt′; *n.* kon′flikt), *v.i.* **1.** to come into collision or disagreement; be contradictory, at variance, or in opposition; clash: *The account of one eyewitness conflicted with that of the other. My class conflicts with my going to the concert.* **2.** to contend; do battle. —*n.* **3.** a battle or struggle, esp. a prolonged struggle; strife. **4.** controversy; a quarrel: *conflicts between church and state.* **5.** discord of action, feeling, or effect; antagonism, as of interests or principles: *a conflict of ideas.* **6.** a striking together; collision. **7.** incompatibility or interference, as of one idea, desire, event, activity, etc., with another: *I have a conflict between French and music theory classes at that hour. There is a conflict in performances scheduled for the theater.* [< L *conflict(us)* a striking together, n. use of *conflictus* thrown together (ptp. of *confligere*), equiv. to *con-* CON- + *flic-* (var. s. of *fligere* to strike) + *-tus* ptp. suffix] —**con·flict′ing·ly,** *adv.* —**con·flic′tion,** *n.* —**con·flic′tive, con·flic·to·ry** (kən flik′tə rē), *adj.*
—**Syn. 1.** collide, oppose. **3.** encounter, siege. See **fight. 5.** contention, opposition. —**Ant. 4.** accord.

con′flict of in′terest, **1.** the circumstance of a person who finds that one of his activities, interests, etc., can be forwarded only at the expense of another of them. **2.** the circumstance of a public office holder whose private financial interests might benefit from his official actions or political influence: *The senator placed all his stocks in trust to avoid possible conflict of interest.*

con′flict of laws′, **1.** dissimilarity or discrepancy between the laws of different municipalities, states, or nations with regard to the rights of a person in a matter falling within two or more jurisdictions. **2.** the branch of law dealing with the determination of the applicable law, the jurisdiction, and the competent court in cases involving such conflict.

con·flu·ence (kon′flo͞o əns), *n.* **1.** a flowing together of two or more streams, rivers, or the like: *the confluence of the Missouri and Mississippi rivers.* **2.** their place of junction: *St. Louis is at the confluence of the Missouri and Mississippi rivers.* **3.** the body of water so formed. **4.** the rate at which fluid flow converges along an axis perpendicular to the direction of flow at a given point. Cf. **convergence** (def. 5), **diffluence** (def. 3). **5.** a coming together of people or things; concourse. **6.** a crowd or throng; assemblage. Also, **con·flux** (kon′fluks). [< LL *confluentia,* equiv. to *confluent-* CONFLUENT + *-ia;* see -ENCE]

con·flu·ent (kon′flo͞o ənt), *adj.* **1.** flowing or running together; blending into one: *confluent rivers; confluent ideas.* **2.** *Pathol.* **a.** running together: *confluent efflorescences.* **b.** characterized by confluent efflorescences: *confluent smallpox.* —*n.* **3.** one of two or more confluent streams. **4.** a tributary stream. [< L *confluent-* (s. of *confluēns,* prp. of *confluere*), equiv. to *con-* CON- + *flu-* (s. of *fluere* to flow) + *-ent-* -ENT; see FLUENT, FLUID]

con·fo·cal (kon fō′kəl), *adj. Math.* having the same focus or foci. [CON- + FOCAL]

con·form (kən fôrm′), *v.i.* **1.** to act in accord or harmony; comply (usually fol. by *to*): *Being obstinate, she refused to conform to the town's social pattern.* **2.** to be or become similar in form, nature, or character. **3.** to comply with the usages of an established church, esp. the Church of England. —*v.t.* **4.** to make similar in form, nature, or character. **5.** to bring into agreement, correspondence, or harmony. —*adj.* **6.** *Archaic.* conformable. [ME *confo(u)rme(n)* < MF *conforme(r)* < L *conformāre* to shape. See CON-, FORM] —**con·form′er,** *n.* —**con·form′ing·ly,** *adv.*
—**Syn. 1.** yield, agree, consent. **2.** correspond, agree, tally. **5.** adapt, adjust, accommodate. —**Ant. 1, 3.** dissent. **2.** differ.

con·form·a·ble (kən fôr′mə bəl), *adj.* **1.** corresponding in form, nature, or character; similar. **2.** compliant; acquiescent; submissive: *a conformable disposition.* **3.** *Geol.* (of strata or beds) having the same dip and strike as a result of successive depositions uninterrupted by crustal movement. [CONFORM + -ABLE] —**con·form′a·bil′i·ty, con·form′a·ble·ness,** *n.* —**con·form′a·bly,** *adv.*

Conformable and unconformable strata; A and B, two sets of unconformable strata; CD, line of junction of A and B

con·for·mal (kon fôr′məl), *adj.* of, pertaining to, or noting a map or transformation in which angles and scale are preserved. [< LL *conformāl(is)* of the same shape. See CON-, FORMAL¹]

confor′mal projec′tion, *Cartog.* a projection in which angles formed by lines are preserved, with every small triangle represented by a similar triangle. Also called **orthomorphic projection.**

con·form·ance (kən fôr′məns), *n.* the act of conforming; conformity. [CONFORM + -ANCE]

con·for·ma·tion (kon′fôr mā′shən), *n.* **1.** manner of formation; structure; form, as of a physical entity. **2.** symmetrical disposition or arrangement of parts. **3.** the act or process of conforming; adaptation; adjustment. **4.** the state of being conformed. [< L *conformātiōn-* (s. of *conformātiō*), equiv. to *conformāt(us)* made, ptp. of *conformāre* (*con-* CON- + *forma* FORM + *-tus* ptp. suffix) + *-iōn-* -ION]
—**Syn. 1.** configuration, shape.

con·form·ism (kən fôr′miz əm), *n.* the policy, practice, or attitude of conforming. [CONFORM + -ISM]

con·form·ist (kən fôr′mist), *n.* **1.** a person who conforms, esp. unquestioningly, to the usual usage or practice of a group, society, etc. **2.** (*often cap.*) a person who conforms to the usages of an established church, esp. the Church of England. —*adj.* **3.** of or characterized by conforming, esp. in action or appearance. [CONFORM + -IST]

con·form·i·ty (kən fôr′mi tē), *n., pl.* **-ties. 1.** correspondence in form, nature, or character; agreement, congruity, or accordance: *a face with a nice conformity of feature.* **2.** compliance or acquiescence. **3.** (*often cap.*) compliance with the usages of an established church, esp. the Church of England. [late ME *conformite* < MF < LL *conformitāt-* (s. of *conformitās*). See CONFORM, -ITY]

con·found (kon found′, kən-; *for 7 usually* kon′found′), *v.t.* **1.** to perplex or amaze, esp. by a sudden disturbance or surprise; bewilder; confuse: *The complicated directions confounded him.* **2.** to throw into confusion or disorder: *The revolution confounded the people.* **3.** to throw into increased confusion or disorder. **4.** to contradict or refute: *to confound their arguments.* **5.** to treat or regard erroneously as identical; mix or associate by mistake: *truth confounded with error.* **6.** to mingle so that the elements cannot be distinguished or separated. **7.** to damn (used in mild imprecations): *Confound it!* **8.** *Archaic.* to put to shame; abash. **9.** *Archaic.* **a.** to defeat or overthrow. **b.** to bring to ruin or naught. **10.** *Obs.* to spend uselessly; waste. [ME *conf(o)und(e)* < AF *confoundre)* < L *confundere* to mix, equiv. to *con-* CON- + *fundere* to pour] —**con·found′a·ble,** *adj.* —**con·found′er,** *n.* —**con·found′ing·ly,** *adv.*
—**Syn. 1.** bewilder, daze, nonplus, astound.

con·found·ed (kon foun′did, kən-), *adj.* damned (used euphemistically): *That is a confounded lie.* [ME; see CONFOUND, -ED²] —**con·found′ed·ly,** *adv.* —**con·found′ed·ness,** *n.*

con·fra·ter·ni·ty (kon′frə tûr′ni tē), *n., pl.* **-ties. 1.** a lay brotherhood devoted to some purpose, esp. to religious or charitable service. **2.** a society or body of men united for some purpose or in some profession. [late ME *confraternite* < ML *confrāternitās*, equiv. to *confrāter* (*con-* CON- + *frāter* brother, fellow-member) + (*frater*)-*nitās* FRATERNITY] —**con′fra·ter′nal,** *adj.*

con·frere (kon′frâr), *n.* a fellow member of a fraternity, profession, etc.; colleague: *my confreres in the medical profession.* [late ME < MF < ML *confrāter* colleague, equiv. to L *con-* CON- + *frāter* brother]

con·fric·a·men·tum (kon frik′ə men′təm), *n., pl.* **-ta** (-tə). (in prescriptions) a liniment. [< L]

con·front (kən frunt′), *v.t.* **1.** to stand or come in front of; stand or meet facing: *The two long-separated brothers confronted each other speechlessly.* **2.** to be in one's way: *the numerous obstacles that still confronted him.* **3.** to face in hostility or defiance; oppose: *The feuding factions confronted one another on the field.* **4.** to present for acknowledgment, contradiction, etc.; set face to face: *They confronted him with evidence of his crime.* **5.** to bring together for examination or comparison. [< ML *confront(ārī)*, equiv. to L *con-* CON- + *front-* (see FRONT) + *-ārī* inf. suffix] —**con·fron·ta·tion** (kon′frən tā′shən), **con·front′ment,** *n.* —**con·front′er,** *n.*

Con·fu·cian (kən fyōō′shən), *n.* **1.** a believer in or advocate of the doctrines of Confucius. **2.** Also called **Ju.** a member of the school of philosophers, founded by Confucius, who codified in their doctrines the traditional Chinese principles of ethics, morals, and politics. —*adj.* **3.** of, pertaining to, or resembling the doctrines of Confucius. [CONFUCI(US) + -AN] —**Con·fu′cian·ism,** *n.* —**Con·fu′cian·ist,** *n.*

Con·fu·cius (kən fyōō′shəs), *n.* (*K'ung Ch'iu*) 551? B.C.–478? B.C., Chinese philosopher and teacher. Chinese, **K'ung Fu-tzŭ.**

con fuo·co (kon fwô′kō, fōō ô′-, kōn; *It.* kôn fōō-ô′kô), with great vigor and speed (used as a musical direction). [< It: lit., with fire]

con·fuse (kən fyōōz′), *v.t.,* **-fused, -fus·ing. 1.** to make unclear or indistinct: *The great volume of the evidence tended to confuse the issue.* **2.** to combine without order; jumble; disorder: *Try not to confuse the papers on his desk.* **3.** to fail to distinguish between; associate by mistake; confound: *to confuse dates; He always confuses the twins.* **4.** to perplex or bewilder: *The sudden light confused him.* **5.** to disconcert or abash: *His candor confused her.* **6.** *Obs.* to bring to ruin or naught. [back formation from CONFUSED < L *confūs(us)* mixed up (ptp. of *confundere* to CONFOUND), equiv. to *con-* CON- + *-fūsus* (see FUSE²) + -ED²] —**con·fus′a·bil′i·ty,** *n.* —**con·fus′a·ble,** *adj.* —**con·fus′a·bly,** *adv.* —**con·fus·ed·ly** (kən fyōō′zid lē, -fyōōzd′-), *adv.* —**con·fus′ed·ness,** *n.* —**con·fus′ing·ly,** *adv.*
—**Syn. 2.** disarray, disarrange, disturb. **4.** mystify, nonplus, disarm, shock. CONFUSE, DISCONCERT, EMBARRASS imply temporary interference with the clear working of one's mind. To CONFUSE is to produce a general bewilderment: *to confuse by giving complicated directions.* To DISCONCERT is quickly or violently to disturb one's mind by irritation, perplexities, etc., making it difficult for him to collect his thoughts: *to disconcert by asking irrelevant questions.* To EMBARRASS is to cause one to be ill at ease or uncomfortable, so that his usual judgment and presence of mind desert him: *to embarrass by treating with unexpected rudeness.* **5.** mortify, shame.

confused′ flour′ bee′tle, a brown flour beetle, *Tribolium confusum*, that feeds on stored grain and grain products.

con·fu·sion (kən fyōō′zhən), *n.* **1.** the act of confusing. **2.** the state of being confused. **3.** disorder; upheaval; chaos: *The army retreated in confusion.* **4.** lack of clearness or distinctness: *There was some confusion in her mind between what was right and what was wrong.* **5.** embarrassment or abashment: *She kissed him suddenly, and he blushed in confusion.* **6.** perplexity; bewilderment: *The more difficult questions left him in complete confusion.* **7.** *Psychiatry.* a disturbed mental state; a clouding of consciousness; disorientation. **8.** *Archaic.* defeat, overthrow, or ruin. [ME < L *confūsiōn-* (s. of *confūsiō*). See CONFUSE, -ION] —**con·fu′sion·al,** *adj.*
—**Syn. 2.** distraction. **3.** turmoil, jumble, mess, disarray. **5.** shame, mortification.

con·fu·ta·tion (kon′fyŏŏ tā′shən), *n.* **1.** the act of confuting. **2.** something that confutes. **3.** *Classical Oratory.* the fourth section of a speech, given over to direct refutation. [< L *confūtātiōn-* (s. of *confūtātiō*), equiv. to *confūtāt(us)* silenced (ptp. of *confūtāre;* see CONFUTE, -ATE¹) + *-iōn-* -ION] —**con·fut·a·tive** (kən-fyōō′tə tiv), *adj.*

con·fute (kən fyōōt′), *v.t.,* **-fut·ed, -fut·ing. 1.** to prove to be false, invalid, or defective; disprove: *to confute an argument.* **2.** to prove to be wrong; convict of error by argument or proof: *to confute one's opponent.* **3.** *Obs.* to bring to naught; confound. [< L *confūt(āre)* (to) repress, put to silence, refute, equiv. to *con-* CON- + *-fūtāre*, perh. akin to FUTILE] —**con·fut′a·ble,** *adj.* —**con·fut′er,** *n.*

Cong., 1. Congregational. **2.** Congregationalist. **3.** Congress. **4.** Congressional.

cong., gallon. [< L *congius*]

con·ga (koŋ′gə), *n., pl.* **-gas,** *v.,* **-gaed, -ga·ing.** —*n.* **1.** a Cuban dance that consists of three steps forward followed by a kick, characteristically performed by a group following a leader in a single line. **2.** the music for this dance. —*v.i.* **3.** to dance a conga. [< AmerSp, fem. of *Congo* CONGO]

con′ game′, *Slang.* See **confidence game.**

con·gé (kon′zhā, -jā; *Fr.* kôN zhā′), *n., pl.* **-gés** (-zhāz, -jāz; *Fr.* -zhā′). **1.** leave-taking; farewell. **2.** permission to depart. **3.** dismissal. **4.** a bow or obeisance. **5.** *Archit.* a concave molding, as an apophyge, formed by a quadrant curving away from a given surface and terminating perpendicular to a fillet parallel to that surface. Also, **congee.** [< F; see CONGEE]

con·geal (kən jēl′), *v.t., v.i.* **1.** to change from a soft or fluid state to a rigid or solid state, as by cooling or freezing: *The fat congealed on the top of the stew.* **2.** to curdle; coagulate, as a fluid. **3.** to make or become fixed, as sentiments, principles, etc.: *Some philosophic systems lost their vitality and became wholly congealed.* [ME *congele(n)* < L *congelā(re)*, equiv. to *con-* CON- + *gelāre* to freeze; see GELID] —**con·geal′a·bil′i·ty, con·geal′a·ble·ness,** *n.* —**con·geal′a·ble,** *adj.* —**con·gealed′ness,** *n.* —**con·geal′er,** *n.* —**con·geal′ment,** *n.*

con·gee (kon′jē), *n., v.,* **-geed, -gee·ing.** —*n.* **1.** congé. —*v.i. Obs.* **2.** to take one's leave. **3.** to bow ceremoniously. [late ME *congie* < MF < L *commeāt(us)* furlough, equiv. to *com-* COM- + *meātus* motion, passage, n. use of *meātus* passed (ptp.) (*meā(re)* (to) pass + *-tus* ptp. suffix)]

con·ge·la·tion (kon′jə lā′shən), *n.* **1.** the act or process of congealing; the state of being congealed. **2.** the product of congealing; a concretion; coagulation. [late ME < L *congelātiōn-* (s. of *congelātiō*). See CONGEAL, -ATION]

con·gel·i·fract (kən jel′ə frakt′), *n. Geol.* a rock fragment split from a rock surface by the action of frost. [< L *congel(āre)* (to) cause to freeze up (see CONGEAL) + -I- + L *fract(us)* broken (ptp. of *frangere;* see BREAK)]

con·gel·i·frac·tion (kən jel′ə frak′shən), *n. Geol.* the shattering or splitting of rock material due to the action of frost. [CONGELIFRACT + -ION]

con·gel·i·tur·ba·tion (kən jel′i tûr bā′shən), *n. Geol.* the churning, heaving, and thrusting of soil material due to the action of frost. [< L *congel(āre)* (to) cause to freeze up (see CONGEAL) + -I- + L *turbāt(us)* (ptp. of *turbāre*), equiv. to *turb-* DISTURB + *-ātus* -ATE¹]

con·ge·ner (kon′jə nər), *n.* **1.** one of the same kind or class. **2.** a plant or animal belonging to the same genus as another. **3.** Also, **congeneric.** a secondary product formed in alcohol during fermentation that determines largely the character of the final liquor. [< L, equiv. to *con-* CON- + *gener-* (s. of *genus*); see GENUS, GENERAL]

con·ge·ner·ic (kon′jə ner′ik), *adj.* **1.** Also, **con·gen·er·ous** (kən jen′ər əs). of the same kind or genus. —*n.* **2.** congener (def. 3). [CONGENER + -IC; see GENERIC]

con·gen·ial (kən jēn′yəl), *adj.* **1.** suited or adapted in spirit, feeling, temper, etc.; compatible: *a congenial couple.* **2.** agreeable or pleasing in nature or character: *congenial surroundings; a congenial atmosphere.* [< L *con-* CON- + *geni(us)* GENIUS + -AL¹] —**con·ge·ni·al·i·ty** (kən jē′nē al′i tē), **con·gen′ial·ness,** *n.* —**con·gen′ial·ly,** *adv.*
—**Syn. 2.** favorable, pleasant, complaisant, sympathetic. —**Ant. 1, 2.** disagreeable.

con·gen·i·tal (kən jen′i tᵊl), *adj.* existing at or from one's birth: *a congenital defect.* [< L *congenit(us)* connate (*con-* CON- + *geni-*, ptp. s. of *gignere* to give birth + *-tus* ptp. suffix) + -AL¹] —**con·gen′i·tal·ly,** *adv.* —**con·gen′i·tal·ness,** *n.*
—**Syn.** innate, inborn, hereditary, inherited.

con·ger (koŋ′gər), *n.* **1.** a large, marine eel, *Conger conger*, sometimes reaching a length of 10 feet, used for food in Europe. **2.** any other eel of the family *Congridae*. Also called **con′ger eel′.** [ME *kunger*, *congre* < OF *congre* < L *conger* < Gk *góngros* sea-eel, gnarl, protuberance; akin to COCK³]

con·ge·ries (kon jēr′ēz), *n.* (*construed as sing. or pl.*) a collection of several particles or bodies in one mass; assemblage; aggregation; heap: *From the airplane the town resembled a congeries of tiny boxes. Here and there, congeries of tiny shells punctuated the beach.* [< L: a heap, equiv. to *conger-* (s. of *congerere* to collect, heap up, equiv. to *con-* CON- + *gerere* to bear, carry) + *-iēs* n. suffix as in *rabies, series*]

con·gest (kən jest′), *v.t.* **1.** to fill to excess; overcrowd or overburden: *The subway entrance was so congested that no one could move. The cold congested his sinuses.* **2.** *Pathol.* to cause an unnatural accumulation of blood in the vessels of (an organ or part). **3.** *Obs.* to heap together. —*v.i.* **4.** to become congested: *His throat congested with phlegm.* [< L *congest(us)* (ptp. of *congerere;* see CONGERIES), equiv. to *con-* CON- + *ges-* (var. s. of *gerere*) + *-tus* ptp. suffix] —**con·gest′i·ble,** *adj.* —**con·ges′tion,** *n.* —**con·ges′tive,** *adj.*

conges′tive heart′ fail′ure. See **heart failure** (def. 2).

con·ges·tus (kən jes′təs), *adj. Meteorol.* (of a cloud) characterized by dense, sharply defined, cauliflowerlike upper parts and sometimes by great verticality. [< L; see CONGEST]

con·gi·us (kon′jē əs), *n., pl.* **-gi·i** (-jē ī′). **1.** (in prescriptions) a gallon. **2.** an ancient Roman unit of liquid measure equal to about 0.8 U.S. gallon. [< L, alter. of Gk *konchíon*, equiv. to *kónch(ē)* CONCH + *-ion* dim. suffix]

con·glo·bate (kon glō′bāt, koŋ′glō bāt′), *adj., v.,* **-bat·ed, -bat·ing.** —*adj.* **1.** formed into a ball. —*v.t., v.i.* **2.** to collect or form into a ball or rounded mass. [< L *conglobāt(us)*, ptp. of *conglobāre.* See CONGLOBE, -ATE¹] —**con·glo′bate·ly,** *adv.* —**con′glo·ba′tion,** *n.*

con·globe (kon glōb′), *v.t., v.i.,* **-globed, -glob·ing.** to conglobate. [< L *conglob(āre)*, equiv. to *con-* CON- + *glob(us)* ball, sphere + *-āre* inf. ending]

con·glom·er·ate (*n., adj.* kən glom′ər it; *v.* kən glom′ə rāt′), *n., adj., v.,* **-at·ed, -at·ing.** —*n.* **1.** anything composed of heterogeneous materials or elements. **2.** Also called **pudding stone.** *Geol.* a rock consisting of rounded and waterworn pebbles or the like embedded in a finer cementing material; consolidated gravel. **3.** a company consisting of a number of subsidiary companies or divisions in a variety of unrelated industries, usually as a result of merger or acquisition. —*adj.* **4.** gathered into a rounded mass; consisting of parts so gathered; clustered. **5.** *Geol.* of the nature of a conglomerate. **6.** noting or pertaining to a corporate conglomerate or conglomerates. —*v.t.* **7.** to bring together into a cohering mass. **8.** to gather into a ball or rounded mass. —*v.i.* **9.** to collect or cluster together. [< L *conglomerāt(us)* (ptp. of *conglomerāre*), equiv. to *con-* CON- + *glomer-* (s. of *glomus*) ball of yarn + *-ātus* -ATE¹] —**con·glom·er·at·ic** (kən glom′ə rat′ik), **con·glom·er·it·ic** (kən glom′ə rit′ik), *adj.*

con·glom·er·a·tion (kən glom′ə rā′shən), *n.* **1.** the act of conglomerating; the state of being conglomerated. **2.** a cohering mass; cluster. **3.** a heterogeneous combination: *a conglomeration of ideas.* [< LL *conglomerātiōn-* (s. of *conglomerātiō*), equiv. to *conglomerāt(us)* CONGLOMERATE + *-iōn-* -ION]
—**Syn. 2, 3.** agglomeration, aggregate, aggregation, conglomerate.

con·glu·ti·nate (kən glōōt′ᵊnāt′), *v.,* **-nat·ed, -nat·ing,** *adj.* —*v.t., v.i.* **1.** to join or become joined with or as if with glue. —*adj.* **2.** glued together; adhering. [< L *conglūtināt(us)* (ptp. of *conglūtināre*), equiv. to *con-* CON- + *glūtin-* (var. s. of *glūten*) glue + *-ātus* -ATE¹] —**con·glu′ti·na′tion,** *n.* —**con·glu′ti·na′tive,** *adj.*

Con·go (koŋ′gō), *n.* congou.

Con·go (koŋ′gō), *n.* **1. Republic of.** Formerly, **French Congo, Middle Congo.** a republic in central Africa, W of Zaire: formerly an overseas territory in French Equatorial Africa; now an independent member of the French Community. 1,300,000 (est. 1974); 132,046 sq. mi. *Cap.:* Brazzaville. **2. Democratic Republic of the,** a former name of **Zaire.** Formerly, **Belgian Congo, Congo Free State. 3.** a river in central Africa, flowing in a great loop from SE Zaire to the Atlantic. ab. 3000 mi. long.

Con′go col′or, *Chem.* any of a group of azo dyes derived from benzidine which will dye cotton and other vegetable fibers without the aid of a mordant. Also called **Con′go dye′.**

Con′go Free′ State′, a former name of **Zaire.**

Con·go·lese (koŋ′gə lēz′, -lēs′), *adj., n., pl.* **-lese.** —*adj.* **1.** of or pertaining to either of the Congo republics, its inhabitants, or their language. —*n.* **2.** an inhabitant or native of either of the Congo republics. [< F *congolais*, irreg. formation; see -ESE]

Con′go red′, *Chem.* a water-soluble powder, $C_{32}H_{22}O_6N_6S_2Na_2$, one of the Congo colors that is not acid-fast or lightfast: used chiefly as a dye, biological stain, and as a chemical indicator.

con′go snake′, any of several eel-shaped salamanders, as the amphiuma or siren. Also called **con′go eel′.**

con·gou (koŋ′gōō), *n.* a kind of black tea from China. Also, **congo.** [perh. < dial. Chin *kong-hu* for Mandarin *kung-fu* work, with reference to care involved in growing and processing it]

con·grat·u·lant (kən grach′ə lənt), *adj.* **1.** expressing or conveying congratulation. —*n.* **2.** a person who congratulates. [< L *congrātulant-* (s. of *congrātulāns*, prp. of *congrātulārī*), equiv. to *con-* CON- + *grātul-* (*grāt-*, s. of *grātus* pleasing + *-ul-* adj. suffix) + *-ant-* -ANT]

con·grat·u·late (kən grach′ə lāt′), *v.t.,* **-lat·ed, -lat·ing. 1.** to express one's pleasure and joy to (a person), as on a happy occasion: *They congratulated him on his marriage.* **2.** *Obs.* **a.** to express sympathetic joy or satisfaction at (an event). **b.** to salute. [< L *congrātulāt(us)*, ptp. of *congrātulārī.* See CONGRATULANT, -ATE¹] —**con·grat′u·la′tor,** *n.*

con·grat·u·la·tion (kən grach′ə lā′shən), *n.* **1.** the act of congratulating. —*interj.* **2. congratulations!** (used to express joy or satisfaction in the success or good fortune of another): *Congratulations! You have just become the father of twins!* [< LL *congrātulātiōn-* (s. of *congrātulātiō*), equiv. to *congrātulāt(us)* (see CONGRATULATE) + *-iōn-* -ION] —**con·grat′u·la′tion·al,** *adj.*

con·grat·u·la·to·ry (kən grach′ə lə tôr′ē, -tōr′ē), *adj.* conveying congratulations: *a congratulatory telegram.* [< ML *congrātulātōri(us)*, equiv. to L *congrātulāt(us)* (see CONGRATULATE) + *-ōrius* -ORY¹]

con·gre·gate (*v.* koŋ′grə gāt′; *adj.* koŋ′grə git, -gāt′), *v.,* **-gat·ed, -gat·ing,** *adj.* —*v.i.* **1.** to come together; assemble, esp. in large numbers: *The people congregated in the theatre.* —*v.t.* **2.** to bring together in a crowd, body, or mass; assemble; collect. —*adj.* **3.** congregated; assembled. **4.** formed by collecting; collective. [< L *congregāt(us)* (ptp. of *congregāre* to flock together), equiv. to *con-* CON- + *greg-* (s. of *grex*) flock + *-ātus* -ATE¹] —**con′gre·ga′tive,** *adj.* —**con′gre·ga′tive·ness,** *n.* —**con′gre·ga′tor, con′gre·gant,** *n.*

con·gre·ga·tion (koŋ′grə gā′shən), *n.* **1.** the act or state of congregating or the state of being congregated. **2.** a congregated body; assemblage. **3.** an assembly of persons brought together for common religious worship. **4.** an organization formed for the purpose of providing for worship of God, for religious education, and for other church activities; a local church society. **5.** the people of Israel. Ex. 12:3,6; Lev. 4:13. **6.** *New Testament.* the Christian church in general. **7.** *Rom. Cath. Ch.* **a.** a committee of cardinals or other ecclesiastics. **b.** a community of men or women, either with or without vows, observing a common rule. **8.** (at English universities) the general assembly of the doctors, fellows, etc. **9.** (in colonial North America) a parish, hundred, town, plantation, or other settlement. [ME *congregacio(u)n* < L *congregātiōn-* (s. of *congregātiō*)]

con·gre·ga·tion·al (koŋ′grə gā′shə nᵊl), *adj.* **1.** of or pertaining to a congregation: *congregational singing.* **2.** (*cap.*) pertaining or adhering to a form of church government in which each congregation or local church acts as an independent, self-governing body, while maintaining fellowship with like congregations. [CONGREGATION + -AL¹] —**con′gre·ga′tion·al·ly,** *adv.*

con·gre·ga·tion·al·ism (koŋ′grə gā′shə nᵊliz′əm), *n.* **1.** a form of church government in which each local religious society is independent and self-governing. **2.** (*cap.*) the system of government and doctrine of Congregational churches. —**con′gre·ga′tion·al·ist,** *n., adj.*

con·gress (*n.* koŋ′gris; *v.* kən gres′), *n.* **1.** (*cap.*) *Govt.* **a.** the national legislative body of the U.S., consisting of the Senate, or upper house, and the House of Representatives, or lower house, as a continuous institution. **b.** this body as it exists for a period of two years during which it has the same membership: *the 69th Congress.* **c.** a session of this body: *to speak in Congress.* **2.** the national legislative body of a nation, esp. of a republic. **3.** a formal meeting or assembly of representatives, as envoys of independent states, for the discussion, arrangement, or promotion of some matter of common interest. **4.** the act of coming together; an encounter. **5.** familiar relations; dealings; intercourse. **6.** coitus; sexual intercourse. —*v.i.* **7.** to assemble together; meet in congress. [< L *congress(us)* a coming together, n. use of *congressus* (ptp. of *congredī*), equiv. to *con-* CON- + *gred-* (var. s. of *gradī* to step; see GRADE) + *-tus* ptp. ending]
—**Syn. 3.** conference, council, convention.

con′gress boot′, *U.S.* a high shoe with elastic sides, worn by men in the late 19th and early 20th centuries.

con·gres·sion·al (kən gresh′ə nəl), *adj.* **1.** of or pertaining to a congress. **2.** (*usually cap.*) of or pertaining to the Congress of the U.S. [< L *congressiōn-* (s. of *congressiō*) a coming together, equiv. to *congress(us)* (see CONGRESS) + *-iōn-* -ION] —**con·gres′sion·al·ist,** *n.* —**con·gres′sion·al·ly,** *adv.*

Congres′sional dis′trict, *U.S. Govt.* one of a fixed number of districts into which a State is divided, each district electing one member to the national House of Representatives. Cf. **assembly district, senatorial district.**

Congres′sional Med′al of Hon′or. See **Medal of Honor.**

Congres′sional Rec′ord, *U.S.* the record of the proceedings of Congress, with a transcript of the discussion, published daily by the government while Congress is in session.

con·gress·man (kong′gris mən), *n., pl.* **-men.** (*often cap.*) a male member of the U.S. Congress, esp. of the House of Representatives. [CONGRESS + MAN[1]]

con·gress·man-at-large (kong′gris mən ət lärj′), *n., pl.* **con·gress·men-at-large** (kong′gris mən ət lärj′). *U.S.* a congressman who is elected from a State as a whole and not from a district.

Con′gress of Indus′trial Organiza′tions, a federation of affiliated industrial labor unions; founded 1935 within the American Federation of Labor but independent of it 1938–55. *Abbr.:* C.I.O., CIO

Con′gress of Vien′na, an international conference (1814–15) held at Vienna after Napoleon's banishment to Elba, with Metternich as the dominant figure, aimed at territorial resettlement and restoration to power of the crowned heads of Europe.

con·gress·wom·an (kong′gris wo͝om′ən), *n., pl.* **-wom·en.** (*often cap.*) a female member of the U.S. Congress, esp. of the House of Representatives. [CONGRESS + WOMAN]

Con·greve (kon′grēv, kong′-), *n.* **1. William,** 1670–1729, English dramatist. **2. Sir William,** 1772–1828, English engineer and inventor.

con·gru·ence (kong′gro͞o əns), *n.* **1.** the quality or state of agreeing or corresponding. **2.** *Math.* a relation between two numbers indicating that the numbers give the same remainder when divided by some given number. Cf. **residue** (def. 4b). [ME < L *congruentia*, deriv. of *congruent-* CONGRUENT; see -ENCE]

con·gru·en·cy (kong′gro͞o ən sē), *n., pl.* **-cies.** congruence. [ME < L *congruentia*. See CONGRUENCE, -CY]

con·gru·ent (kong′gro͞o ənt), *adj.* **1.** agreeing; accordant; congruous. **2.** *Math.* of or pertaining to two numbers related by a congruence. **3.** *Geom.* coinciding at all points when superimposed: *congruent triangles.* [< L *congruent-* (s. of *congruēns*, prp. of *congruere* to go or come together, agree), equiv. to *con-* CON- + *gru-* move + *-ent-* -ENT] —**con′gru·ent·ly,** *adv.*

con·gru·i·ty (kən gro͞o′i tē, kon-), *n., pl.* **-ties.** **1.** the state or quality of being congruous; agreement; harmony; appropriateness: *a congruity of ideas.* **2.** the state or quality of being geometrically congruent. **3.** a point of agreement. **4.** *Scholasticism.* merit bestowed as a divine gift rather than earned. Cf. **condignity.** [late ME *congruite* < MF < LL *congruitāt-* (s. of *congruitās*), equiv. to L *congru(us)* CONGRUOUS + *-itāt-* -ITY]

con·gru·ous (kong′gro͞o əs), *adj.* **1.** exhibiting harmony of parts. **2.** appropriate or fitting. [< L *congruus*, equiv. to *con-* CON- + *gru-* (see CONGRUENT) + *-us* -OUS] —**con′gru·ous·ly,** *adv.* —**con′gru·ous·ness,** *n.*

con·ic (kon′ik), *adj.* **1.** Also, **con′i·cal.** having the form of, resembling, or pertaining to a cone. —*n.* **2.** *Geom.* See **conic section.** [< Gk *kōnik(ós)*, equiv. to *kôn(os)* CONE + *-ikos* -IC] —**con′i·cal·ly,** *adv.* —**co·nic·i·ty** (ko nis′i tē), **con′i·cal·ness,** *n.*

con′ical pen′dulum, *Horol.* a clock pendulum oscillating in a circle rather than in a straight line.

con·i·coid (kon′ə koid′, kō′nə-), *n.* *Geom.* a quadric, esp. a hyperboloid, paraboloid, or ellipsoid. [CONIC + -OID]

con′ic projec′tion, *Cartog.* a map projection based on the concept of projecting the earth's surface on a conical surface, which is then unrolled to a plane surface.

con·ics (kon′iks), *n.* (*construed as sing.*) the branch of geometry that deals with conic sections. [see CONIC, -ICS]

con′ic sec′tion, *Geom.* a curve formed by the intersection of a plane with a right circular cone; an ellipse, a parabola, or a hyperbola. Also called **conic.**

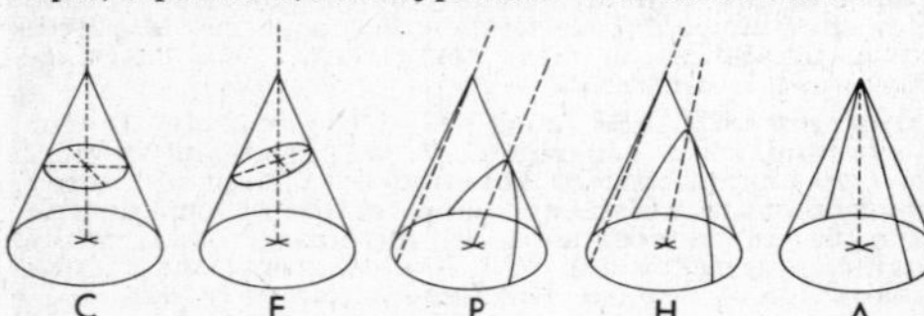

Conic sections

The two principal forms are E, ellipse, and H, hyperbola; P, parabola, is an intermediate case; C, circle, is an ellipse perpendicular to the axis of the cone; A, angle, is a hyperbola whose axis coincides with that of the cone

con′ic sec′tions, the branch of geometry that deals with the ellipse, the parabola, and the hyperbola.

co·nid·i·o·phore (kō nid′ē ə fōr′, -fôr′, kə-), *n.* *Bot.* (in fungi) a special stalk or branch of the mycelium, bearing conidia. [*conidio-* (comb. form of CONIDIUM) + -PHORE] —**co·nid·i·oph·o·rous** (kə nid′ē of′ər əs), *adj.*

co·nid·i·um (kō nid′ē əm, kə-), *n., pl.* **-nid·i·a** (-nid′ē ə). *Bot.* (in fungi) an asexual spore formed by abstriction at the top of a hyphal branch. [< Gk *kón(is)* dust + -IDIUM] —**co·nid′i·al, co·nid′i·an,** *adj.*

co·ni·fer (kō′nə fər, kon′ə-), *n.* **1.** any of numerous, chiefly evergreen trees or shrubs of the gymnospermous order or group *Coniferales* or *Coniferae*, including the pine, fir, spruce, and other cone-bearing trees and shrubs, and also the yews and their allies which bear drupelike seeds. **2.** a plant producing naked seeds in cones, or single naked seeds as in yews, but with pollen always borne in cones. [< L, equiv. to *cōn(us)* CONE + -I- + *-fer* -FER]

co·nif·er·in (kō nif′ər in, kə-), *n.* *Chem.* a grayish-white, water-soluble powder, $C_{16}H_{22}O_8 \cdot 2H_2O$, obtained from the cambium of coniferous trees and from asparagus: used chiefly in the manufacture of vanillin. [CONIFER + -IN[2]]

co·nif·er·ous (kō nif′ər əs, kə-), *adj.* *Bot.* belonging or pertaining to the conifers. Cf. **conifer** (def. 1). [CONIFER + -OUS]

co·ni·ine (kō′nē ēn′, -in, -nēn), *n.* a volatile, highly poisonous alkaloid, $C_8H_{17}N$, constituting the active principle of the poison hemlock. Also, **co·nin** (kō′nin), **co·nine** (kō′nēn, -nin). [CONI(UM) + -INE[2]]

co·ni·ol·o·gy (kō′nē ol′ə jē), *n.* koniology.

co·ni·ros·tral (kō′ni ros′trəl, kon′i-), *adj.* *Ornith.* having a conical bill, as a finch. [*coni-* (comb. form of L *cōnus* CONE) + ROSTRAL] —**co·ni·ros·ter** (kō′ni ros′tər, kon′i-), *n.*

co·ni·um (kō′nē əm), *n.* the poison hemlock, *Conium masculatum.* [< LL < Gk *kṓneion*]

conj., 1. conjugation. **2.** conjunction. **3.** conjunctive.

con·jec·tur·al (kən jek′chər əl), *adj.* **1.** of, of the nature of, or involving conjecture; problematical: *Theories of the origin of the earth are highly conjectural.* **2.** given to making conjectures: *a conjectural thinker.* [< L *conjectūrāl(is)*, equiv. to *conjectūr(a)* CONJECTURE + *-ālis* -AL[1]] —**con·jec′tur·al·ly,** *adv.*

con·jec·ture (kən jek′chər), *n., v.,* **-tured, -tur·ing.** —*n.* **1.** the formation or expression of an opinion without sufficient evidence for proof. **2.** an opinion so formed or expressed; speculation. **3.** *Obs.* the interpretation of signs or omens. —*v.t.* **4.** to conclude or suppose from grounds or evidence insufficient to ensure reliability. —*v.i.* **5.** to form conjectures. [< L *conjectūr(a)* (an opinion based on) a putting together of facts, equiv. to *con-* CON- + *jec-* (var. s. of *jacere* to throw) + *-t(us)* ptp. suffix + *-ūra* -URE] —**con·jec′tur·a·ble,** *adj.* —**con·jec′tur·a·bly,** *adv.* —**con·jec′tur·er,** *n.*
—**Syn. 2.** surmise, inference, supposition, theory, hypothesis. **4.** surmise, suppose, presume. See **guess.**

con·join (kən join′), *v.t., v.i.* to join together; unite; combine; associate. [ME *conjoigne(n)* < MF *conjoign-* (s. of *conjoindre*) < L *conjung(ere)*. See CON-, JOIN] —**con·join′er,** *n.*
—**Ant.** disjoin.

con·joined (kən joind′), *adj.* **1.** linked. **2.** *Numis.* accolated. [CONJOIN + -ED[2]] —**con·join·ed·ly** (kən joi′nid lē, -joind′lē), *adv.*

con·joint (kən joint′), *adj.* **1.** joined together; united; combined; associated. **2.** pertaining to or formed by two or more in combination; joint. —*n.* **3. conjoints,** husband and wife, esp. as joint owners of property. [ME < MF < L *conjunct(us)* (ptp. of *conjungere*). See CON-, JOINT] —**con·joint′ly,** *adv.* —**con·joint′ness,** *n.*

con·ju·gal (kon′jə gəl), *adj.* **1.** of, pertaining to, or characteristic of marriage: *conjugal understanding.* **2.** pertaining to the relation of husband and wife. [< L *conjugāl(is)*, equiv. to *con-* CON- + *jug(um)* YOKE + *-ālis* -AL[1]] —**con′ju·gal′i·ty,** *n.* —**con′ju·gal·ly,** *adv.*
—**Syn. 1.** matrimonial, nuptial, connubial. **2.** marital.

con·ju·gate (*v.* kon′jə gāt′; *adj., n.* kon′jə git, -gāt′), *v.,* **-gat·ed, -gat·ing,** *adj., n.* —*v.t.* **1.** *Gram.* **a.** to inflect (a verb). **b.** to recite or display all or some subsets of the inflected forms of (a verb), in a fixed order: *One conjugates the present-tense verb "be" as I am, you are, he is, we are, you are, they are.* **2.** *Obs.* to join together, esp. in marriage. —*v.i.* **3.** *Biol.* to unite; to undergo conjugation. **4.** *Gram.* to be characterized by conjugation: *The Latin verb esse does not conjugate in the passive voice.* —*adj.* **5.** joined together, esp. in a pair or pairs; coupled. **6.** *Bot.* (of a pinnate leaf) having only one pair of leaflets. **7.** *Gram.* (of words) having a common derivation. **8.** *Bibliog.* (of two leaves in a book) forming one sheet. **9.** *Math.* **a.** (of two points, lines, etc.) so related as to be interchangeable in the enunciation of certain properties. **b.** (of an element) so related to a second element of a group that there exists a third element of the group which, multiplying one element on the right and the other element on the left, results in equal elements. **10.** *Chem.* **a.** of or noting two or more liquids in equilibrium with one another. **b.** (of an acid and a base) related by the loss or gain of a proton: *NH_3 is a base conjugate to NH_4^+. NH_4^+ is an acid conjugate to NH_3.* **c.** Also, **con′ju·gat′ed.** (of an organic compound) containing two or more double bonds each separated from the other by a single bond. —*n.* **11.** one of a group of conjugate words. **12.** *Math.* **a.** either of two conjugate points, lines, etc. **b.** See **conjugate axis. c.** the number corresponding to a given complex number which represents the given number's reflection with respect to the real axis. **d.** the dyad or dyadic with antecedents and consequents of a given dyad or dyadic interchanged. [< L *conjugāt(us)* (ptp. of *conjugāre* to yoke together), equiv. to *con-* CON- + *jug(um)* YOKE + *-ātus* -ATE[1]] —**con·ju·ga·ble** (kon′jo͝o gə bəl), *adj.* —**con′ju·ga·bly,** *adv.* —**con′ju·ga′tive,** *adj.* —**con′ju·ga′tor,** *n.*

con′jugate ax′is, *Geom.* **1.** the axis of a hyperbola perpendicular to the transverse axis at a point equidistant from the foci. **2.** the segment of this axis equal to one side of a rectangle which has its other side equal to the transverse axis and diagonals that are along the asymptotes of the hyperbola. See diag. under **hyperbola.**

con′jugate num′bers, *Math.* the set of roots of an algebraic equation that cannot be factored.

con′jugate solu′tion, *Chem.* a system of liquids, each partially miscible in the other, existing with a common interface, consisting of a saturated solution of one in the other.

con·ju·ga·tion (kon′jə gā′shən), *n.* **1.** *Gram.* **a.** the inflection of verbs. **b.** the whole set of inflected forms of a verb or the recital or display thereof in a fixed order: *The conjugation of the Latin verb* amo *begins* amō, amas, amat. **c.** a class of verbs having similar sets of inflected forms: *the Latin second conjugation.* **2.** an act of joining: *a conjugation of related ideas.* **3.** the state of being joined together; union; conjunction. **4.** *Biol.* **a.** the sexual process in ciliate protozoans in which two animals adhere and exchange nuclear material through a temporary area of fusion. **b.** the temporary union or fusion of two cells or organisms as a form of sexual reproduction in certain lower plants. [< LL *conjugātiōn-* (s. of *conjugātiō*), equiv. to *conjugāt(us)* (see CONJUGATE) + *-iōn-* -ION] —**con′ju·ga′tion·al,** *adj.* —**con′ju·ga′tion·al·ly,** *adv.*

con·junct (kən jungkt′, kon′jungkt), *adj.* **1.** conjoined; bound in close association: *conjunct melodic ideas in the sonata's two movements.* **2.** formed by conjunction. **3.** *Gram.* **a.** occurring only in combination with an immediately preceding or following form of a particular class, and constituting with this form a single phonetic unit, as *'ll* in English *he'll*, and *n't* in *isn't.* **b.** (of a pronoun) having enclitic or proclitic form and occurring with a verb, as French *me, le, se.* **c.** pertaining to a word so characterized. **4.** *Music.* progressing melodically by intervals of a second: *conjunct motion of an ascending scale.* —*n.* **5.** *Logic.* either of the propositions in a conjunction. [< L *conjunct(us)* joined, connected (ptp. of *conjungere*), equiv. to *con-* CON- + *junc-* (var. s. of *jungere* to JOIN) + *-tus* ptp. suffix] —**con·junct′ly,** *adv.*

con·junc·tion (kən jungk′shən), *n.* **1.** the act of conjoining; combination. **2.** the state of being conjoined; union; association: *The police, in conjunction with the army, established order.* **3.** a combination of events or circumstances. **4.** *Logic.* **a.** a compound proposition having a truth-value that is true if and only if both of its terms are true. **b.** the relation between terms of such a proposition, usually shown by simple juxtaposition, or a connective symbol as ·, and usually read as "and." **5.** *Gram.* **a.** any member of a small class of words distinguished in many languages by their function as connectors between words, phrases, clauses, or sentences, as *and, because, but, however.* **b.** any other word or expression of similar function, as *in any case.* **c.** a link or marker in a conjoining transformation, or an introductory word in a subordinate clause. **6.** *Astron.* **a.** the coincidence of two or more heavenly bodies at the same celestial longitude. **b.** the state of two or more such coinciding heavenly bodies. [ME *conjunccio(u)n* < L *conjunctiōn-* (s. of *conjunctiō*). See CONJUNCT, -ION] —**con·junc′tion·al,** *adj.* —**con·junc′tion·al·ly,** *adv.*

con·junc·ti·va (kon′jungk tī′və), *n., pl.* **-vas, -vae** (-vē). *Anat.* the mucous membrane which lines the inner surface of the eyelids. See diag. under **eye.** [short for NL *membrāna conjunctīva* conjunctive membrane; see CONJUNCTIVE] —**con′junc·ti′val,** *adj.*

con·junc·tive (kən jungk′tiv), *adj.* **1.** serving to connect; connective: *conjunctive tissue.* **2.** conjoined; joint: *a conjunctive action.* **3.** *Gram.* **a.** (of a mode) subjunctive. **b.** (of a pronoun) conjunct. **c.** of the nature of a conjunction. **4.** *Logic.* characterizing propositions that are conjunctions. —*n.* **5.** *Gram.* a conjunctive word; a conjunction. [< LL *conjunctīv(us).* See CONJUNCT, -IVE] —**con·junc′tive·ly,** *adv.*

con·junc·ti·vi·tis (kən jungk′tə vī′tis), *n.* *Ophthalm.* inflammation of the conjunctiva. [CONJUNCTIV(A) + -ITIS]

con·junc·ture (kən jungk′chər), *n.* **1.** a combination of circumstances or affairs; a particular state of affairs. **2.** a critical state of affairs; crisis. **3.** conjunction; joining; meeting. [CONJUNCT + -URE] —**con·junc′tur·al,** *adj.*

con·ju·ra·tion (kon′jo͝o rā′shən), *n.* **1.** the act of calling on or invoking by a sacred name. **2.** an incantation; magical spell or charm. **3.** supernatural accomplishment by invocation or spell. **4.** the practice of legerdemain. **5.** *Archaic.* supplication; solemn entreaty. [ME *conjuracio(u)n* < L *conjūrātiōn-* (s. of *conjūrātiō*), equiv. to *conjūrāt(us)*, ptp. of *conjūrāre* to swear together, (*con-* CON- + *jūr-* (s. of *jūs*) right, justice, duty + *-ātus* -ATE[1]) + *-iōn-* -ION]

con·jur·a·tor (kon′jə rā′tər), *n.* **1.** one who practices conjuration. **2.** *Law.* a conspirator. [< L *conjūrāt(us)* (ptp. of *conjūrāre*; see CONJURE, -ATE[1]) + -OR[2]]

con·jure (kon′jər *or, esp. Brit.,* kun′- *for 1–5, 8–10;* kən jo͝or′ *for 6, 7, 11*), *v.,* **-jured, -jur·ing.** —*v.t.* **1.** to call upon or command (a devil or spirit) by invocation or spell. **2.** to affect or influence by or as if by invocation or spell. **3.** to effect, produce, bring, etc., by or as by magic: *to conjure a miracle.* **4.** to call, raise up, or bring into existence by or as if by magic (usually fol. by *up*): *She seemed to have conjured up the person she was talking about.* **5.** to bring to mind; recall (usually fol. by *up*): *to conjure up the happy past.* **6.** to appeal to solemnly or earnestly: *I conjure you to hear my plea.* **7.** *Obs.* to charge solemnly. —*v.i.* **8.** to call upon or command a devil or spirit by invocation or spell. **9.** to practice magic. **10.** to practice legerdemain. **11.** *Obs.* to conspire. [ME *conjure(n)* < OF *conjure(r)* < L *conjūrāre*, equiv. to *con-* CON- + *jūrāre* to swear]

con′jure man′ (kon′jər), (in the southern U.S. and the West Indies) a conjurer; witch doctor.

con·jur·er (kon′jər ər *or, esp. Brit.,* kun′- *for 1, 2;* kən jo͝or′ər *for 3*), *n.* **1.** one who conjures spirits or practices magic; magician. **2.** one who practices legerdemain; juggler. **3.** one who solemnly charges or entreats. Also, **con′ju·ror.** [ME; see CONJURE, -ER[1]]

conk[1] (kongk, kôngk), *n.* **1.** *Slang.* the head. **2.** *Slang.* a blow on the head. **3.** *Brit. Slang.* the nose. —*v.t.* **4.** *Slang.* to hit or strike on the head. [? alter. of CONCH]

conk[2] (kongk, kôngk), *n.* *Bot.* the shelflike fructification of certain wood-decaying fungi; bracket. [? alter. of CONCH]

conk·er (kong′kər, kông′-), *n.* *Brit. Informal.* **1.** a horse chestnut. **2.** the hollowed-out shell of a horse chestnut. **3. conkers,** a game in which a child swings a horse chestnut shell on a string in an attempt to break that of his opponent. [*conk* CONCH (alter. by influence of CONQUER) + -ER[1]]

conk′ out′, *Slang.* **1.** to break or fail, as a machine, engine, etc. **2.** to slow down or stop; lose energy. **3.** to lose consciousness; faint. **4.** to die: *The old man conked out and left them his fortune.* [*conk*, of imit. orig.]

con mae·stà (kon mī stä′; *It.* kôn mä es tä′), majestically (used as a musical direction). [< It: lit., with majesty]

con′ man′, *Slang.* See **confidence man.**

con mo·to (kon mō′tō, kōn; *It.* kôn mô′tô), with spirited drive; animatedly (used as a musical direction). [< It: with animation]

conn (kon), *v.t.* **1.** con[3]. —*n.* **2.** responsibility for the steering of a ship. **3.** con[3].

Conn., Connecticut.

Con·nacht (*Irish.* kon′əKHt, -ət), *n.* Irish name of **Connaught.**

con·nate (kon′āt), *adj.* **1.** existing in a person or thing from birth or origin; inborn; congenital: *a connate sense of right and wrong.* **2.** associated in birth or origin. **3.** allied or agreeing in nature; cognate. **4.** *Biol.* congenitally or firmly united into one body. **5.** *Geol.* trapped in sediment at the time the sediment was deposited: *connate water.* [< LL *connāt(us)* (ptp. of *con-nāscī* to be born at the same time with), equiv. to L *con-* CON- + *nā-* (short s. of *nāscī*) + *-tus* ptp. suffix] —**con/nate·ly,** *adv.* —**con/nate·ness,** *n.* —**con·na·tion** (kə nā/shən), *n.*

con·nat·u·ral (kə nach/ər əl), *adj.* **1.** belonging to a person or thing by nature or from birth or origin; inborn. **2.** of the same or a similar nature. [< ML *connātūrāl(is),* equiv. to L *con-* CON- + *nātūrālis* NATURAL] —**con·nat/u·ral·ly,** *adv.* —**con·nat/u·ral·ness,** *n.*

Con·naught (kon/ôt), *n.* a province in the NW Republic of Ireland. 419,465 (1961); 6611 sq. mi. Irish, **Connacht.**

con·nect (kə nekt/), *v.t.* **1.** to bind or fasten together; join or unite; link: *to connect the two cities by a bridge.* **2.** to establish communication between; put in communication (often fol. by *with*): *The telephone operator connected us. Will you please connect me with Mr. Jones?* **3.** to have as an accompanying or associated feature: *the pleasures that are connected with music.* **4.** to cause to be associated, as in a personal or business relationship: *to connect oneself with a group of like-minded persons; Our bank is connected with major foreign banks the world over.* **5.** to associate mentally or emotionally: *She connects all telegrams with bad news.* —*v.i.* **6.** to become connected; join or unite: *These two parts connect at the sides.* **7.** (of trains, buses, etc.) to run so as to make connections (often fol. by *with*): *This bus connects with a northbound bus at York Avenue.* [< L *connect(ere),* equiv. to *con-* CON- + *nectere* to tie; see NEXUS] —**con·nect/i·ble, con·nect/a·ble,** *adj.*
—**Syn. 1.** See **join.** —**Ant. 1.** divide. **4.** dissociate.

con·nect·ed (kə nek/tid), *adj.* **1.** united, joined, or linked. **2.** having a connection. **3.** *Math.* pertaining to a set for which no cover exists, consisting of two open sets whose intersections with the given set are disjoint and nonempty. [CONNECT + -ED²] —**con·nect/ed·ly,** *adv.* —**con·nect/ed·ness,** *n.*

Con·nect·i·cut (kə net/ə kət), *n.* **1.** a State in the NE United States. 2,535,234 (1960); 5009 sq. mi. *Cap.:* Hartford. *Abbr.:* Conn. **2.** a river flowing S from N New Hampshire along the boundary between New Hampshire and Vermont and then through Massachusetts and Connecticut into Long Island Sound. 407 mi. long.

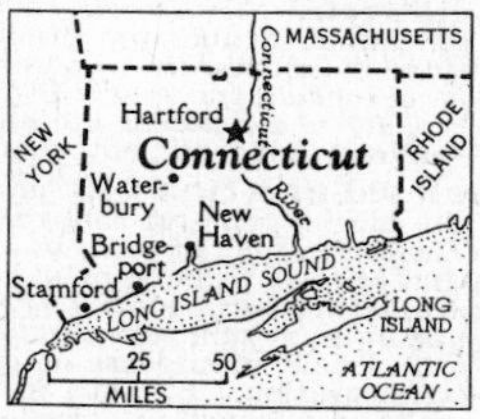

Connect/icut chest/, *U.S. Furniture.* a chest made in Connecticut in the late 17th and early 18th centuries, having three front panels of which the center panel has a conventional sunflower design in low relief and the end panels have tulip designs. Also called **sunflower chest.**

Connect/icut Com/promise, *Amer. Hist.* a compromise adopted at the Constitutional Convention, providing the States with equal representation in the Senate and proportional representation in the House of Representatives. Cf. **New Jersey plan, Virginia plan.**

Connect/icut war/bler, a North American wood warbler, *Oporornis agilis,* olive-green above with a gray head and throat and yellow below.

Connect/icut Yan/kee in King/ Ar/thur's Court/, a novel (1889) by Mark Twain.

connec/ting rod/, *Mach.* a rod or link for transmitting motion and force between a rotating and a reciprocating part. See diag. under **piston.**

con·nec·tion (kə nek/shən), *n.* **1.** the act or state of connecting. **2.** the state of being connected: *the connection between cause and effect.* **3.** anything that connects; connecting part; link; bond: *a pipe connection.* **4.** association; relationship: *the connection between crime and poverty; no connection with any other firm of the same name.* **5.** a circle of friends or associates or a member of such a circle. **6.** association with or development of something observed, imagined, discussed, etc.: *to make a connection between the smell of smoke and the presence of fire; I have a few thoughts in connection with your last remarks.* **7.** contextual relation; context, as of a word. **8.** the meeting of trains, planes, etc., for transfer of passengers: *There are good connections between buses in Chicago.* **9.** Often, **connections.** a transfer between means of transportation made by a passenger: *to miss connections.* **10.** a specific vehicle, airplane, ship, etc., boarded in making connections: *My connection for Hartford is the 10:58 out of New Haven.* **11.** a relative, esp. by marriage or distant blood relationship. **12.** *Slang.* one who supplies narcotics directly to addicts. **13.** a group of persons connected as by political or religious ties. **14.** Usually, **connections.** associates, relations, acquaintances, or friends, esp. representing or having some influence or power: *She has European connections. He has connections in the Senate.* **15.** a religious denomination: *the Methodist connection.* **16.** a channel of communication: *a bad telephone connection.* **17.** sexual intercourse. Also, *Brit.,* **connexion.** [var. sp. of *connexion* < L *connexiōn-* (s. of *connexiō*), equiv. to *connex(us)* (ptp. of *connectere* to CONNECT) + *-iōn-* -ION] —**con·nec/tion·al,** *adj.*
—**Syn. 1.** junction, conjunction, union. **3.** tie, coupling, yoke. **5.** affiliation, alliance, combination. **11.** relation, kinsman.

con·nec·tion·ism (kə nek/shə niz/əm), *n.* *Psychol.* the theory that all mental processes can be described as the operation of inherited or acquired bonds between stimulus and response. [CONNECTION + -ISM]

con·nec·tive (kə nek/tiv), *adj.* **1.** serving or tending to connect: *connective statements between chapters.* —*n.* **2.** something that connects: *The tissue serves as a connective between the bones.* **3.** *Gram.* a word used to connect words, phrases, clauses, and sentences, as a conjunction. **4.** *Bot.* the tissue joining the two cells of the anther. [CONNECT + -IVE] —**con·nec/tive·ly,** *adv.* —**con·nec·tiv·i·ty** (kon/ek tiv/i tē), *n.*

connec/tive tis/sue, *Anat.* a tissue, usually of mesoblastic origin, that connects, supports, or surrounds other tissues, organs, etc., and occurs in various forms throughout the body.

con·nec·tor (kə nek/tər), *n.* **1.** one who or that which connects. **2.** a person who couples railroad cars. **3.** a person who connects metal structural members. **4.** any of various devices for connecting one object to another. Also, **con·nect/er.** [CONNECT + -OR²]

Con·nee (kon/ē), *n.* a girl's given name. Also, **Connie.**

Con·nells·ville (kon/əlz vil/), *n.* a town in SW Pennsylvania. 12,814 (1960).

Con·nel·ly (kon/əlē), *n.* **Marc(us Cook),** born 1890, U.S. journalist and dramatist.

Con·ners·ville (kon/ərz vil/), *n.* a city in E Indiana. 17,698 (1960).

con·nex·ion (kə nek/shən), *n.* *Brit.* connection. —**con·nex/ion·al,** *adj.*

Con·nie (kon/ē), *n.* **1.** a boy's given name, form of **Conrad** or **Cornelius.** **2.** Also, **Connee.** a girl's given name, form of **Constance.**

conn/ing tow/er (kon/ing), **1.** the low observation tower of a submarine, constituting the main entrance to the interior. **2.** the low, dome-shaped, armored pilothouse of a warship, used esp. during battle. [CON³ + -ING²]

con·nip·tion (kə nip/shən), *n.* Often, **conniptions.** *U.S. Informal.* a fit of hysterical excitement or anger. Also called **connip/tion fit/.** [?]

con·niv·ance (kə nī/vəns), *n.* **1.** the act of conniving. **2.** *Law.* **a.** tacit encouragement or assent (without participation) to wrongdoing by another. **b.** the consent by a person to a spouse's conduct, esp. adultery, that is later made the basis of a divorce proceeding or other complaint. Also, **con·niv/ence.** [earlier *connivence* < L *connīventia.* See CONNIVE, -ENCE, -ANCE] —**con·niv/ant, con·niv/ent,** *adj.* —**con·niv/ant·ly, con·niv/ent·ly,** *adv.*

con·nive (kə nīv/), *v.i.,* **-nived, -niv·ing.** **1.** to avoid noticing something that one is expected to oppose or condemn; give aid to wrongdoing by forbearing to act or speak (usually fol. by *at*): *The policeman connived at traffic violations.* **2.** to be indulgent toward something others oppose or criticize (usually fol. by *at*): *to connive at childlike exaggerations.* **3.** to cooperate secretly; conspire (often fol. by *with*): *They connived with army chiefs to take over the government.* [< L *connīv(ēre)* (to) blink, wink at, equiv. to *con-* CON- + *-nīvēre,* perh. akin to *nicere* to beckon] —**con·niv/er,** *n.* —**con·niv/ing·ly,** *adv.*

con·ni·vent (kə nī/vənt), *adj.* *Bot., Zool.* converging, as petals. [< L *connīvent-* (s. of *connīvēns,* prp. of *connīvēre*). See CONNIVE, -ENT]

con·nois·seur (kon/ə sûr/, -sŏŏr/), *n.* **1.** a person who is especially competent to pass critical judgments in an art, esp. one of the fine arts, or in matters of taste: *a connoisseur of modern art; a connoisseur of French cuisine.* **2.** a discerning judge of the best in any field: *a connoisseur of social behavior.* [< F; OF *conoiseor* < L *cognōscitōr-* (s. of *cognōscitor*) knower. See COGNOSCIBLE, -OR²] —**con/nois·seur/ship,** *n.*
—**Syn.** critic, aesthete.

Con·nor (kon/ər), *n.* **Ralph** (*Charles William Gordon*), 1860–1937, Canadian novelist and clergyman.

con·no·ta·tion (kon/ə tā/shən), *n.* **1.** an act or instance of connoting. **2.** the associated or secondary meaning of a word or expression in addition to its explicit or primary meaning: *A possible connotation of "home" is "a place of warmth, comfort, and affection."* Cf. **denotation** (def. 1). **3.** *Logic.* the set of attributes constituting the meaning of a term and thus determining the range of objects to which that term may be applied; comprehension; intension. [< ML *connotātiōn-* (s. of *connotātiō*), equiv. to *connotāt(us)* (ptp. of *connotāre;* see CONNOTE, -ATE¹) + *-iōn-* -ION] —**con·no·ta·tive** (kon/ə tā/tiv, kə nō/tə-), **con·no/tive,** *adj.* —**con/no·ta·tive·ly, con·no/tive·ly,** *adv.*

con·note (kə nōt/), *v.,* **-not·ed, -not·ing.** —*v.t.* **1.** to signify or suggest (certain meanings, ideas, etc.) in addition to the explicit or primary meaning: *The word "fireplace" often connotes hospitality, warm comfort, etc.* **2.** to involve as a condition or accompaniment: *Injury connotes pain.* —*v.i.* **3.** to have significance only by association, as with another word: *Adjectives can only connote, nouns can denote.* [< ML *connot(āre),* equiv. to L *con-* CON- + *notāre* to NOTE]

con·nu·bi·al (kə nōō/bē əl, -nyōō/-), *adj.* of marriage or wedlock; matrimonial; conjugal: *connubial love.* [< L *cōnūbiāl(is),* equiv. to *cōnūbi(um)* (*cō-* co- + *nūb(ēre)* (to) marry + *-ium* n. suffix) + *-ālis* -AL¹] —**con·nu/bi·al/i·ty,** *n.* —**con·nu/bi·al·ly,** *adv.*
—**Syn.** nuptial, marital.

co·noid (kō/noid), *adj.* **1.** Also, **co·noi/dal.** resembling a cone in shape; cone-shaped. —*n.* **2.** a geometrical solid formed by the revolution of a conic section about one of its axes. [< Gk *kōnoeid(ḗs).* See CONE, -OID] —**co·noi/dal·ly,** *adv.*

Co·non (kō/non), *n.* died A.D. 687, pope 686–687.

Con·on (kon/ən), *n.* a crater in the first quadrant of the face of the moon: about 13 miles in diameter.

co·no·scen·ti (kō/nə shen/tē, kon/ə-; *It.* kô/nô shen/tē), *n.pl., sing.* **-te** (-tē; *It.* -te). cognoscenti.

co·no·scope (kō/nə skōp/, kon/ə-), *n.* *Optics.* a polarizing microscope for giving interference figures and for determining the principal axis of a crystal. [< Gk *kōno(s)* CONE + -SCOPE] —**co·no·scop·ic** (kō/nə skop/ik, kon/ə-), *adj.*

con·quer (kong/kər), *v.t.* **1.** to acquire by force of arms; win in war: *to conquer a foreign land.* **2.** to overcome by force; subdue: *to conquer an enemy.* **3.** to gain or obtain by effort: *She conquered the man she loved.* **4.** to gain the victory over; surmount: *to conquer disease and poverty.* —*v.i.* **5.** to make conquests; gain the victory: *Despite their differences, their love will conquer.* [ME *conquer(en)* < OF *conquer(re)* < VL **conquērere* to acquire (alter. of L *conquīrere* to seek out). See CON-, QUERY] —**con/quer·a·ble,** *adj.* —**con/quer·a·ble·ness,** *n.* —**con/quer·ing·ly,** *adv.*
—**Syn. 2.** vanquish, overpower, overthrow, subjugate. See **defeat.**

con·quer·or (kong/kər ər), *n.* a person who conquers; victor. [ME *conquerour* < AF; OF *conquereor,* equiv. to *conquer-* CONQUER + *-eor* -OR²]

con·quest (kon/kwest, kong/-), *n.* **1.** the act or state of conquering or the state of being conquered; vanquishment. **2.** the winning of favor, affection, love, etc.: *the conquest of Antony by Cleopatra.* **3.** a person whose favor, affection, etc., has been won: *He's another one of her conquests.* **4.** anything acquired by conquering, as a nation, a territory, spoils, etc. **5. the Conquest.** See **Norman Conquest.** [ME *conqueste* < MF < VL **conquēsta* (alter. of L *conquīsīta,* fem. ptp. of *conquīrere*). See CON-, QUEST]
—**Syn. 1.** subjugation, overthrow, defeat, mastery. **2.** seduction, enchantment. **3.** See **victory.** —**Ant. 1, 2.** surrender.

con·qui·an (kong/kē ən), *n.* *Cards.* a variety of rummy for two players. [< Sp *con quién?* with whom?]

con·quis·ta·dor (kon kwis/tə dôr/; *Sp.* kông kēs/tä-ᵺôr/), *n., pl.* **-dors,** *Sp.* **-do·res** (-ᵺô/res). one of the Spanish conquerors of Mexico and Peru in the 16th century. [< Sp, equiv. to *conquistad(o)* (ptp. of *conquistar* to conquer; see CONQUEST, -ADE¹) + *-or* -OR²]

Con·rad (kon/rad), *n.* **1. Joseph** (*Teodor Józef Konrad Korzeniowski*), 1857–1924, English novelist and short-story writer, born in Poland. **2.** a town in N Montana. 2665 (1960). **3.** a boy's given name.

Con·ral (kon/ral), *n.* a boy's given name.

con/ rod/, *Mach. Slang.* See **connecting rod.**

Con·roe (kon/rō), *n.* a town in E Texas. 9192 (1960).

Con·roy (kon/roi), *n.* a boy's given name.

Cons., **1.** Constable. **2.** Constitution. **3.** Consul.

cons., **1.** consecrated. **2.** (in prescriptions) conserve; keep. [< L *conservā*] **3.** consolidated. **4.** consonant. **5.** constable. **6.** constitution. **7.** constitutional. **8.** construction. **9.** consul.

con·san·guin·e·ous (kon/sang gwin/ē əs), *adj.* having the same ancestry or descent; related by blood. Also, **con·san·guine** (kon sang/gwin). [< L *consanguineus,* equiv. to *con-* CON- + *sanguin-* (s. of *sanguis*) blood + *-eus* -EOUS] —**con/san·guin/e·ous·ly,** *adv.*

con·san·guin·i·ty (kon/sang gwin/i tē), *n.* **1.** relationship because of the same ancestry or descent; kinship (distinguished from *affinity*). **2.** close relationship or connection. [late ME *consanguinite* < L *consanguinitās.* See CONSANGUINEOUS, -ITY]

con·sarned (kon/särnd/, kən-), *adj.* *Dial.* confounded; damned. [alter. of CONCERNED, used as a euphemism for *confounded*]

con·science (kon/shəns), *n.* **1.** the sense of what is right or wrong in one's conduct or motives, impelling one toward right action: *Let your conscience be your guide.* **2.** the complex of ethical and moral principles that controls or inhibits the actions or thoughts of an individual. **3.** an inhibiting sense of what is prudent: *I'd eat another piece of pie but my conscience would bother me.* **4.** conscientiousness. **5.** *Obs.* consciousness; self-knowledge. **6.** *Obs.* strict and reverential observance. **7. have something on one's conscience,** to feel guilty about something, as an act that one considers wrong: *She behaves as if she had something on her conscience.* **8. in all conscience, a.** in all reason and fairness. **b.** certainly; assuredly. Also, **in conscience.** [ME < OF < L *conscientia* knowledge, awareness, conscience. See CON-, SCIENCE] —**con/science·less,** *adj.* —**con/science·less·ly,** *adv.* —**con/science·less·ness,** *n.*

con/science clause/, a clause or article in an act or law that exempts persons whose conscientious or religious scruples forbid their compliance.

con/science mon/ey, money paid to relieve one's conscience, as for an obligation previously evaded or a wrong done.

con·science-strick·en (kon/shəns strik/ən), *adj.* greatly troubled or disturbed by the knowledge of having acted wrongfully.

con·sci·en·tious (kon/shē en/shəs, kon/sē-), *adj.* controlled by or done according to conscience; scrupulous: *a conscientious judge; conscientious application to the work at hand.* [< ML *conscientiōs(us),* equiv. to L *conscienti(a)* CONSCIENCE + *-ōsus* -OUS] —**con/sci·en/tious·ly,** *adv.* —**con/sci·en/tious·ness,** *n.*
—**Syn.** just, upright, honest, faithful, careful, particular, painstaking, devoted, dedicated.

conscien/tious objec/tor, one who refuses to perform military service for his country for moral or religious reasons.

con·scion·a·ble (kon/shə nə bəl), *adj.* being in conformity with one's conscience; just. [*conscion-* (back formation from *conscions,* var. of CONSCIENCE, the final *-s* taken for pl. sign) + -ABLE] —**con/scion·a·ble·ness,** *n.* —**con/scion·a·bly,** *adv.*

con·scious (kon/shəs), *adj.* **1.** aware of one's own existence, sensations, thoughts, surroundings, etc.; cognizant. **2.** fully aware of or sensitive to something (often fol. by *of*): *conscious of one's own faults.* **3.** having the mental faculties fully active: *He was conscious during the operation.* **4.** known to oneself; felt: *conscious guilt.* **5.** aware of what one is doing: *a conscious liar.* **6.** aware of oneself; self-conscious. **7.** deliberate; intentional: *a conscious insult.* **8.** *Obs.* inwardly sensible of wrongdoing. —*n.* **9. the conscious,** *Psychoanal.* the part of the mind containing the psychic material of which the ego is aware. [< L *conscius* sharing knowledge with, equiv. to *con-* CON- + *sci-* (s. of *scīre* to know; see SCIENCE) + *-us* -OUS] —**con/scious·ly,** *adv.*
—**Syn. 2.** knowing, percipient. CONSCIOUS, AWARE, COGNIZANT refer to an individual sense of recognition of something within or without oneself. CONSCIOUS implies to be awake or awakened to an inner realization of a fact, a truth, a condition, etc.: *to be conscious of an extreme weariness; to be conscious of one's inadequacy.* AWARE lays the emphasis on sense perceptions insofar as they are the object of conscious recognition: *He was aware of the odor of tobacco.* COGNIZANT lays the emphasis on an outer recognition more on the level of reason and knowledge than on the sensory level alone: *He was cognizant of their drawbacks, their advantages, our plans.*

con·scious·ness (kon/shəs nis), *n.* **1.** the state of being conscious; awareness of one's own existence, sensations, thoughts, surroundings, etc. **2.** the thoughts and feelings, collectively, of an individual or of an aggregate of people: *the moral consciousness of a nation.* **3.** full activity of the mind and senses: *to regain consciousness after fainting.* **4.** awareness of something for what it is: *consciousness of wrongdoing.* [CONSCIOUS + -NESS]

con·script (*v.* kən skript/; *n., adj.* kon/skript), *v.t.* **1.** to draft for military or naval service. —*n.* **2.** a recruit obtained by conscription. —*adj.* **3.** enrolled or formed by conscription; drafted: *a conscript soldier.* [< L *conscrīpt(us)* (ptp. of *conscrībere* to write together, list, enroll; see SCRIBE¹), equiv. to *con-* CON- + *scrīp-* (perf. s. of *scrībere*) + *-tus* ptp. suffix]

con/script fa/thers, **1.** the senators of ancient Rome. **2.** any legislators.

con·scrip·tion (kən skrip′shən), *n.* **1.** compulsory enrollment of men for military or naval service; draft. **2.** a compulsory contribution of money to a government during a time of war. [< LL *conscrīptiōn-* (s. of *conscrīptiō*) a levying of troops (L: a drawing up in writing), equiv. to *conscrīpt(us)* (see CONSCRIPT) + *-iōn-* -ION] —**con·scrip′tion·al,** *adj.*

con·scrip·tion·ist (kən skrip′shə nist), *n.* an advocate or supporter of conscription. [CONSCRIPTION + -IST]

con·se·crate (kon′sə krāt′), *v.,* **-crat·ed, -crat·ing,** *adj.* —*v.t.* **1.** to make or declare sacred; set apart or dedicate to the service of the Deity: *to consecrate a building as a place of worship.* **2.** to devote or dedicate to some purpose: *a life consecrated to science.* **3.** to make (something) an object of honor or veneration; hallow: *a custom consecrated by time.* —*adj.* **4.** *Archaic.* consecrated; sacred. [< L *consecrāt(us)* (ptp. of *consecrāre*), equiv. to *con-* CON- + *secr-* (var. s. of *sacer*) sacred, holy + *-ātus* -ATE[1]] —**con′se·crat′ed·ness,** *n.* —**con′se·cra′tor, con′se·crat′er,** *n.* —**con·se·cra·to·ry** (kon′sə krə tôr′ē, -tōr′ē), **con′se·cra′tive,** *adj.*
—**Syn. 3.** sanctify, venerate. **4.** See **holy.** —**Ant. 1.** desecrate.

con·se·cra·tion (kon′sə krā′shən), *n.* **1.** the act of consecrating; dedication to the service and worship of God. **2.** the act of giving the sacramental character to the Eucharistic elements of bread and wine, esp. in the Roman Catholic Church. **3.** ordination to a sacred office, esp. to the episcopate. [ME *consecracio(u)n* < L *consecrātiōn-* (s. of *consecrātiō*). See CONSECRATE, -ION]

con·se·cu·tion (kon′sə kyōō′shən), *n.* **1.** succession; sequence. **2.** logical sequence; chain of reasoning. [< L *consecūtiōn-* (s. of *consecūtiō*), equiv. to *con-* CON- + *secūt(us)*, ptp. of *sequī* to follow (*secū-*, ptp. s. + *-tus* ptp. suffix) + *-iōn-* -ION]

con·sec·u·tive (kən sek′yə tiv), *adj.* **1.** following one another in uninterrupted succession or order; successive: *six consecutive numbers.* **2.** marked by logical sequence. **3.** *Gram.* expressing consequence or result: *a consecutive clause.* [CONSECUT(ION) + -IVE] —**con·sec′u·tive·ly,** *adv.* —**con·sec′u·tive·ness,** *n.*
—**Syn. 1.** continuous. See **successive.**

con·sen·su·al (kən sen′shōō əl), *adj.* **1.** formed or existing merely by consent: *a consensual transaction.* **2.** *Physiol.* (of an action) involuntarily correlative with a voluntary action, as the contraction of the iris when the eye is opened. [CONSENSU(S) + -AL[1]] —**con·sen′su·al·ly,** *adv.*

con·sen·sus (kən sen′səs), *n., pl.* **-sus·es. 1.** general agreement or concord; harmony. **2.** majority of opinion: *The consensus of the group was that they should meet twice a month.* [< L, n. use of *consensus* (ptp. of *consentīre*), equiv. to *con-* CON- + *sent-* (s. of *sentīre* to think, hold an opinion) + *-tus* ptp. suffix]
—**Usage.** CONSENSUS OF OPINION is felt by many grammarians and teachers to be a redundancy, but it is so only if CONSENSUS is taken in sense of "majority of opinion," rather than its equally valid—and, according to available evidence, earlier—sense of "accord or general agreement."

con·sen·sus gen·ti·um (kōn sen′sōōs gen′tē ōōm′; *Eng.* kən sen′səs jen′shē əm), *Latin.* agreement of the people.

con·sent (kən sent′), *v.i.* **1.** to permit, approve, or agree; comply or yield (often fol. by *to* or an infinitive): *He consented to the proposal. She consented to go. We asked her permission, and she consented.* **2.** *Obs.* to agree in sentiment, opinion, etc.; be in harmony. —*n.* **3.** permission, approval, or agreement; compliance; acquiescence: *He gave his consent to his daughter's request to marry.* **4.** agreement in sentiment, opinion, a course of action, etc.: *By common consent he was appointed official delegate.* **5.** *Archaic.* accord; concord; harmony. [ME *consent(en)* < OF *consent(ir)* < L *consentīre.* See CON-, SCENT] —**con·sent′er,** *n.*
—**Syn. 1.** See **agree.**

con·sen·ta·ne·ous (kon′sen tā′nē əs), *adj.* **1.** agreeing; accordant. **2.** done by common consent; unanimous. [< L *consentāneus*, equiv. to *consent-* (s. of *consentīre* to CONSENT) + *-āneus* (*-ān(us)* -AN + *-eus* -EOUS)] —**con′sen·ta′ne·ous·ly,** *adv.* —**con·sen·ta·ne·i·ty** (kən sen′tə nē′i tē), **con′sen·ta′ne·ous·ness,** *n.*

con·sen·tience (kən sen′shəns), *n.* nonintellectual sense of unity. [CONSENTI(ENT) + -ENCE]

con·sen·tient (kən sen′shənt), *adj.* **1.** agreeing; accordant. **2.** acting in harmonious agreement. **3.** unanimous, as an opinion. **4.** characterized by or having consentience. [< L *consentient-* (s. of *consentiēns*, prp. of *consentīre*). See CONSENT, -ENT] —**con·sen′tient·ly,** *adv.*

con·se·quence (kon′sə kwens′, -kwəns), *n.* **1.** the effect, result, or outcome of something occurring earlier: *The wreckage showed the consequences of reckless driving.* **2.** an act or instance of following something as an effect, result or outcome: *Failure was a matter of inevitable consequence.* **3.** the conclusion reached by a line of reasoning; inference. **4.** importance or significance: *a matter of no consequence.* **5.** importance in rank or position; distinction: *a man of great consequence in art.* **6. in consequence,** consequently; as a result; hence: *He withdrew from the world, and in consequence was forgotten.* **7. in consequence of,** as a result of; on account of: *An investigation was initiated in consequence of the naval disaster.* [late ME < L *consequentia.* See CONSEQUENT, -ENCE]
—**Syn. 1.** outcome, issue, upshot, sequel. See **effect. 4.** moment, weight. See **importance.** —**Ant. 1.** cause.

con·se·quent (kon′sə kwent′, -kwənt), *adj.* **1.** following as an effect or result; resulting (often fol. by *on, upon,* or *to*): *a rise in production cost and a consequent fall in price; a fall in price consequent to a rise in production.* **2.** following as a logical conclusion: *a consequent law.* **3.** following or progressing logically: *consequent reasoning.* —*n.* **4.** anything that follows upon something else, with or without a causal relationship. **5.** *Logic.* the second member of a conditional proposition, as "Caesar was a great general" in "If Caesar conquered Gaul, he was a great general." **6.** *Math.* **a.** the second term of a ratio. **b.** the second of two vectors in a dyad. [< L *consequent-* (s. of *consequēns*, prp. of *consequī* to follow closely). See CON-, SEQUENT]

con·se·quen·tial (kon′sə kwen′shəl), *adj.* **1.** following as an effect, result, or outcome; resultant; consequent. **2.** following as a logical conclusion or inference; logically consistent. **3.** of consequence or importance: *a consequential man in the field of international diplomacy.* **4.** self-important; pompous. [< L *consequenti(a)* CONSEQUENCE + -AL[1]] —**con′se·quen′ti·al′i·ty, con′se·quen′tial·ness,** *n.* —**con′se·quen′tial·ly,** *adv.*

con·se·quent·ly (kon′sə kwent′lē, -kwənt-), *adv.* as a result, effect, or outcome; therefore: *He wrote many best-selling books and consequently became very rich.* [late ME; see CONSEQUENT, -LY]
—**Syn.** See **therefore.**

con′sequent stream′, *Geol.* a stream the course of which was determined by the original slope of the land. Cf. **obsequent stream.**

con·serv·a·ble (kən sûr′və bəl), *adj.* capable of being conserved: *conservable fruits.* [< L *conservābil(is).* See CONSERVE, -ABLE]

con·serv·an·cy (kən sûr′vən sē), *n., pl.* **-cies. 1.** *Brit.* a commission regulating navigation, fisheries, etc. **2.** conservation of natural resources. [< ML *conservantia* (see CONSERVE, -ANCY); r. *conservacy* < ML *conservātia;* see -ACY] —**con·serv′ant,** *adj.*

con·ser·va·tion (kon′sər vā′shən), *n.* **1.** the act of conserving; preservation from loss, injury, decay, or waste: *conservation of wildlife.* **2.** official supervision of rivers, forests, and other natural resources. **3.** a district, river, forest, etc., under such supervision. [< L *conservātiōn-* (s. of *conservātiō*), equiv. to *conservāt(us)* (ptp. of *conservāre;* see CONSERVE, -ATE[1]) + *-iōn-* -ION] —**con′ser·va′tion·al,** *adj.*

con·ser·va·tion·ist (kon′sər vā′shə nist), *n.* one who advocates or promotes conservation, esp. of the natural resources of a country. [CONSERVATION + -IST]

conserva′tion of an′gular momen′tum, *Physics.* the principle that the total angular momentum of a system has constant magnitude and direction if the system is subjected to no external force. Also called **law of conservation of angular momentum.**

conserva′tion of charge′, *Physics.* the principle that the total electric charge of a system is constant. Also called **law of conservation of charge.**

conserva′tion of en′ergy, *Physics.* the principle that in a system that does not undergo any force from outside the system, the amount of energy is constant, irrespective of its changes in form. Also called **law of conservation of energy.**

conserva′tion of lin′ear momen′tum, *Physics.* the principle that the linear momentum of a system has constant magnitude and direction if the system is subjected to no external force. Also called **law of conservation of linear momentum.**

conserva′tion of mass′, *Physics.* the principle that in any closed system subjected to no external forces, the mass is constant irrespective of its changes in form; the principle that matter cannot be created or destroyed. Also called **law of conservation of mass, conserva′tion of mat′ter.**

con·serv·a·tism (kən sûr′və tiz′əm), *n.* **1.** the disposition to preserve what is established and to promote gradual development rather than abrupt change. **2.** the principles and practices of political conservatives, esp. of the British Conservative party; Toryism. [CONSERVAT(IVE) + -ISM]

con·serv·a·tive (kən sûr′və tiv), *adj.* **1.** disposed to preserve existing conditions, institutions, etc., and to agree with gradual rather than abrupt change. **2.** cautiously moderate: *a conservative estimate.* **3.** traditional in style or manner; avoiding showiness: *a suit of conservative cut.* **4.** (*often cap.*) of or pertaining to the Conservative party. **5.** (*cap.*) of, pertaining to, or characteristic of Conservative Jews or Conservative Judaism. **6.** having the power or tendency to conserve; preservative. **7.** *Math.* (of a vector or vector function) having curl equal to zero; irrotational; lamellar. —*n.* **8.** a person who is conservative in principles, actions, habits, etc. **9.** a member of a conservative political party, esp. the Conservative party in Great Britian. **10.** a preservative. [< LL *conservātīv(us)*, equiv. to L *conservāt(us)* (see CONSERVATION) + *-īvus* -IVE; r. ME *conservatif* < MF] —**con·serv′a·tive·ly,** *adv.* —**con·serv′a·tive·ness,** *n.*

Conserv′ative Bap′tist, a member of a Protestant denomination **(Conserv′ative Bap′tist Associa′tion of Amer′ica)** organized in Milwaukee, Wisconsin, in 1948.

Conserv′ative Jew′, a Jew who adheres for the most part to the principles and practices of traditional Judaism with the reservation that, taking into account contemporary conditions, certain modifications or rejections are permissible. Cf. **Orthodox Jew, Reform Jew.**

Conserv′ative Ju′daism, Judaism as observed by Conservative Jews.

Conserv′ative par′ty, a political party in Great Britain founded about 1832 as successor to the Tory party and characterized chiefly by moderate progressivism.

con·ser·va·toire (kən sûr′və twär′, -sûr′və twär′; *Fr.* kôn ser va twar′), *n., pl.* **-toires** (-twärz′, -twärz′; *Fr.* -twar′). a conservatory, as of music, theatrical arts, etc. [< F < It *conservator(io)* CONSERVATORY]

con·ser·va·tor (kon′sər vā′tər, kən sûr′və-), *n.* **1.** a person who conserves or preserves; preserver. **2.** *Law.* a guardian; a custodian. **3.** *Brit.* a person employed by the conservancy commission; a conservation worker. [< L, equiv. to *conservāt(us)* (ptp. of *conservāre;* see CONSERVE, -ATE[1]) + *-or* -OR[2]]

con·serv·a·to·ry (kən sûr′və tôr′ē, -tōr′ē), *n., pl.* **-ries,** *adj.* —*n.* **1.** a greenhouse, usually attached to a dwelling, for growing and displaying plants. **2.** a school giving instruction in one or more of the fine or dramatic arts; specifically, a school of music. **3.** *Obs.* a place where things are preserved. —*adj.* **4.** serving or adapted to conserve; preservative. [< L *conservāt(us)* (ptp. of *conservāre;* see CONSERVE, -ATE[1]) + -ORY[2]]

con·serve (*v.* kən sûrv′; *n.* kon′sûrv, kən sûrv′), *v.,* **-served, -serv·ing,** *n.* —*v.t.* **1.** to keep from loss, decay, waste, or injury; preserve: *Conserve your strength for the race.* **2.** to preserve (fruit) by cooking with sugar or syrup. [ME < L *conserv(āre)* (to) preserve, equiv. to *con-* CON- + *servāre* to watch over, akin to OE *searu* armor] —*n.* **3.** Often, **conserves.** a mixture of several fruits cooked to jamlike consistency with sugar and often garnished with nuts and raisins. [ME < MF < LL **conserv(a)*, deriv. of L *conservāre* to preserve] —**con·serv′er,** *n.*

con·sid·er (kən sid′ər), *v.t.* **1.** to think carefully about, esp. in order to make a decision; contemplate; reflect on: *He considered the cost before buying the new car.* **2.** to regard as or deem to be: *I consider the story improbable.* **3.** to think, believe, or suppose: *We consider his reply unsatisfactory.* **4.** to bear in mind; make allowance for: *The arrest was justified if you consider his scandalous behavior.* **5.** to pay attention to; regard: *He considered the man for some time before speaking to him.* **6.** to regard with respect, thoughtfulness, honor, etc.; esteem. **7.** to think about (something that one might do, accept, buy, etc.): *to consider a job in Guatemala.* **8.** *Archaic.* to view attentively; scrutinize. **9.** *Obs.* to recompense or remunerate. —*v.i.* **10.** to think deliberately or carefully; reflect. **11.** to view carefully or thoughtfully. [ME *consid(e)re* < L *considerāre* to examine, equiv. to *con-* CON- + *sīder-* (s. of *sīdus*) star-group, sky + *-āre* inf. suffix] —**con·sid′er·er,** *n.*
—**Syn. 1.** ponder, deliberate, weigh, revolve. See **study.**

con·sid·er·a·ble (kən sid′ər ə bəl), *adj.* **1.** rather large or great, as in size, distance, extent, etc.: *It cost a considerable amount. We took a considerable length of time to decide.* **2.** worthy of respect, attention, etc.; important; distinguished: *The mayor is a considerable citizen.* —*n.* **3.** *U.S. Informal.* much; not a little: *He has done considerable for the community. I found considerable to detain me.* [late ME < ML *consīderābil(is)*, equiv. to *considerā-* (see CONSIDER) + *-bilis* -BLE] —**con·sid′er·a·bly,** *adv.*

con·sid·er·ance (kən sid′ər əns), *n.* *Obs.* consideration. [late ME < L *consīderantia.* See CONSIDER, -ANCE]

con·sid·er·ate (kən sid′ər it), *adj.* **1.** showing kindly awareness or regard for another's feelings, circumstances, etc.: *a very considerate critic.* **2.** carefully considered; deliberate. **3.** *Archaic.* marked by consideration or reflection; deliberate; prudent. [< L *consīderāt(us)* (ptp. of *consīderāre* to CONSIDER), equiv. to *considerā-* (s. of *consīderāre*) + *-tus* ptp. suffix] —**con·sid′er·ate·ly,** *adv.* —**con·sid′er·ate·ness,** *n.*
—**Syn. 1.** kind, patient, concerned. See **thoughtful.**

con·sid·er·a·tion (kən sid′ə rā′shən), *n.* **1.** the act of considering; careful thought; meditation; deliberation: *I will give your project full consideration.* **2.** something that is or is to be kept in mind in making a decision, evaluating facts, etc.: *The judge said the prisoner's age was an important consideration.* **3.** a thought or reflection. **4.** a recompense or payment, as for work done; compensation. **5.** *Law.* **a.** something that suffices to make an informal promise legally binding, usually some value given in exchange for the promise. **b.** the hearing of a case by a tribunal. **6.** thoughtful or sympathetic regard or respect; thoughtfulness for others: *They showed no consideration for his feelings.* **7.** importance or consequence. **8.** estimation; esteem: *He is held in great consideration by the community.* **9. in consideration of, a.** in view of. **b.** in return or recompense for: *The organization offered him a sum of money in consideration of his efforts.* **10. take into consideration,** to take into account; consider: *We failed to take into consideration the large number of tourists attending the exhibition.* [< L *consīderātiōn-* (s. of *consīderātiō*), equiv. to *consīderāt(us)* (see CONSIDERATE) + *-iōn-* -ION]
—**Syn. 1.** reflection, contemplation, rumination; attention. **4.** payment, remuneration, fee. **6.** kindness, kindliness, patience, concern. **7.** weight, significance, moment. **8.** See **honor.**

con·sid·ered (kən sid′ərd), *adj.* **1.** thought about or decided upon with care: *a considered opinion.* **2.** regarded with respect or esteem: *a highly considered person.* [CONSIDER + -ED[2]]

con·sid·er·ing (kən sid′ər ing), *prep.* **1.** taking into account; in view of: *The campaign was a great success, considering the strong opposition.* —*adv.* **2.** *Informal.* with all things considered (used only after the statement it modifies): *He paints very well, considering.* —*conj.* **3.** taking into consideration that: *Considering they are newcomers, they've adjusted very well.* [ME; see CONSIDER, -ING[2]]

con·sign (kən sīn′), *v.t.* **1.** to hand over or deliver formally; commit (often fol. by *to*). **2.** to transfer to another's custody or charge; entrust. **3.** to set apart for or devote to (a special purpose or use): *to consign two afternoon hours to a siesta.* **4.** to banish or set apart in one's mind; relegate: *to consign unpleasant thoughts to oblivion.* **5.** *Com.* **a.** to ship, as by common carrier, esp. for sale or custody. **b.** to address for such shipment. **6.** *Obs.* to confirm or ratify, as with a seal or other token. —*v.i.* **7.** to agree or assent. **8.** *Obs.* to yield or submit. [appar. < ML *consign(āre)* (to) mark with sign of cross, L: to mark with a seal. See CON-, SIGN] —**con·sign′a·ble,** *adj.* —**con·sig·na·tion** (kon′sig nā′shən), *n.*
—**Syn. 1.** relegate, assign. **2.** confide.

con·sign·ee (kon′sī nē′, -si-, kən sī-), *n.* the person or party to whom something, usually merchandise, is consigned. [CONSIGN + -EE]

con·sign·ment (kən sīn′mənt), *n.* **1.** the act of consigning. **2.** something that is consigned. **3.** *Com.* property sent to an agent for sale, storage, or shipment. **4. on consignment,** (of goods) sent to an agent for sale, with title being held by the consignor until a sale is made. [CONSIGN + -MENT]

consign′ment note′, *Chiefly Brit.* See **air waybill.**

con·sign·or (kən sī′nər, kon′sī nôr′), *n.* a person or company that consigns goods, merchandise, etc. Also, **con·sign·er** (kən sī′nər). [CONSIGN + -OR[2]]

con·sist (*v.* kən sist′; *n.* kon′sist), *v.i.* **1.** to be made up or composed (usually fol. by *of*): *This cake consists mainly of sugar, flour, and butter.* **2.** to be comprised or contained (usually fol. by *in*): *Her charm does not consist only in her beauty.* **3.** to be compatible, consistent, or harmonious (usually fol. by *with*): *Their opinions consisted with one another.* **4.** *Archaic.* to exist together or be capable of existing together. **5.** *Obs.* to insist; urge. —*n. Railroads.* **6.** the rolling stock, exclusive of the locomotive, making up a train. **7.** a record made of this rolling stock. [< L *consist(ere)* (to) stand together, stand firm, equiv. to *con-* CON- + *sistere*, redup. v. akin to *stāre* to STAND]
—**Syn. 1, 2.** CONSIST OF, CONSIST IN are often confused. With CONSIST OF, parts, materials, or ingredients are spoken of: *Bread consists of flour, yeast, etc.* With CONSIST IN, something resembling a definition is given: *Cooperation consists in helping one another and in sharing losses or gains.*

con·sist·en·cy (kən sis′tən sē), *n., pl.* **-cies. 1.** the condition of cohering or holding together and retaining form; solidity or firmness. **2.** degree of density, firmness, viscosity, etc.: *The liquid has the consistency of cream.* **3.** steadfast adherence to the same principles, course, form, etc.: *There is consistency in his pattern of behavior.* **4.** agreement, harmony, or compatibility; agreement among themselves of the parts of a complex thing: *consistency of colors throughout the house.* Also, **con·sist′ence.** [CONSIST(ENT) + -ENCY]

con·sist·ent (kən sis′tənt), *adj.* **1.** agreeing or accordant; compatible; not self-opposed or self-contradictory. **2.** constantly adhering to the same principles, course, form, etc.: *a consistent opponent of political change.* **3.** holding firmly together; cohering. **4.** *Archaic.* fixed, firm; solid. [< L *consistent-* (s. of *consistēns,* prp. of *consistere*). See CONSIST, -ENT] —**con·sist′ent·ly,** *adv.* —**Syn. 1.** congruous, consonant, harmonious, conformable.

con·sis·to·ry (kən sis′tə rē), *n., pl.* **-ries. 1.** any of various ecclesiastical councils or tribunals. **2.** the place where such a council or tribunal meets. **3.** the meeting of any such body. **4.** *Rom. Cath. Ch.* a solemn assembly of the whole body of cardinals, summoned and presided over by the pope. **5.** *Ch. of Eng.* a diocesan court for dealing with ecclesiastical and spiritual questions, held in the cathedral church and presided over by the bishop, the bishop's chancellor, or the commissary. **6.** (in certain Reformed churches) the governing board of a local church or congregation. **7.** any assembly or council. **8.** *Obs.* a council chamber. [ME *consistorie* < LL *consistōri(um).* See CONSIST, -ORY²] —**con·sis·to·ri·al** (kon′si stôr′ē əl, -stōr′-), **con′sis·to′ri·an,** *adj.*

con·so·ci·ate (*adj., n.* kən sō′shē it, -āt′; *v.* kən sō′shē āt′), *adj., n., v.i.,* **-at·ed, -at·ing.** associate. [< L *consociāt(us)* (ptp. of *consociāre*), equiv. to *con-* CON- + *soci(us)* fellow, partner + *-ātus* -ATE¹] —**con·so·ci·a·tion** (kən sō′sē ā′shən, -shē-), *n.*

con·sol (kon′sol, kən sol′), *n.* Usually, **consols.** the funded government securities of Great Britain that originated in the consolidation in 1751 of various public securities, chiefly in the form of annuities, into a single debt issue without maturity. Also called **bank annuities.** [short for *consolidated annuities*]

consol., consolidated.

con·so·la·tion (kon′sə lā′shən), *n.* **1.** the act of consoling; comfort; solace. **2.** the state of being consoled. **3.** someone or something that consoles: *His religious faith was a consolation during his troubles. Her devoted daughters are a consolation to her.* **4.** *Sports.* a game, match, or race for entrants in a tournament eliminated before the final round, as a basketball game between the losing semifinalists. [ME *consolacion* < L *consōlātiōn-* (s. of *consōlātiō*), equiv. to *consōlāt(us),* ptp. of *consōlārī* (*con-* CON- + *sōlā-,* s. of *sōlārī* to comfort, + *-tus* ptp. suffix) + *-iōn-* -ION]

Consola′tion of Philos′ophy, The, a philosophical work (A.D. 523?) by Boethius. Latin, **De Consolatione Philosophiae.**

consola′tion prize′, a prize, usually of minor value, given to the loser or runner-up in a contest, competition, etc.

Con·so·la·to del Ma·re (kôn sô lä′tô del mä′re), a code of maritime law compiled in the Middle Ages: it drew upon ancient law and has influenced modern law.

con·sol·a·to·ry (kən sol′ə tôr′ē, -tōr′ē), *adj.* giving solace or comfort; consoling. [late ME < L *consōlātōri(us),* equiv. to *consōlāt(us)* (see CONSOLATION) + *-ōrius* -ORY¹] —**con·sol′i·to′ri·ly,** *adv.* —**con·sol′i·to′ri·ness,** *n.*

con·sole¹ (kən sōl′), *v.t.,* **-soled, -sol·ing.** to alleviate or lessen the grief, sorrow, or disappointment of; give solace or comfort; cheer up: *Only his children could console him when his wife died.* [< L *consō-l(ārī),* equiv. to *con-* CON- + *sōlārī* to soothe; perh. akin to SALVE¹] —**con·sol′a·ble,** *adj.* —**con·sol′er,** *n.* —**con·sol′ing·ly,** *adv.* —**Syn.** See **comfort.**

Console² (def. 1)

con·sole² (kon′sōl), *n.* **1.** a desklike structure containing the keyboards, pedals, etc., by means of which an organ is played. **2.** a radio, phonograph, or television cabinet that stands on the floor. **3.** See **console table. 4.** a small cabinet standing on the floor and having doors. **5.** *Archit.* an ornamental corbel or bracket, esp. one high in relation to its projection. **6.** the monitoring unit or units of a computer, containing most of the keys, switches, and indicators used by an operator to control a computer system. **7.** the control unit of a switchboard or other electrical or electronic system: *a console for generating a theater's lighting system.* [< F < ?]

Console² (def. 5)

con′sole ta′ble (kon′sōl), **1.** a table supported by consoles or brackets fixed to a wall. **2.** a table, often with bracketlike legs, designed to fit against a wall.

con·so·lette (kon′sə let′), *n.* a small console radio, phonograph, or television set. [CONSOLE² + -ETTE]

con·sol·i·date (kən sol′i dāt′), *v.,* **-dat·ed, -dat·ing,** *adj.* —*v.t.* **1.** to bring together (separate parts) into a single whole; unite; combine: *They consolidated their three companies.* **2.** *Mil.* to strengthen by rearranging the position of ground combat troops after a successful attack. **3.** to make solid or firm; solidify; strengthen: *to consolidate gains.* —*v.i.* **4.** to unite or combine. **5.** to become solid or firm. —*adj.* **6.** consolidated. [< L *consolidāt(us)* (ptp. of *consolidāre*), equiv. to *con-* CON- + *solid(us)* SOLID + *-ātus* -ATE¹] —**con·sol′i·da′tor,** *n.*

Consol′idated Fund′, a British national fund created to pay grants to the royal family, interest on public debt, etc., by consolidating various public securities. Cf. **consol.**

consol′idated school′, a public school formed from the pupils and teachers of a number of discontinued smaller schools, esp. in a rural district. Also called **centralized school.**

con·sol·i·da·tion (kən sol′i dā′shən), *n.* **1.** an act or instance of consolidating; the state of being consolidated; unification: *consolidation of companies.* **2.** solidification; strengthening: *consolidation of principles and beliefs.* **3.** something that is or has been consolidated; a consolidated whole. **4.** *Law.* **a.** a statutory combination of two or more corporations. **b.** the union of two or more claims or actions at law for trial or appeal. **5.** (*cap.*) a steam locomotive having a two-wheeled front truck, eight driving wheels, and no rear truck. [< LL *consolidātiōn-* (s. of *consolidātiō*), equiv. to L *consolidāt(us)* (see CONSOLIDATE) + *-iōn-* -ION] —**con·sol′i·da′tive,** *adj.*

con·sol·ute (kon′sə lo͞ot′), *adj. Chem.* **1.** (of two liquids) mutually soluble in all proportions. **2.** soluble in each of two or more conjugate liquids. **3.** of or pertaining to two partially miscible liquids capable of becoming totally miscible under certain conditions. [< LL *consolūt(us)* dissolved together, equiv. to L *con-* CON- + *solūtus,* ptp. of *solvere* to SOLVE (*solū-,* ptp. s. + *-tus* ptp. suffix)]

con·som·mé (kon′sə mā′; *Fr.* kôɴ sô mā′), *n.* a strong clear soup made by boiling meat and bones long and slowly to extract their nutritive properties. [< F, n. use of *consommé* (ptp. of *consommer* to finish) < L *consummāt(us)* CONSUMMATE] —**Syn.** broth.

con·so·nance (kon′sə nəns), *n.* **1.** accord or agreement. **2.** correspondence of sounds; harmony of sounds. **3.** *Music.* a simultaneous combination of tones conventionally accepted as being in a state of repose. Cf. **dissonance** (def. 2). **4.** *Pros.* **a.** the correspondence of consonants, esp. those at the end of a word, in a passage of prose or verse. Cf. **alliteration** (def. 1). **b.** the use of the repetition of consonants or consonant patterns as a rhyming device. **5.** *Physics.* the property of two sounds the frequencies of which have a ratio equal to a small whole number. Also, **con′so·nan·cy.** [late ME < L *consonantia* concord. See CONSONANT, -ANCE] —**Syn. 1.** concord, harmony, correspondence. —**Ant. 1.** dissonance.

con·so·nant (kon′sə nənt), *n.* **1.** *Phonet.* **a.** (in English articulation) a speech sound produced by occluding with or without releasing (p, b; t, d; k, g), diverting (m, n, ng), or obstructing (f, v; s, z, etc.) the flow of air from the lungs (opposed to *vowel*). **b.** (in a syllable) any sound other than the sound of greatest sonority in the syllable, as *b, r,* and *g* in *brig* (opposed to *sonant*). Cf. **vowel** (def. 1b). **c.** (in linguistic function) a concept empirically determined as a phonological element in structural contrast with vowel, as the *b* of *be,* the *w* of *we,* the *y, s,* and *t* of *yeast,* etc. **2.** a letter which usually represents a consonant sound. —*adj.* **3.** in agreement; agreeable; in accord; consistent (usually fol. by *to* or *with*): *behavior consonant with his character.* **4.** corresponding in sound, as words. **5.** harmonious, as sounds. **6.** *Music.* constituting a consonance. **7.** *Physics.* noting or pertaining to sounds exhibiting consonance. **8.** consonantal. [late ME *consona(u)nt* < L *consonant-* (s. of *consonāns,* prp. of *consonāre* to sound with or together). See CON-, SONANT] —**con′so·nant·ly,** *adv.* —**Syn. 3.** concordant, congruous, conformant. —**Ant. 6.** dissonant.

con·so·nan·tal (kon′sə nan′tᵊl), *adj.* **1.** of, or of the nature of, a consonant. **2.** marked by consonant sounds. Also, **con′so·nan′tic.** [CONSONANT + -AL¹] —**con′so·nan′tal·ly,** *adv.*

consonan′tal allitera′tion. See under **alliteration** (def. 1).

con·so·nan·tal·ize (kon′sə nan′tᵊlīz′), *v.t., v.i.,* **-ized, -iz·ing.** *Phonet.* to change into or become changed into a consonant (contrasted with *vocalize*). [CONSONANTAL + -IZE]

con·so·nan·tise (kon′sə nən tīz′), *v.t., v.i.,* **-tised, -tis·ing.** *Chiefly Brit.* consonantize.

con·so·nant·ism (kon′sə nən tiz′əm), *n.* the body of facts concerning the distribution or phonology of the consonants of a word, group of words, or language. [CONSONANT + -ISM]

con·son·an·tize (kon′sə nən tīz′), *v.t., v.i.,* **-tized, -tiz·ing.** consonantalize.

con′sonant sys′tem, *Ling.* the consonant phonemes of a language, esp. when considered as forming an interrelated and interacting group. Cf. **vowel system.**

con sor·di·no (kon sôr dē′nō, kōn; *It.* kôn sôʀ dē′nô), with the mute (used as a direction in music to a string player). [< It: lit., with mute]

con·sort (*n.* kon′sôrt, *v.* kən sôrt′), *n.* **1.** a husband or wife; spouse. **2.** the spouse of a royal person. Cf. **prince consort, queen consort. 3.** one vessel or ship accompanying another. **4.** *Music.* **a.** a group of instrumentalists and singers who perform music, esp. old music. **b.** a group of instruments of the same family, as viols, played in concert. **5.** *Obs.* **a.** a companion or partner. **b.** company or association. **c.** accord or agreement. **d.** harmony of sounds. —*v.i.* **6.** to associate; keep company: *to consort with known criminals.* **7.** to agree or harmonize. —*v.t.* **8.** to associate, join, or unite. **9.** *Obs.* **a.** to accompany; espouse. **b.** to sound in harmony. [late ME < MF < L *consort-* (s. of *consors*) sharer, orig. sharing (adj.). See CON-, SORT] —**con·sort′a·ble,** *adj.* —**con·sort′er,** *n.* —**con·sor′tion,** *n.*

con·sor·ti·um (kən sôr′shē əm), *n., pl.* **-ti·a** (-shē ə). **1.** a combination of financial institutions, capitalists, etc., for carrying into effect some financial operation requiring large resources of capital. **2.** any association, partnership, or union. [< L: partnership, equiv. to *consort-* CONSORT + *-ium* n. suffix] —**con·sor′ti·al,** *adj.*

con·spe·cif·ic (kon′spi sif′ik), *adj. Bot., Zool.* belonging to the same species. [*conspeci(es)* (see CON-, SPECIES) + -FIC]

con·spec·tus (kən spek′təs), *n., pl.* **-tus·es. 1.** a general or comprehensive view; survey. **2.** a digest; summary; résumé. [< L: survey n. use of *conspectus* (ptp. of *conspicere*), equiv. to *con-* CON- + *spec-* (s. of *specere* to look) + *-tus* ptp. ending] —**Syn. 2.** compendium, brief, abstract, epitome.

consperg., (in prescriptions) dust; sprinkle. [< L *consperge*]

con·spic·u·ous (kən spik′yo͞o əs), *adj.* **1.** easily seen or noticed; readily observable: *a conspicuous road sign; a conspicuous error.* **2.** attracting special attention, as by outstanding qualities, eccentricities, etc.: *He was conspicuous by his booming laughter.* [< L *conspicuus* visible, conspicuous, equiv. to *con-* CON- + *spicu-* (var. s. of *spicere, specere;* see CONSPECTUS) + *-us* -OUS] —**conspic′u·ous·ly,** *adv.* —**con·spic′u·ous·ness, con·spi·cu·i·ty** (kon′spi kyo͞o′i tē), *n.* —**Syn. 1.** visible, manifest, noticeable, clear, marked, salient. **2.** prominent, striking, noteworthy.

conspic′uous consump′tion, public enjoyment of possessions that are known to be costly so that one's ability to pay for such things is emphasized.

conspic′uous waste′, public demonstration that one need not economize, made through extravagant waste of goods, the retention of superfluous servants, etc.

con·spir·a·cy (kən spir′ə sē), *n., pl.* **-cies. 1.** the act of conspiring. **2.** an evil, unlawful, treacherous, or surreptitious plan formulated in secret by two or more persons; plot. **3.** a combination of persons for a secret, unlawful, or evil purpose: *He joined the conspiracy to overthrow the government.* **4.** *Law.* an agreement by two or more persons to commit a crime, fraud, or other wrongful act. **5.** any concurrence in action; combination in bringing about a given result. [ME *conspiracie* (see CONSPIRE, -ACY); r. ME *conspiracioun* < AF; MF *conspiration* < L] —**con·spir′a·tive,** *adj.* —**con·spir·a·to·ri·al** (kən spir′ə tôr′ē əl, -tōr′-), **con·spir·a·to·ry** (kən spir′ə tôr′ē, -tōr′ē), *adj.* —**con·spir′a·to′ri·al·ly,** *adv.*

con·spire (kən spīᵊr′), *v.,* **-spired, -spir·ing.** —*v.i.* **1.** to agree together, esp. secretly, to do something wrong, evil, or illegal: *They conspired to kill the king.* **2.** to act or work together toward the same result or goal. —*v.t.* **3.** to plot (something wrong, evil, or illegal). [ME < L *conspīr(āre)* (to) plot (lit., breathe) together, equiv. to *con-* CON- + *spīrāre* to breathe; see SPIRANT, SPIRIT] —**con·spir′er, con·spir·a·tor** (kən spir′ə tər); *referring to a woman,* **con·spir′a·tress,** *n.* —**con·spir′ing·ly,** *adv.* —**Syn. 1.** complot, intrigue. See **plot**¹. **2.** combine, concur, cooperate.

con spir·i·to (kon spir′i tō′, kōn; *It.* kôn spē′ʀē tô), with lively spirit; vigorously (used as a direction in music). [< It: lit., with spirit]

Const., 1. constable. **2.** constant. **3.** constitution.

con·sta·ble (kon′stə bəl *or, esp. Brit.,* kun′-), *n.* **1.** any of various officers of the peace, as one who executes the processes of a justice of the peace. **2.** *Chiefly Brit.* a policeman. **3.** an officer of high rank in medieval monarchies, usually the commander of all armed forces esp. in the absence of the ruler. **4.** the keeper or governor of a royal fortress or castle. [ME *conestable* < OF < LL *comes stabulī* COUNT² of the STABLE¹] —**con′sta·ble·ship′,** *n.*

Con·sta·ble (kun′stə bəl, kon′-), *n.* **John,** 1776–1837, English painter.

con′stable glass′, a drinking glass of the 18th century, having a heavy foot, a tall body, and a quart capacity.

con·stab·u·lar·y¹ (kən stab′yə ler′ē), *n., pl.* **-lar·ies. 1.** the body of constables of a district or locality. **2.** a body of officers of the peace organized on a military basis. [< ML *constabulāri(a),* fem. of *constabulārius* CONSTABULARY²]

con·stab·u·lar·y² (kən stab′yə ler′ē), *adj.* pertaining to constables or their duties. Also, **con·stab·u·lar** (kən stab′yə lər). [< ML *constabulāri(us),* equiv. to *comes stabul(i)* CONSTABLE + *-ārius* -ARY]

Con·stance (kon′stəns), *n.* **1. Lake,** German, **Boden See.** a lake in W Europe, bounded by Germany, Austria, and Switzerland. 46 mi. long; 207 sq. mi. **2.** German, **Konstanz.** a city in S West Germany, on this lake: important church council 1414–18. 55,100 (1963). **3.** a girl's given name.

con·stan·cy (kon′stən sē), *n.* **1.** the quality of being unchanging or unwavering, as in purpose, love, loyalty, etc.; firmness of mind; faithfulness. **2.** uniformity or regularity, as in qualities, conditions, etc.; stability; invariableness. [< L *constantia.* See CONSTANT, -ANCY] —**Syn. 1.** resolution; steadfastness, fidelity, fealty, loyalty, devotion. **2.** permanence, regularity, dependability. —**Ant. 1.** irresolution; infidelity. **2.** fickleness.

Con·stans I (kon′stanz), (*Flavius Julius Constans*) A.D. c323–350, emperor of Rome 337–350 (son of Constantine I).

con·stant (kon′stənt), *adj.* **1.** not changing or varying; uniform; regular; invariable: *All conditions during the three experiments were constant.* **2.** continuing without pause or letup; unceasing: *constant noise.* **3.** regularly recurrent; continual; persistent: *He found it impossible to work with constant interruption.* **4.** faithful; unswerving in love, devotion, etc.: *a constant lover.* **5.** steadfast; firm in mind or purpose; resolute. **6.** *Obs.* certain; confident. —*n.* **7.** something that does not or cannot change or vary. **8.** *Physics.* a number expressing a property, quantity, or relation that remains unchanged under specified conditions. **9.** *Math.* a quantity assumed to be unchanged throughout a given discussion. [ME < L *constant-* (s. of *constāns,* prp. of *constāre* to stand firm), equiv. to *con-* CON- + *stā-* stand + *-nt* prp. suffix] —**con′stant·ly,** *adv.*
—**Syn. 1.** unchanging, immutable, permanent. **2.** perpetual, unremitting, uninterrupted. **3.** incessant, ceaseless. See **continual. 4.** loyal, stanch, true. See **faithful. 5.** steady, unwavering, unswerving, unshaken. —**Ant. 1.** changeable. **2.** fitful. **3.** sporadic. **4.** unreliable. **5.** wavering.

Con·stant (kôɴ stäɴ′), *n.* **1. Paul Hen·ri Ben·ja·min Bal·luat** (pôl äɴ ʀē′ baɴ zha maɴ′ ba lwa′). See **Estournelles de Constant, Paul. 2. Jean Jo·seph Ben·ja·min** (zhäɴ zhô zef′ baɴ zha maɴ′), 1845–1902, French painter. **3.** a girl's given name.

Con·stan·ța (kôn stän′tsä), *n.* a seaport in SE Rumania, on the Black Sea. 110,485 (est. 1959).

con·stant·an (kon′stən tan′), *n.* an alloy containing 60 percent copper and 40 percent nickel, used for electrical resistance heating and thermocouples. [CONSTANT + -AN]

Con·stant de Re·becque (kôn stän′ də rə bek′), **Hen·ri Ben·ja·min** (äN rē′ baN zhA maN′), (*Benjamin Constant*), 1767–1830, French statesman and author, born in Switzerland.

Con·stan·tia (kon stan′shə, -shē ə), *n.* a girl's given name, form of **Constance.**

Con·stan·tine (kon′stən tēn′ *or, for 1, 3,* -tīn′; *for 2, 3, also Fr.* kôn stan tēn′), *n.* **1.** died A.D. 715, pope 708–715. **2.** a city in NE Algeria. 143,334 (1954). **3.** a boy's given name.

Con·stan·tine I (kon′stən tēn′, -tīn′), **1.** (*Flavius Valerius Aurelius Constantinus*) ("*the Great*") A.D. 288?–337, Roman emperor 324–337: named Constantinople as the new capital; legally sanctioned Christian worship. **2.** 1868–1923, king of Greece 1913–17, 1920–22. —**Con·stan·tin·i·an** (kon′stən tin′ē ən), *adj.*

Constantine II, **1.** (*Flavius Claudius Constantinus*) A.D. 317–340, emperor of Rome 337–340 (son of Constantine I). **2.** born 1940, king of Greece since 1964.

Con·stan·ti·no·ple (kon′stan tᵊnō′pəl), *n.* former name of **Istanbul.**

Con·stan′ti·no·pol′i·tan Creed′ (kon stan′tᵊnō-pol′i tᵊn, -stan′-). See under **Nicene Creed** (def. 2). [< LL *Constantinopolitān(us)*, equiv. to *Constantinopol(is)* CONSTANTINOPLE (with Gk *polît(ēs)* citizen r. *pōlis* city) + *-ānus* -AN]

Constan′tinopol′itan rite′. See **Greek rite.**

con′stant of gravita′tion, *Physics.* the proportionality constant appearing in the equation for the attraction between bodies, equal to 6.67×10^{-8} dyne centimeter^2/gram^2. *Symbol:* G Also called **gravitational constant.**

con′stant of integra′tion, *Math.* a constant that is added to the function obtained by evaluating the indefinite integral of a given function, indicating that all indefinite integrals of the given function differ by, at most, a constant.

con·stel·late (kon′stə lāt′), *v.i., v.t.,* **-lat·ed, -lat·ing.** to cluster together, as stars in a constellation. [< LL *constellāt(us)*, equiv. to L *con-* CON- + *stell(a)* star + *-ātus* -ATE[1]]

con·stel·la·tion (kon′stə lā′shən), *n.* **1.** *Astron.* **a.** any of various groups of stars to which definite names have been given, as Ursa Major, Ursa Minor, Boötes, Cancer, Orion. **b.** the section of the heavens occupied by such a group. **2.** *Astrol.* **a.** the grouping or relative position of the stars as supposed to influence events, esp. at a person's birth. **b.** *Obs.* character as presumed to be determined by the stars. **3.** any brilliant, outstanding group or assemblage: *a constellation of great artists.* [ME *constellacioun* < L *constellātiōn-* (s. of *constellātiō*). See CONSTELLATE, -ION] —**con·stel·la·to·ry** (kən stel′ə-tôr′ē, -tōr′ē), *adj.*

con·ster (kon′stər), *v.t., v.i. Obs.* construe.

con·ster·nate (kon′stər nāt′), *v.t.,* **-nat·ed, -nat·ing.** to dismay, confuse, or terrify: *She was consternated by the large crowd.* [< L *consternāt(us)* (ptp. of *consternāre* to alarm, dismay), equiv. to *con-* CON- + *sternā-* make to shy or dodge, startle + *-tus* ptp. suffix; akin to STRATUM]

con·ster·na·tion (kon′stər nā′shən), *n.* a sudden, alarming amazement or dread that results in utter confusion; paralyzing dismay. [< L *consternātiōn-* (s. of *consternātiō*). See CONSTERNATE, -ION]
—**Syn.** bewilderment, alarm, terror, fear, panic, fright, horror. —**Ant.** composure, equanimity.

con·sti·pate (kon′stə pāt′), *v.t.,* **-pat·ed, -pat·ing.** **1.** to cause constipation in; make costive. **2.** *Obs.* to crowd or pack closely together. [late ME (ptp.) < L *constīpāt(us)* (ptp. of *constīpāre*), equiv. to *con-* CON- + *stīpā-* (s. of *stīpāre* to crowd, press) + *-tus* ptp. suffix]

con·sti·pa·tion (kon′stə pā′shən), *n.* **1.** a condition of the bowels in which the feces are dry and hardened and evacuation is difficult and infrequent. **2.** *Obs.* the act of crowding anything into a smaller compass; condensation. [late ME *constipacioun* < LL *constipātiōn-* (s. of *constīpātiō*). See CONSTIPATE, -ION]

con·stit·u·en·cy (kən stich′o͞o ən sē), *n., pl.* **-cies.** **1.** a body of constituents; the voters or residents in a district represented by an elective officer. **2.** the district itself. **3.** any body of supporters, customers, etc.; a clientele. [CONSTITU(ENT) + -ENCY]

con·stit·u·ent (kən stich′o͞o ənt), *adj.* **1.** serving to compose or make up a thing; component: *the constituent parts of a motor.* **2.** having power to frame or alter a political constitution or fundamental law, as distinguished from lawmaking power: *a constituent assembly.* —*n.* **3.** a constituent element, material, etc.; component. **4.** one who authorizes another to act for him, as a voter in a district represented by an elected official. **5.** *Gram.* an element considered as part of a construction. Cf. **immediate constituent, ultimate constituent.** [< L *constituent-* (s. of *constituēns*, prp. of *constituere* to set up, found, constitute), equiv. to *con-* CON- + *-stitu-* (var. s. of *status* STATUS) + *-ent-* -ENT] —**con·stit′u·ent·ly,** *adv.*
—**Syn. 3.** See **element.**

Constit′uent Assem′bly, *Fr. Hist.* the legislature of France 1789–91.

con·sti·tute (kon′sti to͞ot′, -tyo͞ot′), *v.t.,* **-tut·ed, -tut·ing.** **1.** to compose; form: *mortar constituted of lime and sand; Golf constitutes his work and play both.* **2.** to appoint to an office or function; make or create: *He was constituted chairman of the assembly.* **3.** to set up or establish (laws, an institution, etc.). **4.** to give legal form to (an assembly, court, etc.). **5.** to create or be tantamount to: *Cheap imports constitute a menace to our sales.* **6.** *Archaic.* to set or place. [late ME < L *constitūt(us)* (ptp. of *constituere*; see CONSTITUENT), equiv. to *con-* CON- + *-stitūtum*, comb. form of *statūtum*, ptp. of *statuere* to set up. See STATUTE] —**con′sti·tut′er, con′sti·tu′tor,** *n.*

con·sti·tu·tion (kon′sti to͞o′shən, -tyo͞o′-), *n.* **1.** the way in which a thing is composed or made up; make-up; composition: *the physical constitution of the moon.* **2.** the physical character of the body as to strength, health, etc.: *Plenty of exercise has given him a strong constitution.* **3.** character or condition of mind; disposition; temperament. **4.** the act or process of constituting; establishment. **5.** the state of being constituted; formation. **6.** any established arrangement or custom. **7.** (*cap.*) See **Constitution of the United States.** **8.** the system of fundamental principles according to which a nation, state, corporation, or the like, is governed. **9.** the document embodying these principles. [ME *constitucion* < L *constitūtiōn-* (s. of *constitūtiō*). See CONSTITUTE, -ION]

Constitution, The, an American 44-gun frigate, famous for its exploits in the War of 1812 and popularly called "Old Ironsides."

con·sti·tu·tion·al (kon′sti to͞o′shə nᵊl, -tyo͞o′-), *adj.* **1.** belonging to or inherent in a person's constitution of body or mind: *a constitutional weakness for rich foods.* **2.** beneficial to one's constitution; healthful: *daily constitutional exercise.* **3.** pertaining to the constitution or composition of a thing; essential. **4.** of or pertaining to the constitution of a state, organization, etc. **5.** subject to the provisions of such a constitution: *a constitutional monarchy.* **6.** provided for, in accordance with, or not prohibited by, such a constitution: *the constitutional powers of the President; a law held to be constitutional.* —*n.* **7.** a walk or other exercise taken for the benefit of one's health. [CONSTITUTION + -AL[1]]

Constitu′tional Conven′tion, the convention in Philadelphia (1787) of representatives from each of the Colonies except Rhode Island, at which the Constitution of the United States was framed.

Constitu′tional Democrat′ic par′ty, a former Russian political party that advocated a right-wing policy in foreign and domestic affairs.

con·sti·tu·tion·al·ism (kon′sti to͞o′shə nᵊliz′əm, -tyo͞o′-), *n.* **1.** the principles of constitutional government or adherence to them. **2.** constitutional rule or authority. [CONSTITUTIONAL + -ISM]

con·sti·tu·tion·al·ist (kon′sti to͞o′shə nᵊlist, -tyo͞o′-), *n.* **1.** an adherent or advocate of constitutionalism or of an existing constitution. **2.** a student of or writer on a political constitution. [CONSTITUTIONAL + -IST]

con·sti·tu·tion·al·i·ty (kon′sti to͞o′shə nal′i tē, -tyo͞o′-), *n.* **1.** the quality of being constitutional. **2.** accordance with the constitution of a country, State, etc. [CONSTITUTIONAL + -ITY]

con·sti·tu·tion·al·ly (kon′sti to͞o′shə nᵊlē, -tyo͞o′-), *adv.* **1.** in respect to physical make-up: *He is constitutionally fitted for heavy labor.* **2.** in respect to mental or emotional make-up: *She is constitutionally unable to stand up before an audience.* **3.** with respect to a constitution: *The proposed bill was constitutionally invalid.* [CONSTITUTIONAL + -LY]

constitu′tional mon′archy. See **limited monarchy.** —**constitu′tional mon′arch.**

Constitu′tional Un′ion par′ty, *U.S. Hist.* the political party formed in 1859 chiefly by former Whigs to rally moderates desirous of preserving the Union. In 1860 it nominated John Bell for President and Edward Everett for Vice-President.

Constitu′tion clock′, an American banjo clock having depicted on its lower part the battle in the War of 1812 between the U.S. frigate *Constitution* and the British frigate *Guerrière.*

Constitu′tion mir′ror, *U.S. Furniture.* an oblong Chippendale mirror, usually of mahogany or walnut with gilt detail, having a frame with a fanciful outline emphasized by a raised molding which is topped with a scrolled broken pediment with a central finial, often in the form of a bird. Also called **Martha Washington mirror.**

Constitu′tion of the Unit′ed States′, the fundamental or organic law of the U.S., framed in 1787 by the Constitutional Convention. It went into effect March 4, 1789.

Con′stitu′tion State′, Connecticut (used as a nickname).

con·sti·tu·tive (kon′sti to͞o′tiv, -tyo͞o′-), *adj.* **1.** constituent; making a thing what it is; essential. **2.** having power to establish or enact. **3.** *Physics, Chem.* pertaining to a molecular property determined primarily by the arrangement of atoms in the molecule rather than by their nature or number. [CONSTITUTE + -IVE] —**con′sti·tu′tive·ly,** *adv.*

constr., **1.** construction. **2.** construed.

con·strain (kən strān′), *v.t.* **1.** to force, compel, or oblige; bring about by compulsion: *His conscience constrained him to admit the mistake.* **2.** to confine forcibly, as by bonds. **3.** to repress or restrain: *Cold weather constrained the plant's growth.* [ME *constrei(g)ne* < MF *constrei(g)n-* (s. of *constreindre*) < L *constringere.* See CON-, STRAIN[1]] —**con·strain′a·ble,** *adj.* —**con·strain′er,** *n.* —**con·strain′ing·ly,** *adv.*
—**Syn. 1.** coerce. **2.** check, bind, confine, curb. —**Ant. 2.** free.

con·strained (kən strānd′), *adj.* **1.** forced, compelled, or obliged: *a constrained confession.* **2.** stiff or unnatural; uneasy or embarrassed: *a constrained smile or manner.* [CONSTRAIN + -ED[2]] —**con·strain·ed·ly** (kən strā′nid-lē), *adv.*

con·straint (kən strānt′), *n.* **1.** confinement or restriction. **2.** repression of natural feelings and impulses: *I know you're angry, but have a little constraint before company.* **3.** unnatural restraint in manner, conversation, etc.; embarrassment. **4.** something that constrains. **5.** the act of constraining. **6.** the condition of being constrained. [ME *constreinte* < MF, equiv. to *constrein-* (see CONSTRAIN) + *-te* fem. suffix < L *-ta*]

con·strict (kən strikt′), *v.t.* **1.** to draw or press in; cause to contract or shrink; compress. **2.** to slow or stop the natural course or development of: *Greed and aggressiveness constricted the nation's cultural life.* [< L *constrict(us)* (ptp. of *constringere* to draw together, tie up), equiv. to *con-* CON- + *stric-* (ptp. s. of *stringere* to tie; see STRICT) + *-tus* ptp. suffix]
—**Syn. 1.** cramp, squeeze, bind, tighten. —**Ant. 1.** expand.

con·stric·tion (kən strik′shən), *n.* **1.** the act of constricting. **2.** the state of being constricted; tightness or inward pressure. **3.** a constricted part. **4.** something that constricts. **5.** *Phonet.* an articulated narrowing of the vocal tract which in consonants audibly obstructs the flow of air and in vowels defines an interconnection between or among resonance cavities. Cf. **closure** (def. 6). [< LL *constrictiōn-* (s. of *constrictiō*), equiv. to L *constrict(us)* (see CONSTRICT) + *-iōn-* -ION]

con·stric·tive (kən strik′tiv), *adj.* **1.** constricting; tending to constrict. **2.** pertaining to constriction. [< LL *constrictīv(us)*, equiv. to *constrict(us)* (see CONSTRICT) + *-īvus* -IVE]

con·stric·tor (kən strik′tər), *n.* **1.** a snake that kills its prey by coiling tightly around it, preventing normal circulation of the blood and causing suffocation. **2.** *Anat.* a muscle that constricts a hollow part of the body, as the pharynx. **3.** one who or that which constricts. [< NL, equiv. to L *constrict(us)* (see CONSTRICT) + *-or* -OR[2]]

con·stringe (kən strinj′), *v.t.,* **-stringed, -string·ing.** to constrict; compress; cause to contract. [< L *constringe(re)* (to) draw tight, tie up, equiv. to *con-* CON- + *stringere* to draw; see CONSTRICT]

con·strin·gent (kən strin′jənt), *adj.* **1.** constricting. **2.** causing constriction. [< L *constringent-* (s. of *constringēns*, prp. of *constringere*). See CONSTRINGE, -ENT] —**con·strin′gen·cy,** *n.*

con·struct (*v.* kən strukt′; *n.* kon′strukt), *v.t.* **1.** to form by putting together parts; build; frame; devise. **2.** *Geom.* to draw (a figure) fulfilling certain given conditions. —*n.* **3.** something constructed. **4.** a complex image or idea formed from a number of simpler images or ideas. [< L *construct(us)* (ptp. of *construere* to CONSTRUE), equiv. to *con-* CON- + *struc-* (ptp. s. of *struere* to build) + *-tus* ptp. suffix] —**con·struct′i·ble,** *adj.* —**con·struc′tor, con·struct′er,** *n.*
—**Syn. 1.** erect, form. See **make.**

con·struc·tion (kən struk′shən), *n.* **1.** the act or art of constructing. **2.** the way in which a thing is constructed; structure: *a building of solid and ingenious construction.* **3.** something that is constructed; a structure. **4.** *Gram.* **a.** the arrangement of two or more forms in a grammatical unit. Constructions involving bound forms are often called morphological, as the bound forms *fif-* and *-teen.* Those involving only free forms are often called syntactic, as *the good man, in the house.* Cf. **bound form, free form.** **b.** a word or phrase consisting of two or more forms arranged in a particular way. **c.** a group of words or morphemes for which there is a rule in some part of the grammar. **5.** explanation or interpretation, as of a law, a text, an action, etc. [ME < L *constructiōn-* (s. of *constructiō*) a putting together, building, equiv. to *construct(us)* (see CONSTRUCT) + *-iōn-* -ION] —**con·struc′tion·al,** *adj.* —**con·struc′tion·al·ly,** *adv.*

construc′tional homonym′ity, *Gram.* the property of a string of morphemes that is susceptible of two or more syntactic analyses, as in *Flying planes can be dangerous, planes* may be either the object of *flying* or the subject of *can.*

con·struc·tion·ist (kən struk′shə nist), *n.* one who construes or interprets, esp. laws or the like, in a specific manner: *a broad constructionist.* [CONSTRUCTION + -IST] —**con·struc′tion·ism,** *n.*

con·struc·tive (kən struk′tiv), *adj.* **1.** constructing or tending to construct; helping to improve (opposed to *destructive*): *constructive criticism.* **2.** of, pertaining to, or of the nature of construction; structural. **3.** deduced by inference or interpretation; inferential: *constructive permission.* **4.** *Law.* noting a legal relation based on facts other than those normally essential to such a relation but in this instance having the same effect: *a constructive contract.* [< ML *constructīv(us)*, equiv. to L *construct(us)* (see CONSTRUCT) + *-īvus* -IVE] —**con·struc′tive·ly,** *adv.* —**con·struc′tive·ness,** *n.*

construc′tive interfer′ence, *Physics.* the interference of two or more waves of equal frequency and phase, resulting in their mutual reinforcement and producing a single amplitude equal to the sum of the amplitudes of the individual waves. Cf. **destructive interference.**

Con·struc·tiv·ism (kən struk′tə viz′əm), *n.* **1.** (*sometimes l.c.*) *Fine Arts.* a nonrepresentational style of art developed by a group of Russian artists principally in the early 20th century, characterized chiefly by a severely formal organization of mass, volume, and space, and by the employment of modern industrial materials and techniques. Cf. **Suprematism.** **2.** (*often l.c.*) *Theat.* a style of scenic design characterized by abstraction, simplification, and stylization rather than realistic imitation. [CONSTRUCTIVE + -ISM] —**Con·struc′tiv·ist,** *n., adj.*

con·strue (*v.* kən stro͞o′ *or, esp. Brit.,* kon′stro͞o; *n.* kon′stro͞o), *v.,* **-strued, -stru·ing,** *n.* —*v.t.* **1.** to show the meaning or intention of; explain; interpret; invest with a particular interpretation: *He construed from her expression that she was furious.* **2.** to deduce by inference or interpretation; infer. **3.** to translate, esp. orally. **4.** to explain the syntax of; to rehearse the applicable grammatical rules of: *to construe a sentence.* **5.** to arrange or combine (words, phrases, etc.) syntactically. —*v.i.* **6.** to admit of grammatical analysis or interpretation. —*n.* **7.** the act of construing. **8.** something that is construed. [ME *construe(n)* < L *construe(re)* (to) put together, build, equiv. to *con-* CON- + *struere* to pile up, arrange, akin to *sternere* to spread; see STRATUM] —**con·stru′a·ble,** *adj.* —**con·stru′a·bil′i·ty,** *n.* —**con·stru′er,** *n.*

con·sub·stan·tial (kon′səb stan′shəl), *adj.* of one and the same substance, essence, or nature. [late ME < LL *consubstantiāl(is)*, equiv. to *con-* CON- + *substanti(a)* SUBSTANCE + *-ālis* -AL[1]] —**con′sub·stan′tial·ism,** *n.* —**con′sub·stan′tial·ist,** *n.* —**con′sub·stan′ti·al′i·ty,** *n.* —**con′sub·stan′tial·ly,** *adv.*

con·sub·stan·ti·ate (kon′səb stan′shē āt′), *v.,* **-at·ed, -at·ing.** —*v.i.* **1.** to profess the doctrine of consubstantiation. **2.** to become united in one common substance or nature. —*v.t.* **3.** to unite in one common substance or nature. **4.** to regard as so united. [< NL *consubstantiāt(us)* (ptp. of *consubstantiāre*), equiv. to *con-* CON- + *substanti(a)* SUBSTANCE + *-ātus* -ATE[1]]

con·sub·stan·ti·a·tion (kon′səb stan′shē ā′shən), *n.* *Theol.* the doctrine that the substance of the body and blood of Christ coexist in and with the substance of bread and wine of the Eucharist. [< NL *consubstantiātiōn-* (s. of *consubstantiātiō*), equiv. to *con-* CON- + *(trans)substantiātiōn-* TRANSUBSTANTIATION]

Con·sue·la (kon swā′lə; *It., Sp.* kôn swe′lä), *n.* a girl's given name. Also, **Con·sue·lo** (kon swā′lō; *It., Sp.,* kôn swe′lô).

con·sue·tude (kon′swi to͞od′, -tyo͞od′), *n.* custom, esp. as having legal force. [ME < L *consuētūd(ō)*, equiv. to *con-* CON- + *suē-* (short s. of *suēscere* to become accustomed, akin to refl. pron. adj. *suus* one's own) + *-tūdō* -TUDE]

con·sue·tu·di·nar·y (kon′swi to͞od′ᵊner′ē, -tyo͞od′-), *adj.* customary or traditional. [late ME < LL *consuētūdināri(us)*, equiv. to *consuētūdin-* (s. of *consuētūdō*) CONSUETUDE + *-ārius* -ARY]

con·sul (kon′səl), *n.* **1.** an official appointed by the government of one country to look after its commercial interests in another. **2.** either of the two chief magistrates of the ancient Roman republic. **3.** *Fr. Hist.* one of the three supreme magistrates of the First Republic during the period 1799–1804. [ME < L < ?] —**con′-su·lar,** *adj.* —**con′sul·ship′,** *n.*

con′sular a′gent, an officer performing the duties of a consul at a place of small commercial importance.

con·su·late (kon′sə lit), *n.* **1.** the premises officially occupied by a consul. **2.** the position, work, authority, or term of service of a consul. **3.** (*often cap.*) a government by consuls, as in France from 1799 to 1804. [< L *consulāt(us),* equiv. to *consul* CONSUL + *-ātus* -ATE[1]]

con′sulate gen′eral, *pl.* **consulates general.** the office or establishment of a consul general.

con′sul gen′eral, *pl.* **consuls general.** a consular officer of the highest rank, as one stationed at a place of considerable commercial importance.

con·sult (*v.* kən sult′; *n.* kon′sult, kən sult′), *v.t.* **1.** to seek advice or information from; ask guidance from: *Consult your lawyer before signing the contract.* **2.** to refer to for information: *Consult your dictionary for the spelling of the word. He consulted his watch for the time.* **3.** to have regard for (a person's interest, convenience, etc.) in making plans. **4.** *Obs.* to meditate, plan, or contrive. **—***v.i.* **5.** to consider or deliberate; take counsel; confer (usually fol. by *with*): *He consulted with his doctor.* **—***n. Archaic.* **6.** a consultation. **7.** a council. [< L *consult(āre)* (to) deliberate, consult, equiv. to *consul(ere)* in same sense (*con-* CON- + *-sulere* < ?) + *-t-* freq. suffix + *-āre* inf. suffix] **—con·sult′a·ble,** *adj.* **—con·sult′er,** *n.*

—Syn. 1. CONSULT, CONFER imply talking over a situation or a subject with someone to decide points in doubt. To CONSULT is to seek from a presumably qualified personal or an impersonal source advice, opinion, etc.: *to consult an authority.* To CONFER is to interchange views in order to throw light on a subject under consideration: *The partners conferred concerning their business.*

con·sult·ant (kən sul′tᵊnt), *n.* **1.** one who consults someone or something. **2.** one who gives professional or expert advice: *a consultant on business methods.* [< L *consultant-* (s. of *consultāns,* prp. of *consultāre*). See CONSULT, -ANT]

con·sul·ta·tion (kon′səl tā′shən), *n.* **1.** the act of consulting; conference. **2.** a meeting for deliberation, discussion, or decision. **3.** *Eng. Law.* a writ returning a case to an ecclesiastical court from a temporal one. [< L *consultātiōn-* (s. of *consultātiō*), equiv. to *consultāt(us)* (ptp. of *consultāre;* see CONSULT, -ATE[1]) + *-iōn-* -ION]

con·sult·a·tive (kən sul′tə tiv), *adj.* of consultation; advisory. Also, **con·sul·ta·to·ry** (kən sul′tə tôr′ē, -tōr′ē), **consultive.** [CONSULTAT(ION) + -IVE] **—con·sult′a·tive·ly,** *adv.*

con·sult·ing (kən sul′ting), *adj.* employed in giving professional advice to the public or to those practicing the profession: *a consulting physician.* [CONSULT + -ING[2]]

con·sul·tive (kən sul′tiv), *adj.* advisory; consultative. [CONSULT + -IVE]

con·sume (kən sōōm′), *v.,* **-sumed, -sum·ing.** **—***v.t.* **1.** to destroy or expend by use; use up. **2.** to eat or drink up; devour. **3.** to destroy, as by decomposition or burning: *Fire consumed the forest.* **4.** to spend (money, time, etc.) wastefully. **5.** to absorb; engross: *She was consumed with curiosity.* **—***v.i.* **6.** to undergo destruction; waste away. [ME < L *consūm(ere),* equiv. to *con-* CON- + *sūmere* to take up (*sub-* SUB- + *emere* to take, get)] **—con·sum′a·ble,** *adj.* **—con·sum′ing·ly,** *adv.* **—con·sum′ing·ness,** *n.*

—Syn. 1. exhaust, expend. **4.** squander, dissipate.

con·sum·ed·ly (kən sōō′mid lē), *adv.* excessively; extremely: *a consumedly decent thing.* [CONSUMED + -LY]

con·sum·er (kən sōō′mər), *n.* **1.** one who or that which consumes. **2.** *Econ.* one who uses a commodity or service. **3.** *Ecol.* an organism, usually an animal, that feeds on plants or other animals. [CONSUME + -ER[1]]

consum′er cred′it, credit extended by a retail store, bank, finance company, or other lender, chiefly for the purchase of consumer goods.

consum′er goods′, *Econ.* goods that are ready for consumption in satisfaction of human wants, as clothing, food, etc., and are not utilized in any further production.

con·sum·er·ism (kən sōō′mər iz′əm), *n.* a modern movement for the protection of the consumer against useless, inferior, or dangerous products, misleading advertising, unfair pricing, etc.

consum′er price′ in′dex, an index of the changes in the cost of goods and services to a typical consumer, based on the costs of the same goods and services at a base period. Also called **cost-of-living index.**

consum′er strike′, a boycott of a product by consumers, often in protest over a raise in its price.

con·sum·mate (*v.* kon′sə māt′; *adj.* kən sum′it, kon′sə mit), *v.,* **-mat·ed, -mat·ing,** *adj.* **—***v.t.* **1.** to bring to completion or perfection. **2.** to complete (a marriage) by sexual intercourse. **—***adj.* **3.** complete or perfect; supremely skilled; superb: *a consummate master of the violin.* [late ME (adj.) < L *consummāt(us)* (ptp. of *consummāre* to complete, bring to perfection), equiv. to *con-* CON- + *summ(a)* SUM + *-ātus* -ATE[1]] **—con·sum′mate·ly,** *adv.* **—con′sum·ma′tive, con·sum·ma·to·ry** (kən sum′ə tôr′ē, -tōr′ē), *adj.* **—con′sum·ma′tor,** *n.*

—Syn. 1. complete, perfect, fulfill, accomplish, achieve. **3.** excellent. **—Ant. 3.** imperfect, unfinished.

con·sum·ma·tion (kon′sə mā′shən), *n.* **1.** the act of consummating; completion. **2.** the state of being consummated; perfection; fulfillment. [ME *consummacion* < L *consummātiōn-* (s. of *consummātiō*). See CONSUMMATE, -ION]

con·sump·tion (kən sump′shən), *n.* **1.** the act of consuming, as by use, decay, or destruction. **2.** the amount consumed: *This automobile has a high consumption of gasoline.* **3.** *Econ.* the using up of goods and services having an exchangeable value. **4.** *Pathol.* **a.** a wasting disease, esp. tuberculosis of the lungs. **b.** progressive wasting of the body. [ME *consumpcyon* < L *consumptiōn-* (s. of *consumptiō*) a consuming, wasting, equiv. to *consumpt(us)* (ptp. of *consūmere* to CONSUME (*con-* CON- + *sump-* (var. s. of *sūmere* to take up, spend) + *-tus* ptp. suffix) + *-iōn-* -ION]

consump′tion weed′, a low, perennial herb, *Pyrola americana,* of eastern North America, having thick, glossy leaves and numerous, sweet-scented, waxy, white flowers. Also called **canker lettuce, Indian lettuce.**

con·sump·tive (kən sump′tiv), *adj.* **1.** tending to consume; destructive; wasteful. **2.** pertaining to consumption by use. **3.** *Pathol.* **a.** pertaining to or of the nature of consumption. **b.** disposed to or affected with consumption. **—***n.* **4.** one who suffers from consumption. [CONSUMPT(ION) + -IVE] **—con·sump′tive·ly,** *adv.* **—con·sump′tive·ness,** *n.*

Con·sus (kon′səs), *n.* the ancient Roman god of horse racing, good counsel, and the protection of grain: often associated with Ops.

Cont., Continental.

cont., **1.** containing. **2.** contents. **3.** continent. **4.** continental. **5.** continue. **6.** continued. **7.** contra. **8.** contract. **9.** (in prescriptions) bruised. [< L *contūsus*]

con·tact (kon′takt), *n.* **1.** the act or state of touching; a touching or meeting, as of two things, people, etc. **2.** immediate proximity or association. **3.** an acquaintance or relative through whom one can gain access to information, favors, and the like. **4.** *Elect.* a junction of electric conductors, usually metal, that controls current flow, often completing or interrupting a circuit. **5.** *Med.* **a.** one who has lately been exposed to an infected person. **b.** inflammation of the skin due to contact with an irritating agent. **6.** *Sociol.* a condition in which two or more individuals or groups are placed in communication with each other. Cf. **categoric contact, primary contact, secondary contact, sympathetic contact.** **—***v.t.* **7.** to put or bring into contact. **8.** to communicate with (a person): *We'll contact you by mail or telephone.* **—***v.i.* **9.** to enter into or be in contact. **—***adj.* **10.** *Aeron.* made in sight of land or water: *contact flight; contact flying.* Cf. **instrument** (def. 8). [< L *contāct(us)* a touching, n. use of *contactus* (ptp. of *contingere*), equiv. to *con-* CON- + *tac-* (var. of *tag-,* var. s. of *tangere, -tingere* to touch) + *-tus* ptp. suffix] **—con·tac·tu·al** (kon tak′chōō əl), *adj.* **—con·tac′tu·al·ly,** *adv.*

—Usage. 7, 8. Many verbs in English have derived from nouns, and, grammatically at least, there is no justification for the criticism commonly heard of CONTACT used in these senses: *He contacted us about the shipments.* Despite the many objections of teachers and editors to this use on personal, stylistic grounds, its currency is so widespread simply because there is no other single verb in the language to express the same idea, that there is little doubt of its becoming universally acceptable in the future.

con·tac·tant (kən tak′tənt), *n. Med.* any substance that might induce an allergy by coming in contact with the skin or a mucous membrane. [CONTACT + -ANT]

con′tact dermati′tis, *Pathol.* inflammation of the skin caused by an allergic reaction to animal, vegetable, or chemical substances.

con′tact lens′, one of a pair of small lenses of glass or plastic that aid defective vision inconspicuously and are held in place over the cornea by surface tension of the eye fluid.

con′tact metamor′phism, *Geol.* metamorphism in rocks that occurs at or near the contact with an igneous intrusion.

con′tact mine′, a naval mine designed to explode on contact with the hull of a ship. Cf. **acoustic mine, magnetic mine.**

con·tac·tor (kon′tak tər, kən tak′tər), *n. Elect.* a mechanically operated switch for continuously establishing and interrupting an electric power circuit. [CONTACT + -OR[2]]

con′tact pa′per, *Photog.* sensitized paper on which a contact print is made.

con′tact poten′tial, *Elect.* the potential generated by the contact of two dissimilar materials in air or in a vacuum. Also called **Volta effect.**

con′tact print′, *Photog.* a print made by placing a negative directly upon sensitized paper and exposing to light.

con′tact print′ing, *Photog.* the process of making contact prints. Cf. **projection printing.**

con′tact proc′ess, *Chem.* a method for producing sulfuric acid by the interaction of sulfur dioxide and oxygen in the presence of a catalyst to form sulfur trioxide, that on hydration yields sulfuric acid.

con·ta·gion (kən tā′jən), *n.* **1.** the communication of disease by direct or indirect contact. **2.** a disease so communicated. **3.** the medium by which a contagious disease is transmitted. **4.** harmful or undesirable contact or influence. **5.** the ready transmission or spread as of an idea, attitude, emotion, etc., from person to person: *A contagion of fear spread through the hall.* [ME < L *contāgiōn-* (s. of *contāgiō*) contact, infection, equiv. to *con-* CON- + *tāg-* (var. s. of *tangere* to touch) + *-iōn-* -ION] **—con·ta′gioned,** *adj.*

con·ta·gious (kən tā′jəs), *adj.* **1.** capable of being transmitted, as from one person to another, by bodily contact with an infected person or object: *contagious diseases.* **2.** carrying or spreading a contagious disease. **3.** tending to spread from person to person: *contagious laughter.* [ME < LL *contāgiōs(us),* equiv. to *contāgi(ō)* CONTAGION + *-ōsus* -OUS] **—con·ta′gious·ly,** *adv.* **—con·ta′gious·ness, con·ta·gi·os·i·ty** (kən tā′jē os′i tē), *n.*

—Syn. 1. catching. **3.** CONTAGIOUS, INFECTIOUS have scientific uses in which they are precisely defined; but in popular use in referring to disease, the words are often confused. In popular figurative use, in which both have favorable connotations, they are differentiated to some extent. CONTAGIOUS emphasizes the rapidity with which the contagion spreads: *Contagious laughter ran through the hall.* INFECTIOUS suggests the pleasantly irresistible quality of the source of contagion: *His infectious humor stimulated applause.*

conta′gious ec′thyma, *Vet. Pathol.* ecthyma.

conta′gious epithelio′ma, *Vet. Pathol.* See **fowl pox.**

conta′gious mag′ic, magic that attempts to affect a person through something once connected with him, as nail clippings, a cloth containing the sweat from his body, or a footprint left in the sand; a branch of sympathetic magic based on the belief that things once in contact are in some way permanently so, however separated physically they may subsequently become. Cf. **imitative magic.**

con·ta·gium (kən tā′jəm, -jē əm), *n., pl.* **-gia** (-jə, -jē ə). *Pathol.* the causative agent of a contagious or infectious disease, as a virus. [< L, equiv. to *contāg-* (see CONTAGION) + *-ium* n. suffix]

con·tain (kən tān′), *v.t.* **1.** to hold or include within its volume or area: *This glass contains water. This paddock contains some of our best horses.* **2.** to be capable of holding; have capacity for: *The room will contain 75 persons safely.* **3.** to have as contents or constituent parts; comprise; include. **4.** to keep under proper control; restrain: *He could not contain his amusement with the ridiculous situation.* **5.** *Math.* (of a number) to be a multiple of; be divisible by, without a remainder: *Ten contains five.* **6.** to be equal to: *A quart contains two pints.* [ME *conte(y)ne* < OF *contenir(r)* < L *continēre,* equiv. to *con-* CON- + *tenēre* to hold] **—con·tain′a·ble,** *adj.*

—Syn. 1. CONTAIN, ACCOMMODATE, HOLD, express the idea that something is so designed that something else can exist or be placed within it. CONTAIN refers to what is actually within a given container. HOLD emphasizes the idea of causing to remain in position, or keeping within bounds; it refers also to the greatest amount or number that can be kept within a given container. ACCOMMODATE means to contain comfortably or conveniently, or to meet the needs of a certain number. A passenger plane which ACCOMMODATES fifty passengers may be able to HOLD sixty, but at a given time may CONTAIN only thirty. **3.** embody, embrace.

con·tained (kən tānd′), *adj.* showing restraint or calmness; controlled; poised: *She was contained throughout the ordeal.* [late ME *conteynyd.* See CONTAIN, -ED[2]] **—con·tain·ed·ly** (kən tā′nid lē), *adv.*

con·tain·er (kən tā′nər), *n.* anything that contains or can contain something, as a carton, box, crate, can, etc. [CONTAIN + -ER[1]]

con·tain·er·board (kən tā′nər bōrd′, -bôrd′), *n.* any paperboard used in making containers, as corrugated paper, cardboard, etc. Also, **contain′er board′.** [CONTAINER + BOARD]

contain′er car′, a flatcar or gondola car for carrying a number of standard, separate, removable containers.

con·tain·er·i·za·tion (kən tā′nər i zā′shən), *n.* shipment of freight in uniform, sealed, reusable containers. [CONTAINERIZE + -ATION]

con·tain·er·ize (kən tā′nə rīz′), *v.t.,* **-ized, -iz·ing.** **1.** to package (freight) in uniform, sealed containers for shipment. **2.** to perform (a materials-handling operation) with the help of containerization. [CONTAINER + -IZE]

contain′er ship′, a ship built to hold containerized cargoes. Also, **contain′ership′.**

con·ta·ki·on (kôn tä′kē ôn; *Eng.* kən tä′kē on′), *n., pl.* **-ki·a** (-kē ä; *Eng.* -kē ə). *Gk. Orth. Ch.* kontakion.

contam., contamination.

con·tam·i·nant (kən tam′ə nənt), *n.* something that contaminates: *to eliminate contaminants in the air and drinking water.* [< L *contāminant-* (s. of *contāmināns*), prp. of *contāmināre.* See CONTAMINATE, -ANT]

con·tam·i·nate (*v.* kən tam′ə nāt′; *adj.* kən tam′ə nit, -nāt′), *v.,* **-nat·ed, -nat·ing,** *adj.* **—***v.t.* **1.** to render impure or unsuitable by contact or mixture with something unclean, bad, etc.: *to contaminate a well with sewage.* **2.** to render harmful or unusable by adding radioactive material to: *to contaminate a laboratory.* **—***adj.* **3.** *Archaic.* contaminated. [< L *contāmināt(us)* (ptp. of *contāmināre*), equiv. to *con-* CON- + *tāmin-* (? for **tagmin-,* s. of **tagmen* a touch, akin to *tangere* to touch; see CONTAGION) + *-ātus* -ATE[1]] **—con·tam′i·na·ble,** *adj.* **—con·tam′i·na′tive,** *adj.* **—con·tam′i·na′tor,** *n.* **—con·tam′i·nous,** *adj.*

—Syn. 1. defile, pollute, befoul, sully, taint, infect, poison, corrupt.

con·tam·i·na·tion (kən tam′ə nā′shən), *n.* **1.** the act of contaminating. **2.** the state of being contaminated. **3.** something that contaminates. [< LL *contāminātiōn-* (s. of *contāminātiō*), equiv. to *contāmināt(us)* (see CONTAMINATE) + *-iōn-* -ION]

con·tang·o (kən tang′gō), *n., pl.* **-gos, -goes.** (on the London stock exchange) a fee paid by a buyer of securities to the seller for the privilege of deferring his payment. Also called **continuation.** Cf. **backwardation.** [said to be m. of CONTINUE OR CONTINGENT]

contd., continued.

conte (kônt), *n., pl.* **contes** (kônt; *Eng.* kônts). *French.* a tale or short story, esp. of extraordinary and usually imaginary events.

con·té (kôn tā′, kon′tē; *Fr.* kôN tā′), *n., pl.* **-tés** (-tāz′, -tēz; *Fr.* -tā′). a hard crayon of graphite and clay, usually made in black, red, or brown colors. Also called **conté′ cray′on.** [named after N. J. *Conté,* 18th-century French chemist, who invented it]

con·temn (kən tem′), *v.t.* to treat or regard with disdain, scorn, or contempt. [late ME *contempne* < L *contem(p)nā(re)* to despise, scorn, equiv. to *con-* CON- + *temnere* to slight] **—con·temn·er** (kən tem′ər, -tem′nər), **con·tem·nor** (kən tem′nər), *n.* **—con·tem·ni·ble** (kən tem′nə bəl), *adj.* **—con·tem′ni·bly,** *adv.* **—con·temn′ing·ly,** *adv.*

—Syn. scorn, disdain, despise.

contemp., contemporary.

con·tem·pla·ble (kən tem′plə bəl), *adj.* fit to be or capable of being contemplated. [< LL *contemplābil(is),* equiv. to L *contemplā(re), contemplārī* (see CONTEMPLATE) + *-bilis* -BLE]

con·tem·plate (kon′təm plāt′, kən tem′plāt), *v.,* **-plat·ed, -plat·ing.** **—***v.t.* **1.** to look at or view with continued attention; observe thoughtfully: *to contemplate the stars.* **2.** to consider thoroughly; think fully or deeply about: *to contemplate a problem.* **3.** to have as a purpose; intend. **4.** to have in view as a future event: *to contemplate buying a new car.* **—***v.i.* **5.** to think studiously; meditate; consider deliberately. [< L *contemplāt(us)* (ptp. of *contemplāre, contemplārī* to survey, observe, equiv. to *con-* CON- + *templ(um)* space in heavens marked off for augural observation (possibly akin to Gk *témnein* to cut; see -TOMY) + *-ātus* -ATE[1]] **—con′tem·plat′ing·ly,** *adv.* **—con′tem·pla′tor,** *n.*

—Syn. 1. observe, regard, survey. **2.** study, ponder. **3.** design, plan.

con·tem·pla·tion (kon′təm plā′shən), *n.* **1.** the act of contemplating; thoughtful observation. **2.** full or deep consideration; reflection: *religious contemplation.* **3.** purpose or intention. **4.** prospect or expectation. [< L *contemplātiōn-* (s. of *contemplātiō*); see CONTEMPLATE, -ION; r. ME *contemplaci(o)un* < AF]

con·tem·pla·tive (kən tem′plə tiv, kon′təm plā′-), *adj.* **1.** given to or characterized by contemplation: *a contemplative mind.* **—***n.* **2.** one inclined or devoted to contemplation, as a monk. [< L *contemplātīv(us),* equiv. to *contemplāt(us)* (see CONTEMPLATE) + *-īvus* -IVE; r. ME *contemplatif* < MF] **—con·tem′pla·tive·ly,** *adv.* **—con·tem′pla·tive·ness,** *n.*

—Syn. 1. thoughtful, reflective, meditative. **—Ant. 1.** active.

con·tem·po·ra·ne·ous (kən tem′pə rā′nē əs), *adj.* contemporary: *This is a musical form contemporaneous with romantic art.* Also, **cotemporaneous.** [< L *contemporāneus*, equiv. to *con-* CON- + *tempor-* (s. of *tempus* time) + *-āneus* (*-ān(us)* -AN + *-eus* -EOUS)] —**con·tem·po·ra·ne·i·ty** (kən tem′pər ə nē′i tē), **con·tem′po·ra′ne·ous·ness,** *n.* —**con·tem′po·ra′ne·ous·ly,** *adv.*
—**Syn.** simultaneous, concurrent.

con·tem·po·rar·y (kən tem′pə rer′ē), *adj., n., pl.* **-rar·ies.** —*adj.* **1.** existing, occurring, or living at the same time; belonging to the same time: *Newton's discovery of the calculus was contemporary with that of Leibnitz.* **2.** of the same age or date: *a Georgian table with a contemporary wig stand.* **3.** of the present time: *a lecture on the contemporary novel.* —*n.* **4.** one belonging to the same time or period with another or others. **5.** a person of the same age as another. Also, **cotemporary.** [< LL *contempor-* (see CONTEMPORIZE) + -ARY] —**con·tem′po·rar′i·ly,** *adv.* —**con·tem′po·rar′i·ness,** *n.*
—**Syn. 1.** coeval, coexistent; concurrent, simultaneous.

con·tem·po·rise (kən tem′pə rīz′), *v.t., v.i.,* **-rised, -ris·ing.** *Chiefly Brit.* contemporize.

con·tem·po·rize (kən tem′pə rīz′), *v.,* **-rized, -riz·ing.** —*v.t.* **1.** to place in or regard as belonging to the same age or time. —*v.i.* **2.** to be contemporary. [< LL *contempor-* (s. of *contemporāre* to be at the same time), equiv. to *con-* CON- + *tempor-* (s. of *tempus* time) + -IZE]

con·tempt (kən tempt′), *n.* **1.** the feeling with which one regards anything considered mean, vile, or worthless; disdain; scorn. **2.** the state of being despised; dishonor; disgrace. **3.** *Law.* **a.** willful disobedience to or open disrespect for the rules or orders of a court (**contempt′ of court′**) or legislative body. **b.** an act showing such disrespect. [< L *contempt(us)* a slighting, n. use of *contemptus* scorned (ptp. of *contemnere* to CONTEMN), equiv. to *con-* CON- + *temp-* (var. s. of *temnere* to scorn) + *-tus* ptp. ending]
—**Syn. 1.** contumely. CONTEMPT, DISDAIN, SCORN imply strong feelings of disapproval combined with disgust or derision. CONTEMPT is disapproval tinged with disgust for what seems mean, base, or worthless: *to feel contempt for a weakling.* DISDAIN is a feeling that something is beneath the level of one's own dignity or is unworthy of one's notice or acceptance: *disdain for crooked dealing.* SCORN denotes derisive, open, or undisguised contempt, as for a thing thought unworthy of considerate treatment: *He showed only scorn for those who had not been as ambitious as himself.* —**Ant. 1.** respect.

con·tempt·i·ble (kən temp′tə bəl), *adj.* **1.** deserving of or held in contempt; despicable. **2.** *Obs.* contemptuous. [< LL *contemptibil(is)*, equiv. to *contempt(us)* (see CONTEMPT) + *-ibilis* -IBLE] —**con·tempt′i·bil′i·ty, con·tempt′i·ble·ness,** *n.* —**con·tempt′i·bly,** *adv.*
—**Syn. 1.** mean, abject, low, base. —**Ant. 1.** admirable.

contempt′ of Con′gress, *U.S.* contempt of a Congressional body, as an investigating committee, shown by a witness summoned or appearing before it.

con·temp·tu·ous (kən temp′cho͞o əs), *adj.* manifesting or expressing contempt or disdain; scornful. [< L *contemptu(s)* CONTEMPT + -OUS] —**con·temp′tu·ous·ly,** *adv.* —**con·temp′tu·ous·ness,** *n.*
—**Syn.** disdainful, sneering, insolent, arrogant, supercilious, haughty. —**Ant.** respectful.

con·tend (kən tend′), *v.i.* **1.** to struggle in opposition: *to contend with the enemy for control of the port.* **2.** to strive in rivalry; compete; vie: *to contend for first prize.* **3.** to strive in debate; dispute earnestly: *to contend against falsehood.* —*v.t.* **4.** to assert or maintain earnestly: *He contended that taxes were too high.* [< L *contend(ere)* (to) stretch vigorously, strive, equiv. to *con-* CON- + *tendere* to stretch; see TEND[1]] —**con·tend′ing·ly,** *adv.*
—**Syn. 1.** wrestle, grapple, battle, fight. **2.** See **compete. 3.** argue, wrangle. **4.** hold, claim. —**Ant. 3.** agree.

con·tent[1] (kon′tent; *rarely* kən tent′), *n.* **1.** Usually, **contents. a.** something that is contained: *the contents of a box.* **b.** the subjects or topics covered in a book or document. **c.** the chapters or other formal divisions of a book or document: *a table of contents.* **2.** that which is to be expressed through some medium, as speech, writing, or any of various arts: *a poetic form adequate to a poetic content.* **3.** significance or profundity: *a clever play that lacks content.* **4.** that which may be perceived in something: *the latent versus the manifest content of a dream.* **5.** *Philos., Logic.* the sum of the attributes or notions comprised in a given conception; the substance or matter of cognition. **6.** power of containing; holding capacity: *The bowl's content is three quarts.* **7.** volume, area, or extent; size. **8.** the amount contained. **9.** *Ling.* the system of meanings or semantic values specific to a language (opposed to *expression*). **10.** *Math.* the greatest common divisor of all the coefficients of a given polynomial. Cf. **primitive polynomial.** [< L *content(um)*, n. use of neut. of *contentus* contained (ptp. of *continēre*), equiv. to *con-* CON- + *ten-* hold + *-tus* ptp. suffix]

con·tent[2] (kən tent′), *adj.* **1.** satisfied with what one is or has; not wanting more or anything else; satisfied. **2.** *Brit.* agreeing; assenting. **3.** *Archaic.* willing. —*v.t.* **4.** to make content: *These things content me.* —*n.* **5.** the state or feeling of being contented; contentment: *His content was threatened.* **6.** (in the British House of Lords) an affirmative vote or voter. [late ME < MF < L *content(us)* satisfied, special use of ptp. of *continēre*; see CONTENT[1]] —**con·tent′a·ble,** *adj.* —**con·tent′ly,** *adv.* —**con·tent′ness,** *n.*
—**Syn. 4.** appease, gratify. See **satisfy.** —**Ant. 4.** dissatisfy.

con′tent anal′ysis, analysis to determine the meaning, purpose, or effect of any type of communication, as literature, newspapers, broadcasts, etc., by studying and evaluating the details, innuendoes, and implications of the content, recurrent themes, etc.

con·tent·ed (kən ten′tid), *adj.* satisfied, as with what one has or with something mentioned; content. [CONTENT[2] + -ED[2]] —**con·tent′ed·ly,** *adv.* —**con·tent′ed·ness,** *n.*

con·ten·tion (kən ten′shən), *n.* **1.** a struggling together in opposition; strife. **2.** a striving in rivalry; competition; contest. **3.** strife in debate; dispute; controversy. **4.** a point contended for or affirmed in controversy. [ME < L *contentiōn-* (s. of *contentiō*), equiv. to *content(us)*, ptp. of *contendere* to CONTEND (*con-* CON- + *tentus*, alter. of *tensus*; see TENSE[1]) + *-iōn-* -ION] —**con·ten′tion·al,** *adj.*
—**Syn. 1.** struggle, conflict, combat. **3.** disagreement, dissension, debate, wrangle, altercation. —**Ant. 3.** agreement.

con·ten·tious (kən ten′shəs), *adj.* **1.** tending to argument or strife; quarrelsome: *a contentious crew.* **2.** causing, involving, or characterized by argument or controversy: *contentious issues.* **3.** *Law.* pertaining to causes between contending parties. [late ME *contencious* < L *contentiōs(us)*, equiv. to *contenti(ō)* CONTENTION + *-ōsus* -OUS] —**con·ten′tious·ly,** *adv.* —**con·ten′tious·ness,** *n.*
—**Syn. 1.** competitive.

con·tent·ment (kən tent′mənt), *n.* **1.** the state of being contented; satisfaction; ease of mind. **2.** *Archaic.* the act of making contentedly satisfied. [late ME *contentement* < MF. See CONTENT[2], -MENT]
—**Syn. 1.** See **happiness.**

con·ter·mi·nous (kən tûr′mə nəs), *adj.* **1.** having a common boundary; bordering; contiguous. **2.** meeting at the ends; without an intervening gap: *In our calendar system, the close of one year is conterminous with the beginning of the next.* **3.** having the same boundaries or limits; coextensive. Also, **con·ter′mi·nal, coterminous.** [< L *conterminus* having a common border with, equiv. to *con-* CON- + *terminus* TERMINUS] —**con·ter′mi·nous·ly,** *adv.* —**con·ter′mi·nous·ness,** *n.*

con·test (*n.* kon′test; *v.* kən test′), *n.* **1.** struggle for victory or superiority. **2.** a race, conflict, or other competition between rivals, as for a prize. **3.** strife in argument; dispute; controversy: *Their marriage was marred by perpetual contest.* —*v.t.* **4.** to struggle or fight for, as in battle. **5.** to argue against; dispute: *to contest a controversial question; to contest a will.* **6.** to call in question: *They contested his right to speak.* **7.** to contend for in rivalry. —*v.i.* **8.** to dispute; contend; compete. [< legal L *contest(ārī)* (to) call to witness (in a lawsuit), equiv. to *con-* CON- + *testārī* to testify, deriv. of *testis* witness] —**con·test′a·ble,** *adj.* —**con·test′a·ble·ness,** *n.* —**con·test′a·bly,** *adv.* —**con·test′er,** *n.* —**con·test′ing·ly,** *adv.*
—**Syn. 1.** battle, encounter. See **fight. 2.** contention, rivalry, match, tournament, tourney, game. **3.** debate, argument, altercation. **4.** See **compete. 5.** controvert, oppose. **6.** challenge. **7.** strive, compete, vie.

con·test·ant (kən tes′tənt), *n.* **1.** one who takes part in a contest or competition. **2.** one who contests the results of an election. **3.** *Law.* the party who, in proceedings in the probate court, contests the validity of a will. [< F; see CONTEST, -ANT]

con·tes·ta·tion (kon′te stā′shən), *n.* **1.** the act of contesting; controversy; dispute. **2.** an assertion contended for. [< L *contestātiōn-* (s. of *contestātiō*). See CONTEST, -ATION]

con·text (kon′tekst), *n.* **1.** the parts of a written or spoken statement that precede or follow a specific word or passage, usually influencing its meaning or effect: *You have misinterpreted my sentence because you took it out of context.* **2.** the set of circumstances or facts that surround a particular event, situation, etc. [late ME < L *context(us)* a joining together, n. use of *contextus* (ptp. of *contexere*), equiv. to *con-* CON- + *tex-* (s. of *texere* to plait, interweave) + *-tus* ptp. ending]

con·tex·tu·al (kən teks′cho͞o əl), *adj.* of, pertaining to, or depending on the context. [< L *contextu(s)* CONTEXT + -AL[1]] —**con·tex′tu·al·ly,** *adv.*

contex′tual defini′tion, *Logic, Philos.* definition of a word or symbol by explaining the meaning of the phrase or statement in which it occurs.

con·tex·ture (kən teks′chər), *n.* **1.** the arrangement and union of the constituent parts of anything; constitution; structure. **2.** an interwoven structure; fabric. **3.** the act of weaving together. **4.** the process or manner of being woven together. [< F; see CONTEXT, -URE] —**con·tex′tur·al,** *adj.* —**con·tex′tured,** *adj.*

contg., containing.

con·ti·gu·i·ty (kon′tə gyo͞o′i tē), *n., pl.* **-ties. 1.** the state of being contiguous; contact or proximity. **2.** a series of things in continuous connection; a continuous mass or extent. [< LL *contiguitās*. See CONTIGUOUS, -ITY]

con·tig·u·ous (kən tig′yo͞o əs), *adj.* **1.** touching; in contact. **2.** in close proximity without actually touching; near. [< L *contiguus* bordering upon, equiv. to *con-* CON- + *tig-* (perf. s. of *-tingere*, comb. form of *tangere* to touch; see TANGENT, CONTINGENT, CONTAGION) + *-uus* -OUS] —**con·tig′u·ous·ly,** *adv.* —**con·tig′u·ous·ness,** *n.*
—**Syn. 1.** bordering, adjoining, abutting. **2.** adjacent.

contin., continued.

con·ti·nence (kon′tᵊnəns), *n.* self-restraint, esp. in regard to sexual passion or activity; temperance; moderation. Also, **con′ti·nen·cy.** [ME < L *continentia*. See CONTINENT, -ENCE]

con·ti·nent (kon′tᵊnənt), *n.* **1.** one of the main land masses of the globe, usually reckoned as seven in number (Europe, Asia, Africa, North America, South America, Australia and Antarctica). **2.** the mainland, as distinguished from islands or peninsulas. **3. the Continent,** the mainland of Europe, as distinguished from the British Isles. **4.** a continuous tract or extent, as of land. **5.** *Archaic.* something that serves as a container or boundary. —*adj.* **6.** exercising or characterized by restraint in relation to the desires or passions and esp. to sexual desires; temperate. **7.** *Archaic.* containing; being a container; capacious. **8.** *Obs.* restraining or restrictive. **9.** *Obs.* continuous; forming an uninterrupted tract, as land. [ME < L *continent-* (s. of *continēns*, prp. of *continēre* to CONTAIN), equiv. to *con-* CON- + *tin-*, var. of *ten-* hold + *-ent-* -ENT]

con·ti·nen·tal (kon′tᵊnen′tᵊl), *adj.* **1.** of or of the nature of a continent. **2.** (*usually cap.*) of or pertaining to the mainland of Europe. **3.** (*cap.*) of or pertaining to the 13 original American colonies during and immediately after the American Revolution. **4.** of or pertaining to the continent of North America. —*n.* **5.** (*cap.*) a soldier of the Continental army in the American Revolution. **6.** a piece of paper currency issued by the Continental Congress during the American Revolution. **7.** a small amount: *advice that's not worth a continental.* **8.** an inhabitant of a continent. **9.** (*usually cap.*) an inhabitant of the mainland of Europe. [CONTINENT + -AL[1]] —**con′ti·nen′tal·ly,** *adv.*

con′tinen′tal break′fast, a breakfast consisting of bread and a hot beverage, as croissants and café au lait.

Con′tinen′tal Cel′tic, Celtic as spoken and written in ancient times on the mainland of Europe. Gaulish is the only known language that fits this description. Cf. **Insular Celtic.**

con′tinen′tal code′. See **international Morse code.**

Con′tinen′tal Con′gress, *Amer. Hist.* one of two legislative congresses during and after the Revolutionary War. The first was in session from September 5 to October 26, 1774, to petition the British government for a redress of grievances. The second existed from May 10, 1775 to 1789, and issued the Declaration of Independence and established the Articles of Confederation.

continen′tal divide′, 1. a divide separating river systems which flow to opposite sides of a continent. **2.** (*caps.*) (in North America) the line of summits of the Rocky Mountains, separating streams flowing toward the Gulf of California and the Pacific from those flowing toward the Gulf of Mexico, Hudson Bay, and the Arctic Ocean.

con′tinen′tal drift′, the hypothetical tendency or ability of continents to drift on the earth's surface because of the weakness of the suboceanic crust.

con·ti·nen·tal·ism (kon′tᵊnen′tᵊliz′əm), *n.* **1.** an attitude, expression, etc., characteristic of a continent, esp. of Europe. **2.** an attitude or policy of favoritism or partiality to a continent: *American continentalism.* [CONTINENTAL + -ISM] —**con′ti·nen′tal·ist,** *n.*

con·ti·nen·tal·i·ty (kon′tᵊnən tal′i tē), *n.* the degree to which the climate of a region typifies that of the interior of a large land mass. Cf. **oceanicity.** [CONTINENTAL + -ITY]

con′tinen′tal shelf′, *Phys. Geog.* the part of a continent that is submerged in relatively shallow sea.

con′tinen′tal slope′, *Phys. Geog.* a steep slope separating a continental shelf and a deep ocean basin.

continen′tal sys′tem. See **French system.**

con·ti·nent·ly (kon′tᵊnənt lē), *adv.* in a continent manner; temperately. [CONTINENT + -LY]

con·tin·gence (kən tin′jəns), *n.* contact or tangency. [CONTING(ENT) + -ENCE]

con·tin·gen·cy (kən tin′jən sē), *n., pl.* **-cies. 1.** dependence on chance or on the fulfillment of a condition; uncertainty; fortuitousness: *Nothing was left to contingency.* **2.** a contingent event; a chance, accident, or possibility, conditional on something uncertain: *He was prepared for every contingency.* **3.** something incidental to a thing. [CONTING(ENT) + -ENCY]

contin′gency fund′, *Accounting.* money or securities set aside to cover unexpected conditions or losses in business, usually supplementing a contingency reserve. Also, **contin′gent fund′.**

contin′gency reserve′, *Accounting.* an amount of money established from retained earnings to allow for unforeseen losses in business. Also, **contin′gent reserve′.**

contin′gency ta′ble, *Statistics.* the frequency distribution for a two-way statistical classification.

con·tin·gent (kən tin′jənt), *adj.* **1.** dependent for existence, occurrence, character, etc., on something not yet certain; conditional (often fol. by *on* or *upon*): *Our plans are contingent on the weather.* **2.** liable to happen or not; uncertain; possible: *They had to plan for contingent expenses.* **3.** happening by chance or without known cause; fortuitous; accidental: *contingent occurrences that cannot be foreseen.* **4.** *Logic.* (of a proposition) neither logically necessary nor logically impossible, so that its truth or falsity can be established only by sensory observation. —*n.* **5.** the proportion that falls to one as a share to be contributed or furnished. **6.** a quota of troops furnished. **7.** any one of the representative groups composing an assemblage: *the New York contingent at a national convention.* **8.** something contingent; contingency. [late ME < L *contingent-* (s. of *contingēns*, prp. of *contingere*), equiv. to *con-* CON- + *ting-*, var. s. of *tangere* to touch + *-ent-* -ENT] —**con·tin′gent·ly,** *adv.*

contin′gent benefi′ciary, *Insurance.* a person who becomes the beneficiary if the primary beneficiary dies or is otherwise disqualified.

contin′gent fee′, a fee paid to a lawyer conducting a suit, esp. a suit for damages, in the event that the suit is successful and generally based on a percentage of the sum recovered.

contin′gent liabil′ity, a liability dependent upon the occurrence of a particular event, as default by the maker of a guaranteed loan.

con·tin·u·al (kən tin′yo͞o əl), *adj.* **1.** happening without interruption or cessation; continuous in time. **2.** of regular or frequent recurrence; often repeated; very frequent: *These buses make continual runs between Boston and New York.* [< ML *continuāl(is)*, equiv. to L *continu(us)* CONTINUOUS + *-ālis* -AL[1]; r. ME *continuel* < MF] —**con·tin′u·al′i·ty, con·tin′u·al·ness,** *n.*
—**Syn. 1.** unceasing, ceaseless, incessant, uninterrupted, unremitting, unbroken, permanent, unending. **1, 2.** CONTINUAL, CONSTANT, CONTINUOUS all refer to a succession of occurrences. CONTINUAL implies that successive recurrences are very close together, with only small breaks between them, or none at all: *continual misunderstanding between nations.* CONSTANT implies always recurring in the same way, under uniform conditions, with similar results, and the like: *constant repetition of the same mistakes.* CONTINUOUS emphasizes the idea that the succession is unbroken: *the continuous life of the universe.* **2.** successive, recurrent, repetitive, repetitious.

con·tin·u·al·ly (kən tin′yo͞o ə lē), *adv.* **1.** without cessation or intermission; unceasingly. **2.** very often; at regular or frequent intervals; habitually. [ME *continuelli, continueliche*. See CONTINUAL, -LY]

con·tin·u·ance (kən tin′yo͞o əns), *n.* **1.** an act or instance of continuing; continuation: *a continuance of war.* **2.** a remaining in the same place, condition, etc. **3.** sequel. **4.** *Law.* adjournment of a step in a proceeding to a future day. [ME < MF; see CONTINUE, -ANCE]

con·tin·u·ant (kən tin′yo͞o ənt), *n.* *Phonet.* a consonant, as *f* or *s*, that may be prolonged without change of quality. Cf. **stop** (def. 37a). [< L *continuant-*, s. of *continuāns*, prp. of *continuāre* to CONTINUE; see -ANT]

con·tin·u·ate (kən tin′yo͞o āt′), *adj.* *Obs.* continuing; uninterrupted. [< L *continuāt(us)*, ptp. of *continuāre* to CONTINUE; see -ATE[1]] —**con·tin′u·ate′ly,** *adv.* —**con·tin′u·ate′ness,** *n.*

con·tin·u·a·tion (kən tin′yo͞o ā′shən), *n.* **1.** the act or state of continuing; the state of being continued. **2.** extension or carrying on to a further point: *to request the continuation of a loan.* **3.** that which continues some preceding thing by being of the same kind or having a sim-

CONCISE ETYMOLOGY KEY: <, descended or derived from; >, whence; b., blend of, blended; c., cognate with; deriv., derivative; equiv., equivalent; imit., imitative; m., modification of; obl., oblique; r., replacing; s., stem; sp., spelling; trans., translation; ?, origin unknown, perhaps; *, hypothetical. See the full key inside the front cover.

ilar content: *Today's weather will be a continuation of yesterday's. A sequel is a continuation of a previously published story.* **4.** *Library Science.* a publication issued more or less regularly over an indefinite period. **5.** *Stock Exchange Brit.* contango. [ME *continuacio(u)n* < L *continuātiōn-* (s. of *continuātiō*). See CONTINUATE, -ION]

continua′tion school′, a school providing extension courses for people who have left school in the elementary grades to go to work.

con·tin·u·a·tive (kən tin′yo͞o ā′tiv, -ə tiv), *adj.* **1.** tending or serving to continue; causing continuation or prolongation. **2.** expressing continuance of thought. **3.** expressing a following event. In *They arrested a suspect, who gave his name as John Doe,* the second clause is continuative. **4.** (of a verbal form or aspect) expressing continuation. —*n.* **5.** something continuative. **6.** a continuative word or expression. [< LL *continuātīv(us)* connecting, copulative. See CONTINUATE, -IVE] —**con·tin′u·a′tive·ly,** *adv.* —**con·tin′u·a′tive·ness,** *n.*

con·tin·u·a·tor (kən tin′yo͞o ā′tər), *n.* one who or that which continues. [CONTINUATE + -OR[2]]

con·tin·ue (kən tin′yo͞o), *v.,* **-ued, -u·ing.** —*v.i.* **1.** to go on or keep on, as in some course or action; extend: *The road continues for three miles.* **2.** to go on after suspension or interruption: *The program continued after an intermission.* **3.** to last or endure: *The famine continued for two months.* **4.** to remain in a place; abide; stay: *Let us continue in this house forever.* **5.** to remain in a particular state or capacity: *The general agreed to continue in command of the army.* —*v.t.* **6.** to go on with or persist in: *to continue an action.* **7.** to extend from one point to another in space; prolong. **8.** to carry on from the point of suspension or interruption: *He continued the poem after the latecomers were seated.* **9.** to say in continuation. **10.** to cause to last or endure; maintain or retain, as in a position. **11.** to carry over, postpone, or adjourn; keep pending, as a legal proceeding. [ME *continue(n)* < L *continuāre* to make all one, deriv. of *continuus* CONTINUOUS] —**con·tin′u·a·ble,** *adj.* —**con·tin′ued·ly,** *adv.* —**con·tin′ued·ness,** *n.* —**con·tin′u·er,** *n.* —**con·tin′u·ing·ly,** *adv.*

—**Syn. 3.** CONTINUE, ENDURE, PERSIST, PERSEVERE, LAST, REMAIN imply existing uninterruptedly for an appreciable length of time. CONTINUE implies duration or existence without break or interruption: *The rain continued two days.* ENDURE, used of people or things, implies persistent continuance against influences that tend to weaken, undermine, or destroy: *The family endured years of poverty. Brass endures through many years.* PERSIST and PERSEVERE, used principally of people, both imply firm and steadfast continuance in the face of opposition. PERSIST suggests human opposition: *He persisted after he had been warned;* and PERSEVERE suggests opposition from any source, often an impersonal one: *He persevered despite fatigue, heat and cold, and general disbelief.* LAST often applies to that which holds out to a desired end, fresh, unimpaired, or unexhausted, sometimes under conditions that tend to produce the opposite effect: *They had provisions enough to last all winter.* REMAIN is esp. applied to what continues without change in its essential state: *He remained a bachelor.* —**Ant. 1.** cease.

contin′ued frac′tion, *Math.* a fraction whose denominator contains a fraction whose denominator contains a fraction, and so on, as

$$\cfrac{2}{7+\cfrac{1}{9+\cfrac{3}{4+\cdots}}}$$

contin′ued propor′tion, *Math.* an ordered set of numbers such that the ratio between any two successive terms is the same, as 1:3:9:27:81.

con·ti·nu·i·ty (kon′ti no͞o′i tē, -nyo͞o′-, kon′tənoo′-, -tənyo͞o′-), *n., pl.* **-ties** for 3, 4, 5. **1.** the state or quality of being continuous. **2.** a continuous or connected whole. **3.** a motion-picture scenario giving the complete action, scenes, etc., in detail and in the order in which they are to be shown on the screen. **4.** the spoken part of a radio script that serves as introductory or transitional material on a nondramatic program. **5.** *Math.* the property of a continuous function. [late ME *continuite* < MF < L *continuitāt-* (s. of *continuitās*), equiv. to *continu(us)* CONTINUOUS + *-itāt-* -ITY]

continu′ity equa′tion, *Mech.* the mathematical statement in fluid mechanics, that, for a fluid passing through a tube in a steady flow, the mass flowing through any section of the tube in a unit of time is constant.

continu′ity girl′, *Motion Pictures.* a secretary whose records of the details of each take are of special use in determining or directing the process of editing the film. Also called **continu′ity clerk′.**

con·tin·u·o (kən tin′yo͞o ō′), *n., pl.* **-tin·u·os.** *Music.* a keyboard accompanying part consisting originally of a figured bass, which in modern scores is usually realized, and serving to provide or fill out the harmonic texture. [< It: lit., continuous]

con·tin·u·ous (kən tin′yo͞o əs), *adj.* **1.** being in immediate connection or relation: *a continuous series of blasts.* **2.** uninterrupted in time; without cessation: *continuous coughing during the concert.* **3.** *Math.* **a.** (of a function at a point in its domain) having limit equal to the value of the function at the point; having the property that for any small number, a second number can be found such that when the distance between any other point in the domain and the given point is less than the second number, the difference in the functional values at the two points is less in absolute value than the first number. **b.** (of a function at a point in a topological space) having the property that for any open set containing the image of the point, an open set about the given point can be found such that the image of the set is contained in the first open set. **c.** (of a function on a set in its domain or in a topological space) continuous at every point of the set. [< L *continuus* holding together, equiv. to *continu-* (perf. s. of *continēre,* equiv. to *con-* CON- + *-tinēre,* var. of *tenēre* to hold) + *-us* -OUS] —**con·tin′u·ous·ly,** *adv.* —**con·tin′u·ous·ness,** *n.*

—**Syn. 2.** See **continual.**

contin′uous brake′, (in a railroad train, or the like) a system of interconnected brakes controlled from a single point.

contin′uous cast′ing, *Foundry.* a technique of casting of ingots, bars, etc., in which the metal is poured into an open-ended mold, being withdrawn as it solidifies so that the solid portion of the piece retains the fluid portion within the mold.

con·tin′u·ous-ex·pan′sion en′gine (kən tin′-yo͞o əs ik span′shən), a steam engine in which a high-pressure cylinder is partly exhausted into a low-pressure cylinder during each stroke.

contin′uous spec′trum, *Physics.* a spectrum apparently having all wavelengths over a comparatively wide range, usually characteristic of solids and other substances at high temperatures.

contin′uous tone′, a photographic image the tones of which vary continuously in depth.

contin′uous waves′, *Radio.* electric waves that are not intermittent or broken up into damped wave trains, but, unless intentionally interrupted, follow one another without any interval of time between.

con·tin·u·um (kən tin′yo͞o əm), *n., pl.* **-tin·u·a** (-tin′-yo͞o ə). **1.** a continuous extent, series, or whole. **2.** *Math.* **a.** a set of elements such that between any two of them there is a third element. **b.** the set of all real numbers. **c.** any compact, connected set containing at least two elements. [< L, neut. of *continuus* CONTINUOUS]

contin′uum hypoth′esis, *Math.* a conjecture of set theory that the first infinite cardinal number greater than the cardinal number of the set of all positive integers is the cardinal number of the set of all real numbers.

con·to (kon′tō; *Port.* kôn′to͞o), *n., pl.* **-tos** (-tōz; *in Portugal* -to͞osh; *in Brazil* -to͞os). **1.** a money of account in Portugal equal to 1000 escudos. **2.** a former money of account in Portugal and Brazil equal to 1000 milreis. [< Pg < LL *computus* reckoning, deriv. of L *computāre* to COMPUTE; see COUNT[1]]

con·toid (kon′toid), *Phonet.* —*adj.* **1.** consonantlike. —*n.* **2.** a consonantlike sound. Cf. **vocoid.** [CON(SO-NAN)T + -OID]

con·to·ise (kon′tō ēz′), *n.* (loosely) a cointise.

con·tort (kən tôrt′), *v.t.* to twist; bend or draw out of shape; distort. [< L *contort(us)* twisted together, ptp. of *contorquēre.* See CON-, TORT]

con·tort·ed (kən tôr′tid), *adj.* **1.** twisted in a violent manner; distorted. **2.** twisted back on itself; convoluted. [CONTORT + -ED[2]] —**con·tort′ed·ly,** *adv.* —**con·tort′ed·ness,** *n.*

con·tor·tion (kən tôr′shən), *n.* **1.** the act or process of contorting. **2.** the state of being contorted. **3.** a contorted position: *When the fit was on him, he would go into alarming contortions.* **4.** something contorted or twisted, as in position, meaning, etc.: *His account of the incident was a complete contortion of fact.* [< L *contortiōn-* (s. of *contortiō*) a whirling around. See CONTORT, -ION] —**con·tor′tion·al,** *adj.* —**con·tor′tioned,** *adj.*

con·tor·tion·ist (kən tôr′shə nist), *n.* **1.** one who performs gymnastic feats involving contorted postures. **2.** one who practices contortion: *a verbal contortionist.* [CONTORTION + -IST] —**con·tor′tion·is′tic,** *adj.*

con·tor·tive (kən tôr′tiv), *adj.* characterized by, tending toward, or causing contortions or twisting: *contortive movements; contortive pain; contortive alleyways.* [CONTORT + -IVE] —**con·tor′tive·ly,** *adv.*

con·tour (kon′to͝or), *n.* **1.** the outline of a figure or body; the line that defines or bounds anything. **2.** See **contour line.** —*v.t.* **3.** to mark with contour lines. **4.** to make or form the contour or outline of. **5.** to build (a road, railroad track, etc.) in conformity with the contour of the land. —*adj.* **6.** of or used in a system of plowing, cultivating, sowing, etc., along the contour lines of the land in order to prevent erosion. [< F, equiv. to *con-* CON- + *tour* a turn (see TOUR), modeled on It *contorno,* deriv. of *contornare* to outline; see TURN]

—**Syn. 1.** configuration, shape; boundary.

con′tour cur′tain, *Theat.* a curtain having lines attached to several points for drawing up into folds of various shapes.

con′tour feath′er, *Ornith.* one of the feathers that form the surface plumage of a bird, including those of the wings and tail but excluding such specialized types as downs and filoplumes.

con′tour integra′tion, *Math.* integration in the complex plane about a simple closed curve of finite length.

con′tour in′terval, the difference in elevation represented by each contour line on a map.

con′tour line′, **1.** a line joining points of equal elevation on a surface. **2.** the representation of such a line on a map. **3.** *Math.* a line parallel to a trace. Cf. **trace[1]** (def. 11). Also called **level curve, level line.**

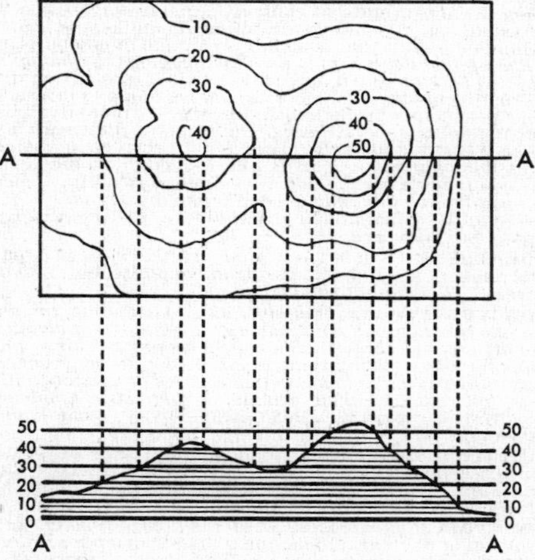

Contour map showing profile (below) through A-A

con′tour map′, a map on which irregularities of land surface are shown by contour lines, the relative spacing of the lines indicating the relative slope of the surface.

con′tour sheet′, a bed sheet designed to fit closely over a mattress or the like, often having elastic material to hold down the corners.

contr., **1.** contract. **2.** contracted. **3.** contraction. **4.** contralto. **5.** contrary. **6.** contrasted. **7.** control. **8.** controller.

con·tra[1] (kon′trə), *prep.* **1.** against; in opposition or contrast to. —*adv.* **2.** contrariwise; on or to the contrary. [ME < L *contrā*]

con·tra[2] (kon′trə; *Sp.* kôn′trä), *n., pl.* **-tras** (-trəz; *Sp.* -träs). (*often cap.*) a member of a counterrevolutionary group seeking to overthrow the Sandinista government of Nicaragua. [AmerSp, shortened form of *contrarrevolucionario* COUNTERREVOLUTIONARY]

contra-, a learned borrowing from Latin meaning "against," "opposite," "opposing," used in the formation of compound words: *contradistinction.* [< L, comb. form of adv. and prep. *contrā*]

con·tra·band (kon′trə band′), *n.* **1.** anything prohibited by law from being imported or exported. **2.** goods imported or exported illegally. **3.** illegal or prohibited trade; smuggling. **4.** *Internat. Law.* See **contraband of war.** **5.** (during the American Civil War) a Negro slave who escaped to or was brought within the Union lines. —*adj.* **6.** prohibited from export or import. [earlier *contrabanda* < Sp < It *contrabando* (now *contrabbando*), equiv. to *contra-* CONTRA- + ML *bandum,* var. of *bannum* BAN[2]]

con·tra·band·ist (kon′trə ban′dist), *n.* a person engaged in contraband trade; smuggler. [< Sp *contrabandista.* See CONTRABAND, -IST]

con′traband of war′, *Internat. Law.* goods that a neutral nation cannot supply to a belligerent nation except at the risk of seizure and confiscation.

con·tra·bass (kon′trə bās′), *Music.* —*n.* **1.** (in any family of instruments) the member below the bass. **2.** (in the violin family) the double bass. —*adj.* **3.** of, pertaining to, or characteristic of such instruments: *a contrabass trombone.* [< It *contrabasso* (now *contrabbasso*). See CONTRA-, BASS[1]] —**con·tra·bass·ist** (kon′trə bā′sist, -bas′ist), *n.*

con·tra·bas·soon (kon′trə ba so͞on′, -bə-), *n.* a bassoon larger in size and an octave lower in pitch than the ordinary bassoon; a double bassoon. [CONTRA- + BASSOON] —**con′tra·bas·soon′ist,** *n.*

con·tra·cep·tion (kon′trə sep′shən), *n.* the prevention of conception or impregnation by any of various techniques or devices; birth control. [CONTRA- + (CON)CEPTION]

con·tra·cep·tive (kon′trə sep′tiv), *adj.* **1.** tending or serving to prevent conception or impregnation. **2.** pertaining to contraception. —*n.* **3.** a contraceptive device, drug, etc. [CONTRA- + (CON)CEPTIVE]

con·tra·clock·wise (kon′trə klok′wīz′), *adj., adv.* counterclockwise. [CONTRA- + CLOCKWISE]

con·tract (*n. and usually for v. 13* kon′trakt; *otherwise v.* kən trakt′), *n.* **1.** an agreement between two or more parties for the doing or not doing of something specified. **2.** an agreement enforceable by law. **3.** the written form of such an agreement. **4.** the division of law dealing with contracts. **5.** the formal agreement of marriage; betrothal. **6.** Also called **con′tract bridge′.** a variety of bridge in which the side that wins the bid can earn toward game only that number of tricks named in the contract, additional points being credited above the line. Cf. **auction bridge.** **7.** (in auction or contract bridge) **a.** a commitment by the declarer and his partner to take six tricks plus the number specified by the final bid made. **b.** the final bid itself. **c.** the number of tricks so specified, plus six. —*v.t.* **8.** to draw together or into smaller compass; draw the parts of together: *to contract a muscle.* **9.** to wrinkle: *to contract the brows.* **10.** to shorten (a word, phrase, etc.) by combining or omitting some of its elements: *Contracting "do not" yields "don't."* **11.** to get or acquire, as by exposure to something contagious: *to contract a disease; to contract a habit.* **12.** to incur, as a liability or obligation: *to contract a debt.* **13.** to settle or establish by agreement: *to contract an alliance.* **14.** to enter into (friendship, acquaintance, etc.). **15.** to betroth. —*v.i.* **16.** to become drawn together or reduced in compass; become smaller; shrink: *The pupils of his eyes contracted in the light.* **17.** to enter into an agreement: *to contract for snow removal.* [ME < L *contract(us)* transaction, hence, agreement, n. use of *contractus* drawn together (ptp. of *contrahere*), equiv. to *con-* CON- + *-trac-* (ptp. s. of *trahere* to draw) + *-tus* ptp. suffix] —**con·tract′i·ble,** *adj.* —**con·tract′i·bil′i·ty, con·tract′i·ble·ness,** *n.* —**con·tract′i·bly,** *adv.*

—**Syn. 1.** See **agreement.** **8.** reduce, shorten, lessen, narrow, shrivel, shrink. CONTRACT, COMPRESS, CONCENTRATE, CONDENSE imply retaining original content but reducing the amount of space occupied. CONTRACT means to cause to draw more closely together: *to contract a muscle.* COMPRESS suggests fusing to become smaller by means of fairly uniform external pressure: *to compress gases into liquid form or clay into bricks.* CONCENTRATE implies causing to gather around a point, or eliminating nonessentials: *to concentrate troops near an objective; to concentrate the attention; to concentrate one's strength.* CONDENSE implies increasing the compactness, or thickening the consistency of a homogeneous mass: *to condense milk.* It is also used to refer to the reducing in length of a book or the like: *to condense a novel; to condense a play.* —**Ant. 8.** expand.

con·tract·ed (kən trak′tid), *adj.* **1.** drawn together; reduced in compass or size; made smaller; shrunken. **2.** condensed; abridged. **3.** (of the mind, outlook, etc.) narrow or illiberal; restricted: *a contracted view of minority rights.* [CONTRACT + -ED[2]] —**con·tract′ed·ly,** *adv.* —**con·tract′ed·ness,** *n.*

con·trac·tile (kən trak′təl, -til), *adj.* capable of contracting or producing contraction. [CONTRACT + -ILE] —**con·trac·til·i·ty** (kon′trak til′i tē), *n.*

con·trac·tion (kən trak′shən), *n.* **1.** an act or instance of contracting. **2.** the quality or state of being contracted. **3.** a shortened form of a word or group of words, as *e'er* for *ever, can't* for *cannot, dep't* for *department.* **4.** *Physiol.* the change in a muscle by which it becomes thickened and shortened. **5.** a restriction or withdrawal, as of currency or of funds available as call money. [< L *contractiōn-* (s. of *contractiō*), equiv. to *contract(us)* drawn together (see CONTRACT) + *-iōn-* -ION] —**con·trac′tion·al,** *adj.*

—**Usage. 3.** In some kinds of writing and particularly in correspondence, contractions serve as an excellent device to inject informality. But teachers and careful editors who are concerned with a more formal style generally require that full forms be retained unless, of course, direct discourse is being transcribed.

contrac′tion joint′, a joint between two parts of a structure, designed to compensate for the contraction to which either part may be subject.

con·trac·tive (kən trak′tiv), *adj.* **1.** serving or tending to contract. **2.** capable of contracting. [CONTRACT + -IVE] —**con·trac′tive·ly,** *adv.* —**con·trac′tive·ness,** *n.*

con·trac·tor (kon′trak tər, kən trak′tər), *n.* **1.** one who contracts to furnish supplies or perform work at a certain price or rate. **2.** that which contracts, esp. a muscle. **3.** *Bridge.* **a.** the player who makes the final bid. **b.** this player's partner. [< LL; see CONTRACT, -OR[2]]

con′tract prac′tice, the medical treatment of a group of persons by a physician or physicians with fees and services mutually agreed upon in advance.

con·trac·tu·al (kən trak′cho͞o əl), *adj.* of, pertaining to, or secured by a contract. [< L *contractu(s)* CONTRACT + -AL[1]] —**con·trac′tu·al·ly,** *adv.*

con·trac·ture (kən trak′chər, -shər), *n.* *Pathol.* a shortening or distortion of muscular tissue due to spasm, scar, or paralysis of the antagonist of the contracting muscle. [< L *contractūra,* equiv. to *contract(us)* drawn together (ptp. of *contrahere;* see CONTRACT) + *-ūra* -URE] —**con·trac′tured,** *adj.*

con·tra·dance (kon′trə dans′, -däns′), *n.* contredanse.

con·tra·dict (kon′trə dikt′), *v.t.* **1.** to assert the contrary or opposite of; deny directly and categorically. **2.** to speak contrary to the assertions of: *to contradict oneself.* **3.** (of an action or event) to imply a denial of: *His way of life contradicts his stated principles.* **4.** *Obs.* to speak or declare against; oppose. —*v.i.* **5.** to utter a contrary statement. [< L *contrādict(us)* spoken against (ptp. of *contrādīcere*), equiv. to *contrā-* CONTRA- + *dic-* (ptp. s. of *dīcere* to speak) + *-tus* ptp. suffix] —**con′tra·dict′a·ble,** *adj.* —**con′tra·dict′er, con′tra·dic′tor,** *n.*
—**Syn. 1, 2.** gainsay, impugn, controvert, dispute. See **deny.** —**Ant. 1.** support.

con·tra·dic·tion (kon′trə dik′shən), *n.* **1.** the act of contradicting; gainsaying or opposition. **2.** assertion of the contrary or opposite; denial. **3.** a statement or proposition that contradicts or denies another or itself and is logically incongruous. **4.** direct opposition between things compared; inconsistency. **5.** a contradictory act, fact, etc. [ME *contradiccioun* < L *contrādictiōn-* (s. of *contrādictiō*). See CONTRADICT, -ION]

con·tra·dic·tious (kon′trə dik′shəs), *adj.* **1.** inclined to contradict; disputatious. **2.** *Archaic.* self-contradictory. [CONTRADICT + -IOUS] —**con′tra·dic′tious·ly,** *adv.* —**con′tra·dic′tious·ness,** *n.*

con·tra·dic·tive (kon′trə dik′tiv), *adj.* tending to contradict; involving contradiction. [CONTRADICT(IOUS) + -IVE] —**con′tra·dic′tive·ly,** *adv.* —**con′tra·dic′tive·ness,** *n.*

con·tra·dic·to·ry (kon′trə dik′tə rē), *adj., n., pl.* **-ries.** —*adj.* **1.** asserting the contrary or opposite; contradicting; inconsistent; logically opposite: *contradictory statements.* **2.** tending or inclined to contradict. —*n.* **3.** *Logic.* a proposition so related to a second that it is impossible for both to be true or both to be false. [ME < LL *contrādictōri(us).* See CONTRADICT, -ORY[1]] —**con′tra·dic′to·ri·ly,** *adv.* —**con′tra·dic′to·ri·ness,** *n.*
—**Syn. 1.** opposing, antagonistic, irreconcilable, paradoxical.

con·tra·dis·tinc·tion (kon′trə di stiŋgk′shən), *n.* distinction by opposition or contrast: *plants and animals in contradistinction to man.* [CONTRA- + DISTINCTION] —**con′tra·dis·tinc′tive,** *adj.* —**con′tra·dis·tinc′tive·ly,** *adv.*

con·tra·dis·tin·guish (kon′trə di stiŋ′gwish), *v.t.* to distinguish by contrasting opposite qualities. [CONTRA- + DISTINGUISH]

con′tra-guide rud′der (kon′trə gīd′), *Naut.* a rudder having a horizontal offset of its upper and lower halves to improve the flow characteristics of the propeller race.

con·trail (kon′trāl), *n.* a visible condensation of water droplets or ice crystals from the atmosphere, occurring in the wake of an aircraft, rocket, or missile under certain conditions. Also called **condensation trail, vapor trail.** [CON(DENSATION) TRAIL]

con·tra·in·di·cate (kon′trə in′də kāt′), *v.t.,* **-cat·ed, -cat·ing.** *Med.* (of a symptom or condition) to give indication against the advisability of (a particular or usual remedy or treatment). [prob. back formation from *contraindication.* See CONTRA-, INDICATION] —**con′tra·in′di·cant** (kon′trə in′də kənt), *n.* —**con′tra·in′di·ca′tion,** *n.*

con·tral·to (kən tral′tō), *n., pl.* **-tos,** *adj.* *Music.* —*n.* **1.** the lowest female voice or voice part, intermediate between soprano and tenor. **2.** the alto, or highest male voice or voice part. **3.** a singer with a contralto voice. —*adj.* **4.** pertaining to the contralto voice or its compass. [< It; see CONTRA-, ALTO]

con·tra·oc·tave (kon′trə ok′tiv, -tāv), *n.* *Music.* the octave between the second and third C's below middle C. [CONTRA- + OCTAVE]

con·tra·or·bi·tal (kon′trə ôr′bi təl), *adj.* of or pertaining to flight in the orbit of, but in a direction contrary to, a given rocket, ballistic missile, satellite, etc. [CONTRA- + ORBITAL] —**con′tra·or′bi·tal·ly,** *adv.*

con·tra·plete (kon′trə plēt′), *n.* *Philos.* either of two opposed and complementary elements in a relationship. [CONTRA- + (COM)PLETE] —**con′tra·ple′tal,** *adj.*

con·tra·pose (kon′trə pōz′), *v.t.,* **-posed, -pos·ing.** to place in contraposition. [back formation from *contraposed* < L *contrāpositus,* ptp. of *contrāpōnere* to place against, with -ED[2] for L *-itus* ptp. suffix]

con·tra·po·si·tion (kon′trə pə zish′ən), *n.* **1.** placement opposite or against. **2.** opposition, contrast, or antithesis. **3.** *Logic.* the inference drawn from a proposition by negating its terms and changing their order, as by inferring "Not B implies not A" from "A implies B." [< LL *contrāpositiōn-* (s. of *contrāpositiō*). See CONTRA-, POSITION]

con·tra·pos·i·tive (kon′trə poz′i tiv), *Logic.* —*adj.* **1.** of or pertaining to contraposition. —*n.* **2.** a contrapositive statement of a proposition. [CONTRAPOSIT(ION) + -IVE]

con·trap·pos·to (kōn′trə pos′tō), *n., pl.* **-tos.** *Fine Arts.* a representation of the human body in which the forms are organized on a varying or curving axis to provide an asymmetrical balance to the figure. [< It < L *contrāpositus* placed against. See CONTRA-, POSIT]

con·tra·prop (kon′trə prop′), *n.* See **contrarotating propeller.** [CONTRA- + PROP[3]]

con′tra·pro·pel′ler construc′tion (kon′trə prə pel′ər), construction of a ship's stern with the propeller post and rudder post inclined to the vertical in opposite directions.

con·trap·tion (kən trap′shən), *n.* *Informal.* a mechanical contrivance; gadget; device: *He's invented a contraption that peels bananas automatically.* [? CONTR(IVANCE) + *(ad)aption,* var. of ADAPTATION] —**con·trap′tious,** *adj.*

con·tra·pun·tal (kon′trə pun′təl), *adj.* *Music.* **1.** of or pertaining to counterpoint. **2.** composed of two or more relatively independent melodies sounded together. [< It *contrappunt(o)* + -AL[1]. See COUNTERPOINT] —**con′tra·pun′tal·ly,** *adv.*

con·tra·pun·tist (kon′trə pun′tist), *n.* one skilled in the practice of counterpoint. [< It *contrappuntista.* See COUNTERPOINT, -IST]

con·tra·ri·a con·tra·ri·is cu·ran·tur (kōn trä′rē ä′ kōn trä′rē is ko͞o rän′to͞or; *Eng.* kən trâ′rē ə kən trâ′rē is kyo͞o ran′tər), *Latin.* opposites are cured by opposites: the principle of allopathy.

con·tra·ri·e·ty (kon′trə rī′i tē), *n., pl.* **-ties** for 2. **1.** the quality or state of being contrary. **2.** something contrary or of opposite character; a contrary fact or statement. **3.** *Logic.* the relation between contraries. [late ME *contrariete* < LL *contrārietās.* See CONTRARY, -ITY]

con·trar·i·ous (kən trâr′ē əs), *adj.* *Archaic.* **1.** perverse; refractory. **2.** adverse; unfavorable. [ME < L *contrārius* CONTRARY] —**con·trar′i·ous·ly,** *adv.* —**con·trar′i·ous·ness,** *n.*

con·tra·ri·wise (kon′trer ē wīz′), *adv.* **1.** in the opposite way. **2.** on the contrary; in direct opposition to a statement, attitude, etc. **3.** perversely. [ME *contrary-wyse.* See CONTRARY, -WISE]

con·tra·ro′tat·ing propel′ler (kon′trə rō′tā tiŋ), one of a pair of propellers on an aircraft or ship mounted on concentric drive shafts geared to rotate in opposite directions. Also called **contraprop, counterrotating propeller.** [CONTRA- + ROTATING]

con·tra·ry (kon′trer ē; *for 5 also* kən trâr′ē), *adj., n., pl.* **-ries,** *adv.* —*adj.* **1.** opposite in nature or character; diametrically or mutually opposed: *contrary to fact; contrary propositions.* **2.** opposite in direction or position: *departures in contrary directions.* **3.** being the opposite one of two: *I will make the contrary choice.* **4.** unfavorable or adverse. **5.** perverse; stubbornly opposed or willful. **6.** *Bot.* at right angles. —*n.* **7.** something that is contrary or opposite: *to prove the contrary of a statement.* **8.** either of two contrary things. **9.** *Logic.* a proposition so related to another proposition that both may not be true though both may be false, as with the propositions "All judges are male" and "No judges are male." **10. by contraries,** contrary to expectation. **11. on the contrary, a.** in opposition to what has been stated. **b.** from another point of view: *On the contrary, there may be some who would agree with you.* **12. to the contrary, a.** to the opposite effect: *She may have a kind heart, but her behavior points to the contrary.* **b.** to a different effect. —*adv.* **13.** in opposition; oppositely; counter: *to act contrary to one's own principles.* [ME *contrarie* < L *contrāri(us).* See CONTRA-, -ARY] —**con′tra·ri·ly,** *adv.* —**con′tra·ri·ness,** *n.*
—**Syn. 1.** contradictory, conflicting, discordant, counter. See **opposite. 4.** unfriendly, hostile. CONTRARY, ADVERSE both describe that which unfavorably opposes. CONTRARY conveys an idea of something impersonal and objective whose opposition happens to be unfavorable: *contrary winds.* ADVERSE suggests something more personally unfriendly or even hostile; it emphasizes the idea of the resulting misfortune to that which is opposed: *The judge rendered a decision adverse to the defendant.* **5.** intractable, obstinate, refractory, headstrong, stubborn, pig-headed, contumacious. —**Ant. 4.** favorable. **5.** obliging.

con′trary mo′tion, *Music.* melodic motion in which one part rises in pitch while the other descends.

con·trast (*v.* kən trast′; *n.* kon′trast), *v.t.* **1.** to compare in order to show unlikeness or differences; note the opposite natures, purposes, etc., of: *Contrast the rights of free men and slaves.* —*v.i.* **2.** to exhibit unlikeness on comparison with something else; form a contrast. [< F *contrast(er)* < It *contrastare* to contest < L *contrā-* CONTRA- + *stāre* to stand]
—*n.* **3.** act or state of contrasting; state of being contrasted. **4.** a striking exhibition of unlikeness. **5.** a thing or person that is strikingly unlike in comparison: *The weather down here is a welcome contrast to what we're having back home.* **6.** opposition or juxtaposition of different forms, lines, or colors in a work of art to intensify each element's properties and produce a more dynamic expressiveness. **7.** *Photog.* the relative difference between light and dark areas of a print or negative. [earlier *contraste* < F < It *contrasto* conflict; see verb] —**con·trast′a·ble,** *adj.* —**con·trast′a·bly,** *adv.* —**con·trast′ed·ly,** *adv.* —**con·trast′ing·ly,** *adv.*
—**Syn. 1.** differentiate, discriminate, distinguish, oppose. See **compare.**

con·traste (*Fr.* kôn trast′), *n.* (in the western Mediterranean) a wind blowing from opposite but nearby areas. [< F; see CONTRAST]

con·tras·tive (kən tras′tiv), *adj.* **1.** tending to contrast; contrasting: *He spoke with a meekness contrastive to his previous behavior. She wore a beautiful dress of contrastive colors.* **2.** studying or exhibiting the congruences and differences between two languages or dialects without reference to their origins: *a contrastive grammar; contrastive linguistics.* [CONTRAST + -IVE] —**con·tras′tive·ly,** *adv.*

con′trast me′dium, *Med.* a radiopaque substance injected into a part of the body, as the stomach, duodenum, etc., to provide a contrasting background for the tissues in an x-ray or fluoroscopic examination.

con·trast·y (kən tras′tē, kon′tras-), *adj.* *Photog.* (of a subject or photograph) having coarse or sharp gradations of tone, esp. between dark and light areas. [CONTRAST + -Y[1]]

con·trate (kon′trāt), *adj.* *Horol.* (of a gear) having teeth at right angles to the plane of rotation. [CON-TR(A)- + -ATE[1]]

con·tra·val·la·tion (kon′trə və lā′shən), *n.* *Fort.* a more or less continuous chain of redoubts and breastworks raised by besiegers outside the line of circumvallation of a besieged place to protect the besiegers from attacks from the outside, as by a relieving force. [CONTRA- + VALLATION; cf. F *contrevallation,* It *contravvallazione*]

con·tra·vene (kon′trə vēn′), *v.t.,* **-vened, -ven·ing.** **1.** to come or be in conflict with; go or act counter to; oppose: *to contravene a statement.* **2.** to violate, infringe, or transgress: *to contravene the law.* [< LL *contrāven(īre),* equiv. to L *contrā* against + *venīre* to come] —**con′tra·ven′er,** *n.*

con·tra·ven·tion (kon′trə ven′shən), *n.* an act of contravening; action counter to something; violation; opposition. [CONTRAVENE + -TION; cf. MF *contrevention*]

con·tra·yer·va (kon′trə yûr′və), *n.* the root of certain tropical American, moraceous plants of the genus *Dorstenia,* esp. *D. contrayerva,* used as a stimulant, tonic, and diaphoretic. [< Sp *contrayerba, contrahierba* < L *contrā* CONTRA- + *herba* HERB; so called from its being thought an antidote to poison]

con·tre·coup (kon′trə ko͞o′; *Fr.* kôn trə ko͞o′), *n.* *Med.* injury of one point of an organ or part resulting from a blow on the opposite point. Also called **counterstroke.** [< F *contre-coup.* See COUNTER-, COUP[1]]

con·tre·danse (kon′tri dans′, -däns′; *Fr.* kôn trə däns′), *n., pl.* **-dans·es** (-dan′siz, -dän′-; *Fr.* -däns′). **1.** a variation of the quadrille in which the dancers face each other. **2.** a piece of music suitable for such a dance. Also, **contradance.** [< F, equiv. to *contre-* COUNTER- + *danse* DANCE, mistranslation of COUNTRY-DANCE]

cont. rem., (in prescriptions) let the medicines be continued. [< L *continuantur remedia*]

con·tre-par·tie (*Fr.* kôn trə par tē′), *n.* *Furniture.* (in buhlwork) an inlay composed of a design in tortoise shell on a background of brass. Also called **counterboulle.** Cf. **première partie.** [< F: counterpart]

con·tre·temps (kon′trə tän′; *Fr.* kôn trə tän′), *n., pl.* **-temps** (-tänz′; *Fr.* -tän′). an inopportune occurrence; an embarrassing mischance: *He caused a minor contretemps by knocking over his highball.* [< F, equiv. to *contre-* COUNTER- + *temps* time (< L *tempus*); perh. alter. (by folk etymology) of MF *contrestant,* prp. of *contrester* to oppose; see CONTRAST]

contrib., **1.** contribution. **2.** contributor.

con·trib·ute (kən trib′yo͞ot), *v.,* **-ut·ed, -ut·ing.** —*v.t.* **1.** to give (money, time, knowledge, assistance, etc.) along with others to a common supply, fund, etc., as for charitable purposes. **2.** to furnish (an original written work) for publication: *He contributes a story or poem every month to our magazine.* —*v.i.* **3.** to give (money, food, etc.) to a common supply, fund, etc.: *He contributes to many charities.* **4.** to furnish works for publication: *He contributes to many magazines.* [< L *contribūt(us)* classified together, ptp. of *contribuere.* See CON-, TRIBUTE] —**con·trib′ut·a·ble,** *adj.* —**con·trib′u·tive,** *adj.* —**con·trib′u·tive·ly,** *adv.* —**con·trib′u·tive·ness,** *n.*
—**Syn. 1.** provide, furnish, donate.

con·tri·bu·tion (kon′trə byo͞o′shən), *n.* **1.** the act of contributing. **2.** something contributed. **3.** an article, story, etc., furnished to a magazine or other publication. **4.** an impost or levy. **5.** *Insurance.* the method of distributing liability, in case of loss, among several insurers whose policies attach to the same risk. [ME *contribucio(u)n* < LL *contribūtiōn-* (s. of *contribūtiō*). See CONTRIBUTE, -ION] —**con′tri·bu′tion·al,** *adj.*

con·trib·u·tor (kən trib′yə tər), *n.* **1.** one who contributes. **2.** one who contributes an article, story, etc., to a newspaper, magazine, or the like. [late ME *contributour* < AF. See CONTRIBUTE, -OR[2]] —**con·trib·u·to·ri·al** (kən trib′yə tôr′ē əl, -tōr′-), *adj.*

con·trib·u·to·ry (kən trib′yə tôr′ē, -tōr′ē), *adj., n., pl.* **-ries.** —*adj.* **1.** pertaining to or of the nature of contribution; contributing. **2.** furnishing something toward a result: *a contributory factor.* **3.** of, pertaining to, or constituting an insurance or pension plan the premiums of which are paid partly by an employer and partly by his employees. **4.** subject to contribution or levy. —*n.* **5.** one who or that which contributes. [late ME *contributorie* < ML *contribūtōri(us).* See CONTRIBUTE, -ORY[1]]
—**Syn. 2.** accessory, ancillary, auxiliary; secondary, incidental.

contrib′utory neg′ligence, *Law.* negligence on the part of an injured party that combines with the negligence of another in causing the injury, sometimes so as to diminish or bar the recovery of damages for the injury.

con·trite (kən trīt′, kon′trīt), *adj.* **1.** overcome by a sense of guilt and the desire for atonement; penitent: *a contrite sinner.* **2.** caused by or showing sincere remorse. [ME *contrit* < L *contrīt(us)* worn down, crushed, ptp. of *conterere.* See CON-, TRITE] —**con·trite′ly,** *adv.* —**con·trite′ness,** *n.*

con·tri·tion (kən trish′ən), *n.* **1.** sincere penitence or remorse. **2.** *Theol.* sorrow for and detestation of sin with a true purpose of amendment, arising from a love of God for His own perfections **(perfect contrition),** or from some inferior motive, as fear of divine punishment **(imperfect contrition).** [ME *contricio(u)n* < LL *contrītiōn-* (s. of *contrītiō*). See CONTRITE, -ION]
—**Syn. 1.** compunction, regret.

con·triv·ance (kən trī′vəns), *n.* **1.** something contrived; a device, esp. a mechanical one. **2.** the act or manner of contriving; the faculty or power of contriving. **3.** a plan or scheme; expedient. [CONTRIVE + -ANCE]

con·trive (kən trīv′), *v.,* **-trived, -triv·ing.** —*v.t.* **1.** to plan with ingenuity; devise; invent: *The author contrived a clever but unrealistic plot.* **2.** to plot (evil, treachery, etc.). **3.** to bring about or effect by a device, stratagem, plan, or scheme; manage: *He contrived to gain their votes.* —*v.i.* **4.** to form schemes or designs; plan. **5.** to plot. [ME *contreve(n)* < MF *contreuv-,* tonic s. of *controver* < LL *contropāre* to compare. See CON-, TROVER] —**con·triv′a·ble,** *adj.* —**con·triv′er,** *n.*
—**Syn. 1.** design, concoct. See **prepare. 2.** complot, conspire, scheme.

con·trived (kən trīvd′), *adj.* obviously planned or forced; artificial; strained: *The expensive dress, tailored to severe lines, had a look of contrived simplicity.* [late ME *contrevede.* See CONTRIVE, -ED[2]]

con·trol (kən trōl′), *v.,* **-trolled, -trol·ling,** *n.* —*v.t.* **1.** to exercise restraint or direction over; dominate; command. **2.** to hold in check; curb: *to control a horse; to control one's emotions.* **3.** to test or verify (a scientific experiment) by a parallel experiment or other standard

of comparison. **4.** to eliminate or prevent the flourishing or spread of: *to control a forest fire; to control rats.* **5.** *Obs.* to check or regulate (transactions) originally by means of a duplicate register. —*n.* **6.** the act or power of controlling; regulation; domination or command: *If only a better person were in control here!* **7.** the situation of being under the regulation, domination, or command of another: *The car is out of control.* **8.** check or restraint: *Her tears are under control.* **9.** a standard of comparison in scientific experimentation; check. **10.** a person who acts as a check; controller. **11.** a device for regulating and guiding a machine, as a motor, airplane, etc. **12. controls,** a coordinated arrangement of such devices. **13.** prevention of the flourishing or spread of something undesirable: *rodent control.* **14.** *Baseball.* the ability of a pitcher to throw the ball into the strike zone consistently: *The rookie pitcher has great power but no control.* **15.** *Philately.* any device printed on a postage or revenue stamp to authenticate it as a government issue or to identify it for bookkeeping purposes. **16.** a spiritual agency believed to assist a medium at a seance. [late ME *co(u)ntrolle* (v.) < AF *contreroll(er),* deriv. of *contrerolle* (n.). See COUNTER-, ROLL] —**con·trol′la·bil′i·ty, con·trol′la·ble·ness,** *n.* —**con·trol′la·ble,** *adj.* —**con·trol′la·bly,** *adv.* —**con·trol′less,** *adj.* —**con·trol′ling·ly,** *adv.*
—**Syn. 1.** manage, govern, rule. **2.** restrain, bridle, constrain. **6.** management, government, reign, rule, mastery. See **authority.**

control′ account′, a general account showing totals of transactions with detailed figures appearing in subsidiary ledgers. Also called **control′ling account′.**

control′ board′, a panel, usually insulated, containing switches, dials, and other equipment for regulating electrical devices, lights, etc. Also called **control panel.**

control′ cen′ter, an administrative or operational center for a group of related activities: *the control center for the new military offensive.*

control′ chart′, *Statistics.* a chart on which observations are plotted as ordinates in the order in which they are obtained and on which control lines are constructed to indicate whether the population from which the observations are being drawn is remaining the same: used esp. in industrial quality control.

control′ elec′trode, *Electronics.* an electrode to which a varying signal is applied to vary the output of a vacuum tube or transistor.

control′ exper′iment, an experiment in which the variables are controlled so that the effects of varying one factor at a time may be observed.

con·trol·la·ble-pitch (kən trō′lə bəl pich′), *adj.* (of a marine or aircraft propeller) having blades whose pitch can be changed during navigation or flight; variable-pitch. Cf. **adjustable-pitch.**

con·trol·ler (kən trō′lər), *n.* **1.** an employee, often an officer, of a business firm who checks expenditures, finances, etc.; comptroller. **2.** a person who regulates, directs, or restrains. **3.** *Brit. Aeron.* a dispatcher. **4.** a regulating mechanism. [late ME *co(u)nt(re)rollo(u)r* < AF *countrero(u)llour,* MF *contrerolleur,* equiv. to *contrerolle* duplicate roll (see CONTROL) + *-eur, -our* -OR[2]] —**con·trol′ler·ship′,** *n.*

control′ling depth′, *Naut.* the depth of water that establishes the maximum draft of vessels that can navigate in a given area.

control′ pan′el, 1. *Computer Technol.* plugboard (def. 2). **2.** See **control board.**

control′ room′, a room housing control equipment, as in a recording studio.

control′ stick′, *Aeron.* a lever by which a pilot controls the ailerons and elevator of an aircraft.

control′ sur′face, any movable airfoil, as a rudder, flap, or aileron, for guiding or controlling an aircraft or missile in flight.

control′ sur′vey, an accurate survey of a region forming a basis for more detailed surveys.

control′ tow′er, a glass-enclosed, elevated structure for the visual observation and control of the air and ground traffic at an airport.

con·tro·ver·sial (kon′trə vûr′shəl), *adj.* **1.** of, pertaining to, or characteristic of controversy; polemical. **2.** subject to controversy; debatable: *a controversial book.* **3.** given to controversy; disputatious. [< LL *contrōversiāl(is),* equiv. to L *contrōversi(a)* CONTROVERSY + *-ālis* -AL[1]] —**con′tro·ver′sial·ism,** *n.* —**con′tro·ver′sial·ist,** *n.* —**con′tro·ver′sial·ly,** *adv.*

con·tro·ver·sy (kon′trə vûr′sē), *n., pl.* **-sies. 1.** dispute, debate, or contention; disputation concerning a matter of opinion. **2.** contention, strife, or argument. [ME *controversie* < L *contrōversia,* equiv. to *contrōvers(us)* turned against, disputed (*contro-,* var. of *contrā* against, + *versus,* ptp. of *vertere* to turn) + *-ia* -Y[3]]
—**Syn. 1.** disagreement, altercation. **2.** quarrel, wrangle. See **argument.**

con·tro·vert (kon′trə vûrt′, kon′trə vûrt′), *v.t.* **1.** to argue against; dispute; deny; oppose. **2.** to argue about; debate; discuss. [alter. of earlier *controverse* (< L *contrōversus;* see CONTROVERSY) with *-vert* from ADVERT[1], CONVERT, etc.] —**con′tro·vert′er, con′tro·vert′ist,** *n.* —**con′tro·vert′i·ble,** *adj.* —**con′tro·vert′i·bly,** *adv.*
—**Syn. 1.** refute, rebut.

con·tu·ma·cious (kon′to͝o mā′shəs, -tyo͝o-), *adj.* stubbornly perverse or rebellious; willfully and obstinately disobedient. [CONTUMACY + -OUS] —**con′tu·ma′cious·ly,** *adv.* —**con′tu·ma′cious·ness, con·tu·mac·i·ty** (kon′to͝o mas′i tē, -tyo͝o-), *n.*
—**Syn.** contrary, pig-headed, factious, refractory, headstrong, intractable.

con·tu·ma·cy (kon′to͝o mə sē, -tyo͝o-), *n., pl.* **-cies.** stubborn perverseness or rebelliousness; willful and obstinate resistance or disobedience to authority. [< L *contumācia* arrogance, stubbornness, equiv. to *contumāc-* (s. of *contumāx* defiant, lit., puffed up; see CONTUMOR) + *-ia* -Y[3]]

con·tu·me·ly (kon′to͝o mə lē, -tyo͝o-; kən to͞o′mə lē, -tyo͞o′-; kon′təm lē; *formerly* kon′tyo͝o mē′lē), *n., pl.* **-lies. 1.** insulting display of contempt in words or actions; contemptuous or humiliating treatment. **2.** a humiliating insult. [ME *contumelie* < L *contumēlia* insult, abuse, equiv. to *con-* CON- + *tumē(re)* (to) be swollen (with rage) + *-l-* (< ?) + *-ia* -Y[3]] —**con·tu·me·li·ous** (kon′to͝o mē′lē əs, -tyo͝o-), *adj.* —**con′tu·me′li·ous·ly,** *adv.* —**con′tu·me′li·ous·ness,** *n.*

con·tuse (kən to͞oz′, -tyo͞oz′), *v.t.,* **-tused, -tus·ing.** to injure (tissue), esp. without breaking the skin; bruise. [late ME < L *contūs(us)* bruised, crushed (ptp. of *contundere*), equiv. to *con-* CON- + *tūd-* (ptp. s. of *tundere* to beat) + *-tus* ptp. suffix] —**con·tu·sive** (kən to͞o′siv, -tyo͞o′-), *adj.*

con·tu·sion (kən to͞o′zhən, -tyo͞o′-), *n.* an injury, as from a blow with a blunt instrument, in which the subsurface tissue is injured but the skin is not broken; a bruise. [late ME < L *contūsiōn-* (s. of *contūsiō*). See CONTUSE, -ION] —**con·tu′sioned,** *adj.*

co·nun·drum (kə nun′drəm), *n.* **1.** a riddle, the answer to which involves a pun or play on words. **2.** anything that puzzles. [?]
—**Syn. 1.** puzzle, enigma.

con·ur·ba·tion (kon′ər bā′shən), *n.* a large, continuous system of suburbs surrounding a city. [CON- + L *urb-* (s. of *urbs*) city + -ATION]

con·ure (kon′yər), *n.* any of several long-tailed New World parrots of the genus *Aratinga,* certain species of which are kept as pets. [< NL *Conurus* name of genus < Gk *kōn(os)* cone + *our(á)* tail (see URO-[2]) + L *-us* masc. n. ending]

con·va·lesce (kon′və les′), *v.i.,* **-lesced, -lesc·ing.** to grow stronger after illness; make progress toward recovery of health. [< L *convalesce(re)* (to) grow fully strong, equiv. to *con-* CON- + *valescere* to grow strong (*val-* strong + *-escere* -ESCE)]

con·va·les·cence (kon′və les′əns), *n.* **1.** the gradual recovery of health and strength after illness. **2.** the period during which one is convalescing. [< LL *convalescentia.* See CONVALESCE, -ENCE]

con·va·les·cent (kon′və les′ənt), *adj.* **1.** convalescing. **2.** of or pertaining to convalescence or convalescing persons. —*n.* **3.** a convalescent person. [< L *convalescent-* (s. of *convalescēns*), prp. of *convalescere* to CONVALESCE; see -ENT] —**con′va·les′cent·ly,** *adv.*

con·val·lar·i·a·ceous (kon′və lâr′ē ā′shəs), *adj.* belonging to the *Convallariaceae,* a family of plants including the lily-of-the-valley, asparagus, etc. [< NL *Convallāri(a)* genus name (L *convall(is)* shut-in valley (see CON-, VALE[1]) + *-āria* -ARIA) + -ACEOUS]

con·vect (kən vekt′), *v.t.* **1.** to transfer (heat or a fluid) by convection. —*v.i.* **2.** (of a fluid) to transfer heat by convection. [back formation from *convected* < L *convect(us)* carried together (ptp. of *convehere;* see CONVECTOR) + -ED[2]] —**con·vec′tive,** *adj.* —**con·vec′tive·ly,** *adv.*

con·vec·tion (kən vek′shən), *n.* **1.** *Physics.* the transfer of heat by the circulation or movement of the heated parts of a liquid or gas. **2.** *Meteorol.* the vertical transport of atmospheric properties, esp. upward (distinguished from *advection*). **3.** the act of conveying or transmitting. [< LL *convectiōn-* (s. of *convectiō*) a bringing together. See CONVECT, -ION] —**con·vec′tion·al,** *adj.*

convec′tive activ′ity, *Meteorol.* any manifestation of convection in the atmosphere, as hail, thunderstorms, etc.

convec′tive dis′charge, *Physics.* the repulsion of ions of a gas by a highly charged body, creating a discernible wind. Also called **electric wind.**

con·vec·tor (kən vek′tər), *n.* any fluid or device transferring heat by convection. [CONVECT + -OR[2]]

con·ve·nance (kon′və näns′; *Fr.* kôɴvᵊ näɴs′), *n., pl.* **-nanc·es** (-nän′siz; *Fr.* -näɴs′). **1.** suitability; expediency; propriety. **2. convenances,** the social proprieties or conventionalities. [< F, equiv. to *conven(ir)* (to) be proper + *-ance* -ANCE]

con·vene (kən vēn′), *v.,* **-vened, -ven·ing.** —*v.i.* **1.** to come together; assemble, usually for some public purpose. —*v.t.* **2.** to cause to assemble; convoke. **3.** to summon to appear, as before a judicial officer. [late ME < L *conven(īre)* (to) come together, equiv. to *con-* CON- + *venīre* to come] —**con·ven′a·ble,** *adj.* —**con·ven′a·bly,** *adv.* —**con·ven′er,** *n.*
—**Syn. 1.** congregate, meet, collect, gather.

con·ven·ience (kən vēn′yəns), *n.* **1.** the quality of being convenient; suitability. **2.** a convenient situation or time: *to await one's convenience; at your convenience.* **3.** advantage or accommodation: *a shelter for the convenience of travelers.* **4.** anything that saves or simplifies work, adds to one's ease or comfort, etc., as an appliance, utensil, or the like. **5.** *Chiefly Brit.* See **water closet** (def. 1). [ME < L *convenientia* harmony, agreement. See CONVENIENT, -ENCE]

con·ven·ien·cy (kən vēn′yən sē), *n., pl.* **-cies.** *Archaic.* convenience. [ME < L *convenientia.* See CONVENIENCE, -CY]

con·ven·ient (kən vēn′yənt), *adj.* **1.** agreeable to the needs or purpose; well-suited with respect to facility or ease in use; favorable, easy, or comfortable for use. **2.** at hand; easily accessible: *Their house is convenient to all transportation.* **3.** *Obs.* fitting; suitable. [ME < L *convenient-* (s. of *conveniēns*), prp. of *convenīre* to be suitable. See CONVENE, -ENT] —**con·ven′ient·ly,** *adv.*
—**Syn. 1.** suitable, adapted, serviceable, useful, helpful, advantageous. **2.** handy.

con·vent (kon′vent), *n.* **1.** a community of persons devoted to religious life under a superior. **2.** a society or association of monks, friars, or nuns: now usually used of a society of nuns. **3.** the building or buildings occupied by such a society; a monastery or nunnery. **4.** *Obs.* assembly; meeting. [late ME < L *convent(us)* assembly (ML: convent, n. use of *conventus* assembled, ptp. of *convenīre* to CONVENE); r. ME *covent* < AF]
—**Syn. 1.** abbey, priory. **2, 3.** cloister.

con·ven·ti·cle (kən ven′ti kəl), *n.* **1.** a secret or unauthorized meeting, esp. for religious worship, as those held by Protestant dissenters in England in the 16th and 17th centuries. **2.** a place of meeting or assembly, esp. a Nonconformist meetinghouse. **3.** *Obs.* a meeting or assembly. [ME < L *conventicul(um)* (place of) assembly. See CONVENT, -I-, -CLE] —**con·ven′ti·cler,** *n.* —**con·ven·tic·u·lar** (kon′ven tik′yə lər), *adj.*

con·ven·tion (kən ven′shən), *n.* **1.** a meeting or formal assembly, as of representatives or delegates, for discussion of and action on particular matters of common concern. **2.** *U.S. Pol.* a representative party assembly to nominate candidates and adopt platforms and party rules. **3.** an agreement, compact, or contract. **4.** an international agreement, esp. one dealing with a specific matter, as postal service, copyright, etc. **5.** general agreement or consent; accepted usage, esp. as a standard of procedure. **6.** conventionalism. **7.** a rule, method, or practice established by general consent or usage; custom. [late ME *convencio(u)n* < L *conventiōn-* (s. of *conventiō*) agreement, lit., a coming together. See CONVENT, -ION]
—**Syn. 1.** CONVENTION, ASSEMBLY, CONFERENCE, CONVOCATION name meetings for particular purposes. CONVENTION usually suggests a meeting of delegates representing political, church, social, or fraternal organizations. ASSEMBLY usually implies a meeting for a settled or customary purpose, as for discussion, legislation, or participation in a social function. CONFERENCE suggests a meeting for consultation and discussion about business or professional problems. CONVOCATION denotes a (church) assembly, the members of which have been summoned for a special purpose; chapel services at some colleges are called CONVOCATIONS. **3.** pact, treaty.

con·ven·tion·al (kən ven′shə nəl), *adj.* **1.** conforming or adhering to accepted standards, as of conduct or taste: *conventional behavior.* **2.** pertaining to convention or general agreement; established by general consent or accepted usage; arbitrarily determined: *conventional symbols.* **3.** ordinary rather than different or original: *conventional phraseology.* **4.** *Art.* **a.** in accordance with accepted manner, model, or tradition. **b.** (of figurative art) represented in a generalized or simplified manner. **5.** of or pertaining to a convention, agreement, or compact. **6.** *Law.* resting on consent, express or implied. **7.** of or pertaining to a convention or assembly. [< LL *conventiōnāl(is).* See CONVENTION, -AL[1]] —**con·ven′tion·al·ist,** *n.* —**con·ven′tion·al·ly,** *adv.*
—**Syn. 1.** See **formal**[1]. **2.** usual, habitual, customary.

con·ven·tion·al·ise (kən ven′shə nəlīz′), *v.t.,* **-ised, -is·ing.** *Chiefly Brit.* conventionalize. —**con·ven′tion·al·i·sa′tion,** *n.*

con·ven·tion·al·ism (kən ven′shə nəliz′əm), *n.* **1.** adherence to or advocacy of conventional attitudes or practices. **2.** something conventional, as an expression or attitude. **3.** *Philos.* the view that fundamental principles are validated by definition, agreement, or convention. [CONVENTIONAL + -ISM]

con·ven·tion·al·i·ty (kən ven′shə nal′i tē), *n., pl.* **-ties** for 3, 4. **1.** conventional quality or character. **2.** adherence to convention. **3.** a conventional practice, principle, form, etc. **4. conventionalities,** conventional rules of behavior. [CONVENTIONAL + -ITY]

con·ven·tion·al·ize (kən ven′shə nəlīz′), *v.t.,* **-ized, -iz·ing. 1.** to make conventional. **2.** *Art.* to represent in a conventional manner. [CONVENTIONAL + -IZE] —**con·ven′tion·al·i·za′tion,** *n.*

con·ven·tio·neer (kən ven′shə nēr′), *n.* a person attending a convention. [CONVENTION + -EER]

con·ven·tion·er (kən ven′shə nər), *n.* **1.** a conventioneer. **2.** a member of a convention. [CONVENTION + -ER[1]]

con·ven·tu·al (kən ven′cho͞o əl), *adj.* **1.** of, belonging to, or characteristic of a convent. —*n.* **2.** See **Friar Minor Conventual. 3.** a member of a convent or monastery. [late ME < ML *conventuāl(is),* equiv. to *conventu(s)* CONVENT + *-ālis* -AL[1]] —**con·ven′tu·al·ly,** *adj.*

Conven′tual Mass′, 1. the Mass celebrated daily in a convent church and attended by all members of the conventual community. **2.** *Rom. Cath. Ch., Anglican Ch.* the Mass said daily in a cathedral or collegiate chapter.

con·verge (kən vûrj′), *v.,* **-verged, -verg·ing.** —*v.i.* **1.** to tend to meet in a point or line; incline toward each other, as lines that are not parallel. **2.** to tend to a common result, conclusion, etc. **3.** *Math.* **a.** (of a sequence) to have values eventually arbitrarily close to some number; to have a finite limit. **b.** (of an infinite series) to have a finite sum; to have a sequence of partial sums which converges. **c.** (of an improper integral) to have a finite value. **d.** (of a net) to be residually in every neighborhood of some point. —*v.t.* **4.** to cause to converge. [< LL *converge(re)* (to) incline together. See CON-, VERGE[2]]

con·ver·gence (kən vûr′jəns), *n.* **1.** an act or instance of converging. **2.** a convergent state or quality. **3.** the degree or point at which lines, objects, etc., converge. **4.** *Physiol.* a coordinated turning of the eyes to bear upon a near point. **5.** *Meteorol.* **a.** the contraction of a vector field. **b.** a measure of this. **c.** a net flow of air into a given region. Cf. **confluence** (def. 4), **divergence** (def. 2). **6.** *Biol.* similarity of form or structure caused by environment rather than heredity. Also, **con·ver′gen·cy** (for defs. 1–3). [CONVERG(ENT) + -ENCE]

con·ver·gent (kən vûr′jənt), *adj.* characterized by convergence; tending to come together; merging. [< ML *convergent-* (s. of *convergēns,* prp. of *convergere*). See CONVERGE, -ENT] —**con·ver′gent·ly,** *adv.*

conver′gent evolu′tion, the appearance of apparently similar structures in organisms of different lines of descent.

conver′gent squint′, *Ophthalm.* strabismus in which one or both eyes are turned inward toward the nose; cross-eye. Also called **conver′gent strabis′mus, esotropia.** Cf. **divergent squint.**

converg′ing lens′, *Optics.* a lens that converts parallel rays of light to convergent rays and produces a real image. Cf. **diverging lens.**

con·vers·a·ble (kən vûr′sə bəl), *adj.* **1.** easy and pleasant to talk with; agreeable. **2.** able or disposed to converse. **3.** pertaining to or proper for conversation. [< ML *conversābil(is).* See CONVERSE[1], -ABLE] —**convers′a·ble·ness,** *n.* —**con·vers′a·bly,** *adv.*

con·ver·sant (kən vûr′sənt, kon′vər-), *adj.* **1.** familiar by use or study (usually fol. by *with*): *conversant with Spanish history.* **2.** having regular or frequent conversation; intimately associating; acquainted. [ME *conversa(u)nt* < L *conversant-* (s. of *conversāns*), prp. of *conversārī* to associate with. See CONVERSE[1], -ANT] —**conver′sance, con·ver′san·cy,** *n.* —**con·ver′sant·ly,** *adv.*
—**Syn. 1.** versed, learned, skilled, practiced, well-informed; proficient.

con·ver·sa·tion (kon′vər sā′shən), *n.* **1.** informal interchange of thoughts, information, etc., by spoken words; oral communication between persons; talk; colloquy. **2.** an instance of this. **3.** association or social intercourse; intimate acquaintance. **4.** See **criminal conversation. 5.** the ability to talk socially with others: *She dresses well, but she has no conversation.* **6.** *Archaic.* behavior or manner of living. **7.** *Obs.* close familiarity; intimate acquaintance, as from constant use or study. [ME *conversacio(u)n* < L *conversātiōn-* (s. of *conversātiō*) society, intercourse, equiv. to *conversāt(us)* associated with (ptp. of *conversārī;* see CONVERSE[1]) + *-iōn-* -ION]

con·ver·sa·tion·al (kon′vər sā′shə nəl), *adj.* **1.** of, pertaining to, or characteristic of conversation: *a conversational tone of voice.* **2.** able or ready to converse; given to conversation. [CONVERSATION + -AL[1]] —**con′ver·sa′tion·al·ly,** *adv.*
—**Syn. 1.** See **colloquial.**

con·ver·sa·tion·al·ist (kon′vər sā′shə nəlist), *n.* a person who enjoys and contributes to good conversation; an interesting person in conversation. [CONVERSATIONAL + -IST]

con′versa′tional qual′ity, (in public speaking) a manner of utterance that resembles the spontaneity and informality of direct conversation.

conversa′tion chair′, an English chair of the 18th century designed to be straddled facing the back of the chair with the elbows resting on the crest rail: an English imitation of the voyeuse.

conversa′tion piece′, **1.** group portraiture representing more or less fashionable people either in an interior or landscape setting. **2.** any object that arouses comment because of some striking or unusual quality.

con·ver·sa·zi·o·ne (kôn′ver sä tsyô′ne; *Eng.* kon′vər sät′sē ō′nē), *n., pl.* **-zio·ni** (-tsyô′nē), *Eng.* **-zi·o·nes.** *Italian.* a social gathering for conversation, esp. on literary or scholarly subjects. [lit., conversation]

con·verse[1] (*v.* kən vûrs′; *n.* kon′vûrs), *v.,* **-versed, -vers·ing,** *n.* —*v.i.* **1.** to talk informally with another or others; exchange views, opinions, etc., by talking. **2.** *Obs.* **a.** to maintain a familiar association (usually fol. by *with*). **b.** to have sexual intercourse (usually fol. by *with*). **c.** to commune spiritually (usually fol. by *with*). —*n.* **3.** familiar discourse or talk; conversation. **4.** *Obs.* spiritual communion. [ME *converse(n)* < L *conversārī* to associate with. See CON-, VERSED] —**con·vers′er,** *n.*
—**Syn. 1.** talk, chat, discuss. See **speak.**

con·verse[2] (*adj.* kən vûrs′, kon′vûrs; *n.* kon′vûrs), *adj.* **1.** opposite or contrary in direction, action, sequence, etc.; turned around. —*n.* **2.** something that is the opposite or contrary of another. **3.** *Logic.* **a.** a proposition obtained from another proposition by conversion. **b.** the relation between two terms, one of which is related to the other in a given manner, as "younger than" to "older than." **4.** a group of words correlative with a preceding group but having a significant pair of terms interchanged, as "hot in winter but cold in summer" and "cold in winter but hot in summer." [< L *convers(us)* turned around, ptp. of *convertere;* see CONVERT] —**con·verse·ly** (kən vûrs′lē, kon′vûrs-), *adv.*

Con·verse (kon′vûrs), *n.* **Frederick Shep·herd** (shep′ərd), 1871–1940, U.S. composer.

con·ver·sion (kən vûr′zhən, -shən), *n.* **1.** act or state of converting; state of being converted. **2.** change in character, form, or function. **3.** spiritual change from sinfulness to righteousness. **4.** change from one religion, political party, viewpoint, etc., to another. **5.** a change of attitude, emotion, or viewpoint from one of indifference, disbelief, or antagonism to one of acceptance, faith, or enthusiastic support, esp. such a change in a person's religion. **6.** a physical transformation from one material or state to another: *conversion of coal, water, and air into nylon.* **7.** a change from one form to another: *conversion of securities into cash; conversion of francs into dollars.* **8.** a physical, structural, or design change or transformation from one state or condition to another, esp. to effect a change in function: *conversion of the basement into a rumpus room; conversion of a freighter into a passenger liner.* **9.** a substitution of one component to another so as to effect a change: *conversion from oil heat to gas heat.* **10.** *Math.* a change in the form or units of an expression. **11.** *Logic.* the transposition of the subject and predicate of a proposition, as "No good man is unhappy" becomes by conversion "No unhappy man is good." **12.** *Law.* **a.** unauthorized assumption and exercise of rights of ownership over personal property belonging to another. **b.** change from realty into personalty, or vice versa, as in the sale or purchase of land, mining coal, etc. **13.** *Football.* a score made on a try for point after touchdown by place-kicking or drop-kicking the ball over the bar between the goal posts or by completing a pass in or running the ball into the end zone. **14.** *Psychoanal.* the process by which a repressed psychic event, idea, feeling, memory, or impulse is represented by a bodily change or symptom, thus simulating a physical illness or its symptoms. **15.** *Physics.* the production of radioactive material in a process in which one nuclear fuel is converted into a second nuclear fuel by the capture of neutrons. Cf. **breeding** (def. 6). **16.** *Computer Technol.* **a.** a change from one code or symbolic system to another, as a change in number base. **b.** a change from one physical or recording system to another, as from paper tape to punch cards. [ME *conversio(u)n* < L *conversiōn-* (s. of *conversiō*) a complete change. See CONVERSE[2], -ION] —**con·ver′sion·al, con·ver·sion·ar·y** (kən vûr′zhə ner′ē, -shə-), *adj.*

conver′sion ra′tio, *Physics.* (in a reactor) the number of fissionable atoms produced by each fissionable atom that is destroyed.

conver′sion ta′ble, a tabular arrangement of the equivalent values of the weight or measure units of different systems.

con·ver·sus (kən vûr′səs), *n., pl.* **-si** (-sī, -sē). *Eccles.* a lay brother. [< L, ptp. of *convertere;* see CONVERT]

con·vert (*v.* kən vûrt′; *n.* kon′vûrt), *v.t.* **1.** to change (something) into something of different form or properties; transmute; transform. **2.** *Chem.* to cause (a substance) to undergo a chemical change: *to convert sugar into alcohol.* **3.** to cause to adopt a different religion, party, opinion, etc.: *When the war came along, he was converted from a pacifist to a jingoist.* **4.** to change in character; cause to turn from an evil life to a righteous one: *to convert a criminal.* **5.** to turn to another or a particular use or purpose; divert from the proper or intended use: *They converted the study into a nursery when the baby was born.* **6.** to modify (something) so as to make it serve a different function: *to convert an underwear factory to the manufacture of army uniforms.* **7.** to appropriate wrongfully to one's own use. **8.** to exchange for an equivalent: *to convert bank notes into gold.* **9.** to invert or transpose. **10.** *Law.* **a.** to assume unlawful rights of ownership of (personal property). **b.** to change the form of (property), as from realty to personalty or vice versa. **11.** *Logic.* to transpose the subject and predicate of (a proposition) by conversion. **12.** *Finance.* to exchange voluntarily (a bond or preferred stock) into another security, usually common stock, because of the greater value of the latter. **13.** *Computer Technol.* to subject to conversion. —*v.i.* **14.** to become converted. **15.** *Football.* to make a conversion. —*n.* **16.** one who has been converted, as to a religion or an opinion. [ME *converte(n)* < L *convertere* to change completely, equiv. to *con-* CON- + *vertere* to turn round] —**con·ver′tive,** *adj.*
—**Syn. 1.** See **transform. 3.** proselytize. **16.** proselyte, neophyte, disciple.

con·vert·ed (kən vûr′tid), *adj.* **1.** noting a specified type of person who has been converted from the religion, beliefs, or attitudes characteristic of that type: *The mission school was run by converted natives. The most pious man there was a converted thief.* **2.** noting anything, formerly of the type specified, that has been converted to something else: *His yacht is a converted destroyer escort.* [CONVERT + -ED[2]]

convert′ed steel′, *Metall.* See **cement steel.**

con·vert·er (kən vûr′tər), *n.* **1.** one who or that which converts. **2.** one engaged in converting textile fabrics, esp. cotton cloths, from the raw state into the finished product ready for the market, as by bleaching, dyeing, etc. **3.** *Elect.* a device that converts alternating current to direct current or vice versa. Cf. **synchronous converter. 4.** *Metall.* a chamber or vessel through which an oxidizing blast of air is forced, as in making steel by the Bessemer process or in refining matte. **5.** *Physics.* a reactor for converting one kind of fuel into another kind. Also, **con·ver′tor.** [CONVERT + -ER[1]]

con·vert·i·ble (kən vûr′tə bəl), *adj.* **1.** capable of being converted. **2.** having a folding top, as an automobile, pleasure boat, etc. —*n.* **3.** an automobile or boat having such a top. [ME < ML *convertibil(is).* See CONVERT, -IBLE] —**con·vert′i·bil′i·ty, con·vert′i·ble·ness,** *n.* —**con·vert′i·bly,** *adv.*

con·ver·tin (kən vûr′tin), *n.* *Biochem.* See **serum prothrombin accelerator.** [CONVERT + -IN[2]]

con·vert·i·plane (kən vûr′tə plān′), *n.* a plane capable of both vertical flight like a helicopter and fast, forward speed like a conventional airplane. Also, **con·ver′ta·plane′, con·ver′to·plane′.** [CONVERT + -I- + PLANE[1]]

con·vert·ite (kon′vər tīt′), *n.* *Archaic.* **1.** a convert. **2.** a reformed prostitute. [CONVERT + -ITE[1]]

con·vex (*adj.* kon veks′, kən-; *n.* kon′veks), *adj.* **1.** having a surface that is curved or rounded outward. Cf. **concave** (def. 1). **2.** *Math.* **a.** (of a polygon) having all interior angles less than or equal to 180°. **b.** (of a set) having the property that for each pair of points in the set the line joining the points is wholly contained in the set. —*n.* **3.** a convex surface, part, or thing. [< L *convex(us)* vaulted, arched, rounded (appar. var. ptp. of *convehere*), equiv. to *con-* CON- + *vec-* (ptp. s. of *vehere* to carry) + *-sus,* var. of *-tus* ptp. suffix] —**con·vex′ly, con·vex·ed·ly** (kən vek′sid lē), *adv.* —**con·vex′ed·ness,** *n.*

A B C

A, Convex or plano-convex lens; B, Convexo-concave lens; C, Convexo-convex lens

con′vex hull′, *Math.* the smallest convex set containing a given set; the intersection of all convex sets that contain a given set.

con·vex·i·ty (kən vek′si tē), *n., pl.* **-ties** for 2. **1.** the state of being convex. **2.** a convex surface or thing. [< L *convexitās.* See CONVEX, -ITY]

convexo-, a combining form of **convex:** *convexoconcave.*

con·vex·o-con·cave (kən vek′sō kon kāv′), *adj.* **1.** convex on one side and concave on the other. **2.** *Optics.* pertaining to or noting a lens in which the convex face has a greater radius of curvature than the concave face. [CONVEXO- + CONCAVE]

con·vex·o-con·vex (kən vek′sō kon veks′), *adj.* convex on both sides; biconvex. [CONVEXO- + CONVEX]

con·vex·o-plane (kən vek′sō plān′), *adj.* plano-convex. [CONVEXO- + PLANE[1]]

con·vey (kən vā′), *v.t.* **1.** to carry, bring, or take from one place to another; transport; bear. **2.** to lead or conduct, as a channel or medium; transmit. **3.** to communicate; impart; make known. **4.** *Law.* to transfer; pass the title to. **5.** *Archaic.* steal; purloin. **6.** *Obs.* to take away secretly. [ME *convey(en)* < AF *conveie(r)* < VL **conviāre,* equiv. to *con-* CON- + *-viāre,* deriv. of *via* way; see VIA] —**con·vey′a·ble,** *adj.*
—**Syn. 1.** bring. See **carry.**

con·vey·ance (kən vā′əns), *n.* **1.** the act of conveying; transmission; communication. **2.** a means of transporting, esp. a vehicle, as a carriage, automobile, etc. **3.** *Law.* **a.** the transfer of property from one person to another. **b.** the instrument or document by which this is effected. [CONVEY + -ANCE]

con·vey·anc·er (kən vā′ən sər), *n.* a person engaged in conveyancing. [CONVEYANCE + -ER[1]]

con·vey·anc·ing (kən vā′ən siṅg), *n.* the branch of law practice consisting of examining titles, giving opinions as to their validity, and drawing of deeds, etc., for the conveyance of property from one person to another. [CONVEYANCE + -ING[1]]

con·vey·or (kən vā′ər), *n.* **1.** one who or that which conveys. **2.** *Mach.* an endless chain or belt adapted for carrying objects or materials. Also, **con·vey′er.** [CONVEY + -OR[2]]

convey′or belt′, *Mach.* an endless belt or chain, set of rollers, etc., for carrying materials or objects short distances, as from one part of a building to another.

convey′or chain′, *Mach.* an endless chain used as a conveyor.

con·vey·or·ize (kən vā′ə rīz′), *v.t.,* **-ized, -iz·ing.** to equip (a factory or the like) with conveyor belts. [CONVEYOR + -IZE] —**con·vey′or·i·za′tion,** *n.* —**con·vey′or·iz′er,** *n.*

con·vict (*v., adj.* kən vikt′; *n.* kon′vikt), *v.t.* **1.** to prove or declare guilty of an offense, esp. after a legal trial: *to convict a prisoner of felony.* **2.** to impress with a sense of guilt. —*n.* **3.** a person proved or declared guilty of an offense. **4.** a person serving a prison sentence. —*adj.* **5.** *Archaic.* convicted. [ME *convict(e)* (ptp.) < L *convict(us)* proved guilty (ptp. of *convincere*), equiv. to *con-* CON- + *vic-* (ptp. s. of *vincere* to overcome) + *-tus* ptp. suffix] —**con·vict′a·ble, con·vict′i·ble,** *adj.* —**con·vic′tive,** *adj.* —**con·vic′tive·ly,** *adv.*

con·vict·fish (kon′vikt fish′), *n., pl.* **-fish·es,** (*esp. collectively*) **-fish.** See **painted greenling.** [CONVICT + FISH, so called from the fancied resemblance of its stripings to a convict's uniform]

con·vic·tion (kən vik′shən), *n.* **1.** the act of convicting. **2.** the state of being convicted. **3.** the act of convincing. **4.** the state of being convinced. **5.** a fixed or firm belief. [late ME < LL *convictiōn-* (s. of *convictiō*) proof (of guilt). See CONVICT, -ION] —**con·vic′tion·al,** *adj.*
—**Syn. 5.** See **belief.** —**Ant. 4.** doubt, uncertainty.

con·vince (kən vins′), *v.t.,* **-vinced, -vinc·ing. 1.** to persuade by argument or proof; cause to believe in the truth of what is alleged (often fol. by *of*): *to convince a man of his errors.* **2.** *Obs.* to prove or find guilty. **3.** *Obs.* overcome; vanquish. [< L *convince(re)* (to) prove (something) false or true, (somebody) right or wrong, equiv. to *con-* CON- + *vincere* to overcome] —**con·vinc′ed·ly,** *adv.* —**con·vinc′ed·ness,** *n.* —**con·vinc′er,** *n.* —**con·vinc′i·bil′i·ty,** *n.* —**con·vin′ci·ble,** *adj.* —**con·vinc′ing·ly,** *adv.* —**con·vinc′ing·ness,** *n.*
—**Syn. 1.** satisfy. See **persuade.**

con·vive (kon′vīv; *Fr.* kôN vēv′), *n., pl.* **-vives** (-vīvz; *Fr.* -vēv′). an eating companion; fellow diner. [< F < L *convīv(a)* one who lives with another, hence table-companion, equiv. to *con-* CON- + *vīv(ere)* (to) live. See REVIVE]

con·viv·i·al (kən viv′ē əl), *adj.* **1.** fond of feasting, drinking, and merry company; jovial. **2.** of or befitting a feast; festive. **3.** friendly; agreeable: *convivial atmosphere.* [< LL *convīviāl(is)* festal, equiv. to L *convīvi(um)* feast (*convīvere* to feast with, equiv. to *con-* CON- + *vīvere* to live well + *-ium* n. suffix) + *-ālis* -AL[1]] —**con·viv′i·al·ist,** *n.* —**con·viv′i·al′i·ty,** *n.* —**con·viv′i·al·ly,** *adv.*

con·vo·ca·tion (kon′və kā′shən), *n.* **1.** the act of convoking. **2.** the state of being convoked. **3.** a group of people gathered in answer to a summons; assembly. **4.** *Ch. of Eng.* one of the two provincial synods or assemblies of the clergy. **5.** *Prot. Episc. Ch.* **a.** an assembly of the clergy of part of a diocese. **b.** the area represented at such an assembly. [ME *convocacio(u)n* < L *convocātiōn-* (s. of *convocātiō*). See CONVOKE, -ATION] —**con′vo·ca′tion·al,** *adj.* —**con′vo·ca′tion·al·ly,** *adv.*
—**Syn. 3.** See **convention.**

con·vo·ca·tor (kon′və kā′tər), *n.* **1.** one who convokes a meeting. **2.** one who takes part in a convocation. [< ML, equiv. to *convocāt(us)* called together (ptp. of *convocāre* to CONVOKE; see -ATE[1]) + *-or* -OR[2]]

con·voke (kən vōk′), *v.t.,* **-voked, -vok·ing.** to call together; summon to meet; assemble by summons. [< L *convoc(āre),* equiv. to *con-* CON- + *vocāre* to call] —**con·voc·a·tive** (kən vok′ə tiv), *adj.* —**con·vok′er, con′vo·cant,** *n.*
—**Syn.** convene.

con·vo·lute (kon′və lo͞ot′), *v.,* **-lut·ed, -lut·ing,** *adj.* —*v.t., v.i.* **1.** to coil up; form into a twisted shape. —*adj.* **2.** rolled up together or with one part over another. **3.** *Bot.* coiled up longitudinally so that one margin is within the coil and the other without, as the petals of cotton. [< L *convolūt(us)* rolled up, equiv. to *convolū-* (ptp. s. of *convolvere* to CONVOLVE) + *-tus* ptp. suffix] —**con′vo·lute′ly,** *adv.*

con·vo·lut·ed (kon′və lo͞o′tid), *adj.* **1.** twisted; coiled. **2.** complicated; intricately involved: *a convoluted way of presenting an argument.* [CONVOLUTE + -ED[2]] —**con′vo·lut′ed·ly,** *adj.* —**con′vo·lut′ed·ness,** *n.*

con·vo·lu·tion (kon′və lo͞o′shən), *n.* **1.** a rolled up or coiled condition. **2.** a rolling or coiling together. **3.** a turn of anything coiled; whorl; sinuosity. **4.** *Anat.* one of the sinuous folds or ridges of the surface of the brain. [< L *convolūt-* (see CONVOLUTE) + -ION] —**con′vo·lu′tion·al, con·vo·lu·tion·ar·y** (kon′və lo͞o′shə ner′ē), *adj.*

con·volve (kən volv′), *v.i., v.t.,* **-volved, -volv·ing.** to roll or wind together; coil; twist. [< L *convolve(re),* equiv. to *con-* CON- + *volvere* to roll, turn, twist] —**con·volve′ment,** *n.*

con·vol·vu·la·ceous (kən vol′vyə lā′shəs), *adj.* belonging to the *Convolvulaceae,* or morning-glory family of plants, including the convolvuluses, ipomoeas, etc. [CONVOLVUL(US) + -ACEOUS]

con·vol·vu·lus (kən vol′vyə ləs), *n., pl.* **-lus·es, -li** (-lī′). any plant of the genus *Convolvulus,* which comprises erect, twining, or prostrate herbs having trumpet-shaped flowers. Cf. **morning-glory.** [< NL, L: bindweed, equiv. to *convolv(ere)* (to) CONVOLVE + *-ulus* -ULE]

con·voy (*v.* kon′voi, kən voi′; *n.* kon′voi), *v.t.* **1.** to accompany or escort, usually for protection: *A destroyer convoyed the merchant ship.* —*n.* **2.** the act of convoying. **3.** the protection provided by an escort. **4.** an armed force, warship, etc., that escorts, esp. for protection. **5.** a ship, fleet, group of vehicles, etc., accompanied by a protecting escort. **6.** any group of military vehicles traveling together under the same orders. **7.** *Obs.* a drag or friction brake, as for a wagon. [ME *convoy(en)* < MF *convoie(r)* < AF *conveier* to CONVEY]
—**Syn. 1.** See **accompany.**

con·vul·sant (kən vul′sənt), *adj.* **1.** causing convulsions; convulsive. —*n.* **2.** a convulsant agent. [CONVULSE + -ANT]

con·vulse (kən vuls′), *v.t.,* **-vulsed, -vuls·ing. 1.** to shake violently; agitate. **2.** to cause to shake violently with laughter, anger, pain, etc. **3.** to cause to suffer violent, spasmodic contractions of the muscles. [< L *convuls(us)* shattered, torn loose (ptp. of *convellere*), equiv. to *con-* CON- + *vul-* (ptp. s. of *vellere* to pull, tear) + *-sus,* var. of *-tus* ptp. suffix] —**con·vuls′ed·ly,** *adv.* —**con·vuls′i·ble,** *adj.* —**con·vuls′i·bil′i·ty,** *n.*

con·vul·sion (kən vul′shən), *n.* **1.** *Pathol.* contortion of the body caused by violent, involuntary muscular contractions of the extremities, trunk, and head. **2.** violent agitation or disturbance; commotion. **3.** an outburst of great, uncontrollable laughter. [< medical L *convulsiōn-* (s. of *convulsiō*). See CONVULSE, -ION]

con·vul·sion·ar·y (kən vul′shə ner′ē), *adj., n., pl.* **-ar·ies.** —*adj.* **1.** of or affected with convulsion. —*n.* **2.** a person who has convulsions, esp. as a result of religious experience. [CONVULSION + -ARY]

con·vul·sive (kən vul′siv), *adj.* **1.** of the nature of or characterized by convulsions or spasms. **2.** producing or accompanied by convulsion: *convulsive rage.* [< medical L *convulsīv(us).* See CONVULSE, -IVE] —**con·vul′sive·ly,** *adv.* —**con·vul′sive·ness,** *n.*
—**Syn. 1.** spasmodic.

Con·way (kon′wā), *n.* **1.** a town in central Arkansas. 9791 (1960). **2.** a town in E South Carolina. 8563 (1960). **3.** a boy's given name.

co·ny (kō′nē, kun′ē), *n., pl.* **-nies.** **1.** the fur of a rabbit, esp. when dyed to simulate Hudson seal. **2.** the daman or some other animal of the same genus. **3.** the pika. **4.** a rabbit. Also, **coney.** [ME, back formation from *conyes* < OF *conis,* pl. of *conil* < L *cunīcul(us)* rabbit, burrowing, mine]

Con·yers (kon′yərz), *n.* a town in central Georgia. 2881 (1960).

coo[1] (ko͞o), *v.,* **cooed, coo·ing,** *n.* —*v.i.* **1.** to utter or imitate the soft, murmuring sound characteristic of pigeons or doves. **2.** to murmur or talk fondly or amorously. —*v.t.* **3.** to utter by cooing. —*n.* **4.** a cooing sound. [imit.] —**coo′er,** *n.* —**coo′ing·ly,** *adv.*

coo[2] (ko͞o), *interj. Brit. Slang.* (used to express surprise or amazement.) [?]

Co·o (kô′ô), *n.* Italian name of **Kos.**

coo·boo (ko͞o′bo͞o), *n., pl.* **-boos.** *Australian Informal.* an aborigine child. [< native Austral]

cooch[1] (ko͞och), *n.* a sinuous, quasi-Oriental dance performed by a woman and characterized chiefly by suggestive gyrating and shaking of the body. Also, **cootch.** Also called **cooch′ dance′, hootchy-kootchy.** [short for HOOTCHY-KOOTCHY]

cooch[2] (ko͞och), *n. Mach.* a roller forcing a semiliquid material against a receiving surface. [var. of COUCH]

Cooch Be·har (ko͞och′ bə här′), **1.** a former state in NE India; now part of West Bengal. 1334 sq. mi. **2.** a city in NE India. 33,242 (1951).

coo·ee (ko͞o′ē), *n., v.,* **coo·eed, coo·ee·ing.** —*n.* **1.** a prolonged, shrill, clear call or cry used as a signal by Australian aborigines and adopted by the settlers in the country. —*v.i.* **2.** to utter the call "cooee." [< native Austral]

coo·ey (ko͞o′ē), *n., pl.* **-eys,** *v.i.,* **-eyed, -ey·ing.** cooee.

coof (ko͝of), *n. Chiefly Scot.* a silly or stupid person. [?]

cook[1] (ko͝ok), *v.t.* **1.** to prepare (food) by the action of heat, as by boiling, baking, roasting, etc. **2.** to subject (anything) to the action of heat. **3.** *Slang.* **a.** to ruin; spoil. **b.** to falsify, as accounts: *to cook the books.* —*v.i.* **4.** to prepare food by the action of heat. **5.** (of food) to undergo cooking. **6.** *Informal.* to take place; occur: *What's cooking at the club?* **7. cook off,** (of a shell or cartridge) to explode or fire without being triggered as a result of overheating in the chamber of the weapon. **8. cook one's goose.** See **goose** (def. 8). **9. cook up,** *Informal.* **a.** to concoct; contrive: *She hastily cooked up an excuse.* **b.** to falsify: *Someone had obviously cooked up the financial records.* [v. use of n.] —*n.* **10.** one who cooks, esp. one employed by another to prepare food for the table: *She has hired a new cook.* [ME *cok(e),* OE *cōc* (cf. Icel *kokkr,* G *Koch,* D *kok*) < L *coc(us),* var. of *coquus,* deriv. of *coquere* to cook; akin to Gk *péptein* to cook] —**cook′a·ble,** *adj.* —**cook′less,** *adj.*

cook[2] (ko͞ok, ko͝ok), *v.i. Scot.* to hide, esp. outdoors, as by crouching down behind a hedge. [? b. ME *couche* bend, stoop (see COUCH) and ME *croke* bend, stoop (see CROOKED)]

Cook (ko͝ok), *n.* **1. Frederick Albert,** 1865–1940, U.S. physician and polar explorer. **2. George Cram** (kram), 1873–1924, U.S. novelist, dramatist, and poet. **3. Captain James,** 1728–79, English navigator and explorer in the S Pacific, Antarctic Ocean, and along the coasts of Australia and New Zealand. **4. Sir Joseph,** 1860–1947, Australian statesman, born in England: prime minister 1913–14. **5. Mount.** Also called **Aorangi.** a mountain in New Zealand, on South Island. 12,349 ft. **6.** a walled plain in the fourth quadrant of the face of the moon, having a dark floor: about 26 miles in diameter.

cook·book (ko͝ok′bo͝ok′), *n.* a book containing recipes and instructions for cooking. Also, *Brit.,* **cookery book.** [COOK[1] + BOOK]

Cooke (ko͝ok), *n.* **1.** See **Coke, Sir Edward. 2. Jay,** 1821–1905, U.S. financier.

cook·er (ko͝ok′ər), *n.* **1.** an appliance or utensil for cooking: *pressure cooker; fireless cooker.* **2.** one employed in certain industrial processes, as in brewing, distilling, etc., to operate cooking apparatus. [COOK[1] + -ER[1]]

cook·er·y (ko͝ok′ə rē), *n., pl.* **-er·ies.** **1.** the art or practice of cooking. **2.** a place equipped for cooking. [ME *cokerie.* See COOK[1], -ERY]

cook′ery book′, *Brit.* cookbook.

cook′ery stove′, *Brit.* cookstove.

Cooke·ville (ko͝ok′vil), *n.* a town in central Tennessee. 7805 (1960).

cook-gen·er·al (ko͝ok′ jen′ər əl), *n., pl.* **cooks-gen·er·al.** *Brit.* a servant who does both cooking and general housework.

cook·house (ko͝ok′hous′), *n., pl.* **-hous·es** (-hou′ziz). a building or place for cooking, esp. a ship's galley or a camp kitchen. [COOK[1] + HOUSE]

cook·ie (ko͝ok′ē), *n.* **1.** *U.S.* a small cake made from stiff, sweet dough dropped, rolled, or sliced and then baked. **2.** *Scot.* a bun. **3.** *Informal.* dear; sweetheart: a term of address, usually connoting affection. **4.** *Slang.* a person, esp. a man: *a smart cookie; a tough cookie.* **5. cookies,** *Slang.* the contents of a person's stomach: *She got seasick and spilled her cookies over the side.* Also, **cooky.** [< D *koekie,* var. of *koekje,* equiv. to *koek* cake (MD *coeke*) + *-je* -Y[2]. See CAKE]

Cook·ie (ko͝ok′ē), *n.* a boy's or girl's given name. Also, **Cook′y.**

cook′ie cut′ter, a device, usually of metal, for cutting shaped forms, as circles, stars, etc., for cookies from dough that has been rolled flat.

cook′ie press′, a device, operating in a manner similar to that of a syringe, in which dough is inserted in a chamber and extruded, by means of a plunger, through one of a number of interchangeable dies to form a shaped cylinder which is sliced into cookies.

cook·ing (ko͝ok′ing), *n.* **1.** the act of one who or that which cooks. **2.** the art or practice of preparing food; cookery. —*adj.* **3.** used in preparing foods: *a cooking utensil.* **4.** fit to eat when cooked (distinguished from *eating*): *cooking apples.* [COOK[1] + -ING[1], -ING[2]]

Cook′ In′let, an inlet of the Gulf of Alaska. 150 mi. long.

Cook′ Is′lands, a group of islands in the S Pacific belonging to New Zealand. 19,214 (1963); 99 sq. mi.

cook·out (ko͝ok′out′), *n.* **1.** a party or entertainment featuring the cooking and eating of a meal out of doors. **2.** the process of cooking and eating a meal outdoors. **3.** a meal cooked and eaten in the open. —*adj.* **4.** of, pertaining to, or intended for use or consumption at a cookout. Also, **cook′-out′.** [n. use of v. phrase *cook out*]

cook·shop (ko͝ok′shop′), *n.* a place where prepared food is sold or served; restaurant. [COOK[1] + SHOP]

Cook's′ tour′ (ko͝oks), an organized but cursory tour of the major features of a place or situation. [after Thomas *Cook* (1808–92), English travel agent]

cook·stove (ko͝ok′stōv′), *n.* a stove for use in cooking. [COOK[1] + STOVE[1]]

Cook′ Strait′, a strait in New Zealand between North and South Islands.

cook·ware (ko͝ok′wâr′), *n.* cooking utensils. [COOK[1] + WARE[1]]

cook·y (ko͝ok′ē), *n., pl.* **cook·ies.** cookie.

cool (ko͞ol), *adj.* **1.** moderately cold; neither warm nor cold. **2.** feeling comfortably or moderately cold: *I'm perfectly cool, but open the window if you feel hot.* **3.** imparting a sensation of moderate coldness: *a cool breeze.* **4.** permitting such a sensation: *a cool dress.* **5.** not excited; calm; unmoved: *to remain cool in the face of disaster; to remain cool to the music.* **6.** not hasty; deliberate: *a cool and calculated action.* **7.** deficient in ardor or enthusiasm: *a cool invitation.* **8.** lacking in cordiality: *a cool reception.* **9.** calmly audacious or impudent: *a cool lie.* **10.** aloof; dissassionate; unfeeling: *He was cool to her passionate advances.* **11.** *Informal.* (of a number or sum) without exaggeration or qualification: *a cool million dollars.* **12.** (of colors) with green, blue, or violet predominating. **13.** *Slang.* great; fine; excellent: *a real cool comic.* —*adv.* **14.** *Informal.* coolly. —*n.* **15.** something that is cool; a cool part, place, time, etc.: *in the cool of the evening.* **16.** coolness. —*v.i.* **17.** to become cool (sometimes fol. by *down* or *off*): *The soup cooled in five minutes. We cooled off in the mountain stream.* **18.** to become less ardent, cordial, etc.; become moderate. —*v.t.* **19.** to make cool; impart a sensation of coolness to. **20.** to lessen the ardor or intensity of; allay; calm; moderate: *They cooled his early zealousness.* **21. cool it,** *Slang.* calm down; take it easy. **22. cool off,** *Informal.* to become calmer or more reasonable: *Wait until he cools off before you approach him again.* **23. cool one's heels.** See **heel**[1] (def. 17). [ME *cole,* OE *cōl;* c. MLG *kōl,* OHG *kuoli* (G *kuhl*). See COLD, CHILL] —**cool′ing·ly,** *adv.* —**cool′ing·ness,** *n.* —**cool′ly,** *adv.* —**cool′ness,** *n.*
—**Syn. 1.** See **cold. 5.** composed, collected, self-possessed, unruffled, placid, quiet. See **calm. 7.** distant, apathetic, indifferent, lukewarm. **8.** quiet. **20.** temper, abate. —**Ant. 1, 5, 7, 8.** warm.

coo·la·mon (ko͞o′lə mon′, -mən), *n.* a basinlike dish made from wood or bark by Australian aborigines. [< native Austral]

cool·ant (ko͞o′lənt), *n.* **1.** a substance, usually a liquid or a gas, used to reduce the temperature of a system below a specified value by conducting away the heat produced in the operation of the system, as the liquid in an automobile cooling system. **2.** a lubricant that dissipates the heat caused by friction. [COOL + -ANT]

cool·er (ko͞o′lər), *n.* **1.** a container or apparatus in which something may be cooled or kept cool: *We'll take the beer to the picnic in a cooler.* **2.** anything that cools or makes cool; refrigerant. **3.** an air-conditioner. **4.** a tall, iced drink: *a grape cooler; a rum cooler.* **5.** See **water cooler. 6.** *Slang.* jail: *He was in the cooler for three months for petty theft.* **7.** *Ice Hockey Slang.* See **penalty box. 8.** a light blanket or similar covering put over a horse being walked after a workout, race, etc., to ensure that the horse cools off gradually. [COOL + -ER[1]]

Coo·ley (ko͞o′lē), *n.* **Charles Hor·ton** (hôr′tən), 1864–1929, U.S. author and pioneer in the field of sociology.

cool-head·ed (ko͞ol′hed′id), *adj.* not easily excited; calm. —**cool′-head′ed·ly,** *adv.* —**cool′-head′ed·ness,** *n.*

Cool·idge (ko͞o′lij), *n.* **1. Calvin,** 1872–1933, 30th president of the U.S. 1923–29. **2.** a town in central Arizona. 4990 (1960).

Cool′idge tube′, *Physics.* a cathode ray tube, used for x-ray production, in which a beam of thermoelectrons is produced by heating a wire cathode. [named after William D. *Coolidge* (b. 1873), American physicist and chemist who devised it]

coo·lie (ko͞o′lē), *n.* **1.** (in India, China, etc.) an unskilled native laborer. **2.** an unskilled laborer employed cheaply, esp. one brought from the Orient. Also, **cooly.** [< Urdu *kūlī* < Tamil *kūli* hire, hireling]

cool′ing degree′-day, a degree-day above the standard temperature of 75°F, used in estimating the energy requirements for air conditioning and refrigeration. Cf. **growing degree-day, heating degree-day.**

cool·ing-off (ko͞o′ling ôf′, -of′), *adj.* intended to allow feelings to become more moderate, usually in order to permit more level-headed discussion of a point in contention: *a cooling-off arrangement; a cooling-off provision in the bill under consideration.*

cool′ing-off′ pe′riod, a period arranged by agreement to allow for negotiation and an abatement of tension between disputing parties: *The Taft-Hartley Act calls for an 80-day cooling-off period.*

cool·ish (ko͞o′lish), *adj.* somewhat cool. [COOL + -ISH[1]]

cool′ jazz′, a style of modern jazz marked by the use of intricate harmonic structures, a de-emphasis of dynamic contrast and tone production, and by carefully controlled phrasing and ensemble playing.

coolth (ko͞olth), *n. Informal.* coolness. [COOL + -TH[1]]

coo·ly (ko͞o′lē), *n., pl.* **-lies.** coolie.

coom (ko͞om), *n. Chiefly Scot. and North Eng.* **1.** soot; coal dust; smut. **2.** dust, esp. sawdust or dust from a gristmill. **3.** grease from bearings, axles, etc. Also, **coomb.** [var. of CULM[1]]

Coo·ma (ko͞o′mä, -mə), *n.* a city in SE Australia. 8716 (1961).

coomb[1] (ko͞om, kōm), *n.* combe. Also, **coombe.**

coomb[2] (ko͞om), *n.* coom.

coon (ko͞on), *n.* **1.** raccoon. **2.** *Offensive and Disparaging.* a Negro. **3.** *U.S. Dial.* a rustic or undignified person. [aph. form]

coon·can (ko͞on′kan′), *n. Cards.* a variety of rummy for two players. [popular alter. of CONQUIAN]

coon′ dog′, any dog trained to hunt raccoons.

coon·er (ko͞o′nər), *n.* See **coon dog.** [COON + -ER[1]]

coon·hound (ko͞on′hound′), *n.* **1.** See **coon dog. 2.** a hound of any of several breeds developed esp. for hunting raccoons. [COON + HOUND[1]]

coon's′ age′, *Informal.* a long time: *I haven't seen you in a coon's age!*

coon·skin (ko͞on′skin′), *n.* **1.** the pelt of a raccoon. **2.** an article of clothing made of coonskin, esp. a cap with a tail. —*adj.* **3.** made of coonskin: *a coonskin cap.* [COON + SKIN]

coon·tie (ko͞on′tē), *n.* **1.** either of two arrowroots, *Zamia integrifolia* or *Z. floridana,* of Florida. **2.** the flour produced from its starch. [< Seminole *kunti* the flour (from the plant)]

co-op (kō′op, kō op′), *n.* a cooperative store, society, dwelling, etc. Also, **co′op.** [shortened form]

coop (ko͞op, ko͝op), *n.* **1.** an enclosure, cage, or pen, usually with bars or wires on at least one side, in which fowls or other small animals are confined for fattening, transportation, etc. **2.** any small or narrow place. **3.** *Slang.* a prison. **4. fly the coop,** *Slang.* to escape, as from a prison; flee: *The robbery suspect had flown the coop despite police surveillance.* —*v.t.* **5.** to place in or as if in a coop; confine narrowly (often fol. by *up* or *in*). [ME *coupe* basket, perh. < Scand; cf. Norw *kaup* wooden can; akin to OE *cȳpa* basket]

Coop (ko͞op), *n.* a boy's given name.

coop., cooperative. Also, **co-op., coöp.**

coop·er (ko͞o′pər, ko͝op′ər), *n.* **1.** one who makes or repairs casks, barrels, etc. —*v.t.* **2.** to make or repair (casks, barrels, etc.). **3.** to furnish or fix (usually fol. by *up*). —*v.i.* **4.** to work as a cooper. [ME *couper* < MLG *kūper* or MD *cūper* < ML *cūpār(ius)* (L *cūp(a)* cask, vat + *-ārius* -ER[2])]

Coo·per (ko͞o′pər, ko͝op′ər), *n.* **1. Anthony Ashley.** See **Shaftesbury, Anthony Ashley Cooper. 2. Hugh Lincoln,** 1865–1937, U.S. hydraulic engineer. **3. James Fen·i·more** (fen′ə mōr′, -môr′), 1789–1851, U.S. novelist. **4. Peter,** 1791–1883, U.S. inventor, manufacturer, reformer, and philanthropist.

coop·er·age (ko͞o′pər ij, ko͝op′ər-), *n.* **1.** the work or business of a cooper. **2.** the place where such work is carried on. **3.** the price paid or charged for coopers' work. **4.** articles made by a cooper, as barrels or casks. [COOPER + -AGE]

co·op·er·ate (kō op′ə rāt′), *v.i.,* **-at·ed, -at·ing.** **1.** to work or act together or jointly for a common purpose or benefit. **2.** to work or act with another or other persons willingly and agreeably. **3.** to practice economic cooperation. Also, **co-op′er·ate′, co·öp′er·ate′.** [< LL *cooperāt(us)* busied with, ptp. of *cooperārī.* See CO-, OPERATE] —**co·op′er·a′tor, co-op′er·a′tor, co·öp′er·a′tor,** *n.*

co·op·er·a·tion (kō op′ə rā′shən), *n.* **1.** an act or instance of working or acting together for a common purpose or benefit; joint action. **2.** more or less active assistance from a person, organization, etc.: *We sought the cooperation of various civic leaders.* **3.** willingness to cooperate: *We can be through soon if you show a little cooperation.* **4.** *Econ.* the combination of persons for purposes of production, purchase, or distribution for their joint benefit: *producers' cooperation; consumers' cooperation.* **5.** *Sociol.* activity shared for mutual benefit. **6.** *Ecol.* mutually beneficial interaction among organisms living in a limited area. Also, **co-op′er·a′tion, co·öp′er·a′tion.** [< LL *cooperātiōn-* (s. of *cooperātiō*). See COOPERATE, -ION] —**co·op′er·a′tion·ist, co-op′er·a′tion·ist, co·öp′er·a′tion·ist,** *n.*

co·op·er·a·tive (kō op′ə rā′tiv, -ər ə tiv), *adj.* **1.** working or acting together willingly for a common purpose or benefit. **2.** demonstrating a willingness to cooperate: *The librarian was most cooperative when I had trouble finding the book.* **3.** pertaining to economic cooperation: *a cooperative business.* —*n.* **4.** a jointly owned means of production or distribution of goods or services operated by the consumers for their mutual benefit: *a farmers' cooperative; a new housing cooperative.* Also, **co-op′er·a′tive, co·öp′er·a′tive.** [< LL *cooperātīv(us).* See COOPERATE, -IVE] —**co·op′er·a·tive·ly, co-op·er·a·tive·ly, co·öp′er·a′tive·ly** (kō op′ə rā′tiv lē, -ər ə tiv-), *adv.* —**co·op′er·a′tive·ness, co-op′er·a′tive·ness, co·öp′er·a′tive·ness,** *n.*

coop′erative bank′. See **savings and loan association.**

coop′erative cred′it un′ion. See **credit union.**

coop′erative store′, **1.** a retail store owned and managed by consumer-customers who supply the capital and share in the profits by patronage dividends. **2.** a store operated by a farmers' cooperative organization or by a cooperative chain.

coop′ered joint′, *Joinery.* a joint made between pieces in a polygonal or curved construction, using either splines or dowels.

coop·er·ite (ko͞o′pə rīt′), *n.* a mineral, sulfide and arsenide of platinum, occurring in igneous rocks in the form of steel-gray crystals. [named after R. A. *Cooper,* who described it in 1920; see -ITE[1]]

Coo′per's hawk′, a North American hawk, *Accipiter cooperii,* having a bluish-gray back and a rusty breast. [named after William *Cooper* (d. 1864), American ornithologist]

Coo·pers·town (ko͞o′pərz toun′, ko͝op′ərz-), *n.* a town in central New York: location of the baseball Hall of Fame. 2553 (1960).

coop·er·y (ko͞o′pə rē, ko͝op′ə-), *n., pl.* **-ries.** **1.** the work of a cooper. **2.** a cooper's shop. **3.** articles made by a cooper. [COOPER + -Y[3]]

co-opt (kō opt′), *v.t.* to elect into a body by the votes of the existing members. Also, **co·öpt′.** [< L *coopt(āre).* See CO-, OPT] —**co′-op·ta′tion, co′öp·ta′tion, co-op·tion, co·öp·tion** (kō op′shən), *n.* —**co-op·ta·tive, co·öp·ta·tive** (kō op′tə tiv), *adj.*

co-or·di·nal (kō ôr′dənəl), *adj. Bot., Zool.* belonging to the same order. Also, **co·ör′di·nal.** [CO- + ORDINAL[1]]

co·or·di·nate (*adj., n.* kō ôr′dənit, -dənāt′; *v.* kō ôr′dənāt′), *adj., n., v.,* **-nat·ed, -nat·ing.** —*adj.* **1.** of the same order or degree; equal in rank or importance. **2.** involving coordination. **3.** *Math.* using or pertaining to systems of coordinates. —*n.* **4.** *Gram.* of the same grammatical construction, as "*Jack*" and "*Jill*" in the phrase "*Jack and Jill,*" or "*got up*" and "*shook*" in the sentence "*He got up and shook hands.*" **5.** one who or that which is equal in rank or importance; an equal. **6.** *Math.* any of the magnitudes that serve to define the position of a point, line, or the like, by reference to a fixed figure, system of lines, etc. **7. coordinates,** *Clothing.* women's outer garments, harmonizing in color, fabric, and style, designed to be worn together. Cf. **separate** (def. 19). —*v.t.* **8.** to place or class in the same order, rank, division, etc. **9.** to place or arrange in proper order or position. **10.** to combine in harmonious relation or action. —*v.i.* **11.** to become coordinate. **12.** to assume proper order or relation. **13.** to act in harmonious combination. Also, **co-or′di·nate, co·ör′di·nate.** [co- + (SUB)ORDINATE] —**co·or′di·nate·ly, co-or′di·nate·ly, co·ör′di·nate·ly,** *adv.* —**co·or′di·nate·ness, co-or′di·nate·ness, co·ör′di·nate·ness,** *n.* —**co·or·di·na·tive, co-or·di·na·tive, co·ör·di·na·tive** (kō ôr′dᵊnā′tiv, -ôr′dᵊnə-), *adj.* —**co·or′di·na′tor, co-or′di·na′tor, co·ör′di·na′tor,** *n.*

coor′dinate pa′per. See **graph paper.**

coor′dinate sys′tem, a system that uses coordinates to establish position.

coor′dinating conjunc′tion, *n.* **1.** *Gram.* a conjunction that connects two grammatical elements of identical construction, as "*and*" in "*Sue and Andrea*" or "*or*" in "*He can't decide if he should stay or go.*" Cf. **subordinating conjunction. 2.** *Ling.* a link or marker in a conjoining transformation.

co·or·di·na·tion (kō ôr′dᵊnā′shən), *n.* **1.** the act or state of coordinating or of being coordinated. **2.** proper order or relationship. **3.** harmonious combination or interaction, as of functions or parts. Also, **co-or′di·na′tion, co·ör′di·na′tion.** [< LL *coordinātiōn-* (s. of *coordinātiō*). See co-, ORDINATION]

coordina′tion num′ber, *Crystall.* the number of anions surrounding a single cation in a stable crystal structure.

Coorg (kŏŏrg), *n.* a former province in SW India; now part of Mysore state. 1593 sq. mi. Also, **Kurg.**

Coos (kōōs), *n.* a language of a group of American Indians indigenous to the coast of Oregon.

Coos′ Bay′, a town in SW Oregon. 7084 (1960).

coot (kōōt), *n.* **1.** any aquatic bird of the genus *Fulica,* as *F. americana,* of North America, and *F. atra,* of the Old World, characterized by lobate toes and short wings and tail. **2.** any of various other swimming or diving birds, esp. the scoters. **3.** *Informal.* a foolish or crotchety man, esp. one who is rather old. [ME *cote;* c. D *koet*]

American coot, *Fulica americana* (Length 16 in.)

cootch (kōōch), *n.* cooch[1].

coot·er (kōō′tər), *n.* any of several large aquatic turtles of the southeastern U.S. and Mexico, esp. *Pseudemys floridana.* [*coot* to copulate (said of tortoises; perh. of Afr orig.; cf. Mandingo *kuta* turtle) + -ER[1]]

coot·ie[1] (kōō′tē), *n.* a louse, esp. the body louse. Also, **cooty.** [? < Malay *kut(u)* louse + -IE]

coot·ie[2] (kōō′tē), *n. Scot.* a wooden container, esp. a wooden bowl, for storing or serving food or drink. Also, **cooty.**

coot′ie garage′, *Slang.* either of a pair of coils of hair worn by a woman on the sides of the head, over the ears; popular esp. during the 1920's.

coot·y[1] (kōō′tē), *n., pl.* **coot·ies.** cootie[1].

coot·y[2] (kōō′tē), *n., pl.* **coot·ies.** *Scot.* cootie[2].

cop[1] (kop), *v.t.,* **copped, cop·ping.** *Slang.* **1.** to catch; nab. **2.** to steal; filch. **3. cop out, a.** to be apprehended for a crime. **b.** Also, **cop a plea.** to plead guilty to a charge, esp. with the intention of escaping more serious punishment which might result from standing trial. [akin to OE *copian* to plunder, steal, hence modern take, lay hold of]

cop[2] (kop), *n. Informal.* a policeman. [back formation from COPPER[2]]

cop[3] (kop), *n.* **1.** a conical mass of thread, yarn, etc., wound on a spindle. **2.** *Brit. Dial.* crest; tip. [ME, OE *cop* tip, top (in ME also head), prob. c. D *kop,* G *Kopf* head; see CUP]

Cop., 1. Copernican. **2.** Coptic.

cop., 1. copper. **2.** copyright; copyrighted.

co·pa·cet·ic (kō′pə set′ik, -sē′tik), *adj. Slang.* fine; completely satisfactory; O.K. Also, **copasetic, copesetic.** [?]

co·pai·ba (kō pā′bə, -pī′bə), *n.* an oleoresin obtained from several tropical, chiefly South American, caesalpiniaceous trees of the genus *Copaifera:* used chiefly in varnishes and lacquers, for removing old oil varnish from or for brightening oil paintings, and formerly in medicine in the treatment of certain mucous-membrane conditions. Also called **balsam capivi, copai′ba bal′sam, copai′ba res′in, Jesuits' resin.** [< Sp < Pg < Tupi]

copai′ba oil′, a colorless, yellowish, or bluish liquid having a pepperlike odor and bitter taste, obtained from copaiba by distillation: used chiefly in the manufacture of perfumes and soaps.

co·pal (kō′pəl, -pal), *n.* a hard, lustrous resin obtained from various tropical trees and used chiefly in making varnishes. [< Sp < Nahuatl *copal(li)* kind of resin]

co·pal·ite (kō′pə līt′), *n. Mineral.* a pale-yellow, amberlike substance composed mainly of hydrocarbons and found in some clays in the Congo. Also, **co·pal·ine** (kō′pə lēn′, -lin). [COPAL + -ITE[1]]

co·palm (kō′päm′), *n.* See **sweet gum** (defs. 1, 2). [? < MexSp *copalme* < LaF **copalmé,* b. *copal* COPAL and *palmé* PALMATE]

Co·pán (*Sp.* kō pän′), *n.* See **Santa Rosa de Copán.**

co·par·ce·nar·y (kō pär′sə ner′ē), *n. Law.* a special kind of joint ownership arising esp. under common law upon the descent of real property to several female heirs. Also, **co·par·ce·ny** (kō pär′sə nē). [co- + PARCENARY]

co·par·ce·ner (kō pär′sə nər), *n.* a member of a coparcenary. [co- + PARCENER]

co·part·ner (kō pärt′nər, kō′pärt′-), *n.* a fellow partner or associate, as in a business. [co- + PARTNER] —**co·part′ner·ship′,** *n.*

co·pa·set·ic (kō′pə set′ik, -sē′tik), *adj.* copacetic.

cope[1] (kōp), *v.,* **coped, cop·ing.** —*v.i.* **1.** to struggle or contend, esp. on fairly even terms or with some degree of success (usually fol. by *with*): *I will try to cope with his rudeness.* **2.** *Archaic.* to come into contact; meet (usually fol. by *with*). —*v.t.* **3.** *Brit. Informal.* to cope with. **4.** *Obs.* to come into contact with; encounter. [ME *coupe(n)* < MF, OF *coupe(r)* (to) strike, deriv. of *coup* COUP[1]]

cope[2] (kōp), *n., v.,* **coped, cop·ing.** —*n.* **1.** a long mantle of silk or other material worn by ecclesiastics over the alb or surplice in processions and on other occasions. **2.** any cloaklike or canopylike covering. **3.** the vault of heaven; the sky. **4.** a coping. **5.** *Foundry.* the upper half of a flask. Cf. **drag** (def. 28). —*v.t.* **6.** to furnish with or as if with a cope or coping. [ME, OE *cāp* < ML *cāp(a),* var. of *cappa* CAP[1]]

A, Cope; B, Crosier

cope[3] (kōp), *v.t.,* **coped, cop·ing. 1.** *Building Trades.* **a.** to join (two molded wooden members) by undercutting the end of one of them to the profile of the other so that the joint produced resembles a miter joint (usually fol. by *in* or *together*). **b.** to form (a joint between such members) in this way. **c.** to undercut the end of (a molded wooden member) in order to form a coped joint. **d.** to cut away (a flange of a metal member) so that it may be joined to another member at an angle. **2.** *Falconry.* to clip or dull (the beak or talons of a hawk). [< F *coup(er)* (to) cut; see COPE[1]]

cope[4] (kōp), *v.t.,* **coped, cop·ing.** *Brit.* to barter; trade; exchange. [late ME *cope(n)* < LG; cf. MD *côpen* to buy]

co·peck (kō′pek), *n.* kopeck.

cope·mate (kōp′māt′), *n. Obs.* **1.** an antagonist; opponent. **2.** a comrade; partner. Also, **copesmate.** [COPE[1] + MATE[1]]

Co·pen·ha·gen (kō′pən hā′gən, -hä′-, kō′pən hā′-, -hä′-), *n.* a seaport in and the capital of Denmark, on the E coast of Zeeland. 923,974 (1960); with suburbs, 1,348,454 (1960). Danish, **København.**

co′penha′gen blue′, gray-blue.

co·pe·pod (kō′pə pod′), *n.* **1.** any minute, fresh-water or marine crustacean of the subclass *Copepoda.* —*adj.* **2.** belonging or pertaining to the *Copepoda.* [< NL *Copepod(a)* name of the order < Gk *kṓpē* a handle, oar + *-poda* -PODA]

cop·er (kō′pər), *n. Brit.* a horse dealer. Also called **horse-coper.** [COPE[4] + -ER[1]]

Co·per·ni·can (kō pûr′ni kən, kə-), *adj.* **1.** of or pertaining to Copernicus or his theories. **2.** important and radically different; thoroughgoing: *the Copernican revolution of Kant in philosophy.* [COPERNIC(US) + -AN]

Co·per·ni·cus (kō pûr′nə kəs, kə-), *n.* **1. Nic·o·la·us** (nik′ə lā′əs), (*Mikolaj Kopernik*), 1473–1543, Polish astronomer who promulgated the now accepted theory that the earth and the other planets move around the sun (the **Coper′nican Sys′tem**). **2.** a crater in the second quadrant of the face of the moon, having an extensive ray system: about 56 miles in diameter from crest to crest with walls rising about 12,000 feet from its floor; having several central mountains the highest being about 2400 feet.

co·pe·set·ic (kō′pə set′ik, -sē′tik), *adj.* copacetic.

copes·mate (kōps′māt′), *n. Obs.* copemate.

cope·stone (kōp′stōn′), *n.* **1.** the top stone of a building or other structure. **2.** a stone used for or in coping. **3.** the crown or completion; finishing touch. [COPE[2] + STONE]

Co·piague (kō′pāg, -peg), *n.* a town on SW Long Island, in SE New York. 14,081 (1960).

Co·pia·pó (kō′pyä pō′), *n.* a city in N Chile. 19,535 (1960).

cop·i·er (kop′ē ər), *n.* one who or that which copies; copyist. [COPY + -ER[1]]

co·pi·lot (kō′pī′lət), *n.* a pilot who is second in command of an aircraft. Also called **first officer.** [co- + PILOT]

cop·ing (kō′piṅg), *n.* **1.** a finishing or protective course or cap to an exterior masonry wall or the like. **2.** a piece of woodwork having its end shaped to fit together with a molding. [COPE[2] + -ING[1]]

A

B

Coping
A, Stone; B, Tile

cop′ing saw′, a saw consisting of a light, ribbonlike blade held, under tension, in a three-sided, U-shaped frame that has a handle: used for cutting small curves in wood.

Coping saw

co·pi·ous (kō′pē əs), *adj.* **1.** large in quantity or number; abundant: *copious amounts of food.* **2.** having or yielding an abundant supply: *a copious larder; a copious harvest.* **3.** exhibiting abundance or fullness, as of thoughts or words. [ME < L *cōpiōs(us)* plentiful, rich, equiv. to *cōpi(a)* wealth (*co-* co- + *op-* (s. of *ops;* see OPS) + *-ia* -IA) + *-ōsus* -OUS] —**co′pi·ous·ly,** *adv.* —**co′pi·ous·ness, co·pi·os·i·ty** (kō′pē os′i tē), *n.*
—**Syn. 1.** plentiful. **2.** See **ample.** —**Ant. 1.** scanty. **2.** scarce. **3.** meager.

co·pla·nar (kō plā′nər), *adj. Math.* being or operating in the same plane. [co- + *planar* < LL *plānār(is);* see PLANE[1], -AR[1]] —**co·pla·nar·i·ty** (kō′plə nar′i tē), *n.*

Cop·land (kōp′lənd), *n.* **Aaron,** born 1900, U.S. composer.

Cop·lay (kop′lē), *n.* a town in E Pennsylvania. 3701 (1960).

Cop·ley (kop′lē), *n.* **John Sin·gle·ton** (siṅg′gəl tən), 1738–1815, U.S. painter.

co·pol·y·mer (kō pol′ə mər), *n. Chem.* a compound of high molecular weight produced by polymerizing two or more different monomers together. [co- + POLYMER]

co·pol·y·mer·ize (kō pol′ə mə rīz′), *v.i., v.t.,* **-ized, -iz·ing.** *Chem.* to subject to or undergo a change analogous to polymerization but with a union of two or more different monomers. [COPOLYMER + -IZE] —**co·pol′y·mer·i·za′tion,** *n.*

Cop·pard (kop′ərd), *n.* **A(lfred) E(dgar),** 1878–1957, English poet and short-story writer.

Cop·pée (kô pā′), *n.* **Fran·çois** (fräN swa′), 1842–1908, French poet, dramatist, and novelist.

Cop·pel·ia (kō pāl′yə), *n.* a ballet (1870) by Délibes.

cop·per[1] (kop′ər), *n.* **1.** *Chem.* a malleable, ductile, metallic element having a characteristic reddish-brown color: used in large quantities as an electrical conductor and in the manufacture of alloys, as brass and bronze. *Symbol:* Cu; *at. wt.:* 63.54; *at. no.:* 29; *sp. gr.:* 8.92 at 20°C. **2.** a coin composed of copper, bronze, or the like, as the U.S. cent or the British penny. **3.** a container made of copper. **4.** a tool partly or wholly made of copper: *a soldering copper.* **5.** *Brit.* a large kettle, now usually made of iron, used for cooking or to boil laundry. **6.** a metallic reddish brown. **7.** any of several butterflies of the family *Lycaenidae,* as *Lycaena hypophleas* **(American copper),** having copper-colored wings spotted and edged with black. —*v.t.* **8.** to cover, coat, or sheathe with copper. **9.** *Informal.* hedge (def. 7). —*adj.* **10.** made of copper: *copper kettles.* **11.** coppery: *The copper sun sank into the sea.* [ME *coper,* OE *copor, copor* (c. Icel *koparr,* G *Kupfer*) < LL *cuprum* for L (*aes*) *Cyprium* CYPRIAN (metal)]

cop·per[2] (kop′ər), *n. Slang.* a policeman. [COP[1] + -ER[1]]

cop′per ac·e·to·ar′se·nite (as′i tō är′sə nīt′, ə sē′tō-), *Chem.* See **Paris green** (def. 1). [ACETO- + ARSENITE]

Cop′per Age′, a cultural period intermediate between the Neolithic and the Bronze Ages, marked by the limited development and use of copper tools.

cop·per·ah (kop′ər ə), *n.* copra.

cop′per ar′senite, *Chem.* a yellowish-green, water-insoluble, poisonous powder, $CuHAsO_3$, used chiefly as a pigment and as an insecticide.

cop·per·as (kop′ər əs), *n.* See **ferrous sulfate.** [late ME *coperas,* var. of ME *coperose* < ML (*aqua*) *cuprōsa* copperish (water). See COPPER[1], -OSE[1]]

Cop′per·as Cove′ (kop′ər əs), a town in central Texas. 4567 (1960).

cop′per beech′, a variety of the European beech, *Fagus sylvatica cuprea,* having bright copper-colored leaves.

cop′per cy′anide, *Chem.* See **cuprous cyanide.**

cop·per·head (kop′ər hed′), *n.* **1.** a venomous snake, *Ancistrodon contortrix,* of the eastern and south-eastern U.S., having a brown to copper-red body marked with darker bands. **2.** (*cap.*) a Northerner who sympathized with the South during the American Civil War. [COPPER[1] + HEAD]

Copperhead (Length to 3 ft.)

Cop·per·head·ism (kop′ər hed iz′əm), *n.* advocacy by a Northerner of the Confederate cause in the American Civil War. [COPPERHEAD + -ISM]

cop′per hydrox′ide, *Chem.* a blue, water-insoluble, poisonous powder, $Cu(OH)_2$, used in the manufacture of rayon, as a source for copper salts, and as a mordant. Also called **cupric hydroxide.**

cop′per i′ris, an iris, *Iris fulva,* found from the Gulf Coast to southern Illinois, having copper-colored or tawny flowers with blue or green variegation.

cop·per-leaf (kop′ər lēf′), *n., pl.* **-leaves.** a plant, *Acalypha wilkesiana,* of the Pacific Islands, having showy, bronzy-green, usually red-mottled foliage.

Cop·per·mine (kop′ər mīn′), *n.* a river in N Canada, in the central Northwest Territories, flowing N to the Arctic Ocean. 525 mi. long.

cop·per·plate (kop′ər plāt′), *n.* **1.** a plate of polished copper on which a writing, picture, or design is made by engraving or etching. **2.** a print or impression from such a plate. **3.** engraving or printing of this kind. [COPPER[1] + PLATE[1]]

cop′per pyri′tes, chalcopyrite.

cop·per·smith[1] (kop′ər smith′), *n.* one who makes utensils, jewelry, etc., out of copper. [ME *copresmythe.* See COPPER[1], SMITH]

cop·per·smith[2] (kop′ər smith′), *n.* a crimson-breasted barbet, *Megalaima haemacephala,* of India, southeast Asia, and adjacent islands, characterized by the ringing, metallic sound of its note. [special use of COPPERSMITH[1]]

cop′per spot′, *Plant Pathol.* a disease of grasses characterized by coppery or orange spore masses covering the blades and caused by a fungus, *Gloeocercospora Sorghi.*

cop′per sul′fate, *Chem.* See **blue vitriol.**

cop·per·y (kop′ə rē), *adj.* of, resembling, or containing copper. [COPPER[1] + -Y[1]]

cop·pice (kop′is), *n. Chiefly Brit.* copse. [late ME *copies* < MF *copeis,* OF *copeiz* < VL **colpātīc(ium)* cut-over area, equiv. to **colpāt(us)* cut (ptp. of **colpāre;* see COPE[1]) + *-īcium* -ICE] —**cop′piced,** *adj.*

cop·ping (kop′iṅg), *n.* the winding of yarn into a cap from a cone, bobbin, etc. Also called **quilling.** [COP[2] + -ING[1]]

copr-, var. of **copro-** before a vowel: *copremia.*

co·pra (kop′rə), *n.* the dried kernel or meat of the coconut from which coconut oil is expressed. Also, **copperah.** [< Pg < Malayalam *koppara* < Hindi *khoprā* coconut]

co·pre·cip·i·tate (kō′pri sip′i tāt′), *v.,* **-tat·ed, -tat·ing.** *Chem.* —*v.t.* **1.** to cause to precipitate together. —*v.i.* **2.** to precipitate together in the same reaction. [co- + PRECIPITATE] —**co′pre·cip′i·ta′tion,** *n.*

cop·re·mi·a (ko prē′mē ə), *n. Pathol.* poisoning due to the presence of fecal matter in the blood. Also, **cop·rae′mi·a.** [COPR- + -EMIA] —**cop·re·mic, cop·rae·mic** (ko prē′mik), *adj.*

Cop·re·us (kop′rē əs, -rōōs), *n. Class. Myth.* the herald of Eurystheus.

copro-, a learned borrowing from Greek meaning "dung," used in the formation of compound words: *coprophagous.* Also, *esp. before a vowel,* **copr-.** [< Gk *kopro-,* comb. form of *kópros*]

cop·ro·lag·ni·a (kop′rə lag′nē ə), *n. Psychiatry.* sexual arousal produced by the thought or sight of feces. [COPRO- + -LAGNIA] —**cop·ro·lag·nist** (kop′rə lag′nist), *n.*

cop·ro·la·li·a (kop′rə lā′lē ə), *n. Psychiatry.* the obsessive use of obscene language. [COPRO- + -LALIA] —**cop·ro·la′li·ac** (kop′rə lā′lē ak′), *adj.*

cop·ro·lite (kop′rə līt′), *n.* a roundish, stony mass consisting of petrified fecal matter of animals. [COPRO- + -LITE] —**cop·ro·lit·ic** (kop′rə lit′ik), *adj.*

cop·rol·o·gy (ko prol′ə jē), *n.* scatology. [COPRO- + -LOGY]

cop·roph·a·gous (ko prof′ə gəs), *adj.* feeding on dung, as certain beetles. [COPRO- + -PHAGOUS] —**cop·roph·a·gist** (ko prof′ə jist), *n.* —**cop·roph′a·gy,** *n.*

cop·ro·phil·i·a (kop′rə fil′ē ə, -fēl′yə), *n.* *Psychiatry.* an extreme interest in feces. [COPRO- + -PHILIA] —**cop′ro·phil′ic,** *adj.* —**co·proph·i·lism** (kə prof′ə liz′əm), *n.*

co·proph·i·lous (kə prof′ə ləs), *adj.* **1.** living or growing on dung, as certain fungi. **2.** coprophilic. [COPRO- + -PHILOUS]

cop·ro·pho·bi·a (kop′rə fō′bē ə), *n.* *Psychiatry.* an abnormal fear of feces. [COPRO- + -PHOBIA] —**cop′ro·pho′bic,** *adj.*

co·pros·ter·ol (kə pros′tə rōl′, -rôl′, -rol′), *n.* *Biochem.* a sterol, $C_{27}H_{48}O$, found in feces and formed in the intestine by bacterial hydrogenation of cholesterol. Also called **co·pros·ta·nol** (kə pros′tə nōl′, -nôl′, -nol′). [COPRO- + STEROL]

cops′ and rob′bers, a children's game in which a group of players imitate the behavior of policemen and of thieves, as in pursuing, capturing, etc.

copse (kops), *n.* a thicket of small trees or bushes; a small wood. Also, *esp. Brit.,* **coppice.** [alter. of COPPICE]

Copt (kopt), *n.* **1.** one of the natives of Egypt descended from the ancient Egyptians. **2.** a member of the Coptic Church. [< Ar *qubt,* back formation from *qubtī* < Coptic *kyptios*), var. of *gyptios* < Gk *Aigýptios* EGYPTIAN]

cop·ter (kop′tər), *n.* *Informal.* helicopter. Also, **′cop′ter.** [short form]

Cop·tic (kop′tik), *n.* **1.** the extinct language of Egypt that developed from ancient Egyptian, now used liturgically by the Coptic Church. —*adj.* **2.** of or pertaining to Coptic or the Copts. [COPT + -IC]

Cop′tic Church′, the native Christian church in Egypt, governed by a patriarch and characterized by an adherence to Monophysitism and the use of the Coptic language in its liturgy.

cop·u·la (kop′yə lə), *n., pl.* **-las, -lae** (-lē′). **1.** something that connects or links together. **2.** *Gram., Logic.* a word or set of words, as the English verbs *be* and *seem,* that acts as a connecting link between subject and predicate complement; an equational verb. [< L, equiv. to *co-* CO- + *ap-* fasten (see APT) + *-ula* -ULE] —**cop′u·lar,** *adj.*

cop·u·late (*v.* kop′yə lāt′; *adj.* kop′yə lit), *v.,* **-lat·ed, -lat·ing,** *adj.* —*v.i.* **1.** to unite in sexual intercourse. —*adj.* **2.** connected; joined. [late ME < L *copulāt(us)* bound together. See COPULA, -ATE¹]

cop·u·la·tion (kop′yə lā′shən), *n.* **1.** a joining together or coupling. **2.** sexual union or intercourse. [ME *copulacion* < L *copulātiōn-* (s. of *copulātiō*) a binding together. See COPULATE, -ION]

cop·u·la·tive (kop′yə lā′tiv, -lə tiv), *adj.* **1.** serving to unite or couple. **2.** *Gram.* **a.** involving or consisting of connected words or clauses: *a copulative sentence.* **b.** serving to connect subject and predicate complement: *a copulative verb.* **c.** serving to connect nouns, noun phrases, verbs, clauses, etc.: *a copulative conjunction.* **d.** of the dvandva type: *"Bittersweet" is a copulative compound.* **3.** of or pertaining to copulation. —*n.* **4.** *Gram.* a copulative word. [ME *copulatif* < LL *copulātīv(us).* See COPULATE, -IVE] —**cop′u·la′tive·ly,** *adv.*

cop′ulative asyn′deton, *Rhet.* a staccato effect produced by omitting copulative connectives from between two or more items forming a group, as in "Friends, Romans, countrymen." Cf. **adversative asyndeton.**

cop·y (kop′ē), *n., pl.* **cop·ies,** *v.,* **cop·ied, cop·y·ing.** —*n.* **1.** an imitation, reproduction, or transcript of an original: *a copy of a famous painting.* **2.** *Journalism.* a person, thing, or event with respect to his or its newsworthiness (often prec. by *good* or *bad*): *The President is always good copy.* Cf. **news** (def. 4). **3.** written matter or art work to be reproduced in printed form: *The editor sent the copy for the next issue to the printer.* **4.** one of the various examples or specimens of the same book, engraving, or the like. **5.** *Brit. Informal.* (in schools) a composition; a written assignment. **6.** Also called **draft.** *Brit.* a size of drawing or writing paper, 16 × 20 inches. **7.** *Archaic.* something that is to be reproduced; an example or pattern, as of penmanship to be copied by a pupil. —*v.t.* **8.** to make a copy of; transcribe; reproduce: *to copy a set of figures from a book.* **9.** to follow as a pattern or model; imitate. —*v.i.* **10.** to make a copy or copies. **11.** to make or do something in imitation of something else: *to copy after bad precedents.* [ME *copie* < ML *cōpia* abundance, something written, L: wealth, abundance; see COPIOUS]
—**Syn. 1.** duplicate, carbon, facsimile. **9.** See **imitate.**
—**Ant. 9.** originate.

cop·y·book (kop′ē bo͝ok′), *n.* **1.** a book containing models, usually of penmanship, for learners to imitate. **2.** a book containing copies, as of documents. —*adj.* **3.** commonplace; stereotyped: *a copybook sort of phrase.* [COPY + BOOK]

cop·y·boy (kop′ē boi′), *n.* an office boy employed by a newspaper. [COPY + BOY]

cop′y cam′era, a camera for photographing pictures, maps, printed pages, or the like.

cop·y·cat (kop′ē kat′), *n., v.,* **-cat·ted, -cat·ting.** *Informal.* —*n.* **1.** one who imitates or reproduces the actions or work of another. —*v.t.* **2.** to copy slavishly: *The clothes were copycatted straight from designer originals.* [COPY + CAT¹]

cop·y·cut·ter (kop′ē kut′ər), *n.* *Journalism.* an employee of a newspaper who separates copy into takes to facilitate printing. [COPY + CUTTER]

cop′y desk′, *Journalism.* the desk, typically U-shaped, at which copy is edited and prepared for printing by the copyreaders. Cf. **slot¹** (def. 3).

cop·y-ed·it (kop′ē ed′it), *v.t.* to edit (a manuscript, document, text, etc.) for publication, esp. for punctuation, spelling, grammatical structure, etc. [back formation from COPY EDITOR]

cop′y ed′itor, **1.** one who edits a manuscript, text, etc., for publication, esp. to find and correct errors in style, punctuation, and grammar. **2.** See **slot man.**

cop·y·fit·ting (kop′ē fit′ing), *n.* *Print.* the determining of the area to be occupied by given copy when set in type. [COPY + FITTING] —**cop′y·fit′ter,** *n.*

cop·y·hold (kop′ē hōld′), *n.* (formerly) a type of ownership of land in England, evidenced by a copy of the manor roll establishing the title. [late ME; see COPY, HOLD¹]

cop·y·hold·er (kop′ē hōl′dər), *n.* **1.** one who or that which holds copy. **2.** a device for holding copy in its place, as on a printer's frame or on a typewriter. **3.** a proofreader's assistant who reads copy aloud or follows it while proof is read for the detection of deviations from it in proof. **4.** one who holds an estate in copyhold. [COPYHOLD + -ER¹]

cop·y·ist (kop′ē ist), *n.* **1.** a person who transcribes copies, esp. of documents. **2.** an imitator. [COPY + -IST]

cop′y pa′per, paper specially prepared for the writing of advertising copy, newspaper copy, etc., usually having guide lines to indicate margins and the number of spaces per line.

cop·y·read (kop′ē rēd′), *v.t.,* **-read** (-red), **-read·ing.** to work on (copy) as a copyreader. [back formation from COPYREADER]

cop·y·read·er (kop′ē rē′dər), *n.* *Journalism.* **1.** an editor concerned with the preparation of copy for the typesetter and printer. **2.** Also called **rim man.** one who edits copy and writes headlines for a newspaper. Cf. **slot man.** [COPY + READER]

cop·y·right (kop′ē rīt′), *n.* **1.** the exclusive right, granted by law for a certain number of years, to make and dispose of and otherwise to control copies of a literary, musical, or artistic work. —*adj.* **2.** Also, **cop′y·right′ed.** protected by copyright. —*v.t.* **3.** to secure a copyright on. [COPY + RIGHT] —**cop′y·right′a·ble,** *adj.* —**cop′y·right′er,** *n.*

cop·y·writ·er (kop′ē rī′tər), *n.* a writer of copy, esp. for advertisements or publicity releases. [COPY + WRITER] —**cop′y·writ′ing,** *n.*

coq au vin (*Fr.* kôk ō vaN′), chicken stewed in a sauce of red wine, diced pork, onions, garlic, and mushrooms. [< F: lit., cock with wine]

coque·li·cot (kok′lə kō′, kōk′-), *n.* See **corn poppy.** [< F: corn poppy, cock, orig. var. of *cocorico* crow of a cock (imit.); flower so named from its color, likened to that of a cock's comb]

Co·que·lin (kôk laN′), *n.* **Be·noît Con·stant** (bə nwA′ kôN stäN′), 1841–1909, French actor.

co·quet (kō ket′), *v.,* **-quet·ted, -quet·ting,** *adj., n.* —*v.i.* **1.** to try to attract the attention and admiration of men for mere self-gratification; flirt. **2.** to act without seriousness; trifle; dally. —*adj.* **3.** coquettish. —*n.* **4.** *Obs.* a male flirt. [< F; lit., cockerel, equiv. to *coq* cock + *-et* -ET]
—**Syn. 1.** dally, tease.

co·quet·ry (kō′ki trē, kō ke′trē), *n., pl.* **-ries. 1.** the behavior or arts of a coquette; flirtation. **2.** dalliance; trifling. [< F *coquetterie.* See COQUETTE, -ERY]

co·quette (kō ket′), *n.* a girl or woman who flirts lightheartedly with men to win their admiration and affection; flirt. [< F, fem. of COQUET] —**co·quet′tish,** *adj.* —**co·quet′tish·ly,** *adv.* —**co·quet′tish·ness,** *n.*

Co·quil·hat·ville (kô kē yA vēl′), *n.* former name of **Mbandaka.**

co·quil·lage (kō′ki läzh′; *Fr.* kô kē yäzh′), *n.* an ornamental shell motif. [< F: a shellfish. See COQUILLE, -AGE]

co·quil′la nut′ (ko kēl′yə, -kē′yə), the elongated oval fruit or nut of a South American palm, *Attalea funifera,* having a very hard brown shell used in turnery. [< Pg *coquilho,* dim. of *côco* coco]

co·quille (kō kil′; *Fr.* kô kē′yə), *n., pl.* **-quilles** (-kilz′; *Fr.* -kē′yə). **1.** any of various meat or fish dishes baked with a sauce and usually served in a shell or a shell-shaped serving dish. **2.** the cooking utensil for baking such dishes, usually a scallop shell or small casserole resembling a shell. **3.** a cooking utensil, filled with charcoal, for roasting meat on a spit. **4.** the shell of an escargot. [< F: lit., shell. See COCKLE¹]

Co·quille (kō kēl′), *n.* a town in SW Oregon. 4730 (1960).

co·qui·na (kō kē′nə), *n.* a soft, whitish rock made up of fragments of marine shells and coral, used as a building material. [< Sp: lit., shellfish, equiv. to OSp *coc(a)* shellfish (< L *concha;* see CONCH) + *-ina* -INE¹]

co·qui·to (kō kē′tō), *n., pl.* **-tos.** a palm, *Jubaea spectabilis,* of Chile, from whose sap a honey is prepared and whose small, hard, edible nuts yield a useful oil. Also called **coqui′to palm′.** [< Sp, dim. of *coco* coco palm < Pg *côco* coco]

cor¹ (kôr), *interj.* *Brit. Dial.* gor. [euphemistic for GOD]

cor² (kôr), *n.* *Chiefly Brit.* the tenor oboe; the English horn. [prob. < F *cor (anglais)* (English) horn]

cor³ (kôr, kōr), *n., pl.* **cor·di·a** (kôr′dē ə, kōr′-). (in prescriptions) the heart. [< L]

cor-, var. of **com-** before *r: correlate.*

Cor., **1.** Corinthians. **2.** Coroner.

cor., **1.** corner. **2.** cornet. **3.** coroner. **4.** corpus. **5.** correct. **6.** corrected. **7.** correction. **8.** correlative. **9.** correspondence. **10.** correspondent. **11.** corresponding.

Co·ra (kôr′ə, kōr′ə), *n.* **1.** Also, **Core, Kore.** *Class. Myth.* Persephone, esp. as a symbol of virginity. **2.** a girl's given name.

cor·a·ci·i·form (kôr′ə sī′ə fôrm′, kor′-), *adj.* belonging or pertaining to the *Coraciiformes,* the order of birds that includes the kingfishers, motmots, rollers, bee eaters, and hornbills. [back formation from NL *Coraciiformēs,* equiv. to *Coraci(as)* genus name (< Gk *korakías* grackle) + *-i-* -I- + *-formēs,* pl. of *-formis* -FORM]

cor·a·cle (kôr′ə kəl, kor′-), *n.* a small, round or very broad boat made of wickerwork or interwoven laths covered with a waterproof layer of skin, canvas, tarred or oiled cloth, or the like: used in Wales, Ireland, and parts of western England. [< Welsh *corwgl,* equiv. to *corwg* (earlier *corwc*) coracle + *-l* suffix; akin to Ir *curach* boat]

cor·a·coid (kôr′ə koid′, kor′-), *Anat., Zool.* —*adj.* **1.** pertaining to the bone that in reptiles, birds, and monotremes articulates with the scapula and the sternum and that in man and other higher mammals is a reduced bony process of the scapula having no connection with the sternum. —*n.* **2.** a coracoid bone or process. [back formation from NL *coracoidēs* < Gk *korakoeidēs* ravenlike, hooked like a raven's beak, equiv. to *korak-* (s. of *kórax*) raven + *-oeidēs* -OID]

co·ra·ji (kə rä′jē), *n.* *Australian.* boyla. [< Austral native name]

cor·al (kôr′əl, kor′-), *n.* **1.** the hard, variously colored, calcareous skeleton secreted by certain anthozoan animals. **2.** such skeletons collectively, forming reefs, islands, etc. **3.** an anthozoan animal, as a solitary or colonial polyp, secreting this calcareous skeleton. **4.** something made of coral, as an ornament or a child's toy. **5.** a reddish yellow; light yellowish red; pinkish yellow. **6.** the unimpregnated roe or eggs of the lobster that when boiled take on the color of red coral. —*adj.* **7.** made of coral: *a coral reef; coral ornamentation.* **8.** making coral: *a coral polyp.* **9.** resembling coral, esp. in color; yellowish-red. [ME *coral(l)* < L *corāll(i)um* < Gk *korállion* red coral, equiv. to *korall-* (< Sem; cf. Heb *gōrāl* pebble) + *-ion* dim. suffix] —**cor′al·like′,** *adj.*

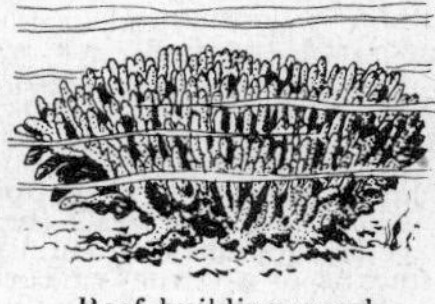
Reef-building coral

Cor·al (kôr′əl, kor′-), *n.* a girl's given name.

cor′al bells′, an alumroot, *Heuchera sanguinea,* of southwestern North America, having red, bell-shaped flowers, cultivated in many varieties.

cor·al·ber·ry (kôr′əl ber′ē, kor′-), *n., pl.* **-ries.** See **Indian currant.** [CORAL + BERRY]

Cor·al Ga·bles (kôr′əl gā′bəlz, kor′-), a city in SE Florida, near Miami. 34,793 (1960).

cor′al hon′eysuckle. See **trumpet honeysuckle.**

cor′al jas′mine, a vinelike shrub, *Cestrum purpureum,* of Mexico, having hairy branches, clustered, red-purple flowers, and red fruit. Also called **purple cestrum.**

coralli-, a combining form of **coral:** *coralliferous.* [repr. L *corāllium* CORAL]

cor·al·lif·er·ous (kôr′ə lif′ər əs, kor′-), *adj.* containing or bearing coral; producing coral. [CORALLI- + -FEROUS]

cor′al lil′y, a bulbous herb, *Lilium pumilum,* of eastern Asia, having scarlet flowers with recurved petals.

cor·al·line (kôr′ə lin, -līn′, kor′-), *adj.* **1.** consisting of or containing deposits of calcium carbonate. **2.** coral-like. **3.** coral-colored; reddish-yellow; light-yellowish red; pinkish-yellow. —*n.* **4.** any red alga that is impregnated with lime. **5.** any of various corallike animals or calcareous algae. [< LL *corallīn(us)* coral-red. See CORAL, -INE¹]

cor·al·li·ta (kôr′ə lē′tə, kor′-), *n.* See **coral vine.** [alter. Sp *coralito,* dim. of *coral* CORAL]

cor·al·lite (kôr′ə līt′, kor′-), *n.* the coral skeleton of a single polyp. [CORALL(I)- + -ITE¹]

cor·al·loid (kôr′ə loid′, kor′-), *adj.* having the form or appearance of coral. Also, **cor′al·loi′dal.** [CORALL(I)- + -OID]

cor′al plant′, **1.** a tree, *Jatropha multifida,* of South America, having showy, scarlet flowers. **2.** See **fountain plant** (def. 1).

cor′al reef′, a reef composed mainly of coral and other organic matter of which parts have solidified into limestone.

cor′al root′, any orchidaceous plant of the genus *Corallorrhiza,* of the Northern Hemisphere.

Cor′al Sea′, a part of the S Pacific, bounded by NE Australia, New Guinea, the Solomon Islands, and the New Hebrides: U.S. naval victory over the Japanese, May, 1942.

cor′al snake′, **1.** any of numerous venomous elapid snakes, found chiefly in the New World tropics, as *Micrurus fulvius* (**east′ern cor′al snake′**), of the southeastern U.S., often brilliantly marked with bands of red, yellow, and black. **2.** any of several other snakes, as of the genus *Callophis,* of Asia, having red markings.

cor′al tree′, any of several tropical, leguminous shrubs or trees of the genus *Erythrina,* having large clusters of pealike flowers.

cor′al vine′, a climbing vine, *Antigonon leptopus,* of Mexico, having arrow- or heart-shaped leaves and pink or white flowers. Also called **Confederate vine, corallita, mountain rose, pink vine.**

Co·ra·lye (kôr′ə lē′, kor′-, kôr′ə lē′, kor′-), *n.* a girl's given name.

Cor·a·mine (kôr′ə mēn′, -min, kor′-), *n.* *Pharm., Trademark.* nikethamide.

co·ram ju·di·ce (kôr′am jo͞o′di sē, kôr′am), *Law.* before a court having the authority to hear and decide (the case in question). [< L: in the presence of a judge]

co·ram no·bis (kôr′am nō′bis, kôr′am), *Law.* a writ to correct an injury caused by a mistake of the court. [< L: before us]

co·ram non ju·di·ce (kôr′am non jo͞o′di sē, kôr′am), *Law.* before a court lacking the authority to hear and decide the case in question. [< L: in the presence of one not a judge]

co·ram po·pu·lo (kō′räm pō′po͝o lō′; *Eng.* kôr′am pop′yə lō′, kôr′-), *Latin.* before the public; publicly.

cor an·glais (kôr′ ôn glā′, ông-, än-, äng-). See **English horn.** [< F, equiv. to *cor* horn + *anglais* English]

co·ran·to (kə ran′tō, -rän′-, kō-), *n., pl.* **-tos, -toes.** courante. [earlier *carranta* < It *cor(r)anta* < F *courante* COURANTE]

Cor·a·op·o·lis (kôr′ē op′ə lis, kôr′-), *n.* a town in W Pennsylvania. 9643 (1960).

cor·ban (kôr′bən; *Heb.* kôR bän′), *n.* *Chiefly Biblical.* an offering of any kind made to God, esp. in fulfillment of a vow. [< Heb *qorbān,* lit., a drawing near]

cor·beil (kôr′bəl; *Fr.* kôr bā′), *n.* a sculptured ornament, esp. on a capital, having the form of a basket. [< F *corbeille* < LL *corbicul(a)*, equiv. to L *corbi(s)* basket + *-cula* -CULE]

cor·beille (kôr′bəl; *Fr.* kôr be′yə), *n., pl.* **-beilles** (bəlz; *Fr.* -be′yə). corbeil.

cor·bel (kôr′bəl), *n., v.,* **-beled, -bel·ing** or (*esp. Brit.*) **-belled, -bel·ling.** *Archit.* —*n.* **1.** any bracket, esp. one of brick or stone, usually of slight extent. **2.** a short horizontal timber supporting a girder. —*v.t.* **3.** to set (bricks, stones, etc.) so as to form a corbel or corbels (usually fol. by *out*). **4.** to support by means of a corbel or corbels. [ME < MF < LL *corvell(us)*, equiv. to L *corv(us)* RAVEN[1] + *-ellus* dim. suffix]

Corbel (def. 1)

cor′bel arch′, a construction like an arch but composed of masonry courses corbeled until they meet.

cor·bel·ing (kôr′bə liṅg), *n.* *Archit.* **1.** the construction of corbels. **2.** a system of corbels. Also, *esp. Brit.,* **cor′bel·ling.** [CORBEL + -ING[1]]

cor′bel step′, corbiestep.

cor′bel ta′ble, a horizontal masonry construction, as a cornice or part of a wall, supported on corbels or on arches supported on corbels.

cor′bel vault′, a structure having the form of a vault but constructed on the principle of a corbel arch.

Cor·bet (kôr′bit), *n.* a boy's given name.

Cor·bett (kôr′bit), *n.* **James John** ("*Gentleman Jim*"), 1866–1933, U.S. boxer: world heavyweight champion 1892–97.

cor·bic·u·la (kôr bik′yə lə), *n., pl.* **-lae** (-lē′). See **pollen basket.** [< NL, little basket, dim. of *corbis* basket] —**cor·bic·u·late** (kôr bik′yə lit, -lāt′), *adj.*

cor·bie (kôʀ′bē), *n.* *Scot.* a raven or crow. Also, **corby.** [ME *corbin* < OF < L *corvīn(us)* CORVINE]

cor′bie ga′ble, a gable with corbiesteps.

cor·bie·step (kôr′bē step′), *n.* any of a series of steplike portions of a masonry gable that terminate the gable above the surface of the roof. Also called **corbel step, crowstep.** [CORBIE + STEP]

Cor·bin (kôr′bin), *n.* a town in SE Kentucky. 7119 (1960).

cor·bi·na (kôr bī′nə), *n.* **1.** a game fish, *Menticirrhus undulatus*, of the croaker family, found along the Pacific coast of North America. **2.** any of various related fish. [< Sp *corvina*, fem. of *corvino* < L *corvīn(us)* CORVINE; so named from its color]

cor·bli·mey (kôr blī′mē), *interj.* *Brit. Slang.* blimey. Also, **cor·bli′my.** Cf. **gor.**

cor·by (kôʀ′bē), *n., pl.* **-bies.** *Scot.* corbie.

Cor·by (kôr′bē), *n.* a town in NE Northamptonshire, in S England. 35,880 (1961).

Cor·co·ran (kôr′kər ən, kôrk′rən), *n.* a town in central California. 4976 (1960).

Cor·co·va·do (kôʀ′kô vä′do͞o *for 1;* kôʀ′kô vä′tħô *for 2*), *n.* **1.** a mountain in SE Brazil, S of Rio de Janeiro: statue of Christ on peak. 2310 ft. **2.** a volcano in S Chile. 7550 ft.

Cor·cy·ra (kôr sī′rə), *n.* ancient name of **Corfu.** —**Cor·cy·rae·an** (kôr′si rē′ən), *adj., n.*

cord (kôrd), *n.* **1.** a string or thin rope made of several strands braided, twisted, or woven together. **2.** *Elect.* a small, flexible, insulated cable. **3.** a ribbed fabric, esp. corduroy. **4.** a cordlike rib on the surface of cloth. **5.** any influence that binds or restrains: *cord of marriage; the silver cord.* **6.** *Anat.* a cordlike structure: *the spinal cord; umbilical cord.* **7.** a unit of volume used chiefly for fuel wood, now generally equal to 128 cubic feet, usually specified as 8 feet long, 4 feet wide, and 4 feet high. *Abbr.:* cd, cd. **8.** a hangman's rope. —*v.t.* **9.** to bind or fasten with a cord or cords. **10.** to pile or stack up (wood) in cords. **11.** to furnish with a cord. [ME *coord(e)*, OE **corde* (see CORDED) < L *chord(a)* < Gk *chordḗ* gut] —**cord′er,** *n.*

cord·age (kôr′dij), *n.* **1.** fiber and wire ropes, lines, hawsers, etc., taken as a whole, esp. with reference to the rigging and other equipment of a vessel. **2.** a quantity of wood measured in cords. [CORD + -AGE]

cor·date (kôr′dāt), *adj.* **1.** heart-shaped: *a cordate shell.* **2.** (of leaves) heart-shaped, with the attachment at the notched end. [< NL *cordāt(us)* heart-shaped, equiv. to L *cord-* (s. of *cor*) heart + *-ātus* -ATE[1]] —**cor′date·ly,** *adv.*

Cordate leaf

Cor·day d'Ar·mont (kôr dā′ där môɴ; *Fr.* kôʀ de dar môɴ′), **(Ma·rie Anne) Char·lotte** (mə rē′ an shär′lət; *Fr.* ma rē′ an shar lôt′), 1768–93, French revolutionary heroine who assassinated Jean Paul Marat.

cord·ed (kôr′did), *adj.* **1.** furnished with, made of, or in the form of cords. **2.** ribbed, as a fabric. **3.** bound with cords. **4.** (of wood) stacked up in cords. **5.** stringy, or ribbed, in appearance, esp. from the prominence of the muscles, veins, etc.: *a corded throat.* [ME; OE *gecorded.* See CORD, -ED[3]]

Cord′ed cul′ture. See **Battle-Ax culture.**

Cor·del·ia (kôr dēl′yə), *n.* **1.** (in Shakespeare's *King Lear*) the youngest of Lear's three daughters and the only one who remains loyal to her father. Cf. **Goneril, Regan. 2.** a girl's given name.

Cor·de·lier (kôr′dᵊlēr′), *n.* **1.** a Franciscan friar: so called from the knotted cord worn as a girdle. **2. Cordeliers,** a political club in Paris which met at an old Cordelier convent at the time of the French Revolution. [< MF; r. ME *cordeler.* See CORDELLE, -ER[2]]

cor·delle (kôr del′), *n., v.,* **-delled, -dell·ing.** —*n.* **1.** a heavy rope formerly used for towing boats or barges on rivers in Canada and the U.S. —*v.t.* **2.** to tow (a boat) by means of a cordelle. [< F, dim. of *corde* CORD]

cord′ foot′, a quantity of wood four feet high, four feet wide, and one foot long, or sixteen cubic feet.

cor·dial (kôr′jəl *or, esp. Brit.,* -dē əl), *adj.* **1.** courteous and gracious; friendly; warm: *a cordial reception.* **2.** invigorating the heart; stimulating. **3.** *Obs.* of or pertaining to the heart. —*n.* **4.** anything that invigorates or exhilarates. **5.** a strong, sweetened, aromatic alcoholic liquor; a liqueur. **6.** a stimulating medicine. [ME < ML *cordiāl(is)*, equiv. to L *cordi-* (s. of *cor*) heart + *-ālis* -AL[1]] —**cor′dial·ly,** *adv.* —**cor′dial·ness,** *n.* —**Syn. 1.** affectionate, genial. **2.** cheering.

cor·dial·i·ty (kôr jal′i tē, kôr′jē al′- *or, esp. Brit.,* -dē al′-), *n., pl.* **-ties** for 2. **1.** cordial quality or feeling. **2.** an expression of cordial feeling. [CORDIAL + -ITY]

cor·di·er·ite (kôr′dē ə rīt′), *n.* a strongly dichroic blue mineral consisting of a silicate of magnesium, aluminum, and iron. Also called **dichroite, iolite.** [named after Pierre L. A. *Cordier* (1777–1861), French geologist; see -ITE[1]]

cor·di·form (kôr′də fôrm′), *adj.* heart-shaped. [< L *cordi-* (s. of *cor*) heart + -FORM]

cor·dil·le·ra (kôr′dil yâr′ə, kôr dil′ər ə), *n.* a chain of mountains, usually the principal mountain system or mountain axis of a large land mass. [< Sp, deriv. of *cordilla*, dim. of *cuerda* string, mountain range (< L *chorda*); see CORD] —**cor′dil·le′ran,** *adj.*

Cor·dil·le·ras (kôr′dil yâr′əz, kôr dil′ər əz; *Sp.* kôʀ′dē ye′ʀäs), *n.* **1.** a mountain system in W South America: the Andes and its component ranges. **2.** a mountain system in W North America, including the Sierra Nevada, Coast Range, Cascade Range, Rocky Mountains, etc. **3.** the entire chain of mountain ranges parallel to the Pacific coast, extending from Cape Horn to Alaska. —**Cor′dil·le′ran,** *adj.*

cord·ing (kôr′diṅg), *n.* cord covered with threads, yarns, or fabric, used decoratively. [CORD + -ING[1]]

cor·dis (kôr′dis, kôr′-), *adj.* (in prescriptions) of the heart. [< L]

cord·ite (kôr′dīt), *n.* a smokeless, slow-burning powder composed of 30–58 percent nitroglycerin, 65–37 percent nitrocellulose, and 5–6 percent mineral jelly. [CORD + -ITE[1], so called from its cordlike form]

cord·less (kôrd′lis), *adj.* **1.** lacking a cord or cords. **2.** (of an electrical appliance) requiring no wire leading to an external source of electricity because of a self-contained, often rechargeable power supply: *a cordless electric toothbrush.* [CORD + -LESS]

Cór·do·ba (kôʀ′dô vä), *n.* **1.** Also, **Cordova.** a city in S Spain on the Guadalquivir River: the capital of Spain under Moorish rule; cathedral. 189,566 (est. 1960). **2.** a city in central Argentina. 589,153 (1965). **3.** (*l.c.*) a silver coin and monetary unit of Nicaragua equal to 100 centavos and equivalent to about .14 of a U.S. dollar.

cor·don (kôr′dᵊn), *n.* **1.** a cord or braid worn for ornament or as a fastening. **2.** a ribbon worn usually diagonally across the breast as a badge of a knightly or honorary order. **3.** a line of sentinels, military posts, police, warships, or the like, enclosing or guarding an area. **4.** *Fort.* **a.** a projecting course of stones at the base of a parapet. **b.** the coping of a scarp. **5.** *Archit.* **a.** a stringcourse, esp. one having little or no projection. **b.** a cut-stone riser on a stepped ramp or the like. **6.** a fruit tree or shrub with one branch or opposing branches trained to grow along a support that is parallel to the ground or is perpendicular to or at an oblique angle with a series of such supports. [< MF, dim. of *corde*]

cor·do·na·zo (kôr′dᵊnä′sō), *n., pl.* **-zos.** a hurricane occurring off the Pacific coast of Central America. [< MexSp, short for Sp *cordonazo de San Francisco* equinoctial storm, lit., lash of St. Francis, referring to the *cordón* or rope (see CORDON) worn by Franciscan friars; the suffix *-azo* is pejorative]

cor·don bleu (*Fr.* kôʀ dôɴ blœ′), *pl.* **cor·dons bleus** (*Fr.* kôʀ dôɴ blœ′). **1.** the sky-blue ribbon worn as a badge by knights of the highest order of French knighthood under the Bourbons. **2.** some similar high distinction. **3.** one entitled to wear the cordon bleu. **4.** any person of great distinction in his field, esp. a distinguished chef. [< F: lit., blue ribbon]

cor·don sa·ni·taire (*Fr.* kôʀ dôɴ sa nē teʀ′), *pl.* **cor·dons sa·ni·taire** (*Fr.* kôʀ dôɴ sa nē teʀ′). **1.** a line around a quarantined area guarded to prevent the spread of a disease by restricting passage into or out of the area. **2.** a group of neighboring, generally neutral states forming a geographical barrier between two states having aggressive military or ideological aims against each other. [< F; see CORDON, SANITARY]

Cor·do·va (kôr′də və), *n.* a coarse wool from Argentina used chiefly for carpet stock.

Cor·do·va (kôr′də və), *n.* **1.** Córdoba (def. 1). **2.** a town in central Alabama. 3184 (1960).

Cor·do·van (kôr′də vən) *n.* **1.** a native or inhabitant of Córdoba, Spain. **2.** (*l.c.*) a soft, smooth leather originally made at Córdoba of goatskin but later made also of split horsehide, pigskin, etc. —*adj.* **3.** of Córdoba, Spain. **4.** (*l.c.*) designating or made of cordovan. [CORDOV(A) + -AN]

cords (kôrdz), *n.pl.* clothing of corded fabric.

cor·du·roy (kôr′də roi′, kôr′də roi′), *n.* **1.** a cotton-filling pile fabric with lengthwise cords or ridges. —*adj.* **2.** of, pertaining to, or resembling corduroy. **3.** constructed of logs laid together transversely, as a road across swampy ground. —*v.t.* **4.** to form (a road or the like) by laying logs transversely. **5.** to make a corduroy road across or along. [? orig. proper name]

cor·du·roys (kôr′də roiz′, kôr′də roiz′), *n.* (*construed as pl.*) trousers made of corduroy.

cord·wain (kôrd′wān), *n.* *Archaic.* cordovan leather. [ME *cordewan* < MF < Sp *cordován* CORDOVAN]

cord·wain·er (kôrd′wā nər), *n.* *Archaic.* **1.** one who makes shoes from cordovan leather. **2.** shoemaker; cobbler. [ME *cordewaner* < OF *cordewan(i)er.* See CORDWAIN, -ER[2]] —**cord′wain·er·y,** *n.*

cord·wood (kôrd′wo͝od′), *n.* **1.** wood stacked in cords for use as fuel. **2.** logs cut to a length of four feet to facilitate stacking in cords. **3.** trees intended for timber but of a quality suitable only for fuel. [CORD + WOOD[1]]

core[1] (kôr, kōr), *n., v.,* **cored, cor·ing.** —*n.* **1.** the central part of a fleshy fruit, containing the seeds. **2.** the central, innermost, or most essential part of anything. **3.** Also called **magnetic core.** the piece of iron, bundle of iron wires, or other ferrous material forming the central or inner portion in an electromagnet, induction coil, transformer, or the like. See diag. under **electromagnet. 4.** *Foundry.* a specially formed refractory object inserted into a mold to produce cavities or depressions in the casting that cannot be readily formed on the pattern. **5.** (in mining, geology, etc.) a cylindrical sample of earth, mineral, or rock extracted from the ground by means of a corer so that the strata are undisturbed in the sample. **6.** the inside wood of a tree. **7.** *Anthropol.* a lump of stone, as flint, from which prehistoric man struck flakes for fashioning into tools. **8.** *Carpentry.* **a.** a thickness of wood forming a base for a veneer or veneers. **b.** a wooden construction, as in a door, forming a backing for veneers. **9.** *Engineering.* kern[4]. **10.** *Metall.* **a.** a thickness of base metal beneath a cladding. **b.** the softer interior of a piece of casehardened metal. **11.** *Geol.* the central portion of the earth, having a radius of about 2100 miles and believed to be composed mainly of iron and nickel in a molten state. Cf. **crust** (def. 6), **mantle** (def. 8). **12.** *Physics.* the region in a reactor that contains its fissionable material. **13.** Also called **magnetic core.** *Computer Technol.* a small ring or loop of ferromagnetic material with two states of polarization that can be changed by changing the direction of the current applied in wires wound around the ring, used to store one bit of information or to perform switching or logical functions. **14.** *Ropemaking.* heart (def. 16). —*v.t.* **15.** to remove the core of (fruit). **16.** to cut from the central part. **17.** to remove a cylindrical sample from the interior, as of the earth, a tree trunk, etc.: *The geologists will core the ocean bottom for testing.* **18.** to form a cavity in (a molded object) by placing a core, as of sand or the like, in the mold before pouring. [ME, perh. var. of *coren*, itself var. of CORN[2]] —**core′less,** *adj.*

core[2] (kôr, kōr), *n.* *Chiefly Scot.* a small company or team of men, esp. a gang of miners or a small corps of workers. [ME *chor(e)*, OE *chor(a)* dance, company of dancers or singers. See CHORUS]

Co·re (kôr′ē, kōr′ē), *n.* **1.** Korah. **2.** *Class. Myth.* Cora (def. 1).

CORE (kôr, kōr), *n.* Congress of Racial Equality. Also, **C.O.R.E.**

core′ bar′rel, (in a core drill) a length of pipe for holding mineral cores while they are being extracted from the drill hole.

core′ curric′ulum, *Educ.* a curriculum in which all or some of the subjects or courses are based on a central theme in order to correlate the subjects and the theme.

core′ draw′ing, *Metalworking.* drawing of fine tubing using wire as a mandrel.

co·re·la·tion (kôr′ə lā′shən, kōr′rə-), *n.* *Chiefly Brit.* correlation. [CO- + RELATION]

co·rel·a·tive (kə rel′ə tiv), *adj., n.* *Chiefly Brit.* correlative. [CO- + RELATIVE] —**co·rel′a·tive·ly,** *adv.*

co·re·li·gion·ist (kō′ri lij′ə nist), *n.* an adherent of the same religion as another. [CO- + RELIGIONIST]

Co·rel·li (kō rel′ē, kô-; *for 1 also It.* kô rel′lē), *n.* **1. Ar·can·ge·lo** (är kän′je lō′), 1653–1713, Italian violinist and composer. **2. Marie** (*Mary Mackay*), 1854?–1924, English novelist.

core·mak·er (kōr′mā′kər, kôr′-), *n.* *Foundry.* one who makes cores for foundry molds. [CORE[1] + MAKER]

co·re·mi·um (kō rē′mē əm, kô-, kə-), *n., pl.* **-mi·a** (-mē ə). *Bot.* the fructification of certain fungi, consisting of a loosely bound fascicle of conidiophores. [< NL < Gk *korēm(a)* bosom, broom + -IUM]

co·re·op·sis (kôr′ē op′sis, kōr′-), *n.* any composite plant of the genus *Coreopsis*, including familiar garden species having yellow, brownish, or yellow and red flowers. [< NL < Gk *kore-* (s. of *kóris*) bedbug + *-opsis* -OPSIS; so named from the shape of seed]

cor·er (kôr′ər, kōr′-), *n.* **1.** one who or that which cores. **2.** a knife for coring apples, pears, etc. **3.** a device having a hollow cylindrical drill or tube, used for taking samples of earth, rock, etc., from below the surface of the ground or ocean bottom. [CORE[1] + -ER[1]]

co·re·spond·ent (kō′ri spon′dənt, kôr′i-, kôr′-, kor′-), *n.* *Law.* a joint defendant, charged along with the respondent, esp. a person charged with adultery, along with the respondent, in a divorce proceeding. [CO- + RESPONDENT]

Co·re·sus (kôr′i səs), *n.* *Class. Myth.* a priest of Dionysus who loved Callirrhoë, a maiden of Calydon: when she rejected Coresus, Dionysus inflicted a plague on Calydon.

Cor·ey (kôr′ē, kōr′ē), *n.* a boy's given name.

corf (kôrf), *n., pl.* **corves** (kôrvz). *Brit.* **1.** *Mining.* **a.** a small wagon for carrying coal, ore, etc. **b.** a wicker basket formerly used for this purpose. **2.** a basket, cage, or boxlike structure with perforations for keeping lobsters or fish alive in water. [ME < MD (c. G *Korb*) < L *corb(is)* basket. See CORBEIL]

Cor·fam (kôr′fam), *n.* *Trademark.* a man-made flexible, microporous material, used as a leather substitute for shoes, handbags, belts, luggage, etc. [coined by computer]

Cor·fu (kôr′fo͞o, -fyo͞o; *It.* kôʀ fo͞o′), *n.* **1.** Ancient, **Corcyra.** one of the Ionian Islands, off the NW coast of Greece. 101,770 (1961); 229 sq. mi. **2.** a seaport on this island. 26,991 (1961). Greek, **Kerkyra.**

cor·gi (kôr′gē), *n.* See **Welsh corgi.** [< Welsh, equiv. to *cor* dwarf + *-gi*, var. of *ci* dog; c. Ir *cu*; see HOUND[1]]

Co·ri (kôr′ē, kōr′ē), *n.* **Carl Ferdinand,** born 1896, and his wife, **Gerty Theresa,** 1896–1957, U.S. biochemists, born in Czechoslovakia: Nobel prize for medicine 1947.

co·ri·a·ceous (kôr′ē ā′shəs, kōr′-, kor′-), *adj.* of or like leather. [< LL *coriāceus* leathern. See CORI(UM), -ACEOUS]

co·ri·an·der (kôr′ē an′dər, kōr′-, kor′-), *n.* **1.** a herbaceous plant, *Coriandrum sativum*, bearing aromatic seedlike fruit used in cookery and medicine. **2.** Also called **corian′der seed′.** the seed of the coriander, used esp. as a flavoring. [ME *coriandre* < L *coriandr(um)* < Gk *koríandron*, var. of *koríannon*]

Cor·i·ci·din (kôr′i sīd′ᵊn, -sēd′-, kô ris′i din), *n.* *Pharm., Trademark.* an antihistaminic compound consisting of chlorprophenpyridamine maleate, aspirin, acetophenetidine, and caffeine, used in treating the symptoms of a cold or of an allergy.

cor·ing (kôr′iṅg, kōr′-), *n.* **1.** the act of removing a core or of cutting from a central part. **2.** *Geol.* a cylindrical section of rock cut out of underground strata and extracted for examination. [CORE[1] + -ING[1]]

Co·rin·na (kō rin′ə, kō-), *n.* a girl's given name, form of Cora. Also, **Co·rinne** (kō rin′, -rēn′, kō-), **Corynne.**

Cor·inth (kôr′inth, kor′- *or, for 5,* kō rinth′), *n.* **1.** an ancient city in Greece, on the Isthmus of Corinth: one of the wealthiest and most powerful of the ancient Greek

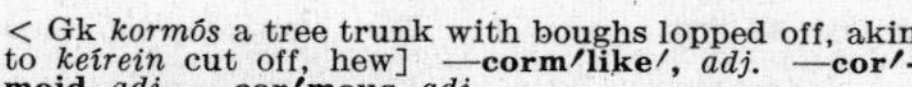

cities. **2.** a port in the NE Peloponnesus, in S Greece: NE of the site of ancient Corinth. **3. Gulf of.** Also called **Gulf of Lepanto.** an arm of the Ionian Sea, N of the Peloponnesus. **4. Isthmus of,** an isthmus at the head of the Gulf of Corinth, connecting the Peloponnesus with central Greece: traversed by a ship canal. **5.** a town in E New York. 3193 (1960).

Co·rin·thi·an (kə rin′thē ən), *adj.* **1.** of, pertaining to, or characteristic of Corinth. **2.** luxurious or licentious. **3.** ornate, as literary style. **4.** *Archit.* noting or pertaining to one of the five classical orders invented in ancient Greece and similar in most respects to the Ionic but usually of slenderer proportions, and characterized by a deep capital with a round bell decorated with acanthus leaves and a square abacus with concave sides. The Corinthian capital has typically two distinct rows of acanthus leaves above which appear eight fluted sheaths, or cauliculi, from each of which spring two scrolls, or helices, of which one curls beneath a corner of the abacus as half of a volute and the other curls beneath the center of the abacus. Cf. **composite** (def. 3), **Doric** (def. 3), **Ionic** (def. 1), **Tuscan** (def. 2). See illustration under **order. 5.** pertaining to or designating a style of vase painting developed in Corinth, in the 7th and early 6th centuries B.C., characterized chiefly by human, animal, and ornamental motifs, painted boldly in a black figure style on a terra-cotta ground, often arranged in tiers around the vase. —*n.* **6.** a native or inhabitant of Corinth. **7.** a man about town, esp. one who lives luxuriously or, sometimes, dissolutely. **8.** an amateur yachtsman. **9.** *Manège.* a horse-show class in which each contestant must be a member of a recognized hunt and wear regulation hunt livery. Cf. **appointment** (def. 6). [ME *Corinthi(es)* men of Corinth (< L *Corinthiī* < Gk *Korínthioi;* see CORINTH) + -AN]

Co·rin·thi·ans (kə rin′thē ənz), *n.* (*construed as sing.*) either of two books of the New Testament, I Corinthians or II Corinthians, written by Paul.

Cor·in·thus (kə rin′thəs, kō-), *n. Class. Myth.* a son of either Zeus or Marathon, the eponymous founder of Corinth.

Co·ri·o·la·nus (kôr′ē ə lā′nəs, kor′-), *n.* **1. Ga·ius** (or **Gnae·us**) **Mar·ci·us** (gā′əs *or* nē′əs, mär′shē əs), fl. late 5th century B.C., legendary Roman military hero. **2.** (*italics.*) a tragedy (1608?) by Shakespeare.

Co·ri·o′lis effect′ (kôr′ē ō′lis), the apparent deflection (**Corio′lis accelera′tion**) of a body in motion with respect to the earth, as seen by an observer on the earth, attributed to a hypothetical force (**Corio′lis force′**) but actually caused by the rotation of the earth and appearing as a deflection to the right in the Northern Hemisphere and a deflection to the left in the Southern Hemisphere. Also called **compound centrifugal force, deflecting force.** [named after Gaspard G. *Coriolis* (d. 1843), French civil engineer]

co·ri·ta (kə rē′tə), *n.* a boat resembling a large, woven basket, used by Indians of the Southwestern U.S. [< MexSp]

co·ri·um (kōr′ē əm, kôr′-), *n., pl.* **co·ri·a** (kōr′ē ə, kôr′-). **1.** *Anat.* the sensitive vascular layer of the skin beneath the epidermis; derma. **2.** *Entomol.* the thickened, leathery, basal portion of a hemelytron. [< L: skin, hide, leather]

cork (kôrk), *n.* **1.** the outer bark of an oak, *Quercus Suber,* of Mediterranean countries, used for making stoppers for bottles, floats, etc. **2.** Also called **cork oak.** the tree itself. **3.** something made of cork. **4.** a piece of cork, rubber, or the like used as a stopper, as for a bottle. **5.** *Angling.* a small float to buoy up a fishing line or to indicate that a fish is biting. **6.** Also called **phellem.** *Bot.* an outer tissue of bark produced by an exterior to the phellogen. —*v.t.* **7.** to provide or fit with cork or a cork. **8.** to stop with or as if with a cork (often fol. by *up*). **9.** to blacken with burnt cork. [ME *cork(e)* < Ar *qurq* < L *querc(us)* oak] —**cork′like′,** *adj.*

Cork (kôrk), *n.* **1.** a county in Munster province, in S Republic of Ireland. 330,443 (1961); 2881 sq. mi. **2.** a seaport in and the county seat of Cork, in the S part. 77,980 (1961).

cork·age (kôr′kij), *n.* a fee charged, as in a restaurant, for serving wine or liquor brought in by the patron. [CORK + -AGE]

cork·board (kôrk′bōrd′, -bôrd′), *n.* an insulating material made of cork, used in building, for industrial purposes, etc. [CORK + BOARD]

cork′ cam′bium, *Bot.* phellogen.

corked (kôrkt), *adj.* **1.** stopped or closed with a cork. **2.** (of wine) corky. **3.** blackened with burnt cork. [CORK + -ED[3]]

cor·ker (kôr′kər), *n.* **1.** one who or that which corks. **2.** *Slang.* something that closes a discussion or settles a question. **3.** *Slang.* someone or something of astonishing or excellent quality: *That show was a corker!* [CORK + -ER[1]]

cork·ing (kôr′king) *Informal.* —*adj.* **1.** excellent; fine. —*adv.* **2.** very: *a corking good time.* [CORK + -ING[2]]

cork′ oak′, cork (def. 2).

cork·screw (kôrk′skrōō′), *n.* **1.** an instrument typically consisting of a metal spiral with a sharp point at one end and a transverse handle at the other, used for drawing corks from bottles. —*adj.* **2.** resembling a corkscrew; helical; spiral. —*v.t., v.i.* **3.** to move in a spiral or zigzag course. [CORK + SCREW]

cork′screw flow′er, snailflower.

cork′ tree′, 1. the cork oak, *Quercus Suber.* **2.** any of several Asian, rutaceous trees of the genus *Phellodendron,* having a corky bark.

cork·wood (kôrk′wŏŏd′), *n.* **1.** a stout shrub or small tree, *Leitneria floridana,* having shiny deciduous leaves, densely pubescent aments, and a drupaceous fruit. **2.** any of certain trees and shrubs yielding a light and porous wood, as the balsa. [CORK + WOOD[1]]

cork·y (kôr′kē), *adj.,* **cork·i·er, cork·i·est. 1.** of the nature of cork; corklike. **2.** *Informal.* buoyant, lively, or skittish. **3.** (of wine) tasting of the cork; having the flavor spoiled by poor corking. [CORK + -Y[1]] —**cork′i·ness,** *n.*

Cor·liss (kôr′lis), *n.* **George Henry,** 1817–88, U.S. engineer and inventor.

Corm of crocus

corm (kôrm), *n. Bot.* an enlarged, fleshy, bulblike base of a stem, as in the crocus. [< NL *corm(us)* < Gk *kormós* a tree trunk with boughs lopped off, akin to *keírein* cut off, hew] —**corm′like′,** *adj.* —**cor′moid,** *adj.* —**cor′mous,** *adj.*

cor·mo·phyte (kôr′mə fīt′), *n.* any of the *Cormophyta,* an old primary division or group of plants having an axis differentiated into stem and root and including all phanerogams and the higher cryptogams. [CORM + -O- + -PHYTE] —**cor·mo·phyt·ic** (kôr′mə fit′ik), *adj.*

cor·mo·rant (kôr′mər ənt), *n.* **1.** any of several voracious, totipalmate sea birds of the family *Phalacrocoracidae,* as *Phalacrocorax carbo,* of America, Europe, and Asia, having a long neck and a distensible pouch under the bill for holding captured fish, used in China for catching fish. **2.** a greedy or rapacious person. —*adj.* **3.** greedy; rapacious; gluttonous. [ME *cormera(u)nt* < MF *cormorant,* OF *cormareng* < LL *cor(vus) marinus* searaven. See CORBEL, MARINE]

Cormorant, *Phalacrocorax carbo* (Length 3 ft.)

corn[1] (kôrn), *n.* **1.** Also called **Indian corn;** *esp. technical and Brit.,* **maize.** *U.S., Canadian, Australian.* **a.** a tall, annual cereal plant, *Zea Mays,* cultivated in many varieties, having a jointed, solid stem and bearing the grain, seeds, or kernels on large ears. **b.** the grain, seeds, or kernels of this plant, used for food by man or for fodder. **c.** the ears of this plant. **2.** the edible seed of certain other cereal plants, esp. wheat in England and oats in Scotland. **3.** the plants themselves. **4.** *U.S.* (loosely) sweet corn. **5.** See **corn whiskey. 6.** *Skiing.* See **corn snow. 7.** *Informal.* old-fashioned, trite, or mawkishly sentimental entertainment material, as a joke, a story, or music. —*v.t.* **8.** to granulate, as gunpowder. **9.** to preserve and season with salt in grains. **10.** to preserve and season with brine. **11.** to plant (land) with corn. **12.** to feed with corn. [ME, OE; c. D *koren,* Icel, G *Korn,* Goth *kaúrn;* akin to L *grānum,* Russ *zerno* GRAIN]

corn[2] (kôrn), *n. Pathol.* a horny induration or callosity of the epidermis, usually with a central core, formed esp. on the toes or feet and caused by undue pressure or friction. [late ME *corne* < MF < L *corn(ū)* horn, hence a horny hardening of the cuticle. See HORN]

Corn., **1.** Cornish. **2.** Cornwall.

-corn, a learned borrowing from Latin meaning "horn," used in the formation of compound words: *longicorn.* [repr. L *-cornis* horned]

cor·na·ceous (kôr nā′shəs), *adj.* belonging to the *Cornaceae,* a family of plants, mostly shrubs and trees, including the dogwood. [< NL *Cornāce(ae)* name of the order (*Corn(us)* CORNEL + *-āceae* -ACEAE) + -OUS]

corn·ball (kôrn′bôl′), *n.* **1.** popcorn rolled into a ball and flavored with molasses or caramel. **2.** a country bumpkin; hick. —*adj.* **3.** corny. [CORN[1] + BALL[1]; defs. 2, 3, influenced by slang sense of *corn.* Cf. SCREWBALL, ODDBALL]

Corn′ Belt′, a region in the midwestern U.S., esp. Iowa, Illinois, and Indiana, excellent for raising corn and cornfed livestock.

corn′ bor′er, any of several pyralid moths, as *Pyrausta nubilalis* (**European corn borer**), the larvae of which bore into the stem and crown of corn and other plants.

corn′ bread′, a bread made of corn meal. Also called **Indian bread.**

corn′ cake′, *U.S.* a cake made of corn meal.

corn·cob (kôrn′kob′), *n.* **1.** the elongated woody core in which the grains of an ear of corn are embedded. **2.** Also called **corn′cob pipe′.** a tobacco pipe with a bowl made from a corncob. [CORN[1] + COB[1]]

corn′ cock′le, a caryophyllaceous plant, *Agrostemma Githago,* having red or white flowers and occurring commonly as a weed among crops of grain. Also called **corn rose, rose campion.**

corn′ col′or, light yellow. —**corn′-col′ored,** *adj.*

corn·crack·er (kôrn′krak′ər), *n. Disparaging.* one of a poor class of white people in the southern U.S.; cracker. [CORN[1] + CRACKER]

corn′ crake′, a short-billed, Eurasian rail, *Crex crex,* found in grain fields. Also called **land rail.**

corn·crib (kôrn′krib′), *n.* a ventilated structure for the storage of unhusked corn. [CORN[1] + CRIB]

corn′ dodg′er, *Chiefly Southern U.S.* a stiff or hard bread made of fried or baked corn meal.

cor·ne·a (kôr′nē ə), *n. Anat.* the transparent anterior part of the external coat of the eye covering the iris and the pupil and continuous with the sclera. See diag. under **eye.** [< ML *cornea* (*tēla,* later *tunica*) horny (web or tunic), fem. of *corneus* CORNEOUS] —**cor′ne·al,** *adj.*

cor′neal re′flex, **1.** *Physiol.* the closing of the eyelids induced by touching the cornea lightly. **2.** *Ophthalm.* the reflection of a keratoscope, as Placido's disk, on the surface of the cornea.

corn′ ear′worm, a noctuid moth, *Heliothis zea,* the larvae of which are highly destructive to crops of corn, cotton, tomatoes, etc.

corned (kôrnd), *adj.* preserved or cured with salt: *corned beef.* [CORN[1] + -ED[2]]

corne de vache (*Fr.* kôrn də vȧsh′), *pl.* **cornes de vache** (*Fr.* kôrn də vȧsh′). *Building., Archit.* a splayed area of an arch soffit, both arrises of which diverge from the crown so that the outer one falls farther from the center. [< F: lit., cow's horn]

Cor·neille (kôr nā′; *Fr.* kôr ne′yə), *n.* **Pierre** (pē âr′; *Fr.* pyer), 1606–84, French dramatist and poet.

cor·nel (kôr′nəl), *n.* any tree or shrub of the genus *Cornus;* dogwood. [late ME *corneille* < MF < VL **corniculu(a),* equiv. to L *corn(um)* cornel + *-cula,* pl. of *-culum* -CULE; r. OE *corn-treōw* cornel-tree]

Cor·nel·ia (kôr nēl′yə), *n.* **1.** fl. 2nd century B.C., Roman matron: mother of Gaius and Tiberius Gracchus. **2.** fl. 1st century B.C., first wife of Julius Caesar 83–67? Cf. **Pompeia, Calpurnia** (def. 1). **3.** a town in NE Georgia. 2936 (1960). **4.** a girl's given name.

cor·nel·ian (kôr nēl′yən), *n.* carnelian.

cornel′ian cher′ry, **1.** a shrub or small tree, *Cornus Mas,* of Europe and Asia. **2.** the tart, scarlet, edible berry of this plant. [CORNEL + -IAN]

Cor·ne·li·us (kôr nēl′yəs, -nē′lē əs; *for 2, 3, also Ger.* kôr nā′lē ōōs′), *n.* **1. Saint,** died A.D. 253, Italian ecclesiastic: pope 251–253. **2. Pe·ter von** (pā′tər fən), 1783–1867, German painter. **3.** a boy's given name.

Cor·nell (kôr nel′), *n.* **1. Ezra,** 1809–74, U.S. capitalist and philanthropist. **2. Katharine,** born 1898, U.S. actress. **3.** a boy's given name.

cor·ne·muse (kôr′nə myōōz′), *n.* a bagpipe used in Italy and France. [ME < OF, back formation from *cornemuser* (v.), equiv. to *corne* HORN + *muse(r)* < VL *mus(a)* pipe]

cor·ne·ous (kôr′nē əs), *adj.* consisting of a horny substance; horny. [< L *corneus* horny, equiv. to *corn(ū)* horn + *-eus* -EOUS]

cor·ner (kôr′nər), *n.* **1.** the meeting place of two converging lines or surfaces. **2.** the space between two converging lines or surfaces near their intersection; angle: *a chair in the corner of the room.* **3.** a projecting angle, esp. of a rectangular figure or object: *He bumped into the corner of the table.* **4.** the point where two streets meet: *the corner of Market and Main Streets.* **5.** an end; margin; edge. **6.** any narrow, secluded, or secret place. **7.** an awkward or embarrassing position, esp. one from which escape is impossible. **8.** *Finance.* a monopolizing or a monopoly of the available supply of a stock or commodity to a point permitting control of price (applied only when monopoly price is exacted). **9.** region; part; quarter: *every corner of his empire.* **10.** a piece to protect the corner of anything. **11. cut corners, a.** to use a shorter route. **b.** to reduce costs or care in execution: *cutting corners to meet the foreign competition.* **12. rough corners,** rude, boorish, or unsophisticated characteristics, manners, or the like: *Despite his rough corners, he was very likable.* **13. the four corners of the earth,** the most distant or remote regions of the earth: *They traveled to the four corners of the earth.* **14. turn the corner,** to pass through a crisis safely: *When the fever passed, we knew he had turned the corner.* —*adj.* **15.** situated on or at a corner where two streets meet: *a corner drug store.* **16.** made to fit or be used in a corner: *a corner cabinet.* —*v.t.* **17.** to furnish with corners. **18.** to place in or drive into a corner. **19.** to force into an awkward or difficult position or one from which escape is impossible: *He finally cornered the hoodlum. She cornered him with a perfectly timed retort.* **20.** to gain control of (a stock, commodity, etc.). —*v.i.* **21.** to meet in or be situated on or at a corner. **22.** to form a corner in a stock or commodity. **23.** (of an automobile) to turn, esp. at a speed relatively high for the angle of the turn involved. [ME < AF (equiv. to OF *cornier*), equiv. to OF *corne* corner, horn (< L *corn(ū)* horn) + *-er* -ER[2]]

cor′ner acces′sory, *Survey.* accessory (def. 5).

cor′ner bead′, a bent and perforated sheet-metal strip for reinforcing plasterwork at an outside corner.

cor′ner cab′inet, a cabinet usually triangular in design so as to fit into a corner of a room.

cor′ner chair′, *Eng. and U.S. Furniture.* a chair having an approximately square seat with a leg at each corner and a back extending around two adjacent sides. Also called **roundabout chair.**

cor′ner chis′el, a woodworking chisel having a blade with a right-angled cross section, used for cutting and finishing interior angles of 90° or more.

cor′ner cup′board, a cupboard usually triangular in design so as to fit into a corner of a room.

cor·nered (kôr′nərd), *adj.* **1.** having corners (usually used in combination): *a six-cornered room.* **2.** having a given number of positions; sided (usually used in combination): *a three-cornered debate.* **3.** forced into an awkward, embarrassing, or inescapable position: *a cornered debater; a cornered fox.* [ME; see CORNER, -ED[3]]

cor′ner man′, *Theat. Brit.* See **end man.**

cor·ner·stone (kôr′nər stōn′), *n.* **1.** a stone uniting two masonry walls at an intersection. **2.** a stone representing the nominal starting place in the construction of a monumental building, usually carved with the date and laid with appropriate ceremonies. **3.** something that is essential, indispensable, or basic: *The cornerstone of democratic government is a free press.* **4.** the chief foundation on which something is constructed or developed: *The cornerstone of his argument was that all men are created equal.* [ME; see CORNER, STONE]

cor′ner ta′ble, a table of the 18th century having a triangular top with a triangular drop leaf of the same size. Also called **handkerchief table.**

cor·ner·wise (kôr′nər wīz′), *adv.* **1.** with the corner in front. **2.** so as to form a corner. **3.** from corner to corner; diagonally. Also, **cor·ner·ways** (kôr′nər wāz′). [late ME; see CORNER, -WISE]

cor·net (kôr net′ *for 1;* kôr′nit, kôr net′ *for 2–7*), *n.* **1.** *Music.* **a.** Also called **cornetto.** a valved wind instrument of the trumpet family. **b.** cornett. **2.** a small cone of paper twisted at the end and used for holding candy, nuts, etc. **3.** *Brit.* a conical wafer, as for ice cream; cone. **4.** a large white headdress worn by the members of the Sisters of Charity. **5.** Also, **cor′nette.** a woman's headdress, often cone-shaped, usually of delicate fabrics and having lappets of lace or other material, worn by women from the 14th to the 18th century. **6.** a pennant or flag used for signaling in a navy. **7.** (formerly) the officer who carried the colors in a troop of cavalry: *the cornet of horse.* [late ME < MF, OF, equiv. to *corn* horn (< L *cornū*) + *-et* -ET]

Cornet (def. 1a)

cor·net-à-pis·tons (kôr net′ə pis′tənz; *Fr.* kôr ne′ȧ pē stôN′), *n., pl.* **cor·nets-à-pis·tons** (kôr nets′ə pis′tənz; *Fr.* kôr ne′zȧ pē stôN′). cornet (def. 1a). [< F: lit., cornet with valves]

cor·net·cy (kôr′nit sē, kôr net′-), *n., pl.* **-cies.** the rank, office, or commission of a cornet. [CORNET + -CY]

cor·net·fish (kôr net′fish′), *n., pl.* (*esp. collectively*) **-fish,** (*esp. referring to two or more kinds or species*) **-fish·es.** any of several slender fishes of the family *Fistulariidae,* found in tropical waters, that are covered with bony plates and have an elongated snout. [CORNET + FISH]

cor·net·ist (kôr net′ist), *n.* a musician who plays the cornet. Also, **cor·net′tist.** [CORNET + -IST]

cor·nett (kôr net′), *n.* a woodwind instrument of the Renaissance having six finger holes and a cup-shaped mouthpiece. Also, **cornet, cornetto.** [ME *cornette* < OF, dim. of *corn* HORN]

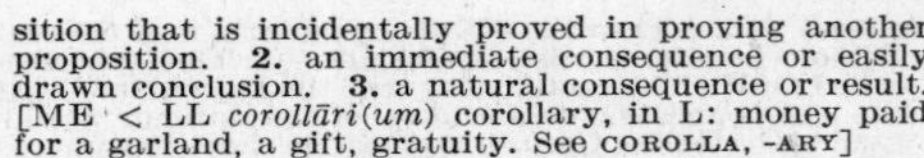

cor·net·to (kôr net′ō; *It.* kōʀ net′tō), *n., pl.* **-net·ti** (-net′ē; *It.* -net′tē). **1.** cornet (def. 1a). **2.** cornett. [< It, dim. of *corno* horn < L *cornū*]

corn·fed (kôrn′fed′), *adj.* **1.** fed on corn: *cornfed cattle.* **2.** having a well-fed, healthy, and guileless appearance: *the open enthusiasm of these handsome, cornfed youngsters.* [CORN¹ + FED]

corn·field (kôrn′fēld′), *n.* a field where corn is grown. [ME *cornfeld.* See CORN¹, FIELD]

corn′field ant′, a small, brown ant, *Lasius alienus,* that lives in cornfields and feeds on honeydew of the corn root aphid.

corn·flag (kôrn′flag′), *n.* an herb, *Gladiolus segetum,* of the Mediterranean region, having one-sided spikes of purple flowers. [CORN¹ + FLAG²]

corn·flakes (kôrn′flāks′), *n.pl.* a breakfast cereal in the form of small toasted flakes made from corn, for serving cold with milk, sugar, etc. Also, **corn′ flakes′.** [CORN¹ + *flakes,* pl. of FLAKE¹]

corn′ flour′, **1.** flour prepared from corn. **2.** *Chiefly Brit.* cornstarch.

corn·flow·er (kôrn′flou′ər), *n.* **1.** Also called **blue-bottle.** a European, composite plant, *Centaurea cyanus,* found in grainfields, having blue to white flowers, often cultivated as an ornamental. **2.** Also called **corn′-flower blue′.** a deep, vivid blue. **3.** See **corn cockle. 4.** strawflower (def. 2). [ME *cornflor.* See CORN¹, FLOWER]

corn′ grits′, *U.S.* (*construed as sing. or pl.*) hominy grits.

corn·husk (kôrn′husk′), *n.* *U.S.* the husk of an ear of corn. [CORN¹ + HUSK]

corn·husk·ing (kôrn′hus′king), *n.* *U.S.* **1.** the removing of the husks from corn. **2.** See **husking bee.** [CORNHUSK + -ING¹] —**corn′husk′er,** *n.*

cor·nice (kôr′nis), *n., v.,* **-niced, -nic·ing.** —*n.* **1.** *Archit.* **a.** any prominent, continuous, horizontally projecting feature surmounting a wall or other construction, or dividing it horizontally for compositional purposes; a more prominent feature than a coping or stringcourse. **b.** the uppermost member of a classical entablature, consisting of a bed molding, a corona, and a cymatium, with rows of dentils, modillions, etc., often placed between the bed molding and the corona. **2.** any of the various other ornamental horizontal moldings or bands, as for concealing hooks or rods from which curtains are hung or for supporting picture hooks. **3.** a mass of snow, ice, etc., projecting over a mountain ridge. —*v.t.* **4.** to furnish or finish with or as if with a cornice. [< It: lit., crow (< L *cornix*); for the meaning, cf. Gk *korṓnē* crow, CROWN]

Cor·ni·chon (kôr′ni shon′), *n.* **1.** a black vinifera grape grown for table use. **2.** the vine bearing this fruit. **3.** (*l.c.*) a cucumber pickle; gherkin. [< F: lit., little horn, equiv. to *corne* horn + *-ichon* dim. suffix]

cor·ni·cle (kôr′ni kəl), *n.* (in aphids) one of a pair of tubes at the posterior end of the abdomen from which a waxy fluid is emitted. [< L *corniculum* little horn, equiv. to *corn-* (s. of *cornū*) HORN + *-i-* -I- + *-culum* -CLE]

cor·nic·u·late (kôr nik′yə lāt′, -lit), *adj.* **1.** resembling a small horn in appearance. **2.** having horns or hornlike parts; horned. [< L *corniculāt(us)* horned, equiv. to *cornicul(um)* little horn (see CORN², -CULE) + *-ātus* -ATE¹]

Cor·ning (kôr′ning), *n.* **1.** a city in S New York. 17,085 (1960). **2.** a town in N California. 3006 (1960).

Corn′ is Green′, The, a play (1938) by Emlyn Williams.

Cor·nish (kôr′nish), *adj.* **1.** of, pertaining to, or characteristic of Cornwall, England, its inhabitants, or the Cornish language. —*n.* **2.** the Celtic language of Cornwall, extinct since c1800. **3.** one of an English breed of chickens raised chiefly for crossing with other breeds to produce roasters. [late ME *Cornyssh,* appar. syncopated var. of ME *Cornwelisse.* See CORNWALL, -ISH¹]

Cor′nish en′gine, a single-acting steam engine working a lift pump by means of a walking beam, the weight of the moving part of the pump giving the return stroke. [so called because first used in Cornwall]

Cor·nish·man (kôr′nish mən), *n., pl.* **-men.** a native or inhabitant of Cornwall. [CORNISH + MAN¹]

Cor′nish stone′, rock consisting mainly of feldspar and quartz, used as a flux in the manufacture of English ceramic ware.

Corn′ Law′, *Eng. Hist.* any of the laws regulating domestic and foreign trading of grain, the last of which was repealed in 1846.

corn′ lil′y, any of several iridaceous plants of the genus *Ixia,* of southern Africa, grown as an ornamental.

corn′ liq′uor. See **corn whiskey.**

corn′ mar′igold, an annual herb, *Chrysanthemum segetum,* of Eurasia, having daisylike, solitary, white or yellowish flowers.

corn′ may′weed. See **scentless camomile.**

corn′ meal′, **1.** meal made of corn or grain; Indian meal. **2.** *Scot.* oatmeal. —**corn′meal′,** *adj.*

corn′ mint′, a perennial herb, *Mentha arvensis,* of Eurasia and North America, having downy leaves and flowers that grow in circles in the leaf axils. Also called **field mint, wild pennyroyal.**

corn′ muf′fin, a muffin, shaped like a cupcake, made from corn meal.

corn′ oil′, a pale-yellow, water-insoluble liquid oil obtained by expressing the germs of corn kernels, used in the preparation of foodstuffs, lubricants, soaps, and hair dressings. Also called **maize oil.**

Cor·no·pi·on (kôr nō′pē on′), *n.* *Class. Myth.* Hercules: so called because he dispelled a plague of locusts in Euboea. [< Gk *Kornōpíon* locust scarer]

corn′ pick′er, a machine for picking the ears of corn from standing stalks and removing the husks. —**corn′ pick′ing.**

corn′ pone′, *Southern U.S.* **1.** corn bread, esp. of a plain or simple kind. **2.** a cake or loaf of this.

corn′ pop′py, a common, Old World poppy, *Papaver Rhoeas,* having bright-red flowers. [so called from its growing in grainfields]

corn′ root′ a′phid, an aphid, *Anuraphis maidiradicis,* that is a common pest in the corn-growing regions of the U.S. and that lives as a symbiont in colonies of cornfield ants.

corn′ rose′, **1.** See **corn poppy. 2.** See **corn cockle.**

corn′ sal′ad, any of several plants of the genus *Valerianella,* esp. *V. olitoria* and *V. eriocarpa,* that is sometimes found wild in grainfields and is used in salads.

corn′ shock′, a stack of upright cornstalks.

corn′ silk′, the long, threadlike, silky styles on an ear of corn.

corn′ smut′, a disease of corn that is characterized by blackish, powdery masses of spores on the affected parts and is caused by a fungus, *Ustilago maydis.*

corn′ snake′, a North American rat snake, *Elaphe guttata,* yellow or gray with dark-red blotches, often found in cornfields. Also called **red rat snake.**

corn′ snow′, *Skiing.* snow in the form of small pellets or grains produced by the alternate melting and freezing of a snow layer. Also called **corn.**

corn·stalk (kôrn′stôk′), *n.* the stalk or stem of corn, esp. Indian corn. [CORN¹ + STALK¹]

Corn·stalk (kôrn′stôk′), *n.* *Australian Informal.* a white person, esp. one from New South Wales.

corn·starch (kôrn′stärch′), *n.* a starch or a starchy flour made from corn and used for thickening gravies and sauces, making puddings, etc. [CORN¹ + STARCH]

corn′ sug′ar, dextrose.

corn′ syr′up, the syrup prepared from corn.

cor·nu (kôr′nyōō, -nōō), *n., pl.* **-nu·a** (-nyōō ə). a horn, esp. a bony part that resembles a horn. [< L: a horn] —**cor′nu·al,** *adj.*

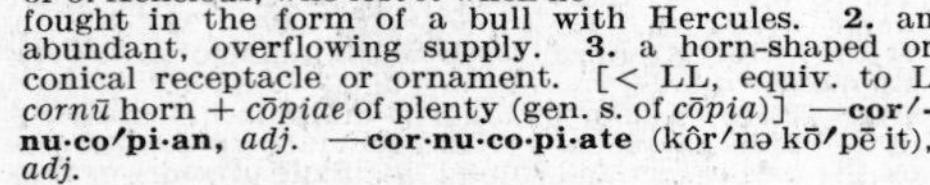

Cornucopia

cor·nu·co·pi·a (kôr′nə kō′pē ə), *n.* **1.** *Class. Myth.* a horn containing food, drink, etc., in endless supply, said to have been a horn of the goat Amalthaea or of the goat belonging to the nymph Amalthaea, or of Achelous, who lost it when he fought in the form of a bull with Hercules. **2.** an abundant, overflowing supply. **3.** a horn-shaped or conical receptacle or ornament. [< LL, equiv. to L *cornū* horn + *cōpiae* of plenty (gen. s. of *cōpia*)] —**cor′nu·co′pi·an,** *adj.* —**cor·nu·co·pi·ate** (kôr′nə kō′pē it), *adj.*

cornuco′pia leg′, *Furniture.* a leg used on pieces in the Directoire and Empire styles, curving downward from the piece and curving upward again to a point and having a foot or caster at the lowest part of the curve.

cornuco′pia so′fa, an Empire sofa having cornucopia designs carved on its visible wooden parts.

cor·nute (kôr nōōt′, -nyōōt′), *v.,* **-nut·ed, -nut·ing,** *adj.* —*v.t.* **1.** *Archaic.* to cuckold. —*adj.* **2.** cornuted. [< L *cornūt(us)* horned, equiv. to *cornū* horn + *-tus* adj. suffix]

cor·nut·ed (kôr nōō′tid, -nyōō′-), *adj.* **1.** having horns. **2.** shaped like a horn. **3.** *Archaic.* cuckolded. Also, **cornute.** [CORNUTE + -ED²]

cor·nu·to (kôr nōō′tō, -nyōō′-), *n., pl.* **-tos.** *Archaic.* a cuckold. [< It: lit., one who is horned < L *cornūt(us)* horned. See CORNUTE]

Corn·wall (kôrn′wôl *or, esp. Brit.,* -wəl), *n.* **1.** a county in SW England. 341,746 (1961); 1357 sq. mi. *Co. seat:* Bodmin. **2.** a town in SE New York. 2785 (1960).

Corn·wal·lis (kôrn wô′lis, -wol′is), *n.* **Charles, 1st Marquis,** 1738–1805, British general and statesman: surrendered to Washington at Yorktown, Virginia, October 19, 1781.

Corn′wall Southwest′, a town in SE New York. 2824 (1960).

corn′ whis′key, whiskey made from at least 80 percent corn. Also called **corn, corn liquor.**

corn·y¹ (kôr′nē), *adj.,* **corn·i·er, corn·i·est. 1.** of or abounding in corn. **2.** *Informal.* **a.** old-fashioned; lacking in subtlety and full of clichés: *corny jokes; corny dinner music.* **b.** mawkishly sentimental: *as corny a soap opera as any we've seen.* [ME; see CORN¹, -Y¹]

corn·y² (kôr′nē), *adj.,* **corn·i·er, corn·i·est.** pertaining to or affected with corns of the feet. [CORN² + -Y¹]

Co·ro (kô′rô), *n.* a city in NW Venezuela. 39,053 (est. 1955).

cor·o·dy (kôr′ə dē, kor′-), *n., pl.* **-dies.** *Old Eng. Law.* **1.** a right to receive maintenance in the form of housing, food, or clothing, esp. the right enjoyed by the sovereign or a private benefactor to receive such maintenance from a religious house. **2.** the housing, food, or clothing so received. Also, **corrody.** [late ME < ML *corrōdi(um)* outfit, provision, var. of *conrēdium* < VL **conrēdāre* to outfit, provide with, equiv. to *con-* CON- + **rēdāre* < Gmc; cf. OE *rǣdan* to equip, provide for, REDE]

Co·roe·bus (kə rē′bəs), *n.* *Class. Myth.* **1.** a son of Mygdon, slain by Diomedes in the Trojan War. **2.** an Argive hero who in penance for having slain the monster Poena built a temple to Apollo.

cor·o·lit·ic (kôr′ə lit′ik, kor′-), *adj.* *Archit.* (of a column or the like) ornamented with foliage. [< F *corollitique,* equiv. to *corolle* COROLLA + *-itique* -ITIC]

coroll., corollary. Also, **corol.**

co·rol·la (kə rol′ə), *n.* *Bot.* the internal envelope of floral leaves of a flower, usually of delicate texture and of some color other than green; the petals considered collectively. [< L: little garland, equiv. to *corōn(a)* garland (see CORONA) + *-ula* -ULE]

cor·ol·la·ceous (kôr′ə lā′shəs, kor′-), *adj.* of, pertaining to, or resembling a corolla. [COROLL(A) + -ACEOUS]

A B C D E F

Corollas
Polypetalous corollas:
A, Papilionaceous;
B, Cruciate;
Gamopetalous corollas:
C, Personate;
D, Tubular;
E, Bilabiate;
F, Rotate

cor·ol·lar·y (kôr′ə ler′ē, kor′-; *esp. Brit.,* kə rol′ə rē), *n., pl.* **-lar·ies. 1.** *Math.* a proposition that is incidentally proved in proving another proposition. **2.** an immediate consequence or easily drawn conclusion. **3.** a natural consequence or result. [ME < LL *corollāri(um)* corollary, in L: money paid for a garland, a gift, gratuity. See COROLLA, -ARY]

co·rol·late (kə rol′āt, -it, kôr′ə lāt′, -lit, kor′-), *adj.* *Bot.* having a corolla. Also, **co·rol·lat·ed** (kə rol′ā tid, kôr′ə lā′, kor′-). [COROLL(A) + -ATE¹]

Cor′o·man′del Coast′ (kôr′ə man′dᵊl, kor′-, kôr′-, kor′-), a coastal region in SE India, extending from Point Calimere to the Kistna River.

Coroman′del work′, lacquer work popular in England c1700 and marked by an incised design filled in with gold and color. Also called **Bantam work.**

cor·o·mell (kôr′ə mel′), *n.* (at La Paz, Mexico) a land breeze blowing from the south during the winter and early spring, setting in at night, and usually lasting until mid-morning. [?]

co·ro·na (kə rō′nə), *n., pl.* **-nas, -nae** (-nē). **1.** a white or colored circle or set of concentric circles of light seen around a luminous body, esp. the sun or moon. **2.** *Meteorol.* such a circle or set of circles having a small radius and ranging in color from blue inside to red outside, attributable to the diffraction caused by thin clouds, mist, or sometimes dust (distinguished from *halo*). **3.** Also called **aureola, aureole.** *Astron.* a faintly luminous envelope outside of the sun's chromosphere, the inner part consisting of highly ionized elements. **4.** *Archit.* the projecting, slablike member of a classical cornice supported by the bed molding or by modillions, dentils, etc., and supporting the cymatium. **5.** *Anat.* the upper portion or crown of a part, as of the head. **6.** *Bot.* a crownlike appendage, esp. one on the inner side of a corolla, as in the narcissus. **7.** *Elect.* See **corona discharge. 8.** *Rom. Cath. Ch.* the five mysteries of the rosary. **9.** the tonsure of a cleric. **10.** *Eccles.* a gold-colored stripe around the lower edge of a clerical headdress, as of a miter. **11.** a chandelier of wrought metal, having the form of one or more concentric hoops. **12.** a ridge surrounding the nugget of a spot-weld. **13.** a long, straight cigar. [< L *corōna* garland, crown < Gk *korṓnē* crown, curved object; akin to *korōnís* wreath, *kórax* crow, raven]

Co·ro·na Aus·tra·lis (kə rō′nə ô strā′lis), *gen.* **Co·ro·nae Aus·tra·lis** (kə rō′nē ô strā′lis). the Southern Crown, a southern constellation touching the southern part of Sagittarius. [< L: lit., southern crown]

Co·ro·na Bo·re·a·lis (kə rō′nə bōr′ē al′is, -ā′lis, -bôr′-), *gen.* **Co·ro·nae Bo·re·al·is** (kə rō′nē bōr′ē al′is, -ā′lis, -bôr′-). the Northern Crown, a northern constellation between Hercules and Boötes. [< L: lit., northern crown]

cor·o·nach (kôʀ′ə naᴋʜ, kor′-), *n.* (in Scotland and Ireland) a song or lamentation for the dead; dirge. [< ScotGael *corranach,* Ir *corānach* dirge (cf. Ir *rān* cry, *rānadh* act of crying), lit., a crying out together; *co-,* c. *co-*]

coro′na dis′charge, *Elect.* a discharge, frequently luminous, at the surface of a conductor or between two conductors of the same transmission line, accompanied by ionization of the surrounding atmosphere and often by a power loss. Also called **corona, electric glow, St. Elmo's fire.** Cf. **brush discharge.**

Co·ro·na·do (kôr′ə nä′dō, kor′-, *Sp.* kô′rô nä′ᴛʜô *for def. 1;* kôr′ə nä′dō, kor′- *for 2*), *n.* **1. Fran·cis·co Vás·ques de** (fran sis′kō vas kwez′ də; *Sp.* frän thēs′kô väs′keth the), 1510–54?, Spanish explorer in North America. **2.** a city in SW California, near San Diego. 18,039 (1960).

co·ro·na·graph (kə rō′nə graf′, -gräf′), *n.* *Astron.* an instrument for observing and often photographing the sun's corona, consisting of a telescope fitted with lenses, filters, and diaphragms which simulate an eclipse. Also, **coronograph.** [earlier *coronograph.* See CORONA, -GRAPH] —**co·ro·na·graph·ic** (kə rō′nə graf′ik), *adj.*

cor·o·nal (*n.* kôr′ə nᵊl, kor′-; *adj.* kə rōn′ᵊl, kôr′ə nᵊl, kor′-), *n.* **1.** a crown; coronet. **2.** a garland. —*adj.* **3.** of or pertaining to a coronal. **4.** *Anat.* **a.** of or pertaining to a corona. **b.** situated in the direction of the coronal suture. **5.** (of a speech sound) articulated with the tip of the tongue, esp. in a retroflex position. **6.** of or pertaining to the tip of the tongue. [< LL *corōnālis*), equiv. to L *corōn(a)* crown + *-ālis* -AL¹] —**cor′o·naled;** *esp. Brit.,* **cor′o·nalled,** *adj.* —**co·ro′nal·ly,** *adv.*

coro′nal su′ture, *Anat.* a suture extending across the skull between the frontal bone and the parietal bones.

co·ro·na ra·di·a·ta (kə rō′nə rā′dē ā′tə), *pl.* **co·ro·nae ra·di·a·tae** (kə rō′nē rā′dē ā′tē). *Anat.* the layer of follicle cells surrounding an ovum and remaining attached to it following ovulation. [< NL; see CORONA, RADIATE]

cor·o·nar·y (kôr′ə ner′ē, kor′-), *adj., n., pl.* **-nar·ies.** —*adj.* **1.** *Med.* **a.** encircling like a crown, as certain blood vessels. **b.** pertaining to the arteries that supply the heart tissues and originate in the root of the aorta. **2.** of or pertaining to the human heart, with respect to health. **3.** of or like a crown. —*n.* **4.** *Med.* an attack of coronary occlusion, esp. coronary thrombosis. **5.** a coronary artery. [< L *corōnāri(us),* equiv. to *corōn(a)* crown + *-ārius* -ARY]

cor′onary cush′ion, *Vet. Med.* a thick band of vascular tissue in the coronet of hoofed animals that secretes the horny wall of the hoof. Also called **cor′onary ring′, cor′onary band′.**

cor′onary occlu′sion, *Pathol.* partial or total obstruction of a coronary artery, as by a thrombus, usually resulting in infarction of the myocardium.

cor′onary thrombo′sis, *Pathol.* a coronary occlusion in which there is blockage of a coronary arterial branch by a blood clot within the vessel, usually at a site narrowed by arteriosclerosis.

cor·o·nate (kôr′ə nāt′, kor′-), *adj.* having or wearing a crown, coronet, or the like. [< L *corōnāt(us)* crowned (ptp. of *corōnāre*), equiv. to *corōn(a)* crown + *-ātus* -ATE¹]

cor·o·na·tion (kôr′ə nā′shən, kor′-), *n.* the act or ceremony of crowning a king, queen, or other sovereign. [late ME *coronacio(u)n* < MF *coronation* < L *corōnāt(us)* crowned (see CORONATE) + MF *-ion* -ION]

cor·o·nel (kôr′ə nᵊl, kor′-), *n.* (in jousting) a crownlike head for a lance of courtesy. [ME *coronell* < AF **coronal* < LL *corōnāl(is)* CORONAL]

CONCISE ETYMOLOGY KEY: <, descended or derived from; >, whence; b., blend of, blended; c., cognate with; deriv., derivative; equiv., equivalent; imit., imitative; m., modification of; obl., oblique; r., replacing; s., stem; sp., spelling; trans., translation; ?, origin unknown, perhaps; *, hypothetical. See the full key inside the front cover.

cor·o·ner (kôr′ə nər, kor′-), *n.* an officer, as of a county or municipality, whose chief function is to investigate by inquest, as before a jury, any death not clearly resulting from natural causes. [ME < AF *corouner* supervisor of the Crown's pleas, equiv. to *coroune* CROWN + *-er* -ER[2]] —**cor′o·ner·ship′,** *n.*

cor′oner's in′quest, inquest (def. 2).

cor·o·net (kôr′ə nit, -net′, kor′-, kôr′ə net′, kor′-), *n.* 1. a small crown. 2. a crown worn by noblemen or peers. 3. a crownlike ornament for the head, as of gold or jewels. 4. an ornament, more or less pedimental in form, situated over a door or window. 5. the lowest part of the pastern of a horse, just above the hoof. 6. Also called **crest coronet.** *Heraldry.* a crownlike support for a crest, used in place of a torse. [alter. of ME *crownet.* See CROWN, -ET] —**cor′o·net·like′,** *adj.*

cor′onet braid′, a braid of hair wound around the head to resemble a coronet.

cor·o·net·ed (kôr′ə nit id, -net′id, kor′-, kôr′ə net′id, kor′-), *adj.* 1. wearing or entitled to wear a coronet. 2. of noble birth. Also, **cor′o·net′ted.** [CORONET + -ED[3]]

cor′onet of rank′, *Heraldry.* a coronet indicating by its form the rank in the peerage of the person wearing or displaying it.

Co·ro·nis (kə rō′nis), *n.* *Class. Myth.* 1. a princess killed by Apollo for being unfaithful to him. Hermes saved Asclepius, her unborn child by Apollo. 2. one of the nymphs who cared for the infant Dionysus.

cor·o·ni·tis (kôr′ə nī′tis, kor′-), *n.* *Vet. Pathol.* inflammation of the coronary cushion of hoofed animals. [CORON(A) + -ITIS]

co·ro·no·graph (kə rō′nə graf′, -gräf′), *n.* *Astron.* coronagraph. —**co·ro·no·graph·ic.** (kə rō′nə graf′ik), *adj.*

Co·ro·nus (kə rō′nəs), *n.* *Class. Myth.* a companion of Jason who became king of the Lapiths.

cor·o·plast (kôr′ə plast′, kor′-), *n.* *Gk. Antiq.* a sculptor of figurines, esp. in terra cotta. [< Gk *koroplást(ēs),* equiv. to *kor(ē)* maiden + *-o-* -O- + *-plastēs* molder; see -PLAST] —**cor′o·plas′tic,** *adj.*

Co·rot (kô rō′, kə-; *Fr.* kô rō′), *n.* **Jean Bap·tiste Ca·mille** (zhäN bA tēst′ kA mē′yə), 1796–1875, French painter.

corp., 1. corporal. 2. corporation. Also, **Corp.**

corpl., corporal. Also, **Corpl.**

corpn., corporation.

cor·po·ra (kôr′pər ə), *n.* pl. of **corpus.**

cor·po·ral[1] (kôr′pər əl, -prəl), *adj.* 1. of the human body; bodily; physical: *corporal pleasure.* 2. personal: *corporal possession.* 3. *Zool.* of the body proper, as distinguished from the head and limbs. 4. *Obs.* corporeal; belonging to the material world. [late ME *corporall* < L *corporāl(is)* bodily, equiv. to *corpor-* (s. of *corpus* CORPUS) + *-ālis* -AL[1]] —**cor′po·ral′i·ty,** *n.* —**cor′po·ral·ly,** *adv.*
—**Syn.** 1. material. See **physical.**

cor·po·ral[2] (kôr′pər əl, -prəl), *n.* 1. (in the army) a noncommissioned officer of lowest rank. 2. *Brit. Navy.* (formerly) a petty officer charged with assisting the master-at-arms. 3. (*cap.*) *U.S.* a surface-to-surface, single-stage ballistic missile. [< MF, var. of *caporal* < It *caporal(e),* appar. contr. of phrase *capo corporale* corporal head, i.e., head of a body (of soldiers). See CAPUT, CORPORAL[1]] —**cor′po·ral·cy, cor′po·ral·ship′,** *n.*

cor·po·ral[3] (kôr′pər əl, -prəl), *n.* *Eccles.* a fine cloth, usually of linen, on which the consecrated elements are placed or with which they are covered during the celebration of the Eucharist. Also called **communion cloth.** [ME *corporalle* < ML *corporale (pallium)* eucharistic (altar cloth); r. earlier *corporas* < OF]

cor′poral pun′ishment, *Law.* physical injury, as flogging, inflicted on the body of one convicted of a crime: formerly included the death penalty, sentencing to a term of years, etc.

cor′poral's guard′, 1. *Mil. Informal.* any small detachment. 2. any small group, as of followers.

cor·po·rate (kôr′pər it, -prit), *adj.* 1. forming a corporation. 2. of or belonging to a corporation. 3. united or combined into one. 4. pertaining to a united group, as of persons: *We did it for the corporate good.* 5. corporative. [< L *corporāt(us)* made into a body, equiv. to *corporā-* (s. of *corporāre* to incorporate; see CORPUS) + *-tus* ptp. suffix] —**cor′po·rate·ly,** *adv.* —**cor′po·rate·ness,** *n.*

cor′porate arms′, *Heraldry.* the armorial achievement of a corporate body, whether civic, religious, professional, or commercial.

cor′porate im′age, the impression of the policies, personnel, and operations of a corporation that is imparted to its employees and the public.

cor·po·ra·tion (kôr′pə rā′shən), *n.* 1. an association of individuals, created by law or under authority of law, having a continuous existence independent of the existences of its members and powers and liabilities distinct from those of its members. 2. (*cap.*) the group of principal officials of a borough or other municipal division in England. 3. any group of persons united or regarded as united in one body. 4. *Informal.* a paunch; potbelly. [late ME < LL *corporātiōn-* (s. of *corporātiō*). See CORPORATE, -ION] —**cor′po·ra′tion·al,** *adj.*

Corpora′tion Act′, *Eng. Hist.* a statute (1661) requiring all members of the governing bodies of municipalities to take an oath of allegiance to the crown and to receive communion in the Church of England: it was repealed in 1828. Cf. **test act** (def. 2).

corpora′tion cock′, a cock controlling the flow of water or gas from mains to individual consumers. Also called **corpora′tion stop′.**

cor·po·rat·ism (kôr′pə rə tiz′əm, -prə tiz′-), *n.* the principles, doctrine, or system of corporative organization of a political unit, as a city or state. Also, **cor·po·rat·iv·ism** (kôr′pə rā′tə viz′əm, -pər ə tə-). [CORPORATE + -ISM] —**cor′po·rat·ist,** *adj.*

cor·po·ra·tive (kôr′pə rā′tiv, -pər ə tiv, -prə-), *adj.* 1. of or pertaining to a corporation. 2. of or pertaining to a political system under which the principal economic functions, as banking, industry, labor, etc., are organized as corporate unities. Also, **corporate.** [< LL *corporātīv(us),* equiv. to L *corporāt(us)* CORPORATE + *-īvus* -IVE]

cor·po·ra·tor (kôr′pə rā′tər), *n.* a member of a corporation, esp. one of the original members. [CORPORATE + -OR[2]]

cor·po·re·al (kôr pōr′ē əl, -pôr′-), *adj.* 1. of the nature of the physical body; bodily. 2. material; tangible: *corporeal property.* [< L *corpore(us)* bodily (*corpor-* (s. of *corpus*) body + *-eus* adj. suffix + -AL[1]] —**cor·po′re·al′i·ty, cor·po′re·al·ness,** *n.* —**cor·po′re·al·ly,** *adv.*
—**Syn.** 1. See **physical.** —**Ant.** 1. spiritual. 2. intangible.

cor·po·re·i·ty (kôr′pə rē′i tē), *n.* material or physical nature or quality; materiality. [< ML *corporeitās,* equiv. to L *corpore(us)* CORPOREAL + *-itās* -ITY]

cor·po·sant (kôr′pə zant′), *n.* See **corona discharge.** [< Pg *corpo-sant(o)* < L *corpus sanctum,* lit., holy body. See CORPS, SAINT]

corps (kōr, kôr), *n., pl.* **corps** (kōrz, kôrz). 1. *Mil.* a. a military organization consisting of officers and men or of officers alone: *the U.S. Marine Corps; corps of cadets.* b. a military unit of ground combat forces consisting of two or more divisions and other troops. 2. a group of persons associated or acting together: *the diplomatic corps.* 3. a continental designation that, preceded by a number, indicates size of type in Didot points of .0148 inches: *14 corps.* 4. *Obs.* corpse. [late ME < MF, sp. var. of *cors* < L *corp(us)* body]

corps′ ar′ea, *Mil.* (formerly) one of the nine military subdivisions of the continental U.S.

corps de bal·let (kôr′ də ba lā′, bal′ā; *Fr.* kôr də bA le′), the dancers in a ballet company who perform as a group and have no solo parts. [< F; see CORPS, BALLET]

corpse (kôrps), *n.* 1. a dead body, usually of a human being. 2. *Obs.* a human or animal body, whether alive or dead. [orig. sp. var. of CORSE but the *p* is now sounded]
—**Syn.** 1. remains. See **body.**

corps·man (kōr′mən, kôr′-), *n., pl.* **-men.** 1. *U.S. Navy.* an enlisted man working as a pharmacist or hospital assistant. 2. *U.S. Army.* an enlisted man in the Medical Corps who accompanies combat troops into battle to give first aid, carry off the wounded, etc. 3. a member of any corps. [CORPS + MAN[1]]

cor·pu·lence (kôr′pyə ləns), *n.* bulkiness or largeness of body; fatness; fleshiness; portliness. Also, **cor′pu·len·cy.** [late ME < L *corpulentia.* See CORPULENT, -ENCE]

cor·pu·lent (kôr′pyə lənt), *adj.* large or bulky of body; portly; stout; fat. [ME < L *corpulent(us),* equiv. to *corp(u)s* body + *-lentus* -LENT] —**cor′pu·lent·ly,** *adv.*

cor pul·mo·na·le (kôr′ po͝ol′mə nal′ē, -nā′lē, -nä′-, pul′-), *pl.* **cor·di·a pul·mo·na·li·a** (kôr′dē ə po͝ol′mə nal′ē ə, -nā′lē ə, -nä′-, pul′-). *Pathol.* a heart condition resulting from disease of the lungs or of their blood vessels. [< NL: pulmonary heart]

cor·pus (kôr′pəs), *n., pl.* **-po·ra** (-pər ə). 1. a large or complete collection of writings: *the entire corpus of Old English poetry.* 2. the body of a man or animal, esp. when dead. 3. *Anat.* a body, mass, or part having a special character or function. 4. *Ling.* a body of utterances or sentences assumed to be representative of and used for grammatical analysis of a given language or dialect. 5. a principal or capital sum, as opposed to interest or income. [< L]

cor·pus al·la·tum (kôr′pəs ə lā′təm), *pl.* **cor·po·ra al·la·ta** (kôr′pər ə ə lā′tə). *Entomol.* one of a pair of small, ductless, hormone-secreting glands in the head of an insect behind the brain. [< NL: lit., body added]

cor·pus cal·lo·sum (kôr′pəs kə lō′səm), *pl.* **cor·po·ra cal·lo·sa** (kôr′pər ə kə lō′sə). *Anat., Zool.* a great band of deeply situated transverse white fibers uniting the two halves of the cerebrum in man and other mammals. [< NL: lit., firm body]

cor·pus car·di·a·cum (kôr′pəs kär dī′ə kəm), *pl.* **cor·po·ra car·di·a·ca** (kôr′pər ə kär dī′ə kə). *Entomol.* one of a pair of bodies in the head of an insect, behind the brain, secreting a hormone that influences growth and metamorphosis. [< NL: lit., cardiac body]

Cor·pus Chris·ti (kôr′pəs kris′tē), *Rom. Cath. Ch.* a festival in honor of the Eucharist, celebrated on the Thursday after Trinity Sunday. [ME < ML: lit., body of Christ]

Cor·pus Chris·ti (kôr′pəs kris′tē, -tī), a seaport in S Texas. 167,690 (1960).

Cor′pus Chris′ti Bay′, a bay in S Texas, at the mouth of the Nueces River.

cor·pus·cle (kôr′pə səl, -pus əl), *n.* 1. *Anat.* a cell, esp. a blood cell. 2. a minute body forming a more or less distinct part of an organism. 3. *Physical Chem.* a minute or elementary particle of matter, as an electron, proton, or atom. 4. any minute particle. Also, **cor·pus·cule** (kôr pus′kyo͞ol). [< L *corpuscul(um),* equiv. to *corp(us)* body + *-culum* -CLE] —**cor·pus·cu·lar** (kôr pus′kyə lər), **cor·pus·cu·lat·ed** (kôr pus′kyə lā′tid), **cor·pus′cu·lous,** *adj.* —**cor·pus·cu·lar·i·ty** (kôr pus′kyə lar′i tē), *n.*

corpus′cular the′ory, *Physics.* the theory that light is transmitted as a stream of particles. Cf. **wave theory.**

cor·pus de·lic·ti (kôr′pəs di lik′tī), *Law.* the basic element of a crime, as, in murder, the death of the murdered person. [< NL: lit., body of the offense]

cor·pus ju·ris (kôr′pəs jo͝or′is), a compilation of law, or the collected law of a nation, state, etc. [< LL: lit., body of law]

Cor·pus Ju·ris Ca·no·ni·ci (kôr′pəs jo͝or′is kə non′i sī′), the collection of church law which remained in force until it was replaced in 1918 by the Codex Juris Canonici. [< ML: lit., body of canon law]

Cor·pus Ju·ris Ci·vi·lis (kôr′pəs jo͝or′is si vī′lis), the collective title of the body of ancient Roman law as collected and codified under the emperor Justinian in the 6th century A.D.: comprises the Digest, the Institutes, the Codes, and the Novels. [< NL: lit., body of civil law]

cor·pus lu·te·um (kôr′pəs lo͞o′tē əm), *pl.* **cor·po·ra lu·te·a** (kôr′pər ə lo͞o′tē ə). 1. *Anat., Zool.* a ductless gland developed within the ovary by the reorganization of a Graafian follicle following ovulation. 2. *Pharm.* an extract of this gland of the hog or cow, the chief principle of which is progesterone. [< NL: yellow body]

cor·pus stri·a·tum (kôr′pəs strī ā′təm), *pl.* **cor·po·ra stri·a·ta** (kôr′pər ə strī ā′tə). *Anat.* a mass of gray matter beneath the cortex and in front of the thalamus in each cerebral hemisphere. [< NL: striated body]

corr., 1. corrected. 2. correspond. 3. correspondence. 4. correspondent. 5. corresponding. 6. corrupt. 7. corrupted. 8. corruption.

cor·rade (kə rād′, kô-), *v.,* **-rad·ed, -rad·ing.** —*v.i.* 1. (of a moving agent, as running water, wind, a glacier, etc.) to erode by the abrasion of materials carried along. 2. to disintegrate as a result of corrasion, as the rock underlying the brink of a waterfall. —*v.t.* 3. to wear down by corrasion; abrade. [< L *corrāde(re)* (to) scrape together, equiv. to *cor-* COR- + *rādere* to scrape. See ERASE, RAZE]

cor·ral (kə ral′), *n., v.,* **-ralled, -ral·ling.** —*n.* 1. an enclosure or pen for horses, cattle, etc. 2. an enclosure formed of wagons during an encampment, for defense against attack. —*v.t.* 3. to confine in or as if in a corral. 4. *U.S. Informal.* to seize; capture. 5. to form (wagons) into a corral. [< Sp < LL *currāl(e) enclosure for carts, equiv. to L *curr(us)* wagon, cart (deriv. of *currere* to run) + *-āle,* neut. of *-ālis* -AL[1]]

cor·ra·sion (kə rā′zhən), *n.* the process in which the surface of the earth is abraded by the action of water, wind, etc. [< L *corrās(us)* scraped together (ptp. of *corrādere*) + -ION. See CORRADE] —**cor·ra·sive** (kô rā′siv), *adj.*

cor·rect (kə rekt′), *v.t.* 1. to set or make right; remove the errors or faults from: *The native guide corrected our pronunciation. The new glasses corrected his eyesight.* 2. to point out or mark the errors in: *The teacher corrected the examination papers.* 3. to scold, rebuke, or punish in order to improve: *A mother should correct her children when they develop bad habits.* 4. to counteract the operation or effect of (something hurtful): *The medicine corrected his arthritis.* 5. *Math., Physics.* to alter or adjust so as to bring into accordance with a standard or with a required condition. —*adj.* 6. conforming to fact or truth; free from error; accurate: *a correct statement.* 7. in accordance with an acknowledged or accepted standard; proper: *correct behavior.* [ME *correct(en)* < L *corrēct(us)* made straight (ptp. of *corrigere,* equiv. to *cor-* COR- + *rēc-* (var. of *rēg-,* past s. of *regere* to direct) + *-tus* ptp. suffix] —**cor·rect′a·ble, cor·rect′i·ble,** *adj.* —**cor·rect′ed·ness,** *n.* —**cor·rect′ing·ly,** *adv.* —**cor·rect′ly,** *adv.* —**cor·rect′ness,** *n.*
—**Syn.** 1. rectify, amend, emend, reform, remedy. 3. warn, chasten, castigate. See **punish.** 6. faultless, perfect, exact. CORRECT, ACCURATE, PRECISE imply conformity to fact, standard, or truth. A CORRECT statement is one free from error, mistakes, or faults. An ACCURATE statement is one which, as a result of an active effort to comprehend and verify, shows careful conformity to fact, truth, or spirit. A PRECISE statement shows scrupulously strict and detailed (sometimes excessive) conformity to fact. —**Ant.** 6. faulty, inaccurate. 7. unconventional, solecistic.

correct′ing plate′, *Optics.* the thin lens used to correct incoming light rays in special forms of reflecting telescopes. Also, **corrector plate.**

cor·rec·tion (kə rek′shən), *n.* 1. the act of correcting. 2. something that is substituted or proposed for what is wrong; emendation. 3. punishment; chastisement; discipline; reproof. 4. *Math., Physics.* a subordinate quantity that is applied in order to increase accuracy, as in the use of an instrument or the solution of a problem. [ME *correccio(u)n* < L *corrēctiōn-* (s. of *corrēctiō*) a setting straight. See CORRECT, -ION] —**cor·rec′tion·al,** *adj.*

cor·rect·i·tude (kə rek′ti to͞od′, -tyo͞od′), *n.* correctness, esp. of manners and conduct. [b. CORRECT and RECTITUDE]

cor·rec·tive (kə rek′tiv), *adj.* 1. tending to correct or rectify; remedial: *Corrective measures were taken.* —*n.* 2. a means of correcting; corrective agent. [< ML *corrēctīv(us).* See CORRECT, -IVE] —**cor·rec′tive·ly,** *adv.*

cor·rec·tor (kə rek′tər), *n.* one who or that which corrects. [ME *correctour* < AF < L *corrēct(us)* (see CORRECT) + *-or* -OR[2]]

correc′tor plate′, *Optics.* See **correcting plate.**

Cor·reg·gio (kə rej′ō, -rej′ē ō′; *It.* kôr red′jô), *n.* **An·to·nio Al·le·gri da** (än tô′nyô äl le′grē dä), 1494–1534, Italian painter.

cor·reg·i·dor (kə reg′i dôr′, -dōr′; *Sp.* kôr re′hē dôr′), *n., pl.* **-dors, -do·res** (-dôr′ēz, -dōr′-; *Sp.* -dô′res). 1. the chief magistrate of a town in Spain. 2. *Hist.* (in Spanish America) a. a minor administrative unit. b. the chief officer of a corregimiento. [< Sp, deriv. of *corregir* to CORRECT]

Cor·reg·i·dor (kə reg′i dôr′, -dōr′; *Sp.* kôr re′hē dôr′), *n.* an island in Manila Bay, in the Philippines: Americans defeated by the Japanese May, 1942. 2 sq. mi.

cor·reg·i·mi·en·to (kə rej′ə mē en′tō; *Sp.* kôr re′hē myen′tô), *n., pl.* **-tos** (-tōz; *Sp.* -tôs). *Hist.* an administrative division in a remote province of Spanish America; the district of a corregidor. [< Sp; see CORREGIDOR, -MENT]

correl., correlative.

cor·re·late (kôr′ə lāt′, kor′-), *v.,* **-lat·ed, -lat·ing,** *adj., n.* —*v.t.* 1. to place in or bring into mutual or reciprocal relation; establish in orderly connection: *to correlate facts.* —*v.i.* 2. to have a mutual or reciprocal relation; stand in correlation: *Her research results correlate with his.* —*adj.* 3. mutually or reciprocally related; correlated. —*n.* 4. either of two related things, esp. when one implies the other. [prob. back formation from CORRELATION and CORRELATIVE] —**cor′re·lat′a·ble,** *adj.*

cor·re·la·tion (kôr′ə lā′shən, kor′-), *n.* 1. mutual relation of two or more things, parts, etc. 2. the act or state of correlating or of being correlated. 3. *Statistics.* the degree of correlation between two or more attributes or measurements on the same group of elements. 4. *Physiol.* the interdependence or reciprocal relations of organs or functions. Also, *esp. Brit.,* **corelation.** [< ML *correlātiōn-* (s. of *correlātiō*). See COR-, RELATION] —**cor′re·la′tion·al,** *adj.*

correla′tion coeffi′cient, *Statistics.* one of a number of measures of correlation, usually assuming values from +1 to −1.

correla′tion ra′tio, *Statistics.* the ratio of the variance between arrays of data within a sample to the variance of the whole sample.

cor·rel·a·tive (kə rel′ə tiv), *adj.* 1. so related that each implies or complements the other. 2. being in correlation; mutually related. 3. *Gram.* having a mutual relation; answering to or complementing one another, as *either* and *or*, *where* and *there*. 4. *Biol.* (of a typical structure of an organism) found in correlation with another. —*n.* 5. either of two things, as two terms, that are correlative. 6. *Gram.* a correlative expression. Also, *esp. Brit.*, **corelative.** [< ML *correlātīv(us).* See COR-, RELATIVE] —**cor·rel′a·tive·ly,** *adv.* —**cor·rel′a·tive·ness, cor·rel′a·tiv′i·ty,** *n.*

correl′ative conjunc′tion, *Gram.* a conjunction grammatically similar to a coordinating conjunction but occurring as a member of a matched pair, as *either . . . or, neither . . . nor, both . . . and.*

cor·ren·te (kə ren′tē, kô-; *It.* kôʀ ʀen′te), *n.* courante. [< It < MF *courante*]

corresp., correspondence.

cor·re·spond (kôr′i spond′, kor′-), *v.i.* 1. to be in agreement or conformity (often fol. by *with* or *to*): *His actions do not correspond with his words.* 2. to be similar or analogous; be equivalent in function, position, amount, etc., (usually fol. by *to*): *The U.S. Congress corresponds to the British Parliament.* 3. to communicate by exchange of letters: *We have corresponded but never met. I corresponded with her while she was away.* [< ML *corrēspond(ēre).* See COR-, RESPOND] —**cor′re·spond′ing·ly,** *adv.*

—**Syn.** 1. harmonize, match, tally. CORRESPOND, AGREE, ACCORD imply comparing persons or things and finding that they harmonize. CORRESPOND suggests having an obvious similarity, though not agreeing in every detail: *Part of this report corresponds with the facts.* AGREE implies having or arriving at a condition in which no essential difference of opinion or detail is evident: *All the reports agree.* ACCORD emphasizes agreeing exactly, both in fact and in point of view: *This report accords with the other.*

cor·re·spond·ence (kôr′i spon′dəns, kor′-), *n.* 1. Also, **correspondency.** an act or instance of corresponding. 2. similarity or analogy. 3. agreement; conformity. 4. communication by exchange of letters. 5. letters that pass between correspondents. 6. *Math.* function (def. 4a). [late ME < ML *corrēspondentia.* See CORRESPONDENT, -ENCE]

—**Syn.** 3. accord, concord, consonance. —**Ant.** 2. difference.

correspond′ence course′, a course of instruction provided by a correspondence school.

correspond′ence prin′ciple, *Physics.* the principle that the laws of quantum mechanics and of any new theory that may be developed reduce to the laws of Newtonian mechanics and electromagnetic theory when applied to systems in which Planck's constant can be regarded as negligible, wavelengths are comparatively small, dimensions are relatively large, etc. Also called **principle of complementarity, principle of correspondence.**

correspond′ence school′, a school operating on a system in which study materials and tests are mailed to the students who in turn mail their work back to the school for grading.

correspond′ence the′ory, *Philos.* the theory of truth that a statement is rendered true by the existence of a fact with corresponding elements and a similar structure. Cf. **coherence theory, pragmatic theory.**

cor·re·spond·en·cy (kôr′i spon′dən sē, kor′-), *n., pl.* **-cies.** correspondence (def. 1).

cor·re·spond·ent (kôr′i spon′dənt, kor′-), *n.* 1. one who communicates by letters. 2. a person employed by a news agency, periodical, or the like, to gather, report, or contribute news, articles, etc., regularly from a distant place: *a London correspondent.* 3. one who contributes a letter or letters to a newspaper, magazine, etc. 4. one who has regular business relations with another, esp. at a distance. 5. a thing that corresponds to something else. —*adj.* 6. corresponding; conforming, similar, or analogous. [late ME < ML *corrēspondent-* (s. of *corrēspondēns*), prp. of *corrēspondēre* to CORRESPOND; see -ENT] —**cor′re·spond′ent·ly,** *adv.*

cor·re·spon·sive (kôr′i spon′siv, kor′-), *adj.* responsive to effort or impulse; answering; corresponding. [< ML *corrēspōns(us)* (ptp. of *corrēspondēre* to CORRESPOND) + -IVE] —**cor′re·spon′sive·ly,** *adv.*

Cor·rèze (kô ʀez′), *n.* a department in central France. 237,926 (1962); 2273 sq. mi. *Cap.:* Tulle.

cor·ri·da (kô rē′də), *n.* a bullfight. [< Sp, short for *corrida de toros,* lit., chasing of bulls; *corrida,* fem. of *corrido,* ptp. of *correr* < L *currere* to run]

cor·ri·dor (kôr′i dər, -dôr′, kor′-), *n.* 1. a gallery or passage connecting parts of a building. 2. a passage into which several rooms or apartments open. 3. a passageway in a railroad passenger car permitting access to separate compartments. 4. a narrow tract of land forming a passageway, as one belonging to an inland country and affording an outlet to the sea: *the Polish Corridor.* [< MF < It *corridor(e)* < Sp *corredor,* lit., runner, deriv. of *correr* to run < L *currere*] —**cor′ri·dored,** *adj.*

cor·rie (kôr′ē, kor′ē), *n.* *Scot.* a circular hollow in the side of a hill or mountain. [< Gael *coire* cauldron, whirlpool, hollow]

Cor·rie·dale (kôr′ē dāl′, kor′-), *n.* one of a breed of sheep raised originally in New Zealand and noted for its high-quality wool and good market lambs.

Cor·ri·en·tes (kôʀ′ʀē en′tes), *n.* a port in NE Argentina, on the Paraná River. 112,725 (1965).

cor·ri·gen·dum (kôr′i jen′dəm, kor′-), *n., pl.* **-da** (-də). 1. an error to be corrected, esp. an error in print. 2. **corrigenda,** a list of corrections of errors in a book or other publication. [< L: lit., (something) to be corrected (neut. ger. of *corrigere*); see CORRECT]

cor·ri·gi·ble (kôr′i jə bəl, kor′-), *adj.* 1. that can be corrected or reformed: *a corrigible criminal.* 2. submissive to correction. 3. subject to being revised, improved, or made more accurate: *a corrigible theory; a corrigible process.* [late ME < ML *corrigibil(is),* equiv. to L *corrig(ere)* (to) CORRECT + *-ibilis* -IBLE] —**cor′ri·gi·bil′i·ty, cor′ri·gi·ble·ness,** *n.* —**cor′ri·gi·bly,** *adv.*

cor·ri·val (kə rī′vəl), *Rare.* —*n.* 1. a rival; competitor. —*adj.* 2. rival; competitive. [< L *corrīvāl(is)* joint rival. See COR-, RIVAL] —**cor·ri′val·ry,** *n.*

cor·rob·bo·ree (kə rob′ə rē), *n.* *Australian.* corroboree.

cor·rob·o·rant (kə rob′ər ənt), *adj.* 1. corroborating; confirming. 2. *Archaic.* strengthening; invigorating: *a corroborant medicine.* —*n.* 3. something that corroborates or strengthens. 4. *Archaic.* a strengthening medicine. [< L *corrōborant-* (s. of *corrōborāns*) strengthening, prp. of *corrōborāre.* See CORROBORATE, -ANT]

cor·rob·o·rate (*v.* kə rob′ə rāt′; *adj.* kə rob′ər it), *v.,* **-rat·ed, -rat·ing,** *adj.* —*v.t.* 1. to make more certain; confirm: *He corroborated my account of the accident.* —*adj.* 2. *Archaic.* corroborated. [< L *corrōborāt(us)* strengthened (ptp. of *corrōborāre*), equiv. to *cor-* COR- + *rōbor(āre)* (to) make strong (deriv. of *rōbor, rōbur* oak, hence strength) + *-ātus* -ATE[1]] —**cor·rob·o·ra·tive** (kə rob′ə rā′tiv, -ər ə tiv-), **cor·rob·o·ra·to·ry** (kə rob′ər ə tôr′ē, -tōr′ē), *adj.* —**cor·rob·o·ra·tive·ly** (kə rob′ə rā′tiv lē, -ər ə tiv-), **cor·rob′o·ra·to′ri·ly,** *adv.* —**cor·rob′o·ra′tor,** *n.*

—**Syn.** 1. verify, substantiate, authenticate, support, validate.

cor·rob·o·ra·tion (kə rob′ə rā′shən), *n.* 1. the act of corroborating. 2. a corroboratory fact, statement, etc. [< L *corrōborātiōn-* (s. of *corrōborātiō*). See CORROBORATE, -ION]

cor·rob·o·ree (kə rob′ə rē), *n.* *Australian.* 1. a sacred, festive, or warlike assembly among the aborigines. 2. any large or noisy gathering. 3. (among the aborigines, esp. of Arnhem Land) a primitive rite in which adolescent boys are elevated to young manhood. Also, **corrobboree.** [< Austral native word]

cor·rode (kə rōd′), *v.,* **-rod·ed, -rod·ing.** —*v.t.* 1. to eat away gradually as if by gnawing, esp. by chemical action. 2. to impair; deteriorate: *Jealousy corroded his character.* —*v.i.* 3. to become corroded. [late ME < L *corrōde(re)* (to) gnaw to pieces, equiv. to *cor-* COR- + *rōdere* to gnaw; akin to RAT] —**cor·rod′ant,** *n.* —**cor·rod′er,** *n.* —**cor·rod′i·bil′i·ty,** *n.* —**cor·rod′i·ble,** *adj.*

—**Syn.** 1. gnaw, eat, consume, erode. 3. canker, rust, crumble.

cor·ro·dy (kôr′ə dē, kor′-), *n., pl.* **-dies.** *Old Eng. Law.* corody.

cor·ro·sion (kə rō′zhən), *n.* 1. the act or process of corroding; condition of being corroded. 2. a product of corroding, as rust. [late ME < LL *corrōsiōn-* (s. of *corrōsiō*) a gnawing away, equiv. to L *corrōs(us),* ptp. of *corrōdere* to CORRODE + *-iōn-* -ION] —**cor·ro′sion·al,** *adj.*

cor·ro·sive (kə rō′siv), *adj.* 1. having the quality of corroding, eating away, or consuming. —*n.* 2. something corrosive, as an acid, drug, etc. [late ME < ML *corrōsīv(us),* equiv. to L *corrōs(us)* (see CORROSION) + *-īvus* -IVE; r. ME *corosif* < MF] —**cor·ro′sive·ly,** *adv.* —**cor·ro′sive·ness, cor·ro·siv·i·ty** (kôr′ō siv′i tē, kor′-), *n.*

corro′sive mer′cury chlo′ride. See **mercuric chloride.**

corro′sive sub′limate. See **mercuric chloride.**

cor·ru·gate (*v.* kôr′ə gāt′, kor′-; *adj.* kôr′ə git, -gāt′, kor′-), *v.,* **-gat·ed, -gat·ing,** *adj.* —*v.t., v.i.* 1. to draw or bend into folds or alternate furrows and ridges. 2. to wrinkle, as the skin or face. —*adj.* 3. corrugated; wrinkled; furrowed. [late ME < L *corrūgāt(us)* wrinkled (ptp. of *corrūgāre*), equiv. to *cor-* COR- + *rūg(āre)* (to) wrinkle + *-ātus* -ATE[1]]

cor′rugated i′ron, a type of sheet iron or steel strengthened for use in construction by having a series of alternating grooves and ridges forced into it, and usually galvanized for weather resistance.

cor′rugated pa′per, heavy paper with alternating ridges and grooves used in packing to protect fragile articles.

cor·ru·ga·tion (kôr′ə gā′shən, kor′-), *n.* 1. the act or state of corrugating or of being corrugated. 2. a wrinkle; fold; furrow; ridge. [< ML *corrūgātiōn-* (s. of *corrūgātiō*) a wrinkling. See CORRUGATE, -ION]

cor·rupt (kə rupt′), *adj.* 1. guilty of dishonest practices, as bribery; without integrity; crooked: *a corrupt judge.* 2. debased in character; depraved; perverted; wicked; evil: *a corrupt society.* 3. decayed; putrid. 4. infected; tainted. 5. made inferior by errors or alterations, as a text. —*v.t.* 6. to destroy the integrity of; cause to be dishonest, disloyal, etc., esp. by bribery. 7. to lower morally; pervert; deprave: *to corrupt youth.* 8. to infect; taint. 9. to make putrid or putrescent. 10. to alter (a language, text, etc.) for the worse; debase. 11. to mar; spoil. —*v.i.* 12. to become corrupt. [ME < L *corrupt(us)* broken in pieces, corrupted (ptp. of *corrumpere*), equiv. to *cor-* COR- + *rup-* (ptp. s. of *rumpere* to break) + *-tus* ptp. suffix] —**cor·rupt′ed·ly,** *adv.* —**cor·rupt′ed·ness,** *n.* —**cor·rupt′er, cor·rup′tor,** *n.* —**cor·rupt′ful,** *adj.* —**cor·rup′tive,** *adj.* —**cor·rup′tive·ly,** *adv.* —**cor·rupt′ly,** *adv.* —**cor·rupt′ness,** *n.*

—**Syn.** 1. false, untrustworthy. CORRUPT, DISHONEST, VENAL apply to one, esp. in public office, who acts on mercenary motives, without regard to honor, right, or justice. A CORRUPT politician is one originally honest who has succumbed to temptation and begun questionable practices. A DISHONEST politician is one lacking native integrity and thoroughly untrustworthy. VENAL is a strongly opprobrious term; a VENAL politician is one so debased that he frankly sells his patronage. 3, 4. putrescent, rotten, spoiled. 4, 5. contaminated. 6. demoralize, bribe. 7. debase, vitiate. 8. contaminate, pollute, spoil, defile. 9. putrefy.

cor·rupt·i·ble (kə rup′tə bəl), *adj.* that can or might be corrupted. [ME < LL *corruptibil(is)* < L *corrupt(us)* (see CORRUPT) + *-ibilis* -IBLE] —**cor·rupt′i·bil′i·ty, cor·rupt′i·ble·ness,** *n.* —**cor·rupt′i·bly,** *adv.*

cor·rup·tion (kə rup′shən), *n.* 1. the act or state of corrupting or of being corrupt. 2. moral perversion; depravity. 3. perversion of integrity. 4. corrupt or dishonest proceedings. 5. bribery. 6. debasement or alteration, as of language or a text. 7. a debased form of a word. 8. putrefactive decay; rottenness. 9. any corrupting influence or agency. [ME *corrupcio(u)n* < L *corruptiōn-* (s. of *corruptiō*). See CORRUPT, -ION]

—**Syn.** 2. abandon, dissolution, immorality. 4. baseness, dishonesty. 8. rot, putrefaction, putrescence, foulness, pollution, contamination. —**Ant.** 3, 7. purity. 3–6. honesty.

cor·rup·tion·ist (kə rup′shə nist), *n.* one who practices or endorses corruption, esp. in politics. [CORRUPTION + -IST]

corrup′tion of blood′, *Eng. Law.* the impurity before law that results from attainder and disqualifies the attainted person from inheriting, retaining, or bequeathing lands or interests in lands: abolished in 1870.

corrupt′ prac′tices act′, *U.S.* any of several statutes for ensuring the purity of elections by forbidding the purchase of votes, restricting the amount and source of political contributions, limiting campaign expenditures, and requiring the submission of an itemized statement of such expenditures.

Cor·ry (kôr′ē, kor′ē), *n.* a town in NW Pennsylvania. 7744 (1960).

cor·sage (kôr säzh′), *n.* 1. a small bouquet worn at the waist, on the shoulder, etc., by a woman. 2. the body or waist of a dress; bodice. [late ME < MF: bodily shape (later: bust, bodice, corsage), equiv. to *cors* body (< L *corpus*) + *-age* -AGE]

cor·sair (kôr′sâr), *n.* 1. a privateer, esp. one of the Barbary Coast. 2. a pirate. 3. a fast vessel used for piracy. [< MF *corsaire* < Pr *corsari* < ML *cursāri(us),* equiv. to L *curs(us)* COURSE + *-ārius* -ARY]

corse (kôrs), *n.* *Obs.* corpse. [ME *cors* < OF < L *corp(us)* body]

Corse (kôʀs), *n.* French name of **Corsica.**

cor·se·let (kôr′sə let′ *for 1;* kôrs′lit *for 2*), *n.* 1. a supporting undergarment with very few or no bones, worn by women. 2. Also, **corslet.** *Armor.* **a.** a suit of light half armor or three-quarter armor of the 16th century or later. **b.** cuirass (def. 1). [< MF, equiv. to *cors* bodice, body + *-elet* -LET]

C, Corselet of English pikeman (17th century) M, Morion

cor·set (kôr′sit), *n.* 1. Often, **corsets.** a close-fitting inner garment, stiffened with whalebone or similar material and capable of being tightened by lacing, enclosing the trunk: worn, esp. by women, to shape and support the body; stays. —*v.t.* 2. to dress or furnish with or as if with a corset. 3. to regulate strictly; constrict. [ME < OF, equiv. to *cors* bodice, body + *-et* -ET] —**cor′set·less,** *adj.*

cor′set cov′er, an undergarment, as a camisole, worn over the upper part of a corset.

Cor·si·ca (kôr′si kə), *n.* an island in the Mediterranean, SE of and forming a department of France. 275,465 (1962); 3367 sq. mi. *Cap.:* Ajaccio. French, **Corse.** —**Cor′si·can,** *adj., n.*

Cor·si·can·a (kôr′sə kan′ə), *n.* a city in E Texas. 20,344 (1960).

Cor′sican sand′-wort, a mosslike sandwort, *Arenaria balearica,* of the Balearic Islands, having numerous small, thick, glossy leaves and solitary, white flowers and growing in moist, rocky sites.

cors·let (kôrs′lit), *n.* corselet (def. 2).

cort., (in prescriptions) the bark. [< L *cortex*]

cor·tege (kôr tezh′, -tāzh′), *n.* 1. a line or train of attendants; retinue. 2. a procession, esp. a ceremonial one. [< F < It *cortegg(io)* courtly retinue, deriv. of *corte* COURT]

cor·tège (kôr tezh′, -tāzh′; *Fr.* kôʀ tezh′), *n., pl.* **-tèg·es** (-tezh′iz, -tā′zhiz; *Fr.* -tezh′). cortege.

Cor·te·gia·no, Il (*It.* ēl kôʀ′te jä′nô). See **Courtier, The.**

Cor·tel·you (kôr′tᵊl yōō′), *n.* **George Bruce,** 1862–1940, U.S. cabinet officer and public utility director.

Cor·te Ma·der·a (kôr′tā mə dâr′ə), a town in W California. 5962 (1960).

Cor·tes (kôr′tiz; *Sp.* kôʀ′tes), *n.* (in Spain or Portugal) the two houses constituting the national legislative body. [< Sp, pl. of *corte* COURT]

Cor·tés (kôr tez′; *Sp.* kôʀ tes′), *n.* **Her·nan·do** (ʀʀ nän′dô) or **Her·nán** (ʀʀ nän′), 1485–1547, Spanish conqueror of Mexico. Also, **Cor·tez′.**

cor·tex (kôr′teks), *n., pl.* **-ti·ces** (-ti sēz′). 1. *Bot.* the portion of a stem between the epidermis and the vascular tissue; bark. 2. *Anat., Zool.* **a.** the rind of an organ, as the outer wall of the kidney. **b.** the layer of gray matter that invests the surface of the cerebral hemispheres and the cerebellum. [< L: bark, rind, shell, husk]

Cor·tez (kôr′tez, kôr tez′), *n.* a town in SW Colorado. 6764 (1960).

Cor·ti (kôr′tē), *n.* **Al·fon·so** (al fon′sō; *It.* äl fôn′sô), 1822–76, Italian anatomist.

cor·ti·cal (kôr′ti kəl), *adj.* 1. *Anat.* of, pertaining to, resembling, or consisting of cortex. 2. *Physiol., Pathol.* resulting from the function or condition of the cerebral cortex. 3. *Bot.* of or pertaining to the cortex. [< NL *corticāl(is),* equiv. to L *cortic-* (s. of *cortex*) CORTEX + *-ālis* -AL[1]] —**cor′ti·cal·ly,** *adv.*

cor·ti·cate (kôr′tə kit, -kāt′), *adj.* having a cortex. Also, **cor′ti·cat′ed.** [< L *corticāt(us),* equiv. to *cortic-* (s. of *cortex*) CORTEX + *-ātus* -ATE[1]] —**cor′ti·ca′tion,** *n.*

cor·tic·o·lous (kôr tik′ə ləs), *adj.* *Bot., Zool.* living or growing on or in bark. [< L *cortic-* (s. of *cortex*) CORTEX + -COLOUS]

cor·ti·co·ster·oid (kôr′tə kō ster′oid, -stēr′-), *n.* *Biochem.* any of a class of steroids, as aldosterone, hydrocortisone, or cortisone, occurring in nature, esp. as a product of the adrenal cortex, or synthesized. Also called **cor·ti·coid** (kôr′tə koid′). [< L *cortic-* (s. of *cortex*) CORTEX + -O- + STEROID]

cor·tin (kôr′tᵊn, -tin), *n.* *Biochem.* a hormone essential to life, secreted by the adrenal glands. [CORT(EX) + -IN[2]]

cor·ti·sol (kôr′ti sôl′, -sōl′), *n.* *Pharm.* hydrocortisone. [CORTIS(ONE) + -OL[1]]

cor·ti·sone (kôr′ti sōn′, -zōn′), *n.* 1. *Biochem.* a steroid hormone of the adrenal cortex, $C_{21}H_{28}O_5$, active in carbohydrate and protein metabolism. 2. *Pharm.* a commercial form of this compound, obtained by extraction from the adrenal glands of certain domesticated animals or produced synthetically, used chiefly as its acetate in the treatment of arthritis, rheumatic fever, certain allergies, and other systemic conditions. Also called **Compound E.** [CORT(EX) + -I- + S(TEROL) + -ONE]

Cort·land (kôrt′lənd), *n.* a city in central New York. 19,181 (1960).

Cor·to·na (kôʀ tô′nä), *n.* **Pie·tro da** (pye′tʀô dä), (*Pietro Berrettini*), 1596–1669, Italian painter and architect.

Co·rum·bá (kô/ro͞onm bä/), *n.* a city in W Brazil. 38,841 (1960).

Co·ru·ña (kô ro͞o/nyä), *n.* See **La Coruña.**

co·run·dum (kə run/dəm), *n.* a common mineral, aluminum oxide, Al_2O_3, notable for its hardness: transparent varieties used as gems, other varieties, as abrasives; often made synthetically. [< Tamil *kuruntam, kurundam;* akin to Skt *kuruvinda* ruby]

Co·run·na (kə run/ə), *n.* **1.** a town in central Michigan. 2764 (1960). **2.** See **La Coruña.**

co·rus·cant (kə rus/kənt, kôr/əs-, kor/-), *adj.* sparkling or gleaming; scintillating; coruscating. [late ME < L *coruscant-* (s. of *coruscāns*) quivering, flashing (prp. of *coruscāre*). See CORUSCATE, -ANT]

cor·us·cate (kôr/ə skāt/, kor/-), *v.i.*, **-cat·ed, -cat·ing.** to emit vivid flashes of light; sparkle; scintillate; gleam. [< L *coruscāt(us)* quivered, flashed, ptp. of *coruscāre*] **—Syn.** glitter, flash.

cor·us·ca·tion (kôr/ə skā/shən, kor/-), *n.* **1.** the act of coruscating. **2.** a sudden gleam or flash of light. **3.** a striking display of brilliance or wit. [late ME < LL *coruscātiōn-* (s. of *coruscātiō*). See CORUSCATE, -ION]

Cor·val·lis (kôr val/is), *n.* a city in W Oregon. 20,669 (1960).

cor·vée (kôr vā/), *n.* **1.** unpaid labor for one day, as on the repair of roads, exacted by a feudal lord. **2.** an obligation imposed on inhabitants of a district to perform services, as repair of roads, bridges, etc., for little or no remuneration. [ME < MF < LL *corrogāta* contribution, collection, n. use of fem. of L *corrogātus,* ptp. of *corrogāre* to collect by asking, equiv. to *cor-* COR- + *rogāre* to ask]

corves (kôrvz), *n.* pl. of **corf.**

cor·vette (kôr vet/), *n.* **1.** a warship of the old sailing class, having a flush deck and usually one tier of guns. **2.** *Brit.* a small, lightly armed, fast vessel used mostly for convoy escort and ranging between a destroyer and a gunboat in size. Also, **cor·vet** (kôr vet/, kôr/vet). [< MF < Pg *corvet(a),* irreg. < L *corbīta* merchant-vessel, short for *corbīta nāvis,* lit., basketed ship; said to be so named from the basket hoisted as an ensign, marking it a cargo vessel]

cor·vi·na (kôr vē/nə), *n.* any of several sciaenoid fishes, as *Cynoscion parvipinnis* **(shortfin corvina),** a food fish found off the coast of California. [< MexSp, Sp: kind of fish, special use of *corvino* CORVINE; so called from its color]

cor·vine (kôr/vīn, -vin), *adj.* **1.** pertaining to or resembling a crow. **2.** belonging or pertaining to the *Corvidae,* a family of birds including the crows, ravens, and jays. [< L *corvīn(us),* equiv. to *corv(us)* raven + *-īnus* -INE[1]]

cor·vo (kôr/vō), *n.* a dry red or white wine of Sicily.

Cor·vus (kôr/vəs), *n., gen.* **-vi** (-vī). *Astron.* the Crow, a southern constellation between Virgo and Hydra.

Cor·win (kôr/win), *n.* **Norman (Lewis),** born 1910, U.S. dramatist and novelist.

Cor·y·ate (kôr/ē it), *n.* **Thomas,** 1577–1617, English traveler and author. Also, **Cor·y·at** (kôr/ē it, kôr/yit).

Cor·y·bant (kôr/ə bant/, kor/-), *n., pl.* **Cor·y·ban·tes** (kôr/ə ban/tēz, kor/-), **Cor·y·bants.** **1.** *Class. Myth.* any of the spirits or secondary divinities attending Cybele. **2.** an ancient Phrygian priest of Cybele. [ME < L *Corybant-* (s. of *Corybās*) < Gk *Korybant-* (s. of *Korýbas*)]

cor·y·ban·tic (kôr/ə ban/tik, kor/-), *adj.* **1.** frenzied; agitated; unrestrained. **2.** *(cap.)* Also, **Cor·y·ban·tian** (kôr/ə ban/shən, kor/-), **Cor·y·ban·tine** (kôr/ə ban/tin, -tīn, kor/-). of or pertaining to a Corybant. [CORYBANT + -IC]

Co·ry·cia (kə rish/ə), *n.* *Class. Myth.* a nymph who bore a son to Apollo.

co·ryd·a·lis (kə rid/əlis), *n.* any papaveraceous plant of the genus *Corydalis* (*Capnoides*), comprising erect or climbing herbs with divided leaves, tuberous or fibrous roots, and very irregular spurred flowers. [< NL < Gk *korydallís,* extended var. of *korydós* crested lark, deriv. of *koryd-,* var. of *koryth-* (s. of *kórys*) helmet, head, crest; akin to *kára* head]

Cor·y·don (kôr/i dən, -don/, kor/-), *n.* **1.** a town in S Indiana. 2701 (1960). **2.** (in pastoral literature) a name for a shepherd or rustic. **3.** a boy's given name.

Cor·yell (kôr yel/), *n.* **John Russell,** 1848–1924, U.S. author of detective and adventure stories.

cor·ymb (kôr/imb, -im, kor/-), *n.* *Bot.* a form of inflorescence resembling a raceme but having a relatively shorter rachis and longer lower pedicles so that the flowers form a flat-topped or convex cluster, the outermost flowers being the first to expand. [< L *corymb(us)* < Gk *kórymbos* head, top, cluster of fruit or flowers] **—cor/ymbed,** *adj.* **—cor/ymb-like/,** *adj.*

co·rym·bose (kə rim/bōs), *adj.* characterized by or growing in corymbs; corymblike. [< NL *corymbōs(us),* equiv. to *corymb(o)* CORYMB + *-ōsus* -OSE[1]] **—co·rym/bose·ly,** *adv.*

co·ry·ne·bac·te·ri·um (kə rī/nə nē bak tēr/ē əm), *n., pl.* **-te·ri·a** (-tēr/ē ə). *Bacteriol.* any of several rod-shaped, aerobic or anaerobic bacteria of the genus *Corynebacterium,* pathogenic for man, animals, or plants. [< NL < Gk *korýnē* club + *bacterium* BACTERIUM] **—cor/y·ne·bac·te/ri·al,** *adj.*

Co·ry·ne·tes (kôr/ə nē/tēz), *n.* *Class. Myth.* an epithet of Periphetes meaning "cudgel bearer." Cf. **Periphetes** (def. 1).

Co·rynne (kō rin/, kō-), *n.* a girl's given name, form of Cora. Also, **Corinna, Corinne.**

Cor·y·phae·a (kôr/ə fē/ə, kor/-), *n.* *Class. Myth.* an epithet meaning "of the peak," applied to goddesses inhabiting mountaintops.

cor·y·phae·us (kôr/ə fē/əs, kor/-), *n., pl.* **-phae·i** (-fē/ī). **1.** the leader of the chorus in the ancient Greek drama. **2.** (in modern use) the leader of an operatic chorus or any group of singers. **3.** *(cap.)* *Class. Myth.* an epithet of Zeus, meaning "highest." [< L < Gk *koryphaîos* leader (n.), leading (adj.), equiv. to *koryph(ḗ)* head, top + *-aîos* adj. suffix]

Cor·y·pha·sia (kôr/ə fā/shə, kor/-), *n.* *Class. Myth.* an epithet of Athena. [< Gk *Koryphasía,* from her worship at *Coryphasium* in Messenia]

cor·y·phée (kôr/ə fā/, kor/-; *Fr.* kô rē fā/), *n., pl.* **-phées** (-fāz/; *Fr.* -fā/). a member of a ballet company who dances usually as part of a small group and who ranks above the members of the corps de ballet but below the soloists. [< F < L *coryphae(us)* CORYPHAEUS]

Co·ryph·o·don (kə rif/ə don/), *n.* *Paleontol.* a genus of amblypods from the early Eocene epoch, having a long, thick-set body, short legs, and five-toed feet, each toe ending in a small hoof. [< NL < Gk *koryph(ḗ)* peak, top + *odṓn* tooth]

Cor·y·thus (kôr/ə thəs, kor/-), *n.* *Class. Myth.* **1.** a king who raised the abandoned Telephus as his own son. **2.** the son of Priam and Oenone who was killed by his father for falling in love with Helen. **3.** (in the *Aeneid*) birthplace of Dardanus.

co·ry·za (kə rī/zə), *n.* **1.** *Pathol.* acute inflammation of the mucous membrane of the nasal cavities; cold in the head. **2.** *Vet. Pathol.* a contagious disease of birds, esp. poultry, characterized by the secretion of a thick mucus in the mouth and throat. [< LL < Gk *kóryza* catarrh]

cos[1] (kos, kôs), *n.* romaine (def. 1). [named after Kos from which it originally came]

cos[2] (kōs), *n.* cosine.

Cos (kôs), *n.* Kos.

cos., **1.** companies. **2.** counties.

C.O.S., cash on shipment. Also, **c.o.s.**

Co·sa Nos·tra (kō/zə nōs/trə), a secret association engaged in organized crime in the U.S., modeled after and affiliated with the Mafia.

Cosecant
ACB being the angle, the ratio of BC to BA, or that of CL to CD, is the cosecant; or, CD being taken as unity, the cosecant is LC

cose (kōs), *v.i.*, **cosed, cos·ing,** *n.* coze.

co·sec (kō/sēk/), *n.* cosecant.

co·se·cant (kō sē/kənt, -kant), *n.* *Trig.* **1.** (in a right triangle) the ratio of the hypotenuse to the side opposite a given angle. **2.** the secant of the complement, or the reciprocal of the sine, of a given angle or arc. *Abbr.:* cosec, csc [< NL *cosecant-* (s. of *cosecāns*). See CO-, SECANT]

co·seis·mal (kō sīs/məl, -sīz/-), *adj.* of, pertaining to, or being in a line, curve, etc., connecting or comprising points on the earth's surface at which an earthquake wave arrives simultaneously. Also, **co·seis/mic.** [CO- + SEISMAL]

Co·sen·za (kô zen/tsä), *n.* a city in S Italy. 78,941 (1961).

co·set (kō/set), *n.* *Math.* a subset of a group, formed by the consistent operation of a given element of the group on the left or right of all the elements of a subgroup of the group. [CO- + SET]

co·sey (kō/zē), *adj.*, **-si·er, -si·est,** *n., pl.* **-seys.** cozy.

Cos·grave (koz/grāv), *n.* **William Thomas,** 1880–1965, Irish political leader: president of the executive council of the Irish Free State 1922–32.

cosh (kosh), *Chiefly Brit. Slang.* **—n.** **1.** a blackjack; bludgeon. **—v.t.** **2.** to hit (someone) on the head with a blackjack. [perh. < Romany *kosh, koshter* stick]

cosh (kosh), hyperbolic cosine. [COS(INE) + H(YPERBOLIC)]

cosh·er (kosh/ər), *v.t.* to pamper. [< Ir *cōisir* entertainment, feast]

co·sie (kō/zē), *adj.*, **-si·er, -si·est,** *n.* cozy. **—co/si·ly,** *adv.* **—co/si·ness,** *n.*

Co·sì fan tut·te (*It.* kô zē/ fän to͞ot/te), a comic opera (1790) by Wolfgang Amadeus Mozart.

co·sig·na·to·ry (kō sig/nə tôr/ē, -tōr/ē), *adj., n., pl.* **-ries.** **—adj.** **1.** signing jointly with another or others. **—n.** **2.** one who signs a document jointly with another or others. [CO- + SIGNATORY]

co·sign·er (kō/sī/nər, kō/sī/-), *n.* a comaker.

Co·si·mo (kō/zə mō/; *It.* kô/zē-mô), *n.* **Pie·ro di** (pye/rô dē). See **Piero di Cosimo.**

co·sine (kō/sīn), *n.* *Trig.* **1.** (in a right triangle) the ratio of the side adjacent to a given angle to the hypotenuse. **2.** the sine of the complement of a given angle or arc. *Abbr.:* cos [< NL *cosin(us).* See CO-, SINE[1]]

Cosine
ACB being the angle, the ratio of AC to BC is the cosine; or, BC being taken as unity, the cosine is AC

cos/ let/tuce, romaine (def. 1).

cosm-, var. of **cosmo-** before a vowel: *cosmic.*

-cosm, var. of **cosmo-** as final element of a compound word: *microcosm.*

Cos·me·tas (koz mē/təs), *n.* *Class. Myth.* an epithet of Zeus, meaning "orderer."

cos·met·ic (koz met/ik), *n.* **1.** a powder, lotion, or other preparation for beautifying the complexion, skin, hair, nails, etc. **—adj.** **2.** serving to beautify; imparting or improving beauty, esp. of the face. [< Gk *kosmētik(ós)* relating to adornment, equiv. to *kosmēt(ós)* adorned, arranged (verbal of *kosmein,* deriv. of *kósmos* order, arrangement) + *-ikos* -IC] **—cos·met/i·cal·ly,** *adv.*

cos·me·ti·cian (koz/mi tish/ən), *n.* **1.** one who manufactures or sells cosmetics. **2.** an expert, usually professional, in the application of cosmetics. [COSMETIC + -ICIAN]

cosmet/ic sur/gery, plastic surgery for improvement of the appearance of a person by restoration of damaged areas of skin, removal of blemishes, etc. Also called **decorative surgery.**

cos·me·tol·o·gy (koz/mi tol/ə jē), *n.* the art or profession of applying cosmetics. [< Gk *kosmēt(ós)* adorned, arranged (see COSMETIC) + -LOGY, appar. modeled on F *cosmétologie*] **—cos·me·to·log·i·cal** (koz/mi təloj/i kəl), *adj.* **—cos/me·tol/o·gist,** *n.*

cos·mic (koz/mik), *adj.* **1.** of or pertaining to the cosmos: *cosmic laws.* **2.** characteristic of the cosmos or its phenomena: *cosmic events.* **3.** immeasurably extended in time and space; vast. **4.** forming a part of the material universe, esp. outside of the earth. Also, **cos/mi·cal.** [< Gk *kosmik(ós)* worldly, universal, equiv. to *kósm(os)* world + *-ikos* -IC] **—cos·mi·cal·i·ty** (koz/mi kal/i tē), *n.* **—cos/mi·cal·ly,** *adv.*

cos/mic dust/, *Astron.* fine particles of matter in space.

cos/mic ray/, *Astron.* a radiation of extremely high penetrating power that originates in outer space and consists partly of high-energy atomic nuclei.

cos·mism (koz/miz əm), *n.* the philosophy of cosmic evolution. [COSM- + -ISM] **—cos/mist,** *n.*

Cos·mo (koz/mō; *It.,* kôz/mô), *n.* a boy's given name.

cosmo-, a learned borrowing from Greek meaning "world," "universe," used in the formation of compound words: *cosmonaut.* Also, **cosm-, -cosm.** [< Gk *kosmo-,* comb. form of *kósmos* COSMOS]

cos·mo·chem·is·try (koz/mō kem/i strē), *n.* the science dealing with the occurrence and distribution of the chemical elements in the universe. [COSMO- + CHEMISTRY]

cos·mog·o·ny (koz mog/ə nē), *n., pl.* **-nies.** a theory or story of the genesis and development of the universe, of the solar system, or of the earth-moon system. [< Gk *kosmogonía* the creation of the world. See COSMO-, -GONY] **—cos·mog/o·nal, cos·mo·gon·ic** (koz/mə-gon/ik), **cos/mo·gon/i·cal,** *adj.* **—cos·mog/o·nist,** *n.*

cos·mog·ra·phy (koz mog/rə fē), *n., pl.* **-phies.** **1.** a science that describes and maps the main features of the heavens and the earth, including astronomy, geography, and geology. **2.** a description or representation of the main features of the universe. [< Gk *kosmographía* description of the world. See COSMO-, -GRAPHY] **—cos·mog/ra·pher, cos·mog/ra·phist,** *n.* **—cos·mo·graph·ic** (koz/mə graf/ik), **cos/mo·graph/i·cal,** *adj.* **—cos/mo·graph/i·cal·ly,** *adv.*

cos·mo·line (koz/mə lēn/), *n., v.,* **-lined, -lin·ing.** **—n.** **1.** heavy grease used to preserve weapons from the elements. **—v.t.** **2.** to grease (weapons) against the elements. [COSM(ETIC) + -OL[2] + -INE[2]]

cos/molog/ical ar/gument, *Philos.* an argument for the existence of God, asserting that the contingency of each entity, and of the universe composed wholly of such entities, demands the admission of an adequate external cause, which is God. Also called **cos/molog/ical proof/.** Cf. **first-cause argument.**

cos·mol·o·gy (koz mol/ə jē), *n.* **1.** the branch of philosophy dealing with the origin and general structure of the universe, with its parts, elements, and laws, and esp. with such of its characteristics as space, time, causality, and freedom. **2.** *Astron.* the branch of astronomy that deals with the general structure and evolution of the universe. [< NL *cosmologia.* See COSMO-, -LOGY] **—cos·mo·log·i·cal** (koz/mə loj/i kəl), **cos/mo·log/ic,** *adj.* **—cos/mo·log/i·cal·ly,** *adv.* **—cos·mol/o·gist,** *n.*

cos·mo·naut (koz/mə nôt/, -not/), *n.* astronaut. [COSMO- + *-naut,* as in *Argonaut,* first coined in Russian]

cos·mo·nau·tic (koz/mə nô/tik, -not/ik), *adj.* of or pertaining to cosmonautics or cosmonauts. Also, **cos/mo·nau/ti·cal.** [COSMONAUT + -IC] **—cos/mo·nau/ti·cal·ly,** *adv.*

cos·mo·nau·tics (koz/mə nô/tiks, -not/iks), *n.* *(construed as sing.)* astronautics, esp. as applied to space flight. [see COSMONAUTIC, -ICS]

cos·mop·o·lis (koz mop/ə lis), *n.* an internationally important city inhabited by many different peoples. [COSMO- + -POLIS, modeled on *metropolis*]

cos·mo·pol·i·tan (koz/mə pol/i tən), *adj.* **1.** belonging to all the world; not limited to just one part of the political, social, commercial, or intellectual world. **2.** *Bot., Zool.* widely distributed over the globe. **3.** free from local, provincial, or national ideas, prejudices, or attachments; at home all over the world. **4.** of or characteristic of a cosmopolite. **—n.** **5.** one who is free from local, provincial, or national prejudices, etc.; citizen of the world; cosmopolite. [COSMOPOLITE + -AN] **—cos/mo·pol/i·tan·ism,** *n.* **—cos/mo·pol/i·tan·ly,** *adv.*

cos·mo·pol·i·tan·ise (koz/mə pol/i tənīz/), *v.t.,* **-ised, -is·ing.** *Chiefly Brit.* cosmopolitanize. **—cos/mo·pol/i·tan·i·sa/tion,** *n.*

cos·mo·pol·i·tan·ize (koz/mə pol/i tənīz/), *v.t.,* **-ized, -iz·ing.** to make cosmopolitan. [COSMOPOLITAN + -IZE] **—cos/mo·pol/i·tan·i·za/tion,** *n.*

cos·mop·o·lite (koz mop/ə līt/), *n.* **1.** a person who is cosmopolitan in his ideas, life, etc.; citizen of the world. **2.** an animal or plant of world-wide distribution. [< Gk *kosmopolítē(s)* citizen of the world, equiv. to *kosmo-* COSMO- + *polítēs* citizen (*pól(is)* a city, state + *-ītēs* -ITE[1])] **—cos·mop/o·lit/ism,** *n.*

cos·mo·ra·ma (koz/mə ram/ə, -rä/mə), *n.* an exhibition of pictures of different parts of the world. [COSM- + (PAN)ORAMA] **—cos/mo·ram/ic,** *adj.*

cos·mos (koz/məs, -mōs), *n., pl.* **-mos, -mos·es** for 2, 4. **1.** the world or universe regarded as an orderly, harmonious system. **2.** a complete, orderly, harmonious system. **3.** order; harmony. **4.** any composite plant of the genus *Cosmos,* of tropical America, some species of which, as *C. bipinnatus* and *C. sulphureus,* are cultivated for their showy flowers. **5.** *(cap.)* name of a series of satellites orbited by the Soviet Union, for observing the upper atmosphere and outer space. [ME *cosmos* world < Gk *kósmos* order, form, arrangement, the world or universe]

Cos·mo·tron (kos/mə tron/), *n.* *Physics.* a proton accelerator. [*cosmo-* (repr. COSMIC RAY) + -TRON]

coss (kōs), *n.* kos.

Cos·sack (kos/ak, -ək), *n.* a person belonging to any of certain groups of Slavs living chiefly in the southern part of the Soviet Union in Europe and forming an elite corps of horsemen, chiefly in czarist Russia. [< Russ *kazak* < Turk: tribal name, appar. special use of *kazak* masterful husband]

cos·set (kos/it), *v.t.* **1.** to treat as a pet; pamper; coddle. **—n.** **2.** a lamb brought up without its dam; pet lamb. **3.** any pet. [akin to OE *cossetung* kissing, verbal n. based on **cossettan* to kiss, deriv. of *coss* kiss; c. Icel *koss,* G *Kuss*]

cost[1] (kôst, kost), *n., v.,* **cost, cost·ing.** **—n.** **1.** the price paid to acquire, produce, accomplish, or maintain anything. **2.** a sacrifice, loss, or penalty: *to work at the cost of one's health.* **3.** outlay or expenditure of money, time, labor, trouble, etc.: *What will the cost be to me?* **4. costs,** *Law.* **a.** money allowed to a successful party in a lawsuit in compensation for his legal expenses, chargeable to the unsuccessful party. **b.** money due to a court or one of its officers for services in a cause. **5. at all costs,** regardless of the effort involved; by any means necessary: *The stolen painting must be recovered at all costs.* Also, **at any cost.** **—v.t.** **6.** to require the payment of (money or something else of value in an exchange): *That camera cost $40.* **7.** to result in or entail the loss of: *Carelessness costs lives.* **8.** to result in or entail (an injury or the like): *His impertinence cost him a broken nose.* **9.** to entail (effort or inconvenience): *Courtesy costs little.* **10.** to estimate or determine the cost of (manufactured arti-

cles, new processes, etc.). —*v.i.* **11.** to estimate or determine costs, as of manufacturing something. [ME *cost(en)* < MF *coste(r)* < L *constāre* to stand with, cost; see CONSTANT] —**cost′less,** *adj.* —**cost′less·ness,** *n.*
—**Syn. 1.** charge, expense, expenditure, outlay. See **price. 2.** detriment.

cost[2] (kôst, kost), *n.* *Heraldry.* cotise (def. 1). [< MF *coste,* lit., rib. See COAST]

cost-, var. of **costo-** before a vowel: *costate.*

cos·ta (kos′tə, kô′stə), *n., pl.* **cos·tae** (kos′tē, kô′stē). **1.** a rib or riblike part. **2.** the midrib of a leaf in mosses. **3.** a ridge. **4.** *Entomol.* **a.** Also called **cos′tal vein′.** a vein, usually marginal, in the anterior portion of the wing of certain insects. **b.** Also called **cos′tal mar′gin.** the anterior edge or border of the wing of certain insects. [< L: rib, side. See COAST]

Cos·ta Bra·va (kos′tə brä′və, kô′stə, kō′-; *Sp.* kôs′tä brä′vä), a coastal region in NE Spain, extending NE along the Mediterranean from Barcelona to the border of France. [< Sp: lit., wild coast]

cost-ac·count (kôst′ə kount′, kost′-), *v.t.* **1.** to estimate or determine the exact expenditure required, as for a process, program, etc., by or as if by application of the principles of cost accounting. **2.** to trace (items) back to a precise source and ascribe to each an appropriate measure or proportion in a total: *No one can cost-account the total of human suffering which results both from too-rapid change and from too-slow progress.*

cost′ account′ing, **1.** an accounting system indicating the cost items involved in production. **2.** the operation of such an accounting system. —**cost′ account′ant.**

Cos·tain (kos′tān), *n.* **Thomas Bertram,** 1885–1965, U.S. novelist, historian, and editor; born in Canada.

cos·tal (kos′tᵊl, kôs′tᵊl), *adj.* **1.** *Anat.* pertaining to the ribs or the side of the body: *costal nerves.* **2.** *Bot., Zool.* pertaining to, involving, or situated near a costa. [< ML *costāl(is)* of the ribs, equiv. to L *cost(a)* rib, side + *-ālis* -AL[1]] —**cos′tal·ly,** *adv.*

Cos·ta Me·sa (kos′tə mā′sə, kô′stə, kō′-), a city in SW California, near Los Angeles. 37,550 (1960)

cost′ and freight′. See **C. & F.**

co-star (*n.* kō′stär′; *v.* kō′stär′), *n., v.,* **-starred, -star·ring.** —*n.* **1.** an actor or actress who shares star billing with another. **2.** an actor or actress whose status is slightly less than that of a star. —*v.i.* **3.** to share star billing with another actor or actress. **4.** to receive billing of slightly less status than that of a star. —*v.t.* **5.** to present (two or more stars) as having equal billing or prominence: *The movie co-starred Theda Bara and Rudolph Valentino.* **6.** to present as having slightly less status than that of a star. [CO- + STAR]

cos·tard (kos′tərd, kô′stərd), *n.* **1.** *Hort.* **a.** a large, English variety of apple. **b.** the tree bearing this fruit. **2.** *Archaic.* the head. [ME, perh. *cost* quality (in OE: choice) + -ARD]

Cos·ta Ri·ca (kos′tə rē′kə, kô′stə, kō′-; *Sp.* kôs′tä rē′kä), a republic in Central America, between Panama and Nicaragua. 1,199,116 (est. 1961); 19,238 sq. mi. *Cap.:* San José. —**Cos′ta Ri′can.**

Cos′ta Ri′ca night′shade, a climbing, prickly shrub, *Solanum wendlandi,* of Costa Rica, having showy, lilac-blue flowers. Also called **paradise flower.**

cos·tate (kos′tāt, kô′stāt), *adj.* **1.** *Anat.* having ribs. **2.** (of mosses) having a midrib or costa. [< L *costāt(us)* having ribs, ribbed, equiv. to *cost(a)* rib + *-ātus* -ATE[1]]

cost′ card′. See **cost sheet.**

cost′ cen′ter, a group, as of employees, machines, or both, or any unit of activity arranged in order to allocate and assign costs more easily.

cos·tec·to·my (ko stek′tə mē, kô-), *n., pl.* **-mies.** *Surg.* excision of part of or all of a rib. Also called **thoracectomy.** [COST- + -ECTOMY]

Cos·tel·lo (ko stel′ō, kos′tᵊlō′), *n.* **John Al·o·y·sius** (al′ō ish′əs, -ē əs), born 1891, Irish political leader: prime minister of the Republic of Ireland 1948–51, 1954–57.

Cos·ten (kos′tən, kô′stən), *n.* a boy's given name.

cos·ter (kos′tər, kô′stər), *n., v.i.* costermonger.

Cos·ter·mans·ville (kos′tər mənz vil′, kô′stər-), *n.* former name of **Bukavu.**

cos·ter·mon·ger (kos′tər mung′gər, -mong′-, kô′stər-), *Chiefly Brit.* —*n.* **1.** Also called **coster.** a hawker of fruit, vegetables, fish, etc. —*v.i.* **2.** to sell fruit, vegetables, fish, etc., from a cart, barrow, or stall in the streets; coster. [earlier *costerdmonger.* See COSTARD, MONGER]

cost′, insur′ance, and freight′. See **C.I.F.**

cos·tive (kos′tiv, kô′stiv), *adj.* **1.** suffering from constipation; constipated. **2.** *Archaic.* slow in action or in expressing ideas, opinions, etc. [late ME < MF *costive* constipated (ptp. of *costiver*) < L *constip(ātus)* (see CONSTIPATE); MF *-ive* (modern *-ivé*) was taken as fem. adj. suffix *-ive* -IVE] —**cos′tive·ly,** *adv.* —**cos′tive·ness,** *n.*

cost′ keep′er, a cost accountant. —**cost′ keep′ing.**

cost′ ledg′er, a subsidiary ledger in which are recorded the costs of goods produced or services supplied.

cost·ly (kôst′lē, kost′-), *adj.,* **-li·er, -li·est.** **1.** costing much; high in price: *Emerald bracelets are costly.* **2.** resulting in great expense. **3.** resulting in great detriment: *It was a costly mistake, for it landed him in prison.* **4.** of great value; very valuable; sumptuous. **5.** *Archaic.* lavish; extravagant. [COST[1] + -LY] —**cost′li·ness,** *n.*
—**Syn. 1.** dear, high-priced. See **expensive.**

cost·mar·y (kost′mâr′ē, kôst′-), *n., pl.* **-mar·ies.** a perennial plant, *Chrysanthemum Balsamita,* that has fragrant leaves and is used in salads and as a flavoring. Also called **mint geranium.** [ME *costmarie,* equiv. to *cost* (OE *cost* costmary < L *cost(um)* some oriental aromatic plant < Gk *kóstos*) + *Marie* (the Virgin) Mary]

costo-, a learned borrowing from Latin meaning "rib," used in the formation of compound words: *costoclavicular.* Also, *esp. before a vowel,* **cost-.** [comb. form repr. L *costa*]

cos·to·cla·vic·u·lar (kos′tō klə vik′yə lər, kô′stō-), *adj.* pertaining to the ribs and the clavicle. [COSTO- + CLAVICULAR]

cost′ of liv′ing, the average cost of food, clothing, and other necessities paid by a person, family, etc.

cost′-of-liv′ing in′dex (kôst′əv liv′ing, kost′-). See **consumer price index.**

cos·to·scap·u·lar (kos′tō skap′yə lər, kô′stō-), *adj.* pertaining to the ribs and the scapula. [COSTO- + SCAPULAR]

cos·to·tome (kos′tə tōm′), *n.* *Surg.* an instrument, as shears or a knife, for incising or dividing a rib, as in costotomy. [COSTO- + -TOME]

cos·tot·o·my (ko stot′ə mē), *n., pl.* **-mies.** *Surg.* incision of a rib. [COSTO- + -TOMY]

cost-plus (kôst′plus′, kost′-), *n.* the cost of production plus an agreed rate of profit: often used as a basis of payment in government contracts.

cos·trel (kos′trəl, kô′strəl), *n.* a flask made of leather, earthenware, or wood, usually with an ear or ears by which to suspend it, as from the waist. [ME < MF *costerel,* equiv. to *costier* at the side (< VL **costār(ius);* see COSTA, -ARY) + *-el* dim. suffix]

cost′ sheet′, a summary of costs involved in the production of a product. Also called **cost card.**

cos·tume (*n.* kos′to͞om, -tyo͞om; *v.* ko sto͞om′, -styo͞om′), *n., v.,* **-tumed, -tum·ing.** —*n.* **1.** a style of dress, including accessories and hairdos, esp. that peculiar to a nation, social class, or historical period. **2.** dress or garb belonging to another period, place, etc., as worn on the stage, at balls, etc. **3.** a set of garments, esp. women's garments, selected for wear at a single time; outfit; ensemble. **4.** fashion of dress appropriate to a particular occasion or season: *dancing costume; winter costume.* —*v.t.* **5.** to dress; furnish with a costume; provide appropriate dress for: *to costume a play.* [< F <It: usage, habit, dress; in origin, doublet of CUSTOM]
—**Syn. 1.** See **dress.**

cos′tume jew′elry, jewelry made of nonprecious metals, sometimes gold-plated or silver-plated, often set with imitation or semiprecious stones.

cos·tum·er (ko sto͞o′mər, -styo͞o′-), *n.* one who makes, sells, or rents costumes, as for theaters, masquerade parties, etc. [COSTUME + -ER[1]]

cos·tum·i·er (ko sto͞o′mē ər, -styo͞o′-; *Fr.* kôs ty myā′), *n., pl.* **cos·tum·i·ers** (ko sto͞o′mē ərz, -styo͞o′-; *Fr.* kôs ty myā′). costumer.

cos·tum·ing (kos′to͞o ming, -tyo͞o-), *n.* **1.** material for costumes. **2.** costumes collectively. **3.** the act of furnishing or designing costumes. [COSTUME + -ING[1]]

cost′ u′nit, a quantity or unit of a product or service whose cost is computed, used as a standard for comparison with other costs.

cos·tus·root (kô′stəs ro͞ot′, -ro͝ot′, kos′təs-), *n.* the fragrant root of a composite herb, *Saussurea Lappa,* native to Kashmir, yielding an essential oil used in the manufacture of perfumes. [< NL *Costus,* specific name of the plant (< Gk *kóstos*) + ROOT[1]]

co-sure·ty (kō sho͝or′tē, -sho͝or′i tē), *n., pl.* **-ties.** one who joins one or more others in a surety bond. —**co-sure′ty·ship′,** *n.*

co·sy (kō′zē), *adj.,* **-si·er, -si·est,** *n., pl.* **-sies.** cozy. —**co′si·ly,** *adv.* —**co′si·ness,** *n.*

Co·sy·ra (kō sī′rə), *n.* ancient name of **Pantelleria.**

cot[1] (kot), *n.* **1.** a light portable bed, esp. one of canvas stretched on a frame. **2.** *Brit.* a crib for a child. **3.** a light bedstead. **4.** *Naut.* a hammocklike bed stiffened by a suspended frame. [< AInd < Hindi *khāt* < Prakrit *khaṭṭā;* akin to Tamil *kaṭṭil* bedstead]

cot[2] (kot), *n.* **1.** a small house; cottage; hut. **2.** a small place of shelter or protection. **3.** a sheath or protective covering, as for an injured finger. [ME, OE *cot(e);* c. Icel *kot* hut]

Cot (kot), *n.* a boy's given name, form of **Cotton.**

cot, cotangent.

Co·ta·ba·to (kō′tä bä′tō), *n.* a city on SW Mindanao, in the S Philippines. 44,100 (est. 1965).

co·tan·gent (kō tan′jənt, kō′tan′-), *n.* *Trig.* **1.** (in a right triangle) the ratio of the side adjacent to a given angle to the side opposite. **2.** the tangent of the complement, or the reciprocal of the tangent, of a given angle or arc. *Abbr.:* cot, ctn [< NL *cotangent-* (s. of *cotangēns*). See CO-, TANGENT] —**co·tan·gen·tial** (kō′tan jen′shəl), *adj.*

Cotangent
ACB being the angle, the ratio of DL to DC, or that of AC to AH, is the cotangent; or DC being taken as unity, it is the line DL

cote[1] (kōt), *n.* **1.** a shelter for sheep, pigs, pigeons, etc. **2.** *Brit. Dial.* a cottage; small house. [var. of COT[2]]

cote[2] (kōt), *v.t.,* **cot·ed, cot·ing.** *Obs.* to pass by; outstrip; surpass. [?]

co·teau (kō tō′, kō-; *Fr.* kô tō′), *n., pl.* **-teaux** (-tōz′; *Fr.* -tō′). *Canadian.* **1.** a hilly, upland region. **2.** the side of a valley. [< CanF, F: slight hill; OF *costel,* dim. of *coste* slope, side]

Côte d'A·zur (kōt da zyr′), French name of the **Riviera.**

Côte-d'Or (kōt dôr′), *n.* a department in E France. 387,869 (1962); 3393 sq. mi. *Cap.:* Dijon.

cote·har·die (kōt′är′dē, -här′-), *n.* (in the Middle Ages) a close-fitting outer garment with long sleeves, hip-length for men and full-length for women, often laced or buttoned down the front or back. [ME < OF: lit., bold coat]

co·tem·po·ra·ne·ous (kō tem′pə rā′nē əs), *adj.* *Archaic.* contemporaneous. —**co·tem′po·ra′ne·ous·ly,** *adv.*

co·tem·po·rar·y (kō tem′pə rer′ē), *adj., n., pl.* **-rar·ies.** *Archaic.* contemporary. —**co·tem′po·rar′i·ly,** *adv.*

co·ten·ant (kō ten′ənt), *n.* a tenant in common with another or others; a joint tenant. [CO- + TENANT] —**co·ten′an·cy, co·ten·ure** (kō ten′yər), *n.*

co·te·rie (kō′tə rē), *n.* **1.** a group of people who associate closely because of common social purposes, interests, etc. **2.** a clique. [< F, MF: an association of tenant-farmers < ML *coter(ius)* COTTER[2] + *-ie* -Y[3]]
—**Syn. 1.** See **circle.**

co·ter·mi·nous (kō tûr′mə nəs), *adj.* conterminous.

Côtes-du-Nord (kōt dy nôr′), *n.* a department in NW France. 501,923 (1962); 2787 sq. mi. *Cap.:* Saint-Brieuc.

coth, hyperbolic cotangent. [COT(ANGENT) + H(YPERBOLIC)]

coth·a·more (kō′thə mōr′, -môr′), *n.* a frieze fabric, often used in the manufacture of overcoats. [< Ir *cōta mōr,* lit., greatcoat]

co·thur·nus (kō thûr′nəs), *n., pl.* **-ni** (-nī). **1.** a grave and elevated style of acting; tragic acting; tragedy. **2.** buskin (def. 2). Also, **co·thurn** (kō′thûrn, kō thûrn′). [< L < Gk *kóthornos* buskin] —**co·thur′nal,** *adj.*

cot·ice (kot′is), *n., v.t.,* **-iced, -ic·ing.** cotise.

co·tid·al (kō tīd′ᵊl), *adj.* **1.** pertaining to a coincidence of tides. **2.** indicating a line connecting points at which high tide occurs at the same time. [CO- + TIDAL]

co·til·lion (kō til′yən, kə-), *n.* **1.** a lively French social dance originating in the 18th century, consisting of a variety of steps and figures and performed by couples. **2.** any of various dances resembling the quadrille. **3.** music arranged or played for these dances. **4.** a complex, formalized dance for a large number of people, in which a head couple lead the other dancers through elaborate and stately figures. **5.** a formal ball given esp. for debutantes. [< F *cotillon* kind of dance, in OF: petticoat, equiv. to *cote* COAT + *-illon* dim. suffix]

co·til·lon (kō til′yən, kō-; *Fr.* kô tē yôn′), *n., pl.* **-til·lons** (-til′yənz; *Fr.* -tē yôn′). cotillion.

co·tin·ga (kō ting′gə, kə-), *n.* any of several chiefly tropical passerine birds of the family *Cotingidae,* of North, Central, and South America. [< NL < F < Tupi]

cot·ise (kot′is), *n., v.,* **-ised, -is·ing.** *Heraldry.* —*n.* **1.** Also called **cost.** a very narrow diminutive of an ordinary, usually one of a pair flanking an ordinary, or a number of charges arranged in the manner of an ordinary. —*v.t.* **2.** to border (an ordinary, or a number of charges arranged in the manner of an ordinary) with a cotise or cotises. Also, **cotice.** [var. of *cotice* < MF *co(s)tice,* equiv. to *coste* rib (< L *costa*) + *-ice* -ICE]

co·to·ne·as·ter (kə tō′nē as′tər, kot′ən ē′stər), *n.* any rosaceous shrub or small tree of the genus *Cotoneaster,* having white to reddish flowers and bearing a red or black, berrylike fruit, grown as an ornamental. [< NL, equiv. to L *cotōne(a)* QUINCE + *-aster* -ASTER[2]]

Co·to·nou (kō′tə no͞o′), *n.* a seaport in SE Dahomey. 58,000 (est. 1960).

Co·to·pax·i (kō′tə pak′sē; *Sp.* kô′tô pä′hē), *n.* a volcano in central Ecuador, in the Andes: the highest active volcano in the world. 19,498 ft.

cot·quean (kot′kwēn′), *n.* **1.** *Archaic.* a man who busies himself with women's household affairs. **2.** *Obs.* a coarse woman. [COT[2] + QUEAN]

Cots·wold (kots′wōld, -wəld), *n.* one of an English breed of large sheep having coarse, long wool. [named after the COTSWOLDS, where the breed originated]

Cots·wolds (kots′wōldz, -wəldz), *n.* (*construed as pl.*) a range of hills in SW England, in Gloucestershire: sheep-herding. Also called **Cots′wold Hills′.**

cot·ta (kot′ə, kô′tə), *n.* *Eccles.* **1.** a surplice. **2.** a short surplice, sleeveless or with short sleeves, worn esp. by choristers. [< ML, var. of *cota* kind of tunic. See COAT]

cot·tage (kot′ij), *n.* **1.** a small house, usually of only one story. **2.** a small, modest house at a lake, mountain resort, etc., owned or rented as a vacation home. **3.** one of a group of small, separate houses, as for patients at a hospital or students at a boarding school. [ME *cotage.* See COT[2], -AGE; cf. ML *cotagium,* said to be < AF] —**cot′taged,** *adj.*
—**Syn. 1, 2.** COTTAGE, CABIN, LODGE, SHACK, HUT, SHANTY formerly meant small, simple, often crude dwellings. During recent years, the first four words have gained great currency as terms for the often elaborate structures maintained by the well-to-do for recreational purposes. HUT and SHANTY, however, still have the former meaning as their most frequent one. —**Ant. 1.** palace, castle.

cot′tage cheese′, an extremely soft, or loose, white, mild-flavored cheese made from skim-milk curds, usually without rennet.

cot′tage fried′ pota′toes. See **home fries.**

Cot′tage Grove′, a town in W Oregon. 3895 (1960).

Cot′tage Hills′, a town in SW Illinois. 3976 (1960).

cot′tage loaf′, *Brit.* a round loaf of bread made by placing one lump of dough on a larger one before baking.

cot·tage or·né (*Fr.* kô tazh ôr nā′), *pl.* **cot·tages or·nés** (*Fr.* kô tazh ôr nā′). (in the early 19th century) a villa having the form of a cottage with a more or less ornate design. [< F: lit., ornate cottage]

cot′tage pud′ding, a pudding made by covering plain cake with a sweet sauce, often of fruit.

cot·tag·er (kot′i jər), *n.* **1.** one who lives in a cottage. **2.** Also, **cotter, cottier.** *Brit.* a rural worker; a laborer on a farm or in a small village. **3.** a person having a private house at a vacation resort. [COTTAGE + -ER[1]]

cot′tage win′dow, a double-hung window with an upper sash smaller than the lower. Also called **front window.**

cot·tar (kot′ər), *n.* cottier.

Cott·bus (kot′bəs; *Ger.* kôt′bo͝os), *n.* a city in E East Germany, on the Spree River. 65,350 (1958).

cotte (kot, kôt), *n.* a close-fitting tunic worn in the Middle Ages as an undergarment. [< OF *cote,* cotte. See COAT]

cot·ter[1] (kot′ər), *Mach.* —*n.* **1.** a pin, wedge, key, or the like, fitted or driven into an opening to secure something or hold parts together. **2.** See **cotter pin.** —*v.t.* **3.** to secure with a cotter. [late ME *coter;* akin to *coterel* (late ME *coterell* iron bracket) < ?]

C, Cotter; G, Gib

cot·ter[2] (kot′ər), *n.* **1.** *Scot.* a person occupying a plot of land under a system similar to cottier tenure. **2.** cottier. **3.** cottager (def. 2). Also, **cot′tar.** [ME *cotere.* See COT[2], -ER[1]]

cot′ter pin′, *Mach.* a cotter having a split end that is spread after being pushed through a hole to prevent the cotter from working loose. Also called **cot′ter way′.**

cot′ter slot′, *Mach.* a slot cut into the end of a rod for the reception of another rod or part to be attached by a cotter.

Cot′ter's Sat′urday Night′, The (kot′ərz), a poem (1786) by Robert Burns.

Cot′ti·an Alps′ (kot′ē ən), a mountain range in SW Europe, on the boundary between France and Italy: a part of the Alps. Highest peak, Monte Viso, 12,602 ft.

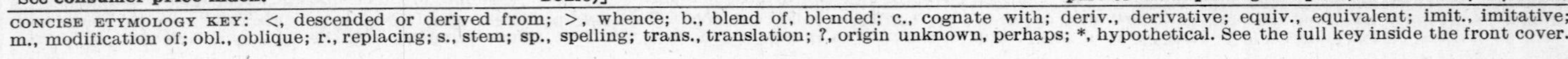
CONCISE ETYMOLOGY KEY: <, descended or derived from; >, whence; b., blend of, blended; c., cognate with; deriv., derivative; equiv., equivalent; imit., imitative; m., modification of; obl., oblique; r., replacing; s., stem; sp., spelling; trans., translation; ?, origin unknown, perhaps; *, hypothetical. See the full key inside the front cover.

cot·ti·er (kot′ē ər), *n.* **1.** (formerly, in Ireland) a tenant renting land directly from the landowner, the rental price being fixed by public competition. **2.** *Brit.* cottager (def. 2). Also, **cottar, cotter.** [ME *cotier* < OF < ML *cotār(ius)*, equiv. to *cot(a)* COTE[1] (< Gmc) + *-ārius* -ER[2]]

cot·ton (kot′ən), *n.* **1.** a soft, white, downy substance consisting of the hairs or fibers attached to the seeds of malvaceous plants of the genus *Gossypium*, used in making fabrics, thread, wadding, etc. **2.** the plant itself, having an upright manner of growth, spreading branches, and broad, lobed leaves. **3.** such plants collectively as a cultivated crop. **4.** cloth, thread, a garment, etc., of cotton. **5.** any soft, downy substance resembling cotton, but growing on some other plant. —*v.i.* **6.** *Informal.* to get on well together; agree. **7.** *Obs.* to prosper or succeed. **8. cotton to** or **with,** *Informal.* **a.** to become fond of; begin to like. **b.** to approve of; agree with: *to cotton to a suggestion.* [ME *coton* < MF < OIt *coton(e)* < Ar *quṭun,* var. of *quṭn*] —**cot′ton·less,** *adj.*

Cotton boll

Cot·ton (kot′ən), *n.* **1. John,** 1584–1652, U.S. clergyman, colonist, and author. **2.** a boy's given name.

cot·ton·ade (kot′ənād′), *n.* a heavy, coarse fabric made of cotton or mixed fibers and often resembling wool, used in the manufacture of work clothes. [< F *cotonnade.* See COTTON, -ADE[1]]

cot′ton bat′ting, absorbent cotton pressed into pads or layers for use in dressing wounds, filling quilts, etc.

cot′ton belt′, the part of the Southern U.S. where cotton is grown.

cot′ton cake′, a mass of compressed cottonseed after the oil has been extracted; used chiefly to feed cattle. Also called **cottonseed cake, seed oil cake.**

cot′ton can′dy, a fluffy, sweet confection whipped from white or colored spun sugar and gathered or wound around a stick or cone-shaped paper holder.

cot′ton flan′nel. See **Canton flannel.**

cot′ton gin′, a machine for separating the fibers of cotton from the seeds.

cot′ton grass′, any rushlike, cyperaceous plants of the genus *Eriophorum,* common in swampy places and bearing spikes resembling tufts of cotton. [so called from its cottonlike heads]

cot′ton gum′. See **sour gum.** [so called from the seeds' cottonlike hairs]

cot′ton mill′, a factory for producing cotton fabrics, thread, etc.

cot·ton mouth (kot′ən mouth′), *n., pl.* **-mouths** (-mouths′, -mouthz′). a venomous snake, *Ancistrodon piscivorous,* of swamps of the southeastern U.S., that grows to a length of about six feet. Also called **water moccasin.** [COTTON + MOUTH, so called from the whiteness of lips and mouth]

cot′ton pick′er, a machine for removing the ripe cotton fiber from the standing plant.

cot·ton·pick·in′ (kot′ən pik′ən), *adj. U.S. Slang.* **1.** fit for nothing better than picking cotton; unworthy: *Get your cottonpickin' hands off me.* **2.** damned; confounded: *That's a cottonpickin' lie.* Also, **cot·ton·pick·ing** (kot′ən pik′ən, -pik′ing).

cot′ton press′, a press for baling cotton.

cot′ton rose′, a shrub, *Hibiscus mutabilis,* of China, having hairy flowers from three to four inches wide that change from white or pink to deep red soon after opening, and round, hairy fruit. Also called **Confederate rose.**

cot·ton·seed (kot′ən sēd′), *n., pl.* **-seeds,** (*esp. collectively*) **-seed.** the seed of the cotton plant, yielding an oil. [COTTON + SEED]

cot′tonseed cake′. See **cotton cake.**

cot′tonseed meal′, cotton cake when pulverized.

cot′tonseed oil′, a brown-yellow, viscid oil with a nutlike odor, obtained from the seed of the cotton plant: used in the manufacture of soaps, hydrogenated fats, lubricants, and cosmetics, as a cooking and salad oil, and in medicine chiefly as a laxative.

cot′ton stain′er, any of several bugs of the genus *Dysdercus,* esp. *D. suturellus,* that feed on cotton, staining the fibers an indelible reddish or yellowish color.

Cot′ton State′, Alabama (used as a nickname).

cot·ton·tail (kot′ən tāl′), *n.* any of several North American rabbits of the genus *Sylvilagus,* having a fluffy white tail. [COTTON + TAIL[1]]

Cottontail, *Sylvilagus floridanus* (Total length 15 in.; tail 2 in.)

cot′ton this′tle, a thistle, *Onopordon Acanthium,* of Eurasia, characterized by cottony stems and leaves and heads of purple flowers. Also called **Scotch thistle.**

cot′ton tie′, a light, narrow strip of metal for binding together bales of cotton, hemp, jute, etc.

cot′ton tree′, a spiny tree, *Bombax malabaricum,* of Indian and Malaysian regions, having large, red flowers that appear when the tree is leafless, and fruit with seeds embedded in cottonlike hairs.

cot·ton·weed (kot′ən wēd′), *n.* any of certain plants having stems and leaves covered with a soft, hoary pubescence, as those of the composite genus *Gnaphalium* or of various allied genera. [COTTON + WEED[1]]

cot·ton·wick (kot′ən wik′), *n. Ichthyol.* a grunt, *Haemulon melanurum,* found in the warm waters of the Atlantic Ocean. [COTTON + WICK[1]]

cot·ton·wood (kot′ən wo͝od′), *n.* any of several American poplars, as *Populus deltoides,* having cottonlike tufts on the seeds. [COTTON + WOOD[1]]

cot′ton wool′, **1.** cotton in its raw state, as on the boll or gathered but unprocessed. **2.** *Brit.* See **absorbent cotton.**

cot·ton·y (kot′ənē), *adj.* **1.** of or like cotton; soft. **2.** covered with a down or nap resembling cotton. [COTTON + -Y[1]]

cot′ton·y-cush′ion scale′ (kot′ənē ko͝osh′ən), a scale insect, *Icerya purchasi,* native to Australia, now a common pest in the citrus-growing regions of California.

cot′tony ju′jube. See **Indian jujube.**

Cot·tus (kot′əs), *n. Class. Myth.* one of the Hecatonchires.

co·tu·la (kō tul′ə, kə-), *n., pl.* **-tu·lae** (-tul′ē). (in prescriptions) a measure. [< L]

Co·tu·la (kə tul′ə), *n.* a town in SW Texas. 3960 (1960).

cot·wal (kōt′wäl), *n.* kotwal.

Co·ty (kō tē′; *Fr.* kô tē′), *n.* **Re·né Jules Gus·tave** (rə nā′ zhyl gys·tav′), 1882–1962, president of France 1954–59.

cot·y·le·don (kot′əlēd′ən), *n. Bot.* the primary or rudimentary leaf of the embryo of seed plants. [< L: navelwort (a plant) < Gk *kotylēdṓn* a plant (prob. navelwort), lit., a cuplike hollow, deriv. of *kotýlē* cup] —**cot′y·le′don·al, cot·y·le·don·ar·y** (kot′əlēd′ənër′ē), **cot′y·le′do·noid′, cot′y·le′don·ous,** *adj.*

A, Cotyledons of a bean plant; B, Epicotyl; C, Hypocotyl; D, Root

Cot·y·leus (kot′əlo͞os′), *n. Class. Myth.* an epithet of Asclepius, meaning "of the hip joint," in reference to a hip wound suffered by Hercules which Asclepius cured.

co·type (kō′tīp), *n.* a syntype. [CO- + TYPE]

cou·cal (ko͞o′kəl), *n.* any of several Old World cuckoos of the genus *Centropus,* having harsh-textured plumage and a long, daggerlike hind claw. [< F, equiv. to *cou-c(ou)* CUCKOO + *-al* < ?]

couch (kouch *or, for 6, 14,* ko͞och), *n.* **1.** a piece of furniture accommodating usually from two to four seated people, typically in the form of a bench with a back, sometimes having an armrest at one or each end, and, depending on its style and period, partly or wholly upholstered and often fitted with springs, tailored cushions, skirts, etc.; sofa. **2.** a similar article of upholstered furniture, with a headrest at one end, on which patients of psychiatrists or psychoanalysts lie while undergoing treatment. **3.** a bed or other place of rest; a lounge; any place used for repose. **4.** the lair of a wild beast. **5.** *Brewing.* the frame on which barley is spread to be malted. **6.** *Papermaking.* the board or felt blanket on which wet pulp is laid for drying into paper sheets. **7.** *Obs.* a coat of paint, etc. [ME *couche* < MF, OF, deriv. of *coucher* to couch] —*v.t.* **8.** to arrange or frame (words, a sentence, etc.); put into words; express: *a simple request couched in respectful language.* **9.** to express indirectly or obscurely: *the threat couched under his polite speech.* **10.** to lower or bend down, as the head. **11.** to lower (a spear, lance, etc.) to a horizontal position, as for attack. **12.** to put or lay down, as for rest or sleep; cause to lie down. **13.** to lay or spread flat. **14.** *Papermaking.* to transfer (a sheet of pulp) from the wire to the couch. **15.** to embroider by couching. **16.** *Surg.* **a.** to remove (a cataract) by inserting a needle and pushing the opaque crystalline lens downward in the vitreous humor below the axis of vision. **b.** to remove a cataract from (a person) in this manner. **17.** *Obs.* hide; conceal. —*v.i.* **18.** to lie at rest or asleep; repose; recline. **19.** to crouch; bend; stoop. **20.** to lie in ambush or in hiding; lurk. **21.** to lie in a heap for decomposition or fermentation, as leaves. [ME *couchen* < MF, OF *couche(r),* OF *colche(r)* < L *collocāre* to put into place, equiv. to *col-* COL- + *locāre* to put, place; see LOCATE]

couch·ant (kou′chənt), *adj.* **1.** lying down; crouching. **2.** *Heraldry.* (of an animal) represented as lying on its stomach with its hind legs and forelegs pointed forward. [ME < MF, prp. of *coucher* to lay or lie. See COUCH, -ANT]

cou·ché (ko͞o shā′), *adj. Heraldry.* (of an escutcheon) depicted in a diagonal position, the sinister chief uppermost. [< F, ptp. of *coucher* to lay down. See COUCH]

couch·er (kou′chər, kou′-), *n. Papermaking.* the craftsman who transfers sheets of wet pulp to the couch. [COUCH + -ER[1]]

couch′ grass′ (kouch, ko͞och), any of various grasses, esp. *Agropyron repens,* known chiefly as troublesome weeds and characterized by creeping rootstocks which spread rapidly. Also called **quitch, scutch grass.** [var. of QUITCH (GRASS)]

couch·ing (kou′ching), *n.* **1.** the act of one who or that which couches. **2.** a method of embroidering in which a thread, often heavy, laid upon the surface of the material, is caught down at intervals by stitches taken with another thread through the material. **3.** work so made. [COUCH + -ING[1]]

couch′ pota′to, *Slang.* a person whose leisure time is chiefly spent at home watching television.

couch′ roll′ (ko͞och, kouch), *Papermaking.* the roll on which a wet web is transferred from the paper machine to the couch.

Cou·ders·port (kou′dərz pōrt′, -pôrt′), *n.* a town in N Pennsylvania. 2889 (1960).

cou·é (ko͞o′ā), *adj. Heraldry.* coward (def. 4). [< F: tailed]

Cou·é (ko͞o ā′), *n.* **É·mile** (ā mēl′), 1857–1926, French psychotherapist.

Cou·é·ism (ko͞o ā′iz əm, ko͞o′ā iz′-), *n.* a method of self-help stressing autosuggestion, popular esp. in the U.S. c1920 and featuring the slogan, "Every day in every way I am getting better and better." [< F *couéisme.* See COUÉ, -ISM]

Cou·ette′ flow′ (ko͞o et′), *Mech.* the flow of a fluid between two surfaces that have tangential relative motion, as of a liquid between two coaxial cylinders that have different angular velocities. [< F *couette,* lit., feather bed (in machinery, a bearing). See QUILT]

cou·gar (ko͞o′gər), *n., pl.* **-gars,** (*esp. collectively*) **-gar.** a large, tawny cat, *Felis concolor,* of North and South America. Also called **mountain lion, panther, puma.** [var. of *couguar* < F, alter. of NL *cuguacuara* < Pg < Tupi *çuçu ara* + Guarani *guaçu ara*]

Cougar (Total length 8 ft.; tail to 3 ft.)

cough (kôf, kof), *v.i.* **1.** to expel air from the lungs suddenly with a harsh noise, often involuntarily. **2.** (of an internal-combustion engine) to make a similar noise as a result of the failure of one or more cylinders to fire in sequence. **3.** to make a similar sound, as a machine gun firing in spurts. —*v.t.* **4.** to expel by coughing (usually fol. by *up* or *out*): *to cough up a fish bone.* **5. cough up,** *Slang.* **a.** (esp. of money) to find among one's resources and hand over, esp. reluctantly; contribute; give. **b.** to blurt out; state, as by way of making a confession: *After several hours of questioning, he finally coughed up the information.* —*n.* **6.** the act or sound of coughing. **7.** an illness characterized by frequent coughing. **8.** a sound, similar to that made by coughing, of a machine gun, an engine firing improperly, etc. [ME *cogh(en),* back formation from OE *cohhetan* to cough; akin to D *kuchen* to cough, G *keuchen* to wheeze] —**cough′er,** *n.*

cough′ drop′, a small, medicinal lozenge for relieving a cough, sore throat, etc.

could (ko͝od; *unstressed* kəd), *v.* pt. of **can**[1]. [ME *coude,* OE *cūthe;* modern *-l-* from *would, should*]

could·n't (ko͝od′ənt), contraction of *could not.*

couldst (ko͝odst), *v. Archaic.* 2nd pers. sing. of **could.**

cou·lee (ko͞o′lē), *n.* **1.** *Western North America.* a deep ravine or gulch, usually dry, that has been worn away by running water. **2.** a small valley. **3.** a low-lying area. **4.** a small intermittent stream. **5.** a stream of lava. [< CanF, F: a flowing, n. use of fem of *coulé,* ptp. of *couler* to flow < L *cōlāre* to filter, strain, deriv. of *cōlum* strainer, sieve]

cou·lée (ko͞o lā′), *n. French.* coulee.

cou·lisse (ko͞o lēs′), *n.* **1.** a timber or the like having a groove for guiding a sliding panel. **2.** *Theat.* **a.** the space between two wing flats, leg drops, or the like. **b.** any space or area backstage. **c.** See **wing flat.** [< F: groove, something that slides in a groove; see PORTCULLIS]

cou·loir (ko͞ol wär′; *Fr.* ko͞o lwar′), *n., pl.* **cou·loirs** (ko͞ol wärz′; *Fr.* ko͞o lwar′). a steep gorge or gully on the side of a mountain. [< F: lit., colander < LL *cōlātōr(ium)* strainer, equiv. to L *cōlāt(us)* strained (ptp. of *cōlāre*) + *-ōrium* -ORY[2]. See COULEE]

cou·lomb (ko͞o′lom, ko͞o lom′), *n.* the meter-kilogram-second unit of quantity of electricity, equal to the quantity of charge transferred in one second across a conductor in which there is a constant current of one ampere. *Abbr.:* C [named after COULOMB]

Cou·lomb (ko͞o′lom, ko͞o lom′; *Fr.* ko͞o lôN′), *n.* **Charles Au·gus·tin de** (sharl ō gys taN′ də), 1736–1806, French physicist and inventor.

Cou′lomb's law′, *Elect.* the principle that the force of attraction between two point charges or two magnetic poles is proportional to the quotient of the product of the charges or strengths of the poles divided by the square of the distance between them. [named after COULOMB]

cou·lom·e·ter (ko͞o lom′i tər, kə-), *n.* voltameter. Also, **cou·lomb·me·ter** (ko͞o′lom mē′tər). [COULO(MB) + -METER]

coul·ter (kōl′tər), *n.* colter.

Coul·ter (kōl′tər), *n.* **1. Ellis Merton,** born 1890, U.S. historian. **2. John Merle** (mûrl), 1851–1928, U.S. botanist.

Coul′ter pine′, a California pine, *Pinus Coulteri,* bearing cones 9 to 14 inches long. Also called **big-cone pine.** [named after Thomas *Coulter* (d. 1843), Irish botanist]

cou·ma·rin (ko͞o′mə rin), *n. Chem.* a white, crystalline substance, having a vanillalike odor, $C_9H_6O_2$, obtained from the tonka bean and certain other plants or prepared synthetically: used chiefly for flavoring and in perfumery. Also, **cumarin.** Also called **tonka bean camphor.** [< F *coumarine,* equiv. to *coumar(ou)* tonka-bean tree (< Sp *cumarú* < Pg < Tupi) + *-ine* -IN[2]]

cou·ma·rone (ko͞o′mə rōn′), *n. Chem.* a colorless liquid, C_6H_4OCHCH, derived from a naphtha distilled from coal tar: used chiefly in the synthesis of coumarone resins. Also, **cumarone.** Also called **benzofuran.** [COUMAR(IN) + -ONE]

cou′marone res′in, *Chem.* any of the group of thermoplastic resins derived by the polymerization of mixtures of coumarone and indene: used chiefly in the manufacture of paints, varnishes, and printing inks. Also called **cou′ma·rone-in′dene res′in** (ko͞o′mərōn′in′dēn, kyo͞o′-).

coun·cil (koun′səl), *n.* **1.** an assembly of persons summoned or convened for consultation, deliberation, or advice. **2.** an ecclesiastical assembly for deciding matters of doctrine or discipline. **3.** *New Testament.* the Sanhedrin or other authoritative body. **4.** a body of persons specially designated or selected to act in an advisory, administrative, or legislative capacity: *the governor's council on housing.* **5.** (in certain British colonies or dependencies) an executive or legislative body assisting the governor. [ME *co(u)nsile* (< OF *concile* < L *concil(ium)* assembly, equiv. to *con-* CON- + *cil-,* var. of *cal-* call + *-ium* n. suffix) + *counseil* < AF < L *consil(ium)* council of war, body of advisers; see COUNSEL]

Coun′cil Bluffs′, a city in SW Iowa, across the Missouri River from Omaha, Nebraska. 54,361 (1960).

coun′cil fire′, a fire kept burning continually during a council of American Indians.

Coun′cil Grove′, a town in central Kansas. 2664 (1960).

coun′cil house′, (in Britain) a low-rent house or apartment building built to provide housing for low-income families by a local governing authority, as a county council or urban or rural district council; a low-income housing project sponsored by the government.

coun·cil·lor (koun′sə lər, -slər), *n.* **1.** a member of a council. **2.** counselor. Also, **councilor.** [COUNCIL + -OR[2]; r. ME *conseiler* < AF: adviser; see COUNSELOR] —**coun′cil·lor·ship′,** *n.*

coun·cil·man (koun′səl mən), *n., pl.* **-men.** a member of a council, esp. the local legislative body of a city. [COUNCIL + MAN[1]] —**coun·cil·man·ic** (koun′səl man′ik), *adj.*

coun′cil-man′ag·er plan′ (koun′səl man′ə jər), a system of municipal government in which the administrative powers of the city are entrusted to a manager selected by the city council.

Coun′cil of Econom′ic Advis′ers, *U.S. Govt.* a board, consisting of five members, established in 1946 to advise the President on economic matters. *Abbr.:* CEA

Coun′cil of National′ities. See under **Supreme Soviet.**

coun′cil of state′, a council that deliberates on high-level policies of a government.

Coun′cil of Ten′, the governing council of Venice from 1310 until its overthrow in 1797, composed originally of 10 and later 17 members having unlimited power.

Coun′cil of the Reich′, *Ger. Hist.* the Reichsrat.

Coun′cil of the Un′ion. See under **Supreme Soviet.**

coun′cil of war′, **1.** a conference of high-ranking military or naval officers, usually for discussing major war problems. **2.** any conference for discussing or deciding upon a course of action.

coun·ci·lor (koun′sə lər, -slər), *n.* **1.** councillor. **2.** counselor. —**coun′ci·lor·ship′,** *n.*

coun′cil school′, (in Britain) a school provided by public tax moneys, similar to a U.S. public school.

coun·cil·wom·an (koun′səl wo͝om′ən), *n., pl.* **-wom·en** (-wim′ən). a female councilman. [COUNCIL + WOMAN]

coun·sel (koun′səl), *n., v.,* **-seled, -sel·ing** or (*esp. Brit.*) **-selled, -sel·ling.** —*n.* **1.** advice; opinion or instruction given in directing the judgment or conduct of another. **2.** interchange of opinions as to future procedure; consultation; deliberation. **3.** deliberate purpose; plan; design. **4.** *Law.* (*construed as sing. or pl.*) the advocate or advocates engaged in the direction of a cause in court; a legal adviser or counselor: *Is counsel for the defense present? Are counsel ready?* **5.** *Theol.* one of the advisory declarations of Christ, considered by some Christians as not universally binding but as given for aid in attaining moral perfection. **6.** *Archaic.* wisdom; prudence. **7.** *Obs.* a private or secret opinion or purpose. **8. keep one's own counsel,** to conceal one's ideas or opinions; keep silent. **9. take counsel,** to ask for or exchange advice, ideas, or opinions; deliberate; consult. —*v.t.* **10.** to give advice to; advise. **11.** to urge the adoption of, as a course of action; recommend (a plan, policy, etc.): *He counseled patience during the crisis.* —*v.i.* **12.** to give counsel or advice. **13.** to get or take counsel or advice. [ME *counseil* < AF (equiv. to OF *conseil*) < L *consilium* a taking counsel, consultative body, advice; akin to CONSUL, CONSULT] —**coun′sel·a·ble;** *esp. Brit.,* **coun′sel·la·ble,** *adj.*
—**Syn. 1.** recommendation, suggestion, admonition, warning, caution. See **advice. 4.** lawyer, attorney.

coun·se·lor (koun′sə lər), *n.* **1.** one who counsels; an adviser. **2.** a faculty member, as in a high school, who advises students on personal and academic problems. **3.** one of a number of assistants at a children's camp, usually high-school or college students, who supervise the children and each of whom, usually, directs a particular activity, as nature study or a sport. **4.** a lawyer, esp. a trial lawyer; counselor-at-law. **5.** an official of an embassy or legation who ranks below an ambassador or minister. Also, *esp. Brit.,* **coun′sel·lor.** [ME *counseiler* < AF < OF *conseilleor.* See COUNSEL, -OR[2]] —**coun′se·lor·ship′;** *esp. Brit.,* **coun′sel·lor·ship′,** *n.*
—**Syn. 4.** counsel, advocate, attorney.

coun·se·lor-at-law (koun′sə lər ət lô′), *n., pl.* **coun·se·lors-at-law.** counselor (def. 4).

count[1] (kount), *v.t.* **1.** to check over (the separate units or groups of a collection) one by one to determine their total number; enumerate: *He counted his tickets and found he had ten. We counted the people in the theater.* **2.** to reckon up; calculate; compute. **3.** to list or name the numerals up to: *He counted five fingers on each hand.* **4.** to include in a reckoning; take into account: *Count me in if you want to know how many are going.* **5.** to reckon to the credit of another; ascribe; impute. **6.** to consider or regard: *He counted himself lucky to have survived the crash.* —*v.i.* **7.** to count the items of a collection one by one in order to know the total: *She counted three times before she was satisfied that none was missing.* **8.** to list or name numerals in order: *Count up to 100 by fives.* **9.** to reckon numerically. **10.** to have a specified numerical value. **11.** to be accounted or worth something: *This book counts as a masterpiece. This box of groceries counts for 500 trading stamps.* **12.** to have merit, importance, value, etc.; deserve consideration: *Every bit of help counts.* **13.** to have worth; amount (usually fol. by *for*): *Intelligence counts for something.* **14. count down,** to count backward, usually by ones, from a given integer to zero. **15. count off,** (often used imperatively, as in the army) to count aloud by turns, as to arrange positions within a group of persons; divide or become divided into groups: *Close up ranks and count off from the left by threes.* **16. count on** or **upon,** to depend or rely on: *You can always count on him to lend you money.* **17. count out, a.** *Boxing.* to declare (a boxer) a loser because of inability to stand up before the referee has counted 10 seconds. **b.** to disqualify (ballots) illegally in counting, in order to control the election. **c.** to exclude: *When it comes to flag-pole sitting, count me out.* —*n.* **18.** the act of counting; enumeration; reckoning; calculation: *A count of hands showed 23 in favor and 16 opposed.* **19.** the number representing the result of a process of counting; the total number. **20.** an accounting. **21.** *Baseball.* the number of balls and strikes, usually designated in that order, that have been called on a batter during his turn at bat: *a count of two balls and one strike; a count of two and one; a full count.* **22.** *Law.* a distinct charge or theory of action in a declaration or indictment: *The defendant was found guilty on two of the three counts contained in the grand jury's indictment.* **23.** *Textiles.* **a.** a number representing the size or quality of yarn, esp. the number based on the relation of weight to length of the yarn and indicating its degree of coarseness. **b.** the number of warp and filling threads per inch in woven material, representing the texture of the fabric. **24.** *Bowling.* the number of pins struck down by the first ball rolled by a bowler in the frame following a spare and included in the score for the frame in which the spare was made. **25.** *Physics.* **a.** a single ionizing reaction registered by an ionization chamber, as in a Geiger counter. **b.** the indication of the total number of ionizing reactions registered by an ionization chamber in a given period of time. **26.** *Archaic.* regard; notice. **27. the count,** *Boxing.* the calling aloud by the referee of the seconds from 1 to 10 while a downed boxer remains off his feet. Completion of the count signifies a knockout, which the referee then declares: *In the eighth round, a series of hard rights finally sent him down for the count.* Also, **the full count.** —*adj.* **28.** noting a number of items determined by an actual count: *The box is labeled 50 count.* [ME *count(en)* < AF *counte(r),* equiv. to MF *conter* < L *computāre* to COMPUTE]

count[2] (kount), *n.* (in some European countries) a nobleman equivalent in rank to an English earl. [< AF *counte* < MF *conte, comte* < L *comitem* (acc. of *comes* companion), lit., he who goes with (someone), equiv. to *com-* COM- + *-it(us),* ptp. of *īre* to go + *-em* acc. ending]

count·a·ble (koun′tə bəl), *adj.* **1.** able to be counted. **2.** *Math.* **a.** (of a set) having a finite number of elements. **b.** (of a set) having elements that form a one-to-one correspondence with the natural numbers; denumerable; enumerable. [COUNT[1] + -ABLE] —**count′a·ble·ness,** *n.* —**count′a·bly,** *adv.*

count′ably ad′ditive func′tion, *Math.* a set function that upon operating on the union of a countable number of disjoint sets gives the same result as the sum of the functional values of each set. Cf. **finitely additive function.**

count′ably compact′ set′, *Math.* a set for which every cover consisting of a countable number of sets has a subcover consisting of a finite number of sets.

count·down (kount′doun′), *n.* the final check prior to the firing of a missile, detonation of an explosive, or the like, with the precise moment of firing or detonation designated as zero, the days, hours, minutes, and seconds are counted backward from the initiation of the project. [n. use of v. phrase *count down*]

coun·te·nance (koun′tᵊnəns), *n., v.,* **-nanced, -nanc·ing.** —*n.* **1.** appearance, esp. the look or expression of the face: *a sad countenance.* **2.** the face; visage. **3.** calm facial expression; composure. **4.** approval or favor; encouragement; moral support. **5.** *Obs.* bearing; behavior. **6. out of countenance,** visibly disconcerted; abashed: *He was somewhat out of countenance at the prospect of an apology.* —*v.t.* **7.** to permit or tolerate: *She should not have countenanced his rudeness.* **8.** to approve, support, or encourage. [ME *cuntenaunce* behavior, bearing, self-control < AF (OF *contenance*) < L *continentia;* see CONTINENCE] —**coun′te·nanc′er,** *n.*
—**Syn. 2.** See **face. 4.** assistance, sanction, approbation. **7.** abet, patronize, sanction, approve.

count·er[1] (koun′tər), *n.* **1.** a table or display case on which goods can be shown, business transacted, etc., the seller and buyer usually being on opposite sides of it. **2.** (in restaurants, lunchrooms, etc.) a long, narrow table with stools or chairs along one side for the patrons, behind which refreshments or meals are prepared and served. **3.** a surface for the preparation of food in a kitchen, esp. on a low cabinet. **4.** anything used in keeping account, as a disk of metal, ivory, wood, or other material used in some games, as checkers. **5.** an imitation coin or token. **6.** a coin; money. **7. over the counter, a.** (of the sale of stock) through a broker's office rather than through the stock exchange. **b.** (of the sale of merchandise) through a retail store rather than through a wholesaler. **8. under the counter,** in a clandestine manner, esp. illegally: *The banned book was sold under the counter.* [ME *countour* < AF (MF *comptoir*) < ML *computātōr(ium)* place for computing, equiv. to L *computāt(us)* computed (ptp. of *computāre*) + *-ōrium* -ORY[2]; see COUNT[1], COMPUTE]

count·er[2] (koun′tər), *n.* **1.** one who counts. **2.** a device for counting revolutions of a wheel, items produced, etc. **3.** *Electronics.* scaler (def. 2). **4.** *Physics.* an instrument for detecting ionizing radiations and for registering counts. Cf. **Geiger counter.** [ME *countour* < AF (MF *conteor*) < L *computātor.* See COMPUTE, -OR[2]]

coun·ter[3] (koun′tər), *adv.* **1.** in the wrong way; contrary to the right course; in the reverse direction. **2.** contrary; in opposition (usually prec. by *run* or *go*): *to run counter to the rules.* —*adj.* **3.** opposite; opposed; contrary. —*n.* **4.** something that is opposite or contrary to something else. **5.** a blow delivered in receiving or parrying another blow, as in boxing. **6.** *Fencing.* a circular parry. **7.** *Naut.* the part of a stern that overhangs and projects aft of the sternpost of a vessel. **8.** Also called **void.** *Typography.* any part of the face of a type that is less than type-high and is therefore not inked. **9.** a piece of leather or other material inserted between the lining and outside leather of a shoe or boot quarter to keep it stiff. **10.** the part of a horse's breast that lies between the shoulders and under the neck. **11.** *Engineering, Building Trades.* a truss member subject to stress only under certain partial loadings of the truss. —*v.t.* **12.** to meet or answer (a move, blow, etc.) by another in return. **13.** to go counter to; oppose; controvert. —*v.i.* **14.** to make a counter or opposing move. **15.** to give a blow while receiving or parrying one, as in boxing. [late ME *countre* < AF (MF *contre*) < L *contrā* against. See COUNTER-]

coun·ter[4] (koun′tər), *v.t. Obs.* to encounter in opposition or combat. [ME *countre,* aph. var. of *acountre* < MF *acontre* (n.), *acontrer* (v.). See A-[5], ENCOUNTER]

counter-, a combining form of **counter**[3]: *counteract.* [ME *countre-* < AF (MF *contre*) < L *contrā* against]

coun·ter·ac·cu·sa·tion (koun′tər ak′yo͞o zā′shən), *n.* an accusation made in response to an accusation. [COUNTER- + ACCUSATION]

coun·ter·act (koun′tər akt′), *v.t.* to act in opposition to; frustrate by contrary action. [COUNTER- + ACT] —**coun′ter·act′er, coun′ter·ac′tor,** *n.* —**coun′ter·act′ing·ly,** *adv.* —**coun′ter·ac′tion,** *n.* —**coun′ter·ac′tive,** *adj.* —**coun′ter·ac′tive·ly,** *adv.*
—**Syn.** neutralize, counterbalance, contravene, thwart, check, countervail. —**Ant.** support.

coun′ter apse′, an apse situated at the end of a church opposite that of the principal apse.

coun·ter·ar·gu·ment (koun′tər är′gyə mənt), *n.* a contrasting, opposing, or refuting argument. [COUNTER- + ARGUMENT]

coun·ter·at·tack (*n.* koun′tər ə tak′; *v.* koun′tər ə tak′), *n.* **1.** an attack made as an offset or reply to another attack. **2.** *Mil.* an attack by a ground combat unit to stop and drive back an enemy attack. —*v.t., v.i.* **3.** to deliver a counterattack. [COUNTER- + ATTACK]

coun·ter·at·trac·tion (koun′tər ə trak′shən), *n.* a rival or opposite attraction. [COUNTER- + ATTRACTION] —**coun′ter·at·trac′tive,** *adj.* —**coun′ter·at·trac′tive·ly,** *adv.*

coun·ter·bal·ance (*n.* koun′tər bal′əns; *v.* koun′tər bal′əns), *n., v.,* **-anced, -anc·ing.** —*n.* **1.** a weight balancing another weight; an equal weight, power, or influence acting in opposition; counterpoise. —*v.t., v.i.* **2.** to act against or oppose with an equal weight, force, or influence; offset. [COUNTER- + BALANCE]

coun·ter·blast (koun′tər blast′, -bläst′), *n.* an unrestrained and vigorously powerful response to an attacking statement. [COUNTER- + BLAST]

coun·ter·blow (koun′tər blō′), *n.* a blow given in retaliation, as in boxing. Also called **counterpunch.** [COUNTER- + BLOW[1]]

coun·ter·bore (koun′tər bōr′, -bôr′; koun′tər bōr′, -bôr′), *n., v.,* **-bored, -bor·ing.** —*n.* **1.** a tool for enlarging a drilled hole for a portion of its length, as to permit sinking of a screw head. **2.** the portion of the hole so enlarged. —*v.t.* **3.** to enlarge (a drilled hole) along part of its length by drilling with a bit having a diameter greater than that of the hole. [COUNTER- + BORE[1]] —**coun′ter·bor′er,** *n.*

coun·ter·boulle (koun′tər bo͞ol′), *n.* contre-partie. [COUNTER- + BOULLE]

coun·ter·brace (koun′tər brās′), *n. Engineering, Building Trades.* a web member of a truss subject to tension or compression under varying conditions. [COUNTER- + BRACE]

coun·ter·brac·ing (koun′tər brā′sing), *n.* a system of counterbraces. [COUNTER- + BRACING]

coun·ter·brand (koun′tər brand′), *n.* a brand put on an animal that replaces the original brand. [COUNTER- + BRAND]

coun·ter·change (koun′tər chānj′), *v.t.,* **-changed, -chang·ing. 1.** to cause to change places, qualities, etc.; interchange. **2.** to diversify; checker. [COUNTER- + CHANGE]

coun·ter·changed (koun′tər chānjd′), *adj. Heraldry.* (of a charge or charges on a parted escutcheon of two tinctures) having the same tincture as that of an area adjacent to its own; countercolored: *quarterly argent and gules, a cross counterchanged.*

coun·ter·charge (*n.* koun′tər chärj′; *v.* koun′tər chärj′), *n., v.,* **-charged, -charg·ing.** —*n.* **1.** a charge by an accused person against his accuser. **2.** *Mil.* a retaliatory charge. —*v.t.* **3.** to make an accusation against (one's accuser). **4.** *Mil.* to charge in retaliation. [COUNTER- + CHARGE]

count′er check′, a blank check available in a bank for the use of a depositor in making a withdrawal from that bank.

coun·ter·check (*n.* koun′tər chek′; *v.* koun′tər chek′), *n.* **1.** a check that opposes or restrains. **2.** a check controlling or confirming another check. —*v.t.* **3.** to oppose or restrain (a tendency, force, trend, etc.) by contrary action. **4.** to control or confirm by a second check. [COUNTER- + CHECK]

coun·ter·claim (*n.* koun′tər klām′; *v.* koun′tər klām′), *n.* **1.** a claim made to offset another claim, esp. one made by the defendant in a legal action. —*v.t., v.i.* **2.** to claim so as to offset a previous claim. [COUNTER- + CLAIM] —**coun′ter·claim′ant,** *n.*

coun·ter·clock·wise (koun′tər klok′wīz′), *adj., adv.* in a direction opposite to that of the normal rotation of the hands of a clock; not clockwise. Also, **contraclockwise.** [COUNTER- + CLOCKWISE]

coun·ter·col·ored (koun′tər kul′ərd), *adj. Heraldry.* counterchanged. [COUNTER- + COLORED]

coun·ter·cul·ture (koun′tər kul′chər), *n.* the culture of those people, esp. among the young, who reject the traditional values and behavior of society. —**coun′ter·cul′tur·al,** *adj.*

coun·ter·cur·rent (koun′tər kûr′ənt), *n.* a current running in an opposite direction to another current. [COUNTER- + CURRENT] —**coun′ter·cur′rent·ly,** *adv.*

coun·ter·dec·la·ra·tion (koun′tər dek′lə rā′shən), *n.* a declaration that opposes another declaration. [COUNTER- + DECLARATION]

coun·ter·dem·on·stra·tion (koun′tər dem′ən strā′shən), *n.* a demonstration intended to offset the effect of a preceding demonstration. [COUNTER- + DEMONSTRATION]

coun·ter-earth (koun′tər ûrth′), *n.* (in Pythagorean astronomy) a planet, out of sight from our part of the earth, whose shadow upon the sun and moon, cast by a central fire which is also out of sight, causes the eclipses. Also called **antichthon.**

coun′ter electromo′tive force′, *Elect.* an electromotive force that is created by a chemical or magnetic effect upon a circuit and that acts in opposition to the applied electromotive force of the circuit. Also called **back electromotive force.**

coun·ter·es·pi·o·nage (koun′tər es′pē ə näzh′, -nij), *n.* the detection and frustration of enemy espionage. [COUNTER- + ESPIONAGE]

coun·ter·fac·tu·al (koun′tər fak′cho͞o əl), *n. Logic.* a conditional statement the first clause of which expresses something contrary to fact, as "If I had known." [COUNTER- + FACTUAL] —**coun′ter·fact′,** *n.* —**coun′ter·fac′tu·al·ly,** *adv.*

coun·ter·feit (koun′tər fit′), *adj.* **1.** made in imitation to be passed off fraudulently or deceptively as genuine; not genuine; forged: *counterfeit dollar bills.* **2.** pretended; unreal: *counterfeit grief.* —*n.* **3.** an imitation intended to be passed off as genuine; forgery. **4.** *Archaic.* a copy. **5.** *Archaic.* a close likeness; portrait. **6.** *Obs.* impostor; pretender. —*v.t.* **7.** to make a counterfeit of; imitate fraudulently; forge. **8.** to resemble. **9.** to simulate. —*v.i.* **10.** to make counterfeits, as of money. **11.** to feign; dissemble. [ME *countrefeten* (v.), *countrefet* (adj.), var. of *contrefet* false, forged < MF *contrefait,* ptp. of *contrefaire* to copy, imitate, equiv. to *contre-* COUNTER- + *faire* to make, do < L *facere*] —**coun′ter·feit′er,** *n.* —**coun′ter·feit′ly,** *adv.* —**coun′ter·feit′ness,** *n.*
—**Syn. 1.** spurious, bogus. See **false. 2.** sham, feigned, simulated, fraudulent; mock, fake, ersatz. **3.** falsification, sham. **7.** copy; falsify. —**Ant. 1.** genuine.

Counterfeiters, The, a novel (1926) by André Gide. French, **Les Faux-Monnayeurs.**

coun·ter·flash·ing (koun′tər flash′ing), *n. Building Trades.* flashing, as on a chimney, covering the upper edge of other flashing, as on a roof. [COUNTER- + FLASHING]

coun·ter·foil (koun′tər foil′), *n. Chiefly Brit.* a part of a bank check, money order, etc., which is kept by the issuer and on which a record of the transaction is made; stub. [COUNTER- + FOIL[2]]

coun·ter·force (koun′tər fōrs′, -fôrs′), *n.* a contrary or opposing force, tendency, etc. [COUNTER- + FORCE]

coun·ter·fort (koun′tər fōrt′, -fôrt′), *n.* **1.** a buttress, esp. one for strengthening a basement wall against the pressure of earth. **2.** a cantilevered weight, as in a retaining wall, having the form of a pier built on the side of the material to be retained. [partial trans. of OE *contrefort,* equiv. to *contre* COUNTER- + *fort* strength (deriv. of *fort* (adj.) strong)]

coun·ter·glow (koun′tər glō′), *n.* *Astron.* gegenschein. [trans. of G *Gegenschein.* See COUNTER-, GLOW]

coun′ter im′age, *Math.* See **inverse image.**

coun·ter·in·sur·gen·cy (koun′tər in sûr′jən sē), *n.* **1.** a program or an act of combating guerrilla warfare and subversion. —*adj.* **2.** of, pertaining to, or designed for combating guerrilla warfare and subversion. [COUNTER- + INSURGENCY]

coun·ter·in·sur·gent (koun′tər in sûr′jənt), *n.* **1.** a person who fights or is trained to fight guerrilla forces. —*adj.* **2.** counterinsurgency. [COUNTER- + INSURGENT]

coun·ter·in·tel·li·gence (koun′tər in tel′i jəns), *n.* **1.** the activity of an intelligence service employed in thwarting the efforts of an enemy's intelligence agents to gather information or commit sabotage. **2.** an organization engaged in counterintelligence. [COUNTER- + INTELLIGENCE]

coun·ter·i·on (koun′tər ī′ən, -ī′on), *n.* *Physical Chem.* an ion in solution that associates itself with an ion of opposite charge on the surface of a member of a solute. Also called **gegen-ion.** [COUNTER- + ION]

coun·ter·ir·ri·tant (koun′tər ir′i tənt), *Med.* —*n.* **1.** an agent for producing irritation in one part to counteract irritation or relieve pain or inflammation elsewhere. —*adj.* **2.** of or acting as a counterirritant. [COUNTER- + IRRITANT]

count·er·jump·er (koun′tər jum′pər), *n.* *Slang.* a clerk in a retail store. [COUNTER[1] + JUMPER[1]]

coun·ter·light (*v.* koun′tər līt′; *n.* koun′tər līt′), *v.*, **-light·ed** or **-lit, -light·ing,** *n.* —*v.t.* **1.** to light (an interior) with windows or lights on opposite sides. **2.** to light (an object) with a window or light directly opposite. —*n.* **3.** a light or window so placed as to counterlight an interior or object. Cf. **crosslight.** [COUNTER- + LIGHT[1]]

count·er·man (koun′tər man′), *n.*, *pl.* **-men.** a man who waits on customers from behind a counter, esp. as in a cafeteria or other eating place. [COUNTER[1] + MAN[1]]

coun·ter·mand (*v.* koun′tər mand′, -mänd′; *n.* koun′tər mand′, -mänd′), *v.t.* **1.** to revoke or cancel (a command, order, etc.). **2.** to recall or stop by a contrary order. —*n.* **3.** a command, order, etc., revoking a previous one. [late ME *countermaund(en)* < MF *contremande(r),* equiv. to *contre-* COUNTER + *mander* to command < L *mandāre;* see MANDATE] —**coun′ter·mand′a·ble,** *adj.*

coun·ter·man·i·fes·to (koun′tər man′ə fes′tō), *n.*, *pl.* **-toes.** a manifesto that opposes another manifesto. [COUNTER- + MANIFESTO]

coun·ter·march (*n.* koun′tər märch′; *v.* koun′tər-märch′), *n.* **1.** a march back over the same ground. **2.** a complete reversal of conduct or measures. —*v.i.* **3.** to turn about and march back along the same route; execute a countermarch. —*v.t.* **4.** to cause to countermarch. [COUNTER- + MARCH[1]]

coun·ter·mark (*n.* koun′tər märk′; *v.* koun′tər-märk′), *Numis.* —*n.* **1.** Also called **counterstamp.** a sign or device stamped on a coin after its minting. —*v.t.* **2.** to stamp (a coin) with a countermark; counterstamp. [< MF *contremarque* (> *contremarquer* (v.)), equiv. to *contre* COUNTER- + *marque* MARK[1]]

coun·ter·meas·ure (koun′tər mezh′ər), *n.* an opposing or retaliatory measure. [COUNTER- + MEASURE]

coun·ter·mine (*n.* koun′tər mīn′; *v.* koun′tər mīn′), *n.*, *v.*, **-mined, -min·ing.** —*n.* **1.** *Mil.* a mine intended to intercept or destroy an enemy mine. **2.** a counterplot. —*v.t.* **3.** to oppose by a countermine. —*v.i.* **4.** to make a countermine. **5.** *Mil.* to intercept or destroy enemy mines. [late ME; see COUNTER-, MINE[2]]

coun·ter·move (*n.* koun′tər mo͞ov′; *v.* koun′tər-mo͞ov′), *n.*, *v.*, **-moved, -mov·ing.** —*n.* **1.** an opposing or retaliatory move. —*v.t.*, *v.i.* **2.** to move in opposition or retaliation. [COUNTER- + MOVE] —**coun′ter·move′ment,** *n.*

coun·ter·of·fen·sive (koun′tər ə fen′siv), *n.* *Mil.* an attack by an army against an attacking enemy force. [COUNTER- + OFFENSIVE]

coun·ter·of·fer (koun′tər ô′fər, -of′ər, koun′tər ô′fər, -of′ər), *n.* an offer or proposal made to offset or substitute for a preceding one. [COUNTER- + OFFER]

coun·ter·pane (koun′tər pān′), *n.* a quilt or coverlet for a bed; bedspread. [COUNTER- + PANE (in obs. sense bedspread); r. late ME *counterpoynte* < MF *contre-pointe* quilt, alter. of *coute pointe* < L *culcita puncta* pricked pillow. See QUILT, POINT] —**coun′ter·paned′,** *adj.*

coun·ter·part (koun′tər pärt′), *n.* **1.** a copy; duplicate. **2.** a part that answers to another, as each part of a document executed in duplicate. **3.** one of two parts that fit, complete, or complement one another. **4.** a person or thing closely resembling another. [late ME; see COUNTER-, PART]

coun·ter-pas·sant (koun′tər pas′ənt), *adj.* *Heraldry.* (of two animals) represented as passant in pale in opposite directions: *two lions counter-passant.* [partial trans. of MF *contre-passant.* See COUNTER-, PASSANT]

coun·ter·plot (*n.*, *v.* koun′tər plot′; *v. also* koun′tər-plot′), *n.*, *v.*, **-plot·ted, -plot·ting.** —*n.* **1.** a plot directed against another plot. **2.** *Literature.* a secondary theme in a play or other literary work, used as a contrast to or variation of the main theme. Cf. **subplot.** —*v.i.* **3.** to devise a counterplot; plot in opposition. —*v.t.* **4.** to plot against (a plot or plotter); frustrate by a counterplot. [COUNTER- + PLOT[1]]

coun·ter·point (koun′tər point′), *n.* **1.** *Music.* the art of combining melodies. **2.** *Music.* the texture resulting from the combining of individual melodic lines. **3.** a melody composed to be combined with another melody. **4.** Also called **coun′terpoint rhythm′.** *Pros.* syncopation (def. 2). —*v.t.* **5.** to emphasize or clarify by contrast or juxtaposition. [late ME, appar. trans. of ML (*cantus*) *contrapunctus,* lit., (song) pricked against. See COUNTER-, POINT]

coun·ter·poise (koun′tər poiz′), *n.*, *v.*, **-poised, -pois·ing.** —*n.* **1.** a counterbalancing weight. **2.** any equal and opposing power or force. **3.** the state of being in equilibrium. **4.** *Radio.* a network of wires or other conductors connected to the base of an antenna, used as a substitute for the ground connection. —*v.t.* **5.** to balance by an opposing weight; counteract by an opposing force. **6.** to bring into equilibrium. **7.** *Archaic.* to weigh (one thing) against something else; consider carefully. [COUNTER- + POISE[1]; r. late ME *countrepets* < AF, equiv. to MF *contrepois*]

coun·ter·poi·son (koun′tər poi′zən), *n.* **1.** an agent for counteracting a poison; an antidote. **2.** a poison that counteracts another poison. [COUNTER- + POISON, modeled on MF *contrepoison*]

coun·ter·po·tent (koun′tər pōt′ənt), *n.* *Heraldry.* a fur similar to potent except that the potents of like tincture face both ways in pale. Cf. **potent**[2]. [COUNTER- + POTENT[2]]

coun·ter·pres·sure (koun′tər presh′ər), *n.* pressure in the opposite direction or with opposing intentions. [COUNTER- + PRESSURE]

coun·ter·proof (koun′tər pro͞of′), *n.* an impression taken from a fresh proof in order to study the progress on an engraved plate. [COUNTER- + -PROOF]

coun·ter·prop·a·gan·da (koun′tər prop′ə gan′də), *n.* propaganda to combat unfriendly or enemy propaganda. [COUNTER- + PROPAGANDA]

coun·ter·pro·pos·al (koun′tər prə pō′zəl), *n.* a proposal offered to offset or substitute for a preceding one. [COUNTER- + PROPOSAL]

coun·ter·prop·o·si·tion (koun′tər prop′ə zish′ən), *n.* a proposition made in place of or in opposition to a preceding one. [COUNTER- + PROPOSITION]

coun·ter·punch (koun′tər punch′), *n.* counterblow. [COUNTER- + PUNCH[1]]

coun·ter·ramp·ant (koun′tər ram′pənt), *adj.* *Heraldry.* (of two beasts) represented as rampant and facing each other; combatant: *two lions counter-rampant.*

Coun′ter Reforma′tion, the movement within the Roman Catholic Church that followed the Protestant Reformation of the 16th century.

coun·ter·ref·or·ma·tion (koun′tər ref′ər mā′shən), *n.* a reformation opposed to or counteracting a previous reformation. [COUNTER- + REFORMATION, modeled on G *Gegenreformation*]

coun·ter·re·ply (*n.* koun′tər ri plī′; *v.* koun′tər ri plī′), *n.*, *pl.* **-plies,** *v.*, **-plied, -ply·ing.** —*n.* **1.** a reply made in response to a reply; rejoinder. —*v.i.* **2.** to make a reply in response to a reply. —*v.t.* **3.** to reply with (a statement) in response to a reply. [COUNTER- + REPLY]

coun·ter·rev·o·lu·tion (koun′tər rev′ə lo͞o′shən), *n.* **1.** a revolution against a government recently established by a revolution. **2.** a political movement that resists revolutionary tendencies. [COUNTER- + REVOLUTION, modeled on F *contre-révolution*]

coun·ter·rev·o·lu·tion·ar·y (koun′tər rev′ə lo͞o′shə ner′ē), *adj.*, *n.*, *pl.* **-ar·ies.** —*n.* **1.** Also, **counterrevolutionist.** one who advocates or engages in a counterrevolution. —*adj.* **2.** characteristic of or resulting from a counterrevolution. **3.** opposing a revolution or revolutionary government.

coun·ter·ro·tat·ing (koun′tər rō′tā ting, koun′-), *adj.* *Mach.* (of two corresponding or similar moving parts) rotating in opposite directions: *counterrotating propellers.* [COUNTER- + ROTATING]

coun′terro′tating propel′ler. See **contrarotating propeller.**

coun·ter·sa·li·ent (koun′tər sā′lē ənt, -sāl′yənt), *adj.* *Heraldry.* (of two animals) represented back to back and leaping in opposite directions: *two lions countersalient.* [trans. of F *contre-saillant.* See COUNTER-, SALIENT]

coun·ter·scarp (koun′tər skärp′), *n.* *Fort.* **1.** the exterior slope or wall of the ditch of a fort, supporting the covered way. See diag. under **bastion.** **2.** this slope with the covered way and glacis. [COUNTER- + SCARP[1] (modeled on It *contrascarpa*); r. *counterscarfe;* see SCARF[2]]

coun·ter·shad·ing (koun′tər shā′ding), *n.* *Zool.* the development of dark colors on parts usually exposed to the sun and of light colors on parts usually shaded, esp. as serving for protection or concealment. [COUNTER- + SHADING]

coun·ter·shaft (koun′tər shaft′, -shäft′), *n.* jackshaft (def. 1). [COUNTER- + SHAFT] —**coun′ter·shaft′ing,** *n.*

coun·ter·sign (*n.*, *v.* koun′tər sīn′; *v. also* koun′tər-sīn′), *n.* **1.** *Mil.* a secret sign that must be given by authorized persons seeking admission through a guarded area. **2.** a sign used in reply to another sign. **3.** a signature added to another signature, esp. for authentication. —*v.t.* **4.** to sign (a document that has been signed by someone else), esp. in confirmation or authentication. [COUNTER- + SIGN, modeled on MF *contresigne,* or its source, OIt *contrasegno*]

coun·ter·sig·na·ture (koun′tər sig′nə chər), *n.* a signature added by way of countersigning. [COUNTER- (SIGN) + SIGNATURE]

coun·ter·sink (*v.*, *n.* koun′tər singk′; *v. also* koun′tər singk′), *v.*, **-sank, -sunk, -sink·ing,** *n.* —*v.t.* **1.** to enlarge the upper part of (a hole or cavity), esp. by chamfering, to receive the cone-shaped head of a screw, bolt, etc. **2.** to cause (the head of a screw, bolt, etc.) to sink into a prepared depression so as to be flush with or below the surface. —*n.* **3.** a tool for countersinking a hole. **4.** a countersunk hole. [COUNTER- + SINK]

coun·ter·spy (koun′tər spī′), *n.*, *pl.* **-spies.** a person who spies against or investigates spies of an enemy nation, competing organization, etc. [COUNTER- + SPY]

coun·ter·stain (*n.* koun′tər stān′; *v.* koun′tər stān′), *n.* **1.** a second stain of a different color applied to a microscopic specimen and used to color and contrast those parts not retaining the first stain. —*v.t.* **2.** to treat (a microscopic specimen) with a counterstain. —*v.i.* **3.** to become counterstained; take a counterstain. [COUNTER- + STAIN]

coun·ter·stamp (*n.* koun′tər stamp′; *v.* koun′tər-stamp′), *n.* **1.** a stamp added to a stamped paper or document as a qualifying mark. **2.** *Numis.* countermark (def. 1). —*v.t.* **3.** to stamp (a paper or document) already stamped. **4.** *Numis.* countermark (def. 2). [COUNTER- + STAMP]

coun·ter·state·ment (koun′tər stāt′mənt), *n.* a statement made to deny or refute another. [COUNTER- + STATEMENT]

coun′ter stern′, *Naut.* See **fantail stern.**

coun·ter·stroke (koun′tər strōk′), *n.* **1.** a stroke or blow given in return. **2.** *Med.* a contrecoup. [COUNTER- + STROKE[1]]

coun·ter·sub·ject (koun′tər sub′jikt), *n.* *Music.* a theme in a fugue that occurs simultaneously with the second and often the subsequent themes of the main subject. [COUNTER- + SUBJECT]

count′er ta′ble, a medieval English table having a top divided into appropriately marked spaces for various denominations of money.

coun·ter·tend·en·cy (koun′tər ten′dən sē), *n.*, *pl.* **-cies.** an opposing tendency. [COUNTER- + TENDENCY]

coun·ter·ten·or (koun′tər ten′ər), *n.* *Music.* **1.** an adult male voice or voice part higher than the tenor. **2.** a singer with such a voice; a high tenor. [ME *countreturnur,* appar. < AF; cf. MF *contreteneur,* OIt *contratenore.* See COUNTER-, TENOR]

coun·ter·thrust (koun′tər thrust′), *n.* a thrust made in opposition or return. [COUNTER- + THRUST]

coun·ter·trans·fer·ence (koun′tər trans fûr′əns, -trans′fer əns), *n.* *Psychoanal.* transference on the part of the analyst of the repressed feelings aroused by the analysand. [COUNTER- + TRANSFERENCE]

coun·ter·turn (koun′tər tûrn′), *n.* **1.** a turn in an opposing or contrary direction. **2.** an unexpected twist or turn of events in the plot of a story, play, or the like. [COUNTER- + TURN]

coun·ter·type (koun′tər tīp′), *n.* **1.** a corresponding type. **2.** an opposite type. [COUNTER- + TYPE]

coun·ter·vail (koun′tər vāl′), *v.t.* **1.** to act or avail against with equal power, force, or effect; counteract. **2.** to furnish an equivalent of or a compensation for; offset. **3.** *Archaic.* to equal. —*v.i.* **4.** to be of equal force in opposition; avail. [ME *contrevail(en)* (v.), late ME *countrevaile* (n.) < AF *countrevail-,* tonic s. (subj.) of *countrevaloir* < L phrase *contrā valēre* to be worth against. See COUNTER, -VALENT]
—**Syn. 1.** counterbalance, counterpoise, neutralize.

coun·ter·vair (koun′tər vâr′), *n.* *Heraldry.* a fur similar to vair except that forms of like tincture face both ways in pale. [COUNTER- + VAIR, modeled on F *contrevair*]

coun·ter·view (koun′tər vyo͞o′), *n.* an opposing or contrasting view or opinion. [COUNTER- + VIEW]

coun′ter wall′, a side wall of a house built to the property line but not serving as a party wall.

coun·ter·weigh (koun′tər wā′), *v.t.*, *v.i.* to counterbalance. [late ME *countrewey(en)*]

coun·ter·weight (koun′tər wāt′), *n.* a weight that equals or balances another; counterpoise. [COUNTER- + WEIGHT] —**coun′ter·weight′ed,** *adj.*

coun′terweight sys′tem, *Theat.* a rigging system by which counterweighted scenery, curtains, etc., suspended from the gridiron are raised and lowered.

coun·ter·word (koun′tər wûrd′), *n.* a word that has come to be used with a meaning much less specific than that which it had originally, as *swell, awful,* or *terrific.* [COUNTER[1] + WORD]

coun·ter·work (*n.* koun′tər wûrk′; *v.* koun′tər-wûrk′), *n.* **1.** work or action to oppose some other work or action. —*v.i.* **2.** to work in opposition. —*v.t.* **3.** to work in opposition to; hinder or frustrate. [COUNTER- + WORK] —**coun′ter·work′er,** *n.*

count·ess (koun′tis), *n.* **1.** the wife or widow of a count in the nobility of Continental Europe or of an earl in the British peerage. **2.** a woman having the rank of a count or earl in her own right. [ME *c(o)untesse* < AF. See COUNT[2], -ESS]

count′ing house′, *Chiefly Brit.* a building or office used by the accounting and bookkeeping department of a business.

count′ing num′ber, *Arith.* a positive integer or zero.

count′ing room′, a room used as a counting house.

count·less (kount′lis), *adj.* too numerous to count; innumerable: *the countless stars.* [COUNT[1] + -LESS]

count′ noun′, *Gram.* a noun that typically refers to a countable thing and that in English can be used with the indefinite article and in the plural, as *apple, table, birthday.* Cf. **mass noun.**

Count′ of Mon′te Cris′to, The (mon′tē kris′tō), a novel (1884–45) by Alexandre Dumas *père.* French, **Le Comte de Monte-Cristo.**

count′ pal′atine, *pl.* **counts palatine. 1.** (formerly, in Germany) a count having jurisdiction in his fief or province. **2.** Also called **earl palatine.** *Eng. Hist.* an earl or other county proprietor who exercised royal prerogatives within his county.

coun·tri·fied (kun′tri fīd′), *adj.* rustic or rural in appearance, conduct, etc.: *a countrified person; a countrified stretch of land.* Also, **countryfied.** [*countrify* (COUNTRY + -FY) + -ED[2]] —**coun′tri·fied′ness,** *n.*

coun·try (kun′trē), *n.*, *pl.* **-tries,** *adj.* —*n.* **1.** a tract of land considered apart from geographical or political limits; region; district. **2.** any considerable territory demarcated by topographical conditions, by a distinctive population, etc.: *mountainous country; the Amish country of Pennsylvania.* **3.** the territory of a nation. **4.** a state. **5.** the people of a district, state, or nation: *The whole country backed the President in his decision.* **6.** the public. **7.** *Law.* the public at large, as represented by a jury. **8.** the land of one's birth or citizenship. **9.** rural districts, as opposed to cities or towns: *Many Easterners spend the summer in the country and the winter in the city.* **10.** *Naut.* an area of a vessel reserved for a certain group of persons: *officer country; steerage country.* **11. go to the country,** *Brit.* to dissolve a Parliament that has cast a majority vote disagreeing with the Prime Minister and cabinet and to call for the election of a new House of Commons. **12. put oneself upon the** (or **one's**) **country,** *Law.* to present one's cause formally before a jury. —*adj.* **13.** of the country; rural: *a winding country road.* **14.** rude; unpolished; rustic: *country manners.* **15.** of a country. **16.** *Dial.* of one's own country. [ME *cuntree* < OF < LL *contrāta,* lit., that which is opposite, hence landscape, equiv. to L *contr(ā)* against, opposite + *-āta,* fem. of *-ātus* -ATE[1]]

coun·try-and-west·ern (kun′trē ən wes′tərn), *n.* a generally simple and straightforward style of music native to the southern U.S., derived from folk music, cowboy songs, spirituals, and blues, and played chiefly on stringed instruments, as guitar, banjo, and fiddle, often electronically amplified. Also called **country music.**

coun·try-bred (kun′trē bred′), *adj.* raised or bred in the country.

coun′try club′, a club, usually in a suburban district, with a clubhouse and grounds, offering various social activities and having facilities for tennis, golf, swimming, etc.

coun′try cous′in, a person from the country, to whom the sights and activities of a large city are novel and bewildering.

coun·try-dance (kun′trē dans′, -däns′), *n.* a dance of rural English origin in which the dancers form circles or squares or in which they face each other in two rows.

coun·try·fied (kun′tri fīd′), *adj.* countrified. —**coun′try·fied′ness,** *n.*

coun·try·folk (kun′trē fōk′), *n.* **1.** people living or raised in the country; rustics. **2.** people from the same country; compatriots. Also called **countrypeople.** [COUNTRY + FOLK]

coun′try gen′tleman, a wealthy man living in his country home or estate.

coun′try house′, a house, usually large and impressive, on an estate in the country.

coun·try·man (kun′trē mən), *n., pl.* **-men.** **1.** a native or inhabitant of one's own country. **2.** a native or inhabitant of a particular region. **3.** a person who lives in the country. [ME *contre man.* See COUNTRY, MAN[1]] —**Syn. 1.** compatriot, fellow citizen. **3.** rustic, farmer, peasant. —**Ant. 1.** foreigner.

coun′try mile′, a long distance: *He can hit a baseball a country mile.*

coun′try mu′sic, country-and-western.

coun·try·peo·ple (kun′trē pē′pəl), *n.* countryfolk. [COUNTRY + PEOPLE]

coun′try rock′, *Geol.* the rock surrounding and penetrated by mineral veins or igneous intrusions.

coun·try·seat (kun′trē sēt′), *n. Brit.* a country mansion or estate, esp. one belonging to a distinguished family and large enough to accommodate house parties, hunt meetings, etc. [COUNTRY + SEAT[2]]

coun·try·side (kun′trē sīd′), *n.* **1.** a particular section of a country, esp. a rural section. **2.** its inhabitants. [COUNTRY + SIDE[1]]

coun′try store′, a general store, esp. one that caters to the tourists in a resort area.

coun′try wal′lah, *Naut. Slang.* a sailing ship having largely the appearance and rig of a European vessel but built in India by natives and manned by native crews.

coun·try-wide (kun′trē wīd′), *adj.* extending across the whole country: *a country-wide reaction.* Also, **coun′try·wide′.** [COUNTRY + WIDE]

coun·try·wom·an (kun′trē wo͝om′ən), *n., pl.* **-wom·en.** **1.** a woman who is a native or inhabitant of one's own country. **2.** a woman who lives in the country. [late ME; see COUNTRY, WOMAN]

count·ship (kount′ship), *n.* **1.** the rank or position of a count. **2.** the territory or jurisdiction of a count. [COUNT[2] + -SHIP]

coun·ty[1] (koun′tē), *n., pl.* **-ties.** **1.** *U.S.* an administrative division of a State. **2.** one of the chief administrative divisions of a country or state, as in Great Britain and Ireland. **3.** one of the larger divisions for purposes of local administration, as in Canada and New Zealand. **4.** the inhabitants of a county. **5.** *Obs.* the domain of a count or earl. [ME *counte* < AF (MF *comte*) < L *comitāt(us)* retinue, in LL: office of a count, whence jurisdiction, territory, equiv. to *comitāt-* (ptp. s. of *comitārī* to go with, deriv. of *comes* companion) + *-us* n. suffix (4th decl.)]

coun·ty[2] (koun′tē), *n. Obs.* count[2]. [< AF *counte* COUNT[2]; -*y*, by confusion with COUNTY[1]]

coun′ty a′gent, *U.S.* a governmental official employed chiefly to advise farmers on farming and marketing techniques and to promote educational programs fitted to the needs of rural people. Also called **agricultural agent.**

coun′ty board′, *U.S.* the governing body of a county consisting usually of three or more elected members.

coun′ty clerk′, *U.S.* an elective county official in most States who generally keeps records of property titles, distributes ballots, issues licenses, etc.

coun′ty col′lege, (in England) a part-time continuation school with compulsory attendance for boys and girls from 15 to 18 years of age, created under the Education Act (1944).

coun′ty commis′sioner, *U.S.* one of the members of a county board who administers the collection and disbursement of funds and other affairs of the county.

coun′ty court′, **1.** *U.S.* **a.** an administrative board in counties in some States. **b.** a judicial tribunal in some States with jurisdiction extending over one or more counties. **2.** (in England) **a.** the lowest civil tribunal, having limited jurisdiction, mostly for the recovery of small debts. **b.** (formerly) the assembly of local residents who met periodically in each county under the presidency of the sheriff to transact the judicial and administrative business of the county.

coun′ty fair′, a competitive exhibition of farm products, livestock, etc., often held annually in the same place in the county.

coun′ty farm′, a farm maintained for the poor by a county.

coun′ty home′, a county poorhouse. Also called **coun′ty house′.**

coun′ty pal′atine, *pl.* **counties palatine.** the territory under the jurisdiction of a count palatine.

coun′ty seat′, the seat of government of a county. Also called **coun′ty town′.**

coup[1] (ko͞o), *n., pl.* **coups** (ko͞oz; *Fr.* ko͞o). a highly successful stroke, act, or move; a clever action or accomplishment. [< F: lit., blow, stroke, OF *colp* < LL *colp(us),* L *colaphus* < Gk *kólaphos*]

coup[2] (kōp, ko͞op), *Scot.* —*v.t.* **1.** to turn (something) upside down; upset. —*v.i.* **2.** to fall over; capsize; spill. [ME *coupe* to pay for < Scand; cf. Icel *kaupa* to buy, barter; c. OE *cēapian,* G *kaufen,* etc. See CHEAP]

coup de grace (ko͞odᵊ gräs′), *pl.* **coups de grace** (ko͞odᵊ gräs′). *French.* **1.** a death blow, esp. one delivered mercifully to end suffering. **2.** any finishing or decisive stroke. [lit., blow of mercy]

coup de main (ko͞odᵊ maN′), *pl.* **coups de main** (ko͞odᵊ maN′). *French.* a surprise attack; a sudden development. [lit., blow from the hand]

coup de maî·tre (ko͞odᵊ me′trᵊ), *pl.* **coups de maî·tre** (ko͞odᵊ me′trᵊ). *French.* a master stroke.

coup de plume (ko͞odᵊ plYm′), *pl.* **coups de plume** (ko͞odᵊ plYm′). *French.* a literary attack; satire. [lit., stroke of the pen]

coup de poing (*Fr.* ko͞odᵊ pwaN′), *pl.* **coups de poing** (*Fr.* ko͞odᵊ pwaN′). *Archaeol.* a paleolithic tool of stone, held in the hand and having an axlike striking edge. [< F: lit., blow from the fist]

coup d'es·sai (ko͞o de se′), *pl.* **coups d'es·sai** (ko͞o de se′). *French.* a first attempt. [lit., (a) trial stroke]

coup d'é·tat (ko͞o′ dā tä′; *Fr.* ko͞o dā tA′), *pl.* **coups d'é·tat** (ko͞oz′ dā tä′; *Fr.* ko͞o dā tA′). a sudden and decisive action in politics, esp. one effecting a change of government illegally or by force. [< F: lit., stroke concerning the state]

coup de thé·â·tre (ko͞odᵊ tā ä′trᵊ), *pl.* **coups de thé·â·tre** (ko͞odᵊ tā ä′trᵊ). *French.* **1.** a surprising or unexpected turn of events in a play. **2.** a sensational and unexpected turn in the plot of a drama. **3.** any theatrical trick intended to have a sensational effect. [lit., stroke concerning the theater]

coup d'oeil (ko͞o dœ′yᵊ), *pl.* **coups d'oeil** (ko͞o dœ′yᵊ). *French.* a quick glance. [lit., stroke of the eye]

coupe[1] (ko͞op), *n.* **1.** Also, **coupé.** a closed, two-door automobile with a body shorter than that of a sedan of the same model. **2.** coupé (defs. 1–3). [see COUPÉ]

coupe[2] (ko͞op), *n.* **1.** ice cream or ice mixed or topped with fruit, liqueur, whipped cream, etc. **2.** a glass container for serving such a dessert, usually having a stem and a wide, deep bowl. **3.** any rimless plate. [ME < OF *coupe* < LL *cupp(a)* cup]

cou·pé (ko͞o pā′ *or, for 1, 5,* ko͞op), *n.* **1.** a short, four-wheeled, closed carriage, usually with a single seat for two passengers and with an outside seat for the driver. **2.** the end compartment in a European diligence or railroad car. **3.** *Ballet.* an intermediary step to transfer the weight from one foot to the other. **4.** (in Continental heraldry) party per fess. **5.** coupe[1] (def. 1). Also, **coupe** (for defs. 1–3). [< F *coupé,* short for *carrosse coupé* cut (i.e., shortened) coach; see COUPED]

couped (ko͞opt), *adj. Heraldry.* **1.** (of a charge) cut off square so as not to touch the edge of the escutcheon: *a cross couped.* **2.** (of part of an animal) represented as cut off from the rest of the body with an even line: *a demi-lion couped.* Cf. **erased** (def. 2). [< F *coup(é)* cut off (ptp. of *couper*) + -ED[2]]

Cou·pe·rin (ko͞opᵊ RaN′), *n.* **Fran·çois** (fRäN swA′), ("*Couperin the Grand*"), 1668–1733, French organist, harpsichordist, and composer.

Cou·pe·rus (ko͞o pā′rəs), *n.* **Lou·is** (lo͞o ē′), 1863–1923, Dutch novelist.

cou·ple (kup′əl), *n., v.,* **-pled, -pling.** —*n.* **1.** a combination of two; a pair. **2.** two of the same sort connected or considered together. **3.** two persons of opposite sex considered together, as a married or engaged pair, lovers, dance partners, etc.: *They make a handsome couple.* **4.** *Mech.* a pair of equal, parallel forces acting in opposite directions and tending to produce rotation. **5.** Also called **couple-close.** a pair of rafters connected by a tie beam or collar beam. **6.** a leash for holding two hounds together. **7.** *Fox Hunting.* two hounds: *25 hounds or 12½ couple.* **8. a couple of,** *Informal.* more than two, but not many, of; a small number of: *It will take a couple of days to get there.* —*v.t.* **9.** to fasten, link, or associate together in a pair or pairs. **10.** to join; connect. **11.** to unite in marriage or in sexual union. **12.** *Radio.* to join or associate by means of a coupler. —*v.i.* **13.** to join in a pair; unite. **14.** to copulate. [ME < MF < L *copula* a tie, bond. See COPULA] —**Syn. 1.** See **pair.**

cou·ple-close (kup′əl klōs′), *n.* **1.** *Heraldry.* a narrow chevron, one quarter the usual breadth. **2.** couple (def. 5).

cou′pled roof′, a double-pitched roof having a narrow span and often depending upon the mass of the walls rather than upon tie beams or collar beams to resist its outward thrust.

cou·ple·ment (kup′əl mənt), *n. Obs.* the act or result of coupling; union. [< MF; see COUPLE, -MENT]

cou·pler (kup′lər), *n.* **1.** one who or that which couples or links together. **2.** a device in an organ or harpsichord for connecting keys, manuals, or a manual and pedals, so that they are played together when one is played. **3.** *Radio.* a device for transferring electrical energy from one circuit to another, as a transformer which joins parts of a radio apparatus together by induction. **4.** *Mach.* a rod or link transmitting force and motion between a rotating part and a rotating or oscillating part. **5.** (in color photography) a chemical that reacts with the developer to produce one of the colors in a print or transparency. **6.** Also called **coupling.** *Railroads.* a device for joining pieces of rolling stock. [COUPLE + -ER[1]]

cou·plet (kup′lit), *n.* **1.** a pair of successive lines of verse, esp. a pair that rhyme and are of the same length. **2.** a pair; couple. **3.** *Music.* any of the contrasting sections of a rondo occurring between statements of the refrain. [< MF; see COUPLE, -ET]

cou·pling (kup′ling), *n.* **1.** the act of one who or that which couples. **2.** *Mach.* **a.** a device for joining two rotating shafts semipermanently at their ends so as to transmit torque from one to the other. Cf. **clutch[1]** (def. 12a). **b.** a part with an inside thread for connecting two pipes of the same diameter. **c.** a fitting at the end of a length of hose into which the end of another such length can be screwed or fitted. **3.** *Railroads.* coupler (def. 6). **4.** *Elect.* **a.** the association of two circuits or systems in such a way that power may be transferred from one to the other. **b.** a device or expedient to insure this. **5.** a short length of plumbing pipe having each end threaded on the inside. **6.** the part of the body between the tops of the shoulder blades and the tops of the hip joints in a dog, horse, etc. [ME; see COUPLE, -ING[1]]

cou·pon (ko͞o′pon, kyo͞o′-), *n.* **1.** a portion of a certificate, ticket, label, advertisement, or the like, set off from the main body by dotted lines or the like to emphasize its separability, entitling the holder to something, as a gift or discount, or for use as an order blank, a contest entry form, etc. **2.** a separate certificate, ticket, etc., for the same purpose. **3.** one of a number of small certificates calling for periodical interest payments on a bond. Cf. **coupon bond.** **4.** *Metall.* a sample of metal or metalwork submitted to a customer or testing agency for approval. **5.** *Brit. Slang.* a party leader's official endorsement of a parliamentary candidate. [< F, OF *colpon* piece cut off, equiv. to *colp(er)* (to) cut (see COPE[1]) + *-on* n. suffix] —**cou′pon·less,** *adj.*

cou′pon bond′, a bond which pays interest by means of coupons with specific cash values.

cou′pon clip′per, a well-to-do person whose main work consists of clipping and cashing coupons from coupon bonds.

cour·age (kûr′ij, kur′-), *n.* **1.** the quality of mind or spirit that enables one to face difficulty, danger, pain, etc., with firmness and without fear; bravery. **2.** *Obs.* the heart as the source of emotion. **3. have the courage of one's convictions,** to act in accordance with one's beliefs, esp. in spite of criticism. [ME *corage* < OF, equiv. to *cuer* heart (< L *cor*) + *-age* -AGE]
—**Syn. 1.** fearlessness, dauntlessness, intrepidity, fortitude, pluck, spirit, heroism, daring, audacity, hardihood, gallantry. COURAGE, BRAVERY, VALOR, BRAVADO refer to qualities of spirit and conduct. COURAGE permits one to face extreme dangers and difficulties without fear: *to take (or lose) courage.* BRAVERY implies true courage together with daring and an intrepid boldness: *bravery in a battle.* VALOR implies continuous, active bravery in the face of personal danger and a noble and lofty quality of courage: *valor throughout a campaign, valor in fighting for the right.* BRAVADO is now usually a boastful and ostentatious pretense of courage or bravery: *empty bravado.*
—**Ant. 1.** cowardice.

cou·ra·geous (kə rā′jəs), *adj.* possessing or characterized by courage; brave; valiant: *a courageous speech against the dictator.* [ME *corageous* < OF *corageus,* equiv. to *corage* COURAGE + *-eus* -EOUS] —**cou·ra′geous·ly,** *adv.* —**cou·ra′geous·ness,** *n.*
—**Syn.** See **brave.**

cou·rant (ko͝or′ənt *for 1;* ko͝o ränt′, *Fr.* ko͞o RäN′ *for 2*), *adj.* **1.** *Heraldry.* (of an animal) represented in the act of running: *a greyhound courant.* —*n.* **2.** courante. [< F: lit., running, masc. prp. of *courir* to run]

cou·rante (ko͝o ränt′; *Fr.* ko͞o RäNt′), *n., pl.* **-rantes** (-ränts′; *Fr.* -RäNt′). **1.** an old-fashioned dance dating back to the 17th century and characterized by a running or gliding step. **2.** a piece of music for or suited to this dance. **3.** *Music.* a movement following the allemande in the classical suite. Also, **courant, corrente.** [< MF; lit., running, fem. prp. of *courir* to run]

Cour·bet (ko͞oR be′), *n.* **Gus·tave** (gYs tAv′), 1819–77, French painter.

Cour·be·voie (ko͞oR bə vwA′), *n.* a city in N France, WNW of Paris. 59,941 (1962).

cour d'hon·neur (ko͞oR dô nœR′), *pl.* **cours d'hon·neur** (ko͞oR dô nœR′). *French.* the forecourt of a castle, palace, government building, or the like. [lit., court of honor]

cou·reur de bois (ko͞o RœR də bwä′), *pl.* **cou·reurs de bois** (ko͞o RœR də bwä′). *French.* a French or French-Indian trapper of North America, esp. of Canada. [lit., runner, hunter of (the) woods]

cour·i·er (kûr′ē ər, ko͝or′-), *n.* **1.** a messenger, usually traveling in haste, bearing urgent news, important reports, etc. **2.** any means of carrying news, messages, etc., regularly. **3.** the conveyance used by a courier, as an airplane, ship, etc. **4.** *Chiefly Brit.* a person hired by travelers to take charge of the arrangements of a journey. [< MF *cour(r)ier* < It *corrier(e),* equiv. to *corr(ere)* (to) run (< L *currere*) + *-iere* -ER[2]; r. ME *corour* < OF *coreor* < LL *currītor* runner]

cour·lan (ko͝or′lən), *n.* the limpkin. [< F *courlan* < Carib; akin to Carib *kurliri* (Galibi dial.)]

Cour·land (ko͝or′lənd), *n.* a former duchy on the Baltic: later, a province of Russia and, in 1918, incorporated into Latvia. Also, **Kurland.**

Cour·nand (ko͝or′nand, -nənd; *Fr.* ko͞oR näN′), *n.* **An·dré Fré·dé·ric** (äN dRā′ frā dā Rēk′), born 1895, U.S. physiologist, born in France: Nobel prize for medicine 1956.

course (kōrs, kôrs), *n., v.,* **coursed, cours·ing.** —*n.* **1.** advance or progression in a particular direction; onward movement. **2.** a direction or route taken or to be taken. **3.** the path, route, or channel along which anything moves: *the course of a stream; the course of a ball.* **4.** the ground, water, etc., on which a race is run, sailed, etc. **5.** the continuous passage or progress through time or a succession of stages: *in the course of a year; in the course of a battle.* **6.** a customary manner of procedure; regular or natural order of events: *as a matter of course; the course of a disease.* **7.** a mode of conduct; behavior. **8.** a particular manner of proceeding: *Try another course of action.* **9.** a systematized or prescribed series: *a course of lectures; a course of medical treatments.* **10.** a program of instruction, as in a college or university. **11.** a prescribed number of instruction periods or classes in a particular field of study. **12.** a part of a meal served at one time: *The main course was steak.* **13.** *Navig.* **a.** the line along the earth's surface upon or over which a vessel, an aircraft, etc., proceeds: described by its bearing with relation to true or magnetic north. **b.** *Obs.* a point of the compass. **14.** *Naut.* the lowermost sail on a fully square-rigged mast: designated by a special name, as foresail or mainsail, or by the designation of the mast itself, as fore course or main course. **15.** *Building Trades.* a continuous and usually horizontal range of bricks, stones, clapboards, shingles, etc., as in a wall or roof. **16.** one of the pairs of strings on an instrument of the lute family, tuned in unison or in octaves to increase the volume. **17.** *Knitting.* the row of stitches going across from side to side (opposed to *wale*). **18.** Often, **courses.** the menses. **19.** a charge by knights in a tournament. **20.** a pursuit of game with dogs by sight rather than by scent. **21.** See **golf course.** **22.** *Archaic.* a race. **23. in due course,** in the proper or natural order of events; eventually: *They will get their comeuppance in due course.* **24. of course, a.** certainly; definitely: *Of course you are welcome.* **b.** in the usual or natural order of things: *Extra services are charged for, of course.* —*v.t.* **25.** to run through or over. **26.** to chase; pursue. **27.** to hunt (game) with dogs by sight rather than by scent. **28.** to cause (dogs) to pursue game by sight rather than by scent. **29.** *Masonry.* to lay (bricks, stones, etc.) in courses. —*v.i.* **30.** to follow a course; direct one's course. **31.** to run, race, or move swiftly: *The blood of ancient emperors courses through his veins.* **32.** to take part in a hunt with hounds, a tilting match, etc. [ME *co(u)rs* < OF < L *curs(us)* a running, course, n. use of ptp. of *currere* to run]
—**Syn. 1, 13a.** bearing. **3.** way, road, track, passage. **6.** process, career. **8.** method, mode. **15.** row, layer.

coursed (kōrst, kôrst), *adj. Masonry.* (of stonework) laid in courses of more or less uniform height from end to end; ranged. [COURSE + -ED[2]]

course′ protrac′tor, a navigational instrument for measuring the bearing of a course as given on a chart, having a disk calibrated in degrees and an arm pivoted about the center of the disk.

cours·er[1] (kōr′sər, kôr′-), *n.* **1.** one who or that which courses. **2.** a dog for coursing. [COURSE + -ER[1]]

cours·er[2] (kōr′sər, kôr′-), *n.* *Literary.* a swift horse. [ME < OF *coursier*, equiv. to *course* run + *-ier* -ER[2]]

cours·er[3] (kōr′sər, kôr′-), *n.* any of several swift-footed, ploverlike birds of the genera *Cursorius* and *Pluvianus*, chiefly of the desert regions of Asia and Africa. [irreg. < L *cursōr(ius)* fitted for running, equiv. to *curs(us)* a running (see COURSE) + *-ōrius* -ORY[1]]

cours·ing (kōr′sing, kôr′-), *n.* **1.** the act of one who or that which courses. **2.** the sport of pursuing game with dogs that follow by sight rather than by scent. [COURSE + -ING[1]]

court (kōrt, kôrt), *n.* **1.** an area open to the sky and mostly or entirely surrounded by buildings, walls, etc. **2.** a high interior usually having a glass roof and surrounded by several stories of galleries or the like. **3.** *Brit.* a stately dwelling. **4.** a short street. **5.** a smooth, level quadrangle on which to play tennis, handball, basketball, etc. **6.** one of the divisions of such an area. **7.** the residence of a sovereign or other high dignitary; palace. **8.** the collective body of persons forming his retinue. **9.** a sovereign and his councilors as the political rulers of a state. **10.** a formal assembly held by a sovereign. **11.** homage paid, as to a king. **12.** special or devoted attention in order to win favor, affection, etc.: *to pay court to a pretty woman.* **13.** *Law.* **a.** a place where justice is administered. **b.** a judicial tribunal duly constituted for the hearing and determination of cases. **c.** a session of a judicial assembly. **14.** the body of qualified members of a corporation, council, board, etc. **15.** a branch or lodge of a fraternal society. **16.** **out of court, a.** without a hearing; privately: *The case will be settled out of court.* **b.** out of the question; undeserving of discussion: *This wild scheme is entirely out of court.* —*v.t.* **17.** to try to win the favor, preference, or good will of: *to court the rich.* **18.** to seek the affections of; woo. **19.** to attempt to gain (applause, favor, a decision, etc.). **20.** to hold out inducements to; invite. **21.** to act in such a manner as to cause, lead to, or provoke: *to court disaster by reckless driving.* —*v.i.* **22.** to seek another's love; woo. [ME *co(u)rt* < OF < L *cohort-* (s. of *cohors*) courtyard; see COHORT]

court-bar·on (kōrt′bar′ən, kôrt′-), *n.* *Old Eng. Law.* a court presided over by the lord of a manor or his steward, for the redress of misdemeanors within the manor and the adjudication of disputes between tenants of land held by copyhold.

court′ card′, *Brit.* See **face card.**

court′ Chris′tian, *pl.* **courts Christian.** See **ecclesiastical court.**

court′ cup′board, *Eng. Furniture.* a sideboard of the 16th and 17th centuries, having three open tiers, the middle of which sometimes has a small closed cabinet with oblique sides. Cf. **press cupboard.**

court′ dance′, a dignified dance for performance at a court. Cf. **folk dance** (def. 1).

court′ dress′, the formal costume worn at a royal court, including, for men, silk knee breeches and stockings.

Courte·nay (kōrt′nē, kôrt′-), *n.* a boy's given name. Also, **Courte′ney.**

cour·te·ous (kûr′tē əs), *adj.* having or showing good manners; polite. [COURT + -EOUS; r. ME *co(u)rteis* < AF; see COURT, -ESE] —**cour′te·ous·ly,** *adv.* —**cour′te·ous·ness,** *n.*
—**Syn.** mannerly, gracious, courtly. See **civil.** —**Ant.** rude.

cour·te·san (kōr′ti zən, kôr′-, kûr′-), *n.* a prostitute or paramour, esp. one associating with noblemen or men of wealth. Also, **cour′te·zan.** [< MF *courtisane* < OIt *cortigian(a)*, equiv. to *corte* COURT + *-igiana* (*-igi-* -ESE + *-ana*, fem. of *-ano* -AN)]

cour·te·sy (kûr′ti sē *or, for 5,* kûrt′sē), *n., pl.* **-sies.** **1.** excellence of manners or social conduct; polite behavior. **2.** a courteous, respectful, or considerate act or expression. **3.** indulgence, consent, or acquiescence: *a "colonel" by courtesy rather than by right.* **4.** favor, help, or generosity: *The costumes for the play were by courtesy of the museum.* **5.** a curtsy. [ME *curteisie* < OF *curteis* COURTEOUS + *-ie* -Y[3]]
—**Syn. 1.** courteousness, civility, urbanity.

cour′tesy card′, a card identifying the bearer and making him eligible for special consideration, as at a club, hotel, or bank.

cour′tesy ti′tle, *Brit.* a title allowed by custom, as to the children of dukes.

court′ hand′, a style of handwriting formerly used in the English law courts.

court·house (kōrt′hous′, kôrt′-), *n., pl.* **-hous·es** (-hou′ziz). **1.** a building in which courts of law are held. **2.** *U.S.* a county seat. [late ME; see COURT, HOUSE]

cour·ti·er (kōr′tē ər, kôr′-), *n.* **1.** a person who is often in attendance at the court of a king or other royal personage. **2.** one who seeks favor by flattery, charm, etc. [< MF < OF *cortei(er)* (to) be at court + *-ier* -ER[2]; r. ME *courteour* < AF]

Courtier, The, a prose work (1528) by Baldassare Castiglione, written in the form of a dialogue and dealing with the education of the courtier. Italian, **Il Cortegiano.**

court′ing chair′. See **love seat.**

court′ing mir′ror, *U.S. Furniture.* a small mirror of c1800 having a border and cresting of glass painted with leaves and flowers in imitation of a Chinese style.

Court·land (kōrt′lənd, kôrt′-), *n.* a boy's given name.

court·ly (kōrt′lē, kôrt′-), *adj.,* **-li·er, -li·est,** *adv.* —*adj.* **1.** polite, refined, or elegant: *courtly manners.* **2.** flattering; obsequious: *His courtly manner was obvious.* **3.** noting, pertaining to, or suitable for the court of a sovereign. —*adv.* **4.** in a courtly manner; politely or flatteringly. [late ME; see COURT, -LY] —**court′li·ness,** *n.*

court′ly love′, a highly stylized code of behavior popular chiefly from the 12th to the 14th century which prescribed the rules of conduct between lovers, advocating idealized but illicit love, and which fostered an extensive medieval literature based on this tradition.

court-mar·tial (kōrt′mär′shəl, -mär′-, kôrt′-), *n., pl.* **courts-mar·tial,** *v.,* **-tialed, -tial·ing** or (*esp. Brit.*) **-tialled, -tial·ling.** —*n.* **1.** a court consisting of military or naval personnel appointed by a commander to try charges of offenses by soldiers, sailors, etc., against military or naval law. **2.** a trial by such a court. **3.** a conviction by such a court: *He lost his privileges because of his court-martial.* **4.** a session of such a court: *He attended the court-martial this morning.* —*v.t.* **5.** to arraign and try by court-martial. [alter. of phrase *martial court*]

Court·ney (kōrt′nē, kôrt′-), *n.* a boy's given name, form of **Courtenay.**

court′ of appeals′, *Law.* **1.** (in the federal court system and some State court systems) an appellate court intermediate between the trial courts and the court of last resort. **2.** the highest appellate court of New York State. **3. Court′ of Appeal′.** *Brit.* See under **Supreme Court of Judicature.** Also, **Court′ of Appeals′** (for defs. 1, 2).

Court′ of Awards′, a ceremony for awarding junior and cadette girl scouts insignia for the specific activities which they have completed.

court′ of chan′cery, *Law.* chancery (def. 4a).

court′ of com′mon pleas′, *Law.* **1.** (formerly in England) a court to hear civil cases between common citizens. **2.** (in some States) a court with general civil jurisdiction. Also, **Court′ of Com′mon Pleas′.**

court′ of domes′tic rela′tions, *Law.* a court, usually with a limited jurisdiction, that handles legal cases involving a family, esp. controversies between parent and child or husband and wife. Also called **domestic-relations court, family court.** Cf. **juvenile court.**

Court′ of Excheq′uer, exchequer (def. 2c).

court′ of hon′or, *Philately.* a noncompetitive exhibit of outstanding stamps forming part of a large exhibition.

Court′ of Hon′or, 1. the planning body of a girl-scout troop, composed of patrol leaders, the troop scribe, the troop treasurer, and the adult troop leader. **2.** a body of officials of a boy-scout organization that awards honor medals and certificates of promotion to members.

court′ of love′, a court, supposed to have existed in medieval France, composed esp. of ladies who decided on questions of gallantry and courtly love.

court′ of rec′ord, a court whose judgments and proceedings are kept on permanent record and which has the power to impose penalties for contempt.

Court′ of Ses′sion, (in Scotland) the highest civil court.

Court′ of St. James′s, the British royal court: so called from St. James's Palace, London, the former scene of royal receptions. Also, **Court′ of Saint James′.**

court′ of wards′, an English court of record created during the reign of Henry VIII, charged with the management of wardships and other profits accruing to the king: abolished during the reign of Charles II. Also called **court′ of wards′ and liv′eries.**

court′ plas′ter, cotton or other fabric coated on one side with an adhesive preparation, as of isinglass and glycerin, used on the skin for medical and cosmetic purposes. [so called because used in courtly circles for making beauty spots]

Cour·trai (*Fr.* ko͞or trε′), *n.* a city in W Belgium, on the Lys River: important medieval city. 44,814 (est. 1964). Flemish, **Kortrijk.**

court′ report′er, a stenographer employed to record and transcribe an official verbatim record of the legal proceedings of a court.

court·room (kōrt′ro͞om′, -ro͝om′, kôrt′-), *n.* a room in which the sessions of a law court are held. [COURT + ROOM]

court·ship (kōrt′ship, kôrt′-), *n.* **1.** the wooing of a woman by a man. **2.** the period during which such wooing takes place. **3.** solicitation of favors, applause, etc. **4.** *Obs.* courtly behavior; courtesy; gallantry. [COURT + -SHIP]

Court′ship of Miles′ Stan′dish, The, a narrative poem (1858) by Longfellow.

court′ shoe′, *Brit.* pump[2]. [so called from the fact that high-heeled shoes were first worn in royal courts]

court′ ten′nis, a variety of tennis played indoors on a specially constructed court having high cement walls off which the ball may be played, points being made chiefly by stroking the ball into any of three openings in the walls of the court. Cf. **penthouse** (def. 6), **tambour** (def. 7), **winning opening.**

court·yard (kōrt′yärd′, kôrt′-), *n.* a court open to the sky, esp. one enclosed on all sides. [COURT + YARD[2]]

cous·cous (ko͞os′ko͞os′), *n.* a North African dish consisting of steamed semolina, served with vegetables and meat as a main course, or with fruit or the like as a dessert, cereal, etc. [< F < Ar *kuskus*, deriv. of *kaskasa* to beat, pulverize]

cous·in (kuz′ən), *n.* **1.** Also called **first cousin, full cousin, cousin-german.** the son or daughter of an uncle or aunt. **2.** one related by descent in a diverging line from a known common ancestor, as from one's grandparent or from one's father's or mother's sister or brother. **3.** a kinsman or kinswoman. **4.** a person or thing related to another by similar natures, languages, geographical proximity, etc.: *Our Canadian cousins are a friendly people.* **5.** a term of address used by a sovereign in speaking, writing, or referring to another sovereign or a high-ranking noble. [ME *cosin* < OF < L *consōbrīn(us)*, equiv. to *con-* CON- + *sōbrīnus*, contr. of **sorōrīnus* cousin on the mother's side (*soror* sister + *-īnus* -INE[1])] —**cous′in·age, cous′in·hood′, cous′in·ship′,** *n.*

Cou·sin (ko͞o zaN′), *n.* **Vic·tor** (vēk tôr′), 1792–1867, French philosopher and educational reformer: founder of the method of eclecticism in French philosophy.

cous·in-ger·man (kuz′ən jûr′mən), *n., pl.* **cous·ins-ger·man** (kuz′ənz jûr′mən). cousin (def. 1). [COUSIN + GERMAN]

Cous′in Jack′, *pl.* **Cousin Jacks.** a man who is a native of Cornwall or is of Cornish descent, esp. a Cornish miner: *We have a lot of Cousin Jacks in the Upper Peninsula.*

cous·in·ly (kuz′ən lē), *adj.* **1.** like or befitting a cousin. —*adv.* **2.** in the manner of a cousin; as a cousin. [COUSIN + -LY]

cous·in·ry (kuz′ən rē), *n., pl.* **-ries.** cousins or kinsfolk collectively. [COUSIN + -RY]

Cous·teau (ko͞o stō′), *n.* **Jacques Yves** (zhäk ēv), born 1910, French naval officer and underseas explorer: developed the aqualung.

Cou·sy (ko͞o′zē), *n.* **Robert Joseph** (*Bob*), born 1928, U.S. basketball player.

cou·teau (ko͞o tō′), *n., pl.* **-teaux** (-tōz′; *Fr.* -tō′). a knife, esp. a large double-edged one formerly carried as a weapon. [< F; OF *coutel* < L *cultell(us)*, equiv. to *cult(er)* knife + *-ellus* dim. suffix]

coûte que coûte (ko͞ot kə ko͞ot′), *French.* cost what it may.

cou·ter (ko͞o′tər), *n.* *Armor.* a piece of plate armor for the elbow. Also called **cubitiere, elbow cop.** See diag. under **armor.** [ME < AF, equiv. to **coute* (c. OF *coute* elbow < L *cubit(um)*, n. use of neut. of ptp. of *cubāre* to lie down) + *-er* -ER[2]]

couth·ie (ko͞o′thē), *adj.* *Scot.* agreeable; genial; kindly. [*couth* (OE *cūth* known, friendly, ptp. of *cunnan* to know; see CAN[1]) + *-ie*, Scot var. of *-Y*[1]] —**couth′i·ly,** *adj.* —**couth′i·ness,** *n.*

cou·til (ko͞o tēl′, -til′), *n.* a sturdy fabric constructed of a compactly woven herringbone twill. [< F, OF, equiv. to *coute* QUILT + *-il* n. suffix]

cou·ture (ko͞o to͝or′; *Fr.* ko͞o TYR′), *n.* **1.** the occupation of a couturier; dressmaking and designing. **2.** fashion designers or couturiers collectively. [< F: lit., sewing, seam]

cou·tu·ri·er (ko͞o to͝or′ē ā′, -ē ər, -to͝or′yā; *Fr.* ko͞o TY-RYĀ′), *n., pl.* **-tu·riers** (-to͝or′ē āz′, -ē ərz, -to͝or′yāz; *Fr.* -TY RYĀ′). a person who designs, makes, and sells fashionable clothes for women. [< F: lit., one who sews]

cou·tu·rière (ko͞o to͝or′ē ər, -ē er′; *Fr.* ko͞o TY RYER′), *n., pl.* **-tu·ri·ères** (-to͝or′ē ərz, -erz′; *Fr.* -TY RYER′). a female couturier. Also called **cou·tu·ri·ere** (ko͞o to͝or′ē-ər, -ē er′). [< F]

cou·vade (ko͞o väd′; *Fr.* ko͞o VAD′), *n.* a practice among some primitive peoples in which a man, immediately preceding the birth of his child, takes to his bed in an enactment of the birth experience and subjects himself to various taboos usually associated with pregnancy. [< F (now obs.), lit., a hatching, sitting on eggs, equiv. to *couv(er)* (to) hatch (< L *cubāre* to lie down) + *-ade* -ADE[1]]

co·va·lence (kō vā′ləns), *n.* *Chem.* **1.** the number of electron pairs that an atom can share with other atoms. **2.** Also called **cova′lent bond′.** the bond formed by the sharing of a pair of electrons by two atoms. [CO- + VALENCE] —**co·va′lent,** *adj.* —**co·va′lent·ly,** *adv.*

co·var·i·ance (kō vâr′ē əns), *n.* *Statistics.* the expectation or mean value of the variable formed by multiplying the differences obtained by subtracting two given variates from their respective means; the product of the standard deviations of two given variates and the coefficient of correlation between them. [CO- + VARIANCE]

co·var·i·ant (kō vâr′ē ənt), *adj.* *Math.* (of one magnitude with respect to another) varying in accordance with a fixed mathematical relationship: *The area of a square is covariant with the length of a side.* [CO- + VARIANT]

Co·var·ru·bias (kō′və ro͞o′bē əs; *Sp.* kō′vär RO͞O′-byäs), *n.* **Mi·guel** (mē gel′), 1904–57, Mexican caricaturist, illustrator, and painter.

cove[1] (kōv), *n., v.,* **coved, cov·ing.** —*n.* **1.** a small indentation or recess in the shoreline of a sea, lake, or river. **2.** a sheltered nook. **3.** a hollow or recess in a mountain; cave; cavern. **4.** a narrow pass between woods or hills. **5.** a sheltered area, usually prairie, between woods or hills. **6.** *Archit.* **a.** a concave surface or molding. **b.** a concave surface forming part of a ceiling at its edge so as to eliminate the usual interior angle between the wall and ceiling. —*v.t., v.i.* **7.** to make or become a cove. [ME; OE *cofa* cave, den, closet; c. Icel *kofi* hut, Gk *gýpē* cave]

cove[2] (kōv), *n.* **1.** *Brit. Slang.* a person; fellow. **2.** *Australian Slang.* a boss or manager, esp. a manager of a sheep station. [said to be < Romany *kova* creature]

coved′ vault′. See **cloistered vault.**

cove′ light′ing, indirect lighting directed upward from an interior cornice or the like toward a cove at the edge of the ceiling.

co·vel·lite (kō vel′īt, kō′və līt′), *n.* a mineral, copper sulfide, CuS, indigo in color and usually occurring as a massive coating on other copper minerals. [named after Nicolò *Covelli* (1790–1829), Italian mineralogist who found it; see -ITE[1]]

cov·en (kuv′ən, kō′vən), *n.* an assembly of witches, esp. a group numbering 13. [ME *covin* band; see COVIN]

cov·e·nant (kuv′ə nənt), *n.* **1.** an agreement, usually formal, between two or more persons to do or not do something specified. **2.** *Law.* an incidental clause in such an agreement. **3.** *Eccles.* a solemn agreement between the members of a church to act together in harmony with the precepts of the gospel. **4.** (*cap.*) *Hist.* **a.** See **National Covenant. b.** See **Solemn League and Covenant. 5.** *Bible.* **a.** the conditional promises made to man by God, as revealed in Scripture. **b.** the agreement between God and the ancient Israelites, in which God promised to protect them if they kept His law and were faithful to Him. **6.** *Law.* **a.** a formal agreement of legal validity, esp. one under seal. **b.** an early English form of action in suits involving sealed contracts. **7.** See **Covenant of the League of Nations.** —*v.i.* **8.** to enter into a covenant. —*v.t.* **9.** to agree to by covenant; pledge. **10.** to stipulate. [ME < OF, n. use of prp. of *covenir* < L *convenīre* to come together, agree; see -ANT] —**cov·e·nan·tal** (kuv′ə nan′təl), *adj.*
—**Syn. 1.** treaty, pact, convention.

cov·e·nan·tee (kuv′ə nən tē′, -nan-), *n.* a person to whom something is promised in a covenant. [COVENANT + -EE]

cov·e·nant·er (kuv′ə nən tər; *for 2 also Scot.* kuv′ə-nan′tər), *n.* **1.** a person who makes a covenant. **2.** (*cap.*) *Scot. Hist.* one who, by solemn agreement, bound himself to uphold Presbyterianism, esp. an adherent of the National Covenant or the Solemn League and Covenant. [COVENANT + -ER[1]]

Cov′enant of the League′ of Na′tions, the covenant or constitution of the League of Nations, included as the first 26 articles in the Treaty of Versailles, in which the organization and purpose of the League was set forth.

cov′enant of war′ranty, *Law.* warranty (def. 2b).

cov·e·nan·tor (kuv′ə nən tər), *n.* *Law.* the party who is to perform the obligation expressed in a covenant. [COVENANT + -OR[2]]

Cov′ent Gar′den (kuv′ənt, kov′-), **1.** a district in central London, England: vegetable and flower market.

2. a theater in this district, first built 1731–32, important in English theatrical history.

Cov·en·try (kuv′ən trē, kov′-), *n.* **1.** a city in NE Warwickshire, in central England: heavily bombed 1940. 305,060 (1961). **2. send to Coventry,** to refuse to associate with; openly ignore: *His friends sent him to Coventry after he made a spectacle of himself.*

Cov′entry bell′, a perennial garden plant, *Campanula Trachelium,* of Eurasia, having coarsely toothed leaves and bluish-purple flowers.

cov·er (kuv′ər), *v.t.* **1.** to place something over or upon, as for protection or concealment. **2.** to be or serve as a covering for; extend over; occupy the surface of: *Snow covered the fields.* **3.** to provide with a covering: *Cover the pot with a lid.* **4.** to protect or conceal (the body, head, etc.) with clothes, a hat, etc. **5.** to bring upon (oneself): *He covered himself with honors at college.* **6.** to shelter; protect; serve as a defense to. **7.** *Mil.* **a.** to be in line with by occupying a position directly before or behind. **b.** to protect (a soldier, force, or military position) during an expected period of ground combat by taking a position from which any hostile troops can be fired upon. **8.** to take charge of or responsibility for: *He tried to persuade someone to cover his post for him.* **9.** to hide from view; screen. **10.** to spread with: *to cover bread with honey.* **11.** to aim at, as with a pistol. **12.** to put all over the surface of: *The boy covered the paper with his scrawl.* **13.** to have within range, as a fortress does adjacent territory. **14.** to include, deal with, or provide for: *The book covers the subject well. The rules cover working conditions.* **15.** to come over and reach a level above: *The river covered the town during the flood.* **16.** to suffice to defray or meet (a charge, expense, etc.). **17.** to offset (an outlay, loss, liability, etc.). **18.** *Insurance.* to insure against risk or loss. **19.** (in short selling) to purchase securities or commodities in order to deliver them to the broker from whom they were borrowed. **20.** to extend between the limits of: *The book covers the 18th century in England.* **21.** to deposit the equivalent of (money deposited), as in wagering. **22.** to accept the conditions of (a bet, wager, etc.). **23.** *Journalism.* **a.** to act as a reporter or reviewer of (an event, a field of interest, a performance, etc.): *He covers sports for the afternoon paper.* **b.** to publish or broadcast a report or reports of (a news item, a series of related events, etc.): *The press covered the incumbent's long campaign.* **24.** to pass or travel over: *We covered 600 miles a day on our trip.* **25.** *Baseball.* to take a position close to or at (a base) so as to catch a ball thrown to the base: *The shortstop covered second on the attempted steal.* **26.** *Sports.* to guard (an opponent on offense) so as to prevent him from scoring or carrying out his assignment: *to cover a potential pass receiver.* **27.** (of a male animal) to copulate with. **28.** (of a hen) to brood or sit on (eggs or chicks). **29.** to play a card higher than (the one led or previously played in the round). —*v.i. Informal.* **30.** to serve as a substitute for someone who is absent: *She covers for the receptionist during lunch hour.* **31.** to play a card higher than the one led or previously played in the round: *She led the eight and I covered with the jack.* **32.** to hide the wrongful or embarrassing action of another by providing an alibi or acting in the other's place: *They covered for him when he missed roll call.* **33. cover up, a.** to cover completely; enfold. **b.** to keep secret; conceal: *She tried to cover up her lack of knowledge.* —*n.* **34.** something that covers, as the lid of a vessel or the binding of a book. **35.** protection; shelter; concealment. **36.** a pretense; feigning. **37.** woods, underbrush, etc., serving to shelter and conceal wild animals or game; a covert. **38.** *Ecol.* vegetation that serves to protect or conceal animals, such as birds, from excessive sunlight, from drying, or from predators. **39.** anything that veils, screens, or shuts from sight: *under cover of darkness.* **40.** a set of eating utensils and the like, as plate, knife, fork, napkin, etc., placed for each person at a table. **41.** See **cover charge. 42.** *Finance.* funds to cover liability or secure against risk of loss. **43.** *Philately.* **a.** an envelope or outer wrapping for mail. **b.** a letter folded so that the address may be placed on the outside and the missive mailed. **44.** Also called **covering.** *Math.* a collection of sets having the property that a given set is contained in the union of the sets in the collection. **45.** *Building Trades.* See **cover plate. 46. break cover,** to emerge, esp. suddenly, from a place of concealment: *The fox broke cover and the chase was on.* **47. take cover,** to seek shelter or safety: *The hikers took cover in a deserted cabin to escape the sudden storm.* **48. under cover, a.** under a pretense; secretly: *Arrangements for the escape were made under cover.* **b.** within an envelope: *The check came under cover in yesterday's mail.* [ME *cover(en)* < OF *covr(ir)* < L *cooperīre* to cover up, equiv. to *co-* co- + *operīre* to cover over (*o-* (var. of *ob-* OB-) + *-perīre* to cover); cf. *aperīre* to uncover] —**cov′er·a·ble,** *adj.* —**cov′er·er,** *n.* —**cov′er·less,** *adj.*

—**Syn. 1.** overlay, overspread, envelop, enwrap. **9.** cloak, conceal. **16.** counterbalance, compensate for. **35, 39.** COVER, PROTECTION, SCREEN, SHELTER mean a defense against harm or danger and a provision for safety. The main idea in COVER is that of concealment, as in darkness, in a wood, behind something, etc.: *Keep under cover. Take cover. The ground troops were left without cover when the air force was withdrawn.* SCREEN refers especially to something behind which one can hide: *A heavy fire formed a screen for ground operations.* PROTECTION and SHELTER emphasize the idea of a guard or defense, a shield against injury or death. A PROTECTION is any such shield: *In World War II, an air cover of airplanes served as a protection for troops.* A SHELTER is something which covers over and acts as a place of refuge: *An abandoned monastery acted as a shelter.*

cov·er·age (kuv′ər ij), *n.* **1.** *Insurance.* protection provided against risks or a risk, often as specified: *a policy affording comprehensive coverage.* **2.** *Finance.* the value of funds held to back up or meet liabilities. **3.** the extent to which something is covered. **4.** *Radio and Television.* the area within the broadcasting range of a station or network, usually calculated by the number of owners of radio or television receivers. **5.** the number of persons in an area served by a newspaper or other communications medium. **6.** *Journalism.* the reporting and subsequent publishing or broadcasting of news: *The fight received inadequate coverage.* [COVER + -AGE]

cov·er·all (kuv′ər ôl′), *n.* Often, **coveralls.** a loose-fitting, one-piece work garment with sleeves and a trouserlike portion, worn over other clothing. [COVER + ALL]

cov′er charge′, a fee, in addition to the cost of food and drink, charged by a restaurant, night club, etc., for entertainment. Also called **cover.** Cf. **minimum** (def. 3).

cov′er crop′, a crop, preferably leguminous, planted to keep nutrients from leaching, soil from eroding, and land from weeding over, as during the winter.

Cov·er·dale (kuv′ər dāl′), *n.* **Miles,** 1488–1569, English divine: translator of the Bible into English 1535.

cov·ered (kuv′ərd), *adj.* **1.** having a cover, covering, or coverage. **2.** wearing a hat or other covering on the head. [COVER + -ED[2]]

cov′ered smut′, *Plant Pathol.* a disease of oats and barley, characterized by masses of spores enclosed in the glumes, caused by a smut fungus, *Ustilago hordei.*

cov′ered wag′on, 1. *U.S.* a large wagon with a high, bonnetlike canvas top, esp. such a wagon used by the pioneers during the westward migrations in the 19th century. **2.** *Railroads Brit.* a boxcar.

cov′er girl′, an attractive girl whose picture is featured on a magazine cover.

cov′er glass′, a thin, round or square piece of glass used to cover an object mounted on a slide for microscopic observation. Also called **cover slip.**

cov·er·ing (kuv′ər ing), *n.* **1.** something laid over or wrapped around a thing, esp. for concealment, protection, or warmth. **2.** *Math.* cover (def. 46). **3.** the buying of securities or commodities that one has sold short, in order to return them to the person from whom they were borrowed. [COVER + -ING[1]]

cov′ering board′, *Naut.* plank-sheer.

cov′ering let′ter, a letter that follows or accompanies another letter, a package, or the like and serves as an explanation, commendation, etc.

cov·er·let (kuv′ər lit), *n.* **1.** the top covering of a bed; bedspread. **2.** any covering or cover. Also, **cov·er·lid** (kuv′ər lid). [ME *coverlite* < AF *cuver-lit* bedspread, equiv. to *cuver* to COVER + *lit* bed < L *lect(us)*]

Cov·er·ley (kuv′ər lē), *n.* **Sir Roger de,** a literary figure representing the ideal of the early 18th-century squire in *The Spectator,* by Addison and Steele.

cov′er plate′, *Building Trades.* a reinforcing plate attached to the outer surface of a flange of a metal beam. Also called **cover, flange plate.**

cov′er point′, 1. *Cricket.* the position and the player stationed near the point. **2.** *Lacrosse.* the position and the player stationed before the point.

covers., coversed sine.

co′versed sine′ (kō′vûrst), *Math.* the versed sine of the complement of an angle or arc. *Abbr.:* covers. Also called **versed cosine.**

cov′er slip′. See **cover glass.**

cov′er sto′ry, a story in a magazine related to an illustration on its cover.

cov·ert (kuv′ərt, kō′vərt), *adj.* **1.** covered; sheltered. **2.** concealed; secret; disguised. **3.** *Law.* (of a woman) under cover or protection of her husband. —*n.* **4.** a covering; cover. **5.** a shelter or hiding place. **6.** concealment or disguise. **7.** *Hunting.* a thicket giving shelter to wild animals or game. **8.** Also called **tectrix.** *Ornith.* one of the small feathers that cover the bases of the large feathers of the wings and tail. See diag. under **bird. 9.** See **covert cloth.** [ME < OF < L *coopert(us),* ptp. of *cooperīre* to cover up, hide; see COVER] —**cov′ert·ly,** *adv.* —**cov′ert·ness,** *n.*

—**Syn. 2.** clandestine, surreptitious, furtive.

co′vert cloth′ (kō′vərt, kuv′ərt), a cotton, woolen, or worsted cloth of twill weave, the warp being of ply yarns one of which may be white. Also called **covert.**

cov′ert coat′, *Brit.* a short, light overcoat of covert cloth; a duster.

cov·er·ture (kuv′ər chər), *n.* **1.** a cover or covering; shelter; concealment. **2.** *Law.* the status of a married woman considered as under the protection and authority of her husband. [ME < OF. See COVERT, -URE]

cov·er-up (kuv′ər up′), *n.* any action or other means of concealing or preventing investigation or exposure. [n. use of v. phrase *cover up*]

cov·et (kuv′it), *v.t.* **1.** to desire inordinately or without due regard for the rights of others; desire wrongfully: *to covet another's property.* **2.** to wish for, esp. eagerly: *He won the prize they all coveted.* —*v.i.* **3.** to have an inordinate or wrongful desire. [ME *coveit(en)* < OF *coveit(i)e(r),* irreg. < VL **cupiditāre* to covet, deriv. of L *cupiditās* CUPIDITY] —**cov′et·a·ble,** *adj.* —**cov′et·er,** *n.* —**cov′et·ing·ly,** *adv.*

—**Syn. 1.** See **envy.** —**Ant. 1.** renounce.

cov·et·ous (kuv′i təs), *adj.* **1.** inordinately or wrongfully desirous. **2.** eagerly desirous. [ME *coveitous* < OF < VL **cupiditōs(us),* equiv. to L *cupidit(ās)* CUPIDITY + *-ōsus* -OUS] —**cov′et·ous·ly,** *adv.* —**cov′et·ous·ness,** *n.*

—**Syn. 1.** greedy, grasping, rapacious, avaricious.

cov·ey (kuv′ē), *n., pl.* **-eys. 1.** a brood or small flock of partridges or similar birds. **2.** a group, set, or company. [ME, var. of *covee* < MF, OF, n. use of fem. of ptp. of *cover* to hatch < L *cubāre* to lie down]

cov·in (kuv′in), *n.* **1.** *Law.* a secret or collusive agreement between two or more persons to the prejudice of another. **2.** *Archaic.* fraud; deception. [ME *covin(e)* < MF < LL *conven(ium)* agreement, L *conven(a)* one coming together (with others), akin to *convenīre* to come together, agree] —**cov′in·ous,** *adj.* —**cov′in·ous·ly,** *adv.*

Co·vi·na (kə vē′nə), *n.* a city in SW California, near Los Angeles. 20,124 (1960).

Cov·ing·ton (kuv′ing tən), *n.* **1.** a city in N Kentucky, on the Ohio River. 60,376 (1960). **2.** a town in central Georgia. 8167 (1960). **3.** a town in SE Louisiana. 6754 (1960). **4.** a town in W Tennessee. 5298 (1960). **5.** a town in W Indiana. 2759 (1960).

cow[1] (kou), *n., pl.* **cows,** (*Archaic*) **kine. 1.** the mature female of a bovine animal, esp. of the genus *Bos.* **2.** the female of various other large animals, as the elephant, whale, etc. **3.** *Slang.* a large, obese, and slovenly woman. **4.** *Vulgar.* a woman who has a large number of children or is frequently pregnant. **5.** *Australian Informal.* an unpleasant or disliked person, object, or task. **6. till the cows come home,** for a long time; forever: *If I don't tell her when to stop, she'll keep on reading till the cows come home.* [ME *cou,* OE *cū;* c. G *Kuh,* D *koe,* Icel *kýr;* akin to L *bōs,* Gk *boûs* ox] —**cow′like′,** *adj.*

cow[2] (kou), *v.t.* to frighten with threats, violence, etc.; intimidate. [< Scand; cf. Icel *kūga* to oppress, tyrannize over, Dan *kue* to cow]

—**Syn. 1.** overawe.

cow[3] (kou; kō), *v.t. Chiefly Scot.* **1.** to cut short the horns of cattle; poll. **2.** to cut short, clip, or thin (any growth); prune. [earlier *coll* < Scand; cf. Icel *kolla* to mow]

cow·age (kou′ij), *n.* **1.** a tropical leguminous vine, *Stizolobium pruritum,* bearing reddish or blackish pods. **2.** the pod itself, covered with bristlelike hairs that are irritating to the skin and cause intense itching. **3.** the hairs of the cowage mixed with a liquid vehicle and used to expel intestinal worms. Also, **cowhage, cowitch.** [< Hindi *kaāwch* (also transliterated *kavāc, kavānc*) by folk etymology]

cow·ard (kou′ərd), *n.* **1.** a person who lacks courage in facing danger, difficulty, pain, etc.; a timid or easily intimidated person. —*adj.* **2.** lacking courage; timid. **3.** proceeding from or expressive of fear or timidity: *a coward cry.* **4.** *Heraldry.* (of an animal) represented with its tail between its legs; coué: *a greyhound coward.* [ME < OF *couard-, couart* cowardly, equiv. to *coue* tail (< L *cauda*) + *-art* -ARD]

—**Syn. 1.** craven, poltroon, dastard, milksop.

Cow·ard (kou′ərd), *n.* **Noel,** born 1899, English playwright, author, actor, and composer.

cow·ard·ice (kou′ər dis), *n.* lack of courage to face danger, difficulty, opposition, etc. [ME *cowardise* < OF *co(u)ardise,* equiv. to *co(u)art* cowardly (see COWARD) + *-ise* -ICE]

—**Syn.** poltroonery, dastardliness, pusillanimity, timidity. —**Ant.** bravery.

cow·ard·ly (kou′ərd lē), *adj.* **1.** lacking courage; contemptibly timid: *a cowardly soldier.* **2.** characteristic of or befitting a coward: *a cowardly attack on the governor's honesty.* —*adv.* **3.** like a coward. [ME (adv.); see COWARD, -LY] —**cow′ard·li·ness,** *n.*

—**Syn. 1.** craven, poltroon, dastardly, pusillanimous, faint-hearted, white-livered, lily-livered, chicken-hearted, fearful, afraid, scared. COWARDLY, TIMID, TIMOROUS refer to a lack of courage or self-confidence. COWARDLY means weakly or basely fearful in the presence of danger: *The cowardly wretch deserted his comrades in battle.* TIMID means lacking in boldness or self-confidence even when there is no danger present: *A timid person stands in the way of his own advancement.* TIMOROUS suggests a timidity based on an exaggeration of dangers or on an imaginary creation of dangers: *timorous as a mouse.* —**Ant. 1.** brave.

cow·bane (kou′bān′), *n.* any of several umbelliferous plants supposed to be poisonous to cattle, as the European water hemlock, *Cicuta virosa,* or an American swamp plant, *Oxypolis rigidior.* [COW[1] + BANE]

cow·bell (kou′bel′), *n.* **1.** a bell hung around a cow's neck to indicate its whereabouts. **2.** *U.S.* the bladder campion. [COW[1] + BELL[1]]

cow·ber·ry (kou′ber′ē, -bə rē), *n., pl.* **-ries. 1.** the berry or fruit of any of various shrubs, as *Vaccinium Vitis-Idaea,* growing in pastures. **2.** any of these shrubs. [COW[1] + BERRY, trans. of L *vaccīnium* plant name, in NL: genus name, deriv. of *vaccīnus* of cows; see VACCINE]

cow·bind (kou′bīnd′), *n.* either the black-berried white bryony, *Bryonia alba,* or the red-berried bryony, *B. dioica.* [COW[1] + *-bind;* see WOODBINE]

cow·bird (kou′bûrd′), *n.* any of several American blackbirds of the genus *Molothrus,* esp. *M. ater,* of North America, that accompany herds of cattle and lay their eggs in the nests of other birds. Also called **cow′ black′bird.** [COW[1] + BIRD]

cow·boy (kou′boi′), *n.* **1.** a man who herds and tends cattle on a ranch, esp. in the western U.S., and who usually goes about his chores on horseback. **2.** a man who exhibits the skills attributed to cowboys, esp. in rodeos, as by roping cattle, riding unbroken horses, etc. **3.** a reckless or speedy automobile driver. **4.** (during the American Revolution) a member of a pro-British guerilla band that operated between the American and British lines near New York City. [COW[1] + BOY]

cow′boy hat′, a broad-brimmed hat, usually of soft felt, conventionally worn by cowboys; a ten-gallon hat.

cow′boys and In′dians, a children's game in which a group of players imitate the supposed behavior of cowboys and Indians in conflict, as in shooting, chasing, capturing, etc.

cow·catch·er (kou′kach′ər), *n.* **1.** Also called **pilot.** *U.S.* a triangular frame at the front of a locomotive, streetcar, etc., designed for clearing the track of obstructions. **2.** *Radio and Television.* a brief commercial advertising a subordinate product or service of a program's sponsor and preceding the main part of the show. [COW[1] + CATCHER]

cow′ col′lege, *U.S. Slang.* **1.** an agricultural college. **2.** a small, obscure rural college.

cow′ cream′er, a silver or ceramic cream pitcher of the 18th century in the form of a cow.

Cow·ell (kou′əl), *n.* **Henry (Dixon)** (dik′sən), 1897–1965, U.S. composer.

cow·er (kou′ər), *v.i.* **1.** to crouch in fear or shame. **2.** *Brit. Dial.* to bend with the knees and back; stand or squat in a bent position. [ME *cour(en)* < Scand; cf. Icel *kūra* to mope, Norw *kura* to cower; c. G *kauern*] —**cow′er·ing·ly,** *adv.*

Cowes (kouz), *n.* a seaport on the Isle of Wight, in S England: resort. 16,974 (1961).

cow·fish (kou′fish′), *n., pl.* (*esp. collectively*) **-fish,** (*esp. referring to two or more kinds or species*) **-fish·es. 1.** any of several marine fishes having hornlike projections over the eyes, esp. a trunkfish, *Lactophrys quadricornus,* found in the warm waters of the Atlantic Ocean. **2.** a sirenian, as the manatee. **3.** any of various small cetaceans, as a porpoise or dolphin or the grampus, *Grampus griseus.* [COW[1] + FISH]

cow·girl (kou′gûrl′), *n.* a girl who assists in herding and handling cattle on a ranch. [COW[1] + GIRL]

cow·hage (kou′ij), *n.* cowage.

cow′ hand′, a person employed on a cattle ranch; cowboy.

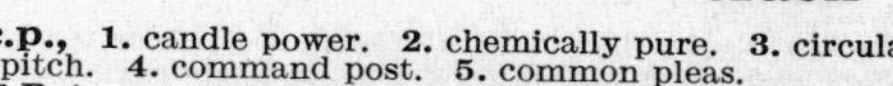

cow·herb (kou′ûrb′, -hûrb′), *n.* a European herb, *Saponaria Vaccaria,* having clusters of pink flowers. Also called **cockle.** [cow[1] + HERB]

cow·herd (kou′hûrd′), *n.* a person whose occupation is tending and herding cows. [ME *couherde,* OE *cūherde.* See cow[1], HERD[2]]

cow·hide (kou′hīd′), *n., v.,* **-hid·ed, -hid·ing.** —*n.* **1.** the hide of a cow. **2.** the leather made from it. **3.** a strong, flexible whip made of rawhide or of braided leather. —*v.t.* **4.** to whip with a cowhide. [cow[1] + HIDE[2]]

cow·itch (kou′ich), *n.* cowage. [cow[1] + ITCH for Hindi *kawach* by folk etymology]

cow′ kil′ler, the wingless female of any of several velvet ants, esp. *Dasymutilla occidentalis,* of the southern U.S., which inflicts a painful sting.

cowl[1] (koul), *n.* **1.** a hooded garment worn by monks. **2.** the hood of this garment. **3.** part of a garment that is draped to resemble a cowl or hood, as at the top of a sleeve or neckline. **4.** a hoodlike covering for increasing the draft of a chimney or ventilator. **5.** the forward part of the automobile body supporting the rear of the hood and the windshield and housing the pedals and instrument panel. **6.** *Aeron.* a cowling. **7.** a wire netting fastened to the top of the smokestack of a locomotive to prevent large sparks from being discharged; a spark arrester. —*v.t.* **8.** to put a monk's cowl on. **9.** to make a monk of. **10.** to cover with or as if with a cowl. [ME *cou(e)le,* OE *cugele* < LL *cucull(a)* monk's hood, var. of L *cucullus* hood]

Cowl

cowl[2] (koul), *n.* *Brit. Dial.* a large tub, often fitted with two handles for convenience in carrying. [ME *coul, couvel,* OE *cūfel* tub < LL *cūpell(us),* equiv. to L *cūp(a)* vat + *-ellus* dim. suffix]

Cowl (koul), *n.* **Jane,** 1884–1950, U.S. actress and playwright.

cowled (kould), *adj.* **1.** wearing a cowl. **2.** shaped like a cowl; cucullate. [COWL[1] + -ED[3]]

Cow·ley (kou′lē, ko͞o′-), *n.* **1. Abraham,** 1618–67, English poet. **2. Malcolm,** born 1898, U.S. writer, critic, and editor.

cow·lick (kou′lik′), *n.* a tuft of hair, usually over the forehead, that grows in a direction different from that of the rest of the hair. [cow[1] + LICK, a humorous American coinage]

cow′ lil′y, the spatterdock, *Nuphar advena.*

cowl·ing (kou′ling), *n.* *Aeron.* a streamlined housing for an aircraft engine, usually forming a continuous line with the fuselage or wing. [COWL[1] + -ING[1]]

cowl·staff (koul′staf′, -stäf′), *n.* *Brit. Dial.* a strong pole thrust through the handles of a cowl and lifted by one person at each end. [ME *cuvelstaf.* See COWL[2], STAFF[1]]

cow·man (kou′mən), *n., pl.* **-men. 1.** (in the western U.S.) one who owns cattle; rancher. **2.** *Brit.* a farmer or farm worker who tends cows. [cow[1] + MAN[1]]

co-work·er (kō wûr′kər, kō′wûr′-), *n.* a fellow worker. [CO- + WORKER]

cow′ pars′nip, any umbelliferous plant of the genus *Heracleum,* as *H. Spondylium,* of Europe, or *H. lanatum,* of North America.

cow·pea (kou′pē′), *n.* **1.** an annual plant, *Vigna sinensis,* extensively cultivated in the southern U.S. for forage, soil improvement, etc. **2.** the seed of this plant, used for food. Also called **black-eyed pea.** [cow[1] + PEA]

Cow·per (ko͞o′pər, kou′-), *n.* **William,** 1731–1800, English poet and hymnologist.

Cow′per's gland′ (kou′pərz, ko͞o′-), *Anat., Zool.* either of two small glands on either side of the urethra in males, that secrete a mucous substance into the urethra. Also called **bulbourethral gland.** [named after William *Cowper* (1666–1709), English anatomist who discovered them]

cow′ pi′lot. See **sergeant major** (def. 2).

cow·poke (kou′pōk′), *n.* a cowboy. [cow[1] + POKE[1] (prob. formed after COWPUNCHER)]

cow′ po′ny, a horse used by cowboys in herding cattle.

cow·pox (kou′poks′), *n.* *Vet. Pathol.* an eruptive disease appearing on the teats and udders of cows in which small pustules form which contain a virus used in the vaccination of man against smallpox. [cow[1] + POX]

cow·punch·er (kou′pun′chər), *n.* a cowboy. [cow[1] + *puncher* (see PUNCH[1], -ER[1])]

cow·rie (kou′rē), *n.* **1.** the highly polished, usually brightly colored shell of a marine gastropod of the genus *Cypraea,* as that of *C. moneta,* used as money in certain parts of Asia and Africa, or that of *C. tigris,* used for ornament. **2.** the gastropod itself. [< Hindi *kaurī,* var. of *kauḍī* < Tamil or Malayalam *kavaṭi*]

cow·ry (kou′rē), *n., pl.* **-ries.** cowrie.

cow′ shark′, any of several sharks of the family *Hexanchidae,* having six or seven gill openings on each side of the head.

cow·shed (kou′shed′), *n.* a shed serving as a shelter for cows. [cow[1] + SHED[1]]

cow·skin (kou′skin′), *n.* **1.** the skin of a cow. **2.** the leather made from it. [cow[1] + SKIN]

cow·slip (kou′slip), *n.* **1.** an English primrose, *Primula officinalis* (*P. veris*), having yellow flowers. **2.** *U.S.* the marsh marigold. **3.** See **shooting star** (def. 2). **4.** See **Virginia cowslip.** [ME *cowslyppe,* OE *cūslyppe.* See cow[1], SLIP[3]] —**cow′slipped,** *adj.*

cow's′ tail′, *Naut.* See **Irish pennant** (def. 1).

cow·tail (kou′tāl′), *n.* a coarse wool of poor quality. [cow[1] + TAIL[1]]

cow-tongue (kou′tung′), *n.* a perennial herb, *Clintonia borealis,* of eastern North America, having greenish-yellow flowers and blue berries. [cow[1] + TONGUE]

cow′ town′, a small, provincial town or center, esp. in a cattle-raising district in the western U.S.

cow′ vetch′, a climbing, perennial herb, *Vicia Cracca,* of Eurasia and North America, having showy, violet-purple flowers.

cox (koks), *Informal.* —*n.* **1.** coxswain. —*v.t.* **2.** to act as coxswain to (a boat). [short form]

Cox (koks), *n.* **James Middleton,** 1870–1957, U.S. journalist and politician.

cox·a (kok′sə), *n., pl.* **cox·ae** (kok′sē). **1.** *Anat.* **a.** See **innominate bone. b.** the joint of the hip. **2.** *Zool.* the first or proximal segment of the leg of insects and other arthropods. [< L: hip] —**cox′al,** *adj.*

A, Coxa of beetle leg; B, Trochanter; C, Femur; D, Tibia; E, Tarsus

cox·al·gi·a (kok sal′jē ə, -jə), *n.* *Pathol.* pain in the hip. Also, **cox·al·gy** (kok′sal jē). [COX(A) + -ALGIA] —**cox·al′gic,** *adj.*

cox·comb (koks′kōm′), *n.* **1.** a conceited, foolish dandy; pretentious fop. **2.** *Archaic.* head; pate. **3.** *Obs.* cockscomb (def. 2). [sp. var. of COCKSCOMB] —**cox·comb·i·cal** (koks kom′i kəl, -kō′mi-), **cox·comb′ic,** *adj.* —**cox·comb′i·cal·ly,** *adv.*
—**Syn. 1.** dude, popinjay, jackanapes.

cox·comb·ry (koks′kōm′rē), *n., pl.* **-ries. 1.** the manners or behavior of a coxcomb. **2.** a foppish trait. [COXCOMB + -ERY]

Cox·ey (kok′sē), *n.* **Jacob Sech·ler** (sech′lər), 1854–1951, U.S. political reformer: led a group of marchers **(Coxey's army)** in 1894 to Washington to petition Congress for legislation to relieve the unemployed.

Cox·sack·ie (ko͝ok sä′kē), *n.* a town in SE New York. 2849 (1960).

Coxsack′ie vi′rus, any of a group of viruses closely related to the virus of poliomyelitis, causing certain diseases of man, as herpangia and epidemic pleurodynia. [named after COXSACKIE, where the first known case appeared]

cox·swain (kok′sən, -swān′), *n.* **1.** the steersman of a racing shell. **2.** a seaman in charge of a ship's boat in the absence of an officer. Also, **cockswain.** [ME *cokeswayne.* See COCKBOAT, SWAIN]

Cox′well chair′ (kok′swəl, -swel). See **Cogswell chair.**

coy (koi), *adj.* **1.** shy; modest. **2.** artfully or affectedly shy or reserved; coquettish. **3.** *Archaic.* quiet; reserved. **4.** *Obs.* disdainful; aloof. —*v.i.* **5.** *Archaic.* to act in a coy manner. —*v.t. Obs.* **6.** to quiet; soothe. **7.** to pat; caress. [ME < MF *coi* calm, earlier *quei* < L *quēt(us), var. of *quiētus* QUIET] —**coy′ish,** *adj.* —**coy′ish·ness,** *n.* —**coy′ly,** *adv.* —**coy′ness,** *n.*
—**Syn. 1.** retiring, diffident, bashful, demure.

Coy (koi), *n.* a boy's given name.

Coy·ol·xauh·qui (koi′ol shō′kē), *n.* (in the Aztec religion) the sister of Uitzilopochtli: beheaded by her brother because she had plotted to kill their mother.

coy·o·te (kī ō′tē, kī′ōt), *n., pl.* **-tes,** (*esp. collectively*) **-te. 1.** Also called **prairie wolf.** a carnivorous, wolflike mammal, *Canis latrans,* of western North America, noted for its loud and prolonged howling at night. **2.** *Amer. Ind. Legend.* the culture hero and trickster of the American Indians of the West. **3.** *Slang.* a contemptible person, esp. a cheat. [< MexSp < Nahuatl *coyotl*]

Coyote (1½ ft. high at shoulder; total length 3½ ft.; tail 1 ft.)

coy·o·te-brush (kī ō′tē brush′, kī′ōt-), *n.* an evergreen shrub, *Baccharis pilularis,* found on dry hills and dunes in the western U.S. Also called **chaparral broom, coy·o·te-bush** (kī ō′tē bo͝osh′, kī′ōt-), **kidneywort, squaw waterweed.**

Coyo′te State′, South Dakota (used as a nickname).

co·yo·til·lo (kō′yō tēl′yō, kī′ō-; *Sp.* kō′yô tē′yô), *n., pl.* **-til·los** (tēl′yōz; *Sp.* -tē′yôs). any rhamnaceous plant of the genus *Karwinskia,* of Mexico, bearing poisonous fruit. [< MexSp, dim. of *coyote* COYOTE]

Coypu (Total length 3½ ft.; tail to 16 in.)

coy·pu (koi′po͞o), *n., pl.* **-pus,** (*esp. collectively*) **-pu.** a large, South American, aquatic rodent, *Myocastor* (or *Myopotamus*) *coypus,* yielding the fur nutria. [< AmerSp *coipú* < Araucanian *coypu*]

Coy·se·vox (kwaz′ vôks′), *n.* **An·toine** (äN twaN′), 1640–1720, French sculptor.

coz (kuz), *n.* *Informal.* cousin. [short form]

Co·zad (kə zad′), *n.* a town in central Nebraska. 3184 (1960).

coze (kōz), *v.,* **cozed, coz·ing,** *n.* —*v.i.* **1.** to converse in a friendly way; chat. —*n.* **2.** a friendly talk; a chat. Also, **cose.** [< F *cause(r)* (to) chat]

coz·en (kuz′ən), *v.t., v.i.* to cheat; deceive; beguile. [?] —**coz′en·er,** *n.* —**coz′en·ing·ly,** *adv.*

coz·en·age (kuz′ə nij), *n.* **1.** the practice of cozening. **2.** the condition of being cozened. [COZEN + -AGE]

Coz·ens (kuz′ənz), *n.* **1. Alexander,** 1717–86, English painter, illustrator, and art theorist, born in Russia. **2.** his son, **John Roberts,** 1752–97?, English painter.

co·zey (kō′zē), *adj.,* **-zi·er, -zi·est,** *n., pl.* **-zeys.** cozy.

co·zy (kō′zē), *adj.,* **-zi·er, -zi·est,** *n., pl.* **-zies.** —*adj.* **1.** snugly warm and comfortable: *a cozy little house.* **2.** convenient or beneficial, usually as a result of dishonesty or connivance: *a very cozy agreement between competing firms.* —*n.* **3.** a padded covering for a teapot, chocolate pot, etc., to retain the heat. Also, **cosey, cosie, cosy, cozey, co′zie.** [orig. Scot; prob. < Scand; cf. Norw *koselig* smug, *kose sig* to make oneself comfortable] —**co′zi·ly,** *adv.* —**co′zi·ness,** *n.*

Coz·zens (kuz′ənz), *n.* **James Gould,** born 1903, U.S. novelist.

cP, centipoise. Also, **cp.**

cp, candlepower.

cp., compare.

C.P., **1.** Chief Patriarch. **2.** Common Prayer. **3.** Communist party.

c.p., **1.** candle power. **2.** chemically pure. **3.** circular pitch. **4.** command post. **5.** common pleas.

C.P.A., **1.** See **certified public accountant. 2.** chartered public accountant.

C.P.C.U., Chartered Property Casualty Underwriter.

cpd., compound.

CPI, Consumer Price Index.

cpl., corporal.

c.p.m., **1.** *Music.* common particular meter. **2.** cycles per minute.

c.p.o., chief petty officer. Also, **C.P.O.**

C power supply. See **C supply.**

CPR, cardiopulmonary resuscitation.

cps, cycles per second.

cpt., counterpoint.

CPU, *Computer Technol.* central processing unit: the main component of a computer, containing the circuitry that coordinates and performs logical operations.

CQ, **1.** *Radio.* a signal sent at the beginning of radiograms of general information or sent by an amateur as an invitation for any other amateur to reply. **2.** *Mil.* charge of quarters.

Cr, *Chem.* chromium.

cr., **1.** credit. **2.** creditor.

C.R., Costa Rica.

craal (kräl), *n.* kraal.

crab[1] (krab), *n., v.,* **crabbed, crab·bing.** —*n.* **1.** any decapod crustacean of the suborder *Brachyura,* having the eyes on short stalks and a short, broad, more or less flattened body, the abdomen being small and folded under the thorax. **2.** any of various other crustaceans, as the hermit crab, or other animals, as the horseshoe crab, resembling the true crabs. **3.** (*cap.*) *Astron., Astrol.* the zodiacal constellation or sign Cancer. **4.** an ill-tempered or grouchy person. **5.** any of various mechanical contrivances for hoisting or pulling. **6.** *Aeron.* the maneuver of crabbing. **7.** Also, **crab louse.** See under **louse** (def. 1). **8. crabs, a.** a losing throw, as two aces, in the game of hazard. **b.** pediculosis. **9. catch a crab,** to make a faulty stroke in rowing, so that the oar strikes the water forcibly on the backstroke. —*v.i.* **10.** to catch crabs. **11.** *Aeron.* (of an aircraft) to head partly into the wind to compensate for drift. **12.** *Naut.* to drift or advance with some movement sideways, esp. when under tow. —*v.t.* **13.** *Aeron.* to head (an aircraft) partly into the wind to compensate for drift. [ME *crabbe,* OE *crabba;* c. D *krab,* Icel *krabbi;* akin to G *Krebs*] —**crab′like′,** *adj.*

Crab, *Callinectes sapidus* (Length 3 in.)

crab[2] (krab), *n.* a crab apple fruit or tree. [ME *crabbe;* perh. special use of CRAB[1]]

crab[3] (krab), *v.,* **crabbed, crab·bing.** —*v.i.* **1.** (of hawks) to claw each other. **2.** to find fault; complain. —*v.t.* **3.** (of a hawk) to claw (another hawk). **4.** *Informal.* to find fault with. **5.** *Slang.* to spoil. [late ME; back formation from CRABBED] —**crab′ber,** *n.*

crab′ ap′ple, **1.** a small, sour, wild apple. **2.** any of various small, tart, cultivated varieties of apple, used for making jelly and preserves. **3.** any tree bearing such fruit.

Crabb (krab), *n.* **George,** 1778–1851, English author and philologist.

Crabbe (krab), *n.* **George,** 1754–1832, English poet.

crab·bed (krab′id), *adj.* **1.** grouchy; ill-natured; irritable; churlish. **2.** perverse; contrary; obstinate. **3.** hard to understand; intricate and obscure. **4.** difficult to read or decipher, as handwriting. [ME; see CRAB[1], -ED[3]] —**crab′bed·ly,** *adv.* —**crab′bed·ness,** *n.*

crab·ber (krab′ər), *n.* **1.** a person who catches crabs. **2.** a boat used in catching crabs. [CRAB[1] + -ER[1]]

crab·bing (krab′ing), *n.* a finishing process for reducing shrinkage and creasing of woolens and worsteds by stretching the fabric on a rotating cylinder and immersing in hot or, sometimes, cold water. [CRAB[1] + -ING[1]]

crab·by (krab′ē), *adj.,* **-bi·er, -bi·est.** grouchy; ill-natured; irritable. [CRAB[1] + -Y[1]]

crab′ cac′tus, a Brazilian cactus, *Zygocactus truncatus,* having broad, leaflike, spineless stems and showy red flowers and fruit. Also called **Christmas cactus.**

crab′ can′on, *Music.* a canon in which the imitating voice is the theme in retrograde motion.

crab·eat·er (krab′ē′tər), *n.* any of various animals that feed on crabs, as the cobia. [CRAB[1] + EATER] —**crab′eat′ing,** *n., adj.*

crab′ grass′, an annual grass, *Digitaria sanguinalis,* common in cultivated and waste grounds and often occurring as a weedy pest in lawns.

crab′ locomo′tive, an electric locomotive having a winch for pulling cars from unelectrified parts of a mine. —**crab′ locomo′tion.**

crab′ louse′. See under **louse** (def. 1). Also called **crab.**

crab-plov·er (krab′pluv′ər, -plō′vər), *n.* a black and white wading bird, *Dromas ardeola,* of the northern and western shores of the Indian Ocean. [so called from its diet]

crab′ spi′der, any crab-shaped spider of the family *Thomisidae,* characterized by its sideways manner of moving.

crab·stick (krab′stik′), *n.* **1.** a stick, cane, or club made of wood, esp. of the crab tree. **2.** an ill-tempered, grouchy person. [CRAB[2] + STICK[1]]

crab′ tree′, a tree bearing crab apples. [ME *crabbe tre*]

crab·wood (krab′wo͝od′), *n.* the carapa. [CRAB[2] + WOOD[1]]

crack (krak), *v.i.* **1.** to make a sudden, sharp sound in or as if in breaking; snap: *The whip cracked.* **2.** to break with a sudden, sharp sound: *The branch cracked under the weight of the ice.* **3.** to break without complete separation of parts; become fissured: *She noticed that the cup had cracked but she used it anyway.* **4.** (of the voice) to break abruptly and discordantly, esp. into an upper register. **5.** *Chem.* to decompose as a result of being subjected to heat. **6.** to fail; give way: *His confidence cracked under the strain.* **7.** to yield; to succumb,

esp. to severe psychological pressure, torture, or the like: *They questioned him for 24 hours before he finally cracked.* **8.** *Chiefly Dial.* to brag; boast. **9.** *Chiefly Scot.* to chat; gossip.
—*v.t.* **10.** to cause to make a sudden sharp sound: *The driver cracked the whip over the horses.* **11.** to strike with a sharp noise: *The man cracked the child with his hand.* **12.** to break without complete separation of parts; break into fissures. **13.** to break with a sudden, sharp sound: *to crack walnuts.* **14.** *Informal.* to break into (a safe, vault, etc.). **15.** *Informal.* to solve; decipher: *to crack the code; to crack a murder case.* **16.** *Informal.* to open and drink (a bottle of wine, liquor, etc.). **17.** to damage, impair, etc.: *The unexpected evidence cracked his composure.* **18.** to make unsound mentally. **19.** to make (the voice) harsh or unmanageable. **20.** to break with grief; affect deeply. **21.** to utter or tell: *to crack jokes.* **22.** to cause to make a cracking sound: *to crack one's knuckles.* **23.** to subject to the process of cracking as in the distillation of petroleum. **24. crack a book,** *Slang.* to open a book in order to read or study: *Everyone wondered how he could have honor grades since he hardly ever cracked a book.* **25. crack a smile,** *Slang.* to smile. **26. crack down,** *U.S. Informal.* to take severe measures, esp. in enforcing obedience to laws or regulations: *Because of the gambling, the police are starting to crack down.* **27. crack off,** to cause (a piece of hot glass) to fall from a blowpipe or punty. **28. crack on,** *Naut.* **a.** (of a sailing vessel) to sail in high winds under sails that would normally be furled. **b.** (of a power vessel) to advance at full speed in heavy weather. **29. crack up,** **a.** *Slang.* to suffer a mental or emotional breakdown. **b.** *Informal.* to crash, as in an automobile or airplane: *He flew into the side of a mountain and cracked up.* **c.** *Informal.* to wreck an automobile, airplane, or other vehicle. **d.** *Informal.* to praise; extol: *That play is not what it is cracked up to be.* **30. crack wise,** *Slang.* to make or attempt to make a witty or humorous remark; wisecrack: *We tried to be serious, but he was always cracking wise.* **31. get cracking,** *Slang.* to begin moving or working; start: *Let's get cracking on these dirty dishes!*
—*n.* **32.** a sudden, sharp noise, as of something breaking. **33.** the snap of or as of a whip. **34.** a shot, as with a rifle: *At the first crack, the deer fell.* **35.** a resounding blow: *He received a terrific crack on the head from the beam.* **36.** a break without complete separation of parts; fissure. **37.** a slight opening, as between boards in a floor or wall, or between a door and its doorpost. **38.** a flaw or defect. **39.** a mental defect or deficiency. **40.** a broken or changing tone of the voice. **41.** *Informal.* opportunity; chance; try: *Give him first crack at the game.* **42.** *Informal.* a witty or cutting remark; wisecrack. **43.** a highly purified and addictive form of cocaine in small, hard pieces used for smoking. **44.** *Chiefly Brit.* one who or that which excels in some respect. **45.** *Informal.* a moment; instant: *He was on his feet again in a crack.* **46.** *Slang.* a burglary, esp. an instance of housebreaking. **47.** *Chiefly Scot.* conversation; chat. **48.** *Brit. Dial.* boasting; braggadocio. **49.** *Archaic.* a burglar.
—*adj.* **50.** *Informal.* first-rate; excellent: *a crack salesman.*
—*adv.* **51.** with a cracking sound. [ME *crakk(en),* var. of *craken,* OE *cracian* to resound; akin to G *krachen,* D *kraken* and perh. also to CREAK] **—crack′a·ble,** *adj.* **—crack′less,** *adj.*

crack·a·jack (krak′ə jak′), *n., adj.* crackerjack.

crack·brain (krak′brān′), *n.* a foolish, senseless, or insane person. [CRACK(ED) + BRAIN]

crack·brained (krak′brānd′), *adj.* foolish, senseless, or insane. [CRACKBRAIN + -ED[3]] **—crack′brained′-ness,** *n.*

crack·down (krak′doun′), *n.* the act of cracking down; a severe enforcing of regulations. [n. use of v. phrase *crack down*]

cracked (krakt), *adj.* **1.** broken: *a container full of cracked ice.* **2.** broken without separation of parts; fissured. **3.** damaged; injured. **4.** *Informal.* eccentric; mad; insane: *a charming old lady who was a bit cracked.* **5.** broken in tone, as the voice. [late ME *crachyd.* See CRACK, -ED[2]] **—cracked′ness,** *n.*

crack·er (krak′ər), *n.* **1.** a thin, crisp biscuit. **2.** a firecracker. **3.** Also called **cracker bonbon.** a small paper roll used as a party favor, that usually contains candy, trinkets, etc., and that pops when pulled sharply at one or both ends. **4.** (*cap.*) a native or inhabitant of Georgia (the **Cracker State**) (used as a nickname). **5.** *Disparaging.* one of a class of poor whites in parts of the southeastern U.S. **6.** *Dial.* braggart; boaster. **7.** one who or that which cracks. **—*adj.*** **8. crackers,** *Brit. Informal.* wild; crazy: *They went crackers over the new styles.* [CRACK + -ER[1]]

crack·er-bar·rel (krak′ər bar′əl), *adj.* of or suggesting the simple rustic informality and directness thought to be characteristic of life in and around a country store: *homespun, cracker-barrel philosophy.* [adj. use of *cracker barrel,* symbol of talkers who supposedly gathered around it in old-style country stores]

crack·er·ber·ry (krak′ər ber′ē), *n., pl.* **-ries.** bunchberry. [so called from the sound made when it is crunched. See CRACKER, BERRY]

crack′er bon′bon, cracker (def. 3).

crack·er·jack (krak′ər jak′), *n.* **1.** *U.S. Slang.* one who or that which shows marked ability or excellence. **—*adj.*** **2.** *Slang.* of marked ability; exceptionally fine. Also, **crackajack.** [earlier *crackajack,* rhyming compound based on CRACK (adj.); *-a-* as in BLACKAMOOR; JACK[1] in sense chap, fellow]

crack·er-on (krak′ər on′, -ôn′), *n., pl.* **crack·ers-on.** *Naut.* a vessel, as a clipper, accustomed to sailing through heavy weather without much reduction of engine power or sail. [CRACKER (with sense of speed) + -ON]

Crack′er State′, Georgia (used as a nickname).

crack·ing (krak′ing), *n.* **1.** (in the distillation of petroleum or the like) the process of breaking down certain hydrocarbons into simpler ones of lower boiling points by means of excess heat, distillation under pressure, etc., in order to give a greater yield of low-boiling products than could be obtained by simple distillation. **—*adv.*** **2.** extremely; unusually: *We saw a cracking good match at the stadium.* **—*adj.*** **3.** done with precision; smart: *A cracking salute from the honor guard.* **4. get cracking.** See **crack** (def. 31). [ME; see CRACK, -ING[1], -ING[2]]

crack·le (krak′əl), *v.,* **-led, -ling,** *n.* **—*v.i.*** **1.** to make slight, sudden, sharp noises, rapidly repeated. **2.** to form a network of fine cracks on the surface. **3.** (of ceramic glaze) to craze. **—*v.t.*** **4.** to cause to crackle. **5.** to break with a crackling noise. **6.** to craze (ceramic glaze). **—*n.*** **7.** the act of crackling. **8.** a crackling noise. **9.** a network of fine cracks, as in the glaze of some kinds of porcelain. **10.** crackleware. [CRACK + -LE]

crack·le·ware (krak′əl wâr′), *n.* ceramic ware having a crackled glaze. Also called **crackle.** [CRACKLE + WARE[1]]

crack·ling (krak′ling), *n.* **1.** the making of slight cracking sounds rapidly repeated. **2.** the crisp browned skin or rind of roast pork. **3.** Usually, **cracklings.** *Dial.* the crisp residue left when fat, esp. hog fat, is rendered. [CRACKLE + -ING[1]]

crack·ly (krak′lē), *adj.,* **-li·er, -li·est.** apt to crackle. [CRACKLE + -Y[1]]

crack·nel (krak′nəl), *n.* **1.** a hard, brittle cake or biscuit. **2. cracknels,** small bits of fat pork fried crisp. [ME *crak(e)nele* < MF **craquenelle,* metathetic alter. of *craquelin* < MD *crākelinc,* equiv. to *crāke(n)* (to) CRACK + *-linc* -LING[1]]

crack′ of dawn′, earliest hour of morning; moment light first appears in the sky: *He awoke at the crack of dawn.*

crack′ of doom′, **1.** the signal that announces the Day of Judgment. **2.** the end of the world; doomsday.

crack-off (krak′ôf′, -of′), *n.* **1.** the operation of cracking off a piece of hot glass. **2.** the place on a piece of blown glass at which it is cracked off. [n. use of v. phrase *crack off*]

crack·pot (krak′pot′), *Informal.* **—*n.*** **1.** a person who is eccentric, unrealistic, or insane. **—*adj.*** **2.** eccentric; impractical; insane: *crackpot ideas.* [CRACK(ED) + POT[1] (referring to the head)]

cracks·man (kraks′mən), *n., pl.* **-men.** *Slang.* burglar; housebreaker. [CRACK + -S[3] + MAN[1]]

crack′ the whip′, **1.** Also called **snap the whip.** a game in which players in a line, each holding the next, run, roller-skate, or ice-skate for a distance until the leader veers suddenly in a new direction, causing the rest of the line to swing around rapidly and the players at the end of the line to lose their balance or to let go of the other players. **2.** to demand obedience, hard work, and efficiency from an employee.

crack-up (krak′up′), *n.* **1.** a crash; collision. **2.** *Informal.* a breakdown in health, esp. a mental breakdown. **3.** collapse or disintegration: *the crack-up of an alliance.* [n. use of v. phrase *crack up*]

crack·y (krak′ē), *n.* See **by cracky.**

cra·co·vi·enne (krə kō′vē en′, krə kō′vē en′), *n.* krakowiak. [< F, fem. of *cracovien* of CRACOW, equiv. to *Cracov(ie)* + *-ien* -IAN]

Crac·ow (krak′ou, krä′kou, krā′kō), *n.* a city in S Poland, on the Vistula: the capital of Poland 1320–1609. 500,000 (est. 1963). German, **Krakau.** Polish, **Kraków.**

-cracy, a word element occurring in loan words from Greek (*aristocracy; democracy*); on this model used, with the meaning "rule," "government," "governing body," to form abstract nouns from stems of other origin: *mobocracy; bureaucracy.* Cf. **-crat.** [< MF *-cracie* (now *-cratie*) < LL *-cratia* < Gk *-kratia,* equiv. to *krat(ós)* rule + *-ia* -Y[3]]

cra·dle (krād′əl), *n., v.,* **-dled, -dling.** **—*n.*** **1.** a little bed or cot for an infant, usually built on rockers. **2.** the place where anything is nurtured during its early existence: *France was the cradle of modern art.* **3.** any of various contrivances similar to a child's cradle, as the framework on which a ship rests during construction or repair, or a frame or case for protecting a broken limb. **4.** *Auto.* creeper (def. 9). **5.** *Agric.* **a.** a frame of wood with a row of long curved teeth projecting above and parallel to a scythe, for laying grain in bunches as it is cut. **b.** a scythe together with the cradle in which it is set. **6.** *Mining.* a box on rockers for washing sand or gravel to separate gold or other heavy metal. **7.** *Aeron.* a docklike structure in which a rigid or semirigid airship is built or is supported during inflation. **8.** a landing platform for ferryboats, rolling on inclined tracks to facilitate loading and unloading at different water levels. **9.** *Painting.* a structure of wooden strips attached to the back of a panel, used as a support and to prevent warping. **10.** an engraver's tool for laying mezzotint grounds. **11.** *Artillery.* the part of a gun carriage on which a recoiling gun slides. **12.** *Med.* a frame that prevents the bedclothes from touching an injured part of a bedridden patient. **13.** *Naut.* **a.** a shaped support for a boat, cast, etc.; chock. **b.** truss (def. 8). **14.** *Shipbuilding.* **a.** a moving framework on which a hull slides down the ways when launched. **b.** a built-up form on which plates of irregular form are shaped. **15. rob the cradle,** *Informal.* to keep company with or marry a person much younger than oneself. **—*v.t.*** **16.** to place or rock in or as in a cradle. **17.** to nurture during infancy. **18.** to cut (grain) with a cradle. **19.** to place (a vessel) on a cradle. **20.** *Mining.* to wash (sand or gravel) in a cradle; rock. **21.** to receive or hold as a cradle. **22.** *Painting.* to support (a panel) with a cradle. **—*v.i.*** **23.** to lie in or as if in a cradle. **24.** to cut grain with a cradle scythe. [ME *cradel,* OE *cradol;* akin to OHG *cratto* basket] **—cra′dler,** *n.*

cra′dle roof′, **1.** a roof having trusses the undersides of which form an arch. **2.** a roof ceiled in the form of a barrel vault.

cra′dle scythe′, cradle (def. 5b).

cra·dle·song (krād′əl sông′, -song′), *n.* a lullaby. [CRADLE + SONG]

cra′dle vault′. See **barrel vault.**

cra·dling (krād′ling), *n.* framework for supporting a coved or vaulted ceiling. [CRADLE + -ING[1]]

craft (kraft, kräft), *n.* **1.** skill; dexterity: *The silversmith worked with great craft.* **2.** skill or ability used for bad purposes; cunning; deceit; guile. **3.** an art, trade, or occupation requiring special skill, esp. manual skill: *the craft of a mason.* **4.** the members of a trade or profession collectively; a guild. **5.** a ship or other vessel. **6.** a number of ships or other vessels taken as a whole: *The craft were warned to beware of squalls.* **7.** aircraft collectively: *The craft were flying over the coast by morning.* **8.** a single aircraft. **—*v.t.*** **9.** to make or manufacture (an object, objects, product, etc.) with skill and careful attention to detail. [ME; OE *cræft* strength, skill; c. G *Kraft,* D *kracht,* Icel *kraptr*] **—craft′less,** *adj.*
—Syn. 1. talent, ability. **2.** craftiness, subtlety, artifice, artfulness, shrewdness, deceitfulness, deception. See **cunning. 3.** vocation, calling, metier.

-craft, a combining form of **craft:** *handicraft.*

Craf·tint (kraf′tint′, kräf′-), *n.* *Print., Trademark.* a set of prepared patterns, printed on clear plastic sheets, for pasting on artwork to produce effects of shading, crosshatching, etc.

Craf·ton (kraf′tən), *n.* a town in SW Pennsylvania. 8418 (1960).

crafts·man (krafts′mən, kräfts′-), *n., pl.* **-men.** **1.** one who practices a craft; artisan. **2.** an artist. [ME *craftes man* man of skill, earlier *craftman;* r. OE *cræftiga* craftsman, workman; see CRAFTY] **—crafts′man·ship′,** *n.*
—Syn. 1. artificer, mechanic, handicraftsman.

craft′ un′ion, a labor union composed only of people in the same craft. **—craft′ un′ionist.**

craft·work (kraft′wûrk′, kräft′-), *n.* **1.** work that requires special skill or artistry, esp. a handicraft. **2.** a piece of such work. [CRAFT + WORK] **—craft′work′er,** *n.*

craft·y (kraf′tē, kräf′-), *adj.,* **craft·i·er, craft·i·est.** **1.** skillful in underhand or evil schemes; cunning; deceitful; sly. **2.** *Archaic.* skillful; ingenious; dexterous. [ME; OE *cræftig* skilled. See CRAFT, -Y[1]] **—craft′i·ly,** *adv.* **—craft′i·ness,** *n.*
—Syn. 1. artful, wily, insidious, tricky, designing, scheming, plotting.

Craf·type (kraf′tīp′, kräf′-), *n.* *Print., Trademark.* type printed on clear plastic sheets for pasting on artwork.

crag[1] (krag), *n.* a steep, rugged rock; a rough, broken, projecting part of a rock. [ME < Celt; cf. Welsh *craig* rock] **—crag′like′,** *adj.*

crag[2] (krag), *n.* *Scot. and North Eng.* the neck, throat, or craw. [late ME *cragge* < MFlem *krage* neck; c. G *Kragen* collar; see CRAW]

crag-and-tail (krag′ən tāl′), *n.* a hill composed of rock or glacial drift, of which one face has a steep, smooth slope and the other a gentle slope.

crag·gy (krag′ē), *adj.,* **-gi·er, -gi·est.** **1.** full of crags. **2.** rugged; harsh; rough. Also, **crag·ged** (krag′id). [ME; see CRAG[1], -Y[1]] **—crag′gi·ly, crag′ged·ly,** *adv.* **—crag′gi·ness, crag′ged·ness,** *n.*

crags·man (kragz′mən), *n., pl.* **-men.** one accustomed to or skilled in climbing crags. [CRAG[1] + -S[3] + MAN[1]]

Craig (krāg), *n.* **1. Edward Gordon,** 1872–1966, English stage designer, producer, and author. **2.** a town in NW Colorado. 3984 (1960). **3.** a boy's given name.

Craig·a·von (krāg ā′vən, -av′ən), *n.* **James Craig, 1st Viscount,** 1871–1940, 1st prime minister of Northern Ireland 1921–40.

Crai·gie (krā′gē), *n.* **Sir William (Alexander),** 1867–1957, Scottish lexicographer and philologist.

Craik (krāk), *n.* **Dinah Maria** (*Dinah Maria Mulock*), 1826–87, English novelist, poet, and author of books for children.

Cra·io·va (krä yô′vä), *n.* a city in SW Rumania. 122,108 (est. 1964).

crake (krāk), *n.* any of several short-billed rails, esp. the corn crake. [ME < Scand; cf. Icel *krāka* crow, *krākr* raven]

cra·kow (krä′kou), *n.* poulaine. [ME *crakowe,* after CRACOW, the place of origin]

cram (kram), *v.,* **crammed, cram·ming,** *n.* **—*v.t.*** **1.** to fill (something) by force with more than it can conveniently hold. **2.** to force or stuff (usually fol. by *into, down,* etc.). **3.** to fill with or as with an excessive amount of food; overfeed. **4.** *Informal.* **a.** to prepare (a person), as for an examination, by storing his memory with facts in a short period of time. **b.** to acquire knowledge of (a subject) by so preparing oneself. **5.** *Archaic.* to tell lies to. **—*v.i.*** **6.** to eat greedily or to excess. **7.** *Informal.* to study for an examination by hastily memorizing facts at the last minute. **—*n.*** **8.** *Informal.* the action of cramming for an examination. **9.** a crammed state. **10.** a dense crowd; throng. [ME *cramm(en),* OE *crammian* to stuff, akin to *crimman* to put in] **—cram′ming·ly,** *adv.*
—Syn. 2. crowd, pack, squeeze, compress, overcrowd. **3.** glut. **6.** gorge.

Cram (kram), *n.* **Ralph Adams,** 1863–1942, U.S. architect and writer.

cram·bo (kram′bō), *n., pl.* **-boes.** **1.** a game in which one person or side must find a rhyme to a word or a line of verse given by another. **2.** inferior rhyme. [earlier *crambe,* lit., cabbage < L (< Gk *krámbē*), short for *crambe repetita* cabbage repeated, i.e., rhyming game]

Cra′mer's rule′ (krā′mərz), *Math.* a method involving the determinant of the coefficients, for calculating a unique solution for a given system of linear equations. [named after Gabriel *Cramer* (1704–72), Swiss mathematician]

Cra·mer·ton (krā′mər tən), *n.* a town in S North Carolina. 3123 (1960).

cram-full (kram′fo͝ol′), *adj.* as full as possible; chock-full: *an argument cram-full of inconsistencies; a box cram-full with toys.*

cram·mer (kram′ər), *n.* **1.** one who or that which crams or stuffs. **2.** *Informal.* **a.** *Brit.* a person or school that prepares a student for an examination or the like by cramming. **b.** a student who crams for an examination or the like. **3.** *Archaic.* a lie or falsehood. [CRAM + -ER[1]]

cram·oi·sy (kram′oi zē, -ə zē), *Archaic.* **—*adj.*** **1.** crimson. **—*n.*** **2.** crimson cloth. Also, **cram′oi·sie.** [< F *cramoisi,* earlier *crameisi* < Sp *carmesí* < Ar *qirmizī,* equiv. to *qirmiz* KERMES + *-ī* suffix of appurtenance; r. late ME *cremesye* < It *crèmisi* < Ar, as above]

cramp[1] (kramp), *n.* **1.** Often, **cramps. a.** a sudden, involuntary, persistent contraction of a muscle or group of muscles, esp. of the extremities, sometimes associated with severe pain. **b.** a piercing pain in the abdomen. **c.** an intermittent, painful contraction of structures of a wall containing involuntary muscle, as in biliary colic or in the uterine contractions of menstruation or of labor. **2.** *Pathol.* See **writer's cramp.** **—*v.t.*** **3.** to affect with or as if with a cramp. [ME *crampe* < MD (whence also MF *crampe*)]

cramp[2] (kramp), *n.* **1.** See **cramp iron. 2.** a portable frame or tool with a movable part which can be screwed up to hold things together; clamp. **3.** anything that confines or restrains. **4.** a cramped state or part. **—*v.t.*** **5.** to fasten or hold with a cramp. **6.** to confine narrowly;

restrict; restrain; hamper. **7.** to steer; to turn the front wheel of a motor vehicle by means of the steering gear. **8. cramp one's style,** *Slang.* to prevent a person from showing his best abilities; thwart: *The routine of library work cramps her style.* —*adj.* **9.** hard to decipher or understand; difficult; knotty. **10.** contracted; narrow. [late ME *crampe* < MD] —**cramped′ness,** *n.* —**cramp′ing·ly,** *adv.*

cramp·fish (kramp′fish′), *n., pl.* **-fish·es,** (*esp. collectively*) **-fish.** See **electric ray.** [CRAMP[1] + FISH]

cramp′ i′ron, a piece of iron with bent ends for holding together building stones or the like.

cram·pon (kram′pən), *n.* **1.** a grappling iron, esp. one of a pair for raising heavy weights. **2.** a spiked iron plate worn on the shoe to prevent slipping on ice, snow, etc. Also, **cram·poon** (kram po͞on′). [ME *cra(u)mpon* < MF *crampon,* equiv. to *crampe* hook (< MD; see CRAMP[2]) + *-on* n. suffix]

cram·pon·née (kram′pə nā′, -nē′), *adj. Heraldry.* noting a cross with equal arms having angular, hooklike terminations. Also, **cram′po·née′.** [< F, fem. of *cramponné,* ptp. of *cramponner* to fasten with cramps, deriv. of *crampon* CRAMPON]

Cra·nach (krä′näkh), *n.* **1. Lucas** ("*the Elder*"), 1472–1553, German painter and graphic artist. **2.** his son, **Lucas the Younger,** 1515–86, German painter and graphic artist. Also, **Kranach, Kronach.**

cran·age (krā′nij), *n. Naut.* **1.** the service performed by a hired crane. **2.** the fee for this service. [ME; see CRANE, -AGE]

Cra·na·us (krā′nā əs), *n. Class. Myth.* a man born of the earth who became a king of Attica.

cran·ber·ry (kran′ber′ē, -bə rē), *n., pl.* **-ries. 1.** the red, acid fruit or berry of any ericaceous plant of the genus *Vaccinium,* as *V. macrocarpus* (**large cranberry** or **American cranberry**), or *V. oxycoccus* (**small cranberry** or **European cranberry**), used in making sauce, jelly, etc. **2.** the plant itself. [< LG *kraanbere.* See CRANE, BERRY]

cran′berry bog′, a bog in which cranberry plants are cultivated.

cran′berry bush′, a shrub, *Viburnum trilobum,* of northern North America, having white flowers nearly four inches wide and scarlet fruit. Also called **high cranberry.**

cran′berry gourd′, 1. a cucurbitaceous vine, *Abora tenuifolia,* of South America, bearing a berrylike scarlet fruit. **2.** the fruit itself.

cran′berry tree′, a caprifoliaceous tree or shrub, *Viburnum Opulus,* bearing red berries and white cymose flowers. Also called **bush cranberry.**

crance′ i′ron (krans), *Naut.* **1.** a metal ring or cap to which bobstays and shrouds are secured, at the forward end of a bowsprit. **2.** an iron mast fitting holding a yard that is not raised or lowered, as those of the foresail or mainsail in a large ship. [cf. D *krans* wreath and CRANCELIN]

cran·ce·lin (kran′sə lin′, krans′lin), *n. Heraldry.* a charge resembling part of the circlet of a coronet. [< early form of G *Kränzlein* little wreath]

cran·dall (kran′dəl), *n.* a tool for dressing stone, having adjustable, pointed, steel rods held in a slot at the end of the handle. [prob. after the proper name]

crane (krān), *n., v.,* **craned, cran·ing.** —*n.* **1.** any of several large wading birds of the family *Gruidae,* having long legs, bill, and neck and an elevated hind toe. **2.** (not used scientifically) any of various similar birds of other families, as the great blue heron. **3.** *Mach.* a device for lifting and moving heavy weights. **4.** any of various similar devices, as a horizontally swinging arm by a fireplace, used for suspending pots, kettles, etc., over the fire. **5.** *Motion Pictures, Television.* a large boom for hoisting and manipulating a camera. **6.** *Naut.* any of a number of supports for a boat or spare spar on the deck or at the side of a vessel. **7.** (*cap.*) *Astron.* the constellation Grus. —*v.t.* **8.** to hoist, lower, or move by or as by a crane. **9.** to stretch (the neck) as a crane does. —*v.i.* **10.** to stretch out one's neck. **11.** *Informal.* to hesitate at danger, difficulty, etc. [ME; OE *cran;* c. G *Kran,* Gk *géranos*] —**crane′like′,** *adj.* —**crane′ly,** *adj.*

Whooping crane, *Grus americana* (Height about 5 ft.; wingspread 7½ ft.)

Crane (krān), *n.* **1.** (**Harold**) **Hart,** 1899–1932, U.S. poet. **2. Stephen,** 1871–1900, U.S. novelist, poet, and short-story writer. **3.** a town in W Texas. 3796 (1960).

crane′ fly′, any of numerous dipterous insects of the family *Tipulidae* that resemble a large mosquito with extremely long legs. —**crane′-fly′,** *adj.*

crane·man (krān′man′, -mən), *n., pl.* **-men** (-men′, -mən). a man who operates a crane. [CRANE + MAN[1]] —**crane′man·ship′,** *n.*

crane's-bill (krānz′bil′), *n.* any plant of the genus *Geranium,* bearing long, slender, beaked fruit. Also, **cranes′bill′, crane′bill′.** [CRANE + 'S[1] + BILL[2], trans. of D *kranebek* geranium (now obs.)]

Cran·ford (kran′fərd), *n.* a town in NE New Jersey. 26,424 (1960).

cra·ni·al (krā′nē əl), *adj.* of or pertaining to the cranium or skull. [CRANI(UM) + -AL[1]] —**cra′ni·al·ly,** *adv.*

cra′nial in′dex, *Craniom.* the ratio of the greatest length from front to back multiplied by 100.

cra′nial nerve′, *Anat.* one member of twelve pairs of nerves that emerge from the brain through openings in the skull and that are sensory, or motor, or both.

Cra·ni·a·ta (krā′nē ā′tə), *n.* Vertebrata. [< NL; see CRANIATE]

cra·ni·ate (krā′nē it, -āt′), *adj.* **1.** having a cranium or skull. **2.** belonging or pertaining to the subphylum *Vertebrata* (or *Craniata*); vertebrate. —*n.* **3.** a craniate animal. [CRANI- + -ATE[1]]

cranio-, a combining form of **cranium:** *craniotomy.* Also, *esp. before a vowel,* **crani-.**

craniol., craniology.

cra·ni·ol·o·gy (krā′nē ol′ə jē), *n.* the science that deals with the size, shape, and other characteristics of human skulls. [CRANIO- + -LOGY] —**cra·ni·o·log·i·cal** (krā′nē ə loj′i kəl), *adj.* —**cra′ni·o·log′i·cal·ly,** *adv.* —**cra′ni·ol′o·gist,** *n.*

craniom., craniometry.

cra·ni·om·e·ter (krā′nē om′i tər), *n.* an instrument for measuring the external dimensions of skulls. [CRANIO- + -METER]

cra·ni·om·e·try (krā′nē om′i trē), *n.* the science of measuring skulls. [CRANIO- + -METRY] —**cra·ni·o·met·ric** (krā′nē ə me′trik), **cra′ni·o·met′ri·cal,** *adj.* —**cra′ni·o·met′ri·cal·ly,** *adv.* —**cra′ni·om′e·trist,** *n.*

cra·ni·o·phore (krā′nē ə fōr′, -fôr′), *n.* a device that holds a skull in place for measuring. [CRANIO- + -PHORE]

cra·ni·os·co·py (krā′nē os′kə pē), *n.* observation, examination, and description of the human skull. [CRANIO- + -SCOPY] —**cra·ni·o·scop·i·cal** (krā′nē ə skop′i kəl), *adj.* —**cra′ni·os′co·pist,** *n.*

cra·ni·ot·o·my (krā′nē ot′ə mē), *n., pl.* **-mies.** *Surg.* the operation of opening the skull, usually for operations on the brain. [CRANIO- + -TOMY] —**cra·ni·o·tome** (krā′nē ə tōm′), *n.*

cra·ni·um (krā′nē əm), *n., pl.* **-ni·ums, -ni·a** (-nē ə). **1.** the skull of a vertebrate. **2.** the part of the skull which encloses the brain. [< ML *crānium* < Gk *krānion* skull]

crank[1] (krangk), *n.* **1.** *Mach.* any of several types of arms or levers for imparting rotary or oscillatory motion to a rotating shaft, one end of the crank being fixed to the shaft and the other end receiving reciprocating motion from hand, connecting rod, etc. **2.** *Informal.* an ill-tempered, grouchy person. **3.** an eccentric person who is overzealous in his advocacy of a private cause. **4.** an eccentric or whimsical notion. **5.** a strikingly clever turn of speech or play of words. **6.** *Obs.* a bend; turn. —*v.t.* **7.** to bend into or make in the shape of a crank. **8.** to furnish with a crank. **9.** *Mach.* to rotate (a shaft) by means of a crank. **10.** to start (an internal-combustion engine) by turning the crankshaft manually or by means of a small motor. **11.** to start the engine of (a motor vehicle) by turning the crankshaft manually. —*v.i.* **12.** to turn a crank, as in starting an automobile engine. **13.** *Archaic.* to turn and twist; zigzag. —*adj.* **14.** unstable; shaky; unsteady. **15.** *Brit. Dial.* cranky[1] (def. 5). [ME *cranke,* OE *cranc-,* in *crancstæf* crank; see STAFF[1]] —**crank′less,** *adj.*

crank[2] (krangk), *adj.* **1.** having a tendency to roll easily, as a boat, ship, etc.; tender (opposed to *stiff*). —*n.* **2.** a crank vessel. [short for *crank-sided;* cf. D *krengd* careened]

crank[3] (krangk), *adj. Dial.* lively; high-spirited. [ME *cranke* < ?] —**crank′ly,** *adv.* —**crank′ness,** *n.*

crank·case (krangk′kās′), *n.* (in an internal-combustion engine) the housing which encloses the crankshaft, connecting rods, and allied parts. [CRANK[1] + CASE[2]]

crank′ disk′. See **disk crank.**

cran·kle (krang′kəl), *n., v.t., v.i.,* **-kled, -kling.** bend; turn. [CRANK[1] + -LE]

crank′ let′ter, a hostile letter, often sent anonymously to a public figure or a newspaper, magazine, etc., and sometimes containing threats of violence.

crank·ous (krang′kəs), *adj. Scot.* irritated; cranky. [CRANK[1] + -OUS]

crank·pin (krangk′pin′), *n. Mach.* a short cylindrical pin at the outer end of a crank, held by and moving with a connecting rod or link. Also, **crank′ pin′.** Cf. **web** (def. 9). [CRANK[1] + PIN]

A, Crankpin B, Disk crank C, Connecting rod

crank·plate (krangk′plāt′), *n.* See **disk crank.** [CRANK[1] + PLATE[1]]

crank·shaft (krangk′shaft′, -shäft′), *n. Mach.* a shaft having one or more cranks, usually formed as integral parts. [CRANK[1] + SHAFT]

Crankshaft W, Web; C, Crankpin

crank·y[1] (krang′kē), *adj.,* **crank·i·er, crank·i·est. 1.** ill-tempered; grouchy; cross: *a cranky old man.* **2.** eccentric; queer. **3.** shaky; unsteady; out of order. **4.** full of bends or windings; crooked. **5.** *Brit. Dial.* sickly; in unsound or feeble condition; infirm. [CRANK[1] + -Y[1]] —**crank′i·ly,** *adv.* —**crank′i·ness,** *n.*
—**Syn. 1.** crotchety, cantankerous, perverse. —**Ant. 1.** good-natured.

crank·y[2] (krang′kē), *adj.* tending to lurch or capsize. [CRANK[2] + -Y[1]]

Cran·mer (kran′mər), *n.* **Thomas,** 1489–1556, 1st Protestant archbishop of Canterbury: leader in the English Protestant Reformation in England.

cran·ne·quin (kran′ə kin), *n.* a portable device for bending a crossbow. See illus. under **crossbow.** [var. of CRANNOG]

cran·nog (kran′əg), *n.* **1.** (in ancient Ireland and Scotland) a lake dwelling, usually built on an artificial island. **2.** a small, artificial, fortified island constructed in bogs in ancient Scotland and Ireland. Also, **cran·noge** (kran′əj). [< Ir: wooden structure, equiv. to *crann* beam, tree + *-ōg* n. suffix]

cran·ny (kran′ē), *n., pl.* **-nies.** a small, narrow opening in a wall, rock, etc.; a chink; crevice; fissure. [late ME *crany* < MF *cran* fissure; see -Y[2]] —**cran′nied,** *adj.*

cran·reuch (krän′rəkh), *n. Scot.* hoarfrost. [appar. < Gael phrase *crann reodhach* frosty tree, equiv. to *crann* tree + *reodh* frost, hoarfrost + *-ach* adj. suffix]

Cran·ston (kran′stən), *n.* a city in E Rhode Island, near Providence. 66,766 (1960).

crap[1] (krap), *n.* **1.** (in craps) a losing throw, in which the total on the two dice is 2, 3, or 12. **2.** craps. —*v.* **3. crap out, a.** *Slang.* to abandon a project, activity, etc., because of fear, cowardice, exhaustion, loss of enthusiasm, etc. **b.** *Slang.* to rest, relax, nap, etc. **c.** *Craps.* to roll a seven rather than make one's point. [back formation from CRAPS]

crap[2] (krap), *n., v.,* **crapped, crap·ping.** *Slang.* —*n.* **1.** *Vulgar.* excrement. **2.** nonsense; drivel: *Man, don't hand me that crap.* **3.** a lie; an exaggeration: *Bah, you don't believe that crap, do you?* **4.** refuse; rubbish; junk; litter: *Will you clean up that crap!* —*v.i.* **5.** *Vulgar.* to defecate. —*v.t.* **6.** to create a mess; cause to fail, esp. by excessive labor, material, etc.: *Boy, did he crap the job up with a lot of junk.* **7. crap around, a.** to behave in a foolish or silly manner. **b.** to avoid work. [late ME *crappe* chaff < MFlem]

crap·au·dine′ door′ (krap′ə dēn′, krap′ə dēn′), a door that rotates on pivots let into the sill and the lintel. [< F, equiv. to *crapaud* toad, OF *crapaut, -ot* (< Gmc) + *-ine* -INE[1]]

crape (krāp), *n., v.t.,* **craped, crap·ing.** crepe. [Anglicized sp.] —**crape′like′,** *adj.*

crape·hang·er (krāp′hang′gər), *n. Slang.* one who sees the gloomy side of things; pessimist. Also, **crepe-hanger.** [CRAPE + HANGER]

crape′ jas′mine, a showy fragrant shrub, *Tabernaemontana coronaria,* of India, having shiny leaves and white flowers. Also called **Adam's apple, East Indian rose-bay, Nero's-crown.**

crape′ myr′tle, a tall Chinese shrub, *Lagerstroemia indica,* having showy pink, purple, red, or white flowers, grown as an ornamental in the southern and western U.S. Also, **crepe myrtle.**

crap·pie (krap′ē), *n.* either of two small sunfishes found in the central U.S., *Pomoxis nigro-maculatus* (**black crappie**) or *P. annularis* (**white crappie**). Also, **croppie.** [< CanF *crapet*]

craps (kraps), *n.* (*usually construed as sing.*) a game in which two dice are thrown and in which a first throw of 7 or 11 wins, a first throw of 2, 3, or 12 loses, and a first throw of 4, 5, 6, 8, 9, or 10 can be won only by repeating the number thrown before a seven appears. [appar. < F *craps,* var. of *crabs* double-ace (lowest throw at hazard) < 18th-century English slang: pl. of CRAB[1]]

crap·shoot·er (krap′sho͞o′tər), *n.* a person who plays the game of craps. [CRAP + SHOOTER]

crap·u·lent (krap′yo͞o lənt, -yə-), *adj.* sick from gross excess in drinking or eating. [< LL *crāpulent(us)* drunk, deriv. of L *crāpula* drunkenness < Gk *kraipálē* a hangover; see -ENT] —**crap′u·lence, crap′u·len·cy,** *n.*

crap·u·lous (krap′yo͞o ləs, -yə-), *adj.* **1.** given to or characterized by gross excess in drinking or eating. **2.** suffering from or due to such excess. [< LL *crāpulōs(us).* See CRAPULENT, -OUS] —**crap′u·lous·ly,** *adv.* —**crap′u·lous·ness,** *n.*

cra·que·lure (krak lo͝or′, krak′lo͝or; *Fr.* krakᵊ lyr′), *n., pl.* **-lures** (-lo͝orz′, -lo͝orz; *Fr.* -lyr′). a network of fine cracks or crackles on the surface of a painting, caused chiefly by shrinkage of paint film or varnish. [< F, equiv. to *craquel(er)* (to) crackle, crack (imit.) + *-ure* -URE]

crare (krâr), *n. Naut.* crayer.

crash[1] (krash), *v.t.* **1.** to break into pieces violently and noisily; shatter. **2.** to force or drive with violence and noise (usually fol. by *in, through, out,* etc.). **3.** *Informal.* **a.** to gain admittance to though uninvited: *to crash a party.* **b.** to enter without a ticket, permission, etc.: *to crash the gate at a football game.* **4.** *Aeron.* to cause (an aircraft) to make a landing in an abnormal manner, usually damaging or wrecking the aircraft. —*v.i.* **5.** to break or fall to pieces with noise. **6.** to make a loud, clattering noise, as of something dashed to pieces. **7.** to collapse or fail suddenly, as a financial enterprise: *The stock market crashed.* **8.** to move or go with a crash; strike with a crash. **9.** *Aeron.* to land in an abnormal manner, usually causing severe damage: *The airliner crashed.* —*n.* **10.** a breaking or falling to pieces with loud noise: *the sudden crash of dishes.* **11.** the shock of collision and breaking. **12.** a collision or crashing, as of automobiles, trains, etc. **13.** a sudden and violent falling to ruin: *the crash of an airplane.* **14.** a sudden collapse of a business enterprise or the like. **15.** a sudden general collapse of business prosperity, the stock market, etc. **16.** a sudden loud noise, as of something being violently smashed or struck: *the crash of thunder.* **17.** *Aeron.* an act or instance of crashing. —*adj.* **18.** *Informal.* characterized by an intensive effort, esp. to meet an emergency: *a crash program to produce vaccine.* [late ME *crasche,* b. *crase* to break (see CRAZE) and MASH] —**crash′er,** *n.*
—**Syn. 1.** smash. **14.** failure, ruin.

crash[2] (krash), *n.* **1.** a plain-weave fabric of rough, irregular, or lumpy yarns, for toweling, dresses, etc. **2.** *Bookbinding.* starched cotton fabric used to reinforce the spine of a bound book. [?]

Crash·aw (krash′ô), *n.* **Richard,** 1613–49, English poet.

crash′ boat′, a small, fast boat used in rescue operations, particularly in connection with airplane crashes.

crash′ dive′, a rapid dive by a submarine made at a steep angle, esp. to avoid attack from a surface vessel or airplane.

crash-dive (krash′dīv′, -dīv′), *v.i., v.t.,* **-dived** or **-dove, -dived, -div·ing.** (of a submarine) to dive rapidly at a steep angle.

crash′ hel′met, a helmet for protecting the head in the event of an accident, worn by motorcyclists, automobile racers, etc.

crash·ing (krash′ing), *adj. Informal.* **1.** unusual; exceptional: *a crashing celebration.* **2.** absolute; complete; utter: *a crashing bore.* [CRASH[1] + -ING[2]] —**crash′ing·ly,** *adv.*

crash-land (krash′land′), *v.t.* **1.** to land (an aircraft), under circumstances where a normal landing is impossible, in such a way as to damage the aircraft. —*v.i.* **2.** to crash-land an aircraft. [CRASH[1] + LAND] —**crash′-land′ing,** *n.*

crash′ pad′, padding inside cars, tanks, or the like, for protecting the passengers in the event of an accident, sudden stop, etc.

crash′ wall′, *Railroads.* a wall for holding derailed rolling stock parallel to the track.

cra·sis (krā′sis), *n., pl.* **-ses** (-sēz). *Archaic.* composition; constitution; makeup. [< Gk *krâsis* mixture, blend, equiv. to *krā-* (root of *kerannýnai* to mix) + *-sis* -SIS]

crass (kras), *adj.* **1.** without refinement, delicacy, or sensitivity; gross; obtuse; stupid: *crass commercialism; a crass misrepresentation of the facts.* **2.** *Archaic.* thick; coarse: *a crass texture.* [< L *crass(us)* thick, dense, fat, heavy] —**crass′ly,** *adv.* —**crass′ness,** *n.*
—**Syn. 1.** dull, boorish, oafish, indelicate.

cras·si·tude (kras′i to͞od′, -tyo͞od′), *n.* **1.** gross ignorance or stupidity. **2.** thickness; grossness. [< L *crassitūd(ō)* thickness. See CRASS, -I-, -TUDE]

cras·su·la·ceous (kras′yŏŏ lā′shəs, -yə-), *adj.* belonging to the *Crassulaceae*, a family of mostly fleshy or succulent herbs, comprising the houseleek, sedum, etc. [< NL *Crassul(a)* genus name (ML *crassula;* see CRASS, -ULE), + -ACEOUS]

Cras·sus (kras′əs), *n.* **Marcus Li·cin·i·us** (li sin′ē əs), c115–53 B.C., Roman general: member of the first triumvirate.

-crat, a learned borrowing from Greek meaning "ruler," "member of a ruling body," "advocate of a particular form of rule," used in the formation of compound words: *autocrat; plutocrat; technocrat.* Cf. **-cracy.** [< Gk *-kratēs* as in *autokratēs* AUTOCRAT; r. *-crate* < F < Gk]

Cra·tae·is (krə tē′is), *n.* (in the *Odyssey*) the mother of Scylla.

cratch (krach), *n.* *Archaic.* a crib to hold fodder; manger. [ME *cracche* manger < OF *crache,* var. of *creche,* CRÈCHE]

crate (krāt), *n., v.,* **crat·ed, crat·ing.** —*n.* **1.** a box or framework, usually made of wooden slats, for packing and transporting fruit, furniture, etc. **2.** a basket of wickerwork, for the transportation of crockery, glassware, etc. **3.** *Informal.* something rickety and dilapidated, esp. an automobile: *She's still driving around in the old crate she bought 20 years ago.* **4.** a quantity, esp. of fruit that is often packed in a crate approximately 2 ft. × 1 ft. × 1 ft.: *a crate of oranges.* —*v.t.* **5.** to put in a crate. [ME < L *crāt(is)* wickerwork, hurdle]

cra·ter (krā′tər), *n., gen.* **Cra·te·ris** (krā tēr′is) for 9, *v.* —*n.* **1.** the cup-shaped depression or cavity in the surface of the earth, moon, or other heavenly body marking the orifice of a volcano . **2.** (in the surface of the earth, moon, etc.) a bowl-shaped depression with a raised rim, formed by the impact of a meteorite. **3.** (on the surface of the moon) a circular or almost circular area having a depressed floor, almost always containing a central mountain and usually completely enclosed by walls that are often higher than those of a walled plain; ring formation; ring. Cf. **walled plain. 4.** the bowllike orifice of a geyser. **5.** the hole or pit in the ground where a military mine, shell, or bomb has exploded. **6.** *Elect.* the cavity formed in a positive carbon electrode by an electric arc. **7.** *Gk. and Rom. Antiquity.* krater. **8.** *Welding.* a depression at the end of a bead. **9.** (*cap.*) *Astron.* the Cup, a small southern constellation east of Corvus and north of Hydra. —*v.t.* **10.** to make craters in: *Bombs had cratered the landscape.* —*v.i.* **11.** to form a crater or craters: *The surface of the concrete cratered and cracked under the repeated impacts.* **12.** (of a lathe tool) to become hollowed on the upper surface, through friction, with chips removed from the work. [< L < Gk *krātēr* mixing bowl, lit., mixer, equiv. to *krā-* (root of *kerannýnai* to mix) + *-tēr* agentive suffix] —**cra′ter·al, cra′ter·ous,** *adj.* —**cra′ter·less,** *adj.* —**cra′ter·like′,** *adj.*

Cra·ter (krā′tər), *n.* **Joseph Force** (fōrs, fôrs), 1889–?, a judge of the New York State Supreme Court: disappeared August 6, 1930.

Cra′ter Lake′, a lake in the crater of an extinct volcano in SW Oregon, in Crater Lake National Park. 20 sq. mi.; 1996 ft. deep.

Cra′ter Lake′ Na′tional Park′, a national park in SW Oregon, in the Cascade Range: Crater Lake. 250 sq. mi.

Cra′ter Mound′, a bowl-shaped depression in the earth in central Arizona: believed to have been made by a meteorite. 4000 ft. wide; 600 ft. deep. Also called **Meteor Crater.**

cra·ton (krā′ton), *n.* *Geol.* a relatively rigid and immobile region of the earth's crust. [< G *Kraton* < Gk *krátos* power]

Cra·tus (krā′təs), *n.* the ancient Greek personification of strength, the son either of Uranus and Gaea or of the Titan Pallas and of Styx.

craunch (krônch, krānch), *v.t., v.i., n.* crunch. [var. of *cranch,* itself perh. nasalized var. of CRASH[1] in its orig. sense of to break up, shatter] —**craunch′ing·ly,** *adv.*

cra·vat (krə vat′), *n., v.,* **-vat·ted, -vat·ting.** —*n.* **1.** necktie (defs. 1, 2). **2.** a cloth, often made of or trimmed with lace, worn about the neck by men esp. in the 17th century. **3.** *Med.* a bandage made by folding a triangular piece of material into a band, used temporarily for a fracture or wound. **4.** *Naut.* a cover at the top of a funnel casing, sloping upward and inward toward the funnel itself. —*v.t.* **5.** to dress or furnish with or as if with a cravat. [< F *cravate* neckcloth, lit., Croat; so called because worn by Croats in French army. See CROAT]

crave (krāv), *v.,* **craved, crav·ing.** —*v.t.* **1.** to long for; want greatly; desire eagerly: *to crave affection.* **2.** to require; need: *a problem craving prompt attention.* **3.** to ask earnestly for (something); beg for. **4.** *Obs.* to ask (a person) earnestly for something or to do something. —*v.i.* **5.** to beg or plead (usually fol. by *for*). **6.** to long (usually fol. by *for* or *after*). [ME *crave(n),* OE *crafian;* akin to Icel *krefja* to demand, lay claim to] —**crav′er,** *n.*
—**Syn. 1.** yearn for, hunger for. **3.** beseech, entreat, implore.

cra·ven (krā′vən), *adj.* **1.** cowardly; contemptibly timid; pusillanimous. —*n.* **2.** a coward. **3. cry craven,** to yield; capitulate; give up. —*v.t.* **4.** to make cowardly. [ME *cravant* overthrown, unexplained alter. of *creant* RECREANT] —**cra′ven·ly,** *adv.* —**cra′ven·ness,** *n.*
—**Ant. 1.** brave.

Cra·ven (krā′vən), *n.* **A·ver·y O·delle** (ā′və rē ō del′), born 1886, U.S. historian.

Crav·en·ette (krav′ə net′, krā′və-), *n., v.,* **-et·ted, -et·ting.** —*n.* **1.** *Trademark.* a finish for wool or cotton fabrics to render them water-repellent. —*v.t.* **2.** (*l.c.*) to render (fabric, a garment, etc.) water-repellent by means of Cravenette.

crav·ing (krā′ving), *n.* deep longing; great or eager desire; yearning. [ME; see CRAVE, -ING[1]] —**crav′ing·ly,** *adv.* —**crav′ing·ness,** *n.*
—**Syn.** See **desire.**

craw (krô), *n.* **1.** the crop of a bird or insect. **2.** the stomach of an animal. **3. stick in one's craw,** to be irritating or intolerable to one: *Her constant complaining just sticks in my craw.* [ME *crawe,* OE **craga;* see CRAG[2]]

craw·fish (krô′fish′), *n., pl.* (*esp. collectively*) **-fish,** (*esp. referring to two or more kinds or species*) **-fish·es,** *v.* —*n.* **1.** crayfish. —*v.i.* **2.** *Informal.* to back out or retreat from a position or undertaking. [var. of CRAYFISH]

Craw·ford (krô′fərd), *n.* **1. Francis Marion,** 1854–1909, U.S. novelist, in Italy after 1885. **2. Thomas,** 1813?–57, U.S. sculptor.

crawl[1] (krôl), *v.i.* **1.** to move in a prone position with the body resting on or close to the ground, as a worm or caterpillar, or on the hands and knees, as a young child. **2.** (of plants or vines) to extend tendrils; creep. **3.** to progress slowly or laboriously: *The work crawled.* **4.** to move stealthily or abjectly. **5.** to be, or feel as if, overrun with crawling things: *The hut crawled with lizards and insects.* **6.** *Ceram.* (of a glaze) to spread unevenly over the surface of a piece. **7.** (of paint) to raise or contract because of an imperfect bond with the underlying surface. —*n.* **8.** act of crawling; a slow, crawling motion. **9.** *Swimming.* a stroke in a prone position, characterized by alternate overarm movements combined with the flutter kick. **10.** Also called **crawl′ box′.** *Motion Pictures, Television.* a revolving drum on which print or lettering is placed for photographing or televising moving titles. [ME *crawl(en)* < Scand; cf. Dan *kravle* to crawl, creep] —**crawl′ing·ly,** *adv.*
—**Syn. 1.** CRAWL, CREEP refer to methods of moving like reptiles or worms, or on all fours. They are frequently interchangeable, but CRAWL is used of a more prostrate movement than CREEP: *A dog afraid of punishment crawls toward his master.* CREEP expresses slow progress: *A baby creeps before walking.* —**Ant. 1.** stride.

crawl[2] (krôl), *n.* an enclosure in shallow water on the seacoast, for confining fish, turtles, etc. [< D *kraal,* by syncope < Sp *corral* CORRAL]

crawl·er (krô′lər), *n.* **1.** one who or that which crawls. **2.** an endless tread for a tractor or the like. **3.** hellgrammite. **4.** Often, **crawlers.** a garment with short sleeves, long pants, and sometimes feet for a baby who does not yet walk, in any of various fibers, as corduroy or denim. [CRAWL[1] + -ER[1]]

crawl′ space′, (in a building) an accessible area having a clearance of much less than human height, used for access, storage, etc.

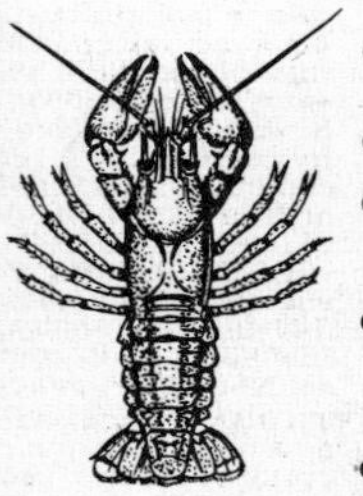

crawl·y (krô′lē), *adj.,* **crawl·i·er, crawl·i·est.** *Informal.* that crawls; noting or describing things, as worms, insects, etc., that crawl, esp. imparting a queasy feeling; creepy. [CRAWL[1] + -Y[1]]

crayer (krâr), *n.* a small sailing vessel formerly used in trade along the coasts of western Europe. Also, **crare.** [ME < AF; OF *croier* < ?]

cray·fish (krā′fish′), *n., pl.* (*esp. collectively*) **-fish,** (*esp. referring to two or more kinds or species*) **-fish·es. 1.** any fresh-water decapod crustacean of the genera *Astacus* and *Cambarus,* closely related to but smaller than the lobsters. **2.** any of several similar marine crustaceans, esp. the spiny lobster. Also, **crawfish.** [alter. (by folk etymology) of ME *crevis* < MF *crevice* < OHG *krebiz* CRAB[1]]

Crayfish, *Cambarus diogenes* (Length 3½ in.)

cray·on (krā′on, -ən), *n., v.,* **-oned, -on·ing.** —*n.* **1.** a pointed stick or pencil of colored clay, chalk, wax, etc., used for drawing. **2.** a drawing in crayons. —*v.t.* **3.** to draw with a crayon or crayons. **4.** to sketch out (a plan, scheme, etc.). [< F, equiv. to *craie* chalk (< L *crēta* clay) + *-on n.* suffix] —**cray′on·ist,** *n.*

craze (krāz), *v.,* **crazed, craz·ing,** *n.* —*v.t.* **1.** to derange or impair the mind of; make insane: *He was crazed by the need for drugs.* **2.** to make small cracks on the surface of (a ceramic glaze, paint, or the like); crackle. **3.** *Brit. Dial.* to crack. **4.** *Archaic.* to weaken; impair: *to craze one's health.* **5.** *Obs.* to break; shatter. —*v.i.* **6.** to become insane. **7.** to become minutely cracked, as a ceramic glaze; crackle. **8.** *Metall.* **a.** (of a casehardened object) to develop reticulated surface markings; worm. **b.** (of an ingot) to develop an alligator skin as a result of being teemed into an old and worn mold. **9.** *Archaic.* to fall to pieces; break. —*n.* **10.** a popular or widespread fad, fashion, etc., usually shortlived; mania: *a dance craze.* **11.** insanity; an insane condition. **12.** a minute crack or pattern of cracks in the glaze of a ceramic object. **13.** *Obs.* flaw; defect. [ME *crase(n)* (to) crush < Scand; cf. Sw, Norw *krasa* to shatter, crush]
—**Syn. 10.** vogue, mode.

crazed (krāzd), *adj.* **1.** insane; demented. **2.** (of a ceramic object) having small cracks in the glaze. [late ME *crasid.* See CRAZE, -ED[2]] —**craz·ed·ly** (krā′zid lē), *adv.* —**craz′ed·ness,** *n.*

cra·zy (krā′zē), *adj.,* **-zi·er, -zi·est. 1.** mentally deranged; demented; insane. **2.** senseless; impractical; totally unsound: *a crazy method for stopping war; a crazy scheme.* **3.** *Informal.* intensely enthusiastic; passionately excited: *crazy about baseball; crazy over a girl.* **4.** very enamored or infatuated (usually fol. by *about*): *He was crazy about her.* **5.** intensely anxious or eager; impatient: *I'm crazy to try those new skis.* **6.** unusual; bizarre; singular: *She always wears a crazy hat. They decorated their home in the craziest combination of colors.* **7.** *Slang.* wonderful; excellent; perfect: *That's crazy, man, crazy.* **8.** likely to break or fall to pieces. **9.** weak; infirm. **10. like crazy,** *Slang.* with great enthusiasm or energy; to an extreme: *She talks like crazy.* [CRAZE + -Y[1]] —**cra′zi·ly,** *adv.* —**cra′zi·ness,** *n.*
—**Syn. 1.** crazed, lunatic. See **mad. 8.** rickety, shaky, tottering. —**Ant. 1.** sane. **3.** calm. **8.** stable. **9.** strong; healthy.

cra′zy bone′. See **funny bone.**

cra′zy house′, 1. *Slang.* an insane asylum. **2.** See **fun house.**

cra′zy pav′ing, a pavement of irregular slabs and fragments of stone, tile, etc., laid in an irregular pattern. Also called **cra′zy pave′ment.**

cra′zy quilt′, 1. a patchwork quilt made of irregular patches combined with little or no regard to pattern. **2.** something which is irregular in pattern or shape, and suggestive of a crazy quilt; patchwork.

cra′zy top′, *Plant Pathol.* a disease of cotton, corn, etc., characterized by abnormal branching and small, misshapen leaves in the upper part of the plant, caused by water shortage, organic deficiencies in the soil, or unknown causes.

cra·zy·weed (krā′zē wēd′), *n.* locoweed. [CRAZY + WEED[1]]

creak (krēk), *v.i.* **1.** to make a sharp, harsh, grating, or squeaking sound. **2.** to move with creaking. —*v.t.* **3.** to cause to creak. —*n.* **4.** a creaking sound. [ME *crek(en)* (to) croak, appar. back formation from OE *crǣcettan,* var. of *crācettan* to CROAK] —**creak′ing·ly,** *adv.*

creak·y (krē′kē), *adj.,* **creak·i·er, creak·i·est. 1.** creaking; apt to creak. **2.** old and rundown; dilapidated: *a creaky shack at the river's edge.* [CREAK + -Y[1]] —**creak′i·ly,** *adv.* —**creak′i·ness,** *n.*

cream (krēm), *n.* **1.** the fatty part of milk, which rises to the surface when the liquid is allowed to stand unless it has been homogenized. **2.** a soft solid or thick liquid containing medicaments or other specific ingredients, applied externally for a prophylactic, therapeutic, or cosmetic purpose. **3.** Usually, **creams.** a soft-centered confection of fondant or fudge coated with chocolate. **4.** a purée or soup containing cream or milk: *cream of tomato soup.* **5.** the best part of anything: *the cream of society.* **6.** yellowish white; light tint of yellow or buff. **7. cream of the crop,** *Informal.* the best or choicest: *a college that accepts only students who are the cream of the crop.* —*v.i.* **8.** to form cream. **9.** to froth; foam. —*v.t.* **10.** to work (butter and sugar, or the like) to a smooth, creamy mass. **11.** to prepare (chicken, oysters, vegetables, etc.) with cream, milk, or a cream sauce. **12.** to allow (milk) to form cream. **13.** to skim (milk). **14.** to separate as cream. **15.** to take the cream or best part of. **16.** to use a cosmetic cream on. **17.** to add cream to (tea, coffee, etc.). **18.** *Slang.* to beat or damage severely; lambaste. —*adj.* **19.** of the color cream; cream-colored. [ME *creme* < MF, OF *cresme* < eccl. L *chrisma* CHRISM] —**cream′less,** *adj.* —**cream′like′,** *adj.*

cream′ bush′, a spreading shrub, *Holodiscus discolor,* of western central North America and the western U.S., having showy, white flowers in clusters about nine inches long.

cream′ cheese′, a soft, white, smooth-textured, unripened cheese made of sweet milk and sometimes cream.

cream-col·ored (krēm′kul′ərd), *adj.* having a yellowish-white color.

cream·cups (krēm′kups′), *n., pl.* **-cups.** (*construed as sing. or pl.*) a papaveraceous plant, *Platystemon californicus,* of California, having small, pale-yellow or cream-colored flowers. [CREAM + CUP + -S[3]]

cream·er (krē′mər), *n.* **1.** one who or that which creams. **2.** a small jug, pitcher, etc., for holding cream. **3.** a refrigerator in which milk is placed to facilitate the formation of cream. **4.** a container or apparatus for separating cream from milk. [CREAM + -ER[1]]

cream·er·y (krē′mə rē), *n., pl.* **-er·ies. 1.** a place where milk and cream are processed and where butter and cheese are produced. **2.** a place for the sale of milk and its products. **3.** a place where milk is set to form cream. [CREAM + -ERY]

cream′ ice′, *Brit.* See **ice cream.**

cream′ of tar′tar, a white, crystalline, water-soluble powder, $KHC_4H_4O_6$, used chiefly as an ingredient in baking powders and in galvanic tinning of metals. Also called **potassium bitartrate, potassium acid tartrate.** Cf. **tartar**[1] (def. 3).

cream′ pail′, an open bowl of silver having a ladle or spoon for serving cream. Also called **piggin.**

cream′ puff′, 1. a baked, hollow pastry made with cream puff paste and filled with custard sauce or whipped cream. **2.** *Slang.* a sissy. **3.** *Slang.* a used car that has been kept in unusually good condition.

cream′ puff′ paste′, paste made with eggs, water or milk, butter, and flour, used in making éclairs, profiteroles, and other kinds of puffs. Also called **chou pastry, pâte à chou.**

cream′ sauce′, a white sauce made of cream or milk, flour, and butter.

cream′ so′da, a soft drink made with vanilla-flavored carbonated water colored brown by caramel.

cream·ware (krēm′wâr′), *n.* earthenware having an opaque, cream-colored lead glaze. [CREAM + WARE[1]]

cream·y (krē′mē), *adj.,* **cream·i·er, cream·i·est. 1.** containing cream. **2.** resembling cream in appearance, consistency, or taste; soft and smooth. **3.** cream-colored. [CREAM + -Y[1]] —**cream′i·ly,** *adv.* —**cream′i·ness,** *n.*

cre·ance (krē′əns), *n.* *Falconry.* a light cord attached to the leg of a hawk to prevent escape during training. [ME < MF < LL **crēdentia* CREDENCE]

crease[1] (krēs), *n., v.,* **creased, creas·ing.** —*n.* **1.** a ridge or groove produced in anything by folding; fold; furrow. **2.** a wrinkle, esp. one on the face. **3.** the sharp, vertical edge or line produced in the front and back of men's trousers by pressing, as with a steam presser, iron, etc. **4.** *Phys. Geog.* the dry channel of a former glacial river in an outwash plain. **5.** *Cricket.* **a.** See **bowling crease. b.** See **popping crease. 6.** *Ice Hockey.* the rectangular area at each end of the rink extending from in front of the goal cages to a distance outside of the posts, into which an offensive player can skate only if he has the puck, if the puck is already within the area, or if the goalie is absent. —*v.t.* **7.** to make a crease or creases in or on; wrinkle. **8.** to wound or stun by a furrowing or superficial shot: *The bullet merely creased his shoulder.* —*v.i.* **9.** to become creased. [late ME *creeste, crest,* appar. special use of CREST] —**crease′less,** *adj.*

crease[2] (krēs), *n.* creese.

crease-re·sis·tant (krēs′ri zis′tənt), *adj.* (of a fabric) resistant to normal wrinkling.

creas·y (krē′sē), *adj.* **creas·i·er, creas·i·est.** full of creases. [CREASE[1] + -Y[1]]

cre·ate (krē āt′), *v.,* **-at·ed, -at·ing,** *adj.* —*v.t.* **1.** to cause to come into being, as something unique that would not naturally evolve or that is not made by ordinary processes: *God created Eve from one of Adam's ribs.* **2.** to evolve from one's own thought or imagination, as a work of art, an invention, etc. **3.** *Theat.* to perform (a role) for the first time or in the first production of a play. **4.** to make by investing with new functions, rank, character, etc.; constitute; appoint: *to create a peer.* **5.** to be the cause or occasion of; give rise to: *Overexplanation creates confusion.* **6.** to cause to happen; bring about; arrange, as by intention or design: *He wanted to create an opportunity to ask for a raise in his allowance; to create a revolution.* —*v.i.* **7.** to do that which is creative or constructive. **8.** *Brit. Informal.* to be conspicuously angry or upset; make a fuss. —*adj.* **9.** *Archaic.* created. [ME *creat* (ptp.) < L *creāt(us),* equiv. to *cre-* (s. of *creāre* to make) + *-tus* ptp. suffix] —**cre·at′a·ble,** *adj.* —**cre·at′ed·ness,** *n.*
—**Syn. 2.** originate, invent.

cre·a·tine (krē′ə tēn′, -tin), *n.* *Biochem.* an alkaloid or amino acid, $HN{=}C(NH_2)N(CH_3)CH_2COOH$, found in the muscles of vertebrates. [creat- (< Gk *kreat-*, s. of *kréas*) flesh + -INE[2]]

cre′atine phos′phate, *Biochem.* phosphocreatine.

cre·at·i·nine (krē at′ənēn′, -at′ənin), *n.* *Biochem.* the white, crystalline, water-soluble anhydride of creatine, $C_4H_7N_3O$, occurring in urine, muscle tissue, blood, and certain grain seeds, usually obtained commercially from creatine and used chiefly in research. [< G *Kreatinin*, equiv. to *kreatin* CREATINE + *-in* -INE[2]]

cre·a·tion (krē ā′shən), *n.* **1.** the act of creating; act of producing or causing to exist. **2.** the fact of being created. **3.** **the Creation,** the original bringing into existence of the universe by God. **4.** that which is or has been created. **5.** the world; universe. **6.** creatures collectively. **7.** an original product of the mind, esp. an imaginative artistic work: *the creations of a poetic genius.* **8.** a specially designed dress, hat, or other article of women's clothing, usually distinguished by imaginative or unique styling and notable for its exciting or sensational effect: *the newest Paris creations.* [ME *creaccion* < L *creātiōn-* (s. of *creātiō*). See CREATE, -ION] —**cre·a′tion·al, cre·a·tion·ar·y** (krē ā′shə ner′ē), *adj.*

cre·a·tion·ism (krē ā′shə niz′əm), *n.* **1.** the doctrine that God immediately creates out of nothing a new human soul for each individual born. Cf. **traducianism.** **2.** the doctrine that matter and all things were created, substantially as they now exist, by an omnipotent Creator, and not gradually evolved or developed. [CREATION + -ISM] —**cre·a′tion·ist,** *n.* —**cre·a′tion·is′tic,** *adj.*

Crea′tion of the World′, The, a ballet (1923) by Milhaud.

cre·a·tive (krē ā′tiv), *adj.* **1.** having the quality or power of creating. **2.** resulting from originality of thought, expression, etc.: *creative writing.* **3.** originative; productive (usually fol. by *of*). [CREATE + -IVE] —**cre·a′tive·ly,** *adv.* —**cre·a′tive·ness,** *n.*

crea′tive evolu′tion, (in the philosophy of Bergson) the continuous formation of the world as the passive, inert product of the élan vital.

crea′tive imagina′tion. See under **imagination** (def. 3).

cre·a·tiv·i·ty (krē′ā tiv′i tē), *n.* **1.** the state or quality of being creative. **2.** creative ability or process: *creativity in the performing arts; the great need for creativity in modern industry.* [CREATIVE + -ITY]

cre·a·tor (krē ā′tər), *n.* **1.** one who or that which creates. **2.** **the Creator,** God. [ME *creato(u)r* < eccl. L *creātor.* See CREAT(E), -OR[2]] —**cre·a′tor·ship′,** *n.*

crea·tur·al (krē′chər əl), *adj.* of, pertaining to, or of the nature of a creature or creatures. [CREATURE + -AL[1]]

crea·ture (krē′chər), *n.* **1.** anything created, whether animate or inanimate. **2.** an animate being. **3.** an animal, esp. an animal other than man: *the creatures of the woods and fields; a creature from outer space.* **4.** person; human being: *She is a charming creature. The driver is an irritable creature.* **5.** a person who owes his position or fortune to someone or something under whose control or influence he continues: *The cardinal was a creature of Louis XI.* **6.** *Dial. and Facetious.* intoxicating liquor, esp. whiskey (usually prec. by *the*): *He drinks a bit of the creature before bedtime.* [ME *creature* < eccl. L *creātūr(a).* See CREATE, -URE]

crea′ture com′forts, those things that contribute to bodily comfort and ease, as food, warmth, shelter, etc.

crea·ture·ly (krē′chər lē), *adj.* creatural. [CREATURE + -LY] —**crea′ture·li·ness,** *n.*

crèche (kresh, krāsh; *Fr.* kresh), *n., pl.* **crèch·es** (kresh′iz, krā′shiz; *Fr.* kresh). **1.** *Brit.* a nursery where children are cared for while their mothers work; day nursery. **2.** a home for foundlings. **3.** a tableau of Mary, Joseph, and others around the crib of Jesus in the stable at Bethlehem, often built for display at Christmas. [< F << OHG *kripja* CRIB]

Cré·cy (kres′ē; *Fr.* krā sē′), *n.* **1.** Also, **Cressy.** a village in N France, NNW of Reims: English victory over the French 1346. 1419 (1962). —*adj.* **2.** (*sometimes l.c.*) (of food) prepared or garnished with carrots.

cre·dence (krēd′əns), *n.* **1.** belief as to the truth of something: *to give credence to a statement.* **2.** something giving a claim to belief or confidence: *letter of credence.* **3.** Also called **cre′dence ta′ble, credenza.** *Eccles.* a small side table, shelf, or niche for holding articles used in the Eucharistic service. **4.** *Furniture.* credenza (def. 1). [ME < ML *crēdentia.* See CREDENT, -ENCE] —**Syn. 1.** credit, faith. —**Ant. 1.** disbelief.

cre·den·dum (kri den′dəm), *n., pl.* **-da** (-də). a doctrine that requires belief; article of faith. [< L, neut. of *crēdendus,* ger. of *crēdere* to believe]

cre·dent (krēd′ənt), *adj.* **1.** believing. **2.** *Obs.* credible. [< L *crēdent-* (s. of *crēdēns*), prp. of *crēdere* to believe] —**cre′dent·ly,** *adv.*

cre·den·tial (kri den′shəl), *n.* Usually, **credentials.** **1.** anything that provides the basis for confidence, belief, credit, etc. **2.** evidence of authority, status, rights, entitlement to privileges, or the like, usually in written form: *Only those with the proper credentials are admitted.* —*adj.* **3.** providing the basis for confidence, belief, credit, etc. [< ML *crēdenti(a)* CREDENCE + -AL[1]] —**cre·den′tialed,** *adj.*

cre·den·za (kri den′zə), *n.* **1.** Also, **credence.** a sideboard or buffet. **2.** *Eccles.* credence (def. 3). [< It, < ML *crēdentia* belief, credit, sideboard; see CREDENCE]

cred·i·ble (kred′ə bəl), *adj.* **1.** capable of being believed; believable: *a credible statement.* **2.** worthy of belief or confidence; trustworthy: *a credible witness.* [< L *crēdibil(is),* equiv. to *crēd(ere)* (to) believe + *-ibilis* -IBLE] —**cred′i·bil′i·ty, cred′i·ble·ness,** *n.* —**cred′i·bly,** *adv.*

cred·it (kred′it), *n.* **1.** trustworthiness; credibility: *a witness of credit.* **2.** commendation or honor given for some action, quality, etc.: *Give credit where it is due.* **3.** a source of commendation or honor: *You are a credit to your school.* **4.** the ascription or acknowledgment of something as due or properly attributable to a person, institution, etc.: *a credit for a photograph; Credit for raising the money in the drive goes to the Kansas chapter.* **5.** *Educ.* **a.** official acceptance and recording of the work of a student in a particular course of study. **b.** a credit hour. **6.** time allowed for payment for goods or services obtained on trust: *90 days' credit.* **7.** confidence in a purchaser's ability and intention to pay, displayed by entrusting him with goods or services without immediate payment: **8.** reputation of solvency and probity, entitling a person to be trusted in buying or borrowing: *Your credit is good.* **9.** a sum of money due to a person; anything valuable standing on the credit side of an account: *He has an outstanding credit of $50.* **10.** *Bookkeeping.* **a.** an entry of payment or value received on an account. **b.** the right-hand side of an account on which such entries are made (opposed to *debit*). **c.** an entry, or the total shown, on the credit side. **11.** any deposit or sum of money against which one may draw. **12.** *Obs.* belief; trust; faith. **13.** *Obs.* influence or authority resulting from the confidence of others or from one's reputation. **14.** *Obs.* repute; reputation; favorable estimation; esteem. **15.** **do someone credit,** to be a source of honor or distinction to someone. Also, **do credit to someone.** **16.** **on credit,** by deferred payment: *Everything they have was bought on credit.* **17.** **to one's credit,** deserving of praise or recognition: *It is to his credit that he admitted his guilt and took the punishment.* —*v.t.* **18.** to believe; put confidence in; trust; have faith in. **19.** to bring honor, esteem, etc., to; reflect credit upon. **20.** *Bookkeeping.* to enter upon the credit side of an account; give credit for or to. **21.** *Educ.* to award educational credits to: *credited with three hours in history.* **22.** **credit to** or **with,** to ascribe to a thing, person, etc.: *In former times many herbs were credited with healing powers. Lindbergh was credited with being the first to solo across the Atlantic.* [< MF < OIt *credit(o)* < L *crēditum* loan, n. use of neut. of *crēditus* believed, credited, ptp. of *crēdere*] —**cred′it·less,** *adj.*
—**Syn. 2.** merit. **8.** CREDIT, REPUTE, REPUTATION, STANDING refer to one's status in the estimation of a community. CREDIT refers to business and financial status and the amount of money for which a man will be trusted: *His credit is excellent at all the stores.* REPUTE is particularly what is reported about someone, the favor in which he is held, etc.: *a man of fine repute among his acquaintances.* REPUTATION is the moral and other character commonly ascribed to someone: *of unblemished reputation.* STANDING is one's position in a community, or rank and condition in life: *a man of good standing and education.*

cred·it·a·ble (kred′i tə bəl), *adj.* bringing or deserving credit, honor, reputation, or esteem. [CREDIT + -ABLE] —**cred′it·a·ble·ness, cred′it·a·bil′i·ty,** *n.* —**cred′it·a·bly,** *adv.*
—**Syn.** praiseworthy, meritorious, estimable, honorable, reputable, respectable.

cred′it a′gency, a business firm that investigates the credit standing of and assigns a credit rating to a client's customers or potential customers.

cred′it card′, a small card which identifies a person as entitled to have food, merchandise, services, etc., billed on a charge account.

cred′it hour′, hour (def. 12b).

cred′it insur′ance, insurance to minimize loss to creditors on defaulted accounts receivable.

cred′it life′ insur′ance, insurance guaranteeing payment of the unpaid portion of a loan if the debtor should die.

cred′it line′, **1.** a line of copy acknowledging the source or origin of published or exhibited material. **2.** Also called **cred′it lim′it, line of credit.** the maximum amount of credit that a customer of a store, bank, etc., is authorized to use. Cf. **revolving credit.**

cred′it man′, a person employed in a business firm to administer credit service for its customers, esp. to evaluate the extension and amount of credit to be granted. Also called **credit manager.**

cred′it man′ager, **1.** an employee who heads and supervises the credit department in a bank or other business organization. **2.** See **credit man.**

cred′it memoran′dum, a memorandum issued to an account allowing a credit or reducing a debit, esp. one posted to a customer's account. Also called **cred′it memo′, credit slip.**

Cred·it Mo·bil·ier (kred′it mō bēl′yər, mō bēl yā′; *Fr.* krā dē mō bē lyā′), *U.S. Hist.* a joint-stock company organized in 1863 and reorganized in 1867 to build the Union Pacific Railroad. It was involved in a scandal in 1872 in which high government officials were accused of accepting bribes.

cred·i·tor (kred′i tər), *n.* **1.** one who gives credit in business transactions. **2.** one to whom money is due (opposed to *debtor*). **3.** *Bookkeeping.* credit (def. 10b, c). [late ME *creditour* < L *crēditor.* See CREDIT, -OR[2]] —**cred′i·tor·ship′,** *n.*

cred′it rat′ing, a classification of credit risk determined by a credit man or credit agency, based on investigation of a customer's or potential customer's financial resources, prior payment pattern, and personal history or degree of personal responsibility for debts incurred.

cred′it slip′, **1.** See **deposit slip.** **2.** See **credit memorandum.**

cred′it stand′ing, reputation for meeting financial obligations.

cred′it un′ion, a cooperative group that makes loans to its members at low rates of interest. Also called **cooperative credit union.**

cre·do (krē′dō, krā′-), *n., pl.* **-dos.** **1.** the Apostles' Creed or the Nicene Creed. **2.** a musical setting of the creed, usually of the Nicene Creed. **3.** any creed or formula of belief. [ME < L: lit., I believe; first word of the Apostles' and Nicene Creeds in Latin]

cre·du·li·ty (krə do͞o′li tē, -dyo͞o′-), *n.* willingness to believe or trust too readily, esp. without proper or adequate evidence; gullibility. [late ME *credulite* < L *crēdulitās.* See CREDULOUS, -ITY]

cred·u·lous (krej′ə ləs), *adj.* **1.** willing to believe or trust too readily, esp. without proper or adequate evidence; gullible. **2.** marked by or arising from credulity: *a credulous rumor.* [< L *crēdulus,* equiv. to *crēd(ere)* (to) believe + *-ulus* adj. suffix denoting a quality or tendency] —**cred′u·lous·ly,** *adv.* —**cred′u·lous·ness,** *n.*
—**Syn. 1.** believing, trustful, unsuspecting. —**Ant. 1.** cautious, suspicious.

Cree (krē), *n., pl.* **Crees,** (*esp. collectively*) **Cree.** **1.** a member of an American Indian people of Ontario, Manitoba, Saskatchewan, and Montana. **2.** an Algonquian language, the language of the Cree Indians, noted for its complex system of verbs.

creed (krēd), *n.* **1.** an authoritative formulated statement of the chief articles of Christian belief, as the Apostles' Creed, the Nicene Creed, or the Athanasian Creed. **2.** **the creed.** See **Apostles' Creed.** **3.** any formula of religious belief, as of a denomination. **4.** an accepted system of religious belief. **5.** any system of belief or of opinion. [ME *crede,* OE *crēda* < L *crēdō* I believe; see CREDO] —**creed′al,** *adj.* —**creed′ed,** *adj.* —**creed′less,** *adj.* —**creed′less·ness,** *n.*

creek (krēk, krik), *n.* **1.** *U.S., Canada, and Australia.* a watercourse smaller than a river. **2.** a watercourse or channel in a coastal marsh. **3.** *Chiefly Brit.* a recess or inlet in the shore of the sea. **4.** *Dial.* an estuary. **5.** *Brit. Dial.* a narrow, winding passage or hidden recess. **6.** **up the creek,** *Slang.* in a predicament; perplexed: *We were really up the creek when the bank foreclosed on our car.* [ME *creke,* var. of *crike* < Scand; cf. Icel *kriki* nook]

Creek (krēk), *n., pl.* **Creeks,** (*esp. collectively*) **Creek.** **1.** a member of a powerful confederacy of Muskogean Indians which in historic times occupied the greater part of Alabama and Georgia. **2.** Also called **Muskogee.** a Muskogean language that is the language of the Creek Indians.

creel (krēl), *n.* **1.** a wickerwork basket worn on the back or suspended from the shoulder, used esp. for carrying fish. **2.** a basket made of wicker or other material, for holding fish, lobsters, etc. **3.** a trap for fish, lobster, etc., esp. one made of wicker. **4.** a framework, esp. one for holding bobbins in a spinning machine. [ME *crele,* perh. < MF *creille,* var. of *greille* GRILLE]

Creel (krēl), *n.* **George,** 1876–1953, U.S. publicist and author.

creep (krēp), *v.,* **crept, creep·ing,** *n.* —*v.i.* **1.** to move with the body close to the ground, as a reptile or an insect, or a child on hands and knees. **2.** to approach slowly, imperceptibly, or stealthily (often fol. by *up*): *We crept up and peeked over the wall.* **3.** to sneak up behind someone or without someone's knowledge (usually fol. by *up on*): *We crept up on the guard and knocked him out.* **4.** to move or behave timidly or servilely. **5.** to slip or move along gradually: *The automobile crept through the heavy traffic. Time just seems to creep along on these hot summer days.* **6.** to enter undetected or unobserved: *The defense of nazism creeps into the book here and there.* **7.** to slip, slide, or shift gradually; become displaced. **8.** to grow along the ground, a wall, etc., as a plant. **9.** (of a metal object) to become deformed, as under continuous loads or at high temperatures. **10.** *Naut.* to grapple (usually fol. by *for*): *The ships crept for their anchor chains.* —*v.t.* **11.** *Archaic.* to creep along or over. **12.** **make one's flesh creep,** to frighten; repel; cause one to experience uneasiness: *The eerie stories made our flesh creep.* —*n.* **13.** the act of creeping. **14.** *Slang.* a boring, disturbingly eccentric, or painfully introverted person. **15.** *Mech.* the gradual, permanent deformation of a body produced by a continued application of heat or stress. **16.** *Firearms.* the slack in a trigger mechanism before it releases the firing pin. **17.** *Geol.* the gradual movement downhill of loose soil, rock, gravel, etc.; solifluction. **18.** See **creep feeder.** **19.** a grappling iron; grapnel. **20.** **the creeps,** *Slang.* a sensation of horror, fear, disgust, etc., suggestive of the feeling induced by something crawling over the skin: *That movie gave me the creeps.* [ME *crep(en),* OE *crēopan;* c. D *kruipen,* Icel *krjūpa*] —**creep′ing·ly,** *adv.*
—**Syn. 1.** See **crawl.**

creep·er (krē′pər), *n.* **1.** one who or that which creeps. **2.** Often, **creepers.** a one-piece garment for an infant, the lower portion resembling briefs and having snaps or buttons across the crotch for convenience in diapering. **3.** a piece of iron or leather with cleats, strapped to the shoe as protection against mud or slipping. **4.** *Bot.* a plant which grows upon or just beneath the surface of the ground, or upon any other surface, sending out rootlets from the stem, as ivy and couch grass. **5.** any of various birds that creep or climb about on trees, esp. of the family *Certhiidae,* as *Certhia familiaris* (**brown creeper** or **tree creeper**), of the Northern Hemisphere. **6.** Also called **creep′er fowl′.** *Vet. Pathol.* one of a breed of domestic fowls having malformed, short legs. **7.** a grappling device for dragging a river, lake, etc. **8.** a spiked iron plate worn on the shoe to prevent slipping on ice, rock, etc. **9.** Also called **cradle.** *Auto.* a flat framework on casters, on which a mechanic lies while working under an automobile or the like. **10.** **creepers,** a pair of small andirons used between a pair of larger ones. [ME *crepere,* OE *crēopere.* See CREEP, -ER[1]]

creep-feed (krēp′fēd′), *v.t.,* **-fed, -feed·ing.** to feed (animals) in a creep feeder.

creep′ feed′er, a pen so constructed as to exclude larger animals while permitting young animals to enter and obtain feed.

creep·ie (krē′pē, krip′ē), *n.* *Brit. Dial.* a low stool. [CREEP + -IE]

creep·ie-peep·ie (krē′pē pē′pē), *n.* a small, portable television camera. [rhyming redupl. of PEEP[1]]

creep′ing bar′berry, a shrub, *Mahonia repens,* found from British Columbia to the southwestern U.S., having spiny, leathery, bluish-green leaves, underground rooting stems, clustered flowers, and small, black fruit.

creep′ing bent′ grass′, a bent grass, *Agrostis palustris,* that spreads by stolons, cultivated in pastures and lawns of coastal areas of North America and Europe. Also called **creeping bent′.**

creep′ing Char′lie, moneywort.

creep′ing cinque′foil. See under **cinquefoil** (def. 1).

creep′ing erup′tion, *Pathol.* a skin condition esp. of dogs, of cats, and also affecting man, caused by the burrowing of hookworm larvae under the dermal tissue, and characterized by a red line that fades behind the invading organism. Also called **larva migrans.**

creep′ing fes′cue. See **red fescue.**

creep′ing forget′-me-not, a perennial herb, *Omphalodes verna,* of Europe, having blue flowers borne in pairs.

creep′ing Jen′nie, moneywort.

creep′ing ju′niper, a prostrate shrub, *Juniperus horizontalis,* of central North America, having bluish-green or gray-blue leaves and blue fruit, growing well in sandy, rocky soil.

creep′ing lil′y-turf, a perennial herb, *Liriope spicata,* of Asia, having pale lilac-colored or nearly white flowers.

creep′ing myr′tle, the periwinkle, *Vinca minor.*

creep′ing snow′berry, an evergreen shrub, *Gaultheria hispidula*, of northern North America, having solitary, bell-shaped, white flowers and aromatic, birch-flavored, berrylike, white fruit.

creep′ing thyme′, mother-of-thyme.

creeps (krēps), *n.* (*construed as sing.*) *Vet. Pathol.* a disease of the bones in sheep and cattle that causes pain in walking, resulting from a deficiency of phosphorus in the diet. [so called from the effect on the animal's gait]

creep·y (krē′pē), *adj.*, **creep·i·er, creep·i·est.** **1.** that creeps, as an insect: *creepy, crawly things.* **2.** having or causing a creeping sensation of the skin, as from horror or fear: *a creepy ghost story.* [CREEP + -Y¹] —**creep′i·ly,** *adv.* —**creep′i·ness,** *n.*

creese (krēs), *n.* a short sword or heavy dagger with a wavy blade, used by the Malays. Also, **crease, kris.** [< Malay *kris* dagger]

creesh (krēsh), *n., v.t. Scot.* grease. [late ME *cresche* < MF *creisse*, var. of *greisse* GREASE]

Cre·feld (krā′feld; *Ger.* krā′felt), *n.* Krefeld.

cre·mas·ter (kri mas′tər), *n.* **1.** *Anat.* the suspensory muscle of the testis. **2.** *Entomol.* a usually hooklike process on the posterior tip of a chrysalis, for attaching the pupa to a stem, twig, etc. [< NL < Gk *kremastḗr*, deriv. of *krema-* hang] —**crem·as·te·ri·al** (krem′ə stēr′ē əl), **crem·as·ter·ic** (krem′ə ster′ik), *adj.*

cre·mate (krē′māt), *v.t.*, **-mat·ed, -mat·ing.** **1.** to reduce (a dead body) to ashes by fire, esp. as a funeral rite. **2.** to consume by fire; burn. [< L *cremāt(us)* burnt to ashes, equiv. to *crem(āre)* + *-ātus* -ATE¹] —**cre·ma·tion** (kri mā′shən), *n.*

cre·ma·tion·ist (kri mā′shə nist), *n.* one who advocates cremation instead of burial of the dead. [CREMATION + -IST] —**cre·ma′tion·ism,** *n.*

cre·ma·tor (krē′mā tər), *n.* **1.** one who cremates. **2.** a furnace for cremating dead bodies. **3.** an incinerator, as for garbage. [< LL; see CREMATE, -OR²]

cre·ma·to·ri·um (krē′mə tōr′ē əm, -tôr′-, krem′ə-), *n., pl.* **-to·ri·ums, -to·ri·a** (-tōr′ē ə, -tôr′-). a crematory. [Latinization of CREMATORY; see -ORIUM]

cre·ma·to·ry (krē′mə tōr′ē, -tôr′ē, krem′ə-), *adj., n., pl.* **-ries.** —*adj.* **1.** of or pertaining to cremation. —*n.* **2.** a place, as a funeral establishment, at which cremation is done. **3.** a furnace for cremating. [CREMATE + -ORY²]

crème (krem, krēm, krām; *Fr.* krem), *n., pl.* **crèmes** (kremz, krēmz, krāmz; *Fr.* krem). **1.** cream. **2.** one of a class of liqueurs of a thickish consistency. [< F; see CREAM]

crème d'a·na·nas (krem′ dä nä nä′, krēm′, krām′; *Fr.* krem da na nä′), a liqueur flavored with pineapple. [< F: lit., cream of pineapples]

crème de ba·nanes (krem′ də bä nän′, krēm′, krām′; *Fr.* krem də ba nan′), a liqueur flavored with bananas. [< F: lit., cream of bananas]

crème de ca·ca·o (krem′ də kō′kō, kä kä′ō, krēm′, krām′; *Fr.* krem də ka ka ō′), a liqueur flavored with cacao and vanilla beans. [< F: lit., cream of cacao]

crème de cas·sis (krem′ də kä sēs′, krēm′, krām′; *Fr.* krem də ka sēs′), a liqueur made from black currants. [< F: lit., cream of blackcurrant]

crème de fraise (krem′ də frez′, krēm′, krām′; *Fr.* krem də frez′), a liqueur flavored principally with strawberries. [< F: lit., cream of strawberry]

crème de la crème (krem′ də la krem′), *French.* the very best; choicest part. [lit., cream of the cream]

crème de menthe (krem′ də menth′, mint′, krēm′, krām′; *Fr.* krem də mänt′), a white or green liqueur flavored with mint. [< F: lit., cream of mint]

crème de vi·o·lette (krem′ də vī′ə lit, krēm′, krām′; *Fr.* krem də vyô let′), a liqueur flavored with vanilla extract and the essential oils of violets. [< F: lit., cream of violet]

Cre·mer (krē′mər), *n.* **Sir William Randal,** 1838–1908, English union organizer: Nobel peace prize 1903.

Crème Y·vette (krem′ ē vet′, krēm′, krām′), *Trademark.* a liqueur, made in the U.S., flavored with the essential oils of violets.

Crem′nitz white′ (krem′nits). See **lead white.** [after *Kremnitz*, in eastern Czechoslovakia]

Cre·mo·na (kri mō′nə; *It.* kre mô′nä), *n.* **1.** a city in N Italy, on the Po River. 74,242 (1961). **2.** one of a class of violins of superior quality made there during the 16th, 17th, and 18th centuries.

cre·morne′ bolt′ (kri môrn′), (on a French window or the like) a pair of rods, moved by a knob mechanism, sliding into sockets in the head and sill of the opening to provide a secure fastening. [< F *crémone*, prob. after CREMONA]

cre·nate (krē′nāt), *adj.* having the margin notched or scalloped so as to form rounded teeth, as a leaf or a shrunken erythrocyte. Also, **cre′nat·ed.** [< NL *crēnāt(us)*, equiv. to *crēn(a)* a notch, groove (? back formation from ML *crenellus* CRENEL) + *-ātus* -ATE¹] —**cre′nate·ly,** *adv.*

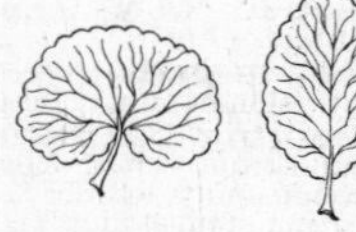

Crenate leaves

cre·na·tion (kri nā′shən), *n.* **1.** a rounded projection or tooth, as on the margin of a leaf. **2.** *Anat.* (in erythrocytes) the state of being or becoming shrunken with a notched or indented edge. **3.** a notch between teeth. [CRENATE + -ION]

cren·a·ture (kren′ə chər, krē′nə-), *n.* **1.** a crenation. **2.** a notch or indentation between crenations. [CRENATE + -URE]

cren·el (kren′əl), *n., v.*, **-eled, -el·ing** or (*esp. Brit.*) **-elled, -el·ling.** —*n.* **1.** any of the open spaces between the merlons of a battlement. See illus. under **battlement.** **2.** a crenature. —*v.t.* **3.** to crenelate. Also, **crenelle.** [late ME < MF, OF, appar. dim. of *cren notch (recorded from 16th century) < ?]

cren·el·ate (kren′əlāt′), *v.*, **-at·ed, -at·ing,** *adj.* —*v.t.* **1.** to furnish with crenels or battlements. —*adj.* **2.** crenelated. Also, *esp. Brit.*, **crenellate.** [< F *crénel(er)* (to) crenelate (see CRENEL) + -ATE¹]

Crenelated molding

cren·el·at·ed (kren′əlā′tid), *adj.* furnished with crenelations, as a parapet or molding, in the manner of a battlement. Also, *esp. Brit.*, **cren′el·lat′ed.** [CRENELATE + -ED²]

cren′elated mold′ing, *Archit.* a molding having a series of indentations resembling a battlement.

cren·el·a·tion (kren′əlā′shən), *n.* **1.** act of crenelating. **2.** state of being crenelated. **3.** a battlement. **4.** a notch; indentation. Also, *esp. Brit.*, **cren′el·la′tion.** [CRENELATE + -ION]

cren·el·et (kren′əlit, -əlet′), *n.* a small crenel. [CRENEL + -ET]

cren·el·late (kren′əlāt′), *v.t.*, **-lat·ed, -lat·ing,** *adj. Chiefly Brit.* crenelate.

cre·nelle (kri nel′), *n., v.t.*, **-nelled, -nel·ling.** crenel.

cre·nel·lé (kren′əlā′, krān′-), *adj. Heraldry.* embattled. [< F *crénelé*, ptp. of *créneler*. See CRENEL]

cren·u·late (kren′yə lāt′, -lit), *adj.* minutely crenate, as the margin of certain leaves. Also, **cren′u·lat′ed.** [< NL *crēnul((ātus)*, equiv. to *crēnul(a)* (dim. of *crēna* notch; see CRENATE) + *-ātus* -ATE¹]

cren·u·la·tion (kren′yə lā′shən), *n.* **1.** a minute crenation. **2.** the state of being crenulate. [CRENULATE + -ION]

cre·o·dont (krē′ə dont′), *n.* one of the primitive carnivorous mammals of the extinct suborder *Creodonta*, from the Paleocene to Pleistocene epochs. [< NL *Creodont(a)* name of the group, equiv. to *cre-* (< Gk *kréas* flesh) + *-odont-* -ODONT + *-a* pl. ending]

Cre·ole (krē′ōl), *n.* **1.** (in the West Indies and Spanish America) one born in the region but of European, usually Spanish, ancestry. **2.** (esp. in Louisiana) a person born in the region but of French ancestry. **3.** a person born in a place but of foreign ancestry, as distinguished from the aborigines and half-breeds. **4.** a creolized language. Cf. **pidgin.** **5.** the creolized French language of the descendants of the original settlers of Louisiana. Cf. **Cajun.** **6.** See **Haitian Creole.** **7.** (*l.c.*) a person of mixed Creole and Negro ancestry speaking a form of French or Spanish. **8.** (*l.c.*) *Archaic.* a native-born Negro, as distinguished from a Negro brought from Africa. —*adj.* **9.** (*sometimes l.c.*) of, pertaining to, or characteristic of a Creole or Creoles. **10.** bred or growing in a country, but of foreign origin, as an animal or plant. **11.** *Cookery.* indicating a sauce or dish made with tomatoes, peppers, seasonings, etc., and often served with rice. [< F < Sp *criollo* < Pg *crioulo* native, deriv. of *criar* to bring up < L *creāre*; see CREATE]

cre·ole-fish (krē′ōl fish′), *n., pl.* **-fish·es,** (*esp. collectively*) **-fish.** a serranid fish, *Paranthias furcifer*, found in the deep waters of the tropical Atlantic Ocean. [CREOLE + FISH]

cre·o·lize (krē′ə līz′), *v.t.*, **-lized, -liz·ing.** to render (a language) creolized. [CREOLE + -IZE] —**cre′o·li·za′tion,** *n.*

cre·o·lized (krē′ə līzd′), *adj.* (of a language) formerly a pidgin but now the native language of a group of speakers, with consequent enrichment of the vocabulary by borrowing and creation. [CREOLIZE + -ED²]

Cre·on (krē′on), *n. Class. Myth.* **1.** a king of Thebes, the brother of Jocasta and the uncle of Eteocles, Polynices, and Antigone. He defeated the Seven against Thebes. **2.** a king of Corinth, father of Creusa and prospective father-in-law of Jason, killed in attempting to save the life of Creusa.

cre·o·sol (krē′ə sōl′, -sôl′, -sol′), *n. Chem.* a colorless oily liquid, $C_8H_{10}O_2$, having an agreeable odor and a burning taste, obtained from wood tar and guaiacum resin. [CREOS(OTE) + -OL²]

cre·o·sote (krē′ə sōt′), *n., v.*, **-sot·ed, -sot·ing.** —*n.* **1.** an oily liquid having a burning taste and a penetrating odor, obtained by the distillation of wood tar, and used as a preservative and antiseptic. **2.** See **coal-tar creosote.** —*v.t.* **3.** to treat with creosote. [< Gk *kré(as)* flesh + -o- + *sōtḗr* preserver] —**cre·o·sot·ic** (krē′ə sot′ik), *adj.*

cre′osote bush′, an evergreen, zygophyllaceous shrub, *Larrea mexicana*, of northern Mexico and adjacent regions, bearing resinous foliage with a strong odor of creosote.

crepe (krāp), *n., v.*, **creped, crep·ing.** —*n.* **1.** a thin, light fabric of silk, cotton, or other fiber, with a finely crinkled or ridged surface. **2.** Also called **crepe paper.** thin paper densely wrinkled to resemble crepe, used for decorating, wrapping, etc. **3.** a black or sometimes white silk fabric for mourning veils, bands, etc. **4.** a band or piece of this material, as for a token of mourning. **5.** See **crepe rubber.** **6.** a thin, light, delicate pancake. —*v.t.* **7.** to cover, clothe, or drape with crepe. Also, **crape.** [< F < L *crisp(us)* curled, wrinkled]

crêpe (krāp; *for 2 also Fr.* krep), *n., pl.* **crêpes** (krāps; *for 2 also Fr.* krep). **1.** crepe (defs. 1, 3, 4). **2.** crepe (def. 6). [< F; see CREPE]

crepe de Chine (krāp′ də shēn′), a light, soft, thin silk or rayon fabric with minute irregularities of surface. [< F: lit., crepe from China]

crepe′ hair′, false hair, usually of plaited wool or vegetable fibers, used in theatrical make-up for making artificial beards, sideburns, etc. Also called **crepe wool.**

crepe′ mar′ocain, marocain.

crepe′ myr′tle. See **crape myrtle.**

crepe′ pa′per, crepe (def. 2). —**crepe′-pa′per,** *adj.*

crepe′ rub′ber, **1.** a type of crude rubber pressed into crinkled sheets. **2.** a similar type of synthetic rubber used esp. in making shoe soles. Also called **crepe.**

crêpe su·zette (krāp′ sōō zet′; *Fr.* krep sy zet′), *pl.* **crêpe su·zettes** (krāp′ sōō zets′), *Fr.* **crêpes su·zette** (krep sy zet′). a thin dessert pancake, usually rolled or folded in quarters, heated in a sauce of orange-flavored liqueur, and flambéed before serving. Also, **crepe′ suzette′.** [< F, equiv. to *crêpe* pancake (see CREPE) + *suzette* special use of proper name]

crepe′ wool′. See **crepe hair.**

crep·i·do·ma (krep′i dō′mə), *n., pl.* **-ma·ta** (-mə tə). the stepped platform forming the floor and substructure of a classical temple, esp. a Greek temple. Also called **crepis, krepis.** [< Gk *krēpídōma*, equiv. to *krēpíd-* (s. of *krēpís*) groundwork + *-o-* -O- + *-ma* n. suffix]

cre·pis (krē′pis), *n., pl.* **-pes** (-pēz). crepidoma. [< Gk *krēpís*]

crep·i·tant (krep′i tənt), *adj.* crackling. [< L *crepitant-* (s. of *crepitāns*) clattering, prp. of *crepitāre*, freq. of *crepāre* to clatter; see -ANT]

crep·i·tate (krep′i tāt′), *v.i.*, **-tat·ed, -tat·ing.** to make a crackling sound; crackle. [< L *crepitāt(us)*, ptp. of *crepitāre*. See CREPITANT, -ATE¹] —**crep′i·ta′tion,** *n.*

cre·pon (krā′pon), *n.* a durable, heavyweight crepe. [< F, equiv. to *crêpe* CREPE + *-on* n. suffix]

crept (krept), *v.* pt. and pp. of **creep.**

cre·pus·cle (kri pus′əl), *n.* crepuscule.

cre·pus·cu·lar (kri pus′kyə lər), *adj.* **1.** of, pertaining to, or resembling twilight; dim; indistinct. **2.** *Zool.* appearing or flying in the twilight. [CREPUSCULE + -AR¹]

crepus′cular light′, a dim light, as of the sky at twilight.

crepus′cular ray′, a twilight ray of sunlight shining through breaks in high clouds and illuminating dust particles in the air.

cre·pus·cule (kri pus′kyōōl, krep′ə skyōōl′), *n.* twilight; dusk. Also, **crepuscle.** [< L *crepuscul(um)*, equiv. to *crepus-* (var. of *creper* dark) + *-culum* -CULE]

cres., *Music.* crescendo. Also, **cresc.**

Cres·cas (kres′kəs), *n.* **Has·dai** (khäs′dī), 1340–1412?, Jewish philosopher and theologian, born in Spain.

cre·scen·do (kri shen′dō, -sen′dō; *It.* kre shen′dô), *n., pl.* **-dos,** *It.* **-di** (-dē), *adj., adv., v.* —*n.* **1.** a gradual increase in force, volume, or loudness: *a crescendo of business activity.* **2.** *Music.* a crescendo passage. —*adj., adv.* **3.** gradually increasing in force, volume, or loudness. —*v.i.* **4.** to grow in force or loudness. [< It: lit., growing < L *crescendum*, ger. of *crescere* to grow] —**Ant. 2.** diminuendo.

cres·cent (kres′ənt), *n.* **1.** *Astron.* **a.** the figure of the moon in its first or last quarter, resembling a segment of a ring tapering to points at the ends. See diag. under **moon.** **b.** the similar figure of Mercury and Venus on either side of inferior conjunction, when seen through a telescope. **2.** a representation of this. **3.** the emblem of Turkey or of Islam. **4.** *Heraldry.* a representation of a crescent moon, horns upward unless otherwise specified, used as the cadency mark of a second son. Cf. **decrescent, increscent.** **5.** the power of Turkey or of Islam. **6.** any crescent-shaped object, as a bun or roll. **7.** Also called **Chinese crescent, Chinese pavilion, jingling Johnny, pavillon Chinois, Turkish crescent.** a musical percussion instrument of Turkish origin, consisting of a pole bearing a crescent-shaped metal plate, topped with a pavillon, and hung with small bells. **8.** *Horol.* (in a lever escapement) a concave indentation in the safety roller, on the same radius with the ruby pin, allowing passage of the guard pin. **9.** *Chiefly Brit.* **a.** a curved street having solid façades of unified architectural design. **b.** the curve or curved portion of a street. —*adj.* **10.** shaped like the moon in its first quarter. **11.** increasing; growing. [< L *crescent-* (s. of *crescēns*) growing, prp. of *crescere*; r. late ME *cressaunt* < AF] —**cres′cent·like′, cres′cen·toid′,** *adj.*

Cres·cent (kres′ənt), *n.* a boy's given name.

Cres′cent Cit′y, a town in NW California. 2958 (1960).

Cres′cent Cit′y Northwest′, a town in NW California. 3086 (1960).

cres·cen·tic (krə sen′tik), *adj.* shaped like a crescent. [CRESCENT + -IC]

cres′cent truss′, a roof truss having upper and lower chords curving upward from a common point at each side. Also called **camelback truss.**

cre·scit e·un·do (kres′kit e ōōn′dō; *Eng.* kres′it ē un′dō), *Latin.* it grows as it goes: motto of New Mexico.

cres·cive (kres′iv), *adj.* increasing; growing. [< L *cresc(ere)* (to) increase + -IVE]

Cres·co (kres′kō), *n.* a town in N Iowa. 3809 (1960).

Cre·si·us (krē′shē əs), *n. Class. Myth.* an epithet of Dionysus, meaning "Cretan."

cre·sol (krē′sōl, -sôl, -sol), *n. Chem.* any of three isomeric compounds having the formula $CH_3C_6H_4OH$, usually derived from coal tar and wood tar, and used chiefly as a disinfectant. Also called **methyl phenol.** Cf. **tricresol.** [*cres-* (irreg. from CREOSOTE) + -OL²]

Cres·phon·tes (kres fon′tēz), *n. Class. Myth.* a Heraclid who gained control of Messenia after helping lead the invasion of Peloponnesus by the Heraclidae.

cress (kres), *n.* **1.** any of various plants of the mustard family, esp. the water cress, having pungent-tasting leaves often used for salad and as a garnish. **2.** any of various similar plants. [ME *cresse*, OE *cress(a)*, *cresse*; c. D *kers*, G *Kresse*]

cres·set (kres′it), *n.* a metal cup or basket often mounted on a pole or suspended from above, containing oil, pitch, a rope steeped in rosin, etc., used as a light or beacon. [ME < MF; OF *craisset*, equiv. to *craisse* GREASE + *-et* -ET]

Cresset

Cres·si·da (kres′i də), *n.* (in medieval adaptations of the story of the Trojan wars) a new character developed from the characters of Chryseis and Bryseis and portrayed as the lover of the Trojan hero, Troilus, whom she deserts for Diomedes, a Greek. Also, **Criseyde.**

Cres·sie (kres′ē), *n.* a girl's given name.

Cress·kill (kres′kil), *n.* a town in NE New Jersey. 7290 (1960).

Cres·son (kres′ən), *n.* a town in central Pennsylvania. 2659 (1960).

cress·y (kres′ē), *adj.*, **cress·i·er, cress·i·est.** abounding in cresses. [CRESS + -Y¹]

Cres·sy (kres′ē), *n.* Crécy (def. 1).

crest (krest), *n.* **1.** a tuft or other natural growth on the top of the head of an animal, as the comb of a cock. **2.** anything resembling or suggesting such a tuft. **3.** the ridge of the neck of a horse, dog, etc. **4.** the mane growing from this ridge. **5.** an ornament or heraldic device surmounting a helmet. **6.** (loosely) a helmet. **7.** a ridge running from front to back along the top of a helmet; comb. **8.** *Heraldry.* a figure borne above the escutcheon in an achievement of arms, often on a helmet or the like, or else by itself as a distinguishing device. **9.** the head or top of anything. **10.** the highest part of a hill or mountain range. **11.** a ridge or ridgelike formation. **12.** the foamy top of a wave. **13.** the point of highest flood, as of a river. **14.** the highest or best of the kind. **15.** *Archit.* a cresting. **16.** *Mach.* (in a screw or other threaded object) the ridge or surface farthest from the body of the object and defined by the flanks of the thread. Cf. **root** (def. 13a). **17.** *Anat.* a ridge, esp. on a bone. **18.** a ridge or other prominence on any part of the body of an animal. **—*v.t.* 19.** to furnish with a crest. **20.** to serve as a crest for; crown or top. **21.** to reach the crest or summit of (a hill, mountain, etc.). **—*v.i.* 22.** to form or rise to a crest, as a wave or river. [ME *creste* < MF < L *crist(a)*] **—crest′ed,** *adj.* **—crest′less,** *adj.*

crest′ cloud′, a stationary cloud parallel to and near the top of a mountain ridge. Cf. **cap cloud** (def. 1).

crest′ cor′onet, *Heraldry.* coronet (def. 6).

crest′ed auk′let. See under **auklet.**

crest′ed dog's′-tail. See under **dog's-tail.**

crest′ed fly′catcher, a North American flycatcher, *Myiarchus crinitus,* noted for its use of the castoff skins of snakes in building its nest.

crest′ed i′ris. See **dwarf crested iris.**

crest′ed liz′ard. See **desert iguana.**

crest′ed pop′py, an herb, *Argemone platyceras,* of tropical America, having bluish-gray leaves and white flowers, densely covered with white spines.

crest′ed swift′. See **tree swift.**

crest·fall·en (krest′fô′lən), *adj.* **1.** dejected; dispirited; depressed. **2.** with drooping crest. [CREST + FALLEN] **—crest′fall′en·ly,** *adv.* **—crest′fall′en·ness,** *n.*

crest·fish (krest′fish′), *n., pl.* **-fish·es,** (*esp. collectively*) **-fish.** a deep-sea fish, *Lophotus capelli,* having an elongated, ribbonlike shape. [CREST + FISH]

Crest′ Hill′, a town in NE Illinois. 5887 (1960).

crest·ing (kres′ting), *n.* **1.** *Archit.* a decorative coping, balustrade, etc., usually designed to give an interesting skyline. **2.** *Furniture.* ornamentation either carved or sawed in the top rail of a piece or else added to it. **3.** a system of ornamental ridges or flutes on a piece of plate armor. [CREST + -ING[1]]

Crest·line (krest′līn′), *n.* a town in central Ohio. 5521 (1960).

Cres·ton (kres′tən), *n.* a town in S Iowa. 7667 (1960).

crest′ rail′, the carved or profiled top rail of a chair, settee, or sofa.

crest′ ta′ble, an ornamented coping.

Crest·view (krest′vyo͞o′), *n.* a town in NW Florida. 7467 (1960).

cres·yl (kres′il, krē′sil), *adj. Chem.* tolyl. Also, **cre·syl·ic** (kri sil′ik). [CRES(OL) + -YL]

Cre·ta (krē′tə), *n. Class. Myth.* the mother, by Helius, of Pasiphaë.

cre·ta·ceous (kri tā′shəs), *adj.* **1.** of the nature of, resembling, or containing chalk. **2.** (*cap.*) *Geol.* noting or pertaining to a period of the Mesozoic era occurring from 70,000,000 to 135,000,000 years ago and characterized by the extinction of giant reptiles and the advent of modern insects. See table under **era. —*n.* 3.** (*cap.*) *Geol.* the Cretaceous period or system. [< L *crētāceus,* equiv. to *crēt(a)* chalk (lit., Cretan earth) + *-āceus* -ACEOUS] **—cre·ta′ceous·ly,** *adv.*

Cre·tan (krēt′ən), *adj.* **1.** of or pertaining to the Island of Crete or its inhabitants. **—*n.* 2.** a native or inhabitant of Crete, esp. one of the indigenous Greeks. [< L *Crētān(us).* See CRETE, -AN]

Cre′tan bear's′-tail (bârz′tāl′), an erect herb, *Celsia Arcturus,* of Crete and Asia Minor, having yellow flowers with purple anthers.

Cre′tan bull′, *Gk. Legend.* a savage bull, sometimes held to be the father of the Minotaur, captured on Crete by Hercules as one of his labors, driven by him to Greece, and there released and allowed to roam the area around Marathon until captured by Theseus. Also called **Marathonian bull.**

Cre′tan mul′lein, an herb, *Celsia cretica,* of the Mediterranean region, having purple-marked, yellow flowers.

Cre′tan spike′nard, a stout, perennial herb, *Valeriana Phu,* of the Caucasus, having white or flesh-pink flowers.

Crete (krēt), *n.* **1.** Also called **Candia.** a Greek island in the Mediterranean, SE of Greece. 483,258 (1961); 3235 sq. mi. *Cap.:* Canea. **2.** a town in SE Nebraska. 3546 (1960). **3.** a town in NE Illinois. 3463 (1960).

Cre·the·is (krē′thē is), *n. Class. Myth.* the wife of Acastus. She was slain and dismembered by Peleus in revenge for her treacherous scheming to make him her lover, even though he had rejected her advances.

Cre·the·us (krē′thē əs, -tho͞os), *n. Class. Myth.* **1.** the founder of Iolcus and a son of Aeolus. **2.** (in the *Aeneid*) a companion of Aeneas beloved by the Muses.

cre·tin (krēt′ən, krē′tin), *n.* **1.** a person suffering from cretinism. **2.** *Informal.* a stupid, obtuse, or mentally defective person. [< F; SwissF *creitin, crestin* human being (though an idiot); see CHRISTIAN] **—cre′ti·noid′,** *adj.* **—cre′tin·ous,** *adj.*

cre·tin·ism (krēt′əniz′əm), *n. Pathol.* a chronic disease due to absence or deficiency of the normal thyroid secretion, characterized by physical deformity, dwarfism, idiocy, and often by goiter. [< F *crétinisme.* See CRETIN, -ISM]

cre·tonne (kri ton′, krē′ton), *n.* a heavy cotton material in printed designs, used esp. for drapery and slip covers. [< F, after *Creton,* Norman village where it was produced]

Cre·ü·sa (krē o͞o′sə), *n. Class. Myth.* **1.** Also called **Glauce.** the bride of Jason, slain by the magic of the jealous Medea. **2.** a daughter of Priam and the wife of Aeneas, lost in the flight from Troy.

Creuse (krœz), *n.* a department in central France. 163,515 (1962); 2165 sq. mi. *Cap.:* Guéret.

Creu·sot (*Fr.* krœ zō′), *n.* **Le.** See **Le Creusot.**

cre·val·le (krə val′ē, -val′ə), *n., pl.* (*esp. collectively*) **-le,** (*esp. referring to two or more kinds or species*) **-les.** any of several marine fishes of the jack family, *Carangidae.* [var. of CAVALLA]

creval′le jack′. See under **jack**[1] (def. 16).

cre·vasse (krə vas′), *n., v.,* **-vassed, -vas·sing. —*n.* 1.** a fissure, or deep cleft, in glacial ice, the earth's surface, etc., as one resulting from an earthquake. **2.** *U.S.* a breach in an embankment or levee. **—*v.t.* 3.** to fissure with crevasses. [< F; see CREVICE]

Creve Coeur (krēv′ ko͝or′), *n.* **1.** a town in central Illinois. 6684 (1960). **2.** a town in E Missouri. 5122 (1960).

Crève·coeur (krev kœr′), *n.* **Mi·chel Guil·laume Jean de** (mē shel′ gē yōm′ zhäN də), ("*J. Hector St. John*"), 1735–1813, French writer, statesman, and agriculturalist; in U.S. after 1754.

crev·ice (krev′is), *n.* a crack forming an opening; cleft; rift; fissure. [ME *crevace* < MF, OF < LL *crepātia* cracked state, equiv. to L *crepā(re)* (to) crack + *-tia* n. suffix] **—crev′iced,** *adj.*

crew[1] (kro͞o), *n.* **1.** a group of persons involved in a particular kind of work or working together: *the crew of a train; a wrecking crew.* **2.** *Naut.* **a.** the company of men who man a ship or boat. **b.** the common sailors of a ship's company. **c.** a particular gang of a ship's company. **3.** the team that mans a racing shell: *varsity crew.* **4.** the sport of racing with racing shells: *He went out for crew in his freshman year.* **5.** any force or band of armed men. **6.** *Often Derogatory.* a company; crowd: *that rough, brawling crew.* **—*v.t.* 7.** to serve as a member of (a ship). **8.** to obtain or employ a crew for (a ship). **—*v.i.* 9.** to serve as a member of a ship's crew. [late ME *crewe* augmentation, hence reinforcements, body of soldiers < MF *creue* increase, n. use of fem. of OF *creu,* ptp. of *creistre* to grow < L *crescere;* see CRESCENT] **—crew′less,** *adj.*

crew[2] (kro͞o), *v.* a pt. of **crow**[2].

crew′ cut′, a man's haircut in which the hair is closely cropped.

crew·el (kro͞o′əl), *n.* **1.** Also called **crew′el yarn′.** a worsted yarn for embroidery and edging. **2.** crewelwork. [late ME *crule*] **—crew′el·ist,** *n.*

crew·el·work (kro͞o′əl wûrk′), *n.* decorative embroidery done with crewel yarn on cotton or linen, using simple stitches worked in floral or pastoral designs. [CREWEL + WORK]

crew·man (kro͞o′mən), *n., pl.* **-men.** a member of a crew. [CREW[1] + MAN[1]] **—crew′man·ship′,** *n.*

crew′ neck′, a collarless neckline, as on a sweater or jersey, that fits snugly at the base of the neck. **—crew′neck′, crew′-necked′,** *adj.*

crib (krib), *n., v.,* **cribbed, crib·bing. —*n.* 1.** a child's bed with enclosed sides. **2.** a stall or pen for cattle. **3.** a rack or manger for fodder, as in a stable or barn. **4.** a small house or room where a low-priced prostitute plies her trade; a cheap, ill-kept brothel. **5.** a room, closet, etc., in a factory or the like, in which tools are kept and issued to workmen. **6.** a shallow, separate section of a bathing area, reserved for small children. **7.** any confined space. **8.** *Slang.* a house, shop, etc., frequented by thieves or regarded by thieves as a likely place for burglarizing. **9.** a wicker basket. **10.** *Building Trades, Civil Engineering.* any of various cellular frameworks of logs, squared timbers, or steel or concrete objects of similar form assembled in layers at right angles, often filled with earth and stones and used in the construction of foundations, dams, retaining walls, etc. **11.** a lining for a well or other shaft. **12.** a bin for storing grain, salt, etc. **13.** a barrier projecting part of the way into a river and then upward, acting to reduce the flow of water and as a storage place for logs being floated downstream. **14.** *Brit., Australian.* lunch, esp. a cold lunch carried from home to work and eaten by a laborer on the job; snack. **15.** *Informal.* a petty theft, plagiarism, etc. **16.** *Informal.* a translation, list of correct answers, or other illicit aid used by students while reciting, taking exams, or the like; pony. **17.** *Cribbage.* a set of cards made up by equal contributions from each player's hand, and belonging to the dealer. **—*v.t.* 18.** to confine in or as in a crib. **19.** to provide with a crib or cribs. **20.** to line with timber or planking. **21.** *Informal.* to pilfer or steal, esp. to plagiarize (another's writings or ideas). **—*v.i.* 22.** *Informal.* to use a crib in translating. **23.** (of a horse) to practice cribbing. **24.** *Informal.* to steal; plagiarize. [ME *cribbe,* OE *crib(b);* c. D *krib,* G *Krippe*]

crib·bage (krib′ij), *n.* a card game, basically for two, but also played by three or four players, a characteristic feature of which is the crib, and in which the object is to make counting combinations for points that are scored on a cribbage board. [CRIB + -AGE]

crib′bage board′, a board for keeping score in cribbage, having holes into which pegs are placed to mark the progress of the players.

crib·ber (krib′ər), *n.* **1.** one who cribs. **2.** a horse that cribs. [CRIB + -ER[1]]

crib·bing (krib′ing), *n.* **1.** *Vet. Med.* Also called **crib-biting, wind-sucking.** an injurious habit in which a horse bites its manger and as a result swallows air. **2.** *Mining.* **a.** a timber lining, closely spaced, as in a shaft or raise. **b.** pieces of timber for lining a shaft, raise, etc. **3.** a system of cribs, as for retaining earth or for a building or the like being moved or having its foundations rebuilt. [CRIB + -ING[1]]

crib-bite (krib′bīt′), *v.i.,* **-bit, -bit·ten** or **-bit, -bit·ing.** *Vet. Med.* to practice cribbing. [back formation from *crib-biting, crib-biter;* see CRIBBING] **—crib′-bit′er,** *n.*

crib′ death′, death from the cessation of breathing in a healthy seeming infant, usually during sleep, sometimes traceable to a chronic oxygen deficiency.

cri·blé (krē blā′), *adj.* **1.** (of certain areas on an engraving plate) textured in a pattern of minute dots so as to reduce the contrast between solid black areas and areas of type. **2.** *Fine Arts.* (of an engraved plate) having a dotted surface or pattern made by small punctures. [< F: lit., made sievelike, deriv. of *crible* sieve < LL *crībl(um),* dissimilated var. of L *crībrum* sieve]

crib·ri·form (krib′rə fôrm′), *adj.* sievelike. Also, **crib·rous** (krib′rəs). [< L *crībr(um)* a sieve + -I- + -FORM]

crib·work (krib′wûrk′), *n. Building Trades, Civil Engineering.* a system of cribs; cribbing. [CRIB + WORK]

Crich·ton (krīt′ən), *n.* **James** ("*the Admirable Crichton*"), 1560?–82, Scottish scholar and linguist.

crick[1] (krik), *n.* **1.** a sharp, painful spasm of the muscles, as of the neck or back, making it difficult to move the part. **—*v.t.* 2.** to give a crick or wrench to (the neck, back, etc.). [late ME *crikke,* perh. akin to CRICK[2]]

Cricket, *Gryllus domesticus* (Length ¾ in.)

crick[2] (krik), *n. U.S. Dial.* creek (def. 1).

Crick (krik), *n.* **Francis Harry Compton,** born 1916, English biophysicist: Nobel prize for medicine 1962.

crick·et[1] (krik′it), *n.* **1.** any of several saltatorial, orthopterous insects of the family *Gryllidae,* characterized by long antennae and stridulating organs on the forewings of the male, as one of those species commonly found in pastures and meadows (**field cricket**) or on trees and shrubs (**tree cricket**). **2.** a metal toy consisting of a convex metal piece with a flat metal spring fastened to it at one side that snaps back and forth with a clicking, cricketlike noise when pressed. [ME *criket* insect < MF *criquet,* equiv. to *criqu(er)* (to) creak (imit.) + *-et* -ET] **—crick′et·like′,** *adj.*

crick·et[2] (krik′it), *n.* **1.** a game for two teams of 11 members each that is played on a large field having two wickets 22 yards apart, the object being to score runs by batting the ball far enough so that one is enabled to exchange wickets with the batsman defending the opposite wicket before the ball is recovered. **2.** fair play; gentlemanly conduct: *It wouldn't be cricket to give away his secret.* **—*v.i.* 3.** to play cricket. [< MF *criquet* goal post < MFlem *krick* kind of stick; see -ET] **—crick′et·er,** *n.*

crick·et[3] (krik′it), *n.* a small, low stool. [?]

crick·et[4] (krik′it), *n.* (on a sloping roof) a small roof for diverting rain water around an obstruction, as a chimney. [?]

crick′et frog′, a tree frog, *Acris gryllus,* of eastern North America, having a call that resembles the chirping of a cricket.

crick′et ta′ble, a three-legged table of the Jacobean period.

cri·coid (krī′koid), *Anat.* **—*adj.* 1.** pertaining to a ring-shaped cartilage at the lower part of the larynx. **—*n.* 2.** the cricoid cartilage. See diag. under **larynx.** [< NL *cricoīd(es)* < Gk *krikoeidēs* ring-shaped. See CIRCLE, -OID]

cri·co·pha·ryn·ge·al (krī′kō fə rin′jē əl, -jəl, -far′in jē′əl), *adj. Anat.* of, pertaining to, or involving the cricoid cartilage and the pharynx. [*crico-* (see CRICOID) + PHARYNGEAL]

cri de guerre (krē′ də gâr′), *pl.* **cris de guerre** (krēz′də gâr′). *Scot. Heraldry.* a martial expression, used instead of or in addition to a motto, and placed at the top of the achievement. [< F: lit., cry of war]

cried (krīd), *v.* pt. of **cry.**

cri·er (krī′ər), *n.* **1.** one who cries. **2.** a court or town official who makes public announcements. **3.** a hawker. [ME *criere* < OF. See CRY, -ER[1]]

Crile (krīl), *n.* **George Washington,** 1864–1943, U.S. surgeon.

crim., criminal.

crim. con., *Civil Law.* See **criminal conversation.**

crime (krīm), *n.* **1.** an action or an instance of negligence that is deemed injurious to the public welfare or morals, or to the interests of the state and that is legally prohibited. **2.** the habitual or frequent performance of crimes: *a life of crime.* **3.** criminal activity and those engaged in it: *to oppose crime and vice.* **4.** any offense, esp. one of grave character. **5.** serious wrongdoing; sin. **6.** *Informal.* a foolish, senseless, or shameful act: *It's a crime to overfeed a dog like that.* [ME < OF < L *crīmin-* (s. of *crīmen*) charge, guilt, crime] **—crime′less,** *adj.* **—crime′less·ness,** *n.*

—Syn. 1. wrong; misdemeanor, tort, felony. CRIME, OFFENSE, SIN agree in meaning a breaking of law. CRIME usually means any serious violation of human laws: *the crime of treason, of robbery.* OFFENSE is used of an infraction of either human or divine law, and does not necessarily mean a serious one: *an offense leading to a jail sentence; an offense against morals.* SIN means a serious breaking of moral or divine law: *the sin of hating one's neighbor.*

SOVIET UNION
Odessa
SEA OF AZOV
Crimea
RUMANIA
Yalta
BLACK SEA

Cri·me·a (krī mē′ə, kri-), *n.* **the, 1.** a peninsula in SE Ukraine, between the Black Sea and the Sea of Azov. **2.** a former autonomous republic of the Soviet Union, now a region of Ukraine, ab. 10,000 sq. mi. Russian, **Krim, Krym. —Cri·me′an,** *adj.*

crime′ against′ na′ture, *Law.* any unnatural sexual relationship or act.

Crime′ and Pun′ishment, a novel (1866) by Feodor Dostoevsky.

Crime′an War′, a war between Great Britain, France, Turkey, and Sardinia on one side, and Russia on the other, fought chiefly in the Crimea 1853–56.

crime d'é·tat (krēm dā tȧ′), *pl.* **crimes d'é·tat** (krēm dā tȧ′). *French.* treason. [lit., crime concerning the State]

crime pas·si·o·nel (krēm′ pä sē ə nel′; *Fr.* krēm pä syō nel′), a crime committed in passion, esp. a murder committed out of sexual motives. [< F: lit., passionate crime]

crim·i·nal (krim′ə nəl), *adj.* **1.** *Law.* of or pertaining to crime or its punishment (distinguished from *civil*): *a criminal proceeding.* **2.** of the nature of or involving crime. **3.** guilty of crime. **4.** *Informal.* **a.** senseless; foolish: *It is criminal to have a steak like that wasted.* **b.** exorbitant; grossly over-priced: *They charge absolutely criminal prices.* **—*n.* 5.** a person guilty or convicted of a crime. [late ME < LL *crīmināl(is),* equiv. to L *crīmin-* (s. of *crīmen;* see CRIME) + *-ālis* -AL[1]] **—crim′i·nal·ly,** *adv.*

—Syn. 2. felonious, unlawful, illegal, nefarious, flagitious, iniquitous, wicked, sinful, wrong. **5.** convict, malefactor, evildoer, transgressor, culprit, delinquent, felon, crook, hoodlum, gangster. **—Ant. 2.** lawful. **3.** innocent.

crim′inal assault′, *Law.* **1.** an attack by physical force on a person for which the attacker is liable to criminal prosecution. **2.** a similar act with intent to commit rape.

crim′inal contempt′, *Law.* any seriously disrespectful act committed against the dignity or authority of a court.

crim′inal conversa′tion, *Civil Law.* adultery. *Abbr.:* crim. con.

crim·i·nal·ist (krim′ə nəlist), *n.* **1.** an expert in criminal law. **2.** one who studies or practices criminology; criminologist. [CRIMINAL + -IST]

crim·i·nal·is·tics (krim′ə nəlis′tiks), *n.* (*construed as sing.*) the science dealing with the detection of crime and the apprehension of criminals. [CRIMINALIST + -ICS]

crim·i·nal·i·ty (krim′ə nal′i tē), *n., pl.* **-ties** for 2. **1.** the quality or state of being criminal. **2.** a criminal act or practice. [< ML *crīminālitās.* See CRIMINAL, -ITY]

crim′inal law′, the laws of a state or country dealing with criminal offenses and their punishments.

crim′inal syn′dicalism, *Law.* the doctrine of recourse to acts of violence or terrorism, or the advocacy of such acts, as a means of effecting economic or political change: proscribed by statute in many States.

crim·i·nate (krim′ə nāt′), *v.t.,* **-nat·ed, -nat·ing. 1.** to charge with a crime. **2.** to incriminate. **3.** to censure (something) as criminal; condemn. [< L *crīmināt(us)* accused, ptp. of *crīminārī.* See CRIME, -ATE[1]] —**crim′i·na′tion,** *n.* —**crim′i·na′tor,** *n.*

crim·i·na·tive (krim′ə nā′tiv), *adj.* tending to or involving crimination; accusatory. Also, **crim·i·na·to·ry** (krim′ə nə tôr′ē, -tōr′ē). [CRIMINATE + -IVE]

crim·i·nol·o·gy (krim′ə nol′ə jē), *n.* the study of crime and criminals. [< L *crīmin-* (s. of *crīmen;* see CRIME) + -O- + -LOGY] —**crim·i·no·log·i·cal** (krim′ə-nᵊloj′i kəl), **crim′i·no·log′ic,** *adj.* —**crim′i·no·log′i·cal·ly,** *adv.* —**crim′i·nol′o·gist,** *n.*

crim·mer (krim′ər), *n.* krimmer.

crimp[1] (krimp), *v.t.* **1.** to press into small regular folds; make wavy: *to crimp the edges of a pie shell.* **2.** to bend (leather) into shape. **3.** to curl (hair), esp. with the use of a curling iron. **4.** *Metalworking.* **a.** to bend the edges of (skelp) before forming into a tube. **b.** to fold the edges of (sheet metal) to make a lock seam. **5.** to produce a corrugated surface in; corrugate, as sheet metal, cardboard, etc. **6.** to press or draw together, as the ends of something. **7.** *Cookery.* to gash (the flesh of a live fish or of one just killed) with a knife to make it more crisp when cooked. **8.** to check; arrest; hinder: *The shortage of labor and materials is crimping production.* —*n.* **9.** the act of crimping. **10.** a crimped condition or form. **11.** Usually, **crimps.** waves or curls, esp. in hair that has been crimped or that displays a crimped pattern. **12.** the waviness of wool fibers as naturally grown on sheep. **13.** a crease formed in sheet metal or plate metal to make the material less flexible, or for fastening purposes. **14. put a crimp in,** *Slang.* to interfere with; hinder: *The accident put a crimp in their vacation plans.* [ME *crymp(en),* OE *(ge)crympan* to curl, deriv. of *crump* crooked] —**crimp′er,** *n.* —**crimp′ness,** *n.*

crimp[2] (krimp), *n.* **1.** a person engaged in enlisting seamen, soldiers, etc., by persuasion, swindling, or coercion. —*v.t.* **2.** to enlist (seamen, soldiers, etc.) by such means. [special use of CRIMP[1]]

crim·ple (krim′pəl), *v.t., v.i.,* **-pled, -pling.** to wrinkle, crinkle, or curl. [ME *crymple.* See CRIMP[1], -LE]

crimp·y (krim′pē), *adj.,* **crimp·i·er, crimp·i·est.** of a crimped form or appearance. [CRIMP[1] + -Y[1]]

crim·son (krim′zən, -sən), *adj.* **1.** deep purplish-red. **2.** sanguinary. —*n.* **3.** a crimson color, pigment, or dye. —*v.t., v.i.* **4.** to make or become crimson. [late ME *crym(e)syn* < OSp *cremesin* < Ar *qirmizī* (*qirm(iz)* KERMES + *-ī* suffix of appurtenance) + OSp *-in* -INE[1]; see CRAMOISY] —**crim′son·ly,** *adv.* —**crim′son·ness,** *n.*

crim′son clo′ver, a European clover, *Trifolium incarnatum,* having heads of crimson flowers, cultivated as a forage plant in the U.S. Also called **Italian clover.**

crim′son flag′, a perennial herb, *Schizostylis coccinea,* of South Africa, having tubular, red flowers. Also called **Kafir lily.**

crim′son sage′, a perennial herb, *Audibertia grandiflora,* having arrow-shaped leaves and crimson-purple or red flowers. Also called **bee sage.**

crine (krīn), *n.* hair; head of hair. [< L *crīn(ia)* hair] —**cri′nal,** *adj.* —**cri·nat·ed** (krī′nā tid), *adj.*

crined (krīnd), *adj. Heraldry.* (of a human being) depicted with hair of a specified tincture: *a head affronté couped at the neck proper, crined gules.* [CRINE + -ED[3]]

crin·et (krin′it), *n. Armor.* a piece composed of articulated lames for protecting the upper part of a horse's neck, attached to a chanfron. Also called **cri·nière** (krin yâr′). [< MF *crinete,* equiv. to OF *crin* hair, mane (< L *crīnis*) + *-ete* -ET]

cringe (krinj), *v.,* **cringed, cring·ing,** *n.* —*v.i.* **1.** to shrink, bend, or crouch, esp. from fear or servility; cower. **2.** to fawn. —*n.* **3.** servile or fawning deference. [ME *crenge(n),* OE **crengan,* causative of *cringan* to yield, fall (in battle)] —**cring′er,** *n.* —**cring′ing·ly,** *adv.* —**cring′ing·ness,** *n.*

crin·gle (kriŋ′gəl), *n. Naut.* **1.** an eye or grommet formed on the boltrope of a sail to permit the attachment of lines, usually consisting of a thimble surrounded by a strop of rope or wire. **2.** the thimble itself. [< LG *kringel,* equiv. to *kring* circle + *-el* dim. suffix; c. ME *Cringle* (in place-names), Icel *kringla* circle]

cri·nite[1] (krī′nīt), *adj.* **1.** hairy. **2.** *Bot., Entomol.* having long hairs, or tufts of long, weak hairs. [< L *crīnīt(us),* equiv. to *crīn(is)* hair + *-ītus* -ITE[2]]

cri·nite[2] (krī′nīt, krin′īt), *n.* a fossil crinoid. [< Gk *krīn(on)* lily + -ITE[1]]

crin·kle (kriŋ′kəl), *v.,* **-kled, -kling,** *n.* —*v.t., v.i.* **1.** to turn or wind in many little bends and twists. **2.** to wrinkle; crimple; ripple. **3.** to make slight, sharp sounds; rustle. —*n.* **4.** a turn or twist; wrinkle; ripple. **5.** a crinkling sound. [ME *crinkle(n);* akin to OE *crincan* to bend, yield, D *krinkelen* to crinkle; see CRINGLE, CRINGE, CRANK]

crin′kle leaf′, *Plant Pathol.* a disease of plants, characterized by puckering, mottling, and distortion of the leaves, caused by any of several viruses.

crin·kle·root (kriŋ′kəl ro͞ot′, -ro͝ot′), *n.* any of several North American, cruciferous plants of the genus *Dentaria,* esp. *D. diphylla.* [CRINKLE + ROOT[1]]

crin·kly (kriŋ′klē), *adj.,* **-kli·er, -kli·est. 1.** having crinkles. **2.** making a rustling noise. [CRINKLE + -Y[1]]

crin·kum-cran·kum (kriŋ′kəm kraŋ′kəm), *n. Archaic.* something full of twists and turns. [humorous var. of *crinkle-crankle,* gradational compound based on CRINKLE; see CRANK]

cri·no·gen·ic (krī′nə jen′ik, krin′ə-), *adj.* stimulating secretion. [< Gk *krīn(ein)* (to) separate + -O- + -GENIC]

cri·noid (krī′noid, krin′oid), *adj.* **1.** belonging or pertaining to the *Crinoidea.* **2.** lilylike. —*n.* **3.** any echinoderm of the class *Crinoidea,* having a cup-shaped body to which are attached branched, radiating arms, comprising the sea lilies, feather stars, and various fossil forms. [< Gk *krinoeid(ēs),* equiv. to *krín(on)* lily + *-oeidēs* -OID]

Cri·noi·de·a (krī noi′dē ə, kri-), *n.* the class comprising the crinoids. [< NL; see CRINOID]

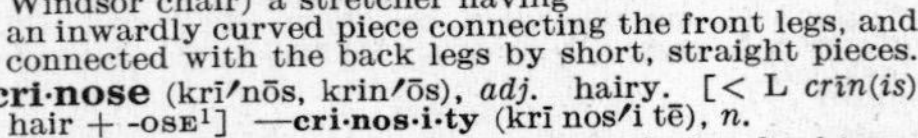

Crinoid (def. 3) Sea lily

crin·o·line (krin′ᵊlin, -ᵊlēn′), *n.* **1.** a petticoat of haircloth or other stiff material, worn by women under a full skirt to keep it belled out. **2.** a hoop skirt. **3.** a stiff, coarse cotton material for interlining. **4.** a reinforcement of iron straps for holding together brickwork, as of a furnace or chimney. [< F < It *crinolin(o),* equiv. to *crino* horse-hair (< L *crīn(is)* hair) + *lino* flax < L *līnum*]

crin′oline stretch′er, (on a Windsor chair) a stretcher having an inwardly curved piece connecting the front legs, and connected with the back legs by short, straight pieces.

cri·nose (krī′nōs, krin′ōs), *adj.* hairy. [< L *crīn(is)* hair + -OSE[1]] —**cri·nos·i·ty** (krī nos′i tē), *n.*

cri·num (krī′nəm), *n.* any of the tropical and subtropical, amaryllidaceous plants of the genus *Crinum,* usually having umbels of large, showy flowers. [< NL < Gk *krīnon* lily]

cri·ol·la (krē ō′lə; *Sp.* krē ô′yä), *n., pl.* **-ol·las** (-ō′ləz; *Sp.* -ô′yäs). a female criollo. [< Sp; fem. of CRIOLLO]

cri·ol·lo (krē ō′lō; *Sp.* krē ô′yô), *n., pl.* **-ol·los** (-ō′lōz; *Sp.* -ô′yôs), *adj.* —*n.* **1.** (in Spanish America) one born in the region but of European, usually Spanish, ancestry. Cf. **Creole** (def. 1). **2.** a domestic animal of any of several strains or breeds developed in Latin America. —*adj.* **3.** of, pertaining to, or characteristic of a criollo or criollos. [< Sp; see CREOLE]

Cri·oph·o·rus (krī of′ər əs), *n. Class. Myth.* an epithet of Hermes, meaning "ram-bearer."

cri·o·sphinx (krī′ə sfiŋks′), *n., pl.* **-sphinx·es, -sphin·ges** (-sfin′jēz). a sphinx with the head of a ram. [< Gk *kriō(s)* a ram + SPHINX]

crip·ple (krip′əl), *n., v.,* **-pled, -pling,** *adj.* —*n.* **1.** one who is partially or totally unable to use one or more of his limbs; a lame person. **2.** one who is disabled or impaired in any way: *a mental cripple.* **3.** *U.S. Dial.* a swampy, densely overgrown tract of land. **4.** *Carpentry.* any structural member shorter than usual, as a stud beneath a window sill. —*v.t.* **5.** to make a cripple of; lame. **6.** to disable; impair. —*adj.* **7.** *Carpentry.* jack[1] (def. 27). [ME *cripel,* OE *crypel;* akin to CREEP] —**crip′pler,** *n.* —**crip′pling·ly,** *adv.*

—**Syn. 5, 6.** maim. CRIPPLE, DISABLE mean to injure permanently or temporarily, to a degree which interferes with normal activities. To CRIPPLE is to injure in such a way as to deprive of the use of a member, particularly a leg or arm: *A broken arm cripples but does not disable a judge.* DISABLE, a more general word, implies such illness, injury, or impairment as makes a person incapable of engaging in his normal activities: *disabled by an attack of malaria; disabled by a wound.*

Crip′ple Creek′, a town in central Colorado: gold rush 1891. 614 (1960); 9600 ft. above sea level.

crip′ple raft′er, a jack rafter, as one between a hip and a valley, meeting neither a wall plate nor a ridgepole.

Cripps (krips), *n.* **Sir Stafford,** 1889–1952, British statesman and socialist leader.

Cri·ses (krī′sēz), *n.* **Sea of.** See **Mare Crisium.**

Cri·sey·de (kri sā′də), *n.* Cressida.

Cris·field (kris′fēld′), *n.* a town in SE Maryland. 3540 (1960).

cri·sis (krī′sis), *n., pl.* **-ses** (-sēz). **1.** a stage in a sequence of events at which the trend of all future events, esp. for better or for worse, is determined; turning point. **2.** the point in a play or story at which hostile elements are most tensely opposed to each other. **3.** *Med.* **a.** the point in the course of a serious disease at which a decisive change occurs, leading either to recovery or to death. **b.** the change itself. **4.** a condition of instability, as in social, economic, political, or international affairs, leading to a decisive change. [< L < Gk *krísis* decision, equiv. to *krī(nein)* (to) decide + *-sis* -SIS] —**cri′sic,** *adj.*

—**Syn. 1.** climax, juncture, exigency, strait, pinch. See **emergency.**

cri′sis theol′ogy, a neoorthodox theology, advocated by Karl Barth and others, emphasizing the absolute necessity of faith and divine revelation in transcending the personal crisis, common to all men, that arises from the contradictions inherent in human nature and in the social order. Also called **theology of crisis.** —**cri′sis theolo′gian.**

Cri·si·um (krē′sē əm), *n.* **Mare.** See **Mare Crisium.**

crisp (krisp), *adj.* **1.** hard but easily breakable; brittle: *crisp toast.* **2.** firm and fresh; not soft or wilted: *a crisp leaf of lettuce.* **3.** brisk; sharp; decided: *a crisp manner; a crisp reply.* **4.** lively; pithy; sparkling: *crisp repartee.* **5.** clean, neat, and well-pressed; well-groomed. **6.** bracing; invigorating: *crisp air.* **7.** crinkled, wrinkled, or rippled, as skin or water. **8.** in small, stiff, or firm curls; curly. —*v.t., v.i.* **9.** to make or become crisp. **9.** to curl. —*n.* **10.** *Chiefly Brit.* See **potato chip.** [ME, OE < L *crisp(us)* curled] —**crisp′ly,** *adv.* —**crisp′ness,** *n.*

cris·pate (kris′pāt), *adj.* crisped or curled. Also, **cris′pat·ed.** [< L *crispāt(us)* curled, ptp. of *crispāre.* See CRISP, -ATE[1]]

cris·pa·tion (kri spā′shən), *n.* **1.** the act or state of crisping or the state of being crisped. **2.** a slight contraction or undulation. [CRISPATE + -ION]

crisp·en (kris′pən), *v.t., v.i.* to make or become crisp. [CRISP + -EN[1]]

crisp·er (kris′pər), *n.* **1.** one who or that which crisps corrugates, or curls. **2.** a closed drawer or compartment in a refrigerator for keeping lettuce, celery, etc., crisp. **3.** *Textiles.* an auxiliary finishing machine for curling pile. [CRISP + -ER[1]]

Cri·spi (krē′spē), *n.* **Fran·ce·sco** (frän che′skô), 1819–1910, prime minister of Italy 1887–91, 1893–96.

Cris·pin (kris′pin), *n.* **1. Saint,** with his brother, Saint Crispinian, martyred A.D. c285, Roman Christian missionaries in Gaul: patron saints of shoemakers. **2.** (*l.c.*) a shoemaker.

Cris·pin·i·an (kri spin′ē ən), *n.* **Saint.** See **Crispin, Saint.**

crisp·y (kris′pē), *adj.,* **crisp·i·er, crisp·i·est. 1.** brittle crisp. **2.** curly or wavy. **3.** brisk. [CRISP + -Y[1]] —**crisp′i·ly,** *adv.* —**crisp′i·ness,** *n.*

cris·sal (kris′əl), *adj.* of or pertaining to the crissum. [< NL *crissāl(is).* See CRISSUM, -AL[1]]

criss·cross (kris′krôs′, -kros′), *adj.* **1.** having many crossing lines, paths, etc. —*n.* **2.** a crisscross mark, pattern, etc. **3.** tick-tack-toe. —*adv.* **4.** in a crisscross manner; crosswise. —*v.t., v.i.* **5.** to mark with or form crossing lines. **6.** to move or cause to move in a crisscross manner. [var. of *christ-cross*]

criss·cross-row (kris′krôs rō′, -kros′-), *n. Archaic.* the alphabet. [CRISSCROSS + ROW[1]]

cris·sum (kris′əm), *n., pl.* **cris·sa** (kris′ə). *Ornith.* **1.** the region surrounding the cloacal opening beneath the tail of a bird. **2.** the feathers of this region collectively. [< NL, equiv. to L *criss(āre)* (to) move the haunches + *-um* n. suffix]

cris·ta (kris′tə), *n., pl.* **-tae** (-tē). *Anat., Zool.* a crest or ridge. [< L: a crest, tuft, comb]

cris·tate (kris′tāt), *adj.* **1.** having a crest; crested. **2.** forming a crest. Also, **cris′tat·ed.** [< L *cristāt(us),* equiv. to *crist(a)* CRISTA + *-ātus* -ATE[1]]

Cris·to·bal (kri stō′bəl), *n.* a seaport in the Canal Zone at the Atlantic end of the Panama Canal, adjacent to Colón. 817 (1960). Spanish, **Cris·tó·bal** (krēs tô′bäl).

cris·to·bal·ite (kri stō′bə līt′), *n. Mineral.* a polymorph of quartz occurring in volcanic rock in the form of colorless, translucent crystals. [named after San *Cristóbal,* a hill near Pachuca de Soto, Mexico; see -ITE[1]]

Cris·tophe (krē stôf′), *n.* **Henri.** See **Christophe, Henri.**

crit., **1.** critical. **2.** criticism. **3.** criticized.

cri·te·ri·on (krī tēr′ē ən), *n., pl.* **-te·ri·a** (-tēr′ē ə), **-te·ri·ons.** a standard of judgment or criticism; an established rule or principle for testing anything. [< Gk *kritērion* a standard, equiv. to *krit-* (verbid s. of *krīnein* to separate, decide) + *-ērion* neut. suffix of means] —**cri·te·ri·on·al** (krī tēr′ē ə nᵊl), *adj.*

—**Syn.** measure, touchstone, test. See **standard.**

crit·ic (krit′ik), *n.* **1.** one who judges, evaluates, or criticizes: *a poor critic of men.* **2.** a person skilled in judging the qualities or merits of some class of things esp. of literary or artistic works, dramatic or musical performances, etc. **3.** a person who tends too readily to make captious, trivial, or harsh judgments. **4.** *Obs.* **a.** criticism. **b.** critique. [< L *critic(us)* < Gk *kritikós* skilled in judging (adj.), critic (n.), equiv. to *krī(nein)* (to) separate, decide + *-tikos* -TIC]

—**Syn. 2.** reviewer, censor, judge. **3.** censurer, carper.

crit·i·cal (krit′i kəl), *adj.* **1.** inclined to find fault or to judge with severity, often too readily. **2.** occupied with or skilled in criticism. **3.** involving skillful judgment as to truth, merit, etc.; judicial: *a critical analysis.* **4.** of or pertaining to critics or criticism: *critical essays.* **5.** providing textual variants, proposed emendations, etc.: *a critical edition of Chaucer.* **6.** pertaining to or of the nature of a crisis; of decisive importance with respect to the outcome; crucial: *a critical moment.* **7.** involving grave uncertainty, risk, peril, etc.; dangerous: *a critical wound.* **8.** *Physics.* pertaining to a state, value, or quantity at which one or more properties of a substance or system undergo a change. **9.** *Math.* indicating a point on a curve at which a transition or change takes place. [CRITIC + -AL[1]] —**crit′i·cal·ly,** *adv.* —**crit′i·cal·ness,** *n.*

—**Syn. 1.** captious, censorious, carping, faultfinding, caviling. **3.** discriminating, fastidious, nice, exact, precise. **6.** decisive, climacteric. **7.** hazardous, precarious, risky, perilous. —**Ant. 6.** unimportant.

crit′ical an′gle, 1. *Optics.* the minimum angle of incidence beyond which total internal reflection occurs for light traveling from a medium of higher to one of lower index of refraction; the angle of incidence for which refracted rays emerge tangent to the surface separating two media, the light traveling from the medium of higher to the medium of lower index of refraction. **2.** Also called **crit′ical an′gle of attack′, stall angle, stall angle of attack, stalling angle.** *Aeron.* the angle of attack, greater than or equal to the angle of attack for maximum lift, at which there is a sudden change in the airflow around an airfoil with a subsequent decrease in lift and increase in drag.

crit′ical con′stant, *Physics.* any of three constants associated with the critical point of a pure element or compound. Cf. **critical density, critical pressure, critical temperature.**

crit′ical den′sity, *Physics.* the density of a pure element or compound at a critical point. Cf. **critical constant.**

crit′ical mass′, *Physics.* the amount of a given radioactive material necessary to sustain a chain reaction at a constant rate.

crit′ical philos′ophy, the mature philosophy of Kant.

crit′ical point′, *Physics.* the point at which a substance in one phase, as the liquid, has the same density, pressure, and temperature as in another phase, as the gaseous.

crit′ical pres′sure, *Physics.* the pressure of a pure element or compound at a critical point. Cf. **critical constant.**

crit′ical ra′tio, *Statistics.* a ratio associated with the probability of a sample, usually the ratio of the deviation from the mean to the standard deviation.

crit′ical state′, *Physics.* the state of a pure element or compound when it is at a critical point.

crit′ical tem′perature, *Physics.* the temperature of a pure element or compound at a critical point. Cf. **critical constant.**

crit′ical vol′ume, *Physics.* the volume occupied by a certain mass, usually one gram molecule of a liquid or gaseous substance at its critical point.

crit·ic·as·ter (krit′i kas′tər), *n.* an inferior or incompetent critic. [CRITIC + -ASTER[1]] —**crit′ic·as′try, crit′ic·as′ter·ism,** *n.*

crit·i·cise (krit′i sīz′), *v.i., v.t.,* **-cised, -cis·ing.** *Chiefly Brit.* criticize. —**crit′i·cis′a·ble,** *adj.* —**crit′i·cis′er,** *n.* —**crit′i·cis′ing·ly,** *adv.*

crit·i·cism (krit′i siz′əm), *n.* **1.** the act or art of analyzing and judging the quality of a literary or artistic work, musical performance, art exhibit, dramatic production, etc. **2.** the act of passing judgment as to the merits of anything. **3.** the act of passing severe judgment; censure; faultfinding. **4.** a critical comment,

article, or essay; critique. **5.** any of various methods of studying texts or documents for the purpose of dating or reconstructing them, evaluating their authenticity, analyzing their content or style, etc.: *historical criticism; verbal criticism; literary criticism.* **6.** investigation of the text, origin, etc., of literary, esp. Biblical, documents: *textual criticism.* [CRITIC + -ISM]
—**Syn. 3.** stricture, animadversion. **4.** See **review.**

crit·i·cize (krit′i sīz′), *v.,* **-cized, -ciz·ing.** —*v.i.* **1.** to make judgments as to merits and faults. **2.** to find fault. —*v.t.* **3.** to judge or discuss the merits and faults of: *to criticize three novels in one review.* **4.** to censure or find fault with. Also, *esp. Brit.,* **criticise.** [CRITIC + -IZE] —**crit′i·ciz′a·ble,** *adj.* —**crit′i·ciz′er,** *n.* —**crit′i·ciz′ing·ly,** *adv.*
—**Syn. 2.** carp, cavil, censure. **3.** appraise, evaluate. **4.** condemn, blame.

cri·tique (kri tēk′), *n.* **1.** an article or essay criticizing a literary or other work; review. **2.** a criticism or critical comment on some problem, subject, etc. **3.** the art or practice of criticism. [< F < Gk *kritikḗ* the art of criticism, n. use of fem. of *kritikós* critical; r. CRITIC]

Critique′ of Pure′ Rea′son, a philosophical work (1781) by Immanuel Kant.

Crit′ten·den Com′promise (krit′ᵊn dən), *U.S. Hist.* a compromise proposed in December, 1860, to avert civil war, but never adopted, stipulating that slavery be permitted south of latitude 36°30′N, and forbidden north of that line. [named after J. J. *Crittenden* (1787–1863), American lawyer]

crit·ter (krit′ər), *n. Dial.* **1.** a domesticated animal. **2.** creature. Also, **crit′tur.** [var. of CREATURE]

Cri·us (krī′əs), *n. Class. Myth.* a Titan, the son of Uranus and Gaea, and the father of Astraeus, Pallas, and Perses.

cri·vetz (krē vyets′), *n.* a cold north or northeast wind in Rumania. Also, **cri·văţ** (krē vœts′), **krivu.** Cf. **bora**¹. [< Rum *crivaţ* < Slav; cf. Bulg *krivec*]

criz·zle (kriz′əl), *v.t., v.i.,* **-zled, -zling.** *Chiefly Dial.* to make or become rough, wrinkled, or irregular: *The cold crizzled the ground. The glass crizzled during cooling.* [?]

croak (krōk), *v.i.* **1.** to utter a low, hoarse, dismal cry, as a frog or a raven. **2.** to speak with a low, rasping voice. **3.** to talk despondingly; forebode evil; grumble. **4.** *Slang.* to die. —*v.t.* **5.** to utter or announce by croaking. **6.** *Slang.* to kill. —*n.* **7.** act or sound of croaking. [? ME *croke(n), *crake, back formation from OE *crācettan* to croak]

croak·er (krō′kər), *n.* **1.** one who or that which croaks. **2.** any of several sciaenoid fishes that make a croaking noise, esp. *Micropogon undulatus* **(Atlantic croaker),** found off the Atlantic coast of the southern U.S. **3.** a person who grumbles or forebodes evil. **4.** *Slang.* doctor.

croak·y (krō′kē), *adj.,* **croak·i·er, croak·i·est.** low and hoarse: *the croaky call of a frog.* [CROAK + -Y¹] —**croak′i·ly,** *adv.* —**croak′i·ness,** *n.*

Cro·at (krō′at), *n.* a native or inhabitant of Croatia; Croatian.

Cro·a·tia (krō ā′shə, -shē ə), *n.* a republic in SE Europe: includes the historical regions of Dalmatia, Istria, and Slavonia; formerly a part of Yugoslavia. 4,660,000, 21,835 sq. mi. *Cap.:* Zagreb, Serbo-Croatian, **Hrvatska.**

Cro·a·tian (krō ā′shən, -shē ən), *adj.* **1.** of or pertaining to Croatia, its people, or their language. —*n.* **2.** a Croat. **3.** Serbo-Croatian as spoken and written in Croatia, differing from Serbian chiefly in its use of the Latin alphabet. [CROATI(A) + -AN]

Cro·ce (krô′che), *n.* **Be·ne·det·to** (be′ne det′tô), 1866–1952, Italian statesman, philosopher, and historian.

Cro·ce·a·tas (krō′sē ā′təs), *n. Class. Myth.* an epithet of Zeus.

cro·ce·in (krō′sē in), *n. Chem.* any of several acid azo dyes producing orange or scarlet colors. Also, **cro·ce·ine** (krō′sē in, -ēn′). [< L *croce(us)* saffron-colored (see CROCUS, -EOUS) + -IN²]

cro·chet (krō shā′; *Brit.* krō′shā, -shē), *n., v.,* **-cheted** (-shād′; *Brit.* -shād, -shēd), **-chet·ing** (-shā′ing; *Brit.* -shā ing, -shē ing). —*n.* **1.** needlework done with a needle having a small hook at one end for drawing the thread or yarn into intertwined loops. —*v.t., v.i.* **2.** to form by crochet. [< F: knitting needle, lit., small hook, dim. of *croche, croc* < ME or Scand. See CROOK¹, -ET] —**cro·chet·er** (krō shā′ər; *Brit.* krō′shā ər, -shē-), *n.*

crochet′ hook′, a needle with a hook at one end, used in crochet. Also called **crochet′ nee′dle.**

cro·cid·o·lite (krō sid′ᵊlīt′), *n.* a bluish asbestos mineral, essentially a sodium iron silicate. Also called **blue asbestos.** [< Gk *krokid-* (s. of *krokís*) nap, wool + -o- + -LITE]

crock¹ (krok), *n.* **1.** an earthen pot, jar, or other container. **2.** *Brit. Dial.* a metal pot, esp. an iron cooking pot. **3.** a fragment of earthenware; potsherd. [ME *crokke,* OE *croc(c), crocca* pot; c. Icel *krukka* jug]

crock² (krok), *n.* **1.** an old ewe. **2.** an old worn-out horse. **3.** *Disparaging.* an old person, esp. if feeble, disabled, or ugly. —*v.t.* **4.** *Brit. Slang.* to disable or injure. [late ME *crok* old ewe, perh. akin to obs. *crack* whore and CRACK (v.); cf. LG *krakke* broken-down horse]

crock³ (krok), *n.* **1.** *Dial.* soot; smut. **2.** soil or marking from imperfectly dyed cloth. —*v.t.* **3.** *Dial.* to soil with soot. —*v.i.* **4.** (of cloth) to give off crock when rubbed. [?]

crocked (krokt), *adj. Slang.* drunk. [CROCK² + -ED²]

crock·er·y (krok′ə rē), *n.* crocks collectively; earthenware. [CROCK¹ + -ERY]

Crockets on coping of a gable

crock·et (krok′it), *n. Archit.* a medieval ornament, almost always suggesting a plant form and used esp. on vertical and steeply inclined surfaces, as the bells of capitals, the coves of cornices, or the copings of gables, which curves up and away from the supporting surface and returns partially upon itself in a knoblike termination. [late ME *croket* hook < AF, equiv. to *croc* hook (< Gmc; see CROOK¹) + *-et* -ET. See CROCHET]

Crock·ett (krok′it), *n.* **1. David** (*Davy*), 1786–1836, U.S. frontiersman, politician, and folklore hero. **2.** a town in E Texas. 5356 (1960).

crock·ing (krok′ing), *n. Textiles.* the rubbing off of excess surface dye. [metathetic var. of *corking, equiv. to late ME *corke* to dye with *cork* (< Gael *corcur* lichen yielding purple dye, hence, the dye < L *purpura* PURPLE) + -ING¹]

croc·o·dile (krok′ə dīl′), *n.* **1.** any of several crocodilians of the genus *Crocodylus,* found in sluggish waters and swamps of the tropics, having a pointed snout. **2.** any reptile of the order *Crocodilia;* crocodilian. **3.** the tanned skin or hide of these animals, used in the manufacture of luggage and accessories, as belts, shoes, wallets, etc. **4.** one who makes a hypocritical show of sorrow. **5.** *Brit. Informal.* a file of persons, usually schoolgirls, out for a walk. [< L *crocodīl(us)* < Gk *krokódeilos* lizard; r. ME *cocodrille* < ML *cocodrill(us)*] —**croc·o·dil·oid** (krok′ə dil′oid, krok′ə dī′loid), *adj.*

Nile crocodile, *Crocodylus niloticus* (Length 20 ft.)

croc′odile bird′, an African courser, *Pluvianus aegyptius,* which often sits upon basking crocodiles and feeds on their insect parasites.

Croc′odile Riv′er, Limpopo.

croc′odile tears′, a hypocritical show of sorrow; false or insincere tears: *She wept crocodile tears when they told her she had to leave school for a week.* [so called from the tears crocodiles were thought to shed while eating their victims]

croc·o·dil·i·an (krok′ə dil′ē ən), *n.* **1.** any reptile of the order *Crocodilia,* comprising the true crocodiles and the alligators, caimans, and gavials. —*adj.* **2.** of or pertaining to the crocodiles. **3.** hypocritical; insincere. [CROCODILE + -IAN]

cro·co·ite (krō′kō īt′), *n.* a mineral, lead chromate, $PbCrO_4$; red lead ore. Also called **cro·co·i·site** (krō′kō i zīt′). [< Gk *krokó(eis)* saffron-colored + -ITE¹; see CROCUS]

cro·cus (krō′kəs), *n., pl.* **-cus·es. 1.** any of the small, bulbous, iridaceous plants of the genus *Crocus,* cultivated for their showy, solitary flowers. **2.** the flower or bulb of the crocus. **3.** a deep yellow; orangish yellow; saffron. **4.** Also called **cro′cus mar′tis** (mär′tis). a polishing powder consisting of iron oxide. [< L < Gk *krókos* saffron, crocus < Sem; cf. Ar *kurkum* saffron] —**cro′cused,** *adj.*

Cro·cus (krō′kəs), *n. Class. Myth.* a youth who was changed into a saffron plant.

cro′cus sack′, *Southern U.S.* a burlap bag. Also called **croker sack.**

Croe·sus (krē′səs), *n., pl.* **-sus·es, -si** (-sī) for 2. **1.** died 546 B.C., king of Lydia 560–546: noted for his great wealth. **2.** a very rich man.

croft¹ (krôft, kroft), *n. Brit.* **1.** a small plot of ground adjacent to a house and used as a kitchen garden, to pasture one or two cows, etc.; a garden large enough to feed a family or have commercial value. **2.** a very small farm, as one worked by a Scottish crofter. [ME, OE: small field]

croft² (krôft, kroft), *n.* a small, portable filing cabinet of table height, having drop leaves for use as a table. [named after the Rev. Sir Herbert *Croft* (1757–1816), lexicologist, its inventor]

croft·er (krôf′tər, krof′-), *n. Brit.* one who rents and works a very small farm. [ME; see CROFT, -ER¹]

croi·sette (krô set′, kro-), *n.* crossette.

crois·sant (*Fr.* krwä säN′), *n., pl.* **-sants** (-säN′). a roll of leavened dough or puff paste shaped into a crescent and baked. [< F: lit., CRESCENT]

Croix de Feu (krwädᵊ fœ′), a reactionary political party in France, organized in 1927, suppressed in 1936, and re-formed as the French Social party, which was suppressed in 1945. [< F: lit., cross of fire]

Croix de Guerre (krwädᵊ ger′), a French military award for heroism in battle. [< F: lit., cross of war]

cro·jack (kroj′ik), *n. Naut.* crossjack.

cro′ker sack′ (krō′kər). See **crocus sack.** [alter. of CROCUS]

Cro-Mag·non (krō mag′nən, -non, -man′yən; *Fr.* krō ma nyôN′), *n.* **1.** an Upper Paleolithic race of men, regarded as the prototype of modern European man. Skeletal remains found in an Aurignacian cave in southern France indicate that the Cro-Magnon had long heads, broad faces, and sunken eyes, and reached a height of approximately 5 feet 9 inches. See illus. under **Pithecanthropus. 2.** a member of the Cro-Magnon race. [named after the cave (near Périgueux, France) where the first remains were found]

Cro·mer (krō′mər), *n.* **1st Earl of.** See **Baring, Evelyn.**

Cro·me·ri·an (krō mēr′ē ən), *adj.* of or pertaining to the prehistoric Stone Age culture in eastern England, known from the stone implements found at Cromer. [*Cromer,* Norfolk, England + -IAN]

crom·lech (krom′lek), *n. Archaeol.* **1.** a circle of upright stones or monoliths. **2.** a dolmen. [< Welsh, equiv. to *crom* bent, curved, crooked (fem. of *crwm*) + *llech* flat stone]

Crom·my·o·ni·an sow (krom′ē ō′nē ən sou′), *Class. Myth.* a wild sow killed by Theseus. Also called **Phaea.**

cro·morne (krō môrn′, krə-), *n.* a Renaissance musical reed instrument consisting of a narrow cylindrical tube curved at the end. Also, **crumhorn.** [< F, alter. of G *Krumhorn* crooked horn, equiv. to *krumm* crooked (OHG *krump*) + *Horn* HORN]

Cromp·ton (kromp′tən), *n.* **Samuel,** 1753–1827, English inventor of the spinning mule.

Crom·well (krom′wəl, -wel, krum′-), *n.* **1. Oliver,** 1599–1658, British general, Puritan statesman, and Lord Protector of England 1653–58. **2.** his son, **Richard,** 1626–1712, British soldier, politician, Lord Protector of England 1658–59. **3. Thomas, Earl of Essex,** 1485?–1540, British statesman. **4.** a town in central Connecticut. 2889 (1960).

Crom·wel·li·an (krom wel′ē ən, krum-), *adj.* **1.** of, pertaining to, or characteristic of the politics, practices, etc., of Oliver Cromwell or of the Commonwealth and Protectorate. **2.** noting or pertaining to the style of English furnishings of the middle 17th century, characterized by austerity and utilitarianism, by the use of oak and leather, and by simple, decorative moldings. [CROMWELL + -IAN]

Cromwel′lian chair′, *Eng. Furniture.* an upright oaken chair, often with arms, having all pieces turned and a seat and back panel of leather or cloth attached with brass-headed nails.

crone (krōn), *n.* an ugly, withered, witchlike, old woman. [ME < MD *croonie* old ewe < ONF *caronie* CARRION] —**cron′ish,** *adj.*

Cro·ni·a (krō′nē ə), *n.* (*sometimes construed as pl.*) an annual festival held in ancient Athens in honor of Cronos. [< Gk *Krónia*] —**Cro′ni·an,** *adj.*

Cro·nin (krō′nin), *n.* **A(rchibald) J(oseph),** born 1896, Scottish novelist and physician in the U.S.

Cron·jé (*Du.* krôn′yā), *n.* **Piet Ar·nol·dus** (*Du.* pēt är nôl′dōōs), 1835?–1911, Boer general.

cronk (krongk, krôngk), *adj. Australian Slang.* sick. [< Yiddish or G *krank,* MHG *kranc* weak]

Cro·nus (krō′nəs), *n. Class. Myth.* a Titan, son of Uranus and Gaea, who dethroned his father and was in turn dethroned by his own son, Zeus: identified by the Romans with the god Saturn. Also, **Cro·nos** (krō′nos), **Kronos.** —**Cro′ni·an,** *adj.*

cro·ny (krō′nē), *n., pl.* **-nies.** an intimate friend or companion; chum. [?]

cro·ny·ism (krō′nē iz′əm), *n.* the practice of favoring one's friends, esp. in political appointments. [CRONY + -ISM]

Cro·nyn (krō′nin), *n.* **Hume,** born 1911, Canadian actor, director, and writer in the U.S.

crood (krōōd), *v.i. Scot.* to make the murmuring sounds of a dove; coo. [imit.]

crook¹ (krŏŏk), *n.* **1.** a bent or curved implement, piece, appendage, etc.; hook. **2.** the hooked part of anything. **3.** an instrument or implement having a bent or curved part, as a shepherd's staff hooked at one end or as the crosier of a bishop or abbot. **4.** *Brit. Dial.* one of a pair of wooden frames, slung across a pack horse, to which loads are fastened. **5.** *Scot.* a pothook. **6.** act of crooking or bending. **7.** any bend, turn, or curve: *a crook in the road.* **8.** *Informal.* a dishonest person, esp. a sharper, swindler, or thief. **9.** Also called **shank.** a device on some musical wind instruments for changing the pitch, consisting of a piece of tubing inserted into the main tube. —*v.t.* **10.** to bend; curve; make a crook in. **11.** *Slang.* to steal; cheat; swindle: *He crooked that contract away from me. She crooked a ring from that shop.* —*v.i.* **12.** to bend; curve. [ME *crok(e),* appar. back formation from *croked* CROOKED, but perh. < Scand; cf. Icel *krōkr* hook]

crook² (krŏŏk), *adj. Australian.* **1.** sick. **2.** ill-humored; angry. **3.** out of order; functioning improperly. **4.** unsatisfactory; disappointing. [perh. alter. of CRONK]

crook·back (krŏŏk′bak′), *n.* a humpback. [CROOK¹ + BACK¹] —**crook′-backed′,** *adj.*

crook·ed (krŏŏk′id), *adj.* **1.** not straight; bending; curved: *a crooked path.* **2.** askew; awry: *The picture seems to be crooked.* **3.** deformed: *a man with a crooked back.* **4.** not straightforward; dishonest. **5.** (of a coin) polygonal: *a crooked sixpence.* [ME *croked,* OE *crōcod* curved, bent] —**crook′ed·ly,** *adv.* —**crook′ed·ness,** *n.*
—**Syn. 1.** winding, devious, sinuous, flexuous, tortuous, spiral, twisted, askew, awry. **3.** misshapen. **4.** unscrupulous, knavish, tricky, fraudulent.
—**Ant. 1.** straight. **4.** honorable.

Crookes (krŏŏks), *n.* **Sir William,** 1832–1919, English chemist and physicist: discovered the element thallium and the cathode ray.

Crookes′ dark′ space′, *Physics.* the dark space between the cathode glow and the negative glow in a vacuum tube, occurring when the pressure is low. [named after Sir William CROOKES]

crookes·ite (krŏŏk′sīt), *n.* a rare mineral, selenide of copper, thallium, and silver, occurring in steel-gray, compact masses. [named after Sir William CROOKES; see -ITE¹]

Crookes′ tube′, *Electronics.* a form of cathode ray tube. [named after Sir William CROOKES]

crook·neck (krŏŏk′nek′), *n.* **1.** any of several varieties of squash having a long, recurved neck. **2.** any plant bearing such fruit. [CROOK¹ + NECK]

crook′ raf′ter. See **knee rafter.**

Crooks·ton (krŏŏk′stən), *n.* a town in NW Minnesota. 8546 (1960).

Crooks·ville (krŏŏks′vil), *n.* a town in central Ohio. 2958 (1960).

croon (krōōn), *v.i.* **1.** to sing in a low, soothing voice: *to croon to a baby.* **2.** to sing in an evenly modulated, slightly exaggerated manner: *Popular singers began crooning in the 1930's.* **3.** to utter a low murmuring sound. **4.** to sing or hum softly. **5.** *Scot. and North Eng.* **a.** to bellow; low. **b.** to lament; mourn. —*v.t.* **6.** to sing (a song) in a crooning manner: *The singer became famous crooning hit tunes.* **7.** to lull by singing to in a low, soothing voice: *to croon a child to sleep.* —*n.* **8.** act or sound of crooning. [late ME *croyn* < MD *kron(en)* (to) murmur] —**croon′er,** *n.* —**croon′ing·ly,** *adv.*

crop (krop), *n., v.,* **cropped, crop·ping.** —*n.* **1.** the cultivated produce of the ground, while growing or when gathered: *the wheat crop; the orange crop.* **2.** the yield of such produce for a particular season. **3.** the yield of some other product in a season: *the crop of diamonds.* **4.** a supply produced. **5.** a collection or group of persons or things appearing or occurring together: *this year's crop of students; a crop of lies.* **6.** the stock or handle of a whip. **7.** Also called **riding crop.** a short riding whip consisting of a stock without a lash. **8.** an entire tanned hide of an animal. **9.** the act of cropping. **10.** a mark produced by clipping the ears, as of an animal. **11.** a close-cropped hair style. **12.** a head of hair so cut. **13.** an outcrop of a vein or seam. **14.** a special pouchlike enlargement of the gullet of many birds, in which food is held and may undergo partial preparation for digestion. **15.** a digestive organ in other animals; craw. **16. cream of the crop.** See **cream** (def. 7). —*v.t.* **17.** to cut off or remove the head or top of (a plant,

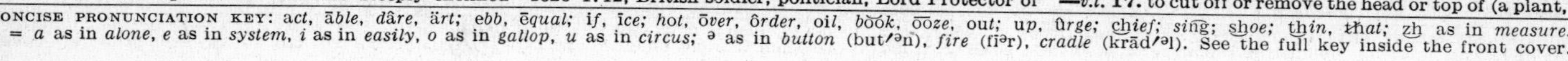

CONCISE PRONUNCIATION KEY: act, āble, dâre, ärt; ebb, ēqual; if, īce; hot, ōver, ôrder, oil, bŏŏk, ōōze, out; up, ûrge; chief; sing; shoe; thin, that; zh as in measure. ə = *a* as in *alone,* *e* as in *system,* *i* as in *easily,* *o* as in *gallop,* *u* as in *circus;* ᵊ as in *button* (butᵊn), *fire* (fīᵊr), *cradle* (krādᵊl). See the full key inside the front cover.

grass, etc.). **18.** to cut off the ends or a part of. **19.** to cut short. **20** to clip the ears, hair, etc., of. **21.** *Photog.* to cut off or mask the unwanted parts of (a print or negative). **22.** to cause to bear a crop or crops. **23.** to graze off the tops of plants, grass, etc.: *His sheep cropped the lawn.* —*v.i.* **24.** to bear or yield a crop or crops. **25.** *Mining.* to come to the surface of the ground, as a vein of ore (usually fol. by *up* or *out*). **26. crop out, a.** to rise to the surface: *A vein of gold was seen cropping out of the ore.* **b.** to become evident or visible; occur: *A few cases of tuberculosis still crop out every now and then.* **27. crop up,** to appear, esp. suddenly or unexpectedly; occur: *A new problem cropped up.* [ME, OE; c. G *Kropf;* basic meaning, protuberance. See CROUP[2]] —**crop′less,** *adj.*

—**Syn. 1.** CROP, HARVEST, PRODUCE, YIELD refer to the return in food for men and animals obtained from land at the end of a season of growth. CROP, the term common in agricultural and commercial use, denotes the amount produced at one cutting or for one particular season: *the wheat crop; potato crop.* HARVEST denotes either the time of reaping and gathering, or the gathering, or that which is gathered: *the season of harvest; to work in a harvest; a ripe harvest.* PRODUCE esp. denotes household vegetables: *Produce from the fields and gardens was taken to market.* YIELD emphasizes what is given by the land in return for expenditure of time and labor: *There was a heavy yield of grain this year.*

crop-dust (krop′dust′), *v.t.* to subject (a field) to crop-dusting.

crop′ dust′er, a pilot employed in crop-dusting from an airplane.

crop-dust·ing (krop′dus′ting), *n.* the spraying of powdered fungicides or insecticides on crops, usually from an airplane.

crop-eared (krop′ērd′), *adj.* **1.** having the ears cropped. **2.** having the hair cropped short, so that the ears are conspicuous.

crop·land (krop′land′), *n.* land suitable for or used for the cultivation of crops. [CROP + LAND]

crop·per (krop′ər), *n.* **1.** one who or that which crops. **2.** a person who raises a crop. **3.** a person who cultivates a land for its owner in return for part of the crop. **4.** a plant which furnishes a crop. **5.** a cloth-shearing machine. **6. come** or **get a cropper,** *Informal.* **a.** to fall headlong, esp. from a horse. **b.** to fail; be struck by some misfortune: *His big deal came a cropper.* [CROP + -ER[1]]

crop·pie (krop′ē), *n., pl.* **-pies,** (*esp. collectively*) **-pie.** crappie.

crop′ rota′tion, the system of varying successive crops in a definite order on the same ground, esp. to maintain crop yields and to control weeds, diseases, and pests.

crop′ shear′, *Metalworking.* a machine for cutting the ends from metal bars, ingots, and blooms.

cro·quet (krō kā′; *Brit.* krō′kā, -kē), *n., v.,* **-queted** (-kād′; *Brit.* -kād, -kēd), **-quet·ing** (-kā′ing; *Brit.* -kā-ing, -kē ing). —*n.* **1.** an outdoor game played by knocking wooden balls through a series of wire wickets by means of mallets. **2.** (in croquet) the act of driving away an opponent's ball by striking one's own when the two are in contact. —*v.t.* **3.** to drive away (a ball) by a croquet. [< F (dial.): hockey stick, lit., little hook; see CROCKET]

cro·quette (krō ket′), *n.* a small mass of minced meat or fish, or of rice, potato, or other material, often coated with beaten egg and bread crumbs, and fried in deep fat. [< F, equiv. to *croqu(er)* (to) crunch (imit.) + *-ette* -ETTE]

cro·qui·gnole (krō′kə nōl′, -kin yōl′), *n.* a method of waving the hair by curling it about metal rods from the ends inward toward the scalp. Also called **cro′quignole wave′.** [< F, perh. alter. of *craquenelle* CRACKNEL, influenced by *croquer* to crunch]

cro·quis (krō kē′; *Eng.* krō kē′), *n., pl.* **-quis** (-kē′; *Eng.* -kēz′). *French.* a sketch.

crore (krōr, krôr), *n.* (in India) ten millions; one hundred lacs. [< Hindi *k(a)rōr* < Prakrit *kroḍi*]

Cros·by (krôz′bē, kroz′-), *n.* **1. Bing** (*Harry Lillis Crosby*) born 1904, U.S. singer and actor. **2.** a town in central Minnesota. 2629 (1960).

cro·sette (krō set′, kro-), *n.* crossette.

cro·sier (krō′zhər), *n.* **1.** the pastoral staff of a bishop or an abbot, hooked at one end like a shepherd's crook. See illus. under **cope**[2]. **2.** *Bot.* the circinate young frond of a fern. Also, **crozier.** [short for *crosier-staff;* late ME *crosier* staff-bearer < MF; r. ME *crocer* < AF. See CROSSE, -ER[2]] —**cro′siered,** *adj.*

cro′sier back′, a back of a chair or the like, curling backward in a partial spiral at the top.

cross (krôs, kros), *n.* **1.** a structure consisting essentially of an upright and a transverse piece, upon which persons were formerly put to death. **2. the Cross,** the cross upon which Jesus died. **3.** a figure of the Cross as a Christian emblem, badge, etc. **4.** the Cross as the symbol of Christianity. **5.** a small cross with a human figure attached to it, as a representation of Jesus crucified; crucifix. **6.** the sign of the Cross made with the right hand as an act of devotion. **7.** a structure or monument in the form of a cross, set up for prayer, as a memorial, etc. **8.** any of various conventional representations or modifications of the Christian emblem as used symbolically or for ornament, as in heraldry, art, etc.: *a Latin cross; a Maltese cross.* **9.** the crucifixion of Jesus as the culmination of His redemptive mission. **10.** any suffering borne for Jesus' sake. **11.** the teaching of redemption gained by Jesus' death. **12.** Christian religion, or those who accept it; Christianity; Christendom. **13.** any object, figure, or mark resembling a cross, as two intersecting lines. **14.** a mark resembling a cross made instead of a signature by a person unable to write. **15.** *Plumbing.* a four-way joint or connection. **16.** See **cross guard. 17.** *Mach.* spider (def. 6b). **18.** a crossing. **19.** a place of crossing. **20.** an opposition; thwarting; frustration. **21.** any misfortune; trouble. **22.** a crossing of animals or plants; a mixing of breeds. **23.** an animal, plant, breed, etc., produced by crossing; crossbreed. **24.** a person or thing that is intermediate in character between two others. **25.** *Boxing.* a punch thrown across and over the lead of an opponent. **26.** *Slang.* a contest the result of which is dishonestly arranged beforehand. **27.** (*cap.*) *Astron.* See **Southern Cross. 28. bear one's cross,** to accept trials or troubles patiently. **29. take the cross,** to make the vows of a crusader.

—*v.t.* **30.** to make the sign of the cross upon or over, as in devotion: *to cross oneself.* **31.** to mark with a cross. **32.** to cancel by marking with a cross or with a line or lines (often fol. by *off* or *out*). **33.** to place in the form of a cross or crosswise. **34.** to put or draw (a line, lines, etc.) across. **35.** *Naut.* **a.** to set (a yard) in its proper position on a mast. **b.** *Obs.* to set (a square sail). **36.** to lie or pass across; intersect. **37.** to move, pass, or extend from one side to the other side of (a street, river, etc.). **38.** to transport across something. **39.** to meet and pass. **40.** *Slang.* to betray; double-cross. **41.** to oppose openly; thwart; frustrate. **42.** *Biol.* to cause (members of different genera, species, breeds, varieties, or the like) to interbreed. **43.** *Archaic.* to confront in a hostile manner.

—*v.i.* **44.** to lie or be athwart; intersect. **45.** to move, pass, or extend from one side or place to another: *Cross at the intersection.* **46.** to meet and pass. **47.** to interbreed. **48.** *Theat.* to move from one side of the stage to the other, esp. by passing downstage of another actor. **49. cross one's heart.** See **heart** (def. 21). **50. cross one's mind.** See **mind** (def. 19). **51. cross one's path.** See **path** (def. 5). **52. cross over,** *Biol.* (of a chromosome segment) to undergo crossing over. **53. cross someone's palm.** See **palm**[1] (def. 11). **54. cross up,** *Slang.* **a.** to change arrangements made with; deceive: *He crossed me up after we had agreed to tell the police the same story.* **b.** to confuse: *I was supposed to meet him at the station, but got crossed up.*

—*adj.* **55.** lying or passing crosswise or across each other; athwart; transverse: *cross timbers.* **56.** involving interchange; reciprocal. **57.** contrary; opposite: *They were at cross purposes with each other.* **58.** adverse; unfavorable. **59.** angry and annoyed; ill-humored; snappish: *She was cross with him; a cross word.* **60.** crossbred; hybrid. **61.** *Australian Slang.* stolen. [ME, OE *cros* < OIr < L *crux.* See CRUX] —**cross′a·bil′i·ty,** *n.* —**cross′a·ble,** *adj.*

—**Syn. 36.** traverse, span, bridge. **41.** baffle, foil, contradict. **59.** petulant, fractious, irascible, waspish, crabbed, churlish, sulky, cantankerous, cranky, curmudgeonly, ill-tempered, impatient, irritable, fretful, touchy, testy. CROSS, ILL-NATURED, PEEVISH, SULLEN refer to being in a bad mood or ill temper. CROSS means temporarily in an irritable or fretful state, and sometimes somewhat angry: *a cross reply; cross and tired.* ILL-NATURED implies a more permanent condition, without definite cause, and means unpleasant, unkind, inclined to snarl or be spiteful: *an ill-natured dog; ill-natured spite.* PEEVISH means complaining and snappish: *a peevish and whining child.* SULLEN suggests a kind of glowering silent gloominess and means refusing to speak because of bad humor, anger, or a sense of injury or resentment: *sullen and vindictive.* —**Ant. 41.** aid. **59.** good-natured, agreeable.

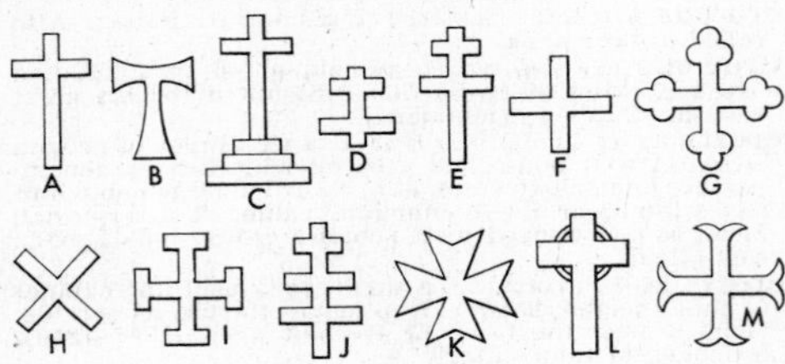

Crosses
A, Latin cross; B, Tau cross or St. Anthony's cross; C, Cross of Calvary; D, Cross of Lorraine; E, Patriarchal cross; F, Greek cross; G, Botonée; H, St. Andrew's cross; I, Jerusalem cross; J, Papal cross; K, Maltese cross; L, Celtic cross; M, Moline

Cross (krôs, kros), *n.* **Wilbur Lucius,** 1862–1948, U.S. educator: governor of Connecticut 1931–39.

cross-, a combining form of **cross:** *crosscurrent.*

cross·arm (krôs′ärm′, kros′-), *n.* a horizontal arm, bar, line, etc., that crosses or is fastened to a vertical counterpart. [CROSS- + ARM[2]] —**cross′-armed′,** *adj.*

cross·band (*n.* krôs′band′, kros′-; *v.* krôs′band′, kros′-), *n.* **1.** crossbanding. —*v.t.* **2.** to assemble (veneers) into plywood with each layer at right angles to the one beneath it. [CROSS- + BAND[2]]

cross·band·ed (krôs′ban′did, kros′-), *adj.* (of a wooden surface) having a border of inlaid veneer with its grain running crosswise. [CROSSBAND + -ED[2]]

cross·band·ing (krôs′ban′ding, kros′-), *n.* **1.** any of the veneers in a sheet of plywood having its grain at right angles to the face veneer. **2.** decorative banding, as on a piece of furniture, having the grain laid crosswise to the grain of the principal surface. Also called **crossband.** [CROSS- + *banding* (see BAND[2], -ING[1])]

cross·bar (krôs′bär′, kros′-), *n.* **1.** a transverse bar, line, or stripe. **2.** the transverse bar between goal posts, as in football, soccer, etc. **3.** a horizontal bar used for gymnastics. **4.** a transverse bar that rests on uprights and that an athlete must clear in performing the pole vault or high jump. **5.** a horizontal line in some letters of the alphabet, as in capital *H.* **6.** the transverse top bar on the frame of a man's bicycle. [CROSS- + BAR[1]]

cross·beam (krôs′bēm′, kros′-), *n.* a transverse beam in a structure, as a joist. [CROSS- + BEAM]

cross-bear·er (krôs′bâr′ər, kros′-), *n.* a person who carries or holds a cross, as in a religious procession. [CROSS- + BEARER]

cross′-beat escape′ment (krôs′bēt′, kros′-), *Horol.* an obsolete escapement having two counterweighted pallets, each on one of two counterrotating, flexible arms, so geared together that they arrest one another by alternately engaging the escape wheel.

cross-bed·ded (krôs′bed′id, kros′-), *adj.* *Geol.* having irregular laminations, as strata of sandstone, inclining in various directions not coincident with the general stratification. [CROSS- + *bedded* (see BED, -ED[2])] —**cross′-bed′ding,** *n.*

cross-bench (krôs′bench′, kros′-), *Brit.* —*n.* **1.** a section of seats at the back of each house of Parliament, for members who are not aligned to any national political party. —*adj.* **2.** impartial; open-minded; objective. Also, **cross′bench′.** —**cross′-bench′er, cross′bench′er,** *n.*

cross-bi·as (krôs′bī′əs, kros′-), *n.* a bias that crosses another bias.

cross·bill (krôs′bil′, kros′-), *n.* any fringilline bird of the genus *Loxia,* characterized by mandibles curved so that the tips cross each other when the bill is closed. [CROSS- + BILL[2]]

cross·birth (krôs′bûrth′, kros′-), *n.* *Obstet.* See **transverse presentation.** [CROSS- + BIRTH]

cross′bolt lock′ (krôs′bōlt′, kros′-), a lock controlling two bolts moving in opposite directions, as to the top and bottom of a doorframe. [CROSS- + BOLT[1]] —**cross′bolt′ed,** *adj.*

cross′ bond′, a brickwork bond having courses of headers, or of Flemish bond, alternating with courses of stretchers in such a way that the joints of each course of stretchers are in line with the centers of the next courses of stretchers above and below.

cross·bones (krôs′bōnz′, kros′-), *n. pl.* two bones placed crosswise, usually below a skull, symbolizing death. [CROSS- + BONE[1] + -S[3]]

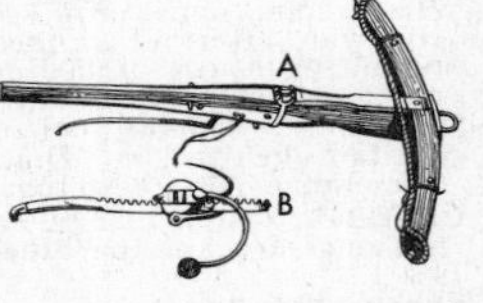

A, Crossbow (15th century)
B, Crannequin

cross·bow (krôs′bō′, kros′-), *n.* a weapon consisting of a bow fixed transversely on a stock having a trigger mechanism to release the bowstring, and often incorporating or accompanied by a mechanism for bending the bow. [late ME *crossebowe.* See CROSS, BOW[2]]

cross·bow·man (krôs′bō′mən, -bō′-, kros′-), *n., pl.* **-men. 1.** one equipped with or skilled in the use of a crossbow. **2.** (in medieval warfare) a soldier armed with a crossbow. [CROSSBOW + MAN[1]]

cross·bred (krôs′bred′, kros′-), *adj.* **1.** produced by crossbreeding. —*n.* **2.** an animal or group of animals produced by hybridization. [CROSS- + BRED]

cross·breed (krôs′brēd′, kros′-), *v.,* **-bred, -breeding,** *n.* —*v.t.* **1.** to produce (a hybrid) within a species, using two breeds or varieties. —*v.i.* **2.** to undertake or engage in hybridizing, esp. within a single species. —*n.* **3.** a crossbred. [CROSS- + BREED]

cross′ bridg′ing, *Carpentry.* bridging composed of crisscross pieces of wood. Also called **herringbone bridging, herringbone strutting.**

cross′ buck′, *Football.* an offensive play in which two backs cross paths and charge into the line on opposite sides, one back receiving the ball from a teammate and the other back faking possession.

cross′ bun′, *Chiefly Brit.* See **hot cross bun.**

cross-check (*v.* krôs′chek′, kros′-; *n.* krôs′chek′, -chek′, kros′-), *v.t.* **1.** to determine the accuracy of (something) by checking it from various sources. **2.** *Ice Hockey.* to execute a cross-check on (an opponent). —*n.* **3.** the act of cross-checking. **4.** a means of cross-checking: *I examined contemporary newspaper reports as a cross-check on his account.* **5.** *Ice Hockey.* an obstructing or impeding of the movement or progress of an opponent by placing the stick, with both hands, across his body or face. Cf. **check** (def. 40).

cross-com·pound (krôs′kom′pound, kros′-), *adj.* (of a compound engine or turbine) having the high-pressure and low-pressure units side by side. Cf. **tandem-compound.**

cross-coun·try (*adj.* krôs′kun′trē, kros′-; *n.* krôs′-kun′trē, -kun′-, kros′-), *adj.* **1.** directed or proceeding over fields, through woods, etc., rather than on a road or path: *a cross-country race.* **2.** from one end of the country to the other: *a cross-country flight.* —*n.* **3.** a cross-country sport or sports: *to go out for cross-country.*

cross′-coun′try mill′, *Metalworking.* a rolling mill the stands of which are so widely spaced that the work passes through only one piece at a time.

cross-cous·in (krôs′kuz′ən, kros′-), *n.* a cousin who is the child either of one's mother's brother or one's father's sister. Cf. **parallel cousin.**

cross′-cousin mar′riage, marriage between the children of a brother and sister. Cf. **parallel cousin marriage.**

cross-cross·let (krôs′krôs′lit, kros′kros′-), *n., pl.* **-cross·lets.** *Heraldry.* a cross the arms of which have crosslike terminations. Also, **cross′cross′let.**

cross·cur·rent (krôs′kûr′ənt, -kur′-, kros′-), *n.* a current, as in a stream, moving across the main current. [CROSS- + CURRENT] —**cross′cur′rent·ed,** *adj.*

cross·cut (krôs′kut′, kros′-), *adj., n., v.,* **-cut, -cut·ting.** —*adj.* **1.** made or used for cutting crosswise. **2.** cut across the grain or on the bias: *crosscut crepe.* **3.** *Naut.* (of a sail) having the seams of the cloth at right angles to the leech. —*n.* **4.** a short cut by way of an area not ordinarily traversed, as grass, open country, etc.; a route which cuts diagonally across a road or path network. **5.** a transverse cut or course. **6.** *Mining.* an underground passageway, usually from a shaft to a vein of ore or crosswise of a vein of ore. **7.** *Motion Pictures, Television.* act or instance of crosscutting. —*v.t.* **8.** to cut or go across. —*v.i.* **9.** *Motion Pictures, Television.* to cut from one scene or action to another in order to present two events as taking place simultaneously or to heighten suspense. [CROSS- + CUT] —**cross′cut′ter,** *n.*

cross′cut saw′, a saw for cutting wood perpendicular to the grain.

crosse (krôs, kros), *n.* a long-handled racket used in the game of lacrosse. [< F: lit., hooked stick, OF *croce* < Gmc; see CRUTCH, CROOK[1]]

crossed (krôst, krost), *adj.* *Math.* (of partial derivatives) mixed, esp. of order two. [CROSS + -ED[2]]

Cros·sett (krô′sit, kros′it), *n.* a town in SE Arkansas. 5370 (1960).

cross·ette (krô set′, kro-), *n.* *Archit.* **1.** Also called **elbow.** a projection at a corner of a door or window architrave. **2.** *Masonry.* a lug on a joggled voussoir. Also, **croisette, crosette.** Also called **dog-ear, dog's-ear.** [< F, dim. of *crosse.* See CROSSE, -ETTE]

cross-ex·am·ine (krôs′ig zam′in, kros′-), *v.t.*, **-ined, -in·ing.** 1. to examine by questions intended to check a previous examination; examine closely or minutely. 2. *Law.* to examine (a witness called by the opposing side), as for the purpose of discrediting his testimony. Cf. **direct-examine.** —**cross-ex·am·i·na·tion** (krôs′ig-zam′ə nā′shən, kros′-), *n.* —**cross′-ex·am′in·er,** *n.*

cross-eye (krôs′ī′, kros′ī′), *n.* strabismus, esp. the form in which both eyes turn toward the nose.

cross-eyed (krôs′īd′, kros′-), *adj.* suffering from cross-eye or strabismus. —**cross′-eyed′ness,** *n.*

cross-fade (*v.* krôs′fād′, kros′-; *n.* krôs′fād′, kros′-), *v.*, **-fad·ed, -fad·ing,** *n.* *Motion Pictures, Television.* —*v.t.* 1. to fade out (an image or sound) while simultaneously fading in a different image or sound. —*n.* 2. an act or instance of cross-fading.

cross-feed (krôs′fēd′, kros′-), *n.* (in a machine tool) a mechanism feeding either work or a tool in a direction other than parallel to the bed.

cross-fer·ti·li·za·tion (krôs′fûr′tᵊli zā′shən, kros′-), *n.* 1. *Biol.* the fertilization of an organism by the fusion of an egg from one individual with a sperm or male gamete from a different individual. 2. *Bot.* fertilization of the flower of one plant by a gamete from the flower of a closely related plant (opposed to *self-fertilization*). 3. (not used technically) cross-pollination.

cross-fer·ti·lize (krôs′fûr′tᵊlīz′, kros′-), *v.t.*, **-lized, -liz·ing.** to cause the cross-fertilization of. —**cross′-fer′ti·liz′a·ble,** *adj.*

cross-file (krôs′fīl′, kros′-), *v.i.*, **-filed, -fil·ing.** to register as a candidate in the primary elections of more than one party.

cross′ fire′, 1. a brisk exchange, as of words or opinions: *a cross fire of repartee.* 2. a predicament arising from conflicting claims on one's attention, help, sympathy, etc. 3. *Mil.* lines of fire from two or more positions, crossing one another, or a single one of such lines. 4. *Furniture.* a mottled, translucent figure occurring in certain polished woods, as mahogany or satinwood. Also, **cross′fire′.**

cross′ fox′, a red fox in the color phase in which the fur is reddish brown with a dark stripe down the back and another over the shoulders.

cross′ gamma′dion, *Heraldry.* a cross potent rebated; swastika.

cross-gar·net (krôs′gär′nit, kros′-), *n.* a T-shaped strap hinge with the crosspiece as the stationary member. Also called **crosstail, garnet hinge, T hinge.** See illus. under **hinge.**

cross-grained (krôs′grānd′, kros′-), *adj.* 1. having the grain running transversely or diagonally, or having an irregular or gnarled grain, as timber. 2. stubborn; perverse. —**cross′-grained′ly,** *adv.* —**cross′-grained′ness,** *n.*

cross′ guard′, a straight, transverse guard for a sword. Also called **cross.**

cross′ hairs′, fine wires, strands of spider web, or the like, crossing in a focal plane of an optical instrument to define a line of sight. Also called **cross wires.**

cross-hand·ed (krôs′han′did, kros′-), *adj., adv.* with the hands crossed one over the other: *to paddle cross-handed.*

cross·hatch (krôs′hach′, kros′-), *v.t.* to hatch or shade with two or more intersecting series of parallel lines. [CROSS- + HATCH³] —**cross′hatch′er,** *n.*

cross·head (krôs′hed′, kros′-), *n.* 1. *Print.* a title or heading filling a line or group of lines the full width of the column. 2. *Mach.* a sliding member of a reciprocating engine for keeping the motion of the joint between a piston rod and a connecting rod in a straight line. 3. *Naut.* a crosspiece on a rudder post by which the rudder is turned. 4. *Engineering, Building Trades.* a transverse timber for transmitting the lifting effort of two or more jackscrews supporting it to the foot of a shore that it supports. [CROSS- + HEAD]

cross′ in′dex, a note or group of notes referring the reader to material elsewhere.

cross-in·dex (krôs′in′deks, kros′-), *v.t.* 1. to provide with cross references. —*v.i.* 2. to refer by appropriate note or indication of location to related material, as in a book, article, etc.; contain cross references: *Footnotes cross-index to the appendix and bibliography.*

cross·ing (krô′sing, kros′ing), *n.* 1. the act of one who or that which crosses. 2. a place where lines, streets, tracks, etc., cross each other. 3. the intersection of nave and transept in a cruciform church. 4. a place at which a road, river, etc., may be crossed. 5. the act of opposing or thwarting; frustration; contradiction. 6. *Railroads.* a track structure composed of four connected frogs, permitting two tracks to cross one another at grade with sufficient clearance for wheel flanges. 7. hybridization; crossbreeding. [CROSS + -ING¹]

cross′ing o′ver, *Genetics.* the interchange of corresponding chromatid segments of homologous chromosomes with their linked genes.

cross·jack (krôs′jak′, kros′-; *Naut.* krô′jik, kroj′ik), *n.* *Naut.* 1. the lowermost square sail set on the mizzenmast of a ship or of a barque with four or more masts; mizzen course. See diag. under **ship.** 2. Also called **cross′jack yard′.** the yard on which this sail is set. [CROSS- + JACK¹]

cross·lap (krôs′lap′, kros′-), *n.* a joint between two crossing timbers halved together. Also, **cross′-lap′, cross′-lap joint′.** [CROSS- + LAP²]

cross-leg·ged (krôs′leg′id, -legd′, kros′-), *adj.* having the legs crossed; having one leg laid across the other. —**cross′-leg′ged·ly,** *adv.* —**cross′-leg′ged·ness,** *n.*

cross·let (krôs′lit, kros′-), *n.* a small cross, as one used as a heraldic charge. [late ME *croslet.* See CROSS, -LET] —**cross′let·ed,** *adj.*

cross′ li′cense, a license that one patent holder grants to a second patent holder in return for a license from the second patent holder, as in the automobile and oil industries.

cross-li·cense (krôs′lī′səns, kros′-), *v.*, **-censed, -cens·ing.** —*v.t.* 1. to grant a license to another to utilize (a patent) in exchange for another such license. —*v.i.* 2. to cross-license a patent.

cross·light (krôs′līt′, kros′-), *n.* 1. a light shone across the path of another to illuminate an area left dark by the first light. 2. light originating from sources not facing each other, as from windows in two adjacent walls. 3. light originating from counterlights. Cf. **counterlight.** [CROSS- + LIGHT¹] —**cross′light′ed,** *adj.*

cross·line (krôs′līn′, kros′-), *n.* 1. a line crossing another line or connecting two separated points: *The main lines are linked at intervals by crosslines.* 2. *Journalism.* a headline or bank consisting of a single line running across a column of type, usually centered and sometimes full width. —*adj.* 3. of or pertaining to the offspring produced by crossbreeding two linebred individuals. [CROSS- + LINE¹]

cross-link (*n.* krôs′lingk′, kros′-; *v.* krôs′lingk′, kros′-), *Chem.* —*n.* a bond, atom, or group linking the chains of atoms in a polymer, protein, or other complex organic molecule. —*v.t.* 2. to attach by a cross-link.

cross′-lot brac′ing (krôs′lot′, kros′-), *Engineering, Building Trades.* bracing extending from one side of an excavation to the opposite to retain the earth on both sides.

cross·ly (krôs′lē, kros′-), *adv.* in a cross or angry manner. [CROSS + -LY]

cross-mate (krôs′māt′, kros′-), *v.t., v.i.*, **-mat·ed, -mat·ing.** to crossbreed.

cross·ness (krôs′nis, kros′-), *n.* the quality or condition of being cross or irritable; irritability; snappishness. [CROSS + -NESS]

cross′ of Cal′vary, a Latin cross with a representation of steps beneath it. See illus. under **cross.**

cross′ of Lorraine′, a cross having two crosspieces, the upper shorter than the lower. See illus. under **cross.**

cros·sop·te·ryg·i·an (kro sop′tə rij′ē ən), *n.* any fish of the group *Crossopterygii*, extinct except for the coelacanth, regarded as being ancestral to amphibians and other land vertebrates. [< NL *crossopterygi(i)* group name (< Gk *krosso(i)* tassels, fringe + *pterýgi(on)* little wing or fin, equiv. to *pteryg-* (s. of *ptéryx*) wing, fin + *-ion* dim. suffix) + -AN]

cross-o·ver (krôs′ō′vər, kros′-), *n.* a bridge or other structure for crossing over a river, highway, etc. [n. use of v. phrase *cross over*]

cross·o·ver (krôs′ō′vər, kros′-), *n.* 1. *Genetics.* **a.** See **crossing over. b.** a genotype resulting from crossing over. 2. *Bowling.* a ball that strikes the side of the head pin opposite to the bowling hand of the bowler. 3. *Railroads.* a track structure composed of two or more turnouts, permitting movement of cars from either of two parallel and adjacent tracks to the other. 4. (in plumbing) a U-shaped pipe for bypassing another pipe. 5. *Dance.* **a.** a step in which dancers exchange places. **b.** a step involving partners in which the woman moves from one side of her partner to the other, crossing in front of him. [CROSS- + OVER]

cross′over net′work, an audio circuit device in a radio or phonograph which sorts the impulses received and channels them into high- or low-frequency loudspeakers.

cross·patch (krôs′pach′, kros′-), *n.* *Informal.* a bad-tempered person. [CROSS- + PATCH¹]

cross-pawl (krôs′pôl′, kros′-), *n.* cross-spall.

cross·piece (krôs′pēs′, kros′-), *n.* a piece of any material placed across something; transverse piece. [CROSS- + PIECE]

cross-pol·li·nate (krôs′pol′ə nāt′, kros′-), *v.t.*, **-nat·ed, -nat·ing.** to subject to cross-pollination.

cross-pol·li·na·tion (krôs′pol′ə nā′shən, kros′-), *n.* *Bot.* the transfer of pollen from the flower of one plant to the flower of a plant having a different genetic constitution. Cf. **self-pollination.**

cross′ prod′uct, *Math.* a vector perpendicular to two given vectors, *u* and *v*, and having magnitude equal to the product of the magnitudes of the two given vectors multiplied by the sine of the angle between the two given vectors, usually represented by $u \times v$. Also called **outer product, vector product.**

cross-pur·pose (krôs′pûr′pəs, kros′-), *n.* 1. an opposing or contrary purpose. 2. **cross-purposes,** (*construed as sing.*) a kind of conversational game in which words are taken in different senses. 3. **at cross-purposes,** in a way that involves or produces mutual misunderstanding or frustration, usually unintentionally: *We must be talking at cross-purposes.*

cross-ques·tion (krôs′kwes′chən, kros′-), *v.t.* 1. to cross-examine. —*n.* 2. a question asked by way of cross-examination. —**cross′-ques′tion·a·ble,** *adj.*

cross·rail (krôs′rāl′, kros′-), *n.* a horizontal slat forming part of the back of a chair or the like. [CROSS- + RAIL¹]

cross′ ra′tio, *Geom.* a ratio relating four points in the real or complex plane, expressed as $\frac{(x_1 - x_4)\ (x_3 - x_2)}{(x_1 - x_2)\ (x_3 - x_4)}$ where x_1, x_2, x_3, x_4, are the abscissas of the points. It is invariant under projections. Also called **anharmonic ratio.** —**cross′-ra′ti·o′,** *adj.*

cross-re·fer (krôs′ri fûr′, kros′-), *v.t., v.i.*, **-ferred, -fer·ring.** to refer by a cross reference.

cross′ ref′erence, a reference from one part of a book, index, or the like, to a word, item, etc., in another part.

cross′ rela′tion, *Music.* a relationship between two successive tones in different voices that normally occurs in one voice. Also called **false relation.**

cross·road (krôs′rōd′, kros′-), *n.* 1. a road that crosses another road, or one that runs transversely to main roads. 2. a by-road. 3. Often, **crossroads.** (*construed as sing. or pl.*) **a.** the place where roads intersect. **b.** a point at which a vital decision must be made. **c.** a main center of activity. [CROSS- + ROAD]

cross·row (krôs′rō′, kros′-), *n.* *Obs.* the alphabet. [CROSS + ROW¹, so called because marked by the figure of a cross]

cross·ruff (*n.* krôs′ruf′, -ruf′, kros′-; *v.* krôs′ruf′, kros′-), *Bridge. Whist.* —*n.* 1. a play in which each hand of a partnership alternately trumps a different suit in consecutive plays. —*v.t., v.i.* 2. to play by means of a crossruff. [CROSS- + RUFF²]

cross′ sec′tion, 1. a section made by a plane cutting anything transversely, esp. at right angles to the longest axis. 2. a piece so cut off. 3. a photograph, diagram, or other pictorial representation of such a section. 4. the act of cutting anything across. 5. a typical selection; a sample showing all characteristic parts, relationships, etc.: *a cross section of American opinion.* 6. *Survey.* a vertical section of the ground surface taken at right angles to a survey line. 7. *Naval Archit.* station (def. 15). 8. Also called **nuclear cross section.** *Physics.* a quantity expressing the effective area that a given nucleus presents as a target to a bombarding particle, giving a measure of the probability that the particle will induce a reaction.

cross-sec·tion (krôs′sek′shən, kros′-), *adj.* 1. Also, **cross′-sec′tion·al.** of or pertaining to a cross section. —*v.t.* 2. to make or divide into a cross section.

cross-shave (krôs′shāv′, kros′-), *n.* *Carpentry.* a shave for working across grain.

cross-spall (krôs′spôl′, kros′-), *n.* *Shipbuilding.* a timber nailed to the upper extremities of a wooden frame to keep the ribs properly spaced until the deck beams are in place. Also, **cross-pawl, cross-spale** (krôs′spāl′, kros′-).

cross-staff (krôs′staf′, -stäf′, kros′-), *n.*, *pl.* **-staffs, -staves.** an instrument for measuring the angle of elevation of heavenly bodies, consisting of a calibrated staff with another shorter staff perpendicular to and sliding on it. Also called **forestaff, Jacob's staff.**

cross-stitch (krôs′stich′, kros′-), *n.* 1. a stitching using pairs of diagonal stitches of the same length crossing each other in the middle at right angles. —*v.t., v.i.* 2. to work in cross-stitch.

cross′ street′, a street crossing another street, or one running transversely to main streets.

cross-string (krôs′string′, kros′-), *v.t.*, **-strung, -strung** or (*Rare*) **-stringed; -string·ing.** overstring.

cross′ stroke′, *Typography.* the horizontal line through the vertical of a *t* or *f.*

cross·tail (krôs′tāl′, kros′-), *n.* cross-garnet. [CROSS- + TAIL¹]

cross′ talk′, 1. incidental conversation; chatter, as opposed to formal discussion: *The meeting was slowed by cross talk between some of the board members.* 2. *Brit.* witty, fast-paced dialogue, esp. in a play, comic act, etc.; repartee. 3. interference by or reception of other sound, radio, or similar waves or frequencies on a telephone, radio, or other receiving set or electrical apparatus.

cross·tie (krôs′tī′, kros′-), *n.* 1. a transverse timber forming a foundation or support; sleeper. 2. *Railroads.* a tie. [CROSS- + TIE] —**cross′tied′,** *adj.*

cross·town (krôs′toun′, kros′-), *adj.* 1. situated or traveling in a direction extending across a town or city: *a crosstown street; a crosstown bus.* —*adv.* 2. in a direction extending across a town or city: *The car sped crosstown.* —*n.* 3. *Informal.* a bus or streetcar having a route running primarily in a crosstown direction. [CROSS- + TOWN]

cross·tree (krôs′trē′, kros′-), *n.* 1. *Naut.* either of a pair of timbers or metal bars placed either athwart the trestletrees at a masthead to spread the shrouds leading to the mast above, or on the head of a lower mast to support the platform or top. 2. *Carpentry.* a heavy crossbeam. [CROSS- + TREE]

C, Crosstree

cross-val·i·da·tion (krôs′val i dā′shən, kros′-), *n.* *Statistics.* a process by which a method that works for one sample of a population is checked for validity by applying the method to another sample from the same population.

cross-vein (krôs′vān′, kros′-), *n.* a transverse vein which connects adjacent longitudinal veins in the wing of an insect.

Cross·ville (krôs′vil, kros′-), *n.* a town in central Tennessee. 4668 (1960).

cross-vine (krôs′vīn′, kros′-), *n.* a climbing or creeping, woody vine, *Bignonia capreolata*, the stem of which shows a crosslike arrangement in cross section.

cross·walk (krôs′wôk′, kros′-), *n.* a lane, usually marked, for pedestrians crossing a street or highway. [CROSS- + WALK]

cross·way (krôs′wā′, kros′-), *n.* a crossroad. [ME *crosswey.* See CROSS, WAY]

cross·ways (krôs′wāz′, kros′-), *adv.* crosswise.

cross′ wind′ (wind), a wind blowing across the course or path of a ship, aircraft, etc. —**cross′-wind′,** *adj.*

cross′ wires′. See **cross hairs.**

cross·wise (krôs′wīz′, kros′-), *adv.* 1. across; transversely. 2. in the form of a cross. 3. contrarily. Also, **crossways.** [ME *a crosse wise* in the form of a cross. See A-¹, CROSS, WISE²]

cross′word puz′zle (krôs′wûrd′, kros′-), a puzzle in which words corresponding to numbered clues or definitions are supplied and fitted into correspondingly numbered sets of squares, one letter per square, the words being arranged horizontally or vertically so that most letters form part of two words. [CROSS- + WORD]

cro·ta·lar·i·a (krōt′ᵊlâr′ē ə, krot′-), *n.* any of several chiefly tropical, leguminous herbs or shrubs of the genus *Crotalaria.* [< NL, equiv. to *crotal-* (< Gk *krótal(on)* a rattle) + *-aria* -ARIA; so named from rattling of seeds in pod]

cro·ta·lin (krōt′ᵊlin), *n.* *Biochem.* a substance prepared from the venom obtained from the venom sac of the rattlesnakes *Crotalus horridus* and *C. adamanteus*, formerly used in the treatment of epilepsy. [< NL *Crotal(us)* name of the genus (< L *crotal(um)* < Gk *krótalon* rattle) + -IN²]

crotch (kroch), *n.* 1. a forked piece, part, support, etc., as a staff with a forked top. 2. a forking or place of forking, as of the human body between the legs. 3. the part of a pair of trousers, panties, or the like, formed by the joining of the two legs. 4. a piece of material serving to form a juncture between the legs of trousers, panties, etc. 5. *Billiards.* **a.** an area 4½ inches square at each corner of a billiard table. **b.** the situation in which both balls to be struck by the cue ball are within this area. 6. *Naut.* crutch (def. 6). [var. of CRUTCH] —**crotched** (krocht), *adj.*

crotch·et (kroch′it), *n.* 1. a small hook. 2. a hooklike device or part. 3. *Entomol.* a small, hooklike process. 4. a curved surgical instrument with a sharp hook. 5. an odd fancy or whimsical notion. 6. *Music, Chiefly Brit.* a quarter note. See illus. under **note.** [ME *crochet* hook, staff with hook at end; doublet of CROCKET] —**Syn.** 5. caprice, whimsy, humor; eccentricity, quirk, oddity.

crotch·et·y (kroch′i tē), *adj.* 1. given to odd notions, whims, grouchiness, etc.: *a crotchety old miser.* 2. of the nature of a crotchet. [CROTCHET + -Y¹] —**crotch′et·i·ness,** *n.*

crotch′ veneer′, a piece of crotchwood.

crotch·wood (kroch′wo͝od′), *n.* veneer wood from a tree crotch. [CROTCH + WOOD[1]]

cro·ton (krōt′ən), *n.* **1.** any of the chiefly tropical, euphorbiaceous plants of the genus *Croton*, many species of which, as *C. Tiglium*, have important medicinal properties. **2.** (among florists) any plant of the related genus *Codiaeum* (or *Phyllaurea*) cultivated for the ornamental foliage. [< NL < Gk *krotōn* a tick, also the castor-oil plant, which has berries likened to ticks]

Cro′ton bug′ (krōt′ən). See **German cockroach.** Also, **cro′ton·bug′.** [named after the *Croton* Aqueduct water, introduced into New York City in 1842]

cro·ton′ic ac′id (krō ton′ik, -tō′nik), *Chem.* a colorless, crystalline, water-soluble solid, $CH_3CH{=}CHCOOH$, used chiefly in organic synthesis. [CROTON + -IC]

cro′ton oil′, a brownish-yellow oil expressed from the seeds of the croton, *Croton Tiglium*, that is a drastic purgative and counterirritant.

Cro·ton-on-Hud·son (krōt′ən on hud′sən, -ôn-), *n.* a town in SE New York. 6812 (1960).

Cro·to·pus (krə tō′pəs, krō-), *n.* *Class. Myth.* a king of Argos who murdered his daughter Psamathe for bearing a son to Apollo.

Cro·tus (krō′təs), *n.* *Class. Myth.* a son of Pan who was skilled in archery and who served as a companion of the Muses.

crouch (krouch), *v.i.* **1.** to stoop or bend low. **2.** to bend close to the ground, as an animal preparing to spring or shrinking with fear. **3.** to bow or stoop servilely; cringe. —*v.t.* **4.** to bend low. —*n.* **5.** act of crouching; a stooping or bending low. [ME *crouche(n)*, perh. b. *couchen* to lie down (see COUCH) and *croken* to CROOK[1]] —**crouch′er,** *n.* —**crouch′ing·ly,** *adv.*

croup[1] (kro͞op), *n.* *Pathol.* any condition of the larynx or trachea characterized by a hoarse cough and difficult breathing. [n. use of *croup* to cry hoarsely (now dial.), b. CROAK and WHOOP]

croup[2] (kro͞op), *n.* the highest part of the rump of a quadruped, esp. a horse. See diag. under **horse.** [ME *croupe* < OF < Gmc; see CROP]

crou·pade (kro͞o pād′, kro͞o′pād), *n.* *Dressage.* a movement in which a horse jumps up from a pesade with all four legs drawn up under him and lands on four legs in the same place. [< F (trans. of It *groppata*), equiv. to *croupe* CROUP[2] + *-ade* -ADE[1]]

crou·pi·er (kro͞o′pē ər, -pē ā′; *Fr.* kro͞o pyā′), *n., pl.* **-pi·ers** (-pē ərz, -pē āz′; *Fr.* -pyā′). **1.** an attendant who collects and pays the money at a gaming table. **2.** one who, at a public dinner, sits at the lower end of the table as assistant chairman. [< F: lit., one who sits behind another on horseback, equiv. to *croupe* rump (see CROUP[2]) + *-ier* -ER[2]]

croup·ous (kro͞o′pəs), *adj.* *Pathol.* pertaining to, of the nature of, or resembling croup. [CROUP[1] + -OUS]

croup′ous pneumo′nia, *Pathol.* pneumonia (def. 2).

croup·y (kro͞o′pē), *adj.,* **croup·i·er, croup·i·est. 1.** pertaining to or resembling croup. **2.** affected with croup. [CROUP[1] + -Y[1]] —**croup′i·ly,** *adv.* —**croup′i·ness,** *n.*

crouse (kro͞os), *adj.* *Scot. and North Eng.* bold; brisk; lively. [ME *crus, crous* fierce, bold, violent < MLG or Fris *krūs* crisp; c. G *kraus*] —**crouse′ly,** *adv.*

Crouse (krous), *n.* **Russel,** 1893–1966, U.S. dramatist and author.

crous·tade (kro͞o städ′), *n.* a shell of bread or pastry, sometimes of noodles, rice, or mashed potatoes, baked or fried and filled with ragout or the like. [< F < Pr *crustad(o)* < L *crustāt(us)*, ptp. of *crustāre* to encrust, deriv. of *crūsta* CRUST]

croûte (kro͞ot), *n.* crust. [< F]

crou·ton (kro͞o′ton, kro͞o ton′), *n.* a small piece of fried or toasted bread, used in soups and for garnishing other dishes. [< F, equiv. to *croûte* CRUST + *-on* dim. suffix]

crow[1] (krō), *n.* **1.** any of several oscine birds of the genus *Corvus*, of the family *Corvidae*, having lustrous black plumage, as the common *C. brachyrhynchos*, of North America. **2.** any of several other birds of the family *Corvidae*. **3.** any of various similar birds of other families. **4.** (*cap.*) *Astron.* the constellation Corvus. **5.** crowbar. **6. as the crow flies,** in a straight line; by the most direct route: *The next town is thirty miles from here, as the crow flies.* **7. eat crow,** *Informal.* to be forced to accept or perform something embarrassing to one, as to retract an emphatic statement; suffer humiliation: *His prediction was completely wrong, and he had to eat crow.* **8. have a crow to pick or pluck with someone,** to have a reason to disagree or argue with someone. [ME *crowe*, OE *crāwe, crāwa*; c. OHG *krāwa*; akin to D *kraai*, G *Krähe*]

Crow, *Corvus brachyrhynchos* (Length 19 in.; wingspread 3 ft.)

crow[2] (krō), *v.,* **crowed** or, for 1, (*esp. Brit.*), **crew; crowed; crow·ing;** *n.* —*v.i.* **1.** to utter the characteristic cry of a rooster. **2.** to utter an inarticulate cry of pleasure, as an infant does. **3.** to exult loudly; boast. —*n.* **4.** the characteristic cry of the cock. **5.** an inarticulate cry of pleasure. [ME *crow(en)*, OE *crāwan*; c. D *kraaien*, G *krähen*] —**crow′er,** *n.* —**crow′ing·ly,** *adv.*
—**Syn. 3.** vaunt, brag.

Crow (krō), *n.* **1.** a member of a Siouan people of eastern Montana. **2.** a Siouan language closely related to Hidatsa. [trans. (through F (*gens de*) *corbeaux* (the people) of the crow) of their own name *Absaroke* crow, sparrow-hawk, bird people]

crow·bar (krō′bär′), *n.* a steel bar, usually flattened and slightly bent at one or both ends, used as a lever. Also called **crow.** [CROW[1] + BAR[1]; r. ME *crowe*, so called because one end was beak-shaped]

crow·ber·ry (krō′ber′ē, -bə rē), *n., pl.* **-ries. 1.** the black or reddish berry of a heathlike, evergreen shrub, *Empetrum nigrum*, of northern regions. **2.** the plant itself. **3.** any of certain other fruits or the plants bearing them, as the bearberry. [CROW[1] + BERRY, prob. trans. of G *Krähenbeere*]

crow′ black′bird, any of several North American grackles of the genera *Quiscalus* and *Cassidix*, esp. the purple grackle.

crow·boot (krō′bo͞ot′), *n.* *Canadian Dial.* a moccasin-like boot made of soft leather. [prob. after CROW]

crowd[1] (kroud), *n.* **1.** a large number of persons gathered closely together; throng: *a crowd of angry people.* **2.** any large number of persons. **3.** the common people; the masses: *The crowd needs leadership.* **4.** any group or set of persons: *They cater to a society crowd.* **5.** a large number of things gathered or considered together. **6.** *Sociol.* a temporary gathering of people responding to common stimuli and engaged in any of various forms of collective behavior. **7.** audience; attendance: *Opening night drew a good crowd.* —*v.i.* **8.** to gather in large numbers; throng; swarm. **9.** to press forward; advance by pushing. —*v.t.* **10.** to push; shove. **11.** to press closely together; force into a confined space; cram: *to crowd clothes into a suitcase.* **12.** to fill to excess; fill by pressing or thronging into. **13.** *Informal.* to place under pressure or stress by constant solicitation: *to crowd a debtor for payment; to crowd someone with embarrassing questions.* **14. crowd on sail,** *Naut.* to carry a press of sail. [ME *crowd(en)*, OE *crūden* to press, hurry; c. MD *crūden* to push (D *kruien*)]
—**Syn. 1.** horde, herd. CROWD, MULTITUDE, SWARM, THRONG are terms referring to large numbers of people. CROWD suggests a jostling, uncomfortable, and possibly disorderly company: *A crowd gathered to listen to the speech.* MULTITUDE emphasizes the great number of persons or things but suggests that there is space enough for all: *a multitude of people at the market on Saturdays.* SWARM as used of people is usually contemptuous, suggesting a moving, restless, often noisy, crowd: *A swarm of dirty children played in the street.* THRONG suggests a company that presses together or forward, often with some common aim: *The throng pushed forward to see the cause of the excitement.* **3.** proletariat, plebeians, people, populace. **8.** assemble, herd. **9.** shove, press. **11.** pack, squeeze, cramp.

crowd[2] (kroud), *n.* an ancient Celtic musical instrument with the strings stretched over a rectangular frame, played with a bow. Also, **crwth.** [ME *crowd(e)*, var. of *crouth* < Welsh *crwth* CRWTH]

crowd·ed (krou′did), *adj.* **1.** filled to excess; filled with a crowd; packed: *crowded streets.* **2.** uncomfortably close together: *crowded passengers on a bus.* [CROWD[1] + -ED[2]] —**crowd′ed·ly,** *adv.* —**crowd′ed·ness,** *n.*

crow·dy (kro͞o′dē, krō′-, kro͝od′ē), *n., pl.* **-dies.** *Scot. and North Eng.* a dish of meal, esp. oatmeal and water, or sometimes milk, stirred together; gruel; brose; porridge. Also, **crow′die.** [?]

crow·foot (krō′fo͝ot′), *n., pl.* **-foots** for 1, 2, **-feet** for 3–6. **1.** any plant of the genus *Ranunculus*, esp. one with divided leaves suggestive of a crow's foot; buttercup. **2.** any of various other plants with leaves or other parts suggestive of a bird's foot, as certain species of the genus *Geranium*. **3.** caltrop (def. 2). **4.** *Naut.* an arrangement of several bridlelike ropes rove through a suspended euphroe to support the backbone of an awning at a number of points. **5.** *Motion Pictures, Television.* a three-legged device placed under a tripod to keep the camera from slipping. **6.** (on an architectural or engineering drawing) a V-shaped mark the apex of which is a reference point. [late ME *crowefote*. See CROW[1], FOOT]

crow·hop (krō′hop′), *n.* **1.** a short hop. **2.** a hop made by a horse with its legs stiffened and its back arched. [CROW[1] + HOP[1]] —**crow′hop′per,** *n.*

crow·keep·er (krō′kē′pər), *n.* *Brit. Dial.* a person employed to frighten away crows from crops. [CROW[1] + KEEPER]

Crow·ley (krou′lē), *n.* a city in S Louisiana. 15,617 (1960).

crown (kroun), *n.* **1.** any of various types of symbolic headgear worn by a king, queen, emperor, etc., as a symbol of sovereignty. **2.** a similar form of headgear worn by a person designated king or queen in a pageant, contest, etc. **3.** an ornamental wreath or circlet for the head, conferred by the ancients as a mark of victory, athletic or military distinction, etc. **4.** the distinction that comes from a great achievement. **5.** the power or dominion of a sovereign. **6. the crown,** the sovereign as head of the state, or the supreme governing power of a state under a monarchical government. **7.** any crownlike emblem or design, as in a heraldic crest. **8.** any of various coins bearing the figure of a crown or crowned head. **9.** a silver coin of the United Kingdom, equal to five shillings and equivalent to about .60 of a U.S. dollar. **10.** the monetary unit of Denmark, Iceland, Norway, or Sweden: a krona or krone. **11.** the koruna of Czechoslovakia. **12.** something having the form of a crown, as the corona of a flower. **13.** *Bot.* **a.** the leaves and living branches of a tree. **b.** the point at which the root of a seed plant joins the stem. **c.** a circle of appendages on the throat of the corolla; corona. **14.** the top or highest part of anything, as of the head, a hat, a mountain, etc. **15.** a crownpiece. **16.** *Archit.* **a.** a termination of a tower consisting of a lanternlike steeple supported entirely by a number of flying buttresses. **b.** any ornamental termination of a tower or turret. **17.** the highest point of any construction of convex section or outline, as an arch, vault, deck, road, etc. **18.** the top of the head: *He broke his crown.* **19.** the crest, as of a bird. See diag. under **bird. 20.** *Dentistry.* **a.** the part of a tooth that is covered by enamel. See diag. under **tooth. b.** an artificial substitute, as of gold or porcelain, for the crown of a tooth. **21.** See **crown cap. 22.** a drill bit consisting of a metal matrix holding diamond chips. **23.** the highest or most nearly perfect state of anything. **24.** an exalting or chief attribute. **25.** the acme or supreme source of honor, excellence, beauty, etc. **26.** Also called **button.** *Horol.* a knurled knob for winding a watch. **27.** See **crown glass. 28.** Also called **head.** *Naut.* the part of an anchor at which the arms join the shank. **29.** Also called **bezel, top.** *Jewelry.* the part of a cut gem above the girdle. **30.** *Mach.* **a.** a slight convexity given to a pulley supporting a flat belt in order to center the belt. **b.** a slight convexity given to the outer faces of the teeth of two gears so that they mesh toward their centers rather than at the ends. **31.** a size of printing paper, 15 × 20 inches. Cf. **double crown. 32.** *Naut., Mach.* swallow[1] (def. 12). **33.** *Knots.* a knot made by interweaving the strands at the end of a rope, often made as the beginning of a back splice or as the first stage in tying a more elaborate knot. —*v.t.* **34.** to place a crown or garland upon the head of. **35.** to invest with a regal crown, or with regal dignity and power. **36.** to honor as with a crown; reward; invest with honor, dignity, etc. **37.** to surmount as with a crown. **38.** to complete worthily; bring to a successful or triumphant conclusion: *The Nobel prize crowned his career as an author.* **39.** *Informal.* to hit on the top of the head: *His wife crowned him with a rolling pin.* **40.** to give to (a construction) an upper surface of convex section or outline. **41.** to cap (a tooth) with a false crown. **42.** *Checkers.* to change (a checker) into a king after it has safely reached the last row by putting another checker of the same color on top of it. **43.** *Knots.* to form a crown on (the end of a rope). [ME *c(o)roune* < AF < L *corōn(a)* wreath; see CORONA] —**crown′less,** *adj.*

Crowns of British royalty and nobility
A, Sovereign; B, Duke; C, Earl; D, Viscount

crown′ ant′ler, the topmost prong of a stag's antler. Also called **sur-royal.** See diag. under **antler.**

crown′ block′, a stationary block for supporting a hoisting tackle from above.

crown′ cam′, *Mach.* a cam having the form of a rotating disk having one shaped face. See illus. under **cam.**

crown′ cap′, a crimped metal bottle cap, usually lined with cork. Also called **crown′ cork′.** —**crown′-cap′ping,** *adj.*

crown′ col′ony, a colony in which the crown has the entire control of legislation and administration, as distinguished from one having a constitution and representative government.

crown′ cut′ter, a hollow, thin-walled cylinder having teeth formed radially on the end and used for cutting round holes out of thin, flat stock; crown saw.

crown′ dai′sy, a garden plant, *Chrysanthemum coronarium*, of southern Europe, having numerous yellowish-white flower heads.

crowned (kround), *adj.* **1.** characterized by or having a crown (often used in combination): *a crowned signet ring; a low-crowned fedora.* **2.** originating from or founded on the royal crown or its associated dignity, sovereignty, etc.: *crowned despotism.* [ME *crouned*. See CROWN, -ED[2]]

crown·er[1] (krou′nər), *n.* **1.** one who or that which crowns. **2.** a crowning event or occurrence. [late ME; see CROWN, -ER[1]]

crown·er[2] (krou′nər, kro͞o′-), *n.* *Brit. Dial.* coroner. [late ME; see CROWN, -ER[2]]

crown·et (krou′net, -nit), *n.* *Archaic.* a coronet. [late ME; see CROWN, -ET]

crown′ fire′, a forest fire that spreads along the treetops, often at great speeds.

crown′ gall′, *Plant Pathol.* **1.** a disease of peaches, apples, roses, grapes, etc., characterized by the formation of galls on the roots or stems usually at or below ground level, caused by a bacterium, *Agrobacterium tumefaciens*. **2.** the gall itself.

crown′ gear′, a bevel gear having a flat pitch surface bounded by two circles.

crown′ glass′, **1.** an optical glass of low dispersion and generally low index of refraction. **2.** an old form of window glass formed by blowing a globe and whirling it into a disk: composed essentially of soda, lime, and silica.

crown′ graft′, *Hort.* a graft in which the scion is inserted at the crown of the stock. —**crown′ graft′ing.**

crown′ impe′rial, a rank-smelling herb, *Fritillaria imperialis*, of Iran, having a purple-spotted stem and purplish, yellow-red, or brownish-orange flowers, grown as an ornamental.

crown·ing (krou′ning), *adj.* **1.** representing a level of surpassing achievement, attainment, etc.; supreme: *the crowning accomplishment of his administration.* **2.** forming or providing a crown, top, or summit: *a crowning star on a Christmas tree.* [CROWN + -ING[2]]

crown′ jew′els, the ceremonial objects of a sovereign, as the crown, scepter, etc., that are heavily ornamented with jewels and highly prized for their symbolic value.

crown′ land′, **1.** land belonging to the crown, the revenue of which goes to the reigning sovereign. **2.** Also, **crown′land′.** one of the provinces or great administrative divisions of the former empire of Austria-Hungary.

crown′ lens′, *Optics.* a lens made of crown glass, usually used as the converging lens component of an achromatic lens.

crown′ mold′ing, *Archit.* a corona, esp. one having the form of a cyma recta.

crown′ octa′vo, a size of book, about 5 × 7½ inches, untrimmed. *Abbr.:* crown 8vo

crown-of-jew·els (kroun′əv jo͞o′əlz), *n., pl.* **-jew·els.** an annual herb, *Lopezia coronata*, of Mexico, having lilac-colored flowers with a red base.

crown′ of thorns′, a climbing spurge, *Euphorbia splendens*, of Madagascar, having stems covered with spines.

crown·piece (kroun′pēs′), *n.* **1.** a piece or part forming or fitting the crown or top of anything. **2.** the strap of a bridle that fits across the head of a horse. See illus. under **harness.** [CROWN + PIECE]

Crown′ Point′, **1.** a village in NE New York, on Lake Champlain: the site of a strategic fort in the French and Indian and the Revolutionary wars. **2.** a town in NW Indiana. 8443 (1960).

crown′ post′, any vertical member in a roof truss, esp. a king post.

crown′ prince′, the heir apparent of a monarch.

crown′ prin′cess, **1.** the wife of a crown prince. **2.** a female heir presumptive.

crown′ quar′to, *Chiefly Brit.* a size of book, about 7½ × 10 inches, untrimmed. *Abbr.:* crown 4to

crown′ rot′, *Plant Pathol.* a disease of plants, characterized by the rotting of the stem at ground level, caused by any of several fungi.

crown′ rust′, *Plant Pathol.* a disease of oats and other grasses, characterized by the formation, on the leaves, of orange or black spores, caused by a rust fungus, *Puccinia coronata.*

crown′ saw′, a rotary saw consisting of a hollow cylinder with teeth formed on one end or edge, as a trephine or trepanning saw.

crown′ val′la·ry (val′ə rē), *Heraldry.* **1.** a representation of a circlet continued upward in a number of flat rays, the tops of the rays and the spaces between being terminated in angular points. **2.** (loosely) a palisado crown. [*vallary* L *vallār(is)* (*vall(um)* rampart + *-āris* -ARY), from the fact that it was given to the first over the ramparts]

crown′ vetch′, axseed.

crown′ wart′, *Plant Pathol.* a disease of alfalfa and clover, characterized by galls around the base of the stem, caused by several fungi of the genus *Urophlyctis.*

crown′ wheel′, *Horol.* **1.** a wheel next to the winding knob, having two sets of teeth, one at right angles to its plane. **2.** any of various wheels having the form of a hoop or short cylinder with a serrated edge, as the escape wheel in a verge escapement.

crown·work (kroun′wûrk′), *n.* *Fort.* an outwork containing a central bastion with a curtain and demibastions. [CROWN + WORK]

crow-pheas·ant (krō′fez′ənt), *n.* a large coucal, *Centropus sinensis,* of Asia, having black and brown plumage and a long tail.

crow's-foot (krōz′fo͝ot′), *n., pl.* **-feet. 1.** Usually, **crow's-feet.** wrinkles at the outer corner of the eye. **2.** *Aeron.* a method by which one main cord exerts pressure or pull at several points simultaneously through smaller ropes. **3.** *Tailoring.* a three-pointed embroidered design used as a finish, as at the end of a seam or opening. [CROW[1] + 'S[1] + FOOT, so called because likened to a crow's foot or footprint]

crow's-nest (krōz′nest′), *n.* **1.** *Naut.* a platform or shelter for a lookout at or near the top of a mast. **2.** any similar station ashore, as for a traffic officer. Also, **crow's′ nest′.**

crow's′-nest mod′el, *Naval Archit.* See **hawk's nest model.**

crow·step (krō′step′), *n.* corbiestep. [CROW[1] + STEP]

Croy·don (kroid′ən), *n.* a city in N Surrey, in SE England, near London: airport. 252,387 (1961).

croze (krōz), *n.* **1.** the groove at either end of the staves of a barrel, cask, etc., into which the edge of the head fits. **2.** a tool for cutting such a groove. [? special use of *crose, croze* (var. of CROSS) in sense cross-groove]

cro·zier (krō′zhər), *n.* crosier.

Cro·zier (krō′zhər), *n.* a crater in the fourth quadrant of the face of the moon: about 15 miles in diameter.

crs., 1. creditors. **2.** credits.

CRT, cathode ray tube.

cru (kro͞o; *Fr.* kʀʏ), *n., pl.* **crus** (kro͞oz; *Fr.* kʀʏ). a wine-producing vineyard in France. [< F, n. use of *crû,* ptp. of *croître* to grow]

cru·ces (kro͞o′sēz), *n.* a pl. of **crux.**

cru·cial (kro͞o′shəl), *adj.* **1.** involving a final and supreme decision; decisive; critical: *a crucial experiment.* **2.** severe; trying. **3.** of the form of a cross; cross-shaped. [< L *cruci-* (s. of *crux*) CROSS + -AL[1]] —**cru·ci·al·i·ty** (kro͞o′shē al′i tē, kro͞o shal′-), *n.* —**cru′cial·ly,** *adv.*
—**Syn. 1.** climacteric, determining, momentous, vital, important.

cru·ci·ate (kro͞o′shē it, -āt′), *adj.* **1.** cross-shaped. **2.** *Bot.* having the form of a cross with equal arms, as the flowers of mustard. **3.** *Entomol.* crossing diagonally when at rest, as the wings of certain insects. [< NL *cruciāt(us),* equiv. to L *cruci-* (s. of *crux*) CROSS + *-ātus* -ATE[1]] —**cru′ci·ate·ly,** *adv.*

cru·ci·ble (kro͞o′sə bəl), *n.* **1.** a vessel of metal or refractory material employed for heating substances to high temperatures. **2.** *Metall.* a hollow area at the bottom of a furnace in which the metal collects. **3.** a severe, searching test. [late ME *crusible* pot for melting metals < ML *crūcibul(um), -bulum* crucible, earlier, night lamp, perh. orig. whaleoil cruse. See CRUSE, BALEEN]

Crucible, The, a play (1953) by Arthur Miller.

cru′cible steel′, steel made in a crucible, esp. a high-grade steel prepared by melting selected materials.

cru·ci·fer (kro͞o′sə fər), *n.* **1.** one who carries a cross, as in ecclesiastical processions. **2.** *Bot.* a cruciferous plant. [< LL, equiv. to L *cruci-* (s. of *crux*) CROSS + *-fer* -FER]

cru·cif·er·ous (kro͞o sif′ər əs), *adj.* **1.** bearing a cross. **2.** *Bot.* belonging or pertaining to the *Cruciferae* or *Brassicaceae,* a family of plants having flowers with a crosslike, four-petaled corolla; brassicaceous. [< LL *crucifer* CRUCIFER + -OUS]

cru·ci·fix (kro͞o′sə fiks), *n.* **1.** a cross with the figure of Jesus crucified upon it. **2.** any cross. **3.** *Gymnastics.* a stunt performed on the parallel rings in which the athlete holds himself rigid with his arms extended horizontally from the shoulders. [ME < eccl. L *crucifix(us)* the crucified one (i.e., Christ), n. use of masc. of ptp. of *crucifigere* to CRUCIFY] —**cru·ci·fi·cial** (kro͞o′sə fish′əl), *adj.*

cru·ci·fix·ion (kro͞o′sə fik′shən), *n.* **1.** the act of crucifying. **2.** (*cap.*) the death of Jesus by exposure upon a cross. **3.** a picture or other representation of this. [late ME < eccl. L *crucifixiōn-* (s. of *crucifixiō*). See CRUCIFIX, -ION]

cru·ci·form (kro͞o′sə fôrm′), *adj.* cross-shaped. [< L *cruci-* (s. of *crux*) cross + -FORM] —**cru′ci·for′mi·ty,** *n.* —**cru′ci·form′ly,** *adv.*

cru·ci·fy (kro͞o′sə fī′), *v.t.,* **-fied, -fy·ing. 1.** to put to death by nailing or binding a person to a cross. **2.** to treat with gross injustice; persecute. **3.** to subdue (passion, sin, etc.). [ME *crucifie(n)* < OF *crucifie(r)* < LL *crucifigere,* equiv. to L *cruci-* (s. of *crux*) CROSS + *figere* to fix, bind fast] —**cru′ci·fi′er,** *n.*

Cru·cis (kro͞o′sis), *n.* *Astron.* gen. of **Crux.** [L]

cruck (kruk), *n.* (in old English building) one of a pair of naturally curved timbers forming one of several rigid arched frames supporting the roof of a cottage or farm building. [ME *crokke,* prob. var. of *crok* CROOK[1]]

crud (krud), *v.,* **crud·ded, crud·ding,** *n.* —*v.t., v.i.* **1.** *Dial.* to curd. —*n.* **2.** *Slang.* **a.** a deposit or coating of refuse or of an impure or alien substance. **b.** a filthy, repulsive, or contemptible person. **3.** *Dial.* curd. [ME; earlier form of CURD]

crude (kro͞od), *adj.,* **crud·er, crud·est. 1.** in a raw or unprepared state; unrefined: *crude oil.* **2.** lacking in intellectual subtlety, perceptivity, etc.; rudimentary; undeveloped. **3.** lacking finish, polish, proper arrangement, or completeness: *a crude summary.* **4.** lacking culture, refinement, tact, etc.: *a crude person; crude behavior.* **5.** undisguised; blunt; bare: *a crude answer.* **6.** *Archaic.* unripe; not mature. [ME < L *crūd(us)* (for **cruidus;* see CRUOR, -ID[4]) bloody, hence, raw, ruthless, unripe; see RAW] —**crude′ly,** *adv.* —**crude′ness,** *n.*
—**Syn. 1.** unprepared, unfinished, coarse. See **raw. 3.** unpolished. **4.** uncouth, rough, rude, coarse, clumsy, awkward. —**Ant. 1, 4.** refined. **4.** cultivated.

crude′ oil′, petroleum as it is before refining. Also called **crude′ petro′leum.**

cru·di·ty (kro͞o′di tē), *n., pl.* **-ties** for 2. **1.** state or quality of being crude. **2.** an instance of this; anything crude. [late ME *crudite* < L *crūditās.* See CRUDE, -ITY]

cru·el (kro͞o′əl), *adj.* **1.** willfully or knowingly causing pain or distress to others. **2.** enjoying the pain or distress of others: *the cruel spectators of the gladiatorial contests.* **3.** causing or marked by great pain or distress: *a cruel remark; a cruel affliction.* **4.** rigid; stern; strict; unrelentingly severe. [ME < OF < L *crūdēl(is),* equiv. to *crūd(us)* bloody, ruthless (see CRUDE) + *-ēlis* adj. suffix] —**cru′el·ly,** *adv.* —**cru′el·ness,** *n.*
—**Syn. 1.** barbarous, bloodthirsty, ferocious, merciless, relentless, implacable. CRUEL, PITILESS, RUTHLESS, BRUTAL, SAVAGE imply readiness to cause pain to others, and being unmoved by their suffering. CRUEL implies willingness to cause pain, and indifference to suffering: *a cruel stepfather; cruel to animals.* PITILESS adds the idea of hard-heartedness and positive refusal to show compassion: *pitiless to captives.* RUTHLESS implies cruelty and unscrupulousness, letting nothing stand in one's way, and using any methods necessary: *ruthless in pressing an advantage.* BRUTAL implies cruelty which takes the form of physical violence: *a brutal master.* SAVAGE suggests fierceness and brutality: *savage battles, jealousy.* —**Ant. 1.** kind. **2.** sympathetic, compassionate.

cru·el·heart·ed (kro͞o′əl här′tid), *adj.* having a cruel heart; lacking kindness, compassion, etc.

cru·el·ty (kro͞o′əl tē), *n., pl.* **-ties. 1.** state or quality of being cruel. **2.** cruel disposition or conduct. **3.** a cruel act. [ME *cruelte* < OF < L *crūdēlitāt-* (s. of *crūdēlitās*). See CRUEL, -ITY]
—**Syn. 1.** harshness, brutality, ruthlessness, barbarity, inhumanity, atrocity. —**Ant. 2, 3.** kindness.

cru·et (kro͞o′it), *n.* a glass bottle, esp. one for holding vinegar, oil, etc., for the table. [ME < AF, equiv. to OF *crue* pot (< Gmc; cf. OE *crūce* pot) + *-et* -ET]

Crü·ger (kro͞o′gər), *n.* a crater in the third quadrant of the face of the moon: about 30 miles in diameter.

Cruik·shank (kro͝ok′shangk′), *n.* **George,** 1792–1878, English illustrator, caricaturist, and painter.

cruise (kro͞oz), *v.,* **cruised, cruis·ing,** *n.* —*v.i.* **1.** to sail about without proceeding directly from one point to another, as a yacht on a pleasure trip or a warship in search of hostile vessels. **2.** to travel about without a particular purpose or destination. **3.** *Aeron.* to fly at moderate speed, esp. at the speed which permits maximum operating efficiency. **4.** to travel about slowly, looking for customers or for something demanding attention: *Taxis and police cars cruise in the downtown area.* **5.** to travel along at a moderately fast, easily controllable speed: *cruising along the highway enjoying the scenery.* **6.** *Informal.* to go about on the streets or in public areas in search of a sexual partner. —*v.t.* **7.** to cruise in (a specified area): *patrol cars cruising the neighborhood; to cruise the Caribbean.* **8.** to inspect (a tract of forest) to estimate its lumber potential. —*n.* **9.** act of cruising; a voyage made by cruising. [< D *kruise(n)* (to) cross, cruise, deriv. of *kruis* CROSS] —**cruis′ing·ly,** *adv.*

cruise′ car′. See **squad car.**

cruise′ mis′sile, a small, winged, rocket- or jet-propelled guided missile that travels in the lower atmosphere and that may be launched from aircraft, ships, or submarines.

cruis·er (kro͞o′zər), *n.* **1.** one who or that which cruises, as a person or a ship. **2.** one of a class of warships of medium tonnage, designed for high speed and long cruising radius. **3.** a vessel, esp. a power-driven one, intended for cruising. **4.** See **squad car. 5.** Also called **timber cruiser.** one who estimates the value of the timber in a tract of forest. **6.** *Slang.* a prostitute who walks the street soliciting customers. [< D *kruiser,* equiv. to *kruis(en)* (to) CRUISE + *-er* -ER[1]]

cruis·er·weight (kro͞o′zər wāt′), *n.* *Brit.* a light-heavyweight boxer. [so called by metaphor, since a cruiser is the second heaviest naval ship, as the boxer is the second heaviest fighter]

cruise′ ship′, a passenger ship used for pleasure cruises primarily, taking the same passengers on an extended circuit with calls in various places and ultimately returning them to their ports of embarkation.

crul·ler (krul′ər), *n.* a light, sweet cake cut from a rolled dough and fried in deep fat, often having a ring-shaped or twisted form. Also, **kruller.** [< D *krulle* kind of cake (deriv. of *krullen* to curl) + -ER[1]]

crum (krum), *n. v.t.,* **crummed, crum·ming.** *Archaic.* crumb.

crumb (krum), *n.* **1.** a small particle of bread, cake, etc., such as breaks or falls off. **2.** a small particle or portion of anything. **3.** the soft inner portion of a bread (distinguished from *crust*). **4. crumbs,** a cake topping made of sugar, flour, butter, and spice, usually crumbled on top of the raw batter and baked with the cake. **5.** *Slang.* an objectionable or worthless person. —*v.t.* **6.** *Cookery.* to dress or prepare with crumbs. **7.** to break into crumbs or small fragments. **8.** *Informal.* to remove crumbs from: *The waiter crumbed the table.* [ME *crome, crume,* OE *cruma;* akin to D *kruim,* G *Krume* crumb, L *grūmus* small heap of earth] —**crumb′a·ble,** *adj.* —**crumb′er,** *n.*

crum·ble (krum′bəl), *v.,* **-bled, -bling,** *n.* —*v.t.* **1.** to break into small fragments or crumbs. —*v.i.* **2.** to fall into small pieces; break or part into small fragments. **3.** to decay or disintegrate gradually: *The ancient walls had crumbled.* —*n.* **4.** a crumbly or crumbled substance. **5.** *Dial.* crumb; particle; fragment. [late ME *crymme* (var. of *crimme,* OE *gecrymman,* deriv. of *cruma* CRUMB) + -LE] —**crum′bling·ness,** *n.*
—**Syn. 1.** mash, shatter. **2.** disintegrate.

crum·bly (krum′blē), *adj.,* **-bli·er, -bli·est.** apt to crumble; friable. [CRUMBLE + -Y[1]] —**crum′bli·ness,** *n.*

crum·bum (krum′bum′), *n.* *Slang.* crumb (def. 5). [playful variation]

crumb·y (krum′ē), *adj.,* **crumb·i·er, crumb·i·est. 1.** full of crumbs. **2.** soft. [CRUMB + -Y[1]]

crum·horn (krum′hôrn′), *n.* cromorne.

crum·mie (krum′ē, kro͝om′ē), *n.* *Chiefly Scot.* a cow with crooked horns. Also, **crummy.** [obs. *crum* crooked (ME, OE *crumb;* c. G *Krumm*) + -IE]

crum·my[1] (krum′ē), *adj.,* **-mi·er, -mi·est,** *n., pl.* **-mies.** —*adj.* **1.** *Slang.* **a.** maintained in a dirty, run-down condition; shabby; seedy: *a crummy fleabag of a hotel.* **b.** of little or no value; cheap; worthless: *crummy furniture that falls apart after a month of use.* **c.** wretchedly inadequate; measly; picayune: *They pay crummy salaries.* **2.** *Brit. Slang.* (of a woman) agreeably buxom; plump. —*n.* **3.** *Railroads Slang.* a caboose. [perh. obs. *crum* crooked (see CRUMMIE) + -Y[1] (orig. adj.)]

crum·my[2] (krum′ē, kro͝om′ē), *n., pl.* **-mies.** *Chiefly Scot.* crummie.

crump (krump, kro͝omp), *v.t.* **1.** to crunch with the teeth. —*v.i.* **2.** (of an artillery shell) to land and explode with a heavy, muffled sound. **3.** to make a crunching sound, as in walking over snow, or as snow when trodden on. —*n.* **4.** a crunching sound. **5.** a large explosive shell or bomb. **6.** *Brit. Informal.* a heavy blow. —*adj.* **7.** *Brit. Dial.* brittle; friable. [imit.]

crum·pet (krum′pit), *n.* **1.** *Chiefly Brit.* a kind of light, soft bread resembling a muffin, cooked on a griddle or the like, and often toasted. **2.** *Slang.* **a.** sex appeal. **b.** a sexually attractive girl or woman. [short for *crumpetcake* curled cake, equiv. to ME *crompid* (ptp. of obs. *crump,* var. of CRIMP) + CAKE]

crum·ple (krum′pəl), *v.,* **-pled, -pling,** *n.* —*v.t.* **1.** to press into irregular folds; rumple; wrinkle. **2.** to cause to collapse or give way suddenly: *That right hook to the midsection crumpled him.* —*v.i.* **3.** to contract into wrinkles; shrink; shrivel. **4.** to give way suddenly; collapse: *At the third punch, his opponent crumpled to the floor.* —*n.* **5.** an irregular fold or wrinkle produced by crumpling. [ME; var. of CRIMPLE] —**crum′ply,** *adj.*

crum·pled (krum′pəld), *adj.* **1.** rumpled; wrinkled. **2.** bent in a spiral curve: *a crumpled ram's horn.* [ME; var. of *crimpled,* ptp. of CRIMPLE]

crunch (krunch), *v.t.* **1.** to crush with the teeth; chew with a crushing noise. **2.** to crush or grind noisily. —*v.i.* **3.** to chew with a crushing sound. **4.** to produce, or proceed with, a crushing noise. —*n.* **5.** act or sound of crunching. **6.** *Slang.* a shortage or reduction of something needed or wanted: *a monetary crunch; the energy crunch.* **7.** *Slang.* distress or depressed conditions due to such a shortage or reduction: *a budget crunch.* **8.** *Slang.* a situation of extreme stress or danger; critical test: *When the crunch comes, just do your best.* Also, **craunch.** [b. CRAUNCH and CRUSH] —**crunch′a·ble,** *adj.* —**crunch′ing·ly,** *adv.* —**crunch′ing·ness,** *n.*

crunch·y (krun′chē), *adj.,* **crunch·i·er, crunch·i·est.** that crunches; crispy. [CRUNCH + -Y[1]] —**crunch′i·ly,** *adv.* —**crunch′i·ness,** *n.*

cru·node (kro͞o′nōd), *n.* *Geom.* a point at which two branches of a curve intersect and have different tangents. [irreg. < L *cru(x)* cross + NODE] —**cru·no′dal,** *adj.*

cru·or (kro͞o′ôr), *n.* *Obs.* coagulated blood, or that portion of the blood which forms the clot. [< L: blood (that flows from a wound), gore; akin to CRUDE]

crup·per (krup′ər, kro͝op′-), *n.* **1.** a leather strap that fastens to the back of the saddle of a harness and passes in a loop under the tail of a horse to prevent the harness from slipping forward. See illus. under **harness. 2.** the rump or buttocks of a horse. **3.** armor for the rump of a horse. [ME *cro(u)per,* var. of *cruper* < AF. See CROUP[2], -ER[2]]

cru·ral (kro͝or′əl), *adj.* **1.** of or pertaining to the leg or the hind limb. **2.** *Anat., Zool.* of or pertaining to the leg proper, or crus. [< L *crūrāl(is)* belonging to the legs, equiv. to *crūr-* (s. of *crūs*) leg + *-ālis* -AL[1]]

crus (krus, kro͞os), *n., pl.* **cru·ra** (kro͝or′ə). *Anat., Zool.* **1.** the part of the leg or hind limb between the femur or thigh and the ankle or tarsus; shank. **2.** a limb or process, as of a bone or other structure. **3.** any of various parts likened to a leg or to a pair of legs. [< L: leg, shank]

cru·sade (kro͞o sād′), *n., v.,* **-sad·ed, -sad·ing.** —*n.* **1.** (*often cap.*) any of the military expeditions undertaken by the Christians of Europe in the 11th, 12th, and 13th centuries for the recovery of the Holy Land from the Muslims. **2.** any war carried on under papal sanction. **3.** any vigorous, aggressive movement for the defense or advancement of an idea, cause, etc.: *a crusade against polio.* —*v.i.* **4.** to go on or engage in a crusade. [earlier *crusada* < Sp *cruzada;* r. 16th century *croisade* < MF. See CROSS, -ADE[1]] —**cru·sad′er,** *n.*

cru·sa·do (kro͞o sā′dō, -zā′-), *n., pl.* **-does, -dos.** an early Portuguese coin of gold or silver, bearing the figure of a cross. Also, **cruzado.** [< Pg *cruzada* crossed, marked with a cross. See CROSS, -ADE[1]]

cruse (kro͞oz, kro͞os), *n.* an earthen pot, bottle, etc., for liquids. [ME *crouse* (OE *crūse;* c. G *Krause* pot with lid) + ME *croo* (OE *crōg, crōh;* c. G *Krug* jug)]

crush (krush), *v.t.* **1.** to press with a force that destroys or deforms. **2.** to squeeze or pound into small fragments or particles, as ore, stone, etc. **3.** to force out by pressing or squeezing; extract: *to crush the juice from an orange.* **4.** to hug or embrace forcibly or strongly: *He crushed her in his arms.* **5.** to destroy, subdue, or suppress utterly: *to crush a revolt.* **6.** to overwhelm with confusion, chagrin, or humiliation, as by argumentation or a slighting action or remark; squelch. **7.** to oppress grievously: *to crush the poor.* **8.** *Archaic.* to drink (wine, ale, etc.). —*v.i.* **9.** to become crushed. **10.** to advance with crushing; press or crowd forcibly. —*n.* **11.** the act of crushing; state of being crushed. **12.** a great crowd. **13.** *Informal.* **a.** a short-lived but intense infatuation, as of a girl for a boy. **b.** the object of such an infatuation: *Who is your latest crush?* [ME *crusche(n)* < MF *cruis(ir)* < Gmc; cf. OSw *krusa, krosa,* MLG *krossen* to crush] —**crush′a·bil′i·ty,** *n.* —**crush′a·ble,** *adj.* —**crush′er,** *n.*
—**Syn. 1.** crumple. **2.** shatter, pulverize, granulate, powder, mash, crumble. See **break. 5.** quell, quash.

crush·ing (krush′ing), *adj.* **1.** overwhelming; humiliating; squelching: *His crushing reply silenced the heckler.* **2.** conclusive; decisive: *a crushing victory.* [CRUSH + -ING[2]] —**crush′ing·ly,** *adv.*

cru·si·ly (krōō′sə lē, -zə-), *adj. Heraldry.* **1.** semé of cross-crosslets: *argent, crusily gules.* **2.** semé of crosses of a specified type: *crusily botonée; crusily paty.* [< MF *crusillie,* var. of *croisille,* equiv. to *croisille* little cross + *-e* ptp. suffix; see -EE]

cru·si·ly-fitch·y (krōō′sə lē fich′ē, -zə-), *adj. Heraldry.* semé of cross-crosslets fitchy.

Cru·soe (krōō′sō), *n.* **Robinson.** See **Robinson Crusoe.**

crust (krust), *n.* **1.** the hard outer portion of a loaf of bread (distinguished from *crumb*). **2.** a piece of this. **3.** the outside covering of a pie. **4.** any more or less hard external covering or coating: *a crust of snow.* **5.** the hard outer shell or covering of an animal. **6.** *Geol.* the outer portion of the earth, about 22 miles deep under the continents and 6 miles deep under the oceans. Cf. **mantle**[1] (def. 8), **core**[1] (def. 11). **7.** a scab or eschar. **8.** deposit from wine, as it ripens, on the interior of bottles, consisting of tartar and coloring matter. **9.** *Slang.* unabashed self-assertiveness; nerve; gall: *It takes a lot of crust to invite yourself to a party.* —*v.t.* **10.** to cover with or as with a crust; encrust. **11.** to form (something) into a crust. —*v.i.* **12.** to form or contract a crust. **13.** to form into a crust. [ME < L *crūst(a)* hard surface (of a body); r. ME *cro(u)ste* < MF < L *crūst(a)*] —**crust′less,** *adj.*

Crus·ta·ce·a (kru stā′shē ə, -shə), *n.* the class comprising the crustaceans. [< NL; see CRUSTACEAN]

crus·ta·cean (kru stā′shən), *n.* **1.** any chiefly aquatic arthropod of the class *Crustacea,* typically having the body covered with a hard shell or crust, including the lobsters, shrimps, crabs, barnacles, wood lice, etc. —*adj.* **2.** belonging or pertaining to the *Crustacea.* [< NL *Crūstāce(a)* (neut. pl.) hard-shelled ones (see CRUST, -ACEA) + -AN]

crus·ta·ceous (kru stā′shəs), *adj.* **1.** of the nature of or pertaining to a crust or shell. **2.** crustacean. **3.** having a hard covering or crust. [< NL *crūstāceus* (adj.) hard-shelled. See CRUST, -ACEOUS]

crus·tal (krus′təl), *adj.* of or pertaining to a crust, as that of the earth. [< L *crūst(a)* shell, crust + -AL[1]]

crust·ed (krus′tid), *adj.* **1.** having a crust; encrusted. **2.** (of a wine) containing a hardened deposit accumulated during aging in the bottle: *crusted port.* **3.** having the accruals of age; antique. [ME; see CRUST, -ED[3]] —**crust′ed·ly,** *adv.*

crust·y (krus′tē), *adj.,* **crust·i·er, crust·i·est. 1.** of the nature of or resembling a crust; having a crust. **2.** harsh; surly; rude: *a crusty person; a crusty remark.* [late ME; see CRUST, -Y[1]] —**crust′i·ly,** *adv.* —**crust′i·ness,** *n.* —**Syn. 2.** testy, prickly, touchy; curt, brusque.

crutch (kruch), *n.* **1.** a staff or support to assist a lame or infirm person in walking, now usually with a crosspiece at one end to fit under the armpit. **2.** any of various devices resembling this in shape or use. **3.** a forked support or part. **4.** a forked device on the left side of a sidesaddle, consisting of two hooks one of which is open at the bottom and serves to clamp the left knee and the other of which is open at the top and serves to support the right knee. **5.** the crotch of the human body. **6.** Also, **crotch.** *Naut.* **a.** a forked support for a boom or spar when not in use. **b.** a forked support for an oar on the sides or stern of a rowboat. **c.** a horizontal knee reinforcing the stern frames of a wooden vessel. **7.** anything that serves as an expedient to supplement insufficient resources: *He uses liquor as a psychological crutch. This works program is basically a crutch for the economy.* —*v.t.* **8.** to support on crutches; prop; sustain. [ME *crucche,* OE *cryce* (obl. *crycce*); c. Norw *krykkja,* Dan *krykke,* G *Krücke,* D *kruk.* See CROOK[1]] —**crutch′like′,** *adj.*

crutched (krucht), *adj.* having or bearing a cross: *a crutched friar.* [earlier *crouched,* equiv. to *crouch* cross (ME *cruche,* OE *crūc* < L *cruci-,* s. of *crux*) + -ED[3]]

crux (kruks), *n., pl.* **crux·es, cru·ces** (krōō′sēz). **1.** a vital, basic, or decisive point: *the crux of the matter.* **2.** a cross. **3.** something that torments by its puzzling nature; a perplexing difficulty. [< L: a cross, torment, trouble]

Crux (kruks), *n., gen.* **Cru·cis** (krōō′sis). *Astron.* See **Southern Cross.** [< L: a cross]

crux an·sa·ta (kruks′ an sā′tə), *pl.* **cru·ces an·sa·tae** (krōō′sēz an sā′tē). a T-shaped cross with a loop at the top; ankh. [< L: cross with a handle]

Cruz (krōōz; *Sp.* krōōth), *n.* **San Juan de la** (sän hwän de lä). See **John of the Cross, Saint.**

cru·za·do (krōō zā′dō; *Port.* krōō zä′thōō), *n., pl.* **-does, -dos.** crusado.

Cruz Al·ta (krōōz äl′tə), a city in S Brazil. 34,236 (1960).

cru·zei·ro (krōō zâr′ō; *Port.* krōō ze′rōō), *n., pl.* **-zei·ros** (-zâr′ōz; *Port.* -ze′rōōs). a monetary unit of Brazil equal to 100 centavos and equivalent to about .312 of a U.S. dollar. [< Pg, equiv. to *cruz* CROSS + *-eiro* -ER[2]]

crwth (krōōth), *n. Music.* crowd[2]. [< Welsh; c. Ir *cruit* harp, lyre]

cry (krī), *v.,* **cried, cry·ing,** *n., pl.* **cries.** —*v.i.* **1.** to utter inarticulate sounds, esp. of lamentation, grief, or suffering, usually with tears. **2.** to weep; shed tears, with or without sound. **3.** to call loudly; shout; yell (sometimes fol. by *out*). **4.** to give forth vocal sounds or characteristic calls, as animals; yelp; bark. **5.** (of a hound or pack) to bay continuously and excitedly in following a scent. **6.** (of tin) to make a noise, when bent, like the crumpling of paper. —*v.t.* **7.** to utter or pronounce loudly; call out. **8.** to announce publicly as for sale: *to cry one's wares.* **9.** to beg or plead for; implore: *to cry quarter.* **10.** to bring (oneself) by weeping: *She cried herself to sleep.* **11. all the cry,** the vogue; the latest style; fad: *Elaborate hair styles are all the cry.* **12. cry down,** to disparage; belittle: *She cries down everyone except the rich and educated.* **13. cry havoc.** See **havoc** (def. 2). **14. cry off,** to break a promise, agreement, etc.: *We made arrangements to purchase a house, but the owner cried off at the last minute.* **15. cry one's eyes** or **heart out,** to cry excessively or inconsolably: *The little girl cried her eyes out when her cat was run over by a car.* **16. cry over spilled** or **spilt milk.** See **milk** (def. 4). **17. cry up,** to praise; extol: *to cry up one's profession.* —*n.* **18.** act or sound of crying; any loud utterance or exclamation; a shout, scream, or wail. **19.** clamor; outcry. **20.** an entreaty; appeal. **21.** an oral proclamation or announcement. **22.** a call of wares for sale, services available, etc., as by a street vendor. **23.** public report. **24.** an opinion generally expressed. **25.** See **battle cry. 26.** a political or party slogan. **27.** a fit of weeping: *to have a good cry.* **28.** the utterance or call of an animal. **29.** *Fox Hunting.* **a.** a pack of hounds. **b.** a continuous baying of a hound or a pack in following a scent. **30. a far cry, a.** quite some distance; a long way. **b.** only remotely related; very different: *This treatment is a far cry from that which we received before.* **31. in full cry,** in hot pursuit: *The pack followed in full cry.* [ME *crie(n)* < OF *crie(r)* < VL **crītāre* for L *quirītāre* to cry for aid (from a Roman citizen), deriv. of *Quirīt-* (s. of *Quirīs*) a citizen of Rome, orig. an inhabitant of the Sabine town Cures]

—**Syn. 1.** wail, keen, moan. **2.** sob, bawl, squall, blubber, whimper, mewl, pule. **3.** yell, yowl, bawl, clamor, vociferate, exclaim, ejaculate, scream. CRY, SHOUT, BELLOW, ROAR refer to kinds of loud articulate or inarticulate sounds. CRY is the general word: *to cry out.* To SHOUT is to raise the voice loudly in uttering words or other articulate sounds: *He shouted back to his companions.* BELLOW especially refers to the loud, deep cry of a bull, moose, etc., or, somewhat in deprecation, to human utterance which suggests such a sound: *The speaker bellowed his answer.* ROAR refers to a deep, hoarse, rumbling or vibrant cry; it often implies tumultuous volume: *The crowd roared approval.*

cry·ba·by (krī′bā′bē), *n., pl.* **-bies. 1.** a person who cries readily for very little reason. **2.** a person who complains too much, usually in a whining manner, about losses, defeats, etc. [CRY + BABY]

cry·ing (krī′ing), *adj.* **1.** that cries; clamorous; wailing; weeping. **2.** demanding attention or remedy: *a crying evil.* [ME *cryenge.* See CRY, -ING[2]] —**cry′ing·ly,** *adv.* —**Syn. 2.** flagrant, notorious, urgent. —**Ant. 2.** trifling.

cry·mo·ther·a·py (krī′mō ther′ə pē), *n. Med.* cryotherapy. [< Gk *krȳmó(s)* frost, cold + THERAPY]

cryo-, a learned borrowing from Greek meaning "icy cold," "frost," used in the formation of compound words: *cryogenics.* [< Gk *kryo-* comb. form of *krýos*]

cry·o·gen (krī′ə jən), *n.* a substance for producing low temperatures; freezing mixture. [CRYO- + -GEN]

cry·o·gen·ics (krī′ō jen′iks), *n.* (*construed as sing.*) the branch of physics that deals with very low temperatures. [CRYO- + -GENICS] —**cry′o·gen′ic,** *adj.*

cry·o·hy·drate (krī′ō hī′drāt), *n.* a mixture of ice and another substance in definite proportions such that a minimum melting or freezing point is attained. [CRYO- + HYDRATE] —**cry·o·hy·dric** (krī′ō hī′drik), *adj.*

cry·o·lite (krī′ə līt′), *n.* a mineral, sodium aluminum fluoride, Na_3AlF_6, occurring in white masses, used as a flux in the electrolytic production of aluminum. [CRYO- + -LITE]

cry·ol·o·gy (krī ol′ə jē), *n.* the study of snow and ice. [CRYO- + -LOGY]

cry·om·e·ter (krī om′i tər), *n.* a thermometer for measuring low temperatures. [CRYO- + -METER] —**cry·om′e·try,** *n.*

cry·os·co·py (krī os′kə pē), *n., pl.* **-pies. 1.** the determination of the freezing points of liquids or solutions, or of the lowering of the freezing points by dissolved substances. **2.** *Med.* the determination of the freezing points of certain bodily fluids, as urine, for diagnosis. [CRYO- + -SCOPY] —**cry·o·scop·ic** (krī′ə skop′ik), *adj.*

cry·o·stat (krī′ə stat′), *n.* an apparatus, usually automatic, maintaining a very low constant temperature. [CRYO- + STAT]

cry·o·sur·ger·y (krī′ō sûr′jə rē), *n.* the use of extreme cold to destroy tissue for therapeutic purposes.

cry·o·ther·a·py (krī′ō ther′ə pē), *n. Med.* treatment by means of applications of cold. Also, **crymotherapy.** [CRYO- + THERAPY]

crypt (kript), *n.* **1.** a subterranean chamber or vault, esp. one beneath the main floor of a church, used as a burial place, a location for secret meetings, etc. **2.** *Anat.* a slender pit or recess; a small glandular cavity. [< L *crypt(a)* < Gk *krýptē* hidden place, n. use of fem. of *kryptós* hidden, verbid of *krýptein* to hide] —**crypt′al,** *adj.*

crypt·a·nal·y·sis (krip′tə nal′i sis), *n.* **1.** the procedures, processes, methods, etc., used to translate or interpret secret writings, as codes and ciphers, for which the key is unknown. **2.** the science or study of such procedures; cryptanalytics. Cf. **cryptography** (def. 1). [CRYPT(OGRAM) + ANALYSIS] —**crypt·an·a·lyt·ic** (krip′tan′əlit′ik), *adj.* —**crypt′an·a·lyt′i·cal·ly,** *adv.* —**crypt·an·a·lyst** (krip tan′əlist), *n.*

crypt·an·a·lyt·ics (krip′tan′əlit′iks), *n.* (*construed as sing.*) cryptanalysis (def. 1). [formation from CRYPTANALYSIS, modeled after *analysis, analytics*]

crypt·an·a·lyze (krip tan′əlīz′), *v.t.,* **-lyzed, -lyz·ing.** to study (a cryptogram) for the purpose of discovering the clear meaning; break (a code, cipher, etc.). [back formation from CRYPTANALYSIS]

cryp·tic (krip′tik), *adj.* Also, **cryp′ti·cal. 1.** hidden; secret; occult: *a cryptic writing.* **2.** mysterious; puzzling; ambiguous: *a cryptic message.* **3.** *Zool.* fitted for concealing. **4.** abrupt; terse; short: *a cryptic note.* **5.** involving or using cipher, code, etc. —*n.* **6.** a cryptogram, esp. one designed as a puzzle. [< LL *cryptic(us)* < Gk *kryptikós* hidden. See CRYPT, -IC] —**cryp′ti·cal·ly,** *adv.* —**Syn. 1.** enigmatic, mysterious, perplexing, puzzling.

crypto-, a learned borrowing from Greek meaning "hidden," "secret," used in the formation of compound words: *cryptograph.* [comb. form repr. Gk *kryptós* hidden. See CRYPT]

cryp·to·a·nal·y·sis (krip′tō ə nal′i sis), *n.* cryptanalysis. [CRYPTO- + ANALYSIS] —**cryp·to·an·a·lyt·ic** (krip′tō an′əlit′ik), *adj.* —**cryp′to·an′a·lyt′i·cal·ly,** *adv.* —**cryp·to·an·a·lyst** (krip′tō an′əlist), *n.*

cryp·to·clas·tic (krip′tə klas′tik), *adj. Geol.* composed of fragments invisible to the unaided eye. [CRYPTO- + CLASTIC]

cryp·to·cli·mate (krip′tō klī′mit), *n.* See under **microclimate.** [CRYPTO- + CLIMATE]

cryp·to·cli·ma·tol·o·gy (krip′tō klī′mə tol′ə jē), *n.* See under **microclimatology.** [CRYPTO- + CLIMATOLOGY]

cryp·to·coc·co·sis (krip′tō ko kō′sis), *n. Pathol.* a disease of man and animals caused by the fungus *Cryptococcus neoformans,* which is found chiefly in soil contaminated by pigeon droppings, and characterized by lesions, esp. of the nervous system and lungs. Also called **European blastomycosis, torulosis.** [< NL, equiv. to *Cryptococc(us)* name of the genus (see CRYPTO-, COCCUS) + *-ōsis* -OSIS]

cryp·to·crys·tal·line (krip′tō kris′təlin, -təlīn′), *adj. Mineral.* having a microscopic crystalline structure. [CRYPTO- + CRYSTALLINE]

cryp·to·gam (krip′tə gam′), *n.* **1.** any of the *Cryptogamia,* an old primary division of plants comprising those without true flowers and seeds, as the ferns, mosses, and thallophytes. **2.** a plant without a true seed (opposed to *phanerogam*). [back formation from NL *cryptogamia.* See CRYPTO-, -GAMY] —**cryp′to·gam′ic, cryp·tog·a·mous** (krip tog′ə məs), **cryp′to·gam′i·cal,** *adj.* —**cryp·tog′a·mist,** *n.* —**cryp·tog′a·my,** *n.*

cryp·to·gen·ic (krip′tə jen′ik), *adj.* of obscure or unknown origin, as a disease. [CRYPTO- + -GENIC]

cryp·to·gram (krip′tə gram′), *n.* **1.** a message or writing in code or cipher; cryptograph. **2.** an occult symbol or representation. [CRYPTO- + -GRAM[1]] —**cryp′to·gram′mic, cryp·to·gram·mat·ic** (krip′tə grə mat′ik), **cryp′to·gram·mat′i·cal,** *adj.* —**cryp′to·gram′ma·tist,** *n.*

cryp·to·graph (krip′tə graf′, -gräf′), *n.* **1.** cryptogram (def. 1). **2.** a system of secret writing; cipher. **3.** a device for translating clear text into cipher. [CRYPTO- + -GRAPH]

cryp·tog·ra·phy (krip tog′rə fē), *n.* **1.** the science or study of secret writing, esp. code and cipher systems, methods, and the like. Cf. **cryptanalysis** (def. 1). **2.** the procedures, processes, methods, etc., of making and using secret writing, as codes, ciphers, and the like. **3.** anything written in a secret code, cipher, or the like. [CRYPTO- + -GRAPHY] —**cryp·tog′ra·pher, cryp·tog′ra·phist,** *n.* —**cryp·to·graph·ic** (krip′tə graf′ik), **cryp′to·graph′i·cal, cryp·tog′ra·phal,** *adj.* —**cryp′to·graph′i·cal·ly,** *adv.*

cryp·to·lith (krip′təlith′), *n. Pathol.* a concretion in the follicle of a gland. [CRYPTO- + -LITH]

cryp·tol·o·gy (krip tol′ə jē), *n.* **1.** cryptography. **2.** the science and study of cryptanalysis and cryptography. [< NL *cryptologia.* See CRYPTO-, -LOGY] —**cryp·tol′o·gist,** *n.*

cryp·to·mer·i·a (krip′tə mēr′ē ə), *n.* the Japan cedar, *Cryptomeria japonica.* [< NL; see CRYPTO-, -MERE, -IA]

cryp·tom·e·ter (krip tom′i tər), *n.* an instrument for measuring the degree to which a coat of paint hides the surface beneath. [CRYPTO- + -METER]

cryp·to·nym (krip′tə nim), *n.* a secret name. [CRYPT- + -ONYM]

cryp·ton·y·mous (krip ton′ə məs), *adj.* having a cryptonym; anonymous. [CRYPTONYM + -OUS]

cryp·to·phyte (krip′tə fīt′), *n.* a plant that forms its reproductive structures, as corms or bulbs, underground or underwater. [CRYPTO- + -PHYTE] —**cryp·to·phyt·ic** (krip′tə fit′ik), *adj.*

cryp·to·por·ti·cus (krip′tə pōr′tə kəs, -pôr′-), *n., pl.* **-cus. 1.** a covered passage, as one underground, lighted on one side. **2.** a portico at the entrance to a crypt. [< L: covered passage; see CRYPTO-, PORTICO]

cryp·tor·chid (krip tôr′kid), *Med.* —*adj.* **1.** characterized by or affected with cryptorchidism. —*n.* **2.** Also, **cryp·tor·chis** (krip tôr′kis). a person affected with cryptorchidism. [< NL *cryptorchid-* (s. of *cryptorchis*). See CRYPTO-, ORCHIS]

cryp·tor·chi·dism (krip tôr′ki diz′əm), *n. Med.* failure of one or both testes to descend into the scrotum. Also, **cryp·tor·chism** (krip tôr′kiz əm). [< NL *cryptorchidism(us),* equiv. to *crypt-* CRYPTO- + *orchid-* (< Gk *orchid-;* see ORCHID) + *-ismus* -ISM]

cryp·to·vol·can·ic (krip′tō vol kan′ik), *adj. Geol.* of or pertaining to a rock structure believed to have been produced by volcanic activity that occurred deep within the earth. [CRYPTO- + VOLCANIC] —**cryp·to·vol·can·ism** (krip′tō vol′kə niz′əm), *n.*

cryp·to·zo·ic (krip′tə zō′ik), *adj.* **1.** Precambrian. **2.** *Zool.* living in concealed or secluded places. —*n.* **3.** Precambrian. [CRYPTO- + ZO- + -IC]

cryp·to·zo·ite (krip′tə zō′īt), *n.* a malarial parasite in the stage of development during which it lives in tissue cells prior to invading the blood cells. [CRYPTO- + ZO- + -ITE[1]]

Cryp·to·zo·on (krip′tə zō′on), *n.* an extinct form genus of algae from the Cambrian and Precambrian periods, forming irregular, hemispherical colonies composed of layers of limy precipitate. [< NL; see CRYPTO-, -ZOON]

cryp·to·zy·gous (krip′tə zī′gəs), *adj. Craniol.* having the skull broad and the face narrow. [CRYPTO- + Gk *-zygos* yoked] —**cryp′to·zy′gy,** *n.*

cryst., 1. crystalline. **2.** crystallography.

crys·tal (kris′təl), *n., adj., v.,* **-taled, -tal·ing** or (*esp. Brit.*) **-talled, -tal·ling.** —*n.* **1.** a clear, transparent mineral or glass resembling ice. **2.** the transparent form of crystallized quartz. **3.** *Chem., Mineral.* a solid body having a characteristic internal structure and enclosed by symmetrically arranged plane surfaces, intersecting at definite and characteristic angles. **4.** anything made of or resembling such a substance. **5.** a single grain or mass of a crystalline substance. **6.** glass of a high degree of brilliance. **7.** the glass or plastic cover over the face of a watch. **8.** *Radio.* **a.** the piece of germanium, silicon, galena, or the like, forming the essential part of a crystal detector. **b.** the crystal detector itself. **9.** a quartz crystal ground in the shape of a rectangular parallelepiped, which vibrates strongly at one frequency when electric voltages of that frequency are placed across opposite sides: it is used to control the frequency of an oscillator, as of a radio transmitter. —*adj.* **10.** composed of crystal. **11.** resembling crystal; clear; transparent. **12.** *Radio.* pertaining to or employing a crystal detector. **13.** indicating the 15th event of a series, as a wedding anniversary. —*v.t.* **14.** to make into crystal; crystallize. **15.** to cover or coat with, or as with, crystal (usually fol. by *over*): *The stream had been crystaled over with ice.* [ME *cristal(le),* OE *cristalla* < ML *cristall(um),* L *crystallum* < Gk *krýstallos* clear ice, rock crystal, deriv. of *krystaínein* to freeze] —**crys′tal·like′,** *adj.*

Crys·tal (kris′təl), *n.* **1.** a city in SE Minnesota, near Minneapolis. 24,283 (1960). **2.** Also, **Chrystal.** a girl's given name.

crys′tal ball′, a ball of clear crystal, glass, or the like, used in crystal gazing.

Crys′tal Cit′y, 1. a town in SW Texas. 9101 (1960). **2.** a town in E Missouri. 3678 (1960).

crys′tal detec′tor, *Radio.* a device for rectifying the alternating current in a receiving apparatus, consisting essentially of a crystal of germanium, silicon, galena, or the like, permitting a current to pass freely in one direction only.

crys′tal gaz′ing, the practice of staring into a crystal ball in order to arouse visual perceptions, as of distant happenings, future events, etc. —**crys′tal-gaz·er** (kris′tᵊl gā′zər), *n.*

crystall-, var. of **crystallo-** before a vowel: *crystallite.*

crystall., crystallography.

Crys′tal Lake′, a town in NE Illinois. 8314 (1960).

crys′tal lat′tice, lattice (def. 4).

crystalli-, var. of **crystallo-** before an element of Latin origin: *crystalliferous.*

crys·tal·lif·er·ous (kris′tᵊlif′ər əs), *adj.* bearing, containing, or yielding crystals. Also, **crys·tal·lig·er·ous** (kris′tᵊlij′ər əs). [CRYSTALLI- + -FEROUS]

crys·tal·line (kris′tᵊlin, -tᵊlīn′), *adj.* **1.** of or like crystal; clear; transparent. **2.** formed by crystallization. **3.** composed of crystals, as rocks. **4.** pertaining to crystals or their formation. [< L *crystallin(us)* < Gk *krystállinos.* See CRYSTAL, -INE[1]] —**crys·tal·lin·i·ty** (kris′tᵊlin′i tē), *n.*

crys′talline lens′, *Anat.* a doubly convex, transparent, lenslike body in the eye, situated behind the iris and serving to focus the rays of light on the retina. See diag. under **eye.**

crys·tal·li·sa·tion (kris′tᵊli zā′shən), *n. Chiefly Brit.* crystallization.

crys·tal·lise (kris′tᵊlīz′), *v.t., v.i.,* **-lised, -lis·ing.** *Chiefly Brit.* crystallize. —**crys′tal·lis′a·bil′i·ty,** *n.* —**crys′tal·lis′a·ble,** *adj.*

crys·tal·lite (kris′tᵊlīt′), *n. Mineral.* a minute body in igneous rock, showing incipient crystallization. [CRYSTALL- + -ITE[1]] —**crys·tal·lit·ic** (kris′tᵊlit′ik), *adj.*

crys·tal·li·za·tion (kris′tᵊli zā′shən), *n.* **1.** the act or process of crystallizing. **2.** a crystallized body or formation. Also, *esp. Brit.,* **crystallisation.** [CRYSTALL- + -IZATION]

crys·tal·lize (kris′tᵊlīz′), *v.,* **-lized, -liz·ing.** —*v.t.* **1.** to form into crystals; cause to assume crystalline form. **2.** to give definite or concrete form to: *to crystallize an idea.* **3.** to coat with sugar. —*v.i.* **4.** to form crystals; become crystalline in form. **5.** to assume definite or concrete form. Also, *esp. Brit.,* **crystallise.** [CRYSTALL- + -IZE] —**crys′tal·liz′a·bil′i·ty,** *n.* —**crys′tal·liz′a·ble,** *adj.*

crystallo-, a learned borrowing from Greek meaning "crystal," used in the formation of compound words: *crystallography.* Also, **crystall-, crystalli-.** [< Gk *krystallo-,* comb. form of *krýstallos* CRYSTAL]

crys·tal·lo·graph·ic (kris′tᵊlə graf′ik), *adj.* of, pertaining to, or dealing with crystals or crystallography. Also, **crys′tal·lo·graph′i·cal.** [CRYSTALLO- + -GRAPHIC] —**crys′tal·lo·graph′i·cal·ly,** *adv.*

crys′tallograph′ic ax′is, *Crystall.* the imaginary reference lines passing through the center of an ideal crystal, designated a, b, and c for all crystal systems except the hexagonal.

crys·tal·log·ra·phy (kris′tᵊlog′rə fē), *n.* the science dealing with crystallization and the forms and structure of crystals. [CRYSTALLO- + -GRAPHY] —**crys′tal·log′ra·pher,** *n.*

crys·tal·loid (kris′tᵊloid′), *adj.* **1.** resembling a crystal; of the nature of a crystalloid. —*n.* **2.** a usually crystallizable substance which, when dissolved in a liquid, will diffuse readily through vegetable or animal membranes. Cf. **colloid** (def. 1). **3.** *Bot.* one of certain minute crystallike granules of protein, found in the tissues of various seeds. [< Gk *krystalloeid(ēs).* See CRYSTALL-, -OID] —**crys′tal·loi′dal,** *adj.*

Crys·tal·lose (kris′tᵊlōs′), *n. Trademark.* See **saccharin sodium.**

Crys′tal Pal′ace, **1.** a structure of prefabricated iron units, glass, and wood, built at London to house the Exhibition of 1851: moved and enlarged 1854, destroyed by fire 1936. **2.** any of several iron-and-glass exhibition buildings in imitation of this.

crys′tal pick′up, a phonograph pickup that generates an electric current through deformation by the stylus of a substance having piezoelectric properties, as a crystal. Cf. **magnetic pickup.**

crys′tal set′, *Radio.* a tubeless receiving set with a crystal detector.

Crys′tal Springs′, a town in SW Mississippi. 4496 (1960).

crys′tal sys′tem, *Crystall.* any of the six main classifications of crystals and of crystal lattices according to their symmetry.

crys′tal tea′. See **wild rosemary.**

crys′tal vi′olet. See **gentian violet.**

crys′tal vi′sion, **1.** visual perception, as of distant happenings, the future, etc., supposed to be aroused by crystal gazing. **2.** that which seems to be perceived; the vision itself.

Cs, *Chem.* cesium.

cS, centistoke. Also, **cs**

cs., case; cases.

C.S., **1.** Christian Science. **2.** civil service. **3.** Confederate States.

c.s., **1.** capital stock. **2.** civil service.

C.S.A., Confederate States of America.

CSC, Civil Service Commission.

csc, cosecant.

csch, hyperbolic cosecant.

C-scroll (sē′skrōl′), *n.* an ornamental motif in the form of the letter C, used chiefly on furniture.

csk., cask.

CSO, See **Commissioners Standard Ordinary Table.**

C.S.O., **1.** Chief Signal Officer. **2.** Chief Staff Officer. **3.** See **Commissioners Standard Ordinary Table.**

CST, Central Standard Time. Also, **C.S.T.**

C supply, *Electronics.* a battery or other source of power for supplying a constant voltage bias to a control electrode of a vacuum tube. Also called **C power supply.** Cf. **A supply, B supply.**

Ct., **1.** Connecticut. **2.** Count.

ct., **1.** carat. **2.** cent. **3.** centum. **4.** certificate. **5.** county. **6.** court.

C.T., Central Time.

C.T.A., *Law.* with the will annexed: *an administrator C.T.A.* [< L *cum testamentō annexō*]

CTC, Citizens' Training Corps.

Cte·a·tus (tē′ə təs), *n.* (in the *Iliad*) a son of Actor and Molione. Cf. **Molionidae.**

cte·nid·i·um (ti nid′ē əm), *n., pl.* **-nid·i·a** (-nid′ē ə). *Zool.* any of various comblike or featherlike structures, as the row of stiff bristles on the legs of a psocid. [< NL; see CTENO-, -IDIUM] —**cte·nid′i·al,** *adj.*

cten·i·zid (ten′i zid), *n.* **1.** a spider of the family *Ctenizidae,* comprising the trap-door spiders. —*adj.* **2.** belonging or pertaining to the family *Ctenizidae.* [< NL *Ctenizid(ae)* name of the family < Gk *ktenìz(ein)* (to) comb (see CTENO-) + NL *-idae* -ID[2]]

cteno-, a learned borrowing from Greek meaning "comb," used in the formation of compound words: *Ctenophora.* [< Gk *kteno-,* comb. form of *kteis* comb (gen. *ktenós*)]

cte·noid (tē′noid, ten′oid), *adj. Zool.* **1.** comblike or pectinate; rough-edged. **2.** having rough-edged scales. [< Gk *ktenoeid(ēs)* like a comb. See CTEN(O)-, -OID]

Cte·noph·o·ra (ti nof′ər ə), *n.* the phylum comprising the ctenophores. [< NL, neut. pl. of *ctenophorus* CTENOPHORE]

cte·noph·o·ran (ti nof′ər ən), *n.* **1.** ctenophore. —*adj.* **2.** Also, **cten·o·phor·ic** (ten′ə fôr′ik), **cte·noph·o·rous** (ti nof′ər əs). belonging or pertaining to the *Ctenophora.* [CTENOPHOR(A) + -AN]

cten·o·phore (ten′ə fôr′, -fōr′, tē′nə-), *n.* any marine, swimming invertebrate of the phylum *Ctenophora,* having rounded, oval, or band-shaped, gelatinous bodies and eight meridional rows of ciliated plates; a comb jelly. [< NL *ctenophor(us).* See CTENO-, -PHORE]

Ctes·i·phon (tes′ə fon′), *n.* a ruined city in Iraq, on the Tigris, near Baghdad: an ancient capital of Parthia.

Cte·sip·pus (ti sip′əs), *n. Class. Myth.* **1.** a son of Hercules. **2.** (in the *Odyssey*) one of Penelope's suitors.

Cte·si·us (tē′sē əs), *n. Class. Myth.* an epithet of Zeus, meaning "god of gain."

ctg., cartridge.

ctn, cotangent.

ctr., center.

cts., **1.** centimes. **2.** cents. **3.** certificates.

CT scan′ner. See **CAT scanner.**

CU, close-up.

Cu, *Chem.* copper. [< L *cuprum*]

Cu., cumulus.

cu., **1.** cubic. **2.** cumulus.

cua·dri·lla (kwä drē′yə, -drēl′yə; *Sp.* kwä thrē′lyä, -thrē′yä), *n., pl.* **-dri·llas** (-drē′yəz, -drēl′yəz; *Sp.* -thrē′lyäs, -thrē′yäs). the group of assistants serving a matador in a bullfight, consisting of three banderilleros and two picadors. [< Sp: group, gang (orig. one of four groups), dim. of *cuadra* < L *quadra* something square]

cua·mu·chil (kwə mo͞o′chil), *n.* guamachil.

cub (kub), *n.* **1.** the young of certain animals, as the fox, bear, etc. **2.** a young and inexperienced person, esp. a callow, youth or young man. **3.** a young person serving as an apprentice. **4.** See **cub scout. 5.** *Aeron.* any small, light monoplane with a high wing, a single engine, and an enclosed cabin. [perh. < Scand; cf. Icel *kobbi* young seal, *kubbr* stump, hence, short, thick-set person] —**cub′bish,** *adj.* —**cub′bish·ly,** *adv.* —**cub′bish·ness,** *n.*

cub., cubic.

Cu·ba (kyo͞o′bə; *Sp.* ko͞o′vä), *n.* a republic in the Caribbean, S of Florida: largest island in the West Indies. 6,743,000 (est. 1960); 44,218 sq. mi. *Cap.:* Havana. —**Cu′ban,** *adj., n.*

cub·age (kyo͞o′bij), *n.* cubic content, displacement, or volume. [CUBE[1] + -AGE]

Cu·ba li·bre (kyo͞o′bə lē′brə), a drink consisting of rum and a kola drink. [< Sp: lit., free Cuba (a toast once given with the drink by revolutionists)]

Cu′ban heel′, a broad heel of medium height, straight in front and slightly tapered toward the bottom in the rear, used on women's shoes.

Cu′ban lil′y, a showy squill, *Scilla peruviana,* of the Mediterranean region, having purple or reddish flowers.

Cu′ban pine′, a tree, *Pinus caribaea,* of the southeastern U.S. and the Caribbean area, having glossy needles and black seeds in cones with prickle-tipped scales.

Cu′ban roy′al palm′, a feather palm, *Roystonea regia,* of tropical America, having drooping leaves from 10 to 15 feet long and small, round fruit.

cu·ba·ture (kyo͞o′bə chər), *n.* **1.** the determination of the cubic contents of a thing. **2.** cubic contents. [CUBE[1] + *-ature,* after *quadrature*]

cub·bing (kub′ing), *n. Chiefly Brit.* See **cub hunting.** [CUB + -ING[1]]

cub·by (kub′ē), *n., pl.* **-bies.** a cubbyhole. [dial. *cub* stall, shed (akin to COVE[1]) + -Y[2]]

cub·by·hole (kub′ē hōl′), *n.* a small, snug place, room, or cabin. [CUBBY + HOLE]

cub·by·u (kub′ē yo͞o′), *n.* a sciaenid fish, *Equetus acuminatus,* found among coral reefs. [var. of *cobia* kind of fish < ?]

cube[1] (kyo͞ob), *n., v.,* **cubed, cub·ing.** —*n.* **1.** a solid bounded by six equal squares, the angle between any two adjacent faces being a right angle. **2.** a cubical piece of anything: *a cube of cheese.* **3.** *Math.* the third power of a quantity, expressed as $a^3 = a \cdot a \cdot a$. **4.** *Slang.* one of a pair of dice; die. —*v.t.* **5.** to make into a cube or cubes. **6.** to measure the cubic contents of. **7.** *Math.* to raise to the third power. **8.** to tenderize (a thin cut or slice of meat) by scoring the fibers in a pattern of squares. [ME *cub(us)* < LL < Gk *kýbos* cube, die] —**cub′er,** *n.*

Cube

cu·be[2] (kyo͞o′bā), *n.* any of several tropical, leguminous plants used in making fish poisons and insecticides. [< AmerSp *cubé* < ?]

cu·beb (kyo͞o′beb), *n.* the spicy fruit or drupe of an East Indian, piperaceous, climbing shrub, *Piper Cubeba,* dried in an unripe but fully grown state and used in the treatment of urinary and bronchial disorders. [< ML *cubēb(a)* < Ar *kubābah* (classical Ar *kabābah*); r. ME *cucube, quibibe* < MF]

cube′ root′, *Math.* a quantity of which a given quantity is the cube: *The cube root of 64 is 4.*

cube′ steak′, a square or round cut of beef tenderized by cubing. Also, **cubed′ steak′.**

cub′ hunt′ing, the hunting of fox cubs using puppies and trained hounds, practiced for the purpose of training the puppies and for scattering or thinning the litters of fox cubs. Also, **cub′-hunt′ing,** *esp. Brit.,* **cubbing.**

cu·bic (kyo͞o′bik), *adj.* **1.** having three dimensions; solid. **2.** having the form of a cube; cubical. **3.** pertaining to the measurement of volume: *the cubic contents of a vessel.* **4.** pertaining to a unit of linear measure that is multiplied by itself twice to form a unit of measure for volume: *a cubic foot; a cubic centimeter.* **5.** *Math.* of or pertaining to the third degree. **6.** *Crystall.* belonging or pertaining to the isometric system of crystallization. —*n.* **7.** *Math.* a cubic polynomial or equation. [late ME *cubike* < L *cubic(us)* < Gk *kybikos.* See CUBE[1], -IC] —**cu·bic·i·ty** (kyo͞o bis′i tē), *n.*

cu·bi·cal (kyo͞o′bi kəl), *adj.* **1.** having the form of a cube. **2.** of or pertaining to volume. [CUBIC + -AL[1]] —**cu′bi·cal·ly,** *adv.* —**cu′bi·cal·ness,** *n.*

cu·bi·cle (kyo͞o′bi kəl), *n.* **1.** a bedroom, esp. one of a number of small ones in a divided dormitory, as in English public schools. **2.** any small space or compartment partitioned off. **3.** carrel. [late ME < L *cubicul(um)* bed chamber, equiv. to *cub(āre)* (to) lie down + *-i-* -I- + *-culum* -CLE]

cu′bic meas′ure, **1.** the measurement of volume or space, by means of cubic units. **2.** a system of such units, esp. that in which 1728 cubic inches = 1 cubic foot, and 27 cubic feet = 1 cubic yard.

cu·bic·u·lum (kyo͞o bik′yə ləm), *n., pl.* **-la** (-lə). *Archaeol.* a burial chamber, as in catacombs. [< L: bed chamber. See CUBICLE]

cu′bic u′nit, a three-dimensional unit or standard of measure; a unit of measurement for volume or space: *a cubic mile; a cubic centimeter.*

cu·bi·form (kyo͞o′bə fôrm′), *adj.* shaped like a cube. [CUBE[1] + -I- + -FORM]

Cub·ism (kyo͞o′biz əm), *n.* (*often l.c.*) *Fine Arts.* a style of painting and sculpture developed in the early 20th century, characterized chiefly by an emphasis on the formal structure of a work of art, the reduction of natural forms to their geometrical equivalents, and the organization of the planes of a represented object independently of representational requirements. Cf. **Analytical Cubism, Synthetic Cubism.** [CUBE[1] + -ISM] —**cub′ist,** *n.* —**cu·bis′tic,** *adj.* —**cu·bis′ti·cal·ly,** *adv.*

cu·bit (kyo͞o′bit), *n.* an ancient linear unit based on th length of the forearm, usually from 17 to 21 inches. [ME, OE < L *cubit(um)* elbow, cubit, special use of neut. of *cubitus,* ptp. of *cubāre* to lie down]

cu·bi·tal (kyo͞o′bi tᵊl), *adj.* **1.** *Anat., Zool.* pertaining to, involving, or situated near the cubitus. —*n.* **2.** *Ornith. Rare.* a secondary feather. [late ME < L *cubitāl(is).* See CUBIT, -AL[1]]

cu′bital fur′row, (in certain insects) a crease, between the cubital and anal veins, along which the wing folds.

cu·bi·tiere (kyo͞o′bi tyâr′), *n. Armor.* couter.

cu·bi·tus (kyo͞o′bi təs), *n., pl.* **-ti** (-tī′). **1.** a longitudinal vein in the rear portion of the wing of an insect. **2.** *Anat.* **a.** the forearm. **b.** *Rare.* the ulna. [< NL, L, var. of *cubitum* CUBIT]

cub·mas·ter (kub′mas′tər, -mä′stər), *n.* the man who supervises a cub-scout pack. [CUB + MASTER]

cu·boid (kyo͞o′boid), *adj.* Also, **cu·boi′dal. 1.** resembling a cube in form. **2.** *Anat.* noting or pertaining to the outermost bone of the distal row of tarsal bones. —*n.* **3.** *Math.* a rectangular parallelepiped. **4.** *Anat.* the cuboid bone. [< Gk *kyboeid(ēs)* cubelike. See CUBE[1], -OID]

cuboi′dal epithe′lium, *Biol.* epithelium consisting of one or more layers of cells of cuboid or polyhedral shape.

cub′ report′er, a young person apprenticing as a newspaper reporter.

cub′ scout′, a member of the junior division (ages 8–11) of the Boy Scouts.

cub′ shark′. See **bull shark.**

Cu·chul·ainn (ko͞o kul′in, ko͞o′kho͝o lin), *n. Irish Legend.* a hero of Ulster and the subject of many legends. Also, **Cu·chul′lain.**

cuck′ing stool′ (kuk′ing), a former instrument of punishment consisting of a chair in which an offender was strapped, to be jeered at and pelted by his neighbors, or, sometimes, to be ducked. [ME *cucking stol,* lit., defecating stool, equiv. to *cucking,* prp. of *cukken* to defecate (< Scand; cf. dial Sw *kukka*) + *stol* STOOL]

cuck·old (kuk′əld), *n.* **1.** the husband of an unfaithful wife. —*v.t.* **2.** to make a cuckold of (a husband). [ME *cokewold, cukeweld*] —**cuck′old·ly,** *adv.*

cuck·old·ry (kuk′əl drē), *n.* **1.** the act of making one a cuckold. **2.** the state or quality of being a cuckold. [CUCKOLD + -RY]

cuck′old's knot′, *Naut.* a hitch, as for holding a spar, consisting of a single loop with the overlapping parts of the rope seized together. Also called **cuck′old's neck′, ring seizing, throat seizing.** [so called because the noose so made is insecure]

cuck·oo (ko͞o′ko͞o, ko͝ok′o͞o), *n., pl.* **-oos,** *v.,* **-ooed, -oo·ing,** *adj.* —*n.* **1.** a common, European bird, *Cuculus canorus,* of the family *Cuculidae,* noted for its characteristic call and its habit of laying its eggs in the nests of other birds, which hatch and rear the young cuckoos. **2.** any of several other birds of the family *Cuculidae.* **3.** the call of the cuckoo, or an imitation of it. **4.** a fool; simpleton. —*v.i.* **5.** to utter the call of the cuckoo or an imitation of it. —*v.t.* **6.** to repeat monotonously. —*adj.* **7.** *Slang.* crazy; silly; foolish. **8.** of, pertaining to, or like a cuckoo. [ME *cuc(c)u, cuccuk(e)* (imit.); cf. L *cucūlus,* F *coucou,* G *Kuckuk,* D *koekoek,* ModGk *koúko,* etc.]

cuck′oo clock′, a clock which announces the hours by a sound like the call of the cuckoo, often accompanied by the appearance of an imitation bird through a little door.

cuck·oo·flow·er (ko͞o′ko͞o flou′ər, ko͝ok′o͞o-), *n.* any of various plants, as the lady's-smock or the ragged robin. [CUCKOO + FLOWER, so called because it is found in bloom when the cuckoo is heard]

cuck·oo·pint (kōō′kōō pīnt′, kŏŏk′ōō-), *n.* a common European arum, *Arum maculatum.* Also called **lords-and-ladies.** [apocopated var. of obs. *cuckoopintle,* late ME *cokkupyntel* (see CUCKOO, PINTLE); its spadix is pintle shaped]

cuck·oo-shrike (kōō′kōō shrīk′, kŏŏk′ōō-), *n.* any of numerous Old World, passerine birds of the family *Campephagidae,* certain species of which superficially resemble cuckoos and have hooked bills like shrikes.

cuck·oo-spit (kōō′kōō spit′, kŏŏk′ōō-), *n.* **1.** a frothy secretion found on plants, exuded as a protective covering by the young of certain insects, as the froghoppers. **2.** an insect that produces this secretion. [late ME *cokkowespitle* cuckoopint; so called from the spitlike secretion found on the plant and thought to be left by the bird]

cuck′oo wasp′, any of several small, metallic green or blue wasps of the family *Chrysididae* that deposit their eggs in nests of other wasps.

cu. cm., cubic centimeter; cubic centimeters.

cu·cu·li·form (kyōō kyōō′lə fôrm′), *adj.* pertaining to or resembling the order *Cuculiformes,* comprising the cuckoos, roadrunners, anis, etc. [< L *cucūl(us)* cuckoo + -I- + -FORM]

cu·cul·late (kyōō′kə lāt′, kyōō kul′āt), *adj.* **1.** cowled; hooded. **2.** resembling a cowl or hood. Also, **cu·cul·lat·ed** (kyōō′kə lā′tid, kyōō kul′ā-). [< LL *cucullāt(us)* hooded, having a hood, equiv. to L *cucull(us)* a covering, hood + *-ātus* -ATE[1]] —**cu′cul·late′ly,** *adv.*

cu·cum·ber (kyōō′kum bər), *n.* **1.** a creeping plant, *Cucumis sativus,* occurring in many cultivated forms. **2.** the edible, fleshy, usually long, cylindrical fruit of this plant. **3.** any of various allied or similar plants. **4.** the fruit of any such plant. [late ME *cucumbre,* ME, OE *cucumer* < L *cucumer-* (s. of *cucumis*) < ?]

cu′cumber bee′tle, any leaf beetle of the genus *Diabrotica* and related genera that feeds on cucumbers and other cucurbitaceous plants and is a vector of cucurbit wilt.

cu′cumber tree′, **1.** any of several American magnolias, esp. *Magnolia acuminata.* **2.** any of certain other trees, as an East Indian tree of the genus *Averrhoa.* [so called from the resemblance of its fruit to cucumbers]

cu·cu·mi·form (kyōō kyōō′mə fôrm′), *adj.* shaped like a cucumber; approximately cylindrical, with rounded or tapering ends. [< L *cucumi(s)* cucumber + -FORM]

cu·cur·bit (kyōō kûr′bit), *n.* **1.** a gourd. **2.** any cucurbitaceous plant. **3.** *Chem.* a gourd-shaped, matrass-like vessel formerly used in distilling. [ME *cucurbit(a)* gourd < L]

cu·cur·bi·ta·ceous (kyōō kûr′bi tā′shəs), *adj.* belonging to the *Cucurbitaceae,* or gourd family of plants, which includes the pumpkin, squash, cucumber, muskmelon, watermelon, etc. [CUCURBIT + -ACEOUS; cf. NL *Cucurbitāceae* gourd family]

cucur′bit wilt′, *Plant Pathol.* a disease of cucumbers and other cucurbitaceous plants, characterized by wilted leaves, caused by a bacterium, *Erwinia tracheiphila.*

Cú·cu·ta (kōō′kōō tä′), *n.* a city in E Colombia. 142,230 (est. 1961).

cud (kud), *n.* **1.** the portion of food which a ruminant returns from the first stomach to the mouth to chew a second time. **2. chew one's** or **the cud,** to meditate on; muse; ruminate: *He didn't reply immediately, but seemed rather to be chewing his cud.* [ME; OE *cudu,* var. of *curidu, cwidu;* akin to OHG *quiti* glue, Skt *jatu* resin, gum. See QUID[1]]

cu·da (kōō′də), *n. Slang.* a barracuda. [by aphesis]

Cud·a·hy (kud′ə hē), *n.* a city in SE Wisconsin, near Milwaukee. 17,975 (1960).

cud·bear (kud′bâr′), *n.* a violet coloring matter obtained from various lichens, esp. *Lecanora tartarea.* [coinage based on his own name by Dr. *Cuthbert* Gordon, 18th-century Scottish chemist; see CUDDY[2]]

cud·dle (kud′əl), *v.,* **-dled, -dling,** *n.* —*v.t.* **1.** to draw or hold close in an affectionate manner; hug tenderly; fondle. —*v.i.* **2.** to lie close and snug; nestle; curl up in going to sleep. —*n.* **3.** act of cuddling; hug; embrace. [? back formation from ME *cudliche* intimate, affectionate, OE *cūthlīc,* or from ME *cuthlechen,* OE *cūthlǣcan* to make friends with] —**cud·dle·some** (kud′əl səm), **cud′dly,** *adj.*
—**Syn. 1.** caress. **2.** snuggle.

cud·dy[1] (kud′ē), *n., pl.* **-dies. 1.** a small room, cabin, or enclosed space at the bow or stern of a vessel, esp. one under the poop. **2.** a galley or pantry in a small vessel. **3.** a small locker in an open boat, esp. one at the bow. **4.** a small room, cupboard, or closet. **5.** (on a fishing boat) a platform on which a net is coiled when not in use. [?]

cud·dy[2] (kud′ē, kŏŏd′ē), *n., pl.* **-dies.** *Chiefly Scot.* **1.** a donkey. **2.** a stupid fellow. [? special use of *Cuddy,* short for *Cuthbert,* man's name]

cud·dy[3] (kud′ē), *n., pl.* **-dies,** (*esp. collectively*) **-dy.** *Chiefly Scot.* **1.** a coalfish, esp. a young or small one. **2.** a hedge sparrow. [< ScotGael *cudaig,* c. *cudainn* young coalfish]

cudg·el (kuj′əl), *n., v.,* **-eled, -el·ing,** or (*esp. Brit.*) **-elled, -el·ling.** —*n.* **1.** a short, thick stick used as a weapon; club. **2. take up the cudgels,** to undertake a defense; come to the aid of something: *Several faculty members took up the cudgels for a revision of the policy on admissions.* —*v.t.* **3.** to strike with a cudgel; beat. **4. cudgel one's brains,** to try to comprehend or remember something; think hard: *I cudgeled my brains to recall her name.* [ME *cuggel,* OE *cycgel;* akin to G *Kugel* ball] —**cudg′el·er;** *esp. Brit.,* **cud′gel·ler,** *n.*

cud·weed (kud′wēd′), *n.* **1.** any of the woolly, composite herbs of the genus *Gnaphalium.* **2.** any of various plants of allied genera. [CUD + WEED[1]]

cue[1] (kyōō), *n., v.,* **cued, cu·ing.** —*n.* **1.** *Theat.* anything said or done, on or behind the stage, that is followed by a specific line or action: *An off-stage door slam was his cue to enter.* **2.** a hint; intimation; guiding suggestion. **3.** the part one is to play; a prescribed or necessary course of action. **4.** anything that excites to action; stimulus. **5.** *Archaic.* frame of mind; mood. **6. miss a cue, a.** to fail to respond to a cue. **b.** *Informal.* to miss the point: *You could tell by his expression that he had missed a cue.* —*v.t.* **7.** to provide with a cue or indication; give a cue to: *Will you cue me on my lines?* **8.** to insert, or direct to come in, in a specific place in a musical or dramatic performance (usually fol. by *in* or *into*): *to cue in a lighting effect; to cue in a violin section.* **9. cue (someone) in,** *Informal.* to inform; give instructions, information, news, etc., to: *Cue him in on the plans for the dance.* [name of the letter *q* as an abbreviation (found in acting scripts) of L *quando* when]

cue[2] (kyōō), *n., v.,* **cued, cu·ing.** —*n.* **1.** a long, tapering rod, tipped with a soft leather pad, used to strike the ball in billiards, pool, etc. **2.** a long, usually wooden stick with a concave head, used to propel the disks in shuffleboard. **3.** a queue of hair. **4.** a queue or file, as of persons awaiting their turn. —*v.t.* **5.** to tie into a queue or tail. [< F *queue* tail, OF *coue* < L *cōda,* var. of *cauda* tail; see COWARD]

cue′ ball′, *Billiards, Pool.* the ball struck by the cue as distinguished from the other balls on the table. [CUE[2] + BALL[1]]

cue′ bid′, *Bridge.* a bid in a suit showing control of the suit, as having an assured winner or a void.

cue-bid (kyōō′bid′), *v.,* **-bid, -bid·den** or **-bid, -bid·ding.** —*v.t.* **1.** to show control of (a suit) by a cue bid. —*v.i.* **2.** to make a cue bid.

cue·ca (kwā′kə; *Sp.* kwe′kä), *n., pl.* **-cas** (-kəz; *Sp.* -käs). a courtship dance of Chile. [< AmerSp, aph. var. of *zamercueca*]

cue·ist (kyōō′ist), *n.* a billiard player. [CUE[2] + -IST]

Cuen·ca (kweng′kä), *n.* a city in SW Ecuador. 66,860 (est. 1959).

Cue·ro (kwâr′ō), *n.* a town in S Texas. 7338 (1960).

cue′ sheet′, a detailed listing of cues for use by a stage manager or the technicians during the production of a play, radio broadcast, television program, etc.

cues·ta (kwes′tə), *n. U.S.* a long low ridge with a relatively steep face or escarpment on one side and a long, gentle slope on the other. [< Sp: shoulder, sloping land < L *costa* side (of a hill), rib; see COAST]

cuff[1] (kuf), *n.* **1.** a fold, band, or variously shaped piece serving as a trimming or finish for the bottom of a sleeve. **2.** a turned-up fold, as at the bottom of a trouser leg. **3.** the part of a gauntlet or long glove that extends over the wrist. **4.** a separate or detachable band or piece of linen or other material worn about the wrist, inside or outside of the sleeve. **5.** an elasticized, ribbed, or reinforced band at the top of a sock or stocking. **6.** a band of leather or other material, wider than a collar, sewed around the outside of the top of a shoe or boot to serve as a trimming or finish. **7.** a handcuff. **8.** *Furniture.* a horizontal strip of veneer used as an ornament on a leg. **9. off the cuff,** *Slang.* **a.** extemporaneously; on the spur of the moment. **b.** imparting information unofficially or informally: *I'm giving this to you strictly off the cuff.* **10. on the cuff,** *Slang.* **a.** with the promise of future payment; on credit. **b.** without charge; with no payment expected: *He enjoyed his meal the more because it was on the cuff.* —*v.t.* **11.** to make a cuff or cuffs on: *to cuff a pair of trousers.* **12.** to put handcuffs on. [ME *cuffe* mitten, OE *cuffie* cap < ML *cuphia* COIF]

cuff[2] (kuf), *v.t.* **1.** to strike with the open hand; beat; buffet. —*n.* **2.** a blow with the fist or the open hand; buffet. [? < Scand; cf. Sw *kuffa* to thrust]

cuff′ but′ton, the button for a shirt cuff.

cuff′ link′, a pair of linked buttons or a piece of jewelry for fastening the cuff, esp. a French cuff, of a shirt. Also called, *esp. Brit.,* **sleeve link.**

Cu·fic (kyōō′fik), *adj., n.* Kufic.

cu. ft., cubic foot; cubic feet.

Cu·i (*Fr.* kʏ ē′), *n.* **Cé·sar** (*Fr.* sā zar′) **An·to·no·vich** (än tô′no vich), 1835–1918, Russian composer.

Cu·ia·bá (kōō′yə bä′), *n.* **1.** a river in SW Brazil. ab. 300 mi. **2.** a port in W Brazil, on the Cuiabá River. 45,875 (1960). Also, **Cuyabá.**

cu·i bo·no (kōō′ē bō′nō; *Eng.* kwē′ bō′nō, kī′-), *Latin.* **1.** for whose benefit? **2.** for what use? of what good?

Cui·cuil·co (kwē kwēl′kō), *n.* a massive oval mound near Tlalpan, Mexico, erected by a prehistoric people.

cu·ié·jo (kōō yā′hō), *n., pl.* **-jos.** the pauraque. [m. AmerSp *cuyeo*]

cuif (kōōf, kœf), *n. Scot. and North Eng.* coof.

cu. in., cubic inch; cubic inches.

cui·rass (kwi ras′), *n.* **1.** Also called **corselet.** defensive armor for the torso comprising a breastplate and backplate, originally made of leather. **2.** either of the plates forming such armor. **3.** any similar covering, as the protective armor of a ship. **4.** *Zool.* a hard shell or other covering forming an indurated defensive shield. —*v.t.* **5.** to equip or cover with a cuirass. [< F *cuirasse* < LL *coriācea,* n. use of fem. of *coriāceus* (adj.) leathern, equiv. to L *cori(um)* leather + *-āceus* -ACEOUS; r. late ME *curas* < MF *curasse,* var. of *cuirasse*]

cui·ras·sier (kwēr′ə sēr′), *n.* a cavalry soldier wearing a cuirass. [< F; see CUIRASS, -ER[2]]

cuir-bouil·li (kwēr bōō yē′), *n. French.* leather hardened by soaking it in hot water or heated wax and allowing it to dry, often after being molded or pressed into a specific shape, as for armor, bookbindings, etc. [lit., boiled leather]

cuir·ie (kwēr′ē), *n. Armor.* a piece for protecting the breast, worn over mail and made of *cuir-bouilli.* [late ME *quyrre* < OF *quiree, quirie, cuirie;* see CUIRASS]

cui·sine (kwi zēn′), *n.* **1.** a style or quality of cooking; cookery: *This restaurant has an excellent cuisine.* **2.** *Archaic.* the kitchen or culinary department of a house, hotel, etc. [< F: lit., kitchen < LL *coquīn(a);* see KITCHEN]

cuisse (kwis), *n. Armor.* a piece of armor or padding for defending the thigh. Also, **cuish** (kwish). See diag. under **armor.** [back formation from *cuisses* (pl.), ME *quyssewes, quysseaux* < MF *cuisseaux* thigh pieces, equiv. to *cuisse* thigh (< L *coxa* hipbone) + *-eaux,* pl. of *-el* n. suffix]

cui·tle (kōōt′əl, kut′-), *v.t.,* **-tled, -tling.** *Scot.* cuittle.

cuit·tle (kʏ′təl), *v.t.,* **-tled, -tling.** *Scot.* to wheedle, cajole, or coax. [?]

cui-ui (kwē′wē), *n.* a fresh-water sucker, *Chasmistes cujus,* of Nevada, having a thin-lipped mouth. [< AmerInd (north)]

cuj., (in prescriptions) of which; of any. [< L *cūjus*]

Cu·kor (kōō′kər, -kôr, kyōō′-), *n.* **George,** born 1899, U.S. motion-picture director.

Cul·bert·son (kul′bərt sən), *n.* **E·ly** (ē′lī), 1893–1955, U.S. authority and writer on contract bridge.

culch (kulch), *n.* **1.** the stones, old shells, etc., forming an oyster bed and furnishing points of attachment for the spawn of oysters. **2.** the spawn. **3.** *Dial.* rubbish; refuse. —*v.t.* **4.** to prepare (an oyster bed) with culch. Also, **cultch.** [perh. metathetic var. of CLUTCH; but note OF *culche* COUCH]

Cul·dee (kul′dē), *n.* a member of a monastic community, never canonically organized, that appeared in Ireland and Scotland from about the 8th to 10th centuries. [< NL *Culdei* (pl.), repr. *Cultōres Deī* worshipers of God, alter. of ML *keldei* < OIr *cēle dé,* equiv. to *cēle* vassal + *dé* of God (gen. of *dia* God)]

cul de lampe (kul′ də lamp′; *Fr.* kʏdə länp′), *pl.* **culs de lampe** (kulz′ də lamp′; *Fr.* kʏdə länp′). **1.** a small corbel having a form approximating an inverted pyramid or cone. **2.** a pyramidal or conical termination to a pendant. [< F: lit., lamp bottom]

cul-de-sac (kul′də sak′, -sak′, kŏŏl′-; *Fr.* kʏdə-sak′), *n., pl.* **culs-de-sac** (kulz′də sak′, -sak′, kŏŏlz′-; *Fr.* kʏdə sak′). **1.** saclike cavity, tube, or the like, open only at one end, as the caecum. **2.** a street, lane, etc., closed at one end; blind alley. **3.** *Mil.* the situation of a military force hemmed in on all sides except behind. **4.** any situation in which further progress is impossible. [< F: lit., bottom of the sack]

-cule, a suffix with the meaning "small," occurring in loan words from Latin (*ridicule*); used as a diminutive in the formation of compound words: *animalcule.* Also, **-cle, -culum, -culus.** [repr. L *-culus, -cula, -culum* dim. suffix]

Cu·le′bra Cut′ (kōō lā′brə; *Sp.* kōō le′vrä), former name of **Gaillard Cut.**

cu·let (kyōō′lit), *n.* **1.** *Jewelry.* a small face forming the bottom of a faceted gem. **2.** *Armor.* a piece below the backplate, composed of lames and corresponding to the fauld in front. [< F (obs.), equiv. to *cul* bottom (< L *cūl(us)* buttocks) + *-et* -ET]

cu·lex (kyōō′leks), *n., pl.* **-li·ces** (-li sēz′). any mosquito of the genus *Culex,* as the common house mosquito, *C. pipiens.* [< L: gnat, midge]

Cu·lia·cán (kōō′lyä kän′), *n.* a city in W Mexico. 48,963 (1960).

cu·lic·id (kyōō lis′id), *n.* **1.** any of numerous dipterous insects of the family *Culicidae,* comprising the mosquitoes. —*adj.* **2.** belonging or pertaining to the family *Culicidae.* [back formation from NL *Culicidae* name of the family, equiv. to L *culic-* (s. of *culex*) CULEX + *-idae* -IDAE]

cu·li·nar·i·an (kyōō′lə nâr′ē ən, kul′ə-), *n.* a cook or chef. [CULINARY + -AN]

cu·li·nar·y (kyōō′lə ner′ē, kul′ə-), *adj.* pertaining to or used in the kitchen or cookery. [< L *culīnāri(us)* of the kitchen, equiv. to L *culīn(a)* kitchen, food + *-ārius* -ARY] —**cu′li·nar′i·ly,** *adv.*

Cu·lion (kōō lyōn′), *n.* an island of the Philippines, in the W part of the group, N of Palawan: leper colony. 150 sq. mi.

cull[1] (kul), *v.t.* **1.** to choose; select; pick; gather the choice things or parts from. **2.** to collect; gather; pluck. —*n.* **3.** act of culling. **4.** something culled, esp. something picked out and put aside as inferior. [ME *cul(en)* (late ME *culle*) < OF *cuill(ir)* < L *colligere* to gather; see COLLECT[1]] —**cull′er,** *n.*
—**Syn. 4.** reject.

cull[2] (kul), *n. Brit. Dial.* dupe; fool. [perh. shortened from CULLY]

Cul·len (kul′ən), *n.* **1. Coun·tee** (koun tā′), 1903–46, U.S. poet. **2.** a boy's given name.

cul·len·der (kul′ən dər), *n.* colander.

cul·let (kul′it), *n.* broken or waste glass suitable for remelting. [var. of *collet* < It *collett(o)* glass blower's term, lit., little neck. See COL, -ET]

Cul′li·nan di′amond (kul′ə nən), the largest diamond found to date, weighing 3106 carats, discovered in the Transvaal in 1905 and cut into 105 pieces.

cul′lin stone′ (kul′ən), a millstone made from a certain kind of stone quarried near Cologne. [after G *Köln* Cologne]

cul·lion (kul′yən), *n. Archaic.* a base or vile fellow. [ME *culyon,* var. of *coil(i)on* < MF *coillon* testicle < L *cole(us)* bag, scrotum (< Gk *koleós* sheath) + F *-on* dim. suffix]

cul·lis (kul′is), *n.* a gutter, as at the eaves of a roof. [< F *coulisse* groove; see PORTCULLIS]

Cull·man (kul′mən), *n.* a city in N Alabama. 10,883 (1960).

cul·ly (kul′ē), *n., pl.* **-lies,** *v.,* **-lied, -ly·ing.** —*n.* **1.** *Archaic.* a dupe. **2.** *Slang.* fellow; companion. —*v.t.* **3.** to trick; cheat; dupe. [? shortening of CULLION]

culm[1] (kulm), *n.* **1.** coal dust; slack. **2.** anthracite, esp. of inferior grade. **3.** (*cap.*) Also called **Culm Measures.** *Geol.* a series of Lower Carboniferous rocks, mainly developed in parts of Europe and mostly dark-colored and siliceous. [ME *colme,* prob., equiv. to *col* COAL + *-m* suffix]

culm[2] (kulm), *n.* **1.** a stem or stalk, esp. the jointed and usually hollow stem of grasses. —*v.i.* **2.** to grow or develop into a culm. [< L *culm(us)* stalk; akin to CALAMUS, HAULM]

cul·mic·o·lous (kul mik′ə ləs), *adj.* (of a fungus) growing on grass culms. [CULM[2] + -I- + -COLOUS]

cul·mif·er·ous (kul mif′ər əs), *adj.* having or producing culms. [CULM[2] + -I- + -FEROUS]

cul·mi·nant (kul′mə nənt), *adj.* culminating; topmost. [< ML *culminant-* (s. of *culmināns*) coming to a peak, prp. of *culmināre.* See CULMINATE, -ANT]

cul·mi·nate (kul′mə nāt′), *v.,* **-nat·ed, -nat·ing.** —*v.i.* **1.** to terminate at the highest point, summit, or highest development (usually fol. by *in*). **2.** to end or conclude; arrive at a final stage (usually fol. by *in*): *The argument culminated in a fistfight.* **3.** to rise to or form an apex; terminate (usually fol. by *in*): *The tower culminates in a forty-foot spire.* **4.** *Astron.* (of a celestial body) to be on the meridian, or reach the highest or the lowest altitude. —*v.t.* **5.** to bring to a close; complete; climax: *A reading from Shakespeare culminates the performance.* [< ML *culmināt(us)* brought to a peak (ptp. of *culmināre*), equiv. to L *culmin-* (s. of *culmen*) peak, top + *-ātus* -ATE[1]]

cul·mi·na·tion (kul′mə nā′shən), *n.* **1.** act or fact of culminating. **2.** that in which anything culminates; highest point; acme. **3.** *Astron.* the position of a celestial body when it is on the meridian. [CULMIN(ANT) + -ATION]
—**Syn. 2.** climax, zenith, peak.

Culm′ Meas′ures, *Geol.* culm[1] (def. 3).

cu·lottes (ko͞o lots′, kyo͞o-), *n.pl.* women's casual trousers cut full to resemble a skirt. Also, **cu·lotte′.** [< F: lit., breeches, equiv. to *cul* rump + *-ottes,* pl. of *-otte,* fem. of *-ot* n. suffix. See CULET]

cul·pa (kul′pə; *Lat.* ko͝ol′pä), *n., pl.* **-pae** (-pē; *Lat.* -pī). **1.** *Roman and Civil Law.* negligence; neglect (distinguished from *dolus*): *One is not always liable before law for culpa resulting in damages.* **2.** guilt; sin. [OE < L: fault, liability, blame]

cul·pa·ble (kul′pə bəl), *adj.* deserving blame or censure; blameworthy. [ME < L *culpābil(is),* equiv. to *culpā(re)* (to) hold liable (see CULPA) + *-bilis* -BLE; r. ME *coupable* < MF] —**cul′pa·bil′i·ty, cul′pa·ble·ness,** *n.* —**cul′pa·bly,** *adv.*
—**Syn.** censurable, reprehensible. —**Ant.** praiseworthy.

Cul·pep·er (kul′pep′ər), *n.* **Thomas** (*2nd Baron Culpeper of Thoresway*), 1635–89, British colonial governor of Virginia 1680–83.

Culottes

cul·prit (kul′prit), *n.* **1.** a person arraigned for an offense. **2.** a person or other agent guilty of or responsible for an offense or fault. [traditionally explained as made up of *cul* (repr. L *culpābilis* guilty) + *prit* (repr. AF *prest* ready), marking the prosecution as ready to prove the defendant's guilt. See CULPABLE, PRESTO]

cult (kult), *n.* **1.** a particular system of religious worship, esp. with reference to its rites and ceremonies. **2.** an instance of great veneration of a person, ideal, or thing, esp. as manifested by a body of admirers: *a cult of Napoleon.* **3.** the object of such devotion. **4.** a group or sect bound together by devotion to or veneration of the same thing, person, ideal, etc. **5.** *Sociol.* a group having a sacred ideology and a set of rites centering around their sacred symbols. **6.** a religion that is considered or held to be false or unorthodox, or its members. **7.** any system for treating human sickness that originated by one usually claiming to have sole insight into the nature of disease, and that employs methods generally regarded as being unorthodox and unscientific. [< L *cult(us)* tilling, care, refinement, worship, n. use of ptp. of *colere* to cultivate, worship, dwell] —**cul′tic, cul·tu·al** (kul′cho͞o əl), *adj.* —**cult′ish,** *adj.*

cultch (kulch), *n., v.t.* culch.

cul·tel·lus (kul tel′əs), *n., pl.* **-tel·li** (-tel′ī). *Zool.* a sharp, knifelike structure, as the mouthparts of certain blood-sucking flies. [< L: small knife, equiv. to *cult(er)* knife, COLTER + *-ellus* dim. suffix]

cul·ti·gen (kul′ti jən), *n.* a cultivated plant whose taxonomic origin is unknown or obscure. [CULTI(VATED) + -GEN]

cult·ism (kul′tiz əm), *n.* the practices and devotions of a cult. [CULT + -ISM] —**cult′ist,** *n.*

cul·ti·va·ble (kul′tə və bəl), *adj.* capable of being cultivated. Also, **cul·ti·vat·a·ble** (kul′tə vā′tə bəl). [CULTIV(ATE) + -ABLE] —**cul′ti·va·bil′i·ty,** *n.* —**cul′ti·va·bly,** *adv.*

cul·ti·var (kul′tə vär′, -vər), *n.* a variety of plant that has been produced only under cultivation. [CULTI(VATED) + VAR(IETY)]

cul·ti·vate (kul′tə vāt′), *v.t.,* **-vat·ed, -vat·ing.** **1.** to prepare and work on (land) in order to raise crops; till. **2.** to use a cultivator on. **3.** to promote or improve the growth of (a plant, crop, etc.) by labor and attention. **4.** to produce by culture. **5.** to develop or improve by education or training; train; refine. **6.** to promote the growth or development of (an art, science, etc.); foster. **7.** to devote oneself to (an art, science, etc.). **8.** to seek to promote or foster (friendship, love, etc.). **9.** to seek the acquaintance or friendship of (a person). [< ML *cultivāt(us)* tilled (ptp. of *cultivāre*), equiv. to *cultīv(us)* (L *cult(us),* ptp. of *colere* to care for, till + *-īvus* -IVE) + *-ātus* -ATE[1]]
—**Ant. 8.** neglect. **9.** ignore.

cul·ti·vat·ed (kul′tə vā′tid), *adj.* **1.** subjected to cultivation. **2.** produced or improved by cultivation, as a plant. **3.** educated; refined; cultured. [CULTIVATE + -ED[2]]

cul·ti·va·tion (kul′tə vā′shən), *n.* **1.** act or art of cultivating. **2.** state of being cultivated. **3.** culture; refinement. [CULTIVATE + -ION]

cul·ti·va·tor (kul′tə vā′tər), *n.* **1.** one who or that which cultivates. **2.** an implement drawn between rows of growing plants to loosen the earth and destroy weeds. [CULTIVATE + -OR[2]]

cul·trate (kul′trāt), *adj.* sharp-edged and pointed, as a leaf. Also, **cul′trat·ed.** [< L *cultrāt(us)* knife-shaped, equiv. to *cultr-* (s. of *culter*) knife + *-ātus* -ATE[1]]

cul·tur·al (kul′chər əl), *adj.* of or pertaining to culture or cultivation. [CULTURE + -AL[1]] —**cul′tur·al·ly,** *adv.*

cul′tural anthropol′ogy, the branch of anthropology dealing with the origins, history, and development of human culture, and including in its scope the fields of archaeology, ethnology, ethnography, and linguistics. Also called **social anthropology.** Cf. **physical anthropology.** —**cul′tural anthropol′ogist.**

cul′tural lag′, *Sociol.* slowness in the rate of change of one part of a culture in relation to another part, resulting in a maladjustment within society, as from the failure of the nonmaterial culture to keep abreast of developments in the material culture. Also, **culture lag.**

cul·ture (kul′chər), *n., v.,* **-tured, -tur·ing.** —*n.* **1.** the quality in a person or society that arises from an interest in and acquaintance with what is generally regarded as excellent in arts, letters, manners, scholarly pursuits, etc. **2.** that which is excellent in the arts, manners, etc. **3.** a particular form or stage of civilization, as that of a certain nation or period: *Greek culture.* **4.** *Sociol.* the sum total of ways of living built up by a group of human beings and transmitted from one generation to another. **5.** *Biol.* **a.** the cultivation of microorganisms, as bacteria, or of tissues, for scientific study, medicinal use, etc. **b.** the product or growth resulting from such cultivation. **6.** the act or practice of cultivating the soil; tillage. **7.** the raising of plants or animals, esp. with a view to their improvement. **8.** the product or growth resulting from such cultivation. **9.** development or improvement of the mind by education or training. —*v.t.* **10.** to subject to culture; cultivate. **11.** *Biol.* **a.** to develop (microorganisms, tissues, etc.) in an artificial medium. **b.** to introduce (living material) into a culture medium. [ME: tilling, place tilled < L *cultūr(a).* See CULT, -URE] —**cul′ture·less,** *adj.*
—**Syn. 9.** See **education.**

Cul′ture and An′archy, a collection of essays (1869) by Matthew Arnold, criticizing English political and social conditions.

cul′ture ar′ea, *Sociol.* a region having a distinct pattern of culture.

cul′ture cen′ter, *Anthropol.* the part of a culture area in which the most distinctive traits of the area are concentrated.

cul′ture com′plex, *Sociol.* a group of culture traits all interrelated and dominated by one essential trait: *Nationalism is a culture complex.*

cul·tured (kul′chərd), *adj.* **1.** cultivated. **2.** enlightened; refined. **3.** artificially nurtured or grown: *experimentally cultured bacteria.* [CULTURE + -ED[3]]

cul′tured pearl′, a pearl formed by a pearl oyster or mussel around an object, as around a seed pearl, bead, or piece of mantle tissue, inserted in its body. Also, **cul′ture pearl′.**

cul′ture fac′tor, *Sociol.* culture as a causative agent, esp. in contrast to biological factors.

cul′ture he′ro, 1. a mythical or mythicized historical figure who embodies the aspirations or ideals of a society. **2.** a mythical figure who is considered by a people to have furnished it the means of existence or survival, as by inventing their alphabet, teaching them the art of husbandry, or stealing fire, as from the gods or a volcano, and giving it to them.

cul′ture lag′. See **cultural lag.**

cul′ture me′dium, *Bacteriol.* medium (def. 8).

cul′ture pat′tern, *Sociol.* a group of interrelated culture traits of some continuity.

cul′ture trait′, *Sociol.* any trait of human activity acquired in social life and transmitted by communication.

cul′ture vul′ture, *Slang.* one who shows an extravagant and often pretentious interest in artistic or intellectual pursuits.

cul·tur·ist (kul′chər ist), *n.* **1.** a cultivator. **2.** an advocate or devotee of culture. [CULTURE + -IST]

cul·tus[1] (kul′təs), *n., pl.* **-tus·es, -ti** (-tī). a cult. [< L; see CULT]

cul·tus[2] (kul′təs), *n., pl.* **-tus·es,** (*esp. collectively*) **-tus.** lingcod. Also called **cul′tus cod′.** [< Chinook *kultus* of little worth]

-culum, a suffix occurring in loan words from Latin, where it denoted result, means or instrument, place, or meant "small": *curriculum; osculum.* Also, **-cule.** [< L, neut. dim. suffix]

-culus, a suffix meaning "small," occurring in loan words from Latin or in scientific names based on Latin roots: *ventriculus.* Also, **-cule.** [< L, masc. dim. suffix]

cul·ver (kul′vər), *n.* *Brit. Dial.* a dove or pigeon. [ME; OE *culfer, culfre* < VL **columbra,* var. of L *columbula,* equiv. to *columb(a)* dove + *-ula* dim. suffix]

Cul′ver Cit′y (kul′vər), a city in SW California, W of Los Angeles. 32,163 (1960).

cul′ver hole′, *Masonry.* a hole for receiving a timber.

cul·ver·in (kul′vər in), *n.* **1.** a medieval form of musket. **2.** a kind of heavy cannon used in the 16th and 17th centuries. [late ME < MF *coulevrine* < L *colubrīna,* fem. of *colubrīnus* COLUBRINE]

Cul′ver's root′, 1. the root of a tall, scrophulariaceous herb, *Veronicastrum virginicum,* used in medicine as a cathartic and emetic. **2.** the plant. [named after Dr. *Culver,* 17th–18th century American physician]

cul·vert (kul′vərt), *n.* a drain or channel crossing under a road, sidewalk, etc.; sewer; conduit. [?]

cum (kum, ko͝om), *prep.* with; together with; along with (usually used in combination): *My garage-cum-workshop is well equipped.* [< L: with, together (prep.)]

Cu·mae (kyo͞o′mē), *n.* an ancient city in SW Italy, on the coast of Campania: believed to be the earliest Greek colony in Italy or in Sicily. —**Cu·mae′an,** *adj.*

Cumae′an sib′yl, *Class. Myth.* a famous prophetess at Cumae who guided Aeneas through the underworld and who was believed in the Middle Ages to have foretold the coming of Christ.

Cu·ma·ná (ko͞o′mä nä′), *n.* a seaport in N Venezuela: earthquake 1766, 1929.

cu·ma·rin (ko͞o′mə rin), *n.* *Chem.* coumarin.

cu·ma·rone (ko͞o′mə rōn′, kyo͞o′-), *n.* *Chem.* coumarone.

cum·ber (kum′bər), *v.t.* **1.** to hinder; hamper. **2.** to overload; burden. **3.** to inconvenience; trouble. —*n.* **4.** a hindrance. **5.** that which cumbers. **6.** *Archaic.* embarrassment; trouble. [ME *cumbren* (v.), aph. var. of *acumbren* to harass, defeat; see ENCUMBER] —**cum′ber·er,** *n.* —**cum′ber·less,** *adj.* —**cum′ber·ment,** *n.*

Cum·ber·land (kum′bər lənd), *n.* **1.** a county in NW England. 294,162 (1961); 1520 sq. mi. *Co. seat:* Carlisle. **2.** a city in NW Maryland, on the Potomac River. 33,415 (1960). **3.** a town in SE Kentucky. 4271 (1960). **4.** a river flowing W from SE Kentucky through N Tennessee into the Ohio River. 687 mi. long.

Cum′berland Gap′, a pass in the Cumberland Mountains at the junction of the Virginia, Kentucky, and Tennessee boundaries. 1315 ft. high.

Cum′berland Moun′tains, a plateau largely in Kentucky and Tennessee, a part of the Appalachian Mountains: highest point, ab. 4000 ft. Also called **Cum′berland Plateau′.**

cum·ber·some (kum′bər səm), *adj.* **1.** burdensome; troublesome. **2.** unwieldy; clumsy. [ME *cummyrsum.* See CUMBER, -SOME[1]] —**cum′ber·some·ly,** *adv.* —**cum′ber·some·ness,** *n.*
—**Syn. 1.** heavy, weighty, onerous. **2.** awkward.

cum·brance (kum′brəns), *n.* **1.** trouble; bother. **2.** burden; encumbrance. [ME *combraunce,* aph. var. of *acombraunce* defeat, harassment; see ENCUMBRANCE]

cum·brous (kum′brəs), *adj.* cumbersome. [ME *cumberous.* See CUMBER, -OUS] —**cum′brous·ly,** *adv.* —**cum′brous·ness,** *n.*

cum′ div′idend, *Stock Exchange.* with or including the dividend which has been previously declared. Cf. **ex dividend.**

cum gra·no sa·lis (ko͝om grä′nō sä′lis; *Eng.* kum grā′nō sā′lis), *Latin.* with a grain of salt; not too seriously.

cum·in (kum′ən), *n.* **1.** a small, apiaceous plant, *Cuminum Cyminum,* bearing aromatic, seedlike fruit, used in cookery and medicine. **2.** the fruit or seeds. [ME *comin,* OE *cymen* << L *cumīn(um)* < Gk *kýminon* < Sem; cf. Ar *kammūn,* Heb *kammōn* cumin]

cum lau·de (ko͝om lou′dā, -də, -dē; kum lô′dē), with honor: used in diplomas to grant the lowest of three special honors for grades above the average. Cf. **magna cum laude, summa cum laude.** [< L: with praise]

cum·mer (kum′ər), *n.* *Scot.* **1.** a godmother. **2.** a female companion. **3.** a girl or woman. Also, **kimmer.** [ME *commare* godmother < MF *commere* < eccl. L *commāter,* equiv. to L *com-* COM- + *māter* mother]

cum·mer·bund (kum′ər bund′), *n.* **1.** a wide sash with horizontal pleats, worn at the waist beneath a dinner jacket. **2.** any shawl or sash worn at the waist, esp. by men in India. Also, **kummerbund.** [< Urdu *kamarband* loin-band < Pers]

Cum·mings (kum′ingz), *n.* **Edward Est·lin** (est′lin), ("*e e cummings*"), 1894–1962, U.S. poet, writer, and painter.

cum·ming·ton·ite (kum′ing tə nīt′), *n.* an amphibole mineral, magnesium iron silicate, similar to anthophyllite but richer in iron. [named after *Cummington,* Mass., where it is found; see -ITE[1]]

cum·quat (kum′kwot), *n.* kumquat.

cum·shaw (kum′shô), *n.* (in Chinese ports) a present; gratuity; tip. [< Chin (Amoy dial.) *kam siā,* c. Mandarin *kan hsieh* grateful thanks]

cu·mu·late (*v.* kyo͞o′myə lāt′; *adj.* kyo͞o′myə lit, -lāt′), *v.,* **-lat·ed, -lat·ing,** *adj.* —*v.t.* **1.** to heap up; amass; accumulate. —*adj.* **2.** heaped up. [< L *cumulāt(us)* heaped up, piled up, accumulated (ptp. of *cumulāre*), equiv. to *cumul(us)* a heap, pile, mass + *-ātus* -ATE[1]] —**cu′mu·late·ly,** *adv.*

cu·mu·la·tion (kyo͞o′myə lā′shən), *n.* **1.** the act of cumulating; accumulation. **2.** a heap; mass. [CUMULATE + -ION]

cu·mu·la·tive (kyo͞o′myə lā′tiv, -lə tiv), *adj.* **1.** increasing or growing by accumulation or successive additions: *the cumulative effect of more evidence.* **2.** formed by or resulting from accumulation or the addition of successive parts or elements. **3.** of or pertaining to interest or dividends which, if not paid when due, become a prior claim for payment in the future: *cumulative preferred stocks.* [CUMULATE + -IVE] —**cu·mu·la·tive·ly** (kyo͞o′myə lā′tiv lē, -lə tiv-), *adv.* —**cu·mu·la·tive·ness** (kyo͞o′myə lā′tiv nis, -lə tiv-), *n.*

cu′mulative ev′idence, 1. evidence of which the parts reinforce one another, producing an effect stronger than any part taken by itself. **2.** *Chiefly Law.* **a.** testimony repetitive of testimony given earlier. **b.** evidence that confirms or adds to evidence already given.

cu′mulative scor′ing, *Duplicate Bridge.* a method of scoring in which the score of a partnership is taken as the sum of their plus and minus scores on all hands played.

cu′mulative vot′ing, a system which gives each voter as many votes as there are persons to be elected from one representative district, allowing him to accumulate them on one candidate or to distribute them.

cu·mu·li·form (kyo͞o′myə lə fôrm′), *adj.* having the appearance or character of cumulus clouds. [< NL *cumuli-,* comb. form of CUMULUS + -FORM]

cu·mu·lo·cir·rus (kyo͞o′myə lō sir′əs), *n., pl.* **-rus.** cirrocumulus. [< NL *cumulo-,* comb. form of CUMULUS + CIRRUS]

cu·mu·lo·nim·bus (kyo͞o′myə lō nim′bəs), *n., pl.* **-bus.** a cloud of a class indicative of thunderstorm conditions, characterized by large, dense, and very tall towers, cumuliform except for their tops, which appear fibrous because of the presence of ice crystals: occurs as a single cloud or as a group with merged bases and separate tops, and may range in vertical length from 3000–20,000 feet above the earth. Also called **thundercloud, thunderclouds.** [< NL *cumulo-,* comb. form of CUMULUS + NIMBUS]

cu′mulonim′bus cal′vus, *pl.* **cumulonimbus calvus.** *Meteorol.* a cumulonimbus cloud evolving from cumulus congestus, its upper portion changing from a cumuliform shape into a diffuse whitish mass having vertical striations.

cu′mulonim′bus capilla′tus, *pl.* **cumulonimbus capillatus.** *Meteorol.* a cumulonimbus cloud the upper portion of which has developed distinctively cirriform shapes often resembling large, disorderly masses of hair.

cu·mu·lo·stra·tus (kyo͞o′myə lō strā′təs, -strat′əs), *n., pl.* **-tus.** stratocumulus. [< NL *cumulo-,* comb. form of CUMULUS + STRATUS]

cu·mu·lous (kyo͞o′myə ləs), *adj.* (formerly) of the form of a cumulus cloud. [< L *cumul(us)* CUMULUS + -OUS]

cu·mu·lus (kyo͞o′myə ləs), *n., pl.* **-lus. 1.** a heap; pile. **2.** a cloud of a class exhibiting great vertical development and characterized by dense individual elements in the form of puffs, mounds, or towers, with flat bases and tops that often resemble cauliflower: vertical length often ranges from about 3000–20,000 feet above the ground. [< NL (L: mass, pile)]

cu′mulus conges′tus, *pl.* **cumulus congestus.** *Meteorol.* a cumulus cloud having very great height and a cauliflower-shaped summit.

cu′mulus frac′tus, *pl.* **cumulus fractus.** a cumulus cloud that is ill-formed, ragged, usually small, and rapidly changing.

cu′mulus hu′milis, *pl.* **cumulus humilis.** *Meteorol.* a cumulus cloud having a small, generally flattened appearance. Also called **fair-weather cumulus.**

cu′mulus medio′cris, *pl.* **cumulus mediocris.** *Meteorol.* a cumulus cloud of medium height and often lacking a distinctive summit: intermediate between cumulus humilis and cumulus congestus.

Cu·nax·a (kyo͞o nak′sə), *n.* an ancient town in Babylonia, near the Euphrates: famous battle between Cyrus the Younger and Artaxerxes II in 401 B.C.

cunc·ta·tion (kungk tā′shən), *n.* delay; tardiness. [< L *cunctātiōn-* (s. of *cunctātiō*) delay, equiv. to *cunctāt(us)* delayed (ptp. of *cunctārī*) + *-iōn-* -ION] —**cunc·ta′tious, cunc·ta·to·ry** (kungk′tə tôr′ē, -tōr′ē), *adj. Rare.* **cunc·ta·tive** (kungk′tə tiv), *adj.*

cunc·ta·tor (kungk tā′tər), *n.* a procrastinator. [< L, equiv. to *cunctāt(us)* delayed (ptp. of *cunctārī*) + *-or* -OR[2]] —**cunc·ta′tor·ship′,** *n.*

cu·ne·al (kyo͞o′nē əl), *adj.* wedgelike; wedge-shaped. [< L *cune(us)* a wedge + -AL¹]

cu·ne·ate (kyo͞o′nē it, -āt′), *adj.* **1.** wedge-shaped. **2.** (of leaves) triangular and tapering to a point at the base. Also, **cu′ne·at′ed.** [< L *cuneāt(us),* equiv. to *cune(us)* a wedge + *-ātus* -ATE¹] —**cu′ne·ate·ly,** *adv.*

Cuneate leaf

cu·ne·at·ic (kyo͞o′nē at′ik), *adj.* cuneiform; cuneate. [CUNEATE + -IC]

cu·ne·i·form (kyo͞o nē′ə fôrm′, kyo͞o′nē ə-), *adj.* **1.** having the form of a wedge; wedge-shaped. **2.** composed of slim triangular elements, as the characters used in writing by the ancient Akkadians, Assyrians, Babylonians, Persians, and others. **3.** written in cuneiform characters: *cuneiform inscription.* **4.** *Anat.* noting or pertaining to any of various wedge-shaped bones, as of the tarsus. —*n.* **5.** cuneiform characters or writing. **6.** a cuneiform bone. Also, **cuniform.** [< L *cune(us)* a wedge + -I- + -FORM]

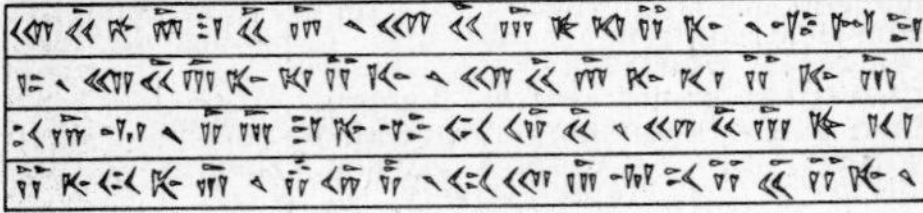

Cuneiform inscription (Persian)

cu·ne·i·form·ist (kyo͞o nē′ə fôr′mist, kyo͞o′nē ə-), *n.* one who studies or deciphers cuneiform writing. [CUNEIFORM + -IST]

Cu·ne·o (ko͞o′ne ô), *n.* a city in NW Italy. 46,287 (1961).

cu·ne·us (kyo͞o′nē əs), *n., pl.* **-ne·i** (-nē ī′). **1.** *Anat.* a wedge-shaped convolution on the medial surface of the occipital lobe of the cerebrum. **2.** *Entomol.* a wedge-shaped segment of the corium of certain hemipterous insects. [< L: wedge]

cu·nic·u·lus (kyo͞o nik′yə ləs), *n., pl.* **-li** (-lī′). **1.** a small conduit or burrow, as an underground drain or rabbit hole. **2.** a low tunnel, as to a burial chamber. **3.** *Pathol.* a burrow in the skin caused by the itch mite. [< L: rabbit, burrow; see CONY] —**cu·nic′u·lar,** *adj.*

cu·ni·form (kyo͞o′nə fôrm′), *adj., n.* cuneiform.

Cu·ni·na (kyŏŏ nī′nə), *n.* an ancient Roman deity, the guardian of sleeping infants.

cun·ner¹ (kun′ər), *n.* a small labroid fish, *Tautogolabrus adspersus,* commonly found on the North Atlantic coast of the U.S. Also called **bergall.** [?]

cun·ner² (kun′ər), *n.* a log canoe of lower Chesapeake Bay, used for fishing and oystering and having one mast with a jib-headed mainsail and a headsail. Also called **kinoo, Virginia log canoe.** [prob. alter. of CANOE]

cun·ni·lin·gus (kun′ᵊling′gəs), *n.* act, practice, or technique of orally stimulating the female genitalia. Also, **cun·ni·linc·tus** (kun′ᵊlingk′təs). [< NL, L: one who licks the vulva, equiv. to *cunni-* (comb. form of *cunnus* vulva) + *-lingus* (deriv. of *lingere* to lick)]

cun·ning (kun′ing), *n.* **1.** skill employed in a crafty manner, as in deceiving; craftiness; guile. **2.** adeptness in performance; dexterity: *His hand lost its cunning.* —*adj.* **3.** showing or made with ingenuity. **4.** artfully subtle or shrewd; crafty; sly. **5.** *Informal.* charmingly cute: *a cunning little baby; cunning spring hats.* **6.** *Archaic.* skillful; expert. —*v.* **7.** *Obs.* ppr. of **can¹**. [(n.) ME; OE *cunnung,* equiv. to *cunn(an)* (to) know (see CAN¹) + *-ung* -ING¹; (adj., v.) ME, prp. of *cunnan* to know (see CAN¹ def. 6, -ING²)] **cun′ning·ly,** *adv.* —**cun′ning·ness,** *n.*

—**Syn. 1.** shrewdness, artfulness, wiliness, trickery, finesse, intrigue, slyness, deception. CUNNING, ARTIFICE, CRAFT imply an inclination toward deceit, slyness, and trickery. CUNNING implies a shrewd, often instinctive skill in concealing or disguising the real purposes of one's actions: *not intelligence but a low kind of cunning.* An ARTIFICE is a clever, unscrupulous ruse, used to mislead others: *a successful artifice to conceal one's motives.* CRAFT suggests underhand methods and the use of deceptive devices and tricks to attain one's ends: *craft and deceitfulness in every act.* **2.** adroitness. **3.** ingenious, skillful. **4.** artful, wily, tricky, foxy. —**Ant. 2.** inability, stupidity. **4.** dull, gullible.

cup (kup), *n., v.,* **cupped, cup·ping.** —*n.* **1.** a small, open container, of china, glass, metal, etc., usually having one handle and used chiefly as a vessel from which to drink tea, soup, etc. **2.** an ornamental vessel, esp. of precious metal, offered as a prize for a contest. **3.** the bowllike part of a goblet or the like. **4.** a cup with its contents. **5.** the quantity contained in a cup. **6.** a unit of capacity, equal to 8 fluid ounces or 16 tablespoons. **7.** any of various beverages, as a mixture of wine and various ingredients: *claret cup.* **8.** the chalice used in the Eucharist. **9.** the wine of the Eucharist. **10.** something to be partaken of or endured; one's portion, as of joy or suffering. **11. cups,** the drinking of intoxicating liquors. **12.** any cuplike utensil, organ, part, cavity, etc. **13.** *Golf.* **a.** the metal receptacle within the hole. **b.** the hole itself. **14.** (*cap.*) *Astron.* the constellation Crater. **15.** See **cupping glass. 16.** *Metalworking.* a cylindrical shell closed at one end, esp. one produced in the first stages of a deep-drawing operation. **17. in one's cups,** intoxicated; drunk: *He is very belligerent when in his cups.* —*v.t.* **18.** to take or cause to be in, or as in, a cup: *He cupped his ear with the palm of his hand to hear better.* **19.** to form into a cuplike shape: *He cupped his hands.* **20.** to use a cupping glass on. **21.** *Metalworking.* to form (tubing, containers, etc.) by punching hot strip or sheet metal and drawing it through a die. Cf. **deep-draw.** [ME, OE *cuppe* < LL *cuppa,* var. of L *cūpa* tub, cask] —**cup′like′,** *adj.*

cup′ and cov′er, *Eng. Furniture.* a turning used in Elizabethan and Jacobean furniture and resembling a goblet with a domed cover: similar to the melon-bulb, but narrower.

cup′-and-sau′cer vine′ (kup′ən sô′sər), a woody vine, *Cobaea scandens,* of Mexico, having violet-colored or greenish-purple flowers with an inflated, leaflike calyx and protruding, curved stamens. Also called **Mexican ivy.**

Cu·pa·vo (kyŏŏ pä′vō), *n.* (in the *Aeneid*) a companion of Aeneas in the war against Turnus.

cup′ barom′eter. See **cistern barometer.**

cup·bear·er (kup′bâr′ər), *n.* an attendant who fills and hands the cups in which drink is served. [late ME *cupberer.* See CUP, BEARER]

cup·board (kub′ərd), *n.* **1.** a closet with shelves for dishes, cups, etc. **2.** *Chiefly Brit.* any small closet or cabinet, as for clothes, food, or the like. [ME *cuppebord.* See CUP, BOARD]

cup′board love′, a personal attachment that appears to be motivated by love but in fact stems from the hope of gain. —**cup′board lov′er.**

cup·cake (kup′kāk′), *n.* a small cake baked in a cup-shaped pan. [CUP + CAKE]

cu·pel (kyo͞o′pəl, kyo͞o pel′), *n., v.,* **-peled, -pel·ing** or (*esp. Brit.*) **-pelled, -pel·ling.** —*n.* **1.** a small, cuplike, porous vessel, usually made of bone ash, used in assaying, as for separating gold and silver from lead. **2.** a receptacle or furnace bottom in which silver is refined. —*v.t.* **3.** to heat or refine in a cupel. [< ML *cūpell(a),* equiv. to L *cūp(a)* tub + *-ella* dim. suffix] —**cu·pel·er** (kyo͞o′pə lər), **cu·pel·ler** (kyo͞o pel′ər), *n.* —**cu·pel·la·tion** (kyo͞o′pə lā′shən), *n.*

Cu·per·ti·no (ko͞o′pər tē′nō, kyo͞o′-), *n.* a town in W California. 3664 (1960).

cup·ful (kup′fo͝ol′), *n., pl.* **-fuls. 1.** the amount a cup can hold. **2.** *Cookery.* a volumetric measure equal to eight fluid ounces; half pint. [ME *cuppefulle.* See CUP, -FUL]

cup′ fun′gus, any ascomycetous fungus of the family *Pezizaceae,* characterized by a fructification resembling a cup.

cup·hold·er (kup′hōl′dər), *n.* a competitor who has succeeded in defending or winning a specific cup, trophy, championship, etc. [CUP + HOLDER]

Cu·pid (kyo͞o′pid), *n.* **1.** Also called **Amor.** the ancient Roman god of love and the son of either Mars or Mercury and Venus, identified with Eros and commonly represented as a winged, naked, infant boy with a bow and arrows. **2.** (*l.c.*) a similar winged being, or a representation of one, esp. as symbolic of love. [ME *Cupide,* var. of *Cupido* < L: lit., desire, love, equiv. to *cup(ere)* (to) long for, desire + *-īdō* n. suffix]

cu·pid·i·ty (kyo͞o pid′i tē), *n.* eager or inordinate desire, esp. to possess something; greed; avarice. [late ME *cupidite* < L *cupiditās,* equiv. to *cupid(us)* eager, desirous + *-itās* -ITY] —**cu·pid·i·nous** (kyo͞o pid′ᵊnəs), *adj.*

Cu′pid's ar′rows. See **love arrows.**

Cu′pid's bow′ (bō), **1.** a classical bow; the bow Cupid is traditionally pictured as bearing. **2.** a line or shape resembling it, esp. the line of the upper lip. —**cu′pid's-bow′,** *adj.*

Cu·pid's-dart (kyo͞o′pidz därt′, -därt′), *n.* See **blue succory.**

cup′ of Eli′jah. See **Elijah's cup.**

cup′ of tea′, *Informal.* **1.** a task, topic, person, or object well-suited to one's experience, taste, or liking: *Chemistry, not art, is my cup of tea.* **2.** *Brit.* **a.** one's fate or destiny: *He has a sad life, but that's his cup of tea.* **b.** something or someone to be warned against or suspicious of: *The investment seems secure, but be careful of that cup of tea.*

Cupola

cu·po·la (kyo͞o′pə lə), *n.* **1.** *Archit.* **a.** a light structure on a dome or roof, serving as a belfry, lantern, or belvedere. **b.** a dome, esp. one covering a circular or polygonal area. **2.** any of various domelike structures. **3.** *Foundry.* a vertical furnace for melting iron to be cast. [< It < L *cūpula,* equiv. to *cūp(a)* tub + *-ula* -ULE. See CUP]

cu·po·lat·ed (kyo͞o′pə lā′tid), *adj.* **1.** having a cupola or cupolas. **2.** having the form of a cupola. [CUPOL(A) + -ATE¹ + -ED²]

cupped (kupt), *adj.* hollowed out like a cup; cup-shaped. [CUP + -ED³]

cup·per (kup′ər), *n.* one who performs the operation of cupping. [CUP + -ER¹]

cup·ping (kup′ing), *n.* the process of drawing blood from the body by scarification and the application of a cupping glass, or by the application of a cupping glass without scarification, as for relieving internal congestion. [ME *cuppinge.* See CUP, -ING¹]

cup′ping glass′, a glass vessel, used in cupping, in which a partial vacuum is created, as by heat.

cup′ plant′, a hardy, herbaceous perennial, *Silphium perfoliatum,* of eastern North America, having yellow flower heads nearly three inches wide. Also called **Indian cup.**

cup·py (kup′ē), *adj.* **-pi·er, -pi·est. 1.** cup-shaped; hollow. **2.** having indentations or depressions. [CUP + -Y¹]

cupr-, var. of **cupri-** before a vowel: *cupreous.*

cu·pram·mo·ni·um (kyo͞o′prə mō′nē əm, -mōn′yəm, ko͞o′-), *n.* *Chem.* any cation containing copper and ammonia. [CUPR- + AMMONIUM]

cu·pre·ous (kyo͞o′prē əs, ko͞o′-), *adj.* **1.** copper-colored; metallic reddish-brown. **2.** consisting of or containing copper; copperlike. [< LL *cupreus,* equiv. to *cupr(um)* COPPER¹ + *-eus* -EOUS]

cupri-, a learned borrowing from Latin meaning "copper," used in the formation of compound words: *cupriferous.* Also, **cupr-, cupro-.** [comb. form of LL *cuprum* COPPER¹]

cu·pric (kyo͞o′prik, ko͞o′-), *adj.* *Chem.* of or containing copper, esp. in the bivalent state: *cupric oxide,* CuO. [CUPR- + -IC]

cu′pric hydrox′ide, *Chem.* See **copper hydroxide.**

cu′pric sul′fate, *Chem.* See **blue vitriol.**

cu·prif·er·ous (kyo͞o prif′ər əs, ko͞o-), *adj.* containing or yielding copper. [CUPRI- + -FEROUS]

cu·prite (kyo͞o′prīt, ko͞o′-), *n.* a mineral, cuprous oxide, Cu_2O, occurring in red crystals and brown to black granular masses: an ore of copper. [CUPR- + -ITE¹]

cupro-, var. of **cupri-:** *cupronickel.*

cu·pro·nick·el (kyo͞o′prə nik′əl, ko͞o′-), *Metall.* —*n.* **1.** any of various alloys of copper with up to 40 percent nickel. —*adj.* **2.** containing copper and nickel. [CUPRO- + NICKEL]

cu·prous (kyo͞o′prəs, ko͞o′-), *adj.* *Chem.* containing copper in the univalent state, as cuprous oxide, Cu_2O. [CUPR- + -OUS]

cu′prous cy′anide, *Chem.* a creamy white, highly poisonous, water-insoluble powder, $CuCN$, used chiefly in electroplating and in organic synthesis. Also called **copper cyanide.**

cu·prum (kyo͞o′prəm, ko͞o′-), *n.* *Chem.* copper. [< LL]

cup′ shake′. See **wind shake.** [so called from the fact that the wood separated into round pieces]

cup′ turn′ing, (in furniture) turning of legs to give the form of an inverted cup.

cu·pu·late (kyo͞o′pyə lāt′, -lit), *adj.* shaped like a cupule. Also, **cu·pu·lar** (kyo͞o′pyə lər). [CUPULE + -ATE¹]

cu·pule (kyo͞o′pyo͞ol), *n.* **1.** *Bot.* **a.** a cup-shaped involucre consisting of indurated, cohering bracts, as in the acorn. See illus. under **acorn. b.** a cup-shaped outgrowth of the thallus of certain liverworts. **c.** the apothecium of a cup fungus. **2.** *Zool.* a small cup-shaped sucker or similar organ or part. [< NL *cūpul(a),* LL: small tub, equiv. to L *cūp(a)* tub + *-ula* -ULE]

cur (kûr), *n.* **1.** a mongrel dog, esp. a worthless or unfriendly one. **2.** a low, despicable person. [ME *curre,* appar. shortened from *curdogge.* See CURR, DOG] —**cur′-like′,** *adj.*

cur., **1.** currency. **2.** current.

cur·a·ble (kyŏŏr′ə bəl), *adj.* that can be cured. [ME < L *cūrābil(is),* equiv. to *cūrā(re)* (to) care for (deriv. of *cūra* care) + *-bilis* -BLE] —**cur′a·bil′i·ty, cur′a·ble·ness,** *n.* —**cur′a·bly,** *adv.*

CARIBBEAN SEA
COLOMBIA
ARUBA
Curaçao
BONAIRE
LAKE MARACAIBO
Caracas
VENEZUELA

Cu·ra·çao (ko͞o′rä sä′ō; *Eng.* kŏŏr′ə sou′, kyŏŏr′ə sō′), *n.* **1.** the main island of the Netherlands Antilles, off the NW coast of Venezuela. 131,000 (est. 1963); 173 sq. mi. *Cap.:* Willemstad. **2.** See **Netherlands Antilles. 3.** (*l.c.*) Also, **cu·ra·çoa** (kyŏŏr′ə sō′, -sō′ə). a cordial or liqueur flavored with the peel of the sour orange.

cu·ra·cy (kyŏŏr′ə sē), *n., pl.* **-cies.** the office or position of a curate. [CURATE + -CY, modeled on pairs like *primate, primacy*]

cur·age (kyŏŏr′ij, kyŏŏ räzh′), *n.* *Surg.* curettage. [< F, equiv. to *cur(er)* (to) cleanse (< L *cūrāre* to attend to; see CURE) + *-age* -AGE]

cur·agh (kur′əkʜ, kur′ə), *n.* *Scot., Irish.* currach.

cu·ra·re (kyŏŏ rär′ē), *n.* **1.** a blackish, resinlike substance derived from tropical plants of the genus *Strychnos,* esp. *S. toxifera,* and from the root of pareira, used by South American Indians for poisoning arrows and employed in physiological experiments, medicine, etc., for arresting the action of the motor nerves. **2.** a plant yielding this substance. Also, **cu·ra′ri.** [< Pg < Carib *kurari*]

cu·ra·rize (kyŏŏr′ə rīz′, kyŏŏ rär′īz), *v.t.,* **-rized, -riz·ing.** to administer curare to, as in vivisection. [CURAR(E) + -IZE] —**cu′ra·ri·za′tion,** *n.*

cu·ras·sow (kyŏŏr′ə sō′, kyŏŏ ras′ō), *n.* any of several large, arboreal, gallinaceous birds of the family *Cracidae,* of South and Central America. [after CURAÇAO]

cu·rate (kyŏŏr′it), *n.* **1.** *Chiefly Brit.* a clergyman employed as assistant or deputy of a rector or vicar. **2.** any ecclesiastic entrusted with the cure of souls, as a parish priest. [ME *curat* < ML *cūrāt(us),* equiv. to L *cūr(a)* care + *-ātus* -ATE¹] —**cu·rat·ic** (kyŏŏ rat′ik), **cu·rat′i·cal,** *adj.* —**cu′rate·ship′,** *n.*

cur·a·tive (kyŏŏr′ə tiv), *adj.* **1.** serving to cure or heal; pertaining to curing or remedial treatment; remedial. —*n.* **2.** a curative agent; remedy. [late ME < L *cūrāt(us)* cared for, attended to (ptp. of *cūrāre;* see CURE); see -IVE] —**cur′a·tive·ly,** *adv.* —**cur′a·tive·ness,** *n.*

—**Syn. 1.** healing, ameliorative, restorative.

cu·ra·tor (kyŏŏ rā′tər, kyŏŏr′ā- *for 1, 2;* kyŏŏr′ə tər *for 3*), *n.* **1.** the person in charge of a museum, art collection, etc. **2.** a manager; overseer; superintendent. **3.** *Law.* a guardian of a minor, lunatic, or other incompetent, esp. with regard to his property. [< L, equiv. to *cūrāt(us)* cared for (ptp. of *cūrāre;* see CURE) + *-or* -OR²; r. ME *curatour* < AF] —**cu·ra·to·ri·al** (kyŏŏr′ə tôr′ē əl, -tōr′-), *adj.* —**cu·ra′tor·ship′,** *n.*

cu·ra·trix (kyŏŏ rā′triks), *n., pl.* **cu·ra·tri·ces** (kyŏŏ-rā′tri sēz′, kyŏŏr′ə trī′sēz), a female curator. [< LL, fem. of L *cūrātor* CURATOR; see -TRIX]

curb (kûrb), *n.* **1.** a rim of joined stones, concrete, metal, or the like, forming an edge for a sidewalk. **2.** the framework around the top of a well. **3.** Also called **curb′ mar′ket;** *Brit.,* **kerb market, kerb′stone mar′ket.** a market, originally on the sidewalk or street, for the sale of securities not listed on a stock exchange. Cf. **American Stock Exchange. 4.** Also called **curb bit.** a bit used with a bridoon for surer control of a horse, having a port in the center and an eyelet at each end to which a chain (**curb chain**), passing beneath the chin, is hooked. **5.** an enclosing framework or border. **6.** anything that restrains or controls; a restraint; check. **7.** the arris between an upper and a lower slope on a gambrel or mansard roof. **8.** (in a windmill) the track on which the cap turns. **9.** a belt of metal, masonry, etc., for abutting a dome at its base. **10.** See **purlin plate. 11.** *Vet. Pathol.* a swelling on the lower part of the back of the hock of a horse, often causing lameness. **12.** *Engineering.* the cutting edge at the bottom of a caisson. —*v.t.* **13.** to control as with a curb; restrain; check. **14.** to put a curb on (a horse). **15.** to furnish with or protect by a curb. **16.** to cause to keep near the curb: *curb your dog.* Also, *Brit.,* **kerb** (for defs. 1, 15). [ME *curb, courbe* curved piece of wood (n.), stooped, hunchbacked (adj.) < MF *courbe* < L *curv(us)* crooked, bent, curved. See CURVE] —**curb′a·ble,** *adj.* —**curb′less,** *adj.* —**curb′like′,** *adj.*

—**Syn. 13.** bridle, repress. See **check.** —**Ant. 13.** encourage.

curb′ ball′, stoop ball played off a street curb.

curb′ bit′, curb (def. 4).

curb′ chain′. See under **curb** (def. 4).

curb·ing (kûr′bing), *n.* **1.** the material forming a curb, as along a street. **2.** curbstones collectively. **3.** a curb, or a section of a curb. Also, *Brit.,* **kerbing.** [CURB + -ING¹]

curb′ pin′, *Horol.* See **regulator pin.**

curb′ roof′, a roof divided on each side of the ridge into two or more slopes, as a gambrel or mansard.

curb′ serv′ice, service given to people seated in parked cars, as at a roadside eating place.

curb·stone (kûrb′stōn′), *n.* one of the stones, or a range of stones, forming a curb, as along the outer edge of a sidewalk, path, etc. Also, *Brit.,* **kerbstone.** [CURB + STONE]

curb′ string′. See **closed string.**

curch (kûrch), *n.* **1.** a simple, close-fitting cap worn by women in colonial America. **2.** a kerchief worn by Scottish women. [late ME *kerche, c(o)urche,* back formation from *courche(i)s* (pl.) < MF *couvrech(i)es,* pl. of *couvrechef* KERCHIEF; the final *e* of the sing. form, orig. long, was later lost]

cur·cu·li·o (kûr kyōō′lē ō′), *n., pl.* **-li·os.** any of several weevils, esp. one of the genus *Conotrachelus,* as *C. nenuphar* **(plum curculio),** which feeds on plums, cherries, and other fruits. [< L: weevil, corn worm]

cur·cu·ma (kûr′kyŏŏ mə), *n.* any chiefly Old World, zingiberaceous plant of the genus *Curcuma,* as *C. longa,* yielding turmeric, or *C. Zedoaria,* yielding zedoary. [< NL < Ar *kurkum* saffron, turmeric]

curd (kûrd), *n.* **1.** Often, **curds.** a substance consisting mainly of casein and the like, obtained from milk by coagulation, and used as food or made into cheese. **2.** any substance resembling this. **3.** the edible flower heads of various brassicaceous plants, as cauliflower and broccoli. —*v.t., v.i.* **4.** to turn into curd; coagulate; congeal. [ME *crud;* see CROWD¹]

curd′ cheese′, *Chiefly Brit.* See **cottage cheese.**

cur·dle (kûr′dəl), *v.t., v.i.,* **-dled, -dling. 1.** to change into curd; coagulate; congeal. **2. curdle the** or **one's blood,** to fill with horror or fear; terrify: *Walking through those streets at night is enough to curdle my blood.* [CURD + -LE] —**cur′dler,** *n.*

curd·y (kûr′dē), *adj.,* **curd·i·er, curd·i·est.** like curd; full of or containing curd; coagulated. [CURD + -Y¹] —**curd′i·ness,** *n.*

cure (kyŏŏr), *n., v.,* **cured, cur·ing.** —*n.* **1.** a method or course of remedial treatment, as for disease. **2.** successful remedial treatment; restoration to health. **3.** a means of healing or restoring to health; remedy. **4.** the act or a method of preserving meat, fish, etc., by smoking, salting, or the like. **5.** spiritual charge of the people in a certain district. **6.** the office or district of a curate or parish priest. [ME < OF *cure* and its source L *cūra* care; in religious sense < ML *cūra*] —*v.t.* **7.** to restore to health. **8.** to relieve or rid of something troublesome or detrimental, as an illness, a bad habit, etc. **9.** to prepare (meat, fish, etc.) for preservation by salting, drying, etc. **10.** to promote hardening of (fresh concrete or mortar) by keeping it damp. —*v.i.* **11.** to effect a cure. **12.** to become cured. [ME *cure(n)* < MF *cure(r)* and its source L *cūrāre* to take care of, deriv. of *cūra* care] —**cure′less,** *adj.* —**cure′less·ly,** *adv.* —**cur′er,** *n.*

—**Syn. 1.** remedy, restorative, specific, antidote. **8.** CURE, HEAL, REMEDY imply making well, whole, or right. CURE is especially applied to the eradication of disease or sickness: *to cure a fever, a headache.* HEAL suggests the making whole of wounds, sores, etc.: *to heal a cut or a burn.* REMEDY is a more general word which includes both the others and applies also to making wrongs right: *to remedy a mistake, a misunderstanding.*

cu·ré (kyŏŏ rā′, kyŏŏr′ā; *Fr.* KY RĀ′), *n., pl.* **cu·rés** (kyŏŏ rāz′, kyŏŏr′āz; *Fr.* KY RĀ′). (in France) a parish priest. [< F, OF; modeled on eccl. L *cūrātus* parish priest; see CURATE]

cure-all (kyŏŏr′ôl′), *n.* a cure for all ills; panacea.

cu·ret (kyŏŏ ret′), *n., v.t.,* **-ret·ted, -ret·ting.** curette.

Cu·re·tes (kyŏŏ rē′tēz), *n.pl. Class. Myth.* a group of demigods attending the infant Zeus in Crete.

cu·ret·tage (kyŏŏ ret′ij, kyŏŏr′i täzh′), *n. Surg.* the process of curetting. Also, **curage, cu·rette·ment** (kyŏŏ ret′mənt). [< F, equiv. to *curette* CURETTE + *-age* -AGE]

cu·rette (kyŏŏ ret′), *n., v.,* **-ret·ted, -ret·ting.** —*n.* **1.** a scoop-shaped surgical instrument for removing diseased tissue from body cavities, as the uterus, brain, etc. —*v.t.* **2.** to scrape with a curette. Also, **curet.** [< F, equiv. to *cur(er)* (to) cleanse + *-ette* -ETTE. See CURE]

curf (kûrf), *n.* kerf.

cur·few (kûr′fyōō), *n.* **1.** (in medieval Europe) the ringing of a bell at a fixed hour in the evening as a signal for covering or extinguishing fires. **2.** an order establishing a specific time in the evening after which certain regulations apply, as that no children may still be outdoors. **3.** a signal, usually made with a bell, announcing the start of the time of restrictions under the curfew. **4.** the time of sounding a curfew. **5.** a bell for sounding a curfew. **6.** a metal cover for shielding a banked or unattended fire. [ME < MF *cuevre-feu,* lit., cover (the) fireplace (impv.). See COVER, FOCUS]

cu·ri·a (kyŏŏr′ē ə), *n., pl.* **cu·ri·ae** (kyŏŏr′ē ē′). **1.** one of the political subdivisions of each of the three tribes of ancient Rome. **2.** the building in which such a division or group met, as for worship or public deliberation. **3.** the senate house in ancient Rome. **4.** the senate of an ancient Italian town. **5.** (*sometimes cap.*) See **Curia Romana. 6.** the papal court. **7.** the administrative aides of a bishop. [< L, contr. of **coviria,* equiv. to *co-* CO- + *vir* man + *-ia* -IA] —**cu′ri·al,** *adj.*

Cu·ri·a Re·gis (kyŏŏr′ē ə rē′jis), (*often l.c.*) *Eng. Hist.* **1.** a small, permanent council, composed chiefly of officials in the household of a Norman king, that served in an advisory and administrative capacity. **2.** See **great council** (def. 1). [< ML: lit., (the) king's curia]

Cu′ria Ro·ma′na (rō mā′nə, -mä′-), *Roman Cath. Ch.* the body of congregations, offices, permanent commissions, etc., that assist the pope in the government and administration of the church. [< ML, L: lit., (the) Roman curia]

Cu·ri·a·ti·i (kyŏŏr′ē ā′shē ī′), *n. pl. Rom. Legend.* See under **Horatii.**

cu·rie (kyŏŏr′ē, kyŏŏ rē′), *n. Physics, Chem.* the unit of radioactivity, equivalent to 3.70×10^{10} disintegrations per second. *Abbr.:* Ci, c [named after Marie CURIE]

Cu·rie (kyŏŏr′ē, kyŏŏ rē′; *Fr.* KY RĒ′), *n.* **1. I·rène** (*Fr.* ē REN′). See **Joliot-Curie, Irène. 2. Ma·rie** (mə rē′; *Fr.* MA RĒ′), 1867–1935, Polish physicist and chemist in France: co-discoverer of radium 1898; Nobel prize for physics 1903, for chemistry 1911. **3.** her husband, **Pierre** (pē âr′; *Fr.* PYER), 1859–1906, French physicist and chemist: co-discoverer of radium; Nobel prize for physics 1903.

Cu′rie point′, *Physics.* the temperature beyond which a ferromagnetic substance exhibits paramagnetism. Also called **Cu′rie tem′perature.** [named after Pierre CURIE]

Cu′rie's law′, *Physics.* the law that the susceptibility of a paramagnetic substance is inversely proportional to its absolute temperature. [named after Pierre CURIE]

Cu′rie-Weiss′ law′ (kyŏŏr′ē wīs′, -vīs′), *Physics.* the law that the susceptibility of a paramagnetic substance is inversely proportional to the difference of its temperature and the Curie point and that the substance ceases to be paramagnetic below the Curie point. [named after Pierre CURIE and Pierre *Weiss* (1865–1940), French physicist]

cu·ri·o (kyŏŏr′ē ō′), *n., pl.* **-ri·os.** any article, object of art, etc., valued as a curiosity. [shortened from CURIOSITY]

cu·ri·o·sa (kyŏŏr′ē ō′sə), *n.pl.* **1.** books, pamphlets, etc., dealing with unusual subjects. **2.** (in selling and collecting books) books, pamphlets, etc., containing pornographic literature or art; erotica. [< NL: unusual things, special use of neut. pl. of L *cūriōsus* careful, inquisitive. See CURIOUS]

cu·ri·os·i·ty (kyŏŏr′ē os′i tē), *n., pl.* **-ties. 1.** the desire to learn or know about anything; inquisitiveness. **2.** curious or interesting quality, as from strangeness. **3.** a curious, rare, or novel thing. **4.** *Obs.* carefulness; fastidiousness. [ME *curiosite* < L *cūriōsitās.* See CURIOUS, -ITY]

—**Syn. 3.** curio, rarity, wonder, marvel, phenomenon, freak.

cu·ri·ous (kyŏŏr′ē əs), *adj.* **1.** desirous of learning or knowing; inquisitive. **2.** prying; meddlesome. **3.** arousing or exciting speculation, interest, or attention through being inexplicable or highly unusual; odd; strange: *a curious sort of person; a curious scene.* **4.** (of books) indelicate, indecent, or obscene. **5.** *Archaic.* **a.** made or prepared skillfully. **b.** done with painstaking accuracy or attention to detail: *a curious inquiry.* **6.** *Obs.* **a.** careful; fastidious. **b.** marked by intricacy or subtlety. [ME < L *cūriōsus* careful, inquisitive, equiv. to *cūri-* (comb. form of *cūra* care) + *-ōsus* -OUS. See CURE] —**cu′ri·ous·ly,** *adv.* —**cu′ri·ous·ness,** *n.*

—**Syn. 1.** inquiring, interested. **2.** spying, peeping. CURIOUS, INQUISITIVE, MEDDLESOME, PRYING refer to taking an undue (and petty) interest in others' affairs. CURIOUS implies a desire to know what is not properly one's concern: *curious about a neighbor's habits.* INQUISITIVE implies asking impertinent questions in an effort to satisfy curiosity: *inquisitive in asking about a neighbor's habits.* MEDDLESOME implies thrusting oneself into and taking an active part in other people's affairs (or handling their possessions) entirely unasked and unwelcomed: *a meddlesome aunt who tries to run the affairs of a family.* PRYING implies a meddlesome and persistent inquiring into others' affairs: *a prying reporter inquiring into the secrets of a business firm.* **3.** unusual, singular, novel, rare, exotic. —**Ant. 1, 2.** indifferent.

Cu·ri·ti·ba (kōō′RĒ tē′bə; *Eng.* kŏŏr′i tē′bə), *n.* a city in and the capital of Paraná, in SE Brazil. 351,259 (1960). Also, **Cu′ri·ty′ba.**

Cu·ri·tis (kyŏŏ rī′tis), *n. Rom. Religion.* an epithet of Juno, meaning "of the spear."

cu·ri·um (kyŏŏr′ē əm), *n. Chem.* a radioactive element not found in nature but discovered in 1944 among the products of plutonium after bombardment by high-energy helium ions. *Symbol:* Cm; *at. no.:* 96. [< NL; named after Marie and Pierre CURIE; see -IUM]

curl (kûrl), *v.t.* **1.** to form into coils or ringlets, as the hair. **2.** to form into a spiral or curved shape; coil. **3.** *Obs.* to adorn with, or as with, curls or ringlets. —*v.i.* **4.** to grow in or form curls or ringlets, as the hair. **5.** to coil. **6.** to become curved or undulated. **7.** to play at the game of curling. **8.** to progress in a curving direction or path; move in a curving or spiraling way: *The ball curled toward the plate.* **9. curl one's lip,** to assume or display an expression of contempt: *He curled his lip in disdain.* **10. curl up, a.** to sit or lie down cozily: *to curl up with a good book.* **b.** *Informal.* to falter or droop with fatigue. —*n.* **11.** a coil or ringlet of hair. **12.** anything of a spiral or curved shape, as a lettuce leaf, wood shaving, etc. **13.** a coil. **14.** the act of curling or state of being curled. **15.** *Plant Pathol.* **a.** the distortion, fluting, or puffing of a leaf, resulting from the unequal development of its two sides. **b.** a disease so characterized. **16.** Also called **rotation.** *Math.* **a.** a vector obtained from a given vector by taking its cross product with the vector whose coordinates are the partial derivative operators with respect to each coordinate. **b.** the operation that produces this vector. [appar. back formation from *curled,* metathetic var. of ME *crulled* (ptp.) *crul* (adj.); cf. MD *crullen* to curl] —**curl·ed·ly** (kûr′lid lē, kûrld′-), *adv.* —**curl′edness,** *n.*

curled′ mal′low, 1. a rank-growing, annual herb, *Malva crispa,* of Europe, having a treelike stem, leaves with curled edges, and white flowers in dense clusters. **2.** a weedy, related herb, *M. verticillata,* of Eurasia, having pink, stalkless flowers.

curl·er (kûr′lər), *n.* **1.** one who or that which curls. **2.** any of various pins, clasps, or rollers on which locks of hair are wound or clamped for curling. **3.** a player at the game of curling. [CURL + -ER¹]

cur·lew (kûr′lōō), *n.* **1.** any of several shore birds of the genus *Numenius,* having a long, slender, downward curved bill, as the common *N. arquatus,* of Europe. **2.** any of various similar birds. [ME < AF *curleu,* c. MF *corleu;* ? imit.]

Curlew, *Numenius arquatus* (Length 23 in.; wingspread 3¼ ft.)

Cur·ley (kûr′lē), *n.* **James M(ichael),** 1874–1958, U.S. politician.

curl·i·cue (kûr′lə kyōō′), *n.* an ornamental, fancy curl or twist. Also, **curlycue.** [CURLY + CUE²]

curl·ing (kûr′ling), *n.* a game played on ice in which two teams of four players each compete in sliding large stones toward a mark in the center of a circle. Cf. **house** (def. 20). [?] —**curl′ing·ly,** *adv.*

curl′ing i′ron, a rod of iron, used when heated for curling the hair, which is twined around it. Also, **curl′ing i′rons.** Also called **curl′ing tongs′.**

curl′ing stone′, a large, heavy, ellipsoidal stone or a similar object made of iron, usually having one rough side and one smooth side with a hole in the center of each for screwing in a handle by which the stone is released, for use in the game of curling.

Curling stone

curl·pa·per (kûrl′pā′pər), *n.* a piece of paper on which a lock of hair is rolled up tightly, to remain until the hair has become fixed in a curl. [CURL + PAPER]

curl·y (kûr′lē), *adj.,* **curl·i·er, curl·i·est. 1.** curling or tending to curl: *curly blond hair.* **2.** having curls (usually used in combination): *curlyheaded.* [CURL + -Y¹] —**curl′i·ness,** *n.*

curl′y clem′atis. See **blue jasmine.**

cur·ly·cue (kûr′lə kyōō′), *n.* curlicue.

cur·ly·head (kûr′lē hed′), *n.* **1.** one whose hair is curly. **2. curlyheads,** (*construed as sing. or pl.*) a shrubby clematis, *Clematis ochroleuca,* of the eastern U.S. [CURLY + HEAD]

curl′y palm′, a feather palm, *Howea belmoreana,* of Lord Howe Island, having plumy leaves about seven feet long.

cur′ly top′, *Plant Pathol.* a disease of plants, esp. beets, characterized by puckered or cupped leaves and stunting or distortion, caused by a virus, *Ruga verrucosans.*

cur·mudg·eon (kər muj′ən), *n.* an irascible, churlish person. [unexplained; perh. *cur-* repr. CUR] —**cur·mudg′eon·ly,** *adj.*

curn (kûrn), *n. Scot.* **1.** a grain. **2.** a small quantity or number. [ME; akin to CORN¹, KERNEL]

curr (kûr), *v.i.* to make a low, murmuring sound, like the purring of a cat. [akin to Icel *kurra* to grumble, murmur, MHG *kurren,* MD *curren* to growl]

cur·rach (kur′əKH, kur′ə), *n. Scot., Irish.* a coracle. Also, **curagh, cur′ragh.** [late ME *currok* < ScotGael *curach,* IrGael *currach* boat; see CORACLE]

cur·ra·jong (kur′ə jong′), *n.* kurrajong.

cur·rant (kûr′ənt, kur′-), *n.* **1.** a small seedless raisin, produced chiefly in California and in the Levant, and used in cookery and confectionery. **2.** the small, edible, acid, round fruit or berry of certain wild or cultivated shrubs of the genus *Ribes.* **3.** the shrub itself. **4.** any of various similar fruits or shrubs. [shortened from ME *raysons of Coraunte* raisins of CORINTH, the port in Greece whence they chiefly came]

cur′rant bor′er, the larva of a clearwing moth, *Ramosia tipuliformis,* that bores into the stems of currants.

cur′rant toma′to, an herb, *Lycopersicum pimpinellifolium,* of Peru, having numerous, bell-shaped, yellow flowers and small, currantlike, red fruit.

cur·rant·worm (kûr′ənt wûrm′, kur′-), *n.* the larva of any of several insects, as a sawfly, *Nematus ribesii* **(imported currantworm),** which infests and feeds on the leaves and fruit of currants. [CURRANT + WORM]

cur·ren·cy (kûr′ən sē, kur′-), *n., pl.* **-cies. 1.** that which is used as a medium of exchange; money. **2.** the fact or quality of being widely accepted and circulated from person to person. **3.** general acceptance; prevalence; vogue. **4.** a time or period during which something is widely accepted and circulated. **5.** circulation, as of coin. [< ML *currentia.* See CURRENT, -ENCY]

cur′rency bond′, a bond payable in legal tender.

cur′rency prin′ciple, the principle that banks should be permitted to issue notes only against bullion or coin. Also called **cur′rency doc′trine.** Cf. **banking principle.**

cur·rent (kûr′ənt, kur′-), *adj.* **1.** passing in time, or belonging to the time actually passing: *the current month.* **2.** passing from one to another; circulating, as a coin. **3.** publicly reported or known: *a rumor that is current.* **4.** prevalent; customary: *the current practice.* **5.** popular; in vogue: *the current fashions.* **6.** new; present; most recent: *their current film together; the current issue of a publication.* **7.** *Archaic.* running; flowing. **8.** *Obs.* genuine; authentic. —*n.* **9.** a flowing; flow, as of a river. **10.** that which flows, as a stream. **11.** a large portion of air, large body of water, etc., moving in a certain direction. **12.** the speed at which such flow moves; velocity of flow. **13.** Also called **electric current.** *Elect.* **a.** the movement or flow of electricity. **b.** the time rate of flow, usually measured in amperes. **14.** course, as of time or events; the main course; the general tendency. [< L *current-* (s. of *currēns*) running (prp. of *currere*); r. ME *curraunt* < AF; see -ENT]

—**Syn. 4.** common, widespread, popular, rife. CURRENT, PRESENT, PREVAILING, PREVALENT refer to something generally or commonly in use. That which is CURRENT is in general circulation or a matter of common knowledge or acceptance: *current usage in English.* PRESENT refers to that which is in general use now; it is more limited than current, as to time: *present customs.* That which is PREVAILING is that which has superseded others: *prevailing fashion.* That which is PREVALENT exists or is spread widely: *a prevalent idea.* **5.** stylish, fashionable, modish. **10.** See **stream.** —**Ant. 4.** obsolete. **5.** old-fashioned.

cur′rent account′, 1. Also called **open account.** an account of credits, debits, receipts, and expenditures between two individuals or companies, usually providing for settlement at the end of specified accounting periods. **2.** (in certain foreign countries) a checking account.

cur′rent as′sets, *Com.* assets that are readily convertible into cash, usually within one year, without loss in value.

cur′rent cost′, a cost based on the prevailing price paid for material, labor, etc.

cur′rent den′sity, *Elect.* the current flowing per unit area, equal to a vector with the same direction as the current and having magnitude equal to the ratio of the current flowing perpendicular to a given point and through a given infinitesimal area to the area.

cur·ren·te ca·la·mo (ko͞o ren′te kä′lä mō′; *Eng.* kə ren′tē kal′ə mō′), *Latin.* fluently; offhand. [lit., with running (hurrying) pen]

cur′rent expens′es, regularly continuing expenditures for the maintenance and the carrying on of business.

cur′rent liabil′ities, *Com.* indebtedness maturing within one year.

cur′rent lim′iter, *Elect.* a device, as a resistor or fuse, that limits the flow of current to a prescribed amount, independent of the voltage applied.

cur·rent·ly (kûr′ənt lē, kur′-), *adv.* **1.** at the present moment; now: *He is currently working on the project.* **2.** easily; smoothly. [CURRENT + -LY]

cur·rent·ness (kûr′ənt nis, kur′-), *n.* the state or quality of being current; currency. [CURRENT + -NESS]

cur′rent ra′tio, the ratio between current assets and current liabilities.

cur′rent rip′ple, *Geol.* an asymmetrical ripple mark on the surface of sand beds or rocks, caused by the action of a current flowing over the surface.

cur·ri·cle (kûr′i kəl), *n.* a light, two-wheeled, open carriage drawn by two horses abreast. [< L *curricul(um)* racing chariot, equiv. to *curr(us)* chariot, wagon (deriv. of *currere* to run) + *-i-* -I- + *-culum* -CLE]

cur·ric·u·lum (kə rik′yə ləm), *n., pl.* **-lums, -la** (-lə). **1.** the aggregate of courses of study given in a school, college, university, etc. **2.** the regular or a particular course of study in a school, college, etc. [< L: course, career (lit., a running), equiv. to *curri-* (s. of *currere* to run) + *-culum* -CULE] —**cur·ric′u·lar,** *adj.*

cur·ric·u·lum vi·tae (kə rik′yə ləm vī′tē; *Lat.* ko͞or rik′o͞o lo͞om′ wē′tī), *pl.* **cur·ric·u·la vi·tae** (kə rik′yə lə vī′tē; *Lat.* ko͞or rik′o͞o lä′ wē′tī). **1.** Also called **vita, vitae.** a brief biographical résumé of one's career. **2.** (*italics*) *Latin.* the course of one's life or career.

cur·rie (kûr′ē, kur′ē), *n., v.t.,* **-ried, -ry·ing.** curry[1].

cur·ri·er (kûr′ē ər, kur′-), *n.* **1.** a person who dresses and colors leather after it is tanned. **2.** a person who curries horses. [CURRY[2] + -ER[1]; r. ME *corayour,* etc. < AF << *coriār(ius),* equiv. to *cori(um)* leather + *-ārius* -ARY]

Cur·ri·er (kûr′ē ər, kur-), *n.* **Nathaniel,** 1813–88, U.S. lithographer. Cf. **Ives** (def. 4).

Cur′rier and Ives′, the lithography firm of Nathaniel Currier and James Merritt Ives, founded originally by Currier (1835), which produced prints of American history, life, and manners.

cur·ri·er·y (kûr′ē ə rē, kur′-), *n., pl.* **-er·ies.** **1.** the occupation or business of a currier. **2.** the place where it is carried on. [CURRY[2] + -ERY]

cur·ri·jong (kur′i jông′), *n.* kurrajong.

cur·rish (kûr′ish), *adj.* **1.** of or pertaining to a cur. **2.** curlike; snarling; quarrelsome. **3.** contemptible; base. [late ME *kuresshe.* See CUR, -ISH[1]] —**cur′rish·ly,** *adv.* —**cur′rish·ness,** *n.*

cur·ry[1] (kûr′ē, kur′ē), *n., pl.* **-ries,** *v.,* **-ried, -ry·ing.** —*n.* **1.** *East Indian Cookery.* a pungent dish of vegetables, onions, meat or fish, etc., flavored with various spices or curry powder, and often eaten with rice. **2.** any dish flavored with curry powder or the like: *a lamb curry.* **3.** See **curry powder.** —*v.t.* **4.** to prepare (food) as a curry: *to curry eggs.* Also, **currie.** [< Tamil *kari* sauce]

cur·ry[2] (kûr′ē, kur′ē), *v.t.,* **-ried, -ry·ing.** **1.** to rub and clean (a horse) with a currycomb. **2.** to dress (tanned hides) by soaking, scraping, beating, coloring, etc. **3.** to beat; thrash. **4. curry favor,** to seek to advance oneself or gain some benefit through flattery or fawning: *His fellow workers despised him for attempting to curry favor with the boss.* [ME *cor(r)ay(en), cor(r)ey(en),* etc. < AF *curreier,* c. OF *correer,* earlier *conreer* to make ready, equiv. to *con-* CON- + *-reer* < VL **rēdāre* < Gmc; cf. OE *rǣdan* to equip, provide for, put in order, READ[1]]

Cur·ry (kûr′ē, kur′ē), *n.* **John Steu·art** (sto͞o′ərt, styo͞o′-), 1897–1946, U.S. painter.

cur·ry·comb (kûr′ē kōm′, kur′-), *n.* **1.** a comb, usually with rows of metal teeth, for currying horses. —*v.t.* **2.** to rub or clean with such a comb. [CURRY[2] + COMB[1]]

cur′ry pow′der, a powdered preparation of spices and other ingredients, usually including turmeric and coriander, used for making curry or for seasoning food. [CURRY[1] + POWDER[1]]

cur′ry sauce′, a sauce containing curry powder as a flavoring.

curse (kûrs), *n., v.,* **cursed** or **curst, curs·ing.** —*n.* **1.** the expression of a wish that misfortune, evil, doom, etc., befall another. **2.** a formula or charm intended to cause such misfortune to another. **3.** the act of reciting such a formula. **4.** an ecclesiastical censure or anathema. **5.** a profane oath. **6.** an evil that has been invoked upon one. **7.** something accursed. **8.** the cause of evil, misfortune, or trouble. **9.** *Slang.* the menstrual period; menstruation (usually prec. by *the*). —*v.t.* **10.** to wish or invoke evil, calamity, injury, or destruction upon. **11.** to swear at. **12.** to blaspheme. **13.** to afflict with great evil. **14.** to excommunicate. —*v.i.* **15.** to utter curses; swear profanely. [ME *curs* (n.), *cursen* (v.), OE *curs* (n.), *cursian* (v.), of disputed orig.; cf. OIr *cūrsagim* I blame] —**curs′er,** *n.*

—**Syn. 1, 4.** imprecation, execration, fulmination, malediction. **6.** misfortune, calamity, trouble. **6, 8.** bane, scourge, plague, affliction, torment. **10–12.** CURSE, BLASPHEME, SWEAR are often interchangeable in the sense of using profane language. However, CURSE is the general word for the heartfelt invoking or violent or angry calling down of evil on another: *They called down curses on their enemies.* To BLASPHEME is to speak contemptuously or with abuse of God or of sacred things: *to blaspheme openly.* To SWEAR is to use the name of God or of some holy person or thing as an exclamation to add force or show anger: *to swear in every sentence.* **13.** plague, scourge, afflict, doom. —**Ant. 1, 4.** blessing, benediction. **10.** bless.

curs·ed (kûr′sid, kûrst), *adj.* **1.** under a curse; damned. **2.** deserving a curse; hateful; abominable. **3.** *Chiefly Dial.* cantankerous; ill-tempered; cross. [ME; see CURSE, -ED[2]] —**curs′ed·ly,** *adv.* —**curs′ed·ness,** *n.*

—**Syn. 1.** accursed. **2.** damnable, execrable.

curse′ word′, **1.** a profane or obscene word, esp. as used in anger or for emphasis: *His speech was richly garnished with curse words.* **2.** any term conceived of as obscene or offensive: *He dared not admit to being a teacher, since "academic" had become a curse word.*

cur·sive (kûr′siv), *adj.* **1.** *Print.* in flowing strokes resembling handwriting. **2.** (of handwriting) in flowing strokes with the letters joined together. —*n.* **3.** a cursive letter or printing type. [< ML *cursīv(us)* flowing (said of penmanship), equiv. to L *curs(us)* (ptp. of *currere* to run) + *-īvus* -IVE] —**cur′sive·ly,** *adv.* —**cur′sive·ness,** *n.*

cur·sor (kûr′sər), *n.* **1.** a movable marker, as a blinking bar of light, that indicates the current position for entry of data on a computer screen. **2.** a sliding object, as the lined glass on a slide rule, able to be set at any point on a scale. [ME < L: a runner, racer, courier, equiv. to *curs(us)* (ptp. of *currere* to run) + *-or* -OR[2]]

cur·so·ri·al (kûr sôr′ē əl, -sōr′-), *adj.* *Zool.* **1.** adapted for running, as the feet and skeleton of dogs, horses, etc. **2.** having limbs adapted for running, as certain birds, insects, etc. [< LL *cursōri(us)* of running (see CURSORY) + -AL[1]]

cur·so·ry (kûr′sə rē), *adj.* going rapidly over something, without noticing details; hasty; superficial. [< LL *cursōri(us)* running, equiv. to L *curs(us)* a running (see COURSE) + *-ōrius* -ORY[1]] —**cur′so·ri·ly,** *adv.* —**cur′so·ri·ness,** *n.*

curst (kûrst), *v.* **1.** a pt. and pp. of **curse.** —*adj.* **2.** cursed. —**curst′ly,** *adv.* —**curst′ness,** *n.*

curt (kûrt), *adj.* **1.** short; shortened. **2.** brief; concise; terse; laconic. **3.** rudely brief in speech, abrupt in manner, or the like. [< L *curt(us)* shortened, short, cut short] —**curt′ly,** *adv.* —**curt′ness,** *n.*

—**Syn. 1.** abbreviated. **2.** See **blunt. 3.** snappish, sharp, rude.

Curt (kûrt), *n.* a boy's given name, form of **Curtis.**

cur·tail[1] (*v.* kər tāl′; *n.* kûr′tāl′), *v.t.* to cut short; cut off a part of; abridge; reduce; diminish. [late ME *curtayle* to restrict (said of inheritance), appar. CURT + TAIL[2]] —**cur·tailed′ly,** *adv.* —**cur·tail′er,** *n.* —**cur·tail′ment,** *n.*

—**Syn.** lessen, dock. See **shorten.**

cur·tail[2] (kûr′tāl), *n.* *Archit.* **1.** a horizontal, spiral termination to the lower end of a stair railing. **2.** Also called **cur′tail step′.** a starting step having a scroll termination to one or both ends of the tread. [? CUR + TAIL[1]]

cur·tain (kûr′tən, -tin), *n.* **1.** a hanging piece of fabric used to shut out the light from a window, adorn a room, etc. **2.** *Theat.* **a.** a set of hanging drapery for concealing all or part of the stage or set from the view of the audience. **b.** the act or time of raising or opening a curtain at the start of a performance: *an 8:30 curtain.* **c.** the end of a scene or act indicated by the closing or falling of a curtain: *first-act curtain.* **d.** an effect, line, or plot solution at the conclusion of a performance: *a strong curtain; weak curtain.* **e.** music signaling the end of a radio or television performance. **f.** (used as a direction in a script of a play to indicate that a scene or act is concluded.) **3.** anything that shuts off, covers, or conceals: *a curtain of artillery fire.* **4.** *Archit.* a relatively flat or featureless extent of wall between two pavilions or the like. **5.** *Fort.* the part of a wall or rampart connecting two bastions, towers, or the like. See diag. under **bastion. 6. curtains,** *Slang.* the end; death, esp. by violence: *It looked like curtains for another mobster.* **7. draw the curtain on or over, a.** to bring to a close: *to draw the curtain on a long career of public service.* **b.** to keep secret. **8. lift the curtain on, a.** to commence; start. **b.** to make known or public; disclose: *to lift the curtain on a new scientific discovery.* —*v.t.* **9.** to provide, shut off, conceal, or adorn with, or as with, a curtain. [ME *co(u)rtine* < OF < LL *cortīn(a)* < ?] —**cur′tain·less,** *adj.*

—**Syn. 1.** drapery, portiere, lambrequin, valance. CURTAIN, BLIND, SHADE, SHUTTER agree in being covers for a window, to shut out light or keep persons from looking in. CURTAIN, BLIND, and SHADE may mean a cover, usually of cloth, which can be rolled up and down inside the window. CURTAIN, however, may also refer to a drapery at a window; and a Venetian BLIND consists of slats mounted on tapes for drawing up or down and varying the pitch of the slats. BLIND and SHUTTER may mean a cover made of two wooden frames with movable slats, attached by hinges outside a window and pulled together or opened at will. SHUTTERS may mean also a set of panels (wooden or iron) put up outside small shops or stores at closing time.

cur′tain call′, **1.** the appearance of the performers at the conclusion of a theatrical or other performance in response to the applause of the audience. **2.** each individual appearance of a performer at the end of a performance when prolonged applause causes him to appear more than once.

cur′tain lec′ture, a scolding administered in private by a wife to her husband.

cur′tain line′, *Theat.* the last line of a scene, act, etc., as in a play; tag line.

cur′tain mu′sic, *Theat.* music played immediately before opening or raising the curtain, as before the beginning of a performance or act.

cur′tain rais′er, a short play acted before a main play.

cur′tain shut′ter, *Photog.* a focal-plane shutter consisting of a curtain on two rollers, moved at a constant speed past the lens opening so as to expose the film to one of several slots in the curtain, the width of which determines the length of exposure. Also called **roller-blind shutter.**

cur′tain speech′, *Theat.* **1.** the final speech of an act, scene, or play. **2.** a brief speech by an actor, producer, author, or the like, immediately following a performance, usually delivered in front of the closed curtains on the stage.

cur′tain wall′, (in a framed building) an exterior wall having no structural function.

cur·tal (kûr′tᵊl), *adj.* **1.** *Archaic.* wearing a short frock: *a curtal friar.* **2.** *Obs.* brief; curtailed. —*n.* **3.** a 16th-century bassoon. **4.** *Obs.* an animal with a docked tail. [earlier *courtault* < MF, equiv. to *court* short (see CURT) + *-ault,* var. of *-ald* n. suffix < Gmc]

cur·tal·ax (kûr′tᵊl aks′), *n.* *Archaic.* cutlass. Also, **curtle ax.** [var. (by folk etymology) of earlier *curtilace,* appar. < dial. It *cortelaz(o),* metathetic var. of It *coltellaccio* hunting knife, equiv. to *coltell(o)* (< L; see CULTELLUS) + *-accio* n. suffix. See CUTLASS]

cur·tate (kûr′tāt), *adj.* shortened; abbreviated. [< L *curtāt(us)* shortened, ptp. of *curtāre.* See CURT, -ATE[1]]

cur·te·sy (kûr′ti sē), *n., pl.* **-sies.** *Law.* the life tenure formerly enjoyed by a husband in his wife's land inheritance after her death, provided they had issue able to inherit: *a tenancy by the curtesy.* [var. of COURTESY]

cur·ti·lage (kûr′tᵊlij), *n.* *Law.* the area of land occupied by a dwelling and its yard and outbuildings, actually enclosed or considered as enclosed. [ME *courtelage* < OF *cortillage,* equiv. to *cortil* yard (*cort* COURT + *-il* dim. suffix) + *-age* -AGE]

Cur·tin (kûr′tin), *n.* **John,** 1885–1945, Australian statesman: prime minister 1941–45.

Cur·tis (kûr′tis), *n.* **1. Charles,** 1860–1936, vice-president of the U.S. 1929–33. **2. Cyrus Her·mann Kotzsch·mar** (hûr′mən koch′mär), 1850–1933, U.S. publisher. **3. George Tick·nor** (tik′nər), 1812–94, U.S. attorney and writer. **4. George William,** 1824–92, U.S. essayist, editor, and reformer. **5.** a boy's given name.

Cur·tiss (kûr′tis), *n.* **Glenn Hammond,** 1878–1930, U.S. inventor: pioneer in the field of aviation.

Cur·ti·us (ko͝or′tsē o͝os′ *for 1;* kûr′tē əs *for 2, 3*), *n.* **1. Ernst** (ernst), 1814–96, German archaeologist and historian. **2. Marcus,** *Rom. Legend.* a young Roman who, on learning that a sacrificial victim was needed to close a crevice formed in the floor of the Roman forum, voluntarily plunged himself and his horse into it. **3.** a walled plain in the fourth quadrant of the face of the moon: about 50 miles in diameter.

cur′tle ax′ (kûr′tᵊl), curtalax.

curt·sey (kûrt′sē), *n., pl.* **-seys,** *v.i.,* **-seyed, -sey·ing.** curtsy.

curt·sy (kûrt′sē), *n., pl.* **-sies,** *v.,* **-sied, -sy·ing.** —*n.* **1.** a bow by women in recognition or respect, consisting of bending the knees and lowering the body. —*v.i.* **2.** to make a curtsy. [var. of COURTESY]

cu·rule (kyo͞or′o͞ol), *adj.* **1.** privileged to sit in a curule chair. **2.** of the highest rank. [< L *curūl(is),* var. of *currūlis,* equiv. to *currū-* (s. of *currus* triumphal car) + *-lis,* var. of *-ālis* -AL[1]]

cu′rule chair′, (in ancient Rome) a folding seat with curved legs and no back, often ornamented with ivory, used only by certain high officials.

cur·va·ceous (kûr vā′shəs), *adj.* *Informal.* (of a woman) having a well-shaped figure with pronounced, voluptuous curves: *the curvaceous blond in the knitted dress.* Also, **cur·va′cious.** [CURVE + -ACEOUS]

cur·va·ture (kûr′və chər), *n.* **1.** act of curving. **2.** curved condition, often abnormal: *curvature of the spine.* **3.** the degree of curving of a line or surface. **4.** *Geom.* **a.** (at a point on a curve) the derivative of the inclination of the tangent with respect to arc length. **b.** the absolute value of this derivative. **5.** something curved. [< L *curvātūr(a),* equiv. to *curvāt(us)* bent, curved (ptp. of *curvāre*) + *-ūra* -URE. See CURVE, -ATE[1]]

cur′vature of field′, *Optics.* a monochromatic aberration of a lens or other optical system in which the focal surface is curved, the refracted image of an object oriented perpendicular to the axis of the lens lying on a curved surface rather than in a plane perpendicular to the axis.

curve (kûrv), *n., v.,* **curved, curv·ing,** *adj.* —*n.* **1.** a continuously bending line, without angles. **2.** a curving movement or path. **3.** any curved outline, form, thing, or part. **4.** a curved guide used by draftsmen. **5.** Also called **curve′ ball′.** *Baseball.* **a.** a pitch delivered with a spin that causes the ball to veer from a normal straight path, away from the side from which it was thrown. **b.** the course of such a pitched ball. **6.** *Math.* a collection of points whose coordinates are continuous functions of a single independent variable. **7.** a graphic representation of the variations effected in something by the influence of changing conditions; graph. **8.** a misleading or deceptive trick; cheat; deception. **9.** *Educ.* a grading system based on the scale of performance of a group, so that those performing better, regardless of their knowledge of a given subject, receive higher marks: *The new English professor marks on the curve.* Cf. **absolute** (def. 10). —*v.t., v.i.* **10.** to bend in a curve; take or cause to take the course of a curve. —*adj.* **11.** curved. [< L *curv(us)* crooked, bent, curved] —**curv·ed·ly** (kûr′vid lē), *adv.* —**curv′ed·ness,** *n.*

curve′ of buoy′ancy, *Naval Archit.* a graphic representation of the distribution of buoyancy in a hull, drawn as a curve connecting the tops of a series of ordinates representing the amount of buoyancy in each of the various sections of the hull from stem to stern. Cf. **curve of loads.**

curve′ of displace′ment, *Naval Archit.* a graphic representation of the displacement in long tons of a given vessel at various drafts.

curve′ of flota′tion, *Naval Archit.* a line uniting the centers of flotation of a hull, at a given draft, for a certain range of angles of heel.

curve′ of loads′, *Naval Archit.* a graphic representation of the discrepancies between the distribution of buoyancy in the hull of a vessel, as indicated by the curve of buoyancy, and the distribution of dead weight for the vessel, as indicated by the curve of weights: used to determine longitudinal structural requirements.

curve′ of longitu′dinal shear′ing stress′es, *Naval Archit.* a graphic representation of the shearing stresses on a hull structure from stem to stern based on the buoyancy and the weight, when fully loaded, of each section.

curve′ of resist′ance, *Naval Archit.* a graphic representation of the resistance, in tons, of a given hull to being moved through the water at various progressive speeds.

curve′ of weights′, *Naval Archit.* a graphic representation of the distribution of dead weight of the structure and contents of a fully loaded and equipped vessel, drawn as a curve connecting the tops of ordinates representing the amount of weight in each section of the hull from stem to stern. Cf. **curve of loads.**

cur·vet (*n.* kûr′vit; *v.* kər vet′, kûr′vit), *n., v.,* **-vet·ted** or **-vet·ed, -vet·ting** or **-vet·ing.** —*n.* **1.** *Dressage.* a leap of a horse from a rearing position, in which it springs up with the hind legs outstretched as the forelegs descend. —*v.i.* **2.** to leap in a curvet, as a horse; cause one's horse to do this. **3.** to leap and frisk. —*v.t.* **4.** to cause to make a curvet. [earlier *curvetto* < It *corvetta* leap (of a horse), equiv. to *corv(o), corv(a)* bent, arched (see CURVE) + *-etta* -ET]

cur·vette (kûr vet′), *n.* *Jewelry.* cuvette (def. 2).

cur·vi-, a combining form of **curve:** *curvilinear.* [< LL, comb. form of *curvus* curved]

cur·vi·lin·e·ar (kûr′və lin′ē ər), *adj.* **1.** consisting of or bounded by curved lines: *a curvilinear figure.* **2.** forming or moving in a curved line. **3.** formed or characterized by curved lines. Also, **cur′vi·lin′e·al.** [CURVI- + LINEAR] —**cur·vi·lin·e·ar·i·ty** (kûr′və lin′ē ar′i tē), *n.* —**cur′vi·lin′e·ar·ly,** *adv.*

curvilin′ear coor′dinate sys′tem, *Math.* a system of coordinates in which the coordinates are determined by three families of surfaces, usually perpendicular.

curv·y (kûr′vē), *adj.,* **curv·i·er, curv·i·est.** curved, esp. curvaceous. Also, **curv′ey.** [CURVE + -Y[1]]

Cur·wens·ville (kûr′wənz vil′), *n.* a town in central Pennsylvania. 3231 (1960).

Cur·zon (kûr′zən), *n.* **George Nathaniel, 1st Marquis Curzon of Ked·le·ston** (ked′əl stən), 1859–1925, British statesman: viceroy of India 1899–1905.

Cu·san·us (ko͞o san′əs), *n.* a crater in the first quadrant of the face of the moon: about 30 miles in diameter.

Cus·co (ko͞os′kō), *n.* Cuzco.

cu·sec (kyo͞o′sek), *n.* one cubic foot per second. [*cu(bic foot per) sec(ond)*]

Cush (kush), *n.* **1.** the eldest son of Ham. Gen. 10:6. **2.** an area mentioned in the Bible, sometimes identified with Upper Egypt. Also, **Kush.**

cush·at (kush′ət, ko͝osh′-), *n. Brit. Dial.* the ringdove, *Colomba palumbus.* [ME *couschot,* OE *cūscote* wood pigeon]

cu·shaw (kə shô′), *n.* any of several squashes having long, curved necks, esp. varieties of *Cucurbita moschata.* [? < Algonquian]

cush-cush (ko͝osh′ko͝osh′), *n.* yampee. [?]

Cush·ing (ko͝osh′ing), *n.* **1. Caleb,** 1800–79, U.S. statesman and diplomat. **2. Harvey (Williams),** 1869–1939, U.S. surgeon and author. **3. Richard James,** born 1895, U.S. Roman Catholic clergyman: cardinal since 1958; archbishop of Boston since 1944. **4.** a town in central Oklahoma. 8619 (1960).

cush·ion (ko͝osh′ən), *n.* **1.** a soft bag of cloth, leather, or rubber, filled with feathers, air, etc., on which to sit, kneel, or lie. **2.** anything similar in form, used to dampen shocks or to prevent excessive pressure or chafing. **3.** a pillow used in lacemaking. **4.** a leather pad on which gold leaf is placed preparatory to gilding. **5.** a pad worn under the hair by women. **6.** the elastic raised rim encircling the top of a billiard table. **7.** something to absorb or counteract a shock, jar, or jolt, as a body of air or steam. **8.** *Anat., Zool.* any part or structure resembling a cushion. **9.** a portion of a radio or television script that can be adjusted in length or cut out altogether in order to end the program on time. **10.** *Ice Hockey, Canadian.* the iced surface of a rink. —*v.t.* **11.** to place on or support by a cushion. **12.** to furnish with a cushion or cushions. **13.** to cover or conceal with, or as with, a cushion. **14.** to check the motion of (a piston or the like) by a cushion, as of steam. **15.** to form (steam or the like) into a cushion. **16.** to suppress (complaints, lamentations, etc.) by quietly ignoring. **17.** to lessen or soften the effects of: *to cushion the blow to his pride.* [ME *cuisshin* < MF *coussin* << L *cox(a)* hip + *-īnus* -INE[1]; see COXA] —**cush′ion·less,** *adj.* —**cush′ion·like′,** *adj.*
—**Syn. 1.** pad. CUSHION, PILLOW, BOLSTER agree in being cases filled with a material more or less resilient, intended to be used as supports for the body or parts of it. A CUSHION is a soft pad used to sit, lie, or kneel on, or to lean against: *a number of cushions on a sofa; cushions on pews in a church.* A PILLOW is a bag or case filled with feathers, down, or other soft material, usually to support the head: *to sleep with a pillow under one's head.* A BOLSTER is a firm pillow, long enough to extend the width of a bed and used as head support, with or without a pillow. **7.** shock absorber. **16.** quieten, check, forestall.

cush′ion cut′, *Jewelry.* a variety of brilliant cut in which the girdle has the form of a square with rounded corners.

cush′ion pink′, a perennial herb, *Silene acaulis,* of Europe and North America, having purplish-red, solitary flowers. Also called **moss campion.**

cush′ion raft′er. See **auxiliary rafter.**

cush′ion spurge′, a perennial herb, *Euphorbia epithymoides,* of Europe, having showy foliage, grown as an ornamental.

cush·ion·y (ko͝osh′ə nē), *adj.* **1.** soft like a cushion; easy; comfortable. **2.** having or provided with cushions. **3.** used as a cushion. [CUSHION + -Y[1]]

Cush·it·ic (kə shit′ik), *n.* **1.** a subfamily of the Afro-Asiatic family of languages, including Somali, Galla, and other languages of Somalia and Ethiopia. —*adj.* **2.** of or pertaining to Cushitic. [*Cushite* (see CUSH, -ITE[1]) + -IC]

Cush·man (ko͝osh′mən), *n.* **Charlotte Saun·ders** (sôn′dərz, sän′-), 1816–76, U.S. actress.

cush·y (ko͝osh′ē), *adj.,* **cush·i·er, cush·i·est.** *Slang.* easy; pleasant: *He got a cushy job as restaurant editor.* [CUSH(ION) + -Y[1]]

cusk (kusk), *n., pl.* **cusks,** (*esp. collectively*) **cusk. 1.** an edible marine fish, *Brosmius brosme,* found along both coasts of the North Atlantic. **2.** the burbot. [prob. var. of *tusk* kind of fish < Scand; cf. Norw *tosk,* var. of *torsk,* c. Icel *thorskr* codfish]

cusk-eel (kusk′ēl′), *n., pl.* (*esp. collectively*) **-eel,** (*esp. referring to two or more kinds or species*) **-eels.** any of several eellike, marine fishes of the family *Ophidiidae,* having the ventral fins located under the throat and so modified as to resemble barbels.

cusp (kusp), *n.* **1.** a point; pointed end. **2.** *Anat., Zool., Bot.* a point, projection, or elevation, as on the crown of a tooth. **3.** Also called **spinode.** *Geom.* a point where two branches of a curve meet, end, and are tangent. **4.** *Archit.* a decorative device, used esp. in Gothic architecture to vary the outlines of intradoses or to form architectural foils, consisting of a pair of curves tangent to the real or imaginary line defining the area decorated and meeting at a point within the area. **5.** *Astron.* a point of a crescent, esp. of the moon. **6.** *Astrol.* the first part of a house, esp. in nativity calculations. [< L *cusp(is)* a point] —**cusp′al,** *adj.*

cusped (kuspt), *adj.* having a cusp or cusps; cusplike. Also, **cus·pate** (kus′pit, -pāt), **cus′pat·ed.** [CUSP + -ED[3]]

cus·pid (kus′pid), *n.* (in man) a tooth with a single projection point or elevation; canine. [< L *cuspid-* (s. of *cuspis*) point]

cus·pi·dal (kus′pi dəl), *adj.* of, like, or having a cusp; cuspidate. [< L *cuspid-* (s. of *cuspis*) point + -AL[1]]

cus·pi·date (kus′pi dāt′), *adj.* **1.** having a cusp or cusps. **2.** furnished with or ending in a sharp and stiff point or cusp: *cuspidate leaves; a cuspidate tooth.* Also, **cus′pi·dat′ed.** [< NL *cuspidāt(us),* equiv. to L *cuspid-* (see CUSPID) + *-ātus* -ATE[1]]

cus·pi·da·tion (kus′pi dā′shən), *n.* decoration with cusps, as in architecture. [CUSPIDATE + -ION]

cus·pi·dor (kus′pi dôr′), *n.* a bowl used as a receptacle for spit, tobacco ash, etc. [< Pg: lit., spitter, equiv. to *cuspid-* (ptp. s. of *cuspir* to spit < L *conspuere* to cover with spit) + *-or* -OR[2]]

cuss (kus), *U.S. Informal.* —*n.* **1.** curseword; oath. **2.** a person or animal: *a strange but likable cuss.* —*v.t.* **3.** to swear at; curse: *He cussed the pedestrian for getting in his way.* **4.** to criticize or reprimand in harsh terms (often fol. by *out*): *The coach cussed out the team for its poor showing.* —*v.i.* **5.** to use profanity; curse; swear: *He left the room cussing to himself.* [early var. of CURSE]

cuss·ed (kus′id), *adj. U.S. Informal.* **1.** cursed. **2.** obstinate; perverse. [CUSS + -ED[3]] —**cuss′ed·ly,** *adv.*

cuss·ed·ness (kus′id nis), *n. Informal.* intractable temperament; obstinacy: *Nothing can touch that donkey for sheer cussedness.* [CUSSED + -NESS]

cus·so (ko͞os′ō, kus′ō, ko͞o′sō), *n. Pharm.* brayera. [< Amharic *kussu*]

cuss·word (kus′wûrd′), *n. U.S. Informal.* See **curse word.** [CUSS + WORD]

cus·tard (kus′tərd), *n.* a dish made of eggs and milk, sweetened and baked, boiled, or frozen. [late ME, var. of *crustade* kind of pie. See CRUST, -ADE[1] and cf. OPr *cr(o)ustado*]

cus′tard ap′ple, 1. the fruit of any of various shrubs and trees native to tropical America, having a soft, edible pulp, esp. *Annona reticulata.* **2.** the shrub or tree itself. **3.** some related tree, as *Asimina triloba,* the North American papaw, or its fruit. Also called **bullock's-heart.**

cus′tard cup′, a heat-resistant, porcelain or glass cup in which custard is baked.

Cus·ter (kus′tər), *n.* **George Arm·strong** (ärm′strông, -strong), 1839–76, U.S. general and Indian fighter.

cus·to·des (ku stō′dēz; *Lat.* ko͝os tō′des), *n.* pl. of **custos.**

cus·to·di·al (ku stō′dē əl), *adj.* **1.** of or pertaining to custody. —*n.* **2.** a vessel or receptacle for something sacred, as the Host. [< L *custōdi(a)* CUSTODY + -AL[1]]

cus·to·di·an (ku stō′dē ən), *n.* a person who has custody; keeper; guardian. [< L *custōdi(a)* watchman (see CUSTODY) + -AN] —**cus·to′di·an·ship′,** *n.*

cus·to·dy (kus′tə dē), *n., pl.* **-dies. 1.** keeping; guardianship; care: *in the custody of her father.* **2.** the keeping or charge of officers of the law: *The car was held in the custody of the police.* **3.** imprisonment; legal restraint: *He was taken into custody.* [late ME *custodye* < L *custōdia* a watching, watchman, equiv. to *custōd-* (s. of *custōs*) keeper + *-ia* -Y[3]]
—**Syn. 1.** safekeeping, charge, watch. CUSTODY, KEEPING, POSSESSION imply a guardianship or care for something. CUSTODY denotes a strict keeping, as by a formally authorized and responsible guardian or keeper: *in the custody of the sheriff.* KEEPING denotes having in one's care or charge, as for guarding or preservation: *in a bank for safekeeping.* POSSESSION means holding, ownership, or mastery: *Leave it in possession of its owner.* **3.** confinement, detention.

cus·tom (kus′təm), *n.* **1.** a habitual practice; the usual way of acting in given circumstances. **2.** habits or usages collectively; convention. **3.** a long-continued habit that is so established that it has the force of law. **4.** such habits collectively. **5.** a customary tax, tribute, or service due by feudal tenants to their lord. **6.** *Sociol.* a group pattern of habitual activity usually transmitted from one generation to another. **7.** toll; duty. **8. customs, a.** (*construed as sing. or pl.*) duties imposed by law on imported or, less commonly, exported goods. **b.** (*construed as sing.*) the government department that collects these duties. **9.** habitual patronage of a particular shop, restaurant, etc.; business patronage. **10.** the customers or patrons of a business firm, collectively. **11.** the aggregate of customers. —*adj.* **12.** made specially for individual customers: *custom shoes.* **13.** dealing in things so made, or doing work to order: *a custom tailor.* [ME *custume* < OF, var. of *costume* < LL **co(n)s(uē)tūmin-,* r. L *consuētūdin-* (s. of *consuētūdō*), equiv. to *consuēt(us)* accustomed, ptp. of *consuēscere* (*con-* CON- + *suē-* (akin to *suus* one's own) + *-tus* ptp. suffix) + *-ūdin-* n. suffix]
—**Syn. 1, 2.** CUSTOM, HABIT, PRACTICE mean an established way of doing things. CUSTOM, applied to a community or to an individual, implies a more or less permanent continuance of a social usage: *It is the custom to give gifts at Christmas time.* HABIT, applied particularly to an individual, implies such repetition of the same action as to develop a natural, spontaneous, or rooted tendency or inclination to perform it: *to make a habit of reading the newspapers.* PRACTICE applies to a set of fixed habits or an ordered procedure in conducting activities: *It is his practice to verify all statements; secret practice of a cult.*

cus·tom·a·ble (kus′tə mə bəl), *adj. Rare.* subject to customs or duties; dutiable. [ME < MF *costumable.* See CUSTOM, -ABLE] —**cus′tom·a·ble·ness,** *n.*

cus·tom·ar·y (kus′tə mer′ē), *adj., n., pl.* **-ar·ies.** —*adj.* **1.** according to or depending on custom; usual; habitual. **2.** of or established by custom rather than law. **3.** *Law.* defined by long continued practices: *the customary service due from land in a manor.* —*n.* **4.** a book or document containing the legal customs or customary laws of a locality. **5.** any body of such customs or laws. [ML *customāri(us),* equiv. to *costum(i)a* custom (also in VL; see CUSTOM) + *-ārius* -ARY] —**cus·tom·ar·i·ly** (kus′tə mer′ə lē; *for emphasis,* kus′tə mâr′ə lē), *adv.* —**cus′tom·ar′i·ness,** *n.*
—**Syn. 1.** wonted, accustomed, conventional, common, regular. See **usual.** —**Ant. 1.** uncommon.

cus·tom-built (kus′təm bilt′), *adj.* made to individual order: *a custom-built limousine.*

cus·tom·er (kus′tə mər), *n.* **1.** one who purchases goods from another; a buyer; patron. **2.** *Informal.* a person one has to deal with; fellow: *a tough customer; a cool customer.* [late ME; see CUSTOM, -ER[1]; cf. ME *customer* collector of customs < AF; OF *costumier,* c. ML *custumārius;* see CUSTOMARY]

cus′tomer's man′, *Stock Exchange.* See **registered representative.**

cus′tom house′, a government office, often at a seaport, for collecting customs, clearing vessels, etc. Also, **cus′tom·house′, cus′toms house′, cus′toms·house′.**

cus·tom-made (kus′təm mād′), *adj.* made to individual order: *custom-made shoes.*

cus′toms bro′ker, a person or firm whose business is to clear goods or merchandise through customs for a consignee or shipper. Also called **cus′tom·house bro′ker** (kus′təm hous′).

cus′toms un′ion, an arrangement between independent nations or tariff areas to remove customs barriers between them and to adopt a uniform tariff policy.

cus·tos (kus′tos; *Lat.* ko͝os′tōs), *n., pl.* **cus·to·des** (ku stō′dēz; *Lat.* ko͝os tō′des). **1.** (*italics.*) *Latin.* a custodian. **2.** a superior in the Franciscan order. [late ME < ML]

cus·tos mo·rum (ko͝os′tōs mō′ro͞om; *Eng.* kus′tos mōr′əm, môr′-), *pl.* **cus·to·des mo·rum** (ko͝os tō′des mō′ro͞om; *Eng.* ku stō′dēz mōr′əm, môr′-). *Latin.* a custodian or guardian of morals; censor. [lit., guardian of established usages, laws, etc.]

cus·tu·mal (kus′cho͞o məl), *n.* a customary. [< ML *custumāl(is),* a Latinization of OF *costumel* customary, usual, equiv. to *costume* CUSTOM + *-el* -AL[1]]

cut (kut), *v.,* **cut, cut·ting,** *adj., n.* —*v.t.* **1.** to penetrate with or as with a sharp-edged instrument: *He cut his finger.* **2.** to strike sharply, as with a whip. **3.** to wound severely the feelings of. **4.** to divide with or as with a sharp-edged instrument; sever; carve: *to cut a rope; to cut bread into slices.* **5.** to hew or saw down; fell: *to cut timber.* **6.** to detach with or as with a sharp-edged instrument; separate from the main body; lop off: *to cut the heel from a loaf of bread.* **7.** to reap; mow; harvest: *to cut grain or hay.* **8.** to trim by clipping, shearing, paring, or pruning: *to cut the hair; to cut the nails.* **9.** to intersect; cross: *One line cuts another at right angles.* **10.** to abridge or shorten; edit by omitting a part or parts: *to cut a speech.* **11.** *Radio and Television.* **a.** to stop recording or transmitting (a scene, broadcast, orchestra number, etc.). **b.** to eliminate (a part of a program) so that it will end on time. **12.** to lower; reduce; diminish (sometimes fol. by *down*): *to cut prices; to cut down the TV sound.* **13.** to dissolve; dilute; make less thick: *to cut wine; to cut phlegm.* **14.** to make or fashion by cutting, as a statue, jewel, garment, etc. **15.** *Glassmaking.* to produce a pattern (in glass) by grinding and polishing. **16.** to hollow out; excavate; dig: *to cut a trench.* **17.** to grow (a tooth or teeth) through the gum: *He is cutting his permanent teeth.* **18.** to stop; halt the running of, as a liquid, an engine, etc. (often fol. by *off*): *The pilot cut the engines and glided in for a landing. Cut off the water.* **19.** *Informal.* to cease; discontinue (often fol. by *out*): *Cut the kidding. Let's cut out the pretense.* **20.** (in motion pictures, television, etc.) **a.** to suspend or terminate (a program, motion picture, or scene) by stopping the action of the cameras or players. **b.** to edit (motion picture or television film) by deleting unwanted footage, rearranging segments, and splicing. **21.** to refuse to recognize socially; shun ostentatiously: *Her friends began to cut her as the season progressed.* **22.** to absent oneself from: *allowed to cut three classes per semester.* **23.** *Cards.* **a.** to divide (a pack of cards) at random into two or more parts, by removing cards from the top. **b.** to take (a card) from a deck. **24.** *Sports.* to hit (a ball) either with the hand or some instrument so as to change its course and often to cause it to spin. **25.** *Cricket.* to strike and send off (a ball) in front of the batsman, and parallel to the wicket. **26.** to record a selection on (a phonograph record or tape); make a recording of. **27.** to switch off or reduce the speed of (an engine or motor).
—*v.i.* **28.** to penetrate or divide something, as with a sharp-edged instrument; make an incision: *The scissors cut well.* **29.** to admit of being cut: *Butter cuts easily.* **30.** to pass, go, or come, esp. in the most direct way (usually fol. by *across, through, in,* etc.): *to cut across an empty lot.* **31.** to shift suddenly from one shot to another, as in film making or television: *Cut to the barroom interior.* **32.** to make a sudden or sharp turn in direction; change direction suddenly; swerve: *We cut to the left to avoid hitting that child.* **33.** to strike a person, animal, etc., sharply, as with a whip. **34.** to wound the feelings severely: *His criticism cut deep.* **35.** (of the teeth) to grow through the gums. **36.** *Cards.* to cut the cards. **37.** *Informal.* to leave hastily: *to cut for the hills.* **38.** (of a horse) to interfere. **39. cut a caper** or **figure,** to perform a spirited, brief, outlandish dance step, esp. as a result of euphoria: *When I told him he could go to the movies, he cut a caper.* **40. cut across,** to precede or go beyond considerations of; transcend: *The gross injustice of the situation cut across their personal prejudices.* **41. cut a figure, a.** See **cut a caper. b.** to give a certain impression of oneself: *He cut a distinguished figure in his tuxedo. She cut quite a figure in her new hat.* **42. cut and run, a.** *Naut.* to cut the anchor cable and set sail, as in an emergency. **b.** to leave as hurriedly as possible: *After breaking the window, they cut and ran.* **43. cut back, a.** to shorten by cutting off the end. **b.** to return to an earlier episode or event, as in the plot of a novel. **c.** *Football.* to reverse direction suddenly by moving in the diagonally opposite course. **d.** to curtail or discontinue: *Steel production has been cut back in recent months.* **44. cut both ways,** to have, produce, or result in advantages as well as disadvantages: *This decision will inevitably cut both ways.* **45. cut down, a.** Also, **cut down on.** to lessen; decrease: *She cut down her between-meal snacks.* **b.** to strike and cause to fall: *The first force to attempt an advance was swiftly cut down.* **c.** to destroy, kill, or disable: *The hurricane cut down everything in its path. He was cut down in the prime of life.* **d.** to remodel, remake, or reduce in size, as a garment: *She had her old evening wrap cut down to fit her daughter. I cut down Mother's old linen dress and made a suit out of it.* **46. cut in, a.** to move or thrust oneself, a

vehicle, etc., abruptly between or in: *A speeding car cut in and nearly caused an accident.* **b.** to interpose; interrupt: *to cut in with a remark.* **c.** *Informal.* (of a man) to stop a dancing couple in order to take the woman for one's own partner. **47. cut it out,** *Slang.* to stop doing something: *You're making too much noise and I wish you'd cut it out.* **48. cut no ice.** See **ice** (def. 11). **49. cut off, a.** to intercept. **b.** to interrupt. **c.** to bring to a sudden end; stop. **d.** to shut off or shut out. **e.** to disinherit or leave an unexpectedly small sum to someone. **f.** to sever; separate: *Since leaving the city she has been cut off from her college friends.* **50. cut out, a.** to omit; delete; excise. **b.** to oust and replace a rival; supplant. **c.** to part an animal from a herd. **d.** to plan; contrive; arrange. **e.** to move out of one's lane of traffic. **f.** *Slang.* to leave suddenly. **g.** *Informal.* to refrain from; stop: *to cut out smoking.* **51. cut up, a.** to cut into pieces or sections. **b.** to lacerate; wound. **c.** to distress mentally; injure. **d.** *Informal.* to play pranks; misbehave: *They received a scolding for cutting up during church services.* **52. cut up rough,** to become unpleasant and ill-tempered. Also, **cut up nasty, cut up bad.**
—*adj.* **53.** that has been subjected to cutting; divided into pieces by cutting; detached by cutting: *cut flowers.* **54.** *Bot.* incised; cleft. **55.** fashioned by cutting; having the surface shaped or ornamented by grinding, polishing, or the like: *cut diamonds.* **56.** reduced by or as by cutting: *cut whiskey; cut prices.* **57.** castrated; gelded. **58.** *Slang.* drunk. **59. cut and dried, a.** fixed or settled in advance. **b.** lacking freshness, original thought, or spontaneity: *a lecture that was cut and dried.* **60. cut out for,** *Informal.* fitted for; capable of: *He wasn't cut out for military service.*
—*n.* **61.** the act of cutting; a stroke or a blow, as with a knife, whip, etc. **62.** a piece cut off: *a cut of a pie.* **63.** *Butchering.* part of an animal usually cut as one piece. **64.** *Informal.* share: *His agent's cut is 20 percent.* **65.** a quantity cut, esp. of lumber. **66.** the result of cutting, as an incision, wound, a passage, channel, etc. **67.** manner or fashion in which anything is cut: *the cut of a dress; I don't like the cut of that chair.* **68.** style; manner; kind: *We need a man of his cut in this firm.* **69.** a passage or course straight across or through: *a cut through the woods.* **70.** an excision or omission of a part. **71.** a part or quantity of text deleted or omitted. **72.** a reduction in price, salary, etc. **73.** an act, speech, etc., which wounds the feelings. **74.** an engraved plate or block used for printing. **75.** a printed picture or illustration. **76.** a refusal to recognize an acquaintance. **77.** an absence, as from a school class, at which attendance is required. **78.** *Sports.* **a.** act of cutting a ball. **b.** the spin of the ball. **79.** *Cards.* a cutting of the cards. **80.** one of several pieces of straw, paper, etc., used in drawing lots. **81.** *Fencing.* a blow with the edge of the blade instead of the tip. **82.** *Motion Pictures, Television.* a sudden shift from one shot to another. **83. a cut above,** *Informal.* somewhat superior to another (thing, person, etc.) in some respect: *Her pies are a cut above any others I've tasted.* [ME *cutten, kytten, kitten,* OE **cyttan;* akin to OSw *kotta* to cut, Icel *kuti* little knife] —**cut′ta·ble,** *adj.*
—**Syn. 1.** gash, slash, slit, lance. **3.** hurt, touch, slight, insult. **4.** cleave, sunder, bisect. CUT, CHOP, HACK, HEW refer to giving a sharp blow or stroke. CUT is a general word for this: *to cut the grass.* To CHOP is to cut by giving repeated blows with something sharp, as an ax. To CHOP and to HEW are practically interchangeable, but CHOP may refer to a more or less undirected action, whereas HEW, more formal, suggests keeping to a definite purpose: *to chop or hew down a tree; to hew a line.* To HACK is to cut or chop roughly and unevenly: *to hack off a limb.* **10.** abbreviate, curtail. **13.** thin. **66.** gash, slash, slit.

cut-and-cov·er (kut′ən kuv′ər), *n.* a method for digging a tunnel, laying pipe, etc., by cutting a trench, constructing the tunnel or laying the pipe in it, and covering with the excavated material.

cu·ta·ne·ous (kyōō tā′nē əs), *adj.* of, pertaining to, or affecting the skin. [< ML *cutāne(us),* equiv. to L *cut(is)* the skin + *-āneus* (*-ān(us)* -AN + *-eus* -EOUS). See HIDE²] —**cu·ta′ne·ous·ly,** *adv.*

cuta′neous quit′tor, *Vet. Pathol.* a purulent infection of horses and other hoofed animals, characterized by an acute inflammation of soft tissue above the hoof and resulting in suppuration and sloughing of the skin and usually lameness.

cut·a·way (kut′ə wā′), *adj.* **1.** (of a coat) having the front portion of the skirt cut away from the waist in a curve or slope. **2.** having a part cut away, as an outer section of something illustrated so that the inside may be shown. —*n.* **3.** a cutaway coat, as that worn by a man for formal dress. **4.** a switch from one scene to another, as in a motion picture, for showing simultaneous or related action, creating suspense, etc. [adj., n. use of v. phrase *cut away*]

Cutaway coat

cut·back (kut′bak′), *n.* **1.** a return in the course of a story, motion picture, etc., to earlier events. **2.** reduction in rate, quantity, etc.: *a cutback in production.* **3.** *Football.* a play in which the ball-carrier abruptly reverses direction, esp. by starting to make an end run and then turning suddenly to run toward the middle of the line. [n. use of v. phrase *cut back*]

Cut′ Bank′, a town in N Montana. 4539 (1960).

cut·bank (kut′bangk′), *n.* *Geol.* a nearly vertical slope produced by erosion along the side of a stream. [CUT + BANK¹]

cut′-card′ work′ (kut′kärd′), silver leaf cut in ornamental shapes and soldered to a silver vessel as ornament.

cutch (kuch), *n.* catechu.

Cutch (kuch), *n.* **1.** a former state in W India, now part of Gujarat state. 8461 sq. mi. **2. Rann of** (ren), a salt marsh NE of this area. 9000 sq. mi. Also, **Kutch.**

cut·cha (kuch′ə), *adj.* kutcha.

cut·cher·ry (kə cher′ē, kuch′ə rē), *n., pl.* **-ries. 1.** (in India) a public administrative or judicial office. **2.** any administrative office. [< Hindi *kacerī,* var. of *kacahrī* audience house, court-house, office]

cut·cher·y (kə cher′ē, kuch′ə rē), *n., pl.* **-ries.** cutcherry.

cut·down (kut′doun′), *n.* **1.** reduction; decrease; diminution: *a cutdown in profits; a cutdown in sales.* **2.** *Surg.* the incision of a superficial vein in order to effect direct insertion of a catheter. [n. use of v. phrase *cut down*]

cut′ drop′, *Theat.* a drop scene cut to reveal part of the upstage area.

cute (kyōōt), *adj.,* **cut·er, cut·est. 1.** *Chiefly U.S. Informal.* pleasingly pretty or dainty: *a cute child; a cute hat.* **2.** affectedly or mincingly pretty or clever; precious: *The child has acquired some intolerably cute mannerisms.* **3.** *Informal.* mentally keen; clever; shrewd. [aph. var. of ACUTE] —**cute′ly,** *adv.* —**cute′ness,** *n.*

cut·ey (kyōō′tē), *n., pl.* **-eys.** cutie.

cut′ glass′, glass ornamented or shaped by cutting or grinding with abrasive wheels. —**cut′-glass′,** *adj.*

cut-grass (kut′gras′, -gräs′), *n.* any of several grasses having blades with rough edges, esp. grasses of the genus *Leersia* (*Homalocenchrus*).

Cuth·bert (kuth′bərt), *n.* **1. Saint,** A.D. c635–687, English monk and bishop. **2.** a town in SW Georgia. 4300 (1960). **3.** a boy's given name.

cut′ hunt′er, *Horol.* demi-hunter.

cu·ti·cle (kyōō′ti kəl), *n.* **1.** the epidermis. **2.** a superficial integument, membrane, or the like. **3.** the nonliving epidermis which surrounds the edges of the fingernail or toenail. **4.** *Bot.* a very thin hyaline film covering the surface of plants, derived from the outer surfaces of the epidermal cells. [< L *cuticul(a)* the skin, equiv. to *cuti(s)* skin + *-cula* -CLE] —**cu·tic·u·lar** (kyōō tik′yə lər), *adj.*

cu·ti·col·or (kyōō′tə kul′ər), *adj.* of the color of flesh. [< NL, equiv. to L *cuti(s)* skin + *color* COLOR]

cu·tic·u·la (kyōō tik′yə lə), *n., pl.* **-lae** (-lē′). *Zool.* the outer, noncellular layer of the arthropod integument, composed of a mixture of chitin and protein, but commonly containing other hardening substances. [< NL, L; see CUTICLE]

cut·ie (kyōō′tē), *n.* **1.** *Informal.* a charmingly pretty or cute girl (often used as a form of address): *Hi, cutie.* **2.** *Slang.* **a.** one who tries to outsmart an opponent, as an athlete who outmaneuvers an opposing player: *The tackle was a real cutie when blocking on trap plays.* **b.** a clever or cunning maneuver: *He pulled a cutie.* [CUTE + -IE]

cut′ie pie′, *Informal.* a beloved person; darling; sweetheart; sweetie (often used as a term of endearment).

cut-in (kut′in), *n.* **1.** *Motion Pictures.* a still, as of a scene or an object, inserted in a film and interrupting the action or continuity: *We will insert a cut-in of the letter after she reads it.* **2.** *Radio and Television.* a commercial or other announcement inserted by a local station into a network broadcast. **3.** the act of cutting in, as on a dancing couple. [n. use of v. phrase *cut in*]

cu·tin (kyōō′tin), *n.* a transparent, waxy substance constituting, together with cellulose, the cuticle of plants. [< L *cut(is)* skin + -IN²]

cu·tin·ise (kyōōt′ənīz′), *v.t., v.i.,* **-ised, -is·ing.** *Chiefly Brit.* cutinize. —**cu′tin·i·sa′tion,** *n.*

cu·tin·ize (kyōōt′ənīz′), *v.t., v.i.,* **-ized, -iz·ing.** to make into or become cutin. [CUTIN + -IZE] —**cu′tin·i·za′tion,** *n.*

cu·tis (kyōō′tis), *n., pl.* **-tes** (-tēz), **-tis·es.** the corium or true skin. [< L: skin; akin to Gk *skŷtos* HIDE²]

cu′tis an·se·ri′na (an′sə rī′nə), *Med.* See **goose flesh.** [< NL: goose flesh; see CUTIS, ANSERINE]

cu·tis ve·ra (kyōō′tis vēr′ə), *pl.* **cu·tes ve·rae** (kyōō′tēz vēr′ē). cutis. [< L: lit., true skin]

cut·lass (kut′ləs), *n.* a short, heavy, slightly curved sword. Also, **cut′las.** [earlier *coutelace* < MF *coutelas,* equiv. to *coutel* knife (now *couteau*) (< L *cultell(us),* dim. of *culter* COLTER) + *-as* aug. suffix; c. It *coltellaccio* big knife]

cut·lass·fish (kut′ləs fish′), *n., pl.* (*esp. collectively*) **-fish,** (*esp. referring to two or more kinds or species*) **-fish·es.** any of several silvery marine fishes of the family *Trichiuridae,* having a slender, elongated body ending in a hairlike tail. Also called **hairtail.** [CUTLASS + FISH]

cut′leaf black′berry (kut′lēf′), an arching or trailing, perennial, evergreen blackberry, *Rubus laciniatus,* of Europe, having leaflets with fine, toothed segments, white or pinkish flowers, and small, round, black fruit. Also called **evergreen blackberry.** [CUT + LEAF]

cut·ler (kut′lər), *n.* one who makes, sells, or repairs knives and other cutting instruments. [ME *cuteler* < AF, c. MF *coutelier* < LL *cultellār(ius),* equiv. to L *cultell(us)* (dim. of *culter* COLTER) + *-ārius* -ER²]

cut·ler·y (kut′lə rē), *n.* **1.** the trade or business of a cutler. **2.** cutting instruments collectively, esp. those for serving or eating food. [ME *cutellerie* < MF *coutelerie,* equiv. to *coutel* knife. See CUTLER, -Y³]

cut·let (kut′lit), *n.* **1.** a slice of meat, esp. of veal or mutton, for broiling or frying: originally one, as of mutton, containing a rib, but now commonly one cut from the leg. **2.** a flat croquette of minced chicken, lobster, or the like. [< F *côtelette,* OF *costelette* double dim. of *coste* rib < L *costa.* See -LET]

cut·line (kut′līn′), *n.* *Journalism.* a caption or legend accompanying a cut. [CUT + LINE¹]

cut′lips min′now (kut′lips′), a cyprinid fish, *Exoglossum maxillingua,* found in the eastern U.S., having a trilobate lower lip. [so called from the shape of its lower lip]

cut′ nail′, a nail having a tapering rectangular form with a blunt point, made by cutting from a thin rolled sheet of iron or steel. See illus. under **nail.**

cut·off (kut′ôf′, -of′), *n.* **1.** an act or instance of cutting off. **2.** something that cuts off. **3.** a road, passage, etc., that leaves another, usually providing a short cut: *There is the cutoff to Baltimore.* **4.** a new and shorter channel formed in a river by the water cutting across a bend in its course. **5.** *Mach.* arrest of the steam moving the pistons of an engine, usually occurring before the completion of a stroke. **6.** *Accounting.* a selected point at which records are considered complete for the purpose of settling accounts, taking inventory, etc. **7.** *Electronics.* (in a vacuum tube) the minimum grid potential preventing an anode current. [n. use of v. phrase *cut off*]

cut·out (kut′out′), *n.* **1.** something cut out from something else. **2.** a valve in the exhaust pipe of an internal-combustion engine, which when open permits the engine to exhaust directly into the air ahead of the muffler. [n. use of v. phrase *cut out*]

cut·o·ver (kut′ō′vər), *adj.* **1.** (esp. of timberland) cleared of trees. —*n.* **2.** land, esp. timberland, cleared of trees. [adj., n. use of v. phrase *cut over*]

cut·purse (kut′pûrs′), *n.* **1.** a pickpocket. **2.** (formerly) one who steals by cutting purses from the belt. [ME *cutte-purs.* See CUT, PURSE]

cut′ rate′, *U.S.* a price, fare, or rate below the standard charge. —**cut′-rate′,** *adj.*

cut′ stone′, *Masonry.* a stone or stonework dressed to a relatively fine finish with tools other than hammers.

cut·tage (kut′ij), *n.* the process of propagating plants from separate vegetative parts. [CUT + -AGE]

cut·ter (kut′ər), *n.* **1.** one who or that which cuts. **2.** a single-masted sailing vessel, very similar to a sloop but having its mast set somewhat farther astern, about two-fifths of the way aft measured on the water line. **3.** a ship's boat having double-banked oars and one or two lugsails. **4.** Also called **revenue cutter.** a lightly armed governmental vessel used to prevent smuggling and enforce the customs regulations. **5.** a small, light sleigh, usually single-seated and pulled by one horse. **6.** Also called **rubber.** a brick suitable for cutting and rubbing. [ME *kittere, cuttere.* See CUT, -ER¹]

cut′ter bar′, **1.** (in a mower, binder, or combine) a bar with triangular guards along which the knife or blade runs. **2.** a bar holding the cutting tool in a boring machine or lathe.

cut·ter-rigged (kut′ər rigd′), *adj.* fore-and-aft-rigged on one mast in the manner of a cutter.

cut·throat (kut′thrōt′), *n.* **1.** one who cuts throats; murderer. —*adj.* **2.** murderous. **3.** ruthless: *cutthroat competition.* **4.** pertaining to a game, as of cards, participated in by three or more persons, each acting and scoring as an individual. [CUT + THROAT]

cut′throat trout′, a spotted trout, *Salmo clarkii,* found in coastal streams of western North America, having a reddish streak on each side of the throat.

cut′ time′, *Music.* See **alla breve.**

cut·ting (kut′ing), *n.* **1.** act of one who or that which cuts. **2.** something cut off. **3.** *Hort.* a piece, as a root, stem, or leaf, cut from a plant and used for propagation. **4.** *Chiefly Brit.* a clipping from a newspaper, magazine, etc. **5.** *Brit.* a trenchlike excavation, esp. through a hill, as one made in constructing a highway. —*adj.* **6.** that cuts; penetrating or dividing by, or as by, a cut. **7.** piercing, as a wind. **8.** wounding the feelings severely; sarcastic. [ME; see CUT, -ING¹, -ING²] —**cut′ting·ly,** *adv.* —**cut′ting·ness,** *n.*
—**Syn. 8.** caustic, biting, mordant, bitter, acid, sardonic.

cut′ting flu′id, a liquid or gas for cooling or lubricating a cutting tool and a piece of work at their point of contact.

cut′ting horse′, a saddle horse trained to separate calves, steers, etc., from a herd.

cut·tle¹ (kut′əl), *n.* **1.** cuttlefish. **2.** cuttlebone. [apocopated form]

cut·tle² (kut′əl), *v.t.,* **-tled, -tling.** *Textiles.* **1.** to fold (cloth) face to face after finishing. **2.** to allow (cloth) to lie without further treatment after fulling, milling, scouring, etc. [?]

cut·tle·bone (kut′əl bōn′), *n.* the calcareous internal shell or plate of true cuttlefishes, used to make powder for polishing and fed to canaries to supply their diet with lime. [CUTTLE(FISH) + BONE¹]

cut·tle·fish (kut′əl fish′), *n., pl.* (*esp. collectively*) **-fish,** (*esp. referring to two or more kinds or species*) **-fish·es.** any of several decapod, dibranchiate cephalopods, esp. of the genus *Sepia,* having arms with suckers and ejecting a black, inklike fluid when in danger. [late ME *codel,* OE *cudele* cuttlefish (akin to COD¹) + FISH]

Cuttlefish, *Sepia officinialis* (Length 5 in.)

cut·ty (kut′ē), *adj., n., pl.* **-ties.** *Chiefly Scot.* —*adj.* **1.** cut short; short; stubby. **2.** irritable; impatient; short-tempered. —*n.* **3.** a short spoon. **4.** a short-stemmed tobacco pipe. **5.** *Informal.* an immoral woman; a worthless woman. [CUT + -Y¹, -Y²]

cut·ty·hunk (kut′ē hungk′), *n.* a twisted, linen fishline, esp. one laid by hand. [after *Cuttyhunk* Island, Massachusetts]

cut′ty stool′, *Scot.* **1.** a low stool. **2.** a seat in old churches, where offenders against chastity, or other delinquents, sat and received public rebuke.

cut·up (kut′up′), *n.* *Informal.* a showoff or prankster. [n. use of v. phrase *cut up*]

cut′ vel′vet, **1.** a fabric in which the looped pile has been cut with a trivet. Cf. **velvet. 2.** a fabric having a pattern of figured velvet with a backing of chiffon or voile. **3.** carpeting with a cut-pile effect.

cut·wa·ter (kut′wô′tər, -wot′ər), *n.* **1.** *Naut.* **a.** the forward edge of the stem of a vessel, dividing the water as the vessel advances. **b.** a vertical timber construction set forward of and following the stem of a wooden vessel below the water line, usually curving forward above the water line to support a beak-head or figurehead. **2.** a sharply pointed upstream face of a bridge pier, for resisting the effects of moving water or ice. [CUT + WATER]

cut·work (kut′wûrk′), *n.* **1.** openwork embroidery in which the ground fabric is cut out about the pattern. **2.** fretwork formed by perforation or cut in low relief. **3.** ornamental needlework in which spaces are cut from a ground material into which are inserted decorative figures that were made separately. **4.** See **point coupé** (def. 1). [CUT + WORK]

cut′work lace′. See **point coupé** (def. 2).

cut·worm (kut′wûrm′), *n.* the caterpillar of any of several noctuid moths, which feeds at night on the stems of young herbaceous plants, cutting them off at the ground. [CUT + WORM]

cu·vée (ko͞o vā′; *Fr.* kʏ vā′), *n.* **1.** wine in vats or casks, blended, often from different vintages, for uniform quality. **2.** a blend resulting from the mixing of wines, esp. of champagnes produced by several vineyards in the same district. [< F, equiv. to *cuve* cask, vat (<< L *cūpa*) + *-ée* ptp. suffix; see -EE]

cu·vette (ko͞o vet′, kyo͞o-), *n.* **1.** *Chem.* a tube or vessel used in laboratory experimentation. **2.** Also, **curvette.** Also called **chevee.** a carving on stone similar to a cameo, having a raised figure on a hollowed background. [< F, dim. of *cuve* vat << L *cūpa*. See CUP, -ETTE]

Cu·vi·er (kyo͞o′vē ā′, ko͞ov yā′; *Fr.* kʏ vyā′), *n.* **1.** **Georges Lé·o·pold Chré·tien Fré·dé·ric Da·go·bert** (zhôʀzh lā ô pôld′ kʀā tyaN′ fʀā dā ʀēk′ dA gō beʀ′), **Baron,** 1769–1832, French naturalist: pioneer in the fields of paleontology and comparative anatomy. **2.** a walled plain in the fourth quadrant of the face of the moon: about 50 miles in diameter.

Cux·ha·ven (ko͝oks′hä′fən), *n.* a seaport in N West Germany, at the mouth of the Elbe River. 44,900 (1963).

Cu·ya·bá (ko͞o′yä bä′), *n.* Cuiabá.

Cuy′a·hog′a Falls′ (kī′ə hog′ə; *older* kī′ə hō′gə), a city in NE Ohio, near Akron. 47,922 (1960).

Cuyp (koip), *n.* **Ael·bert** (äl′bəʀt), 1620–91, Dutch painter. Also, **Kuyp.**

Cuz·co (ko͞os′kō; *Sp.* ko͞os′kô), *n.* a city in S Peru: ancient Inca ruins. 78,289 (1961). Also, **Cusco.**

C.V.O., Commander of the Royal Victorian Order.

CW, *Radio.* continuous wave.

CWA, Civil Works Administration.

cwm (ko͞om), *n.* cirque (def. 1). [< Welsh: valley. See COMBE]

Cwm·bran (ko͝om brän′), *n.* a town in central Monmouthshire, in SE Wales. 30,043 (1961).

CWO, *Mil.* chief warrant officer.

c.w.o., cash with order.

cwt., hundredweight.

Cy (sī), *n.* a boy's given name, form of **Cyrus.**

CY, cycle; cycles.

-cy, **1.** a suffix used to form abstract nouns from adjectives with stems in *-t, -te, -tic,* and esp. *-nt* (*democracy; accuracy; expediency; stagnancy; necromancy*); also paired with other adjectives (*fallacy*) and nouns (*lunacy*), and sometimes used to form action nouns (*vacancy; occupancy*). **2.** a suffix of nouns denoting rank or office, sometimes attached to the stem of a word rather than to the word itself: *captaincy; colonelcy; magistracy.* [repr. F *-cie, -tie,* L *-cia, -tia,* Gk *-kia, -keia, -tia, -teia;* in most cases to be analyzed as consonant + *-y*³: the consonant making the whole or the last member of the preceding morpheme]

Cy., county.

cy., **1.** capacity. **2.** currency. **3.** cycle; cycles.

cy·an (sī′an, sī′ən), *n.* a hue between blue and green. [< Gk *kýan(os)* dark blue]

cyan-¹, var. of **cyano-¹,** usually before a vowel or *h: cyanamide.*

cyan-², var. of **cyano²,** before a vowel.

cyan-³, var. of **cyano-³,** before a vowel.

cy·an·a·mide (sī an′ə mid, -mīd′, sī′ə nam′īd, -id), *n.* *Chem.* **1.** Also called **amidocyanogen, carbimide, cyanogenamide.** a white, crystalline, unstable, deliquescent solid, HN=C=NH, usually produced by the action of ammonia on cyanogen chloride or by the action of sulfuric acid on calcium cyanamide. **2.** (not in technical use) See **calcium cyanamide.** Also, **cy·an·a·mid** (sī an′ə mid, sī′ə nam′id). [CYAN-² + AMIDE]

cy·a·nate (sī′ə nāt′), *n.* *Chem.* a salt or ester of cyanic acid. [CYAN-³ + -ATE²]

cy′an blue′, a moderate greenish-blue to bluish-green color.

Cy·a·ne (sī′ə nē′), *n.* *Class. Myth.* **1.** a princess who was violated by her father, who did not recognize her. **2.** a nymph who unsuccessfully attempted to keep Hades from taking Persephone to the underworld.

Cy·an·e·ë (sī an′ē ē′), *n.* *Class. Myth.* the mother, by Miletus, of Caunus and Byblis.

cy·an·e·ous (sī an′ē əs), *adj.* deep blue; azure; cerulean. [< L *cyaneus* < Gk *kyáneos.* See CYANO-¹, -EOUS]

cy·an·ic (sī an′ik), *adj.* blue: applied esp. to a series of colors in flowers, including the blues and colors tending toward blue. [CYAN-¹ + -IC]

cyan′ic ac′id, *Chem.* an unstable, poisonous, liquid acid, HOCN, isomeric with fulminic acid.

cy·a·nide (sī′ə nīd′, -nid), *n., v.,* **-nid·ed, -nid·ing.** —*n.* **1.** Also, **cy·a·nid** (sī′ə nid). *Chem.* **a.** a salt of hydrocyanic acid, as potassium cyanide, KCN. **b.** a nitrile, as methyl cyanide, CH_3CN. —*v.t.* **2.** to treat with a cyanide, as an ore in order to extract gold. [CYAN-³ + -IDE]

cy′anide proc′ess, a process for extracting gold or silver from ore by dissolving the ore in an alkaline solution of sodium cyanide or potassium cyanide and precipitating the gold or silver from the solution.

cy·a·nine (sī′ə nēn′, -nin), *n.* any of several groups of dyes which make silver halide photographic plates sensitive to a wider color range. Also, **cy·a·nin** (sī′ə nin). [CYAN-¹ + -INE²]

cy·a·nite (sī′ə nīt′), *n.* a mineral, aluminum silicate, Al_2SiO_5, occurring in blue or greenish bladed crystals, used as a refractory. Also, **kyanite.** [CYAN-¹ + -ITE¹] —**cy·a·nit·ic** (sī′ə nit′ik), *adj.*

cy·a·no (sī′ə nō′), *adj.* *Chem.* containing the cyano group. [independent use of CYANO-³]

cyano-¹, a learned borrowing from Greek, indicating dark-blue coloring, used in the formation of compound words: *cyanotype.* Also, *esp. before a vowel,* **cyan-¹.** [< Gk *kýano(s)* dark blue (adj.), dark-blue substance (n.)]

cyano-², a combining form of **cyanide:** *cyanogen.* Also, *esp. before a vowel,* **cyan-².**

cyano-³, *Chem.* a word element referring to the cyanogen group, CN. Also, *esp. before a vowel,* **cyan-³.** [comb. form repr. CYANOGEN]

cy·a·no·chroi·a (sī′ə nō kroi′ə), *n.* *Pathol.* cyanosis. [CYANO-¹ + Gk *chroía* skin]

cy·a·no·co·bal·a·min (sī′ə nō kō bal′ə min), *n.* *Biochem.* See **vitamin B_{12}.** [CYANO-³ + COBAL(T) + (VIT)AMIN]

cy·a·no·der·ma (sī′ə nō dûr′mə), *n.* *Pathol.* cyanosis. [CYANO-¹ + DERMA]

cy·an·o·gen (sī an′ə jən), *n.* *Chem.* **1.** Also called **ethane dinitrile.** a colorless, poisonous, flammable, water-soluble gas, $(CN)_2$, having an almondlike odor: used chiefly in organic synthesis. **2.** See **cyano group.** [CYANO-¹ + -GEN; so named from the fact that CN makes part of the pigment Prussian blue]

cy·a·no·gen·a·mide (sī′ə nō jen′ə mīd′, -mid), *n.* *Chem.* cyanamide. [CYANOGEN + AMIDE]

cyan′ogen bro′mide, *Chem.* a colorless, slightly water-soluble, poisonous, volatile, crystalline solid, BrCN, used chiefly as a fumigant and a pesticide.

cyan′ogen chlo′ride, *Chem.* a colorless, volatile, poisonous liquid, CNCl, used chiefly in the synthesis of compounds containing the cyano group.

cy·a·no·gen·ic (sī′ə nō jen′ik), *adj.* *Biol., Chem.* capable of producing hydrogen cyanide. Also, **cy·a·no·ge·net·ic** (sī′ə nō jə net′ik). [CYANOGEN + -IC]

cy′ano group′, *Chem.* the univalent group, –C≡N; cyanogen.

cy·a·no·guan·i·dine (sī′ə nō gwä′ni dēn′, -din), *n.* *Chem.* dicyandiamide. [CYANO-² + GUANIDINE]

cy·a·no·hy·drin (sī′ə nō hī′drin), *n.* *Chem.* any of a class of organic compounds that contains both the –CN and the –OH group, usually linked to the same carbon atom. [CYANO-³ + HYDR-² + -IN²]

cy·a·nom·e·ter (sī′ə nom′i tər), *n.* an instrument for measuring the amount and intensity of blue present in a phenomenon, as in the sky. [CYANO-¹ + -METER]

cy·a·nop·a·thy (sī′ə nop′ə thē), *n.* cyanosis. [CYANO-¹ + -PATHY] —**cy·a·no·path·ic** (sī′ə nō path′ik), *adj.*

cy·a·no·plat·i·nite (sī′ə nō plat′ənīt′), *n.* *Chem.* platinocyanide. [CYANO-² + PLATINITE]

cy′ano rad′ical. See **cyano group.**

cy·a·no·sis (sī′ə nō′sis), *n.* *Pathol.* blueness or lividness of the skin, as from imperfectly oxygenated blood. Also called **cyanopathy, cyanoderma, cyanochroia.** [< NL < Gk *kyánōsis* dark-blue color. See CYAN-¹, -OSIS] —**cy·a·not·ic** (sī′ə not′ik), *adj.*

cy·an·o·type (sī an′ə tīp′), *n.* **1.** a process of photographic printing, used chiefly in copying architectural and mechanical drawings, which produces a blue line on a white background. **2.** a print made by this process. [CYANO-¹ + -TYPE]

cy·a·nu·ric (sī′ə no͝or′ik, -nyo͝or′-), *adj.* *Chem.* of or derived from cyanuric acid. [CYAN-³ + URIC]

cy′anu′ric ac′id, *Chem.* a white, crystalline, water-soluble solid, $C_3H_3O_3N_3{\cdot}2H_2O$, used chiefly in organic synthesis. Also called **tricyanic acid.**

cy·ath·i·form (sī ath′ə fôrm′), *adj.* *Bot., Zool.* shaped like a cup. [CYATH(IUM) + -I- + -FORM]

cy·ath·i·um (sī ath′ē əm), *n., pl.* **-ath·i·a** (-ath′ē ə). *Bot.* an inflorescence consisting of a cup-shaped involucre enclosing an apetalous, pistillate flower surrounded by several staminate flowers. [< NL < Gk *kyáthion,* dim. of *kýathos* cup]

cy·a·thus (sī′ə thəs), *n., pl.* **-thi** (-thī′). kyathos. [< L]

Cyb·e·le (sib′ə lē′), *n.* a nature goddess of Phrygia and Asia Minor, identified by the Greeks with Rhea and by the Romans with Ops. Also, **Cy·be·be** (sī bē′bē). Also called **Berecyntia, Dindymean Mother, Dindymene, Great Idaean Mother.**

cy·ber·net·ics (sī′bər net′iks), *n.* (*construed as sing.*) the study of human control functions and of mechanical and electric systems designed to replace them, involving the application of statistical mechanics to communication engineering. [< Gk *kybernḗt(ēs)* helmsman, steersman (*kybern(ân)* (to) steer + *-ētēs* agent suffix) + -ICS] —**cy′ber·net′ic,** *adj.* —**cy′ber·net′i·cist, cy·ber·ne·ti·cian** (sī′bər ni tish′ən), *n.*

cyc (sīk), *n.* *Informal.* cyclorama (def. 2). [shortened form]

cy·cad (sī′kad), *n.* any gymnospermous plant of the order *Cycadales,* intermediate in appearance between ferns and the palms, many species having a thick, unbranched, columnar trunk bearing a crown of large, leathery, pinnate leaves. [< NL *Cycad-* (s. of *Cycas*) genus name < Gk *kýkas,* dial. var. of *kóïkas,* acc. pl. of *kóïx* kind of palm, but taken as a synonym (s. *kykad-*) in nom. sing.] —**cy′cad·like′,** *adj.*

cyc·a·da·ceous (sik′ə dā′shəs), *adj.* belonging or pertaining to the order *Cycadales.* [< NL *Cycad-* (see CYCAD) + -ACEOUS]

Cy·chre·us (sī′krē əs, -kro͞os), *n.* *Class. Myth.* a son of Poseidon who became king of Salamis.

cycl-, var. of **cyclo-,** before a vowel: *cycloid.*

Cyc·la·des (sik′lə dēz′), *n.* a group of Greek islands in the S Aegean. 99,959 (1961). 1023 sq. mi.

Cy·clad·ic (si klad′ik, sī-), *adj.* **1.** of or pertaining to the Cyclades. **2.** of or pertaining to the Bronze Age culture of the Cyclades, c3000–c1100 B.C. [CYCLAD(ES) + -IC]

cy·cla·mate (sī′klə māt′, sik′lə-), *n.* any of a group of artificial sweetening agents, as calcium cyclamate or sodium cyclamate.

cyc·la·men (sik′lə mən, -men′), *n.* any low, primulaceous herb of the genus *Cyclamen,* having tuberous rootstocks and nodding white, purple, pink, or crimson flowers with reflexed petals. [< ML < Gk *kykláminos* bulbous plant, akin to *kýklos* CYCLE]

cyc′lamen al′dehyde, *Chem.* a colorless to light-yellow alcohol-soluble, synthetic liquid, $(CH_3)_2CHC_6H_4CH(CH_3)CH_2CHO$, having a strong floral odor, used chiefly in perfumes, esp. those of soap.

Cy·cla·my·cin (sī′klə mī′sin), *n.* *Pharm., Trademark.* triacetyloleandomycin.

cyc·las (sik′ləs), *n., pl.* **-la·des** (-lə dēz′). **1.** a tunic or surcoat, longer in back than in front, worn over armor in the Middle Ages. **2.** a similar, full-length garment worn by women. **3.** a round robe with an elaborately ornamented border, worn by women in ancient Rome. [< ML, L < Gk *kyklás,* n. use of *kyklás* around, akin to *kýklos* CYCLE]

cy·cle (sī′kəl), *n., v.,* **-cled, -cling.** —*n.* **1.** a round of years or a recurring period of time, esp. one in which certain events or phenomena repeat themselves in the same order and at the same intervals. **2.** any complete round or series of occurrences that repeats or is repeated: *the gasoline-engine cycle; a cycle of alternating current.* **3.** any long period of years; age. **4.** any group of poems, dramas, prose narratives, etc., about a central theme, figure, or the like: *an Arthurian cycle.* **5.** a bicycle, tricycle, etc. **6.** *Physics.* **a.** a sequence of changing states that, upon completion, produces a final state identical to the original one. **b.** one of a succession of periodically recurring events. **c.** a complete alteration in which a phenomenon attains a maximum and minimum value, returning to a final value equal to the original one. **7.** *Math.* a permutation of a set of elements which leaves the original cyclic order of the elements unchanged. **8.** *Computer Technol.* **a.** the smallest interval of time required to complete an action in a computer. **b.** a series of computer operations repeated as a unit. *Abbr.:* c, c., cy, cy. —*v.i.* **9.** to ride or travel by bicycle, tricycle, etc. **10.** to move or revolve in cycles; pass through cycles. [ME *cicle* < LL *cycl(us)* < Gk *kýklos* cycle, circle, wheel, ring, disk, orb, etc.; see WHEEL]

cy′cle bill′ing, a method of billing customers at monthly intervals in which statements are prepared on each working day of the month and mailed to a designated fraction of the total number of customers.

cy·cle·car (sī′kəl kär′), *n.* a light automobile, open like a motorcycle but having three or four wheels. [(MOTOR)CYCLE + CAR¹]

cy′cle of indic′tion, indiction (def. 3).

cy·clic (sī′klik, sik′lik), *adj.* **1.** of, pertaining to, or constituting a cycle or cycles. **2.** revolving or recurring in cycles; characterized by recurrence in cycles. **3.** *Chem.* of or pertaining to a compound whose structural formula contains a closed chain or ring of atoms. **4.** *Bot.* **a.** arranged in whorls, as the parts of a flower. **b.** (of a flower) having the parts so arranged. **5.** *Math.* **a.** pertaining to an algebraic system in which all the elements of a group are powers of one element. **b.** (of a set of elements) arranged as if on a circle, so that the first element follows the last. Also, **cy′cli·cal.** [< L *cyclic(us)* < Gk *kyklikós* circular. See CYCLE, -IC] —**cy′cli·cal·ly,** *adv.* —**cy·clic·i·ty** (sī klis′i tē), **cy·cli·cal·i·ty** (sī′klə kal′i tē), *n.*

cy′clic shift′, *Computer Technol.* a transfer of digits from one end of a machine word to the other end of the word, retaining the same order in both places.

cy·cling (sī′kling), *n.* **1.** the act or sport of riding or traveling by bicycle, tricycle, etc. **2.** Also called **bicycle race, bicycle racing.** *Sports.* a race on lightweight bicycles with low handle bars, conducted for specified distances or against time on a dirt or board track or over public roads between cities. [CYCLE + -ING¹]

cy·clist (sī′klist), *n.* one who rides or travels by bicycle, tricycle, etc. Also, **cy′cler.** [CYCLE + -IST]

cy·cli·za·tion (sī′kli zā′shən, sik′li-), *n.* *Chem.* the formation of a ring or rings. [CYCLIZE + -ATION]

cy·clize (sī′klīz, sik′līz), *v.,* **-clized, -cliz·ing.** *Chem.* —*v.t.* **1.** to cause cyclization. —*v.i.* **2.** to undergo cyclization. [CYCLE + -IZE]

cyclo-, a learned borrowing from Greek meaning "cycle," used in the formation of compound words: *cyclohexane.* Also, *esp. before a vowel,* **cycl-.** [< Gk *kyklo-,* comb. form of *kýklos* circle, ring; c. Skt *cakra,* WHEEL]

cyclo., **1.** cyclopedia. **2.** cyclotron.

cy·clo·a·cet·y·lene (sī′klō ə set′əlin, -əlēn′, sik′lō-), *n.* *Chem.* any of the homologous series of unsaturated, alicyclic hydrocarbons containing one triple bond in the ring and having the general formula, C_nH_{2n-4}. [CYCLO- + ACETYLENE]

cy·clo·ceph·a·ly (sī′klə sef′ə lē, sik′lə-), *n.* *Med.* a congenital defect characterized by fusion of the orbits into a single cavity containing a rudimentary eye, and usually complete absence of the olfactory organs. [CYCLO- + -CEPHALY]

cy·clo·gen·e·sis (sī′klə jen′i sis, sik′lə-), *n.* *Meteorol.* the intensification or development of a cyclone. Cf. **cyclolysis.** [CYCLO(NE) + GENESIS]

cy·clo·graph (sī′klə graf′, -gräf′, sik′lə-), *n.* arcograph. [CYCLO- + -GRAPH]

cy·clo·hex·ane (sī′klə hek′sān, sik′lə-), *n.* *Chem.* a colorless, pungent, flammable liquid, C_6H_{12}, composed of a ring of six methylene groups, derived from crude petroleum by distillation or from benzene by hydrogenation: used chiefly as a solvent and in the manufacture of adipic acid. Also called **hexahydrobenzene, hexamethylene, hexanaphthene.** [CYCLO- + HEXANE]

cy·clo·hex·a·tri·ene (sī′klə hek′sə trī′ēn, sik′lə-), *n.* *Chem.* benzene. [CYCLOHEXA(NE) + TRI- + -ENE]

Y P C O X

Cycloid (def. 6) P, Point on rolling circle tracing out cycloid C

cy·cloid (sī′kloid), *adj.* **1.** resembling a circle; circular. **2.** (of the scale of a fish) smooth-edged, more or less circular in form, and having concentric striations. **3.** (of a fish) having such scales. **4.** *Psychiatry.* of or noting a personality type characterized by wide fluctuation in mood within the normal range. —*n.* **5.** a cycloid fish. **6.** *Geom.* a curve generated by a point on the circumference of a circle which rolls, without slipping, on a straight line. Equation: $x = a(\theta - \sin\theta)$, $y = 2a\ (1 - \cos\theta)$. [< Gk *kykloeid(ēs)* like a circle. See CYCL-, -OID] —**cy·cloi′dal,** *adj.* —**cy·cloi′dal·ly,** *adv.*

cycloi′dal propul′sion, *Naut.* propulsion of a vessel by propellers of controllable pitch that steer as well as propel.

cy·clol·y·sis (sī klol′i sis), *n.* *Meteorol.* the weakening or extinction of a cyclone. Cf. **cyclogenesis.** [CYCLO(NE) + -LYSIS]

cy·clom·e·ter (sī klom′i tər), *n.* **1.** an instrument which measures circular arcs. **2.** a device for recording the revolutions of a wheel and hence the distance traversed by a wheeled vehicle; odometer. [CYCLO- + -METER]

cy·clo·nal (sī klōn′əl), *adj.* of or like a cyclone. [CYCLONE + -AL¹]

cy·clone (sī′klōn), *n.* **1.** a large-scale, atmospheric wind-and-pressure system characterized by low pressure at its center and by circular wind motion, counterclockwise in the Northern Hemisphere, clockwise in the Southern Hemisphere. Cf. **anticyclone, extratropical cyclone, tropical cyclone.** **2.** (not in technical use) tornado. **3.** Also called **cy′clone collec′tor, cy′clone sep′arator.** a device for removing small or powdered solids from air, water, or other gases or liquids by centrifugal force. [< Gk *kyklôn* revolving (prp. of *kyklóein* to revolve), equiv. to *kýkl(os)* a circle + *-ōn* prp. suffix] —**cy·clon·ic** (sī klon′ik), **cy·clon′i·cal,** *adj.* —**cy·clon′i·cal·ly,** *adv.*

cy′clone cel′lar, a cellar or underground place for refuge from tornadoes.

cy′clone fur′nace, a furnace burning liquid or pulverized fuel in a whirling air column.
cy·clo·nite (sī′klə nīt′, sik′lə-), *n. Chem.* See **RDX.** [CYCLO- + (TRI)NIT(RO- + AMIN)E]
cy·clo·o·le·fin (sī′klō ō′lə fin, sik′lō-), *n. Chem.* any of the homologous series of unsaturated, alicyclic hydrocarbons containing one double bond in the ring and having the general formula, C_nH_{2n-2}. [CYCLO- + OLEFIN]
cy·clo·par·af·fin (sī′klə par′ə fin, sik′lə-), *n. Chem.* any of the homologous series of saturated, alicyclic hydrocarbons having the general formula, C_nH_{2n}. [CYCLO- + PARAFFIN]
Cy·clo·pe·an (sī′klə pē′ən), *adj.* **1.** of or characteristic of the Cyclops. **2.** (*sometimes l.c.*) gigantic; vast. **3.** (*usually l.c.*) *Archit., Building Trades.* formed with, or containing, large, undressed stones: *a cyclopean wall.* [< L *Cyclōpe(us)* (< Gk *Kyklṓpeios,* equiv. to *Kýklōp(s)* CYCLOPS + *-eios* -EOUS) + -AN]
Cy′clope′an con′crete, concrete containing stones weighing 100 pounds or more.
cy·clo·pe·di·a (sī′klə pē′dē ə), *n.* an encyclopedia. Also, **cy′clo·pae′di·a.** [by aphesis] —**cy′clo·pe′dist, cy′clo·pae′dist,** *n.*
cy·clo·pe·dic (sī′klə pē′dik), *adj.* like a cyclopedia in character or contents; broad and varied; exhaustive. Also, **cy′clo·pae′dic.** [aph. var. of ENCYCLOPEDIC] —**cy′clo·pe′di·cal·ly, cy′clo·pae′di·cal·ly,** *adv.*
cy·clo·pen·ta·di·ene (sī′klə pen′tə dī′ēn, sik′lə-), *n. Chem.* a colorless liquid, C_5H_6, derived by the distillation of coal tar: used chiefly in the manufacture of insecticides and resins. [CYCLO- + *pentadiene;* see PENTA-, -DIENE]
cy·clo·pen·tane (sī′klə pen′tān, sik′lə-), *n. Chem.* a colorless, water-insoluble liquid, C_5H_{10}, obtained from petroleum and used chiefly as a solvent. Also called **pentamethylene.** [CYCLO- + PENTANE]
cy·clo·pi·a (sī klō′pē ə), *n. Med.* a congenital defect characterized by fusion of the orbits into a single cavity containing one eye. Also called **synophthalmia.** [< NL < Gk *Kýklōp(s)* CYCLOPS + *-ia* -IA]
cy·clo·ple·gi·a (sī′klə plē′jē ə, -jə, sik′lə-), *n. Pathol.* paralysis of the intraocular muscles. [CYCLO- + -PLEGIA] —**cy′clo·ple′gic,** *adj., n.*
cy·clo·pro·pane (sī′klə prō′pān, sik′lə-), *n. Chem., Pharm.* a colorless, flammable gas, C_3H_6, used in organic synthesis and in medicine as an anesthetic. Also called **trimethylene.** [CYCLO- + PROPANE]
Cy·clops (sī′klops), *n., pl.* **Cy·clo·pes** (sī klō′pēz). **1.** *Class. Myth.* a member of a family of giants having a single round eye in the middle of the forehead. **2.** (*l.c.*) a fresh-water copepod of the genus *Cyclops,* having a median eye in the front of the head. [< Gk *Kýklōps,* lit., round-eye, equiv. to *Kýkl(os)* a circle, round + *ṓps* EYE]
cy·clo·ram·a (sī′klə ram′ə, -rä′mə), *n.* **1.** a pictorial representation, in perspective, of a landscape, battle, etc., on the inner wall of a cylindrical room or hall, the spectators occupying a position in the center. **2.** *Theat.* a curved wall or drop at the back of a stage, used for creating an illusion of unlimited space or distance in the background of exterior scenes or for obtaining lighting effects. [CYCL- + Gk *(h)órama* view] —**cy′clo·ram′ic,** *adj.*
cy·clo·sil·i·cate (sī′klə sil′ə kit, -kāt′), *n. Mineral.* any silicate involving more than two tetrahedral SiO_3 groups in a ring. Cf. **inosilicate, nesosilicate, sorosilicate, tektosilicate.** [CYCLO- + SILICATE]
cy·clo·sis (sī klō′sis), *n., pl.* **-ses** (-sēz). *Biol.* the movement of protoplasm within a cell. [< Gk *kýklōsis* an encircling. See CYCL-, -OSIS]
cy·clo·stom·a·tous (sī′klə stom′ə təs, -stō′mə-, sik′lə-), *adj.* **1.** having a circular mouth. **2.** belonging or pertaining to the cyclostomes. Also, **cy·clos·to·mate** (sī klos′tə mit, -māt′). [CYCLO- + STOMATOUS]
cy·clo·stome (sī′klə stōm′, sik′lə-), *adj.* **1.** belonging or pertaining to the *Cyclostomata,* a subclass of eellike, aquatic, agnathous vertebrates comprising the lampreys and hagfishes. **2.** having a circular mouth. —*n.* **3.** a cyclostome vertebrate; a lamprey or hagfish. [CYCLO- + -STOME]
cy·clo·stroph·ic (sī′klə strof′ik, sik′le-), *adj. Meteorol.* pertaining to atmospheric motion in which the centripetal acceleration exactly balances the horizontal pressure force. [CYCLO- + LGk *strophik(ós)* turned, equiv. to Gk *stroph-* (s. of *stréphein* to turn) + *-ikos* -IC; see STROPHE]
cy·clo·style (sī′klə stīl′, sik′lə-), *n.* **1.** a manifolding device consisting of a kind of pen with a small toothed wheel at the end which cuts minute holes in a specially prepared paper stretched over a smooth surface: used to produce a stencil from which copies are printed. **2.** *Archit.* a circular colonnade or columned building open at the center. [formerly trademark] —**cy′clo·sty′lar,** *adj.*
cy·clo·thy·mi·a (sī′klə thī′mē ə, sik′lə-), *n. Psychiatry.* a mild, manic-depressive psychosis involving recurring cycles of exhilaration and depression. [CYCLO- + *-thymia* < Gk *thȳm(ós)* spirit + *-ia* -IA] —**cy′clo·thy′mic,** *adj.*
cy·clo·thy·mi·ac (sī′klə thī′mē ak′, sik′lə-), *n.* a person affected with cyclothymia. [CYCLOTHYMI(A) + -AC]
cy·clo·tome (sī′klə tōm′, sik′lə-), *n. Surg.* a type of scalpel for performing a cyclotomy. [CYCLO- + -TOME]
cy·clo·tom·ic (sī′klə tom′ik, sik′lə-), *adj.* **1.** of or pertaining to cyclotomy. **2.** *Math.* (of a polynomial) irreducible and of the form $x^{p-1} + x^{p-2} \pm \ldots \pm 1$, where *p* is a prime number. [CYCLOTOM(Y) + -IC]
cy·clot·o·my (sī klot′ə mē), *n., pl.* **-mies.** **1.** *Surg.* incision of the ciliary muscle. **2.** *Geom.* the process of dividing a circle into a specific number of equal parts. [CYCLO- + -TOMY]
cy·clo·tri·meth·yl·ene·tri·ni·tra·mine (sī′klō trī meth′ə lēn′trī nī′trə mēn′, -nī tram′in, sik′lō-), *n. Chem.* See **RDX.** [CYCLO- + TRI- + METHYLENE + TRI- + NITR- + AMINE]
cy·clo·tron (sī′klə tron′, sik′lə-), *n. Physics.* an accelerator in which particles are propelled in spiral paths by the use of a constant magnetic field. [CYCLO- + -TRON]
Cyc·nus (sik′nəs), *n. Class. Myth.* **1.** any of several men transformed into swans. **2.** a son of Ares killed in a duel with Hercules.
Cyd (sid), *n.* a girl's given name.
cy·der (sī′dər), *n. Brit.* cider.
Cy·dip·pe (sī dip′ē), *n. Class. Myth.* a priestess of Hera at Argos and the mother of Biton and Cleobis.
Cyd·nus (sid′nəs), *n.* a river in SE Asia Minor, in Cilicia.
cy·e·sis (sī ē′sis), *n., pl.* **-ses** (-sēz). pregnancy. [< NL < Gk *kýēsis* pregnancy, equiv. to *kyē-* (var. s. of *kyéin* to be pregnant) + *-sis* -SIS] —**cy·et·ic** (sī et′ik), *adj.*
cyg·net (sig′nit), *n.* a young swan. [late ME *signet* < L *cygn(us),* var. of *cycnus* (< Gk *kýknos* swan); see -ET]
Cyg·nus (sig′nəs), *n., gen.* **-ni** (-nī). *Astron.* the Swan, a northern constellation southwest of Draco, containing the bright star Deneb. [< L: swan; see CYGNET]
cyke (sīk), *n. Informal.* cyclorama (def. 2). [short var. of CYCLORAMA; cf. BIKE]
cyl., cylinder.
cyl·in·der (sil′in dər), *n.* **1.** *Geom.* a surface or solid bounded by two parallel planes and generated by a straight line moving parallel to the given planes and tracing a curve bounded by the planes and lying in a plane perpendicular or oblique to the given planes. **2.** any cylinderlike object or part, whether solid or hollow. **3.** the rotating part of a revolver, containing the chambers for the cartridges. **4.** (in a pump) a cylindrical chamber in which a piston slides to move or compress a fluid. **5.** (in an engine) a cylindrical chamber in which the pressure of a gas or liquid moves a sliding piston. **6.** (in certain printing presses) **a.** a rotating cylinder which produces the impression and under which a flat form to be printed from passes. **b.** either of two cylinders, one carrying a curved form or plate to be printed from, which rotate against each other in opposite directions. **7.** (in certain locks) a cylindrical device for retaining the bolt until tumblers have been pushed out of its way. **8.** (in a screw or cylindrical gear) an imaginary cylindrical form, concentric to the axis, defining the pitch or the inner or outer ends of the threads or teeth. **9.** *Textiles.* the main roller on a carding machine, esp. the roller covered with card clothing that works in combination with the worker and stripper rollers in carding fibers. **10.** *Archaeol.* a cylindrical or somewhat barrel-shaped stone or clay object bearing a cuneiform inscription or a carved design, worn by the Babylonians, Assyrians, and kindred peoples as a seal and amulet. —*v.t.* **11.** to furnish with a cylinder or cylinders. **12.** to subject to the action of a cylinder or cylinders. [< L *cylindr(us)* < Gk *kýlindros* roller, cylinder, akin to *kylíndein* to roll] —**cyl′in·der·like′,** *adj.*

Cylinder (Right circular)

cyl′inder desk′, a desk having a cylinder front, usually a tambour but occasionally of solid wood.
cyl′inder escape′ment, *Horol.* an escapement in which an escape wheel, having teeth with a wedgelike section set around the rim at right angles, engages with an oscillating, hollow, semicylindrical part on the balance staff.
cyl′inder front′, *Furniture.* a front cover for a desk or the like, consisting either of a solid piece or of a tambour sliding up and back in quadrantal grooves.
cyl′inder glass′, a sheet of glass formed originally in the shape of a cylinder and then divided lengthwise and flattened. Also called **broad glass.**
cyl′inder head′, (in a reciprocating engine or pump) a detachable plate or cover on the end opposite to that from which the piston rod or connecting rod projects.
cyl′inder press′, a printing press in which paper is impressed by a cylinder against type on a flat plane.
cyl·in·dra·ceous (sil′in drā′shəs), *adj.* resembling a cylinder. [CYLIND(E)R + -ACEOUS]
cy·lin·dri·cal (si lin′dri kəl), *adj.* of, pertaining to, or having the form of a cylinder. Also, **cy·lin′dric.** [< NL *cylindric(us)* (< Gk *kylindrikós;* see CYLINDER, -IC) + -AL[1]] —**cy·lin′dri·cal′i·ty** (si lin′dri kal′i tē), **cy·lin′dri·cal·ness,** *n.* —**cy·lin′dri·cal·ly,** *adv.*
cylin′drical coeffi′cient, *Naval Archit.* See **longitudinal coefficient.**
cylin′drical coor′dinates, *Math.* a system of coordinates for locating a point in space by its polar coordinates and its perpendicular distance to the polar plane.
cyl·in·drite (sil′in drīt′, si lin′-), *n.* a mineral, a complex sulfide of lead, tin, and antimony, occurring in cylindrical form. [CYLIND(E)R + -ITE[1]]
cyl·in·droid (sil′in droid′), *n.* **1.** a solid having the form of a cylinder, esp. one with an elliptical, as opposed to a circular, cross section. —*adj.* **2.** resembling a cylinder. [< Gk *kylindroeidḗs* cylinderlike. See CYLINDER, -OID]
cyl·in·dro·ma (sil′in drō′mə), *n. Pathol.* a type of epithelial tumor containing small plugs or cylinders of connective tissue, usually involving salivary glands, bronchi, or skin. [< NL < Gk *kýlindr(os)* CYLINDER + *-ōma* -OMA] —**cyl·in·drom·a·tous** (sil′in drom′ə təs), *adj.*
cy·lix (sī′liks, sil′iks), *n., pl.* **cyl·i·ces** (sil′ə sēz′). kylix.
Cyl·le·ne (si lē′nē), *n. Class. Myth.* a nymph who nursed Hermes.
Cyl·le·ni·an (si lē′nē ən), *adj.* of or pertaining to Mount Cyllene in Arcadia, Greece, or to the god Hermes, reputed to have been born there. [< LL *Cyllēni(us)* (< Gk *Kyllḗnios,* equiv. to *Kyllḗn(ē)* in Arcadia + *-ios* -IOUS) + -AN]
Cyl·vi·a (sil′vē ə), *n.* a girl's given name. Also, **Sylvia.**
Cym., Cymric.
cy·ma (sī′mə), *n., pl.* **-mae** (-mē), **-mas.** **1.** *Archit.* either of two moldings having a partly convex and partly concave curve for an outline: used esp. in classical architecture. Cf. **cyma recta, cyma reversa.** **2.** *Bot.* a cyme. [< NL < Gk *kŷma* something swollen, a wave, wavy molding, sprout, equiv. to *ký(ein)* (to) be pregnant, swollen with child + *-ma* n. suffix]
cy·maise (sē mez′), *n.* a pewter wine jar having a spout, a fixed handle on the side opposite the spout, and a bail for carrying. Also, **cimaise, semaise.** [< F < L *cymat(ium)* an ogee; see CYMATIUM]
cy·mar (si mär′), *n.* simar (def. 1).
cy′ma rec′ta (rek′tə), *Archit.* a cyma whose concave part projects beyond the convex part. See illus. under **molding.** [< NL: lit., straight cyma]
cy′ma re·ver′sa (ri vûr′sə), *Archit.* a cyma whose convex part projects beyond the concave part. Also called **Lesbian cyma, Lesbian cymatium.** See illus. under **molding.** [< NL: lit., reversed cyma]
cy·ma·ti·on (si mā′shē on′), *n., pl.* **-ti·a** (-shē ə). cymatium.
cy·ma·ti·um (si mā′shē əm), *n., pl.* **-ti·a** (-shē ə). *Archit.* **1.** the uppermost member of a classical cornice or of a cornice of similar form: usually a cyma recta in classical examples. Cf. **sima**[2]. **2.** echinus (def. 2c). [< L < Gk *kymátion,* equiv. to *kymat-* (s. of *kŷma* wave; see CYMA) + *-ion* dim. suffix]
cym·bal (sim′bəl), *n.* a concave plate of brass or bronze which produces a sharp, ringing sound when struck: played either in pairs, by being struck together, or singly, by being struck with a drumstick or the like. [ME; OE *cymbala* < ML, var. of *cymbalum* < L < Gk *kýmbalon,* var. of *kýmbos, kýmbē* hollow object] —**cym′bal·er, cym′bal·eer′, cym′bal·ist,** *n.* —**cym′bal·like′,** *adj.*

Cymbals

cym·ba·lom (sim′bə ləm), *n.* a complex zither of Hungary. Also, **cimbalom.** [< Hung *cimbalom* < It *cembal(o)* < L *cymbalum* CYMBAL]
Cym·be·line (sim′bə lēn′), *n.* a girl's given name.
Cym·be·line (sim′bə lēn′), *n.* a romantic drama (1610?) by Shakespeare.
cym·bi·form (sim′bə fôrm′), *adj. Bot., Zool.* boat-shaped. [< L *cymb(a)* (< Gk *kýmbē* hollow object) + -I- + -FORM]
cym·bo·ceph·a·ly (sim′bō sef′ə lē), *n. Med.* a condition of the human skull in which the forehead recedes sharply and the back of the head projects outward. [< Gk *kýmbo(s)* hollow object + -CEPHALY] —**cym·bo·ce·phal·ic** (sim′bō sə fal′ik), **cym′bo·ceph′a·lous,** *adj.*
cyme (sīm), *n.* **1.** an inflorescence in which the primary axis bears a single terminal flower which develops first, the inflorescence being continued by secondary, tertiary, and other axes. **2.** a flat or convex inflorescence of this type. [< L *cȳma* cabbage sprout < Gk *kŷma;* see CYMA]
cy·mene (sī′mēn), *n. Chem.* a colorless, pleasant-smelling benzene derivative, $CH_3C_6H_4CH(CH_3)_2$, occurring in the volatile oil of the common cumin, *Cuminum cyminium,* and existing in three forms, the ortho, meta, and para isomers. Cf. **para-cymene.** [< Gk *kýmīn(on)* CUMIN + -ENE]
cymo-, a learned borrowing from Greek meaning "wave," used in the formation of compound words: *cymometer.* [< Gk *kymo-,* comb. form of *kŷma* wave. See CYMA]
Cy·mod·o·ce (sī mod′ə sē′), *n.* (in the *Aeneid*) a sea nymph who was at first a ship in the fleet of Aeneas. When Turnus set the fleet on fire, Cybele turned the ships into nymphs.
cy·mo·gene (sī′mə jēn′), *n. Chem.* a mixture of very volatile, flammable hydrocarbons, constituting the fraction boiling at about 0°C, obtained in distilling crude petroleum and containing a large percentage of butane. [CYM(ENE) + -O- + -GENE]
cy·mo·graph (sī′mə graf′, -gräf′), *n.* kymograph. —**cy·mo·graph·ic** (sī′mə graf′ik), *adj.*
cy·moid (sī′moid), *adj.* **1.** resembling a cyma. **2.** resembling a cyme. [CYME + -OID]
cy·mom·e·ter (sī mom′i tər), *n. Elect. Obs.* an instrument for measuring electromagnetic waves. [CYMO- + -METER]
cy·mo·phane (sī′mə fān′), *n. Mineral.* chrysoberyl. [CYMO- + -PHANE]
cy·mose (sī′mōs, sī mōs′), *adj. Bot.* **1.** bearing a cyme or cymes. **2.** of or of the nature of a cyme. [< L *cymōs(us)* full of shoots. See CYME, -OSE[1]] —**cy′mose·ly,** *adv.*
cy·mot·ri·chous (sī mo′trə kəs), *adj.* having wavy hair. [CYMO- + TRICH(O)- + -OUS] —**cy·mot′ri·chy,** *n.*
Cym·ric (kim′rik, sim′-), *adj.* **1.** of or pertaining to the Cymry. —*n.* **2.** Welsh (def. 3). Also, **Kymric.** [CYMR(Y) + -IC]
Cym·ry (kim′rē), *n.* (*construed as pl.*) the Welsh, or the branch of the Celtic race to which the Welsh belong, comprising also the Cornish people and the Bretons. Also, **Kymry.** [< Welsh *Cymry* Welshmen, pl. of *Cymro,* prob. repr. OWelsh *combrox compatriot, equiv. to *com-* COM- + *brox (Welsh *bro* district, region); akin to L *margo* margin; see MARK[1]]
Cyn (sin), *n.* a girl's given name, form of **Cynthia.**
Cyn·a·ra (sin′ər ə), *n.* a girl's given name.
Cyn·e·wulf (kin′ə wo͝olf′), *n.* fl. early 9th century A.D., Anglo-Saxon poet. Also, **Cynwulf, Kynewulf.**
cyn·ic (sin′ik), *n.* **1.** a person who believes that only selfishness motivates human actions and who disbelieves in or minimizes selfless acts or disinterested points of view. **2.** (*cap.*) one of a sect of Greek philosophers, 4th century B.C., who advocated the doctrines that virtue is the only good, that the essence of virtue is self-control, and that surrender to any external influence is beneath the dignity of man. —*adj.* **3.** cynical. **4.** (*cap.*) Also, **Cynical.** of or pertaining to the Cynics or their doctrines. **5.** *Astron. Rare.* of or pertaining to the Dog Star. **6.** *Med. Rare.* resembling the actions of a dog: *cynic spasm.* [< L *Cynic(us)* < Gk *Kynikós* Cynic, lit., doglike, currish, equiv. to *kyn-* (s. of *kýōn*) dog + *-ikos* -IC]
cyn·i·cal (sin′i kəl), *adj.* **1.** like or characteristic of a cynic; distrusting or disparaging the motives of others. **2.** showing contempt for accepted standards of honesty or morality by one's actions, esp. by actions that exploit the scruples of others. **3.** (*cap.*) cynic (def. 4). [CYNIC + -AL[1]] —**cyn′i·cal·ly,** *adv.* —**cyn′i·cal·ness,** *n.*
—**Syn. 1.** distrustful, disbelieving, sneering, contemptuous, derisive. CYNICAL, PESSIMISTIC, SARCASTIC, SATIRICAL imply holding a low opinion of mankind. CYNICAL suggests a disbelief in the sincerity of human motives: *cynical about honesty.* PESSIMISTIC implies a more or less habitual disposition to look on the dark side of things, and to believe that the worst will happen: *pessimistic as to the future.* SARCASTIC refers to sneering or making cutting jibes: *sarcastic about a profession of faith.* SATIRICAL suggests expressing scorn or ridicule by saying the opposite of what one means: *satirical about the way in which actions differ.* —**Ant. 1.** optimistic.

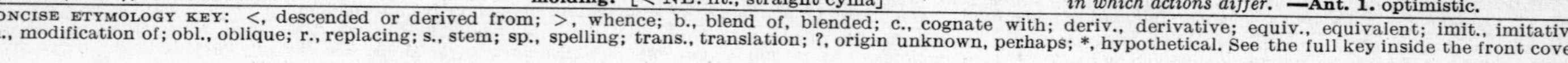

cyn·i·cism (sin′i siz′əm), *n.* **1.** cynical disposition character, or belief. **2.** a cynical remark. **3.** (*cap.*) any of the doctrines or practices of the Cynics. [CYNIC + -ISM]

cyn′ic spasm′, a spasm of the muscles of the face producing a snarling expression.

Cy·nor·tes (sī nôr′tēz), *n.* *Class. Myth.* a son of Amyclas and Diomede.

Cy·no·su·ra (sī′nə sho͝or′ə), *n.* *Class. Myth.* one of the nurses of the infant Zeus.

cy·no·sure (sī′nə sho͝or′, sin′ə-), *n.* **1.** something that strongly attracts attention by its brilliance, interest, etc.: *the cynosure of all eyes.* **2.** something serving for guidance or direction. **3.** (*cap.*) *Astron. Obs.* **a.** See **Ursa Minor.** **b.** Polaris. [< L *Cynosūra* < Gk *Kynósoura* the constellation Ursa Minor, equiv. to *kyn*(*ós*) dog's (gen. of *kýōn*) + *ourá* tail] —**cy′no·sur′al,** *adj.*

Cyn·thi·a (sin′thē ə), *n.* **1.** Artemis: so called from her birth on Mt. Cynthus, on Delos. **2.** *Poetic.* the moon, the emblem of Artemis. **3.** a girl's given name.

Cyn·thi·an·a (sin′thē an′ə), *n.* a town in N Kentucky. 5641 (1960).

Cyn·thi·us (sin′thē əs), *n.* *Class. Myth.* an epithet of Apollo.

Cy·nu·rus (sī no͝or′əs, -nyo͝or′-), *n.* *Class. Myth.* a son of Perseus.

Cyn·wulf (kin′wo͝olf), *n.* Cynewulf.

Cyp·a·ris·si·a (sip′ə ris′ē ə), *n.* *Class. Myth.* an epithet of Athena, meaning "cypress-goddess."

Cyp·a·ris·sus (sip′ə ris′əs), *n.* *Rom. Legend.* a youth who grieved for having accidentally killed his stag: the gods turned him into a cypress tree.

cy·per·a·ceous (sī′pə rā′shəs, sip′ə-), *adj.* belonging or pertaining to the *Cyperaceae* or sedge family of monocotyledonous plants, with solid, often triangular, stems and small, coriaceous, achenial fruit. [< NL *Cypēr*(*us*) the typical genus (L: kind of rush < Gk *kýpeiros* a marsh plant) + -ACEOUS]

cy·phel·la (si fel′ə, sī-), *n., pl.* **-phel·lae** (-fel′ē). (in certain lichens) a cuplike pit in the under surface of the thallus. [< NL < Gk *kýphella* (pl.) hollows of the ears]

cy·phel·late (si fel′it, -āt, sī-), *adj.* *Bot.* having cyphellae. [CYPHELL(A) + -ATE[1]]

cy·pher (sī′fər), *n., v.i., v.t.* *Chiefly Brit.* cipher.

cy pres (sē′ prā′), *Law.* **1.** as near as possible. **2.** the doctrine, applied esp. to cases of charitable trusts or donations, which, in place of an impossible or illegal condition, limitation, or object, allows the nearest practicable one to be substituted. Also, **cy′pres′.** [< AF: lit., as near (c. F *si près*)]

cy·press[1] (sī′prəs), *n.* **1.** any of several evergreen coniferous trees of the genus *Cupressus*, having dark-green, scalelike, overlapping leaves. **2.** any of various other coniferous trees allied to the true cypress, as the bald cypress. **3.** any of various unrelated plants resembling the true cypress. **4.** the wood of these trees or plants. [ME, OE *cypresse* < LL *cypress*(*us*), appar. b. L *cupressus* and *cyparissus* < Gk *kypárissos;* r. ME *cipres* < OF]

cy·press[2] (sī′prəs), *n.* *Obs.* a fine, thin fabric resembling lawn or crepe, which was formerly much used in black for mourning garments and trimmings. Also, **cyprus.** [ME *cipre*(*s*), *cyprus*, after CYPRUS]

cy′press spurge′, a perennial herb, *Euphorbia Cyparissias*, of Eurasia, having small, greenish-yellow flowers in dense clusters.

cy′press vine′, a convolvulaceous plant, *Quamoclit pennata*, having finely parted leaves and scarlet or white, tubular flowers.

Cyp·ri·an (sip′rē ən), *adj.* **1.** noting or pertaining to the worship of Aphrodite or to conduct inspired by Aphrodite. **2.** lewd; licentious. **3.** Cypriote. —*n.* **4.** Cypriote. **5.** a lewd person, esp. a prostitute. **6. the Cyprian,** Aphrodite: so called because her cult was centered on Cyprus. [< L *Cypri*(*us*) of Cyprus (< Gk *Kýprios*, deriv. of *Kýpros* CYPRUS) + -AN]

Cyp·ri·an (sip′rē ən), *n.* **Saint** (*Thascius Caecillus Cyprianus*), A.D. c200–258, early church father, bishop, and martyr.

cy·pri·nid (si prī′nid, sip′rə nid), *n.* **1.** any fish belonging to the *Cyprinidae*, or minnow family. —*adj.* **2.** carplike in form or structure. [back formation from NL *Cyprinidae* name of family, equiv. to *Cyprīn*(*us*) genus name (< L < Gk *kyprînos* carp) + *-idae* -IDAE]

cy·prin·o·dont (si prin′ə dont′, si prī′nə-), *n.* any soft-rayed fish of the order *Cyprinodontes*, found esp. in fresh and brackish waters of North America, including the killifishes, topminnows, guppies, etc. [< L *cyprīn*(*us*) < Gk *kyprînos* carp + -ODONT]

cyp·ri·noid (sip′rə noid′, si prī′noid), *adj.* **1.** resembling a carp; belonging to the *Cyprinoidea*, a group of fishes including the carps, suckers, loaches, etc. —*n.* **2.** a cyprinoid fish. [< L *cyprīn*(*us*) < Gk *kyprînos* carp + -OID]

Cyp·ri·ote (sip′rē ōt′, -ət), *n.* **1.** a native or inhabitant of Cyprus. **2.** the Greek dialect of Cyprus. —*adj.* **3.** of, pertaining to, or characteristic of Cyprus, its people, or their language. Also, **Cyp·ri·ot** (sip′rē ət). [< Gk *Kypriṓtē*(*s*)]

Cyp′riote syl′labary, a syllabic script in use on Cyprus in the first millennium B.C., used for the writing of Greek and of an unknown language.

cyp·ri·pe·di·um (sip′rə pē′dē əm), *n.* any plant of the genus *Cypripedium*, comprising the lady's-slippers. [< NL, equiv. to L *Cypri*(*a*) Venus + *-pedi-* -PED + *-um* neut. ending]

Cypro-, a combining form of **Cyprian:** *Cypro-Minoan.*

cy·prus (sī′prəs), *n.* cypress[2].

Cy·prus (sī′prəs), *n.* an island republic in the Mediterranean, S of Turkey: formerly a British colony; independent since 1960. 562,000 (est. 1960); 3572 sq. mi. *Cap.:* Nicosia.

cyp·se·la (sip′sə lə), *n., pl.* **-lae** (-lē′). *Bot.* an achene with an adherent calyx, as in the composite plants. [< NL < Gk *kypsélē* hollow vessel, chest, box]

Cyp·se·lus (sip′sə ləs), *n.* *Class. Myth.* a son of Aepytus and king of Arcadia. By marrying his daughter to Cresphontes, Cypselus protected his kingdom from the Heraclidae invasion of the Peloponnesus.

Cy·ra (sī′rə), *n.* a girl's given name.

Cyr·a·no (sir′ə nō′), *n.* a boy's given name.

Cyr·a·no de Ber·ge·rac (sir′ə nō′ də bûr′jə rak′, -zhə rak′, bâr′-; *Fr.* sē RA nō′ də ber zhə RAK′). **1.** See **Bergerac, Savinien Cyrano de.** **2.** (*italics.*) a play in verse (1897) by Edmond Rostand.

Cy·re·na (sī rē′nə), *n.* a girl's given name. Also, **Cyrene.**

Cyr·e·na·ic (sir′ə nā′ik, sī′rə-), *adj.* **1.** of or pertaining to Cyrenaica, or its chief city, Cyrene. **2.** noting or pertaining to a school of philosophy founded by Aristippus of Cyrene, who taught that pleasure is the only rational aim of life. —*n.* **3.** a native or inhabitant of Cyrenaica. **4.** a disciple of the Cyrenaic school of philosophy. [< L *Cyrēnaic*(*us*) < Gk *Kyrēnaïkós*, equiv. to *Kyrēna-* (comb. form of *Kyrḗnē* CYRENE) + *-ikos* -IC]

Cyr·e·na·i·ca (sir′ə nā′ə kə, sī′rə-), *n.* an ancient district in N Africa, W of the present United Arab Republic. Also, **Cirenaica.** Also called **Barca.**

Cy·re·ne (sī rē′nē), *n.* **1.** an ancient Greek city and colony in N Africa, in Cyrenaica. **2.** *Class. Myth.* a huntress and a mistress of Apollo. **3.** Also, **Cyrena.** a girl's given name.

Cyr·il (sir′əl), *n.* **1. Saint** ("*Apostle of the Slavs*"), A.D. 827–869, Greek missionary to the Moravians. **2.** a boy's given name.

Cy·ril·lic (si ril′ik), *adj.* **1.** noting or pertaining to a script derived from Greek uncials and traditionally supposed to have been invented by St. Cyril, first used for the writing of Old Church Slavonic and adopted with minor modifications for the writing of Russian, Bulgarian, Serbian, and also Mongolian, Tajik, and many other languages of the USSR. **2.** of or pertaining to St. Cyril. —*n.* **3.** Cyrillic script. [< L *Cyrill*(*us*) (Saint) CYRIL + -IC]

Cy·ril·lus (si ril′əs), *n.* a walled plain in the fourth quadrant of the face of the moon: about 55 miles in diameter.

cyr·to·sis (sər tō′sis), *n.* *Pathol.* any abnormal curvature of the spine or of the extremities. [< NL < Gk *kyrt*(*ós*) curved, arched, round + *-ōsis* -OSIS]

cyr·to·style (sûr′tə stīl′), *n.* a convex portico, as at an entrance. [< Gk *kyrtó*(*s*) curved + *stŷl*(*os*) pillar]

Cy·rus (sī′rəs), *n.* **1.** ("*the Elder*" or "*the Great*") c600–529 B.C., king of Persia 558?–529: founder of the Persian empire. **2.** ("*the Younger*") 424?–401 B.C., Persian prince and satrap: leader of the armed conspiracy against his brother King Artaxerxes II. **3.** a boy's given name.

Cys·a·tus (sis′ə təs, -ātəs), *n.* a walled plain in the third quadrant of the face of the moon: about 28 miles in diameter.

cyst (sist), *n.* **1.** *Pathol.* a closed, bladderlike sac formed in animal tissues, containing fluid or semifluid matter. **2.** a bladder, sac, or vesicle. **3.** *Bot.* **a.** a sporelike cell with a resistant, protective wall. **b.** a cell or cavity enclosing reproductive bodies. **4.** *Zool.* **a.** a sac, usually spherical, surrounding an animal that has passed into a dormant condition. **b.** such a sac plus the contained animal. **c.** a capsule or resistant covering. [< NL *cyst*(*is*) < Gk *kýstis* bag, pouch, the bladder]

cyst-, var. of **cysto-,** before a vowel: *cystectomy.*

-cyst, var. of **cysto-,** as final element in a compound word: *statocyst.*

cys·tec·to·my (si stek′tə mē), *n., pl.* **-mies.** *Surg.* excision of a cyst or bladder, usually the urinary bladder. [CYST- + -ECTOMY]

cys·te·ine (sis′tē ēn′, -in), *n.* *Biochem.* a crystalline amino acid, $HSCH_2CH(NH_2)COOH$, a component of nearly all proteins, obtained by the reduction of cystine. [alter. of CYSTINE] —**cys′te·in′ic,** *adj.*

cysti-, var. of **cysto-:** *cysticercus.*

cyst·ic (sis′tik), *adj.* **1.** pertaining to, of the nature of, or having a cyst or cysts; encysted. **2.** *Anat.* belonging or pertaining to the urinary bladder or gall bladder. [CYST + -IC]

cys·ti·cer·coid (sis′ti sûr′koid), *n.* *Zool.* the larva of certain tapeworms, a bladderlike structure with a retracted head or scolex and often with a taillike appendage. [CYSTICERC(US) + -OID]

cys·ti·cer·cus (sis′ti sûr′kəs), *n., pl.* **-cer·ci** (-sûr′sī). *Zool.* the larva of certain tapeworms, a fluid-filled, bladderlike structure with an invaginated head or scolex. [< NL < Gk *kýsti*(*s*) bladder + *kérkos* tail]

cys′tic fibro′sis, *Pathol.* a hereditary, chronic disease of the pancreas, lungs, etc., beginning in infancy, in which there is an inability to digest foods and difficulty in breathing, characterized by failure of normal growth and development. Also called **mucoviscidosis, pancreatic fibrosis.**

cys·tid·i·um (si stid′ē əm), *n., pl.* **cys·tid·i·a** (si stid′ē ə). *Bot.* (in certain basidiomycetous fungi) one of the large, inflated, sterile cells growing between the basidia and usually projecting beyond them. [< NL; see CYST-, -IDIUM]

cys·tine (sis′tēn, -tin), *n.* *Biochem.* a crystalline amino acid, $C_6H_{12}O_4N_2S_2$, occurring in most proteins, esp. the keratins in hair, wool, and horn, and yielding cysteine on reduction. [CYST- + -INE[2]; so called because found in stone of the bladder]

cys·ti·tis (si stī′tis), *n.* *Pathol.* inflammation of the urinary bladder. [CYST- + -ITIS]

cysto-, a combining form of **cyst:** *cystolith.* Also, **cyst-, -cyst, cysti-.**

cys·to·carp (sis′tə kärp′), *n.* the mass of carpospores formed as a result of fertilization in red algae, with or without a special envelope. [CYSTO- + -CARP] —**cys′to·car′pic,** *adj.*

cys·to·cele (sis′tə sēl′), *n.* *Pathol.* hernia in which the urinary bladder protrudes into the vagina. [CYSTO- + -CELE[1]]

cyst·oid (sis′toid), *adj.* **1.** resembling a cyst. —*n.* **2.** a cystlike structure or formation. [CYST + -OID]

cys·to·lith (sis′tə lith), *n.* *Bot.* a mass of calcium carbonate on the cellulose wall. [CYSTO- + -LITH] —**cys′to·lith′ic,** *adj.*

cys·to·ma (si stō′mə), *n., pl.* **-mas, -ma·ta** (-mə tə). *Pathol.* a cystic tumor. [CYST- + -OMA] —**cys·tom·a·tous** (si stom′ə təs), *adj.*

cys·tom·e·ter (si stom′i tər), *n.* *Med.* a device for determining the reaction of the urinary bladder to increased internal pressure. [CYSTO- + -METER]

cys·to·scope (sis′tə skōp′), *n.* *Med.* a slender, cylindrical instrument for examining the interior of the urinary bladder and for the introduction of medication therein. [CYSTO- + -SCOPE]

cys·tos·co·py (si stos′kə pē), *n., pl.* **-pies.** *Med.* an examination by means of a cystoscope. [CYSTO- + -SCOPY] —**cys·to·scop·ic** (sis′tə skop′ik), *adj.*

cys·tos·to·my (si stos′tə mē), *n., pl.* **-mies.** *Surg.* formation of a permanent or semipermanent opening in the urinary bladder. [CYSTO- + -STOMY]

cys·tot·o·my (si stot′ə mē), *n., pl.* **-mies.** *Surg.* the operation of cutting into the urinary bladder. [CYSTO- + -TOMY] —**cys·to·tome** (sis′tə tōm′), *n.*

cy·tas·ter (sī tas′tər, sī′tas-), *n.* *Biol.* aster. [CYT(O)- + -ASTER[2]]

-cyte, var. of **cyto-** as final element in a compound word: *leucocyte.*

Cyth·er·a (sith′ər ə, si thēr′ə), *n.* Cerigo.

Cyth·er·e·a (sith′ə rē′ə), *n.* Aphrodite: so called because of her birth in the sea near Cythera. —**Cyth′er·e′an,** *adj.*

Cy·tis·sor·us (sī′ti sôr′əs), *n.* *Class. Myth.* a son of Phrixus and Chalciope.

cyto-, a learned borrowing from Greek used, with the meaning "cell," in the formation of compound words: *cytoplasm.* Also, **-cyte.** [< Gk *kyto-*, comb. form of *kýtos* container, receptacle, body]

cy·to·ar·chi·tec·ture (sī′tō är′ki tek′chər), *n.* the cellular structure of a tissue or part. [CYTO- + ARCHITECTURE] —**cy′to·ar′chi·tec′tur·al,** *adj.* —**cy′to·ar′chi·tec′tur·al·ly,** *adv.*

cy·to·chem·is·try (sī′tə kem′i strē), *n.* the branch of cytology dealing with the chemistry of living cells. [CYTO- + CHEMISTRY] —**cy′to·chem′i·cal,** *adj.*

cy·to·chrome (sī′tə krōm′), *n.* *Biochem.* any of several oxidoreductase enzymes found in plants and animals, composed of iron, a protein, and a porphyrin, that catalyze intracellular oxidations. [CYTO- + -CHROME]

cy′tochrome sys′tem, *Biochem.* the system of respiratory enzymes, found in plants and animals, that includes the cytochromes and that serves in oxidation reactions to transfer electrons and ions.

cy·toc·la·sis (sī tok′lə sis, sī′tə klā′sis), *n.* *Pathol.* destruction of cells. [CYTO- + Gk *klásis* a breaking]

cy·to·clas·tic (sī′tə klas′tik), *adj.* *Pathol.* **1.** of or pertaining to cytoclasis. **2.** destructive to cells. [CYTO- + CLASTIC]

cy·to·gen·e·sis (sī′tə jen′i sis), *n.* the origin and development of cells. [CYTO- + -GENESIS]

cy·to·ge·net·ics (sī′tō jə net′iks), *n.* (*construed as sing.*) the branch of biology dealing with the study of heredity from the points of view of cytology and genetics. [CYTO- + GENETICS] —**cy′to·ge·net′ic, cy′to·ge·net′i·cal,** *adj.* —**cy′to·ge·net′i·cal·ly,** *adv.* —**cy′to·ge·net′i·cist,** *n.*

cy·toid (sī′toid), *adj.* resembling a cell. [CYT(O)- + -OID]

cy·to·ki·ne·sis (sī′tō ki nē′sis, -kī-), *n.* the changes in the cytoplasm during mitosis, meiosis, and fertilization. [CYTO- + Gk *kínēsis* motion]

cy·tol·o·gist (sī tol′ə jist), *n.* a specialist in cytology. [CYTOLOG(Y) + -IST]

cy·tol·o·gy (sī tol′ə jē), *n.* **1.** the branch of biology dealing with the study of cells, esp. their formation, structure, and functions. **2.** cytological phenomena, processes, etc.: *the cytology of cancer.* [CYTO- + -LOGY] —**cy·to·log·ic** (sīt′əloj′ik), **cy′to·log′i·cal,** *adj.* —**cy′to·log′i·cal·ly,** *adv.*

cy·tol·y·sin (sī tol′i sin, sīt′əlī′sin), *n.* *Biochem.* an antibody that partially or completely destroys animal cells. [CYTOLYS(IS) + -IN[1]]

cy·tol·y·sis (sī tol′i sis), *n.* *Physiol.* the dissolution or degeneration of cells. [CYTO- + -LYSIS] —**cy·to·lyt·ic** (sīt′əlit′ik), *adj.*

cy·ton (sīt′ən), *n.* the body of a nerve cell. [CYT(O)- + *-on* (Gk neut. ending), modeled on *proton*]

cy·to·path·o·gen·ic (sī′tō path′ə jen′ik), *adj.* *Pathol.* **1.** of or pertaining to an agent that is pathologic for or destructive to cells. **2.** of or pertaining to the cellular changes produced by such an agent. [CYTO- + PATHOGENIC]

cy·to·pa·thol·o·gy (sī′tō pə thol′ə jē), *n.* *Pathol.* the science dealing with the study of the diseases of cells. [CYTO- + PATHOLOGY] —**cy·to·path·o·log·ic** (sī′tō-path′ə loj′ik), **cy′to·path′o·log′i·cal,** *adj.* —**cy′to·path′o·log′i·cal·ly,** *adv.*

cy·to·pe·ni·a (sī′tə pē′nē ə), *n.* *Pathol.* the condition of having a decreased number of cellular elements in the blood; hypocytosis. [CYTO- + Gk *penía* poverty, want]

cy·toph·a·gy (sī tof′ə jē), *n.* the ingestion of cells by other cells. [CYTO- + -PHAGY] —**cy·to·phag·ic** (sī′tə-faj′ik), **cy·toph′a·gous,** *adj.*

cy·to·phar·ynx (sī′tə far′ingks), *n., pl.* **-pha·ryn·ges** (-fə rin′jēz), **-phar·ynx·es.** the gullet of a protozoan. [CYTO- + PHARYNX]

cy·to·plasm (sī′tə plaz′əm), *n.* *Biol.* the protoplasm of a cell exclusive of the nucleus. [CYTO- + -PLASM] —**cy′to·plas′mic,** *adj.*

cy·to·plast (sī′tə plast′), *n.* *Biol.* the intact, cytoplasmic content of a cell. [CYTO- + -PLAST] —**cy′to·plas′tic,** *adj.*

cy·to·sine (sī′tə sēn′, -zēn′, -sin), *n.* *Biochem.* a white, crystalline, slightly water-soluble pyrimidine, $C_4H_5N_3O$, derived from the hydrolysis of nucleic acids, esp. RNA and DNA, or made synthetically and used in biochemical research in the study of cell metabolism. [CYT(O)- + -OSE[2] + -INE[2]]

cy·to·some (sī′tə sōm′), *n.* *Biol.* the cytoplasmic part of a cell. [CYTO- + -SOME[3]]

cy·tost (sī′tost), *n.* *Biochem.* any cellular substance liberated because of injury to the cell or cells. [CYT(O)- + Gk *ost*(*éon*) bone]

cy·to·stome (sī′tə stōm′), *n.* the mouth of a protozoan. [CYTO- + -STOME] —**cy′to·sto′mal,** *adj.*

cy·to·tax·is (sī′tə tak′sis), *n.* *Biol.* the mutual attraction or repulsion of cells or groups of motile cells. [CYTO- + -TAXIS] —**cy·to·tac·tic** (sī′tə tak′tik), *adj.*

cy·to·tox·in (sī′tə tok′sin), *n.* *Immunol.* a substance in the blood having a toxic effect on certain cells. [CYTO- + TOXIN] —**cy′to·tox′ic,** *adj.*

cy·to·troph·o·blast (sī′tə trof′ə blast′), *n.* *Embryol.* the inner, cellular layer of the trophoblast. Also called **Langhan's layer.** Cf. **syntrophoblast.** [CYTO- + TROPHOBLAST] —**cy′to·troph′o·blas′tic,** *adj.*

cy·to·trop·ic (sī′tə trop′ik), *adj.* *Biol.* **1.** (of cells or groups of cells) growing or moving toward or away from each other. **2.** having an affinity for cells, as certain viruses. [CYTO- + -TROPIC]

cy·tot·ro·pism (sī to′trə piz′əm), *n.* cytotropic tendency or behavior. [CYTO- + -TROPISM]

cy·to·zo·on (sī′tə zō′on, -ən), *n., pl.* **-zo·a** (-zō′ə). *Biol.* a parasite, esp. a protozoon, living within a cell. [CYTO- + -ZOON] —**cy′to·zo′ic,** *adj.*

Cyz·i·cus (siz′ə kəs), *n.* an ancient city in NW Asia Minor, in Mysia, on a peninsula in the Sea of Marmara.

C.Z., Canal Zone.

czar (zär), *n.* **1.** an emperor or king. **2.** (*often cap.*) the former emperor of Russia. **3.** (*often cap.*) an autocratic ruler or leader. Also, **tsar, tzar.** [< Russ *tsar′*, ORuss *tsĭsarĭ* emperor, king (c. OSlav *tsĕsarĭ*) < Goth *kaisar* emperor (< Gk or L); Gk *kaisar* < L *Caesar*]

czar·das (chär′däsh), *n.* a Hungarian national dance in two movements, one slow and the other fast. [< Hung *csárdás*]

czar·dom (zär′dəm), *n.* **1.** the domain of a czar. **2.** the authority or position of a czar. Also, **tsardom, tzardom.** [CZAR + -DOM]

czar·e·vitch (zär′ə vich), *n.* **1.** the son of a czar. **2.** the eldest son of a czar. Also, **tsarevitch, tzarevitch.** [< Russ *tsarevich*, equiv. to *tsar′* CZAR + *-evich* patronymic suffix]

cza·rev·na (zä rev′nə), *n.* **1.** a daughter of a czar. **2.** the wife of the son of a czar. Also, **tsarevna, tzarevna.** [< Russ *tsarevna*, equiv. to *tsar′* CZAR + *-evna* fem. patronymic suffix]

cza·ri·na (zä rē′nə), *n.* the wife of a czar; Russian empress. Also, **tsarina, tzarina.** [CZAR + *-ina* fem. suffix (as in *Christina*), modeled on G *Zarin* empress, equiv. to *Zar* Czar + *-in* fem. suffix]

czar·ism (zär′iz əm), *n.* dictatorship; autocratic government. Also, **tsarism, tzarism.** [CZAR + -ISM]

czar·ist (zär′ist), *adj.* Also, **czar·is·tic** (zä ris′tik), **tsaristic, tzaristic. 1.** of, pertaining to, or characteristic of a czar or the system and principles of government under a czar. **2.** autocratic; dictatorial. —*n.* **3.** an adherent of a czar or of czarism. Also, **tsarist, tzarist.** [CZAR + -IST]

cza·rit·za (zä rit′sə), *n.* a czarina. Also, **tsaritza, tzaritza.** [< Russ *tsaritsa* (fem. of *tsar′*)]

Czech (chek), *n.* **1.** a member of the most westerly branch of the Slavs, comprising the Bohemians, or Czechs proper, and, sometimes, the Moravians. **2.** the language of Bohemia and Moravia, a Slavic language similar to Slovak. **3.** (loosely) Czechoslovak. —*adj.* **4.** Also **Czech′ish.** of or pertaining to Czechoslovakia, its people, or their language.

Czech., Czechoslovakia. Also, **Czechosl.**

Czech·o·slo·vak (chek′ə slō′vak, -väk), *n.* **1.** a member of the branch of the Slavic peoples comprising the Czechs proper, the Moravians, and the Slovaks. **2.** a native or inhabitant of Czechoslovakia. —*adj.* **3.** of or pertaining to Czechoslovakia, its people, or their language. Also **Chech′o-Slo′vak.**

Czech·o·slo·va·ki·a (chek′ə slə vä′kē ə, -vak′ē ə), *n.* a former republic in central Europe: formed after World War I; comprised Bohemia, Moravia, Slovakia, and part of Silesia: a federal republic 1968–92. 49,383 sq. mi. *Cap.:* Prague. Official name, **Chech′ and Slo′vak Fed′erative Repub′lic.** Formerly (1948–89). **Czech′o·slo′vak So′cialist Repub′lic.** —**Czech′o·slo·va′ki·an, Czech′o-Slo·va′ki·an,** *adj., n.*

Czech′ Repub′lic, a republic in central Europe: includes the regions of Bohemia, Moravia, and part of Silesia; formerly part of Czechoslovakia. 10,343,398; 30,449 sq. mi. *Cap.:* Prague.

Czer·no·witz (cher′nô vits), *n.* German name of **Cernăuţi.**

Czer·ny (cher′nē), *n.* **Carl,** 1791–1857, Austrian composer, esp. of exercises in piano technique.

Czę·sto·cho·wa (chen′stô hô′vä), *n.* a city in S Poland. 170,000 (est. 1963).

D

D, d (dē), *n., pl.* **D's** or **Ds, d's** or **ds.** **1.** the fourth letter of the English alphabet, a consonant. **2.** any spoken sound represented by the letter *D* or *d*, as in *dog, ladder, ladle, pulled,* etc. **3.** something having the shape of a D. **4.** a written or printed representation of the letter *D* or *d*. **5.** a device, as a printer's type, for reproducing the letter *D* or *d*.

d'[1], *prep.* **1.** de (used in French names as an elided form of *de*): *Charles Louis d'Albert.* **2.** di (used in Italian names as an elided form of *di*): *Gabriele d'Annunzio.*

d'[2], *Informal.* contraction of the second person sing. and pl. of *do* or *did: D'you go to the movies last night? How d'you like your eggs cooked?*

'd, **1.** contraction of *had: I was glad they'd gone.* **2.** contraction of *did: Where'd they go?* **3.** contraction of *should* or *would: He'd like to go. I'd like to remind you of your promise.*

D, **1.** *Elect.* debye. **2.** *Physics.* D-state. **3.** Dutch.

D, **1.** the fourth in order or in a series. **2.** (*sometimes l.c.*) (in some grading systems) a grade or mark, as in school or college, indicating the quality of a student's work as poor or just passing. **3.** (*sometimes l.c.*) a classification, rating, or the like, indicating poor quality. **4.** *Music.* **a.** the second tone in the scale of C major, or the fourth tone in the relative minor scale, A minor. **b.** a string, key, or pipe tuned to this tone. **c.** a written or printed note representing this tone. **d.** (in the fixed system of solmization) the second tone of the scale of C major, called *re.* **e.** the tonality having D as the tonic note. **5.** (*sometimes l.c.*) the Roman numeral for 500. Cf. **Roman numerals.** **6.** *Chem.* deuterium. **7.** a symbol for a shoe width size narrower than E and wider than C. **8.** a proportional brassiere cup size, smaller than DD and larger than C. **9.** (in men's pajama sizes) extra large.

D., **1.** day. **2.** December. **3.** Democrat. **4.** Democratic. **5.** *Physics.* density. **6.** Deus. **7.** Deuteronomy. **8.** *Optics.* diopter. **9.** Dutch.

d., **1.** (in prescriptions) give. [< L *dā*] **2.** date. **3.** daughter. **4.** degree. **5.** delete. **6.** *Brit.* pence. [< L *denarii*] **7.** *Brit.* penny. [< L *denarius*] **8.** *Physics.* density. **9.** dialect. **10.** dialectal. **11.** diameter. **12.** died. **13.** dime. **14.** dividend. **15.** dollar; dollars. **16.** dose. **17.** dyne.

da., **1.** daughter. **2.** day; days.

D/A, **1.** (*sometimes l.c.*) days after acceptance. **2.** deposit account. **3.** documents against acceptance. **4.** documents for acceptance.

D.A., **1.** Delayed Action. **2.** direct action. **3.** District Attorney. **4.** documents against acceptance. **5.** documents for acceptance. **6.** doesn't answer; don't answer.

dab[1] (dab), *v.,* **dabbed, dab·bing,** *n.* **—***v.t.* **1.** to pat or tap gently, as with something soft or moist: *She dabbed her eyes with the handkerchief.* **2.** to apply (a substance) by light strokes: *He dabbed the salve on his burned finger.* **3.** to strike, esp. lightly, as with the hand. **4.** to dress (stonework) with a pointed tool. **—***v.i.* **5.** to strike lightly; make a dab; pat: *She dabbed at the stain on her dress.* **—***n.* **6.** a quick or light blow; a pat, as with the hand or something soft. **7.** a small moist lump or mass: *a dab of mustard.* **8.** a small quantity: *a dab of powder.* [ME *dabbe(n)*; cf. OIcel *dabba* to tap, slap, G *Tappe* paw, fist, slap]

dab[2] (dab), *n.* **1.** a European flatfish, *Limanda limanda.* **2.** any of several other flatfishes of the genus *Limanda.* [? special use of DAB[1]]

DAB, Dictionary of American Biography.

dab·ber (dab′ər), *n.* **1.** one who or that which dabs. **2.** a cushionlike article used for applying ink, as by printers and engravers. [DAB[1] + -ER[1]]

dab·ble (dab′əl), *v.,* **-bled, -bling.** **—***v.t.* **1.** to wet slightly in or with a liquid; splash; spatter. **—***v.i.* **2.** to play and splash in or as if in water, as with the hands. **3.** to work at anything in an irregular or superficial manner: *to dabble in literature.* [prob. DAB[1] + -LE; cf. D *dabbelen, dabben*] **—dab′bler,** *n.*

dab·chick (dab′chik′), *n.* any of various small grebes, as the pied-billed grebe. [earlier *dapchick* (see DAP, CHICK); cf. *dopp(ened)* moorhen (lit., dipping duck)]

dab′ hand′, *Chiefly Brit. Informal.* a person adept in a particular occupation or situation; expert.

dab·ster (dab′stər), *n.* **1.** *Brit. Dial.* an expert. **2.** *Informal.* a person who works in a superficial or clumsy manner; dabbler. [*dab* expert (< ?) + -STER]

da ca·po (dä kä′pō; *It.* dä kä′pō), repeated from the beginning (used as a musical direction). [< It: lit., from the head]

Dac·ca (dak′ə), *n.* a city in and the capital of the provinces of East Pakistan, in Pakistan. 558,000 (est. 1961).

d'ac·cord (dA kôR′), *adv. French.* agreed; granted.

dace (dās), *n., pl.* (*esp. collectively*) **dace,** (*esp. referring to two or more kinds or species*) **dac·es.** **1.** a small, fresh-water cyprinoid fish, *Leuciscus leuciscus,* of Europe, having a stout, fusiform body. **2.** any of several similar or related fishes of the U.S. [ME *darce, darse* < OF *dars* < LL *dars(us)*]

da·cha (dä′chə), *n.* (in Russia) a country house or villa. Also, **datcha.** [< Russ *dacha,* lit., payment, a giving]

Da·chau (dä′kou; *Ger.* dä′KHOU), *n.* a city in SE West Germany, near Munich: site of Nazi concentration camp. 30,000 (1963).

Da·ché (da shā′; *Fr.* dA-shā′), *n.* **Lil·ly,** born 1914?, U.S. hat designer, born in France.

Dachshund
(8 in. high at shoulder)

dachs·hund (däks′ho͝ond′, -ənd, dash′-; *Ger.* däks′-ho͝ont′), *n.* one of a German breed of dogs having short legs, a long body and ears, and a usually tan or black-and-tan coat. [< G, equiv. to *Dachs* badger + *Hund* dog]

Da·ci·a (dā′shē ə, -shə), *n.* **1.** an ancient kingdom and later a Roman province in S Europe between the Carpathian Mountains and the Danube, corresponding generally to modern Rumania and adjacent regions. **2.** a girl's given name.

dack·er (dak′ər; *Scot.* dä′kəR), *v.i. Scot. and North Eng.* **1.** to totter, stagger; waver or shake. **2.** to saunter; move slowly or idly. **3.** to vacillate; act irresolutely or indecisively. Also, **daiker.** [appar. c. MFlem *daeckeren*]

Dack·o (dak′ō, dä′kō), *n.* **David,** born 1930, African statesman: president of the Central African Republic since 1959.

da·coit (də koit′), *n.* (in India and Burma) one of a class of criminals who engage in organized robbery and murder. Also, **dakoit.** [< Hindi *ḍakait,* deriv. of *ḍākā* dacoity < Skt *dashṭaka* crowded]

da·coit·y (də koi′tē), *n., pl.* **-coit·ies.** (in India and Burma) gang robbery; robbery by dacoits. Also, **dakoity.** [< Hindi *ḍakaitī,* deriv. of *ḍakait* DACOIT]

Da·cron (dā′kron, -krən, dak′ron, -rən), *n. Trademark.* a synthetic textile fiber that is wrinkle-resistant and strong.

dac·ry·a·gogue (dak′rē ə gôg′, -gog′), *Med.* **—***adj.* **1.** stimulating the secretion of tears. **—***n.* **2.** a dacryagogue agent. [DACRY- + -AGOGUE]

dacryo-, a learned borrowing from Greek meaning "tear," used in the formation of compound words: *dacryorrhea.* Also, *esp. before a vowel,* **dacry-.** [< Gk *dakryo-,* comb. form repr. *dákry* or *dákryon* TEAR[1]]

dac·ry·on (dak′rē on′), *n., pl.* **-ry·a** (-rē ə). *Anat.* the point of junction of the maxillary, lacrimal, and frontal bones. [< NL < Gk *dákryon* a tear (sp. var. of *dákry*); see DACRYO-]

dac·ry·or·rhe·a (dak′rē ə rē′ə), *n. Med.* excessive flow of tears. [DACRYO- + -RRHEA]

dac·tyl (dak′təl, -til), *n.* **1.** *Pros.* a foot of three syllables, one long followed by two short in quantitative meter, or one stressed followed by two unstressed in accentual meter, as in *gently and humanly.* **2.** a finger or toe. [< L *dactyl(us)* < Gk *dáktylos* finger, a dactyl, referring to the three joints of the finger]

Dac·tyl (dak′til), *n., pl.* **-tyls, -tyl·i** (-ti lī′). *Class. Myth.* any of a number of beings dwelling on Mount Ida and working as craftsmen and magicians. Also, **Daktyl.** Also called **Idaean Dactyl.** [< Gk *Dáktyloi* (Idaean) craftsmen or wizards (pl. of *dáktylos;* see DACTYL)]

-dactyl, var. of **dactylo-** as final element in a compound word: *pterodactyl.*

dac·tyl·ic (dak til′ik), *adj.* **1.** of, containing, or characterized by dactyls: *dactylic hexameter; a dactylic line.* **2.** of a dactyl. **—***n.* **3.** a dactylic verse. [< L *dactylic(us)* < Gk *daktylikós.* See DACTYL, -IC] **—dac·tyl′i·cal·ly,** *adv.*

dactylo-, a learned borrowing from Greek meaning "finger," "toe," used in the formation of compound words: *dactylomegaly.* Also, **dactyl-, -dactyl, -dactyly.** [< Gk, comb. form repr. *dáktylos* finger, toe]

dac·tyl·o·gram (dak til′ə gram′), *n.* a fingerprint. [DACTYLO- + -GRAM[1]]

dac·ty·log·ra·phy (dak′tᵊlog′rə fē), *n.* the study of fingerprints for purposes of identification. [DACTYLO- + -GRAPHY] **—dac′ty·log′ra·pher,** *n.* **—dac·tyl·o·graph·ic** (dak til′ə graf′ik, dak′tᵊ lə-), *adj.*

dac·ty·lol·o·gy (dak′tᵊlol′ə jē), *n., pl.* **-gies.** the technique of communicating by signs made with the fingers, as in the manual alphabets used by the deaf. [DACTYLO- + -LOGY]

dac·ty·lo·meg·a·ly (dak′tᵊlō meg′ə lē), *n. Med.* the abnormal enlargement of a finger or fingers. [DACTYLO- + MEGAL- + -Y[3]]

-dactyly, a combination of **-dactyl** and **-y**[3], used to form nouns to stems in **-dactyl:** *tetradactyly.* [< NL *-dactylia.* See -DACTYL, -Y[3]]

dad[1] (dad), *n. Informal.* **1.** father. **2.** fellow; buddy; pal (usually used in addressing a stranger). [childish alter.]

dad[2] (dad), *n. Scot. and North Eng.* **1.** a solid blow or knock. **2.** a large slice, lump, or portion. Also, **daud.** [prob. var. of DAB[1]]

dad[3] (dad), *interj. U.S. Informal.* God (used in combination in mild oaths): *dad-blasted; dad-blamed.* [euphemism for *God*]

dad (däd), *n.* the 15th letter of the Arabic alphabet. [< Ar]

Da·da (dä′dä), *n.* (*sometimes l.c.*) the style and techniques of a group of artists, writers, etc., of the early 20th century who exploited accidental and incongruous effects in their work and who programmatically challenged established canons of art, thought, morality, etc. [< F: hobby horse, childish redupl. of *da* giddap] **—Da′da·ism,** *n.* **—Da′da·ist,** *n.* **—Da′da·is′tic,** *adj.* **—Da′da·is′ti·cal·ly,** *adv.*

dad-blamed (dad′blāmd′), *adj., adv.* damned (used as a euphemism in expressions of surprise, disgust, anger, etc.): *The dad-blamed car got stuck in a snowdrift. He's so dad-blamed sure of himself.*

dad-blast·ed (dad′blas′tid, -bläs′-), *adj., adv.* damned (used as a euphemism in expressions of surprise, disgust, anger, etc.): *The dad-blasted door won't lock. What makes her so dad-blasted uppity?*

dad-burned (dad′bûrnd′), *adj., adv.* damned (used as a euphemism in expressions of surprise, disgust, anger, etc.): *I ruined the whole dad-burned batch. Well I'll be dad-burned! You're dad-burned right I do!*

Dad·dah (dad′ə, dä′dä), *n.* **Mokh·tar Ould** (mo͞oKH-tär′ o͞old), born 1925, Mauritanian statesman: president of the Republic of Mauritania since 1961.

dad·dy (dad′ē), *n., pl.* **-dies.** **1.** a diminutive of **dad**[1]. **2.** *Slang.* See **sugar daddy.** [DAD[1] + -Y[2]]

dad·dy-long·legs (dad′ē lông′legz′, -long′-), *n.* (*construed as sing. or pl.*) **1.** harvestman (def. 2). **2.** *Brit.* a crane fly. [DADDY + LONG[1] + LEG + -S[3]]

Dade (dād), *n.* a town in central Florida. 4759 (1960).

Dade·ville (dād′vil), *n.* a town in E Alabama. 2940 (1960).

da·do (dā′dō), *n., pl.* **-does, -dos,** *v.* **—***n.* **1.** Also called **die.** *Archit.* the part of a pedestal between the base and the cornice or cap. **2.** the lower broad part of an interior wall finished in wallpaper, a fabric, paint, etc. **3.** *Carpentry.* a groove or rectangular section for receiving the end of a board. —*v.t.* **4.** to provide with a dado. **5. dado in,** to insert (a board or the like) into a dado. [< It: die, cube, pedestal, perh. < Ar *dad* game]

da′do head′, a rotary cutter composed of several sawlike blades side by side, for cutting dadoes in wood.

Dado (def. 2)

D.A.E., Dictionary of American English. Also, **DAE**

dae·dal (dēd′əl), *adj.* **1.** skillful; ingenious. **2.** cleverly intricate. **3.** diversified. [< L *daedal(us)* skillful < Gk *daídalos,* equiv. to *daidáll(ein)* (to) work with skill + *-os* adj. suffix]

Dae·da·la (dēd′ələ), *n.* (*sometimes construed as pl.*) either of two festivals held in ancient Boeotia in honor of the reconciliation of Hera with Zeus, one **(Little Daedala)** being held every 6 years, the other **(Great Daedala),** every 59 years. [< Gk *Daídala* (neut. pl.), n. use of *daídalos* DAEDAL]

Daed·a·lid (ded′əlid *or, esp. Brit.,* dēd′əlid), *adj.* **1.** pertaining to or designating a style of vase painting developed in Attica from the middle to the end of the 7th century B.C., characterized chiefly by the use of the black-figure style in painting and a narrative treatment of subject matter. Cf. **Idaean** (def. 2). **2.** pertaining to or designating a style of terra-cotta sculpture developed in Greece during the 7th century B.C. [DAEDAL + -ID²]

Dae·da·li·on (dē dā′lē on′), *n.* *Class. Myth.* a son of Phosphorus who, despondent over the death of his daughter Chione, leaped off Parnassus: Apollo changed him into a hawk.

Daed·a·lus (ded′ələs *or, esp. Brit.,* dēd′ələs), *n.* *Class. Myth.* an Athenian architect who built the labyrinth for Minos and made wings for himself and his son Icarus to escape from Crete. [< L < Gk *Daídalos;* see DAEDAL] —**Dae·da·li·an, Dae·da·le·an** (di dā′lē ən, -dāl′yən), **Dae·dal·ic** (di dal′ik), *adj.*

dae·mon (dē′mən), *n.* **1.** *Class. Myth.* **a.** a god. **b.** a subordinate deity, as the genius of a place or a man's attendant spirit. **2.** a demon. Also, **daimon.** [< L: a spirit, an evil spirit < Gk *daímōn* a deity, fate, fortune, cf. *daíesthai* to distribute] —**dae·mon·ic** (di mon′ik), **dae·mon·is·tic** (dē′mə nis′tik), *adj.*

dae·mo·ni·an (di mō′nē ən), *n.* demonian.

dae·mon·ol·o·gy (dē′mə nol′ə jē), *n.* demonology.

daff¹ (daf), *v.i.* *Scot. and North Eng.* to make sport; dally; play. [v. use of *daff* (obs.) a fool, ME *daffe* (n.); see DAFT]

daff² (daf), *v.t.* **1.** *Archaic.* to turn or thrust aside. **2.** *Obs.* to doff. [alter. of DOFF]

daf·fa·dil·ly (daf′ə dil′ē), *n., pl.* **-lies.** *Chiefly Dial.* daffodil. [by alter.; see -Y²]

daf·fa·down·dil·ly (daf′ə doun′dil′ē), *n., pl.* **-lies.** *Chiefly Dial.* daffodil. [by alter.]

daf·fing (daf′ing), *n.* *Scot. and North Eng.* **1.** merriment; playful behavior; foolishness. **2.** *Archaic.* insanity. [DAFF¹ + -ING¹]

daf·fo·dil (daf′ə dil), *n.* **1.** a plant, *Narcissus Pseudo-Narcissus,* having single or double, yellow, nodding flowers that bloom in the spring. **2.** (formerly) any plant of this genus. **3.** clear yellow; canary. —*adj.* **4.** having the color daffodil. [unexplained var. of ME *affodile* < VL *affodill(us),* var. of *asphodelus* < Gk: ASPHODEL]

Daffodil, *Narcissus Pseudo-Narcissus*

Daf·fo·dil (daf′ə dil), *n.* a girl's given name.

daf′fodil gar′lic, a large herb, *Allium neapolitanum,* of Europe, that has clusters of white flowers and is grown as an ornamental.

daf·fo·dil·ly (daf′ə dil′ē), *n., pl.* **-lies.** *Chiefly Dial.* daffodil. [see DAFFADILLY]

daf·fo·down·dil·ly (daf′ə doun′dil′ē), *n., pl.* **-lies.** daffodil. [see DAFFADOWNDILLY]

daff·y (daf′ē), *adj.,* **daff·i·er, daff·i·est.** *Informal.* silly; weak-minded; crazy. [*daff* (obs.; see DAFF¹) + -Y¹]

daft (daft, däft), *adj.* **1.** insane; crazy. **2.** simple or foolish. **3.** *Scot.* merry; playful; frolicsome. [ME *dafte* uncouth, awkward; earlier, gentle, meek, OE *dæfte;* cf. DEFT] —**daft′ly,** *adv.* —**daft′ness,** *n.*

Da·fydd ap Gwi·lym (dä′vith äp gwi′lim), c1340–c1400, Welsh poet.

dag (dag), *n., v.,* **dagged, dag·ging.** —*n.* **1.** one of a series of decorative scallops or foliations along the edge of a garment, cloth, etc. **2.** *Scot.* daglock. —*v.t.* **3.** to edge (a garment, cloth, etc.) with decorative scallops or the like. [ME *dagge* < ?; cf. OF *dague* dagger]

Da·gan (dä′gän), *n.* the Mesopotamian god of agriculture and the earth: a counterpart of the Phoenician and Philistine Dagon.

Dag·da (däg′də, -thə), *n.* *Irish Myth.* a god, the chief of the Tuatha De Danann, the father of Angus Og and Brigit, and the leader of the battle against the Fomorians. Also, **Daghda.**

Dag·en·ham (dag′ə nəm), *n.* a city in SE England, part of greater London. 108,363 (1961).

Da·ge·stan (dä′gə stän′, dag′ə stan′; *Russ.* də gyi stän′), *n.* **1.** an autonomous republic in the SW Russian Federation on the W shore of the Caspian Sea. 1,800,000; 19,421 sq. mi. *Cap.:* Makhachkala. Formerly, **Dagestan′ Auton′omous So′viet So′cialist Repub′lic.** **2.** a closely woven carpet of this region with a floral design and zigzag border, usually in pastels.

Dagger with scabbard

dag·ger (dag′ər), *n.* **1.** a short, swordlike weapon with a pointed blade and a handle, used for stabbing. **2.** Also called **obelisk.** *Print.* a mark (†) used esp. for references. **3. look daggers,** to look at angrily, threateningly, or with hate: *The teacher looked daggers at the two boys who were passing notes.* —*v.t.* **4.** to stab with or as if with a dagger. **5.** *Print.* to mark with a dagger. [ME, prob. < MF *dague* < OPr or OIt *daga*]

dag·ger·board (dag′ər bōrd′, -bôrd′), *n.* *Naut.* a removable board on a small sailboat, typically of small dimension fore and aft, lowered into the water through a trunk to serve as a keel. Cf. **centerboard.** [DAGGER + BOARD]

dag·gle (dag′əl), *v.t., v.i.,* **-gled, -gling.** *Archaic.* to drag or trail through mud, water, etc.; draggle; bemire. [*dag* to bemire + -LE]

Dagh·da (däg′də, -thə), *n.* *Irish Myth.* Dagda.

dag·lock (dag′lok′), *n.* *Scot.* a dangling, matted lock of wool on a sheep. [DAG + LOCK²]

Dag·mar (dag′mär), *n.* a girl's given name.

Dag·na (dag′nə), *n.* a girl's given name.

Dag·ney (dag′nē), *n.* a girl's given name, form of **Dagna.** Also, **Dagny.**

Dag·ny (dag′nē), *n.* a girl's given name, form of **Dagna.** Also, **Dagney.**

da·go (dā′gō), *n., pl.* **-gos, -goes.** (*often cap.*) *Disparaging and Offensive.* a person of Spanish or esp. of Italian origin or descent. [alter. of *Diego* < Sp: a given name]

Dag·ö (däg′œ′), *n.* Danish name of **Hiiumaa.**

da·go·ba (dä′gə bə), *n.* a dome-shaped memorial alleged to contain relics of Buddha or a Buddhist saint; stupa; chaitya. [< Singhalese *dāgoba* < Pali *dhātugabbha* < Skt *dhātugarbha,* equiv. to *dhātu* relics + *garbha* womb, inside]

Dag·o·bert I (dag′ə bərt; *Fr.* dA gô beʀ′), A.D. 602?–639, Merovingian king of the Franks 628–639.

Da·go·ber·to (dag′ə bûr′tō), *n.* a boy's given name.

Da·gon (dā′gon), *n.* a Phoenician and Philistine god of agriculture and the earth: the national god of the Philistines. [< L < Gk < Heb *dāghōn* little fish]

Da′go red′, *Slang* (*offensive*). a cheap red wine, esp. a Chianti.

D.Agr., Doctor of Agriculture.

Da·guerre (də gâr′; *Fr.* dA geʀ′), *n.* **1. Louis Jacques Man·dé** (lwē zhäk mäN dā′), 1789–1851, French painter and inventor of the daguerreotype. **2.** a walled plain in the fourth quadrant of the face of the moon: about 30 miles in diameter.

da·guerre·o·type (də ger′ə tīp′, -ē ə tīp′), *n., v.,* **-typed, -typ·ing.** —*n.* **1.** an obsolete photographic process, invented in 1839, in which a picture made on a silver surface sensitized with iodine was developed by exposure to mercury vapor. **2.** a picture made by this process. —*v.t.* **3.** to photograph by this process. [named after L. J. M. DAGUERRE; see -O-, -TYPE] —**da·guerre′o·typ′er, da·guerre′o·typ′ist,** *n.* —**da·guerre·o·typ·ic** (də ger′ə tip′ik), *adj.* —**da·guerre′o·typ′y,** *n.*

Dag·wood (dag′wŏŏd), *n.* **1.** See **Dagwood sandwich.** **2.** a boy's given name.

Dag′wood sand′wich, a huge sandwich in which a large quantity of varied meats, cheeses, dressings, and condiments have been used for a filling. [named after *Dagwood* Bumstead, a character in comic strip *Blondie,* who makes and eats such sandwiches]

dah (dä), *n.* an echoic word, the referent of which is a tone interval approximately three times the length of the dot, used to designate the dash of Morse code, International Morse code, etc. Cf. **dit.**

da·ha·be·ah (dä′hə bē′ə), *n.* a large boat used on the Nile as a houseboat or for conveying passengers. Also, **da′ha·bee′yah, da′ha·bi′ah, da′ha·bi′eh, da′ha·bi′ya.** [< Ar *dhahabīyah,* lit., the golden]

Dahl·gren (dal′grən), *n.* **John Adelphus Bernard,** 1809–70, U.S. naval officer and inventor.

dahl·ia (dal′yə, däl′- *or, esp. Brit.,* dāl′-), *n.* **1.** any composite plant of the genus *Dahlia,* native to Mexico and Central America and widely cultivated for its showy, variously colored flowers. **2.** the flower or tuberous root of a dahlia. **3.** a violet, coal-tar color. —*adj.* **4.** having the color dahlia. [< NL, named after Anders *Dahl* (d. 1789), Swedish botanist; see -IA]

Dahl·ia (dal′yə, däl′-), *n.* a girl's given name.

Dah·lon·e·ga (də lon′ə gə), *n.* a town in N Georgia. 2604 (1960).

Dah·na (däKH′nä), *n.* **1.** an area in the NE Rub' al Khali desert, comprising a region of E central Saudi Arabia. **2.** See **Rub' al Khali.**

Da·ho·mey (də hō′mē; *Fr.* dA ô mā′), *n.* former name of **Benin** (def. 1). —**Da·ho′me·an, Da·ho·man** (də hō′mən), *adj., n.*

da·hoon (də hōōn′), *n.* a shrub or small tree, *Ilex Cassine,* of the southern U.S. [?]

Da·hu′ri·an larch′ (də hŏŏr′ē ən, -hyŏŏr′-), a pine tree, *Larix gmelini,* of northern Asia, that has wide-spreading branches and small, oval cones which are pink when young, with downy scales, and that is grown for timber and as an ornamental. [after *Dahuria,* in southern Siberia; see -AN]

Dai·bu·tsu (dī′bŏŏ tsōō), *n.* *Japanese.* a large representation of the Buddha. [lit., great Buddha]

Dai·gle·ville (dā′gəl vil), *n.* a town in SE Louisiana. 5906 (1960).

dai·ker (dā′kər), *v.i.* *Scot. and North Eng.* dacker.

Dail Eir·eann (dôl âr′ən; *Irish* thōl ār′ən), the lower house of the parliament of the Republic of Ireland. Also called **Dail.** Cf. **Oireachtas.** [< IrGael: assembly of Eire]

dai·ly (dā′lē), *adj., n., pl.* **-lies,** *adv.* —*adj.* **1.** of, done, occurring, or issued each day or each weekday: *daily attendance; a daily newspaper.* **2.** computed by the day: *daily quota; a daily wage.* —*n.* **3.** a newspaper appearing each day or each weekday: *a strike against the city's dailies.* **4.** Often, **dailies.** *Motion Pictures.* rush (def. 21). **5.** *Brit.* **a.** a nonresident servant who comes to work every day; a permanently employed servant who sleeps out. **b.** a woman employed to do cleaning or other household work by the day. —*adv.* **6.** every day; day by day: *She phoned the hospital daily to find out how I was.* [ME *daily,* OE *dæglīc.* See DAY, -LY] —**dai′li·ness,** *n.*

dai·ly-bread·er (dā′lē bred′ər), *n.* *Brit.* a commuter. [from the phrase *daily bread* + -ER¹]

dai′ly dou′ble, a betting system in horse racing and dog racing in which the bettor makes one bet on the winners of two races, usually the first and second, and collects only if both of his choices win.

dai′ly doz′en, *Informal.* a set of 12 or more calisthenic exercises to be done each day.

dai·men (dā′min), *adj.* *Scot.* rare; occasional. [?]

dai·mon (dī′mōn), *n.* daemon. —**dai·mon·ic** (dī-mon′ik), **dai·mon·is·tic** (dī′mə nis′tik), *adj.*

dai·myo (dī′myō), *n., pl.* **-myo, -myos.** *Japanese Hist.* one of the great feudal lords who were vassals of the emperor. Also, **dai′mio.** [< Jap, equiv. to *dai* great + *mio* name]

Dain·ger·field (dān′jər fēld′), *n.* a town in NE Texas. 3133 (1960).

dain·ty (dān′tē), *adj.,* **-ti·er, -ti·est,** *n., pl.* **-ties.** —*adj.* **1.** of delicate beauty; exquisite: *a dainty lass.* **2.** pleasing to the taste; delicious: *dainty pastries.* **3.** of delicate discrimination or taste; particular; fastidious: *a dainty eater.* **4.** overly particular; finical: *a dainty attitude toward eating lobster.* —*n.* **5.** something delicious to the taste; a delicacy. [ME *deinte* worthiness, happiness, delicacy < AF (OF *deint(i)e*) < L *dignitāt-* (s. of *dignitās*); see DIGNITY] —**dain′ti·ly,** *adv.* —**dain′ti·ness,** *n.*
—**Syn. 1.** fine. See **delicate. 2.** tender, delectable. **3.** scrupulous. See **particular. 4.** overnice. **5.** tidbit, sweetmeat.

dai·qui·ri (dī′kə rē, dak′ə-), *n., pl.* **-ris.** a cocktail consisting of rum, lemon or lime juice, and sugar. [after *Daiquirí,* town on the east coast of Cuba]

Da·i·ra (dā ī′rə), *n.* *Class. Myth.* a daughter of Oceanus.

Dai·ren (dī′ren′), *n.* a city in S Liaoning, in NE China: capital of the former Japanese leased territory of Kwantung in S Manchuria. 1,508,000 with Port Arthur (est. 1957). Chinese, **Talien.** Formerly, **Dalny.**

dair·y (dâr′ē), *n., pl.* **dair·ies.** **1.** an establishment, as a room, building, or buildings, where milk and cream are kept and butter and cheese are made. **2.** a shop or company that sells milk, butter, etc. **3.** the business of a dairy farm, concerned with the production and treatment of milk and cream and the manufacture of butter and cheese. **4.** See **dairy farm. 5.** the cows on a dairy farm. [ME *daierie,* equiv. to *daie, deie* dairymaid (OE *dǣge* bread maker; c. Icel *deigja;* see LADY) + *-erie* -ERY]

dair′y cat′tle, cows raised mainly for their milk.

dair′y farm′, a farm devoted chiefly to the production of milk and the manufacture of butter and cheese.

dair·y·ing (dâr′ē ing), *n.* the business of a dairy. [DAIRY + -ING¹]

dair·y·maid (dâr′ē mād′), *n.* a girl or woman employed in a dairy. [DAIRY + MAID]

dair·y·man (dâr′ē mən), *n., pl.* **-men.** **1.** an owner or manager of a dairy. **2.** an employee in a dairy. [DAIRY + MAN¹]

Dair′y Val′ley, a town in SW California. 3508 (1960).

dair·y·wom·an (dâr′ē wŏŏm′ən), *n., pl.* **-wom·en.** a woman who works in a dairy or sells its produce. [DAIRY + WOMAN]

da·is (dā′is, dī′-, dās), *n.* a raised platform, as at the end of a room, for a throne, seats of honor, a lecturer's desk, etc. [ME *deis* < AF (OF *dois*) < L *disc(us)* quoit; see DISCUS]

dai·sho (dī′shō; *Jap.* dī′shô′), *n., pl.* **-sho.** the pair of swords of a Japanese samurai, comprising a katana and a wakizashi. [< Jap]

dai·sy (dā′zē), *n., pl.* **-sies.** **1.** any of various composite plants the flowers of which have a yellow disk and white rays, as the English daisy and the oxeye daisy. **2.** Also called **daisy ham.** a small section of pork shoulder, usually smoked, boned, and weighing from two to four pounds. Cf. **picnic** (def. 5). **3.** *Slang.* someone or something of first-rate quality: *That new car is a daisy.* **4.** a Cheddar cheese of cylindrical shape, weighing about 20 pounds. **5. push up daisies,** *Informal.* to be dead: *Another year of this and I'll be pushing up daisies.* [ME *dayesye,* OE *dægesēge* the day's eye] —**dai′sied,** *adj.*

Dai·sy (dā′zē), *n.* a girl's given name. Also, **Daysie.**

dai·sy-cut·ter (dā′zē kut′ər), *n.* **1.** *Sports Slang.* a batted or served ball that skims along near the ground. **2.** *Mil. Slang.* an antipersonnel fragmentation bomb.

dai′sy ham′, daisy (def. 2).

Dai′sy Mil′ler, a short novel (1879) by Henry James.

dai′sy wheel′, a printing mechanism used in a computer printer or electronic typewriter, consisting of a wheellike disk with raised characters on spokes.

dak (dôk, däk), *n.* **1.** transportation by relays of men or horses, esp. in the East Indies. **2.** mail delivered by such transportation. Also, **dauk, dawk.** [< Hindi *dāk*]

Dak., Dakota.

Da·kar (dä kär′), *n.* a seaport in and the capital of Senegal; capital of former French West Africa. 234,500 (1957); 68 sq. mi.

da·ker-hen (dā′kər hen′), *n.* *Brit. Dial.* the corn crake. [?]

Dakh·la (däKH′lä), *n.* an oasis in the S United Arab Republic: source of ocher.

dakh·ma (däk′mə), *n.* See **tower of silence.** [< Pers; MPers *dakhmak,* Avestan *daxma-* funeral site]

Da′kin's solu′tion (dā′kinz), *Pharm.* a liquid antiseptic that consists of an approximately neutral solution containing about 0.5 percent of sodium hypochlorite and is used in treating infected wounds. [named after Henry Drysdale *Dakin* (1880–1952), English biochemist who compounded it]

da·koit (də koit′), *n.* dacoit.

da·koit·y (də koi′tē), *n., pl.* **-koit·ies.** dacoity.

Da·ko·ta (də kō′tə), *n.* **1.** a former territory in the United States: divided into the states of North Dakota and South Dakota 1889. **2.** North Dakota or South Dakota. **3. the Dakotas,** North Dakota and South Dakota. **4.** a Sioux Indian. **5.** a division of the Siouan stock of North American Indians, whose former habitat was in and near North and South Dakota. **6.** a Siouan language spoken by the Dakota and Assiniboin Indians. —**Da·ko′tan,** *adj., n.*

Dak·tyl (dak′til), *n., pl.* **-tyls, -tyl·i** (-ti lī′). Dactyl.

dāl (däl), *n.* the eighth letter of the Arabic alphabet. [< Ar]

dal., decaliter.

Da·la·dier (dA lA dyā′), *n.* **É·douard** (ā dwAʀ′), born 1884, premier of France 1933, 1934, 1938–40.

Da·lai La·ma (dä′lī lä′mə), the former ruler and chief monk of Tibet, believed to be a reincarnation of Avalokitesvara and sought for among new babies after the death of the former Dalai Lama: title assumed since the middle of the 17th century. [< Mongolian, equiv. to *dalai* ocean + *lama* a celibate priest]

da·lan (də län′), *n.* (in Persian and Indian architecture) a veranda or open hall for reception of visitors. Also, **dallan.** [< Pers]

d'Al·bert (dal′bərt; *Ger.* däl′bert), *n.* **Eu·gen** (oigān′) (or **Eugene**) **Francis Charles.** See **Albert, d', Eugen** (or **Eugene**) **Francis Charles.**

Dal·croze (*Fr.* dal krōz′), *n.* Jaques-Dalcroze.

dale (dāl), *n.* **1.** a valley, esp. a broad valley. **2.** *Phys. Geog., U.S.* a small open river valley partly enclosed by low hills. [ME *dal,* OE *dæl;* c. G *Tal,* Icel *dalr,* Goth *dals*]

Dale (dāl), *n.* **1. Sir Henry Hal·lett** (hal′it), 1875–1968, English physiologist: Nobel prize for medicine 1936. **2. Sir Thomas,** died 1619, British colonial administrator in America: governor of Virginia 1614–16. **3.** a town in central Pennsylvania. 2807 (1960). **4.** a boy's or girl's given name.

D'Al′em·bert Moun′tains (dal′əm bâr′, dal′əmbâr′), a mountain range in the third quadrant of the face of the moon in the libration area, having peaks as high as 20,000 feet.

d'A′lem·bert's′ test′ (dal′əm bârz′, dal′-), *Math.* See **ratio test.** [named after Jean Le Rond *d'Alembert* (1717?–83), French mathematician who formulated it]

Da·lén (də lān′, da-), *n.* **Gus·taf** (gōōs′täf), 1869–1937, Swedish inventor: Nobel prize for physics 1912.

dales·man (dālz′mən), *n., pl.* **-men.** a person living in a dale or valley, esp. in the northern counties of England. [DALE + 's[1] + MAN[1]]

da·leth (dä′led, dä′ləth), *n.* **1.** the fourth letter of the Hebrew alphabet. **2.** the consonant sound represented by this letter. [< Heb *dāleth,* prob. var. of *deleth* door, as pronounced before a pause]

Dal·hart (dal′härt), *n.* a town in N Texas. 5160 (1960).

Dal·hou·sie (dal hōō′zē, -hou′-), *n.* **1. George Ramsay, Earl of,** 1770–1838, British general: governor of the Canadian colonies 1819–28. **2. James Andrew Broun Ramsay, 1st Marquis and 10th Earl of,** 1812–60, British statesman: viceroy of India 1848–56.

Da·li (dä′lē), *n.* **Sal·va·dor** (sal′və dôr′; *Sp.* säl′vä-thôr′), born 1904, Spanish painter, illustrator, and writer: in U.S. since 1940.

Dal·ia (dāl′yə), *n.* a girl's given name.

Dal·i·la (dal′ə lə), *n. Douay Bible.* Delilah (def. 1).

dal·lan (də län′), *n.* dalan.

Dal·la·pic·co·la (dä′lä pē′kō lə; *It.* däl′lä pēk′kō-lä), *n.* **Lu·i·gi** (lōō ē′jē), born 1904. Italian composer.

Dal·las (dal′əs), *n.* **1. George Miff·lin** (mif′lin), 1792–1864, lawyer and diplomat, vice-president of the U.S. 1845–49. **2.** a city in NE Texas. 904,078. **3.** a town in NW Oregon. 5072 (1960). **4.** a town in S North Carolina. 3270 (1960). **5.** a town in central Pennsylvania. 2586 (1960). **6.** a boy's given name.

Dal·las·town (dal′əs toun′), *n.* a town in S Pennsylvania. 3615 (1960).

dalles (dalz), *n.pl.* the rapids of a river running between the walls of a canyon or gorge. Also, **dells.** [< CanF, pl. of F *dalle* flagstone, throat, gutter << Gmc; cf. OE *dæl* DALE]

dal·li·ance (dal′ē əns, dal′yəns), *n.* **1.** a trifling away of time; dawdling. **2.** amorous toying; flirtation. [ME *daliaunce.* See DALLY, -ANCE]

Dal·lin (dal′in), *n.* **Cyrus Earle,** 1861–1944, U.S. sculptor.

Dall's′ sheep′ (dôlz), a white-haired wild sheep, *Ovis dalli,* of mountainous regions of northwestern North America, having curved horns. [named after William H. *Dall* (1845–1927), American naturalist]

dal·ly (dal′ē), *v.,* **-lied, -ly·ing.** —*v.i.* **1.** to sport or play, esp. amorously. **2.** to play mockingly; trifle: *to dally with danger.* **3.** to waste time; loiter; delay. —*v.t.* **4.** to waste (time) (usually fol. by *away*). [ME *dali(en)* < AF *dalier* to chat << LG *dallen* to talk foolishly] —**dal′li·er,** *n.* —**dal′ly·ing·ly,** *adv.*
—**Syn. 1.** fondle, caress, pet. **2.** toy. **3.** See **loiter.** —**Ant. 3.** hasten.

Dal·ma·tia (dal mā′shə), *n.* **1.** a historic region along the Adriatic coast of Yugoslavia, now part of Croatia. **2.** a Roman province formed by Emperor Tiberius and called after the tribe inhabiting the area.

Dal·ma·tian (dal mā′shən), *adj.* **1.** of or pertaining to Dalmatia or its people. —*n.* **2.** an inhabitant of Dalmatia, esp. a member of the native Slavic-speaking people of Dalmatia. **3.** Also called **coach dog, Dalma′tian dog′.** one of a breed of short-haired dogs having a white coat marked with black or liver-colored spots. **4.** a Romance language of Dalmatia, extinct since 1898. [DALMATI(A) + -AN]

Dalmatian (21 in. high at shoulder)

dal·mat·ic (dal mat′ik), *n.* **1.** *Eccles.* a vestment worn over the alb by the deacon, as at the celebration of the Mass, and worn by bishops on some occasions, as at a coronation. **2.** a similar vestment worn by the king of England at his coronation. [< LL *dalmatic(a),* special use of L *Dalmatica,* fem. of *Dalmaticus* Dalmatian. See DALMATIA, -IC]

Dal·ny (däl′nē), *n.* former name of **Dairen.**

Dal·rym·ple (dal rim′pəl, dal′rim-), *n.* **Sir James, 1st Viscount Stair,** 1619–95, Scottish jurist.

dal se·gno (däl sān′yō; *It.* däl se′nyô), go back to the sign marking the beginning of a repeat (used as a musical direction). [< It: from the sign]

Dal·ton (dôl′tən), *n.* **1. John,** 1766–1844, English chemist and physicist. **2.** a city in NW Georgia. 17,868 (1960). **3.** a town in W Massachusetts. 6436 (1960).

Dal·to·ni·an (dôl tō′nē ən), *adj.* **1.** of John Dalton or his atomic theory. **2.** of or pertaining to daltonism.

dal·ton·ism (dôl′tən iz′əm), *n.* (*sometimes cap.*) *Pathol.* color blindness, esp. the inability to distinguish red from green. [J. DALTON + -ISM] —**dal·ton·ic** (dôl ton′ik), *adj.*

Dal′ton's law′, *Physics, Chem.* the law that the total pressure exerted by a mixture of gases is equal to the sum of the partial pressures of the gases of the mixture. Also called **Dal′ton's law′ of par′tial pres′sures, law of additive pressures, law of partial pressures.** [named after J. DALTON]

Dal′ton Sys′tem, a method of progressive education whereby students contract to carry through on their own responsibility the year's work as divided up into monthly assignments. [named after *Dalton,* Massachusetts where it was used in the high schools]

Da·ly (dā′lē), *n.* **(John) Au·gus·tin** (ô gus′tin), 1838–99, U.S. playwright, critic, and theatrical manager.

Dal·yce (dal′is), *n.* a girl's given name.

Da′ly Cit′y, a city in central California, S of San Francisco. 44,791 (1960).

Dal·y·more (dal′ē mōr′, -môr′), *n.* a boy's given name.

dam[1] (dam), *n., v.,* **dammed, dam·ming.** —*n.* **1.** a barrier to obstruct the flow of water, esp. one of earth, masonry, etc., built across a stream. **2.** a body of water confined by a dam. **3.** any barrier resembling a dam. —*v.t.* **4.** to furnish with a dam; obstruct or confine with a dam. **5.** to stop up; block up. [ME, prob. < ON; cf. OIcel *damm(a);* akin to OE *demman* to stop up, block]

Dam[1] (def. 1)
A, Trash rack
B, Penstock
C, Powerhouse

dam[2] (dam), *n.* a female parent (used esp. of four-footed animals). [ME; var. of DAME]

Dam (dam, däm), *n.* **(Carl Pe·ter) Hen·rik** (kärl pē′tər hen′rik; *Dan.* käRl pā′təR hen′Rik), born 1895, Danish biochemist: Nobel prize for medicine 1943.

dam·age (dam′ij), *n., v.,* **-aged, -ag·ing.** —*n.* **1.** injury or harm that impairs value or usefulness: *The storm did considerable damage to the crops.* **2. damages,** *Law.* the estimated money equivalent for detriment or injury sustained. **3.** Often, **damages.** *Informal.* cost; expense; charge: *What are the damages for the lubrication job on my car?* —*v.t.* **4.** to cause damage to; injure or harm; impair the usefulness of: *He damaged the saw on a nail.* —*v.i.* **5.** to become damaged: *Soft wood damages easily.* [ME < OF, equiv. to *dam* (< L *damnum* damage, fine) + *-age* -AGE; see DAMN] —**dam′age·a·ble,** *adj.* —**dam′age·a·ble·ness, dam′age·a·bil′i·ty,** *n.* —**dam′ag·er,** *n.*
—**Syn. 1.** loss. DAMAGE, DETRIMENT, HARM, MISCHIEF refer to injuries of various kinds. DAMAGE is the kind of injury or the effect of injury which directly impairs appearance, value, usefulness, soundness, etc.: *Fire causes damage to property. Property suffers damage.* DETRIMENT is a falling off from an original condition as the result of damage, depreciation, devaluation, etc.: *detriment to health because of illness, to property because of neglect.* HARM is the kind of injury which connotes sorrow or a sense of evil; it may denote either physical hurt or mental, moral, or spiritual injury: *bodily harm; harm to one's self-confidence.* MISCHIEF may be damage, harm, trouble, or misfortune caused by a person, esp. if maliciously: *an enemy who would do one mischief.* **4.** hurt, mar. —**Ant. 1.** improvement. **4.** improve.

dam·ag·ing (dam′i jing), *adj.* causing or capable of causing damages; harmful; injurious: *a damaging statement.* [DAMAGE + -ING[2]] —**dam′ag·ing·ly,** *adv.*

Dam·a·lis (dam′ə lis), *n.* a girl's given name.

dam·an (dam′ən), *n.* **1.** a hyrax, *Procavia syriaca,* of Syria, Palestine, etc.: the cony of the Bible. **2.** any hyrax. [< Ar *damān* (*Isrā'īl*), lit., lamb (of Israel)]

Da·man (də män′), *n.* **1.** a union territory in W India: formerly a district of Portuguese India; annexed by India December, 1961. 23,093 (1961); 176 sq. mi. **2.** the capital of this territory. 22,390 (1961). Portuguese, **Da·mão** (dä moun′).

Da·man·hur (dä′män hōōr′), *n.* a city in N United Arab Republic, near Alexandria. 110,521 (est. 1957).

dam·ar (dam′är, -ər, də mär′), *n.* dammar.

Da·ma·ra·land (də mär′ə land′), *n.* a region in the central part of SW Africa.

Dam·ar·is (dam′ər is), *n.* a girl's given name.

Da·mas (da mä′), *n.* French name of **Damascus.**

Dam·a·scene (dam′ə sēn′, dam′ə sēn′), *adj., n., v.,* **-scened, -scen·ing.** —*adj.* **1.** of or pertaining to the city of Damascus. **2.** (*l.c.*) of or pertaining to the art of damascening. —*n.* **3.** an inhabitant of Damascus. **4.** (*l.c.*) work or patterns produced by damascening. —*v.t.* **5.** (*l.c.*) Also, **damaskeen.** to produce wavy lines on (watered steel). [ME < L *Damascēn(us)* of Damascus < Gk *Damaskēnós,* equiv. to *Damask(ós)* DAMASCUS + *-ēnos* -ENE]

Da·mas·cus (də mas′kəs), *n.* a city in and the capital of Syria, in the SW part: reputed to be the oldest continuously existing city in the world. 526,454 (1962). French, **Damas.**

Damas′cus steel′. See **watered steel.**

dam·ask (dam′əsk), *n.* **1.** a reversible fabric of linen, silk, cotton, or wool, woven with patterns. **2.** napery of this material. **3.** Also called **damask steel.** See **watered steel. 4.** the pattern or wavy appearance peculiar to the surface of such steel. **5.** the pink color of the damask rose. —*adj.* **6.** made of or resembling damask: *damask cloth.* **7.** of the pink color of the damask rose. —*v.t.* **8.** to damascene. **9.** to weave or adorn with elaborate design, as damask cloth. [ME *damaske* < ML *damasc(us),* after DAMASCUS where fabrics were first made]

dam·a·skeen (dam′ə skēn′), *v.t.* Damascene (def. 5).

dam·a·skeen·ing (dam′ə skē′ning), *n.* **1.** the act of a person who damaskeens. **2.** *Horol.* snailing. [DAMASKEEN + -ING[1]]

dam′ask rose′, a fragrant pink rose, *Rosa damascena.*

dam′ask steel′. See **watered steel.**

Da·mas·tes (də mas′tēz), *n. Class. Myth.* Procrustes.

Dam·a·sus I (dam′ə səs), **Saint,** pope A.D. 366–384.

Damasus II, died 1048, pope 1048.

D'Am·boise (*Fr.* dän bwaz′), *n.* **Jacques** (*Fr.* zhäk) **(Jo·seph),** born 1934, U.S. ballet dancer and choreographer.

dame (dām), *n.* **1.** a form of address to any woman of rank or authority. **2.** (*cap.*) (in Britain) **a.** the official title of the wife of a knight or baronet. **b.** the official title of a female member of the Order of the British Empire. **3.** *Eccles.* a title of a nun in certain orders **4.** a matronly woman of advanced age; matron. **5.** *Slang.* a woman; female: *dating a good-looking dame.* **6.** *Brit.* a mistress of a dame-school. **7.** *Archaic.* the mistress of a household. **8.** *Archaic.* a woman of rank or authority, as a woman ruler. [ME < OF < L *domina,* fem. of *dominus* lord, master]

Dame aux Ca·mé·lias, La (*Fr.* la dam ō ka mā-lya′). See **Lady of the Camellias, The.**

dame-school (dām′skōōl′), *n.* (formerly in Britain) a school in which the rudiments of reading, writing, and arithmetic were taught to neighborhood children by a woman in her own home.

dame's′ rock′et, a rocket, *Hesperis matronalis,* of Europe and Asia, having showy purple or white fragrant flowers. Also called **dame's′ vi′olet, garden rocket.**

dam·fool (dam′fōōl′), *Informal.* —*n.* **1.** a person who is exceptionally foolish. —*adj.* **2.** Also, **dam·fool·ish** (dam′fōō′lish). extraordinarily stupid or foolish: *That was a damfool thing to do.* [alter. of *damned fool* or *foolish*]

Dam·i·a (dam′ē ə), *n. Class. Myth.* a spirit of fertility.

dam·i·an·a (dam′ē an′ə, -ä′nə), *n.* the dried leaves of the Mexican plant *Turnera aphrodisiaca,* containing bitter principles believed to be effective in the treatment of sexual impotence. [< AmerSp]

Da·mien (dā′myen; *Fr.* da myan′), *n.* **Father (Jo·seph de Veu·ster)** (*Fr.* zho zef′ də vœ steR′), 1840–89, Belgian Roman Catholic missionary to the lepers of Molokai.

Dam·i·et·ta (dam′ē et′ə), *n.* a city in NE United Arab Republic, in the Nile delta. 391,000 (est. 1960). Arabic, **Dumyat.**

dam·mar (dam′är, -ər, də mär′), *n.* **1.** Also called **gum dammar.** a copallike resin derived largely from dipterocarpaceous trees of southern Asia, esp. Malaya and Sumatra, and used chiefly for making colorless varnish. **2.** any of various similar resins from trees of other families. Also, **damar, dam·mer** (dam′ər). [< Malay *damar*]

dam·mit (dam′it), *interj. Informal.* damn it (used as a mild expletive). [by alter.]

damn (dam), *v.t.* **1.** to declare (something) to be bad, unfit, invalid, or illegal. **2.** to condemn as a failure: *to damn a play.* **3.** to bring condemnation upon; ruin. **4.** to doom to eternal punishment or condemn to hell. **5.** to swear at or curse, using the word "damn": *Damn the torpedoes! Full speed ahead!* —*v.i.* **6.** to use the word "damn"; swear. **7. damn with faint praise,** to condemn in effect by praising too moderately or indifferently: *The critics damned the opera with faint praise when they termed the production adequate.* —*interj.* **8.** (used as an expletive to express anger, annoyance, disgust, etc.) —*n.* **9.** the utterance of "damn" in swearing or for emphasis. **10.** something of negligible value: *not worth a damn.* **11. give a damn,** *Informal.* to care; be concerned; consider as important: *You shouldn't give a damn for their opinions. He doesn't give a damn about cards.* Also, **give a darn.** —*adj.* **12.** damned (def. 2). —*adv.* **13.** damned. [ME *dam(p)n(en)* < OF *dam(p)ne(r)* < L *damnāre* to condemn, deriv. of *damnum* damage, fine, harm] —**damn′-er,** *n.*

dam·na·ble (dam′nə bəl), *adj.* **1.** worthy of damnation. **2.** detestable, abominable, or outrageous. [ME *dam(p)nable* < MF *damnable* < LL *damnābil(is),* equiv. to L *damn(āre)* (see DAMN) + *-ābilis* -ABLE] —**dam′na·ble·ness, dam′na·bil′i·ty,** *n.* —**dam′na·bly,** *adv.*

dam·nant quod non in·tel·li·gunt (däm′nänt kwōd nōn in tel′i gōōnt′; *Eng.* dam′nənt kwod non in tel′ə gənt), *Latin.* they condemn what they do not understand.

dam·na·tion (dam nā′shən), *n.* **1.** the act or state of damning or of being damned. **2.** a cause or occasion of being damned. **3.** *Theol.* condemnation to eternal punishment as a consequence of sin. **4.** an oath expressing anger, disappointment, etc. —*interj.* **5.** (used in exclamatory phrases to express anger, disappointment, etc.) [ME *dam(p)nacioun* < OF *damnation* < L *damnātiōn-* (s. of *damnātiō*), equiv. to *damnāt(us)* (ptp. of *damnāre;* see DAMN) + *-iōn-* -ION]

Damna′tion of Faust′, The, a dramatic cantata (1846) by Hector Berlioz.

dam·na·to·ry (dam′nə tōr′ē, -tôr′ē), *adj.* conveying, expressing, or causing condemnation; damning. [< L *damnātōri(us),* equiv. to *damnāt(us)* (see DAMNATION) + *-ōrius* -ORY[1]]

damned (damd), *adj., superl.* **damned·est, damnd·est,** *adv.* —*adj.* **1.** condemned or doomed, esp. to eternal punishment: *The wailing of damned souls.* **2.** detestable; loathsome: *Get that damned dog out of the room!* **3.** extraordinary; amazing: *It was the damnedest thing I'd ever seen.* —*n.* **4. the damned,** those condemned to suffer eternal punishment: *In his dream he journeyed through the regions of the damned.* —*adv.* **5.** extremely; very; absolutely: *He had damned bad luck. She's a damned good singer. She is just too damned fussy.* [ME *dam(p)ned.* See DAMN, -ED[2]]

damned·est (dam′dist), *n. Informal.* best; utmost: *They did their damnedest to finish on time.* [DAMNED + -EST[1]]

dam·ni·fy (dam′nə fī′), *v.t.,* **-fied, -fy·ing.** *Law.* to cause loss or damage to. [< MF *damnifi(er),* OF < LL *damnificāre,* deriv. of L *damnific(us)* harmful, equiv. to *damn(um)* damage + *-ificus* (see -I-, -FIC); see -IFY]

damn·ing (dam′ing, dam′ning), *adj.* causing incrimination: *damning evidence.* [DAMN + -ING[2]] —**damn′ing·ly,** *adv.* —**damn′ing·ness,** *n.*

damn·yan·kee (dam′yang′kē), *n. Informal.* damyankee.

Dam·o·cles (dam′ə klēz′), *n.* a flatterer who, having extolled the happiness of Dionysius, tyrant of Syracuse, was seated at a banquet with a sword suspended over his head by a single hair to show him the perilous nature of that happiness. —**Dam·o·cle·an** (dam′ə klē′ən), *adj.*

dam·oi·selle (dam′ə zel′), *n. Archaic.* damsel. Also, **dam′o·sel′, dam′o·zel′.**

Da·mon (dā′mən), *n.* a boy's given name.

Da′mon and Pyth′ias, *Class. Myth.* two young friends whose extreme loyalty to one another was shown by Damon's offer of his life as pledge that Pythias would return from handling his affairs to be executed for rebelling against Dionysius, the tyrant of Syracuse. At the time set for the execution, Pythias returned, and Dionysius relented and pardoned them both.

damp (damp), *adj.* **1.** moderately wet; moist: *damp weather; a damp towel.* **2.** unenthusiastic; dejected; depressed; lifeless: *The welcoming committee gave them a rather damp reception.* —*n.* **3.** moisture; humidity; moist air: *damp that goes through your warmest clothes.* **4.** a noxious or stifling vapor or gas, esp. in a mine. **5.** depression of spirits; dejection. **6.** a restraining or discouraging force or factor. —*v.t.* **7.** to make damp; moisten. **8.** to check or retard the energy, action, etc., of: *Continued failures damped her enthusiasm.* **9.** to stifle or suffocate; extinguish: *to damp a furnace.* **10.** *Acoustics, Music.* to check or retard the action of (a vibrating string); dull; deaden. **11.** *Physics.* to cause a decrease in amplitude of (successive oscillations or waves). **12. damp off,** to undergo damping-off. [ME; cf. MD *damp*, MHG *dampf* vapor, smoke] —**damp′ish,** *adj.* —**damp′ish·ly,** *adv.* —**damp′ish·ness,** *n.* —**damp′ly,** *adv.* —**damp′ness,** *n.*

—**Syn. 1.** dank, steamy. DAMP, HUMID, MOIST mean slightly wet. DAMP usually implies slight and extraneous wetness, generally undesirable or unpleasant unless the result of intention: *a damp cellar; to put a damp cloth on a patient's forehead.* HUMID is a literary or scientific word, applied to that which is so permeated with moisture that the moisture seems a part of it, esp. unpleasant dampness in the air in either hot or cold weather: *The air is oppressively humid today.* MOIST denotes that which is slightly wet, naturally or properly: *moist ground; moist leather.* **3.** dankness, dampness, fog, vapor. **7.** humidify. **8.** slow, inhibit, restrain, moderate, abate. —**Ant. 1.** dry.

damp′ box′, *Ceram.* a box that is lined with moist material for keeping clay in a plastic state.

damp·en (dam′pən), *v.t.* **1.** to make damp; moisten: *to dampen a sponge.* **2.** to dull or deaden; depress: *to dampen one's spirits.* **3.** damp (def. 10). —*v.i.* **4.** to become damp. [DAMP + -EN[1]] —**damp′en·er,** *n.*

damp·er (dam′pər), *n.* **1.** a movable plate for regulating the draft in a stove, furnace, etc. **2.** one who or that which damps: *His glum mood put a damper on their party.* **3.** *Music.* **a.** a device in stringed keyboard instruments to deaden the vibration of the strings. **b.** the mute of a brass instrument, as a horn. **4.** *Elect.* an attachment to keep the indicator of a measuring instrument from oscillating excessively, usually a set of vanes in an air space or fluid or a short-circuited winding in a magnetic field. **5.** *Australian.* **a.** a round, flat cake made of flour, water, and baking powder, and cooked over a campfire by bushmen and swagmen. **b.** the dough for such cakes. [DAMP + -ER[1]]

damp′er ped′al, *Music.* a pedal on a piano that when depressed with the foot raises the dampers and permits the strings to vibrate and sustain the tone. Also called **loud pedal.**

Dam·pi·er (dam′pē ər, damp′yər), *n.* **William,** 1652–1715, English navigator, explorer, buccaneer, and writer.

damp·ing-off (dam′ping ôf′, -of′), *n.* *Plant Pathol.* a disease of seedlings, occurring either before or immediately after emerging from the soil, characterized by wilting and collapse of the plant and caused by several soil fungi.

damp·proof (damp′pro͞of′), *adj.* **1.** resistant to dampness or the effects of dampness. —*v.t.* **2.** to make dampproof. [DAMP + -PROOF]

Dam·rosch (dam′rosh), *n.* **Walter Jo·han·nes** (jō han′əs), 1862–1950, U.S. conductor and composer, born in Germany.

dam·sel (dam′zəl), *n.* a young woman; a girl; a maiden, originally one of gentle or noble birth. [ME *damisel* < AF (OF *damoisele*) < VL **domicella*, equiv. to L *domin(a)* lady (see DAME) + *-cella* fem. dim. suffix]

dam·sel·fish (dam′zəl fish′), *n., pl.* (*esp. collectively*) **-fish,** (*esp. referring to two or more kinds or species*) **-fish·es.** any of several chiefly tropical, brilliantly colored, marine fishes of the family *Pomacentridae*, found among coral reefs. Also called **demoiselle.** [DAMSEL + FISH]

dam·sel·fly (dam′zəl flī′), *n., pl.* **-flies.** any of numerous slender, slow-flying insects of the order *Odonata* (suborder *Zygoptera*), distinguished from the dragonflies by having the wings held together over the body when at rest. [DAMSEL + FLY[2]]

dam·son (dam′zən), *n.* **1.** Also called **dam′son plum′.** the small dark-blue or purple fruit of a plum, *Prunus insititia*, introduced into Europe from Asia Minor. **2.** the tree bearing it. **3.** a medium to dark violet. —*adj.* **4.** having the color damson. [ME *damascene, damson* < L (*prūnum*) *Damascēn(um)* (plum) of Damascus; see DAMASCENE]

dam·yan·kee (dam′yang′kē), *n.* *Informal.* (in the southern U.S.) a person native to the northern States of the U.S. Also, **damnyankee.** [alter. of *damned Yankee*]

Dam·y·sus (dam′i səs), *n.* *Class. Myth.* one of the Gigantes.

Dan (dan), *n.* **1.** a son of Jacob and Bilhah. Gen. 30:6. **2.** one of the 12 tribes of Israel. **3.** the northernmost city of ancient Palestine. **4. from Dan to Beersheba,** from one outermost extreme or limit to the other. Judges 20:1. **5.** a boy's given name, form of **Daniel.**

Dan (dan), *n.* *Archaic.* a title of honor equivalent to *master* or *sir: Dan Chaucer; Dan Cupid.* [ME < MF *dan(z)* < OF < ML *domn(us)*, contr. of L *dominus* lord, master]

Dan., **1.** Daniel. **2.** Also **Dan** Danish. **3.** Danzig.

Da·na (dā′nə), *n.* **1. Charles Anderson,** 1819–97, U.S. journalist, editor, and publisher. **2. Edward Salisbury,** 1849–1935, U.S. mineralogist and physicist. **3.** his father, **James Dwight,** 1813–95, U.S. geologist and mineralogist. **4. Richard Henry Jr.,** 1815–82, U.S. jurist, author, and sailor: specialist in admiralty law. **5.** a boy's or girl's given name.

Da·na (thä′nə, dä′-), *n.* *Irish Myth.* Danu.

Dan·a·ë (dan′ə ē′), *n.* *Class. Myth.* a maiden who became the mother of Perseus after Zeus, disguised as a golden rain, visited her in the tower where she had been imprisoned by her father, the king of Argos. —**Dan·a·än** (dan′ē ən), *adj.*

Dan·a·i (dan′ā ī′), *n.pl.* *Class. Myth.* **1.** the Argives. **2.** the Greeks.

Da·na·i·des (də nā′i dēz′), *n.pl.* *Class. Myth.* the 50 daughters of Danaus, 49 of whom were condemned to pour water forever into a leaky vessel for having murdered their husbands. Also, **Da·na·i·dae** (də nā′i dē′), **Da·na·ids** (də nā′idz). Cf. **Hypermnestra.** —**Dan·a·id·e·an** (dan′ē id′ē ən, dan′ē i dē′ən), *adj.*

da·na·ite (dā′nə īt′), *n.* *Mineral.* a variety of arsenopyrite having cobalt in place of some of the iron. [named after J. F. *Dana* (1793–1827), American chemist; see -ITE[1]]

Da·nang (dä′näng′, də nang′), *n.* a seaport in E South Vietnam. 121,400 (est. 1962). Also, **Da′ Nang′.** Formerly, **Tourane.**

Dan·a·us (dan′ē əs), *n.* *Class. Myth.* the ruler of Argos who married his 50 daughters to the 50 sons of his brother, Aegyptus, and ordered them to kill their husbands on the wedding night. Cf. **Danaides.**

Da·na·va (dä′nə və), *n.* *Hinduism.* one of the Vedic demons. Cf. **Asura, Vrita.**

dan′ buoy′ (dan), a temporary buoy having a staff for carrying a flag or light. [?]

dan·bur·ite (dan′bə rīt′), *n.* a rare mineral, calcium borosilicate, $CaB_2Si_2O_8$, occurring in pegmatite in yellow or colorless crystals resembling topaz. [named after DANBURY, where it was discovered in 1839; see -ITE[1]]

Dan·bur·y (dan′ber′ē, -bə rē), *n.* a city in SW Connecticut. 22,928 (1960).

dance (dans, däns), *v.,* **danced, danc·ing,** *n.* —*v.i.* **1.** to move one's feet, or body, or both, rhythmically in a pattern of steps, esp. to the accompaniment of music. **2.** to leap, skip, etc., as from excitement or emotion; move nimbly or quickly: *to dance with joy.* **3.** to bob up and down: *The toy sailboats danced on the pond.* —*v.t.* **4.** to perform or take part in (a dance): *to dance a waltz.* **5.** to cause to dance: *He danced her around the ballroom.* **6.** to cause to be in a specified condition by dancing: *She danced her shoes to shreds.* **7. dance attendance.** See **attendance** (def. 4). **8. dance on air,** *Slang.* to be hanged. **9. dance to another tune,** to change one's opinion, attitude, or behavior: *Now that he is well-to-do, he dances to another tune.* —*n.* **10.** a successive group of rhythmical steps or bodily motions, or both, usually executed to music. **11.** an act or round of dancing; set: *May I have this dance?* **12.** a social gathering for dancing; ball: *It was a great dance.* **13.** a piece of music suited in rhythm or style to a particular form of dancing: *He liked the composer's country dances.* **14.** a stylized, instinctive pattern of movements performed by an animal, as a bird in courtship display, or an insect, as a honeybee in indicating a source of nectar. **15. the dance,** ballet, interpretive dancing, and other dancing of an artistic nature performed by professional dancers before an audience. [ME *da(u)nce(n)* < OF *dancie(r)*, perh. < VL **deantiāre*, equiv. to LL *deante* before (see DE-, ANTE-) + *-āre* inf. suffix] —**danc′ing·ly,** *adv.*

dance·a·ble (dan′sə bəl, dän′-), *adj.* appropriate for dancing: *danceable music.* [DANCE + -ABLE] —**dance′a·bil′i·ty,** *n.*

dance′ band′, a musical group that varies in size from a combo to an orchestra and that specializes in playing music for dancing.

dance′ form′, *Music.* the binary form used in most of the movements of the 18th-century suite.

dance′ hall′, a public establishment that, for an admission fee, provides its patrons with music and space for dancing and, sometimes, dancing partners and refreshments.

dance′ of death′, **1.** a symbolic dance in which Death, represented as a skeleton, leads people or skeletons to their grave. **2.** a representation of this theme in art. Also called **danse macabre.**

danc·er (dan′sər, dän′-), *n.* **1.** a person who dances. **2.** a person who dances professionally, as on the stage. [ME; see DANCE, -ER[1]]

dan·cette (dan set′), *n.* *Archit.* an ornamental zigzag, as in a molding. [var. of DANCETTÉ]

dan·cet·té (dan set′ē), *adj.* *Heraldry.* noting a partition line or charge, as an ordinary, formed in a series of deep or broad zigzags. Also, **dan·cet′tée, dan·cet′ty.** Cf. **indented.** [prob. m. F *denché* < LL *denticāt(us)*, equiv. to L *dent-* (s. of *dēns*) tooth + *-icātus* -IC, -ATE[1]]

danc′ing step′. See **balanced step.** Also called **danc′ing wind′er.**

D and C, *Med.* a surgical method for the removal of tissue from the lining of the uterus by means of scraping. [*d(ilation) and c(urettage)*]

dan·de·li·on (dan′dᵊlī′ən), *n.* **1.** a weedy composite plant, *Taraxacum officinale*, having deeply toothed or notched leaves and golden-yellow flowers. **2.** any other plant of the genus *Taraxacum.* [< MF, m. *dent de lion*, lit., tooth of (a) lion, trans. of ML *dēns leōnis*, in allusion to the toothed leaves]

dan·der[1] (dan′dər), *n.* *Informal.* anger; temper: *You're getting your dander up over a trifle.* [alter. of DANDRUFF]

dan·der[2] (dan′dər), *n.* **1.** *Scot.* a stroll; saunter. **2.** *Brit. Dial.* a fit of shivering. [?]

Dan·die Din·mont (dan′dē din′mont), one of a breed of small terriers having short legs, pendulous ears, and a long, wiry, pepper- or mustard-colored coat. [after a character in Scott's novel, *Guy Mannering*, who owned two terriers]

dan·di·fy (dan′də fī′), *v.t.,* **-fied, -fy·ing.** to make into a dandy or fop. [DANDY + -FY] —**dan′di·fi·ca′tion,** *n.*

dan·di·prat (dan′dē prat′), *n.* **1.** a silver coin of 16th-century England, equal to about twopence. **2.** *Archaic.* **a.** a diminutive person; a person who is not developed to adult stature; child; midget. **b.** a person of small or childish mind; a person who is silly, finical, or puerile. [?]

dan·dle (dan′dᵊl), *v.t.,* **-dled, -dling.** **1.** to move (a baby, child, etc.) lightly up and down, as on one's knee or in one's arms. **2.** to pet; pamper. [prob. < It *dandol(are)*] —**dan′dler,** *n.*

dan·druff (dan′drəf), *n.* a seborrheic scurf that forms on the scalp and comes off in small scales. Also, **dan·driff** (dan′drif). [?] —**dan′druff·y, dan′driff·y,** *adj.*

dan·dy (dan′dē), *n., pl.* **-dies,** *adj.,* **-di·er, -di·est.** —*n.* **1.** Also called **jack-a-dandy.** a man who is excessively concerned about clothes and appearance; a fop. **2.** *Informal.* something or someone of exceptional or first-rate quality: *Your remark was a dandy.* **3.** *Naut. Brit.* **a.** a yawl or ketch. **b.** the jigger or mizzen sail of this vessel. —*adj.* **4.** characteristic of a dandy; foppish. **5.** *U.S. Informal.* fine; first-rate: *a dandy vacation spot.* [?] —**dan′di·ly, dan·di·a·cal·ly** (dan dī′ək lē), *adv.* —**dan′dy·ish, dan·di′a·cal,** *adj.* —**dan′dy·ism,** *n.*

Dan·dy (dan′dē), *n.* a boy's given name, form of **Andrew.** Also, **Dan′die.**

dan′dy brush′, a brush with stiff, short bristles that is used for grooming animals, esp. horses.

dan′dy fe′ver, *Pathol.* (in the West Indies) dengue. [prob. < West Indian Creole, of Afr orig.]

dan′dy roll′, *Papermaking.* a light, open cylinder of wire gauze in a papermaking machine, for smoothing wet pulp and for impressing a watermark. Also called **dan′dy roll′er.**

Dane (dān), *n.* **1.** a native or inhabitant of Denmark. **2.** a person of Danish descent. **3.** See **Great Dane.** [ME *Dane-*, OE *Dene* (pl.), influenced by ON *Danir* (pl.)]

Da·neen (də nēn′), *n.* a girl's given name. Also, **Danene.**

Dane·geld (dān′geld′), *n.* (in medieval England) an annual tax believed to have been levied originally as a tribute to the Danish invaders but later continued for other purposes. Also, **dane′geld′, Dane·gelt, dane·gelt** (dān′gelt′). [ME; see DANE, GELD[2]]

Dane·law (dān′lô′), *n.* **1.** the body of laws in force in the northeast of England where the Danes settled in the 9th century A.D. **2.** the part of England under this law. Also, **Dane·la·ge** (dān′lä′gə, dä′nə lä′gə), **Dane·lagh** (dān′lô′). [ME *Dane-lawe*, earlier *Dene-lawe*, OE *Dena lagu.* See DANE, LAW[1]]

Da·nel·la (də nel′ə), *n.* a girl's given name, form of **Daniela.** Also, **Danelle.**

Da·nelle (də nel′), *n.* a girl's given name, form of **Daniela.** Also, **Danella.**

Da·nene (də nēn′), *n.* a girl's given name. Also, **Daneen.**

Da·nette (də net′), *n.* a girl's given name, form of **Daniela.**

Dan·ford (dan′fərd), *n.* a boy's given name.

dang (dang), *v.t., adj., n.* damn (used euphemistically).

danged (dangd), *adj.* damn (used euphemistically).

dan·ger (dān′jər), *n.* **1.** liability or exposure to harm or injury; risk; peril. **2.** an instance or cause of peril. **3.** *Obs.* power; jurisdiction; domain. [ME *da(u)nger* < AF, c. OF *dangier*, alter. of *dongier* (by influence of *dam* DAMAGE) < VL **domniār(ium)*, equiv. to L *domini-(um)* DOMINION + *-ārium*, neut. of *-ārius* -ARY] —**dan′ger·less,** *adj.*

—**Syn. 1.** DANGER, HAZARD, PERIL, JEOPARDY imply some evil or harm which one may encounter. DANGER is the general word for liability to all kinds of injury or evil consequences, either near at hand and certain, or remote and doubtful: *to be in danger of catching cold or of being killed.* HAZARD suggests a danger which one can foresee but cannot avoid: *An aviator is exposed to many hazards.* PERIL usually denotes great and imminent danger: *The passengers on the disabled ship were in great peril.* JEOPARDY, a less common word, has essentially the same meaning as peril, but emphasizes exposure to the chances of a situation: *To save his friend he put his life in jeopardy.* —**Ant. 1.** safety.

dan′ger an′gle, *Navig.* a horizontal or vertical angle, subtended by two points on shore, that provides a maximum or minimum angle between the points as observed from a vessel if it is to steer a safe course.

dan·ger·ous (dān′jər əs), *adj.* full of danger or risk; causing danger; perilous; hazardous; unsafe. [ME *da(u)ngerous* domineering, fraught with danger < OF *dangereus* threatening, difficult, equiv. to *dangier* (see DANGER) + *-eus* -OUS] —**dan′ger·ous·ly,** *adv.* —**dan′ger·ous·ness,** *n.*

dan·gle (dang′gəl), *v.,* **-gled, -gling,** *n.* —*v.i.* **1.** to hang loosely, esp. with a jerking or swaying motion: *A rope dangles in the breeze.* **2.** to hang around or follow a person, as if seeking favor. —*v.t.* **3.** to cause to dangle; hold or carry swaying loosely: *He dangled a bone in front of the dog.* —*n.* **4.** the act of dangling. **5.** something that dangles. [< Scand; cf. Dan *dangle* to bob up and down] —**dan′gler,** *n.* —**dan′gling·ly,** *adv.*

dan·gle·ber·ry (dang′gəl ber′ē), *n., pl.* **-ries.** tangleberry.

dan′gling par′ticiple, *Gram.* a participle or participial phrase, often found at the beginning of a sentence, that appears from its position to modify an element of the sentence other than the one it was intended to modify, as *plunging* in *Plunging 1000 feet into the gorge, we saw Yosemite Falls.* Cf. **misplaced modifier.**

Dan·i (dan′ē), *n.* a boy's or girl's given name. Also, **Danny.**

Da·ni·a (dā′nē ə), *n.* a town in S Florida. 7065 (1960).

Dan·i·ca (dan′ə kə), *n.* a girl's given name.

Dan·iel (dan′yəl), *n.* **1.** *Bible.* **a.** a prophet living in Babylon during the Captivity. **b.** the book of the Bible bearing his name. **2. Samuel,** 1562–1619, English poet and historian: poet laureate 1599–1619. **3.** a boy's given name.

Dan·iel·a (dan yel′ə), *n.* a girl's given name.

Dan·iell (dan′yəl), *n.* a crater in the first quadrant of the face of the moon: about 19 miles in diameter.

Dan′iell cell′, *Elect.* a cell having an approximate electromotive force of one volt and consisting of a copper electrode immersed in a copper-sulfate solution which is separated by a porous partition from a zinc-sulfate solution in which a zinc electrode is immersed. [named after John F. *Daniell* (1790–1845), English chemist and physicist who invented it]

Dan·iels (dan′yəlz), *n.* **1. Jonathan Worth,** born 1902, U.S. journalist, editor, and author. **2.** his father, **Jo·se·phus** (jō sē′fəs), 1862–1948, U.S. editor and statesman.

Dan·iel·son (dan′ᵊl sən, dan′yəl-), *n.* a town in NE Connecticut. 4642 (1960).

Da·nil·o (də nil′ō), *n.* a boy's given name, form of **Daniel.**

Da·ni·lo·va (də nē′lə və, -lō-; *Russ.* dä nē′lo vä), *n.* **Al·ex·an·dra** (al′ig zan′drə, -zän′-; *Russ.* ä′le ksän′drə), born 1904?, Russian ballet dancer.

dan·i·o (dā′nē ō′), *n., pl.* **-i·os.** any of several cyprinid fishes of the genus *Danio*, found in India and Ceylon and often kept in aquariums. [< NL *Danio* name of a genus]

Dan·ish (dā′nish), *adj.* **1.** of or pertaining to the Danes, their country, or their language. **—*n.* 2.** a Germanic language, the language of Denmark, closely related to Norwegian, Swedish, and Icelandic. **3.** *Informal.* See **Danish pastry.** [ME, alter. of *Danish* (by influence of *Dan* DANE), OE *Denisc,* equiv. to *Den* Danes + *-isc* -ISH[1]]

Dan′ish pas′try, a light pastry leavened with yeast and often filled with cheese, nuts and raisins, custard, or fruit.

Dan′ish West′ In′dies, former name of the **Virgin Islands of the United States.** Also called **Dan′ish Vir′gin Is′lands.**

Da·ni·ta (də nē′tə), *n.* a girl's given name, form of **Daniela.**

Dan·ite (dan′īt), *n.* **1.** a member of the tribe of Dan. **2.** a member of an alleged secret order of Mormons supposed to have been formed about 1837. [DAN + -ITE[1]]

dank (dangk), *adj.* unpleasantly moist or humid; damp: *a dank cellar or dungeon.* [ME (adj. and n.), prob. < Scand; cf. OIcel *dökk* pool] **—dank′ly,** *adv.* **—dank′ness,** *n.*

dan·ke (däng′kə), *interj. German.* thank you.

dan′ke schön′ (shœn), *German.* thank you very much.

Danl., Daniel.

Dann (dan), *n.* a boy's given name.

Dan·ne·mo·ra (dan′ə mōr′ə, -môr′ə), *n.* a town in NE New York. 4835 (1960).

D'An·nun·zio (də no͞on′sē ō; *It.* dän no͞on′tsyô), *n.* **Ga·bri·e·le** (*It.* gä′brē e′le), (*Duca Minimo*), 1863–1938, Italian soldier, novelist, and poet.

Dan·ny (dan′ē), *n.* a boy's or girl's given name, form of **Daniel.** Also, **Dani.**

Da·no-Nor·we·gian (dā′nō nôr wē′jən), *n.* Bokmål. [< LL *Dan(i)* DANE(S) + -o- + NORWEGIAN]

dan·sant (dän sän′), *n., pl.* **-sants** (-sän′). *French.* See **thé dansant.**

danse du ven·tre (*Fr.* däns dy vän′trə), *pl.* **danses du ven·tre** (*Fr.* däns dy vän′trə). See **belly dance.** [< F]

danse ma·ca·bre (*Fr.* däns ma ka′brə). See **dance of death.** [< F]

dan·seur (*Fr.* dän sœr′), *n., pl.* **-seurs** (*Fr.* -sœr′). a male ballet dancer. [< F: lit., dancer. See DANCE, -OR[2]]

dan·seur no·ble (*Fr.* dän sœr nô′blə), *pl.* **dan·seurs no·bles** (*Fr.* dän sœr nô′blə). a male dancer who is the partner of a ballerina, as in a pas de deux. [< F; lit., noble dancer]

dan·seuse (*Fr.* dän sœz′), *n., pl.* **-seuses** (*Fr.* -sœz′). a female ballet dancer. [< F; fem. of DANSEUR]

Dans·ville (danz′vil), *n.* a town in central New York. 5460 (1960).

Dan·te (dan′tē, dän′tā; *It.* dän′te), *n.* **1.** (*Dante Alighieri*), 1265–1321, Italian poet: author of the *Divine Comedy.* **2.** a boy's given name.

Dan·te·an (dan′tē ən, dan tē′ən), *adj.* **1.** of or pertaining to Dante or his writings. **2.** Dantesque. **—*n.* 3.** a person who studies the works of Dante. [DANTE + -AN]

Dan′te chair′, *Ital. Furniture.* a chair of the Renaissance having two transverse pairs of curved legs crossing beneath the seat and rising to support the arms and back. Also called **Dan·tes′ca chair′** (dan tes′kə, dän tes′kä). Cf. **Savonarola chair.** [named after DANTE]

Dante chair

Dan·tesque (dan tesk′), *adj.* in the style of Dante; characterized by impressive elevation of style with deep solemnity or somberness of feeling. [< It *dantesc(o).* See DANTE, -ESQUE]

Dan·ton (dan′tᵊn; *Fr.* dän tôn′), *n.* **Georges Jacques** (zhôrzh zhäk), 1759–94, French Revolutionary leader.

Da·nu (thä′no͞o, dä′-), *n. Irish Myth.* the mother of the Tuatha De Danann: identified with the Welsh Don. Also, **Dana.**

Dan·ube (dan′yo͞ob), *n.* a river in central and SE Europe, flowing E from SW West Germany to the Black Sea. 1725 mi. long. German, **Donau.** Hungarian, **Duna.** Rumanian, **Dunărea.**

Dan′ube rud′der, *Naut.* See **salmon tail.**

Dan·u·bi·an (dan yo͞o′bē ən), *adj.* of, pertaining to, or characteristic of a Neolithic culture of the Danube basin. [DANUBE + -IAN]

Da·nu·ta (da no͞o′tə, də nyo͞o′tə), *n.* a girl's given name.

Dan·vers (dan′vərz), *n.* a town in NE Massachusetts, near Boston. 21,926 (1960).

Dan·ville (dan′vil), *n.* **1.** a city in S Virginia. 46,577 (1960). **2.** a city in E Illinois. 41,856 (1960). **3.** a town in central Kentucky. 9010 (1960). **4.** a town in central Pennsylvania. 6889 (1960). **5.** a town in W California. 3585 (1960). **6.** a town in central Indiana. 3287 (1960).

Dan·zig (dan′sig; *Ger.* dän′tsikh), *n.* **1.** a seaport in N Poland, on the Bay of Danzig. 306,000 (est. 1963). **2.** **Free City of,** a former self-governing territory including the seaport of Danzig: constituted by the treaty of Versailles 1920; a part of Germany 1939–45; now in Poland. 754 sq. mi. Polish, **Gdańsk.**

dap (dap), *v.,* **dapped, dap·ping,** *n.* **—*v.i.* 1.** to fish by letting the bait fall lightly on the water. **2.** to dip lightly or suddenly into water: *The bird dapped for the fish.* **3.** to bounce or skip, as on the surface of a body of water: *The stone dapped along the surface of the pond.* **—*v.t.* 4.** to cause to dip in and out of water: *to dap one's bait.* **5.** to cause to skip along the surface of water: *to dap stones.* **6.** *Carpentry.* to notch (a timber) to receive part of another timber. **—*n.* 7.** *Carpentry.* a notch in a timber for receiving part of another timber. [prob. var. of DAB[1]]

Daph·nae·a (daf nē′ə), *n. Class. Myth.* an epithet of Artemis, meaning "of the laurel."

Daph·ne (daf′nē), *n.* **1.** *Class. Myth.* a nymph who, when pursued by Apollo, was saved by being changed into a laurel tree. **2.** (*l.c.*) *Bot.* **a.** the laurel, *Laurus nobilis.* **b.** any thymelaeaceous shrub of the genus *Daphne,* of Europe and Asia, certain species of which, as *D. Mezereum,* are cultivated for their fragrant flowers. **3.** a girl's given name. [< L < Gk *dáphnē* laurel]

Daph·ne·pho·ri·a (daf′nə fōr′ē ə, -fôr′-), *n.* an ancient Greek festival in honor of Apollo.

Daph·ni·a (daf′nē ə), *n.* a genus of tiny, fresh-water water fleas having a transparent body, used in biological research and as food for tropical fish. [< NL, perh. after DAPHNE; see -IA]

Daph·nis (daf′nis), *n. Class. Myth.* a son of Hermes and a nymph: he was regarded by the Greeks as the originator of pastoral poetry.

Daph′nis and Chlo′e, 1. two lovers in pastoral literature, esp. in a Greek romance attributed to Longus. **2.** (*italics.*) a ballet (1912) with music by Maurice Ravel and scenario and choreography by Michel Fokine. **3.** (*italics.*) either of two orchestral suites by Ravel based on the music of this ballet.

dap·per (dap′ər), *adj.* **1.** neat; trim; smart: *He looked very dapper in his new suit.* **2.** small and active. [ME *daper* < MD *dapper* nimble, strong; cf. G *tapfer* brave] **—dap′per·ly,** *adv.* **—dap′per·ness,** *n.*

dap·ple (dap′əl), *n., adj., v.,* **-pled, -pling. —*n.* 1.** a spot or mottled marking, usually occurring in clusters. **2.** an animal with a mottled skin or coat. **—*adj.* 3.** dappled; spotted: *a dapple horse.* **—*v.t., v.i.* 4.** to mark or become marked with spots. [prob. back formation from DAPPLED]

dap·pled (dap′əld), *adj.* having spots of a different shade, tone, or color from the background; mottled. [ME, prob. < ON; akin to OIcel *depill* spot]

dap·ple-gray (dap′əl grā′), *adj.* gray with ill-defined mottling of a darker shade. [ME, perh. **appelgrei,* with *d-* from DAPPLED; cf. OIcel *apal-grār, apli* dapple-gray horse]

Dap·sang (dəp sung′), *n.* See **K2.**

DAR, Defense Aid Reports.

D.A.R., See **Daughters of the American Revolution.**

Dar·a (dar′ə), *n.* a girl's given name.

dar·bies (där′bēz), *n.pl. Brit. Slang.* handcuffs; manacles. [prob. from the phrase *Darby's bonds* a rigid bond, ? after a noted 16th-century usurer]

dar·by (där′bē), *n., pl.* **-bies.** a float having two handles, used by plasterers. [? after a proper name or the city *Derby* in England]

Dar′by and Joan′ (där′bē; jōn), a happily married elderly couple who lead a placid, uneventful life. [after a couple mentioned in an 18th-century song]

Dar′by and Joan′ settee′, a settee having a back resembling two chair backs.

Dar·by·ite (där′bē īt′), *n.* a member of the Plymouth Brethren. [after John N. *Darby* (1800–82), English theologian; see -ITE[1]]

Dar·cy (där′sē), *n.* a boy's given name.

Dar·dan (där′dᵊn), *adj., n.* Trojan. Also, **Dar·da·ni·an** (där dā′nē ən).

Dar·da·nelles (där′dᵊnelz′), *n.* (*construed as pl.*) the strait between Europe and Asian Turkey, connecting the Aegean Sea with the Sea of Marmara. 40 mi. long; 1–5 mi. wide. Ancient, **Hellespont.**

Dar·da·nus (där′dᵊnəs), *n. Class. Myth.* the ancestor of the Trojans.

dare (dâr), *v.,* **dared** or (*Archaic*) **durst, dared, dar·ing,** *n.* **—*v.i.* 1.** to have the necessary courage or boldness for something; be bold enough: *You wouldn't dare!* **—*v.t.* 2.** to have the necessary courage (to do something): *She dared to jump over the barbed-wire fence.* **3.** to meet defiantly. **4.** to challenge or provoke (a person) into a demonstration of courage; defy: *to dare a man to fight.* **—*n.* 5.** an act of daring; defiance; challenge. [ME *dar,* OE *dear(r),* 1st and 3rd pers. sing. pres. indic. of *durran;* akin to OHG *(gi)tarran*] **—dar′er,** *n.*

—Syn. 1. DARE, VENTURE imply involvement in risks and dangers. DARE emphasizes the state of mind that makes one willing to meet danger: *He dared to do what he knew was right.* VENTURE emphasizes the act of doing something that involves risk: *He ventured into deep water.* **2.** hazard, risk, brave.

Dare (dâr), *n.* **Virginia,** 1587–?, first child born of English parents in the Western Hemisphere.

dare·dev·il (dâr′dev′əl), *n.* **1.** a recklessly daring person. **—*adj.* 2.** recklessly daring. [DARE + DEVIL]

dare·dev·il·try (dâr′dev′əl trē), *n.* reckless daring; venturesome boldness. Also, **dare·dev·il·ry** (dâr′dev′əl rē). [DARE + DEVILTRY]

dare·n't (dâr′ənt), contraction for *dare not.*

Dar·es (dâr′ēz), *n.* (in the *Aeneid*) one of the companions of Aeneas, noted for his boxing skill.

dare·say (dâr′sā′), *v.i., v.t.* to venture to say (something); assume (something) as probable: *I daresay we will soon finish.* [ME *dar sayen* I dare to say]

Dar·es Phryg·i·us (dâr′ēz frij′ē əs), (in the *Iliad*) a priest of Hephaestus.

Dar es Sa·laam (där′ es sə läm′), a seaport in and the capital of Tanzania, on the Indian Ocean. 128,742 (1957). Also, **Dar′-es-Sa·laam′.**

Dar·fur (där fo͝or′), *n.* a province in the W Sudan. 1,328,765 (1956); 191,650 sq. mi. *Cap.:* El Fasher.

darg (därg), *n.* **1.** *Scot. and North Eng.* a day's work. **2.** *Australian.* a fixed or definite amount of work; a work quota. [ME *dawerk, daiwerk,* OE *dægweorc,* equiv. to *dæg* DAY + *weorc* WORK]

Da·ri·a (də rī′ə), *n.* a girl's given name.

dar·ic (dar′ik), *n.* a gold coin and monetary unit of ancient Persia. [< Gk *Dāreik(ós)* (*statḗr*) Persian stater < Pers]

Da·rice (də rēs′), *n.* a girl's given name, form of **Daria.**

Dar·i·en (dâr′ē en′, dâr′ē en′), *n.* **1.** **Gulf of,** an arm of the Caribbean between NE Panama and NW Colombia. **2.** **Isthmus of,** former name of the **Isthmus of Panama.** Spanish, **Da·rién** (dä ryen′).

dar·ing (dâr′ing), *n.* **1.** adventurous courage; boldness. **—*adj.* 2.** bold; intrepid; adventurous. [DARE + -ING[1], -ING[2]] **—dar′ing·ly,** *adv.* **—dar′ing·ness,** *n.*

—Syn. 1. audacity, bravery. **2.** dauntless, undaunted, venturesome, audacious, brave, courageous. **—Ant. 1.** caution. **2.** timid.

Da·rí·o (dä rē′ô), *n.* **Ru·bén** (ro͞o ven′), (*Félix Rubén García Sarmiento*), 1867–1916, Nicaraguan poet and diplomat.

dar·i·ole (dar′ē ōl′), *n. French Cookery.* a small round mold. [ME < OF *dariole*]

Da·ri·us (də rī′əs, dar′ē əs), *n.* a boy's given name.

Da·ri·us I (də rī′əs), (*Darius Hystaspes*) (*"the Great"*) 558?–486? B.C., king of Persia 521–486.

Darius II, (*Ochus*) died 404 B.C., king of Persia 424–404 (son of Artaxerxes I).

Darius III, (*Codomannus*) died 330 B.C., king of Persia 336–330.

Dar·jee·ling (där jē′ling), *n.* **1.** a town in West Bengal, in NE India: mountain resort. 40,700 (1961). **2.** Also called **Darjee′ling tea′.** a tea grown in mountainous areas around the town of Darjeeling.

dark (därk), *adj.* **1.** having very little or no light: *a dark room.* **2.** radiating, admitting, or reflecting little light: *a dark color; dark windowshades.* **3.** approaching black in hue: *a dark brown.* **4.** not pale or fair; swarthy: *a dark complexion.* **5.** brunette; dark-haired: *dark eyebrows.* **6.** having brunette hair: *She's dark but her children are blond.* **7.** gloomy; cheerless; dismal: *the dark days of World War II.* **8.** sullen; frowning: *a dark expression.* **9.** evil; iniquitous; wicked: *a dark plot.* **10.** destitute of knowledge or culture; unenlightened: *Will our own age be called dark?* **11.** hard to understand; obscure: *There was an occasional dark passage in his poetry.* **12.** hidden; secret: *He kept his plans dark.* **13.** silent; reticent. **14.** *Phonet.* **a.** (of an *l*-sound) having back-vowel resonance; situated after a vowel in the same syllable. Cf. **clear** (def. 26a). **b.** (of a speech sound) of dull quality; acoustically damped. **15. keep dark,** to keep as a secret; conceal: *He kept his political activities dark.* **—*n.* 16.** the absence of light; darkness: *He couldn't see well in the dark.* **17.** night; nightfall: *Dark fell over the countryside. Please come home before dark.* **18.** a dark place. **19.** a dark color. **20. in the dark, a.** in ignorance; uninformed: *As usual, he was in the dark about our plans for the evening.* **b.** in secrecy; concealed; obscure: *The family disgrace remained in the dark for many years.* **—*v.t.* 21.** *Archaic.* to make dark; darken. **—*v.i.* 22.** *Obs.* to grow dark; darken. [ME *derk,* OE *deorc;* cf. MHG *terken* to darken, hide] **—dark′ish,** *adj.* **—dark′ish·ness,** *n.*

—Syn. 1. DARK, DIM, OBSCURE, GLOOMY, MURKY refer to absence or insufficiency of light. DARK implies a more or less complete absence of light: *a dark night.* DIM implies faintness of light or indistinctness of form (resulting from the lack of light or from imperfect vision): *a dim outline.* OBSCURE implies dimness that may arise also from factors that interfere with light or vision: *obscure because of haze, smoke, fog.* GLOOMY means cloudy, ill-lighted, dusky: *a gloomy hall.* MURKY implies a thick, cloudy, or misty darkness: *a murky cave.* **4.** dusky, black. **11.** recondite, abstruse. **—Ant. 1.** lighted. **2.** bright. **7.** cheerful. **8.** pleasant. **11.** clear.

dark′ adapta′tion, *Ophthalm.* the reflex adaptation of the eye to dim light, consisting of a dilatation of the pupil and an increase in the number of functioning rods accompanied by a decrease in the number of functioning cones (opposed to *light adaptation*).

Dark′ Ag′es, 1. the period in European history from about A.D. 476 to about 1000. **2.** the whole of the Middle Ages, from about A.D. 476 to the Renaissance.

dark′ choc′olate, chocolate to which little or no milk has been added.

Dark′ Con′tinent, The, Africa: so called because little was known about it.

dark·en (där′kən), *v.t.* **1.** to make dark or darker. **2.** to make obscure. **3.** to make less white or clear in color. **4.** to make gloomy; sadden: *darkened festivities by his presence.* **5.** to make blind. **—*v.i.* 6.** to become dark or darker. **7.** to become obscure: *The scene was darkened beyond comprehension.* **8.** to become less white or clear in color. **9.** to grow clouded, as with gloom or anger. **10.** to become blind. **11. darken one's door,** to come to visit a person; appear: *Never darken my door again!* [ME *derknen.* See DARK, -EN[1]] **—dark′en·er,** *n.*

dark·ey (där′kē), *n., pl.* **-eys.** *Offensive.* darky.

dark-field (därk′fēld′), *adj. Optics.* of or pertaining to the illumination of an object by which it is seen, through a microscope, as bright against a dark background.

dark′ horse′, 1. a race horse, competitor, etc., about whom little is known or who unexpectedly wins. **2.** a person unexpectedly nominated, esp. in a political convention.

dark·ie (där′kē), *n. Offensive.* darky.

dark·ish (där′kish), *adj.* slightly dark: *a darkish color.* [ME; see DARK, -ISH[1]]

Dark′ is Light′ Enough′, The, a drama in verse (1954) by Christopher Fry.

dark′ lan′tern, a lantern having an opening with a shutter that can be slid across the opening to obscure the light.

dar·kle (där′kəl), *v.i.,* **-kled, -kling. 1.** to appear dark; show indistinctly. **2.** to grow dark, gloomy, etc. [back formation from DARKLING, adv. taken as prp.]

dark·ling (därk′ling), *Chiefly Literary.* **—*adv.* 1.** in the dark. **—*adj.* 2.** being or occurring in the dark; dark; obscure. [ME *derkeling.* See DARK, -LING[2]]

dark′ling bee′tle, any brown or black beetle of the family *Tenebrionidae,* the larvae of which feed on dead or decaying plant material, fungi, stored grain, etc.

dark·ly (därk′lē), *adv.* **1.** so as to appear dark. **2.** vaguely; mysteriously: *His appearance was darkly sinister.* **3.** in a vaguely threatening or menacing manner: *He hinted darkly that we had not heard the last of the matter.* **4.** imperfectly; faintly. [ME *derkly,* OE *deorclīce* (in fig. sense only). See DARK, -LY]

dark′ meat′, meat that is dark in appearance after cooking, as a leg or thigh of chicken or turkey (distinguished from *white meat*).

dark′ min′eral, *Geol.* any rock-forming mineral that has a specific gravity greater than 2.8 and that is generally dark in color. Cf. **light mineral.**

dark·ness (därk′nis), *n.* **1.** the state or quality of being dark: *The room was in darkness.* **2.** absence or deficiency of light: *the darkness of night.* **3.** wickedness or evil: *Satan, the prince of darkness.* **4.** obscurity; concealment: *The darkness of the metaphor destroyed its effectiveness.* **5.** lack of knowledge or enlightenment: *heathen darkness.* **6.** lack of sight; blindness. [ME *derknesse*, OE *deorcnysse*. See DARK, -NESS]

Dark′ness at Noon′, a novel (1941) by Arthur Koestler.

dark′ of the moon′, the period during which the moon is not visible.

dark·room (därk′ro͞om′, -ro͝om′), *n.* *Photog.* a room in which film or the like is made, handled, or developed and from which the actinic rays of light are excluded. [DARK + ROOM]

dark′ seg′ment, a relatively dark band, just below the antitwilight arch, along the horizon opposite the rising or setting sun.

dark·some (därk′səm), *adj.* dark; darkish. [DARK + -SOME[1]] —**dark′some·ness,** *n.*

dark′ star′, *Astron.* an invisible member of a binary or multiple star system.

dark·town (därk′toun′), *n.* *Usually Offensive.* a part of a town or city inhabited largely by Negroes. [DARK + TOWN]

dark′-trace′ tube′ (därk′trās′), *Electronics.* a cathode ray tube having a screen coated with a halide of sodium or potassium which shows a dark spot at the point where it is struck by a beam of electrons. Also called **skiatron.**

dark·y (där′kē), *n., pl.* **dark·ies.** *Offensive.* a Negro. Also, **darkey, darkie.** [DARK + -Y[2]]

Dar·lan (dar län′), *n.* **Jean Louis Xa·vier Fran·çois** (zhäN lwē gza vyā′ fräN swa′), 1881–1942, French naval officer and politician.

Dar·lene (där lēn′), *n.* a girl's given name.

dar·ling (där′ling), *n.* **1.** a person very dear to another; one dearly loved. **2.** a person or thing in great favor: *He was the darling of café society.* —*adj.* **3.** very dear; dearly loved: *my darling child.* **4.** favorite; cherished: *He is the darling member of the horsy set.* **5.** *Informal.* charming; cute; lovable: *What a darling baby! She has a darling red sports car.* [ME *derling*, OE *dēorling*. See DEAR, -LING[1]] —**dar′ling·ly,** *adv.* —**dar′ling·ness,** *n.*

Dar·ling (där′ling), *n.* **Jay Nor·wood** (nôr′wo͝od), ("*Ding*"), 1876–1962, U.S. cartoonist.

Dar′ling Range′, a range of low mountains along the SE coast of Australia. Highest peak, Mt. Cooke, 1910 ft.

Dar′ling Riv′er, a river in SE Australia, flowing SW into the Murray River. 1160 mi. long.

Dar·ling·ton (där′ling tən), *n.* **1.** a city in S Durham, in NE England. 84,162 (1961). **2.** a town in NE South Carolina. 6710 (1960).

Darm·stadt (därm′stat; *Ger.* därm′shtät′), *n.* a city in central West Germany, S of Frankfort: former capital of Hesse. 139,600 (1963).

darn[1] (därn), *v.t.* **1.** to mend, as torn clothing, with rows of stitches, sometimes by crossing and interweaving rows to span a gap. —*n.* **2.** a darned place, as in a garment: *He found darns in the toes and heels of both socks.* [? ME *dern(en)*, OE *dernan* to hide] —**Syn. 1.** See **mend.**

darn[2] (därn), *Informal.* —*adj., adv.* **1.** darned. —*v.t.* **2.** to curse; damn: *Darn that pesky kid!* —*n.* **3. give a darn.** See **damn** (def. 11). [var. of DAMN]

darned (därnd), *U.S. Informal.* —*adj.* **1.** irritating; damned; confounded: *Get that darned bicycle out of the driveway!* —*adv.* **2.** extremely; remarkably: *She's a darned good tennis player. He came darned near breaking a leg.* [var. of DAMNED]

dar·nel (där′nəl), *n.* any of several annual or perennial grasses of the genus *Lolium*, having simple culms, flat leaves, and terminal spikes. [ME; cf. F (Walloon) *darnelle*, prob. < Gmc]

Dar·nell (där′nəl, där nel′), *n.* a boy's or girl's given name.

darn·er (där′nər), *n.* **1.** one who or that which darns. **2.** dragonfly. [DARN[1] + -ER[1]]

darn·ing (där′ning), *n.* **1.** the act of one who or that which darns. **2.** the result produced. **3.** articles darned or to be darned. [DARN[1] + -ING[1]]

darn′ing egg′, a smooth, egg-shaped piece of wood, ivory, marble, jade, or the like, for holding under a hole or tear to serve as a backing while darning.

darn′ing nee′dle, **1.** a long needle with a long eye used in darning. **2.** *U.S. Dial.* a dragonfly.

Darn·ley (därn′lē), *n.* **Lord Henry Stewart** or **Stuart,** 1545–67, Scottish nobleman: second husband of Mary Queen of Scots (father of James I of England).

Dar·rell (dar′əl), *n.* a boy's given name. Also, **Derrel.**

Dar·row (dar′ō), *n.* **Clarence (Seward),** 1857–1938, U.S. lawyer, lecturer, and author.

darś·a·na (dur′shə nə), *n.* *Hinduism.* any of the six principal systems of philosophy. [< Skt: lit., act of seeing]

D'Ar′son·val galvanom′eter (dar′sən vôl′, -val′), *Elect.* a galvanometer consisting of a large, fixed magnet and a light coil that swings in the magnetic field. Also, **d'Ar′sonval galvanom′eter.** [named after Jacques A. *D'Arsonval* (1851–1940), French physicist]

dart (därt), *n.* **1.** a small, slender missile that is pointed at one end and usually feathered at the other and is propelled by hand, as in the game of darts, or by a blowgun for use as a weapon. **2.** something resembling such a weapon, as the stinging member of an insect. **3. darts,** (*construed as sing.*) a game in which darts are thrown at a target usually marked with concentric circles divided into segments and with a bull's-eye in the center. **4.** an act of darting; a sudden swift movement. **5.** a tapered seam of fabric for adjusting the fit of a garment. —*v.i.* **6.** to move swiftly; spring or start suddenly and run swiftly: *A mouse darted out of the closet and ran across the room.* —*v.t.* **7.** to thrust or move suddenly or rapidly: *He darted his eyes around the room.* **8.** to throw with a sudden thrust, as a dart. [ME < MF < Gmc] —**dart′ing·ly,** *adv.* —**dart′ing·ness,** *n.* —**Syn. 1.** arrow, barb. **6.** dash, bolt, shoot.

dart·board (därt′bōrd′, -bôrd′), *n.* the target used in the game of darts. [DART + BOARD]

dart·er (där′tər), *n.* **1.** one who or that which darts or moves swiftly. **2.** snakebird. **3.** any of several small, darting, fresh-water fishes of the perch family of eastern North America. [DART + -ER[1]]

dar·tle (där′tᵊl), *v.t., v.i.,* **-tled, -tling.** to dart or shoot forth repeatedly. [DART + -LE]

Dart·moor (därt′mo͝or, -mōr, -môr), *n.* **1.** a rocky plateau in SW England, in Devonshire. ab. 20 mi. long. **2.** a prison on this plateau. **3.** one of an English breed of sheep having coarse, long wool.

Dar·von (där′von), *n.* *Pharm., Trademark.* See **dextro propoxyphene.**

Dar′von Com′pound, *Pharm., Trademark.* a combination of Darvon, phenacetin, aspirin, and caffeine used chiefly in the treatment of pain.

Dar·win (där′win), *n.* **1. Charles (Robert),** 1809–82, English naturalist and author. **2.** his grandfather, **Erasmus,** 1731–1802, English naturalist and poet. **3.** a seaport in and the capital of Northern Territory, in N Australia. 12,326 (1961). **4.** a walled plain in the third quadrant of the face of the moon: about 75 miles in diameter. **5.** a boy's given name.

Dar·win·i·an (där win′ē ən), *adj.* **1.** pertaining to Charles Darwin or his doctrines. —*n.* **2.** a follower of Charles Darwin; a person who accepts Darwinism. [DARWIN + -IAN]

Darwin′ian the′ory. Darwinism.

Dar·win·ism (där′wə niz′əm), *n.* the Darwinian theory that the origin of species is derived by descent, with variation, from parent forms, through the natural selection of those best adapted to survive in the struggle for existence. [DARWIN + -ISM] —**Dar′win·ist, Dar·win·ite** (där′wə nīt′), *n., adj.* —**Dar′win·is′tic,** *adj.*

Dar′win tu′lip, a class of tulips having a tall stem and broad, bright-colored flowers with a flat base. [named after C. R. DARWIN]

Dar·yl (dar′əl), *n.* a boy's or girl's given name.

Das·cy·lus (das′kə ləs), *n.* *Class. Myth.* a member of the Argonauts and son of Lycus.

Da·se·hra (dus′ər ə), *n.* a Hindu festival symbolizing the triumph of good over evil, celebrated for ten days in October. Also, **Da·sa·ha·ra** (dus′ə hur′ə), **Da′sa·hra, Da′sa·ra, Da·sha·ha·ra** (dush′ə hur′ə), **Dusehra, Dushehra, Dussehra, Dussera, Dusserah.** Also called **Durga Puja.** [< Skt *daśaharā*: lit., taking away the tensions]

da·sein (dä′zīn), *n.* *Existentialism.* the sensation of existence with a full awareness of the conditions of one's existence. [< G: existence (n.), to be present (v.), equiv. to *da* here + *Sein* being]

dash[1] (dash), *v.t.* **1.** to strike violently, esp. so as to break to pieces: *He dashed the plate into smithereens against the wall.* **2.** to throw or thrust violently or suddenly: *to dash one stone against another.* **3.** to splash violently; bespatter (with water, mud, etc.): *He recovered consciousness when they dashed water in his face.* **4.** to apply roughly, as by splashing: *to dash paint here and there on the wall.* **5.** to mix or adulterate by adding another substance: *to dash wine with water.* **6.** to ruin or frustrate (hopes, plans, etc.): *The rain dashed our hopes for a picnic.* **7.** to depress; dispirit: *The failure of the experiment dashed his spirits.* **8.** to confound or abash: *His rejection dashed and humiliated him.* **9.** to accomplish quickly: *to dash off a letter.* —*v.i.* **10.** to strike with violence: *The waves dashed against the cliff.* **11.** to move with violence; rush: *The horses dashed out of the burning stable.* **12. dash off, a.** to hurry away; leave: *I must dash off now.* **b.** Also, **dash down.** to write, make, sketch, etc., hastily: *We dashed off a letter to announce the news. He dashed down a memo.* —*n.* **13.** the throwing or splashing of liquid against something: *the dash of the waves against the dock.* **14.** the sound of such splashing: *The dash of the waves on the beach could be heard from afar.* **15.** a small quantity of anything thrown into or mixed with something else: *a dash of salt; a dash of lemon juice.* **16.** a hasty stroke, esp. of a pen. **17.** the sign (—) used to note an abrupt break or pause in a sentence or hesitation in an utterance, to begin and end a parenthetic word, phrase, or clause, to indicate the omission of letters or words, to divide a line, to substitute for certain uses of the colon, and to separate any of various elements of a sentence or series of sentences, as a question from its answer. **18.** an impetuous movement; a rush; a sudden onset: *At the cry, "Fire!," they all made a dash for the door.* **19.** *Track.* a short race: *a 100-yard dash.* **20.** spirited action; élan; vigor in action or style: *The dancer performed with spirit and dash.* **21.** a dashboard: *The headlight switch is on the dash.* **22.** *Telegraphy.* a signal of longer duration than a dot, used in groups of dots, dashes, and spaces to represent letters, as in Morse code. **23.** *Archaic.* a violent and rapid blow or stroke. **24. cut a dash,** *Informal.* to make a striking impression; be ostentatious or showy: *He cut a dash on the ski slopes last winter.* [ME *dassh(en)*, prob. < ON; cf. Dan *daske* slap, flap, Sw *daska*] —**Syn. 11.** dart, bolt. See **rush**[1]. **15.** pinch, bit; touch, tinge; suggestion, soupçon; sprinkle, sprinkling. **20.** flourish.

dash[2] (dash), *v.t.* *Chiefly Brit.* to damn (usually used interjectionally). [euphemism based on *d—n*, printed form of DAMN]

dash·board (dash′bōrd′, -bôrd′), *n.* **1.** (in an automobile or similar vehicle) a panel beneath the front window having various gauges and accessories for the use of the driver; instrument panel. **2.** a board or panel at the front of an open carriage or the like to protect the occupants from mud or dirt cast up by the hoofs of the animals drawing the vehicle. [DASH[1] + BOARD]

dashed[1] (dasht), *adj.* made up of dashes: *a dashed line down the middle of the road.* [DASH[1] + -ED[2]]

dashed[2] (dasht), *adj., adv.* *Chiefly Brit.* (used as a euphemism) damned: *dashed impudence; dashed bad luck.* [DASH[2] + -ED[2]] —**dash·ed·ly** (dash′id lē), *adv.*

da·sheen (da shēn′), *n.* the taro plant, *Colocasia esculenta*, native to tropical Asia, now cultivated in the southern U.S. for its edible tubers. [m. F *de Chine* of China]

dash·er (dash′ər), *n.* **1.** one who or that which dashes. **2.** a kind of plunger with paddles at one end, for stirring and mixing liquids or semisolids in a churn, ice-cream freezer, or the like. **3.** *Slang, Chiefly Brit.* a fashionable, sophisticated man or woman. [DASH[1] + -ER[1]]

dash′er block′, *Naut.* See **jewel block.**

dash·ing (dash′ing), *adj.* **1.** impetuous; spirited; lively: *a dashing hero.* **2.** brilliant; showy; stylish: *the dashing lines of the carriage.* [DASH[1] + -ING[2]] —**dash′ing·ly,** *adv.*

dash·pot (dash′pot′), *n.* a device for cushioning, damping, or reversing the motion of a piece of machinery, consisting of a cylinder in which a piston operates to create a pressure or vacuum on an enclosed gas or to force a fluid in or out of the chamber through narrow openings. [DASH[1] + POT[1]]

Dasht-i-Ka·vir (däsht′ē kä vēr′; *Eng.* dasht′ē kə vēr′), *n.* a salt desert in N central Iran. 200 mi. wide. ab. 18,000 sq. mi. Also called **Kavir Desert, Great Salt Desert.**

Dasht-i-Lut (däsht′ē lo͞ot′), *n.* a desert in E central Iran. 200 mi. long; 100 mi. wide. ab. 20,000 sq. mi. Also called **Lut Desert.**

dash·y (dash′ē), *adj.,* **dash·i·er, dash·i·est.** showy; stylish; dashing. [DASH[1] + -Y[1]]

Das Ka·pi·tal (*Ger.* däs kä′pi täl′), a theoretical and polemical work (1867) by Karl Marx, dealing systematically with economic, social, and political relations within society and containing the tenets on which modern communism is based.

Das Schloss (*Ger.* däs shlôs′). See **Castle, The.**

Das·sin (das′in, da sin′; *Fr.* da saN′), *n.* **Jules** (jo͞olz; *Fr.* zhyl), born 1911, French motion-picture director, born in the U.S.

dass·n't (das′ənt), *U.S. Dial.* contraction for *dare not.* Also, **das′n't.**

das·tard (das′tərd), *n.* **1.** a mean, sneaking coward. —*adj.* **2.** of or befitting a dastard; mean and cowardly. [late ME, prob. < ON *dasat, neut. ptp. of *dasa* to get tired; see -ARD]

das·tard·ly (das′tərd lē), *adj.* cowardly; meanly base; sneaking: *a dastardly act.* [DASTARD + -LY] —**das′tard·li·ness,** *n.*

da·stur (də sto͝or′), *n.* a Parsee chief priest. Also, **dustoor, dustour.** [< Pers *dastūr*]

dasy-, a learned borrowing from Greek meaning "hairy," "shaggy," "dense," used in the formation of compound words: *dasyphyllous.* [< Gk, comb. form repr. *dasýs*; see DENSE]

da·sym·e·ter (da sim′i tər), *n.* an instrument for determining the density of a gas. [DASY- + -METER]

das·y·phyl·lous (das′ə fil′əs), *adj.* *Bot.* having very hairy leaves. [DASY- + -PHYLLOUS]

das·y·ure (das′ē yo͝or′), *n.* **1.** any of several nocturnal, carnivorous marsupials of the genus *Dasyurus* and related genera, of Australia, Tasmania, etc., typically having a reddish or olive-brown coat marked with white spots. **2.** any of several related animals, as the Tasmanian devil or ursine dasyure. [< NL *Dasyūr(us)* name of the genus < Gk *dasý(s)* DASY- + *our(á)* tail + NL *-us* n. suffix] —**das·y·u·rine** (das′i yo͝or′in, -in), *adj.* —**das′y·u′roid,** *adj., n.*

Das·yus (dus′yo͞os), *n.* *Hinduism.* (in Vedic mythology) a race of Asuras defeated by Indra. [< Skt: lit., enemy, barbarian]

dat., dative.

da·ta (dā′tə, dat′ə, dä′tə), *n.* pl. of **datum.**

da′ta bank′, **1.** the total fund of information gathered and stored by an organization for access and use, generally by computer, and contained in data bases, files, libraries, etc. **2.** See **data base.**

da′ta base′, a comprehensive collection of related data organized for quick access, generally by computer. Also, **da·ta-base** (dā′tə bās′), **da′ta·base′.**

da′ta proc′essing, processing of information, esp. the handling of information by computers in accordance with strictly defined systems of procedure.

da·ta·ry (dā′tə rē), *n., pl.* **-ries.** *Rom. Cath. Ch.* **1.** the office of the Curia Romana that investigates candidates for papal benefices. **2.** the cardinal who heads this office. [< ML *datāria the office (where documents were dated); *datārius* the officer (who gave the dates), equiv. to LL *dat(a)* DATE[1] + L *-āria, -ārius* -ARY]

dat·cha (dä′chə), *n.* dacha.

date[1] (dāt), *n., v.,* **dat·ed, dat·ing.** —*n.* **1.** a particular point or period of time at which some event has happened or will happen: *July 4, 1776 was the date of the signing of the Declaration of Independence.* **2.** an inscription on a writing, coin, etc., that shows the time, or time and place, of writing, casting, delivery, etc.: *a letter bearing the date January 16.* **3.** the time or period to which any event or thing belongs; period in general: *at a late date.* **4.** the time during which anything lasts; duration: *The pity is that childhood has so short a date.* **5.** an appointment for a particular time: *They have a date with their accountant at ten o'clock.* **6.** a social appointment, engagement, or occasion arranged beforehand with a person of the opposite sex: *to make a date for the dance; to go out on a date on Saturday night.* **7.** a person of the opposite sex with whom one has such a social appointment or engagement: *Eve's my date for the apple-blossom festival.* **8. dates,** the birth and death dates, usually in years, of a person: *Dante's dates are 1265 to 1321.* **9. down** or **up to date,** in agreement with or inclusive of the latest information; modern: *His news commentary is always up to date.* **10. to date,** up to the present time; up to now: *This is his best book to date.* —*v.i.* **11.** to have a date: *The letter dates from 1873.* **12.** to belong to a particular period; have its origin: *That dress dates from the 19th century. The architecture dates as far back as 1830.* **13.** to reckon from some point in time: *The custom dates from the days when women wore longer skirts.* **14.** to go out on dates with persons of the opposite sex: *She dated a lot during high school.* **—v.t.** **15.** to mark or furnish with a date: *Please date the check as of today.* **16.** to ascertain or fix the period or point in time of; assign a period or point in time to: *The archaeologist dated the ruins as belonging to the early Minoan period.* **17.** to show the age of; show to be old-fashioned: *Wearing spats certainly dates him!* **18.** to make a date with; go out on dates with: *I'll date Eve for the dance.* [ME < MF < LL *dat(a)*, n. use of *data* (fem. of *datus*, ptp. of *dare* to give), from the phrase *data (Romae)* written, given (at Rome)] **—dat′a·ble, date′a·ble,** *adj.* **—dat′a·ble·ness, date′a·ble·ness,** *n.* **—dat′er,** *n.*

date[2] (dāt), *n.* **1.** the oblong, fleshy fruit of the date palm, a staple food in northern Africa, Arabia, etc., and an important export. **2.** See **date palm.** [ME < OF < OPr *dat(il)* < L *dactyl(us)*; see DACTYL]

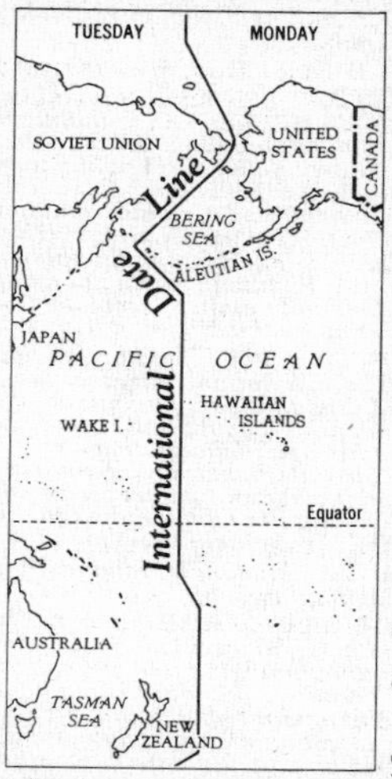

dat·ed (dā′tid), *adj.* **1.** having or showing a date: *a faithful dated record of facts.* **2.** out-of-date; old-fashioned: *Spats are considered dated today.* [DATE[1] + -ED[3]]

date·less (dāt′lis), *adj.* **1.** without a date; undated. **2.** endless; limitless: *the dateless night of death.* **3.** so old as to be undatable: *a dateless rock formation.* **4.** of permanent interest regardless of age: *a dateless work of art.* [DATE[1] + -LESS]

date′ line′, a theoretical line following approximately the 180° meridian, the regions on the east of which are counted as being one day earlier in their calendar dates than the regions on the west. Also called **international date line.**

date·line (dāt′līn′), *n., v.,* **-lined, -lin·ing.** **—n.** **1.** a line giving the place of origin and usually the date of a story, news dispatch, or the like. **—v.t.** **2.** to furnish (a news story) with a dateline: *a dispatch datelined Berlin; He datelines his stories Djakarta.* [DATE[1] + LINE[1]]

date′ mus′sel, a rock-boring, marine mussel of the genus *Lithophaga*, having a horny, brown shell.

date′ of rec′ord, the final date a registered stockholder of a corporation has the right to receive a dividend or other benefit.

date′ palm′, the date-bearing palm, *Phoenix dactylifera*, having a stem reaching a height of 60 feet and terminating in a crown of pinnate leaves.

date′ plum′, a tree, *Diospyros Lotus*, of the Himalayas, China, and Asia Minor, having glossy leaves and globular, yellow or purplish fruit.

date′ slip′, a record pasted to the endpaper of a library book on which are registered the dates the book was borrowed and is due back.

date′ stamp′, **1.** a device for stamping dates and frequently the place of origin or receipt, as on postal matter. **2.** the information stamped by this instrument.

date-stamp (dāt′stamp′), *v.t.* to stamp the date on, as with a date stamp: *He date-stamped his correspondence as he opened the mail in the morning.*

dat′ing nail′, a nail driven into a wooden tie, pole, etc., bearing on its head the date of installation or last treatment of the timber.

da·tive (dā′tiv), *Gram.* **—adj.** **1.** (in certain inflected languages, as Latin and German) noting a case having as a distinctive function indication of the indirect object of a verb. **—n.** **2.** the dative case. **3.** a word or form in that case, as Latin *regī* in *regī haec dīcite* meaning "tell this to the king." [ME *datif* < L *dativ(us)* (*casus*) dative (case), lit., the belonging to giving case, equiv. to *dat(us)* given (see DATE[1]) + *-īvus* -IVE; trans. of Gk *dotikḗ* (*ptôsis*)] **—da·ti·val** (dā tī′vəl), *adj.* **—da′tive·ly,** *adv.*

da·to (dä′tō; *Sp.* dä′tô), *n., pl.* **-tos** (-tōz; *Sp.* -tôs). **1.** (in the Philippines) a native chief. **2.** the headman of a barrio or of a Malay tribe. Also, **datto.** [< Sp < Tagalog *datū* < Malay *dāto(q)* title of respect]

dat·o·lite (dat′əlīt′), *n.* a mineral, calcium and boron silicate, $CaB(SiO_4)(OH)$, usually occurring in rock cavities in the form of colorless, prismatic crystals. [< G *Datolith* < Gk *dat(eîsthai)* (to) divide, share out; see -O-, -LITE] **—dat·o·lit·ic** (dat′əlit′ik), *adj.*

dat·to (dä′tō), *n., pl.* **-tos** (-tōz). dato.

da·tum (dā′təm, dat′əm, dä′təm), *n., pl.* **da·ta** (dā′tə, dat′ə, dä′tə) for 1–3, **da·tums** for 4, 5. **1.** **data,** (*usually construed as sing.*) facts, information, statistics, or the like, either historical or derived by calculation or experimentation: *Additional data is available from the president of the firm. These data represent the results of our analyses.* **2.** *Philos.* **a.** any fact assumed to be a matter of direct observation. **b.** any proposition assumed or given, from which conclusions may be drawn. **3.** Also called **sense datum.** *Epistemology.* the object of knowledge as presented to the mind. Cf. **ideatum. 4.** *Survey., Civ. Eng.* any level surface, line, or point used as a reference in measuring elevations. **5.** *Survey.* a basis for horizontal control surveys, consisting of the longitude and latitude of a certain point, the azimuth of a certain line from this point, and two constants used in defining the terrestrial spheroid. [< L: a thing given, neut. ptp. of *dare* to give]

da′tum plane′, *Survey.* See **tidal datum.**

da·tu·ra (də tŏŏr′ə, -tyŏŏr′ə), *n.* any solanaceous plant of the genus *Datura*, the species having funnel-shaped flowers, prickly pods, and narcotic properties. [< NL < Hindi *dhatūra* Jimson weed < Skt *dhattūra*] **—da·tu′ric,** *adj.*

dau (dou), *n.* dhow.

dau., daughter.

daub (dôb), *v.t.* **1.** to cover or coat with soft, adhesive matter, such as plaster, mud, etc.: *to daub a canvas with paint; to daub stone walls with mud.* **2.** to spread (plaster, mud, etc.) on or over something: *to daub plaster on a brick wall.* **3.** to smear, soil, or defile. **4.** to paint unskillfully. **—v.i.** **5.** to daub something. **6.** to paint unskillfully. **—n.** **7.** material, esp. of an inferior kind, for daubing walls. **8.** anything daubed on. **9.** an act of daubing. **10.** a crude, inartistic painting: *It was an exhibition of daubs.* [ME *daube(n)* < OF *daube(r)* (to) whiten, paint < L *dealbāre*, equiv. to *de-* DE- + *albāre* to whiten, equiv. to *alb(us)* white + *-āre* inf. suffix] **—daub′er,** *n.* **—daub′ing·ly,** *adv.* **—daub′y,** *adj.*

daube (dōb), *n.* a stew of braised meat, vegetables, herbs, and seasonings. [< F, prob. < It *addobbo* seasoning, sauce]

daub·er·y (dô′bə rē), *n.* unskillful painting or work. Also, **daub·ry** (dô′brē). [DAUB + -ERY]

Dau·bi·gny (dō bē nyē′), *n.* **Charles Fran·çois** (sharl fräN swa′), 1817–78, French painter.

daud (dôd, däd), *n. Scot. and North Eng.* dad[2].

Dau·det (dō dā′, dō-; *Fr.* dō de′), *n.* **1. Al·phonse** (al fôNs′), 1840–97, French novelist and short-story writer. **2.** his son, **Lé·on** (lā ôN′), 1867–1942, French journalist and novelist.

dau·er·schlaf (dou′ər shläf′), *n.* psychotherapy by means of prolonged sleep induced by drugs. [< G, equiv. to *dauer* long lasting + *Schlaf* sleep]

Dau·ga·va (dou′gä vä′), *n.* Lettish name of **Dvina.**

Dau·gav·pils (dou′gäf pēls′), *n.* a city in SE Latvia, in the W Soviet Union in Europe. 65,000 (1959). German, **Dünaburg.** Russian, **Dvinsk.**

daugh·ter (dô′tər), *n.* **1.** a female child or person in relation to her parents. **2.** a female child or person adopted as a daughter; a person in the legal position of a daughter. **3.** any female descendant. **4.** one related as if by the ties binding daughter to parent: *daughter of the church.* **5.** anything personified as female and considered with respect to its origin: *The United States is the daughter of the 13 original colonies.* [ME *doughter*, OE *dohtor*; c. G *Tochter*, Gk *thygátēr*, Skt *duhitā*] **—daugh′ter·less,** *adj.* **—daugh′ter·like′,** *adj.*

daugh·ter-in-law (dô′tər in lô′), *n., pl.* **daugh·ters-in-law.** the wife of one's son. [ME *doughter in lawe*]

daugh·ter·ly (dô′tər lē), *adj.* pertaining to, befitting, or like a daughter. [DAUGHTER + -LY] **—daugh′ter·li·ness,** *n.*

daugh′ter of Eve′, any girl or woman.

Daugh′ters of the Amer′ican Revolu′tion, a patriotic society of women descended from Americans of the Revolutionary period, organized in 1890. *Abbr.:* D.A.R.

dauk (dôk), *n.* dak.

Dau·mier (dō myā′), *n.* **Ho·no·ré** (ô nô rā′), 1808–79, French painter, caricaturist, and lithographer.

daunt (dônt, dänt), *v.t.* **1.** to overcome with fear; intimidate: *to daunt one's adversaries.* **2.** to lessen the courage of; dishearten: *He was daunted by the amount of work still to be done.* [ME *da(u)nte(n)* < OF *dante(r)*, alter. of *donter* (prob. by influence of *dangier* power, authority) < L *domitāre* to tame, deriv. of *domitus*, ptp. of *domāre* to tame] **—daunt′ing·ly,** *adv.* **—daunt′ing·ness,** *n.*

—Syn. 1. overawe, subdue, dismay, frighten. **2.** discourage, dispirit. **—Ant. 2.** encourage.

daunt·less (dônt′lis, dänt′-), *adj.* not to be daunted; fearless; intrepid; bold: *The dauntless platoon captured five machine-gun emplacements.* [DAUNT + -LESS] **—daunt′less·ly,** *adv.* **—daunt′less·ness,** *n.*

—Syn. undaunted, daring, indomitable, brave, courageous. **—Ant.** fearful, timid.

dau·phin (dô′fin; *Fr.* dō faN′), *n., pl.* **-phins** (-finz; *Fr.* -faN′). the eldest son of a king of France, used as a title from 1349 to 1830. [< F; MF *dalphin*, after *Dauphiné* from an agreement to thus honor the province after its cession to France]

dau·phine (dô′fēn; *Fr.* dō fēn′), *n., pl.* **-phines** (-fēnz; *Fr.* -fēn′). dauphiness. [< F; MF *dalfine*, fem. of *dalphin* DAUPHIN]

Dau·phi·né (dō fē nā′), *n.* a historical region and former province of SE France.

dau·phin·ess (dô′fi nis), *n.* the wife of a dauphin. Also, **dauphine.** [earlier *daulphiness*. See DAUPHIN, -ESS]

daut (dôt, dät), *v.t. Scot.* to fondle; caress. Also, **dawt.** [?]

daut·ie (dô′tē, dä′-), *n. Scot.* a darling; a favored person. Also, **dawtie.** [DAUT + -IE]

D.A.V., Disabled American Veterans. Also, **DAV**

Da·vao (dä vou′), *n.* a seaport on SE Mindanao, in the S Philippines. 138,899 (est. 1960).

Dave (dāv), *n.* a boy's given name, form of **David.**

D'Av·e·nant (dav′ə nənt), *n.* **Sir William,** 1606–68, English dramatist and producer: poet laureate 1638–68. Also, **Dav′e·nant, Davy.**

Da·vene (dä vēn′), *n.* a girl's given name.

dav·en·port (dav′ən pōrt′, -pôrt′), *n.* **1.** *U.S.* a large sofa, often one convertible into a bed. **2.** *Chiefly Brit.* a small writing desk. [the desk is said to be named after a Captain *Davenport* who first commissioned it]

Dav·en·port (dav′ən pōrt′, -pôrt′), *n.* **1. John,** 1597–1670, Puritan clergyman: one of the founders of New Haven. **2.** a city in E Iowa, on the Mississippi River. 88,981 (1960).

dav′enport ta′ble, a narrow table with drawers, having drop leaves at both ends, placed in front of or behind a sofa. Also called **sofa table.**

Dav·ey (dā′vē), *n.* a boy's given name, form of **David.** Also, **Da′vie, Davy.**

Da·vid (dā′vid *for 1, 2, 5;* dA vēd′ *for 3;* dä vēth′ *for 4*), *n.* **1.** died c970 B.C., the second king of Israel, reigned c1010–c970, successor to Saul. **2. Saint.** Also called **Saint Dewi.** A.D. c510–601?, Welsh bishop: patron saint of Wales. **3. Jacques Louis** (zhäk lwē), 1748–1825, French painter. **4.** a city in SW Panama. 14,969 (1950). **5.** a boy's given name.

Da·vid I (dā′vid), 1084–1153, king of Scotland 1124–53.

Da·vi·da (də vē′də), *n.* a girl's given name. Also, **Davita.**

Da′vid Cop′per·field (kop′ər fēld′), a novel (1850) by Charles Dickens.

Da·vid·ic (də vid′ik), *adj.* of or pertaining to the Biblical David or his descendants. [DAVID + -IC]

Da·vid·son (dā′vid sən), *n.* **1. Jo** (jō), 1883–1952, U.S. sculptor. **2.** a town in S North Carolina. 2573 (1960).

Da·vies (dā′vēz), *n.* **1. Arthur Bow·en** (bō′ən), 1862–1928, U.S. painter. **2. Joseph Edward,** 1876–1958, U.S. lawyer and diplomat.

Da·vi·na (də vē′nə), *n.* a girl's given name, form of **Davida.**

da Vin·ci (də vin′chē; *for 1 also It.* dä vēn′chē), **Le·o·nar·do** (lē′ə när′dō; *It.* le′ô när′dô). **1.** See **Vinci, Leonardo da. 2.** a walled plain in the first quadrant of the face of the moon: about 21 miles in diameter.

Da·vis (dā′vis), *n.* **1. Alexander Jackson,** 1803–92, U.S. architect. **2. Elmer (Holmes),** 1890–1958, U.S. radio commentator and author. **3. Jefferson,** 1808–89, U.S. statesman: president of the Confederate States of America 1861–65. **4. John.** Also, **Davys.** c1550–1605, English navigator and explorer. **5. John William,** 1873–1955, U.S. lawyer, politician, and diplomat. **6. Owen,** 1874–1956, U.S. playwright. **7. Richard Harding,** 1864–1916, U.S. journalist, novelist, and playwright. **8. Stuart,** 1894–1964, U.S. painter and illustrator. **9.** a town in central California. 8910 (1960). **10.** a boy's given name.

Da·vi·son (dā′vi sən), *n.* a town in central Michigan. 3761 (1960).

Da·vis·son (dā′vi sən), *n.* **Clinton Joseph,** 1881–1958, U.S. physicist: Nobel prize 1937.

Da′vis·son-Ger′mer exper′iment (dā′vi sən-gûr′mər), *Physics.* an experiment that verified the wave properties of matter by showing that a beam of electrons is diffracted by a crystal at an angle dependent upon the velocity of the electrons. [named after C. J. DAVISSON and L. H. *Germer* (b.1896), American physicists]

Da′vis's quad′rant, *Navig.* See **back staff.** [named after John DAVIS, who invented it]

Da′vis Strait′, a strait between Canada and Greenland, connecting Baffin Bay and the Atlantic. 200–500 mi. wide.

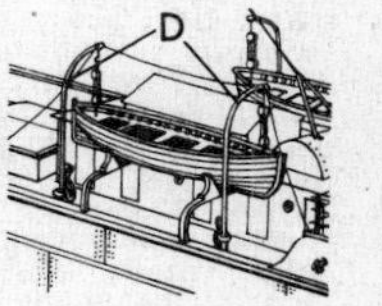

dav·it (dav′it, dā′vit), *n. Naut.* any of various cranelike devices used singly or in pairs for supporting, raising, and lowering boats, anchors, etc. [ME *daviot* < AF, appar. dim. of *Davi* David]

D, Davit

Da·vi·ta (də vē′tə), *n.* a girl's given name. Also, **Davida.**

Da·vout (dA vōō′), *n.* **Louis Ni·co·las** (lwē nē kô lä′), **Duke of Au·er·stadt** (ou′ər stat′), **Prince of Eck·mühl** (ek′myōōl), 1770–1823 marshal of France: one of Napoleon's leading generals.

Da·vy (dā′vē), *n.* **1. Sir Humphry,** 1778–1829, English chemist. **2.** a crater in the third quadrant of the face of the moon: about 20 miles in diameter. **3.** Also, **Davey, Davie.** a boy's given name, form of **David.**

Da′vy Jones′ (jōnz), *Naut.* the spirit of the sea; the sailors' devil. [?]

Da′vy Jones′s lock′er, the ocean's bottom, esp. as the grave of all who perish at sea.

Da′vy lamp′, a safety lamp formerly used by miners. [named after Sir H. DAVY]

Da·vys (dā′vis), *n.* **John.** See **Davis, John.**

daw (dô), *n.* **1.** jackdaw. **2.** *Obs.* simpleton; fool. [ME *dawe;* cf. OHG *taha*]

daw·dle (dôd′əl), *v.,* **-dled, -dling.** **—v.i.** **1.** to waste time; idle; trifle; loiter: *Stop dawdling and help me with these packages!* **—v.t.** **2.** to waste (time) by trifling (usually fol. by *away*): *Instead of working, he dawdled away four years painting in Europe.* [var. of *daddle* to TODDLE] **—daw′dler,** *n.* **—daw′dling·ly,** *adv.*

—Syn. 1. See **loiter.**

Dawes (dôz), *n.* **1. Charles Gates,** 1865–1951, U.S. financier and diplomat: vice-president of the U.S. 1925–29: Nobel peace prize 1925. **2.** a crater in the first quadrant of the face of the moon: about 14 miles in diameter.

Dawes′ plan′, a plan to ensure payments of reparations by Germany after World War I, devised by an international committee headed by Charles Gates Dawes and put into effect in 1924. Cf. **Young plan.**

dawk (dôk, däk), *n.* dak.

dawn (dôn), *n.* **1.** the first appearance of daylight in the morning: *Dawn broke over the valley.* **2.** the beginning or rise of anything; advent: *the dawn of civilization.* **3.** *Informal.* a sudden realization, understanding, or enlightenment: *After my three-hour explanation, the dawn finally came and he saw what I meant.* **—v.i.** **4.** to begin to grow light in the morning: *The day dawned with a cloudless sky.* **5.** to begin to open or develop: *By the time the Roman civilization dawned and began to flourish, the Minoans had become a legend.* **6.** to begin to be perceived (usually fol. by *on*): *The idea dawned on him.* [ME *dawen*, OE *dagian;* c. OIcel *daga*, MHG *tagen;* akin to DAY] **—dawn′like′,** *adj.*

—Syn. 1. daybreak, sunrise. **6.** appear, occur, break. **—Ant. 1.** sunset.

Dawn (dôn), *n.* a girl's given name.

dawn′ patrol′, **1.** a military flight undertaken at dawn or early morning in order to reconnoiter enemy positions. **2.** the personnel of a radio or television station who prepare and perform early-morning programs.

Daw·son (dô′sən), *n.* **1. Sir John William,** 1820–99, Canadian geologist and educator. **2.** a town in NW Canada, at the confluence of the Yukon and Klondike rivers: former capital of the Yukon Territory. 881 (1961). **3.** a town in SW Georgia. 5062 (1960).

Daw′son Creek′, a village in NE British Columbia, Canada, at the SE terminus of the Alaska Highway. 10,946 (1961).

Daw′son Springs′, a town in W Kentucky. 3002 (1960).

dawt (dôt, dät), *v.t. Scot.* daut.

dawt·ie (dô′tē, dä′-), *n. Scot.* dautie.

Dax (däks), *n.* a city in SW France: mineral hot springs. 18,422 (1962).

day (dā), *n.* **1.** the interval of light between two successive nights; the time between sunrise and sunset: *Since there was no artificial illumination, all activities had* *to be carried on during the day.* **2.** the light of day; daylight: *The owl sleeps by day and feeds at night.* **3.** *Astron.* **a.** Also called **mean solar day.** a division of time equal to 24 hours and representing the average length of the period during which the earth makes one revolution on its axis. **b.** Also called **solar day.** a division of time equal to the time elapsed between two consecutive returns of the same terrestrial meridian to the sun. **c.** Also called **civil day.** a division of time equal to 24 hours but reckoned from one midnight to the next. Cf. **astronomical day, lunar day, sidereal day.** **4.** an analogous division of time for a planet other than the earth: *the Martian day.* **5.** the portion of a day allotted to labor: *an eight-hour day.* **6.** a day on which something occurs: *the day we met.* **7.** (*often cap.*) a day assigned to a particular purpose or observance: *New Year's Day.* **8.** a time considered as propitious or opportune: *His day will come. Every dog has his day.* **9.** a day of contest or the contest itself: *to win the day.* **10.** Often, **days.** a particular time or period: *the present day; in days of old.* **11.** Usually, **days.** period of life or activity: *His days are numbered.* **12.** period of existence, power, or influence: *in the day of the dinosaurs.* **13.** light[1] (def. 16a). **14. call it a day,** to stop one's activity for the day or for the present; quit temporarily: *After typing the paper for the third time, she decided to call it a day.* **15. day in, day out,** every day without fail; continuously: *They endured the noise, dirt, and turbulence of the city day in, day out.* Also, **day in and day out.** [ME; OE *dæg;* c. G *Tag;* akin to Skt *dāhas* heat]

Day (dā), *n.* **Clarence (Shep·ard)** (shep′ərd), 1874–1935, U.S. author.

Day·ak (dī′ak, -ək), *n., pl.* **-aks,** (*esp. collectively*) **-ak.** a member of any of the Malay peoples of interior Borneo. Also, **Dyak.**

da·yan (dä yän′, -yôn′), *n., pl.* **-ya·nim** (-yä nēm′, -yô′nim). *Hebrew.* **1.** a judge in a Jewish religious court. **2.** a person knowledgeable in Talmudic law whose advice on religious questions is often sought by rabbis.

Da·yan (dä yän′), *n.* **Mo·she** (mô she′), 1915–81, Israeli political leader; foreign minister 1977–79.

day·bea·con (dā′bē′kən), *n.* *Navig.* an unlighted beacon used as a daymark. [DAY + BEACON]

day′ bed′, an elongated couch for reclining or sleeping, esp. during the day. Also, **day′bed′.**

day·bill (dā′bil′), *n.* a poster advertising a play or other form of entertainment. Cf. **playbill.** [DAY + BILL[1]]

day′ blind′ness, hemeralopia (def. 1).

day·book (dā′bo͝ok′), *n.* **1.** *Bookkeeping.* a book in which the transactions of the day are entered in the order of their occurrence. **2.** a diary. [DAY + BOOK]

day′ boy′, *Chiefly Brit.* a boarding school student who lives at home.

day·break (dā′brāk′), *n.* the first appearance of daylight in the morning; dawn: *After a long, cold night, we finally rode off at daybreak.* [DAY + BREAK]

day-by-day (dā′bī dā′), *adj.* taking place each day; daily: *a day-by-day account.*

day′ camp′, a camp for children providing no sleeping facilities and attended only during the day on weekdays. Cf. **summer camp.**

day′-care cen′ter, a day nursery, esp. one operated by private or public funds to provide child care at low cost.

day′ coach′, an ordinary railroad passenger car, as distinguished from a sleeping car, parlor car, etc.

day·dream (dā′drēm′), *n.* **1.** a visionary fancy indulged in while awake; reverie. —*v.i.* **2.** to indulge in such reveries. [DAY + DREAM] —**day′dream′er,** *n.* —**day′dream′y,** *adj.*

day·flow·er (dā′flou′ər), *n.* any plant of the genus *Commelina,* of the spiderwort family, usually bearing cymes of small, blue flowers. [DAY + FLOWER]

day·fly (dā′flī′), *n., pl.* **-flies.** a mayfly. [DAY + FLY[2]]

Day-Glow (dā′glō′), *n.* *Trademark.* a highly luminous printing ink.

day′ in court′, **1.** the day on which one involved in a lawsuit is to be afforded the opportunity to appear and be heard in court. **2.** a chance to present one's defense or argument: *Each candidate has been given his day in court.*

day′ jas′mine, a shrub, *Cestrum diurnum,* of the West Indies, having clusters of white flowers that are very fragrant by day.

day′ la′bor, **1.** workers hired on a daily basis only, esp. unskilled labor. **2.** work done by a day laborer.

day′ la′borer, an unskilled worker paid by the day.

day′ let′ter, a telegram with a minimum charge for 50 words or less, sent day or night and cheaper and slower than a regular telegram.

day·light (dā′līt′), *n.* **1.** the light of day: *At the end of the tunnel they could see daylight.* **2.** openness; publicity: *Some of his inventions never saw daylight.* **3.** the time of day; daytime. **4.** daybreak; dawn. **5.** a clear space between any two parts that should be close together, as between the jambs of the opening of a doorway or the knees of a horseback rider and a saddle. —*adj.* **6.** *Photog.* noting film made for exposure by the natural light of day, usually limited to the interval between two hours after sunrise and two hours before sunset. **7. beat, frighten,** or **scare the (living) daylights out of someone,** to beat, frighten, or scare a person into a state of senselessness. [ME; see DAY, LIGHT[1]]

day′light-sav′ing time′ (dā′līt′sā′viŋ), time one or more hours later than the standard time for a country or community, usually used during summer months to give more hours of daylight to the working day.

day′ lil′y, **1.** any liliaceous plant of the genus *Hemerocallis,* having yellow or orange flowers that commonly last only for a day. **2.** any liliaceous plant of the genus *Hosta* (*Funkia*), having white or blue flowers. **3.** the flower of any of these plants.

day′ loan′, a bank loan to finance the purchase of securities which is repayable within the calendar day on which it is made. Also called **clearing loan, morning loan.**

day·long (dā′lông′, -long′), *adj.* during the entire day; lasting all day: *a daylong trip.* [DAY + LONG[1]]

day′ man′, *Naut.* **1.** a seaman who is a member of a deck gang. **2.** Also called **idler.** a member of a ship's company who does not stand watch and who ordinarily works only during the day, as a carpenter, sailmaker, etc.

day·mark (dā′märk′), *n.* **1.** a navigational aid distinctively marked for visibility by day. **2.** See **day shape.** [DAY + MARK[1]]

day′ nurs′ery, a nursery for the care of small children during the day, esp. while their mothers are at work.

Day′ of Atone′ment, *Judaism.* See **Yom Kippur.**

Day′ of Judg′ment, the day of the Last Judgment, at the end of the world.

day′ of reck′oning, **1.** the time when one is called to account for one's actions, to pay one's debts, or to fulfill one's promises or obligations. **2.** See **Day of Judgment.**

Day′ of the Lord′, **1.** Also called **Day′ of Yah′weh.** (in Old Testament eschatology) a day of final judgment. Amos 5:18-21; Ezek. 30. **2.** Also called **Day′ of Christ′, Day of Je′sus Christ′.** the day of the Second Advent. II Peter 3:10; I Cor. 1:14; Phil. 1:10; 2:16.

day′ room′, a room on a military or air base for the leisure activities of enlisted personnel.

days (dāz), *adv.* in or during the day regularly: *They slept days rather than nights.* [DAY + -S[1]]

Days′ and Nights′, a novel (1944) by Konstantin Simonov.

day′ school′, **1.** a school open for instruction on weekdays only, usually from 9 A.M. until 3 P.M. **2.** a school conducted in the daytime (distinguished from *night school*). **3.** a private school for pupils living outside the school (distinguished from *boarding school*).

day′ shape′, *Naut.* an unlighted buoy or shape used as a day signal.

day′ shift′, **1.** the work force, as of a factory, scheduled to work during the daytime. **2.** the scheduled period of labor for this work force.

day·side (dā′sīd′), *n.* *Journalism.* the day shift of a newspaper. Cf. **nightside.** [DAY + SIDE[1]]

Day·sie (dā′zē), *n.* a girl's given name. Also, **Daisy.**

days·man (dāz′mən), *n., pl.* **-men.** *Archaic.* an umpire; mediator. [ME *dayesman.* See DAY, 'S[1], MAN[1]]

days′ of grace′, days, usually three, allowed by law or custom for payment after a bill or note falls due. [trans. of L *diēs grātiae*]

day·spring (dā′spriŋ′), *n.* *Archaic.* dawn; daybreak. [ME; see DAY, SPRING]

day·star (dā′stär′), *n.* **1.** See **morning star.** **2.** *Archaic.* the sun. [ME *daysterre,* OE *daegsteorra.* See DAY, STAR]

day's′ work′, *Naut.* the work of computing the navigation of a vessel for the succeeding nautical day.

day′ tank′, a tank in which a batch of glass is melted in a sufficient quantity for one day's work.

day·time (dā′tīm′), *n.* the time between sunrise and sunset. [DAY + TIME]

day-to-day (dā′tə dā′), *adj.* **1.** occurring each day; daily: *day-to-day chores; day-to-day worries.* **2.** involving concern only with immediate needs or desires; limited to the demands of one day at a time without preparation for the future: *He led a hand-to-mouth and day-to-day existence.*

Day·ton (dāt′ᵊn), *n.* **1. Jonathan,** 1760–1824, U.S. politician, Speaker of the House 1795–99. **2.** a city in SW Ohio. 262,332 (1960). **3.** a town in N Kentucky. 9050 (1960). **4.** a town in E Tennessee. 3500 (1960). **5.** a town in E Texas. 3367 (1960). **6.** a town in SE Washington. 2913 (1960).

Day·to′na Beach′ (dā tō′nə), a city in NE Florida: seashore resort. 37,395 (1960).

day·work (dā′wûrk′), *n.* work done and paid for by the day. [ME *dai-werk* the amount of land worked by a team in one day, OE *dæg-weorc* day's work. See DAY, WORK] —**day′work′er,** *n.*

daze (dāz), *v.,* **dazed, daz·ing,** *n.* —*v.t.* **1.** to stun or stupefy with a blow, shock, etc.: *He was dazed by a blow on the head.* **2.** to confuse; bewilder; dazzle: *The splendor of the palace dazed him.* —*n.* **3.** a dazed condition: *After meeting the movie star, she was in a daze for a week.* [ME *dase(n)* < OIcel *dasa-* (as in *dasask* to become weary); cf. Dan *dase* to doze, mope] —**daz·ed·ly** (dā′zid lē), *adv.*

daz·zle (daz′əl), *v.,* **-zled, -zling,** *n.* —*v.t.* **1.** to overpower or dim the vision of by intense light: *Coming from the dark house, he was dazzled by the sudden sunlight.* **2.** to bewilder, impress, or confuse by brilliancy, splendor, etc.: *The glorious palace dazzled him.* —*v.i.* **3.** to shine or reflect brilliantly: *polished gems dazzling in the sunlight.* **4.** to be overpowered by light: *Her eyes dazzled in the glare.* **5.** to excite admiration by brilliance: *Once one is accustomed to such splendor, it no longer dazzles.* —*n.* **6.** an act or instance of dazzling: *the dazzle of the spotlights.* **7.** something that dazzles; bewildering brightness, brilliance, or splendor. [DAZE + -LE] —**daz′zler,** *n.* —**daz′zling·ly,** *adv.*

dB, decibel; decibels. Also, **db**

D.B., **1.** Bachelor of Divinity. **2.** Domesday Book.

d.b., daybook.

DBA, doing business as. Also, **dba**

dBa, decibels above reference noise, adjusted. Also, **dba**

D.B.A., Doctor of Business Administration.

D.B.E., Dame Commander of the Order of the British Empire.

DBI, *Pharm. Trademark.* a compound, $C_{10}H_{15}N_5$, used in the form of its hydrochloride for the treatment of diabetes. Also called **phenformin.**

D.Bib., Douay Bible.

dbl., double.

dBm, decibel referred to one milliwatt. Also, **dbm**

dBm/m^2, decibel referred to one milliwatt per square meter. Also, **dbm/m^2**

D.B.O., *Theat.* See **dead blackout.**

dBrn, decibels above reference noise. Also, **dbrn**

dBV, decibel referred to one volt. Also, **dbv**

dBW, decibel referred to one watt. Also, **dbw**

DC, **1.** dental corps. **2.** Also, **D.C., dc, d-c, d.c.** *Elect.* direct current: an electric current of constant direction, having a magnitude that does not vary or varies only slightly. Cf. **AC** (def. 2).

D.C., **1.** *Music.* da capo. **2.** See **District of Columbia.** **3.** See **DC** (def. 2).

D.Ch.E., Doctor of Chemical Engineering.

D.C.L., Doctor of Civil Law.

D.C.M., *Brit.* Distinguished Conduct Medal.

D.Cn.L., Doctor of Canon Law.

D.C.S., **1.** Deputy Clerk of Sessions. **2.** Doctor of Christian Science. **3.** Doctor of Commercial Science.

DD, dishonorable discharge.

DD, the largest proportional brassiere cup size.

dd, **1.** *Law.* today's date. [< L *dē datō*] **2.** degree-day. **3.** delayed delivery. **4.** delivered. **5.** demand draft. **6.** double deck. **7.** *Shipbuilding.* dry dock.

dd., delivered.

D.D., **1.** Doctor of Divinity. **2.** demand draft.

D-day (dē′dā′), *n.* **1.** *Mil.* the day, usually unspecified, set for the beginning of a planned attack. **2.** June 6, 1944, the day of the invasion of western Europe by Allied forces in World War II. Also, **D-Day.** [D (for *day*) + DAY; the same pattern as H-HOUR]

D.D.S., **1.** Doctor of Dental Science. **2.** Doctor of Dental Surgery.

D.D.Sc., Doctor of Dental Science.

DDT, a white, crystalline, water-insoluble solid, $(ClC_6H_4)_2CHCCl_3$, usually derived from chloral by reaction with chlorobenzene in the presence of fuming sulfuric acid: used as an insecticide and as a scabicide and pediculicide. Also called **dichlorodiphenyltrichloroethane, chlorophenothane, dicophane.** [*d(ichloro)d(iphenyl)t(richloroethane)*]

de (də; *Fr.* də; *Sp.* de), *prep.* from; of: used in French and Spanish personal names, originally to indicate place of origin: *Comte de Rochambeau; Don Ricardo de Aragón.* [< F, Sp < L]

de (de), *prep.* *Latin.* of; from.

de-, a formal element occurring in loan words from Latin (*decide*); also used as a prefix to indicate privation, removal, and separation (*dehumidify*), negation (*demerit; derange*), descent (*degrade; deduce*), reversal (*detract*), intensity (*decompound*). Cf. **di-**[2], **dis-**[1]. [ME < L, comb. form repr. *de* (prep.) from, away from, of, out of, etc.; in some words, < F < L *dē-* or *dis-* DIS-[1]]

DE, destroyer escort.

D.E., Doctor of Engineering.

Dea., Deacon.

de·a·cet·y·late (dē′ə setᵊlāt′), *v.t.,* **-lat·ed, -lat·ing.** *Chem.* to remove the acetyl group from (an organic compound). [DE- + ACETYLATE] —**de′a·cet′y·la′tion,** *n.*

dea·con (dē′kən), *n.* **1.** (in hierarchical churches) a member of the clerical order next below that of a priest. **2.** (in other churches) an appointed or elected officer having variously defined duties. **3.** (in Freemasonry) one of two officers in a masonic lodge. —*v.t.* **4.** to pack (vegetables or fruit) with only the finest pieces or the most attractive sides visible. **5.** to falsify (something); doctor. **6.** *New Eng.* to castrate (a pig or other animal). **7.** *Archaic.* to read aloud (a line of a psalm, hymn, etc.) before singing it. [ME *deken,* OE *diacon* < LL *diācon(us)* < Gk *diákonos* servant, minister, deacon, equiv. to *diā-* DIA- + *-konos* service] —**dea′con·ship′,** *n.*

dea·con·ess (dē′kə nis), *n.* **1.** (in certain Protestant churches) a woman belonging to an order or sisterhood dedicated to the care of the sick or poor or who is engaging in other social-service duties, as teaching or missionary work. **2.** a woman elected by a church to assist the clergy. [earlier *deaconisse,* m. LL *diāconissa,* fem. of *diāconus* DEACON; see -ESS]

dea·con·ry (dē′kən rē), *n., pl.* **-ries.** **1.** the office of a deacon. **2.** deacons collectively. [ME *dekenry.* See DEACON, -RY]

de·ac·ti·vate (dē ak′tə vāt′), *v.,* **-vat·ed, -vat·ing.** —*v.t.* **1.** to cause to be inactive; remove the effectiveness of. **2.** to demobilize or disband (a military unit). **3.** to render (a bomb, shell, or the like) inoperative, esp. by disconnecting, removing, or otherwise interfering with the action of the fuze. **4.** *Chem.* to render (a chemical, enzyme, catalyst, etc.) inactive. —*v.i.* **5.** *Physical Chem.* to lose radioactivity. [DE- + ACTIVATE] —**de·ac′ti·va′tion,** *n.* —**de·ac′ti·va′tor,** *n.*

dead (ded), *adj.* **1.** no longer living; deprived of life: *dead people; dead flowers; dead animals.* **2.** not endowed with life; inanimate: *dead stones.* **3.** resembling death; deathlike: *a dead sleep; a dead faint.* **4.** bereft of sensation; numb: *She was half dead with fright. My leg feels dead.* **5.** lacking sensitivity of feeling; insensitive: *dead to all sense of shame; dead to the needs of others.* **6.** incapable of being emotionally moved; unresponsive: *dead to his attentions; dead to the nuances of the music.* **7.** (of an emotion) no longer felt; ended; extinguished: *a dead passion; dead affections.* **8.** *Law.* deprived of civil rights so that one is in the state of civil death, esp. deprived of the rights of property. **9.** no longer current or prevalent, as in effect, significance, or practice; obsolete: *a dead law; a dead controversy.* **10.** (of a language) no longer in use as a sole means of oral communication among a people: *Latin is a dead language.* **11.** utterly tired; exhausted: *They felt dead from the six-hour trip.* **12.** infertile; barren: *dead land.* **13.** not moving or circulating; stagnant; stale: *dead water; dead air.* **14.** no longer functioning, operating, or productive: *a dead motor; a dead oil well; a dead battery.* **15.** put out; extinguished: *a dead cigarette; a dead fire.* **16.** tasteless or flat, as liquor: *dead wine; The beer is dead.* **17.** flat rather than glossy, bright, or brilliant: *The house was painted dead white.* **18.** without resonance; anechoic: *dead sound; a dead wall surface of a recording studio.* **19.** without resilience or bounce: *a dead tennis ball.* **20.** lacking the customary activity; dull; inactive: *a dead market.* **21.** without vitality, spirit, enthusiasm, or the like: *a dead party.* **22.** complete; absolute: *The plan was a dead loss. A dead silence ensued.* **23.** sudden or abrupt, as the complete stoppage of an action: *The workmen came to a dead stop.* **24.** accurate; sure; unerring: *a dead shot.* **25.** direct; straight: *a dead line.* **26.** exact; precise: *the dead center of a circle.* **27.** not fruitful; unproductive: *dead capital.* **28.** *Sports.* out of play: *a dead ball.* **29.** (of a golf ball) lying so close to the hole as to make holing on the next stroke a virtual certainty. **30.** (of type or copy) having been used or rejected: *dead matter from the printer.* **31.** *Elect.* **a.** free from any electric connection to a source of potential difference and from electric charge. **b.** not having a potential different from that of the earth. **32.** *Metall.* (of steel) **a.** fully killed. **b.** unresponsive to heat treat-

ment. **33.** (of a lock or bolt) not closing automatically. **34.** (of the mouth of a horse) no longer sensitive to the pressure of a bit. **35.** noting any rope in a tackle that does not pass over a pulley or is not rove through a block.
—*n.* **36.** the period of greatest darkness, coldness, etc.: *the dead of night; the dead of winter.* **37. the dead,** dead persons collectively: *Prayers were recited for the dead.*
—*adv.* **38.** absolutely; completely: *dead right; dead tired.* **39.** with abrupt and total stoppage of motion, action, or the like: *He stopped dead.* **40.** directly; exactly; diametrically: *The island lay dead ahead.* [ME *deed,* OE *dēad;* c. Goth *dauths,* G *tot,* OIcel *daudh(r);* orig. ptp. See DIE¹] —**dead′ness,** *n.*
—**Syn. 1.** DEAD, DECEASED, EXTINCT, LIFELESS refer to something which does not have or appear to have life. DEAD is usually applied to that which had life but from which life is now gone: *dead trees, animals; They recovered the dead bodies.* DECEASED, a more formal word than dead, is applied to human beings who no longer have life: *a deceased member of the church.* EXTINCT is applied esp. to a race, species, or the like, no member of which is any longer alive: *Mastodons are now extinct.* LIFELESS is applied to that which may or may not have had life but which does not have it or appear to have it now: *The lifeless body of a child was taken out of the water. Minerals consist of lifeless materials.* **5.** unfeeling, indifferent, callous, cold. **12.** sterile. **14.** still, motionless, inert, inoperative. **22.** utter, entire, total. —**Ant. 1.** living, alive.

dead-an·neal (ded′ə nēl′), *v.t.* to anneal (steel) very slowly to improve its softness and ductility.

dead′-ball line′ (ded′bôl′), *Rugby.* the line at each end of the field parallel to and not over 25 yards behind the goal line.

dead′ beat′, *Informal.* very tired; exhausted.

dead·beat (*adj.* ded′bēt′; *n.* ded′bēt′), *adj.* **1.** *Horol.* noting any of various escapements acting without recoil of the locking parts from the shock of contact. **2.** *Elect.* (of the indicator of an electric meter and the like) coming to a stop with little or no oscillation. —*n.* *Informal.* **3.** a person who deliberately avoids paying his debts. **4.** a loafer; sponger. [DEAD + BEAT]

dead′ black′out, *Theat.* a total blackout.

dead′ cen′ter, **1.** Also called **dead point.** (in a reciprocating engine) either of two positions at which the crank cannot be turned by the connecting rod, occurring at each end of a stroke when the crank and connecting rod are in the same line. **2.** See under **center** (def. 16a). —**dead′-cen′ter,** *adj.*

dead·en (ded′ən), *v.t.* **1.** to make less sensitive, active, energetic, or forcible; dull; weaken: *to deaden sound; to deaden the senses; to deaden the force of a ball.* **2.** to lessen the velocity of; retard: *to deaden the headway of a ship.* **3.** to make impervious to sound, as a floor. —*v.i.* **4.** to become dead. [DEAD + -EN¹] —**dead′en·er,** *n.*

dead′ end′, **1.** a street, water pipe, etc., that is closed at one end. **2.** a position that offers no hope of progress; blind alley; cul-de-sac: *His theory led him to a dead end.* —**dead′-end′,** *adj.*

dead·en·ing (ded′ə ning), *n.* **1.** a device or material employed to deaden or render dull. **2.** a device or material preventing the transmission of sound. **3.** a woodland in which the trees are killed by girdling prior to being cleared. [DEADEN + -ING¹]

dead·eye (ded′ī′), *n., pl.* **-eyes.** *Naut.* either of a pair of disks of hardwood having holes through which a lanyard is rove and concave rims to receive a strop from a shroud, stay, etc., or from a chain or chain plate, the disks and lanyard being used to tighten the shroud or stay. [DEAD + EYE]

Deadeyes

dead·fall (ded′fôl′), *n.* **1.** a trap, esp. for large game, in which a weight falls on and crushes the prey. **2.** a mass of brush and fallen trees. [DEAD + FALL]

dead′ fir′ing, firing of a furnace or boiler at less than normal operating temperature in order to maintain conditions desirable during a period of idleness.

dead′ flat′, *Naut.* **1.** Also called **parallel middle body, square body.** a middle body or portion of the middle body having sides absolutely parallel to the fore-and-aft center line. **2.** a bottom of a hull having no deadrise. Also, **dead′flat′.**

dead′ hand′, *Law.* mortmain.

dead·head (ded′hed′), *Informal.* —*n.* **1.** a person who uses a ticket, as for a play or a train ride, without having paid for it. **2.** one who is unfit for or unable to achieve advancement, as in rank, position, etc.; dullard. **3.** *Foundry Slang.* excess metal in the riser of a mold. **4.** *Railroads.* a car or train being moved while empty. —*v.t.* **5.** to transport (someone) as a deadhead. **6.** *Railroads.* to move (an empty car or train). —*v.i.* **7.** to act or serve as a deadhead. [DEAD + HEAD]

dead′ heat′, a race in which two or more competitors finish in a tie.

De·a Di·a (dē′ə dī′ə), an ancient Roman goddess of agriculture, sometimes identified with Acca Laurentia, whose priests were the Arval Brothers.

dead′ let′ter, **1.** a law, ordinance, etc., that has lost its force but has not been formally repealed or abolished. **2.** a letter that cannot reach the addressee or be returned to the sender, usually because of incorrect address, and that is sent to and handled in a special division or department (**dead′-let′ter of′fice**) of a general post office. —**dead′-let′ter,** *adj.*

dead′ lift′, **1.** a direct lifting without any mechanical advantage. **2.** a situation that requires all one's strength or ingenuity.

dead·light (ded′līt′), *n.* *Naut.* **1.** a strong shutter able to be screwed against the interior of a porthole in heavy weather. **2.** a thick pane of glass set in the hull or deck to admit light. [DEAD + LIGHT¹]

dead·line (ded′līn′), *n.* **1.** the latest time for finishing something: *The reporter had to file his story before the five o'clock deadline.* **2.** a line or limit that must not be passed. [DEAD + LINE¹]

dead′ load′. See under **load** (def. 8).

dead·lock (ded′lok′), *n.* **1.** a state in which progress is impossible; complete standstill, as in a dispute, produced by the counteraction of opposing forces: *The union and management reached a deadlock over fringe benefits.* —*v.t.* **2.** to bring to a deadlock: *The proposal deadlocked the parley.* —*v.i.* **3.** to come to a deadlock: *The meeting deadlocked over the wage issue.* [DEAD + LOCK¹]

dead·ly (ded′lē), *adj.,* **-li·er, -li·est,** *adv.* —*adj.* **1.** causing or tending to cause death; fatal: *a deadly poison.* **2.** aiming to kill or destroy; implacable: *a deadly enemy.* **3.** like death: *a deadly pallor.* **4.** excessive; inordinate: *deadly haste.* **5.** extremely accurate: *Sammy Baugh was a deadly passer.* **6.** excruciatingly boring: *The formal dinner party was absolutely deadly.* —*adv.* **7.** in a manner resembling or suggesting death: *deadly pale.* **8.** excessively; completely: *deadly dull.* [ME *deedli(ch),* OE *dēadlīce.* See DEAD, -LY] —**dead′li·ness,** *n.*
—**Syn. 1.** See **fatal.**

dead′ly night′shade, **1.** belladonna (def. 1). **2.** See **black nightshade.**

dead′ly sins′, the seven sins of pride, covetousness, lust, anger, gluttony, envy, and sloth. Also called **seven deadly sins.** [ME *deedly synnes*]

dead′ mail′, undeliverable and unreturnable mail that is handled in the dead-letter office of the general post office.

dead·man (ded′man′, -mən), *n., pl.* **-men** (-men′, -mən). **1.** *Building Trades.* a log, concrete block, etc., buried in the ground as an anchor. **2.** a crutchlike prop temporarily supporting a pole or mast being erected. **3.** *Naut.* **a.** an object fixed on shore to hold a mooring line temporarily. **b.** a rope for hauling the boom of a derrick inboard after discharge of a load of cargo. [ME *ded man.* See DEAD, MAN¹]

dead′ man's′ control′, *Railroads.* a pedal, handle, or combination of both that must be held down by an engineer to keep a train in motion.

dead′-man's float′ (ded′manz′), *Swimming.* a floating position, esp. of a beginning swimmer, with face downward, legs extended backward, and arms stretched forward. Also called **prone float.**

dead′ man's′ hand′, *Poker Slang.* a hand containing two aces and two eights.

dead′ man's′ han′dle, a handle for operating a powered machine such that constant hand pressure is needed to keep the power supply open.

dead′ march′, a piece of solemn music for a funeral procession, esp. one played at a military funeral.

dead′ mat′ter, *Print.* type that has been set and used for printing or platemaking and is of no further use.

dead-melt (ded′melt′), *v.t.* *Metall.* to melt (steel) until it is killed.

dead′ men′, *Naut. Slang.* See **Irish pennant** (def. 1).

dead′ met′al, *Print.* furniture (def. 3).

dead′ muz′zler, *Naut.* muzzler (def. 2).

dead pan (ded′ pan′, pan′ *for 1;* ded′ pan′ *for 2*), **1.** *Slang.* a face completely lacking in expression. **2.** a style of comedy that relies on the comedian's maintaining such a face.

dead·pan (ded′pan′), *adj., adv., v.,* **-panned, -pan·ning.** —*adj.* **1.** marked by or accomplished with a careful pretense of seriousness or calm detachment: *deadpan humor; a relentless deadpan teasing.* **2.** displaying no emotional or personal involvement: *a deadpan style.* —*adv.* **3.** in a deadpan manner: *He spoke his lines utterly deadpan.* —*v.i., v.t.* **4.** to behave or perform in a deadpan manner. [adj., adv., v. use of DEAD PAN]

dead′ point′. See **dead center** (def. 1).

dead′ reck′oning, *Navig.* **1.** calculation of one's position on the basis of distance run on various headings since the last precisely observed position, with as accurate allowance as possible being made for wind, currents, compass errors, etc. **2.** position as so calculated.

dead·rise (ded′rīz′), *n.* *Naut.* the angle with the horizontal made by the outboard rise of the bottom of a vessel at the widest frame. Also called **rise of floor, rise of bottom.** [DEAD + RISE]

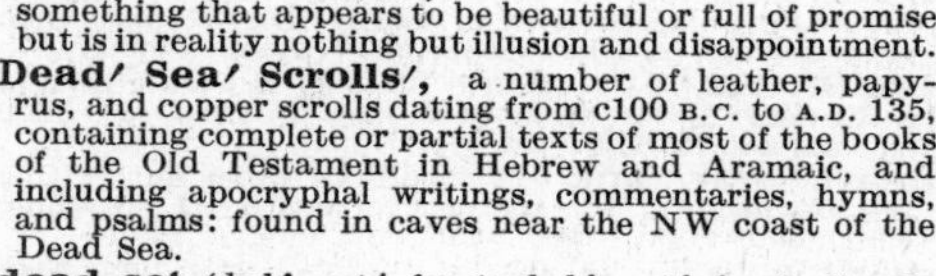

Dead′ Sea′, a salt lake between Israel and Jordan: the lowest lake in the world. 46 mi. long; 10 mi. wide; 1293 ft. below sea level.

Dead′ Sea′ fruit′, something that appears to be beautiful or full of promise but is in reality nothing but illusion and disappointment.

Dead′ Sea′ Scrolls′, a number of leather, papyrus, and copper scrolls dating from c100 B.C. to A.D. 135, containing complete or partial texts of most of the books of the Old Testament in Hebrew and Aramaic, and including apocryphal writings, commentaries, hymns, and psalms: found in caves near the NW coast of the Dead Sea.

dead set (ded′ set′ *for 1;* ded′ set′ *for 2, 3*), **1.** *Hunting.* the stiff posture assumed by a hunting dog in indicating the presence and location of game. **2.** a serious or determined attempt; firm effort: *He made a dead set at winning the championship.* —*adj.* **3.** determined; resolute: *His family was dead set against the marriage.*

dead′ sheave′, *Naut.* a half sheave having no rotating parts.

dead′ slow′, *Naut.* as slow as possible without losing steerageway.

dead-smooth (ded′smōōth′), *adj.* noting a double-cut metal file having the minimum commercial grade of coarseness; smoother than smooth; super-smooth.

dead′ sol′dier, *Slang.* an empty beer, liquor, or wine bottle.

Dead′ Souls′, a novel (1842) by Gogol.

dead′ spin′dle. See under **spindle** (def. 5).

dead′ spot′. See **blind spot** (defs. 3, 4).

dead′-stick land′ing (ded′stik′), *Aeron.* a landing made with the engine not functioning.

dead′ time′, downtime.

dead′ wa′ter, **1.** *Naut.* water eddying beside a moving hull, esp. directly astern. **2.** *Phys. Geog.* a part of a stream where there is a slack current.

dead′ weight′, **1.** the heavy, unrelieved weight of anything inert: *The dead weight of the bear's body was over 300 pounds.* **2.** a heavy or oppressive burden: *Supporting his ailing mother was a dead weight on his resources.* **3.** the weight of a railroad car, etc., as distinct from its load.

dead′weight ton′nage (ded′wāt′), *Naut.* the capacity in long tons of cargo, passengers, fuel, stores, etc. (**dead′ weight′ tons′**), of a vessel: the difference between the loaded and light displacement tonnage of the vessel. Also called **dead′weight capac′ity.**

dead·wood (ded′wŏŏd′), *n.* **1.** the dead branches on a tree; dead branches or trees. **2.** *Bowling.* pins remaining on the alley after having been knocked down by the ball. **3.** *Cards.* **a.** *Rummy.* cards in a hand that have not been included in sets and are usually counted as points against the holder. **b.** *Poker.* cards that have been discarded. **4.** anything useless and burdensome: *He cut the deadwood from his staff of advisers.* **5.** *Naut.* **a.** the relatively narrow, vertical, solid construction serving only as reinforcement and filling for the space between the keel of a vessel and the stem or sternpost and not as an integral part of the structure of the hull. **b.** relative fullness of form at the stern of a vessel. [DEAD + WOOD¹]

Dead·wood (ded′wŏŏd′), *n.* a town in W South Dakota. 3045 (1960).

dead·work (ded′wûrk′), *n.* *Mining.* necessary work other than the actual extraction of minerals, as the removal of overburden. [DEAD + WORK]

de·aer·ate (dē âr′āt, -ā′ə rāt′), *v.t.,* **-at·ed, -at·ing.** **1.** to remove air or gas from. **2.** to remove bubbles from (a liquid, as boiler feedwater), as by mechanical agitation in a vacuum or by heating at atmospheric pressure. Also, **de·a′ër·ate′, de·aer′ate.** [DE- + AERATE] —**de′aer·a′tion,** *n.* —**de·aer·a·tor** (dē âr′ā tər, -ā′ə rā′-), *n.*

deaf (def), *adj.* **1.** partially or wholly lacking or deprived of the sense of hearing; unable to hear. **2.** refusing to listen; heedless of; inattentive: *deaf to all advice.* [ME *deef,* OE *dēaf;* c. MLG *dōf,* D *doof,* OHG *toub*] —**deaf′ly,** *adv.* —**deaf′ness,** *n.*

deaf-and-dumb (def′ən dum′), *adj.* unable to hear or speak.

deaf′-and-dumb′ al′phabet, the manual alphabet used by deaf-mutes for communicating with others.

deaf·en (def′ən), *v.t.* **1.** to make deaf: *The operation deafened him for life.* **2.** to stun with noise: *The pounding of the machines deafened us.* **3.** *Archaic.* to render (a sound) inaudible, esp. by a louder sound: *His cries for help were deafened by the noise of the railroad.* **4.** deaden (def. 3). [DEAF + -EN¹]

deaf·en·ing (def′ə ning), *n.* deadening (def. 2). [DEAFEN + -ING¹] —**deaf′en·ing·ly,** *adv.*

deaf-mute (def′myōōt′, -myōōt′), *n.* a deaf-and-dumb person, esp. one in whom inability to speak is due to congenital or early deafness. [trans. of F *sourd-muet*] —**deaf′mute′ness, deaf′-mut′ism,** *n.*

Dea·kin (dē′kin), *n.* **Alfred,** 1856–1919, Australian statesman: prime minister 1903–04; 1905–08; 1909–10.

deal¹ (dēl), *v.,* **dealt, deal·ing,** *n.* —*v.i.* **1.** to occupy oneself or itself (usually fol. by *with* or *in*): *He dealt with the first question. Botany deals with the study of plants. He deals in generalities.* **2.** to take action with respect to a thing or person (usually fol. by *with*): *Law courts must deal with lawbreakers.* **3.** to conduct oneself toward persons: *He deals fairly.* **4.** to trade or do business: *to deal with a firm; to deal in an article.* **5.** to distribute, esp. the cards in a game (often fol. by *out*): *to deal out five hands of six cards each; your turn to deal.* **6.** *Archaic.* to have dealings or commerce, often in a secret or underhand manner (often fol. by *with*): *to deal with the Devil.* —*v.t.* **7.** to give to one as his share; apportion: *Deal me in.* **8.** to distribute among a number of recipients, as the cards required in a game: *Deal five cards to each player.* **9.** *Cards.* to give a player (a specific card) in dealing: *You dealt yourself four aces.* **10.** to deliver; administer: *to deal a blow; to deal someone a scolding.* **11. deal off,** *Poker.* to deal the final hand of a game. **12. deal someone in,** *Slang.* to include: *He was making a lot of dough in the construction business so I asked him to deal me in.* —*n.* **13.** *Informal.* **a.** a business transaction: *They closed the deal after a week of negotiating.* **b.** a bargain or arrangement for mutual advantage: *The best deal in town.* **c.** a secret or underhand agreement or bargain: *His supporters worked a number of deals to help his campaign.* **14.** (*cap.*) an economic and social policy pursued by a political administration: *the Fair Deal; the New Deal.* **15.** *Informal.* treatment received in dealing with another: *He got a raw deal.* **16.** an indefinite but large quantity, amount, extent, or degree (usually prec. by *good* or *great*): *a good deal of work; a great deal of money; There is a deal of good in him.* **17.** an act of dealing or distributing. **18.** *Cards.* **a.** the distribution of cards to the players in a game. **b.** the set of cards in one's hand. **c.** the turn of a player to deal. **d.** the period of time during which a deal is played. **19.** *Archaic.* portion; share. [ME *dele(n),* OE *dǣlan* (c. G *teilen,* etc.), deriv. of *dǣl* part (c. G *Teil*)]
—**Syn. 3.** act, behave. **4.** traffic. **8.** allot, assign, dole; mete, dispense. **13.** pact, contract. —**Ant. 8.** collect.

deal² (dēl), *n.* **1.** a board or plank, esp. of fir or pine, cut to any of various standard sizes. **2.** such boards collectively. **3.** fir or pine wood. —*adj.* **4.** made of deal. [ME *dele* < MLG or MD; see THILL]

de·a·late (dē′ā lāt′, -lit), *Entomol.* —*adj.* **1.** Also, **de·a·lat·ed** (dē′ā lā′tid). having no wings as a result of having bitten or rubbed them off. —*n.* **2.** a dealate insect. [DE- + ALATE] —**de′a·la′tion,** *n.*

deal·er (dē′lər), *n.* **1.** one who conducts himself toward another or others in a specified manner: *a plain dealer.* **2.** one who buys and sells articles without altering their condition; trader or merchant, esp. a wholesaler: *I got a dealer's discount on this coat.* **3.** *Cards.* the player distributing the cards. [ME *delere,* OE *dǣlere.* See DEAL¹, -ER¹]

deal·er·ship (dē′lər ship′), *n.* **1.** authorization to sell a commodity: *He got the dealership for the area after a long investigation into his credit status.* **2.** a sales agency or distributor having such authorization. [DEALER + -SHIP]

deal·fish (dēl′fish′), *n., pl.* **-fish·es,** (*esp. collectively*) **-fish.** a ribbonfish, esp. *Trachipterus arcticus.* [DEAL[2] + FISH]

deal·ing (dē′ling), *n.* **1.** Usually, **dealings.** relations; business: *frequent dealings; commercial dealings.* **2.** conduct in relation to others; treatment: *honest dealing.* [ME *deling.* See DEAL[1], -ING[1]]

dealt (delt), *v.* pt. and pp. of **deal**[1].

De′a Mari′ca (dē′ə), Marica.

de·am·bu·la·to·ry (dē am′byə lə tōr′ē, -tôr′ē), *n., pl.* **-ries.** ambulatory (def. 6). [ME < LL *deambulātōri(um),* equiv. to L *deambulāt(us)* (ptp. of *deambulāre* to walk about) + *-ōrium* -ORY[2]]

de·am·i·dase (dē am′i dās′), *n. Biochem.* an enzyme that releases the amido group from a compound. Also, **desamidase.** [DE- + AMIDASE]

de·am·i·nase (dē am′ə nās′), *n. Biochem.* an enzyme that releases the amino group from a compound. Also, **desaminase.** [DE- + AMIN(O)- + -ASE]

de·am·i·nate (dē am′ə nāt′), *v.t.,* **-nat·ed, -nat·ing.** *Chem.* to remove the amino from (a compound). [DE- + AMINATE] **—de·am′i·na′tion,** *n.*

de·am·i·nize (dē am′ə nīz′), *v.t.,* **-nized, -niz·ing.** *Chem.* deaminate. [DE- + AMIN(O)- + -IZE] **—de·am·i·ni·za·tion** (dē am′ə ni zā′shən), *n.*

dean[1] (dēn), *n.* **1.** *Educ.* **a.** the head of a faculty, or sometimes its registrar or secretary, in a university or college. **b.** the official in charge of undergraduate students at an English university. **c.** an official in an American college or university having charge of student personnel services, such as counseling or discipline: *the dean of men.* **2.** *Eccles.* **a.** the dean of the chapter of a cathedral or a collegiate church. **b.** Also called **vicar forane.** a priest in the Roman Catholic Church appointed by a bishop to take care of the affairs of a division of a diocese. **3.** the senior member, in length of service, of any body: *the dean of jurists.* [ME *deen* < MF *deien* < LL *decān(us)* chief of ten, equiv. to L *dec(em)* ten + *-ānus* -AN] **—dean′ship,** *n.*

dean[2] (dēn), *n. Brit.* dene.

Dean (dēn), *n.* a boy's given name.

dean·er·y (dē′nə rē), *n., pl.* **-er·ies. 1.** the office, jurisdiction, or district of a dean. **2.** the residence of a dean. [ME *denerie.* See DEAN[1], -ERY]

De·an·na (dē an′ə), *n.* a girl's given name, form of **Diana.**

dean's′ list′, a list of students of high scholastic standing, compiled by a college or university usually at the end of each semester or academic year. Cf. **honor roll** (def. 1).

de·an·thro·po·mor·phism (dē an′thrə pə môr′fiz-əm), *n.* the ridding of philosophy or religion of anthropomorphic beliefs and doctrines. [DE- + ANTHROPOMORPHISM] **—de·an′thro·po·morph′ic,** *adj.*

dear[1] (dēr), *adj.* **1.** beloved or loved: *a dear friend of mine.* **2.** (in the salutation of a letter) highly esteemed: *Dear Sir.* **3.** precious in one's regard: *our dearest possessions.* **4.** heartfelt; earnest: *one's dearest wish.* **5.** high-priced; expensive: *The silk dress was too dear and I couldn't afford it.* **6.** charging high prices: *That shop is too dear for my budget.* **7.** excessive; high: *a dear price to pay for one's independence.* **8.** *Obs.* difficult to get; scarce. **9.** *Obs.* worthy; honorable. **—*n.* 10.** one who is dear: *You're a dear to bring such a nice present.* **11.** a beloved one (often used in direct address): *my dear.* **—*adv.* 12.** dearly; fondly. **13.** at a high price: *That painting cost me dear.* **—*interj.* 14.** an exclamation of surprise, distress, etc.: *Oh dear, what a disappointment! Dear me! What a catastrophe!* [ME *dere,* OE *dēore;* c. OHG *tiuri,* OIcel *dȳrr*] **—dear′ly,** *adv.* **—dear′ness,** *n.*
—Syn. 1. darling, cherished. **5.** See **expensive.**

dear[2] (dēr), *adj. Archaic.* hard; grievous. Also, **dere.** [ME *dere,* OE *dēor* wild; cf. OHG *tiorīh* wild]

Dear·born (dēr′bərn, -bôrn), *n.* **1. Henry,** 1751–1829, U.S. soldier and diplomat: Secretary of War 1801–09. **2.** a city in SE Michigan, near Detroit. 112,007 (1960). **3.** See **Fort Dearborn.**

Dear′ John′, *Slang.* a letter from a girl or woman informing her boyfriend or fiancé that she is jilting him. [after the proper name]

dearth (dûrth), *n.* **1.** a scanty supply; scarcity; lack: *There is a dearth of good engineers.* **2.** scarcity and dearness of food; famine. [ME *derthe.* See DEAR[1], -TH[1]]

dear·y (dēr′ē), *n., pl.* **dear·ies.** *Informal.* darling (usually used by women as a term of address): *Mabel, deary, you just don't understand men.* Also, **dear′ie.** [DEAR[1] + -Y[2]]

death (deth), *n.* **1.** the act of dying; the end of life; the total and permanent cessation of all the vital functions of an animal or plant: *The death of the dog upset the boy.* **2.** an instance of this: *a death in the family; They published the letters after his death.* **3.** (*usually cap.*) the agent of death personified, usually represented as a man or a skeleton carrying a scythe. Cf. **Grim Reaper. 4.** the state of being dead: *to lie still in death.* **5.** extinction; destruction: *It will mean the death of our hopes.* **6.** manner of dying: *a hero's death.* **7.** *Law.* See **civil death. 8.** Also called **spiritual death.** loss or absence of spiritual life. **9.** *Christian Science.* the illusory destruction or end of life. **10.** bloodshed or murder: *Hitler was responsible for the death of millions.* **11.** a cause or occasion of death: *You'll be the death of me yet!* **12.** *Archaic.* pestilence; plague. Cf. **Black Death. 13. at death's door,** in serious danger of death; gravely ill: *Two survivors of the crash are still at death's door.* **14. be death on,** *Informal.* **a.** to be excessively strict about: *That publisher is death on sloppily typed manuscripts.* **b.** to be snobbish about or toward: *She's death on his friends from the office.* **c.** *Baseball.* to be able to cope with easily: *He's death on curves.* **15. do to death, a.** to kill, esp. to murder. **b.** to repeat too often, to the point of becoming monotonous and boring: *That theme has been done to death.* **16. in at the death, a.** *Fox Hunting.* present at the kill. **b.** present at the climax or conclusion of a situation. **17. put to death,** to kill; execute: *Many persons were put to death for their religious beliefs.* **18. to death,** to an extreme degree; thoroughly: *sick to death of the heat.* [ME *deeth,* OE *dēath;* c. G *Tod,* Goth *dauth(us);* akin to OIcel *deya* to die]
—Syn. 1. decease, demise, passing, departure. **—Ant. 1.** life.

Death (deth), *n.* **Lake of.** See **Lacus Mortis.**

death′ ad′der, a highly venomous elapid snake, *Acanthophis antarcticus,* of Australasia, having a stout body and broad head.

death·bed (deth′bed′), *n.* **1.** the bed on which a person dies: *On his deathbed he sent for his son.* **2.** the last few hours before death. [ME *deethbed.* See DEATH, BED]

death′ bell′, the bell that announces a death.

death′ ben′efit, the amount of money to be paid under the terms of an insurance policy to the designated beneficiary upon the death of the insured.

Death′, Be′ Not′ Proud′, a sonnet (1617–20?) by John Donne, published in 1633.

death·blow (deth′blō′), *n.* a blow causing death. [DEATH + BLOW[1]]

death′ cam′as, 1. any of several liliaceous herbs of the genus *Zygadenus,* of the Southern and Western U.S. and Canada. **2.** the root of any of these plants, poisonous to sheep and other animals.

death′ certif′icate, a certificate signed by a doctor, giving pertinent information, as age, sex, etc., about a deceased person and certifying the time, place, and cause of death.

death′ chair′. See **electric chair.**

death′ cham′ber, 1. a room in which a person is dying or has died. **2.** a place, as in a prison, in which executions take place.

Death′ Comes′ for the Archbish′op, a novel (1927) by Willa Cather.

death′ cup′, 1. a poisonous mushroom of the genus *Amanita,* part of which persists around the base of the stipe as a definite membranous cup. **2.** the cup itself.

death·day (deth′dā′), *n.* the day or the anniversary of the day of a person's death. [ME *deth day,* OE *dēothdæge.* See DEATH, DAY]

death′ dut′y, *Brit. Law.* an inheritance tax.

death·ful (deth′fəl), *adj.* **1.** deadly; fatal. **2.** resembling death; deathlike. [ME *deethful.* See DEATH, -FUL]

death′ house′, a building or part of a prison in which persons condemned to death await execution.

death′ in′stinct, suicidal tendency or inclination; predisposition to self-destruction.

Death′ in Ven′ice, a short story (1913) by Thomas Mann. German, **Der Tod in Venedig.**

death′ knell′, 1. a harbinger of the end, death, or destruction of something. **2.** See **passing bell.**

death·less (deth′lis), *adj.* **1.** not subject to death; immortal: *the belief that the human soul is deathless.* **2.** unceasing; perpetual: *his deathless devotion to the cause.* **3.** likely to endure because of superior quality, timelessness, etc. (sometimes used ironically): *deathless prose.* [DEATH + -LESS] **—death′less·ly,** *adv.* **—death′less·ness,** *n.*

death·like (deth′līk′), *adj.* resembling death. [DEATH + -LIKE; r. OE *dēath -līc* DEATHLY]

death·ly (deth′lē), *adj.* **1.** causing death; deadly; fatal. **2.** like death. **3.** of, pertaining to, or indicating death: *a deathly odor from the sepulcher.* **—*adv.* 4.** in the manner of death. **5.** very; utterly: *deathly afraid.* [ME *dethlich,* OE *dēathlīc.* See DEATH, -LY] **—death′li·ness,** *n.*

death′ mask′, a cast taken of a person's face after death. Cf. **life mask.**

Death′ of a Sales′man, a play (1949) by Arthur Miller.

Death′ of Gen′eral Wolfe′, The, a painting (1770) by Benjamin West.

Death′ of I·van′ Il·yich′, The, (i vän′ il yēch′, ī′vən), a short novel (1884) by Leo Tolstoy.

death′ rate′, the number of deaths per unit, usually 1000, of population in a given place and time.

death′ rat′tle, a sound produced by a person immediately preceding death, resulting from the passage of air through the mucus in the throat.

death′ ray′, a hypothetical ray that destroys life from a distance.

death′ row′, a row of prison cells for prisoners awaiting execution.

death′ sen′tence, a sentence condemning a convicted felon to execution by the state. Cf. **life sentence.**

death's-head (deths′hed′), *n.* a human skull, esp. as a symbol of mortality.

death's′-head moth′, a European hawk moth, *Acherontia atropos,* having markings on the back of the thorax that resemble a human skull.

deaths·man (deths′mən), *n., pl.* **-men.** *Archaic.* an executioner. [DEATH + 'S[1] + MAN[1]]

death·trap (deth′trap′), *n.* a structure or situation involving imminent risk of death: *They escaped from the deathtrap just before it exploded.* [DEATH + TRAP[1]]

Death′ Val′ley, an arid basin in E California and S Nevada: lowest land in North America. ab. 1500 sq. mi.; 280 ft. below sea level.

death′ war′rant, 1. an official order authorizing the execution of the sentence of death. **2.** anything which ends hope, expectation, etc.

death·watch (deth′woch′, -wôch′), *n.* **1.** a vigil beside a dying or dead person. **2.** a guard set over a condemned person before execution. **3.** Also called **death′watch bee′tle.** any of several beetles of the family *Anobiidae* that make a ticking sound as they bore through wood: the sound is believed to be an omen of death. [DEATH + WATCH]

death′ wish′, desire for one's own death or for the death of another.

death·y (deth′ē), *adj., adv. Archaic.* deathly. [DEATH + -Y[1]] **—death′i·ness,** *n.*

Deau·ville (dō′vil; *Fr.* dō vēl′), *n.* a coastal resort in NW France, S of Le Havre. 5239 (1962).

deave (dēv), *v.t.,* **deaved, deav·ing.** *Chiefly Scot.* to make deaf; deafen. [ME *deve(n),* OE (*ā*)*dēafian* to grow DEAF]

deb (deb), *n.* **1.** *Informal.* a debutante. **2.** *Slang.* an adolescent girl who belongs to a street gang. [by shortening]

Deb (deb), *n.* a girl's given name, form of **Deborah.**

deb., debenture.

de·ba·cle (dā bä′kəl, -bak′əl, də-), *n.* **1.** a general breakup or dispersion; sudden downfall or collapse: *The revolution ended in a debacle.* **2.** a breaking up of ice in a river. Cf. **embacle. 3.** a violent rush of waters or ice. [< F *débâcle,* deriv. of *débâcler* to unbar, clear, equiv. to *dé-* DIS-[1] + *bâcler* to bar << L *bacul(um)* stick, rod]

de·bag (dē bag′), *v.t.,* **-bagged, -bag·ging.** *Brit. Slang.* **1.** to divest of trousers as a joke or punishment. **2.** to debunk. [DE- + BAG]

de·bar (di bär′), *v.t.,* **-barred, -bar·ring. 1.** to shut out or exclude from a place or condition: *to debar all those who are not members.* **2.** to hinder or prevent; prohibit: *to debar an action.* [late ME < MF, OF *desbarr(er)* (to) lock out, bar. See DIS-[1], BAR[1]] **—de·bar′ment,** *n.*
—Syn. 1. See **exclude. 2.** interdict. **—Ant. 1.** admit. **2.** permit.

de·bark (di bärk′), *v.t., v.i.* to disembark. [< F *débarque(r),* equiv. to *dé-* DIS-[1] + *barque* BARK[3] + *-er* inf. suffix] **—de·bar·ka·tion** (dē′bär kā′shən), *n.*

de·base (di bās′), *v.t.,* **-based, -bas·ing. 1.** to reduce in quality or value; adulterate: *They debased the value of the dollar.* **2.** to lower in rank, dignity, or significance: *He wouldn't debase himself by doing manual labor. They debased the purpose of a free press.* [DE- + BASE[2]; cf. ABASE] **—de·bas·ed·ness** (di bā′sid nis, -bāst′-), *n.* **—de·base′ment,** *n.* **—de·bas′er,** *n.* **—de·bas′ing·ly,** *adv.*
—Syn. 1. lower, vitiate, corrupt; contaminate, pollute, defile. **2.** degrade, abase, demean, reduce.

de·bat·a·ble (di bā′tə bəl), *adj.* **1.** capable of being debated: *to be willing to discuss debatable issues.* **2.** in dispute; open to question; doubtful: *Whether or not he is qualified for the job is debatable.* [late ME < MF *debatable.* See DEBATE, -ABLE]

de·bate (di bāt′), *n., v.,* **-bat·ed, -bat·ing. —*n.* 1.** a discussion, esp. of a public question in an assembly: *a debate in the Senate on farm price supports.* **2.** deliberation; consideration. **3.** a contest in which the affirmative and negative sides of a proposition are advocated by opposing speakers. **4.** *Archaic.* strife; contention. **—*v.i.* 5.** to engage in discussion, esp. in a legislative or public assembly: *When we left, the men were still debating.* **6.** to deliberate; consider; discuss or argue: *Although the point was settled, they continued to debate far into the night.* **7.** *Obs.* to fight; quarrel. **—*v.t.* 8.** to discuss or argue (a question, issue, or the like), as in a legislative or public assembly: *They debated the matter of free will.* **9.** to dispute about: *The homeowners debated the value of a road on the island.* **10.** to engage in formal argumentation or disputation with (another person, group, etc.): *Jones will debate Smith. Harvard will debate Oxford.* **11.** to deliberate upon; consider: *The park commissioner debated the homeowner's demands. He debated his decision in the matter.* **12.** *Archaic.* to contend for or over. [ME *debate(n)* < MF *debat(re),* equiv. to *de-* DE- + *batre* to beat < L *battere,* alter. of *battuere*] **—de·bat′er,** *n.* **—de·bat′ing·ly,** *adv.*
—Syn. 1. argument, controversy, disputation, contention. **6.** dispute, contend. See **argue.**

de·bauch (di bôch′), *v.t.* **1.** to corrupt by sensuality, intemperance, etc.; seduce. **2.** to corrupt or pervert; deprave: *His honesty was debauched by the prospect of easy money.* **3.** *Archaic.* to lead away, as from allegiance or duty. **—*v.i.* 4.** to indulge in debauchery. **—*n.* 5.** a period of debauchery. **6.** intemperance; debauchery: *a wild debauch.* [< F *débauche(r),* OF *desbaucher* to seduce from duty, corrupt, equiv. to *des-* DE- + *baucher* < ?] **—de·bauch′er,** *n.* **—de·bauch′ment,** *n.*

de·bauched (di bôcht′), *adj.* **1.** displaying the effect of excessive indulgence in sensual pleasure: *a flabby and debauched face.* **2.** corrupt; debased: *debauched morals; a debauched nation.* [DEBAUCH + -ED[2]] **—de·bauch·ed·ly** (di bô′chid lē), *adv.* **—de·bauch′ed·ness,** *n.*

deb·au·chee (deb′ô chē′, -shē′), *n.* one addicted to excessive indulgence in sensual pleasures; one given to debauchery. [< F *débauché* (ptp. of *débaucher*). See DEBAUCH, -EE]

de·bauch·er·y (di bô′chə rē), *n., pl.* **-er·ies. 1.** excessive indulgence in sensual pleasures; intemperance. **2.** *Archaic.* seduction from duty, allegiance, or virtue. [DEBAUCH + -ERY]

Deb·bie (deb′ē), *n.* a girl's given name, form of **Deborah.** Also, **Debby.**

Deb·bo·ra (deb′ər ə), *n. Douay Bible.* Deborah.

Deb·by (deb′ē), *n.* a girl's given name, form of **Deborah.** Also, **Debbie.**

de·beak (dē bēk′), *v.t. Vet. Med.* to remove the beak from (a bird). [DE- + BEAK[1]] **—de·beak′er,** *n.*

de be·ne es·se (dē bē′nē es′ē), *Law.* of validity for the time being but subject to objection or nullification at a later date; provisionally: *to take evidence de bene esse to ensure against its loss.* [< ML: of well-being]

de·ben·ture (di ben′chər), *n.* **1.** See **certificate of indebtedness. 2.** a certificate of drawback issued at a custom house. [ME *debentur* < L *dēbentur (mihi)* there are owing (to me), equiv. to *dēb-* owe + *-entur* 3rd pers. pl. indic. pass. suffix] **—de·ben′tured,** *adj.*

deben′ture bond′, a corporation bond unsecured by any mortgage, dependent on the credit of the issuer.

Deb·es (deb′is), *n.* a walled plain in the first quadrant of the face of the moon: about 17 miles in diameter.

de·bil·i·tate (di bil′i tāt′), *v.t.,* **-tat·ed, -tat·ing.** to make weak or feeble; enfeeble: *The siege of pneumonia debilitated her completely.* [< L *dēbilitāt(us)* (ptp. of *dēbilitāre*), equiv. to *dēbili(s)* weak + *-ātus* -ATE[1]] **—de·bil′i·tant,** *n.* **—de·bil′i·ta′tion,** *n.* **—de·bil′i·ta′tive,** *adj.*

de·bil·i·ty (di bil′i tē), *n., pl.* **-ties. 1.** the state of being weak or feeble; weakness: *The old man's debility prevented him from getting out of bed.* **2.** *Pathol.* a condition of the body in which there is weakening of the vital functions. [ME *debylite* < MF *debilite* < L *dēbilitās,* equiv. to *dēbil(is)* weak + *-itās* -ITY]

De·bir (dē′bər), *n.* a royal city in the vicinity of Hebron, conquered by Othniel.

deb·it (deb′it), *n.* **1.** the recording or an entry of debt in an account. **2.** *Bookkeeping.* **a.** that which is entered in an account as a debt; a recorded item of debt. **b.** any entry or the total shown on the debit side. **c.** the left-hand side of an account on which such entries are made (opposed to *credit*). **—*v.t.* 3.** to charge with a debt: *The store debited her account for the pur-*

chase. **4.** to charge as a debt: *The store debited the purchase to her account.* **5.** *Bookkeeping.* to enter upon the debit side of an account. [ME < OF < L *dēbit(um)* something owed; see DEBT]

deb·i·tor (deb′i tər), *n. Obs.* a debtor. [late ME *debytour* < OF < L *dēbitor;* see DEBTOR]

dé·boî·té (*Fr.* dā bwȧ tā′), *n., pl.* **-tés** (*Fr.* -tā′). *Ballet.* a step in which the dancer stands on the toes with legs together and then springs up, swinging one foot out and around to the back of the other. Cf. **emboîté.** [< F: dislocated (n. use of ptp.)]

deb·o·nair (deb′ə nâr′), *adj.* **1.** of pleasant manners; courteous, gracious, and charming: *a debonair and well-dressed gentleman.* **2.** gay; carefree; sprightly: *He's so debonair since he married.* Also, **deb′o·naire′, deb′o·naire′.** [ME *debonaire, debonere,* OF *debonaire,* orig. phrase *de bon aire* of good disposition] —**deb′o·nair′ly,** *adv.* —**deb′o·nair′ness,** *n.*

de bo·nis non ad·min·i·stra·tis (dē bō′nis non ad min′i strā′tis, dā), *Law.* of the part of the estate of a deceased person that has not been administered: *administration or an administrator de bonis non administratis.* Also, **de′ bo′nis non′.** [< L]

de bonne grâce (də bôn gräs′), *French.* graciously; willingly. [lit., with good grace]

Deb·o·rah (deb′ər ə), *n.* **1.** Also, *Douay Bible,* **Deb′bo·ra.** a prophetess and judge of Israel. Judges 4, 5. **2.** Also, **Deb′o·ra.** a girl's given name.

de·bouch (di bo͞osh′, -bouch′), *v.i.* **1.** to march out from a narrow or confined place into open country, as a body of troops: *The platoon debouched from the defile into the plain.* **2.** *Phys. Geog.* **a.** to emerge from a relatively narrow valley upon an open plain: *A river or glacier debouches on the plains.* **b.** to flow from a small valley into a larger one. **3.** to come forth; emerge. —*n.* **4.** débouché. [< F *déboucher,* equiv. to *dé-* DIS-[1] + *boucher* to stop up, deriv. of *bouche* mouth < L *bucca* cheek, mouth]

dé·bou·ché (dā bo͞o shā′), *n.* **1.** *Fort.* an opening in works for passing troops. **2.** an outlet; an exit. [< F n. use of ptp. of *déboucher* to DEBOUCH]

de·bouch·ment (di bo͞osh′mənt, -bouch′-), *n.* **1.** an act or instance of debouching. **2.** Also, **de·bou·chure** (di bo͞o′sho͝or, di bo͞o sho͝or′). *Geol.* a mouth or outlet, as of a river or pass. [< F *débouchement,* deriv. of *déboucher.* See DEBOUCH, -MENT]

Deb·ra (deb′rə), *n.* a girl's given name, form of **Deborah.**

De·bre·cen (de′bre tsen′), *n.* a city in E Hungary. 129,671 (1960).

de·bride·ment (di brēd′mənt, dā-), *n.* surgical removal of foreign matter and dead tissue from a wound. [< F *débridement,* equiv. to *débrid(er)* (to) take away the bridle, MF *desbrider* (*des-* DE- + *brider,* deriv. of *bride* BRIDLE) + *-ment* -MENT]

de·brief (dē brēf′), *v.t.* to interrogate (a soldier, astronaut, diplomat, etc.) on return from a mission in order to assess the conduct and results of the mission. [DE- + BRIEF]

de·bris (də brē′, dā′brē *or, esp. Brit.,* deb′rē), *n.* **1.** the remains of anything broken down or destroyed; ruins; fragments; rubbish: *the debris of buildings after an air raid.* **2.** *Geol.* an accumulation of loose fragments of rock, etc. Also, **dé·bris′.** [< F *débris,* MF *debris,* deriv. of *debriser* to break up (in pieces), OF *debrisier* (*de-* DE- + *brisier* to break; see BRUISE)]

de Bro·glie (*Fr.* də brô′yə), **Louis Vic·tor** (*Fr.* lwē vēk tôr′). See **Broglie, Louis Victor de.**

de Bro′glie equa′tion, *Physics.* the postulate of wave mechanics that a particle of mass *m* moving at a velocity *v* will have the properties of a wave of wavelength **(de Bro′glie wave′length)** equal to *h/mv* where *h* is Planck's constant. [named after L.V. DE BROGLIE]

de Bro′glie wave′, *Physics.* one of a set of waves that represent the wave properties, as diffraction by a crystal diffraction grating, of a given particle and that have wavelengths assigned by the de Broglie equation.

de·bruise (də bro͞oz′, dē-), *v.t.,* **-bruised, -bruis·ing.** *Heraldry.* to overlay (a charge) other than an ordinary with an ordinary. [ME *debrusen, debrise(n)* (to) break down, crush < OF *debr(u)is(ier),* equiv to *de-* DE- + *bruisier* to break; see BRUISE]

Debs (debz), *n.* **1. Eugene Victor,** 1855–1926, U.S. labor leader: Socialist candidate for president 1900–20. **2.** a boy's given name.

debt (det), *n.* **1.** something that is owed; something that one person is bound to pay to or perform for another: *a debt of five dollars.* **2.** a liability or obligation to pay or render something: *My debt to her for advice is not to be discharged easily.* **3.** the condition of being under such an obligation: *His gambling losses put him deeply in debt.* **4.** *Theol.* an offense requiring reparation; a sin; a trespass. [ME *dette* < OF < VL *débit(a)* (neut. pl.), L *dēbit(um)* (neut. sing.), n. use of *dēbitus* (ptp. of *dēbere* to owe), equiv. to *dē-* DE- + *(ha)bere* to have] —**debt′less,** *adj.*
—**Syn. 1.** obligation, duty, due.

debt′ lim′it, (in public finance) the legal maximum debt permitted a municipal, State, or national government.

debt′ of hon′or, a gambling debt.

debt·or (det′ər), *n.* **1.** one who is in debt or under financial obligation to another (opposed to *creditor*). **2. debtors,** receivables. [ME *detto(u)r* < OF *detor* < L *dēbitor.* See DEBT, -OR[2]]

debt′ serv′ice, the amount set aside annually in a fund to pay the interest and the part of the principal due on a debt.

de·bug (dē bug′), *v.t.,* **-bugged, -bug·ging.** *Informal.* **1.** to detect and remove defects or errors from. **2.** to remove electronic bugs from (a room or building). [DE- + BUG[1]]

de·bunk (di bungk′), *v.t. Informal.* to strip or divest of pretentious, false, or exaggerated opinions, sentiments, or claims: *to debunk advertising slogans.* [DE- + BUNK[2]] —**de·bunk′er,** *n.*

de·burr (dē bûr′), *v.t.* to remove burrs from (a piece of metal); burr. [DE- + BURR[1]]

de·bus (dē bus′), *v.t., v.i.,* **-bused, -bus·ing** or **-bussed, -bus·sing.** to get out of a bus; alight from a bus. [DE- + BUS]

De·bus·sy (deb′yo͝o sē′, dā′byo͝o-, də byo͞o′sē; *Fr.* də bʏ sē′), *n.* **Claude A·chille** (klōd ə shēl′; *Fr.* klōd ȧ shēl′), 1862–1918, French composer. —**De·bus·sy·an** (di byo͞o′sē ən), *adj.*

de·but (dā byo͞o′, di-, dā′byo͞o, deb′yo͞o), *n.* **1.** a first public appearance on a stage, over the radio, etc. **2.** (of a girl or woman) a formal introduction and entrance into society. **3.** the beginning of a profession, career, etc. —*v.i.* **4.** to make a debut, as in society, in a performing art, etc.: *She decided to debut with several of her friends.* —*v.t.* **5.** to perform (something) for the first time before an audience; introduce: *He didn't know when the orchestra would debut his new symphony.* Also, **dé·but′.** [< F *début,* deriv. of *débuter* to make the first stroke in a game, make one's first appearance, equiv. to *dé-* DE- + *but* goal; see BUTT[2]]

deb·u·tant (deb′yo͝o tänt′, -yə-), *n.* a person who makes a debut into a professional career or before the public. Also, **déb′u·tant′.** [< F *débutant,* prp. of *débuter.* See DEBUT, -ANT]

deb·u·tante (deb′yo͝o tänt′, -tant′), *n.* a girl making a debut, esp. into society. Also, **déb′u·tante′.** [< F; fem. of DEBUTANT]

de·bye (di bī′), *n. Elect.* a unit of measure for electric dipole moments, equal to 10^{-18} statcoulomb-centimeters. *Abbr.:* D [named after P. J. W. DEBYE]

De·bye (de bī′), *n.* **Pe·ter Jo·seph Wil·helm** (pā′tər yō′sef vil′helm), 1884–1966, Dutch physicist, in the U.S. after 1940: Nobel prize for chemistry 1936.

dec-, var. of **deca-** before a vowel: *decare.*

Dec., December.

dec., **1.** (in prescriptions) pour off. [< L *dēcantā*] **2.** deceased. **3.** decimeter. **4.** declension. **5.** decrease **6.** *Music.* decrescendo.

deca-, a learned borrowing from Greek meaning "ten," used in the formation of compound words (*decapod*); specialized in the metric system so that *deca-* gives the multiplication by 10 (*decaliter*) and *deci-* the division by 10 (*deciliter*). Also, **dec-, dek-, deka-.** Cf. **deci-.** [< Gk *deka-,* comb. form of *déka* TEN; c. L *decem*]

dec·a·dal (dek′ə dᵊl), *adj.* of or pertaining to a decade. [DECADE + -AL[1]] —**dec′a·dal·ly,** *adv.*

dec·ade (dek′ād), *n.* **1.** a period of ten years: *the three decades from 1921 to 1951.* **2.** a group, set, or series of ten. [ME < MF < LL *decad-* (s. of *decas*) < Gk *dekad-* (s. of *dekás*) group of ten, equiv. to *dék(a)* ten + *-ad* -ADE[2]]

dec·a·dence (dek′ə dəns, di kād′ᵊns), *n.* **1.** the act or process of falling into an inferior condition or state; decay; deterioration: *Some historians hold that the fall of Rome can be attributed to internal decadence.* **2.** (*often cap.*) the decadent movement in literature. Also, **dec·a·den·cy** (dek′ə dən sē, di kād′ᵊn-). [< MF < ML *dēcadentia,* equiv. to LL *dēcadent-* (s. of *dēcadēns*), prp. of *dēcadere* to fall away (*de-* DE- + *cad-* fall + *-ent-* -ENT) + *-ia;* see -ENCE]
—**Syn. 1.** decline, degeneration, retrogression.

dec·a·dent (dek′ə dənt, di kād′ᵊnt), *adj.* **1.** characterized by decadence; decaying; deteriorating: *a decadent life of excessive money and no sense of responsibility.* **2.** of or like the decadents. —*n.* **3.** one who is decadent. **4.** (*often cap.*) one of a group of French and English writers of the latter part of the 19th century whose works were characterized by great refinement or subtlety of style and a marked tendency toward the artificial and abnormal in content. [back formation from DECADENCE] —**dec·a·dent·ly** (dek′ə dənt lē, di-kā′dᵊnt-), *adv.*

dec·a·drachm (dek′ə dram′), *n.* a silver coin of ancient Greece equal to 10 drachmas. Also, **dekadrachm, dec·a·drach·ma** (dek′ə drak′mə). [DECA- + DRACHM]

Dec·a·dron (dek′ə dron′), *n. Pharm., Trademark.* dexamethasone.

de·caf·fein·ate (dē kaf′ə nāt′, -kaf′ē ə-), *v.t.,* **-at·ed, -at·ing.** to extract caffeine from: *They decaffeinated the coffee.* [DE- + CAFFEIN + -ATE[1]]

dec·a·gon (dek′ə gon′), *n. Geom.* a polygon having 10 angles and 10 sides. [< ML *decagōn(um).* See DECA-, -GON] —**de·cag·o·nal** (də kag′ə nᵊl), *adj.*

144°
Decagon

dec·a·gram (dek′ə gram′), *n. Metric System.* a unit of 10 grams, equivalent to 0.3527 ounce avoirdupois. Also, **dekagram;** *esp. Brit.,* **dec′a·gramme′.** [< F *décagramme.* See DECA-, -GRAM[2]]

dec·a·he·dron (dek′ə hē′drən), *n., pl.* **-drons, -dra** (-drə). *Geom.* a solid figure having 10 faces. [< NL; see DECA-, HEDRON] —**dec·a·he·dral** (dek′ə hē′drəl), *adj.*

dec·a·hy·drate (dek′ə hī′drit, -drāt), *n. Chem.* a hydrate that contains 10 molecules of water, as washing soda, $Na_2CO_3 \cdot 10H_2O$. [DECA- + HYDRATE] —**dec′a·hy′drat·ed,** *adj.*

de·cal (dē′kal, di kal′, dek′əl), *n.* **1.** the art or process of transferring pictures or designs from specially prepared paper to wood, metal, china, glass, etc. **2.** the paper bearing such a picture or design. [shortened form of DECALCOMANIA]

de·cal·ci·fy (dē kal′sə fī′), *v.t.,* **-fied, -fy·ing.** to deprive of lime or calcareous matter, as a bone. [DE- + CALCIFY] —**de·cal·ci·fi·ca·tion** (dē kal′sə fə kā′shən), *n.* —**de·cal′ci·fi′er,** *n.*

de·cal·co·ma·ni·a (di kal′kə mā′nē ə, -mān′yə), *n.* decal. [< F *décalcomanie,* equiv. to *décalco-* (repr. *décalquer* to transfer a tracing of, equiv. to *dé-* DE- + *calquer* to trace) + *-manie* -MANIA]

de·ca·les·cence (dē′kə les′əns), *n. Metall.* absorption of heat at an increased rate by a piece of metal being heated because of a transformation of the metal that is taking place: appears as a darkening of the red color of the metal. [< L *dēcalēscent-* (s. of *dēcalēscēns*) becoming warm. See DE-, CALESCENT, -ENCE] —**de′ca·les′cent,** *adj.*

dec·a·li·ter (dek′ə lē′tər), *n. Metric System.* a unit of 10 liters equivalent to 9.08 quarts U.S. dry measure or 2.64 gallons U.S. liquid measure. Also, **dekaliter;** *esp. Brit.,* **dec′a·li′tre.** [< F *décalitre.* See DECA-, LITER]

Dec·a·logue (dek′ə lôg′, -log′), *n.* See **Ten Commandments.** Ex. 20:2–17. Also, **dec′a·logue′, Dec′a·log′, dec′a·log′.** [ME *decalog* < LL *decalog(us)* < MGk, Gk *dekálogos.* See DECA-, -LOGUE]

De·cam·er·on, The (di kam′ər ən), a collection of 100 tales (1353) by Boccaccio. —**De·cam·er·on·ic** (di kam′ə ron′ik), *adj.*

de·cam·er·ous (di kam′ər əs), *adj.* consisting of 10 parts or divisions. [DECA- + -MEROUS]

dec·a·me·ter (dek′ə mē′tər), *n. Metric System.* a measure of length equal to 10 meters. Also, **dekameter;** *esp. Brit.,* **dec′a·me′tre.** [< F *décamètre.* See DECA-, METER[1]]

de·camp (di kamp′), *v.i.* **1.** to depart from a camp; to pack up equipment and leave a camping ground: *We decamped before the rain began.* **2.** to depart quickly, secretly, or unceremoniously: *The band of thieves decamped in the night.* [< F *décamp(er),* equiv. to *dé-* DIS-[1] + *camper* to encamp; see CAMP[1]] —**de·camp′ment,** *n.*

dec·an (dek′ən), *n.* any of three divisions of 10° within a sign of the zodiac. [ME < LL *decān(us)* chief of ten; see DEAN[1]]

dec·a·nal (dek′ə nᵊl, di kān′ᵊl), *adj.* of or pertaining to a dean or deanery: *decanal responsibilities.* [< LL *decān(us)* DEAN[1] + -AL[1]] —**dec′a·nal·ly, de·can·i·cal·ly** (di kan′ik lē), *adv.*

de·can·cel·late (dē kan′sə lāt′), *v.t.,* **-lat·ed, -lat·ing.** to remove cancellate bone from. [DE- + CANCELLATE] —**de·can′cel·la′tion,** *n.*

dec·ane (dek′ān), *n. Chem.* a hydrocarbon, $C_{10}H_{22}$, of the methane series, occurring in several isomeric forms. [DEC- + -ANE]

de·ca·ni (di kā′nī), *adj.* of or pertaining to the epistle or liturgical south side of a church (opposed to *cantoris*). [< ML *decānī* of the dean (gen. of *decānus*); see DEAN[1]]

dec·a·nor·mal (dek′ə nôr′məl), *adj. Chem.* (of a solution) containing 10 equivalent weights of solute per liter of solution. [DECA- + NORMAL]

de·cant (di kant′), *v.t.* **1.** to pour (wine or other liquid) gently so as not to disturb the sediment. **2.** to pour (a liquid) from one container to another. [< ML *dēcanth(āre),* equiv. to L *dē-* DE- + ML *canthāre,* deriv. of L *canthus* iron band round a wheel < Gk *kánthos* corner of the eye, tire] —**de·can·ta·tion** (dē′kan tā′shən), *n.*

de·cant·er (di kan′tər), *n.* **1.** a bottle used for decanting. **2.** a vessel, usually an ornamental glass bottle, for holding and serving wine, brandy, or the like. [DECANT + -ER[1]]

Decanter

de·cap·i·tate (di kap′i tāt′), *v.t.,* **-tat·ed, -tat·ing.** to cut off the head of; behead: *The dog was decapitated by the wheel of the railroad car.* [< LL *dēcapitāt(us),* ptp. of *dēcapitāre* (see -ATE[1]), equiv. to *dē-* DE- + *capitāre,* deriv. of L *capit-* (s. of *caput*) head] —**de·cap′i·ta′tion,** *n.* —**de·cap′i·ta′tor,** *n.*

dec·a·pod (dek′ə pod′), *n.* **1.** any crustacean of the order *Decapoda,* having five pairs of walking legs, including the crabs, lobsters, crayfish, prawns, shrimps, etc. **2.** any dibranchiate cephalopod having 10 arms, as the cuttlefish, squid, etc. **3.** (*cap.*) a steam locomotive having a two-wheeled front truck, 10 driving wheels, and no rear truck. —*adj.* **4.** belonging or pertaining to the *Decapoda.* **5.** having 10 feet or legs. [< NL *Decapod(a)* name of the order. See DECA-, -POD] —**de·cap·o·dous** (də kap′ə dəs), *adj.*

De·cap·o·da (də kap′ə də), *n.* the order comprising the decapods. [< NL: DECAPOD]

De·cap·o·lis (di kap′ə lis), *n.* a region in the NE part of ancient Palestine: confederacy of 10 cities in the 1st century B.C.

de·car·bon·ate (dē kär′bə nāt′), *v.t.,* **-at·ed, -at·ing.** to remove carbon dioxide from. [DE- + CARBONATE] —**de·car′bon·a′tion,** *n.*

de·car·bon·ise (dē kär′bə nīz′), *v.t.,* **-ised, -is·ing.** *Chiefly Brit.* decarbonize. —**de·car′bon·i·sa′tion,** *n.* —**de·car′bon·is′er,** *n.*

de·car·bon·ize (dē kär′bə nīz′), *v.t.,* **-ized, -iz·ing.** decarburize. [DE- + CARBONIZE] —**de·car′bon·i·za′tion,** *n.* —**de·car′bon·iz′er,** *n.*

de·car·bo·nyl·ate (dē kär′bə nᵊlāt′), *v.t.,* **-lat·ed, -lat·ing.** *Chem.* to remove the carbonyl group from (an organic compound). [DE- + CARBONYLATE] —**de′car·bon′yl·a′tion,** *n.*

de·car·box·yl·ase (dē′kär bok′sə lās′), *n. Biochem.* any of the class of enzymes that catalyze the release of carbon dioxide from the carboxyl group of certain organic acids. Also called **carboxylase.** [DECARBOXYL(ATE) + -ASE]

de·car·box·yl·ate (dē′kär bok′sə lāt′), *v.t.,* **-at·ed, -at·ing.** *Chem.* to remove the carboxyl group from (an organic compound). [DE- + CARBOXYLATE] —**de′car·box′yl·a′tion,** *n.*

de·car·bu·rise (dē kär′bə rīz′, -byə-), *v.t.,* **-rised, -ris·ing.** *Chiefly Brit.* decarburize. —**de·car′bu·ri·sa′tion,** *n.*

de·car·bu·rize (dē kär′bə rīz′, -byə-), *v.t.,* **-rized, -riz·ing.** to remove carbon from (molten steel, automobile cylinders, etc.). [DE- + CARBURIZE] —**de·car′bu·ri·za′tion, de·car′bu·ra′tion,** *n.*

dec·are (dek′âr, de kâr′), *n. Metric System.* a unit of area equal to 10 ares. Also, **dekare.** [< F *décare.* See DECA-, ARE[2]]

de·car·te·lize (di kär′tᵊlīz′), *v.t.,* **-lized, -liz·ing.** to break up or dissolve (a business cartel). [DE- + CARTELIZE] —**de·car′te·li·za′tion,** *n.*

dec·a·stere (dek′ə stēr′), *n. Metric System.* a unit of volume equal to 10 steres. Also, **dekastere.** [< F *décastère.* See DECA-, STERE]

dec·a·style (dek′ə stīl′), *adj. Archit.* **1.** having 10 columns. **2.** (of a classical temple) having 10 columns on one front or on each front. Also, **dec′a·styl′ar.** [< L *decastȳl(os)* < Gk *dekástylos,* equiv. to *déka* DECA- + *stŷlos* pillar]

dec·a·sty·los (dek′ə stī′los), *n.* a decastyle building, as a classical temple. [< L; see DECASTYLE]

de·cas·u·al·ise (dē kazh′o͞o ə līz′), *v.t.,* **-ised, -is·ing.** *Chiefly Brit.* decasualize. —**de·cas′u·al·i·sa′tion,** *n.*

de·cas·u·al·ize (dē kazh′o͞o ə līz′), *v.t.,* **-ized, -iz·ing.** to reduce or eliminate the employment of (casual labor). [DE- + CASUAL + -IZE] —**de·cas′u·al·i·za′tion,** *n.*

dec·a·syl·lab·ic (dek′ə si lab′ik), *adj.* having 10 syllables: *a decasyllabic verse.* [DECA- + SYLLABIC; cf. F *décasyllabique*]

dec·a·syl·la·ble (dek′ə sil′ə bəl), *n.* a word or line of verse of 10 syllables. [DECA- + SYLLABLE]

de·cath·lon (di kath′lon), *n.* an athletic contest comprising 10 different track-and-field events and won by the contestant amassing the highest total score. [DEC- + Gk *âthlon* a contest]

dec·at·ing (dek′ə ting), *n.* a finishing process for making fabric more lustrous, for improving the tactile quality of the nap, and for setting the material to reduce shrinkage. Also, **dec·a·tiz·ing** (dek′ə tī′zing). [< F *décat(ir)* (to) sponge, remove gloss (*dé-* DE- + *catir* to press, add gloss to < VL *coactire* to drive together, equiv. to L *coact(us)*, ptp. of *coagere* (*co-* CO- + *agere* to drive) + *-ire* inf. suffix) + -ING[1]]

De·ca·tur (di kā′tər), *n.* **1. Stephen,** 1779–1820, U.S. naval officer. **2.** a city in central Illinois. 78,004 (1960). **3.** a city in N Alabama. 29,217 (1960). **4.** a city in N Georgia, near Atlanta. 22,026 (1960). **5.** a town in E Indiana. 8327 (1960). **6.** a town in N Texas. 3563 (1960).

de·cay (di kā′), *v.i.* **1.** to decline in excellence, prosperity, health, etc.; deteriorate: *the decay of civilizations in tropical zones.* **2.** to become decomposed; rot: *vegetation that was decaying.* **3.** *Physics.* (of a radioactive nucleus) to change spontaneously into one or more different nuclei in a process in which particles, as alpha particles, are emitted from the nucleus, electrons are captured or lost, or fission takes place. —*v.t.* **4.** to cause to decay or decompose; rot: *The dampness of the climate decayed the books.* —*n.* **5.** a gradual falling into an inferior condition; progressive decline: *the decay of international relations; the decay of the Aztec civilizations after the conquest of Mexico.* **6.** loss of strength, health, intellect, etc.: *His mental decay is distressing.* **7.** decomposition; rot: *Decay made the wood unsuitable for use.* **8.** Also called **disintegration, radioactive decay.** *Physics.* a radioactive process in which a nucleus undergoes spontaneous transformation into one or more different nuclei and simultaneously emits radiation, loses electrons, or undergoes fission. [ME *decay(en)* < ONF *decai(ir)*, equiv. to *de-* DE- + *cair* to fall < LL *cadēre*, L *cadere*] —**de·cay′a·ble,** *adj.* —**de·cayed·ness** (di kād′nis, -kā′id-), *adj.* —**de·cay′less,** *adj.*

—**Syn. 1.** degenerate, wither. **2.** putrefy. DECAY, DECOMPOSE, DISINTEGRATE, ROT imply a deterioration or falling away from a sound condition. DECAY implies either entire or partial dissolution or deterioration by progressive natural changes: *Teeth decay.* DECOMPOSE suggests the reducing of a substance, through natural change or human agency, to its component elements: *Moisture makes some chemical compounds decompose.* DISINTEGRATE emphasizes the breaking up, going to pieces, or wearing away of anything, so that its original wholeness is impaired: *Rocks disintegrate.* ROT is a stronger word than decay and is esp. applied to decaying vegetable matter, which may or may not emit offensive odors: *Potatoes rot.* **5.** deterioration, decadence, impairment, dilapidation, degeneration. **7.** putrefaction. —**Ant. 1.** flourish.

De·cay (di kā′), **Marsh of.** See **Palus Putredinis.**

decay′ se′ries, *Physics.* See **radioactive series.**

Dec·ca (dek′ə), *n.* a British radio navigational aid by which a fix is obtained by determining phase difference between continuous-wave signals from two synchronized fixed signals. Cf. **loran.**

Dec·can (dek′ən), *n.* **1.** the entire peninsula of India S of the Narbada River. **2.** a plateau region in S India between the Narbada and Kristna rivers.

decd., deceased.

de·cease (di sēs′), *n., v.,* **-ceased, -ceas·ing.** —*n.* **1.** departure from life; death. —*v.i.* **2.** to depart from life; die. [ME *deces* < OF < L *dēcess(us)* departure, death, ptp. of *dēcēdere* to go away, equiv. to *dē-* DE- + *cēdere* to go; see CEDE]

—**Syn. 2.** See **die**[1].

de·ceased (di sēst′), *adj.* **1.** no longer living; dead. **2. the deceased, a.** the particular dead person referred to. **b.** dead persons collectively: *It behooves one to speak well of the deceased.* [DECEASE + -ED[2]]

—**Syn. 1.** See **dead.**

de·ce·dent (di sēd′ᵊnt), *n. Law.* a deceased person. [< L *dēcēdent-* (s. of *dēcēdēns*) departing, withdrawing, prp. of *dēcēdere.* See DECEASE, -ENT]

dece′dent estate′, *Law.* the estate left by a decedent.

de·ceit (di sēt′), *n.* **1.** the act or practice of deceiving; concealment or distortion of the truth for the purpose of misleading; fraud; cheating: *Once she'd acquired a reputation for deceit, no one ever trusted her again.* **2.** an act or device intended to deceive; a trick, stratagem. **3.** the quality of being deceitful; falseness: *a man full of deceit.* [ME *deceite* < OF < LL *dēcepta*, n. use of fem. of L *dēceptus* having deceived; see DECEPTION]

—**Syn. 1.** deception, dissimulation. **1, 3.** DECEIT, GUILE, HYPOCRISY, FRAUD, DUPLICITY, TRICKERY refer, with greater or lesser degrees of opprobrium, either to practices designed to mislead or to the qualities that produce those practices. DECEIT is the quality that prompts intentional concealment or perversion of truth for the purpose of misleading: *honest and without deceit.* The quality of GUILE leads to craftiness in the use of deceit: *using guile and trickery to attain one's ends.* HYPOCRISY is the pretense of possessing qualities of sincerity, goodness, devotion, etc.: *It was sheer hypocrisy for him to go to church.* DUPLICITY is the form of deceitfulness which leads one to give two impressions, either or both of which may be false: *the duplicity of a spy working for two governments.* FRAUD refers usually to the practice of subtle deceit or duplicity by which one may benefit himself at another's expense: *an advertiser convicted of fraud.* TRICKERY is the quality which leads to the use of tricks and habitual deception: *notorious for his trickery in business deals.* —**Ant. 3.** honesty, sincerity.

de·ceit·ful (di sēt′fəl), *adj.* **1.** full of deceit; given to deceiving: *A deceitful person cannot keep friends for long.* **2.** misleading; fraudulent; deceptive: *a deceitful action.* [ME; see DECEIT, -FUL] —**de·ceit′ful·ly,** *adv.* —**de·ceit′ful·ness,** *n.*

—**Syn. 1.** insincere, disingenuous, false, hollow, designing, tricky, wily. **2.** illusory, fallacious. —**Ant. 1.** honest. **2.** genuine.

de·ceive (di sēv′), *v.,* **-ceived, -ceiv·ing.** —*v.t.* **1.** to mislead by a false appearance or statement; delude: *They deceived the enemy by disguising their destroyer as a whaler.* **2.** *Archaic.* to beguile or while away (time, etc.). —*v.i.* **3.** to practice deceit; act deceitfully: *an engaging manner that easily deceives.* [ME *deceive(n)* < OF *deceiv(re)* < L *dēcipere*, lit., to ensnare, equiv. to *dē-* DE- + *-cipere*, comb. var. of *capere* to take] —**de·ceiv′a·ble·ness, de·ceiv′a·bil′i·ty,** *n.* —**de·ceiv′a·bly,** *adv.* —**de·ceiv′er,** *n.* —**de·ceiv′ing·ly,** *adv.*

—**Syn. 1.** cozen, dupe, fool, gull, hoodwink, trick, defraud, outwit, entrap, ensnare, betray, bamboozle. See **cheat.**

de·cel·er·ate (dē sel′ə rāt′), *v.t., v.i.,* **-at·ed, -at·ing.** to decrease in velocity: *He decelerates the racer when he nears a curve. The plane decelerated just before landing.* [DE- + (AC)CELERATE] —**de·cel′er·a′tion,** *n.* —**de·cel′er·a′tor,** *n.*

de·cel·er·on (dē sel′ə ron′), *n. Aeron.* an aileron that acts as a brake. [DECELER(ATE + AILER)ON]

de·cem (dā′kem; *Eng.* des′em), *adj. Latin.* ten.

De·cem·ber (di sem′bər), *n.* the 12th month of the year, containing 31 days. [ME *decembre* < OF < L *december* the tenth month of the early Roman year, equiv. to *decem* ten + *-ber* < ?]

De·cem·brist (di sem′brist), *n. Russ. Hist.* a participant in the conspiracy and insurrection against Nicholas I on his accession in December, 1825. [trans. of Russ *dekabrist.* See DECEMBER, -IST]

de·cem·vir (di sem′vər), *n., pl.* **-virs, -vi·ri** (-və rī′). **1.** a member of a permanent board or a special commission of 10 members in ancient Rome, esp. the commission that drew up Rome's first code of law. **2.** a member of any council or ruling body of 10. [< L, orig. pl. *decemvirī*, equiv. to *decem* ten + *virī* men] —**de·cem′vi·ral,** *adj.*

de·cem·vi·rate (di sem′və rit, -rāt′), *n.* **1.** a body of decemvirs. **2.** the office or government of decemvirs. [< L *decemvirāt(us).* See DECEMVIR, -ATE[1]]

de·cen·cy (dē′sən sē), *n., pl.* **-cies. 1.** the state or quality of being decent. **2.** conformity to the recognized standard of propriety, good taste, modesty, etc. **3.** something decent or proper. **4. decencies,** the requirements or amenities of decent living and conduct: *The least you can expect from her is some respect for the decencies.* [< L *dēcentia* comeliness, decency, equiv. to *dēcent-* (s. of *dēcēns*) fitting (see DECENT) + *-ia* n. suffix]

de·cen·na·ry (di sen′ə rē), *n., pl.* **-ries,** *adj.* —*n.* **1.** a decennium. —*adj.* **2.** pertaining to a period of 10 years; decennial. [< L *decenn(is)* of ten years (*dec(em)* ten + *-ennis*, comb. form of *annus* a year) + -ARY]

de·cen·ni·al (di sen′ē əl), *adj.* **1.** of or for 10 years. **2.** occurring every 10 years. —*n.* **3.** a decennial anniversary. **4.** its celebration. [< LL *decenni(um)* a period of ten years (L *decenn(is)* DECENNARY + *-ium* n. suffix) + -AL[1]] —**de·cen′ni·al·ly,** *adv.*

de·cen·ni·um (di sen′ē əm), *n., pl.* **-cen·ni·ums, -cen·ni·a** (-sen′ē ə). a period of 10 years; a decade. [< L; see DECENNIAL]

de·cent (dē′sənt), *adj.* **1.** fitting; appropriate: *She did not have a decent dress for the ball.* **2.** conforming to the recognized standard of propriety, good taste, modesty, etc., as in behavior or speech. **3.** respectable; worthy: *a decent family.* **4.** of fairly attractive appearance: *a decent face.* **5.** adequate; fair; passable: *a decent wage.* **6.** kind; obliging; generous: *Very decent of him to lend me his watch.* **7.** *Informal.* wearing enough clothing to be seen in public: *After knocking on the dressing-room door, he called, "Are you decent?"* [< L *dēcent-* (s. of *dēcēns*) fitting, (prp. of *decēre*; see -ENT), akin to *decus* honor] —**de′cent·ly,** *adv.* —**de′cent·ness,** *n.*

—**Syn. 1.** suitable, apt, fit, becoming. **2.** seemly, proper, decorous. —**Ant. 1.** inappropriate. **2.** unseemly.

de·cen·ter (dē sen′tər), *v.t.* **1.** to put out of center. **2.** to make eccentric. Also, *esp. Brit.,* **decentre.** [DE- + CENTER]

de·cen·tral·ise (dē sen′trə līz′), *v.t.,* **-ised, -is·ing.** *Chiefly Brit.* decentralize. —**de·cen′tral·i·sa′tion,** *n.*

de·cen·tral·ize (dē sen′trə līz′), *v.t.,* **-ized, -iz·ing. 1.** to distribute the administrative powers or functions of over a less concentrated area: *to decentralize the national government.* **2.** to disperse (something) from an area of concentration: *to decentralize the nation's industry.* [DE- + CENTRALIZE] —**de·cen′tral·ist,** *n.* —**de·cen′tral·i·za′tion,** *n.*

de·cen·tre (dē sen′tər), *v.t.,* **-tred, -tring.** *Chiefly Brit.* decenter.

de·cep·tion (di sep′shən), *n.* **1.** the act or state of deceiving or the state of being deceived. **2.** something that deceives or is intended to deceive; fraud; artifice. [ME *decepcioun* < OF < LL *dēceptiōn-* (s. of *dēceptiō*), equiv. to L *dēcept(us)* (ptp. of *dēcipere*; see DECEIVE) + *-iōn-* -ION]

—**Syn. 2.** trick, stratagem, ruse, wile, hoax, imposture, subterfuge, treachery.

decep′tion bed′, any of various kinds of concealed or disguised beds designed in the 18th century.

decep′tion ta′ble, a table of the 18th century made so as to conceal its true function.

de·cep·tive (di sep′tiv), *adj.* apt or tending to deceive: *The enemy's peaceful overtures may be deceptive.* [< NL *dēceptīv(us)*, equiv. to L *dēcept(us)* (see DECEPTION) + *-īvus* -IVE] —**de·cep′tive·ly,** *adv.* —**de·cep′tive·ness,** *n.*

—**Syn.** misleading, delusive, fallacious, specious, false.

decep′tive ca′dence, *Music.* a cadence consisting of a dominant harmony followed by a resolution to a harmony other than the tonic.

de·cer·e·brate (*v.* dē ser′ə brāt′; *n.* dē ser′ə brāt′, -brit), *v.,* **-brat·ed, -brat·ing,** *n.* —*v.t.* **1.** *Surg.* to remove the brain or a section of the brain from the spinal cord. —*n.* **2.** a decerebrated animal. **3.** a patient who, because of brain injury, exhibits behavior characteristic of a decerebrated animal. [DE- + CEREBR- + -ATE[1]] —**de·cer′e·bra′tion,** *n.*

de·cern (di sûrn′), *v.i.* **1.** *Scots Law.* to enter a judicial decree. —*v.t.* **2.** *Obs.* to discern. [ME *decern(en)*, *discern(en)* (to) decide < OF *decerne(r)* < L *dēcernere*, equiv. to *dē-* DE- + *cernere* to separate, decide]

de·cer·ti·fy (dē sûr′tə fī′), *v.t.,* **-fied, -fy·ing.** to withdraw certification from. [DE- + CERTIFY] —**de·cer·ti·fi·ca·tion** (dē sûr′tə fə kā′shən, dē′sər tif′ə-), *n.*

De·chen (dā′kin), *n.* a crater in the second quadrant of the face of the moon: about 7 miles in diameter.

dech·e·nite (dek′ə nīt′), *n.* a rare mineral, lead vanadate, occurring in red, massive aggregates. [named after Heinrich von *Dechen* (1800–89), German geologist; see -ITE[1]]

de·chlo·ri·da·tion (dē klôr′i dā′shən, -klôr′-), *n. Med.* the reduction of the amount of sodium chloride in the body by removing salt from the diet. [DE- + CHLORIDE + -ATION]

de·chlo·ri·dize (dē klôr′i dīz′, -klôr′-), *v.t.,* **-dized, -diz·ing.** *Med.* to lessen body chlorides by the removal of salt from the diet. [DE- + CHLORIDE + -IZE]

deci-, a learned borrowing from French meaning "tenth," introduced as part of the various units of the metric system (*deciliter*); on this model, extended to other systems (*decibel*). Cf. **deca-.** [< F *déci-* < L *decimus* tenth]

dec·i·are (des′ē âr′, -är′; *Fr.* dā sē AR′), *n., pl.* **-ares** (-ârz′, -ärz′; *Fr.* -AR′). *Metric System.* a metric unit of area equivalent to 10 square meters or 11.96 square yards; $^1/_{10}$ are. [< F *déciare.* See DECI-, ARE[2]]

dec·i·bar (des′ə bär′), *n.* a centimeter-gram-second unit of pressure, equal to $^1/_{10}$ bar or 100,000 dynes per square centimeter. [DECI- + BAR[1]]

dec·i·bel (des′ə bel′), *n. Physics.* **1.** a unit of power ratio, the number of units being equal to a constant times the logarithm to the base 10 of the intensities of two sources. **2.** a unit used to compare two voltages or currents, equal to 20 times the common logarithm of the ratio of the voltages or currents measured across equal resistances. **3.** a unit used to express the intensity of a sound wave, equal to 20 times the common logarithm of the ratio of the pressure produced by the sound wave to a reference pressure, usually .0002 microbar or 1 microbar. *Abbr.:* dB, db [DECI- + BEL]

de·cid·a·ble (di sī′də bəl), *adj.* **1.** capable of being decided. **2.** *Logic.* (of an axiom, proposition, etc.) having the property that its consistency or inconsistency with the axioms of a given logical system is determinable. [DECIDE + -ABLE]

de·cide (di sīd′), *v.,* **-cid·ed, -cid·ing.** —*v.t.* **1.** to determine or settle (a question, controversy, or struggle) by giving victory to one side: *The judge decided the case in favor of the plaintiff.* **2.** to adjust or settle (anything in dispute or doubt): *to decide an argument.* **3.** to bring (a person) to a decision: *The new evidence decided him.* —*v.i.* **4.** to settle something in dispute or doubt: *The judge decided in favor of the plaintiff.* **5.** to pronounce a judgment; come to a conclusion: *We arrived too late: they had already decided.* [ME *decide(n)* < MF *decide(r)* < L *dēcīdere*, lit., to cut off, equiv. to *dē-* DE- + *-cīdere* (comb. var. of *caedere* to cut); see SCISSORS] —**de·cid′er,** *n.*

—**Syn. 1.** conclude. DECIDE, RESOLVE, DETERMINE imply settling upon a purpose and being able to adhere to it. To DECIDE is to make up one's mind promptly, clearly, and firmly as to what shall be done and the way to do it: *He decided to go today.* To RESOLVE is usually positively or actively to show firmness of purpose: *He resolved to ask for a promotion.* To DETERMINE is to make up one's mind and then doggedly, and sometimes obstinately, to stick to a fixed or settled purpose: *determined to maintain his position at all costs.* —**Ant. 1.** hesitate.

de·cid·ed (di sī′did), *adj.* **1.** free from ambiguity; unquestionable; unmistakable: *a decided victory.* **2.** free from hesitation or wavering; resolute; determined: *a decided approach to a problem.* [DECIDE + -ED[2]] —**de·cid′ed·ly,** *adv.* —**de·cid′ed·ness,** *n.*

—**Syn. 1.** undeniable, indisputable, positive, certain, emphatic, pronounced, definite, sure, indubitable. **2.** resolved, unhesitating, unwavering. —**Ant. 1, 2.** uncertain.

de·cid·u·a (di sij′o͞o ə), *n., pl.* **-cid·u·as, -cid·u·ae** (-sij′o͞o ē′). *Embryol.* the uterine mucosa that in many of the higher mammals is cast off at parturition. [< NL (fem. n.), L *dēcidu(us)* falling down (n. and adj.); see DECIDUOUS] —**de·cid′u·al,** *adj.*

de·cid·u·ate (di sij′o͞o it), *adj. Anat., Zool.* **1.** having or characterized by a decidua. **2.** (of a placenta) partly formed from the decidua. [< NL *deciduāt(us)*, equiv. to *decidu(a)* DECIDUA + L *-ātus* -ATE[1]]

de·cid·u·i·tis (di sij′o͞o ī′tis), *n. Pathol.* inflammation of the decidua. [< NL; see DECIDUA, -ITIS]

de·cid·u·ous (di sij′o͞o əs), *adj.* **1.** shedding the leaves annually, as trees, shrubs, etc. **2.** falling off or shed at a particular season, stage of growth, etc., as leaves, horns, teeth, etc. **3.** not permanent; transitory. [< L *dēcidu(us)* (adj.) falling down, equiv. to *dēcid(ere)* (to) fall down (*dē-* DE- + *-cidere*, comb. form of *cadere* to fall) + *-us* -OUS] —**de·cid′u·ous·ly,** *adv.* —**de·cid′u·ous·ness,** *n.*

decid′uous tooth′. See **milk tooth.**

dec·i·gram (des′ə gram′), *n. Metric System.* a unit of weight of $^1/_{10}$ gram, equivalent to 1.543 grains. *Abbr.:* dg Also, *esp. Brit.,* **dec′i·gramme′.** [< F *décigramme.* See DECI-, -GRAM[2]]

dec·ile (des′il, -īl), *n. Statistics.* one of the values of a variable which divides the distribution of the variable into 10 groups having equal frequencies. [DEC- + -ILE]

dec·i·li·ter (des′ə lē′tər), *n. Metric System.* a unit of capacity of $^1/_{10}$ liter, equivalent to 6.102 cubic inches, or 3.381 U.S. fluid ounces. *Abbr.:* dl Also, *esp. Brit.,* **dec′i·li′tre.** [< F *décilitre.* See DECI-, LITER]

de·cil·lion (di sil′yən), *n.* **1.** a cardinal number represented in the U.S. and France by the number one followed by 33 zeros, and, in Great Britain and Germany, by the number one followed by 60 zeros. —*adj.* **2.** amounting to one decillion in number. [< L *dec(em)* ten + *-illion*, as in *million*] —**de·cil′lionth,** *adj., n.*

Dec·i·ma (des′ə mə), *n.* a girl's given name.

dec·i·mal (des′ə məl), *adj.* **1.** pertaining to tenths or to the number 10. **2.** proceeding by tens: *a decimal system.* —*n.* **3.** See **decimal fraction.** [< ML *decimāl(is)* of tenths, equiv. to L *decim(a)* tenth (deriv. of *decem* ten) + *-ālis* -AL[1]] —**dec′i·mal·ly,** *adv.*

dec′imal classifica′tion. See **Dewey decimal classification.**

dec′imal frac′tion, *Arith.* a fraction whose denominator is some power of 10, usually indicated by a dot **(decimal point)** written before the numerator: as 0.4 = 4/10; 0.126 = 126/1000. Cf. **common fraction.**

dec·i·mal·ise (des′ə mə līz′), *v.t.*, **-ised, -is·ing.** *Chiefly Brit.* decimalize. —**dec′i·mal·i·sa′tion,** *n.*

dec·i·mal·ize (des′ə mə līz′), *v.t.*, **-ized, -iz·ing.** to reduce to a decimal system. [DECIMAL + -IZE] —**dec′i·mal·i·za′tion,** *n.*

dec′imal point′. See under **decimal fraction.**

dec′imal sys′tem, a system of counting or measurement, the units of which are powers of 10: the numerical system in common worldwide use.

dec·i·mate (des′ə māt′), *v.t.*, **-mat·ed, -mat·ing.** **1.** to destroy a great number or proportion of: *The population was decimated by a plague.* **2.** to select by lot and kill every tenth man of. **3.** to take a tenth of or from. [< L *decimāt(us)* (ptp. of *decimāre*), equiv. to *decim(us)* tenth (deriv. of *decem* ten) + *-ātus* -ATE[1]] —**dec′i·ma′tion,** *n.* —**dec′i·ma′tor,** *n.*

dec·i·me·ter (des′ə mē′tər), *n.* *Metric System.* a unit of length equal to 1/10 meter. *Abbr.:* dm Also, *esp. Brit.*, **dec′i·me′tre.** [< F *décimètre.* See DECI-, METER[1]]

dec·i·mus (des′ə məs; *Lat.* dek′i mŏŏs′), *adj.* (in prescriptions) tenth. [< L]

dec·i·nor·mal (des′ə nôr′məl), *adj.* *Chem.* (of a solution) containing 1/10 the equivalent weight of solute per liter of solution. [DECI- + NORMAL]

de·ci·pher (di sī′fər), *v.t.* **1.** to make out the meaning of (poor or partially obliterated writing, etc.): *to decipher a manuscript.* **2.** to discover the meaning of (anything obscure or difficult to trace or understand): *to decipher hieroglyphics.* **3.** to interpret by the use of a key, as something written in cipher: *to decipher a secret message.* **4.** *Obs.* to depict; portray. [trans. of F *déchiffrer.* See DE-, CIPHER] —**de·ci′pher·a·bil′i·ty,** *n.* —**de·ci′pher·a·ble,** *adj.* —**de·ci′pher·er,** *n.* —**de·ci′pher·ment,** *n.*

de·ci·sion (di sizh′ən), *n.* **1.** the act of deciding; determination, as of a question or doubt, by making a judgment: *He must make a decision between these two contestants.* **2.** a judgment, as one formally pronounced by a court: *The decision is final.* **3.** the act of making up one's mind: *This is a difficult decision.* **4.** something that is decided; a resolution: *He made a poor decision.* **5.** the quality of being decided; firmness: *He spoke with decision.* [< MF < L *dēcīsiōn-* (s. of *dēcīsiō*), lit., a cutting off, equiv. to *dēcīs(us)* (ptp. of *dēcīdere;* see DECIDE) + *-iōn-* -ION] —**de·ci′sion·al,** *adj.*

deci′sion proce′dure, *Logic.* a procedure, as an algorithm, for determining in a finite number of steps the validity of any of a certain class of propositions.

de·ci·sive (di sī′siv), *adj.* **1.** having the power or quality of determining; putting an end to controversy: *The decisive test of the missile was whether or not it would work. His argument was the decisive one.* **2.** characterized by or displaying decision; resolute; determined: *The general was known for his decisive manner.* [< ML *dēcīsīv(us)*, equiv. to L *dēcīs(us)* (see DECISION) + *-īvus* -IVE] —**de·ci′sive·ly,** *adv.* —**de·ci′sive·ness,** *n.*
—**Syn. 1.** conclusive, final. **2.** firm.

dec·i·stere (des′i stēr′), *n.* *Metric System.* a unit of volume equal to 1/10 stere. *Abbr.:* ds [< F *décistère.* See DECI-, STERE]

De·cius (dē′shəs, desh′əs), *n.* (*Gaius Messius Quintus Trajanus Decius*) A.D. c201–251, emperor of Rome 249?–251.

De Ci·vi·ta·te De·i (dē siv′i tā′tē dē′ī; dā chē′vē tä′tä dā′ē). See **City of God, The.**

deck (dek), *n.* **1.** *Naut.* **a.** a floorlike surface wholly or partially occupying one level of a hull, superstructure, or deckhouse, generally cambered, and often serving as a member for strengthening the structure of a vessel. **b.** the space between such a surface and the next such surface above: *Our stateroom was on B deck, not on the promenade deck.* **2.** any open platform suggesting an exposed deck of a ship. **3.** See **flight deck** (def. 2). **4.** a flat or nearly flat watertight surface, as at the top of a French roof. **5.** a floor or roof surface composed of decking units. **6.** a pack of playing cards. **7.** bank[3] (def. 7). **8.** *Slang.* a small packet of a narcotic, esp. heroin. **9.** **clear the decks, a.** to prepare for combat, as by removing all unnecessary gear. **b.** to prepare for some activity or work, as by getting rid of hindrances. **10.** **hit the deck,** *Slang.* **a.** to rise from bed. **b.** to fall or be knocked to the ground or floor. **11.** **on deck,** *Informal.* **a.** prepared to act or work; ready. **b.** next in line, coming up: *a batter on deck; What's on deck for the next meeting?* —*adj.* **12.** (of a bridge truss) having a deck or floor upon or above the structure. Cf. **through** [ME *dekke* material for covering < MD *dec* roof, (def. 20). covering]
—*v.t.* **13.** to clothe or attire (people) or array (rooms, houses, etc.) in something ornamental or decorative (often fol. by *out*): *She was all decked out in her Sunday best. The church was decked with holly for the holiday season.* **14.** to furnish with a deck. **15.** *Informal.* to knock down; floor: *The challenger decked him in the first round.* [< D, MD *dekke(n)*; c. MLG *decken;* cf. THATCH] —**deck′er,** *n.*
—**Syn. 13.** bedeck, garnish, trim, bedizen, adorn, embellish; dress.

deck′ bolt′, *Shipbuilding.* a flat-headed bolt for fastening down deck planking.

deck′ chair′, a folding chair, usually with arms and a full-length leg rest, commonly used on the decks of ships. Also called **steamer chair.**

deck′ depart′ment, *Naut.* the part of a merchant vessel's crew that is responsible for navigation, cargo handling, maintenance of deck gear and lifesaving equipment, and mooring.

deck·el (dek′əl), *n.* deckle.

Deck·er (dek′ər), *n.* **Thomas.** See **Dekker, Thomas.**

deck′ gang′, *Naut.* **1.** (on a ship) the seamen who are on duty but not on watch. **2.** the longshoremen working on board a ship during loading and unloading.

deck′ hand′, **1.** *Naut.* a seaman belonging to the deck department of a vessel. **2.** *Theat.* a stagehand.

deck·head (dek′hed′), *n.* *Naut.* the under surface of a deck. [DECK + HEAD]

deck′ hook′, *Naut.* hook (def. 13).

deck′ horse′, *Naut.* a transverse metal rod on which the traveler of a boom slides. Also called **leefang, leefange.**

deck·house (dek′hous′), *n., pl.* **-hous·es** (-hou′ziz). *Naut.* any enclosed structure projecting above the weather deck of a vessel and surrounded by exposed deck area on all sides. Cf. **superstructure** (def. 3). [DECK + HOUSE]

deck·ing (dek′ing), *n.* **1.** material, as paper or fiberboard, treated in various ways as a waterproof covering for a roof or deck. **2.** material of concrete, asbestos, steel, or the like, in the form of self-supporting flooring or roofing units laid between joists or rafters. [DECK + -ING[1]]

deck·le (dek′əl), *n.* **1.** *Papermaking.* a board, usually of stainless steel, fitted under part of the wire in a Fourdrinier machine for supporting the pulp stack before it is sufficiently formed to support itself on the wire. **2.** See **deckle edge.** Also, **deckel.** [< G *Deckel* cover, lid, equiv. to *deck(en)* (to) cover (see DECK) + *-el* -LE]

deck′le edge′, the irregular, untrimmed edge of handmade paper, often used for ornamental effect in fine books and stationery, now often produced artificially on machine-made paper. Also called **deckle.**

deck·le-edged (dek′əl ejd′), *adj.* having a deckle edge: *deckle-edged paper for stationery.*

deck′ light′, *Naut.* a skylight for a 'tween deck, built flush with the upper deck.

deck′ load′, *Naut.* cargo carried on an open deck of a ship.

deck′ log′, *Naut.* a log filled in by the officer of the watch at the end of each watch, giving details of weather, navigation, unusual happenings, etc. Also called **rough log, scrap log.**

deck′ of′ficer, *Naut.* any officer whose responsibilities include navigation, cargo handling, etc.

deck·pipe (dek′pīp′), *n.* *Naut.* spillpipe. [DECK + PIPE[1]]

deck′ plate′, *Carpentry.* a purlin plate at the edge of a deck.

deck′ ten′nis, a variety of tennis played usually on the deck of a ship, in which a ring, generally of rubber or Manila rope, is thrown and caught, using only one hand, between two opponents standing on opposite sides of a net.

deck′ watch′, (on a ship) a precision watch used on deck for navigational purposes to avoid disturbing the chronometer. Also called **hack watch.**

decl., declension.

de·claim (di klām′), *v.i.* **1.** to speak aloud rhetorically; make a formal speech: *Brutus declaimed from the steps of the Roman senate building.* **2.** to inveigh (usually fol. by *against*): *He declaimed against the high rents in slums.* **3.** to speak or write for oratorical effect, without sincerity or sound argument. —*v.t.* **4.** to utter aloud in a rhetorical manner: *to declaim a speech.* [ME *declam(en)* < L *dēclām(āre)*, equiv. to *dē-* DE- + *clāmāre* to cry, shout; see CLAIM] —**de·claim′er,** *n.*

dec·la·ma·tion (dek′lə mā′shən), *n.* **1.** the act or art of declaiming. **2.** exercise in oratory or elocution, as in the recitation of a classic speech. **3.** speech or writing for oratorical effect. **4.** *Music.* the proper enunciation of the words, as in recitative. [< L *dēclāmātiōn-* (s. of *dēclāmātiō*), equiv. to *dēclāmāt(us)* (ptp. of *dēclāmāre* to DECLAIM; see -ATE[1]) + *-iōn-* -ION]

de·clam·a·to·ry (di klam′ə tôr′ē, -tôr′ē), *adj.* **1.** pertaining to or characterized by declamation. **2.** merely rhetorical; stilted: *a pompous, declamatory manner of speech.* [< L *dēclāmātōr(ius)*, equiv. to *dēclāmāt(us)* (see DECLAMATION) + *-ōrius* -ORY[1]]

de·clar·ant (di klâr′ənt), *n.* **1.** one who declares or makes a declaration or statement. **2.** *Law.* an alien who has formally declared his intention before a court of record to become a citizen of the U.S. [DECLARE + -ANT]

dec·la·ra·tion (dek′lə rā′shən), *n.* **1.** the act of declaring; announcement: *a declaration of a dividend.* **2.** a positive, explicit, or formal statement; proclamation: *a declaration of war.* **3.** something that is announced, avowed, or proclaimed: *The declaration will affect everyone.* **4.** a document embodying an announcement or proclamation: *He posted the declaration in a public place.* **5.** *Law.* **a.** a formal statement in which a plaintiff presents his claim in an action. **b.** a complaint. **c.** a statement, esp. by a witness. **d.** a statement made to an official. **6.** *Cards.* **a.** *Bridge.* a bid, esp. the successful bid. **b.** the statement during the game of the points earned by a player, in bezique or other games. **7.** a statement of goods, income, etc., esp. for the assessment of duty, tax, or the like. [ME *declaracioun* < L *dēclārātiōn-* (s. of *dēclārātiō*) explanation, equiv. to *dēclārāt(us)* (ptp. of *dēclārāre* to explain, DECLARE; see -ATE[1]) + *-iōn-* -ION]

Declara′tion of Indepen′dence, **1.** the public act by which the Second Continental Congress, on July 4, 1776, declared the Colonies to be free and independent of England. **2.** the document embodying it.

de·clar·a·tive (di klar′ə tiv), *adj.* serving to declare, make known, or explain: *a declarative statement.* Also, **de·clar·a·to·ry** (di klar′ə tôr′ē, -tôr′ē). [< LL *dēclārātīv(us)* explanatory, equiv. to L *dēclārāt(us)* (see DECLARATION) + *-īvus* -IVE] —**de·clar′a·tive·ly,** *adv.*

declar′atory judg′ment, *Law.* a judgment that merely decides the rights of the parties in a given transaction, situation, or dispute, but does not order any action.

de·clare (di klâr′), *v.*, **-clared, -clar·ing.** —*v.t.* **1.** to make known clearly, esp. in explicit or formal terms: *to declare one's position in a controversy.* **2.** to announce officially; proclaim: *to declare a state of emergency; to declare someone winner.* **3.** to state emphatically: *He declared that her allegation was a lie.* **4.** to manifest; reveal; show: *His attendance at the rally declared his political allegiance.* **5.** to make due statement of: *to declare goods for duty, income for taxation, etc.* **6.** to make (a dividend) payable. **7.** *Bridge.* to name (a certain suit) as trumps or to establish the bid at no-trump. —*v.i.* **8.** to make a declaration. **9.** to proclaim oneself (usually fol. by *for* or *against*): *He declared against the proposal.* **10.** *Cricket.* (of a team) to surrender a turn at bat in an innings before 10 players are put out. [ME *declare(n)* < L *dēclār(āre)* (to) explain, equiv. to *dē-* DE- + *clārāre* to make clear (*clār(us)* CLEAR + *-āre* inf. suffix)] —**de·clar′a·ble,** *adj.*
—**Syn. 3.** aver, asseverate, state. DECLARE, AFFIRM, ASSERT, PROTEST imply making something known emphatically, openly, or formally. To DECLARE is to make known, sometimes in the face of actual or potential contradiction: *to declare someone the winner of a contest.* To AFFIRM is to make a statement based on one's reputation for knowledge or veracity, or so related to a generally recognized truth that denial is not likely: *to affirm the necessity of high standards.* To ASSERT is to state boldly, usually without other proof than personal authority or conviction: *to assert that the climate is changing.* To PROTEST is to affirm publicly, as if in the face of doubt: *to protest that a newspaper account is misleading.* **4.** disclose, publish. —**Ant. 3.** deny.

de·clared (di klârd′), *adj.* avowed; professed: *a declared liberal.* [DECLARE + -ED[2]] —**de·clar·ed·ly** (di klâr′id lē), *adv.*

de·clar·er (di klâr′ər), *n.* **1.** one who or that which declares. **2.** *Bridge.* the player who plays the contract; dummy's partner. [DECLARE + -ER[1]]

de·class (dē klas′, -kläs′), *v.t.* to remove or degrade from one's social class, rank, or the like. [trans. of F *déclasser.* See DE-, CLASS]

dé·clas·sé (dā′klə sā′, -kla-; *Fr.* dā klȧ sā′), *adj.* reduced or belonging to or characteristic of a lower or low social class: *a déclassé neighborhood.* Also, *referring to a woman,* **dé·clas·sée′.** [< F, ptp. of *déclasser.* See DE-, CLASS]

de·clas·si·fy (dē klas′ə fī′), *v.t.*, **-fied, -fy·ing.** *U.S. Govt., Mil.* to remove the classification from (information, a document, etc.). Cf. **classification** (def. 5). [DE- + CLASSIFY] —**de·clas·si·fi·ca·tion** (dē klas′ə fə kā′shən), *n.*

de·clen·sion (di klen′shən), *n.* **1.** *Gram.* **a.** the inflection of nouns and of words similarly inflected for categories such as case and number. **b.** the whole set of inflected forms of such a word, or the recital therof in a fixed order. **c.** a class of such words having similar sets of inflected forms, as the Latin second declension. **2.** an act or instance of declining. **3.** a bending, sloping, or moving downward: *land with a gentle declension toward the sea.* **4.** deterioration; decline. **5.** deviation, as from a standard. [irreg. < L *dēclīnātiōn-*, lit., a turning aside; see DECLINATION] —**de·clen′sion·al·ly,** *adv.*

de·clen·sion·al (di klen′shə nᵊl), *adj.* of or pertaining to the grammatical declension. [DECLENSION + -AL[1]] —**de·clen′sion·al·ly,** *adv.*

de·clin·a·ble (di klī′nə bəl), *adj.* *Gram.* able to be declined. [ME < MF, equiv. to *decline(r)* (to) DECLINE + *-able* -ABLE]

dec·li·nate (dek′lə nāt′, -nit), *adj.* having a downward curve or slope; bending away, as from the horizontal: *a declinate flower.* [< L *dēclīnāt(us)*, ptp. of *dēclīnāre.* See DECLINE, -ATE[1]]

dec·li·na·tion (dek′lə nā′shən), *n.* **1.** a bending, sloping, or moving downward. **2.** deterioration; decline. **3.** a swerving or deviating, as from a standard. **4.** a polite refusal. **5.** *Astron.* the angular distance of a heavenly body from the celestial equator, measured on the great circle passing through the celestial pole and the body. **6.** the horizontal angle between the direction of true north and magnetic north: variable according to geographic location. **7.** the formal refusal by a nominee of a nomination to public office. [ME *declinacioun* < OF *declinacion* < L *dēclīnātiōn-* (s. of *dēclīnātiō*), equiv. to *dēclīnāt(us)*, lit., turned aside (ptp. of *dēclīnāre;* see DECLINE, -ATE[1]) + *-iōn-* -ION] —**dec′li·na′tion·al,** *adj.*

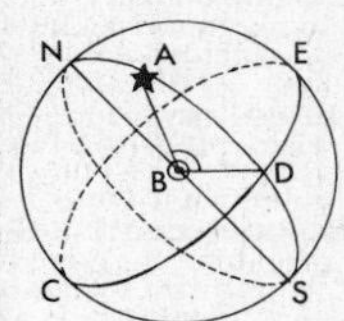

Declination
A, Star; B, Earth; Angle DBA, Declination of star; N, North celestial pole; S, South celestial pole; CDE, Celestial equator

de·clin·a·to·ry (di klī′nə tôr′ē, -tôr′ē), *adj.* expressing refusal; implying declination. [< ML *dēclīnātōri(us)*, equiv. to *dēclīnāt(us)* (see DECLINATION) + *-ōrius* -ORY[1]]

de·clin·a·ture (di klī′nə chər), *n.* the act of refusing. [alter. of earlier *declinatour*, influenced by L *dēclīnātūra.* See DECLINATION, -URE]

de·cline (di klīn′), *v.*, **-clined, -clin·ing,** *n.* —*v.t.* **1.** to withhold or deny consent to do, enter into or upon, etc.; refuse: *He declined to say more about it. He declined the offer with thanks.* **2.** to express inability or reluctance to accept; refuse with courtesy: *to decline an invitation or an offer.* **3.** to cause to slope or incline downward. **4.** *Gram.* **a.** to inflect (a noun, pronoun, or adjective), as Latin *puella*, declined *puella, puellae, puellae, puellam, puellā* in the five cases of the singular. **b.** to recite or display all or some subset of the inflected forms of a noun, pronoun, or adjective in a fixed order. —*v.i.* **5.** to express courteous refusal; refuse: *We sent him an invitation but he declined.* **6.** to bend or slant down; slope downward; descend: *The hill declines to the lake.* **7.** to follow a downward course or path: *The road declines sharply. The sun declined in the skies.* **8.** to draw toward the close, as the day. **9.** to stoop; condescend, as to an unworthy object or level: *He has declined to a disgraceful state.* **10.** to fail in strength, vigor, character, value, etc.; deteriorate. **11.** to fail or dwindle; sink or fade away: *to decline in popularity; The plot declined toward the end of the novel.* **12.** *Gram.* to be characterized by declension. —*n.* **13.** a downward slope; declivity. **14.** a failing or gradual loss, as in strength, character, value, etc.; deterioration: *the decline of the Roman Empire; a mental decline.* **15.** a downward movement, as of prices, population, etc.; diminution: *the decline of the stock market.* **16.** progress downward or toward the close, as of the sun or the day. **17.** a gradual deterioration of the physical powers, as in later life or in disease: *After his seventieth birthday he went into a decline.* **18.** the last part: *World War II started its decline during March, 1945.* [ME *decline(n)* < OF: to inflect, turn aside, sink < L *dēclīn(āre)* (to) slope, incline, bend; c. Gk *klínein*] —**de·clin′a·ble,** *adj.* —**de·clin′er,** *n.*
—**Syn. 1.** reject. See **refuse**[1]. **10.** degenerate, decay, weaken, diminish, languish. **13.** hill. **14.** retrogression, degeneration, enfeeblement, weakening. —**Ant. 6.** rise. **10.** improve.

Decline′ and Fall′ of the Ro′man Em′pire, The, a history in six volumes (1776–88) by Edward Gibbon.

dec·li·nom·e·ter (dek′lə nom′i tər), *n.* an instrument for measuring declination. [comb. form repr. L *dēclīnāre* (see DECLINE) + -O- + -METER]

de·clive (di klīv′), *adj. Obs.* declivous. [< L *dēclīv(is)* sloping downwards; see DECLIVITY]

de·cliv·i·tous (di kliv′i təs), *adj.* having a somewhat steep downward slope. [DECLIVIT(Y) + -OUS] **—de·cliv′i·tous·ly,** *adv.*

de·cliv·i·ty (di kliv′i tē), *n., pl.* **-ties.** a downward slope, as of ground (opposed to *acclivity*). [< L *dēclīvitāt-* (s. of *dēclīvitās*) a slope, hill, equiv. to *dēclīvus* sloping downwards (*dē-* DE- + *clīv(us)* slope, hill) + *-itāt-* -ITY]

de·cli·vous (di klī′vəs), *adj.* sloping downward. Also, **de·cli′vent.** [< L *dēclīv(us)* (see DECLIVITY) + -OUS]

Dec·lo·my·cin (dek′lō mī′sin), *n. Pharm., Trademark.* demethylchlortetracycline.

de·coct (di kokt′), *v.t.* to extract the flavor or essence of by boiling. [< L *dēcoct(us)* boiled down; see DECOCTION]

de·coc·tion (di kok′shən), *n.* **1.** the act of decocting. **2.** *Pharm.* **a.** an extract obtained by decocting. **b.** water in which a crude vegetable drug has been boiled and which therefore contains the constituents or principles of the substance soluble in boiling water. [ME *decoccioun* < OF *decoction* < LL *dēcoctiōn-* (s. of *dēcoctiō*) a boiling down, equiv. to *dēcoct(us)*, ptp. of *dēcoquere* (*dē-* DE- + *coquere* to COOK) + *-iōn-* -ION] **—de·coc′tive,** *adj.*

de·code (dē kōd′), *v.,* **-cod·ed, -cod·ing.** **—***v.t.* **1.** to translate (a message) from code into the original language or form. **—***v.i.* **2.** to work at decoding: *He learned to decode while assigned to the embassy.* [DE- + CODE]

de·cod·er (dē kō′dər), *n.* **1.** one who decodes messages or the like. **2.** a device for decoding cryptograms, codes, or the like, as an electric or electronic apparatus which transforms arbitrary input signals into letters, words, etc. **3.** *Navigation, Radio.* an electronic circuit designed to respond only to a certain signal or signals and to reject others. **4.** *Electronics.* (in a computer) a circuit designed to produce a single output when actuated by a certain combination of inputs. [DE- + CODER]

de·col·late (di kol′āt), *v.t.,* **-lat·ed, -lat·ing.** to behead; decapitate. [< L *dēcollāt(us)* beheaded (ptp. of *dēcoll(āre)*, equiv. to *dē-* DE- + *coll(āre)* (see COLLAR) + *-ātus* -ATE[1]] **—de·col·la·tion** (dē′kə lā′shən), *n.* **—de′col·la′tor,** *n.*

dé·colle·tage (dā′kol täzh′, -kol ə-, dek′ə lə-; *Fr.* dā kôl tazh′), *n.* **1.** the neckline of a dress cut low in the front or back and often across the shoulders. **2.** a décolleté garment or costume. Also, **de′colle·tage′.** [< F, equiv. to *décollet(er)* (see DÉCOLLETÉ) + *-age* -AGE]

dé·colle·té (dā′kol tā′, -kol ə-, dek′ə lə-; *Fr.* dā kôl tā′), *adj.* **1.** (of a garment) low-necked. **2.** wearing a low-necked garment. Also, **de′colle·te′.** [< F, ptp. of *décolleter* to bare the neck, equiv. to *dé-* DE- + *collet* COLLAR (see -ET) + *-er* inf. suffix]

de·col·o·nise (dē kol′ə nīz′), *v.t.,* **-nised, -nis·ing.** *Chiefly Brit.* decolonize. **—de·col′o·ni·sa′tion,** *n.*

de·col·o·nize (dē kol′ə nīz′), *v.t.,* **-nized, -niz·ing.** **1.** to release from the status of a colony. **2.** to free a colony or colonies to become self-governing or independent. [DE- + COLONIZE] **—de·col′o·ni·za′tion,** *n.*

de·col·or (dē kul′ər), *v.t.* to deprive of color; bleach. Also, *esp. Brit.,* **de·col′our.** [< L *dēcolōr(āre)*, equiv. to *dē-* DE- + *colōrāre* to COLOR] **—de′col·or·a′tion, de′col·our·a′tion,** *n.*

de·col·or·ant (dē kul′ər ənt), *adj.* **1.** having the property of removing color; bleaching. **—***n.* **2.** a decolorant substance or agent. Also, *esp. Brit.,* **de·col′our·ant.** [DECOLOR + -ANT]

de·col·or·ise (dē kul′ə rīz′), *v.t.,* **-ised, -is·ing.** *Chiefly Brit.* decolorize. **—de·col′or·i·sa′tion,** *n.* **—de·col′or·is′er,** *n.*

de·col·or·ize (dē kul′ə rīz′), *v.t.,* **-ized, -iz·ing.** to decolor. [DE- + COLORIZE] **—de·col′or·i·za′tion,** *n.* **—de·col′or·iz′er,** *n.*

de·col·our·ise (dē kul′ə rīz′), *v.t.,* **-ised, -is·ing.** *Chiefly Brit.* decolorize. **—de·col′our·i·sa′tion,** *n.* **—de·col′our·is′er,** *n.*

de·col·our·ize (dē kul′ə rīz′), *v.t.,* **-ized, -iz·ing.** *Chiefly Brit.* decolorize. **—de·col′our·i·za′tion,** *n.* **—de·col′our·iz′er,** *n.*

de·com·mis·sion (dē′kə mish′ən), *v.t.* to retire (a ship, airplane, etc.) from active service. [DE- + COMMISSION]

de·com·pen·sa·tion (dē′kom pən sā′shən), *n. Med.* the inability of a diseased heart to compensate for its defect. [DE- + COMPENSATION]

de·com·pose (dē′kəm pōz′), *v.,* **-posed, -pos·ing.** **—***v.t.* **1.** to separate or resolve into constituent parts or elements; disintegrate: *The bacteria decomposed the milk into its solid and liquid elements.* **—***v.i.* **2.** to rot; putrefy: *The egg began to decompose after a day in the sun.* [< F *décompose(r)*, equiv. to *dé-* DIS-[1] + *composer* to COMPOSE] **—de′com·pos′a·bil′i·ty,** *n.* **—de′com·pos′a·ble,** *adj.*
—Syn. 1. distill, fractionate, analyze. **2.** See **decay.**

de·com·posed (dē′kəm pōzd′), *adj.* **1.** having undergone decomposition. **2.** (of a feather) having the barbs separate, hanging loosely, and not interconnected by barbules. [DECOMPOSE + -ED[2]]

de·com·pos·er (dē′kəm pō′zər), *n.* **1.** one who or that which decomposes. **2.** *Ecol.* an organism, usually a bacterium or fungus, that breaks down the cells of dead plants and animals into simpler substances. [DECOMPOSE + -ER[1]]

de·com·po·si·tion (dē′kom pə zish′ən), *n.* **1.** the act or process of decomposing. **2.** the state of being decomposed; disintegration; decay. [prob. < F *décomposition*, deriv. of *décomposer* to DECOMPOSE; see COMPOSITION]

de·com·pound (dē′kəm pound′), *v.t.* **1.** to decompose. **2.** *Obs.* to compound a second or further time. **—***adj.* **3.** *Bot.* divided into compound divisions. **4.** composed of things which are themselves compound. [DE- + COMPOUND[1]]

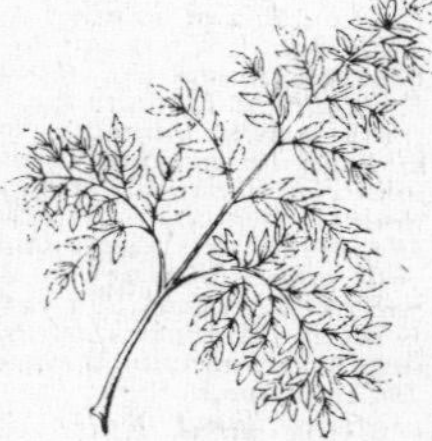
Decompound leaves

de·com·press (dē′kəm pres′), *v.t., v.i.* to undergo or cause to undergo decompression. [trans. of F *décomprimer.* See DE-, COMPRESS] **—de′com·pres′sive,** *adj.*

de·com·pres·sion (dē′kəm presh′ən), *n.* **1.** the act or process of releasing from pressure. **2.** the gradual return of persons, as divers or construction workers, to normal atmospheric pressure after working in deep water or in air under compression. **3.** *Surg.* the procedure of relieving increased cranial, cardiac, or orbital pressure. [prob. < F *décompression.* See DE-, COMPRESSION]

decompres′sion sick′ness, *Pathol.* See **caisson disease.**

de·con·cen·trate (dē kon′sən trāt′), *v.t.,* **-trat·ed, -trat·ing.** to diminish or end the concentration of or within (a group, organization, etc.). [DE- + CONCENTRATE]

de·con·gest (dē′kən jest′), *v.t.* to diminish or end the congestion of. [DE- + CONGEST]

de·con·ges·tant (dē′kən jes′tənt), *n. Med.* an agent that relieves congestion. [DECONGEST + -ANT]

de·con·ges·tive (dē′kən jes′tiv), *adj. Med.* relieving or tending to relieve congestion. [DE- + CONGESTIVE]

de·con·se·crate (dē kon′sə krāt′), *v.t.,* **-crat·ed, -crat·ing.** to deprive (a place or object) of sanctity acquired through consecration. [< F *déconsacrer.* See DE-, CONSECRATE] **—de·con′se·cra′tion,** *n.*

De Con·so·la·ti·o·ne Phi·lo·so·phi·ae (dā kōn′sō lä′tē ō′ne fē′lō sō fē′ī). See **Consolation of Philosophy, The.**

de·con·tam·i·nate (dē′kən tam′ə nāt′), *v.t.,* **-nat·ed, -nat·ing.** **1.** to make free of contamination; purify: *to decontaminate a sickroom.* **2.** to make (an object or area) safe for unprotected personnel by removing, neutralizing, or destroying any harmful substance, as poisonous gas, radioactive material, etc. [DE- + CONTAMINATE] **—de′con·tam′i·na′tion,** *n.* **—de′con·tam′i·na′tive,** *adj.* **—de′con·tam′i·na′tor,** *n.*

de·con·trol (dē′kən trōl′), *v.,* **-trolled, -trol·ling,** *n.* **—***v.t.* **1.** to remove controls from: *to decontrol prices or rents.* **—***n.* **2.** the removal of control. [DE- + CONTROL]

dé·cor (dā kôr′, di-, dā′kôr), *n.* **1.** style or mode of decoration, as of a room, building, or the like: *modern office décor; a bedroom having a Spanish décor.* **2.** decoration in general; ornamentation: *beads, baubles, and other décor.* **3.** *Theat.* scenic decoration; scenery. Also, **de·cor′.** [< F, deriv. of *décorer* to DECORATE]

De·co·rah (də kôr′ə, -kōr′-), *n.* a town in NE Iowa. 6435 (1960).

dec·o·rate (dek′ə rāt′), *v.t.,* **-rat·ed, -rat·ing.** **1.** to furnish or adorn with something ornamental or becoming; embellish: *to decorate walls with murals.* **2.** to plan and execute the design, furnishings, and ornamentation of the interior of (a house, office, apartment, etc.) esp. by selecting colors, fabrics, styles of furniture, by making minor structural changes, etc.: *Their house is decorated in French Provincial style.* **3.** to confer distinction upon by a badge, a medal of honor, etc.: *to decorate a soldier for valor.* [ME (adj.) < L *decorāt(us)* (ptp. of *decorāre*), equiv. to *decor-* (s. of *decus*) an ornament, splendor, honor (see DECENT) + *-ātus* -ATE[1]]

Dec·o·rat·ed (dek′ə rā′tid), *adj.* noting or pertaining to the English Gothic architecture of the late 13th through the late 14th centuries, characterized by curvilinear tracery, elaborate ornamental sculpture and vaulting, and by refinement of stonecutting techniques. [DECORATE + -ED[2]]

dec·o·ra·tion (dek′ə rā′shən), *n.* **1.** the act of decorating: *His profession involves the decoration of interiors as well as the design of buildings.* **2.** adornment; embellishment: *Ornate decoration of picture frames is an art in itself.* **3.** See **interior decoration.** **4.** a badge, medal, etc., conferred and worn as a mark of honor: *a decoration for bravery.* [< LL *decorātiōn-* (s. of *decorātiō*) an ornament. See DECORATE, -ION]

Decora′tion Day′. See **Memorial Day.**

dec·o·ra·tive (dek′ər ə tiv, dek′rə-, dek′ə rā′-), *adj.* **1.** serving or tending to decorate. **2.** *Fine Arts.* serving only to decorate, in contrast to providing a meaningful experience. [DECORATE + -IVE] **—dec′o·ra·tive·ly,** *adv.* **—dec′o·ra·tive·ness,** *n.*

dec′orative sur′gery. See **cosmetic surgery.**

dec·o·ra·tor (dek′ə rā′tər), *n.* **1.** one who decorates. **2.** See **interior decorator.** [DECORATE + -OR[2]]

dec·o·rous (dek′ər əs, di kōr′əs, -kôr′-), *adj.* characterized by propriety in conduct, manners, appearance, character, etc. [< L *decōr(us)* seemly, equiv. to *decōr-* (see DECORE) + -OUS] **—dec′o·rous·ly,** *adv.* **—dec′o·rous·ness,** *n.*
—Syn. proper, seemly, becoming, decent, sedate, conventional. **—Ant.** undignified.

de·cor·ti·cate (dē kôr′tə kāt′), *v.t.,* **-cat·ed, -cat·ing.** **1.** to remove the bark, husk, or outer covering from. **2.** *Surg.* to remove the cortex from (an organ or structure). [< L *dēcorticāt(us)* peeled (ptp. of *dēcorticāre*), equiv. to *dē-* DE- + *corticātus* having bark, shell; see CORTICATE] **—de·cor′ti·ca′tor,** *n.*

de·cor·ti·ca·tion (dē kôr′tə kā′shən), *n.* **1.** the act or process of decorticating. **2.** Also, **de·cor·ti·za·tion** (dē kôr′ti zā′shən). *Surg.* the removal of the cortex, the enveloping membrane, or a fibrinous covering from an organ or structure. [< L *dēcorticātiōn-* (s. of *dēcorticātiō*) the act of peeling off bark. See DECORTICATE, -ION]

de·co·rum (di kōr′əm, -kôr′-), *n.* **1.** dignified propriety of behavior, speech, dress, etc. **2.** something that is proper or suitable; fitness; congruity; propriety. **3.** an observance or requirement of polite society. [< L *decōrum* (neut. of *decōrus* used as n.). See DECOROUS]
—Syn. 1. politeness, manners, dignity. See **etiquette.**

dé·cou·page (dā′ko͞o päzh′), *n.* **1.** the art, technique, or method of decorating something with paper cutouts. **2.** something produced by this technique. Also, **dé·cou·page** (dā′ko͞o päzh′; *Fr.* dā ko͞o pȧzh′). [< F *découpage* a cutting out, equiv. to MF *decoup(er)* (to) cut out (*de-* from, out of (see DE-) + *couper* to cut) + *-age* -AGE]

de·cou·ple (dē kup′əl), *v.t.,* **-pled, -pling.** to absorb the shock of (a nuclear explosion): *a surrounding mass of earth and rock can decouple a nuclear blast.* [DE- + COUPLE]

de·coy (*n.* di koi′, dē′koi; *v.* di koi′), *n.* **1.** one who entices or lures, as into danger, a trap, etc. **2.** anything used as a lure. **3.** a trained bird or other animal used to entice game into a trap or within gunshot. **4.** an image of a bird used for the same purpose. **5.** a pond into which wild fowl are lured for capture. **6.** an object capable of reflecting radar waves, used as a spurious aircraft, missile, chaff, etc., for the deception of radar detectors. **—***v.t.* **7.** to lure by or as if by a decoy: *They decoyed the ducks to an area right in front of the blind.* **—***v.i.* **8.** to become decoyed: *Ducks decoy more easily than most other waterfowl.* [var. of *coy* (now dial.) < D, m. (*de*) *kooi* (the) cage, MD *côie* < L *cavea* CAGE] **—de·coy′er,** *n.*

de·crease (*v.* di krēs′; *n.* dē′krēs, di krēs′), *v.,* **-creased, -creas·ing,** *n.* **—***v.i.* **1.** to diminish gradually in extent, quantity, strength, power, etc.: *During the 10-day march across the desert their supply of water decreased rapidly.* **—***v.t.* **2.** to make less; cause to diminish: *The commander decreased each soldier's water allotment.* **—***n.* **3.** the act or process of decreasing; condition of being decreased; gradual reduction: *a decrease in volume of sales; a decrease in intensity.* **4.** the amount by which a thing is lessened: *The decrease in sales was almost 20 percent.* [ME *decrese(n)* < OF *descreiss-,* long s. of *decreistre* < L *dēcresc(ere)* (*dē-* DE- + *crescere* to grow); see CRESCENT]
—Syn. 1. wane, lessen, fall off, decline, contract, abate. DECREASE, DIMINISH, DWINDLE, SHRINK imply becoming smaller or less in amount. DECREASE commonly implies a gradual and sustained reduction, esp. of bulk, size, volume, or quantity, often from some imperceptible cause or inherent process: *The swelling decreased daily.* DIMINISH usually implies the action of some external cause which keeps taking away: *Disease caused the number of troops to diminish steadily.* DWINDLE implies an undesirable reduction by degrees, resulting in attenuation: *His followers dwindled to a mere handful.* SHRINK esp. implies contraction through an inherent property under specific conditions: *Many fabrics shrink in hot water.* **3.** abatement, decline, subsidence, shrinking, dwindling, ebbing. **—Ant. 1.** increase, expand.

de·creas·ing (di krē′sing), *adj.* **1.** becoming less; lessening; diminishing. **2.** *Math.* (of a function) having the property that for any two points in the domain such that one is larger than the other, the image of the larger point is less than or equal to the image of the smaller point; nonincreasing. Cf. **increasing** (def. 2). [DECREASE + -ING[2]] **—de·creas′ing·ly,** *adv.*

de·cree (di krē′), *n., v.,* **-creed, -cree·ing.** **—***n.* **1.** an ordinance or edict promulgated by civil or other authority: *to issue a decree.* **2.** *Law.* a judicial decision or order. **3.** *Theol.* one of the eternal purposes of God, by which events are foreordained. **—***v.t., v.i.* **4.** to ordain or decide by decree. [ME *decre* < OF (var. of *decret*) < L *dēcrēt(um)*, n. use of neut. of *dēcrētus,* ptp. of *dēcernere;* see DECERN]

decree′ ni′si (nī′sī), *Law.* a decree, esp. of divorce, that will become absolute at a later date.

dec·re·ment (dek′rə mənt), *n.* **1.** the act or process of decreasing; gradual reduction. **2.** the amount lost by reduction. **3.** *Math.* a negative increment. [< L *dēcrēment(um)*, equiv. to *dēcrē(tus)* (see DECREASE) + *-mentum* -MENT]

dec·re·me·ter (dek′rə mē′tər, di krem′i tər), *n.* an instrument for measuring the damping of an electromagnetic wave train. [DECRE(MENT) + -METER]

de·crep·it (di krep′it), *adj.* **1.** weakened by old age; feeble; infirm: *a decrepit man who can hardly walk.* **2.** worn out by long use; dilapidated: *a decrepit stove.* [ME < L *dēcrepit(us)*, lit., broken down, equiv. to *dē-* DE- + *crepitus,* ptp. of *crepāre* to crack] **—de·crep′it·ly,** *adv.*
—Syn. 1. enfeebled. See **weak.** **—Ant.** vigorous.

de·crep·i·tate (di krep′i tāt′), *v.,* **-tat·ed, -tat·ing.** **—***v.t.* **1.** to roast or calcine (salt, minerals, etc.) so as to cause crackling or until crackling ceases. **—***v.i.* **2.** to make a crackling noise, as salt in roasting. [< NL *dēcrepitāt(us)* crackled, ptp. of *dēcrepitāre,* equiv. to L *dē-* DE- + *crepitāre* to crackle (freq. of *crepāre* to crackle); see -ATE[1]] **—de·crep′i·ta′tion,** *n.*

de·crep·i·tude (di krep′i to͞od′, -tyo͞od′), *n.* decrepit condition; dilapidated state; feebleness, esp. from old age. [< F *décrépitude* < L *dēcrepit(us)* DECREPIT; see -TUDE]

decresc., *Music.* decrescendo.

de·cre·scen·do (dē′kri shen′dō, dā′-; *It.* de′kre-shen′dô), *adj., adv., n., pl.* **-dos.** *Music.* **—***adj. adv.* **1.** gradually reducing force of loudness; diminuendo (opposed to *crescendo*). **—***n.* **2.** a gradual reduction in force or loudness. **3.** a decrescendo passage. [< It, prp. of *decrescere;* see DECREASE]

de·cres·cent (di kres′ənt), *adj.* **1.** diminishing; decreasing. **2.** waning, as the moon. **3.** *Heraldry.* (of a crescent) having the horns toward the sinister side. Cf. **increscent** (def. 2). [< L *dēcrescent-* (s. of *dēcrescēns*), prp. of *dēcrescere* to DECREASE; see -ENT] **—de·cres′cence,** *n.*

de·cre·tal (di krēt′əl), *adj.* **1.** pertaining to, of the nature of, or containing a decree or decrees. **—***n.* **2.** a papal decree authoritatively determining some point of doctrine or church law. **3. Decretals,** the body or collection of such decrees as a part of the canon law. [ME *decretal* < OF < LL *dēcrētāl(is)*, equiv. to *dēcrēt(um)* DECREE + *-ālis* -AL[1]]

de·cre·tist (di krē′tist), *n.* (in medieval universities) **1.** a student in the faculty of law. **2.** a student of the Decretals; one versed in the canon law. [< ML *decretist(a)*, equiv. to L *dēcrēt(um)* DECREE + *-ista* -IST]

de·cre·tive (di krē′tiv), *adj.* having the force of a decree; pertaining to a decree. [< L *dēcrēt(um)* DECREE + -IVE] **—de·cre′tive·ly,** *adv.*

dec·re·to·ry (dek′ri tôr′ē, -tōr′ē), *adj.* **1.** pertaining to or following a decree. **2.** established by a decree; judicial; definitive. [< L *dēcrētōri(us)*, equiv. to *dēcrē-t(us)* decided (see DECREE) + *-ōrius* -ORY[1]]

de·cri·al (di krī′əl), *n.* the act of decrying; noisy censure. [DECRY + -AL[2]]

de·crim·i·nal·ize (dē krim′ə nəlīz′), *v.t.,* **-ized, -iz·ing.** to eliminate criminal penalties for possession or use of: *to decriminalize marijuana.* [DE- + CRIMINAL + -IZE] **—de·crim′i·nal·i·za′tion,** *n.*

de·cry (di krī′), *v.t.,* **-cried, -cry·ing.** **1.** to speak disparagingly of; denounce as faulty or worthless; express open censure of: *She decried the state of creative art in the country.* **2.** to condemn or depreciate by proclamation, as foreign or obsolete coins. [< F *décri(er)*, OF *descrier.* See DIS-[1], CRY] **—de·cri′er,** *n.*
—Syn. 1. belittle, disparage, discredit, depreciate, minimize.

de·crypt (dē kript′, di-), *v.t.* to decode or decipher. [DE- + CRYPT(OGRAM)]

CONCISE ETYMOLOGY KEY: <, descended or derived from; >, whence; b., blend of, blended; c., cognate with; deriv., derivative; equiv., equivalent; imit., imitative; m., modification of; obl., oblique; r., replacing; s., stem; sp., spelling; trans., translation; ?, origin unknown, perhaps; *, hypothetical. See the full key inside the front cover.

de·cub·i·tus (di kyo͞o′bi təs), *n., pl.* **-ti** (-tī′). *Med.* **1.** any position assumed by a patient when lying in bed. **2.** Also called **decu′bitus ul′cer.** *Pathol.* a bedsore. [< NL, deriv. of L *dēcumbere* to lie down, equiv. to *dē-* DE- + *cumbere*, deriv. of *cubāre* to lie down; after L *accubitus*] —**de·cu′bi·tal,** *adj.*

dec·u·man (dek′yo͞o mən), *adj.* **1.** large or immense, as a wave. **2.** (in ancient Rome) **a.** of or pertaining to the 10th cohort of a legion. **b.** Also called **dec′uman gate′.** the main gate of a military camp, facing away from the enemy and near which the 10th cohort of the legion was usually stationed. [< L *decumān(us)* of the tenth, var. of *decimānus*; by metonymy: large, equiv. to *decim(us)* tenth (see DECIMATE) + *-ānus* -AN]

de·cum·bent (di kum′bənt), *adj.* **1.** lying down; recumbent. **2.** *Bot.* (of stems, branches, etc.) lying or trailing on the ground with the extremity tending to ascend. [< L *dēcumbent-* (s. of *dēcumbēns*), prp. of *dēcumbere*. See DECUBITUS, -ENT] —**de·cum′bence, de·cum′ben·cy,** *n.* —**de·cum′bent·ly,** *adv.*

dec·u·ple (dek′yo͝o pəl), *adj., n., v.,* **-pled, -pling.** —*adj.* **1.** tenfold; ten times as great. —*n.* **2.** a tenfold quantity or multiple. —*v.t.* **3.** to make ten times as great. [< F < L *decupl(us)* tenfold, equiv. to *dec(em)* ten + *-uplus*, as in *quadruplus* QUADRUPLE]

de·cu·ri·on (di kyo͝or′ē ən), *n. Rom. Hist.* **1.** the head of a decury. **2.** a member of the senate of an ancient Roman colony or municipality. [ME < L *decuriōn-* (s. of *decuriō*), equiv. to *decuri(a)* a division of ten (*dec(em)* ten + *-uria* -URE) + *-iōn-* -ION]

de·cur·rent (di kûr′ənt, -kur′-), *adj. Bot.* extending down the stem below the place of insertion, as certain leaves. [< L *dēcurrent-* (s. of *dēcurrēns*) running down (prp. of *dēcurrere*, equiv. to *dē-* DE- + *currere* to run); see CURRENT] —**de·cur′rence, de·cur′ren·cy,** *n.* —**de·cur′rent·ly,** *adv.*

Decurrent leaf of thistle

de·curved (dē kûrvd′), *adj.* curved downward, as the bill of a bird. [DE- + CURVED]

dec·u·ry (dek′yo͞o rē), *n., pl.* **-ries.** *Rom. Hist.* **1.** a division, company, or body of 10 men. **2.** any larger body of men, esp. the curiae. [< L *decuria* a company of ten. See DECURION, -Y³]

de·cus·sate (*v.* di kus′āt, dek′ə sāt′; *adj.* di kus′āt, -it), *v.,* **-sat·ed, -sat·ing,** *adj.* —*v.t., v.i.* **1.** to cross in the form of the letter X; intersect. —*adj.* **2.** in the form of the letter X; crossed; intersected. **3.** *Bot.* arranged along the stem in pairs, each pair at right angles to the pair next above or below, as leaves. [< L *decussāt(us)* divided in the form of an X (ptp. of *decussāre*), equiv. to *decuss(is)* the number ten (*dec(em)* ten + *-ass* AS²) + *-ātus* -ATE¹] —**de·cus′sate·ly,** *adv.* —**de·cus·sa·tion** (dē′kə sā′shən, dek′ə-), *n.*

Decussate leaves

D.Ed., Doctor of Education.

de·dal (dēd′əl), *adj. Archaic.* daedal.

de·dans (də dāN′), *n., pl.* **-dans** (-dāN′). (*construed as sing.*) *Court Tennis.* **1.** a netted winning opening of rectangular shape at the service side of the court. Cf. **grille** (def. 3), **winning gallery. 2.** the body of spectators behind this opening at a court-tennis match. [< F: (the) inside, MF (adv. and prep.), OF *dedenz*, equiv. to *de-* of (< L *dē-* DE-) + *denz* in (< LL *deint(us)*, equiv. to L *dē-* DE- + *-intus* IN)]

De·de A·gach (*Turk.* de de′ a äch′), former name of **Alexandroupolis.**

De·de·kind (dā′də kind; *Ger.* dā′də kint), *n.* **Ju·li·us Wil·helm Rich·ard** (jo͞ol′yəs wil′helm rich′ərd; *Ger.* yo͞o′lē o͝os′ vil′helm riкн′ärt), 1831–1916, German mathematician.

De′dekind cut′, *Math.* two nonempty subsets of an ordered field, as the rational numbers, such that one subset is the collection of upper bounds of the second and the second is the collection of lower bounds of the first. [named after J.W.R. DEDEKIND]

de·den·dum (di den′dəm), *n., pl.* **-da** (-də). *Mach.* (on a gear or rack) the radial distance between the pitch circle or line and the root circle or line. Cf. **addendum** (def. 3a). [< L: to be given up, ger. of *dedere*, equiv. to *dē-* DE- + *-dere* give; see ADDENDUM]

Ded·ham (ded′əm), *n.* a town in E Massachusetts, near Boston. 23,869 (1960).

ded·i·cate (ded′ə kāt′), *v.,* **-cat·ed, -cat·ing,** *adj.* —*v.t.* **1.** to set apart and consecrate to a deity or to a sacred purpose: *The ancient Greeks dedicated many shrines to Aphrodite.* **2.** to devote wholly and earnestly, as to some person or purpose: *He dedicated his life to fighting corruption.* **3.** to inscribe (a book, piece of music, etc.) to a person, cause, or the like, in testimony of affection or respect. —*adj.* **4.** *Archaic.* dedicated. [< L *dēdicāt(us)* declared, devoted, ptp. of *dēdicāre*, equiv. to *dē-* DE- + *dicāre* to proclaim, var. of *dicere* to say, speak (see DICTATE)] —**ded′i·ca′tor,** *n.*

ded·i·cat·ed (ded′ə kā′tid), *adj.* wholly committed to something, as to an ideal, political cause, personal goal, etc.: *a dedicated artist; a dedicated purist.* [DEDICATE + -ED²]

ded·i·ca·tion (ded′ə kā′shən), *n.* **1.** the act of dedicating. **2.** the state of being dedicated: *Her dedication to medicine was so great that she had time for little else.* **3.** an inscription prefixed or attached to a book, piece of music, etc., dedicating it to a person, cause, or the like. [ME *dedicacioun* < L *dēdicātiōn-* (s. of *dēdicātiō*), equiv. to *dēdicāt(us)* (see DEDICATE) + *-iōn-* -ION] —**ded′i·ca′tion·al,** *adj.*

ded·i·ca·to·ry (ded′ə kə tôr′ē, -tōr′ē), *adj.* of or pertaining to dedication; serving as a dedication. Also, **ded·i·ca·tive** (ded′ə kā′tiv). [DEDICATE + -ORY¹] —**ded′i·ca·to′ri·ly,** *adv.*

de·dif·fer·en·ti·ate (dē′dif ə ren′shē āt′), *v.i.,* **-at·ed, -at·ing.** *Biol.* to undergo dedifferentiation. [back formation from DEDIFFERENTIATION]

de·dif·fer·en·ti·a·tion (dē dif′ə ren′shē ā′shən), *n. Biol.* (of cells or tissues) reversion to a more primitive or general state. [DE- + DIFFERENTIATION]

de d. in d., (in prescriptions) from day to day. [< L *dē diē in diem*]

de·do·lo·mit·ize (dē dō′lə mi tīz′, -mi-, -dol′ə-), *v.t.,* **-ized, -iz·ing.** to transform (dolomite or dolomitic limestone) by separating the dolomite into calcium carbonate and magnesium carbonate. [DE- + DOLOMITE + -IZE] —**de·do′lo·mit′i·za′tion,** *n.*

de·duce (di do͞os′, -dyo͞os′), *v.t.,* **-duced, -duc·ing. 1.** to derive as a conclusion from something known or assumed; infer: *From the evidence the detective deduced that the butler had done it.* **2.** to trace the derivation of; trace the course of: *to deduce one's lineage.* [< L *dēdūc(ere)* (to) lead down, derive, equiv. to *dē-* DE- + *dūcere* to lead, bring] —**de·duc′i·bil′i·ty, de·duc′i·ble·ness,** *n.* —**de·duc′i·ble,** *adj.* —**de·duc′i·bly,** *adv.*

de·duct (di dukt′), *v.t.* **1.** to take away, as from a sum or amount: *Once you deduct your expenses, there is nothing left.* **2.** detract; abate (usually fol. by *from*): *The rocky soil deducts from the value of his property.* [< L *dēduct(us)* brought down, withdrawn, ptp. of *dēdūcere*; see DEDUCE] —**Syn. 1.** See **subtract.** —**Ant.** add.

de·duct·i·ble (di duk′tə bəl), *adj.* **1.** that can be deducted. **2.** *U.S.* allowable as a tax deduction: *Church dues and charitable contributions are deductible expenses.* —*n.* **3.** an insurance policy having a deductible clause: *He has a $50 deductible on his car.* [DEDUCT + -IBLE] —**de·duct′i·bil′i·ty,** *n.*

deduct′ible clause′, a clause in an insurance policy stipulating that the insured will be liable for a specified initial amount of each loss, injury, etc., and that the insurance company will be liable for any excess up to the insured amount. Cf. **franchise clause.**

de·duc·tion (di duk′shən), *n.* **1.** the act or process of deducting; subtraction. **2.** something that is deducted: *He made three deductions before paying the bill. Please credit the deduction to my account.* **3.** the act or process of deducing: *His deduction seemed to lead him to the wrong conclusion.* **4.** something that is deduced: *His deduction was that the butler had done it.* **5.** *Logic.* **a.** a process of reasoning in which a conclusion follows necessarily from the premises presented, so that the conclusion cannot be false if the premises are true. **b.** a conclusion reached by this process. Cf. **induction.** [ME < L *dēductiōn-* (s. of *dēductiō*) a leading away. See DEDUCT, -ION]

de·duc·tive (di duk′tiv), *adj.* based on deduction from accepted premises: *deductive argument; deductive reasoning.* [< L *dēductīv(us)* derivative. See DEDUCT, -IVE] —**de·duc′tive·ly,** *adv.*

—**Syn.** DEDUCTIVE and INDUCTIVE refer to two distinct logical processes. DEDUCTIVE reasoning is a logical process in which a conclusion drawn from a set of premises contains no more information than the premises taken collectively. *All dogs are animals; this is a dog; therefore, this is an animal:* The truth of the conclusion is dependent only on the method. *All men are apes; this is a man; therefore, this is an ape:* The conclusion is logically true, although the premise is absurd. INDUCTIVE reasoning is a logical process in which a conclusion is proposed that contains more information than the observations or experience on which it is based. *Every crow ever seen was black; all crows are black:* The truth of the conclusion is verifiable only in terms of future experience and certainty is attainable only if all possible instances have been examined. In the example, there is no certainty that a white crow won't be found tomorrow, although past experience would make such an occurrence seem unlikely.

dee (dē), *n.* **1.** a metal loop attached to tack, for fastening gear: *to hang wirecutters from a dee on a saddle.* **2.** *Physics.* a hollow electrode for accelerating particles in a cyclotron. [so called from its shape which resembles the letter D]

Dee (dē), *n.* **1. John,** 1527–1608, English mathematician and astrologer. **2.** a river in NE Scotland, flowing E into the North Sea at Aberdeen. 90 mi. long. **3.** a river in N Wales and W England, flowing E and N into the Irish Sea. ab. 70 mi. long. **4.** a boy's or girl's given name.

deed (dēd), *n.* **1.** something that is done, performed, or accomplished; an act: *Do a good deed every day.* **2.** an exploit or achievement: *Brave men's deeds live after them.* **3.** action or performance, esp. as illustrative of intentions, promises, or the like: *His deeds speak for themselves.* **4.** *Law.* a writing or document executed under seal and delivered to effect a conveyance, esp. of real estate. **5.** to convey or transfer by deed. [ME *dede*, OE *dēd*, var. of *dǣd*; c. G *Tat*, Goth *(ga)dēth(s)*; see DO¹] —**deed′less,** *adj.*
—**Syn. 1.** See **action.**

dee·jay (dē′jā, -jā′), *n. Slang.* See **disk jockey.** [pronunciation of initials D.J.]

deem (dēm), *v.i.* **1.** to form or have an opinion; judge; think: *He did not deem lightly of the issue.* —*v.t.* **2.** to hold as an opinion; think; regard: *He deemed it wise to refuse the offer.* [ME *dem(en)*, OE *dēman*; c. Goth *dōmjan*, OHG *tuomen*; see DOOM]
—**Syn. 2.** consider, hold, believe.

de-em·pha·sis (dē em′fə sis), *n., pl.* **-ses** (-sēz′). **1.** a reduction in emphasis: *There has been de-emphasis on social activities at the school.* **2.** the act or process of de-emphasizing. **3.** *Electronics.* a process of reducing the relative amplitude of certain frequencies in a signal which have been exaggerated by preemphasis, restoring the signal to its original form. Also, **de·em′pha·sis, de·ëm′pha·sis.** [DE- + EMPHASIS]

de-em·pha·size (dē em′fə sīz′), *v.t.,* **-sized, -siz·ing.** to place less emphasis upon; reduce in importance, size, scope, etc.: *In that year the stylists de-emphasized the use of make-up.* [DE- + EMPHASIZE]

Deems (dēmz), *n.* a boy's given name.

deem·ster (dēm′stər), *n.* a judge of the Isle of Man. Also, **dempster.** [ME *demestre*, fem. form of *demere* judge. See DEEM, -STER] —**deem′ster·ship′,** *n.*

deep (dēp), *adj.* **1.** extending far down from the top or surface: *a deep well; a deep lake.* **2.** extending far in or back from the front or from an edge considered as the front: *a deep shelf; a deep piece of land.* **3.** extending far in width; broad: *deep lace; a deep border.* **4.** ranging far from the earth and sun: *a deep space probe.* **5.** having a specified dimension in depth: *a tank eight feet deep.* **6.** extending far down relative to the surface of a given object: *The knife made a deep scratch in the table.* **7.** situated far down, in, or back: *deep below the surface; deep in the woods; deep behind the frontier.* **8.** reaching or advancing far down: *a deep dive.* **9.** coming from far down: *a deep breath.* **10.** made with the body bent or lowered to a considerable degree: *a deep bow or curtsy.* **11.** lying below a given surface or layer; submerged: *a road deep in mud.* **12.** difficult to penetrate or understand; abstruse: *deep allegory.* **13.** not superficial; profound: *deep truth; deep insight.* **14.** grave or serious: *deep disgrace.* **15.** heartfelt; sincere: *deep affections.* **16.** absorbing; engrossing: *deep study.* **17.** great in measure; intense; extreme: *deep sorrow; deep concentration.* **18.** sound and heavy; profound: *deep sleep.* **19.** (of colors) dark and vivid: *a deep red.* **20.** low in pitch, as sound, a voice, or the like: *He has a deep voice for a little boy.* **21.** having penetrating intellectual powers: *a deep scholar.* **22.** profoundly cunning or artful: *a deep and crafty scheme.* **23.** mysterious; obscure: *deep, dark secrets.* **24.** immersed or involved; enveloped: *a man deep in debt.* **25.** absorbed; engrossed: *deep in thought; deep in a book.* **26.** *Baseball.* relatively far from home plate: *He hit the ball into deep center field.* **27. in deep water,** in difficult or serious circumstances; in trouble: *He's been in deep water ever since he stole his first candy bar.* —*n.* **28.** the deep part of the sea, a river, etc. **29.** a vast extent, as of space, time, etc. **30.** the part of greatest intensity, as of winter. **31.** *Naut.* any of the unmarked levels, one fathom apart, called by the number of fathoms distant from the lead. Cf. **mark¹** (def. 18). **32. the deep,** *Chiefly Literary.* the sea or ocean: *He was laid to rest in the deep.* —*adv.* **33.** to or at a considerable or specified depth: *The boat rode deep in the water.* **34.** far on in time: *He claimed he could see deep into the future.* **35.** profoundly; intensely: *He went deep into the matter.* **36.** *Baseball.* at or to a deep place or position: *The outfielders played deep, knowing the batter's reputation as a slugger.* **37. in deep,** inextricably involved. [ME *dep*, OE *dēop*; akin to Goth *diup(s)*, OIcel *djup(r)*, OHG *tiof*] —**deep′ness,** *n.*
—**Syn. 12.** recondite, mysterious, obscure, profound. **21.** sagacious, wise, profound, shrewd. —**Ant. 1, 8, 13–15, 21.** shallow.

deep-chest·ed (dēp′ches′tid), *adj.* **1.** having a large, broad chest: *a deep-chested man.* **2.** coming from deep in the chest: *a deep-chested laugh.*

deep-dish (dēp′dish′), *adj. Cookery.* baked in a deep dish, often with a pastry top: *a deep-dish peach pie.*

deep-draw (dēp′drô′), *v.t.,* **-drew, -drawn, -draw·ing.** *Metalworking.* to form (tubing, containers, etc.) by pulling strip or sheet metal between suitably formed and spaced dies. Cf. **cup** (def. 21).

deep-dyed (dēp′dīd′), *adj.* thorough; unmitigated: *a deep-dyed villain.*

deep·en (dē′pən), *v.t., v.i.* **1.** to make or become deep or deeper: *They deepened the shallow pool. The shadows deepened toward late afternoon.* **2.** *Meteorol.* to decrease in atmospheric pressure: *a deepening cyclone.* [DEEP + -EN¹] —**deep′en·er,** *n.* —**deep′en·ing·ly,** *adv.*

deep′-etch plate′ (dēp′ech′), an offset printing plate with an intaglio image filled with a substance that attracts ink to make it planographic. Cf. **albumen plate.**

deep′ fat′, hot fat used for deep-frying food.

deep′ floor′, *Naut.* any of the floors toward the ends of a vessel, deeper than those of standard depth amidships. Also called **rising floor.**

Deep·freeze (dēp′frēz′), *n. Trademark.* a freezer designed for the quick-freezing and cold storage of food.

deep-freeze (dēp′frēz′), *v.t.,* **-freezed** or **-froze, -freezed** or **-fro·zen, -freez·ing.** to quick-freeze (food). [DEEP + FREEZE]

deep-fry (dēp′frī′), *v.t.,* **-fried, -fry·ing.** to fry in a quantity of fat sufficient to cover the food being cooked.

deep′ fry′er, a deep pan or pot with a basket, usually of mesh, inside, for deep-frying.

Deep·ha·ven (dēp′hā′vən), *n.* a town in E Minnesota. 3286 (1960).

Deep·ing (dē′ping), *n.* **(George) War·wick** (wôr′ik, wor′-), 1877–1950, English novelist.

deep′ kiss′. See **soul kiss.**

deep-kiss (dēp′kis′), *v.t., v.i.* to soul-kiss.

deep-laid (dēp′lād′), *adj.* carefully, cunningly, or secretly made: *deep-laid plot.*

deep·ly (dēp′lē), *adv.* **1.** at or to a considerable extent downward; well within or beneath a surface. **2.** to a thorough extent or profound degree: *deeply pained; deeply committed.* **3.** with depth of color, tone, sound, etc. **4.** with great cunning, skill, and subtlety. [ME *deply*, OE *dēoplīce* (adv.), deriv. of *dēoplīc* (adj.), equiv. to *dēop* DEEP + *-līc* -LY]

deep′ mourn′ing, completely black mourning clothes made of a drab material: *After her brother died, she was in deep mourning for a year.*

deep-root·ed (dēp′ro͞o′tid, -ro͝ot′id), *adj.* deeply rooted; firmly implanted: *a deep-rooted patriotism; deep-rooted suspicions.* —**deep′-root′ed·ness,** *n.*

deep-sea (dēp′sē′), *adj.* of, pertaining to, in, or associated with the deeper parts of the sea: *deep-sea fishing; deep-sea diver.*

deep′-sea smelt′, any of several bathypelagic fishes of the family *Bathylagidae.* Cf. **smoothtongue.**

deep-seat·ed (dēp′sē′tid), *adj.* firmly implanted: *a deep-seated sense of propriety.*

deep′ sensibil′ity, *Med.* sensibility within the deeper structures of the body, as the muscles, joints, etc.

deep′ six′, **1.** *U.S. Navy Informal.* burial at sea. **2.** *Slang.* complete rejection: *The agency gave his ideas the deep six.*

deep-six (dēp′siks′), *v.t. Slang.* to get rid of; abandon; jettison. [v. use of DEEP SIX]

Deep′ South′, the southeastern part of the U.S., including esp. those States that border the Gulf of Mexico.

deep′ space′, space beyond the limits of the solar system. Cf. **outer space.**

deep-voiced (dēp′ voist′), *adj.* having a voice that is low in pitch: *a deep-voiced young man.*

deep·wa·ter (dēp′wô′tər, -wot′ər), *adj.* **1.** of or pertaining to water of fairly great depth. **2.** deep-sea. [DEEP + WATER]

deer (dēr), *n., pl.* **deer,** (*occasionally*) **deers. 1.** any of several ruminants of the family *Cervidae*, most of the males of which have solid, deciduous horns or antlers. 2. any of the smaller species of this family, as distinguished from the moose, elk, etc. [ME *der*, OE *dēor* beast; akin to Goth *dius* beast, OHG *tior*]

deer′ fern′, an evergreen fern, *Blechnum Spicant*, of Eurasia and western North America, having densely clustered fronds. Also called **hard fern.** [so called because it is often cultivated for deer]

Deer′field Beach′ (dēr′fēld′), a town in S Florida. 9573 (1960).

deer′ fly′, any of several tabanid flies of the genus *Chrysops*, the female of which bites and sucks the blood of deer, livestock, and man.

Virginia deer, *Odocoileus virginianus* (3½ ft. high at shoulder; length 6½ ft.)

deer′ fly′ fe′ver, *Med., Vet. Med.* tularemia.

deer′ grass′, a perennial herb, *Rhexia virginica*, found in sandy bogs in eastern North America, having hairy, fringed leaves and purple flowers. Also called **handsome Harry.**

deer·hound (dēr′hound′), *n.* one of a Scottish breed of large dogs having a shaggy, gray or brindled coat. [DEER + HOUND[1]]

deer′ lick′, a spot of ground, naturally or artificially salty, where deer come to lick the earth.

Scottish deerhound (2½ ft. high at shoulder)

Deer′ Lodge′, a town in SW Montana. 4681 (1960).

deer′ mouse′. See **white-footed mouse.**

Deer′ Park′, 1. a town on central Long Island, in SE New York. 16,726 (1960). 2. a town in SW Ohio. 8423 (1960). 3. a town in S Texas. 4865 (1960).

deer·skin (dēr′skin′), *n.* 1. the skin of a deer. 2. leather made from this. 3. a garment made of such leather. —*adj.* 4. made of deerskin: *a deerskin jacket.* [ME *dereskin*, var. of *deres skin*. See DEER, SKIN]

Deer·slay·er, The (dēr′slā′ər), a historical novel (1841) by James Fenimore Cooper. Cf. **Leather-Stocking Tales.**

deer·stalk·er (dēr′stô′kər), *n.* 1. one who stalks deer. 2. Also called **fore-and-after.** a close-fitting cap having peaks in front and back, with earflaps usually raised and tied on top of the crown; worn as a hunting cap and associated with Sherlock Holmes. [DEER + STALKER] —**deer′stalk′ing,** *n.*

deer's-tongue (dērz′tung′), *n.* an herb, *Frasera speciosa*, of the northwestern U.S., having purple-spotted, greenish-white flowers.

de·es·ca·late (dē es′kə lāt′), *v.t., v.i.,* **-lat·ed, -lat·ing.** to decrease in intensity, magnitude, etc.: *to deescalate a war.* Also, **de-es′ca·late′, de·ës′ca·late′.** [DE- + ESCALATE] —**de·es′ca·la′tion, de-es′ca·la′tion, de·ës′ca·la′tion.**

de·e·sis (dē ē′sis), *n., pl.* **-ses** (-sēz). a representation in Byzantine art of Christ enthroned and flanked by the Virgin Mary and St. John the Baptist, often found on an iconostasis. Also, **de·ë′sis.** [< Gk *déēsis* entreaty; cf. *déomai* I beg]

de·ex·cite (dē′ik sīt′), *v.t.,* **-cit·ed, -cit·ing.** *Physics.* to cause (an atom) to fall from an excited energy level to a lower energy level.

def., 1. defective. 2. defendant. 3. deferred. 4. defined. 5. definite. 6. definition.

de·face (di fās′), *v.t.,* **-faced, -fac·ing.** 1. to mar the face or appearance of; disfigure: *to deface a wall by writing on it.* 2. to efface, obliterate, or injure the surface of, as to make illegible, invalid, etc.: *to deface a bond.* [ME *deface(n)* < OF *desfacie(r)*, equiv. to *des-* DIS-[1] + *facier* (*face* FACE + *-ier* inf. suffix)] —**de·face′a·ble,** *adj.* —**de·face′ment,** *n.* —**de·fac′er,** *n.*
—**Syn. 1.** spoil. See **mar.**

de fac·to (dē fak′tō), 1. in fact; in reality: *Although his title was prime minister, he was de facto president of the country. Although the schools were open to all qualified registrants, the city still practiced de facto segregation.* 2. actually existing, esp. when without lawful authority (distinguished from *de jure*). [< L: lit., from the fact]

de·fal·cate (di fal′kāt, -fôl′-), *v.i.,* **-cat·ed, -cat·ing.** *Law.* to be guilty of defalcation. [< ML *dēfalcāt(us)* cut off (ptp. of *dēfalcāre*), equiv. to *dē-* DE- + *falcātus*; see FALCATE] —**de·fal′ca·tor,** *n.*

de·fal·ca·tion (dē′fal kā′shən, -fôl-), *n. Law.* 1. misappropriation of money, etc., held by an official, trustee, or other fiduciary. 2. the sum misappropriated. [< ML *dēfalcātiōn-* (s. of *dēfalcātiō*) a taking away, equiv. to *dēfalcāt(us)* (see DEFALCATE) + *-iōn-* -ION]

def·a·ma·tion (def′ə mā′shən, dē′fə-), *n.* the act of defaming; false or unjustified injury of the good reputation of another as by slander or libel; calumny: *She sued the magazine for defamation of character.* [ME *defamatioun*; r. (by analogy with DEFAME) ME *diffamacioun* < ML *diffāmātiōn-* (s. of *diffāmātiō*), equiv. to L *diffāmāt(us)* (ptp. of *diffāmāre*) + *-iōn-* -ION]

de·fam·a·to·ry (di fam′ə tōr′ē, -tôr′ē), *adj.* containing defamation; injurious to reputation; slanderous: *She claimed that the article in the magazine was defamatory.* [ML *diffāmātōri(us)*, equiv. to L *diffāmāt(us)* (ptp. of *diffāmāre*; see DEFAME) + *-ōrius* -ORY[1]]

de·fame (di fām′), *v.t.,* **-famed, -fam·ing.** 1. to attack the good name or reputation of, as by uttering or publishing maliciously or falsely anything injurious; slander or libel; calumniate: *The newspaper editorial defamed the politician.* 2. *Archaic.* to disgrace; bring dishonor upon. 3. *Archaic.* to accuse. [ME *defame(n)* < L *dēfām(āre)*, equiv. to *dē-* DE- + *fāmāre*, deriv. of *fāma* a report, rumor, reputation (see FAME); r. ME *diffame(n)* < OF *diffame(r)* < L *diffāmāre*, equiv. to *dif-* DIF- + *fāmāre*] —**de·fam′er,** *n.* —**de·fam′ing·ly,** *adv.*

de·fang (dē fang′), *v.t.* to remove the fangs of: *to defang a snake.* [DE- + FANG]

de·fault (di fôlt′), *n.* 1. failure to act; neglect: *They lost their best client by sheer default.* 2. failure to meet financial obligations. 3. *Law.* failure to perform an act or obligation legally required, esp. to appear in court or to plead at a time assigned. 4. *Sports.* failure to participate in or complete a scheduled match. 5. want; lack; absence: *owing to default of water.* —*v.i.* 6. to fail in fulfilling or satisfying an engagement, claim, or obligation. 7. to fail to meet financial obligations or to account properly for money in one's care: *When he defaulted in his payments, the bank foreclosed on the car.* 8. *Law.* to fail to appear in court. 9. *Sports.* a. to fail to participate in or complete a match. b. to lose a match by default. —*v.t.* 10. to fail to perform or pay: *to default a debt.* 11. to declare to be in default, esp. legally: *The judge defaulted the defendant.* 12. *Sports.* a. to fail to compete in (a game, race, etc.). b. to lose by default. 13. *Law.* to lose by failure to appear in court. [ME *defau(l)te* < OF *defaute* (AF *defalte*), deriv. of *defaillir*, after *faute, faillir*. See DE-, FAULT, FAIL]

de·fault·er (di fôl′tər), *n.* 1. one who defaults or fails to fulfill an obligation, esp. a legal or financial one. 2. *Brit.* a soldier convicted by court martial. [DEFAULT + -ER[1]]

de·fea·sance (di fē′zəns), *n. Law.* 1. a rendering null and void. 2. a condition on the performance of which a deed or other instrument is defeated or rendered void. 3. a collateral deed or other writing embodying such a condition. [ME *defesance* < AF *defesaunce*, OF *defesance*, equiv. to *desfes-* (ptp. s. of *desfaire* to undo; see DEFEAT) + *-ance* -ANCE]

de·fea·si·ble (di fē′zə bəl), *adj.* that may be annulled or terminated. [< AF *defesible*. See DEFEASANCE, -IBLE] —**de·fea′si·ble·ness, de·fea′si·bil′i·ty,** *n.*

de·feat (di fēt′), *v.t.* 1. to overcome in a contest, battle, etc.; vanquish; win over: *They defeated the enemy. He defeated her at tennis.* 2. to frustrate; thwart: *This kind of problem always defeats him.* 3. to deprive of something expected: *The early returns defeated his hopes of election.* 4. *Law.* to annul. —*n.* 5. the act of overcoming in a contest: *an overwhelming defeat of all opposition.* 6. an overthrow; vanquishment: *the defeat of a government.* 7. an instance of defeat: *He considered his defeat a personal affront.* 8. a bringing to naught; frustration: *the defeat of all his hopes and dreams.* 9. *Obs.* undoing; destruction; ruin. [ME *defete(n)* < OF *desfait*, ptp. of *desfaire* to undo, destroy < ML *disfacere*, equiv. to L *dis-* DIS-[1] + *facere* to do] —**de·feat′er,** *n.*
—**Syn. 1.** overwhelm, overthrow, rout, check. DEFEAT, CONQUER, OVERCOME, SUBDUE imply gaining a victory or control over an opponent. DEFEAT suggests temporarily, and often permanently, beating or frustrating: *to defeat an enemy in battle.* CONQUER, more formal, implies finally gaining control over, usually after a series of efforts or against systematic resistance: *to conquer a country, one's inclinations.* OVERCOME emphasizes surmounting difficulties in prevailing over an antagonist: *to overcome opposition, bad habits.* SUBDUE means to conquer so completely that the spirit of resistance is broken: *to subdue an uprising or a rebellious spirit.* 2. foil, baffle, balk. 6. downfall. 8. bafflement.

de·feat·ism (di fē′tiz əm), *n.* the attitude, policy, or conduct of one who admits or expects defeat, usually resulting from a premature decision that further struggle or effort is futile: *His failure to win election was attributable more to his defeatism than to the voters' lack of enthusiasm for him.* [DEFEAT + -ISM, modeled on F *défaitisme*]

de·feat·ist (di fē′tist), *n.* 1. one who surrenders easily or is subject to defeatism. 2. an advocate or follower of defeatism as a public policy. —*adj.* 3. marked by defeatism. [DEFEAT + -IST, modeled on F *défaitiste*]

de·fea·ture[1] (di fē′chər), *n. Archaic.* disfigurement. [DE- + FEATURE]

de·fea·ture[2] (di fē′chər), *n. Obs.* defeat; ruin. [DEFEAT + -URE]

def·e·cate (def′ə kāt′), *v.,* **-cat·ed, -cat·ing.** —*v.i.* 1. to void excrement from the bowels through the anus. 2. to become clear of dregs, impurities, etc. —*v.t.* 3. to clear of dregs, impurities, etc.; purify; refine. [< L *dēfaecāt(us)* cleansed, refined (ptp. of *dēfaecāre*), equiv. to *dē-* DE- + *faec-* (s. of *faex* dregs, sediment) + *-ātus* -ATE[1]] —**def′e·ca′tion,** *n.*

de·fect (*n.* dē′fekt, di fekt′; *v.* di fekt′), *n.* 1. a falling short; a fault or imperfection: *a defect in an argument; a defect in a machine.* 2. want or lack, esp. of something essential to perfection or completeness; deficiency: *a defect in hearing.* —*v.i.* 3. to desert a cause, country, etc., esp. in order to adopt another (often fol. by *to*): *He defected to the West.* [ME *defect* a falling short < L *dēfectus*, equiv. to *dēfect-* (ptp. s. of *dēficere* to fall short; see DEFICIENT) + *-us*, 4th decl. suffix] —**de·fect′i·bil′i·ty,** *n.* —**de·fect′i·ble,** *adj.* —**de·fect′less,** *adj.*
—**Syn. 1.** DEFECT, BLEMISH, FLAW refer to faults which detract from perfection. DEFECT is the general word for any kind of shortcoming or imperfection, whether literal or figurative: *a defect in eyesight, in character, in a plan.* A BLEMISH is usually a defect on a surface, which mars the appearance: *A mole or scar on a cheek (or a scratch on a table) is a blemish.* FLAW is applied to a defect in quality, caused by imperfect structure (as in a diamond) or brought about during manufacture (as in texture of cloth, in tensile strength of metals, in clearness of glass, etc.).

de·fec·tion (di fek′shən), *n.* 1. desertion from allegiance, loyalty, duty, or the like; apostasy: *His defection to East Germany was regarded as treasonable.* 2. failure; lack; loss: *He was overcome by a sudden defection of courage.* [< L *dēfectiōn-* (s. of *dēfectiō*), equiv. to *dēfect(us)* (see DEFECT) + *-iōn-* -ION]
—**Ant. 1.** loyalty.

de·fec·tive (di fek′tiv), *adj.* 1. having a defect; faulty; imperfect: *a defective machine.* 2. *Psychol.* characterized by subnormal intelligence or behavior. 3. *Gram.* (of an inflected word or its inflection) lacking one or more of the inflected forms proper to most words of the same class in the language, as English *must*, which occurs only in the present tense. —*n.* 4. a defective person or thing. [< LL *dēfectīvus* (see DEFECT, -IVE), r. ME *defectif* < MF] —**de·fec′tive·ly,** *adv.* —**de·fec′tive·ness,** *n.*
—**Syn. 1.** incomplete, deficient. —**Ant. 1.** perfect, complete.

defec′tive num′ber, *Math.* See **deficient number.**

defec′tive year′. See under **Jewish calendar.**

de·fec·tor (di fek′tər), *n.* one who defects from a cause, country, etc. [< L: deserter. See DEFECT, -OR[2]]

de·fem·i·nise (dē fem′ə nīz′), *v.t.,* **-nised, -nis·ing.** *Chiefly Brit.* defeminize. —**de·fem′i·ni·sa′tion,** *n.*

de·fem·i·nize (dē fem′ə nīz′), *v.t.,* **-nized, -niz·ing.** to remove or strip feminine qualities or characteristics from; make masculine in character, appearance, etc. [DE- + FEMIN(INE) + -IZE] —**de·fem′i·ni·za′tion,** *n.*

de·fence (di fens′), *n. Chiefly Brit.* defense. —**de·fence′a·ble,** *adj.* —**de·fence′less,** *adj.* —**de·fence′less·ly,** *adv.* —**de·fence′less·ness,** *n.*

Defence′ of Po′e·sie (pō′i sē, -zē). See **Apologie for Poetrie.**

Defence′ of Po′etry, an essay (1821) by Shelley in defense of the elements of love and imagination in poetry.

de·fend (di fend′), *v.t.* 1. to ward off attack from; guard against assault or injury (usually fol. by *from* or *against*): *She defended her children from the mad dog. The sentry defended the platoon against sudden attack.* 2. to maintain by argument, evidence, etc.; uphold: *He defended his point successfully.* 3. to contest (a legal charge, claim, etc.). 4. *Law.* to serve as attorney for (a defendant): *He has defended some of the most notorious criminals ever brought to trial.* 5. to support (an argument, theory, etc.) in the face of criticism; prove the validity of (a dissertation, thesis, or the like) by answering arguments and questions put by a committee of specialists. —*v.i.* 6. *Law.* to enter or make a defense. [ME *defende(n)* < OF *defendre* < L *dēfendere* to ward off, equiv. to *dē-* DE- + *-fendere* to strike] —**de·fend′a·ble,** *adj.* —**de·fend′er,** *n.*
—**Syn. 1.** shelter, screen, shield; garrison, fortify. DEFEND, GUARD, PRESERVE, PROTECT all mean to keep safe. To DEFEND is to strive to keep safe by resisting attack: *to defend a position in battle; to defend one's country.* To GUARD is to watch over in order to keep safe: *to guard a camp, a secret.* To PRESERVE is to keep safe in the midst of danger, either in a single instance or continuously: *to preserve a city, a spirit of conciliation.* To PROTECT is to keep safe by interposing a shield or barrier: *to protect books by means of heavy paper covers, the reputation of a friend.* 2. vindicate. —**Ant.** 1. attack.

de·fend·ant (di fen′dənt), *n.* 1. *Law.* one against whom a claim or charge is brought in a court (opposed to *plaintiff*). 2. *Obs.* defender. —*adj.* 3. defending; making one's defense: *a defendant corporation.* 4. *Obs.* defensive. [ME *defendaunt* < AF, OF *defendant*). See DEFEND, -ANT]

defend′er of the bond′, *Rom. Cath. Ch.* an official appointed in each diocese to uphold marriages of disputed validity. Also called **defend′er of the mar′riage bond′.**

Defend′er of the Faith′, a title originally conferred on Henry VIII by Pope Leo X in 1521, later withdrawn but restored by Parliament and used ever since by English sovereigns. [trans. of NL *Fidei defensor*]

de·fen·es·tra·tion (dē fen′i strā′shən), *n.* the act of throwing a person or thing out of a window: *the defenestration of the commissioners at Prague.* [DE- + L *fenestr(a)* a window + -ATION]

de·fense (di fens′ *or, for 1, 6,* dē′fens), *n.* 1. resistance against attack; protection: *They brought two more regiments to the defense of the island.* 2. something that defends, esp. a fortification: *This fort was once the main defense of the island. There is no defense against such a disease.* 3. the defending of a cause or the like by speech, argument, etc.: *He spoke in defense of the nation's foreign policy.* 4. a speech, argument, etc., in vindication: *He delivered a defense of free enterprise.* 5. *Law.* a. the denial or pleading of the defendant in answer to the claim or charge against him. b. the proceedings adopted by a defendant, or his legal agents, for defending himself. c. a defendant and his legal agents collectively. 6. *Sports.* a. the practice or art of defending oneself or one's goal against attack, as in fencing, boxing, soccer, football, etc. b. the team attempting to thwart the attack of the team having the ball or puck. c. the players of a team who line up in their own defensive zone. d. the positions on the field, ice, etc., taken by such players. Also, *esp. Brit.,* **defence.** [ME < OF < LL *dēfensa* a forbidding, n. use of fem. of ptp. of L *dēfendere* to DEFEND; r. ME *defens* < OF < ML *dēfens(um)* (thing) forbidden, neut. ptp. of L *dēfendere*] —**de·fense′less,** *adj.* —**de·fense′less·ly,** *adv.* —**de·fense′less·ness,** *n.*

de·fense·man (di fens′mən, -man′), *n., pl.* **-men** (-mən, -men′). *Sports.* a player in certain games, as ice hockey or lacrosse, who lines up in his own defensive zone. [DEFENSE + MAN[1]]

defense′ mech′anism, 1. *Physiol.* the defensive reaction of an organism, as against a pathogenic microorganism. 2. an unconscious process that opposes the entrance into consciousness or the acting out of unacceptable or painful ideas and impulses.

de·fen·si·ble (di fen′sə bəl), *adj.* 1. capable of being defended against assault or injury: *The troops were bivouacked in a defensible position.* 2. that may be defended in argument; justifiable. [ME < LL *dēfensibil(is)*, equiv. to L *dēfens(us)* (see DEFENSE) + *-ibilis* -IBLE; r. ME *defensable* < OF < LL *dēfensābil(is)*, equiv. to *dēfens(āre)* (freq. of *dēfendere* to DEFEND) + *-ābilis* -ABLE] —**de·fen′si·bil′i·ty, de·fen′si·ble·ness,** *n.* —**de·fen′si·bly,** *adv.*

de·fen·sive (di fen′siv), *adj.* 1. serving to defend; protective: *defensive armament.* 2. made or carried on for the purpose of resisting attack: *defensive treaty; a defensive attitude.* 3. of or pertaining to defense: *He plays defensive positions brilliantly.* —*n.* 4. a position or attitude of defense: *to play the defensive in a game; to be on the defensive about one's mistakes.* 5. *Obs.* something that serves to defend. [< ML *dēfensīvus* (see DEFENSE, -IVE), r. ME *defensif* < MF] —**de·fen′sive·ly,** *adv.* —**de·fen′sive·ness,** *n.*

de·fer[1] (di fûr′), *v.,* **-ferred, -fer·ring.** —*v.t.* 1. to put off (action, consideration, etc.) to a future time: *The decision has been deferred by the board until next week.* 2. to exempt temporarily from induction into military service. —*v.i.* 3. to put off action; delay. [ME *deferre(n)*, var. of *differre(n)* to DIFFER] —**de·fer′rer,** *n.*
—**Syn. 1.** DEFER, DELAY, POSTPONE imply keeping something from occurring until a future time. To DEFER is to decide deliberately to do something later on: *to defer making a decision, a payment.* To DELAY is

sometimes equivalent to DEFER, but usually it is to act in a dilatory manner and thus lay something aside until some indefinite future time: *to delay one's departure, answering a letter.* To POSTPONE a thing is to put it off to (usually) some particular time in the future, with the intention of beginning or resuming it then; the word is esp. used of official business, formal meetings, or the like: *to postpone an election.* **3.** procrastinate. **—Ant. 1.** accelerate.

de·fer[2] (di fûr′), *v.t.*, **-ferred, -fer·ring. 1.** to yield in judgment or opinion (usually fol. by *to*): *We all defer to him in these matters.* **2.** to submit for decision; refer: *We defer questions of this kind to him.* [late ME *deferre(n)* < L *dēferre* to carry from or down, report, accuse, equiv. to *dē-* DE- + *ferre* to bear]

de·fer·a·ble (di fûr′ə bəl), *adj.*, *n.* deferrable.

def·er·ence (def′ər əns), *n.* **1.** submission or yielding to the judgment, opinion, will, etc., of another. **2.** respectful or courteous regard: *in deference to his wishes.* [< F *déférence*, MF, equiv. to *defer(er)* (to) DEFER[2] + *-ence* -ENCE]

def·er·ent[1] (def′ər ənt), *adj.* marked by or showing deference: *She was always deferent to her elders.* [DEFER[2] + -ENT]

def·er·ent[2] (def′ər ənt), *adj.* *Anat.* **1.** conveying away; efferent. **2.** of or pertaining to the vas deferens. **—*n.* 3.** *Astron.* (in the Ptolemaic system) the circle around the earth in which a celestial body or the center of the epicycle of its orbit was thought to move. [< L *dēferent-* (s. of *dēferēns*), prp. of *dēferre*. See DEFER[2], -ENT]

def·er·en·tial (def′ə ren′shəl), *adj.* deferent; respectful. [after DEFERENCE, by analogy with such sets as *residence, residential*] **—def′er·en′tial·ly,** *adv.*

de·fer·ment (di fûr′mənt), *n.* **1.** the act of deferring or putting off; postponement. **2.** a temporary exemption from induction into military service. [DEFER[1] + -MENT]

de·fer·ra·ble (di fûr′ə bəl), *adj.* **1.** capable of being deferred or postponed: *deferrable demands; a deferrable project.* **2.** qualified or eligible to receive a military deferment. **—*n.* 3.** one eligible for deferment from compulsory military service. Also, **deferable.** [DEFER[1] + -ABLE]

de·fer·ral (di fûr′əl), *n.* a deferment. [DEFER[1] + -AL[2]]

de·ferred (di fûrd′), *adj.* **1.** postponed or delayed, as property rights which do not vest until some future event has occurred. **2.** suspended or withheld for or until a certain time: *a deferred payment.* **3.** classified as temporarily exempt from induction into military service. [DEFER[1] + -ED[2]]

deferred′ annu′ity, *Insurance.* an annuity which is bought either with a single premium or with periodic premiums in which the initial payment to the annuitant is to begin after a stated period of time has elapsed but not earlier than one year. Cf. **immediate annuity.**

deferred′ share′, *Chiefly Brit.* a share of stock on which a dividend is not paid until some fixed date or until some conditional event.

de·fer·vesce (dē′fər ves′, def′ər-), *v.i.*, **-vesced, -vesc·ing.** to undergo defervescence. [back formation from DEFERVESCENCE]

de·fer·ves·cence (dē′fər ves′əns, def′ər-), *n.* *Med.* the abatement of fever. [< G *Deferveszenz* < L *dēfervēscent-* (s. of *dēfervēscēns*, prp. of *dēfervēscere*), equiv. to *dē-* DE- + *fervēsce* to begin to boil; see EFFERVESCENT] **—de′fer·ves′cent,** *adj.*

de·fi·ance (di fī′əns), *n.* **1.** a daring or bold resistance to authority or to any opposing force. **2.** open disregard; contempt (often fol. by *of*): *defiance of danger; His refusal amounted to defiance.* **3.** a challenge to meet in combat or in a contest. **4. bid defiance to,** to offer resistance; defy: *to bid defiance to an oppressor.* **5. in defiance of,** in spite of; notwithstanding: *There was a splendid audience in defiance of the rainstorm.* **6. set at defiance,** to disregard or flout; defy: *He sets conventions at defiance.* [ME < OF, equiv. to *defi(er)* (to) DEFY + *-ance* -ANCE]

de·fi·ant (di fī′ənt), *adj.* characterized by defiance, bold opposition, or antagonism: *a defiant attitude.* [< F *défiant*, OF, prp. of *defi(er)* (to) DEFY + *-ant* -ANT] **—de·fi′ant·ly,** *adv.* **—de·fi′ant·ness,** *n.*
—Syn. insubordinate, contumacious, refractory, recalcitrant, rebellious, insolent; daring. **—Ant.** obedient.

de·fi·bril·late (dē fī′brə lāt′, -fib′rə-), *v.t.*, **-lat·ed, -lat·ing.** *Med.* to arrest fibrillation of. [DE- + *fibrillate*, back formation from FIBRILLATION] **—de·fi′bril·la′tion,** *n.*

de·fi·bril·la·tor (dē fī′brə lā′tər, -fib′rə-), *n.* *Med.* an agent or device for arresting fibrillation of the auricular or ventricular muscles of the heart. [DE- + FIBRILLAT(ION) + -OR[2]]

de·fi·cience (di fish′əns), *n.* *Obs.* deficiency.

de·fi·cien·cy (di fish′ən sē), *n.*, *pl.* **-cies. 1.** the state of being deficient; lack; incompleteness; insufficiency. **2.** the amount lacked; a deficit. [< LL *dēficientia*, L *dēficient-* (s. of *dēficiēns*). See DEFICIENT, -ENCY]

defi′ciency account′, an account summarizing the financial condition of an individual or company in danger of bankruptcy. Also called **defi′ciency state′ment.**

defi′ciency disease′, *Pathol.* an illness due to an insufficient supply of one or more essential dietary constituents.

defi′ciency judg′ment, *Law.* a judgment in favor of a creditor who has not satisfied the full amount of his claim against a debtor.

de·fi·cient (di fish′ənt), *adj.* **1.** lacking some element or characteristic; defective: *deficient in taste.* **2.** insufficient; inadequate: *deficient knowledge.* [< L *dēficient-* (s. of *dēficiēns*, prp. of *dēficere*), equiv. to *dē-* DE- + *fic-* make, do (sp. var. of *fac-*) + thematic *-i-* + *-ent-* -ENT] **—de·fi′cient·ly,** *adv.*

defi′cient num′ber, *Math.* a positive number that is greater than the sum of all positive integers which are submultiples of it, as 10, which is greater than the sum of 1, 2, and 5. Also called **defective number.** Cf. **abundant number, perfect number.**

def·i·cit (def′i sit; *Brit. also* di fis′it), *n.* the amount by which a sum of money falls short of the required amount. [< L: there is wanting, 3rd pers. sing. pres. indic. of *dēficere*; see DEFICIENT]
—Syn. shortage, deficiency. **—Ant.** surplus.

def′icit finan′cing, (esp. of a government) expenditures in excess of public revenues, made possible typically by borrowing.

def′icit spend′ing, the practice of spending funds in excess of income, esp. by a government.

de fi·de (de fē′de; *Eng.* dē fī′dē), *Latin.* of the faith: a phrase used in the Roman Catholic Church to qualify certain teachings as being divinely revealed, belief in them therefore being obligatory.

de·fi·er (di fī′ər), *n.* one who defies. [DEFY + -ER[1]]

def·i·lade (def′ə lād′), *n.*, *v.*, **-lad·ed, -lad·ing. —*n.* 1.** protection or shielding from hostile ground observation and flat projecting fire provided by an artificial or natural obstacle, as a hill. **—*v.t.* 2.** to shield from enemy fire by using natural or artificial obstacles. [< F *défil(er)*, orig. to unthread, equiv. to *dé-* DIS-[1] + *(en)filer* to thread << L *fil(um)* thread + F *-ade* -ADE[1]]

de·file[1] (di fīl′), *v.t.*, **-filed, -fil·ing. 1.** to make foul, dirty, or unclean; pollute; taint. **2.** to violate the chastity of. **3.** to make impure for ceremonial use; desecrate. **4.** to sully, as a person's reputation. [ME *defile(n)*, *defele(n)*, alter. of *defoilen* (by assoc. with *filen* to FILE[3]) < OF *defoule(r)* (to) trample on, violate; cf. OE *befȳlan* to befoul] **—de·fil′a·ble,** *adj.* **—de·file′ment,** *n.* **—de·fil′er,** *n.* **—de·fil′ing·ly,** *adv.*

de·file[2] (di fīl′, dē′fīl), *n.*, *v.*, **-filed, -fil·ing. —*n.* 1.** any narrow passage, esp. between mountains. **—*v.i.* 2.** to march in a line or by files; file off. [< F *défilé*, n. use of ptp. of *défiler* to file off; see DEFILADE]

de·fine (di fīn′), *v.t.*, **-fined, -fin·ing. 1.** to state or set forth the meaning of (a word, phrase, etc.): *A careful person always defines his terms.* **2.** to explain the nature or essential qualities of; describe: *to define judicial functions.* **3.** to determine or fix the boundaries or extent of: *to define property with stakes.* **4.** to make clear the outline or form of: *The artist defined the roof of the barn boldly against the sky.* **5.** to fix or lay down definitely; specify distinctly: *to define one's responsibilities.* [ME *def(f)ine(n)* < AF, OF *define(r)* (to) put an end to < L *dēfīnīre* to limit, explain, equiv. to *dē-* DE- + *fīnīre* to FINISH] **—de·fin′a·ble,** *adj.* **—de·fin′a·bil′i·ty,** *n.* **—de·fin′a·bly,** *adv.* **—de·fin′er,** *n.*

de·fin·i·en·dum (di fin′ē en′dəm), *n.*, *pl.* **-da** (-də). **1.** that which is or is to be defined, esp. the term at the head of a dictionary entry. **2.** *Logic.* an expression to be defined in terms of another expression previously defined. Cf. **definiens.** [< L, neut. ger. of *dēfīnīre* to terminate, decide, DEFINE]

de·fin·i·ens (di fin′ē ənz), *n.*, *pl.* **de·fin·i·en·tia** (di fin′ē en′chə, -chē ə). **1.** that which defines, esp. the defining part of a dictionary entry. **2.** *Logic.* an expression in terms of which another may be adequately defined. Cf. **definiendum.** [< L, prp. of *dēfīnīre*; see DEFINE]

def·i·nite (def′ə nit), *adj.* **1.** clearly defined or determined; not vague or general; fixed; precise; exact: *a definite quantity; definite directions.* **2.** having fixed limits; bounded with precision: *a definite area.* **3.** positive; certain; sure: *It is definite that he will take the job.* **4.** defining; limiting. **5.** *Bot.* (of an inflorescence) determinate. [< L *dēfīnīt(us)* bounded, precise, ptp. of *dēfīnīre*; see DEFINE] **—def′i·nite·ness,** *n.*
—Syn. 1. specific, particular. **2.** certain, clear, express. **—Ant. 1.** inexact. **2.** uncertain.

def′inite ar′ticle, an article, as English *the*, which classes as identified or definite the noun it modifies.

def′inite in′tegral, *Math.* the representation, usually in symbolic form, of the difference in values of a primitive of a given function evaluated at two designated points. Cf. **indefinite integral.**

def·i·nite·ly (def′ə nit lē), *adv.* **1.** in a definite manner. **2.** unequivocally; positively. **—*interj.* 3.** (in expressions of complete agreement or strong affirmation) certainly; to be sure. [DEFINITE + -LY]

def·i·ni·tion (def′ə nish′ən), *n.* **1.** the act of defining or making definite or clear. **2.** the formal statement of the meaning or significance of a word, phrase, etc. **3.** condition of being definite. **4.** *Optics.* sharpness of the image formed by an optical system. **5.** *Radio and Television.* the accuracy of sound reproduction through a receiver or of picture reproduction in a television receiver. [ME *diffinicioun* < OF *diffinition* < L *dēfīnītiōn-* (s. of *dēfīnītiō*), equiv. to *dēfīnīt(us)* (see DEFINITE) + *-iōn-* -ION]

de·fin·i·tise (di fin′i tīz′), *v.t.*, **-tised, -tis·ing.** *Chiefly Brit.* definitize.

de·fin·i·tive (di fin′i tiv), *adj.* **1.** most reliable or complete, as of a text, author, criticism, study, or the like: *a definitive biography; a definitive performance of a Beethoven sonata.* **2.** serving to define; fix or specify definitely: *to clarify with a definitive statement.* **3.** having its fixed and final form; providing a solution or final answer: *the definitive treatment for an infection; a definitive answer to a dilemma.* **4.** *Biol.* complete; fully developed or formed. **—*n.* 5.** a defining or limiting word, as an article, a demonstrative, or the like. [ME *diffinitif* < OF < L *dēfīnītīv(us)*, equiv. to *dēfīnīt(us)* (see DEFINITE) + *-īvus* -IVE] **—de·fin′i·tive·ly,** *adv.* **—de·fin′i·tive·ness,** *n.*

defin′itive plum′age, *Ornith.* the plumage or plumages of a bird which, once attained, do not change significantly in color or pattern for the rest of the bird's life.

def·i·nit·ize (def′ə ni tīz′), *v.t.*, **-ized, -iz·ing.** to cause to become definite; crystallize. Also, *esp. Brit.*, **definitise.** [DEFINITE + -IZE]

de·fin·i·tude (di fin′i to͞od′, -tyo͞od′), *n.* definiteness; exactitude; precision. [DEFINITE + -TUDE]

def·la·grate (def′lə grāt′, dē′flə-), *v.t.*, *v.i.*, **-grat·ed, -grat·ing.** to burn, esp. suddenly and violently. [< L *dēflagrāt(us)* burned down (ptp. of *dēflagrāre*), equiv. to *dē-* DE- + *flagr(āre)* to burn + *-ātus* -ATE[1]] **—def′la·gra·bil′i·ty,** *n.* **—def′la·gra·ble,** *adj.* **—def′la·gra′tion,** *n.*

de·flate (di flāt′), *v.*, **-flat·ed, -flat·ing. —*v.t.* 1.** to release the air or gas from (something inflated, as a balloon): *They deflated the tires to allow the truck to drive under the overpass.* **2.** to reduce (currency, prices, etc.) from an inflated condition. **3.** to depress or reduce (a person or a person's ego, hopes, spirits, etc.); puncture; dash: *Her rebuff thoroughly deflated him.* **—*v.i.* 4.** to become deflated. [< L *dēflāt(us)* blown off, away (ptp. of *dēflāre*), equiv. to *dē-* DE- + *fl(āre)* (to) blow + *-ātus* -ATE[1]] **—de·fla′tor,** *n.*

de·fla·tion (di flā′shən), *n.* **1.** the act of deflating or the state of being deflated. **2.** an abnormal decline in the level of commodity prices, esp. one not accompanied by an equal reduction in the costs of production. **3.** the erosion of sand, soil, etc., by the action of the wind. [DEFLATE + -ION] **—de·fla·tion·ar·y** (di flā′shə ner′ē), *adj.* **—de·fla′tion·ist,** *n.*, *adj.*

defla′tionary spi′ral, *Econ.* See **spiral** (def. 7).

de·flect (di flekt′), *v.t.*, *v.i.* to bend or turn aside; turn from a true course or straight line; swerve. [< L *dēflect(ere)* (to) bend down, turn aside, equiv. to *dē-* DE- + *flectere* to bend, turn] **—de·flect′a·ble,** *adj.*

de·flect·ed (di flek′tid), *adj.* *Biol.* **1.** curved or bent downward. **2.** deflexed. [DEFLECT + -ED[2]]

deflect′ing force′. See **coriolis effect.**

de·flec·tion (di flek′shən), *n.* **1.** the act or state of deflecting or the state of being deflected. **2.** amount of deviation. **3.** *Physics.* the deviation of the indicator of an instrument from the position taken as zero. **4.** *Optics.* deviation (def. 5a). **5.** *Mil.* the angle formed by the line of sight to the target and the line of sight to the point at which a gun is aimed so as to strike the target. **6.** *Electronics.* (in a cathode ray tube) the bending by a magnetic field of the beam of electrons leaving the electron gun. Also, *Brit.*, **deflexion.** [< LL *dēflexiōn-* (s. of *dēflexiō*), equiv. to L *dēflex(us)* (ptp. of *dēflectere*; see DEFLECT) + *-iōn-* -ION]

deflec′tion yoke′, *Electronics.* an assembly of one or more coils through which a controlled current is passed to produce a magnetic field for deflecting a beam of electrons. Also called **yoke.**

de·flec·tive (di flek′tiv), *adj.* causing deflection. [DEFLECT + -IVE]

de·flec·tor (di flek′tər), *n.* **1.** one who or that which deflects. **2.** an instrument for measuring the deviation caused in a compass by surrounding metal and by electrical currents. [DEFLECT + -OR[2]]

de·flexed (di flekst′), *adj.* *Biol.* **1.** bent abruptly downward. **2.** deflected. [< L *dēflex(us)* bent down; see DEFLECTION, -ED[2]]

de·flex·ion (di flek′shən), *n.* *Brit.* deflection.

de·floc·cu·lant (dē flok′yə lənt), *n.* *Ceram.* a chemical added to slip to increase fluidity. [DEFLOCCU(LATE) + -ANT]

de·floc·cu·late (dē flok′yə lāt′), *v.t.*, **-lat·ed, -lat·ing.** *Physical Chem.* to reduce from a flocculent state by dispersing the flocculated particles. [DE- + FLOCCULATE] **—de·floc′cu·la′tion,** *n.*

def·lo·ra·tion (def′lə rā′shən, dē′flə-), *n.* the act of deflowering. [ME *defloracioun* < OF *defloracion*, LL *dēflōrātiōn-* (s. of *dēflōrātiō*) a plucking of flowers, equiv. to *dēflōrāt(us)*, lit., deprived of flowers, ptp. of *dēflōr(āre)* (to) DEFLOWER + *-ātiōn-* -ATION]

de·flow·er (di flou′ər), *v.t.* **1.** to deprive or strip of flowers: *The deer had deflowered an entire section of the field.* **2.** to deprive (a woman) of virginity; ravish; violate. **3.** to despoil of beauty, freshness, sanctity, etc. [ME *defloure(n)* < OF *desflore(r)* < L *dēflōrāre*, equiv. to *dē-* DE- + *flōrāre* to FLOWER] **—de·flow′er·er,** *n.*

de·flux·ion (di fluk′shən), *n.* *Pathol.* a copious discharge of fluid matter, as in catarrh. [< LL *dēfluxiōn-* (s. of *dēfluxiō*) a flowing down, discharge, equiv. to L *dē-* DE- + *fluxiōn-* FLUXION]

De·foe (di fō′), *n.* **Daniel** (*Daniel Foe*), 1659?–1731, English novelist and political journalist. Also, **De Foe′.**

de·fo·li·ant (dē fō′lē ənt), *n.* a preparation for defoliating plants. [DEFOLI(ATE) + -ANT]

de·fo·li·ate (*v.* dē fō′lē āt′; *adj.* dē fō′lē it, -āt′), *v.*, **-at·ed, -at·ing,** *adj.* **—*v.t.* 1.** to strip (a tree, bush, etc.) of leaves. **2.** to destroy (an area of jungle, forest, etc.), as by chemical sprays or incendiary bombs, in order to give enemy troops or guerrilla forces no place of concealment. **—*v.i.* 3.** to lose leaves. **—*adj.* 4.** (of a tree) having lost its leaves, esp. by a natural process. [< ML *dēfoliāt(us)*, ptp. of *dēfoliāre*, equiv. to L *dē-* DE- + *foli(um)* leaf + *-ātus* -ATE[1]] **—de·fo′li·a′tion,** *n.* **—de·fo′li·a′tor,** *n.*

de·force (di fôrs′, fōrs′), *v.t.*, **-forced, -forc·ing.** *Law.* to withhold (property, esp. land) by force or violence, as from the rightful owner. [ME < AF *deforc(er)*, OF *de(s)forc(ier)*, equiv. to *de(s)-* DE- + *forc(i)er* to FORCE] **—de·force′ment,** *n.* **—de·forc′er,** *n.*

de·for·ciant (di fôr′shənt, -fōr′-), *n.* *Law.* one who deforces. [< AF, prp. of *deforcer.* See DEFORCE, -ANT]

De For·est (di fôr′ist, for′-), **Lee,** 1873–1961, U.S. inventor, esp. in the field of electronics.

de·for·est (dē fôr′ist, -for′-), *v.t.* to divest of forests or trees: *Poor planning deforested the area in 10 years.* [DE- + FOREST] **—de·for′est·a′tion,** *n.* **—de·for′est·er,** *n.*

de·form[1] (di fôrm′), *v.t.* **1.** to mar the natural form or shape of; put out of shape; disfigure: *In cases where the drug was taken during pregnancy, it deformed the infants.* **2.** to make ugly, ungraceful, or displeasing; mar the beauty of; spoil: *The trees had been completely deformed by the force of the wind.* **3.** to change the form of; transform. **4.** *Mech.* to subject to deformation: *The metal was deformed under stress.* [ME *deform(en)* < L *dēform(āre)*, equiv. to *dē-* DE- + *formāre* to FORM] **—de·form′a·bil′i·ty,** *n.* **—de·form′a·ble,** *adj.* **—de·form′a·tive,** *adj.* **—de·form′er,** *n.*
—Syn. 1. misshape. See **mar. 2.** ruin.

de·form[2] (di fôrm′), *adj.* *Archaic.* deformed; ugly. [ME *defo(u)rme* < L *dēform(is)*, equiv. to *dē-* DE- + *-formis* -FORM]

de·for·ma·tion (dē′fôr mā′shən, def′ər-), *n.* **1.** the act of deforming; distortion; disfigurement. **2.** result of deforming; change of form, esp. for the worse. **3.** *Mech.* a change in the shape or dimensions of a body, resulting from stress; strain. **4.** an altered form. [ME *deformacioun* < L *dēformātiōn-* (s. of *dēformātiō*), equiv. to *dēformāt(us)* (ptp. of *dēformāre*; see DEFORM[1]) + *-iōn-* -ION] **—de′for·ma′tion·al,** *adj.*

de·formed (di fôrmd′), *adj.* **1.** having the form changed, with loss of beauty, etc.; misshapen; disfigured: *After the accident his arm was deformed.* **2.** hateful; offensive: *a deformed personality.* [ME; see DEFORM[1], -ED[2]] **—de·form·ed·ly** (di fôr′mid lē), *adv.* **—de·form′ed·ness,** *n.*
—Syn. 1. malformed, crippled.

deformed′ bar′, a rod for reinforcing concrete, having surface irregularities, as transverse ridges, to improve the bond.

de·for·me·ter (di fôr′mē tər), *n.* a gauge used to determine stresses in a structure by tests on a model of the structure. [DEFOR(MATION) + -METER]

de·form·i·ty (di fôr′mi tē), *n., pl.* **-ties.** **1.** the quality or state of being deformed, disfigured, or misshapen. **2.** *Pathol.* an abnormally formed part of the body. **3.** a deformed person or thing. **4.** hatefulness; ugliness. [ME *deformite* < OF < L *dēformitās,* equiv. to *dēform(is)* DEFORM² + *-itās* -ITY]

de·fraud (di frôd′), *v.t.* to deprive of a right or property by fraud; cheat: *They were defrauded of their money in an old confidence game.* [ME *defraud(en)* < OF *defraud(er)* < L *dēfraudāre,* equiv. to *dē-* DE- + *fraudāre* to cheat; see FRAUD] —**de·frau·da·tion** (dē′frô dā′shən), **de·fraud′ment,** *n.* —**de·fraud′er,** *n.*

de·fray (di frā′), *v.t.* to bear or pay (the costs, expenses, etc.): *The grant helped defray the expenses of the trip.* [< F *défray(er),* OF *deffroier* to pay costs, equiv. to *de-* DIS-¹ + *frai* cost] —**de·fray′a·ble,** *adj.* —**de·fray′er,** *n.*

de·fray·al (di frā′əl), *n.* payment of charges or expenses. Also, **de·fray′ment.** [DEFRAY + -AL²]

de·frock (dē frok′), *v.t.* to unfrock. [< F *défroqu(er),* equiv. to *dé-* DIS-¹ + *froque* FROCK + *-er* inf. suffix]

de·frost (di frôst′, -frost′), *v.t.* **1.** to remove the frost or ice from. —*v.i.* **2.** to become free of ice or frost; thaw: *The refrigerator defrosted quickly. The meat took two hours to defrost.* [DE- + FROST]

de·frost·er (di frô′stər, -fros′tər), *n.* **1.** one who or that which defrosts. **2.** a blower device for evaporating moisture condensed on the inside of a windshield or other window of an automobile, airplane, or other vehicle. [DEFROST + -ER¹]

defs., definitions.

deft (deft), *adj.* dexterous; nimble; skillful; clever: *deft hands; a deft mechanic.* [ME; var. of DAFT] —**deft′ly,** *adv.* —**deft′ness,** *n.*

de·funct (di fungkt′), *adj.* **1.** deceased; dead; extinct: *a defunct person; a defunct tribe of Indians.* **2.** no longer in effect or use; not operating or functioning: *a defunct law; a defunct practice; a defunct style.* **3. the defunct,** the dead person referred to: *the survivors of the defunct.* [< L *dēfunct(us)* discharged, dead (ptp. of *dēfungī*), equiv. to *dē-* DE- + *functus* performed; see FUNCTION] —**de·funct′ness,** *n.*

de·func·tive (di fungk′tiv), *adj.* of or pertaining to the dead; funereal. [< L *dēfunct(us)* DEFUNCT + -IVE]

De Fu′ni·ak Springs′ (də fyōō′nē ak′), a town in NW Florida. 5282 (1960).

de·fuse (dē fyōōz′), *v.t.,* **-fused, -fus·ing.** defuze.

de·fu·sion (dē fyōō′zhən), *n.* *Psychoanal.* separation of the life instinct from the death instinct, a process often accompanying maturity. [DE- + FUSION]

de·fuze (dē fyōōz′), *v.t.,* **-fuzed, -fuz·ing.** to remove the fuze from (a bomb, mine, etc.). Also, **defuse.** [DE- + FUZE]

de·fy (*v.* di fī′; *n.* di fī′, dē′fī), *v.,* **-fied, -fy·ing,** *n., pl.* **-fies.** —*v.t.* **1.** to challenge the power of; resist boldly or openly: *to defy a judge's order; to defy the authority of one's father.* **2.** to offer effective resistance to: *a fort that defies attack.* **3.** to challenge (one) to do something deemed impossible: *They defied him to jump off the bridge.* **4.** *Archaic.* to challenge to a combat or contest. —*n.* **5.** *Informal.* a challenge; a defiance. [ME *defie(n)* < OF *desfi(er),* equiv. to *des-* DE- + *fier* to trust < VL **fīdāre,* var. of L *fīdere*] —**de·fi′a·ble,** *adj.* —**de·fy′ing·ly,** *adv.*
—**Syn. 1.** dare, brave, flout, scorn.

deg., degree; degrees.

dé·ga·gé (dā ga zhā′), *adj.* *French.* **1.** unconstrained; easy, as in manner. **2.** without emotional involvement, as in causes or questions of public interest. [lit., disengaged]

de·gas (di gas′), *v.t.,* **-gassed, -gas·sing.** **1.** to free from gas. **2.** to treat (a gas or its harmful properties) with chemical agents. **3.** to complete the evacuation of gases in (a vacuum tube). [DE- + GAS]

De·gas (də gä′), *n.* **Hi·laire Ger·main Ed·gar** (ē ler′ zher man′ ed gar′), 1834–1917, French impressionist painter.

De Gas·pa·ris (di gas′par is), *n.* a walled plain in the third quadrant of the face of the moon: about 20 miles in diameter.

De Gas·pe·ri (de gäs′pe rē), **Al·ci·de** (äl chē′de), 1881–1954, Italian statesman: premier 1945–53.

de Gaulle (də gōl′, gôl′), **Charles An·dré Jo·seph Ma·rie** (chärlz än′drā jō′zəf mə rē′; *Fr.* sharl än drā′ zhō zef′ ma rē′), 1890–1970, French general and statesman: president 1959–69.

de Gaull·ism (də gō′liz əm, gô′-), Gaullism.

de Gaull·ist (də gō′list, gô′-), Gaullist.

de·gauss (dē gous′), *v.t.* to neutralize (the magnetic field of a ship's hull, electrical equipment, etc.) by means of electric coils that create a magnetic field cancelling that of the hull, chassis, etc. Cf. **deperm.** [DE- + GAUSS] —**de·gauss′er,** *n.*

de·gen·er·a·cy (di jen′ər ə sē), *n.* degenerate state or character; degeneration. [DEGENERA(TE) + -CY]

de·gen·er·ate (*v.* di jen′ə rāt′; *adj., n.* di jen′ər it), *v.,* **-at·ed, -at·ing,** *adj., n.* —*v.i.* **1.** to decline in physical, mental, or moral qualities; deteriorate: *The morale of the soldiers degenerated, and they were unable to fight.* **2.** *Biol.* to revert to a less highly organized or simpler type. —*adj.* **3.** having declined in physical or moral qualities; deteriorated; degraded: *a degenerate king.* **4.** having lost, or become impaired with respect to, the qualities proper to the race or kind: *a degenerate plant.* **5.** characterized by or associated with degeneracy: *degenerate times.* **6.** *Physics.* **a.** pertaining to a vibrating system with several degrees of freedom such that with two or more degrees of freedom, the same frequency is or may be associated. **b.** obeying the laws of quantum mechanics and having several equal energy levels. —*n.* **7.** one who has declined, as in morals or character, from a type or standard considered normal. **8.** a sexual deviate. **9.** *Pathol.* a person exhibiting morbid physical or mental traits or tendencies. [< L *dēgenerāt(us)* departed from its race (ptp. of *dēgenerāre*), equiv. to *dēgener-* (s. of *dēgener*) not genuine + *-ātus* -ATE¹; see DE-, GENERATE] —**de·gen′er·ate·ly,** *adv.* —**de·gen′er·ate·ness,** *n.*

degen′erate state′, Usually, **degenerate states.** a quantum state of a system, having the same energy level as, but a different wave function from, another state of the system.

de·gen·er·a·tion (di jen′ə rā′shən), *n.* **1.** the process of degenerating. **2.** the condition or state of being degenerate. **3.** *Biol.* reversion to a less highly organized or simpler type. **4.** *Pathol.* **a.** a process by which a tissue deteriorates, loses functional activity, and may become converted into or replaced by other kinds of tissue. **b.** the condition produced by such a process. [< LL *dēgenerātiōn-* (s. of *dēgenerātiō*). See DE-, GENERATION]

de·gen·er·a·tive (di jen′ə rā′tiv, -ər ə tiv), *adj.* **1.** tending to degenerate. **2.** characterized by degeneration. [DEGENERATE + -IVE]

degen′erative joint′ disease′, *Pathol.* osteoarthritis.

de Ghel·de·rode (də gel də rōd′), *n.* **Mi·chel** (mē shel′), 1898–1962, Belgian dramatist.

de·gla·ci·a·tion (dē glā′sē ā′shən, -shē-), *n.* the gradual melting away of a glacier from the surface of a land mass. [DE- + GLACIATION]

de·glam·or·ize (dē glam′ə rīz′), *v.t.,* **-ized, -iz·ing.** to take away the glamor of; treat so as to reduce the attractiveness or status of. [DE- + GLAMORIZE] —**de·glam′or·i·za′tion,** *n.*

deglut., (in prescriptions) may be swallowed; let it be swallowed. [< L *dēglutiātur*]

de·glu·ti·nate (dē glōōt′ənāt′), *v.t.,* **-nat·ed, -nat·ing.** to extract the gluten from. [< L *dēglūtinātus* (ptp. of *dēglūtināre*), equiv. to *dē-* DE- + *glūtināre* to GLUE (*glūtin-* (see GLUTEN) + *-ātus* -ATE¹)] —**de·glu′ti·na′tion,** *n.*

de·glu·ti·tion (dē′glōō tish′ən), *n.* *Physiol.* the act or process of swallowing. [< F *déglutition* < L *dēglūt(us)* swallowed down, ptp. of *dēglūt(īre),* equiv. to *dē-* DE- + *glūt(īre)* (to) swallow (see GLUTTON¹) + *-itus* ptp. suffix; see -ION] —**de′glu·ti′tious,** *adj.*

de·gold (dē gōld′), *v.t.* *Metall.* to remove gold from (lead in base bullion form). [DE- + GOLD]

deg·ra·da·tion (deg′rə dā′shən), *n.* **1.** the act of degrading. **2.** the state of being degraded. **3.** *Phys. Geog.* the wearing down of the land by the action of water, wind, or ice; erosion. **4.** *Chem.* the breakdown of a compound, esp. an organic hydrocarbon. [< LL *dēgradātiōn-* (s. of *dēgradātiō*), equiv. to *dēgradāt(us)* (ptp. of *dēgradāre* to DEGRADE) + *-iōn-* -ION] —**deg′ra·da′tion·al,** *adj.* —**deg′ra·da′tive,** *adj.*
—**Syn. 2.** humiliation, disgrace, dishonor, debasement.

degrada′tion of en′ergy, *Thermodynamics.* the principle that during any irreversible process the total energy available to do work decreases.

de·grade (di grād′; *also, for 1,* dē grād′), *v.,* **-grad·ed, -grad·ing.** —*v.t.* **1.** to reduce (someone) to a lower rank, degree, etc.; deprive of office, rank, degree, or title, esp. as a punishment: *degraded from public office.* **2.** to lower in character or quality; debase; deprave. **3.** to lower in dignity or estimation; bring into contempt: *He felt they were degrading him by making him wash the dishes.* **4.** to reduce in amount, strength, intensity, etc. **5.** *Phys. Geog.* to wear down by erosion, as hills (opposed to *aggrade*). **6.** *Chem.* to break down (a compound, esp. an organic hydrocarbon). —*v.i.* **7.** *Chem.* (esp. of an organic hydrocarbon compound) to break down or decompose. [ME *degrade(n)* < LL *dēgrad(āre),* equiv. to L *dē-* DE- + *grad(us)* GRADE + *-āre* inf. suffix] —**de·grad′er,** *n.*
—**Syn. 1.** demote, depose, downgrade, lower, cashier, break. **2.** abase, vitiate. **3.** disgrace, dishonor, discredit. See **humble.** —**Ant. 1.** promote. **2, 3.** exalt.

de·grad·ed (di grā′did), *adj.* **1.** reduced in rank, position, reputation, etc.: *He felt degraded by the mental tasks assigned to him.* **2.** reduced in quality or value; debased; vulgarized: *the degraded level of the modern novel.* [late ME; see DEGRADE, -ED²] —**de·grad′ed·ly,** *adv.* —**de·grad′ed·ness,** *n.*

de·grad·ing (di grā′ding), *adj.* that degrades; debasing: *degrading submission.* [DEGRADE + -ING²] —**de·grad′ing·ly,** *adv.* —**de·grad′ing·ness,** *n.*

de gra·ti·a (dē grā′shē ə; *Lat.* de grä′tē ä′), *Law.* by favor or grace. [< L]

de·grease (dē grēs′, -grēz′), *v.t.,* **-greased, -greas·ing.** **1.** to remove grease, oil, or the like, from: *to degrease a stove.* **2.** *Chem.* to remove the grease from (metal, wool, etc.) by treating with a chemical. [DE- + GREASE] —**de·greas′er,** *n.*

de·gree (di grē′), *n.* **1.** any of a series of steps or stages, as in a process or course of action; a point in any scale. **2.** a stage or point, in or as if in progression or retrogression: *She finished the assignment by degrees. He grew weaker by degrees.* **3.** a stage in a scale of rank or station; relative standing in society, business, etc.: *His uncouth behavior showed him to be a man of low degree.* **4.** a stage in a scale of intensity or amount: *a high degree of mastery.* **5.** extent, measure, scope, or the like: *To what degree will he cooperate? Each of us in varying degrees has learned this for himself.* **6.** *Geom.* the 360th part of a complete angle or turn, often indicated by the sign°, as 45°. **7.** a unit in the measurement of temperature: *He has a temperature of 101 degrees.* **8.** a unit of measure, as of temperature or pressure, marked off on the scale of a measuring instrument: *This thermometer only shows a scale of degrees between 20° and 40° C.* **9.** *Geog., Astron.* a line or point on the earth or the celestial sphere, the position of which is defined by its angular distance from the equator, the equinoctial, or from a given meridian. **10.** the distinctive classification of a crime according to its gravity: *murder in the first degree.* **11.** *Educ.* an academic title conferred by universities and colleges as an indication of the completion of a course of study, or as an honorary recognition of achievement. **12.** *Gram.* one of the parallel formations of adjectives and adverbs used to express differences in quality, quantity, or intensity. In English, *low* and *careful* are the positive degree, *lower* and *more careful* are the comparative degree, *lowest* and *most careful* are the superlative degree. **13.** *Math.* **a.** the sum of the exponents of the variables in an algebraic expression: *x^3 and $2x^2y$ are terms of degree three.* **b.** the term of highest degree of a given equation or polynomial: *The expression $3x^2y + y^2 + 1$ is of degree three.* **c.** the exponent of the derivative of highest order appearing in a given differential equation. **14.** *Music.* a tone or step of the scale. **15.** *Genetics.* a certain distance or remove in the line of descent, determining the proximity of relationship: *a cousin of the second degree.* **16.** *Obs.* a step, as of a stair. **17. by degrees,** by easy stages; gradually: *He grew angrier by degrees.* **18. to a degree, a.** to a considerable extent; exceedingly. **b.** to a small extent; somewhat: *He is to a degree difficult to get along with.* [ME *degre* < OF < L *dē-* DE- + *grad(us)* GRADE] —**de·gree′less,** *adj.*

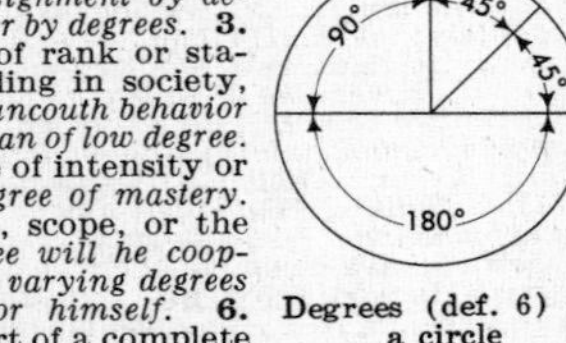

Degrees (def. 6) of a circle

de·gree-day (di grē′dā′), *n.* one degree of deviation, on a single day, of the daily mean temperature from a given standard temperature: five degrees above or below the standard temperature would be recorded as five degree-days. *Abbr.:* dd Cf. **cooling degree-day, growing degree-day, heating degree-day.**

degree′ of free′dom, *Physics, Chem.* one of the independent variables designating a way in which the configuration in space of a system can change. Also called **degree′ of var′iance.**

de·gres·sion (di gresh′ən), *n.* **1.** a downward movement; descent. **2.** the decrease in rate in degressive taxation. [late ME < ML *dēgressiōn-* (s. of *dēgressiō*) descent, equiv. to L *dēgress(us)* having gone aside, down (ptp. of *dēgredī*; *dē-* DE- + *gre-* go (ptp. s. of *gradī*) + *-ss-* ptp. suffix) + *-iōn-* -ION]

de·gres·sive (di gres′iv), *adj.* pertaining to a form of taxation in which the rate diminishes gradually on sums below a certain fixed amount. [DEGRESS(ION) + -IVE] —**de·gres′sive·ly,** *adv.*

de Groot (də khrōt′), **Huig** (hoikh). See **Grotius, Hugo.**

de·gum (dē gum′), *v.t.,* **-gummed, -gum·ming.** **1.** to free from gum. **2.** to remove sericin from (silk filaments or yarn) by boiling the silk in a soap solution; boil off. [DE- + GUM¹] —**de·gum′mer,** *n.*

de·gust (di gust′), *v.t.* taste; savor. Also, **de·gus·tate** (di gus′tāt). [< L *dēgust(āre)* (to) taste, try, equiv. to *dē-* DE- + *gustāre* to taste (*gust(us)* a tasting + *-āre* inf. suffix)] —**de·gus·ta·tion** (dē′gu stā′shən), *n.*

de gus·ti·bus non est dis·pu·tan·dum (de gōōs′ti bōōs′ nōn est dis′pōō tän′dōōm; *Eng.* dē gus′tə bəs non est dis′pyōō tan′dəm), *Latin.* there is no disputing about tastes.

de Haas (də häz′), **Jacob,** 1872–1937, English Zionist leader, in U.S. after 1902.

de·hisce (di his′), *v.i.,* **-hisced, -hisc·ing.** to gape; burst open, as capsules of plants. [< L *dēhisc(ere)* (to) gape, part, equiv. to *dē-* DE- + *hiscere* to gape, yawn (*hi(āre)* (to) yawn + *-sc(ere)* inceptive suffix)]

de·his·cence (di his′əns), *n.* **1.** the natural bursting open of capsules, fruits, anthers, etc., for the discharge of their contents. **2.** *Biol.* the release of materials by the splitting open of an organ or tissue. [< NL *dēhiscentia,* equiv. to L *dēhiscent-* DEHISCENT + *-ia*; see -ENCE]

de·his·cent (di his′ənt), *adj.* gaping open; characterized by dehiscence. [< L *dēhiscent-* (s. of *dēhiscēns*) gaping, prp. of *dēhiscere.* See DEHISCE, -ENT]

de·horn (dē hôrn′), *v.t.* **1.** to deprive (cattle) of horns. **2.** *Mil. Slang.* to defuze (a bomb, mine, etc.). [DE- + HORN] —**de·horn′er,** *n.*

De Hor′sey rig′ (də hôr′sē), *Naut.* a British two-masted rig composed of a jib-headed foresail and a loose-footed gaff mainsail.

de·hort (di hôrt′), *v.t.* *Archaic.* to seek to dissuade. [< L *dēhort(ārī)* (to) dissuade, equiv. to *dē-* DE- + *hortārī* to urge (*hor(īrī)* (to) urge + *-t-* freq. suffix + *-ārī* passive inf. suffix)] —**de·hor·ta·tion** (dē′hôr tā′shən), *n.* —**de·hor′ta·tive, de·hor′ta·to·ry,** *adj., n.* —**de·hort′er,** *n.*

Deh·ra Dun (dā′rə dōōn′), a city in NW Uttar Pradesh, in N India. 126,900 (1961).

de·hu·man·ise (dē hyōō′mə nīz′ *or, often,* -yōō′-), *v.t.,* **-ised, -is·ing.** *Chiefly Brit.* dehumanize. —**de·hu′man·i·sa′tion,** *n.*

de·hu·man·ize (dē hyōō′mə nīz′ *or, often,* -yōō′-), *v.t.,* **-ized, -iz·ing.** to deprive of human qualities or attributes; divest of individuality: *Conformity dehumanized him.* [DE- + HUMANIZE] —**de·hu′man·i·za′tion,** *n.*

de·hu·mid·i·fi·er (dē′hyōō mid′ə fī′ər, *or, often,* -yōō-), *n.* an electrical appliance for removing moisture from the air, as for lowering the humidity in a storage room. [DE- + HUMIDIFIER]

de·hu·mid·i·fy (dē′hyōō mid′ə fī′ *or, often,* -yōō-), *v.t.,* **-fied, -fy·ing.** to remove moisture from. [DE- + HUMIDIFY] —**de′hu·mid′i·fi·ca′tion,** *n.*

de·hy·drate (dē hī′drāt), *v.,* **-drat·ed, -drat·ing.** —*v.t.* **1.** to deprive (a chemical compound) of water or the elements of water. **2.** to free (fruit, vegetables, etc.) from moisture for preservation. **3.** to remove water from (the body or a tissue). —*v.i.* **4.** to lose water or moisture: *Milk dehydrates easily.* [DE- + HYDRATE] —**de′hy·dra′tion,** *n.* —**de·hy′dra·tor,** *n.*
—**Syn. 2.** See **evaporate.**

de·hy·dro·freeze (dē hī′drə frēz′), *v.t.,* **-froze, -fro·zen, -freez·ing.** to subject (food) to partial dehydration and quick-freezing for refrigerated storage. [DE- + HYDRO-¹ + FREEZE]

de·hy·dro·gen·ase (dē hī′drə jə nās′), *n.* *Biochem.* any of a class of oxide-reductase enzymes that catalyze the removal of hydrogen. [DE- + HYDROGEN + -ASE]

de·hy·dro·gen·ate (dē hī′drə jə nāt′, -hī droj′ə-), *v.t.,* **-at·ed, -at·ing.** *Chem.* to remove hydrogen from (a compound). [DE- + HYDROGENATE] —**de·hy′dro·gen·a′tion,** *n.*

de·hy·dro·gen·ise (dē hī′drə jə nīz′, -hī droj′ə-), *v.t.,* **-ised, -is·ing.** *Chiefly Brit.* dehydrogenize. —**de·hy′dro·gen·i·sa′tion,** *n.* —**de·hy′dro·gen·is′er,** *n.*

de·hy·dro·gen·ize (dē hī′drə jə nīz′, -hī droj′ə-), *v.t.,* **-ized, -iz·ing.** *Chem.* dehydrogenate. [DE- + HYDROGENIZE] —**de·hy′dro·gen·i·za′tion,** *n.* —**de·hy′dro·gen·iz′er,** *n.*

de·hyp·no·tise (dē hip′nə tīz′), *v.t.,* **-tised, -tis·ing.** *Chiefly Brit.* dehypnotize.

de·hyp·no·tize (dē hip′nə tīz′), *v.t.,* **-tized, -tiz·ing.** to bring out of the hypnotic state. [DE- + HYPNOTIZE]

D.E.I., Dutch East Indies.

De·ia·ni·ra (dē′yə nī′rə), *n.* *Class. Myth.* a sister of Meleager and wife of Hercules, whom she killed unwittingly by giving him a shirt that had been dipped in the poisoned blood of Nessus. Also, **De′ia·nei′ra.**

de·ice (dē īs′), *v.t.*, **-iced, -ic·ing. 1.** to free or keep free of ice. **2.** to prevent or remove ice formation on (the wing of an airplane or the like). Also, **de-ice′.** [DE- + ICE]

de·ic·er (dē ī′sər), *n.* a mechanical or exhaust-heat device or a chemical substance for preventing or removing ice. Also, **de-ic′er.** [DEICE + -ER[1]]

de·i·cide (dē′i sīd′), *n.* **1.** one who kills a god. **2.** the act of killing a god. [< NL *deicīd(a)*, equiv. to L *dei-* (comb. form of *deus* god) + *-cīd-* -CIDE + *-a* fem. n. suffix] **—de′i·ci′dal,** *adj.*

De·ic·o·ön (dē ik′ō on′), *n.* *Class. Myth.* a son of Megara and Hercules, killed by his father in a fit of madness.

deic·tic (dīk′tik), *adj.* **1.** *Logic.* proving directly. **2.** *Gram.* pointing; demonstrative. [< Gk *deiktik(ós)* relating to proof, *deikt(ós)* able to be proved + *-ikos* -IC] **—deic′ti·cal·ly,** *adv.*

De·i·da·mi·a (dē′i də mī′ə), *n.* *Class. Myth.* a daughter of Lycomedes who bore a son, Neoptolemus, to Achilles.

de·if·ic (dē if′ik), *adj.* making divine; deifying. [< LL *deific(us)*, equiv. to L *dei-* (comb. form of *deus* god) + *fic-* -FIC- + *-us* adj. suffix]

de·i·fi·ca·tion (dē′ə fə kā′shən), *n.* **1.** the act of deifying. **2.** the state of being deified. **3.** the result of deifying: *Buddha is a deification of the human intellect.* [ME *deificacion* < LL *deificātiōn-* (s. of *deificātiō*), equiv. to *deificāt(us)* (ptp. of *deificāre*; *deific(us)* DEIFIC + *-ātus* -ATE[1]) + *-iōn-* -ION]

de·i·form (dē′ə fôrm′), *adj.* godlike; divine. [< ML *deiform(is)*, equiv. to L *dei-* (comb. form of *deus* god) + *-formis* -FORM] **—de′i·form′i·ty,** *n.*

de·i·fy (dē′ə fī′), *v.t.*, **-fied, -fy·ing. 1.** to make a god of; exalt to the rank of a deity; personify as a deity: *The people deified their beloved king. Buddhists deify the human intellect.* **2.** to adore or regard as a deity: *to deify prudence.* [ME *deifi(en)* < OF *deifi(er)* < LL *deificāre*. See DEIFICATION, -IFY] **—de′i·fi′er,** *n.*

deign (dān), *v.i.* **1.** to think fit or in accordance with one's dignity; condescend: *He would not deign to discuss the matter with us.* **—***v.t.* **2.** to condescend to give or grant: *He deigned no reply.* **3.** *Obs.* to condescend to accept. [ME *dein(en)* < OF *deign(ier)* < L *dignārī* to judge worthy, equiv. to *dign(us)* worthy + *-ārī* pass. inf. suffix]

De·i gra·ti·a (de′ē grä′tē ä′; *Eng.* dē′ī grā′shē ə), *Latin.* by the grace of God.

deil (dēl), *n.* *Scot.* devil. [ME *del, dule*]

De I·mi·ta·ti·o·ne Chris·ti (dē im′i tā′shē ō′nē kris′tī; *Lat.* de im′i tä′tē ō′ne kris′tē). See **Imitation of Christ, The.**

Dei·mos (dī′mos), *n.* **1.** an ancient Greek personification of fear, a son of Ares and brother of Phobus. **2.** *Astron.* one of the two satellites of Mars, having a diameter of about five miles and orbiting the planet at an altitude of 12,500 miles. Cf. **Phobos.**

De·i·on (dē′ē on′), *n.* *Class. Myth.* a son of Aeolus and Enarete who became king of Phocis.

de·i·on·ize (dē ī′ə nīz′), *v.t.*, **-ized, -iz·ing.** *Chem.* **1.** to remove ions from. **2.** to reassociate the ions of (an ionized gas). [DE- + IONIZE] **—de·i′on·i·za′tion,** *n.* **—de·i′on·iz′er,** *n.*

De·i·o·pe (dē ī′ə pē′), *n.* *Class. Myth.* a woman believed to be the daughter of Triptolemus.

De·iph·i·lus (dē if′ə ləs), *n.* *Class. Myth.* Thoas (def. 2).

De·iph·o·be (dē if′ə bē′), *n.* (in the *Aeneid*) a daughter of Glaucus.

De·iph·o·bus (dē if′ə bəs), *n.* *Class. Myth.* a son of Priam and Hecuba who married Helen after the death of Paris and was slain by Menelaus.

De·i·phon·tes (dē′ə fon′tēz), *n.* *Class. Myth.* the son-in-law of Temenus and husband of Hyrnetho. Temenus willed his kingdom to Deiphontes rather than to his own sons.

deip·nos·o·phist (dīp nos′ə fist), *n.* a person who is an adept conversationalist at table. [after a literary work by Athenaus *Deipnosophistēs*, an expert in affairs of the kitchen, equiv. to *deipno(n)* meal + *sophistēs* SOPHIST]

De·ip·y·le (dē ip′ə lē), *n.* *Class. Myth.* a daughter of Adrastus who became the mother, by Tydeus, of Diomedes.

De·ip·y·lus (dē ip′ə ləs), *n.* *Class. Myth.* a grandson of Priam.

Deir·dre (dēr′drē, -drə; *Irish* dâr′drə), *n.* **1.** *Irish Legend.* a woman, raised with the intention that she should be the bride of Conchobar, King of Ulster. Instead she married Naoise, a son of Usnach and the nephew of Conchobar. When Conchobar treacherously killed Naoise and his brothers, she killed herself, thereby provoking a dissension among the followers of Conchobar that brought ruin to Ireland, as had once been prophesied. **2.** a girl's given name.

Deir′dre of the Sor′rows, a verse play (1910) by John Millington Synge.

de·ism (dē′iz əm), *n.* **1.** belief in the existence of a God on the evidence of reason and nature only, with rejection of supernatural revelation (distinguished from *theism*). **2.** belief in a God who created the world but has since remained indifferent to his creation. [< F *déisme* < L *de(us)* god + F *-isme* -ISM]

de·ist (dē′ist), *n.* one who believes in deism. [< F *déiste* < L *de(us)* god + F *-iste* -IST] **—de·is′tic, de·is′ti·cal,** *adj.* **—de·is′ti·cal·ly,** *adv.* **—de·is′ti·cal·ness,** *n.*

de·i·ty (dē′i tē), *n.*, *pl.* **-ties. 1.** a god or goddess. **2.** divine character or nature; divinity: *Her deity is manifest in her actions.* **3.** the estate or rank of a god: *The king attained deity after his death.* **4.** the character or nature of the Supreme Being: *the deity of Christ.* **5.** a person or thing revered as a god or goddess: *a society in which money is the only deity.* **6. the Deity,** God; Supreme Being. [ME *deite* < OF < LL *deitāt-* (s. of *deitās*), equiv. to L *dei-* (comb. form of *deus* god) + *-itāt-* -ITY, formed after L *dīvīnitās* divinity]

dé·jà vu (dā zhä vy′), **1.** (*italics.*) *French.* already seen; unoriginal, as a trite story situation or a dated film technique. **2.** *Psychol.* the illusion of having previously experienced something actually being encountered for the first time.

de·ject (di jekt′), *v.t.* **1.** to depress the spirits of; dispirit; dishearten: *Such news dejects me.* **—***adj.* **2.** *Archaic.* dejected; downcast. [ME < L *dēject(us)* thrown down (ptp. of *dējicere*), equiv. to *dē-* DE- + *jec-* throw (ptp. s. of *jacere*) + *-t-* ptp. suffix]

de·jec·ta (di jek′tə), *n.pl.* waste discharged from the body; excrements. [< NL, neut. pl. of L *dēject(us)*; see DEJECT]

de·ject·ed (di jek′tid), *adj.* depressed in spirits; disheartened; low-spirited: *The dejected expression on the face of the loser spoiled my victory.* [DEJECT + -ED[2]] **—de·jec′ted·ly,** *adv.* **—de·jec′ted·ness,** *n.*
—Syn. discouraged, despondent, dispirited, downhearted, unhappy, miserable. See **sad. —Ant.** happy.

de·jec·tion (di jek′shən), *n.* **1.** depression or lowness of spirits. **2.** *Med., Physiol.* **a.** evacuation of the bowels; fecal discharge. **b.** excrement. [ME *dejeccion* < L *dējectiōn-* (s. of *dējectiō*) a throwing down, equiv. to *dēject(us)* (see DEJECT) + *-iōn-* -ION]
—Ant. 1. exhilaration.

dé·jeu·ner (dā zhœ nā′; *Eng.* dā′zhə nā′), *n.*, *pl.* **-ners** (-nā′; *Eng.* -nāz′). *French.* lunch; luncheon.

dé·jeu·ner à la four·chette (dā zhœ nā′ a la fōōr shet′), *pl.* **dé·jeu·ners à la four·chette** (dā zhœ nā′ a la fōōr shet′). *French.* a luncheon or light meal, esp. one at which eggs, meat, etc., are served. Cf. **petit dejeuner.** [lit., lunch with the fork]

Dé·jeu·ner sur l'Herbe, Le (lə dā zhœ nā syr lerb′), a painting (1863) by Édouard Manet. Also called **Luncheon on the Grass.**

de ju·re (dē jŏŏr′ē; *Lat.* de yōō′re), by right; according to law (distinguished from *de facto*). [< L]

dek-, var. of **dec-.**

deka-, var. of **deca-.**

dek·a·drachm (dek′ə dram′), *n.* decadrachm.

dek·a·gram (dek′ə gram′), *n.* decagram. *Abbr.:* dkg

de Kalb (di kalb′), **1. Baron.** See **Kalb, Johann. 2.** a city in N Illinois. 18,486 (1960).

dek·a·li·ter (dek′ə lē′tər), *n.* decaliter. *Abbr.:* dkl

dek·a·me·ter (dek′ə mē′tər), *n.* decameter. *Abbr.:* dkm

dek·are (dek′âr, de kâr′), *n.* decare.

dek·a·stere (dek′ə stēr′), *n.* decastere. *Abbr.:* dks

deki-, var. of **deci-.**

Dek·ker (dek′ər), *n.* **Thomas,** 1572?–1632?, English dramatist. Also, **Decker.**

dek·ko (dek′ō), *n.*, *pl.* **-kos.** *n.* *Brit. Slang.* a look or glance. [< Hindi *dekho* look (impv.)]

de Koo·ning (də kōō′ning), **Wil·lem** (vil′əm, wil′-), born 1904, U.S. painter, born in the Netherlands.

De Ko·ven (di kō′vən), **(Henry Louis) Reginald,** 1861–1920, U.S. composer, conductor, and music critic.

de Kruif (də krīf′), **Paul,** born 1890, U.S. bacteriologist and author.

del[1] (del), **1.** (in names of Spanish derivation) a contraction of *de* and the article *el: Estanislao del Campo.* **2.** (in names of Italian derivation) a contraction of *di* and the article *il: Giovanni del Monte.*

del[2] (del), *Math.* a differential operator. *Symbol:* ∇ Cf. **gradient** (def. 4), **Laplace operator.** [short form of DELTA]

Del (del), *n.* a boy's given name, form of **Delmore.**

Del., Delaware.

del., 1. delegate. 2. *delineavit.*

de·la·bi·a·li·za·tion (dē lā′bē ə li zā′shən), *n.* *Phonet.* **1.** the result or process of delabializing. **2.** the historical progression in which labial sounds delabialize, as the *kw*-sound in Latin words in *quin-* "five" becoming a *k*-sound as in Spanish *quince* "fifteen." [DE- + LABIALIZATION]

de·la·bi·al·ize (dē lā′bē ə līz′), *v.*, **-ized, -iz·ing.** *Phonet.* **—***v.t.* **1.** to deprive (a sound) of labial character, as in unrounding a vowel. **—***v.i.* **2.** (of a speech sound) to lose its labial character. [DE- + LABIALIZE]

De·la·croix (də la krwä′), *n.* **(Fer·di·nand Vic·tor) Eu·gène** (fer dē nän′ vēk tôr′ œ zhen′), 1798–1863, French painter.

Del′a·go·a Bay′ (del′ə gō′ə, del′-), an inlet of the Indian Ocean, in S Mozambique. 55 mi. long.

de·laine (də lān′), *n.* **1.** (*cap.*) See **Delaine Merino. 2.** a combing wool of high quality often used in worsteds. **3.** a high-grade worsted dress goods formerly in use. [< F *(mousseline) de laine* (muslin) of wool]

Delaine′ Meri′no, one of an American strain of Merino sheep.

de la Mare (də lə mâr′, del′ə mâr′), **Walter (John),** 1873–1956, English poet, novelist, playwright, and short-story writer.

De·lam·bre (də läm′brə), *n.* a walled plain in the fourth quadrant of the face of the moon: about 32 miles in diameter.

de·lam·i·nate (dē lam′ə nāt′), *v.i.*, **-nat·ed, -nat·ing.** to split into laminae or thin layers. [DE- + LAMINATE]

de·lam·i·na·tion (dē lam′ə nā′shən), *n.* **1.** a splitting apart into layers. **2.** *Embryol.* the separation of a primordial cell layer into two layers by a process of cell migration. [DE- + LAMINATION]

De·land (di land′), *n.* **Margaret** (*Mrs. Margaretta Wade Campbell Deland*), 1857–1945, U.S. novelist.

Del·a·no (del′ə nō′), *n.* a boy's given name.

De·lan·noy (də la nwa′), *n.* **Mar·cel** (mar sel′), born 1898, French composer.

De·la·roche (də la rôsh′), *n.* **(Hip·po·lyte) Paul** (ē pô lēt′ pôl), 1797–1856, French historical and portrait painter.

de la Rue (del′ə rōō′, del′ə rōō′), **Warren,** 1815–89, English astronomer and inventor.

De la Rue (del′ə rōō′), a walled plain in the first quadrant of the face of the moon: about 80 miles in diameter.

de·late (di lāt′), *v.t.*, **-lat·ed, -lat·ing. 1.** *Chiefly Scot.* to inform against; denounce or accuse. **2.** *Archaic.* to relate; report: *to delate an offense.* [< L *dēlāt(us)* brought down, reported, accused (ptp. of *dēferre*), equiv. to *dē-* DE- + *lā-* carry (ptp. s. of *ferre*) + *-t-* ptp. suffix] **—de·la′tion,** *n.* **—de·la′tor, de·lat′er,** *n.* **—del·a·to·ri·an** (del′ə tōr′ē ən, -tôr′-), *adj.*

de·la·tive (di lā′tiv), *Gram.* **—***adj.* **1.** noting a case whose distinctive function is to indicate place down from which. **—***n.* **2.** the delative case. [< L *dēlāt(us)* (see DELATE) + -IVE]

De·lau·nay (də lō ne′), *n.* **Ro·bert** (rō ber′), 1885–1941, French painter.

De·lau·nay (də lô′nā), *n.* a walled plain in the fourth quadrant of the face of the moon: about 30 miles in diameter.

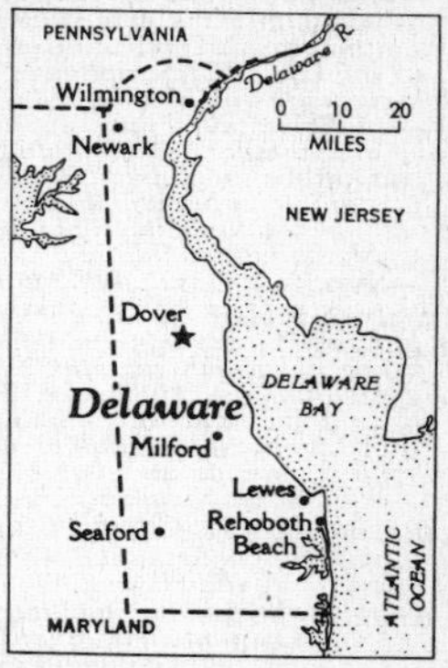

Del·a·van (del′ə van′), *n.* a town in SE Wisconsin. 4846 (1960).

De·la·vigne (də la vēn′yə), *n.* **(Jean Fran·çois) Ca·si·mir** (zhän fräN swa′ ka zē mēr′), 1793–1843, French poet and dramatist.

Del·a·ware (del′ə wâr′), *n.*, *pl.* **-wares,** (*esp. collectively*) **-ware** for 4. **1. Baron.** See **De La Warr, Baron. 2.** a State in the eastern United States, on the Atlantic coast. 446,292 (1960); 2057 sq. mi. *Cap.:* Dover. *Abbr.:* Del. **3.** a river flowing S from SE New York, along the boundary between Pennsylvania and New Jersey into Delaware Bay. 296 mi. long. **4.** a member of an Indian people formerly occupying the drainage basin of the Delaware River and the greater part of New Jersey. **5.** the Algonquian language of the Delaware Indians. **6.** *Hort.* **a.** a red vinifera grape that is grown for table use and that yields a white wine. **b.** the vine bearing this fruit.

Del·a·war·e·an (del′ə wâr′ē ən), *n.* **1.** a native or inhabitant of Delaware. **—***adj.* **2.** of or pertaining to Delaware or Delawareans. [DELAWARE + -AN]

Del′aware Bay′, an inlet of the Atlantic between E Delaware and S New Jersey. ab. 70 mi. long.

Del′aware Wa′ter Gap′, a gorge on the boundary between E Pennsylvania and NW New Jersey.

De La Warr (del′ə wâr′; *Brit.* del′ə wər), **Baron** (*Thomas West*), 1577–1618, 1st British colonial governor of Virginia. Also, **Delaware.**

de·lay (di lā′), *v.t.* **1.** to put off to a later time; defer; postpone: *The pilot delayed the flight until the weather cleared.* **2.** to impede the progress of; retard; hinder: *The dense fog delayed the plane's landing.* **—***v.i.* **3.** to put off action; linger; loiter: *He delayed until it was too late.* **—***n.* **4.** the act of delaying; procrastination; loitering: *There has been too much delay already. What we need is action!* **5.** an instance of being delayed: *There were five delays before the train left.* [ME *delai(en)* < OF *delaie(r)*] **—de·lay′a·ble,** *adj.* **—de·lay′er,** *n.* **—de·lay′ing·ly,** *adv.*
—Syn. 1. See **defer. 2.** slow, detain. **3.** procrastinate, tarry. **4.** tarrying, dawdling. **5.** deferment, postponement, respite.

de·layed-ac·tion (di lād′ak′shən), *adj.* (of an explosive projectile) exploding some time after hitting the target. Also, **de·lay-ac·tion** (di lā′ak′shən).

delayed′ al′pha par′ticle, *Physics.* an alpha particle emitted from an excited nucleus formed in a radioactive process, as fission, the emission occurring some time after the process is terminated.

delayed′ neu′tron, *Physics.* a neutron emitted from an excited nucleus formed in a radioactive process, the emission occurring some time after the process is terminated.

delayed′ speech′, *Speech Pathol.* a speech disorder of children in which the levels of intelligibility, vocabulary, complexity of utterance, etc., are significantly below the levels considered standard.

delay′ing ac′tion, *Mil.* a maneuver in which a defensive force delays the advance of a superior enemy force by withdrawing while inflicting the maximum destruction possible without becoming involved in decisive combat: *They fought a delaying action for four days.*

delay′ screen′, *Electronics.* (in a cathode ray tube) a sensitized screen with a phosphorescent coating that retains the image formed by the electron beam for an appreciable time.

Del·bert (del′bərt), *n.* a boy's given name, form of **Albert.**

Del·cas·sé (del ka sā′), *n.* **Thé·o·phile** (tā ô fēl′), 1852–1923, French statesman.

de·le (dē′lē), *v.*, **de·led, de·le·ing,** *n.* *Print.* **—***v.t.* **1.** to delete. **—***n.* **2.** a mark, as ₰ or ₰, used to indicate matter to be deled. [< L *dēle* (2nd pers. sing. pres. act. impv. of *dēlēre*), equiv. to *dēl-* destroy + *-e-* impv. suffix]

de·lead (dē led′), *v.t.* *Metalworking.* to remove lead adhering to (a metal object) after cold drawing through a die in which the lead served as a lubricant. [DE- + LEAD[2]]

de·lec·ta·ble (di lek′tə bəl), *adj.* delightful; highly pleasing; enjoyable: *a delectable dinner; a delectable witticism.* [ME < L *dēlectābil(is)* delightful, equiv. to *dēlectāre* to delight (*dēlic(ere)* + *-t-* freq. suffix) + *-ābilis* -ABLE] **—de·lec′ta·ble·ness, de·lec′ta·bil′i·ty,** *n.* **—de·lec′ta·bly,** *adv.*
—Ant. disagreeable, distasteful.

de·lec·tate (di lek′tāt), *v.t.*, **-tat·ed, -tat·ing.** to please; charm; delight. [< L *dēlectāt(us)* delighted, ptp. of *dēlect(āre)*. See DELECTABLE, -ATE[1]]

de·lec·ta·tion (dē′lek tā′shən), *n.* delight; enjoyment. [ME *delectacioun* < L *dēlectātiōn-* (s. of *dēlectātiō*), equiv. to *dēlectāt(us)* (see DELECTATE) + *-iōn-* -ION]

De·led·da (de led′dä), *n.* **Gra·zia** (grä′tsyä), 1875–1936, Italian novelist.

del·e·ga·cy (del′ə gə sē), *n.*, *pl.* **-cies. 1.** the position or commission of a delegate. **2.** the appointing or sending of a delegate. **3.** a body of delegates; delegation. **4.** (at Oxford University) a permanent committee charged with certain duties. [DELEGA(TE) + -CY]

de·le·gal·ize (dē lē′gə līz′), *v.t.*, **-ized, -iz·ing.** to revoke the statutory authorization of. [DE- + LEGALIZE]

del·e·gate (*n.* del′ə gāt′, -git; *v.* del′ə gāt′), *n., v.,* **-gat·ed, -gat·ing.** —*n.* **1.** one designated to act for or represent another or others; a deputy; a representative, as in a political convention. **2.** *U.S. Govt.* **a.** the representative of a Territory in the House of Representatives of the U.S. **b.** a member of the lower house of the State legislatures of Maryland, Virginia, and West Virginia. —*v.t.* **3.** to send or appoint (a person) as deputy or representative. **4.** to commit (powers, functions, etc.) to another as agent or deputy. [ME < ML *dēlēgāt(us)*, n. use of L: assigned (ptp. of *dēlēgāre*), equiv. to *dē-* DE- + *lēgātus* disputed; see LEGATE] —**del·e·ga·ble** (del′ə gə bəl), *adj.*
—**Syn. 1.** envoy. **4.** depute, entrust, commission.

del·e·ga·tion (del′ə gā′shən), *n.* **1.** the act of delegating. **2.** the state of being delegated. **3.** a group or body of delegates: *Our firm sent a delegation to the convention.* **4.** the body of delegates chosen to represent a political unit in an assembly. Cf. **deputation** (def. 2). [< L *dēlēgātiōn-* (s. of *dēlēgātiō*), equiv. to *dēlēgāt(us)* (see DELEGATE) + *-iōn-* -ION]
—**Syn. 4.** commission.

de·len·da est Car·tha·go (de len′dä est kär tä′gō; *Eng.* di len′də est kär thā′gō), *Latin.* Carthage must be destroyed.

de Les·seps (də les′eps; *Fr.* də le seps′), **Vicomte Fer·di·nand Ma·rie** (fûr′dᵊnand′ mə rē′; *Fr.* fer dē-näN′ ma rē′). See **Lesseps, Ferdinand Marie, Vicomte de.**

de·lete (di lēt′), *v.t.,* **-let·ed, -let·ing.** to strike out or remove (something written or printed); cancel; erase; expunge. [< L *dēlēt(us)* destroyed (ptp. of *dēlēre*), equiv. to *dēl-* destroy + *-ē-* thematic vowel + *-t-* ptp. suffix]
—**Syn.** eradicate. See **cancel.**

del·e·te·ri·ous (del′i tēr′ē əs), *adj.* **1.** injurious to health: *deleterious gases.* **2.** hurtful; harmful; injurious: *deleterious influences.* [< NL *dēlētēri(us)* < Gk *dēlētḗrios* destructive, deriv. of *dēlētḗr* destroyer, equiv. to *dēlé(esthai)* (to) hurt, injure + *-tēr* agent suffix + -OUS] —**del′e·te′ri·ous·ly,** *adv.* —**del′e·te′ri·ous·ness,** *n.*
—**Syn. 2.** pernicious, destructive; noxious. —**Ant. 2.** beneficial.

de·le·tion (di lē′shən), *n.* **1.** an act or instance of deleting. **2.** the state of being deleted. **3.** a deleted word, passage, etc. [< L *dēlētiōn-* (s. of *dēlētiō*) a destroying, equiv. to *dēlēt(us)* (see DELETE) + *-iōn-* -ION]

delft (delft), *n.* **1.** an earthenware having an opaque white glaze with an overglaze decoration, usually blue. **2.** any pottery resembling this. Also, **delf** (delf). Also called **delft′ ware′.** [after DELFT]

Delft (delft), *n.* a city in the W Netherlands. 75,125 (1962).

Del·ga·do (del gä′dō), *n.* **Cape,** a cape at the NE extremity of Mozambique.

Del·hi (del′ē *or, for 2,* del′hī), *n.* **1.** a union territory in N India. 2,658,612 (1961); 574 sq. mi. **2.** Also called **Old Delhi.** a city in and the capital of this territory: former capital of the old Mogul Empire; administrative headquarters of British India 1912–29. 2,061,800 (1961). Cf. **New Delhi. 3.** a town in NE Louisiana. 2514 (1960).

del·i (del′ē), *n., pl.* **del·is** (del′ēz). *Informal.* a delicatessen. [by shortening]

Del·ia (dēl′yə), *n.* **1.** (*sometimes construed as pl.*) a festival of Apollo held on Delos every five years in ancient times. **2.** a girl's given name.

De·li·an (dē′lē ən, dēl′yən), *adj.* **1.** pertaining to Delos. —*n.* **2.** a native or inhabitant of Delos. [< L *Dēli(us)* < Gk *Dḗlios* + -AN]

de·lib·er·ate (*adj.* di lib′ər it; *v.* di lib′ə rāt′), *adj., v.,* **-at·ed, -at·ing.** —*adj.* **1.** carefully weighed or considered; studied; intentional: *a deliberate lie.* **2.** characterized by deliberation; careful or slow in deciding: *a deliberate decision.* **3.** leisurely and steady in movement or action; slow and even; unhurried: *a deliberate step; He took deliberate aim and fired, killing the mad dog.* —*v.t.* **4.** to weigh in the mind; consider: *to deliberate a question.* —*v.i.* **5.** to think carefully or attentively; reflect: *He deliberated for a long time before giving his decision.* **6.** to consult or confer formally: *The jury deliberated for three hours.* [ME < L *dēlīberāt(us)* considered (ptp. of *dēlīberāre*), equiv. to *dē-* DE- + *lībr(āre)* (to) balance, weigh (deriv. of *lībra* balance, scales) + *-ātus* -ATE¹] —**de·lib′er·ate·ly,** *adv.* —**de·lib′er·ate·ness,** *n.* —**de·lib′er·a′tor,** *n.*
—**Syn. 1.** purposeful; willful. DELIBERATE, INTENTIONAL, PREMEDITATED, VOLUNTARY refer to something not happening by chance. DELIBERATE is applied to what is done not hastily but with full realization of what one is doing: *a deliberate attempt to evade justice.* INTENTIONAL is applied to what is definitely intended or done on purpose: *an intended omission.* PREMEDITATED is applied to what has been planned in advance: *a premeditated crime.* VOLUNTARY is applied to what is done by a definite exercise of the will and not because of outward pressures: *a voluntary enlistment.* **2.** methodical, thoughtful, circumspect, cautious. **3.** See **slow. 4.** ponder. **5.** cogitate, ruminate. —**Ant. 1.** accidental. **2.** impulsive, precipitate.

de·lib·er·a·tion (di lib′ə rā′shən), *n.* **1.** careful consideration before decision. **2.** formal consultation or discussion. **3.** deliberate quality; leisureliness of movement or action; slowness. [ME *deliberacion* < L *dēlīberātiōn-* (s. of *dēlīberātiō*), equiv. to *dēlīberāt(us)* (see DELIBERATE) + *-iōn-* -ION]

de·lib·er·a·tive (di lib′ə rā′tiv, -ər ə tiv), *adj.* **1.** having the function of deliberating, as a legislative assembly: *a deliberative body.* **2.** having to do with policy; dealing with the wisdom and expediency of a proposal: *a deliberative speech.* [< L *dēlīberātīv(us),* equiv. to *dēlīberāt(us)* (see DELIBERATE) + *-īvus* -IVE] —**de·lib′er·a′tive·ly,** *adv.* —**de·lib′er·a′tive·ness,** *n.*

De·libes (də lēb′), *n.* **Clé·ment Phi·li·bert Lé·o** (klā mäN′ fē lē ber′ lā ō′), 1836–91, French composer, esp. of operas, operettas, and ballets.

del·i·ca·cy (del′ə kə sē), *n., pl.* **-cies. 1.** fineness of texture, quality, etc.; softness: *the delicacy of lace.* **2.** something delightful or pleasing; esp. a choice food considered with regard to its rarity, costliness, or the like: *Caviar is a great delicacy.* **3.** fineness of perception or feeling; sensitiveness: *the delicacy of her taste in music.* **4.** quality of being easily broken or damaged; fragility: *Because of its delicacy, the instrument was packed in cotton batting.* **5.** the quality of requiring or involving great care or tact: *negotiations of great delicacy.* **6.** extreme sensitivity; precision of action or operation; minute accuracy: *the delicacy of a skillful surgeon's touch; a watch mechanism of unusual delicacy.* **7.** fineness of feeling with regard to what is fitting, proper, etc.: *Delicacy would not permit her to be rude.* **8.** sensitivity with regard to the feelings of others: *She criticized him with such delicacy that he was not offended.* **9.** bodily weakness; liability to sickness; frailty: *The doctor commented on the delicacy of her condition.* **10.** *Obs.* sensuous indulgence; luxury. [ME *delicasie.* See DELICATE, -CY]
—**Ant. 1, 3.** coarseness.

del·i·cate (del′ə kit), *adj.* **1.** fine in texture, quality, construction, etc. **2.** fragile; easily damaged; frail: *delicate porcelain; a delicate child.* **3.** so fine as to be scarcely perceptible; subtle: *a delicate flavor.* **4.** soft or faint, as color: *a delicate shade of pink.* **5.** exquisite or refined in perception or feeling; sensitive: *a delicate taste in clothes.* **6.** distinguishing subtle differences: *a delicate eye; a delicate sense of smell.* **7.** fine or precise in action or execution; capable of responding to the slightest influence: *a delicate instrument.* **8.** requiring great care, caution, or tact: *a delicate situation.* **9.** regardful of what is becoming, proper, etc.: *a delicate sense of propriety.* **10.** mindful of or sensitive to the feelings of others: *a delicate refusal.* **11.** dainty or choice, as food: *delicate tidbits.* **12.** primarily fastidious; squeamish: *not a movie for the delicate viewer.* **13.** *Obs.* sensuous; voluptuous. —*n.* **14.** *Archaic.* a choice food; delicacy. **15.** *Obs.* a source of pleasure; luxury. [ME *delicat* < L *dēlicāt(us)* delightful, dainty; akin to DELICIOUS] —**del′i·cate·ly,** *adv.* —**del′i·cate·ness,** *n.*
—**Syn. 1.** DELICATE, DAINTY, EXQUISITE imply beauty such as belongs to rich surroundings or which needs careful treatment. DELICATE, used of an object, suggests fragility, small size, and often very fine workmanship: *a delicate piece of carving.* DAINTY, in concrete references, suggests a smallness, gracefulness, and beauty which forbid rough handling; there is a connotation of attractiveness: *a dainty handkerchief;* of persons, it refers to fastidious sensibilities: *dainty in eating habits.* EXQUISITE suggests an outstanding beauty, daintiness, and elegance, or a discriminating sensitivity and ability to perceive fine distinctions: *an exquisite sense of humor.* **2.** tender, slight, weak. **7.** exact, accurate. **8.** critical, precarious. **12.** discriminating, careful, painstaking. —**Ant. 1, 2.** coarse. **3.** hard, crude.

del·i·ca·tes·sen (del′ə kə tes′ən), *n.* **1.** a store selling foods already prepared or requiring little preparation for serving, as cooked meats, cheese, relishes, and the like. **2.** the food products sold in such a store: *To save time, we're having delicatessen for dinner.* [< G, pl. of *Delikatesse* dainty < F *délicatesse*]

De·li·cia (də lish′ə), *n.* a girl's given name.

de·li·cious (di lish′əs), *adj.* **1.** highly pleasing to the senses, esp. to taste or smell: *a delicious dinner; a delicious aroma.* **2.** very pleasing; delightful: *a delicious sense of humor.* —*n.* **3.** (*cap.*) a red variety of apple. **4.** (*cap.*) the tree bearing this fruit, grown in the U.S. [ME < OF < LL *dēliciōs(us),* equiv. to *dēlici(ae)* delight + *-ōsus* -OUS] —**de·li′cious·ly,** *adv.* —**de·li′cious·ness,** *n.*
—**Syn. 1.** palatable, savory, delectable, dainty, delicate. DELICIOUS, LUSCIOUS refer to that which is especially agreeable to the senses. That which is DELICIOUS is highly agreeable to the taste or sometimes to the smell: *a delicious meal.* LUSCIOUS implies such a luxuriant fullness or ripeness as to make an object sweet and rich, sometimes to excess, it is often used in transferred or humorous senses: *a luscious banana; a luscious beauty; luscious music.* —**Ant. 1.** unpleasant.

de·lict (di likt′), *n.* **1.** *Law.* a misdemeanor; offense. **2.** *Roman Law.* a civil wrong permitting compensation or punitive damages. [< L *dēlict(um)* a fault, n. use of neut. of *dēlict(us)* having done wrong (ptp. of *dēlinquere*), equiv. to *dēlic-* fail (ptp. s. of *dēlinquere;* see DELINQUENCY) + *-t-* ptp. suffix + *-um* n. suffix]

de·light (di līt′), *n.* **1.** a high degree of pleasure or enjoyment; joy; rapture: *We accepted with delight.* **2.** something that gives great pleasure: *The dance was a delight to see. She takes great delight in teasing the boys.* —*v.t.* **3.** to give great pleasure, satisfaction, or enjoyment to; please highly: *The first issue of the magazine delighted everyone.* —*v.i.* **4.** to have great pleasure; take pleasure (fol. by *in* or an infinitive): *She delights in teasing the boys.* [erroneous 16th-century sp. after *light;* r. ME *delit* < OF < *delit(ier)* < L *dēlectāre;* see DELECTABLE] —**de·light′er,** *n.* —**de·light′ing·ly,** *adv.* —**de·light′less,** *adj.*
—**Syn. 1.** transport, delectation. See **pleasure. 3.** charm, enrapture. —**Ant. 1.** distress. **2.** disappointment.

De·light (də līt′), *n.* a girl's given name.

de·light·ed (di lī′tid), *adj.* **1.** highly pleased. **2.** *Obs.* delightful. [DELIGHT + -ED²] —**de·light′ed·ly,** *adv.* —**de·light′ed·ness,** *n.*

de·light·ful (di līt′fəl), *adj.* affording delight; highly pleasing: *a delightful surprise.* [DELIGHT + -FUL] —**de·light′ful·ly,** *adv.* —**de·light′ful·ness,** *n.*
—**Syn.** pleasant, pleasurable, enjoyable; charming, enchanting, delectable, agreeable. —**Ant.** disagreeable.

de·light·some (di līt′səm), *adj.* highly pleasing; delightful. [DELIGHT + -SOME¹] —**de·light′some·ly,** *adv.* —**de·light′some·ness,** *n.*

De·li·lah (di lī′lə), *n.* **1.** Also, *Douay Bible,* **Dalila.** Samson's mistress, who betrayed him to the Philistines. Judges 16. **2.** a seductive and treacherous woman. **3.** a girl's given name.

de·lim·it (di lim′it), *v.t.* to fix or mark the limits of; demarcate: *A ravine delimited the property on the north. The subjects on which he could converse were delimited by the conventions of materialism and puritanism.* [< F *délimit(er)* < L *dēlimitāre,* equiv. to *dē-* DE- + *limitāre* to LIMIT]

de·lim·i·tate (di lim′i tāt′), *v.t.,* **-tat·ed, -tat·ing.** delimit. [< L *dēlimitāt(us),* ptp. of *dēlimitāre.* See DELIMIT, -ATE¹] —**de·lim′i·ta′tion,** *n.* —**de·lim′i·ta′tive,** *n.*

de·lin·e·ate (di lin′ē āt′), *v.t.,* **-at·ed, -at·ing. 1.** to trace the outline of; sketch or trace in outline; represent pictorially: *He delineated the State of Texas on the map with a red pencil.* **2.** to portray in words; describe or outline with precision: *In his speech he delineated the ideal suburban dwelling. He delineated the plan with great care.* [< L *dēlīneāt(us),* equiv. to *dē-* DE- + *līneātus* LINEATE] —**de·lin·e·a·ble** (di lin′ē ə bəl), *adj.*

de·lin·e·a·tion (di lin′ē ā′shən), *n.* **1.** the act or process of delineating. **2.** a chart or diagram; a sketch; a rough draft. **3.** a description. [< LL *dēlīneātiōn-* (s. of *dēlīneātiō*) a sketch, equiv. to L *dēlīneāt(us)* (see DELINEATE) + *-iōn-* -ION] —**de·lin·e·a·tive** (di lin′ē ā′tiv, -ē ə tiv), *adj.*

de·lin·e·a·tor (di lin′ē ā′tər), *n.* **1.** one who or that which delineates. **2.** a tailor's pattern which can be adjusted for cutting garments of different sizes. [DELINEATE + -OR²]

de·li·ne·a·vit (de lin′e ä′wit; *Eng.* di lin′ē ā′vit), *Latin.* he drew (this); she drew (this). *Abbr.:* del.

de·lin·quen·cy (di liŋ′kwən sē), *n., pl.* **-cies. 1.** failure in or neglect of duty or obligation; dereliction; fault; guilt. **2.** a misdeed or offense; a misdemeanor. Cf. **juvenile delinquency.** [< LL *dēlinquentia* fault, crime, equiv. to L *dēlinquent-* (s. of *dēlinquēns,* prp. of *dēlinquere; dē-* DE- + *linqu(ere)* (to) leave) + *-entia* -ENCY]

de·lin·quent (di liŋ′kwənt), *adj.* **1.** failing in or neglectful of a duty or obligation; guilty of a misdeed or offense. **2.** (of an account, tax, debt, etc.) past due; overdue. **3.** of or pertaining to delinquents or delinquency: *delinquent attitudes.* —*n.* **4.** one who is delinquent, esp. a juvenile delinquent. [< L *dēlinquent-;* see DELINQUENCY] —**de·lin′quent·ly,** *adv.*

del·i·quesce (del′ə kwes′), *v.i.,* **-quesced, -quesc·ing. 1.** to melt away. **2.** to become liquid by absorbing moisture from the air, as certain salts. **3.** *Bot.* to form many small divisions or branches. [< L *dēliquesce(re)* (to) become liquid, equiv. to *dē-* DE- + *liquescere;* see LIQUESCENT]

del·i·ques·cence (del′ə kwes′əns), *n.* **1.** the act or process of deliquescing. **2.** the liquid produced when something deliquesces. [DELIQUESCE + -ENCE] —**del′i·ques′cent,** *adj.*

del·i·ra·tion (del′ə rā′shən), *n. Obs.* mental derangement; raving; delirium. [< L *dēlīrātiōn-* (s. of *dēlīrātiō*) folly, equiv. to *dēlī(rāre)* (to) be silly, lit., go out of the furrow (*dē-* DE- + *līr(a)* furrow) + *-ātiōn-* -ATION]

de·lir·i·ous (di lēr′ē əs), *adj.* **1.** *Pathol.* affected with or characteristic of delirium. **2.** wild with excitement, enthusiasm, etc.: *She was delirious with joy at the news of the birth of a son.* [DELIRI(UM) + -OUS] —**de·lir′i·ous·ly,** *adv.* —**de·lir′i·ous·ness,** *n.*

de·lir·i·um (di lēr′ē əm), *n., pl.* **-lir·i·ums, -lir·i·a** (-lēr′ē ə). **1.** *Pathol.* a more or less temporary disorder of the mental faculties, as in fevers, disturbances of consciousness, or intoxication, characterized by restlessness, excitement, delusions, hallucinations, etc. **2.** a state of violent excitement or emotion. [< L *dēlīrium* frenzy, lit., going out of the furrow, equiv. to *dēlīr(āre)* (see DELIRATION) + *-ium* (neut. n. suffix)]

delir′ium tre′mens (trē′mənz), *Pathol.* a violent restlessness due to excessive indulgence in alcoholic beverages, characterized by trembling, terrifying visual hallucinations, etc. [< NL: trembling delirium]

De·lisle (də lēl′), *n.* a crater in the second quadrant of the face of the moon: about 16 miles in diameter.

de·list (dē list′), *v.t.* **1.** to delete from a list. **2.** to withdraw or remove (a security) from the group listed with a particular exchange. [DE- + LIST¹]

del·i·tes·cent (del′i tes′ənt), *adj.* concealed; hidden; latent. [< L *dēlitescent-* (s. of *dēlitescēns*) hiding away (prp. of *dēlitescere*), equiv. to *dē-* DE- + *latescent-* LATESCENT] —**del′i·tes′cence, del′i·tes′cen·cy,** *n.*

De·li·um (dē′lē əm), *n.* an ancient seaport in Greece, in Boeotia: the Boeotians defeated the Athenians here 424 B.C.

De·li·us (dē′lē əs, dēl′yəs), *n.* **1. Frederick,** 1862–1934, English composer. **2.** *Class. Myth.* an epithet of Apollo: so called because he was born in Delos.

de·liv·er (di liv′ər), *v.t.* **1.** to carry and turn over (letters, goods, etc.) to the intended recipient or recipients: *to deliver mail; to deliver a package.* **2.** to give into another's possession or keeping; surrender: *to deliver a prisoner to the police; to deliver a bond.* **3.** *Informal.* to bring (votes) to the support of a candidate or a cause. **4.** to give forth in words; utter or pronounce: *to deliver a verdict; to deliver a speech.* **5.** to give forth or emit; *The oil well delivers 500 barrels a day.* **6.** to direct; throw: *to deliver a blow; deliver a fast ball.* **7.** to set free or liberate: *They were delivered from bondage.* **8.** to release or save: *Deliver me from such tiresome people!* **9.** to assist (a female) in bringing forth young: *The doctor delivered Mrs. Jones of twins. The veterinarian delivered the mare of a foal.* **10.** to assist at the birth of: *The doctor delivered three sets of twins last year.* **11.** to give birth to: *She delivered twins at 4 a.m.* **12.** to disburden (oneself) of thoughts, opinions, etc. **13.** *Obs.* to make known; assert. —*v.i.* **14.** to give birth: *She delivered exactly when the doctor had predicted she would.* **15.** to provide a delivery service for goods and products: *You don't have to go out into the rain since the store delivers free of charge.* —*adj.* **16.** *Archaic.* agile; quick. [ME *delivre(n)* < OF *delivr(er)* < LL *dēlīberāre* to set free, equiv. to *dē-* DE- + *līber(āre)* (to) LIBERATE] —**de·liv′er·a·ble,** *adj.* —**de·liv′er·er,** *n.*
—**Syn. 1.** hand over, transfer, cede, yield. **4.** communicate, impart, announce, proclaim, publish. **7.** emancipate, release. **8.** redeem, rescue. —**Ant. 1, 7, 8.** confine.

de·liv·er·ance (di liv′ər əns), *n.* **1.** an act or instance of delivering. **2.** the state of being delivered. **3.** a thought or judgment expressed; a formal or authoritative pronouncement. [ME *deliveraunce* < OF *delivrance,* equiv. to *delivr(er)* (to) DELIVER + *-ance* -ANCE]

deliv′ered price′, a quoted price of merchandise, as steel, that includes freight charges from the basing point to the point of delivery, usually f.o.b.

de·liv·er·ly (di liv′ər lē), *adv. Archaic.* quickly; deftly. [ME; see DELIVER, -LY]

de·liv·er·y (di liv′ə rē), *n., pl.* **-er·ies. 1.** the delivering of letters, goods, etc. **2.** a giving up or handing over; surrender. **3.** the utterance or enunciation of words. **4.** vocal and bodily behavior during the presentation of a speech: *a speaker's fine delivery.* **5.** the act or manner of giving or sending forth: *the pitcher's fine delivery of the ball.* **6.** release or rescue; liberation. **7.** the state of being delivered of or giving birth to a child; parturition. **8.** something delivered: *The delivery is late today.* **9.** *Com.* a shipment of goods from the seller to the buyer. **10.** *Law.* a formal act performed to make a transfer of property legally effective: *a delivery of* *deed.* [ME < AF *delivrée* (n.), equiv. to *delivré*, ptp. of *delivr(er)* (to) DELIVER + *-é* -Y[3]]

de·liv′ery boy′, a boy or young man who delivers merchandise for a store, as to the homes, offices, etc., of customers.

de·liv·er·y·man (di liv′ə rē man′, -mən), *n., pl.* **-men** (-men′, -mən). a man employed to make deliveries of merchandise to purchasers, usually by means of a truck, as a milkman, iceman, etc. [DELIVERY + MAN[1]]

de·liv′ery room′, 1. an area in a hospital equipped for delivering babies. 2. a room or area in which deliveries are made or received, as the section of a public library where books are taken out or returned.

dell (del), *n.* a small valley; a vale. [ME *delle*, OE *dell;* akin to DALE]

Dell (del), *n.* a boy's or girl's given name.

dell' (del), (in names of Italian derivation) an elided form of *della: Giovanni dell' Anguillara.*

del·la (del′lä), (in names of Italian derivation) a contraction of *di* and the article *la: Andrea della Robbia.*

Del·la (del′ə), *n.* a girl's given name, form of **Delia.**

del·la Rob·bia (del′ə rō′bē ə; *It.* del′lä rôb′byä), **Lu·ca** (lo͞o′kä). See **Robbia, Luca della.**

Del·lo Joi·o (del′ō joi′ō), **Norman,** born 1913, U.S. composer and pianist.

dells (delz), *n.pl.* dalles. [by folk etymology]

Del·ma (del′mə), *n.* a girl's given name.

Del Mar (del′ mär′), a town in S California. 3124 (1960).

Del·mar′va Penin′sula (del mär′və), a peninsula between Chesapeake and Delaware bays including most of Delaware and those parts of Maryland and Virginia E of Chesapeake Bay. Cf. **Eastern shore.**

Del·motte (del mot′), *n.* a walled plain in the first quadrant of the face of the moon: about 19 miles in diameter.

de·lo·cal·ise (dē lō′kə līz′), *v.t.,* **-ised, -is·ing.** *Chiefly Brit.* delocalize. —**de·lo′cal·i·sa′tion,** *n.*

de·lo·cal·ize (dē lō′kə līz′), *v.t.,* **-ized, -iz·ing.** 1. to remove from the proper or usual locality. 2. to free or remove from the restrictions of locality; free of localism, provincialism, or the like: *to delocalize an industry; to delocalize a person's accent.* [DE- + LOCALIZE] —**de·lo′cal·i·za′tion,** *n.*

De·lo·res (də lôr′is, -lôr′-), *n.* a girl's given name. Also, **Dolores.**

De·lorme (də lôrm′), *n.* **Phi·li·bert** (fē lē ber′), 1515?–70, French architect.

De·los (dē′los, del′ōs), *n.* 1. a Greek island in the Cyclades, in the SW Aegean: site of an oracle of Apollo. 2. a boy's given name.

de los An·ge·les (dā lôs an′jə ləs, -lēz′, los; *Sp.* de lôs än′he les), **Vic·to·ria** (vik tôr′ē ə, -tōr′-; *Sp.* bēk tō′ryä), born 1923?, Spanish operatic soprano.

de·louse (dē lous′, -louz′), *v.t.,* **-loused, -lous·ing.** to free of lice; remove lice from. [DE- + LOUSE]

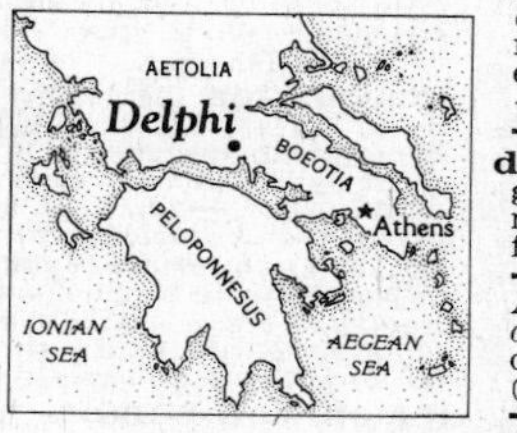

Del·phi (del′fī), *n.* 1. an ancient city in central Greece, in Phocis: the site of an oracle of Apollo. 2. a town in central Indiana. 2517 (1960).

Del·phi·an (del′fē ən), *n.* 1. a native or inhabitant of Delphi. —*adj.* 2. Delphic. [DELPHI + -AN]

Del·phic (del′fik), *adj.* 1. of or pertaining to Delphi. 2. of or pertaining to Apollo, or to his temples or oracles. 3. oracular; obscure; ambiguous: *She was known for her Delphic prognostications.* [< L *Delphic(us)* < Gk *Delphikós*, equiv. to *Delph(oí)* DELPHI + *-ikos* -IC]

Del′phic or′acle, the oracle of Apollo at Delphi, noted for giving ambiguous answers.

Del·phine (del fēn′), *n.* a girl's given name.

Del·phin·i·a (del fin′ē ə), *n.* an ancient Greek festival in honor of Apollo.

del·phi·nin (del′fə nin), *n.* *Chem.* a violet anthocyanin, $C_{41}H_{38}O_{21}$, found in the flowers of the larkspur, *Delphinium consolida.* [DELPHIN(IUM) + -IN[2]]

del·phi·nine (del′fə nēn′, -nin), *n.* *Chem.* a bitter, poisonous, crystalline alkaloid, $C_{33}H_{45}NO_9$, obtained from various species of larkspur, esp. *Delphinium, Staphisagria.* [DELPHIN(IUM) + -INE[2]]

del·phin·i·um (del fin′ē əm), *n., pl.* **-i·ums, -i·a** (-ē ə). any of numerous ranunculaceous plants of the genus *Delphinium*, esp. a cultivated one, comprising the larkspurs. [< NL < Gk *delphínion* larkspur, deriv. of *delphin-* DOLPHIN; so called from the shape of the nectary]

Del·phin·i·us (del fin′ē əs), *n.* *Class. Myth.* an epithet of Apollo, meaning "dolphin."

Del·phi·nus (del fī′nəs), *n., gen.* **-ni** (-nī) for 2. 1. *Class. Myth.* an intermediary who convinced Amphitrite to marry Poseidon and who was placed among the stars for his success. 2. *Astron.* the Dolphin, a northern constellation between Aquila and Pegasus. [< L: dolphin]

Del·phos (del′fəs), *n.* a town in W Ohio. 6961 (1960).

Del·phus (del′fəs), *n.* *Class. Myth.* a son of Poseidon and Melantho.

Del·phy·ne (del fī′nē), *n.* *Class. Myth.* 1. Python. 2. a monster, half woman and half beast, that guarded Zeus during his imprisonment by Typhon.

Del Ri·o (del rē′ō), a city in S Texas, on the Rio Grande. 18,612 (1960).

Del·sarte (del särt′; *Fr.* del sart′), *n.* **Fran·çois** (fran swä′; *Fr.* fräN swa′), 1811–71, French musician and teacher.

Delsarte′ meth′od, a theory or system devised by Delsarte for improving musical and dramatic expression through the mastery of various bodily attitudes and gestures. Also called **Delsarte′ sys′tem.**

Del·sar·ti·an (del sär′tē ən), *adj.* of, pertaining to, or characteristic of François Delsarte or the Delsarte method. [DELSARTE + -IAN]

del·ta (del′tə), *n.* 1. the fourth letter of the Greek alphabet (Δ, δ). 2. the consonant sound represented by this letter. 3. anything triangular, like the Greek capital delta (Δ). 4. a nearly flat plain of alluvial deposit between diverging branches of the mouth of a river, often, though not necessarily, triangular: *the delta of the Nile.* 5. a word used in communications to represent the letter D. 6. (*cap.*) *U.S.* the upper stage of a Thor-boosted vehicle, for placing satellites into orbit and spacecraft into trajectories to escape the earth's atmosphere. 7. (*cap.*) *Astron.* a star that is usually the fourth brightest of a constellation: *The fourth brightest star in the Southern Cross is Delta Crucis.* [ME *deltha* < L *delta* < Gk *délta;* akin to Heb *dāleth*]

Del·ta (del′tə), *n.* 1. a town in W Colorado. 3832 (1960). 2. a girl's given name.

del′ta connec′tion, *Elect.* the series connection of three elements in a three-phase circuit forming a triangle.

del′ta func′tion, *Physics, Math.* a generalized function having the value 0 except at 0, the value infinity at 0, and an integral from minus infinity to plus infinity of 1, used in thermodynamics and quantum mechanics. Also called **Dirac delta function.**

del·ta·ic (del tā′ik), *adj.* 1. pertaining to or like a delta. 2. forming or having a delta. [DELTA + -IC]

del′ta i′ron, *Metall.* an allotrope of iron, stable above 1400°C, having a body-centered cubic lattice structure.

del′ta ray′, *Physics.* a low-energy electron emitted by a substance after bombardment by higher-energy particles, as alpha particles.

del′ta wing′, the triangular surface that serves as both wing and horizontal stabilizer of some supersonic aircraft.

del·toid (del′toid), *n.* 1. *Anat.* a large, triangular muscle covering the joint of the shoulder, the action of which raises the arm away from the side of the body. —*adj.* 2. Also, **del·toi·dal.** in the shape of a Greek capital delta (Δ); triangular. [< Gk *deltoeid(ḗs)* delta-shaped, equiv. to *délt(a)* DELTA + *-oeidēs* -OID]

Deltoid leaf

del·toi·dal (del toid′əl), *adj.* 1. of or pertaining to a river delta. 2. deltoid. [DELTOID + -AL[1]]

de·lu·brum (də lo͞o′brəm), *n., pl.* **-bra** (-brə). (in ancient Rome) a temple, shrine, or sanctuary. [< L *dēlu(ere)* (to) wash off (see DELUGE) + *-brum* instrumental suffix]

De·luc (də luk′, -lo͝ok′), *n.* a walled plain in the third quadrant of the face of the moon: about 28 miles in diameter.

de·lude (di lo͞od′), *v.t.,* **-lud·ed, -lud·ing.** 1. to mislead the mind or judgment of; deceive: *His own conceit deluded him into believing he was important.* 2. *Obs.* to mock or frustrate the hopes or aims of. 3. *Obs.* to elude; evade. [ME < L *dēlūde(re)* (to) play false, equiv. to *dē-* DE- + *lūdere* to play] —**de·lud′er,** *n.* —**de·lud′ing·ly,** *adv.*
—**Syn.** 1. beguile, cozen, dupe, cheat, defraud, gull.

del·uge (del′yo͞oj), *n., v.,* **-uged, -ug·ing.** —*n.* 1. a great flood of water; inundation; flood. 2. a drenching rain; downpour. 3. anything that overwhelms like a flood: *a deluge of mail.* 4. **the Deluge.** See **flood** (def. 2). —*v.t.* 5. to flood; inundate. 6. to overrun; overwhelm: *After winning the beauty contest, she was deluged with offers of modeling jobs.* [ME < OF < L *dīluv(ium)* flood, deriv. of *dīluere* to wash off, equiv. to *dī-* DIS-[1] + *-luere* (var. of *lavere* to wash)]
—**Syn.** 1. See **flood.** 3. cataclysm, catastrophe.

de·lu·sion (di lo͞o′zhən), *n.* 1. an act or instance of deluding. 2. the state of being deluded. 3. a false belief or opinion: *delusions of grandeur.* 4. *Psychiatry.* a fixed, dominating, or persistent false mental conception resistant to reason with regard to actual things or matters of fact: *a paranoiac delusion.* [ME < L *dēlūsiōn-* (s. of *dēlūsiō*), equiv. to *dēlūs(us)* (ptp. of *dēlūdere;* see DELUDE) + *-iōn-* -ION] —**de·lu′sion·al,** *adj.*
—**Syn.** 2. deception See **illusion.**

de·lu·sive (di lo͞o′siv), *adj.* 1. tending to delude; deceptive: *a delusive reply.* 2. of the nature of a delusion; false; unreal: *a delusive belief.* Also, **de·lu·so·ry** (di lo͞o′sə rē). [DELUS(ION) + -IVE] —**de·lu′sive·ly,** *adv.* —**de·lu′sive·ness,** *n.*

de·lus·ter·ant (dē lus′tər ənt), *n.* a chemical agent, as titanium dioxide, used in reducing the sheen of a yarn or fabric. Also, **de·lus′trant.** [DE- + LUSTER[1] + -ANT]

de·lust·er·ing (dē lus′tər ing), *n.* a chemical process for reducing the luster of rayon yarns by adding a finely divided pigment to the spinning solution. [DE- + LUSTER[1] + -ING[1]]

de·luxe (də lo͝oks′, -luks′; *Fr.* də lyks′), *adj.* 1. of special elegance, sumptuousness, or fineness. —*adv.* 2. in a luxurious or sumptuous manner: *We always travel deluxe.* Also, **de luxe′.** [< F *de luxe* of luxury]

delve (delv), *v.,* **delved, delv·ing.** —*v.i.* 1. to carry on intensive and thorough research for data, information, or the like. 2. *Archaic.* to dig, as with a spade. —*v.t.* 3. *Archaic.* to dig; excavate. 4. *Archaic.* to obtain by digging. [ME *delve(n)*, OE *delfan;* c. D *delven*, OHG *telban*] —**delv′er,** *n.*

Dem., 1. Democrat. 2. Democratic.

de·mag·net·ise (dē mag′ni tīz′), *v.t.,* **-ised, -is·ing.** *Chiefly Brit.* demagnetize. —**de·mag′net·is′a·ble,** *adj.* —**de·mag′net·i·sa′tion,** *n.* —**de·mag′net·is′er,** *n.*

de·mag·net·ize (dē mag′ni tīz′), *v.t.,* **-ized, -iz·ing.** to remove magnetization from. [DE- + MAGNETIZE] —**de·mag′net·iz′a·ble,** *adj.* —**de·mag′net·i·za′tion,** *n.* —**de·mag′net·iz′er,** *n.*

dem·a·gog·ic (dem′ə goj′ik, -gog′-), *adj.* of, pertaining to, or characteristic of a demagogue. Also, **dem′a·gog′i·cal.** [< Gk *dēmagōgik(ós)*, equiv. to *dēmagōg(ós)* (see DEMAGOGUE) + *-ikos* -IC] —**dem′a·gog′i·cal·ly,** *adv.*

dem·a·gogue (dem′ə gôg′, -gog′), *n.* 1. a person, esp. an orator or political leader, who gains power and popularity by arousing the emotions, passions, and prejudices of the people. 2. (in ancient times) a leader of the people. Also, **dem′a·gog′.** [< Gk *dēmagōg(ós)* a leader of the people, popular leader, equiv. to *dêm(os)* people + *agōgós* -AGOGUE]

dem·a·gogu·er·y (dem′ə gô′gə rē, -gog′ə rē), *n.* the methods or practices of a demagogue. [DEMAGOGUE + -RY]

dem·a·gogu·ism (dem′ə gô′giz əm, -gog′iz əm), *n.* demagoguery. Also, **dem′a·gog′ism.** [DEMAGOGUE + -ISM]

dem·a·go·gy (dem′ə gō′jē, -gō′jē, -goj′ē), *n.* 1. *Chiefly Brit.* demagoguery. 2. the character of a demagogue. 3. a body of demagogues. [< Gk *dēmagōgía* leadership of the people, equiv. to *dēmagōg(ós)* DEMAGOGUE + *-ia* -Y[3]]

de mal en pis (də mal äN pē′), *French.* from bad to worse.

de·mand (di mand′, -mänd′), *v.t.* 1. to ask for with authority; claim as a right: *He demanded payment of the debt.* 2. to ask for peremptorily or urgently: *He demanded sanctuary. She demanded that we let her in.* 3. to call for or require as just, proper, or necessary: *This task demands patience. Justice demands objectivity.* 4. *Law.* **a.** to lay formal legal claim to. **b.** to summon, as to court. —*v.i.* 5. to make a demand; inquire; ask. —*n.* 6. the act of demanding. 7. something that is demanded. 8. an urgent or pressing requirement: *demands upon one's time.* 9. *Econ.* **a.** the desire to purchase, coupled with the power to do so. **b.** the quantity of goods that buyers will take at a particular price. 10. a requisition; a legal claim: *The demands of the client could not be met.* 11. the state of being in request for purchase or use: *an article in great demand.* 12. *Archaic.* inquiry; question. 13. **on demand,** subject to payment upon presentation and demand: *The fee is payable on demand.* [ME *demaund(en)* < AF *demaund(er)* < ML *dēmandāre* to demand, L: to entrust, equiv. to *dē-* DE- + *mandāre* to commission, order; see MANDATE] —**de·mand′a·ble,** *adj.* —**de·mand′er,** *n.*
—**Syn.** 1. exact. DEMAND, CLAIM, REQUIRE imply making an authoritative request. To DEMAND is to ask in a bold, authoritative way: *to demand an explanation.* To CLAIM is to assert a right to something: *He claimed it as his due.* To REQUIRE is to ask for something as being necessary; to compel: *The Army requires absolute obedience of its soldiers.*

de·mand·ant (di man′dənt, -män′-), *n.* *Law.* 1. the plaintiff in a real action. 2. any plaintiff. [ME < AF *demandaunt*, n. use of prp. of *demaunder* to DEMAND; see -ANT]

demand′ bid′, *Bridge.* a bid to which one's partner is obliged to respond.

demand′ bill′, a bill payable upon presentation.

demand′ depos′it, *Banking.* a deposit subject to withdrawal at the demand of the depositor without prior notice.

de·mand·ing (di man′ding), *adj.* requiring or claiming more than is generally felt by others to be due: *Her childishness makes her the most demanding person I know.* [DEMAND + -ING[2]] —**de·mand′ing·ly,** *adv.*

demand′ loan′. See **call loan.**

demand′ note′, a note payable upon presentation.

de·man·toid (di man′toid), *n.* *Mineral.* a brilliant green variety of andradite, used as a gem. Also called **Uralian emerald.** [< G, equiv. to (obs.) *Demant* DIAMOND (< MHG *diemant* < OF *diamant*) + *-oid* -OID]

de·mar·cate (di mär′kāt, dē′mär kāt′), *v.t.,* **-cat·ed, -cat·ing.** 1. to determine or mark off the boundaries of: *to demarcate a piece of property.* 2. to separate distinctly: *to demarcate the lots with fences.* [back formation from DEMARCATION] —**de·mar′ca·tor,** *n.*

de·mar·ca·tion (dē′mär kā′shən), *n.* 1. the determining and marking off of the boundaries of something. 2. separation by distinct boundaries: *line of demarcation.* Also, **de′mar·ka′tion.** [Latinization of Sp *demarción*, deriv. of *demarcar* to mark out the bounds of, equiv. to *de-* DE- + *marcar* < It *marcare* < Gmc; see MARK[1], -TION]

dé·marche (dā marsh′), *n., pl.* **-marches** (-marsh′). *French.* 1. a plan or mode of procedure. 2. a change in a course of action. [lit., gait]

Dem·a·rest (dem′ə rest′), *n.* a town in NE New Jersey. 4231 (1960).

de·mark (di märk′), *v.t.* demarcate. [DE- + MARK[1]]

de·mas·cu·lin·ise (dē mas′kyə lə nīz′), *v.t.,* **-nised, -nis·ing.** *Chiefly Brit.* demasculinize. —**de·mas′cu·lin·i·sa′tion,** *n.*

de·mas·cu·lin·ize (dē mas′kyə lə nīz′), *v.t.,* **-nized, -niz·ing.** to remove or strip masculine qualities or characteristics from. [DE + MASCULIN(E) + -IZE] —**de·mas′cu·lin·i·za′tion,** *n.*

de·ma·te·ri·al·ise (dē′mə tēr′ē ə līz′), *v.t., v.i.,* **-ised, -is·ing.** *Chiefly Brit.* dematerialize. —**de′ma·te′ri·al·i·sa′tion,** *n.*

de·ma·te·ri·al·ize (dē′mə tēr′ē ə līz′), *v.t., v.i.,* **-ized, -iz·ing.** to deprive of or lose material character. [DE- + MATERIALIZE] —**de′ma·te′ri·al·i·za′tion,** *n.*

Dem·a·vend (dem′ə vend′), *n.* a mountain in N Iran, in the Elburz Mountains. 18,606 ft.

Dem·bow·ski (dem bou′skē), *n.* a walled plain in the first quadrant of the face of the moon: about 16 miles in diameter.

deme (dēm), *n.* one of the administrative divisions of ancient Attica and of modern Greece. [< Gk *dêmos* a district, the people, commons]

de·mean[1] (di mēn′), *v.t.* to lower in dignity or standing; debase: *He demeaned himself by accepting the bribe.* [DE- + MEAN[2], modeled on *debase*]

de·mean[2] (di mēn′), *v.t.* to conduct or behave (oneself) in a specified manner: *He demeaned himself with great charm.* [ME *deme(i)n(en)* < OF *demen(er)*, equiv. to *de-* DE- + *mener* to lead, conduct < L *mināre* to drive, *minārī* to threaten]

de·mean·or (di mē′nər), *n.* 1. conduct; behavior; deportment. 2. facial appearance; mien. Also, *esp. Brit.,* **de·mean′our.** [ME *demenure.* See DEMEAN[2], -OR[1]]

de·ment (di ment′), *v.t.* *Obs.* to make mad or insane. [< LL *dēment(āre)* (to) deprive of mind, L *dēment-* (s. of *dēmēns*) out of one's mind, equiv. to *dē-* DE- + *ment-* (s. of *mēns*) mind + *-āre* inf. suffix]

de·ment·ed (di men′tid), *adj.* affected with dementia; insane; mad. [DEMENT + -ED[2]] —**de·ment′ed·ly,** *adv.* —**de·ment′ed·ness,** *n.*

dé·men·ti (dā män tē′; *Fr.* dā mäN tē′), *n., pl.* **-tis** (-tēz; *Fr.* -tē′). an official denial by a government of actions, aims, etc., ascribed to it. [< F *démenti* contradiction < OF *desmenti(r)* (to) deny, *des-* DIS-[1] + *mentir* to lie < LL *mentire*, equiv. to L *mentīrī*, orig. to invent]

de·men·tia (di men′shə, -shē ə), *n.* *Psychiatry.* severe impairment or loss of intellectual capacity and personality integration. [< L: madness, equiv. to *dēment-* out of one's mind (see DEMENT) + *-ia* n. suffix]

demen′tia prae′cox (prē′koks), *Psychiatry.* schizophrenia. [< NL: precocious dementia]

de·mer·it (dē mer′it), *n.* **1.** the quality of being censurable or punishable; fault; culpability: *There is no demerit inherent in such an action.* **2.** a mark against a person for misconduct or deficiency: *He already has three demerits on his record.* **3.** *Obs.* merit or desert. [ME < L *dēmerit(um)* (in ML: fault), prob. n. use of neut. of ptp. of *dēmerērī* to deserve (esp. well). See DE-, MERIT] —**de·mer·i·to·ri·ous** (dē mer′i tôr′ē əs, -tôr′-), *adj.* —**de·mer′i·to′ri·ous·ly,** *adv.*

Dem·e·rol (dem′ə rōl′, -rôl′, -rol′), *n. Pharm., Trademark.* meperidine.

de·mesne (di mān′, -mēn′), *n.* **1.** possession of land as one's own: *land held in demesne.* **2.** an estate or part of an estate occupied and controlled by the owner and worked exclusively for his use. **3.** land belonging to and adjoining a manor house; estate. **4.** the dominion or territory of a sovereign or state; a domain. **5.** a district; region. [ME *demeine* < AF *demesne*, OF *demein*; see DOMAIN] —**de·mesn′i·al,** *adj.*

De·me·ter (di mē′tər), *n.* the ancient Greek goddess of the fertility of the earth and the protectress of marriage and the social order, identified by the Romans with Ceres.

de·meth·yl·chlor·tet·ra·cy·cline (dē meth′əl-klôr′te trə sī′klēn, -klōr′-), *n. Pharm.* a broad-spectrum antibiotic compound, $C_{21}H_{21}ClN_2O_8 \cdot 1\frac{1}{2}H_2O$, used in the treatment of infections. [DE- + METHYL + CHLOR-[2] + TETRA- + CYCL- + -INE[2]]

De·me·tra (də mē′trə), *n.* a girl's given name, form of **Demetria.**

De·me·tri·a (də mē′trē ə), *n.* a girl's given name.

De·me·tri·as (də mē′trē əs), *n.* an ancient city in NE Greece, in Thessaly.

De·me·tri·us (də mē′trē əs), *n.* a boy's given name.

Demetrius I, (*Poliorcetes*) 337?–283 B.C., king of Macedonia 294–286 (son of Antigonus I).

demi-, a word element appearing in loan words from French meaning "half" (*demilune*), "lesser" (*demitasse*), or sometimes used with a pejorative sense (*demimonde*); on this model, also prefixed to words of English origin (*demigod*). [< F, comb. form repr. *demi* (adj.; also n. and adv.) < L *dīmedius*, r. *dīmidius* half]

dem·i·bas·tion (dem′ē bas′chən), *n. Fort.* a work consisting of half a bastion, and hence having one face and one flank. [DEMI- + BASTION] —**dem′i·bas′tioned,** *adj.*

dem·i·can·non (dem′ē kan′ən), *n.* a large cannon of the 16th century, having a bore of about 6½ inches and firing a shot of from 30 to 36 pounds. [< F; see DEMI-, CANNON]

dem·i·can·ton (dem′ē kan′tən, -ton, -kan ton′), *n.* either of the two political divisions in Switzerland into which the cantons of Basel, Appenzell, and Unterwalden are each divided. [< F *demi-canton.* See DEMI-, CANTON]

De·mi·chev (de′mi chef), *n.* **Pyotr** (pyô′tər), born 1917, Russian government official: alternate member of the Presidium since 1964.

dem·i·cul·ver·in (dem′ē kul′vər in), *n.* a culverin having a bore of about 4½ inches and firing a shot of about 10 pounds. Also, **dem′i·cul′ver·in.** [< F *demi-coulevrine.* See DEMI-, COULVERIN]

dem·i·god (dem′ē god′), *n.* **1.** a mythological being who is partly divine and partly human; an inferior deity. **2.** a deified mortal. Also, *referring to a woman,* **dem·i·god·dess** (dem′ē god′is). [trans. of L *semideus.* See DEMI-, GOD]

dem·i·hunt·er (dem′ē hun′tər), *n.* a watch having a hunting case with a hole in the lid permitting the time to be told when the lid is closed. Also called **cut hunter, half hunter.**

dem·i·john (dem′i jon′), *n.* a large bottle having a short, narrow neck, and usually being encased in wickerwork. [< F *dame-jeanne* (by folk etymology), appar. special use of proper name]

de·mil·i·ta·rise (dē mil′i tə rīz′), *v.t.,* **-rised, -ris·ing.** *Chiefly Brit.* demilitarize. —**de·mil′i·ta·ri·sa′tion,** *n.*

de·mil·i·ta·rize (dē mil′i tə rīz′), *v.t.,* **-rized, -riz·ing.** **1.** to deprive of military character; free from militarism. **2.** to place under civil instead of military control. **3.** to forbid military use of (a border zone). [DE- + MILITARIZE] —**de·mil′i·ta·ri·za′tion,** *n.*

De Mille (də mil′), **1. Agnes (George),** born 1908, U.S. choreographer and dancer. **2.** her uncle, **Cecil B(lount)** (blunt), 1881–1959, U.S. motion-picture producer and director.

dem·i·lune (dem′i lo͞on′), *n.* **1.** a crescent. **2.** *Fort.* an outwork resembling a bastion with a crescent-shaped gorge. **3.** a crescent or half-moon shape, as of the top of a piece of furniture. —*adj.* **4.** shaped like a crescent. [< F: half moon. See DEMI-, LUNE[1]]

dem·i·met·o·pe (dem′ē met′ə pē′, -met′ōp), *n.* the space between the end of a Doric frieze and the first triglyph. [DEMI- + METOPE]

dem·i·mon·daine (dem′ē mon dān′; *Fr.* də mē môn-den′), *n., pl.* **-daines** (-dānz′; *Fr.* -den′), *adj.* —*n.* **1.** a woman of the demimonde. —*adj.* **2.** of or pertaining to the demimonde. [< F, equiv. to *demimonde* DEMIMONDE + *-aine* fem. adj. suffix < L *-āna* -AN]

dem·i·monde (dem′ē mond′; *Fr.* də mē mônd′), *n.* a class of women who have lost their standing in respectable society, usually because of their indiscreet behavior or sexual promiscuity. [< F: lit., half-world]

de·min·er·al·ize (dē min′ər ə līz′), *v.t.,* **-ized, -iz·ing.** to deprive of mineral content. [DE- + MINERALIZE] —**de·min′er·al·i·za′tion,** *n.*

Dem·ing (dem′ing), *n.* a town in SW New Mexico. 6764 (1960).

Dem·i·phon (dem′ə fon′), *n. Class. Myth.* a king who, at the suggestion of an oracle, annually drew by lot the name of a noble maiden to be sacrificed in order to avert a plague. His daughters were murdered when it was discovered that their names were never placed among the lots.

dem·i·pique (dem′i pēk′), *n.* an 18th-century military saddle with a low pommel. [DEMI- + *pique* (pseudo-F sp. of PEAK[1])]

dem·i·re·lief (dem′ē ri lēf′), *n.* mezzo-relievo. [DEMI- + RELIEF[2]]

dem·i·rep (dem′ē rep′), *n.* a woman of doubtful or compromised reputation. [short for *demi-reputation*]

de·mise (di mīz′), *n., v.,* **-mised, -mis·ing.** —*n.* **1.** death or decease. **2.** termination of existence or operation: *the demise of the French monarchy; the demise of the coach-and-four.* **3.** *Law.* **a.** a death or decease occasioning the transfer of an estate. **b.** a conveyance or transfer of an estate. **4.** *Govt.* transfer of sovereignty, as by the death or deposition of the sovereign. —*v.t.* **5.** *Law.* to transfer (an estate or the like) for a limited time; lease. **6.** *Govt.* to transfer (sovereignty), as by the death or abdication of the sovereign. —*v.i.* **7.** *Law.* to pass to the king by bequest, inheritance, or succession. [ME *dimise, demise, dimisse* < OF *demis* (ptp. of *desmetre*), L *dīmiss(um)* (ptp. of *dīmittere*); see DEMIT, DISMISS] —**de·mis′a·bil′i·ty,** *n.* —**de·mis′a·ble,** *adj.*

dem·i·sec (dem′ē sek′), *adj.* (of wines) semi-dry; sweeter than sec but drier than doux. [< F; see DEMI-, SEC[1]]

dem·i·sem·i·qua·ver (dem′ē sem′ē kwā′vər), *n. Music, Chiefly Brit.* a thirty-second note. See illus. under **note.** [DEMI- + SEMIQUAVER]

de·mis·sion (di mish′ən), *n. Archaic.* **1.** abdication. **2.** dismissal. [ME *dimissioun* < AF < L *dīmissiōn-* (s. of *dīmissiō*), equiv. to *dīmiss(us)* (see DISMISS) + *-iōn* -ION]

de·mit (di mit′), *v.,* **-mit·ted, -mit·ting.** *Chiefly Scot.* —*v.t.* **1.** to resign (a job, public office, etc.); relinquish; give up. **2.** *Archaic.* to dismiss, fire. —*v.i.* **3.** to resign. [< L *dīmitt(ere)* (to) send down, equiv. to *dī-* DI-[2] + *mittere* to send]

dem·i·tasse (dem′i tas′, -täs′; *Fr.* də mē täs′), *n., pl.* **-tass·es** (-tas′iz, -tä′siz; *Fr.* -täs′). **1.** a small cup for serving strong black coffee after dinner. **2.** the coffee contained in such a cup. [< F: lit., half-cup]

dem·i·urge (dem′ē ûrj′), *n.* **1.** *Philos.* **a.** *Platonism.* the artificer of the world. **b.** (in the Gnostic and certain other systems) a supernatural being imagined as creating or fashioning the world in subordination to the Supreme Being, and sometimes regarded as the originator of evil. **2.** (in many states of ancient Greece) a public official or magistrate. [< Gk *dēmiourg(ós)* a worker for the people, skilled worker, equiv. to *dḗmio(s)* of the people (deriv. of *dêmos* the people) + *-ergos* a worker, deriv. of *érgon* work] —**dem·i·ur·geous** (dem′ē ûr′jəs), **dem′i·ur′gic, dem′i·ur′gi·cal,** *adj.* —**dem′i·ur′gi·cal·ly,** *adv.*

dem·i·volt (dem′ē vōlt′), *n.* a half turn made by a horse with forelegs raised. Also, **dem′i·volte′.** [< F *demi-volte.* See DEMI-, VOLT[1]]

dem·o (dem′ō), *n., pl.* **dem·os.** *Informal.* **1.** demonstration (def. 6). **2.** demonstrator (def. 5). **3.** a phonograph record of a new song or made by an unknown singer, singing group, or band, for sending to disk jockeys, recording companies, etc., to demonstrate the merits of the song or performer, sample the reactions of the audience, or gain popularity. [by shortening]

Dem·o (dem′ō), *n., pl.* **Dem·os.** *U.S. Informal.* a member of the Democratic party; Democrat.

demo-, a prefix occurring in loan words from Greek, where it meant "people" (*democratic*); on this model, used in the formation of compound words (*demography*). [< Gk, comb. form of *dêmos*]

de·mob (dē mob′), *n., v.,* **-mobbed, -mob·bing.** *Brit. Informal.* —*n.* **1.** demobilization. **2.** one who has an honorable discharge from the armed forces; one who has been demobilized. —*v.t.* **3.** to discharge or demobilize (a person) from the armed forces. [orig. short for DEMOBILIZE]

de·mo·bi·lise (dē mō′bə līz′), *v.t.,* **-lised, -lis·ing.** *Chiefly Brit.* demobilize. —**de·mo′bi·li·sa′tion,** *n.*

de·mo·bi·lize (dē mō′bə līz′), *v.t.,* **-lized, -liz·ing.** **1.** to disband (an army, etc.). **2.** to discharge (a person) from military service. [DE- + MOBILIZE] —**de·mo′bi·li·za′tion,** *n.*

De·moc·o·on (də mok′ō on′), *n.* (in the *Iliad*) an illegitimate son of Priam slain by Odysseus.

de·moc·ra·cy (di mok′rə sē), *n., pl.* **-cies.** **1.** government by the people; a form of government in which the supreme power is vested in the people and exercised directly by them or by their elected agents under a free electoral system. **2.** a state having such a form of government. **3.** a state of society characterized by formal equality of rights and privileges. **4.** political or social equality; democratic spirit. **5.** the common people of a community as distinguished from any privileged class; the common people with respect to their political power. [< F *démocratie*, LL *democratia* < Gk *dēmokratía* popular government, equiv. to *dēmo-* DEMO- + *-kratia* -CRACY]

Democ′racy in Amer′ica, a study (1835) by Alexis de Tocqueville of American political institutions. French, **Dé·mo·cra·cie en A·mé·rique** (dā mô krä-sē′ än nä mā rēk′).

dem·o·crat (dem′ə krat′), *n.* **1.** an advocate of democracy. **2.** one who maintains the political or social equality of men. **3.** (*cap.*) *Politics.* **a.** a member of the Democratic party. **b.** a member of the former Democratic-Republican party. **4.** Also called **dem′ocrat wag′on.** a high, lightweight, horse-drawn wagon, usually having two seats. [< F *démocrate*, back formation from *démocratie* DEMOCRACY. See DEMO-, -CRAT]

dem·o·crat·ic (dem′ə krat′ik), *adj.* **1.** pertaining to or of the nature of democracy or a democracy. **2.** pertaining to or characterized by the principle of political or social equality for all. **3.** advocating or upholding democracy. **4.** (*cap.*) *Govt.* **a.** of, pertaining to, or characteristic of the Democratic party. **b.** of, pertaining to, or belonging to the Democratic-Republican party. Also, **dem′o·crat′i·cal.** [< F *démocratique*, ML *dēmocratic(us)* < Gk *dēmokratikós*, equiv. to *dēmokrat(ía)* (see DEMOCRACY) + *-ikos* -IC] —**dem′o·crat′i·cal·ly,** *adv.*

Dem′ocrat′ic par′ty, one of the two major political parties in the U.S., founded in 1828.

Democrat′ic-Repub′lican par′ty, *U.S. Hist.* a political party opposed to the old Federalist party.

de·moc·ra·tise (di mok′rə tīz′), *v.t., v.i.,* **-tised, -tis·ing.** *Chiefly Brit.* democratize. —**de·moc′ra·ti·sa′tion,** *n.*

de·moc·ra·tize (di mok′rə tīz′), *v.t., v.i.,* **-tized, -tiz·ing.** to make or become democratic. [< F *démocratis(er)*, equiv. to *démocrate* DEMOCRAT + *-iser* -IZE] —**de·moc′ra·ti·za′tion,** *n.*

De·moc·ri·tus (di mok′ri təs), *n.* **1.** ("*the Laughing Philosopher*") c460–370 B.C., Greek philosopher. **2.** a walled plain in the first quadrant of the face of the moon: about 25 miles in diameter. —**De·moc·ri·te·an** (di mok′ri tē′ən), *adj.*

Democ′ritus Jun′ior, pen name of Robert Burton.

dé·mo·dé (dā mô dā′), *adj. French.* no longer in fashion; out of date; outmoded.

de·mod·ed (dē mō′did), *adj.* out of date; outmoded. [trans. of F *démodé*]

De·mod·o·cus (də mod′ə kəs), *n.* (in the *Odyssey*) a blind minstrel of Alcinoüs.

de·mod·u·late (dē moj′ə lāt′, -mod′yə-), *v.t.,* **-lat·ed, -lat·ing.** *Radio.* detect (def. 4). [DE- + MODULATE]

de·mod·u·la·tion (dē moj′ə lā′shən, -mod′yə-), *n. Radio.* detection (def. 4b). [DE- + MODULATION]

de·mod·u·la·tor (dē moj′ə lā′tər, -mod′yə-), *n. Radio.* a device that demodulates or extracts a signal from a carrier wave. [DEMODULATE + -OR[2]]

De·mo·gor·gon (dē′mə gôr′gən, dem′ə-), *n.* a vague, mysterious, infernal power or divinity of ancient mythology, variously represented and regarded as an object of awe or fear. [< LL < Gk; see DEMO-, GORGON]

de·mog·ra·phy (di mog′rə fē), *n.* the science of vital and social statistics, as of the births, deaths, diseases, marriages, etc., of populations. [DEMO- + -GRAPHY] —**de·mog′ra·pher, de·mog′ra·phist,** *n.* —**de·mo·graph·ic** (dē′mə graf′ik, dem′ə-), **de′mo·graph′i·cal,** *adj.* —**de′mo·graph′i·cal·ly,** *adv.*

dem·oi·selle (dem′wä zel′; *Fr.* də mwa zel′), *n., pl.* **-selles** (-zelz′; *Fr.* -zel′). **1.** an unmarried girl or young woman. **2.** See **demoiselle crane.** **3.** a damselfly, esp. of the genus *Agrion.* **4.** damselfish. **5.** *Furniture.* a lady's wig stand of the 18th century, in the form of a pedestal table. [< F; see DAMSEL]

demoiselle′ crane′, a gray crane, *Anthropoides virgo*, of northern Africa, Europe, and Asia, having long, white plumes behind each eye.

de Moi·vre (də mwäv′, mwä′vrə, moi′vər; *Fr.* də mwä′vrᵊ), **A·bra·ham** (A BRA AM′), 1667–1754, French mathematician in England.

de Moi′vre's the′orem, *Math.* the theorem that a complex number raised to a given power is equal to the modulus of the number raised to the power and multiplied by the amplitude times the given power, expressed in the formula $[r(\cos\theta + i\sin\theta)]^n = r^n(\cos n\theta + i\sin n\theta)$. [named after A. DE MOIVRE]

de·mol·ish (di mol′ish), *v.t.* **1.** to destroy or ruin (a building or other structure), esp. on purpose; tear down; raze. **2.** to put an end to; destroy; explode: *The results of his research demolished many theories.* **3.** to lay waste to; ruin utterly: *The fire demolished the area.* **4.** *Informal.* to devour completely: *We simply demolished that turkey.* [< F *démoliss-*, s. of *démolir* < L *dēmōlīrī* to destroy, equiv. to *dē-* DE- + *mōlīrī* to set in motion, struggle (*mōl(ēs)* mass, bulk + *-īrī* pass. inf. suffix)] —**de·mol′ish·er,** *n.* —**de·mol′ish·ment,** *n.*

dem·o·li·tion (dem′ə lish′ən, dē′mə-), *n.* **1.** the act or an instance of demolishing. **2.** the state of being demolished; destruction. **3.** destruction or demolishment by explosives. **4. demolitions,** explosives, esp. as used in war. —*adj.* **5.** of, pertaining to, or working with explosives: *A specially trained demolition squad attempted to blow up the bridge before the enemy captured it.* **6.** of or pertaining to tearing down or demolishing: *Demolition work had begun on the old building.* [< L *dēmōlītiōn-* (s. of *dēmōlītiō*), equiv. to *dēmōlīt(us)* (ptp. of *dēmōlīrī*; see DEMOLISH) + *-iōn-* -ION]

demoli′tion bomb′, *Mil.* a bomb containing a relatively large charge, used to destroy structures and other large objects.

de·mon (dē′mən), *n.* **1.** an evil spirit; devil. **2.** an evil passion or influence. **3.** a person considered extremely wicked, evil, or cruel. **4.** a person with great energy, drive, etc.: *He's a demon for work.* **5.** daemon. —*adj.* **6.** of, pertaining to, characteristic of, or noting a demon. **7.** possessed or controlled by a demon. [defs. 1–4: ME, for L *daemōn(ium)* < Gk *daimónion*, thing of divine nature (in Jewish and Christian writers, evil spirit), neut. of *daimónios*, deriv. of *daímōn*; def. 5: < L; see DAEMON]

demon-, var. of **demono-** before a vowel: *demonism.*

De·mo·nas·sa (dē′mə nas′ə), *n. Class Myth.* a daughter of Amphiaraus and Eriphyle, the wife of Thersander, and the mother of Tisamenus.

De·mo·nax (dē′mə naks′), *n.* a walled plain in the fourth quadrant of the face of the moon in the libration area: about 75 miles in diameter.

de·mon·e·tise (dē mon′i tīz′, -mun′-), *v.t.,* **-tised, -tis·ing.** *Chiefly Brit.* demonetize. —**de·mon′e·ti·sa′tion,** *n.*

de·mon·e·tize (dē mon′i tīz′, -mun′-), *v.t.,* **-tized, -tiz·ing.** **1.** to divest (a monetary standard or the like) of value. **2.** to withdraw (money or the like) from use. **3.** to deprive (an issue of postage stamps) of validity by legal methods and without marking the stamps themselves. Also, *esp. Brit.,* **demonetise.** [< F *démonétise(r).* See DE-, MONETIZE] —**de·mon′e·ti·za′tion,** *n.*

de·mo·ni·ac (di mō′nē ak′, dē′mə nī′ak), *adj.* Also, **de·mo·ni·a·cal** (dē′mə nī′ə kəl). **1.** of, pertaining to, or like a demon; demonic: *demoniac laughter.* **2.** possessed by or as by an evil spirit; raging; frantic. —*n.* **3.** one seemingly possessed by a demon or evil spirit. [ME *demoniak* < LL *daemoniac(us)* < Gk *daimoniakos*, equiv. to *daimon-* DEMON- + adj. suffix *-i-* -I- + *-akos* -AC] —**de·mo·ni·a·cal·ly** (dē′mə nī′ik lē), *adv.*
—**Ant. 1.** angelic.

de·mo·ni·an (di mō′nē ən), *adj.* demoniac (def. 1). Also, **daemonian.** [DEMON + -IAN]

de·mon·ic (di mon′ik), *adj.* **1.** inspired as if by a demon, indwelling spirit, or genius. **2.** demoniac (def. 1). Also, **daemonic, de·mon′i·cal.** [< LL *daemonic(us)* < Gk *daimonikós*, equiv. to *daimon-* DEMON- + *-ikos* -IC]

de·mon·ise (dē′mə nīz′), *v.t.,* **-ised, -is·ing.** *Chiefly Brit.* demonize.

de·mon·ism (dē′mə niz′əm), *n.* **1.** belief in demons. **2.** the study of demons; demonology. [DEMON- + -ISM] —**de′mon·ist,** *n.*

de·mon·ize (dē′mə nīz′), *v.t.,* **-ized, -iz·ing.** **1.** to turn into a demon or make demonlike. **2.** to subject to the influence of demons. Also, *esp. Brit.,* **demonise.** [< ML *daemoniz(āre)*, equiv. to LL *daemon* DEMON + *-izāre* -IZE]

demono-, a combining form of **demon:** *demonology.* Also, *esp. before a vowel,* **demon-.**

de·mon·og·ra·phy (dē′mə nog′rə fē), *n., pl.* **-phies.** a treatise on demons. [DEMONO- + -GRAPHY] —**de′mon·og′ra·pher,** *n.*

de·mon·ol·a·ter (dē′mə nol′ə tər), *n.* one who worships demons. [back formation from DEMONOLATRY]

de·mon·ol·a·try (dē′mə nol′ə trē), *n.* the worship of demons. [DEMONO- + -LATRY] —**de′mon·ol′a·trous,** *adj.* —**de′mon·ol′a·trous·ly,** *adv.*

de·mon·ol·o·gy (dē′mə nol′ə jē), *n.* **1.** the study of demons or of beliefs about demons. **2.** the doctrine of demons. Also, **daemonology.** [DEMONO- + -LOGY] —**de·mon·o·log·ic** (dē′mə nᵊloj′ik), **de′mon·o·log′i·cal,** *adj.* —**de′mon·o·log′i·cal·ly,** *adv.* —**de′mon·ol′o·gist,** *n.*

de·mon·stra·ble (di mon′strə bəl, dem′ən-), *adj.* capable of being demonstrated. [ME < OF < L *dēmonstrābil(is),* equiv. to *dēmonstr(āre)* (see DEMONSTRATE) + *-ābilis* -ABLE] —**de·mon′stra·bil′i·ty, de·mon′stra·ble·ness,** *n.* —**de·mon′stra·bly,** *adv.*

de·mon·strant (də mon′strənt), *n.* demonstrator (def. 2). [< L *dēmonstrant-* (s. of *dēmonstrāns*) showing, prp. of *dēmonstrāre.* See DEMONSTRATE, -ANT]

dem·on·strate (dem′ən strāt′), *v.,* **-strat·ed, -strat·ing.** —*v.t.* **1.** to make evident or establish by arguments or reasoning; prove: *to demonstrate a philosophical principle.* **2.** to describe, explain, or illustrate by examples, specimens, experiments, or the like: *to demonstrate the force of gravity by dropping an object.* **3.** to manifest or exhibit; show: *He demonstrated his courage by his actions in battle.* **4.** to display publicly, as feelings: *to demonstrate one's anger by slamming a door.* **5.** to exhibit the operation or use of (a device, machine, process, product, or the like) usually to a purchaser or prospect: *to demonstrate an automobile.* —*v.i.* **6.** to make, give, or take part in, a demonstration: *To show what he meant, he demonstrated. The pickets required a license to demonstrate.* **7.** *Mil.* to attack or make a show of force to deceive an enemy. [< L *dēmonstrāt(us),* ptp. of *dēmonstrāre* to show, point out, equiv. to *dē-* DE- + *monstrāre* to show (*monstr(um)* a portent (see MONSTER) + *-ātus* -ATE[1])] —**dem′on·strat′ed·ly,** *adv.*

dem·on·stra·tion (dem′ən strā′shən), *n.* **1.** the act or circumstance of proving or being proven conclusively, as by reasoning or a show of evidence: *a belief incapable of demonstration.* **2.** something serving as proof or supporting evidence: *His speech was a demonstration of his patriotism.* **3.** a description or explanation, as of a process, illustrated by examples, specimens, or the like: *a demonstration of methods of refining ore.* **4.** the act of exhibiting the operation or use of a device, machine, process, product, or the like, as to a prospective buyer: *The salesman gave Mrs. Jones a demonstration of the new vacuum cleaner.* **5.** an exhibition, as of feeling; display; manifestation: *His demonstration of affection was embarrassing.* **6.** a public exhibition of the attitude of a group of persons toward a controversial issue, or other matter, made by picketing, parading, etc. **7.** a show of military force or of offensive operations made to deceive an enemy. **8.** *Math.* a logical presentation of the way in which given assumptions imply a certain result; proof. [ME *demonstracion* < L *dēmonstrātiōn-* (s. of *dēmonstrātiō,* equiv. to *dēmonstrāt(us)* (see DEMONSTRATE) + *-iōn-* -ION] —**dem′on·stra′tion·al,** *adj.*

de·mon·stra·tive (də mon′strə tiv), *adj.* **1.** characterized by or given to open exhibition or expression of one's emotions, attitudes, etc., esp. of love or affection: *She wished her fiancé was more demonstrative.* **2.** serving to demonstrate; explanatory or illustrative. **3.** serving to prove the truth of anything; indubitably conclusive. **4.** *Gram.* indicating or singling out the thing referred to. *This* is a demonstrative pronoun. —*n.* **5.** *Gram.* a demonstrative word, as *this* or *there.* [ME *demonstratif* < L *dēmonstrātīv(us),* equiv. to *dēmonstrāt(us)* (see DEMONSTRATE) + *-īvus* -IVE] —**de·mon′stra·tive·ly,** *adv.* —**de·mon′stra·tive·ness,** *n.*

dem·on·stra·tor (dem′ən strā′tər), *n.* **1.** one who or that which demonstrates. **2.** Also, **demonstrant.** one who takes part in a public demonstration, as by marching or picketing. **3.** one who explains or teaches by practical demonstrations. **4.** one who exhibits the use and application of (a product, service, etc.) to a prospective customer. **5.** the product, device, machine, etc., actually used in demonstrations to prospective customers: *They sold the demonstrator at half price.* [< L *dēmonstrātor,* equiv. to *dēmonstrāt(us)* (see DEMONSTRATE) + *-or* -OR[2]]

De·mo·phon (dē′mə fon′), *n.* *Class. Myth.* a son of Theseus.

De·moph·o·ön (də mof′ō on′), *n.* *Class. Myth.* a son of Celeus and Metanira, nursed by Demeter.

De·mop·o·lis (də mop′ə lis), *n.* a town in W Alabama. 7377 (1960).

de·mor·al·ise (di môr′ə līz′, -mor′-), *v.t.,* **-ised, -is·ing.** *Chiefly Brit.* demoralize. —**de·mor′al·i·sa′tion,** *n.* —**de·mor′al·is′er,** *n.*

de·mor·al·ize (di môr′ə līz′, -mor′-), *v.t.,* **-ized, -iz·ing.** **1.** to deprive (a person or persons) of spirit, courage, discipline, etc.; destroy the morale of: *The continuous barrage demoralized the infantry.* **2.** to throw (a person) into disorder or confusion; bewilder: *Although she knew the subject, she was so demoralized by the teacher's criticism that she failed the examination.* **3.** to corrupt or undermine the morals of. Also, *esp. Brit.,* **demoralise.** [< F *démoralise(r).* See DE-, MORAL, -IZE] —**de·mor′al·i·za′tion,** *n.* —**de·mor′al·iz′er,** *n.*

De Mor·gan (di môr′gən), **1. Augustus,** 1806–71, English mathematician and logician. **2. William Frend** (frend), 1839–1917, English novelist and ceramist.

De Mor′gan's Laws′, **1.** *Logic.* two laws, one stating that the denial of the conjunction of a class of propositions is equivalent to the disjunction of the denials of a proposition, and the other stating that the denial of the disjunction of a class of propositions is equivalent to the conjunction of the denials of the propositions. **2.** *Math.* **a.** the theorem of set theory that the complement of the union of two sets is equal to the intersection of the complements of the sets. **b.** the theorem of set theory that the complement of the intersection of two sets is equal to the union of the complements of the sets. [named after A. DE MORGAN]

de mor·tu·is nil ni·si bo·num (dā mōr′tōō is′ nil nē′sē bō′nōōm; *Eng.* dē môr′chōō is nil nī′sī bō′nəm), *Latin.* of the dead (say) nothing unless (it is) good.

de·mos (dē′mos), *n.* **1.** the people or commons of an ancient Greek state. **2.** the common people; populace. **3.** *Sociol.* a people viewed as a political unit. [< Gk: district, people]

De·mos·the·nes (di mos′thə nēz′), *n.* 384?–322 B.C., Athenian statesman and orator.

de·mote (di mōt′), *v.t.,* **-mot·ed, -mot·ing.** to reduce to a lower grade or class (opposed to *promote*): *They demoted the careless waiter to busboy.* [DE- + *-mote,* modeled on *promote*] —**de·mo′tion,** *n.*

de·moth·ball (dē môth′bôl′, -moth′-), *v.t.* to remove (a naval vessel) from storage or reserve, usually for active duty; reactivate. [DE- + MOTHBALL]

de·mot·ic (di mot′ik), *adj.* **1.** of or pertaining to the common people; popular. **2.** of, pertaining to, or noting the simplified form of hieratic writing used in ancient Egypt. —*n.* **3.** demotic script. **4.** (*cap.*) Also called **Romaic.** the Modern Greek vernacular (opposed to *Katharevusa*). [< Gk *dēmotik(ós)* popular, plebeian, equiv. to *dēmót(ēs)* a plebeian (see DEMO-) + *-ikos* -IC]

de·mount (dē mount′), *v.t.* **1.** to remove from a mounting, setting, or place of support, as a gun. **2.** to take apart; disassemble. [DE- + MOUNT[1]] —**de·mount′a·bil′i·ty,** *n.* —**de·mount′a·ble,** *adj.*

Demp·sey (demp′sē), *n.* **Jack** (*William Harrison Dempsey*), 1895–1983, U.S. boxer: world heavyweight champion 1919–26.

demp·ster (demp′stər), *n.* deemster.

Demp·ster (demp′stər, dem′-), *n.* **Arthur Jeffrey,** 1886–1950, U.S. physicist.

de·mul·cent (di mul′sənt), *adj.* **1.** soothing or mollifying, as a medicinal substance. —*n.* **2.** a demulcent substance or agent, often mucilaginous, as for soothing or protecting an irritated mucous membrane. [< L *dēmulcent-* (s. of *dēmulcēns,* prp. of *dēmulcēre*) stroking down, softening, equiv. to *dē-* DE- + *mulc(ere)* (to) soothe + *-ent-* -ENT]

de·mul·si·fy (dē mul′sə fī′), *v.t.,* **-fied, -fy·ing.** *Physical Chem.* to break down (an emulsion) into separate substances incapable of re-forming the same emulsion. [DE- + (E)MULSIFY] —**de·mul′si·fi·ca′tion,** *n.* —**de·mul′si·fi′er,** *n.*

de·mur (di mûr′), *v.,* **-murred, -mur·ring,** *n.* —*v.i.* **1.** to make objection, esp. on the grounds of scruples; take exception; object: *They wanted to make him the chairman but he demurred.* **2.** *Law.* to interpose a demurrer. **3.** *Archaic.* to linger; hesitate. —*n.* **4.** the act of making objection. **5.** an objection raised. **6.** *Law. Obs.* a demurrer. **7.** *Archaic.* hesitation. [ME *demur(en)* < OF *demur-, demuer,* var. s. of *demorer* < L *dēmorārī* to linger, equiv. to *dē-* DE- + *morārī* to delay (*mor(a)* delay + *-ārī* pass. inf. suffix)] —**de·mur′ra·ble,** *adj.*
—**Ant. 1.** agree, accede.

de·mure (di myŏŏr′), *adj.,* **-mur·er, -mur·est. 1.** characterized by shyness and modesty; reserved. **2.** affectedly or coyly decorous, sober, or sedate. [ME, prob. < AF; cf. OF *mëur* ripe, mature < L *matūr(us)*] —**de·mure′ly,** *adv.* —**de·mure′ness,** *n.*
—**Syn. 1.** retiring. See **modest.** —**Ant. 1, 2.** indecorous.

de·mur·rage (di mûr′ij), *n.* *Com.* **1.** the detention of a vessel, as in loading or unloading, beyond the time agreed upon. **2.** the similar detention of a railroad car, truck, etc. **3.** a charge for such detention. [DEMUR + -AGE]

de·mur·ral (di mûr′əl), *n.* the act of demurring; demur. [DEMUR + -AL[2]]

de·mur·rer (di mûr′ər), *n.* **1.** one who demurs; objector. **2.** *Law.* a pleading in effect that even if the facts are as alleged by the opposite party, they do not sustain the contention based on them. **3.** an objection or demur. [< AF, var. of OF *demourer.* See DEMUR, -ER[1]]

De·mus (dē′məs), *n.* a boy's given name.

De·muth (di mōōth′), *n.* **Charles,** 1883–1935, U.S. painter and illustrator.

de·my (di mī′), *n., pl.* **-mies. 1.** a foundation scholar at Magdalen College, Oxford: so called because such a scholar originally received half the allowance of a fellow. **2.** (in England) a size of printing paper, 17½ × 22½ inches. **3.** a size of drawing or writing paper, 15½ or 15 × 20 inches in England, 16 × 21 inches in the U.S. **4.** Also called **demy′ octa′vo.** a size of book, about 5½ × 8¾ inches, untrimmed. *Abbr.:* demy 8vo **5.** Also called **demy′ quar′to.** *Chiefly Brit.* a size of book, about 8¾ × 11 inches, untrimmed. *Abbr.:* demy 4to [ME *demi, demy;* see DEMI-]

de·my·thol·o·gise (dē′mi thol′ə jīz′), *v.t.,* **-gised, -gis·ing.** *Chiefly Brit.* demythologize. —**de′my·thol′o·gi·sa′tion,** *n.*

de·my·thol·o·gize (dē′mi thol′ə jīz′), *v.,* **-gized, -giz·ing.** —*v.t.* **1.** to divest (a writing, work of art, author, artist, etc.) of mythological or legendary attributes in an attempt to appraise its or his merit more accurately: *scholars who are intent on demythologizing Shakespeare.* —*v.i.* **2.** to separate mythological, legendary, or apocryphal elements from a writing, work of art, historical figure, etc. [DE- + MYTHOLOGIZE] —**de′my·thol′o·gi·za′tion,** *n.*

den (den), *n., v.,* **denned, den·ning.** —*n.* **1.** a secluded place, as the lair of a predatory animal. **2.** a cave used as a place of shelter or concealment. **3.** a squalid or vile abode or place: *dens of misery.* **4.** a small, secluded room in a house or apartment, designed to provide a quiet, comfortable, and informal atmosphere for conversation, reading, writing, etc. **5.** one of the units of a cub scout pack, analogous to a patrol in the Boy Scouts. —*v.i.* **6.** to live in or as in a den. [ME; OE *denn;* cf. early D *denne* floor, cave, den, G *Tenne* floor]

Den (den), *n.* a boy's given name, form of **Dennis.**

Den., Denmark.

de·nar·i·us (di nâr′ē əs), *n., pl.* **-nar·i·i** (-nâr′ē ī′). **1.** a silver coin and monetary unit of ancient Rome, first issued in the latter part of the 3rd century B.C., which fluctuated in value and sometimes appeared as a bronze coin. **2.** a gold coin of ancient Rome equal to 25 silver denarii; aureus. [< L, orig. adj.: containing ten (asses). See DENARY]

den·a·ry (den′ə rē, dē′nə-), *adj.* **1.** containing ten; tenfold. **2.** proceeding by tens; decimal. [< L *dēnāri(us)* containing ten, equiv. to *dēn(ī)* ten at a time (deriv. of *dec(em)* ten) + *-ārius* -ARY]

de·na·sal·ize (dē nā′zə līz′), *v.t.,* **-ized, -iz·ing.** *Phonet.* to diminish the nasal resonance of (speech or a speech sound). [DE- + NASALIZE]

de·na·tion·al·ise (dē nash′ə nᵊlīz′), *v.t.,* **-ised, -is·ing.** *Chiefly Brit.* denationalize. —**de·na′tion·al·i·sa′tion,** *n.*

de·na·tion·al·ize (dē nash′ə nᵊlīz′), *v.t.,* **-ized, -iz·ing. 1.** to remove (an industry or the like) from government for return to or placement in private ownership or control. **2.** to deprive of national status, attachments, or characteristics. [DE- + NATIONALIZE] —**de·na′tion·al·i·za′tion,** *n.*

de·nat·u·ral·ise (dē nach′ər ə līz′), *v.t.,* **-ised, -is·ing.** *Chiefly Brit.* denaturalize. —**de·nat′u·ral·i·sa′tion,** *n.*

de·nat·u·ral·ize (dē nach′ər ə līz′), *v.t.,* **-ized, -iz·ing. 1.** to deprive (someone or something) of his or its proper or true nature; make unnatural. **2.** to deprive of the rights and privileges of citizenship or of naturalization. [DE- + NATURALIZE] —**de·nat′u·ral·i·za′tion,** *n.*

de·na·ture (dē nā′chər), *v.t.,* **-tured, -tur·ing. 1.** to deprive (something) of its natural character, properties, etc. **2.** to render (any of various alcohols) unfit for drinking by adding an unwholesome substance that does not alter the alcohol's usefulness for other purposes. **3.** *Biochem.* to treat (a protein or the like) by chemical or physical means so as to alter its original state. **4.** to make (fissionable material) impure for use in an atomic weapon by mixing it with unfissionable material. [DE- + NATURE] —**de·na′tur·ant,** *n.* —**de·na′tur·a′tion,** *n.*

dena′tured al′cohol, *Chem.* alcohol, esp. ethyl alcohol, that has been denatured: used chiefly as a solvent and in chemical synthesis.

de·na·tur·ise (dē nā′chə rīz′), *v.t.,* **-ised, -is·ing.** *Chiefly Brit.* denaturize.

de·na·tur·ize (dē nā′chə rīz′), *v.t.,* **-ized, -iz·ing.** denature. [DE- + NATURE + -IZE] —**de·na′tur·i·za′tion,** *n.* —**de·na′tur·iz′er,** *n.*

de·na·zi·fy (dē nä′tsə fī′, -nat′sə-), *v.t.,* **-fied, -fy·ing.** to rid of Nazism or Nazi influences. [DE- + NAZI- + -FY] —**de·na′zi·fi·ca′tion,** *n.*

Den·bigh (den′bē), *n.* **1.** a municipal borough in and the county seat of Denbighshire, in N Wales. 8044 (1963). **2.** Denbighshire.

Den·bigh·shire (den′bē shēr′, -shər), *n.* a county in N Wales. 173,843 (1961); 669 sq. mi. *Co. seat:* Denbigh. Also called **Denbigh.**

den′ chief′, (in the Boy Scouts) a boy scout who supervises a cub scout den in cooperation with a den mother.

den′ dad′, (in the Boy Scouts) a man who serves as an adult leader of a cub scout den.

dendr-, var. of **dendro-** before a vowel: *dendrite.*

dendri-, var. of **dendro-** before elements of Latin origin: *dendriform.*

den·dri·form (den′drə fôrm′), *adj.* treelike in form. [DENDRI- + -FORM]

Dendrite

den·drite (den′drīt), *n.* **1.** *Geol.* **a.** a branching figure or marking, resembling moss or a shrub or tree in form, found on or in certain stones or minerals due to the presence of a foreign material. **b.** any arborescent crystalline growth. **2.** *Anat.* the branching process of a neuron which conducts impulses toward the cell. See diag. under **neuron.** [< Gk *dendrít(ēs)* pertaining to a tree, equiv. to *dendr-* DENDR- + *-itēs* -ITE[1]]

Den·dri·tes (den drī′tēz), *n.* *Class. Myth.* an epithet of Dionysus, meaning "tree-youth."

den·drit·ic (den drit′ik), *adj.* **1.** formed or marked like a dendrite. **2.** of a branching form; arborescent. Also, **den·drit′i·cal.** [DENDRITE + -IC] —**den·drit′i·cal·ly,** *adv.*

dendro-, a learned borrowing from Greek meaning "tree," used in the formation of compound words: *dendrology.* Also, **dendr-, dendri-, -dendron.** [< Gk, comb. form of *déndron*]

den·dro·chro·nol·o·gy (den′drō krə nol′ə jē), *n.* the science dealing with the study of the annual rings of trees in determining the dates and chronological order of past events. [DENDRO- + CHRONOLOGY] —**den·dro·chron·o·log·i·cal** (den′drō kron′ᵊloj′i kəl), *adj.* —**den′dro·chron′o·log′i·cal·ly,** *adv.* —**den′dro·chro·nol′o·gist,** *n.*

den·droid (den′droid), *adj.* treelike; branching like a tree; arborescent. Also, **den·droi′dal.** [< Gk *dendroeid(ēs)* treelike, equiv. to *dendr-* DENDR- + *-eidēs* -OID]

den·drol·o·gy (den drol′ə jē), *n.* the branch of botany dealing with trees and shrubs. [DENDRO- + -LOGY] —**den·dro·log·i·cal** (den′drə loj′i kəl), **den′dro·log′ic, den·drol·o·gous** (den drol′ə gəs), *adj.* —**den·drol·o·gist** (den drol′ə jist), *n.*

den·dron (den′dron), *n., pl.* **-drons, -dra** (-drə). *Anat.* a dendrite. [< NL < Gk *déndron* a tree] —**den′dric,** *adj.*

-dendron, var. of **dendro-** as final element of a compound word: *rhododendron.*

den·droph·a·gous (den drof′ə gəs), *adj.* feeding on the wood of trees, as certain insects. [DENDRO- + -PHAGOUS]

den·droph·i·lous (den drof′ə ləs), *adj.* *Zool.* living in or on trees; arboreal. [DENDRO- + -PHILOUS]

dene (dēn), *n.* *Brit.* a bare, sandy tract or low sand hill near the sea. Also, **dean.** [ME; OE *denu* valley]

Den·eb (den′eb), *n.* *Astron.* a first-magnitude star in the constellation Cygnus. [< Ar *dhanab* a tail]

den·e·ga·tion (den′ə gā′shən), *n.* denial; contradiction. [late ME *denegacion* < LL *dēnegātiōn-* (s. of *dēnegātiō*). See DE-, NEGATION]

D.Eng., Doctor of Engineering.

D.Eng.S., Doctor of Engineering Science.

den·gue (deng′gā, -gē), *n.* *Pathol.* an infectious, eruptive fever of warm climates, usually epidemic, characterized esp. by severe pains in the joints and muscles. Also called **den′gue fe′ver, breakbone fever.** [< Sp; ? of Afr orig.]

Deng Xiao·ping (dœng′ shyou′ping′), born 1904, chairman of the Chinese Central Advisory Commission since 1982.

Den′ham Springs′, a town in SE Louisiana. 5991 (1960).

de·ni·a·ble (di nī′ə bəl), *adj.* capable of being or liable to be denied or contradicted. [DENY + -ABLE]

de·ni·al (di nī′əl), *n.* **1.** an assertion that an allegation or something considered true is false: *Despite his denials, we knew he had taken the purse. The politician issued a denial of his opponent's charges.* **2.** refusal to believe a doctrine, theory, or the like. **3.** disbelief in the existence or reality of a thing. **4.** the refusal of or the refusal to satisfy a claim, request, desire, etc., or of a person making a request. **5.** refusal to recognize or acknowledge; a disowning or disavowal: *a traitor's denial of his country; Peter's denial of Christ.* **6.** *Law.* refusal to acknowledge the validity of a claim, suit, or the like; a plea that denies allegations of fact in an adversary's plea: *Although she sued for libel, he entered a general denial.* **7.** sacrifice of one's own wants or needs; self-denial. [DENY + -AL[2]]

De·nice (də nēs′), *n.* a girl's given name. Also, **Denise, Denys.**

de·nic·o·tin·ize (dē nik′ə ti nīz′), *v.t.*, **-ized, -iz·ing.** to remove nicotine from (tobacco). [DE- + NICOTINE + -IZE]

de·ni·er[1] (di nī′ər), *n.* one who denies. [ME; see DENY, -ER[1]]

de·nier[2] (də nēr′ *or, esp. for 1,* den′yər; *Fr.* də nyā′), *n.* **1.** a unit of weight indicating the fineness of fiber filaments and yarns, both silk and synthetic, and equal to a yarn weighing one gram per each 9000 meters: used esp. in indicating the fineness of women's hosiery. **2.** any of various coins issued in French-speaking regions, esp. a coin of France, originally of silver but later of copper, introduced in the 8th century and continued until 1794. [ME < OF < L *denār(ius)* DENARIUS]

den·i·grate (den′ə grāt′), *v.t.*, **-grat·ed, -grat·ing.** **1.** to speak damagingly of; criticize in a derogatory manner; sully; defame: *to denigrate someone's good reputation.* **2.** to make black; blacken: *rain clouds denigrating the sky.* [< L *dēnigrāt(us)* blackened (ptp. of *dēnigrāre*), equiv. to *dē-* DE- + *nigr(āre)* (to) make black + *-ātus* -ATE[1]] —**den′i·gra′tion,** *n.* —**den′i·gra′tor,** *n.*

De·ni·ker (de nē ker′), *n.* **Jo·seph** (zhō zef′), 1852–1918, French anthropologist and naturalist.

den·im (den′əm), *n.* **1.** a heavy, Z-twist, twill cotton for overalls, jeans, and other work and leisure garments. **2.** a similar fabric of finer quality, for covering cushions, furniture, etc. **3. denims,** (*construed as pl.*) a garment, esp. overalls or trousers, made of denim. [< F: short for *serge de Nîmes* serge of NÎMES]

Den·is (den′is; *Fr.* də nē′), *n.* **1. Saint,** died A.D. c280, 1st bishop of Paris: patron saint of France. **2.** Also, **Dennis.** a boy's given name. Also, **Denys.**

De·nise (də nēs′, -nēz′), *n.* a girl's given name. Also, **Denice, Denys.**

Den·i·son (den′i sən), *n.* **1.** a city in NE Texas. 22,748 (1960). **2.** a town in W Iowa. 4930 (1960).

de·ni·trate (dē nī′trāt), *v.t.*, **-trat·ed, -trat·ing.** to free from nitric acid or nitrates; remove oxides of nitrogen from. [DE- + NITRATE] —**de′ni·tra′tion,** *n.*

de·ni·tri·fy (dē nī′trə fī′). *v.t.*, **-fied, -fy·ing.** to reduce (nitrates) to nitrites, ammonia, and free nitrogen, as in soil by microorganisms. [DE- + NITRIFY] —**de·ni′tri·fi·ca′tion,** *n.* —**de·ni′tri·fi′er, de·ni′tri·fi·ca′tor,** *n.*

den·i·zen (den′i zən), *n.* **1.** an inhabitant; resident. **2.** *Brit.* an alien admitted to residence and to certain rights of citizenship in a country. **3.** anything adapted to a new place, condition, etc., as an animal or plant not indigenous to a place but successfully naturalized. —*v.t.* **4.** to make a denizen of. [ME *denisein* < AF, equiv. to *deinz* within (< L *de intus*) + *-ein* -AN] —**den′i·za′tion, den′i·zen·a′tion,** *n.* —**den′i·zen·ship′,** *n.*

Den·mark (den′märk), *n.* **1.** a kingdom in N Europe, on the Jutland peninsula and adjacent islands. 4,585,256 (1960); 16,576 sq. mi. *Cap.:* Copenhagen. **2.** a town in central South Carolina. 3221 (1960).

Den′mark Strait′, a strait between Iceland and Greenland. 130 mi. wide.

den′ moth′er, (in the Boy Scouts) a woman who serves as an adult leader of a cub-scout den.

Den·nis (den′is), *n.* **1. John,** 1657–1734, English dramatist and critic. **2.** Also, **Denis, Denys.** a boy's given name.

Den·ni·son (den′i sən), *n.* **1.** a town in E Ohio. 4158 (1960). **2.** a boy's given name.

Den·ny (den′ē), *n.* a boy's given name, form of **Dennis.**

denom., denomination.

de·nom·i·nate (di nom′ə nāt′), *v.t.*, **-nat·ed, -nat·ing.** to give a name to; denote; designate. [< L *dēnōmināt(us)* (ptp. of *dēnōmināre*), equiv. to *dē-* DE- + *nōminātus*; see NOMINATE]

de·nom·i·na·tion (di nom′ə nā′shən), *n.* **1.** a name or designation, esp. one for a class of things. **2.** a class or kind of persons or things distinguished by a specific name. **3.** a religious group, usually including many local churches, often larger than a sect: *the Lutheran denomination.* **4.** the act of naming or designating a person or thing. **5.** one of the grades or degrees in a series of designations of quantity, value, measure, weight, etc.: *He paid $500 in bills of small denomination.* [ME *denominacioun* < LL *dēnōminātiōn-* (s. of *dēnōminātiō*), in L: metonymy, equiv. to *dēnōmināt(us)* (see DENOMINATE) + *-iōn-* -ION]

de·nom·i·na·tion·al (di nom′ə nā′shə n(ə)l), *adj.* **1.** of or pertaining to a denomination or denominations. **2.** founded, sponsored, or controlled by a particular religious denomination or sect: *denominational schools.* **3.** limited, conditioned, originating in, or influenced by the beliefs, attitudes, or interests of a religious sect, political party, etc.: *denominational prejudice; denominational opposition.* [DENOMINATION + -AL[1]] —**de·nom′i·na′tion·al·ly,** *adv.*

de·nom·i·na·tion·al·ism (di nom′ə nā′shə n(ə)liz′əm), *n.* denominational or sectarian spirit or policy; the tendency to divide into denominations or sects. [DENOMINATIONAL + -ISM] —**de·nom′i·na′tion·al·ist,** *n.*

de·nom·i·na·tive (di nom′ə nā′tiv, -nə tiv), *adj.* **1.** conferring or constituting a distinctive designation or name. **2.** *Gram.* (esp. of verbs) formed from a noun, as English *to man* from the noun *man.* —*n.* **3.** *Gram.* a denominative verb or other word. [< LL *dēnōminātīv(us)*, equiv. to *dēnōmināt(us)* (see DENOMINATE) + *-īvus* -IVE] —**de·nom·i·na·tive·ly** (di nom′ə nā′tiv lē, -nə tiv-), *adv.*

de·nom·i·na·tor (di nom′ə nā′tər), *n.* **1.** *Arith.* that term of a fraction, usually written under the line, that indicates the number of equal parts into which the unit is divided; divisor. **2.** something shared or held in common; standard. **3.** *Archaic.* one who or that which denominates. [< ML *dēnōminātor*, equiv. to *dēnōmināt(us)* (see DENOMINATE) + *-or* -OR[2]]

de·no·ta·tion (dē′nō tā′shən), *n.* **1.** the association or set of associations that a word or expression usually elicits for most speakers of a language, as distinguished from those elicited for any individual speaker because of personal experience. Cf. **connotation. 2.** a word that names or signifies something specific: *"Wind" is the denotation for air in natural motion. "Poodle" is the denotation for a certain breed of dog.* **3.** the act or fact of denoting; indication. **4.** something that denotes; mark; symbol. **5.** *Logic.* **a.** the class of particulars to which a term is applicable. **b.** that which is represented by a sign. [< L *dēnotātiōn-* (s. of *dēnotātiō*) a marking out, equiv. to L *dēnotāt(us)* (ptp. of *dēnotāre*; see DENOTE) + *-iōn-* -ION]

de·no·ta·tive (dē′nō tā′tiv, di nō′tə tiv), *adj.* **1.** having power to denote. **2.** denoting or tending to denote: *the denotative meaning of a word.* [DENOTATE + -IVE] —**de′no·ta′tive·ly,** *adv.* —**de·no′ta·tive·ness,** *n.*

de·note (di nōt′), *v.t.*, **-not·ed, -not·ing.** **1.** to be a mark or sign of; indicate: *A quick pulse often denotes fever.* **2.** to be a name or designation for; mean. **3.** to represent by a symbol; stand as a symbol for. [< F *dénot(er)*, L *dēnot(āre)* (to) mark out, equiv. to *dē-* DE- + *notāre* to mark; see NOTE] —**de·not′a·ble,** *adj.* —**de·note′ment,** *n.*

de·no·tive (di nō′tiv), *adj.* used or serving to denote; denotative. [DENOTE + -IVE]

de·noue·ment (dā′no͞o mäN′), *n.* **1.** the final resolution of the intricacies of a plot, as of a drama or novel. **2.** the place in the plot at which this occurs. **3.** the outcome or resolution of a doubtful series of occurrences. [< F: lit., an untying, equiv. to *dénou(er)* (to) untie < OF *desnoer* (*des-* DE- + *noe(r)* (to) knot < L *nodāre*, deriv. of *nod(us)* knot) + *-ment* -MENT]

de·nounce (di nouns′), *v.t.*, **-nounced, -nounc·ing.** **1.** to censure or condemn openly or publicly: *to denounce a politician as morally corrupt.* **2.** to make a formal accusation against, as to the police or in a court. **3.** to give formal notice of the termination or denial of (a treaty, pact, agreement, or the like). **4.** *Archaic.* to announce or proclaim, esp. as something evil or calamitous. **5.** *Obs.* to portend. [ME *denounce(n)* < OF *denonc(ier)* (to) speak out < L *dēnuntiāre* to threaten (*dē-* DE- + *nuntiāre* to announce, deriv. of *nunti(us)* messenger)] —**de·nounce′ment,** *n.* —**de·nounc′er,** *n.* —**de·nun·ci·a·ble** (di nun′sē ə bəl), *adj.*
—**Syn. 1.** attack, stigmatize, blame, brand. —**Ant. 1.** praise, commend.

de no·vo (de nō′wō; *Eng;* dē nō′vō), *Latin.* anew; afresh; again; from the beginning.

Den·pa·sar (den pä′sär), *n.* a city on S Bali, in S Indonesia. Also, **Den Pa′sar.**

dens (denz), *n., pl.* **den·tes** (den′tēz). *Zool.* a tooth or toothlike part. [< L]

dense (dens), *adj.*, **dens·er, dens·est.** **1.** having the component parts closely compacted together; crowded or compact: *a dense forest; dense population.* **2.** stupid; slow-witted; dull. **3.** intense; extreme: *dense ignorance.* **4.** relatively opaque; transmitting little light, as a photographic negative, optical glass, color, etc. **5.** *Math.* of or pertaining to a subset of a topological space in which every neighborhood of every point in the space contains at least one point of the subset. [< L *dens(us)* thick; c. Gk *dasýs*] —**dense′ly,** *adv.* —**dense′ness,** *n.*

den·si·fy (den′sə fī′), *v.t.*, **-fied, -fy·ing.** to impregnate (wood) with additives under heat and pressure to harden it. [DENSE + -IFY] —**den′si·fi·ca′tion,** *n.* —**den′si·fi′er,** *n.*

den·sim·e·ter (den sim′i tər), *n.* *Chem., Physics.* any instrument for measuring density. [< L *dens(us)* DENSE + -I- + -METER] —**den·si·met·ric** (den′sə me′trik), *adj.* —**den′si·met′ri·cal·ly,** *adv.* —**den·sim′e·try,** *n.*

den·si·tom·e·ter (den′si tom′i tər), *n.* **1.** *Photog.* an instrument for measuring the density of negatives. **2.** a densimeter. [DENSIT(Y) + -O- + -METER] —**den·si·to·met·ric** (den′si tə me′trik), *adj.* —**den′si·tom′e·try,** *n.*

den·si·ty (den′si tē), *n., pl.* **-ties.** **1.** the state or quality of being dense; compactness; closely set or crowded condition. **2.** stupidity; obtuseness. **3.** *Physics.* mass per unit volume. **4.** *Elect.* **a.** the quantity of electricity per unit of volume at a point in space, or the quantity per unit of area at a point on a surface. **b.** See **current density. 5.** the degree of opacity of a substance, medium, etc., that transmits light. **6.** *Photog.* the relative degree of opacity of an area of a negative or transparency, often expressed logarithmically. [< L *densitāt-* (s. of *densitās*), equiv. to *dens(us)* DENSE + *-itāt-* -ITY]

den′sity cur′rent, *Geol.* See **turbidity current.**

den·sus (den′səs), *adj.* *Meteorol. Obs.* spissatus. [< L: dense]

dent[1] (dent), *n.* **1.** a hollow or depression in a surface, as from a blow. **2. to make a dent, a.** to cause to take heed; make an impression: *The doctor told him to stop smoking, but it didn't make a dent.* **b.** to show initial progress; pass an initial stage (of work, thought, solving a problem, etc.): *I haven't even made a dent in this job of painting the house.* —*v.t.* **3.** to make a dent in or on; indent: *The impact dented the fender of the automobile.* **4.** to injure or hurt slightly: *The caustic remark dented his ego.* —*v.i.* **5.** to sink in, making a dent: *Nails dent into metal.* **6.** to show dents; become indented: *Tin dents more easily than steel.* [ME *dente*, var. of DINT]

dent[2] (dent), *n.* **1.** a toothlike projection, as a tooth of a gearwheel. **2.** *Textiles.* the space between two wires through which the warp ends are drawn in the reed of a loom. [< F < L *dent-* (s. of *dēns*) tooth]

dent-, var. of **denti-** before a vowel: *dentin.*

dent., **1.** dentist. **2.** dentistry.

den·tal (den′t(ə)l), *adj.* **1.** of or pertaining to the teeth. **2.** of or pertaining to dentistry or a dentist. **3.** *Phonet.* **a.** (of a speech sound) articulated with the tongue tip touching the back of the upper front teeth or immediately above them, as French *t.* **b.** alveolar, as English *t.* —*n.* **4.** *Phonet.* a dental sound. [< ML *dentāl(is)*, equiv. to L *dent-* (s. of *dēns*) tooth + *-ālis* -AL[1]] —**den·tal′i·ty,** *n.*

den′tal floss′, *Dentistry.* a soft, waxed thread for cleaning between the teeth.

den·tal·ise (den′t(ə)līz′), *v.t.*, **-ised, -is·ing.** *Chiefly Brit.* dentalize. —**den′tal·i·sa′tion,** *n.*

den·ta·li·um (den tā′lē əm), *n., pl.* **-li·ums, -li·a.** any tooth shell of the genus *Dentalium.* [< NL < ML *dentāl(is)* DENTAL + *-ium* neut. n. suffix]

den·tal·ize (den′t(ə)līz′), *v.t.*, **-ized, -iz·ing.** *Phonet.* to change into or pronounce as a dental sound. Also, *esp. Brit.*, **dentalise.** [DENTAL + -IZE] —**den′tal·i·za′tion,** *n.*

den′tal lisp′, *Phonet.* See under **lisp** (def. 2).

den·tal·man (den′t(ə)l mən), *n., pl.* **-men.** *U.S. Navy.* an enlisted man working as a dental assistant. [DENTAL + MAN[1]]

den′tal pulp′. See under **pulp** (def. 4).

den′tal techni′cian, a skilled worker who makes dentures, bridges, etc., as specified by dentists for their patients.

den·ta·ry (den′tə rē), *n., pl.* **-ta·ries.** *Zool.* one member of the pair of membrane bones that in lower vertebrates form the distal part of the lower jaws and in mammals comprise the mandible. [< L *dentāri(us)* of the teeth, equiv. to *dent-* (s. of *dēns*) tooth + *-ārius* -ARY]

den·tate (den′tāt), *adj.* *Bot., Zool.* having a toothed margin or toothlike projections or processes. [< L *dentāt(us)*, equiv. to *dent-* (s. of *dēns*) tooth + *-ātus* -ATE[1]] —**den′tate·ly,** *adv.*

Dentate leaf

den·ta·tion (den tā′shən), *n.* *Bot., Zool.* **1.** dentate state or form. **2.** an angular projection of a margin. [DENTATE + -ION]

den·telle (den tel′, dän-), *n.* a lacelike, tooled pattern used in decorating book covers. [< F: lace, lit., little tooth < OF *dentele*, dim. of *dent* tooth < L *dent-* (s. of *dēns*)]

denti-, a learned borrowing from Latin meaning "tooth," used in the formation of compound words: *dentiform.* Also, *esp. before a vowel,* **dent-.** Cf. **odont-.** [< L, comb. form *dēns, dent-* (s. of obl.)]

den·ti·cle (den′ti kəl), *n.* a small tooth or toothlike part. [ME < L *denticul(us)*, equiv. to *denti-* DENTI- + *-culus* -CLE]

den·tic·u·late (den tik′yə lit, -lāt′), *adj.* **1.** *Bot., Zool.* finely dentate, as a leaf. **2.** *Archit.* having dentils. Also, **den·tic′u·lat′ed.** [< L *denticulāt(us)* having small teeth, equiv. to *denticul(us)* DENTICLE + *-ātus* -ATE[1]] —**den·tic′u·late·ly,** *adv.*

den·tic·u·la·tion (den tik′yə lā′shən), *n.* **1.** denticulate state or form. **2.** a denticle. **3.** a series of denticles. [DENTICULATE + -ION]

den·ti·form (den′tə fôrm′), *adj.* having the form of a tooth; tooth-shaped. [DENTI- + -FORM]

den·ti·frice (den′tə fris), *n.* a powder, paste, or other preparation for cleaning the teeth. [< F < L *dentifric(ium)* tooth powder. See DENTI-, FRICTION]

den·til (den′t(ə)l, -til), *n.* *Archit.* any of a series of closely spaced, small, rectangular blocks, used esp. in classical architecture beneath the coronas of Ionic, Corinthian, and Composite cornices. [< F < *dentille* (obs.), fem. dim. of *dent* tooth] —**den′tiled,** *adj.*

den·ti·la·bi·al (den′ti lā′bē əl), *adj., n.* *Phonet.* labiodental. [DENTI- + LABIAL]

den′til band′, (in classical architecture) a molding occupying the position of a row of dentils and often cut to resemble one.

den·ti·lin·gual (den′ti liṉg′gwəl), *Phonet.* —*adj.* **1.** interdental (def. 2). —*n.* **2.** a dentilingual sound. [DENTI- + LINGUAL]

den·tin (den′t(ə)n, -tin), *n.* *Dentistry.* the hard, calcareous tissue, similar to but denser than bone, that forms the major portion of a tooth, surrounds the pulp cavity, and is situated beneath the enamel and cementum. See diag. under **tooth.** Also, **den·tine** (den′tēn). [DENT- + -IN[2]] —**den′tin·al,** *adj.*

den·ti·phone (den′tə fōn′), *n.* an instrument held against the teeth to assist hearing by transmitting sound vibrations to the auditory nerve. [DENTI- + -PHONE]

den·ti·ros·tral (den′ti ros′trəl), *adj.* *Ornith.* having a toothlike projection on the cutting edge of the bill, as in falcons and shrikes. [DENTI- + ROSTRAL]

den·tist (den′tist), *n.* one whose profession is dentistry. [< F *dentiste*, equiv. to *dent* tooth (see DENT[2]) + *-iste* -IST]

den·tist·ry (den′ti strē), *n.* the profession or science dealing with the prevention and treatment of diseases and malformations of the teeth, gums, and oral cavity and the removing, correcting, and replacing of decayed, damaged, or lost parts, including such operations as the filling and crowning of teeth, straightening teeth, the construction of artificial dentures, etc. [DENTIST + -RY]

den·ti·tion (den tish′ən), *n.* **1.** the kind, number, and arrangement of the teeth of man and animals. **2.** the eruption or cutting of the teeth; teething; odontiasis. [< L *dentītiōn-* (s. of *dentītiō*) a teething, equiv. to *dentīt(us)* teethed (ptp. of *dentīre*) + *-iōn-* -ION]

den·toid (den′toid), *adj.* resembling a tooth; toothlike. [DENT- + -OID]

Den·ton (den′tən), *n.* **1.** a city in N Texas. 26,844 (1960). **2.** a boy's given name.

D'En·tre·cas·teaux′ Is′lands (däN trə ka stō′), a group of islands SE of New Guinea belonging to Australia: part of the Territory of Papua.

den·ture (den′chər), *n.* an artificial replacement of one or several of the teeth **(partial denture),** or all of the teeth **(full denture)** of either or both jaws. [< F, equiv. to *dent* tooth (see DENT[2]) + *-ure* -URE]

de·nu·date (*v.* den′yo͝o dāt′, di no͞o′dāt, -nyo͞o′-; *adj.* di no͞o′dāt, -nyo͞o′-, den′yo͞o dāt′), *v.*, **-dat·ed, -dat·ing,** *adj.* —*v.t.* **1.** to make bare; strip; denude. —*adj.* **2.** denuded; bare. [< L *dēnūdāt(us)*, ptp. of *dēnūdāre* to DENUDE; see -ATE[1]]

de·nu·da·tion (den′yo͝o dā′shən, dē′no͞o-, -nyo͞o-), *n.* **1.** the act of denuding. **2.** the state of being denuded. **3.** *Geol.* **a.** the laying bare of rock by erosive processes. **b.** (not in technical use) erosion. [< LL *dēnūdātiōn-* (s. of *dēnūdātiō*) = L *dēnūdāt(us)* (see DENUDATE) + *-iōn-* -ION] —**de·nu·da·tive** (di no͞o′də tiv, -nyo͞o′-), *adj.*

de·nude (di no͞od′, -nyo͞od′), *v.t.*, **-nud·ed, -nud·ing.** **1.** to make naked or bare; strip: *The storm completely denuded the trees.* **2.** *Geol.* to subject to denudation. [< L *dēnūd(āre)*, equiv. to *dē-* DE- + *nūdāre* to lay bare; see NUDE] —**de·nud′er,** *n.*

de·nu·mer·a·ble (di no͞o′mər ə bəl, -nyo͞o′-), *adj.* countable (def. 2b). [DE- + NUMERABLE] —**de·nu′mer·a·bly,** *adv.*

de·nun·ci·ate (di nun′sē āt′, -shē-), *v.t., v.i.*, **-at·ed, -at·ing.** to denounce; condemn openly. [< L *dēnuntiāt(us)* declared (ptp. of *dēnuntiāre*). See DENOUNCE, -ATE¹] —**de·nun′ci·a′tor,** *n.*

de·nun·ci·a·tion (di nun′sē ā′shən, -shē-), *n.* **1.** an act or instance of denouncing; public censure or condemnation. **2.** an accusation of crime before a public prosecutor or tribunal. **3.** notice of the termination or the renouncement of an international agreement or part thereof. **4.** *Archaic.* warning of impending evil; threat. [< L *dēnuntiātiōn-* (s. of *dēnuntiātiō*) < *dēnuntiāt(us)* (see DENUNCIATE) + *-iōn-* -ION]

de·nun·ci·a·to·ry (di nun′sē ə tôr′ē, -tōr′ē, -shē-), *adj.* characterized by or given to denunciation. Also, **de·nun·ci·a·tive** (di nun′sē ā′tiv, -shē-) [DENUNCIATE + -ORY¹] —**de·nun′ci·a′tive·ly,** *adv.*

Den·ver (den′vər), *n.* a city in and the capital of Colorado, in the central part. 493,887 (1960).

Den′ver Cit′y, a town in NW Texas. 4302 (1960).

de·ny (di nī′), *v.t.*, **-nied, -ny·ing.** **1.** to state that (something declared or believed to be true) is not true: *to deny an accusation; to deny that the earth is flat.* **2.** to refuse to agree or accede to: *to deny a petition.* **3.** to withhold the possession, use, or enjoyment of: *to deny access to secret information; to deny a man his rights.* **4.** to withhold something from, or refuse to grant a request of: *to deny a beggar; to deny a petitioner.* **5.** to refuse to recognize or acknowledge; disown; disavow; repudiate: *to deny one's gods.* **6.** to withhold (someone) from accessibility to a visitor: *The secretary denied her employer to all those without appointments.* **7.** *Obs.* **a.** to refuse to take or accept. **b.** to refuse (to do something). [ME *deni(en)* < OF *deni(er)* < L *dēnegāre.* See DENEGATION]
—**Syn. 1.** dispute, controvert, oppose, gainsay. DENY, CONTRADICT both imply objecting to or arguing against something. To DENY is to say that something is not true, or that it would not hold in practice: *to deny an allegation.* To CONTRADICT is to declare that the contrary is true: *to contradict a statement.* **5.** renounce, abjure. —**Ant. 1.** admit, accept. **3.** allow.

Den·ys (den′is; *Fr.* də nē′), *n.* **1. Saint.** See **Denis, Saint. 2.** Also, **Denis, Dennis.** a boy's given name. **3.** Also, **Denice, Denise.** a girl's given name.

de·o·dand (dē′ə dand′), *n.* *Eng. Law.* (formerly) an animal or article which, having been the immediate occasion of the death of a human being, was forfeited to the crown to be applied to pious uses. [< ML *deōdand-(um)* (a thing) to be given to God < L *deō* to God (dat. sing. of *deus*) + *dandum* to be given (neut. ger. of *dare* to give)]

de·o·dar (dē′ə där′), *n.* a large Himalayan cedar, *Cedrus Deodara*, yielding a durable wood. [< Hindi *deodār* < Skt *devadāru* wood of the gods, equiv. to *deva* god + *dāru* wood]

de·o·dor·ant (dē ō′dər ənt), *n.* **1.** an agent for destroying odors. **2.** a substance, often combined with an antiperspirant, for inhibiting or masking perspiration or other bodily odors. —*adj.* **3.** capable of destroying odors: *a deodorant cream.* [DE- + ODOR + -ANT]

de·o·dor·ise (dē ō′də rīz′), *v.t.*, **-ised, -is·ing.** *Chiefly Brit.* deodorize. —**de·o′dor·i·sa′tion,** *n.* —**de·o′dor·is′er,** *n.*

de·o·dor·ize (dē ō′də rīz′), *v.t.*, **-ized, -iz·ing.** to rid of odor, esp. of unpleasant odor. Also, *esp. Brit.*, **deodorise.** [DE- + ODOR + -IZE] —**de·o′dor·i·za′tion,** *n.* —**de·o′dor·iz′er,** *n.*

De·o fa·ven·te (dā′ō fä ven′tā), *Latin.* with God's favor.

De·o gra·ti·as (dā′ō grä′tsē äs′), *Latin.* thanks to God.

De·o ju·van·te (dā′ō yo͞o vän′tā), *Latin.* with God's help.

deon′tolog′ical eth′ics, the branch of ethics dealing with right action and the nature of duty, without regard to the goodness or value of motives or the desirability of the ends of any act. Cf. **axiological ethics.**

de·on·tol·o·gy (dē′on tol′ə jē), *n.* ethics, esp. that branch dealing with duty, moral obligation, and right action. [< Gk *deont-* that which is binding (s. of *déon*, neut. prp. of *dein*), equiv. to *de-* binding + *-ont-* (prp. suffix) + *-o-* + -LOGY] —**de·on·to·log·i·cal** (dē on′tᵊloj′i kəl), *adj.* —**de′on·tol′o·gist,** *n.*

De·o Op·ti·mo Max·i·mo (de′ō ōp′ti mō′ mäk′si-mō′; *Eng.* dē′ō op′tə mō′ mak′sə mō′). *Latin.* See **D.O.M.**

De·o vo·len·te (dā′ō vō len′tā), *Latin.* God willing.

de·ox·i·dise (dē ok′si dīz′), *v.t.*, **-dised, -dis·ing.** *Chiefly Brit.* deoxidize.

de·ox·i·dize (dē ok′si dīz′), *v.t.*, **-dized, -diz·ing.** to remove oxygen from; reduce from the state of an oxide. [DE- + OXIDIZE] —**de·ox′i·di·za′tion,** *n.* —**de·ox′i·diz′er,** *n.*

de·ox·y·gen·ate (dē ok′si jə nāt′), *v.t.*, **-at·ed, -at·ing.** to remove oxygen from. [DE- + OXYGENATE] —**de·ox′y·gen·a′tion,** *n.*

de·ox·y·gen·ize (dē ok′si jə nīz′), *v.t.*, **-ized, -iz·ing.** to deoxygenate. [DE- + OXYGENIZE] —**de·ox′y·gen·i·za′tion,** *n.*

de·ox·y·ri·bo·nu·cle·ase (dē ok′si rī′bō no͞o′klē-ās′, -nyo͞o′-), *n.* *Biochem.* an enzyme, found esp. in the pancreas, that serves to hydrolyze DNA to nucleotides. Also, **desoxyribonuclease.** [DE- + OXY-² + RIBONUCLEASE]

de·ox·y·ri′bo·nu·cle′ic ac′id (dē ok′si rī′bō no͞o-klē′ik, -nyo͞o-, -rī′-), *Biochem.* See **DNA.** [DE- + OXY-² + RIBONUCLE(IC ACID)]

de·ox·y·ri·bo·nu·cle·o·pro·tein (dē ok′si rī′bō-no͞o′klē ə prō′tēn, -tē in, -nyo͞o′-), *n.* *Biochem.* any of a class of nucleoproteins that yield DNA upon partial hydrolysis. Also, **desoxyribonucleoprotein.** [DE- + OXY-² + RIBONUCLE(IC ACID) + -O- + PROTEIN]

de·ox·y·ri·bose (dē ok′si rī′bōs), *n.* *Biochem.* **1.** any of certain carbohydrates having the formula $C_5H_{10}O_4$, derived from ribose by the replacement of a hydroxyl group with a hydrogen atom. **2.** the sugar, $HOCH_2(CHOH)_2CH_2CHO$, obtained from DNA by hydrolysis. Also, **desoxyribose.** [DE- + OXY-² + RIBOSE]

dep., **1.** department. **2.** departs. **3.** departure. **4.** deponent. **5.** depot. **6.** deputy.

de·paint (di pānt′), *v.t.* *Obs.* to depict; portray. [ME *depeint(en)* < OF *depeint*, ptp. of *depeindre* < L *dēpingere* to DEPICT]

de·part (di pärt′), *v.i.* **1.** to go away; leave: *He departed from Paris at noon. The train departs at 10:52.* **2.** to diverge or deviate (usually fol. by *from*): *The new method departs from the old in several respects.* **3.** to pass away, as from life or existence. —*v.t.* **4.** to go away from, leave: *to depart this life.* —*n.* **5.** *Archaic.* departure; death. [ME *depart(en)* < OF *departir*, equiv. to *de-* DE- + *partir* to go away; see PART (v.)]
—**Syn. 1.** DEPART, RETIRE, RETREAT, WITHDRAW imply leaving a place. DEPART is a somewhat literary word, implying going away from a definite place: *to depart on a journey.* RETIRE emphasizes the reason or purpose for absenting oneself or drawing back from a place: *to retire from a position in battle.* RETREAT implies a necessary withdrawal, esp. as a result of adverse fortune in war: *to retreat to secondary lines of defense.* WITHDRAW suggests leaving some specific place or situation, usually for some definite and often unpleasant reason: *to withdraw from a hopeless task.* **3.** die. **4.** quit. —**Ant. 1.** arrive.

de·part·ed (di pär′tid), *adj.* **1.** deceased; dead. **2.** gone; past. **3. the departed, a.** the dead person referred to. **b.** dead persons collectively. [DEPART + -ED²]

dé·par·te·ment (dā PAR tə mäN′), *n., pl.* **-ments** (mäN′). *French.* department (def. 3).

de·part·ment (di pärt′mənt), *n.* **1.** a distinct part of anything arranged in divisions; a division of a complex whole or organized system. **2.** a division of official business, duties, or functions: *judicial departments.* **3.** one of the large districts into which certain countries, as France, are divided for administrative purposes. **4.** one of the principal branches of a governmental organization: *The sanitation department says we can't use this lot for a dump.* **5.** a division of a business enterprise dealing with a particular area of activity: *the production department of a publishing house; personnel department.* **6.** a section of a retail store selling a particular class or kind of goods: *the sportswear department; luggage department.* **7.** one of the sections of a school or college dealing with a particular field of knowledge: *the department of English.* **8.** (*usually cap.*) *U.S. Army.* (formerly) a large geographical division of the U.S. or its possessions as divided for military and defense purposes: *the Hawaiian Department.* **9.** a sphere or province of activity, knowledge, or responsibility: *I'd like to buy a dress for my wife, but picking out her clothes isn't in my department.* [< F *département*, equiv. to *départ(ir)* (see DEPART) + *-ment* -MENT] —**de·part·men·tal** (di pärt men′tᵊl, dē′pärt-), *adj.* —**de·part·men′tal·ly,** *adv.*

de·part·men·tal·ism (di pärt men′tᵊliz′əm, dē′-pärt-), *n.* **1.** division into departments, as in a university. **2.** advocacy of or partiality for such division. [DEPARTMENTAL + -ISM]

de·part·men·tal·ize (di pärt men′tᵊlīz′, dē′pärt-), *v.t.*, **-ized, -iz·ing.** to divide into departments. Also, *esp. Brit.*, **de·part·men′tal·ise′.** [DEPARTMENTAL + -IZE]—**de′part·men′tal·i·za′tion,** *n.*

departmen′tal store′, *Brit.* a department store.

Depart′ment of Ag′riculture, *U.S.* the department of the federal government that institutes and administers all federal programs dealing with agriculture.

Depart′ment of Com′merce, *U.S.* the department of the federal government that promotes and administers domestic and foreign commerce.

Depart′ment of Defense′, *U.S.* the department of the federal government charged with ensuring that the military capacity of the U.S. is adequate to safeguard the national security.

Depart′ment of Educa′tion, *U.S.* the department of the federal government that institutes and administers all federal programs dealing with education: created in 1980 by transfer from part of the former Department of Health, Education, and Welfare.

Depart′ment of En′ergy, *U.S.* the department of the federal government that sets forth and maintains the national energy policy, including energy conservation, environmental protection, etc.

Depart′ment of Health′ and Hu′man Serv′ices, *U.S.* the department of the federal government that institutes and administers all federal programs dealing with public health and welfare: created in 1980 from the reorganized Department of Health, Education, and Welfare.

Depart′ment of Hous′ing and Ur′ban Devel′opment, *U.S.* the department of the federal government that institutes and administers all federal programs dealing with better housing, urban renewal, and metropolitan planning.

Depart′ment of Jus′tice, *U.S.* the department of the federal government charged with the responsibility for the enforcement of federal laws.

Depart′ment of La′bor, *U.S.* the department of the federal government that promotes and improves the welfare, opportunities, and working conditions of wage earners.

Depart′ment of State′, *U.S.* the department of the federal government that sets forth and maintains the foreign policy of the U.S., esp. in negotiations with foreign governments and international organizations.

Depart′ment of the Inte′rior, *U.S.* the department of the federal government charged with the conservation and development of the natural resources of the U.S. and its possessions.

Depart′ment of the Treas′ury, *U.S.* the department of the federal government that collects revenue and administers the national finances.

Depart′ment of Trans′porta′tion, *U.S.* the department of the federal government that coordinates and institutes national transportation programs.

department store′, a large retail store carrying several lines of merchandise and organized into various departments for sales and administrative purposes.

de·par·ture (di pär′chər), *n.* **1.** an act or instance of departing: *the time of departure; a hasty departure.* **2.** divergence or deviation, as from a standard, rule, etc.: *a departure from accepted teaching methods.* **3.** *Navig.* **a.** the distance due east or west made by a vessel or aircraft. **b.** See **point of departure. 4.** *Survey.* the length of the projection, on the east-west reference line, of a survey line. **5.** *Archaic.* death. [ME < OF *departëure*; cf. AF *departir* (n. use of inf.). See DEPART, -URE]

de·pau·per·ate (di pô′pər it), *adj.* *Biol.* poorly or imperfectly developed. [< LL *dēpauperāt(us)* made poor (ptp. of *dēpauperāre*), equiv. to *dē-* DE- + *pauper(āre)* (to) make poor (*pauper-* poor (see PAUPER) + *-ātus* -ATE¹)] —**de·pau′per·a′tion,** *n.*

de·pend (di pend′), *v.i.* **1.** to rely; place trust (usually fol. by *on* or *upon*): *You may depend on the accuracy of the report.* **2.** to rely for support, maintenance, help, etc. (usually fol. by *on* or *upon*): *Children depend on their parents.* **3.** to be conditioned or contingent (usually fol. by *on* or *upon*): *His success here depends upon effort and ability.* **4.** *Gram.* (of a word or other linguistic form) to be subordinate to another linguistic form in the same construction; to form a part of a construction other than the head. **5.** to hang down; be suspended (usually fol. by *from*): *The chandelier depends from the ceiling of the ballroom.* **6.** to be undetermined or pending: *I may go to Europe or I may not, it all depends.* [ME *depend(en)* < OF *depend(re)* < L *dēpendēre* to hang down = *dē-* DE- + *pendere* to hang]

de·pend·a·ble (di pen′də bəl), *adj.* worthy of trust; reliable; capable of being depended on: *a dependable employee.* [DEPEND + -ABLE] —**de·pend′a·bil′i·ty, de·pend′a·ble·ness,** *n.* —**de·pend′a·bly,** *adv.*

de·pend·ence (di pen′dəns), *n.* **1.** the state of depending on or needing someone or something for aid, support, or the like. **2.** reliance; confidence; trust: *He proved himself unworthy of her dependence.* **3.** the state of being conditional or contingent on something, as through a natural or logical sequence: *the dependence of an effect upon a cause.* **4.** subordination or subjection: *the dependence of Martinique upon France.* **5.** an object of reliance or trust. Also, **de·pend′ance.** [ME *dependaunce* < ML *dēpendentia*, OF *dependance*, equiv. to *depend(re)* (see DEPEND) + *-ance* -ENCE]

de·pend·en·cy (di pen′dən sē), *n., pl.* **-cies. 1.** the state of being dependent; dependence. **2.** something dependent or subordinate; appurtenance. **3.** an outbuilding or annex. **4.** a subject territory that is not an integral part of the ruling country. Also, **de·pend′an·cy.** [DEPENDENCE + -Y³]

de·pend·ent (di pen′dənt), *adj.* **1.** depending on someone or something else for aid, support, etc. **2.** conditioned or determined by something else; contingent: *Our trip is dependent on the weather.* **3.** subordinate; subject: *a dependent territory.* **4.** *Gram.* not used in isolation; used only in connection with other forms. In *I walked out when the bell rang, when the bell rang* is a dependent clause. Cf. **independent** (def. 12), **main¹** (def. 4). **5.** hanging down; pendent. —*n.* **6.** a person who depends on or needs someone or something for aid, support, favor, etc. **7.** a person, including oneself, one's spouse, children, and certain other relations, to whom one contributes all or a major amount of necessary financial support: *He listed four dependents on his income-tax form.* **8.** *Archaic.* a subordinate part. Also, **de·pend′ant.** [ME *dependaunt*. See DEPEND, -ENT] —**de·pend′ent·ly, de·pend′ant·ly,** *adv.*

depend′ent var′iable, *Math.* a variable in a functional relation whose value is determined by the values assumed by other variables in the relation, as *y* in the relation $y = 3x^2$. Cf. **independent variable.**

de·peo·ple (dē pē′pəl), *v.t.*, **-pled, -pling.** to depopulate. [DE- + PEOPLE]

de·perm (dē pûrm′), *v.t.* *Naut.* to reduce the permanent magnetism of (a vessel) by wrapping an electric cable around it vertically athwartships and energizing the cable. Cf. **degauss.** [DE- + PERM(ANENT)]

de·per·son·al·ise (dē pûr′sə nᵊlīz′), *v.t.*, **-ised, -is·ing.** *Chiefly Brit.* depersonalize.

de·per·son·a·li·za·tion (dē pûr′sə nᵊli zā′shən), *n.* **1.** the act of depersonalizing. **2.** the state of being depersonalized. **3.** *Psychiatry.* a state in which an individual no longer perceives the reality of self or of his environment. Also, *esp. Brit.*, **de·per′son·al·i·sa′tion.** [DEPERSONALIZE + -ATION]

de·per·son·al·ize (dē pûr′sə nᵊlīz′), *v.t.*, **-ized, -iz·ing. 1.** to make impersonal. **2.** to deprive of personality or individuality: *a mechanistic society which is depersonalizing its members.* Also, *esp. Brit.*, **depersonalise.** [DE- + PERSONALIZE]

dep·e·ter (dep′i tər), *n.* an exterior wall finish composed of mortar into which pebbles are pressed by means of a board while the mortar is still wet. Also, **depreter.** Cf. **pebble dash, roughcast** (def. 1). [?]

De·pew (də pyo͞o′), *n.* **Chauncey Mitchell,** 1834–1928, U.S. lawyer, legislator, and orator.

de·phlo·gis·ti·cat·ed (dē′flə jis′tə kā′tid), *adj.* *Archaic.* lacking phlogiston. [DE- + PHLOGIST(ON) + -IC + -ATE¹ + -ED²]

de·pict (di pikt′), *v.t.* **1.** to represent by or as by painting; portray; delineate. **2.** to represent or characterize in words; describe. [< L *dēpict(us)* (ptp. of *dēpingere*), equiv. to *dē-* DE- + *pic-* paint (ptp. s. of *pingere*) + *-t-* ptp. suffix] —**de·pict′er, de·pic′tor,** *n.* —**de·pic′tion,** *n.* —**de·pic′tive,** *adj.*
—**Syn. 1.** reproduce, draw, paint, limn. **1, 2.** DEPICT, PORTRAY, SKETCH imply an actual reproduction of an object or scene by colors or lines, or by words. DEPICT emphasizes vividness of detail: *to depict the confusion of departure.* PORTRAY emphasizes faithful representation: *We could not portray the anguish of the exiles.* SKETCH suggests the drawing of the outlines of the most prominent features, or of the fundamental details, often in a preparatory way: *to sketch a scene so that it can later be painted; to sketch the plans for a community development.*

de·pic·ture (di pik′chər), *v.t.*, **-tured, -tur·ing.** to picture; depict. [< L *dēpict(us)* (see DEPICT) + -URE]

dep·i·late (dep′ə lāt′), *v.t.*, **-lat·ed, -lat·ing.** to remove the hair from (hides, skin, etc.). [< L *dēpilāt(us)* plucked (ptp. of *dēpilāre*), equiv. to *dē-* DE- + *pil(āre)* (to) deprive of hair (deriv. of *pilus* a hair) + *-ātus* -ATE¹] —**dep′i·la′tion,** *n.* —**dep′i·la′tor,** *n.*

de·pil·a·to·ry (di pil′ə tôr′ē, -tōr′ē), *adj., n., pl.* **-ries.** —*adj.* **1.** capable of removing hair. —*n.* **2.** a depilatory agent. **3.** such an agent in a mild liquid or cream form for temporarily removing unwanted hair from the body. [< ML *dēpilātōr(ius)* < L *dēpilāt(us)* (see DEPILATE) + *-ōrius* -ORY[1]]

de·plane (dē plān′), *v.i.*, **-planed, -plan·ing.** to disembark from an airplane. [DE- + PLANE[1]]

de pla·no (dē plā′nō), *Chiefly Law.* **1.** without argument. **2.** by manifest right; plainly. [< L]

de·plete (di plēt′), *v.t.*, **-plet·ed, -plet·ing.** **1.** to decrease seriously or exhaust the abundance or supply of: *The fire had depleted the wild game in the forest. Wasteful errors depleted the supply of office stationery.* **2.** *Surg.* to empty or relieve (overcharged vessels), as by bloodletting or purging. [< L *dēplēt(us)* emptied out (ptp. of *dēplēre*), equiv. to *dē-* DE- + *pl(ēre)* (to) fill + *-ē* thematic vowel + *-t-* ptp. suffix] —**de·ple′tion,** *n.* —**de·ple′tive, de·ple·to·ry** (di plē′tə rē), *adj.*

de·plor·a·ble (di plōr′ə bəl, -plôr′-), *adj.* **1.** causing or being a subject for grief or regret; lamentable: *the deplorable death of a friend.* **2.** causing or being a subject for censure, reproach, or disapproval; wretched; bad: *This room is in deplorable order. You have deplorable manners!* [< F *déplorable* < MF, equiv. to *deplor(er)* (see DEPLORE) + *-able* -ABLE] —**de·plor′a·ble·ness, de·plor′a·bil′i·ty,** *n.* —**de·plor′a·bly,** *adv.*

de·plore (di plōr′, -plôr′), *v.t.*, **-plored, -plor·ing.** **1.** to regret deeply or strongly; lament: *to deplore the present state of morality.* **2.** to feel or express deep grief for or in regard to: *The class deplored the death of their teacher.* [< L *dēplōr(āre)* (to) weep bitterly, complain, equiv. to *dē-* DE- + *plōrāre* to wail, prob. of imit. orig.] —**dep·lo·ra·tion** (dep′lə rā′shən, dē′plə-), *n.* —**de·plor′er,** *n.* —**de·plor′ing·ly,** *adv.*
—**Syn. 1.** bemoan, bewail. **2.** lament, mourn.

de·ploy (di ploi′), *v.t.* **1.** *Mil.* to spread out (troops) so as to form an extended front or line. **2.** to arrange, place, or move strategically or appropriately: *He deployed his chessmen in a classic defense.* —*v.i.* **3.** to spread out strategically or in an extended front or line. [< F *déploy(er)*, equiv. to *dé-* DIS-[1] + *ployer* to fold; see PLOY] —**de·ploy′ment,** *n.*

de·plume (dē plōōm′), *v.t.*, **-plumed, -plum·ing.** **1.** to deprive of feathers; pluck. **2.** to strip of honor, wealth, etc. [ME < ML *dēplūmāre* < L *dē-* DE- + *plūm(a)* feather (see PLUME) + *-āre* inf. suffix] —**de′plu·ma′tion,** *n.*

de·po·lar·ise (dē pō′lə rīz′), *v.t.*, **-ised, -is·ing.** *Chiefly Brit.* depolarize. —**de·po′lar·i·sa′tion,** *n.* —**de·po′lar·is′er,** *n.*

de·po·lar·ize (dē pō′lə rīz′), *v.t.*, **-ized, -iz·ing.** to deprive of polarity or polarization. [DE- + POLARIZE] —**de·po′lar·i·za′tion,** *n.* —**de·po′lar·iz′er,** *n.*

de·po·lym·er·ize (dē′pə lim′ə rīz′, dē pol′ə mə-), *v.t.*, **-ized, -iz·ing.** *Chem.* to break down (a polymer) into monomers. [DE- + POLYMERIZE] —**de·po·lym·er·i·za·tion** (dē′pə lim′ər i zā′shən, dē pol′ə mər i-), *n.*

de·pone (di pōn′), *v.t., v.i.*, **-poned, -pon·ing.** to testify under oath; depose. [< L *dēpōne(re)* (to) put away, down, aside (ML: to testify), equiv. to *dē-* DE- + *pōn-* put + *-e* thematic vowel + *-re* inf. suffix]

de·po·nent (di pō′nənt), *adj.* **1.** *Classical Gk. and Lat. Gram.* (of a verb) appearing only in the passive or Greek middle-voice forms, but with active meaning. —*n.* **2.** *Law.* a person who testifies, esp. under oath. **3.** *Classical Gk. and Lat. Gram.* a deponent verb, as Latin *loquor.* [< L *dēpōnent-* (s. of *dēpōnēns*) putting away (ML: testifying), prp. of *dēpōnere.* See DEPONE, -ENT]

de·pop·u·late (*v.* dē pop′yə lāt′; *adj.* dē pop′yə lit, -lāt′), *v.*, **-lat·ed, -lat·ing,** *adj.* —*v.t.* **1.** to remove or reduce the number of inhabitants of, as by destruction or expulsion. —*adj.* **2.** *Archaic.* depopulated. [< L *dēpopulāt(us)* devastated (ptp. of *dēpopulārī*), equiv. to *dē-* DE- + *populātus*; see POPULATE] —**de·pop′u·la′tion,** *n.* —**de·pop′u·la′tive,** *adj.* —**de·pop′u·la′tor,** *n.*

de·port (di pōrt′, -pôrt′), *v.t.* **1.** to expel (an alien) from a country; banish. **2.** to carry off; transport, esp. forcibly: *The country deported its criminals to penal colonies.* **3.** to bear, conduct, or behave (oneself) in a particular manner. —*n.* **4.** *Obs.* deportment. [< F *déport(er)*, L *dēport(āre)* to carry away, banish oneself, equiv. to *dē-* DE- + *portāre* to carry; see PORT[5]] —**de·port′a·ble,** *adj.* —**de·port′er,** *n.*

de·por·ta·tion (dē′pōr tā′shən, -pôr-), *n.* **1.** the lawful expulsion of an undesired alien or other person from a state. **2.** the act or an instance of deporting. [< L *dēportātiōn-* (s. of *dēportātiō*), equiv. to *dēportāt(us)* (ptp. of *dēportāre*; see DEPORT, -ATE[1]) + *-iōn-* -ION]

de·por·tee (dē′pōr tē′, -pôr-), *n.* one who is or who is about to be deported, as from a country. [DEPORT + -EE]

de·port·ment (di pōrt′mənt, -pôrt′-), *n.* **1.** demeanor; conduct; behavior. **2.** the conduct or obedience of a child in school, as graded by a teacher. [< F *déportement*, equiv. to *déporte(r)* (see DEPORT) + *-ment* -MENT]
—**Syn.** See **behavior.**

de·pos·al (di pō′zəl), *n.* the act of deposing or removing, as from office; deposition. [ME; see DEPOSE, -AL[2]]

de·pose (di pōz′), *v.*, **-posed, -pos·ing.** —*v.t.* **1.** to remove from office or position, esp. high office: *The people deposed the dictator.* **2.** to declare or testify, esp. under oath, usually in writing: *to depose that an event took place.* —*v.i.* **3.** to bear witness; give sworn testimony, esp. in writing. [ME *depos(en)* < OF *depos(er)* (to) put down, equiv. to *de-* DE- + *poser* < VL *posāre*, LL *pausāre*; see POSE[1]] —**de·pos′a·ble,** *adj.* —**de·pos′er,** *n.*

de·pos·it (di poz′it), *v.t.* **1.** to put, place, or set down, esp. carefully or exactly: *She deposited the baby in the crib.* **2.** to insert (a coin) in a coin-operated device: *Deposit a quarter and push the button.* **3.** to lay or throw down by a natural process; precipitate: *The river deposited soil at its mouth.* **4.** to deliver and leave (an item): *Please deposit your returned books with the librarian.* **5.** to place for safekeeping or in trust, esp. in a bank account: *He deposited his paycheck every Friday.* **6.** to give as security or in part payment. —*v.i.* **7.** to be placed, inserted, precipitated, left for safekeeping, given as security or in partial payment, etc. —*n.* **8.** something precipitated, delivered and left, or thrown down, as by a natural process: *a deposit of soil.* **9.** the natural sediment of wine in a bottle. **10.** a coating of metal deposited on something, usually by an electric current. **11.** a natural accumulation or occurrence, esp. of oil or ore: *a mountain range with many rich deposits of gold.* **12.** anything laid away or entrusted to another for safekeeping: *A large deposit of jewels was stolen from the hotel safe.* **13.** money placed in a bank account or an instance of placing money in a bank account. **14.** anything given as security or in part payment: *The boy returned the pop bottle and got his two-cent deposit back. He made a deposit on the house and signed a ten-year mortgage.* **15.** a place for safekeeping; depository. [< L *dēposit(us)* laid down, ptp. of *dēpōn(ere)* (see DEPONE), equiv. to *dēpos-* + *-i-* thematic vowel + *-t-* ptp. suffix]
—**Syn. 3.** deposition, silt, alluvium. **5.** bank, save, hoard, store. **11.** lode, vein, pocket.

de·pos·i·tar·y (di poz′i ter′ē), *n., pl.* **-tar·ies.** **1.** one to whom anything is given in trust. **2.** depository. [< LL *dēpositāri(us)* a trustee, equiv. to L *dēposit(us)* (see DEPOSIT) + *-ārius* -ARY]

dep·o·si·tion (dep′ə zish′ən, dē′pə-), *n.* **1.** removal from an office or position. **2.** the act or process of depositing. **3.** the state of being deposited: *deposition of the documents with the Library of Congress; deposition of soil at the mouth of a river.* **4.** that which is deposited. **5.** *Law.* **a.** the giving of testimony under oath. **b.** the testimony so given. **c.** a statement under oath, taken down in writing, to be used in court in place of the spoken testimony of the witness. **6.** *Eccles.* **a.** the interment of the body of a saint. **b.** the reinterment of the body or the relics of a saint. **c.** a festival commemorating either of these. **7.** (*cap.*) See **Descent from the Cross.** [ME < OF, LL *dēpositiōn-* (s. of *dēpositiō*) a putting aside, testimony, burial, equiv. to *dēposit(us)* degraded < L (see DEPOSIT) + *-iōn-* -ION] —**dep′o·si′tion·al,** *adj.*

depos′it mon′ey, *Banking.* checks, letters of credit, etc., that circulate and are payable on demand.

depos′it of faith′, *Rom. Cath. Ch.* the body of truths held to be revealed in Scripture and tradition.

de·pos·i·tor (di poz′i tər), *n.* **1.** one who or that which deposits. **2.** a person who deposits money in a bank or who has a bank account. [< LL, equiv. to L *dēposit(us)* (see DEPOSIT) + *-or* -OR[2]]

de·pos·i·to·ry (di poz′i tōr′ē, -tôr′ē), *n., pl.* **-ries.** **1.** a place where anything is deposited or stored, as for safekeeping, future shipment, etc.: *the night depository of a bank.* **2.** a depositary; trustee. [< ML *dēpositōrium*, equiv. to L *dēposit(us)* (see DEPOSIT) + *-ōrium* -ORY[2]]

depos′it slip′, a printed slip for a bank depositor to fill out, listing all the items being deposited, as cash, coupons, and checks, for credit to his account. Also called **credit slip.**

de·pot (dē′pō; *Mil. or Brit.* dep′ō), *n.* **1.** *U.S.* **a.** a railroad station. **b.** a bus station. **2.** *Mil.* **a.** a place to which supplies and materials are shipped and stored for distribution. **b.** (formerly) a place where recruits are assembled for classification, initial training, and assignment to active units. **3.** a storehouse or warehouse, as a building where freight is deposited. **4.** *Physiol.* a place where body products not actively involved in metabolic processes are accumulated, deposited, or stored. [< F *dépôt* < L *dēposit(um)* (neut.), n. use of *dēpositus*; see DEPOSIT]
—**Syn. 1.** terminal. See **station.**

de·prave (di prāv′), *v.t.*, **-praved, -prav·ing.** **1.** to make bad or worse; vitiate; corrupt. **2.** *Obs.* to defame. [ME *deprave(n)* < L *dēprāv(āre)* (to) pervert, corrupt, equiv. to *dē-* DE- + *prāv(us)* crooked + *-āre* inf. suffix] —**dep·ra·va·tion** (dep′rə vā′tion), *n.* —**de·prav′er,** *n.* —**de·prav′ing·ly,** *adv.*

de·praved (di prāvd′), *adj.* corrupt, wicked, or perverted. [DEPRAVE + -ED[2]] —**de·praved·ly** (di prāvd′lē, -prā′vid-), *adv.* —**de·praved′ness,** *n.*
—**Syn.** evil, sinful, iniquitous, debased, reprobate, degenerate; dissolute, profligate; licentious, lascivious, lewd. See **immoral.** —**Ant.** decorous.

de·prav·i·ty (di prav′i tē), *n., pl.* **-ties.** **1.** the state of being depraved. **2.** a depraved act or practice. [DEPRAVE + -ITY]

dep·re·cate (dep′rə kāt′), *v.t.*, **-cat·ed, -cat·ing.** **1.** to express earnest disapproval of. **2.** to urge reasons against; protest against (a scheme, purpose, etc.). **3.** to depreciate; belittle. **4.** *Archaic.* to pray for deliverance from. [< L *dēprecāt(us)* prayed against, warded off (ptp. of *dēprecārī*), equiv. to *dē-* DE- + *prec(ārī)* (to) PRAY + *-ātus* -ATE[1]] —**dep′re·cat′ing·ly,** *adv.* —**dep′re·ca′tion,** *n.* —**dep′re·ca′tor,** *n.*

dep·re·ca·tive (dep′rə kā′tiv, -kə tiv), *adj.* serving to deprecate; deprecatory. [< LL *dēprecātīv(us)*, equiv. to *dēprecāt(us)* (see DEPRECATE) + *-īvus* -IVE] —**dep′re·ca′tive·ly,** *adv.*

dep·re·ca·to·ry (dep′rə kə tōr′ē, -tôr′ē), *adj.* **1.** of the nature of or expressing disapproval, protest, or depreciation. **2.** apologetic; making apology. [< L *dēprecātōri(us)*, equiv. to *dēprecāt(us)* (see DEPRECATE) + *-ōrius* -ORY[1]] —**dep′re·ca·to′ri·ly,** *adv.* —**dep′re·ca·to′ri·ness,** *n.*

de·pre·ci·a·ble (di prē′shē ə bəl), *adj.* **1.** capable of depreciating or being depreciated in value. **2.** *U.S.* capable of being depreciated for tax purposes. [DEPRECI(ATE) + -ABLE]

de·pre·ci·ate (di prē′shē āt′), *v.*, **-at·ed, -at·ing.** —*v.t.* **1.** to reduce the purchasing value of (money). **2.** to lessen the value or price of. **3.** *U.S.* to claim depreciation on (a property) for tax purposes. **4.** to represent as of little value or merit; belittle. —*v.i.* **5.** to decline in value. [< LL *dēpretiāt(us)* undervalued (ptp. of *dēpretiāre*, sp. var. of *dēpreciāre*), equiv. to L *dē-* DE- + *preti(um)* PRICE + *-ātus* -ATE[1]] —**de·pre′ci·at′ing·ly,** *adv.* —**de·pre′ci·a′tor,** *n.*
—**Syn. 4.** disparage, decry, minimize.

de·pre·ci·a·tion (di prē′shē ā′shən), *n.* **1.** decrease in value due to wear and tear, decay, decline in price, etc. **2.** *U.S.* such a decrease as allowed in computing the value of property for tax purposes. **3.** a decrease in the purchasing or exchange value of money. **4.** a lowering in estimation; disparagement. [DEPRECIATE + -ION]

de·pre·ci·a·to·ry (di prē′shē ə tōr′ē, -tôr′ē), *adj.* tending to depreciate. Also, **de·pre·ci·a·tive** (di prē′shē ā′tiv). [DEPRECIATE + -ORY[1]] —**de·pre·ci·a·tive·ly** (di prē′shē ā′tiv lē, -shə tiv-), *adv.*

dep·re·date (dep′ri dāt′), *v.*, **-dat·ed, -dat·ing.** —*v.t.* **1.** to plunder or lay waste to; pillage; ravage; prey upon. —*v.i.* **2.** to plunder; pillage. [< LL *dēpraedāt(us)* plundered (ptp. of *dēpraedārī*), equiv. to L *dē-* DE- + *praed(ārī)* (to) plunder (see PREY) + *-ātus* -ATE[1]] —**dep′re·da′tor,** *n.* —**dep·re·da·to·ry** (dep′ri dā′tə rē, di pred′ə tōr′ē, -tôr′ē), *adj.*

dep·re·da·tion (dep′ri dā′shən), *n.* the act of preying upon or plundering; robbery; ravage. [ME *depredacion* < LL *dēpraedātiōn-* (s. of *dēpraedātiō*) a plundering, equiv. to *dēpraedāt(us)* (see DEPREDATE) + *-iōn-* -ION] —**dep′re·da′tion·ist,** *n.*

de·press (di pres′), *v.t.* **1.** to lower in spirits; deject; dispirit; make sad or gloomy. **2.** to lower in force, vigor, activity, etc.; weaken; make dull. **3.** to lower in amount or value. **4.** to put into a lower position: *to depress the muzzle of a gun.* **5.** to press down. **6.** *Music.* to lower in pitch. [ME *depress(en)* < OF *depress(er)* < L *dēpress(us)* pressed down (ptp. of *dēprimere*, equiv. to *dē-* DE- + *-primere*, comb. form of *premere* to press); see PRESSURE] —**de·press′i·bil′i·ty,** *n.* —**de·press′i·ble,** *adj.* —**de·press′ing·ly,** *adv.*
—**Syn. 1.** dishearten, discourage, sadden. See **oppress.** **3.** devalue, cheapen. —**Ant. 4.** raise, elevate.

de·pres·sant (di pres′ənt), *adj.* **1.** *Med.* having the quality of depressing or lowering the vital activities; sedative. **2.** causing a lowering in spirits; dejecting. **3.** causing a drop in value; economically depressing. —*n.* **4.** *Med.* a sedative. Cf. **stimulant** (def. 1). **5.** *Chem.* any agent capable of diminishing a specific property of a substance. [DEPRESS + -ANT]

de·pressed (di prest′), *adj.* **1.** dejected; downcast; sad; gloomy. **2.** pressed down, or situated lower than the general surface. **3.** lowered in force, amount, etc. **4.** undergoing economic hardship, esp. poverty and unemployment. **5.** *Bot., Zool.* flattened down; greater in width than in height. [DEPRESS + -ED[2]]
—**Syn. 1.** saddened, morose, despondent, miserable; blue; morbid. See **sad.** —**Ant. 1.** happy.

depressed′ arch′. See **drop arch** (def. 1).

depressed′ ar′ea, a region where unemployment and a low standard of living prevail.

de·pres·sion (di presh′ən), *n.* **1.** the act of depressing. **2.** the state of being depressed. **3.** a depressed or sunken place or part; an area lower than the surrounding surface. **4.** dejection; sadness; gloom. **5.** *Psychiatry.* a condition of general emotional dejection and withdrawal; sadness greater and more prolonged than that warranted by any objective reason. **6.** dullness or inactivity, as of trade. **7.** a period during which business, employment, and stock-market values decline or remain at a low level of activity. **8. the Depression.** See **Great Depression.** **9.** *Pathol.* a low state of vital powers or functional activity. **10.** *Astron.* the angular distance of a celestial body below the horizon; negative altitude. **11.** *Survey.* **a.** the angle between the line from an observer or instrument to an object below him or it and a horizontal line. **b.** an area completely surrounded by higher ground. **12.** *Meteorol.* an area of low atmospheric pressure. [ME < ML *dēpressiōn-* (s. of *dēpressiō*), LL: a pressing down, equiv. to L *dēpress(us)* (see DEPRESS) + *-iōn-* -ION]
—**Syn. 4.** discouragement, despondency.

de·pres·sive (di pres′iv), *adj.* **1.** tending to depress. **2.** characterized by depression, esp. mental depression. [DEPRESS + -IVE] —**de·pres′sive·ly,** *adv.* —**de·pres′sive·ness,** *n.*

de·pres·so·mo·tor (di pres′ō mō′tər), *adj.* *Physiol., Med.* causing a retardation of motor activity: *depressomotor nerves.* [DEPRESS + -O- + MOTOR]

de·pres·sor (di pres′ər), *n.* **1.** one who or that which depresses. **2.** *Surg.* an instrument for pressing down a protruding part. Cf. **tongue depressor.** **3.** *Anat.* **a.** a muscle that draws down some part of the body. **b.** a nerve, the stimulation of which decreases the heartbeat and blood pressure. [< LL < L *dēpress(us)* (see DEPRESS) + *-or* -OR[2]]

dep·re·ter (dep′ri tər), *n.* depeter.

de·priv·al (di prī′vəl), *n.* the act of depriving; deprivation. [DEPRIVE + -AL[2]]

dep·ri·va·tion (dep′rə vā′shən), *n.* **1.** the act of depriving. **2.** the fact of being deprived. **3.** dispossession; loss. **4.** removal from office. **5.** privation. [< ML *dēprīvātiōn-* (s. of *dēprīvātiō*), equiv. to *dēprīvāt(us)* deprived (ptp. of *dēprīvāre*; see DEPRIVE) + *-iōn-* -ION]

de·prive (di prīv′), *v.t.*, **-prived, -priv·ing.** **1.** to remove or withhold something from the enjoyment or possession of (a person or persons): *to deprive a man of life; to deprive a baby of candy.* **2.** to remove from office. [ME *deprive(n)* < OF *depriv(er)* < ML *dēprīvāre*, equiv. to L *dē-* DE- + *prīvāre* to deprive (*prīv(us)* PRIVATE) + *-āre* inf. suffix] —**de·priv′a·ble,** *adj.* —**de·priv·a·tive** (di priv′ə tiv), *adj.* —**de·priv′er,** *n.*

de pro·fun·dis (dā prō fōōn′dis), *Latin.* out of the depths (of sorrow, despair, etc.).

de pro·pri·o mo·tu (dā prō′prē ō′ mō′tōō; *Eng.* dē prō′prē ō′ mō′tōō, -tyōō), *Latin.* of one's or its own motion.

dep·side (dep′sīd, -sid), *n.* *Chem.* any of a group of esters formed from two or more phenol carboxylic acid molecules. [< Gk *déps(ein)* (to) tan, soften + -IDE]

dept., department.

Dept·ford (det′fərd), *n.* a borough of London, England, S of the Thames River. 68,267 (1961).

depth (depth), *n.* **1.** a dimension taken through an object or body of material, usually downward from an outer surface, horizontally inward from an outer surface, or from top to bottom of something regarded as one of several layers. **2.** the quality of being deep; deepness. **3.** complexity or obscurity, as of a subject: *a question of great depth.* **4.** gravity; seriousness. **5.** emotional profundity: *the depth of someone's feelings.* **6.** intensity, as of silence, color, etc. **7.** lowness of tonal pitch: *the depth of a voice.* **8.** the amount of knowledge, intelligence, wisdom, insight, feeling, etc. present in a person's mind or evident either in some product of his mind, as a learned paper, argument, work of art, etc., or in his behavior. **9.** a high degree of such knowledge, insight, etc. **10.** Often, **depths.** a deep part or place: *from the depths of the ocean.* **11.** an unfathomable space; abyss: *the depth of time.* **12.** Sometimes, **depths.** the farthest, innermost, or extreme part or state: *the depth of space; the depths of the forest; the depths of despair.* **13.** Usually, **depths.** a low intellectual or moral condition: *How could he sink to such depths?* **14.** the part of greatest intensity, as of night or winter. **15.** *Sports.* the strength of a team in

terms of the number and quality of its substitute players: *With no depth in the infield, an injury to any of the regulars would be costly.* **16. in depth,** extensively or thoroughly: *Make a survey in depth of the conditions.* **17. out of** or **beyond one's depth,** beyond one's knowledge or capability: *The child is being taught subjects that are beyond his depth.* [ME *depthe,* equiv. to *dep* (OE *dēop* DEEP) + *-the* -TH[1]]
—Ant. 2. shallowness. **9.** superficiality.

depth′ bomb′, a depth charge, esp. when dropped from an airplane.

depth′ charge′, an explosive device that is used against submarines and other underwater targets and is usually set to detonate at a predetermined depth.

depth-charge (depth′chärj′), *v.t.,* **-charged, -charg·ing.** to attack or destroy with depth charges: *to depth-charge a submarine.*

depth′ in′terview, a detailed interview used in polling public opinion, designed to elicit more information about views, attitudes, etc., than may be disclosed by responses to a standardized list of questions.

depth′ of field′, *Optics.* the range of distances along the axis of an optical instrument, usually a camera lens, through which an object will produce a relatively distinct image. Also called **depth′ of fo′cus, penetration.**

depth′ of hold′, *Naut.* See **registered depth.**

depth′ psychol′ogy, any approach to psychology that postulates and studies personality from the standpoint of dynamic and unconscious motivation.

dep·u·rate (dep′yə rāt′), *v.t., v.i.,* **-rat·ed, -rat·ing.** to make or become free from impurities; purify; cleanse. [< ML *dēpūrāt(us)* purified (ptp. of *dēpūrāre*), equiv. to L *dē-* DE- + *pūr(āre)* (to) purify (*pūr(us)* PURE) + *-ātus* -ATE[1]] **—dep′u·ra′tion,** *n.* **—dep′u·ra′tor,** *n.*

dep·u·ra·tive (dep′yə rā′tiv), *adj.* **1.** serving to depurate; purifying. **—***n.* **2.** a depurative agent or substance. [DEPURATE + -IVE]

dep·u·ta·tion (dep′yə tā′shən), *n.* **1.** the act of appointing a person or persons to represent or act for another or others. **2.** the person or body of persons so appointed or authorized. Cf. **delegation** (def. 4). [ME *deputacioun* < ML *dēputātiōn-* (s. of *dēputātiō*), LL: delegation, equiv. to *dēputāt(us)* (ptp. of *dēputāre;* see DEPUTE, -ATE[1]) + *-iōn-* -ION]

de·pute (də pyōōt′), *v.t.,* **-put·ed, -put·ing. 1.** to appoint as one's substitute or agent. **2.** to assign (authority, a function, etc.) to a deputy. [ME *depute(n)* < OF *deput(er)* (to) assign < LL *dēputāre* to allot, L: to consider, equiv. to *dē-* DE- + *putāre* to think (*pu-,* lit., cleanse; see PURE)] **—dep·u·ta·ble** (dep′yə tə bəl, də pyōō′-), *adj.*

dep·u·tise (dep′yə tīz′), *v.t., v.i.,* **-tised, -tis·ing.** *Chiefly Brit.* deputize.

dep·u·tize (dep′yə tīz′), *v.,* **-tized, -tiz·ing. —***v.t.* **1.** to appoint as deputy. **—***v.i.* **2.** to act as a deputy; substitute. [DEPUT(Y) + -IZE]

dep·u·ty (dep′yə tē), *n., pl.* **-ties. 1.** a person appointed or authorized to act as a substitute for another or others. **2.** See **deputy sheriff. 3.** a person appointed or elected as assistant to a public official, serving as successor in the event of a vacancy. **4.** a person representing a constituency in certain legislative bodies. **—***adj.* **5.** appointed, elected, or serving as an assistant or second-in-command. [ME *depute* < OF, n. use of ptp. of *deputer.* See DEPUTE, -Y[3]] **—dep′u·ty·ship′,** *n.*

dep′uty sher′iff, a peace officer subordinate to a sheriff; a member of a sheriff's law-enforcement staff.

De Queen (di kwēn′), a town in SW Arkansas. 2859 (1960).

De Quin·cey (di kwin′sē), **1. Thomas,** 1785–1859, English essayist. **2.** a town in SW Louisiana. 3928 (1960).

der., 1. derivation. **2.** derivative. **3.** derive. **4.** derived.

de·rac·in·ate (di ras′ə nāt′), *v.t.,* **-nat·ed, -nat·ing. 1.** to pull up by the roots; uproot; extirpate; eradicate. **2.** to isolate or alienate (a person or persons) from a native or customary culture or environment. [< F *déracin(er),* equiv. to *dé-* DIS-[1] + *racine* root < LL *rādīcīn(a)* (dim. of L *rādīc-,* s. of *rādīx*) + -ATE[1]] **—de·rac′i·na′tion,** *n.*

de·raign (di rān′), *v.t.* **1.** *Law.* **a.** to dispute or contest (a claim, suit, etc., of another). **b.** to maintain or vindicate a claim to (something). **2.** *Hist.* to dispose troops for (battle). [ME *derein(er)* < OF *deraisn(ier)* (to) render an account, equiv. to *de-* DE- + *raisnier* to discourse < VL **ratiōnāre;* see REASON. Cf. ARRAIGN] **—de·raign′ment,** *n.*

de·rail (dē rāl′), *v.t.* **1.** to cause (a train, streetcar, etc.) to run off the rails of a track. **—***v.i.* **2.** (of a train, streetcar, etc.) to run off the rails of a track. **—***n.* **3.** a track device for derailing rolling stock in an emergency. [< F *déraill(er),* equiv. to *dé-* DIS-[1] + *rail* RAIL[1] (< E)] **—de·rail′ment,** *n.*

De·rain (də RAN′), *n.* **An·dré** (äN drā′), 1880–1954, French painter.

de·range (di rānj′), *v.t.,* **-ranged, -rang·ing. 1.** to throw into disorder; disarrange. **2.** to disturb the condition, action, or function of. **3.** to make insane. [< F *dérang(er)* < OF *desrengier,* equiv. to *des-* DIS-[1] + *rengier;* see RANGE] **—de·range′a·ble,** *adj.* **—de·rang′er,** *n.*

de·ranged (di rānjd′), *adj.* **1.** disordered; disarranged. **2.** insane. [DERANGE + -ED[2]]

de·range·ment (di rānj′mənt), *n.* **1.** the act of deranging. **2.** disarrangement; disorder. **3.** insanity or a mental disturbance. [< F *dérangement.* See DERANGE, -MENT]

de·ra·tion (dē rā′shən), *v.t.* to discontinue the rationing of (something). [DE- + RATION]

de·rat·i·za·tion (dē rat′i zā′shən), *n. Naut.* extermination of rats, esp. aboard a merchant vessel. [DERATIZE + -ATION]

de·rat·ize (dē rat′īz), *v.t.,* **-ized, -iz·ing.** to carry out the deratization of (a vessel). [DE- + RAT + -IZE]

de·ray (di rā′), *n. Archaic.* disorderly merrymaking. [ME *derai, drai(e), desrai* < AF *de(s)rei* (OF *desroi*), deriv. of *desrē(er)* (to) put out of order (*des-* DIS-[1] + *rēer* to arrange); cf. ARRAY]

Der·bent (der bent′), *n.* a seaport in the SW RSFSR in the S Soviet Union in Europe, on the Caspian Sea. 38,000 (1959). Also, **Der·bend** (der bend′).

Der·by (dûr′bē; *Brit.* där′bē), *n., pl.* **-bies. 1.** a horse race for three-year-old horses that is run annually at Epsom Downs, near London, England: first run in 1780. **2.** any of certain other important annual horse races, usually for three-year-old horses, esp. the Kentucky Derby. **3.** (*l.c.*) a race or contest, usually one open to all who wish to enter and offering a prize for the winner. **4.** (*l.c.*) Also called, *esp. Brit.,* **bowler.** a stiff felt hat with rounded crown and narrow brim, worn chiefly by men. [after Edward Stanley, 12th Earl of *Derby* (d. 1834), who instituted the race]

Der·by (dûr′bē; *for 1, 2 also Brit.* där′bē), *n.* **1.** a city in and the county seat of Derbyshire, in central England. 132,325 (1961). **2.** Derbyshire. **3.** a town in S Kansas. 6458 (1960). **4.** a boy's given name.

Der·by·shire (dûr′bē shēr′, -shər; *Brit.* där′bi shēr′, -shər), *n.* a county in central England. 877,548 (1961); 1006 sq. mi. *Co. seat:* Derby. Also called **Derby.**

Der′byshire chair′, *Eng. Furniture.* a chair of the mid-17th century, made of oak, usually without arms, and having a back of two carved rails between square uprights. Also called **Yorkshire chair.**

dere (dēr), *adj.* dear[2].

de rè·gle (də RE′glə), *French.* according to rule; following a pattern, principle, or law.

de·re·ism (dē rē′iz əm, dā rā′-), *n. Psychol.* autism. [< L *dē rē,* lit., away from the matter + -ISM] **—de′re·is′tic,** *adj.* **—de′re·is′ti·cal·ly,** *adv.*

Der·ek (der′ik), *n.* a boy's given name, form of **Theodoric.**

der·e·lict (der′ə likt), *adj.* **1.** left or abandoned, as by the owner or guardian: *a derelict ship.* **2.** neglectful of duty; delinquent; negligent. **—***n.* **3.** personal property abandoned or thrown away by the owner. **4.** *Naut.* a vessel abandoned in open water by its crew without any hope or intention of returning. **5.** a person abandoned by society; vagrant; bum. **6.** one guilty of neglect of duty. **7.** *Law.* land left dry by a change of the water line. [< L *dērelict(us)* forsaken (ptp. of *dērelinquere*), equiv. to *dē-* DE- + *relict-* left behind; see RELICT] **—der′e·lict·ly,** *adv.* **—der′e·lict·ness,** *n.*

der·e·lic·tion (der′ə lik′shən), *n.* **1.** deliberate or conscious neglect; negligence; delinquency: *dereliction of duty.* **2.** the act of abandoning something. **3.** the state of being abandoned. **4.** *Law.* a leaving dry of land by recession of the water line. [< L *dērelictiōn-* (s. of *dērelictiō*) an abandoning, equiv. to *dērelict(us)* (see DERELICT) + *-iōn-* -ION]
—Syn. 1. See **neglect. 2.** desertion.

de·req·ui·si·tion (dē rek′wi zish′ən), *Brit.* **—***n.* **1.** a freeing of requisitioned property, esp. from military to civilian control. **—***v.i.* **2.** to free requisitioned property. **—***v.t.* **3.** to return (property, a business, or the like, that has been requisitioned by the military) to civilian control. [DE- + REQUISITION]

de re·rum na·tu·ra (dā RĀ′ROOm nä tōō′Rä; *Eng.* dē rēr′əm nə tŏŏr′ə, -tyŏŏr′ə), **1.** *Latin.* on the nature of things. **2.** (*caps.*) a poem in six books, of the 1st century B.C., by Lucretius, setting forth the theories of Epicurus, esp. as a means of explicating natural phenomena and as offering an alternative to a supernaturalistic view of reality.

De Rid·der (də rid′ər), a town in W Louisiana. 7188 (1960).

de·ride (di rīd′), *v.t.,* **-rid·ed, -rid·ing.** to laugh at in contempt; scoff or jeer at; mock. [< L *dērīd(ere)* (to) mock, equiv. to *dē-* DE- + *rīdere* to laugh] **—de·rid′er,** *n.* **—de·rid′ing·ly,** *adv.*
—Syn. taunt, flout, gibe, banter, rally. See **ridicule.**

de ri·gueur (də RĒ gœR′; *Eng.* də ri gûr′), *French.* strictly required, as by etiquette, usage, or fashion.

der·in·ger (der′in jər), *n.* derringer.

de·ris·i·ble (di riz′ə bəl), *adj.* subject to or worthy of derision. [DERIS(ION) + -IBLE]

de·ri·sion (di rizh′ən), *n.* **1.** the act of deriding; ridicule; mockery. **2.** an object of ridicule. [ME *derisioun* < OF *derision* < LL *dērīsiōn-* (s. of *dērīsiō*), equiv. to L *dērīs(us)* mocked (ptp. of *dērīdere;* see DERIDE) + *-iōn-* -ION]

de·ri·sive (di rī′siv), *adj.* characterized by or expressing derision; ridiculing; mocking. Also, **de·ri·so·ry** (di rī′sə rē, -zə-). [DERIS(ION) + -IVE] **—de·ri′sive·ly,** *adv.* **—de·ri′sive·ness,** *n.*

deriv., 1. derivation. **2.** derivative. **3.** derive. **4.** derived.

der·i·va·tion (der′ə vā′shən), *n.* **1.** the act or fact of deriving or of being derived. **2.** the process of deriving. **3.** the source from which something is derived; origin. **4.** something that is or has been derived; derivative. **5.** *Math.* **a.** development of a theorem. **b.** differentiation. **6.** *Gram.* **a.** the process or device of adding affixes to or changing the shape of a base, thereby assigning the result to a form class that may undergo further inflection or participate in different syntactic constructions. **b.** the systematic description of such processes in a given language, as in *service* from *serve, song* from *sing,* and *hardness* from *hard* (contrasted with *inflection*). [ME < L *dērīvātiōn-* (s. of *dērīvātiō*) a turning away, equiv. to *dērīvāt(us)* (ptp. of *dērīvāre;* see DERIVE, -ATE[1]) + *-iōn-* -ION] **—der′i·va′tion·al,** *adj.* **—der′i·va′tion·al·ly,** *adv.*

de·riv·a·tive (di riv′ə tiv), *adj.* **1.** derived. **2.** not original; secondary. **—***n.* **3.** something derived or derivative. **4.** *Gram.* a form that has undergone derivation from another, as *atomic* from *atom.* **5.** *Chem.* a substance or compound obtained from, or regarded as derived from, another substance or compound. **6.** Also called **derived function, differential quotient.** *Mathematics.* the limit of the ratio of the increment of a function to the increment of a variable in it, as the latter tends to 0; the instantaneous change of one quantity with respect to another, as velocity which is the instantaneous change of distance with respect to time. Cf. **first derivative, second derivative. 7.** *Psychoanal.* behavior which allows expression of an id impulse with a minimum of anxiety. [ME < LL *dērīvātīv(us),* equiv. to *dērīvāt(us)* (see DERIVATION) + *-īvus* -IVE] **—de·riv′a·tive·ly,** *adv.* **—de·riv′a·tive·ness,** *n.*

de·rive (di rīv′), *v.,* **-rived, -riv·ing. —***v.t.* **1.** to receive or obtain from a source or origin (usually fol. by *from*). **2.** to trace from a source or origin. **3.** to reach or obtain by reasoning; deduce; infer. **4.** *Chem.* to produce or obtain (a substance) from another. **—***v.i.* **5.** to come from a source or origin; originate (often fol. by *from*). [ME *dirive(n), derive(n)* (to) flow, draw from, spring < OF *derive(r)* < L *dērīvāre* to lead off, equiv. to *dē-* DE- + *rīv(us)* a stream + *-āre* inf. suffix] **—de·riv′a·ble,** *adj.* **—de·riv′er,** *n.*

derived′ curve′, *Math.* a curve whose equation is the derivative of the equation of a given curve. Also called **first derived curve.**

derived′ func′tion, *Math.* derivative (def. 6).

derived′ set′, *Math.* the set of all accumulation points of a given set. Also called **weak derived set.**

derived′ u′nit, (in physics, chemistry, etc.) a unit derived from fundamental units of length, mass, and time.

Der·leth (dûr′leth, -ləth), *n.* **August (William),** born 1909, U.S. novelist, poet, and short-story writer.

derm (dûrm), *n. Navig.* a device for making a nearby object conspicuous on a radarscope. [*d(elayed) e(cho) r(adar) m(arker)*]

derm-, var. of **dermato-:** *dermoid.*

-derm, var. of **dermato-** as final element of compound words: *endoderm.*

der·ma[1] (dûr′mə), *n. Anat., Zool.* **1.** the corium or true skin. **2.** skin; integument. [NL < Gk *dérma* skin, equiv. to *dér(ein)* (to) skin + *-ma* n. suffix] **—der′mal, der·mat·ic** (dûr mat′ik), *adj.*

der·ma[2] (dûr′mə), *n.* **1.** beef or fowl intestine used as a casing in preparing certain savory dishes, esp. kishke. **2.** kishke. [< Yiddish *derme,* pl. of *darm* intestine < MHG < OHG; akin to OE *thearm* gut]

derm·a·bra·sion (dûrm′ə brā′zhən), *n. Surg.* the removal of acne scars, dermal nevi, or the like, by abrading with wire brushes, sandpaper, or other abrasives. Also called **skin planing.** [DERM- + ABRASION]

dermat-, var. of **dermato-** before a vowel: *dermatitis.*

der·ma·therm (dûr′mə thûrm′), *n. Med.* an instrument for measuring skin temperature. Also, **dermotherm.** [DERMA[1] + THERM]

der·ma·ti·tis (dûr′mə tī′tis), *n. Pathol.* inflammation of the skin. [DERMAT- + -ITIS]

dermato-, a learned borrowing from Greek meaning "skin," used in the formation of compound words: *dermatology.* Also, **derm-, -derm, dermat-, dermo-.** [< Gk, comb. form of *dérmat-,* s. of *dérma*]

der·mat·o·gen (dər mat′ə jən, dûr′mə tə jən), *n. Bot.* a thin layer of meristem in embryos and growing ends of stems and roots, which gives rise to the epidermis. [DERMATO- + -GEN]

der·mat·o·glyph·ics (dər mat′ə glif′iks, dûr′mə tə-), *n.* **1.** (*construed as pl.*) the patterns of ridges on the inner surface of the hands and feet. **2.** (*construed as sing.*) the science dealing with the study of these patterns. [DERMATO- + Gk *glýph(ein)* (to) carve + -ICS]

der·mat·o·graph·i·a (dər mat′ə graf′ē ə, dûr′mə-tə-), *n. Med.* a condition in which touching or lightly scratching the skin causes raised, reddish marks. Also, **der·ma·tog·ra·phism** (dûr′mə tog′rə fiz′əm), **dermographia, dermographism.** [< NL; see DERMATO-, -GRAPHY] **—der·mat′o·graph′ic,** *adj.*

der·ma·toid (dûr′mə toid′), *adj.* resembling skin; skinlike. [DERMAT- + -OID]

der·ma·tol·o·gist (dûr′mə tol′ə jist), *n.* a specialist in dermatology, esp. a doctor who specializes in the treatment of diseases of the skin. [DERMATOLOG(Y) + -IST]

der·ma·tol·o·gy (dûr′mə tol′ə jē), *n.* the science dealing with the skin and its diseases. [DERMATO- + -LOGY] **—der·ma·to·log·i·cal** (dûr′mə tᵊloj′i kəl), *adj.*

der·ma·tome (dûr′mə tōm′), *n.* **1.** *Anat.* an area of skin that is supplied with the nerve fibers of a single, posterior, spinal root. **2.** *Surg.* a mechanical instrument for cutting thin sections of skin for grafting. **3.** *Embryol.* the part of a mesodermal somite contributing to the development of the dermis. [DERMA[1] + -TOME] **—der·ma·tom·ic** (dûr′mə tom′ik), *adj.*

der·ma·to·phyte (dûr′mə tə fīt′, dər mat′ə-), *n. Pathol.* any fungus parasitic on the skin causing a skin disease, as ringworm, in man or animals. [DERMATO- + -PHYTE] **—der·mat·o·phyt·ic** (dûr′mə tə fit′ik, -dər-mat′ə fit′-), *adj.* **—der·mat′o·phy·to′sis,** *n.*

der·ma·to·plas·ty (dûr′mə tə plas′tē, dər mat′ə-), *n. Surg.* See **skin grafting.** [DERMATO- + -PLASTY] **—der′ma·to·plas′tic,** *adj.*

der·ma·to·sis (dûr′mə tō′sis), *n., pl.* **-to·ses** (-tō′sēz). *Pathol.* any disease of the skin. [< NL; see DERMAT-, -OSIS]

der·ma·to·zo·on (dûr′mə tə zō′on, -ən, dər mat′ə-), *n., pl.* **-zo·a** (-zō′ə). *Biol.* a microscopic animal living as a parasite on or in the skin of the host. Also, **der′ma·to·zo′ön.** [DERMATO- + -ZOON]

der·ma·trop·ic (dûr′mə trop′ik, -trō′pik), *adj.* (esp. of viruses) attracted toward, localizing in, or affecting the skin. Also, **der′mo·trop′ic, der·mat·o·trop·ic** (dûr-mat′ə trop′ik). [DERMA[1] + -TROPIC]

der·mis (dûr′mis), *n. Anat., Zool.* derma. [< NL; abstracted from EPIDERMIS] **—der′mic,** *adj.*

dermo-, var. of **dermato-:** *dermographic.*

der·mo·graph·i·a (dûr′mə graf′ē ə), *n. Med.* dermatographia. Also, **der·mog·ra·phism** (dûr mog′rə fiz′əm). [< NL; see DERMO-, -GRAPHY] **—der′mo·graph′ic,** *adj.*

der·moid (dûr′moid), *adj.* skinlike; dermatoid. [DERM- + -OID]

Der·mop·ter·a (dər mop′tər ə, -trə), *n.* the order comprising the flying lemurs. [< NL, equiv. to *dermo-* DERMO- + Gk *pterá,* pl. of *pterón* wing]

der·mo·therm (dûr′mə thûrm′), *n.* dermatherm.

Der·mott (dûr′mət), *n.* a town in SE Arkansas. 3665 (1960).

dern (dûrn), *adj., adv., v.t. Dial.* darn[2].

der·nier (der nyā′; *Eng.* dûr′nē ər, dern yā′), *adj. French.* last; final; ultimate.

der·nier cri (der nyā krē′), *French.* **1.** the latest word. **2.** the latest fashion; the newest style. [lit., last cry]

der·nier res·sort (der nyā rə sôr′), *French.* the last resort.

der·o·gate (*v.* der′ə gāt′; *adj.* der′ə git, -gāt′), *v.,* **-gat·ed, -gat·ing,** *adj.* **—***v.i.* **1.** to detract, as from authority, estimation, etc. (usually fol. by *from*). **2.** to stray in character or conduct; degenerate (usually fol. by *from*). **—***v.t.* **3.** *Archaic.* to take away (a part) so as to impair the whole. **—***adj.* **4.** *Archaic.* debased. [ME < L *dērogāt(us)* repealed, restricted (ptp. of *dērogāre*), equiv. to *dē-* DE- + *rog(āre)* (to) ask + *-ātus* -ATE[1]] —*Rare.* **der′o·gate′ly,** *adv.* —**der′o·ga′tion,** *n.*

de·rog·a·tive (di rog′ə tiv), *adj.* lessening; belittling; derogatory. [< OF *derogatif* < L *dērogāt(us).* See DEROGATE, -IVE] —**de·rog′a·tive·ly,** *adv.*

de·rog·a·to·ry (di rog′ə tôr′ē, -tōr′ē), *adj.* tending to derogate or detract, as from authority or estimation; disparaging; depreciatory: *a derogatory remark.* [< L *dērogātōri(us)* of a derogation, equiv. to *dērogāt(us)* (see DEROGATE) + *-ōrius* -ORY[1]] —**de·rog·a·to·ri·ly** (di rog′-ə tôr′ə lē, -tōr′-, -rog′ə tôr′-, -tōr′-), *adv.* —**de·rog′a·to′ri·ness,** *n.*

Der·on (der′ən), *n.* a boy's given name.

Der Pro·zess (*Ger.* der prō tses′). See **Trial, The.**

Der·rel (der′əl), *n.* a boy's given name. Also, **Darrell.**

Der Rich·ter und sein Hen·ker (*Ger.* der riKH′tər ōōnt zīn heng′kər). See **Judge and His Hangman, The.**

der·rick (der′ik), *n.* **1.** *Mach.* a jib crane having a boom hinged near the base of the mast so as to rotate about the mast, for moving a load toward or away from the mast by raising or lowering the boom. **2.** the tower-like framework over an oil well or the like. **3.** *Naut.* a boom for lifting cargo or the like, pivoted at its inner end to a mast or kingpost, and raised and supported at its outer end by topping lifts. —*v.t., v.i.* **4.** *Mach.* luff. [after *Derrick,* 17th-century hangman at Tyburn, London]

der·ri·ère (der′ē âr′; *Fr.* de ryer′), *n.* the buttocks; rump; behind. Also, **der′ri·ere′.** [< F < OF *deriere* < L *de retrō* from the back, backwards; see ARREAR]

der·ring-do (der′ing-dōō′), *n.* daring deeds; heroic daring: *a knight renowned for derring-do.* [ME *durring-do,* lit., daring to do, erroneously taken as n. phrase. See DARE, DO[1]]

Derringer

der·rin·ger (der′in jər), *n. U.S.* a short-barreled pocket pistol. Also, **deringer.** [named after Henry *Deringer,* mid-19th-century American gunsmith who invented it]

der·ris (der′is), *n.* any East Indian, leguminous plant of the genus *Derris,* esp. *D. elliptica,* the roots of which contain rotenone and are used as an insecticide. [NL < Gk: a covering, deriv. of *déros* skin, hide; see -DERM]

der·ry (der′ē), *n., pl.* **-ries.** a meaningless refrain or chorus in old songs. Also called **der·ry-down** (der′ē-doun′).

Der·ry (der′ē), *n.* **1.** Londonderry. **2.** a town in central Pennsylvania. 3426 (1960).

der Tag (der täKH′), *German.* the day: used by German nationalists to refer to the day on which Germany would begin the *Drang nach Osten;* later, the day on which she would undertake a plan of conquest.

Der Tod in Ve·ne·dig (*Ger.* der tōt′ in ve nā′-diKH). See **Death in Venice.**

der·trum (dûr′trəm), *n., pl.* **-tra** (-trə). *Ornith.* the extremity of the maxilla of a bird's bill, esp. when hooked or differentiated from the rest of the bill, as in pigeons and plovers. [< NL < Gk *dértron* membrane, deriv. of *dér(ein)* (to) skin, c. *dérma* DERMA]

de·rust (dē rust′), *v.t.* to remove rust from (an iron or steel piece). [DE- + RUST]

der·vish (dûr′vish), *n.* a member of any of various Muslim ascetic orders, some of which carry on ecstatic observances, such as violent dancing and whirling or vociferous chanting or shouting. [< Turk: beggar < Pers *darvīsh* religious mendicant] —**der′vish·hood′,** *n.* —**der′vish·ism,** *n.* —**der′vish·like′,** *adj.*

Der·went (dûr′wənt), *n.* **1.** a river flowing N and W into Solway Firth, in N England. **2.** a river flowing S and SE past Derby to the Trent, in central England. **3.** a river flowing into the Ouse, in Yorkshire in NE England. **4.** a river flowing NE to the Tyne, in N England. **5.** a river in S Australia, in S Tasmania, flowing SE to the Tasman Sea. 107 mi. long.

Der Zau·ber·berg (*Ger.* der tsou′bər berKH′). See **Magic Mountain, The.**

des (de), *prep.* used in French names as a contraction of *de* and the article *les: François des Adrets.*

-des, a plural suffix appearing in loan words from Greek: *proboscides.* [< Gk, nom. pl. of *d*-stem nouns]

De·saix de Vey·goux (de ze′ də vā gōō′), **Louis Charles An·toine** (lwē sharl än twan′), 1768–1800, French general.

de·sal·i·nate (dē sal′ə nāt′), *v.t.,* **-nat·ed, -nat·ing.** desalt. [DE- + SALINE + -ATE[1]] —**de·sal′i·na′tion,** *n.*

de·sa·lin·ize (dē sā′lə nīz′, -lī-, -sal′ə-), *v.t.* **-ized, -iz·ing.** desalt. Also, **desalinate.** [DE- + SALINE + -IZE] —**de·sa′lin·i·za′tion,** *n.*

de·salt (dē sôlt′), *v.t.* to remove the salt from (esp. sea water), usually to make it drinkable. [DE- + SALT] —**de·salt′er,** *n.*

des·am·i·dase (des am′i dās′), *n. Biochem.* deamidase.

des·am·i·nase (des am′ə nās′), *n. Biochem.* deaminase.

De·sargues (dā zarg′, *Eng.* dā zärg′), *n.* **Gé·rard** (zhā rar′), 1593–1662, French mathematician.

Desargues′s the′orem, *Geom.* the theorem that if two triangles are so related that the lines joining corresponding vertices meet in a point, then the extended corresponding lines of the two triangles meet in three points, all on the same line. [named after G. DESARGUES]

desc., descendant.

de·scale (dē skāl′), *v.t.,* **-scaled, -scal·ing.** to remove scale from (rolled steel, a boiler, etc.). [DE- + SCALE[1]]

des·ca·mi·sa·do (des′kam i sä′dō; *Sp.* des′kä mē-sä′thō), *n., pl.* **-dos** (-dōz; *Sp.* -thōs). **1.** an extreme liberal of the Spanish revolution 1820–23. **2.** (in Argentina) a worker, esp. one who is poor. [< Sp: lit., shirtless]

des·cant (*n., adj.* des′kant; *v.* des kant′, dis-), *n.* **1.** *Music.* **a.** a melody or counterpoint accompanying a simple musical theme and usually written above it. **b.** (in part music) the soprano. **c.** a song or melody. **2.** a variation upon anything; comment on a subject. —*adj.* **3.** *Music, Chiefly Brit.* **a.** soprano: *a descant recorder.* **b.** treble: *a descant viol.* —*v.i.* **4.** *Music.* to sing. **5.** to comment or discourse at great length. Also, **discant.** [ME *discant, descaunt* < ONF, ML *discanth(us),* equiv. to L *dis-* DIS-[1] + *canthus* song; see CHANT] —**des·cant′er,** *n.*

Des·cartes (dā kärt′; *Fr.* de kart′), *n.* **1. Re·né** (rə-nā′; *Fr.* rə nā′), 1596–1650, French philosopher and mathematician. **2.** a walled plain in the fourth quadrant of the face of the moon: about 30 miles in diameter.

Descartes′ law′, *Optics.* See **Snell's law.** [named after René DESCARTES]

de·scend (di send′), *v.i.* **1.** to move or pass from a higher to a lower place; climb or come down: *to descend from the mountaintop.* **2.** to pass from higher to lower in any scale or series. **3.** to go from generals to particulars, as in a discussion. **4.** to slope, tend, or lead downward: *The path descends to the pond.* **5.** to be inherited or transmitted, as through succeeding generations of a family: *The title descends through eldest sons. This clock has descended through five generations.* **6.** to have a specific person or family among one's ancestors (usually fol. by *from*): *He is descended from Cromwell.* **7.** to be derived from something remote in time, esp. through continuous transmission: *This festival descends from a druidic rite.* **8.** to approach or pounce upon, esp. in a greedy or hasty manner (fol. by *on* or *upon*): *Heirs descended upon the rich man's estate. Thrill-seekers descended upon the scene of the crime.* **9.** to settle, as a cloud or vapor. **10.** to appear or become manifest, as a supernatural being, state of mind, etc.: *Jupiter descended to mankind. Fear descended into his soul.* **11.** to attack, esp. with violence and suddenness (usually fol. by *on* or *upon*): *to descend upon enemy soldiers; to descend on one's opponent in a debate.* **12.** to sink or come down from a certain intellectual, moral, or social standard: *He would never descend to baseness.* **13.** *Astron.* to move toward the horizon, as the sun or a star. —*v.t.* **14.** to move downward upon or along; go or climb down (stairs, a hill, etc.). **15.** to extend or lead down along: *The path descends the hill.* [ME *descend(en)* < OF *descend(re)* < L *dēscendere,* equiv. to *dē-* DE- + *scend-* climb (sp. var. of *scandere;* see SCAN) + *-ere* inf. suffix] —**de·scend′ing·ly,** *adv.*

de·scend·ant (di sen′dənt), *n.* **1.** one who is descended from a specific ancestor; an offspring. **2.** something deriving in appearance, function, or general character from an earlier form. **3.** an adherent who follows closely the teachings, methods, practices, etc., of an earlier master, as in art, music, philosophy, etc.; disciple. —*adj.* **4.** descending; descendent. [ME *descendaunt* (adj.) < OF *descendant,* prp. of *descendre.* See DESCEND, -ANT]

de·scend·ent (di sen′dənt), *adj.* **1.** descending; going or coming down. **2.** deriving or descending from an ancestor. [< L *dēscendent-* (s. of *dēscendēns*), prp. of *dēscend(ere).* See DESCEND, -ENT]

de·scend·er (di sen′dər), *n.* **1.** one who or that which descends. **2.** *Print.* **a.** (in any of most lower-case letters) the part that goes below the body. **b.** a letter having such a part, as *p, q, j,* or *y.* [DESCEND + -ER[1]]

de·scend·i·ble (di sen′də bəl), *adj.* capable of being transmitted by inheritance. Also, **de·scend′a·ble.** [ME *descendable* < OF, equiv. to *descend(re)* (to) DESCEND + *-able* -ABLE] —**de·scend′i·bil′i·ty, de·scend′a·bil′i·ty,** *n.*

descend′ing node′, *Astron.* the node through which an orbiting body passes as it moves to the south (opposed to *ascending node*).

de·scen·sion (di sen′shən), *n.* **1.** *Astrol.* the part of the of the zodiac in which the influence of a planet is weakest. Cf. **exaltation** (def. 6). **2.** *Archaic.* descent. [ME *descensioun* < OF *descension,* L *dēscensiōn-* (s. of *dēscensiō*), equiv. to *dēscēns(us)* (ptp. of *dēscendere* to DESCEND) + *-iōn-* -ION]

de·scen·so·ry (di sen′sə rē), *n., pl.* **-ries.** *Alchemy.* a still in which, by applying heat to the top and sides, the vapors are made to descend through the perforations in its base into a receiver. [ME *descensorie* < ML **dēscensōri(um)* (cf. OF *descensoire*) < L *dēscēns* (pp. of *descendere* to DESCEND) + *-ōrium* -ORY[2]]

de·scent (di sent′), *n.* **1.** the act, process, or fact of descending. **2.** a downward inclination or slope. **3.** a passage or stairway leading down. **4.** derivation from an ancestor; lineage; extraction. **5.** any passing from higher to lower in degree or state; decline. **6.** a sudden raid or hostile attack. **7.** *Law.* transmission of real property by intestate succession. [ME < OF *descente,* deriv. of *descend(re)* to DESCEND]
—**Syn. 1.** falling, sinking. **2.** decline, grade, declivity. **4.** ancestry, parentage. **6.** assault, foray. —**Ant. 1, 2.** ascent, rise.

Descent′ from the Cross′, *Fine Arts.* a representation of Christ being lowered from the Cross. Also called **Deposition.**

Des·chutes (dā shōōt′), *n.* a river flowing N from the Cascade Range in central Oregon to the Columbia River. 250 mi. long.

des·cloi·zite (dā kloi′zīt, di-), *n.* a mineral, lead zinc vanadate. [< F, named after A.L.O. *Des Cloizeaux* (1817–97), French mineralogist; see -ITE[1]]

de·scribe (di skrīb′), *v.t.,* **-scribed, -scrib·ing. 1.** to tell or depict in written or spoken words; give an account of: *He described the monument very carefully.* **2.** to pronounce, as by a designating term, phrase, or the like; label: *There are few men who may be described as geniuses.* **3.** to indicate; be a sign of; denote: *Promiscuity, in many cases, describes a state of serious emotional insecurity.* **4.** to represent or delineate by a picture or figure. **5.** *Geom.* to draw or trace the outline of: *to describe an arc.* [ME *describe(n)* < L *dēscrībere,* equiv. to *dē-* DE- + *scrībere* to write] —**de·scrib′a·bil′i·ty,** *n.* —**de·scrib′a·ble,** *adj.* —**de·scrib′a·bly,** *adv.* —**de·scrib′er,** *n.*
—**Syn. 1.** portray, characterize, represent; recount, tell, relate. DESCRIBE, NARRATE agree in the idea of giving an account of something. TO DESCRIBE is to convey an image or impression in words designed to reveal the appearance, nature, attributes, etc., of the thing described. The word applies primarily to what exists in space (by extension, to what occurs in time) and often implies the vividness of personal observation: *to describe a scene, a sensation, a character, a room.* TO NARRATE is to recount the occurrence of something, usually by giving the details of an event or events in the order of their happening. NARRATE thus applies only to that which happens in time: *to narrate an incident.*

de·scrip·tion (di skrip′shən), *n.* **1.** a statement, account, or picture in words that describes; descriptive representation. **2.** the act or method of describing. **3.** sort; kind; variety: *dogs of every description.* **4.** *Geom.* the act or process of describing a figure. [ME *descripcioun* < L *dēscrīptiōn-* (s. of *dēscrīptiō*), equiv. to *dēscrīpt(us)* (ptp. of *dēscrībere* to DESCRIBE) + *-iōn-* -ION]
—**Syn. 3.** species; nature, character, condition; ilk.

de·scrip·tive (di skrip′tiv), *adj.* **1.** having the quality of describing; characterized by description: *a descriptive passage in an essay.* **2.** *Gram.* (of an adjective or other modifier) expressing a quality of the word it modifies, as *fresh* in *fresh milk.* Cf. **limiting. 3.** noting, concerned with, or based upon the fact or experience. **4.** characterized by or based upon the classification and description of material in a given field: *descriptive botany.* [< LL *dēscrīptīv(us),* equiv. to L *dēscrīpt(us)* (see DESCRIPTION) + *-īvus* -IVE] —**de·scrip′tive·ly,** *adv.* —**de·scrip′tive·ness,** *n.*

descrip′tive clause′, a relative clause that describes or supplements but does not identify the antecedent, and that is usually set off by commas in English; a nonrestrictive clause. In *This year, which has been dry, is bad for crops* the clause *which has been dry* is a descriptive clause. Cf. **restrictive clause.**

descrip′tive geom′etry, 1. the theory of making projections of any accurately defined figure such that from them can be deduced not only its projective, but also its metrical, properties. **2.** geometry in general, treated by means of projections.

descrip′tive linguis′tics, the study of the grammar, classification, and arrangement of the features of language or of a language, without reference to their history or origin.

de·scry (di skrī′), *v.t.,* **-scried, -scry·ing. 1.** to make out (something unclear or distant) by looking carefully; discern; espy: *The lookout descried land.* **2.** to discover; perceive; detect. [ME *descrie(n)* < OF *decri(er)* (to) proclaim. See DECRY] —**de·scri′er,** *n.*
—**Syn. 1.** notice.

Des·de (dez′də), *n.* a girl's given name, form of **Desdemona.**

Des·de·mo·na (dez′də mō′nə), *n.* **1.** (in Shakespeare's *Othello*) Othello's wife, murdered by her husband as a result of jealousy instilled by Iago. **2.** a girl's given name.

de·seam (dē sēm′), *v.t. Foundry.* to remove surface defects from (ingots, blooms, etc.) [DE- + SEAM]

des·e·crate (des′ə krāt′), *v.t.,* **-crat·ed, -crat·ing. 1.** to divest of sacred or hallowed character or office. **2.** to divert from a sacred to a profane use or purpose. **3.** to treat with sacrilege; profane. [DE- + *-secrate,* modeled on *consecrate*] —**des′e·crat′er, des′e·cra′tor,** *n.* —**des′e·cra′tion,** *n.*

de·seg·re·gate (dē seg′rə gāt′), *v.,* **-gat·ed, -gat·ing.** —*v.t.* **1.** to eliminate racial segregation in: *to desegregate all schools.* —*v.i.* **2.** to eliminate racial segregation. [DE- + SEGREGATE]

de·seg·re·ga·tion (dē′seg rə gā′shən, dē seg′-), *n.* the elimination of laws, customs, or practices under which different races, groups, etc., are restricted to specific or separate public facilities, neighborhoods, schools, organizations, or the like. [DE- + SEGREGATION]

Des·eil·lig·ny (des′ə lēn′yē), *n.* a crater in the first quadrant of the face of the moon: about 4 miles in diameter.

de·sen·si·tize (dē sen′si tīz′), *v.t.,* **-tized, -tiz·ing. 1.** to lessen the sensitiveness of. **2.** to make indifferent, unaware, or the like, in feeling. **3.** *Physiol.* to eliminate the natural or acquired reactivity or sensitivity of (an animal, organ, tissue, etc.) to an external stimulus, as an allergen. **4.** *Photog.* to make less sensitive or wholly insensitive to light, as the emulsion on a film. **5.** *Print.* to treat (the design on a lithographic plate) with an etch in order to increase the capacity to retain moisture, and to remove traces of grease. **6.** *Chem.* to reduce the sensitivity of (an explosive) to those stimuli capable of detonating it. [DE- + SENSITIZE] —**de·sen′si·ti·za′tion,** *n.* —**de·sen′si·tiz′er,** *n.*

des·ert[1] (dez′ərt), *n.* **1.** a region so arid that it supports only sparse and widely spaced vegetation or no vegetation at all. **2.** any area in which few forms of life can exist because of lack of water, permanent frost, or absence of soil. **3.** an area of the ocean in which it is believed no marine life exists. **4.** (formerly) any unsettled area between the Mississippi and the Rocky Mountains thought to be unsuitable for human habitation. **5.** any place lacking in something: *The town was a cultural desert.* —*adj.* **6.** of, pertaining to, or like a desert; desolate; barren. **7.** occurring, living, or flourishing in the desert: *a desert tribe; a desert palm.* [ME < OF < eccl. L *dēsert(um)* (neut.), n. use of ptp. of *dēserere* to abandon, forsake, equiv. to *dē-* DE- + *serere* to join together (in a line); cf. SERIES] —**de·ser·tic** (di zûr′tik), *adj.* —**des′ert·like′,** *adj.*
—**Syn. 1.** DESERT, WASTE, WILDERNESS refer to areas which are uninhabited. DESERT emphasizes lack of water; it refers to a dry, barren, treeless region, usually sandy: *an oasis in a desert; the Sahara Desert.* WASTE emphasizes lack of inhabitants and of cultivation; it is used of wild, barren land, but figuratively the word is also applied to turbulent seas: *a desolate waste; a terrifying waste of water.* WILDERNESS emphasizes the difficulty of finding one's way, whether because of barrenness or of luxuriant vegetation; it is also applied to the ocean, especially in stormy weather: *a trackless wilderness.* **6.** forsaken, wild, uninhabited.

de·sert[2] (di zûrt′), *v.t.* **1.** to leave (a person, place, etc.) without intending to return, esp. in violation of a duty, promise, or the like; abandon; forsake: *He deserted his wife.* **2.** (of military personnel) to leave or run away from (service, duty, etc.) with the intention of never returning. **3.** to fail (one) at a time of need: *All friends had deserted him.* —*v.i.* **4.** to forsake or leave one's duty, obligations, etc. (sometimes fol. by *from, to,* etc.): *Many deserted during the food shortage.* **5.** (of military personnel) to leave or run away from service, duty, etc., with no intention of returning: *Troops were deserting to the enemy.* [< F *désert(er)* < LL *dēsertāre,* freq. of L *dēserere;* see DESERT[1]] —**de·sert′ed·ly,** *adv.* —**de·sert′ed·ness,** *n.* —**de·sert′er,** *n.*
—**Syn. 1.** DESERT, ABANDON, FORSAKE mean to leave behind persons, places, or things. DESERT implies intentionally violating an oath, formal obligation, or duty: *to desert campaign pledges.* ABANDON suggests

giving up wholly and finally, whether of necessity, unwillingly, or through shirking responsibilities: *to abandon a hopeless task.* FORSAKE has emotional connotations, since it implies violating obligations of affection or association: *to forsake a noble cause.*

de·sert[3] (di zûrt′), *n.* **1.** Often, **deserts.** reward or punishment that is deserved: *to get one's just deserts.* **2.** the state or fact of deserving reward or punishment. **3.** the fact of deserving well; merit; virtue. [ME < OF *deserte*, n. use of fem. ptp. of *deservir* to DESERVE] —**Syn. 3.** See **merit.**

de·sert·ed (di zûr′tid), *adj.* **1.** abandoned; forsaken: *the miserable lot of deserted wives and children.* **2.** untenanted; without inhabitants: *a deserted village; a deserted farmhouse.* **3.** unfrequented; lonely: *the victim was lured to a deserted spot.* [DESERT[2] + -ED[2]]

Desert′ed Vil′lage, The, a poem (1770) by Oliver Goldsmith.

des′ert fa′thers, those monks, as Saint Anthony or Saint Pachomius, who lived as hermits in the deserts of Egypt and founded the first Christian monasteries.

des·er·tic·o·lous (dez′ər tik′ə ləs), *adj. Biol.* living or growing in a desert. [DESERT[1] + -I- + -COLOUS]

des′ert igua′na, any of several long-tailed iguanid lizards of the genus *Dipsosaurus*, having a ridge of enlarged scales down the middle of the back, as the grayish-brown *D. dorsalis*, of arid parts of the southwestern U.S. and northwestern Mexico. Also called **crested lizard.**

de·ser·tion (di zûr′shən), *n.* **1.** the act of deserting or the state of being deserted. **2.** *Law.* willful abandonment, esp. of one's wife or husband without consent, in violation of legal or moral obligations. **3.** *Mil.* leaving or running away from service or duty without the intention of returning. Cf. **A.W.O.L.** [< LL *dēsertiōn-* (s. of *dēsertiō*) < L *dēsert(us)* (see DESERT[1]) + *-iōn-* -ION]

des′ert rat′, **1.** any of various small rodents, as the kangaroo rat, found in arid regions. **2.** *Chiefly Western U.S.* one who lives in the desert, esp. in order to prospect for gold or other valuable minerals. **3.** *Informal.* a soldier fighting in the N African desert in World War II, esp. a British soldier.

des′ert var′nish, the dark, lustrous coating or crust, usually of manganese and iron oxides, that forms on rocks, pebbles, etc., in the desert. Also called **des′ert pol′ish.**

de·serve (di zûrv′), *v.*, **-served, -serv·ing.** —*v.t.* **1.** to merit, be qualified for, or have a claim to (reward, assistance, punishment, etc.) because of one's acts, qualities, or situation: *to deserve exile; to deserve charity; The theory deserves considering.* —*v.i.* **2.** to be worthy of, qualified for, or have a claim to reward, punishment, recompense, etc.: *to reward someone as he deserves; an idea deserving of study.* [ME *deserve(n)* < OF *deserv(ir)*, L *dēservīre* to serve zealously, equiv. to *dē-* DE- + *servīre* to SERVE] —**de·serv′er,** *n.*

de·served (di zûrvd′), *adj.* justly earned; merited: *a deserved increase in salary.* [DESERVE + -ED[2]] —**de·serv·ed·ness** (di zûr′vid nis), *n.*

de·serv·ed·ly (di zûr′vid lē), *adv.* according to desert; justly; rightly. [DESERVED + -LY]

de·serv·ing (di zûr′ving), *adj.* qualified for or having a claim to reward, assistance, etc., because of one's actions, qualities, or situation: *the deserving poor; a deserving applicant.* [DESERVE + -ING[2]] —**de·serv′ing·ly,** *adv.* —**de·serv′ing·ness,** *n.*

de·sex (dē seks′), *v.t.* **1.** to castrate or spay. **2.** to deprive of sex, sex appeal, or sexual interest.

des·ha·bille (dez′ə bēl′, -bē′), *n.* dishabille.

De Si·ca (də sē′kə; *It.* de sē′kä), **Vit·to·rio** (vi tôr′ē ō′, -tōr′-; *It.* vēt tô′ryô), 1901–74, Italian motion-picture director, producer, and actor.

des·ic·cant (des′ə kənt), *adj.* **1.** desiccating or drying, as a medicine. —*n.* **2.** a desiccant substance or agent. [< L *dēsiccant-* s. of *dēsiccāns*, prp. of *dēsiccāre* to dry up. See DESICCATE, -ANT]

des·ic·cate (des′ə kāt′), *v.*, **-cat·ed, -cat·ing.** —*v.t.* **1.** to dry thoroughly; dry up. **2.** to preserve (food) by removing moisture; dehydrate. —*v.i.* **3.** to become thoroughly dried or dried up. [< L *dēsiccāt(us)* dried up, ptp. of *dēsiccāre*, equiv. to *dē-* DE- + *siccāre*, deriv. of *siccus* dry; see -ATE[1]] —**des′ic·ca′tion,** *n.* —**des′ic·ca′tive,** *adj.*

des·ic·cat·ed (des′ə kā′tid), *adj.* dehydrated or powdered: *desiccated milk or soup.* [DESICCATE + -ED[2]]

des·ic·ca·tor (des′ə kā′tər), *n.* **1.** one who or that which desiccates. **2.** an apparatus for drying fruit, milk, etc. **3.** *Chem.* **a.** an apparatus for absorbing the moisture present in a chemical substance. **b.** an airtight, usually glass container containing calcium chloride or some other drying agent for absorbing the moisture of another substance placed in the container. [DESICCATE + -OR[2]]

de·sid·er·a·ta (di sid′ə rā′tə), *n.* pl. of **desideratum.**

de·sid·er·ate (di sid′ə rāt′), *v.t.*, **-at·ed, -at·ing.** to wish or long for; want; desire. [< L *dēsīderāt(us)* longed for (ptp. of *dēsīderāre*), equiv. to *dē-* DE- + *sīder-* (s. of *sīdus*) star + *-ātus* -ATE[1]] —**de·sid′er·a′tion,** *n.*

de·sid·er·a·tive (di sid′ə rā′tiv, -ər ə tiv), *adj.* **1.** having or expressing desire. **2.** *Gram.* (of a verb derived from another verb) expressing desire to perform the action denoted by the underlying verb, as, Sanskrit *pi-pat-iṣ-ati* "he wishes to fly" from *pāt-ati*, "he flies." —*n.* **3.** *Gram.* a desiderative verb. [< LL *dēsīderātīv(us)*. See DESIDERATE, -IVE]

de·sid·er·a·tum (di sid′ə rā′təm), *n.*, *pl.* **-ta** (-tə). something wanted or needed. [< L, n. use of neut. ptp. of *dēsīderāre;* see DESIDERATE]

Des·i·der·i·i (des′i der′ē ē′), *n.* **Mare.** See **Mare Desiderii.**

de·sign (di zīn′), *v.t.* **1.** to prepare the preliminary sketch or the plans for (a work to be executed), esp. to plan the form and structure of: *to design a new bridge.* **2.** to plan and fashion artistically or skillfully. **3.** to intend for a definite purpose: *a scholarship designed for medical students.* **4.** to form or conceive in the mind; contrive; plan: *The prisoner designed an intricate escape.* **5.** to assign in thought or intention; purpose: *He designed to be a doctor.* **6.** *Archaic.* to mark out, as by a sign; indicate. —*v.i.* **7.** to make drawings, preliminary sketches, or plans. **8.** to plan and fashion the form and structure of an object, work of art, decorative scheme, etc. —*n.* **9.** an outline, sketch, or plan, as of the form and structure of a work of art, an edifice, or a machine to be executed or constructed. **10.** organization or structure of formal elements in a work of art; composition. **11.** the combination of details or features of a picture, building, etc.; the pattern or motif of artistic work: *the design on a bracelet.* **12.** the art of designing: *a school of design.* **13.** a plan or project: *a design for a new process.* **14.** a plot or intrigue, esp. an underhand, deceitful, or treacherous one: *His political rivals formulated a design to unseat him.* **15. designs,** a hostile or aggressive project or scheme having evil or selfish motives: *He had designs on his partner's stock. The ranchers had designs against the stream running through their neighbor's land.* **16.** intention; purpose; end. **17.** adaptation of means to a preconceived end. **18.** an artistic work. [ME *design(en)* < L *dēsignāre* to mark out. See DE-, SIGN] —**Syn. 4.** devise, project. **5.** See **intend. 9.** drawing, blueprint. **13.** See **plan. 16.** intent, aim, object; purport, drift.

des·ig·nate (*v.* dez′ig nāt′; *adj.* dez′ig nit, -nāt′), *v.*, **-nat·ed, -nat·ing,** *adj.* —*v.t.* **1.** to mark or point out; indicate; show; specify. **2.** to denote; indicate; signify. **3.** to name; entitle; style. **4.** to nominate or select for a duty, office, purpose, etc.; appoint; assign. —*adj.* **5.** named or selected for an office, position, etc., but not yet installed (often used in combination following the noun it modifies): *ambassador-designate.* [ME < L *dēsignāt(us)*, ptp. of *dēsignāre.* See DESIGN, -ATE[1]] —**des′ig·na′tive, des·ig·na·to·ry** (dez′ig nə tôr′ē, -tōr′ē, dez′ig nā′tə rē), *adj.* —**des′ig·na′tor,** *n.*

des′ignated′ hit′ter, *Baseball.* a hitter selected prior to the start of the game to bat for the starting pitcher and all subsequent pitchers without otherwise affecting the status of the pitchers in the game.

des·ig·na·tion (dez′ig nā′shən), *n.* **1.** the act of designating. **2.** the fact of being designated. **3.** that which designates; a distinctive name or title; appellation. **4.** nomination, appointment, or election to an office, position, etc.: *His designation as treasurer has been confirmed.* [ME *designacioun* < L *dēsignātiōn-* (s. of *dēsignātiō*) a marking out, equiv. to *dēsignāt(us)* (see DESIGNATE) + *-iōn-* -ION]

de·signed (di zīnd′), *adj.* made or done by design; intended; planned. [DESIGN + -ED[2]] —**de·sign·ed·ness** (di zī′nid nis), *n.*

de·sign·ed·ly (di zī′nid lē), *adv.* intentionally; purposely; deliberately. [DESIGNED + -LY]

des·ig·nee (dez′ig nē′), *n.* one who is designated. [DESIGN(ATE) + -EE]

de·sign·er (di zī′nər), *n.* **1.** one who devises or executes designs, esp. one who creates forms, structures, and patterns, as for works of art, dresses, machines, stage sets, etc. **2.** a schemer, intriguer, or plotter. [DESIGN + -ER[1]]

de·sign·ing (di zī′ning), *adj.* **1.** scheming; intriguing; artful; crafty. **2.** showing or using forethought. —*n.* **3.** the act or art of making designs. [DESIGN + -ING[2], -ING[1]] —**de·sign′ing·ly,** *adv.* —**Syn. 1.** wily, cunning, tricky, sly. —**Ant. 1.** artless.

de·sign·ment (di zīn′mənt), *n. Obs.* design; plan.

de·silt (dē silt′), *v.t.* to remove the silt from (a river, stream, etc.). [DE- + SILT]

de·sil·ver (dē sil′vər), *v.t.* to remove silver from (lead in base bullion form). [DE- + SILVER]

de·sil·ver·ize (dē sil′və rīz′), *v.t.*, **-ized, -iz·ing.** to desilver. [DESILVER + -IZE]

des·i·nence (des′ə nəns), *n.* **1.** a termination or ending, as the final line of a verse. **2.** *Gram.* a termination, ending, or suffix of a word. [< F < ML *dēsinentia*, equiv. to L *dēsinent-* (s. of *dēsinēns*), prp. of *dēsinere* to put down, leave (*dē-* DE- + *sinere* to leave) + *-ia;* see -ENCE] —**des′i·nent, des·i·nen·tial** (des′ə nen′shəl), *adj.*

de·sir·a·ble (di zīər′ə bəl), *adj.* **1.** worth desiring; pleasing, excellent, or fine: *a desirable apartment; a desirable award.* **2.** arousing desire or longing: *a desirable woman.* **3.** advisable; recommendable: *a desirable law.* —*n.* **4.** one who or that which is desirable. [ME *desirable* < OF. See DESIRE, -ABLE] —**de·sir′a·bil′i·ty, de·sir′a·ble·ness,** *n.* —**de·sir′a·bly,** *adv.*

de·sire (di zīər′), *v.*, **-sired, -sir·ing,** *n.* —*v.t.* **1.** to wish or long for; crave; want. **2.** to express a wish to obtain; ask for; request: *I desire that you shall come here.* —*n.* **3.** a longing or craving, as for something that brings satisfaction or enjoyment: *a desire for fame.* **4.** an expressed wish; request. **5.** something desired. **6.** sexual appetite or a sexual urge. [ME *desire(n)* < OF *desir(er)* < L *dēsīderāre;* see DESIDERATE] —**de·sired·ly** (di zīərd′lē, -zī′rid-), *adv.* —**de·sired′ness,** *n.* —**de·sire′less,** *adj.* —**de·sir′er,** *n.* —**de·sir′ing·ly,** *adv.*

—**Syn. 1.** covet, fancy. See **wish. 2.** solicit. **3.** aspiration, hunger, appetite, thirst. DESIRE, CRAVING, LONGING, YEARNING suggest feelings which impel one to the attainment or possession of something. DESIRE is a strong feeling, worthy or unworthy, that impels to the attainment or possession of something which is (in reality or imagination) within reach: *a desire for success.* CRAVING implies a deep and imperative wish for something, based on a sense of need and hunger (literally or figuratively): *a craving for food, companionship.* A LONGING is an intense wish, generally repeated or enduring, for something that is at the moment beyond reach but may be attainable at some future time: *a longing to visit Europe.* YEARNING suggests persistent, uneasy, and sometimes wistful or tender longing: *a yearning for one's native land.* —**Ant. 1.** reject, loathe.

de·sired (di zīərd′), *adj.* **1.** coveted; yearned or wished for. **2.** deemed correct or proper; selected; required: *The chef added stock until the sauce reached the desired consistency.* [ME; see DESIRE, -ED[2]]

Dé·si·rée (dez′ə rā′; *Fr.* dā zē rā′), *n.* a girl's given name.

Desire′ Un′der the Elms′, a play (1924) by Eugene O'Neill.

de·sir·ous (di zīər′əs), *adj.* having or characterized by desire; desiring: *desirous of high political office.* [ME < OF *desireus.* See DESIRE, -OUS] —**de·sir′ous·ly,** *adv.* —**de·sir′ous·ness,** *n.*

de·sist (di zist′, -sist′), *v.i.* to cease, as from some action or proceeding; stop. [ME < OF *desist(er)* < L *dēsistere* to leave off, equiv. to *dē-* DE- + *sistere* to stand, place, redupl. form of *stare* to stand] —**de·sist′ance, de·sist′ence,** *n.*

de Sit·ter (də sit′ər), **Wil·lem** (wil′əm). See **Sitter.**

desk (desk), *n.* **1.** an article of furniture having a broad, usually level, writing surface, as well as drawers or compartments for papers, writing materials, etc. **2.** a frame for supporting a book from which the service is read in a church. **3.** a pulpit. **4.** the section of a large organization, as a governmental bureau, newspaper, etc., having authority over and responsibility for particular operations within the organization: *city desk; foreign desk.* **5.** a stand used to support sheet music; music stand. **6.** (in an orchestra) a seat or position assigned by rank (usually used in combination): *a first-desk flutist.* —*adj.* **7.** of or pertaining to a writing desk: *a desk drawer.* **8.** of a size or form suitable for use on a desk: *a desk dictionary.* **9.** done at or based on a desk, as in an office or schoolroom: *He used to be a traveling salesman, but now he has a desk job.* [ME *deske* < ML *desc(a)* table < L *disc(us)* desk, dish]

desk·bound (desk′bound′), *adj.* **1.** doing sedentary, as opposed to active, work; assigned to or capable of working exclusively at a desk. **2.** preoccupied with detailed records, reports, etc.; unfamiliar with actualities or practical matters outside one's own job: *deskbound executives who can't grasp production problems.* **3.** noncombatant, as a member of the armed forces, esp. in wartime: *chair-borne commandos and deskbound dough-boys.* [DESK + -BOUND[1]]

desk′ job′ber. See **drop shipper.**

desk·man (desk′man′, -mən), *n.*, *pl.* **-men** (-men′, -mən). **1.** *Journalism.* a member of a newspaper staff, often a subeditor, who processes news and prepares copy, usually from information telephoned in by reporters. **2.** one who works at a desk, esp. in a managerial capacity. [DESK + MAN[1]]

desk′ pad′, **1.** a cushioned pad, often topped with a blotter, for the surface of a desk. **2.** a tablet, scratch pad, or the like, kept on or in a desk, often having the user's name or initials printed on each sheet.

desk′top pub′lishing (desk′top′), the writing and production of publications, as newsletters or books, using a small computer, esp. a microcomputer.

desk′ work′, **1.** work done at a desk. **2.** habitual writing, as that of a clerk or a literary man.

D. ès L., Doctor of Letters. [< F *Docteur ès Lettres*]

Des·lan·dres (də län′drə), *n.* a walled plain in the third quadrant of the face of the moon: about 140 miles in diameter.

Des·ma (dez′mə), *n.* a girl's given name.

des·man (des′mən), *n.*, *pl.* **-mans.** either of two aquatic, insectivorous mammals, *Myogale moschata*, of southeastern Russia, or *M. pyrenaica*, of the Pyrenees, related to shrews. [< Sw, short for *desman-råtta* muskrat]

des·mid (des′mid), *n.* any of the microscopic freshwater algae belonging to the family *Desmidiaceae.* [< NL *Desmid(ium)* name of the genus < Gk *desm(ós)* a band, chain (cf. *deîn* to fasten) + NL *-id-* dim. suffix] —**des·mid′i·an,** *adj.*

des·mi·tis (des mī′tis, dez-), *n. Pathol.* inflammation of a ligament. [< NL < Gk *desm(ós)* (see DESMID) + *-itis* -ITIS]

des·moid (des′moid), *adj. Anat., Zool.* **1.** resembling a fascia or fibrous sheet. **2.** resembling a ligament; ligamentous. —*n.* **3.** *Pathol.* a firm and tough tumor of fibrous tissue. [< Gk *desm(ós)* (see DESMID) + -OID]

Des Moines (də moin′, moinz′), **1.** a city in and the capital of Iowa, in the central part, on the Des Moines River. 208,982 (1960). **2.** a river flowing SE from SW Minnesota through Iowa to the Mississippi River. ab. 530 mi. long.

des·mo·lase (des′mə lās′), *n. Biochem.* any of the class of enzymes comprising the carboxylases and carboligases that serve to form or break up chains of carbon atoms. [< NL *desmol(ysis)* (< Gk *desmó(s)* bond, band + *-lysis* -LYSIS) + -ASE]

Des·mo·na (dez mō′nə), *n.* a girl's given name, form of **Desdemona.**

Des·mond (dez′mənd), *n.* a boy's given name.

des·mot·ro·py (dez mo′trə pē), *n. Chem.* tautomerism. Also, **des·mot′ro·pism.** [< Gk *desmó(s)* (see DESMID) + -TROPY] —**des·mo·trop·ic** (dez′mə trop′ik), *adj.*

Des·mou·lins (de mo͞o laN′), *n.* **(Lu·cie Sim·plice) Ca·mille (Be·noît)** (ly sē′ saN plēs′ ka mē′yə bə nwa′), 1760–94, journalist, pamphleteer, and leader in the French Revolution.

des·o·late (*adj.* des′ə lit; *v.* des′ə lāt′), *adj.*, *v.*, **-lat·ed, -lat·ing.** —*adj.* **1.** barren or laid waste; devastated. **2.** deprived or destitute of inhabitants; deserted; uninhabited. **3.** solitary; lonely: *a desolate place.* **4.** having the feeling of being abandoned by friends or by hope; forlorn. **5.** dreary; dismal; gloomy: *desolate prospects.* —*v.t.* **6.** to lay waste; devastate. **7.** to deprive of inhabitants; depopulate. **8.** to make disconsolate. **9.** to forsake or abandon. [ME < L *dēsōlāt(us)* forsaken, ptp. of *dēsōlāre*, equiv. to *dē-* DE- + *sōlāre* to make lonely, deriv. of *sōlus* SOLE[1]; see -ATE[1]] —**des′o·late·ly,** *adv.* —**des′o·late·ness,** *n.* —**des′o·lat′er, des′o·la′tor,** *n.* —**des′o·lat′ing·ly,** *adv.*

—**Syn. 1.** ravaged. **2.** desert. **4.** lonesome, lost; miserable, wretched, woebegone, woeful, inconsolable, cheerless, hopeless. DESOLATE, DISCONSOLATE, FORLORN suggest one who is in a sad and wretched condition. The DESOLATE person or place gives a feeling or impression of isolation or of being deprived of human consolation, relationships, or presence: *desolate and despairing.* The DISCONSOLATE person is aware of the efforts of others to console and comfort him, but is unable to be relieved or cheered by them: *She remained disconsolate even in the midst of friends.* The FORLORN person has the feeling or gives the impression of being lost, deserted, or forsaken by friends: *wretched and forlorn in a strange city.* **6.** ravage, ruin. **8.** sadden, depress. **9.** desert. —**Ant. 4.** delighted, happy.

des·o·la·tion (des′ə lā′shən), *n.* **1.** the act or an instance of desolating. **2.** the state of being desolated. **3.** devastation; ruin. **4.** depopulation. **5.** dreariness; barrenness. **6.** deprivation of companionship; loneliness. **7.** sorrow; grief; woe. **8.** a desolate place. [ME < LL *dēsōlātiōn-* (s. of *dēsōlātiō*) a desolating, equiv. to *dēsōlāt(us)* (see DESOLATE) + *-iōn-* -ION]

de·sorb (dē sôrb′, -zôrb′), *v.t. Physical. Chem.* to remove an absorbate or adsorbate from (an absorbent or adsorbent). [DE- + *-sorb*, modeled on *absorb*] —**de·sorp·tion** (dē sôrp′shən, -zôrp′-), *n.*

De So·to (di sō′tō; *Sp.* de sō′tō), **1. Her·nan·do** (hər nan′dō; *Sp.* er nän′dō) or **Fer·nan·do** (fər nan′dō; *Sp.* fer nän′dō), c1500–42, Spanish soldier and explorer in America. **2.** a town in E Missouri. 5804 (1960).

des·ox·y·ri·bo·nu·cle·ase (des ok′si rī′bō no͞o′klē-ās′, -nyo͞o′-), *n. Biochem.* deoxyribonuclease.

des·ox′y·ri′bo·nu·cle′ic ac′id (des ok′si rī′bō-no͞o klē′ik, -nyo͞o-, -rī′), *Biochem.* See **DNA.**

des·ox·y·ri·bo·nu·cle·o·pro·tein (des ok′si rī′-bō no͞o′klē ə prō′tēn, -tē in, -nyo͞o′-), *n. Biochem.* deoxyribonucleoprotein.

des·ox·y·ri·bose (des ok′si rī′bōs), *n. Biochem.* deoxyribose.

de·spair (di spâr′), *n.* **1.** loss of hope; hopelessness. **2.** that which causes hopelessness; that of which there is no hope: *He is his mother's despair.* —*v.i.* **3.** to lose, give up, or be without hope (often fol. by *of*): *to despair of humanity.* —*v.t.* **4.** *Obs.* to give up hope of. [ME *despeir* (n.), *despeir(en)* (v.) < AF *despeir,* OF *despoir* (n.), *despeir-,* tonic s. of *desperer* < L *dēspērāre* to be without hope, equiv. to *dē-* DE- + *spērāre* to hope, akin to *spes* hope] —**de·spair′er,** *n.* —**de·spair′ful,** *adj.* —**de·spair′ful·ly,** *adv.* —**de·spair′ful·ness,** *n.*

—**Syn. 1.** gloom, disheartenment. DESPAIR, DESPERATION, DESPONDENCY, DISCOURAGEMENT, HOPELESSNESS refer to a state of mind caused by circumstances which seem too much to cope with. DESPAIR suggests total loss or abandonment of hope, which may be passive or may drive one to furious efforts, even if at random: *in the depths of despair; courage born of despair.* DESPERATION is usually an active state, the abandonment of hope impelling to a furious struggle against adverse circumstances, with utter disregard of consequences: *an act of desperation when everything else had failed.* DESPONDENCY is usually a temporary state of deep gloom and disheartenment: *a spell of despondency.* DISCOURAGEMENT is a temporary loss of courage, hope, and ambition because of obstacles, frustrations, etc.: *His optimism yielded to discouragement.* HOPELESSNESS is a loss of hope so complete as to result in a more or less permanent state of passive despair: *a state of hopelessness and apathy.* —**Ant. 1.** hope.

de·spair·ing (di spâr′ing), *adj.* **1.** given to despair or hopelessness. **2.** indicating despair: *a despairing look.* [DESPAIR + -ING²] —**de·spair′ing·ly,** *adv.* —**de·spair′ing·ness,** *n.*

—**Syn. 1.** See **hopeless.** —**Ant. 1.** hopeful.

des·patch (di spach′), *v.t., v.i., n.* dispatch. —**des·patch′er,** *n.*

des·per·a·do (des′pə rä′dō, -rā′-), *n., pl.* **-does, -dos.** a bold, reckless criminal or outlaw, esp. in the early days of the American West. [< Sp: lit., DESPERATE]

des·per·ate (des′pər it, -prit), *adj.* **1.** reckless or dangerous because of despair or urgency: *a desperate killer.* **2.** having an urgent need, desire, etc.: *desperate for attention.* **3.** leaving little or no hope; very serious or dangerous: *a desperate illness.* **4.** extremely bad; intolerable or shocking: *clothes in desperate taste.* **5.** extreme or excessive. **6.** making a final, ultimate effort; giving all: *The doctor made a last, desperate attempt to save the child's life.* **7.** actuated by a feeling of hopelessness. **8.** having no hope; giving in to despair. [ME < L *dēspērāt(us),* ptp. of *dēspērāre* to DESPAIR; see -ATE¹] —**des′per·ate·ly,** *adv.* —**des′per·ate·ness,** *n.*

—**Syn. 1.** rash, frantic. **3.** grave. See **hopeless. 8.** forlorn, desolate. —**Ant. 1.** careful. **3, 8.** hopeful.

des·per·a·tion (des′pə rā′shən), *n.* **1.** the state of being desperate or of having the recklessness of despair. **2.** the act or fact of despairing; despair. [ME *desperacioun* < L *dēspērātiōn-* (s. of *dēspērātiō*). See DESPERATE, -ION]

—**Syn. 1.** See **despair.**

Des Peres (də pâr′), a town in E Missouri. 4362 (1960).

Des·piau (des′pē ō′; *Fr.* des pyō′), *n.* **Charles** (chärlz; *Fr.* sharl), 1874–1946, French sculptor.

des·pi·ca·ble (des′pi kə bəl; *for emphasis* di spik′ə-bəl), *adj.* deserving to be despised; contemptible. [< LL *dēspicābil(is),* equiv. to L *dēspic(ārī)* (to) despise, *dēspic(ere)* (to) look down (*dē-* DE- + *spic-* look, comb. form of *specere*) + *-ābilis* -ABLE] —**des′pi·ca·bil′i·ty, des′pi·ca·ble·ness,** *n.* —**des′pi·ca·bly,** *adv.*

—**Syn.** worthless, base, vile, mean, abject, low. —**Ant.** admirable.

de·spise (di spīz′), *v.t.,* **-spised, -spis·ing.** to regard with contempt, distaste, disgust, or disdain; scorn; loathe. [ME *despise(n)* < OF *despis-,* s. of *despire* < L *dēspicere;* see DESPICABLE] —**de·spis′a·ble,** *adj.* —**de·spis′a·ble·ness,** *n.* —**de·spis′er,** *n.* —**de·spis′ing·ly,** *adv.*

—**Syn.** contemn, detest. —**Ant.** admire.

de·spite (di spīt′), *prep., n., v.,* **-spit·ed, -spit·ing.** —*prep.* **1.** in spite of; notwithstanding. —*n.* **2.** contemptuous treatment; insult. **3.** *Archaic.* malice, hatred, or spite. **4. in despite of,** in defiance of; in spite of; notwithstanding: *He was tolerant in despite of his background and education.* —*v.t.* **5.** *Obs.* to anger or annoy (someone) out of spite. [orig. *in despite of;* ME *despit* < OF < L *dēspect(us)* a looking down upon, ptp. of *dēspicere;* see DESPICABLE]

—**Syn. 1.** See **notwithstanding.**

de·spite·ful (di spīt′fəl), *adj.* **1.** malicious; spiteful. **2.** *Obs.* contemptuous; insolent. [DESPITE + -FUL] —**de·spite′ful·ly,** *adv.* —**de·spite′ful·ness,** *n.*

des·pit·e·ous (di spit′ē əs), *adj. Archaic.* **1.** malicious; spiteful. **2.** contemptuous. [var. of ME *despitous* < AF; OF *despiteus,* equiv. to *despit* DESPITE + *-eus* -EOUS] —**des·pit′e·ous·ly,** *adv.*

Des Plaines (des plānz′), a city in NE Illinois, near Chicago. 34,886 (1960).

Des·poe·na (des pē′nə), *n.* an ancient Greek deity, the daughter of Poseidon and Demeter, usually associated with Persephone.

de·spoil (di spoil′), *v.t.* to strip of possessions, things of value, etc.; rob; plunder; pillage. [ME *despoil(en)* < OF *despoill(ier)* < L *dēspoliāre* to strip, rob, plunder, equiv. to *dē-* DE- + *spoliāre* to plunder; see SPOIL] —**de·spoil′er,** *n.* —**de·spoil′ment,** *n.*

—**Syn.** dispossess, divest; rifle, sack; fleece.

de·spo·li·a·tion (di spō′lē ā′shən), *n.* **1.** the act of despoiling. **2.** the fact or circumstance of being despoiled. [< LL *dēspoliātiōn-* (s. of *dēspoliātiō*), equiv. to L *dēspoliāt(us)* (ptp. of *dēspoliāre;* see DESPOIL) + *-iōn-* -ION]

de·spond (di spond′ *or, esp. for 2,* des′pond), *v.i.* **1.** to be depressed by loss of hope, confidence, or courage. —*n.* **2.** despondency. [< L *dēspond(ēre)* (to) give up, lose heart, promise, equiv. to *dē-* DE- + *spondēre* to promise] —**de·spond′er,** *n.* —**de·spond′ing·ly,** *adv.*

de·spond·en·cy (di spon′dən sē), *n.* state of being despondent; depression of spirits from loss of courage or hope; dejection. Also, **de·spond′ence.** [DESPOND + -ENCY]

—**Syn.** discouragement, melancholy, gloom, desperation. See **despair.** —**Ant.** joy.

de·spond·ent (di spon′dənt), *adj.* feeling or showing profound hopelessness, dejection, discouragement, or gloom; depressed; dispirited: *He was despondent about his failing health.* [< L *dēspondent-* (s. of *dēspondēns*), prp. of *dēspondēre.* See DESPOND, -ENT] —**de·spond′ent·ly,** *adv.*

—**Syn.** discouraged, disheartened, downhearted, melancholy, low-spirited, sad, blue. See **hopeless.** —**Ant.** happy, hopeful.

des·pot (des′pət, -pot), *n.* **1.** a ruler with absolute, unlimited power; autocrat. **2.** any tyrant or oppressor. **3.** *Hist.* an honorary title applied to a Byzantine emperor, afterward to members of his family, and later to Byzantine vassal rulers and governors. [< Gk *despót(ēs)* master]

des·pot·ic (di spot′ik), *adj.* of, pertaining to, or of the nature of a despot or despotism; autocratic; arbitrary; tyrannical. Also, **des·pot′i·cal.** [< F *despotique* < Gk *despotik(ós).* See DESPOT, -IC] —**des·pot′i·cal·ly,** *adv.* —**des·pot′i·cal·ness,** *n.*

despot′ic mon′archy. See **absolute monarchy.** —**despot′ic mon′arch.**

des·pot·ism (des′pə tiz′əm), *n.* **1.** the rule of a despot; the exercise of absolute authority. **2.** absolute power or control; tyranny. **3.** an absolute or autocratic government. **4.** a country ruled by a despot. [< F *despotisme.* See DESPOT, -ISM]

Des Prés (də prā′; *Fr.* dā PRĀ′), **Jos·quin** (zhus′-kan; *Fr.* zhôs KAN′), c1445–1521, Flemish composer. Also, **De·près** (də PRE′), **De·prez** (də PRĀ′).

de·spu·mate (di spyo͞o′māt, des′pyo͞o māt′), *v.,* **-mat·ed, -mat·ing.** *Archaic.* —*v.t.* **1.** to skim impurities or scum from (a liquid). —*v.i.* **2.** to throw off froth. [< L *dēspūmāt(us)* skimmed, ptp. of *dēspūmāre,* equiv. to *dē-* DE- + *spūmāre* to foam, deriv. of *spūma* SPUME; see -ATE¹] —**des′pu·ma′tion,** *n.*

des·qua·mate (des′kwə māt′), *v.i.,* **-mat·ed, -mat·ing.** *Pathol.* to come off in scales, as the skin in certain diseases; peel off. [< L *dēsquāmāt(us)* scaled (ptp. of *dēsquāmāre*). See DE-, SQUAMATE] —**des′qua·ma′tion,** *n.*

D. ès S., Doctor of Sciences. [< F *Docteur ès Sciences*]

Des·sa·lines (dā SA lēn′), *n.* **Jean Jacques** (zhäN zhäk), 1758–1806, Haitian revolutionary: emperor of Haiti as Jacques I 1804–06.

Des·sau (des′ou), *n.* a city in central East Germany, SW of Berlin: formerly the capital of Anhalt. 94,300 (est. 1959).

des·sert (di zûrt′), *n.* **1.** *U.S.* pastry, pudding, ice cream, etc., served as the final course of a meal. **2.** *Brit.* (formerly) a serving of fruit, nuts, candy, etc., after the final course of a meal. [< F, deriv. of *desserv(ir)* (to) clear the table. See DIS-¹, SERVE]

dessert′ fork′, a fork used for eating cake or pie, usually somewhat smaller than a dinner fork.

dessert′ knife′, a knife used during the dessert course, usually somewhat smaller than a dinner knife.

des·sert·spoon (di zûrt′spo͞on′), *n.* a spoon intermediate in size between a tablespoon and a teaspoon, used in eating pudding, ice cream, etc. [DESSERT + SPOON]

des·sert·spoon·ful (di zûrt′spo͞on′fo͝ol′), *n., pl.* **-fuls.** as much as a dessertspoon can hold: 2½ fluid drams. [DESSERTSPOON + -FUL]

dessert′ wine′, a sweet wine, as port, served with dessert or sometimes between meals.

des·sia·tine (des′yə tēn′), *n.* a Russian unit of land measure equal to 2.7 U.S. acres. [< Russ *dessyatina,* lit., tithe, tenth, deriv. of *dessyat′* ten]

Des·ta (des′tə), *n.* a girl's given name, form of **Desde.**

de-Sta·lin·i·za·tion (dē stä′li ni zā′shən), *n.* the policy, pursued in most Communist areas and among most Communist groups since 1956, of eradicating the memory or influence of Stalin and Stalinism, as by alteration of governmental policies or the elimination of monuments, place names, etc., named for Stalin. Also, **de·sta′lin·i·za′tion.** [DE-STALINIZE + -ATION]

de-Sta·lin·ize (dē stä′lə nīz′, -stal′ə-), *v.,* **-ized, -iz·ing.** —*v.i.* **1.** to divest of the influence or memory of Stalin, esp. by means of a systematic campaign. —*v.t.* **2.** to remove the influence of Stalin from (culture, sports, etc.). Also, **de·sta′lin·ize′.** [DE- + STALIN + -IZE]

de·ster·i·lize (dē ster′ə līz′), *v.t.,* **-lized, -liz·ing.** to utilize an idle fund or commodity, as when a nation issues currency against gold previously unused. [DE- + STERILIZE] —**de·ster′i·li·za′tion,** *n.*

Des·ter·ro (*Port.* des teʀ′ʀo͞o), *n.* former name of **Florianópolis.**

des·ti·na·tion (des′tə nā′shən), *n.* **1.** the place to which a person or thing travels or is sent: *His destination was Rome. What is the destination of that letter?* **2.** the purpose for which anything is destined; ultimate end or design. [ME < L *dēstinātiōn-* (s. of *dēstinātiō*) an establishing, purpose, equiv. to *dēstināt(us)* (ptp. of *dēstināre;* see DESTINE) + *-iōn-* -ION]

des·tine (des′tin), *v.t.,* **-tined, -tin·ing.** **1.** to set apart for a particular use, purpose, etc.; design; intend. **2.** to appoint or ordain beforehand, as by divine decree; foreordain; predetermine. [ME *destin(en)* < OF *destin(er)* < L *dēstināre* to establish, determine, equiv. to *dē-* DE- + **stanāre,* deriv. of *stare* to stand]

des·tined (des′tind), *adj.* **1.** bound for a certain destination: *a ship destined for the Orient.* **2.** ordained, appointed, or predetermined to be or do something. **3.** liable, planning, or intending to be or do something. [DESTINE + -ED²]

des·ti·ny (des′tə nē), *n., pl.* **-nies.** **1.** that which is to happen or has happened to a particular person or thing; lot or fortune. **2.** the predetermined, usually inevitable or irresistible course of events. **3.** the power or agency which determines the course of events. **4.** (*cap.*) this power personified or represented as a goddess. **5. the Destinies,** the Fates. [ME *destinee* < OF (n. use of ptp. of *destiner*) < L *dēstināta,* fem. ptp. of *dēstināre.* See DESTINE, -EE]

—**Syn. 1.** fate, karma, kismet. **2.** future. See **fate.**

des·ti·tute (des′ti to͞ot′, -tyo͞ot′), *adj., v.,* **-tut·ed, -tut·ing.** —*adj.* **1.** without means of subsistence; completely poverty-stricken. **2.** deprived of, devoid of, or lacking (often fol. by *of*): *destitute of children.* **3.** *Obs.* abandoned; deserted. —*v.t.* **4.** to leave destitute. **5.** *Obs.* to forsake; abandon. **6.** to deprive, as of office; depose. [ME < L *dēstitūt(us)* put away, abandoned (ptp. of *destituere*), equiv. to *dē-* DE- + *stit-* place, put (sp. var. of *statuere;* see STATUTE) + *-ū-* thematic vowel + *-t-* ptp. suffix] —**des′ti·tute′ly,** *adv.* —**des′ti·tute′ness,** *n.*

—**Syn. 1.** needy, poor, indigent, necessitous, penniless, impoverished. **2.** deficient. —**Ant. 1.** affluent.

des·ti·tu·tion (des′ti to͞o′shən, -tyo͞o′-), *n.* **1.** lack of the means of subsistence; utter poverty. **2.** deprivation, lack, or absence. [ME < L *dēstitūtiōn-* (s. of *dēstitūtiō*) an abandoning, equiv. to *dēstitūt(us)* (see DESTITUTE) + *-iōn-* -ION]

—**Syn. 1.** See **poverty.** —**Ant. 1.** affluence.

de·stool (dē sto͞ol′), *v.t.* to remove (a West African ruler) from office. [DE- + STOOL] —**de·stool′ment,** *n.*

des·tri·er (des′trē ər, de strēr′), *n. Archaic.* a war horse; charger. [ME *destrer* < AF, var. of OF *destrier* < LL *dextrāt(ius),* lit., (horse) led at the right hand, equiv. to L *dexter* right + *-ārius* -ARY]

de·stroy (di stroi′), *v.t.* **1.** to reduce (an object) to useless fragments, a useless form, or remains, as by rending, burning, or dissolving. **2.** to put an end to; extinguish. **3.** to kill; slay. **4.** to render ineffective or useless; nullify; neutralize; invalidate. **5.** to defeat completely. —*v.i.* **6.** to engage in destroying things. [ME *destroy(en)* < OF *destruire* < LL **dēstrūgere,* var. of L *dēstruere* (*dē-* DE- + *struere* to pick up, build)] —**de·stroy′a·ble,** *adj.*

—**Syn. 1.** smash, level, waste, ravage, devastate. DESTROY, DEMOLISH, RAZE imply reducing a thing to uselessness. To DESTROY is to reduce something to nothingness or to take away its powers and functions so that restoration is impossible; the action is usually violent or sudden, but may be gradual and slow, esp. when it entails a reversal of natural processes: *Fire destroys a building. Disease destroys tissues.* To DEMOLISH is to destroy an organized body or structure by complete separation of parts: *to demolish a machine.* To RAZE is to level down to the ground: *to raze a fortress.* **2.** extirpate, annihilate, uproot. —**Ant. 1, 2.** create.

de·stroy·er (di stroi′ər), *n.* **1.** one who or that which destroys. **2.** a fast, relatively small, warship armed mainly with five-inch guns, originally designed to destroy torpedo boats, now used as an escort in convoys, in antisubmarine duties, etc. [ME *destroiere* (cf. OF *destruiere*). See DESTROY, -ER¹]

destroy′er es′cort, a warship somewhat smaller than a destroyer, designed especially for antisubmarine action. *Abbr.:* DE

destroy′ing an′gel, any of several deadly poisonous mushrooms of the genus *Amanita,* having a white pileus, stipe, and spores, and a conspicuous volva at the base of the stem.

de·struct (di strukt′), *adj.* **1.** serving or designed to destroy: *A test missile is often provided with a destruct mechanism which can explode it in flight if it leaves its predetermined course.* —*n.* **2.** the act or process of intentional destruction: *Three out of ten launchings ended in destructs.* —*v.t.* **3.** to destroy. [back formation from DESTRUCTION]

de·struct·i·ble (di struk′tə bəl), *adj.* capable of being destroyed; liable to destruction. [< LL *dēstructibil(is),* equiv. to L *dēstruct(us)* pulled down (see DESTRUCTION) + *-ibilis* -IBLE] —**de·struct′i·bil′i·ty, de·struct′i·ble·ness,** *n.*

de·struc·tion (di struk′shən), *n.* **1.** the act of destroying: *the wanton destruction of a town.* **2.** the fact or condition of being destroyed; demolition; annihilation. **3.** a cause or means of destroying. [ME < L *dēstructiōn-* (s. of *dēstructiō*), equiv. to *dēstruct(us)* (ptp. of *dēstruere;* see DESTROY) + *-iōn-* -ION]

—**Syn. 1.** extinction, extermination, eradication, devastation. See **ruin.**

de·struc·tion·ist (di struk′shə nist), *n. Obs.* an advocate of the destruction of an existing political institution or the like. [DESTRUCTION + -IST]

de·struc·tive (di struk′tiv), *adj.* **1.** tending to destroy; causing destruction or much damage (often fol. by *of* or *to*): *a very destructive windstorm.* **2.** tending to overthrow, disprove, or discredit (opposed to *constructive*): *destructive criticism.* [< MF < LL *dēstructīv(us),* equiv. to L *dēstruct(us)* (see DESTRUCTION) + *-or* -OR²] —**de·struc′tive·ly,** *adv.* —**de·struc′tive·ness, de·struc·tiv·i·ty** (dē′struk tiv′i tē), *n.*

—**Syn. 1.** ruinous, baleful, pernicious, deleterious, fatal, deadly, lethal. **2.** unfavorable, unfriendly, adverse, negative. —**Ant. 1.** creative. **2.** constructive.

destruc′tive distilla′tion, *Chem.* the decomposition of a substance, as wood, coal, etc., by heating with a minimal exposure to air, and the collection of the volatile products formed.

destruc′tive interfer′ence, *Physics.* the interference of two waves of equal frequency and opposite phase, resulting in their cancellation where the negative displacement of one always coincides with the positive displacement of the other. Cf. **constructive interference.**

de·struct′ line′ (di strukt′), *Rocketry.* a line on a chart or map indicating the limit of tolerance allowed in the trajectory of a missile before it must be destroyed.

de·struc·tor (di struk′tər), *n. Brit.* a furnace for the burning of refuse; incinerator. [< LL *dēstructor,* equiv. to L *dēstruct(us)* (see DESTRUCTION) + *-or* -OR²]

des·ue·tude (des′wi to͞od′, -tyo͞od′), *n.* the state of being no longer used or practiced. [ME < L *dēsuētūdo,* equiv. to *dēsuēt(us),* ptp. of *dēsuescere* to lay aside (*dē-* DE- + *suescere* to become accustomed) + *-ūdo* n. suffix]

de·sul·fur (dē sul′fər), *v.t.* to free from sulfur; desulfurize. Also, **de·sul′phur.** [DE- + SULFUR]

de·sul·fur·ate (dē sul′fyə rāt′, -fə-), *v.t.,* **-at·ed, -at·ing.** *Chem.* to desulfurize. Also, **desulphurate.** [DE- + SULFURATE] —**de·sul′fu·ra′tion,** *n.*

de·sul·fu·rise (dē sul′fyə rīz′, -fə-), *v.t.,* **-ised, -is·ing.** *Chiefly Brit.* desulfurize. —**de·sul′fu·ri·sa′tion,** *n.* —**de·sul′fu·ris′er,** *n.*

de·sul·fu·rize (dē sul′fyə rīz′, -fə-), *v.t.*, **-rized, -riz·ing.** to free from sulfur. Also, **desulphurize.** [DE- + SULFURIZE] —**de·sul′fu·ri·za′tion,** *n.* —**de·sul′fu·riz′er,** *n.*

de·sul·phur·ate (dē sul′fyə rāt′, -fə-), *v.t.*, **-at·ed, -at·ing.** desulfurate. —**de·sul′phu·ra′tion,** *n.*

de·sul·phu·rise (dē sul′fyə rīz′, -fə-), *v.t.*, **-rised, -ris·ing.** *Chiefly Brit.* desulfurize.

de·sul·phu·rize (dē sul′fyə rīz′, -fə-), *v.t.*, **-rized, -riz·ing.** desulfurize.

des·ul·to·ry (des′əl tōr′ē, -tôr′ē), *adj.* **1.** lacking in consistency, constancy, or visible order, as in performing a series of actions, giving one's attention to some subject, etc.; disconnected; fitful: *desultory attempts at getting a job; desultory conversation.* **2.** digressing from the main subject; random: *a desultory remark.* [< L *dēsultōri(us)* of a jumper, superficial, equiv. to *dēsult(us)* (ptp. of *dēsilīre* to leap down, equiv. to *dē-* DE- + *sul-* leap, var. of *sal-* leap, + *-tus* ptp. suffix) + *-ōrius* -ORY[1]] —**des′ul·to′ri·ly,** *adv.* —**des′ul·to′ri·ness,** *n.*
—**Ant. 1.** methodical. **2.** pertinent.

de·su·per·heat·er (dē sōō′pər hē′tər), *n.* an apparatus in a boiler for cooling and controlling the temperature of superheated steam or for converting it to saturated steam. [DE- + SUPERHEAT + -ER[1]]

det., **1.** detachment. **2.** (in prescriptions) let it be given. [< L *dētur*]

de·tach (di tach′), *v.t.* **1.** to unfasten and separate; disengage; disunite. **2.** *Mil.* to send away (a regiment, ship, etc.) on a special mission: *Men were detached to defend to pass.* [< F *détach(er),* OF *destachier,* equiv. to *des-* DIS-[1] + *tache* (<< Romanic *tacca* nail). Cf. ATTACH] —**de·tach′a·ble,** *adj.* —**de·tach′a·bil′i·ty,** *n.* —**de·tach′er,** *n.*

de·tached (di tacht′), *adj.* **1.** separated; not attached: *a detached ticket stub.* **2.** having no wall in common with another building (opposed to *attached*): *a detached house.* **3.** disinterested; objective; unbiased: *a detached judgment.* **4.** aloof; not involved or concerned. [DETACH + -ED[2]] —**de·tached·ly** (di tach′id lē, -tacht′lē), *adv.* —**de·tach·ed·ness** (di tach′id nis, -tacht′-), *n.*
—**Syn. 3.** uninvolved, uninterested, impartial, dispassionate, unprejudiced. —**Ant. 1.** attached. **3.** involved; partial.

detached′ escape′ment, *Horol.* an escapement having a balance or pendulum that moves independently of the mechanism during a large part of each oscillation.

de·tach·ment (di tach′mənt), *n.* **1.** the act of detaching. **2.** the condition of being detached. **3.** aloofness, as from worldly affairs or from the concerns of others. **4.** freedom from prejudice or partiality. **5.** the act of sending out a detached force of troops or naval ships. **6.** the body of troops or ships so detached. [< F *détachement.* See DETACH, -MENT]

de·tail (*n.* di tāl′, dē′tāl; *v.* di tāl′), *n.* **1.** an individual or minute part; an item or particular. **2.** particulars collectively; minutiae. **3.** attention to or treatment of a subject in individual or minute parts: *to postpone detail and concentrate on a subject as a whole.* **4.** intricate, finely wrought decoration. **5.** See **detail drawing. 6.** any small section of a larger structure or whole, considered as a unit. **7.** *Mil.* **a.** an appointment or assignment, as of a small group of men or an officer, for a special task. **b.** the party or person so selected: *the kitchen detail.* **c.** a particular assignment of duty. **8.** the property of an image or of a method of image production to make small, closely spaced image elements individually distinguishable. **9.** *Archaic.* a narrative or report of particulars. **10. in detail,** item by item; with particulars: *The résumé stated his qualifications in detail.* —*v.t.* **11.** to relate or report with complete particulars; tell fully and distinctly. **12.** to mention one by one; specify; list: *He detailed the events leading up to the robbery.* **13.** *Mil.* to appoint or assign for some particular duty: *We were detailed to patrol the border.* **14.** to provide with intricate, finely wrought decoration: *lingerie detailed with lace and embroidery.* [< F *détail,* deriv. of OF *detailler* to cut in pieces, equiv. to *de-* DIS-[1] + *tailler* to cut; see TAILOR]

de′tail draw′ing, a drawing, at relatively large scale, of a part of a building, machine, etc., with dimensions or other information for use in construction.

de·tailed (di tāld′, dē′tāld), *adj.* **1.** having numerous details: *a detailed problem.* **2.** thorough in the treatment of details; minute: *a detailed report.* [DETAIL + -ED[2]] —**de·tailed·ly** (di tāld′lē, -tā′lid-), *adv.* —**de·tailed′ness,** *n.*
—**Syn. 1.** involved, complex, complicated. **2.** itemized, particularized; exhaustive, thorough, comprehensive; intricate.

de′tail man′, a promotional representative of a manufacturer of drugs or medical supplies, who calls on doctors, hospital administrators, pharmacists, etc.

de·tain (di tān′), *v.t.* **1.** to keep from proceeding; keep waiting; delay. **2.** to keep under restraint or in custody. **3.** *Archaic.* to keep back or withhold, as from a person. [ME *detain(en)* < OF *deten(ir)* < L *dētinēre,* equiv. to *dē-* DE- + *-tinēre,* comb. form of *tenēre* to hold] —**de·tain′a·ble,** *adj.* —**de·tain′ment,** *n.*
—**Syn. 1.** retard, stop, slow, stay, check. **2.** confine, arrest. **3.** retain. —**Ant. 1.** promote, advance.

de·tain·er (di tā′nər), *n.* *Law.* **1.** the wrongful detaining or withholding of what belongs to another. **2.** a writ for the further detention of a person already in custody. [< AF *detener* (n. use of inf.), var. of OF *detenir;* see DETAIN]

de·tect (di tekt′), *v.t.* **1.** to discover or catch (a person) in the performance of some act: *to detect someone cheating.* **2.** to find out the true character or activity of: *to detect a spy.* **3.** to discover the presence, existence, or fact of: *to detect the odor of gas.* **4.** *Radio.* to subject to the action of a detector; demodulate. [ME *detect* (ptp.) < L *dētect(us)* (ptp. of *dētegere*), equiv. to *dē-* DE- + *teg-* cover (var. of *tegere*) + *-t-* ptp. suffix] —**de·tect′a·ble, de·tect′i·ble,** *adj.*
—**Syn. 1.** descry, find. **3.** See **learn.**

de·tec·ta·phone (di tek′tə fōn′), *n.* a device for overhearing telephone conversations secretly. [DETECT + *-a-,* var. of *-o-* + -PHONE]

de·tec·tion (di tek′shən), *n.* **1.** the act of detecting. **2.** the fact of being detected. **3.** discovery, as of error or crime: *chance detection of smuggling.* **4.** *Radio.* **a.** rectification of alternating currents in a radio receiver. **b.** Also called **demodulation.** the conversion of an alternating carrier wave or current into a direct pulsating current equivalent to the transmitted signal. [ME < LL *dētectiōn-* (s. of *dētectiō*), equiv. to L *dētect(us)* (see DETECT) + *-iōn-* -ION]

de·tec·tive (di tek′tiv), *n.* **1.** a member of the police force or a private investigator whose function it is to obtain information and evidence, as of offenses against the law. —*adj.* **2.** of or pertaining to detection or detectives: *a detective story.* **3.** serving to detect; detecting: *various detective devices.* [DETECT + -IVE]

de·tec·tor (di tek′tər), *n.* **1.** one who or that which detects. **2.** *Radio.* **a.** a device for detecting electric oscillations or waves. **b.** a device, as a crystal detector or a vacuum tube, which rectifies the alternating currents in a radio receiver. [< LL *dētector* an uncoverer, equiv. to L *dētect(us)* uncovered (see DETECT) + *-or* -OR[2]]

de·tent (di tent′), *n.* *Mach.* a mechanism for temporarily keeping one part in a certain position relative to that of another, released by application of force to one of the parts. [< F *détente,* OF *destente,* deriv. of *destendre* to relax, equiv. to *des-* DIS-[1] + *tendre;* see TENDER[2]]

dé·tente (dā tänt′; *Fr.* dā täɴt′), *n., pl.* **-tentes** (-tänts′; *Fr.* -täɴt′). a relaxing, esp. of international tension. [< F; see DETENT]

detent′ escape′ment. See **chronometer escapement.**

de·ten·tion (di ten′shən), *n.* **1.** the act of detaining. **2.** the state of being detained. **3.** maintenance of a person in custody or confinement, esp. while awaiting a court decision. **4.** the withholding of what belongs to or is claimed by another. —*adj.* **5.** of or pertaining to detention or used to detain: *the detention room of a police station.* [ME < L *dētentiōn-* (s. of *dētentiō*), equiv. to *dētent(us)* detained (ptp. of *dētinēre;* see DETAIN) + *-iōn-* -ION]

deten′tion home′, a house of correction or detention for juvenile offenders or delinquents, usually under the supervision of a juvenile court.

dé·te·nu (dātᵊ ny′), *n., pl.* **-nus** (-ny′). *French.* one who is detained; prisoner.

dé·te·nue (dātᵊ ny′), *n., pl.* **-nues** (-ny′). *French.* a female prisoner.

de·ter (di tûr′), *v.t.*, **-terred, -ter·ring.** **1.** to discourage or restrain from acting or proceeding through fear, doubt, etc.: *The large dog deterred trespassers.* **2.** to prevent; check; arrest: *Timber is often treated with creosote to deter rot.* [< L *dēterr(ēre)* (to) prevent, hinder, equiv. to *dē-* DE- + *terrēre* to frighten] —**de·ter′ment,** *n.*
—**Syn. 1.** dissuade, hinder, stop.

de·terge (di tûrj′), *v.t.*, **-terged, -terg·ing.** **1.** to wipe or wash away; cleanse. **2.** to cleanse of impurities or undesirable matter, as a wound. [< L *dēterg(ēre)* (to) wipe off, equiv. to *dē-* DE- + *tergere* to wipe]

de·ter·gen·cy (di tûr′jən sē), *n.* cleansing or purging power. Also, **de·ter′gence.** [DETERG(ENT) + -ENCY]

de·ter·gent (di tûr′jənt), *adj.* **1.** cleansing; purging. —*n.* **2.** any of a group of synthetic, organic, liquid or water-soluble cleaning agents that, unlike soap, are not prepared from fats and oils, are inactivated by hard water, and have wetting-agent and emulsifying-agent properties. **3.** a similar substance that is oil-soluble and capable of holding insoluble foreign matter in suspension, used in lubricating oils, dry-cleaning preparations, etc. **4.** any cleansing agent, including soap. Cf. **anionic detergent, cationic detergent, synthetic detergent.** [< L *dētergent-* (s. of *dētergēns*) wiping off (prp. of *dētergēre*). See DETERGE, -ENT]

de·te·ri·o·rate (di tēr′ē ə rāt′), *v.t., v.i.*, **-rat·ed, -rat·ing.** **1.** to make or become worse; make or become lower in character, quality, value, etc. **2.** to disintegrate or wear away. [< LL *dēteriōrāt(us)* made worse (ptp. of *dēteriōrāre*), equiv. to L *dēterior* worse, comp. of **dēter* poor + *-ātus* -ATE[1]] —**de·te′ri·o·ra′tive,** *adj.*
—**Syn. 1.** degenerate, decline, weaken, retrogress, worsen, diminish.

de·te·ri·o·ra·tion (di tēr′ē ə rā′shən), *n.* **1.** the act or process of deteriorating. **2.** the state or condition of having deteriorated. **3.** a gradual decline, as in quality, serviceability, vigor, etc. [< LL *dēteriōrātiōn-* (s. of *dēteriōrātiō*), equiv. to *dēteriōrāt(us)* (see DETERIORATE) + *-iōn-* -ION]

de·te·ri·o·ra·tion·ist (di tēr′ē ə rā′shə nist), *n.* one who believes that society and mankind are in a state of deterioration. [DETERIORATION + -IST]

de·ter·mi·na·ble (di tûr′mə nə bəl), *adj.* **1.** capable of being determined. **2.** *Law.* subject to termination. [ME: fixed < OF < LL *dēterminābil(is),* equiv. to L *dētermin(āre)* (to) bound, DETERMINE + *-ābilis* -ABLE] —**de·ter′mi·na·bil′i·ty, de·ter′mi·na·ble·ness,** *n.* —**de·ter′mi·na·bly,** *adv.*

de·ter·mi·nant (di tûr′mə nənt), *n.* **1.** a determining agent or factor. **2.** *Math.* an algebraic expression of the sum of products of elements, usually written in a square array and used in the solution of systems of linear equations, Jacobians, etc. **3.** *Genetics. Archaic.* a gene. [< L *dēterminant-* (s. of *dēterminans*), prp. of *dētermināre.* See DETERMINE, -ANT]
—**Syn. 1.** cause, condition, antecedent.

deter′minant rank′, *Math.* rank[1] (def. 14).

de·ter·mi·nate (*adj.* di tûr′mə nit; *v.* di tûr′mə nāt′), *adj., v.*, **-nat·ed, -nat·ing.** —*adj.* **1.** having defined limits; definite. **2.** settled; positive. **3.** conclusive; final. **4.** resolute. **5.** *Bot.* (of an inflorescence) having the primary and each secondary axis ending in a flower or bud, thus preventing further elongation. **6.** *Engineering.* **a.** (of a structure) able to be analyzed completely by means of the principles of statics. **b.** (of a member of a structure) subject only to definite, known stresses. **c.** (of a stress) able to be determined through the principles of statics. —*v.t.* **7.** to make certain of. **8.** to identify. [ME < L *dētermināt(us),* ptp. of *dētermināre.* See DETERMINE, -ATE[1]] —**de·ter′mi·nate·ly,** *adj.* —**de·ter′mi·nate·ness,** *n.*

de·ter·mi·na·tion (di tûr′mə nā′shən), *n.* **1.** the act of coming to a decision or of fixing or settling a purpose. **2.** ascertainment, as after observation or investigation: *determination of a ship's latitude.* **3.** the information ascertained; solution. **4.** the settlement of a dispute, question, etc., as by authoritative decision. **5.** the decision or settlement arrived at or pronounced. **6.** the quality of being resolute; firmness of purpose. **7.** a fixed purpose or intention: *It is my determination to suppress vice.* **8.** the fixing or settling of amount, limit, character, etc.: *the determination of a child's allowance.* **9.** fixed direction or tendency toward some object or end. **10.** *Chiefly Law.* conclusion or termination. **11.** *Embryol.* the fixation of the nature of morphological differentiation in a group of cells before actual, visible differentiation. **12.** *Logic.* **a.** the act of rendering a notion more precise by the addition of differentiating characteristics. **b.** definition of a concept in terms of its constituent elements. [ME *determinacioun* < L *dēterminātiōn-* (s. of *dēterminātiō*) a boundary, conclusion, equiv. to *dētermināt(us)* (see DETERMINATE) + *-iōn-* -ION]

de·ter·mi·na·tive (di tûr′mə nā′tiv, -nə tiv), *adj.* **1.** serving to determine; determining. —*n.* **2.** something that determines. **3.** a graphic symbol used in ideographic writing to denote a semantic class and written next to a word to indicate in what semantic category that word is to be understood, thus at times distinguishing homographs. [prob. < ML *dēterminātīv(us)* fixed, LL: crucial (of a disease), equiv. to L *dētermināt(us)* (see DETERMINATE) + *-īvus* -IVE] —**de·ter′mi·na′tive·ly,** *adv.* —**de·ter′mi·na′tive·ness,** *n.*
—**Syn. 1.** concluding, conclusive, deciding, settling. **2.** precipitant, determinant, determiner.

de·ter·mine (di tûr′min), *v.*, **-mined, -min·ing.** —*v.t.* **1.** to settle or decide (a dispute, question, etc.) by an authoritative or conclusive decision. **2.** to conclude or ascertain, as after reasoning, observation, etc. **3.** *Geom.* to fix the position of. **4.** to cause, affect, or control; fix or decide causally: *Demand for a product usually determines supply.* **5.** to give direction or tendency to; impel. **6.** *Logic.* to limit (a notion) by adding differentiating characteristics. **7.** *Chiefly Law.* to put an end to; terminate. **8.** to lead or bring (a person) to a decision. **9.** to decide upon. —*v.i.* **10.** to come to a decision or resolution; decide. **11.** *Chiefly Law.* to come to an end. [ME *determine(n)* < OF *determin(er)* < L *dētermināre,* equiv. to *dē-* DE- + *termināre* to bound, limit; see TERMINATE]
—**Syn. 1.** resolve, adjust. See **decide. 2.** verify. **4.** influence. **5.** induce, lead, incline.

de·ter·mined (di tûr′mind), *adj.* **1.** resolute; unwaveringly decided; staunch: *the determined defenders of the Alamo.* **2.** decided; settled; resolved. **3.** *Gram.* (of a phonetic feature) predictable from its surrounding context. [DETERMINE + -ED[2]] —**de·ter′mined·ly,** *adv.* —**de·ter′mined·ness,** *n.*
—**Syn. 1.** inflexible, rigid, unfaltering, unwavering.

de·ter·min·er (di tûr′mə nər), *n.* **1.** one who or that which determines. **2.** *Gram.* a member of a subclass of English adjectival words that limits the nouns it modifies in a special way and that usually is placed before descriptive adjectives, as *a, an, the, your, their.* [DETERMINE + -ER[1]]

de·ter·min·ism (di tûr′mə niz′əm), *n.* **1.** the doctrine that all facts and events exemplify natural laws. **2.** the doctrine that all events, including human choices and decisions, have sufficient causes. [DETERMINE + -ISM] —**de·ter′min·ist,** *n., adj.* —**de·ter′min·is′tic,** *adj.*

de·ter·rent (di tûr′ənt, -tur′-, -ter′-), *adj.* **1.** serving or tending to deter. —*n.* **2.** something that deters: *a deterrent to crime.* **3.** military strength or an ability to retaliate sufficiently to frighten an enemy from attacking. [< L *dēterrent-* (s. of *dēterrēns*), prp. of *dēterrēre.* See DETER, -ENT] —**de·ter′rence,** *n.*

de·ter·sive (di tûr′siv), *adj.* **1.** cleansing; detergent. —*n.* **2.** a detergent, esp. a detersive agent or medicine. [< F *détersif* < L (medical) *dētersīv(us),* equiv. to L *dēters(us)* (ptp. of *dētergēre;* see DETERGE) + *-īvus* -IVE] —**de·ter′sive·ly,** *adv.* —**de·ter′sive·ness,** *n.*

de·test (di test′), *v.t.* to feel abhorrence of; hate; dislike intensely. [< MF *detest(er)* < L *dētestārī,* lit., to curse while calling a deity to witness, equiv. to *dē-* DE- + *testārī* to bear witness; see TESTATE] —**de·test′er,** *n.*
—**Syn.** abhor, loathe, abominate, execrate, despise. See **hate.** —**Ant.** love, like.

de·test·a·ble (di tes′tə bəl), *adj.* deserving to be detested; abominable; hateful. [ME < OF < L *dētestābil(is),* equiv. to *dētest(ārī)* (to) DETEST + *-ābilis* -ABLE] —**de·test′a·bil′i·ty, de·test′a·ble·ness,** *n.* —**de·test′a·bly,** *adv.*
—**Syn.** execrable, abhorrent, loathsome, odious, vile.

de·tes·ta·tion (dē′te stā′shən), *n.* **1.** abhorrence; hatred. **2.** a person or thing detested. [ME *detestacion* < L *dētestātiōn-* (s. of *dētestātiō*), equiv. to *dētestāt(us)* (ptp. of *dētestārī* to DETEST; see -ATE[1]) + *-iōn-* -ION]

de·throne (dē thrōn′), *v.t.*, **-throned, -thron·ing.** to remove from a throne; depose. [DE- + THRONE] —**de·throne′ment,** *n.* —**de·thron′er,** *n.*

det. in dup., (in prescriptions) let twice as much be given. [< L *dētur in duplō*]

det·i·nue (det′ᵊnōō′, -ᵊnyōō′), *n.* *Law.* an old common-law form of action to recover possession of personal property wrongfully detained. [ME *detenu* < OF *detenue* detention, orig. fem. ptp. of *detenir* to DETAIN]

det·o·nate (det′ᵊnāt′), *v.*, **-nat·ed, -nat·ing.** —*v.i.* **1.** to explode with suddenness and violence. —*v.t.* **2.** to cause (something explosive) to explode. [< L *dētonāt(us)* thundered forth (ptp. of *dētonāre*), equiv. to *dē-* DE- + *ton(āre)* (to) THUNDER + *-ātus* -ATE[1]] —**det·o·na·bil·i·ty** (det′ᵊnə bil′i tē), **det′o·nat′a·bil′i·ty,** *n.* —**det′o·na·ble,** *adj.*

det·o·na·tion (det′ᵊnā′shən), *n.* **1.** the act of detonating. **2.** an explosion. [< ML *dētonātiōn-* (s. of *dētonātiō*), equiv. to L *dētonāt(us)* (see DETONATE) + *-iōn-* -ION] —**det′o·na′tive,** *adj.*

det·o·na·tor (det′ᵊnā′tər), *n.* **1.** a device, as a percussion cap or an explosive, used to make another substance explode. **2.** something that explodes. [DETONATE + -OR[2]]

de·tour (dē′tŏŏr, di tŏŏr′), *n.* **1.** a roundabout or circuitous way or course, esp. one used temporarily instead of the main route. **2.** an indirect or roundabout procedure, path, etc. —*v.i.* **3.** to make a detour; go by way of a detour. —*v.t.* **4.** to cause to make a detour; send by way of a detour. **5.** to make a detour around: *We detoured Birmingham.* [< F *détour,* OF *destor,* deriv. of *destorner* to turn aside, equiv. to *des-* DE- + *torner* to TURN]

de·tox·i·cate (dē tok′sə kāt′), *v.t.*, **-cat·ed, -cat·ing.** to detoxify. [DE- + L *toxic(um)* poison (see TOXIC) + -ATE[1]] —**de·tox·i·cant** (dē tok′sə kənt), *adj., n.* —**de·tox′i·ca′tor,** *n.*

de·tox·i·ca·tion (dē tok′sə kā′shən), *n.* detoxification. [DETOXICATE + -ION]

de·tox·i·fi·ca·tion (dē tok′sə fə kā′shən), *n.* **1.** *Biochem.* the metabolic process by which toxins are changed into less toxic or more readily excretable substances. **2.** the act of detoxifying. **3.** the state of being detoxified. [alter. of DETOXICATION]

de·tox·i·fy (dē tok′sə fī′), *v.t.*, **-fied, -fy·ing.** to rid of poison or the effect of poison. [back formation from DETOXIFICATION]

de·tract (di trakt′), *v.t.* **1.** to draw away or divert; distract: *to detract another's attention from more important issues.* **2.** *Archaic.* to take away (a part); abate: *The dilapidated barn detracts charm from the landscape.* —*v.i.* **3.** to take away a part, as from quality, value, or reputation (usually fol. by *from*). [ME < L *dētract(us)* drawn away (ptp. of *dētrahere*), equiv. to *dē-* DE- + *tractus* drawn; see TRACT[1]] —**de·tract′ing·ly,** *adv.* —**de·trac′tor,** *n.*

de·trac·tion (di trak′shən), *n.* the act of disparaging or belittling the reputation or worth of a person, work, etc. [ME *detraccion* < LL *dētractiōn-* (s. of *dētractiō*), equiv. to L *dētract(us)* (see DETRACT) + *-iōn-* -ION]
—**Syn.** defamation, vilification, aspersion, depreciation, calumny, slander, abuse. —**Ant.** praise.

de·trac·tive (di trak′tiv), *adj.* tending or seeking to detract; depreciative. Also, **de·trac·to·ry** (di trak′tə rē). [ME < OF *detractif.* See DETRACT, -IVE] —**de·trac′tive·ly,** *adv.* —**de·trac′tive·ness,** *n.*

de·train (dē trān′), *v.i.* **1.** to alight from a railway train; arrive by train. **2.** *Meteorol.* to transfer air from an organized air current to the surrounding atmosphere (opposed to *entrain*). [DE- + TRAIN] —**de·train′ment,** *n.*

de·trib·al·ize (dē trī′bə līz′), *v.t.*, **-ized, -iz·ing.** to cause to lose tribal allegiances and customs, chiefly through contact with another culture: *an attempt to detribalize African native.* [DE- + TRIBAL + -IZE] —**de·trib′al·i·za′tion,** *n.*

det·ri·ment (de′trə mənt), *n.* **1.** loss, damage, disadvantage, or injury. **2.** a cause of loss or damage. [ME < L *dētrīment(um)* loss, damage, equiv. to *dētrī(tus)* (see DETRITUS) + *-mentum* -MENT]
—**Syn. 1.** harm, hurt, impairment, prejudice. See **damage.** —**Ant. 1.** advantage.

det·ri·men·tal (de′trə men′tᵊl), *adj.* causing detriment; damaging, harmful, disadvantageous, or injurious. [DETRIMENT + -AL[1]] —**det·ri·men·tal·i·ty** (de′trə men tal′i tē), **det′ri·men′tal·ness,** *n.* —**det′ri·men′tal·ly,** *adv.* —**Syn.** hurtful; deleterious, noxious.

de·tri·tal (di trīt′ᵊl), *adj.* composed of detritus. [DETRIT(US) + -AL[1]]

de·tri·tion (di trish′ən), *n.* the act of wearing away by rubbing. [< ML *dētrītiōn-* (s. of *dētrītiō*), equiv. to L *dētrīt(us)* (see DETRITUS) + *-iōn-* -ION]

det·ri·tiv·or·ous (de′tri tiv′ər əs), *adj.* feeding on organic waste, as certain insects. Also, **de·triv·or·ous** (di triv′ər əs). [DETRIT(US) + -I- + -VOROUS]

de·tri·tus (di trī′təs), *n.* **1.** rock in small particles or other material worn or broken away from a mass, as by the action of water or glacial ice. **2.** any disintegrated material; debris. [< F *détritus* < L: a rubbing away, n. use of *dētrītus*, ptp. of *dēterere*, equiv. to *dē-* DE- + *terere* to rub]

De·troit (di troit′), *n.* **1.** a city in SE Michigan, on the Detroit River. 1,670,144 (1960). **2.** a river in SE Michigan, flowing S from Lake St. Clair to Lake Erie, forming part of the boundary between the U.S. and Canada. ab. 32 mi. long.

Detroit′ Lakes′, a town in W Minnesota. 5633 (1960).

de trop (də trō′), *French.* **1.** too much; too many. **2.** in the way; not wanted.

de·trude (di tro͞od′), *v.t.*, **-trud·ed, -trud·ing. 1.** to thrust out or away. **2.** to thrust or force down. [ME < L *dētrūd(ere)* (to) thrust down, drive away, equiv. to *dē-* DE- + *trūdere* to thrust, drive, force]

de·trun·cate (di trung′kāt), *v.t.*, **-cat·ed, -cat·ing.** to reduce by cutting off a part; cut down. [< L *dētruncāt(us)* (ptp. of *dētruncāre*). See DE-, TRUNCATE] —**de′trun·ca′tion,** *n.*

de·tru·sion (di tro͞o′zhən), *n.* the act of detruding. [< LL *dētrūsiōn-* (s. of *dētrūsiō*) a thrusting down, equiv. to L *dētrūs(us)* (ptp. of *dētrūdere*; see DETRUDE) + *-iōn-* -ION] —**de·tru′sive,** *adj.*

de·tu·mes·cence (dē′to͞o mes′əns, -tyo͞o-), *n.* subsidence of swelling. [< L *dētumesc(ere)* (to) cease swelling (*dē-* DE- + *tumescere* to swell + -ENCE; see TUMESCENCE]

Deu·ca·li·on (do͞o kā′lē ən, dyo͞o-), *n.* *Class. Myth.* a son of Prometheus who survived the deluge with his wife, Pyrrha, to become the founder of the renewed human race.

deuce[1] (do͞os, dyo͞os), *n.* **1.** *Cards.* a card having two pips; a two, or two spot. **2.** *Dice.* **a.** the face of a die having two pips. **b.** a cast or point of two. **3.** *Tennis.* a situation, as a score of 40–40 in a game or 5–5 in a match, in which a player must score two successive points to win the game or two successive games to win the set. **4.** *U.S. Slang.* **a.** a two-dollar bill. **b.** the sum of two dollars. —*adj.* **5.** (esp. in games, sports, and gambling) two. [< MF *deus* two < L *duos* (m. acc. of *duo*)]

deuce[2] (do͞os, dyo͞os), *n.* *Informal.* devil; dickens (used as a mild oath): *Where the deuce did they hide it?* [ME *deus*, special use of DEUCE[1]]

deuc·ed (do͞o′sid, dyo͞o′-; do͞ost, dyo͞ost), *Chiefly Brit. Informal.* —*adj.* **1.** devilish; confounded; damned. —*adv.* **2.** deucedly. [DEUCE[2] + -ED[3]]

deuc·ed·ly (do͞o′sid lē, dyo͞o′-), *adv.* *Chiefly Brit. Informal.* devilishly; confoundedly; damnably. [DEUCED + -LY]

deuc′es wild′, *Cards.* a variety or method of playing certain poker and other games in which a deuce represents any suit or denomination that the holder chooses: *We're playing five-card stud, deuces wild.*

De·us·ded·it (dē′əs ded′it, -dē′dit), *n.* **Saint,** died A.D. 618, Italian ecclesiastic: pope 615–618. Also called **Adeodatus I.**

de·us ex ma·chi·na (de′o͝os eks mä′ki nä′; *Eng.* dē′əs eks mak′ə nə, dā′-), *Latin.* **1.** (in Greek drama) a god who resolves the entanglements of the play by his supernatural intervention. **2.** any artificial, forced, or improbable device used to resolve the difficulties of a plot. [lit., god from a machine]

De·us Mi·se·re·a·tur (dā′o͝os mē′sā rā ä′to͝or), *Latin.* (May) God have mercy; God be merciful: title of Psalm 67.

De·us Ra·mos (de′o͞osh rä′mo͞osh), **Jo·ão de** (zhwoun də), 1830–96, Portuguese poet.

De·us vo·bis·cum (dā′o͝os vō bis′ko͝om), *Latin.* God be with you.

De·us vult (dā′o͝os vo͝olt′), *Latin.* God wills (it): cry of the Crusaders.

deut-, var. of **deuto-** before a vowel.

Deut., Deuteronomy.

deuter-, var. of **deutero-** before a vowel: *deuteron.*

deu·ter·ag·o·nist (do͞o′tə rag′ə nist, dyo͞o′-), *n.* (in classical Greek drama) the character second in importance to the protagonist, esp. one serving as antagonist. [< Gk *deuteragōnist(ḗs).* See DEUTER-, AGONIST]

deu·ter·a·nom·a·ly (do͞o′tər ə nom′ə lē, dyo͞o′-), *n.* *Ophthalm.* a defect of vision characterized by a diminished response of the retina to green. [< NL *deuteranomalia.* See DEUTER-, ANOMALY] —**deu′ter·a·nom′a·lous,** *adj.* —**deu·ter·an·o·mal** (do͞o′tər an′ə məl, dyo͞o′-), *n.*

deu·ter·an·ope (do͞o′tər ə nōp′, dyo͞o′-), *n.* *Ophthalm.* a person who has deuteranopia. [back formation from DEUTERANOPIA]

deu·ter·a·no·pi·a (do͞o′tər ə nō′pē ə, dyo͞o′-), *n.* *Ophthalm.* a defect of vision in which the retina fails to respond to green. [< NL; see DEUTER-, ANOPIA] —**deu·ter·an·op·ic** (do͞o′tər ə nop′ik, dyo͞o′-), *adj.*

deu·te·ri·um (do͞o tēr′ē əm, dyo͞o-), *n.* *Chem.* an isotope of hydrogen, having twice the mass of ordinary hydrogen; heavy hydrogen. *Symbol:* D; *at. no.:* 1; *at. wt.:* 2.01. [< NL < Gk *deuter(eion)* of second quality (neut. of *deutereîos*), equiv. to *deúter(os)* second (see DEUTER-) + *-ei* adj. suffix + *-on* neut. sing. suffix]

deute′rium ox′ide, *Chem.* heavy water, D_2O.

deutero-, a learned borrowing from Greek, where it meant "second," used in the formation of compound words (*deuterocanonical*), sometimes specialized as a combining form of **deuterium** (*deuteron*). Also, **deut-, deuter-, deuto-.** [< Gk, comb. form of *deúteros*]

deu′ter·o·ca·non′ical books′ (do͞o′tə rō kə non′i kəl, dyo͞o′-, do͞o′-, dyo͞o′-), the books of the Bible regarded by the Roman Catholic Church as canonical but not universally acknowledged as such in the early church, including, in the Old Testament, most of the Protestant Apocrypha. [DEUTERO- + CANONICAL]

deu·ter·og·a·my (do͞o′tə rog′ə mē, dyo͞o′-), *n.* a second marriage, after the death or divorce of a first husband or wife. Cf. **monogamy** (def. 3). [< Gk *deuterogamía* a second marriage. See DEUTERO-, -GAMY] —**deu′ter·og′a·mist,** *n.*

deu·ter·on (do͞o′tə ron′, dyo͞o′-), *n.* *Physics.* a positively charged particle consisting of a proton and a neutron, equivalent to the nucleus of an atom of deuterium. Cf. **triton.** [DEUTER- + -ON[1]]

Deu·ter·o·nom·ic (do͞o′tər ə nom′ik, dyo͞o′-), *adj.* of, pertaining to, or resembling Deuteronomy, esp. the laws contained in that book. [DEUTERONOM(Y) + -IC]

Deu·ter·on·o·my (do͞o′tə ron′ə mē, dyo͞o′-), *n.* the fifth book of the Pentateuch, containing a second statement of the Mosaic law. [< LL *Deuteronomi(um)* < Gk *Deuteronómion* (see DEUTERO-, -NOMY); earlier *Deutronome*, ME *Deutronomie* < LL]

deu·ter·ot·o·ky (do͞o′tə rot′ə kē, dyo͞o′-), *n.* production of both males and females parthenogenetically. [DEUTERO- + Gk *-tokia*, equiv. to *-tok(os)* child (akin to *tíktein* to bear) + *-ia* -Y[3]]

deuto-, var. of **deutero-:** *deutoplasm.* Also, *esp. before a vowel,* **deut-.**

deu·ton (do͞o′ton, dyo͞o′-), *n.* *Physics.* (no longer current) deuteron.

deu·to·plasm (do͞o′tə plaz′əm, dyo͞o′-), *n.* *Embryol.* the nonliving, nutritive material, as a yolk granule, in the ovarian cytoplasm. [DEUTO- + -PLASM] —**deu′to·plas′mic,** *adj.*

Deutsch (doich), *n.* **Babette,** born 1895, U.S. poet, novelist, and critic.

Deut·sche blu·men (doi′chə blo͞o′mən), a form of porcelain decoration of the mid-18th century, derived from botanical engravings of European flowers. [< G: German flowers]

Deut′sche mark′ (doi′chə, doich), a cupronickel coin, the monetary unit of Germany, equal to 100 pfennigs: replaced the reichsmark in 1948. *Abbr.:* DM. Also, **Deut′sche·mark′.** Cf. **ostmark.** [< G: German mark]

Deut·scher (doi′chər), *n.* **Isaac,** 1907–1967, English journalist and author, born in Poland.

Deut·sches Reich (doi′chəs rīkh′), former official name of **Germany.**

Deutsch·land (doich′länt′), *n.* German name of **Germany.**

Deutsch′land ü′ber al′les (Y′bər ä′ləs), *German.* Germany over all.

deut·zi·a (do͞ot′sē ə, dyo͞ot′-, doit′-), *n.* any saxifragaceous shrub of the genus *Deutzia*, having showy white, bluish, pink, or purplish flowers, grown as an ornamental. [< NL, named after Jean *Deutz*, 18th-century Dutch botanical patrod; see -IA]

Deux-Sè·vres (dœ seʹvrᵊ), *n.* a department in W France. 321,118 (1962); 2338 sq. mi. *Cap.:* Niort.

de·va (dā′və), *n.* *Hindu Myth.* a god or divinity; one of an order of good spirits. [< Skt]

De·va (dē′və), *n.* a girl's given name.

de·va·da·si (dā′və dä′sē), *n.* (formerly, in India) **1.** a member of an ancient caste whose daughters were offered to the temples as dancing girls. **2.** a temple dancer. **3.** a temple courtesan. [< Skt *devadāsī*: lit., servant of a god]

De Va·le·ra (dev′ə lâr′ə, -lēr′ə; *Irish.* de vä lā′rä), **Ea·mon** (ā′mən), 1882–1975, Irish political leader and statesman, born in the U.S.: prime minister of the Republic of Ireland 1932–48, 1951–54, 1957–59; president 1959–73.

de Val·ois (də val′wä), **Dame Ni·nette** (ni net′), (*Edris Stannus*), born 1898, English ballet dancer and choreographer.

de·val·u·ate (dē val′yo͞o āt′), *v.t.*, **-at·ed, -at·ing. 1.** to deprive of value; reduce the value of. **2.** to fix a lower legal value on (a currency). [DE- + VALUE + -ATE[1]]

de·val·u·a·tion (dē val′yo͞o ā′shən), *n.* **1.** an official lowering of the legal exchange value of a country's currency by reducing the currency's gold equivalency. **2.** a reduction of a value, status, etc. [DEVALUATE + -ION]

de·val·ue (dē val′yo͞o), *v.t.*, **-val·ued, -val·u·ing.** to devaluate. [DE- + VALUE]

De·va·na·ga·ri (dā′və nä′gə rē′), *n.* an alphabetical script with some syllabic features derived from Brahmi, used for the writing of Hindi and many other languages of India including Sanskrit. Also called **Nagari.** [< Skt: lit., Nagari (an alphabet of India) of the gods]

dev·as·tate (dev′ə stāt′), *v.t.*, **-tat·ed, -tat·ing. 1.** to lay waste; render desolate: *The invaders devastated the city.* **2.** to overwhelm. [< L *dēvastāt(us)* laid waste (ptp. of *dēvastāre*), equiv. to *dē-* DE- + *vast(āre)* (to) lay waste (akin to *vastus* empty) + *-ātus* -ATE[1]] —**dev′as·ta′tive,** *adj.* —**dev′as·ta′tor,** *n.*
—**Syn. 1.** destroy, sack, despoil. See **ravage.**

dev·as·tat·ing (dev′ə stā′ting), *adj.* **1.** tending or threatening to devastate: *a devastating fire.* **2.** satirical, ironic, or caustic in an effective way: *a devastating reply to an impudent remark; a devastating portrayal of society between the World Wars.* [DEVASTATE + -ING[2]]

dev·as·ta·tion (dev′ə stā′shən), *n.* **1.** the act of devastating; destruction. **2.** devastated state; desolation. [ME < LL *dēvastātiōn-* (s. of *dēvastātiō*), equiv. to L *dēvastāt(us)* (see DEVASTATE) + *-iōn-* -ION]

de Ve·ga (də vā′gə; *Sp.* de be′gä), *n.* **Lo·pe** (lō′pā, -pē; *Sp.* lô′pe), (*Lope Félix de Vega Carpio*), 1562–1635, Spanish dramatist and poet.

dev·el (dev′əl), *n.* *Scot.* a heavy blow. [?]

devel., development.

de·vel·op (di vel′əp), *v.t.* **1.** to bring out the capabilities or possibilities of; bring to a more advanced or effective state: *to develop natural resources.* **2.** to cause to grow or expand: *to develop one's muscles.* **3.** to elaborate or expand in detail: *to develop a theory.* **4.** to bring into being or activity; generate; evolve. **5.** to transfer the details of (a more or less two-dimensional design, pattern, or the like) from one surface, esp. one that is prismatic or cylindrical, onto another, usually planar, in such a way that the distances between points remain the same. **6.** *Biol.* to cause to go through the process of natural evolution from a previous and lower stage, or from an embryonic state to a later and more complex or perfect one. **7.** *Math.* **a.** to express in an extended form, as in a series. **b.** to project (a surface) onto a plane. **8.** *Music.* to unfold, by various technical means, the inherent possibilities of (a theme). **9.** *Photog.* **a.** to render visible (the latent image on an exposed film or the like). **b.** to treat (an exposed film or the like) with chemicals so as to render the latent image visible. **10.** *Chess.* to bring (a piece) into effective play, esp. during the initial phase of a game when pieces are moved from their original position on the board: *He developed his rook by castling.* **11.** *Mining.* to prepare (a new mine) for working by digging access openings and building necessary structures. —*v.i.* **12.** to grow into a more mature or advanced state; advance; expand: *He is developing into a good citizen.* **13.** to come gradually into existence or operation; be evolved. **14.** to be disclosed; become evident or manifest: *The plot of the novel developed slowly.* **15.** *Biol.* to undergo differentiation in ontogeny or progress in phylogeny. **16.** to undergo developing, as a photographic plate. Also, **develope.** [< F *développ(er)*, OF *desveloper*, equiv. to *des-* DIS-[1] + *veloper* to wrap up; see ENVELOP] —**de·vel′op·a·bil′i·ty,** *n.* —**de·vel′op·a·ble,** *adj.*

de·vel·ope (di vel′əp), *v.i., v.t.*, **-oped, -op·ing.** develop.

de·vel·op·er (di vel′ə pər), *n.* **1.** one who or that which develops. **2.** *Photog.* a reducing agent or solution for developing a film or the like. **3.** a person who invests in and develops the urban or suburban potentialities of real estate, esp. by subdividing the land into home sites and then building houses and selling them. **4.** *Shipbuilding.* one who lays out at full size the lines of a vessel and prepares templates from them; loftsman. [DEVELOP + -ER[1]]

de·vel·op·ing (di vel′ə ping), *adj.* (of a nation or geographical area) having a standard of living and a level of industrial production that are rising fairly rapidly but that are still considerably below the potential levels obtainable with the continuing aid of capital and skilled technicians to develop resources and industries. [DEVELOP + -ING[2]]

de·vel′op·ing-out′ pa′per (di vel′ə ping out′, -vel′-), *Photog.* a sensitized printing paper requiring development in order to bring out the image. *Abbr.:* D.O.P. Cf. **print-out paper.**

de·vel·op·ment (di vel′əp mənt), *n.* **1.** the act or process of developing; progress. **2.** a developed state, form, or product. **3.** *Music.* the part of a movement or composition in which a theme or themes are developed. **4.** a large group of private houses or of apartment houses of similar design, constructed as a unified community, esp. by a government organization. **5.** *Chess.* the act or process of developing chess pieces. **6.** *Mining.* the act of digging openings, as tunnels, raises, and winzes, to give access to new workings, and of erecting necessary structures. Also, **de·vel′ope·ment.** [DEVELOP + -MENT] —**de·vel′op·men′tal, de·vel′op·men′ta·ry,** *adj.* —**de·vel′op·men′tal·ly,** *adv.*
—**Syn. 1.** expansion, elaboration, growth, evolution; unfolding, opening, maturing, maturation. **2.** maturity, ripeness. **4.** community, subdivision. —**Ant. 1.** deterioration, disintegration.

de·vel·op·pé (di vel′ə pā′; *Fr.* devᵊ lô pā′), *n., pl.* **-pés** (-pāz′; *Fr.* -pā′). a movement in ballet in which the free leg is drawn up beside the working leg and then extended into the air. [< F, ptp. of *développer* to DEVELOP]

De·ven·ter (dā′vən tər), *n.* a city in the E Netherlands. 57,973 (1962).

Dev·e·reux (dev′ə ro͞o′), *n.* **Robert, 2nd Earl of Essex,** 1566–1601, British statesman, soldier, and courtier of Queen Elizabeth I.

de·vest (di vest′), *v.t.* **1.** *Law.* to divest. **2.** *Obs.* to remove the clothes from; undress. [< MF *desvest(er)*, var. of OF *desvestir*, equiv. to *des-* DIS-[1] + *vestir* to clothe < L *vestīr(e)*; see DIVEST]

De·vi (dā′vē), *n.* *Hinduism.* **1.** a mother goddess of which Durga, Kali, etc., are particular forms. **2.** Also called **Annapurna, Parvati.** the consort of Shiva, identified with Shakti and Kali as a goddess of love, maternity, and death. [< Skt, fem. of *deva* DEVA]

de·vi·ant (dē′vē ənt), *adj.* **1.** deviating from the norm; characterized by deviation: *deviant social behavior.* —*n.* **2.** one who or that which deviates markedly from the accepted norm: *an intellectual deviant; a mathematical deviant.* [ME < L *dēviant-* (s. of *dēviāns,* prp. of *dēviāre*), equiv. to *dē-* DE- + *via* road, way + *-ant-* -ANT]

de·vi·a·scope (dē′vē ə skōp′), *n.* a device for simulating different types of compass deviation. [DEVIA(TION) + -SCOPE]

de·vi·ate (*v.* dē′vē āt′; *adj., n.* dē′vē it), *v.,* **-at·ed, -at·ing,** *adj., n.* —*v.i.* **1.** to turn aside, as from a route, way, course, etc. **2.** to depart or swerve, as from a procedure, course of action, or acceptable norm. **3.** to digress, as from a line of thought or reasoning. —*v.t.* **4.** to cause to swerve; turn aside. —*adj.* **5.** characterized by deviation from an accepted norm or standard, as of behavior. —*n.* **6.** a person or thing that departs from the accepted norm or standard. **7.** a sexual pervert. **8.** *Statistics.* a variable equal to the difference between a variate and some fixed value, often the mean. [< LL *dēviāt(us)* turned from the straight road, ptp. of *dēviāre.* See DEVIANT, -ATE[1]] —**de·vi·a·bil·i·ty** (dē′vē ə bil′i tē), *n.* —**de′vi·a·ble,** *adj.* —**de′vi·a′tor,** *n.*

—**Syn. 1.** veer, wander, stray. DEVIATE, DIGRESS, DIVERGE, SWERVE imply turning or going aside from a path. To DEVIATE is to turn or wander, often by slight degrees, from what is considered the most direct or desirable approach to a given physical, intellectual, or moral end: *Fear caused him to deviate from the truth.* To DIGRESS is primarily to wander from the main theme or topic in writing or speaking, esp. for explanation or illustration: *Some authors digress to relate entertaining episodes.* Two paths DIVERGE when they proceed from a common point in such directions that the distance between them increases: *The sides of an angle diverge from a common point. Their interests gradually diverged.* To SWERVE is to make a sudden or sharp turn from a line or course (and then, often, return to it): *The car swerved to avoid striking a pedestrian.*

de·vi·a·tion (dē′vē ā′shən), *n.* **1.** the act of deviating. **2.** departure from a standard or norm. **3.** *Statistics.* the difference between one of a set of values and some fixed value, usually the mean of the set. **4.** *Navig.* the error of a magnetic compass, as that of a ship, on a given heading as a result of local magnetism; the angle between the compass meridian and the magnetic meridian, expressed in plus degrees east or minus degrees west of magnetic north. Cf. **variation** (def. 7). **5.** *Optics.* **a.** Also called **deflection.** the bending of rays of light away from a straight line. **b.** See **angle of deviation. 6.** departure or divergence from an established dogma or ideology, esp. a Communist one. [ME < ML *dēviātiōn-* (s. of *dēviātiō*), equiv. to LL *dēviāt(us)* (see DEVIATE) + *-iōn-* -ION] —**de·vi·a·to·ry** (dē′vē ə tôr′ē, -tōr′ē), **de′vi·a′tive,** *adj.*

devia′tion card′, a card recording the deviation of the compass of a vessel or aircraft on various headings.

de·vi·a·tion·ism (dē′vē ā′shə niz′əm), *n.* (in Communist ideology) departure from accepted party policies or practices; deviation from the party line. [DEVIATION + -ISM] —**de′vi·a′tion·ist,** *n.*

de·vice (di vīs′), *n.* **1.** a thing that is made, usually for a particular working purpose; an invention or contrivance, esp. a mechanical or electrical one. **2.** a plan or scheme for effecting a purpose. **3.** a crafty scheme; trick. **4.** a representation or design used as a heraldic charge or as an emblem, badge, trademark, or the like. **5.** a motto. **6.** something elaborately or fancifully designed. **7.** a particular word pattern, figure of speech, combination of word sounds, etc., used in a literary work to evoke a desired effect or arouse a desired reaction in the reader. **8.** *Archaic.* devising; invention. **9. leave to one's own devices,** to leave alone to do as one pleases. [b. ME *devis* division, discourse and *devise* heraldic device, will; both < OF < L *dīvīs(a),* fem. of *dīvīsus;* see DIVISION] —**de·vice′ful,** *adj.* —**de·vice′ful·ly,** *adv.* —**de·vice′ful·ness,** *n.*

—**Syn. 1.** gadget. **2.** project, design. **3.** wile, ruse, artifice, stratagem, maneuver. **5.** slogan, legend.

De Vi·co (də vē′kō), a crater in the third quadrant of the face of the moon: about 13 miles in diameter.

dev·il (dev′əl), *n., v.,* **-iled, -il·ing** or (*esp. Brit.*) **-illed, -il·ling.** —*n.* **1.** *Theol.* **a.** (*sometimes cap.*) the supreme spirit of evil; Satan. **b.** a subordinate evil spirit at enmity with God, and having power to afflict man both with bodily disease and with spiritual corruption. **2.** an atrociously wicked, cruel, or ill-tempered person. **3.** a person of great cleverness, energy, or recklessness. **4.** *Print.* an errand boy or the youngest apprentice in a printing office. **5.** a person, usually one in unfortunate or pitiable circumstances: *The poor devil kept losing jobs through no fault of his own.* **6.** any of various mechanical devices, as a machine for tearing rags, a machine for manufacturing wooden screws, etc. **7.** *Naut.* (in deck or hull planking) any of various seams difficult to pay because of form or position, as between deck planking and the adjacent waterway, or between the keel and a garboard strake. **8.** any of various portable furnaces or braziers used in construction and foundry work. **9. between the devil and the deep blue sea,** between two undesirable alternatives; in an unpleasant dilemma: *His headache was bad, but as he was allergic to aspirin, he was between the devil and the deep blue sea.* **10. devil of a,** damned; hellishly: *I had a devil of a time getting home through the snow last night.* **11. give the devil his due,** to give deserved credit even to a person one dislikes: *To give the devil his due, you must admit that she is competent in her field.* **12. go to the devil, a.** to fail completely; lose all hope or chance of succeeding. **b.** to become depraved. **c.** (an expletive expressing annoyance, disgust, impatience, etc.) **13. let the devil take the hindmost,** to leave the least able or fortunate persons to suffer adverse consequences; leave behind or to one's fate: *We failed to come to their defense as we had promised and let the devil take the hindmost.* **14. play the devil with,** *Informal.* to ruin completely; spoil: *The financial crisis played the devil with our investment plans.* **15. raise the devil, a.** to cause a commotion or disturbance. **b.** to celebrate wildly; revel. **c.** to make an emphatic protest or take drastic measures: *His father warned him that he would raise the devil if his grades did not improve.* **16. the devil!** an emphatic expletive or mild oath used to express disgust, anger, astonishment, negation, etc. **17. the devil to pay,** trouble to be faced; mischief in the offing: *If inflation becomes much worse there will be the devil to pay.* —*v.t.* **18.** *Informal.* to annoy; harass; pester: *to devil Dad for a new car.* **19.** to tear (rags, cloth, etc.) with a devil. **20.** *Cookery.* to prepare (food, usually finely chopped) with hot or savory seasoning. [ME *devel,* OE *dēofol* < L *diabolus* < Gk *diábolos* slanderer]

Dev′il and Dan′iel Web′ster, The, a short story (1937) by Stephen Vincent Benét.

dev′il dog′, *Informal.* a United States Marine.

dev·iled (dev′əld), *adj. Cookery.* prepared with hot or savory seasoning, usually after being finely chopped: *deviled eggs; deviled crab.* [DEVIL + -ED[2]]

dev·il·fish (dev′əl fish′), *n., pl.* (*esp. collectively*) **-fish,** (*esp. referring to two or more kinds or species*) **-fish·es. 1.** any of several huge rays of the family *Mobulidae,* esp. of the genus *Manta,* found in tropical waters, having a pair of fleshy horns on the head. **2.** an octopus. [DEVIL + FISH]

Devilfish,
Manta hamiltoni
(18 ft. across "wing tips"; total length 20 ft.; tail 6 ft.)

dev′il grass′. See **Bermuda grass.**

dev·il-in-the-bush (dev′əl in thə bo͝osh′, -bo͝osh′), *n.* love-in-a-mist.

dev·il·ish (dev′ə lish, dev′lish), *adj.* **1.** of, like, or befitting a devil; diabolical; fiendish. **2.** *Informal.* excessive; very great: *He's in a devilish mess.* —*adv.* **3.** *Informal.* excessively; extremely: *He's devilish proud of himself.* [DEVIL + -ISH[1]] —**dev′il·ish·ly,** *adv.* —**dev′il·ish·ness,** *n.*

—**Syn. 1.** satanic, demoniac, infernal.

dev·il·kin (dev′əl kin), *n.* a little devil; imp. [DEVIL + -KIN]

dev·il-may-care (dev′əl mā kâr′), *adj.* reckless; careless; rollicking.

dev·il·ment (dev′əl mənt), *n.* devilish action or conduct; mischief. [DEVIL + -MENT]

dev·il·ry (dev′əl rē), *n., pl.* **-ries.** deviltry. [ME; see DEVIL, -RY]

dev′il's ad′vocate, 1. one who advocates an opposing or bad cause, esp. for the sake of argument. **2.** Also called **promoter of the faith.** *Rom. Cath. Ch.* an official appointed to present arguments against a proposed beatification or canonization of a beatus. **3.** an adverse critic, esp. of what is deemed good; detractor. [trans. of NL *advocātus diabolī*]

dev·il's-bit (dev′əlz bit′), *n.* gay-feather (def. 2).

dev′il's claw′, *Naut.* a hook on deck for holding an anchor chain by one of its links.

dev′il's darn′ing nee′dle, a dragonfly.

Dev′il's Disci′ple, The, a play (1900) by G. B. Shaw.

dev′il's dung′, asafetida.

dev′il's food′ cake′, a rich, chocolate cake. [modeled on ANGEL FOOD CAKE]

dev′il's grip′, *Pathol.* pleurodynia (def. 2).

Dev′il's Is′land, one of the Safety Islands, off the coast of French Guiana: former French penal colony. French, **Île du Diable.**

dev′il's i′vy. See **hunter's robe.**

Dev′ils Lake′, a town in central North Dakota. 6299 (1960).

dev′il's mark′, (in witchcraft) a mark, as a scar or blemish, on the body of a person who has made a compact with a devil. Also called **witch's mark.**

dev′il's paint′brush. See **orange hawkweed.**

dev·il's-pin·cush·ion (dev′əlz pin′ko͝osh′ən), *n.* a small, globe-shaped cactus, *Coryphantha robustispina,* of southwestern North America, having numerous, interlocking spines and salmon-pink flowers. Also called **pineapple cactus.**

dev′il's tattoo′, a meaningless beating or drumming with the hands or feet: *to beat the devil's tattoo.*

dev·il's-tongue (dev′əlz tung′), *n.* a foul-smelling, fleshy herb, *Hydrosme rivieri,* of the Old World tropics, having flowers on a spadix surrounded by a dark-red spathe. Also called **snake palm.**

dev·il's-walk·ing-stick (dev′əlz wô′king stik′), *n.* Hercules'-club (def. 2).

dev·il·try (dev′əl trē), *n., pl.* **-tries. 1.** reckless or unrestrained mischievous behavior; mischief. **2.** extreme or utter wickedness. **3.** an act or instance of mischievous or wicked behavior. **4.** diabolic magic or art. **5.** demonology. Also, **devilry.** [var. of DEVILRY]

dev·il·wood (dev′əl wo͝od′), *n.* a small, oleaceous tree, *Osmanthus americanus,* of the U.S., yielding a hard wood. [DEVIL + WOOD[1]]

De·vine (də vīn′), *n.* a town in SW Texas. 2522 (1960).

de·vi·ous (dē′vē əs), *adj.* **1.** departing from the shortest way; circuitous; indirect: *a devious course.* **2.** without definite course; vagrant: *a devious current.* **3.** departing from the proper or accepted way; roundabout: *a devious procedure for accomplishing a very simple result.* **4.** not straightforward; shifty or crooked; using unexpected or unfair methods; tricky; deceptive; deceitful: *a devious person; a devious scheme to acquire sudden wealth.* [< L *dēvi(us)* lying off the road, equiv. to *dē-* DE- + *vi(a)* road, way + -OUS] —**de′vi·ous·ly,** *adv.* —**de′vi·ous·ness,** *n.*

—**Syn. 1.** roundabout, tortuous, involved. **4.** subtle, cunning, crafty, artful, sly, underhand; insidious; surreptitious, secret; stealthy, furtive.

de·vis·a·ble (di vī′zə bəl), *adj.* **1.** capable of being devised, invented, or contrived. **2.** *Law.* capable of being transferred. [ME < AF: assignable by will, OF: that which may be divided, equiv. to *devis(er)* (see DEVISE) + *-able* -ABLE]

de·vis·al (di vī′zəl), *n.* the act of devising; contrivance. [DEVISE + -AL[2]]

de·vise (di vīz′), *v.,* **-vised, -vis·ing,** *n.* —*v.t.* **1.** to contrive, plan, or elaborate; invent from existing principles or ideas: *to devise a method.* **2.** *Law.* to assign or transmit (property, esp. real property) by will. **3.** *Archaic.* to imagine; suppose. —*v.i.* **4.** to form a plan; contrive. —*n.* **5.** *Law.* **a.** the act of disposing of property, esp. real property, by will. **b.** a will or clause in a will disposing of property, esp. real property. **c.** the property disposed of. [ME *devise(n)* < OF *devis(er)* < VL **dīvīsāre,* freq. of *dīvidere* to DIVIDE] —**de·vis′er,** *n.*

—**Syn. 1.** concoct, scheme, project, design. See **prepare.**

de·vi·see (di vī zē′, dev′i zē′), *n. Law.* one to whom a devise is made. [DEVISE + -EE]

de·vi·sor (di vī′zər), *n. Law.* one who makes a devise. [ME < AF *devisour* (OF *deviseur*). See DEVISE, -OR[2]]

de·vi·tal·ise (dē vīt′əlīz′), *v.t.,* **-ised, -is·ing.** *Chiefly Brit.* devitalize. —**de·vi′tal·i·sa′tion,** *n.*

de·vi·tal·ize (dē vīt′əlīz′), *v.t.,* **-ized, -iz·ing.** to deprive of vitality or vital properties; make lifeless; weaken. [DE- + VITALIZE] —**de·vi′tal·i·za′tion,** *n.*

—**Ant.** invigorate.

de·vit·ri·fy (dē vi′trə fī′), *v.t.,* **-fied, -fy·ing.** to deprive, wholly or partly, of vitreous character or properties. [DE- + VITRIFY] —**de·vit′ri·fi·ca′tion,** *n.*

de·vo·cal·ise (dē vō′kə līz′), *v.t.,* **-ised, -is·ing.** *Chiefly Brit.* devocalize. —**de·vo′cal·i·sa′tion,** *n.*

de·vo·cal·ize (dē vō′kə līz′), *v.t.,* **-ized, -iz·ing.** *Phonet.* to unvoice. [DE- + VOCALIZE] —**de·vo′cal·i·za′tion,** *n.*

de·voice (dē vois′), *v.t., v.i.,* **-voiced, -voic·ing.** *Phonet.* unvoice. [DE- + VOICE]

de·void (di void′), *adj.* not possessing, untouched by, void, or destitute (usually fol. by *of*). [ME, orig. ptp. < OF *desvuid(ier)* (to) empty out, equiv. to *des-* DIS-[1] + *vuidier* to empty, VOID]

de·voir (də vwär′, dev′wär; *Fr.* də VWAR′), *n., pl.* **de·voirs** (də vwärz′, dev′wärz; *Fr.* də VWAR′). **1.** an act of civility or respect. **2. devoirs,** respects or compliments. **3.** something for which one is responsible; duty. [ME *devoir, deveir, dever* < OF *devoir* (AF *deveir, dever*) < L *dēbēre* to owe; see DEBT]

de·vol·a·til·ise (dē vol′ə təlīz′), *v.t., v.i.,* **-ised, -is·ing.** *Chiefly Brit.* devolatilize. —**de·vol′a·til·i·sa′tion,** *n.*

de·vol·a·til·ize (dē vol′ə təlīz′), *v.,* **-ized, -iz·ing.** *Chem.* —*v.t.* **1.** to cause (a vapor) to liquefy. —*v.i.* **2.** (of a vapor) to liquefy. [DE- + VOLATILIZE] —**de·vol′a·til·i·za′tion,** *n.*

dev·o·lu·tion (dev′ə lo͞o′shən), *n.* **1.** the act or fact of devolving; passage onward from stage to stage. **2.** the passing on to a successor of an unexercised right. **3.** *Law.* the passing of property upon death, as to an heir. **4.** *Biol.* degeneration; retrograde evolution. **5.** the transfer of power or authority from a central government to a local government. [< ML *dēvolūtiōn-* (s. of *dēvolūtiō*) a rolling down, equiv. to L *dēvolūt(us)* rolled down (ptp. of *dēvolvere;* see DEVOLVE) + *-iōn-* -ION]

de·volve (di volv′), *v.,* **-volved, -volv·ing.** —*v.t.* **1.** to transfer or delegate (a duty, responsibility, etc.) to or upon another; pass on. **2.** *Archaic.* to cause to roll downward. —*v.i.* **3.** to be transferred or passed on from one to another: *The responsibility devolved on me.* **4.** *Archaic.* to roll or flow downward. [ME *devolve(n)* < L *dēvolv(ere)* (to) roll down, equiv. to *dē-* DE- + *volvere* to roll] —**de·volve′ment,** *n.*

Dev·on (dev′ən), *n.* **1.** Devonshire. **2.** one of an English breed of red cattle, bred for beef and milk.

De·vo·na (də vō′nə), *n.* a girl's given name.

De·vo·ni·an (də vō′nē ən), *adj.* **1.** *Geol.* noting or pertaining to a period of the Paleozoic era, occurring from 350,000,000 to 400,000,000 years ago and characterized by the dominance of fishes and the advent of amphibians and ammonites. See table under **era. 2.** of or pertaining to Devonshire, England. —*n.* **3.** *Geol.* the Devonian period or system. [DEVON + -IAN]

Dev·on·port (dev′ən pōrt′, -pôrt′), *n.* a city in N Tasmania. 13,068 (1961).

Dev·on·shire (dev′ən shēr′, -shər), *n.* a county in SW England. 822,906 (1961); 2612 sq. mi. *Co. seat:* Exeter. Also called **Devon.**

Dev′onshire cream′, *Brit.* cream that has been clotted by cooking; clotted cream.

de·vote (di vōt′), *v.,* **-vot·ed, -vot·ing,** *adj.* —*v.t.* **1.** to give up or appropriate to or concentrate on a particular pursuit, occupation, purpose, cause, etc.: *devoting himself to science; to devote one's time to reading.* **2.** to appropriate by or as by a vow; set apart or dedicate by a solemn or formal act; consecrate. **3.** *Archaic.* to commit to evil or destruction; doom. —*adj.* **4.** *Archaic.* devoted. [< L *dēvōt(us)* vowed (ptp. of *dēvovēre*), equiv. to *dē-* DE- + *vōtus;* see VOTE, VOW]

—**Syn. 1.** assign, apply, consign.

de·vot·ed (di vō′tid), *adj.* **1.** zealous or ardent in attachment: *a devoted friend.* **2.** dedicated; consecrated. **3.** *Archaic.* accursed or doomed. [DEVOTE + -ED[2]] —**de·vot′ed·ly,** *adv.* —**de·vot′ed·ness,** *n.*

—**Syn. 1.** faithful, constant, loyal, devout.

dev·o·tee (dev′ə tē′), *n.* **1.** a person who is devoted to something. **2.** a person who is extremely devoted to religion. **3.** an enthusiastic follower or fan: *He's a devotee of jazz.* [DEVOTE + -EE]

de·vote·ment (di vōt′mənt), *n.* devotion; dedication. [DEVOTE + -MENT]

de·vo·tion (di vō′shən), *n.* **1.** profound dedication; consecration. **2.** earnest attachment to a cause, person, etc. **3.** an assignment or appropriation to any purpose, cause, etc.: *the devotion of one's wealth and time to scientific advancement.* **4.** *Theol.* the ready will to perform that which belongs to the service of God. **5.** Often, **devotions.** *Eccles.* religious observance or worship; a form of prayer or worship for special use. [ME *devocioun* < LL *dēvōtiōn-* (s. of *dēvōtiō*), equiv. to L *dēvōt(us)* (see DEVOTE) + *-iōn-* -ION]

—**Syn. 2.** zeal, ardor. See **love. 4.** piety, faith, devoutness.

de·vo·tion·al (di vō′shə nəl), *adj.* characterized by devotion; used in devotions. [DEVOTION + -AL[1]] —**de·vo′tion·al′i·ty, de·vo′tion·al·ness,** *n.* —**de·vo′tion·al·ly,** *adv.*

De Vo·to (də vō′tō), **Bernard (Augustine),** 1897–1955, U.S. novelist and critic.

de·vour (di vour′), *v.t.* **1.** to swallow or eat up hungrily, voraciously, or ravenously. **2.** to consume destructively, recklessly, or wantonly: *Fire devoured the old museum.* **3.** to engulf or swallow up. **4.** to take in greedily with the senses or intellect: *to devour the works of Dumas.* **5.** to absorb or engross wholly: *a mind devoured by fears.* [ME *devour(en)* < OF *devour(er)* < L *dēvorāre* to swallow down, equiv. to *dē-* DE- + *vorāre* to eat up] —**de·vour′er,** *n.* —**de·vour′ing·ly,** *adv.* —**de·vour′ing·ness,** *n.*

de·vout (di vout′), *adj.* **1.** devoted to divine worship or service; pious; religious: *a devout Catholic.* **2.** expressing devotion or piety: *devout prayer.* **3.** earnest or sincere; hearty: *He had a devout allegiance to the political regime.* [ME < OF *devo(u)t* < LL *dēvōt(us),* L: devoted; see DEVOTE] —**de·vout′ly,** *adv.* —**de·vout′ness,** *n.*
—**Syn. 1.** worshipful; holy, saintly. See **religious.** —**Ant. 1.** irreverent.

De Vries (də vrēs′; *Du.* də vres′), **Hu·go** (hy o͞o′gō; *Du.* hy′gō), 1848–1935, Dutch botanist and student of organic heredity: developed the concept of mutation as a factor in the process of evolution.

dew (do͞o, dyo͞o), *n.* **1.** moisture condensed from the atmosphere, esp. at night, and deposited in the form of small drops upon any cool surface. **2.** something like or compared to such drops of moisture, as in purity, delicacy, refreshing quality, etc. **3.** moisture in small drops on a surface, as tears, perspiration, etc. **4.** *Informal.* **a.** See **Scotch whisky. b.** See **mountain dew.** —*v.t.* **5.** to wet with or as with dew. [ME; OE *dēaw;* c. G *Tau,* OIcel *dögg*] —**dew′less,** *adj.*

Dew (do͞o, dyo͞o), *n.* **Bay of.** See **Sinus Roris.**

DEW (do͞o, dyo͞o), distant early warning. Cf. **DEW line.**

De·wa·li (də wä′lē), *n.* Diwali.

de·wan (di wän′, -wôn′), *n.* (in India) any of certain officials, as a financial minister, prime minister of a native colony, etc. Also, **diwan.** [< Hindi: minister (of state) < Pers *dēvan* register; see DIVAN]

Dew·ar (do͞o′ər, dyo͞o′-), *n.* **Sir James,** 1842–1923, Scottish chemist and physicist.

Dew′ar ves′sel, a container with an evacuated space between two walls that are highly reflective, capable of maintaining its contents at a near-constant temperature over relatively long periods of time; thermos. Also called **Dewar, Dew′ar flask′.** [named after Sir James DEWAR, its inventor]

de·wa·ter (dē wô′tər, -wot′ər), *v.t.* to remove the water from; dehydrate. [DE- + WATER]

dew·ber·ry (do͞o′ber′ē, -bə rē, dyo͞o′-), *n., pl.* **-ries. 1.** (in North America) the fruit of any of several trailing blackberries of the genus *Rubus.* **2.** (in England) the fruit of a bramble, *Rubus caesius.* **3.** a plant bearing either fruit. [DEW + BERRY]

dew′ cell′, an electrical instrument for measuring the dew point.

dew·claw (do͞o′klô′, dyo͞o′-), *n.* **1.** a functionless inner claw or digit in the foot of some dogs, not reaching the ground in walking. **2.** an analogous false hoof of deer, hogs, etc. [DEW + CLAW] —**dew′clawed′,** *adj.*

D, Dewclaw

dew·drop (do͞o′drop′, dyo͞o′-), *n.* a drop of dew. [DEW + DROP]

De Wet (*Du.* də wet′), **Chris·ti·an Ru·dolph** (*Du.* kris′tē än′ ry′dolf), 1854–1922, Boer general and politician.

Dew·ey (do͞o′ē, dyo͞o′ē), *n.* **1. George,** 1837–1917, U.S. admiral: defeated Spanish fleet in Manila Bay during the Spanish-American War. **2. John,** 1859–1952, U.S. philosopher and educator. **3. Mel·vil** (mel′vil), (*Melville Louis Kossuth Dewey*), 1851–1931, U.S. educator, administrator, and innovator in the field of library science. **4. Thomas E(dmund),** born 1902, U.S. lawyer and political leader. **5.** a town in NE Oklahoma. 3994 (1960). **6.** a boy's given name, form of **David. 7.** a girl's given name.

Dew·ey·an (do͞o′ē ən, dyo͞o′-), *adj.* of, pertaining to, or characteristic of the philosophy of John Dewey. [DEWEY + -AN]

Dew′ey dec′imal classifica′tion, *Library Science.* a system of classifying books and other publications into ten main classes of knowledge with further subdivision in these classes by use of the numbers of a decimal system, devised by Melvil Dewey in 1876 and used in most libraries in the United States. Also called **decimal classification, Dew′ey dec′imal sys′tem.**

dew·fall (do͞o′fôl′, dyo͞o′fôl′), *n.* **1.** formation of dew. **2.** the time at which dew begins to form. [DEW + FALL]

De·wi (dā′wē), *n.* **Saint.** See **David, Saint.**

De Witt (də wit′), **1. Jan** (yän), 1625–72, Dutch statesman. **2.** a town in E Iowa. 3224 (1960). **3.** a town in central Arkansas. 3019 (1960). **4.** a boy's given name.

dew·lap (do͞o′lap′, dyo͞o′-), *n.* **1.** a pendulous fold of skin under the throat of a bovine animal **2.** any similar part, as the loose skin under the throat of some dogs, the wattle of fowls, etc. [ME *dew(e)lappe; -lappe,* OE *læppa* pendulous piece; *dew(e)-* prob. akin to DEW; cf. Dan *dog-læp,* D (dial.) *dauw-zwengel*] —**dew′lapped′,** *adj.*

DEW′ line′ (do͞o, dyo͞o), a 3,000-mile-long network of radar stations north of the Arctic Circle, maintained by the U.S. and Canada for providing advance warning of the approach of hostile planes, missiles, etc.

dew′ plant′, 1. See **ice plant. 2.** sundew.

dew′ point′, the temperature to which air must be cooled, at a given pressure and water-vapor content, for it to reach saturation; the temperature at which dew begins to form. Also called **dew′-point tem′perature.** Cf. **absolute humidity, mixing ratio, relative humidity, specific humidity.**

dew′-point spread′ (do͞o′point′, dyo͞o′-), the number of degrees of difference between the air temperature and the dew point. Also called **dew′-point def′icit, dew′-point depres′sion.**

dew·y (do͞o′ē, dyo͞o′ē), *adj.* **dew·i·er, dew·i·est. 1.** moist with or as with dew. **2.** having the quality of dew: *dewy tears.* **3.** *Poetic.* falling gently or refreshing like dew: *dewy sleep.* **4.** of dew. [DEW + -Y¹] —**dew′i·ly,** *adv.* —**dew′i·ness,** *n.*

dew·y-eyed (do͞o′ē īd′, dyo͞o′-), *adj.* romantically naïve or credulous; sentimental, innocent, and trusting: *dewy-eyed, aspiring young actresses.*

Dex·a·me·nus (dek sä′mə nəs), *n. Class. Myth.* a centaur, king of Olenus.

dex·a·meth·a·sone (dek′sə meth′ə sōn′), *n. Pharm.* a crystalline, water-soluble steroid, $C_{22}H_{29}FO_5$, used in the treatment of certain allergic or inflammatory conditions, as of rheumatoid arthritis, bronchial asthma, and dermatosis. [DEX(TRO-) + METH(YL) + (CORTI)SONE]

Dex·a·myl (dek′sə mil), *n. Pharm., Trademark.* a mixture of dextroamphetamine and amobarbitol that curbs the appetite and raises the spirits, used in the treatment of obesity and mental depression.

Dex·e·drine (dek′si drēn′, -drin), *n. Pharm., Trademark.* dextroamphetamine.

dex·i·o·car·di·a (dek′sē ō kär′dē ə), *n. Pathol.* dextrocardia. [< Gk *dexió(s)* on the right hand or side + -CARDIA]

dex·ter (dek′stər), *adj.* **1.** on the right side; right. **2.** *Heraldry.* noting the side of an escutcheon or achievement of arms which is to the right of one who bears the escutcheon and to the left of one who looks at it (opposed to *sinister*). **3.** *Obs.* favorable. [< L: right, favorable; c. Gk *dexiós*]

Dex·ter (dek′stər), *n.* **1.** a town in SE Missouri. 5519 (1960). **2.** a town in central Maine. 2720 (1960). **3.** a boy's given name.

dex·ter·i·ty (dek ster′i tē), *n.* **1.** skill or adroitness in using the hands or body; agility. **2.** mental adroitness or skill; cleverness. **3.** right-handedness. [< L *dexteritās* readiness, equiv. to *dexter-* (s. of *dexter*) skillful + *-itās* -ITY]

dex·ter·ous (dek′strəs, -stər əs), *adj.* **1.** skillful or adroit in the use of the hands or body. **2.** having mental adroitness or skill; clever. **3.** done with dexterity. **4.** right-handed. Also, **dextrous.** [< L *dexter* right, skillful + -OUS] —**dex′ter·ous·ly,** *adv.* —**dex′ter·ous·ness,** *n.*
—**Syn. 1.** deft, nimble, handy. **1, 2.** expert, apt, able, quick. —**Ant. 1.** clumsy. **2.** inept. **3.** awkward.

dextr-, var. of **dextro-** before a vowel: *dextral.*

Dex·tra (dek′strə), *n.* a girl's given name.

dex·trad (dek′strad), *adv. Anat., Zool.* toward the right side; dextrally. [DEXTR- + L *ad* (prep.) towards]

dex·tral (dek′strəl), *adj.* **1.** of, pertaining to, or on the right side; right (opposed to *sinistral*). **2.** right-handed. **3.** *Zool.* (of certain gastropod shells) coiling from left to right, as seen from the apex. [DEXTR- + -AL¹] —**dex′tral·ly,** *adv.*

dex·tral·i·ty (dek stral′i tē), *n.* **1.** the state or quality of having the right side or its parts or members different from and, usually, more efficient than the left side or its parts or members; right-handedness (opposed to *sinistrality*). **2.** preference for using the right hand or side (opposed to *sinistrality*). **3.** *Zool.* the state of being dextral. [DEXTRAL + -ITY]

dex·tran (dek′strən), *n. Chem., Pharm.* a white, gummy material, produced from milk, molasses, etc., by bacterial action, used in confections and lacquers and in medicine chiefly as a substitute for blood plasma. [DEXTR- + -AN(E)]

dex·trin (dek′strin), *n.* a soluble, gummy substance, formed from starch by the action of heat, acids, or ferments, occurring in various forms and having dextrorotatory properties: used chiefly as a thickening agent in printing inks and food, as a mucilage, and as a substitute for gum arabic and other natural substances. Also, **dex·trine** (dek′strin, -strēn). Also called **British gum.** [< F *dextrine.* See DEXTR-, -IN²]

dex·tro (dek′strō), *adj. Chem.* dextrorotatory. [by shortening]

dextro-, 1. a learned borrowing from Latin meaning "right," used in the formation of compound words: *dextrogyrate.* **2.** *Chem.* a word element meaning "turning clockwise": *dextroglucose.* Also, *esp. before a vowel,* **dextr-.** [< L, comb. form of *dexter*]

dex·tro·am·phet·a·mine (dek′strō am fet′ə mēn′, -min), *n. Pharm.* a white, crystalline, water-soluble solid, $C_6H_5CH_2CH(NH_2)CH_3$, which stimulates the central nervous system: used in medicine, usually in the form of its sulfate, chiefly to lift the mood in depressive states and to control the appetite in the treatment of obesity. [DEXTRO- + AMPHETAMINE]

dex·tro·car·di·a (dek′strō kär′dē ə), *n. Pathol.* **1.** an abnormal condition in which the heart is displaced to the right side of the chest. **2.** dextral displacement of the heart with complete transposition of the cardiac chambers, the right chambers being on the left side and the left chambers being on the right side. Also, **dexiocardia.** [< NL; see DEXTRO-, -CARDIA] —**dex′tro·car′di·al,** *adj.*

dex·troc·u·lar (dek strok′yə lər), *adj. Ophthalm.* favoring the right eye, rather than the left, by habit or for effective vision (opposed to *sinistrocular*). [DEXTR- + OCULAR] —**dex·troc·u·lar·i·ty** (dek strok′yə lar′i tē), *n.*

dex·tro·glu·cose (dek′strō glo͞o′kōs), *n. Chem.* See under **glucose** (def. 1). [DEXTRO- + GLUCOSE]

dex·tro·gy·rate (dek′strō jī′rit, -rāt), *adj. Optics, Crystall.* dextrorotatory. Also, **dex·tro·gyre** (dek′strō jīər′). [DEXTRO- + GYRATE]

dex·tron′ic ac′id (dek stron′ik), *Chem.* See **gluconic acid.** [DEXTR- + (GLUC)ONIC ACID]

dex′tro propox′yphene, *Pharm.* a nonnarcotic compound, $C_{22}H_{29}NO_2$, used in the form of its hydrochloride as an analgesic.

dex·tro·ro·ta·tion (dek′strō rō tā′shən), *n. Optics, Crystall.* a turning to the right of the plane of polarization. [DEXTRO- + ROTATION]

dex·tro·ro·ta·to·ry (dek′strō rō′tə tōr′ē, -tôr′ē), *adj. Optics, Chem. Crystall.* turning to the right, as the rotation to the right of the plane of polarization of light in certain crystals and the like; dextrogyrate. Also, **dex·tro·ro·ta·ry** (dek′strō rō′tə rē). [DEXTRO- + ROTATORY]

dex·trorse (dek′strôrs, dek strôrs′), *adj. Bot.* (of a climbing plant) rising helically from right to left, as seen from outside the helix (opposed to *sinistrorse*). Also, **dex·tror′sal.** [< L *dextrors(um)* toward the right, contr. of *dextro-* DEXTRO- + *vors(us)* turned (ptp. of *vortere,* var. of *vertere*) + *-um* adv. suffix] —**dex′trorse·ly,** *adv.*

Dextrorse stem of morning glory vine

dex·trose (dek′strōs), *n. Chem.* dextroglucose, commercially obtainable from starch by acid hydrolysis. Also called **corn sugar, grape sugar.** Cf. **glucose** (def. 1). [DEXTR- + -OSE²]

dex·tro·sin·is·tral (dek′strō sin′i strəl), *adj.* **1.** passing or extending from the right to the left. **2.** left-handed, but having the right hand trained for writing. [DEXTRO- + SINISTRAL] —**dex′tro·sin′is·tral·ly,** *adv.*

dex·trous (dek′strəs), *adj.* dexterous. —**dex′trous·ly,** *adv.* —**dex′trous·ness,** *n.*

dey (dā), *n.* **1.** the title of the governor of Algiers before the French conquest in 1830. **2.** a title sometimes used by the former rulers of Tunis and Tripoli. [< F < Turk *dayi,* orig. maternal uncle]

Dezh·nev (dezh nyôf′), *n.* **Cape,** a cape in the NE Soviet Union in Asia, on the Bering Strait: the northeasternmost point of Asia. Also called **East Cape.**

de·zinc·i·fi·ca·tion (dē ziŋ′kə fə kā′shən), *n. Metall.* a process of corrosion in which the zinc of copper-zinc alloys becomes absorbed by the environment. [DE- + ZINCIFICATION]

D/F, direction finding.

D.F., 1. Defender of the Faith. [< L *Defensor Fidei*] **2.** Distrito Federal. **3.** Doctor of Forestry.

D.F.A., Doctor of Fine Arts.

D.F.C., Distinguished Flying Cross.

dg, decigram; decigrams.

d-glu·cose (dē′glo͞o′kōs), *n. Chem.* See under **glucose** (def. 1).

DH., dirham.

D.H., 1. Doctor of Humanics. **2.** Doctor of Humanities.

Dhah·ran (dä rän′), *n.* a city in E Saudi Arabia: oil center. 75,000 (est. 1952).

Dha·ka (dak′ə, dä′kə), *n.* Dacca.

dhal (thäl), *n.* the ninth letter of the Arabic alphabet. [< Ar]

Dham·ma·pa·da (dum′ə pə də), *n. Buddhism.* a Hinayana text on the spiritual life, said to have been written by Buddha. [< Skt]

dha·ra·na (där′ə nä), *n. Hinduism.* complete concentration upon one thing in a spiritual exercise. [< Skt: a holding]

dhar·ma (där′mə, dur′-), *n. Hinduism, Buddhism.* **1.** essential quality or character, as of the cosmos or one's own nature. **2.** conformity to religious law, custom, duty, or one's own qualitp or character. **3.** virtue. **4.** religion. **5.** law, esp. religious law. **6.** the doctrine or teaching of the Buddha. Pali, **dham·ma** (dum′ə). [< Skt: decree, custom, akin to *dhārāyati* he holds]

Dhar·ma·pa·da (dûr′mə pə də, dur′-), *n. Sanskrit.* Dhammapada.

Dhar·ma·sas·tra (där′mə shä′strə, dur′-), *n.* a Hindu text of the law dealing mainly with social life from the moral viewpoint. Also, **Dhar′ma·shas′tra.**

Dhar·ma·su·tra (där′mə so͞o′trə, dur′-), *n.* a Hindu text of the law dealing chiefly with religion and ethics.

dhar·na (där′nə, dur′-), *n.* (in India) the practice of exacting justice or compliance with a just demand by sitting and fasting at the doorstep of an offender until death or until the demand is granted. Also, **dhurna.** [< Hindi: placing]

Dhau·la·gi·ri (dou′lə gēr′ē), *n.* a mountain in W central Nepal: a peak of the Himalayas. 26,826 ft.

dhikr (dik′ər), *n., pl.* **dhikrs, dhikr.** *Islam.* **1.** a meeting of dervishes at which certain passages from the Koran are chanted rhythmically to induce a state of ecstasy. **2.** each set of passages from the Koran so chanted, with its accompanying ritual. [< Ar: recitation]

D.H.L., 1. Doctor of Hebrew Letters. **2.** Doctor of Hebrew Literature.

dho·bi (dō′bē), *n., pl.* **-bis.** *Anglo-Indian.* a laundryboy; washerman. Also, **dho′bie.** [< Hindi]

dhole (dōl), *n.* a fierce, wild, Indian dog, *Cuon rutilus,* which hunts in packs that attack large game. [?]

dhoo·ly (do͞o′lē), *n., pl.* **-lies.** dooly.

dho·ti (dō′tē), *n., pl.* **-tis. 1.** a loincloth worn by Hindu men in India. **2.** the cotton fabric, sometimes patterned, of which the loincloth is made. Also, **dhoo·ti, dhoo·tie, dhu·ti** (do͞o′tē). [< Hindi]

Dhow

dhow (dou), *n.* any of various types of sailing vessels used by Arabs on the east African, the Arabian, and the Indian coasts, generally lateen-rigged on two or three masts. Also, **dau, dow.** [< Ar *dāwa*]

dhur·na (dûr′nə), *n.* dharna.

dhur·rie (dûr′ē), *n.* durrie.

dhya·na (dyä′nə), *n. Hinduism, Buddhism.* meditation upon a single object. [< Skt, akin to *dhyāti* he thinks]

di¹ (dē), *prep.* from; of: used in Italian personal names, originally to indicate place of origin: *Conte di Savòia.* Also, **Di.** [< It < L *dē*]

di² (dē), *n. Music.* a tone in the ascending chromatic scale between do and re. [? alter. of DO²]

Di (dī), *n.* a girl's given name, form of **Diana.**

DI, 1. Department of the Interior. **2.** drill instructor.

Di, *Chem.* didymium.

di-¹, a prefix occurring in loan words from Greek, where it meant "two," "twice," "double" (*diphthong*); on this model, freely used in the formation of compound words (*dicotyledon; dipolar*) and in chemical terms (*diatomic; disulfide*). Also, **dis-².** Cf. **mono-.** [ME < L < Gk, comb. form repr. *dís* twice, double, akin to *dýo* two. See BI-, TWI-]

di-², var. of **dis-¹** before *b, d, l, m, n, r, s, v,* and sometimes *g* and *j*: *digest; divide.*

di-³, var. of **dia-** before a vowel: *diorama.*

di., diameter. Also, **dia.**

dia-, a prefix occurring in loan words from Greek (*diabetes; dialect*) and used, in the formation of compound words, to mean "passing through" (*diathermy*), "thoroughly," "completely" (*diagnosis*), "going apart" (*dialysis*), and "opposed in moment" (*diamagnetism*). Also, *esp. before a vowel,* **di-.** [< Gk, comb. form repr. *diá* (prep.) through, between, across, by, of, akin to *dýo* two and *di-* DI-¹]

di·a·base (dī′ə bās′), *n.* **1.** *U.S.* a dark igneous rock occurring as minor intrusives composed essentially of labradorite and pyroxene. **2.** *Brit.* a dark igneous rock consisting essentially of augite and feldspar; an altered dolerite. **3.** *Obs.* diorite. [< F, equiv. to *dia-* (error for *di-* two) + *base* BASE[1]] —**di′a·ba′sic,** *adj.*

Di·a·bel·li (dē′ä bel′ē), *n.* **An·to·ni·o** (än tô′nē ô′), 1781–1858, Austrian composer and music publisher.

di·a·be·tes (dī′ə bē′tis, -tēz), *n.* *Pathol.* **1.** Also called **diabe′tes mel·li′tus** (mə lī′təs). a disease that impairs the ability of the body to use sugar and causes sugar to appear abnormally in the urine. **2.** Also called **diabe′tes in·sip′i·dus** (in sip′i dəs), a disease in which there is a persistent, abnormal amount of urine. [< NL, L < Gk: lit., a passer through, equiv. to *diabē-* (var. s. of *diabaínein,* equiv. to *dia-* DIA- + *baínein* to pass) + *-tēs* agent suffix]

di·a·bet·ic (dī′ə bet′ik, -bē′tik), *adj.* **1.** of, pertaining to, or for diabetes or persons having diabetes. **2.** having or resulting from diabetes. —*n.* **3.** a person who has diabetes. [< L *diabēticus*). See DIABETES, -IC]

di·a·ble·rie (dē ä′blə rē; *Fr.* dyȧ blə ʀē′), *n., pl.* **-ries** (-rēz; *Fr.* -ʀē′). **1.** diabolic magic or art; sorcery; witchcraft. **2.** the domain or realm of devils. **3.** the lore of devils; demonology. **4.** reckless mischief; deviltry. [< F, OF, equiv. to *diable* DEVIL + *-erie* -ERY]

di·a·ble·ry (dē ä′blə rē), *n., pl.* **-ries.** diablerie.

di·a·bol·ic (dī′ə bol′ik), *adj.* **1.** having the qualities of a devil; fiendish; outrageously wicked: *a diabolic plot.* **2.** pertaining to or actuated by the devil or a devil. Also, **di′a·bol′i·cal.** [ME *diabolik* < LL *diabolic(us)* < Gk *diabolikós,* equiv. to *diábol(os)* DEVIL + *-ikos* -IC] —**di′a·bol′i·cal·ly,** *adv.* —**di′a·bol′i·cal·ness,** *n.*

di·ab·o·lise (dī ab′ə līz′), *v.t.,* **-lised, -lis·ing.** *Chiefly Brit.* diabolize. —**di·ab′o·li·sa′tion,** *n.*

di·ab·o·lism (dī ab′ə liz′əm), *n.* **1.** *Theol.* **a.** action aided or caused by the devil; sorcery; witchcraft. **b.** the character or condition of a devil. **c.** a doctrine concerning devils. **d.** a belief in or worship of devils. **2.** action befitting the devil; deviltry. [< Gk *diábol(os)* DEVIL + -ISM] —**di·ab′o·list,** *n.*

di·ab·o·lize (dī ab′ə līz′), *v.t.,* **-lized, -liz·ing.** **1.** to make diabolical or devilish. **2.** to represent as diabolical. **3.** to subject to diabolical influences. Also, *esp. Brit.,* **diabolise.** [< Gk *diábol(os)* DEVIL + -IZE] —**di·ab′o·li·za′tion,** *n.*

di·ab·o·lo (dē ab′ə lō′), *n., pl.* **-los** for 2. **1.** a game in which a toplike object is spun, thrown, and caught by or balanced on and whirled along a string the ends of which are fastened to the ends of two sticks that are manipulated by hand. **2.** the top used in this game. Cf. **yoyo.** [coinage by Gustave Phillipart, 19th-century French engineer]

di·a·caus·tic (dī′ə kô′stik), *Math., Optics.* —*adj.* **1.** noting a caustic surface or curve formed by the refraction of light. —*n.* **2.** a diacaustic surface or curve. Cf. **catacaustic.** [DIA- + CAUSTIC]

di·a·ce·tyl (dī′ə sēt′ᵊl, -as′i tᵊl), *n.* *Chem.* biacetyl. [DI-[1] + ACETYL]

di·a·ce·tyl·mor·phine (dī′ə sēt′ᵊl môr′fēn, dī as′i-tᵊl-), *n.* *Pharm.* heroin. [DIACETYL + MORPHINE]

di·a·chron·ic (dī′ə kron′ik), *adj.* *Ling.* of or pertaining to the changes in a linguistic system between successive points in time; historical: *diachronic analysis; diachronic linguistics.* Cf. **synchronic.** [DIA- + CHRONIC]

di·ach·y·lon (dī ak′ə lon′), *n.* an adhesive plaster consisting chiefly of litharge and oil. Also, **di·ach·y·lum** (dī ak′ə ləm). [< L < Gk *diàchylōn* (something) made of juices, equiv. to *dia-* DIA- + *chylós* juice (also Latinized as *diachȳlum* whence E sp. with *-um*); r. ME *diaculon* < ML, and ME *diaquilon* < MF, both < L *diachȳlōn*]

di·ac·id (dī as′id), *adj.* *Chem.* **1.** capable of combining with two molecules of a monobasic acid. **2.** (of an acid or a salt) having two replaceable hydrogen atoms. [DI-[1] + ACID]

di·ac·o·nal (dī ak′ə nᵊl), *adj.* pertaining to a deacon. [< LL *diāconāl(is).* See DEACON, -AL[1]]

di·ac·o·nate (dī ak′ə nit, -nāt′), *n.* **1.** the office or dignity of a deacon. **2.** a body of deacons. [< LL *diāconāt(us).* See DEACON -ATE[1]]

di·a·con·i·con (dī′ə kon′ə kon′, -kən), *n., pl.* **-ca** (-kə). a sacristy in an Eastern or early Christian church, usually on the south side of the bema. Also, **diaconicum, diakonikon.** [< LGk *diākonikón* (LL *diāconicum*), neut. of *diākonikós* of a DEACON; see -IC]

di·a·con·i·cum (dī′ə kon′ə kəm), *n., pl.* **-ca** (-kə). diaconicon.

di·a·crit·ic (dī′ə krit′ik), *n.* **1.** Also called **diacrit′ical mark′.** a mark, point, or sign added or attached to a letter or character to distinguish it from another of similar form, to give it a particular phonetic value, to indicate stress, etc., as a cedilla, tilde, circumflex, macron, etc. —*adj.* **2.** diacritical. **3.** *Med.* diagnostic. [< Gk *diakritik(ós)* distinctive, equiv. to *dia-* DIA- + *kritikós;* see CRITIC]

di·a·crit·i·cal (dī′ə krit′i kəl), *adj.* **1.** serving to distinguish; distinctive. **2.** capable of distinguishing. **3.** *Phonet.* serving as a diacritic. [DIACRITIC + -AL[1]] —**di′a·crit′i·cal·ly,** *adv.*

di·ac·tin·ic (dī′ak tin′ik), *adj.* *Physics.* capable of transmitting actinic rays. [DI-[3] + ACTINIC] —**di·ac′tin·ism,** *n.*

di·a·del·phous (dī′ə del′fəs), *adj.* *Bot.* **1.** (of stamens) united into two sets by their filaments. **2.** (of plants) having the stamens so united. [DI-[1] + Gk *adelph(ós)* brother + -OUS]

di·a·dem (dī′ə dem′), *n.* **1.** a crown. **2.** a cloth headband, sometimes adorned with jewels, formerly worn by Oriental kings. **3.** royal dignity or authority. —*v.t.* **4.** to adorn with or as if with a diadem; crown. [ME *diademe* < L *diadēma* < Gk *diádēma* fillet, band, equiv. to *diadē-* (verbid s. of *diadeîn* to bind round + *-ma* n. suffix]

Di·ad·o·chi (dī ad′ə kī′), *n.pl.* the Macedonian generals under Alexander the Great who, after his death, divided his empire. [< NL < Gk *diádochoi,* pl. of *diádochos* successor (n. use of adj.), akin to *diadéchesthai* to succeed; see DIADOCHOKINESIA] —**Di·a·do·chi·an** (dī′ə dō′kē ən), *adj.*

di·ad·o·cho·ki·ne·sia (dī ad′ə kō ki nē′zhə, -zhē ə, -zē ə, -kī-), *n.* *Med.* the normal ability to perform rapidly alternating muscular movements, as flexion and extension. Also, **di·ad·o·cho·ki·ne·sis** (dī ad′ə kō ki-nē′sis), **di·ad′o·ko·ki·ne′sia, di·ad′o·ko·ki·ne′sis.** Cf. **adiadochokinesia.** [< NL < Gk *diádoch(os)* succeeding, equiv. to *diadéch(esthai)* (to) succeed (*dia-* DIA- + *déchesthai* to take up) + NL *kinesia* < Gk, equiv. to *kinē(sis)* motion (*kin(ein)* (to) move + *-ē-* thematic vowel + *-sis* -SIS) + *-ia* -IA]

di·ad·o·chy (dī ad′ə kē), *n.* *Crystall.* the ability of certain different elements to exist in place of each other in certain points of a space lattice; isomorphism. [irreg. < Gk *diadochē* succession; see DIADOCHOKINESIA] —**di·a·doch·ic** (dī′ə dok′ik), *adj.*

di·ad·ro·mous (dī ad′rə məs), *adj.* **1.** *Bot.* (of a leaf) having a fanlike venation. **2.** (of fish) migrating between fresh and salt waters. Cf. **anadromous, catadromous.** [DIA- + -DROMOUS]

di·aer·e·sis (dī er′i sis), *n., pl.* **-ses** (-sēz′). dieresis. —**di·ae·ret·ic** (dī′ə ret′ik), *adj.*

diag., diagram.

di·a·gen·e·sis (dī′ə jen′i sis), *n.* *Geol.* the physical and chemical changes occurring in sediments between the times of deposition and solidification. [< NL; see DIA-, GENESIS] —**di·a·ge·net·ic** (dī′ə jə net′ik), *adj.*

di·a·ge·o·trop·ic (dī′ə jē′ə trop′ik), *adj.* *Bot.* (of a plant part) growing at a right angle to the direction of gravity. [DIA- + GEOTROPIC]

di·a·ge·ot·ro·pism (dī′ə jē o′trə piz′əm), *n.* *Bot.* diageotropic tendency or growth. [DIA- + GEOTROPISM]

Dia·ghi·lev (dyä′gi lef′), *n.* **Ser·gei Pa·vlo·vich** (seʀ ge′i pä vlô′vich), 1872–1929, Russian ballet producer and art critic.

di·ag·nose (dī′əg nōs′, -nōz′, dī′əg nōs′, -nōz′), *v.,* **-nosed, -nos·ing.** —*v.t.* **1.** to determine the identity of (a disease, illness, etc.) by a medical examination: *The doctor diagnosed her illness as diabetes mellitus.* **2.** to ascertain the cause or nature of (a disorder, malfunction, etc.) from the symptoms: *The mechanic diagnosed the trouble that caused the engine knock.* **3.** to classify or determine on the basis of scientific examination. **4.** to ascertain or analyze the cause or nature of (a problem or situation), esp. when such presents an obvious answer: *He diagnosed the increase in crime as due to too few foot patrolmen.* —*v.i.* **5.** to make a diagnosis. [back formation from DIAGNOSIS] —**di′ag·nos′a·ble,** *adj.*

di·ag·no·sis (dī′əg nō′sis), *n., pl.* **-ses** (-sēz). **1.** *Med.* **a.** the process of determining by examination the nature and circumstances of a diseased condition. **b.** the decision reached from such an examination. **2.** *Biol.* scientific determination; a description which classifies precisely. **3.** a determining or analysis of the cause or nature of a problem or situation. **4.** an answer or solution to a problematic situation. [< NL < Gk *diágnōsis* a distinguishing. See DIA-, -GNOSIS]

di·ag·nos·tic (dī′əg nos′tik), *adj.* **1.** of or pertaining to diagnosis. **2.** having value in diagnosis; constituting a symptom or syndrome of a disease. —*n.* **3.** diagnosis (def. 1). **4.** a symptom or characteristic of value in diagnosis. **5.** *Med.* a compound administered for the diagnosis of an abnormal condition of the body or mind, that when excreted and analyzed indicates a specific pathology. [< Gk *diagnōstik(ós),* equiv. to *diagnōst(ós)* to be distinguished (deriv. of *diágnōsis;* see DIAGNOSIS) + *-ikos* -IC] —**di′ag·nos′ti·cal·ly,** *adv.*

di·ag·nos·ti·cate (dī′əg nos′tə kāt′), *v.t., v.i.,* **-cat·ed, -cat·ing.** to diagnose. [DIAGNOSTIC + -ATE[1]] —**di′ag·nos′ti·ca′tion,** *n.*

di·ag·nos·ti·cian (dī′əg no stish′ən), *n.* an expert in making diagnoses. [DIAGNOSTIC + -IAN]

di·ag·nos·tics (dī′əg nos′tiks), *n.* (*construed as sing.*) the art or science of diagnosis. [see DIAGNOSTIC, -ICS]

di·ag·o·nal (dī ag′ə nᵊl), *adj.* **1.** *Math.* **a.** connecting two nonadjacent angles or vertices of a polygon or polyhedron, as a straight line. **b.** extending from one edge of a solid figure to an opposite edge, as a plane. **2.** having an oblique direction. **3.** having oblique lines, ridges, markings, etc. —*n.* **4.** a diagonal line or plane. **5.** virgule. **6.** a diagonal row, part, pattern, etc. **7.** *Manège.* (of a horse at a trot) the foreleg and the hind leg, diagonally opposite, which move forward simultaneously. **8.** See **diagonal cloth.** **9.** *Math.* a set of entries in a square matrix running either from upper left to lower right **(main** or **principal diagonal)** or lower left to upper right **(secondary diagonal).** **10.** *Chess.* one of the oblique lines of squares on a chessboard: *He advanced his bishop along the open diagonal.* **11.** Also called **diag′onal line′.** *Naval Archit.* any of a series of lines on the lines plan of a hull, used for fairing, esp. in the area of the bilge, and representing the intersection of a series of planes sloping downward from the midship fore-and-aft vertical plane, which they intersect in a series of horizontal lines, with the hull surface, the inner surface being the one most commonly used: such a line appears as a sloping line on the body plan, and as a curved line on the half-breadth and sheer plans. **12. to post on a diagonal,** *Manège.* (of a rider posting to a trot) to sit in the saddle as one diagonal strikes the ground, rising as the other diagonal strikes (named after the appropriate foreleg): *to post on the left diagonal.* [< L *diagonāl(is)* < Gk *diagṓn(ios)* from angle to angle (see DIA-, -GON) + L *-ālis* -AL[1]] —**di·ag′o·nal·ly,** *adv.*

diag′onal bond′, a brickwork bond in which the exposed brickwork is bonded to the heart of the wall by concealed courses of parallel bricks set diagonally to the face of the wall; a form of raking bond.

di·ag·o·nal-built (dī ag′ə nᵊl bilt′), *adj.* *Naut.* (of a wooden vessel) built with one layer of planking at an angle of 45° to the frames and with another layer over it either at right angles to the first layer or in a fore-and-aft direction.

diag′onal cloth′, a twilled fabric woven with distinctly diagonal lines. Also called **diagonal.**

di·ag·o·nal-cut (dī ag′ə nᵊl kut′), *adj.* *Naut.* noting any of various triangular sails formed of a head section having seams at right angles to the leech and a foot section having seams at right angles to the foot, the two sections meeting in a last running diagonally upward from the clew.

diag′onal ma′trix, *Math.* a square matrix in which all the entries except those along the diagonal from upper left to lower right are zero.

di·a·gram (dī′ə gram′), *n., v.,* **-gramed, -gram·ing** or (*esp. Brit.*) **-grammed, -gram·ming.** —*n.* **1.** a figure, usually consisting of a simple line drawing, made to accompany and illustrate a geometrical theorem, mathematical demonstration, etc. **2.** a drawing or plan that outlines and explains the parts, operation, etc., of something: *a diagram of an engine.* **3.** a chart, plan, or scheme. —*v.t.* **4.** to represent by a diagram; make a diagram of. [< L *diagram(ma)* < Gk: that which is marked out by lines. See DIA-, -GRAM[1]]

di·a·gram·mat·ic (dī′ə grə mat′ik), *adj.* **1.** in the form of a diagram. **2.** pertaining to diagrams. Also, **di′a·gram·mat′i·cal.** [DIAGRAM + *-atic* as in *problem, problematic*] —**di′a·gram·mat′i·cal·ly,** *adv.*

di·a·graph (dī′ə graf′, -gräf′), *n.* **1.** a device for drawing, used in reproducing outlines, plans, etc., mechanically on any desired scale. **2.** a combined protractor and scale. [< F *diagraphe* < Gk *diagráph(ein)* (to) draw. See DIA-, -GRAPH]

Di·ahann (dī an′), *n.* a girl's given name, form of **Diana.**

di·a·ki·ne·sis (dī′ə ki nē′sis, -kī-), *n.* *Biol.* the last stage in prophase, prior to the dissolution of the nuclear membrane. [< NL, equiv. to *dia-* DIA- + Gk *kinēsis* movement, equiv. to *kin(ein)* (to) move + *-ē-* thematic vowel + *-sis* -SIS]

di·a·kon·i·kon (dī′ə kon′ə kon′, -kən), *n., pl.* **-ka** (-kə). diaconicon.

di·al (dī′əl, dīl), *n., v.,* **di·aled, di·al·ing** or (*esp. Brit.*) **di·alled, di·al·ling.** —*n.* **1.** a plate, disk, face, or other surface containing graduations or figures upon which time is indicated by hands, pointers, or shadows, as of a clock or sundial. **2.** a plate or disk with graduations or figures for indicating or registering some measurement or number, as of pressure, number of revolutions, the frequency to which a radio is tuned, etc., usually by means of a pointer. **3.** a rotatable plate or disk having a knob used for regulating a mechanism, making and breaking electrical connections, etc., as in tuning a radio station in or out. **4.** a rotatable plate or disk on a telephone, fitted with finger holes that are marked with letters and numbers or numbers only, used in making calls through an automatic switchboard. **5.** Also called **miner's dial.** *Mining.* a compass used for underground surveying. —*v.t.* **6.** to indicate or register on or as on a dial. **7.** to regulate, select, or tune to by means of a dial, as on a radio. **8.** to work the dial of (a telephone) so that a call can be made to another telephone: *Put a dime in the slot and then dial the phone.* **9.** to form (the number of another telephone) by dialing one's own telephone, in order to make a call: *Dial 502 for long distance to Louisville.* **10.** to make a telephone call to: *Dial me at home.* **11.** *Mining.* to survey with the aid of a dial or compass. —*v.i.* **12.** to use a telephone dial. **13.** to tune in or regulate by means of a dial. [ME < ML *diāl(is)* daily (L *di(ēs)* day + *-ālis* -AL[1])] —**di′al·er;** *esp. Brit.,* **di′al·ler,** *n.*

dial., **1.** dialect. **2.** dialectal.

di·a·lect (dī′ə lekt′), *n.* **1.** *Ling.* a variety of a language that is distinguished from other varieties of the same language by features of phonology, grammar, and vocabulary, and by its use by a group of speakers who are set off from others geographically or socially. **2.** a provincial, rural, or socially distinct variety of a language that differs from the standard language, esp. when considered as substandard. **3.** a special variety of a language: *The literary dialect is usually taken as the standard language.* **4.** a language considered as one of a group that have a common ancestor: *Persian, Latin, and English are Indo-European dialects.* **5.** jargon or cant. [< L *dialect(us)* < Gk *diálekt(os)* discourse, language, dialect, equiv. to *dialég(esthai)* (to) converse (*dia-* DIA- + *lég(ein)* (to) speak) + *-t-* ptp. suffix]
—**Syn. 2.** idiom, patois. **3.** tongue, speech. See **language.**

di·a·lec·tal (dī′ə lek′tᵊl), *adj.* **1.** of a dialect. **2.** characteristic of a dialect. Also, **dialectic, dialectical.** [DIALECT + -AL[1]] —**di′a·lec′tal·ly,** *adv.*

di′alect at′las, *Ling.* a collection of maps of a certain area indicating the distribution of various phonological, morphological, lexical, or other features of the dialects of that area.

di′alect geog′raphy, *Ling.* the study of regional dialect variation. —**di′alect geog′rapher.**

di·a·lec·tic (dī′ə lek′tik), *adj.* Also, **dialectical. 1.** of, pertaining to, or of the nature of logical argumentation. **2.** dialectal. —*n.* **3.** the art or practice of logical discussion as employed in investigating the truth of a theory or opinion. **4.** logical argumentation. **5.** Often, **dialectics. a.** logic or any of its branches. **b.** any formal system of reasoning or thought. **6.** See **Hegelian dialectic.** **7. dialectics,** (*often construed as sing.*) the arguments or bases of dialectical materialism, including the elevation of matter over mind and a constantly changing reality with a material basis. **8.** (in Kantian epistemology) a fallacious metaphysical system arising from the attribution of objective reality to the perceptions by the mind of external objects. Cf. **transcendental dialectic.** [< L *dialectic(a)* < Gk *dialektikḗ* (*téchnē*) argumentative (art), fem. of *dialektikós.* See DIALECT, -IC] —**di′a·lec′ti·cal·ly,** *adv.*

di·a·lec·ti·cal (dī′ə lek′ti kəl), *adj.* **1.** dialectic. **2.** dialectal. [DIALECTIC + -AL[1]]

dialec′tical mate′rialism, a form of materialism, developed chiefly by Karl Marx, noted especially for the application of the Hegelian dialectic in its philosophy of history. —**dialec′tical mate′rialist.**

dialec′tical theol′ogy, a form of neoorthodox theology emphasizing the infinite tensions, paradoxes, and basic ambiguities inherent in Christian existence, and holding, against rationalism, that God is unknowable to man except through divine grace and revelation.

di·a·lec·ti·cian (dī′ə lek tish′ən), *n.* **1.** one skilled in dialectic; logician. **2.** a dialectologist. [< F *dialecticien* < L *dialectic(us)* DIALECTIC + F *-ien* -IAN]

di·a·lec·ti·cism (dī′ə lek′ti siz′əm), *n.* **1.** dialectal speech or influence. **2.** a dialectal word or expression. [DIALECTIC + -ISM]

di·a·lec·tol·o·gist (dī′ə lek tol′ə jist), *n.* a specialist in the study of dialect or dialects. [DIALECTOLOG(Y) + -IST]

di·a·lec·tol·o·gy (dī′ə lek tol′ə jē), *n., pl.* **-gies** for 2. **1.** *Ling.* the study dealing with dialects and dialect features. **2.** the linguistic features of a dialect or of the dialects of a language. [DIALECT + -O- + -LOGY] —**di·a·lec·to·log·ic** (dī′ə lek′tə loj′ik), **di′a·lec′to·log′i·cal,** *adj.* —**di′a·lec′to·log′i·cal·ly,** *adv.* —**di′a·lec·tol′o·gist,** *n.*

di·al·ing (dī′ə ling, dī′ling), *n.* **1.** the act of one who dials. **2.** the art of constructing dials. **3.** measurement of time by dials. **4.** surveying, as in a mine, by means of a dial. [DIAL + -ING¹]

di·al·lage (dī′ə lij), *n. Mineral.* a variety of diopside with a laminated structure, found in gabbro and other igneous rocks. [< F < Gk *diallagḗ* interchange, equiv. to *diallag-*, aorist stem of *diallássein* to interchange (*dia-* DIA- + *allássein* to change < *állos* other)]

di·al′lyl group′ (dī al′il), *Chem.* See **allyl sulfide.**

di·a·log·ic (dī′ə loj′ik), *adj.* **1.** of, pertaining to, or characterized by dialogue. **2.** participating in dialogue. Also, **di′a·log′i·cal.** [< ML *dialogic(us)* < Gk *dialogikós*, equiv. to *diálog(os)* DIALOGUE + *-ikos* -IC] —**di′a·log′i·cal·ly,** *adv.*

di·al·o·gise (dī al′ə jīz′), *v.i.,* **-gised, -gis·ing.** *Chiefly Brit.* dialogize.

di·al·o·gism (dī al′ə jiz′əm), *n.* the discussion of a subject in an imaginary dialogue. [< LL *dialogism(os)* < Gk *dialogismós* a consideration. See DIALOGIZE, -ISM]

di·al·o·gist (dī al′ə jist), *n.* **1.** a speaker in a dialogue. **2.** a writer of dialogue. [< LL *dialogist(a)* < Gk *dialogist(ḗs)*, equiv. to *diálog(os)* DIALOGUE + *-istēs* -IST] —**di·a·lo·gis·tic** (dī′ə lō jis′tik), *adj.* —**di′a·lo·gis′ti·cal·ly,** *adv.*

di·al·o·gite (dī al′ə jīt′), *n. Mineral.* rhodocrosite. [< Gk *dialog(ḗ)* selection, deriv. of *dialég(ein)* (to) select (*dia-* DIA- + *légein* to speak) + -ITE¹]

di·al·o·gize (dī al′ə jīz′), *v.i.,* **-gized, -giz·ing.** to carry on a dialogue. Also, *esp. Brit.,* **dialogise.** [< Gk *dialogíz(esthai)* (to) converse, equiv. to *diálog(os)* DIALOGUE + *-iz-* -IZE]

di·a·logue (dī′ə lôg′, -log′), *n., v.* **-logued, -logu·ing.** —*n.* **1.** conversation between two or more persons. **2.** the conversation between characters in a novel, drama, etc. **3.** an exchange of ideas or opinions on a particular issue, esp. a political or religious issue, with a view to reaching an amicable agreement or settlement. **4.** a literary work in the form of a conversation: *a dialogue of Plato.* —*v.i.* **5.** to carry on a dialogue; converse. —*v.t.* **6.** to put into the form of a dialogue. Also, **di′a·log′.** [ME < OF *dialogue*, L *dialog(us)* < Gk *diálogos.* See DIA-, -LOGUE] —**di′a·logu′er,** *n.*

Di′alogue Mass′, *Rom. Cath. Ch.* a Low Mass at which the responses are recited by the congregation instead of by the server.

di′al tel′ephone, a telephone that has a dial with letters and numbers or numbers only, permitting the user to be connected automatically to another telephone without the aid of an operator.

di′al tone′, (in a dial or push-button telephone) a steady humming sound which indicates that the line is ready for dialing.

di′al train′, *Horol.* the part of a going train that drives the minute and hour hands.

di·al·y·sate (dī al′i sāt′), *n. Chiefly Brit.* dialyzate.

di·a·lyse (dī′ə līz′), *v.t., v.i.,* **-lysed, -lys·ing.** *Chiefly Brit.* dialyze. —**di′a·lys′a·bil′i·ty,** *n.* —**di′a·lys′a·ble,** *adj.* —**di′a·ly·sa′tion,** *n.*

di·a·lys·er (dī′ə lī′zər), *n. Chiefly Brit.* dialyzer.

di·al·y·sis (dī al′i sis), *n., pl.* **-ses** (-sēz′). *Physical Chem., Physiol.* the separation of crystalloids from colloids in a solution by diffusion through a membrane. [< LL < Gk *diálysis* a separation. See DIA-, -LYSIS]

di·a·lyt·ic (dī′ə lit′ik), *adj. Physical Chem.* **1.** of or pertaining to dialysis. **2.** characterized by or displaying dialysis. [< Gk *dialytik(ós)*; see DIA-, -LYTIC] —**di′a·lyt′i·cal·ly,** *adv.*

di′alyt′ic meth′od, *Math.* a procedure for eliminating a variable or power of a variable from two equations in powers of the same unknown. Also called **Sylvester's dialytic method.**

di·al·y·zate (dī al′i zāt′), *n. Physical Chem.* (in dialysis) **1.** the remaining, or colloidal, portion of a solution. **2.** the solution, or the crystalline material which passes into it through the semipermeable membrane; diffusate. Also, *esp. Brit.,* **dialysate.**

di·a·lyze (dī′ə līz′), *v.,* **-lyzed, -lyz·ing.** *Physical Chem., Physiol.* —*v.t.* **1.** to subject to dialysis; separate or procure by dialysis. —*v.i.* **2.** to undergo dialysis. Also, *esp. Brit.,* **dialyse.** [DIA- + -LYZE] —**di′a·lyz′a·bil′i·ty,** *n.* —**di′a·lyz′a·ble,** *adj.* —**di′a·ly·za′tion,** *n.*

di·a·lyz·er (dī′ə lī′zər), *n.* **1.** Also, **di·al·y·za·tor** (dī al′i zā′tər). *Physical Chem.* an apparatus containing a semipermeable membrane for dialysis. **2.** *Med.* an apparatus substituted for the kidney to filter waste products from the blood artificially. Also, *esp. Brit.,* **dialyser.** [DIALYZE + -ER¹]

diam., diameter.

di·a·mag·net (dī′ə mag′nit), *n. Physics.* a diamagnetic substance. [back formation from DIAMAGNETIC]

di·a·mag·net·ic (dī′ə mag net′ik), *adj. Physics.* noting or pertaining to a class of substances, as bismuth and copper, whose permeability is less than that of a vacuum: in a magnetic field, their induced magnetism is in a direction opposite to that of iron. Cf. **antiferromagnetic, ferromagnetic, paramagnetic.** [DIA- + MAGNETIC] —**di′a·mag·net′i·cal·ly,** *adv.* —**di·a·mag·net·ism** (dī′ə mag′ni tiz′əm), *n.*

Di·a·man·ta (dī′ə man′tə), *n.* a girl's given name.

di·a·man·tif·er·ous (dī′ə man tif′ər əs), *adj.* containing diamonds. [< F *diamantifère*, equiv. to *diamant* DIAMOND + *-ifère*; see -I-, -FEROUS]

di·am·e·ter (dī am′i tər), *n.* **1.** *Geom.* **a.** a straight line passing through the center of a circle or sphere and meeting at each end the circumference or surface. **b.** a straight line passing from side to side of any figure or body, through its center. **2.** the length of such a line. **3.** the width of a circular or cylindrical object. **4.** *Math.* the least upper bound of distances between points of a given set. **5.** (in Renaissance architectural theory) a unit of dimension equal to the diameter of the lower half of a column, usually divided into two parts **(modules),** which are subdivided into other parts **(minutes),** numbering 12 in the Doric and Tuscan orders and 18 in the Ionic, Corinthian, and Composite orders. [ME *diametre* < OF < L *diametr(os)* < Gk: diagonal, diameter < *dia-* DIA- + *métr(on)* METER¹]

di·am·e·tral (dī am′i trəl), *adj.* **1.** of a diameter. **2.** forming a diameter. [ME < ML *diametrāl(is)* < L *diametr(os)* DIAMETER + *-ālis* -AL¹] —**di·am′e·tral·ly,** *adv.*

di·a·met·ri·cal (dī′ə me′tri kəl), *adj.* **1.** of, pertaining to, or along a diameter. **2.** direct; complete; absolute: *diametrical opposites.* Also, **di′a·met′ric.** [< Gk *diametrik(ós)*, equiv. to *diámetr(os)* DIAMETER + *-ikos* -IC + -AL¹] —**di′a·met′ri·cal·ly,** *adv.*

di·am·ine (dī′ə mēn′, -min, dī am′ēn), *n. Chem.* a compound containing two amino groups. [DI-¹ + AMINE]

di·a·mi·no·pro·pyl·tet·ra·meth·yl·ene·di·a·mine (dī′ə mē′nō prō′pil te′trə meth′ə lēn′dī′ə mēn′, -am′in, dī am′ə nō-), *n. Biochem.* spermine. [DI-¹ + AMINO- + PROPYL + TETRA- + METHYLENE + DIAMINE]

dia·mond (dī′mənd, dī′ə-), *n.* **1.** a pure or nearly pure form of carbon, naturally crystallized in the isometric system, of extreme hardness. **2.** a piece of this stone. **3.** a transparent, flawless or almost flawless piece of this stone, esp. when cut and polished, valued as a precious gem. **4.** a ring or other piece of jewelry containing such a precious stone, esp. an engagement ring. **5.** a piece of this stone used in a drill or cutting tool. **6.** a tool provided with such an uncut stone, used for cutting glass. **7.** crystallized carbon, or a piece of it, artificially produced. **8.** *Geom.* an equilateral quadrilateral, esp. as placed with its diagonals vertical and horizontal; a lozenge or rhombus. **9.** a red lozenge-shaped figure on a playing card. **10.** a card of the suit bearing such figures. **11. diamonds,** (*construed as sing. or pl.*) the suit so marked: *Diamonds is trump. Diamonds are trump.* **12.** *Baseball.* **a.** the space enclosed by home plate and the three bases; infield. **b.** the entire playing field. **13.** *Print.* a 4½-point type of a size between brilliant and pearl. **14. diamond in the rough,** a person of fine character but lacking refined manners or graces. Also called **rough diamond.** —*adj.* **15.** made of or set with a diamond or diamonds: *a diamond ring; a diamond necklace.* **16.** having the shape of a diamond: *a dress with a diamond print.* **17.** indicating the 75th, or sometimes the 60th, event of a series, as of a wedding anniversary. —*v.t.* **18.** to adorn with or as with diamonds. [ME *diamant* < OF < LL *diamant-* (s. of *diamas*), alter. of L *adamas* ADAMANT, diamond] —**dia′mond·like′,** *adj.*

Diamond (def. 4)

Dia·mond (dī′mənd, dī′ə-), *n.* **Cape,** a hill in Canada, in S Quebec, on the St. Lawrence River.

dia·mond·back (dī′mənd bak′, dī′ə-), *n.* **1.** See **diamondback rattlesnake. 2.** See **diamondback terrapin. 3.** See **diamondback moth.** [DIAMOND + BACK¹]

dia′mondback moth′, a moth, *Plutella maculipennis,* having brownish wings marked with diamond-shaped, yellow spots in the male, the larvae of which feed on the leaves of cabbages and other cruciferous plants. Also called **cabbage moth.**

dia′mondback rat′tlesnake, any of several large, highly venomous rattlesnakes having diamond-shaped markings on the back. Cf. **eastern diamondback rattlesnake, western diamondback rattlesnake.**

dia′mondback ter′rapin, any of several edible turtles of the genus *Malaclemys,* found in tidewaters of the eastern and southern U.S., having diamond-shaped markings on the back.

dia′mond drill′, a drill having a hollow, cylindrical bit set with diamonds, used for obtaining cores of rock samples.

dia′mond dust′, **1.** pulverized diamonds, used as an abrasive. **2.** See **ice crystals.**

Dia′mond Head′, a promontory on SE Oahu Island, in central Hawaii. 761 ft.

dia′mond jubilee′. See under **jubilee** (def. 1).

dia′mond-leaf lau′rel (dī′mənd lēf′, dī′ə-), a tree, *Pittosporum rhombifolium,* of Australia, having coarsely toothed, ovalish or diamond-shaped leaves and white flowers.

dia·mond-matched (dī′mənd macht′, dī′ə-), *adj.* (of a veneer) composed of straight-grained flitches cut and assembled to form a diamond pattern.

dia′mond plate′, *Shipbuilding.* a diamond-shaped metal plate for uniting and reinforcing the angles between members meeting in one place.

dia′mond point′, **1.** *Furniture.* a faceted, low-relief ornamental motif giving the effect of a cut gem. **2.** an acute, pyramidal point on a nail or spike.

dia′mond-point spoon′ (dī′mənd point′, dī′ə-), a spoon having a handle terminating in a polygonal, pointed knob. Also called **spear-head spoon.**

dia′mond ring′ effect′, *Astron.* a phenomenon, sometimes observed immediately before and after a total eclipse, in which one of Baily's beads is much brighter than the others, resembling a diamond ring around the moon.

dia′mond skin′ disease′, *Vet. Pathol.* a form of swine erysipelas in which diamond-shaped skin inflammations appear, usually accompanied by swollen joints which later become arthritic.

Dia′mond State′, Delaware (used as a nickname).

di·a·mor·phine (dī′ə môr′fēn), *n. Pharm.* heroin. [DIA(CETYL) + MORPHINE]

Di·a·mox (dī′ə moks′), *n. Pharm., Trademark.* acetazolamide.

di·am′yl sul′fide (dī am′əl), *Chem.* a yellow liquid consisting of a mixture of isomers having the formula $(C_5H_{11})_2S$, used chiefly in the preparation of organic sulfur compounds. Also, **amyl sulfide.** [DI-¹ + AMYL + SULFIDE]

Di·an·a (dī an′ə), *n.* **1.** an ancient Italian deity, goddess of the moon and of hunting, and protectress of women, identified by the Romans with the Greek Artemis. **2.** the moon personified as a goddess. **3.** Also, **Diane, Dyana, Dyane.** a girl's given name.

Diana

di·an·drous (dī an′drəs), *adj. Bot.* **1.** (of a flower) having two stamens. **2.** (of a plant) having flowers with two stamens. [< NL *diandrus.* See DI-¹, -ANDROUS]

Di·ane (dī an′), *n.* a girl's given name. Also, **Diana, Dyana, Dyane.**

di·a·net·ics (dī′ə net′iks), *n.* (*construed as sing.*) a nonscientific theory of personality explaining behavior in terms of an individual's experiences prior to birth. [alter. of DIANOETIC; see -ICS]

di·a·no·et·ic (dī′ə nō et′ik), *adj.* pertaining to thought or reasoning, esp. discursive reasoning. [< Gk *dianoētik(ós)*, equiv. to *diáno(ia)* DIANOIA + *-ē-* thematic vowel + *-tikos* -TIC] —**di′a·no·et′i·cal·ly,** *adv.*

di·a·noi·a (dī′ə noi′ə), *n. Greek Philos.* the mental faculty used in discursive reasoning. [< Gk *diánoia* the intellect, a thought, notion, belief, equiv. to *dia-* DIA- + *nó(ein)* to think + *-ia* -IA]

Di·an·tha (dī an′thə), *n.* a girl's given name.

di·an·thus (dī an′thəs), *n., pl.* **-thus·es.** any caryophyllaceous plant of the genus *Dianthus,* as the carnation or sweet william. [< NL < Gk *Di(ós)* of Zeus (gen. of *Zeús*) + *ánthos* flower]

di·a·pa·son (dī′ə pā′zən, -sən), *n. Music.* **1.** a melody or strain. **2.** the compass of a voice or instrument. **3.** a fixed standard of pitch. **4.** either of two principal timbres or stops of a pipe organ, one of full, majestic tone **(open diapason)** and the other of strong, flutelike tone **(stopped diapason). 5.** any of several other organ stops. **6.** a tuning fork. [< L *diapāsōn* the whole octave < Gk *dià pāsôn (chordôn)* through all (the notes), short for *hē dià pāsôn chordôn symphōnía* the concord through all the notes of the scale] —**di′a·pa′son·al,** *adj.*

diapa′son nor′mal pitch′, *Music.* a standard of pitch in which A above middle C is established at 435 vibrations per second. Also called **French pitch, international pitch, low pitch.**

di·a·pause (dī′ə pôz′), *n., v.* **-paused, -paus·ing.** *Zool.* —*n.* **1.** a period of quiescence during the development of insects and other arthropods, characterized by a cessation of growth in immature stages. **2.** a period of quiescence of reproductive activity in adults of annelids. —*v.i.* **3.** to undergo diapause. [< Gk *diápausis*; see DIA-, PAUSE]

di·a·pe·de·sis (dī′ə pi dē′sis), *n. Physiol.* the passage of blood cells, esp. leukocytes, through the unruptured walls of the capillaries into the tissues. [< NL < Gk *diapḗdēsis* a leaping through, equiv. to *diapēdē-* (verbid s. of *diapēdân* to leap through) + *-sis* -SIS] —**di·a·pe·det·ic** (dī′ə pi det′ik), *adj.*

di·a·per (dī′pər, dī′ə pər), *n.* **1.** a piece of cloth or other absorbent material that forms part of a baby's underclothing; a baby's breechcloth. **2.** a linen or cotton fabric with a woven pattern of small, constantly repeated figures, as diamonds. **3.** Also, **dia′per pat′tern.** such a pattern, originally used in the Middle Ages in weaving silk and gold. —*v.t.* **4.** to put a diaper on (a baby). **5.** to ornament with a diaperlike pattern. [ME *diapre* < MF, var. of *diaspre* < ML *diaspr(us)* made of diaper < MGk *díaspros* pure white, equiv. to *dia-* DIA- + *áspros* white]

dia′per rash′, a reddish inflammation of the buttocks occurring in infants usually as a result of irritation by ammonia formed as a breakdown product of urine.

dia′per serv′ice, a customer-service enterprise which delivers regular supplies of fresh diapers for babies, picking up used diapers to be washed.

di·a·phane (dī′ə fān′), *Microscopy.* a substance used to embed tissues for cutting and microscopic examination. [< MF < ML *diaphan(us)* DIAPHANOUS]

di·aph·a·ne·i·ty (di af′ə nē′i tē, dī′ə fə-), *n.* quality of being diaphanous; transparency. [< Gk *diaphanḗ(s)* showing through + *-ity*]

di·aph·a·nom·e·ter (dī af′ə nom′i tər), *n.* an instrument for measuring the transparency of a solid, liquid, or gas. [DIAPHAN(OUS) + -O- + -METER] —**di·aph·a·no·met·ric** (dī af′ə nə me′trik), *adj.* —**di·aph′a·nom′e·try,** *n.*

di·aph·a·nous (dī af′ə nəs), *adj.* **1.** very sheer and light; almost completely transparent or translucent. **2.** delicately hazy. [< ML *diaphanus* < Gk *diaphanḗs* transparent, equiv. to *diaphan-* (s. of *diaphaínein* to show through; see DIA-, -PHANE) + -OUS] —**di·aph′a·nous·ly,** *adv.* —**di·aph′a·nous·ness,** *n.*

di·a·phone (dī′ə fōn′), *n.* **1.** a foghorn producing a low-pitched, penetrating signal. **2.** *Phonet.* **a.** a phoneme in one dialect corresponding to a similar but phonetically different phoneme in a related dialect. **b.** the aggregation of all the variants of a single phoneme in a given language. **3.** *Ling.* a group of sounds comprising all the phonetically different dialectal variants of a given phoneme: *The broad-a and flat-a of "half" are members of a single diaphone.* [DIA- + -PHONE]

di·a·pho·re·sis (dī′ə fə rē′sis), *n. Med.* perspiration, esp. when artificially produced. [< LL < Gk: a sweating, equiv. to *diaphorē-* (verbid s. of *diaphorein* to carry off or through) + *-sis* -SIS]

di·a·pho·ret·ic (dī′ə fə ret′ik), *Med.* —*adj.* **1.** producing perspiration. —*n.* **2.** a diaphoretic medicine. [< LL *diaphorētic(us)* < Gk *diaphorētikós* promoting perspiration: *diaphorē-* (see DIAPHORESIS) + *-tikos* -TIC]

di·a·phragm (dī′ə fram′), *n.* **1.** *Anat.* **a.** a muscular, membranous or ligamentous wall separating two cavities or limiting a cavity. **b.** the partition separating the thoracic cavity from the abdominal cavity in mammals. **2.** *Physical Chem.* **a.** a porous plate separating two liquids, as in a galvanic cell. **b.** a semipermeable membrane. **3.** a thin disk that vibrates when receiving or producing sound waves, as in a telephone, microphone, or the like. **4.** Also called **pessary.** a thin, dome-shaped device, usually of rubber, for wearing over the uterine cervix to prevent conception during sexual intercourse. **5.** *Optics.* a ring or a plate with a hole in the center which is placed on the axis of an optical instrument, as a camera, and which controls the amount of light entering the instrument. **6.** a plate or web for stiffening metal-framed constructions. —*v.t.* **7.** to furnish with a diaphragm. **8.** *Optics.* to reduce the aperture of (a lens, camera, etc.) by means of a diaphragm. [< LL *diaphragm(a)* < Gk *diáphragma* the diaphragm, midriff, equiv. to *dia-* DIA- + *phrágma* a fence]

di·a·phrag·mat·ic (dī′ə frag mat′ik), *adj.* **1.** of the diaphragm. **2.** like a diaphragm. [< Gk *diaphragmat-* (s. of *diáphragma* DIAPHRAGM) + -IC] —**di′a·phrag·mat′i·cal·ly,** *adv.*

di·aph·y·sis (dī af′i sis), *n., pl.* **-ses** (-sēz′). *Anat.* the shaft of a long bone. [< NL < Gk, equiv. to *diaphý(es-thai)* to grow between + *-sis* -SIS] —**di·a·phys·i·al** (dī′ə fiz′ē əl), *adj.*

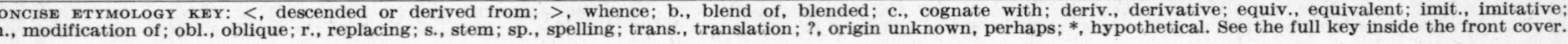
CONCISE ETYMOLOGY KEY: <, descended or derived from; >, whence; b., blend of, blended; c., cognate with; deriv., derivative; equiv., equivalent; imit., imitative; m., modification of; obl., oblique; r., replacing; s., stem; sp., spelling; trans., translation; ?, origin unknown, perhaps; *, hypothetical. See the full key inside the front cover.

di·ap·la·sis (dī ap′lə sis), *n., pl.* **-ses** (-sēz′). *Surg.* the setting of a fracture or the reduction of a dislocated bone. Also called **diorthosis.** [DIA- + -PLASIS]

di·a·poph·y·sis (dī′ə pof′i sis), *n., pl.* **-ses** (-sēz′). *Anat., Zool.* the upper part of the transverse process of a vertebra. [< NL; see DI-³, APOPHYSIS] —**di·ap·o·phys·i·al** (dī′ap ə fiz′ē əl), *adj.*

Di·ar·bek·r (dē är bek′ər), *n.* Diyarbekir.

di·ar·chy (dī′är kē), *n., pl.* **-chies.** government or a government in which power is vested in two rulers or authorities. Also, **dyarchy.** [DI-¹ + -ARCHY] —**di·ar′chi·al, di·ar′chic,** *adj.*

di·a·rist (dī′ə rist), *n.* a person who keeps a diary [DIAR(Y) + -IST] —**di′a·ris′tic,** *adj.*

di·ar·rhe·a (dī′ə rē′ə), *n. Pathol.* an intestinal disorder characterized by abnormal frequency and fluidity of fecal evacuations. Also, **di′ar·rhoe′a.** [< LL *diarrhoea* < Gk *diárrhoia* a flowing through, equiv. to *diarrho-* (var. s. of *diarrheîn* to flow through) + *-ia* -IA] —**di′ar·rhe′al, di′ar·rhe′ic, di·ar·rhet·ic** (dī′ə ret′ik), **di′ar·rhoe′al, di′ar·rhoe′ic, di′ar·rhoet′ic,** *adj.*

di·ar·thro·sis (dī′är thrō′sis), *n., pl.* **-ses** (-sēz). *Anat.* a form of articulation which permits maximal motion, as the knee joint. [< NL < Gk; see DI-³, ARTHROSIS] —**di·ar·thro·di·al** (dī′är thrō′dē əl), *adj.*

di·a·ry (dī′ə rē), *n., pl.* **-ries. 1.** a daily record, esp. of the writer's own experiences, observations, attitudes, etc. **2.** a book for keeping such a record. **3.** a book or pad containing pages marked and arranged in calendar order, in which to note appointments and the like. [< L *diāri(um)* daily allowance, journal, equiv. to *di(ēs)* day + *-ārium* -ARY]

Di′ary of Sam′uel Pepys′, The. See **Pepys' Diary.**

Di·as (dē′əs; *Port.* dē′əsh), *n.* **Bar·tho·lo·me·u** (bär′to͝o lo͞o me′o͞o), c1450–1500, Portuguese navigator and discoverer of the Cape of Good Hope. Also, **Diaz.**

di·as·chi·sis (dī as′ki sis), *n. Med.* a disturbance or loss of function in one part of the brain due to a localized injury in another part. [< NL < Gk *diáskhisis* a division; see DIA-, SCHI(ZO)-, -SIS]

Di·a·si·a (dī ā′sē ə), *n.* an ancient Greek festival in honor of Zeus.

Di·as·po·ra (dī as′pər ə), *n.* **1.** the scattering of the Jews to countries outside of Palestine after the Babylonian captivity. **2.** the body of Jews living in such countries. **3.** such countries collectively: *the return of the Jews from the Diaspora.* **4.** (*l.c.*) any religious group living as a minority among people of the prevailing religion. [< Gk *diasporá* a dispersion. See DIA-, SPORE]

di·a·spore (dī′ə spōr′, -spôr′), *n.* **1.** a mineral, aluminum hydroxide, $HAlO_2$, occurring in crystals, or more usually in lamellar or scaly masses. **2.** *Bot.* a disseminule, esp. one that undergoes dispersal. [< Gk *diasporá*; see DIASPORA]

di·a·stase (dī′ə stās′), *n. Biochem.* an enzyme that converts starch into dextrin and maltose, present in germinated barley, potatoes, etc. [< F < Gk *diástasis*; see DIASTASIS]

di·as·ta·sis (dī as′tə sis), *n., pl.* **-ses** (-sēz′). **1.** *Med.* the separation of normally joined parts, as in the dislocation of bones, without fracture. **2.** *Physiol.* the diastolic rest period immediately preceding systole. [< NL < Gk *diástasis* a separation. See DIA-, STASIS]

di·a·stat·ic (dī′ə stat′ik), *adj.* **1.** *Biochem.* **a.** of or pertaining to diastase. **b.** having the properties of diastase: *diastatic action.* **2.** *Med., Physiol.* of or pertaining to diastasis. Also, **di·a·sta·sic** (dī′ə stā′sik). [< Gk *diastatik(ós)* separative. See DIA-, STATIC]

di·a·ste·ma (dī′ə stē′mə), *n., pl.* **-ma·ta** (-mə tə). **1.** *Biol.* the modified protoplasm at the equator of a cell, which exists previous to the mitotic division of the cell. **2.** *Dentistry.* a space between two teeth, esp. a space between a canine and an incisor of the upper jaw into which a lower canine occludes. [< LL < Gk: interval, equiv. to *diastḗ(nai)* to stand apart + *-ma* n. suffix]

di·as·ter (dī as′tər), *n. Biol.* the stage in mitosis at which the chromosomes, after their division and separation, are grouped near the poles of the spindle. [DI-¹ + ASTER²] —**di·as′tral,** *adj.*

di·as·to·le (dī as′tᵊlē′), *n.* **1.** *Physiol.* the normal rhythmical dilatation of the heart during which the chambers are filling with blood. Cf. **systole** (def. 1). **2.** *Pros.* the lengthening of a syllable regularly short, esp. before a pause or at the ictus. [< LL *diastolē* < Gk *diastolḗ* a putting asunder, dilation, lengthening; cf. *diastéllein* to set apart < *dia-* DIA- + *stéllein* to put, place]

di·as·tol·ic (dī′ə stol′ik), *adj.* pertaining to or produced by diastole. [DIASTOLE + -IC]

di·as·tro·phism (dī as′trə fiz′əm), *n. Geol.* **1.** the action of the forces which cause the earth's crust to be deformed, producing continents, mountains, changes of level, etc. **2.** any such deformation. [< Gk *diastroph(ḗ)* a distortion. See DIA-, STROPHE, -ISM] —**di·a·stroph·ic** (dī′ə strof′ik), *adj.*

di·a·style (dī′ə stīl′), *adj. Archit.* having an intercolumniation of three diameters. See illus. under **intercolumniation.** [< L *diastȳl(os)* < Gk *diástylos* with columns far apart, equiv. to *dia-* DIA- + *stŷl(os)* column + *-os* adj. suffix]

di·a·sys·tem (dī′ə sis′təm), *n. Gram.* a linguistic system forming a common denominator for a group or set of dialects. [DIA(LECT) + SYSTEM]

di·a·tes·sa·ron (dī′ə tes′ə ron′), *n.* **1.** (*sometimes cap.*) a harmony of the four Gospels, arranged to form a single narrative. **2.** *Gk. and Medieval Music.* the interval of a fourth. [< LL: the interval of a fourth, L, (a medicine) made of four < Gk *dià tessárōn* through four]

di·a·ther·mic (dī′ə thûr′mik), *adj.* **1.** of or pertaining to diathermy. **2.** capable of conducting heat. [< F *diathermique*; see DIA-, THERM-, -IC]

di·a·ther·my (dī′ə thûr′mē), *n. Med.* the production of heat in body tissues by electric currents, for therapeutic purposes. Also, **di·a·ther·mi·a** (dī′ə thûr′mē ə). [< NL *diathermia.* See DIA-, -THERMY]

di·ath·e·sis (dī ath′i sis), *n., pl.* **-ses** (-sēz′). **1.** *Pathol.* a constitutional predisposition or tendency, as to a particular disease or affection. **2.** *Gram. Rare.* voice (def. 15). [< NL < Gk *diáthesis* arrangement, disposition. See DIA-, THESIS] —**di·a·thet·ic** (dī′ə thet′ik), *adj.*

di·a·tom (dī′ə təm, -tom′), *n.* any of numerous microscopic, unicellular, marine or fresh-water algae having siliceous cell walls. [< NL *Diatom(a)* name of the genus < Gk *diátom(os)* cut in two. See DIA-, -TOME]

di·a·to·ma·ceous (dī′ə tə mā′shəs), *adj.* consisting of or containing diatoms or their fossil remains. [< NL *Diatomace(ae)* name of the family < *Diatom(a)* DIATOM + -ACE(AE); see -ACEOUS]

di′atoma′ceous earth′, a fine siliceous earth composed chiefly of the cell walls of diatoms: used in filtration, as an abrasive, etc. Also called **di·at·o·mite** (dī at′ə mīt′), **kieselguhr.**

di·a·tom·ic (dī′ə tom′ik), *adj. Chem.* **1.** having two atoms in the molecule. **2.** containing two replaceable atoms or groups; binary. [DI-¹ + ATOMIC] —**di·at·o·mic·i·ty** (dī′at ə mis′i tē), *n.*

di·a·ton·ic (dī′ə ton′ik), *adj. Music.* **1.** noting a scale that contains five whole tones and two semitones, as the major, minor, and certain modal scales **2.** of or pertaining to the tones, intervals, or harmonies of such a scale. [< LL *diatonic(us)* < Gk *diatonikós*; see DIA-, TONIC] —**di′a·ton′i·cal·ly,** *adv.*

di·a·ton·i·cism (dī′ə ton′i siz′əm), *n.* the use of diatonic harmony; composition in a diatonic idiom.

di·a·treme (dī′ə trēm′), *n. Geol.* a volcanic vent produced in a solid rock structure by the explosive energy of gases in magmas. [DIA- + Gk *trêma* hole]

di·a·tribe (dī′ə trīb′), *n.* a bitter, sharply abusive denunciation, attack, or criticism. [< L *diatrib(a)* < Gk *diatribḗ* pastime, study, discourse, deriv. of *diatrī́b(ein)* (to) rub away (*dia-* DIA- + *trī́bein* to rub)]

di·at·ro·pism (dī a′trə piz′əm), *n. Bot.* the tendency of some plant organs to take a transverse position to the line of action of an outside stimulus. [DIA- + TROPISM] —**di·a·trop·ic** (dī′ə trop′ik), *adj.*

Di·az (dē′əs; *Port.* dē′əsh), *n.* **Bar·tho·lo·me·u** (bär′to͝o lo͞o me′o͞o). See **Dias, Bartholomeu.**

Dí·az (dē′äs), *n.* **(Jo·sé de la Cruz) Por·fi·rio** (hô se′ *th*e lä kro͞os′ pôr fē′ryô), 1830–1915, president of Mexico 1877–80, 1884–1911.

diaz-, var. of **diazo-** before a vowel: *diazine.*

Dí·az de Bi·var (dē′äth *th*e bē vär′), **Ro·dri·go** (rô *th*rē′gô) or **Ruy** (rwē). See **Cid, The.** Also, **Dí·az de Vi·var** (dē′äth *th*e bē vär′).

Dí·az del Cas·til·lo (dē′äth *th*el käs tē′lyô), **Ber·nal** (ber näl′), 1492–1581, Spanish soldier-historian of the conquest of Mexico.

di·a·zine (dī′ə zēn′, dī az′ēn, -in), *n. Chem.* any of three isomeric compounds having the formula $C_4H_4N_2$, containing a ring of four carbon and two nitrogen atoms. [DIAZ- + -INE²]

Dí·az Mi·rón (dē′äs mē rôn′), **Sal·va·dor** (säl′vä-*th*ôr′), 1853–1928, Mexican poet.

di·az·o (dī az′ō, -ā′zō), *adj. Chem.* containing the diazo group. [DI-¹ + AZO-]

diazo-, *Chem.* a combining form of **diazo:** *diazotype.* Also, *esp. before a vowel,* **diaz-.**

di·az·o·al·kane (dī az′ō al′kān, -ā′zō-), *n. Chem.* any diazo compound having the general formula, R_2CN_2, where R is hydrogen or any saturated organic group, as diazoethane, CH_3CHN_2. [DIAZO- + ALKANE]

di·az·o·a·mi·no (dī az′ō ə mē′nō, -am′ə nō′, -ā′zō-), *adj. Chem.* containing the diazoamino group. [DIAZO- + AMINO]

diazoami′no group′, *Chem.* the divalent group, –N=NNH–. Also called **diazoami′no rad′ical.**

diaz′o group′, *Chem.* the bivalent group, –N=N–, united with one hydrocarbon group and another atom or group, as in benzenediazo hydroxide, $C_6H_5N{=}NOH$, or the bivalent group =N=N united with one hydrocarbon group, as in diazomethane, $CH_2{=}N{=}N$. Also called **diaz′o rad′ical.**

di·a·zole (dī′ə zōl′, dī az′ōl), *n. Chem.* any of a group of organic compounds containing three carbon and two nitrogen atoms arranged in a ring. [DIAZ- + -OLE]

di·az·o·meth·ane (dī az′ō meth′ān, -ā′zō-), *n. Chem.* a yellow, odorless, toxic, explosive gas, CH_2N_2, used chiefly as a methylating agent and in organic synthesis. [DIAZO- + METHANE]

di·a·zo·ni·um (dī′ə zō′nē əm), *adj. Chem.* of or derived from a diazonium compound. [DIAZ- + *-onium,* as in *ammonium*]

diazo′nium com′pound, *Chem.* any of a series of compounds that contain the group Ar≡N–, in which Ar represents an aryl group.

diazo′nium salt′, *Chem.* any of a group of salts of the general formula ArN_2X, in which Ar represents an aryl group and X an anion, as benzenediazonium chloride, $(C_6H_5N{\equiv}N)Cl$, many of which are important intermediates in the manufacture of azo dyes.

diaz′o proc′ess, *Photog.* a method for printing on paper treated with a diazo compound that disintegrates upon exposure to light and developing the unexposed areas by the use of diazo dyes.

diaz′o rad′ical. See **diazo group.**

Dí·az Or·daz (dē′äs ôr däs′), *n.* **Gus·ta·vo** (go͞os-tä′vô), born 1911, Mexican teacher, jurist, and public official: president since 1964.

di·az·o·ti·za·tion (dī az′ə ti zā′shən), *n. Chem.* the preparation of a diazonium salt by treatment of an arylamine with nitrous acid. [DIAZOTIZE + -ATION]

di·az·o·tize (dī az′ə tīz′), *v.t.,* **-tized, -tiz·ing.** *Chem.* to cause diazotization. [DI-¹ + AZOTE + -IZE] —**di·az′o·tiz′a·bil′i·ty,** *n.* —**di·az′o·tiz′a·ble,** *adj.*

di·az·o·type (dī az′ə tīp′), *n. Photog.* a print produced by the diazo process. [DIAZO- + -TYPE]

Dí·az Ro·drí·guez (dē′äs rô *th*rē′ges), **Ma·nuel** (mä nwel′), 1868–1927, Venezuelan novelist, poet, and essayist.

dib (dib), *v.i.,* **dibbed, dib·bing.** to fish by letting the bait bob lightly on the water. [b. DI(P + BO)B¹]

Di·bai (di bī′), *n.* Dubai.

di·ba·sic (dī bā′sik), *adj. Chem.* **1.** containing two replaceable or ionizable hydrogen atoms: *dibasic acid.* **2.** having two univalent, basic atoms, as dibasic sodium phosphate, Na_2HPO_4. [DI-¹ + BASIC] —**di·ba·sic·i·ty** (dī′bā sis′i tē), *n.*

diba′sic so′dium phos′phate, *Chem.* See **sodium phosphate** (def. 2).

dib·a·tag (dib′ə tag′), *n.* a small gazelle, *Ammodorcas clarkei,* of Somaliland, having a long neck. Also called **Clarke's gazelle.** [< Somali]

dib·ble (dib′əl), *n., v.,* **-bled, -bling.** —*n.* **1.** Also, **dib·ber** (dib′ər). a small, curved, hand-held, pointed implement for making holes in the ground for planting seeds, bulbs, etc. —*v.t.* **2.** to make a hole (in the ground) with or as with a dibble. **3.** to set (plants) in holes made with a dibble. [? akin to DIB]

dib·buk (dib′ək; *Heb.* dē bo͞ok′), *n., pl.* **dib·buks dib·buk·im** (di bo͞ok′im; *Heb.* dē′bo͞o kēm′). *Jewish Folklore.* dybbuk.

Di·be·li·us (di bā′lē əs, -bāl′yəs; *Ger.* dē bā′lē o͝os′), *n.* **Mar·tin** (mär′tᵊn; *Ger.* mär′tēn), 1883–1947, German theologian.

D'I·ber·ville (dī′bər vil′), *n.* a town in SE Mississippi. 3005 (1960).

Di·boll (dī′bəl), *n.* a town in E Texas. 2506 (1960).

di·brach (dī′brak), *n. Pros.* pyrrhic¹ (def. 3). [< L *dibrach(ys)* < Gk *díbrachys* a foot of two short syllables, equiv. to *di-* DI-¹ + *brachýs* short; see BRACHY-]

di·bran·chi·ate (dī brang′kē it, -kē āt′), *adj.* **1.** belonging or pertaining to the *Dibranchiata,* a subclass or order of cephalopods with two gills, including the decapods and octopods. —*n.* **2.** a dibranchiate cephalopod. [< NL *Dibranchiāt(a)* name of the order; see DI-¹, BRANCHIATE]

di·bro·mide (dī brō′mīd, -mid), *n. Chem.* a compound containing two bromine atoms, as ethylene dibromide, CH_2BrCH_2Br. [DI-¹ + BROMIDE]

dibs (dibz), *n.pl. Slang.* **1.** money in small amounts. **2. dibs on (something),** a declaration of one's rights or claims regarding the possession or use of (something): *I have dibs on the telephone when you finish your call.* [shortening of earlier *dibstones* a children's game, a deriv. of DIB]

di·bu·caine (dī byo͞o′kān), *n. Pharm.* a compound, $C_{20}H_{29}N_3O_2$, used in the form of its hydrochloride as a local and spinal anesthetic. [DI-¹ + BU(TYL) + (CO)-CAINE]

di·bu′tyl ox′alate (dī byo͞ot′ᵊl), *Chem.* a colorless liquid, $H_9C_4OOCCOOC_4H_9$, used chiefly in organic synthesis and as a solvent. Also called **butyl oxalate.** [DI-¹ + BUTYL]

di·cac·o·dyl (dī kak′ə dil), *n. Chem.* cacodyl (def. 2). [DI-¹ + CACODYL]

di·car′box·yl′ic ac′id (dī kär′bok sil′ik, -kär′-), *Chem.* any of the organic compounds that contain two carboxyl groups. [DI-¹ + CARBOXYLIC ACID]

di·cast (dī′kast, dik′ast), *n.* (in ancient Athens) one of 6000 citizens over 30 years old, eligible to be chosen by lot to sit as a judge. [< Gk *dikast(ḗs)* a juryman < *dikáz(ein)* (to) judge, determine (deriv. of *díkē* right, law, order) + agentive prefix *-tēs*] —**di·cas′tic,** *adj.*

di·cas·ter·y (dī kas′tə rē), *n., pl.* **-ter·ies.** (in ancient Athens) **1.** a court of dicasts. **2.** the place where this court was held. [< Gk *dikastḗri(on)* a hall of justice, equiv. to *dikast(ḗs)* (see DICAST) + *-erion* a place for]

dice (dīs), *n.pl., sing.* **die,** *v.,* **diced, dic·ing.** —*n.* **1.** small cubes of plastic, ivory, bone, or wood, marked on each side with one to six spots, usually used in pairs in games of chance or in gambling. **2.** See **poker dice. 3.** any of various games, esp. gambling games, played by shaking and throwing from two to six dice or poker dice onto a flat surface. Cf. **craps. 4.** any small cubes. **5. no dice,** *Slang.* a negative response; refusal; being without success: *He asked for a raise, but it was no dice.* —*v.t.* **6.** to cut into small cubes. **7.** to decorate with cubelike figures. —*v.i.* **8.** to play at dice. [ME *dice* (sing. and pl.), var. of *de;* see DIE²] —**dic′er,** *n.*

Di·ce (dī′sē), *n. Class. Myth.* Dike.

dice′ cup′, a container, usually cylindrical and open at the top, in which dice are shaken to give them a random position and from which they are then thrown or rolled.

di·cen·tra (dī sen′trə), *n.* any plant of the genus *Dicentra,* having racemes of drooping flowers, as the Dutchman's-breeches or the bleeding heart. [< NL < Gk *díkentr(os)* with two stings or spurs, equiv. to *di-* DI-¹ + *kéntr(on)* a spur, point, sting (deriv. of *kent(ein)* (to) prick, sting) + L *-a* n. suffix]

di·ceph·a·lous (dī sef′ə ləs), *adj.* having two heads; two-headed. [< Gk *diképhal(os)* two-headed. See DI-¹, CEPHALOUS] —**di·ceph′a·lism,** *n.*

di·cha·si·um (dī kā′zhē əm, -zē əm), *n., pl.* **-si·a** (-zhē ə, -zē ə). *Bot.* a form of cymose inflorescence in which each axis produces a pair of lateral axes. [< NL < Gk *díchas(is)* a division, deriv. of *dicház(ein)* (to) cleave (equiv. to *dích(a)* apart + *-az(ein)* (to) subject to) + L *-ium* n. suffix] —**di·cha′si·al,** *adj.*

di·chla·myd·e·ous (dī′klə mid′ē əs), *adj.* (of a flower) having both a calyx and a corolla. [DI-¹ + CHLAMYDEOUS]

di·chlo·ride (dī klôr′īd, -id, -klôr′-), *n.* (chiefly in organic chemistry) bichloride. [DI-¹ + CHLORIDE]

di·chlo′ro·di·eth′yl sul′fide (dī klôr′ō dī eth′əl -klōr′-, -klôr′-, -klōr′-), *Chem.* See **mustard ga**[DI-¹ + CHLORO-² + DI-¹ + ETHYL + SULFIDE]

di·chlo·ro·di·flu·o·ro·meth·ane (dī klôr′ō flo͞o′ə rō meth′ān, -flo͞or′ō-, -flôr′-, -flōr′-, dī klôr′-) *Chem.* a colorless, slightly water-soluble, nonflamma gas, CCl_2F_2, that boils at −29°C: used chiefly as a pellant in aerosols and as a refrigerant. [DI-¹ + CHLO + DI-¹ + FLUORO-¹ + METHANE]

di·chlo·ro·di·phen·yl·tri·chlor·o·eth·ane klôr′ō dī fen′il trī klôr′ō eth′ān, -trī klôr′-, dī k *n. Chem.* See **DDT.** [DI-¹ + CHLORO-² + DI-¹ + P + TRI- + CHLORO-² + ETHANE]

di·chlo·ro·eth′yl for′mal (dī klôr′ō -klôr′-), *Chem.* a colorless liquid, $CH_2(OCH_2C$ used chiefly as a solvent and in the manufa certain synthetic rubbers. Also, **dichlo′ro for′mal.** [DI- + CHLORO-² + ETHYL]

di·chlo·ro·meth·ane (dī klôr′ə meth′ān, *n. Chem.* See **methylene chloride.** [DI-¹ + METHANE]

di·chlo′ro·phe·nox′y·a·ce′tic ac′id nok′sē ə sē′tik, -ə set′ik, -ə sē′tik, -ə set′ dī klôr′-, dī klôr′-), *Chem.* a white to yell line, slightly water-soluble powder, C_6H_3(O Cl_2, used for killing weeds. Also called **2,** CHLORO-² + PHEN- + OXY-² + ACETIC ACI

dicho-, a prefix occurring in loan word (*dichotomy*); on this model used, with th two parts," "in pairs," in the formatio words: (*dichogamy*). [< Gk, comb. fo two, asunder]

di·chog·a·mous (dī kog′ə məs), *adj.* stamens and pistils maturing at differ fore preventing self-pollination, as a monoclinous flower (opposed to *homogamous*). Also, **di·cho·gam·ic** (dī/kō-gam/ik). [DICHO- + -GAMOUS]

di·chog·a·my (dī kog/ə mē), *n.* a dichogamous condition. [< G *Dichogamie.* See DICHO-, -GAMY]

di·chon·dra (dī kon/drə), *n.* any of several prostrate, creeping, tropical vines of the genus *Dichondra*, esp. *D. repens*, often used as a ground cover. [< NL, equiv. to *di-* DI-[1] + *-chondra* (< Gk *chóndr(os)* grain, granule (see CHONDRIA-) + *-a* n. suffix)]

di·chot·o·mise (dī kot/ə mīz/), *v.t., v.i.*, **-mised, -mis·ing.** *Chiefly Brit.* dichotomize. —**di·chot/o·mi·sa/tion,** *n.*

di·chot·o·mize (dī kot/ə mīz/), *v.*, **-mized, -miz·ing.** —*v.t.* **1.** to divide or separate into two parts, kinds, etc. —*v.i.* **2.** to become divided into two parts; form a dichotomy. [< LL *dichotom(os)* DICHOTOMOUS + -IZE] —**di·chot·o·mist** (dī kot/ə mist), *n.* —**di·chot/o·mis/tic,** *adj.* —**di·chot/o·mi·za/tion,** *n.*

di·chot·o·mous (dī kot/ə məs), *adj.* **1.** divided or dividing into two parts. **2.** of or pertaining to dichotomy. [< LL *dichotomos* < Gk *dichótomos.* See DICHO-, -TOME, -OUS] —**di·chot/o·mous·ly,** *adv.*

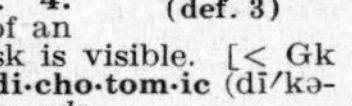

Dichotomy (def. 3)

di·chot·o·my (dī kot/ə mē), *n., pl.* **-mies. 1.** division into two parts, kinds, etc.; subdivision into halves or pairs. **2.** *Logic.* classification by division into two mutually exclusive and exhaustive groups. **3.** *Bot.* a mode of branching by constant bifurcation, as in some stems, in veins of leaves, etc. **4.** *Astron.* the phase of the moon or of an inferior planet when half of its disk is visible. [< Gk *dichotomía.* See DICHO-, -TOMY] —**di·cho·tom·ic** (dī/kə-tom/ik), *adj.* —**di/cho·tom/i·cal·ly,** *adv.*

di·chro·ic (dī krō/ik), *adj.* **1.** characterized by dichroism: *dichroic crystal.* **2.** dichromatic. Also, **di·chro·it·ic** (dī/krō it/ik). [< Gk *díchro(os)* of two colors. See DI-[1], -CHROIC]

di·chro·i·scope (dī krō/i skōp/), *n.* dichroscope. —**di·chro·i·scop·ic** (dī krō/i skop/ik), *adj.*

di·chro·ism (dī/krō iz/əm), *n.* **1.** *Crystall.* pleochroism of a uniaxial crystal such that it exhibits two different colors when viewed from two different directions under transmitted light. **2.** *Chem.* the exhibition of essentially different colors by certain solutions in different degrees of dilution or concentration. [< Gk *díchro(os)* (see DICHROIC) + -ISM]

di·chro·ite (dī/krō īt/), *n.* *Mineral.* cordierite. [< F < Gk *díchro(os)* (see DICHROIC) + F *-ite* -ITE[1]]

di·chro·mat (dī/krō mat/), *n.* *Ophthalm.* a person who has dichromatism. Also, **dichromate.** [back formation from DICHROMATIC]

di·chro·mate (dī krō/māt *for 1;* dī/krō māt/ *for 2*), *n.* **1.** Also, **bichromate.** *Chem.* a salt of a hypothetical acid, $H_2Cr_2O_7$, as potassium dichromate, $K_2Cr_2O_7$. **2.** dichromat. [DI-[1] + CHROMATE]

di·chro·mat·ic (dī/krō mat/ik, -krə-), *adj.* **1.** having or showing two colors; dichromic. **2.** *Zool.* exhibiting two color phases within a species not due to age or season. [DI-[1] + CHROMATIC]

di·chro·mat·i·cism (dī/krō mat/i siz/əm, -krə-), *n.* dichroism (def. 1). [DICHROMATIC + -ISM]

di·chro·ma·tism (dī krō/mə tiz/əm), *n.* **1.** the quality or state of being dichromatic. **2.** Also, **di·chro·ma·top·si·a** (dī krō/mə top/sē ə). *Ophthalm.* a defect of vision in which the retina responds to only two of the three primary colors. Cf. **monochromatism, trichromatism** (def. 3). [DICHROMAT(IC) + -ISM]

di·chro·mic[1] (dī krō/mik), *adj.* pertaining to or involving two colors only: *dichromic vision.* [DI-[1] + CHROMIC]

di·chro·mic[2] (dī krō/mik), *adj.* *Chem.* (of a compound) containing two atoms of chromium. [DI-[1] + CHROM(IUM) + -IC]

dichro/mic ac/id, *Chem.* the hypothetical acid, $H_2Cr_2O_7$, from which dichromates are derived.

di·chro·scope (dī/krə skōp/), *n.* an instrument for observing the dichroism or pleochroism of crystals. Also, **dichroiscope, di·chro·o·scope** (dī krō/ə skōp/). [DICHRO(ISM) + -SCOPE] —**di·chro·scop·ic** (dī/krə-skop/ik), **di·chro·o·scop·ic** (dī krō/ə skop/ik), *adj.*

Dich·ter·lie·be (*Ger.* diKH/tər lē/bə), *n.* a song cycle (1840) by Robert Schumann, consisting of 16 songs set to poems of Heinrich Heine.

dic·ing (dī/sing), *n.* **1.** gambling or playing with dice. **2.** ornamentation, especially of leather, with squares or diamonds. [DICE + -ING[1]]

dick (dik), *n.* **1.** *U.S. Slang.* a detective. **2.** *Slang (vulgar).* penis. **3.** *Chiefly Brit.* man; fellow. [generic use of the proper name]

Dick (dik), *n.* **1. George Frederick,** 1881–1967, U.S. internist. **2.** a boy's given name, form of **Richard.**

dick·cis·sel (dik sis/əl), *n.* a bunting, *Spiza americana*, of the eastern and central U.S., having a brownish back streaked with black, a black patch on the throat, and a yellowish breast. [imit. of its call]

dick·ens (dik/inz), *n.* devil; deuce (usually prec. by *the* and often used in exclamations as a mild imprecation): *The dickens take you! What the dickens!* [prob. substitute for *devil;* ? special use of *Dicken*, earlier form of *Dick*, proper name]

Dick·ens (dik/inz), *n.* **Charles (John Huf·fam)** (huf/əm), ("*Boz*"), 1812–70, English novelist. —**Dick·en·si·an** (di ken/zē ən), *adj.*

dick·er[1] (dik/ər), *v.i.* **1.** to swap or trade with petty bargaining; bargain; haggle. **2.** to barter. **3.** to try to arrange matters by mutual bargaining: *They dickered for hours over some of the finer points of the contract.* —*v.t.* **4.** to swap or trade, esp. with bargaining or haggling. —*n.* **5.** a petty bargain. **6.** a barter or swap. **7.** an item or goods bartered or swapped. **8.** a deal, esp. a political deal. [? v. use of DICKER[2]]

dick·er[2] (dik/ər), *n.* the number or quantity ten, esp. a lot of ten hides or skins. [ME *diker* < OF *dacre*, ML *dicria*; cf. L *decuria* DECURY]

dick·ey (dik/ē), *n., pl.* **-eys. 1.** a waist for women, without sides or sleeves, to be worn under a dress or jacket. **2.** a detachable, usually starched, insert worn to simulate the front of a shirt in clerical dress, formal attire, service uniforms, or the like. Cf. **vest** (def. 2), **tee. 3.** a detachable linen shirt collar. **4.** a bib or pinafore worn by a child. **5.** a small bird. **6.** a donkey, esp. a male. **7.** *Brit. Dial.* an outside seat on a carriage, as the driver's seat in front or seats for servants or guards in the rear. Also, **dicky, dickie.** [application of *Dicky*, dim. of *Dick*, proper name]

dick·ey·bird (dik/ē bûrd/), *n.* dickey (def. 5). [DICKEY + BIRD]

dick·ie (dik/ē), *n.* dickey.

Dick·ie (dik/ē), *n.* a boy's given name, form of **Richard.**

Dick·in·son (dik/in sən), *n.* **1. Emily (Elizabeth),** 1830–86, U.S. poet. **2. John,** 1732–1808, U.S. statesman and publicist. **3.** a town in W North Dakota. 9971 (1960). **4.** a town in S Texas. 4715 (1960).

dick·ite (dik/īt), *n.* *Mineral.* a polymorph of kaolinite, occurring as the result of igneous solutions. [named after A. B. *Dick* (d. 1926), English mineralogist + -ITE[1]]

Dick·son (dik/sən), *n.* **1. Leonard Eugene,** 1874–1954, U.S. mathematician. **2.** a town in central Tennessee. 5028 (1960).

Dick/son Cit/y, a town in NE Pennsylvania. 7738 (1960).

Dick/ test/, *Med.* a test for determining immunity or susceptibility to scarlet fever in which scarlet fever toxin is injected into the skin, susceptibility being characterized by redness at the injection area. [named after G. F. DICK who devised it]

dick·y (dik/ē), *n., pl.* **dick·ies.** dickey.

di·cli·nous (dī/klə nəs, dī klī/-), *adj* *Bot.* **1.** (of a plant species, variety, etc.) having the stamens and the pistils in separate flowers, either on the same plant or on different plants; either monoecious or dioecious. **2.** (of a flower) having only stamens or only pistils; unisexual. [DI-[1] + Gk *klín(ē)* couch, bed + -OUS] —**di/cli·nism,** *n.*

di·co·phane (dī/kə fān/), *n.* See **DDT.** [DI-[1] + C(HLORO-[2]) + -O- + PH(ENYL) + (ETH)ANE]

di·cot (dī/kot), *n.* a dicotyledon. Also, **di·cot·yl** (dī-kot/əl). [by shortening]

di·cot·y·le·don (dī kot/əlēd/ən, dī/kotəlēd/-), *n.* an angiospermous plant of the subclass *Dicotyledoneae*, characterized by producing seeds with two cotyledons and an exogenous manner of growth. Cf. **monocotyledon.** [< NL *Dicotyledon(ēs)* name of the class. See DI-[1], COTYLEDON]

di·cot·y·le·don·ous (dī kot/əlēd/ənəs, -əled/-; dī/-kotəlēd/ənəs, -kotəled/-), *adj.* belonging or pertaining to the subclass *Dicotyledoneae;* having two cotyledons. [DICOTYLEDON + -OUS]

di·cou·ma·rin (dī ko͞o/mər in, -kyo͞o/-), *n.* *Pharm.* a white, crystalline, almost water-insoluble powder, $C_{19}H_{12}O_6$, originally obtained from spoiled clover, and now synthesized: used chiefly to prevent the coagulation of blood and in the treatment of arterial thrombosis. Also, **di·cou·ma·rol** (dī ko͞o/mə rôl/, -rōl/, -kyo͞o/-). Also called **bishydroxycoumarin.** [DI-[1] + COUMARIN]

di·crot·ic (dī krot/ik), *adj.* *Physiol.* **1.** having two arterial beats for one heartbeat, as certain pulses. **2.** pertaining to such a pulse. [< Gk *díkrot(os)* double-beating (*di-* DI-[1] + *krótos* a clapping, rattling noise) + -IC] —**di·cro·tism** (dī/krə tiz/əm), *n.*

dict., 1. dictation. **2.** dictator. **3.** dictionary.

dic·ta (dik/tə), *n.* a pl. of **dictum.**

dic·ta·graph (dik/tə graf/, -gräf/), *n.* Dictograph.

Dic·ta·phone (dik/tə fōn/), *n.* *Trademark.* a phonographic instrument that records and reproduces dictation.

dic·tate (*v.* dik/tāt, dik tāt/; *n.* dik/tāt), *v.*, **-tat·ed, -tat·ing,** *n.* —*v.t.* **1.** to say or read aloud (something) for another to transcribe or for a machine to record: *to dictate some letters to a secretary.* **2.** to prescribe positively; command with authority: *to dictate peace terms to a conquered enemy.* —*v.i.* **3.** to say or read aloud something to be taken down. **4.** to give orders. —*n.* **5.** an authoritative order or command. **6.** a guiding or governing principle, requirement, etc.: *to follow the dictates of one's conscience.* [< L *dictāt(us)* pronounced, repeated, dictated (ptp. of *dictāre*), equiv. to *dīc(ere)* (to) say, speak + *-t-* freq. suffix + *-ātus* -ATE[1]] —**dic/tat·ing·ly,** *adv.*

dic·ta·tion (dik tā/shən), *n.* **1.** the act or manner of dictating for reproduction in writing. **2.** the act or manner of transcribing words uttered by another. **3.** words that are dictated or that are reproduced from dictation. **4.** the act of ordering or commanding authoritatively. **5.** something commanded. [< LL *dictātiōn-* (s. of *dictātiō*) a dictating < L *dictāt(us)* (see DICTATE) + *-iōn-* -ION] —**dic·ta/tion·al,** *adj.*

dic·ta·tor (dik/tā tər, dik tā/tər), *n.* **1.** a person exercising absolute power, esp. one who assumes absolute control in a government without hereditary right or the free consent of the people. **2.** (in ancient Rome) a person constitutionally invested with supreme authority during a crisis, the regular magistracy being subordinated to him until the crisis was met. **3.** a person who authoritatively prescribes conduct, usage, etc.: *a dictator of fashion.* **4.** one who dictates, as to a secretary. Also, *referring to a woman,* **dic·ta·tress** (dik tā/tris). [ME < L *dictātor* a chief magistrate, dictator, equiv. to *dictāt-(us)* (see DICTATE) + *-or* -OR[2]]

dic·ta·to·ri·al (dik/tə tōr/ē əl, -tôr/-), *adj.* **1.** of or pertaining to a dictator or dictatorship. **2.** appropriate to, or characteristic of, a dictator; absolute; unlimited: *dictatorial powers in wartime.* **3.** inclined to dictate or command; imperious; overbearing: *a dictatorial attitude.* [< L *dictātōri(us)*, equiv. to *dictāt(us)* (see DICTATE) + *-ōrius* -ORY[1] + -AL[1]] —**dic/ta·to/ri·al·ly,** *adv.* —**dic/ta·to/ri·al·ness,** *n.*
—**Syn. 2.** totalitarian. **3.** despotic, tyrannical, autocratic.

dic·ta·tor·ship (dik tā/tər ship/, dik/tā-), *n.* **1.** a country, government, or the form of government in which absolute power is exercised by a dictator. **2.** absolute, imperious, or overbearing power or control. **3.** the office or position held by a dictator. [DICTATOR + -SHIP]

dicta/torship of the proletar/iat, (in Marxism) the absolute rule by the proletariat, preceding the establishment of a classless society.

dic·tion (dik/shən), *n.* **1.** style of speaking or writing as dependent upon choice of words: *good diction; a Latin diction.* **2.** the accent, inflection, intonation, and speech-sound quality manifested by an individual speaker, usually judged in terms of prevailing standards of acceptability; enunciation. [ME *diccion* < LL *dictiōn-* (s. of *dictiō*) word < L: rhetorical delivery, equiv. to *dict(us)* said, spoken (ptp. of *dīcere*) + *-iōn-* -ION]
—**Syn. 1.** usage, language. DICTION, PHRASEOLOGY, WORDING refer to the means and the manner of expressing ideas. DICTION usually implies a high level of usage; it refers chiefly to the choice of words, their arrangement, and the force, accuracy, and distinction with which they are used: *The speaker was distinguished for his excellent diction; poetic diction.* PHRASEOLOGY refers more to the manner of combining the words into related groups, and esp. to the peculiar or distinctive manner in which certain technical, scientific, and professional ideas are expressed: *legal phraseology.* WORDING refers to the exact words or phraseology used to convey thought: *the wording of a will.*

dic·tion·ar·y (dik/shə ner/ē), *n., pl.* **-ar·ies. 1.** a book containing a selection of the words of a language, usually arranged alphabetically, giving information about their meanings, pronunciations, etymologies, inflected forms, etc., expressed in either the same or another language; lexicon; glossary: *a dictionary of English; a French-English dictionary.* **2.** a book giving information on particular subjects or on a particular class of words, names, or facts, usually arranged alphabetically: *a biographical dictionary; a dictionary of mathematics.* [< ML *dictiōnāri(um)*, lit., a wordbook < LL *dictiōn-* word (see DICTION) + *-ārium* -ARY]

dic/tionary cat/alog, a library catalog having all its entries, including authors, titles, subjects, etc., in one alphabetical list.

Dic·to·graph (dik/tə graf/, -gräf/), *n.* *Trademark.* a telephonic device with a highly sensitive transmitter obviating the necessity of a mouthpiece, used for listening to conversations secretly or obtaining a record of them.

dic·tum (dik/təm), *n., pl.* **-ta** (-tə), **-tums. 1.** an authoritative pronouncement; judicial assertion. **2.** a saying; maxim. **3.** See **obiter dictum.** [< L: something said, a saying, command, word (n. use of neut. ptp. of *dīcere*), equiv. to *dic-* say, speak + *-t-* ptp. suffix + *-um* neut. adj. and n. suffix]

Dic·tyn·na (dik tin/ə), *n.* an ancient Cretan goddess of the sea, often associated with Britomartis.

Dic·tys (dik/tis), *n.* *Class. Myth.* a fisherman who found the chest in which Danaë and Perseus were cast out to sea.

Di·cu·ma·rol (dī ko͞o/mə rôl/, -rōl/, -kyo͞o/-), *n.* *Pharm., Trademark.* dicoumarin.

di·cy·an·di·am·ide (dī sī/ən dī am/īd), *n.* *Chem.* a white, crystalline, sparingly water-soluble solid, $H_2NC(=NH)NHCN$, produced from cyanamide by polymerization: used in the manufacture of plastics and pharmaceuticals. Also, **di·cy·an·o·di·am·ide** (dī sī/ə nō/dī am/-īd). Also called **cyanoguanidine.** [DI-[1] + CYAN(O)-[2] + DI-[1] + AMIDE]

di·cy·clo·pen·ta·di·en·yl·i·ron (dī sī/klō pen/tə dī-en/əlī/ərn), *n.* ferrocene (def. 1).

di·cy·clo·pen·ta·di·en/yl met/al (dī sī/klō pen/-tə dī en/əl), ferrocene (def. 2).

did (did), *v.* pt. of **do**[1].

Did·a·che (did/ə kē/), *n.* an anonymous Christian treatise of the 2nd century A.D.: called in full *The Teaching of the Twelve Apostles.*

Did·a·chist (did/ə kist), *n.* the name for the anonymous author of the *Didache.* Also called **Did·a·chog·ra·pher** (did/ə kog/rə fər). [DIDACH(E) + -IST]

di·dac·tic (dī dak/tik), *adj.* **1.** intended for instruction; instructive: *didactic poetry.* **2.** inclined to teach or lecture others too much: *a didactic old lady.* **3.** teaching or intended to teach a moral lesson. **4. didactics,** (*construed as sing.*) the art or science of teaching. Also, **di·dac/ti·cal.** [< Gk *didaktik(ós)* apt at teaching, instructive, equiv. to *didakt(ós)* that may be taught + *-ikos* -IC] —**di·dac/ti·cal·ly,** *adv.* —**di·dac/ti·cism,** *n.*

di·dap·per (dī/dap/ər), *n.* *U.S. Dial.* a dabchick. [ME *dydoppar;* shortened form of *dive-dapper;* see DAP]

did·di·kai (did/ə kī/), *n.* a person of partial Gypsy extraction. [< Romany]

did·dle[1] (did/əl), *v.*, **-dled, -dling.** *Informal.* —*v.t.* **1.** to cheat; swindle; victimize. —*v.i.* **2.** to waste time. [? akin to OE *dydrian* to deceive] —**did/dler,** *n.*

did·dle[2] (did/əl), *v.t., v.i.*, **-dled, -dling.** *Informal.* to move rapidly up and down or backward and forward. [akin to DODDER]

Di·de·rot (dē/də rō/; *Fr.* dēdə rō/), *n.* **De·nis** (də-nē/), 1713–84, French philosopher, critic, and encyclopedist.

Did·love (did/luv/), *n.* a boy's given name.

did·n't (did/ənt), contraction of *did not.*

di·do (dī/dō), *n., pl.* **-dos, -does.** Usually, **didos, didoes.** *Informal.* a prank; an antic. [?]

Di·do (dī/dō), *n.* **1.** Phoenician, **Elissa.** *Class. Myth.* a queen of Carthage who killed herself when abandoned by Aeneas. **2.** a girl's given name.

Di/do and Aene/as, an opera (1689) by Henry Purcell.

Di/do's prob/lem, *Math.* the problem of finding a curve of specified length which encloses the maximum area, the curve being a circle. [so called from a tale told of DIDO who is said to have bargained for an area a skin could cover and to have then cut the skin to enclose a larger area]

Di·dot/ point/ sys/tem (dē dō/), *Print.* a Continental system of measurement for type, based on a unit of .0148 inches. [named after François Ambroise *Didot* (1730–1804), French printer who devised it]

di·drachm (dī/dram/), *n.* a silver coin of ancient Greece equal to two drachmas. Also, **di·drach·ma** (dī drak/mə). [< LL *didrachmon* < Gk *dídrachmon* worth two drachmas. See DI-[1], DRACHMA]

Did·rik·son (did/rik sən), *n.* **Mildred** ("*Babe*"), 1913?–56, U.S. athlete.

didst (didst), *v.* *Archaic.* 2nd pers. sing. pt. of **do.**

di·dy (dī/dē), *n., pl.* **-dies.** diaper (def. 1). [by alter. (baby-talk)]

Did·y·mae·a (did/ə mē/ə), *n.* an ancient Greek festival in honor of Zeus and Apollo.

di·dym·i·um (dī dim/ē əm, di-), *n.* *Chem.* a mixture of neodymium and praseodymium, formerly thought to be an element: called the "twin brother of lanthanum." *Symbol:* Di [< NL < Gk *dídym(os)* twin (see DIDYMOUS) + -IUM]

did·y·mous (did′ə məs), *adj.* *Bot.* occurring in pairs; paired; twin. [< Gk *dídym(os)* twin, double, (akin to *dís* twice, double) + -OUS]

di·dyn·a·mous (dī din′ə məs), *adj.* (of a flower) having four stamens in two pairs of different length. [< NL *Didynam(ia)* name of the class, equiv. to *di-* DI-¹ + Gk *dýnam(is)* power (see DYNAMIC) + -OUS] —**di·dyn′a·my,** *n.*

die¹ (dī), *v.i.,* **died, dy·ing. 1.** to cease to live; undergo the complete and permanent cessation of all vital functions. **2.** (of something inanimate) to cease to exist: *The laughter died on their lips. The secret died with him.* **3.** to lose force, strength, or active qualities: *Superstitions die slowly.* **4.** to cease to function; stop: *The motor died.* **5.** to be no longer subject; become indifferent: *to die to worldly matters.* **6.** to pass gradually; fade or subside gradually (usually fol. by *away, out,* or *down*): *The storm slowly died down.* **7.** *Theol.* to lose spiritual life. **8.** to faint or languish. **9.** to suffer as if dying: *I'm dying of boredom!* **10.** to pine with desire, love, longing, etc. **11.** *Informal.* to desire or want keenly or greatly: *I'm dying for a cup of coffee.* **12. die away,** (of a sound) to become weaker or fainter and then cease: *The drumbeats gradually died away.* **13. die down,** to become calm or quiet; subside. **14. die hard, a.** to die only after a bitter struggle. **b.** to cling stubbornly to a belief, theory, etc.; refuse to yield: *Racial prejudice dies hard.* **15. die off,** to die one after another until the number is greatly reduced: *Her friends are dying off.* **16. die standing up,** *Theat.* to act, as in a play, without receiving applause. **17. never say die,** never give up hope; never abandon one's efforts. [ME *dien, deien* < ON; c. OIcel *deyja.* Cf. DEAD, DEATH]

—**Syn. 1.** expire, depart. DIE, PASS AWAY (PASS ON), PERISH mean to relinquish life. To DIE is to become dead from any cause and in any circumstances. It is the simplest, plainest, and most direct word for this idea, and is used figuratively of anything that has once displayed activity: *An echo, flame, storm, rumor dies.* PASS AWAY (or PASS ON) is a commonly used euphemism implying a continuation of life after death: *Grandfather passed away (passed on).* PERISH, a more literary term, implies death under harsh circumstances such as hunger, cold, neglect, etc.; figuratively, PERISH connotes utter extinction: *Hardship caused many pioneers to perish. Ancient Egyptian civilization has perished.* **2.** end, vanish, disappear. **3.** weaken, fail. **6.** decline, wither, decay.

Die² (def. 2) A, Greek drachm, 4th century B.C.; B, Die

die² (dī), *n., pl.* **dies** for 1, 2, 4, **dice** for 3; *v.,* **died, die·ing.** —*n.* **1.** *Mach.* **a.** any of various devices for cutting or forming material in a press or a stamping or forging machine. **b.** a hollow device of steel, often composed of several pieces to be fitted into a stock, for cutting the threads of bolts or the like. **c.** one of the separate pieces of such a device. **d.** a steel block or plate with small conical holes through which wire, plastic rods, etc., are drawn. **2.** an engraved stamp for impressing a design upon some softer material, as in coining money. **3.** sing. of **dice. 4.** *Archit.* dado (def. 1). **5. the die is cast,** the irrevocable decision has been made: *The die was cast when war was declared.* —*v.t.* **6.** to impress, shape, or cut with a die. [b. ME *de* + *dice* (see DICE); *de* < OF < L *dat(um),* orig. neut. ptp. of *dare* to give (appar. in the sense of given by fortune)]

die·back (dī′bak′), *n.* *Plant Pathol.* a condition in a plant in which the branches or shoots die from the tip inwards, caused by any of several bacteria, fungi, or viruses or by certain environmental conditions. [DIE¹ + BACK²]

dieb. alt., (in prescriptions) every other day. [< L *diebus alternis*]

dieb. secund., (in prescriptions) every second day. [< L *diebus secundis*]

dieb. tert., (in prescriptions) every third day. [< L *diebus tertius*]

die′ cast′, to shape or form by die casting.

die′ cast′ing, *Metall.* **1.** a process in which molten metal is forced into metallic molds under hydraulic pressure to shape it, form objects, etc. **2.** an article made by this process. —**die′-cast′ing,** *adj.*

di·e·cious (dī ē′shəs), *adj.* *Biol.* dioecious. —**di·e′cious·ly,** *adv.*

Die Drei·gro′schen·o·per (dē drī grō′shən ō′pər). See **Threepenny Opera, The.**

Die·fen·ba·ker (dē′fən bā′kər), *n.* **John George,** 1895–1979, prime minister of Canada 1957–63.

Die·go-Sua·rez (dyā′gō swär′es), *n.* a seaport in N Madagascar. 28,772 (1960). Also called **Antsirane.**

die-hard (dī′härd′), *n.* **1.** one who vigorously maintains or defends a hopeless position, outdated attitude, lost cause, or the like. —*adj.* **2.** resisting vigorously and stubbornly to the last. Also, **die′hard′.** [n., adj. use of v. phrase *die hard*] —**die′-hard′ism,** *n.*

diel·drin (dēl′drin), *n.* *Chem.* a light tan, crystalline, water-insoluble, poisonous solid, $C_{12}H_8OCl_6$, used as an insecticide. [DIEL(S-AL)D(E)R (REACTION) + -IN²]

di·e·lec·tric (dī′i lek′trik), *Elect.* —*n.* **1.** a nonconducting substance; insulator. **2.** a substance in which an electric field can be maintained with a minimum loss of power. —*adj.* **3.** of or pertaining to a dielectric substance. [DI-³ + ELECTRIC] —**di′e·lec′tri·cal·ly,** *adv.*

di′elec′tric con′stant, *Elect.* a measure of the storage capability of a given dielectric, equal to the ratio of the capacitance of a capacitor when its plates are separated by the given dielectric to the capacitance when the plates are separated by a vacuum. Also called **relative permittivity, specific inductive capacity, dielec′tric coeffi′cient.**

di′elec′tric heat′ing, *Elect.* the heating of a nonconducting substance caused by dielectric loss when the material is placed in a variable electric field.

di′elec′tric loss′, *Elect.* the loss of power in a dielectric caused by the loss of energy in the form of heat generated by an electric field.

di′elec′tric strength′, *Elect.* the maximum voltage that can be applied to a given material without causing it to break down, usually expressed in volts or kilovolts per unit of thickness. Cf. **breakdown voltage.**

Die Lei·den des Jung·en Wer·ther (*Ger.* dē līd′ən des yŏŏng′ən ver′tər). See **Sorrows of Werther, The.**

Diels (dēlz; *Ger.* dēls), *n.* **Ot·to** (ot′ō; *Ger.* ôt′ō), 1876–1954, German chemist: Nobel prize 1950.

Diels′-Al′der reac′tion (dēlz′äl′dər), *Chem.* the reaction in which a conjugated diene combines with a double or triple bond of a given compound to form a ring of six carbon atoms. [named after O. *Diels* and K. *Alder*]

di·en·ceph·a·lon (dī′en sef′ə lon′), *n., pl.* **-lons, -la** (-lə). *Anat.* the posterior section of the forebrain. [< NL; see DI-³, ENCEPHALON] —**di·en·ce·phal·ic** (dī′en sə fal′ik), *adj.*

di·ene (dī′ēn, dī ēn′), *n.* *Chem.* any compound containing two double bonds, as 1, 3-butadiene, $CH_2{=}CH{-}CH{=}CH_2$. [DI-¹ + -ENE]

-dienes, *Chem.* a combining form of **diene.** [DIENE + -S³]

die′ plate′, diestock.

Di·eppe (dē ep′; *Fr.* dyep), *n.* a seaport in N France, on the English Channel: raided by an Allied expeditionary force August 1942. 30,327 (1962).

di·er·e·sis (dī er′i sis), *n., pl.* **-ses** (-sēz′). **1.** the separation of two adjacent vowels, dividing one syllable into two. **2.** a sign (¨) placed over the second of two adjacent vowels to indicate separate pronunciation, as in *naïve.* **3.** *Pros.* the division made in a line or verse by coincidence of the end of a foot and the end of a word. Also, **diaeresis.** [< L *diaerēsis* the division of a syllable into two < Gk *diaíresis* a dividing, division, equiv. to *diair(eîn)* (to) divide (*di-* DI-³ + *hair(eîn)* (to) take) + *-e-* thematic vowel + *-sis* -SIS] —**di·e·ret·ic** (dī′ə ret′ik), *adj.*

Dies (dīz), *n.* **Martin,** 1901–72, U.S. politician: member of the House of Representatives 1931–44; chairman of a special House committee investigating subversive activities 1938–44.

die·sel (dē′zəl), *n.* **1.** See **diesel engine.** —*adj.* **2.** noting a machine, vehicle, etc., powered by a diesel engine: *diesel locomotive.* **3.** of or pertaining to a diesel engine: *diesel fuel.* Also, **Diesel.** [named after Rudolf DIESEL]

Die·sel (dē′zəl), *n.* **Ru·dolf** (rōō′dolf; *Ger.* rōō′dôlf), 1858–1913, German automotive engineer.

die′sel cy′cle, *Mach.* a theoretical heat cycle for an engine in which combustion occurs at a constant pressure and cooling at a constant volume.

die·sel-e·lec·tric (dē′zəl i lek′trik), *adj.* having an electric motor powered by a diesel engine: *a diesel-electric locomotive.* Also, **Die′sel-e·lec′tric.**

die′sel en′gine, a compression-ignition engine in which a spray of fuel, introduced into air compressed to a heat of 1000°F, ignites at a virtually constant pressure.

die·sel·ize (dē′zə līz′), *v.,* **-ized, -iz·ing.** —*v.t.* **1.** to equip with diesel machinery. —*v.i.* **2.** to become equipped with diesel machinery or vehicles, as a railroad. [DIESEL + -IZE] —**die′sel·i·za′tion,** *n.*

die·sink·er (dī′siŋg′kər), *n.* an engraver of dies for stamping or embossing. [DIE² + SINKER] —**die′-sink′ing,** *n.*

Di·es I·rae (dē′äs ēr′ä), a Latin hymn on the Day of Judgment, commonly sung in a Requiem Mass.

di·e·sis (dī′i sis), *n., pl.* **-ses** (-sēz′). See **double dagger.** [ME < L < Gk *díesis* a quarter-tone, a sending through < *dii(énai)* (to) send through, equiv. to *di-* DI-³ + *hi(énai)* (to) send + *-e-* thematic vowel + *-sis* -SIS]

di·es non (dī′ēz non′), *Law.* a day on which no courts can be held. [short for L *diēs non jūridicus* a day not juridical (for legal business)]

die·stock (dī′stok′), *n.* a frame for holding a number of standard threaded dies for cutting screw threads. Also, **die′ stock′.** Also called **die plate, screw stock.** [DIE² + STOCK]

di·et¹ (dī′it), *n., v.,* **-et·ed, -et·ing.** —*n.* **1.** food and drink considered in terms of its qualities, composition, and its effects on health: *Milk is a wholesome article of diet.* **2.** a particular selection of food, esp. as prescribed to improve the physical condition or cure a disease: *a diet low in sugar.* **3.** such a selection or a limitation on the amount a person eats for reducing weight: *No pie for me, I'm on a diet.* **4.** the usual or regular food or foods a person eats most frequently: *He would be happy on a diet of meat and potatoes. Many Chinese exist on a diet of rice.* **5.** food or feed habitually provided: *The rabbits were fed a diet of carrots and lettuce.* **6.** anything that is habitually provided or partaken of: *Television has given us a steady diet of quiz shows and murder mysteries.* —*v.t.* **7.** to regulate the food of, esp. in order to improve the physical condition. **8.** to feed. —*v.i.* **9.** to select or limit the food one eats to improve one's physical condition or lose weight: *I've dieted all month and lost only one pound.* **10.** *Archaic.* to eat; feed. [ME *diete* < OF < L *diaet(a)* < Gk *díaita* way of living, diet, equiv. to *dia-* DIA- + *-aita* (akin to *aisa* share, lot)] —**di′et·er,** *n.*

di·et² (dī′it), *n.* a formal assembly for discussing or acting upon public or state affairs, as the general assembly of the estates of the former Holy Roman Empire, the German Reichstag, Japan, etc. [late ME < ML *diēt(a)* public assembly, appar. the same word as L *diaeta* (see DIET¹) with sense affected by L *diēs* day]

di·e·tar·y (dī′i ter′ē), *adj., n., pl.* **-tar·ies.** —*adj.* **1.** of or pertaining to diet: *a dietary deficiency in protein.* —*n.* **2.** a regulated allowance of food. **3.** *Obs.* a system or course of diet. [ME *dietarie* system of diet. See DIET¹, -ARY]

di′etary law′, *Judaism.* any of the body of laws dealing with the foods and combinations of foods permitted or forbidden to be eaten, the vessels to be used in preparing and serving different types of foods, and the procedure to be followed in treating certain foods prior to use.

di·e·tet·ic (dī′i tet′ik), *adj.* Also, **di′e·tet′i·cal. 1.** pertaining to diet or to regulation of the use of food. **2.** prepared or suitable for special diets, esp. those requiring a restricted sugar intake: *a jar of dietetic jelly.* —*n.* **3. dietetics,** (*construed as sing.*) the science concerned with the nutritional planning and preparation of foods. [< L *diaeteticus* < Gk *diaitētikós,* equiv. to *diait(a)* (see DIET¹) + *-ē-* thematic vowel + *-tikos* -TIC]

di·eth·yl·ac·e·tal (dī eth′əl as′i tal′), *n.* *Chem.* acetal (def. 1). [DI-¹ + ETHYL + ACETAL]

di·eth·yl·am·i·no·eth·a·nol (dī eth′əl ə mē′nō eth′ə nōl′, -nôl′, -nol′, -am′ə nō-), *n.* *Chem.* a colorless, hygroscopic, water-soluble liquid, $(C_2H_5)_2NCH_2CH_2OH$, used for the synthesis of local anesthetics, in anti-rust compounds, and in photographic emulsions. Also, **diethylethanolamine.** [DI-¹ + ETHYL + AMINO- + ETHANOL]

di·eth′yl·bar·bi·tu′ric ac′id (dī eth′əl bär′bi tŏŏr′ik, -tyŏŏr′-, dī eth′-), *Pharm.* barbital. [DI-¹ + ETHYL + BARBITURIC ACID]

di·eth·yl·eth·a·nol·a·mine (dī eth′əl eth′ə nō′lə mēn′, -nô′-, -nol′ə-), *n.* *Chem.* diethylaminoethanol.

di·eth′yl e′ther (dī eth′əl), *Chem.* ether (def. 1). Also called **diethyl oxide.** [DI-¹ + ETHYL]

dieth′yl mal′onate (mal′ə nāt′, -nit), *Chem.* See **ethyl malonate.** [DI-¹ + ETHYL + MALON(IC ACID) + -ATE²]

di·eth·yl·mal·o·nyl·u·re·a (dī eth′əl mal′ə nil yŏŏ rē′ə), *n.* *Pharm.* barbital. [DI-¹ + ETHYL + MALON(IC ACID) + -YL + UREA]

dieth′yl ox′ide, *Chem.* ether (def. 1).

di·eth·yl·stil·bes·trol (dī eth′əl stil bes′trōl, -trôl, -trol), *n.* *Pharm.* a white, crystalline, almost water-insoluble solid, $[HOC_6H_4C(C_2H_5){=}]_2$, a nonsteroidal synthetic estrogen: used in medicine chiefly in the treatment of menopausic symptoms and in animal feeds for chemical caponization. Also, **di·eth′yl·stil·boes′trol.** Also called **stilbestrol, stilboestrol.** [DI-¹ + ETHYL + STILBESTROL]

dieth′yl sul′fide. See **ethyl sulfide.**

di·e·ti·tian (dī′i tish′ən), *n.* a person who is an expert in nutrition or dietetics. Also, **di′e·ti′cian.** [DIET¹ + *-itian;* see -ICIAN]

di′et kitch′en, a kitchen for preparing special diets, as in a hospital.

Die·trich (dē′trik, -triкн), *n.* **Mar·le·ne** (mär lā′nə), born 1904, U.S. actress and singer, born in Germany.

Die′trich von Bern (dē′triкн fən bern′), Theodoric of Verona: the name of the eastern Gothic emperor Theodoric as it appears in German legends.

Dieu a·vec nous (dyœ′ a vek nōō′), *French.* God with us.

Dieu dé·fend le droit (dyœ′ dā fäɴ lə drwa′), *French.* God defends the right.

Dieu et mon droit (dyœ′ ā môɴ drwa′), *French.* God and my right: motto on the royal arms of England.

Dieu vous garde (dyœ′ vōō gard′), *French.* God keep you.

Die Ver·wand·lung (*Ger.* dē fer vänd′lŏŏng). See **Metamorphosis, The.**

dif-, var. of **dis-¹** before *f: differ.*

diff., 1. difference. **2.** different.

dif·fer (dif′ər), *v.i.* **1.** to be unlike, dissimilar, or distinct in nature or qualities (often fol. by *from*). **2.** to disagree in opinion, belief, etc.; be at variance; disagree (often fol. by *with* or *from*): *His wife always differs with him.* **3.** *Obs.* to dispute; quarrel. [ME *differr(en)* (to) distinguish < MF *differ(er)* (to) put off, distinguish, L *differre* to bear apart, put off, delay (see DEFER¹) be different, equiv. to *dif-* DIF- + *ferre* to bear]

dif·fer·ence (dif′ər əns, dif′rəns), *n., v.,* **-enced, -enc·ing.** —*n.* **1.** the state or relation of being different; dissimilarity. **2.** an instance or point of unlikeness or dissimilarity. **3.** a significant change in or effect on a situation: *What you eat for breakfast makes a difference in how you feel all day long.* **4.** a distinguishing characteristic; distinctive quality, feature, etc. **5.** the degree in which one person or thing differs from another. **6.** the act of distinguishing; discrimination; distinction. **7.** a disagreement in opinion. **8.** a dispute or quarrel. **9.** *Math.* **a.** the amount by which one quantity is greater or less than another. **b.** See **relative complement. 10.** *Logic.* a differentia. **11.** *Heraldry.* See **cadency mark. 12. split the difference, a.** to compromise, esp. to make equal concessions. **b.** to divide the remainder equally: *Let's take half of the cake and let the three of them split the difference.* —*v.t.* **13.** to cause or constitute a difference in or between; make different. **14.** to perceive the difference in or between; discriminate. **15.** *Heraldry.* to add a charge to (a coat of arms) to identify a particular branch of a family. [ME, OE < L *differentia,* equiv. to *different-* carrying different ways (see DIFFERENT) + *-ia;* see -ENCE]

—**Syn. 1.** inconsistency, variation, diversity, imbalance, inequality, divergence, contrast, contrariety. DIFFERENCE, DISCREPANCY, DISPARITY, DISSIMILARITY imply perceivable unlikeness, variation, or diversity. DIFFERENCE refers to a complete or partial lack of identity or a degree of unlikeness: *a difference of opinion; a difference of six inches.* DISCREPANCY usually refers to the difference or inconsistency between things that should agree, balance, or harmonize: *a discrepancy between the statements of two witnesses.* DISPARITY implies inequality, often where a greater approximation to equality might reasonably be expected: *a great disparity between the ages of husband and wife.* DISSIMILARITY indicates an essential lack of resemblance between things in some respect comparable: *a dissimilarity between the customs in Asia and America.* **6.** See **distinction.** —**Ant. 1.** similarity, agreement.

dif′ference ring′, *Math.* See **quotient ring.**

dif·fer·ent (dif′ər ənt, dif′rənt), *adj.* **1.** differing in character or quality; not alike; dissimilar. **2.** not identical; separate or distinct: *three different answers.* **3.** various; several: *Different people told me the same story.* **4.** unusual; not ordinary. [ME < MF < L *different-* (s. of *differēns*), prp. of *differre.* See DIFFER, -ENT] —**dif′fer·ent·ly,** *adv.*

—**Syn. 1.** unlike, diverse, divergent, altered, changed, contrary, deviant, variant. **3.** sundry, divers, miscellaneous. See **various.**

—**Usage.** Many speakers, on the analogical use of

THAN with other adjectives (*He is older than I. His handwriting is better than mine.*), extend its use to follow DIFFERENT. But most grammarians, chiefly on semantic grounds, regard any preposition but FROM after DIFFERENT as a solecism: *He is different from me. His handwriting is different from mine.* DIFFERENT TO, acceptable in England as standard, is rarely heard in the U.S. In the comparative of the sense "unusual; not ordinary," DIFFERENT is used in the same way as other adjectives: *He is more different than you are.*

dif·fer·en·ti·a (dif′ə ren′shē ə), *n., pl.* **-ti·ae** (-shē ē′). **1.** the character or attribute by which one species is distinguished from all others of the same genus. **2.** the character or basic factor by which one entity is distinguished from another. [< L: *difference*]

dif·fer·en·ti·a·ble (dif′ə ren′shē ə bəl), *adj.* capable of being differentiated. [DIFFERENTI(ATE) + -ABLE]

dif·fer·en·tial (dif′ə ren′shəl), *adj.* **1.** of or pertaining to difference or diversity. **2.** constituting a difference; distinguishing; distinctive: *a differential feature.* **3.** exhibiting or depending upon a difference or distinction. **4.** *Physics, Mach.* pertaining to or involving the difference of two or more motions, forces, etc. **5.** *Math.* pertaining to or involving a derivative or derivatives. —*n.* **6.** a difference or the amount of difference, as in rate, cost, quantity, degree, or quality, between things that are comparable. **7.** Also called **differential gear.** *Mach.* an epicyclic train of gears designed to permit two or more shafts to revolve at different speeds, as a set of gears in an automobile permitting the rear wheels to revolve at different speeds when the car is turning. **8.** *Math.* **a.** a function of two variables that is obtained from a given function, $y = f(x)$, and that expresses the approximate increment in the given function as the derivative of the function times the increment in the independent variable, written as $dy = f^1(x)dx$. **b.** any generalization of this function to higher dimensions. Cf. **total differential. 9.** *Com.* **a.** the difference involved in a differential rate. **b.** See **differential rate. 10.** *Physics.* the quantitative difference between two or more forces, motions, etc.: *a pressure differential.* [< ML *differentiāl(is)*, equiv. to *differenti(a)* DIFFERENCE + *-ālis* -AL] —**dif′fer·en′tial·ly,** *adv.*

Differential (def. 7) A, Ring gear; B, Axle; C, Drive shaft gear; D, Drive shaft; E, Pinion gear

dif′feren′tial an′alyzer, an analog computer designed for solving certain differential equations.

dif′feren′tial cal′culus, the branch of mathematics that deals with differentials and derivatives, with the rate of change of a function with respect to its variables.

differen′tial coeffic′ient, *Chiefly Brit.* derivative (def. 6).

differen′tial equa′tion, *Math.* an equation involving differentials or derivatives.

dif′feren′tial gear′, *Mach.* **1.** differential (def. 7). **2.** any of various comparable arrangements of gears, as an epicyclic train.

differen′tial geom′etry, *Math.* the branch of mathematics that deals with the application of the principles of differential and integral calculus to the study of curves and surfaces.

dif′feren′tial lev′eling, *Survey.* leveling to establish bench marks or other elevation control points.

dif′feren′tial op′erator, *Math.* a function, usually expressed as a polynomial, that indicates linear combinations of the derivatives of the expression on which it operates.

differen′tial psychol′ogy, the branch of psychology dealing with the study of characteristic differences or variations of groups or individuals, esp. through the use of analytic techniques and statistical methods.

dif′feren′tial quo′tient, derivative (def. 6).

dif′feren′tial rate′, a special lower rate, as one charged by one of two or more competing businesses.

dif′feren′tial tone′, *Music.* a combination tone with a frequency equal to the difference between the frequencies of the two tones producing it.

dif′feren′tial weath′ering, the difference in degree of discoloration, disintegration, etc., of minerals of rocks of different kinds of structures exposed to the same environment.

dif′feren′tial wind′lass, a pair of hoisting drums of different diameter turning at the same rate, such that a pulley suspended below them on a line wound on the larger drum and unwound from the smaller drum is raised with mechanical advantage.

dif·fer·en·ti·ate (dif′ə ren′shē āt′), *v.,* **-at·ed, -at·ing.** —*v.t.* **1.** to form or mark differently from other such things; distinguish. **2.** to change; alter. **3.** to perceive the difference in or between. **4.** to make different by modification, as a biological species. **5.** *Math.* to obtain the differential or the derivative of. —*v.i.* **6.** to become unlike or dissimilar; change in character. **7.** to make a distinction. **8.** *Biol.* (of cells or tissues) to change from relatively generalized to specialized kinds, during development. [< ML *differentiāt(us)* distinguished (ptp. of *differentiāre*), equiv. to L *different(ia)* DIFFERENCE + *-ātus* -ATE[1]] —**dif′fer·en′ti·a′tion,** *n.*
—**Syn. 1.** set off. See **distinguish. 3.** separate.

dif·fer·en·ti·a·tor (dif′ə ren′shē ā′tər), *n.* **1.** one who or that which differentiates. **2.** *Computer Technol.* an electronic device the output signal of which is proportional to the derivative of its input signal. **3.** *Elect., Electronics.* a transducer or circuit **(differen′tiator cir′cuit)** the output of which is proportional to the rate of change of the input signal. [DIFFERENTIATE + -OR[2]]

dif·fi·cile (dif′i sēl′; *Fr.* dē fē sēl′), *adj.* **1.** hard to deal with, satisfy, or please. **2.** hard to do; difficult. [< F < L *difficilis* difficult; see DIF-, FACILE]

dif·fi·cult (dif′ə kult′, -kəlt), *adj.* **1.** requiring much labor, skill, or planning to be performed successfully; not readily done; hard. **2.** hard to understand or solve: *a difficult problem.* **3.** hard to deal with or get on with: *a difficult pupil.* **4.** hard to please or satisfy: *a difficult employer.* **5.** hard to persuade or induce; stubborn: *a difficult old man.* **6.** disadvantageous; trying; hampering: *The operation was performed under the most difficult conditions.* **7.** fraught with hardship, esp. financial hardship: *We saw some difficult times during the depression years.* [back formation from DIFFICULTY] —**dif′fi·cult′ly,** *adv.*
—**Syn. 1.** arduous. See **hard. 2.** obscure, complex, intricate, perplexing, involved, knotty. **4.** particular, finical, fussy. **5.** obdurate, uncompromising. —**Ant. 1.** easy. **2.** simple.

dif·fi·cul·ty (dif′ə kul′tē, -kəl tē), *n., pl.* **-ties. 1.** the fact or condition of being difficult. **2.** Often, **difficulties.** an embarrassing situation, esp. of financial affairs. **3.** a trouble. **4.** a cause of trouble or embarrassment. **5.** reluctance; unwillingness. **6.** a demur; objection. **7.** that which is hard to do, understand, or surmount; an impediment or obstacle. [ME *difficulte* < L *difficultās,* b. of *diffic(ilis)* DIFFICILE and *(fac)ultas* FACULTY]
—**Syn. 2.** dilemma, predicament, quandary, plight, fix, exigency, strait. **3.** problem.

dif·fi·dence (dif′i dəns), *n.* **1.** lack of confidence in one's own ability, worth, or fitness; timidity; shyness. **2.** restraint or reserve in manner, conduct, etc. [ME < L *diffidentia* mistrust, want of confidence. See DIFFIDENT, -ENCE]

dif·fi·dent (dif′i dənt), *adj.* **1.** lacking confidence in one's own ability, worth, or fitness; timid; shy. **2.** restrained or reserved in manner, conduct, etc. **3.** *Archaic.* distrustful. [ME < L *diffident-,* (s. of *diffidēns* mistrusting, despairing prp. of *diffidere*) equiv. to *dif-* DIF- + *fīd-* trust + *-ent-* -ENT] —**dif′fi·dent·ly,** *adv.* —**dif′fi·dent·ness,** *n.*
—**Syn. 1.** self-conscious, self-effacing, abashed, embarrassed, modest, unassuming, unconfident. See **shy**[1]. —**Ant. 1.** self-confident, forward.

dif·flu·ence (dif′lo͞o əns), *n.* **1.** the act of flowing off or away. **2.** the act or process of dissolving into a liquid; liquefaction; deliquescence. **3.** the rate at which fluid flow diverges along an axis perpendicular to the direction of flow at a given point. Cf. **confluence, divergence.** [DIFFLU(ENT) + -ENCE]

dif·flu·ent (dif′lo͞o ənt) *adj.* **1.** tending to flow off or away. **2.** easily dissolving. [< L *diffluent-* (s. of *diffluēns,* prp. of *diffluere*), equiv. to *dif-* DIF- + *fluent-* flowing; see FLUENT]

Dif·flu·gi·a (di flo͞o′jē ə), *n.* a genus of amoeboid protozoans that construct a shell of cemented sand grains. [< NL, equiv. to L *diffluere* (to) flow away (see DIFFLUENT) + *-g-* (unexplained) + *-ia* -IA]

dif·fract (di frakt′), *v.t.* to break up or bend by diffraction. [back formation from DIFFRACTION]

dif·frac·tion (di frak′shən), *n.* *Physics.* **1.** the phenomenon exhibited by wave fronts that, passing the edge of an opaque body, are modulated, thereby causing a redistribution of energy within the front: it is detectable in light waves by the presence of minute dark and light bands at the edge of a shadow. **2.** the bending of waves, esp. sound and light waves, around obstacles in their path. [< NL *diffractiōn-* (s. of *diffractiō*) a breaking up, equiv. to L *diffract(us)* broken up (ptp. of *diffringere*) + *-iōn-* -ION. See DIF-, FRACTION]

diffrac′tion grat′ing, *Physics.* a band of equidistant, parallel lines, usually more than 5000 to the inch, ruled on a glass or polished metal surface for diffracting light to produce optical spectra. Also called **grating.**

dif·frac·tive (di frak′tiv), *adj.* causing or pertaining to diffraction. [DIFFRACT + -IVE] —**dif·frac′tive·ly,** *adv.* —**dif·frac′tive·ness,** *n.*

dif·fu·sate (di fyo͞o′zāt), *n.* *Physical Chem.* (in dialysis) the solution, or the crystalline material which passes into it through the semipermeable membrane; dialyzate. [DIFFUS(ION) + -ATE[1]]

dif·fuse (*v.* di fyo͞oz′; *adj.* di fyo͞os′), *v.,* **-fused, -fus·ing,** *adj.* —*v.t.* **1.** to pour out and spread, as a fluid. **2.** to spread or scatter widely or thinly; disseminate. **3.** *Physics.* to spread by diffusion. —*v.i.* **4.** to spread. **5.** *Physics.* to intermingle by diffusion. —*adj.* **6.** characterized by great length or discursiveness in speech or writing; wordy. **7.** widely spread or scattered; dispersed. **8.** *Bot.* widely or loosely spreading. [ME < L *diffūs(us)* spread, poured forth. See DIF-, FUSE[2]] —**diffus′ed·ly,** *adv.* —**dif·fus′ed·ness,** *n.* —**dif·fuse·ly** (di fyo͞os′lē), *adv.* —**dif·fuse′ness,** *n.*

diffuse′ neb′ula, *Astron.* nebula (def. 1a).

dif·fus·er (di fyo͞o′zər), *n.* **1.** one who or that which diffuses. **2.** (in any of various machines or mechanical systems, as centrifugal pumps or compressors) a device for utilizing part of the kinetic energy of a fluid passing through a machine by gradually increasing the cross-sectional area of the channel or chamber through which it flows so as to decrease its speed and increase its pressure. **3.** (in a lighting fixture) any of a variety of translucent materials for filtering glare from the light source. **4.** a pierced plate or similar device for distributing compressed air for aeration of sewage. Also, **dif·fu′sor.** [DIFFUSE + -ER[1]]

dif·fus·i·ble (di fyo͞o′zə bəl), *adj.* capable of being diffused. [DIFFUSE + -IBLE] —**dif·fus′i·bil′i·ty, dif·fus′i·ble·ness,** *n.* —**dif·fus′i·bly,** *adv.*

dif·fu·sion (di fyo͞o′zhən), *n.* **1.** act of diffusing; state of being diffused. **2.** diffuseness or prolixity of speech or writing; discursiveness. **3.** *Physics.* **a.** an intermingling of molecules, ions, etc., resulting from random thermal agitation, as permeation of a solid by a liquid. **b.** a reflection or refraction of light or other electromagnetic radiation from an irregular surface or an erratic dispersion through a surface; scattering. **4.** *Meteorol.* the spreading of atmospheric constituents or properties by turbulent as well as molecular motions of the air. **5.** *Anthropol., Sociol.* the transmission of elements or features of one culture to another. [ME < L *diffūsiōn-* (s. of *diffūsiō*) a spreading out, equiv. to *diffūs(us)* (see DIFFUSE) + *-iōn-* -ION]

dif·fu·sive (di fyo͞o′siv), *adj.* **1.** tending to diffuse. **2.** characterized by diffusion. **3.** diffuse; prolix. [DIFFUSE + -IVE] —**dif·fu′sive·ly,** *adv.* —**dif·fu′siveness,** *n.*

dif·fu·siv·i·ty (dif′yo͞o siv′i tē), *n.* *Physics.* the property of a substance indicative of the rate at which a thermal disturbance, as a rise in temperature, will be transmitted through the substance. [DIFFUSIVE + -ITY]

dif·lu·ence (dif′lo͞o əns), *n.* diffluence. [DI-[2] + *-fluence* (as in *confluence*). See DIFFLUENT]

dig (dig), *v.,* **dug** or (*Archaic*) **digged; dig·ging;** *n.* —*v.i.* **1.** to break up, turn over, or remove earth, sand, etc., as with a spade; make an excavation. **2.** to make one's way or work by or as by removing or turning over material: *to dig through the files.* **3.** *Brit. Informal.* to reside, esp. as a renter or lodger: *He digs in London now.* —*v.t.* **4.** to break up, turn over, or loosen (earth, sand, etc.), as with a spade (often fol. by *up*). **5.** to form or excavate (a hole, tunnel, etc.) by removing material. **6.** to unearth, obtain, or remove by digging (often fol. by *up* or *out*). **7.** to find or discover by effort or search. **8.** to poke, thrust, or force (usually fol. by *in* or *into*): *He dug his heel into the ground.* **9.** *Slang.* **a.** to understand and appreciate; find to one's taste: *He just doesn't dig modern jazz.* **b.** to take notice of; give attention to; note: *Hey, dig those alligator shoes he's wearing.* **10. dig in, a.** to dig trenches, as in order to defend a position in battle. **b.** to maintain one's opinion or position. **c.** *Informal.* to dig into. **11. dig into,** *Informal.* to attack, work, or apply oneself voraciously, vigorously, or energetically: *to dig into one's work; to dig into a meal.* **12. dig up, a.** to discover in the course of digging. **b.** *Informal.* to obtain or find by chance or after a haphazard search: *Could you dig up a date for my friend?* —*n.* **13.** thrust; poke: *He gave me a dig in the ribs with his elbow.* **14.** a cutting, sarcastic remark. **15.** *Informal.* an archaeological site undergoing excavation. **16.** *U.S. Slang.* a diligent student. **17. digs,** *Chiefly Brit. Informal.* diggings (def. 4). [ME *digg(en),* prob. < MF *digu(er)* < Gmc]

dig., digest.

Di·gam·ba·ra (di gum′bər ə), *n.* the earlier of the two principal Jain sects whose members went naked. Cf. **Svetambara.** [< Skt: naked]

di·gam·ma (dī gam′ə), *n.* a letter of the early Greek alphabet that generally fell into disuse in Attic Greek before the classical period and that represented a sound similar to English *w.* [< L < Gk *digamma,* equiv. to *di-* DI-[1] + *gámma* GAMMA; from its likeness to two gammas (Γ)] —**di·gam·mat·ed** (dī gam′ā tid), *adj.*

dig·a·my (dig′ə mē), *n.* a second marriage, after the death or divorce of the first husband or wife; deuterogamy. Cf. **monogamy** (def. 3). [< LL *digamia* < Gk *digamía,* equiv. to *di-* DI-[1] + *-gamia* -GAMY] —**dig′a·mous,** *adj.*

di·gas·tric (dī gas′trik), *Anat.* —*adj.* **1.** (of a muscle) having two bellies with an intermediate tendon. —*n.* **2.** a muscle of the lower jaw, the action of which assists in lowering the jaw. [< NL *digastric(us).* See DI-[1], GASTRIC]

Dig·by (dig′bē), *n.* **Sir Kenelm,** 1603–65, English writer, naval commander, and diplomat.

di·gen·e·sis (dī jen′i sis), *n.* *Zool.* See **alternation of generations.** [< NL; see DI-[1], GENESIS] —**di·ge·net·ic** (dī′jə net′ik), *adj.*

di·gest (*v.* di jest′, dī-; *n.* dī′jest), *v.t.* **1.** to prepare and convert (food) in the alimentary canal into absorbable form for assimilation into the system. **2.** to promote the digestion of (food). **3.** to assimilate mentally; obtain information, ideas, or principles from: *to digest a pamphlet.* **4.** to arrange methodically in the mind; think over: *to digest a plan.* **5.** to bear with patience; endure. **6.** to arrange in convenient or methodical order; reduce to a system; classify. **7.** to condense, abridge, or summarize. —*v.i.* **8.** *Chem.* to soften or disintegrate a substance by means of moisture, heat, chemical action, or the like. **9.** to digest food. **10.** to undergo digestion, as food. [ME *digest(en)* < L *dīgest(us)* separated, dissolved (ptp. of *dīgerere*), equiv. to *dī-* DI-[2] + *ges-* carrry, bear (perf. s. of *gerere*) + *-t-* ptp. suffix]
—*n.* **11.** a collection or compendium, usually of literary, historical, legal, or scientific matter, esp. when classified or condensed. **12.** *Law.* **a.** a systematic abstract of some body of law. **b. the Digest,** a collection in fifty books of excerpts compiled by order of Justinian in the 6th century A.D., the largest part of the Corpus Juris Civilis; the Pandects. [ME: collection of laws < LL *dīgest(a)* (pl.) < L: collection of writings deriv. of *dīgest(us),* as above] —**di·gest′ed·ly,** *adv.* —**di·gest′edness,** *n.*
—**Syn. 4.** understand; study, ponder. **6.** systematize, codify. **11.** epitome, abridgment. See **summary.**

di·gest·ant (di jes′tənt, dī-), *n.* *Med.* an agent that promotes digestion. [DIGEST + -ANT]

di·gest·er (di jes′tər, dī-), *n.* **1.** one who or that which digests. **2.** Also, **digestor.** *Chem.* an apparatus in which substances are softened or disintegrated by moisture, heat, chemical action, or the like. [DIGEST + -ER[1]]

di·gest·i·ble (di jes′tə bəl, dī-), *adj.* capable of being digested; readily digested. [ME < LL *dīgestibil(is)* < L *dīgest(us)* (see DIGEST) + *-ibilis* -IBLE] —**di·gest′i·bil′i·ty, di·gest′i·ble·ness,** *n.* —**di·gest′i·bly,** *adv.*

di·ges·tif (dē zhe stēf′), *n.* *French.* a digestive, esp. brandy, liqueur, or the like, taken after a meal.

di·ges·tion (di jes′chən, -jesh′-, dī-), *n.* **1.** the process in the alimentary canal by which food is broken up physically, as by the action of the teeth, and chemically, as by the action of enzymes, and converted into a substance suitable for absorption and assimilation into the body. **2.** the function or power of digesting food: *My digestion is bad.* **3.** the act of digesting. **4.** the resulting state. [ME *digestioun* < MF *digestion* < L *dīgestiōn-* (s. of *dīgestiō*), equiv. to *dīgest(us)* (see DIGEST) + *-iōn-* -ION] —**di·ges′tion·al,** *adj.*

di·ges·tive (di jes′tiv, dī-), *adj.* **1.** serving for or pertaining to digestion; having the function of digesting food: *the digestive system.* **2.** promoting digestion. —*n.* **3.** an agent or medicine promoting digestion. [ME < MF *digestif,* L *dīgestīv(us),* equiv. to *dīgest(us)* (see DIGEST) + *-īvus* -IVE] —**di·ges′tive·ly,** *adv.*

diges′tive bis′cuit, *Brit.* a large, round, semisweet, dessert cookie, similar to a graham cracker.

di·ges·tor (di jes′tər, dī-), *n.* digester (def. 2).

digged (digd), *v.* a pt. of **dig.**

dig·ger (dig′ər), *n.* **1.** a person or an animal that digs. **2.** a tool, part of a machine, etc., for digging. **3.** (*cap.*) Also called **Dig′ger In′dian.** a member of any of several Indian peoples of western North America, esp. of a tribe that dug roots for food. **4.** an Australian or New Zealand soldier of World War I. **5.** (*cap.*) *Eng. Hist.* a member of a group that advocated the abolition of private property and began in 1649 to cultivate certain common lands. **6.** *Slang.* an illicit speculator who purchases theater tickets for resale at higher prices; scalper. [late ME; see DIG, -ER[1]]

dig′ger wasp′, any of numerous solitary wasps of the family *Sphecidae* that excavate a nest in soil, wood, etc., which they provision with prey paralyzed by stinging.

dig·gings (dig′ingz *for 1–3;* dig′ənz *for 4*), *n.* **1.** (*usually construed as sing.*) a place where digging is carried on. **2.** (*construed as sing. or pl.*) a mining operation or locality. **3.** (*construed as pl.*) that which is removed from an excavation. **4.** Also called **digs.** (*construed as pl.*) *Chiefly Brit. Informal.* living quarters; lodgings. [DIG + -ING[1] + -S[3]]

dight (dīt), *v.t.*, **dight** or **dight·ed, dight·ing. 1.** *Chiefly Scot.* to clean. **2.** *Archaic.* **a.** to equip; furnish **b.** to dress; adorn. **3.** *Obs.* to make ready; prepare. [ME *dight(en)*, OE *dihtan* to arrange, compose < L *dictāre* (see DICTATE); c. G *dichten*]

dig·it (dij′it), *n.* **1.** a finger or toe. **2.** the breadth of a finger used as a unit of linear measure, usually equal to ¾ inch. **3.** any of the Arabic figures of 1 through 9 and 0. **4.** index (def. 6). **5.** *Astron.* the twelfth part of the sun's or moon's diameter: used to espress the magnitude of an eclipse. [ME < L *digit(us)* finger, toe]

dig·it·al (dij′i tᵊl), *adj.* **1.** of or pertaining to a digit. **2.** resembling a digit or finger. **3.** *Computer Technol.* involving or using numerical digits expressed in a scale of notation to represent discretely all variables occurring in a problem. **4.** having digits or digitlike parts. **—***n.* **5.** one of the keys or finger levers of keyboard instruments. [ME < L *digitāl(is)*, equiv. to *digit(us)* (see DIGIT) + *-ālis* -AL[1]] **—dig′it·al·ly,** *adv.*

dig′ital comput′er, a computer that processes information in digital form. Cf. **analog computer.**

dig·i·tal·in (dij′i tal′in, -tā′lin), *n.* *Pharm.* **1.** a glucoside obtained from digitalis. **2.** any of several extracts of mixtures of glucosides obtained from digitalis. [DIGITAL(IS) + -IN[2]]

dig·i·tal·is (dij′i tal′is, -tā′lis), *n.* **1.** any scrophulariaceous plant of the genus *Digitalis*, esp. the common foxglove, *D. purpurea.* **2.** the dried leaves of the foxglove, *Digitalis purpurea*, used in medicine as a heart stimulant. [< NL < L *digitālis;* see DIGITAL]

dig·i·tal·ism (dij′i tᵊliz′əm), *n.* *Pathol.* the abnormal condition resulting from an overconsumption of digitalis. [DIGITAL(IS) + -ISM]

dig·i·tal·i·za·tion (dij′i tᵊli zā′shən), *n.* *Med.* **1.** (in the treatment of heart disease) the administration of digitalis, usually in a regimen, to produce a desired physiological effect. **2.** the effect produced. [DIGITALIZE + -ATION]

dig·i·tal·ize (dij′i tᵊlīz′, dij′i tal′īz), *v.t.*, **-ized, -iz·ing.** *Med.* to cause (a person) to undergo digitalization. [DIGITAL(IS) + -IZE]

dig·i·tate (dij′i tāt′), *adj.* **1.** *Zool.* having digits or digitlike processes. **2.** *Bot.* having radiating divisions or leaflets resembling the fingers of a hand. **3.** like a digit or finger. Also, **dig′i·tat′ed.** [< L *digitāt(us).* See DIGIT, -ATE[1]] **—dig′i·tate′ly,** *adv.*

Digitate leaf

dig·i·ta·tion (dij′i tā′shən), *n.* *Biol.* **1.** digitate formation. **2.** a digitlike process or division. [DIGITATE + -ION]

digiti-, a learned borrowing from Latin meaning "finger," used in the formation of compound words: *digitinervate.* [comb. form repr. L *digitus*]

dig·i·ti·form (dij′i tə fôrm′), *adj.* like a finger. [DIGITI- + -FORM]

dig·i·ti·grade (dij′i tə grād′), *adj.* **1.** walking on the toes, as most quadruped mammals. **—***n.* **2.** a digitigrade animal. [< F; see DIGITI-, -GRADE]

dig·i·ti·nerv·ate (dij′i tə nûr′vāt), *adj.* *Bot.* (of a leaf) having veins that radiate from the petiole like the fingers of a hand. Also, **dig·i·ti·nerved** (dij′i tə nûrvd′). [DIGITI- + NERVATE]

dig·i·ti·pin·nate (dij′i tə pin′āt), *adj.* *Bot.* (of a compound leaf) digitate with pinnate leaflets. [DIGITI- + PINNATE]

dig·i·tise (dij′i tīz′), *v.t.*, **-tised, -tis·ing.** *Chiefly Brit.* digitize. **—dig′i·ti·sa′tion,** *n.*

dig·i·tize (dij′i tīz′), *v.t.*, **-tized, -tiz·ing.** *Computer Technol.* **1.** to convert (data) to digital form for use in a computer. **2.** to convert (analogous physical measurements) to digital form. [DIGIT + -IZE] **—dig′i·ti·za′tion,** *n.*

dig·i·tox·in (dij′i tok′sin), *n.* *Pharm.* a white, crystalline, water-insoluble cardiac glycoside, $C_{41}H_{64}O_{13}$, or a mixture of cardiac glycosides of which this is the chief constituent, obtained from digitalis and used as a heart stimulant. [DIGI(TALIS) + TOXIN]

di·glot (dī′glot), *adj.* **1.** bilingual. **—***n.* **2.** a bilingual book or edition. [< Gk *díglōtt(os)*, equiv. to *di-* DI-[1] + *glōtt(a)* tongue, language (sp. var of *glôssa*); see GLOSS[2]] **—di·glot′tic,** *adj.*

di·glyc·er·ide (dī glis′ə rīd′, -ər id), *n.* *Chem.* an ester obtained from glycerol by the esterification of two hydroxyl groups with fatty acids. Cf. **glyceride.** [DI-[1] + GLYCERIDE]

di′gly·col′ic ac′id (dī′glī kol′ik, dī′-), *Chem.* a white, crystalline, water-soluble solid, $O(CH_2COOH)_2$, used chiefly in the manufacture of resins and plasticizers. Also, **di′glycol′lic ac′id.** Also called **oxydiacetic acid.** [DI-[1] + GLYCOLIC]

di·glyph (dī′glif), *n.* an architectural ornament similar to the triglyph but having no chamfers at the edges. [< Gk *díglyph(os)*, lit., twice carved, equiv. to *di-* DI-[1] + *-glyphos* < *glýphein* to carve]

dig·ni·fied (dig′nə fīd′), *adj.* marked by dignity of aspect or manner; noble; stately: *dignified conduct.* [DIGNIFY + -ED[2]] **—dig·ni·fied·ly** (dig′nə fīd′lē, -fī′id-), *adv.* **—dig′ni·fied′ness,** *n.*
—Syn. grave, august.

dig·ni·fy (dig′nə fī′), *v.t.*, **-fied, -fy·ing. 1.** to confer honor or dignity upon; honor; ennoble. **2.** to give a high-sounding title or name to; confer unmerited distinction upon: *to dignify pedantry by calling it scholarship.* [ME < OF *dignefi(er)* < ML *dignificāre* < L *dign(us)* worthy + *-ificāre* -IFY]

dig·ni·tar·y (dig′ni ter′ē), *n.*, *pl.* **-tar·ies.** a person who holds a high rank or office, as in the government. [DIGNIT(Y) + -ARY] **—dig·ni·tar·i·al** (dig′ni târ′ē əl), *adj.*

dig·ni·ty (dig′ni tē), *n.*, *pl.* **-ties. 1.** bearing, conduct, or speech indicative of self-respect or appreciation of the formality or gravity of an occasion. **2.** nobility or elevation of character; worthiness: *dignity of sentiments.* **3.** elevated rank, office, station, etc. **4.** degree of excellence, either in estimation or in the order of nature: *Man is superior in dignity to brutes.* **5.** relative standing; rank. **6.** a sign or token of respect: *an impertinent question unworthy of the dignity of an answer.* **7.** *Archaic.* **a.** person of high rank or title. **b.** such persons collectively. [ME *dignite* < OF < L *dignitāt-* (s. of *dignitās*) worthiness, equiv. to *dign(us)* worthy + *-itāt-* -ITY]
—Syn. 1. decorum.

di·graph (dī′graf, -gräf), *n.* a pair of letters representing a single speech sound, as *ea* in *meat*, or *th* in *path.* [DI-[1] + -GRAPH] **—di·graph′ic,** *adj.*

di·gress (di gres′, dī-), *v.i.* **1.** to deviate or wander away from the main topic or purpose in speaking or writing, or from the principal line of argument, study, etc. **2.** *Archaic.* to turn aside. [< L *dīgress(us)* having departed or gone aside (ptp. of *dīgredī*), equiv. to *dī-* DI-[2] + *gre-* go (perf. s. of *grad(ī)* (to) go) + *-ss-* ptp. suffix] **—di·gress′er,** *n.* **—di·gress′ing·ly,** *adv.*
—Syn. 1. ramble, stray. See **deviate.**

di·gres·sion (di gresh′ən, dī-), *n.* **1.** the act of digressing. **2.** a passage or section that deviates from the central theme of a discourse or writing. [ME *digression* < MF < L *dīgressiōn-* (s. of *dīgressiō*) a going away, aside, equiv. to *dīgress(us)* (see DIGRESS) + *-iōn-* -ION] **—di·gres′sion·al,** *adj.*

di·gres·sive (di gres′iv, dī-), *adj.* tending to digress; departing from the main subject. [< L *dīgressīv(us).* See DIGRESS, -IVE] **—di·gres′sive·ly,** *adv.* **—di·gres′sive·ness,** *n.*

di·he·dral (dī hē′drəl), *adj.* **1.** having or formed by two planes. **2.** of or pertaining to a dihedron. **—***n.* **3.** dihedron. **4.** *Aeron.* the angle at which the right and left wings of an airplane or the like are inclined upward or downward with reference to the center horizontal section. [DI-[1] + -HEDRAL]

D, Dihedral angle included between planes AA and BB

dihe′dral an′gle, *Math.* **1.** the angle between two planes in a dihedron. **2.** dihedron.

di·he·dron (dī hē′drən), *n.* *Geom.* a figure formed by two intersecting planes. Also called **dihedral, dihedral angle.** [DI-[1] + -HEDRON]

di·hy·brid (dī hī′brid), *Biol.* **—***n.* **1.** the offspring of parents differing in two specific pairs of genes. **—***adj.* **2.** of or pertaining to such an offspring. [DI-[1] + HYBRID] **—di·hy′brid·ism,** *n.*

di·hy·drate (dī hī′drāt), *n.* *Chem.* a hydrate that contains two molecules of water, as potassium sulfite, $K_2SO_3{\cdot}2H_2O$. [DI-[1] + HYDRATE] **—di·hy′drat·ed,** *adj.*

di·hy·dric (dī hī′drik), *adj.* *Chem.* (esp. of alcohols and phenols) dihydroxy. [DI-[1] + -HYDRIC]

di·hy·dro·mor·phi·none (dī hī′drō môr′fə nōn′), *n.* *Pharm.* a narcotic compound, $C_{17}H_{19}O_3N$, prepared from morphine and used chiefly as an analgesic. [DI-[1] HYDRO-[2] + MORPHINE + -ONE]

di·hy·dro·sphin·go·sine (dī hī′drō sfing′gə sēn′, -sin), *n.* *Biochem.* the completely saturated sphingosine compound. [DI-[1] + HYDRO-[2] + SPHINGOSINE]

di·hy·dro·strep·to·my·cin (dī hī′drō strep′tə mī′-sin), *n.* *Pharm.* an antibiotic, $C_{21}H_{41}N_7O_{12}$, derived by organic synthesis from and believed to be less toxic than streptomycin: used in the form of its sulfate chiefly in the treatment of tuberculosis. [DI-[1] + HYDRO-[2] + STREPTOMYCIN]

di·hy·dro·ta·chys·ter·ol (dī hī′drō tə kis′tə rōl′, -rôl′, -rol′), *n.* *Pharm.* a white, crystalline, water-insoluble sterol, $C_{28}H_{46}O$, derived from ergosterol: used chiefly in the treatment of hypoparathyroidism. [DI-[1] + HYDRO-[2] + TACHY- + STEROL]

di·hy·drox·y (dī′hī drok′sē), *adj.* *Chem.* (of a molecule) containing two hydroxyl groups. [DI-[1] + HYDROXY]

Di·ip·o·li·a (dī ip′ə lē′ə), *n.* (*sometimes construed as pl.*) Dipolia.

di·i·so·bu·tyl phthal·ate (dī ī′sō byōōt′ᵊl thal′āt, -ī′sō-), *Chem.* a clear, colorless liquid, $C_6H_4[COOCH_2CH(CH_3)_2]_2$, used chiefly as a plasticizer for nitrocellulose. [DI-[1] + ISO- + BUTYL + PHTHAL- (from PHTHALIC ACID) + -ATE[2]]

Di·jon (dē zhôN′), *n.* a city in and the capital of Côte d'Or, in E central France. 141,104 (1962).

dik-dik (dik′dik′), *n.* any of several small antelopes of the genera *Madoqua* and *Rhynchotragus*, of eastern and southwestern Africa, being about 14 inches high at the shoulder. [native EAfr name]

dike[1] (dīk), *n.*, *v.*, **diked, dik·ing. —***n.* **1.** an embankment for controlling or holding back the waters of the sea or a river. **2.** a ditch. **3.** a bank of earth formed of material being excavated. **4.** a causeway. **5.** *Brit. Dial.* a low wall or fence, esp. of earth or stone, for dividing or enclosing land. **6.** an obstacle; barrier. **7.** *Geol.* **a.** a long, narrow, cross-cutting mass of igneous or eruptive rock intruded into a fissure in older rock. **b.** a similar mass of rock composed of other kinds of material, as sandstone. **—***v.t.* **8.** to furnish or drain with a dike. **9.** to enclose, restrain, or protect by a dike: *to dike a tract of land.* Also, **dyke.** [ME *dik(e)*, OE *dīc* < ON *dīki;* akin to DITCH] **—dik′er,** *n.*

dike[2] (dīk), *n.* *Slang.* dyke[2].

Di·ke (dī′kē), *n.* *Class. Myth.* one of the Horae, the personification of natural law or justice, sometimes identified with Astraea. Also, **Dice.**

di·ke·tone (dī kē′tōn), *n.* *Chem.* a compound containing two C=O groups, as $CH_3COCOCH_3$. [DI-[1] + KETONE]

dil., **1.** dilute. **2.** diluted.

di·lac·er·ate (di las′ə rāt′, dī-), *v.t.*, **-at·ed, -at·ing.** to tear apart or to pieces. [ME < L *dīlacerāt(us)* torn to pieces (ptp. of *dīlacerāre*), equiv. to *dī-* DI-[2] + *lacerāre* to tear; see LACERATE]

di·lac·er·a·tion (di las′ə rā′shən, dī-), *n.* **1.** the act of dilacerating. **2.** the state of being dilacerated. **3.** *Dentistry.* displacement in the position of a developing tooth, resulting in angulation or distortion. [ME < LL *dīlacerātiōn-* (s. of *dīlacerātiō*) a tearing to pieces, equiv. to *dīlacerāt(us)* (see DILACERATE) + *-iōn-* -ION]

Di·lan·tin (di lan′tin), *n.* *Pharm.*, *Trademark.* diphenylhydantoin.

di·lap·i·date (di lap′i dāt′), *v.*, **-dat·ed, -dat·ing.** **—***v.t.* **1.** to bring (a building, automobile, etc.) into a state of disrepair, as by misuse or neglect. **2.** *Archaic.* to squander; waste. **—***v.i.* **3.** to fall into ruin or decay. [< L *dīlapidāt(us)* thrown away, consumed, scattered (ptp. of *dīlapidāre*), equiv. to *dī-* DI-[2] + *lapidātus* having thrown stones; see LAPIDATE] **—di·lap′i·da′tion,** *n.* **—di·lap′i·da′tor,** *n.*

di·lap·i·dat·ed (di lap′i dā′tid), *adj.* reduced to or fallen into partial ruin or decay, as from age, wear, misuse, or neglect: *a dilapidated cabin in the woods.* [DILAPIDATE + -ED[2]]

di·lat·ant (di lāt′ᵊnt, dī-), *adj.* **1.** dilating; expanding. **2.** *Physical Chem.* exhibiting an increase in volume on being changed in shape, owing to a wider spacing between particles. [< L *dīlātant-* (s. of *dīlātāns*), prp. of *dīlātāre* to DILATE; see -ANT] **—di·lat′an·cy,** *n.*

di·lat·ate (di lā′tāt, dil′ə tāt′), *adj.* dilated; broadened. [ME < L *dīlātāt(us)*, ptp. of *dīlātāre* to DILATE; see -ATE[1]]

dil·a·ta·tion (dil′ə tā′shən, dī′lə-), *n.* **1.** act of dilating; the state of being dilated. **2.** a dilated formation or part. **3.** *Pathol.* an abnormal enlargement of an aperture or a canal of the body. **4.** *Med.* an enlargement made in a body aperture or canal for surgical or medical treatment. **5.** *Surg.* a restoration to normal patency of an abnormally small body opening or passageway, as of the anus or esophagus. **6.** *Mech.* increase in volume per unit volume of a homogeneous substance. Also, **dilation.** [ME *dilatacioun* < OF *dilatacion* < L *dīlātātiōn-* (s. of *dīlātātiō*), equiv. to *dīlātāt(us)* spread out (ptp. of *dīlātāre* to DILATE) + *-iōn-* -ION]

di·late (dī lāt′, di-), *v.*, **-lat·ed, -lat·ing. —***v.t.* **1.** to make wider or larger; cause to expand. **2.** *Archaic.* to describe or develop at length. **—***v.i.* **3.** to spread out; expand. **4.** to speak at length; expatiate (often fol. by *on* or *upon*). [ME *dilate(n)* < MF *dilat(er)*, L *dīlāt(āre)* (to) spread out, equiv. to *dī-* DI-[2] + *lāt(us)* broad + *-āre* inf. suffix] **—di·lat′a·bil′i·ty, di·lat′a·ble·ness,** *n.* **—di·lat′a·ble,** *adj.* **—di·lat′a·bly,** *adv.* **—di·lat′ing·ly,** *adv.*
—Syn. 1. enlarge, widen, extend. **3.** swell. **—Ant. 1.** constrict.

di·lat·er (dī lā′tər, di-), *n.* dilator.

di·la·tion (dī lā′shən, di-), *n.* **1.** dilatation. **2.** *Mech.* dilatation, esp. when produced by deformation. [DILATE + -ION]

di·la·tive (dī lā′tiv, di-), *adj.* serving or tending to dilate. [DILATE + -IVE]

dil·a·tom·e·ter (dil′ə tom′i tər), *n.* *Physics.* a device for measuring expansion caused by changes in temperature in substances. [DILATE + -O- + -METER] **—dil·a·to·met·ric** (dil′ə tə me′trik), *adj.* **—dil′a·to·met′ri·cal·ly,** *adv.* **—dil′a·tom′e·try,** *n.*

di·la·tor (dī lā′tər, di-), *n.* **1.** one who or that which dilates. **2.** *Anat.* a muscle that dilates some cavity of the body. **3.** *Surg.* an instrument for dilating body canals, orifices, or cavities. [DILATE + -OR[2]]

dil·a·to·ry (dil′ə tōr′ē, -tôr′ē), *adj.* **1.** inclined to delay or procrastinate; slow; tardy; not prompt. **2.** intended to bring about delay, gain time, or defer decision: *a dilatory strategy.* [ME < LL *dīlātōri(us)* delaying < L *dīlātōr-* (s. of *dīlātor*) a delayer < *dīlāt(us)* put off, delayed (ptp. of *differre;* see DIFFER), equiv. to *dī-* DI-[2] + *lā* (ptp. s. of *ferre* to bear, carry) + *-t-* ptp. suffix + *-ōrius* -ORY[1]] **—dil′a·to′ri·ly,** *adv.* **—dil′a·to′ri·ness,** *n.*

Di·lau·did (dī lô′did, di-), *n.* *Pharm., Trademark.* the hydrochloride salt of dihydromorphinone.

dil·do (dil′dō), *n.*, *pl.* **-dos.** *Slang.* an artificial erect penis. Also, **dil′doe.** [?]

di·lem·ma (di lem′ə), *n.* **1.** a situation requiring a choice between equally undesirable alternatives. **2.** any difficult or perplexing situation or problem. **3.** *Logic.* a form of syllogism in which the major premise is formed of two or more hypothetical propositions and the minor premise is an exhaustive disjunctive proposition, as "If A, then B; if C then D. Either A or C. Therefore, either B or D." [< LL < Gk *dílēmma*, equiv. to *di-* DI-[1] + *lêmma* an assumption, premise deriv. of *lambán(ein)* (to) take] **—dil·em·mat·ic** (dil′ə mat′ik), **dil′em·mat′i·cal,** **di·lem′mic,** *adj.* **—dil′em·mat′i·cal·ly,** *adv.*
—Syn. 1. See **predicament. 2.** question, difficulty.

dil·et·tan·te (dil′i tan′tē, -tän′tä, -i tänt′, dil′i tänt′), *n.*, *pl.* **-tan·tes, -tan·ti** (-tän′tē), *adj.* **—***n.* **1.** a person who takes up an art, activity, or subject merely for amusement, esp. in a desultory or superficial way; dabbler. **2.** a lover of an art or science, esp. of a fine art. **—***adj.* **3.** of or pertaining to dilettantes. [< It, n. use of prp. of *dilettare* < L *dēlectāre* to DELIGHT] **—dil′et·tan′tish, dil′et·tan′te·ish,** *adj.*
—Syn. 1. amateur.

dil·et·tant·ism (dil′i tan′tiz əm, -tän′-), *n.* the practices or characteristics of a dilettante. Also, **dil·et·tan·te·ism** (dil′i tan′tē iz′əm, -tän′-). [DILETTANTE + -ISM]

dil·i·gence[1] (dil′i jəns), *n.* **1.** constant and earnest effort to accomplish what is undertaken; persistent exertion of body or mind. **2.** *Obs.* care; caution. [ME *diligence* < MF, L *dīligentia*, equiv. to *dīligent-* (s. of *dīligēns*) DILIGENT + *-ia;* see -ENCE]
—Syn. 1. application, industry, assiduity, perseverance.

dil·i·gence[2] (dil′i jəns; *Fr.* dē lē zhäNs′), *n.*, *pl.* **-gen·ces** (-jən siz; *Fr.* -zhäNs′). a public stagecoach, esp. in France. [short for F *carosse de diligence* speed coach]

Diligence[2]

dil·i·gent (dil′i jənt), *adj.* **1.** constant in effort to accomplish something; attentive and persistent in doing anything: *a diligent student.* **2.** done or pursued with persevering attention; painstaking: *a diligent search.* [ME < MF, L *dīligent-* (s. of *dīligēns*), prp. of *dīligere* to choose, like, equiv. to *dī-* DI-[2] + *-ligere* (sp. var. of *legere* to choose, read); see -ENT] **—dil′i·gent·ly,** *adv.* **—dil′i·gent·ness,** *n.*
—Syn. 1. industrious, assiduous, sedulous, occupied. See **busy. 2.** persevering, indefatigable, untiring, tireless, unremitting.

dill[1] (dil), *n.* **1.** an apiaceous plant, *Anethum graveolens,* bearing a seedlike fruit used in medicine, in cookery, for flavoring pickles, etc. **2.** its aromatic seeds or leaves used as a common food flavoring. **3.** See **dill pickle.** [ME *di(l)le,* OE *dile;* akin to G *Dill,* Sw *dill*]

dill[2] (dil), *Brit., Australian.* —*v.t.* to sooth or assuage; lull to sleep. —*n.* **2.** *Informal.* simpleton; fool. —*adj.* **3.** *Informal.* stupid; dull. [ME *dill(en),* akin to *dil* (adj.) sluggish, slow < ON *dilla* to lull]

Dil·lin·ger (dil′in jər), *n.* **John,** 1902–34, U.S. bank robber and murderer.

Dil·lon (dil′ən), *n.* **1. C(larence) Douglas,** born 1909, U.S. lawyer and government official, born in Switzerland: Secretary of the Treasury 1961–65. **2. John Forrest,** 1831–1914, U.S. jurist and legal scholar. **3.** a town in NE South Carolina. 6173 (1960).

dill′ pick′le, a cucumber pickle flavored with dill.

dil·ly (dil′ē), *n., pl.* **-lies.** *Informal.* something remarkable of its kind: *a dilly of a movie.* [obs. dial.: cranky; perh. alter. of *delightful*]

Dil·ly (dil′ē), *n.* a girl's given name, form of **Dolly.** Also, **Dil′lie.**

dil′ly bag′ (dil′ē), *Australian.* a bag, usually for collecting and carrying food and other articles, made by the aborigines from reeds, grasses, or hair. [< Austral *dhilla* hair]

dil·ly·dal·ly (dil′ē dal′ē, -dal′-), *v.i.,* **-lied, -ly·ing.** to waste time, esp. by indecision; vacillate; trifle; loiter. [gradational redupl. of DALLY]

dil·u·ent (dil′yo͞o ənt), *adj.* **1.** serving to dilute; diluting. —*n.* **2.** a diluting substance. [< L *dīluent-* (s. of *dīluēns*), prp. of *dīluere* to DILUTE; see -ENT]

di·lute (di lo͞ot′, dī-; *adj. also* dī′lo͞ot), *v.,* **-lut·ed, -lut·ing,** *adj.* —*v.t.* **1.** to make (a liquid) thinner or weaker by the addition of water or the like. **2.** to make fainter, as a color. **3.** to reduce the strength, force, or efficiency of by admixture. —*v.i.* **4.** to become diluted. —*adj.* **5.** reduced in strength, as a chemical by admixture; weak: *a dilute solution.* [< L *dīlūt(us)* washed away, dissolved (ptp. of *dīluere*), equiv. to *dī-* DI-[2] + *lu(ere)* (to) wash + *-t-* ptp. suffix] —**di·lute′ly,** *adv.* —**di·lute′ness,** *n.*

di·lu·tion (di lo͞o′shən, dī-), *n.* **1.** the act or state of diluting; the state of being diluted. **2.** something diluted; a diluted form of anything. [DILUTE + -ION]

di·lu·vi·al (di lo͞o′vē əl), *adj.* **1.** pertaining to or caused by a flood or deluge, esp. the Biblical flood. **2.** *Geol.* pertaining to or consisting of diluvium. Also, **di·lu′vi·an.** [< LL *dīluviāl(is),* equiv. to *dīluvi(um)* flood (see DILUVIUM) + *-ālis* -AL[1]]

di·lu·vi·um (di lo͞o′vē əm), *n., pl.* **-vi·a** (-vē ə), **-vi·ums.** *Geol.* a coarse superficial deposit formerly attributed to a general deluge but now regarded as glacial drift. Also, **di·lu′vi·on.** [< L *dīluvium* flood (sp. var. of *dīluviēs,* equiv. to *dīlu(ere)* (to) DILUTE + connecting *-v-* + *-ium* n. suffix]

dim (dim), *adj.,* **dim·mer, dim·mest,** *v.,* **dimmed, dim·ming.** —*adj.* **1.** not bright; obscure from lack of light or emitted light: *a dim room; a dim flashlight.* **2.** not seen clearly or in detail; indistinct: *a dim object in the distance.* **3.** not clear to the mind; vague: *a dim idea.* **4.** not brilliant; dull in luster: *a dim color.* **5.** not clear or distinct to the senses; faint: *a dim sound.* **6.** not seeing clearly: *eyes dim with tears.* **7.** tending to be unfavorable; not likely to happen, succeed, be favorable, etc.: *Chances of rain are dim.* **8.** not understanding clearly. **9. take a dim view of,** to regard with pessimism, apathy, skepticism, or dismay: *Her mother takes a dim view of her choice of clothes.* —*v.t.* **10.** to make dim or dimmer. **11.** to switch (the headlights of a vehicle) from the high to the low beam. —*v.i.* **12.** to become or grow dim or dimmer. **13. dim out,** to reduce the night illumination (of a city, ship, etc.) to make it less visible from the air or sea, as a protection from enemy aircraft or ships. [ME, OE *dimm;* c. OFris *dim,* Icel *dimm(r)*] —**dim′ly,** *adv.* —**dim′ness,** *n.*
—**Syn. 1.** See **dark. 10.** darken, cloud. **12.** blur, dull, fade.

dim., **1.** (in prescriptions) one-half. [< L *dīmidius*] **2.** diminuendo. **3.** diminutive. Also, **dimin.**

Di·Mag·gi·o (də mä′jē ō′, -maj′ē ō′), *n.* **Joseph Paul** (*Joe*), born 1914, U.S. baseball player.

dime (dīm), *n.* **1.** a silver coin of the U.S., the 10th part of a dollar, equal to 10 cents. **2. a dime a dozen,** *Slang.* so abundant or readily obtainable that the value becomes decreased; common; cheap: *Actors are a dime a dozen in the city.* [ME < OF (var. of *disme*) < L *decima* tenth part, tithe, prop. fem. of *decim(us)* tenth, deriv. of *dec(em)* ten]

di·men·hy·dri·nate (dī′men hī′drə nāt′), *n. Pharm.* a synthetic, crystalline, antihistamine powder, $C_{17}H_{22}NO{\cdot}C_7H_6ClN_4O_2$, used in the treatment of allergic disorders and as a preventive for seasickness and airsickness. [DIME(THYL) + (AMI)N(E) + HYDR(A-M)INE + -ATE[2]]

dime′ nov′el, a cheap melodramatic or sensational novel, usually in paperback, esp. such an adventure novel popular from c1850 to c1920.

di·men·sion (di men′shən), *n.* **1.** magnitude measured in a particular direction, or along a diameter or principal axis. **2.** Usually, **dimensions. a.** measurement in width, length, and thickness. **b.** scope; importance: *the dimensions of a problem.* **3.** magnitude; size: *Matter has dimension.* **4.** *Topology.* **a.** a magnitude that, independently or in conjunction with other such magnitudes, serves to define the location of an element within a given set, as of a point on a line, an object in a space, or an event in space-time. **b.** the number of elements in a finite basis of a given vector space. **5. dimensions,** *Informal.* the measurements of a woman's bust, waist, and hips, in that order: *The chorus girl's dimensions were 38-24-36.* [ME *dimensioun* < MF *dimension,* L *dīmensiōn-* (s. of *dīmensiō*) a measuring, equiv. to *dīmens(us)* measured out (ptp. of *dīmetīrī,* equiv. to *dī-* DI-[2] + *mētīrī* to measure) + *-iōn-* -ION] —**di·men′sion·al,** *adj.* —**di·men′sion·al′i·ty,** *n.* —**di·men′sion·al·ly,** *adv.* —**di·men′sion·less,** *adj.*

dimen′sion lum′ber, **1.** building lumber cut to standard or specified sizes. **2.** sawed lumber between two and five inches thick and from four to twelve inches wide.

dimen′sion stone′, quarried and squared stone two feet or more in length and width and of specified thickness.

di·mer (dī′mər), *n. Chem.* **1.** a molecule composed of two identical, simpler molecules. **2.** a polymer derived from two identical monomers. [DI-[1] + -MER]

di·mer·cap·rol (dī′mər kap′rōl, -rôl, -rol), *n. Chem.* a colorless, oily, viscous liquid, $CH_2(SH)CH(SH)CH_2OH$, originally developed as an antidote to lewisite and now used in treating bismuth, gold, mercury, and arsenic poisoning. Also called **BAL, British anti-lewisite.** [alter. of *di-mercapto-propanol* (*mercapto-* comb. form of MERCAPTAN)]

di·mer·ize (dī′mə rīz′), *v.i., v.t.* **-ized, -iz·ing.** *Chem.* to form a dimer, as in polymerization. [back formation from *dimerization;* see DIMER, -IZE]

dim·er·ous (dim′ər əs), *adj.* **1.** consisting of or divided into two parts. **2.** *Bot.* (of flowers) having two members in each whorl. [< NL *dimerus* < Gk *dimer(ḗs)* bipartite. See DI-[1], -MEROUS] —**dim′er·ism,** *n.*

Dimerous flower

dime′ store′, **1.** five-and-ten (def. 1). **2.** *Bowling Slang.* a split in which the five and ten pins remain standing.

dim·e·ter (dim′i tər), *n. Pros.* a verse or line of two measures or feet, as *He is gone on the mountain,/He is lost to the forest.* [< LL *dimeter* < Gk *dímetr(os)* of two measures, a dimeter, equiv. to *di-* DI-[1] + *métr(on)* -METER]

di·me·thox·y·meth·ane (dī′mə tho̵k′sē meth′ān), *n. Chem.* methylal. [DI-[1] + METH(YL) + OXY-[2] + METHANE]

di·meth·yl (dī meth′əl), *n. Chem.* ethane. [DI-[1] + METHYL]

di·meth·yl·an·thran·i·late (dī meth′əl an thran′əlāt′, -əlit, -an′thrə nəlāt′), *n. Chem.* a colorless or pale-yellow liquid, $CH_3COOC_6H_4NHCH_3$, having a grape odor: used chiefly in perfumes, flavorings, and drugs. [DIMETHYL + ANTHR(ACENE) + ANIL(INE) + -ATE[2]]

dimeth′yl arsin′ic ac′id, *Chem.* See **cacodylic acid.**

di·meth·yl·ben·zene (dī meth′əl ben′zēn, -ben-zēn′), *n. Chem.* xylene. [DI-[1] + METHYL + BENZENE]

di·meth·yl·car·bi·nol (dī meth′əl kär′bə nōl′, -nôl′, -nol′), *n. Chem.* See **isopropyl alcohol.** [DI- + METHYL + CARBINOL]

di·meth·yl·di·ke·tone (dī meth′əl dī kē′tōn), *n. Chem.* biacetyl. [DIMETHYL + DI-[1] + KETONE]

di·meth·yl·gly·ox·al (dī meth′əl glī ok′sal), *n. Chem.* biacetyl. [DIMETHYL + GLYOXAL(IN)]

di·meth·yl·ke·tol (dī meth′əl kē′tôl, -tōl), *n. Chem.* acetoin. [DI-[1] + METHYL + KET(ONE) + -OL[1]]

di·meth·yl·ke·tone (dī meth′əl kē′tōn), *n. Chem.* acetone. [DIMETHYL + KETONE]

di·meth·yl·meth·ane (dī meth′əl meth′ān), *n. Chem.* propane. [DI-[1] + METHYL + METHANE]

dimeth′yl sul′fate, *Chem.* a colorless or yellow, slightly water-soluble, poisonous liquid, $(CH_3)_2SO_2$, used chiefly in organic synthesis. Also, **methyl sulfate.**

dimeth′yl sulf·ox′ide (sul fok′sīd), *Chem.* See **DMSO.**

di·met·ric (dī me′trik), *adj. Crystall.* tetragonal. [DI-[1] + METRIC[2]]

di·mid·i·ate (di mid′ē āt′, dī-), *v.,* **-at·ed, -at·ing,** *adj.* —*v.t.* **1.** *Heraldry.* to combine (two coats of arms, as those of a husband and wife or of a person and the office held by him) so that the dexter half of one coat is placed beside the sinister half of the other. Cf. **impale** (def. 6). **2.** *Obs.* to divide into halves; reduce to half. —*adj.* **3.** divided into halves. [< L *dīmidiāt(us)* divided in half (ptp. of *dīmidiāre*), equiv. to *dīmidi(us)* half or *dīmidi(um)* a half (*dī-* DI-[2] + *medi(us)* middle or *medi(um)* the middle) + *-ātus* -ATE[1]] —**di·mid′i·a′tion,** *n.*

di·min·ish (di min′ish), *v.t.* **1.** to make or cause to seem smaller, less, less important, etc.; lessen; reduce. **2.** *Archit.* to give (a column) a form tapering inward from bottom to top. **3.** *Music.* to make (an interval) smaller by a chromatic half step than the corresponding perfect or minor interval. **4.** to detract from the authority, honor, stature, or reputation of; disparage. —*v.i.* **5.** to lessen; decrease. [ME; b. *diminue* (< ML *dīminuere* for L *dēminuere* to make smaller) + MINISH] —**di·min′ish·a·ble,** *adj.* —**di·min′ish·a·ble·ness,** *n.* —**di·min′ish·ing·ly,** *adv.*
—**Syn. 1.** shrink, abate, contract, decrease. **5.** subside, ebb, dwindle, shrink, abate, contract. See **decrease.**

di·min·ished (di min′isht), *adj. Music.* **1.** (of an interval) smaller by a half tone than the corresponding perfect or minor interval. **2.** (of a triad) having a minor third and a diminished fifth above the root. [DIMINISH + -ED[2]]

dimin′ished dove′tail, *Joinery.* a housed joint in which the end being housed is partly cut away to form a dovetail tapering from the full thickness of the board at the inner end to a lesser thickness at the edge.

dimin′ished stile′, (in a door or the like) a stile having different breadths above and below the middle rail, as to accommodate a wide sash and narrower paneling. Also, **dimin′ishing stile′.**

dimin′ishing returns′, **1.** *Econ.* the fact, often stated as a law or principle, that when any factor of production, as labor, is increased while other factors, as capital and land, are held constant in amount, the output per unit of the variable factor will eventually diminish. **2.** any rate of profit, production, benefits, etc. that, beyond a certain point, fails to increase proportionately with added investment, effort, or skill.

dimin′ishing rule′, *Masonry.* a templet for determining the entasis of a column.

di·min·u·en·do (di min′yo͞o en′dō), *adj., n., pl.* **-dos.** *Music.* —*adj.* **1.** gradually reducing in force or loudness; decrescendo (opposed to *crescendo*). —*n.* **2.** a gradual reduction of force or loudness. **3.** a diminuendo passage. *Symbol:* > [< It, prp. of *diminuire;* see DIMINISH]

dim·i·nu·tion (dim′ə no͞o′shən, -nyo͞o′-), *n.* **1.** the act, fact, or process of diminishing; lessening; reduction. **2.** *Music.* the repetition or imitation of a subject or theme in notes of shorter duration than those first used. [ME *diminucion* < AF *diminucium* < L *dēminūtiōn-* (s. of *dīminūtiō*) for *dēminūtiōn-* (s. of *dēminūtiō*) (by influence of *dimunuere;* see DIMINISH), equiv. to *dēminūt(us)* (ptp. of *dēminuere,* equiv. to *dē-* DE- + *minuere* to lessen) + *-iōn-* -ION]

di·min·u·tive (di min′yə tiv), *adj.* **1.** small; little; tiny: *a diminutive house.* **2.** *Gram.* pertaining to or productive of a form denoting smallness, familiarity, affection, or triviality, as the suffix *-let,* in *droplet* from *drop.* —*n.* **3.** a small thing or person. **4.** *Gram.* a diminutive element or formation. **5.** *Heraldry.* a charge, as an ordinary, smaller in length or breadth than the usual. [ME < ML *dīminūtīv(us)* < L *dīminūt(us)* lessened (for *dēminūtus;* see DIMINUTION) + *-īvus* -IVE] —**di·min′u·tive·ly,** *adv.* —**di·min′u·tive·ness,** *n.*
—**Syn. 1.** See **little.**

dim·is·so·ry (dim′i sôr′ē, -sōr′ē), *adj.* dismissing or giving permission to depart. [< LL *dīmissōri(us)* relating to leaving, equiv. to L *dīmiss(us)* sent away (ptp. of *dīmittere;* see DEMIT) + *-ōrius* -ORY[1]]

dim′issory let′ter, a letter issued by a bishop, abbot, etc., permitting a subject to be ordained by another bishop. Also, **dim′is·so′ri·al, dim′isso′rial let′ter.** [trans. of LL *dīmissōriae litterae*]

Di·mi·trov (di mē′trôf), *n.* **Ge·or·gi** (ge ôr′gi), 1882–1949, Bulgarian political leader: premier 1946–49.

Di·mi·tro·vo (di mē′trô vo), *n.* a city in W Bulgaria, near Sofia. 59,721 (1956). Formerly, **Pernik.**

dim·i·ty (dim′i tē), *n., pl.* **-ties.** a thin, cotton fabric, white, dyed, or printed, woven with a stripe or check of heavier yarn. [< ML *dimit(um)* (< Gk *dímiton,* n. use of neut. of *dímitos* double-threaded, equiv. to *di-* DI-[1] + *mít(os)* warp thread + *-os* adj. suffix) + -Y[2]; r. ME *demyt*]

dim·mer (dim′ər), *n.* **1.** one who or that which dims. **2.** a rheostat or similar device by which the intensity of illumination, esp. in stage lighting, is varied. **3. dimmers, a.** the low-beam headlights of an automobile or truck. **b.** the small, parking lights of an automobile. [DIM + -ER[1]]

Dim·mitt (dim′it), *n.* a town in NW Texas. 2935 (1960).

Dimorphism (def. 2)
Submerged and floating leaves of fanwort, genus *Cabomba*

di·morph (dī′môrf), *n. Crystall.* either of the two forms assumed by a substance exhibiting dimorphism. [< Gk *dímorph(os)* having two shapes, equiv. to *di-* DI-[1] + *morphḗ* -MORPH]

di·mor·phism (dī môr′fiz əm), *n.* **1.** *Zool.* the occurrence of two forms distinct in structure, coloration, etc., among animals of the same species. **2.** *Bot.* the occurrence of two different forms of flowers, leaves, etc., on the same plant or on distinct plants of the same species. **3.** *Crystall.* the property of some substances of crystallizing in two chemically identical but crystallographically distinct forms. [DIMORPH + -ISM]

di·mor·phite (dī môr′fīt), *n.* a mineral, arsenic sulfide, yellow-orange in color and similar in its properties to orpiment. [DIMORPH + -ITE[1]]

di·mor·phous (dī môr′fəs), *adj.* exhibiting dimorphism. Also, **di·mor′phic.** [< Gk *dímorph(os)* (see DIMORPH) + -OUS]

dim-out (dim′out′), *n.* a reduction or concealment of night lighting, as of a city, a ship, etc., to make it less visible to an enemy from the air or sea. Also, **dim′out′.** [n. use of v. phrase *dim out*]

dim·ple (dim′pəl), *n., v.,* **-pled, -pling.** —*n.* **1.** a small, natural hollow area, permanent or transient, in some soft part of the human body, esp one formed in the cheek in smiling. **2.** any similar slight depression. —*v.t.* **3.** to mark with or as with dimples; produce dimples in: *A smile dimpled her face.* **4.** *Metalworking.* **a.** to dent (a metal sheet) so as to permit use of bolts or rivets with countersunk heads. **b.** to mark (a metal object) with a drill point as a guide for further drilling. **c.** to remove surface defects from (a metal object); scarf. **d.** to press a shallow sunken area into (a piece of sheet metal). —*v.i.* **5.** to form or show dimples. [ME *dimpel,* OE **dympel;* c. G *Tümpel* pool] —**dim′ply,** *adj.*

dim·wit (dim′wit′), *n. Slang.* a stupid or slow-thinking person. [DIM + WIT[1]] —**dim′-wit′ted,** *adj.*

din[1] (din), *n., v.,* **dinned, din·ning.** —*n.* **1.** a loud, confused noise; a continued, loud or tumultuous sound; noisy clamor. —*v.t.* **2.** to assail with din. **3.** to sound or utter with clamor or persistent repetition. —*v.i.* **4.** to make a din. [ME *din(e),* OE *dyne, dynn;* c. OIcel *dynr* noise, OHG *tuni,* Skt *dhuni* roaring]
—**Syn. 1.** uproar. See **noise.**

din[2] (din), *n.* (*construed as pl.*) *Islam.* the religious observances of a Muslim. Also called **Pillars of Islam, Pillars of the Faith.** [< Ar: lit., pillars]

Din., dinar; dinars.

Di·nah (dī′nə), *n.* **1.** Also, *Douay Bible,* **Di′na.** the daughter of Jacob and Leah. Gen. 30:21. **2.** a girl's given name.

di·nan·de·rie (di nan′də rē, dē′nän drē′), *n.* fine brassware, esp. that made in Belgium in the Middle Ages. [< MF, after *Dinand, Dinant* town in Belgium noted for brassware; see -ERY]

di·nar (di när′), *n.* **1.** any of various former coins of the Near East, esp. gold coins issued by Islamic governments. **2.** a money of account of Iran, the 100th part of a rial, equivalent to about .00013 of a U.S. dollar. **3.** an aluminum coin and monetary unit of Yugoslavia, equal to 100 paras and equivalent to about .00125 of a U.S. dollar. *Abbr.:* Din. **4.** a paper money and monetary unit of Iraq, equal to 100 fils and equivalent to about 2.80 U.S. dollars. *Abbr.:* ID. **5.** a paper money and monetary unit of Jordan, equal to 100 fils and equivalent to about 2.80 U.S. dollars. *Abbr.:* JD. **6.** a paper money and monetary unit of Kuwait, equal to 10 dirhem or 1000 fils, and equivalent to about 2.79 U.S. dollars. *Abbr.:* KD. **7.** a paper money and monetary unit of Tunisia, equal to 10 dirhams or 1000 millums, and equivalent to about 2.40 U.S. dollars. [< Ar, Pers < LGk *dēnár(ion)* < L *dēnāri(us)* a ten-as coin, equiv. to *dēn(ī)* ten at a time + *-ārius* -ARY]

din·ar·chy (din′är kē), *n., pl.* **-chies.** duarchy. [< F (obs.) *dinarchie,* equiv. to *din-* erroneous for DI-[1] (after *bi-, bin-*) + *-archie* -ARCHY]

Di·nard (dē NAR′), *n.* a city in W France: seaside resort. 9432 (1962).

Di·nar·ic (di nar′ik), *adj.* **1.** of or pertaining to the Alpine region of Yugoslavia. **2.** of, pertaining to, or characteristic of a Caucasoid subracial type with a long face and round, often flattened head, found chiefly in eastern Europe, esp. in Yugoslavia and Albania. [*Dinar(a)* mountain in Yugoslavia + -IC]

Dinar′ic Alps′, a mountain range in W Yugoslavia: part of the Alps.

din·dle (din′dᵊl, din′ᵊl), *v.t., v.i.,* **-dled, -dling,** *n. Scot. and North Eng.* —*v.t., v.i.* **1.** to thrill; tremble. —*n.* **2.** a tremor; quiver; tingle. [late ME *dindle(n),* of imit. orig.]

d'In·dy (daN dē′), **Vin·cent** (vaN säN′). See **Indy,d' Vincent.**

Din·dy·me·ne (din′də mē′nē), *n.* Cybele. Also called **Din′dy·me′an Moth′er.**

dine (dīn), *v.,* **dined, din·ing,** *n.* —*v.i.* **1.** to eat the principal meal of the day; have dinner. **2.** to take any meal. —*v.t.* **3.** to entertain at dinner. **4. dine out,** to take a meal, esp. the principal or more formal meal of the day, away from home, as in a hotel or restaurant: *They dine out at least once a week.* —*n.* **5.** *Scot.* dinner. [ME *dine(n)* < OF *di(s)n(er)* < VL **disjējūnāre* to break one's fast, equiv. to *dis-* DIS-[1] + *jējūnāre;* see JEJUNE]

din·er (dī′nər), *n.* **1.** one who dines. **2.** a railroad dining car. **3.** a restaurant built like such a car. [DINE + -ER[1]]

di·ner·gate (dī nûr′git), *n.* a soldier ant. [DIN(O)- + ERGATE]

di·ner·ic (dī ner′ik, di-), *adj. Physics.* of or pertaining to the face of separation of two immiscible liquid phases. [DI-[1] + LGk *nēr(on)* water + -IC]

Din·e·sen (din′i sən), *n.* **I·sak** (ī′zək), [*Baroness Karen Blixen* (*Finecke*)], 1885–1962, Danish author.

di·nette (dī net′), *n.* **1.** a small space or alcove, often in or near the kitchen, serving as an informal dining room. **2.** Also called **dinette′ set′,** a small table and set of matching chairs for such a space or alcove, usually inexpensive, made of or covered with metal or plastic, and accommodating four people. [DINE + -ETTE]

ding[1] (ding), *v.t., v.i.* **1.** to sound as a bell; ring, esp. with wearisome continuance. **2.** *Informal.* to keep repeating, impress by reiteration. —*n.* **3.** the sound of a bell or the like. [see DING-DONG]

ding[2] (ding), *v.t., v.i.* **1.** *Australian.* to hit; strike; knock. **2.** *Scot., Australian.* to fall, flow, or throw down heavily. [ME *ding(en), deng(en),* etc., prob. OE **dingan;* akin to OE *dencgan,* Icel *dengja*]

ding an sich (ding′ än ziKH′), *pl.* **ding·e an sich** (ding′ə än ziKH′). *German.* thing-in-itself.

ding·bat (ding′bat′), *n.* **1.** *Informal.* an object of unknown or unspecified description; thingumbob; dingus. **2.** *Print.* an ornamental piece of type for borders, separators, decorations, etc. **3.** *Archaic.* an object, as a brick, serving as a missile. [?]

ding-dong (ding′dông′, -dong′), *n.* **1.** the sound of a bell. **2.** any similar sound of repeated strokes. —*adj.* **3.** characterized by or resembling the sound of a bell. **4.** marked by rapid alternation of retaliatory action: *a ding-dong struggle between the two teams.* [gradational compound based on *ding,* appar. b. DIN[1] and RING[2]]

din·gey (ding′gē), *n., pl.* **-geys.** dinghy.

din·ghy (ding′gē), *n., pl.* **-ghies.** **1.** any small boat designed as a tender, esp. a small ship's boat, rowed, sailed, or driven by a motor. **2.** a boat used by warships, having four single-banked oars and a spritsail. **3.** any of various rowing or sailing boats used in sheltered waters along the Indian coasts to transport passengers and freight. Also, **dingey, dingy, dinky.** [< Bengali *dingi,* Hindi *ḍiṅgī,* dim. of *ḍiṅgā* boat]

Dingo, *Canis dingo* (21 in. high at shoulder; total length 3½ ft.; tail 14 in.)

din·gle (ding′gəl), *n.* a deep, narrow cleft between hills; a shady dell. [ME: a deep dell, hollow; akin to OE *dung* dungeon, OHG *tunc* cellar]

din·go (ding′gō), *n., pl.* **-goes.** a wolflike, wild dog, *Canis dingo,* of Australia, having a reddish- or yellowish-brown coat, believed to have been introduced by the aborigines. [< native Austral]

ding·us (ding′əs), *n., pl.* **-us·es.** *Informal.* a gadget or object whose name is unknown or forgotten. [< D *dinges,* c. G *Dings,* gen. of *Ding* THING[1]]

din·gy[1] (din′jē), *adj.,* **-gi·er, -gi·est.** **1.** of a dark, dull, or dirty color or aspect; lacking brightness or freshness. **2.** shabby; dismal. [?] —**din′gi·ly,** *adv.* —**din′gi·ness,** *n.*

din·gy[2] (ding′gē), *n., pl.* **-gies.** dinghy.

din′ing car′, a railroad car equipped as a restaurant and supplied with a kitchen, pantry, etc.

din′ing hall′, a large, private room in which meals are served to a number of persons belonging to the same group, class, etc., as at a college, in a castle, etc.

din′ing room′, a room in which meals are eaten, as in a home or hotel, esp. the room in which the major or more formal meals are eaten.

din′ing ta′ble, a table, esp. one seating several persons, where meals are served and eaten, esp. the major or more formal meals.

di·ni·tro·ben·zene (dī nī′trō ben′zēn, -ben zēn′), *n. Chem.* any of three isomeric benzene derivatives having the formula $C_6H_4(NO_2)_2$, made by nitration of benzene or nitrobenzene, the most important of which is the meta form: used chiefly in the manufacture of dyes. [DI-[1] + NITROBENZENE]

dink[1] (dingk), *Scot.* —*adj.* **1.** neatly dressed; dressed in one's finest or newest clothes. —*v.t.* **2.** to decorate; array. [?] —**dink′ly,** *adv.*

dink[2] (dingk), *n.* dinghy. [by apocope and unvoicing]

dink[3] (dingk), *n.* a small close-fitting cap, often worn by college freshmen; beanie. [? back formation from DINKY[1]]

Din·ka (ding′kä), *n., pl.* **-kas,** (*esp. collectively*) **-ka.** **1.** a member of a tall, pastoral, Negroid people of Sudan. **2.** the language of the Dinka. [< Dinka *jieng* people]

dink·ey (ding′kē), *n., pl.* **-eys.** anything small, esp. a small locomotive. Also, **dinky.** [perh. DINK[1] + -EY[2]]

din·kum (ding′kəm), *Australian.* —*adj.* **1.** genuine; authentic. **2.** honest; fair. —*adv.* **3.** honestly, truly. [dial. E: work]

dink·y[1] (ding′kē), *adj.,* **dink·i·er, dink·i·est,** *n., pl.* **dink·ies.** —*adj.* **1.** *Informal.* of small size or importance. **2.** *Brit. Informal.* fashionable; well dressed; smart. —*n.* **3.** dinkey. [DINK[1] + -Y[1]]

dink·y[2] (ding′kē), *n., pl.* **dink·ies.** dinghy. [DINK[2] + -Y[2]]

din·mont (din′mont), *n. Scot. and North Eng.* a castrated male sheep, between one and two years old, that has been shorn only once. [ME *dinmouth, dinmoth* (Scot *dinmont*) < ?]

din·ner (din′ər), *n.* **1.** the main meal of the day, eaten in the evening or at midday. **2.** a formal meal in honor of some person or occasion. **3.** See **table d'hôte.** [ME *diner* < OF *disner* (n. use of v.); see DINE] —**din′ner·less,** *adj.*

din′ner clothes′, formal or semiformal clothing worn for formal dinners or similar social occasions.

din′ner dress′, a dress, often long and having sleeves or a jacket, more elaborate than one designed for daytime wear but less formal than an evening gown.

din′ner fork′, a fork used by an individual in eating his portion of the main course of a meal.

din′ner jack′et, **1.** a man's jacket for semiformal evening dress; tuxedo. **2.** the complete semiformal outfit, including this jacket, dark trousers, often with silk stripes down the sides, a bow tie, and usually a cummerbund.

din′ner knife′, a knife used by an individual to cut up his own portion of the main course of a meal.

din′ner plate′, a plate from which an individual eats his portions during the main course of a meal.

din′ner ring′, a ring, usually with a large setting, worn by women in the afternoon and evening.

din′ner ta′ble. See **dining table.**

din·ner·ware (din′ər wâr′), *n.* china, glasses, and silver used for table service. [DINNER + WARE[1]]

dino-, a learned borrowing from Greek, where it meant "terrible"; used in the formation of compound words: *dinothere.* [< Gk *deino-,* comb. form of *deinós*]

Di·noc·er·as (dī nos′ər əs), *n.* an extinct genus of huge, horned, ungulate mammals of the Eocene epoch of North America. [< NL, equiv. to *dino-* DINO- + Gk *kéras* horn]

di·no·flag·el·late (din′ə flaj′ə lāt′), *n.* any of numerous chiefly marine, plantlike flagellates of the order *Dinoflagellata,* which are important elements of plankton and have usually two flagella, one being in a groove around the body and the other extending from the center of the body. [DINO- + FLAGELLATE]

di·no·saur (dī′nə sôr′), *n.* any chiefly terrestrial, herbivorous, or carnivorous reptile of the extinct orders *Saurischia* and *Ornithischia,* from the Mesozoic era, certain species of which are the largest known land animals. [< NL *dinosaur(us).* See DINO-, -SAUR]

Dinosaur *Tyrannosaurus rex* (Height 20 ft.; length 50 ft.)

di·no·sau·ri·an (dī′nə sôr′ē ən), *adj.* **1.** pertaining to or of the nature of a dinosaur. —*n.* **2.** a dinosaur. [< NL *Dinosauria* name of the group. See DINO-, SAURIAN]

di·no·there (dī′nə thēr′), *n.* any elephantlike mammal of the extinct genus *Dinotherium,* from the later Tertiary period of Europe and Asia, having downward curving tusks in the lower jaw. [< NL *dinother(ium),* equiv. to *dino-* DINO- + Gk *thērion* a wild beast, deriv. of *thēr-* (s. of *thḗr*) a beast, wild animal]

d. in p. aeq., (in prescriptions) let it be divided into equal parts. [< L *dīvidātur in partēs aequālēs*]

dint (dint), *n.* **1.** force; power: *by dint of argument.* **2.** a dent. **3.** *Archaic.* a blow; stroke. —*v.t.* **4.** to make a dent or dents in. **5.** to impress or drive in with force. [ME; OE *dynt;* c. OIcel *dyntr*] —**dint′less,** *adj.*

Di·nu·ba (di nōō′bə, -nyōō′-), *n.* a town in central California. 6103 (1960).

Din·wid·die (din wid′ē, din′wid ē), *n.* **1. Robert,** 1693–1770, British colonial administrator in America: lieutenant governor of Virginia 1751–58. **2.** a boy's given name.

di·oc·e·san (dī os′i sən), *adj.* **1.** of or pertaining to a diocese. —*n.* **2.** one of the clergy or people of a diocese. **3.** the bishop in charge of a diocese. [ME < ML *dioecēsān(us).* See DIOCESE, -AN]

di·o·cese (dī′ə sēs′, -sis), *n.* an ecclesiastical district under the jurisdiction of a bishop. [ME *diocise, diocese* < OF < LL *diocēsis,* var. of *dioecēsis,* L: a governor's jurisdiction < Gk *dioíkēsis* housekeeping, administration, province, diocese, equiv. to *dioik(eîn)* (to) keep house, administer, govern (*di-* DI-[3] + *oikeîn* to dwell, occupy, manage, deriv. of *oîkos* house) + *-ē-* thematic vowel + *-sis* -SIS]

Di·o·cle·tian (dī′ə klē′shən), *n.* (*Gaius Aurelius Valerius Diocletianus*), A.D. 245–316, Illyrian soldier: emperor of Rome 284–305.

Di′ocle′tian win′dow. See **Palladian window.**

di·ode (dī′ōd), *n. Electronics.* a device, as a two-element electron tube or a semiconductor, through which current can pass freely in only one direction. [DI-[1] + -ODE[2]]

Di·o·do·rus Sic·u·lus (dī′ō dōr′əs sik′yə ləs, -dôr′-), late 1st century B.C., Greek historian.

di·oe·cious (dī ē′shəs), *adj. Biol.* (esp. of plants) having the male and female organs in separate and distinct individuals; having separate sexes. Also, **dioicous.** [< NL *Dioeci(a)* name of the genus (*di-* DI-[1] + Gk *oikía* a house, dwelling, sp. var. of *oîkos*) + -OUS] —**di·oe′cious·ly,** *adv.* —**di·oe′cious·ness,** *n.*

di·oes·trum (dī es′trəm, -ē′strəm), *n.* the period between the rutting periods, esp. of female animals. [< NL; see DI-[1], ESTRUM] —**di·oes′trous,** *adj.*

Di·og·e·nes (dī oj′ə nēz′), *n.* 412?–323 B.C., Greek Cynic philosopher. —**Di·o·gen·ic** (dī′ə jen′ik), **Diog′e·ne′an,** *adj.*

di·oi·cous (dī oi′kəs), *adj. Biol.* dioecious. —**di·oi′cous·ly,** *adv.* —**di·oi′cous·ness,** *n.*

Di′o·mede Is′lands (dī′ə mēd′), two islands in Bering Strait, one belonging to the Soviet Union (**Big Diomede**), ab. 15 sq. mi., and one belonging to the U.S. (**Little Diomede**), ab. 4 sq. mi.: separated by the international date line and the U.S.-Soviet Union boundary.

Di·o·me·des (dī′ə mē′dēz), *n. Class. Myth.* **1.** the son of Tydeus, one of the Epigoni, counted next in prowess to Achilles among those at the siege of Troy. **2.** a Thracian king who fed his wild mares on human flesh and was himself fed to them by Hercules. Also, **Di·o·mede** (dī′ə mēd′).

Di·on (dī′on, -ən), *n.* a boy's given name, form of **Dionysus.**

di·o·nae·a (dī′ə nē′ə), *n.* the Venus's-flytrap. [< NL < Gk *Diṓnē* a name for Venus + L *-aea* adj. and n. suffix]

Di·o·ne (dī ō′nē), *n.* **1.** *Class. Myth.* a Titaness and consort of Zeus: sometimes believed to be the mother of Aphrodite, later replaced as consort by Hera. **2.** *Astron.* one of the nine satellites of Saturn. **3.** Also, **Dionne.** a girl's given name, form of **Dion.**

Di·on·ne (dī ō′nē), *n.* a girl's given name. Also, **Dione.**

Di·o·ny·si·a (dī′ə nish′ē ə, -nis′-), *n.pl.* the orgiastic and dramatic festivals held periodically in honor of Dionysus, esp. those in Attica, from which Greek comedy and tragedy developed. Cf. **Anthesteria, Greater Dionysia, Lenea, Lesser Dionysia.** [< L < Gk]

Di·o·nys·i·ac (dī′ə nis′ē ak′), *adj.* **1.** pertaining to the Dionysia or to Dionysus; Bacchic. **2.** Dionysian (def. 2). [< L *Dionȳsiac(us)* < Gk *Dionysiakós,* equiv. to *Diónys(os)* DIONYSUS + *-i-* connective vowel + *-akos* -AC] —**Di·o·ny·si·a·cal·ly** (dī′ə ni sī′ik lē), *adv.*

Di·o·ny·sian (dī′ə nish′ən, -nis′ē ən), *adj.* **1.** pertaining to Dionysus or Bacchus. **2.** recklessly uninhibited; unrestrained; undisciplined; frenzied; orgiastic. Cf. **Apollonian** (def. 2). **3.** *Anthropol.* characterized by behavior that is individualistic, uninhibited, and reckless, often through the influence of drugs or alcohol: *a primitive, Dionysian society.* [DIONYS(US) + -IAN]

Di·o·ny·si·us (dī′ə nish′ē əs, -nis′-), *n.* **1.** ("*the Elder*") 431?–367B.C., Greek soldier: tyrant of Syracuse 405–367. **2. Saint,** died A.D. 268, pope 259–268. **3.** a crater in the first quadrant of the face of the moon: about 12 miles in diameter.

Diony′sius Ex·ig′u·us (eg zig′yōō əs, ek sig′-), died A.D. 556?, Scythian monk, deviser of the current system of reckoning the Christian era.

Diony′sius of Alexan′dria, Saint ("*the Great*"), A.D. c190–265, patriarch of Alexandria 247?–265?.

Diony′sius of Halicarnas′sus, died 7? B.C., Greek rhetorician and historian in Rome.

Diony′sius the Areop′agite, 1st century A.D., Athenian scholar: converted to Christianity by Saint Paul c50.

Di·o·ny·sus (dī′ə nī′səs), *n. Class. Myth.* the god of fertility, wine, and drama; Bacchus. Also, **Di′o·ny′sos.**

di·o·phan′tine equa′tion (dī′ə fan′tīn, -tēn, -fan′tᵊn, dī′-), *Math.* an equation involving more than one variable in which the coefficients of the variables are integers and for which integral solutions are sought. [named after *Diophantus* 3rd-century A.D. Greek mathematician; see -INE[1]]

Di·oph·an·tus (dī of′ən təs), *n.* a crater in the second quadrant of the face of the moon: about 13 miles in diameter.

di·op·side (dī op′sīd, -sid), *n. Mineral.* a common variety of pyroxene, occurring in various colors, usually in crystals. [DI-[3] + Gk *óps(is)* appearance + -IDE]

di·op·sim·e·ter (dī′əp sim′i tər), *n. Ophthalm.* an instrument that measures the field of vision. [DI-[3] + Gk *ops-* (s. of *ópsis*) sight, vision + -I- + -METER]

di·op·tase (dī op′tās), *n.* a mineral, hydrous copper silicate, $CuSiO_3 \cdot H_2O$, occurring in emerald-green crystals. [< F, equiv. to *di-* DI-[3] + Gk *optasía* view]

di·op·ter (dī op′tər), *n.* **1.** *Optics.* a unit of measure of the refractive power of a lens, having the dimension of the reciprocal of length and a unit equal to the reciprocal of one meter. *Abbr.:* D. **2.** an instrument, invented by Hipparchus, to measure the apparent diameter of the sun or moon or to estimate the size or elevation of distant objects. Also, *esp. Brit.,* **di·op′tre.** [< L *dioptra* < Gk: instrument for measuring height or levels, equiv. to *di-* DI-[3] + **op-* (for *ópsesthai* to see) + *-tra* n. suffix of means] —**di·op′tral,** *adj.*

di·op·tom·e·ter (dī′op tom′i tər), *n.* an instrument for measuring the refraction of the eye. [DI-[3] + OPT(IC) + -O- + -METER]

di·op·tric (dī op′trik), *adj.* **1.** *Optics.* pertaining to dioptrics: *dioptric images.* **2.** *Optics, Ophthalm.* noting or pertaining to refraction or refracted light. Also, **di·op′tri·cal.** [< Gk *dioptrik(ós).* See DIOPTER, -IC] —**di·op′tri·cal·ly,** *adv.*

di·op·trics (dī op′triks), *n.* (*construed as sing.*) the branch of geometrical optics dealing with the formation of images by lenses. [see DIOPTRIC, -ICS]

Di·or (dē ôr′; *Fr.* dē ôR′), *n.* **Chris·tian** (kris′chən; *Fr.* krēs tyäN′), 1905–57, French fashion designer.

di·o·ram·a (dī′ə ram′ə, -rä′mə), *n.* **1.** a scene, often in miniature, reproduced in three dimensions by placing objects, figures, etc., in front of a painted background. **2.** a spectacular picture, partly translucent, for exhibition through an aperture, made more realistic by various illuminating devices. **3.** a building for exhibiting such a scene or picture. [< F, equiv. to *di-* DI-[3] + Gk *(h)órama* view (*hor(ân)* (to) see, look + *-a-* thematic vowel + *-ma* n. suffix)] —**di′o·ram′ic,** *adj.*

Di·o·res (dī ôr′ēz, -ōr′-), *n.* (in the *Iliad*) a son of Amarynceus who fought against the Trojans.

di·o·rite (dī′ə rīt′), *n.* a granular igneous rock consisting essentially of plagioclase feldspar and hornblende. [< F, irreg. < Gk *dior(ízein)* (to) distinguish; see -ITE[1]] —**di·o·rit·ic** (dī′ə rit′ik), *adj.*

di·or·tho·sis (dī′ôr thō′sis), *n., pl.* **-ses** (-sēz). *Surg.* diaplasis. [< NL < Gk: a making straight, correcting,

CONCISE PRONUNCIATION KEY: *act, āble, dâre, ärt; ebb, ēqual; if, īce; hot, ōver, ôrder, oil, bŏŏk, ōōze, out; up, ûrge; chief; sing; shoe; thin, that;* zh *as in measure.* ə = *a* as in *alone,* e as in *system,* i as in *easily,* o as in *gallop,* u as in *circus;* ᵊ as in *button* (but′ᵊn), *fire* (fīᵊr), *cradle* (krād′ᵊl). See the full key inside the front cover.

equiv. to *diorth(oûn)* (to) set right + *-ōsis* -OSIS] —**di·or·thot·ic** (dī′ôr thot′ik), *adj.*

Di·os·cu·ri (dī′ə skyŏŏr′ī), *n.pl. Class. Myth.* Castor and Pollux, the twin sons of Zeus and Leda.

di·os·gen·in (dī′oz jen′in, dī oz′jə nin), *n. Biochem.* a crystalline compound, $C_{27}H_{42}O_3$, obtained chiefly from Mexican yams: used in the synthesis of steroidal hormones, as of progesterone. [< NL *Dios(corea)* name of the genus, irreg. after *Dioscorides* 1st-century A.D. Greek physician + -GEN + -IN[1]]

di·o·tic (dī ō′tik, -ot′ik), *adj. Med.* pertaining to or affecting both ears; binaural. [DI-[1] + OTIC]

di·ox·ane (dī ok′sān), *n. Chem.* a colorless, flammable, liquid cyclic ether, $C_4H_8O_2$, having a faint, pleasant odor: used chiefly in the varnish and silk industries and as a dehydrator in histology. Also, **di·ox·an** (dī ok′-san, -sən). [DI-[1] + OX(Y)-[2] + -ANE]

di·ox·ide (dī ok′sīd, -sid), *n. Chem.* an oxide containing two atoms of oxygen, each of which is bonded directly to an atom of a second element, as manganese dioxide, MnO_2, or nitrogen dioxide, NO_2. [DI-[1] + OXIDE]

di·ox·in (dī ok′sən), *n. Chem.* a highly toxic chlorinated hydrocarbon, 2,3,7,8 tetrachlorodibenzo-p-dioxin, formed by acid runoff and as an impurity or byproduct in herbicide manufacture and other industrial processes: believed to be carcinogenic.

dip[1] (dip), *v.*, **dipped** or (*Archaic*) **dipt; dip·ping;** *n.* —*v.t.* **1.** to plunge temporarily into a liquid, as to wet, color, or take up some of the liquid: *He dipped her pigtails into the inkwell.* **2.** to raise or take up by a plunging or up-and-down action; lift by bailing, scooping, or ladling: *to dip water out of a boat; to dip ice cream from a container.* **3.** to lower and raise: *to dip a flag in salutation.* **4.** to immerse (a sheep, hog, etc.) in a solution to destroy germs, parasites, or the like. **5.** to make (a candle) by repeatedly plunging a wick into melted tallow. **6.** *Naut.* to lower the shorter end of (a yard of a lugsail) to shift it from one side of the mast to the other in tacking. **7.** *Archaic.* to baptize by immersion. **8.** *Obs.* to moisten or wet as if by immersion. —*v.i.* **9.** to plunge into water or other liquid and emerge quickly: *The boat dipped into the waves.* **10.** to put the hand, a dipper, etc., down into a liquid or a container, esp. in order to remove something: *He dipped into the jar for an olive.* **11.** to sink or drop down: *The sun dipped below the horizon.* **12.** to incline or slope downward: *At that point the road dips into a valley.* **13.** to decrease slightly or temporarily: *Stock-market prices often dip on Fridays.* **14.** to engage slightly in a subject: *to dip into astronomy.* **15.** to read here and there in a book. —*n.* **16.** the act of dipping or plunging into or as into a liquid. **17.** that which is taken up by dipping. **18.** a quantity taken up by dipping, as much as a scoop, ladle, dipper, etc., will hold. **19.** a scoop of ice cream. **20.** a liquid or soft substance into which something is dipped. **21.** a creamy mixture of savory foods for scooping with potato chips, crackers, and the like, often served as an hors d'oeuvre, esp. with cocktails. **22.** a momentary lowering; a sinking down. **23.** a moderate or temporary decrease: *a dip in stock-market prices.* **24.** a downward extension, inclination, slope, or course. **25.** the amount of such extension. **26.** a hollow or depression in the land. **27.** a brief swim: *She took a dip in the ocean and then sat on the beach for an hour.* **28.** *Geol., Mining.* the downward inclination of a vein or stratum with reference to a horizontal plane. **29.** the angular amount by which the horizon lies below the level of the eye. **30.** Also called **angle of dip, inclination, magnetic dip.** the angle which a freely-rotating magnetic needle makes with the plane of the horizon. **31.** a short, downward plunge, as of an airplane. **32.** a candle made by repeatedly dipping a wick into melted tallow. **33.** *Gymnastics.* an exercise on the parallel bars in which a person bends his elbow until his chin is on a level with the bars, then elevates himself by straightening out his arms. **34.** *Theat. Brit.* See **stage pocket. 35.** *Slang.* a pickpocket. **36.** *Slang.* a dipsomaniac. **37. at the dip,** *Naut.* not fully raised; halfway up the halyard: *an answering pennant flown at the dip.* Cf. **close** (def. 55). [ME *dipp(en),* OE *dyppan;* akin to G *taufen* to baptize, and to DEEP]
—**Syn. 1.** duck. DIP, IMMERSE, PLUNGE refer literally to putting something into water (or any liquid). To DIP is to put down into a liquid quickly or partially and lift out again: *to dip a finger into water to test the temperature.* IMMERSE denotes a gradual lowering into a liquid until covered by it, sometimes for a moment only (as in one mode of baptism): *to immerse meat in salt water.* PLUNGE adds a suggestion of force or suddenness to the action of dipping: *to plunge a chicken into boiling water before stripping off the feathers.* **2.** scoop. **9.** dive.

dip[2] (dip), *n. Slang.* dipsomaniac. [by shortening]

di·pep·tide (dī pep′tīd, dī-), *n. Biochem.* a peptide which yields two amino acids on hydrolysis. [DI-[1] + PEPTIDE]

di·pet·al·ous (dī pet′əl əs), *adj. Bot.* bipetalous.

di·phase (dī′fāz′), *adj. Elect.* having two phases; two-phase. Also, **di·phas·ic** (dī fā′zik). [DI-[1] + PHASE]

di·phen·hy·dra·mine (dī′fen hī′drə mēn′), *n. Pharm.* a white, crystalline, antihistaminic compound, $(C_6H_5)_2CHOCH_2CH_2N(CH_3)_2$, used in the form of its hydrochloride orally, topically, and parenterally, esp. for allergies. [DIPHEN(YL) + HYDR-[2] + AMINE]

di·phen·yl (dī fen′əl, -fēn′-), *n. Chem.* biphenyl.

di·phen·yl·a·ce·ty·lene (dī fen′əl ə set′əl ēn′, -fēn′-), *n. Chem.* tolan. [DIPHENYL + ACETYLENE]

di·phen·yl·a·mine (dī fen′əl ə mēn′, -am′in, -fēn′-), *n. Chem.* a colorless, crystalline, slightly water-soluble benzene derivative, $(C_6H_5)_2NH$, used chiefly in the preparation of various dyes, as a stabilizer for nitrocellulose propellants, and for the detection of oxidizing agents in analytical chemistry. [DIPHENYL + AMINE]

di·phen·yl·a·mine·chlo·rar·sine (dī fen′əl ə mēn′-klō rär′sēn, -klō-, -am′ən-, -fēn′-), *n. Chem.* adamsite. [DIPHENYLAMINE + CHLOR-[2] + ARSINE]

di·phen·yl·hy·dan·to·in (dī fen′əl hī dan′tō in, -fēn′-), *n. Pharm.* a white, slightly water-soluble powder, $C_{15}H_{11}N_2O_2$, used in the form of its sodium salt to prevent or arrest convulsions in epilepsy. [DIPHENYL + HYDANTOIN]

diphen′yl ke′tone, *Chem.* benzophenone.

di·pho·ni·a (dī fō′nē ə), *n. Pathol.* diplophonia.

di·phos·gene (dī fos′jēn), *n. Chem.* a colorless liquid, $ClOOCCl_3$, usually derived from methyl formate or methyl chloroformate by chlorination: a World War I poison gas now used chiefly in organic synthesis. Also called **trichloromethyl chloroformate.** [DI-[1] + PHOSGENE]

di·phos·phate (dī fos′fāt), *n. Chem.* **1.** a pyrophosphate. **2.** a phosphate containing two phosphate groups. [DI-[1] + PHOSPHATE]

diph·the·ri·a (dif thēr′ē ə, dip-), *n. Pathol.* a febrile, infectious disease caused by the bacillus *Corynebacterium diphtheriae,* and characterized by the formation of a false membrane in the air passages, esp. the throat. [< NL < F *diphthérie* < Gk *diphthéra* skin, leather + *-ia* -IA]

diph·the·rit·ic (dif′thə rit′ik, dip′-), *adj. Pathol.* **1.** pertaining to diphtheria. **2.** affected by diphtheria. Also, **diph·the·ri·al** (dif thēr′ē əl, dip-), **diph·ther·ic** (dif ther′ik, dip-). [earlier *diphtherit(is)* (see DIPHTHERIA, -ITIS) + -IC] —**diph′the·rit′i·cal·ly,** *adv.*

diph·the·roid (dif′thə roid′, dip′-), *adj. Pathol.* resembling diphtheria. [DIPHTHER(IA) + -OID]

diph·thong (dif′thông, -thong, dip′-), *n.* **1.** *Phonet.* an unsegmentable, gliding speech sound varying continuously in phonetic quality but held to be a single sound or phoneme and identified by its apparent beginning and ending sound, as the *oi*-sound of *toy* or *boil,* or the *ch*-sound of *chip.* **2.** (not in technical use) **a.** a digraph, as the *ea* of *meat.* **b.** a ligature, as *æ.* [< LL *diphthong(us)* < Gk *díphthongos,* lit., having two sounds (*di-* DI-[1] + *phthóngos* voice, sound)] —**diph·thon·gal** (dif thông′gəl, -thong′-, dip-), **diph·thon′gic, diph·thon′gous,** *adj.*

diph·thon·gi·a (dif thông′ē ə, -gē ə, -thong′-, dip-), *n. Pathol.* diplophonia. [DIPHTHONG + -IA]

diph·thong·ise (dif′thông īz′, -gīz′, -thong-, dip′-), *v.t., v.i.,* **-ised, -is·ing.** *Chiefly Brit.* diphthongize. —**diph′thong·i·sa′tion,** *n.*

diph·thong·ize (dif′thông īz′, -gīz′, -thong-, dip′-), *v.,* **-ized, -iz·ing.** *Phonet.* —*v.t.* **1.** to change into or pronounce as a diphthong. —*v.i.* **2.** to become a diphthong. Also, *esp. Brit.,* **diphthongise.** [DIPHTHONG + -IZE] —**diph′thong·i·za′tion,** *n.*

di·phyl·lous (dī fil′əs), *adj. Bot.* having two leaves. [< NL *diphyllus.* See DI-[1], -PHYLLOUS]

diph·y·o·dont (dif′ē ə dont′), *adj. Zool.* having two successive sets of teeth, as most mammals. [< Gk *diphy(ḗs)* double, twofold (*di-* DI-[1] + *phyḗ* growth, nature, deriv. of *phýein* to produce, grow) + -ODONT]

dipl., 1. diplomat. **2.** diplomatic.

dip·la·cu·sis (dip′lə kyōō′sis), *n., pl.* **-ses** (-sēz). *Pathol.* a difference in hearing by the two ears so that one sound is heard as two. [< NL, equiv. to *dipl(o)-* DIPLO- + Gk *akoûsis* hearing (*akoú(ein)* (to) hear, listen to + *-sis* -SIS)]

di·ple·gia (dī plē′jə, -jē ə), *n. Pathol.* paralysis of the identical part on both sides of the body. [< NL; see DI-[1], -PLEGIA] —**di·ple′gic,** *adj.*

di·pleu·ru·la (dī plŏŏr′yŏŏ lə, -ŏŏ-), *n., pl.* **-las, -le** (-lē′). the hypothetical ancestor of modern echinoderms. [< NL, neut. pl. of *dipleurulus* < Gk *di-* DI-[1] + *pleur(á)* rib, side + L *-ula* -ULE]

di·plex (dī′plex), *adj.* pertaining to or noting a telegraphic or telephonic system permitting the sending or receiving of two signals or messages simultaneously in the same direction over a single communications channel. [DI-[1] + *-plex,* modeled on *duplex*]

diplo-, a learned borrowing from Greek meaning "double," "in pairs," used in the formation of compound words: *diplococcus.* [< Gk, comb. form of *diplóos* twofold]

dip·lo·blas·tic (dip′lə blas′tik), *adj.* having two germ layers, the ectoderm and entoderm, as the embryos of sponges and coelenterates. [DIPLO- + -BLAST + -IC]

dip·lo·car·di·ac (dip′lə kär′dē ak′), *adj. Zool.* having the right and left sides of the heart somewhat or completely divided, as in birds and mammals. [DIPLO- + CARDIAC]

dip·lo·coc·cus (dip′lə kok′əs), *n., pl.* **-coc·ci** (-kok′-sī). *Bacteriol.* any of several spherical bacteria occurring in pairs, as *Diplococcus pneumoniae.* [< NL; see DIPLO-, COCCUS] —**dip′lo·coc′cal, dip·lo·coc·cic** (dip′lə kok′sik), *adj.*

di·plod·o·cus (di plod′ə kəs), *n., pl.* **-cus·es.** a huge, herbivorous dinosaur of the genus *Diplodocus,* from the upper Jurassic period of western North America, growing to a length of about 87 feet. [< NL, equiv. to *diplo-* DIPLO- + Gk *dok(ós)* beam, bar, shaft + L *-us* n. suffix]

dip·lo·ë (dip′lō ē′), *n. Anat.* the cancellate bony tissue between the hard inner and outer walls of the bones of the cranium. [< Gk: a fold, deriv. of *diplóos* DIPLO-] —**di·plo·ic** (di plō′ik), **dip·lo·et·ic** (dip′lō et′ik), *adj.*

dip·loid (dip′loid), *adj.* **1.** double; twofold. **2.** *Biol.* having two similar complements of chromosomes. —*n.* **3.** *Biol.* an organism or cell having double the basic or haploid number of chromosomes. **4.** *Crystall.* a solid belonging to the isometric system and having 24 trapezoidal planes. [DIPL(O)- + -OID] —**dip·loi′dic,** *adj.*

di·plo·ma (di plō′mə), *n., pl.* **-mas,** *Lat.* **-ma·ta** (-mə-tə), *v.,* **-maed, -ma·ing.** —*n.* **1.** a document given by an educational institution conferring a degree on a person or certifying his satisfactory completion of a course of study. **2.** a document conferring some honor, privilege, or power. **3.** a public or official document, esp. one of historical interest: *a diploma from Carolingian times.* —*v.t.* **4.** to furnish with a diploma. [< L *diplōma* a letter of recommendation, an official document < Gk *díplōma* a letter folded double, equiv. to *dipló(os)* DIPLO- + *-ma* n. suffix]

di·plo·ma·cy (di plō′mə sē), *n.* **1.** the conduct by government officials of negotiations and other relations between nations. **2.** the art or science of conducting such negotiations. **3.** skill in managing negotiations, handling people, etc., so that there is little or no ill will; tact: *She showed considerable diplomacy in seating her guests.* [< F *diplomatie* (with *t* pronounced as *s*), equiv. to *diplomate* DIPLOMAT + *-ie* -Y[3]]

diplo′ma mill′, 1. a pretended institution of higher learning existing for profit only and granting degrees without demanding proper qualifications of the recipients. **2.** *Informal.* a college or university having such a large number of students that none receives individual attention from the teachers.

dip·lo·mat (dip′lə mat′), *n.* **1.** a person employed by a national government to conduct official negotiations and maintain political, economic, and social relations with another country or countries. **2.** a person who is tactful and skillful in managing a delicate situation, a sensitive person, or the like. [< F *diplomate,* back formation from *diplomatique* DIPLOMATIC]

dip·lo·mate (dip′lə māt′), *n.* a person who has received a diploma, esp. a doctor, engineer, etc., who has been certified as a specialist by a board within his profession. [DIPLOM(A) + -ATE[1]]

dip·lo·mat·ic (dip′lə mat′ik), *adj.* **1.** of, pertaining to, or engaged in diplomacy: *diplomatic officials; diplomatic immunity.* **2.** skilled in diplomacy; tactful. [< F *diplomatique* < NL *diplōmatic(us),* equiv. to L *diplōmat-* (s. of *diplōma*) DIPLOMA + *-icus* -IC] —**dip′lo·mat′i·cal·ly,** *adv.*
—**Syn. 2.** DIPLOMATIC, POLITIC, TACTFUL imply ability to avoid offending others or hurting their feelings, esp. in situations where this ability is important. DIPLOMATIC suggests a smoothness and skill in handling others, usually in such a way as to attain one's own ends and yet avoid any unpleasantness or opposition: *By diplomatic conduct he avoided antagonizing anyone.* POLITIC emphasizes expediency or prudence in looking out for one's own interests, thus knowing how to treat people of different types and on different occasions: *a truth which it is not politic to insist on.* TACTFUL suggests a nice touch in the handling of delicate matters or situations, and, unlike the other two, often suggests a sincere desire not to hurt the feelings of others: *a tactful wife.* —**Ant. 2.** blunt, blundering, tactless.

diplomat′ic corps′, the entire body of diplomats accredited to and resident at a court or capital. Also called **diplomatic body.**

diplomat′ic immu′nity, exemption from taxation, searches, seizures, arrest, customs duties, etc., enjoyed by diplomatic officials and their dependent families under international law, and usually on a reciprocal basis.

dip′lomat′ic pouch′, a sealed mailbag containing diplomatic correspondence that is sent free of inspection between a foreign office and its diplomatic or consular post abroad or from one such post to another.

dip·lo·mat·ics (dip′lə mat′iks), *n.* (*construed as sing.*) the science of deciphering old official documents, as charters and codicils, and of determining their authenticity, age, or the like. [see DIPLOMATIC, -ICS]

di·plo·ma·tist (di plō′mə tist), *n.* **1.** *Brit.* a Foreign Office employee officially engaged as a diplomat. **2.** a person who is astute and tactful in any negotiation. [DIPLOMAT(IC) + -IST]

dip·lo·pho·ni·a (dip′lə fō′nē ə), *n. Pathol.* a condition in which the voice simultaneously produces two sounds of different pitch. Also, **diphonia.** Also called **diphthongia.** [< NL, equiv. to *diplo-* DIPLO- + Gk *phōn(ḗ)* sound, tone, voice + L *-ia* -IA] —**dip·lo·phon·ic** (dip′lə fon′ik), *adj.*

di·plo·pi·a (di plō′pē ə), *n. Ophthalm.* a pathological condition of vision in which a single object appears double (opposed to *haplopia*). [< NL; see DIPLO-, -OPIA] —**di·plop·ic** (di plop′ik), *adj.*

dip·lo·pod (dip′lə pod′), *adj.* **1.** belonging or pertaining to the *Diplopoda.* —*n.* **2.** any arthropod of the class *Diplopoda,* comprising the millipedes. [< NL *Diplopod(a).* See DIPLO-, -POD]

di·plo·sis (di plō′sis), *n. Biol.* the doubling of the chromosome number by the union of the haploid sets in the union of gametes. [< Gk *díplōsis* a doubling, equiv. to *dipl(oûn)* (to) double (deriv. of *diplóos* DIPLO-) + *-sis* -SIS]

dip·lo·ste·mo·nous (dip′lə stē′mə nəs, -stem′ə-), *adj. Bot.* having two series of stamens, or twice as many stamens as petals. [DIPLO- + Gk *stēmon-* (s. of *stḗmōn*) the warp (see STAMEN) + -OUS] —**dip′lo·ste′mo·ny,** *n.*

dip′ nee′dle, a magnetic needle pivoted through its center of gravity and having its axis through the vertical plane of the earth's magnetic meridian so as to point in the direction of maximum magnetic intensity. Also called **dipping needle.** —**dip′-nee′dling,** *n.*

dip·no·an (dip′nō ən), *adj.* **1.** belonging or pertaining to the group *Dipnoi,* comprising the lungfishes. —*n.* **2.** a dipnoan fish. [< NL *Dipno(i)* name of the class < Gk *dípno(os)* double-breathing (*di-* DI-[1] + *pno(ḗ)* breathing, breath, air, deriv. of *phein* to breathe) + -AN]

dipod′ic rhythm′, *Pros.* a rhythmical pattern frequently employed in ballads, created by a succession of accentual dipodies.

dip·o·dy (dip′ə dē), *n., pl.* **-dies.** *Pros.* a group of two feet, esp., in accentual verse, in which one of the two accented syllables bears primary stress and the other bears secondary stress. [< LL *dipodia* < Gk: the quality of having two feet, equiv. to *dipod-* (s. of *dípous*) two-footed (*di-* DI-[1] + *-pod* -POD) + *-ia* -Y[3]] —**di·pod·ic** (dī pod′ik), *adj.*

di·pole (dī′pōl′), *n.* **1.** *Physics, Elect.* a pair of electric point charges or magnetic poles of equal magnitude and opposite signs, separated by an infinitesimal distance. **2.** *Physical Chem.* a molecule in which the centroid of the positive charges is different from the centroid of the negative charges. **3.** Also called **di′pole anten′na.** *Radio, Television.* an antenna of a transmitter or receiving set consisting of two equal rods extending in opposite direction from the connection to the lead-in wire. [DI-[1] + POLE[2]] —**di·po′lar,** *adj.*

di′pole mo′ment, 1. See **electric dipole moment. 2.** See **magnetic moment.**

Di·pol·i·a (dī pol′ē ə), *n.* (*sometimes construed as pl.*) an annual festival held in ancient Athens in honor of Zeus, consisting of the slaughter of an ox, ordinarily taboo, followed by a mock inquest and trial. Also, **Dipolia.** Also called **Bouphonia, Buphonia.**

dip·per (dip′ər), *n.* **1.** one who or that which dips. **2.** a cuplike container with a long, straight handle, used for dipping liquids. **3.** (*cap.*) *Astron.* **a.** Also called **Big Dipper.** the group of seven bright stars in Ursa Major resembling such a vessel in outline. **b.** Also called **Little Dipper.** a similar group in Ursa Minor. **4.** any of various diving birds, esp. the water ouzels. [ME: diving bird; see DIP, -ER[1]]

dip′ping lug′sail, *Naut.* a lugsail the yard of which is dipped in going about, having about one fourth of its area forward of the mast.

dip′ping nee′dle. See **dip needle.**

dip·py (dip′ē), *adj.*, **-pi·er, -pi·est.** *Slang.* **1.** somewhat mad or obsessed: *dippy about peanuts; dippy with love for her.* **2.** silly; unreasonable; preposterous: *He has a dippy notion that the moon is inhabited.* [?]

di·prot·ic (dī prot′ik), *adj. Chem.* (of an acid) having two transferable protons. [DI-[1] + PROT(ON) + -IC]

dip·sa·ca·ceous (dip′sə kā′shəs), *adj.* belonging to the *Dipsacaceae*, or teasel family of plants. [< NL *Dipsacac(ae)* name of the family (*Dipsac(us)* the typical genus < Gk *dípsakos* teasel (deriv. of *dípsa* thirst) + NL *-aceae* -ACEAE) + -OUS]

dip·so (dip′sō), *n., pl.* **-sos.** *Slang.* a dipsomaniac; habitual drunk. [by shortening]

dip·so·ma·ni·a (dip′sə mā′nē ə), *n.* an irresistible, typically periodic, craving for intoxicating drink. [< NL < Gk *díps(a)* thirst + *-o-* -O- + *manía* -MANIA]

dip·so·ma·ni·ac (dip′sə mā′nē ak′), *n.* a person with an abnormal, irresistible, and insatiable craving for alcoholic liquor. [DIPSOMANI(A) + -AC] —**dip·so·ma·ni·a·cal** (dip′sə mə nī′ə kəl), *adj.*

dip·sy·doo·dle (dip′sē do͞od′əl), *n. Slang.* shady dealings; chicanery. [?]

dipt (dipt), *v.* a pt. of **dip.**

Dip·ter·a (dip′tər ə, -trə), *n.* **1.** (*italics.*) the order comprising the dipterous insects. **2.** (*l.c.*) pl. of **dipteron.** [< NL < Gk, neut. pl. of *dípteros* two-winged, equiv. to *di-* DI-[1] + *-pteros*; see -PTEROUS]

dip·ter·al (dip′tər əl), *adj.* **1.** (of a classical temple) having a double row of columns on all sides. **2.** *Biol.* dipterous. [< L *dipter(us)* (< Gk *dípteros*; see DIPTERA) + -AL[1]]

dip·ter·an (dip′tər ən), *adj.* **1.** dipterous (def. 1). —*n.* **2.** a dipterous insect. [DIPTER(A) + -AN]

dip·ter·o·car·pa·ceous (dip′tə rō kär pā′shəs), *adj.* belonging to the *Dipterocarpaceae*, a family of trees, chiefly of tropical Asia. [< NL *Dipterocarpace(ae)* name of the family (*Dipterocarp(us)* (see DIPTERA, -O-, -CARP) + *-aceae* -ACEAE) + -OUS]

dip·ter·on (dip′tə ron′), *n., pl.* **-ter·a** (-tər ə). a dipterous insect; a fly. [< Gk, neut. of *dípteros*; see DIPTERA]

dip·ter·os (dip′tə ros′), *n., pl.* **-ter·oi** (-tə roi′). *Archit.* a dipteral building. [< Gk; see DIPTERA]

dip·ter·ous (dip′tər əs), *adj.* **1.** *Entomol.* belonging or pertaining to the order *Diptera*, comprising the houseflies, mosquitoes, gnats, etc., characterized typically by a single, anterior pair of membranous wings with the posterior pair reduced to small, knobbed structures. **2.** *Bot.* having two winglike appendages, as seeds, stems, etc. [< NL *dipter(us)* < Gk *dípter(os)* (see DIPTERA) + -OUS]

dip·tote (dip′tōt), *n.* a substantive declined in only two cases, esp. when occurring in a language in which this is less than the normal number. [< LL *diptōt(a)* nouns with only two cases < Gk, equiv. to *di-* DI-[1] + *ptōt(ós)* a falling (for *ptṓsis*) + *-a* n. suffix]

dip·tych (dip′tik), *n.* **1.** a hinged two-leaved tablet used in ancient times for writing on with a stylus. **2.** Usually, **diptychs. a.** a similar tablet of wood or metal containing on one leaf the names of those among the living, and on the other those among the dead, for whom prayers and Masses are said. **b.** the lists of such persons. **c.** the intercession in the course of which these names were introduced. **3.** a pair of pictures or carvings on two panels, usually hinged together. [< LL *diptych(a)* writing tablet with two leaves < Gk *díptycha*, neut. pl. of *díptychos* folded together, equiv. to *di-* DI-[1] + *ptych(ḗ)* a fold (deriv. of *ptýssein* to fold) + *-a* n. suffix]

dip·y·lon (dip′ə lon′), *n.* (in ancient Greek architecture) a double gateway. [< Gk *dípylon*, n. use of *dípylos* with two gates. See DI-[1], PYLON]

Dip′ylon vase′, a Greek funerary vase (8th century B.C.) with holes in the bottom through which libations were poured for the dead, decorated in the geometric style of vase painting. [after *Dipylon*, cemetery near Athens, Greece, where vases were found]

di·pyr·a·mid (dī pir′ə mid), *n.* bipyramid. —**di·py·ram·i·dal** (dī′pi ram′i dəl), *adj.*

dir., direxit.

Di·rac (di rak′), *n.* **Paul Adrien Maurice,** born 1902, English physicist: Nobel prize 1933.

Dirac′ del′ta func′tion, *Physics, Math.* See **delta function.** Also called **Dirac′ func′tion.** [named after P.A.M. DIRAC]

Di·rae (dī′rē), *n.pl. Class. Myth.* the furies. Also called **Furiae.**

dir·dum (dir′dəm, dûr′-), *n. Scot. and North Eng.* blame. [late ME (dial.) *durdan* uproar]

dire (dīər), *adj.,* **dir·er, dir·est. 1.** causing or involving great fear or suffering; dreadful; terrible: *a dire calamity.* **2.** indicating trouble, disaster, misfortune, or the like: *his dire predictions about the stock market.* **3.** urgent; desperate: *in dire need of food.* [< L *dīr(us)* fearful, unlucky] —**dire′ly,** *adv.* —**dire′ness,** *n.*

direc. prop., (in prescriptions) with a proper direction. [< L *dīrectiōne prōpriā*]

di·rect (di rekt′, dī-), *v.t.* **1.** to guide by advice, helpful information, instruction, etc.: *He directed the company through a difficult time.* **2.** to regulate the course of; control: *History is directed by the men who make it.* **3.** to administer; manage; supervise: *He directs the affairs of the estate.* **4.** to give authoritative instructions to; command; order or ordain (something): *I directed him to leave the room.* **5.** to serve as a director in the production or performance of (a musical work, play, motion picture, etc.). **6.** to guide, tell, or show (a person) the way to a place: *I directed him to the post office.* **7.** to point, aim, or send toward a place or object: *to direct radio waves around the globe.* **8.** to cause to move, act, or work toward a given result, object, or end (often fol. by *to* or *toward*): *He directed all his energies toward the accomplishment of the work.* **9.** to address (words, a speech, a written report, etc.) to a person or persons: *The chairman directed his remarks to two of the committee members.* **10.** to mark (a letter, package, etc.) with the name and address of the intended recipient. —*v.i.* **11.** to act as a guide. **12.** to give commands or orders. **13.** to serve as the director of a play, orchestra, etc. —*adj.* **14.** proceeding in a straight line or by the shortest course; straight; undeviating; not oblique: *a direct route.* **15.** proceeding in an unbroken line of descent; lineal rather than collateral: *a direct descendant.* **16.** *Math.* **a.** (of a proportion) containing terms of which an increase (or decrease) in one results in an increase (or decrease) in another: a term is said to be in direct proportion to another term if one increases (or decreases) as the other increases (or decreases). **b.** (of a function) the function itself, in contrast to its inverse. Cf. **inverse** (def. 2). **17.** without intervening persons, influences, factors, etc.; immediate; personal: *direct contact with the voters; direct exposure to a disease.* **18.** straightforward; frank; candid: *the direct remarks of a forthright man.* **19.** absolute; exact: *the direct opposite.* **20.** consisting exactly of the words originally used: *direct quotation.* **21.** *Govt.* of or by action of voters, which takes effect without any intervening agency such as representatives. **22.** inevitable; consequential: *War will be a direct result of such political action.* **23.** allocated for or arising from a particular known agency, process, job, etc.: *The new machine was listed by the accountant as a direct cost.* **24.** *Elect.* of or pertaining to direct current. **25.** *Astron.* **a.** moving in an orbit in the same direction as the earth in its revolution round the sun. **b.** appearing to move on the celestial sphere in the direction of the natural order of the signs of the zodiac, from west to east. Cf. **retrograde** (def. 4). **26.** *Survey.* (of a telescope) in its normal position; not inverted or transited. **27.** (of dye colors) working without the use of a mordant; substantive. —*adv.* **28.** in a direct manner; directly; straight: *Answer me direct.* [ME *direct(en)* < L *dīrect(us)* made straight (sp. var. of *dērectus* and ptp. of *dīrigere*, sp. var. of *dērigere*), equiv. to *dī-* DI-[2] + *rec-* rule (sp. var. of *regere*) + *-t-* ptp. suffix] —**di·rect′a·ble,** *adj.* —**di·rect′ness,** *n.*

—**Syn. 1.** See **guide. 4.** DIRECT, ORDER, COMMAND mean to issue instructions. DIRECT suggests also giving explanations or advice; the emphasis is not on the authority of the director, but on steps necessary for the accomplishing of a purpose. ORDER connotes a personal relationship, in which one in a superior position imperatively instructs a subordinate (or subordinates) to do something. COMMAND, less personal and, often, less specific in detail suggests greater formality and, sometimes, a more fixed authority on the part of the superior. **17.** DIRECT, IMMEDIATE imply relationships which are readily to be observed. A DIRECT result is one which is easily traceable to its cause or causes; there may be a number of steps in between, but the line from one to another is unbroken, simple, and quite evident. An IMMEDIATE result is one in which there is no medium or step (or practically none) intervening between cause and result; these are consecutive or side by side, so that it is possible to pass at once from one to the other. **18.** plain, categorical, unequivocal, unambiguous, open, sincere, outspoken. —**Ant. 1.** mislead. **18.** devious, roundabout.

di·rect-act·ing (di rekt′ak′tiŋ, dī-), *adj.* (of a steam pump) having the steam pistons connected directly to the pump pistons without a crankshaft or flywheel.

direct′ ac′tion, any method of acting directly against an established authority or powerful group, institution, etc., as by strikes, picketing, etc. —**direct′ ac′tionist.**

direct′ carv′ing, *Sculpture.* the art of carving directly in stone or wood without a design from a finished model. Cf. **pointing.**

direct′ cur′rent. See **DC** (def. 2). —**di·rect′-cur′rent,** *adj.*

direct′ dis′course, quotation of a speaker in which his exact words are repeated. Cf. **indirect discourse.**

di·rect·ed (di rek′tid, dī-), *adj.* **1.** having direction; guided; regulated; managed: *a carefully directed program.* **2.** subject to direction, guidance, regulation, etc. **3.** *Math.* **a.** having positive or negative direction or orientation assigned. **b.** (of a set) having a reflexive and transitive relation defined on it such that for any two elements in the set, there is a third element that is related to both elements. [DIRECT + -ED[2]]

direct′ ev′idence, evidence of a witness who testifies to the truth of the fact to be proved (contrasted with *circumstantial evidence*).

direct′ examina′tion, *Law.* the first interrogation of a witness by the side that has called him.

di·rect-ex·am·ine (di rekt′ig zam′in, dī-), *v.t.,* **-ined, -in·ing.** *Law.* to subject to direct examination. Cf. **cross-examine** (def. 2).

direct′ grant′ school′, *Brit.* a private school that receives government support in return for taking in a certain number of students without fee.

di·rec·tion (di rek′shən, dī′-), *n.* **1.** the act or an instance of directing. **2.** the line along which anything lies, faces, moves, etc., with reference to the point or region toward which it is directed: *The storm moved in a northerly direction.* **3.** the point or region itself: *The direction is north.* **4.** a position on a line extending from a specific point toward a point of the compass or toward the nadir or the zenith. **5.** a line of thought or action or a tendency or inclination: *the direction of contemporary thought.* **6.** instruction or guidance for making, using, etc.: *directions for baking a cake.* **7.** order; command. **8.** management; control; guidance; supervision: *a company under good direction.* **9.** a directorate. **10.** the name and address of the intended recipient as written on a letter, package, etc. **11.** decisions in a stage or film production as to stage business, speaking of lines, lighting, and general presentation. **12.** the technique, act, or business of making such decisions, managing and training a cast of actors, etc. **13.** the technique, act, or business of directing an orchestra, concert, or other musical presentation or group. **14.** *Music.* a symbol or phrase which indicates in a score the proper tempo, style of performance, mood, etc. [ME *direccioun* < L *dīrectiōn-* (s. of *dīrectiō*) a making straight. See DIRECT, -ION] —**di·rec′tion·less,** *adj.*

—**Syn. 5.** See **tendency.**

di·rec·tion·al (di rek′shə nəl, dī-), *adj.* **1.** of or pertaining to direction in space. **2.** *Radio.* adapted for determining the direction of signals received, or for transmitting signals in a given direction: *a directional antenna.* [DIRECTION + -AL[1]]

direc′tional deriv′ative, *Math.* the limit, as a function of several variables moving along a given line from one specified point to another on the line, of the difference in the functional values at the two points divided by the distance between the points.

direc′tion an′gle, *Math.* an angle made by a given vector and a coordinate axis. Cf. **direction cosine.**

direc′tion co′sine, *Math.* the cosine of the angle made by a given vector and a coordinate axis. Cf. **direction angle.**

direc′tion di′al, a sundial utilizing the direction of the sun with reference to the meridian as a means of telling the time. Cf. **altitude dial.**

direc′tion find′er, *Radio.* a contrivance on a receiver, usually based on a loop antenna rotating on a vertical axis, which ascertains the direction of incoming radio waves. —**direc′tion find′ing.**

direc′tion num′ber, *Math.* the component of a vector along a given line; any number proportional to the direction cosines of a given line.

direc′tion theod′olite, *Survey.* a theodolite having a horizontal circle not capable of rotating with the alidade. Cf. **repeating theodolite.**

di·rec·tive (di rek′tiv, dī-), *adj.* **1.** serving to direct; directing: *a directive board.* —*n.* **2.** an authoritative instruction or direction: *the directives of the bishop; a new directive by the President on foreign aid.* [ME < ML *dīrectīv(us)*. See DIRECT, -IVE] —**di·rec′tive·ly,** *adv.* —**di·rec′tive·ness, di·rec·tiv′i·ty,** *n.*

direct′ la′bor, labor performed, as by workers on a production line, and considered in computing costs per unit of production. Cf. **indirect labor.**

direct′ light′ing, lighting in which most of the light is cast directly from the fixture or source to the illumined area.

di·rect·ly (di rekt′lē, dī-), *adv.* **1.** in a direct line, way, or manner; straight: *The path leads directly to the lake.* **2.** at once; without delay; immediately: *Do that directly.* **3.** presently; shortly; soon: *They will be here directly.* **4.** absolutely; exactly; precisely: *directly opposite the store.* **5.** without intervening space; next in order: *The truck was parked directly behind my car.* **6.** *Math.* in direct proportion. —*conj.* **7.** as soon as: *Directly he arrived, he mentioned the subject.* [ME *directli.* See DIRECT, -LY]

—**Syn. 2.** See **immediately.**

direct′ mail′, mail, usually consisting of advertising matter, appeals for donations, or the like, sent individually to large numbers of people: *a fund-raising campaign by direct mail.* —**di·rect′-mail′,** *adj.*

direct′ ob′ject, a word or group of words representing the person or thing upon which the action of a verb is performed or toward which it is directed: in English, generally coming after the verb, without a preposition. In *He saw it* the pronoun *it* is the direct object of *saw.*

Di·rec·toire (dē rek twär′), *adj.* **1.** noting or pertaining to the style of French furnishings and decoration of the mid-1790's, characterized by an increasing use of Greco-Roman forms, along with an introduction, toward the end, of Egyptian motifs: usually includes the Consulate period. **2.** (of costume) in the style of the period of the French Directory. —*n.* **3.** *Fr. Hist.* directory (def. 4). [< F; see DIRECTORY]

di·rec·tor (di rek′tər, dī-), *n.* **1.** one who or that which directs. **2.** one of a body of persons chosen to control or govern the affairs of a company or corporation: *a board of directors.* **3.** the person responsible for the interpretive aspects of a stage, film, television, or radio production; the person who supervises the integration of all the elements, as acting, staging, lighting, etc., required to realize a playwright's conception. Cf. **producer** (def. 3). **4.** the musical conductor of an orchestra, chorus, etc. **5.** the manager or chief executive of certain schools, institutes, government bureaus, etc. **6.** *Mil.* a mechanical or electronic device that continuously calculates firing data for use against an airplane or other moving target. [< LL; see DIRECT, -OR[2]] —**di·rec′tor·ship′,** *n.*

di·rec·to·rate (di rek′tər it, dī-), *n.* **1.** the office of a director. **2.** a body of directors. [< F *directorat* < LL *dīrector* DIRECTOR + F *-at* -ATE[1]]

direc′tor gen′eral, *pl.* **directors general.** the executive head of an organization, or of a major subdivision, as a branch, agency, etc., of government.

di·rec·to·ri·al (di rek tôr′ē əl, -tōr′-, dī′rek-), *adj.* pertaining to a director or directorate. [< LL *dīrectōri(us)*. See DIRECTOR, -ORY[1], -AL[1]] —**di·rec·to′ri·al·ly,** *adv.*

direc′tor's chair′, a folding armchair with transversely crossed legs and having a canvas seat and back panel, as traditionally used by motion-picture directors.

di·rec·to·ry (di rek′tə rē, -trē, dī-), *n., pl.* **-ries,** *adj.* —*n.* **1.** a book containing an alphabetical index of the names and addresses of persons in a city, district, organization, etc., or of a particular class of people. **2.** a board or tablet on a wall of a building listing the room and floor numbers of the occupants. **3.** a book of directions. **4. the Directory,** *Fr. Hist.* the body of five directors forming the executive power of France from 1795 to 1799. —*adj.* **5.** serving to direct; directing; directive. [defs. 1, 2, 3, 5: < ML *dīrectōrium*, n. use of LL *dīrectōrius* DIRECTORIAL; def. 4: trans. of F *Directoire* < ML, as above]

direct′ pos′itive, *Photog.* a positive obtained from another positive without an intermediate step.

direct′ pri′mary, *U.S. Politics.* a primary in which members of a party nominate its candidates by direct vote. Cf. **indirect primary.**

direct′ prod′uct, *Math.* a group, or other such system, every element of which can be written uniquely as the product of elements of disjoint groups, each group contributing one element to the product.

di·rec·tress (di rek′tris, dī-), *n.* a woman who serves as a director, as in a business firm or theater. [DIRECT(O)R + -ESS]

di·rec·trix (di rek′triks, dī-), *n., pl.* **di·rec·trix·es, di·rec·tri·ces** (di rek′tri sēz′, -dī-; dī′rek trī′sēz). **1.** *Math.* a fixed line used in the description of a curve or surface. See diag. under **parabola. 2.** *Archaic.* a female director. [< NL; see DIRECT, -TRIX]

direct′ sum′, *Math.* a composition of two disjoint sets, as vector spaces, such that every element in the composition can be written uniquely as the sum of two elements, one from each of the given sets.

direct′ tax′, *Govt.* a tax exacted directly from the persons who will bear the burden of it (not reimbursing themselves at the expense of others), as a poll tax, a general property tax, or an income tax.

di·rect′-vi′sion prism′ (di rekt′vizh′ən, dī-), *Optics.* a prism combination which spreads out incident white light into a spectrum but produces no deviation of the central color of the dispersed beam.

direct′-vi′sion spec′troscope, *Optics.* a simple spectroscope consisting of a collimating lens and a direct-vision prism.

Di·re·da·wa (dē′rä də wä′), *n.* a city in E Ethiopia. ab. 30,000. Also, **Di′re Da·wa′.**

dire·ful (dīər′fəl), *adj.* **1.** dreadful; awful; terrible. **2.** indicating trouble, disaster, misfortune, or the like: *his direful business forecasts.* [DIRE + -FUL] —**dire′ful·ly,** *adv.* —**dire′ful·ness,** *n.*

direx., direxit.

di·rex·it (dē rek′sit; *Eng.* dī rek′sit), *Latin.* he supervised (this); she supervised (this). *Abbr.:* dir., direx.

dirge (dûrj), *n.* **1.** a funeral song or tune, or one expressing mourning in commemoration of the dead. **2.** *Eccles.* the office of the dead, or the funeral service as sung. **3.** any composition resembling such a song or tune in character, as a poem of lament for the dead or solemn, mournful music: *Tennyson's dirge for the Duke of Wellington.* **4.** a mournful sound resembling a dirge: *The autumn wind sang the dirge of summer.* [ME *dir(i)ge* < L: DIRECT, syncopated var. of *dīrige* (impv. of *dīrigere*), first word of the antiphon sung in the Latin office of the dead (Psalm V, 8)] —**dirge′like′,** *adj.*

dirge·ful (dûrj′fəl), *adj.* funereal; mournful. [DIRGE + -FUL]

dir·ham (dir ham′), *n.* **1.** a money of account of Kuwait, the 10th part of a dinar, equal to 100 fils and equivalent to about .28 of a U.S. dollar. **2.** the monetary unit of Morocco, equal to 100 francs and equivalent to about .20 of a U.S. dollar. *Abbr.:* DH. **3.** a money of account of Tunisia, the 10th part of a dinar, equal to 100 millums and equivalent to about .24 of a U.S. dollar. [< Ar *dirham* < L *drachm(a)*; see DRACHMA]

dir·hem (dir hem′), *n.* any of various fractional silver coins issued in Islamic countries at different periods. [var. of DIRHAM]

di·rhin·ous (dī rī′nəs), *adj. Zool.* having paired nostrils. [DI-¹ + RHIN- + -OUS]

Di·ri·chlet (dir′ə klā′; *Ger.* dē′rē klā′), *n.* **Pe·ter Gus·tav Le·jeune** (pā′tər gōōs′täf lə zhœn′), 1805–59, German mathematician.

Dirichlet′ in′tegral, *Math.* an integral that gives the *n*th partial sum for a given Fourier series. [named after P.G.L. DIRICHLET]

dir·i·gi·ble (dir′ə jə bəl, di rij′ə-), *n.* **1.** an airship. —*adj.* **2.** designed for or capable of being directed, controlled, or steered. [< L *dīrig(ere)* (to) DIRECT + -IBLE] —**dir′i·gi·bil′i·ty,** *n.*

di·ri·go (dē′ri gō′; *Eng.* dir′i gō′), *Latin.* I direct: motto of Maine.

dir′i·ment imped′iment (dir′ə mənt), *Law.* a fact or circumstance that renders a marriage void from the beginning. [< L *diriment-* (s. of *dirimēns,* prp. of *dirimere*) parting, dividing, equiv. to *dir-* (var. of *dis-* DIS-¹) + *emere* to buy, acquire, take; see -ENT]

dirk (dûrk), *n.* **1.** a dagger. —*v.t.* **2.** to stab with a dirk. [?]

Dirk (dûrk), *n.* a boy's given name, form of **Derek.** Also, **Dirck.**

dirl (dirl, dûrl), *v.i. Scot.* to vibrate; shake. [akin to DRILL]

dirn·dl (dûrn′dəl), *n.* **1.** a woman's dress with a close-fitting bodice and full skirt, commonly of colorful and strikingly patterned material, fashioned after Tyrolean peasant wear. **2.** a full skirt in such a colorful style. [< G *Dirndl* girl (deriv. of *Dirne*), OHG *thiorna* + *-(d)l* Bavarian dim. suffix]

dirt (dûrt), *n.* **1.** any foul or filthy substance, as mud, grime, dust, excrement, etc. **2.** earth or soil, esp. when loose. **3.** something or someone vile, mean, or worthless: *After that last trick of hers I thought she was dirt.* **4.** moral filth; vileness; corruption: *a sexy novel full of dirt.* **5.** obscene or licentious language: *to talk dirt.* **6.** gossip, esp. of a malicious nature: *Give me all the dirt, dearie.* **7.** an element or elements of a story withheld, esp. by an official agency, usually for the purpose of protecting a person or persons, a nation or its prestige, etc. **8.** *Mining.* **a.** crude, broken ore or waste. **b.** (in placer mining) the material from which gold is separated by washing. **9. do someone dirt,** *Slang.* to cause another to lose status, an opportunity, or the like, esp. deliberately: *He had done his brother dirt just once too often.* **10. eat dirt,** *Slang.* to accept criticism or insults without complaint; humble oneself: *His creditors made him eat dirt by forcing him into bankruptcy.* [ME *dirt, drit* < Scand; cf. OIcel *drit* excrement; c. OE *drītan*]

dirt-cheap (dûrt′chēp′), *adj.* **1.** very inexpensive: *The house was dirt-cheap.* —*adv.* **2.** very inexpensively: *They got it dirt-cheap.*

dirt′ farm′, *Informal.* a tract of land on which a dirt farmer works.

dirt′ farm′er, *Informal.* a farmer who works on the soil, distinguished from one who operates a farm with hired hands or tenants. —**dirt′ farm′ing.**

dirt′ poor′, without material means or resources; poverty-stricken, esp. over a long period of time and without prospect of improvement; chronically impecunious: *Many Japanese fishermen are dirt poor.*

dirt·y (dûr′tē), *adj.,* **dirt·i·er, dirt·i·est,** *v.,* **dirt·ied, dirt·y·ing.** —*adj.* **1.** soiled with dirt; foul; unclean: *dirty clothes.* **2.** spreading or imparting dirt; soiling: *a dirty wind.* **3.** vile; mean; sordid; contemptible: *dirty flattery.* **4.** obscene; pornographic; lewd: *a dirty joke.* **5.** undesirable or unpleasant; tedious: *He left the dirty work for me.* **6.** very unfortunate or regrettable: *That's a dirty shame!* **7.** not fair or sportsmanlike; unscrupulous: *a dirty fighter; to play a dirty trick.* **8.** insulting, contemptuous, or resentful: *She gave me a dirty look. He made a dirty crack about the cooking.* **9.** *Physics.* (of a nuclear weapon) producing a relatively large amount of radioactive fallout. **10.** (of the weather) stormy; squally: *It looks dirty to windward.* **11.** appearing as if soiled; dark-colored; dingy; murky. —*v.t., v.i.* **12.** to make or become dirty. [DIRT + -Y¹] —**dirt′i·ly,** *adv.* —**dirt′i·ness,** *n.*

—**Syn. 1.** grimy, defiled. DIRTY, FILTHY, FOUL, SQUALID refer to that which is not clean. DIRTY is applied to that which is filled or covered with dirt so that it is unclean or defiled: *dirty streets; dirty clothes.* FILTHY is an emphatic word suggesting that which is offensively defiled or is excessively soiled or dirty: *a filthy hovel.* FOUL implies an uncleanness that is grossly offensive to the senses: *a foul odor.* SQUALID, applied usually to dwellings or surroundings, implies dirtiness that results from the slovenly indifference often associated with poverty: *a whole family living in one squalid room.* **3.** base, vulgar, low, shabby, groveling. **4.** nasty, lascivious, lecherous. **9.** contaminated, radioactive. **10.** rainy, foul, sloppy, disagreeable, nasty. **11.** dull, dark, sullied, clouded. **12.** soil, befoul, sully. —**Ant. 1, 11, 12.** clean.

dir·ty-faced (dûr′tē fāst′), *adj.* having a soiled or unclean face.

dir·ty-mind·ed (dûr′tē mīn′did), *adj.* tending to have lewd thoughts, interpretations, etc.

Dis (dis), *n. Class. Myth.* **1.** Also called **Dis Pater.** a god of the underworld, identified with Orcus or the Greek god Pluto. **2.** the underworld; Orcus; Hades.

dis-¹, a learned borrowing from Latin meaning "apart," "asunder," "away," "utterly," or having a privative, negative, or reversing force (see **de-, un-²**); used freely, esp. with these latter significations, as an English formative: *disability; disaffirm; disbar; disbelief; discontent; dishearten; dislike; disown.* Also, **di-.** [< L (akin to *bis,* Gk *dís* twice); before *f, dif-;* before some consonants, *di-;* often r. obs. *des-* < OF]

dis-², var. of **di-¹** before *s: dissyllable.*

dis., **1.** distance. **2.** distant. **3.** distribute.

dis·a·bil·i·ty (dis′ə bil′i tē), *n., pl.* **-ties** for 2. **1.** lack of competent power, strength, or physical or mental ability; incapacity. **2.** a permanent physical flaw, weakness, or handicap, which prevents one from living a full, normal life or from performing any specific job. **3.** the state or condition of being disabled. **4.** legal incapacity; legal disqualification. [DIS-¹ + ABILITY]

—**Syn. 1.** disqualification, incompetence, incapability, impotence. DISABILITY, INABILITY imply a lack of power or ability. A DISABILITY is some disqualifying deprivation or loss of power, physical or other: *excused because of a physical disability; a temporary disability.* INABILITY is a lack of ability, usually because of an inherent lack of talent, power, etc.: *inability to talk, to do well in higher mathematics.* —**Ant. 1.** ability, capacity.

disabil′ity clause′, *Insurance.* a clause in a life-insurance policy providing for waiver of premium and sometimes payment of monthly income if the policyholder becomes totally and permanently disabled.

disabil′ity insur′ance, insurance providing income to a policyholder who is disabled and cannot work.

dis·a·ble (dis ā′bəl), *v.t.,* **-bled, -bling.** **1.** to make unable; weaken or destroy the capability of; cripple; incapacitate: *He was disabled by blindness.* **2.** to make legally incapable; disqualify. [ME; see DIS-¹, ABLE] —**dis·a′ble·ment,** *n.* —**dis·a′bler,** *n.*

—**Syn. 1.** enfeeble, paralyze. See **cripple. 2.** eliminate.

dis·a·bled (dis ā′bəld), *adj.* crippled; injured; incapacitated. [DISABLE + -ED²]

dis·a·buse (dis′ə byōōz′), *v.t.,* **-bused, -bus·ing.** to free (a person) from deception or error; set right: *His travels disabused him of many fond illusions about human nature.* [< F *désabuse(r).* See DIS-¹, ABUSE] —**dis′a·bus′al,** *n.*

di·sac·cha·ride (dī sak′ə rīd′, -rid), *n. Chem.* any of a group of carbohydrates, as sucrose or lactose, which hydrolyze into simple sugars or monosaccharides. [DI-¹ + SACCHARIDE]

dis·ac·cord (dis′ə kôrd′), *v.i.* **1.** to be out of accord; disagree: *Your theory disaccords with my experience.* —*n.* **2.** lack of accord; disagreement: *grave disaccords among nations.* [ME *disaccord(en)* < OF *desaccord(er),* deriv. of *desacort.* See DIS-¹, ACCORD]

dis·ac·cred·it (dis′ə kred′it), *v.t.* to take away the accreditation or authorization of: *to disaccredit a diplomat.* [DIS-¹ + ACCREDIT]

dis·ac·cus·tom (dis′ə kus′təm), *v.t.* to cause to lose a habit: *In the country I was disaccustomed of rising late.* [< MF *desacoustum(er),* OF *desacostumer.* See DIS-¹, ACCUSTOM] —**dis′ac·cus′tomed·ness,** *n.*

dis·ad·van·tage (dis′əd van′tij, -vän′-), *n., v.,* **-taged, -tag·ing.** —*n.* **1.** absence or deprivation of advantage or equality. **2.** the state or an instance of being in an unfavorable circumstance or condition: *to be at a disadvantage.* **3.** injury to interest, reputation, credit, profit, etc.; loss: *Your behavior is a disadvantage to your family's good name.* —*v.t.* **4.** to subject to disadvantage: *I was disadvantaged by illness.* [ME *disavauntage* < OF *desavantage.* See DIS-¹, ADVANTAGE]

—**Syn. 1.** drawback, inconvenience, hindrance. **3.** detriment, hurt, harm, damage.

dis·ad·van·taged (dis′əd van′tijd, -vän′-), *adj.* lacking the normal or usual advantages, as good homes, wholesome friends, etc.: *disadvantaged children.* [DISADVANTAGE + -ED²]

dis·ad·van·ta·geous (dis ad′vən tā′jəs, dis′ad-), *adj.* characterized by or involving disadvantage; unfavorable; detrimental. [DIS-¹ + ADVANTAGEOUS] —**dis·ad′van·ta′geous·ly,** *adv.* —**dis·ad′van·ta′geous·ness,** *n.*

dis·af·fect (dis′ə fekt′), *v.t.* to alienate the affection of; make discontented or disloyal: *The dictator's policies had soon disaffected the people.* [DIS-¹ + AFFECT²] —**dis′af·fect′ed·ly,** *adv.* —**dis′af·fect′ed·ness,** *n.*

dis·af·fec·tion (dis′ə fek′shən), *n.* absence or alienation of affection or good will; estrangement; disloyalty: *Disaffection often leads to outright treason.* [DIS-¹ + AFFECTION¹]

dis·af·fil·i·ate (dis′ə fil′ē āt′), *v.,* **-at·ed, -at·ing.** —*v.t.* **1.** to sever affiliation with; disassociate: *He disaffiliated himself from the church.* —*v.i.* **2.** to sever an affiliation. [DIS-¹ + AFFILIATE] —**dis′af·fil′i·a′tion,** *n.*

dis·af·firm (dis′ə fûrm′), *v.t.* **1.** to deny; contradict. **2.** *Law.* to annul; reverse; repudiate. [DIS-¹ + AFFIRM] —**dis·af·fir·ma·tion** (dis′af ər mā′shən), **dis′af·fir′mance,** *n.*

dis·af·for·est (dis′ə fôr′ist, -for′-), *v.t.* **1.** to reduce from the legal status of a forest. **2.** to strip of forests. [< ML *disafforest(āre).* See DIS-¹, AFFOREST] —**dis′af·for′es·ta′tion, dis′af·for′est·ment,** *n.*

dis·a·gree (dis′ə grē′), *v.i.,* **-greed, -gree·ing.** **1.** to fail to agree; differ: *The conclusions disagree with the facts. The theories disagree in their basic premises.* **2.** to differ in opinion; dissent: *Three of the judges disagreed with the verdict.* **3.** to quarrel: *They disagreed violently and parted company.* **4.** to cause physical discomfort or ill effect (usually fol. by *with*): *The oysters disagreed with her. Cold weather disagrees with me.* [ME < MF *desagre(er).* See DIS-¹, AGREE]

dis·a·gree·a·ble (dis′ə grē′ə bəl), *adj.* **1.** contrary to one's taste or liking; unpleasant; offensive; repugnant. **2.** unpleasant in manner or nature; unamiable: *a thoroughly disagreeable person.* —*n.* **3.** an unpleasant or repugnant circumstance, attribute, etc.: *Bent upon being cheerful, he suppressed any mention of the disagreeable in the other's nature.* **4. disagreeables,** the disagreeable aspects or concomitants of a situation, course of action, etc.: *The pleasant features of the arrangement far outweigh the disagreeables.* [ME < MF *desagreable.* See DIS-¹, AGREEABLE] —**dis′a·gree′a·ble·ness, dis′a·gree′a·bil′i·ty,** *n.* —**dis′a·gree′a·bly,** *adv.*

dis·a·gree·ment (dis′ə grē′mənt), *n.* **1.** the act, state, or fact of disagreeing. **2.** lack of agreement; diversity; unlikeness: *a disagreement of colors.* **3.** difference of opinion; dissent. **4.** quarrel; dissension; argument. [DISAGREE + -MENT]

dis a·li·ter vi·sum (dēs ä′li ter′ wē′sōōm; *Eng.* dis al′i tər vī′səm), *Latin.* the gods have deemed otherwise.

dis·al·low (dis′ə lou′), *v.t.* **1.** to refuse to allow; reject; veto: *to disallow a proposal.* **2.** to refuse to admit the truth or validity of: *to disallow the veracity of a report.* [ME < OF *desallou(er).* See DIS-¹, ALLOW] —**dis′al·low′a·ble,** *adj.* —**dis′al·low′a·ble·ness,** *n.* —**dis′al·low′ance,** *n.*

dis·an·nul (dis′ə nul′), *v.t.,* **-nulled, -nul·ling.** to annul utterly; make void: *to disannul a contract.* [DIS-¹ + ANNUL] —**dis′an·nul′ler,** *n.* —**dis′an·nul′ment,** *n.*

dis·a·noint (dis′ə noint′), *v.t.* to invalidate the consecration of. [DIS-¹ + ANOINT]

dis·ap·pear (dis′ə pēr′), *v.i.* **1.** to cease to be seen; vanish from sight. **2.** to cease to exist or be known; pass away; end gradually: *One by one the symptoms disappeared.* [DIS-¹ + APPEAR]

—**Syn. 1.** DISAPPEAR, FADE, VANISH suggest that something passes from sight. DISAPPEAR is used of whatever suddenly or gradually goes out of sight: *We watched him turn down a side street and then disappear.* FADE suggests a (complete or partial) disappearance that proceeds gradually and often by means of a blending into something else: *Colors in the sky at sunrise quickly fade.* VANISH suggests complete, generally rapid, and often mysterious disappearance: *A mirage can vanish as suddenly as it appears.*

dis·ap·pear·ance (dis′ə pēr′əns), *n.* the act of disappearing; a ceasing to be seen or to exist. [DISAPPEAR + -ANCE]

dis·ap·point (dis′ə point′), *v.t.* **1.** to fail to fulfill the expectations or wishes of (a person): *His conduct disappointed us.* **2.** to defeat the fulfillment of (hopes, plans, etc.); thwart; frustrate: *to be disappointed in love.* [ME < MF *desappoint(er).* See DIS-¹, APPOINT] —**dis′ap·point′er,** *n.* —**dis′ap·point′ing·ly,** *adv.* —**dis′ap·point′ing·ness,** *n.*

dis·ap·point·ed (dis′ə poin′tid), *adj.* **1.** depressed or discouraged by the failure of one's hopes or expectations: *a disappointed suitor.* **2.** *Obs.* inadequately appointed; ill-equipped. [DISAPPOINT + -ED²] —**dis′ap·point′ed·ly,** *adv.*

dis·ap·point·ment (dis′ə point′mənt), *n.* **1.** the act or fact of disappointing: *All of his efforts only led to the disappointment of his supporters.* **2.** the state or feeling of being disappointed: *His disappointment was very great when the job failed to come through.* **3.** one who or that which disappoints: *The play was a disappointment.* [DISAPPOINT + -MENT]

—**Syn. 1.** failure, defeat, frustration. **2.** mortification, frustration, chagrin.

dis·ap·pro·ba·tion (dis′ap rə bā′shən), *n.* disapproval; condemnation. [DIS-¹ + APPROBATION]

dis·ap·prov·al (dis′ə prōō′vəl), *n.* the act or state of disapproving; a condemnatory feeling, look, or utterance; censure: *stern disapproval.* [DIS-¹ + APPROVAL]

—**Syn.** disapprobation, dislike, condemnation.

dis·ap·prove (dis′ə prōōv′), *v.,* **-proved, -prov·ing.** —*v.t.* **1.** to think (something) wrong or reprehensible; censure or condemn in opinion. **2.** to withhold approval from; decline to sanction: *The court disapproved the verdict.* —*v.i.* **3.** to have an unfavorable opinion (usually fol. by *of*). [DIS-¹ + APPROVE] —**dis′ap·prov′er,** *n.* —**dis′ap·prov′ing·ly,** *adv.*

—**Ant. 1.** praise.

dis·arm (dis ärm′), *v.t.* **1.** to deprive of a weapon or weapons. **2.** to deprive of means of attack or defense: *The lack of logic disarmed his argument.* **3.** to divest of hostility, suspicion, etc.; make friendly: *His smile disarmed us.* —*v.i.* **4.** to lay down one's weapons. **5.** (of a country) to reduce or limit the size, equipment, armament, etc., of the army, navy, or air forces. [ME < OF *desarm(er).* See DIS-¹, ARM²] —**dis·arm′er,** *n.*

dis·ar·ma·ment (dis är′mə mənt), *n.* **1.** the act or an instance of disarming. **2.** the reduction or limitation of the size, equipment, armament, etc., of the army, navy, or air forces of a country. [DISARM + *-ament,* modeled on *armament*]

dis·arm·ing (dis är′ming), *adj.* removing or capable of removing hostility, suspicion, etc.; charming: *a disarming smile.* [DISARM + -ING²] —**dis·arm′ing·ly,** *adv.*

dis·ar·range (dis′ə rānj′), *v.t.,* **-ranged, -rang·ing.** to disturb the arrangement of; disorder; unsettle. [DIS-¹ + ARRANGE] —**dis′ar·range′ment,** *n.* —**dis′ar·rang′er,** *n.*

dis·ar·ray (dis′ə rā′), *v.t.* **1.** to put out of array or order; throw into disorder. **2.** to undress. —*n.* **3.** disorder; confusion: *The army retreated in disarray.* **4.** disorder of apparel; disorderly dress. [ME *disaraie(n)* < OF *desarroy,* deriv. of *desarroyer, desareer.* See DIS-¹, ARRAY]

dis·ar·tic·u·late (dis′är tik′yə lāt′), *v.t., v.i.,* **-lat·ed, -lat·ing.** to make or become disjointed, as the bones of a body, stems of a plant, etc. [DIS-¹ + ARTICULATE] —**dis′ar·tic′u·la′tion,** *n.* —**dis′ar·tic′u·la′tor,** *n.*

dis·as·sem·ble (dis′ə sem′bəl), *v.t.*, **-bled, -bling.** to take apart. [DIS-[1] + ASSEMBLE]

dis·as·sem·bly (dis′ə sem′blē), *n.* **1.** the act of disassembling. **2.** the state of being disassembled. [DIS-[1] + ASSEMBLY]

dis·as·so·ci·ate (dis′ə sō′shē āt′, -sē-), *v.t.*, **-at·ed, -at·ing.** to dissociate. [DIS-[1] + ASSOCIATE] **—dis′as·so′ci·a′tion,** *n.*

dis·as·ter (di zas′tər, -zä′stər), *n.* **1.** a calamitous event, esp. one occurring suddenly and causing great damage or hardship. **2.** *Obs.* an unfavorable aspect of a star or planet. [< MF *desastre,* It *disastr(o),* equiv. to *dis-* DIS-[1] + *astro* star < L *astrum* < Gk *ástron*]
—Syn. 1. mischance, misfortune, misadventure, mishap, accident, blow, reverse, adversity, affliction. DISASTER, CALAMITY, CATASTROPHE, CATACLYSM refer to adverse happenings often occurring suddenly and unexpectedly. A DISASTER may be caused by carelessness, negligence, bad judgment, or the like; or by natural forces, as a hurricane, flood, etc.: *a railway disaster.* CALAMITY suggests great affliction, either personal or general; the emphasis is on the grief or sorrow caused: *the calamity of losing a dear child.* CATASTROPHE refers esp. to the tragic outcome of a personal or public situation; the emphasis is on the destruction or irreplaceable loss: *the catastrophe of a defeat in battle.* CATACLYSM, physically an earth-shaking change, refers to a personal or public upheaval of unparalleled violence: *a cataclysm that turned his life in a new direction.* **—Ant. 1.** success.

disas′ter ar′ea, *U.S.* **1.** a region or locality in which the population is generally affected by the occurrence of a major disaster, as a widespread flood, an explosion causing extensive damage, or the like. **2.** such a region or locality officially determined to be eligible, under statutory provisions, for emergency governmental relief.

dis·as·trous (di zas′trəs, -zä′strəs), *adj.* **1.** causing great distress or injury; ruinous; unfortunate; calamitous: *The rain and cold proved disastrous to his health.* **2.** *Archaic.* foreboding disaster. [< MF *desastreux,* It *disastros(o).* See DISASTER, -OUS] **—dis·as′trous·ly,** *adv.* **—dis·as′trous·ness,** *n.*

dis·a·vow (dis′ə vou′), *v.t.* to disclaim knowledge of, connection with, or responsibility for; disown; repudiate: *He disavowed the statement that had been attributed to him.* [ME *disavou(en),* *desavou(en)* < OF *desavou(er).* See DIS-[1], AVOW] **—dis′a·vow′ed·ly,** *adv.* **—dis′a·vow′er,** *n.*

dis·a·vow·al (dis′ə vou′əl), *n.* a disowning; repudiation; denial. [DISAVOW + -AL[2]]

dis·band (dis band′), *v.t.* **1.** to break up or dissolve (an organization): *They disbanded the corporation.* **2.** to dissolve (a military body) by dismissing it from service. **—*v.i.*** **3.** to break up or disperse, as a band or company. [< MF *desband(er),* equiv. to *des-* DIS-[1] + *bander* to tie; see BAND[2]] **—dis·band′ment,** *n.*
—Syn. 1. disperse, dismiss, scatter. **2.** demobilize. **—Ant. 1.** organize, unite.

dis·bar (dis bär′), *v.t.*, **-barred, -bar·ring.** *Law.* to expel from the legal profession or from the bar of a particular court. [DIS-[1] + BAR[1]] **—dis·bar′ment,** *n.*
—Syn. debar, suspend, exclude.

dis·be·lief (dis′bi lēf′), *n.* refusal to believe or to accept as true. [DIS-[1] + BELIEF]
—Syn. unbelief, incredulity.

dis·be·lieve (dis′bi lēv′), *v.t.*, **-lieved, -liev·ing.** to refuse or reject belief in: *When you say you will go, I disbelieve you.* [DIS-[1] + BELIEVE] **—dis′be·liev′er,** *n.* **—dis′be·liev′ing·ly,** *adv.*

dis·bos·om (dis bo͝oz′əm, -bo͞o′zəm), *v.t.* to make known; reveal; confess. [DIS-[1] + BOSOM]

dis·bow·el (dis bou′əl), *v.t.*, **-eled, -el·ing** or (*esp. Brit.*) **-elled, -el·ling.** to disembowel. [ME; see DIS-[1], BOWEL]

dis·branch (dis branch′, -bränch′), *v.t.* **1.** to deprive of branches, as a tree. **2.** to cut or break off, as a branch. [< MF *desbranch(er).* See DIS-[1], BRANCH]

dis·bud (dis bud′), *v.t.*, **-bud·ded, -bud·ding.** *Hort.* **1.** to remove leaf buds or shoots from (a plant) to produce a certain shape or effect. **2.** to remove certain flower buds from (a plant) to improve the quality and size of the remaining flowers. [DIS-[1] + BUD[1]]

dis·bur·den (dis bûr′dən), *v.t.* **1.** to remove a burden from; rid of a burden. **2.** to relieve of anything oppressive or annoying: *Action disburdened his mind of doubt.* **3.** to get rid of (a burden); discharge. **—*v.i.*** **4.** to unload a burden. [DIS-[1] + BURDEN[1]] **—dis·bur′den·ment,** *n.*

dis·burse (dis bûrs′), *v.t.*, **-bursed, -burs·ing.** **1.** to pay out (money); expend. **2.** to distribute or scatter: *Our troops were disbursed over a wide area. She disbursed the flowers to the children.* [< MF *desbours(er),* OF *desborser,* equiv. to *des-* DIS-[1] + *-borser,* deriv. of *borse* PURSE < LL *bursa* bag] **—dis·burs′a·ble,** *adj.* **—dis·burs′er,** *n.*
—Syn. 1. lay out. See **spend.**

dis·burse·ment (dis bûrs′mənt), *n.* **1.** the act or an instance of disbursing. **2.** money paid out or spent. [< MF *desboursement.* See DISBURSE, -MENT]

dis·bur·then (dis bûr′thən), *v.t., v.i.* *Obs.* to disburden.

disc (disk), *n., v.t.* disk.

disc., **1.** discount. **2.** discovered.

dis·calced (dis kalst′), *adj.* without shoes; unshod; barefoot: applied esp. to members of certain religious orders. Also, **dis·cal·ce·ate** (dis kal′sē it, -āt′). Cf. **calced.** [part trans. of L *discalceātus,* equiv. to *dis-* DIS-[1] + *calceātus* shod, ptp. of *calceāre* (*calce(us)* a shoe, deriv. of *calc-* (s. of *calx*) heel + *-ātus* -ATE[1])]

dis·cant (*n.* dis′kant; *v.* dis kant′), *n.* **1.** Also, **dis·can·tus** (dis kan′təs). *Music.* a 13th-century polyphonic style with strict mensural meter in all the voice parts, in contrast to the metrically free organum of the period. **2.** descant. **—*v.i.*** **3.** descant. [ME < ML *discanth(us);* see DESCANT] **—dis·cant′er,** *n.*

dis·card (*v.* di skärd′; *n.* dis′kärd), *v.t.* **1.** to cast aside; reject; dismiss, esp. from use: *to discard an old hat.* **2.** *Cards.* **a.** to throw out (a card or cards) from one's hand. **b.** to play (a card, not a trump, of a different suit from that of the card led). **—*v.i.*** **3.** *Cards.* to discard a card or cards. **—*n.*** **4.** the act of discarding. **5.** one who or that which is cast out or rejected. **6.** *Cards.* a card or cards discarded. [DIS-[1] + CARD[1]] **—dis·card′er,** *n.* **—Ant. 1.** retain.

dis·car·nate (dis kär′nit, -nāt), *adj.* without a physical body; incorporeal. [DIS-[1] + *-carnate,* as in *incarnate*] **—dis′car·na′tion,** *n.*

dis·case (dis kās′), *v.t.*, **-cased, -cas·ing.** to take the case or covering from; uncase. [DIS-[1] + CASE[2]]

disc′ brake′, a brake system, as on an automobile, that is activated when a caliper is pressed against the disc of a wheel.

dis·cept (di sept′), *v.t.* *Rare.* to dispute; debate. [< L *discept(āre)* (to) dispute, discuss, decide, equiv. to *dis-* DIS-[1] + *cep-* take (sp. var. of *capere*) + *-t-* freq. suffix] **—dis′cep·ta′tion,** *n.*

dis·cern (di sûrn′, -zûrn′), *v.t.* **1.** to perceive by the sight or some other sense or by the intellect; see, recognize, or apprehend clearly: *They discerned a sail on the horizon.* **2.** to distinguish mentally; recognize as distinct or different; discriminate: *He is incapable of discerning right from wrong.* **—*v.i.*** **3.** to distinguish or discriminate. [ME *discern(en)* < L *discernere* to separate, equiv. to *dis-* DIS-[1] + *cernere* to separate] **—dis·cern′er,** *n.*
—Syn. 1. discover, descry, espy. See **notice. 2, 3.** differentiate, judge.

dis·cern·i·ble (di sûr′nə bəl, -zûr′-), *adj.* capable of being discerned; distinguishable. Also, **dis·cern′a·ble.** [< L *discernibil(is)* (see DISCERN, -IBLE); r. earlier *discernable* < MF, equiv. to *discern(er)* to discern + *-able* -ABLE] **—dis·cern′i·ble·ness, dis·cern′a·ble·ness,** *n.* **—dis·cern′i·bly, dis·cern′a·bly,** *adv.*

dis·cern·ing (di sûr′ning, -zûr′-), *adj.* showing good judgment and understanding: *a discerning critic of poetry.* [DISCERN + -ING[2]] **—dis·cern′ing·ly,** *adv.*

dis·cern·ment (di sûrn′mənt, -zûrn′-), *n.* **1.** the faculty of discerning; discrimination; acuteness of judgment and understanding. **2.** the act or an instance of discerning. [< MF *discernement,* equiv. to *discern(er)* (to) DISCERN + *-ment* -MENT]
—Syn. 1. judgment, perspicacity, penetration, insight.

dis·cerp (di sûrp′, -zûrp′), *v.t.* *Rare.* to pull apart; tear into pieces; disarticulate. [late ME *discerp(en)* < L *discerp(ere),* equiv. to *dis-* DIS-[1] + *-cerpere* (var. of *carpere* to pluck)]

dis·cerp·ti·ble (di sûrp′tə bəl, -zûrp′-), *adj.* capable of being torn apart; divisible. [< L *discerpt(us)* torn to pieces, scattered (ptp. of *discerpere;* see DISCERP) + -IBLE] **—dis·cerp′ti·bil′i·ty, dis·cerp′ti·ble·ness,** *n.*

dis·charge (*v.* dis chärj′; *n.* dis′chärj, dis chärj′), *v.,* **-charged, -charg·ing,** *n.* **—*v.t.*** **1.** to relieve of a charge or load; unload: *to discharge a ship.* **2.** to remove or send forth: *They discharged the cargo at New York.* **3.** to fire or shoot (a firearm or missile): *to discharge a gun.* **4.** to pour forth; emit: *to discharge oil; to discharge oaths.* **5.** to relieve oneself of (an obligation, burden, etc.). **6.** to relieve of obligation, responsibility, etc. **7.** to fulfill, perform, or execute (a duty, function, etc.). **8.** to relieve or deprive of office, employment, etc.; dismiss from service. **9.** to release, send away, or allow to go (often fol. by *from*): *The children were discharged early from school. They discharged him from prison.* **10.** to pay (a debt). **11.** *Law.* **a.** to release (a defendant, esp. one under confinement). **b.** to release (a bankrupt) from former debts. **c.** to cancel (a contract). **d.** to release (bail). **12.** *Elect.* to rid (a battery, capacitor, etc.) of a charge of electricity. **13.** *Dyeing.* to free from a dye, as by chemical bleaching. **—*v.i.*** **14.** to get rid of a burden or load. **15.** to deliver a charge or load. **16.** to pour forth. **17.** to blur or run, as a color or dye. **18.** *Elect.* to lose, or give up, a charge of electricity. **—*n.*** **19.** the act of discharging a ship, load, etc. **20.** the act of firing a weapon, as a bow by drawing and releasing the string, or a gun by exploding the charge of powder. **21.** a sending or coming forth, as of water from a pipe; ejection; emission. **22.** the rate or amount of such issue. **23.** something sent forth or emitted. **24.** a relieving, ridding, or getting rid of something of the nature of a charge. **25.** *Law.* **a.** an acquittal or exoneration. **b.** an annulment, as of a court order. **c.** the freeing of one held under legal process. **26.** a relieving or being relieved of obligation or liability; fulfillment of an obligation. **27.** the payment of a debt. **28.** a release or dismissal, as from prison, an office, employment, etc. **29.** a certificate of such a release or a certificate of release from obligation or liability. **30.** *Mil.* **a.** the separation of a person from military service. **b.** a certificate of such separation. **31.** *Elect.* **a.** the removal or transference of an electric charge, as by the conversion of chemical energy to electrical energy. **b.** the equalization of a difference of potential, as between two terminals. [ME *descharge(n)* < OF *descharg(ier)* < LL *discarricāre,* equiv. to *dis-* DIS-[1] + *carricāre* to load; see CHARGE] **—dis·charge′a·ble,** *adj.* **—dis·charg′er,** *n.*
—Syn. 1. unburden, disburden. **2.** expel, eject. **4.** exude. **6.** See **release. 7.** See **perform. 8.** cashier.

dis′charge print′ing, a fabric-printing method in which all the material is dyed and then certain specified areas are discharged so as to permit the original hue or its color replacement to act as a pattern against the colored ground. Also called **extract printing.** Cf. **resist printing.**

discharg′ing arch′, an arch for taking some of the weight from a structural member beneath it. Also called **relieving arch.**

discharg′ing pal′let, *Horol.* the second and last pallet engaging with a tooth of an escape wheel. Also called **exit pallet.** Cf. **receiving pallet.**

disci-, a combining form of **disk:** *discifloral.*

dis·ci·flo·ral (dis′i flôr′əl, -flōr′-), *adj.* *Bot.* having flowers in which the receptacle is expanded into a conspicuous disk, as in composite plants. [DISCI- + FLORAL]

dis·ci·ple (di sī′pəl), *n., v.,* **-pled, -pling.** **—*n.*** **1.** *Relig.* **a.** one of the 12 personal followers of Christ. **b.** one of the 70 followers sent forth by Christ. Luke 10:1. **c.** any other professed follower of Christ in His lifetime. **2.** any follower of Christ. **3.** (*cap.*) a member of the Disciples of Christ. **4.** one who is a pupil or an adherent of the doctrines of another; follower: *a disciple of Freud.* **—*v.t.*** **5.** *Archaic.* to convert into a disciple. **6.** *Obs.* to teach; train. [ME < OF < L *discipul(us),* equiv. to **discip(ere)* (to) grasp (*dis-* DIS-[1] + *-cipere,* sp. var. of *capere* to take + *-ulus* -ULE); r. ME *deciple* < OF; r. OE *discipul* < L, as above] **—dis·ci′ple·like′,** *adj.* **—dis·ci′ple·ship′,** *n.* **—Syn. 4.** See **pupil**[1].

Disci′ples of Christ′, a Christian denomination, founded in the U.S. by Alexander Campbell in the early part of the 19th century, that rejects all creeds, holds the Bible as a sufficient rule of faith and practice, administers baptism by immersion, celebrates the Lord's Supper every Sunday, and has a congregational polity.

dis·ci·plin·a·ble (dis′ə plin′ə bəl), *adj.* **1.** subject to or meriting disciplinary action: *a disciplinable breach of rules.* **2.** capable of being instructed. [ME < MF < LL *disciplīnābil(is).* See DISCIPLINE, -ABLE] **—dis′ci·plin′a·bil′i·ty, dis′ci·plin′a·ble·ness,** *n.*

dis·ci·pli·nal (dis′ə plə nəl, -plin′əl, dis′ə plīn′əl), *adj.* of, pertaining to, or of the nature of discipline: *disciplinal rigor.* [DISCIPLINE + -AL[1]]

dis·ci·plin·ant (dis′ə plə nənt, -plin′ənt), *n.* **1.** a person who subjects himself to discipline. **2.** (*cap.*) one of a former Spanish religious order whose members scourged themselves publicly and inflicted upon themselves other severe tortures. [< Sp *disciplinant(e)* < It < ML *disciplīnant-* (s. of *disciplīnāns*), prp. of *disciplīnāre* (deriv. of *disciplīna* DISCIPLINE); see -ANT]

dis·ci·pli·nar·i·an (dis′ə plə nâr′ē ən), *n.* **1.** a person who enforces or advocates discipline: *The teacher was a formidable disciplinarian.* **—*adj.*** **2.** disciplinary. [DISCIPLINE + -ARIAN]

dis·ci·pli·nar·y (dis′ə plə ner′ē), *adj.* of, for, or constituting discipline; promoting discipline: *disciplinary action.* [DISCIPLINE + -ARY]

dis·ci·pline (dis′ə plin), *n., v.,* **-plined, -plin·ing.** **—*n.*** **1.** training to act in accordance with rules; drill: *military discipline.* **2.** instruction and exercise designed to train to proper conduct or action: *A daily stint at the typewriter is excellent discipline for a writer.* **3.** punishment inflicted by way of correction and training. **4.** the training effect of experience, adversity, etc.: *the harsh discipline of poverty.* **5.** behavior in accord with rules of conduct; behavior and order maintained by training and control: *good discipline in an army.* **6.** a set or system of rules and regulations. **7.** *Eccles.* the system of government regulating the practice of a church as distinguished from its doctrine. **8.** an instrument of punishment, esp. a whip or scourge, used in the practice of self-mortification or as an instrument of chastisement in certain religious communities. **9.** a branch of instruction or learning: *the disciplines of history and economics.* **—*v.t.*** **10.** to train by instruction and exercise; drill. **11.** to bring to a state of order and obedience by training and control. **12.** to punish or penalize in order to train and control; correct; chastise. [ME < L *disciplīna* instruction, tuition, equiv. to *discipul(us)* DISCIPLE + *-ina* -INE[2]] **—dis′ci·plin′er,** *n.*
—Syn. 3. chastisement, castigation. **12.** See **punish.**

dis·cis·sion (di sizh′ən), *n.* *Surg.* an incision of the lens of the eye, as for removal of cataract. [< LL *discissiōn-* (s. of *discissiō*) division, separation, equiv. to L *disciss(us)* torn apart, ptp. of *discindere* (*dī-* DI-[2] + *scissus*) + *-iōn-;* see SCISSION]

disc′ jock′ey. See **disk jockey.**

dis·claim (dis klām′), *v.t.* **1.** to repudiate or deny interest in or connection with; disavow; disown: *disclaiming all participation.* **2.** *Law.* to renounce a claim or right to. **3.** to reject the claims or authority of. **—*v.i.*** **4.** *Law.* to renounce or repudiate a legal claim or right. **5.** *Obs.* to disavow interest. [ME < AF *disclaim(er),* *desclam(er).* See DIS-[1], CLAIM]

dis·claim·er (dis klā′mər), *n.* **1.** the act of disclaiming; the renouncing, repudiating, or denying of a claim; disavowal. **2.** a person who disclaims. **3.** a statement, document, or the like, that disclaims. [ME < AF: to DISCLAIM]

dis·cla·ma·tion (dis′klə mā′shən), *n.* the act of disclaiming; renunciation; disavowal. [< ML *disclamā-t(us)* (ptp. of *disclamāre* to DISCLAIM, prob. < AF *disclaimer;* see -ATE[1]) + -ION] **—dis·clam·a·to·ry** (dis klam′ə tôr′ē, -tōr′ē), *adj.*

dis·cli·max (dis klī′maks), *n.* *Ecol.* a stable community that has replaced the normal climax in a given area, owing to disturbance by man or domestic animals. [DIS-[1] + CLIMAX]

dis·close (di sklōz′), *v.,* **-closed, -clos·ing,** *n.* **—*v.t.*** **1.** to make known; reveal or uncover: *to disclose a secret.* **2.** to cause to appear; allow to be seen; lay open to view: *In spring the violets disclose their fragrant petals.* **3.** *Obs.* to open up; unfold. **—*n.*** **4.** *Obs.* disclosure. [ME *disclose(n),* *desclosen* < OF *desclos-,* s. of *desclore,* equiv. to *des-* DIS-[1] + *clore* to close < L *claudere;* see CLOSE] **—dis·clos′er,** *n.*
—Syn. 1. show, tell, unveil. See **reveal. 2.** expose.

dis·clo·sure (di sklō′zhər), *n.* **1.** the act or an instance of disclosing; exposure; revelation. **2.** that which is disclosed; a revelation. **3.** *Patent Law.* (in a patent application) the descriptive information imparted by the specification claims, drawings, and models submitted. [DISCLOSE + -URE]

dis·co (dis′kō), *n., pl.* **-cos.** *Informal.* **1.** discotheque. **2. a.** a style of popular music for dancing, usually recorded and with complex electronic instrumentation, in which simple, repetitive lyrics are subordinated to a heavy, pulsating rhythmic beat. **b.** any of various forms of dance, often improvisational, performed to such music.

dis·cob·o·lus (di skob′ə ləs), *n., pl.* **-li** (-lī′, -lē′) for 1. **1.** *Chiefly Class. Antiq.* a discus thrower. **2.** (*cap., italics.*) a statue of a discus thrower (5th century B.C.) by the Greek sculptor Myron. [< L, equiv. to Gk *diskobólos,* deriv. of *dísk(os)* DISCUS + *-o-* -O- + *-bolos* thrower, *bállein* to throw]

dis·cog·ra·pher (di skog′rə fər), *n.* a person who compiles discographies. [DISCOGRAPH(Y) + -ER[1]]

dis·cog·ra·phy (di skog′rə fē), *n.* **1.** a selective or complete list of phonograph recordings, typically of one composer, performer, or group of performers. **2.** the analysis, history, or classification of phonograph recordings. **3.** the methods of analyzing or classifying phonograph recordings. Also, **diskography.** [< F *discographie.* See DISC, -O-, -GRAPHY] **—dis·co·graph·i·cal** (dis′kə graf′i kəl), *adj.* **—dis′co·graph′i·cal·ly,** *adv.*

dis·coid (dis′koid), *adj.* Also, **dis·coi′dal.** **1.** having the form of a discus or disk; flat and circular. **2.** *Bot.* (of a composite flower) consisting of a disk only, without rays. **—*n.*** **3.** something in the form of a disk. **4.** *Dentistry.* an excavator with a disklike blade. [< LL *discoīd(ēs)* < Gk *diskoeidēs* quoit-shaped]

dis·col·or (dis kul′ər), *v.t.* **1.** to change or spoil the color of; fade or stain: *The sun gradually discolored the* rug. —*v.i.* **2.** to change color; become faded or stained. Also, *esp. Brit.,* **dis·col′our.** [ME *discolour(en)* < OF *descolor(er)* < LL *discolōrā(re)* (to) change color, deriv. of L *discolor* of another color. See DIS-[1], COLOR]

dis·col·or·a·tion (dis kul′ə rā′shən), *n.* **1.** the act or fact of discoloring or the state of being discolored. **2.** a discolored marking or area; stain. Also, *esp. Brit.,* **dis·col′our·a′tion.** Also called **dis·col′or·ment.** [DISCOLOR + -ATION]

dis·com·bob·u·late (dis′kəm bob′yə lāt′), *v.t.,* **-lat·ed, -lat·ing.** *Informal.* to upset; confuse; frustrate: *Her plans were discombobulated by the turn of events.* [? by alter. from DISCOMPOSE or DISCOMFORT]

dis·com·fit (dis kum′fit), *v.t.* **1.** to defeat utterly; rout: *The army was discomfited in every battle.* **2.** to frustrate the plans of; thwart; foil. **3.** to confuse and deject; disconcert: *to be discomfited by a question.* —*n.* **4.** *Archaic.* rout; defeat. [ME < OF *desconfit,* ptp. of *desconfire,* equiv. to *des-* DIS-[1] + *confire* to make, accomplish < L *conficere;* see CONFECT] —**dis·com′fit·er,** *n.*
—**Syn. 3.** discompose, embarrass, disturb.

dis·com·fi·ture (dis kum′fi chər), *n.* **1.** defeat in battle; rout. **2.** frustration of hopes or plans. **3.** discomcertion; confusion. [ME *desconfiture* < OF: defeat. See DISCOMFIT, -URE]

dis·com·fort (dis kum′fərt), *n.* **1.** an absence of comfort or ease; uneasiness, hardship, or mild pain. **2.** anything that disturbs the comfort. —*v.t.* **3.** to disturb the comfort or happiness of; make uncomfortable or uneasy. [ME *discomfort(en)* < OF *desconfort(er).* See DIS-[1], COMFORT] —**dis·com′fort·ing·ly,** *adv.*

dis·com·fort·a·ble (dis kum′fər tə bəl, -kumf′tə-), *adj. Archaic.* **1.** physically uncomfortable; comfortless. **2.** causing unease or discouragement. [ME < OF *desconfortable.* See DISCOMFORT, -ABLE] —**dis·com′fort·a·bly,** *adv.*

dis·com·mend (dis′kə mend′), *v.t.* **1.** to express disapproval of: *The diners discommended the wine.* **2.** to bring into disfavor: *He was discommended for his negligence.* [DIS-[1] + COMMEND] —**dis′com·mend′er,** *n.*

dis·com·mode (dis′kə mōd′), *v.t.,* **-mod·ed, -mod·ing.** to cause inconvenience to; disturb, trouble, or incommode. [< MF *discommod(er),* equiv. to *dis-* DIS-[1] + *commode* convenient; see COMMODE] —**dis′com·mo′di·ous,** *adj.* —**dis′com·mo′di·ous·ly,** *adv.* —**dis′com·mo′di·ous·ness,** *n.*

dis·com·mod·i·ty (dis′kə mod′i tē), *n., pl.* **-ties.** *Archaic.* **1.** inconvenience; disadvantageousness. **2.** a source of inconvenience or trouble; disadvantage. [DIS-[1] + COMMODITY]

dis·com·mon (dis kom′ən), *v.t.* **1.** (at Oxford and Cambridge) to prohibit (a tradesman or townsman who has violated the regulations of the university) from dealing with the undergraduates. **2.** *Law.* to deprive of the character of a common, as by enclosing a piece of land. [DIS-[1] + obs. *common* to participate, associate]

dis·com·pose (dis′kəm pōz′), *v.t.,* **-posed, -pos·ing.** **1.** to upset the order of; disarrange; disorder; unsettle: *The breeze discomposed the bouquet.* **2.** to disturb the composure of; agitate; perturb: *The bad news discomposed us.* [DIS-[1] + COMPOSE] —**dis′com·pos′ed·ly,** *adv.* —**dis′com·pos′ing·ly,** *adv.*
—**Syn. 2.** discomfit, disconcert.

dis·com·po·sure (dis′kəm pō′zhər), *n.* the state of being discomposed; disorder; agitation; perturbation. [DIS-[1] + COMPOSURE]

dis·con·cert (dis′kən sûrt′), *v.t.* **1.** to disturb the self-possession of; perturb; ruffle. **2.** to throw into disorder or confusion; disarrange: *She changed her mind and disconcerted everybody's plans.* [< obs. F *disconcert(er).* See DIS-[1], CONCERT] —**dis′con·cert′ing·ly,** *adv.* —**dis′con·cert′ing·ness,** *n.* —**dis′con·cer′tion, dis′con·cert′ment,** *n.*
—**Syn. 1.** discompose, perplex, bewilder, abash, discomfit. See **confuse.** —**Ant. 1.** calm. **2.** arrange.

dis·con·cert·ed (dis′kən sûr′tid), *adj.* confused, ruffled, abashed, or uneasy. [DISCONCERT + -ED] —**dis′con·cert′ed·ly,** *adv.* —**dis′con·cert′ed·ness,** *n.*

dis·con·form·i·ty (dis′kən fôr′mi tē), *n., pl.* **-ties.** **1.** *Geol.* the surface of a division between parallel rock strata, indicating interruption of sedimentation: a type of unconformity. **2.** *Archaic.* nonconformity. [DIS-[1] + CONFORMITY]

dis·con·nect (dis′kə nekt′), *v.t.* to sever or interrupt the connection of or between; detach: *They disconnected the telephone. We were disconnected.* [DIS-[1] + CONNECT] —**dis′con·nect′er,** *n.* —**dis′con·nec′tive,** *adj.* —**dis′con·nec′tive·ness,** *n.*

dis·con·nect·ed (dis′kə nek′tid), *adj.* **1.** disjointed; broken. **2.** not coherent; seemingly irrational: *a disconnected argument.* **3.** *Math.* pertaining to a set for which there exists cover consisting of two open sets whose intersections with the given set are disjoint and nonempty. Cf. **connected** (def. 3). [DISCONNECT + -ED[2]] —**dis′con·nect′ed·ly,** *adv.* —**dis′con·nect′ed·ness,** *n.*

dis·con·nec·tion (dis′kə nek′shən), *n.* **1.** the act of disconnecting. **2.** the state of being disconnected; lack of connection. Also, *Brit.,* **dis′con·nex′ion.** [DIS-[1] + CONNECTION]

dis·con·sid·er (dis′kən sid′ər), *v.t.* to discredit. [DIS-[1] + CONSIDER] —**dis′con·sid′er·a′tion,** *n.*

dis·con·so·late (dis kon′sə lit), *adj.* **1.** without consolation or solace; hopelessly unhappy; inconsolable: *Loss of her beauty made her disconsolate.* **2.** characterized by or causing dejection; cheerless; gloomy: *disconsolate prospects.* [ME < ML *disconsōlāt(us),* equiv. to L *dis-* DIS-[1] + *consōlātus* consoled, ptp. of *consōlārī* to CONSOLE; see -ATE[1]] —**dis·con′so·late·ly,** *adv.* —**dis·con·so·la·tion** (dis kon′sə lā′shən), **dis·con′so·late·ness,** *n.*
—**Syn. 1.** heart-broken, dejected. **1, 2.** cheerless; sad, melancholy, sorrowful, miserable. See **desolate.**
—**Ant. 1.** delighted. **1, 2.** happy.

dis·con·tent (dis′kən tent′), *adj.* **1.** not content; dissatisfied; discontented. —*n.* **2.** Also, **dis′con·tent′ment.** lack of content; dissatisfaction. **3.** a restless desire or craving for something one does not have. **4.** a malcontent. —*v.t.* **5.** to make discontented; dissatisfy; displease. [DIS-[1] + CONTENT[2]]
—**Syn. 2.** uneasiness, inquietude, restlessness, displeasure. See **dissatisfaction.**

dis·con·tent·ed (dis′kən ten′tid), *adj.* uneasy in mind; dissatisfied; restlessly unhappy: *For all their wealth, or perhaps because of it, they were discontented.* [DISCONTENT + -ED[2]] —**dis′con·tent′ed·ly,** *adv.* —**dis′con·tent′ed·ness,** *n.*

dis·con·tin·u·ance (dis′kən tin′yo͞o əns), *n.* **1.** the act or state of discontinuing or the state of being discontinued; cessation: *the discontinuance of a business.* **2.** *Law.* the termination of a suit by the act of the plaintiff, as by notice in writing, or by neglect to take the proper adjournments to keep it pending. [ME; see DIS-[1], CONTINUANCE]

dis·con·tin·u·a·tion (dis′kən tin′yo͞o ā′shən), *n.* breach or interruption of continuity or unity: *Progress was delayed by repeated discontinuations of work.* [< MF < ML *discontinuātiōn-* (s. of *discontinuātiō*), equiv. to *discontinuāt(us)* (ptp. of *discontinuāre* to DISCONTINUE; see -ATE[1]) + *-iōn-* -ION]

dis·con·tin·ue (dis′kən tin′yo͞o), *v.,* **-tin·ued, -tin·u·ing.** —*v.t.* **1.** to cause to cease; put an end to; stop: *to discontinue nuclear testing.* **2.** to cease to take, use, etc.: *to discontinue a newspaper.* **3.** *Law.* to terminate or abandon (a suit, claim, or the like). —*v.i.* **4.** to come to an end or stop; cease; desist. [ME < MF *discontinu(er)* < ML *discontinuāre.* See DIS-[1], CONTINUE] —**dis′con·tin′u·er,** *n.*
—**Syn. 1.** See **interrupt.** —**Ant. 1.** resume.

dis·con·ti·nu·i·ty (dis′kon tᵊno͞o′i tē, -tᵊnyo͞o′-), *n., pl.* **-ties.** **1.** lack of continuity; absence of uninterrupted connection; irregularity: *The plot was marred by discontinuity.* **2.** a break or gap: *The surface of the moon is characterized by major discontinuities.* **3.** *Math.* a point at which a function is not continuous. Cf. **continuous** (def. 3). **4.** *Geol.* a zone between layers within the earth where the velocity of earthquake waves changes radically. [< ML *discontinuitās.* See DISCONTINUOUS, -ITY]

dis·con·tin·u·ous (dis′kən tin′yo͞o əs), *adj.* **1.** not continuous; broken; interrupted; intermittent: *a discontinuous argument.* **2.** *Math.* (of a function at a point) not continuous at the point. Cf. **continuous** (def. 3). [< ML *discontinuus.* See DIS-[1], CONTINUOUS] —**dis′con·tin′u·ous·ly,** *adv.* —**dis′con·tin′u·ous·ness,** *n.*

dis·co·phile (dis′kə fīl′), *n.* a person who zealously studies and collects phonograph records, esp. those of a rare or specialized nature. Also, **diskophile.** [DISC + -O- + -PHILE]

dis·cord (*n.* dis′kôrd; *v.* dis kôrd′), *n.* **1.** lack of concord or harmony between persons or things; disagreement. **2.** difference of opinion. **3.** strife; dispute; war: *marital discord.* **4.** *Music.* an inharmonious combination of musical tones sounded together. **5.** any confused or harsh noise; dissonance. [ME *descorde, discorde* < OF *descort* (deriv. of *descorder*), *descorde* < L *discord(ia),* deriv. of *discord-* (s. of *discors*) discordant (*dis-* DIS-[1] + *cord-,* s. of *cors* heart)] —*v.i.* **6.** to disagree; be at variance. [ME *discord(en)* < OF *descord(er)* < L *discordāre* deriv. of *discord-,* as above]
—**Syn. 3.** conflict, struggle, controversy, antagonism, argument, contention, quarreling.

dis·cord·ance (dis kôr′dᵊns), *n.* **1.** a discordant state; disagreement; discord. **2.** an instance of this: *Efforts to arbitrate their discordance quickly failed.* **3.** dissonance. **4.** *Geol.* lack of parallelism between superjacent strata, as in an angular unconformity. [ME < OF *descord(er)* (see DISCORD) + *-ance* -ANCE]

dis·cor·dan·cy (dis kôr′dᵊn sē), *n., pl.* **-cies.** discordance (defs. 1–3). [DISCORDANCE + -Y[3]]

dis·cord·ant (dis kôr′dᵊnt), *adj.* **1.** being at variance; disagreeing; incongruous: *discordant opinions.* **2.** disagreeable to the ear; dissonant; harsh. [ME *discordaunt* < OF *discordant* < L *discordant-* (s. of *discordāns*), prp. of *discordāre.* See DISCORD, -ANT] —**dis·cord′ant·ly,** *adv.*

Dis·cor·di·a (dis kôr′dē ə), *n.* the ancient Roman goddess of discord, identified with the Greek goddess Eris. [< L: DISCORD]

dis·co·theque (dis′kō tek′), *n.* a cabaret in which the patrons dance to recorded music usually played on high-fidelity equipment. Also, **dis′co·thèque′.** [< F *discothèque.* See DISC, -O-, THECA]

dis·count (*v.* dis′kount, dis kount′; *n.* dis′kount), *v.t.* **1.** to deduct (a certain amount) from a bill, charge, etc.: *All bills that are paid promptly will be discounted at two percent.* **2.** to offer for sale or sell at a reduced price: *The store discounted all clothing for the sale.* **3.** to advance or lend money with deduction of interest on (commercial paper not immediately payable). **4.** to purchase or sell (a bill or note) before maturity at a reduction based on the interest for the time it still has to run. **5.** to leave out of account; disregard: *Even if we discount the irrelevant material, the thesis remains mediocre.* **6.** to allow for exaggeration in (a statement, opinion, etc.): *Knowing his political bias they discounted most of his story.* **7.** to take into account in advance, often so as to diminish the effect of: *They had discounted the effect of a decline in the stock market.* —*v.i.* **8.** to advance or lend money after deduction of interest. —*n.* **9.** the act or an instance of discounting. **10.** an amount deducted for prompt payment or other special reason. **11.** any deduction from the nominal value. **12.** a payment of interest in advance upon a loan of money. **13.** the amount of interest obtained by one who discounts. **14.** an allowance made for exaggeration or bias, as in a report, story, etc.: *Even after all the discounts are taken, his story sounds phony.* **15. at a discount, a.** *Com.* below par. **b.** below the usual list price. **c.** in low esteem or regard: *His excuses were taken at a discount by all who knew him.* **d.** not in demand; unwanted: *His ancient superstitions are at a discount in a civilized society.* [< F *décompt(er),* OF *desconter* < ML *discomputāre.* See DIS-[1], COUNT[1]] —**dis·count·a·ble,** *adj.*

dis′count bro′ker, an agent who discounts commercial paper.

dis·coun·te·nance (dis koun′tᵊnəns), *v.,* **-nanced, -nanc·ing,** *n.* —*v.t.* **1.** to disconcert, embarrass, or abash: *With his composure, he survived every attempt to discountenance him.* **2.** to show disapproval of; treat with disfavor: *The teachers discountenanced smoking by the students.* —*n.* **3.** disapproval; disapprobation. [DIS-[1] + COUNTENANCE] —**dis·coun′te·nanc·er,** *n.*

dis·count·er (dis′koun tər), *n.* **1.** a person who discounts. **2.** a person who operates a discount house. [DISCOUNT + -ER[1]]

dis′count house′, a store that sells much of its merchandise at a price considerably below the usual price.

dis′count mar′ket, a trading market in which notes, bills, and other negotiable instruments are discounted.

dis′count rate′, *Finance.* **1.** the rate of interest charged in discounting commercial paper. **2.** the rediscount rate.

dis′count store′. See **discount house.**

dis·cour·age (di skûr′ij, -skur′-), *v.t.,* **-aged, -ag·ing.** **1.** to deprive of courage, hope, or confidence; dishearten; dispirit. **2.** to dissuade (usually fol. by *from*). **3.** to obstruct by opposition or difficulty; hinder: *Low prices discourage industry.* **4.** to express disapproval of: *to discourage the expression of enthusiasm.* [ME *discorage(n)* < MF *descorag(er),* OF *descoragier.* See DIS-[1], COURAGE] —**dis·cour′ag·er,** *n.* —**dis·cour′age·a·ble,** *adj.* —**dis·cour′ag·ing·ly,** *adv.*
—**Syn. 1.** daunt, depress, deject, overawe, cow, abash. DISCOURAGE, DISMAY, INTIMIDATE may imply the attempt to dishearten or frighten one so as to prevent some action, or any further action. To DISCOURAGE is to dishearten by expressing disapproval or by suggesting that a contemplated action or course will probably fail: *He was discouraged from giving up his job.* To DISMAY is to dishearten completely, by the disclosure of unsuspected facts, so that the action contemplated seems useless or dangerous: *to dismay a prosecutor by revealing his brother's connection with a crime.* To INTIMIDATE is to frighten, as by threats of force, violence, or dire consequences: *to intimidate a witness.* —**Ant. 1.** encourage.

dis·cour·age·ment (di skûr′ij mənt, -skur′-), *n.* **1.** the act or an instance of discouraging. **2.** the state of being discouraged. **3.** something that discourages: *Poor health and poverty are grave discouragements.* [< MF *descouragement,* OF *descoragement.* See DISCOURAGE, -MENT]
—**Syn. 2.** depression, dejection, hopelessness. See **despair. 3.** deterrent, damper, impediment, obstacle, obstruction. —**Ant. 1–3.** encouragement.

dis·course (*n.* dis′kōrs, -kôrs, dis kōrs′, -kôrs′; *v.* dis kōrs′, -kôrs′), *n., v.,* **-coursed, -cours·ing.** —*n.* **1.** communication of thought by words; talk; conversation: *earnest and intelligent discourse.* **2.** a formal discussion of a subject in speech or writing, as a dissertation, treatise, sermon, etc. —*v.i.* **3.** to communicate thoughts orally; talk; converse. **4.** to treat of a subject formally in speech or writing. —*v.t.* **5.** to utter or give forth (musical sounds). [ME *discours* < ML *discurs(us)* (sp. by influence of ME *cours* course), LL: conversation, L: a running to and fro (n. use of ptp. of *discurrere*), equiv. to *dis-* DIS-[1] + *cursus* ran; see COURSE] —**dis·course′less,** *adj.* —**dis·cours′er,** *n.*

Dis′course on Meth′od, a philosophical work (1637) by Descartes, containing an exposition of the basic concepts of his system, the formulation of the method of reasoning known as *Cartesian doubt,* and his famous statement *Cogito, ergo sum.* French, **Dis·cours de la Mé·thode** (dēs ko͞or′ də lA mā tôd′).

dis·cour·te·ous (dis kûr′tē əs), *adj.* impolite; uncivil; rude: *a discourteous salesman.* [DIS-[1] + COURTEOUS] —**dis·cour′te·ous·ly,** *adv.* —**dis·cour′te·ous·ness,** *n.*

dis·cour·te·sy (dis kûr′ti sē), *n., pl.* **-sies.** **1.** lack or breach of courtesy; incivility; rudeness. **2.** a discourteous or impolite act. [DIS-[1] + COURTESY]

dis·cov·er (di skuv′ər), *v.t.* **1.** to see, get knowledge of, learn of, find, or find out; gain sight or knowledge of (something previously unseen or unknown): *to discover America; to discover electricity.* **2.** *Archaic.* to make known; reveal; disclose. **3.** *Archaic.* to make manifest unintentionally; give away; betray. [ME *discover(en)* < OF *descovr(ir)* < LL *discooperīre.* See DIS-[1], COVER] —**dis·cov′er·a·ble,** *adj.* —**dis·cov′er·a·bly,** *adv.*
—**Syn. 1.** detect, espy, descry, discern, ascertain, unearth, ferret out, notice. DISCOVER, INVENT, ORIGINATE suggest bringing to light something previously unknown. To DISCOVER may be to find something that had previously been in existence but had hitherto been unknown: *to discover a new continent, a planet, electricity;* it may also refer to devising a new use for something already known: *to discover how to make synthetic rubber.* To INVENT is to make or create something new, esp. something ingeniously devised to perform mechanical operations: *to invent a device for detecting radioactivity.* To ORIGINATE is to begin something new, esp. new ideas, methods, etc.: *to originate a religious or political movement, the use of deep-freezing units.* See **learn.**

discov′ered check′, *Chess.* a check that is effected by moving an intervening piece from the line of attack of a queen, rook, or bishop.

dis·cov·er·er (di skuv′ər ər), *n.* **1.** a person who discovers. **2.** (*cap.*) *U.S.* a cylindrical earth satellite, usually launched by a Thor-Agena or Atlas-Agena booster with a smaller engine (**Hustler**) as sustainer, to carry out military and scientific experiments: it carries a capsule that is released from the satellite in orbit, reenters the earth's atmosphere, and is recovered. [ME < OF *descovreur.* See DISCOVER, ER[1]]

dis·cov·ert (dis kuv′ərt), *adj. Law.* (of a woman) not covert; not under the protection of a husband. [DIS-[1] + COVERT]

dis·cov·er·ture (dis kuv′ər chər), *n. Law.* the state of being discovert; freedom from coverture. [DISCOVERT + -URE]

dis·cov·er·y (di skuv′ə rē), *n., pl.* **-er·ies.** **1.** the act or an instance of discovering. **2.** something discovered. **3.** *Law.* compulsory disclosure, as of facts or documents. [DISCOVER + -Y[3]]

Discov′ery Day′. See **Columbus Day.**

Discov′ery In′let, an inlet of the Ross Sea, Antarctica.

discov′ery proce′dure, *Ling.* any vigorous method by the application of which a grammar might be constructed from a corpus of utterances in a language; an algorithm leading from data to a formulation.

dis·cre·ate (dis′krē āt′), *v.t.,* **-at·ed, -at·ing.** to reduce to nothing; annihilate. [DIS-[1] + CREATE] —**dis′cre·a′tion,** *n.*

dis·cred·it (dis kred′it), *v.t.* **1.** to injure the credit or reputation of: *an effort to discredit certain politicians.* **2.** to show to be undeserving of trust or belief; destroy confidence in: *Later research discredited earlier theories.* **3.** to give no credence to; disbelieve: *There was good reason to discredit the witness.* —*n.* **4.** loss or lack of belief or confidence; disbelief; distrust: *His theories met with general*

discredit. **5.** loss or lack of repute or esteem; disrepute. **6.** something that damages a good reputation: *This behavior will be a discredit to your good name.* [DIS-[1] + CREDIT]
—Syn. 1. disparage.

dis·cred·it·a·ble (dis kred′i tə bəl), *adj.* bringing, capable of bringing, or liable to bring discredit; disgraceful. [DISCREDIT + -ABLE] **—dis·cred′it·a·bil′i·ty,** *n.* **—dis·cred′it·a·bly,** *adv.*

dis·creet (di skrēt′), *adj.* **1.** judicious in one's conduct or speech, esp. with regard to maintaining silence about something of a delicate nature; prudent; circumspect. **2.** showing prudence and circumspection: *a discreet silence.* [ME *discret* < OF < ML *discrēt(us),* L: separated (ptp. of *discernere;* see DISCERN), equiv. to *dis-* DIS-[1] + *crē-* separate, distinguish (sp. var. of *cernere*) + *-t-* ptp. suffix] **—dis·creet′ly,** *adv.* **—dis·creet′ness,** *n.*
—Syn. 1. considerate. See **careful. —Ant. 1.** indiscreet.

dis·crep·an·cy (di skrep′ən sē), *n., pl.* **-cies. 1.** the state or quality of being discrepant; difference; inconsistency: *a discrepancy between two versions of a story.* **2.** an instance of difference or inconsistency: *There are obvious discrepancies between what you practice and what you preach.* Also, **dis·crep′ance.** [< L *discrepantia,* equiv. to *discrepant-* (see DISCREPANT) + *-ia;* see -ANCY]
—Syn. 1. incongruity, disagreement, discordance, contrariety, variance. See **difference. 2.** variation. **—Ant. 1.** consistency.

dis·crep·ant (di skrep′ənt), *adj.* differing; disagreeing; discordant; inconsistent: *discrepant accounts.* [ME < L *discrepant-* (s. of *discrepāns*), prp. of *discrepāre* to sound discordant, equiv. to *dis-* DIS-[1] + *crepāre* to crack, creak; see -ANT] **—dis·crep′ant·ly,** *adv.*

dis·crete (di skrēt′), *adj.* **1.** detached from others; separate; distinct: *six discrete parts.* **2.** consisting of or characterized by distinct or individual parts; discontinuous. **3.** *Math.* (of a topology or topological space) having the property that every subset is an open set. Cf. **trivial** (def. 4). [ME < L *discrēt(us)* separated; see DISCREET] **—dis·crete′ly,** *adv.* **—dis·crete′ness,** *n.*

dis·cre·tion (di skresh′ən), *n.* **1.** the power or right to decide or act according to one's own judgment; freedom of judgment or choice: *It is entirely in my discretion whether I will go or stay.* **2.** quality of being discreet; discernment of what is judicious or expedient, esp. with reference to one's own actions or speech; prudence: *Throwing all discretion to the winds, he blurted out the truth.* **3. at discretion,** at one's option or pleasure: *They were allowed to work overtime at discretion.* [ME *discrecioun* < LL *discrētiōn-* (s. of *discrētiō*). See DISCREET, -ION]

dis·cre·tion·al (di skresh′ə nəl), *adj.* discretionary. [DISCRETION + -AL[1]] **—dis·cre′tion·al·ly,** *adv.*

dis·cre·tion·ar·y (di skresh′ə ner′ē), *adj.* subject or left to one's own discretion. [DISCRETION + -ARY] **—dis·cre′tion·ar′i·ly,** *adv.*

dis·crim·i·nant (di skrim′ə nənt), *n.* *Math.* a relatively simple expression that determines some of the properties, as the nature of the roots, of a given equation or function. [< L *discrīminant-* (s. of *discrīmināns*) separating (prp. of *discrīmināre*), equiv. to *discrīmin-,* s. of *discrīmen* (*dis-* DIS-[1] + *crīmin-,* perf. s. of *cernere* to distinguish) + *-ant-* -ANT] **—dis·crim·i·nan·tal** (dis krim′ə nan′təl), *adj.*

dis·crim·i·nate (*v.* di skrim′ə nāt′; *adj.* di skrim′ə nit), *v.,* **-nat·ed, -nat·ing,** *adj.* **—v.i. 1.** to make a distinction in favor of or against a person or thing on the basis of the group, class, or category to which the person or thing belongs, rather than according to actual merit: *He discriminates against foreigners. He discriminates in favor of his relatives.* **2.** to note or observe a difference; distinguish accurately: *to discriminate between things.* **—v.t. 3.** to make or constitute a distinction in or between; differentiate: *a mark that discriminates the original from the copy.* **4.** to note or distinguish as different: *He can discriminate minute variations in tone.* **—adj. 5.** marked by discrimination; making nice distinctions: *Discriminate people choose carefully.* [< L *discrīmināt(us)* separated, ptp. of *discrīmināre.* See DISCRIMINANT, -ATE[1]] **—dis·crim′i·nate·ly,** *adv.*
—Syn. 3. See **distinguish.**

dis·crim·i·nat·ing (di skrim′ə nā′ting), *adj.* **1.** differentiating; analytical. **2.** noting differences or distinctions with nicety; possessing discrimination: *a discriminating interpreter of events.* **3.** having excellent taste or judgment: *a discriminating interior designer.* **4.** differential, as a tariff. **5.** possessing distinctive features; capable of being differentiated; discriminative. [DISCRIMINATE + -ING[2]] **—dis·crim′i·nat′ing·ly,** *adv.*

dis·crim·i·na·tion (di skrim′ə nā′shən), *n.* **1.** the act or an instance of discriminating. **2.** the resulting state. **3.** treatment or consideration of, or making a distinction in favor of or against, a person or thing based on the group, class, or category to which that person or thing belongs rather than on individual merit: *racial and religious intolerance and discrimination.* **4.** the power of making fine distinctions; discriminating judgment: *She chose her colors with great discrimination.* **5.** *Archaic.* something that serves to differentiate. [< L *discrīminātiōn-* (s. of *discrīminātiō*) a distinguishing. See DISCRIMINATE, -ION] **—dis·crim′i·na′tion·al,** *adj.*

dis·crim·i·na·tive (di skrim′ə nā′tiv, -nə tiv), *adj.* **1.** distinctive; constituting a difference; characteristic: *the discriminative features of men.* **2.** making distinctions; discriminating. **3.** reflecting preferential treatment; differential: *discriminative tariff.* Also, **dis·crim·i·na·to·ry** (di skrim′ə nə tôr′ē, -tōr′ē). [DISCRIMINATE + -IVE] **—dis·crim′i·na′tive·ly,** *adv.*

dis·crim·i·na·tor (di skrim′ə nā′tər), *n.* **1.** one who or that which discriminates. **2.** *Electronics.* a circuit in which the output is a function of some variation of an input signal from a fixed characteristic. [< LL; see DISCRIMINATE, -OR[2]]

dis·crown (dis kroun′), *v.t.* to deprive of a crown; depose. [DIS-[1] + CROWN]

dis·cur·sion (di skûr′shən), *n.* **1.** an instance of discursive writing, speech, etc.; a wandering or logically unconnected statement. **2.** the quality or characteristic of ranging from topic to topic; irrelevance; discursiveness. **3.** the process or procedure of rigorous formal analysis or demonstration, as distinguished from immediate or intuitive formulation. [< LL *discursiōn-* (s. of *discursiō*) a running to and fro. See DISCOURSE, -ION]

dis·cur·sive (di skûr′siv), *adj.* **1.** passing aimlessly from one subject to another; digressive; rambling. **2.** proceeding by reasoning or argument; not intuitive. [< ML *discursīv(us).* See DISCOURSE, -IVE] **—dis·cur′sive·ly,** *adv.* **—dis·cur′sive·ness,** *n.*

Discus

dis·cus (dis′kəs), *n., pl.* **dis·cus·es, dis·ci** (dis′ī). **1.** a circular wooden disk having a metal rim and thicker in the center than at the edge, for throwing for distance in athletic competition. **2.** the sport of throwing this disk for distance. [< L < Gk *dískos* a quoit, discus, disk, deriv. of *dikeîn* to throw]

dis·cuss (di skus′), *v.t.* **1.** to consider or examine by argument, comment, etc.; talk over or write about; debate: *to discuss the proposed law on taxes.* **2.** to consume (food or drink) enthusiastically: *They discussed a bottle of excellent wine.* **3.** *Civil Law.* **a.** to collect a debt from (the person primarily liable) before proceeding against the person secondarily liable. **b.** to execute against the movable property of (a debtor) before proceeding against his immovable property, as land. **4.** *Obs.* to make known; reveal. [ME *discuss(en)* < L *discuss(us)* struck asunder, shaken, scattered, ptp. of *discutere,* equiv. to *dis-* DIS-[1] + *-cutere* (comb. form of *quatere* to shake, strike)] **—dis·cuss′er,** *n.* **—dis·cuss′i·ble, dis·cuss′a·ble,** *adj.*
—Syn. 1. reason, deliberate. See **argue.**

dis·cus·sant (di skus′ənt), *n.* a person who participates in a formal discussion or symposium. [DISCUSS + -ANT]

dis·cus·sion (di skush′ən), *n.* the act or an instance of discussing; consideration or examination by argument, comment, etc.; debate. [ME < OF *discucion* < LL *discussiōn-* (s. of *discussiō*) inquiry, examination, L: a shaking. See DISCUSS, -ION] **—dis·cus′sion·al,** *adj.*

Dis′cus Throw′er, The, discobolus (def. 2).

dis·cu·ti·ent (di skyōō′shē ənt), *n.* *Pharm.* an agent that causes the resolution of tumors, swellings, or the like. [< L *discutient-* (s. of *discutiēns*) shattering, scattering, prp. of *discutere* to DISCUSS; see -ENT]

dis·dain (dis dān′), *v.t.* **1.** to look upon or treat with contempt; despise; scorn. **2.** to think unworthy of notice, performance, etc.; consider beneath oneself: *to disdain to reply to an insult.* **—n. 3.** a feeling of contempt for anything regarded as unworthy; haughty contempt; scorn. [ME *disdain(en)* < OF *desdeign(ier).* See DIS-[1], DEIGN]
—Syn. 1. contemn, spurn. **3.** contemptuousness, haughtiness, arrogance, superciliousness, contumely. See **contempt. —Ant. 1.** accept. **3.** admiration.

dis·dain·ful (dis dān′fəl), *adj.* full of or showing disdain; scornful. [DISDAIN + -FUL] **—dis·dain′ful·ly,** *adv.* **—dis·dain′ful·ness,** *n.*
—Syn. contemptuous, haughty, supercilious, contumelious.

dis·ease (di zēz′), *n., v.,* **-eased, -eas·ing. —n. 1.** *Pathol.* a condition of an organ, part, structure, or system of the body in which there is incorrect function resulting from the effect of heredity, infection, diet, or environment; illness; sickness; ailment. **2.** any abnormal condition in a plant that interferes with its normal, vital physiological processes, caused by pathogenic microorganisms, parasites, unfavorable environmental, genetic, or nutritional factors, etc. **3.** any deranged or depraved condition, as of the mind, society, etc.: *Excessive melancholy is a disease.* **4.** decomposition of a material under special circumstances: *tin disease.* **—v.t. 5.** to affect with disease; make ill. [ME *disese* < OF *desaise,* equiv. to *des-* DIS-[1] + *aise* EASE] **—dis·eas′ed·ly,** *adv.* **—dis·eas′ed·ness,** *n.*
—Syn. 1. morbidity, complaint, derangement, distemper, indisposition, infirmity. DISEASE, AFFECTION, DISORDER, MALADY imply a deviation of the body, or an organ of it, from health or normality. DISEASE and MALADY apply to organic deviations involving structural change. A DISEASE is a serious, active, prolonged, and deep-rooted condition. A MALADY is a lingering, chronic disease, usually painful and often fatal. An AFFECTION is a seriously abnormal state of body or mind, esp. one that interferes with their functions. A DISORDER is usually a physical or mental derangement, frequently a slight or transitory one. **—Ant. 1.** health. **5.** cure.

dis·eased (di zēzd′), *adj.* having or affected with disease. [ME *disesed.* See DISEASE, -ED[2]]

di·se·gno (dē se′nyô), *n.* *Italian.* drawing or design: used during the 16th and 17th centuries to designate the formal discipline required for the representation of the ideal form of an object in the visual arts, esp. as expressed in the linear structure of a work of art.

dis·em·bar·go (dis′em bär′gō), *v.t.,* **-goed, -go·ing.** to remove an embargo from. [DIS-[1] + EMBARGO]

dis·em·bark (dis′em bärk′), *v.t., v.i.* to put or go on shore from a ship; land. [< MF *desembarqu(er),* equiv. to *des-* DIS-[1] + *embarquer* to EMBARK] **—dis·em·bar·ka·tion** (dis em′bär kā′shən), **dis′em·bark′ment,** *n.*

dis·em·bar·rass (dis′em bar′əs), *v.t.* **1.** to free from embarrassment. **2.** to relieve; rid. **3.** to disentangle or extricate from something troublesome, embarrassing, or the like. [DIS-[1] + EMBARRASS] **—dis′em·bar′rass·ment,** *n.*

dis·em·bod·y (dis′em bod′ē), *v.t.,* **-bod·ied, -bod·y·ing.** to divest (a soul, spirit, etc.) of a body. [DIS-[1] + EMBODY] **—dis′em·bod′i·ment,** *n.*

dis·em·bogue (dis′em bōg′), *v.,* **-bogued, -bogu·ing. —v.i. 1.** to discharge contents by pouring forth. **2.** to discharge water, as at the mouth of a stream: *a river that disembogues into the ocean.* **3.** *Phys. Geog.* debouch (def. 2). **—v.t. 4.** to discharge; cast forth. [< Sp *desemboc(ar),* equiv. to *des-* DIS-[1] + *embocar* to enter by the mouth (*en-* in (< L *in-* IN-[2] + *boc(a)* mouth (< L *bucca* + *-ar* inf. suffix)] **—dis′em·bogue′ment,** *n.*

dis·em·bos·om (dis′em bŏŏz′əm, -bōō′zəm), *v.t.* **1.** to reveal; divulge. **2.** to unburden (oneself) of a secret. [DIS-[1] + EMBOSOM]

dis·em·bow·el (dis′em bou′əl), *v.t.,* **-eled, -el·ing** or (*esp. Brit.*) **-elled, -el·ling.** to remove the bowels or entrails from; eviscerate. [DIS-[1] + EMBOWEL] **—dis′em·bow′el·ment,** *n.*

dis·em·broil (dis′em broil′), *v.t.* to free from embroilment, entanglement, or confusion. [DIS-[1] + EMBROIL]

dis·en·a·ble (dis′en ā′bəl), *v.t.,* **-bled, -bling.** to deprive of ability; make unable; prevent. [DIS-[1] + ENABLE]

dis·en·chant (dis′en chant′, -chänt′), *v.t.* to deprive of or to free from enchantment; disillusion: *The harshness of everyday reality disenchanted him of his idealistic hopes.* [< MF *desenchant(er),* equiv. to *des-* DIS-[1] + *enchanter* to ENCHANT] **—dis′en·chant′er,** *n.* **—dis′en·chant′ment,** *n.*

dis·en·cum·ber (dis′en kum′bər), *v.t.* to free from encumbrance; disburden. [< MF *desencombr(er),* equiv. to *des-* DIS-[1] + *encombrer* to ENCUMBER]
—Syn. disentangle, disembarrass, unburden.

dis·en·dow (dis′en dou′), *v.t.* to deprive (a church, school, etc.) of endowment. [DIS-[1] + ENDOW] **—dis′en·dow′er,** *n.* **—dis′en·dow′ment,** *n.*

dis·en·fran·chise (dis′en fran′chīz), *v.t.,* **-chised, -chis·ing.** to disfranchise. [DIS-[1] + ENFRANCHISE] **—dis·en·fran·chise·ment** (dis′en fran′chiz mənt), *n.*

dis·en·gage (dis′en gāj′), *v.,* **-gaged, -gag·ing. —v.t. 1.** to release from attachment or connection; loosen; unfasten: *to disengage a clutch.* **2.** to free from engagement, a pledge, obligation, etc.: *He accepted the invitation, but was later forced to disengage himself.* **3.** *Mil.* to break off action with (an enemy). **—v.i. 4.** to become disengaged; free oneself. [< MF *desengag(er),* equiv. to *des-* DIS-[1] + *engager* to ENGAGE] **—dis·en·gag·ed·ness** (dis′en gā′jid nis, -gājd′-), *n.*

dis·en·gage·ment (dis′en gāj′mənt), *n.* **1.** the act or process of disengaging or the state of being disengaged. **2.** freedom from obligation or occupation; leisure: *He filled his hours of disengagement with reading.* **3.** *Obstet.* (during childbirth) the emergence of the head or the presenting part of the fetus from the vulva. [DISENGAGE + -MENT]

dis·en·tail (dis′en tāl′), *v.t.* *Law.* to free (an estate) from entail. [DIS-[1] + ENTAIL] **—dis′en·tail′ment,** *n.*

dis·en·tan·gle (dis′en tang′gəl), *v.t., v.i.,* **-gled, -gling.** to free or become free from entanglement; untangle; extricate (often fol. by *from*). [DIS-[1] + ENTANGLE] **—dis′en·tan′gle·ment,** *n.* **—dis′en·tan′gler,** *n.*
—Syn. disembarrass, disencumber.

dis·en·thral (dis′en thrôl′), *v.t.,* **-thralled, -thral·ling.** disenthrall. **—dis′en·thral′ment,** *n.*

dis·en·thrall (dis′en thrôl′), *v.t.* to free from bondage; liberate: *to be disenthralled from morbid fantasies.* [DIS-[1] + ENTHRALL] **—dis′en·thrall′ment,** *n.*

dis·en·throne (dis′en thrōn′), *v.t.,* **-throned, -thron·ing.** to dethrone. [DIS-[1] + ENTHRONE] **—dis′en·throne′ment,** *n.*

dis·en·ti·tle (dis′en tīt′əl), *v.t.,* **-tled, -tling.** to deprive of title or right. [DIS-[1] + ENTITLE]

dis·en·tomb (dis′en tōōm′), *v.t.* to take from the tomb; disinter. [DIS-[1] + ENTOMB] **—dis′en·tomb′ment,** *n.*

dis·en·trance (dis′en trans′, -träns′), *v.t.,* **-tranced, -tranc·ing.** to bring out of an entranced condition; disenchant: *The necessity of making a living disentranced him from his idleness.* [DIS-[1] + ENTRANCE[2]] **—dis′en·trance′ment,** *n.*

dis·en·twine (dis′en twīn′), *v.t., v.i.,* **-twined, -twin·ing.** to bring or come out of an entwined or intertwined state; untwine. [DIS-[1] + ENTWINE]

di·sep·a·lous (dī sep′ə ləs), *adj.* *Bot.* having two sepals. [DI-[1] + -SEPALOUS]

dis·e·qui·lib·ri·um (dis ē′kwə lib′rē əm, dis′ē-), *n.* lack of equilibrium; imbalance. [DIS-[1] + EQUILIBRIUM]

dis·es·tab·lish (dis′e stab′lish), *v.t.* **1.** to deprive of the character of being established: *to disestablish the authority of an outdated moral code.* **2.** to withdraw exclusive state recognition or support from (a church). [DIS-[1] + ESTABLISH] **—dis′es·tab′lish·ment,** *n.*

dis·es·tab·lish·men·tar·i·an (dis′e stab′lish mən târ′ē ən), *n.* **1.** one who favors the separation of church and state, esp. the withdrawal of special rights, status, and support granted an established church by a state; an advocate of disestablishing a state church. **—adj. 2.** of, pertaining to, or favoring the disestablishment of a state church. [DISESTABLISHMENT + -ARIAN] **—dis′es·tab′lish·men·tar′i·an·ism,** *n.*

dis·es·teem (dis′ə stēm′), *v.t.* **1.** to hold in low regard; think unfavorably of. **—n. 2.** lack of esteem; disfavor; low regard. [DIS-[1] + ESTEEM]

di·seur (dē zûr′; *Fr.* dē zœr′), *n., pl.* **-seurs** (-zûrz′; *Fr.* -zœr′). a professional public entertainer who talks, recites, etc. [< F: lit., speaker, OF, equiv. to *dis-* (s. of *dire* < L *dīcere;* see DICTION) + *-eur* -OR[2]]

di·seuse (*Fr.* dē zœz′), *n., pl.* **-seuses** (-zœz′). a female diseur. [< F]

dis·fa·vor (dis fā′vər), *n.* **1.** unfavorable regard; displeasure; disesteem; dislike: *The minister incurred the king's disfavor.* **2.** lack of favor; state of being regarded unfavorably: *The fashions of one year are in disfavor the next.* **3.** an unkind or detrimental act: *The pianist did himself the disfavor of singing.* **—v.t. 4.** to regard or treat with disfavor. Also, *esp. Brit.,* **dis·fa′vour.** [prob. < obs. F *desfaveur,* equiv. to *des-* DIS-[1] + *faveur* FAVOR] **—dis·fa′vor·er;** *esp. Brit.,* **dis·fa′vour·er,** *n.*

dis·fea·ture (dis fē′chər), *v.t.,* **-tured, -tur·ing.** to mar the features of; disfigure. [DIS-[1] + FEATURE] **—dis·fea′ture·ment,** *n.*

dis·fig·ure (dis fig′yər), *v.t.,* **-ured, -ur·ing. 1.** to mar the appearance or beauty of; deform; deface: *Our old towns are increasingly disfigured by tasteless new buildings.* **2.** to mar the effect or excellence of: *His reputation as an able administrator is disfigured by instances of political favoritism.* [ME *disfigur(en)* < OF *desfigur(er),* equiv. to *des-* DIS-[1] + *figurer* (*figure* FIGURE + *-er* inf. suffix)] **—dis·fig′ur·er,** *n.*
—Syn. 1. spoil, blemish. See **mar. —Ant. 1.** beautify.

dis·fig·ure·ment (dis fig′yər mənt), *n.* **1.** the act or an instance of disfiguring. **2.** a disfigured condition. **3.** something that disfigures, as a scar. Also called **dis·fig′ur·a′tion.** [DISFIGURE + -MENT]

dis·for·est (dis fôr′ist, -for′-), *v.t.* *Law.* to disafforest. **—dis·for′est·a′tion,** *n.*

dis·fran·chise (dis fran′chīz), *v.t.,* **-chised, -chis·ing. 1.** to deprive (a person) of a right of citizenship, as of the right to vote. **2.** to deprive of a franchise, privilege, or right. [ME; see DIS-[1], FRANCHISE] **—dis·fran·chise·ment** (dis fran′chiz mənt), *n.*

dis·frock (dis frok′), *v.t.* *Eccles.* to unfrock. [DIS-[1] + FROCK]

dis·fur·nish (dis fûr′nish), *v.t.* to deprive of something with which a person or thing is furnished; strip. [< MF *desfourniss-,* s. of *desfournir,* equiv. to *des-* DIS-[1] + *fournir* to FURNISH] **—dis·fur′nish·ment,** *n.*

dis·gav·el (dis gav′əl), *v.t.*, **-eled, -el·ing** or (*esp. Brit.*) **-elled, -el·ling.** *Eng. Law.* to free from the tenure of gavelkind: *to disgavel an estate.* [DIS-¹ + GAVEL²]

dis·gorge (dis gôrj′), *v.*, **-gorged, -gorg·ing.** —*v.t.* **1.** to eject or throw out from the throat, mouth, or stomach; vomit forth. **2.** to surrender or yield (something, esp. something illicitly obtained). **3.** to discharge forcefully or as a result of force. —*v.i.* **4.** to eject, yield, or discharge something. [late ME < MF *desgorg(er)*, equiv. to *des-* DIS-¹ + *gorge* throat (see GORGE) + *-er* inf. suffix] —**dis·gorge′ment,** *n.* —**dis·gorg′er,** *n.*

dis·grace (dis grās′), *n.*, *v.*, **-graced, -grac·ing.** —*n.* **1.** the state of being in dishonor; ignominy; shame: *the disgrace of criminals.* **2.** a person, act, or thing that causes shame, reproach, or dishonor or is dishonorable or shameful. **3.** the state of being out of favor; exclusion from favor, confidence, or trust: *courtiers and ministers in disgrace.* —*v.t.* **4.** to bring or reflect shame or reproach upon: *to be disgraced by cowardice.* **5.** to dismiss with discredit; put out of grace or favor; treat with disfavor: *to be disgraced at court.* [< MF < OIt *disgrazia*, equiv. to *dis-* -DIS¹ + *grazia* < L *gratia*; see GRACE] —**dis·grac′er,** *n.*

—**Syn. 1.** disapproval, disapprobation, notoriety, taint. DISGRACE, DISHONOR, IGNOMINY, INFAMY imply a very low position in the opinion of others. DISGRACE implies the disfavor, with a greater or less degree of reproachful disapprobation, of others: *He brought disgrace on his family; to be in disgrace.* DISHONOR implies a stain on honor or honorable reputation; it relates esp. to the conduct of the person himself: *He preferred death to dishonor.* IGNOMINY is disgrace in which one's situation invites contempt: *the ignominy of being discovered cheating.* INFAMY is shameful notoriety, or baseness of action or character which is widely known and recognized: *The children never outlived the father's infamy.* **3.** disfavor, odium, obloquy, degradation. **4.** dishonor, defame, stain, sully, taint. **5.** humiliate, degrade, disapprove. —**Ant. 1.** honor.

dis·grace·ful (dis grās′fəl), *adj.* bringing or deserving disgrace; shameful; dishonorable; disreputable. [DISGRACE + -FUL] —**dis·grace′ful·ly,** *adv.* —**dis·grace′ful·ness,** *n.*

dis·gre·gate (dis′grə gāt′), *v.t.*, *v.i.*, **-gat·ed, -gat·ing.** to separate; disintegrate; scatter. [ME < LL *disgregāt(us)* separated (ptp. of *disgregāre*), equiv. to L *dis-* DIS-¹ + *greg(āre)* (to) assemble, collect, deriv. of *greg-* (s. of *grex*) flock, herd, crowd + *-ātus* -ATE¹] —**dis′gre·ga′tion,** *n.*

dis·grun·tle (dis grun′tᵊl), *v.t.*, **-tled, -tling.** to put into a state of sulky dissatisfaction; make discontent. [DIS-¹ + *gruntle*, freq. of GRUNT] —**dis·grun′tle·ment,** *n.*

dis·guise (dis gīz′, di skīz′), *v.*, **-guised, -guis·ing,** *n.* —*v.t.* **1.** to change the appearance or guise of so as to conceal identity or mislead, as by means of deceptive garb: *The king was disguised as a peasant.* **2.** to conceal or cover up the real state or character of by a counterfeit form or appearance; misrepresent: *to disguise one's intentions.* —*n.* **3.** that which disguises; something that serves or is intended for concealment of identity, character, or quality; a deceptive covering, condition, manner, etc.: *Noble words can be the disguise of base intentions.* **4.** the make-up, mask, or costume of an entertainer: *a clown's disguise.* **5.** the act of disguising: *to speak without disguise.* **6.** the state of being disguised: *The gods appeared in disguise to men. His illness proved to be a blessing in disguise.* [ME *disg(u)ise(n)* < OF *desguis(er)*, equiv. to *des-* DIS-¹ + *guise* GUISE + *-er* inf.] —**dis·guis′a·ble,** *adj.* —**dis·guis′ed·ly,** *adv.* —**dis·guis′ed·ness,** *n.* —**dis·guis′er,** *n.*
—**Syn. 2.** cloak, mask.

dis·gust (dis gust′, di skust′), *v.t.* **1.** to cause nausea or loathing in. **2.** to offend the good taste, moral sense, etc., of; cause aversion or impatient dissatisfaction in: *Your vacillations disgust me.* —*n.* **3.** strong distaste; nausea; loathing. **4.** repugnance caused by something offensive; strong aversion; impatient dissatisfaction: *He left the room in disgust over their petty quarrel.* [< MF *desgoust(er)*, equiv. to *des-* DIS-¹ + *gouster* to taste, relish, deriv. of *goust* taste < L *gust(a)*; see CHOOSE] —**dis·gust′ed·ly,** *adv.* —**dis·gust′ed·ness,** *n.*
—**Syn. 1.** sicken, nauseate. **2.** repel, revolt. **4.** abhorrence, detestation, antipathy. See **dislike.** —**Ant. 1.** delight. **4.** relish.

dis·gust·ful (dis gust′fəl, di skust′-), *adj.* causing disgust; nauseous; offensive. [DISGUST + -FUL] —**dis·gust′ful·ly,** *adv.*

dis·gust·ing (dis gus′ting, di skus′-), *adj.* causing disgust; offensive to the physical, moral, or aesthetic taste. [DISGUST + -ING²] —**dis·gust′ing·ly,** *adv.* —**dis·gust′ing·ness,** *n.*
—**Syn.** loathsome, sickening, nauseous, repulsive, revolting, repugnant, abhorrent, detestable.

dish (dish), *n.* **1.** an open, more or less shallow container of pottery, glass, metal, wood, etc., used for various purposes, esp. for holding or serving food. **2.** any container used at table: *dirty dishes.* **3.** that which is served or contained in a dish: *The meal consisted of several dishes.* **4.** a particular article or preparation of food: *Rice is an inexpensive dish.* **5.** the quantity held by a dish; dishful: *a dish of applesauce.* **6.** anything like a dish in form or use. **7.** concavity or the degree of concavity, as of a wheel. **8.** *Slang.* an attractive girl or woman: *The receptionist is quite a dish.* **9.** an antenna with a dish-shaped reflector, used in transmitting or receiving television, radio, or microwave signals. —*v.t.* **10.** to put into or serve in a dish, as food: *to dish food onto plates.* **11.** to fashion like a dish; make concave. **12.** *Slang.* to defeat; frustrate; cheat. **13. dish it out,** *Informal.* to dispense abusive language, punishment or praise, enthusiastic approval, etc. **14. dish out,** *Informal.* to deal out; distribute. [ME; OE *disc*, dish, plate, bowl (akin to G *Tisch* table) < L *disc(us)* dish, DISCUS]

dis·ha·bille (dis′ə bēl′), *n.* **1.** the state of being dressed in a careless, disheveled, or disorderly style or manner; undress; negligee. **2.** a garment worn in undress. **3.** a loose morning dress. **4.** a disorderly or disorganized state of mind or way of thinking. Also, **deshabille.** [< F *déshabillé*, n. use of ptp. of *déshabiller* to undress, equiv. to *dés-* DIS-¹ + *habiller* to dress; see HABILIMENT]

dis·ha·bit·u·ate (dis′hə bich′o͞o āt′), *v.t.*, **-at·ed, -at·ing.** to cause to be no longer habituated or accustomed. [DIS-¹ + HABITUATE]

dis·hal·low (dis hal′ō), *v.t.* to profane; desecrate. [DIS-¹ + HALLOW¹]

dis·har·mo·ni·ous (dis′här mō′nē əs), *adj.* inharmonious; discordant. [DIS-¹ + HARMONIOUS]

dis·har·mo·nize (dis här′mə nīz′), *v.t.*, *v.i.*, **-nized, -niz·ing.** to make or be inharmonious. [DIS-¹ + HARMONIZE] —**dis·har·mo·nism** (dis här′mə niz′əm), *n.*

dis·har·mo·ny (dis här′mə nē), *n.*, *pl.* **-nies. 1.** lack of harmony; discord. **2.** something discordant. [DIS-¹ + HARMONY]

dish·cloth (dish′klôth′, -kloth′), *n.*, *pl.* **-cloths** (-klôthz′, -klothz′, -klôths′, -kloths′). a cloth for use in washing dishes; a dishrag. Also, *Brit.*, **dish·clout** (dish′klout′). [DISH + CLOTH]

dish′cloth gourd′, luffa (def. 1).

dish′ cross′, a metal stand having pieces sliding on four radially placed arms to support a dish.

dis·heart·en (dis här′tᵊn), *v.t.* to depress the hope, courage, or spirits of; discourage. [DIS-¹ + HEARTEN] —**dis·heart′en·er,** *n.* —**dis·heart′en·ing·ly,** *adv.* —**dis·heart′en·ment,** *n.*

dished (disht), *adj.* **1.** concave: *a dished face.* **2.** *Slang.* (no longer current) exhausted; worn out. **3.** (of a parallel pair of vehicle wheels) farther apart at the top than at the bottom. [DISH + -ED³]

dished′ keel′, *Naut.* a plate keel bent upward at the edges, as at the forefoot of a hull.

dis·her·it (dis her′it), *v.t.* to disinherit. [ME *deserit(en)* < OF *deserit(er)*, equiv. to *des-* DIS-¹ + *heriter* to INHERIT] —**dis·her′i·tor,** *n.*

di·shev·el (di shev′əl), *v.t.*, **-eled, -el·ing** or (*esp. Brit.*) **-elled, -el·ling. 1.** to let down, as hair, or wear or let hang in loose disorder, as clothing. **2.** to cause untidiness and disarray in: *The wind disheveled the papers on the desk.* [back formation from DISHEVELED] —**di·shev′el·ment,** *n.*

di·shev·eled (di shev′əld), *adj.* **1.** hanging loosely or in disorder; unkempt: *disheveled hair.* **2.** untidy; disarranged: *disheveled appearance.* Also, *esp. Brit.*, **di·shev′elled.** [ME *discheveled* < OF *deschevele*, ptp. of *descheveler* to dishevel the hair, equiv. to *des-* DIS-¹ + *chevel* hair < L *capill(us)*, dim. akin to *caput* head]

dish·ful (dish′fo͝ol), *n.*, *pl.* **-fuls.** the amount that a dish will hold. [ME; see DISH, -FUL]

dish′ gra′vy, meat juices, as from a roast, served as a gravy without seasoning or thickening. Cf. **pan gravy.**

dish′ night′, *U.S.* (formerly) a weekday night, usually held weekly, when local movie theaters distribute free dishes to all patrons as an inducement to visit the theater.

dis·hon·est (dis on′ist), *adj.* **1.** not honest; disposed to lie, cheat, or steal; not worthy of trust or belief: *a dishonest person.* **2.** proceeding from or exhibiting lack of honesty; fraudulent. [ME *dishoneste* < OF *deshoneste*, equiv. to *des-* DIS-¹ + *honeste* HONEST] —**dis·hon′est·ly,** *adv.*
—**Syn. 1.** unscrupulous, knavish, thievish, deceitful, perfidious. See **corrupt. 2.** false. —**Ant. 1, 2.** honest.

dis·hon·es·ty (dis on′i stē), *n.*, *pl.* **-ties. 1.** lack of honesty; a disposition to lie, cheat, or steal. **2.** a dishonest act; fraud. [ME *deshonestee*. See DIS-¹, HONESTY]

dis·hon·or (dis on′ər), *n.* **1.** lack or loss of honor; disgraceful or dishonest character or conduct. **2.** disgrace; ignominy; shame: *His arrest brought him to dishonor.* **3.** an indignity; insult: *to do someone a dishonor.* **4.** a cause of shame or disgrace: *He is a dishonor to his family.* **5.** *Com.* failure or refusal of the drawee or intended acceptor of a bill of exchange or note to accept it or, if it is accepted, to pay and retire it. —*v.t.* **6.** to deprive of honor; disgrace; bring reproach or shame on. **7.** *Com.* to fail or refuse to honor or pay (a draft, check, etc.). **8.** to rape or seduce. Also, *esp. Brit.*, **dis·hon′our.** [ME *dishonour* < OF *deshonor*, equiv. to *des-* DIS-¹ + *honor* HONOR] —**dis·hon′or·er,** *esp. Brit.*, **dis·hon′our·er,** *n.*

dis·hon·or·a·ble (dis on′ər ə bəl), *adj.* **1.** showing lack of honor; ignoble; base; disgraceful; shameful: *Cowardice is dishonorable.* **2.** having no honor or good repute, unprincipled; disreputable: *Only a dishonorable man will break his oath without shame.* Also, *esp. Brit.*, **dis·hon′our·a·ble.** [DIS-¹ + HONORABLE] —**dis·hon′or·a·ble·ness;** *esp. Brit.*, **dis·hon′our·a·ble·ness,** *n.* —**dis·hon′or·a·bly;** *esp. Brit.*, **dis·hon′our·a·bly,** *adv.*
—**Syn. 1.** shameless, false. **2.** infamous, unscrupulous, disgraceful, scandalous, ignominious.

dishon′orable dis′charge, *U.S. Mil.* **1.** the discharge of a person from military service for an offense more serious than one for which a bad conduct discharge is given. **2.** a certificate of such a discharge.

dish·pan (dish′pan′), *n.* a large pan in which dishes, pots, etc., are washed. [DISH + PAN¹]

dish′pan hands′, hands, esp. of a housewife, that are red and rough, as from scrubbing, frequent exposure to strong cleaning agents, etc.

dish·rag (dish′rag′), *n.* a dishcloth. [DISH + RAG¹]

dish′ top′, a circular table top upturned at the edge.

dish·tow·el (dish′tou′əl), *n.* a towel for drying dishes. [DISH + TOWEL]

dish·wash·er (dish′wosh′ər, -wô′shər), *n.* **1.** a person who washes dishes. **2.** a machine for washing dishes, kitchen utensils, etc., automatically. [DISH + WASHER]

dish·wa·ter (dish′wô′tər, -wot′ər), *n.* **1.** water in which dishes are, or have been, washed. **2. dull as dishwater,** extremely dull; boring. Also, **dull as ditchwater.** [DISH + WATER]

dis·il·lu·sion (dis′i lo͞o′zhən), *v.t.* **1.** to free from or deprive of illusion; disenchant. —*n.* **2.** a freeing or a being freed from illusion; disenchantment. [DIS-¹ + ILLUSION] —**dis′il·lu′sion·ment,** *n.* —**dis·il·lu·sive** (dis′i lo͞o′siv), *adj.*

dis·il·lu·sion·ise (dis′i lo͞o′zhə nīz′), *v.t.*, **-ised, -is·ing.** *Chiefly Brit.* disillusionize. —**dis′il·lu′sion·is′er,** *n.*

dis·il·lu·sion·ize (dis′i lo͞o′zhə nīz′), *v.t.*, **-ized, -iz·ing.** to disillusion. [DISILLUSION + -IZE] —**dis′il·lu′sion·iz′er,** *n.* **dis′il·lu′sion·ist,** *n.*

dis·im·pas·sioned (dis′im pash′ənd), *adj.* calm; dispassionate. [DIS-¹ + IMPASSIONED]

dis·im·pris·on (dis′im priz′ən), *v.t.* to release from imprisonment. [DIS-¹ + IMPRISON] —**dis′im·pris′on·ment,** *n.*

dis·in·cli·na·tion (dis in′klə nā′shən, dis′in-), *n.* the absence of inclination; aversion; distaste; unwillingness. [DIS-¹ + INCLINATION]

dis·in·cline (dis′in klīn′), *v.t.*, *v.i.*, **-clined, -clin·ing.** to make or be averse or unwilling: *Your rudeness disinclines me to grant your request.* [DIS-¹ + INCLINE]

dis·in·clined (dis′in klīnd′), *adj.* unwilling; averse. [DISINCLINE + -ED²]
—**Syn.** reluctant, loath.

dis·in·fect (dis′in fekt′), *v.t.* to cleanse (rooms, clothing, etc.) of infection; destroy disease germs in. [< MF *desinfect(er)*, equiv. to *des-* DIS-¹ + *infecter* to INFECT] —**dis′in·fec′tive,** *adj.* —**dis′in·fec′tor,** *n.*

dis·in·fect·ant (dis′in fek′tənt), *n.* **1.** any chemical agent used chiefly on inanimate objects to inhibit the growth of or destroy harmful organisms. —*adj.* **2.** serving as a disinfectant. [< F *désinfectant*, n. use of prp. of *désinfect(er)*, MF. See DISINFECT, -ANT]

dis·in·fec·tion (dis′in fek′shən), *n.* the process of disinfecting. [DISINFECT + -ION]

dis·in·fest (dis′in fest′), *v.t.* to rid of insects, rodents, etc. [DIS-¹ + INFEST] —**dis′in·fes·ta′tion,** *n.*

dis·in·flate (dis′in flāt′), *v.t.*, **-flat·ed, -flat·ing.** to reduce (the general price level) from an inflated state. [DIS-¹ + INFLATE] —**dis′in·fla′tion,** *n.*

dis·in·for·ma·tion (dis′in fər mā′shən, di sin′-), *n.* false information about a country's military, political, or economic strength and plans, publicly announced or planted in the news media of other countries to mislead or to discredit foreign intelligence agents, leaders, or institutions. [< Russ *dezinformatsiya* disinformation, used in name of department in Soviet intelligence]

dis·in·gen·u·ous (dis′in jen′yo͞o əs), *adj.* not ingenuous; lacking in frankness, candor, or sincerity; insincere: *Disingenuous persons are often betrayed by their attempts to seem candid.* [DIS-¹ + INGENUOUS] —**dis′in·gen′u·ous·ly,** *adv.* —**dis′in·gen′u·ous·ness,** *n.*

dis·in·her·it (dis′in her′it), *v.t.* **1.** *Law.* to exclude from inheritance (an heir or a next of kin). **2.** to deprive of a heritage, country, right, privilege, etc.: *the disinherited people of communist countries.* [DIS-¹ + INHERIT] —**dis′in·her′i·tance,** *n.*

dis·in·hi·bi·tion (dis in′i bish′ən, -in′hi-, dis′in-), *n.* *Psychol.* a temporary loss of inhibition caused by an outside, often unrelated, stimulus. [DIS-¹ + INHIBITION]

dis·in·hume (dis′in hyo͞om′), *v.t.*, **-humed, -hum·ing.** to disinter. [DIS-¹ + INHUME]

dis·in·te·grate (dis in′tə grāt′), *v.*, **-grat·ed, -grat·ing.** —*v.i.* **1.** to separate into component parts; break up: *The house is gradually disintegrating with age.* **2.** *Physics.* **a.** to decay. **b.** (of a nucleus) to change into one or more different nuclei after being bombarded by high energy particles, as alpha particles or gamma rays. —*v.t.* **3.** to reduce to particles, fragments, or parts; break up or destroy the cohesion of: *Rocks are disintegrated by frost and rain.* [DIS-¹ + INTEGRATE] —**dis·in·te·gra·ble** (dis in′tə grə bəl), *adj.* —**dis·in′te·gra·tive,** **dis·in·te·gra·to·ry** (dis in′tə grə tôr′ē, -tōr′ē, -grā′tə rē), *adj.* —**dis·in′te·gra′tor,** *n.*
—**Syn. 2.** See **decay.**

dis·in·te·gra·tion (dis in′tə grā′shən), *n.* **1.** the act or process of disintegrating. **2.** *Physics.* decay (def. 8). [DISINTEGRATE + -ION]

dis·in·ter (dis′in tûr′), *v.t.*, **-terred, -ter·ring. 1.** to take out of the place of interment; exhume; unearth. **2.** to bring from obscurity into view: *The actor's autobiography disinterred a past era.* [DIS-¹ + -INTER] —**dis′in·ter′ment,** *n.*

dis·in·ter·est (dis in′tər ist, -trist), *n.* **1.** absence of interest; indifference. —*v.t.* **2.** to divest of interest or concern. [DIS-¹ + INTEREST]

dis·in·ter·est·ed (dis in′tə res′tid, -tri stid), *adj.* **1.** unbiased by personal interest or advantage; not influenced by selfish motives: *a disinterested decision.* **2.** not interested; indifferent. [DIS-¹ + INTERESTED] —**dis·in′ter·est′ed·ly,** *adv.* —**dis·in′ter·est′ed·ness,** *n.*
—**Syn.** DISINTERESTED, UNINTERESTED are not properly synonyms. DISINTERESTED today stresses absence of prejudice or of selfish interests: *a disinterested report.* UNINTERESTED suggests aloofness and indifference: *completely uninterested and taking no part in proceedings.* See **fair**¹. —**Ant. 1.** partial, biased.

dis·jas·ked (dis jas′kit), *adj.* *Scot.* dilapidated; decayed; broken. Also, **dis·jas′ket, dis·jas′kit.** [perh. alter. of DEJECTED]

dis·ject (dis jekt′), *v.t.* to scatter; disperse. [< L *disject(us)*, ptp. of *disjicere*, equiv. to *dis-* DIS-¹ + *-jicere* (comb. form of *jacere* to throw); see JET¹] —**dis·jec′tion,** *n.*

dis·jec·ta mem·bra (dis jek′tä mem′brä; *Eng.* dis jek′tə mem′brə), *Latin.* scattered members; disjointed portions or parts.

dis·join (dis join′), *v.t.* **1.** to undo or prevent the junction or union of; disunite; separate. —*v.i.* **2.** to become disunited; separate. [ME *disjoin(en)* < OF *desjoind(re)* < L *disjungere*, equiv. to *dis-* DIS-¹ + *jungere* to JOIN] —**dis·join′a·ble,** *adj.*

dis·joined (dis joind′), *adj.* **1.** separated; disunited. **2.** *Entomol.* disjunct (def. 3). [DISJOIN + -ED²]

dis·joint (dis joint′), *v.t.* **1.** to separate or disconnect the joints or joinings of. **2.** to put out of order; derange. —*v.i.* **3.** to come apart. **4.** to be dislocated; be out of joint. **5.** *Math.* **a.** (of two sets) having no common elements. **b.** (of a system of sets) having the property that every pair of sets is disjoint. —*adj.* **6.** *Obs.* disjointed; out of joint. [ME *disjoint* < OF *desjoint*, ptp. of *desjoindre* to DISJOIN]

dis·joint·ed (dis join′tid), *adj.* **1.** having the joints or connections separated: *a disjointed fowl.* **2.** disconnected; incoherent: *a disjointed discourse.* **3.** *Entomol.* disjunct (def. 3). [DISJOINT + -ED²] —**dis·joint′ed·ly,** *adv.* —**dis·joint′ed·ness,** *n.*

dis·junct (dis jungkt′), *adj.* **1.** disjoined; separated. **2.** *Music.* progressing melodically by intervals larger than a second. **3.** *Entomol.* having the head, thorax, and abdomen separated by deep constrictions; disjoined; disjointed. [ME < L *disjunct(us)* separated, ptp. of *disjungere* to DISJOIN; see JUNCTION]

dis·junc·tion (dis jungk′shən), *n.* **1.** the act of disjoining or the state of being disjoined: *a disjunction between thought and action.* **2.** *Logic.* **a.** a proposition asserting either that at least one of a number of alternatives is true **(inclusive disjunction)**, or that one and only one of a number of alternatives is true **(exclusive disjunction)**. **b.** the relation between the terms of such a proposition. [late ME *disjunccioun* < L *disjunctiōn-* (s. of *disjunctiō*) separation, equiv. to *disjunct(us)* (see DISJUNCT) + *-iōn-* -ION]

dis·junc·tive (dis jungk′tiv), *adj.* **1.** serving or tending to disjoin; separating; dividing; distinguishing. **2.** *Gram.* **a.** syntactically setting two or more expressions in opposition to each other, as *but* in *poor but happy*, or expressing an alternative, as *or* in *this or that*. **b.** not syntactically dependent upon some particular expression. **3.** *Logic.* **a.** characterizing propositions which are disjunctions. **b.** (of a syllogism) containing at least one disjunctive proposition as a premise. **—n. 4.** a statement, course of action, etc., involving alternatives. **5.** *Logic.* disjunction (def. 2a). [ME < LL *disjunctīv(us)* placed in opposition, equiv. to L *disjunct(us)* (see DISJUNCT) + *-īvus* -IVE] **—dis·junc′tive·ly,** *adv.*

dis·junc·ture (dis jungk′chər), *n.* the act of disjoining or the state of being disjoined. [ME < ML *disjunctūr(a)*, equiv. to L *disjunct(us)* (see DISJUNCT) + *-ūra* -URE]

disk (disk), *n.* **1.** any thin, flat, circular plate or object. **2.** any surface that is flat and round, or seemingly so: *the disk of the sun.* **3.** a phonograph record. **4.** *Bot., Zool.* any of various roundish, flat structures or parts. **5.** See **intervertebral disk. 6.** *Bot.* (in the daisy and other composite plants) the central portion of the flower head, composed of tubular florets. **7.** *Math.* the domain bounded by a circle. **8.** *Computer Technol.* **a.** a thin, round plate of plastic or metal with magnetic recording surfaces on one or both sides, used to store and retrieve data. **b.** See **disk pack. 9.** *Archaic.* discus. **—v.t. 10.** to make (a recording) on a phonograph disk. **11.** to cultivate (soil) with a disk harrow. Also, **disc.** [< L *disc(us)* DISCUS] **—disk′like′,** *adj.*

disk′ crank′, *Mach.* a crank having the form of a disk with a crankpin mounted off center. Also called **crankdisk, crankplate.** See diag. under **crankpin.**

disk·ette (dis′ket, dis ket′), *n.* See **floppy disk.**

disk′ flow′er, *Bot.* one of a number of small tubular flowers composing the disk of certain composite plants. Also called **disk′ flo′ret.** Cf. **ray flower.**

disk′ har′row, a harrow having a number of sharp-edged, concave disks set at such an angle that as the harrow is drawn along the ground they turn the soil, pulverize it, and destroy weeds.

disk′ jock′ey, a performer who conducts a radio broadcast consisting of recorded music, informal talk, commercial announcements, etc.

dis·kog·ra·phy (di skog′rə fē), *n.* discography.

dis·ko·phile (dis′kə fīl′), *n.* discophile.

disk′ pack′, *Computer Technol.* a cylinder containing several magnetic disks that can be handled as a unit: used for data storage and retrieval.

disk′-seal tube′ (disk′sēl′), *Electronics.* See **lighthouse tube.**

disk′ wheel′, a spokeless vehicular wheel, esp. on motor cars, having a heavy circular pressed-steel disk mounted on the wheel hub and supporting the tire rim on its outer edge.

dis·like (dis līk′), *v.,* **-liked, -lik·ing,** *n.* **—v.t. 1.** to regard with displeasure, antipathy, or aversion: *I dislike working. I dislike him.* **—n. 2.** a feeling of aversion; antipathy: *a strong dislike for Bach.* [DIS-[1] + LIKE[2]] **—dis·lik′a·ble,** *adj.*
—Syn. 2. disrelish. DISLIKE, DISGUST, DISTASTE, REPUGNANCE imply antipathy toward something. DISLIKE is a general word, the strength of the feeling being indicated by the context. It expresses a positive (not necessarily strong), sometimes inherent or permanent feeling of antipathy for something: *to have a dislike for crowds, for someone, for noise.* DISGUST is a very strong word, expressing a feeling of loathing for what is offensive to the physical taste or to the feelings and sensibilities: *The taste of spoiled food fills one with disgust. He feels disgust at seeing snobbery and ostentation.* DISTASTE, though etymologically equal to disgust, is weaker; it implies a more or less settled dislike for what is naturally uncongenial or has been made so by association: *to have distaste for certain foods, for hard work, for unconventional art or music.* REPUGNANCE is a strong feeling of aversion for, and antagonism toward, something: *to feel repugnance for (or toward) low criminals, or a kind of conduct.*

dis·lo·cate (dis′lō kāt′), *v.t.,* **-cat·ed, -cat·ing. 1.** to put out of place; displace; put out of proper relative position: *The glacier dislocated great stones. The earthquake dislocated several buildings.* **2.** *Surg.* to put out of joint or out of position, as a limb or an organ. **3.** to throw out of order; derange; upset; disorder: *Frequent strikes dislocated the economy.* [< ML *dislocāt(us)* (ptp. of *dislocāre*), equiv. to L *dis-* DIS-[1] + *locātus* placed]

dis·lo·ca·tion (dis′lō kā′shən), *n.* **1.** the act or an instance of dislocating. **2.** the state of being dislocated. **3.** *Crystall.* (in a crystal lattice) a line about which there is a discontinuity in the lattice structure. [ME *dislocacioun*; see DISLOCATE, -ION]

dis·lodge (dis loj′), *v.,* **-lodged, -lodg·ing. —v.t. 1.** to remove or force out of a particular place: *to dislodge a stone with one's foot.* **2.** to drive out of a hiding place, a military position, etc. **—v.i. 3.** to go from a place of lodgment. [late ME *dislogg(en)* < OF *deslog(er),* equiv. to *des-* DIS-[1] + *loger* to LODGE] **—dis·lodg′ment;** *esp. Brit.,* **dis·lodge′ment,** *n.*

dis·loy·al (dis loi′əl), *adj.* not loyal; false to one's obligation or allegiance. [< MF *desloial* < OF *desleal,* equiv. to *des-* DIS[1] + *leal* LOYAL] **—dis·loy′al·ly,** *adv.*
—Syn. unfaithful, perfidious, traitorous, treasonable.
—Ant. constant.

dis·loy·al·ty (dis loi′əl tē), *n., pl.* **-ties. 1.** the quality of being disloyal; lack of loyalty; unfaithfulness. **2.** violation of allegiance or duty, as to a government. **3.** a disloyal act. [ME < MF *desloiauté* < OF *desleauté,* equiv. to *desleal* DISLOYAL + *-te* -TY[2]]
—Syn. 1. faithlessness, subversion. DISLOYALTY, PERFIDY, TREACHERY, TREASON imply betrayal of trust, and esp. traitorous acts against one's country or its government. DISLOYALTY applies to any violation of loyalty, whether to a person, a cause, or one's country, and whether in thought or in deeds: *to suspect disloyalty in a friend.* PERFIDY implies deliberate breaking of faith or of one's pledges and promises, on which others are relying: *It is an act of perfidy to cheat innocent persons.* TREACHERY implies being secretly traitorous but seeming friendly and loyal: *In treachery deceit is added to disloyalty.* TREASON is definitely wishing harm to one's country or government and performing overt acts to help its enemies: *Acting to aid a hostile power is treason.*
—Ant. 1. loyalty.

dis·mal (diz′məl), *adj.* **1.** causing gloom or dejection; gloomy; dreary; cheerless; melancholy: *dismal weather; dismal news.* **2.** characterized by ineptness or lack of talent, skill, training, imagination, or interest: *Our team played a dismal game.* **3.** *Obs.* **a.** disastrous; calamitous. **b.** unlucky; sinister. **—n. 4. dismals,** *Informal.* low spirits, the dumps. **5.** *Southern U.S.* a tract of swampy land along the coast. [ME < OF phrase *dis mal unlucky days, trans. of L *diēs malī*] **—dis′mal·ly,** *adv.* **—dis′mal·ness, dis·mal′i·ty,** *n.*
—Ant. 1. gay.

Dis′mal Swamp′, a swamp in SE Virginia and NE North Carolina. ab. 30 mi. long; ab. 600 sq. mi.

dis·man·tle (dis man′t^{ə}l), *v.t.,* **-tled, -tling. 1.** to deprive or strip of apparatus, furniture, equipments, defenses, etc.: *to dismantle a ship or a fortress.* **2.** to pull down; take apart; take to pieces: *They dismantled the machine and shipped it in pieces.* **3.** to divest of dress, covering, etc.: *The wind dismantled the trees of their leaves.* [< MF *desmantel(er).* See DIS-[1], MANTLE] **—dis·man′tle·ment,** *n.* **—dis·man′tler,** *n.*

dis·mast (dis mast′, -mäst′), *v.t.* to deprive (a ship) of masts; break off the masts of. [DIS-[1] + MAST[1]] **—dis·mast′ment,** *n.*

dis·may (dis mā′), *v.t.* **1.** to break down the courage of completely, as by sudden danger or trouble; dishearten thoroughly; daunt: *The surprise attack dismayed the enemy.* **2.** to surprise in such a manner as to disillusion: *She was dismayed to learn of their disloyalty.* **3.** to alarm; perturb: *The new law dismayed some of the more conservative politicians.* **—n. 4.** sudden or complete loss of courage; utter disheartenment. **5.** sudden disillusionment. **6.** agitation of mind; perturbation; alarm. [ME *dismai(en),* prob. < OF *desmai(er); cf. OF *esmaier* to dismay] **—dis·may·ed·ness** (dis mād′nis, -mā′id-), *n.*
—Syn. 1. appall, terrify, horrify, frighten, scare, intimidate, disconcert. See **discourage. 4.** consternation, terror, panic, horror, fear. **—Ant. 1.** hearten. **4.** confidence.

dis·mem·ber (dis mem′bər), *v.t.* **1.** to deprive of members or limbs; divide limb from limb: *The ogre dismembered his victims before he ate them.* **2.** to divide into parts; cut to pieces; mutilate: *The revolution dismembered the country.* [ME *dismembr(en)* < OF *desmembr(er),* equiv. to *des-* DIS-[1] + *membre* MEMBER + *-er* inf. suffix] **—dis·mem′ber·er,** *n.* **—dis·mem′ber·ment,** *n.*

dis·miss (dis mis′), *v.t.* **1.** to direct (an assembly of persons) to disperse: *She dismissed the class early.* **2.** to bid or allow (a person) to go; give permission or a request to depart. **3.** to discharge or remove, as from office or service: *to dismiss an employee.* **4.** to discard or reject: *to dismiss a suitor.* **5.** to put off or away; lay aside; esp., to put aside from consideration: *He dismissed the story as mere rumor.* **6.** to have done with (a subject) after summary treatment: *After a perfunctory discussion, he dismissed the idea.* **7.** *Law.* to put out of court, as a complaint or appeal. [ME < ML *dismiss(us)* sent away (for L *dīmissus,* ptp. of *dīmittere*), equiv. to L *dis-* DIS-[1] + *mi-* send (s. of *mittere*) + *-ss-* ptp. suffix] **—dis·miss′i·ble,** *adj.*
—Syn. 2. See **release. 3.** fire. **—Ant. 2.** recall. **3.** hire. **4.** accept.

dis·miss·al (dis mis′əl), *n.* **1.** the act or an instance of dismissing. **2.** the state of being dismissed. **3.** a spoken or written order of discharge from employment, service, enrollment, etc. Also, **dis·mis·sion** (dis mish′ən). [DISMISS + -AL[2]]

dis·mis·sive (dis mis′iv), *adj.* **1.** indicating dismissal or rejection; having the purpose or effect of dismissing, as from one's presence, from consideration, etc.: *a curt, dismissive gesture.* **2.** indicating lack of interest or approbation; scornful; disdainful. [DISMISS + -IVE]

dis·mount (dis mount′), *v.i.* **1.** to get off or alight from a horse, bicycle, etc. **—v.t. 2.** to bring or throw down, as from a horse; unhorse: *The horse twisted, bucked, kicked, and finally dismounted its rider.* **3.** to remove (a thing) from its mounting, support, setting, etc.: *to dismount a picture.* **4.** to take (a mechanism) to pieces. **—n. 5.** the act or manner of dismounting. [prob. modeled on ML *dismontāre* or F *démonter.* See DIS-[1], MOUNT[1]] **—dis·mount′a·ble,** *adj.*

dis·na·ture (dis nā′chər), *v.t.,* **-tured, -tur·ing.** to deprive (something) of its proper nature or appearance; make unnatural. [late ME < MF *desnatur(er),* equiv. to *des-* DIS-[1] + *nature* NATURE + *-er* inf. suffix]

Dis·ney (diz′nē), *n.* **Walt(er E.),** 1901–66, U.S. creator and producer of animated cartoons, motion pictures, etc.

dis·o·be·di·ence (dis′ə bē′dē əns), *n.* lack of obedience; neglect or refusal to obey. [ME < OF *desobedience,* equiv. to *des-* DIS-[1] + *obedience* OBEDIENCE]

dis·o·be·di·ent (dis′ə bē′dē ənt), *adj.* neglecting or refusing to obey; refractory. [ME < OF *desobedient,* equiv. to *des-* DIS-[1] + *obedient* OBEDIENT] **—dis′o·be′di·ent·ly,** *adv.*
—Syn. insubordinate, contumacious, defiant, unruly, rebellious, unsubmissive, uncompliant. **—Ant.** obedient.

dis·o·bey (dis′ə bā′), *v.t., v.i.* to neglect or refuse to obey. [ME *disobei(en)* < OF *desobeir,* equiv. to *des-* DIS-[1] + *obeir* to OBEY] **—dis′o·bey′er,** *n.*
—Syn. violate; defy.

dis·o·blige (dis′ə blīj′), *v.t.,* **-bliged, -blig·ing. 1.** to refuse or neglect to oblige; act contrary to the desire or convenience of; fail to accommodate. **2.** to give offense to; affront: *to be disobliged by a tactless remark.* **3.** to cause inconvenience to; incommode: *to be disobliged by an uninvited guest.* [< MF *desoblig(er),* equiv. to *des-* DIS-[1] + *obliger* to OBLIGE] **—dis′o·blig′ing·ly,** *adv.* **—dis′o·blig′ing·ness,** *n.*

dis·oc·clude (dis′ə klōōd′), *v.t.,* **-clud·ed, -clud·ing.** *Dentistry.* to grind a tooth so that it does not articulate with its antagonist during mastication. [DIS-[1] + OCCLUDE]

dis·op·er·a·tion (dis op′ə rā′shən, dis′op ə-), *n.* *Ecol.* interaction among organisms living in a limited area that is mutually harmful or disadvantageous. [DIS-[1] + OPERATION]

dis·or·der (dis ôr′dər), *n.* **1.** lack of order or regular arrangement; disarrangement; confusion: *Your papers are in disorder.* **2.** an irregularity: *a disorder in legal proceedings.* **3.** breach of order; disorderly conduct; a public disturbance. **4.** a derangement of physical or mental health or functions: *a mild stomach disorder.* **—v.t. 5.** to destroy the order or regular arrangement of; disarrange. **6.** to derange the physical or mental health or functions of. [DIS-[1] + ORDER]
—Syn. 1. disorderliness, disarray, jumble, litter, clutter. **3.** riot, turbulence. DISORDER, BRAWL, DISTURBANCE, UPROAR are disruptions or interruptions of a peaceful situation. DISORDER refers to unrest within a city or state, and to any scene in which there is confusion or fighting among individuals or groups: *The police went to the scene of the disorder.* A BRAWL is a noisy, unseemly quarrel, usually in a public place: *a tavern brawl.* A DISTURBANCE is disorder of such size as to inconvenience many people: *to cause a disturbance.* An UPROAR is a tumult, a bustle and clamor of many voices, often because of a disturbance: *a mighty uproar.* **4.** ailment, malady, illness, complaint, sickness, indisposition. See **disease. 5.** disarray, mess up, disorganize. **6.** disturb, upset, confuse.

dis·or·dered (dis ôr′dərd), *adj.* **1.** in confusion; disarranged. **2.** suffering from a physical or mental disorder: *a disordered liver.* [DISORDER + -ED[2]] **—dis·or′dered·ly,** *adv.* **—dis·or′dered·ness,** *n.*

dis·or·der·ly (dis ôr′dər lē), *adj.* **1.** characterized by disorder; irregular; untidy; confused: *a disorderly desk.* **2.** unruly; turbulent; tumultuous: *the disorderly course of a storm.* **3.** *Law.* violating or opposing constituted order; contrary to public order or morality. **—adv. 4.** without order, rule, or method; irregularly; confusedly. [DIS-[1] + ORDERLY] **—dis·or′der·li·ness,** *n.*

disor′derly con′duct, *Law.* any of various petty misdemeanors, generally including nuisances, breaches of the peace, offensive or immoral conduct in public, etc.

disor′derly house′, 1. a house of prostitution; brothel. **2.** a gambling place.

disor′derly per′son, *Law.* a person guilty of disorderly conduct.

dis·or·gan·ise (dis ôr′gə nīz′), *v.t.,* **-ised, -is·ing.** *Chiefly Brit.* disorganize. **—dis·or′gan·is′er,** *n.*

dis·or·gan·i·za·tion (dis ôr′gə ni zā′shən), *n.* **1.** a breaking up of order or system; disunion or disruption of constituent parts. **2.** the absence of organization or orderly arrangement; disarrangement; disorder. Also, *esp. Brit.,* **dis·or′gan·i·sa′tion.** [< F *désorganisation,* equiv. to *désorganis(er)* (to) DISORGANIZE + *-ation* -ATION]

dis·or·gan·ize (dis ôr′gə nīz′), *v.t.,* **-ized, -iz·ing.** to destroy the organization, systematic arrangement, or orderly connection of; throw into confusion or disorder. Also, *esp. Brit.,* **disorganise.** [< F *désorganis(er),* equiv. to *dés-* DIS-[1] + *organiser* to ORGANIZE] **—dis·or′gan·iz′er,** *n.*

dis·o·ri·ent (dis ōr′ē ent′, -ôr′-), *v.t.* **1.** to cause to lose one's way: *The strange streets disoriented him.* **2.** to confuse by removing or obscuring something that has guided a person, group, or culture, as customs, moral standards, etc.: *a society disoriented by changing values.* **3.** *Psychiatry.* to cause to lose perception of time, place, or one's personal identity. [< F *désorient(er),* equiv. to *dés-* DIS-[1] + *orienter* to ORIENT]

dis·o·ri·en·tate (dis ōr′ē ən tāt′, -ôr′-), *v.t.,* **-tat·ed. -tat·ing.** to disorient. [DIS-[1] + ORIENTATE] **—dis·o′ri·en·ta′tion,** *n.*

dis·own (dis ōn′), *v.t.* to refuse to acknowledge as belonging or pertaining to oneself; deny the ownership of or responsibility for; repudiate; renounce: *to disown one's heirs; to disown a statement.* [DIS-[1] + OWN]

dis·par·age (di spar′ij), *v.t.,* **-aged, -ag·ing. 1.** to bring reproach or discredit upon; lower the estimation of: *Your behavior will disparage the whole family.* **2.** to speak of or treat slightingly; depreciate; belittle: *Do not disparage good manners.* [ME *disparage(n)* < OF *desparag(ier)* (to) match unequally, equiv. to *des-* DIS-[1] + *parage* equality, equiv. to *par(er)* (to) equalize (< L *parāre;* see PEER[1]) + *-age* -AGE] **—dis·par′ag·er,** *n.* **—dis·par′ag·ing·ly,** *adv.*
—Syn. 2. decry, minimize.

dis·par·age·ment (di spar′ij mənt), *n.* **1.** the act of disparaging. **2.** something that causes loss of dignity or reputation. [< MF *desparagement,* equiv. to *desparag(ier)* (to) DISPARAGE + *-ment* -MENT]

dis·pa·rate (dis′pər it, di spar′-), *adj.* distinct in kind; essentially different; dissimilar; unlike: *disparate ideas.* [< L *disparāt(us)* separated (ptp. of *disparāre*), equiv. to *dis-* DIS-[1] + *par(āre)* (to) prepare (see PARE) + *-ātus* -ATE[1]] **—dis′pa·rate·ly,** *adv.* **—dis′pa·rate·ness,** *n.*
—Syn. separate, divergent, incommensurable, inconsonant.

dis·par·i·ty (di spar′i tē), *n., pl.* **-ties.** lack of similarity or equality; inequality; difference: *a disparity in age; disparity in rank.* [< MF *desparite* < LL *disparitāt-* (s. of *disparitās*), equiv. to L *dis-* DIS-[1] + LL *paritāt-* (s. of *paritās*) PARITY[1]]
—Syn. See **difference.**

dis·part (dis pärt′), *v.t., v.i.* to part asunder; separate; divide into parts. [appar. < It *dispart-,* s. of *dispartire* < L *dispartīre* to part, separate, divide, equiv. to *dis-* DIS-[1] + *partīre* to share out, deriv. of *part-* PART] **—dis·part′ment,** *n.*

dis·pas·sion (dis pash′ən), *n.* freedom from passion; state or quality of being unemotional. [DIS-[1] + PASSION]

dis·pas·sion·ate (dis pash′ə nit), *adj.* free from or unaffected by passion; devoid of personal feeling or bias; impartial; calm: *a dispassionate critic.* [DIS-[1] + PASSIONATE] **—dis·pas′sion·ate·ly,** *adv.* **—dis·pas′sion·ate·ness,** *n.*
—Syn. cool, unemotional, uninvolved; fair, just.

dis·patch (di spach′), *v.t.* **1.** to send off or away with speed, as a messenger, telegram, body of troops, etc. **2.** to dismiss (a person), as after an audience. **3.** to put to death; kill: *The spy was promptly dispatched.* **4.** to transact or dispose of (a matter) promptly or speedily. **—v.i. 5.** *Archaic.* to hasten; be quick. **—n. 6.** the sending off of a messenger, letter, etc., to a destination. **7.** act of putting to death; killing; execution. **8.** prompt or speedy transaction, as of business. **9.** expeditious performance; promptness or speed: *Proceed with all possible dispatch.* **10.** *Com.* **a.** a method of effecting a speedy delivery of goods, money, etc. **b.** a conveyance or organization for the expeditious transmission of goods, money, etc. **11.** a written message sent in haste. **12.** an official communication sent by special messenger. **13.** *Journalism.* a news account hastily transmitted by a reporter to his newspaper, wire service, or the like, or by a wire service to a newspaper or other news agency. **14. mentioned in dispatches,** *Brit.* honored by being named in official military reports for special bravery or acts of service. Also, **despatch.** [< It *dispacci(are)* (to) hasten, speed, or < Sp *despach(ar)*]

dispatch′ boat′, *Naut.* a small, fast boat used for delivering dispatches.

dispatch′ case′. See **attaché case.**

dis·patch·er (di spach′ər), *n.* **1.** a person who dispatches. **2.** a person who oversees the departure of trains, planes, buses, etc., as for a transportation company, railroad, etc. **3. dispatchers,** *Slang.* a fraudulently made pair of dice; loaded dice. Also, **despatcher.** [DISPATCH + -ER[1]]

Dis′ Pa′ter, *Class. Myth.* Dis (def. 1).

dis·pau·per (dis pô′pər), *v.t. Law.* to divest of the status of a person having the privileges of a pauper, as of public support or the right to proceed at law in forma pauperis. [DIS-[1] + PAUPER]

dis·pel (di spel′), *v.t.,* **-pelled, -pel·ling.** to drive off in various directions; scatter; disperse; dissipate: *to dispel vapors, fear, etc.* [< L *dispell(ere)* (to) drive asunder, equiv. to *dis-* DIS-[1] + *pell(ere)* (to) drive + *-e* thematic vowel + *-re* inf. suffix] —**dis·pel′la·ble,** *adj.* —**dis·pel′ler,** *n.*
—**Syn.** See **scatter.** —**Ant.** gather.

dis·pend (di spend′), *v.t. Obs.* to pay out; expend; spend. [ME *dispend(en)* < OF *despend(re)* < L *dispendere* to weigh out; see DISPENSE]

dis·pen·sa·ble (di spen′sə bəl), *adj.* **1.** capable of being dispensed with or done without; not necessary or essential. **2.** capable of being dispensed or administered: *The money is not dispensable at present.* **3.** *Rom. Cath. Ch.* capable of being remitted, as an offense or sin. [< ML *dispensābil(is)*, equiv. to L *dispens(āre)* (to) distribute by weight (see DISPENSE) + *-ābilis* -ABLE] —**dis·pen′sa·bil′i·ty, dis·pen′sa·ble·ness,** *n.*

dis·pen·sa·ry (di spen′sə rē), *n., pl.* **-ries.** **1.** a place where something is dispensed, esp. medicines. **2.** a charitable or public institution where medicines are furnished and medical advice is given gratuitously or for a small fee. [< ML *dispensāria* storeroom, equiv. to L *dispens(āre)* (to) DISPENSE + *-āria* -ARY]

dis·pen·sa·tion (dis′pən sā′shən, -pen-), *n.* **1.** the act or an instance of dispensing; distribution. **2.** that which is distributed or given out. **3.** a certain order, system, or arrangement: administration or management: *Things were managed differently under the dispensation of the last ministry.* **4.** *Theol.* **a.** the divine ordering of the affairs of the world. **b.** an appointment, arrangement, or favor, as by God. **c.** a divinely appointed order or age: *the old Mosaic, or Jewish, dispensation; the new gospel, or Christian, dispensation.* **5.** a dispensing with, doing away with, or doing without something: *Total dispensation of cigarettes can be difficult for a habitual smoker.* **6.** *Rom. Cath. Ch.* **a.** a relaxation of law in a particular case granted by a competent superior or his delegate in laws which he has the power to make and enforce: *a dispensation regarding the Lenten fast.* **b.** an official document authorizing such a relaxation of law. [ME *dispensacioun* < ML *dispensātion-* (s. of *dispensātiō*) a pardon, relaxation, LL: order, system, L: distribution, equiv. to *dispensāt(us)* (ptp. of *dispensāre* to DISPENSE; see -ATE[1]) + *-iōn-* -ION] —**dis′pen·sa′tion·al,** *adj.* —**dis·pen·sa·to·ri·ly** (di spen′sə tôr′ə lē, -tōr′-), *adv.*

dis·pen·sa·tion·al·ism (dis′pən sā′shə nəliz′əm, -pen-), *n.* the interpreting of history as a series of divine dispensations. [DISPENSATIONAL + -ISM]

dis·pen·sa·tor (dis′pən sā′tər, -pen-), *n. Archaic.* one who dispenses; distributor; administrator. [ME *dispensatour* < ML *dispensātor*, L: manager, steward, equiv. to *dispensāt(us)* (see DISPENSATION) + *-or* -OR[2]]

dis·pen·sa·to·ry (di spen′sə tôr′ē, -tōr′ē), *n., pl.* **-ries.** **1.** a book in which the composition, preparation, and uses of medicinal substances are described; a nonofficial pharmacopoeia. **2.** a dispensary. [< ML *dispensātōri(um)*, LL *dispensātōri(us)* of management, equiv. to L *dispensāt(us)* (see DISPENSATION) + *-ōrium* -ORY[2]]

dis·pense (di spens′), *v.,* **-pensed, -pens·ing,** *n.* —*v.t.* **1.** to deal out; distribute: *to dispense wisdom.* **2.** to administer: *to dispense the law without bias.* **3.** *Pharm.* to put up and distribute (medicine), esp. on prescription. **4.** *Rom. Cath. Ch.* to grant dispensation. —*v.i.* **5.** to grant dispensation. **6. dispense with, a.** to do without; forgo: *to dispense with preliminaries.* **b.** to do away with; rid of. **c.** to grant exemption from a law or promise. —*n.* **7.** *Obs.* expenditure. [ME *dispens(en)* < ML *dispens(āre)* to pardon, exempt, LL: (to) distribute (by weight), freq. of *dispendere* to weigh out, equiv. to *dis-* DIS-[1] + *pend-* weigh]
—**Syn. 1.** apportion, allot, dole. See **distribute.**

dis·pens·er (di spen′sər), *n.* **1.** one who or that which dispenses. **2.** a container, package, device, or vending machine for holding and dispensing something in small amounts, as facial tissue, paper cups, candy, etc. [ME; see DISPENSE, -ER[1]]

dis·pen·si·ble (di spen′sə bəl), *adj. Obs.* dispensable.

dis·peo·ple (dis pē′pəl), *v.t.,* **-pled, -pling.** to deprive of people; depopulate. [DIS-[1] + PEOPLE] —**dis·peo′ple·ment,** *n.* —**dis·peo′pler,** *n.*

di·sper·mous (dī spûr′məs), *adj. Bot.* having two seeds. [DI-[1] + SPERMOUS]

di·sper·my (dī′spûr′mē), *n.* the fertilization of an ovum by two spermatozoa. [DI-[1] + *-spermy* < Gk *-spermia.* See -SPERM, -Y[3]] —**di·sper′mic,** *adj.*

dis·per·sal (di spûr′səl), *n.* dispersion (def. 1). [DISPERSE + -AL[2]]

dis·per·sant (di spûr′sənt), *n.* **1.** that which disperses. **2.** *Physical Chem.* any admixture to a dispersion capable of maintaining the dispersed particles in suspension. [DISPERSE + -ANT]

dis·perse (di spûrs′), *v.,* **-persed, -pers·ing,** *adj.* —*v.t.* **1.** to drive or send off in various directions; scatter: *to disperse a crowd.* **2.** to spread abroad; disseminate: *to disperse knowledge.* **3.** to dispel; cause to vanish: *The wind dispersed the fog.* **4.** *Chem.* to cause (particles) to separate uniformly throughout a solid, liquid, or gas. **5.** *Optics.* to subject (light) to dispersion. —*v.i.* **6.** to separate and move apart in different directions without order or regularity; become scattered: *The crowd dispersed after the speech.* **7.** to be dispelled; be scattered out of sight; vanish: *The smoke dispersed into the sky.* —*adj.* **8.** *Physical Chem.* noting that phase of a dispersion consisting of the dispersed particles. [< L *dispers(us)* (ptp. of *dispergere*), equiv. to *di-* DI-[2] + *sper-* scatter (s. of *-spergere*, comb. form of *spargere* to SPARGE) + *-sus* ptp. suffix; r. ME *disparse* < MF < L] —**dis·pers′ed·ly,** *adv.* —**dis·pers′er,** *n.* —**dis·pers′i·bil′i·ty,** *n.* —**dis·pers′i·ble,** *adj.*
—**Syn. 1.** See **scatter. 2.** sow, broadcast. **7.** disappear, evanesce. —**Ant. 1.** combine, collect.

dispersed′ el′ement, *Geol.* any widely distributed element in rocks, minerals, etc., occurring as a minor, nonconcentrated constituent with another element or elements.

disperse′ dye′, *Chem.* any of the class of slightly water-soluble dyes dispersed in aqueous solution for dyeing synthetic textile fibers.

dis·per·sion (di spûr′zhən, -shən), *n.* **1.** Also, **dispersal.** the act, state, or an instance of dispersing; state of being dispersed. **2.** *Optics.* **a.** the variation of the index of refraction of a transparent substance, as glass, with the wavelength of light, the index of refraction increasing as the wavelength decreases. **b.** the separation of white or compound light into its respective colors, as in the formation of a spectrum by a prism. **3.** *Statistics.* the scattering of values of a variable around the mean or median of a distribution. **4.** *Mil.* a scattered pattern of hits of bombs dropped under identical conditions, or of shots fired from the same gun with the same firing data. **5.** *Chem.* a system of dispersed particles suspended in a solid, liquid, or gas. **6.** (*cap.*) Diaspora (def. 1). [< L *dispersiōn-* (s. of *dispersiō*), equiv. to *dispers(us)* (see DISPERSE) + *-iōn-* -ION]

dis·per·sive (di spûr′siv), *adj.* serving or tending to disperse. [DISPERSE + -IVE] —**dis·per′sive·ly,** *adv.* —**dis·per′sive·ness,** *n.*

disper′sive pow′er, *Optics.* a measure of the ability of a substance to disperse light, equal to the quotient of the difference in refractive indices of the substance for two representative wavelengths divided by the difference of the refractive index for an intermediate wavelength and 1. Cf. **Abbe number.**

dis·per·soid (di spûr′soid), *n. Physical Chem.* the suspended particles in a dispersion. [DISPERSE + -OID]

di·sphe·noid (dī sfē′noid), *n.* bisphenoid.

dis·pir·it (di spir′it), *v.t.* to deprive of spirit, hope, enthusiasm, etc.; depress; discourage; dishearten. [DI-[2] + SPIRIT]

dis·pir·it·ed (di spir′i tid), *adj.* discouraged; dejected; disheartened; gloomy. [DISPIRIT + -ED[2]] —**dis·pir′it·ed·ly,** *adv.* —**dis·pir′it·ed·ness,** *n.*

dis·pit·e·ous (dis pit′ē əs), *adj. Archaic.* malicious; cruel; pitiless. [var. of *despiteous*, with *dis-* (< L) for *des-* (< F)] —**dis·pit′e·ous·ly,** *adv.* —**dis·pit′e·ous·ness,** *n.*

dis·place (dis plās′), *v.t.,* **-placed, -plac·ing.** **1.** to compel (a person or persons) to leave home, country, etc. **2.** to move or put out of the usual or proper place. **3.** to take the place of; replace; supplant: *Fiction displaces fact.* **4.** to remove from a position, office, or dignity. **5.** *Obs.* to make oneself rid of; banish from oneself. [DIS-[1] + PLACE, perh. modeled on MF *desplacer*] —**dis·place′a·ble,** *adj.*
—**Syn. 2.** relocate. DISPLACE, MISPLACE mean to put something in a different place from where it should be. To DISPLACE now often means to shift something solid and comparatively immovable, more or less permanently from its place: *The flood displaced houses from their foundations.* To MISPLACE is to put an object, usually an easily portable one, in a wrong place, so that it is difficult to find: *Papers belonging in the safe were misplaced and temporarily lost.* **4.** depose, oust, dismiss.

displaced′ per′son, a person driven or expelled from his homeland by war or tyranny. *Abbr.:* DP, D.P.

dis·place·ment (dis plās′mənt), *n.* **1.** the act of displacing. **2.** the state of being displaced or the amount or degree to which something is displaced. **3.** *Physics.* **a.** the displacing in space of one mass by another. **b.** the weight or the volume of fluid displaced by a floating or submerged body. Cf. **Archimedes' principle. c.** the linear or angular distance in a given direction between a body or point and a reference position. **4.** *Mach.* the volume of the space through which a piston travels. **5.** the distance of an oscillating body from its central position or point of equilibrium at any given moment. **6.** *Geol.* the offset of rocks caused by movement along a fault. **7.** *Psychoanal.* the transfer of an emotion from the object about which it was originally experienced to another object or a person. [DISPLACE + -MENT]

displace′ment hull′, *Naut.* a hull that displaces a significant volume of water when under way. Cf. **planing hull.**

displace′ment ton′, *Naut.* a unit for measuring the displacement of a vessel, equal to a long ton of 2240 pounds or 35 cubic feet of sea water.

displace′ment ton′nage, *Naut.* the number of long tons of water displaced by a vessel, light or load displacement being specified.

dis·plac·er (dis plā′sər), *n.* **1.** one who or that which displaces. **2.** plum (def. 10). [DISPLACE + -ER[1]]

dis·plant (dis plant′, -plänt′), *v.t. Obs.* **1.** to dislodge. **2.** to transplant. [DIS-[1] + PLANT, modeled on MF *desplanter*]

dis·play (di splā′), *v.t.* **1.** to show; exhibit; make visible: *to display a sign.* **2.** to reveal; betray: *to display fear.* **3.** to unfold; open out; spread out: *to display a sail.* **4.** to show ostentatiously; flaunt: *to display a new automobile.* **5.** *Print.* to give special prominence to (words, captions, etc.) by choice and arrangement of type. —*n.* **6.** the act or an instance of displaying; exhibition: *a display of courage.* **7.** an ostentatious show: *a vulgar display of wealth.* **8.** *Print.* **a.** the giving of prominence to particular words, sentences, etc., by the choice and arrangement of types and position, as in an advertisement, headline, or news story. **b.** printed matter thus displayed. **9.** an arrangement, as of merchandise, art objects, flowers, etc., designed to please the eye, advertise, induce buyers, etc. **10.** the visual representation of the output of an electronic device, as the screen of a cathode ray tube. [ME *desplay(en)* < AF *desplei(er)* < LL *displicāre* to unfold. See DIS-[1], PLICATE] —**dis·play′er,** *n.*
—**Syn. 1.** DISPLAY, EVINCE, EXHIBIT, MANIFEST mean to show or bring to the attention of another or others. To DISPLAY is literally to spread something out so that it may be most completely and favorably seen: *to display goods for sale.* To EXHIBIT is to put something in plain view and usually in a favorable position for particular observation: *to exhibit the best flowers at a special show.* They may both be used of showing (off) one's qualities or feelings: *He displayed his wit, his ignorance. He exhibited great surprise.* To EVINCE and to MANIFEST have only this latter reference, MANIFEST being the stronger word: *to evince or manifest surprise, interest, sympathy.* **4.** flourish, parade, air. **6.** See **show.** —**Ant. 1.** conceal.

display′ ad′, a printed advertisement, in a newspaper or other publication, using any and typically several of the available attention-getting devices, as magnitude, display type, illustrations, white space, and color, and usually not classified with other advertisements in the issue (distinguished from *classified ad*).

display′ ad′vertising, display ads taken collectively.

dis·played (di splād′), *adj. Heraldry.* (of a bird) represented with wings and legs spread: *an eagle displayed.* [ME; see DISPLAY, -ED[2]]

display′ type′, *Print.* type larger than body type used in headings, advertisements, etc. Cf. **body type.**

dis·please (dis plēz′), *v.,* **-pleased, -pleas·ing.** —*v.t.* **1.** to incur the dissatisfaction, dislike, or disapproval of; offend; annoy: *His reply displeased the king.* —*v.i.* **2.** to be unpleasant; cause displeasure: *Bad weather displeases.* [ME *desplese(n)* < AF, MF *desplais(ir)* < VL **displacēre.* See DIS-[1], PLEASE] —**dis·pleas′ing·ly,** *adv.* —**dis·pleas′ing·ness,** *n.*

dis·pleas·ure (dis plezh′ər), *n., v.,* **-ured, -ur·ing.** —*n.* **1.** dissatisfaction, disapproval, or annoyance. **2.** *Archaic.* discomfort, uneasiness, or pain. **3.** *Archaic.* a cause of offense, annoyance, or injury. —*v.t.* **4.** *Archaic.* to displease. [DIS-[1] + PLEASURE; r. late ME *desplaisir* < MF (n. use of inf.); see DISPLEASE] —**dis·pleas′ure·a·ble,** *adj.* —**dis·pleas′ure·a·bly,** *adv.*
—**Syn. 1.** distaste, dislike; indignation, vexation. See **dissatisfaction.** —**Ant. 1.** pleasure.

dis·plode (dis plōd′), *v.t., v.i.,* **-plod·ed, -plod·ing.** *Archaic.* to explode. [< L *displōd(ere)*, equiv. to *dis-* DIS-[1] + *plaudere* to make a sudden loud noise]

dis·plume (dis plo͞om′), *v.t.,* **-plumed, -plum·ing.** **1.** to strip of plumes; deplume. **2.** to strip of honors. [DIS-[1] + PLUME; cf. DEPLUME]

dis·plu·vi·ate (dis plo͞o′vē āt′), *adj.* (of the atrium of an ancient Roman house) having roofs sloping downward and outward from a central opening. [< L *displuviāta*, equiv. to *dis-* DIS-[1] + *pluvi(a)* rain + *-āta*, fem. of *-ātus* -ATE[1]]

dis·port (di spôrt′, -spōrt′), *v.t.* **1.** to divert or amuse (oneself). **2.** to display (oneself) in a sportive manner: *Wearing a bikini, she danced and disported herself on the beach.* —*v.i.* **3.** to divert oneself; sport. —*n.* **4.** diversion; amusement; play; sport. [ME *disporte, desporte* < AF *desport(er)*, equiv. to *des-* DIS-[1] + *porter* to PORT[5]]

dis·pos·a·ble (di spō′zə bəl), *adj.* **1.** designed for or capable of being disposed of: *a disposable paper plate.* **2.** free for use; available: *Every disposable vehicle was sent.* [DISPOSE + -ABLE] —**dis·pos′a·bil′i·ty, dis·pos′a·ble·ness,** *n.*

dispos′able in′come, **1.** the part of a person's income remaining after deducting personal income taxes. **2.** (in national income accounting) the total disposable income of all consumers.

dis·pos·al[1] (di spō′zəl), *n.* **1.** the act or an instance of disposing; arrangement: *the disposal of the troops.* **2.** a disposing of or getting rid of something: *the disposal of waste material.* **3.** a disposing of, as by gift or sale; bestowal or assignment: *She left no will to indicate the disposal of her possessions.* **4.** power or right to dispose of a thing; control: *left at his disposal.* [DISPOSE + -AL[2]]

dis·pos·al[2] (di spō′zəl), *n.* an electrical device in the drain of a sink, for grinding up garbage to be washed down the drain. Also called **disposer.** [short for *garbage-disposal;* see DISPOSAL[1]]

dis·pose (di spōz′), *v.,* **-posed, -pos·ing,** *n.* —*v.t.* **1.** to put in a particular or the proper order or arrangement; adjust by arranging the parts. **2.** to put in a particular or suitable place: *The lamp was disposed on a table nearby.* **3.** to give a tendency or inclination to; incline: *His temperament disposed him to dislike many people.* **4.** to make fit or ready; prepare: *Your words of cheer dispose me for the task.* —*v.i.* **5.** to arrange or decide matters: *to do as God disposes.* **6.** *Obs.* to make terms. **7. dispose of, a.** to deal with conclusively; settle. **b.** to get rid of; discard. **c.** to transfer or give away, as by gift or sale. **d.** to do away with; destroy: *We will have to dispose of the mice in our attic.* —*n.* **8.** *Archaic.* disposition; habit. **9.** *Obs.* arrangement; regulation; disposal. [ME < MF *dispos(er)*, equiv. to L *dis-* DIS-[1] + *pos-* perf. s. of *pōnere* to place] —**dis·pos′ing·ly,** *adv.*

dis·posed (di spōzd′), *adj.* having a certain inclination or disposition; inclined (usually fol. by *to* or an infinitive): *a man disposed to like others.* [DISPOSE + -ED[2]] —**dis·pos′ed·ly,** *adv.* —**dis·pos′ed·ness,** *n.*

dis·pos·er (di spō′zər), *n.* **1.** one who or that which disposes. **2.** disposal[2]. [DISPOSE + -ER[1]]

dis·po·si·tion (dis′pə zish′ən), *n.* **1.** the predominant or prevailing tendency of one's spirits; mental outlook or mood: *a girl with a pleasant disposition.* **2.** state of mind regarding something; inclination: *a disposition to gamble.* **3.** physical inclination or tendency: *the disposition of ice to melt when heated.* **4.** arrangement or placing, as of troops or buildings. **5.** final settlement of a matter. **6.** bestowal, as by gift or sale. **7.** power to dispose of a thing; control: *funds at one's disposition.* **8.** *Archaic.* regulation; appointment; dispensation: *the disposition of God.* [< L *dispositiōn-* (s. of *dispositiō*), equiv. to *disposit(us)* (ptp. of *dispōnere* to

distribute; *dispos-* (see DISPOSE) + *-itus* ptp. suffix) + *-iōn-* -ION; r. ME *disposicioun* < AF] —**dis′po·si′tion·al,** *adj.*
—**Syn. 1.** nature, character, humor. DISPOSITION, TEMPER, TEMPERAMENT refer to the aspects and habits of mind which one displays over a length of time. DISPOSITION is the natural or prevailing aspect of one's mind as shown in behavior and in relationships with others: *a happy disposition; a selfish disposition.* TEMPER sometimes denotes the essential quality of one's nature: *a temper of iron;* usually it has to do with propensity toward anger: *an even temper; a quick or hot temper.* TEMPERAMENT suggests the delicate balance of one's emotions, the disturbance of which determines one's moods: *an artistic temperament; an unstable temperament.* **2.** bent, tendency, predisposition, proclivity. **4.** order, grouping, location, placement. **5.** outcome, result. **7.** management, control, direction. —**Ant. 2.** unwillingness.

dis·pos·sess (dis′pə zes′), *v.t.* **1.** to put (a person) out of possession, esp. of real property; oust. **2.** to banish. [DIS-[1] + POSSESS; r. ME *dispossessen,* equiv. to DIS-[1] + MF *posseder* < L *possidēre* (*por-* (?) + *sedēre* to SIT)] —**dis′pos·ses′sion,** *n.* —**dis′pos·ses′sor,** *n.* —**dis·pos·ses·so·ry** (dis′pə zes′ə rē), *adj.*
—**Syn.** See **strip**[1].

dis·pos·sessed (dis′pə zest′), *adj.* **1.** evicted, as from a dwelling, land, etc.; ousted. **2.** without property, status, etc., as wandering or displaced persons; rootless; disfranchised. **3.** having suffered the loss of expectations, prospects, relationships, etc.; disinherited; disaffiliated; alienated: *Modern man is spiritually dispossessed.* [DISPOSSESS + -ED[2]]

dis·po·sure (di spō′zhər), *n. Archaic.* disposal; disposition. [DISPOSE + -URE]

dis·praise (dis prāz′), *v.,* **-praised, -prais·ing,** *n.* —*v.t.* **1.** to speak of as undeserving or unworthy; censure; disparage. —*n.* **2.** the act or an instance of dispraising; censure. [ME < OF *despreis(i)er,* equiv. to *des-* DIS-[1] + *preis(i)er* to PRAISE] —**dis·prais′er,** *n.* —**dis·prais′ing·ly,** *adv.*

dis·pread (di spred′), *v.t., v.i.,* **-pread, -pread·ing.** *Archaic.* to spread out; extend. Also, **disspread.** [DI-[2] + SPREAD] —**dis·pread′er,** *n.*

dis·prize (dis prīz′), *v.t.,* **-prized, -priz·ing.** *Archaic.* to hold in small esteem; disdain. [ME *disprise(n)* < MF *despris(er),* late var. of *despreis(i)er* to DISPRAISE]

dis·proof (dis prōōf′), *n.* **1.** the act of disproving. **2.** proof to the contrary; refutation. [DIS-[1] + -PROOF]

dis·pro·por·tion (dis′prə pōr′shən, -pôr′-), *n.* **1.** lack of proportion; lack of proper relationship in size, number, etc.: *architectural disproportions.* **2.** something out of proportion: *the disproportions of an awkward body.* —*v.t.* **3.** to make disproportionate. [DIS-[1] + PROPORTION] —**dis′pro·por′tion·a·ble,** *adj.* —**dis′pro·por′tion·a·ble·ness,** *n.* —**dis′pro·por′tion·a·bly,** *adv.*

dis·pro·por·tion·al (dis′prə pōr′shə nəl, -pôr′-), *adj.* not in proportion; disproportionate. [DIS-[1] + PROPORTIONAL] —**dis′pro·por′tion·al′i·ty, dis′pro·por′tion·al·ness,** *n.* —**dis′pro·por′tion·al·ly,** *adv.*

dis·pro·por·tion·ate (dis′prə pōr′shə nit, -pôr′-), *adj.* not proportionate; out of proportion, as in size, number, etc: *The door is disproportionate to the windows.* [DIS-[1] + PROPORTIONATE] —**dis′pro·por′tion·ate·ly,** *adv.* —**dis′pro·por′tion·ate·ness,** *n.*

dis·pro·por·tion·a·tion (dis′prə pōr′shə nā′shən, -pôr′-), *n. Chem.* the simultaneous oxidation and reduction of a substance reacting with itself, to form two dissimilar molecules, as $2C_2H_4 \rightarrow C_2H_6 + C_2H_2$. [DISPROPORTION + -ATION]

dis·prove (dis prōōv′), *v.t.,* **-proved, -prov·ing.** to prove (an assertion, claim, etc.) to be false or wrong; refute; invalidate: *I disproved his claim.* [ME *disprove(n)* < OF *desprov(er),* equiv. to *des-* DIS-[1] + *prover* to PROVE] —**dis·prov′a·ble,** *adj.* —**dis·prov′er,** *n.*

dis·put·a·ble (di spyōō′tə bəl, dis′pyŏŏ tə bəl), *adj.* capable of being disputed; debatable; questionable. [< L *disputābil(is),* equiv. to *disput-* (see DISPUTE) + *-ābilis* -ABLE] —**dis·put′a·bil′i·ty, dis·put′a·ble·ness,** *n.* —**dis·put′a·bly,** *adv.*

dis·pu·tant (di spyōōt′ᵊnt), *n.* **1.** a person who disputes; debater. —*adj.* **2.** engaged in dispute; disputing. [< L *disputant-* (s. of *disputāns,* prp. of *disputāre*), equiv. to *disput-* (see DISPUTE) + *-ant-* -ANT]

dis·pu·ta·tion (dis′pyŏŏ tā′shən), *n.* **1.** the act of disputing or debating; verbal controversy; discussion or debate. **2.** an academic exercise consisting of the arguing of a thesis between its maintainer and his opponents. **3.** *Obs.* conversation. [< L *disputātiōn-* (s. of *disputātiō*), equiv. to *disputāt(us)* (ptp. of *disputāre; disput-* (see DISPUTE) + *-ātus* -ATE[1]) + *-iōn-* -ION; r. ME *desputisoun* < OF]

dis·pu·ta·tious (dis′pyŏŏ tā′shəs), *adj.* given to disputation; argumentative; contentious: *disputatious litigants.* Also, **dis·put·a·tive** (di spyōō′tə tiv). [DISPUTATI(ON) + -OUS] —**dis′pu·ta′tious·ly,** *adv.* —**dis′pu·ta′tious·ness,** *n.*

dis·pute (di spyōōt′), *v.,* **-put·ed, -put·ing,** *n.* —*v.i.* **1.** to engage in argument or debate. **2.** to argue vehemently; wrangle or quarrel. —*v.t.* **3.** to argue or debate about; discuss. **4.** to argue against; call in question: *to dispute a proposal.* **5.** to quarrel or fight about; contest. **6.** to strive against; oppose: *to dispute an advance.* —*n.* **7.** a debate or controversy. **8.** a wrangling argument; quarrel. [ME < LL *disput(āre)* (to) dispute (in L: to discuss), equiv. to *dis-* DIS-[1] + *putāre* to argue] —**dis·pute′less,** *adj.* —**dis·put′er,** *n.*
—**Syn. 2.** bicker, squabble. **8.** disputation, altercation, wrangle, bickering, squabble. See **argument.**

dis·qual·i·fi·ca·tion (dis kwol′ə fə kā′shən), *n.* **1.** the act or an instance of disqualifying. **2.** the state of being disqualified. **3.** something that disqualifies. [*disqualific-,* comb. form of DISQUALIFY + -ATION]

dis·qual·i·fy (dis kwol′ə fī′), *v.t.,* **-fied, -fy·ing.** **1.** to deprive of qualification or fitness; render unfit; incapacitate. **2.** to deprive of legal or other rights or privileges; declare ineligible or unqualified. **3.** *Sports.* to deprive of the right to participate in or win a contest because of a violation of the rules. [DIS-[1] + QUALIFY] —**dis·qual′i·fi′a·ble,** *adj.*

dis·qui·et (dis kwī′it), *n.* **1.** lack of calm, peace, or ease; anxiety; uneasiness. —*v.t.* **2.** to deprive of quiet, rest, or peace; disturb; make uneasy: *The news disquieted him.* —*adj.* **3.** *Archaic.* uneasy; disquieted. [DIS-[1] + QUIET] —**dis·qui′et·ed·ly,** *adv.* —**dis·qui′et·ed·ness,** *n.* —**dis·qui′et·ly,** *adv.*

dis·qui·et·ing (dis kwī′i ting), *adj.* causing anxiety or uneasiness; disturbing: *disquieting news.* [DISQUIET + -ING[2]] —**dis·qui′et·ing·ly,** *adv.*

dis·qui·e·tude (dis kwī′i tōōd′, -tyōōd′), *n.* the state of disquiet; uneasiness. [DIS-[1] + QUIETUDE]

dis·qui·si·tion (dis′kwi zish′ən), *n.* a formal discourse or treatise in which a subject is examined and discussed; dissertation. [< L *disquīsītiōn-* (s. of *disquīsītiō*), equiv. to *disquīsīt(us)* (ptp. of *disquīrere; dis-* DIS-[1] + *quaerere* to seek, ask), equiv. to *disquīs-* investigate + *-ītus* ptp. suffix + *-iōn-* -ION] —**dis′qui·si′tion·al,** *adj.*

Dis·rae·li (diz rā′lē), *n.* **Benjamin, 1st Earl of Beaconsfield** ("*Dizzy*"), 1804–81, British statesman and novelist: prime minister 1867, 1874–80.

dis·rate (dis rāt′), *v.t.,* **-rat·ed, -rat·ing.** to reduce to a lower rating, as a petty officer, or a noncommissioned officer of the marines. [DIS-[1] + RATE[1]]

dis·re·gard (dis′ri gärd′), *v.t.* **1.** to pay no attention to; leave out of consideration: *Disregard the footnotes.* **2.** to treat without due regard, respect, or attentiveness; slight: *to disregard an invitation.* —*n.* **3.** lack of regard or attention; neglect. **4.** lack of due or respectful regard. [DIS-[1] + REGARD] —**dis′re·gard′er,** *n.*
—**Syn. 1.** ignore. **2.** insult. See **slight. 3.** inattention, oversight. **4.** disrespect, slight, indifference. —**Ant. 1.** notice.

dis·re·gard·ful (dis′ri gärd′fəl), *adj.* neglectful; careless. [DIS-[1] + REGARDFUL] —**dis′re·gard′ful·ly,** *adv.* —**dis′re·gard′ful·ness,** *n.*

dis·rel·ish (dis rel′ish), *v.t.* **1.** to have a distaste for; dislike. —*n.* **2.** distaste; dislike. [DIS-[1] + RELISH]

dis·re·mem·ber (dis′ri mem′bər), *v.t. Chiefly Southern U.S.* to fail to remember; forget. [DIS-[1] + REMEMBER]

dis·re·pair (dis′ri pâr′), *n.* the condition of needing repair; an impaired or neglected state. [DIS-[1] + REPAIR]

dis·rep·u·ta·ble (dis rep′yə tə bəl), *adj.* **1.** not reputable; having a bad reputation. **2.** discreditable; dishonorable. [DIS-[1] + REPUTABLE] —**dis·rep′u·ta·bil′i·ty, dis·rep′u·ta·ble·ness,** *n.* —**dis·rep′u·ta·bly,** *adv.*

dis·rep·u·ta·tion (dis rep′yə tā′shən), *n. Archaic.* disrepute. [DIS-[1] + REPUTATION]

dis·re·pute (dis′ri pyōōt′), *n.* bad repute; discredit; low regard (usually prec. by *in* or *into*): *Isolationism is in disrepute. These early theories have fallen into disrepute.* [DIS-[1] + REPUTE]
—**Syn.** disfavor, disgrace.

dis·re·spect (dis′ri spekt′), *n.* **1.** lack of respect; discourtesy; rudeness. —*v.t.* **2.** to regard or treat without respect; regard or treat with contempt or rudeness. [DIS-[1] + RESPECT]

dis·re·spect·a·ble (dis′ri spek′tə bəl), *adj.* not respectable. [DIS-[1] + RESPECTABLE] —**dis′re·spect′a·bil′i·ty,** *n.*

dis·re·spect·ful (dis′ri spekt′fəl), *adj.* characterized by, having, or showing disrespect; lacking courtesy or esteem: *a disrespectful remark about teachers.* [DIS-[1] + RESPECTFUL] —**dis′re·spect′ful·ly,** *adv.* —**dis′re·spect′ful·ness,** *n.*
—**Syn.** discourteous, uncivil, impolite, rude, impudent, impertinent, irreverent.

dis·robe (dis rōb′), *v.t., v.i.,* **-robed, -rob·ing.** to undress. [DIS-[1] + ROBE; cf. MF *desrober*] —**dis·robe′ment,** *n.* —**dis·rob′er,** *n.*

dis·root (dis rōōt′, -rŏŏt′), *v.t.* to uproot; dislodge. [DIS-[1] + ROOT[1]]

dis·rupt (dis rupt′), *v.t.* **1.** to cause disorder or turmoil in: *The news disrupted their conference.* **2.** to destroy, usually temporarily, the normal continuance or unity of; interrupt: *Telephone service was disrupted for hours.* **3.** to break apart: *to disrupt a connection.* —*adj.* **4.** disrupted; broken apart. [< L *disrupt(us)* (var. of *dīruptus,* ptp. of *dīrumpere; di-* DI-[2] + *rumpere* to break), equiv. to *dis-* DIS-[1] + *rup-* break + *-tus* ptp. suffix] —**dis·rupt′er, dis·rup′tor,** *n.*

dis·rup·tion (dis rup′shən), *n.* **1.** forcible separation or division into parts: *the disruption of rock.* **2.** a disrupted condition: *The state was in disruption.* [< L *disruptiōn-* (s. of *disruptiō*), equiv. to *disrupt-* (see DISRUPT) + *-iōn-* -ION]

dis·rup·tive (dis rup′tiv), *adj.* causing, tending to cause, or caused by disruption; disrupting: *the disruptive effect of their rioting.* [DISRUPT + -IVE] —**dis·rup′tive·ly,** *adv.*

disrup′tive dis′charge, *Elect.* the sudden, large increase in current through an insulating medium resulting from complete failure of the medium under electrostatic stress.

dis·rup·ture (dis rup′chər), *n.* interruption; disruption. [DISRUPT + -URE]

dis·sat·is·fac·tion (dis′sat is fak′shən, dis sat′-), *n.* the state or attitude of not being satisfied; discontent; displeasure. [DIS-[1] + SATISFACTION]
—**Syn.** disappointment, disapproval, uneasiness. DISSATISFACTION, DISCONTENT, DISPLEASURE imply a sense of dislike for, or unhappiness in, one's surroundings and a wish for other conditions. DISSATISFACTION results from contemplating what falls short of one's wishes or expectations and is usually only temporary: *dissatisfaction with results of an afternoon's work.* DISCONTENT is a sense of lack and a general feeling of uneasy dislike for the conditions of one's life, which colors one's entire outlook: *feeling a continual vague discontent.* DISPLEASURE, a more positive word, suggests a certain amount of anger as well as dissatisfaction: *displeasure at being kept waiting.* —**Ant.** satisfaction.

dis·sat·is·fac·to·ry (dis′sat is fak′tə rē, dis sat′-), *adj.* causing dissatisfaction; unsatisfactory: *dissatisfactory service.* [DIS-[1] + SATISFACTORY] —**dis′sat·is·fac′to·ri·ness,** *n.*

dis·sat·is·fied (dis sat′is fīd′), *adj.* **1.** not satisfied or pleased; discontented. **2.** showing dissatisfaction: *a dissatisfied look.* [DISSATISFY + -ED[2]] —**dis·sat′is·fied′ly,** *adv.* —**dis·sat′is·fied′ness,** *n.*

dis·sat·is·fy (dis sat′is fī′), *v.t.,* **-fied, -fy·ing.** to cause to be displeased, esp. by failing to provide something expected or desired. [DIS-[1] + SATISFY]

dis·seat (dis sēt′), *v.t.* to unseat. [DIS-[1] + SEAT]

dis·sect (di sekt′, dī-), *v.t.* **1.** to cut apart (an animal body, plant, etc.) to examine the structure, relation of parts, or the like. **2.** to examine minutely part by part; analyze: *to dissect an idea.* [< L *dissect(us)* (ptp. of *dissecāre* to cut up), equiv. to *dis-* DIS-[1] + *sec-* cut + *-tus* ptp. suffix] —**dis·sec′ti·ble,** *adj.* —**dis·sec′tor,** *n.*
—**Syn. 1, 2.** anatomize.

dis·sect·ed (di sek′tid, dī-), *adj.* **1.** *Bot.* deeply cut into numerous segments, as a leaf. **2.** *Phys. Geog.* separated, by erosion, into many closely spaced valleys, as a plateau. [DISSECT + -ED[2]]

dis·sec·tion (di sek′shən, dī-), *n.* **1.** the act of dissecting. **2.** something that has been dissected. **3.** a detailed, part-by-part analysis. [< L *dissectiōn-* (s. of *dissectiō*), equiv. to *dissect-* DISSECT + *-iōn-* -ION]

dissec′tor tube′. See **image dissector.**

dis·seise (dis sēz′), *v.t.,* **-seised, -seis·ing.** *Chiefly Brit.* disseize. —**dis·sei′sor,** *n.*

dis·seize (dis sēz′), *v.t.,* **-seized, -seiz·ing.** *Law.* to deprive (a person) of seizin, or of the possession, of a freehold interest in land, esp. wrongfully or by force; oust. [ME *disseise* < AF *disseis(ir),* equiv. to *dis-* DIS-[1] + *seisir* to SEIZE] —**dis·sei′zor,** *n.*

dis·sei·zee (dis′sē zē′, dis sē zē′), *n.* a person who is disseized. Also, *esp. Brit.,* **dis′sei·see′.** [DISSEIZE + -EE]

dis·sei·zin (dis sē′zin), *n. Law.* **1.** the act of disseizing. **2.** the state of being disseized. Also, *esp. Brit.,* **dis·sei′sin.** [ME *disseisine* < AF. See DIS-[1], SEIZIN]

dis·sem·blance[1] (di sem′bləns), *n.* dissimilarity; unlikeness. [late ME < MF *dessemblance.* See DIS-[1], SEMBLANCE]

dis·sem·blance[2] (di sem′bləns), *n.* dissembling; dissimulation. [DISSEMBLE + -ANCE]

dis·sem·ble (di sem′bəl), *v.,* **-bled, -bling.** —*v.t.* **1.** to give a false appearance to; conceal the real nature of: *to dissemble one's incompetence with industry.* **2.** to put on the appearance of; feign: *to dissemble innocence.* **3.** *Archaic.* to let pass unnoticed; ignore. —*v.i.* **4.** to conceal one's true motives, thoughts, etc., under some pretense; speak or act hypocritically. [alter. (? by assoc. with obs. *semble* to RESEMBLE) of ME *dissimulen* < L *dissimulāre.* See DIS-[1], SIMULATE] —**dis·sem′bler,** *n.* —**dis·sem′bling·ly,** *adv.*

dis·sem·i·nate (di sem′ə nāt′), *v.t.,* **-nat·ed, -nat·ing.** to scatter or spread widely, as though sowing seed; promulgate extensively; broadcast; disperse: *to disseminate Christianity among primitive peoples.* [< L *dissēmināt(us)* (ptp. of *dissēmināre; dis-* DIS-[1] + *sēmināre* to sow), equiv. to *dis-* + *sēmin-* (s. of *sēmen* seed) + *-ātus* -ATE[1]] —**dis·sem′i·na′tion,** *n.* —**dis·sem′i·native,** *adj.* —**dis·sem′i·na′tor,** *n.*

dis·sem·i·nule (di sem′ə nyōōl′), *n. Bot.* any propagative part of a plant, as a bud, seed, or spore, that is capable of disseminating the plant. [prob. DISSEMIN(ATE) + -ULE]

dis·sen·sion (di sen′shən), *n.* **1.** strong disagreement; discord; a contention or quarrel. **2.** difference in sentiment or opinion; disagreement. [< L *dissēnsiōn-* (s. of *dissēnsiō*), equiv. to *dissēns(us)* (ptp. of *dissentīre; dis-sent-* (see DISSENT) + *-tus* ptp. suffix) + *-iōn-* -ION; r. ME *dissencioun* < AF]
—**Syn. 1.** strife. See **quarrel**[1].

dis·sent (di sent′), *v.i.* **1.** to differ in sentiment or opinion, esp. from the majority; disagree; withhold assent (often fol. by *from*). **2.** to differ in religious opinion; reject the doctrines or authority of an established church. —*n.* **3.** difference in sentiment or opinion. **4.** separation from an established church, esp. the Church of England; nonconformity. [ME *dissent(en)* < L *dissent(īre),* equiv. to *dis-* DIS-[1] + *sentīre* to feel; cf. ASSENT, CONSENT] —**dis·sent′ing·ly,** *adv.*
—**Syn. 3.** disagreement, dissatisfaction, opposition. DISSENT, DISSIDENCE mean disagreement with the majority opinion. DISSENT may express either withholding of agreement or open disagreement. DISSENTERS may withdraw from a group, but if so, they merely go their own way. DISSIDENCE, formerly much the same as DISSENT, has come to suggest not only strong dissatisfaction but a determined opposition. If DISSIDENTS withdraw, they continue actively to oppose the original group.

dis·sent·er (di sen′tər), *n.* **1.** a person who dissents, as from an established church; nonconformist. **2.** (*sometimes cap.*) an English Protestant who dissents from the Church of England. [DISSENT + -ER[1]]

dis·sen·tient (di sen′shənt), *adj.* **1.** dissenting, esp. from the opinion of the majority. —*n.* **2.** one who dissents. [< L *dissentient-* (s. of *dissentiēns,* prp. of *dissentīre*), equiv. to *dissenti-* (see DISSENT) + *-ent-* -ENT] —**dis·sen′tience, dis·sen′tien·cy,** *n.* —**dis·sen′tient·ly,** *adv.*

dissent′ing opin′ion, *Law.* (in appellate courts) an opinion filed by a judge who disagrees with the majority decision of a case and states his own views of it.

dis·sen·tious (di sen′shəs), *adj.* contentious; quarrelsome. [DISSENT + -IOUS]

dis·sep·i·ment (di sep′ə mənt), *n.* **1.** a partition or septum. **2.** *Bot.* one of the partitions formed within ovaries and fruits by the coherence of the sides of the constituent carpels. [< L *dissaepīment(um),* equiv. to *dis-* DIS-[1] + *saepīmentum* hedge (*saepī(re)* (to) fence + *-mentum* -MENT)] —**dis·sep′i·men′tal,** *adj.*

D, Dissepiment

dis·sert (di sûrt′), *v.i. Archaic.* to discourse on a subject. [< L *dissert(āre)* to set forth at length (freq. of *disserere* to arrange in order), equiv. to *dis-* DIS-[1] + *ser-* put together + freq. *-t-* + *-āre* inf. suffix]

dis·ser·tate (dis′ər tāt′), *v.i.,* **-tat·ed, -tat·ing.** to discuss a subject fully and learnedly; discourse. [prob. back formation from DISSERTATION] —**dis′ser·ta′tor,** *n.*

dis·ser·ta·tion (dis′ər tā′shən), *n.* **1.** a written essay, treatise, or thesis, esp. one written by a candidate for the degree of Doctor of Philosophy. **2.** any formal discourse in speech or writing. [< L *dissertātiōn-* (s. of *dissertātiō*), equiv. to *dissertāt(us)* (ptp. of *dissertāre; dissert-* (see DISSERT) + *-ātus* -ATE[1]) + *-iōn-* -ION] —**dis′ser·ta′tion·al,** *adj.* —**dis′ser·ta′tion·ist,** *n.*

dis·serve (dis sûrv′), *v.t.*, **-served, -serv·ing.** to serve harmfully or injuriously. [DIS-¹ + SERVE]

dis·serv·ice (dis sûr′vis), *n.* harmful or injurious service; an ill turn. [DIS-¹ + SERVICE]

dis·sev·er (di sev′ər), *v.t.* **1.** to sever; separate: *A quarrel dissevered the two friends.* **2.** to divide into parts: *to dissever a chicken.* —*v.i.* **3.** to part; separate. [ME *des(s)ever(en)* < OF *dessevr(er)* < LL *dissēparāre*, equiv. to L *dis-* DIS-¹ + *sēparāre* to SEPARATE] —**dis·sev′er·ance, dis·sev′er·ment, dis·sev′er·a′tion,** *n.*

dis·si·dence (dis′i dəns), *n.* disagreement. [< L *dissidentia*, equiv. to *dissid-* (see DISSIDENT) + *-entia* -ENCE]
—**Syn.** See **dissent.**

dis·si·dent (dis′i dənt), *adj.* **1.** disagreeing or dissenting, as in opinion or attitude. —*n.* **2.** a person who dissents. [< L *dissident-* (s. of *dissidēns*, prp. of *dissidēre* to sit apart), equiv. to *dis-* DIS-¹ + *sid-* (var. of *sed-* SIT) + *-ēnt-* -ENT] —**dis′si·dent·ly,** *adv.*

dis·sil·i·ent (di sil′ē ənt), *adj.* flying or bursting apart; bursting open. [< L *dissilient-* (s. of *dissiliēns*, prp. of *dissilīre* to leap apart), equiv. to *dis-* DIS-¹ + *sili-* (var. of *sali-* leap; see SALLY) + *-ent-* -ENT] —**dis·sil′i·en·cy, dis·sil′i·ence,** *n.*

dis·sim·i·lar (di sim′ə lər, dis sim′-), *adj.* not similar; unlike; different. [DIS-¹ + SIMILAR] —**dis·sim′i·lar·ly,** *adv.*

dis·sim·i·lar·i·ty (di sim′ə lar′i tē), *n., pl.* **-ties.** **1.** unlikeness; difference. **2.** a point of difference: *There are dissimilarities in our outlooks.* [DIS-¹ + SIMILARITY]

dis·sim·i·late (di sim′ə lāt′), *v.t.*, **-lat·ed, -lat·ing.** *Phonet.* to modify by dissimilation. [DIS-¹ + (AS)SIMILATE] —**dis·sim′i·la′tive,** *adj.* —**dis·sim·i·la·to·ry** (di sim′ə lə tôr′ē, -tōr′ē), *adj.*

dis·sim·i·la·tion (di sim′ə lā′shən), *n.* **1.** the act of making or becoming unlike. **2.** *Phonet.* the phonetic process by which a speech sound becomes different from or less like a neighboring sound, as *pilgrim* (pil′grim) from Latin *peregrīnus* (peʀ′e grē′nŏŏs), and *purple* (pûr′pəl) from Old English *purpure* (pŏŏʀ′pŏŏ ʀe), or disappears entirely because of a like sound in another syllable, as in the pronunciation (guv′ə nər) for *governor*. Cf. **assimilation** (def. 5). **3.** *Biol.* catabolism. [DIS-¹ + (AS)SIMILATION]

dis·si·mil·i·tude (dis′si mil′i to͞od′, -tyo͞od′), *n.* **1.** unlikeness; difference; dissimilarity. **2.** a point of difference; dissimilarity. [< L *dissimilitūdō*, equiv. to *dis-* DIS-¹ + *similitūdō* SIMILITUDE]

dis·sim·u·late (di sim′yə lāt′), *v.*, **-lat·ed, -lat·ing.** —*v.t.* **1.** to disguise or conceal under a false appearance; dissemble. —*v.i.* **2.** to conceal one's true motives, thoughts, etc., under some pretense; speak or act hypocritically. [< L *dissimulāt(us)* (ptp. of *dissimulāre* to feign). See DIS-¹, SIMULATE] —**dis·sim′u·la′tive,** *adj.* —**dis·sim′u·la′tor,** *n.*

dis·sim·u·la·tion (di sim′yə lā′shən), *n.* **1.** the act of dissimulating; feigning; hypocrisy. **2.** *Psychiatry.* the ability or the tendency to appear mentally normal when actually suffering from disorder: a characteristic of the paranoiac. [< L *dissimulātiōn-* (s. of *dissimulātiō* a feigning); see DIS-¹, SIMULATION; r. ME *dissimulacioun* < AF]

dis·si·pate (dis′ə pāt′), *v.*, **-pat·ed, -pat·ing.** —*v.t.* **1.** to scatter in various directions; disperse; dispel. **2.** to scatter or spread wastefully or extravagantly; squander: *to dissipate one's creative energy.* —*v.i.* **3.** to become scattered or dispersed; be dispelled; disintegrate: *The sun shone and the mist dissipated.* **4.** to indulge in extravagant, intemperate, or dissolute pleasure: *They dissipate all night and sleep all day.* [< L *dissipāt(us)* (ptp. of *dissipāre* to scatter), equiv. to *dis-* DIS-¹ + *sip-* (root of *sipāre* to throw) + *-ātus* -ATE¹] —**dis′si·pat′er, dis′si·pa′tor,** *n.* —**dis′si·pa′tive,** *adj.* —**dis·si·pa·tiv·i·ty** (dis′ə pə tiv′i tē), *n.*
—**Syn. 1.** See **scatter. 3.** disappear, vanish. —**Ant. 1, 3.** unite.

dis·si·pat·ed (dis′ə pā′tid), *adj.* indulging in or characterized by excessive devotion to pleasure; intemperate; dissolute. [DISSIPATE + -ED²] —**dis′si·pa′ted·ly,** *adv.* —**dis′si·pa′ted·ness,** *n.*

dis·si·pa·tion (dis′ə pā′shən), *n.* **1.** the act of dissipating. **2.** the state of being dissipated; dispersion; disintegration. **3.** a wasting by misuse: *the dissipation of a fortune.* **4.** mental distraction; amusement; diversion. **5.** dissolute mode of living, esp. excessive drinking of liquor; intemperance. **6.** *Physics, Mech.* a process in which energy is used or lost without accomplishing useful work, as friction causes loss of mechanical energy. [< L *dissipātiōn-* (s. of *dissipātiō*), equiv. to *dissipāt(us)* (see DISSIPATE) + *-iōn-* -ION]

dissipa′tion trail′, a clear rift left behind an aircraft flying through a thin cloud layer.

dis·so·ci·a·ble (di sō′shē ə bəl, -shə bəl *or, for 1,* -sē ə-), *adj.* **1.** capable of being dissociated; separable: *Worthy and unworthy motives are often not dissociable.* **2.** not sociable; unsociable. **3.** incongruous; not reconcilable. [< L *dissociābil(is)*, equiv. to *dis-* DIS-¹ + *sociābilis* SOCIABLE] —**dis·so′ci·a·bil′i·ty, dis·so′ci·a·ble·ness,** *n.*

dis·so·cial (di sō′shəl), *adj.* unsocial; disinclined to or unsuitable for society: *solitary, dissocial habits.* [< L *dissociāl(is)* irreconcilable, equiv. to *dis-* DIS-¹ + *sociālis* sociable (see SOCIAL)] —**dis·so′ci·al′i·ty,** *n.*

dis·so·ci·ate (di sō′shē āt′, -sē-), *v.*, **-at·ed, -at·ing.** —*v.t.* **1.** to sever the association of; disunite; separate: *He tried to dissociate himself from the evil in his past.* **2.** *Physical Chem.* to subject to dissociation. —*v.i.* **3.** to withdraw from association. **4.** *Physical Chem.* to undergo dissociation. [DIS-¹ + (AS)SOCIATE, modeled on L *dissociātus*, ptp. of *dissociāre* to divide, sever] —**dis·so′ci·a′tive,** *adj.*

dis·so·ci·a·tion (di sō′sē ā′shən, -shē ā′-), *n.* **1.** the act or an instance of dissociating. **2.** the state of being dissociated; disunion: *the dissociation of church and state.* **3.** *Physical Chem.* **a.** the reversible resolution or decomposition of a complex substance into simpler constituents caused by variation in physical conditions, as when water gradually decomposes into hydrogen and oxygen under great heat in such a way that when the temperature is lowered the liberated elements recombine to form water. **b.** See **electrolytic dissociation. 4.** *Psychiatry.* the splitting off of certain mental processes from the main body of consciousness, with varying degrees of autonomy resulting. [DIS-¹ + (AS)SOCIATION, modeled on L *dissociātiō* separation]

dis·sog·e·ny (di soj′ə nē), *n. Zool.* the condition in ctenophores in which an individual has two periods of sexual maturity, one in the larval and one in the adult stage. Also, **dis·sog·o·ny** (di sog′ə nē). [< Gk *dissó(s)* twofold + -GENY]

dis·sol·u·ble (di sol′yə bəl), *adj.* capable of being dissolved. [< L *dissolūbil(is)*, equiv. to *dissolū-*, perf. s. of *dissolvere* to DISSOLVE + *-bilis* -BLE. See DIS-¹, SOLUBLE] —**dis·sol′u·bil′i·ty, dis·sol′u·ble·ness,** *n.*

dis·so·lute (dis′ə lo͞ot′), *adj.* indifferent to moral restraints; given to immoral or improper conduct; licentious; dissipated. [< L *dissolūt(us)* (ptp. of *dissolvere* to DISSOLVE). See DIS-¹, SOLUTE] —**dis′so·lute′ly,** *adv.* —**dis′so·lute′ness,** *n.*

dis·so·lu·tion (dis′ə lo͞o′shən), *n.* **1.** the act or process of resolving or dissolving into parts or elements. **2.** the resulting state. **3.** the undoing or breaking of a bond, tie, union, partnership, etc. **4.** the breaking up of an assembly or organization; dismissal; dispersal. **5.** *Govt.* an order issued by the head of a state terminating a parliament and necessitating a new election. **6.** death; decease. **7.** a bringing or coming to an end; disintegration; decay; termination: *the dissolution of the body.* **8.** legal termination, esp. of business activity, with the final distribution of assets, the fixing of liabilities, etc. **9.** *Chem.* the act by which a solid, gas, or liquid is dispersed homogeneously in a gas, solid, or, esp., a liquid. [< L *dissolūtiōn-* (s. of *dissolūtiō*); r. ME *dissolucioun* < AF. See DIS-¹, SOLUTION] —**dis′so·lu′tive,** *adv.*

dis·solve (di zolv′), *v.*, **-solved, -solv·ing,** *n.* —*v.t.* **1.** to make a solution of, as by mixing with a liquid; pass into solution: *to dissolve salt in water.* **2.** to melt; liquefy: *to dissolve sugar into syrup.* **3.** to undo (a tie or bond); break up (a connection, union, etc.). **4.** to break up (an assembly or organization); dismiss; disperse. **5.** *Govt.* to order the termination of (a parliament or other legislative body). **6.** to bring to an end; terminate; destroy: *to dissolve one's hopes.* **7.** to separate into parts or elements; disintegrate: *Time dissolves all things.* **8.** to destroy the binding power or influence of: *to dissolve a spell.* **9.** *Law.* to deprive of force; abrogate; annul: *to dissolve a marriage or injunction.* —*v.i.* **10.** to become dissolved, as in a solvent. **11.** to become melted or liquefied. **12.** to disintegrate, break up, or disperse. **13.** to lose force, intensity, or strength. **14.** to disappear gradually; fade away. **15.** to become emotionally weakened; to lose one's composure completely: *She dissolved in tears.* **16.** *Motion Pictures.* to fade out one shot or scene while simultaneously fading in the next, overlapping the two during the process. —*n.* **17.** Also called **lap dissolve.** *Motion Pictures.* a scene made by dissolving. [< L *dissolv(ere)*, equiv. to *dis-* DIS-¹ + *solvere* to SOLVE] —**dis·solv′a·bil′i·ty, dis·solv′a·ble·ness,** *n.* —**dis·solv′a·ble,** *adj.* —**dis·solv′er,** *n.* —**dis·solv′ing·ly,** *adv.*
—**Syn. 1.** See **melt. 3.** sever, loosen. **5.** adjourn.

dis·sol·vent (di zol′vənt), *adj.* **1.** capable of dissolving another substance. —*n.* **2.** a solvent. [< L *dissolvent-* (s. of *dissolvēns*, prp. of *dissolvere*). See DIS-¹, SOLVENT]

dissolv′ing view′, an effect created by the projection of slides on a screen in such a way that each picture seems to dissolve into the succeeding one without an interval in between.

dis·so·nance (dis′ə nəns), *n.* **1.** an inharmonious or harsh sound; discord. **2.** *Music.* a simultaneous combination of tones conventionally accepted as being in a state of unrest and needing completion. Cf. **consonance** (def. 3). **3.** disagreement or incongruity. [< LL *dissonantia*, equiv. to *disson-* (see DISSONANT) + *-antia* -ANCE]

dis·so·nan·cy (dis′ə nən sē), *n., pl.* **-cies.** dissonance.

dis·so·nant (dis′ə nənt), *adj.* **1.** disagreeing or harsh in sound; discordant. **2.** out of harmony; incongruous; at variance. [< L *dissonānt-* (s. of *dissonāns*, prp. of *dissonāre* to sound harsh), equiv. to *disson-* (deriv. of *dissonus* discordant; see DIS-¹, SOUND) + *-ānt-* -ANT; r. ME *dissonaunte* < AF] —**dis′so·nant·ly,** *adv.*

dis·spread (di spred′), *v.t., v.i.*, **-spread, -spread·ing.** dispread.

dis·suade (di swād′), *v.t.*, **-suad·ed, -suad·ing.** **1.** to deter by advice or persuasion; persuade not to do something (usually fol. by *from*): *She dissuaded him from leaving home.* **2.** *Archaic.* to advise or urge against: *to dissuade an action.* [< L *dissuād(ēre)*, equiv. to *dis-* DIS-¹ + *suādēre* to persuade] —**dis·suad′a·ble,** *adj.*

dis·sua·sion (di swā′zhən), *n.* the act or an instance of dissuading. [< L *dissuāsiōn-* (s. of *dissuāsiō*) a speaking against, equiv. to *dissuās(us)* (ptp. of *dissuādēre*; *dissuād-* (see DISSUADE) + *-tus* ptp. suffix) + *-iōn-* -ION]

dis·sua·sive (di swā′siv), *adj.* tending or liable to dissuade. [DISSUAS(ION) + -IVE] —**dis·sua′sive·ly,** *adv.* —**dis·sua′sive·ness,** *n.*

dis·syl·la·bise (di sil′ə bīz′, dis sil′-, dī sil′-), *v.t.*, **-bised, -bis·ing.** *Chiefly Brit.* dissyllabize.

dis·syl·la·bize (di sil′ə bīz′, dis sil′-, dī sil′-), *v.t.*, **-bized, -biz·ing.** disyllabize. —**dis·syl·la·bism** (di sil′ə biz′əm, dis sil′-), *n.*

dis·syl·la·ble (di sil′ə bəl, dis′sil′-, dī′sil-), *n.* disyllable. —**dis·syl·lab·ic** (dis′i lab′ik, dis′si-), *adj.*

dis·sym·me·try (di sim′i trē, dis sim′-), *n.* absence or lack of symmetry. [DIS-¹ + SYMMETRY] —**dis·sym·met·ric** (dis′i me′trik, dis′si-), **dis′sym·met′ri·cal,** *adj.* —**dis′sym·met′ri·cal·ly,** *adv.*

dist., **1.** distance. **2.** distinguish. **3.** distinguished. **4.** district.

di·stad (dis′tad), *adv.* toward or at the distal end or part. [DIST(ANT) + *-ad* (< L *ad*; see AD-)]

dis·taff (dis′taf, -täf), *n.* **1.** a staff with a cleft end for holding wool, flax, etc., from which the thread is drawn in spinning by hand. **2.** a similar attachment on a spinning wheel. **3.** the female sex. **4.** a woman. —*adj.* **5.** noting, pertaining to, characteristic of, or suitable for a woman; female. [ME *distaf*, OE *distæf*, equiv. to *dis-* (c. LG *diesse* bunch of flax on a distaff; cf. DIZEN) + *stæf* STAFF]

dis′taff side′, the female side of a family (opposed to *spear side*).

dis·tain (di stān′), *v.t. Archaic.* to discolor; stain; sully. [ME *desteigne*, < MF *destein(dre)*, equiv. to *des-* DIS-¹ + *teindre* < L *tingere* to dye, TINGE]

dis·tal (dis′tᵊl), *adj.* **1.** situated away from the point of origin or attachment, as of a limb or bone; terminal. Cf. **proximal. 2.** *Dentistry.* directed away from the sagittal plane or midline of the face, along the dental arch. Cf. **buccal** (def. 3), **mesial** (def. 2). [DIST(ANT) + -AL¹] —**dis′tal·ly,** *adv.*

dis′tal con′voluted tu′bule, *Anat.* that part of a nephron between the loop of Henle and the collecting tubule that concentrates the urine. Cf. **proximal convoluted tubule.**

dis·tance (dis′təns), *n., v.*, **-tanced, -tanc·ing.** —*n.* **1.** the extent or amount of space between two things, points, lines, etc. **2.** the state or fact of being apart in space, as of one thing from another; remoteness. **3.** a linear extent of space: *Three miles is a distance too great to walk in an hour.* **4.** an expanse; area: *A vast distance of water surrounded the ship.* **5.** the interval between two points of time or an extent of time: *His vacation period was a good distance away.* **6.** remoteness or difference in any respect: *We agree on a few things, but our philosophies are a long distance apart.* **7.** an amount of progress: *There's still a lot to be done, but we've come a long distance since last year.* **8.** a distant point, place, or region. **9.** the distant part of a field of view: *Can you see that barn in the distance?* **10.** reserve; absence of warmth: *Their first meeting in several years was hampered by a certain distance between them.* **11.** *Music.* interval (def. 7). **12.** *Horse Racing.* (in a heat race) the space measured back from the winning post which a horse must reach by the time the winner passes the winning post or be eliminated from subsequent heats. **13.** *Math.* the greatest lower bound of differences between points, one from each of two given sets. **14.** *Obs.* disagreement or dissension; a quarrel. **15. keep one's distance,** to avoid becoming familiar with; remain cool or aloof. Also, **keep at a distance.** —*v.t.* **16.** to leave behind at a distance, as at a race; surpass. **17.** to place at a distance. **18.** to cause to appear distant. [ME < L *distantia*, equiv. to *distant-* (see DISTANT) + *-ia* -Y³ (L *-āntia* > E -ANCE); r. ME *destaunce* < AF] —**dis′tance·less,** *adj.*

dis′tance made′ good′, *Navig.* the distance between a point where a vessel has been and a point where it is at present, measured in nautical miles along the rhumb line connecting the two points.

dis′tance med′ley, *Track.* a medley relay in which the first member of a team runs 440 yards, the second runs 880 yards, the third runs 1320 yards, and the fourth runs 1760 yards. Cf. **sprint medley.**

dis·tant (dis′tənt), *adj.* **1.** far off or apart in space; not near at hand; remote or removed (often followed by *from*): *a distant place; a town three miles distant from here.* **2.** separate or apart; distinct; not joined: *distant leaves.* **3.** apart or far off in time: *distant centuries past.* **4.** remote or far apart in any respect: *a distant relative.* **5.** reserved or aloof; not familiar or cordial: *a distant greeting.* **6.** arriving from or going to a distance, as a communication, journey, etc.: *I have here a distant letter from Japan.* [ME < L *distānt-* (s. of *distāns*, prp. of *distāre* to stand apart), equiv. to *di-* DI-¹ + *stā-* stand + *-nt-* prp. suffix; r. ME *distaunt* < AF] —**dis′tant·ly,** *adv.* —**dis′tant·ness,** *n.*
—**Syn. 5.** cool, withdrawn.

dis·taste (dis tāst′), *n., v.*, **-tast·ed, -tast·ing.** —*n.* **1.** dislike; disinclination. **2.** dislike for food or drink. —*v.t.* **3.** *Archaic.* to dislike. [DIS-¹ + TASTE]
—**Syn. 1.** aversion, repugnance, disgust. See **dislike.**

dis·taste·ful (dis tāst′fəl), *adj.* **1.** unpleasant, offensive, or causing dislike. **2.** unpleasant to the taste: *a distasteful medicine.* [DISTASTE + -FUL] —**dis·taste′ful·ly,** *adv.* —**dis·taste′ful·ness,** *n.*
—**Syn. 1.** disagreeable, displeasing; repugnant, repulsive. **2.** unpalatable, unsavory.

Dist. Atty., District Attorney.

Dist. Ct., District Court.

dis·tel·fink (dis′tᵊl fingk′), *n.* a stylized bird motif traditional in Pennsylvania-Dutch art. [< G *Distel* thistle + *Fink* finch]

dis·tem·per¹ (dis tem′pər), *n.* **1.** *Vet. Pathol.* **a.** Also called **canine distemper.** a specific infectious disease of young dogs, caused by a filterable virus and characterized by lethargy, fever, loss of appetite, vomiting, and a dry, hot nose. **b.** Also called **colt distemper, equine distemper, strangles.** an infectious febrile disease of horses, caused by the organism *Streptococcus equi* and characterized by catarrh of the upper air passages and the formation of pus by the submaxillary and other lymphatic glands. **c.** Also called **cat distemper, cat fever, cat plague, cat typhoid, feline agranulocytosis, feline distemper, feline enteritis, feline infectious enteritis, feline panleucopenia, feline panleukopenia, panleucopenia, panleukopenia.** a highly fatal disease of cats, caused by a virus and characterized by fever, refusal of food, vomiting, and diarrhea. **d.** (formerly) any of several diseases characterized by fever and catarrhal symptoms. **2.** a deranged condition of mind or body; a disorder or disease: *a feverish distemper.* **3.** disorder or disturbance, esp. of a political nature. —*v.t.* **4.** to derange physically or mentally. [ME *distemp(e)re(n)* < ML *distemper(āre)*, equiv. to L *dis-* DIS-¹ + *temperāre* to TEMPER; r. ME *destempre* < MF] —**dis·tem′pered·ly,** *adv.* —**dis·tem′pered·ness,** *n.*

dis·tem·per² (dis tem′pər), *n.* **1.** *Art.* **a.** a technique of decorative painting in which glue or gum is used as a binder or medium to achieve a mat surface and rapid drying. **b.** (formerly) the tempera technique. **2.** a painting executed by this method. **3.** *Brit.* whitewash; calcimine. —*v.t.* **4.** to paint in distemper. **5.** *Brit.* to whitewash a wall, cottage, etc.; calcimine. [ME *distempere(n)* < ML *distemper(āre)* (to) dissolve, dilute, equiv. to L *dis-* DIS-¹ + *temperāre* to blend, TEMPER]

dis·tem·per·a·ture (dis tem′pər ə chər), *n.* a distempered or disordered condition; disturbance of health, mind, or temper. [obs. *distemperate* (DIS-¹ + TEMPERATE) + -URE]

dis·tend (di stend′), *v.t., v.i.* **1.** to spread in all directions; expand; swell: *The sea distended about them.* **2.** to expand by stretching, as something hollow or elastic: *Habitual overeating had distended his stomach.* [< L *distend(ere)*, equiv. to *dis-* DIS-¹ + *tendere* to stretch] —**dis·tend′er,** *n.*
—**Syn. 1.** enlarge, bloat. —**Ant. 1, 2.** shrink, contract.

dis·tend·ed (di sten′did), *adj.* **1.** expanded; increased, as in size, volume, etc.; dilated: *the distended nostrils of the terrified horse.* **2.** swollen, by or as by internal pressure, out of normal size or shape; protuberant: *distended wineskins; His anger showed in the distended arteries of his neck.* [DISTEND + -ED[2]] —**dis·tend′ed·ly,** *adv.* —**dis·tend′ed·ness,** *n.*

dis·ten·si·ble (di sten′sə bəl), *adj.* capable of being distended. [< L *distens(us)* (ptp. of *distendere; distend-* DISTEND + *-tus* ptp. suffix) + -IBLE] —**dis·ten′si·bil′i·ty,** *n.*

dis·ten·sile (di sten′sil), *adj.* 1. distensible. 2. serving to distend. [< L *distens(us)* (ptp. of *distendere* to DISTEND) + -ILE]

dis·tent (di stent′), *adj.* *Obs.* distended. [< L *distent(us)* distended (ptp. of *distennere,* var. of *distendere* to DISTEND), equiv. to *distenn-* + *-tus* ptp. suffix]

dis·ten·tion (di sten′shən), *n.* the act of distending or the state of being distended. Also, **dis·ten′sion.** [< L *distentiōn-* (s. of *distentiō*), equiv. to *distent(us)* DISTENT + *-iōn-* -ION]

dis·tich (dis′tik), *n.* *Pros.* 1. a group of two lines of verse, usually making complete sense; couplet. 2. a rhyming couplet. [< L *distich(on),* n. use of neut. of Gk *dístichos* having two lines, equiv. to *di-* DI-[1] + *stíchos* row] —**dis′ti·chal,** *adj.*

dis·ti·chous (dis′tə kəs), *adj.* 1. *Bot.* arranged alternately in two vertical rows on opposite sides of an axis, as leaves. 2. *Zool.* divided into two parts, as antennae. [< L *distichus* (< Gk *dístichos* (adj.); see DISTICH), with -OUS for L *-us* adj. suffix] —**dis′ti·chous·ly,** *adv.*

dis·til (di stil′), *v.t., v.i.* **-tilled, -til·ling.** *Chiefly Brit.* distill.

dis·till (di stil′), *v.t.* 1. to subject to a process of vaporization and subsequent condensation, as for purification or concentration. 2. to extract the volatile components of by distillation; transform by distillation. 3. to concentrate, purify, or obtain by or as by distillation: *to distill whiskey from mash.* 4. to remove by distillation (usually fol. by *off* or *out*): *to distill out impurities.* 5. to let fall in drops; give forth in or as in drops: *The cool of the night distills the dew.* —*v.i.* 6. to undergo or perform distillation. 7. to become vaporized and then condensed in distillation. 8. to drop, pass, or condense as a distillate. 9. to fall in drops; trickle; exude. [ME *distille(n)* < L *distill(āre),* var. of *dēstillāre,* equiv. to *dē-* DE- + *stillāre* to drop] —**dis·till′a·ble,** *adj.*

dis·til·land (dis′tᵊland′), *n.* a substance that undergoes distillation. Cf. **distillate.** [< L *distillānd(um),* neut. ger. of *distillāre* to DISTILL]

dis·til·late (dis′tᵊlit, -tᵊlāt′, di stil′it), *n.* 1. the product obtained from the condensation of vapors in distillation. 2. any concentration, essence, or abstraction. [< L *distillāt(us)* (ptp. of *distillāre* to trickle down), equiv. to *distill-* DISTILL + *-ātus* -ATE[1]]

dis·til·la·tion (dis′tᵊlā′shən), *n.* 1. the volatilization or evaporation and subsequent condensation of a liquid, as when water is boiled in a retort and the steam is condensed in a cool receiver. 2. the purification or concentration of a substance, the obtaining of the essence or volatile properties contained in it, or the separation of one substance from another, by such a process. 3. a product of distilling; distillate. 4. the act or fact of distilling or the state of being distilled. [< L *distillātiōn-* (s. of *distillātiō*), equiv. to *distillāt(us)* DISTILLATE + *-iōn-* -ION; r. ME *distillacioun* < AF] —**dis·til·la·to·ry** (di stil′ə tôr′ē, -tōr′ē), *adj.*

dis·tilled (di stild′), *adj.* obtained or produced by distillation. [DISTILL + -ED[2]]

distilled′ wa′ter, water from which impurities, as dissolved salts, colloidal particles, etc., have been removed by one or more processes of distillation; chemically pure water.

dis·till·er (di stil′ər), *n.* 1. an apparatus for distilling, as a condenser; a still. 2. one whose business it is to extract alcoholic liquors by distillation. [DISTILL + -ER[1]]

dis·till·er·y (di stil′ə rē), *n., pl.* **-er·ies.** a place or establishment where distilling, esp. the distilling of liquors, is done. [DISTILL + -ERY]

dis·till·ment (di stil′mənt), *n.* *Archaic.* distillation. Also, *esp. Brit.,* **dis·til′ment.** [DISTILL + -MENT]

dis·tinct (di stingkt′), *adj.* 1. distinguished as not being the same; not identical; separate (sometimes fol. by *from*): *His private and public lives are distinct.* 2. different in nature or quality; dissimilar (sometimes fol. by *from*): *Gold is distinct from iron.* 3. clear to the senses or intellect; plain; definite; unmistakable: *The ship appeared as a distinct silhouette.* 4. distinguishing or perceiving clearly: *distinct vision.* 5. unusual; rare; notable: *His praise is a distinct honor.* 6. *Archaic.* distinctively decorated or adorned. [ME < L *distinct(us)* (ptp. of *distinguere* to DISTINGUISH), equiv. to *di-* DI-[2] + *sting-* prod, mark + *-tus* ptp. suffix] —**dis·tinct′ness,** *n.*
—**Syn.** 1. individual. See **various.** 3. well-defined, clear, unconfused. —**Ant.** 3. indistinct.

dis·tinc·tion (di stingk′shən), *n.* 1. a marking off or distinguishing as different: *His distinction of sounds is excellent.* 2. the recognizing or noting of differences; discrimination: *to make a distinction between right and wrong.* 3. a discrimination made between things as different: *Death comes to all without distinction.* 4. condition of being different; difference: *There is a distinction between what he says and what he does.* 5. a distinguishing quality or characteristic: *It has the distinction of being the oldest house in the town.* 6. a distinguishing or treating with special honor, attention, or favor. 7. an act of bestowing, or a mark of, honor or favor. 8. marked superiority; note; eminence. 9. distinguished appearance. 10. *Obs.* division; separation. [< L *distinctiōn-* (s. of *distinctiō*), equiv. to *distinct(us)* (see DISTINCT) + *-iōn-* -ION; r. ME *distinccioun* < AF] —**dis·tinc′tion·less,** *adj.*
—**Syn.** 3. DISTINCTION and DIFFERENCE may both refer to perceivable dissimilarities and, in this meaning, may be used interchangeably: *There is a distinction (difference) between the two.* DISTINCTION, however, usually suggests the perception of dissimilarity, as the result of analysis and discrimination: *a carefully made distinction between two treatments of the same theme;* whereas DIFFERENCE refers only to the condition of being dissimilar: *the difference between Gothic and Roman architecture.* "A distinction without a difference" is a way of referring to an artificial or false discrimination. 7. See **honor.** 8. renown, importance. —**Ant.** 4. resemblance.

dis·tinc·tive (di stingk′tiv), *adj.* distinguishing; serving to distinguish; characteristic: *the distinctive stripes of the zebra.* [< ML *distinctīv(us),* equiv. to L *distinct(us)* DISTINCT + *-īvus* -IVE] —**dis·tinc′tive·ly,** *adv.* —**dis·tinc′tive·ness,** *n.*
—**Syn.** individual.

distinc′tive fea′ture, *Ling.* 1. a feature of the sound system of a language that serves as the crucial distinguishing mark between two phonemes, as the distinctive feature of voicing, which distinguishes *b* from *p* in English, or nasality, which distinguishes *m* from *b* and *p.* 2. one of a set of universally valid phonetic dimensions which are intended to be sufficient to distinguish the phonemes of any language. 3. a component or phonetic feature characterizing a phoneme.

dis·tinct·ly (di stingkt′lē), *adv.* 1. in a distinct manner; clearly. 2. without doubt; unmistakably. [DISTINCT + -LY]
—**Syn.** 1. See **clearly.**

dis·tin·gué (dis′tang gā′, di stang′gā; *Fr.* dē staN gā′), *adj.* distinguished; having an air of distinction. Also, *referring to a woman,* **dis′tin·guée′.** [< F, adj. use of ptp. of *distinguer* to DISTINGUISH]

dis·tin·guish (di sting′gwish), *v.t.* 1. to mark off as different (often fol. by *from*): *He was distinguished from the other boys by his height.* 2. to recognize as distinct or different; recognize the individual features or characteristics of: *It is hard to distinguish her from her sister.* 3. to perceive clearly by sight or other sense; discern; recognize: *I cannot distinguish things so far away. He could not distinguish many of the words.* 4. to serve to separate as different; be a distinctive characteristic of; characterize: *It is his Italian accent that distinguishes him.* 5. to make prominent, conspicuous, or eminent: *to distinguish oneself in battle.* 6. to divide into classes; classify: *Let us distinguish the various types of metaphor.* 7. *Archaic.* to single out for or honor with special attention: *He was distinguished for bravery.* —*v.i.* 8. to indicate or show a difference (usually fol. by *between*). 9. to recognize or note differences; discriminate. [< ME *distingu(en)* (< L *distinguere*) + -ISH[2]; r. ME *distingen* < MF *distinguer;* see DISTINCT] —**dis·tin′guish·a·ble,** *adj.* —**dis·tin′guish·a·ble·ness, dis·tin′guish·a·bil′i·ty,** *n.* —**dis·tin′guish·a·bly,** *adv.* —**dis·tin′guish·er,** *n.* —**dis·tin′guish·ing·ly,** *adv.* —**dis·tin′guish·ment,** *n.*
—**Syn.** 2. DISTINGUISH, DIFFERENTIATE, DISCRIMINATE suggest a positive attempt to analyze characteristic features or qualities of things. To DISTINGUISH is to recognize the characteristic features belonging to a thing: *to distinguish a light cruiser from a heavy cruiser.* To DISCRIMINATE is to perceive the particular, nice, or exact differences between things, to determine wherein these differences consist, and to estimate their significance: *to discriminate prejudiced from unprejudiced testimony.* To DIFFERENTIATE is especially to point out exactly and in detail the differences (usually) between two things: *The symptoms of some diseases are so familiar that it is hard to differentiate one from another.* —**Ant.** 2. confuse.

dis·tin·guished (di sting′gwisht), *adj.* 1. conspicuous; marked. 2. noted; eminent; famous; made conspicuous by excellence: *a distinguished scholar.* 3. having an air of distinction, dignity, or eminence; distingué: *a distinguished old gentleman.* [DISTINGUISH + -ED[2]] —**dis·tin′guished·ly,** *adv.*
—**Syn.** 2. renowned, illustrious. See **famous.**

Distin′guished Con′duct Med′al, *Brit. Mil.* a decoration awarded for distinguished conduct in operations in the field against an enemy. *Abbr.:* D.C.M.

Distin′guished Fly′ing Cross′, 1. *U.S. Mil.* a decoration awarded for heroic or extraordinary achievement while on aerial duty. 2. *Brit. Mil.* a decoration awarded for similar achievement while in flying operations against an enemy. *Abbr.:* D.F.C.

Distin′guished Serv′ice Cross′, *U.S. Army.* a bronze medal awarded to an officer or enlisted man for extraordinary heroism in military action against an armed enemy. *Abbr.:* D.S.C.

Distin′guished Serv′ice Med′al, 1. *U.S. Mil.* a decoration awarded for exceptionally meritorious performance of a duty of great responsibility. 2. *Brit. Mil.* a decoration awarded for distinguished conduct in war. *Abbr.:* D.S.M.

Distin′guished Serv′ice Or′der, *Brit. Mil.* a decoration awarded for distinguished service in action. *Abbr.:* D.S.O.

dis·tin·guish·ing (di sting′gwi shing), *adj.* distinctive; characteristic, as a definitive feature of an individual or group: *Contrived rhyme is a distinguishing mark of her undistinguished poetry.* [DISTINGUISH + -ING[2]]

di·sto·ma·to·sis (dī stō′mə tō′sis), *n.* *Vet. Pathol.* liverrot. [< NL *Distomat(a)* name of a suborder of trematode worms (see DI-[1], STOMATA) + -OSIS]

dis·tort (di stôrt′), *v.t.* 1. to twist awry or out of shape; make crooked or deformed: *Arthritis had distorted his wrists.* 2. to pervert; misrepresent: *to distort the facts.* 3. *Electronics.* to reproduce or amplify (a signal) inaccurately by changing the frequencies or unequally changing the delay or amplitude of the components of the output wave. [< L *distort(us)* (ptp. of *distorquēre* to distort), equiv. to *dis-* DIS-[1] + *tor(qu)-* (s. of *torquēre* to twist) + *-tus* ptp. suffix] —**dis·tort′er,** *n.* —**dis·tor′tive,** *adj.*

dis·tort·ed (di stôr′tid), *adj.* 1. twisted; deformed; misshapen. 2. misrepresented; altered; twisted out of true meaning: *He supported the lie with distorted facts.* 3. mentally or morally twisted, as with an aberration or bias: *He has a distorted sense of values.* [DISTORT + -ED[2]] —**dis·tort′ed·ly,** *adv.* —**dis·tort′ed·ness,** *n.*

dis·tor·tion (di stôr′shən), *n.* 1. the act or an instance of distorting. 2. the state of being distorted or the relative degree or amount by which something is distorted or distorts. 3. anything that is distorted, as a sound, image, fact, etc. 4. *Optics.* an aberration of a lens or system of lenses in which the magnification of the object varies with the lateral distance from the axis of the lens. Cf. **barrel distortion, pincushion distortion.** [< L *distortiōn-* (s. of *distortiō*). See DISTORT, -ION] —**dis·tor′tion·al,** *adj.*

distr., 1. distribute. 2. distribution. 3. distributor

dis·tract (di strakt′), *v.t.* 1. to draw away or divert, as the mind or attention: *The music distracted him from his work.* 2. to divide (the mind, attention, etc.) between objects. 3. to disturb or trouble greatly in mind: *Grief distracted him.* 4. to amuse; entertain; provide a pleasant diversion for: *I'm bored with bridge, but golf still distracts me.* 5. to separate or divide by dissension or strife. —*adj.* 6. *Obs.* distracted. [< L *distract(us)* (ptp. of *distrahere* to draw apart), equiv. to *dis-* DIS-[1] + *trac-* (perf. s. of *trahere* to draw) + *-tus* ptp. suffix] —**dis·tract′er,** *n.* —**dis·tract′i·bil′i·ty,** *n.* —**dis·tract′i·ble,** *adj.* —**dis·tract′ing·ly,** *adv.*
—**Syn.** 3. bewilder.

dis·tract·ed (di strak′tid), *adj.* 1. having the attention diverted: *He tossed several rocks to the far left and slipped past the distracted sentry.* 2. irrational; rendered incapable of behaving, reacting, etc., in a normal manner, as by worry, remorse, or the like: *The distracted mother was unable to tell them how the child had got the poison.* [DISTRACT + -ED[2]] —**dis·tract′ed·ly,** *adv.* —**dis·tract′ed·ness,** *n.*

dis·trac·tion (di strak′shən), *n.* 1. the act of distracting. 2. the state of being distracted. 3. mental distress or derangement: *That child will drive me to distraction.* 4. that which distracts, divides the attention, or prevents concentration: *The distractions of the city hinder my studies.* 5. that which amuses, entertains, or diverts; amusement; entertainment: *Fishing is his major distraction.* 6. division or disorder caused by dissension; tumult. [< L *distractiōn-* (s. of *distractiō*) separation. See DISTRACT, -ION]

dis·trac·tive (di strak′tiv), *adj.* tending to distract. [DISTRACT + -IVE] —**dis·trac′tive·ly,** *adv.*

dis·trail (dis′trāl′), *n.* See **dissipation trail.** [by shortening]

dis·train (di strān′), *Law.* —*v.t.* 1. to constrain by seizing and holding goods, etc., in pledge for rent, damages, etc., or in order to obtain satisfaction of a claim. 2. to levy a distress upon. —*v.i.* 3. to levy a distress. [ME *distreine(n)* < OF *destreind(re)* < L *distringere* to stretch out, equiv. to *di-* DI-[2] + *stringere* to draw tight; see STRAIN[1]] —**dis·train′a·ble,** *adj.* —**dis·train′ment,** *n.* —**dis·trai′nor, dis·train′er,** *n.*

dis·traint (di strānt′), *n.* *Law.* the act of distraining; a distress. [DISTRAIN + *-t,* modeled on *constraint, restraint*]

dis·trait (di strā′; *Fr.* dēs tre′), *adj.* inattentive because of distracting worries, fears, etc.; absent-minded. Also, *referring to a female,* **dis·traite** (di strāt′; *Fr.* dēs tret′). [< F < L *distract(us);* see DISTRACT]

dis·traught (di strôt′), *adj.* 1. distracted; bewildered; deeply agitated. 2. mentally deranged; crazed. [var. of obs. *distract* distracted, by assoc. with *straught,* old ptp. of STRETCH]

dis·tress (di stres′), *n.* 1. great pain, anxiety, or sorrow; acute physical or mental suffering; affliction; trouble. 2. a state of extreme necessity or misfortune. 3. the state of a ship requiring immediate assistance, when on fire at sea. 4. that which causes pain, suffering, trouble, danger, etc. 5. danger; liability or exposure to pain, suffering, trouble, etc.: *It was an old story of a damsel in distress.* 6. *Law.* a. the act of distraining; the legal seizure and detention of the goods of another as security or satisfaction for debt, etc. b. the thing seized in distraining. [ME *destresse* < OF < LL *districtia, equiv. to L *district(us)* (see DISTRICT) + *-ia* -Y[3]]
—*v.t.* 7. to afflict with great pain, anxiety, or sorrow; trouble; worry; bother. 8. to subject to pressure, stress, or strain; embarrass or exhaust by strain: *to be distressed by excessive work.* 9. to compel by pain or force of circumstances: *His suffering distressed him into committing suicide.* [ME *destress(en)* < AF *destresser* (OF *destrecier*) < LL *districtiāre,* deriv. of *districtia distress (n.)] —**dis·tress′ing·ly,** *adv.*
—**Syn.** 1. agony, anguish, adversity, hardship, tribulation. See **sorrow.** 2. need, destitution. —**Ant.** 1. comfort.

distress′ call′, 1. a prearranged communication code sign indicating that the sender is in a situation of peril, distress, or the like, as SOS, Mayday, etc. Cf. **distress signal** (def. 1). 2. a communication prompted by or indicating distress: *The hospital sent out distress calls for all available stocks of the antitoxin.*

dis·tressed (di strest′), *adj.* 1. affected with distress. 2. of or pertaining to distress merchandise: *distressed prices.* [DISTRESS + -ED[2]] —**dis·tress·ed·ly** (di stres′id lē, -strest′lē), *adv.* —**dis·tress′ed·ness,** *n.*

distressed′ ar′ea, 1. a region so severely damaged by a flood, hurricane or other natural catastrophe that its inhabitants need food, clothing, shelter, and economic aid from national charities or the federal government. 2. See **depressed area.**

distress′ flag′, any flag flown by a vessel to show that it is in distress, as an ensign flown at half-mast or upside down.

distress′ fre′quency, a radio frequency band reserved for emergency signals from aircraft or ships in distress.

dis·tress·ful (di stres′fəl), *adj.* 1. causing or involving distress: *the distressful circumstances of poverty and sickness.* 2. full of distress; feeling or indicating distress: *a distressful cry.* [DISTRESS + -FUL] —**dis·tress′ful·ly,** *adv.* —**dis·tress′ful·ness,** *n.*

distress′ gun′, *Naut.* a gun fired at one-minute intervals as a signal of distress.

distress′ mer′chandise, *Com.* 1. goods sold below the prevailing price in order to raise cash quickly to pay overdue bills or to meet some other financial emergency. 2. damaged goods sold below fair-trade prices.

distress′ sig′nal, 1. a signal used, or designed to be used, by persons in peril, for the purpose of summoning aid, indicating their position, etc., as a radio code sign, pyrotechnic rocket, flag hoist, or the like. Cf. **distress call** (def. 1). 2. an indication, esp. nonverbal, that assistance, cooperation, or the like, is needed: *He correctly interpreted the hostess' upturned eyes as a distress signal and hastily changed the subject.*

dis·trib·u·tar·y (di strib′yo͞o ter′ē), *n., pl.* **-tar·ies.** a branch of a river flowing away from the main stream and not rejoining it (opposed to *tributary*). [DISTRIBUTE + -ARY]

dis·trib·ute (di strib′yo͞ot), *v.t.,* **-ut·ed, -ut·ing.** 1. to divide and give out in shares; deal out; allot. 2. to disperse through a space or over an area; spread; scatter. 3. to pass out or deliver (mail, newspapers, etc.)

to intended recipients. **4.** to divide into parts of distinct character: *The process was distributed into three stages.* **5.** to divide into classes: *These plants are distributed into 22 classes.* **6.** *Logic.* to employ (a term) so as to refer to all individuals denoted by it. **7.** *Physical Chem.* to dissolve uniformly in a solvent consisting of layers of immiscible or partially miscible substances. **8.** *Print.* **a.** to roll out (ink) on the table to attain the proper consistency. **b.** to return (type) to its proper place in a case after printing. [< L *distribūt(us)*, ptp. of *distribuere* to divide up. See DIS-[1], TRIBUTE] —**dis·trib′ut·a·ble,** *adj.*

—**Syn. 1.** assign, mete, apportion. DISTRIBUTE, DISPENSE apply to giving out something. DISTRIBUTE implies apportioned, individualized, and, often, personal giving, esp. of something that is definite or limited in amount or number: *The prizes were distributed among ten winners.* DISPENSE formerly implied indiscriminate, general, and liberal giving, esp. of something that was more or less indefinite or unmeasured in amount: *to dispense largess.* It now applies chiefly to giving according to need or deserts, from an organized and official source: *to dispense medicines and food to the victims, justice to criminals.* **5.** dispose, sort, arrange, categorize.

dis·trib·u·tee (di strib′yo͞o tē′), *n.* *Law.* a person who shares in a decedent estate. [DISTRIBUTE + -EE]

dis·tri·bu·tion (dis′trə byo͞o′shən), *n.* **1.** the act or an instance of distributing. **2.** the state or manner of being distributed. **3.** arrangement; classification. **4.** that which is distributed. **5.** the frequency of occurrence or the natural geographic range or place where any item or category of items occur: *That particular pronunciation has too wide a distribution to be considered as part of an accent. What is the distribution of coniferous forests in the world?* **6.** placement, location, arrangement, or disposition: *The distribution of our troops is a military secret. Every doctor knows the distribution of the nerves in the body.* **7.** apportionment: *The court decided the distribution of the property among the heirs.* **8.** the delivery or giving out of an item or items to the intended recipients, as mail, newspapers, etc. **9.** the total number of an item delivered, sold, or given out: *The distribution of our school paper is now 3000.* **10.** the marketing, transporting, merchandising, and selling of any item: *We have a good product but our distribution is bad.* **11.** (in bridge and other card games) the way in which the suits of a deck of cards are, or one specific suit is, divided or apportioned in one player's hand or among the hands of all the players: *My distribution was six spades, four hearts, two clubs, and a singleton diamond. The distribution was such that each of the players had one void suit.* **12.** *Econ.* **a.** the division of the aggregate income of any society among its members, or among the factors of production. **b.** the system of dispersing goods throughout a community. **13.** *Statistics.* a set of values or measurements of a set of elements, each measurement being associated with an element. **14.** *Math.* a generalized function used esp. in solving differential equations. [< L *distribūtiōn-* (s. of *distribūtiō*). See DISTRIBUTE, -ION] —**dis′tri·bu′tion·al,** *adj.*

distribu′tion curve′, *Statistics.* the curve or line of a graph in which cumulative frequencies are plotted as ordinates and values of the variate as abscissas.

distribu′tion func′tion, *Statistics.* a function of a variate for which the functional value corresponding to a given value of the variate is the number of or the proportion of values of the variate equal to or less than the given value.

dis·trib·u·tive (di strib′yə tiv), *adj.* **1.** serving to distribute, assign, allot, or divide; characterized by or pertaining to distribution. **2.** *Gram.* treating the members of a group individually, as the adjectives *each* and *every*. **3.** *Logic.* (of a term) distributed in a given proposition. **4.** *Math.* **a.** (of a binary operation) having the property that terms in an expression may be expanded in a particular way to form an equivalent expression, as $a(b + c) = ab + ac$. **b.** having reference to this property: *distributive law for multiplication over addition.* **c.** (of a lattice) having the property that for any three elements, the intersection of the first element with the union of the others is equal to the intersection of the first element with each of the others. —*n.* **5.** a distributive word or expression. [< LL *distribūtīv(us)* (see DISTRIBUTE, -IVE); r. ME *distributif* < MF] —**dis·trib′u·tive·ly,** *adv.* —**dis·trib′u·tive·ness,** *n.*

dis·trib·u·tor (di strib′yə tər), *n.* **1.** one who or that which distributes. **2.** *Com.* **a.** one engaged in the general distribution or marketing of some article or class of goods. **b.** a wholesaler who has exclusive rights to market, within a given territory, the goods of a manufacturer or company. **3.** *Mach.* a device in a multicylinder engine which distributes the igniting voltage to the spark plugs in a definite sequence. **4.** *Print.* **a.** (in a press) one of the rollers for spreading ink on the table, rolling it to a proper consistency, and transferring it to rollers that ink the form or plate. **b.** Also called **distrib′utor bar′.** (in a Linotype) a bar with keylike cuts along its length, for sorting matrices into their proper magazines after type has been cast. Also, **dis·trib′ut·er.** [< L *distribūtor*. See DISTRIBUTE, -OR[2]]

dis·trib·u·tor·ship (di strib′yə tər ship′), *n.* *Com.* a franchise held by a distributor: *He was granted sole distributorship for the New England States.* [DISTRIBUTOR + -SHIP]

dis·trict (dis′trikt), *n.* **1.** a division of territory, as of a country, state, county, etc., marked off for administrative, electoral, or other purposes. **2.** a region or locality: *the Lake District.* **3.** *Brit.* a subdivision of a county or a town, roughly equal to a U.S. ward or precinct. —*v.t.* **4.** to divide into districts. [< ML *district(us)* exercise of justice, (area of) jurisdiction, n. use of L ptp. of *distringere* to stretch out (see DISTRAIN), equiv. to *di-* DI-[2] + *strig-* (root of *stringere* to bind, tie) + *-tus* ptp. suffix]

dis′trict attor′ney, an officer who acts as attorney for the people or government within a specified district.

dis′trict coun′cil, *Brit.* the local ruling body of an urban or rural district.

dis′trict court′, *U.S. Law.* **1.** (in many States) the court of general jurisdiction. **2.** the federal trial court sitting in each district of the United States.

Dis′trict Heights′, a town in central Maryland. 7524 (1960).

dis′trict man′, a legman who covers a beat for a newspaper.

Dis′trict of Colum′bia, a federal area in the E United States, on the Potomac, coextensive with the federal capital, Washington: governed by Congress. 763,957 (1960); 69 sq. mi. *Abbr.:* D.C.

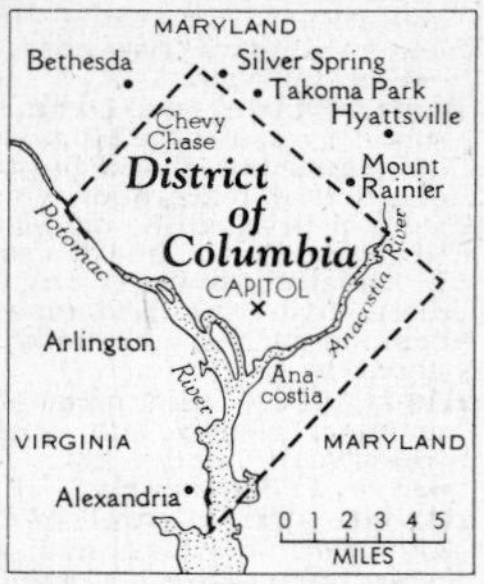

Dis·tri·to Fe·de·ral (dēs trē′tô fe′de räl′), *Spanish.* See **Federal District.** *Abbr.:* D.F.

dis·trust (dis trust′), *v.t.* **1.** to regard with doubt or suspicion; have no trust in. —*n.* **2.** lack of trust; doubt; suspicion. [DIS-[1] + TRUST] —**dis·trust′er,** *n.*

—**Syn. 2.** See **suspicion.**

dis·trust·ful (dis trust′fəl), *adj.* unable or unwilling to trust; doubtful; suspicious: *An alert scientist is distrustful of coincidences. A distrustful dog is the best watchdog.* [DISTRUST + -FUL] —**dis·trust′ful·ly,** *adv.* —**dis·trust′ful·ness,** *n.*

dis·turb (di stûrb′), *v.t.* **1.** to interrupt the quiet, rest, or peace of. **2.** to interfere with; interrupt; hinder: *Please do not disturb me while I am working.* **3.** to throw into commotion or disorder; agitate; disorder; disarrange; unsettle. **4.** to perplex; trouble: *to be disturbed by strange behavior.* —*v.i.* **5.** to cause disturbance to someone's sleep, rest, etc.: *Do not disturb.* [ME *disturbe(n)* < L *disturb(āre)* (to) destroy, equiv. to *dis-* DIS-[1] + *turbāre* to confuse; r. ME *disto(u)rben* < OF *desto(u)rb(er)*] —**dis·turb′er,** *n.*

dis·turb·ance (di stûr′bəns), *n.* **1.** the act of disturbing. **2.** the state of being disturbed. **3.** an instance of this; commotion. **4.** something that disturbs. **5.** an outbreak of disorder; a breach of public peace: *Political disturbances shook the city.* **6.** *Meteorol.* any cyclonic storm or low-pressure area, usually a small one. **7.** *Geol.* a crustal movement of moderate intensity, somewhat restricted in area. [ME *disto(u)rbance*, etc. < OF. See DISTURB, -ANCE]

—**Syn. 2.** perturbation, confusion. See **agitation. 5.** confusion, tumult, riot. See **disorder.** —**Ant. 3.** order.

dis·turbed (di stûrbd′), *adj.* marked by symptoms of neurosis or psychosis: *a disturbed personality.* [DISTURB + -ED[2]]

dis·turb·ing (di stûr′biŋ), *adj.* causing a loss of tranquillity; upsetting or troubling; disquieting: *The rumor of war had a disturbing effect on him.* [DISTURB + -ING[2]]

disty., distillery.

dis·tyle (dis′tīl, dī′stīl), *adj.* *Archit.* **1.** having two columns. **2.** (of a classical temple or building in the style of one) having two columns on one or either front; dyostyle. Also, **di·sty·lar** (dī stī′lər). [DI-[1] + Gk *stŷl(os)* column, pillar]

di·sub·sti·tut·ed (dī sub′sti to͞o′tid, -tyo͞o′-), *adj.* *Chem.* containing two substituents. [DI-[1] + SUBSTITUTED]

di·sul·fate (dī sul′fāt), *n.* *Chem.* a salt of pyrosulfuric acid, as sodium disulfate, $Na_2S_2O_7$. Also, **di·sul′phate.** [DI-[1] + SULFATE]

di·sul·fide (dī sul′fīd, -fid), *n.* *Chem.* **1.** (in inorganic chemistry) a sulfide containing two atoms of sulfur, as carbon disulfide, CS_2. **2.** (in organic chemistry) a sulfide containing the bivalent group –SS–, as diethyl disulfide, $C_2H_5SSC_2H_5$. Also, **di·sul′phide.** [DI-[1] + SULFIDE]

di·sul·fir·am (dī′sul fēr′əm), *n.* *Pharm.* a cream-colored, water-insoluble solid, $C_{10}H_{20}N_2S_4$, used chiefly in the treatment of chronic alcoholism, producing highly unpleasant symptoms when alcohol is taken following its administration. Also called **tetraethylthiuram disulfide.** [DISULFI(DE + *thiu*)*ram*; see THIO-, UREA, AMYL]

di·sul·fu·ric (dī′sul fyo͝or′ik), *adj.* *Chem.* pyrosulfuric. Also, **di′sul·phu′ric.** [DI-[1] + SULFURIC]

dis·u·ni·fy (dis yo͞o′nə fī′), *v.t.,* **-fied, -fy·ing.** to destroy the unity of. [DIS-[1] + UNIFY]

dis·un·ion (dis yo͞on′yən), *n.* **1.** a severance of union; separation; disjunction. **2.** lack of unity; dissension. [DIS-[1] + UNION]

dis·un·ion·ist (dis yo͞on′yə nist), *n.* **1.** one who advocates or causes disunion. **2.** *U.S. Hist.* a secessionist during the period of the Civil War. [DISUNION + -IST] —**dis·un′ion·ism,** *n.*

dis·u·nite (dis′yo͞o nīt′), *v.,* **-nit·ed, -nit·ing.** —*v.t.* **1.** to sever the union of; separate; disjoin. **2.** to set at variance; alienate: *The issue disunited the party members.* —*v.i.* **3.** to part; fall apart. [DIS-[1] + UNITE] —**dis·u·nit′er,** *n.*

dis·u·ni·ty (dis yo͞o′ni tē), *n., pl.* **-ties.** lack of unity or accord. [DIS-[1] + UNITY]

dis·use (*n.* dis yo͞os′; *v.* dis yo͞oz′), *n., v.,* **-used, -us·ing.** —*n.* **1.** discontinuance of use or practice: *Traditional customs are falling into disuse.* —*v.t.* **2.** to cease to use. [DIS-[1] + USE]

dis·u·til·i·ty (dis′yo͞o til′i tē), *n.* the quality of causing inconvenience, harm, distress, etc. [DIS-[1] + UTILITY]

dis·val·ue (dis val′yo͞o), *v.,* **-ued, -u·ing,** *n.* —*v.t.* **1.** *Archaic.* to depreciate; disparage. —*n.* **2.** disesteem; disparagement. [DIS-[1] + VALUE]

di·syl·lab·ic (dī′si lab′ik, dis′i-), *adj.* consisting of or pertaining to two syllables. Also, **dissyllabic.** [DI-[1] + SYLLABIC]

di·syl·la·bism (dī sil′ə biz′əm, di-), *n.* the state of being dysyllabic. Also, **dissyllabism.** [DI-[1] + SYLLABISM]

di·syl·la·bize (dī sil′ə bīz′, di-), *v.t.,* **-bized, -biz·ing.** to make disyllabic. Also, **dissyllabize.** [DISYLLABLE + -IZE]

di·syl·la·ble (dī′sil ə bəl, di sil′-), *n.* a word of two syllables. Also, **dissyllable.** [DI-[1] + SYLLABLE; cf. Gk *disýllabos*; var. *dissyllable* has *ss* < MF *dissilabe*]

dis·yoke (dis yōk′), *v.t.,* **-yoked, -yok·ing.** to free from or as from a yoke. [DIS-[1] + YOKE]

dit (dit), *n.* an echoic word, the referent of which is a click or brief tone interval, used to designate the dot of Morse code, International Morse code, etc. Cf. **dah.**

di·tat De·us (dē′tät de′o͞os; *Eng.* dī′tat dē′əs), *Latin.* God enriches: motto of Arizona.

ditch (dich), *n.* **1.** a long, narrow excavation made in the ground by digging, as for draining or irrigating land; trench. **2.** any open passage or trench, as a natural channel or waterway. —*v.t.* **3.** to dig a ditch or ditches in or around. **4.** to derail (a train) or drive or force (an automobile, bus, etc.) off the road. **5.** to crash-land (a land-based aircraft) on water and abandon it. **6.** *Slang.* **a.** to get rid of: *I ditched that old hat of yours.* **b.** to escape from: *He ditched the cops by turning off his lights and driving down an alley.* —*v.i.* **7.** to dig a ditch. **8.** (of an aircraft or its crew) to crash-land in water and abandon the sinking aircraft. [ME *dich*, OE *dīc*; c. G *Teich.* See DIKE[1]] —**ditch′less,** *adj.*

ditch·dig·ger (dich′dig′ər), *n.* **1.** a worker whose usual occupation is digging ditches, esp. with pick and shovel. **2.** a person engaged in exhausting manual work, esp. work that requires little or no originality. **3.** Also called **ditcher.** a power excavating machine designed to remove earth in a continuous line and to a predetermined width and depth, as by means of a rotating belt equipped with scoops. [DITCH + DIGGER] —**ditch′dig′ging,** *n., adj.*

ditch·er (dich′ər), *n.* **1.** a person who digs ditches. **2.** a person who ditches. **3.** ditchdigger (def. 3). [DITCH + -ER[1]]

ditch-moss (dich′môs′, -mos′), *n.* waterweed.

ditch·wa·ter (dich′wô′tər, -wot′ər), *n.* **1.** water, esp. stagnant and dirty water, that has collected in a ditch. **2. dull as ditchwater.** See **dishwater** (def. 2). [DITCH + WATER]

di·the·ism (dī′thē iz′əm), *n.* **1.** the doctrine of or belief in two supreme gods. **2.** belief in the existence of two independent antagonistic principles, one good and the other evil. [DI-[1] + THEISM] —**di′the·ist,** *n.* —**di′the·is′tic, di′the·is′ti·cal,** *adj.*

dith·er (dith′ər), *n.* **1.** a trembling; vibration. **2.** *Informal.* a state of flustered excitement or fear. —*v.i.* **3.** to act irresolutely; vacillate. **4.** *Northern England.* to tremble with excitement or fear. [var. of *didder* (ME *diddere*); cf. DODDER]

di·thi·o·nate (dī thī′ə nāt′, -nit), *n.* *Chem.* a salt of dithionic acid. [DITHION(IC) + -ATE[2]]

di·thi·on·ic (dī′thī on′ik, dith′ē-), *adj.* *Chem.* of or derived from dithionic acid. [DI-[1] + THIONIC]

di′thion′ic ac′id, *Chem.* an unstable acid, $H_2S_2O_6$, known only in solution and in the form of its salts.

di·thi·o·nite (dī thī′ə nīt′), *n.* *Chem.* hyposulfite (def. 1). [DI-[1] + Gk *theîon* sulfur + -ITE[1]]

di·thi·on·ous (dī′thī on′əs, dith′ē-, dī thī′ə nəs), *adj.* *Chem.* hyposulfurous. [DI-[1] + Gk *theîon* sulfur + -OUS]

dith·y·ramb (dith′ə ram′, -ramb′), *n.* **1.** a Greek choral song or chant of vehement or wild character and of usually irregular form, originally in honor of Dionysus or Bacchus. **2.** any poem or other composition having similar characteristics, as an impassioned or exalted theme or irregular form. [< L *dithyramb(us)* < Gk *dithýrambos*]

dith·y·ram·bic (dith′ə ram′bik), *adj.* **1.** of, pertaining to, or of the nature of a dithyramb. **2.** wildly irregular in form. **3.** wildly enthusiastic. [< L *dithyrambic(us)* < Gk *dithyrambikós*. See DITHYRAMB, -IC] —**dith′y·ram′bi·cal·ly,** *adv.*

Dith·y·ram·bus (dith′ə ram′bəs), *n.* *Class. Myth.* an epithet of Dionysus, meaning "child of the double door," in allusion to the fact that he was born twice.

Dit·mars (dit′märz), *n.* **Raymond Lee,** 1876–1942, U.S. zoologist and author.

dit·o·kous (dit′ə kəs), *adj.* **1.** producing two young or laying two eggs at each birth. **2.** producing two kinds of young, as certain worms. [< Gk *ditókos* twin-bearing, equiv. to *di-* DI-[1] + *tókos* child-bearing; see -OUS]

di·tri·glyph (dī trī′glif′), *n.* (in Doric architecture) **1.** the distance, on centers, between a metope and the second one distant. **2.** an intercolumniation having two whole triglyphs. [< F *ditriglyphe*. See DI-[1], TRIGLYPH] —**di′tri·glyph′ic,** *adj.*

dit·ta·ny (dit′ənē), *n., pl.* **-nies. 1.** a labiate plant, *Origanum Dictamnus*, of Crete, formerly believed to have medicinal qualities. **2.** a labiate plant, *Cunila origanoides*, of North America, bearing clusters of purplish flowers. **3.** Also called **burning-bush, fraxinella, gas-plant.** a perennial, rutaceous plant, *Dictamnus albus*, having foliage and flowers which emit an inflammable vapor. [ME *ditane, detany* < OF *ditan* < L *dictamn(us), dictamn(um)* < Gk *díktamnon*, perh. akin to *Diktē*, a mountain in Crete where the herb abounded]

Dit·ters·dorf (dit′ərz dôrf′), *n.* **Karl Dit·ters von** (kärl dit′ərs fən), 1739–99, Austrian violinist and composer.

dit·to (dit′ō), *n., pl.* **-tos,** *adv., v.,* **-toed, -to·ing.** —*n.* **1.** the aforesaid; the above; the same (used in accounts, lists, etc., to avoid repetition). *Abbr.:* do. *Symbol:* ″. Cf. **ditto mark. 2.** another of the same. **3.** *Informal.* a duplicate; copy. —*adv.* **4.** as already stated; likewise. —*v.t.* **5.** to duplicate; copy. [< It, var. of *detto* < L *dictus* said, ptp. of *dīcere* to say; see DICTUM]

dit·to·graph (dit′ə graf′, -gräf′), *n.* an instance of dittography; a passage containing reduplicated syllables, letters, etc. [back formation from DITTOGRAPHY]

dit·tog·ra·phy (di tog′rə fē), *n.* reduplication of letters or syllables in writing, printing, etc., usually through error. Cf. **haplography.** [< Gk *dittographía*, dial. var. of *dissographía*, equiv. to *dissó(s)* double + *-graphia* -GRAPHY] —**dit·to·graph·ic** (dit′ə graf′ik), *adj.*

dit′to machine′, a machine that copies letters, drawings, etc., esp. by an ink-transfer process.

dit′to mark′, Often, **ditto marks.** two small marks (″) indicating the repetition of something, usually placed beneath the thing repeated.

dit·ty (dit′ē), *n., pl.* **-ties,** *v.,* **-tied, -ty·ing.** —*n.* **1.** a poem intended to be sung. **2.** a short, simple song. —*v.i.* **3.** *Obs.* to sing. —*v.t.* **4.** *Obs.* to set or to celebrate in music. [ME *dite* < OF *dit(i)e* poem, n. use of ptp. of *ditier* to compose < L *dictāre* (see DICTATE), freq. of *dīcere* to say]

dit′ty bag′, a bag used by sailors to hold sewing implements and other necessaries. [?]

dit′ty box′, a small box used like a ditty bag.

Di·u (dē′o͞o), *n.* a former district in Portuguese India, comprising a small island and seaport at the extremity of

Kathiawar peninsula: annexed by India in December, 1961. 24,342 (1950); 14 sq. mi.

di·u·re·sis (dī′yŏŏ rē′sis), *n.* increased discharge of urine. [< NL < Gk *diourē-* (verbal s. of *diourein* to urinate) + *-sis* -SIS; see DIURETIC]

di·u·ret·ic (dī′yŏŏ ret′ik), *Med.* —*adj.* **1.** increasing the volume of the urine excreted, as by a medicinal substance. —*n.* **2.** a diuretic medicine or agent. [< NL *diurētic(us)* < Gk *diourētikós*, equiv. to *di-* DI-³ + *ourē-* (verbal s. of *oureîn* to urinate) + *-tikos* -TIC] —**di′u·ret′i·cal·ly,** *adv.* —**di′u·ret′i·cal·ness,** *n.*

Di·ur·il (dī′ər il), *n. Pharm., Trademark.* chlorothiazide.

di·ur·nal (dī ûr′nᵊl), *adj.* **1.** of or pertaining to a day or each day; daily: *the diurnal round of the mailman.* **2.** of or belonging to the daytime (opposed to *nocturnal*). **3.** *Bot.* showing a periodic alteration of condition with day and night, as certain flowers which open by day and close by night. **4.** active by day, as certain birds and insects (opposed to *nocturnal*). —*n.* **5.** *Liturgy.* a service book containing offices for the daily hours of prayer. **6.** *Archaic.* a diary. **7.** *Archaic.* a newspaper, esp. a daily one. [ME < L *diurnāl(is)*, equiv. to *diurn(us)* daily + *-ālis* -AL¹] —**di·ur′nal·ly,** *adv.* —**di·ur′nal·ness,** *n.*

diur′nal arc′, *Astron.* the portion of the diurnal circle that is above the horizon at a given point. Cf. **nocturnal arc.**

diur′nal cir′cle, *Astron.* the apparent circle described by a heavenly body as a result of one rotation by the earth.

diur′nal par′allax. See under **parallax** (def. 2).

Di·us Fi·di·us (dī′əs fid′ē əs), an ancient Roman god of oaths, hospitality, and international affairs, sometimes identified with Sancus.

Diu·sham·be (*Russ.* dyŏŏ shäm′be), *n.* Dyushambe.

Div., **1.** divine. **2.** divinity.

div., **1.** divide. **2.** divided. **3.** dividend. **4.** division. **5.** divisor.

di·va (dē′vä), *n., pl.* **-vas, -ve** (-ve). a distinguished female singer; prima donna. [< It < L *dīva*, fem. of *dīvus* god; cf. DIVINE]

di·va·gate (dī′və gāt′), *v.i.,* **-gat·ed, -gat·ing. 1.** to wander; stray. **2.** to digress in speech. [< L *dīvagāt(us)* (ptp. of *dīvagārī* to wander off), equiv. to *dī-* DI-² + *vag-* (root of *vagārī* to wander) + *-ātus* -ATE¹] —**di′va·ga′tion,** *n.*

di·va·lent (dī vā′lənt), *adj. Chem.* having a valence of two, as the ferrous ion, Fe^{++}. [DI-¹ + -VALENT] —**di·va′lence,** *n.*

Di·va·li (di vä′lē), *n.* Diwali.

di·van (di van′, -vän′ *or, esp. for 1,* dī′van), *n.* **1.** a sofa or couch. **2.** a long, cushioned seat, usually without arms or back, placed against a wall, as in Oriental countries. **3.** a council of state in Turkey and other countries of the Middle East. **4.** any council, committee, or commission. **5.** (in the Middle East) **a.** a council chamber, judgment hall, audience chamber, or bureau of state. **b.** a large building used for some official or public purpose, as a custom house. **6.** a smoking room, as in connection with a tobacco shop. **7.** a collection of poems, esp. a collection in Arabic or Persian of poems by one poet. [< Turk < Pers *dīwān*, orig. *dēvan* booklet (whence account book, office, council, bench)]

di·var·i·cate (*v.* dī var′ə kāt′, di-; *adj.* dī var′ə kit, -kāt′, di-), *v.,* **-cat·ed, -cat·ing,** *adj.* —*v.i.* **1.** to spread apart; branch; diverge. **2.** *Bot., Zool.* to branch at a wide angle. —*adj.* **3.** spread apart; widely divergent. **4.** *Bot., Zool.* branching at a wide angle. [< L *dīvāricāt(us)* (ptp. of *dīvāricāre*), equiv. to *dī-* DI-² + *vāric-* (base of *vāricāre* to straddle; see PREVARICATE) + *-ātus* -ATE¹] —**di·var′i·cate·ly,** *adv.* —**di·var′i·cat′ing·ly,** *adv.* —**di·var′i·ca′tion,** *n.* —**di·var′i·ca′tor,** *n.*

dive (dīv), *v.,* **dived or dove, dived, div·ing,** *n.* —*v.i.* **1.** to plunge, esp. head first, as into water. **2.** to go below the surface of the water, as a submarine. **3.** to plunge, fall, or descend through the air, into the earth, etc.: *The acrobats dived into nets.* **4.** *Aeron.* (of an airplane) to plunge downward at a greater angle than when gliding. **5.** to penetrate suddenly into something, as with the hand: *to dive into a purse.* **6.** to dart: *to dive into a doorway.* **7.** to enter deeply or plunge into a subject, business, activity, etc. —*v.t.* **8.** to cause to plunge, submerge, or descend: *He dived the submarine and gave orders to prepare to fire torpedoes.* —*n.* **9.** the act or an instance of diving. **10.** a jump or plunge into water, esp. in a prescribed way from a diving board. **11.** the vertical or almost vertical descent of an airplane at a speed surpassing the possible speed of the same plane in level flight. **12.** a submerging, as of a submarine, skin-diver, etc. **13.** a dash, plunge, or lunge, as if throwing oneself at or into something: *The right end made a dive for the football.* **14.** a sudden or sharp decline: *Rail stocks took a dive on the stock market.* **15.** *Informal.* a dingy or disreputable bar or nightclub. **16.** *Boxing Slang.* a false show of being knocked out, usually in a bout the result of which has been prearranged: *to take a dive in an early round.* [ME *dīve(n)* (to) dive, dip, OE *dȳfan* to dip (causative of *dūfan* to dive, sink); c. Icel *dȳfa* dip, G *taufen* to baptize; akin to DIP]

dive-bomb (dīv′bom′), *v.i., v.t.* to attack with or as with a dive bomber.

dive′ bomb′er, an airplane of the fighter-bomber type that drops its bombs while diving at the enemy.

dive′ bomb′ing, *Mil.* a technique of bombing in which the bomb load is released when the aircraft is in a steep dive, usually at an angle of 60 degrees or more from horizontal.

div·er (dī′vər), *n.* **1.** one who or that which dives. **2.** a person who makes a business of diving, as for pearl oysters, to examine sunken vessels, etc. **3.** *Brit.* a loon. **4.** any of several other birds noted for their skill in diving. [DIVE + -ER¹]

di·verge (di vûrj′, dī-), *v.,* **-verged, -verg·ing.** —*v.i.* **1.** to move, lie, or extend in different directions from a common point; branch off. **2.** to differ in opinion, character, form, etc.; deviate. **3.** *Math.* (of a sequence, series, etc.) to have no unique limit; to have infinity as a limit. **4.** to turn aside or digress, as from a path, discussion, plan, etc. —*v.t.* **5.** to deflect or turn aside. [< ML *dīverg(ere)*, equiv. to L *dī-* DI-² + *vergere* to incline] —**Syn. 4.** See **deviate.**

di·ver·gence (di vûr′jəns, dī-), *n.* **1.** the act, fact, or amount of diverging: *a divergence in opinion.* **2.** (in physics, meteorology, etc.) the total amount of flux escaping an infinitesimal volume at a point in a vector field, as the net flow of air from a given region. **3.** *Electronics.* the spreading of a stream of electrons resulting from their mutual electrostatic repulsion. **4.** *Math., Mech.* **a.** the limiting ratio of the flux passing through the area surrounding a point to the area as it decreases to zero for a given vector at the point in a vector field; the inner product of the given vector and the vector whose components are the partial derivatives with respect to each coordinate. **b.** the operation of obtaining this quantity. [< ML *dīvergentia.* See DIVERGE, -ENCE] —**Syn. 1.** separation, division, variation, deviation.

di·ver·gen·cy (di vûr′jən sē, dī-), *n., pl.* **-cies.** divergence; deviation. [< ML *dīvergentia.* See DIVERGE, -ENCY]

di·ver·gent (di vûr′jənt, dī-), *adj.* **1.** diverging; differing, deviating. **2.** pertaining to or causing divergence. [< ML *dīvergent-* (s. of *dīvergēns*, prp. of *dīvergere*). See DIVERGE, -ENT] —**di·ver′gent·ly,** *adv.*

diver′gent squint′, *Ophthalm.* strabismus in which one or both eyes are turned outward from the nose. Also called **diver′gent strabis′mus, exotropia.** Cf. **convergent squint.**

diverg′ing lens′, *Optics.* a lens which causes a beam of parallel rays to diverge after refraction, as from a virtual image; a lens that has a negative focal length. Also called **negative lens.** Cf. **converging lens.**

di·vers (dī′vərz), *adj.* **1.** several; sundry: *divers articles.* —*pron.* **2.** (*construed as pl.*) an indefinite number more than one: *He chose divers of them, who were asked to accompany him.* [ME < OF < L *dīvers(us)* DIVERSE]

di·verse (di vûrs′, dī-, dī′vûrs), *adj.* **1.** of a different kind, form, character, etc.; unlike: *He is of a diverse nature from the rest of his family.* **2.** of various kinds or forms; multiform. [ME < L *dīvers(us)* (ptp. of *dīvertere* to DIVERT), equiv. to *dī-* DI-² + *vert-* (base of *vertere* to turn) + *-tus* ptp. suffix] —**di·verse′ly,** *adv.* —**di·verse′ness,** *n.*
—**Syn. 1.** dissimilar, separate. **2.** varied, manifold, divergent. See **various.**

di·ver·si·fi·ca·tion (di vûr′sə fə kā′shən), *n.* **1.** the act or state of diversifying. **2.** the act or practice of manufacturing a variety of products, investing in a variety of securities, selling a variety of merchandise, etc., so that a failure in or an economic slump affecting one will not be disastrous. [< ML *dīversificātiōn-* (s. of *dīversificātiō*). See DIVERSIFY, -FICATION]

di·ver·si·fied (di vûr′sə fīd′, dī-), *adj.* **1.** distinguished by various forms or by a variety of objects: *diversified activity.* **2.** varied; distributed among or producing several types: *diversified investments.* [DIVERSIFY + -ED²]

di·ver·si·form (di vûr′sə fôrm′, dī-), *adj.* differing in form; of various forms. [< L *divers(us)* DIVERSE + -I- + -FORM]

di·ver·si·fy (di vûr′sə fī′, dī-), *v.t.,* **-fied, -fy·ing. 1.** to make diverse, as in form or character; give variety or diversity to; variegate. **2.** to invest in different types of (securities, investments, etc.) or produce different types of (manufactured products, crops, etc.). [late ME < MF *diversifi(er)* < ML *dīversificāre*, equiv. to L *dīvers(us)* DIVERSE + *-ificāre* -IFY] —**di·ver′si·fi′a·bil′i·ty,** *n.* —**di·ver′si·fi′a·ble,** *adj.* —**di·ver′si·fi′er,** *n.*

di·ver·sion (di vûr′zhən, -shən, dī-), *n.* **1.** the act of diverting or turning aside, as from a course or purpose: *a diversion of industry into the war effort.* **2.** a channel made to divert the flow of water from one course to another or to direct the flow of water draining from a piece of ground. **3.** *Brit.* a detour on a highway or road. **4.** distraction from business, care, etc.; recreation; entertainment; amusement; a pastime: *Movies can be a worthwhile diversion.* **5.** *Mil.* a feint intended to draw off attention from the point of main attack. [< ML *dīversiōn-* (s. of *dīversiō*), equiv. to L *dīvers(us)* DIVERSE + *-iōn-* -ION] —**di·ver′sion·al,** *adj.* —**di·ver′sion·ar′y,** *adj.*

di·ver·si·ty (di vûr′si tē, dī-), *n., pl.* **-ties. 1.** the state or fact of being diverse; difference; unlikeness. **2.** variety; multiformity. **3.** a point of difference. [ME *diversite* < MF < L *dīversitās.* See DIVERSE, -ITY]

di·vert (di vûrt′, dī-), *v.t.* **1.** to turn aside or from a path or course; deflect. **2.** *Brit.* to route (traffic) on a detour. **3.** to draw off to a different course, purpose, etc. **4.** to distract from serious occupation; entertain or amuse. [late ME < L *dīvert(ere)*, equiv. to *dī-* DI-² + *vertere* to turn] —**di·vert′ed·ly,** *adv.* —**di·vert′er,** *n.* —**di·vert′i·ble,** *adj.*
—**Syn. 4.** distract, delight. See **amuse.** —**Ant. 4.** bore.

di·ver·tic·u·lum (dī′vər tik′yə ləm), *n., pl.* **-la** (-lə). *Anat.* a blind, tubular sac or process branching off from a canal or cavity. [< L, var. of *dēverticulum*, equiv. to *dēverti-* (comb. form of *dēvertere*, equiv. to *dē-* DE- + *vertere* to turn) + *-culum* -CULE] —**di′ver·tic′u·lar,** *adj.*

di·ver·ti·men·to (di vûr′tə men′tō; *It.* dē ver′tē-men′tô), *n., pl.* **-ti** (-tē). *Music.* an instrumental composition in several movements, light and diverting in character, similar to a serenade. Also called **divertissement.** [< It, equiv. to *diverti(re)* (to) DIVERT + *-mento* -MENT]

di·vert·ing (di vûr′ting, dī-), *adj.* serving to divert; entertaining; amusing. [DIVERT + -ING²] —**di·vert′ing·ly,** *adv.*

di·ver·tisse·ment (di vûr′tis mənt; *Fr.* dē ver tēs-mäN′), *n., pl.* **-ments** (-mənts; *Fr.* -mäN′). **1.** a diversion or entertainment. **2.** *Music.* divertimento. **3.** a short ballet or other performance given between or in the course of acts or longer pieces. **4.** a series of such performances. [< F, equiv. to *divertiss(e)-* (s. of *divertir* to DIVERT) + *-ment* -MENT]

di·ver·tive (di vûr′tiv, dī-), *adj.* diverting; amusing. [DIVERT + -IVE]

Di·ves (dī′vēz), *n.* **1.** the rich man of the parable in Luke 16:19–31. **2.** any rich man. [< L: rich, rich man]

di·vest (di vest′, dī-), *v.t.* **1.** to strip of clothing, ornament, etc.: *The wind divested the trees of their leaves.* **2.** to strip or deprive of anything; dispossess. **3.** to rid of or free from: *He divested himself of all responsibility for the decision.* **4.** *Law.* to take away or alienate (property, rights, etc.). **5.** *Com.* to sell off or rid of through sales: *to divest holdings; to divest oneself of shares.* [< ML *dīvest(īre)*, equiv. to *dī-* DI-² + *vestīre* to VEST]
—**Syn. 1.** unclothe, denude. **2.** See **strip¹.**

di·vest·i·ble (di ves′tə bəl, dī-), *adj.* capable of being divested, as an estate in land. [DIVEST + -IBLE]

di·vest·i·ture (di ves′ti chər, dī-), *n.* **1.** the act of divesting. **2.** the state of being divested. **3.** something, as property or investments, that has been divested. **4.** the sale of business holdings or part of a company, esp. under legal compulsion. [DI-² + (IN)VESTITURE]

divid., (in prescriptions) divide. [< L *dīvide*]

di·vid·a·ble (di vī′də bəl), *adj.* capable of being divided; divisible. [DIVIDE + -ABLE] —**di·vid′a·ble·ness,** *n.*

di·vide (di vīd′), *v.,* **-vid·ed, -vid·ing,** *n.* —*v.t.* **1.** to separate into parts, groups, sections, etc. **2.** to separate or part from something else; sunder; cut off. **3.** to deal out in parts; apportion; distribute in shares. **4.** to cleave; part. **5.** to separate in opinion or feeling; cause to disagree: *The issue divided the senators.* **6.** to distinguish the kinds of; classify. **7.** *Math.* **a.** to separate into equal parts by the process of mathematical division; apply the mathematical process of division to. **b.** to be a divisor of, without a remainder. **c.** to mark a uniform scale on (a ruler, thermometer, etc.). **8.** *Brit. Govt.* to separate (a legislature, assembly, etc.) into two groups in ascertaining the vote on a question. —*v.i.* **9.** to become divided or separated. **10.** to share something with others: *We all divide equally.* **11.** to diverge; branch; fork: *The road divides six miles from here.* **12.** to perform the mathematical process of division: *He could add and subtract, but hadn't learned to divide.* **13.** *Brit. Govt.* to vote by separating into two groups. —*n.* **14.** *Archaic.* the act of dividing; a division. **15.** Also called **height of land.** *Phys. Geog.* the line or zone of higher ground between two adjacent streams or drainage basins. [< L *dīvid(ere)*, equiv. to *dī-* DI-² + a root *vid* found also in *vidua* WIDOW]
—**Syn. 1.** See **separate. 2.** sever, shear. **3.** partition.

di·vid·ed (di vī′did), *adj.* **1.** separated; separate. **2.** disunited. **3.** shared; apportioned. **4.** *Bot.* (of a leaf) cut into distinct portions by incisions extending to the midrib or the base. [DIVIDE + -ED²] —**di·vid′ed·ly,** *adv.* —**di·vid′ed·ness,** *n.*

divid′ed high′way, a superhighway with a broad median strip, designed to prevent collisions, headlight glare, etc., between vehicles moving in opposite directions, and usually having limited or cloverleaf access. Also called **dual highway.** Cf. **Autobahn.**

di·vi·de et im·pe·ra (dē′vi de′ et im′pe rä′; *Eng.* div′ə dē′ et im′pər ə), *Latin.* divide and rule: political maxim of Machiavelli.

div·i·dend (div′i dend′), *n.* **1.** *Math.* a number that is to be divided by the divisor. **2.** *Law.* a sum out of an insolvent estate paid to creditors. **3.** Also called, *Brit.,* **capital bonus.** *Finance.* **a.** a pro-rata share in an amount to be distributed. **b.** a sum of money paid to shareholders of a corporation out of earnings. **4.** *Insurance.* (in participating insurance) a distribution to a policyholder of a portion of the premium not needed by the company to pay claims or to meet expenses. **5.** a share of anything divided. **6.** anything received as a bonus, reward, or in addition to or beyond what is expected: *Swimming is fun, and gives you the dividend of better health.* [< L *dividend-(um)* thing to be divided, neut. ger. of *dīvidere* to DIVIDE]
—**Syn. 5.** allotment, portion.

di·vi·den·dus (dī′vi den′dəs), *adj.* (in prescriptions) meant to be divided. [< L]

di·vid·er (di vī′dər), *n.* **1.** one who or that which divides. **2. dividers,** a pair of compasses, as used for dividing lines, measuring, etc. **3.** a partition between two areas or dividing one area into two, as a piece of cardboard in a box or a bookcase jutting out from a wall. **4.** *Mining.* bunton. [DIVIDE + -ER¹]

Dividers

divid′ing en′gine, a machine for scribing accurately spaced division marks or scales.

divid′ing ridge′, a mountain ridge that separates two or more drainage basins.

di·vi·di·vi (div′ē div′ē), *n., pl.* **di·vi·di·vis, di·vi·di·vi. 1.** a shrub or small tree, *Caesalpinia coriaria*, of tropical America, the astringent pods of which are used in tanning and dyeing. **2.** the related species *C. tinctoria.* **3.** the pods of either plant. [< Sp < Carib]

di·vid·u·al (di vij′ōō əl), *adj. Archaic.* **1.** divisible or divided. **2.** separate; distinct. **3.** distributed; shared. [< L *dīvidu(us)* divisible (see DIVIDE) + -AL¹] —**di·vid′u·al·ly,** *adv.*

Di·vi·na Com·me·dia (*It.* dē vē′nä kôm me′dyä). See **Divine Comedy.**

div·i·na·tion (div′ə nā′shən), *n.* **1.** the practice of attempting to foretell future events or discover hidden knowledge by occult or supernatural means. **2.** augury; prophecy: *The divination of the high priest was fulfilled.* **3.** perception by intuition; instinctive foresight. [< L *dīvīnātiōn-* (s. of *dīvīnātiō*), equiv. to *dīvīnāt(us)*, ptp. of *dīvīnāre* to soothsay (*dīvīn-* DIVINE + *-ātus* -ATE¹) + *-iōn-* -ION; r. ME *divinacioun* < AF] —**di·vin·a·to·ry** (di vin′ə tōr′ē, -tôr′ē), *adj.*

di·vine (di vīn′), *adj., n., v.,* **-vined, -vin·ing.** —*adj.* **1.** of or pertaining to a god, esp. the Supreme Being. **2.** addressed, appropriated, or devoted to God or a god; religious; sacred: *divine worship.* **3.** proceeding from God or a god: *divine laws.* **4.** godlike; characteristic of or befitting a deity: *divine magnanimity.* **5.** heavenly; celestial: *the divine kingdom.* **6.** *Informal.* extremely good; unusually lovely: *She wore the most divine hat.* **7.** being a god; being God: *a divine person.* **8.** of superhuman or surpassing excellence: *Beauty is divine.* **9.** *Archaic.* of or pertaining to divinity or theology. —*n.* **10.** a theologian; scholar in religion. **11.** a priest or clergyman. **12. the Divine, a.** God. **b.** (*sometimes l.c.*) the spiritual aspect of man; the group of attributes and qualities of mankind regarded as Godly or Godlike: *He hated the lust but admired the Divine in man.* —*v.t.* **13.** to discover or declare (something obscure or in the future) by divination; prophesy. **14.** to discover (water, metal, etc.) by means of a divining rod. **15.** to perceive by intuition or insight; conjecture. **16.** *Archaic.* to portend. —*v.i.* **17.** to use or practice divination; prophesy. **18.** to have perception by intuition or insight; conjecture. [ME < L *dīvīn(us)*, equiv. to *dīv(us)* god + *-īnus* -INE¹; r. ME *devin(e)* < OF *devin* < L, as above]

—**di·vin′a·ble,** *adj.* —**di·vine′ly,** *adv.* —**di·vine′ness,** *n.*
—**Syn. 13, 17.** foretell, predict, foresee, forecast. **15, 18.** discern, understand. —**Ant. 5.** earthy, mundane.

Divine′ Com′edy, a narrative epic poem (14th century) by Dante. Italian, **Divina Commedia.**

divine′ heal′ing, 1. healing through divine intervention as in response to prayer or because of faith. **2.** a method employing prayer or faith in the hope of receiving such healing.

Divine′ Lit′urgy, *Chiefly Eastern Ch.* liturgy (def. 5).

Divine′ Mind′, *Christian Science.* mind (def. 16).

Divine′ Moth′er, *Hinduism.* the creative, dynamic aspect of the Godhead, the consort or Shakti of Brahma, Vishnu, or Shiva, variously known as Devi, Durga, Kali, Shakti, etc.

divine′ of′fice, (*sometimes caps.*) *Eccles.* office (def. 12b).

di·vin·er (di vī′nər), *n.* a person who divines; soothsayer; prophet. [DIVINE + -ER[1]; r. ME *divinour* < AF < L *dīvīnātor* soothsayer, equiv. to *dīvīnā(re)* (to) DIVINE + *-tor* -TOR]

divine′ right′ of kings′, the right to rule derived directly from God, not from the consent of the people.

divine′ serv′ice, service[1] (def. 15).

div′ing bee′tle. See **predaceous diving beetle.**

div′ing bell′, a chamber with an open-bottomed chamber in which persons can go underwater without special apparatus, the water being excluded from the upper part of the chamber by the equal pressure of the air.

div′ing board′, a springboard.

div′ing boat′, a boat used as a tender for divers or others working under water.

div′ing suit′, any of various weighted, hermetically sealed costumes, supplied with air under pressure, worn by divers under water. Also called **div′ing dress′.**

divin′ing rod′, a rod, esp. a forked stick, commonly of hazel, supposed to be useful in locating underground water, metal deposits, etc. Also called **dowsing rod.**

Di·vi·ni Re·demp·to·ris (dē vē′nē rā′demp tôr′ēs, -tōr′-), *Latin.* Divine Redemption: the opening words and the title of an encyclical of Pope Pius XI issued in 1937 on Communism.

div·i·nise (div′ə nīz′), *v.t.,* **-nised, -nis·ing.** *Chiefly Brit.* divinize. —**div′i·ni·sa′tion,** *n.*

di·vin·i·ty (di vin′i tē), *n., pl.* **-ties. 1.** the quality of being divine; divine nature. **2.** deity; godhood. **3.** a divine being; God. **4. the Divinity,** (*sometimes l.c.*) the Deity. **5.** a being having divine attributes, ranking below God but above man: *minor divinities.* **6.** the study or science of divine things; theology. **7.** godlike character; supreme excellence: *the divinity of Beethoven's music.* **8.** Also called **divin′ity fudge′.** a fluffy white or artificially tinted fudge made usually of sugar, corn syrup, egg whites and flavoring, often with nuts. [ME *divinite* < MF < L *dīvīnitāt-* (s. of *dīvīnitās*). See DIVINE, -ITY]

divin′ity cir′cuit. See **circuit binding.**

divin′ity school′, a Protestant seminary.

div·i·nize (div′ə nīz′), *v.t.,* **-nized, -niz·ing.** to make divine; deify. Also, *esp. Brit.,* **divinise.** [DIVINE + -IZE; cf. F *diviniser*] —**div′i·ni·za′tion,** *n.*

div. in par. aeq., (in prescriptions) let it be divided into equal parts. [< L *dīvidātur in partes aequāles*]

di·vi′nyl e′ther (dī vī′nil, -vin′əl, -vin′il, -vin′əl), *Pharm.* See **vinyl ether.** [DI-[1] + VINYL]

di·vi·si (di vē′zē), *adj. Music.* divided; separated (used as a musical direction for two or more performers reading a part to begin reading two or more parts). [< It, pl. of *diviso* divided, ptp. of *dividere* to DIVIDE]

di·vis·i·bil·i·ty (di viz′ə bil′i tē), *n. Math.* the capacity of being evenly divided, without remainder. [< L *dīvīsibil(is)* DIVISIBLE + -ITY]

di·vis·i·ble (di viz′ə bəl), *adj.* **1.** capable of being divided. **2.** *Math.* of or pertaining to a group in which given any element and any integer, there is a second element which when raised to the integer equals the first element. [< L *dīvīsibil(is),* equiv. to *dīvīs(us),* ptp. of *dīvidere* (*dī-* DI-[2] + *vid-* (perf. s.) + *-tus* ptp. suffix) + *-ibilis* -IBLE] —**di·vis′i·ble·ness,** *n.* —**di·vis′i·bly,** *adv.*

di·vi·sion (di vizh′ən), *n.* **1.** the act or state of being divided. **2.** *Arith.* the operation inverse to multiplication; the finding of a quantity, the quotient, which, when multiplied by a given quantity, the divisor, gives another given quantity, the dividend; the scientific mathematical process for ascertaining how many times one number or quantity is contained in another. **3.** something that divides or separates; partition. **4.** something that marks a division; dividing line or mark. **5.** one of the parts into which a thing is divided; section. **6.** separation by difference of opinion or feeling; disagreement; dissension. **7.** *Govt.* the separation of a legislature, or the like, into two groups, in taking a vote. **8.** one of the parts into which a country or an organization is divided for political, judicial, military, or other purposes. **9.** *Mil.* **a.** (in the army) a major administrative and tactical unit, larger than a regiment or brigade and smaller than a corps: it is usually commanded by a major general. **b.** (in the navy) a number of ships, usually four, forming a tactical group which is part of a fleet or squadron. **10.** a major autonomous or semi-independent but subordinate administrative unit of an industrial enterprise, government bureau, transportation system, or university: *the sales division of the Ford Motor Co.; the Division of Humanities of the University of Chicago; the eastern division of the Greyhound Bus Lines.* **11.** (in sports) a category or class containing all the teams or competitors grouped together according to standing, skill, weight, age, or the like: *He had never played on a team in the first division. In boxing, the heavyweight division attracts the most fans.* **12.** *Biol.* a major primary subdivision of the plant kingdom, consisting of one or more classes. Cf. **phylum** (def. 1). **13.** *Zool.* any subdivision of a classificatory group or category. **14.** the ornamentation of a melodic line in 17th- and 18th-century music. **15.** *Hort.* a type of propogation in which new plants are grown from segments separated from the parent plant. [ME < L *dīvīsiōn-* (s. of *dīvīsiō*), equiv. to *dīvīs(us)* (see DIVISIBLE) + *-iōn-* -ION; r. ME *devisioun* < AF] —**di·vi′sion·al, di·vi′sion·ar′y,** *adj.* —**di·vi′sion·al·ly,** *adv.*
—**Syn. 1.** separation, apportionment, allotment, distribution. DIVISION, PARTITION suggest the operation of dividing into parts or of one part from another. DIVISION usually means little more than the marking off or separation of a whole into parts. PARTITION often adds the idea of sharing, of an allotting or assigning of parts following division: *partition of an estate, of a country.* **4.** boundary, demarcation. **5.** compartment, segment. **6.** breach, rift, disunion, rupture, estrangement, alienation. —**Ant. 6.** accord, union.

divi′sion al′gebra, *Math.* a linear algebra in which each element of the vector space has a multiplicative inverse.

divi′sion al′gorithm, *Algebra.* the theorem that an integer can be written as the sum of the product of two integers, one a given positive integer, added to a positive integer smaller than the given positive integer. Cf. **Euclidean algorithm.**

Di·vi·sion·ism (di vizh′ə niz′əm), *n.* (*sometimes l.c.*) *Fine Arts.* the theory and technique of the Pointillists. [DIVISION + -ISM] —**Di·vi′sion·ist,** *n., adj.*

divi′sion ring′, *Math.* a ring in which the set of nonzero elements is a group with the operation of multiplication.

divi′sion sign′, *Arith.* the symbol (÷) placed between two expressions and denoting division of the first by the second.

di·vi·sive (di vī′siv), *adj.* **1.** forming or expressing division or distribution. **2.** creating dissension or discord. [< ML *dīvīsīv(us),* equiv. to L *dīvīs(us)* (see DIVISIBLE) + *-īvus* -IVE] —**di·vi′sive·ly,** *adv.* —**di·vi′sive·ness,** *n.*

di·vi·sor (di vī′zər), *n. Math.* **1.** a number by which another number, the dividend, is divided. **2.** a number contained in another given number a certain integral number of times, without a remainder. [< L *dīvīsor,* equiv. to *dīvīs(us)* (see DIVISIBLE) + *-or* -OR[2]]

di·vorce (di vōrs′, -vôrs′), *n., v.* **-vorced, -vorc·ing.** —*n.* **1.** *Law.* a judicial declaration dissolving a marriage in whole or in part, esp. one that releases the husband and wife from all matrimonial obligations. Cf. **judicial separation. 2.** any formal separation of man and wife according to established custom, as among uncivilized tribes. **3.** total separation; disunion: *a divorce between thought and action.* —*v.t.* **4.** to separate by divorce: *The judge divorced the couple.* **5.** to break the marriage contract between oneself and (one's spouse) by divorce: *She divorced her husband.* **6.** to separate; cut off: *Life and art cannot be divorced. He is divorced from society.* —*v.i.* **7.** to get a divorce. [ME < MF < L *dīvort(ium)* separation, equiv. to *divort-* DIVERT + *-ium* -Y[3] (L *-tium* > E *-ce*)] —**di·vorce′a·ble,** *adj.* —**di·vorc′er,** *n.* —**di·vor′cive,** *adj.*

di·vor·cé (di vōr sā′, -vôr-, -vōr′sā, -vôr′-), *n.* a divorced man. [< F, n. use of masc. ptp. of *divorcer* < ML *dīvortiāre* to divorce, deriv. of L *dīvorti(um)* DIVORCE]

divorce′ court′, a court having jurisdiction over termination of marital relations, as actions for divorce, annulment, etc.

di·vor·cee (di vōr sē′, -sā′, -vôr-, -vōr′sē, -vôr′-), *n.* a divorced woman. Also, **di·vor·cée′.** [DIVORCE + -EE]

di·vorce·ment (di vōrs′mənt, -vôrs′-), *n.* divorce; separation. [DIVORCE + -MENT]

divorce′ mill′, *Informal.* a divorce court, esp. such a court in a state or country which does not impose onerous requirements, as a long period of residence, humiliating grounds, etc., on those who wish to dissolve their marriage.

div·ot (div′ət), *n.* **1.** *Golf.* a piece of turf gouged out with a club in making a stroke. **2.** *Scot.* a piece of turf. [?]

di·vul·gate (di vul′gāt), *v.t.,* **-gat·ed, -gat·ing.** *Archaic.* to make publicly known; publish. [< L *dīvulgāt(us)* made common property (ptp. of *dīvulgāre*), equiv. to *dīvulg-* (see DIVULGE) + *-ātus* -ATE[1]] —**di·vul′ga·tor, di·vul′gat·er,** *n.* —**di·vul·ga·tion** (div′əl gā′shən), *n.* —**di·vul·ga·to·ry** (di vul′gə tōr′ē, -tôr′ē), *adj.*

di·vulge (di vulj′), *v.t.,* **-vulged, -vulg·ing.** to disclose or reveal (something private, secret, or previously unknown). [late ME < L *dīvulg(āre),* equiv. to *dī-* DI-[2] + *vulgāre* to make general or common, to spread (*vulg(us)* the masses + *-āre* inf. suffix)] —**di·vulge′ment,** *n.* —**di·vulg′er,** *n.*
—**Syn.** See **reveal.**

di·vul·gence (di vul′jəns), *n.* a divulging. [DIVULGE + -ENCE]

di·vulse (dī vuls′, di-), *v.t.,* **-vulsed, -vuls·ing.** *Surg.* to tear away or apart, as distinguished from cut or dissect. [< L *dīvuls(us)* (ptp. of *dīvellere*), equiv. to *dī-* DI-[2] + *vulsus* plucked (ptp. of *vellere*)]

di·vul·sion (di vul′shən), *n.* a tearing apart; violent separation. [< L *dīvulsiōn-* (s. of *dīvulsiō*), equiv. to *dīvuls(us)* (see DIVULSE) + *-iōn-* -ION] —**di·vul·sive** (di vul′siv), *adj.*

div·vy (div′ē), *v.,* **-vied, -vy·ing,** *n., pl.* **-vies.** *Informal.* —*v.t., v.i.* **1.** divide; distribute (often fol. by *up*): *They divvied up the profits among themselves.* —*n.* **2.** distribution; a sharing. [short for DIVIDEND]

Di·wa·li (di wä′lē), *n.* the Hindu festival of lights, celebrated as a religious holiday throughout India in mid-November. Also, **Dewali, Divali.**

di·wan (di wän′, -wôn′), *n.* dewan.

Dix (diks), *n.* **Dorothea Lynde** (lind), (*Dorothy*), 1802–87, U.S. humanitarian and author of childrens' books: established reforms in prisons and hospitals in the U.S., Europe, and Japan.

dix·ie (dik′sē), *n. Anglo-Indian.* a large iron pot, esp. a 12-gallon camp kettle used by the British Army. [< Hindi *degcī,* dim. of *degcā* pot]

Dix·ie (dik′sē), *n.* **1.** Also called **Dixieland, Dixie Land.** the southern States of the United States, esp. those that were formerly part of the Confederacy. **2.** any of several songs with this name, esp. the minstrel song (1859) by D. D. Emmett, popular as a Confederate war song. —*adj.* **3.** of, from, or characteristic of the southern States of the United States. **4.** a girl's given name. [? (MASON-)DIX(ON LINE) + -IE]

Dix·ie·crat (dik′sē krat′), *n.* a member of a faction of southern Democrats stressing States' rights and opposed to the civil-rights programs of the Democratic party, esp. a southern Democrat who bolted the party in 1948 and voted for the candidates of the States' Rights Democratic party. [DIXIE + (DEMO)CRAT] —**Dix′ie·crat′ic,** *adj.*

Dix′iecrat par′ty. See **States' Rights Democratic party.**

Dix′ie Cup′ (dik′sē), *Trademark.* a disposable paper cup, as for beverages, ice cream, etc.

Dix′ie Land′, Dixie (def. 1).

Dix·ie·land (dik′sē land′), *n.* **1.** a style of jazz, originating in New Orleans, played by a small group of instruments, as trumpet, trombone, clarinet, piano, and drums, and marked by strongly accented four-four rhythm and vigorous, quasi-improvisational solos and ensembles. **2.** Also, **Dix′ie Land′.** Dixie (def. 1). [DIXIE + LAND]

Dix·ie·land·er (dik′sē lan′dər), *n.* a musician who specializes in playing Dixieland jazz. [DIXIELAND + -ER[1]]

dix·it (dik′sit), *n.* an utterance. [< L: he has said]

Dix·moor (diks′mo͝or), *n.* a town in NE Illinois. 3076 (1960).

Dix·on (dik′sən), *n.* **1.** a city in N Illinois. 19,565 (1960). **2.** a town in central California. 2970 (1960). **3.** a boy's given name.

dix·y (dik′sē), *n., pl.* **dix·ies.** *Anglo-Indian.* dixie.

Di·yar·be·kir (dē yär′be kir′), *n.* a city in SE Turkey in Asia, on the Tigris River. 80,645 (1960). Also, **Diarbekr.**

di·zen (dī′zən, diz′ən), *v.t. Archaic.* to deck with clothes or finery; bedizen. [*dis-* bunch of flax on a DISTAFF + -EN[1]] —**di′zen·ment,** *n.*

di·zy·got·ic (dī′zī got′ik), *adj.* developed from two fertilized ova, as fraternal twins. [DI-[1] + ZYGOTIC]

diz·zy (diz′ē), *adj.,* **-zi·er, -zi·est,** *v.,* **-zied, -zy·ing.** —*adj.* **1.** having a sensation of whirling and a tendency to fall; giddy; vertiginous. **2.** bewildered; confused. **3.** causing giddiness or confusion: *a dizzy height.* **4.** heedless; thoughtless. **5.** *Informal.* foolish; featherheaded; silly: *How many drinks has that dizzy blonde had?* —*v.t.* **6.** to make dizzy. [ME *dysy,* OE *dysig* foolish; c. LG *düsig* stupefied] —**diz′zi·ly,** *adv.* —**diz′zi·ness,** *n.*

D.J., 1. disk jockey. **2.** District Judge. **3.** Doctor of Law. [< L *Doctor Juris*]

Dja·kar·ta (jə kär′tə), *n.* a seaport in and the capital of Indonesia, on the NW coast of Java. 2,922,000 (est. 1961). Also, **Jacarta, Jakarta.** Formerly, **Batavia.**

Djam·bi (jäm′bē), *n.* a port on SE Sumatra, in W Indonesia. Also, **Jambi.**

djeb·el (jeb′əl), *n.* (chiefly in Arabic-speaking countries) a mountain: often used as part of a place name to indicate that the place is situated on or near a mountain: *the Djebel Druze of southern Syria.* Also, **jebel.** [< Ar *jebel*]

djel·la·bah (jə lä′bə), *n.* a loose-fitting hooded gown or robe worn by men in North Africa, esp. in Morocco. Also, **djel·lab, dje·lab** (jə lab′), **jellaba, jellab, jelab, jellib, jelib.** [< Ar *jallabah*]

Djer·ba (jer′bə), *n.* an island off the SE coast of Tunisia: Roman ruins. 59,351 (1946); 197 sq. mi. Also, **Jerba.**

djib·bah (jib′ə), *n.* jibba.

Dji·bou·ti (ji bo͞o′tē), *n.* **1.** a republic in E Africa, on the Gulf of Aden: formerly an overseas territory of France; independent since 1977. 110,000; 8492 sq. mi. *Cap.:* Djibouti. Formerly, **French Territory of the Afars and Issas, French Somaliland. 2.** a seaport in and the capital of Djibouti, in the SE part. 102,000. Also, **Jibuti.**

Dji·las (jĭ′läs), *n.* **Mi·lo·van** (mē′lo vän), born 1911, Yugoslavian political leader and author.

djin (jin), *n., pl.* **djins,** (*esp. collectively*) **djin.** *Islam.* jinn. Also, **djinn, dji·nni** (ji nē′).

Djok·ja·kar·ta (jôk′yä kär′tä), *n.* Dutch name of **Jogjakarta.**

D.Journ., Doctor of Journalism.

D.J.S., Doctor of Juridical Science.

D.J.T., Doctor of Jewish Theology.

dk., 1. deck. **2.** dock.

dkg, dekagram; dekagrams.

dkl, dekaliter; dekaliters.

dkm, dekameter; dekameters.

dks, dekastere; dekasteres.

dl, deciliter; deciliters.

D/L, demand loan.

D layer, the lowest region of the ionosphere, characterized by mounting electron and ion density: exists, at night only, from about 70–80 kilometers to about 100–120 kilometers of altitude.

D. Lit., Doctor of Literature. [< L *Doctor Literārum*]

D. Litt., Doctors of Letters. [< L *Doctor Litterārum*]

dlr., dealer.

D.L.S., Doctor of Library Science.

dlvy., delivery.

DM, See **Deutsche mark.** Also, **DM.**

DM, adamsite.

dm, decimeter; decimeters.

Dm., See **Deutsche mark.**

D.M.D., Doctor of Dental Medicine. [< L *Dentariae Medicinae Doctor*]

DMDT, *Chem.* methoxychlor. [*d(i)m(ethoxy)d(iphenyl) t(richloroethane)*]

D.M.L., Doctor of Modern Languages.

D.M.S., 1. Director of Medical Services. **2.** Doctor of Medical Science.

DMSO, *Chem., Pharm.* a colorless, nontoxic, water-soluble liquid, $(CH_3)_2SO$, noted for its unusual capacity for penetrating the skin: obtained from lignin as a by-product in papermaking or prepared by the oxidation of dimethyl sulfide with nitrogen oxide, and used as a solvent, antifreeze, vehicle for insecticides, in hydraulic fluids, in the manufacture of synthetic fibers, and in medicine in the treatment of headache, swelling, bursitis, arthritis, burns, and bruises, and as a vehicle and synergist for drugs. Also called **dimethyl sulfoxide.** [*d(i)m(ethyl) s(ulf)o(xide)*]

D. Mus., Doctor of Music.

DMZ, demilitarized zone.

DNA, *Biochem.* any of the class of nucleic acids that contains deoxyribose, found chiefly in the nucleus of cells, and that functions in the transference of genetic characteristics and in the synthesis of protein. Also called **deoxyribonucleic acid, desoxyribonucleic acid.** Cf. **RNA.** [*d(eoxyribo) n(ucleic) a(cid)*]

D.N.B., *Brit.* Dictionary of National Biography.

Dne·pr (dnye′pər), *n.* Russian name of **Dnieper.**

Dne·pro·dzer·zhinsk (dnye′pro jer zhinsk′), *n.* a city in the E central Ukraine, in the SW Soviet Union in Europe, on the Dnieper River. 658,000 (1959).

Dne·pro·pe·trovsk (dnye′pro pe trôfsk′), *n.* a city in the E central Ukraine, in the SW Soviet Union in Europe, on the Dnieper River. Formerly, **Ekaterinoslav.**

Dnes·tr (dnyes′tər), *n.* Russian name of **Dniester.**

Dnie·per (nē′pər, dnye′pər), *n.* a river in the W Soviet Union in Europe flowing S to the Black Sea. 1400 mi. long. Russian, **Dnepr.**

Dnies·ter (nē′stər, dnyes′tər), *n.* a river in the SW Soviet Union in Europe, flowing SE from the Carpathian Mountains to the Black Sea. ab. 875 mi. long. Russian, **Dnestr.** Rumanian, **Nistru.**

do[1] (dōō; *unstressed* dŏŏ, də), *v., pres. sing. 1st pers.* **do,** *2nd* **do** or (*Archaic*) **do·est** or **dost,** *3rd* **does** or (*Archaic*) **do·eth** or **doth,** *pres. pl.* **do;** *past sing. 1st pers.* **did,** *2nd* **did** or (*Archaic*) **didst,** *3rd* **did,** *past pl.* **did;** *past part.* **done;** *pres. part.* **do·ing;** *n., pl.* **dos, do's.** —*v.t.* **1.** to perform (an act, duty, penance, role, etc.). **2.** to execute (a piece or amount of work): *to do a hauling job.* **3.** to accomplish; finish; complete: *He has already done it.* **4.** to put forth; exert: *Do your best.* **5.** to be the cause of (good, harm, credit, etc.); bring about; effect. **6.** to render, give, or pay (homage, justice, etc.). **7.** to deal with, fix, clean, arrange, move, etc., (anything) as the case may require: *to do the dishes; She did her hair.* **8.** to travel; traverse: *We did 30 miles today.* **9.** to serve, suffice for: *This will do us for the present.* **10.** to travel at the rate of (a specified speed): *He was doing 80 when they arrested him.* **11.** to make or prepare: *I'll do the salad if you'll do the dessert.* **12.** to serve a term (of time) in office or in prison: *He's doing five years in Sing Sing. He's doing a second year as chairman of the charity drive.* **13.** to create, form, or bring into being: *She does lovely oil portraits.* **14.** to translate into or change the form or language of: *MGM did the book into a movie.* **15.** to study or work at or in the field of: *I have to do my math tonight.* **16.** to explore or travel through as a sightseer: *They did Europe in three weeks.* **17.** *Informal.* to wear out; exhaust; tire: *That last set of tennis did me.* **18.** *Informal.* to cheat, trick, or take advantage of: *That crooked dealer did him for $500 at poker.* —*v.i.* **19.** to act or conduct oneself; behave; be in action. **20.** to proceed: *to do wisely.* **21.** to get along; fare; manage: *to do well; to do without an automobile.* **22.** to be as to health: *Mother and child are doing fine.* **23.** to serve or be satisfactory, as for the purpose; suffice; be enough: *Will this do?* **24.** to finish or be finished. **25.** to happen; transpire; take place: *What's doing at the office?* **26.** (used without special meaning in interrogative, negative, and inverted constructions; in imperatives with *you* or *thou* expressed, and occasionally as a metrical expedient in verse): *Do you think so? I don't agree.* **27.** (used to lend emphasis to a principal verb): *Do visit us!* **28.** (used to avoid repetition of a verb or full verb expression): *I think as you do. Did you see him? I did.* **29. do away with, a.** to put an end to; abolish. **b.** to kill: *He is suspected of having done away with his first wife.* **30. do by,** to deal with; treat: *He had always done well by his family.* **31. do for, a.** to cause the defeat, ruin, or death of. **b.** *Chiefly Brit.* to cook and keep house for; manage or provide for: *She does for her father and brother.* **32. do in,** *Slang.* **a.** to kill, esp. to murder. **b.** to injure gravely or exhaust; ruin; wear out: *The tropical climate did them in; all done in after the long hike.* **33. do one proud.** See **proud** (def. 10). **34. do or die,** to make a supreme effort. **35. do out of,** *Slang.* to swindle; cheat: *A furniture store did me out of several hundred dollars.* **36. do over,** *Informal.* to redecorate: *to do a room over in Colonial.* **37. do time,** *Informal.* to serve a term in prison: *It's hard to get a decent job once you've done time.* **38. do to death.** See **death** (def. 15). **39. do up,** *Informal.* **a.** to wrap and tie up. **b.** to pin up or arrange (the hair). **c.** to renovate; launder; clean. **d.** to wear out; tire. **e.** to fasten: *Do up your coat and hurry, or we'll be late.* **f.** to dress: *The waitresses are all done up in funny costumes.* **40. do with,** to gain advantage or benefit from; make use of: *I could do with more leisure time.* **41. do without, a.** to forgo; dispense with: *She did without necessities to be able to pay for her daughter's voice lessons.* **b.** to dispense with the thing mentioned: *The store hasn't any, so you'll have to do without.* **42. have to do with,** to be associated with; have a connection with: *Many are convinced that smoking has a great deal to do with lung cancer.* **43. make do,** to get along with what is at hand, despite its inadequacy: *She can't afford a new coat and so will have to make do with the old one.* —*n.* **44.** *Sometimes Facetious.* action; activity; a burst of frenzied activity; commotion. **45.** *Brit. Slang.* a swindle; hoax. **46.** *Chiefly Brit.* a festive social gathering; a party. **47. dos and don'ts,** customs, rules, or regulations: *The dos and don'ts of polite manners are easy to learn.* [ME, OE *dōn;* c. D *doen,* G *tun;* akin to L *-dere* to put (as in *abdere* to put away)]
—**Syn. 1, 20.** act. **3.** Do, ACCOMPLISH, ACHIEVE mean to bring some action to a conclusion. Do is the general word, carrying no implication of success or failure: *He did a great deal of hard work.* ACCOMPLISH and ACHIEVE both have a connotation of successful completion of an undertaking. ACCOMPLISH emphasizes attaining a desired purpose through effort, skill, and perseverance: *to accomplish what one has hoped for.* ACHIEVE emphasizes accomplishing something important, excellent, or great: *to achieve a beneficial condition for mankind.*

do[2] (dō), *n., pl.* **dos.** *Music.* **1.** the syllable used for the first tone or keynote of a diatonic scale. **2.** (in the fixed system of solmization) the tone C. Cf. **sol-fa,** (def. 1), **ut.** [< It]

do., ditto.

D/O, delivery order. Also, **d.o.**

D.O., 1. Doctor of Optometry. **2.** Doctor of Osteopathy.

D.O.A., dead on arrival.

do·a·ble (dōō′ə bəl), *adj.* capable of being done. [late ME; see DO[1], -ABLE]

do-all (dōō′ôl′), *n.* one employed as a factotum, such as the manager of all the affairs of an individual, a business, etc.

Doane (dōn), *n.* a boy's given name.

Do·an·na (dō an′ə), *n.* a girl's given name.

doat (dōt), *v.i.* dote. —**doat′er,** *n.*

dob·ber (dob′ər), *n.* *U.S. Dial.* a float for a fishing line; bob. [< D: buoy]

dob·bin (dob′in), *n.* **1.** a horse, esp. a quiet, plodding horse for farm work or family use. **2.** a drinking vessel of the 18th century holding a gill. [var. of *Robin,* alter. of *Robert*]

Dobbs′ Fer′ry (dobz), a town in SE New York. 9260 (1960).

dob·by (dob′ē), *n., pl.* **-bies. 1.** *Brit. Dial.* a fatuous person; fool. **2.** *Textiles.* **a.** an attachment on a loom, used in weaving small patterns. **b.** Also called **dob′by weave′.** a small geometric or floral pattern produced by this attachment. **c.** a fabric having such a pattern. [akin to dial. *dovie* stupid, imbecile, deriv. of *dove* to doze, dote, OE *dofian, dobian;* c. G *toben* to rage; cf. OE *dobende* decrepit]

dob′by loom′, a loom equipped with a dobby for weaving small, geometric patterns.

Do′bell's solu′tion (dō′belz), *Pharm.* a clear, yellowish, aqueous solution of sodium borate, sodium bicarbonate, phenol, and glycerol, used chiefly as an antiseptic and astringent for the mucous membranes. [named after H. B. *Dobell* (1828–1917), English physician]

Do·ber·man pin·scher (dō′bər mən pin′shər), one of a German breed of medium-sized, short-haired dogs having a black, brown, or blue coat with rusty brown markings. [named after Ludwig *Dobermann,* 19th-century German, original breeder; *pinscher* terrier, a pseudo-G coinage, perh. based on G *Pinzgau* Austrian district noted for its breeding farms]

Doberman pinscher (27 in. high at shoulder)

do·bie (dō′bē), *n.* adobe.

Do·bie (dō′bē), *n.* **(James) Frank,** 1888–1964, U.S. folklorist, educator, and author.

do·bla (dō′blä), *n.* a former gold coin of Spain. [< Sp < L *dupla,* fem. of *duplus* DOUBLE]

Dö·blin (dœ′blēn), *n.* **Al·fred** (äl′frāt), 1878–1957, German physician and novelist.

do·blón (də blōn′; *Sp.* dô vlôn′), *n., pl.* **-blon·es** (-blō′nēz; *Sp.* -vlô′nes). a former gold coin of Spain and Spanish America, equal to two gold escudos. [< Sp: DOUBLOON]

Do′bos torte′ (dō′bōs, -bōsh), *pl.* **Do·bos tortes.** (*sometimes l.c.*) a cake made of several thin, spongy layers, often with ground hazelnuts, held together with a filling of mocha chocolate and having a glazed caramel topping. [named after J. C. *Dobos* (d. 1928), Hungarian pastrycook]

do·bra (dō′brə), *n.* any of various former Portuguese coins, esp. a gold coin of John V equal to two johannes. [< Pg < L *dupla;* see DOBLA]

Do·bru·ja (dō′brōō jə; *Bulg.* dô′brōō jä′), *n.* a region in SE Rumania and NE Bulgaria, between the Danube River and the Black Sea. 2970 sq. mi. Rumanian, **Do·bro·gea** (dô′brô jä′).

Do·bry·nin (do brē′nin), *n.* **A·na·to·ly F(e·do·ro·vich)** (ä nä tô′li fyô′do rô′vich), born 1919, Russian diplomat.

dob·son (dob′sən), *n.* **1.** dobsonfly. **2.** hellgrammite. [after surname *Dobson*]

Dob·son (dob′sən), *n.* **(Henry) Austin,** 1840–1921, English poet, biographer, and essayist.

dob·son·fly (dob′sən flī′), *n., pl.* **-flies.** a large insect, *Corydalus cornutus,* having membranous wings, the male of which has greatly elongated, hornlike mandibles. Cf. **hellgrammite.** [after surname *Dobson;* see FLY[2]]

Do·bu·an (dō′bōō ən, dō bōō′-), *n., pl.* **-ans,** (*esp. collectively*) **-an.** a member of a Melanesian people inhabiting the island of Dobu, in the Territory of Papua. [*Dobu* + -AN]

doc (dok), *n.* *Informal.* doctor. [by shortening]

doc., *pl.* **docs.** document.

do·cent (dō′sənt; *Ger.* dō tsent′), *n.* **1.** Privatdocent. **2.** a college or university lecturer. [< G *Dozent* < L *docent-* (s. of *docēns,* prp. of *docēre*), equiv. to *doc-* teach + *-ent-* -ENT] —**do′cent·ship′,** *n.*

doch-an-dor·rach (dokh′ən dor′əkh), *n.* *Scot., Irish.* a stirrup cup. Also, **doch′-an-dor′roch, doch-an-dor·ris** (dokh′ən dor′is). [cf. Ir *deoch an dorais* drink of the door]

Do·cil·a (dō sil′ə), *n.* a girl's given name.

doc·ile (dos′əl; *Brit.* dō′sīl), *adj.* **1.** easily managed or handled; tractable: *a docile horse.* **2.** readily trained or taught; teachable. [late ME < L *docile,* neut. of *docilis* readily taught, equiv. to *doc(ēre)* to teach + *-ilis* -ILE] —**doc′ile·ly,** *adv.* —**do·cil·i·ty** (do sil′i tē, dō-), *n.*
—**Syn. 1.** manageable, malleable; dutiful, obedient, submissive.

dock[1] (dok), *n.* **1.** a wharf. **2.** the space or waterway between two piers or wharves, as for receiving a ship while in port. **3.** such a waterway, enclosed or open, together with the surrounding piers, wharves, etc. **4.** See **dry dock. 5.** a platform for loading and unloading trucks, railway freight cars, etc. **6.** an airplane hangar or repair shed. **7.** Also called **scene dock.** a place in a theater near the stage or beneath the floor of the stage for the storage of scenery. —*v.t.* **8.** to bring (a ship or boat) into a dock; lay up in a dock. **9.** to place in dry dock, as for repairs, cleaning, or painting. —*v.i.* **10.** to come or go into a dock or dry dock. **11.** (of two space vehicles) to join together in outer space. [< MD, orig. hollow made in sand or mud by grounded ship; c. Norw, Icel *dokk* hollow, Latvian *danga* muddy hole made by traffic]

dock[2] (dok), *n.* **1.** the solid or fleshy part of an animal's tail, as distinguished from the hair. **2.** the part of a tail left after cutting or clipping. —*v.t.* **3.** to cut off the end of; cut short: *to dock a tail; to dock the ears of cattle.* **4.** to deduct a part from: *to dock one's wages; to dock an allowance.* **5.** to cut short the tail of: *to dock a horse.* **6.** to deduct from the wages of, usually as a punishment: *The boss docked him a day's pay.* **7.** to deduct from (wages): *The boss docked his paycheck $20.* [ME *dok,* OE *-docca,* in *fingirdoccana* (gen. pl.) finger muscles; c. Fris *dok,* LG *docke* bundle, Icel *dokkur* stumpy tail, MHG *tocke* bundle, sheaf]

dock[3] (dok), *n.* the place in a courtroom where a prisoner is placed during trial. [< Flem *dok* cage]

dock[4] (dok), *n.* **1.** any of various weedy, polygonaceous plants of the genus *Rumex,* as *R. obtusifolius* **(bitter dock)** or *R. Acetosa* **(sour dock),** having long taproots. **2.** any of various other plants, mostly coarse weeds. [ME *dokke,* OE *docce;* c. MD *docke,* MHG *tocke*]

dock·age[1] (dok′ij), *n.* **1.** a charge for the use of a dock. **2.** docking accommodations. **3.** the act of docking a vessel. [DOCK[1] + -AGE]

dock·age[2] (dok′ij), *n.* **1.** a curtailment; deduction, as from wages. **2.** waste material in wheat and other grains which is easily removed. [DOCK[2] + -AGE]

dock·er[1] (dok′ər), *n.* a longshoreman; a laborer on shipping docks. [DOCK[1] + -ER[1]]

dock·er[2] (dok′ər), *n.* one who or that which docks or cuts short. [DOCK[2] + -ER[1]]

dock·et (dok′it), *n., v.,* **-et·ed, -et·ing.** —*n.* **1.** a list of causes in court for trial, or the names of the parties who have causes pending. **2.** *Chiefly Brit.* **a.** an official memorandum or entry of proceedings in a legal cause. **b.** a register of such entries. **c.** any of various certificates or warrants giving the holder right to obtain, buy, or move goods which are controlled by the government, as a Custom-House docket certifying duty has been paid. **3.** *U.S.* **a.** the list of business to be transacted by a board, council, legislative assembly, or the like. **b.** Also called **trial docket.** a list or calendar of cases awaiting trial in a court of law. **4.** *Brit.* a writing on a letter or document stating its contents; any statement of particulars attached to a package, envelope, etc.; a label or ticket. —*v.t.* **5.** *Law.* to make an abstract or summary of the heads of, as a document; abstract and enter in a book: *judgments regularly docketed.* **6.** to endorse (a letter, document, etc.) with a memorandum. [late ME *dogget* < ?]

dock′ing bridge′, *Naut.* a raised platform running from one side to the other of a vessel toward the stern, used by officers for supervising docking or warping operations. Also called **warping bridge.**

dock′ing keel′, *Naut.* one of two keellike projections for bracing a hull of a ship against bilge blocks when the ship is in drydock.

dock′ing plan′, *Naut.* a plan of the hull of a vessel used in setting supports beneath it when it is drydocked.

dock′ing tel′egraph, *Naut.* a telegraph transmitting orders from the bridge of a ship to the officers in charge of docking operations.

Dock′ Junc′tion, a town in SE Georgia. 5417 (1960).

dock·mack·ie (dok′mak′ē), *n.* a caprifoliaceous shrub, *Viburnum acerifolium,* of North America, having yellowish-white flowers and ovoid, almost black berries. [< Delaware *dogekumak* + D *-je* -IE]

dock·mas·ter (dok′mas′tər, -mä′stər), *n.* *Naut.* **1.** one who supervises the dry-docking of vessels. **2.** an assistant to a harbor master, responsible for the berthing of vessels at certain docks. [DOCK[1] + MASTER]

dock·side (dok′sīd′), *n.* **1.** land or area adjoining a dock: *We were at the dockside to greet them.* —*adj.* **2.** pertaining to or located at or near a dockside: *dockside slums; a dockside fire.* [DOCK[1] + SIDE[1]]

dock-wal·lop·er (dok′wol′ə pər), *n.* *Slang.* a casual laborer about docks or wharves. [DOCK[1] + WALLOPER] —**dock′-wal′lop·ing,** *n.*

dock·yard (dok′yärd′), *n.* **1.** a waterside area containing docks, workshops, warehouses, etc., for building, outfitting, and repairing ships, for storing naval supplies, etc. **2.** *Brit.* a navy yard. [DOCK[1] + YARD[2]]

doc·o·sa·no·ic (dok′ə sə nō′ik), *adj.* *Chem.* behenic. [*do-* (< Gk, comb. form of *dúo* two) + *-cos-* (abstracted from Gk *eíkosi* twenty) + -ANE + -O- + -IC]

doc·tor (dok′tər), *n.* **1.** a person licensed to practice medicine; physician, dentist, or veterinarian. **2.** a person who has been awarded a doctor's degree. **3.** *Archaic.* a man of great learning. **4.** See **Doctor of the Church. 5.** *Slang.* a cook, as at a camp or on a ship. **6.** *Informal.* a refreshing wind in any of various parts of the world, as the sea breeze in the tropics and the harmattan on the Guinea coast of Africa. **7.** *Print.* See **doctor blade. 8.** *Mach.* any of various minor mechanical devices, esp. one designed to remedy an undesirable characteristic of an automatic process. **9.** *Metall.* (in electroplating) an anode of the metal deposited, wrapped in a cloth or sponge saturated with the plating solution and applied to imperfectly plated areas of the metal to build up the surface. **10.** *Angling.* any of several artificial flies, esp. the silver doctor. **11.** *Archaic.* a loaded die. —*v.t.* **12.** to give medical treatment to; act as a physician to: *He feels he can doctor himself for just a common cold.* **13.** to treat (an ailment); apply remedies to: *He doctored his cold at home.* **14.** to restore to original or working condition; repair; mend: *She was able to doctor the chipped vase with a little plastic cement.* **15.** to tamper with; falsify: *He doctored the facts on his passport.* **16.** to add a foreign substance to; adulterate: *Someone had doctored the drink with a stupefying dose of chloral hydrate.* **17.** to revise, alter, or adapt (a photograph, manuscript, etc.) in order to serve a specific purpose or to improve the material: *to doctor a play.* —*v.i.* **18.** to practice medicine: *He doctored in Europe before coming to the U.S.* **19.** *Dial.* to take medicine; receive medical treatment. **20.** *Metall.* (of an article being electroplated) to receive plating unevenly. [< L, equiv. to *doc(ēre)* (to) teach + *-tor* -TOR; r. ME *doct(o)ur* < AF < L, as above] —**doc′tor·al, doc·to·ri·al** (dok tôr′ē əl, -tōr′-), *adj.* —**doc′tor·al·ly, doc·to′ri·al·ly,** *adv.* —**doc′tor·less,** *adj.* —**doc′tor·ship′,** *n.*

doc·tor·ate (dok′tər it), *n.* **1.** See **Doctor of Philosophy** (def. 1). **2.** See **doctor's degree** (def. 2). [< ML *doctōrāt(us)* degree of doctor. See DOCTOR, -ATE[1]]

doc′tor blade′, *Print.* a sharp blade for wiping excess ink from an intaglio plate in rotogravure process. Also called **doctor.**

Doc′tor Faus′tus, 1. (*italics.*) (*The Tragical History of Doctor Faustus*) a play (c1588) by Christopher Marlowe, based on the medieval legend of Faust. **2.** the hero of this play.

doc·tor·fish (dok′tər fish′), *n., pl.* **-fish·es,** (*esp. collectively*) **-fish.** a surgeonfish, esp. *Acanthurus chirurgus,* found in the West Indies, having a bluish body and black tail. [so named from knifelike rays on tail]

Doc′tor of Philos′ophy, 1. Also called **doctor's degree, doctorate.** the highest degree awarded by a graduate school, usually to a person who has completed at least three years of graduate study and a dissertation approved by a board of professors. 2. a person who has been awarded this degree. *Abbr.:* Ph.D.

Doc′tor of the Church′, a title conferred on an ecclesiastic for great learning and saintliness.

Doc′tors' Com′mons, a building in London, at one time the dining hall of the College of Doctors of Civil Law, and later housing ecclesiastical and Admiralty courts which applied primarily civil law.

doc′tor's degree′, 1. See **Doctor of Philosophy** (def. 1). 2. Also called **doctorate.** an honorary degree conferring the title of doctor upon the recipient, as with the LL.D. degree. 3. a degree awarded to a graduate of a school of medicine, dentistry, or veterinary science.

Doc′tor's Dilem′ma, The, a play (1906) by G. B. Shaw.

doc·tri·naire (dok′trə nâr′), *n.* 1. a person who tries to apply some doctrine or theory without sufficient regard for practical considerations; an impractical theorist. —*adj.* 2. dogmatic about others' acceptance of one's ideas; fanatical: *a doctrinaire preacher.* 3. impractical; merely theoretical. 4. of or pertaining to a doctrinaire. [< F, equiv. to *doctrine* DOCTRINE + *-aire* -ARY] —**doc′tri·nair′ism,** *n.*
—**Syn. 2.** authoritarian.

doc·tri·nal (dok′trə nᵊl; *Brit. also* dok trīn′ᵊl), *adj.* of, pertaining to, or concerned with, doctrine: *a doctrinal dispute.* [< LL *doctrīnāl(is),* equiv. to L *doctrīn(a)* (see DOCTRINE) + *-ālis* -AL[1]] —**doc′tri·nal′i·ty,** *n.* —**doc′tri·nal·ly,** *adv.*

doc′trinal theol′ogy, dogmatics.

doc·trine (dok′trin), *n.* 1. a particular principle, position, or policy taught or advocated, as of a religion, government, etc.: *Catholic doctrines; the Monroe Doctrine.* 2. that which is taught; teachings collectively: *religious doctrine.* 3. a body or system of teachings relating to a particular subject: *the doctrine of the Catholic Church.* [ME < MF < L *doctrīn(a)* teaching, equiv. to *doct(o)r* DOCTOR + *-ina* -INE[2]]
—**Syn. 1.** tenet, dogma, theory, precept, belief.

doc·u·ment (*n.* dok′yə mənt; *v.* dok′yə ment′), *n.* 1. a written or printed paper furnishing information or evidence, as a passport, deed, bill of sale, bill of lading, etc.; a legal or official paper. 2. any written item, as a book, article, letter, etc., esp. of a factual or informative nature. 3. *Archaic.* evidence; proof. —*v.t.* 4. to furnish with documents, evidence, or the like: *a carefully documented biography.* 5. to support by documentary evidence: *to document a case.* 6. *Naut.* to provide (a vessel) with a certificate giving particulars concerning its nationality, ownership, tonnage, dimensions, etc., according to its size and purpose. 7. *Obs.* to instruct. [late ME < L *document(um),* equiv. to *docu-* (perf. s. of *docēre* to teach) + *-mentum* -MENT]

doc·u·men·ta·ry (dok′yə men′tə rē), *adj., n., pl.* **-ries.** —*adj.* 1. Also, **doc·u·men·tal** (dok′yə men′tᵊl). pertaining to, consisting of, or derived from documents: *a documentary history of France.* —*n.* 2. *Motion Pictures, Television.* a dramatically structured film of an actual event or of a play giving the impression of an actual event. [DOCUMENT + -ARY] —**doc′u·men·ta′ri·ly,** *adv.*

doc·u·men·ta·tion (dok′yə men tā′shən), *n.* 1. the use of documentary evidence. 2. a furnishing with documents. [DOCUMENT + -ATION]

do-dad (do͞o′dad), *n.* doodad.

Dodd (dod), *n.* **William Edward,** 1869–1940, U.S. historian and diplomat.

dod·der[1] (dod′ər), *v.i.* to shake; tremble; totter. [cf. DITHER, TOTTER, TEETER, etc.] —**dod′der·er,** *n.*

dod·der[2] (dod′ər), *n.* any of the leafless parasitic plants of the genus *Cuscuta,* having yellowish, reddish, or white, threadlike stems that twine about clover, flax, etc. Also called **love vine.** [ME *doder;* c. D, Dan *dodder,* MLG *dod(d)er,* MHG *toter,* G *Dotter*]

dod·dered (dod′ərd), *adj.* infirm; feeble. [DODDER[1] + -ED[2]]

dod·der·ing (dod′ər ing), *adj.* shaky or trembling, as from old age; tottering: *a doddering old man.* [DODDER[1] + -ING[2]]

dod·die (dod′ē), *n.* a cow or bull having no horns, esp. an Aberdeen Angus. Also, **doddy.** [*dod* to poll (ME *dodden*) + -IE]

Dodds (dodz), *n.* **Warren** ("*Baby*"), 1898–1959, U.S. jazz drummer.

dod·dy (dod′ē), *n., pl.* **-dies.** doddie.

dodeca-, a learned borrowing from Greek meaning "twelve," used in the formation of compound words: *dodecasyllabic.* Also, *esp. before a vowel,* **dodec-.** [< Gk *dōdeka-,* comb. form of *dōdeka* twelve, equiv. to *dō-* TWO + *-deka* TEN]

do·dec·a·gon (dō dek′ə gon′, -gən), *n.* *Geom.* a polygon having 12 angles and 12 sides. Also, **duodecagon.** [DODECA- + -GON] —**do·de·cag·o·nal** (dō′de kag′ə nᵊl), *adj.*

Dodecahedrons
A, Rhombic; B, Pentagonal

do·dec·a·he·dron (dō′dek ə hē′drən, dō′dek-), *n., pl.* **-drons, -dra** (-drə). *Geom.* a solid figure having 12 faces. [DODECA- + -HEDRON] —**do·dec′a·he′dral,** *adj.*

do·dec·a·nal (dō dek′ə nal′), *n.* *Chem.* See **lauric aldehyde.** [*dodecane* (DODEC- + -ANE) + -AL[3]]

Do·dec·a·nese (dō dek′ə nēs′, -nēz′, dō′dek ə-), *n.* a group of 12 Greek islands in the Aegean, off the SW coast of Turkey: belonged to Italy 1911–45. 123,021 (1961); 1035 sq. mi.

do·dec′a·no′ic ac′id (dō dek′ə nō′ik, dō′dek-, dō′dek-′, dō′dek-), *Chem.* See **lauric acid.** [DODEC- + -ANE + -O- + -IC]

do·dec·a·pho·nism (dō dek′ə fə niz′əm, dō′də kaf′ə-), *n.* musical composition using the 12-tone technique. Also, **do·dec·a·pho·ny** (dō dek′ə fō′nē, dō′də kaf′ə nē). [DODECA- + -PHONE + -ISM] —**do·dec·a·phon·ic** (dō dek′ə fon′ik), *adj.* —**do·dec·a·phon·ist** (dō dek′ə fə nist, dō′də kaf′ə-), *n.*

do·dec·a·style (dō dek′ə stīl′), *adj.* *Archit.* 1. having 12 columns. 2. (of a classical temple or building in the style of one) having 12 columns on one or either front. Also, **do·dec′a·sty′lar, duodecastyle.** [< Gk *dōdekástylos,* equiv. to *dōdeka-* DODECA- + *stŷlos* pillar, column]

do·dec·a·sty·los (dō dek′ə stī′los, dō′dek-), *n.* a dodecastyle building, as a classical temple. [< Gk *dōdekástylos.* See DODECASTYLE]

do·dec·a·syl·lab·ic (dō dek′ə si lab′ik, dō′dek-), *adj.* 1. consisting of or pertaining to 12 syllables. —*n.* 2. a dodecasyllable. [DODECA- + SYLLABIC]

do·dec·a·syl·la·ble (dō′dek ə sil′ə bəl), *n.* a word or line of verse containing 12 syllables. [DODECA- + SYLLABLE]

do′de·cyl al′dehyde (dō′di sil), *Chem.* See **lauric aldehyde.** [DODEC- + -YL]

do·de·cyl·phen·ol (dō′di sil fē′nōl, -nôl, -nol), *n.* *Chem.* a thick, straw-colored, water-insoluble liquid mixture of isomers having the formula $C_{12}H_{25}C_6H_4OH$: used chiefly as a solvent and as an intermediate for surface-active agents. [DODECYL + PHENOL]

dodge (doj), *v.,* **dodged, dodg·ing,** *n.* —*v.i.* 1. to move aside or change position suddenly, as to avoid a blow or get behind something. 2. to use evasive methods; prevaricate: *When asked a direct question, he dodges.* —*v.t.* 3. to elude or evade by a sudden shift of position or by strategy: *to dodge a blow; to dodge a question.* 4. *Photog.* (in printing) a. to shade (an area of a print) from the light for a short time in order to lighten or eliminate the area (sometimes fol. by *out*). b. to shade an area of (a print). —*n.* 5. a quick, evasive movement; a sudden jump aside or away in order to avoid a blow or the like. 6. *Informal.* an ingenious expedient or contrivance; a shifty trick: *He said he was rich, but that was only a dodge to win your confidence.* [?]
—**Syn. 2.** equivocate, quibble. 3. elude.

Dodge (doj), *n.* **Mary Elizabeth,** 1831–1905, U.S. editor and author of children's books.

Dodge′ Cit′y, a city in SW Kansas, on the Arkansas River: important frontier town and railhead on the old Santa Fe route. 13,520 (1960).

Dodg·em (doj′əm), *n.* *Trademark.* an attraction at amusement parks, carnivals, or the like, consisting of small electrically-powered automobiles which the patrons drive trying to bump other cars while avoiding being bumped by them.

dodg·er (doj′ər), *n.* 1. a person who dodges. 2. a shifty person, esp. one who persistently evades a specific responsibility: *tax dodger; draft dodger.* 3. *Southern U.S.* a leafhopper. 4. a small handbill; throwaway. 5. *Chiefly Southern U.S.* See **corn dodger.** 6. *Naut.* a screen erected on a flying bridge to protect persons on watch from wind, flying spray, etc. 7. *Australian.* a large slice, lump, or portion of food, esp. of bread. [DODGE + -ER[1]]

Dodge·ville (doj′vil), *n.* a town in S Wisconsin. 2911 (1960).

Dodg·son (doj′sən), *n.* **Charles Lut·widge** (lut′wij), ("*Lewis Carroll*"), 1832–98, English mathematician and writer of books for children.

do·do (dō′dō), *n., pl.* **-dos, -does.** 1. any of several clumsy, flightless, extinct birds of the genera *Raphus* and *Pezophaps,* related to the pigeons, but about the size of a turkey, formerly inhabiting the islands of Mauritius, Réunion, and Rodriguez. 2. *Slang.* a dull-witted, slow-reacting person. [< Pg *dondo,* deriv. of *doudo* silly] —**do′do·ism,** *n.*

Dodo,
Raphus solitarius
(Length 3 ft.)

Do·do·na (də dō′nə), *n.* an ancient town in NW Greece, in Epirus: the site of a famous oracle of Zeus. —**Do·do·nae·an, Do·do·ne·an** (dōd′ᵊnē′ən), *adj.*

Do·do·ni·an (də dō′nē ən), *n.* *Class. Myth.* an epithet of Zeus. [< L *Dodonae(us)* (< Gk *Dōdōnaîos,* deriv. of *Dōdṓn(ē)* DODONA) + -IAN]

do′do split′, *Bowling Slang.* a split in which the head pin and the seven or ten pin remain standing.

Dods·worth (dodz′wûrth), *n.* a novel (1929) by Sinclair Lewis.

doe (dō), *n., pl.* **does,** (*esp. collectively*) **doe.** the female of the deer, antelope, goat, rabbit, and certain other animals. [ME *dō,* OE *dā;* c. Dan *daa,* Alemannic *tē;* akin to OE *dēon* to suck]

Doe of Virginia deer,
Odocoileus virginianus

Doe (dō), *n.* a girl's given name.

Doe·nitz (dœ′nits), *n.* **Karl** (kärl), born 1891, German admiral.

do·er (do͞o′ər), *n.* one who or that which does something, esp. one who gets things done with vigor and efficiency. [DO[1] + -ER[1]]

does (duz), *v.* 3rd pers. sing. pres. ind. of **do**[1].

doe·skin (dō′skin′), *n.* 1. the skin of a doe. 2. leather made from this. 3. **doeskins,** soft leather gloves made of sheepskin. 4. a closely woven woolen cloth made with a satin or a small twill weave. —*adj.* 5. of or made of doeskin. [ME *doskin.* See DOE, SKIN]

does·n't (duz′ənt), contraction of *does not.*
—**Usage.** See **contraction.**

do·est (do͞o′ist), *v.* *Archaic.* 2nd pers. sing. pres. ind. of **do**[1].

do·eth (do͞o′ith), *v.* *Archaic.* 3rd pers. sing. pres. ind. of **do**[1].

doff (dof, dôf), *v.t.* 1. to remove or take off, as clothing. 2. to remove or tip (the hat), as in greeting. 3. to throw off; get rid of: *Doff your stupid habits and live.* 4. *Textiles.* a. to strip (carded fiber) from a carding machine. b. to remove (full bobbins, material, etc.) from a textile machine. —*n.* 5. *Textiles.* a. the act of removing bobbins, material, etc., and stripping fibers from a textile machine. b. the material so doffed. [ME, contr. of *do off;* cf. DON[1]]

doff·er (dof′ər, dôf′ər), *n.* 1. one who or that which doffs. 2. *Textiles.* a. a wire-clothed roller on a carding machine, esp. the roller to which the carded fibers are transferred from the cylinder and then prepared for conversion into sliver. b. any roller that removes the fibers from another roller. [DOFF + -ER[1]]

dog (dôg, dog), *n., v.,* **dogged, dog·ging.** —*n.* 1. a domesticated carnivore, *Canis familiaris,* bred in a great many varieties. 2. any animal belonging to the same family, *Canidae,* including the wolves, jackals, foxes, etc. 3. the male of such an animal. 4. any of various animals resembling a dog. 5. a despicable man or youth. 6. *Informal.* a fellow in general: *a gay dog.* 7. **dogs,** *Slang.* feet: *She's been standing on her dogs all day behind the lingerie counter.* 8. *Slang.* a. something worthless or of extremely poor quality: *That used car you bought is a dog.* b. an utter failure; flop: *a playwright with two dogs and one turkey to his credit.* 9. *Slang.* an ugly, boring, or crude girl or woman. 10. *Slang.* See **hot dog.** 11. (*cap.*) *Astron.* either of two constellations, Canis Major or Canis Minor. 12. *Mach.* a. any of various mechanical devices, as for gripping or holding something. b. a projection on a moving part for moving steadily or for tripping another part with which it engages. 13. Also called **gripper, nipper.** *Metalworking.* a device on a drawbench for drawing the work through the die. 14. a cramp binding together two timbers. 15. an iron bar driven into a stone or timber to provide a means of lifting it. 16. an andiron; firedog. 17. *Meteorol.* a sundog or fogdog. 18. a word formerly used in communications to represent the letter D. 19. **go to the dogs,** *Informal.* to degenerate morally or physically; go to ruin: *Because of the continuing unemployment problem, the area is steadily going to the dogs.* 20. **lead a dog's life,** to have an unhappy or harassed existence: *He maintained that he had led a dog's life while in the army.* 21. **let sleeping dogs lie,** to refrain from action which would alter an existing situation for fear of unfavorable results: *We were furious at her behavior, but decided to keep quiet and let sleeping dogs lie.* 22. **put on the dog,** *U.S. Slang.* to assume an attitude of wealth or importance; put on airs: *They really have nothing, but enjoy putting on the dog.* —*v.t.* 23. to follow or track like a dog, esp. with hostile intent; hound. 24. to drive or chase with a dog or dogs. 25. *Mach.* to fasten with dogs. [ME *dogge,* OE *docga* < ?] —**dog′less,** *adj.* —**dog′like′,** *adj.*

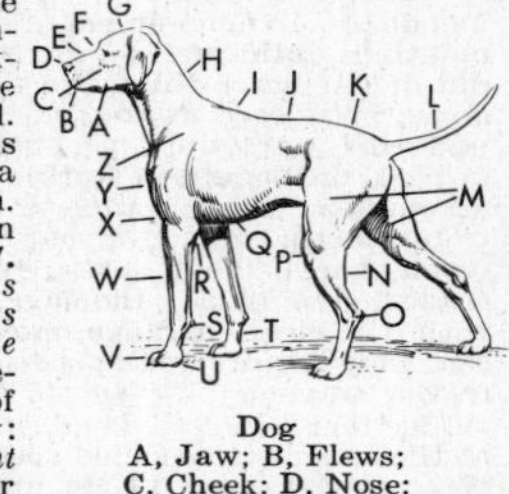

Dog
A, Jaw; B, Flews; C, Cheek; D, Nose; E, Muzzle; F, Stop; G, Forehead; H, Neck; I, Withers; J, Back; K, Croup or rump; L, Tail; M, Thigh; N, Breech; O, Hock; P, Stifle; Q, Chest; R, Elbow; S, Knee; T, Pastern; U, Pad; V, Paw; W, Forearm; X, Upper arm; Y, Brisket; Z, Shoulder

dog′ ape′, a baboon.

dog·bane (dôg′bān′, dog′-), *n.* any plant of the genus *Apocynum,* esp. *A. androsaemifolium,* a perennial herb yielding an acrid milky juice and having an intensely bitter root. [DOG + BANE]

dog′ bent′. See **brown bent.**

dog·ber·ry (dôg′ber′ē, -bə rē, dog′-), *n., pl.* **-ries.** 1. the berry or fruit of any of various plants, as the European dogwood, *Cornus sanguinea,* the chokeberry, *Aronia arbutifolia,* or the mountain ash, *Sorbus americana.* 2. the plant itself. 3. any of several plants, esp. the dog rose, bearberry, and guelder rose. [DOG + BERRY]

Dog·ber·ry (dôg′ber′ē, -bə rē, dog′-), *n., pl.* **-rys** for 2. 1. a foolish constable in Shakespeare's *Much Ado About Nothing.* 2. any foolish, blundering, or stupid official.

dog′ bis′cuit, 1. a hard biscuit for dogs, usually containing ground meat, bones, etc. 2. *Slang.* a hard dry biscuit used as an emergency ration in the armed forces.

dog·bod·y (dôg′bod′ē, dog′-), *n., pl.* **-bod·ies.** a two-masted fishing vessel built mainly at Essex, Massachusetts, in the late 18th and early 19th centuries, similar to the Chebacco boat but shorter and having a square stern. [DOG + BODY]

dog·cart (dôg′kärt′, dog′-), *n.* 1. a light, two-wheeled, horse-drawn vehicle for ordinary driving, with two transverse seats back to back. 2. a cart drawn by a dog or dogs. [DOG + CART]

dog·catch·er (dôg′kach′ər, dog′-), *n.* a person employed by a municipal pound, S.P.C.A., or the like, to find and impound stray or homeless dogs, cats, etc. [DOG + CATCHER]

dog-cheap (dôg′chēp′, dog′-), *Informal.* —*adj.* 1. very inexpensive. —*adv.* 2. very inexpensively.

dog′ clutch′, *Mach.* a clutch in which projections of one of the engaging parts fit into recesses of the other.

dog′ col′lar, 1. a collar used to restrain, identify, etc., a dog. 2. *Informal.* a close-fitting necklace, as a wide band covered with or composed of precious or semiprecious stones; choker. 3. *Slang.* a collar of the type worn by some clergymen, priests, etc., having the opening at the back; clerical collar.

dog′ cur′tain, *Naut.* a flap on a canvas cover for a binnacle, affording a view of the compass when raised.

dog′-day cica′da (dôg′dā′, dog′-), any of several cicadas of the genus *Tibicen,* which have distinctive songs commonly heard during July and August. Also called **harvest fly.**

dog′ days′, a sultry part of the summer supposed to occur during the period that Sirius, the Dog Star, rises at the same time as the sun, now often reckoned from July 3 to August 11. [trans. of L *diēs caniculārēs;* see CANICULAR]

dog·dom (dôg′dəm, dog′-), *n.* 1. the category of all dogs. 2. the state of being a dog. 3. those people, collectively, who are interested in dogs. [DOG + -DOM]

doge (dōj), *n.* the chief magistrate in the former republics of Venice and Genoa. [< It, Venetian var. of *duce* leader < s. of L *dux;* see DUKE] —**doge′dom,** *n.* —**doge′ship,** *n.*

dog-ear (dôg′ēr′, dog′-), *n.* **1.** (in a book) the corner of a page folded over like a dog's ear, as by careless use, or to mark a place. **2.** *Archit.* crossette. —*v.t.* **3.** to fold the corner of (a page). Also, **dog's-ear.**

dog-eared (dôg′ērd′, dog′-), *adj.* **1.** having dog-ears: *a dog-eared book.* **2.** shabby; worn: *dog-eared furniture.*

dog-eat-dog (dôg′ēt dôg′, dog′ēt dog′), *adj.* **1.** marked by destructive or ruthless competition; without self-restraint, ethics, etc. —*n.* **2.** complete egotism; action based on utter cynicism: *The only rule of the marketplace was dog-eat-dog.*

do·gey (dō′gē), *n., pl.* **-geys.** dogie.

dog·face (dôg′fās′, dog′-), *n. Slang.* an enlisted man in the U.S. Army, esp. an infantryman in World War II. [DOG + FACE]

dog′ fen′nel, 1. mayweed. **2.** a composite weed, *Eupatorium capillifolium*, having heads of greenish-white to bronze flowers.

dog·fight (dôg′fīt′, dog′-), *n.* **1.** a violent fight between or as between dogs. **2.** *Mil.* a violent engagement of war planes at close quarters, esp. of small and highly maneuverable planes. **3.** any rough-and-tumble physical battle. —*v.t.* **4.** to engage in a dogfight with. [DOG + FIGHT]

dog·fish (dôg′fish′, dog′-), *n., pl.* (*esp. collectively*) **-fish,** (*esp. referring to two or more kinds or species*) **-fish·es. 1.** any of several small sharks, esp. of the genera *Mustelus* and *Squalus*, that are destructive to food fishes. **2.** any of various other fishes, as the bowfin. [earlier *dokefyche*. See DOG, FISH]

dog′ fox′, a male fox.

dog·ged (dô′gid, dog′id), *adj.* persistent in effort; stubbornly tenacious: *a dogged scholar.* [DOG + -ED[3]] —**dog′ged·ly,** *adv.* —**dog′ged·ness,** *n.*
—**Syn.** mulish, inflexible, unyielding. See **stubborn.**

dog·ger[1] (dô′gər, dog′ər), *n.* a two-masted Dutch fishing vessel with a blunt bow, used in the North Sea. [ME < MD, equiv. to *dogge(boot)* trawler + *-er* -ER[1]; akin to Icel *dugga* fishing vessel]

dog·ger[2] (dô′gər, dog′ər), *n. Metalworking.* an assistant at a drawbench. [DOG + -ER[1]]

Dog′ger Bank′ (dô′gər, dog′ər), a shoal in the North Sea, between N England and Denmark: fishing grounds; naval battle 1915.

dog·ger·el (dô′gər əl, dog′ər-), *adj.* **1.** (of verse) comic or burlesque, and usually loose or irregular in measure. **2.** rude; crude; poor. —*n.* **3.** doggerel verse. Also, **dog·grel** (dô′grəl, dog′rəl). [ME; see DOG, -REL; cf. DOG LATIN]

dog·ger·y (dô′gə rē, dog′ə-), *n., pl.* **-ger·ies. 1.** dog-like behavior or conduct, esp. when surly. **2.** dogs collectively. **3.** rabble; canaille; mob. [DOG + -ERY]

dog·gish (dô′gish, dog′ish), *adj.* **1.** like a dog; canine: *doggish affection.* **2.** surly; mean: *a doggish temper.* **3.** stylish and showy. [ME; see DOG, -ISH[1]] —**dog′gish·ly,** *adv.* —**dog′gish·ness,** *n.*

dog·go (dô′gō, dog′ō), *adv.* **1.** *Informal.* in concealment; out of sight. **2. lie doggo,** *Brit. Slang.* to keep out of sight; hide: *Lie doggo until the excitement blows over.* [DOG + *-o* adv. suffix]

dog·gone (dôg′gôn′, -gon′, dog′-), *v.t.,* **-goned, -gon·ing,** *adj., superl.* **-gon·est,** *adv. Informal.* —*v.t.* **1.** to damn: *Doggone your silly ideas.* —*adj.* **2.** Also, **doggoned.** damned; confounded: *That was a doggone insult. Well, I'll be doggoned.* —*adv.* **3.** Also, **doggoned.** *Informal.* damned: *He's a doggone poor sport.* [euphemistic alter. of *God damn(ed)*]

dog·goned (dôg′gônd′, -gond′, dog′-), *adj., superl.* **-goned·est,** *adv.* doggone.

dog·gy[1] (dô′gē, dog′ē), *n., pl.* **-gies. 1.** a little dog or a puppy. **2.** a pet term for any dog. Also, **dog′gie.** [DOG + -Y[2]]

dog·gy[2] (dô′gē, dog′ē), *adj.,* **-gi·er, -gi·est. 1.** of or pertaining to a dog: *a doggy smell.* **2.** fond of dogs: *tweedy, doggy people.* **3.** pretentious; ostentatious. Also, **dog′gie.** [ME; see DOG, -Y[1]]

dog′ hook′, an iron hook used for handling logs in lumbering.

dog·house (dôg′hous′, dog′-), *n., pl.* **-hous·es** (-hou′ziz). **1.** a small shelter for a dog. **2.** *Rocketry Slang.* a bulge on the surface of a rocket or missile, for scientific instruments. **3.** (on a yacht) a small cabin that presents a relatively high profile and gives the appearance of a box. Cf. **trunk cabin. 4. in the doghouse,** *Slang.* in disfavor or disgrace: *He's in the doghouse because he forgot his wife's birthday.* [DOG + HOUSE]

D, Doghouse (def. 3)
C, Cabin

do·gie (dō′gē), *n. Western U.S.* a motherless calf in a cattle herd. Also, **dogey, dogy.** [perh. contr. of *dough-guts*, or alter. of *doughy*]

dog′ in the man′ger, a person who selfishly keeps something that he does not need or want so that others may not use or enjoy it.

dog′ Lat′in, 1. mongrel or spurious Latin. **2.** a jargon imitating Latin.

dog·leg (dôg′leg′, dog′-), *n.* **1.** a route, way, or course that turns at a sharp angle. —*adj.* **2.** dog-legged. [DOG + LEG]

dog′leg fence′. See **snake fence.**

dog-leg·ged (dôg′leg′id, -legd′, dog′-), *adj.* bent like the hind leg of a dog. Also, **dogleg.**

dog′-leg stair′ (dôg′leg′, dog′-), a half-turn stair the successive flights of which are immediately side by side in plan. Also, **dog′-legged stair′.**

dog·like (dôg′līk′, dog′-), *adj.* **1.** similar to a dog; having the appearance, traits, etc., of a dog. **2.** uncritical; unshakeable, as the attachment of a dog for its master: *doglike devotion.* [DOG + -LIKE]

dog·ma (dôg′mə, dog′-), *n., pl.* **-mas, -ma·ta** (-mə tə), **1.** a system of principles or tenets, as of a church. **2.** a specific tenet or doctrine authoritatively laid down, as by a church: *the dogma of the Assumption.* **3.** prescribed doctrine: *political dogma.* **4.** a settled or established opinion, belief, or principle: *the dogma that might makes right.* [< L < Gk, equiv. to *dok(ein)* (to) seem, think, seem good + *-ma* n. suffix]

dog·mat·ic (dôg mat′ik, dog-), *adj.* **1.** of, pertaining to, or of the nature of a dogma or dogmas; doctrinal. **2.** asserting opinions in a doctrinaire or arrogant manner; opinionated. Also, **dog·mat′i·cal.** [< L *dogmatic(us)* < Gk *dogmatikós*, equiv. to *dogmat-* (s. of *dógma*) + *-ikos* -IC] —**dog·mat′i·cal·ly,** *adv.* —**dog·mat′i·cal·ness,** *n.*
—**Syn. 2.** doctrinaire.

dog·mat·ics (dôg mat′iks, dog-), *n.* (*construed as sing.*) the science that treats of the arrangement and statement of religious doctrines, esp. of the doctrines received in and taught by the Christian church. Also called **dogmat′ic theol′ogy, doctrinal theology.** [see DOGMATIC, -ICS]

dog·ma·tise (dôg′mə tīz′, dog′-), *v.i., v.t.,* **-tised, -tis·ing.** *Chiefly Brit.* dogmatize. —**dog′ma·ti·sa′tion,** *n.* —**dog′ma·tis′er,** *n.*

dog·ma·tism (dôg′mə tiz′əm, dog′-), *n.* dogmatic character; unfounded positiveness in matters of opinion; arrogant assertion of opinions as truths. [< ML *dogmatismus*), equiv. to L *dogmat(icus)* DOGMATIC + *-ismus* -ISM; r. *dogmatisme* < F]

dog·ma·tist (dôg′mə tist, dog′-), *n.* **1.** a person who asserts his opinions in an unduly positive or arrogant manner; a dogmatic person. **2.** a person who lays down dogmas. [< ML *dogmatist(a)*, equiv. to *dogmat(izāre)* (to) DOGMATIZE + *-ista* -IST]

dog·ma·tize (dôg′mə tīz′, dog′-), *v.,* **-tized, -tiz·ing.** —*v.i.* **1.** to make dogmatic assertions; speak or write dogmatically. —*v.t.* **2.** to assert or deliver as a dogma. Also, *esp. Brit.,* **dogmatise.** [< LL *dogmatiz(āre)*, equiv. to L *dogmat(icus)* DOGMATIC + *-izāre* -IZE] —**dog′ma·ti·za′tion,** *n.* —**dog′ma·tiz′er,** *n.*

dog′ nail′, a nail having a head projecting to one side.

do-good·er (do͞o′go͝od′ər), *n.* a well-intentioned but naïve and often clumsily ineffectual social reformer. [*do good* + -ER[1]]

do-good·ism (do͞o′go͝od iz′əm), *n.* attempts at philanthropy or reform, often of a naïve or officious character. [*do good* + -ISM]

dog′ pad′dle, a simple swimming stroke mainly used to stay afloat while remaining almost stationary in the water, executed by paddling both arms underwater while kicking the legs, with the body in a crouching position and the head above water.

dog-pad·dle (dôg′pad′əl, dog′-), *v.i.,* **-dled, -dling.** to swim by use of the dog-paddle stroke.

dog·plum (dôg′plum′, dog′-), *n.* a perennial herb, *Clintonia borealis*, of the mountainous regions of the eastern U.S., having small, white flowers and black fruit.

dog-poor (dôg′po͝or′, dog′-), *adj.* very poor.

dog′ rose′, an Old World wild rose, *Rosa canina*, having pale-red flowers.

dog's′ age′, *Informal.* quite a long time: *I haven't seen you in a dog's age!*

dog′ salm′on. See **chum salmon.**

dog's-ear (dôgz′ēr′, dogz′-), *n., v.t.* dog-ear. —**dog's′-eared′,** *adj.*

dog·shore (dôg′shôr′, -shōr′, dog′-), *n. Shipbuilding.* any of several shores for holding the hull of a small or moderate-sized vessel in place after keel blocks and other shores are removed and until the vessel is launched. [DOG + SHORE[2]]

dog′ sled′, a sled pulled by dogs. Also, **dog′ sledge′.**

dog's′ let′ter, the letter *r*, esp. when representing a trill. [trans. of L *littera canīna*, from the resemblance of the sound of the trill to a dog's snarl]

dog's-tail (dôgz′tāl′, dogz′-), *n.* any Old World grass of the genus *Cynosurus*, the species of which have the spikes fringed on one side only, esp. *C. cristatus* **(crested dog's-tail).** Also called **dog's′-tail grass′.**

Dog′ Star′, 1. the bright star Sirius, in Canis Major. **2.** the bright star Procyon, in Canis Minor.

dog's-tongue (dôgz′tung′, dogz′-), *n.* hound's-tongue.

dog′ tag′, 1. a small disk or strip attached to a dog's harness or collar stating owner, home, etc. **2.** either of a pair of metal identification tags that are worn on a chain around the neck by a member of the armed forces and are stamped with the wearer's name, serial number, blood type, and, often, religious affiliation.

dog-tired (dôg′tīərd′, dog′-), *adj. Informal.* utterly exhausted; worn out.

dog·tooth (dôg′to͞oth′, dog′-), *n.* **1.** Also, **dog′ tooth′,** a canine tooth. **2.** *Archit.* any of a series of small pyramidal ornaments, usually formed by a radiating arrangement of four sculptured leaves, set close together in a concave molding, used esp. in England in the 13th century. [DOG + TOOTH]

dog′tooth vi′olet, 1. a bulbous, liliaceous plant, *Erythronium dens-canis*, of Europe, having purple flowers. **2.** any of several American plants of the genus *Erythronium*, as *E. americanum*, having yellow flowers, or *E. albidum*, having pinkish-white flowers. Also, **dog's′-tooth vi′olet.**

dog·trot (dôg′trot′, dog′-), *n.* a gentle trot, like that of a dog. [DOG + TROT]

dog′ tune′, *Slang.* (in jazz and popular music) a second-rate song.

dog·vane (dôg′vān′, dog′-), *n. Naut.* a small vane that shows the direction of the wind, mounted in a position visible to a helmsman. [DOG + VANE]

dog·watch (dôg′woch′, -wôch′, dog′-), *n.* **1.** *Naut.* either of two two-hour watches, the first from 4 to 6 P.M., the latter from 6 to 8 P.M. **2.** Also called **lobster shift, lobster trick, sunrise watch.** *Journalism Slang.* the period, after the regular editions of a newspaper have gone to press, during which staff personnel remain on duty to await any new developments that may warrant an extra issue. Also, **dog′ watch′.** [DOG + WATCH]

dog′ whelk′, any of several carnivorous, marine gastropods of the family *Nassidae*. Also called **dog·win·kle** (dôg′wing′kəl, dog′-).

dog·wood (dôg′wo͝od′, dog′-), *n.* **1.** any tree or shrub of the genus *Cornus*, esp. *C. sanguinea*, of Europe, or *C. florida*, of America. **2.** the wood of any such tree. **3.** a light to medium brown or a medium yellowish-brown color. —*adj.* **4.** having the color dogwood. [DOG + WOOD[1]]

do·gy (dō′gē), *n., pl.* **-gies.** dogie.

Do·ha (dō′hə, -ha), *n.* a town in and the capital of the sheikdom of Qatar, on the Persian Gulf.

Doh·ná·nyi (dôh′nä nyi), *n.* **Ernst von** (ernst fən) or **Er·nö** (er′nœ), 1877–1960, Hungarian pianist and composer in the U.S.

doiled (doild), *adj. Scot.* stupid; foolish; crazed. [var. of *duled*, ptp. of *dule*, ME < OF *duel-*, tonic s. of *doleir* < L *dolēre* to grieve; see DOLE[2]]

doi·ly (doi′lē), *n., pl.* **-lies. 1.** any small, ornamental mat, as of embroidery or lace. **2.** *Archaic.* a small napkin, as one used during a dessert course. Also, **doyley.** [named after a London draper of the late 17th century]

do·ing (do͞o′ing), *n.* **1.** action; performance; execution: *Your misfortune is not of my doing.* **2. doings,** deeds; proceedings; happenings; events. [ME; see DO[1], -ING[1]]

Doi·sy (doi′zē), *n.* **Edward Ad·el·bert** (ad′əl bərt, ə del′-), born 1893, U.S. biochemist: Nobel prize for medicine 1943.

doit (doit), *n.* **1.** Also, **duit.** a small copper coin of the Netherlands and Dutch colonies, first issued in the 17th century. **2.** a bit or trifle. [< D *duit*; akin to Icel *thveiti* small coin, E *thwait* clearing (< Scand), *thwite* to WHITTLE]

doit·ed (doi′tid, -tit), *adj. Scot.* childish or feeble-minded, esp. because of advanced age; senile. [ME, ptp. of *do(i)ten* to DOTE]

do-it-your·self (do͞o′it yər self′ *or, commonly,* -i chər-), *adj.* **1.** of or designed for construction or use by amateurs without special training: *a do-it-yourself kit for building a radio.* —*n.* **2.** the practice or hobby of building or repairing. —**do′-it-your·self′er,** *n.*

dol (dōl), *n.* a unit for measuring the intensity of pain. Cf. **dolorimetry.** [< L *dol(or)* pain]

dol., 1. *Music.* dolce. **2.** dollar.

do·lab·ri·form (dō lab′rə fôrm′), *adj. Bot., Zool.* shaped like an ax or a cleaver. [< L *dolābr(a)* mattock, pickax + -I- + -FORM]

Dolabriform leaf

dol·ce (dōl′chā; *It.* dôl′che), *Music.* —*adj.* **1.** sweet; soft. —*n.* **2.** an instruction to the performer that the music is to be executed softly and sweetly. **3.** a soft-toned organ stop. [< It < L *dulcis* savory, sweet; see DULCET]

dol·ce far nien·te (dôl′che fär nyen′te), *Italian.* pleasing inactivity. [lit: (it is) sweet to do nothing]

dol·ce vi·ta (dôl′che vē′tä; *Eng.* dōl′chā vē′tə), *Italian.* sweet life; the good life perceived as a mode of existence devoted to the single-minded pursuit of pleasure or dedicated to excessive self-indulgence. (usually prec. by *the* or *la*)

dol·drums (dōl′drəmz, dol′-), *n.* (*construed as pl.*) **1.** a state of inactivity or stagnation, as in business, art, etc.: *August is a time of doldrums for many enterprises.* **2. the doldrums, a.** a belt of calms and light baffling winds north of the equator between the northern and southern trade winds in the Atlantic and Pacific oceans. **b.** the weather prevailing in this area. **3.** a dull, listless, depressed mood; low spirits. [? obs. *dold* stupid (see DOLT) + *-rum(s)* (pl.) n. suffix (see TANTRUM)]

dole[1] (dōl), *n., v.,* **doled, dol·ing.** —*n.* **1.** a portion or allotment of money, food, etc., esp. as given at regular intervals by a charity or for maintenance. **2.** a dealing out or distributing, esp. in charity. **3.** a form of payment to the unemployed instituted by the British government in 1918. **4.** any similar payment by a government to an unemployed person. **5.** *Archaic.* one's fate or destiny. **6. on the dole,** receiving payment from the government, as relief: *They could not go on living on the dole forever.* —*v.t.* **7.** to distribute in charity. **8.** to give out sparingly or in small quantities (usually fol. by *out*): *The last of the water was doled out to the thirsty crew.* [ME *dōl*, OE *(ge)dāl* sharing; cf. DEAL[1]]
—**Syn. 1.** share, pittance. **8.** ration.

dole[2] (dōl), *n. Archaic.* grief or sorrow; lamentation. [ME *do(e)l* < OF < LL *dolus*, var. of *dolor* DOLOR]

dole′ cup′board, a livery cupboard formerly used in churches for holding bread to be distributed to the poor.

dole·ful (dōl′fəl), *adj.* sorrowful; mournful; melancholy. [ME *dolful*. See DOLE[2], -FUL] —**dole′ful·ly,** *adv.* —**dole′ful·ness,** *n.*

dol·er·ite (dol′ə rīt′), *n.* **1.** a coarse-grained variety of basalt. **2.** any of various other igneous rocks, as diabase. **3.** *U.S.* any basaltlike igneous rock whose composition can be determined only by microscopic examination. [< F *dolérite* < Gk *dolerós* deceitful (deriv. of *dólos* wile) + F *-ite* -ITE[1]] —**dol·er·it·ic** (dol′ə rit′ik), *adj.*

dole·some (dōl′səm), *adj. Literary.* doleful. [DOLE[2] + -SOME[1]]

Dolge·ville (dolj′vil), *n.* a town in central New York. 3058 (1960).

dol·i·cho·ce·phal·ic (dol′ə kō sə fal′ik), *adj.* (in cephalometry) **1.** long-headed; having a breadth of head small in proportion to the length from front to back. Cf. **brachycephalic. 2.** having a cephalic index of 75 and under. Also, **dol·i·cho·ceph·a·lous** (dol′ə kō sef′ə ləs). [DOLICHO- + CEPHALIC] —**dol·i·cho·ceph·a·lism** (dol′ə kō sef′ə liz′əm), **dol′i·cho·ceph′a·ly,** *n.*

dol·i·cho·cra·nic (dol′ə kō krā′nik), *adj.* (in craniometry) **1.** long-skulled; having a breadth of skull small in proportion to length from front to back. Cf. **brachycranic. 2.** having a cranial index of 75 and under. [DOLICHO- + *cranic* of the skull (see CRANIUM, -IC)]

Do·lin (dō′lin), *n.* **An·ton** (an′ton), (*Patrick Healey-Kay*), born 1904, English ballet dancer.

do·li·um (dō′lē əm), *n., pl.* **-li·a** (-lē ə). a large earthenware jar used by the ancient Romans. [< L]

Do·li·us (dō′lē əs), *n. Class. Myth.* **1.** (in the *Odyssey*) a slave given to Penelope when she married Odysseus. **2.** an epithet of Hermes, meaning "crafty."

doll (dol), *n.* **1.** a toy representing a baby or other human being, esp. a child's toy. **2.** a pretty but expressionless or unintelligent woman. **3.** *Slang.* **a.** a girl or woman, esp. one who is very attractive. **b.** a boy or man who is considered attractive by a woman. **4.** *Slang.* a generous or helpful person: *Be a doll and pit these dates for me.* **5. doll up,** *Slang.* to dress in an elegant or ostentatiously stylish manner: *You can see her, even on a hot summer day, dolled up in furs and diamonds.* [special use of DOLL] —**doll′ish, doll′-like′,** *adj.* —**doll′ish·ly,** *adv.* —**doll′ish·ness,** *n.*

Doll (dol), *n.* a girl's given name, form of **Dorothy.** Also, **Dollie, Dolly.**

dol·lar (dol′ər), *n.* **1.** a currency bill and monetary unit of the U.S., equal to 100 cents. **2.** a silver coin and monetary unit of Canada, equal to 100 cents and equivalent to about .93 of a U.S. dollar. **3.** any of the monetary units of various other nations and territories as Barbados, British Honduras, Ethiopia, Hong Kong, Liberia, Malaya, Singapore, and Trinidad, equal to 100 cents. **4.** a thaler. **5.** a peso. **6.** See **Levant dollar. 7.** yuan (def. 1). **8.** *Brit. Slang.* **a.** a five-shilling piece; crown. **b.** the sum of five shillings. [earlier *daler* < LG, D *daler;* c. G *Taler,* short for *Joachimsthaler* coin minted in Joachimsthal in Bohemia]

dol′lar-a-year′ man′ (dol′ər ə yēr′), U.S. a federal appointee serving for a token salary.

dol·lar·bird (dol′ər bûrd′), *n.* a common roller, *Eurystomus orientalis,* of Asia and Australia, having a silvery spot the size of a dollar on its wings. [DOLLAR + BIRD]

dol′lar cost′ av′eraging, a system of buying securities at regular intervals, using a fixed amount of cash over a considerable period of time regardless of the prevailing prices of the securities. Also called **dol′lar av′eraging.**

dol′lar diplo′macy, 1. a government policy of promoting the business interests of its citizens in other countries. **2.** diplomacy or foreign relations strengthened by the power of a nation's financial resources.

dol·lar·fish (dol′ər fish′), *n., pl.* (*esp. collectively*) **-fish,** (*esp. referring to two or more kinds or species*) **-fish·es. 1.** the butterfish. **2.** the moonfish. [so called because roundish and silvery]

dol′lar gap′, the difference, measured in U.S. dollars, between the earnings of a foreign country through sales and investments in the U.S. and the payments made by that country to the U.S. Also called **dol′lar short′age, dol′lar def′icit.**

dol·lar·wise (dol′ər wīz′), *adv.* **1.** as expressed in dollars; in dollars and cents: *How much does a million francs amount to, dollarwise?* **2.** on a monetary basis; financially: *The plan has disadvantages, but we will come out ahead dollarwise.* [DOLLAR + -WISE]

doll·face (dol′fās′), *n.* a person having a smooth, unblemished complexion and small, regular features. [DOLL + FACE] —**doll′faced′,** *adj.*

Doll·fuss (dôl′fo͞os), *n.* **Eng·el·bert** (eng′əl bert′), 1892–1934, Austrian statesman: premier, 1932–34.

doll·house (dol′hous′), *n., pl.* **-hous·es** (-hou′ziz). **1.** a miniature house built to the scale of children's dolls. **2.** a cozy, diminutive home, as a small cottage, house-trailer, etc. Also, *esp. Brit.,* **doll's′ house′.** [DOLL + HOUSE]

Dol·lie (dol′ē), *n.* a girl's given name, form of **Doll.** Also, **Dolly.**

Dol·lond (dol′ənd), *n.* a crater in the fourth quadrant of the face of the moon: about 6 miles in diameter.

dol·lop (dol′əp), *n.* **1.** a lump or blob of some substance: *There were dollops of mud on the carpet.* **2.** a small quantity: *Add a dollop of soda water to the mixture.* [cf. Icel *dōlpur* fat man, Norw (dial.) *dolp* lump]

Doll's′ House′, A, a play (1879) by Henrik Ibsen.

dol·ly (dol′ē), *n., pl.* **dol·lies,** *v.,* **dol·lied, dol·ly·ing.** —*n.* **1.** *Baby Talk.* a doll. **2.** a low truck or cart with small wheels for moving loads too heavy to be carried by hand. **3.** *Mach.* a tool for receiving and holding the head of a rivet while the other end is being headed. **4.** a block placed on the head of a pile being driven to receive the shock of the blows. **5.** a small locomotive operating on narrow-gauge tracks, esp. in quarries, construction sites, etc. **6.** a short, wooden pole with a hollow dishlike base for stirring clothes while laundering them. **7.** *Motion Pictures, Television.* a mobile platform for moving a camera about a set. —*v.t.* **8.** to transport or convey (a camera) by means of a dolly. —*v.i.* **9.** to move a camera on a dolly, esp. toward or away from the subject being filmed or televised. **10.** (of a camera) to be transported or conveyed on a dolly. [DOLL + -Y²]

Dol·ly (dol′ē), *n.* a girl's given name, form of **Doll.** Also, **Dollie.**

dol·ly·man (dol′ē mən), *n., pl.* **-men.** *Motion Pictures, Television.* a technician who moves or pushes the camera dolly during or between shots. [DOLLY + MAN¹]

dol′ly shot′, *Motion Pictures, Television.* a camera shot taken from a moving dolly. Also called **tracking shot, track shot, trucking shot, truck shot.**

Dol·ly Var·den (dol′ē vär′dᵊn), **1.** a woman's costume of the late 19th century, including a flower-trimmed, broad-brimmed hat and a dress consisting of a tight bodice and bouffant panniers in a flower print over a calf-length quilted petticoat. **2.** the hat of this costume. **3.** the dress of this costume. **4.** a trout, *Salvelinus malma,* found from Alaska to California. [named after character in Dickens' *Barnaby Rudge;* applied to fish in allusion to its coloring]

Dol′ly Var′den pat′tern, a fabric print consisting of bouquets of flowers.

dol·man (dōl′mən, dol′-), *n., pl.* **-mans. 1.** a woman's mantle with capelike arm pieces instead of sleeves. **2.** a long outer robe worn by Turks. [syncopated var. of *doliman, dolyman* < Turk *dolaman* (obs.), deriv. of *dolamak* to wind round]

dol′man sleeve′, a sleeve tapered from a very large armhole to fit closely at the wrist, used on women's garments.

dol·men (dōl′men, -mən, dol′-), *n.* *Archaeol.* a structure usually regarded as a tomb, consisting of two or more large, upright stones set with a space between and capped by a horizontal stone. Cf. **cromlech** (def. 1). [< F < Cornish, lenited form of *tolmen* hole of stone (taken by French archeologists to mean CROMLECH)] —**dol·men·ic** (dōl men′ik, dol-), *adj.*

Dolmen

do·lo·mite (dō′lə mīt′, dol′ə-), *n.* **1.** a very common mineral, calcium magnesium carbonate, $CaMg(CO_3)_2$, occurring in crystals and in masses. **2.** a rock consisting essentially or largely of this mineral. [< F, named after D. de *Dolom(ieu)* (1750–1801), French mineralogist; see -ITE¹] —**dol·o·mit·ic** (dol′ə mit′ik), *adj.*

dol′omite mar′ble, coarse-grained dolomite.

Do·lo·mites (dō′lə mīts′, dol′ə-), *n.* (*construed as pl.*) a mountain range in N Italy: a part of the Alps. Highest peak, Marmolada, 10,965 ft. Also called **Dol′omite Alps′.**

do·lo·mit·ise (dō′lə mī tīz′, -mi-, dol′ə-), *v.t.,* **-ised, -is·ing.** *Chiefly Brit.* dolomitize.

do·lo·mit·i·za·tion (dō′lə mī′ti zā′shən, -mi-, dol′ə-), *n.* *Geol.* the conversion of limestone into dolomite. Also, *esp. Brit.,* **do′lo·mit′i·sa′tion.** [DOLOMITIZE + -ATION]

do·lo·mit·ize (dō′lə mī tīz′, -mi-, dol′ə-), *v.t.,* **-ized, -iz·ing.** *Geol.* to convert (limestone) into dolomite. Also, *esp. Brit.,* **dolomitise.** [DOLOMITE + -IZE]

Do·lon (dō′lon), *n.* (in the *Iliad*) a son of Eumedes who was killed by Diomedes and Odysseus even though he had given them valuable information about the Trojans.

do·lor (dō′lər), *n.* sorrow; grief; anguish. Also, *esp. Brit.,* **do′lour.** [< L, equiv. to *dol(ēre)* (to) feel pain + *-or* -OR¹; r. ME *dolour* < AF]

Do·lo·res (də lōr′is, -lôr′-), *n.* a girl's given name. Also, **Delores.**

do·lo·rim·e·ter (dō′lə rim′i tər), *n.* *Med.* an instrument used in dolorimetry. [DOLOR + -I- + -METER]

do·lo·rim·e·try (dō′lə rim′i trē, dol′ə-), *n.* *Med.* a technique for measuring the sensitivity to pain produced by heat rays focused on an area of skin and recorded in dols. [DOLOR + -I- + -METRY] —**do·lo·ri·met·ric** (dō′lər ə me′trik, dol′ər-), *adj.* —**do′lo·ri·met′ri·cal·ly,** *adv.*

do·lo·ro·so (dō′lə rō′sō; *It.* dô′lô rô′sô), *adj.* plaintive, as if expressing sorrow (used as a musical direction). [< It; see DOLOR, -OSE¹]

dol·or·ous (dol′ər əs, dō′lər-), *adj.* full of, expressing, or causing pain or sorrow; grievous; mournful: *a dolorous melody; dolorous news.* [DOLOR + -OUS; r. ME *dolerous* < AF] —**dol′or·ous·ly,** *adv.* —**dol′or·ous·ness,** *n.*

Dolph (dolf), *n.* a boy's given name, form of **Adolf.**

dol·phin (dol′fin, dôl′-), *n.* **1.** any of several chiefly marine, cetacean mammals of the family *Delphinidae,* having a fishlike body, numerous teeth, and a head elongated into a beaklike snout. **2.** either of two large, slender fishes, *Coryphaena hippurus* or *C. equisetis,* found in warm and temperate seas. **3.** *Naut.* **a.** a pile, cluster of piles, or buoy to which a vessel may be moored in open water. **b.** a cluster of piles used as a fender, as at the entrance to a dock. **c.** a pudding fender at the nose of a tugboat. **d.** a pudding fender on the side of a vessel. **4.** (*cap.*) *Astron.* the constellation Delphinus. [ME *dolphyn* < OF *dauphin, doffin* < OPr *dalfin* < LL *dalfīn(us),* L *delphīnus* < Gk *delphī́n*]

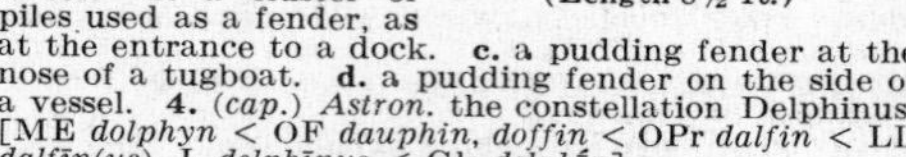

Bottle-nosed dolphin,
Tursiops truncatus
(Length 8½ ft.)

Dol·phin (dol′fin, dôl′-), *n.* a boy's given name.

dol·phin·fish (dol′fin fish′, dôl′-), *n., pl.* **-fish·es,** (*esp. collectively*) **-fish.** dolphin (def. 2). [DOLPHIN + FISH]

dol′phin strik′er, *Naut.* See **martingale boom.**

dols., dollars.

dolt (dōlt), *n.* a dull, stupid person; blockhead. [var. of obs. *dold* stupid, orig. ptp. of ME *dollen, dullen* to DULL] —**dolt′ish,** *adj.* —**dolt′ish·ly,** *adv.* —**dolt′ish·ness,** *n.*

Dol·ton (dôl′tᵊn), *n.* a city in NE Illinois, near Chicago. 18,746 (1960).

do·lus (dō′ləs), *n.* *Roman and Civil Law.* fraud; deceit, esp. involving or evidencing evil intent (distinguished from *culpa*): *One is always liable for dolus resulting in damages.* [< L]

dom (dom), *n.* **1.** (*sometimes cap.*) a title of a monk in the Benedictine, Carthusian, Cistercian, and certain other monastic orders. **2.** a title formerly given to certain Portuguese and Brazilian dignitaries. [short for L *dominus* lord, master]

Dom (dom), *n.* a boy's given name, form of **Dominic.**

-dom, a native English suffix referring to domain (*kingdom*), collection of persons (*officialdom*), rank or station (*earldom*), or general condition (*freedom*). [OE *-dōm;* c. Icel *-dōmr,* G *-tum;* see DOOM]

Dom., 1. Dominica. **2.** Dominican.

dom., 1. domain. **2.** domestic.

D.O.M., to God, the Best, the Greatest. [< L *Deō Optimō Maximō*]

Do·magk (dō′mäk), *n.* **Ger·hard** (geʀ′härt), 1895–1964, German physician: declined 1939 Nobel prize at demand of Nazi government.

do·main (dō mān′), *n.* **1.** *Law.* ultimate ownership and control over the use of land. **2.** the territory governed by a single ruler or government; realm. **3.** a field of action, thought, influence, etc.: *the domain of science.* **4.** a realm or range of personal knowledge, responsibility, etc. **5.** a region characterized by a specific feature, type of growth or wildlife, etc.: *We entered the domain of the pine trees.* **6.** *Math.* **a.** the set of values assigned to the independent variables of a function. **b.** an open set that is connected. **7.** *Physics.* one of many regions of magnetic polarity within a ferromagnetic body, each consisting of a number of atoms having a common polarity, and collectively determining the magnetic properties of the body by their arrangement. **8.** *Crystall.* a connected region with uniform polarization in a twinned ferroelectric crystal. [< F *domaine,* OF *demeine* DEMESNE] —**do·ma′ni·al,** *adj.*

domain′ of integ′rity, *Math.* See **integral domain.**

dome (dōm), *n., v.,* **domed, dom·ing.** —*n.* **1.** *Archit.* **a.** a vault, having a circular plan and usually in the form of a portion of a sphere, so constructed as to exert an equal thrust in all directions. **b.** a domical roof or ceiling. **c.** a polygonal vault, ceiling, or roof. **2.** (in a dam) a semidome having its convex surface toward the impounded water. **3.** something resembling the hemispherical vault of a building or room in form or structure: *the great dome of the sky; the dome formed by the trees' branches.* **4.** anything shaped like a hemisphere or inverted bowl. **5.** *Crystall.* a form having planes that intersect the vertical axis and are parallel to one of the lateral axes. **6.** *Railroads.* a raised, glass-enclosed section of the roof of a passenger car, placed over an elevated section of seats to afford passengers a full view of scenery. **7.** *Horol.* an inner cover for the works of a watch, which snaps into the rim of the case. **8.** a mountain peak having a rounded summit. **9.** *Slang.* a person's head: *I wish I could get the idea into that big dome of yours.* —*v.t.* **10.** to cover with or as with a dome. **11.** to shape like a dome. —*v.i.* **12.** to rise or swell as a dome. [< MF *dome* < It *duomo* < eccl. L *domus (Dei)* house of God, church; akin to TIMBER] —**dome′like′,** *adj.*

dome′ car′, *Railroads.* a passenger car having a dome in its roof.

domed (dōmd), *adj.* **1.** shaped like a dome: *a domed forehead.* **2.** having a dome: *a domed roof.* [DOME + -ED³]

Dom·e·nic (dom′ə nik), *n.* a boy's given name. Also, **Dom′e·nick, Dominic, Dominick.**

domes·day (do͞omz′dā′, dōmz′-), *n.* doomsday. [ME; OE *dōmes dæg* DOOMSDAY]

Domes′day Book′ (do͞omz′dā′, dōmz′-), a record of a survey of the lands of England made by order of William the Conqueror about 1086, giving ownership, extent, value, etc., of the properties. Also, **Doomsday Book.**

do·mes·tic (də mes′tik), *adj.* **1.** of or pertaining to the home, the household, household affairs, or the family: *domestic troubles.* **2.** devoted to home life or household affairs: *a domestic woman.* **3.** tame; domesticated: *a domestic animal.* **4.** of or pertaining to one's own or a particular country as apart from other countries: *domestic trade.* **5.** indigenous to or produced or made within one's own country; not foreign; native: *domestic goods.* —*n.* **6.** a hired household servant. [< L *domestic(us),* equiv. to *domes-* (gradative var. of *domus* house; see DOME) + *-ticus* (cf. RUSTIC); r. *domestique* < F] —**do·mes′ti·cal·ly,** *adv.*

do·mes·ti·cate (də mes′tə kāt′), *v.,* **-cat·ed, -cat·ing.** —*v.t.* **1.** to convert to domestic uses; tame. **2.** to accustom to household life or affairs. **3.** to cause to be or feel at home; naturalize. —*v.i.* **4.** to be domestic. [< ML *domesticāt(us)* (ptp. of *domesticāre*), equiv. to *domestic-* DOMESTIC + *-atus* -ATE¹] —**do·mes·ti·ca·ble** (də mes′tə kə bəl), *adj.* —**do·mes′ti·ca′tion,** *n.* —**do·mes′ti·ca′tive,** *adj.* —**do·mes′ti·ca′tor,** *n.*

domes′tic fowl′, 1. a bird of any breed of chicken. **2.** poultry.

do·mes·tic·i·ty (dō′me stis′i tē), *n., pl.* **-ties. 1.** the state of being domestic; domestic or home life. **2.** a domestic or household act, activity, duty, or chore. [DOMESTIC + -ITY]

do·mes′tic-re·la′tions court′ (də mes′tik ri lā′shənz). See **court of domestic relations.**

domes′tic sci′ence. See **home economics.**

dome′ top′, *Furniture.* a top to a desk, secretary, or the like having the form of a semicircular pediment.

Dom·ett (dom′it), *n.* **Alfred,** 1811–87, British government official and poet: prime minister of New Zealand 1862.

dome′ whis′tle. See **bell whistle.**

do·mi·cal (dō′mi kəl, dom′i-), *adj.* **1.** domelike. **2.** having a dome or domes. Also, **dom′ic.** [DOME + -ICAL] —**dom′i·cal·ly,** *adv.*

dom·i·cile (dom′i sīl′, -səl, dō′mi-), *n., v.,* **-ciled, -cil·ing.** —*n.* **1.** a place of residence; an abode; house or home. **2.** *Law.* a permanent legal residence. —*v.t.* **3.** to establish in a domicile. Also, **dom′i·cil.** [< MF < L *domicil(ium),* equiv. to *domi-* (see DOME) + *-cilium* (*cil-* (see CONCEAL) + *-ium* -Y³)]

dom·i·cil·i·ar (dom′i sil′ē ər, dō′mi-), *n.* *Eccles. Obs.* a canon of a minor order. [< ML *domiciliār(ius).* See DOMICILE, -AR¹]

dom·i·cil·i·ar·y (dom′i sil′ē er′ē), *adj.* of or pertaining to a domicile. [< ML *domiciliārius.* See DOMICILE, -ARY]

dom·i·cil·i·ate (dom′i sil′ē āt′), *v.,* **-at·ed, -at·ing.** —*v.t.* **1.** to domicile. —*v.i.* **2.** to establish a residence for oneself or one's family. [< L *domicili(um)* DOMICILE + -ATE¹] —**dom′i·cil′i·a′tion,** *n.*

Dom·i·na (dom′ə nə, dō′mə-; *It.* dô′mē nä′), *n.* a girl's given name.

dom·i·nance (dom′ə nəns), *n.* **1.** rule; control; authority; ascendancy. **2.** the condition of being dominant. Also, **dom′i·nan·cy.** [< L *domin(us)* master + -ANCE]

dom·i·nant (dom′ə nənt), *adj.* **1.** ruling; governing; controlling; having or exerting authority or influence: *dominant motives in human behavior.* **2.** occupying or being a commanding or elevated position: *the dominant points of the globe; a dominant mountain peak.* **3.** predominant; main; major; chief: *Corn is the dominant crop of Iowa.* **4.** *Genetics.* of or pertaining to a dominant. **5.** *Music.* pertaining to or based on the dominant: *the dominant chord.* —*n.* **6.** *Genetics.* **a.** the one of a pair of alternative alleles that masks the effect of the other when both are present in the same cell or organism. **b.** the trait or character determined by such an allele. Cf. **recessive** (defs. 4, 5). **7.** *Music.* the fifth tone of a scale. **8.** *Ecol.* any of one or more types of plants, or sometimes animals, that by virtue of abundance, size, or habits exert so important an influence on the conditions of an area as to determine, to a great extent, what other organisms can live there. [< L *dominant-* (s. of *domināns,* prp. of *dominārī* to DOMINATE), equiv. to *domin(us)* master + *-ant-* -ANT] —**dom′i·nant·ly,** *adv.*

—**Syn. 1.** prevailing, principal. DOMINANT, PREDOMINANT, PARAMOUNT, PREEMINENT describe something outstanding. DOMINANT describes that which is most influential or important: *the dominant characteristics of monkeys.* PREDOMINANT describes that which is dominant over all others, or is more widely prevalent: *Curiosity is the predominant characteristic of monkeys.* PARAMOUNT applies to that which is first in rank or order: *Safety is of paramount importance.* PREEMINENT applies to a prominence based on recognition of excellence: *His work was of preeminent quality.*

dom′inant ten′ement, *Law.* land in favor of which an easement or other servitude exists over another's land. Cf. **servient tenement.** Also called **dom′inant estate′.**

dom·i·nate (dom′ə nāt′), *v.,* **-nat·ed, -nat·ing.** —*v.t.* **1.** to rule over; govern; control; sway. **2.** to tower above; overlook; overshadow: *A tall pine domi-*

nated the landscape. 3. to predominate, permeate, or characterize. 4. *Math.* (of a series, vector, etc.) to have terms or components greater in absolute value than the corresponding terms or components of a given series, vector, etc. —*v.i.* 5. to rule; exercise control; predominate. 6. to occupy a commanding or elevated position. [< L *dominā̆t(us)* (ptp. of *dominārī* to master, control), equiv. to *domin-* (s. of *dominus*) master + *-ātus* -ATE[1]] —**dom′i·nat′ing·ly,** *adv.* —**dom′i·na′tor,** *n.*

dom·i·na·tion (dom′ə nā′shən), *n.* 1. the act or an instance of dominating. 2. rule or sway; control, often arbitrary. 3. **dominations,** *Theol.* one of the nine orders of celestial attendants of God. Cf. **angel** (def. 1). [ME < L *dominātiōn-* (s. of *dominātiō*), equiv. to *domināt(us)* (see DOMINATE) + *-iōn-* -ION; r. ME *dominacioun* < AF]

dom·i·na·tive (dom′ə nā′tiv, -nə tiv), *adj.* dominating; controlling. [< ML *dominātīv(us).* See DOMINATE, -IVE]

dom·i·ne (dom′ə nē′, dō′mə-), *n.* *Obs.* lord; master (used as a title of address). [voc. of L *dominus* master, lord]

dom·i·ne, di·ri·ge nos (dō′mi ne′, dē′ri ge′ nōs′; *Eng.* dom′i nē′, dir′i jē nōs′), *Latin.* Master, guide us: motto of the city of London.

dom·i·neer (dom′ə nēr′), *v.t., v.i.* 1. to rule arbitrarily or despotically; tyrannize. 2. to tower; to tower over or above: *The castle domineers the town.* [< D *domineer(en)* < F *dominer* < L *dominārī*, equiv. to *domin(us)* lord + *-ārī* inf. suffix]

dom·i·neer·ing (dom′ə nēr′ing), *adj.* inclined to rule arbitrarily or despotically; overbearing; tyrannical: *domineering parents.* [DOMINEER + -ING[2]] —**dom′i·neer′ing·ly,** *adv.* —**dom′i·neer′ing·ness,** *n.*
—**Syn.** arrogant; despotic, oppressive.

Dom·i·nic (dom′ə nik), *n.* 1. **Saint,** 1170–1221, Spanish priest: founder of the Dominican order. 2. Also, **Domenic, Domenick, Dominick.** a boy's given name.

Dom·i·ni·ca (dom′ə nē′kə, də min′ə kə), *n.* 1. one of the Windward Islands, in the E West Indies: a member of the West Indies Associated States; formerly a British colony. 62,696 (est. 1964); 290 sq. mi. *Cap.:* Roseau. 2. a girl's given name.

do·min·i·cal (də min′i kəl), *adj.* 1. of or pertaining to Jesus Christ as Lord. 2. of or pertaining to the Lord's Day, or Sunday. [< LL *dominicāl(is)*, equiv. to L *dominic(us)* of a lord or the Lord (*dominus* lord, Lord + *-icus* -IC) + *-ālis* -AL[1]]

domin′ical al′tar, *Eccles.* a high altar.

do·min·i·ca·le (də min′ə kā′lē), *n.* a veil formerly worn by women during divine service. [< It, var. of *domenicale* DOMINICAL]

domin′ical let′ter, any one of the letters from A to G used in church calendars to mark the Sundays throughout any particular year, serving primarily to aid in determining the date of Easter.

Do·min·i·can (də min′ə kən), *adj.* 1. of or pertaining to St. Dominic or the Dominicans. —*n.* 2. a member of one of the mendicant religious orders founded by St. Dominic; Black Friar. [*Dominic-* (s. of *Dominicus* Latinized form of *Domingo* de Guzman, founder of the order) + -AN]

Do·min·i·can (də min′i kən), *adj.* 1. of or pertaining to the Dominican Republic. —*n.* 2. a native or inhabitant of the Dominican Republic.

Domin′ican Repub′lic, a republic in the West Indies, occupying the E part of the island of Hispaniola. 3,013,525 (est. 1960); 19,129 sq. mi. *Cap.:* Santo Domingo. Also called **Santo Domingo.**

Dom·i·nick (dom′ə nik), *n.* 1. Dominique. 2. Also, **Domenic, Domenick, Dominic.** a boy's given name.

dom·i·nie (dom′ə nē, dō′mə-), *n.* 1. *Chiefly Scot.* a schoolmaster. 2. a pastor in the Dutch Reformed Church. 3. *Dial.* pastor or minister. [var. of DOMINE]

do·min·ion (də min′yən), *n.* 1. the power or right of governing and controlling; sovereign authority. 2. rule; control; domination: *He struggled to escape the dominion of others.* 3. a territory, usually of considerable size, in which a single rulership holds sway. 4. lands or domains subject to sovereignty or control. 5. *Govt.* a territory constituting a self-governing commonwealth and being one of a number of such territories united in a community of nations, or empire: formerly applied to self-governing divisions of the British Empire, as Canada and New Zealand. 6. **the Dominion,** Canada. 7. **dominions,** *Theol.* domination (def. 3). [late ME < MF < ML **dominiōn-* (s. of **dominiō*) lordship, equiv. to L *domin(ium)* DOMINIUM + *-iōn-* -ION]

Domin′ion Day′, (in Canada) a legal holiday, July 1, celebrating the formation of the Dominion on July 1, 1867.

Dom·i·nique (dom′ə nēk′), *n.* one of an American breed of chickens, raised for meat and eggs. [named after *Dominique* or DOMINICA]

Dom·i·nique (dom′ə nēk′), *n.* a girl's given name.

do·min·i·um (də min′ē əm), *n.* *Law.* complete power to use, to enjoy, and to dispose of property at will. [< L, equiv. to *domin(us)* lord, master + *-ium* -Y[3]]

dom·i·no[1] (dom′ə nō′), *n., pl.* **-noes, -nos.** 1. a large, loose cloak, usually hooded, worn with a small mask by persons in masquerade. 2. the mask. 3. a person wearing such dress. [< It: hood and mask costume < ML or MF *domino* black hood worn by priests in winter < L, in some unexplained way]

dom·i·no[2] (dom′ə nō′), *n., pl.* **-noes.** 1. a flat, thumb-sized, rectangular piece of ivory, bone, or wood, the face of which is divided into two parts, each left blank or bearing from one to six pips or dots arranged as on the faces of dice: 28 such pieces form a complete set used in playing various games. 2. **dominoes,** (*construed as sing.*) any of various games played with such pieces, usually by placing the end of a piece from one's hand next to or at right angles to a matching end of a piece already played, played pieces remaining face up between the players and forming specific lines and angular patterns: variations range from simple, children's games in which the player playing all the pieces from his hand first is the winner, to gambling games in which the number of pips or dots, specific patterns, certain combination of pieces, etc., which each player places or completes count toward his score. [? special use of DOMINO[1]]

dom′ino pa′per, a marbleized or figured decorative paper, used as wallpaper, for end papers, etc., printed from wood blocks and colored by hand.

dom′ino the′ory, a theory that if one country, esp. in Southeast Asia, is taken over by communism, nearby nations will be taken over one after another.

Do·mi·nus (dō′mi no͝os′, dom′i-), *n.* *Latin.* God; the Lord.

Do·mi·nus vo·bis·cum (dō′mi no͝os′ vō bis′ko͝om, dom′i-), *Latin.* the Lord be with you.

do·mi·tae na·tu·rae (dom′i tē′ nə to͝or′ē), *Law.* tamed or domesticated animals (distinguished from *ferae naturae*). [< L: lit., of a tamed nature]

Do·mi·tian (də mish′ən, -ē ən), *n.* (*Titus Flavius Domitianus Augustus*) A.D. 51–96, Roman emperor 81–96.

Dom·nus (dom′nəs), *n.* Donus.

Dom·re·my-la-Pu·celle (dôN rə mē′lA py sel′), *n.* a village in NE France, SW of Nancy: birthplace of Joan of Arc. 257 (1962). Also called **Dom·re·my′.**

Dom. Rep., Dominican Republic.

don[1] (don), *n.* 1. (*cap.*) Mr.; Sir: a Spanish title prefixed to a man's Christian name. 2. a Spanish lord or gentleman. 3. (*cap.*) a title of address for an Italian priest. 4. a person of great importance. 5. (in the English universities) a head, fellow, or tutor of a college. [< Sp, It < L *dominus*]

don[2] (don), *v.t.,* **donned, don·ning.** to put on or dress in: *to don one's clothes.* [contr. of DO[1] + ON; cf. DOFF]

don[3] (dōn), *conj.* (in prescriptions) donec. [by shortening]

Don (don; *for 1 also Russ.* dôn), *n.* 1. a river flowing generally S from the central Soviet Union in Europe, to the Sea of Azov. ab. 1200 mi. long. 2. a river in NE Scotland, flowing E from Aberdeen county to the North Sea. 62 mi. long. 3. a river in central England, flowing NE from S Yorkshire to the Humber estuary. 60 mi. long. 4. a boy's or girl's given name, form of **Donald.**

Don (dôn), *n.* *Welsh Myth.* a goddess, the mother of Gwydion and Arianrod: corresponds to the Irish Danu.

do·na (dô′nä), *n.* Portuguese form of **doña.** [< Pg < L *domina,* fem. of *dominus*]

do·ña (dô′nyä), *n.* 1. (*cap.*) Madam: a Spanish title prefixed to a married woman's Christian name. 2. a Spanish lady. [< Sp < L *domina,* fem. of *dominus*]

Don·ald (don′ᵊld), *n.* a boy's given name.

Do·nal·da (də nal′də, -nôl′-), *n.* a girl's given name.

Don·ald·son·ville (don′ᵊld sən vil), *n.* a town in SE Louisiana. 6082 (1960).

Don·al·son·ville (don′ᵊl sən vil), *n.* a town in SW Georgia. 2621 (1960).

Do·nar (dō′när), *n.* *Germanic Myth.* the god of thunder, corresponding to Thor. [< OHG *thonar, donar;* c. OE *Thunor,* Icel *Thōrr;* see THUNDER, THURSDAY]

do·nate (dō′nāt, dō nāt′), *v.,* **-nat·ed, -nat·ing.** —*v.t.* 1. to present as a gift, grant, or contribution; make a donation of, as to a fund or cause. —*v.i.* 2. to make a gift, grant, or contribution of something; give; contribute: *They used to donate to the Red Cross every year.* [prob. back formation from DONATION] —**do′na·tor,** *n.* —**Syn. 1.** contribute.

Don·a·tel·lo (don′ə tel′ō; *It.* dô′nä tel′lô), *n.* (*Donato di Niccolo di Betto Bardi*) 1386?–1466, Italian sculptor. Also, **Do·na·to** (də nä′tō; *It.* dô nä′tô).

Do·na·ti (də nä′tē), *n.* a walled plain in the fourth quadrant of the face of the moon: about 22 miles in diameter.

do·na·tion (dō nā′shən), *n.* 1. the act or an instance of presenting something as a gift, grant, or contribution. 2. a gift, as to a fund; contribution. [< L *dōnātiōn-* (s. of *dōnātiō*), equiv. to *dōnāt(us),* ptp. of *dōnāre* to give (*dōn-,* s. of *dōnum* gift, + *-ātus* -ATE[1]) + *-iōn-* -ION] —**Syn. 2.** offering, benefaction, gratuity. See **present.**

dona′tion land′, *U.S.* land given free or sold on liberal terms by a State or the federal government, esp. to encourage settlement in undeveloped areas.

Dona′tion of Con′stantine, a document of the 8th century A.D., proved spurious in the 15th century, in which Constantine I is supposed to have conferred on the pope extensive privileges and vast possessions.

Don·a·tist (don′ə tist, dō′nə-), *n.* a member of a Christian sect which developed in northern Africa in A.D. 311, and which maintained that it alone constituted the whole and only true church and that baptisms and ordinations of the orthodox clergy were invalid. [DONAT(US) + -IST] —**Don′a·tism,** *n.* —**Don′a·tis′tic, Don′a·tis′ti·cal,** *adj.*

don·a·tive (don′ə tiv, dō′nə-), *n.* a gift or donation. [< L *dōnātīv(um),* n. use of neut. of *dōnātīvus* gratuitous, equiv. to *dōnāt(us)* (see DONATION) + *-īvus* -IVE]

don·a·to·ry (don′ə tôr′ē, -tōr′ē, dō′nə-), *n., pl.* **-ries.** *Chiefly Scots Law.* a donee of the king, esp. one given the right by the king to property obtained by escheat or forfeit. [< ML *dōnātōri(us),* equiv. to *dōnāt(us)* (see DONATION) + *-ōrius* -ORY[1]]

Do·na·tus (dō nā′təs), *n.* early-4th-century bishop of Casae Nigrae in northern Africa: leader of a heretical Afro-Christian group. Cf. **Donatist.**

Do·nau (dō′nou), *n.* German name of **Danube.**

Don Car·los (don kär′lōs), 1. an opera (1867) by Giuseppe Verdi. 2. a drama in blank verse (1787) by Schiller.

Don·cas·ter (dong′kas tər; *Brit.* dong′kə stər), *n.* a city in S Yorkshire, in N England. 86,402 (1961).

Don·di (don′dē), *n.* a boy's given name.

done (dun), *v.* 1. pp. of **do**[1]. 2. **be or have done with,** to break off relations or connections with; stop. —*adj.* 3. completed; finished; through: *Our work is done.* 4. cooked sufficiently. 5. worn out; exhausted; used up. 6. in conformity with fashion, good taste, or propriety; acceptable: *It isn't done.* 7. **done for,** *Informal.* a. tired; exhausted. b. deprived of one's means, position, etc. c. dead, or close to death: *Three days without water and a man is done for.* 8. **done in,** *Informal.* very tired; exhausted: *He was really done in after a close race.*

do·nec (dō′nek), *conj.* (in prescriptions) until. Also, **don.** [< L]

do·nee (dō nē′), *n.* *Law.* 1. one to whom a gift is made. 2. one who has a power of appointment in property. [DON(OR) + -EE]

Don·e·gal (don′i gôl′, don′i gôl′), *n.* 1. a county in the N Republic of Ireland. 113,842 (1961); 1865 sq. mi. *Co. seat:* Lifford. 2. Also called **Don′egal tweed′.** a plain or herringbone tweed with colored slubs.

Don·el·son, Fort (don′ᵊl sən). See **Fort Donelson.**

Do·nets (do nets′), *n.* 1. a river in the SW Soviet Union in Europe, flowing SE to the Don River. ab. 650 mi. long. 2. Also called **Donets′ Ba′sin.** an area S of this river, in the E Ukraine: important coal mining region and recently developed industrial area. 9650 sq. mi.

Do·netsk (do netsk′), *n.* a city in SW Soviet Union, in the Donets Basin. 699,000 (est. 1959). Formerly, **Stalin, Stalino, Yuzovka.**

dong[1] (dông, dong), *n.* a deep sound like that of a large bell. [imit.; see DING-DONG]

dong[2] (dông), *n., pl.* **dong.** piaster (def. 3). [< Annamese]

don·ga (dong′gə, dông′gə), *n.* *Geol.* (in an ice shelf) a small ravine with steep sides. [< SAfrD < Zulu]

Don Gio·van·ni (don′ jō vä′nē, jē ə-), an opera (1787) by Wolfgang Amadeus Mozart.

Don·go·la (dong′gə lə), *n.* a former province in the N Sudan now part of Northern Province.

Don′gola leath′er, a leather similar to kid, made from goatskin, sheepskin, or calfskin. Also called **Don′gola kid′.** [after DONGOLA]

Don′gola proc′ess, the process by which Dongola leather is made.

Don·i·ca (don′ə kə), *n.* a girl's given name, form of **Donata.**

Do·ni·zet·ti (don′i zet′ē; *It.* dô′nē dzet′tē), *n.* **Ga·e·ta·no** (gä′e tä′nô), 1797–1848, Italian operatic composer.

don·jon (dun′jən, don′-), *n.* the inner tower, keep, or stronghold of a castle. [var. of DUNGEON]

Don Ju·an (don wän′ *or, Sp.,* dôn hwän′ *for 1, 2;* don jo͞o′ən *for 1–3*), 1. a legendary Spanish nobleman famous for his many seductions and dissolute life. 2. a libertine or rake. 3. (*italics.*) an unfinished epic satire (1819–24) by Byron.

don·key (dong′kē, dung′-), *n., pl.* **-keys,** *adj.* —*n.* 1. the ass, *Equus asinus.* 2. *U.S.* (since 1874) a representation of this animal as the emblem of the Democratic party. 3. a stupid, silly, or obstinate person. —*adj.* 4. *Mach.* auxiliary: *donkey engine; donkey pump; donkey boiler.* [var. of *Dunkey,* pet var. of *Duncan,* man's name]

don′key ears′, *Informal.* a long time; a coon's age: *I haven't seen him for donkey ears.* Also, **don′key's ears′, donkey's years.** [pun on *donkey ears,* i.e., long ears]

don′key top′sail, *Naut.* a four-sided gaff topsail, used above a gaff sail or lugsail, having its head laced to a small spar.

don·na (don′nä), *n.* 1. (*cap.*) Madam: an Italian title of respect prefixed to the Christian name of a married woman. 2. an Italian lady. [< It < L *domina,* fem. of *dominus*]

Don·na (don′ə), *n.* 1. a town in S Texas. 7522 (1960). 2. a girl's given name.

don·nard (don′ərd), *adj.* *Chiefly Scot.* stunned; dazed. Also, **donnered.** [ptp. of Scot *donnar, donner* to daze, stun, freq. of ME *donen, dinen,* OE *dynian* to make a DIN]

Donn-Byrne (don′bûrn′), *n.* **Brian Oswald** ("*Donn Byrne*"), 1889–1928, U.S. novelist and short-story writer.

Donne (dun), *n.* **John,** 1573–1631, English poet and clergyman.

don·nered (don′ərd), *adj.* *Chiefly Scot.* donnard.

Don·nie (don′ē), *n.* a boy's given name, form of **Donald.** Also, **Donny.**

don·nish (don′ish), *adj.* resembling or characteristic of a university don, esp. stuffily academic. [DON[1] + -ISH[1]] —**don′nish·ly,** *adv.* —**don′nish·ness,** *n.* —**don′nism,** *n.*

Don·ny (don′ē), *n.* a boy's given name, form of **Donald.** Also, **Donnie.**

don·ny·brook (don′ē bro͝ok′), *n.* (*often cap.*) an inordinately wild fight or contentious dispute; brawl; free-for-all: *The party threatened to turn into a donnybrook.* Also called **Donnybrook Fair.** [after DONNYBROOK (FAIR)]

Don′ny·brook Fair′ (don′ē bro͝ok′), 1. a fair which until 1855 was held annually at Donnybrook, County Dublin, Ireland, and which was famous for rioting and dissipation. 2. donnybrook.

do·nor (dō′nər), *n.* 1. one who gives or donates. 2. *Med.* a person or animal furnishing biological tissue, esp. blood for transfusion. 3. *Law.* one who gives property by gift, legacy, or devise, or who confers a power of appointment. [ME *donour* < AF (OF *doneur*) < L *dōnātor,* equiv. to *dōnāt(us)* (see DONATION) + *-or* -OR[2]] —**do′nor·ship′,** *n.*

do-noth·ing (do͞o′nuth′ing), *n.* 1. one who chooses to do nothing; a lazy or worthless person. —*adj.* 2. characterized by inability or unwillingness to initiate action, work toward a goal, assume responsibility, or the like: *a do-nothing administration.*

do-noth·ing·ism (do͞o′nuth′ing iz′əm), *n.* the policy or practice of opposing a specific measure, or a change, simply by refusing to consider or act on proposals, while holding a key position; deliberate obstructionism. [DO-NOTHING + -ISM]

Don Pas·qua·le (don pä skwä′lā, -lē), an opera (1843) by Gaetano Donizetti.

Don Quix·o·te (don′ kē hō′tē, don kwik′sət; *Sp.* dôn kē hô′te), 1. the hero of a romance by Cervantes who was inspired by lofty and chivalrous but impractical ideals. 2. (*italics.*) (*Don Quixote de la Mancha*) the romance itself (1605 and 1615).

don·sie (don′sē), *adj.* 1. *Scot.* unfortunate; ill-fated; unlucky. 2. *Brit. Dial.* fastidious; neat; tidy. Also, **don′sy.** [perh. < ScotGael *donas* harm, ill + -IE]

don't (dōnt), *v.* 1. contraction of *do not.* 2. *Nonstandard.* contraction of *does not.* —*n.* 3. **don'ts,** customs, rules, or regulations that forbid something: *The boss has a long list of don'ts that you had better observe if you want a promotion.* Cf. **do** (def. 47).
—**Usage.** See **contraction.**

Do·nus (dō′nəs), *n.* died A.D. 678, pope 676–678. Also, **Domnus.**

do·nut (dō′nət, -nut′), *n.* doughnut.

don·zel (don′zəl), *n. Archaic.* a young gentleman not yet knighted; squire; page. [< It *donzell(o)* < OPr *donzel* < VL **dom(i)nicell(us),* equiv. to L *domin(us)* lord + *-cellus* dim. suffix]

doo·dad (dōō′dad), *n. Informal.* **1.** a decorative embellishment or article; trinket; bauble: *a dress covered with doodads.* **2.** dingus; gadget: *a kitchen full of the latest doodads.* Also, **do′-dad.** [repetitive compound with gradation, based on dial. *dad* piece, flake]

doo·dle[1] (dōōd′ᵊl), *v.,* **-dled, -dling,** *n.* —*v.t., v.i.* **1.** to draw or scribble idly: *He doodled during the whole lecture.* **2.** *Dial.* to deceive; cheat. **3.** to engage in aimless or foolish activity. —*n.* **4.** a foolish or silly person. **5.** a design, figure, or the like, made by idle scribbling. [orig. sense of fool] —**doo′dler,** *n.*

doo·dle[2] (dōōd′ᵊl), *n. Brit. Informal.* See **buzz bomb.** [short for DOODLEBUG[2]]

doo·dle·bug[1] (dōōd′ᵊl bug′), *n. U.S. Dial.* the larva of an antlion. [DOODLE[1] + BUG[1]]

doo·dle·bug[2] (dōōd′ᵊl bug′), *n.* **1.** a divining rod or similar device supposedly useful in locating underground water, oil, minerals, etc. **2.** *Brit. Informal.* See **buzz bomb.** [? special use of DOODLEBUG[1]]

doo·dle·sack (dōōd′ᵊl sak′), *n.* bagpipe. (def. 1). Also, **dudelsack.** [< G *Dudelsack,* equiv. to *Dudel* (bag)pipe + *Sack* SACK[1]]

doo·hick·ey (dōō′hik′ē), *n., pl.* **-eys.** *Informal.* dingus; thingumbob; gadget. [*do(o)* + HICKEY; cf. DOODAD]

dook (dŏŏk), *n.* plug (def. 8). [?]

doo·lie (dōō′lē), *n. Slang.* a first-year cadet in the U.S. Air Force Academy. [?]

Doo·lit·tle (dōō′lit′ᵊl), *n.* **1. Hilda** ("*H.D.*"), 1886–1961, U.S. poet. **2. James Harold,** born 1896, U.S. aviator and general.

doo·ly (dōō′lē), *n., pl.* **-lies.** (in India) a simple litter, often used to transport sick or wounded persons. Also, **doo′lie, dhooly.** [< Hindi *ḍolī* litter]

doom (dōōm), *n.* **1.** fate or destiny, esp. adverse fate: *His doom was to be poverty.* **2.** ruin; death: *to fall to one's doom.* **3.** a judgment, decision, or sentence, esp. an unfavorable one: *The judge pronounced the defendant's doom.* **4.** the Last Judgment, at the end of the world. —*v.t.* **5.** to destine, esp. to an adverse fate. **6.** to pronounce judgment against; condemn. **7.** to ordain or fix as a sentence or fate. [ME *dome, dōm,* OE *dōm* judgement, law; c. Icel *dōmr,* Goth *dōms;* cf. Skt *dhāman,* Gk *thémis* law; see DO[1], DEEM]
—**Syn. 1.** See **fate. 3.** condemnation. **5.** predestine, foreordain.

doom′ palm′, an African fan palm, *Hyphaene thebaica,* bearing an edible, gingerbread-flavored fruit. Also, **doum palm.** Also called **gingerbread palm.** [< Ar *dum*]

dooms (dōōmz), *adv. Scot. and North Eng.* very; extremely: used as a euphemism for *damned.* [DOOM + -S[1]]

dooms·day (dōōmz′dā′), *n.* **1.** the day of the Last Judgment, at the end of the world. **2.** any day of judgment or sentence. Also, **domesday.** [OE *dōmesdæg* Judgment Day. See DOOM, DAY]

Dooms′day Book′ (dōōmz′dā′). See **Domesday Book.**

Doon (dōōn), *n.* a river in SW Scotland, flowing NW from Ayr county to the Firth of Clyde. ab. 30 mi. long.

door (dōr, dôr), *n.* **1.** a movable, usually solid, barrier for opening and closing an entranceway, cupboard, cabinet, or the like, commonly turning on hinges or sliding in grooves. **2.** a doorway: *to go through the door.* **3.** the building, house, etc., to which a door belongs: *two doors down the street.* **4.** any means of approach, admittance, participation, access, or exit: *the doors to learning.* **5.** *Naut.* a removable cover: *a manhole door.* **6. lay at someone's door,** to hold someone accountable for; blame; impute: *The blame for delinquency may be laid at the door of careless parents.* **7. lie at someone's door,** to be the responsibility of; be imputable to: *One's mistakes generally lie at one's own door.* **8. out of doors,** outside of buildings; in the open: *We couldn't wait to get out of doors again after the long winter.* **9. show someone the door,** to request or order someone to leave; dismiss: *She slapped his face and showed him the door.* [ME *dore,* OE *duru* door, *dor* gate; akin to G *Tür,* Icel *dyrr,* Gk *thýra,* L *foris,* etc.] —**door′less,** *adj.*

door·bell (dōr′bel′, dôr′-), *n.* a bell at a door or connected with a door, rung by persons outside seeking admittance. [DOOR + BELL[1]]

door·brand (dōr′brand′, dôr′-), *n.* **1.** a bar for a door. **2.** a hinge having a long strap holding together the planks of a door. [alter. of obs. *doorband,* ME *dorband,* equiv. to *dor* DOOR + *band* BAND[2]]

door·case (dōr′kās′, dôr′-), *n.* the finish frame of a doorway. [DOOR + CASE[2]]

door′ chain′, a short chain with a removable slide fitting which can be attached between the inside of a door and the doorjamb to prevent the door from being opened more than a few inches while the identity of an arriving visitor is being determined.

door′ check′, a device, usually hydraulic or pneumatic, for controlling the closing of a door and preventing it from slamming. Also called **door′ clos′er.**

do-or-die (dōō′ər dī′), *adj.* **1.** reflecting or characterized by an irrevocable decision to succeed at all costs; desperate; all-out: *a do-or-die attempt to halt the invaders.* **2.** involving a potentially fatal crisis or crucial emergency.

door·frame (dōr′frām′, dôr′-), *n.* the frame of a doorway, including two jambs and a lintel or head. [DOOR + FRAME]

door′ han′dle, *Chiefly Brit.* doorknob.

door′ jack′, a frame for holding a door while its edge is being planed.

door·jamb (dōr′jam′, dôr′-), *n.* either of the two sidepieces of a doorframe. Also called **doorpost.** [DOOR + JAMB[1]]

door·keep·er (dōr′kē′pər, dôr′-), *n.* **1.** one who guards the entrance of a building. **2.** *Brit.* a janitor; hall porter. **3.** *Rom. Cath. Ch.* ostiary (def. 1). [DOOR + KEEPER]

door·knob (dōr′nob′, dôr′-), *n.* the handle or knob by which the latch is released to open a door. [DOOR + KNOB]

door·man (dōr′man′, -mən, dôr′-), *n., pl.* **-men** (-men′, -mən). the door attendant of an apartment house, night club, etc., who performs minor services for entering and departing guests. [DOOR + MAN[1]]

door·mat (dōr′mat′, dôr′-), *n.* a mat, usually placed before a door or other entrance, for scraping mud or dirt from shoes. [DOOR + MAT[1]]

door′ mon′ey, the admission fee to a place of entertainment or recreation.

Doorn (dōrn, dôrn), *n.* a village in the central Netherlands, SE of Utrecht: the residence of Wilhelm II of Germany after his abdication. 9357 (1964).

door·nail (dōr′nāl′, dôr′-), *n.* **1.** a large-headed nail formerly used for strengthening or ornamenting doors. **2. dead as a doornail,** undoubtedly dead: *The fish was dead as a doornail.* [ME *dornail.* See DOOR, NAIL]

door·piece (dōr′pēs′, dôr′-), *n.* an architecturally treated doorframe. [DOOR + PIECE]

door·plate (dōr′plāt′, dôr′-), *n.* a small identification plate on the outside door of a house or room, bearing the occupant's name, the apartment or house number, or the like. [DOOR + PLATE[1]]

door·post (dōr′pōst′, dôr′-), *n.* doorjamb. [DOOR + POST[1]]

door′ prize′, a prize given to a person attending a dance, party, or the like, on the basis of chance, as through a drawing of ticket numbers, as a reward for having created a clever costume, etc.

door·sill (dōr′sil′, dôr′-), *n.* the sill of a doorway. [DOOR + SILL]

door·stead (dōr′sted′, dôr′-), *n. Chiefly Brit.* the structure of a doorway. [DOOR + STEAD]

door·step (dōr′step′, dôr′-), *n.* a step at a door, raised above the level of the ground outside; one of a series of steps leading from the ground to a door. [DOOR + STEP]

door·stone (dōr′stōn′, dôr′-), *n.* a stone serving as the sill of a doorway. [DOOR + STONE]

door·stop (dōr′stop′, dôr′-), *n.* **1.** a device for holding a door open in a desired position. **2.** Also called **slamming stile, stop.** (in a doorframe) a strip or projecting surface against which the door closes. **3.** a device for preventing a door from striking a wall or an object on a wall, as a small rubber-covered projection. [DOOR + STOP]

door-to-door (dōr′tə dōr′, dôr′tə dôr′), *adj.* **1.** canvassing, selling, calling, etc., at each house in an area, town, or the like: *a door-to-door poll.* **2.** sent direct from the point of origin to the point of delivery, as a shipment, order of merchandise, or the like. **3.** covering the complete route of a door-to-door shipment, delivery, etc.: *door-to-door carrying charges; door-to-door insurance.*

door·way (dōr′wā′, dôr′-), *n.* **1.** the passage or opening into a building, room, etc., commonly closed and opened by a door; portal. **2.** a means of access: *a doorway to success.* [DOOR + WAY]

door·yard (dōr′yärd′, dôr′-), *n.* a yard in front of the door of a house. [DOOR + YARD[2]]

doo·ver (dōō′vər), *n. Australian Slang.* thingumbob; thingumajig. [?]

D.O.P., See **developing-out paper.**

dop (dop), *n.* a tool for holding gemstones for cutting or polishing. [< D: shell, cover]

do·pat·ta (dō put′ə), *n.* a silk or muslin shawl, often interwoven with gold or silver threads, worn by men and women in India. [< Hindi]

dope (dōp), *n., v.,* **doped, dop·ing.** —*n.* **1.** any thick liquid or pasty preparation, as a lubricant, used in preparing a surface. **2.** an absorbent material used to absorb and hold a liquid, as in the manufacture of dynamite. **3.** *Aeron.* **a.** any of various varnishlike products for coating a fabric, as of airplane wings, in order to make it waterproof, stronger, etc. **b.** a similar product used to coat the fabric of a balloon to reduce gas leakage. **4.** any narcotic or narcoticlike drug taken solely to induce euphoria or satisfy an addiction. **5.** *Slang.* a person addicted to narcotics. **6.** *Slang.* a narcotic preparation given surreptitiously to a horse to improve or retard its performance in a race. **7.** *Slang.* information or data: *What's the dope on the strike?* **8.** *Slang.* a stupid or unresponsive person. **9.** *Southern U.S.* a carbonated drink, esp. Coca-Cola. —*v.t.* **10.** *Slang.* to affect with dope or drugs. **11.** to apply or treat with dope. **12. dope out,** *Slang.* **a.** to figure out; calculate; devise: *to dope out a plan.* **b.** to deduce or infer from available information: *to dope out a solution to a problem.* [< D *doop* sauce, dipping, gravy, deriv. of *doopen* to DIP] —**dop′er,** *n.*

dope′ fiend′, *Slang.* a person addicted to narcotics; junkie.

dope·sheet (dōp′shēt′), *n.* a bulletin or list including the names of entries in various horse races, and including information on each entry, as the name, jockey, past performances, etc., of each entry. [DOPE + SHEET[1]]

dope·ster (dōp′stər), *n.* a person who undertakes to predict the outcome of elections, sports events, or other contests which hold the public interest. [DOPE + -STER]

dope′ sto′ry. See **think piece.**

dope·y (dō′pē), *adj.,* **dop·i·er, dop·i·est.** *Informal.* **1.** sluggish or befuddled from or as from the use of narcotics or alcohol. **2.** stupid; inane: *It was rather dopey of him to lock himself out.* Also, **dopy.** [DOPE + -Y[1]]

Dop·pel·gäng·er (dop′əl gang′ər; *Ger.* dô′pəl geng′-ər), *n.* a ghostly double or counterpart of a living person. Also, **doubleganger.** [< G: lit., double-walker]

Dop·pel·may·er (dop′əl mā′ər), *n.* a walled plain in the third quadrant of the face of the moon: about 40 miles in diameter.

Dop·pler (dop′lər), *n.* the Doppler effect created by a moving object as observed by a listening device, radar apparatus, or the like.

Dop′pler effect′, *Physics.* the apparent change in the frequency of a wave, as a light wave or sound wave, resulting from a change in the distance between the source of the wave and the receiver. [named after C. J. *Doppler* (1803–53), Austrian physicist]

Dop′pler ra′dar, *Electronics.* a radar tracking system for airborne vehicles which determines their velocity and position by the Doppler shift in the frequency of a radar signal transmitted from the ground to the vehicle and retransmitted by the vehicle to precisely located ground stations. Also called **DOVAP**

Dop′pler shift′, *Physics.* the magnitude of the change in frequency or wavelength of waves, caused by the Doppler effect.

dop·y (dō′pē), *adj.,* **dop·i·er, dop·i·est.** dopey.

dor[1] (dôr), *n.* **1.** Also, **dor·bee·tle** (dôr′bēt′ᵊl). a common European dung beetle, *Geotrupes stercorarius.* **2.** any of several insects, as the June bug, that make a buzzing noise in flight. Also, **dorr.** [ME *dor(r)e,* OE *dora;* cf. MLG *dorte* DRONE[2]]

dor[2] (dôr), *n. Archaic.* mockery; scorn. [< Icel *dār* mockery; cf. G *Tor* fool]

Dor., 1. Dorian. **2.** Doric.

Do·ra (dōr′ə, dôr′ə), *n.* a girl's given name.

do·rab (dōr′ab, də rab′), *n.* See **wolf herring.** [?]

do·ra·do (də rä′dō), *n., pl.* **-dos,** (*esp. collectively*) **-do.** dolphin (def. 2). [< Sp < L *deaurātus,* ptp. of *deaurāre* to gild. See DE-, AURUM, -ATE[1]]

Do·ra·do (də rä′dō), *n., gen.* **-dus** (-dəs). the Swordfish, a small southern constellation between Volans and Horologium. [< Sp; see DORADO]

Dor·al·ice (dōr al′is, dôr-), *n.* a girl's given name.

Dor·al·ynne (dōr al′in, dôr-), *n.* a girl's given name.

Dor·an (dōr′ən, dôr′-), *n.* a boy's given name.

DORAN (dōr′an, dôr′-), *n.* an electronic device for determining range and assisting navigation, employing the principle of the Doppler effect. [*Do(ppler) ran(ge)*]

Do·ra·ti (dō rä′tē, dō-; *Hung.* dô′rô ti), *n.* **An·tal** (än′täl; *Hung.* ôn′tôl), born 1906, Hungarian conductor, in the U.S.

Do·ra·ville (dōr′ə vil, dôr′-), *n.* a town in central Georgia. 4437 (1960).

Dor·cas (dôr′kəs), *n.* **1.** a Christian woman at Joppa who made clothing for the poor. Acts 9:36–41. **2.** a girl's given name.

Dor′cas soci′ety, a society of women of a church whose work it is to provide clothing for the poor. [named after DORCAS]

Dor·ches·ter (dôr′ches′tər, -chi stər), *n.* a town in and the county seat of Dorsetshire: named *Casterbridge* in Thomas Hardy's novels. 12,266 (1961).

Dor·dogne (dôʀ dôn′yᵊ), *n.* **1.** a river in SW France, flowing W to the Gironde estuary. 300 mi. long. **2.** a department in central France. 375,455 (1962); 3561 sq. mi. *Cap.:* Périgueux.

Dor·drecht (dôʀ′dʀeKHt), *n.* a city in the SW Netherlands, on the Waal River. 85,711 (1962). Also called **Dort.**

Dore (dôʀ), *n.* **Monts,** a group of mountains in central France: highest peak, 6188 ft.

do·ré (dō rā′), *n. Canadian Dial.* the walleye or pike perch of North America. [< CanF: lit., gilded < L *deaurāt(us);* see DORADO]

Do·ré (dō rā′; *Fr.* dô ʀā′), *n.* **(Paul) Gus·tave** (pôl gʏ stav′), 1832?–83, French painter, illustrator, and sculptor.

Do·reen (dō rēn′, dô-, dōr′ēn, dôr′-), *n.* a girl's given name. Also, **Do·rene′.**

Do·rette (dō ret′, dô-), *n.* a girl's given name.

Dör′fel Moun′tains (dûr′fəl, dôr′-), a mountain range in the third quadrant of the face of the moon in the libration area, with peaks over 20,000 feet high.

Do·ri (dōr′ē, dôr′ē), *n.* a girl's given name, form of **Dora.**

Do·ri·an (dōr′ē ən, dôr′-), *adj.* **1.** of or pertaining to the ancient Greek region of Doris or to the Dorians. —*n.* **2.** a member of a people who entered Greece about the 12th century B.C., conquered the Peloponnesus, and destroyed the Mycenaean culture: one of the four main divisions of the prehistoric Greeks. Cf. **Achaean** (def. 5), **Aeolian** (def. 2), **Ionian** (def. 4). [< L *Dōri(us)* (< Gk *Dṓrios* Dorian) + -AN]

Do·ri·an (dōr′ē ən, dôr′-), *n.* a boy's or girl's given name.

Do′rian mode′, *Music.* an authentic church mode represented on the white keys of a keyboard instrument by an ascending scale from D to D.

Dor·ic (dôr′ik, dor′-), *adj.* **1.** of or pertaining to Doris, its inhabitants, or their dialect. **2.** rustic, as a dialect. **3.** *Archit.* noting or pertaining to one of the five classical orders, developed in Greece and altered by the Romans. The Greek Doric order consists typically of a channeled column without a base, having as a capital a circular echinus supporting a square abacus, above which come a plain architrave, a frieze of triglyphs and metopes, and a cornice the corona of which has mutules on its soffit. In the Roman Doric order, the columns usually have bases, the channeling is sometimes altered or omitted, and the capital usually consists of three parts: a thick, bandlike necking, an echinus with an ovolo outline, and a molded abacus. Cf. **composite** (def. 3), **Corinthian** (def. 4), **Ionic** (def. 1), **Tuscan** (def. 2). See illus. under **order.** —*n.* **4.** a dialect of ancient Greek spoken in the southern and eastern Peloponnesus, including Sparta, Corinth, and Argos, on Rhodes and other islands of the Dodecanese, in Crete, and in Syracuse. **5.** rustic English speech. [< L *Dōric(us)* < Gk *Dōrikós* Dorian]

Dor·ice (dôr′is, dor′-), *n.* a girl's given name, form of **Doris.**

Dor·i·den (dôr′i dᵊn, -den′), *n. Pharm., Trademark.* glutethimide.

Do·rin (dōr′in, dôr′-), *n.* a boy's given name, form of **Dorian.**

Do·rin·da (dō rin′də, dô-), *n.* a girl's given name.

Do·rine (dō rēn′, dô-, dōr′ēn, dôr′-), *n.* a girl's given name, form of **Doreen.**

Do·ris (dōr′is, dôr′-), *n.* **1.** an ancient region in central Greece: the earliest home of the Dorians. **2.** a region in SW Asia Minor, on the coast of Caria: Dorian settlements.

Do·ris (dōr′is, dôr′-), *n.* **1.** *Class. Myth.* the wife of Nereus and mother of the Nereids. **2.** a girl's given name.

Do·ri·ta (dō rē′tə, dô-), *n.* a girl's given name.

Do·ri·tis (də rī′tis), *n. Class. Myth.* an epithet of Aphrodite, meaning "bountiful."

dor·je (dôr′jə), *n. Lamaism.* a small trident symbolizing power. [< Tibetan]

Dor·king (dôr′kiŋg), *n.* one of an English breed of chickens having five toes on each foot, instead of the usual four. [after *Dorking*, town in Surrey, England]

dorm (dôrm), *n. Informal.* dormitory. [by shortening]

dor·man·cy (dôr′mən sē), *n.* the state of being dormant. [DORM(ANT) + -ANCY]

dor·mant (dôr′mənt), *adj.* **1.** lying asleep or as if asleep; inactive, as in sleep; torpid: *dormant faculties.* **2.** in a state of rest or inactivity; inoperative; in abeyance: *The project is dormant for the time being.* **3.** undisclosed; unasserted: *the girl's dormant talent.* **4.** (of a volcano) not erupting. **5.** *Bot.* temporarily inactive: *dormant buds, dormant seeds.* **6.** *Heraldry.* (of an animal) represented as lying with its head on its forepaws, as if asleep. [ME *dorma(u)nt* < AF, prp. of *dormir* < L *dormīre* to sleep; see -ANT] —**Syn. 1, 2.** quiescent. See **inactive. 3.** latent. —**Ant. 1.** awake, active.

Dormer

dor·mer (dôr′mər), *n.* **1.** Also called **dor′mer win′dow.** a vertical window in a projection built out from a sloping roof. **2.** the entire projecting structure. [< MF *dormoir* DORMITORY]

dor·mered (dôr′mərd), *adj.* having dormer windows. [DORMER + -ED³]

dor·meuse (*Fr.* dôʀ mœz′), *n.* **1.** mobcap. **2.** *Obs.* a nightcap. [< F; fem. of *dormeur* sleeper; see DORMANT]

dor·mie (dôr′mē), *adj. Golf.* (of a player or side) being in the lead by as many holes as are still to be played. Also, **dor′my.** [?]

dor·mi·ent (dôr′mē ənt), *adj.* sleeping; dormant. [< L *dormient-* (s. of *dormiēns,* prp. of *dormīre*), equiv. to *dormi-* sleep + *-ent-* -ENT]

dor·mi·to·ry (dôr′mi tôr′ē, -tōr′ē), *n., pl.* **-ries. 1.** a building, as at a college, containing a number of private or semiprivate rooms for residents, usually along with common bathroom facilities and recreation areas. **2.** a room containing a number of beds and serving as communal sleeping quarters, as in an institution, fraternity house, passenger vessel, etc. [< L *dormītōri(um)* (neut. of *dormītōrius*) equiv. to *dormīt(us)* (ptp. of *dormīre* to sleep) + *-ōrium* -ORY²]

dor′mitory sub′urb, a suburb having little business or cultural activity and occupied mainly by the homes of commuters. Also called **bedroom suburb.**

dor·mouse (dôr′mous′), *n., pl.* **-mice** (-mīs′). any small, furry-tailed, Old World rodent of the family *Gliridae,* resembling small squirrels in appearance and habits. [*dor-* (? < Scand; cf. Icel *dūra* to nap, Sw (dial.) *dorsk* sleepy) + MOUSE]

Dormouse, *Muscardinus avellanarius* (Length 6 in.)

dor·nick¹ (dôr′nik), *n.* a stout linen cloth, esp. one of a damask linen. Also, **dor′neck.** [ME *dornyk,* after *Doornik* (F *Tournai*), where the cloth was first made]

dor·nick² (dôr′nik), *n.* **1.** a boulder, esp. one of iron ore found in limonite deposits. **2.** a small stone that is easy to throw. [? < Ir *dornóg* small casting stone (lit., fistful)]

Do·ro·bo (də rō′bō), *n., pl.* **-bos,** (*esp. collectively*) **-bo.** a member of a Negro people having a hunting economy and living in the uplands of Kenya and Tanganyika. Also called **Wandorobo.**

do·ron·i·cum (də ron′ə kəm), *n.* any plant of the genus *Doronicum,* comprising the leopard's-banes. [< NL < Ar *dorūn(aj)* + L *-icum,* neut. of *-icus* -IC]

Dor·o·the·a (dôr′ə thē′ə, dor′-), *n.* a girl's given name.

Dor·o·thee (dôr′ə thē′, dor′-), *n.* a girl's given name, form of **Dorothea.** Also, **Dorothy.**

Dor·o·thy (dôr′ə thē, dor′-), *n.* a girl's given name, form of **Dorothea.** Also, **Dorothee.**

dorp (dôrp), *n.* a village; hamlet. [< D: village; c. THORP]

Dor·pat (dôʀ′pät), *n.* German name of **Tartu.**

dorr (dôr), *n.* dor¹.

Dorr (dôr), *n.* a boy's given name, form of **Dorrance.**

Dor·rance (dôr′əns, dor′-), *n.* a boy's given name.

Dor·rie (dôr′ē, dor′ē), *n.* a girl's given name, form of **Dora.**

Dorr's′ Rebel′lion (dôrz), an insurrection in Rhode Island (1842) that grew out of dissatisfaction with the existing State constitution, which restricted suffrage to landholders or their eldest sons. [named after Thomas W. *Dorr* (1805–54), state legislator and leader of the insurrection]

dor·sad (dôr′sad), *adv. Anat., Zool.* toward the back or dorsum; dorsally. [< L *dors(um)* back + *ad;* see AD-]

dor·sal¹ (dôr′səl), *adj.* **1.** *Zool., Anat.* of, pertaining to, or situated on the back, as of an organ or part: *dorsal nerves.* **2.** *Bot.* pertaining to the surface away from the axis, as of a leaf; abaxial. **3.** *Phonet.* (of a speech sound) articulated with the dorsum of the tongue. —*n.* **4.** *Phonet.* a dorsal speech sound. [< ML *dorsāl(is),* equiv. to L *dors(um)* back + *-ālis* -AL¹] —**dor′sal·ly,** *adv.*

dor·sal² (dôr′səl), *n.* dossal (def. 1).

dor′sal fin′, the fin or finlike integumentary expansion generally developed on the back of aquatic vertebrates.

dor·sal·is (dôr sal′is, -sā′lis), *adj., n., pl.* **-sal·es** (-sal′ēz, -sā′lēz). *Anat.* —*adj.* **1.** dorsal. —*n.* **2.** a blood vessel or nerve serving the back of the part with which it is associated. [< NL; see DORSAL¹]

dorse (dôrs), *n.* **1.** the back of a book or folded document. **2.** *Eccles. Obs.* dossal (def. 1). [< L *dors(um)* back]

dor·ser (dôr′sər), *n.* dosser.

Dor·set (dôr′sit), *n.* **1. 1st Earl of.** See **Sackville, Thomas. 2.** Dorsetshire.

Dor·set (dôr′sit), *n.* an Eskimo culture that flourished from A.D. 100–1000 in the central and eastern regions of arctic North America. [after Cape *Dorset* in northern Canada]

Dor′set Horn′, one of an English breed of sheep having a close-textured, medium-length wool. [after DORSET, county in England]

Dor·set·shire (dôr′sit shēr′, -shər), *n.* a county in S England. 309,176 (1961); 973 sq. mi. *Co. seat:* Dorchester. Also called **Dorset.**

Dor·sey (dôr′sē), *n.* a boy's given name.

dorsi-, a combining form of **dorsum, dorsal:** *dorsispinal.* Also, **dorso-.**

dor·sif·er·ous (dôr sif′ər əs), *adj. Bot.* borne on the back, as the sori on most ferns. [DORSI- + -FEROUS]

dor·si·flex·ion (dôr′sə flek′shən), *n. Anat.* flexion toward the back. [*dorsiflex* to bend backward (DORSI- + FLEX) + -ION]

dor·si·flex·or (dôr′sə flek′sər), *n. Anat.* a muscle causing dorsiflexion. [DORSI- + FLEXOR]

dor·si·spi·nal (dôr′si spīn′əl), *adj. Anat.* of or pertaining to the back and the spine. [DORSI- + SPINAL]

dor·si·ven·tral (dôr′sə ven′trəl), *adj.* **1.** *Bot.* having distinct dorsal and ventral sides, as most foliage leaves. **2.** *Zool.* dorsoventral. [DORSI- + VENTRAL] —**dor′si·ven·tral′i·ty,** *n.* —**dor′si·ven′tral·ly,** *adv.*

dorso-, var. of **dorsi-:** *dorsoventral.*

dor·so·lat·er·al (dôr′sō lat′ər əl), *adj. Anat., Zool.* of, pertaining to, or affecting the back and the side. [DORSO- + LATERAL]

dor·so·lum·bar (dôr′sō lum′bər), *adj. Anat.* of, pertaining to, or affecting the back in the region of the lumbar vertebrae. [DORSO- + LUMBAR]

dor·so·ven·tral (dôr′sō ven′trəl), *adj.* **1.** *Zool.* pertaining to the dorsal and ventral aspects of the body; extending from the dorsal to the ventral side: *the dorsoventral axis.* **2.** *Bot.* dorsiventral. [DORSO- + VENTRAL] —**dor′so·ven′tral·ly,** *adv.*

dor·sum (dôr′səm), *n., pl.* **-sa** (-sə). **1.** *Anat., Zool.* **a.** the back, as of the body. **b.** the back or outer surface of an organ, part, etc. **2.** *Navig.* the reverse side of an astrolabe, graduated in part or all of its circumference, and often having an alidade, used for taking the angle of elevation of the sun or a fixed star. [< L]

Dort (dôrt), *n.* Dordrecht.

dor·ter (dôr′tər), *n.* a dormitory, esp. in a monastery. Also, **dor′tour.** [ME *dortour* < OF < L *dormītōr(ium)* DORMITORY]

Dor·ti·cós (dôʀ′tē kōs′), *n.* **Os·val·do** (ôs väl′dô), (*Osvaldo Dorticós Torrado*), born 1919, Cuban lawyer and statesman: president since 1959.

Dort·mund (dôrt′mənd; *Ger.* dôʀt′mŏŏnt′), *n.* a city in W West Germany. 650,900 (1963).

dort·y (dôʀ′tē), *adj. Scot.* sullen; sulky. [*dort* sulkiness (< ?) + -Y¹] —**dor′ti·ness,** *n.*

Do·rus (dôr′əs, dōr′-), *n. Class Myth.* **1.** the youngest son of Hellen and Orseis. **2.** a son of Apollo and Phthia, slain by Aetolus.

do·ry¹ (dôr′ē, dōr′ē), *n., pl.* **-ries.** a boat with a narrow, flat bottom, high bow, and flaring sides. [< *dōri,* native name for a dugout on Mosquito Coast of Central America]

do·ry² (dôr′ē, dōr′ē), *n., pl.* **-ries. 1.** the John Dory, *Zeus faber.* **2.** any of several related species of fish. [late ME *dorre, dorray* < MF *doree* (fem. ptp. of *dorer* to gild) < L *deaurāta;* see DORADO]

do·ry·man (dôr′ē mən, dōr′-), *n., pl.* **-men.** a person who uses a dory, esp. a person who engages in fishing, lobstering, etc. [DORY¹ + MAN¹]

do′ry skiff′, *Naut.* an open boat similar to but smaller than a dory.

dos-à-dos (*Fr.* dō zA dō′ *for 1;* dō′sē dō′, -zi- *for 2*), *adv.* **1.** *Archaic.* back to back. —*n.* **2.** a figure in square-dancing, in which two persons advance, pass around each other back to back, and return to their places. [< F: back to back]

dos·age (dō′sij), *n.* **1.** the administration of medicine in doses. **2.** the amount of medicine to be given. **3.** *Physics.* dose. [DOSE + -AGE]

dose (dōs), *n., v.,* **dosed, dos·ing.** —*n.* **1.** a quantity of medicine prescribed to be taken at one time. **2.** a substance, situation, or quantity of anything analogous to medicine, esp. of something nauseous or disagreeable: *Failing the exam was a hard dose to swallow.* **3.** an amount of sugar added in the production of champagne. **4.** *Physics.* the quantity of radiation absorbed by a given mass of material, esp. tissue, being dependent upon the strength and distance of the source and the duration of exposure. **5.** *Slang.* a case of gonorrhea or syphilis. —*v.t.* **6.** to administer in or apportion for doses. **7.** to give a dose of medicine to. **8.** to add sugar to (champagne) during production. —*v.i.* **9.** to take a dose of medicine. [earlier *dos* < ML *dos(is)* < Gk *dósis* a giving]

do·sim·e·ter (dō sim′i tər), *n.* an instrument for measuring the dosage of x-rays or of radiation. [< Gk *dósi(s)* DOSE + -METER]

do·sim·e·try (dō sim′i trē), *n.* **1.** the process or method of measuring the dosage of x-rays or radiation. **2.** the measurement of the doses of medicines. [< Gk *dósi(s)* DOSE + -METRY] —**do·si·met·ric** (dō′sə me′trik), *adj.* —**do·si·me·tri·cian** (dō′sə mi trish′ən), **do·sim′e·trist,** *n.*

Dos Pas·sos (dōs pas′ōs), **John (Rod·er·i·go)** (ro drē′gō), born 1896, U.S. novelist.

doss (dos), *Brit. Slang.* —*n.* **1.** a place to sleep, esp. in a cheap lodging house. **2.** sleep. —*v.i.* **3.** to sleep or lie down in any convenient place. [? < Scand; cf. Sw *dorsk* sleepy]

dos·sal (dos′əl), *n.* **1.** Also, **dorsal.** an ornamental hanging placed at the back of an altar or at the sides of the chancel. **2.** *Archaic.* dosser (def. 2). Also, **dos′sel.** [< ML *dossal(e),* var. of *dorsale,* neut. of L *dorsālis,* equiv. to *dors(um)* back + *-ālis* -AL¹]

dos·ser (dos′ər), *n.* **1.** a basket for carrying objects on the back; pannier. **2.** an ornamental covering for the back of a seat, esp. a throne or the like. **3.** a hanging, sometimes richly embroidered, for the wall of a hall or the back or sides of a chancel. Also, **dorser.** [ME < AF; MF *dossier* < ML *dosser(ium),* var. of *dorserium,* equiv. to *dors(um)* back + *-erium* -ERY; r. ME *dorser* < ML *dorser(ium)*]

dos·se·ret (dos′ə ret′), *n. Archit.* a supplementary capital or thickened abacus, as in Byzantine architecture. Also called **impost block.** [< F, dim. of *dossier* DOSSER]

doss′ house′, *Brit. Slang.* a cheap rooming house; flophouse.

dos·si·er (dos′ē ā′, -ē ər, dô′sē ā′, -sē ər; *Fr.* dô syā′), *n., pl.* **dos·si·ers** (dos′ē āz′, -ē ərz, dô′sē-; *Fr.* dô syā′). a group of documents on the same subject, esp. a complete group containing detailed information. [< F: bundle of papers (late sense of word) < ML; see DOSSER]

dos·sil (dos′əl), *n. Engraving.* a cloth roll for removing excess ink from a plate before printing. [ME *dosil* < MF < ML *ducicul(us),* equiv. to L *duci-* (s. of *dux*) leader + *-culus* dim. suffix]

Dosseret on capital supporting arches

dost (dust), *v. Archaic.* 2nd pers. sing. pres. ind. of **do**¹.

Dos·to·ev·sky (dos′tə yef′skē, -toi-, dus′-; *Russ.* do sto yef′ski), *n.* **Feo·dor Mi·khai·lo·vich** (fyô′dôʀ mi ᴋʜī′lo vich), 1821–81, Russian novelist. Also, **Dos′to·yev′sky, Dos′to·ev′ski, Dos′to·yev′ski, Dos′toi·ev′ski.**

dot¹ (dot), *n., v.,* **dot·ted, dot·ting.** —*n.* **1.** a minute or small spot on a surface; speck: *There were dots of soot on the window sill.* **2.** a small, roundish mark made with or as with a pen. **3.** anything relatively small or specklike. **4.** a small specimen, section, amount, or portion: *a dot of a man; a dot of butter.* **5.** *Music.* **a.** a point placed after a note or rest, to indicate that the duration of the note or rest is to be increased one half. A double dot further increases the duration by one half the value of the single dot. **b.** a point placed under or over a note to indicate that it is to be played staccato. **6.** *Telegraphy.* a signal of shorter duration than a dash, used in groups along with groups of dashes and spaces to represent letters, as in Morse code. **7. on the dot,** *Informal.* precisely on time; prompt; punctual: *The guests arrived at eight o'clock on the dot.* —*v.t.* **8.** to mark with or as with a dot or dots. **9.** to stud or diversify with or as with dots: *Trees dot the landscape.* **10.** to form or cover with dots: *He dotted a line across the page.* —*v.i.* **11.** to make a dot or dots. **12. dot one's i's and cross one's t's,** to be meticulous or precise, even to the smallest detail: *He would dot his i's and cross his t's in letting his employees know what he expected of them.* [OE *dott* head of a boil; c. OHG *tutta* nipple; *dit,* deriv. of OE *dyttan* to stop up (prob. deriv. of *dott*)] —**dot′like′,** *adj.* —**dot′ter,** *n.*

dot² (dot, dôt), *n. Civil Law.* dowry. (def. 1). [< F < L *dōt-,* s. of *dōs* dower, *dōtāre* to endow, akin to *dāre* to give] —**do·tal** (dōt′əl), *adj.*

Dot (dot), *n.* a girl's given name, form of **Dorothea, Dorothee,** and **Dorothy.**

dot·age (dō′tij), *n.* **1.** feebleness of mind, esp. resulting from old age; senility. **2.** excessive fondness; foolish affection. [ME; see DOTE, -AGE]

do·tard (dō′tərd), *n.* one whose mind is feeble, esp. from old age. [ME; see DOTE, -ARD] —**do′tard·ly,** *adv.*

do·ta·tion (dō tā′shən), *n.* an endowment. [< L *dōtātiōn-* (s. of *dōtātiō*), equiv. to *dōtāt(us),* ptp. of *dōtāre* (*dōt-* dower + *-ātus* -ATE¹) + *-iōn-* -ION; r. ME *dotacioun* < AF]

dote (dōt), *v.i.,* **dot·ed, dot·ing. 1.** to bestow or express excessive love or fondness regularly (usually fol. by *on* or *upon*): *She dotes on her youngest son.* **2.** to be weak-minded, esp. from old age. Also, **doat.** [ME *dot(i)e(n)* (obs.), *dote* (n.); c. MD *doten;* see DOTTY¹] —**dot′er,** *n.*

doth (duth), *v. Archaic.* 3rd pers. sing. pres. ind. of **do**¹.

Do·than (dō′thən), *n.* a city in SE Alabama. 31,440 (1960).

dot·ing (dō′tiŋg), *adj.* **1.** excessively fond: *doting parents.* **2.** weak-minded, esp. from old age. [DOTE + -ING²] —**dot′ing·ly,** *adv.* —**dot′ing·ness,** *n.*

dot′ prod′uct, *Math.* See **inner product** (def. 1).

dot·ted (dot′id), *adj.* **1.** marked with a dot or dots. **2.** consisting or constructed of dots. **3.** having objects scattered or placed in a random manner (often fol. by *with*): *a landscape dotted with small houses.* [DOT¹ + -ED³]

dot′ted swiss′. See under **Swiss muslin.**

dot·ter·el (dot′ər əl), *n.* **1.** any of several plovers usually inhabiting upland areas, esp. *Eudromias morinellus,* of Europe and Asia, which is easily captured. **2.** *Brit. Dial.* a silly, stupid person, esp. one who is easily duped. Also, **dot·trel** (do′trəl). [late ME *dotrelle.* See DOTE, -REL]

Dot·tie (dot′ē), *n.* a girl's given name, form of **Dorothea, Dorothee,** and **Dorothy.** Also, **Dotty.**

dot·tle (dot′əl), *n.* the plug of half-smoked tobacco in the bottom of a pipe after smoking. Also, **dot′tel.** [dial. *dot* small lump (prob. identical with DOT¹) + -LE]

dot·ty¹ (dot′ē), *adj.,* **-ti·er, -ti·est.** *Informal.* **1.** crazy; eccentric. **2.** feeble or unsteady in gait. [dial. *dot* to confuse (cf. Icel *dotta* to doze, nap, be half asleep) + -Y¹] —**dot′ti·ly,** *adv.*

dot·ty² (dot′ē), *adj.* marked with dots; dotted. [DOT¹ + -Y¹] —**dot′ti·ness,** *n.*

Dot·ty (dot′ē), *n.* a girl's given name, form of **Dorothea, Dorothee,** and **Dorothy.** Also, **Dottie.**

dot·y (dō′tē), *adj.,* **dot·i·er, dot·i·est.** (of wood) decayed. [DOTE + -Y¹]

Dou (dou), *n.* **Ge·rard** (gā′ʀäʀt), 1613–75, Dutch painter: pupil of Rembrandt. Also, **Douw, Dow.**

Dou·ai (do͞o ā′; *Fr.* dwe), *n.* a city in N France, SE of Calais. 50,104 (1962). Also, **Dou·ay′.**

Dou·a·la (do͞o ä′lä), *n.* a seaport in W Cameroon. 113,212 (1956). Also, **Duala.**

douane (dwan), *n., pl.* **douanes** (dwan). *French.* See **custom house.**

Dou′ay Bi′ble (do͞o′ā), an English translation of the Bible, prepared by Roman Catholic scholars from the Vulgate: the New Testament published at Rheims in 1582 and the Old Testament published at Douai in 1609–10. Also called **Dou′ay Ver′sion, Dou′ay-**

Rheims′ Bi′ble (do͞o′ä rēmz′), **Dou′ay-Rheims′ Ver′sion, Rheims-Douay Bible, Rheims-Douay Version.**

dou·ble (dub′əl), *adj., n., v.,* **-bled, -bling,** *adv.* —*adj.* **1.** twice as large, heavy, strong, etc.: *double pay; a double portion.* **2.** twofold in form, size, amount, number, extent, etc.: *a double blanket.* **3.** composed of two like parts or members; paired: *double doors.* **4.** *Bot.* (of flowers) having many more than the normal number of petals: *double petunias; double hollyhocks.* **5.** (of musical instruments) producing a tone an octave lower than the notes indicate. **6.** twofold in character, meaning, or conduct; dual or ambiguous: *a double interpretation.* **7.** deceitful; hypocritical; insincere. **8.** duple, as time or rhythm. **9.** folded in two; having one half folded over the other.
—*n.* **10.** a twofold size or amount; twice as much. **11.** something that is twice the usual size, amount, strength, etc. **12.** a duplicate or counterpart; something exactly or closely resembling another: *This dress is the double of that. He is the double of his cousin.* **13.** a fold or plait. **14.** a sudden backward turn or bend, as of a fox on the run in fox hunting; reversal. **15.** a trick or artifice, as of argument in a formal debate. **16.** *Motion Pictures.* a substitute who performs feats or actions too hazardous or difficult for a star. **17.** *Theat.* an actor having two roles in one play. **18.** *Baseball.* See **two-base hit. 19.** *Mil.* double time. **20. doubles,** (*construed as sing.*) a game or match in which there are two players on each side, as in tennis. **21.** (in bridge or other card games) **a.** a challenge by an opponent that the declarer cannot fulfill his contract, increasing the points to be won or lost. **b.** a hand which warrants such a challenge. **22.** *Bridge.* a conventional bid informing one's partner that a player's hand is of a certain strength. **23.** See **daily double. 24.** *Bowling.* two strikes in succession: *He needed a double in the tenth frame to win.* **25.** any of certain feasts in the Roman Catholic Church, marked by a doubled antiphon and taking precedence over lesser feasts. **26.** a substitute actor or singer ready to take another's place; understudy. **27.** *Music Rare.* a variation. **28.** a former coin of France, the sixth part of a sol, issued in silver in the 14th century, later made of copper. **29. on the double,** *Informal.* **a.** in double time, as marching troops. **b.** without delay; rapidly: *The fire engines came on the double.*
—*v.t.* **30.** to make double or twice as great; to add an equal amount to: *to double a sum; The baby doubled its weight in a year.* **31.** to be or have twice as much as. **32.** to bend or fold with or as with one part over another (often fol. by *over, up, back,* etc): *Double over the edge before sewing. A left jab doubled him up.* **33.** to clench: *He doubled his fists.* **34.** *Naut.* **a.** to sail around (a projecting area of land): *to double Cape Horn.* **b.** to add a new layer of planking or ceiling to (an old wooden hull). **35.** to pair; couple: *The players were doubled for the tournament.* **36.** *Music.* to reduplicate by means of a tone in another part, either at the unison or at an octave above or below. **37.** (in bridge and other card games) **a.** to challenge (the bid of an opponent) by making a call that increases the value of tricks to be won or lost. **b.** to challenge the bid of (an opponent): *He doubled me into game.* **38.** *Baseball.* **a.** to cause the advance of (a base runner) by a two-base hit: *He doubled him to third.* **b.** to cause (a run) to be scored by a two-base hit (often fol. by *in*): *He doubled in the winning run.* **c.** to put out (a base runner) as the second out of a double play (often fol. by *up*).
—*v.i.* **39.** to become double: *My money doubled in three years.* **40.** to bend or fold (often fol. by *up* or *over*): *to double over with pain.* **41.** to turn back on a course or reverse direction (often fol. by *back*): *He doubled back by another road and surprised us.* **42.** *Mil.* to march at the double-time pace. **43.** to serve in two capacities or in an additional capacity: *The girl doubles as secretary and receptionist.* **44.** *Theat.* to have two roles in one play. **45.** *Music.* to play an instrument besides one's regular instrument (usually followed by *on*): *The saxophonist doubles on drums.* **46.** (in bridge and other card games) to double the bid of an opponent. **47.** *Baseball.* to make a two-base hit. **48.** to double-date. **49. double in brass,** *Slang.* to serve in two capacities; be able to do work different from one's own: *It is a small firm, and everyone doubles in brass when emergencies arise.* **50. double or nothing,** a bet having as its outcome either the doubling of a previous loss or the canceling of that loss. Also, **double or quits. 51. double up, a.** to share quarters planned for only one person or family: *Because of the room shortage, we had to double up.* **b.** to bend over, as from pain: *He doubled up in agony.*
—*adv.* **52.** to twice the amount, number, extent, etc.; twofold; doubly. [ME < OF < L *dupl(us),* equiv. to *du(o)* two + *-plus* -FOLD] —**dou′ble·ness,** *n.* —**dou′bler,** *n.*

Double, The, a short novel (1846) by Dostoevsky.

dou′ble achieve′ment, *Heraldry.* a representation of the arms of a man beside those of his wife such that a difference of rank between them is shown.

dou·ble-act·ing (dub′əl ak′ting), *adj.* **1.** (of a reciprocating engine, pump, etc.) having pistons accomplishing work in both directions, fluid being admitted alternately to opposite ends of the cylinders. Cf. **single-acting. 2.** (of a hinge of a door or the like) permitting movement in either direction from the normal, or closed, position. **3.** having twice the usual effectiveness, strength, use, etc.

dou·ble-ac·tion (dub′əl ak′shən), *adj.* (of a firearm) requiring only one pull of the trigger to cock and fire it.

dou′ble a′gent, 1. a person who spies on a country while pretending to spy for it. **2.** a spy in the service of two rival countries, companies, etc.

dou′ble al′tar, an altar on which the Eucharist may be celebrated from either the liturgical east or the liturgical west side.

dou′ble-armed bolt′ (dub′əl ärmd′). See **double-ended bolt.**

dou·ble-bank (dub′əl bangk′), *v.t. Naut.* **1.** to have two men pull (each of a number of oars). **2.** to have men pull (a rope) from both sides. **3.** to row (a boat) with rowers for both sides on each thwart.

dou′ble bar′, *Music.* a double vertical line on a staff indicating the conclusion of a piece of music or a subdivision of it. See illus. under **bar**[1].

dou·ble-bar·reled (dub′əl bar′əld), *adj.* **1.** having two barrels mounted side by side, as a shotgun. **2.** serving a double purpose or having two parts or aspects: *He launched a double-barreled attack on government policy.*

dou′ble bass′ (bās), the largest instrument of the violin family, having three or, usually, four strings, rested vertically on the floor when played. Also called **bass fiddle, bass viol, string bass.** —**dou′ble-bass′,** *adj.*

dou′ble bassoon′, a bassoon an octave lower in pitch than the ordinary bassoon: the largest and deepest-toned instrument of the oboe class.

dou′ble bat′ten, *Theat.* two wooden battens screwed together for holding the edge of a drop between them. Also called **sandwich batten.**

dou′ble-beat valve′ (dub′əl bēt′). See **balanced valve.**

dou′ble bed′, a bed large enough for two adults.

dou′ble Black′wall hitch′. See **double hitch.**

dou′ble block′, *Mach.* a block having two sheaves or pulleys.

dou′ble blos′som, *Plant Pathol.* a disease of blackberries and dewberries, characterized by witches'-brooms and flower malformations, caused by a fungus, *Cercosporella rubi.*

dou′ble boil′er, a utensil consisting of two pots, one of which fits partway into the other: water is boiled in the lower pot to cook or warm food or melt a substance in the upper.

dou′ble bond′, *Chem.* a chemical linkage consisting of two covalent bonds between two atoms of a molecule, represented in chemical formulas by two lines, two dots, or four dots: $CH_2=CH_2$; $CH_2:CH_2$; $CH_2::CH_2$.

dou·ble-breast·ed (dub′əl bres′tid), *adj.* **1.** (of a coat, jacket, etc.) overlapping sufficiently in front to allow for two rows of buttons. **2.** (of a suit) having a coat or jacket that so overlaps. Cf. **single-breasted.**

dou′ble cen′tering, *Survey.* a method of extending a survey line by taking the average of two foresights, one with the telescope direct and one with it inverted, made each time by transiting the telescope after a backsight.

dou′ble check′, *Chess.* a simultaneous check by two pieces in which the moving of one piece to give check also reveals a check by another piece.

dou·ble-check (dub′əl chek′), *v.t., v.i.* **1.** to check twice or again; recheck. —*n.* **2.** a second examination or verification to assure accuracy, proper functioning, or the like.

dou′ble chin′, a fold of fat beneath the chin. —**dou′ble-chinned′,** *adj.*

dou′ble cloth′, a cloth used in overcoating, blankets, brocade, etc., made of five sets of yarn: face warp, face filling, back warp, back filling, and a set of binder yarns to unite the face and back fabrics.

dou·ble-clutch (dub′əl kluch′), *v.i. Auto.* to shift gears in an automotive vehicle first into neutral and then into the desired gear, releasing the clutch twice, once for each shift.

dou′ble coun′terpoint, *Music.* invertible counterpoint using two transposable voices.

dou·ble-crest·ed cor′morant (dub′əl kres′tid), a North American cormorant, *Phalacrocorax auritus,* having tufts of black and white feathers on each side of the head.

dou·ble-crop (dub′əl krop′), *v.t.,* **-cropped, -crop·ping.** to raise two crops per year on (an area of land).

dou′ble cross′, 1. *Informal.* a betrayal or swindle of a colleague. Cf. **cross** (def. 26). **2.** *Genetics.* a cross in which both parents are first-generation hybrids resulting from single crosses, thus involving four inbred lines.

dou·ble-cross (dub′əl krôs′, -kros′), *v.t. Informal.* to prove treacherous to; betray. —**dou′ble-cross′er,** *n.*

Dou·ble-Cros·tic (dub′əl krô′stik, -kros′tik), *n. Trademark.* a word game in which the player fills out, over respective numbered dashes, words for a given set of definitions and transcribes each letter of these words to correspondingly numbered spaces in an accompanying pattern, so that the properly filled pattern produces a quotation and the first letters of the words over the dashes form an acrostic of the name of the author and title of the book containing the quotation.

dou′ble crown′, *Chiefly Brit.* a size of printing paper, 20 × 30 inches.

dou′ble cup′, (in Renaissance art) a matched pair of metal cups, made so that one can be placed inverted on top of the other.

dou·ble-cut (dub′əl kut′), *adj.* noting a file having parallel cutting ridges crisscrossing in two directions. Cf. **single-cut.**

dou′ble dag′ger, *Print.* a mark (‡) used for references, as footnotes. Also called **diesis.**

dou′ble date′, *Informal.* a date which two couples go on together.

dou·ble-date (dub′əl dāt′), *v.,* **-dat·ed, -dat·ing.** *Informal.* —*v.i.* **1.** to take part in a double date. —*v.t.* **2.** to accompany (someone) on a double date.

Dou·ble·day (dub′əl dā′), *n.* **Abner,** 1819–93, U.S. army officer and reputed inventor of baseball.

dou·ble-deal·ing (dub′əl dē′ling), *n.* **1.** duplicity; deception. —*adj.* **2.** using duplicity; treacherous. —**dou′ble-deal′er,** *n.*

dou·ble-deck·er (dub′əl dek′ər), *n.* **1.** something with two decks, tiers, or the like, as two beds one above the other, a ship with two decks above the water line, or a bus with two decks. **2.** a food item consisting of two main layers, as a sandwich made with three slices of bread and two layers of filling, a cake of two layers, or an ice-cream cone with two scoops of ice cream.

dou′ble decomposi′tion, *Chem.* a reaction whose result is the interchange of two parts of two substances to form two new substances, as $AgNO_3 + NaCl \rightarrow AgCl + NaNO_3$. Also called **metathesis.**

dou·ble-dig·it (dub′əl dij′it), *adj.* of or denoting a percentage greater than ten, esp. with reference to rates traditionally below that level: *double-digit inflation.*

dou′ble di′ode, duodiode.

dou·ble-dip (dub′əl dip′), *v.i.* **-dipped, -dip·ping.** *Informal.* to earn a salary from one position while collecting a pension from the same employer or organization, esp. to be a wage earner on the federal payroll while receiving a military retiree's pension. —**dou′ble-dip′per,** *n.* —**dou′ble-dip′ping,** *n.*

dou′ble dome′, *Slang.* egghead.

dou′ble dress′er, *Furniture.* a dresser having two long drawers across its width for most of its height.

dou′ble drift′, *Navig.* a method of calculating wind direction and velocity by observing the direction of drift of a vessel on two or more headings.

dou′ble ea′gle, 1. a gold coin of the U.S., issued from 1849 to 1933, equal to 2 eagles or 20 dollars. **2.** *Golf.* a score of three strokes under par on a hole.

dou·ble-edged (dub′əl ejd′), *adj.* **1.** having two cutting edges, as a razor blade. **2.** capable of acting two ways or having opposite effects: *a double-edged argument.*

dou′ble el′ephant, *Chiefly Brit.* a size of drawing or writing paper, 26¾ × 40 inches.

dou·ble-end·ed (dub′əl en′did), *adj.* **1.** having the two ends alike. **2.** *Naut.* **a.** operating equally well with either end as the bow, as a ferryboat. **b.** noting a vessel having a stern curved or pointed so as to resemble or suggest a bow. **3.** noting any of various vehicles, as certain streetcars, designed to be operated with either end serving as the front.

dou′ble-ended bolt′, a headless bolt threaded at both ends. Also called **double-armed bolt.**

dou′ble end′er, *Naut.* a double-ended vessel. Also, **dou′ble-end′er.**

dou·ble en·ten·dre (dub′əl än tän′drə, -tänd′; *Fr.* do͞o bläN täN′drᵊ), *pl.* **dou·ble en·ten·dres** (dub′əl än tän′drəz, -tändz′; *Fr.* do͞o bläN täN′drᵊ). **1.** a double meaning. **2.** a word or expression used in a given context so that it can be understood in two ways, esp. when one meaning is indelicate or risqué. [< obs. F; see DOUBLE, INTEND]

dou·ble en·tente (do͞o bläN täNt′), *pl.* **dou·bles en·tentes** (do͞o blə zäN täNt′). *French.* a double meaning; ambiguity.

dou′ble en′try, *Bookkeeping.* a method in which each transaction is entered twice in the ledger, once to the debit of one account, and once to the credit of another. Cf. **single entry.**

dou′ble expo′sure, 1. *Photog.* the act of exposing the same film, frame, plate, etc., twice. **2.** the picture resulting from such exposure.

dou·ble-faced (dub′əl fāst′), *adj.* **1.** practicing duplicity; hypocritical. **2.** having two faces or aspects. —**dou·ble-fac·ed·ly** (dub′əl fā′sid lē, -fāst′-), *adv.* —**dou′ble-fac′ed·ness,** *n.*

dou′ble fault′, (in tennis, squash, handball, etc.) two faults in succession, resulting in the loss of the point, the loss of the serve, or both.

dou′ble fea′ture, a motion-picture program consisting of two features.

dou′ble first′, *Brit. Univ.* **1.** a first in two subjects. **2.** a student who earns a first in two subjects.

dou′ble flat′, *Music.* **1.** a symbol (♭♭) that lowers the pitch of the note following it by two semitones. **2.** a note or tone marked or affected by such a symbol.

dou′ble fools′cap, *Chiefly Brit.* a size of printing paper, 17 × 27 inches.

dou′ble fugue′, *Music.* **1.** a fugue with two subjects developed simultaneously. **2.** a fugue having two subjects that are developed at first independently and then together.

dou·ble·gang·er (dub′əl gang′ər), *n.* Doppelgänger. [half-trans. of G *Doppelgänger*]

dou′ble gen′itive. See **double possessive.**

dou′ble glaz′ing, *Building Trades.* glazing consisting of two thicknesses of glass with a dead air space between them.

dou′ble har′ness, 1. harness for a pair of horses. **2. in double harness,** *Informal.* married.

dou·ble·head·er (dub′əl hed′ər), *n.* **1.** *Sports.* **a.** two games, as of baseball, between the same teams on the same day in immediate succession. **b.** two games, as of basketball, between two different pairs of teams on the same day in immediate succession. **2.** a railroad train pulled by two locomotives. [DOUBLE + HEADER]

dou′ble-hel·i·cal gear′ (dub′əl hel′i kəl), **1.** a gear similar to the herringbone gear but having right-handed and left-handed helical teeth with a gap between them. **2.** See **herringbone gear.**

dou′ble hitch′, a Blackwall hitch with an extra upper loop passed around the hook. Also called **double Blackwall hitch.**

dou·ble-hung (dub′əl hung′), *adj.* **1.** (of a window) having two vertically sliding sashes, each closing a different part of the opening. **2.** (of a window sash) sliding vertically, with a counterweight on each side.

dou′ble indem′nity, a clause in a life-insurance or accident-insurance policy providing for payment of twice the face value of the policy in the event of accidental death.

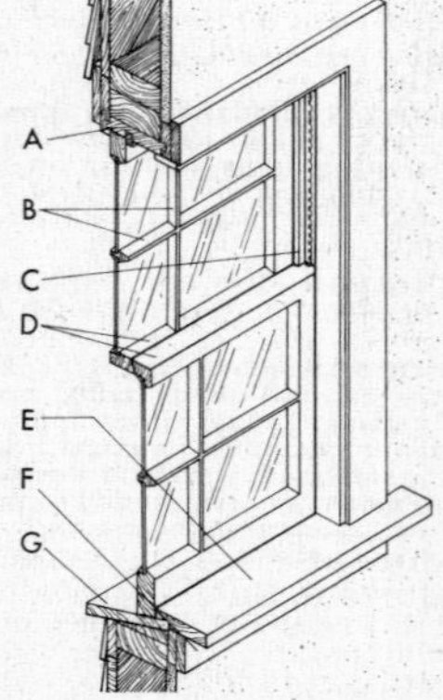

Double-hung window
A, Yoke; B, Muntins; C, Parting strip; D, Meeting rails; E, Stool; F, Apron; G, Sill

dou′ble in′tegral, *Math.* an integral in which the integrand involves a function of two variables and which requires two applications of the integration process to evaluate.

dou′ble jeop′ardy, *Law.* the subjecting of a person to a second trial for the same offense the person has already been tried for.

dou·ble-joint·ed (dub′əl join′tid), *adj.* (of people and animals) having unusually flexible joints which enable the limbs, spine, etc., to curve in extraordinary ways.

dou′ble jump′, **1.** *Chess.* the advance of a pawn, in its original move only, from its initial position on the second rank to the fourth without stopping at the intervening square. **2.** *Checkers.* the capturing of two of the opponent's checkers in two uninterrupted jumps, constituting a single move by one man.

dou·ble-lock (dub′əl lok′), *v.t.* **1.** to lock with two turns of a key, so that a second bolt is engaged. **2.** to fasten with particular care.

dou′ble luff′ tack′le, a tackle composed of a fall rove through a standing double and a running treble block and attached to the double block, the hauling being done upon the treble block and the mechanical advantage being six, neglecting friction.

dou′ble mag′num, Jeroboam (def. 2).

dou·ble-mind·ed (dub′əl mīn′did), *adj.* wavering or undecided in mind. **—dou′ble-mind′ed·ly,** *adv.* **—dou′ble-mind′ed·ness,** *n.*

dou′ble mon′astery, a religious community of both men and women who live in separate establishments under the same superior and who worship in a common church.

dou′ble neg′ative, a syntactic construction in which two negative words are used in the same clause to express a single negation.

dou·ble·ness (dub′əl nis), *n.* **1.** the quality or condition of being double. **2.** deception or dissimulation. [DOUBLE + -NESS]

dou·ble-O (dub′əl ō′), *n., pl.* **-Os.** *Slang.* careful scrutiny or close inspection. [after the two *o*'s in *once-over*]

dou′ble or′ange dai′sy, a perennial herb, *Erigeron aurantiacus,* of southeastern Asia, having orange-yellow flowerheads.

dou′ble pad′dle, *Naut.* a paddle with a blade at each end, as that of the kayak.

dou′ble pair′ roy′al, *Cribbage.* a set of four cards of the same denomination. Cf. **pair royal.**

dou·ble-park (dub′əl pärk′), *v.t., v.i.* to park alongside another automobile that is already parked parallel to the curb.

dou′ble-part′ed and fret′ty (dub′əl pär′tid), *Heraldry.* See **parted and fretty.**

dou′ble piece′, *Armor.* See **piece of exchange.**

dou′ble play′, *Baseball.* a play in which two putouts are made.

dou′ble pneumo′nia, *Pathol.* pneumonia affecting both lungs.

dou′ble posses′sive, *Gram.* a possessive consisting of a prepositional phrase with *of* containing a substantive in the possessive case, as *of father's* in *He is a friend of father's.* Also called **double genitive.**

dou′ble post′, *Chiefly Brit.* a size of printing paper, $19\frac{1}{2} \times 31\frac{1}{2}$ inches.

dou′ble predestina′tion, *Theol.* the doctrine that God has foreordained both those who will be saved and those who will be damned.

dou′ble pur′chase. See **gun tackle.**

dou′ble quat′refoil, *Heraldry.* a charge having the form of a foil with eight leaves, used esp. as the cadency mark of a ninth son. Also called **octofoil.**

dou·ble-quick (*adj., adv.* dub′əl kwik′; *n., v.* dub′əl-kwik′), *adj.* **1.** very quick or rapid. **—***adv.* **2.** in a very quick or rapid manner. **—***n.* **3.** See **double time.** **—***v.t., v.i.* **4.** to double-time.

dou′ble quotes′, quotation marks (" "), as usually appear around quoted material. Cf. **single quotes.**

dou·ble-reed (dub′əl rēd′), *adj. Music.* of or pertaining to wind instruments producing sounds through two reeds fastened and beating together, as the oboe.

dou′ble refrac′tion, *Optics.* the separation of a ray of light into two unequally refracted, plane-polarized rays of orthogonal polarizations, occurring in crystals in which the velocity of light rays is not the same in all directions. Also called **birefringence.**

dou′ble rhyme′. See under **feminine rhyme.**

dou·ble-rip·per (dub′əl rip′ər), *n. New Eng.* bobsled (def. 2). Also called **dou·ble-run·ner** (dub′əl run′ər).

dou′ble roy′al, *Chiefly Brit.* a size of printing paper, 25×40 inches.

dou′ble salt′, *Chem.* a salt that crystallizes as a single substance but ionizes as two distinct salts when dissolved, as carnallite, $KCl \cdot MgCl_2 \cdot 6H_2O$.

dou′ble sculls′, a race for sculls rowed by two oarsmen each using a pair of oars. Cf. **single sculls.**

dou′ble-seat·ed valve′ (dub′əl sē′tid). See **balanced valve.**

dou′ble sharp′, *Music.* **1.** a symbol (× or 𝄪) that raises by two semitones the pitch of the following note. **2.** a note or tone marked or affected by such a symbol.

dou′ble sol′itaire, *Cards.* a game of solitaire for two persons, each usually having his own pack and layout but pooling his foundations with those of his opponent.

dou·ble-space (dub′əl spās′), *v.,* **-spaced, -spac·ing.** **—***v.t.* **1.** to typewrite (text, copy, etc.) leaving a full space between lines: *Always double-space a term paper.* **—***v.i.* **2.** to typewrite leaving a full space between lines: *I can never remember to double-space.*

dou′ble Span′ish bur′ton, a tackle having the load suspended from one of two single running blocks, supported both by the fall, which is rove through it, and by one end of a runner which is rove through the standing block and which supports at its other end the other running block: made in two ways, either with the standing end of the fall attached to a fixed point beside the running block, or with the fall rove through the standing block and attached to the running block supporting the load, with a mechanical advantage of four and five, neglecting friction, for these two types respectively. See diag. under **tackle.**

dou′ble spin′naker, *Naut.* See **parachute spinnaker.**

dou′ble spread′, any pair of facing pages in a completed book, magazine, etc.

dou′ble sprit′, *Naut.* wishbone (def. 2).

dou′ble stand′ard, any code or set of principles containing different provisions for one group of people than for another, esp. the unwritten code of sexual behavior that permits men more freedom than women. Cf. **single standard** (def. 1).

dou′ble star′, *Astron.* two stars that appear as one if not viewed through a telescope with adequate magnification, such as two stars that are separated by a great distance but are nearly in line with each other and an observer **(optical double star),** or those that are relatively close together and comprise a single physical system **(physical double star).** Cf. **binary star.**

dou′ble steal′, *Baseball.* a play in which two base runners steal a base each.

dou′ble stop′, *Music.* two or more notes bowed simultaneously on a stringed instrument, as the violin.

dou·ble-stop (dub′əl stop′), *v.,* **-stopped, -stop·ping.** *Music.* **—***v.t.* **1.** to play a double stop on (a stringed instrument). **—***v.i.* **2.** to play a double stop.

dou′ble sum′mer time′, *Brit.* time made by setting clocks two hours ahead of Greenwich Mean Time during the summer months, similar in purpose to the U.S. daylight-saving time.

dou′ble-sunk di′al (dub′əl sungk′), *Horol.* a dial having sunken areas for the second and hour hands.

dou·blet (dub′lit), *n.* **1.** a close-fitting outer garment, with or without sleeves and sometimes having a short skirt, worn by men in the Renaissance. **2.** an undergarment, quilted and reinforced with mail, worn beneath armor. **3.** a pair of like things; couple. **4.** one of a pair of like things; duplicate. **5.** one of two or more words in a language that are derived from the same source, esp. when one is learned while the other is popular, as *coy* and *quiet,* both taken from the same Latin word, *quiet* directly, and *coy* by way of Old French. **6.** *Print.* an unintentional repetition in printed matter or proof. **7. doublets,** a throw of a pair of dice in which the same number of spots turns up on each die. **8.** *Jewelry.* a counterfeit gem made of two pieces, either of smaller gemstones, inferior stones, or glass. Cf. **imitation doublet, triplet** (def. 6). **9.** *Optics.* a compound lens made of two thin lenses shaped so as to reduce chromatic and spherical aberrations. [ME < MF. See DOUBLE, -ET]

Doublets (def. 1), Elizabethan period

dou′ble tack′le, a pulley with two grooved wheels.

dou·ble-tailed (dub′əl tāld′), *adj. Heraldry.* (of a lion) represented with two tails joined together next to the body. Cf. **queue fourché.**

dou′ble take′, *Informal.* a rapid or surprised second look, either literal or figurative, at a person or situation whose significance had not been completely grasped at first: *His friends did a double take when they saw how much weight he had lost.*

dou·ble-talk (dub′əl tôk′), *n.* **1.** speech using nonsense syllables along with words in a rapid patter. **2.** evasive or ambiguous language: *When you try to get a straight answer, he gives you double-talk.* **—***v.i.* **3.** to engage in double-talk. **—***v.t.* **4.** to accomplish or persuade by double-talk.

dou′ble tape′. See under **magnetic tape.**

dou·ble-team (dub′əl tēm′), *v.t.* to defend against or block (an opposing player) by using two players, as in football or basketball: *By double-teaming the end the safety men left the other receiver in the open.*

dou·ble·think (*v.* dub′əl thingk′; *n., adj.* dub′əl-thingk′), *v.,* **-thought, -think·ing,** *n., adj.* **—***v.i.* **1.** to accept as true two inconsistent versions of a factual matter at the same time, consciously disciplining the mind to ignore the conflict between them. **—***v.t.* **2.** to doublethink about (something). **—***n.* **3.** the technique or process of doublethinking. **—***adj.* **4.** characterized by doublethinking or doublethink. Also, **dou′ble-think′.** [DOUBLE + THINK[1]]

dou′ble tide′, agger (defs. 1, 2).

dou′ble time′, **1.** *U.S. Army.* the fastest rate of marching troops, a slow jog in which 180 paces, each of 3 feet, are taken in a minute. **2.** a slow run by troops in step. **3.** a rate of overtime pay that is twice the regular wage rate.

dou·ble-time (dub′əl tīm′), *v.,* **-timed, -tim·ing.** **—***v.t.* **1.** to cause to move in double time: *Double-time the troops to the mess hall.* **—***v.i.* **2.** to move in double-time: *The platoon double-timed around the company area.*

dou·ble·ton (dub′əl tən), *n. Chiefly Bridge.* a set of only two cards of the same suit in a hand as dealt: *The other player held a doubleton.* [modeled on SINGLETON]

dou·ble-tongue (dub′əl tung′), *v.i.,* **-tongued, -tongu·ing.** *Music.* (in playing the flute, cornet, etc.) to apply the tongue rapidly to the teeth and the hard palate alternately, so as to ensure a brilliant execution of a staccato passage.

dou·ble-tongued (dub′əl tungd′), *adj.* deceitful; hypocritical. [ME *dowble tungid*]

dou′blet pat′tern, *Fine Arts.* a pattern, as on a fabric, in which a figure or group is duplicated in reverse order on the opposite side of a center line.

dou·ble·tree (dub′əl trē′), *n.* a pivoted bar with a whiffletree attached to each end, used in harnessing two horses abreast. See illus. under **whiffletree.** [modeled on SINGLETREE]

dou′ble tri′ode, duotriode.

dou′ble truck′, **1.** a chase for holding the type for a center spread, esp. for a newspaper. **2.** matter occupying a center spread, esp. advertising matter.

dou′ble whip′, See under **whip** (def. 26).

dou′ble wick′et, cricket in which two wickets are used, being the usual form of the game.

dou′ble wing′back forma′tion, *Football.* an offensive formation in which two backs line up at opposite ends of the backfield about one yard outside of the ends and about one yard behind the line of scrimmage. Also called **dou′ble wing′.** Cf. **single wingback formation.**

dou·bling (dub′ling), *n. Naut.* the part of the upper or lower end of one spar of a mast that is overlapped by another spar above or below it. [ME, see DOUBLE, -ING[1]]

dou·bloon (du blo͞on′), *n.* a former gold coin of Spain and Spanish America, originally equal to two escudos but fluctuating in value. [< Sp *doblón,* equiv. to *dobl(a)* DOBLA + *-ón* aug. suffix]

dou·blure (də blo͝or′, do͞o-; *Fr.* do͞o blʏʀ′), *n., pl.* **-blures** (-blo͝orz′; *Fr.* -blʏʀ′). an ornamental lining of a book cover. [< F: a lining, equiv. to *doubl(er)* (to) line (lit., to DOUBLE) + *-ure* -URE]

dou·bly (dub′lē), *adv.* **1.** to a double measure or degree: *to be doubly cautious.* **2.** in a double manner. **3.** *Obs.* with duplicity. [ME; see DOUBLE, -LY]

Doubs (do͞o), *n.* **1.** a river in E France, flowing into the Saône River. ab. 260 mi. long. **2.** a department in E France. 384,881 (1962); 2031 sq. mi. *Cap.:* Besançon.

doubt (dout), *v.t.* **1.** to be uncertain in opinion about; hold questionable; hesitate to believe. **2.** to distrust. **3.** *Archaic.* to fear; be apprehensive about. **—***v.i.* **4.** to be uncertain about something; be undecided in opinion or belief. **—***n.* **5.** a feeling of uncertainty about the truth, reality, or nature of something. **6.** distrust. **7.** a state of affairs such as to occasion uncertainty. **8.** *Obs.* fear; dread. **9. beyond the shadow of a doubt,** with certainty; definitely. Also, **beyond a doubt, beyond doubt. 10. in doubt,** in a state of uncertainty or suspense: *His appointment to the position is still in doubt.* **11. no doubt, a.** probably. **b.** certainly: *There is no doubt an element of truth in what you say.* **12. without doubt,** unquestionably; certainly: *It was without doubt the only reasonable course of action.* [ME *dout(en)* < OF *dout(er)* < L *dubitāre* to waver, hesitate, be uncertain (freq. of OL *dubāre*), equiv. to *dub-* doubt + *-it-* freq. suffix + *-āre* inf. suffix] **—doubt′a·ble,** *adj.* **—doubt′a·bly,** *adv.* **—doubt′er,** *n.* **—doubt′ing·ly,** *adv.* **—doubt′ing·ness,** *n.*

—Syn. 1, 2. mistrust, suspect, question. **5.** indecision, irresolution.

doubt·ful (dout′fəl), *adj.* **1.** admitting of or causing doubt; uncertain; ambiguous. **2.** of uncertain outcome or result. **3.** of equivocal character: *His tactics are highly doubtful.* **4.** unsettled in opinion or belief; undecided; hesitating. [ME *douteful.* See DOUBT, -FUL] **—doubt′ful·ly,** *adv.* **—doubt′ful·ness,** *n.*

—Syn. 1. unsure, indeterminate. **2.** undetermined, unsettled, indecisive, dubious, problematic. **3.** shady, questionable. **4.** irresolute, vacillating, hesitant. DOUBTFUL, DUBIOUS, INCREDULOUS, SKEPTICAL imply reluctance or unwillingness to be convinced. To be DOUBTFUL about something is to feel that it is open to question or that more evidence is needed to prove it: *to be doubtful about the statements of witnesses.* DUBIOUS implies greater vacillation, vagueness, or suspicion: *dubious about suggested methods of manufacture, about future plans.* INCREDULOUS means actively unwilling or reluctant to believe, usually in a given situation: *incredulous at the good news.* SKEPTICAL implies a general disposition to doubt or question: *skeptical of human progress.* **—Ant. 1, 2.** certain.

doubt′ing Thom′as, a person who refuses to believe without proof; skeptic. John 20:24–29.

doubt·less (dout′lis), *adv.* Also, **doubt′less·ly. 1.** without doubt; unquestionably. **2.** probably or presumably. **—***adj.* **3.** free from doubt or uncertainty. [ME *douteles.* See DOUBT, -LESS] **—doubt′less·ness,** *n.*

douce (do͞os), *adj. Scot. and North Eng.* sedate; modest; quiet. [ME < MF, OF < L *dulci-,* s. of *dulcis* (fem.); see DULCET] **—douce′ly,** *adv.* **—douce′ness,** *n.*

douce·pere (do͞os′pēr′, do͞o′sə-), *n.* douzepers.

dou·ceur (do͞o sûr′; *Fr.* do͞o sœʀ′), *n., pl.* **-ceurs** (-sûrz′; *Fr.* -sœʀ′). **1.** a gratuity; tip. **2.** a conciliatory gift or bribe. **3.** *Archaic.* sweetness; agreeableness. [< F: sweetness. See DOUCE, -OR[1]]

douche (do͞osh), *n., v.,* **douched, douch·ing.** **—***n.* **1.** a jet or current of water applied to a body part, organ, or cavity for medicinal or hygienic purposes. **2.** the application of such a jet. **3.** an instrument, as a syringe, for administering it. **4.** a bath administered by such a jet. **—***v.t.* **5.** to apply a douche to. **—***v.i.* **6.** to use a douche or douches; undergo douching. [< F < It *doccia* water pipe, abstracted from *doccione* big drainpipe (where *-one* was taken as aug. suffix) < LL *duction-* (s. of *ductiō*) a leading, conveying, equiv. to L *duct(us)* DUCT + *-iōn-* -ION]

douche′ bag′, a small syringe having detachable nozzles for fluid injections, used chiefly for vaginal lavage and for enemas.

Doug (dug), *n.* a boy's given name, form of **Douglas.**

dough (dō), *n.* **1.** flour or meal combined with water, milk, etc., in a mass for baking into bread, cake, etc.; paste of bread. **2.** any soft, pasty mass. **3.** *Slang.* money. [ME *dowgh,* etc., OE *dāg, dāh;* c. D *deeg,* Icel *deig,* Goth *daigs,* G *Teig*]

dough·bel·ly (dō′bel′ē), *n., pl.* **-lies.** stoneroller (def. 1). [DOUGH + BELLY]

dough′ bird′, *U.S. Dial.* the Eskimo curlew.

dough·boy (dō′boi′), *n.* **1.** *Informal.* an American infantryman in Europe, esp. in World War I. **2.** any infantryman. **3.** a rounded mass of dough, boiled or steamed as a dumpling or deep-fried and served as a hot bread. [DOUGH + BOY; in informal sense, prob. so called from the buttons on the infantry uniforms in the Civil War]

dough·face (dō′fās′), *n. U.S. Hist.* **1.** a Northerner who sympathized with the South during the controversies over new territories and slavery before the Civil War. **2.** a congressman from a Northern State not opposed to slavery in the South. [DOUGH + FACE]

dough·nut (dō′nət, -nut′), *n.* **1.** a small cake of sweetened or, sometimes, of unsweetened dough fried in deep fat, typically shaped like a ring or, when prepared with a filling, a ball. **2.** anything shaped like a thick ring; an annular object; toroid. Also, **donut.** [DOUGH + NUT]

dought (dout), *v.* a pt. of **dow.**

dough·ty (dou′tē), *adj.,* **-ti·er, -ti·est.** steadfastly courageous and resolute. [ME; OE *dohtig* worthy, equiv. to *doht worth (c. OHG *toht;* see DOW[1]) + *-ig* -Y[1]; r. OE *dyhtig,* c. G *tüchtig*] **—dough′ti·ly,** *adv.* **—dough′ti·ness,** *n.*

Dough·ty (dou′tē), *n.* **Charles Mon·ta·gu** (mon′tə gyo͞o′), 1843–1926, English traveler and writer.

dough·y (dō′ē), *adj.,* **dough·i·er, dough·i·est.** of or like dough, esp. in being soft and heavy or pallid and flabby: *a doughy consistency; a fat, doughy face.* [DOUGH + -Y¹] —**dough′i·ness,** *n.*

Doug·las (dug′ləs), *n.* **1. Sir James** ("*the Black Douglas*"), 1286–1330, Scottish military leader. **2. James, 2nd Earl of,** 1358?–88, Scottish military leader. **3. Lloyd C(as·sel)** (kas′əl), 1877–1951, U.S. novelist and clergyman. **4. Stephen A(rnold),** 1813–61, U.S. political leader and statesman. **5. William O(r·ville)** (ôr′vil), 1898–1980, Associate Justice of the U.S. Supreme Court 1939–75. **6.** a city on and the capital of the Isle of Man: resort. 18,837 (1961). **7.** a city in SE Arizona. 11,925 (1960). **8.** a town in central Georgia. 8736 (1960). **9.** a town in central Wyoming. 2822 (1960). **10.** Also, **Douglass.** a boy's given name.

Doug′las fir′, a coniferous tree, *Pseudotsuga taxifolia* (*P. mucronata* or *P. Douglasii*), of western North America, often over 200 feet high, and yielding a strong, durable timber: the State tree of Oregon. Also called **Doug′las pine′, Doug′las spruce′, Oregon fir, Oregon pine.** [named after David Douglas (1798–1834), Scottish botanist and traveler in America]

Doug·las-Home (dug′ləs hyo͞om′), *n.* **Sir Alexander Frederick,** born 1903, British statesman and politician: prime minister 1963–64.

Doug·lass (dug′ləs), *n.* **1. Frederick,** 1817–95, U.S. ex-slave, abolitionist, and orator. **2.** Also, **Douglas.** a boy's given name.

Doug·las·ville (dug′ləs vil), *n.* a town in central Georgia. 4462 (1960).

Dou·kho·bor (do͞o′kō bôr′), *n., pl.* **-bors, -bor·tsy** (-bôrt′sē). a member of an independent religious sect originating in Russia in the 18th century, believing in the supreme authority of the inner voice and in the transmigration of souls, rejecting the divinity of Christ and the establishing of churches, and expressing opposition to civil authority by refusing to pay taxes, do military service, etc. Also, **Dukhobor.** [< Russ *dukhoborets,* equiv. to *dukh* spirit + *borets* wrestler, contender (*bor-,* s. of *borot′sja* to contend, + *-ets* agent suffix)]

dou·ma (do͞o′mä), *n.* duma.

Dou·mergue (do͞o merg′), *n.* **Gas·ton** (gas tôn′), 1863–1937, French statesman: president of France 1924–31.

doum′ palm′ (do͞om). See **doom palm.**

doup (doup), *n. Scot.* **1.** the bottom, end, or butt of something. **2.** the buttocks. [cf. ON *daup*]

doup·pi·o·ni (do͞o′pē ō′nē), *n.* an irregular silk thread reeled from two or more entangled cocoons and producing a coarse yarn generally used in fabrics such as shantung or pongee. Also, **dou·pi·on** (do͞o′pē on′), **dou′pi·o′ni, dupion, dupioni.** [< It *doppione;* see DUPION]

dour (do͝or, dour, dou′ər), *adj.* **1.** sullen; gloomy. **2.** severe; stern. **3.** *Scot.* (of land) barren; rocky, infertile, or otherwise difficult or impossible to cultivate. [ME < L *dūr(us)* DURE¹] —**dour′ly,** *adv.* —**dour′ness,** *n.*

dou·ra (do͝or′ə), *n.* durra. Also, **dou′rah.**

dou·ri·cou·li (do͝or′ē ko͞o′lē), *n.* a small, nocturnal, South American monkey of the genus *Aotus,* having large, owllike eyes. [from some SAmerInd tongue]

dou·rine (do͝o rēn′), *n. Vet. Pathol.* an infectious disease of horses, affecting the genitals and hind legs, caused by a protozoan parasite, *Trypanosoma equiperdum.* [< F; cf. Ar *darin* scabby]

Dou·ro (*Port.* dō′ro͝o), *n.* a river in SW Europe, flowing W from N Spain through N Portugal to the Atlantic. ab. 475 mi. long. Spanish, **Duero.**

Dousch·ka (do͞osh′kə), *n.* a girl's given name.

douse (dous), *v.,* **doused, dous·ing,** *n.* —*v.t.* **1.** to plunge into water or the like; drench: *She doused the clothes in soapy water.* **2.** to splash or throw water or other liquid on: *She doused the thirsty plant with water.* **3.** *Informal.* to extinguish: *She quickly doused the candle's flame with her fingertips.* **4.** *Informal.* to remove; doff. **5.** *Naut.* **a.** to lower or take in (a sail, mast, or the like) suddenly. **b.** to slacken (a line) suddenly. **c.** to stow quickly. —*v.i.* **6.** to plunge or be plunged into a liquid. —*n.* **7.** *Brit. Dial.* a stroke or blow. Also, **dowse.** [?]

dous·er (dou′sər), *n.* **1.** one who or that which douses. **2.** dowser. [DOUSE + -ER¹]

dout·er (dou′tər, do͞o′-), *n.* an implement for snuffing out candles, consisting either of a scissorlike device with two broad flat blades or of a cone at the end of a handle. [dial. *dout* (v.) (D(O)¹ + OUT) + -ER¹]

Douw (*Du.* dou), *n.* **Ger·rard** (*Du.* gä′rärt). See **Dou, Gerard.**

doux (do͞o), *adj.* (of champagne) very sweet. [< F < L *dulc(is)* savory, sweet]

dou·zaine (do͞o zen′), *n., pl.* **-zaines** (-zen′). *French.* a bet in roulette on 12 numbers simultaneously so as to share in any that win. [lit., dozen]

douze·pers (do͞oz′pârz′), *n.pl., sing.,* **douze·per** (do͞oz′pâr′). **1.** *French Legend.* the 12 peers or paladins represented in old romances as attendants of Charlemagne. **2.** *French Hist.* the 12 great spiritual and temporal peers of France, taken to represent those of Charlemagne. Also, **doucepere.** [ME *dusze pers* (pl.) < OF *douze pers* (pl.) twelve equals. See DOZEN¹, PEER¹]

dou·zi·ème (do͞o′zē em′; *Fr.* do͞o zyem′), *n., pl.* **-zi·èmes** (-zē emz′; *Fr.* -zyem′). (in Swiss watchmaking) the 12th part of a ligne, used mainly to gauge the thickness of a movement. [< F: lit., twelfth]

DOVAP (dō′vap), *n.* See **Doppler radar.** [*Do(ppler) V(elocity) a(nd) P(osition)*]

dove¹ (duv), *n.* **1.** any bird of the family *Columbidae,* usually the smaller species with pointed tails. Cf. **pigeon** (def. 1). **2.** a symbol of innocence, gentleness, tenderness, and peace. **3.** (*cap.*) a symbol for the Holy Ghost. **4.** an innocent, gentle, or tender person. **5.** *Informal.* a person, esp. one in public office, who advocates peace or a conciliatory national attitude. **6.** (*cap.*) *Astron.* the constellation Columba. [ME; OE *dūfe-* (in *dūfedoppa* dip-diver); c. D *duif,* G *Taube,* Icel *dúfa,* Goth *dubo,* orig. a diver] —**dov′ish,** *adj.*

dove² (dōv), *v.* a pt. of **dive.**

Dove (duv), *n.* a walled plain in the fourth quadrant of the face of the moon: about 11 miles in diameter.

dove′ col′or (duv), warm gray with a slight purplish or pinkish tint. —**dove′-col′ored,** *adj.*

dove·cote (duv′kōt′), *n.* **1.** a structure, usually at a height above the ground, for housing domestic pigeons. **2. flutter the dovecotes,** to cause a stir in a quiet or conservative institution or group: *The flamboyant manner of the tourists fluttered the dovecotes of the sleepy New England town.* Also, **dove·cot** (duv′kot). [DOVE¹ + COTE]

dove·kie (duv′kē), *n.* **1.** a small, short-billed, black and white auk, *Plautus alle,* of the northern part of the Atlantic and Arctic oceans. **2.** *Brit.* the black guillemot. Also, **dove′key.** [DOVE + *-kie* compound suffix (see -OCK, -IE)]

dove·like (duv′līk′), *adj.* resembling a dove, esp. in gentleness, purity, etc. [DOVE¹ + -LIKE]

Dove′ prism′ (duv), *Optics.* a prism that inverts a beam of light, often used in a telescope to produce an erect image. Also called **erecting prism, reversing prism, rotating prism.** [named after Heinrich W. Dove (1803–79), German physicist]

Do·ver (dō′vər), *n.* **1.** a seaport in E Kent, in SE England: point nearest the coast of France. 35,248 (1961). **2. Strait of.** French, **Pas de Calais.** a strait between England and France, connecting the English Channel and the North Sea: least width 20 mi. **3.** a city in SE New Hampshire. 19,131 (1960). **4.** a town in N New Jersey. 13,034 (1960). **5.** a city in and the capital of Delaware, in the central part. 7250 (1960).

Do′ver Beach′, a poem (1867) by Matthew Arnold.

Do′ver's pow′der, *Pharm.* a powder containing ipecac and opium, used as an anodyne, diaphoretic, and antispasmodic. [named after T. *Dover* (1660–1742), English physician]

dove·tail (duv′tāl′), *n. Carpentry.* **1.** a tenon broader at its end than at its base; pin. **2.** a joint formed of one or more such tenons fitting tightly within corresponding mortises. —*v.t., v.i.* **3.** *Carpentry.* to join or fit together by means of a dovetail or dovetails. **4.** to join or fit together compactly or harmoniously. [so named from its shape] —**dove′tail′er,** *n.*

Dovetail joint

dove·tailed (duv′tāld′), *adj. Heraldry.* noting a partition line or a charge, as an ordinary, having a series of indentations suggesting dovetails. [DOVETAIL + -ED³]

dove′tail hinge′, a strap hinge having leaves which are narrower at their junction than at their other extremities.

dove′tail plane′, *Carpentry.* a plane for cutting tongues and grooves with parallel or inclined sides.

dove′tail saw′, a backsaw for fine woodworking, as dovetailing. Also called **foxtail saw.**

Dov·zhen·ko (dəv zheng′kō; *Russ.* dov zhen′ko), *n.* **A·le·xan·der P.** (ä′le ksän′dər), 1894–1956, Russian motion-picture director.

dow¹ (dou, dō), *v.i.,* **dowed** or **dought** (dout), **dow·ing.** *Scot. and North Eng.* **1.** to be able. **2.** to thrive; prosper; do well. [ME *dowen, doghen,* OE *dugan* to be worthy; c. G *taugen;* cf. DOUGHTY]

dow² (dou), *n.* dhow.

Dow (*Du.* dou), *n.* **Ger·rard** (*Du.* gä′rärt). See **Dou, Gerard.**

Dow., dowager.

dow·a·ble (dou′ə bəl), *adj. Law.* **1.** subject to the provision of a dower: *dowable land.* **2.** entitled to dower. [< AF; see ENDOW, -ABLE]

dow·a·ger (dou′ə jər), *n.* **1.** a woman who holds some title or property from her deceased husband, esp. the widow of a king, duke, etc. (often used as an additional title to differentiate her from the wife of the present king, duke, etc.): *a queen dowager; an empress dowager.* **2.** an elderly woman of stately dignity, esp. one of elevated social position: *a wealthy dowager in her long black limousine.* —*adj.* **3.** noting, pertaining to, or characteristic of a dowager: *the dowager duchess; to prefer a dowager style of dress.* [< MF *douag(i)ere,* equiv. to *douage* dower (see ENDOW, -AGE) + *-ier* -ER²] —**dow′a·ger·ism,** *n.*

Do·wa·giac (də woj′ak), *n.* a town in SW Michigan. 7208 (1960).

Dow·den (doud′ən), *n.* **Edward,** 1843–1913, Irish critic and poet.

dow·dy¹ (dou′dē), *adj.,* **-di·er, -di·est,** *n., pl.* **-dies.** —*adj.* **1.** not tidy, neat, or stylish: *dowdy clothes; a dowdy apartment.* —*n.* **2.** a dowdy woman. [ME *doude* unattractive woman + -Y¹ or -Y²] —**dow′di·ly,** *adv.* —**dow′di·ness,** *n.* —**dow′dy·ish,** *adj.* —**dow′dy·ism,** *n.*
—**Syn. 1.** frumpy, shabby, old-fashioned. —**Ant. 1.** fashionable, chic.

dow·dy² (dou′dē), *n., pl.* **-dies.** pandowdy. [short form]

dow·el (dou′əl), *n., v.,* **-eled, -el·ing** or (*esp. Brit.*) **-elled, -el·ling.** —*n.* **1.** Also called **dowel pin.** *Carpentry.* a pin, usually round, fitting into holes in two adjacent pieces to prevent their slipping or to align them. **2.** a piece of wood driven into a hole drilled in a masonry wall to receive nails, as for fastening woodwork. **3.** *Dentistry.* a peg, usually of metal, set into the root canal of a natural tooth to give additional support to an artificial crown. —*v.t.* **4.** to reinforce or furnish with a dowel or dowels. [ME *dowle* < MLG *dovel* plug; cf. G *Döbel, Dübel,* OHG *tubili*]

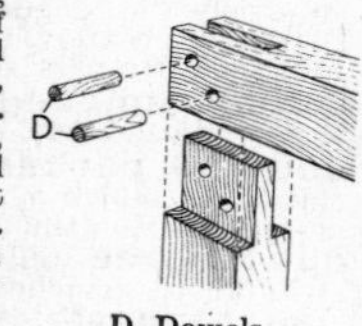

D, Dowels

dow′el pin′, 1. dowel (def. 1). **2.** sprig (def. 7).

dow·er (dou′ər), *n.* **1.** *Law.* the portion of a deceased husband's real property allowed to his widow for her lifetime. **2.** dowry (def. 1). **3.** a natural gift or endowment. —*v.t.* **4.** to provide with a dower or dowry. **5.** to give as a dower or dowry. [ME *dowere* < OF *do(u)aire* < ML *dō(t)ār(ium).* See DOT², -ARY] —**dow′er·less,** *adj.*

dow′er chest′, a Pennsylvania Dutch hope chest bearing the initials of the owner.

dow′er house′, *Brit.* the dwelling of a widow, as part of her dower.

dow·er·y (dou′ə rē), *n., pl.* **-er·ies.** dowry.

dowf (douf, do͞of), *adj. Scot. and North Eng.* dull; stupid. [< Scand; cf. Icel *dauf(u)r* deaf, dull, flat, spiritless]

dow·ie (dou′ē, dō′ē), *adj. Scot. and North Eng.* dull; melancholy; dismal. Also, **dowy.** [var. of *dolly,* equiv. to OE *dol* DULL + -LY] —**dow′i·ly,** *adv.* —**dow′i·ness,** *n.*

dow·itch·er (dou′ich ər), *n.* any of several long-billed, snipelike shore birds of North America, esp. *Limnodromus griseus.* [*dowitch* (cf. Onondaga *tawish*) + -ER¹]

Dow′-Jones′ av′erage (dou′jōnz′), any of the indexes published by Dow-Jones, a financial publishing firm in New York, reflecting the price level of various groups of stocks or bonds, esp. those for the common stocks of 30 industrials, 20 railroads, and 15 utilities. Also called **Dow′-Jones′ in′dex.**

Dow·land (dou′lənd), *n.* **John,** 1563–1626, English lutanist and composer.

dow·las (dou′ləs), *n.* a coarse linen or cotton cloth. [after *Daoulas* in Brittany; r. late ME *douglas,* popular substitution for *dowlas*]

Dow·met·al (dou′met′əl), *n. Trademark.* any of various magnesium alloys containing more than 85 percent magnesium, characterized by extreme lightness.

down¹ (doun), *adv.* **1.** from higher to lower; in descending direction or order; toward, into, or in a lower position. **2.** on or to the ground, floor, or bottom: *He fell down.* **3.** to or in a sitting or lying position. **4.** to or in a position considered lower, esp. from a geographical or cartographic standpoint, as to the south, a business district, etc.: *We drove down from San Francisco to Los Angeles.* **5.** to or at a lower value or rate. **6.** to a lesser pitch or volume: *Turn down the phonograph.* **7.** in or to a calmer, less active, or less prominent state: *The wind went down.* **8.** from an earlier to a later time: *from the 17th century down to the present.* **9.** from a greater to a lesser strength, amount, etc.: *to water down liquor.* **10.** in an attitude of earnest application: *to get down to work.* **11.** on paper or in a book: *Write down the address.* **12.** in cash at the time of purchase; at once: *He paid $40 down and $10 a month.* **13.** to the point of defeat, submission, inactivity, etc.: *They shouted down the opposition.* **14.** in or into a fixed or supine position: *They tied down the struggling animal.* **15.** to the source or actual position: *The repair crew traced down the leak. The dogs tracked down the bear.* **16.** confined to bed with illness: *He's down with a cold.* **17.** in or into a lower status or condition: *Some people are kept down by lack of education.* **18.** *Naut.* toward the lee side, so as to turn a vessel to windward: *Put the helm down!* **19. down with! a.** on or toward the ground or into a lower position: *Down with your rifles!* **b.** away with! cease!: *Down with tyranny!*
—*prep.* **20.** in a descending or more remote direction or place on, over, or along: *They ran off down the street.*
—*adj.* **21.** downward; going or directed downward: *the down elevator.* **22.** being at a low position or on the ground, floor, or bottom. **23.** toward the south, a business district, etc.: *I am taking the down train.* **24.** associated with or serving traffic, transportation, or the like, directed toward the south, a business district, etc.: *the down platform; the down side of the street.* **25.** downcast; depressed; dejected: *His face wore a down expression.* **26.** being the portion of the full price, as of an article bought on the installment plan, that is paid at the time of purchase or delivery: *a payment of $200 down.* **27.** *Football.* (of the ball) not in play because its progress has been stopped or because the officials have halted play. **28.** behind an opponent or opponents in points, games, etc.: *The team won the pennant despite having been down three games in the final week of play.* **29.** *Baseball.* out: *He came to bat with two men down in the ninth inning.* **30.** losing or having lost the amount indicated, esp. at gambling: *After an hour at poker, he was down $10.* **31.** having placed one's bet: *Are you down for the fourth race?* **32.** finished, done, considered, or taken care of: *With five down and one to go, he would finish his term papers at the end of the week.* **33. down and out,** without friends, money, or prospects; destitute. **34. down in the mouth,** discouraged; depressed; sad: *Why do you look so down in the mouth?* **35. down on,** *Informal.* hostile or averse to: *He is down on dancing because he considers it immoral.*
—*n.* **36.** a downward movement; descent. **37.** a turn for the worse; reverse: *The business cycle experienced a sudden down.* **38.** *Football.* **a.** one of a series of four plays during which a team must advance the ball at least ten yards to keep possession of it. **b.** the declaring of the ball as down or out of play, or the play immediately preceding this.
—*v.t.* **39.** to put, knock, or throw down; subdue: *He downed his opponent in the third round.* **40.** to drink down: *to down a tankard of ale.* **41.** to cause to fall from a height, esp. by shooting: *The anti-aircraft downed ten bombers.*
—*v.i.* **42.** to go down; fall.
—*interj.* **43.** (used as a command to a dog to stop attacking, to stop jumping on someone, to get off a couch or chair, etc.): *Down, boy!* **44.** (used as a command or warning to duck, take cover, or the like): *Down! They're starting to shoot!* [ME *doune,* OE *dūne,* aph. var. of *adūne* for *of dūne* off (the hill); see DOWN³]

down² (doun), *n.* **1.** the soft, first plumage of many young birds. **2.** the soft under plumage of birds as distinct from the contour feathers. **3.** a growth of soft, fine hair or the like. **4.** *Bot.* **a.** a fine, soft pubescence on plants and some fruits. **b.** the light, feathery pappus or coma on seeds by which they are borne on the wind, as on the dandelion and thistle. [ME *downe* < Scand; cf. Icel *dúnn*] —**down′less,** *adj.* —**down′like′,** *adj.*

down³ (doun), *n.* **1.** *Archaic.* a hill, esp. a sand hill or dune. **2.** Usually, **downs.** (used esp. in southern England) open, rolling, upland country with fairly smooth slopes usually covered with grass. **3.** (*cap.*) any sheep of several breeds, raised originally in the downs of southern England, as the Southdown, Suffolk, etc. [ME; OE *dūn* hill; c. D *duin* DUNE; not related to Ir *dūn* (see TOWN)]

Down (doun), *n.* a county in SW Northern Ireland. 270,200 (est. 1962), 952 sq. mi. *Co. seat:* Downpatrick.

down-and-out (doun′ənd out′, -ən), *adj.* **1.** without money or means of support; penniless. **2.** without physical strength or stamina; disabled; incapacitated. **3.** too physically weakened by repeated defeats to qualify as a professional boxer. —*n.* **4.** Also, **down′-and-out′er.** one who is down-and-out: *He tried to help some down-and-out.*

down-at-heel (doun′ət hēl′), *adj.* of a shabby, run-down appearance; seedy: *He is rapidly becoming a down-at-heel drifter.* Also, **down′at-the-heel′, down′-at-heels′, down′-at-the-heels′.**

down·beat (doun′bēt′), *n.* *Music.* **1.** the downward stroke of a conductor's arm or baton indicating the first or accented beat of a measure. **2.** the first beat of a measure. —*adj.* **3.** *Informal.* gloomy, pessimistic: *Hollywood movies seldom have downbeat endings.* [DOWN[1] + BEAT (n.)]

down-bow (doun′bō′), *n.* *Music.* (in bowing on a stringed instrument) a stroke bringing the tip of the bow toward the strings, indicated in scores by the symbol ⌐ (opposed to *up-bow*). [DOWN[1] + BOW[2]]

down·cast (doun′kast′, -käst′), *adj.* **1.** dejected in spirit; depressed. **2.** directed downward, as the eyes. —*n.* **3.** overthrow or ruin. **4.** a downward look or glance. **5.** a shaft down which air passes, as into a mine (opposed to *upcast*). [ME *douncaste(n).* See DOWN[1], CAST] —**down′cast′ly,** *adv.* —**down′cast′ness,** *n.*

down·come (doun′kum′), *n.* **1.** *Archaic.* descent or downfall; comedown; humiliation. **2.** a downcomer. [ME *douncome.* See DOWN[1], COME]

down·com·er (doun′kum′ər), *n.* a pipe, tube, or passage for conducting material downward. [DOWN[1] + COMER]

down·draft (doun′draft′, -dräft′), *n.* a downward current, as of air: *a downdraft in a mine shaft.* [DOWN[1] + DRAFT]

down′ East′, 1. in, to, or into New England. **2.** New England. **3.** in, to, or into the State of Maine. **4.** the State of Maine.

down-east·er (doun′ē′stər), *n.* **1.** *Naut.* a full-rigged ship built in New England in the late 19th century, usually of wood and relatively fast, but not so fast as the clippers. **2.** a native or inhabitant of Maine. **3.** a native or inhabitant of New England.

Dow′ners Grove′ (dou′nərz), a city in NE Illinois, near Chicago. 21,154 (1960).

Dow·ney (dou′nē), *n.* **1.** a city in SW California, near Los Angeles. 82,505 (1960). **2.** a boy's given name.

down·fall (doun′fôl′), *n.* **1.** descent to a lower position or standing; overthrow; ruin. **2.** something causing this: *Liquor was his downfall.* **3.** a fall, as of rain, snow, or the like, often sudden or heavy: *What a downfall we had last night!* **4.** a trap using a falling weight for killing, injuring, or imprisoning the prey. [ME; see DOWN[1], FALL] —**down′fall′en,** *adj.*

down·field (doun′fēld′), *adv., adj.* *Football.* past the line of scrimmage and at or toward the goal line of the defensive team: *He sent his receivers downfield. Downfield blocking is important on passes.* [DOWN[1] + FIELD]

down·grade (doun′grād′), *n., adj., adv., v.,* **-grad·ed, -grad·ing.** —*n.* **1.** a downward slope, esp. of a road. **2. on the downgrade,** falling from success, wealth, etc.; failing: *His career has been on the downgrade since his last film two years ago.* —*adj., adv.* **3.** downhill. —*v.t.* **4.** to assign to a lower status with a smaller salary. **5.** to minimize the importance of; denigrate: *He tried to downgrade the findings of the investigation. He always downgrades his colleagues.* **6.** *U.S. Govt., Mil.* to assign a lower security classification to (information, a document, etc.). [DOWN[1] + GRADE]

down·haul (doun′hôl′), *n.* *Naut.* any of various lines for pulling down a sail or a yard, as for securing in a lowered position when not in use. [DOWN[1] + HAUL]

down·heart·ed (doun′här′tid), *adj.* dejected; depressed; discouraged. [DOWN[1] + HEARTED] —**down′heart′ed·ly,** *adv.* —**down′heart′ed·ness,** *n.*
—**Syn.** downcast, despondent, disheartened, dispirited, sad, sorrowful.

down·hill (doun′hil′), *adv.* **1.** down the slope of a hill; downward. **2.** into a worse or inferior condition: *He's been going downhill since he lost his job.* —*adj.* **3.** going or tending downward on or as on a hill. [DOWN[1] + HILL]

Down′ing Street′, 1. a street in W central London, England: government offices; residence of the prime minister. **2.** the British prime minister and cabinet.

Dow·ning·town (dou′ning toun′), *n.* a town in SE Pennsylvania. 5598 (1960).

down′ pay′ment, an initial amount paid at the time of purchase, in installment buying, time sales, etc. Also, **down′-pay′ment.** [DOWN[1] + PAYMENT]

down·pipe (doun′pīp′), *n.* downspout. [DOWN[1] + PIPE[1]]

down·pour (doun′pōr′, -pôr′), *n.* a heavy, drenching rain. [DOWN[1] + POUR]

down·range (*adj.* doun′rānj′; *adv.* doun′rānj′), *adj., adv.* *Rocketry.* in the designated path from a launch pad to the point on a course generally taken as the target: *The signal was picked up by a downrange radar station. The missile was fired downrange.* [DOWN[1] + RANGE]

down·right (doun′rīt′), *adj.* **1.** thorough; absolute; out-and-out: *a downright falsehood.* **2.** frankly direct; straightforward: *a downright person.* **3.** *Archaic.* directed straight downward: *a downright blow.* —*adj.* **4.** completely or thoroughly: *He is downright angry.* [ME; see DOWN[1], RIGHT] —**down′right′ly,** *adv.* —**down′right′ness,** *n.*

Downs, The (dounz), **1.** a range of low ridges in S and SW England. **2.** a roadstead in the Strait of Dover, between SE England and Goodwin Sands.

down·size (doun′sīz′), *v.,* **-sized, -siz·ing,** *adj.* —*v.t.* **1.** to design and manufacture a smaller version of (a standard product, such as a car). —*adj.* **2.** Also, **down·sized** (doun′sīzd′). being or of a smaller version: *a downsized car.* [DOWN[1] + SIZE (v.)]

down·spout (doun′spout′), *n.* a pipe for conveying rain water from a roof or gutter to the ground or to a drain. Also called **downpipe, drainspout.** [DOWN[1] + SPOUT]

Down's′ syn′drome (dounz), *Pathol.* the abnormal condition of a child born whith a wide, flattened skull, epicanthic folds at the eyelids, and usually a moderate to severe mental deficiency and other organic problems: caused by a chromosomal abnormality. Formerly, **Mongolism.** [named after J.L.H. *Down* (1828–96), English physician]

down·stage (*adv., n.* doun′stāj′; *adj.* doun′stāj′), *Theat.* —*adv.* **1.** at or toward the front of the stage. —*adj.* **2.** of or pertaining to the front of the stage. —*n.* **3.** the front half of the stage. [DOWN[1] + STAGE]

down·stairs (*adv., n.* doun′stârz′; *adj.* doun′stârz′), *adv.* **1.** down the stairs. **2.** to or on a lower floor. —*adj.* **3.** Also, **down′stair′.** pertaining to or situated on a lower floor, esp. the ground floor. —*n.* **4.** (*construed as sing.*) the lower floor or floors of a building: *The downstairs is being painted.* **5.** the stairway designated for use by people descending: *Don't try to go up the downstairs.* [DOWN[1] + STAIR + -S[3]]

down·state (*n., adv.* doun′stāt′; *adj.* doun′stāt′), *n.* *U.S.* —*n.* **1.** the southern part of a State. —*adj.* **2.** located in or characteristic of this part: *The downstate precincts reported early.* —*adv.* **3.** in, to, or into the downstate area: *We're going downstate for the holidays.* [DOWN[1] + STATE] —**down′stat′er,** *n.*

down·stream (doun′strēm′), *adv.* with or in the direction of the current of a stream. [DOWN[1] + STREAM]

down·stroke (doun′strōk′), *n.* **1.** a downward stroke, as of a machine part, piston, or the like. **2.** (in handwriting, penmanship, etc.) a downward stroke in writing, often heavier and darker than an upward stroke. [DOWN[1] + STROKE[1]]

down·swing (doun′swing′), *n.* **1.** a downward swing, as of a golf club in driving a ball. **2.** a downward trend or decrease, as of business, a nation's birth rate, etc. [DOWN[1] + SWING[1]]

down·take (doun′tāk′), *n.* a pipe or passage for conducting smoke, a current of air, or the like downward from a furnace, opening, etc. [n. use of v. phrase *take down*]

down-the-line (doun′thə līn′), *adj.* **1.** complete, full, unreserved, or whole-hearted: *a down-the-line endorsement of the party's platform.* —*adv.* **2.** fully; completely; whole-heartedly: *Will you support it down-the-line?*

down·throw (doun′thrō′), *n.* a throwing down or being thrown down; overthrow. [n. use of v. phrase *throw down*]

down·time (doun′tīm′), *n.* **1.** the time during a regular working period when an employee is not productive because of external circumstances, as the breakdown of equipment. **2.** an interval during which a machine is not productive, as during loading, maintenance, repair, or the like. [DOWN[1] + TIME]

down-to-earth (doun′tōō ûrth′, -tə-), *adj.* practical and realistic: *a down-to-earth person; a down-to-earth outlook.*

down·town (doun′toun′), *adv.* **1.** to or in the central business section of a city. —*adj.* **2.** of, pertaining to, or situated in the central business section of a city. —*n.* **3.** the central business section of a city. [DOWN[1] + TOWN]

down·trend (doun′trend′), *n.* a downward or decreasing tendency, movement, or shift. [DOWN[1] + TREND]

down·trod·den (doun′trod′ən), *adj.* **1.** tyrannized over; oppressed: *the downtrodden plebeians of ancient Rome.* **2.** trodden down; trampled upon. Also, **down′trod′.** [adj. use of v. phrase *trodden down*] —**down′trod′den·ness,** *n.*

down·turn (doun′tûrn′), *n.* **1.** an act or instance of turning down or the state of being turned down: *several downturns in the rock folds; the downturn of her lower lip in a permanent pout.* **2.** a turn or trend downward; decrease or decline: *The new year brought a downturn in the cost of living. Paid admissions at the theater were taking a downturn.* [n. use of v. phrase *turn down*]

down′ un′der, *Informal.* **1.** Australia or New Zealand. **2.** in, to, or into Australia or New Zealand.

down·ward (doun′wərd), *adv.* **1.** Also, **down′wards.** from a higher to a lower place or condition. **2.** down from a source or beginning: *As the river flows downward, it widens.* **3.** from a past time, predecessor, or ancestor: *The estate was handed downward from generation to generation.* —*adj.* **4.** moving or tending to a lower place or condition. **5.** descending from a source or beginning. [ME *dounward,* aph. var. of *adounward,* OE *adūnweard.* See DOWN[1], -WARD] —**down′ward·ly,** *adv.* —**down′ward·ness,** *n.*

down·wash (doun′wosh′, -wôsh′), *n.* *Aeron.* a deflection of air downward relative to an airfoil that causes the deflection. [n. use of v. phrase *wash down*]

down·wind (doun′wind′), *adv.* **1.** in the same direction as that in which the wind is blowing; with the wind coming from behind: *We coasted downwind for three hours.* **2.** on or toward the lee side: *The lion was running downwind of us and caught our scent at once.* —*adj.* **3.** moving downwind: *a downwind current.* **4.** situated on or toward the lee side: *The downwind halyard was caught by the breeze and blew outboard.* Cf. **upwind.** [DOWN[1] + WIND[1]]

down·y (dou′nē), *adj.,* **down·i·er, down·i·est. 1.** of the nature of or resembling down; fluffy; soft. **2.** made of down. **3.** covered with down. **4.** soft; soothing. [DOWN[2] + -Y[1]] —**down′i·ly,** *adv.* —**down′i·ness,** *n.*

down′y mil′dew, 1. Also called **false mildew.** any fungus of the family *Peronosporaceae,* which causes many plant diseases and produces a white, downy mass of conidiophores, usually on the under surface of the leaves of the host plant. **2.** *Plant Pathol.* a disease of plants, characterized by mildewed, distorted, and yellowed foliage, caused by any of several fungi of the family *Peronosporaceae,* as of the genera *Peronospora* and *Phytophthora.*

down′y wood′pecker, a small, North American woodpecker, *Dendrocopos pubescens,* having black and white plumage.

dow·ry (dou′rē), *n., pl.* **-ries. 1.** Also, **dower.** the money, goods, or estate which a woman brings to her husband at marriage. **2.** *Obs.* a widow's dower. **3.** a natural gift, endowment, talent, etc. Also, **dowery.** [ME *dowerie* < AF *douarie* < LL *dōtārium.* See DOT[2], -ARY]

dowse[1] (dous), *v.t., v.i.,* **dowsed, dows·ing,** *n.* douse.

dowse[2] (douz), *v.i.,* **dowsed, dows·ing.** to search for underground supplies of water, metal, etc., by the use of a divining rod. [?]

dows·er (dou′zər), *n.* **1.** a rod or wand used in dowsing; divining rod. **2.** a person skilled in its use. [DOWSE[2] + -ER[1]]

dows′ing rod′ (dou′zing). See **divining rod.**

Dow′ the′ory (dou), a method of determining the long-term trend of prices in the stock market by analyzing the fluctuations between the high and low prices in the Dow-Jones averages for industrial and railroad common stocks.

dow·y (dou′ē, dō′ē), *adj.* *Scot. and North Eng.* dowie.

dox·ol·o·gy (dok sol′ə jē), *n., pl.* **-gies. 1.** a hymn or form of words containing an ascription of praise to God. **2. the Doxology,** the metrical formula beginning "Praise God from whom all blessings flow." [< ML *doxologia* < Gk, equiv. to *doxo-* (comb. form of *dóxa* honor, glory) + *-logia* -LOGY] —**dox·o·log·i·cal** (dok′sə loj′i kəl), *adj.* —**dox′o·log′i·cal·ly,** *adv.*

dox·y[1] (dok′sē), *n., pl.* **dox·ies. 1.** opinion; doctrine. **2.** religious views. Also, **dox′ie.** [abstracted from HETERODOXY, ORTHODOXY]

dox·y[2] (dok′sē), *n., pl.* **dox·ies.** *Archaic.* **1.** a mistress or paramour. **2.** a prostitute. [< MFlem *docke* doll + *-sy,* affectionate dim. suffix]

doy·en (doi en′, doi′ən; *Fr.* dwA yaN′), *n., pl.* **doy·ens** (doi enz′, doi′enz; *Fr.* dwA yaN′). the senior member, as in age or rank, of a group, class, profession, etc. [< F; see DEAN[1]]

doy·enne (doi en′; *Fr.* dwA yen′), *n., pl.* **doy·ennes** (doi enz′; *Fr.* dwA yen′). a female doyen. [< F]

Doyle (doil), *n.* **Sir Arthur Co·nan** (kō′nən, kō′-), 1859–1930, British physician, novelist, and detective-story writer.

Doyles·town (doilz′toun′), *n.* a town in SE Pennsylvania. 5917 (1960).

doy·ley (doi′lē), *n., pl.* **-leys.** doily.

D'Oy·ly Carte (doi′lē kärt′), **Richard.** See **Carte, Richard D'Oyly.**

doz., dozen; dozens.

doze[1] (dōz), *v.,* **dozed, doz·ing,** *n.* —*v.i.* **1.** to sleep lightly or fitfully. **2.** to fall into a light sleep unintentionally (often fol. by *off*): *He dozed off during the sermon.* **3.** to be dull or half asleep. —*v.t.* **4.** to pass or spend (time) in drowsiness (often fol. by *away*): *He dozed away the afternoon.* —*n.* **5.** a light or fitful sleep. [< Scand; cf. obs. Dan *daase* to be idle, OIcel *dāsi* lazy, sleepy, dull person, Icel *dosa,* c. *dasa* to exhaust, tire out; cf. DAZE] —**doz′er,** *n.*

doze[2] (dōz), *v.t.,* **dozed, doz·ing.** to move (earth, rubbish, etc.) with a dozer or bulldozer. [shortened form of BULLDOZE]

doz·en[1] (duz′ən), *n., pl.* **doz·ens,** (*as after a numeral*) **doz·en,** *adj.* —*n.* **1.** a group of twelve. —*adj.* **2.** twelve. [ME *dozeine* < OF *do(u)zaine,* equiv. to *do(u)ze* (< L *duodecim*) + *-aine* (< L *-āna*) -AN]

doz·en[2] (dō′zən), *v.t.* *Scot.* to stun. [DOZE[1] + -EN[1]]

doz·enth (duz′ənth), *adj.* twelfth. [DOZEN[1] + -TH[2]]

doz·er (dō′zər), *n.* *Informal.* bulldozer (def. 2). Also, **'doz′er.** [by shortening]

doz·y (dō′zē), *adj.,* **doz·i·er, doz·i·est. 1.** drowsy; half asleep. **2.** decayed, as timber. [DOZE[1] + -Y[1]] —**doz′i·ly,** *adv.* —**doz′i·ness,** *n.*

D/P, documents against payment.

D.P., 1. (in prescriptions) with a proper direction. [< L *dīrectiōne prōpriā*] **2.** displaced person. Also, **DP**

D.P.A., Doctor of Public Administration.

DPC, Defense Plant Corporation.

D.P.H., Doctor of Public Health.

D.P.S., Doctor of Public Service.

dpt., 1. department. **2.** deponent.

D.P.W., Department of Public Works.

dr, door.

Dr., 1. Doctor. **2.** Drive (used in street names). Also, **Dr**

dr., 1. debit. **2.** debtor. **3.** drachma. **4.** dram; drams. **5.** drawer. **6.** drum.

D.R., 1. Daughters of the (American) Revolution. **2.** Dutch Reformed.

drab[1] (drab), *n., adj.,* **drab·ber, drab·best.** —*n.* **1.** dull gray; dull brownish or yellowish gray. **2.** any of several fabrics of this color, esp. of thick wool or cotton. —*adj.* **3.** having a drab color. **4.** dull; cheerless; lacking in spirit, brightness, etc. [< MF *drap* < LL *drapp(us)* piece of cloth] —**drab′ly,** *adv.* —**drab′ness,** *n.*

drab[2] (drab), *n., v.,* **drabbed, drab·bing.** —*n.* **1.** a dirty, untidy woman; slattern. **2.** a prostitute. —*v.i.* **3.** to associate with drabs. [?; cf. D *drab* dregs, lees, obs. D *drablen* to run or tramp about, Ir *drabóg* slattern, equiv. to *drab* spot, stain + *-óg* n. suffix; see DRABBLE, DRAFF]

drab·bet (drab′it), *n.* a coarse, drab linen fabric for smock frocks and similar garments. [DRAB[1] + -ET]

drab·ble (drab′əl), *v.t., v.i.,* **-bled, -bling.** to draggle; make or become wet and dirty. [ME *drabele(n)* < MLG *drabbeln* to wade in liquid mud, bespatter, equiv. to *drabbe* liquid mud + *-eln* freq. v. suffix; see DRAB[2], DRAFF]

drab·bler (drab′lər), *n.* *Naut.* an extra piece of canvas sewn to the foot of a bonnet. [DRABBLE + -ER[1]]

dra·cae·na (drə sē′nə), *n.* **1.** any liliaceous tree of the genus *Dracaena,* of tropical regions. **2.** any tree of the closely related genus *Cordyline.* [< NL < Gk *drákaina,* fem. of *drákōn* DRAGON]

drachm[1] (dram), *n.* *Brit.* a dram in apothecaries' and troy weights, and sometimes in avoirdupois weights. [learned sp. of DRAM]

drachm[2] (dram), *n.* drachma.

drach·ma (drak′mə), *n., pl.* **-mas, -mae** (-mē). **1.** a cupronickel coin and monetary unit of modern Greece, equal to 100 lepta and equivalent to about .033 of a U.S. dollar. *Abbr.:* dr., drch. **2.** the principal silver coin of ancient Greece. **3.** a small unit of weight in ancient Greece, approximately equivalent to the U.S. and British apothecaries' dram. **4.** any of various modern weights, esp. a dram. Also, **drachm.** [< L < Gk *drachmḗ,* prob. equiv. to *drach-* root of *drássesthai* to grasp + *-mē* n. suffix] —**drach′mal,** *adj.*

Dra·co (drā′kō), *n., gen.* **Dra·co·nis** (drā kō′nis). *Astron.* the Dragon, a northern circumpolar constellation between Ursa Major and Cepheus. [< L < Gk *drákōn* DRAGON]

Dra·co (drā′kō), *n.* a late 7th-century B.C. Athenian statesman noted for the severity of his code of laws. Also called **Dra·con** (drā′kon).

Dra·co·ni·an (drā kō′nē ən), *adj.* **1.** of, pertaining to, or characteristic of Draco or his code of laws. **2.** (*sometimes l.c.*) rigorous; severe. Also, **Draconic.** [< L *Dracōn-* (s. of DRACO) + -IAN] —**Dra·co′ni·an·ism,** *n.*

dra·con·ic (drā kon′ik), *adj.* of or like a dragon. [< L *dracōn-* (s. of *dracō*) DRAGON + -IC] —**dra·con′i·cal·ly,** *adv.*

Dra·con·ic (drā kon′ik), *adj.* *(sometimes l.c.)* Draconian. [< L *Dracōn-* (s. of DRACO) + -IC] —**Dra·con′i·cal·ly,** *adv.*

dracon′ic month′. See under **month** (def. 5).

Drac·o·nid (drak′ə nid), *n.* *Astron.* any of several unrelated meteor showers whose radiants are in the constellation Draco. [< Gk *Drákōn* DRACO + -ID[1]]

Drac·u·la (drak′yə lə), *n.* **1.** *(italics.)* a novel (1897) by Bram Stoker, dealing with the supernatural and the grotesque. **2. Count,** the central character in this novel: the archetype of the vampire.

drae·ger·man (drā′gər mən), *n., pl.* **-men.** *Mining.* a miner, usually a member of a special crew, trained in underground rescue work and other emergency procedure. [after Alexander B. *Dräger* (d. 1928), German scientist and inventor of rescue equipment; see MAN[1]]

draff (draf), *n.* dregs, as in a brewing process; lees; refuse. [ME *draf;* c. Icel, D *draf;* akin to D *drab* (see DRAB[2]), G *Treber* draff] —**draff′y,** *adj.*

draft (draft, dräft), *n.* **1.** a drawing, sketch, or design. **2.** a first or preliminary form of any writing, subject to revision, copying, etc. **3.** act of drawing; delineation. **4.** a current of air in any enclosed space, esp. in a room, chimney, or stove. **5.** a device for regulating the current of air in a stove, fireplace, etc. **6.** act of drawing or pulling loads. **7.** that which is drawn or pulled; a haul. **8.** an animal or team of animals used to pull a load. **9.** the force required to pull a load. **10.** the taking of supplies, forces, money, etc., from a given source. **11.** a selection or drawing of persons, by lot or otherwise, from the general body of the people for military service; levy; conscription. **12.** *Sports.* a selecting or drawing of new players from a choice group of amateur players by professional teams, esp. a system of selecting new players so that each team in a professional league receives some of the most promising players. **13.** (formerly) a selection of persons already in military service to be sent from one post or organization to another; detachment. **14.** a written order drawn by one person upon another; a writing directing the payment of money on account of the drawer; bill of exchange. **15.** a drain or demand made on anything. **16.** *Naut.* the depth to which a vessel is immersed when bearing a given load. **17.** Also called **leave.** *Foundry.* the slight taper given to a pattern so that it may be drawn from the sand without injury to the mold. **18.** *Metalworking.* **a.** the change in sectional area of a piece of work caused by a rolling or drawing operation. **b.** a taper on a die or punch permitting it to be withdrawn readily from the work. **19.** *Masonry.* a line or border chiseled at the edge of a stone, to serve as a guide in leveling the surfaces. **20.** *Brit.* copy (def. 6). **21.** *Textiles.* **a.** the degree of attenuation produced in fibers during yarn processing, expressed either by the ratio of the weight of raw to the weight of processed fiber, or by the ratio between the varying surface speeds of the rollers on the carding machine. **b.** the act of attenuating the fibers. **22.** *Chiefly Brit.* a short stream or creek. **23.** *Obs.* an allowance granted to a buyer for waste of goods sold by weight. **24. on draft,** available to be drawn from a cask rather than from a sealed bottle: *imported beer on draft.* —*v.t.* **25.** to draw the outlines or plan of; sketch. **26.** to draw up in written form; compose. **27.** to draw or pull. **28.** to take or select by draft, esp. for military service. **29.** *Masonry.* to cut a draft on. —*adj.* **30.** used or suited for drawing loads: *a draft horse.* **31.** drawn or available to be drawn from a cask rather than served from a sealed bottle. **32.** being a tentative or preliminary outline, version, design, or sketch. Also, *esp. Brit.,* **draught** (for defs. 1, 3–9, 16–19, 22, 23, 25–32). [later sp. of DRAUGHT] —**draft′er,** *n.*

draft′ an′imal, an animal used for pulling heavy loads.

draft′ beer′, beer drawn or available to be drawn from a cask.

draft′ board′, *U.S.* (in a city, county, etc.) a board of civilians charged with registering, classifying, and selecting men for military service.

draft′ chair′, a chair so designed as to fend off drafts from behind, as a wing chair.

draft′ dodg′er, one who evades or attempts to evade compulsory military service.

draft·ee (draf tē′, dräf-), *n.* a person who is drafted into military service. Cf. **enlistee** (def. 1). [DRAFT + -EE]

draft′ horse′, a horse used for pulling heavy loads.

draft′ing yard′, *Australian.* a yard fenced into compartments for the holding and sorting of livestock.

draft′ mark′, *Naut.* any of a series of figures or marks at the stem or stern of a vessel indicating the distance vertically from the lowermost part of the hull.

draft′ mill′, smokejack.

draft′ scale′, *Naut.* See **immersion scale.**

drafts·man (drafts′mən, dräfts′-), *n., pl.* **-men. 1.** one employed in making mechanical drawings, as of machines, structures, etc. **2.** one who draws sketches, plans, or designs. **3.** an artist exceptionally skilled in the fundamentals of drawing: *Picasso is a fine draftsman.* **4.** one who draws up documents. **5.** draughtsman (def. 1). Also, **draughtsman** (for defs. 1–4). [DRAFT + 's[1] + MAN[1]] —**drafts′man·ship′,** *n.*

draft′ tube′, the flared passage leading vertically from a water turbine to its tailrace.

draft·y (draf′tē, dräf′-), *adj.,* **draft·i·er, draft·i·est.** characterized by or admitting drafts of air. Also, **draughty.** [DRAFT + -Y[1]] —**draft′i·ly,** *adv.* —**draft′i·ness,** *n.*

drag (drag), *v.,* **dragged, drag·ging,** *n., adv., adj.* —*v.t.* **1.** to draw with force, effort, or difficulty; pull heavily or slowly along; haul; trail: *They dragged the carpet from mother's house to mine.* **2.** to search or catch with a drag, grapnel, or the like: *They dragged the lake for the body of the missing man.* **3.** to level and smooth (land) with a drag or harrow. **4.** to introduce or bring in, as an irrelevant matter (usually fol. by *in*): *He always drags his Ph.D. into every discussion.* **5.** to protract (something) or pass (time) tediously or painfully (often fol. by *out* or *on*): *They dragged the discussion out for three hours.* —*v.i.* **6.** to be drawn or hauled along. **7.** to trail on the ground. **8.** to move heavily or with effort. **9.** to proceed or pass with tedious slowness: *The parade dragged by endlessly.* **10.** to lag behind. **11.** to use a drag or grapnel; dredge. **12.** *Informal.* to take a puff on a cigarette. —*n.* **13.** *Naut.* **a.** a designed increase of draft toward the stern of a vessel. **b.** resistance to the movement of a hull through the water. **c.** any of a number of weights dragged cumulatively by a vessel sliding down ways to check its speed. **d.** any object dragged in the water, as a sea anchor. **e.** any device for dragging the bottom of a body of water to recover lost objects. **14.** *Agric.* a heavy wooden or steel frame drawn over the ground to smooth it. **15.** *Slang.* a painfully boring person: *Don't invite him—he's a drag.* **16.** *Slang.* something tedious; a bore: *It's a drag having to read this text.* **17.** a stout sledge or sled. **18.** *Aeron.* the aerodynamic force exerted on an airfoil, airplane, or other aerodynamic body which tends to reduce its forward motion and which is proportional to the square of the lift force. **19.** a four-horse sporting and passenger coach with seats inside and on top. **20.** a metal shoe to receive a wheel of heavy wagons and serve as a wheel lock on steep grades. **21.** anything that retards progress. **22.** act of dragging. **23.** slow, laborious movement or procedure; retardation. **24.** *Informal.* a puff or inhalation on a cigarette, pipe, etc. **25.** *Hunting.* **a.** the scent left by a fox or other animal. **b.** something, as aniseed, dragged over the ground to leave an artificial scent. **c.** Also called **drag hunt.** a hunt, esp. a fox hunt, in which the hounds follow an artificial scent. **26.** *Angling.* **a.** a brake on a fishing reel. **b.** the sideways pull on a fishline as caused by a cross current. **27.** *Slang.* transvestite attire. **28.** Also called **comb.** *Masonry.* a steel plate with a serrated edge for dressing a stone surface. **29.** *Foundry.* the lower part of a flask. Cf. **cope**[2] (def. 5). **30.** *Slang.* influence: *He claims he has drag with the school authorities.* **31.** *Slang.* a girl whom one escorts to a dance, party, etc.; date. —*adv.* **32.** with a girl: *Are you going stag or drag?* —*adj.* **33.** *Slang.* of, noting, or pertaining to transvestites or transvestite attire. [both n. and v. prob. < MLG *dragge* grapnel, *draggen* to dredge, deriv. of *drag-* DRAW] —**Syn. 1.** See **draw. 10.** linger, loiter.

drag′ bunt′, *Baseball, Softball.* a light bunt made by drawing the bat back as the ball is struck, causing it to roll on the ground.

drag′ chain′, *Shipbuilding.* one of a number of chains attached to a hull about to be launched in restricted waters in order to slow its motion by dragging along the bottom.

dra·gée (dra zhā′), *n.* **1.** a piece of candy, usually coated with chocolate and having a liquid center. **2.** a small, beadlike piece of candy, usually silver-colored and used for decorating cookies, cake, and the like. **3.** a sugar-coated medicine. [< F; see DREDGE[2]]

Drag·er·ton (drag′ər tən), *n.* a town in central Utah. 2959 (1960).

drag·ger (drag′ər), *n.* **1.** *U.S.* any of various small motor trawlers operating off the North Atlantic Coast of the U.S. **2.** one who or that which drags. [DRAG + -ER[1]]

drag·ging (drag′ing), *adj.* **1.** extremely tired or slow as in movement; lethargic; sluggish: *He was annoyed by her dragging way of walking and talking.* **2.** tediously slow in developing, progressing, terminating, etc.: *a series of dragging speeches; the dragging hot spell.* **3.** used in dragging, hoisting, etc.: *dragging ropes.* [DRAG + -ING[2]] —**drag′ging·ly,** *adv.*

drag′ging piece′, (in a hipped roof) a short beam holding the foot of a hip rafter to counteract its thrust. Also called **drag′ging beam′, dragon beam, dragon piece.**

drag·gle (drag′əl), *v.,* **-gled, -gling.** —*v.t.* **1.** to soil by dragging over damp ground or in mud. —*v.i.* **2.** to trail on the ground; be or become draggled. **3.** to follow slowly; straggle. [DRAG + -LE]

drag·gle·tail (drag′əl tāl′), *n.* **1.** a dirty, untidy person. **2.** slut; slattern. [DRAGGLE + TAIL[1]]

drag·gle·tailed (drag′əl tāld′), *adj.* **1.** untidy; bedraggled. **2.** sluttish. **3.** having wet, dirty clothes, from or as from dragging them through mud. [DRAGGLETAIL + -ED[3]]

drag·hound (drag′hound′), *n.* a hound for use in following a hunting drag, specifically bred for speed and stamina rather than subtlety of sense of smell. [DRAG + HOUND[1]]

drag′ hunt′, drag (def. 25c).

drag·line (drag′līn′), *n.* a rope dragging from something; dragrope. [DRAG + LINE[1]]

drag′line crane′, an excavating crane having a bucket which is dropped from a boom and dragged toward the crane base by a cable.

drag′ link′, *Mach.* a link connecting cranks on parallel shafts.

drag·net (drag′net′), *n.* **1.** a net to be drawn along the bottom of a river, pond, etc., or along the ground, to catch fish, small game, etc. **2.** a system or network for finding or catching someone, as a criminal wanted by the police. [OE *drægnet.* See DRAG, NET[1]]

Dra·go (drä′gō; *Sp.* drä′gō), *n.* **Lu·is Ma·rí·a** (lo͞o′is mə rē′ə; *Sp.* lo͞o ēs′ mä rē′ä), 1859–1921, Argentine jurist and statesman.

Dra′go Doc′trine, the doctrine that debts owed by an American nation to a European nation cannot be collected through armed intervention or occupation. [named after L. M. DRAGO]

drag·o·man (drag′ə mən), *n., pl.* **-mans, -men.** (in the Orient) a professional interpreter. [< F; r. ME *drogman* < MF *drog(o)man, dragoman* < OIt *dragomann(o)* < LGk *dragoúmenos* < OAr *targumān* interpreter] —**drag·o·man·ic** (drag′ə man′ik), **drag′o·man·ish,** *adj.*

drag·on (drag′ən), *n.* **1.** a fabulous monster variously represented, generally as a huge, winged reptile with crested head and terrible claws and teeth, and often spouting fire. **2.** *Archaic.* a huge serpent or snake. **3.** *Bible.* a large animal, possibly a large snake or crocodile. **4. the dragon,** Satan. **5.** a fierce, violent person. **6.** a very watchful and strict female chaperon; duenna. **7.** See **flying dragon. 8.** *Bot.* any of several araceous plants, as *Arisaema Dracontium* **(green dragon** or **dragonroot),** the flowers of which have a long, slender spadix and a green, shorter spathe. **9.** a short musket carried by a mounted infantryman in the 16th and 17th centuries. **10.** a soldier armed with such a musket. **11.** *Mil. Slang.* a heavy vehicle for transporting a tank. **12.** *(cap.) Astron.* the constellation Draco. [ME < OF < L *dracōn-* (s. of *dracō*) < Gk *drákōn* kind of serpent, prob. orig. epithet, the (sharp-)sighted one, akin to *dérkesthai* to look] —**drag′on·ish,** *adj.* —**drag′on·like′,** *adj.*

drag′on beam′. See **dragging piece.** Also called **dragon piece.**

drag·on·ess (drag′ə nis), *n.* a female dragon. [DRAGON + -ESS]

drag·on·et (drag′ə net′, drag′ə nit), *n.* any small, usually brightly colored, shore fish of the genus *Callionymus.* [ME < MF; see DRAGON, -ET]

Dragonfly, *Plathemis lybia* (Length 1½ in.; wingspread 2½ in.)

drag·on·fly (drag′ən flī′), *n., pl.* **-flies.** any of numerous stout-bodied, harmless insects of the order *Odonata* (suborder *Anisoptera*) that prey on mosquitoes and other insects, and are distinguished from the damselflies by the horizontal position of the wings when at rest. [DRAGON + FLY[2]]

drag·on·head (drag′ən hed′), *n.* any of several mints of the genus *Dracocephalum.* Also, **dragon's head.** [trans. of NL *Dracocephalum*]

drag′on liz′ard. See **Komodo dragon.**

drag·on·nade (drag′ə nād′), *n.* **1.** one of a series of persecutions of French Protestants, under Louis XIV, by dragoons quartered upon them. **2.** any persecution with the aid of troops. [< F, equiv. to *dragonne* pertaining to a DRAGOON + *-ade* -ADE]

drag′on piece′. See **dragging piece.**

drag·on·root (drag′ən ro͞ot′, -ro͝ot′), *n.* See under **dragon** (def. 8). [DRAGON + ROOT[1]]

drag′on's blood′, 1. a deep-red, water-insoluble resin exuding from the fruit of a palm, *Daemonorops Draco,* of the Malay Archipelago, formerly used in medicine, now used chiefly in the preparation of varnishes and in photoengraving for protecting certain areas of the metal plate from the acid. **2.** any of various similar resins from other trees.

drag′on's head′, 1. dragonhead. **2.** *Astron. Obs.* the ascending node of the moon or a planet.

drag′on's tail′, *Astron. Obs.* the descending node of the moon or a planet.

drag·on's-tongue (drag′ənz tung′), *n.* See **spotted wintergreen.**

drag′on tree′, a liliaceous tree, *Dracaena Draco,* of the Canary Islands, yielding a variety of dragon's blood.

drag′on withe′, (in the West Indies) a climbing shrub, *Heteropteris laurifolia,* having winged fruits.

dra·goon (drə go͞on′), *n.* **1.** a cavalryman of a heavily armed troop. **2.** a member of a military unit formerly composed of such cavalrymen, as in the British army. **3.** a mounted infantryman armed with a short musket. —*v.t.* **4.** to set dragoons or soldiers upon; persecute by armed force; oppress. **5.** to force by rigorous and oppressive measures; coerce: *The authorities dragooned the peasants into leaving their farms.* [< F *dragon,* special use of *dragon* DRAGON, applied first to a pistol hammer (so named because of its shape), then to the firearm, then to the troops so armed] —**dra·goon′age,** *n.*

drag′ par′achute, a parachute released behind an airplane to serve as a brake during landing.

drag′ race′, a short race between two or more automobiles starting from a standstill, the winner being the car that can accelerate the fastest.

drag′ rake′, a heavy rake with closely set, hooklike teeth, for use in digging for clams

drag·rope (drag′rōp′), *n.* **1.** a rope for dragging something, as a piece of artillery. **2.** a rope dragging from something, as the guide rope from a balloon. [DRAG + ROPE]

drag′ sail′, *Naut.* a sea anchor made of canvas. Also called **drag′ sheet′.**

drag·saw (drag′sô′), *n.* a large power saw having a reciprocating blade, as a power hacksaw for metals or a lumbermill saw. [DRAG + SAW[1]] —**drag′saw′ing,** *n.*

drag·ster (drag′stər), *n.* *Slang.* an automobile stripped down and altered for drag racing. [DRAG + -STER]

drag′ strip′, a straight, paved area or course where drag races are held, as a section of road or airplane runway.

Dra·gui·gnan (dʀa gē nyäN′), *n.* a town in and the capital of Var, in SE France. 16,083 (1962).

draht·haar (drät′här), *n.* one of a German breed of wire-haired pointing dogs. [< G, equiv. to *Draht* wire + *Haar* hair]

drain (drān), *v.t.* **1.** to withdraw or draw off (a liquid) gradually; remove slowly or by degrees, as by filtration: *to drain oil from a crankcase.* **2.** to withdraw liquid gradually from; make empty or dry by drawing off liquid: *to drain a crankcase.* **3.** to draw off or take away completely. **4.** to deprive of possessions, resources, spiritual strength, etc., by gradual withdrawal or exhaustion; exhaust. —*v.i.* **5.** to flow off gradually. **6.** to become empty or dry by the gradual flowing off of liquid or moisture: *This land drains into the Mississippi.* —*n.* **7.** that by which anything is drained, as a pipe or conduit. **8.** *Surg.* a material or appliance for maintaining the opening of a wound to permit free exit of fluid contents. **9.** gradual or continuous outflow, withdrawal, or expenditure. **10.** that which causes a large or continuous outflow, expenditure, or depletion: *Medical expenses were a drain on his bank account.* **11.** act of draining. **12.** *Phys. Geog.* **a.** an artificial watercourse, as a ditch or trench. **b.** a natural watercourse modified to increase its flow of water. **13. go down the drain,** to become worthless or profitless: *When he lost the plans, all his efforts went down the drain.* [ME *dreyne,* OE *drēhn(ian), drēahnian* to strain, filter; akin to DRY] —**drain′a·ble,** *adj.* —**drain′er,** *n.*

drain·age (drā′nij), *n.* **1.** act or process of draining. **2.** a system of drains, artificial or natural. **3.** See **drainage basin. 4.** that which is drained off. **5.** *Surg.* the drainage of fluids, as bile, urine, etc., from the body, or of pus and other diseased products from a wound. [DRAIN + -AGE]

drain′age ba′sin, the area drained by a river and all its tributaries. Also called **drain′age ar′ea.**

drain·age·way (drā′nij wā′), *n.* a conduit, ditch, or the like, for draining water from an area. [DRAINAGE + WAY]

drain′age wind′ (wind). See **gravity wind.**

drain·board (drān′bōrd′, -bôrd′), *n.* a working surface beside or on a kitchen sink, formed and inclined to drain into the sink. [DRAIN + BOARD]
drain·field (drān′fēld′), *n.* an open area, the soil of which absorbs the contents of a septic tank. [DRAIN + FIELD]
drain′ing board′, *Brit.* drainboard.
drain·less (drān′lis), *adj.* *Chiefly Literary.* inexhaustible. [DRAIN + -LESS]
drain·pipe (drān′pīp′), *n.* a large pipe that carries away the discharge of soil pipes, waste pipes, etc. [DRAIN + PIPE[1]]
drain·spout (drān′spout′), *n.* downspout. [DRAIN + SPOUT]
drain·way (drān′wā′), *n.* a course or passage by which something is drained. [DRAIN + WAY]
drake[1] (drāk), *n.* a male duck. Cf. **duck**[1] (def. 2). [ME; c. LG *drake*, dial. HG *drache*; cf. OHG *(an)trahho*, *(anu)trehho* male duck]
drake[2] (drāk), *n.* **1.** a small cannon, used esp. in the 17th and 18th centuries. **2.** *Obs.* a dragon. [ME; OE *drac(a)* < L *dracō* DRAGON]
Drake (drāk), *n.* **1.** **Sir Francis,** c1540–96, English admiral, circumnavigator, and buccaneer. **2.** **Joseph Rod·man** (rod′mən), 1795–1820, U.S. poet.
drake′ fly′, *Angling.* See **May fly.** [? late ME *drake flye* artificial fly dressed with drake feathers]
drake′ foot′, *Furniture.* See **trifid foot.**
Dra·kens·berg (drä′kənz bûrg′), *n.* a mountain range in the E Republic of South Africa: highest peak, 10,988 ft. Also called **Quathlamba.**
Drake′ Pas′sage, a strait between S South America and the South Shetland Islands, connecting the Atlantic and Pacific oceans.
dram (dram), *n.*, *v.*, **drammed, dram·ming.** —*n.* **1.** a unit of apothecaries' weight, equal to 60 grains, or ⅛ ounce. **2.** 1/16 ounce, avoirdupois weight (27.34 grains). **3.** See **fluid dram.** **4.** a small drink of liquor. **5.** a small quantity of anything. —*v.i.* **6.** *Archaic.* to drink drams; tipple. —*v.t.* **7.** *Archaic.* to ply with drink. [ME *dramme*, assimilated var. of *dragme* < OF < LL *dragma*, L *drachma* DRACHMA]
dra·ma (drä′mə, dram′ə), *n.* **1.** a composition in prose or verse presenting in dialogue or pantomime a story involving conflict or contrast of character, esp. one intended to be acted on the stage; a play. **2.** the branch of literature having such compositions as its subject; dramatic art or representation. **3.** the art dealing with the writing and production of plays. **4.** any series of events having vivid, emotional, conflicting, or striking interest or results: *the drama of a murder trial.* [< LL < Gk *drâma* action (of a play), equiv. to *drā(n)* to do + *-ma* n. suffix]
Dram·a·mine (dram′ə mēn′), *n.* *Pharm., Trademark.* dimenhydrinate.
dra·mat·ic (drə mat′ik), *adj.* **1.** of or pertaining to the drama. **2.** employing the form or manner of the drama. **3.** characteristic of or appropriate to the drama, esp. in involving conflict or contrast; vivid; moving: *dramatic colors; a dramatic speech.* **4.** highly effective; striking: *The silence following his impassioned speech was dramatic.* [< LL *drāmatic(us)* < Gk *drāmatikós*, equiv. to *drāmat-* (s. of *drâma*) DRAMA + *-ikos* -IC] —**dra·mat′i·cal·ly,** *adv.*
—**Syn. 1.** theatrical. **4.** startling, sensational.
dramat′ic i′rony, *Theat.* irony that is inherent in speeches or a situation, understood by the audience but not grasped by the characters of the play.
dramat′ic mon′ologue, a poetic form in which a single character, addressing a silent auditor at a critical moment, reveals himself and the dramatic situation. Also called **dramat′ic lyr′ic.**
dra·mat·ics (drə mat′iks), *n.* **1.** (*construed as sing. or pl.*) the art of producing or acting dramas. **2.** (*construed as pl.*) dramatic productions, esp. by amateurs. **3.** (*construed as pl.*) dramatic, overly emotional, or insincere behavior: *His friends are tired of all his phony dramatics.* [see DRAMATIC, -ICS]
dram·a·tise (dram′ə tīz′, drä′mə-), *v.t.*, **-tised, -tis·ing.** *Chiefly Brit.* dramatize. —**dram′a·tis′a·ble,** *adj.* —**dram′a·tis′er,** *n.*
dram·a·tis per·so·nae (dram′ə tis pər sō′nē, drä′mə-), **1.** (*construed as plural*) the characters in a play. **2.** (*construed as sing.*) a list of the characters preceding the text of a play. [< L: characters of the play]
dram·a·tist (dram′ə tist, drä′mə-), *n.* a writer of dramas or dramatic poetry; playwright. [< Gk *drāmat-* (see DRAMATIC) + -IST]
dram·a·ti·za·tion (dram′ə ti zā′shən, drä′mə-), *n.* **1.** act of dramatizing. **2.** construction or representation in dramatic form. **3.** a dramatized version of a novel, a historic incident, etc. Also, *esp. Brit.*, **dram′a·ti·sa′tion.** [DRAMATIZE + -ATION]
dram·a·tize (dram′ə tīz′, drä′mə-), *v.t.*, **-tized, -tiz·ing.** **1.** to put into a form suitable for acting on a stage. **2.** to express or represent vividly, emotionally, or strikingly: *He dramatizes his woes with sobs and sighs.* Also, *esp. Brit.*, **dramatise.** [< Gk *drāmat-* (see DRAMATIC) + -IZE] —**dram′a·tiz′a·ble,** *adj.* —**dram′a·tiz′er,** *n.*
dram·a·turge (dram′ə tûrj′, drä′mə-), *n.* a dramatist. Also, **dram′a·tur′gist.** [? back formation from DRAMATURGY, but cf. F *dramaturge*, G *Dramaturg*]
dram·a·tur·gy (dram′ə tûr′jē, drä′mə-), *n.* **1.** the craft or the techniques of dramatic composition considered collectively. **2.** the dramatic art. [< Gk *drāmatourgía* dramatic composition, equiv. to *drāmaturg(ós)* playwright + *-ia* -Y[3]. See DRAMATIC, -URGY] —**dram′a·tur′gic, dram′a·tur′gi·cal,** *adj.* —**dram′a·tur′gi·cal·ly,** *adv.* —**dram′a·tur′gist,** *n.*
Dram·bu·ie (dram bo͞o′ē), *n.* *Trademark.* a liqueur made from Highland malt Scotch whisky and heather honey.
drame (DRAM), *n.* *French.* tragicomedy (def. 1). [lit., drama]
dram′ glass′. See **joey glass.**
dram·mock (dram′ək), *n.* *Chiefly Scot.* an uncooked mixture of meal, usually oatmeal, and cold water. Also, **dram·mach** (dram′əKH), **drummock.** [cf. Gael *dramag* foul mixture]
dram. pers., dramatis personae.
dram·shop (dram′shop′), *n.* *Archaic.* barroom; saloon. [DRAM + SHOP]
Dran·ces (dran′sēz), *n.* *Class. Myth.* (in the *Aeneid*) an enemy of Turnus.
Drang nach Ost·en (dräŋ′ näKH ôs′tᵊn), *German.* drive to the east: the former German imperialistic foreign policy, esp. during the 12th to 14th centuries, of extending influence to eastern and southeastern Europe.
drank (draŋk), *v.* a pt. and pp. of **drink.**
drape (drāp), *v.*, **draped, drap·ing,** *n.* —*v.t.* **1.** to cover or hang with cloth or other fabric, esp. in graceful folds; adorn with drapery. **2.** to adjust (curtains, clothes, etc.) into graceful folds, attractive lines, etc. **3.** to arrange, hang, or let fall carelessly: *Don't drape your feet over the chair!* **4.** *Med., Surg.* to cover with cloth the area around a part to be operated on or examined. **5.** (in reinforced-concrete construction) to hang (reinforcement) in a certain form between two points before pouring the concrete. —*v.i.* **6.** to hang, fall, or become arranged in folds, as drapery: *This silk drapes well.* —*n.* **7.** a curtain or hanging of heavy fabric and usually considerable length, esp. one of a pair for covering a window or windows and drawn open and shut horizontally. **8.** either of a pair of similar curtains extending or draped at the sides of a window, French doors, or the like and serving a purely decorative purpose. **9.** manner or style of hanging: *the drape of a skirt.* [late ME < MF *drap(er)*, deriv. of *drap* cloth (see DRAB[1])] —**drap′a·ble, drape′a·ble,** *adj.*
drap·er (drā′pər), *n.* *Brit.* **1.** a dealer in cloth; a retail merchant or clerk who sells piece goods. **2.** a retail merchant or clerk who sells clothing and dry goods. [ME < AF; OF *drapier*, equiv. to *drap* cloth + *-ier* -ER[2]]
Dra·per (drā′pər), *n.* **1.** **Charles Stark,** born 1901, U.S. engineer. **2.** **Henry,** 1837–82, U.S. astronomer. **3.** his father, **John William,** 1811–82, U.S. chemist, physiologist, historian, and writer; born in England. **4.** **Ruth,** 1884–1956, U.S. monologist, diseuse, and writer of character sketches. **5.** a town in N North Carolina. 3382 (1960). **6.** a crater in the second quadrant of the face of the moon: about 7 miles in diameter.
dra·per·y (drā′pə rē), *n.*, *pl.* **-per·ies.** **1.** coverings, hangings, clothing, etc., of fabric, esp. as arranged in loose, graceful folds. **2.** long curtains, usually of heavy fabric and often designed to open and close across a window. **3.** the draping or arranging of hangings, clothing, etc., in graceful folds. **4.** *Art.* hangings, clothing, etc., as represented in sculpture or painting. **5.** cloths or textile fabrics collectively. **6.** *Brit.* **a.** See **dry goods.** **b.** the stock, shop, or business of a draper. [ME *draperie* < OF, equiv. to *drap* cloth + *-erie* -ERY] —**dra′per·ied,** *adj.*
dras·tic (dras′tik), *adj.* **1.** acting with force or violence; violent. **2.** extremely severe or extensive: *The legislature passed a drastic tax-reduction measure.* [< Gk *drastik(ós)* active, equiv. to *drast(ós)* (verbal adj. of *drân* to do) + *-ikos* -IC] —**dras′ti·cal·ly,** *adv.*
drat (drat), *v.*, **drat·ted, drat·ting,** *interj.* —*v.t.* **1.** *Informal.* to damn; confound. —*interj.* **2.** (used to express mild disgust, disappointment, or the like): *Drat, there goes another button!* [alter. of *(o)d rot* God rot (i.e., may God rot him, her, it)]
D ration, *U.S. Army.* an emergency field ration consisting of three specially prepared bars of food.
drat·ted (drat′id), *adj.* *Informal.* damned; confounded (used as a mild oath): *This dratted car won't start.* [DRAT + -ED[2]]
draught (draft, dräft), *n.* **1.** the drawing of a liquid from its receptacle, as of ale from a cask: *ale on draught.* **2.** act of drinking or inhaling. **3.** that which is taken in by drinking or inhaling; a drink; dose. **4.** a quantity of fish caught. **5.** **draughts,** (*construed as sing.*) *Brit.* the game of checkers. **6.** *Chiefly Brit.* draft (defs. 1, 3–9, 16–19, 22, 23). —*v.t.* **7.** *Chiefly Brit.* draft (defs. 25–29). —*adj.* **8.** being on draught; drawn as required: *draught ale.* **9.** *Chiefly Brit.* (defs. 30–32). [ME *draht* (c. D *dragt*, G *Tracht*, Icel *drāttr*); akin to OE *dragan* to DRAW, *drōht* a pull (at the oars)] —**draught′er,** *n.*
draught·board (draft′bōrd′, -bôrd′, dräft′-), *n.* *Brit.* checkerboard (def. 1). Also, **draughts·board** (drafts′bōrd′, -bôrd′, dräfts′-). [DRAUGHT + BOARD]
draughts·man (drafts′mən, dräfts′-), *n.*, *pl.* **-men.** **1.** *Brit.* a checker, as used in the game of checkers. **2.** draftsman (defs. 1–4). [DRAUGHT + -S[3] + MAN[1]]
draught·y (draf′tē, dräf′-), *adj.*, **draught·i·er, draught·i·est.** drafty. —**draught′i·ly,** *adv.* —**draught′i·ness,** *n.*
Dra·va (drä′və), *n.* a river in S central Europe, flowing E and SE from S Austria along a part of the boundary between Hungary and SE Slovenia into the Danube. 450 mi. long. Also, **Dra′ve.** German, **Drau** (DROU).
drave (drāv), *v.* a pt. of **drive.**
Dra·vid·i·an (drə vid′ē ən), *n.* **1.** a family of languages, wholly distinct from Indo-European, spoken mostly in southern India and including Tamil, Telugu, Kannada, Malayalam, and, in Baluchistan, Brahui. **2.** a member of an Australoid race occupying much of southern India and parts of Ceylon. —*adj.* **3.** Also, **Dra·vid′ic.** of or pertaining to this people or their language. [< Skt *Draviḍ(a)* folk name + -IAN]
dra·vite (drä′vīt), *n.* a brown variety of magnesium tourmaline. [< G *Dravit.* See DRAVA, -ITE[1]]
Dra·vos·burg (drə vōs′bûrg), *n.* a town in SW Pennsylvania. 3458 (1960).
draw (drô), *v.*, **drew, drawn, draw·ing,** *n.* —*v.t.* **1.** to cause to move in a particular direction by or as by a pulling force; pull; drag (often fol. by *along, away, in, out, off,* etc.). **2.** to bring, take, or pull out, as from a receptacle or source: *to draw water from a well; Draw your gun and start shooting.* **3.** to bring toward oneself or itself, as by inherent force or influence; attract: *The concert drew a large audience.* **4.** to sketch (someone or something) in lines or words; delineate; depict: *to draw a vase.* **5.** to compose or create (a picture) in lines. **6.** to mark or lay out; trace: *to draw perpendicular lines.* **7.** to frame or formulate (as a distinction or the like). **8.** to write out in legal form (sometimes fol. by *up*): *Draw up the contract for the sale.* **9.** to inhale or suck in. **10.** to derive or use, as from a source: *to draw inspiration from Shakespeare.* **11.** to deduce; infer: *to draw a conclusion.* **12.** to get, take, or receive, as from a source: *to draw interest on a savings account; He drew a salary of $100 a week.* **13.** to produce; bring in: *The deposits draw interest.* **14.** to disembowel: *to draw a turkey.* **15.** to drain: *to draw a pond.* **16.** to pull out to full or greater length; stretch; make by attenuating: *to draw filaments of molten glass.* **17.** to bend (a bow) by pulling back its string in preparation for shooting an arrow. **18.** to choose or to have assigned to one at random, by or as by picking an unseen number, item, etc.: *Let's draw straws to see who has to wash the car. My son drew a hard teacher in the fifth grade.* **19.** *Metalworking.* to make or reduce the sectional area of (a wire, tube, etc.) by pulling its material through a die. **20.** to wrinkle or shrink by contraction. **21.** *Med.* to digest and cause to discharge: *to draw an abscess by a poultice.* **22.** *U.S. Army.* to obtain (rations, clothing, equipment, weapons, or ammunition) from an issuing agency, such as the quartermaster. **23.** *Naut.* (of a vessel) to need (a specific depth of water) to float in: *She draws six feet.* **24.** to leave (a contest) undecided; finish with neither side winning, as in a tie. **25.** *Cards.* **a.** to take or be dealt (a card or cards) from the pack. **b.** *Bridge.* to remove the outstanding cards in (a given suit) by leading that suit: *He had to draw spades first in order to make the contract.* **26.** *Billiards.* to cause (a cue ball) to recoil after impact by giving it a backward spin on the stroke. **27.** *Hunting.* to search (a covert) for game. **28.** *Cricket.* to play (a ball) with a bat held at an angle in order to deflect the ball between the wicket and the legs. **29.** *Curling.* to slide (the stone) gently. **30.** to steep (tea) in boiling water. **31.** to form or shape (glass) as it comes from the furnace by stretching.
—*v.i.* **32.** to exert a pulling, moving, or attracting force: *A sail draws by being properly trimmed and filled with wind.* **33.** to move, go, or pass, esp. slowly or continuously, as under a pulling force (often fol. by *on, off, out,* etc.): *The day draws near.* **34.** to take out a sword, pistol, etc., for action (often fol. by *on*): *The sheriff drew on him before he could reach his gun.* **35.** to hold a drawing, lottery, or the like: *to draw for prizes.* **36.** to sketch or to trace figures; create a picture or depict by sketching. **37.** to be skilled in or practice the art of sketching. **38.** to shrink or contract (often fol. by *up*). **39.** to make a draft or demand (usually fol. by *on* or *upon*): *to draw on one's imagination.* **40.** to levy or call on for money, supplies, etc. **41.** *Med.* **a.** to act as an irritant; cause blisters. **b.** to cause blood, pus, or the like to gather at a specific point. **42.** to produce or permit a draft, as a pipe or flue. **43.** to leave a contest undecided; tie. **44.** *Hunting.* (of a hound) **a.** to search a covert for game. **b.** to follow a game animal by its scent. **45.** to attract customers, an audience, etc.: *Our newspaper advertisement drew very well.* **46.** to pull back the string of a bow in preparation for shooting an arrow. **47.** **draw ahead,** *Naut.* (of the wind) to blow from a direction closer to that in which a vessel is moving; haul forward. Cf. **veer**[1] (def. 2). **48.** **draw on, a.** to come nearer; approach: *He felt death drawing on.* **b.** to clothe oneself in: *She drew on her cape and gloves.* **c.** *Naut.* (of a vessel) to gain on (another vessel). **d.** to take (some of one's money) from a place of deposit: *He drew $50 on his checking account.* **49.** **draw oneself up,** to assume an erect posture: *The elderly spinster drew herself up and asserted that she would never sell her family's house.* **50.** **draw out, a.** to pull out; remove: *to draw out a tooth.* **b.** to prolong; lengthen: *He drew out the interview.* **c.** to persuade someone to speak with or confide in one: *You'll find she's a sweet girl if you take the trouble to draw her out.* **d.** *Naut.* (of a vessel) to move away from (sometimes fol. by *from*): *The boat drew out from the wharf.* **e.** to take (money, esp. all one's money) from a place of deposit: *He drew his money out of the bank and invested it in bonds.* **51.** **draw up, a.** to put into position; arrange: *The officer drew up his men.* **b.** to bring or cause to be brought to a stop; halt: *He drew up his car at the curb.*
—*n.* **52.** the act of drawing. **53.** something that attracts customers, an audience, etc. **54.** that which is moved by being drawn, as the movable part of a drawbridge. **55.** that which is chosen or drawn at random, as a lot or chance. **56.** *Informal.* drawing (defs. 5, 6). **57.** a contest that ends in a tie; an undecided contest. **58.** Also called **draw play.** *Football.* a play in which the quarterback fades as if to pass and then hands the ball to a back, usually the fullback, who is running toward the line of scrimmage. **59.** *Poker.* **a.** a card or cards taken or dealt from the pack. **b.** See **draw poker.** **60.** *Phys. Geog.* **a.** a small, natural drainageway with a shallow bed; gully. **b.** the dry bed of a stream. **61.** the pull necessary to draw a bow to its full extent. **62.** *Horol.* **a.** the tendency of a tooth of an escape wheel to force toward the center of the wheel a pallet engaging with it. **b.** the angle made by the locking surface of a pallet, at the moment of engaging an escape wheel, with the radius from the center of the escape wheel which passes through the point of contact. **63.** **beat to the draw,** to outdo someone else by taking advantage of an opportunity before he can: *They beat us to the draw by signing up our potential star.* [ME *draw(en)*, OE *dragan*; c. Icel *draga* to draw, G *tragen* to carry; cf. DRAG] —**draw′a·ble,** *adj.*
—**Syn. 1.** tug, tow. DRAW, DRAG, HAUL, PULL imply causing movement of an object toward one by exerting force upon it. To DRAW is to move by a force, in the direction from which the force is exerted: *A magnet draws iron to it. Horses draw a wagon.* To DRAG is to draw with greater force, necessary to overcome friction between the object drawn and the surface on which it rests: *to drag a sled to the top of a hill, a heavy piece of furniture across a room.* To HAUL is to transport a heavy object slowly by mechanical force or with sustained effort: *to haul a piano up to the seventh floor; to haul a large boat across a portage.* To PULL is to draw or tug, exerting varying amounts of force according to the effort needed: *to pull out an eyelash; to pull fighting dogs apart.* **13.** bear.
draw·a·bil·i·ty (drô′ə bil′i tē), *n.* *Metalworking.* the degree of readiness with which a metal can be drawn. [DRAWABLE + -ITY]

draw·back (drô′bak′), *n.* **1.** a hindrance or disadvantage; an undesirable or objectionable feature. **2.** *Com.* an amount paid back from a charge made. **3.** *Govt.* a refund of tariff or other tax, as when imported goods are reexported. [n. use of v. phrase *draw back*]

draw·bar (drô′bär′), *n.* *Railroads.* a metal rod or bar for connecting two pieces of rolling stock, as a steam locomotive and a tender. [DRAW + BAR[1]]

draw′bar pull′, the force, measured in pounds, available to a locomotive for pulling rolling stock after overcoming its own tractive resistance.

draw·bench (drô′bench′), *n.* *Metalworking.* a bench having apparatus for cold-drawing wires, tubes, etc. [DRAW + BENCH]

draw·bore (drô′bōr′, -bôr′), *n., v.,* **-bored, -bor·ing.** *Carpentry.* —*n.* **1.** a hole in a tenon made eccentric with the corresponding holes to the mortise so that the two pieces being joined will be forced tightly together when the pin (**draw′bore pin′**) is hammered into place. —*v.t.* **2.** to make a drawbore in (a tenon). [DRAW + BORE[1]]

draw·boy (drô′boi′), *n.* **1.** an apparatus for controlling and manipulating the harness cords on a power loom. **2.** *Obs.* a boy who operates and controls the harness cords of a draw-loom. [DRAW + BOY]

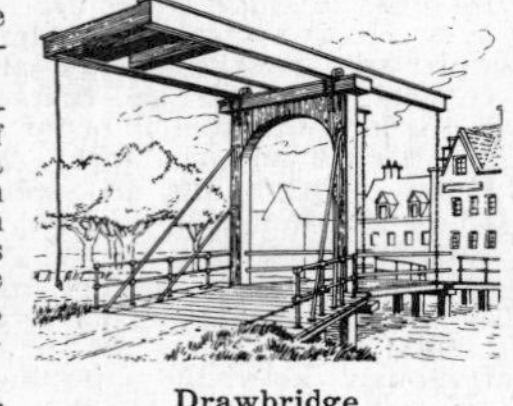

Drawbridge

draw·bridge (drô′brij′), *n.* a bridge of which the whole or a section may be drawn up, let down, or drawn aside, to prevent access or to leave a passage open for boats, barges, etc. [ME *drawebrigge.* See DRAW, BRIDGE[1]]

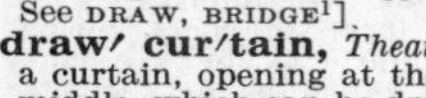

draw′ cur′tain, *Theat.* a curtain, opening at the middle, which can be drawn to the sides of a stage.

draw·ee (drô ē′), *n.* *Finance.* a person on whom an order, draft, or bill of exchange is drawn. [DRAW + -EE]

draw·er (drôr *for 1, 2;* drô′ər *for 3–6*), *n.* **1.** a sliding, lidless, horizontal compartment, as in a piece of furniture, that may be drawn out in order to gain access to it. **2. drawers,** an undergarment, with legs, that covers the lower part of the body. **3.** one who or that which draws. **4.** *Finance.* a person who draws an order, draft, or bill of exchange. **5.** *Metalworking.* one who operates a drawbench. **6.** *Archaic.* a tapster. [ME; see DRAW, -ER[1]]

draw′ game′, *Dominoes.* a game in which a player must keep drawing pieces from the boneyard until he gets one that he can play.

draw′ hole′, (in strip mining) a funnel-shaped raise cut at the bottom of a pit, permitting the loading of cars stationed in drifts below. Also called **glory hole, mill hole.**

draw·ing (drô′ing), *n.* **1.** the act of one who or that which draws. **2.** a representation by lines; a delineation of form without reference to color. **3.** a sketch, plan, or design, esp. one made with pen, pencil, or crayon. **4.** the art or technique of making these. **5.** something decided by drawing lots; lottery. **6.** the selection, or time of selection, of the winning chance or chances sold by lottery or raffle. [ME; see DRAW, -ING[1]]

draw′ing account′, *Com.* **1.** an account used by a partner or employee for cash withdrawals. **2.** an account that is charged with advances of money for expenses, on salaries, against earnings, etc., esp. for salesmen.

draw′ing board′, **1.** a rectangular board on which paper is placed or mounted for drawing. **2.** this board with at least two perfectly straight edges at right angles, used for making relatively precise drawings.

draw′ing card′, **1.** an entertainer, speaker, etc., who attracts a large audience. **2.** a performance, item on sale, advertisement, etc., that attracts many customers, patrons, or the like.

draw′ing chis′el, an obliquely edged wood chisel for working across grain, as in forming the ends of tenons.

draw′ing frame′, *Textiles.* a machine used to attenuate and straighten fibers by having them pass, in sliver form, through a series of double rollers, each pair of which revolves at a slightly greater speed than the preceding pair and reduces the number of strands originally fed into the machine to one extended fibrous strand doubled or redoubled in length.

draw·ing-in (drô′ing in′), *n., pl.* **draw·ings-in.** the act or process of threading warp ends through the heddle eyes of the harness and the dents of the reed according to a given plan for weaving a fabric. [n. use of v. phrase *draw in*]

draw′ing pin′, *Brit.* a thumbtack.

draw′ing room′, **1.** a formal reception room, esp. in an apartment or private house. **2.** *U.S.* (in a railway car) a private room for two or three passengers. **3.** *Brit.* a formal reception, esp. at court. [(*with*)*drawing*] —**draw′ing-room′,** *adj.*

draw′ing ta′ble, a table having a surface consisting of a drawing board adjustable to various heights and angles. Also called **architect's table.**

Drawknife

draw·knife (drô′nīf′), *n., pl.* **-knives.** *Carpentry.* a knife with a handle at each end at right angles to the blade, used by drawing over a surface. Also called **draw′ing knife′, drawshave.** [DRAW + KNIFE]

drawl (drôl), *v.t., v.i.* **1.** to say or speak in a slow manner, usually prolonging the vowels. —*n.* **2.** the act or utterance of one who drawls. [< D or LG *dralen* to linger (cf. *gauze* < F *gaze*)] —**drawl′er,** *n.* —**drawl′ing·ly,** *adv.* —**drawl′ing·ness,** *n.* —**drawl′y,** *adj.*

draw-loom (drô′lo͞om′), *n.* an early handloom used for producing figured fabrics.

drawn (drôn), *v.* **1.** pp. of **draw.** —*adj.* **2.** tense; haggard. **3.** eviscerated, as a fowl. **4.** *Glassmaking.* **a.** of or pertaining to the stem of a drinking glass that has been formed by stretching from a small mass of molten metal left at the base of the bowl of the vessel. **b.** of or pertaining to glass that is drawn over a series of rollers as it comes from the furnace.

drawn′ but′ter, **1.** melted butter, often seasoned with herbs or lemon juice, served on cooked vegetables, fish, etc. **2.** a sauce of melted butter, flour, vegetable or fish stock, and lemon juice.

drawn′ but′ter sauce′, *U.S.* a sauce of melted butter, flour, seasonings, and hot water or stock.

drawn′ work′, ornamental work done by drawing threads from a fabric, the remaining portions usually being formed into lacelike patterns by needlework.

draw′-out ta′ble (drô′out′). See **draw table.**

draw·plate (drô′plāt′), *n.* *Metalworking.* a small plate containing tapered holes used as dies for drawing wire, small tubing, etc. [DRAW + PLATE[1]]

draw′ play′, *Football.* draw (def. 58).

draw′ pok′er, a variety of poker in which each player can, after an initial bet, discard several, usually up to three, of the five cards dealt to him and receive substitutes from the dealer.

draw′ run′ner, *Furniture.* loper. Also called **draw′ slip′.**

draw·shave (drô′shāv′), *n.* *Carpentry.* drawknife. [DRAW + SHAVE]

draw-sheet (drô′shēt′), *n.* a narrow sheet, used on hospital beds, placed under a patient's buttocks and often over a rubber sheet, that can easily be removed if soiled.

draw′ shot′, *Billiards, Pool.* a stroke that imparts a backward spin to the cue ball, causing it to roll back after striking the object ball. Cf. **follow shot** (def. 1).

draw·string (drô′string′), *n.* a string, cord, etc., which tightens or closes an opening, as of a bag, clothing, or the like, when one or both ends are pulled. Also, **draw′ string′.** [DRAW + STRING]

draw′ tab′, *Theat. Chiefly Brit.* a single curtain that is opened by being drawn across to one side of the stage. Also called **French tab.**

draw′ ta′ble, a table having one or more sliding leaves that may be drawn out as an extension. Also called **draw-out table, draw′-top ta′ble** (drô′top′).

draw′ top′, *Furniture.* a table top that can be extended by drawing out and raising leaves suspended from either end.

draw·tube (drô′to͞ob′, -tyo͞ob′), *n.* a tube sliding within another tube, as the tube carrying the eyepiece in a microscope. [DRAW + TUBE]

dray (drā), *n.* **1.** a low, strong cart without fixed sides, for carrying heavy loads. **2.** a sledge or sled. **3.** (loosely) any vehicle, as a truck, used to haul goods, esp. one used to carry heavy loads. —*v.t.* **4.** to convey on a dray. —*v.i.* **5.** to drive or operate a dray, esp. as an occupation. **6.** to convey goods by dray, esp. locally or for short distances. [ME *draye* sledge; cf. OE *draeg-* (in *drægnett* dragnet), akin to *dragan* to DRAW]

dray·age (drā′ij), *n.* **1.** conveyance by dray. **2.** a charge made for it. [DRAY + -AGE]

dray·ing (drā′ing), *n.* the business, occupation, or activities of driving a dray. [DRAY + -ING[1]]

dray·man (drā′mən), *n., pl.* **-men.** a man who drives a dray. [DRAY + MAN[1]]

Dray·ton (drāt′ən), *n.* **1. Michael,** 1563–1631, English poet. **2. William Henry,** 1742–1779, American member of Continental Congress, 1778–79.

drch., drachma. Also, **dr.**

D.R.E., Doctor of Religious Education.

dread (dred), *v.t.* **1.** to fear greatly; be in extreme apprehension of: *to dread death.* **2.** to be reluctant to do, meet, or experience: *I dread going to big parties.* **3.** *Archaic.* to hold in respectful awe. —*v.i.* **4.** to be in great fear. —*n.* **5.** terror or apprehension as to something in the future; great fear. **6.** a person or thing dreaded. **7.** *Archaic.* deep awe or reverence. —*adj.* **8.** greatly feared; frightful; terrible. **9.** held in awe or reverential fear. [ME *drede*(*n*), OE *drǣdan,* aph. var. of *adrǣdan, ondrǣdan;* c. OHG *intrātan* to fear] —**dread′a·ble,** *adj.* —**dread′ness,** *n.*

—**Syn. 5.** See **fear. 8.** dire, dreadful, horrible. —**Ant. 1.** welcome.

dread·ful (dred′fəl), *adj.* **1.** causing great dread, fear, or terror; terrible: *a dreadful storm.* **2.** inspiring awe or reverence. **3.** extremely bad, unpleasant, or ugly: *dreadful cooking; a dreadful hat.* —*n. Brit.* **4.** See **penny dreadful. 5.** a periodical given to highly sensational matter. [ME *dredful.* See DREAD, -FUL] —**dread′ful·ly,** *adv.* —**dread′ful·ness,** *n.*

—**Syn. 1.** frightful, dire.

dread·nought (dred′nôt′), *n.* **1.** a type of battleship armed with heavy-caliber guns in turrets: so called from the British battleship *Dreadnought,* launched in 1906, the first of the type. **2.** an outer garment of heavy woolen cloth. **3.** a thick cloth with a long pile. Also, **dread′naught′.** [DREAD + NOUGHT]

dream (drēm), *n., v.,* **dreamed** or **dreamt, dream·ing.** —*n.* **1.** a succession of images, thoughts, or emotions passing through the mind during sleep. **2.** the sleeping state in which this occurs. **3.** an object seen in a dream. **4.** an involuntary vision occurring to one awake. **5.** a vision voluntarily indulged in while awake; daydream; reverie. **6.** an aspiration; goal; aim: *A trip to Europe is his dream.* **7.** a wild or vain fancy. **8.** something of an unreal beauty or charm. —*v.i.* **9.** to have a dream or dreams. **10.** to indulge in daydreams or reveries: *He dreamed about vacation plans when he should have been working.* **11.** to think or conceive of something in a very remote way (usually fol. by *of*). —*v.t.* **12.** to see or imagine in sleep or in a vision. **13.** to imagine as if in a dream; fancy; suppose. **14.** to pass or spend (time) in dreaming (often fol. by *away*). **15. dream up,** *Informal.* to form an idea or plan of action in the imagination; devise: *They dreamed up the most impossible plan.* [ME *dreem, drēam;* c. OS *drōm* mirth, dream, Icel *draumr,* OHG *troum* dream; modern sense first recorded in ME but presumably current in OE too, as in OS] —**dream′er,** *n.* —**dream′ful,** *adj.* —**dream′ful·ly,** *adv.* —**dream′ful·ness,** *n.* —**dream′ing·ly,** *adv.* —**dream′less,** *adj.* —**dream′less·ly,** *adv.* —**dream′less·ness,** *n.* —**dream′like′,** *adj.*

—**Syn. 1.** DREAM, NIGHTMARE, and VISION refer to the kinds of mental images that form during sleep. DREAM is the general term for any such succession of images. A NIGHTMARE is a dream, sometimes with confused or distorted images, that brings fear or anxiety: *frightened by a nightmare.* VISION, now somewhat archaic in this sense, refers to a series of images of unusual vividness, clarity, order, and significance.

Dream, The, a painting (1910) by Henri Rousseau.

dream′ anal′ysis, *Psychoanal.* the analysis of dreams as a means of gaining access to the unconscious mind, typically consisting of a method involving free association.

dream·boat (drēm′bōt′), *n.* *Slang.* **1.** a highly desirable person of the opposite sex. **2.** anything considered as highly desirable of its kind: *His new car is a dreamboat.* [DREAM + BOAT]

dream′ book′, a book, pamphlet, etc., that lists common dreams and purports to interpret them.

dream·land (drēm′land′), *n.* a pleasant, lovely land that exists only in dreams or the imagination; the region of reverie. [DREAM + LAND]

Dream′ of the Red′ Cham′ber, The, a 17th-century Chinese novel of unknown authorship, published in 24 volumes. Chinese, **Hung Lou Mêng.**

Dreams (drēmz), **Lake of.** See **Lacus Somniorum.**

dreamt (dremt), *v.* a pt. and pp. of **dream.**

dream·time (drēm′tīm′), *n.* *Anthropol.* alcheringa. [? trans. of Austral *alchera, alcheringa.* See DREAM, TIME]

dream′ vi′sion, a conventional device used in narrative verse, employed esp. by medieval poets, that presents a story as told by one who falls asleep and dreams the events of the poem: *Dante's* Divine Comedy *exemplifies the dream vision in its most developed form.* Also called **dream′ al′legory.**

dream′ wish′, *Psychoanal.* the representation in a dream of an unfulfilled, often repressed desire.

dream′ work′, *Psychoanal.* the processes which cause a dream to evolve, as condensation, displacement, etc.

dream′ world′, the world of imagination or illusion rather than of objective reality.

dream·y (drē′mē), *adj.,* **dream·i·er, dream·i·est. 1.** abounding in dreams; characterized by or causing dreams. **2.** of the nature of or characteristic of dreams; visionary. **3.** vague; dim. **4.** soothing; restful; quieting: *dreamy music.* **5.** *Informal.* wonderful; marvelous: *He has a dreamy new convertible.* [DREAM + -Y[1]] —**dream′i·ly,** *adv.* —**dream′i·ness,** *n.*

drear (drēr), *adj.* *Literary.* dreary. [back formation from DREARY]

drear·y (drēr′ē), *adj.,* **drear·i·er, drear·i·est,** *n., pl.* **drear·ies.** —*adj.* **1.** causing sadness or gloom. **2.** dull; boring. **3.** sorrowful; sad. —*n.* **4.** a dull, drab, tedious, or unpleasant person, writer, historical figure, etc.: *Cromwell, Bloody Mary, and those other drearies.* [ME *drery,* OE *drēorig* gory, cruel, sad, equiv. to *drēor* gore + *-ig* -Y[1]; akin to Icel *dreyrigr* bloody, G *traurig* sad] —**drear′i·ly,** *adv.* —**drear′i·ness,** *n.* —**drear′i·some,** *adj.*

—**Syn. 1.** gloomy, dismal, drear, cheerless, depressing, comfortless. **2.** tedious, monotonous, wearisome, tiresome. —**Ant. 1.** cheerful. **2.** interesting.

Dreb·bel (dreb′əl), *n.* a crater in the third quadrant of the face of the moon: about 18 miles in diameter.

dreck (drek), *n.* *Slang.* **1.** excrement; dung. **2.** worthless trash; junk. Also, **drek.** [< Yiddish; c. G *Dreck* filth; cf. Icel *threkkr* excrement]

dredge[1] (drej), *n., v.,* **dredged, dredg·ing.** —*n.* **1.** any of various powerful machines for dredging up or removing earth, as from the bottom of a river, by means of a scoop, a series of buckets, a suction pipe, or the like. **2.** a barge on which such a machine is mounted. **3.** a dragnet or other contrivance for gathering material or objects from the bottom of a river, bay, etc. —*v.t.* **4.** to clear out with a dredge; remove sand, silt, mud, etc., from the bottom of. **5.** to take, catch, or gather with a dredge; obtain or remove by a dredge. —*v.i.* **6.** to use a dredge. [late ME *dreg-* (Scot), OE **drecg*(*e*); see DRAY, DRAW]

dredge[2] (drej), *v.t.* **dredged, dredg·ing.** *Cookery.* to sprinkle or coat with some powdered substance, esp. flour. [ME *drage, dreg*(*g*)*e* < OF *drag*(*i*)*e* << Gk *tragḗmata,* pl. of *trágēma* sweetmeat, dried fruit]

dredg·er[1] (drej′ər), *n.* **1.** *Chiefly Brit.* dredge[1] (def. 1). **2.** a person who uses a dredge. [DREDGE[1] + -ER[1]]

dredg·er[2] (drej′ər), *n.* a container with a perforated top for sprinkling flour, sugar, etc., on food for cooking. [DREDGE[2] + -ER[1]]

dredg′ing machine′, dredge[1] (def. 1).

dree (drē), *adj., v.,* **dreed, dree·ing.** *Scot. and North Eng.* —*adj.* **1.** tedious; dreary. —*v.t.* **2.** to suffer; endure. Also, **dreegh** (drēḵh), **dreigh, driech, driegh.** [ME; OE *drēog*(*an*) (to) endure; c. Goth *driugan* to serve (in arms)]

dreg (dreg), *n.* **1. dregs,** the sediment of liquors; lees; grounds. **2.** Usually, **dregs.** the least valuable part of anything: *the dregs of society.* **3.** a small remnant; any small quantity. [ME < Scand; cf. Icel *dreggjar* dregs; akin to L *fracēs* oil grounds]

D region, the lowest region of the ionosphere, the one in which the D layer develops.

Drei·bund (drī′bo͝ont′), *n.* *German.* See **Triple Alliance** (def. 1).

Dreidel

drei·del (drād′əl), *n., pl.* **-dels, -del.** a four-sided top bearing the Hebrew letters *nun, gimel, he,* and *shin,* each on one side, used chiefly in a children's game traditionally played on the Jewish festival of Hanukkah. [< Yiddish, Galician dial. for standard *dreydl* < G *dreh*(*en*) (to) turn + instrumental suffix *-dl*]

dreigh (drēḵh), *adj., v.t.* *Scot. and North Eng.* dree. [var. of DRIEGH]

drei·kan·ter (drī′kän tər), *n., pl.* **-ters, -ter.** a pebble or boulder having three faces formed by the action of windblown sand. [< G, equiv. to *drei* three + *Kante* edge + *-er* -ER[1]]

Drei·ser (drī′sər, -zər), *n.* **Theodore,** 1871–1945, U.S. novelist.

drek (drek), *n.* dreck.

drench (drench), *v.t.* **1.** to wet thoroughly; soak. **2.** to saturate by immersion in a liquid; steep. **3.** to cover or fill completely; bathe: *trees drenched with sunlight.* **4.** *Vet. Med.* to administer a draft of medicine to (an animal), esp. by force: *to drench a horse.* **5.** *Archaic.* to cause to drink. **—*n.*** **6.** the act of drenching. **7.** something that drenches: *a drench of rain.* **8.** a preparation for drenching or steeping. **9.** a solution, esp. one of fermenting bran, for drenching hides or skins. **10.** a large drink or draft. **11.** a draft of medicine, esp. one administered to an animal by force. [ME *drenche(n)*, OE *drencan*, causative of *drincan* to DRINK; c. D *drenken*, G *tränken* to water, give to drink] **—drench′er,** *n.* **—drench′ing·ly,** *adv.*
—Syn. 1. See **wet.**

Dren·the (dren′tə), *n.* a province in the E Netherlands. 324,517 (1962); 1011 sq. mi. Also, **Dren′te.**

Dres·den (drez′dən; *Ger.* drās′dən), *n.* the capital of Saxony in E Germany, on the Elbe River. 518,057.

Dres′den chi′na, porcelain ware produced at Meissen, Germany, near Dresden, after 1710. Also called **Dres′den por′celain, Dres′den ware′, Meis′sen porcelain.**

dress (dres), *n.* **1.** the most common outer garment of women, consisting of waist and skirt in one piece. **2.** clothing; apparel; garb: *The dress of the 18th century was colorful.* **3.** formal attire. **4.** outer covering, as the plumage of birds. **5.** a particular form of appearance; guise. **—*adj.*** **6.** of or for a dress or dresses. **7.** of or for a formal occasion. **8.** requiring formal dress. **—*v.t.*** **9.** to put clothing upon. **10.** to design clothing for or sell clothes to. **11.** to put formal or evening clothes on. **12.** to trim; ornament; adorn: *to dress a store window.* **13.** *Angling.* **a.** to prepare (a fishhook) for use. **b.** to prepare (bait, esp. an artificial fly) for use. **14.** to cut up, trim, and remove the skin, feathers, viscera, etc., from (an animal, meat, fowl, or flesh of a fowl) for market or for the table (often fol. by *out* when referring to a large animal): *She dressed three chickens for the dinner. He dressed out the deer when he got back to camp.* **15.** to prepare (skins, fabrics, timber, stone, ore, etc.) by special processes. **16.** to comb out and do up (hair). **17.** to cultivate (land, fields, etc.). **18.** to apply medication or a dressing to (a wound or sore). **19.** to make straight; bring (troops) into line: *to dress ranks.* **20.** *Theat.* to arrange (a stage) by effective placement of properties, scenery, actors, etc. **21.** to ornament (a vessel) with ensigns, house flags, code flags, etc.: *The bark was dressed with masthead flags only.* **22.** *Print.* to fit (furniture) around and between pages in a chase prior to locking it up. **—*v.i.*** **23.** to clothe or attire oneself; put on one's clothes: *Wake up and dress, now!* **24.** to put on or wear formal or fancy clothes: *to dress for dinner.* **25.** to come into line, as troops. **26.** to align oneself with the next soldier, marcher, dancer, etc., in line. **27. dress down,** *Informal.* **a.** to reprimand; scold. **b.** to thrash; beat. **28. dress ship, a.** to decorate a ship by hoisting lines of flags running its full length. **b.** *U.S. Navy.* to display the national ensigns at each masthead and a larger ensign on the flagstaff. **29. dress up, a.** to put on one's best or fanciest clothing; dress relatively formally: *They were dressed up for the Easter parade.* [ME *dresse(n)* < MF *dresse(r)* (to) arrange, prepare, OF *drecier* < LL **dīrēctiāre*, deriv. of L *dīrēctus* DIRECT]
—Syn. 1. frock. DRESS, COSTUME, GOWN refer to the outer garment of women. DRESS is the general term, esp. for a garment such as is used not only for covering but for adornment: *a black dress; a summer dress; a becoming dress.* COSTUME is used of the style of dress appropriate to some occasion, purpose, period, or character, esp. as used on the stage, at balls, at court, or the like: *an 18th-century costume; an appropriate costume for the country; costumes worn at an important social event.* GOWN is usually applied to a dress more expensive and elegant than the ordinary, to be worn on a special occasion: *a wedding gown; an evening gown* (or *dress*). **2.** raiment, attire, clothes, habit, garments, vestments, habiliments. **9.** clothe, robe, garb.

dres·sage (drə säzh′; *Fr.* dre sazh′), *n.* **1.** See **haute école** (def. 1). **2.** the art or method of training a horse in obedience and in precision of movement. [< F, equiv. to *dress(er)* (to) DRESS + *-age* -AGE]

dress′ cir′cle, a circular or curving division of seats in a theater, opera house, etc., usually the first gallery, originally set apart for spectators in evening dress.

dress′ coat′. See **tail coat.** **—dress′-coat′ed,** *adj.*

dress·er[1] (dres′ər), *n.* **1.** one who dresses. **2.** one employed to dress actors, care for costumes, etc., at a theater, television studio, or the like. **3.** *Chiefly Brit.* **a.** one who dresses wounds, as an intern, nurse, or medical corpsman. **b.** a surgeon's assistant at a hospital operation. **4.** a person who dresses in a particular manner, as specified: *a fancy dresser; a careful and distinctive dresser.* **5.** any of several tools or devices used in dressing materials. **6.** *Metalworking.* **a.** a block, fitting into an anvil, on which pieces are forged. **b.** a mallet for shaping sheet metal. **7.** a tool for truing the surfaces of grinding wheels. [DRESS + -ER[1]]

dress·er[2] (dres′ər), *n.* **1.** a dressing table or bureau. **2.** a sideboard or set of shelves for dishes and cooking utensils. **3.** *Obs.* a table or sideboard on which food is dressed for serving. [ME *dresso(u)r* sideboard < AF; MF *dresseur*, OF *dreceor(e)*, equiv. to *dreci(er)* (to) DRESS + *-ore* -ORY[2] (F *dressoir*)]

dress′er set′, a set of toilet articles, as comb, brush, mirror, etc., usually of matching design for arrangement and use on a dresser or vanity.

dress′ goods′, cloth or material for dresses.

dress·ing (dres′ing), *n.* **1.** the act of one who or that which dresses. **2.** that with which something is dressed. **3.** a sauce for food: *salad dressing.* **4.** stuffing for a fowl: *turkey dressing.* **5.** material used to dress or cover a wound. **6.** manure, compost, or other fertilizers. **7.** *Archaic.* the ornamental detail of a building, esp. that around openings. [ME; see DRESS, -ING[1]]

dress′ing case′, a small piece of luggage for carrying toilet articles, medicine, etc.

dress′ing down′, **1.** a severe reprimand; scolding. **2.** a thrashing; beating.

dress′ing gown′, a tailored robe worn for lounging or for washing, shaving, applying make-up, etc.

dress′ing room′, a room for use in getting dressed, esp. backstage in a theater, television studio, etc.

dress′ing sack′, a woman's dressing gown.

dress′ing sta′tion, *Mil.* a post or center that gives first aid to the wounded, located near a combat area.

dress′ing ta′ble, **1.** a table or stand, usually surmounted by a mirror, in front of which a person sits while dressing, applying make-up, etc. **2.** *Chiefly Brit.* a side table, similar in appearance to a lowboy, having a shaped apron containing one or two rows of drawers.

Dress·ler (dres′lər), *n.* **Marie** (*Leila Koerber*), 1869–1934, U.S. actress, born in Canada.

dress·mak·er (dres′mā′kər), *n.* **1.** one whose occupation is the making of women's dresses, coats, etc. **—*adj.*** **2.** (of women's clothing) having soft, feminine lines or elaborate detail. Cf. **man-tailored, tailored.** [DRESS + MAKER] **—dress′mak′ing,** *n.*

dres·soir (dres wär′), *n., pl.* **dres·soirs** (dres wär′). *Fr. Furniture.* a cabinet of the 18th century, having a number of shallow shelves for dishes over a base with drawers and closed cupboards. [< F; see DRESSER[2]]

dress′ parade′, the formal, ceremonial parade at which soldiers in dress uniforms take formation under arms.

dress′ rehears′al, a rehearsal of a play in costume and with scenery, properties, and lights arranged and operated as for a performance, often the final rehearsal.

dress′ shield′, a fabric or plastic pad for attaching to the inside of the underarm of a woman's garment to protect the garment from being soiled by perspiration. Also called **shield.**

dress′ shirt′, **1.** a man's white shirt, usually having French cuffs and a stiff or pleated front to be fastened with studs, worn for semiformal or formal evening dress. **2.** a man's white or light-colored shirt, buttoning down the front and typically having long sleeves with barrel or French cuffs, and a soft or starched collar, worn with a necktie, esp. to business. Cf. **sport shirt.**

dress′ suit′, a man's suit for formal evening dress, with dress coat and open-front waistcoat.

dress′ u′niform, **1.** *U.S. Air Force.* a uniform consisting of the coat and trousers of the service uniform, with a white shirt and black bow tie, worn for formal occasions. **2.** *U.S. Army.* a blue uniform worn for formal occasions. **3.** *U.S. Navy.* a dark blue uniform worn in cool seasons or climates.

dress-up (dres′up′), *adj.* being an occasion, situation, etc., for which one must be somewhat formally well-dressed: *the first dress-up dinner of the season.* [adj. use of v. phrase *dress up*]

dress·y (dres′ē), *adj.,* **dress·i·er, dress·i·est.** *Informal.* **1.** showy in dress; stylish: *a rather dressy reception.* **2.** appropriate to somewhat formal occasions: *an outfit that's a little too dressy for office wear.* [DRESS + -Y[1]] **—dress′i·ly,** *adv.* **—dress′i·ness,** *n.*

drest (drest), *v. Obs.* a pt. and pp. of **dress.**

drew (drōō), *v.* pt. of **draw.**

Drew (drōō), *n.* **1. John,** 1827–62, U.S. actor, born in Ireland. **2.** his son, **John,** 1853–1927, U.S. actor. **3.** a boy's given name.

Drey·fus (drā′fəs, drī′-; *Fr.* drĕ fys′), *n.* **Al·fred** (al′frid; *Fr.* al fred′), 1859–1935, French army officer of Jewish descent: convicted of treason 1894, 1899; acquitted 1906.

Drey·fu·sard (drī′fə särd′, -zärd′, -fōō-, drā′-; drī′-fə särd′, -zärd′, -fōō-, drā′-), *n.* a defender or supporter of Alfred Dreyfus. [DREYFUS + -ARD]

drib (drib), *n.* **1.** *Dial.* a small amount, as of water; drop. **2.** a small or minute quantity; bit. [back formation from DRIBLET]

drib·ble (drib′əl), *v.,* **-bled, -bling,** *n.* **—*v.i.*** **1.** to fall or flow in drops or small quantities; trickle. **2.** to drivel; slaver. **3.** *Sports.* to advance a ball or puck by bouncing it or giving it a series of short kicks or pushes. **—*v.t.*** **4.** to let fall in drops. **5.** *Sports.* **a.** *Basketball.* to bounce (the ball) as in advancing or keeping control of it. **b.** (esp. in ice hockey and soccer) to move (the ball or puck) along by a rapid succession of short kicks or pushes. **—*n.*** **6.** a small trickling stream or a drop. **7.** a small quantity of anything: *a dribble of revenue.* **8.** the act or instance of dribbling a ball or puck. **9.** *Scot.* a drizzle; a light rain. [freq. of obs. *drib* (v.), prob. var. of DRIP] **—drib′bler,** *n.*

drib·let (drib′lit), *n.* **1.** a small portion or part. **2.** a small or petty sum. Also, **drib′blet.** [obs. *drib* (v.) (see DRIBBLE) + -LET]

dribs′ and drabs′, small and usually irregular amounts: *He repaid the loan in dribs and drabs.*

driech (drēKH), *adj., v.t. Scot. and North Eng.* dree. [var. of DRIEGH]

dried (drīd), *v.* pt. and pp. of **dry.**

dried′ milk′. See **dry milk.**

dried-up (drīd′up′), *adj.* **1.** depleted of moisture; gone dry: *a dried-up water hole.* **2.** shriveled with age; wizened: *a dried-up old mule skinner.*

driegh (drēKH), *adj., v.t. Scot. and North Eng.* dree. [ME *dregh*, etc., OE *(ge)drēog* patient, serious (of persons), tame (of animals); c. Icel *drjūgr* substantial, lasting, ample; akin to DREE]

dri·er[1] (drī′ər), *n.* **1.** one who or that which dries. **2.** any substance added to paints, varnishes, etc., to make them dry quickly. **3.** a mechanical appliance, contrivance, or apparatus for removing moisture, as by forced ventilation or by heat: *hair drier; clothes drier.* Also, **dryer.** [DRY + -ER[1]]

dri·er[2] (drī′ər), *adj.* comparative of **dry.**

dri·est (drī′ist), *adj.* superlative of **dry.**

drift (drift), *n.* **1.** a driving movement or force; impulse; impetus; pressure. **2.** *Navig.* (of a vessel) the component of the movement that is due to the force of wind and currents. **3.** *Phys. Geog.* a broad, shallow ocean current which advances at the rate of ten or fifteen miles a day. **4.** *Naut.* **a.** the flow or the speed in knots of an ocean current. **b.** the distance between the end of a rope and the part in use. **c.** the distance between two blocks in a tackle at any given time. **d.** the extreme distance possible between two blocks in a tackle. **e.** the difference in diameter between two parts, one of which fits within the other, as a mast and its mast hoops, or a treenail and its hole. **f.** a hance in the bulwarks of a wooden vessel, furnished with a carved, scroll-like piece **(drift′ piece′).** **5.** *Aeron.* the deviation of an aircraft from a set course due to cross winds. **6.** the course along which something moves; tendency; aim: *The drift of political events after the war was toward chaos.* **7.** a meaning; intent; purport: *the drift of a statement.* **8.** something driven, as animals, rain, etc. **9.** a heap of any matter driven together. **10.** a snowdrift. **11.** *Geol.* **a.** a deposit of detritus. **b.** the deposit of a continental ice sheet. **12.** the state or process of being driven. **13.** overbearing power or influence. **14.** *Mil.* a tool used in charging an ordnance piece. **15.** *Electronics.* **a.** a gradual change in some operating characteristic of a circuit, tube, or other electronic device, either during a brief period as an effect of warming up or during a long period as an effect of continued use. **b.** the movement of charge carriers in a semiconductor due to the influence of an applied voltage. **16.** *Mach.* **a.** Also called **driftpin.** a round, tapering piece of steel for enlarging holes in metal, or for bringing holes in line to receive rivets or bolts. **b.** a flat, tapered piece of steel used to drive tools with tapered shanks, as drill bits, from their holders. **17.** *Civ. Eng.* a secondary tunnel between two main tunnels or shafts. **18.** *Mining.* an approximately horizontal passageway in underground mining. **19.** *Physics.* the movement of ions influenced by an electric field. **20.** the gradual deviation of a rocket or guided missile from its intended trajectory. **21.** *Mech.* displacement of the gimbals of a gyroscope due to friction on bearings, unbalance of the gyroscope's mass, and other imperfections. **22.** the thrust of an arched structure. **23.** *Dentistry.* a shift of the teeth from their normal position in the dental arch. **24.** *Dial.* a flock of animals or birds. **—*v.i.*** **25.** to be carried along by currents of water or air, or by the force of circumstances. **26.** to wander aimlessly: *He drifts from town to town.* **27.** to be driven into heaps, as by the wind: *drifting sand.* **28.** to deviate or vary from a set course or adjustment. **—*v.t.*** **29.** to carry along: *The current drifted the boat to sea.* **30.** to drive into heaps: *The wind drifted the snow.* **31.** *Mach.* **a.** to enlarge (a punched or drilled hole) with a drift. **b.** to align or straighten (holes, esp. rivet holes) with a drift. [ME *drift*, verbal abstract of OE *drīfan* to DRIVE; c. D *drift* herd, flock, G *Trift* herd, pasturage, road to pasture] **—drift′ing·ly,** *adv.* **—drift′less,** *adj.* **—drift′less·ness,** *n.*
—Syn. 7. tenor. See **tendency.**

drift·age (drif′tij), *n.* **1.** the action or an amount of drifting. **2.** drifted matter. **3.** *Navig.* the amount of drift away from a set course as a result of wind and currents. **4.** windage. [DRIFT + -AGE]

drift′ an′chor, a sea anchor or drag.

drift′ an′gle, *Naut.* the angle made by the path of a drifting vessel with its heading.

drift′ boat′, drifter (def. 4).

drift·bolt (drift′bōlt′), *n.* **1.** Also called **driftpin.** a spike, having a round shank, for fastening heavy timbers together. **—*v.t.*** **2.** to fasten (timbers) together with a driftbolt. [DRIFT + BOLT[1]]

drift·er (drif′tər), *n.* **1.** one who or that which drifts. **2.** a person who goes from place to place, job to job, etc., remaining in each for a very short period. **3.** a tramp, hobo, or bum. **4.** Also called **drift boat.** a boat used in fishing with a drift net. [DRIFT + -ER[1]]

drift·fish (drift′fish′), *n., pl.* (*esp. collectively*) **-fish,** (*esp. referring to two or more kinds or species*) **-fish·es.** any of several butterfishes of the genus *Psenes*, found in tropical waters. [DRIFT + FISH]

drift′ ice′, detached floating ice in masses which drift with the wind or ocean currents, as in the polar seas.

drift′ in′dicator, *Aeron.* an instrument that indicates the amount of drift of an aircraft. Also called **drift′ me′ter, drift′ sight′.**

Drift′ing Cloud′, The, a novel (1887–89) by Shimei Futabatei. Also called **The Floating Cloud.** Japanese, **Uki Gumo.**

drift′ lead′ (led), *Naut.* a lead indicating, by the angle its line makes with the perpendicular, the movement of a supposedly stationary ship or the movement of water past a stationary ship.

drift′ map′, *Geol.* a map showing the distribution of glacial deposits.

drift′ net′, a fishing net supported upright in the water by floats attached along the upper edge and sinkers along the lower, so as to be carried with the current or tide.

drift′ net′ter, one who uses a drift net in fishing.

drift·pin (drift′pin′), *n.* **1.** driftbolt. **2.** drift (def. 16a). [DRIFT + PIN]

drift′ tube′, *Radio.* a conducting enclosure, usually cylindrical, held at a constant potential so that electrons or charged particles within will experience no force, and therefore no change in velocity. Cf. **Klystron** (def. 1).

drift·wood (drift′wŏŏd′), *n.* **1.** wood floating on or cast ashore by the water. **2.** such wood adapted for use in interior decoration. **—*adj.*** **3.** of, pertaining to, or made of driftwood: *a driftwood lamp.* [DRIFT + WOOD[1]]

drift·y (drif′tē), *adj.,* **drift·i·er, drift·i·est.** of the nature of or characterized by drifts. [DRIFT + -Y[1]]

drill[1] (dril), *n.* **1.** *Mach., Building Trades.* **a.** a shaftlike tool with two or more cutting edges for making holes in firm materials, esp. by rotation. **b.** a tool, esp. a hand tool, for holding and operating such a tool. **2.** *Mil.* **a.** training in formal marching or other precise military or naval movements. **b.** an exercise in such training: *gun drill.* **3.** any strict, methodical training, instruction, or exercise: *a drill in spelling.* **4.** *Chiefly Brit. Informal.* the correct or customary manner of proceeding. **5.** a gastropod, *Urosalpinx cinera*, destructive to oysters. **—*v.t.*** **6.** to pierce or bore a hole in (something). **7.** to make (a hole) by boring. **8.** *Mil.* to instruct and exercise in formation marching and movement, in the carrying of arms during formal marching, and in the formal handling of arms for ceremonies and guard work. **9.** to impart (knowledge) by strict training, discipline, or repetition. **—*v.i.*** **10.** to pierce or bore something with or as with a drill. **11.** to go through exercise in military or other training. [< D *dril* (n.), *drillen* (v.)] **—drill′a·ble,** *adj.* **—drill′er,** *n.*
—Syn. 3. See **exercise.**

drill[2] (dril), *n.* **1.** a small furrow made in the soil in which to sow seeds. **2.** a machine for sowing in rows and for covering the seeds when sown. **3.** a row of seeds or plants thus sown. —*v.t.* **4.** to sow (seed) in drills. **5.** to sow or plant (soil, a plot of ground, etc.) in drills. —*v.i.* **6.** to sow seed in drills. [cf. *drill* rill, G *Rille* furrow, *rillen* to groove] —**drill′er,** *n.*

drill[3] (dril), *n.* a strong, twilled cotton fabric. [short for DRILLING[2]]

drill[4] (dril), *n.* a baboon, *Papio leucophaeus*, of western Africa, smaller than the mandrill. [appar. native name; see MANDRILL]

drill′ bit′, bit[1] (defs. 3a, b).

drill′ chuck′, a chuck for holding a drill bit.

drill′ corps′. See **drill team.**

drill·ing[1] (dril′ing), *n.* act of one who or that which drills. [DRILL[1] + -ING[1]]

drill·ing[2] (dril′ing), *n.* drill[3]. [alter. of G *Drillich*, itself alter. of L *trilīx* triple-twilled (G *dri-* three r. L *tri-*)]

drill′ing mud′, a water-based or oil-based suspension of clays pumped into an oil well during drilling in order to seal off porous rock layers, equalize the pressure, cool the bit, and flush out the cuttings. Also called **drill′ing flu′id.**

drill·mas·ter (dril′mas′tər, -mä′stər), *n.* **1.** a person who trains others in anything, esp. routinely or mechanically. **2.** *Mil.* one who instructs in marching drill.

drill′ pipe′, (in oil-well drilling or the like) any of several coupled tubes for rotating the bit and supplying drilling mud.

drill′ press′, a drilling machine having a single vertical spindle.

drill·stock (dril′stok′), *n.* a device for holding a drill. [DRILL[1] + STOCK]

drill′ team′, a group trained, esp. for exhibition purposes, in precision marching, manual of arms, etc. Also called **drill corps.**

drill′ tow′er, a structure, usually of concrete and steel, that resembles a building and is used by firemen for practicing and improving fire-fighting techniques.

dri·ly (drī′lē), *adv.* dryly.

Drin (drēn), *n.* a river in S Europe, flowing generally NW from SW Macedonia through N Albania into the Adriatic. 180 mi. long.

Dri·na (drē′nə, -nä), *n.* a river in SE Europe, flowing N along the border between Serbia and Bosnia and Herzegovina to the Sava River. 160 mi. long.

drink (dringk), *v.*, **drank** or (*Nonstandard*) **drunk; drunk** or, often, **drank; drink·ing;** *n.* —*v.i.* **1.** to take water or other liquid into the mouth and swallow it; imbibe. **2.** to imbibe alcoholic liquors, esp. habitually or to excess; tipple: *He never drinks.* **3.** to show one's respect, affection, or hopes with regard to a person, thing, or event by ceremoniously taking a swallow of wine or some other drink (often fol. by *to*). —*v.t.* **4.** to take into the mouth and swallow (a liquid). **5.** to take in (a liquid) in any manner; absorb. **6.** to take in through the senses, esp. with eagerness and pleasure (often fol. by *in*): *He drank in the beauty of the scene.* **7.** to swallow the contents of (a cup, glass, etc.). **8.** to drink to (a person, thing, or event): *to drink one's health.* —*n.* **9.** any liquid which is swallowed to quench thirst, for nourishment, etc.; beverage. **10.** alcoholic liquor. **11.** excessive indulgence in alcoholic liquor: *Drink was his downfall.* **12.** a draft of liquid; potion: *He took a drink of water before he spoke.* **13.** a large body of water, as a lake, ocean, river, etc. (usually prec. by *the*): *His teammates threw him in the drink.* [ME *drinke(n)*, OE *drincan*; c. D *drinken*, G *trinken*, Goth *drinkan*, Icel *drekka*]
—**Syn. 2.** tope. **4.** quaff. DRINK, IMBIBE, SIP refer to swallowing liquids. DRINK is the general word: *to drink coffee.* IMBIBE is more formal and today is hardly used in reference to actual drinking except facetiously; it is used figuratively in the meaning to absorb: *to imbibe culture.* SIP implies drinking little by little, at short, succeeding intervals, often in a delicate, toying or idle manner: *to sip a cup of broth.* **8.** toast.

drink·a·ble (dring′kə bəl), *adj.* **1.** suitable for drinking. —*n.* **2.** Usually, **drinkables.** substances that are drinkable; liquids for drinking. [DRINK + -ABLE] —**drink′a·bil′i·ty, drink′a·ble·ness,** *n.* —**drink′a·bly,** *adv.*

drink·er (dring′kər), *n.* **1.** one who drinks. **2.** one who drinks alcoholic liquors habitually or to excess. [ME *drinkere*, OE *drincere*. See DRINK, -ER[1]]

drink·ing (dring′king), *adj.* **1.** suitable or safe to drink: *drinking water.* **2.** used in drinking: *drinking glass.* **3.** addicted to or indulging excessively in alcoholic liquor: *Is he a drinking man?* **4.** of or pertaining to the act of drinking: *a drinking companion.* —*n.* **5.** habitual and excessive consumption of alcoholic liquor: *His drinking caused him to lose his job.* [ME; see DRINK, -ING[2], -ING[1]]

drink′ing foun′tain, a water fountain which ejects a jet of water for drinking without a cup.

drink′ing song′, a song of hearty character suitable for singing by a group engaged in convivial drinking.

Drink·wa·ter (dringk′wô′tər, -wot′ər), *n.* **John,** 1882–1937, English poet, playwright, and critic.

drip (drip), *v.*, **dripped** or **dript, drip·ping,** *n.* —*v.i.* **1.** to let drops fall; shed drops. **2.** to fall in drops, as a liquid. —*v.t.* **3.** to let fall in drops. —*n.* **4.** the act of dripping. **5.** the liquid that drips. **6.** the sound made by falling drops: *the irritating drip of a faucet.* **7.** *Slang.* an unattractive, colorless person. **8.** (in house painting) the accumulation of solidified drops of paint at the bottom of a painted surface. **9.** *Archit., Building Trades.* any device, as a molding, for shedding rain water to keep it from running down a wall, falling onto the sill of an opening, etc. **10.** a pipe for draining off excess water, as condensed steam from radiators. **11.** a pipe for draining condensed steam from a heat exchanger. **12.** Also called **intravenous drip.** *Med.* the continuous, slow introduction of a fluid into a vein of the body. **13.** *Slang.* maudlin sentimentality. [ME *dryppe*, OE *drypp(an)*, denominative of *dropa* DROP]

drip′ cap′, *Carpentry.* a molding over an opening for catching and shedding rain water.

drip′ cof′fee, a beverage prepared in a vessel **(dripolator)** in which boiling water filters from a top compartment through the coffee into a pot below.

drip-dry (*adj.* drip′drī′; *v.* drip′drī′, -drī′), *adj.*, *v.* **-dried, -dry·ing.** —*adj.* **1.** See **wash and wear.** —*v.i.* **2.** (of a cloth item) to dry into its desired form and shape when hung dripping wet after washing. —*v.t.* **3.** to hang (a cloth item) after washing while it is dripping wet and allow it to dry, esp. in anticipation of its assuming its desired form and shape during the drying process.

drip′ grind′, finely ground coffee beans, used in making drip coffee.

drip·o·la·tor (drip′ə lā′tər), *n.* See under **drip coffee.** [DRIP + (PERC)OLATOR]

drip·page (drip′ij), *n.* **1.** a dripping, as of water from a faucet. **2.** an amount formed by dripping: *emptying the drippage from under the icebox.* [DRIP + -AGE]

drip′ pan′, **1.** a pan, tray, etc., for collecting liquid waste: *Put a drip pan under the crankcase.* **2.** See **dripping pan.**

drip·ping (drip′ing), *n.* **1.** the act of anything that drips. **2.** Often, **drippings. a.** the liquid that drips. **b.** fat and juices exuded from meat in cooking, used for basting, for making gravy, or as a cooking fat. [ME; see DRIP, -ING[1]]

drip′ping pan′, a shallow metal pan used under roasting meat to receive the dripping. Also, **drip pan.**

drip·py (drip′ē), *adj.* **-pi·er, -pi·est. 1.** dripping or tending to drip: *a drippy faucet.* **2.** tending to be rainy, wet, or drizzly: *a hot, drippy country; drippy weather.* **3.** *Informal.* revoltingly sentimental; mawkish: *another drippy love story.* [DRIP + -Y[1]]

drip·stone (drip′stōn′), *n.* **1.** *Archit.* a stone molding used as a drip. **2.** calcium carbonate, $CaCO_3$, occurring in the form of stalactites and stalagmites. [DRIP + STONE]

drive (drīv), *v.*, **drove** or (*Archaic*) **drave; driv·en; driv·ing;** *n.*; *adj.* —*v.t.* **1.** to send, expel, or otherwise cause to move by force or compulsion (often fol. by *along, away, off, in, out, back,* etc.): *to drive away the flies; to drive back an attacking army; to drive someone to desperation.* **2.** to force to work or act: *He drove the workers until they collapsed.* **3.** to cause and guide the movement of (a vehicle, an animal, etc.): *to drive a car; to drive a mule.* **4.** to convey in a vehicle: *He drove her to the station.* **5.** to keep (machinery) going. **6.** to impel; constrain; urge; compel. **7.** to carry (business, an agreement, etc.) vigorously through: *He drove a hard bargain.* **8.** (in mining, construction, etc.) to dig (a mine shaft, tunnel, etc.) in a more or less horizontal direction. **9.** *Sports.* **a.** to hit or propel (a ball, puck, shuttlecock, etc.) very hard. **b.** to kick (a ball) with much force. **10.** *Golf.* to hit (a golf ball), esp. from the tee, with a driver or driving iron: *He drove the ball within ten feet of the pin.* **11.** *Baseball.* **a.** to cause the advance of (a base runner) by a base hit or sacrifice fly. **b.** to cause (a run) to be scored by a base hit or sacrifice fly: *He drove him home with a scratch single.* **12.** *Hunting.* **a.** to chase (game). **b.** to search (a district) for game. **13.** to float (logs) down a river or stream. —*v.i.* **14.** to go along before an impelling force; be impelled: *The ship drove before the wind.* **15.** to rush or dash violently. **16.** to cause and guide the movement of a vehicle or animal. **17.** to go or travel in a driven vehicle: *He drives to work with me.* **18.** *Golf.* to hit a golf ball, esp. from the tee, as with a driver or driving iron: *He drove long and straight throughout the match.* **19.** to strive vigorously toward a goal or objective; to work, play, or try wholeheartedly and with determination. **20. drive at,** to attempt or intend to convey; allude to; suggest: *What is he driving at?* **21. let drive,** to aim a blow or missile at; attack: *He let drive at his pursuers.* —*n.* **22.** the act of driving. **23.** a trip in a vehicle, esp. a short, pleasure trip: *a Sunday drive in the country.* **24.** an impelling along, as of game, cattle, or floating logs, in a particular direction. **25.** the animals, logs, etc., thus driven. **26.** *Psychol.* an inner urge that stimulates a response, inciting or repressing action; a basic or instinctive need: *the hunger drive; sex drive.* **27.** a vigorous onset or onward course toward a goal or objective: *the drive toward the goal line.* **28.** a strong military offensive. **29.** a united effort to accomplish some specific purpose, esp. to raise money, as for a charity. **30.** energy and initiative: *a person with great drive.* **31.** vigorous pressure or effort, as in business. **32.** a road for vehicles, esp. a scenic one, as in or along a park, or a short one, as an approach to a house. **33.** *Mach.* a driving mechanism, as of an automobile: *gear drive; chain drive.* **34.** *Auto.* the point or points of power application to the roadway: *front drive; four-wheel drive.* **35.** *Electronics.* excitation (def. 5). **36.** *Sports.* **a.** the act or an instance of driving a ball, puck, shuttlecock, or the like. **b.** the flight of such a ball, puck, shuttlecock, or the like, that has been driven with much force. **37.** *Golf.* a shot, esp. with a driver or driving iron from the tee, that is intended to carry a great distance. **38.** a hunt in which game is driven toward stationary hunters. **39.** *Type Founding.* strike (def. 84). —*adj.* **40.** noting or pertaining to a part of a machine or vehicle used for its propulsion. [ME *drive(n)*, OE *drīfan*; c. D *drijven*, Icel *drīfa*, Goth *dreiban*, G *treiben*] —**driv′a·ble, drive′a·ble,** *adj.*
—**Syn. 1.** push, force. **17.** DRIVE, RIDE are used interchangeably to mean taking a trip in a private horse-drawn vehicle or an automobile. These two words are not synonyms in other connections. To DRIVE is to guide or steer the progress of a vehicle, animal, etc.: *to drive a bus, a truck, an automobile, a horse, oxen.* To RIDE is to sit on the back of, and be carried about by, an animal, or to be carried as a passenger in a vehicle: *to ride a horse, a train, a bus, a public conveyance.* **31.** energy. —**Ant. 1.** lead.

drive′ fit′. See **press fit.**

drive-in (drīv′in′), *n.* **1.** a motion-picture theater, refreshment stand, bank, etc., designed to accommodate patrons in their automobiles. —*adj.* **2.** of, pertaining to, or characteristic of such an establishment or its provision of service to patrons in automobiles: *Drive-in business far exceeded walk-in business.* [n., adj. use of *drive in*]

driv·el (driv′əl), *v.*, **-eled, -el·ing** or (*esp. Brit.*) **-elled, -el·ling,** *n.* —*v.i.* **1.** to let saliva flow from the mouth or mucus from the nose; slaver. **2.** to talk childishly or idiotically. **3.** *Archaic.* to issue like spittle. —*v.t.* **4.** to utter childishly or idiotically. **5.** to waste foolishly. —*n.* **6.** saliva flowing from the mouth, or mucus from the nose; slaver. **7.** childish, silly, or meaningless talk or thinking; nonsense; twaddle. [ME *dryvele*, var. of *drevele(n)*, OE *dreflian*; akin to DRAFF] —**driv′el·er;** *esp. Brit.*, **driv′el·ler,** *n.* —**driv′el·ing·ly;** *esp. Brit.*, **driv′el·ling·ly,** *adv.*

driv·en (driv′ən), *v.* pp. of **drive.**

driv·er (drī′vər), *n.* **1.** one who or that which drives. **2.** a person who drives a vehicle; coachman, chauffeur, etc. **3.** a person who drives an animal or animals, as a drover or cowboy. **4.** *Brit.* a locomotive engineer. **5.** *Mach.* **a.** a part transmitting force or motion. **b.** the member of a pair of connected pulleys, gears, etc., nearest the power source. **6.** See **driving wheel** (def. 2). **7.** *Golf.* a club with a wooden head whose face has almost no slope, for hitting long, low drives from the tee. Also called **number one wood. 8.** *Naut.* **a.** a jib-headed spanker sail. **b.** a designation given to one of the masts abaft the mizzen on a sailing vessel having more than three masts, either the fifth or sixth from forward. Cf. **pusher** (def. 3), **spanker** (def. 1b). —*adj.* *Naut.* **9.** noting or pertaining to a driver mast. **10.** noting or pertaining to a sail, yard, boom, etc., or to any rigging belonging to a driver lower mast or to some upper mast of a driver mast. **11.** noting any stay running aft and upward to the head of a driver lower mast or of some specified upper mast of a driver mast: *driver topmast stay.* [ME *drivere*. See DRIVE, -ER[1]] —**driv′er·less,** *adj.*

driv′er ant′. See **army ant.**

driv′er's seat′, **1.** the position of power, dominance, control, or superiority, as in a situation, dispute, governing body, etc.: *After the election the Democrats were back in the driver's seat.* **2.** the seat or position from which a vehicle is operated.

drive′ screw′, a fastener with a helical thread of coarse pitch that can be driven into wood with a hammer and removed with a screw driver. Also called **screw nail.** See illus. under **nail.**

drive′ shaft′, *Mach.* a shaft for imparting torque from a power source or prime mover to machinery. See diag. under **differential.**

drive·way (drīv′wā′), *n.* **1.** a road, esp. a private one, leading from a street or other thoroughfare to a building, house, garage, etc. **2.** any road for driving on. [DRIVE + WAY]

driv·ing (drī′ving), *adj.* **1.** demanding a high or unreasonable rate of work from subordinates. **2.** energetic; vigorously active: *a driving young salesman.* **3.** having force and violence: *a driving storm.* **4.** relaying or transmitting power. **5.** used while operating a vehicle: *driving gloves.* [ME; see DRIVE, -ING[2]] —**driv′ing·ly,** *adv.*

driv′ing bar′rel, (in a weight-driven clock) the drum turned by the descent of the weight, which drives the clock mechanism.

driv′ing dog′, (on a lathe) a clamp securing a piece of work and engaging with a slot in a faceplate.

driv′ing i′ron, *Golf.* a club with a long shaft and an iron head the face of which has almost no slope, for hitting long, low drives. Also called **number one iron.**

driv′ing range′, *Golf.* a tract of land for practicing golf shots, esp. drives, with clubs and balls rented from the management.

driv′ing sail′, *Naut.* a sail that, when filled, tends to force the hull of a vessel downward (opposed to *lifting sail*).

driv′ing wheel′, **1.** *Mach.* a main wheel which communicates motion to others. **2.** Also called **driver.** *Railroads.* one of the wheels of a locomotive transmitting the power of an engine or motor into tractive effort.

driz·zle (driz′əl), *v.*, **-zled, -zling,** *n.* —*v.t.*, *v.i.* **1.** to rain gently and steadily in fine drops; sprinkle (often used impersonally with *it* as subject): *It drizzled throughout the night.* —*n.* **2.** a very light rain. **3.** *Meteorol.* precipitation consisting of numerous, minute droplets of water less than 1/50 inch in diameter. [? back formation from *dryseling*, dissimilated var. of ME *drysning* fall (of dew); akin to OE *drēosan* to fall; c. OS *driosan*, Goth *driusan*] —**driz′zly,** *adv.*

Dr. Jekyll and Mr. Hyde, (*The Strange Case of Dr. Jekyll and Mr. Hyde*) a novel (1886) by Robert Louis Stevenson.

Drog·he·da (drô′i də), *n.* a seaport in the NE Republic of Ireland, near the mouth of the Boyne River: the town was captured and its inhabitants massacred by Cromwell 1649. 17,085 (1961).

dro·gher (drō′gər), *n.* a freight barge of the West Indies, rigged as a cutter or schooner. [< D *drog(h)er* ship for fishing and drying herring and mackerel, equiv. to *drog(en)* to DRY + *-er* -ER[1]]

drogue (drōg), *n.* **1.** a bucket or canvas bag used as a sea anchor. **2.** *Aeron.* a funnel-shaped device attached to the end of a hose on a tanker aircraft for connecting with the probe of another aircraft to be refueled in flight. [earlier *drug*, common dial. var. of DRAG]

droit (droit; *Fr.* DRWA), *n.*, *pl.* **droits** (droits; *Fr.* DRWA). **1.** a legal right or claim. **2.** the body of rules constituting the law. **3. droits,** *Finance. Rare.* customs duties. [< F < LL *dīrēct(um)* legal right, law (n. use of neut. of *dīrēctus* DIRECT)]

droit des gens (DRWA dā zhäN′), *pl.* **droits des gens** (DRWA dā zhäN′). *French.* law of nations; international law.

droit du sei·gneur (*Fr.* DRWA dY se nyœR′), the supposed right claimable by a feudal lord to have sexual relations with the bride of a vassal on their first night of marriage. [< F: lit., right of the lord]

droi·tu·ral (droi′chər əl), *adj.* *Law.* pertaining to right of ownership as distinguished from right of possession. [< F *droiture* equity, uprightness (see DROIT, -URE) + -AL[1]]

droll (drōl), *adj.* **1.** amusing in an odd way; whimsically humorous; waggish. —*n.* **2.** a droll person; jester; wag. —*v.i.* **3.** *Archaic.* to play the droll or wag; jest; joke. [< MF *drolle* pleasant rascal < MD *drol* a fat little man] —**droll′ness,** *n.* —**drol′ly,** *adv.*
—**Syn. 1.** diverting, odd, witty. See **amusing. 2, 3.** clown. —**Ant. 1.** serious.

droll·er·y (drō′lə rē), *n.*, *pl.* **-er·ies. 1.** something whimsically amusing or funny. **2.** an oddly amusing story or jest. **3.** a droll quality or manner; whimsical humor. **4.** the action or behavior of a droll, waggish person; jesting. **5.** *Archaic.* a comic picture. **6.** *Archaic.* a puppet show. [DROLL + -ERY; cf. F *drôlerie*]

Drôme (drōm), *n.* a department in SE France. 304,227 (1962); 2533 sq. mi. *Cap.:* Valence.

-drome, a suffix occurring in loan words from Greek, meaning "running," "course," "race course," (*hippodrome*); on this model used to refer to other large structures (*airdrome*). [comb. form of Gk *drómos* DROMOS]

Dromedary (6 ft. high at shoulder; length 9½ ft.)

drom·e·dar·y (drom′i der′ē, drum′-), *n., pl.* **-dar·ies.** the single-humped camel, *Camelus dromedarius,* of Arabia and northern Africa. [ME *dromedarie, -ary* < LL *dromedāri(us)* (*camelus*) < Gk *dromad-* (s. of *dromás*) running + L *-ārius* -ARY]

drom·ond (drom′ənd, drum′-), *n.* a large, fast-sailing vessel of the Middle Ages. Also, **drom·on** (drom′ən, drum′-). [ME *dromund* < AF << Gk *drómōn* swift ship, deriv. of *drómos* a running]

drom·os (drom′əs, -os; drō′məs, -mos), *n., pl.* **drom·oi** (drom′oi, drō′moi). **1.** *Archaeol.* a passageway into an ancient subterranean tomb. **2.** a race track in ancient Greece. [< Gk *drómos* a running, course, place for running]

-dromous, a word element used to form adjectives from nouns ending in **-drome.** [-DROME + -OUS]

drone[1] (drōn), *n.* **1.** the male of the honeybee and other bees, stingless and making no honey. See illus. under **bee. 2.** one who lives on the labor of others; parasitic loafer. **3.** a remote control mechanism, as a radio-controlled airplane or boat. [ME *drone, drane,* OE *dran, dron;* akin to OHG *treno,* G *Drohne*] —**dron′ish,** *adj.*

drone[2] (drōn), *v.,* **droned, dron·ing,** *n.* —*v.i.* **1.** to make a dull, continued, monotonous sound; hum; buzz. **2.** to speak in a monotonous tone. —*v.t.* **3.** to say in a dull, monotonous tone. —*n.* **4.** *Music.* **a.** a continuous low tone produced by the bass pipes or bass strings of musical instruments. **b.** the pipes (esp. of the bagpipe) or strings producing this tone. **c.** a bagpipe equipped with such pipes. **5.** a monotonous tone; humming or buzzing sound. **6.** one who speaks in a monotonous tone. [see DRONE[1] and cf. ME *droun* to roar, Icel *drynja* to bellow, Goth *drunjus* noise] —**dron′ing·ly,** *adv.*

dron·go (drong′gō), *n., pl.* **-gos.** any of several passerine birds of the family *Dicruridae,* of Africa and Asia, usually having black plumage and long, forked tails. [< Malagasy]

drool (dro͞ol), *v.i.* **1.** to water at the mouth, as in anticipation of food. **2.** to show excessive pleasure or anticipation of pleasure. **3.** to talk foolishly. —*n.* **4.** drivel. [var. of *driule,* itself var. of DRIVEL]

drool·y (dro͞o′lē), *adj.,* **drool·i·er, drool·i·est. 1.** drooling, tending to drool, or covered with drool. **2.** *Slang.* exceptionally pleasing. [DROOL + -Y[1]]

droop (dro͞op), *v.i.* **1.** to sag, sink, bend, or hang down, as from weakness, exhaustion, or lack of support. **2.** *Literary.* to sink; descend, as the sun. **3.** to fall into a state of physical weakness; flag; fail. **4.** to lose spirit or courage. —*v.t.* **5.** to let sink or drop: *an eagle drooping its wings.* —*n.* **6.** a sagging, sinking, bending, or hanging down, as from weakness, exhaustion, or lack of support. [ME *drupe(n), drowpe(n)* < Icel *drūpa;* akin to DROP] —**droop′i·ness,** *n.* —**droop′ing·ly,** *adv.*
—**Syn. 1.** flag, languish. **3.** weaken, decline, faint, wilt, wither, fade.

droop·y (dro͞o′pē), *adj.,* **droop·i·er, droop·i·est. 1.** hanging down; sagging. **2.** lacking in spirit or courage; disheartened; dejected. [DROOP + -Y[1]]

drop (drop), *n., v.,* **dropped** or **dropt, drop·ping.** —*n.* **1.** a small quantity of liquid that falls or is produced in a more or less spherical mass; a liquid globule. **2.** the quantity of liquid contained in such a globule. **3.** a very small quantity of liquid: *I'll have a little tea, just a drop.* **4.** a minute quantity of anything: *not even a drop of mercy* **5.** Usually, **drops. a.** liquid medicine given in a dose or form of globules from a medicine dropper. **b.** a solution for dilating the pupils of the eyes, administered to the eyes in globules by a medicine dropper. **6.** *Informal.* a more or less limited amount of an alcoholic beverage: *He occasionally takes a drop after dinner.* **7.** something resembling or likened to a liquid globule, as certain ornaments, a spherical earring, etc. **8.** a small, usually spherical, piece of candy; lozenge: *a lemon drop.* **9.** a pendant. **10.** *Archit.* gutta (def. 2). **11.** *Furniture.* an applied ornament resembling a pendant. **12.** the act or an instance of dropping; fall; descent. **13.** the distance or depth to which anything drops: *a 10-foot drop.* **14.** a steep slope: *a short drop to the lake.* **15.** that which drops or is used for dropping. **16.** a central depository where items are left or transmitted: *a mail drop.* **17.** a decline in amount, degree, quality, value, etc.: *a drop in prices.* **18.** *Mil.* **a.** a group of men dropped by parachute in one military action. **b.** an instance of dropping supplies or an amount of supplies dropped by parachute during one action. **c.** a descent by parachute. **19.** *Theat.* **a.** See **drop curtain. b.** See **drop scene. 20.** See **trap door. 21.** a gallows. **22.** a slit or opening into which something can be dropped, as a mailbox. **23.** a small flag, usually of enameled metal, that gives a visual signal in an annunciator. **24.** *Naut.* the vertical dimension amidships of any sail that is bent to a standing yard. Cf. **hoist** (def. 6a). **25.** Also called **drop panel.** (in reinforced-concrete-slab construction) a thickened portion of the ceiling around a column head. **26.** *Horol.* the free motion of an escape wheel between successive checks by the pallet. **27.** the newborn young of an animal. **28. at the drop of a hat,** at the slightest provocation or without delay: *He used to fight at the drop of a hat.* **29. get** or **have the drop on,** *Informal.* **a.** to aim and be ready to shoot a gun at an antagonist before he can draw his gun. **b.** to get or have at a disadvantage. [ME *droppe* (< v.); r. ME *drope,* OE *dropa;* c. Icel *dropi*] —*v.i.* **30.** to fall in globules or small portions, as water or other liquid: *Rain drops from the clouds.* **31.** to fall vertically; have an abrupt descent. **32.** to sink or fall to the ground, floor, or bottom as if inanimate. **33.** to fall wounded, dead, etc.: *A thousand men dropped in the battle.* **34.** to come to an end; cease; lapse: *There the matter dropped.* **35.** to withdraw; quit: *to drop from a race; He chose to drop rather than call the last bet.* **36.** to cease to appear or be seen; vanish: *to drop from sight or notice.* **37.** to squat or crouch, as a dog at the sight of game. **38.** to fall lower in condition, degree, value, etc.; sink; diminish or lessen: *The prices dropped sharply.* **39.** to pass or enter without effort into some condition, activity, or the like: *to drop asleep; to drop into a habit.* **40.** to move gently, as with the tide or a light wind (usually fol. by *down*). **41.** to fall or move to a position that is lower, farther back, inferior, etc.: *to drop back in line; to drop to the rear.* **42.** to make an unexpected or unannounced stop at a place; pay an informal visit or call (usually fol. by *in, by,* or *over*): *Since we're in the neighborhood anyway, why don't we drop in at my brother's house?* —*v.t.* **43.** to let fall in drops or small portions: *to drop lemon juice into tea.* **44.** to let or cause to fall. **45.** to cause or allow to sink to a lower position. **46.** to cause to decrease in value, amount, quality, etc.; reduce. **47.** to utter or express casually or incidentally: *to drop a hint.* **48.** to send or mail (a note, message, etc.): *Drop me a line.* **49.** to bring to the ground by a blow or shot. **50.** to set down or unload, as from a ship, car, etc.: *Drop me at the corner.* **51.** to omit (a letter or syllable) in pronunciation or writing: *He dropped his h's.* **52.** to lower (the voice) in pitch or loudness. **53.** to cease to keep up or have to do with: *I dropped the subject. She dropped her old friends when she married money.* **54.** to cease to employ; to dismiss. **55.** *Sports.* **a.** to throw, shoot, hit, kick, or roll (a ball, puck, etc.) through or into a basket, hole, or other goal: *He dropped the ball through the basket for two points.* **b.** to lose (a game or contest): *Ohio State dropped two games in a row and was eliminated from the tournament.* **56.** *Football.* **a.** to drop-kick (a ball). **b.** to score with a drop kick. **57.** (of animals) to give birth to: *The cat dropped a litter of six kittens.* **58.** to parachute (men, supplies, etc.): *The Marines dropped 300 combat troops into the jungle battlefield.* **59.** to lengthen by lowering or letting out: *to drop the hem of a skirt.* **60.** to lower (the wheels) into position for landing an airplane. **61.** *Naut.* to outdistance; pass out of sight of. **62.** *Cookery.* to poach (an egg). **63. drop behind,** to fall short of the required pace or progress: *Her long illness caused her to drop behind the rest of the class.* **64. drop off, a.** to fall asleep. **b.** to decrease; decline: *Sales have dropped off drastically.* [ME *dropp(en),* OE *droppian*] —**drop′like′,** *adj.*

drop′ arch′, 1. Also called **depressed arch.** a pointed arch having radii of length less than the span. **2.** Also called **surbased arch.** an arch having a rise of less than half its span.

drop′ bis′cuit, a biscuit made by dropping baking powder biscuit dough from a spoon onto a pan for baking.

drop′ black′, *Chem.* carbon, as animal black or lampblack, formed into pellets by mixing with water or glue.

drop′ box′, *Textiles.* a box for holding shuttles on a loom, used on either side of the race plate in weaving cloth having a variety of colors in the filling.

drop′ cloth′, a sheet of cloth, paper, plastic, or the like, laid over furniture, a floor, etc., for protection while the room is being painted.

drop′ cook′y, a cooky made by dropping batter from a spoon onto a greased cooky sheet for baking.

drop′ cur′tain, *Theat.* a curtain that is lowered into position from the flies.

drop′ el′bow, (in plumbing) an elbow having lugs for attaching it to a wall or joist. Also called **drop′ ell′.**

drop′ forge′, a device for making large forgings in which a heavy object is allowed to fall vertically upon a piece of work placed on an anvil or between dies. Also called **drop hammer, drop press.**

drop-forge (drop′fōrj′, -fôrj′), *v.t.,* **-forged, -forg·ing.** *Metalworking.* to form in a drop forge. —**drop′-forg′er,** *n.*

drop′ forg′ing, a drop-forged object.

drop′ front′, *Furniture.* See **fall front.**

drop′ girt′, *Carpentry.* a girt running beneath the ends of joists and at right angles to them. Also, **dropped′ girt′.** Cf. **flush girt.**

drop′ ham′mer. See **drop forge.**

drop′ ini′tial, *Print.* See **inset initial.**

drop′ keel′, *Naut.* centerboard.

drop′ kick′, *Football.* a kick made by dropping a football to the ground and kicking it as it starts to bounce up. Cf. **place kick, punt**[1] (def. 1).

drop-kick (drop′kik′), *Football.* —*v.t.* **1.** to score (a field goal or point after touchdown) by a drop kick. **2.** to kick (the ball as dropped for a drop kick). —*v.i.* **3.** to make a drop kick. —**drop′-kick′er,** *n.*

drop′ leaf′, *Furniture.* an extension attached to the end or side of a table and folded vertically when not needed. —**drop′-leaf′,** *adj.*

drop·let (drop′lit), *n.* a little drop. [DROP + -LET]

drop′ let′ter, *U.S.* a letter to be delivered from or by the same post office in which it is posted.

drop·light (drop′līt′), *n.* an electric or gas lamp suspended from the ceiling or wall by a flexible cord or tube. [DROP + LIGHT[1]]

drop·line (drop′līn′), *n.* *Journalism.* a headline or bank consisting of a top line set flush with the left margin, with each succeeding line indented on the left, and the final line flush with the right margin. Also called **stagger head, staggered head, stephead, stepped line.** [DROP + LINE[1]]

drop-off (drop′ôf′, -of′), *n.* **1.** a vertical or very steep descent: *The trail has a drop-off of several hundred feet.* **2.** a decline; decrease: *Sales have shown a considerable drop-off.* [n. use of v. phrase *drop off*]

drop·out (drop′out′), *n.* **1.** an act or instance of dropping out. **2.** a student who withdraws before completing a course of instruction. **3.** a person who withdraws from high school after having reached the legal age to do so. **4.** *Rugby.* a drop kick made by a defending team from within its own 25-yard line as a result of a touchdown or of the ball's having touched or gone outside of a touch-in-goal line or the dead-ball line. **5.** Also called **facsimile, highlight halftone.** a halftone negative or plate in which dots have been eliminated from highlights by continued etching, burning in, opaquing, or the like. Also, **drop′-out′.** [n. use of v. phrase *drop out*]

drop·page (drop′ij), *n.* **1.** an amount dropped or wasted during application, installation, etc.: *Mix some extra plaster to allow for droppage.* **2.** the amount of fruit that falls from a tree before ripening: *Storms greatly increased the droppage this year.* [DROP + -AGE]

drop′ pan′el, drop (def. 25).

dropped′ scone′, scone (def. 3).

dropped′ seat′, a seat of a chair or the like, having a front dished so as to be lower than the sides or back. Also called **scoop seat.**

drop·per (drop′ər), *n.* **1.** one who or that which drops. **2.** a glass tube with a hollow rubber bulb at one end and a small orifice at the other, for drawing in a liquid and expelling it in drops; medicine dropper. **3.** a short-haired dog that is a cross between a pointer and a setter. [DROP + -ER[1]]

drop·ping (drop′ing), *n.* **1.** the act of one who or that which drops. **2.** that which drops or falls in drops. **3.** **droppings,** dung of animals. [ME; OE *droppung.* See DROP, -ING[1]]

drop′ping bot′tle, a bottle with correlated lengthwise grooves in the neck and in the stopper permitting a controlled flow of the liquid contents in the form of drops.

drop′ press′. See **drop forge.**

drop′ rud′der, *Naut.* a rudder that can be lowered beneath the level of the bottom of a boat.

drop′ scene′, *Theat.* **1.** a drop curtain, often of painted or dyed canvas, located downstage and used as the backdrop for a scene played while the set upstage is being changed. **2.** a scene or act played with less intensity than the preceding one. **3.** the last scene of an act or play.

drop′ ship′ment, *Com.* a shipment of goods made directly from the manufacturer to the retailer but billed through the wholesaler or distributor.

drop′ ship′per, a wholesaler or distributor who conducts business in drop shipments. Also called **desk jobber.**

drop′ shot′, 1. shot made in a shot tower. **2.** (in tennis, badminton, etc.) a ball or shuttlecock so softly hit that it falls to the playing surface just after clearing the net. **3.** (in squash, handball, etc.) a ball so softly hit that it falls suddenly to the ground just after striking the front wall.

drop·si·cal (drop′si kəl), *adj.* of, like, or affected with dropsy. [DROPS(Y) + -ICAL] —**drop′si·cal·ly,** *adv.* —**drop′si·cal·ness,** *n.*

drop′ sid′ing, weatherboarding having its upper edges narrowed to fit into grooves or rabbets in its lower edges, and its backs flat against the sheathing or studs of the wall. Also called **novelty siding.** See illus. under **siding.**

drop·sonde (drop′sond′), *n.* *Meteorol.* an instrument similar to a radiosonde, released from an aircraft and descending by parachute. [DROP + (RADIO)SONDE]

drop·sy (drop′sē), *n.* **1.** *Pathol.* an excessive accumulation of serous fluid in a serous cavity or in the subcutaneous cellular tissue; hydrops. **2.** an infectious disease of fishes, characterized by a swollen, spongelike body and protruding scales, caused by a variety of the bacterium *Pseudomonas punctata.* [ME *drop(e)sie,* aph. var. of *ydropesie* < OF < ML *(h)ydrōpisia,* equiv. to L *hydrōpis(is)* (< Gk *hydrṓps* dropsy (hydr- HYDR- + *-ōpsi-* < ?) + *-sis* -SIS) + *-ia* -Y[3]] —**drop·sied** (drop′sēd), *adj.*

dropt (dropt), *v.* a pt. and pp. of **drop.**

drop′ ta′ble, a table top hinged to a wall, held in a horizontal position by a bracket while in use.

drop′ tee′, (in plumbing) a tee having lugs for attaching it to a wall or joist.

drop′ the hand′kerchief, a children's game in which all the players but one stand in a circle facing inward, while that one player stealthily drops a handkerchief behind a player in the circle who must pursue him around the circle and catch him before he reaches the vacated place.

drop′ valve′, a valve, as for a steam engine, that drops freely to close.

drop′ win′dow, a window with a sash that slides into a space below the sill.

drop·wort (drop′wûrt′), *n.* **1.** a European, rosaceous herb, *Filipendula hexapetala,* bearing small, scentless, white or reddish flowers. **2.** any North American, umbelliferous plant of the genus *Oxypolis,* as *O. rigidior,* found in ditches and marshes. [DROP + WORT[2]]

drosh·ky (drosh′kē), *n., pl.* **-kies. 1.** a light, low, four-wheeled, open vehicle used mainly in Russia, in which the passengers sit astride or sideways on a long, narrow bench. **2.** any of various other carriages, used mainly in Russia. [< Russ *drozhki*]

dros·ky (dros′kē), *n., pl.* **-kies.** droshky.

dro·som·e·ter (drō som′i tər, drə-), *n.* an instrument for measuring the amount of dew formed on a given surface. [< Gk *drósо(s)* dew + -METER]

dro·soph·i·la (drō sof′ə lə, drə-), *n., pl.* **-las, -lae** (-lē′). a fly of the genus *Drosophila,* esp. *D. melanogaster,* used in laboratory studies of heredity. [< Gk *dróso(s)* dew + *phíla,* neut. pl. of *phílos* -PHILE]

dross (drôs, dros), *n.* **1.** *Metall.* a waste product taken off molten metal during smelting, essentially metallic in character. **2.** *Brit. Mining.* coal of little value. **3.** waste matter; refuse. [ME *dros(se),* OE *drōs;* c. MD *droes* dregs; cf. ME *drōsen,* OE *drōsna;* c. MHG *truosen* husks] —**dross′i·ness,** *n.*

dross·y (drô′sē, dros′ē), *adj.,* **dross·i·er, dross·i·est. 1.** containing dross. **2.** resembling dross; worthless. [ME; see DROSS, -Y[1]]

Dro·ste-Hüls·hoff (drôs′tə hyls′hôf′), *n.* **An·net·te E·li·za·beth Frei·in von** (ä net′ə ā lē′zä bet′ frī′in fən), 1797–1848, German poet.

CONCISE PRONUNCIATION KEY: *act, āble, dâre, ärt; ebb, ēqual; if, īce; hot, ōver, ôrder, oil, bo͝ok, o͞oze, out; up, ûrge; chief; sing; shoe; thin, that;* zh *as in measure.* ə = *a* as in *alone, e* as in *system, i* as in *easily, o* as in *gallop, u* as in *circus;* ᵊ as in *button* (but′ᵊn), *fire* (fīᵊr), *cradle* (krād′ᵊl). See the full key inside the front cover.

drought (drout), *n.* **1.** dry weather; lack of rain. **2.** a period of dry weather, esp. one extensive in time and injurious to crops. **3.** an extended shortage: *a drought of good writing.* **4.** *Archaic.* thirst. Also, **drouth** (drouth). [ME; OE *drūgath*, equiv. to *drūg-* (base of *drȳge* DRY) + *-ath* -TH¹; c. D *droogte* dryness]

drought·y (drou′tē), *adj.*, **drought·i·er, drought·i·est.** **1.** dry. **2.** lacking rain. **3.** *Dial.* thirsty. Also, **drouthy.** [DROUGHT + -Y¹] —**drought′i·ness,** *n.*

drouk (dro͝ok), *v.t. Scot.* to drench; wet thoroughly. [< Scand; cf. Icel *drukna* to be drowned; c. OE *druncnian* to drown]

drouth·y (drou′thē), *adj.*, **drouth·i·er, drouth·i·est.** droughty. —**drouth′i·ness,** *n.*

drove¹ (drōv), *v.* pt. of **drive.**

drove² (drōv), *n.*, *v.*, **droved, drov·ing.** —*n.* **1.** a number of oxen, sheep, or swine driven in a group; herd; flock. **2.** a large crowd of human beings, esp. in motion: *They came to Yankee Stadium in droves.* **3.** *Masonry.* **a.** Also called **drove′ chis′el.** a chisel, from two to four inches broad at the edge, for dressing stones to an approximately true surface. **b.** See **drove work.** —*v.t., v.i.* **4.** to drive or deal in (cattle) as a drover; herd. **5.** *Masonry.* to work or smooth (stone) as with a drove. [ME; OE *drāf* that which is driven, i.e., herd, flock; akin to DRIVE]
—**Syn. 1.** See **flock**¹.

dro·ver (drō′vər), *n.* **1.** one who drives cattle, sheep, etc., to market. **2.** a dealer in cattle. [DROVE² + -ER¹]

drove′ work′, *Masonry.* the surface of stone worked with a drove.

drown (droun), *v.i.* **1.** to be suffocated by immersion in water or other liquid. —*v.t.* **2.** to suffocate by immersion in water or other liquid. **3.** to destroy or get rid of, as by immersion: *He drowned his sorrows in drink.* **5.** to overwhelm as by a flood; overpower. **6.** to add too much water or liquid to (a drink, food, or the like). **7.** to slake (lime) by covering it with water and letting it stand. [ME *drounne*, etc., OE *druncnian*, perh. by loss of *c* between nasals and shift of length from *nn* to *ou*] —**drown′er,** *n.*

drowned′ val′ley, a valley that, having been flooded by the sea, now exists as a bay or estuary.

drowse (drouz), *v.*, **drowsed, drows·ing,** *n.* —*v.i.* **1.** to be sleepy or half-asleep. **2.** to be dull or sluggish. —*v.t.* **3.** to pass or spend (time) in drowsing (often fol. by *away*): *He drowsed away the morning.* **4.** to make sleepy. —*n.* **5.** a sleepy condition; state of being half-asleep. [OE *drūsian* to droop, become sluggish; akin to OE *drēosan* to fall]

drow·si·head (drou′zē hed′), *n. Archaic.* drowsiness. [DROWSY + HEAD]

drow·sy (drou′zē), *adj.*, **-si·er, -si·est.** **1.** half-asleep; sleepy. **2.** marked by or resulting from sleepiness. **3.** dull; sluggish. **4.** inducing lethargy or sleepiness: *drowsy spring weather.* [DROWSE + -Y¹] —**drow′si·ly,** *adv.* —**drow′si·ness,** *n.*
—**Syn. 1.** somnolent. **3.** lethargic.

Dru (dro͞o), *n.* a girl's given name, form of **Drusilla.**

drub (drub), *v.*, **drubbed, drub·bing,** *n.* —*v.t.* **1.** to beat with a stick or the like; cudgel; flog; thrash. **2.** to drive as if by flogging: *Latin grammar was drubbed into their heads.* **3.** to defeat decisively, as in a game or contest. **4.** to stamp (the feet). —*n.* **5.** a blow with a stick or the like. [prob. connected with Ar *ḍarb* blow, beating] —**drub′ber,** *n.*

drub·bing (drub′ing), *n.* **1.** a beating; a sound thrashing. **2.** a decisive, humiliating defeat, as in a game or contest. [DRUB + -ING¹]

Dru·cil·la (dro͞o sil′ə), *n.* a girl's given name. Also, **Drusilla.**

drudge (druj), *n.*, *v.*, **drudged, drudg·ing.** —*n.* **1.** a person who does menial, distasteful, dull, or hard work. **2.** a person who works in a routine, unimaginative way. —*v.i.* **3.** to perform menial, distasteful, dull, or hard work. [cf. OE man's name *Drycghelm* helmet-maker, equiv. to *drycg* (akin to *drēogan* to work) + *helm* HELM²] —**drudg′er,** *n.* —**drudg′ing·ly,** *adv.*

drudg·er·y (druj′ə rē), *n.* menial, distasteful, dull, or hard work. [DRUDGE + -ERY]
—**Syn.** See **work.**

Dru·el·la (dro͞o el′ə), *n.* a girl's given name.

drug (drug), *n.*, *v.*, **drugged, drug·ging.** —*n.* **1.** *Pharm.* a chemical substance administered to a person or animal to prevent or cure disease or otherwise enhance physical or mental welfare. **2.** a habit-forming medicinal substance; narcotic. **3. drugs,** *U.S.* any personal hygienic items sold in a drugstore, as toothpaste, mouthwash, etc. **4.** *Obs.* any ingredient used in chemistry, pharmacy, dyeing, or the like. **5. drug on the market,** a commodity that is overabundant or in excess of demand in the market. Also, **drug in the market.** —*v.t.* **6.** to mix (food or drink) with a drug, esp. a stupefying, narcotic, or poisonous drug. **7.** to stupefy or poison with a drug. **8.** to administer a medicinal drug to. **9.** to administer anything nauseous to. [ME *drogges* (pl.) < MF *drogue* < Gmc; cf. MD *droge* DRY]

Drug (dro͝og), *n. Zoroastrianism.* the principle of evil. Cf. **Asa.** [< Parsee]

drug′ ad′dict, a person who is addicted to narcotics.

drug·get (drug′it), *n.* **1.** Also called **India drugget.** a rug from India of coarse hair with cotton or jute. **2.** *Obs.* a fabric woven wholly or partly of wool, used for clothing. [< MF *droguet* worthless stuff (textile), equiv. to *drogue* trash + *-et* -ET]

drug·gist (drug′ist), *n.* **1.** one who compounds or prepares drugs according to medical prescriptions; apothecary; pharmacist; dispensing chemist. **2.** the owner or operator of a drug store. [DRUG + -IST; cf. F *droguiste*]

drug·less (drug′lis), *adj.* without the use of drugs, as certain methods of medical treatment. [DRUG + -LESS]

drug·store (drug′stôr′, -stōr′), *n. U.S.* the place of business of a druggist or pharmacist, usually also selling cosmetics, stationery, toothpaste, mouthwash, cigarettes, etc., and often soft drinks and light meals. Also, **drug′ store′.** [DRUG + STORE]

drug′store cow′boy, *Slang.* **1.** a young man who loafs around drugstores or on street corners. **2.** a person who dresses like a cowboy but has never worked as one.

Dru·id (dro͞o′id), *n.* (*often l.c.*) a member of a pre-Christian religious order of priests among the ancient Celts of Gaul, Britain, and Ireland. Also, *referring to a woman,* **Dru·id·ess** (dro͞o′i dis). [< L *druid(ae)* < Gaulish *druid(es)* (pl.); r. *druide* < F; cf. OIr *drui* (nom.), *druid* (dat., acc.)] —**dru·id′ic, dru·id′i·cal,** *adj.*

dru·id·ism (dro͞o′i diz′əm), *n.* the religion or rites of the Druids. [DRUID + -ISM]

dru·i·dol·o·gy (dro͞o′i dol′ə jē), *n.* the study of the religion, customs, and practices of the Druids. [DRUID + -O- + -LOGY]

Dru′id stone′, sarsen.

drum¹ (drum), *n.*, *v.*, **drummed, drum·ming.** —*n.* **1.** a musical percussion instrument consisting of a hollow, usually cylindrical, body covered at one or both ends with a tightly stretched membrane, or head, which is struck with the hand, a stick, or a pair of sticks, and typically produces a booming, tapping, or hollow sound. **2.** any hollow tree or similar object or device used in this way. **3.** the sound produced by such an instrument, object, or device. **4.** any rumbling or deep booming sound. **5.** a natural organ by which an animal produces a loud or bass sound. **6.** *Anat., Zool.* **a.** See **middle ear. b.** See **tympanic membrane. 7.** any cylindrical object with flat ends. **8.** a cylindrical part of a machine. **9.** a cylindrical box or receptacle, esp. a large, metal one for storing or transporting liquids. **10.** any of several cylindrical or nearly cylindrical stones laid one above the other to form a column or pier. **11.** Also called **tambour.** *Archit.* a cylindrical or faceted construction supporting a dome. **12.** any of several marine and fresh-water fishes of the family *Sciaenidae* that produce a drumming sound. **13.** *Computer Technol.* See **magnetic drum. 14.** *Archaic.* an assembly of fashionable people at a private house in the evening. **15.** *Archaic.* one who plays the drum. **16. beat the drum,** to advertise: *The boss is out beating the drum for a new product.* —*v.i.* **17.** to beat or play a drum. **18.** to beat on anything rhythmically, esp. to tap one's fingers rhythmically on a hard surface. **19.** to make a sound like that of a drum; resound. **20.** (of ruffed grouse and other birds) to produce a sound resembling drumming. —*v.t.* **21.** to beat (a drum) rhythmically; perform by beating a drum: *to drum a rhythm for dancers.* **22.** to call or summon by, or as by, beating a drum. **23.** to drive or force by persistent repetition: *to drum an idea into someone.* **24. drum out, a.** (formerly) to expel or dismiss from a military service in disgrace to the beat of a drum. **b.** to dismiss in disgrace: *He was drummed out of the university for his gambling activities.* **25. drum up,** to obtain or create (customers, trade, interest, etc.) through vigorous effort: *They were unable to drum up enthusiasm for the new policies.* [back formation from *drumslade* drum, drummer, alter. (by mishearing) of D or LG *trommelslag* drumbeat, equiv. to *trommel* drum + *slag* beat (akin to *slagen* to beat; c. SLAY)]

drum² (drum), *n. Scot., Irish Eng.* a long, narrow hill or ridge. [< Ir and ScotGael *druim*]

drum·beat (drum′bēt′), *n.* the sound of a drum. [DRUM¹ + BEAT]

drum·beat·er (drum′bē′tər), *n.* one who vigorously proclaims or publicizes the merits of a product, idea, movie, etc.; press agent. [DRUM¹ + BEATER]

drum·ble (drum′bəl, -əl, dro͝om′-), *v.i.*, **-bled, -bling.** *Archaic.* to move sluggishly. [dial. *drumble* sluggard var. of *dumble.* See DUMB, -LE]

drum′ clock′, a small clock having a cylindrical brass case.

drum′ corps′, a band of drum players under the direction of a drum major.

drum·fire (drum′fīᵊr′), *n.* gunfire so heavy and continuous as to sound like the beating of drums. [DRUM¹ + FIRE]

drum·fish (drum′fish′), *n.*, *pl.* (*esp. collectively*) **-fish,** (*esp. referring to two or more kinds or species*) **-fish·es.** drum¹ (def. 12). [DRUM¹ + FISH]

drum·head (drum′hed′), *n.* **1.** the membrane stretched upon a drum. **2.** the top part of a capstan. —*adj.* **3.** characteristic of a drumhead court-martial; carried out in summary fashion: *a drumhead execution.* [DRUM¹ + HEAD]

drum′head court′-martial, a court-martial held for the summary trial of charges of offenses committed during military operations.

drum·lin (drum′lin), *n. Geol.* a long, narrow or oval, smoothly rounded hill of unstratified glacial drift. [DRUM² + *-lin*, var. of -LING¹]

drum·ly (drum′lē; *Scot.* dro͝om′lē), *adj.*, **-li·er, -li·est.** *Scot.* troubled; gloomy. [nasalized var. of ME *drublie*, *drōblie*, OE *drōflic*, equiv. to *drōf* turbid, troubled (c. G *trüb*) + *-līc* -LY]

drum′ ma′jor, the marching leader of a drum corps or band.

drum′ majorette′, a girl who twirls a baton, esp. while marching with a band or drum corps, as in a parade. Also called **majorette.**

drum·mer (drum′ər), *n.* **1.** one who plays a drum. **2.** *U.S.* a commercial traveler or traveling salesman. [DRUM¹ + -ER¹]

drum·mock (drum′ək), *n. Chiefly Scot.* drammock.

Drum·mond (drum′ənd), *n.* **1. Henry,** 1851–97, Scottish clergyman and writer. **2. William,** 1585–1649, Scottish poet. **3. William Henry,** 1854–1907, Canadian poet, born in Ireland.

Drum′mond light′. See **calcium light.** [named after Capt. T. *Drummond* (1797–1840), British engineer]

drum′ pan′eling, flush paneling in a door.

Drum·right (drum′rīt′), *n.* a town in central Oklahoma. 4190 (1960).

drum·stick (drum′stik′), *n.* **1.** a stick for beating a drum. **2.** the meaty thigh of a chicken, duck, turkey, or other fowl. [DRUM¹ + STICK¹]

drum′stick tree′. See **pudding-pipe tree.**

drum′ ta′ble, a table having a cylindrical top with drawers or shelves in the skirt, rotating on a central post with three or four outwardly curving legs. Also called **capstan table.**

drunk (drungk), *adj.* **1.** being in a temporary state in which one's physical and mental faculties are impaired by an excess of alcoholic liquor; intoxicated: *He is drunk with wine.* **2.** overcome or dominated by a strong feeling or emotion: *He is drunk with power. She is drunk with joy.* **3.** pertaining to or caused by intoxication or inebriated persons. —*n.* **4.** a drunken person. **5.** a spree; drinking party. —*v.* **6.** pp. and a nonstandard pt. of drink. [ME *drunke(n)*, OE *druncen* (n., adj.), ptp. of *drincan* to DRINK]
—**Syn. 1.** drunken, inebriated. —**Ant. 1–3.** sober.

drunk·ard (drung′kərd), *n.* a person who is habitually or frequently drunk. [DRUNK + -ARD]
—**Syn.** toper, sot, tippler, drinker. DRUNKARD and INEBRIATE are terms for a person who drinks hard liquors habitually. DRUNKARD connotes willful indulgence to excess. INEBRIATE, once a more formal word, is now applied only humorously. (DIPSOMANIAC is the term for a person who, because of some psychological or physiological illness, has an irresistible craving for liquor. The DIPSOMANIAC is popularly called an ALCOHOLIC.) —**Ant.** teetotaler.

drunk′ard's chair′, *Eng. Furniture.* a low, deep armchair of the 18th century.

drunk·en (drung′kən), *adj.* **1.** intoxicated; drunk. **2.** given to drunkenness. **3.** pertaining to, proceeding from, or marked by intoxication: *a drunken quarrel.* [var. of DRUNK adj. and ptp.] —**drunk′en·ly,** *adv.* —**drunk′en·ness,** *n.*
—**Syn. 1.** inebriated, tipsy, fuddled, besotted. —**Ant. 1.** sober.

Drunk′en Boat′, The. See **Le Bateau Ivre.**

drunk′en saw′, a circular saw for cutting a wide kerf, having a blade set obliquely on the spindle. Also called **wabble saw, wobble saw.**

drunk·om·e·ter (drung kom′i tər), *n. Med.* a device for measuring the amount of alcohol in a person's breath to determine the amount of alcohol in his blood stream. [DRUNK + -O- + -METER]

dru·pa·ceous (dro͞o pā′shəs), *adj. Bot.* **1.** resembling or relating to a drupe; consisting of drupes. **2.** producing drupes: *drupaceous trees.* [DRUPE + -ACEOUS]

drupe (dro͞op), *n. Bot.* a fruit, as a peach, cherry, plum, etc., consisting of an outer skin or epicarp, a usually pulpy and succulent layer or mesocarp, and a hard and woody inner shell or endocarp usually enclosing a single seed. [< L *drūpa, druppa* overripe olive < Gk *drýppa* olive]

drupe·let (dro͞op′lit), *n. Bot.* a little drupe, as one of the individual pericarps composing the blackberry. [DRUPE + -LET]

Dru′ry Lane′ (dro͝or′ē), **1.** a street in London, England, famous for its theaters, named after the house Sir William Drury built there in the reign of Henry VIII. **2.** a famous theater (founded 1661) on Drury Lane in London, England. **3.** the theatrical district located on or near this street.

druse (dro͞oz), *n.* an incrustation of small crystals on the surface of a rock or mineral. [< G, deriv. of *Drüse* gland (OHG *druos*); or < Czech *druza* bit of crystallized ore]

Druse (dro͞oz), *n.* a member of an independent religious sect living chiefly in the mountainous regions of Syria and Lebanon, founded in the 11th century, having a faith containing elements of Christianity, Judaism, and Islam, and believing in the transmigration of souls and the ultimate perfection of man. —**Dru′se·an, Dru′si·an,** *adj.*

Dru·sil·la (dro͞o sil′ə), *n.* a girl's given name. Also, **Drucilla.**

Dru·sus (dro͞o′səs), *n.* **Nero Claudius** ("*Germanicus*"), 38–9 B.C., Roman general.

druth·ers (druth′ərz), *n.* (*usually construed as sing.*) *Dial.* one's own way, choice, or preference: *If I had my druthers, I'd go swimming.* [pl. of *druther*, alter. of *would rather*]

Druze (dro͞oz), *n.* Druse.

dry (drī), *adj.*, **dri·er, dri·est,** *v.*, **dried, dry·ing,** *n.*, *pl.* **drys.** —*adj.* **1.** free from moisture or excess moisture; not moist; not wet: *a dry towel; dry air.* **2.** having or characterized by little or no rain: *a dry climate; the dry season.* **3.** characterized by absence, deficiency, or failure of natural or ordinary moisture. **4.** not under, in, or on water: *It was good to be on dry land.* **5.** not now containing or yielding water or other liquid; depleted or empty of liquid: *The well is dry.* **6.** not yielding milk: *a dry cow.* **7.** free from tears: *dry eyes.* **8.** drained or evaporated away: *a dry river.* **9.** desiring drink; thirsty: *He was so dry he could hardly speak.* **10.** causing thirst: *dry work.* **11.** served or eaten without butter, jam, etc.: *dry toast.* **12.** (of cooked food) lacking enough moisture or juice to be satisfying or succulent. **13.** (of bread and bakery products) stale. **14.** *Building Trades.* **a.** (of masonry construction) built without fresh mortar or cement. **b.** (of a wall, ceiling, etc., in an interior) finished without the use of fresh plaster. **15.** *Art.* hard and formal in outline, or lacking mellowness and warmth in color. **16.** plain; bald; unadorned: *dry facts.* **17.** dull; uninteresting: *a dry subject.* **18.** expressed in a straight-faced, matter-of-fact way: *dry humor.* **19.** indifferent; cold; unemotional: *a dry answer.* **20.** unproductive: *The greatest of artists have dry years.* **21.** (of wines) not sweet. **22.** (of a cocktail) **a.** made with dry vermouth: *a dry Manhattan.* **b.** made with relatively little dry vermouth: *a dry martini.* **23.** (of British biscuits) not sweet. **24.** *Ceram.* **a.** unglazed. **b.** insufficiently glazed. **25.** of or pertaining to nonliquid substances or commodities: *dry measure.* **26.** characterized by or favoring prohibition of the manufacture and sale of alcoholic liquors for use as beverages: *a dry state.* **27.** (of lumber) fully seasoned. **28. not dry behind the ears,** immature; unsophisticated: *Adult responsibilities were forced on him, although he was still not dry behind the ears.* —*v.t.* **29.** to make dry; free from moisture: *to dry the dishes.* —*v.i.* **30.** to become dry; lose moisture. **31. dry up, a.** to make or become completely dry. **b.** to cease to exist; evaporate. **c.** *Informal.* to stop talking. **d.** (in acting) to forget one's lines or part. —*n.* **32.** *Informal.* a prohibitionist. **33.** a dry place, area, or region. [ME *drie*, OE *drȳge*; akin to D *droog*, G *trocken*; see DROUGHT] —**dry′a·ble,** *adj.* —**dry′ly,** *adv.* —**dry′ness,** *n.*
—**Syn. 1.** DRY, ARID both mean without moisture. DRY is the general word indicating absence of water or freedom from moisture (which may be favorable): *a dry well; dry clothes or land.* ARID suggests great or intense dryness in a region or climate, esp. such as results in bareness or in barrenness: *arid tracts of desert.* **17.** tedious, barren, boring, tiresome, jejune. **29.** See **evaporate. 30.** dehydrate. —**Ant. 1.** wet. **17.** interesting.

dry·ad (drī′əd, -ad), *n., pl.* **-ads, -a·des** (-ə dēz′). *(often cap.) Class. Myth.* a deity or nymph of the woods. Cf. **hamadryad.** [abstracted from Gk *Dryádes,* pl. of *Dryás,* equiv. to *drŷ(s)* tree, oak + *-as* fem. suffix] —**dry·ad·ic** (drī ad′ik), *adj.*

dry·as (drī′əs), *n., pl.* **dry·as.** any rosaceous plant of the genus *Dryas,* comprising the mountain avens. [named after species of wood nymphs; see DRYAD]

Dry·as (drī′əs), *n. Class. Myth.* a son of Lycurgus, killed by his father in a fit of madness.

dry-as-dust (drī′əz dust′), *adj.* dull and boring: *a dry-as-dust biography.*

dry·as·dust (drī′əz dust′), *n.* a person who deals with dull, boring subjects. [after Dr. *Dryasdust,* a creation of Sir Walter Scott]

dry′ bat′tery, *Elect.* a dry cell or a voltaic battery consisting of a number of dry cells.

dry′-bone ore′ (drī′bōn′), a porous variety of smithsonite found near the surface of the earth.

dry·brush (drī′brush′), *n.* a technique of drawing or painting in which a brush having a small quantity of pigment or medium is applied to or dragged across a surface. [DRY + BRUSH[1]]

dry′ cell′, *Elect.* a cell in which the electrolyte exists in the form of a paste, is absorbed in a porous medium, or is otherwise restrained from flowing.

dry-clean (drī′klēn′), *v.t.* to clean (garments, draperies, rugs, etc.) with a liquid other than water, as benzine or gasoline. [back formation from DRY CLEANING]

dry′ clean′er, a person who owns or operates a dry-cleaning establishment.

dry′ clean′ing, 1. the cleaning of garments, fabrics, draperies, etc., with any of various nonaqueous agents. 2. garments for cleaning in this way.

dry-cleanse (drī′klenz′), *v.t.,* **-cleansed, -cleans·ing.** to dry-clean.

dry′ com′pass, *Navig.* a compass having a compass card mounted on pivots. Cf. **wet compass.**

Dry·den (drīd′ən), *n.* **John,** 1631–1700, English poet, dramatist, and critic. —**Dry·de·ni·an** (drī dē′nē-ən, -den′yən), **Dry·den·ic** (drī den′ik), *adj.*

dry′ distilla′tion. See **destructive distillation.**

dry′ dock′, a structure able to contain a vessel and to be drained or lifted so as to leave the vessel free of water with all parts of the hull accessible for repairs, painting, etc. Cf. **floating dock, graving dock.**

dry-dock (drī′dok′), *v.t.* 1. to place (a ship) in a dry dock. —*v.i.* 2. (of a ship) to go into a dry dock.

dry·er (drī′ər), *n.* drier.

dry-eyed (drī′īd′), *adj.* not weeping.

dry-farm (drī′färm′), *v.i.* 1. to engage in dry farming. —*v.t.* 2. to grow (a specified crop) by means of dry farming.

dry′ farm′ing, a mode of farming practiced in regions of slight or insufficient rainfall, depending largely upon tillage methods which render the soil more receptive of moisture and reduce evaporation. —**dry′ farm′er.**

dry′ fly′, *Angling.* an artificial fly designed for use on the surface of the water. Cf. **wet fly.**

dry′ fog′, *Meteorol. Rare.* a haze due principally to the presence of dust or smoke in the air.

dry-foot·ing (drī′fo͝ot′ing), *n. Ceram.* removal of glaze from the rim at the bottom of a piece. [*dry foot* the base of the piece + -ING[1]]

dry′ freeze′, *Meteorol.* the occurrence of freezing temperatures without the formation of hoarfrost.

dry′ fres′co. See **fresco secco.**

Dry·gal·ski (dri gal′skē), *n.* a walled plain in the third quadrant of the face of the moon in the libration area: about 95 miles in diameter.

dry′ goods′, textile fabrics and related merchandise, as distinguished from groceries, hardware, etc.

dry-gulch (drī′gulch′), *v.t.* 1. *Informal.* to ambush with the intent of killing or severely mauling: *The riders were dry-gulched by Indians.* 2. to betray by a sudden change of attitude or allegiance: *The party dry-gulched its chief candidate at the convention.*

dry′ hole′, any well drilled for oil or gas that does not yield enough to be commercially profitable. Also called **duster.**

Dry′ Ice′, *Trademark.* carbon dioxide, CO_2, solidified under great pressure or as a result of cooling by rapid evaporation of the liquid: used as a refrigerant because it passes directly from a solid to a gas at –78.5°C, absorbing a great amount of heat.

dry·ing (drī′ing), *adj.* 1. causing dryness: *a drying breeze.* 2. designed to or capable of becoming dry and hard on exposure to air. [ME; see DRY, -ING[2]]

dry′ing oil′, any of a group of oily, organic liquids occurring naturally, as linseed, soybean, or dehydrated castor oil, or synthesized, that when applied as a thin coating absorb atmospheric oxygen, forming a tough, elastic layer.

dry′ kiln′, an oven for the controlled drying and seasoning of cut lumber.

dry′ lake′, a tract of land in a desert region over which a shallow lake is formed during the rainy season or after prolonged heavy rains. Cf. **playa.**

dry′ law′, *U.S.* a law prohibiting the sale of alcoholic beverages.

dry′ meas′ure, the system of units of capacity ordinarily used in measuring dry commodities, such as grain or fruit. In the U.S. 2 pints = 1 quart; 8 quarts = 1 peck; 4 pecks = 1 bushel (2150.42 cubic inches). In Great Britain 2 pints = 1 quart; 4 quarts = 1 gallon; 8 quarts = 1 peck; 4 pecks = 1 bushel (2219.36 cubic inches); 8 bushels = 1 quarter.

dry′ milk′, dehydrated milk from which about 95 percent of the moisture has been evaporated. Also called **dried milk, milk powder, powdered milk.**

dry′ mop′. See **dust mop.**

dry′ nurse′, 1. a nurse who takes care of but does not suckle another's infant. Cf. **wet nurse.** 2. *Informal.* one who tutors and guides an inexperienced superior officer.

dry-nurse (drī′nûrs′), *v.t.,* **-nursed, -nurs·ing.** to act as a dry nurse to.

dry′ off′set, *Print.* a method for printing by offset in which the original plate is in relief.

Dry·o·pe (drī′ə pē′), *n. Class. Myth.* a nymph who was transformed into a poplar.

Dry·o·pi·the·cus (drī′ō pə thē′kəs, -pith′ə kəs), *n.* an extinct genus of Old World apes of the Miocene and Pliocene epochs, related to man. [< NL < Gk *drŷ(s)* tree, oak + *-o-* -o- + *píthēkos* monkey]

dry′ plate′, 1. a glass photographic plate coated with a sensitive emulsion of silver bromide and silver iodide in gelatin. 2. *Metall.* tin plate having patches of dull finish.

dry·point (drī′point′), *n.* 1. a technique of engraving, esp. on copper, in which a sharp-pointed needle is used for producing furrows having a burr that is often retained in order to produce a print characterized by soft, velvety black lines. 2. a print made by this technique. [DRY + POINT]

dry′ pud′dling, *Metall.* puddling in a furnace with a bottom of sand. Cf. **wet puddling.**

dry′ rent′, *Law.* See **rent seck.**

dry′ rot′, 1. *Plant Pathol.* **a.** a decay of seasoned timber, resulting in its becoming brittle and crumbling to a dry powder, caused by various fungi. **b.** any of various diseases of plants in which the rotted tissues are dry. 2. any concealed or unsuspected inner decay.

dry′ run′, 1. *Mil.* practice in firing arms without using live ammunition. 2. a rehearsal or practice exercise.

dry-sail (drī′sāl′), *v.i. Informal.* (of a yachtsman) to own or cruise a power craft only.

dry′ sail′ing, the practice of keeping a boat on land when it is not in use.

dry′ sail′or, *Informal.* 1. a yachtsman who owns or cruises only on power craft. 2. a yachtsman who keeps his boat on land when it is not in use.

dry-salt (drī′sôlt′), *v.t.* to cure or preserve (meat, hides, etc.) by drying and salting.

dry·salt·er (drī′sôl′tər), *n. Brit.* 1. a dealer in the chemicals and chemical products used in drugs, dyes, gums, etc. 2. *Informal.* a dealer in dried and salted foods, pickles, sauces, oils, etc. [DRY + SALTER]

dry·salt·er·y (drī′sôl′tə rē), *n., pl.* **-er·ies.** *Brit.* the stock, shop, or business of a drysalter. [DRYSALTER + -Y[3]]

Dry′ Sal′vages, The (sal vā′jiz), a poem (1941) by T. S. Eliot. Cf. **Four Quartets.**

dry-shod (drī′shod′), *adj.* having or keeping the shoes dry. [OE *drȳgsceod,* equiv. to *drȳg-* DRY + *sc(e)od,* ptp. of *scōgan* to shoe, deriv. of *sc(e)ōh* SHOE]

Dry′ Tor·tu′gas (tôr to͞o′gəz), a group of ten small islands at the entrance to the Gulf of Mexico: a part of Florida; the site of Fort Jefferson.

dry′ wash′, 1. clothes, curtains, etc., washed and dried but not yet ironed. Cf. **wet wash.** 2. wash (def. 41).

dry′ well′, 1. a drainage pit lined with loose stonework for the leaching of liquid wastes. 2. See **absorbing well.**

Dr. Zhi·va·go (zhi vä′gō), a novel (1958) by Boris Pasternak.

Ds, *Chem.* (formerly) dysprosium. Cf. **Dy**

ds, decistere; decisteres.

D.S., 1. *Music.* dal segno. 2. Doctor of Science.

d.s., 1. daylight saving. 2. *Com.* days after sight.

DSC, Defense Supplies Corporation.

D.Sc., Doctor of Science.

D.S.C., 1. Distinguished Service Cross. 2. Doctor of Surgical Chiropody.

D.S.M., 1. Distinguished Service Medal. 2. Doctor of Sacred Music.

D.S.O., See **Distinguished Service Order.**

D.S.S., Doctor of Social Science.

DST, Daylight Saving Time. Also, **D.S.T.**

D-state (dē′stāt′), *n. Physics.* the energy state of an electron in an atom having an orbital angular momentum of two units: so called because spectral lines from such states in alkali spectra are relatively diffuse. *Symbol:* D

D. Surg., Dental Surgeon.

D.S.W., 1. Doctor of Social Welfare. 2. Doctor of Social Work.

d.t., delirium tremens. Also, **d.t.'s.**

d.t.d., (in prescriptions) give such doses. [< L *dentur tāles doses*]

D.Th., Doctor of Theology. Also, **D.Theol.**

du (do͞o, dyo͞o; *Fr.* dʏ), (in names of French derivation) a contraction of *de* and the article *le: Joachim du Bellay.*

Du., 1. Duke. 2. Dutch.

du·ad (do͞o′ad, dyo͞o′-), *n.* a group of two; pair. [< L *duo* two + -AD[1]]

du·al (do͞o′əl, dyo͞o′-), *adj.* 1. of, pertaining to, or noting two. 2. composed or consisting of two people, items, parts, etc., together; twofold; double: *dual ownership; dual controls on a plane.* 3. having a twofold, or double, character or nature. 4. noting or pertaining to a member of the category of number, as in Old English, Old Russian, or Arabic, that denotes two of the things in question. —*n. Gram.* 5. the dual number. 6. a form in the dual, as Old English *git* "you two," as contrasted with *ge* "you" referring to three or more. [< L *duāl(is)* containing two, relating to a pair, equiv. to *du(o)* two + *-ālis* -AL[1]] —**du′al·ly,** *adv.*

Du·a·la (do͞o ä′lä), *n.* Douala.

Du′al Alli′ance, 1. the alliance between France and Russia (1890–92), strengthened by a military convention (1892–93) and lasting until the Bolshevik Revolution in 1917. 2. the alliance between Germany and Austria-Hungary against Russia 1879–1918.

du′al car′riageway, *Brit.* an express highway on which the lanes of traffic moving in opposite directions are separated by a divider, as a strip of grass, a fence, or the like.

du′al cit′izenship, 1. citizenship of both a state and a nation, in nations consisting of a federation of states, as the U.S. 2. See **dual nationality.**

du′al high′way. See **divided highway.**

du·al·ism (do͞o′ə liz′əm, dyo͞o′-), *n.* 1. state of being dual or consisting of two parts; division into two. 2. *Philos.* a theory that there are two basic substances or principles, as mind and body. Cf. **monism** (def. 1), **pluralism** (def. 1a). 3. *Theol.* **a.** the doctrine that there are two independent divine beings or eternal principles, one good and the other evil. **b.** the belief that man embodies two parts, such as body and soul. [DUAL + -ISM] —**du′al·ist,** *n.*

du·al·is·tic (do͞o′ə lis′tik, dyo͞o′-), *adj.* 1. of, pertaining to, or of the nature of dualism. 2. dual; twofold. [DUAL + -ISTIC] —**du′al·is′ti·cal·ly,** *adv.*

du·al·i·ty (do͞o al′i tē, dyo͞o-), *n.* dual state or quality. [ME *dualitie* < LL *duālitās.* See DUAL, -ITY]

Du′al Mon′archy, the kingdom of Austria-Hungary 1867–1918.

du′al national′ity, the status of a person whose exclusive allegiance is claimed simultaneously by two or more nations.

du′al personal′ity, *Psychol.* a disorder in which an individual possesses two dissociated personalities. Cf. **multiple personality.**

du·al-pur·pose (do͞o′əl pûr′pəs, dyo͞o′-), *adj.* 1. serving two functions. 2. (of cattle) bred for two purposes, as to provide beef and milk.

du′al space′, *Math.* 1. the set of all linear functionals whose domain is a given vector space. 2. Also called **algebraic conjugate.** such a set defined for a vector space with no norm. 3. Also called **normed conjugate.** such a set defined for a normed vector space.

Duane (dwān, do͞o ān′), *n.* a boy's given name.

du·ar·chy (do͞o′är kē, dyo͞o′-), *n., pl.* **-chies.** a government or form of government in which power is vested equally in two rulers. [< L *du(o)* two + -ARCHY]

Duar·te Fuen·tes (dwär′te fwen′tes), **Jo·sé Na·po·le·ón** (hô se′ nä pô le ôn′), born 1926, Salvadoran political leader: president since 1984.

dub[1] (dub), *v.t.,* **dubbed, dub·bing.** 1. to strike lightly with a sword in the ceremony of conferring knighthood; make, or designate as, a knight: *The King dubbed him a knight.* 2. to invest with any name, character, dignity, or title; style; name; call: *He was dubbed a charlatan.* 3. to strike, cut, rub, or make smooth, as leather or timber. 4. *Brit. Angling* dress (def. 10). 5. **dub bright,** *Shipbuilding.* to shave off the outer surface of the planking of (a vessel). [ME *dubb(en),* OE *dubbian,* deriv. of unrecorded n.; c. HG (dial.) *tuppe* big piece of wood, Norw *dubb* peg; cf. Icel *dubba,* OF *adub(b)er* to dub (< E), EFris, LG *dubben* to strike, beat; see DOWEL]

dub[2] (dub), *n. Slang.* an awkward, unskillful person. [?]

dub[3] (dub), *v.,* **dubbed, dub·bing,** *n.* —*v.t., v.i.* 1. to thrust; poke. —*n.* 2. a thrust; poke. 3. a drumbeat. [appar. same word (with older sense) as DUB[1]]

dub[4] (dub), *v.,* **dubbed, dub·bing,** *n.* —*v.t.* 1. to furnish (a film) with a new sound track recorded in the language of the country of import. 2. to add (music, speech, etc.) to a film or tape recording (often fol. by *in*). —*n.* 2. the new sounds added. [short for DOUBLE]

dub[5] (dub), *n. Scot. and North Eng.* a pool of water; puddle. [?; cf. G *Tümpel* pond, puddle]

Du·bai (do͞o bī′), *n.* a seaport in NE Trucial Oman, on the Persian Gulf. ab. 20,000. Also, **Dibai.**

Du Bar·ry (do͞o bar′ē, dyo͞o; *Fr.* dʏ ba rē′), **Comtesse** (*Marie Jeanne Bécu*), 1746–93, mistress of Louis XV.

dub·bel·tje (dub′əl chə, -tyə), *n.* a silver 10-cent piece of the Netherlands, equivalent to about .028 of a U.S. dollar. [< D, equiv. to *dubbel* DOUBLE + *-tje* dim. suffix]

dub·bin (dub′in), *n.* a mixture of tallow and oil used in dressing leather. Also, **dubbing.** [var. of DUBBING]

dub·bing (dub′ing), *n.* 1. the conferring of knighthood; accolade. 2. *Angling.* the material used for the body of an artificial fly. 3. dubbin. [ME; see DUB[1], -ING[1]]

Dub·bo (dub′ō), *n.* a city in E Australia. 14,130.

du Bel·lay (do͞o bə lā′, dyo͞o; *Fr.* dʏ be lā′), **Joachim.** See **Bellay, Joachim du.**

du·bi·e·ty (do͞o bī′i tē, dyo͞o-), *n., pl.* **-ties.** 1. doubtfulness; doubt. 2. a matter of doubt. Also called **dubiosity.** [< L *dubietās,* equiv. to *dubi(us)* DUBIOUS + *-etās,* var. of *-itās;* see -ITY]
—**Syn.** 1. skepticism, mistrust, distrust, suspicion.

Du·bin·sky (do͞o bin′skē), *n.* **David,** born 1892, U.S. labor leader, born in Poland: president of the I.L.G.W.U. 1932–66.

du·bi·os·i·ty (do͞o′bē os′i tē, dyo͞o′-), *n., pl.* **-ties.** dubiety.

du·bi·ous (do͞o′bē əs, dyo͞o′-), *adj.* 1. doubtful; marked by or occasioning doubt: *a dubious reply.* 2. of doubtful quality or propriety; questionable: *a dubious transaction; a dubious compliment.* 3. of uncertain outcome: *in dubious battle.* 4. wavering or hesitating in opinion; inclined to doubt. [< L *dubius,* with -OUS for *-us*] —**du′bi·ous·ly,** *adv.* —**du′bi·ous·ness,** *n.*
—**Syn.** 1. equivocal, ambiguous, obscure, unclear. 4. undecided, uncertain, hesitant. See **doubtful.**

du·bi·ta·ble (do͞o′bi tə bəl, dyo͞o′-), *adj.* open to doubt; doubtful; uncertain. [< L *dubitābil(is),* equiv. to *dubitā(re)* (to) doubt + *-bilis* -BLE] —**du′bi·ta·bly,** *adv.*

du·bi·ta·tion (do͞o′bi tā′shən, dyo͞o′-), *n.* doubt. [late ME < L *dubitātiōn-* (s. of *dubitātiō*), equiv. to *dubitāt(us),* ptp. of *dubitāre* (*dubit-* DOUBT + *-ātus* -ATE[1]) + *-iōn-* -ION]

du·bi·ta·tive (do͞o′bi tā′tiv, dyo͞o′-), *adj.* 1. doubting; doubtful. 2. expressing doubt. [< LL *dubitātīv(us),* equiv. to *dubitāt(us)* (see DUBITATION) + *-īvus* -IVE] —**du′bi·ta′tive·ly,** *adv.*

Dub·lin (dub′lin), *n.* 1. Gaelic, **Baile Átha Cliath.** a seaport in and the capital of the Republic of Ireland, in the E part, on the Irish Sea. 537,448 (1961). 2. a county in E Republic of Ireland. 718,332 (1961); 356 sq. mi. *Co. seat:* Dublin.

Dub·lin·ers (dub′lə nərz), *n.* a collection of short stories (1914) by James Joyce.

Du Bois (do͞o bois′), **William Edward Burg·hardt** (bûrg′härd), 1868–1963, U.S. educator and writer.

Du·bois (dʏ bwä′), *n.* **(Ma·rie) Eu·gène (Fran·çois Tho·mas)** (ma rē′ œ zhen′ frän swa′ tô mä′), 1858–1941, Dutch physical anthropologist and anatomist.

Du·bon·net (do͞o′bə nā′, dyo͞o′-), *n.* 1. *Trademark.* a sweet, red or white, aromatized wine, used chiefly as an apéritif. 2. (*l.c.*) a deep purple-red color. —*adj.* 3. (*l.c.*) of the color dubonnet.

Du·brov·nik (do͞o′brôv nik), *n.* a seaport in S Croatia, on the Adriatic: resort. 58,920. Italian, **Ragusa.**

Du·buf·fet (dʏ bʏ fe′), *n.* **Jean** (zhäN), born 1901, French painter.

Du·buque (də byo͞ok′), *n.* a city in E Iowa, on the Mississippi River. 56,606 (1960).

duc (dʏk), *n., pl.* **ducs** (dʏk). *French.* duke.

du·cal (do͞o′kəl, dyo͞o′-), *adj.* of or pertaining to a duke. [< LL *ducāl(is).* See DUKE, -AL[1]]

du·cal·ly (do͞o′kə lē, dyo͞o′-), *adj.* **1.** in the manner of or pertaining to a duke. **2.** *Heraldry.* with a ducal coronet: *a lion gules ducally gorged.* [DUCAL + -LY]

Du·casse (dʏ kas′), *n.* **Jean Jules A·ma·ble Ro·ger** (zhäN zhʏl A mA′blə Rô zhā′). See **Roger-Ducasse, Jean Jules Amable.**

duc·at (duk′ət), *n.* **1.** any of various gold coins formerly issued in various parts of Europe, esp. that first issued in Venice in 1284. Cf. **sequin** (def. 2). **2.** any of various silver coins formerly issued in various parts of Europe. **3.** *Slang.* a ticket to a public performance. **4. ducats,** *Slang.* money; cash. [ME < MF < OIt *ducat(o)* < LL *ducāt(us)* DUCHY, also name of a coin]

duc·a·toon (duk′ə to͞on′, duk′ə to͞on′), *n.* a former silver coin of the Netherlands, used through the 17th and 18th centuries: equal to three gulden. Also, **duc·a·ton** (duk′ə ton′). [< F *ducaton,* dim. of *ducat* DUCAT]

Duc·cio di Buo·nin·se·gna (do͞ot′chô dē bwô′-nēn se′nyä), c1255–1319?, Italian painter.

du·ce (do͞o′chā; *It.* do͞o′che), *n., pl.* **-ces,** *It.* **-ci** (-chē). **1.** a leader or dictator. **2. il Duce,** the leader: applied esp. to Benito Mussolini as head of the fascist Italian state. [< It < L *dūci-* (s. of *dux*) leader]

du Cer·ceau (dʏ ser sō′), **An·drou·et** (äN dro͞o e′). See **Androuet du Cerceau.**

Du Chail·lu (do͞o shī′yo͞o, -shal′-, dyo͞o-; *Fr.* dʏ shA yʏ′), **Paul Bel·lo·ni** (pôl bə lō′nē; *Fr.* pôl be lô nē′), 1835–1903, U.S. explorer in Africa, traveler, and writer; born in France.

Du·champ (dʏ shäN′), *n.* **Mar·cel** (mAR sel′), 1887–1968, French painter, in U.S. after 1915 (brother of Raymond Duchamp-Villon and Jacques Villon).

Du·champ-Vil·lon (dʏ shäN vē yôN′), *n.* **Ray·mond** (Re môN′), 1876–1918, French sculptor (brother of Jacques Villon and Marcel Duchamp).

duch·ess (duch′is), *n.* **1.** the wife or widow of a duke. **2.** a woman who holds in her own right the sovereignty or titles of a duchy. [ME *duchesse* < MF, fem. of *duc* < L *dūc-* (base of *dux*) leader; see -ESS] —**duch′ess·like′,** *adj.*

du·chesse (*Fr.* dʏ shes′), *n., pl.* **du·chesses** (*Fr.* dʏ shes′). *Fr. Furniture.* a day bed having a rounded, partially enclosed head and usually a similar foot, sometimes made in two or three pieces able to be used separately **(duchesse brisée).** [< F; see DUCHESS]

duchesse′ bed′, *Fr. Furniture.* a bed having a suspended, full-length tester. Cf. **angel bed.**

du·chesse bri·sée (*Fr.* dʏ shes brē zā′), *pl.* **du·chesses bri·sées** (*Fr.* dʏ shes brē zā′). See under **duchesse.** [< F: folding duchesse]

Duch′ess of Mal′fi, The (mal′fē), a tragedy (1614?) by John Webster.

duch·y (duch′ē), *n., pl.* **duch·ies.** the territory ruled by a duke or duchess. [ME *duche, duchie* < MF *duche* < LL *ducāt(us)* dukedom, equiv. to *duc-* (see DUKE) + *-ātus* -ATE[1]]

duck[1] (duk), *n., pl.* **ducks,** (*esp. collectively for 1–3*) **duck. 1.** any of numerous wild or domesticated web-footed swimming birds of the family *Anatidae,* esp. of the genus *Anas* and allied genera, characterized by a broad, flat bill, short legs, and depressed body. **2.** the female of this bird, as distinguished from the male. Cf. **drake**[1]. **3.** the flesh of this bird, eaten as food. **4.** *Informal.* person; individual: *He's the queer old duck with the knee-length gaiters and walrus mustache.* **5.** *Dial.* a playing marble, esp. one that is not used as a shooter. **6.** Often, **ducks.** (*construed as sing.*) *Brit. Slang.* ducky. **7.** *Cricket Slang.* **a.** failure of a batsman to score: *to be out for a duck.* **b.** a player's score of zero: *to be bowled for a duck.* Cf. **goose egg. 8. water off a duck's back,** something that has little or no effect: *Our criticisms of his talk rolled off him like water off a duck's back.* [ME *duk, doke,* OE *dūce* diver, duck; akin to DUCK[2]]

duck[2] (duk), *v.i.* **1.** to plunge the whole body or the head momentarily under water. **2.** to stoop or bend suddenly; bob. **3.** to avoid or evade a blow, unpleasant task, etc.; dodge. **4.** *Cards Informal.* to play a card lower than the card led. —*v.t.* **5.** to plunge or dip in water momentarily. **6.** to lower (the head, body, etc.) suddenly. **7.** to avoid or evade (a blow, unpleasant task, etc.); dodge: *to duck a hard right; to duck an embarrassing question.* **8.** *Cards Informal.* to play a card lower than (the card led). —*n.* **9.** the act or an instance of ducking. [ME *duken, douken;* c. G *tauchen* to dive, *ducken* to duck]
—**Syn. 1.** dive, dip, souse. **2.** bow, dodge.

duck[3] (duk), *n.* **1.** a heavy, plain-weave cotton fabric for tents, clothing, bags, etc., in any of various weights and widths. **2. ducks,** (*construed as pl.*) slacks or trousers made of this material. [< D *doek* cloth, c. G *Tuch*]

duck[4] (duk), *n.* (in World War II) an amphibious military truck. [alter. of DUKW, code name]

duck′ and drake′. See **ducks and drakes** (def. 1).

duck·bill (duk′bil′), *n.* a small, aquatic, egg-laying monotreme, *Ornithorhynchus anatinus,* of Australia and Tasmania, having webbed feet and a bill like that of a duck. Also called **duck′bill plat′ypus, duck′-billed plat′ypus, platypus.** [DUCK[1] + BILL[2]]

Duckbill
(Total length 2 ft.; tail 6 in.)

duck·board (duk′bôrd′, -bōrd′), *n.* a board or boards laid as a track or floor over wet or muddy ground. [DUCK[1] + BOARD]

duck·egg (duk′egg′), *n.* *Cricket.* duck[1] (def. 7).

duck·er (duk′ər), *n.* one who or that which ducks. [late ME; see DUCK[2], -ER[1]]

duck′ foot′, *Furniture.* See **web foot.**

duck′ hawk′, an American subspecies of the peregrine falcon, *Falco peregrinus anatum,* noted for its swift flight.

duck·ie (duk′ē), *adj.* ducky.

duck′ing stool′, a former instrument of punishment consisting of a chair in which offenders were tied to be plunged into water.

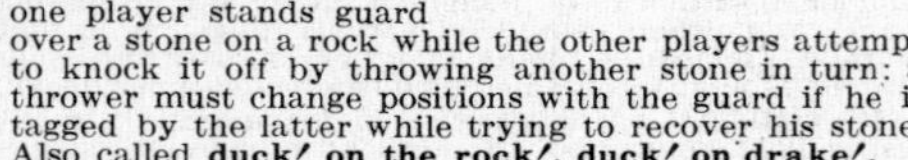

Ducking stool

duck-leg·ged (duk′-leg′id *or, esp. Brit.,* -legd′), *adj.* (of a person or animal) having legs that are unusually short: *Her dress gave her a duck-legged appearance.*

duck·ling (duk′ling), *n.* a young duck. [late ME; see DUCK[1], -LING[1]]

duck′ on a rock′, a children's game in which one player stands guard over a stone on a rock while the other players attempt to knock it off by throwing another stone in turn: a thrower must change positions with the guard if he is tagged by the latter while trying to recover his stone. Also called **duck′ on the rock′, duck′ on drake′.**

duck·pin (duk′pin′), *n.* **1.** *Bowling.* a short pin of relatively large diameter, used in a game resembling tenpins, and bowled at with small balls. **2. duckpins,** (*construed as sing.*) the game played with such pins. [so called from the pin's resemblance to the shape of a duck]

ducks′ and drakes′, 1. Also, **duck and drake.** a pastime in which flat stones or shells are thrown across water so as to skip over the surface several times before sinking. **2. play ducks and drakes with,** to handle recklessly; squander: *He played ducks and drakes with his fortune.* Also, **make ducks and drakes of.** [from a fancied likeness to a waterfowl's movements]

duck′ soup′, *Slang.* something that is easy to accomplish: *Making a fortune is duck soup to him.*

duck·tail (duk′tāl′), *n.* a style of haircut, favored esp. by teenage boys, in which the hair is worn long on the sides and combed to meet at the back. Also called **duck′-tail hair′cut.** [DUCK[1] + TAIL[1]]

duck·weed (duk′wēd′), *n.* any plant of the family *Lemnaceae,* esp. of the genus *Lemna,* comprising small aquatic plants which float free on still water. [late ME *dockewede;* so called because eaten by ducks]

duck·wheat (duk′hwēt′, -wēt′), *n.* See **India wheat.** [DUCK[1] + WHEAT]

duck·y[1] (duk′ē), *adj.,* **duck·i·er, duck·i·est.** *Informal.* dear; darling. [DUCK[1] + -Y[1]]

duck·y[2] (duk′ē), *n., pl.* **duck·ies.** *Brit. Slang.* (used as a term of endearment or familiarity) dear; sweetheart; darling; pet. [DUCK[1] + -Y[2] (? altered by folk etymology < MFlem *docke* doll; see DOXY[2])]

Du·com·mun (dʏ kô mœN′), *n.* **É·lie** (ā lē′), 1833–1906, Swiss author: Nobel peace prize 1902.

duct (dukt), *n.* **1.** any tube, canal, pipe, or conduit by which a fluid, air, or other substance is conducted or conveyed. **2.** *Anat., Zool.* a tube, canal, or vessel conveying a body fluid, esp. a glandular secretion or excretion. **3.** *Bot.* a cavity or vessel formed by elongated cells or by many cells. **4.** *Elect.* a single enclosed runway for conductors or cables. **5.** *Print.* (in a press) the reservoir for ink. [< L *duct(us)* leadership, a conducting, a drawing off (as of water), hence channel (in ML), n. use of ptp. of *dūcere* to lead (*duc-* + *-tus* ptp. suffix)] —**duct′less,** *adj.*

duc·tile (duk′tᵊl, -til), *adj.* **1.** capable of being hammered out thin, as certain metals; malleable. **2.** capable of being drawn out into wire or threads, as gold. **3.** able to undergo change of form without breaking. **4.** capable of being molded or shaped; plastic. [< L *ductile,* neut. of *ductilis,* equiv. to *duct(us)* (ptp of *dūcere* to draw along; see DUCT) + *-ilis* -ILE] —**duc′tile·ly,** *adv.* —**duc·til′i·ty, duc′tile·ness,** *n.*

duct′ keel′, *Naut.* See **box keel.**

duct′less gland′. See **endocrine gland.**

duc·tor (duk′tər), *n.* *Print.* the roller that conveys ink in a press from the ink reservoir to the distributor. [< L: guide, equiv. to *duct(us)* (ptp. of *dūcere* to draw along; see DUCT) + *-or* -OR[2]]

duc·tule (duk′to͞ol, -tyo͞ol), *n.* a small duct. [DUCT + -ULE]

duct·work (dukt′wûrk′), *n.* the ducts of a ventilation system or the like. [DUCT + WORK]

dud (dud), *n.* *Informal.* **1.** a person or enterprise that proves to be a failure. **2.** *Mil.* a shell that fails to explode after being fired. [? special use of *dud,* sing. of DUDS]

dud·dy (dud′ē), *adj.* *Scot.* ragged; tattered. Also, **dud′-die.** [DUD(S) + -Y[1]]

dude (do͞od, dyo͞od), *n.* **1.** a man excessively concerned with his clothes, grooming, and manners. **2.** *Slang.* a person reared in a large city. **3.** *Western U.S.* an Easterner who vacations on a ranch. [?]

du·deen (do͞o dēn′), *n.* *Irish Eng.* a short clay tobacco pipe. [< Ir *dúidín,* equiv. to *dúd* pipe + *-īn* dim. suffix]

du·del·sack (do͞od′ᵊl sak′; *Ger.* do͞od′ᵊl zäk′), *n.* *Music.* doodlesack.

dude′ ranch′, a ranch operated primarily as a vacation resort.

Du·de·vant (*Fr.* dʏdə väN′), *n.* **Madame A·man·dine Lu·cile Au·rore** (*Fr.* A mäN dēn′ lʏ sēl′ ō rôr′), real name of George Sand.

dudg·eon[1] (duj′ən), *n.* a feeling of offense or resentment; anger: *We left in high dudgeon.* [?]
—**Syn.** indignation, pique.

dudg·eon[2] (duj′ən), *n.* *Obs.* **1.** a kind of wood used esp. for the handles of knives, daggers, etc. **2.** a handle or hilt made of this wood. **3.** a dagger having such a hilt. [late ME; cf. AF *digeon*]

dud·ish (do͞o′dish, dyo͞o′-), *adj.* resembling or characteristic of a dude, as in manner or appearance. [DUDE + -ISH[1]] —**dud′ish·ly,** *adv.*

Dud·ley (dud′lē), *n.* **1. Robert, 1st Earl of Leicester,** 1532?–88, British statesman and favorite of Queen Elizabeth. **2. Thomas,** 1576–1653, English governor of Massachusetts Bay Colony, 1634–35, 1640–41, 1645–46, 1650–51. **3.** a city in central England, near Birmingham. 61,748 (1961). **4.** a boy's given name.

duds (dudz), *n.pl.* *Informal.* **1.** clothes, esp. a suit of clothes. **2.** belongings in general. [ME *dudde;* akin to LG *dudel* coarse sackcloth; cf. OE *Dudda,* man's name]

due (do͞o, dyo͞o), *adj.* **1.** immediately owed; having reached the date for payment: *This bill is due.* **2.** owing or owed, irrespective of whether the time of payment has arrived: *This bill is due next month.* **3.** owing or observed as a moral or natural right. **4.** rightful; proper; fitting: *due care; in due time.* **5.** adequate; sufficient: *a due margin for delay.* **6.** under engagement as to time; expected to be ready, be present, or arrive; scheduled: *The plane is due at noon.* **7. due to,** attributable, as to a cause: *The delay was due to heavy traffic.* —*n.* **8.** that which is due, owed, or naturally belongs to someone. **9.** Usually, **dues.** a regular fee or charge payable at specific intervals, esp. to a group or organization: *membership dues.* **10. give someone his due, a.** to give that which justice demands; treat fairly: *Even though he had once cheated me, I gave him his due.* **b.** to credit a disliked or dishonorable person for something that is likable, honorable, or the like. —*adv.* **11.** directly or exactly: *a due east course.* **12.** *Obs.* duly. [ME < MF *deu,* ptp. of *devoir* < L *debēre* to owe; see DEBT] —**due′ness,** *n.*

due′ bill′, a brief written acknowledgment of indebtedness, not payable to order.

du·e·cen·to (do͞o′ə chen′tō, dyo͞o′-; *It.* do͞o′e chen′tô), *n.* (*often cap.*) the 13th century, with reference to Italy, esp. to its art or literature. Also, **dugento.** [< It: lit., two hundred] —**du′e·cen′tist,** *n.*

due′ course′ of law′. See **due process of law.**

du·el (do͞o′əl, dyo͞o′-), *n., v.,* **-eled, -el·ing** or (*esp. Brit.*) **-elled, -el·ling.** —*n.* **1.** a prearranged combat between two persons, fought with deadly weapons according to an accepted code of procedure, esp. to settle a private quarrel. **2.** any contest between two persons or parties. —*v.t., v.i.* **3.** to fight in a duel. [earlier *duell* < ML *duell(um),* L, archaic var. of *bellum* war] —**du′el·is′tic;** *esp. Brit.,* **du′el·lis′tic,** *adj.*

Duel, The, a novel (1905) by Alexander Kuprin.

du·el·ist (do͞o′ə list, dyo͞o′-), *n.* one who participates in a duel. Also, *esp. Brit.,* **du′el·list.** Also called **du′el·er;** *esp. Brit.,* **du′el·ler.** [DUEL + -IST]

du·el·lo (do͞o el′ō, dyo͞o-; *It.* do͞o el′lô), *n., pl.* **-los,** *It.* **-li** (-lē). **1.** the practice or art of dueling. **2.** the code of rules regulating it. [< It; see DUEL]

Due·ña (dwe′nyä), *n.* a girl's given name.

du·en·na (do͞o en′ə, dyo͞o-), *n.* **1.** (in Spain and Portugal) an older woman serving as escort or chaperon of a young lady. **2.** a governess. [< Sp *duenna* (now *dueña*) < L *domina,* fem. of *dominus* master]

due′ proc′ess of law′, a limitation in the U.S. Federal and State constitutions that restrains the actions of the instrumentalities of government within limits of fairness. Also called **due′ proc′ess, due course of law.**

Due·ro (dwe′rô), *n.* Spanish name of **Douro.**

du·et (do͞o et′, dyo͞o-), *n.* *Music.* a composition for two voices or instruments. [earlier *duett* < It *duett(o),* equiv. to *du(o)* duet + *-etto* -ET] —**du·et′tist,** *n.*

Du·fay (dʏ fā′), *n.* **Guil·laume** (gē yōm′), c1400–74, Flemish composer.

duff[1] (duf), *n.* organic matter in various stages of decomposition on the floor of the forest. [fig. use of DUFF[2]]

duff[2] (duf), *n.* a stiff flour pudding, boiled or steamed and often flavored with currants, citron, spices, etc. [var. of DOUGH]

duff[3] (duf), *n.* *Slang.* the buttocks or rump: *If you don't like the way things are, get off your duff and do something about it!* [special use of DUFF[2]]

duff[4] (duf), *v.t.* *Slang.* **1.** to give a deliberately deceptive appearance to; misrepresent; fake. **2.** *Brit.* (in golf) to misplay (a golf ball), esp. to misjudge one's swing so that the club strikes the ground behind the ball before hitting it. **3.** *Australian.* **a.** to steal (cattle). **b.** (formerly) to alter the brand on (stolen cattle). **4.** to cheat someone. [back formation from DUFFER]

Duff (duf), *n.* a boy's given name.

duf·fel (duf′əl), *n.* **1.** a sportsman's or camper's clothing and equipment. **2.** a coarse woolen cloth having a thick nap. Also, **duf′fle.** [after *Duffel,* a town near Antwerp]

duf′fel bag′, a large, cylindrical canvas bag used esp. by military personnel for transporting personal effects.

duff·er (duf′ər), *n.* **1.** *Informal.* **a.** a plodding, clumsy, incompetent person. **b.** a person inept at a specific sport. **c.** a dull, indecisive old man. **2.** *Slang.* **a.** anything inferior, counterfeit, or useless. **b.** a peddler, esp. one who sells cheap, flashy goods as valuable. [? Scot dial. *duffar, dowfart* dull, stupid person, deriv. of DOWF]

duf′fle coat′, a hooded overcoat of sturdy wool, usually knee-length and with frog fasteners. Also, **duf′fel coat′.** [var. of DUFFEL]

Duf·fy (duf′ē), *n.* **1. Sir Charles Gav·an** (gav′ən), 1816–1903, Irish and Australian politician. **2.** a boy's given name, form of **Duff.**

Du·fy (dʏ fē′), *n.* **Ra·oul** (RA o͞ol′), 1877–1953, French painter, lithographer, and decorator.

dug[1] (dug), *v.* a pt. and pp. of **dig.**

dug[2] (dug), *n.* the mamma or the nipple of a female mammal. [< Scand; cf. Dan *dægge* to coddle; c. Goth *daddjan* to give suck]

Du Gard (*Fr.* dʏ gAR′), **Ro·ger Mar·tin** (*Fr.* Rô-zhā′ mAR taN′). See **Martin Du Gard, Roger.**

du·gen·to (do͞o jen′tō, dyo͞o-; *It.* do͞o jen′tô), *n.* duecento.

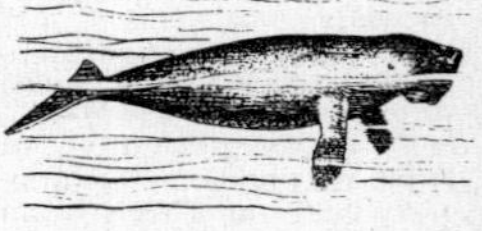

Dugong
(Length 9 ft.)

du·gong (do͞o′gong), *n.* an herbivorous, aquatic mammal, *Dugong dugon,* of the Red Sea and Indian Ocean, having a fishlike body, flipperlike forelimbs, no hind limbs, and a rounded, paddlelike tail. [alter. of Malay *duyong*]

dug·out (dug′out′), *n.* **1.** a rough shelter or dwelling formed by an excavation in the ground, in the face of a bank, in the side of a hill, etc., esp. one used by soldiers. **2.** a boat made by hollowing out a log. **3.** *Baseball.* a roofed structure enclosed on three sides and with the fourth side open and facing the playing field, usually with the floor below ground level, where the players sit when not on the field. [n. use of v. phrase *dug out*]

Du Gues·clin (dʏ ge klaɴ′), **Ber·trand** (beʀ tʀäɴ′), (*"the Eagle of Brittany"*), c1320–80, French military leader: constable of France 1370–80.

Du·ha·mel (do͞o′ə mel′, dyo͞o′-; *Fr.* dʏ a mel′), *n.* **Georges** (zhôʀzh), (*Denis Thévenin*), 1884–1966, French novelist, physician, poet, and essayist.

Du·ha·mel's′ the′orem (do͞o′hə melz′), *Math.* a theorem giving methods for expressing physical quantities by means of integrals. Also called **Duhamel's′ prin′ciple.**

dui·ker (dī′kər), *n., pl.* **-kers,** (*esp. collectively*) **-ker.** any of several small African antelopes of the *Cephalophus, Sylvicapra,* and related genera, of which usually only the males have short, spikelike horns. [< SAfrD, D *duiker* diver, equiv. to *duik(en)* (to) dive (see DUCK[2]) + *-er* -ER[1]]

dui·ker·bok (dī′kər bok′), *n., pl.* **-boks,** (*esp. collectively*) **-bok.** duiker. [< SAfrD: duiker buck]

Dui′no El′egies (dwē′nō), a collection of ten poems (1923) by Rainer Maria Rilke. German, **Dui·ne·ser E·le·gi·en** (dwē nā′zəʀ ā lā gē′ən).

Duis·burg (dʏs′bo͝oʀkh′), *n.* a city in W West Germany, at the junction of the Rhine and Ruhr rivers: the largest river port in Europe; formed 1929 from the cities of Duisburg and Hamborn. 501,100 (1963). Formerly, **Duis·burg-Ham·born** (dʏs′bo͝oʀkh′häm′-bôʀn).

duit (doit, dīt), *n.* doit (def. 1).

du jour (də zho͞or′, do͞o; *Fr.* dʏ zho͞oʀ′), as prepared on the particular day; of the kind being served today: *The soup du jour is split pea.* [< F: of the day]

Du·kas (dʏ kä′), *n.* **Paul (Ab·ra·ham)** (pôl a bʀa-äm′), 1865–1935, French composer.

duke (do͞ok, dyo͞ok), *n.* **1.** (in Continental Europe) the male ruler of a duchy; the sovereign of a small state. **2.** a British nobleman holding the highest hereditary title outside the royal family, ranking immediately below a prince and above a marquis; a member of the highest rank of the British peerage. Cf. **royal duke. 3.** a nobleman of corresponding rank in certain other countries. **4.** a cultivated cherry, a hybrid of the sweet and sour cherry. **5. dukes,** *Slang.* fists; hands: *Put up your dukes.* [ME *duke, duc* < OF *duc* < L *dūc-* (s. of *dux*) leader; akin to TUG, TOW[1]]

Duke (do͞ok, dyo͞ok), *n.* **1. Benjamin Newton,** 1855–1929, and his brother, **James Buchanan,** 1856–1925, U.S. industrialists. **2.** a boy's given name.

duke·dom (do͞ok′dəm, dyo͞ok′-), *n.* **1.** a duchy. **2.** the office or rank of a duke. [late ME; see DUKE, -DOM]

Du·kho·bor (do͞o′kə bôr′), *n., pl.* **Du·kho·bors, Du·kho·bor·tsy** (do͞o′kə bôrt′sē). Doukhobor.

duk·kha (do͞ok′ə), *n. Buddhism.* the suffering of humanity in its common, unenlightened state. Cf. **Three Signs of Being.** [< Pali]

Du·la·ney (də lā′nē), *n.* a boy's given name.

dulc., (in prescriptions) sweet. [< L *dulcis*]

Dul·ce (dul′sē), *n.* a girl's given name.

dul·ce et de·co·rum est pro pa·tri·a mo·ri (do͝ol′ke et de kō′ro͝om est pʀō pä′tʀē ä′ mō′ʀē; *Eng.* dul′sē et di kōr′əm est prō pā′tre ə mōr′ī, môr′ī, -kôr′əm), *Latin.* sweet and fitting it is to die for one's country.

dul·cet (dul′sit), *adj.* **1.** pleasant to the ear; melodious: *the dulcet tones of the cello.* **2.** pleasant or agreeable to the eye or the feelings; soothing. **3.** *Archaic.* sweet to the taste or smell. —*n.* **4.** an organ stop resembling the dulciana but an octave higher. [obs. *dulce* (< L, neut. of *dulcis* sweet) + -ET; r. ME *doucet* < MF; see DOUCE] —**dul′cet·ly,** *adv.* —**dul′cet·ness,** *n.*

dul·ci·an·a (dul′sē an′ə, -ä′nə), *n.* an organ stop having metal pipes and giving thin, incisive, somewhat stringlike tones. [< ML, equiv. to L *dulci(s)* sweet + *-āna,* fem. of *-ānus* -AN]

Dul·ci·belle (dul′sə bel′), *n.* a girl's given name.

Dul·cie (dul′sē), *n.* a girl's given name, form of **Dulce.**

dul·ci·fy (dul′sə fī′), *v.t.,* **-fied, -fy·ing. 1.** to make more agreeable; mollify; appease. **2.** to sweeten. [< LL *dulcificāre,* with -FY for *-ficāre*] —**dul′ci·fi·ca′tion,** *n.*

dul·ci·mer (dul′sə mər), *n.* **1.** a trapezoidal zither with metal strings that are struck with light hammers. **2.** a modern folk instrument related to the guitar and plucked with the fingers. [alter. of ME *dowcemere* < MF *doulcemer,* dissimilated var. of *doulcemele* < OIt *dolcimel(o), dolzemele* < L *dulce melos* sweet song. See DULCET, MELIC]

Dulcimer (def. 1)

dul·cin·e·a (dul sin′ē ə, dul′sə-nē′ə), *n.* a ladylove; sweetheart. [after *Dulcinea* the ladylove of Don Quixote]

Dul·cin·e·a (dul sin′ē ə, dul′sə nē′ə; *Sp.* do͞ol′thē-ne′ä), *n.* a girl's given name.

Dul·ci·tone (dul′si tōn′), *n. Trademark.* a keyboard instrument in which the sound is produced by hammers striking against a set of tuning forks.

Dul·cy (dul′sē), *n.* a girl's given name, form of **Dulce.**

du·li·a (do͞o lī′ə, dyo͞o-), *n. Rom. Cath. Theol.* veneration and invocation given to saints as the servants of God. Cf. **hyperdulia, latria.** [< ML *dūlīa* service, work done < Gk *douleía* slavery, equiv. to *doûl(os)* slave + *-eia* -Y[3]]

dull (dul), *adj.* **1.** mentally slow; lacking brightness of mind; obtuse; somewhat stupid. **2.** lacking keenness of perception in the senses or feelings; insensible; unfeeling. **3.** not intense or acute: *a dull pain.* **4.** slow in motion or action; not brisk; sluggish: *a dull day in the stock market.* **5.** not lively or spirited; listless. **6.** causing boredom; tedious; uninteresting: *a dull sermon.* **7.** not sharp; blunt: *a dull knife.* **8.** having very little depth of color; lacking in richness or intensity of color. **9.** not bright, intense, or clear; dim: *a dull day; a dull sound.* —*v.t., v.i.* **10.** to make or become dull. [ME; akin to OE *dol* foolish, stupid; c. G *toll*] —**dull′ish,** *adj.* —**dull′ness, dul′ness,** *n.* —**dul′ly,** *adv.*

—**Syn. 1.** unimaginative, unintelligent, stolid. DULL, BLUNTED, SLOW, STUPID are applied figuratively to mental qualities. DULL implies obtuseness, inability to receive clear impressions, lack of imagination: *a dull child.* BLUNTED implies loss of original keenness of intelligence through disease, sad experience, and the like: *blunted wits or faculties.* SLOW applies to a sluggish intellect not able rapidly to take in or understand, although its eventual action may be good: *a slow mind.* STUPID implies slowness of mental processes, but also applies to lack of intelligence, wisdom, prudence, etc.: *a stupid person, thing to do.* **5.** apathetic, torpid, inactive, inert. **6.** boring, tiresome, dreary, vapid. **7.** DULL, BLUNT refer to the edge or point of an instrument, tool, or the like. DULL implies a lack or a loss of keenness or sharpness: *a dull razor or saw.* BLUNT may mean the same or may refer to an edge or point not intended to be keen or sharp: *a blunt or stub pen; a blunt foil.* **10.** blunt, deaden, benumb; depress, dishearten, discourage. —**Ant. 1, 5.** bright. **6.** interesting. **7.** sharp, keen.

dull·ard (dul′ərd), *n.* a dull or somewhat stupid person. [DULL + -ARD]

Dul·les (dul′əs), *n.* **John Foster,** 1888–1959, U.S. statesman: Secretary of State 1953–59.

Dul′les Interna′tional Air′port, airport in N Virginia, just west of Washington, D.C., used mainly for international flights.

dull·ish (dul′ish), *adj.* somewhat dull; tending to be dull. [ME; see DULL, -ISH[1]]

du·loc·ra·cy (do͞o lok′rə sē, dyo͞o-), *n.* rule by slaves. [< Gk *doûlo(s)* slave + -CRACY]

du·lo·sis (do͞o lō′sis, dyo͞o-), *n.* the enslavement of an ant colony or its members by ants of a different species. [< Gk *doúlōsis* enslavement, equiv. to *doul(oûn)* (to) enslave + *-ōsis* -OSIS] —**du·lot·ic** (do͞o lot′ik, dyo͞o-), *adj.*

dulse (duls), *n.* a coarse, edible, red seaweed, *Rhodymenia palmata.* [< Scot < Gael *duileasg* (by syncope and loss of final, as in SCOTS, etc.)]

Du·luth (də lo͞oth′), *n.* a port in E Minnesota, on Lake Superior. 106,884 (1960).

du·ly (do͞o′lē, dyo͞o′-), *adv.* **1.** in a due manner; properly; fittingly. **2.** in due season; punctually. [ME *duelich(e).* See DUE, -LY]

du·ma (do͞o′mə; *Russ.* do͞o′mä), *n.* **1.** (in Russia prior to 1917) a council or official assembly. **2.** (*cap.*) an elective legislative assembly, established in 1905 by Nicholas II, constituting the lower house of parliament. Also, **douma.** [< Russ: thought, meditation, council]

Du·ma·gue·te (do͞o′mä ge′te), *n.* a city on S Negros, in the central Philippines. 35,282 (1960).

Du·mas (dʏ mä′ *for 1;* do͞o′məs *for 2, 3*), *n.* **1. A·le·xan·dre** (a lek säɴ′dʀᵊ), (*"Dumas père"*), 1802–70, and his son, **Alexandre** (*"Dumas fils"*), 1824–95, French dramatists and novelists. **2.** a town in N Texas. 8477 (1960). **3.** a town in SE Arkansas. 3540 (1960).

Du Mau·ri·er (do͞o môr′ē ā′, dyo͞o; *Fr.* dʏ mō-ʀyā′), **1. Daphne** (*Lady Browning*), born 1907, English novelist. **2.** her grandfather **George Louis Pal·mel·la Bus·son** (pal mel′ə bo͞o sôn′; *Fr.* bʏ sôɴ′), 1834–96, English illustrator and novelist. **3.** her father, **Sir Gerald (Hubert Edward Bus·son)** (bʏ sôɴ′), 1873–1934, English actor and theatrical manager.

dumb (dum), *adj.* **1.** *Informal.* stupid; dull-witted. **2.** without the power of speech: *a dumb animal.* **3.** temporarily unable to speak: *dumb with astonishment.* **4.** refraining from any or much speech; silent. **5.** made, done, etc., without speech. **6.** lacking some usual property, characteristic, etc. **7.** performed in pantomime; mimed. **8.** *Naut.* **a.** (of a barge) without motors, engines, or sails to propel it. **b.** (of any craft) without means of propulsion, steering, or signaling. [OE; c. Icel *dumbr,* Goth *dumbs,* OS *dumb,* OHG *tump,* G *dumm*] —**dumb′ly,** *adv.* —**dumb′ness,** *n.*

—**Syn. 2, 3.** DUMB, MUTE, SPEECHLESS, VOICELESS describe a condition in which speech is absent. DUMB was formerly used to refer to persons unable to speak; it is now used almost entirely of the inability of animals to speak: *dumb beasts of the field.* The term MUTE is now the one more often applied to persons who, usually because of congenital deafness, have never learned to talk: *With training most mutes learn to speak well enough to be understood.* Either of the foregoing terms or SPEECHLESS may describe a temporary inability to speak, caused by emotion, etc.: *dumb with amazement; mute with terror; left speechless by surprise.* VOICELESS means literally having no voice, either from natural causes or from injury: *Turtles are voiceless. A laryngectomy leaves one voiceless until he has learned esophageal speech.*

dumb′ a′gue, *Pathol.* an irregular form of intermittent malarial fever, lacking the usual chill.

Dum·bar·ton (dum bär′tᵊn), *n.* **1.** Also, **Dunbarton.** Also called **Dum·bar·ton·shire** (dum bär′tᵊn shēr′, -shər). a county in W Scotland. 184,546 (1961); 241 sq. mi. **2.** its county seat, near the Clyde River: shipbuilding. 23,706 (1951).

Dum′bar·ton Oaks′ (dum′bär tᵊn), an estate in the District of Columbia: site of conferences held to discuss proposals for creation of the United Nations August–October, 1944.

dumb′ bar′ter, a form of barter practiced among some primitive peoples, in which the goods for exchange are left at and taken from a preselected spot without the exchanging parties ever coming face-to-face. Also called **silent barter, silent trade.**

dumb·bell (dum′bel′), *n.* **1.** a gymnastic apparatus consisting of two wooden or metal balls connected by a short bar serving as a handle, used as a weight for exercising. **2.** *Slang.* a stupid person. [DUMB + BELL[1]]

Dumbbell

dumb′ bid′, the undisclosed price set by the owner of something to be auctioned, below which no offer will be accepted.

dumb′ cane′, a foliage plant, *Dieffenbachia seguine,* of the West Indies, having yellow-blotched leaves that cause temporary speechlessness when chewed. Also called **mother-in-law plant.**

dumb′ cluck′, *Slang.* a stupid person.

dumb′ com′pass, *Navig.* pelorus.

dumb′ Do′ra, a foolishly simple, stupid, or scatterbrained woman: *She was pretty, but a dumb Dora.*

dumb·head (dum′hed′), *n. Slang.* blockhead. [DUMB + HEAD]

dumb′ sheave′, *Naut.* **1.** a block having no sheave or other part rolling with the movement of a line. **2.** a groove in a spar or other timber, through which a rope can slide.

dumb′ show′, 1. a part of a dramatic representation given in pantomime, common in early English drama. **2.** gestures without speech. —**dumb′-show′,** *adj.*

dumb·struck (dum′struk′), *adj.* temporarily deprived of the power of speech, as by surprise, confusion, etc.; dumfounded. Also, **dumb′-struck′, dumb′struck′, dumb·strick·en** (dum′strik′ən), **dumb′strick′en.** [DUMB + STRUCK]

dumb·wait·er (dum′wā′tər), *n.* **1.** *U.S.* a small elevator, manually or electrically operated, consisting typically of a box with shelves, used in apartment houses, restaurants, and large private dwellings for moving dishes, food, garbage, etc., between floors. **2.** *Brit.* **a.** an auxiliary serving table. **b.** a serving stand with tiers of revolving shelves. **c.** a serving cart. [DUMB + WAITER]

dum·dum (dum′dum′), *n.* a hollow-nosed or soft-nosed bullet that expands greatly on impact, inflicting a severe wound. Also called **dum′dum bul′let.** [after *Dum-Dum,* town in India where the bullets were made]

Dum′dum fe′ver, *Pathol.* kala-azar.

dum·found (dum found′, dum′found′), *v.t.* to make speechless with amazement; astonish. Also, **dumbfound′, dumb·found′er, dumb·found′er.** [DUMB + (CON)FOUND] —**dum·found′er·ment, dumb·found′erment,** *n.*

—**Syn.** amaze, confound, astound, stagger.

Dum·fries (dum frēs′), *n.* **1.** Also called **Dum·fries-shire** (dum frēs′shēr′, -shər, -frēsh′-), a county in S Scotland. 88,423 (1961); 1047 sq. mi. **2.** its county seat: burial place of Robert Burns. 26,320 (1951).

dum·ka (do͝om′kə), *n., pl.* **-ky** (-kē). **1.** a Slavic folk song that alternates in character between sadness and gaiety. **2.** an instrumental composition or movement imitative of such a folk song. [< Czech, equiv. to *dum* (< Gmc; see DOOM) + *-ka* suffix]

dumm·kopf (do͝om′kôf′, -kôpf′, dum′-), *n. Slang.* a stupid person; dumbhead; blockhead. [< G: lit. stupid head]

dum·my (dum′ē), *n., pl.* **-mies,** *adj., v.,* **-mied, -my·ing.** —*n.* **1.** a representation or copy of something, as for displaying to indicate appearance: *a display of lipstick dummies made of colored plastic.* **2.** a representation of a human figure for displaying clothes, as in store windows. **3.** *Informal.* a stupid person; dolt. **4.** one who has nothing to say or who takes no active part in affairs. **5.** one put forward to act for others while ostensibly acting for himself. **6.** *Slang.* a person who lacks the power of speech or is characteristically and habitually silent; mute. **7.** *Cards.* **a.** *Bridge.* the declarer's partner, whose hand is exposed and played by the declarer. **b.** the cards so exposed. **c.** a game so played. **d.** an imaginary player represented by an exposed hand which is played by and serves as partner to one of the players. **8.** *Railroads.* a type of steam locomotive having boiler and running gear completely enclosed, formerly used in city streets. **9.** *Print.* sheets folded and made up to show the size, shape, form, sequence, and general style of a contemplated piece of printing. **10.** a rammer for pushing out dents in lead pipe. **11.** *Computer Technol.* an artificial address, instruction, or other datum fed into a computer only to fulfill prescribed conditions and not affecting operations for solving problems. **12.** *Mil.* a nonexplosive bomb used for practice exercises. **13.** *Dentistry.* pontic. —*adj.* **14.** noting or pertaining to an imitation, representation, or copy. **15.** counterfeit; sham; fictitious. **16.** put forward to act for others while ostensibly acting for oneself. **17.** *Cards.* played with a dummy. —*v.t.* **18.** *Print.* to prepare a dummy of (a contemplated piece of printing) (often fol. by *up*): *The designer dummied up the book so that they could study the format.* **19.** to represent in a dummy (often fol. by *in*). [DUMB + -Y[3]]

dum′my block′, *Metalworking.* a freely moving cylinder for transmitting the pressure of a ram to a piece being extruded.

dum′my joint′, a slot cut into a concrete slab to prevent serious fractures.

dum′my pass′, (in a steel mill or machine shop) a pass in which nothing is done to the work and which is made only to position it for the next operation.

Du·mont (do͞o′mont, dyo͞o′-), *n.* a city in NE New Jersey. 18,882 (1960).

du·mor·ti·er·ite (do͞o môr′tē ə rīt′, dyo͞o-), *n.* a mineral, aluminum borosilicate. [< F, named after Eugène *Dumortier,* 19th-century French paleontologist; see -ITE[1]]

dump[1] (dump), *v.t.* **1.** to drop or let fall in a mass; fling down or drop heavily or suddenly: *Dump the topsoil here.* **2.** to empty out, as from a container by tilting or overturning. **3.** to unload or empty out (a container), as by tilting or overturning. **4.** to be dismissed, fired, or released from a contract: *The first baseman was dumped from the team after hitting .210 for the first half of the season.* **5.** to transfer or rid oneself of suddenly and irresponsibly: *Don't dump your troubles on me!* **6.** *Boxing Slang.* **a.** to knock down: *The champion was dumped twice but won the fight.* **b.** to lose (a match) intentionally: *a bribe to dump a fight.* **7.** *Com.* **a.** to put (goods) on the market in large quantities and at a low price. **b.** to market (goods) thus in a foreign country at a price below that charged in the home country. **8.** *Computer Technol.* **a.** to record (data stored in an internal storage unit at a given instant of time) on an output device, usually as an aid in detecting program errors. **b.** to cut off the electric power of (a computer) accidentally or intentionally. —*v.i.* **9.** to fall or drop down suddenly. **10.** to throw away or dump garbage, refuse, etc. **11.** to offer goods for sale at a low price, esp. in large quantities. —*n.* **12.** an accumulation of discarded garbage, refuse, etc. **13.** a place where garbage, refuse, etc., is deposited. **14.** *Mil.* **a.** a collection of ammunition, stores, etc., deposited at some point, as near a battlefront, to be distributed for use. **b.** the ammunition, stores, etc., so deposited. **15.** the act of dumping. **16.** *Mining.* **a.** a runway or embankment equipped with tripping devices, from which low-grade ore, rock, etc., are dumped. **b.** the pile of ore so dumped. **17.** *Slang.* a place, house, or town that is dilapidated, dirty, or disreputable. **18.** *Computer Technol.* a printed listing of all the information contained in the storage of a computer, or on a computer tape, or both. [ME < Scand; cf. Icel *dumpa* to thump, Dan *dumpe* to fall with a thump] —**dump′er,** *n.*

dump[2] (dump), *n.* **1. dumps,** *Informal.* a depressed state of mind (usually prec. by *in the*): *to be in the dumps over money problems.* **2.** *Obs.* a plaintive melody. **3.** *Obs.* an old dance with a distinctive rhythm. [cf. G *dumpf* dull, MD *domp* haze]

dump[3] (dump), *n.* **1.** *Brit. Dial.* a leaden counter used by boys in certain games. **2.** *Australian.* the center of a Spanish piece of eight reminted in New South Wales, 1813–29, and issued as an Australian coin worth 15 pence. Cf. **holey dollar.** [back formation from DUMPY[2]]

dump·cart (dump′kärt′), *n.* a cart with a body that can be tilted, or a bottom that can be opened downward to discharge the contents. [DUMP[1] + CART]

dump·ish (dum′pish), *adj.* **1.** depressed; sad. **2.** *Obs.* dull; stupid. [DUMP[2] + -ISH[1]] —**dump′ish·ly,** *adv.* —**dump′ish·ness,** *n.*

dump·ling (dump′liṉg), *n.* **1.** a rounded mass of steamed and seasoned dough, often served in soup or with stewed meat. **2.** a kind of pudding consisting of a wrapping of dough enclosing an apple or other fruit, and boiled or baked. **3.** *Informal.* a short or stout person or animal. **4.** *Building Trades.* a mass of earth surrounded with excavations but not removed. [*dump* (< ?) + -LING[1]]

dump′ scow′, See **hopper barge.**

dump′ truck′, a truck having a body that can be tilted to discharge its contents through an open tailgate.

dump·y[1] (dum′pē), *adj.,* **dump·i·er, dump·i·est.** dumpish; dejected; sulky. [DUMP[2] + -Y[1]]

dump·y[2] (dum′pē), *adj.,* **dump·i·er, dump·i·est.** short and stout; squat: *a dumpy woman.* [? akin to DUMPLING] —**dump′i·ly,** *adv.* —**dump′i·ness,** *n.*

dump′y lev′el, *Survey.* an instrument consisting of a spirit level mounted under and parallel to a telescope, the latter being rigidly attached to its supports.

dum spi·ro, spe·ro (dŏŏm spē′rō, spā′rō; *Eng.* dum spī′rō, spēr′ō), *Latin.* while I breathe, I hope: a second motto of South Carolina.

Du·mu·zi (do͞o′mo͞o zē), *n.* the Sumerian god of pastures and vegetation: the consort of Inanna. Cf. **Tammuz.**

dum vi·vi·mus, vi·va·mus (dŏŏm wē′wi mo͞os′, wi-wä′mo͞os; *Eng.* dum viv′i məs, vi vā′məs), *Latin.* while we are living, let us live (to the full).

Dum·yat (dŏŏm yät′), *n.* Arabic name of **Damietta.**

dun[1] (dun), *v.,* **dunned, dun·ning,** *n.* —*v.t.* **1.** to make repeated and insistent demands upon, esp. for the payment of a debt. —*n.* **2.** one who duns, esp. a creditor. **3.** a demand for payment, esp. a written one. [? special use of ME *don(i)e(n)* (to) make a din < Scand; cf. Icel *duna* to make a thundering noise; akin to OE *dynian;* see DIN[1]]

dun[2] (dun), *adj.* **1.** dull, grayish brown. **2.** dark; gloomy. —*n.* **3.** dun color. **4.** a horse of a dun color, with a black mane and tail. **5.** a mayfly. **6.** *Angling.* See **dun fly.** [ME *dun(ne),* OE *dunn;* c. OS *dun*]

Du·na (do͞o′no), *n.* Hungarian name of the **Danube.**

Dü·na (dʏ′nä), *n.* German name of the **Dvina.**

Dü·na·burg (dʏ′nä bo͞orkʜ′), *n.* German name of **Daugavpils.**

Du·naj (do͞o′nī), *n.* Czech and Slovak name of the **Danube.**

Du·nant (*Fr.* dʏ nän′), *n.* **Jean Hen·ri** (*Fr.* zhän än rē′), 1828–1910, Swiss banker and philanthropist; founder of the Red Cross: Nobel peace prize 1901.

Du·nă·rea (do͞o′nə ryä), *n.* Rumanian name of the **Danube.**

Dun·bar (dun′bär *for 1;* dun bär′ *for 2, 3*), *n.* **1. Paul Laurence,** 1872–1906, U.S. poet. **2. William,** c1460–c1520, Scottish poet. **3.** a town in SE Scotland, at the mouth of the Firth of Forth: Cromwell's defeat of the Scots 1650. 4292 (est. 1964).

Dun·bar·ton (dun bär′tᵊn), *n.* Dumbarton.

Dun·can (duṉg′kən), *n.* **1. Isadora,** 1878–1927, U.S. dancer: pioneer in modern dance. **2.** a city in S Oklahoma. 20,009 (1960). **3.** a boy's given name.

Duncan I, died 1040, king of Scotland 1030–40: murdered by Macbeth.

Dun·can Phyfe (duṉg′kən fīf′), of, pertaining to, or resembling the furniture made by Duncan Phyfe, esp. the earlier pieces in the Sheraton and Directoire styles.

Dun·can·ville (duṉg′kən vil′), *n.* a town in N Texas. 3774 (1960).

dunce (duns), *n.* a dull-witted, stupid, or ignorant person; dolt. [after John DUNS SCOTUS, whose writings were attacked by the humanists as foolish] —**dun′ci·cal, dunc′ish,** *adj.* —**dunc′ish·ly,** *adv.*
—**Syn.** dullard, numbskull, blockhead, ignoramus, simpleton, nincompoop, ninny.

dunce′ cap′, a tall, cone-shaped hat formerly worn by slow or lazy students as a punishment in school. Also, **dunce′s cap′.** Also called **fool's cap.**

dunch (dunsh), *n.* *Scot. and North Eng.* a shove; push; jog. [? akin to Icel *dynk(u)r* crashing noise, *dunka* to make a noise, knock, rap; c. Dan *dunke* to thump, knock]

Dun·ci·ad, The (dun′sē ad′), a poem (1728–42) by Pope, satirizing various contemporary writers.

Dun·dalk (dun′dôk), *n.* a town in central Maryland, near Baltimore. 82,428 (1960).

dun·da·voe (dun′də vō′), *n.* See **Irish boat.** [?]

Dun·dee (dun dē′, dun′dē), *n.* a seaport in E Scotland, on the Firth of Tay. 182,959 (1961).

dun·der (dun′dər), *n.* the thick lees from boiled sugar-cane juice, used in the distillation of rum. [alter. of Sp *redundar* to overflow]

dun·der·head (dun′dər hed′), *n.* a dunce; blockhead; numbskull. Also, **dun·der·pate** (dun′dər pāt′). [< D *donderbol* cannon ball, lit., thunder ball; *-bol* means head in D slang; cf. BLOCKHEAD] —**dun′der·head′ed,** *adj.* —**dun′der·head′ed·ness,** *n.*

dune (do͞on, dyo͞on), *n.* a sand hill or sand ridge formed by the wind, usually in desert regions or near lakes and oceans. [< F, OF < OD *dūna;* c. DOWN[3]]

Dun·e·din (dun ē′din), *n.* **1.** a seaport on SE South Island, in New Zealand. 73,245 (1961). **2.** a town in W Florida. 8444 (1960).

dune′ grass′. See **sea lyme grass.**

Dun·el·len (də nel′ən), *n.* a town in NE New Jersey. 6840 (1960).

Dun·ferm·line (dun fûrm′lin, -ferm′-, dum-), *n.* a city in SW Fife, in E Scotland, near the Firth of Forth. 47,159 (1961).

dun′ fly′, *Angling.* a dun-colored artificial fly that resembles the larval stage of certain real flies.

dung (duṉg), *n.* **1.** manure; excrement, esp. of animals. —*v.t.* **2.** to manure (ground) with or as with dung. [ME, OE; c. LG, G *dung;* cf. Icel *dyngja* heap, dung, Sw *dynga* dung, muck, OHG *tunga* manuring] —**dung′y,** *adj.*

dun·ga·ree (duṉg′gə rē′), *n.* **1. dungarees, a.** work clothes, overalls, etc., of blue denim. **b.** See **blue jeans. 2.** *Obsolesc.* blue denim. [< Hindi *dungrī*]

dung′ bee′tle, any of various scarabaeid beetles that feed upon or breed in dung.

Dun′ge·ness crab′ (dun′jə nes′, dun′jə nes′), a small, edible crab, *Cancer magister,* found in the shallow waters of the Pacific coast from northern California to Alaska. [after *Dungeness,* village in NW Washington]

dun·geon (dun′jən), *n.* **1.** any strong; close prison or cell, usually underground, as in a medieval castle. **2.** the keep or stronghold of a castle; donjon. [ME *dungeo(u)n, donjon,* etc. < MF *donjon* < LL *domniōn-* (s. of *domniō*) keep, mastery, syncopated var. of **dominiōn-* DOMINION]

dung·hill (duṉg′hil′), *n.* **1.** a heap of dung. **2.** a repugnantly filthy or degraded place, abode, condition, or person. [ME; see DUNG, HILL]

dun·ie·was·sal (do͞o′nē wos′əl), *n.* a gentleman, esp. a cadet of a ranking family, among the Highlanders of Scotland. [< Gael *duine vasal* man wellborn, gentleman]

du·nite (do͞o′nīt, dun′īt), *n.* a coarse-grained igneous rock, composed almost entirely of olivine. [named after Mt. *Dun* in New Zealand, where it is found; see -ITE[1]]

dunk (duṉgk), *v.t.* **1.** to dip (a doughnut, cake, etc.) into coffee, milk, or the like, before eating. **2.** to submerge in a liquid: *She dunked the curtains in the dye.* —*v.i.* **3.** to dip or submerge something, oneself, etc., in a liquid: *She thinks it's vulgar to dunk. Let's dunk in the pool before dinner.* [< G *dunk(en),* nasalized var. of *ducken* to DUCK[2]] —**dunk′er,** *n.*

Dunk·er (duṉg′kər), *n.* a member of a denomination of Christians founded in Germany in 1708 and later reorganized in the U.S., characterized by the practice of trine immersion, the celebration of a love feast accompanying the Lord's Supper, and opposition to the taking of oaths and to military service. Also, **Dunk·ard** (duṉg′kərd), **Tunker.** Official name, **Church of the Brethren.** [< G: lit., ducker, dipper, i.e., baptizer by immersion]

Dun·kirk (dun′kûrk), *n.* **1.** French, **Dun·kerque** (dœn kerk′). a seaport in N France: scene of the evacuation of a British expeditionary force of over 330,000 men under German fire May 29–June 4, 1940. 28,388 (1962). **2.** a city in W New York, on Lake Erie. 18,205 (1960). **3.** a town in E Indiana. 3117 (1960).

Dun Laoghai·re (dun lâr′ə), a seaport in E Republic of Ireland, near Dublin. 47,792 (1961). Also called **Dun·lea·ry.**

dun·lin (dun′lin), *n.* a common sandpiper, *Erolia alpina,* which breeds in the northern parts of the Northern Hemisphere. [var. of *dunling.* See DUN[2], -LING[1]]

Dun·lop (dun lop′, dun′lop), *n.* **John Boyd,** 1840–1921, Scottish inventor of the pneumatic tire.

Dun·more (dun mōr′, -môr′; dun′mōr, -môr), *n.* **1. John Murray, 4th Earl of,** 1732–1809, Scottish colonial governor in America. **2.** a borough in NE Pennsylvania, near Scranton. 18,917 (1960).

Dunn (dun), *n.* a town in central North Carolina. 7566 (1960).

dun·nage (dun′ij), *n., v.,* **-naged, -nag·ing.** —*n.* **1.** baggage or personal effects. **2.** loose material laid beneath or wedged among objects carried by ship or rail to prevent injury from chafing or moisture, or to provide ventilation. —*v.t.* **3.** to cover or pack with dunnage. [cf. D (*het is*) *dunnetjes* (it is) poor stuff]

Dunne (dun), *n.* **Fin·ley Peter** (fin′lē), 1867–1936, U.S. humorist.

dunn·ite (dun′īt), *n.* an ammonium picrate explosive used as a bursting charge for armor-piercing projectiles and in high-explosive shells; explosive D. [named after Col. B. W. *Dunn* (1860–1936), U.S. Army, the inventor; see -ITE[1]]

dun·no (də nō′), *Eye Dialect.* don't know: *Who did it? I dunno!*

dun·nock (dun′ək), *n.* *Brit. Dial.* the hedge sparrow. [ME *dunoke, donek.* See DUN[2], -OCK]

Du·nois (dʏ nwa′), *n.* **Jean** (zhän), **Count de,** (*"Bastard of Orleans"*), 1403?–68; French military leader: relieved by Joan of Arc and her troops when besieged at Orleans.

du Noü·y ten·si·om·e·ter (də no͞o′ē ten′sē om′i-tər), *Physical Chem.* a device for measuring the surface tension of liquids.

Dun·sa·ny (dun sā′nē), *n.* **Edward John More·ton Drax Plun·kett** (mōr′tᵊn draks pluṉg′ket, -kit, mōr′-), **8th Baron** (*"Lord Dunsany"*), 1878–1957, Irish dramatist, poet, and essayist.

Dun·si·nane (dun′sə nān′, dun′sə nān′), *n.* a hill NE of Perth, in central Scotland: a ruined fort on its summit is traditionally called Macbeth's Castle. 1012 ft.

Duns·muir (dunz′myŏŏr), *n.* a town in N California. 2873 (1960).

Duns Sco·tus (dunz skō′təs), **John** (*"Doctor Subtilis"*), 1265?–1308, Scottish scholastic theologian.

Dun·sta·ble (dun′stə bəl), *n.* **John,** c1390–1453, English composer. Also, **Dun·sta·ple** (dun′stə pəl).

Dun·stan (dun′stən), *n.* **Saint,** A.D. c925–988, English statesman: archbishop of Canterbury 961–978.

dunt[1] (dunt, dŏŏnt), *Scot.* —*n.* **1.** a hard blow or hit, esp. one that makes a dull sound; thump. **2.** a wound from such a blow. —*v.t., v.i.* **3.** to strike, esp. with a dull sound; thump. [ME; c. Sw *dunt* DINT]

dunt[2] (dunt), *v.i.* (of ceramic ware) to crack because of excessively rapid cooling. [?]

Dun·thorne (dun′thôrn), *n.* a crater in the third quadrant of the face of the moon: about 8 miles in diameter.

du·o (do͞o′ō, dyo͞o′ō), *n., pl.* **du·os. 1.** *Music.* duet. **2.** two persons commonly associated with one another; couple. **3.** two animals or objects of the same sort; two things ordinarily placed or found together; a pair: *a duo of lovebirds.* [< It < L: two]

duo-, an element borrowed from Greek and Latin meaning "two," used in the formation of compound words: *duologue.* [comb. form of Gk *dýo,* L *duo* TWO]

du·o·dec·a·gon (do͞o′ə dek′ə gon′, dyo͞o′-), *n.* *Geom.* dodecagon.

du·o·dec·a·style (do͞o′ə dek′ə stīl′, dyo͞o′-), *adj.* dodecastyle.

du·o·de·cil·lion (do͞o′ō di sil′yən, dyo͞o′-), *n., pl.* **-lions,** (*as after a numeral*) **-lion,** *adj.* —*n.* **1.** a cardinal number represented in the U.S. and France by one followed by 39 zeros, and in Great Britain and Germany by one followed by 72 zeros. —*adj.* **2.** amounting to one duodecillion in number. [< L *duodec(im)* twelve + *-illion,* as in *million*] —**du′o·de·cil′lionth,** *n., adj.*

du·o·dec·i·mal (do͞o′ə des′ə məl, dyo͞o′-), *adj.* **1.** pertaining to twelfths or to the number twelve. **2.** proceeding by twelves. —*n.* **3.** one of a system of numbers based on the number 12. **4.** one of twelve equal parts. [< L *duodecim* twelve + -AL[1]] —**du′o·dec′i·mal′i·ty,** *n.* —**du′o·dec′i·mal·ly,** *adv.*

du·o·dec·i·mo (do͞o′ə des′ə mō′, dyo͞o′-), *n., pl.* **-mos,** *adj.* —*n.* **1.** Also called **twelvemo.** a book size of about 5 × 7½ inches, determined by printing on sheets folded to form 12 leaves or 24 pages. *Abbr.:* 12mo, 12° **2.** a book of this size. —*adj.* **3.** in duodecimo; twelvemo. [short for L *in duodecimō* in twelfth]

du·o·dec′u·ple scale′ (do͞o′ə dek′yə pəl, -dek′ə-, dyo͞o′-), *Music.* a scale consisting of the 12 chromatic tones, with each regarded as an individual scale degree and none as an altered or attendant tone of a diatonic scale. [< L *duodec(im)* twelve, modeled on *decuple*]

duoden-, a combining form of **duodenum:** *duodenitis.* Also, *esp. before a consonant,* **duodeno-.**

du·o·de·nal (do͞o′ə dēn′ᵊl, dyo͞o′-; do͞o od′ᵊnᵊl, dyo͞o-), *adj.* of or pertaining to the duodenum. [DUODEN- + -AL[1]]

du·o·den·a·ry (do͞o′ə den′ə rē, -dē′nə rē, dyo͞o′-), *adj.* duodecimal. [DUODEN- + -ARY]

du·o·de·ni·tis (do͞o′ō di nī′tis, dyo͞o′-; do͞o od′ᵊnī′tis, dyo͞o-), *n.* *Pathol.* inflammation of the duodenum. [DUODEN- + -ITIS]

duodeno-, var. of **duoden-** before a consonant: *duodenojejunostomy.*

du·o·de·no·je·ju·nos·to·my (do͞o′ə dē′nō ji jo͞o-nos′tə mē, dyo͞o′-), *n., pl.* **-mies.** *Surg.* the formation of an artificial connection between the duodenum and the jejunum. [DUODENO- + JEJUNOSTOMY]

du·o·de·num (do͞o′ə dē′nəm, dyo͞o′-; do͞o od′ᵊnəm, dyo͞o-), *n., pl.* **du·o·de·na** (do͞o′ə dē′nə, dyo͞o′; do͞o od′ᵊnə, dyo͞o-), **du·o·de·nas.** *Anat., Zool.* the first portion of the small intestine, from the stomach to the jejunum. See diag. under **intestine.** [< ML; L *duodēn(ī)* twelve each, so called from its length, about twelve finger-breadths]

du·o·di·ode (do͞o′ə dī′ōd, dyo͞o′-), *n.* *Electronics.* a vacuum tube having two diodes within the same envelope. Also called **double diode.** [DUO- + DIODE]

du·o·di·ode-pen·tode (do͞o′ō dī′ōd pen′tōd, dyo͞o′-), *n.* *Electronics.* a vacuum tube having two diodes and a pentode within the same envelope.

du·o·logue (do͞o′ə lôg′, -log′, dyo͞o′-), *n.* **1.** a conversation between two persons; dialogue. **2.** a dramatic performance or piece in the form of a dialogue limited to two speakers. [DUO- + (MONO)LOGUE]

duo·mo (dwô′mô), *n., pl.* **-mi** (-mē). *Italian.* cathedral. [lit., dome]

du·op·o·ly (do͞o op′ə lē, dyo͞o-), *n., pl.* **-lies.** the market condition which exists when there are two sellers only. Cf. **monopoly** (def. 1), **oligopoly.** [DUO- + (MONO)POLY]

du·op·so·ny (do͞o op′sə nē, dyo͞o-), *n., pl.* **-nies.** the market condition which exists when there are two buyers only. Cf. **monopsony, oligopsony.** [DU(O)- + *-opsony* < Gk *opsōnía* purchasing of food, equiv. to *ópson* viands + *ōn(eisthai)* (to) buy + *-ia* -Y[3]]

du·o·tone (do͞o′ə tōn′, dyo͞o′-), *adj.* **1.** of two tones or colors. —*n.* **2.** a picture in two tones or colors. **3.** *Print.* **a.** a method of printing an illustration in two shades of the same color from two negatives of a monochrome original made at different screen angles. **b.** an illustration printed by this method. [DUO- + TONE]

du·o·tri·ode (do͞o′ə trī′ōd, dyo͞o′-), *n.* *Electronics.* a vacuum tube having two triodes within the same envelope. Also called **double triode.** [DUO- + TRIODE]

du·o·type (do͞o′ə tīp′, dyo͞o′-), *n.* *Print.* two halftone plates made from a monochrome original but etched differently to create two values of intensity when superimposed in printing. [DUO- + -TYPE]

dup (dup), *v.t.,* **dupped, dup·ping.** *Brit. Dial.* to push or swing open. [contr. of DO[1] + UP, cf. DOFF, DON[2]]

dup., duplicate.

dupe[1] (do͞op, dyo͞op), *n., v.,* **duped, dup·ing.** —*n.* **1.** a person who is easily deceived or fooled; gull. **2.** a person who unquestioningly or unwittingly serves a cause or another person: *a dupe of the communists.* —*v.t.* **3.** to make a dupe of; deceive; delude; trick. [< F; MF *duppe* for **(tête) d'uppe* head of hoopoe, i.e., fool (cf. *tête de fou*) < VL **uppa,* L *upupa* hoopoe, a bird thought to be especially stupid (F *huppe* hoopoe < aspirated var.)] —**dup′a·bil′i·ty,** *n.* —**dup′a·ble,** *adj.* —**dup′er,** *n.*

dupe[2] (do͞op, dyo͞op), *adj., n., v.t.,* **duped, dup·ing.** *Informal.* duplicate. [by shortening]

du·per·y (do͞o′pə rē, dyo͞o′-), *n., pl.* **-er·ies. 1.** the act, practice, or an instance of duping. **2.** the state of one who is duped. [< F *duperie.* See DUPE¹, -ERY]

du·pi·on (do͞o′pē on′), *n.* **1.** a cocoon formed jointly by two silkworms. **2.** douppioni. Also, **du·pi·o·ni** (do͞o′pē ō′nē). [alter. of F *doupion* < It *doppione,* equiv. to *doppi(e)* DOUBLE + *-one* aug. suffix]

du·pla·tion (do͞o plā′shən, dyo͞o-), *n.* multiplication by two; doubling. [< L *duplātiō* a doubling, equiv. to *duplāt(us)* (*dupl(us)* DUPLE + *-ātus* -ATE¹) + *-iō* -ION]

du·ple (do͞o′pəl, dyo͞o′-), *adj.* **1.** having two parts; double; twofold. **2.** *Music.* having two or sometimes a multiple of two beats in a measure: *duple meter.* [< L *dupl(us)* double]

Du·pleix (dʏ pleks′), *n.* **Jo·seph Fran·çois** (zhō zef′ fräN swa′), **Marquis,** 1697–1763, French colonial governor of India 1724–54.

du′ple rhythm′, *Pros.* a rhythmic pattern created by a succession of disyllabic feet.

Du·ples·sis-Mor·nay (dʏ ple sē′môr nā′), *n.* **Phi·lippe** (fē lēp′). See **Mornay, Philippe de.**

du′ple time′, *Music.* characterized by two beats to the measure. Also called **du′ple meas′ure, two-part time.**

du·plex (do͞o′pleks, dyo͞o′-), *adj.* **1.** having two parts; double; twofold. **2.** (of a machine) having two identical working units, operating together or independently, in a single framework or assembly. **3.** pertaining to or noting a telegraphic system permitting the simultaneous transmission of two messages in opposite directions over one channel. —*n.* **4.** See **duplex apartment. 5.** See **duplex house. 6.** paper or cardboard having different colors, finishes, or stocks on opposite sides. **7.** *Print.* a method of reproducing an illustration using two halftone plates, one black and the other in a color. **8.** a printing press equipped to print both sides of a sheet in one pass. **9.** a Linotype matrix having two type molds on the same piece of brass. **10.** the alternative face on a Linotype matrix. [< L: twofold, double, equiv. to *du(o)* two + *-plex* fold (cf. *plexus* interwoven)] —**du·plex′i·ty,** *n.*

du′plex apart′ment, an apartment, or a suite of rooms, on two connected floors or stories. Also called **duplex.**

du·plex·er (do͞o′plek sər, dyo͞o′-), *n. Electronics.* an automatic electronic switching device that permits the use of the same antenna for transmitting and receiving. [DUPLEX + -ER¹]

du′plex escape′ment, *Horol.* an escapement in which the escape wheel has two sets of teeth, one set locked by a roller on the balance staff having a slot releasing the teeth, the other set giving impulses to the balance staff through a pallet projecting from the balance staff.

du′plex house′, a house having separate apartments for two families, esp. a two-story house having a complete apartment on each floor and two separate entrances.

du′plex lock′, a lock capable of being opened either by a master key or a change key, each operating its own mechanism.

du′plex proc′ess, any of several methods for making steel in which the process is begun in one furnace and finished in another.

du′plex pump′, a pair of direct-acting steam pumps so arranged that each pump begins its working stroke just as the other finishes its working stroke, so that the rate of flow of the fluid is nearly continuous.

du·pli·ca·ble (do͞o′plə kə bəl, dyo͞o′-), *adj.* capable of being duplicated. [DUPLIC(ATE) + -ABLE] —**du′pli·ca·bil′i·ty,** *n.*

du·pli·cate (*adj., n.* do͞o′plə kit, dyo͞o′-; *v.* do͞o′plə kāt′, dyo͞o′-), *adj., n., v.,* **-cat·ed, -cat·ing.** —*adj.* **1.** exactly like or corresponding to something else: *duplicate copies of a map.* **2.** double; consisting of or existing in two identical or corresponding parts. **3.** *Cards.* noting a game in which each team plays a series of identical hands, the winner being the team making the best total score: *duplicate bridge.* —*n.* **4.** a copy exactly like an original. **5.** anything corresponding in all respects to something else. **6.** *Cards.* a duplicate game. **7. in duplicate,** in two copies, esp. two identical copies made at one time: *Please type the letter in duplicate.* —*v.t.* **8.** to make an exact copy of. **9.** to repeat; do or perform again: *He duplicated his father's failure.* **10.** to double; make twofold. [< L *duplicāt(us)* (ptp. of *duplicāre* to make double), equiv. to *duplic-* (s. of *duplex*) DUPLEX + *-ātus* -ATE¹] —**du′pli·ca′tive,** *adj.*
—**Syn. 2.** twofold. **4.** facsimile, replica, reproduction. **8.** See **imitate.** —**Ant. 4.** original.

du′plicating machine′, 1. a duplicator, esp. one for making duplicates of documents, letters, etc. **2.** profiler.

du·pli·ca·tion (do͞o′plə kā′shən, dyo͞o′-), *n.* **1.** the act or an instance of duplicating. **2.** the state of being duplicated. **3.** a duplicate. [< L *duplicātiōn-* (s. of *duplicātiō*), equiv. to *duplicāt(us)* (see DUPLICATE) + *-iōn-* -ION; r. ME *duplicacioun* < AF]

duplica′tion of the cube′, *Geom.* the unsolved problem of constructing a cube having twice the volume of a given cube.

du·pli·ca·tor (do͞o′plə kā′tər, dyo͞o′-), *n.* a machine for making duplicates. [< L; see DUPLICATE, -OR²]

du·pli·ca·ture (do͞o′plə kə cho͝or′, -kə chər, -kā′chər, dyo͞o′-), *n.* a folding or doubling of a part on itself, as a membrane. [< NL *duplicātūra.* See DUPLICATE, -URE]

du·pli·ca·tus (do͞o′plə kā′təs, dyo͞o′-), *adj. Meteorol.* (of a cloud) consisting of superposed layers that sometimes partially merge. [< L: doubled; see DUPLICATE]

du·plic·i·ty (do͞o plis′i tē, dyo͞o-), *n., pl.* **-ties. 1.** deceitfulness in speech or conduct; speaking or acting in two different ways concerning the same matter with intent to deceive; double-dealing. **2.** a twofold or double state or quality. [ME *duplicite* < MF < LL *duplicitāt-* (s. of *duplicitās*), equiv. to L *duplic-* (s. of *duplex*) DUPLEX + *-itāt-* -ITY]
—**Syn. 1.** deception, dissimulation. See **deceit.** —**Ant. 1.** straightforwardness.

duplic′ity the′ory, *Physiol.* the theory that the retina in man and other vertebrates contains cone-shaped cells, sensitive both to the color and intensity of light and promoting vision in bright light, and rod-shaped cells, sensitive only to the intensity of light and promoting vision in dim light. Also called **duplic′ity prin′ciple.**

Du·po (do͞o′pō, dyo͞o′-), *n.* a town in SW Illinois. 2937 (1960).

du·pon·di·us (do͞o pon′dē əs, dyo͞o-), *n., pl.* **-di·i** (-dē ī′). a coin of ancient Rome, equal to two asses. [< L, equiv. to *duo* TWO + *pond(us)* weight, POUND² + *-ius* adj. suffix]

Du Pont (do͞o pont′, dyo͞o-, do͞o′pont, dyo͞o′-; *for 1, 2 also Fr.* dʏ pôN′), **1. E·leu·thère I·ré·née** (e lœ tεr′ ē Rā nā′), 1771–1834, U.S. industrialist, born in France. **2. Pierre Samuel** (pē âr′ sam′yo͞o əl; *Fr.* pyεr sa mʏ el′), 1739–1817, French economist and statesman (father of Irénée). **3. Samuel Francis,** 1803–65, Union admiral in the U.S. Civil War.

Du·pont (də pont′), *n.* a town in NE Pennsylvania. 3669 (1960).

Du·pré (dʏ pRā′), *n.* **1. Jules** (zhʏl), 1812–89, French painter. **2. Mar·cel** (maR sel′), born 1886, French organist and composer.

Du·quesne (do͞o kān′, dyo͞o-; *for 1 also Fr.* dʏ ken′), *n.* **1. A·bra·ham** (a bRa am′), 1610–88, French naval commander. **2.** a city in SW Pennsylvania, on the Monongahela River. 15,019 (1960). **3. Fort.** See **Fort Duquesne.**

Du Quoin (do͞o koin′), a town in SW Illinois. 6558 (1960).

dur (do͞oR), *adj. German.* (in music) written in a major key; major.

Dur., Durango.

du·ra (do͝or′ə, dyo͝or′ə), *n.* See **dura mater.** —**du′ral,** *adj.*

du·ra·ble (do͝or′ə bəl, dyo͝or′-), *adj.* **1.** able to resist wear, decay, etc., well; lasting; enduring. —*n.* **2. durables.** See **durable goods.** [ME < MF < L *dūrābil(is).* See DURE², -ABLE] —**du′ra·bil′i·ty, du′ra·ble·ness,** *n.* —**du′ra·bly,** *adv.*
—**Syn. 1.** permanent. —**Ant. 1.** weak, transitory.

du′rable goods′, goods that are not consumed or destroyed in use and can be used over a number of years, as appliances and machinery.

du·rain (do͝or′ān, dyo͝or′-), *n. Mineral.* the coal forming the dull layers in banded bituminous coal. Cf. **clarain, vitrain.** [< L *dūr(us)* hard + *-ain,* as in *clarain, fusain*]

du·ral·u·min (do͝o ral′yə min, dyo͝o-), *n.* an alloy of aluminum that is four percent copper and contains small amounts of magnesium, manganese, iron, and silicon: used for applications requiring lightness and strength, as in airplane construction. [< L *dūr(us)* hard + ALUMIN(UM)]

du′ra ma′ter (mā′tər), *Anat.* the tough, fibrous membrane forming the outermost of the three coverings of the brain and spinal cord. Also called **dura.** Cf. **arachnoid** (def. 6), **pia mater.** [late ME < ML: lit., hard mother]

du·ra·men (do͝o rā′min, dyo͝o-), *n. Bot.* the hard central wood, or heartwood, of an exogenous tree. [< L *dūrāmen* hardness, hardened vine branch, equiv. to *dūrā(re)* (to) harden + *-men* noun suffix]

dur·ance (do͝or′əns, dyo͝or′-), *n.* **1.** imprisonment, esp. long confinement. **2.** *Archaic.* **a.** duration. **b.** endurance. [late ME < MF. See DURE², -ANCE]

Du·rand (də rand′), *n.* a town in central Michigan. 3312 (1960).

Du·ran·go (do͝o rang′gō; *for 1, 2 also Sp.* do͞o Räng′gō), *n.* **1.** a state in N Mexico. 750,220 (1960); 47,691 sq. mi. **2.** a city in and the capital of this state, in the S part. 94,257 (1960). **3.** a city in SW Colorado. 10,530 (1960).

Du·rant (də rant′), *n.* **1. Will(iam James),** born 1885, U.S. author and historian. **2.** a town in central Mississippi. 2617 (1960).

du·ran·te vi·ta (do͞o Rän′te wē′tä; *Eng.* do͝o ran′tē vī′tə, dyo͝o-), *Latin.* during life.

Du·ran·ty (do͝o ran′tē), *n.* **Walter,** 1884–1957, English journalist and author in the U.S.

du·ra·tion (do͝o rā′shən, dyo͝o-), *n.* **1.** continuance in time. **2.** the length of time something continues or exists. **3.** (in the philosophy of Bergson) a temporal continuum, intuitively known, within which the élan vital operates. **4. the duration,** (*sometimes cap.*) *Slang.* (during World War II) the time until the end of the war: *No vacations for the duration.* [< LL *dūrātiōn-* (s. of *dūrātiō*), equiv. to *dūrāt(us)* (ptp. of *dūrāre* to last; see DURE²) + *-iōn-* -ION] —**du·ra′tion·al,** *adj.*

dur·a·tive (do͝or′ə tiv, dyo͝or′-), *adj. Gram.* noting or pertaining to a verb aspect expressing incomplete or continued action. *Beat* and *walk* are durative in contrast with *strike* and *step.* [DURAT(ION) + -IVE]

Du·raz·zo (də rät′sō; *It.* do͞o Rät′tsō), *n.* a seaport in W Albania, on the Adriatic: important ancient city. 32,300 (est. 1958). Albanian, **Durrës.**

Dur·ban (dûr′bən), *n.* a seaport in SE Natal, in the E Republic of South Africa. 655,370 (1960).

dur·bar (dûr′bär), *n.* (in India) **1.** the court of a native ruler. **2.** a public audience or levee held by a native prince or by a British governor or viceroy; an official reception. **3.** the hall or place of audience. **4.** the audience itself. [alter. of Urdu *darbār* court < Pers, equiv. to *dar* door + *bār* entry]

dure¹ (do͝or, dyo͝or), *adj. Archaic.* hard; severe. [ME < MF < L *dūr(us)* hard]

dure² (do͝or, dyo͝or), *v.i., v.t.,* **dured, dur·ing.** *Archaic.* endure. [ME < OF *dur(er)* < L *dūrāre* to last; see DURE¹]

Du·rene (do͝o rēn′, dyo͝o-), *n.* a girl's given name.

Dü·rer (do͝or′ər, dyo͝or′-; *Ger.* dʏ′Rər), *n.* **Al·brecht** (äl′bRεkHt) or **Al·bert** (äl′bert), 1471–1528, German painter and engraver.

du·ress (do͝o res′, dyo͝o-, do͝or′is, dyo͝or′-), *n.* **1.** compulsion by threat; coercion; constraint. **2.** forcible restraint, esp. imprisonment. **3.** *Law.* such constraint or coercion as will render void a contract or other legal act entered or performed under its influence. [ME *duresse* < MF *duresse, -esce, -ece* < L *dūritia* hardness, harshness, oppression, equiv. to *dūr(us)* hard + *-itia* -ICE]

du·ress·or (do͝o res′ər, dyo͝o-), *n. Law.* one who subjects another to duress. [DURESS + -OR²]

D'Ur·fey (dûr′fē), *n.* **Thomas,** 1653–1723, English dramatist.

Dur·ga (do͝or′gä), *n. Hinduism.* the goddess of war, sometimes malignant: an aspect of Devi.

Dur·ga Pu·ja (do͝or′gə po͞o′jə), Dasehra.

Dur·ham (dûr′əm), *n.* **1.** a county in NE England. 1,517,039 (1961); 1015 sq. mi. **2.** its county seat. 20,484 (1961). **3.** a city in N North Carolina. 78,302 (1960). **4.** a town in SE New Hampshire. 4688 (1960). **5.** *Stockbreeding.* Shorthorn.

du·ri·an (do͝or′ē ən), *n.* **1.** the edible fruit of a tree, *Durio zibethinus,* of southeastern Asia, having a hard, prickly rind, a highly flavored, pulpy flesh, and an offensive odor. **2.** the tree itself. Also, **du′ri·on.**

dur·ing (do͝or′ing, dyo͝or′-), *prep.* **1.** throughout the duration, continuance, or existence of: *He lived in Florida during the winter.* **2.** at some time or point in the course of: *They departed during the night.* [ME; orig. DURE² + -ING²]

Durk·heim (dûrk′hīm; *Fr.* dʏR kem′), *n.* **É·mile** (ā mēl′), 1858–1917, French sociologist and philosopher.

dur·mast (dûr′mast′, -mäst′), *n.* a European oak, *Quercus petraea,* yielding a heavy, elastic wood used for furniture and in the construction of buildings. [short for *durmast oak,* i.e. ? oak yielding MAST² even in times of dearth; see DEAR²]

du·ro (do͝or′ō; *Sp.* do͞o′Rō), *n., pl.* **-ros** (-rōz; *Sp.* -Rôs). a peso of Spain or Spanish America.

Du·roc (do͝or′ok, dyo͝or′-), *n.* one of an American breed of hardy red hogs having drooping ears. Also called **Du·roc-Jer·sey** (do͝or′ok jûr′zē, dyo͝or′-). [named after a horse owned by breeder]

dur·ra (do͝or′ə), *n.* a type of grain sorghum with slender stalks, cultivated in Asia and Africa and introduced into the U.S. Also, **doura, dourah.** Also called **Indian millet, Guinea corn.** [< Ar *dhura(h)*]

Dur·rell (do͝or′əl), *n.* **Lawrence (George),** born 1912, English novelist and poet.

Dur·rës (do͞oR′Rəs), *n.* Albanian name of **Durazzo.**

dur·rie (dûr′ē), *n.* a fringed, usually rectangular cotton carpet manufactured in India. Also, **dhurrie.**

durst (dûrst), *v.* a pt. of **dare.**

du′rum wheat′ (do͝or′əm, dyo͝or′-), a wheat, *Triticum durum,* the grain of which yields flour used in making macaroni, spaghetti, etc. Also called **du′rum.**

Dur·yea (do͝or′yā, do͝or′ē ā′), *n.* **1. Charles Edgar,** 1861–1938, U.S. inventor and manufacturer of automobile and automotive devices. **2.** a town in NE Pennsylvania. 5626 (1960).

Du·se (do͞o′ze), *n.* **E·le·o·no·ra** (e′le ô nô′Rä), (*Signora Checchi*), 1859–1924, Italian actress.

Du·se·hra (dus′ər ə), *n.* Dasehra. Also, **Du·she·hra** (dush′ər ə), **Dus·se·hra, Dus·se·ra, Dus·se·rah** (dus′ər ə).

dü·sen·wind (do͞o′zən wind′, dyo͞o′-), *n.* a strong east-northeast wind that blows out of the Dardanelles into the Aegean Sea. [*düsen* (< ?) + WIND¹]

Du·shan·be (do͞o shän′bə, -shäm′-, dyo͞o-; *Russ* do͞o shun bye′), *n.* a city in and the capital of Tadzhikistan, in the SW Russian Federation in Asia, SW of Tashkent. 493,000. Formerly, **Dyushambe** (before 1929), **Stalinabad** (1929–61).

dusk¹ (dusk), *n.* **1.** the state or period of partial darkness between day and night; the dark part of twilight. **2.** partial darkness; shade; gloom: *She was invisible in the dusk of the room.* [back formation from DUSKY]

dusk² (dusk), *adj.* **1.** dark; tending to darkness. —*v.t., v.i.* **2.** to make or become dusk; darken. [ME *duske* (adj.), *dusken* (v.); metathetic alter. of OE *dox* dusky, *doxian* to turn dark; c. L *fuscus* dark] —**dusk′ish,** *adj.*

dusk·y (dus′kē), *adj.,* **dusk·i·er, dusk·i·est. 1.** somewhat dark; having little light; dim; shadowy. **2.** having dark skin. **3.** of a dark color **4.** gloomy. [DUSK² + -Y¹] —**dusk′i·ly,** *adv.* —**dusk′i·ness,** *n.*
—**Syn. 2.** DUSKY, SWARTHY both mean dark in color. They differ more in application than in meaning. DUSKY suggests shadiness or a veiled and dim light, as well as darkness of coloring: *dusky twilight shadows; a dusky grove; a dusky Ethiopian.* SWARTHY, which usually denotes a greater degree of darkness or blackness, is used only of the complexion: *a swarthy skin.*

dusk′y grouse′, a gallinaceous game bird, *Dendragapus obscurus,* of western North America.

dusk′y shark′, a blue-gray shark, *Carcharinus obscurus,* found in the warmer parts of the Atlantic and eastern Pacific oceans, reaching a length of 12 feet.

Düs·sel·dorf (do͝os′əl dôrf′; *Ger.* dʏs′əl dôRf′), *n.* a port in and the capital of North Rhine-Westphalia, in W West Germany, on the Rhine. 704,000. (1963).

dust (dust), *n.* **1.** earth or other matter in fine, dry particles. **2.** any finely powdered substance, as sawdust. **3.** a cloud of finely powdered earth or other matter in the air. **4.** the ground; the earth's surface. **5.** that to which anything, as the human body, is ultimately reduced by disintegration or decay. **6.** *Brit.* **a.** ashes, refuse, etc. **b.** junk¹ (def. 1). **7.** a low or humble condition. **8.** anything worthless. **9.** disturbance; turmoil. **10.** See **gold dust. 11.** *Archaic.* the mortal body of man. **12.** *Archaic.* a single particle or grain. **13.** *Archaic.* money; cash. **14. bite the dust, a.** to be killed, esp. in battle; die. **b.** to suffer defeat; be unsuccessful; fail: *Another manufacturer has bitten the dust.* **15. lick the dust, a.** to be killed; die. **b.** to humble oneself abjectly; grovel: *He will resign rather than lick the dust.* **16. make the dust fly,** to execute with vigor or speed: *We turned them loose on the work, and they made the dust fly.* **17. shake the dust from one's feet,** to depart in anger or disdain; leave decisively: *As the country moved toward totalitarianism, many of the intelligentsia shook its dust from their feet.* **18. throw dust in someone's eyes,** to mislead; deceive: *Certain advertisers are under investigation for throwing dust in the public's eyes.* —*v.t.* **19.** to wipe the dust from: *to dust a table.* **20.** to sprinkle with a powder or dust: *to dust rosebushes with an insecticide.* **21.** to strew or sprinkle (a powder, dust, or other fine particles): *to dust insecticide on a rosebush.* **22.** to soil with dust; make dusty. —*v.i.* **23.** to wipe dust from a table, room, etc. **24.** to become dusty. **25.** to apply dust or powder to a plant, one's body, etc.: *to dust with an insecticide in late spring.* **26. dust off,** *Slang.* **a.** *Baseball.* (of a pitcher) to throw the ball purposely at or dangerously close to (the batter). **b.** to beat up badly: *The gang of hoodlums dusted off a cop.* **c.** to take out or prepare for use again, as after a period of inactivity or storage: *I'm going to dust off that old gun and see if I can still hit a rabbit.* [ME; OE *dūst;* c. G *Dunst* vapor] —**dust′less,** *adj.*

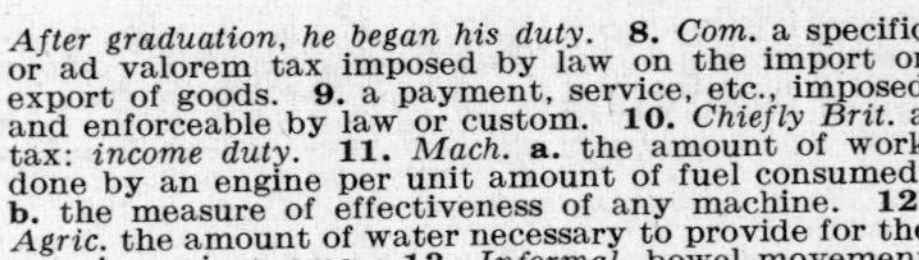

dust′ bin′, *Chiefly Brit.* ash can; garbage can.

dust′ bowl′, an area subject to dust storms, esp. the region in S central U.S. which suffered from such storms in the 1930's.

dust′ cart′, *Brit.* a garbage truck.

dust·cloth (dust′klôth′, -kloth′), *n., pl.* **-cloths** (-klôt͟hz′, -klot͟hz′, -klôths′, -kloths′). a soft, absorbent cloth, as flannel, cheesecloth, or jersey, used for dusting furniture or the like. [DUST + CLOTH]

dust′ count′, the number of dust particles in the atmosphere at a particular time, based on samplings.

dust′ count′er, any instrument used to measure the amount and size of dust particles in the atmosphere. Also called **kern counter, nucleus counter.**

dust′ cov′er, 1. a cloth covering, often of muslin, used to protect furniture or furnishings during an extended period of nonuse. 2. See **book jacket.**

dust′ dev′il, a small whirlwind 10–100 feet in diameter and from several hundred to 1000 feet high, common in dry regions on hot, calm afternoons and made visible by the dust, debris, and sand it picks up from the ground. Also called **dust whirl.**

dust·er (dus′tər), *n.* **1.** one who or that which removes or applies dust. **2.** a cloth, brush, etc., for removing dust. **3.** an apparatus or device for sprinkling dust, powder, insecticide, or the like, esp. on plants. **4.** a person employed in spreading insecticidal dusts or the like on crops from a low-flying plane. **5.** a long, light overgarment, worn esp. in the early days of open automobiles to protect the clothing from dust. **6.** a woman's lightweight housecoat. **7.** a summer-weight coat for women, loose-fitting and often unlined. **8.** See **dust storm. 9.** *Informal.* See **dry hole. 10.** *Baseball Slang.* a ball purposely thrown by a pitcher at or dangerously close to a batter. [DUST + -ER[1]]

dust′ gun′, a hand spray for filling with insecticide, poison, or the like, and dusting plants, treating ratholes, etc.

dust·heap (dust′hēp′), *n.* **1.** a heap or pile of rubbish, refuse, or the like. **2.** oblivion; obscurity; disregard; disuse: *He was consigned to the dustheap after many years of public service.* [DUST + HEAP]

Dus·tin (dus′tin), *n.* a boy's given name.

dust·ing (dus′ting), *n.* **1.** a light application: *a dusting of powder.* **2.** *Slang.* a beating; defeat: *He gave his opponent a good dusting.* [DUST + -ING[1]]

dust′ing pow′der, a powder used on the skin, esp. to relieve irritation or absorb moisture.

dust′ jack′et. See **book jacket.**

dust·man (dust′man′, -mən), *n., pl.* **-men** (-men′, -mən). *Brit.* **1.** a garbage man; one employed to remove or cart away garbage, refuse, ashes, etc. **2.** sandman. [DUST + MAN[1]]

dust′ mop′, a long-handled mop of dry, absorbent material, used for dusting floors. Also called **dry mop.**

du·stoor (də sto͝or′), *n.* dastur. Also, **du·stour′.**

dust·pan (dust′pan′), *n.* a short-handled shovellike utensil into which dust is swept for removal. [DUST + PAN[1]]

dust·proof (dust′pro͞of′), *adj.* impervious to dust. [DUST + -PROOF]

dust′ shot′, the smallest size of shot for use in a shotgun.

dust′ storm′, a storm of strong winds and dust-filled air over an extensive area during a period of drought over normally arable land (distinguished from *sandstorm*). Also, **dust′storm′.** Also called **duster.**

dust·up (dust′up′), *n.* a quarrel; argument; row. [n. use of v. phrase *dust up*]

dust′ well′, a hollow in the surface of a glacier, formed by the melting action of dust or soil deposits.

dust′ whirl′. See **dust devil.**

dust·y (dus′tē), *adj.,* **dust·i·er, dust·i·est. 1.** filled, covered, or clouded with or as with dust. **2.** of the nature of dust; powdery. **3.** of the color of dust; gray. [ME; see DUST, -Y[1]] **—dust′i·ly,** *adv.* **—dust′i·ness,** *n.*

dust′y clo′ver, a bush clover, *Lespedeza capitata.*

dust′y mill′er, **1.** *Angling.* a type of artificial fly used chiefly for trout and salmon. **2.** an herb, *Centaurea cineraria*, of southern Italy, having white foliage and large, yellow or purple flower heads. **3.** a similar, related herb, *C. gymnocarpa*, of Capri, having small, clustered, rose-purple flowers. **4.** a hairy, branching, herbaceous perennial, *Senecio cineraria*, of the Mediterranean region, having cream-colored or yellow flowers. **5.** See **rose campion** (def. 1).

Dutch (duch), *adj.* **1.** of, pertaining to, or characteristic of the natives or inhabitants of the Netherlands or their country or language. **2.** pertaining to or designating the style of painting and subject matter developed in the Netherlands during the 17th century, chiefly characterized by the use of chiaroscuro, muted tones, naturalistic colors or forms, and of genre, landscape, or still-life subjects drawn from contemporary urban and rural life. **3.** *U.S.* of, pertaining to, or characteristic of the Pennsylvania Dutch. **4.** *Slang.* German; Teutonic. **5. go Dutch,** *Informal.* to have each person pay his own expenses: *a trip where everyone goes Dutch.* **—***n.* **6.** the people of the Netherlands and their immediate descendants elsewhere, collectively. **7.** *U.S.* See **Pennsylvania Dutch. 8.** the Germanic language of the Netherlands. **9.** *Obs.* the German language. **10. beat the Dutch,** *Informal.* to be incomprehensible or surprising: *How does he do it? It beats the Dutch.* **11. in Dutch,** *Slang.* **a.** in trouble. **b.** in disfavor (with someone): *in Dutch with the teacher for disturbing the class.* [ME *Du(c)ch* < MD *du(u)tsch*; c. OHG *diutisc* popular (as opposed to learned), trans. of L *vulgāris* vernacular; akin to OE *theodisc* speech]

Dutch 200, *Bowling Slang.* a score of 200 in a game, made by bowling strikes and spares alternately.

Dutch′ auc′tion, a method of auction consisting in the offer of a property at a price above the actual value and then at gradually reduced prices until a buyer is found.

Dutch′ Belt′ed, one of a breed of black dairy cattle, raised originally in the Netherlands, having a broad white belt encircling the body.

Dutch′ bond′, *n.* a brickwork bond of alternate courses of headers and stretchers, the joints between stretchers being over the centers of the stretchers in the next courses above and below; English cross bond.

Dutch′ Bor′neo, the former name of the southern and larger part of the island of Borneo: now part of Indonesia.

Dutch′ chair′, *Eng. Furniture.* a chair of c1700, derived from Dutch models, having curved uprights, a wide splat joined to the seat rail, and cabriole legs.

Dutch′ cheese′. See **cottage cheese.**

Dutch′ cir′cle, *Survey.* circumferentor.

Dutch′ clo′ver. See **white clover.**

Dutch′ cour′age, *Informal.* courage inspired by drunkenness or drinking liquor: *At the time, Dutch courage seemed better than none at all, so he took a few more nips at the bottle.*

Dutch′ cup′board, a buffet with open upper shelves.

Dutch′ door′, a door consisting of two units horizontally divided so that while the upper part is open the lower can remain closed.

Dutch door

Dutch′ East′ Indies, a former name of the Republic of Indonesia.

Dutch′ elm′ disease′, *Plant Pathol.* a disease of elms, characterized by wilting, yellowing, and falling of the leaves, caused by a fungus, *Ceratostomella ulmi,* transmitted by bark beetles.

Dutch′ foot′, *Furniture.* any of several varieties of pad foot.

Dutch′ gold′, an alloy of copper and zinc in the form of thin sheets, used as a cheap imitation of gold leaf. Also called **Dutch′ foil′, Dutch′ leaf′, Dutch metal.**

Dutch′ Guian′a, Surinam.

Dutch′ Har′bor, a U.S. naval base on Unalaska Island, in the Aleutian Islands.

Dutch′ lap′, a method of laying shingles, slates, or the like, in which each shingle or slate overlaps those below and to one side and is itself overlapped by those above and to the other side.

Dutch′ lunch′, an individual portion or serving of cold cuts. Also, **dutch′ lunch′.**

Dutch·man (duch′mən), *n., pl.* **-men. 1.** a native or inhabitant of the Netherlands. **2.** *Building Trades.* a piece or wedge inserted to hide the fault in a badly made joint, to stop an opening, etc. **3.** *Theat.* a narrow strip of canvas to conceal the join between two flats. **4.** *Archaic.* a German. [ME; see DUTCH, MAN[1]]

Dutch·man's-breech·es (duch′mənz brich′iz), *n., pl.* **-breech·es.** an herb, *Dicentra* (or *Bicuculla*) *cucullaria,* having pale-yellow, two-spurred flowers. Also called **white eardrop.** [so called from the shape of the flowers]

Dutch′man's land′, *Naut. Slang.* an illusory land mass on the horizon, caused by the presence of a cloud bank or the like; Cape Flyaway.

Dutch′man's log′, *Naut.* a method of gauging a ship's speed, in which the distance between two shipboard observation stations is divided by the time elapsing between the throwing overboard of an object by the first station and the sighting of it by the second.

Dutch·man's-pipe (duch′mənz-pīp′), *n.* a climbing, aristolochiaceous vine, *Aristolochia Sipho,* having large leaves and flowers of a curved form suggesting a tobacco pipe.

Dutchman's-pipe, *Aristolochia Sipho*

Dutch′ met′al. See **Dutch gold.**

Dutch′ New′ Guin′ea, a former name of **West Irian.**

Dutch′ ov′en, **1.** a heavily constructed kettle with a close-fitting lid, used for pot roasts, stews, etc. **2.** a metal utensil, open in front, for roasting before an open fire. **3.** a brick oven in which the walls are preheated for cooking.

Dutch′ Reformed′, of or pertaining to a Protestant denomination **(Dutch′ Reformed′ Church′),** founded by Dutch settlers in New York in 1628 and renamed the Reformed Church in America in 1867.

Dutch′ rush′. See **scouring rush.**

Dutch′ set′tle, *Furniture.* a settle having a back so hinged that it can be lowered onto the arms to form a table.

Dutch′ straight′, *Poker.* See **skip straight.**

Dutch′ treat′, a meal or entertainment for which each person pays his own way.

Dutch′ un′cle, *Informal.* a person who criticizes or reproves with unsparing severity and frankness: *He talked to her like a Dutch uncle.*

Dutch′ West′ Indies, a former name of **Netherlands Antilles.**

Dutch′ wife′, (in tropical countries) an open framework used in beds as a rest for the limbs.

du·te·ous (do͞o′tē əs, dyo͞o′-), *adj.* dutiful; obedient. [DUTY + -OUS] **—du′te·ous·ly,** *adv.* **—du′te·ous·ness,** *n.*

du·ti·a·ble (do͞o′tē ə bəl, dyo͞o′-), *adj.* subject to duty, as imported goods. [DUTY + -ABLE] **—du′ti·a·bil′i·ty,** *n.*

du·ti·ful (do͞o′ti fəl, dyo͞o′-), *adj.* **1.** performing the duties expected or required of one; characterized by doing one's duty: *a dutiful citizen; a dutiful child.* **2.** required by duty; proceeding from or expressive of a sense of duty: *dutiful attention.* [DUTY + -FUL] **—du′ti·ful·ly,** *adv.*
—Syn. 1. respectful, docile, submissive, duteous.

du·ty (do͞o′tē, dyo͞o′-), *n., pl.* **-ties. 1.** that which one is expected or required to do by moral or legal obligation. **2.** the binding or obligatory force of that which is morally or legally right; moral or legal obligation. **3.** action or a task required by one's position or occupation; function: *the duties of a clergyman.* **4.** the respectful and obedient conduct due to a parent, superior, elder, etc. **5.** an act or expression of respect. **6.** a task or chore which one is expected to perform: *It's your duty to do the dishes.* **7.** *Mil.* **a.** an assigned task, occupation, or place of service: *He was on radar duty for two years.* **b.** the military service required of a citizen by a country: *After graduation, he began his duty.* **8.** *Com.* a specific or ad valorem tax imposed by law on the import or export of goods. **9.** a payment, service, etc., imposed and enforceable by law or custom. **10.** *Chiefly Brit.* a tax: *income duty.* **11.** *Mach.* **a.** the amount of work done by an engine per unit amount of fuel consumed. **b.** the measure of effectiveness of any machine. **12.** *Agric.* the amount of water necessary to provide for the crop in a given area. **13.** *Informal.* bowel movement (used chiefly in reference to children). **14. do duty,** to serve the same function; substitute for: *bookcases that do duty as room dividers.* **15. off duty,** not at one's post or work; at liberty: *They spent their days off duty in hiking and fishing.* **16. on duty,** at one's post or work; occupied; engaged: *He was suspended from the force for being drunk while on duty.* [ME *du(e)te* < AF *duete.* See DUE, -TY[2]]
—Syn. 1. DUTY, OBLIGATION refer to what one feels bound to do. DUTY is what one performs, or avoids doing, in fulfillment of the permanent dictates of conscience, piety, right, or law: *duty to one's country; one's duty to tell the truth, to raise children properly.* An OBLIGATION is what one is bound to do to fulfill the dictates of usage, custom, or propriety, and to carry out a particular, specific, and often personal promise or agreement: *financial or social obligations.* **3.** responsibility, business. **4.** deference, reverence. **8.** impost.

du·ty-free (do͞o′ti frē′, dyo͞o′-), *adj., adv.* free of customs duty: *duty-free cargo; merchandise shipped duty-free.*

du·um·vir (do͞o um′vər, dyo͞o-), *n., pl.* **-virs, -vi·ri** (-və rī′). *Rom. Hist.* one of two officers or magistrates jointly exercising the same public function. [< L, back formation from *duumvirōrum,* gen. pl. of *duovirī* two men, equiv. to *duo-* DUO- + *virī,* pl. of *vir* man, c. OE *wer* (see WEREWOLF)]

du·um·vi·rate (do͞o um′vər it, dyo͞o-), *n.* **1.** a coalition of two men holding the same office, as in ancient Rome. **2.** the office or government of two such persons. [< L *duumvirāt(us).* See DUUMVIR, -ATE[1]]

Du·va·lier (do͞o′väl yā′; *Fr.* dʏ va lyā′), *n.* **François** (fräɴ swa′), born 1907, Haitian physician and statesman: president since 1957.

Du·ve·neck (do͞o′və nek′), *n.* **Frank** (*Frank Decker*), 1848–1919, U.S. painter and teacher.

du·ve·tyn (do͞o′vi tēn′), *n.* a napped fabric, in a twilled or plain weave, of cotton, wool, silk, or rayon. Also, **du′ve·tine′, du′ve·tyne′.** [< F *duvetine,* equiv. to *duvet* down + *-ine* -INE[2]]

Du·vi·da (*Port.* do͞o′vē də), *n.* **Rí·o da** (*Port.* rē′o͞o də). See **Roosevelt, Río.**

du Vi·gneaud (do͞o vēn′yō, dyo͞o), **Vincent,** born 1901, U.S. biochemist: Nobel prize for chemistry 1955.

dux (duks, do͝oks), *n., pl.* **du·ces** (do͞o′sēz, dyo͞o′-, do͞o′kās), **dux·es** (duk′siz, do͝ok′-). **1.** *Chiefly Scot.* the student who is academically first in his class or school. **2.** (in the later Roman Empire) a military chief commanding the troops in a frontier province. [< L: leader]

D.V., 1. Deo volente. **2.** Douay Version (of the Bible).

dvai·ta (dvī′tə), *n. Hinduism.* **1.** any of the pluralistic schools of philosophy. **2.** (*cap.*) (in Vedantic philosophy) one of the two principal schools, asserting that entities have a real existence apart from Brahman. Cf. **Advaita.** [< Skt; akin to TWO]

dvan·dva (dvän′dvä, dvun′dvə), *n. Gram.* a compound word neither element of which is subordinate to the other, as *bittersweet, Anglo-Saxon.* [< Skt, nasalized redupl. of *dva* TWO]

Dva·pa·ra Yu·ga (dvä′pər ə yo͝og′ə), *Hinduism.* the third of the Yugas, not as good as the Treta Yuga but better than the Kali Yuga. [< Skt, equiv. to *dvāpara* third best (*dvā* TWO + *para* ahead) + *yuga* era (lit., YOKE)]

Dvi·na (dvi nä′), *n.* **1.** Lettish, **Daugava.** German, **Düna.** a river in the W Soviet Union in Europe, flowing NW to the Baltic Sea at Riga. ab. 640 mi. long. **2. Northern,** a river in the N Soviet Union in Europe, flowing NW into the White Sea. ab. 470 mi. long.

Dvina′ Bay′, an arm of the White Sea, in the NW Soviet Union in Europe. Formerly, **Gulf of Archangel.**

Dvinsk (dvēnsk), *n.* Russian name of **Daugavpils.**

D.V.M., Doctor of Veterinary Medicine.

D.V.M.S., Doctor of Veterinary Medicine and Surgery.

Dvo·řák (*Eng.* dvôr′zhäk, -zhak; *Czech* dvô′ʀzhäk), *n.* **An·ton** (*Eng.* an′tən, -ton; *Czech* än′tôn), 1841–1904, Czech composer.

D.V.S., Doctor of Veterinary Surgery.

D/W, dock warrant.

dwalm (dwäm, dwam), *n. Chiefly Scot.* a swooning spell; faint. [OE *dwolma* confusion, chaos; c. G *Twalm* giddiness; cf. OE *dwola* madman, *dwolian* to wander, etc.]

dwarf (dwôrf), *n.* **1.** a person who is considerably smaller than the average in stature or size, esp. one who is not normally proportioned. **2.** an animal or plant much below the ordinary size of its kind or species. **3.** a legendary being in the form of a small, often misshapen and ugly, man, usually having magic powers. **4.** See **dwarf star. —***adj.* **5.** of unusually small stature or size; diminutive. **—***v.t.* **6.** to cause to appear or seem small in size, extent, character, etc., as by being much larger or better: *He dwarfed all his rivals in general ability.* **7.** to make dwarf or dwarfish; prevent the due development of. **—***v.i.* **8.** to become stunted or smaller. [ME *dwerf,* OE *dweorh;* r. ME *dwerg,* OE *dweorg;* c. OHG *twerg,* Icel *dvergr*]
—Syn. 1. DWARF, MIDGET, PYGMY are terms for a very small person. A DWARF is one checked in growth, or stunted; he usually has a large head or is in some way not normally formed: *In the past, dwarfs were considered very comical.* A MIDGET is one perfect in form and normal in function, but like a tiny replica of the ordinary species: *Some midgets are like handsome dolls.* A PYGMY is properly a member of one of certain small-sized peoples of Africa and Asia, but the word is often used to mean dwarf or midget. **2.** runt, miniature. **—Ant. 1, 5.** giant.

dwarf′ al′der, **1.** a small buckthorn, *Rhamnus alnifolia,* having leaves resembling those of an alder. **2.** a low shrub, *Fothergilla gardeni,* of the southeastern U.S., having wedge-shaped leaves and white flowers, grown as an ornamental.

dwarf′ banan′a, a large herb, *Musa cavendishi*, of southern China, having bluish-green leaves, yellowish-white flowers with reddish-brown bracts, and fragrant, edible, curved fruit from four to five inches long, often borne in clusters of 200. Also called **Cavendish banana, Chinese banana.**

dwarf′ chest′nut, any low, shrubby chestnut, as the chinquapin.

dwarf′ cor′nel, the bunchberry.

dwarf′ crest′ed i′ris, a low iris, *Iris cristata*, of the eastern and central U.S., having faintly fragrant, yellow-crested, blue flowers. Also called **crested iris.**

dwarf′ door′, a door of approximately half normal height, as the lower half of a Dutch door.

dwarf′ fan′ palm′, a fan palm, *Chamaerops humilis*, of the Mediterranean region, having stiff, bluish-green leaves. Also called **European fan palm.**

dwarf′ gin′seng, a perennial herb, *Panax trifolius*, of eastern North America, having globe-shaped clusters of small, white flowers and yellow fruit.

dwarf′ gold′enrod, an herb, *Solidago nemoralis*, of eastern North America, having one-sided, terminal clusters of yellow flowers. Also called **gray goldenrod.**

dwarf·ish (dwôr′fish), *adj.* like a dwarf, esp. in being abnormally small; diminutive. [DWARF + -ISH[1]] —**dwarf′ish·ly,** *adv.* —**dwarf′ish·ness,** *n.* —**Syn.** pygmy, tiny, stunted, runty.

dwarf·ism (dwôr′fiz əm), *n. Med.* the condition of being a dwarf or dwarfed. [DWARF + -ISM]

dwarf′ Jap′anese quince′, a low, shrubby flowering quince, *Chaenomeles japonica*, of Japan, having orange-to-scarlet flowers and yellow fruit.

dwarf′ June′berry, a sprawling shrub, *Amelanchier stolonifera*, of America, forming patches due to its underground stolons and having sweet, blackish-purple fruit used for making jelly.

dwarf′ lau′rel. See **sheep laurel.**

dwarf′ mal′low, a European herb, *Malva neglecta*, having roundish leaves and small pinkish-white flowers.

dwarf′ morn′ing-glory, a semiprostrate plant, *Convolvulus tricolor*, of southern Europe, having white-margined, blue flowers with yellow throats.

dwarf′ nastur′tium, an annual herb, *Tropaeolum minus*, of South America, having yellow-orange flowers.

dwarf′ palmet′to, an apparently stemless palm, *Sabal minor*, of the southeastern U.S., having stiffish, bluish-green leaves, the leafstalks arising from the ground. Also called **bluestem.**

dwarf′ poincia′na. See **Barbados pride** (def. 2).

dwarf′ star′, *Astron.* a star of relatively small volume but often of very high density. Cf. **white dwarf.**

dwarf′ su′mac, a shrub or small tree, *Rhus copallina*, of the eastern U.S., having greenish flowers.

Dwayne (dwān), *n.* a boy's given name. Also, **Duane.**

dwell (dwel), *v.*, **dwelt** or **dwelled, dwell·ing,** *n.* —*v.i.* **1.** to live or stay as a permanent resident; reside. **2.** to live or continue in a given condition or state: *to dwell in happiness.* **3.** to linger over, emphasize, or ponder in thought, speech, or writing (often fol. by *on* or *upon*): *to dwell on a particular point in an argument.* **4.** (of a moving tool or machine part) to be motionless for a certain interval during operation. —*n. Mach.* **5.** a flat or cylindrical area on a cam for maintaining a tool or part in a certain position during part of a cycle. **6.** a period in a cycle in the operation of a machine during which a given tool or part remains motionless. [ME *dwell(en)* (to) lead astray, stun, abide, OE *dwellan* to lead or go astray, hinder; c. Icel *dvelja*] —**dwell′er,** *n.*

dwell·ing (dwel′ing), *n.* a building or place of shelter to live in; place of residence; abode; home. [ME; see DWELL, -ING[1]] —**Syn.** See **house.**

dwell′ing house′, a house occupied, or intended to be occupied, as a residence.

dwell′ing place′, a dwelling.

dwelt (dwelt), *v.* a pt. and pp. of **dwell.**

Dwight (dwīt), *n.* **1. Timothy,** 1826–1916, U.S. ecclesiastic, pres. Yale Univ., 1886–98. **2.** a town in central Illinois. 3086 (1960). **3.** a boy's given name.

dwin·dle (dwin′dəl), *v.*, **-dled, -dling.** —*v.i.* **1.** to become smaller and smaller; shrink; waste away: *His vast fortune has dwindled away.* **2.** to fall away, as in quality; degenerate. —*v.t.* **3.** to make smaller and smaller; cause to shrink: *Failing health dwindles ambition.* [DWINE + -LE] —**Syn. 1.** diminish, decline, lessen, wane. See **decrease. 3.** lessen. —**Ant. 1.** increase. **3.** magnify.

dwine (dwīn), *v.i.*, **dwined, dwin·ing.** *Chiefly Dial.* to waste away; fade. [ME; OE *dwīn(an)* (to) waste away; c. MD *dwīnen* to languish, Icel *dvína* to pine away]

dwt, pennyweight; pennyweights.

d.w.t., deadweight tonnage.

DX, *Radio.* **1.** distance. **2.** distant. Also, **D.X.**

Dy, *Chem.* dysprosium.

dy·ad (dī′ad), *n.* **1.** a group of two; couple; pair. **2.** *Biol.* **a.** a secondary morphological unit, consisting of two monads: *a chromosome dyad.* **b.** the double chromosomes resulting from the separation of the four chromatids of a tetrad. **3.** *Chem.* an element, atom, or group having a valence of two. Cf. **monad, triad** (def. 2a). **4.** *Math.* two vectors with no symbol connecting them, usually considered as an operator. —*adj.* **5.** of two parts; dyadic. [< Gk *dyad-* (s. of *dyás*) pair, equiv. to *dý(o)* two + *-ad-* n. suffix]

dy·ad·ic (dī ad′ik), *adj.* **1.** of, or consisting of, two parts. **2.** pertaining to the number two. —*n.* **3.** *Math.* two or more dyads added together. [< Gk *dyadik(ós)*. See DYAD, -IC]

dyad′ic sys′tem. See **binary system.**

Dy·ak (dī′ak), *n.* Dayak.

Dy·ane (dī an′), *n.* a girl's given name. Also, **Diana, Diane, Dy·an′a.**

dy·ar·chy (dī′är kē), *n., pl.* **-chies.** diarchy. —**dy·ar′chic, dy·ar′chi·cal,** *adj.*

Dyaus (dyous), *n.* the Vedic god of the sky. Also called **Dyaus-pit·ar** (dyous′pit′ər).

dyb·buk (dib′ək; *Heb.* dē bōōk′), *n., pl.* **dyb·buks, dyb·bu·kim** (di bōōk′im; *Heb.* dē bōō kēm′). *Jewish Folklore.* a demon, or the soul of a dead person, that enters the body of a living person and directs his conduct, exorcism being possible only by a religious ceremony. Also, **dibbuk.** [< Yiddish *dibbūk* devil < Heb *dibbūq*, akin to *dābhaq* to hang on]

Dyce (dīs), *n.* **Alexander,** 1798–1869, Scottish editor.

dye (dī), *n., v.*, **dyed, dye·ing.** —*n.* **1.** a coloring material or matter. **2.** a liquid containing coloring matter, for imparting a particular hue to cloth, paper, etc. **3.** color or hue, esp. as produced by dyeing. **4. of the deepest** or **blackest dye,** of the most extreme or the worst sort: *a prevaricator of the blackest dye.* —*v.t.* **5.** to color or stain; treat with a dye; color (cloth, hair, etc.) with a substance containing coloring matter: *to dye a dress green.* **6.** to impart (color) by means of a dye: *The coloring matter dyed green.* —*v.i.* **7.** to impart color, as a dye: *This brand dyes well.* **8.** to become colored or absorb color when treated with a dye: *This cloth dyes easily.* [ME *die(n)*, OE *dēagian*, deriv. of *dēag* a dye] —**dy′a·ble, dye′a·ble,** *adj.* —**dy′er,** *n.*

dyed-in-the-wool (dīd′ən *th*ə wōōl′), *adj.* **1.** dyed before weaving. **2.** through-and-through; complete: *a dyed-in-the-wool Republican.*

dye·ing (dī′ing), *n.* process of coloring fibers, yarns, or fabrics. [OE *dēagunge.* See DYE, -ING[1]]

dye·line (dī′līn′), *n. Photog.* a contact print of a line drawing, giving brown lines on an off-white background. [DYE + LINE[1]]

Dy·er (dī′ər), *n.* **1. John,** 1700–58, British poet. **2.** a town in NW Indiana. 3993 (1960).

dy·er's-broom (dī′ərz brōōm′, -brōōm′), *n.* woadwaxen.

dy′er's green′weed (grēn′wēd′), woadwaxen. Also called **dy′er's furze′, dy′er's green′wood.**

Dy·ers·ville (dī′ərz vil′), *n.* a town in E Iowa. 2818 (1960).

dy·er's-weed (dī′ərz wēd′), *n.* any of various plants yielding dyes, as the weld, *Reseda Luteola*, the dyeweed, *Genista tinctoria*, or the woad, *Isatis tinctoria.*

dy′er's wood′ruff, a perennial herb, *Asperula tinctoria*, of Europe, having red or pinkish-white flowers and red roots, and growing well in moist soil.

dye′ sen′sitizing, *Photog.* the producing of panchromatic or orthochromatic film by treating it with an emulsion containing dyes that absorb light of all or certain colors.

dye·stuff (dī′stuf′), *n.* a material yielding or used as a dye. [prob. trans. of G *Farbstoff*]

dye′ trans′fer, *Photog.* **1.** a process of color printing in which positives on film from three separation negatives are dyed in cyan, magenta, and yellow, and transferred to a sheet of paper to form the print. **2.** a print made by this process.

dye·weed (dī′wēd′), *n.* a fabaceous shrub, *Genista tinctoria*, of the Old World, having yellow flowers and yielding a yellow dye. [DYE + WEED[1]]

dye·wood (dī′wŏŏd′), *n.* any wood yielding a coloring matter used for dyeing. [DYE + WOOD[1]]

dy·ing (dī′ing), *adj.* **1.** ceasing to live; approaching death: *a dying man.* **2.** of, pertaining to, or associated with death: *a dying hour.* **3.** given, uttered, or manifested just before death: *dying words.* **4.** drawing to a close: *the dying year.* —*n.* **5.** the act or process of ceasing to live, ending, or drawing to a close. [late ME (n., adj.), ME (n.). See DIE[1], -ING[2], -ING[1]]

dyke[1] (dīk), *n., v.*, **dyked, dyk·ing.** dike[1].

dyke[2] (dīk), *n. Slang.* a female homosexual; lesbian. [orig. *bulldyke* < ?]

Dyl·an (dil′ən), *n.* a boy's given name.

Dy·mas (dī′məs), *n.* (in the *Aeneid*) a Trojan who fought with Aeneas against the Greeks.

dyn, dyne; dynes.

dyn., dynamics. Also, **dynam.**

dyna-, a learned borrowing from Greek meaning "power," used in the formation of compound words: *dynamotor.* Also, **dynam-, dynamo-.** [comb. form of Gk *dýnamis* power, *dýnasthai* to be able]

dy·nam·e·ter (dī nam′i tər), *n. Optics.* an instrument for determining the magnifying power of telescopes. [DYNA- + -METER]

dy·nam·ic (dī nam′ik), *adj.* **1.** pertaining to or characterized by energy or effective action; vigorously active or forceful; energetic. **2.** *Physics.* **a.** of or pertaining to force or power. **b.** of or pertaining to force related to motion. **3.** pertaining to dynamics. **4.** of or pertaining to the range of volume of musical sound. Also, **dy·nam′i·cal.** [< F *dynamique* < Gk *dynamik(ós)*, equiv. to *dýnam(is)* force, power + *-ikos* -IC] —**dy·nam′i·cal·ly,** *adv.*

dynam′ical astron′omy, the branch of astronomy that deals with the application of the laws of dynamics and Newton's law of gravitation to the motions of heavenly bodies. Cf. **celestial mechanics.**

dynam′ical stabil′ity, *Naval Archit.* **1.** a measure of the work required to heel a vessel to a specified angle, equal to the product of the displacement and the righting lever, expressed in foot-tons. **2.** a measure of the work required to heel a sailing vessel to a specified angle, equal to the product of the wind pressure on the sails and the vertical distance between the center of effort and the center of lateral resistance.

dynam′ic geol′ogy, the branch of geology dealing with geological change.

dynam′ic meteorol′ogy, the branch of meteorology dealing with the study of atmospheric motion and its causal relation to other forces. Cf. **physical meteorology.**

dynam′ic psychol′ogy, any approach to psychology which emphasizes drives and motives as determinants of behavior.

dy·nam·ics (dī nam′iks), *n.* **1.** (*construed as sing.*) *Physics.* the branch of mechanics that deals with the motion and equilibrium of systems under the action of forces, usually from outside the system. **2.** (*construed as pl.*) the science or principles of forces acting in any field. **3.** (*construed as pl.*) the motivating or driving forces, physical or moral, in any field. **4.** (*construed as pl.*) the pattern or history of growth, change, and development in any field. **5.** (*construed as pl.*) the variations and gradation in the volume of musical sound. [see DYNAMIC, -ICS]

dynam′ic similar′ity, a principle whereby model airplanes, ships, and hydraulic structures are operated for test purposes under conditions exactly simulating full-scale performance.

dynam′ic strength′, resistance of a structure to loads suddenly applied.

dy·na·mism (dī′nə miz′əm), *n.* **1.** any of various theories or philosophical systems which seek to explain phenomena of nature by the action of force. Cf. **mechanism** (def. 7), **vitalism** (def. 1). **2.** great force or power; vigor: *the dynamism of the new opera singer.* **3.** *Psychol.* a habitual mode of reducing or eliminating tension. [DYNAM- + -ISM] —**dy′na·mist,** *n.* —**dy′na·mis′tic,** *adj.*

dy·na·mite (dī′nə mīt′), *n., v.*, **-mit·ed, -mit·ing.** —*n.* **1.** a high explosive, originally consisting of nitroglycerin mixed with an absorbent substance such as kieselguhr, now with ammonium nitrate usually replacing the nitroglycerin. **2.** *Slang.* any person or thing having a spectacular effect. —*v.t.* **3.** to blow up, shatter, or destroy with dynamite: *Saboteurs dynamited the dam.* **4.** to mine or charge with dynamite. [DYNAM- + -ITE[1]] —**dy·na·mit·ic** (dī′nə mit′ik), *adj.* —**dy′na·mit′i·cal·ly,** *adv.*

dy·na·mit·er (dī′nə mī′tər), *n.* a person who uses dynamite, esp. for revolutionary purposes. Also, **dy′na·mit′ist.** [DYNAMITE + -ER[1]]

dy·na·mo (dī′nə mō′), *n., pl.* **-mos. 1.** an electric generator, esp. for direct current. **2.** *Informal.* an energetic, hard-working, forceful person. [short for DYNAMOELECTRIC]

dynamo-, var. of **dyna-:** *dynamometer.* Also, **dynam-.**

dy·na·mo·e·lec·tric (dī′nə mō i lek′trik), *adj.* pertaining to the conversion of mechanical energy into electric energy, or vice versa: *a dynamoelectric machine.* Also, **dy′na·mo·e·lec′tri·cal.** [DYNAMO- + ELECTRIC]

dy·na·mo·gen·e·sis (dī′nə mō jen′i sis), *n., pl.* **-ses** (-sēz′). *Psychol.* the correlation of changes in response with changes in sensory activity. [DYNAMO- + GENESIS] —**dy′na·mo·gen′ic, dy·na·mog·e·nous** (dī′nə moj′ə nəs), *adj.* —**dy′na·mog′e·nous·ly,** *adv.*

dy·na·mom·e·ter (dī′nə mom′i tər), *n. Mech.* **1.** a device for measuring mechanical force, as a balance. **2.** a device for measuring mechanical power, esp. one that measures the output or driving torque of a rotating machine. [DYNAMO- + -METER]

dy·na·mom·e·try (dī′nə mom′i trē), *n.* the act, method, or process of using a dynamometer. [DYNAMO- + -METRY] —**dy·na·mo·met·ric** (dī′nə mō me′trik), **dy′na·mo·met′ri·cal,** *adj.*

dy·na·mo·tor (dī′nə mō′tər), *n.* an electric machine for transforming direct current into alternating current or for altering the voltage of direct current, having two armature windings on the same core and a common magnetic field. [DYNA- + MOTOR]

dy·nast (dī′nast, -nəst; *Brit. also* din′ast), *n.* a ruler or potentate, esp. a hereditary ruler. [< L *dynast(ēs)* < Gk *dynástēs*, equiv. to *dýnas(thai)* (to) rule + *-tēs* agent suffix]

dy·nas·ty (dī′nə stē; *Brit. also* din′ə stē), *n., pl.* **-ties. 1.** a sequence of rulers from the same family, stock, or group: *the Ming dynasty.* **2.** the rule of such a sequence. [late ME < LL *dynastīa* < Gk *dynasteía.* See DYNAST, -Y[3]] —**dy·nas·tic** (dī nas′tik; *Brit. also* di nas′tik), **dy·nas′ti·cal,** *adj.* —**dy·nas′ti·cal·ly,** *adv.*

dy·na·tron (dī′nə tron′), *n. Electronics.* a tetrode, frequently used as an oscillator in radio, in which an increase in the plate voltage results in a decrease in the plate current because of emission of electrons from the plate. [DYNA- + -TRON]

dyne (dīn), *n. Physics.* the standard centimeter-gram-second unit of force, equal to the force that produces an acceleration of one centimeter per second per second on a mass of one gram. *Abbr.:* dyn [< F < Gk *dýn(amis)* force, power]

Dy·nel (dī nel′), *n. Trademark.* **1.** a modacrylic fiber used in textiles, characterized chiefly by its strength, rapid drying rate, and noncombustibility. **2.** yarn or fabric made of this fiber.

dy·node (dī′nōd), *n. Electronics.* an electrode for the emission of secondary electrons in a vacuum tube. [DYN(A)- + -ODE[2]]

Dy·oph·y·site (dī of′i sīt′), *n. Theol.* one who maintains that Christ has two natures, one divine and the other human. Cf. **Monophysite.** [< LGk *dyophysīt(ēs)*, equiv. to *dýo* two + *phýs(is)* nature + *-ītes* -ITE[1]] —**Dy·oph·y·sit·ic** (dī of′i sit′ik), **Dy·oph′y·sit′i·cal,** *adj.*

dy·o·style (dī′ə stīl′), *adj.* distyle.

Dy·oth·e·lite (dī oth′ə līt′), *n. Theol.* one who maintains that Christ has two wills, one divine and the other human. Cf. **Monothelite.** [< Gk *dýo* two + *-thelite* as in *monothelite*] —**Dy·oth′e·lit·ism,** *n.*

dys-, a learned borrowing from Greek meaning "ill," "bad," used in the formation of technical terms: *dysfunction.* [< Gk; c. Icel *tor-*, G *zer-*, Skt *-dus*]

dys·a·cou·sia (dis′ə kōō′zhə, -zhē ə, -zē ə), *n. Pathol.* a condition in which noise produces pain in the ear. Also, **dys·a·cous·ma** (dis′ə kōōz′mə), **dys·a·cu·sia** (dis′ə kyōō′zhə, -zhē ə, -zē ə). [< NL, equiv. to *dys-* DYS- + *-acousia* < Gk *ákou(ein)* ability to hear (*akoú(ein)* (to) hear + *-sis* -SIS) + *-ia* -IA]

dys·ad·ap·ta·tion (dis ad′əp tā′shən), *n. Ophthalm.* faulty adaptation of the iris and retina to light. Also, **dys·ap·ta·tion** (dis′ap tā′shən). [DYS- + ADAPTATION]

dys·an·ag·no·sia (dis an′əg nō′zhə, -zhē ə, -zē ə), *n. Pathol.* an inability to comprehend certain words; dyslexia. [DYS- + Gk *anagnōsía* ability to read (*ana-* ANA- + *gnōsía* knowledge; see GNOSIS)]

dys·an·a·lyte (dis an′ə līt′), *n.* a mineral, titanate and niobate of calcium and iron, found mainly at Baden, Germany, in the form of cubic crystals. [< Gk *dysanályt(os)* hard to analyze, equiv. to *dys-* DYS- + *analý(ein)* (to) ANALYZE + *-tos* ptp. suffix]

dys·ar·thri·a (dis är′thrē ə), *n. Pathol.* any of certain disorders of articulation, as stammering or stuttering, caused by a nerve defect. [< NL, equiv. to *dys-* DYS- + Gk *árthr(on)* joint + *-ia* -IA] —**dys·ar′thric,** *adj.*

dys·bar·ism (dis′bä riz′əm), *n. Med.* the condition resulting from a difference between the atmospheric pressure and the pressure of gases within the body. [DYS- + BAR(O)- + -ISM]

dys·cra·sia (dis krā′zhə, -zhē ə, -zē ə), *n. Pathol.* an undefined disease, malfunction, or abnormal condition, esp. of the blood. [< ML < Gk *dyskrasía* bad mixture, equiv. to *dys-* DYS- + *krâs(is)* a mixing + *-iā* -IA] —**dys·cra′si·al, dys·cras·ic** (dis kraz′ik, -kras′-), **dys·crat′ic,** *adj.*

dys·cri·nism (dis krī′niz əm), *n. Pathol.* any condition caused by defective glandular secretion. [DYS- + Gk *krī́n(ein)* (to) separate + -ISM]

dys·en·ter·y (dis′ən ter′ē), *n.* **1.** *Pathol.* an infectious disease marked by inflammation and ulceration of the lower part of the bowels, with diarrhea that becomes mucous and hemorrhagic. **2.** *Informal.* diarrhea. [< ML *dysenteria* < Gk, equiv. to *dysénter(a)* bad bowels + *-iā* -IA; r. ME *dissenterie* < OF] —**dys′en·ter′ic,** *adj.*

dys·er·gia (di sûr′jə, -jē ə), *n. Pathol.* lack of muscular coordination due to defective nerve conduction. [< NL < Gk *dysergía* difficulty in working, equiv. to *dys* -DYS- + *-ergia;* see ERG, -Y³]

dys·es·the·sia (dis′is thē′zhə, -zhē ə, -zē ə), *n. Pathol.* **1.** any impairment of the senses, esp. of the sense of touch. **2.** a condition in which light physical contact of the skin causes pain. [< NL < Gk *dysaisthēsíā*. See DYS-, ESTHESIA] —**dys·es·thet·ic** (dis′is thet′ik), **dys′aes·thet′ic,** *adj.*

dys·func·tion (dis fungk′shən), *n. Med.* malfunctioning, as of a structure of the body. [DYS- + FUNCTION]

dys·gen·ic (dis jen′ik), *adj.* pertaining to or causing degeneration in the type of offspring produced. Cf. **eugenic.** [DYS- + GENIC]

dys·gen·ics (dis jen′iks), *n.* (*construed as sing.*) *Biol.* the study of the operation of factors that cause degeneration in offspring. [see DYSGENIC, -ICS]

dys·gno·sia (dis nō′zhə, -zhē ə, -zē ə), *n. Psychiatry.* any intellectual impairment. [< Gk *dysgnōsía*. See DYS-, -GNOSIS, -IA]

dys·gon·ic (dis gon′ik), *adj. Bacteriol.* growing poorly on artificial media, as certain bacteria. Cf. **eugonic.** [DYS- + Gk *gón(os)* offspring + -IC]

dys·graph·i·a (dis graf′ē ə), *n. Psychiatry.* inability to write, caused by cerebral lesion. [DYS- + -GRAPH + -IA]

dys·ki·ne·sia (dis′ki nē′zhə, -zhē ə, -zē ə, -kī-), *n. Pathol.* difficulty or abnormality in performing voluntary muscular movements. [< NL < Gk *dyskīnēsía*, equiv. to *dys-* DYS- + *kīnēs(is)* motion + *-iā* -IA] —**dys·ki·net·ic** (dis′ki net′ik, -kī-), *adj.*

dys·la·li·a (dis lā′lē ə, -lal′ē ə), *n. Pathol.* an inability to speak due to a defect of the organs of speech. [< NL; see DYS-, -LALIA]

dys·lex·i·a (dis lek′sē ə), *n. Pathol.* an impairment of the ability to read due to a brain defect. [< NL < Gk *dys-* DYS- + *léx(is)* word + *-ia* -IA]

dys·lo·gia (dis lō′jə, -jē ə), *n. Pathol.* inability to express ideas because of faulty reasoning or speech, due to a mental disorder. [< NL < Gk *dys-* DYS- + *lóg(os)* speech + *-ia* -IA]

dys·lo·gis·tic (dis′lə jis′tik), *adj.* conveying disapproval or censure; not complimentary or eulogistic. [DYS- + (EU)LOGISTIC] —**dys′lo·gis′ti·cal·ly,** *adv.*

dys·men·or·rhe·a (dis′men ə rē′ə), *n. Med.* painful menstruation. Also, **dys′men·or·rhoe′a.** [DYS- + *menorrhea* < Gk *mēn-* (s. of *meís*) month + -O- + -RRHEA] —**dys′men·or·rhe′al, dys′men·or·rhoe′al,** *adj.*

dys·met·ri·a (dis me′trē ə), *n. Pathol.* the inability to conform muscular action to desired movements because of faulty judgment of distance. [< NL < Gk *dys-* DYS- + *métr(on)* a measure + *-ia* -IA]

dys·mne·sia (dis nē′zhə, -zhē ə, -zē ə), *n. Psychiatry.* an impairment of memory. [DYS- + Gk *mnês(is)* a remembering + -IA]

dys·pa·reu·ni·a (dis′pə ro͞o′nē ə), *n. Med.* painful coitus. [DYS- + Gk *páreun(os)* bedfellow + -IA]

dys·pa·thy (dis′pə thē), *n. Archaic.* antipathy. [DYS- + (SYM)PATHY] —**dys′pa·thet′ic,** *adj.*

dys·pep·sia (dis pep′shə, -sē ə), *n.* deranged or impaired digestion; indigestion (opposed to *eupepsia*). Also, **dys·pep·sy** (dis pep′sē). [< L < Gk *dyspepsía*, equiv. to *dys-* DYS- + *péps(is)* digestion + *-ia* -IA]

dys·pep·tic (dis pep′tik), *adj.* Also, **dys·pep′ti·cal. 1.** pertaining to, subject to, or suffering from dyspepsia. **2.** gloomy and irritable. —*n.* **3.** a person subject to or suffering from dyspepsia. [DYS- + Gk *peptik(ós)* pertaining to digestion, equiv. to *pept(ós)* digested (*pep*-cook, digest + *-tos* ptp. suffix) + *-ikos* -IC] —**dys·pep′ti·cal·ly,** *adv.*

dys·pha·gia (dis fā′jə, -jē ə), *n. Pathol.* difficulty in swallowing. [< NL < Gk *dys-* DYS- + *phag(ein)* (to) eat, devour + *-ia* -IA] —**dys·phag·ic** (dis faj′ik), *adj.*

dys·pha·sia (dis fā′zhə, -zhē ə, -zē ə), *n. Pathol.* inability to speak or understand words because of a brain lesion. [DYS- + (A)PHASIA] —**dys·pha′sic,** *adj.*

dys·phe·mi·a (dis fē′mē ə), *n. Psychol.* any neurotic disorder of speech. [< NL < Gk *dys-* DYS- + *phḗm(ē)* utterance + *-ia* -IA]

dys·pho·ni·a (dis fō′nē ə), *n.* any disturbance of normal vocal function. [< NL < Gk *dysphōnía* roughness of sound, equiv. to *dys-* DYS- + *phōn(ḗ)* sound, voice + *-ia* -IA] —**dys·phon·ic** (dis fon′ik), *adj.*

dys·pho·ri·a (dis fôr′ē ə, -fōr′-), *n. Pathol.* a state of dissatisfaction, anxiety, restlessness, or fidgeting. [< NL < Gk *dysphoría* malaise, discomfort, equiv. to *dys-* DYS- + *phor(ós)* bearing + *-ia* -IA] —**dys·phor·ic** (dis fôr′ik, -for′-), *adj.*

dys·pla·sia (dis plā′zhə, -zhē ə, -zē ə), *n. Pathol.* abnormal tissue growth. [< NL < Gk *dys-* DYS- + *plás(is)* a fashioning + *-ia* -IA] —**dys·plas·tic** (dis plas′tik), *adj.*

dysp·ne·a (disp nē′ə), *n. Pathol.* difficult or labored breathing (opposed to *eupnea*). Also, **dysp·noe′a.** [< L *dyspnoea* < Gk *dýspnoia*, equiv. to *dys-* DYS- + *pno(ḗ)* breath + *-ia* -IA] —**dysp·ne′al, dysp·ne′ic, dysp·noe′al, dysp·noe′ic, dysp·no·ic** (disp nō′ik), *adj.*

dys·prax·i·a (dis prak′sē ə), *n. Pathol.* inability to perform coordinated movements. [< Gk: ill success, equiv. to *dys-* DYS- + *prāx(is)* action + *-ia* -IA]

dys·pro·si·um (dis prō′sē əm, -shē-), *n. Chem.* a rare-earth metallic element found in small amounts, together with other rare earths, in certain minerals. *Symbol:* Dy; *at. wt.:* 162.50; *at. no.:* 66. [< NL < Gk *dysprós(itos)* hard to get at (*dys-* DYS- + *pros-* to + *itós*, ptp. of *iénai* to go) + L *-ium*]

dys·rhyth·mi·a (dis rith′mē ə), *n.* a disturbance of rhythm, as of speech or as of brain waves recorded by an electroencephalograph. [< NL < Gk *dys-* DYS- + *rhythm(ós)* RHYTHM + *-ia* -IA]

dys·tel·e·ol·o·gy (dis′tel ē ol′ə jē, -tē lē-), *n.* **1.** *Philos.* a doctrine denying the existence of a final cause or purpose. **2.** the assumed absence of purpose in life or nature. **3.** the evasion or frustration of a natural or normal function or purpose. [DYS- + TELEOLOGY] —**dys·tel·e·o·log·i·cal** (dis′tel ē ə loj′i kəl, -tē lē-), *adj.* —**dys′tel·e·ol′o·gist,** *n.*

dys·thy·mi·a (dis thī′mē ə), *n.* despondency or a tendency to be despondent. [< NL < Gk, equiv. to *dys-* DYS- + *thym(ós)* spirit + *-ia* -IA] —**dys·thy′mic,** *adj.*

dys·to·ni·a (dis tō′nē ə), *n. Pathol.* abnormal tone of any tissue. [< NL < Gk *dys-* DYS- + *tón(os)* a stretching, power of contracting muscles + *-ia* -IA] —**dys·ton·ic** (dis ton′ik), *adj.*

dys·troph·ic (dis trof′ik), *adj.* **1.** *Med.* pertaining to or caused by dystrophy. **2.** *Ecol.* (of a lake) having too low an accumulation of dissolved nutrients to support abundant plant life; having highly acid, brownish waters filled with undecayed plant materials, and eventually developing into a peat bog or marsh. [DYS- + TROPHIC]

dys·tro·phy (dis′trə fē), *n.* **1.** *Med.* faulty or inadequate nutrition or development. **2.** *Pathol.* any of a number of disorders characterized by weakening, degeneration, or abnormal development of muscle. **3.** *Ecol.* the state of being dystrophic. Also, **dys·tro·phi·a** (di strō′fē ə). [< NL *dystrophia.* See DYS-, -TROPHY]

dys·u·ri·a (dis yo͝or′ē ə), *n. Pathol.* difficult or painful urination. [< NL < Gk *dysouríā*. See DYS- UR-¹, -IA] —**dys·u′ric,** *adj.*

Dyu·sham·be (dyo͞o shäm′be), *n.* a city in and the capital of Tadzhikistan, in the SW Soviet Union in Asia. 224,000 (1959). Also, **Diushambe.** Formerly, **Stalinabad.**

dz., dozen; dozens.

Dzer·zhinsk (dzer zhinsk′), *n.* a city in the central Soviet Union in Europe, ENE of Moscow. 163,000 (1959).

dzig·ge·tai (jig′i tī′), *n.* chigetai.

Dzhu·gash·vi·li (*Russ.* jo͞o′gäsh vē′li), *n.* **Io·sif Vis·sa·ri·o·no·vich** (*Russ.* yô′sif vis sä ri ô′no vich). See **Stalin, Joseph.** Also, **Dzu′gash·vi′li.**

Dzun·ga·ri·a (dzo͝ong gâr′ē ə, zo͝ong-), *n.* a region in N Sinkiang, China: a Mongol kingdom during the 11th to 14th centuries.

Dzyu·bin (*Russ.* dzyo͞o′bin), *n.* **E·du·ard Ge·or·gie·vich** (*Russ.* e do͞o ärt′ ge ôr′gyə vich). See **Bagritski, Eduard.**

E

E, e (ē), *n., pl.* **E's** or **Es, e's** or **es.** **1.** the fifth letter of the English alphabet, a vowel. **2.** any spoken sound represented by the letter *E* or *e*, as in *met, meet, mere,* etc. **3.** something having the shape of an E. **4.** a written or printed representation of the letter *E* or *e*. **5.** a device, as a printer's type, for reproducing the letter *E* or *e*. **6.** *U.S.* a flag bearing the letter E, for *Efficiency*, presented during World War II as an award by the army or navy to factories meeting or surpassing their production schedules of war materials.

E, **1.** east. **2.** eastern. **3.** English. **4.** excellent.

E, **1.** the fifth in order or in a series. **2.** (*sometimes l.c.*) (in some grading systems) a grade or mark, as in school or college, indicating the quality of a student's work is in need of improvement in order to be passing. **3.** *Music.* **a.** the third tone in the scale of C major or the fifth tone in the relative minor scale, A minor. **b.** a string, key, or pipe tuned to this tone. **c.** a written or printed note representing this tone. **d.** (in the fixed system of solmization) the third tone of the scale of C major, called *mi.* **e.** the tonality having E as the tonic note. **4.** (*sometimes l.c.*) the medieval Roman numeral for 250. Cf. **Roman numerals. 5.** *Physics, Elect.* electric field strength. **6.** *Physics.* energy. **7.** *Elect.* See **electromotive force. 8.** *Logic.* See **universal negative. 9.** a proportional shoe width size narrower than EE and wider than D.

e, erg.

e, **1.** *Math.* a transcendental constant equal to 2.7182818 . . ., used as the base of natural logarithms; the limit of the expression $\left(1 + \frac{1}{n}\right)^n$ as *n* approaches infinity. **2.** *Logic.* See **universal negative.**

e-, var. of **ex-**[1], occurring in words of Latin origin before consonants other than *c, f, p, q, s,* and *t*: *emit.*

E., **1.** Earl. **2.** east. **3.** eastern. **4.** English.

e., **1.** eldest. **2.** *Football.* end. **3.** entrance. **4.** *Baseball.* error; errors.

E·a (ā′ä), *n.* the Akkadian god of wisdom, the son of Apsu and father of Marduk: the counterpart of Enki.

-ea, a formal element occurring in loan words from Latin, orig. in feminine adjectives: *cornea.* [< L *-ēa, -aea, -ea,* fem. of *-ēus, -aeus, -eus;* see -EAN]

ea., each.

E.A., educational age.

E.A.A., Engineer in Aeronautics and Astronautics.

each (ēch), *adj.* **1.** every one of two or more considered individually or one by one: *each stone in a building; a hallway with a door at each end.* —*pron.* **2.** each one: *Each went his way.* —*adv.* **3.** to, from, or for each; apiece: *They cost a dollar each.* [ME *eche,* OE *ǣlc,* equiv. to *ā* ever (see AY[1]) + *(ge)līc* (A)LIKE; c. OHG *ēo-gilīh,* OFris *ellīk,* D, LG *elk*]
—**Syn. 1.** EACH, EVERY are alike in having a distributive meaning. Of two or more members composing a (usually) definite aggregate, EACH directs attention to the separate members in turn: *Each child* (of those considered and enumerated) *received a large apple.* EVERY emphasizes the idea of inclusiveness or universality; it is also used of an indefinite number, all being regarded singly and separately: *Every child present received an apple* (no child was omitted). *Every child* (of all in existence) *likes to play.*
—**Usage. 2.** Careful speakers make certain that EACH, which is a singular pronoun, is always used with a singular verb: *Each child has his own book. Each of the houses on this street is painted a different color.*

each′ oth′er, **1.** each the other: *to love each other.* **2.** one another (used as a compound reciprocal pronoun in oblique cases): *They struck at each other.* [ME *ech other,* OE *ǣlc ōther.* See EACH, OTHER]

ead., (in prescriptions) the same. [< L *eādem*]

Ea·die (ē′dē), *n.* a girl's given name.

Ead·mund I (ed′mənd). See **Edmund I.**

Eadmund II. See **Edmund II.**

Eads (ēdz), *n.* **James Buchanan,** 1820–87, U.S. engineer and inventor.

Ead·wine (ed′win), *n.* Edwin (def. 1).

-eae, plural of **-ea:** *tracheae.*

ea·ger[1] (ē′gər), *adj.* **1.** keen or ardent in desire or feeling; impatiently longing: *I am eager for news about them. He is eager to sing.* **2.** characterized by or revealing great earnestness: *an eager look.* **3.** *Archaic.* keen; sharp; biting. [ME *egre* < OF *egre, aigre* < L *acer* sharp] —**ea′ger·ly,** *adv.* —**ea′ger·ness,** *n.*
—**Syn. 1.** fervent, zealous, enthusiastic.

ea·ger[2] (ē′gər, ā′gər), *n.* *Chiefly Brit.* eagre.

ea′ger bea′ver (ē′gər), *Informal.* a person who is excessively diligent or zealous, esp. one who appears to be currying favor or seeking advancement: *He would be popular in school if he weren't such an eager beaver.*

ea·gle (ē′gəl), *n., v.,* **-gled, -gling.** —*n.* **1.** any of several large, diurnal, accipitrine birds of prey, noted for their size, strength, and powers of flight and vision. Cf. **bald eagle, golden eagle. 2.** a figure or representation of an eagle, much used as an emblem: *the Roman eagle.* **3.** a standard, seal, or the like bearing such a figure. **4.** one of a pair of silver insignia in the shape of eagles with outstretched wings worn by a colonel in the U.S. Army, Air Force, and Marine corps and by a captain in the U.S. Navy. **5.** a lectern having the form of an eagle. **6.** a gold coin of the U.S., issued until 1933, equal to 10 dollars, having on its reverse the figure of an eagle. **7.** *U.S.* **a.** a representation in green of an eagle, used on playing cards to designate a suit in the pack additional to the four standard suits. **b.** a card of a suit so designated. **c. eagles,** the suit itself. **8.** (*cap.*) *Astron.* the constellation Aquila. **9.** *Golf.* a score of two below par on any hole. —*v.t.* **10.** *Golf.* to make an eagle on (a hole). [ME *egle* < OF *egle, aigle* < OPr *aigla* < L *aquila* n. use of fem. of *aquilus* dark-colored]

ea′gle boat′, a small antisubmarine warship.

ea′gle eye′, **1.** unusually sharp visual powers; keen ability to watch or observe. **2.** a person who has sharp vision or who maintains a keen watchfulness.

ea·gle-eyed (ē′gəl īd′), *adj.* sharp-sighted.

Ea′gle Grove′, a town in central Iowa. 4381 (1960).

Ea′gle Lake′, a town in S Texas. 3565 (1960).

ea′gle owl′, any of several large owls of the genus *Bubo,* having prominent tufts of feathers on each side of the head, esp. *B. bubo,* of Europe and Asia.

Ea′gle Pass′, a city in S Texas, on the Rio Grande. 12,094 (1960).

ea′gle ray′, any of several rays of the family *Myliobatidae,* found in tropical seas and noted for the soaring movements by which they propel themselves through the water.

ea′gle scout′, a boy scout who has earned 21 merit badges.

ea·gle·stone (ē′gəl stōn′), *n.* a concretionary lump of ironstone about the size of a small egg, formerly believed to be carried by eagles to their nests as a magical aid in laying eggs. [EAGLE + STONE]

ea·glet (ē′glit), *n.* a young eagle. [< F *aiglette.* See EAGLE, -ET]

Ea′gle·ton Vil′lage (ē′gəl tən), a town in E Tennessee. 5068 (1960).

ea·gle·wood (ē′gəl wo͝od′), *n.* agalloch. [trans. of Pg *pāo d'aguila* wood of agalloch, by confusion of Pg *águia* eagle with *aguila* < Malayalam *agil* agalloch]

ea·gre (ē′gər, ā′gər), *n.* *Chiefly Brit.* a tidal bore or flood. Also, **eager.** [earlier *eager, eagar,* equiv. to OE *ēa* river + *gār* storm]

Ea·ker (ā′kər), *n.* **Ira Clarence,** born 1896, U.S. Air Force general.

Ea·kins (ā′kinz), *n.* **Thomas,** 1844–1916, U.S. painter.

eal·dor·man (ôl′dər mən), *n., pl.* **-men.** *Obs.* alderman. Also, **eal′der·man.**

Ea·ling (ē′ling), *n.* a city in SE England, part of Greater London. 183,151 (1961).

EAM, National Liberation Front, a Greek underground resistance movement of World War II and political coalition of various leftist groups. [< ModGk *E(thniko) A(pelevtherotiko) M(etōpo)*]

-ean, an element used to form adjectives from nouns with stems in **-ea:** *trachean.* [< L *-ē(us)* (Gk *-eios*), *-ae(us)* (Gk *-aios*), *-e(us)* + -AN]

E.&O.E., errors and omissions excepted.

E. and P., extraordinary and plenipotentiary.

ean·ling (ēn′ling), *n.* *Obs.* a young lamb; kid. [var. of YEANLING]

ear[1] (ēr), *n.* **1.** the organ of hearing in man and other vertebrates, in man usually consisting of an expanded outer portion, the external ear, which receives sound vibrations that are passed into the middle ear, causing a vibration of its bones which in turn causes a movement of the fluid in the internal ear, the hair cells of which stimulate the auditory nerve which transmits the impulse to the brain. **2.** the external part alone: *The teacher seized the student by the ear.* **3.** the sense of hearing: *sounds that are pleasing to the ear.* **4.** keen or sensitive perception of the differences of sound, esp. sensitiveness to the quality and correctness of musical sounds: *an ear for music; a violinist with a good ear.* **5.** attention; heed: *to gain a person's ear.* **6.** any part that resembles or suggests an ear in position or form, as the handle of a teacup. **7.** *Archit.* crossette (def. 1). **8.** *Journalism.* a small box in either upper corner of a newspaper page, usually the front page or split page, containing the name of or a symbol for the edition, a weather bulletin, a slogan, or the like. **9.** *Furniture.* **a.** a decorative feature at the upper end of a leg. **b.** one of the decorative features at each end of a crest rail. **10. be all ears,** to give all one's attention; listen: *She was all ears as the scandal was revealed.* **11. bend an ear,** to listen attentively: *to bend an ear to a request for aid.* **12. bend one's ear,** *Slang.* to talk to someone uninterruptedly and often so as to induce boredom: *Keep away from him because he'll bend your ear for hours if given the chance.* **13. by ear,** without reference to, or dependence upon, written or printed music: *He sat down at the piano and gave a magnificent performance, playing completely by ear.* **14. fall on deaf ears,** to be disregarded; pass unheeded: *Their pleas for an extension of time fell on deaf ears.* **15. give ear,** to pay attention; listen carefully. Also, **lend an ear. 16. go in one ear and out the other,** to be heard but ignored; be put out of mind: *My repeated warnings to her went in one ear and out the other.* **17. have** or **keep one's ear to the ground,** to keep well-informed about current trends; be shrewd or astute: *Because he had his ear to the ground, he made a large fortune in stock speculation.* **18. pin someone's ears back,** *Slang.* to give a person a sound beating; defeat a person utterly: *If he doesn't behave himself I'll pin his ears back.* **19. set by the ears,** to cause to dispute or quarrel: *His choice of a wife set his family by the ears.* **20. turn a deaf ear to,** to refuse to listen to or consider (a request, petition, etc.): *He turns a deaf ear to requests for loans.* **21. up to one's ears,** deeply involved or occupied: *We are up to our ears in work.* **22. wet behind the ears.** See **wet** (def. 12).

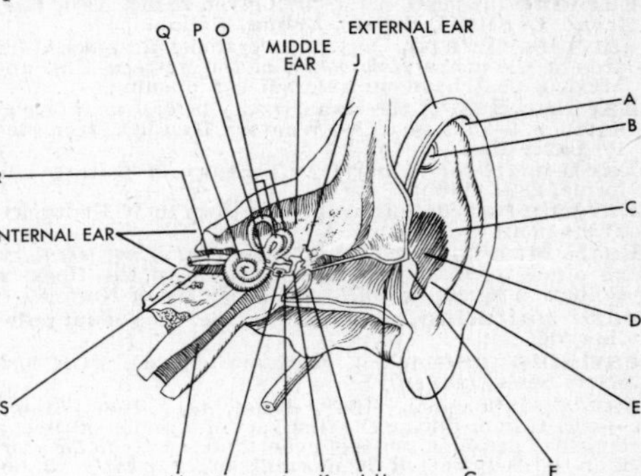

Human ear (Transverse section)
External ear: A, Helix; B, Fossa of antihelix; C, Antihelix; D, Concha; E, Antitragus; F, Tragus; G, Lobe; H, External auditory meatus. Middle ear: I, Tympanic membrane; J, Malleus; K, Incus; L, Tympanic cavity; M, Stapes; N, Eustachian tube. Internal ear; O, Semicircular canals; P, Vestibule; Q, Cochlea; R, Nerves; S, Internal auditory meatus

[ME *ere*, OE *ēare;* c. Icel *eyra*, G *Ohr*, Goth *auso*, L *auris*, Lith *ausis*, Gk *oûs*] —**ear′less,** *adj.* —**ear′like′,** *adj.*

ear[2] (ēr), *n.* **1.** the part of a cereal plant, as corn, wheat, etc., that contains the flowers and hence the fruit, grains, or kernels. —*v.i.* **2.** to form or put forth ears. [ME *ere*, OE *ēar, æhher;* c. G *Ähre*, Icel *ax*, Goth *ahs* ear, L *acus* husk]

ear[3] (ēr), *v.t. Brit. Dial.* to plow; cultivate. [ME *ere(n)*, OE *erian;* c. Icel *erja*, Goth *arjan*, L *arāre*]

ear·ache (ēr′āk′), *n.* pain in the ear or an instance of it. [EAR[1] + ACHE]

ear·bob (ēr′bob′), *n. Dial.* an earring or eardrop. [EAR[1] + BOB[2]]

ear·drop (ēr′drop′), *n.* an earring with a pendant. [EAR[1] + DROP]

ear′ drops′, *Med.* drops for use in the ears.

ear·drum (ēr′drum′), *n.* See **tympanic membrane.** [EAR[1] + DRUM[1]]

eared (ērd), *adj.* having ears or earlike appendages. [ME *ered*, OE *ēarede.* See EAR[1], -ED[3]]

ear·flap (ēr′flap′), *n.* either of a pair of flaps attached to a cap, for covering the ears in cold weather. Also called **earlap.** [EAR[1] + FLAP]

ear·ful (ēr′fo͝ol), *n., pl.* **-fuls. 1.** an amount of oral information or advice, esp. when given without solicitation. **2.** a sharp verbal rebuke; a dressing-down. [EAR[1] + -FUL]

Ear·hart (âr′härt), *n.* **Amelia (Mary),** 1897–1937, U.S. aviator.

ear·ing (ēr′ing), *n. Naut.* any of various short ropes attached to cringles and used for bending a corner of a sail to a yard, boom, or gaff, for reefing a sail, or for bending a corner of an awning to a spar or stanchion. [EAR[1] + -ING[1]]

earl (ûrl), *n.* **1.** a British nobleman of a rank next below that of marquis and next above that of viscount: called counts for a time after the Norman conquest. The wife of an earl is a countess. **2.** (in Anglo-Saxon England) a governor of one of the great divisions of England, including East Anglia, Mercia, Northumbria, and Wessex. [ME *erl*, OE *eorl;* c. OS *erl* man, Icel *jarl* chieftain] —**earl′ship,** *n.*

Earl (ûrl), *n.* a boy's given name. Also, **Earle.**

ear·lap (ēr′lap′), *n.* **1.** earflap. **2.** the lobe of the ear. **3.** the whole external ear. [ME *erelappe*, OE *ēarlæppa* external ear. See EAR[1], LAP[1]]

earl·dom (ûrl′dəm), *n.* **1.** the rank or title of an earl. **2.** *Obs.* the territory or jurisdiction of an earl. [ME *erldom*, OE *eorldōm.* See EARL, -DOM]

Ear·lene (ûr lēn′), *n.* a girl's given name. Also, **Earleen′, Ear·line′, Erlene, Erlina, Erline.**

ear′less liz′ard, any of several slender iguanid lizards of the genus *Holbrookia*, of the western U.S. and Mexico, that have no external ear opening.

Ear′lier Han′, the Han dynasty before the interregnum A.D. 9–25. Also called **Western Han.** Cf. **Han** (def. 1), **Later Han.**

Ear·li·mart (ûr′lē märt′), *n.* a town in central California. 2897 (1960).

Ear·ling·ton (ûr′ling tən), *n.* a town in W Kentucky. 2786 (1960).

Earl′ Mar′shal, *pl.* **Earl Marshals.** *Eng. Heraldry.* an officer of state having supervision of the Heralds' College: a hereditary office of the Dukes of Norfolk.

earl′ pal′atine, *pl.* **earls palatine.** See **count palatine** (def. 2).

earl·ship (ûrl′ship), *n.* earldom (def. 1). [OE *eorlscipe.* See EARL, -SHIP]

ear·ly (ûr′lē), *adv.,* **-li·er, -li·est,** *adj.,* **-li·er, -li·est.** —*adv.* **1.** in or during the first part of a period of time, a course of action, a series of events, etc.: *early in the year.* **2.** in the early part of the morning: *to get up early.* **3.** before the usual or appointed time; ahead of time: *They came early and found their hosts still dressing.* **4.** far back in time: *Man early learned the usefulness of weapons.* **5. early on,** *Chiefly Brit.* with but little time elapsed; early in the course of the process or project in question; early in the game. —*adj.* **6.** occurring in the first part of a period of time, a course of action, a series of events, etc.: *an early hour of the day.* **7.** occurring before the usual or appointed time: *an early dinner.* **8.** belonging to a period far back in time: *early French architecture.* **9.** occurring in the near future: *I look forward to an early reply.* [ME *erlich* (adj.) *erliche* (adv.), OE *ǣrlīc, ǣrlīce,* mutated var. of *ārlīc, ārlīce,* equiv. to *ār-* early (positive of *ǣr* ERE) + *līc(e)* -LY] —**ear′li·ness,** *n.*
—**Ant. 1-3, 6-8.** late.

Ear·ly (ûr′lē), *n.* **Ju·bal Anderson** (jo͞o′bəl), 1816–94, Confederate general in the U.S. Civil War.

Ear′ly Amer′ican, 1. (of furniture, buildings, utensils, etc.) built or made in the U.S. in the colonial period or somewhat later. **2.** built or made in imitation of this style: *a cabinetmaker specializing in Early American tables.*

ear′ly bird′, 1. *Informal.* a person who arises from bed at an early hour of the morning: *She was an early bird who finished her housecleaning by nine o'clock.* **2.** a person who arrives before others, as for the purpose of gaining some advantage: *The early birds got the best seats for the play.*

ear′ly blight′, *Plant Pathol.* a disease of plants characterized by leaf spotting, defoliation, and stunted growth and caused by any of several fungi, as *Alternaria solani* or *Cercospora apii.*

Ear′ly Chris′tian, 1. of or pertaining to the fine and applied arts of Christian content or designating the styles of these arts developed from the 2nd century A.D. either to the beginning of the Byzantine Empire in the 5th century or, in western Europe, to about the 8th century. **2.** noting or pertaining to the style of religious architecture developed chiefly in Italy from the 3rd century A.D. through the 5th century, but evolving in the Eastern Roman Empire into the Byzantine style by the end of this period: characterized by the extensive use of the basilican plan and the atrium, the re-use of columns, capitals, entablatures, etc., from older buildings, the extensive use of timber for ceilings with some limited use of vaulting, a general plainness of exteriors, and the lavish use of mosaic for interior iconographic and decorative schemes.

Ear′ly Eng′lish, noting or pertaining to the first style of Gothic architecture in Great Britain, ending in the latter half of the 13th century, characterized by the use of lancet arches, plate tracery, and narrow openings.

Ear′ly He′brew, noting or pertaining to the alphabetical script used for the writing of Hebrew mainly from the 11th to the 6th centuries B.C.

ear′ly mead′ow rue′. See **meadow rue.**

Ear′ly Mod′ern Eng′lish, the English language represented in printed documents of the period starting with Caxton (1476) and ending with Dryden (1700).

Ear′ly Ren′aissance, a style of art developed principally in Florence during the 15th century and characterized chiefly by the development of linear perspective, chiaroscuro, and geometrically based compositions. Cf. **High Renaissance.**

ear′ly sax′ifrage, a perennial herb, *Saxifraga virginiensis*, of eastern North America, having white flowers. Also called **rock saxifrage.**

ear′ly warn′ing sys′tem, *Mil.* a network of radar installations designed to detect enemy aircraft or missiles in time for the effective deployment of defense systems.

ear′ly wood′, springwood.

ear·mark (ēr′märk′), *n.* **1.** a mark of identification made on the ear of an animal to show ownership. **2.** any identifying or distinguishing mark or characteristic: *The mayor's statement had all the earmarks of Toryism.* —*v.t.* **3.** to mark with an earmark. **4.** to set aside for a specific purpose, use, recipient, etc.: *to earmark some goods for export.* [EAR[1] + MARK[1]]

ear·mind·ed (ēr′mīn′did), *adj.* tending to perceive one's environment in terms of sound and to recall sounds more vividly than sights, smells, etc. Cf. **eye-minded, motor-minded.** —**ear′mind′ed·ness,** *n.*

ear·muff (ēr′muf′), *n. U.S.* one of a pair of adjustable coverings for protecting the ears in cold weather. [EAR[1] + MUFF]

earn[1] (ûrn), *v.t.* **1.** to gain or get in return for one's labor or service: *to earn one's living.* **2.** to merit as compensation, as for service; deserve: *to receive more than one has earned.* **3.** to acquire through merit: *to earn a reputation for honesty.* **4.** to gain as due return or profit: *Savings bonds earn interest.* **5.** to bring about or cause deserved-ly: *His fair dealing earned our confidence.* —*v.i.* **6.** to gain income: *securities that earn on a quarterly basis.* [ME *ern(i)en*, OE *earnian;* akin to OHG *arnēn* to earn] —**earn′er,** *n.*
—**Syn. 1.** procure. See **gain.**

earn[2] (ûrn), *v.i., v.t. Obs.* to yearn.

earned′ in′come, income from wages, salaries, fees, or the like, accruing from labor or services performed by the earner. Cf. **unearned income.**

earned′ run′, *Baseball.* a run yielded by a pitcher in which no error by him or his teammates and no passed ball by the catcher was involved.

earned′ run′ av′erage, *Baseball.* a measure of the effectiveness of a pitcher, obtained by dividing the number of earned runs scored against him by the number of innings pitched and multiplying the result by nine. A pitcher yielding three earned runs in nine innings has an earned run average of 3.00. *Abbr.:* ERA, era

earned′ sur′plus. See **retained earnings.**

ear·nest[1] (ûr′nist), *adj.* **1.** serious in intention, purpose, or effort; sincerely zealous: *an earnest worker.* **2.** showing depth and sincerity of feeling: *earnest words; an earnest entreaty.* **3.** seriously important; demanding or receiving serious attention: *earnest consideration of measures to be adopted.* —*n.* **4.** full seriousness, as of intention or purpose: *to speak in earnest.* [ME *erneste*, OE *eornoste* (adj.); ME *ernest*, OE *eornost* (n.); c. D, G *ernst*] —**ear′nest·ly,** *adv.* —**ear′nest·ness,** *n.*
—**Syn. 1.** fervent. EARNEST, RESOLUTE, SERIOUS, SINCERE imply having qualities of depth, firmness, and stability. EARNEST implies having a purpose and being steadily and soberly eager in pursuing it: *an earnest student.* RESOLUTE adds somewhat more of a quality of determination; a person who is resolute is very difficult to sway or turn aside from a purpose: *resolute in defending the right.* SERIOUS implies having depth and a soberness of attitude which contrasts with gaiety and frivolity; it may include the qualities of both earnestness and resolution: *serious and thoughtful.* SINCERE suggests genuineness, trustworthiness, and absence of superficiality: *a sincere interest in music.* —**Ant. 1.** frivolous.

ear·nest[2] (ûr′nist), *n.* **1.** a portion of something, given or done in advance as a pledge of the remainder. **2.** *Law.* See **earnest money. 3.** anything that gives pledge, promise, assurance, or indication of what is to follow. [ME *ernes(t)*, alter. of OF *erres,* pl. of *erre* earnest money < L *arra,* short for *arrhabō* < Gk *arrhabṓn* < Sem (cf. Heb *'ērābōn* security, pledge). See ARLES]

ear′nest mon′ey, *Law.* money given by a buyer to a seller to bind a contract.

earn·ing (ûr′ning), *n.* **1.** the act of a person who earns. **2. earnings,** money earned; wages; profits. [ME *erning*, OE *earning*, *earnung* merit, pay. See EARN, -ING[1]]

Earp (ûrp), *n.* **Wy·att (Ber·ry Stapp)** (wī′ət ber′ē stap′), 1848–1929, U.S. frontiersman, law officer, and gunfighter.

ear·phone (ēr′fōn′), *n.* the sound receiver in a headset, as of a radio, telephone, etc. [EAR[1] + PHONE[1]]

ear·piece (ēr′pēs′), *n.* **1.** a piece that covers or passes over the ear, as on a cap, eyeglasses, etc. **2.** an earphone. [EAR[1] + PIECE]

ear-pierc·ing (ēr′pēr′sing), *adj.* extremely harsh and irritating to the ears: *an ear-piercing blast of his horn.*

ear·plug (ēr′plug′), *n.* a plug of soft, pliable material, as rubber, wax, etc., inserted into the opening of the outer ear esp. to keep out water or noise. [EAR[1] + PLUG]

ear·reach (ēr′rēch′), *n.* earshot. [EAR[1] + REACH]

ear·ring (ēr′ring′, -ing), *n.* an ornament worn upon or hanging from the lobe of the ear. [ME *erering*, OE *ēarhring.* See EAR[1], RING[1]] —**ear′ringed,** *adj.*

ear′ shell′, abalone.

ear·shot (ēr′shot′), *n.* the range or distance within which a sound, voice, etc., can be heard: *The children were told to go out and play but to stay within earshot.* Also called **earreach.** [EAR[1] + SHOT[1]]

ear·split·ting (ēr′split′ing), *adj.* very loud; deafening: *an earsplitting explosion.* [EAR[1] + SPLITTING]

ear′ stone′, an otolith.

ear′ tag′, an identification tag fastened to the ear of an animal.

earth (ûrth), *n.* **1.** (*often cap.*) the planet third in order from the sun, having an equatorial diameter of 7926 miles and a polar diameter of 7900 miles, a mean distance from the sun of 92.9 million miles, and a period of revolution of 365.26 days, having one satellite, and being the only planet known to sustain life. **2.** the inhabitants of this planet, esp. the human inhabitants: *The whole earth rejoiced.* **3.** this planet as the habitation of man, often in contrast to heaven and hell: *to create a hell on earth.* **4.** the surface of this planet: *to fall to earth.* **5.** the solid matter of this planet; dry land; ground. **6.** soil and dirt, as distinguished from rock and sand; the softer part of the land. **7.** *Chiefly Brit.* the hole of a burrowing animal. **8.** *Fox Hunting.* any hole in the ground in which a fox takes refuge. **9.** worldly matters, as distinguished from spiritual matters. **10.** *Chem.* any of several metallic oxides that are difficult to reduce, as alumina, zirconia, yttria, etc. Cf. **alkaline earth, rare earth. 11.** Also called **earth′ col′or.** *Fine Arts.* any of various pigments consisting chiefly of iron oxides and tending toward brown in hue. **12.** *Elect.* a ground. **13.** *Obs.* a land or country. **14. move heaven and earth,** to try everything possible; employ every means: *They moved heaven and earth to adopt a child.* **15. on earth,** in the world: *Where on earth have you been?* **16. run to earth, a.** *Hunting.* to chase (an animal) to its hole or burrow: *to run a fox to earth.* **b.** to search out; track down: *They ran the fugitive to earth in Algiers.* —*v.t.* **17.** *Brit. Elect.* to ground. [ME *erthe*, OE *eorthe;* c. G *Erde*, D *aarde*, Icel *jörth*, Dan *jord*, Goth *airtha*]
—**Syn. 3.** EARTH, GLOBE, WORLD are terms applied to the planet on which we dwell. EARTH is used esp. in speaking of a condition of existence contrasted with that in heaven or hell: *those who are yet on earth.* GLOBE formerly emphasized merely the roundness of the earth: *to circumnavigate the globe.* It is now coming to be used more like WORLD, with especial application to the inhabitants of the earth and their activities, interests, and concerns. In this sense, both GLOBE and WORLD are more inclusive than EARTH and are used more abstractly: *the politics of the globe; the future of the world; One World.*

Ear·tha (ûr′thə), *n.* a girl's given name. Also, **Ertha.**

earth′ al′mond, chufa.

earth′ au′ger, a drill for boring holes in the ground, as to tap springs.

earth·born (ûrth′bôrn′), *adj.* **1.** born on or sprung from the earth; of earthly origin. **2.** mortal; human. [EARTH + BORN]

earth·bound[1] (ûrth′bound′), *adj.* **1.** firmly set in or attached to the earth. **2.** having only earthly interests. **3.** headed for the earth: *an earthbound astronaut.* Also, **earth′-bound′.** [EARTH + -BOUND[1]]

earth·bound[2] (ûrth′bound′), *adj.* headed for the earth: *an earthbound astronaut.* Also, **earth′-bound′.** [EARTH + -BOUND[2]]

earth·en (ûr′thən), *adj.* **1.** composed of earth. **2.** made of baked clay. **3.** earthly; worldly. [ME *erthen*, OE *eorthen.* See EARTH, -EN[2]]

earth·en·ware (ûr′thən wâr′), *n.* **1.** pottery of baked or hardened clay, esp. any of the coarse, opaque varieties. **2.** clay for making such pottery. [EARTHEN + WARE[1]]

earth-god (ûrth′god′), *n.* a god of fertility and vegetation.

earth-god·dess (ûrth′god′is), *n.* a goddess of fertility and vegetation.

earth′ induc′tor com′pass, *Aeron.* a compass actuated by induction from the earth's magnetic field.

earth·i·ness (ûr′thē nis), *n.* **1.** earthy nature or properties. **2.** the quality of being unaffectedly realistic, direct, or down-to-earth. [ME *erthynesse.* See EARTHY, -NESS]

earth·light (ûrth′līt′), *n. Astron.* earthshine. [EARTH + LIGHT[1]]

earth·ling (ûrth′ling), *n.* **1.** an inhabitant of earth; mortal. **2.** a person attached to earthly or worldly things. [EARTH + -LING[1]; cf. OE *eorthling* plowman]

earth·ly (ûrth′lē), *adj.,* **-li·er, -li·est. 1.** of or pertaining to the earth, esp. as opposed to heaven; worldly. **2.** possible or conceivable in this world: *an invention of no earthly use to anyone.* [ME *erth(e)ly*, OE *eorthlīc.* See EARTH, -LY] —**earth′li·ness,** *n.*
—**Syn. 1.** earthy. EARTHLY, TERRESTRIAL, WORLDLY, MUNDANE refer to that which is concerned with the earth literally or figuratively. EARTHLY now almost always implies a contrast to that which is heavenly: *earthly pleasures; our earthly home.* TERRESTRIAL, from Latin, is the dignified equivalent of EARTHLY, and it applies to the earth as a planet or to the land as opposed to the water, and is contrasted with that which is celestial: *terrestrial areas; the terrestrial globe.* WORLDLY is commonly used in the derogatory sense of being devoted to the vanities, cares, advantages, or gains of this present life to the exclusion of spiritual interests or the life to come: *worldly success; worldly standards.* MUNDANE, from Latin, is a formal equivalent of WORLDLY and suggests that which is bound to the earth, is not exalted, and therefore is commonplace: *mundane affairs, pursuits.*
—**Ant. 1.** spiritual, divine.

earth·man (ûrth′man′, -mən), *n., pl.* **-men** (-men′, -mən). an inhabitant or native of the planet earth. [EARTH + -MAN]

earth′ moth′er, the earth conceived of as the female principle of fertility and the source of all life. Also, **Earth′ Moth′er.**

earth·mov·er (ûrth′mo͞o′vər), *n.* a vehicle, as a bulldozer, for pushing or carrying excavated earth from place to place. [EARTH + MOVER]

earth·nut (ûrth′nut′), *n.* **1.** any of various roots, tubers, or underground growths, as the peanut and the truffle. **2.** any of the plants producing these. [ME *erthenote*, OE *eorthnutu.* See EARTH, NUT]

earth·pea (ûrth′pē′), *n.* the peanut. [EARTH + PEA]

earth′ pil′lar, *Geol.* a pillar of earthy matter left by erosion of the surrounding ground.

earth·quake (ûrth′kwāk′), *n.* a vibration or movement of a part of the earth's surface, due to the faulting of rocks, to volcanic forces, etc. [ME *erthequake* (see EARTH, QUAKE), r. OE *eorthdyne;* see DIN] —**earth′-quaked′, earth′quak′en,** *adj.* —**earth′quak′ing,** *adj.*

earth′ sci′ence, any of various sciences, as geography, geology, meteorology, etc., that deal with the earth, its composition, or any of its changing aspects.

earth·shak·er (ûrth′shā′kər), *n.* something of extreme importance, superlative quality, etc. [EARTH + SHAKER]

earth·shak·ing (ûrth′shā′king), *adj.* imperiling, challenging, or affecting basic beliefs, attitudes, relationships, etc.: *an earthshaking revision of Christian dogma.* [EARTH + SHAKING]

earth·shine (ûrth′shīn′), *n.* *Astron.* the faint illumination of the part of the moon not illuminated by sunlight, as during a crescent phase, caused by the reflection of light from the earth. Also called **earthlight.** [EARTH + SHINE]

earth·star (ûrth′stär′), *n.* a fungus of the genus *Geaster,* having an outer covering which splits into the form of a star. [EARTH + STAR]

earth′ ta′ble, (in a masonry wall) the lowest course or courses appearing above ground, esp. when brought out to the face of a water table. Also called **grass table, ground table.**

earth·ward (ûrth′wərd), *adv.* **1.** Also, **earth′wards.** toward the earth. —*adj.* **2.** directed toward the earth. [ME *ertheward.* See EARTH, -WARD]

earth′ wave′, *Geol.* any elastic wave traveling through the material of the earth, as a wave caused by an earthquake.

earth·work (ûrth′wûrk′), *n.* **1.** excavation and piling of earth in connection with an engineering operation. **2.** *Mil.* a construction formed chiefly of earth for protection against enemy fire, used in both offensive and defensive operations. [EARTH + WORK]

earth·worm (ûrth′wûrm′), *n.* **1.** any one of numerous annelid worms that burrow in soil and feed on soil and decaying organic matter. **2.** *Archaic.* a mean or groveling person. [ME *ertheworm.* See EARTH, WORM]

earth·y (ûr′thē), *adj.,* **earth·i·er, earth·i·est. 1.** of the nature of or consisting of earth or soil. **2.** characteristic of earth: *an earthy smell.* **3.** realistic; practical. **4.** coarse or unrefined: *a very earthy sense of humor.* **5.** direct; robust; unaffected: *an earthy, generous farmer's wife.* **6.** *Archaic.* worldly; pertaining to the earth. [ME *erthy.* See EARTH, -Y[1]] —**earth′i·ly,** *adv.*

ear′ trum′pet, a trumpet-shaped device for collecting and intensifying sounds, held to the ear as an aid to a person with defective hearing.

ear·wax (ēr′waks′), *n.* cerumen. [ME *erewax.* See EAR[1], WAX[1]]

ear·wig (ēr′wig′), *n., v.,* **-wigged, -wig·ging.** —*n.* **1.** any of numerous elongate, nocturnal insects of the order *Dermaptera,* having a pair of large, movable pincers at the rear of the abdomen. —*v.t.* **2.** to fill the mind of with prejudice by insinuations. [ME *erwigge,* OE *ēarwicga* ear insect; from the superstition that they enter people's ears. See WIGGLE]

ear·wig·gy (ēr′wig′ē), *adj.* infested with earwigs. [EARWIG + -Y[1]]

ear·wit·ness (ēr′wit′nis), *n.* *Law.* one who testifies or can testify to what he has heard. [EAR[1] + WITNESS]

ease (ēz), *n., v.,* **eased, eas·ing.** —*n.* **1.** freedom from labor, pain, or physical annoyance; tranquil rest; comfort: *to take one's ease.* **2.** freedom from concern, anxiety, or solicitude; a quiet state of mind: *to be at ease about one's health.* **3.** freedom from difficulty or great effort; facility: *It can be done with ease.* **4.** freedom from financial need; plenty: *a life of ease on a moderate income.* **5.** freedom from stiffness, constraint, or formality; unaffectedness: *ease of manner; at ease with others.* **6.** **at ease,** *Mil.* a position of rest in which soldiers may relax but may not leave their places or talk. —*v.t.* **7.** to give rest or relief to; make comfortable. **8.** to free from anxiety or care: *to ease one's mind.* **9.** to mitigate, lighten, or lessen: *to ease pain.* **10.** to release from pressure, tension, or the like. **11.** to move or shift with great care: *to ease a car into a narrow parking space.* **12.** to render less difficult; facilitate: *I'll help if it will ease your job.* **13.** to provide (an architectural member) with an easement. **14.** *Shipbuilding.* to trim (a timber of a wooden hull) so as to fair its surface into the desired form of the hull. **15.** *Naut.* **a.** to bring (the helm or rudder of a vessel) slowly amidships. **b.** to bring the head of (a vessel) into the wind. **c.** to slacken or lessen the hold upon (a rope). **d.** to lessen the hold of (the brake of a windlass). —*v.i.* **16.** to reduce severity, pressure, tension, etc. (often fol. by *off* or *up*). **17.** to become less painful, burdensome, etc. **18.** to move, shift, or be moved or be shifted with great care. **19. ease out,** to depose from, or relieve of, a position of authority, a job, or the like, esp. by methods intended to be tactful: *Perkins was eased out as division head to make way for the boss's nephew.* [ME *ese, eise* < OF *aise,* perh. < VL **adiaces,* var. of L *adiacēs* ADJACENT]
—**Syn. 1.** repose, contentment, effortlessness. EASE, COMFORT refer to a sense of relaxation or of well-being. EASE implies a relaxed condition with an absence of effort or pressure: *a life of ease; ease after the day's work.* COMFORT suggests a sense of well-being, along with ease, which produces a quiet happiness and contentment: *comfort in one's old age.* **2.** tranquillity, serenity, calmness, peace. **5.** naturalness, informality. **7, 8.** comfort, relieve, disburden. **8.** tranquilize, soothe. **9.** alleviate, assuage, allay, abate, reduce. —**Ant. 1.** discomfort, effort. **2.** disturbance. **5.** constraint.

ease·ful (ēz′fəl), *adj.* comfortable; quiet; peaceful; restful. [ME *eisefull.* See EASE, -FUL] —**ease′ful·ly,** *adv.* —**ease′ful·ness,** *n.*

ea·sel (ē′zəl), *n.* **1.** a stand or frame for supporting an artist's canvas, a blackboard, or the like. **2.** any stand or frame for displaying objects, as paintings, china, etc. [< D *ezel* ass, easel (c. G *Esel,* OE *esel* ass) < VL **asilus,* var. of L *asellus,* dim. of *asinus* ASS[1]] —**ea′seled,** *adj.*

ease·ment (ēz′mənt), *n.* **1.** an easing; relief. **2.** something that gives ease; a convenience. **3.** *Law.* a right held by one person to make use of the land of another for a limited purpose, as right of passage. **4.** Also called **easing.** *Archit.* a curved member joining without angles two members that would otherwise intersect at an angle. [ME *esement* < OF *aisement,* equiv. to *aise* EASE + *-ment* -MENT]

eas·er (ē′zər), *n.* one who or that which eases. [EASE + -ER[1]]

eas·i·er (ē′zē ər), *adj.* comparative of **easy.**

eas·i·est (ē′zē ist), *adj.* superlative of **easy.**

eas·i·ly (ē′zə lē, ēz′lē), *adv.* **1.** in an easy manner; with ease; without trouble: *The traffic moves along easily.* **2.** beyond question; by far: *easily the best.* **3.** likely; well: *He may easily change his mind.* [ME *esily.* See EASY, -LY]

eas·i·ness (ē′zē nis), *n.* **1.** the quality or condition of being easy. **2.** ease of manner; carelessness; indifference. [ME *esinesse.* See EASY, -NESS]

eas·ing (ē′zing), *n.* *Archit.* easement (def. 4). [ME; see EASE, -ING[1]]

Eas·ley (ēz′lē), *n.* a town in NW South Carolina. 8283 (1960).

east (ēst), *n.* **1.** a cardinal point of the compass, 90° to the right of north. **2.** the direction in which this point lies. **3.** (*usually cap.*) a quarter or territory situated in this direction. **4. the East, a.** the parts of Asia collectively lying E of Europe and including Asia Minor, Syria, Arabia, India, China, etc.; the Orient. **b.** the entire eastern or Atlantic portion of the U.S., esp. the part N of Maryland. **c.** New England. **d.** *Ancient and Medieval Hist.* the Eastern Roman Empire. —*adj.* **5.** directed or proceeding toward the east. **6.** coming from the east: *an east wind.* **7.** lying toward or situated in the east: *the east side.* **8.** *Eccles.* being in the end of the church where the high altar is: *an east window.* —*adv.* **9.** toward or in the east: *an island located east of Sumatra; He went east.* [ME *est,* OE *ēast;* c. G *Ost,* Icel *austr;* akin to L *aurora,* Gk *aúōs* dawn. See EASTER] —**east′ness,** *n.*

East., eastern. Also, **east.**

East′ Al′ton, a town in SW Illinois. 7630 (1960).

East′ An′glia, an early English kingdom in SE Britain: modern Norfolk and Suffolk. See map under **Mercia.** —**East′ An′glian.**

East′ Ashtabu′la, a town in NE Ohio. 4179 (1960).

East′ Auro′ra, a town in W New York. 6791 (1960).

East′ Bengal′, a state in Pakistan: formerly part of the Indian province of Bengal; now coextensive with East Pakistan. Cf. **Bengal** (def. 1).

East′ Berlin′. See under **Berlin** (def. 2).

east·bound (ēst′bound′), *adj.* **1.** traveling, proceeding, or headed east: *an eastbound train.* **2.** pertaining to travel eastward. [EAST + -BOUND[2]]

East·bourne (ēst′bôrn, -bərn), *n.* a seaport in E Sussex, in SE England. 60,897 (1961).

East′ Brew′ton, a town in S Alabama. 2511 (1960).

east′ by north′, *Navig., Survey.* a point on the compass 11°15′ north of east. *Abbr.:* EbN

east′ by south′, *Navig., Survey.* a point on the compass 11°15′ south of east. *Abbr.:* EbS

East′ Cape′. See **Dezhnev, Cape.**

East′ Chica′go, a port in NW Indiana, on Lake Michigan, near Chicago. 57,669 (1960).

East′ Chica′go Heights′, a town in NE Illinois. 3270 (1960).

East′ Chi′na Sea′, a part of the N Pacific, bounded by China, Japan, Korea, the Ryukyus, and Formosa. 480,000 sq. mi.

East′ Cleve′land, a city in NE Ohio, near Cleveland. 37,991 (1960).

East′ Cok′er, a poem (1940) by T. S. Eliot. Cf. **Four Quartets.**

East′ Con′e·maugh (kon′ə mô′), a town in central Pennsylvania. 3334 (1960).

East′ Detroit′, a city in SE Michigan. 45,756 (1960).

East′ End′, a section of E London, England.

East·er (ē′stər), *n.* **1.** an annual Christian festival in commemoration of the resurrection of Jesus Christ, observed on the first Sunday after the first full moon after the vernal equinox, as calculated according to tables based in western churches on the Gregorian calendar and in Orthodox churches on the Julian calendar. **2.** the day on which this festival is celebrated. **3.** a girl's given name. [ME *ester,* OE *ēastre;* c. G *Ostern;* orig. name of a goddess and her festival; akin to EAST]

East′er can′dle, *Rom. Cath. Ch.* See **paschal candle.**

East′er dai′sy, a nearly stemless, perennial herb, *Townsendia exscapa,* of the Rocky Mountain regions, having stalkless purplish or white flowers in a rosette of narrow leaves. [so called because its flowers appear at Easter time]

East′er egg′, a chicken egg that is dyed and often given a figure or design or an imitation of such an egg used at Easter as a gift or decoration.

East′er Is′land, an island in the S Pacific, W of and belonging to Chile. ab. 45 sq. mi. Also called **Rapa Nui.** Spanish, **Isla de Pascua.**

East′er lil′y, any of several white-flowered lilies that are artificially brought into bloom in early spring, as the Madonna lily or Bermuda lily.

east·er·ling (ē′stər ling), *n.* a native of a country lying eastward of another country. [ME *esterling,* equiv. to *ester* eastern (? OE *ēastra,* comp. of *ēast* adj.) + -LING[1]]

east·er·ly (ē′stər lē), *adj., adv., n., pl.* **-lies.** —*adj.* **1.** moving, directed, or situated toward the east: *an easterly course.* **2.** (esp. of a wind) coming from the east: *an easterly gale.* —*adv.* **3.** toward the east. **4.** from the east. —*n.* **5.** a wind that blows from the east. [obs. *easter* eastern (see EASTERLING) + -LY] —**east′er·li·ness,** *n.*

east′erly wave′, a westward-moving, wavelike disturbance of low atmospheric pressure embedded in tropical easterly winds.

East′er Mon′day, the day after Easter, a legal holiday in North Carolina, England, Wales, Ireland, Australia, Canada, New Zealand, and the Republic of South Africa.

east·ern (ē′stərn), *adj.* **1.** lying toward or situated in the east: *the eastern half of the island.* **2.** directed or proceeding toward the east: *an eastern route.* **3.** coming from the east: *an eastern wind.* **4.** (*often cap.*) of or pertaining to the East: *an Eastern Congressman.* **5.** (*cap.*) of or pertaining to the Eastern Church or to any of the churches comprising it. **6.** (*usually cap.*) Oriental. [ME *esterne,* OE *ēasterne;* akin to Icel *austroenn,* OHG *ōstrōni.* See EAST, -ERN]

East′ern A′den Protec′torate, a former British protectorate, now the E part of South Yemen: composed of the Arab sheikdoms of Hadhramaut and the island of Socotra. 350,000 (est. 1966).

East′ern Church′, 1. any of the churches originating in countries formerly comprising the Eastern Roman Empire, observing an Eastern rite and adhering to the Niceno-Constantinopolitan Creed; Byzantine Church. **2.** See **Orthodox Church** (def. 2).

east′ern cor′al snake′. See under **coral snake.**

east′ern crown′, *Heraldry.* a coronet, represented as a circlet supporting eight triangular points of which only five are usually visible. Also called **antique crown.**

east′ern di′amondback rat′tlesnake, an extremely venomous diamondback rattlesnake, *Crotalus adamanteus,* of the southeastern U.S.

East′ern Em′pire. See **Eastern Roman Empire.**

east·ern·er (ē′stər nər), *n.* (*often cap.*) a native or inhabitant of an eastern area, esp. of the Eastern U.S. [EASTERN + -ER[1]]

East′ern Ghats′, a low mountain range in S India along the E margin of the Deccan plateau and parallel to the coast of the Bay of Bengal.

East′ern Hem′isphere, the eastern part of the terrestrial globe, including Asia, Africa, Australia, and Europe.

east′ern hem′lock, a hemlock, *Tsuga canadensis,* of eastern North America: the State tree of Pennsylvania.

East′ern Hin′di, the vernacular of the eastern half of the Hindi-speaking area in India.

east·ern·ize (ē′stər nīz′), *v.t.,* **-ized, -iz·ing. 1.** to influence with ideas, customs, etc., characteristic of the Orient. **2.** *U.S.* to influence with ideas, customs, etc., characteristic of the eastern U.S., esp. sophisticated or cosmopolitan ideas or customs. [EASTERN + -IZE]

east′ern king′bird. See under **kingbird.**

east·ern·most (ē′stərn mōst′ *or, esp. Brit.,* -məst), *adj.* farthest east. [EASTERN + -MOST]

East′ern Or′thodox, of or pertaining to the Orthodox Church.

East′ern Or′thodox Church′. See **Orthodox Church** (def. 1).

East′ern Or′thodoxy, the faith, practice, membership, and government of the Eastern Orthodox Church.

East′ern Ques′tion, 1. (formerly) the problem in international relations arising from the instability of the Ottoman Empire. **2.** Also, **Eastern question.** any international political problem in the Middle East.

east′ern red′ ce′dar. See **red cedar** (def. 1).

East′ern rite′, 1. the rite of an Eastern church, usually observed in the national language of the country where the church is located. **2.** a Uniat church.

East′ern Ro′man Em′pire, the eastern division of the Roman Empire after A.D. 395, having its capital at Constantinople: survived the fall of the Western Roman Empire in A.D. 476. Also called **Eastern Empire.** Cf. **Byzantine Empire.**

East′ern Sea′. See **Mare Orientalis.**

East′ern shore′, the eastern shore of Chesapeake Bay, including parts of Maryland, Delaware, and Virginia.

East′ern Slavs′. See under **Slav** (def. 1).

East′ern Thrace′. See under **Thrace** (def. 2).

East′ern time′. See under **standard time.**

East′ern Tur′kestan. See under **Turkestan.**

East′er sep′ulcher, sepulcher (def. 2).

East′er Sun′day, Easter day.

East·er·tide (ē′stər tīd′), *n.* **1.** Easter time. **2.** the week following Easter. **3.** the 50 days between Easter and Whitsuntide. [late ME *Estertyde.* See EASTER, TIDE[1]]

East′ Flan′ders, a province in W Belgium. 1,289,011 (est. 1964); 1150 sq. mi. *Cap.:* Ghent.

East′ Gaff′ney (gaf′nē), a town in N South Carolina. 4779 (1960).

East′ Gar′y, a town in NW Indiana. 9309 (1960).

East′ Gasto′nia, a town in S North Carolina. 3326 (1960).

East′ German′ic, a branch of the Germanic languages no longer extant, comprising Gothic and probably others of which there are no written records.

East′ Ger′many, a former country in central Europe: created in 1949 from the Soviet zone of occupied Germany established in 1945: reunited with West Germany in 1990. 16,340,000; 41,827 sq. mi. *Cap.:* East Berlin. Official name, **German Democratic Republic.** Cf. **Germany.** —**East′ Ger′man.**

East′ Goth′, an Ostrogoth.

East′ Grand′ Forks′, a town in NW Minnesota. 6998 (1960).

east′ Green′land cur′rent, a cold ocean current of low salinity flowing south along the east coast of Greenland.

East′ Ham′, a city in SE England, near London. 105,359 (1961).

East′ Hart′ford, a town in central Connecticut. 43,977 (1960).

East′ Ha′ven, a town in S Connecticut, near New Haven. 21,388 (1960).

East′ Hills′, a town on W Long Island, in SE New York. 7184 (1960).

East′ In′dia Com′pany, 1. the company chartered by the British government in 1600 to carry on trade in the East Indies; dissolved in 1874. **2.** any similar company, as one chartered by the Dutch (1602–1798), the French (1664–1769), or the Danes (1729–1801).

East′ In′diaman, 1. a large sailing ship operated by the British East India Company, used for carrying passengers and freight but constructed, armed, and managed in the manner of a naval vessel. Cf. **Blackwall frigate. 2.** any of the sailing ships of various nations trading with India or the East Indies; Indiaman.

East′ In′dian lo′tus. See **Indian lotus.**

East′ In′dian rose′-bay. See **crape jasmine.**

East′ In′dian wal′nut, lebbek.

East′ In′dies, 1. Also called **the Indies, Indonesia.** SE Asia, including India, Indonesia, and the Malay Archipelago. **2.** the Malay Archipelago. Also called **East′ In′dia.** —**East′ In′dian.**

east·ing (ē′sting), *n.* **1.** *Navig.* the distance due east made good on any course tending eastward; easterly departure. **2.** a shifting eastward; easterly direction. **3.** *Survey.* a distance east from a north-south reference line. [EAST + -ING[1]]

east′ing down′, *Naut.* **1.** the passage eastward from the Cape of Good Hope, as made by a sailing ship bound for Australia or the East Indies. **2.** the passage eastward from Australia, as made by a sailing ship bound for Cape Horn.

East′ Kil′bride (kil′brīd), a town in W Lanark, in E Scotland. 31,972 (1961).

East·lake (ēst′lāk′), *adj.* noting or pertaining to an English and American style of furniture and decoration originally introduced c1870 as a revival of former standards of workmanship and decoration but ending as an adaptation of Gothic and Japanese motifs. [named after Sir Charles *Eastlake* (1796–1865), English art critic]

East·lake (ēst′lāk′), *n.* **Sir Charles Locke,** 1836–1906, English architect, designer, and author.

East·land (ēst′lənd), *n.* a town in central Texas. 3292 (1960).

East′ Lans′downe (lanz′doun′), a town in SE Pennsylvania. 3224 (1960).

East′ Lan′sing, a city in S Michigan. 30,198 (1960).

East′ Liv′erpool, a city in E Ohio, on the Ohio River. 22,306 (1960). —**East′ Liverpud′lian.**

East′ Lon′don, a seaport in the SE Cape of Good Hope province, in the S Republic of South Africa. 106,100 with suburbs (est. 1957). —**East′ Lon′doner.**

East′ Los′ An′geles, a seaport in SW California, near Los Angeles. 104,270 (1960).

East′ Lo′thi·an (lō′thē ən), a county in SE Scotland. 52,653 (1961); 267 sq. mi. *Co. seat:* Haddington. Formerly, **Haddington.**

East·man (ēst′mən), *n.* **1. George,** 1854–1932, U.S. philanthropist and inventor in the field of photography. **2. Max For·res·ter** (fôr′i stər, for′-), 1883–1969, U.S. editor and writer. **3.** a town in central Georgia. 5118 (1960).

East′ Mc·Kees′port (mə kēz′pōrt′, -pôrt′), a town in SW Pennsylvania. 3470 (1960).

East′ Mead′ow, a town on W Long Island, in SE New York. 46,036 (1960).

East′ Moline′, a city in NW Illinois. 16,732 (1960).

east·most (ēst′mōst′ *or, esp. Brit.,* -məst), *adj.* easternmost. [ME *estmest,* OE *ēastmest.* See EAST, -MOST]

east-north·east (ēst′nôrth′ēst′), *Navig., Survey.* —*n.* **1.** the point on a compass midway between east and northeast. —*adj.* **2.** coming from this point: *an east-northeast wind.* **3.** directed toward this point: *an east-northeast course.* —*adv.* **4.** from this point: *The wind is blowing east-northeast.* **5.** toward this point: *sailing east-northeast. Abbr.:* ENE

east-north·east·ward (ēst′nôrth′ēst′wərd; *Naut.* ēst′nôr′ēst′wərd), *adv., adj.* toward the east-northeast. Also, **east′-north′east′ward·ly.**

East′ North′port, a town on NW Long Island, in SE New York. 8381 (1960).

Eas·ton (ē′stən), *n.* **1.** a city in E Pennsylvania, on the Delaware River. 31,955 (1960). **2.** a town in E Maryland. 6337 (1960).

East′ Or′ange, a city in NE New Jersey, near Newark. 77,259 (1960).

East′ Pak′istan, former name of **Bangladesh.**

East′ Pal′estine, a town in E Ohio. 5232 (1960).

East′ Pat′erson, a city in NE New Jersey. 19,344 (1960).

East′ Pitts′burgh, a town in SW Pennsylvania. 4122 (1960).

East′ Point′, a city in N Georgia, near Atlanta. 35,633 (1960).

East·port (ēst′pōrt′, -pôrt′), *n.* a town in E Maine. 2537 (1960).

East′ Por′terville, a town in central California. 3538 (1960).

East′ Prai′rie, a town in SE Missouri. 3449 (1960).

East′ Prov′idence, a town in NE Rhode Island, near Providence. 41,955 (1960).

East′ Prus′sia, a former province in NE Germany: an enclave separated from Germany by the Polish Corridor; now divided between Poland and the Soviet Union. 14,283 sq. mi. *Cap.:* Königsberg. German, **Ostpreussen.** —**East′ Prus′sian.**

East′ Punjab′, the eastern part of the former province of Punjab: now part of Punjab state. —**East′ Punjab′i.**

East′ Ridge′, a city in SE Tennessee, near Chattanooga. 19,570 (1960).

East′ Rid′ing, an administrative division of Yorkshire, in NE England. 527,051 (1961); 1172 sq. mi. *Co. seat:* Beverley.

East′ Riv′er, a strait in SE New York separating Manhattan Island from Long Island and connecting New York Bay and Long Island Sound.

East′ Roch′ester, a town in W New York. 8152 (1960).

East′ Rock′ingham, a town in S North Carolina. 3211 (1960).

East′ Ruth′erford, a town in NE New Jersey. 7769 (1960).

East′ Side′, a town in SE Mississippi. 4304 (1960).

East·side (ēst′sīd′), *adj.* (*sometimes l.c.*) of, pertaining to, or located on the east side of Manhattan, in New York City: *one of the little Eastside shops.*

East-sid·er (ēst′sī′dər), *n.* a native or resident of the east side of Manhattan, in New York City. [EASTSIDE + -ER[1]]

East′ Som′erset, a town in central Kentucky. 3645 (1960).

east-south·east (ēst′south′ēst′), *Navig., Survey.* —*n.* **1.** the point on a compass midway between east and southeast. —*adj.* **2.** coming from this point: *an east-southeast wind.* **3.** directed toward this point: *an east-southeast course.* —*adv.* **4.** from this point: *The wind is blowing east-southeast.* **5.** toward this point: *sailing east-southeast. Abbr.:* ESE

east-south·east·ward (ēst′south′ēst′wərd; *Naut.* ēst′sou′ēst′wərd), *adv., adj.* toward the east-southeast. Also, **east′-south′east′ward·ly.**

East St. Louis, a city in SW Illinois, across the Mississippi River from St. Louis, Missouri. 81,712 (1960). —**East St. Louisan.**

East′ Strouds′burg, a town in E Pennsylvania. 7674 (1960).

East′ Suf′folk, an administrative division of Suffolk county, in E England. 342,696 (1961); 871 sq. mi. *Co. seat:* Ipswich.

East′ Sus′sex, an administrative division of Sussex county, in SE England. 664,669 (1961); 829 sq. mi. *Co. seat:* Lewes.

East′ Syr′acuse, a town in central New York. 4708 (1960).

east·ward (ēst′wərd), *adv.* **1.** Also, **east′wards.** toward the east. —*adj.* **2.** moving, bearing, facing, or situated toward the east. —*n.* **3.** the eastward part, direction, or point. [ME *estward,* OE *ēasteweard.* See EAST, -WARD]

east·ward·ly (ēst′wərd lē), *adj.* **1.** having an eastward direction or situation. **2.** coming from the east: *an eastwardly wind.* —*adv.* **3.** toward the east. **4.** from the east. [EASTWARD + -LY]

East′ Wil′liston, a town on W Long Island, in SE New York. 2940 (1960).

East′ Wil′mington, a town in SE North Carolina. 5520 (1960).

eas·y (ē′zē), *adj.,* **eas·i·er, eas·i·est,** *adv., n., pl.* **eas·ies.** —*adj.* **1.** not difficult; requiring no great labor or effort: *a book that is easy to read; an easy victory.* **2.** free from pain, discomfort, worry, or care: *easy in one's mind.* **3.** providing or conducive to ease or comfort; comfortable: *an easy stance; an easy relationship.* **4.** fond of or given to ease; easygoing: *an easy disposition.* **5.** not harsh or strict; lenient: *an easy master.* **6.** not burdensome or oppressive: *easy terms on a loan.* **7.** not difficult to influence or overcome; compliant: *He was an easy prey to victimizers.* **8.** free from formality, constraint, or embarrassment: *He has an easy manner.* **9.** effortlessly clear and fluent: *an easy style of writing.* **10.** readily comprehended or mastered: *an easy language to learn.* **11.** not tight or constricting: *an easy fit.* **12.** not forced or hurried; moderate: *an easy pace.* **13.** *Com.* **a.** (of a commodity) not difficult to obtain; in plentiful supply and often weak in price. **b.** (of the market) not characterized by eager demand. **14.** *Naut.* **a.** (of a bilge) formed in a long curve so as to make a gradual transition between the bottom and sides of a vessel; slack. **b.** (of the run of a hull) having gently curved surfaces leading from the middle body to the stern; not abrupt. —*adv.* **15.** *Informal.* in an easy manner; comfortably: *to go easy; take it easy.* —*n.* **16.** a word formerly used in communications to represent the letter E. [ME *aisie, esy* < OF *aaisie,* ptp. of *aisier* to put (someone) at his ease (orig. adv. phrase *a aise* at ease)] —**eas′y·like′,** *adj.*
—**Syn. 2.** tranquil, untroubled, comfortable, contented, quiet, satisfied. **7.** accommodating, agreeable. **8.** smooth, unconstrained. —**Ant. 1.** difficult. **2.** agitated. **3.** uncomfortable.

eas′y chair′, **1.** an upholstered chair for lounging. **2.** *Obs.* See **wing chair.**

eas·y·go·ing (ē′zē gō′ing), *adj.* **1.** calm and unworried; relaxed and rather casual: *an easygoing person.* **2.** going easily, as a horse. Also, **eas′y-go′ing.** [EASY + GOING] —**eas′y·go′ing·ness,** *n.*

eas′y mon′ey, **1.** money obtained with a minimum of effort. **2.** money obtained by deception, fraud, artifice, etc.

eas′y street′, *Slang.* a footing of wealth, financial independence, or ease: *If the book sells, next year we'll be on easy street.* Also, **Eas′y Street′.**

eat (ēt), *v.,* **ate** (āt; *esp. Brit.* et) or (*Archaic*) **eat** (et, ēt); **eat·en** or (*Archaic*) **eat** (et, ēt); **eat·ing;** *n.* —*v.t.* **1.** to take into the mouth and swallow for nourishment; chew and swallow (food). **2.** to consume by or as if by devouring gradually; wear away; corrode: *The patient was eaten by disease and pain.* **3.** to ravage or devastate: *a forest eaten by fire.* **4.** to make (a hole, passage, etc.), as by gnawing or corrosion. —*v.i.* **5.** to consume food; take a meal: *We'll eat at 6:00.* **6.** to make a way, as by gnawing or corrosion: *Acid ate through the linoleum.* **7. be eating someone,** to cause someone to be greatly troubled, or in a bad temper: *Something seems to be eating him—he's been wearing a frown all day.* **8. eat away** or **into,** to destroy gradually, as by erosion: *For eons, the pounding waves ate away at the shoreline.* **9. eat high off the hog.** See **hog** (def. 10). **10. eat in,** *Naut.* See **pucker** (def. 2). **11. eat one out of house and home,** to batten on (one) so as to strain one's resources of food or money: *a mob of visiting relatives eating their host out of house and home.* **12. eat one's heart out.** See **heart** (def. 23). **13. eat one's terms.** See **term** (def. 16). **14. eat one's words.** See **word** (def. 15). **15. eat the wind out of,** *Naut.* to blanket (a sailing vessel sailing close-hauled) by sailing close on the weather side of; eat to windward of. **16. eat to windward,** *Naut.* to sail close-hauled in such a way as to utilize all available wind. **17. eat to windward of,** *Naut.* to blanket (a sailing vessel sailing close-hauled) by sailing close on the weather side of; eat the wind out of. **18. eat up, a.** to consume wholly. **b.** to show enthusiasm for; take pleasure in: *The audience ate up everything he said.* **c.** to believe without question. —*n.* **19. eats,** *Slang.* food. [ME *eten,* OE *etan;* c. G *essen,* Goth *itan,* L *edere*] —**eat′er,** *n.*

eat·a·ble (ē′tə bəl), *adj.* **1.** fit to be eaten; edible. —*n.* **2.** Usually, **eatables.** articles of food. [EAT + -ABLE]

eat·en (ēt′ən), *v.* a pp. of **eat.**

eat·er·y (ē′tə rē), *n., pl.* **-er·ies.** *Slang.* a restaurant or other commercial establishment serving food: *We went to the opening of a posh new eatery.* [EAT + -ERY]

eath (ēth, ēth), *Scot.* —*adj.* **1.** easy; not difficult. **2.** comfortable; free from pain. —*adv.* **3.** easily; without difficulty. [ME *ethe,* OE *ēathe* (adv.); c. Icel *auth-,* OHG *-ōdo;* akin to OE *ēadig,* Goth *audags* happy]

eat·ing (ē′ting), *n.* **1.** the act of one who or that which eats. **2.** food with reference to the quality it displays when eaten: *This fish is delicious eating.* —*adj.* **3.** good or fit to eat, esp. raw (distinguished from *cooking*): *eating apples.* [ME; see EAT, -ING[1], -ING[2]]

eat′ing house′, a restaurant, esp. an inexpensive or inferior one.

Ea·ton (ēt′ən), *n.* **1. Theophilus,** 1590–1658, English colonist and colonial administrator in America. **2.** a town in W Ohio. 5034 (1960). **3.** a boy's given name.

Ea′ton Rap′ids, a town in central Michigan. 4052 (1960).

Ea·ton·ton (ēt′ən tən), *n.* a town in central Georgia. 3612 (1960).

eau (ō), *n., pl.* **eaux** (ō). *French.* water.

Eau Claire (ō′ klâr′), a city in W Wisconsin. 37,987 (1960).

eau de Co·logne (ō′ də kə lōn′), cologne.

eau de Ja·velle (ō′ də zha vel′, -zhə-; *Fr.* ōdə zha vel′). See **Javel water.**

eau de vie (ōdə vē′; *Eng.* ō′ də vē′), *French.* brandy, esp. a coarser and less purified variety. [lit., water of life]

eau de vie de marc (ōdə vē də mar′; *Eng.* ō′ də vē′ də märk′), *French.* marc (def. 2).

eau forte (ō′ fôrt′, ō′ fôrt′). See **nitric acid.** [short for *gravure à l'eau forte* etching; lit., engraving (done) with strong water, i.e., acid]

eau mi·né·rale (ō mē ne ral′), *pl.,* **eaux mi·né·rales** (ō mē ne ral′). *French.* See **mineral water** (def 1).

eave (ēv), *n.* Usually, **eaves.** the overhanging lower edge of a roof. [ME *eves,* OE *efes;* c. OHG *obisa,* Goth *ubizwa* hall] —**eaved,** *adj.*

eaves·drop (ēvz′drop′), *v.,* **-dropped, -drop·ping,** *n.* —*v.i.* **1.** to listen secretly to a private conversation (usually followed by *on*). —*v.t.* **2.** to eavesdrop on. —*n.* Also, **eaves·drip** (ēvz′drip′). **3.** water that drips from the eaves. **4.** the ground on which such water falls. [lit., to be on the *eavesdrop* (ME *evesdrope,* var. of *evesdripe,* OE *yfesdrype*) of a house, i.e., on the ground to which falls the drip from the eaves. See EAVES, DROP, DRIP] —**eaves′drop′per,** *n.*

Eb (eb), *n.* a boy's given name, form of **Ebenezer.**

é·bauche (ā bōsh′), *n.* a watch movement supplied by a manufacturer, without jewels, escapement, finish, or a case. [< F, deriv. of *ébaucher* to sketch out, equiv. to OF *es-* EX-[1] + *-bauchier* rough-hew, deriv. of *bauc(h)* beam < Gmc; cf. BALK]

ebb (eb), *n.* **1.** the flowing back of the tide as the water returns to the sea (opposed to *flood, flow*). **2.** a flowing backward or away; decline or decay: *the ebb of a once great nation.* **3.** a point of decline: *His fortunes were at a low ebb.* —*v.i.* **4.** to flow back or away, as the water of a tide (opposed to *flow*). **5.** to decline or decay; waste or fade away: *His life is ebbing.* [ME *eb(be),* OE *ebba;* c. OFris *ebba,* D *eb(be),* OS *ebbia,* G *Ebbe* ebb, Icel *efja* place where water backs up; akin to OFF]
—**Syn. 2.** wane. **4.** subside, abate, recede, retire. **5.** sink, wane.

ebb′ an′chor, *Naut.* an anchor holding a vessel in place at the ebb of a tide (opposed to *flood anchor*).

ebb′ tide′, the reflux of the tide or the tide at ebb.

Eb·en·e·zer (eb′ə nē′zər), *n.* a boy's given name.

é·bé·niste (ā bā nēst′), *n., pl.* **-nistes** (-nēst′). *French.* **1.** a person who does cabinetwork with veneers and inlays. **2.** ebonist.

é·bé·nis·te·rie (ā bā nē stə rē′), *n.* *French.* the work or craft of an *ébéniste.*

Eb·ens·burg (eb′ənz bûrg′), *n.* a town in central Pennsylvania. 4111 (1960).

Eb·er·hard (eb′ər härd′; *Ger.* ā′bər härt′), *n.* a boy's given name.

E·ber·hart (ā′bər härt′, eb′ər-), *n.* **Richard,** born 1904, U.S. poet.

E·bert (ā′bərt; *for 1 also Ger.* ā′bərt), *n.* **1. Friedrich** (frē′drikh), 1871–1925, 1st president of Germany 1919–25. **2.** a boy's given name, form of **Everard.**

Eb·lis (eb′lis), *n.* *Islamic Myth.* an evil spirit or devil, the chief of the wicked jinn. Also, **Iblis.** [< Ar *Iblīs* chief of the wicked jinn < Gk *diábolos* slanderer, the Devil; *di-* lost by confusion with Aram *di-* of]

EbN, See **east by north.**

Eb·ner (eb′nər), *n.* a boy's given name, form of **Abner.**

E-boat (ē′bōt′), *n.* *Brit.* a fast unarmored motorboat armed with torpedoes and small guns. [short for *enemy-boat*]

eb·on (eb′ən), *adj.* ebony. [ME < L *ebenus* < Gk *hébenos, ébenos* EBONY]

eb·on·ise (eb′ə nīz′), *v.t.,* **-ised, -is·ing.** *Chiefly Brit.* ebonize.

eb·on·ist (eb′ə nist), *n.* a worker in ebony. [EBON(Y) + -IST]

eb·on·ite (eb′ə nīt′), *n.* vulcanite. [EBON(Y) + -ITE[1]]

eb·on·ize (eb′ə nīz′), *v.t.,* **-ized, -iz·ing.** to stain or finish black in imitation of ebony. Also, *esp. Brit.,* **ebonise.** [EBON(Y) + -IZE]

eb·on·y (eb′ə nē), *n., pl.* **-on·ies,** *adj.* —*n.* **1.** a hard, heavy, durable wood, most highly prized when black, from various tropical trees of the genus *Diospyros,* as *D. Ebenum* of southern India and Ceylon, used for cabinetwork, ornamental objects, etc. **2.** any tree yielding such wood. **3.** any of various similar woods or trees. **4.** a deep, lustrous black. —*adj.* **5.** Also, **ebon.** made of ebony. **6.** of a deep, lustrous black. [EBON + -Y; r. ME *hebenyf* < L *hebeninus* of ebony (misread as *hebeniuus*) < Gk *ebéninos*]

eb′ony spleen′wort, a fern, *Asplenium platyneuron,* of woody areas of North America.

Eb·o·ra·cum (eb′ə rā′kəm), *n.* ancient name of **York, England.**

e·brac·te·ate (ē brak′tē āt′), *adj.* *Bot.* having no bracts. [< NL *ebracteāt(us).* See E-, BRACTEATE]

E·bro (ē′brō; *Sp.* e′brō), *n.* a river flowing SE from N Spain to the Mediterranean. ab. 470 mi. long.

EbS, See **east by south.**

e·bul·lience (i bul′yəns), *n.* **1.** a boiling over; overflow. **2.** high spirits; exhilaration; enthusiasm; exuberance. Also, **e·bul′lien·cy.** [EBULLI(ENT) + -ENCE]

e·bul·lient (i bul′yənt), *adj.* **1.** overflowing with fervor, enthusiasm, or excitement; high-spirited: *The award winner was in an ebullient mood at the dinner in his honor.* **2.** boiling up; bubbling up like a boiling liquid. [< L *ēbullient-* (s. of *ēbulliēns* boiling up, prp. of *ēbullīre*), equiv. to *ē-* E- + *bulli-* (deriv. of *bulla* a bubble) + *-ent-* -ENT] —**e·bul′lient·ly,** *adv.*

eb·ul·li·tion (eb′ə lish′ən), *n.* **1.** a seething or overflowing, as of passion or feeling; outburst: *ebullition of feeling.* **2.** the state of being ebullient. **3.** the act or process of boiling up. **4.** a rushing forth of water, lava, etc., in a state of agitation. [< L *ēbullītiōn-* (s. of *ēbullītiō*), equiv. to *ēbullīt(us)* (ptp. of *ēbullīre* to boil up), equiv. to *ēbulli-* (see EBULLIENT) + *-t* ptp. suffix + *-iōn-* -ION]

e·bur·na·tion (ē′bər nā′shən, eb′ər-), *n.* *Pathol.* an abnormal condition in which bone becomes hard and dense like ivory. [< L *eburn(us)* of ivory (equiv. to *ebur* ivory + *-nus* adj. suffix) + -ATION]

ec-, var. of **ex-**³ before a consonant: *eccentric.*

E.C., 1. Engineering Corps. 2. Established Church.

e.c., for the sake of example. [< L *exemplī causā*]

ECA, See **Economic Cooperation Administration.** Also, **E.C.A.**

e·cal·ca·rate (ē kal′kə rāt′), *adj. Bot., Zool.* having no spur or calcar. [E- + CALCAR + -ATE¹]

e·car·i·nate (ē kar′ə nāt′), *adj. Bot., Zool.* having no carina or keel. [E- + CARINATE]

é·car·té (ā′kär tā′; *Brit.* ā kär′tā; *Fr.* ā kaʀ tā′), *n.* a card game for two players. [< F (n. use of ptp. of *écarter* to discard), equiv. to *é-* (< L *ex-* EX-¹) + *cart-* CARD¹ + *-é* -EE]

e·cau·date (ē kô′dāt), *adj. Zool.* having no tail. [< NL *ecaudat(us).* See E-, CAUDATE]

Ec·bat·a·na (ek bat′ənə), *n.* ancient name of **Hamadan.**

ec·bol·ic (ek bol′ik), *Med.* —*adj.* 1. promoting labor by increasing uterine contractions. —*n.* 2. an ecbolic agent. [< Gk *ekbol(ḗ)* expulsion (equiv. to *ek-* EC- + *-bolē* a throwing) + -IC]

ec·ce ho·mo (ech′ā hō′mō *for 1;* ek′sē hō′mō, ek′ā *for 2*), *Latin.* 1. "Behold the man!": the words with which Pilate presented Christ, crowned with thorns, to his accusers. John 19:5. 2. *Art.* a representation of Christ crowned with thorns.

ec·cen·tric (ik sen′trik, ek-), *adj.* 1. deviating from the recognized or customary character, practice, etc.; irregular; erratic; peculiar; odd: *eccentric conduct; an eccentric person.* 2. *Geom.* not having the same center; not concentric: used esp. of two circles or spheres at least one of which contains the centers of both. 3. not situated in the center, as an axis. 4. *Mach.* having the axis or support away from the center, as a wheel. 5. *Astron.* deviating from a circular form, as an elliptic orbit. —*n.* 6. a person who has an unusual, peculiar, or odd personality, set of beliefs, or behavior pattern. 7. something that is unusual, peculiar, or odd. 8. *Mach.* a device for converting circular motion into reciprocating rectilinear motion, consisting of a disk fixed somewhat out of center to a revolving shaft, and working freely in a surrounding collar (**eccen′tric strap′**), to which a rod (**eccen′tric rod′**) is attached. Also, *esp. Brit.,* **excentric.** [< LL *eccentric(us)* < Gk *ékkentr(os)* out of center (see EC-, CENTER) + L *-icus* -IC] —**ec·cen′tri·cal,** *adj.* —**ec·cen′tri·cal·ly,** *adv.*
—**Ant. 1.** normal, ordinary.

A
B

Eccentric circles
A, Center of small circle; B, Center of large circle

ec·cen·tric·i·ty (ek′sən tris′i tē, ek′sen-), *n., pl.* **-ties.** 1. an oddity or peculiarity, as of conduct: *an interesting man, known for his eccentricities.* 2. the quality of being eccentric. 3. the amount by which something is eccentric. 4. *Mach.* the distance between the centers of two cylindrical objects one of which surrounds the other, as between an eccentric and the shaft on which it is mounted. 5. *Math.* a constant expressed as the ratio of the distance from a point on a conic to a focus and the distance from the point to the directrix. [< ML *eccentricitās,* equiv. to *eccentric-* (see ECCENTRIC) + *-itās* -ITY]
—**Syn. 2.** queerness, freakishness, aberration.

ec·ce sig·num (ek′e sig′no͝om; *Eng.* ek′sē sig′nəm), *Latin.* behold the sign (or proof).

ec·chy·mo·sis (ek′ə mō′sis), *n., pl.* **-ses** (-sēz). *Pathol.* a discoloration due to extravasation of blood, as in a bruise. [< NL < Gk *ekchýmōsis* extravasation, equiv. to *ek-* EC- + *chym(ós)* juice + *-ōsis* -OSIS] —**ec·chy·mot·ic** (ek′ə mot′ik), *adj.*

Eccl., Ecclesiastes. Also, **Eccles.**

eccl., ecclesiastical. Also, **eccles.**

Ec·cles (ek′əlz), *n.* 1. **Sir John Ca·rew** (kə ro͞o′), born 1903, Australian physiologist: Nobel prize for medicine 1963. 2. **Mar·ri·ner Stod·dard** (mar′ə nər stod′ərd), born 1890, U.S. economist and banker.

ecclesi-, var. of **ecclesio-** before a vowel: *ecclesiarch.*

ec·cle·si·a (i klē′zhē ə, -zē ə), *n., pl.* **-si·ae** (-zhē ē′, -zē ē′). 1. an assembly, esp. the popular assembly of ancient Athens. 2. a congregation; church. [< L < Gk *ekklēsía* assembly, equiv. to *ekklē(tós)* summoned (*ek-* EC- + *klē-,* var. of *kal-,* s. of *kalein* to call, + *-tos* ptp. suffix) + *-ia* n. suffix]

Ec·cle·si·am Su·am (ā klā′zē äm′ so͞o′äm), *Latin.* His Church (opening words and the title of an encyclical of Pope Paul VI issued in 1964 on Christian unity and world problems).

ec·cle·si·arch (i klē′zē ärk′), *n. Eastern Ch.* a sacristan, esp. of a monastery. [< MGk *ekklēsiárchēs.* See ECCLESI-, -ARCH]

Ec·cle·si·as·tes (i klē′zē as′tēz), *n.* a book of the Bible. [< LL < Gk *ekklēsiastḗs* assemblyman, equiv. to *ekklēsí(a)* ECCLESIA + *-astēs,* var. of *-istēs* -IST]

ec·cle·si·as·tic (i klē′zē as′tik), *n.* 1. a clergyman or other person in religious orders. 2. a member of the ecclesia in ancient Athens. —*adj.* 3. ecclesiastical. [< LL *ecclēsiastic(us)* < Gk *ekklēsiastikós.* See ECCLESIASTES, -IC]

ec·cle·si·as·ti·cal (i klē′zē as′ti kəl), *adj.* of or pertaining to the church or the clergy; churchly; clerical; not secular; not lay: *ecclesiastical discipline; ecclesiastical writings.* [late ME; see ECCLESIASTES, -ICAL] —**ec·cle′si·as′ti·cal·ly,** *adv.*

eccle′sias′tical cal′endar, 1. a calendar based on the lunisolar cycle, used by many Christian churches in determining the dates for the movable feasts. 2. Also called **church calendar.** a calendar of the Christian year, indicating the days and seasons for fasts and festivals.

eccle′sias′tical court′, a church court in ecclesiastical matters, presided over by members of the clergy and usually having no compulsory jurisdiction. Also called **court Christian.**

eccle′sias′tical law′, 1. the law made by a church for its own administration. 2. any law applied to a church.

ecclesias′tical mode′, *Music.* See **church mode.**

ecclesias′tical soci′ety, *U.S.* (in Congregational churches) a legal corporation with power to sue and be sued and to administer all of the temporalities of the church.

ec·cle·si·as·ti·cism (i klē′zē as′ti siz′əm), *n.* 1. ecclesiastical principles, practices, or spirit. 2. devotion to the principles or interests of the church. [ECCLESIASTIC + -ISM]

Ec·cle·si·as·ti·cus (i klē′zē as′ti kəs), *n.* a book of the Apocrypha. Also called **Wisdom of Jesus.**

ecclesio-, a combining form meaning "church": *ecclesiology.* Also, *esp. before a vowel,* **ecclesi-.** [repr. MGk *ekklēsía* church (Gk: assembly). See ECCLESIA]

ec·cle·si·ol·a·try (i klē′zē ol′ə trē), *n.* excessive reverence for churchly forms and traditions. [ECCLESIO- + -LATRY] —**ec·cle′si·ol′a·ter,** *n.*

ec·cle·si·ol·o·gy (i klē′zē ol′ə jē), *n.* 1. the study of ecclesiastical adornments and furnishings. 2. the study of church doctrine. [ECCLESIO- + -LOGY] —**ec·cle·si·o·log·ic** (i klē′zē ə loj′ik), **ec·cle′si·o·log′i·cal,** *adj.* —**ec·cle′si·o·log′i·cal·ly,** *adv.* —**ec·cle′si·ol′o·gist,** *n.*

Ecclus., Ecclesiasticus.

ec·cri·nol·o·gy (ek′rə nol′ə jē), *n.* the branch of physiology and anatomy dealing with secretions and the secretory glands. [< Gk *ekkrín(ein)* (to) secrete (*ek-* EC- + *krínein* to separate) + -O- + -LOGY]

ec·dem·ic (ek dem′ik), *adj. Pathol.* noting or pertaining to a disease that originates outside the area in which it occurs but is neither epidemic nor endemic. [EC- + Gk *dêm-* (s. of *dêmos*) people + -IC]

ec·dys·i·ast (ek diz′ē ast′), *n.* stripper (def. 3). [ECDYSI(S) + *-ast,* var. of -IST; coined by H. L. Mencken]

ec·dy·sis (ek′di sis), *n., pl.* **-ses** (-sēz′). the shedding or casting off of an outer coat or integument by snakes, crustaceans, etc. [< NL < Gk *ékdysis* a getting out, equiv. to *ek-* EC- + *dý(ein)* (to) enter + *-sis* -SIS] —**ec·dys·i·al** (ek diz′ē əl, -dizh′-, -dizh′əl), *adj.*

e·ce·sis (i sē′sis), *n. Ecol.* the establishment of an immigrant plant in a new environment. [< Gk *oíkēsis* an inhabiting, equiv. to *oik(ein)* (to) inhabit (akin to *oikos* house, home) + *-ēsis* -ESIS] —**e·ce′sic,** *adj.*

ECG, electrocardiogram. Also, **E.C.G.**

é·chap·pé (ā′shä pā′, ā shap′ā; *Fr.* ā shȧ pā′), *n., pl.* **é·chap·pés** (ā′shä pāz′, ā shap′āz; *Fr.* ā shȧ pā′). a ballet movement in which the dancer jumps from the fifth position and lands on the toes or the balls of the feet in the second position. [< F, ptp. of *échapper* to ESCAPE]

é·chap·pée (ā′shä pā′, ā shap′ā; *Fr.* ā shȧ pā′), *n., pl.* **é·chap·pées** (ā′shä pāz′, ā shap′āz; *Fr.* ā shȧ pā′), *Music.* a melodic ornamental tone following a principal tone by a step above or below and proceeding by a skip. [< F: escape (tone), lit., escaped (fem. ptp. of *échapper*). See ESCAPE]

E, Echappées

eche (ēch), *v.t., v.i.,* **eched, ech·ing.** *Obs.* to enlarge; increase. [ME; var. of EKE¹]

E·che·cles (ē′kə klēz′), *n.* (in the *Iliad*) the husband of Polymela who raised his wife's son by Hermes as his own child.

E·che·ga·ray (e′che gä rī′), *n.* **Jo·sé** (hô se′), (*José Echegaray y Eizaguirre*), 1832–1916, Spanish dramatist and statesman: Nobel prize 1904.

ech·e·lette (esh′ə let′, ā′shə-), *n. Physics.* a diffraction grating that is used for the reflection of infrared radiation and that has grooves spaced comparatively far apart and flattened for the reflection of the radiation into particular orders. Also called **echelette′ grat′ing.** [< F: rack, dim. of *échelle* ladder, scale]

e·chelle (ā shel′), *n.* 1. Also called **echelle′ grat′ing.** *Physics.* a diffraction grating that has comparatively widely-spaced grooves and that has a high resolving power for a small number of incident wavelengths. 2. a vertical row of bows or ribbon lacing on a 17th-century stomacher. 3. any such ladderlike decoration on a garment. [< F: lit., ladder]

ech·e·lon (esh′ə lon′), *n.* 1. a level of command, authority, or rank: *the top echelon of city officials.* 2. a formation of troops, ships, airplanes, etc., in which groups are disposed in parallel lines, each to the right or left of the one in front, so that the whole presents the appearance of steps. 3. one of the groups of a formation so disposed. 4. Also called **ech′elon grat′ing.** *Physics.* a diffraction grating that is used in the resolution of fine structure lines and consists of a series of plates of equal thickness placed together in the shape of a staircase. —*v.t., v.i.* 5. to form in an echelon. [< F *échelon,* orig. rung of a ladder, OF *eschelon,* equiv. to *esch(i)ele* ladder (< L *scāla* SCALE³) + *-on* n. suffix] —**ech′e·lon′ment,** *n.*

E·che·mus (ē′kə məs), *n. Class. Myth.* an Arcadian king who killed Hyllus in a duel and thus temporarily delayed the Heraclidan invasion of the Peloponnesus.

E·che·tus (ē′ki təs), *n. Class. Myth.* a king of Epirus who blinded his daughter. Cf. **Amphissa** (def. 1).

E·che·ver·rí·a (e′che veʀ rē′ä), *n.* **Es·te·ban** (es te′vän), 1805–51, Argentine poet.

e·chid·na (i kid′nə), *n.* 1. Also called **spiny anteater.** any of several insectivorous monotremes of the genera *Tachyglossus,* of Australia, Tasmania, and New Guinea, and *Zaglossus,* of New Guinea, that have claws and a slender snout and are covered with coarse hair and long spines. 2. (*cap.*) *Class. Myth.* a monster, half woman and half serpent, who was the mother of several monsters including the Chimera, the Hydra, the Sphinx, and Cerberus. She was killed by Argus. [< L < Gk *échidna* viper]

Echidna, *Tachyglossus aculeatus* **(Length to 1½ ft.)**

ech·i·nate (ek′ə nāt′, -nit), *adj.* bristly; prickly. Also, **ech′i·nat′ed.** [ECHIN(O)- + -ATE¹]

echino-, a learned borrowing from Greek meaning "sea urchin," used in the formation of compound words: *echinoderm.* Also, *esp. before a vowel,* **echin-.** [< Gk *echîno(s)* ECHINUS]

e·chi·no·derm (i kī′nə dûrm′, ek′i nə-), *n.* any marine animal of the phylum *Echinodermata,* having a radiating arrangement of parts and a body wall stiffened by calcareous pieces that may protrude as spines and including the starfishes, sea urchins, sea cucumbers, etc. [ECHINO- + -DERM]

E·chi·no·der·ma·ta (i kī′nə dûr′mə tə, ek′ə-), *n.* the phylum comprising the echinoderms. [< NL; see ECHINO-, DERMATO-, -A]

e·chi·no·der·ma·tous (i kī′nə dûr′mə təs, ek′i nə-), *adj.* belonging or pertaining to the *Echinodermata.* [ECHINODERMAT(A) + -OUS]

e·chi·noid (i kī′noid, ek′ə noid′), *adj.* 1. belonging or pertaining to the *Echinoidea.* 2. resembling a sea urchin. —*n.* 3. any echinoderm of the class *Echinoidea,* comprising the sea urchins. [ECHIN- + -OID]

Ech·i·noi·de·a (ek′ə noi′dē ə), *n.* the class comprising the sea urchins, sand dollars, etc. [< NL; see ECHINO-, -OIDEA]

e·chi·nus (i kī′nəs), *n., pl.* **-ni** (-nī). 1. a sea urchin of the genus *Echinus.* 2. *Archit.* a. an ovolo molding, esp. one having an outline with several radii or one carved with an egg-and-dart pattern. b. the prominent circular molding supporting the abacus of a Doric or Tuscan capital. c. Also called **cymatium.** the circular molding, usually carved with an egg-and-dart pattern, forming part of an Ionic capital between the volutes and under the balteus. [ME < L < Gk *echînos* hedgehog, sea urchin]

E·chi·on (i kī′on), *n. Class. Myth.* one of the Sparti, the husband of Agave and father of Pentheus.

e·chiu·roid (ē′kyə roid′), *n.* 1. any wormlike invertebrate of the phylum *Echiuroidea,* found in sand and mud of tropical and subtropical seas, having a ciliated, often elongated prostomium. —*adj.* 2. belonging or pertaining to the *Echiuroidea.* [< NL *Echiuroidea* name of phylum, equiv. to *Echiur(us)* name of genus (< Gk *échi(s)* viper + NL *-urus* tail < Gk; see URO-²) + *-oidea* -OID]

ech·o (ek′ō), *n., pl.* **ech·oes,** *v.,* **ech·oed, ech·o·ing.** —*n.* 1. a repetition of sound produced by the reflection of sound waves from an obstructing surface. 2. a sound heard again near its source after being reflected. 3. any repetition or close imitation, as of the ideas or opinions of another. 4. a person who reflects or imitates another. 5. a sympathetic or identical response, as to sentiments expressed. 6. (*cap.*) *Class. Myth.* a mountain nymph who pined away for love of the beautiful youth Narcissus until only her voice remained. 7. (*cap.*) the personification of an echo or of echoes. 8. *Music.* a part (**ech′o or′gan**) or stop (**ech′o stop′**) of a large organ for the production of echolike effects. 9. *Cards.* the play of a high card then a low card in the suit led by one's partner as a signal to continue leading the suit, as in bridge, or to lead a trump, as in whist. 10. *Electronics.* the reflection of a radio wave, as in radar or the like. 11. (*cap.*) *U.S.* one of a series of inflatable passive communications satellites. 12. a word used in communications to represent the letter E. —*v.i.* 13. to emit an echo; resound with an echo: *The hall echoed with cheers.* 14. to be repeated by or as by an echo: *Shouts echoed through the street.* —*v.t.* 15. to repeat by or as by an echo; emit an echo of: *The hall echoes the faintest sounds.* 16. to repeat or imitate the words, sentiments, etc., of (a person). 17. to repeat or imitate (words, sentiments, etc.). [ME *ecco* < L *ēchō* < Gk, akin to *ēchḗ* sound] —**ech′o·er,** *n.* —**ech′o·less,** *adj.*
—**Syn. 13, 15.** reverberate.

ech′o cham′ber, a room or studio with resonant walls for broadcasting or recording echoes or hollow sound effects.

ech·o·gram (ek′ō gram′), *n.* a record produced by the action of an echograph. [ECHO + -GRAM¹]

ech·o·graph (ek′ō graf′, -gräf′), *n.* a device that records oceanic depths by means of sonic waves. [ECHO + -GRAPH]

e·cho·ic (e kō′ik), *adj.* 1. resembling an echo. 2. onomatopoetic. [< L *ēchōic(us).* See ECHO, -IC]

ech·o·ism (ek′ō iz′əm), *n.* onomatopoeia. [ECHO + -ISM]

ech·o·la·li·a (ek′ō lā′lē ə), *n.* 1. *Psychiatry.* the uncontrollable and immediate repetition of words spoken by another person. 2. the imitation by a baby of the vocal sounds produced by others, occurring as a natural phase of childhood development. [ECHO + -LALIA] —**ech·o·lal·ic,** (ek′ō lal′ik, -lā′lik), *adj.*

ech·o·lo·ca·tion (ek′ō lō kā′shən), *n. Electronics.* the general method of locating objects by determining the time for an echo to return and the direction from which it returns, as by radar and sonar. [ECHO + LOCATION]

ech·o·prax·i·a (ek′ō prak′sē ə), *n. Psychiatry.* the abnormal repetition of the actions of another person. [< NL; see ECHO, PRAXIS, -IA] —**ech·o·prac·tic** (ek′ō-prak′tik), *adj.*

echt (eKHt), *adj. German.* real; authentic; genuine: *The performance was echt Bach, with no added instrumentation.*

Eck (ek), *n.* **Jo·hann** (yō′hän), (*Johann Mayer*), 1486–1543, German Roman Catholic theologian: opponent of Martin Luther.

Eck·er·mann (ek′əʀ män), *n.* **Jo·hann Pe·ter** (yō′hän pā′təʀ), 1792–1854, German writer and literary assistant to Goethe.

Eck·hardt (ek′härt), *n.* a boy's given name.

Eck·hart (ek′härt), *n.* **Jo·han·nes** (yō hä′nəs), ("*Meister Eckhart*"), c1260–1327?, Dominican theologian and preacher: founder of German mysticism. Also, **Eck′ardt, Eck′art.**

é·clair (ā klâr′, i klâr′, ā′klâr; *Fr.* ā kleʀ′), *n., pl.* **é·clairs** (ā klârz′, i klârz′, ā′klârz; *Fr.* ā kleʀ′). a finger-shaped cream puff, filled with whipped cream, ice cream, or pastry cream, usually coated with an icing. [< F: lit., lightning (flash), OF *esclair,* appar. back formation from *esclairier* to flash < VL *exclariāre, alter. of L *exclārāre,* equiv. to *ex-* EX-¹ + *clārāre* to make bright, deriv. of *clārus* CLEAR]

é·clair·cisse·ment (ā kleʀ sēs män′), *n., pl.* **-ments** (-män′). *French.* clarification, as of something obscure or troublesome; explanation.

ec·lamp·si·a (i klamp′sē ə), *n. Pathol.* a form of toxemia of pregnancy, characterized by convulsions, albuminuria, and hypertension. [< NL < Gk *éklamps(is)* sudden development (*ek-* EC- + *lámp(ein)* (to) shine + *-sis* -SIS) + *-ia* -IA] —**ec·lamp′tic,** *adj.*

é·clat (ā klä′; *Fr.* ā klȧ′), *n.* 1. brilliance of success, reputation, etc.: *the éclat of a great achievement.* 2. showy or elaborate display; fanfare: *a performance of great éclat.* **3.** acclamation; acclaim. [< F, OF *esclat* splinter, akin to *esclater* to splinter, of disputed orig.]

ec·lec·tic (i klek′tik), *adj.* **1.** selecting; choosing from various sources. **2.** made up of what is selected from different sources. **3.** not following any one system, as of philosophy, medicine, etc., but selecting and using what are considered the best elements of all systems. **4.** noting or pertaining to works of architecture, decoration, landscaping, etc., produced by a certain person or during a certain period, that derive from a wide range of historic styles, the style in each instance often being chosen for its fancied appropriateness to local tradition, local geography, the purpose to be served, or the cultural background of the client. —*n.* **5.** Also, **ec·lec·ti·cist** (i klek′ti sist). a person who follows an eclectic method, as in philosophy or architecture. [< Gk *eklektik(ós)* selective, equiv. to *eklekt(os)* chosen, select (*ekleg(ein)* (to) pick out + *-tos* ptp. suffix; see EC-) + *-ikos* -IC] —**ec·lec′ti·cal·ly,** *adv.*

ec·lec·ti·cism (i klek′ti siz′əm), *n.* **1.** the use or advocacy of an eclectic method. **2.** an eclectic system. [ECLECTIC + -ISM]

e·clipse (i klips′), *n., v.,* **e·clipsed, e·clips·ing.** —*n.* **1.** *Astron.* **a.** the obscuration of the light of the moon by the intervention of the earth between it and the sun **(lunar eclipse)** or the obscuration of the light of the sun by the intervention of the moon between it and a point on the earth **(solar eclipse). b.** a similar phenomenon with respect to any other planet and either its satellite or the sun. **c.** the partial or complete interception of the light of one component of a binary star by the other. **2.** any obscuration of light. **3.** a reduction or loss of splendor, status, reputation, etc.; any obscuration or overshadowing: *Scandal caused the eclipse of his career.* —*v.t.* **4.** to cause to suffer eclipse: *The moon eclipses the sun.* **5.** to cast a shadow upon; obscure; darken. **6.** to make dim or obscure by comparison; surpass: *a soprano whose singing eclipsed that of her rivals.* [ME, back formation (cf. ELLIPSE) from OE *eclypsis* (or its pl.) < L *eclīpsis* < Gk *ékleipsis,* equiv. to *ekleíp(ein)* (to) leave out, forsake, fail to appear (see EC-) + *-sis* -SIS] —**e·clips′er,** *n.*

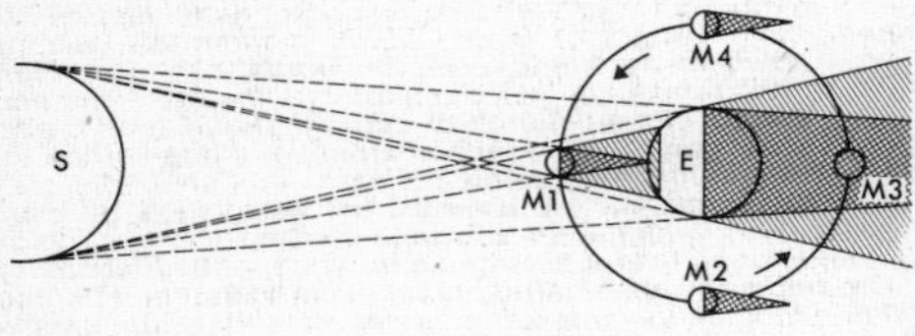

Eclipse
S, Sun; E, Earth; M1, Eclipse of the sun;
M3, Eclipse of the moon; M2, M4, Intermediate phases

eclipse′ plum′age, *Ornith.* the dull plumage developed in some brightly colored birds after the breeding season.

eclips′ing var′iable, *Astron.* a variable star whose changes in brightness are caused by periodic eclipses of two stars in a binary system. [ECLIPSE + -ING²]

e·clip·tic (i klip′tik), *n.* *Astron.* **1.** the great circle formed by the intersection of the plane of the earth's orbit with the celestial sphere; the apparent annual path of the sun in the heavens. **2.** an analogous great circle on a terrestrial globe. —*adj.* Also, **e·clip′ti·cal. 3.** pertaining to an eclipse. **4.** pertaining to the ecliptic. [ME < ML *eclīptic(a),* fem. of *eclīpticus* < Gk *ekleiptikós,* equiv. to *ekleipt-* (verbid s. of *ekleípein;* see ECLIPSE) + *-ikos* -IC] —**e·clip′ti·cal·ly,** *adv.*

ec·lo·gite (ek′lə jīt′), *n.* a rock consisting of granular aggregate of green pyroxene and red garnet, often containing cyanite, silvery mica, quartz, and pyrite. [< Gk *eklog(ḗ)* selection (see ECLOGUE) + -ITE¹]

ec·logue (ek′lôg, -log), *n.* a pastoral or idyllic poem, often in dialogue form. [late ME *eclog* < L *ecloga* < Gk *eklogḗ* selection, akin to *eklégein* to select; see EC-]

Ec·logues (ek′lôgz, -logz), *n.* a collection of pastoral poems (42–37 B.C.) by Vergil. Also called **Bucolics.**

e·clo·sion (i klō′zhən), *n.* *Entomol.* **1.** the emergence of an adult insect from its pupal case. **2.** the hatching of a larva from its egg. [< F *éclosion,* equiv. to *éclos-* (past s. of *éclore* to hatch < LL **exclōdere,* var. of L *exclūdere* to hatch, EXCLUDE) + *-ion* -ION]

ec·o·cide (ek′ə sīd′, ē′kə-), *n.* destruction of the earth's ecology or environment, as by the indiscriminate use of natural resources, dumping of chemical wastes, etc. [ECO- + -CIDE] —**ec′o·cid′al,** *adj.*

ecol., 1. ecological. **2.** ecology.

é·cole (ā kôl′), *n., pl.* **é·coles** (ā kôl′). *French.* a school.

ec′olog′ical niche′, the position that a creature occupies in relation to its environment.

e·col·o·gy (i kol′ə jē), *n.* **1.** the branch of biology dealing with the relations between organisms and their environment. **2.** the branch of sociology concerned with the spacing of people and institutions and the resulting interdependency. Also, **oecology.** [earlier *œcology* < Gk *oîko(s)* house + -LOGY; modeled on G *Okologie*] —**ec·o·log·i·cal** (ek′ə loj′i kəl, ē′kə-), **ec′o·log′ic,** *adj.* —**ec′o·log′i·cal·ly,** *adv.* —**e·col′o·gist,** *n.*

econ., 1. economic. **2.** economics. **3.** economy.

e·con·o·met·rics (i kon′ə me′triks), *n.* (*construed as sing.*) *Econ.* the application of statistical and mathematical techniques in solving problems as well as in testing and demonstrating theories. [see ECONOMY, METRIC¹, -ICS] —**e·con′o·met′ric, e·con′o·met′ri·cal,** *adj.* —**e·con·o·me·tri·cian** (i kon′ə mi trish′ən), **e·con′o·met′rist,** *n.*

e·co·nom·ic (ē′kə nom′ik, ek′ə-), *adj.* **1.** pertaining to the production, distribution, and use of income, wealth, and commodities. **2.** of or pertaining to the science of economics. **3.** pertaining to an economy, or system of organization or operation, esp. of the process of production. **4.** pertaining to one's personal resources of money: *to give up a large house for economic reasons.* **5.** pertaining to use in human economy: *economic entomology; economic botany.* **6.** affecting or apt to affect the welfare of material resources: *weevils, locusts, and other economic pests.* [< L *oeconomic(us)* < Gk *oikonomikós* relating to household management, equiv. to *oikonóm(os)* steward (*oîko(s)* house + *nómos* manager) + *-ikos* -IC]

e·co·nom·i·cal (ē′kə nom′i kəl, ek′ə-), *adj.* **1.** avoiding waste or extravagance; thrifty: *an economical housewife; an economical use of interior space.* **2.** economic. [ECONOMIC + -AL¹]
—**Syn. 1.** saving, provident, sparing, parsimonious. ECONOMICAL, THRIFTY, FRUGAL imply careful and saving use of resources. ECONOMICAL implies prudent planning in the disposition of resources so as to avoid unnecessary waste or expense: *economical in budgeting household expenditures.* THRIFTY is a stronger word than economical, and adds to it the idea of industry and successful management: *a thrifty housewife looking for bargains.* FRUGAL emphasizes being saving, sometimes excessively saving, esp. in such matters as food, dress, or the like: *frugal almost to the point of being stingy.* —**Ant. 1.** wasteful.

e·co·nom·i·cal·ly (ē′kə nom′ik lē, ek′ə-), *adv.* **1.** in a thrifty or frugal manner; with economy. **2.** as regards the efficient use of income and wealth: *economically feasible proposals.* **3.** as regards one's personal resources of money: *He's quite well off economically.* [ECONOMICAL + -LY]

Econom′ic Coopera′tion Administra′tion, the U.S. government agency that administered the European Recovery Program. *Abbr.:* ECA, E.C.A.

e′conom′ic cy′cle. See **business cycle.**

econom′ic deter′minism, the doctrine that all social, cultural, political, and intellectual forms are determined by or result from economic factors such as the quality of natural resources, productive capability, technological development, or the distribution of wealth. —**econom′ic deter′minist.**

econom′ic geog′raphy, a branch of geography that deals with the relation of physical and economic conditions to the production and utilization of raw materials and their manufacture into finished products.

econom′ic geol′ogy, the branch of geology relating to industrial uses of materials from the earth.

e′conom′ic good′, a commodity or service that can be utilized to satisfy human wants and that has exchange value.

e·co·nom·ics (ē′kə nom′iks, ek′ə-), *n.* **1.** (*construed as sing.*) the science treating of the production, distribution, and consumption of goods and services, or the material welfare of mankind. **2.** (*construed as pl.*) financial considerations; economically significant aspects: *What are the economics of such a project?* [see ECONOMIC, -ICS]

e′conom′ic strike′, a strike called in protest over wages, hours, or working conditions.

e·con·o·mist (i kon′ə mist), *n.* **1.** an expert in the science of economics. **2.** *Archaic.* a thrifty or frugal person. [ECONOM(Y) + -IST]

e·con·o·mize (i kon′ə mīz′), *v.,* **-mized, -miz·ing.** —*v.t.* **1.** to manage economically; use sparingly or frugally. —*v.i.* **2.** to practice economy; avoid waste or extravagance. Also, *esp. Brit.,* **e·con′o·mise′.** [ECONOM(Y) + -IZE]

e·con·o·miz·er (i kon′ə mī′zər), *n.* **1.** a person who economizes. **2.** (in a boiler) a device for warming feed water with gases entering the chimney or stack. Also, *esp. Brit.,* **e·con′o·mis′er.** [ECONOMIZE + -ER¹]

e·con·o·my (i kon′ə mē), *n., pl.* **-mies,** *adv.* —*n.* **1.** thrifty management; frugality in the expenditure or consumption of money, materials, etc. **2.** an act or means of thrifty saving; a saving: *He achieved a small economy by walking to work instead of taking a bus.* **3.** the management of the resources of a community, country, etc., esp. with a view to its productivity. **4.** the prosperity or earnings of a place: *Further inflation would endanger the national economy seriously.* **5.** the disposition or regulation of the parts or functions of any organic whole; an organized system or method. **6.** the efficient, sparing, or concise use of something: *an economy of effort; an economy of movement.* **7.** See **economy class. 8.** *Theol.* **a.** the divine plan for man, from creation through redemption to final beatitude. **b.** the method of divine administration, as at a particular time or for a particular race. **9.** *Archaic.* the management of household affairs. —*adv.* **10.** in economy-class accommodations, or by economy-class conveyance: *to travel economy.* [< L *oeconomia* < Gk *oikonomía* household management, equiv. to *oîko(s)* house + *-nomia* -NOMY]
—**Syn. 1.** thriftiness, thrift, saving. —**Ant. 1.** lavishness.

E·con·o·my (i kon′ə mē), *n.* a town in W Pennsylvania. 5925 (1960).

econ′omy class′, a type of lower-priced fare accommodation for travel, esp. on an airplane.

econ′omy wall′, *Masonry.* a bearing wall half a brick thick, thickened at intervals to support floor or roof framing.

E·corse (i kôrs′, ē′kôrs), *n.* a city in SE Michigan, near Detroit. 17,328 (1960).

ec·o·spe·cies (ek′ō spē′shēz, -sēz, ē′kō-), *n.* *Ecol.* a taxon consisting of one or more interbreeding ecotypes; equivalent to a taxonomic species. [ECO(LOGY) + SPECIES] —**ec′o·spe·cif′ic,** *adj.* —**ec′o·spe·cif′i·cal·ly,** *adv.*

ec·o·sphere (ek′ō sfēr′, ē′kō-), *n.* the part of the atmosphere in which it is possible to breathe normally without aid: the portion of the troposphere from sea level to an altitude of about 13,000 feet. Also called **physiological atmosphere.** [ECO(LOGY) + SPHERE]

é·cos·saise (ā′kō sāz′, -kə-), *n.* **1.** an old country-dance in quick duple meter. **2.** a piece of music for this dance. **3.** a short, lively piano piece patterned after the écossaise. [< F, fem. of *écossais* Scottish, equiv. to *Écosse* Scotland + *-ais* -ESE; trans. of G *Schottisch*]

ec·o·sys·tem (ek′ō sis′təm, ē′kō-), *n.* *Ecol.* a system formed by the interaction of a community of organisms with their environment. [ECO(LOGY) + SYSTEM]

ec·o·tone (ek′ə tōn′, ē′kə-), *n.* *Ecol.* the transition zone between two different plant communities, as that between forest and prairie. [ECO(LOGY) + *tone* < Gk *tónos* tension] —**ec′o·ton′al,** *adj.*

ec·o·type (ek′ə tīp′, ē′kə-), *n.* *Ecol.* a subspecies or race that is especially adapted to a particular set of environmental conditions. [ECO(LOGY) + TYPE] —**ec·o·typ·ic** (ek′ə tip′ik, ē′kə-), *adj.* —**ec′o·typ′i·cal·ly,** *adv.*

ec·pho·ne·sis (ek′fō nē′sis), *n.* *Rhet.* the use of an exclamatory phrase, as in "O tempore! O mores!" Also called **exclamation.** [< Gk *ekphṓnēsis,* equiv. to *ekphōn-* (s. of *ekphōneîn* to cry out; see EC-, -PHONE) + *-ēsis* -ESIS]

é·cra·sé (ā′krä zā′), *adj.* (of leather) crushed to produce a grained effect. [< F, ptp. of *écraser* to crush]

é·cra·seur (ā′krä zûr′, *Fr.* ā krä zœr′), *n., pl.* **-seurs** (-zûrz′; *Fr.* zœr′). a surgical instrument used in an operation in which there is danger of hemorrhage, as in the removal of certain types of tumors. [< F, equiv. to *écras(er)* (to) crush (*é-* EX-¹ + *craser* from CRAZE to shatter) + *-eur* -OR²]

ec·ru (ek′ro͞o, ā′kro͞o), *adj.* **1.** very light brown in color, as raw silk, unbleached linen, etc. —*n.* **2.** an ecru color. Also, **é·cru** (*Fr.* ā krʏ′). [< F, equiv. to *é-* completely (< L *ex-* EX-¹) + *cru* raw (< L *crūdus;* see CRUDE)]

Ec·sta·sie, The (ek′stə sē). See **Extasie, The.**

ec·sta·sy (ek′stə sē), *n., pl.* **-sies. 1.** an overpowering emotion or exaltation; a state of sudden, intense feeling. **2.** rapturous delight. **3.** the frenzy of poetic inspiration. **4.** mental transport or rapture from the contemplation of divine things. [ME *extasie* < OF < ML *extasis* < Gk *ékstasis* displacement, trance, equiv. to *ek-* EC- + *stásis* STASIS]
—**Syn. 1.** rapture.

Ecstasy, The. See **Extasie, The.**

Ecstasy of St. Theresa, The, a marble altarpiece (1645–52) by Gianlorenzo Bernini.

ec·stat·ic (ek stat′ik), *adj.* **1.** of, pertaining to, or characterized by ecstasy. **2.** subject to or in a state of ecstasy; rapturous. —*n.* **3.** a person subject to fits of ecstasy. **4. ecstatics,** ecstatic delights; raptures. [< Gk *ekstatik(ós),* equiv. to *ek-* EC- + *statikós* STATIC. See ECSTASY] —**ec·stat′i·cal·ly,** *adv.*

ect-, var. of **ecto-** before a vowel: *ectal.*

ec·tad (ek′tad), *adv.* *Anat., Zool.* outward. [ECT- + L *ad* toward]

ec·tal (ek′təl), *adj.* *Anat., Zool.* external; outer; on the surface of. [ECT- + -AL¹] —**ec′tal·ly,** *adv.*

ec·ta·sis (ek′tə sis), *n., pl.* **-ses** (-sēz′). *Pros.* the lengthening of an ordinarily short syllable. [< LL < Gk *éktasis* a stretching out] —**ec·tat·ic** (ek tat′ik), *adj.*

ec·te·ne (ek′tə nē′, ek′tə nē′), *n.* ektene.

ec·thlip·sis (ek thlip′sis), *n., pl.* **-ses** (-sēz). loss of a consonant, esp., in Latin, loss of a final *m* before a word beginning with a vowel or *h.* [< LL < Gk *ékthlipsis,* equiv. to *ekthlíb(ein)* (to) squeeze out (*ek-* EC- + *thlíbein,* var. of *phlíbein* to squeeze) + *-sis* -SIS]

ec·thy·ma (ek′thə mə), *n.* *Vet. Pathol.* a contagious viral disease of sheep and goats and occasionally of man, marked by vesicular and pustular lesions on the lips. Also called **contagious ecthyma, scabby mouth, sore mouth.** [< Gk *ékthyma* pustule, equiv. to *ek-* EC- + *thý(ein)* (to) be angry + *-ma* n. suffix] —**ec·thym·a·tous** (ek thim′ə təs, -thī′mə-), *adj.*

ecto-, a learned borrowing from Greek meaning "outer," "outside," "external," used in the formation of compound words: *ectoderm.* Also, *esp. before a vowel,* **ect-.** [comb. form of Gk *ektós* outside]

ec·to·blast (ek′tə blast′), *n.* *Embryol.* **1.** the ectoderm. **2.** epiblast (def. 2). [ECTO- + -BLAST] —**ec′to·blas′tic,** *adj.*

ec·to·cor·ne·a (ek′tō kôr′nē ə), *n.* *Anat.* the outer layer of the cornea. [ECTO- + CORNEA]

ec·to·cra·ni·al (ek′tō krā′nē əl), *adj.* *Anat.* of or pertaining to the outside of the skull. [ECTO- + CRANIAL]

ec·to·derm (ek′tə dûrm′), *n.* *Embryol.* the outer germ layer in the embryo of a metazoan. [ECTO- + -DERM] —**ec′to·der′mal, ec′to·der′mic,** *adj.* —**ec′to·der·moi′dal,** *adj.*

ec·to·en·zyme (ek′tō en′zīm), *n.* *Biochem.* exoenzyme. [ECTO- + ENZYME]

ec·to·gen·e·sis (ek′tō jen′i sis), *n.* *Biol.* development outside the body, as of an embryo in an artificial environment. [< NL; see ECTO-, GENESIS] —**ec·to·ge·net·ic** (ek′tō jə net′ik), *adj.*

ec·tog·e·nous (ek toj′ə nəs), *adj.* growing outside the body of the host, as certain bacteria and other parasites. Also, **ec·to·gen·ic** (ek′tō jen′ik). [ECTO- + -GENOUS]

ec·to·mere (ek′tə mēr′), *n.* *Embryol.* any of the blastomeres that participate in the development of the ectoderm. [ECTO- + -MERE] —**ec·to·mer·ic** (ek′tō mer′ik), *adj.*

ec·to·morph (ek′tə môrf′), *n.* *Psychol.* a person of the ectomorphic type. [ECTO- + -MORPH]

ec·to·mor·phic (ek′tə môr′fik), *adj.* *Psychol.* having a thin body build characterized by the relative prominence of structures developed from the embryonic ectoderm (contrasted with *endomorphic, mesomorphic*). [ECTO- + -MORPHIC] —**ec′to·morph′y,** *n.*

-ectomy, a combining form meaning "excision (of a specified part)": *tonsillectomy.* [< NL *-ectomia.* See EC-, -TOMY]

ec·to·par·a·site (ek′tō par′ə sīt′), *n.* an external parasite (opposed to *endoparasite*). [ECTO- + PARASITE] —**ec·to·par·a·sit·ic** (ek′tō par′ə sit′ik), *adj.*

ec·to·phyte (ek′tə fīt′), *n.* a parasitic plant growing on an animal or another plant. [ECTO- + -PHYTE] —**ec·to·phyt·ic** (ek′tō fit′ik), *adj.*

ec·to·pi·a (ek tō′pē ə), *n.* *Med.* the usually congenital displacement of an organ or part. [< NL < Gk *éktop(os)* out of place (*ek-* EC- + *tópos* place) + *-ia* -IA]

ec·top·ic (ek top′ik), *adj.* *Pathol.* occurring in an abnormal position or place; displaced. [ECTOP(IA) + -IC]

ectop′ic preg′nancy, *Med.* the development of a fertilized ovum outside the uterus. Also called **extra-uterine pregnancy.**

ec·to·plasm (ek′tə plaz′əm), *n.* **1.** *Biol.* the outer portion of the cytoplasm of a cell. Cf. **endoplasm. 2.** *Spiritualism.* the supposed emanation from the body of a medium. [ECTO- + -PLASM] —**ec′to·plas′mic, ec·to·plas·mat·ic** (ek′tə plaz mat′ik), *adj.*

ec·to·sarc (ek′tə särk′), *n.* *Biol.* the ectoplasm of a protozoan (opposed to *endosarc*). [ECTO- + SARC-] —**ec′to·sar′cous,** *adj.*

ec·to·sto·sis (ek′to stō′sis, -tə-), *n.* the ossification of cartilage that begins under the perichondrium and proceeds inward. [ECT- + OSTOSIS] —**ec·tos·te·al** (ek tos′tē əl), *adj.* —**ec·tos′te·al·ly,** *adv.*

ec·to·troph·ic (ek′tə trof′ik), *adj.* (of a mycorrhiza) growing outside the root or between the cells. Cf. **endotrophic.** [ECTO- + -TROPHIC]

ec·to·zo·a (ek′tə zō′ə), *n.pl., sing.* **-zo·on** (-zō′on). (*often cap.*) *Biol.* animals living as parasites on the body of the host. [ECTO- + -ZOA] —**ec′to·zo′an,** *adj., n.*

ec·to·zo·ic (ek′tə zō′ik), *adj.* (of a parasitic animal) living on the surface of its host. [ECTOZO(A) + -IC]

ectro-, a combining form indicating the congenital absence of a specified part: *ectrodactylism.* [< NL, comb. form repr. Gk *éktrōsis* abortion, miscarriage, equiv. to *ektrō-* verbid s. of *ektitrṓskein* to miscarry + *-sis* -SIS]

ec·tro·dac·tyl·ism (ek′trō dak′tᵊliz′əm), *n.* *Med.* the congenital absence of part or all of one or more fingers or toes. Also, **ec·tro·dac·tyl·i·a** (ek′trō dak-til′ē ə, -til′yə), **ec·tro·dac·ty·ly** (ek′trō dak′tᵊlē). [ECTRO- + -DACTYL + -ISM] —**ec′tro·dac′ty·lous,** *adj.*

ec·tro·me·li·a (ek′trō mē′lē ə), *n.* **1.** *Med.* the congenital absence or imperfection of a limb or limbs. **2.** Also called **infectious ectromelia, mouse pox.** *Vet. Pathol.* a viral disease of mice, characterized by gangrene of the extremities, swelling and loss of limbs, and mottling of the liver. [ECTRO- + Gk *mél(os)* limb + *-ia* -IA] —**ec·tro·mel·ic** (ek′trō mel′ik), *adj.*

ec·tro·pi·on (ek trō′pē ən), *n.* *Med.* the abnormal eversion of a part, esp. of an eyelid. Also, **ec·tro·pi·um** (ek trō′pē əm). [< Gk *ektrópion* everted eyelid, equiv. to *ek-* EC- + *-tropion* (akin to *trépein* to turn)]

ec·tro·pi·on·ize (ek trō′pē ə nīz′), *v.i.,* **-ized, -iz·ing.** *Pathol.* to undergo ectropion. [ECTROPION + -IZE] —**ec·tro′pi·on·i·za′tion,** *n.*

ec·type (ek′tīp), *n.* a reproduction; copy (opposed to *prototype*). [< Gk *éktyp(os)* wrought in relief, equiv. to *ek-* EC- + *týp(os)* figure (on a wall) + *-os* adj. suffix; akin to TYPE] —**ec·ty·pal** (ek′tə pəl), *adj.*

é·cu (ā kyōō′; *Fr.* ā kʏ′), *n., pl.* **é·cus** (ā kyōōz′; *Fr.* ā kʏ′). **1.** *French.* the shield carried by a mounted man-at-arms in the Middle Ages. **2.** any of various gold and silver coins of France, issued from the reign of Louis IX until 1794, bearing the figure of a shield. [< F; MF OF *escu* < L *scūtum* shield]

E.C.U., English Church Union.

Ecua., Ecuador.

Ec·ua·dor (ek′wə dôr′), *n.* a republic in NW South America. 4,116,451 (est. 1959); 104,510 sq. mi. *Cap.:* Quito. —**Ec′ua·do′ran, Ec′ua·do′re·an, Ec′ua·do′ri·an,** *adj., n.*

é·cuelle (ā kwel′; *Fr.* ā kʏel′), *n., pl.* **é·cuelles** (ā kwelz′; *Fr.* ā kʏel′). a shallow French bowl, introduced in the 17th century, usually having a high cover and two flat, pierced horizontal handles. [< F < < VL **scutella* drinking bowl; see SCUTTLE]

ec·u·men·i·cal (ek′yōō men′i kəl *or, esp. Brit.,* ē′kyōō-), *adj.* **1.** general; universal. **2.** pertaining to the whole Christian church. **3.** promoting or fostering Christian unity throughout the world. **4.** of or pertaining to a movement **(ecumenical movement),** esp. among Protestant groups since the 1800's, aimed at achieving universal Christian unity and church union through international interdenominational organizations that cooperate on matters of mutual concern. Also, **ec′u·men′ic, oecumenic, oecumenical.** [< LL *oecumenic(us)* belonging to the whole inhabited world (< Gk *oikoumenikós,* equiv. to *oikoumen-* (s. of prp. pass. of *oikein* to inhabit) + *-ikos* -IC) + -AL¹] —**ec′u·men′i·cal·ly,** *adv.*

ec′umen′ical coun′cil, a solemn assembly in the Roman Catholic Church, convoked and presided over by the pope, composed of cardinals, bishops, and certain other prelates whose decrees, when confirmed by the pope, become binding. Also, **Ecumen′ical Coun′cil.**

ec·u·men·i·cal·ism (ek′yōō men′i kə liz′əm), *n.* the doctrines and practices of the ecumenical movement. Also, **ecumenicism.** [ECUMENICAL + -ISM]

ec′umen′ical move′ment. See under **ecumenical.**

ec′umen′ical pa′triarch, the patriarch of Constantinople, regarded as the highest dignitary of the Greek Orthodox Church. —**ecumen′ical pa′triarchate.**

ec·u·men·i·cism (ek′yōō men′i siz′əm), *n.* ecumenicalism. [ECUMENIC(AL) + -ISM]

ec·u·men·i·cist (ek′yə men′i sist), *n.* a person who advocates Christian ecumenicity. [ECUMENIC + -IST]

ec·u·me·nic·i·ty (ek′yə mə nis′i tē, -me-), *n.* (in the Christian church) the state of being ecumenically united, esp. in furthering the aims of the ecumenical movement. [ECUMENIC + -ITY]

ec·u·men·ics (ek′yə men′iks), *n.* (*construed as sing.*) the study of the Christian church in its aspect as a world-wide Christian community. [see ECUMENICAL, -ICS]

ec·u·me·nism (ek′yōō mə niz′əm), *n.* ecumenical doctrines and practices, esp. as manifested in the ecumenical movement. [ECUMENIC + -ISM] —**ec′u·me·nist,** *n.*

é·cus·son (ā kʏ sôɴ′), *n., pl.* **-sons** (-sôɴ′). a flat area between the guillons in a sword guard, often having a cusp extending over the end of the blade. [< F; see ESCUTCHEON]

ec·ze·ma (ek′sə mə, eg′zə-, ig zē′-), *n.* *Pathol.* an inflammatory disease of the skin attended with itching and the exudation of serous matter. [< NL < Gk *ékzema,* equiv. to *ek-* EC- + *ze-* (s. of *zein* to boil, ferment) + *-ma* n. suffix] —**ec·zem·a·tous** (ig zem′ə təs), *adj.*

ec·ze·ma·toid (ig zē′mə toid′, ek′sə-), *adj.* *Pathol.* resembling eczema. [< NL *eczemat-* (s. of *eczema*) + -OID]

Ed (ed), *n.* a boy's given name, form of **Edgar** or **Edward.**

-ed¹, a suffix forming the past tense of weak verbs: *he crossed the river.* [OE *-de, -ede, -ode, -ade;* orig. disputed]

-ed², a suffix forming the past participle of weak verbs (*he had crossed the river*), and of participial adjectives indicating a condition or quality resulting from the action of the verb (*inflated balloons*). [OE *-ed, -od, -ad;* orig. disputed]

-ed³, a suffix forming adjectives from nouns: *bearded; moneyed; tender-hearted.* [OE *-ede*]

E.D., **1.** Eastern Department. **2.** election district. **3.** ex dividend.

ed., **1.** edited. **2.** edition. **3.** *pl.* **eds.** editor.

Ed·a (ed′ə), *n.* a girl's given name. Also, **Edda.**

e·da·cious (i dā′shəs), *adj.* devouring; voracious; consuming. [EDACI(TY) + -OUS]

e·dac·i·ty (i das′i tē), *n.* the state of being edacious; voraciousness; appetite. [< L *edācitās,* equiv. to *edāci-* (s. of *edāx*) gluttonous, equiv. to *ed-* EAT + *-āci-* adj. suffix + *-tāt-* -TY²]

E·dam (ē′dəm, ē′dam; *Du.* ā däm′), *n.* a mild, hard, yellow cheese, produced in a round shape and coated with red wax. Also called **E′dam cheese′.** [after *Edam,* town in Netherlands, where it originated]

e·daph·ic (i daf′ik), *adj.* related to or caused by particular soil conditions, as of texture or drainage, rather than by physiographic or climatic factors. [< Gk *édaph(os)* ground, bottom + -IC] —**e·daph′i·cal·ly,** *adv.*

ed·a·phon (ed′ə fon′), *n.* the aggregate of organisms that live in the soil. [< Gk *édaph(os)* ground, base, foundation + *-on,* neut. n. suffix]

Ed.B., Bachelor of Education.

EDC, European Defense Community.

Ed·couch (ed′kouch′), *n.* a town in S Texas. 2814 (1960).

Ed.D., Doctor of Education.

Ed·da (ed′ə), *n.* a girl's given name. Also, **Eda.**

Ed·da (ed′ə), *n., pl.* **Ed·das.** either of two old Icelandic literary works, one a collection of poems on mythical and religious subjects **(Elder** or **Poetic Edda)** erroneously attributed to Saemund Sigfusson (c1055–1133), the other a collection of ancient Scandinavian myths and legends, rules and theories of versification, poems, etc. **(Younger** or **Prose Edda),** compiled and written in part by Snorri Sturluson (1179–1241). —**Ed′dic, Ed·da·ic** (e dā′ik), *adj.*

Ed·die (ed′ē), *n.* a boy's given name, form of **Ed.** Also, **Eddy.**

Ed·ding·ton (ed′ing tən), *n.* **Sir Arthur Stanley,** 1882–1944, English astronomer, physicist, and writer.

ed·do (ed′ō), *n., pl.* **-does.** the edible root of the taro or of any of several related plants. [< a Ghana tongue]

ed·dy (ed′ē), *n., pl.* **-dies,** *v.,* **-died, -dy·ing.** —*n.* **1.** a current at variance with the main current in a stream of liquid or gas, esp. one having a rotary or whirling motion. **2.** a small whirlpool. **3.** any similar current, as of air, dust, or fog. —*v.t., v.i.* **4.** to move or whirl in eddies. [late ME; OE *ed-* turning + *ēa* water; akin to Icel *itha*]

Ed·dy (ed′ē), *n.* **1. Mary (Morse) Baker** (*Mrs. Glover; Mrs. Patterson*), 1821–1910, U.S. founder of the Christian Science Church. **2.** a boy's given name, form of **Ed.** Also, **Eddie.**

Ed·dy·stone (ed′i stōn′), *n.* a town in SE Pennsylvania. 3006 (1960).

Ed′dy·stone Rocks′ (ed′i stən), a group of rocks near the W end of the English Channel, SW of Plymouth, England: lighthouse.

E·de (ā′də), *n.* a city in the central Netherlands. 61,872 (1962).

Ed·e·line (ed′ᵊ lēn′), *n.* a girl's given name.

e·del·weiss (ād′ᵊl vīs′, -wīs′), *n.* a small composite herb, *Leontopodium alpinum,* having white woolly leaves and flowers, growing in the high altitudes of the Alps. [< G, equiv. to *edel* noble + *weiss* WHITE]

e·de·ma (i dē′mə), *n., pl.* **-ma·ta** (-mə tə). *Pathol.* effusion of serous fluid into the interstices of cells in tissue spaces or into body cavities. Also, **oedema.** [< NL *oedēma* < Gk *oídēma* a swelling, equiv. to *oidē-* (s. of *oidein* to swell) + *-ma* n. suffix] —**e·dem·a·tous** (i dem′ə təs), **e·dem·a·tose** (i dem′ə tōs′), *adj.*

E·den (ēd′ᵊn), *n.* **1.** the place where Adam and Eve lived before the fall. Gen. 2:8–24. **2.** any delightful region or abode; a paradise. **3.** a state of perfect happiness. Also called **Garden of Eden.** [< Heb *'ēden* delight, pleasure] —**E·den·ic** (ē den′ik), *adj.*

E·den (ēd′ᵊn), *n.* **(Robert) Anthony, Earl of Avon,** born 1897, British statesman: prime minister 1955–57.

E·den·ta·ta (ē′den tā′tə, -tä′-), *n.* the order comprising the edentate mammals. [< NL, neut. pl. of L *ēdentātus.* See EDENTATE]

e·den·tate (ē den′tāt), *adj.* **1.** belonging or pertaining to the *Edentata,* an order of New World mammals, comprising the armadillos, the sloths, and the South American anteaters. **2.** toothless. —*n.* **3.** an edentate mammal. [< L *ēdentāt(us)* deprived of teeth, equiv. to *ē-* E- + *dent-* (s. of *dēns*) tooth + *-ātus* -ATE¹]

E·den·ton (ēd′ᵊn tən), *n.* a town in NE North Carolina. 4458 (1960).

E·der·le (ā′dər lē), *n.* **Gertrude Caroline,** born 1907?, U.S. swimmer.

EDES, Hellenic National Democratic army, a conservative Greek resistance coalition in World War II. [< ModGk *E(thnikos) D(ēmokratikos) E(llēnikos) S(yndesmos)*]

E·des·sa (i des′ə), *n.* an ancient city in NW Mesopotamia, on the modern site of Urfa: an early center of Christianity; the capital of a principality under the Crusaders. —**E·des′san, E·des·sene** (i des′ēn), *adj.*

Ed·gar (ed′gər), *n.* an award given annually in various categories of mystery writing. [named after Edgar Allan POE]

Ed·gar (ed′gər), *n.* a boy's given name.

Ed·gard (ed′gärd, -gərd), *n.* a boy's given name.

edge (ej), *n., v.,* **edged, edg·ing.** —*n.* **1.** a line or border at which a surface terminates: *Grass grew along the edges of the road. The paper had deckle edges.* **2.** a brink or verge: *the edge of a precipice.* **3.** any of the narrow surfaces of a thin, flat object: *a book with gilt edges.* **4.** a line at which two surfaces of a solid object meet: *an edge of a box.* **5.** the thin, sharp side of the blade of a cutting instrument or weapon. **6.** the sharpness proper to a blade: *The knife has lost its edge.* **7.** sharpness or keenness of language, argument, tone of voice, appetite, desire, etc.: *The snack took the edge off his hunger. Her voice had an edge to it that indicated how strong her feelings were.* **8.** *Brit. Dial.* a hill or cliff. **9.** *Informal.* an improved position; advantage: *He gained the edge on his opponent. He lost the edge he previously had.* **10.** *Cards.* **a.** advantage, esp. the advantage gained by being the age or eldest hand. **b.** See **eldest hand. 11. have an edge on,** to be mildly intoxicated with alcoholic liquor: *He had a pleasant edge on from the sherry.* **12. on edge, a.** (of a person or a person's nerves) acutely sensitive; nervous; tense. **b.** impatient; eager: *The contestants were on edge to learn the results.* **13. set one's teeth on edge.** See **tooth** (def. 18). —*v.t.* **14.** to put an edge on; sharpen. **15.** to provide with an edge or border: *to edge a book in gold; to edge a skirt with lace.* **16.** to make or force (one's way) gradually by moving edgewise or sideways. **17.** *Metalworking.* **a.** to turn (a piece to be rolled) onto its edge. **b.** to roll (a piece set on edge). **c.** to give (a piece) a desired width by passing between vertical rolls. **d.** to rough (a piece being forged) so that the bulk is properly distributed for final forging. —*v.i.* **18.** to move edgewise: *to edge through a crowd.* **19.** to advance gradually: *a car edging up to a curb.* **20. edge out,** to defeat or vanquish (rivals or opponents) by a small margin: *The home team edged out the visitors in an exciting finish.* [ME *egge,* OE *ecg;* c. G *Ecke* corner; akin to L *aciēs,* Gk *akís* point] —**edge′less,** *adj.*

—**Syn. 1.** rim, lip. EDGE, BORDER, MARGIN refer to a boundary. An EDGE is the boundary line of a surface or plane: *the edge of a table.* BORDER is the boundary of a surface or the strip adjacent to it, inside or out: *a border of lace.* MARGIN is a limited strip, generally unoccupied, at the extremity of an area: *the margin of a page.*

edge·bone (ej′bōn′), *n.* aitchbone.

-edged, a combining form of **edge:** *dull-edged.*

edge′ effect′, *Ecol.* the tendency toward greater variety and density of plant and animal populations in an ecotone.

Edge·field (ej′fēld′), *n.* a town in W South Carolina. 2876 (1960).

edge-grained (ej′grānd′), *adj.* (of sawn lumber) having the annual rings at an angle of no less than 45° with the broader surfaces. Cf. **flat-grained.**

edge′ mold′ing, a convexly rounded molding having a fillet or concavity at or near its centerline.

edg·er (ej′ər), *n.* **1.** a person who puts an edge, esp. a finishing edge, on a garment, surface, lens, etc. **2.** a machine for finishing or making an edge, as for stitching, beveling, or trimming. **3.** a gardening tool with a rotary blade for cutting a neat border around a lawn, flower bed, or the like. [EDGE + -ER¹]

Edg·er·ton (ej′ər tᵊn, -tən), *n.* a town in S Wisconsin. 4000 (1960).

edge′ tool′, a tool with a cutting edge. [ME *egge tol*]

Edge·wa·ter (ej′wô′tər, -wot′ər), *n.* **1.** a town in central Colorado. 4314 (1960). **2.** a town in NE New Jersey. 4113 (1960).

edge·wise (ej′wīz′), *adv.* **1.** with the edge forward; in the direction of the edge. **2. get a word in edgewise,** to succeed in entering a conversation or expressing one's opinion in spite of competition or opposition: *There were so many people talking at once that I couldn't get a word in edgewise.* Also, **edge·ways** (ej′wāz′). [EDGE + -WISE]

Edge·wood (ej′wŏŏd′), *n.* **1.** a town in SW Pennsylvania. 5124 (1960). **2.** a town in central Pennsylvania. 3399 (1960).

Edge·worth (ej′wûrth′), *n.* **Maria,** 1767–1849, English novelist.

edg·ing (ej′ing), *n.* **1.** the act of one who edges. **2.** something that forms or is placed along an edge or border. **3.** (in cabinetwork) material, usually a strip of wood, placed along the edges of a veneered surface to provide a protective surface. [EDGE + -ING¹] —**edg′ing·ly,** *adv.*

edg′ing lobel′ia, a trailing, annual herb, *Lobelia Erinus,* of South Africa, having blue flowers.

edg·y (ej′ē), *adj.,* **edg·i·er, edg·i·est. 1.** sharp-edged; sharply defined, as outlines. **2.** nervously irritable; impatient and anxious. [EDGE + -Y¹] —**edg′i·ly,** *adv.* —**edg′i·ness,** *n.*

edh (eth), *n.* eth.

ed·i·ble (ed′ə bəl), *adj.* **1.** fit to be eaten as food; eatable; esculent. —*n.* **2.** Usually, **edibles.** edible articles; food. [< LL *edibil(is),* equiv. to *ed(ere)* (to) EAT + *-ibilis* -IBLE] —**ed′i·bil′i·ty, ed′i·ble·ness,** *n.*

e·dict (ē′dikt), *n.* **1.** a decree issued by a sovereign or other authority. **2.** any authoritative proclamation or command. [< L *ēdictum,* n. use of neut. of *ēdictus* (ptp. of *ēdicere* to say out), equiv. to *ē-* E- + *dictus* said; see DICTUM] —**e·dic′tal,** *adj.* —**e·dic′tal·ly,** *adv.*

ed·i·cule (ed′ə kyōōl′), *n.* aedicule.

E·die (ē′dē), *n.* a girl's given name, form of **Edith.** Also, **Edyie.**

ed·i·fi·ca·tion (ed′ə fə kā′shən), *n.* **1.** an act of edifying. **2.** the state of being edified; uplift; enlightenment. **3.** moral improvement: *sermons offered for a congregation's edification.* [< L *aedificātiōn-* (s. of *aedificātiō*), equiv. to *aedificāt(us)* (ptp. of *aedificāre*) built (*aedi-,* s. of *aedes* house + *-fic,* var. of *fac-* make + *-ātus* -ATE¹) + *-iōn-* -ION]

e·dif·i·ca·to·ry (i dif′ə kə tôr′ē, -tōr′ē, ed′ə fə kā′tə rē), *adj.* intended or serving to edify: *a sermon notable for its edificatory force.* [< LL *aedificātōri(us)* edifying, equiv. to *aedificāt(us)* (ptp. of *aedificāre* to EDIFY; see -ATE¹) + *-ōrius* -ORY¹]

ed·i·fice (ed′ə fis), *n.* a building, esp. one of large size or imposing appearance: *The governor's mansion is a rambling edifice of brick.* [ME < MF < L *aedificium,* equiv. to *aedific(āre)* (to) build (see EDIFY) + *-ium* neut. suffix] —**ed·i·fi·cial** (ed′ə fish′əl), *adj.*

—**Syn.** See **building.**

ed·i·fy (ed′ə fī′), *v.t.,* **-fied, -fy·ing.** to build up or increase the faith, morality, etc., of; instruct or benefit, esp. morally; uplift: *religious paintings that edify the viewer.* [ME *edifie(n)* < OF *edifier* < L *aedificāre* to build, equiv. to *aedi-* (s. of *aedes*) house, temple + *-ficāre* -FY] —**ed′i·fi′er,** *n.* —**ed′i·fy′ing·ly,** *adv.* —**ed′i·fy′ing·ness,** *n.*

e·dile (ē′dīl), *n.* *Rom. Hist.* aedile.

E·di·na (i dī′nə), *n.* a city in SE Minnesota, near Minneapolis. 28,501 (1960).

Ed·in·burg (ed′ᵊn bûrg′), *n.* **1.** a city in S Texas. 18,706 (1960). **2.** a town in central Indiana. 3664 (1960).

Ed·in·burgh (ed′ᵊn bûr′ō, -bur′ō *or, esp. Brit.,* -brə), *n.* **1.** a city in and the capital of Scotland, in the SE part. 468,378 (1961). **2.** former name of **Midlothian.**

E·dir·ne (e dēr′ne), *n.* a city in NW European Turkey. 33,591 (1955). Also called **Adrianople.** Formerly, **Adrianopolis.**

Ed·i·son (ed′i sən), *n.* **1. Thomas Al·va** (al′və), 1847–1931, U.S. inventor, esp. of electrical devices. **2.** a town in central New Jersey. 44,799 (1960). **3.** a boy's given name.

Ed′ison effect′, *Physics.* the phenomenon of the flow of electric current when an electrode sealed inside the bulb of an incandescent lamp is connected to the positive terminal of the lamp. [named after T. A. EDISON]

ed·it (ed′it), *v.t.* **1.** to supervise or direct the preparation of (a newspaper, magazine, etc.); serve as editor of; direct the policies of. **2.** to collect, prepare, and arrange (materials) for publication. **3.** to revise or correct, as a manuscript. **4.** to omit; eliminate (often fol. by *out*): *The author has edited out all references to his own family.* **5.** to prepare (motion-picture or television film) by deleting, arranging, and splicing shots, by synchronizing the sound record with the film, etc. [partly back formation from EDITOR, partly < L *ēdit(us)* published (ptp. of *ēdere* to give out), equiv. to *ē-* E- + *-ditus* (*di-* give, var. of *dā-,* + *-tus* ptp. suffix)]

edit., 1. edited. **2.** edition. **3.** editor.

E·dith (ē′dith), *n.* a girl's given name. Also, **E′dithe, Edyth, Edythe.**

e·di·tion (i dish′ən), *n.* **1.** one of a series of printings of the same book, newspaper, etc., each issued at a different time and differing from another by alterations, additions, etc. (distinguished from *impression*). **2.** the format in which a literary work is published: *a one-volume edition of Shakespeare.* **3.** the whole number of impressions or copies of a book, newspaper, etc., printed from one set of type at one time. **4.** a version of anything, printed or not, presented to the public: *the newest edition of a popular musical revue.* [< L *ēditiōn-* (s. of *ēditiō*) publication, equiv. to *ēdit(us)* (ptp. of *ēdere;* see EDIT) + *-iōn-* -ION]

edi′tion bind′ing, a decorative binding for books, often of leather or simulated leather. Cf. **library binding.**

edi′tion time′, a newspaper's press time.

e·di·ti·o prin·ceps (e dit′i ō′ pring′keps; *Eng.* i dish′ē ō′ prin′seps), *pl.* **e·di·ti·o·nes prin·ci·pes** (e dit′i ō′nes pring′ki pes′; *Eng.* i dish′ē ō′nēz prin′sə pēz′). *Latin.* first edition.

ed·i·tor (ed′i tər), *n.* **1.** a person having managerial and sometimes policy-making responsibility for the editorial part of a publishing firm or of a newspaper, magazine, or the like: *a senior editor; an editor in chief; a managing editor.* **2.** the supervisor or conductor of a department of a newspaper, magazine, etc.: *the music, foreign affairs, and show business editors.* **3.** a person who edits material for publication, films, etc. **4.** a device for examining and splicing film. [< L, equiv. to *ēdit(us)* (see EDIT) + *-or* -OR²]

ed·i·to·ri·al (ed′i tôr′ē əl, -tōr′-), *n.* **1.** an article in a newspaper or other periodical presenting the opinion of the publisher, editor, or editors. **2.** a statement broadcast on radio or television that presents the opinion of the owner, manager, or the like, of the station or channel. **3.** something regarded as resembling such an article or statement, as a lengthy, dogmatic utterance. —*adj.* **4.** of or pertaining to an editor or to editing: *editorial policies; editorial techniques.* **5.** of, pertaining to, or involved in the preparation of an editorial or editorials: *editorial page; editorial writer.* **6.** of or pertaining to the literary and artistic activities or contents of a publication, broadcasting organization, or the like, as distinguished from its business activities, advertisements, etc.: *an editorial employee; an editorial decision, not an advertising one.* [EDITOR + -IAL] —**ed·i·to·ri·al·ist** (ed′i tôr′ē ə list, -tōr′-), *n.*

ed·i·to·ri·al·ize (ed′i tôr′ē ə līz′, -tōr′-), *v.i.,* **-ized, -iz·ing. 1.** to set forth one's position or opinion on some subject in, or as if in, an editorial. **2.** to inject personal interpretations or opinions into an otherwise factual account. [EDITORIAL + -IZE] —**ed′i·to′ri·al·i·za′tion,** *n.* —**ed′i·to′ri·al·iz′er,** *n.*

ed·i·to·ri·al·ly (ed′i tôr′ē ə lē, -tōr′-), *adv.* **1.** in an editorial manner; as an editor does. **2.** in an editorial. [EDITORIAL + -LY]

ed′ito′rial "we", we (def. 6).

ed′itor in chief′, *pl.* **editors in chief.** the policy-making executive or principal editor of a publishing house, publication, etc.

ed·i·tor·ship (ed′i tər ship′), *n.* **1.** the office or function of an editor. **2.** editorial direction. [EDITOR + -SHIP]

ed·i·tress (ed′i tris), *n.* a woman editor. [EDIT(O)R + -ESS]

Ed·ley (ed′lē), *n.* a boy's given name.

Ed.M., Master of Education.

Ed·man (ed′mən), *n.* **Irwin,** 1896–1954, U.S. philosopher and essayist.

Ed·mond (ed′mənd), *n.* **1.** a town in central Oklahoma. 8577 (1960). **2.** Also, **Ed′mund.** a boy's given name.

Ed·monde (ed′mənd), *n.* a girl's given name. Also, **Edmunda.**

Ed·monds (ed′məndz), *n.* a town in NW Washington. 8016 (1960).

Ed·mon·ton (ed′mən tən), *n.* **1.** a city in and the capital of Alberta, in the central part, in SW Canada. 357,696 (1965). **2.** a city in NE Middlesex, in SE England, near London. 92,062 (1961).

Edmund I (ed′mənd), A.D. 921?–946, king of England 940–946. Also, **Eadmund I.**

Edmund II, (*"Ironside"*) A.D. c980–1016, English king defeated by Canute 1016. Also, **Eadmund II.**

Ed·mun·da (ed mun′də), *n.* a girl's given name. Also, **Edmonde.**

Ed·na (ed′nə), *n.* **1.** a town in S Texas. 5038 (1960). **2.** a girl's given name.

Ed·nas (ed′nəs), *n.* *Douay Bible.* Adnah.

Ed·nie (ed′nē), *n.* a girl's given name, form of **Edna.**

E·do (ed′ō; *Jap.* e′dô′), *n.* a former name of **Tokyo.**

E·dom (ē′dəm), *n.* **1.** Esau, the brother of Jacob. **2.** Greek, **Idumaea, Idumea.** an ancient region between the Dead Sea and the Gulf of Aqaba, bordering ancient Palestine. **3.** the kingdom of the Edomites located in this region. See map under **Philistia.**

E·dom·ite (ē′də mīt′), *n.* a descendant of Esau or Edom. Num. 20:14–21. [EDOM + -ITE¹] —**E′dom·it′ish, E·dom·it·ic** (ē′də mit′ik), *adj.*

EDP, See **electronic data processing.**

eds., 1. editions. **2.** editors.

Ed.S., 1. Education Specialist. **2.** Specialist in Education.

Ed·sel (ed′səl), *n.* a boy's given name.

Ed′sel Ford′ Range′, a mountain range in Antarctica, E of the Ross Sea.

EDT, Eastern daylight time. Also, **E.D.T.**

educ., 1. educated. **2.** education. **3.** educational.

ed·u·ca·ble (ej′o͝o kə bəl, ed′yo͝o-), *adj.* capable of being educated. Also, **ed·u·cat·a·ble** (ej′o͝o kā′tə bəl, ed′yo͝o-). [EDUC(ATE) + -ABLE] —**ed′u·ca·bil′i·ty, ed′u·cat′a·bil′i·ty,** *n.*

ed·u·cate (ej′o͝o kāt′, ed′yo͝o-), *v.t.,* **-cat·ed, -cat·ing. 1.** to develop the faculties and powers of (a person) by teaching, instruction, or schooling. **2.** to qualify by instruction or training for a particular calling, practice, etc.; train: *to educate someone for law.* **3.** to provide education for; send to school. **4.** to develop or train (the ear, taste, etc.): *to educate one's palate to appreciate fine food.* —*v.i.* **5.** to educate a person or group: *a television program designed to educate and not merely entertain.* [< L *ēducāt(us)* brought up, taught (ptp. of *ēducāre*), equiv. to *ē-* E- + *-duc-* lead + *-ātus* -ATE¹]
—**Syn. 1.** teach, instruct, school, drill, indoctrinate.

ed·u·cat·ed (ej′o͝o kā′tid, ed′yo͝o-), *adj.* **1.** having undergone education: *the linguistic usage of educated people.* **2.** characterized by or displaying qualities of culture and learning. **3.** based on some information or experience: *an educated estimate of next year's sales.* [EDUCATE + -ED²]

ed·u·ca·tee (ej′o͝o kā tē′, -kə-, ed′yo͝o-), *n.* a person who receives instruction; student. [EDUCATE + -EE]

ed·u·ca·tion (ej′o͝o kā′shən, ed′yo͝o-), *n.* **1.** the act or process of imparting or acquiring general knowledge, developing the powers of reasoning and judgment, and generally of preparing oneself or others intellectually for mature life. **2.** the act or process of imparting or acquiring particular knowledge or skills, as for a trade or profession. **3.** a degree, level, or kind of schooling: *a university education.* **4.** the result produced by instruction, training, or study: *to show one's education.* **5.** the science or art of teaching; pedagogics. [< L *ēducātiōn-* (s. of *ēducātiō*), equiv. to *ēducāt(us)* (see EDUCATE) + *-iōn-* -ION]
—**Syn. 1.** instruction, schooling, tuition. EDUCATION, TRAINING imply a discipline and development by means of study and learning. EDUCATION is the development of the special and general abilities of the mind (learning to know): *a liberal education.* TRAINING is practical education (learning to do) or practice, usually under supervision, in some art, trade, or profession: *training in art, teacher training.* **4.** learning, knowledge, enlightenment. EDUCATION, CULTURE are often used interchangeably to mean the results of schooling. EDUCATION, however, suggests chiefly the information acquired. CULTURE is a mode of thought and feeling encouraged by education (the process and the acquirement). It suggests an aspiration toward, and an appreciation of, high intellectual and esthetic ideals: *The level of culture in a country depends upon the education of its people.* —**Ant. 4.** illiteracy.

ed·u·ca·tion·al (ej′o͝o kā′shə nᵊl, ed′yo͝o-), *adj.* **1.** pertaining to education. **2.** tending or intended to educate: *an educational show on television.* [EDUCATION + -AL¹] —**ed′u·ca′tion·al·ly,** *adv.*

ed·u·ca·tion·ist (ej′o͝o kā′shə nist, ed′yo͝o-), *n.* a specialist in the theory and methods of education. Also, **ed′u·ca′tion·al·ist.** [EDUCATION + -IST]

Educa′tion of Hen′ry Ad′ams, The, (*A Study of Twentieth-Century Multiplicity*) an autobiographical work (1907) by Henry Adams.

ed·u·ca·tive (ej′o͝o kā′tiv, ed′yo͝o-), *adj.* **1.** serving to educate: *educative knowledge.* **2.** pertaining to or productive of education: *the educative process.* [EDUCATE + -IVE]

ed·u·ca·tor (ej′o͝o kā′tər, ed′yo͝o-), *n.* **1.** one who or that which educates, esp. a teacher, principal, or other person involved in planning or directing education. **2.** an educationist. [< L *ēducātor,* equiv. to *ēducāt(us)* (see EDUCATE) + *-or* -OR²]

ed·u·ca·to·ry (ej′o͝o kə tôr′ē, -tōr′ē, ed′yo͝o-), *adj.* serving to educate. [EDUCATE + -ORY¹]

e·duce (i do͞os′, i dyo͞os′), *v.t.,* **e·duced, e·duc·ing. 1.** to draw forth or bring out, as something potential or latent; elicit; develop. **2.** to infer or deduce. [ME < L *ēdūce(re),* equiv. to *ē-* E- + *dūcere* to lead] —**e·duc′i·ble,** *adj.*

e·duct (ē′dukt), *n.* **1.** something educed; eduction. **2.** *Chem.* a substance extracted from a mixture, as distinguished from a product. [< L *ēduct(um)* something educed, n. use of neut. of *ēductus* educed (ptp. of *ēdūcere* to EDUCE), equiv. to *ē-* E- + *-duc-* lead + *-tus* ptp. suffix]

e·duc·tion (i duk′shən), *n.* **1.** the act of educing. **2.** something educed. [< L *ēductiōn-* (s. of *ēductiō*), equiv. to *ēduct(us)* (see EDUCT) + *-iōn-* -ION]

e·duc·tive (i duk′tiv), *adj.* educing; serving to educe. [EDUCT + -IVE]

e·duc·tor (i duk′tər), *n.* ejector (def. 3). [< LL: one who leads forth from. See EDUCT, -OR²]

e·dul·co·rate (i dul′kə rāt′), *v.t.,* **-rat·ed, -rat·ing.** *Chem.* to free from acids, salts, or impurities by washing; to purify. [< NL *ēdulcorāt(us),* equiv. to *ē-* E- + LL *dulcorātus* sweetened (ptp. of *dulcorāre*), equiv. to L *dulcor* sweetness (*dulc(is)* sweet + *-or* -OR¹) + *-ātus* -ATE¹] —**e·dul′co·ra′tion,** *n.* —**e·dul′co·ra′tive,** *adj.*

Ed·ward (ed′wərd), *n.* **1. Prince of Wales** and **Duke of Cornwall** (*"The Black Prince"*), 1330–76, English military leader (son of Edward III). **2. Lake,** a lake in central Africa, between Uganda and the Republic of the Congo: a headwater of the Nile. 830 sq. mi. **3.** a boy's given name.

Edward I, (*"Edward Longshanks"*) 1239–1307, king of England 1272–1307 (son of Henry III).

Edward II, 1. 1284–1327, king of England 1307–27 (son of Edward I). **2.** (*italics.*) a drama (1593?) by Christopher Marlowe.

Edward III, 1312–77, king of England 1327–77 (son of Edward II).

Edward IV, 1442–83, king of England 1461–70, 1471–1483: 1st king of the house of York.

Edward V, 1470–83, king of England 1483 (son of Edward IV).

Edward VI, 1537–53, king of England 1547–53 (son of Henry VIII and Jane Seymour).

Edward VII, (*Albert Edward*) (*"the Peacemaker"*) 1841–1910, king of Great Britain and Ireland 1901–10 (son of Queen Victoria).

Edward VIII, (*Duke of Windsor*) 1894–1972, king of Great Britain 1936 (son of George V; brother of George VI).

Ed·ward·i·an (ed wôr′dē ən, -wär′-), *adj.* **1.** of or pertaining to the reign of Edward VII. **2.** reflecting the self-satisfaction or opulence characteristic of this reign. **3.** noting or pertaining to the castle architecture of Edward I. [EDWARD (VII, I) + -IAN] —**Ed·ward′i·an·ism,** *n.*

Ed·wards (ed′wərdz), *n.* **Jonathan,** 1703–58, American clergyman and theologian.

Ed·ward·si·an·ism (ed wôrd′zē ə niz′əm, -wärd′-), *n.* a modified form of Calvinism taught by Jonathan Edwards. [Jonathan EDWARDS + -IAN + -ISM] —**Ed·ward′si·an,** *adj., n.*

Ed′wards Plateau′, a highland area in SW Texas. 2000–5000 ft. high.

Ed·wards·ville (ed′wərdz vil′), *n.* **1.** a town in SW Illinois. 9996 (1960). **2.** a town in central Pennsylvania. 5711 (1960).

Ed′ward the Confes′sor, Saint, 1002?–66, English king 1042–66: founder of Westminster Abbey.

Ed·win (ed′win), *n.* **1.** Also, **Eadwine.** A.D. 585?–633, king of Northumbria 617–633. **2.** a boy's given name.

Ed·wi·na (ed wē′nə), *n.* a girl's given name.

E·dyie (ē′dē), *n.* a girl's given name, form of **Edith.** Also, **Edie.**

E·dyth (ē′dith), *n.* a girl's given name. Also, **Edith, Edithe, E′dythe.**

-ee, a suffix of nouns denoting one who is the object of some action, or undergoes or receives something (often as opposed to the person acting): *assignee; donee; employee.* [< F *-é,* masc. ending of ptp. < L *-ātus* -ATE¹]

EE, a proportional shoe width size narrower than EEE and wider than E.

E.E., 1. Early English. **2.** Electrical Engineer. **3.** Electrical Engineering.

e.e., errors excepted.

E.E. & M.P., Envoy Extraordinary and Minister Plenipotentiary.

EEC, European Economic Community.

EEE, eastern equine encephalitis.

EEE, the widest proportional shoe size.

EEG, electroencephalogram. Also, **E.E.G.**

eel (ēl), *n., pl.* (*esp. collectively*) **eel,** (*esp. referring to two or more kinds or species*) **eels. 1.** any of numerous elongated, snakelike, marine or fresh-water fishes of the order *Apodes,* having no ventral fins. **2.** any of several similar but unrelated fishes, as the lamprey. [ME *ele,* OE *ēl, ǣl;* c. D, G *Aal,* Icel *āll*]

Eel,
Anguilla rostrata
(Length to 6 ft.)

eel·back (ēl′bak′), *n.* See **smooth flounder.** [so called from its smooth, eellike back]

eel·blen·ny (ēl′blen′ē), *n., pl.* (*esp. collectively*) **-ny,** (*esp. referring to two or more kinds or species*) **-nies.** any of several eellike fishes of the genus *Lumpenus,* of the prickleback family, found in subarctic coastal waters. [EEL + BLENNY]

eel·grass (ēl′gras′, -gräs′), *n.* **1.** a grasslike marine herb, *Zostera marina,* having ribbonlike leaves. **2.** See **tape grass.** [EEL + GRASS]

eel·like (ēl′līk′), *adj.* resembling an eel, as in appearance or movement. [EEL + -LIKE]

eel·pout (ēl′pout′), *n.* **1.** any blennioid fish of the family *Zoarcidae,* esp. *Zoarces viviparus,* of Europe. **2.** the burbot. [OE *ǣlepūte.* See EEL, POUT²]

eel·worm (ēl′wûrm′), *n.* any small nematode worm of the family *Anguillulidae,* including the minute vinegar eel, *Anguillula aceti.* [EEL + WORM]

eel·y (ē′lē), *adj.,* **eel·i·er, eel·i·est.** eellike; wriggling. [EEL + -Y¹]

e'en (ēn), *adv.* *Chiefly Literary.* even¹.

e'er (âr), *adv.* *Chiefly Literary.* ever.

-eer, a suffix of nouns denoting one who is concerned with, or employed in connection with, or busies himself with something: *auctioneer; engineer; profiteer.* Also, **-ier.** [var. of *-ier* < F < L *-ārius* -ARY; see -ER²]

ee·rie (ēr′ē), *adj.,* **-ri·er, -ri·est. 1.** uncanny, so as to inspire superstitious fear; weird: *an eerie midnight scene.* **2.** *Brit. Dial.* affected with superstitious fear. Also, **eery.** [ME *eri,* dial. var. of *argh,* OE *earg* cowardly; c. OFris *erg,* Icel *argr* evil, G *arg* cowardly] —**ee′ri·ly,** *adv.* —**ee′ri·ness,** *n.*
—**Syn. 1.** See **weird.**

ee·ry (ēr′ē), *adj.,* **-ri·er, -ri·est.** eerie.

E·ë·ti·on (ē ē′tē on′), *n.* (in the *Iliad*) a king of Thebes in Cilicia and the father of Andromache.

ef-, var. of **ex-**¹ (by assimilation) before *f: efficient.*

E.F., English finish. Cf. **English** (def. 8).

ef·fa·ble (ef′ə bəl), *adj.* utterable; expressible. [< MF < L *effābil(is),* equiv. to *eff(ārī)* (to) speak out (*ef-* EF- + *fārī* to speak) + *-ābilis* -ABLE]

ef·face (i fās′), *v.t.,* **-faced, -fac·ing. 1.** to wipe out; destroy; do away with: *to efface a memory.* **2.** to rub out, erase, or obliterate (outlines, traces, inscriptions, etc.). **3.** to make (oneself) inconspicuous; withdraw (oneself) modestly or shyly. [< F *effacer.* See EF-, FACE] —**ef·face′a·ble,** *adj.* —**ef·face′ment,** *n.* —**ef·fac′er,** *n.*

ef·fect (i fekt′), *n.* **1.** something that is produced by an agency or cause; result; consequence: *Exposure to the sun had the effect of toughening his skin.* **2.** power to produce results; efficacy; force; validity; influence: *His protest had no effect.* **3.** the state of being effective or operative; operation or execution; accomplishment or fulfillment: *to bring a plan into effect.* **4.** a mental impression produced, as by a painting or a speech. **5.** main idea or meaning; gist (prec. by *to*): *He disapproved of the proposal and wrote to that effect.* **6.** the making of a desired impression: *When she wants her own way she cries just for effect.* **7.** an illusory phenomenon:

a three-dimensional effect. **8.** a real phenomenon (usually named for its discoverer): *the Doppler effect.* **9.** See **special effect. 10.** the result intended; purport; intent. **11. in effect, a.** for practical purposes; virtually: *His silence was in effect a confirmation of the rumor.* **b.** essentially; basically. **12. take effect, a.** to go into operation; begin to function. **b.** to produce a result: *The prescribed medicine failed to take effect.* —*v.t.* **13.** to produce as an effect; bring about; accomplish; make happen: *Their transition to automation was effected last spring.* **14.** to produce or make. [ME < L *effect(us)* (4th decl.), n. use of ptp. of *efficere* to effect, equiv. to *ef-* EF- + *fec-* (var. of *fac-*) do + *-tus* ptp. suffix] —**ef·fect′i·ble,** *adj.* —**ef·fect′less,** *adj.*

—**Syn. 1.** outcome, issue. EFFECT, CONSEQUENCE(S), RESULT refer to something produced by an action or a cause. An EFFECT is that which is produced, usually more or less immediately and directly: *The effect of morphine is to produce sleep. Morphine produces the effect of sleep.* A CONSEQUENCE, something that follows naturally or logically, as in a train of events or sequence of time, is less intimately connected with its cause than is an effect: *Punishment is the consequence of disobedience. Take the consequences.* A RESULT may be near or remote, and often is the sum of effects or consequences as making an end or final outcome: *The English language is the result of the fusion of many different elements.* **13.** achieve, realize, fulfill, perform, consummate. See **affect**[1]. —**Ant. 1.** cause.

ef·fect·er (i fek′tər), *n.* effector.

ef·fec·tive (i fek′tiv), *adj.* **1.** adequate to accomplish a purpose; producing the intended or expected result: *effective measures; effective steps toward peace.* **2.** actually in operation or in force; functioning: *The law becomes effective at midnight.* **3.** producing a deep or vivid impression; striking: *an effective photograph.* **4.** prepared and available for service, esp. military service. —*n.* **5.** a soldier or sailor fit for duty or active service. **6.** the effective total of a military force. [ME < L *effectīv(us)* practical, equiv. to *effect-* (see EFFECT) + *-īvus* -IVE] —**ef·fec′tive·ly,** *adv.* —**ef·fec′tive·ness, ef·fec·tiv′i·ty,** *n.*

—**Syn. 1.** capable, competent. EFFECTIVE, EFFECTUAL, EFFICACIOUS, EFFICIENT refer to that which is able to produce a (desired) effect. EFFECTIVE is applied to that which has the power to, or which actually does, produce an (often lasting) effect: *an effective action, remedy, speech.* EFFECTUAL is used esp. of that which produces the effect desired or intended, or a decisive result: *An effectual bombardment silenced the enemy.* EFFICACIOUS suggests the capability of achieving a certain end, a capability often manifested only when actually employed: *an efficacious plan, medicine.* EFFICIENT (applied also to persons) is the most active of these words, and implies the skillful use of energy or industry to accomplish desired results with little waste of effort: *efficient methods; an efficient manager.* **2.** operative. **3.** telling. —**Ant. 1.** futile.

effec′tive cur′rent, *Elect.* the magnitude of an alternating current having the same heating effect as that of a given magnitude of direct current.

effec′tive electromo′tive force′, *Elect.* (in relation to a given alternating current) the square root of the average of the squares of the values of the electromotive force measured at each instant throughout a time interval of one period.

effec′tive horse′power, *Naval Archit.* a measure of the horsepower required to move a hull at a certain speed, equal to the resistance of the hull, in pounds, times the number of feet traveled per second, divided by 550. Also called **towrope horsepower.**

effec′tive resist′ance, *Elect.* the resistance to an alternating current, expressed as the ratio of the power dissipated to the square of the effective current.

effec′tive sound′ pres′sure, *Physics.* the square root of the mean of the squares of the sound pressures of a sound wave, measured at a given point over a certain time interval. Also called **sound pressure.**

ef·fec·tor (i fek′tər), *n.* **1.** *Physiol.* an organ tissue or cell that carries out a response to a nerve impulse. **2.** one who or that which effects. Also, **effecter.** [< L, equiv. to *effect-* (see EFFECT) + *-or* -OR[2]]

ef·fects (i fekts′), *n.pl.* goods; movables; personal property. [pl. of EFFECT]

ef·fec·tu·al (i fek′cho͞o əl), *adj.* **1.** producing or capable of producing an intended effect; adequate. **2.** valid or binding, as an agreement or document. [late ME < LL *effectuāl(is),* equiv. to L *effectu(s)* (see EFFECT) + *-ālis* -AL[1]; r. ME *effectuel* < MF] —**ef·fec′tu·al·ly,** *adv.* —**ef·fec′tu·al·ness, ef·fec′tu·al′i·ty,** *n.*
—**Syn. 1.** See **effective.**

ef·fec·tu·ate (i fek′cho͞o āt′), *v.t.,* **-at·ed, -at·ing.** to bring about; effect. [< ML *effectuāt(us)* brought to pass (ptp. of *effectuāre*), equiv. to L *effectu(s)* (see EFFECT) + *-ātus* -ATE[1]] —**ef·fec′tu·a′tion,** *n.*

ef·fem·i·na·cy (i fem′ə nə sē), *n.* the state or quality of being effeminate. [EFFEMIN(ATE) + -ACY]

ef·fem·i·nate (*adj.* i fem′ə nit; *v.* i fem′ə nāt′), *adj., v.,* **-nat·ed, -nat·ing.** —*adj.* **1.** (of a man) soft or delicate to an unmanly degree in traits, tastes, habits, etc.; womanish. **2.** characterized by unmanly softness, delicacy, self-indulgence, etc.: *effeminate luxury.* —*v.t., v.i.* **3.** to make or become effeminate. [< L *effēmināt(us),* equiv. to *ef-* EF- + *fēmin(a)* woman + *-ātus* -ATE[1]] —**ef·fem′i·nate·ly,** *adv.* —**ef·fem′i·nate·ness,** *n.* —**ef·fem′i·na′tion,** *n.*
—**Syn. 1.** See **female.**

ef·fem·i·nise (i fem′ə nīz′), *v.t.,* **-nised, -nis·ing.** *Chiefly Brit.* effeminize. —**ef·fem′i·ni·sa′tion,** *n.*

ef·fem·i·nize (i fem′ə nīz′), *v.t.,* **-nized, -niz·ing.** to make effeminate: *Coddling had effeminized the boy.* [EFFEMIN(ATE) + -IZE] —**ef·fem′i·ni·za′tion,** *n.*

ef·fen·di (i fen′dē), *n., pl.* **-dis. 1.** a former Turkish title of respect, esp. for government officials. **2.** (in eastern Mediterranean countries) a man who is well-educated or a member of the aristocracy. [< Turk *efendi* < ModGk *aphentēs* for Gk *authentēs* doer, master. See AUTHENTIC]

ef·fer·ent (ef′ər ənt), *Anat., Physiol.* —*adj.* **1.** conveying or conducting away from an organ or part (opposed to *afferent*). —*n.* **2.** an efferent part, as a nerve or blood vessel. [< L *efferent-* (s. of *efferēns* carrying off, prp. of *efferre*), equiv. to *ef-* EF- + *ferent-* carrying (*fer-* carry + *-ent-* -ENT)] —**ef′fer·ence,** *n.* —**ef′fer·ent·ly,** *adv.*

ef·fer·vesce (ef′ər ves′), *v.i.,* **-vesced, -vesc·ing. 1.** to give off bubbles of gas, as fermenting liquors; bubble and hiss. **2.** to issue forth in bubbles. **3.** to show enthusiasm, excitement, liveliness, etc.: *The parents effervesced with pride over their healthy new baby.* [< L *effervesce(re),* equiv. to *ef-* EF- + *ferv-* hot (see FERVENT) + *-escere* -ESCE] —**ef′fer·ves′cence, ef′fer·ves′cen·cy,** *n.* —**ef′fer·ves′ci·ble,** *adj.*

ef·fer·ves·cent (ef′ər ves′ənt), *adj.* **1.** effervescing; bubbling. **2.** gay; lively; sparkling. [< L *effervescent-* (s. of *effervescēns*), prp. of *effervescere* to EFFERVESCE; see -ENT] —**ef′fer·ves′cent·ly, ef′fer·vesc′ing·ly,** *adv.*

ef·fete (i fēt′), *adj.* **1.** exhausted of vigor or energy; worn out: *an effete political force.* **2.** lacking in wholesome vigor; decadent: *an effete, over-refined society.* **3.** unable to produce; sterile. [< L *effēta* exhausted from bearing, equiv. to *ef-* EF- + *fēta* having brought forth, fem. ptp. of lost v.; see FETUS] —**ef·fete′ly,** *adv.* —**ef·fete′ness,** *n.*

ef·fi·ca·cious (ef′ə kā′shəs), *adj.* having or showing the desired result or effect; effective as a means, measure, remedy, etc.: *An efficacious solution was found to the persistent problem.* [< L *efficāci-* (s. of *efficāx* effectual. See EFFICIENT, -ACIOUS] —**ef′fi·ca′cious·ly,** *adv.* —**ef′fi·ca′cious·ness,** *n.*
—**Syn.** See **effective.**

ef·fi·ca·cy (ef′ə kə sē), *n., pl.* **-cies.** capacity for producing a desired result or effect; effectiveness: *a remedy of great efficacy.* [< L *efficācia,* equiv. to *efficāc-* (see EFFICACIOUS) + *-ia* -Y[3]]

ef·fi·cien·cy (i fish′ən sē), *n., pl.* **-cies. 1.** the state or quality of being efficient; competency in performance. **2.** accomplishment of or ability to accomplish a job with a minimum expenditure of time and effort: *The employees were graded on their efficiency.* **3.** the ratio of the work done or energy developed by a machine, engine, etc., to the energy supplied to it, usually expressed as a percentage. **4.** See **efficiency apartment.** [< L *efficientia,* equiv. to *efficient-* (see EFFICIENT) + *-ia* -Y[3]]

effi′ciency apart′ment, an apartment consisting typically of a combined living room and bedroom area, a bathroom, and a small kitchen alcove. Also called **efficiency.**

effi′ciency engineer′, a person who studies the methods, procedures, and job characteristics of a business or factory with the object of devising ways to increase the efficiency of equipment and personnel. Also called **effi′ciency ex′pert.** Cf. **time and motion study.**

ef·fi·cient (i fish′ənt), *adj.* **1.** performing or functioning in the best possible and least wasteful manner; having and using requisite knowledge, skill, and industry; competent; capable: *a reliable, efficient secretary.* **2.** satisfactory and economical to use: *Our new house is more efficient than our old one.* **3.** producing an effect, as a cause; causative. [< L *efficient-* (s. of *efficiēns*), equiv. to *ef-* EF- + *fic-* (var. of *fac-*) do + *-ent-* -ENT] —**ef·fi′cient·ly,** *adv.*
—**Syn. 1.** effectual. See **effective.**

effi′cient cause′, *Aristotelianism.* See under **cause** (def. 8b).

Ef·fie (ef′ē), *n.* a girl's given name. Also, **Effy, Effye.**

ef·fig·i·ate (i fij′ē āt′), *v.t.,* **-at·ed, -at·ing.** *Archaic.* to make an image or effigy of: *a great statesman effigiated in bronze.* [< LL *effigiāt(us)* imagined (ptp. of *effigiāre*). See EFFIGY, -ATE[1]] —**ef·fig·i·a·tion** (i fij′ē ā′shən), *n.*

ef·fi·gies[1] (ef′i jēz), *n.* pl. of **effigy.**

ef·fig·i·es[2] (e fij′ē ēz′; *Lat.* e fig′i es), *n., pl.* **-i·es.** *Archaic.* effigy.

ef·fi·gy (ef′i jē), *n., pl.* **-gies. 1.** a representation or image, esp. sculptured, as on a monument. **2.** a crude representation of someone disliked, used for purposes of ridicule. **3. burn** or **hang in effigy, a.** to burn or hang an image of a despised person as a public expression of indignation, ridicule, or contempt. **b.** to criticize or ridicule. [< L *effigia,* equiv. to *effig-* (*ef-* EF- + *fig-* shape, form; see FIGURE) + *-ia* -Y[3]] —**ef·fig·i·al** (e fij′ē əl), *adj.*

Ef·fing·ham (ef′ing ham′), *n.* a town in central Illinois. 8172 (1960).

ef·fleu·rage (ef′lə räzh′), *n.* a delicate stroking motion in massage. [< F, equiv. to *effleur(er)* (to) stroke as one would a flower (i.e., lightly; see EF-, FLOWER) + *-age* -AGE]

ef·flo·resce (ef′lə res′), *v.i.,* **-resced, -resc·ing. 1.** to burst into bloom; blossom. **2.** *Chem.* **a.** to change either throughout or on the surface to a mealy or powdery substance upon exposure to air, as a crystalline substance through loss of water of crystallization. **b.** to become incrusted or covered with crystals of salt or the like through evaporation or chemical change. [< L *efflōresce(re)* (to) blossom out, equiv. to *ef-* EF- + *flōrescere* to begin to bloom (*flōr(i)-,* s. of *flōs* flower + *-escere* -ESCE)]

ef·flo·res·cence (ef′lə res′əns), *n.* **1.** the state or a period of flowering. **2.** an example or result of growth and development: *These paintings and drawings are the efflorescence of his mature genius.* **3.** *Chem.* **a.** the act or process of efflorescing. **b.** the resulting powdery substance or incrustation. **4.** *Pathol.* a rash or eruption of the skin. [< MF < ML *efflōrescentia.* See EFFLORESCE, -ENCE]

ef·flo·res·cent (ef′lə res′ənt), *adj.* **1.** efflorescing; blossoming. **2.** *Chem.* **a.** subject to efflorescence. **b.** covered with or forming an efflorescence. [< L *efflōrescent-* (s. of *efflōrescēns*), prp. of *efflōrescere* to EFFLORESCE; see -ENT]

ef·flu·ence (ef′lo͞o əns), *n.* **1.** the process or action of flowing out; efflux. **2.** something that flows out; emanation. [< L *efflu-* outflow (*ef-* EF- + *flu-* flow) + -ENCE]

ef·flu·ent (ef′lo͞o ənt), *adj.* **1.** flowing out or forth. —*n.* **2.** something that flows out or forth; outflow; effluence. **3.** a stream flowing out of a larger stream, lake, reservoir, etc. [< L *effluent-* (s. of *effluēns* flowing out, prp. of *effluere*), equiv. to *ef-* EF- + *flu-* flow + *-ent-* -ENT]

ef·flu·vi·um (i flo͞o′vē əm), *n., pl.* **-vi·a** (-vē ə), **-vi·ums.** a slight or invisible exhalation or vapor, esp. one that is disagreeable or noxious. [< L, equiv. to *ef-* EF- + *fluv-* (var. of *flu-*) flow (see EFFLUENT) + *-ium* -Y[3]] —**ef·flu′vi·al,** *adj.*

ef·flux (ef′luks), *n.* **1.** outward flow, as of water. **2.** something that flows out; effluence. [< L *efflux(us),* ptp. of *effluere* to flow out. See EFFLUVIUM]

ef·fort (ef′ərt), *n.* **1.** deliberate exertion of physical or mental power: *It will take great effort to achieve victory.* **2.** a strenuous attempt: *With a last, all-out effort they gained the top of the hill.* **3.** something done by exertion; an achievement, as in literature or art: *The painting is one of his finest efforts.* **4.** *Chiefly Brit.* **a.** an organized community drive or achievement. **b.** a fund-raising drive, as for charity. **5.** *Mech.* the force or energy that is applied to a machine for the accomplishment of useful work. [late ME < MF; OF *esfort, esforz,* deriv. of *esforcier* to force (*es-* EX-[1] + *forcier* to FORCE)]

—**Syn. 1.** struggle, striving. EFFORT, APPLICATION, ENDEAVOR, EXERTION imply actions directed or force expended toward a definite end. EFFORT is an expenditure of energy to accomplish some usually single and definite object: *He made an effort to control himself.* APPLICATION is continuous effort plus careful attention: *constant application to duties.* ENDEAVOR means a continued and sustained series of efforts to achieve some, often worthy and difficult, end: *a constant endeavor to be useful.* EXERTION is the vigorous and often strenuous expenditure of energy, frequently without conscious reference to a definite end: *out of breath from exertion.*

ef·fort·ful (ef′ərt fəl), *adj.* marked by effort or exertion; labored. [EFFORT + -FUL] —**ef′fort·ful·ly,** *adv.*

ef·fort·less (ef′ərt lis), *adj.* **1.** requiring or involving no effort; easy. **2.** making no effort; passive. [EFFORT + -LESS] —**ef′fort·less·ly,** *adv.* —**ef′fort·less·ness,** *n.*
—**Syn. 1.** smooth, facile, flowing.

ef′fort syn′drome, *Pathol.* See **cardiac neurosis.**

ef·frac·tion (i frak′shən), *n.* *Law.* a breaking into by force; forcible entry. [< F: lit., a breaking open < L *ef-* EF- + *fraction-* FRACTION]

ef·frac·tor (i frak′tər), *n.* *Law.* a burglar; housebreaker. [< LL, equiv. to L *effract(us)* broken open (ptp. of *effringere*), equiv. to *ef-* EF- + *frac-* break + *-t(us)* ptp. suffix + *-or* -OR[2]]

ef·fron·ter·y (i frun′tə rē), *n., pl.* **-ter·ies. 1.** shameless or impudent boldness; barefaced audacity: *She had the effrontery to ask for two free samples.* **2.** an act or instance of this. [< F *effronterie,* equiv. to OF *esfront* shameless (*es-* EX-[1] + *front* brow; see FRONT) + *-erie* -ERY]
—**Syn. 1.** impertinence, impudence, temerity.

ef·fulge (i fulj′), *v.t., v.i.,* **-fulged, -fulg·ing.** to shine or send forth brilliantly. [< L *effulgē(re),* equiv. to *ef-* EF- + *fulgēre* to shine]

ef·ful·gent (i ful′jənt), *adj.* shining forth brilliantly; radiant. [< L *effulgent-* (s. of *effulgēns,* prp. of *effulgēre*), equiv. to *effulg-* (see EFFULGE) + *-ent-* -ENT] —**ef·ful′gence,** *n.* —**ef·ful′gent·ly,** *adv.*

ef·fuse (*v.* i fyo͞oz′; *adj.* i fyo͞os′), *v.,* **-fused, -fus·ing,** *adj.* —*v.t.* **1.** to pour out or forth; shed; disseminate: *The town effuses warmth and hospitality.* —*v.i.* **2.** to exude; flow out. **3.** *Physics.* (of a gas) to flow through a very small orifice. —*adj.* **4.** *Bot.* spread out loosely. **5.** (of certain shells) having the lips separated by a gap or groove. [ME < L *effūs(us)* (ptp. of *effundere*) poured out, equiv. to *ef-* EF- + *fūsus* (**fūd-* + *-tus* ptp. suffix)]

ef·fu·sion (i fyo͞o′zhən), *n.* **1.** the act of effusing or pouring forth. **2.** something that is effused. **3.** an unrestrained expression, as of feelings: *poetic effusions.* **4.** *Pathol.* **a.** the escape of a fluid from its natural vessels into a body cavity. **b.** the fluid that escapes. **5.** *Physics.* the flow of a gas through a small orifice at such density that the mean distance between the molecules is large compared with the diameter of the orifice. [ME < L *effūsiōn-* (s. of *effūsiō*), equiv. to *ef-* EF- + *fūsion-* FUSION]

ef·fu·sive (i fyo͞o′siv), *adv.* **1.** unduly demonstrative; lacking reserve: *effusive greetings; an effusive person.* **2.** pouring out; overflowing. **3.** *Geol.* noting or pertaining to igneous rocks which have solidified near or on the surface of the earth (opposed to *plutonic*). [EFFUSE + -IVE] —**ef·fu′sive·ly,** *adv.* —**ef·fu′sive·ness,** *n.*

Ef·fy (ef′ē), *n.* a girl's given name.

Ef·ik (ef′ik), *n.* a Benue-Congo language of SE Nigeria.

efph, equivalent full-power hour.

eft[1] (eft), *n.* **1.** a newt, esp. the common newt, *Diemictylus viridescens* **(red eft),** in its immature terrestrial stage. **2.** *Obs.* a lizard. [ME *evete,* OE *efete*]

eft[2] (eft), *adv.* *Archaic.* **1.** again. **2.** afterward. [OE *eft;* akin to AFT, AFTER]

EFT, electonic funds transfer: a method of transferring bank funds by electronic means, as from one corporate bank account to another or by withdrawal from one's own account to deposit in a creditor's, esp. so as to pay bills. Also, **EFTS** [e(lectronic) f(unds) t(ransfer) (system)]

eft·soon (eft so͞on′), *adv.* *Archaic.* **1.** soon afterward. **2.** again. **3.** forthwith. Also, **eft·soons′.** [ME *eftsone,* OE *eftsōna.* See EFT[2], SOON]

Eg., **1.** Egypt. **2.** Egyptian.

e.g., for the sake of example; for example. [< L *exemplī grātia*]

e·gad (i gad′, ē′gad′), *interj.* (used as an expletive or mild oath): *Egad, that's true!* [euphemistic alter. of *ah God!*]

E·ga·di (eg′ə dē), *n.* a group of islands in the Mediterranean Sea off the coast of W Sicily. 15 sq. mi. Also called **Aegadian Islands, Aegadean Islands.** Ancient, **Aegates.**

e·gads′ but′ton (i gadz′, ē gadz′), *Rocketry Slang.* a switch that triggers the destruction in flight of a malfunctioning missile. Also called **chicken switch.**

e·gal (ē′gal), *adj.* *Obs.* equal. [ME *egall* < OF *egal* < L *aequālis*]

e·gal·i·tar·i·an (i gal′i târ′ē ən), *adj.* **1.** asserting, resulting from, or characterized by belief in the equality of all men. —*n.* **2.** a person who adheres to egalitarian beliefs. [alter. of EQUALITARIAN with F *égal* r. EQUAL] —**e·gal′i·tar′i·an·ism,** *n.*

é·ga·li·té (ā gȧ lē tā′), *n.* *French.* equality.

Eg·bert (eg′bərt), *n.* **1.** A.D. 775?–839, king of the West Saxons 802–839; 1st king of the English 828–839. **2.** a boy's given name.

Eg·e·de (eg′ə də), *n.* a crater in the second quadrant of the face of the moon: about 30 miles in diameter.

E·ger (ā′gər), *n.* German name of **Ohře.**

E·ge·ri·a (i jēr′ē ə), *n.* **1.** Also, **Aegeria.** *Rom. Legend.* one of the Camenae, the wife and instructress of Numa Pompilius. **2.** a woman counselor.

e·gest (ē jest′), *v.t.* to discharge, as from the body; void (opposed to *ingest*). [< L *ēgest(us)* (ptp. of *ēgerere*) carried out, equiv. to *ē-* E- + *ges-* (var. of *ger-*) carry + *-tus* ptp. suffix] —**e·ges′tive,** *adj.*

e·ges·ta (ē jes′tə), *n.pl.* matter egested from the body, as excrement. [neut. pl. of L *ēgestus* carried out. See EGEST]

E·ges·ta (i jes′tə), *n. Class. Myth.* (in the *Aeneid*) a Trojan woman sold as a slave by Laomedon but rescued by Aphrodite. Also, **Aegesta, Segesta.**

e·ges·tion (ē jes′chən, -jesh′-), *n.* the process of egesting; the voiding of the refuse of digestion. [ME < L *ēgestiōn-* (s. of *ēgestiō*), equiv. to *ēgest-* (see EGEST) + *-iōn-* -ION]

egg[1] (eg), *n.* **1.** the roundish reproductive body produced by the female of animals, consisting of an ovum and its envelopes, being albumen, jelly, membranes, egg case, or shell, according to species. **2.** the body of this sort produced by a bird, esp. the domestic hen. **3.** the contents of an egg or eggs: *raw egg; fried eggs; a bit of egg on one's shirt front.* **4.** anything resembling a hen's egg. **5.** Also called **egg′ cell′.** *Biol.* the ovum or female reproductive cell. **6.** *Slang.* person: *He's a good egg.* **7.** *Slang.* an aerial bomb. **8.** *Brit. Disparaging.* a young, immature, or unworldly person. **9. lay an egg,** *Slang.* to fail wretchedly, esp. to be unsuccessful in front of an audience: *He laid an egg as the romantic hero.* **10. put all one's eggs in one basket,** to venture all of something that one possesses in a single enterprise. **11. teach one's grandmother to suck eggs,** to attempt to teach those older and more experienced than oneself. **12. walk** or **tread upon eggs,** to walk or behave very cautiously: *Clearing up this delicate matter will be a question of walking on eggs.* —*adj.* **13.** noting a size of anthracite coal less than 4 inches and more than 1½ inches in the longest dimension. —*v.t.* **14.** to prepare (food) by dipping in beaten egg. [ME < Scand; cf. Icel egg; c. ME *ey,* OE *æg,* G *Ei* egg; akin to L *ōvum,* Gk *ōiṓn* egg] —**egg′less,** *adj.*

egg[2] (eg), *v.t.* to incite or urge; encourage (usually fol. by *on*). [ME < Scand; cf. Icel *eggja* to incite, deriv. of *egg* EDGE]

Egg and dart

egg′ and dart′, *Archit.* an ornament for enriching an ovolo or echinus, consisting of a closely set, alternating series of oval and pointed forms. Also called **egg′ and an′chor, egg′ and tongue′.**

egg′ and spoon′ race′, a novelty race in which contestants, each equipped with a spoon, run to a point, pick up an egg with the spoon, and carry the egg back to the starting line.

egg·beat·er (eg′bē′tər), *n.* **1.** a small rotary beater, usually operated manually, for beating eggs, whipping cream, etc. **2.** *Slang.* a helicopter. [EGG[1] + BEATER]

egg′ co′zy, a little hood for keeping a boiled egg warm until it is eaten.

egg·crate (eg′krāt′), *n.* **1.** a compartmented box for packing and shipping eggs. **2.** a horizontal construction divided by vertical partitions into cell-like areas, used esp. for directing downward rays of overhead light.

egg·cup (eg′kup′), *n.* a small cup composed usually of two hollow, U-shaped bowls joined together at their bottoms, one for holding upright a soft-boiled egg that is to be eaten from the shell, the other, larger bowl for holding a soft-boiled egg broken into it. [EGG[1] + CUP]

egg′drop soup′ (eg′drop′), a soup made by stirring beaten eggs into a simmering broth. [EGG[1] + DROP]

egg·er (eg′ər), *n.* See **tent caterpillar.** [EGG[1] + -ER[1]; the cocoon is egg-shaped]

Egg′ Har′bor Cit′y, a town in SE New Jersey. 4416 (1960).

egg·head (eg′hed′), *n. Informal.* an intellectual. [EGG[1] (i.e. hairless) + HEAD]

Eg·gle·ston (eg′əl stən), *n.* **Edward,** 1837–1902, U.S. author, editor, and clergyman.

egg·nog (eg′nog′), *n.* a drink made of eggs, milk or cream, sugar, and, usually, wine or spirits. [EGG[1] + NOG[1]]

egg·plant (eg′plant′, -plänt′), *n.* **1.** a plant, *Solanum Melongena,* cultivated for its edible, dark-purple or occasionally white or yellow fruit. **2.** the fruit of this plant used as a table vegetable. [EGG[1] + PLANT]

egg′ roll′, (in Chinese and Chinese-American cuisine) a dish consisting of a cylindrical casing of egg dough filled with a minced mixture of roast pork, bamboo shoots, onions, etc., and fried in deep fat until light brown.

egg′ roll′ing, a contest or race using Easter eggs, usually held as a children's entertainment during the Easter season.

eggs′ Ben′edict, (*sometimes l.c.*) an egg dish consisting of toast or toasted halves of English muffin covered with a thin slice of fried or broiled ham, poached eggs, and a topping of hollandaise sauce.

egg-shaped (eg′shāpt′), *adj.* having an oval form, usually with one end larger than the other.

egg·shell (eg′shel′), *n.* **1.** the shell of a bird's egg, consisting of keratin fibers and calcite crystals. **2.** a pale yellow color. **3.** rather bulky paper having a slightly rough finish. —*adj.* **4.** like an eggshell, as in thinness and delicacy; very brittle. **5.** being pale yellow in color. **6.** having little or no gloss: *eggshell white paint.* [ME *ayschelle.* See EGG[1], SHELL]

egg′shell por′celain, thin, translucent porcelain.

egg′ stone′, oolite (def. 1).

egg′ tim′er, a small hourglass or clock device running about three to five minutes, used to time the boiling of an egg.

egg′ tooth′, a calcareous prominence at the tip of the beak or upper jaw of an embryonic bird or reptile, used to break through the eggshell at hatching.

egg′ white′, the white of an egg, esp. a hen's egg, used in cooking; albumen: *Separate the egg whites from the yolks and beat until they are stiff.*

egg′-white in′jury (eg′hwīt′, -wīt′), *Pathol.* a condition, usually induced in rats as an experiment, caused by the protein avidin that occurs in egg white and that when eaten in excessive amounts prevents the function of the vitamin biotin.

e·gis (ē′jis), *n.* aegis.

Egk (ek), *n.* **Wer·ner** (vɛʀ′nəʀ), born 1901, German composer and conductor.

eg·lan·tine (eg′lən tīn′, -tēn′), *n.* **1.** the sweetbrier. **2.** the Austrian briar, *Rosa foetida.* [ME < MF; OF *aiglent* (< VL **aculentum,* neut. of **aculentus* prickly, equiv. to L *acu(s)* needle + *-lentus* adj. suffix) + *-ine* -INE[1]]

Eg·lev·sky (i glef′skē, eg′lev skē), *n.* **An·dre** (än′drā, än dʀā′), 1917–77, U.S. ballet dancer, born in Russia.

é·glo·mi·sé (ā′glə mi zā′), *adj.* of or pertaining to a technique of decorating glass in which the back is painted or gilded so that the ornamental pattern can be seen from the front. Also, **e′glo·mi·se′.** [< F, ptp. of *églomiser,* equiv. to *é-* E- + *Glomy* (French artist of 18th century) + *-iser* -IZE]

EGmc, East Germanic.

Eg·mont (eg′mont), *n.* a drama (1788) by Goethe.

e·go (ē′gō, eg′ō), *n., pl.* **e·gos. 1.** the "I" or self of any person; a person as thinking, feeling, and willing, and distinguishing itself from the selves of others and from objects of its thought. **2.** (*often cap.*) *Philos.* **a.** the enduring and conscious element that knows experience. **b.** *Scholasticism.* the complete man comprising both body and soul. **3.** *Psychoanal.* the part of the psychic apparatus that experiences and reacts to the outside world and thus mediates between the primitive drives of the id and the demands of the social and physical environment. **4.** egotism, or self-importance: *Her ego becomes more unbearable each day.* **5.** self-esteem or self-image; feelings: *Your criticism injured her ego.* **6.** *Ethnol.* one who serves as the central reference point in the study of organizational and kinship relationships. [< L: I]

EGO, Eccentric Orbiting Geophysical Observatory.

e·go·cen·tric (ē′gō sen′trik, eg′ō-), *adj.* **1.** having or regarding the self as the center of all things, esp. as applied to the known world. **2.** having little or no regard for interests, beliefs, or attitudes other than one's own; self-centered: *an egocentric person; egocentric demands upon the time and patience of others.* —*n.* **3.** an egocentric person. [EGO + CENTRIC] —**e·go·cen·tric·i·ty** (ē′gō sen tris′i tē, eg′ō-), *n.* —**e′go·cen′trism,** *n.*

e′go ide′al, *Psychoanal.* a more or less conscious ideal of personal excellence toward which an individual strives, and which is derived from a composite image of the characteristics of persons, initially those of the parents, with whom the individual identifies himself.

e·go·ism (ē′gō iz′əm, eg′ō-), *n.* **1.** the habit of valuing everything only in reference to one's personal interest; selfishness (opposed to *altruism*). **2.** egotism or self-conceit. **3.** *Ethics.* the view that each person should regard his own welfare as the supreme end of his actions; materialism. [< NL *egōism(us).* See EGO, -ISM]
—**Syn. 1.** See **egotism.**

e·go·ist (ē′gō ist, eg′ō-), *n.* **1.** a self-centered or selfish person. **2.** an egotist; an arrogantly conceited person. **3.** *Obs.* an adherent of the metaphysical principle of the ego, or self; a solipsist. [< NL *egōist(a).* See EGO, -IST]

Egoist, The, a novel (1879) by George Meredith.

e·go·is·tic (ē′gō is′tik, eg′ō-), *adj.* **1.** pertaining to or of the nature of egoism. **2.** being centered in or preoccupied with oneself and the gratification of one's own desires; self-centered (opposed to *altruistic*). Also, **e′go·is′ti·cal.** [EGOIST + -IC] —**e′go·is′ti·cal·ly,** *adv.*

e·go·ma·ni·a (ē′gō mā′nē ə, -mān′yə, eg′ō-), *n.* psychologically abnormal egotism. [EGO + -MANIA; modeled on *monomania*] —**e′go·ma′ni·ac′,** *n.* —**e·go·ma·ni·a·cal** (ē′gō mə nī′i kəl), *adj.*

e·go·tism (ē′gə tiz′əm, eg′ə-), *n.* **1.** excessive and objectionable reference to oneself in conversation or writing; self-conceit; boastfulness. **2.** selfishness; egoism. [alter. of LL *idiotismus* common way of speaking, idiom (see IDIOTISM), with L *ego* r. *idio-*]
—**Syn. 1.** EGOTISM, EGOISM refer to preoccupation with one's ego or self. EGOTISM is the common word for obtrusive and excessive reference to and emphasis upon oneself and one's own importance, in conversation and writing, often to the extent of monopolizing attention and showing disregard for others' opinions: *His egotism alienated all his friends.* EGOISM, a less common word, is used especially in philosophy, ethics, or metaphysics, where it emphasizes the importance of self in relation to other things: *sufficient egoism to understand one's central place in the universe.* See **pride.** —**Ant. 1.** humility, altruism.

e·go·tist (ē′gə tist, eg′ə-), *n.* **1.** a conceited, boastful person. **2.** an egoist. [EGOT(ISM) + -IST]

e·go·tis·tic (ē′gə tis′tik, eg′ə-), *adj.* **1.** pertaining to or characterized by egotism. **2.** given to talking about oneself; vain; boastful; opinionated. **3.** indifferent to the well-being of others; selfish. Also, **e′go·tis′ti·cal.** [EGOTIST + -IC] —**e′go·tis′ti·cal·ly,** *adv.*

e·gre·gious (i grē′jəs, -jē əs), *adj.* **1.** remarkable or extraordinary in some bad way; glaring; flagrant: *an egregious mistake; an egregious liar.* **2.** *Archaic.* distinguished or eminent. [< L *ēgregius* preeminent, equiv. to *ē-* E- + *greg-* (s. of *grex*) flock + *-us* -OUS] —**e·gre′gious·ly,** *adv.* —**e·gre′gious·ness,** *n.*

e·gress (*n.* ē′gres; *v.* i gres′), *n.* **1.** the act or an instance of going, esp. from an enclosed place. **2.** a means or place of going out; an exit. **3.** the right or permission to go out. **4.** *Astron.* emersion (def. 1). —*v.i.* **5.** to go out; emerge. [< L *ēgress(us)* departure, equiv. to *ē-* E- + *gress-* (ptp. s. of *gradī* to step; see -GRADE) + *-us* n. suffix (4th decl.)]

e·gres·sion (i gresh′ən), *n.* a going out; egress. [< L *ēgressiōn-* (s. of *ēgressiō*) a going out, equiv. to *ē-* E- + *gress-* (see EGRESS) + *-iōn-* -ION]

Egret, *Casmerodius albus egretta* (Length 3½ ft.)

e·gret (ē′grit, eg′rit), *n.* **1.** any of several usually white herons that grow long, ornamental plumes during the breeding season, as *Egretta garzetta* **(little egret),** of the Old World. **2.** a plume of an egret; aigrette. —*adj.* **3.** made of or covered with egret plumes. [ME *egrete* < MF < OPr *aigreta,* equiv. to *aigr-* (< OHG *heiger* HERON) + *-eta* -ET]

E·gypt (ē′jipt), *n.* **1. Arab Republic of,** a republic in NE Africa. 40,500,000 (est. 1979); 386,198 sq. mi. *Cap.:* Cairo. **2.** a former kingdom in NE Africa: divided into the Nile Delta **(Lower Egypt)** and the area from Cairo S to the Sudan **(Upper Egypt).** —**E·gyp·ti·ac** (i jip′tē ak′), *adj.*

Egypt, Egyptian (def. 4). Also, **Egypt.**

E·gyp·tian (i jip′shən), *adj.* **1.** of or pertaining to Egypt or its people: *Egyptian architecture.* **2.** *Obs.* of or pertaining to the Gypsies. —*n.* **3.** a native or inhabitant of Egypt. **4.** the extinct, Afro-Asiatic language of the ancient Egyptians. *Abbr.:* Egypt **5.** a printing type having square serifs. **6.** *Obs.* a Gypsy. [ME (see EGYPT, -IAN); r. *Egiptish,* OE *Egiptisc,* equiv. to *Egipt-* + *-isc* -ISH[1]] —**E·gyp′tian·ism, E·gyp·tic·i·ty** (ē′jip-tis′i tē), *n.*

Egyp′tian cal′endar, the calendar of ancient Egypt, having a year consisting of twelve 30-day months, with five additional days at the end, leap year not being considered.

Egyp′tian clo′ver, berseem.

Egyp′tian co′bra, a highly venomous cobra, *Naja haje,* of Egypt, three or four feet long.

Egyp′tian cot′ton, a cotton, *Gossypium barbadense,* having long, silky, strong fibers, raised originally in Central and South America and now grown chiefly in Egypt and the southwestern U.S.

E·gyp·tian·ise (i jip′shə nīz′), *v.t., v.i.,* **-ised, -is·ing.** *Chiefly Brit.* Egyptianize. —**E·gyp′tian·i·sa′tion,** *n.*

E·gyp·tian·ize (i jip′shə nīz′), *v.,* **-ized, -iz·ing.** —*v.t.* **1.** to make Egyptian; assign Egyptian origin or characteristics to. —*v.i.* **2.** to become Egyptian; adopt Egyptian manners or characteristics. [EGYPTIAN + -IZE] —**E·gyp′tian·i·za′tion,** *n.*

Egyp′tian lo′tus, 1. either of two Egyptian wate lilies of the genus *Nymphaea,* as *N. caerulea* **(blue lotus)** having light blue flowers, or *N. Lotus* **(white lotus)** having white flowers. **2.** See **Indian lotus.**

E·gyp·tol·o·gy (ē′jip tol′ə jē), *n.* the scientific study of Egyptian antiquities. [EGYPT + -O- + -LOGY] —**E·gyp·to·log·i·cal** (i jip′tə loj′i kəl), *adj.* —**E′gyp·tol′o·gist,** *n.*

eh (ā, e), *interj.* (an interrogative utterance, usually expressing surprise or doubt or seeking confirmation): *Wasn't it lucky, eh? Eh? What did you say?*

EHF, See **extremely high frequency.**

EHFA, Electric Home and Farm Authority.

Eh·ren·breit·stein (ā′rən brīt′shtīn), *n.* a fortress in Coblenz, West Germany, built in the 12th century.

Eh·ren·burg (ā′rən bo͝orkh′), *n.* **Il·ya Gri·gor·ie·vich** (il yä′ gri gôr′yə vich), 1891–1967, Russian novelist and journalist.

Ehr·lich (âr′likh), *n.* **Paul** (poul), 1854–1915, German physician, bacteriologist, and chemist: Nobel prize for medicine 1908.

E.I., 1. East Indian. **2.** East Indies.

Eich·mann (īk′mən, ikh′-; *Ger.* ikh′män), *n.* **Adolf,** 1906–1962, German Nazi official: executed for war crimes.

Eich·stadt (īk′stät), *n.* a crater in the third quadrant of the face of the moon: about 32 miles in diameter.

ei·der (ī′dər), *n.* **1.** See **eider duck. 2.** eiderdown. [< ModIcel *æthar* (in 18th century spelled *ædar*), gen. sing. of *æthur* eider duck, in phrase *ædar dūnn* down of the eider duck; spelling *eider* < G or Sw]

ei·der·down (ī′dər doun′), *n.* **1.** down, or soft feathers, from the breast of the female eider duck. **2.** a heavy quilt or comforter, esp. one filled with eiderdown. **3.** *U.S.* a fabric of cotton with wool nap. —*adj.* **4.** filled with down, or feathers of the breast of the female eider duck. [EIDER + DOWN[2]]

Eider duck, *Somateria mollissima* (Length 2 ft.)

ei′der duck′, any of several large sea ducks of the genus *Somateria* and allied genera of the Northern Hemisphere, the females of which yield eiderdown.

ei·det·ic (ī det′ik), *adj.* of, pertaining to, or constituting visual imagery retained in the memory and readily reproducible with great accuracy and in great detail. [< Gk *eidētik(ós),* equiv. to *eid(os)* EIDOS + *-ētikos* -ETIC]

ei·do·lon (ī dō′lən), *n., pl.* **-la** (-lə), **-lons.** a phantom; apparition; image. [see IDOL]

ei·dos (ī′dos, ā′-), *n., pl.* **ei·de** (ī′dē, ā′dā). the formal content of a culture, encompassing its system of ideas, criteria for interpreting experience, etc. [< Gk *eidos* something seen, form; akin to Gk *idein,* L *vidēre* to see]

Eif·fel (ī′fəl; *Fr.* e fel′), *n.* **A·le·xan·dre Gus·tave** (A lek sän′dr[a] gys tav′), 1832–1923, French civil engineer and pioneer aerodynamic researcher.

Eif′fel Tow′er, a tower of skeletal iron construction in Paris, France: built for the exposition of 1889. 984 feet high. [named after A. E. EIFFEL, its designer]

ei·gen·func·tion (ī′gən fungk′shən), *n. Math.* a characteristic vector in a vector space in which the elements are functions. Also called **proper function.** [< G *Eigenfunktion,* equiv. to *eigen-* characteristic, particular + *Funktion* FUNCTION]

ei·gen·val·ue (ī′gən val′yo͞o), *n. Math.* See **characteristic root.** [< G *Eigenwert,* equiv. to *eigen-* characteristic, particular + *Wert* VALUE]

ei·gen·vec·tor (ī′gən vek′tər), *n. Math.* See **characteristic vector.** [part. trans. of G *Eigenvektor*]

eight (āt), *n.* **1.** a cardinal number, seven plus one. **2.** a symbol for this number, as 8 or VIII. **3.** a set of this many persons or things, as the crew of an eight-oared racing shell. **4.** a playing card the face of which bears eight pips. —*adj.* **5.** amounting to eight in number. [ME *eighte,* OE *eahta;* c. D, G *acht,* Icel *ātta,* Goth *ahtau,* L *octō,* Gk *oktṓ*]

eight·ball (āt′bôl′), *n.* **1.** *Pool.* **a.** a black ball bearing the number eight. **b.** a game in which one player or side must pocket all of either the solid-color balls or the striped ones before being permitted to attempt the pocketing of the eightball, which wins. **2.** *Slang.* an inept person. **3.** *Electronics Informal.* a knoblike, dynamic, nondirectional microphone at the end of a handle. **4. behind the eightball,** *Slang.* in a disadvantageous or uncomfortable situation: *He didn't study all term and now that it's time for the final exam he's behind the eightball.* [EIGHT + BALL[1]]

eight′ cut′, *Jewelry.* See **single cut.**

eight·een (ā′tēn′), *n.* **1.** a cardinal number, ten plus eight. **2.** a symbol for this number, as 18 or XVIII. **3.** a set of this many persons or things. —*adj.* **4.** amounting to 18 in number. [ME *ehtetene,* OE *eahtatēne;* c. Icel *āttjān,* G *achtzehn.* See EIGHT, -TEEN]

eight·een·mo (ā′tēn′mō), *n., pl.* **-mos,** *adj. Bookbinding.* octodecimo. [EIGHTEEN + -MO]

eight·eenth (ā′tēnth′), *adj.* **1.** next after the seventeenth; being the ordinal number for 18. **2.** being one of 18 equal parts. —*n.* **3.** an eighteenth part, esp. of one (1/18). **4.** the eighteenth member of a series. [ME *eightenthe, eightethe,* OE *eahtatēotha.* See EIGHTEEN + -TH[2]]

eight·fold (āt′fōld′), *adj.* **1.** comprising eight parts or members. **2.** eight times as great or as much. —*adv.* **3.** in eightfold measure. [EIGHT + -FOLD]

Eight′fold Path′, *Buddhism.* the eight activities to be pursued by one seeking enlightenment, including right understanding, motives, speech, action, means of livelihood, effort, intellectual activity, and contemplation.

eighth (ātth), *adj.* **1.** next after the seventh. **2.** being one of eight equal parts. —*n.* **3.** an eighth part, esp. of one (1/8). **4.** the eighth member of a series. **5.** *Music.* octave. [ME *eighthe,* OE *eahtotha;* c. OHG *ahtoda,* Icel *āttandi,* Goth *ahtud-.* See EIGHT, -TH[2]] —**eighth′ly,** *adv.*

eighth′ note′, *Music.* a note having 1/8 of the time value of a whole note; a quaver. See illus. under **note.**

eight·i·eth (ā′tē ith), *adj.* **1.** next after the seventy-ninth; being the ordinal number for 80. **2.** being one of 80 equal parts. —*n.* **3.** an eightieth part, esp. of one (1/80). **4.** the eightieth member of a series. [ME *eightetithe,* OE (*hund*)*eahtatigotha* eightieth. See EIGHTY, -TH[2]]

eight·pen·ny (āt′pen′ē), *adj.* **1.** noting a nail 2½ inches long. *Abbr.:* 8d **2.** costing or amounting to the sum of eight pennies. [EIGHT + -PENNY]

eight-spot (āt′spot′), *n. Slang.* a playing card the face of which bears eight pips.

eight-track (āt′trak′), *n.* a magnetic-tape cartridge, esp. one carrying eight parallel tracks of prerecorded sound or music. Also, **8′-track′.**

eight·y (ā′tē), *n., pl.* **eight·ies,** *adj.* —*n.* **1.** a cardinal number, ten times eight. **2.** a symbol for this number, as 80 or LXXX. **3.** a set of this many persons or things. **4. eighties,** the numbers 80 through 89, esp. the 80th through the 89th years of a lifetime or of a given or implied century. —*adj.* **5.** amounting to 80 in number. [ME *eighteti,* OE *eahtatig.* See EIGHT, -TY[1]]

eight·y-eight (ā′tē āt′), *n.* **1.** a cardinal number, 80 plus 8. **2.** a symbol for this number, as 88 or LXXXVIII. **3.** a set of this many persons or things. —*adj.* **4.** amounting to 88 in number.

eight·y-eighth (ā′tē ātth′), *adj.* **1.** next after the eighty-seventh; being the ordinal number for 88. **2.** being one of 88 equal parts. —*n.* **3.** an eighty-eighth part, esp. of one (1/88). **4.** the eighty-eighth member of a series.

eight·y-fifth (ā′tē fifth′), *adj.* **1.** next after the eighty-fourth; being the ordinal number for 85. **2.** being one of 85 equal parts. —*n.* **3.** an eighty-fifth part, esp. of one (1/85). **4.** the eighty-fifth member of a series.

eight·y-first (ā′tē fûrst′), *adj.* **1.** next after the eightieth; being the ordinal number for 81. **2.** being one of 81 equal parts. —*n.* **3.** an eighty-first part, esp. of one (1/81). **4.** the eighty-first member of a series.

eight·y-five (ā′tē fīv′), *n.* **1.** a cardinal number, 80 plus 5. **2.** a symbol for this number, as 85 or LXXXV. **3.** a set of this many persons or things. —*adj.* **4.** amounting to 85 in number.

eight·y-four (ā′tē fōr′, -fôr′), *n.* **1.** a cardinal number, 80 plus 4. **2.** a symbol for this number, as 84 or LXXXIV. **3.** a set of this many persons or things. —*adj.* **4.** amounting to 84 in number.

eight·y-fourth (ā′tē fōrth′, -fôrth′), *adj.* **1.** next after the eighty-third; being the ordinal number for 84. **2.** being one of 84 equal parts. —*n.* **3.** an eighty-fourth part, esp. of one (1/84). **4.** the eighty-fourth member of a series.

eight·y-nine (ā′tē nīn′), *n.* **1.** a cardinal number, 80 plus 9. **2.** a symbol for this number, as 89 or LXXXIX. **3.** a set of this many persons or things. —*adj.* **4.** amounting to 89 in number.

eight·y-nin·er (ā′tē nī′nər), *n.* a person who began homesteading in Oklahoma in 1889.

eight·y-ninth (ā′tē nīnth′), *adj.* **1.** next after the eighty-eighth; being the ordinal number for 89. **2.** being one of 89 equal parts. —*n.* **3.** an eighty-ninth part, esp. of one (1/89). **4.** the eighty-ninth member of a series.

eight·y-one (ā′tē wun′), *n.* **1.** a cardinal number, 80 plus 1. **2.** a symbol for this number, as 81 or LXXXI. **3.** a set of this many persons or things. —*adj.* **4.** amounting to 81 in number.

eight·y-sec·ond (ā′tē sek′ənd), *adj.* **1.** next after the eighty-first; being the ordinal number for 82. **2.** being one of 82 equal parts. —*n.* **3.** an eighty-second part, esp. of one (1/82). **4.** the eighty-second member of a series.

eight·y-sev·en (ā′tē sev′ən), *n.* **1.** a cardinal number, 80 plus 7. **2.** a symbol for this number, as 87 or LXXXVII. **3.** a set of this many persons or things. —*adj.* **4.** amounting to 87 in number.

eight·y-sev·enth (ā′tē sev′ənth), *adj.* **1.** next after the eighty-sixth; being the ordinal number for 87. **2.** being one of 87 equal parts. —*n.* **3.** an eighty-seventh part, esp. of one (1/87). **4.** the eighty-seventh member of a series.

eight·y-six (ā′tē siks′), *n.* **1.** a cardinal number, 80 plus 6. **2.** a symbol for this number, as 86 or LXXXVI. **3.** a set of this many persons or things. —*adj.* **4.** amounting to 86 in number.

eight·y-sixth (ā′tē siksth′), *adj.* **1.** next after the eighty-fifth; being the ordinal number for 86. **2.** being one of 86 equal parts. —*n.* **3.** an eighty-sixth part, esp. of one (1/86). **4.** the eighty-sixth member of a series.

eight·y-third (ā′tē thûrd′), *adj.* **1.** next after the eighty-second; being the ordinal number for 83. **2.** being one of 83 equal parts. —*n.* **3.** an eighty-third part, esp. of one (1/83). **4.** the eighty-third member of a series.

eight·y-three (ā′tē thrē′), *n.* **1.** a cardinal number, 80 plus 3. **2.** a symbol for this number, as 83 or LXXXIII. **3.** a set of this many persons or things. —*adj.* **4.** amounting to 83 in number.

eight·y-two (ā′tē to͞o′), *n.* **1.** a cardinal number, 80 plus 2. **2.** a symbol for this number, as 82 or LXXXII. **3.** a set of this many persons or things. —*adj.* **4.** amounting to 82 in number.

Eijk·man (īk′män), *n.* **Chris·ti·aan** (krɪs′tē än′), 1858–1930, Dutch physician: Nobel prize 1929.

ei·kon (ī′kon), *n.* icon (defs. 1, 2).

eild (ēld), *adj. Scot.* **1.** Also, **yeld,** (of a cow) not giving milk, from being in calf or from age. —*n.* **2.** eld (defs. 1, 2).

Ei·leen (ī lēn′, ā lēn′), *n.* a girl's given name, form of **Helen.** Also, **Aileen, Alene.**

Ei·lei·thy·ia (ī′lī thī′yə), *n.* the ancient Greek goddess of childbirth, identified by the Romans with Lucina. Also, **Ilithyia.**

Eil·she·mi·us (il shē′mē əs), *n.* **Louis Mi·chel** (mī′kəl), 1864–1941, U.S. painter.

Eim·mart (ī′märt), *n.* a walled plain in the first quadrant of the face of the moon: about 25 miles in diameter.

Ei·nar (ī′nər, ī′när), *n.* a boy's given name.

E. Ind., East Indian.

Eind·ho·ven (īnt′hō′vən), *n.* a city in the S Netherlands. 174,612 (1962).

ein·kan·ter (īn′kän tər), *n.* a pebble or boulder having a single facet formed by the action of windblown sand. [< G, equiv. to *ein* one + *Kante* edge + *-er* -ER[1]]

ein·korn (īn′kôrn), *n.* a wheat, *Triticum monococcum,* having a one-grained spikelet, grown as a forage crop in Europe and Asia. [< G, equiv. to *ein* one + *Korn* grain]

Ein·stein (īn′stīn; *Ger.* īn′shtīn′), *n.* **1. Al·bert** (al′bərt; *Ger.* äl′bert), 1879–1955, German physicist, U.S. citizen from 1940: formulator of the theory of relativity; Nobel prize 1921. **2. Al·fred** (al′frid; *Ger.* äl′fret), 1880–1952, German musicologist in U.S. **3.** (*l.c.*) *Physics, Chem.* a unit of radiant energy, equal to the energy of radiation that is capable of photochemically changing one mol of a photosensitive substance. **4.** a crater in the fourth quadrant of the face of the moon: about 28 miles in diameter.

Ein′stein equa′tion, *Physics.* any of several equations formulated by Albert Einstein, esp. the mass-energy equation.

Ein·stein·i·an (īn stī′nē ən), *adj.* pertaining to Albert Einstein or his theories, esp. the theory of relativity. [EINSTEIN + -IAN]

ein·stein·i·um (īn stī′nē əm), *n. Chem.* a synthetic, radioactive, metallic element. *Symbol:* Es; *at. no.:* 99. [named after Albert EINSTEIN; -IUM]

Ein′stein shift′, *Physics, Astron.* the shift toward longer wavelengths in the spectra of electromagnetic radiation subjected to a strong gravitational force by the body emitting the radiation, as light emitted by the sun or by a star having a high density. Cf. **red shift.** [named after Albert EINSTEIN]

Ein′stein's photoelec′tric equa′tion, *Physics.* the equation that the energy of a photoelectron is equal to the difference of the product of the frequency of the incident radiation times Planck's constant minus the energy needed to remove the photoelectron from the substance. [named after Albert EINSTEIN]

Ein′stein the′ory, *Physics.* relativity (def. 2). Also called **Ein′stein's the′ory of relativ′ity.**

Eint·ho·ven (īnt′hō′vən), *n.* **Wil·lem** (wil′əm), 1860–1927, Dutch physiologist: Nobel prize for medicine 1924.

E·io·ne·us (ī yō′nē əs), *n. Class. Myth.* **1.** the father of Dia. **2.** the father of Rhesus.

Eir·e (âr′ə, ī′rə), *n.* former name of the Republic of Ireland.

eis·e·ge·sis (ī′si jē′sis), *n., pl.* **-ses** (-sēz). an interpretation, esp. of Scripture, that expresses the interpreter's own ideas, bias, or the like, rather than the meaning of the text. [< Gk *eisḗgesis,* equiv. to *eis-* into + (*h*)*ēge-* (s. of *hēgeîsthai* to lead) + *-sis* -SIS] —**ei·se·get·ic** (ī′si jet′ik), **ei′se·get′i·cal,** *adj.*

Ei·sen·ach (ī′zə näkh′), *n.* a city in SW East Germany. 50,038 (est. 1955).

Ei·sen·how·er (ī′zən hou′ər), *n.* **Dwight David,** 1890–1969, U.S. general and statesman: Chief of Staff 1945–48; 34th president of the U.S. 1953–61.

Ei′senhower jack′et. See **battle jacket.**

Ei·sen·stein (ī′zən stīn′; *for 1 also Ger.* ī′zən shtīn′; *for 2 also Russ.* ī zen shtān′), *n.* **1. Fer·di·nand Gott·hold Max** (fer′di nänt′ gôt′hôlt mäks), 1823–52, German mathematician. **2. Ser·gei Mi·khai·lo·vich** (ser gā′ mi khī′lo vich), 1898–1948, Russian theatrical and motion-picture director.

Ei′sen·stein's irreducibil′ity crite′rion, *Math.* a method for determining the irreducibility of a given polynomial, based on the divisibility of the coefficients by a prime number. [named after F.G.M. EISENSTEIN]

Eisk (āsk), *n.* Yeisk.

eis·tedd·fod (ā steth′vod, ī steth′-), *n., pl.* **eis·tedd·fods, eis·tedd·fod·au** (ā′steth vod′ī, ī′steth-). a congress of Welsh bards and minstrels. [< Welsh: lit., session, equiv. to *eistedd* sit(ting) + *fod,* var. (by lenition) of *bod* be(ing)] —**eis′tedd·fod′ic,** *adj.*

ei·ther (ē′thər, ī′thər), *adj.* **1.** one or the other of two: *You may sit at either end of the table.* **2.** each of two; the one and the other: *There are trees on either side of the river.* —*pron.* **3.** one or the other: *There are two roads into the town, and you can take either. Either will do.* —*conj.* **4.** (a coordinating conjunction that, when preceding a word or statement followed by the disjunctive *or,* serves to emphasize the possibility of choice): *Either come or write.* —*adv.* **5.** also; too; as well; to the same degree (used after negative clauses coordinated by *and, or,* or *nor,* or after negative subordinate clauses): *He is not fond of parties, and I am not either. If you do not come, he will not come either.* [ME; OE *ǣgther,* contr. of *ǣghwæther* each of two, both]

—**Usage.** The pronoun EITHER is commonly followed by a singular verb: *Either is good enough.*

e·jac·u·late (*v.* i jak′yə lāt′; *n.* i jak′yə lit), *v.,* **-lat·ed, -lat·ing,** *n.* —*v.t.* **1.** to utter suddenly and briefly; exclaim. **2.** to eject suddenly and swiftly; discharge. **3.** to eject (semen). —*v.i.* **4.** to eject semen. —*n.* **5.** the semen emitted in an ejaculation. [< L *ējaculāt(us)* (ptp. of *ējaculārī*) shot out, equiv. to *ē-* E- + *jacul(um)* javelin (*jac(ere)* (to) throw + *-ulum* -ULE) + *-ātus* -ATE[1]]

e·jac·u·la·tion (i jak′yə lā′shən), *n.* **1.** an abrupt, exclamatory utterance. **2.** the act or process of ejaculating, esp. the discharge of semen by the male reproductive organs. [EJACULATE + -ION]

e·jac·u·la·tor (i jak′yə lā′tər), *n.* **1.** one who or that which ejaculates. **2.** *Stockbreeding.* a device used to obtain semen from a male animal by electrical stimulation of the reproductive organs. [EJACULATE + -OR[2]]

e·jac·u·la·to·ry (i jak′yə lə tōr′ē, -tôr′ē), *adj.* **1.** pertaining to or of the nature of an ejaculation or exclamatory utterance. **2.** *Physiol.* pertaining to ejaculation. Also, **e·jac·u·la·tive** (i jak′yə lā′tiv, -lə tiv). [EJACULATE + -ORY[1]]

e·ject (i jekt′), *v.t.* **1.** to drive or force out; expel, as from a place or position: *The police ejected the hecklers from the meeting.* **2.** to dismiss, as from office, occupancy, etc. **3.** to evict, as from property. **4.** to throw out, as from within; throw off. [< L *ēject(us)* (ptp. of *ēicere*) thrown out, equiv. to *ē-* E- + *jec-* (var. s. of *jacere*) throw + *-tus* ptp. suffix]

—**Syn. 1–3.** oust.

e·jec·ta (i jek′tə), *n.pl.* matter ejected, as from a volcano in eruption. [neut. pl. of L *ējectus.* See EJECT]

e·jec·tion (i jek′shən), *n.* **1.** the act or an instance of ejecting. **2.** the state of being ejected. **3.** something ejected, as lava. [< L *ējectiōn-* (s. of *ējectiō*) a throwing out, equiv. to *eject-* (see EJECT) + *-iōn-* -ION]

ejec′tion cap′sule, a cockpit designed to be ejected from an aircraft in an emergency and usually fitted with survival equipment.

ejec′tion seat′, an airplane seat that can be ejected with the pilot in an emergency. Also called **ejector seat.**

e·jec·tive (i jek′tiv), *adj.* **1.** serving to eject. **2.** *Phonet.* (of a voiceless stop, affricate, or fricative) produced with air compressed above the closed glottis. —*n.* **3.** *Phonet.* an ejective stop, affricate, or fricative. [EJECT + -IVE] —**e·jec′tive·ly,** *adv.*

e·ject·ment (i jekt′mənt), *n.* **1.** the act of ejecting. **2.** *Law.* a possessory action wherein the title to real property may be tried and the possession recovered. [EJECT + -MENT]

e·jec·tor (i jek′tər), *n.* **1.** one who or that which ejects. **2.** (in a firearm or gun) the mechanism that after firing throws out the empty cartridge or shell. **3.** Also called **eductor.** a device for inducing a flow of a fluid from a chamber or vessel by using the pressure of a jet of water, air, steam, etc., to create a partial vacuum in such a way as to entrain the fluid to be removed. **4.** any of various devices for removing work from a machine or die. [EJECT + -OR[2]]

ejec′tor seat′. See **ejection seat.**

e·ji·do (e hē′thō), *n., pl.* **-dos** (-thōs). (in Mexico) a communal farm operated by the inhabitants of a village on an individual or cooperative basis. [< Sp < L *exitus* a going out (4th decl.), n. use of ptp. of *exīre,* equiv. to *ex-* EX-[1] + *-i-* go + *-tus* ptp. suffix]

ejusd., (in prescriptions) of the same. [< L *ējusdem*]

E·ka·te·rin·burg (*Russ.* e kä′te rēn bo͝orkh′), *n.* former name of **Sverdlovsk.**

E·ka·te·ri·no·dar (*Russ.* e kä′te rē′no där′), *n.* former name of **Krasnodar.**

E·ka·te·ri·no·slav (*Russ.* e kä′te rē′no släf′), *n.* former name of **Dnepropetrovsk.**

eke[1] (ēk), *v.t.,* **eked, ek·ing. 1.** *Archaic.* to increase; enlarge; lengthen. **2. eke out, a.** to supply by some expedient what is lacking in; supplement: *to eke out one's knowledge of a subject from encyclopedia articles.* **b.** to make (a living) or support (existence) laboriously: *They managed to eke out a living by farming a small piece of land.* [ME *eke(n),* OE *ēac(i)an* (v.i.), deriv. of *ēaca* (n.) increase; ME *echen,* OE *ēcan,* var. of *īecan* (v.t.) < WGmc **aukjan;* both akin to Icel *auka,* Goth *aukan,* L *augēre,* Gk *auxánein* to increase, amplify]

eke[2] (ēk), *adv. Archaic.* also. [ME *eek,* OE *ēc, ēac;* c. G *auch,* Icel, Goth *auk*]

EKG, electrocardiogram. Also, **E.K.G.** [< G *E(lectro)-k(ardio)g(ramme)*]

ek·te·ne (ek′tə nē′, ek′tə nē′), *n. Eastern Ch.* synapte. Also, **ectene.** [< MGk *ektenḗ,* Gk *ektenḗs* extended, assiduous, abundant, deriv. of *ektéinein* to stretch out, prolong (*ek-* EC- + *teínein* to stretch)]

el[1] (el), *n.* See **elevated railroad.** [by shortening]

el[2] (el), *n.* ell[1].

e·lab·o·rate (*adj.* i lab′ər it; *v.* i lab′ə rāt′), *adj., v.,* **-rat·ed, -rat·ing.** —*adj.* **1.** worked out with great care and nicety of detail; executed with great minuteness: *elaborate preparations; elaborate care.* **2.** marked by intricate and often excessive detail; complicated. —*v.t.* **3.** to work out carefully or minutely; develop to perfection. **4.** to produce or develop by labor. **5.** *Physiol.* to convert (food, plasma, etc.) by means of chemical processes into a substance more suitable for use within the body. —*v.i.* **6.** to add details in writing, speaking, etc.; give additional or fuller treatment (usually fol. by *on* or *upon*): *to elaborate upon a theme or an idea.* [< L *ēlabōrāt(us)* (ptp. of *ēlabōrāre*) worked out, equiv. to *ē-* E- + *labōr-* work + *-ātus* -ATE[1]] —**e·lab′o·rate·ly,** *adv.* —**e·lab′o·rate·ness,** *n.* —**e·lab′o·ra′tive,** *adj.* —**e·lab′o·ra′tor,** *n.*

—**Syn. 1.** perfected, painstaking. **2.** ornate, intricate. ELABORATE, LABORED, STUDIED apply to that which is worked out in great detail. That which is ELABORATE is characterized by great, sometimes even excessive, nicety or minuteness of detail: *elaborate preparations for a banquet; an elaborate apology.* That which is LABORED is marked by excessive, often forced or uninspired, effort: *a labored explanation, style of writing.* That which is STUDIED is accomplished with care and deliberation, and is done purposely, sometimes even having been rehearsed: *a studied pose.* **3, 6.** refine, improve. —**Ant. 1.** simple.

e·lab·o·ra·tion (i lab′ə rā′shən), *n.* **1.** the act or an instance of elaborating. **2.** the state of being elaborated; elaborateness. **3.** something that is elaborated. [< L *ēlabōrātiōn-* (s. of *ēlabōrātiō*), equiv. to *ēlabōrāt-* (see ELABORATE) + *-iōn-* -ION]

e·lab·o·ra·tive (i lab′ə rā′tiv, -ər ə tiv), *adj.* able to elaborate; serving or tending to elaborate: *the mind conceived of as the elaborative faculty.* [ELABORATE + -IVE] —**e·lab′o·ra′tive·ly,** *adv.*

el·ae·op·tene (el′ē op′tēn), *n. Chem.* eleoptene.

el·ae·o·the·si·um (el′ē ō thē′shē əm, -sē əm, ē′lē-), *n., pl.* **-si·a** (-shē ə, -sē ə). [< Gk *elaiothésion* oiling-room, equiv. to *élaio(n)* oil + *-thesion* suffix indicating place (deriv. of *thésis* placing, setting; see THESIS)]

El·a·gab·a·lus (el′ə gab′ə ləs, ē′lə-), *n.* Heliogabalus.

E·laine (i lān′), *n.* **1.** any of several women in Arthurian romance, as the daughter of King Pelles and the mother, by Lancelot, of Sir Galahad. **2.** Also, **Alaine, Alayne, Elena.** a girl's given name, form of **Helen.**

E·la·ïs (ē′lā is), *n. Class. Myth.* a daughter of Anius and Dorippe who had the power to change anything she touched into oil.

El A·la·mein (el ä′lä mān′, -lə-), a town on the N coast of the United Arab Republic, ab. 70 mi. W of Alexandria: decisive British victory October, 1942. Also called **Alamein.**

E·lam (ē′ləm), *n.* **1.** Also called **Susiana.** an ancient kingdom E of Babylonia and N of the Persian Gulf. *Cap.:* Susa. **2.** a boy's given name.

E·lam·ite (ē′lə mīt′), *n.* **1.** a native or inhabitant of ancient Elam. **2.** Also, **Elamitic.** a language of unknown affinities, spoken by the Elamites as late as the 1st century B.C., written c3500–c2500 B.C. in a linear script and thereafter in a cuneiform script. —*adj.* **3.** of or pertaining to Elam, its people, or their language. [ELAM + -ITE^1]

E·lam·it·ic (ē′lə mit′ik), *n.* **1.** Elamite (def. 2). —*adj.* **2.** Elamite. [ELAMITE + -IC]

é·lan (ā län′, ā lan′; *Fr.* ā län′), *n.* dash; impetuous ardor: *a pas de deux performed with great élan.* [< MF *eslan* a dash, rush, appar. back formation from *eslancer* to dart, equiv. to *es-* EX-^{1} + *lancer* to LANCE^1]

é·lan·cé (ā län′sā; *Fr.* ā län sā′), *n., pl.* **-cés** (-sāz; *Fr.* -sā′). *Ballet.* a quick, darting movement. [< F, n. use of ptp. of *élancer* to dart. See ÉLAN]

e·land (ē′lənd), *n., pl.* **e·lands,** (*esp. collectively*) **e·land.** either of two large, African antelopes of the genus *Taurotragus,* having long spirally twisted horns. [< SAfrD, special use of D *eland* elk < obs. G *Elen(d),* prob. < Lith *élnis;* akin to ELK]

Eland, *Taurotragus oryx* (5½ ft. high at shoulder; horns to 3½ ft.; length to 11 ft.)

é·lan vi·tal (*Fr.* ā län vē tal′), (esp. in Bergsonian philosophy) the creative force within an organism that is able to build physical form and to produce growth and necessary or desirable adaptations. [< F: lit., vital ardor]

El·a·phe·bo·li·a (el′ə fē bō′lē ə), *n.* (*sometimes construed as pl.*) an ancient Greek festival held annually in honor of Artemis as goddess of game and hunting. [< Gk: festival of Artemis, neut. pl. of *elaphēbolia* (fem. sing.) a shooting of deer]

el·a·pid (el′ə pid), *n.* **1.** any of numerous cosmopolitan snakes of the family *Elapidae,* having permanently erect fangs in the front of the upper jaw and including the New World coral snakes, the cobras, and most Australian snakes. —*adj.* **2.** belonging or pertaining to the *Elapidae.* [< NL *Elapid(ae),* equiv. to *Elap-* (s. of *Elaps* name of genus << Gk *éllops* a sea-fish) + *-idae* -ID^2]

e·lapse (i laps′), *v.* **-lapsed, -laps·ing,** *n.* —*v.i.* **1.** (of time) to slip by or pass away: *Thirty minutes elapsed before the performance began.* —*n.* **2.** the passage or termination of a period of time; lapse. [< L *ēlaps(us)* (ptp. of *ēlābī* to slip away), equiv. to *e-* E- + *lab-* slip + *-tus* ptp. suffix]

E·la·ra (ē′lər ə), *n. Class. Myth.* the mother of Tityus.

E.L.A.S., Hellenic People's Army of Liberation, the military organization of the EAM: Greek resistance force in World War II. [< Mod Gk *E(thnikos) L(aikos) A(pelephtherotikos) S(tratos)*]

e·las·mo·branch (i las′mə brangk′, i laz′-), *adj.* **1.** belonging or pertaining to the *Elasmobranchii,* the group of cartilaginous fishes comprising the sharks and rays. —*n.* **2.** an elasmobranch fish. [< NL *elasmobranch(ii)* < Gk *elasmó(s)* plate metal + *bránchia* (neut. pl.) gills]

e·las·tance (i las′təns), *n. Elect.* the reciprocal of capacitance. [ELAST(IC) + -ANCE]

e·las·tic (i las′tik), *adj.* **1.** capable of returning to its original length, shape, etc., after being stretched, deformed, or expanded: *an elastic waistband; elastic fiber.* **2.** spontaneously expansive, as gases. **3.** flexible; accommodating; tolerant: *an elastic conscience.* **4.** springing back or rebounding; springy: *He walks with an elastic step.* **5.** readily recovering from depression or exhaustion; buoyant: *an elastic temperament.* **6.** *Econ.* relatively responsive to change, as to a proportionate increase in demand as the result of a decrease in price. Cf. **inelastic** (def. 2). **7.** *Physics.* of, pertaining to, or noting a body having the property of elasticity. —*n.* **8.** webbing, or material in the form of a band, made elastic with strips of rubber. **9.** something made from this material, as a garter. **10.** See **rubber band.** [< NL *elastic(us)* expansive < Gk *elastikós,* equiv. to *elast(ós)* beaten (*elas-,* var. s. of *elaúnein* to beat, + *-tos* ptp. suffix) + *-ikos* -IC] —**e·las′ti·cal·ly,** *adv.*
—**Syn. 3, 4.** resilient.

elas′tic cur′rency, currency that varies in volume in proportion to business activity. Also called **elas′tic mon′ey.**

elas′tic deforma′tion, *Physics.* the temporary change in length, volume, or shape produced in an elastic substance by a stress that is less than the elastic limit of the substance.

e·las·tic·i·ty (i la stis′i tē, ē′la stis′-), *n.* **1.** the state or quality of being elastic. **2.** flexibility; resilience: *a statement that has an elasticity of meaning.* **3.** buoyancy; ability to resist or overcome depression. **4.** *Physics.* the property of a substance that enables it to change its length, volume, or shape in direct response to a force effecting such a change and to recover its original form upon the removal of the force. [ELASTIC + -ITY]

e·las·ti·cize (i las′ti sīz′), *v.t.,* **-cized, -ciz·ing.** to make elastic, as by furnishing with elastic bands: *to elasticize the waistband of a dress.* [ELASTIC + -IZE]

elas′tic lim′it, *Physics.* the greatest stress that can be applied to an elastic body without causing its permanent deformation. Also called **limit of proportionality, proportional limit.**

elas′tic mod′ulus, *Physics.* See **modulus of elasticity.**

elas′tic tis′sue, *Anat.* connective tissue consisting chiefly of yellow, elastic fibers and composing certain ligaments and the walls of the arteries.

elas′tic wave′, *Physics.* a wave propagated by the elastic deformation of a medium.

e·las·tin (i las′tin), *n. Biochem.* a protein constituting the basic substance of elastic tissue. [ELAST(IC) + -IN^2]

e·las·to·mer (i las′tə mər), *n. Chem.* an elastic substance occurring naturally, as natural rubber, or produced synthetically, as butyl rubber or neoprene. [ELAST(IC) + -O- + Gk *mér(os)* a part] —**e·las·to·mer·ic** (i las′tə mer′ik), *adj.*

e·late (i lāt′), *v.,* **e·lat·ed, e·lat·ing,** *adj.* —*v.t.* **1.** to make very happy or proud; cause to be in high spirits: *The news that he was safe elated his parents.* —*adj.* **2.** *Chiefly Literary.* elated. [< L *ēlāt(us)* carried away, lifted up (ptp. of *efferre*), equiv. to *ē-* E- + *lā-* carry, lift (cf. OE *-lō* pulley, strap) + *-tus* ptp. suffix]

e·lat·ed (i lā′tid), *adj.* very happy or proud; jubilant; in high spirits: *an elated winner of a contest.* [ELATE + -ED^2] —**e·lat′ed·ly,** *adv.*
—**e·lat′ed·ness,** *n.*

el·a·ter (el′ə tər), *n.* **1.** *Bot.* an elastic filament serving to disperse spores. **2.** *Zool.* elaterid. **3.** *Obs.* elasticity. [< NL < Gk *elatḗr* driver, equiv. to *ela-* (s. of *elaúnein* to drive; see ELASTIC) + *-tēr* n. suffix]

e·lat·er·id (i lat′ər id), *n.* **1.** any beetle of the family *Elateridae,* comprising the click beetles. —*adj.* **2.** belonging or pertaining to the family *Elateridae.* [ELATER + -ID^2]

e·lat·er·in (i lat′ər in), *n. Chem., Pharm.* a white, crystalline substance obtained from and constituting the active principle of elaterium, used chiefly in medicine as a cathartic. [ELATER + -IN^2]

e·lat·er·ite (i lat′ə rīt′), *n.* an elastic, rubbery, brownish natural asphalt. [ELATER + -ITE^1]

el·a·te·ri·um (el′ə tēr′ē əm), *n. Pharm.* a grayish-green, bitter solid obtained from the juice of *Ecballium elaterium,* the squirting cucumber, and used as a cathartic. [< L < Gk *elatḗrion* squirting cucumber, neut. of *elatḗrios* purgative, equiv. to *elatḗr* (see ELATER) + *-ios* adj. suffix]

e·la·tion (i lā′shən), *n.* a feeling or state of great joy or pride; exultant gladness; high spirits. [< L *ēlātiōn-* (s. of *ēlātiō*), equiv. to *ēlāt(us)* (see ELATE) + *-iōn-* -ION; r. ME *elacioun* < AF]

e·la·tive (ē′lə tiv, el′ə-), *Gram.* —*adj.* **1.** noting a case, as in Finnish, whose function is to indicate motion out of or away from. —*n.* **2.** an elative case. **3.** (in Arabic grammar) an adjectival form denoting intensity or superiority, approximately equivalent to the comparative and superlative of other languages. [< L *ēlāt(us)* (see ELATE) + -IVE]

E·la·tus (ē′lə təs), *n. Class. Myth.* a son of Arcas.

E layer, the radio-reflective ionospheric layer of maximum electron density normally found at an altitude between 100 and 120 kilometers. Also called **Heaviside layer, Kennelly-Heaviside layer.**

el·a·yl (el′ā il), *n.* ethylene (def. 2). [E(THY)L + A(LCOHOL) + -YL]

E·la·zig (e lä zi′), *n.* a city in central Turkey. 41,915 (1955).

El·ba (el′bə), *n.* **1.** an Italian island in the Mediterranean, between Corsica and Italy: the scene of Napoleon's first exile 1814–15. 29,462 (1951); 94 sq. mi. **2.** a town in SE Alabama. 4321 (1960).

El·be (*Ger.* el′bə; *Eng.* elb), *n.* a river in central Europe, flowing from the W Czech Republic NW through Germany to the North Sea. 725 mi. long. Czech, **Labe.**

El·ber·feld (el′bər felt′), *n.* a former city in W West Germany, now incorporated into Wuppertal.

El·bert (el′bərt), *n.* **1. Mount,** a mountain in central Colorado, in the Sawatch range: second highest peak of the Rocky Mountains in the U.S. 14,431 ft. **2.** Also, **Albert.** a boy's given name.

El·ber·ta (el bûr′tə), *n.* **1.** a freestone peach having reddish-yellow skin. **2.** the tree bearing this fruit. **3.** a girl's given name.

El·ber·ton (el′bər tᵊn, -tən), *n.* a town in NE Georgia. 7107 (1960).

El·bie (el′bē), *n.* a boy's given name, form of **Elbert.**

El·bląg (el′blông), *n.* a seaport in N Poland: formerly in Germany. 82,000 (est. 1963). Also, **El·bing** (el′bing).

el·bow (el′bō), *n.* **1.** the bend or joint of the human arm between upper arm and forearm. **2.** the joint at the upper end of the forearm of a quadruped. See diag. under **horse.** **3.** something bent like an elbow, as a sharp turn in a road or river, or a piece of pipe bent at an angle. **4.** *Archit.* crossette (def. 1). **5.** Also called **ell.** a plumbing pipe or pipe connection having a right-angled bend. **6. at one's elbow,** within easy reach; nearby: *A virtue of the cottage is that the ocean is at your elbow.* **7. bend, lift,** or **crook an elbow,** *Slang.* to drink alcoholic beverages, esp. to excess: *He bends an elbow every night at the saloon.* **8. out at the elbows, a.** poorly dressed; shabby. **b.** impoverished. Also, **out at elbows.** **9. rub elbows with,** to mingle socially with; associate with: *a resort where royalty rubs elbows with the common folk.* **10. up to one's elbows,** very busy; engrossed: *I am up to my elbows in answering mail.* Also, **up to the elbows.** —*v.t.* **11.** to push with or as if with the elbow; jostle. **12.** to make (one's way) by so pushing. —*v.i.* **13.** to elbow one's way: *He elbowed through the crowd.* [ME *elbowe,* OE *el(n)boga;* c. G *Ellenbogen,* Icel *ölnbogi.* See ELL^2, BOW^1]

el′bow board′, **1.** a board or strip of millwork forming a window stool. **2.** a board or strip of millwork attached to a partition as an arm rest. Also called **el′bow rail′.**

el′bow catch′, an L-shaped catch, as for a door, having a piece for the thumb on one arm and a hooked end for engaging a hooked plate on the other.

el′bow cop′, *Armor.* couter.

el′bow grease′, *Informal.* strenuous physical exertion, as in manual labor: *Cleaning up this kitchen will take a lot of elbow grease.*

el·bow·room (el′bō ro͞om′, -ro͝om′), *n.* ample room; space in which to move freely. [ELBOW + ROOM]

El·brus (el′bro͞os), *n.* a mountain in the S Soviet Union in Europe, in the Caucasus range: the highest peak in Europe, 18,465 ft. Also, **El′bruz.**

El·burz′ Moun′tains (el bo͝orz′), a mountain range in N Iran, along the S coast of the Caspian Sea. Highest peak, Mt. Demavend, 18,606 ft.

El Ca·jon (el′ kə hōn′), a city in SW California. 37,618 (1960).

El Cam·po (el kam′pō), a town in S Texas. 7700 (1960).

El Cap·i·tan (el kap′i tan′), a mountain in E California, in the Sierra Neveda Mountains: precipice which rises over 3300 ft. above Yosemite Valley.

El Cen·tro (el sen′trō), a city in S California. 16,811 (1960).

El Cer·ri·to (el′ sə rē′tō), a city in W California, on San Francisco Bay. 25,437 (1960).

El·che (el′che), *n.* a city in E Spain. 67,088 (1955).

El Cid Cam·pe·a·dor (*Sp.* el thēd′ käm′pe ä thôr′, sēd′). See **Cid, The.**

eld (eld), *n. Archaic.* **1.** age. **2.** old age. **3.** antiquity. [ME *elde,* OE *eldo, ieldo,* deriv. of *(e)ald* OLD; see WORLD]

El·da (el′də), *n.* a girl's given name. Also, **Alda.**

El·den (el′dᵊn), *n.* a boy's given name.

eld·er^1 (el′dər), *adj.* *a compar. of* **old** *with* **eldest** *as superl.* **1.** of greater age; older. **2.** of higher rank; senior: *an elder officer.* **3.** of or pertaining to former times; earlier: *Much that was forbidden by elder custom is accepted today.* —*n.* **4.** a person who is older or higher in rank than oneself. **5.** an aged person. **6.** one of the older and more influential men of a tribe or community, often a chief or ruler. **7.** a presbyter. **8.** (in certain Protestant churches) a layman who is a governing officer, often assisting the pastor in services. **9.** *Mormon Ch.* a member of the Melchizedek priesthood. [ME; OE *eldra,* comp. of *eald* OLD]
—**Syn. 1.** See **older.** —**Ant. 1.** younger.

el·der^2 (el′dər), *n.* any caprifoliaceous tree or shrub of the genus *Sambucus,* having clusters of white flowers and red or black, berrylike fruit. [ME *eldre, elrene, ellerne,* OE *ellærn;* c. MLG *ellern*]

El·der (el′dər), *n.* a boy's given name.

el·der·ber·ry (el′dər ber′ē, -bə rē), *n., pl.* **-ries.** **1.** the drupaceous fruit of the elder, used in making wine and jelly. **2.** elder^2. [ME *eldreberie.* See ELDER^2, BERRY]

Eld′er Ed′da. See under **Edda.**

eld′er hand. See **eldest hand.**

eld·er·ly (el′dər lē), *adj.* **1.** somewhat old; between middle and old age: *a resort for elderly people.* **2.** of or pertaining to persons in later life. [ELDER^1 + -LY] —**eld′er·li·ness,** *n.*
—**Syn. 1.** See **old.**

eld′er states′man, **1.** an influential elderly citizen, often a retired statesman, whose advice is sought by government leaders. **2.** any influential member of a company, group, etc., whose advice is deeply respected. **3.** *Japanese Hist.* any of the political leaders who retired from official office but continued to exert a strong influence in the government and who controlled the emperor's privy council, esp. in the period 1898–1914.

eld·est (el′dist), *adj.* *a super. of* **old** *with* **elder** *as compar.* oldest; first-born; of greatest age: *eldest brother; eldest sister; eldest born.* [OE *eldesta,* superl. of *(e)ald* OLD]

eld′est hand′, *Cards.* the player on the dealer's left. Also, **elder hand.** Also called **age, edge.** Cf. **pone^2** (def. 1).

el·ding (el′ding), *n. Brit. Dial.* fuel for a fire, esp. wood or peat. [ME < Scand; cf. Icel *elding* act of heating, equiv. to *eld(r)* fire + *-ing* -ING^1; akin to OE *ǣled* fire (brand). See ANNEAL]

El·do (el′dō), *n.* a boy's given name.

El·don (el′dən), *n.* a town in central Missouri. 3158 (1960).

El·do·ra (el dōr′ə, -dôr′ə), *n.* **1.** a town in central Iowa. 3225 (1960). **2.** a girl's given name.

El Do·ra·do (el′ də rä′dō, -rā′- *or, Sp.,* el dō rä′thō *for 1, 2;* el′ də rā′dō *for 3*), **1.** a legendary treasure city of South America, sought by the early Spanish explorers. **2.** any fabulously wealthy place. **3.** a city in S Arkansas. 25,292 (1960).

El·do·ra·do (el′də rā′dō), *n.* a town in SE Illinois. 3573 (1960).

El′dorado Springs′, a town in W Missouri. 2864 (1960).

El·dred (el′drid), *n.* a boy's given name.

El·dridge (el′drij), *n.* a boy's given name. Also, **Elldridge.**

el·dritch (el′drich), *adj.* eerie; weird; spooky. Also, **el′drich, elritch.** [earlier *elrich,* equiv. to OE *el-* foreign, strange, uncanny + *-rīc* creature (as in *gāsrīc*); cf. *ǣlwiht* alien creature]

E·le·a (ē′lē ə), *n.* an ancient Greek city in SW Italy, on the coast of Lucania.

El·ea·nor (el′ə nər, -nôr′), *n.* a girl's given name, form of **Helen.** Also, **El·e·a·nor·a** (el′ē ə nôr′ə), **Elenor, Elenore, Eleonora, Eleonore, Elinor.**

El′eanor of Aq′uitaine, 1122?–1204, queen of Louis VII of France 1137–52; queen of Henry II of England.

El·e·at·ic (el′ē at′ik), *adj.* **1.** of or pertaining to Elea. **2.** noting or pertaining to a school of philosophy, founded by Parmenides, that investigated the phenomenal world, especially with reference to the phenomena of change. —*n.* 3. a philosopher of the Eleatic school. [< L *Eleātic(us)* < Gk *Eleātikós.* See Elea, -tic] —**El/e·at/i·cism,** *n.*

El·e·a·zar (el/ē ā/zər), *n.* a son of Aaron and his successor in the priesthood. Num. 20:28.

el·e·cam·pane (el/ə kam pān/), *n.* a composite plant, *Inula Helenium*, having large yellow flowers and aromatic leaves and root. [ME; OE *ele(ne)*, *eolone* (metathetic alter. of ML *enula*, L *inula* elecampane) + ME *campane* < ML *campāna*, equiv. to *camp(us)* field + *-āna*, fem. of *-ānus* -ane, -an]

e·lect (i lekt/), *v.t.* 1. to select by vote, as for an office: *to elect a mayor.* 2. to determine in favor of (a method, course of action, etc.). 3. to pick out; choose: *First-year students may elect French, Spanish, or German.* 4. *Theol.* (of God) to select for divine mercy or favor, esp. for salvation. —*v.i.* 5. to choose or select someone or something, as by voting. —*adj.* 6. selected for an office, but not yet inducted (usually used in combination following a noun): *the governor-elect.* 7. picked out; chosen. 8. select or choice. 9. *Theol.* chosen by God, esp. for eternal life. —*n.* **the elect,** 10. a person or the persons chosen or worthy to be chosen. 11. *Theol.* a person or persons chosen by God, esp. for eternal life. [< L *ēlect(us)* chosen (ptp. of *ēligere*), equiv. to *ē-* e- + *leg-* choose + *-tus* ptp. suffix; see elite] —**Syn.** 3. See **choose.** —**Ant.** 1, 2. reject.

elect., 1. electric. 2. electrical. 3. electricity. 4. (in prescriptions) electuary. Also, **elec.** [< L *electuārium*]

e·lec·tion (i lek/shən), *n.* 1. the selection of a person or persons for office by vote. 2. a public vote upon a proposition submitted. 3. the act of electing. 4. *Theol.* the choice by God of individuals, as for a particular work, or esp. for salvation or eternal life. [< L *ēlectiōn-* (s. of *ēlectiō*), equiv. to *ēlect(us)* (see elect) + *-iōn-* -ion; r. ME *eleccioun* < AF] —**Syn.** 3. choice.

elec/tion board/. See **board of elections.**

Elec/tion Day/, 1. *U.S.* the first Tuesday after the first Monday in November on which national elections are held for electors of the President and Vice-President in those years evenly divisible by four. On even years constituents elect members of the House of Representatives for two-year terms and one third of the Senate for six-year terms. 2. (*often l.c.*) any day designated for the election of public officials.

elec/tion dis/trict, precinct (def. 2).

e·lec·tion·eer (i lek/shə nēr/), *v.i.* to work for the success of a candidate, party, ticket, etc., in an election. [election + -eer] —**e·lec/tion·eer/er,** *n.*

e·lec·tive (i lek/tiv), *adj.* 1. pertaining to the principle of electing to an office, position, etc. 2. appointed by election, as an official. 3. bestowed by or derived from election, as an office. 4. having the power or right of electing to office, as a body of persons. 5. open to choice; optional; not required: *an elective subject in college.* 6. *Chem.* selecting for combination or action; tending to combine with certain substances in preference to others: *elective attraction.* —*n.* 7. an optional study; a course that a student may select from among alternatives. [< ML *ēlectīv(us)*, equiv. to L *ēlect(us)* (see elect) + *-īvus* -ive] —**e·lec/tive·ly,** *adv.* —**e·lec/tive·ness,** *n.*

e·lec·tor (i lek/tər), *n.* 1. a person who elects or may elect, esp. a qualified voter. 2. *U.S.* a member of the electoral college. 3. (*usually cap.*) one of the German princes entitled to elect the emperor of the Holy Roman Empire. [late ME *electo(u)r* < L *ēlector*, equiv. to *ēlect(us)* (see elect) + *-or* -or[2]]

e·lec·tor·al (i lek/tər əl), *adj.* 1. pertaining to electors or election. 2. consisting of electors. [elector + -al[1]] —**e·lec/tor·al·ly,** *adv.*

elec/toral col/lege, *U.S.* a body of electors chosen by the voters in each State to elect the President and Vice-President.

elec/toral vote/, *U.S.* the vote cast, usually as a formality, by the electoral college to reflect the popular vote of each State in a presidential election.

e·lec·tor·ate (i lek/tər it), *n.* 1. the body of persons entitled to vote in an election. 2. the dignity or territory of an Elector of the Holy Roman Empire. [elector + -ate[3]]

electr-, var. of **electro-** before a vowel: *electrode.*

E·lec·tra (i lek/trə), *n.* 1. *Class. Myth.* the daughter of Agamemnon and Clytemnestra who incited her brother Orestes to kill Clytemnestra and her lover Aegisthus. 2. (*italics*) a tragedy (418?–410? b.c.) by Sophocles. 3. (*italics*) a tragedy (413 b.c.) by Euripides. 4. a town in N Texas. 4759 (1960). 5. a girl's given name.

Elec/tra com/plex, *Psychoanal.* the unresolved desire of a daughter for sexual gratification from her father.

e·lec·tress (i lek/tris), *n.* 1. a female elector. 2. (*usually cap.*) the wife or widow of an Elector of the Holy Roman Empire. [elect(o)r + -ess]

e·lec·tret (i lek/trit), *n.* *Elect.* a dielectric that possesses a permanent or semipermanent electric polarity, analogous to a permanent magnet. [electr(icity + magn)et]

e·lec·tric (i lek/trik), *adj.* 1. pertaining to, derived from, produced by, or involving electricity: *an electric current; an electric shock.* 2. producing, transmitting, or operated by electric currents: *an electric bell.* 3. electrifying; thrilling; exciting; stirring: *The atmosphere was electric with excitement.* —*n.* 4. *Railroads.* a. an electric locomotive. b. *Slang.* a railroad operated by electricity. 5. a truck or the like operated by electricity from storage batteries. 6. *Elect. Archaic.* a substance that is a nonconductor of electricity, as glass or amber, used to store or to excite an electric charge. [< NL *electric(us)*, equiv. to L *ēlectr(um)* amber (< Gk *ēlektron*) + *-icus* -ic]

e·lec·tri·cal (i lek/tri kəl), *adj.* 1. electric. 2. concerned with electricity: *an electrical consultant.* [electric + -al[1]] —**e·lec/tri·cal·ly,** *adv.* —**e·lec/tri·cal·ness,** *n.*

elec/trical degree/, *Elect.* one 360th of a cycle of alternating current.

elec/trical engineer/, a person trained in electrical engineering.

elec/trical engineer/ing, the branch of engineering that deals with the practical application of the theory of electricity to the construction of machinery, power supplies, etc.

elec/trical scan/ning, 1. *Electronics.* a technique for varying the sector covered by a transmitting or receiving antenna by electrical means without moving the antenna. 2. Also called **electronic scanning.** *Television.* the technique used in scanning a surface to reproduce or transmit a picture.

elec/trical storm/, thunderstorm. Also, **electric storm.**

elec/trical transcrip/tion, 1. a radio broadcast from a phonograph record. 2. the phonograph record itself.

elec/tric arc/, arc (def. 2).

elec/tric chair/, 1. an electrified chair used to execute criminals. 2. the penalty of legal electrocution: *The jury felt that he should get the electric chair for the murder.*

elec/tric charge/, *Physics.* charge (def. 40a).

elec/tric cur/rent, *Elect.* current (def. 13).

elec/tric di/pole mo/ment, *Elect.* a vector quantity associated with two equal charges of opposite sign separated by a specified distance, having magnitude equal to the product of the charge and the distance between the charges and having direction from the negative to the positive charge along the line between the charges.

elec/tric eel/, an eellike, fresh-water fish, *Electrophorus electricus*, found in the Amazon and Orinoco rivers and tributaries, sometimes over six feet in length, capable of emitting strong electric discharges.

elec/tric eye/, 1. See **photoelectric cell** (def. 1). 2. See **electron-ray tube.**

elec/tric field/, *Physics.* a condition of space in the vicinity of an electric charge, manifesting itself as a force on an electric charge within that space.

elec/tric fur/nace, a furnace in which the heat required is produced through electricity.

elec/tric glow/, *Elect.* See **corona discharge.**

elec/tric guitar/, a guitar with an electrical attachment on the bridge that transmits the sound through an amplifier to a loudspeaker.

e·lec·tri·cian (i lek trish/ən, ē/lek-), *n.* a person who installs, operates, maintains, or repairs electric devices or electrical wiring. [irreg. electr(icity) + -ician]

elec/tric inten/sity, *Physics.* the magnitude of an electric field at a point in the field, equal to the force that would be exerted on a small unit charge placed at the point. Also called **elec/tric field/ inten/sity, elec/tric field/ strength/.**

e·lec·tric·i·ty (i lek tris/i tē, ē/lek-), *n.* 1. a fundamental physical agency formerly thought to be caused by a kind of fluid but now understood to be caused by the presence and motion of electrons, protons, and other charged particles, manifesting itself as attraction, repulsion, luminous and heating effects, and the like. 2. the science dealing with this agency. 3. electric current: *to install electricity; a machine run by electricity.* 4. a state or feeling of excitement, anticipation, tension, etc. [electric + -ity]

elec/tric nee/dle, *Surg.* an acusector.

elec/tric or/gan, 1. a pipe organ with an action controlled by electrical impulses. 2. (in certain fishes) an organ composed of electroplaques.

elec/tric ray/, any ray of the family *Torpedinidae*, capable of emitting strong electric discharges.

elec/tric reac/tor, reactor (def. 2).

elec/tric storm/. See **electrical storm.**

elec/tric thermom/eter, *Elect.* any of several devices that use electricity for measuring temperature.

elec/tric torch/, *Brit.* torch (def. 4).

elec/tric wave/. See **electromagnetic wave.**

elec/tric wind/ (wind). See **convective discharge.**

E·lec·tri·des (i lek/tri dēz/), *n.pl.* *Class. Myth.* the Amber Islands.

e·lec·tri·fy (i lek/trə fī/), *v.t.*, **-fied, -fy·ing.** 1. to charge with or subject to electricity; apply electricity to. 2. to equip for the use of electric power, as a railroad. 3. to startle greatly; excite or thrill: *to electrify an audience.* [electr- + -ify] —**e·lec/tri·fi·ca/tion,** *n.* —**e·lec/tri·fi/er,** *n.*

e·lec·tro (i lek/trō), *n.*, *pl.* **-tros.** electrotype. [by shortening]

electro-, a combining form of **electric** or **electricity:** *electromagnetic.* Also, *esp. before a vowel,* **electr-.** [< Gk *elektro-*, comb. form of *ēlektron* amber]

e·lec·tro·a·cous·tic (i lek/trō ə kōō/stik), *adj.* of or pertaining to electroacoustics. Also, **e·lec/tro·a·cous/ti·cal.** [electro- + acoustic] —**e·lec/tro·a·cous/ti·cal·ly,** *adv.*

e·lec·tro·a·cous·tics (i lek/trō ə kōō/stiks), *n.* (*construed as sing.*) the branch of electronics that deals with the conversion of electricity into acoustical energy and vice versa. [electro- + acoustics]

e·lec·tro·a·nal·y·sis (i lek/trō ə nal/i sis), *n.* analysis by electrochemical methods. [electro- + analysis] —**e·lec·tro·an·a·lyt·ic** (i lek/trō an/əlit/ik), **e·lec/tro·an/a·lyt/i·cal,** *adj.*

e·lec·tro·bal·lis·tics (i lek/trō bə lis/tiks), *n.* (*construed as sing.*) the measurement of the velocities of projectiles by means of electronic devices. [electro- + ballistics] —**e·lec/tro·bal·lis/tic,** *adj.* —**e·lec/tro·bal·lis/ti·cal·ly,** *adv.* —**e·lec·tro·bal·lis·ti·cian** (i lek/trō bal/i stish/ən), *n.*

e·lec·tro·bi·ol·o·gy (i lek/trō bī ol/ə jē), *n.* the branch of biology dealing with electric phenomena in plants and animals. [electro- + biology] —**e·lec·tro·bi·o·log·i·cal** (i lek/trō bī/ə loj/i kəl), *adj.* —**e·lec/tro·bi/o·log/i·cal·ly,** *adv.* —**e·lec/tro·bi·ol/o·gist,** *n.*

e·lec/tro·ca·lor/ic effect/ (i lek/trō kə lôr/ik), *Thermodynamics.* the temperature change accompanying a change in the electric intensity of a thermally isolated system. [electro- + caloric]

e·lec·tro·car·di·o·gram (i lek/trō kär/dē ə gram/), *n.* the graphic record produced by an electrocardiograph. Also called **EKG, E.K.G., ECG, E.C.G., cardiogram.** [electro- + cardiogram]

e·lec·tro·car·di·o·graph (i lek/trō kär/dē ə graf/, -gräf/), *n.* a galvanometric device that detects and records the minute differences in potential caused by heart action and occurring between different parts of the body: used in the diagnosis of heart disease. Also called **cardiograph.** [electro- + cardiograph] —**e·lec·tro·car·di·o·graph·ic** (i lek/trō kär/dē ə graf/ik), *adj.* —**e·lec/tro·car/di·o·graph/i·cal·ly,** *adv.* —**e·lec·tro·car·di·og·ra·phy** (i lek/trō kär/dē og/rə fē), *n.*

e·lec·tro·cau·ter·y (i lek/trō kô/tə rē), *n.*, *pl.* **-ter·ies.** *Med.* 1. a cautery heated by an electric current. 2. Also, **e·lec/tro·cau/ter·i·za/tion.** the process of cauterizing by means of an electrocautery. [electro- + cautery]

e·lec·tro·chem·is·try (i lek/trō kem/i strē), *n.* the branch of chemistry that deals with the chemical changes produced by electricity and the production of electricity by chemical changes. [electro- + chemistry] —**e·lec·tro·chem·i·cal** (i lek/trō kem/i kəl), *adj.* —**e·lec/tro·chem/i·cal·ly,** *adv.* —**e·lec/tro·chem/ist,** *n.*

e·lec·tro·co·ag·u·la·tion (i lek/trō kō ag/yə lā/shən), *n.* *Med., Surg.* the hardening or coagulation of a tumor or other diseased tissue by means of diathermy. [electro- + coagulation]

e·lec·tro·crat·ic (i lek/trə krat/ik), *adj.* *Physical Chem.* noting a colloid owing its stability to the electric charge of the particles on its surface. Cf. **lyocratic.** [electro- + -crat + -ic]

e·lec·tro·cute (i lek/trə kyōōt/), *v.t.*, **-cut·ed; -cut·ing.** 1. to kill by electricity. 2. to execute (a criminal) by electricity, as in an electric chair. [electro- + (exe)cute] —**e·lec/tro·cu/tion,** *n.*

e·lec·trode (i lek/trōd), *n.* *Elect.* a conductor, not necessarily metallic, through which a current enters or leaves a conductor of the nonmetallic class, as an electrolytic cell, arc generator, vacuum tube, gaseous discharge tube, etc. [electr- + -ode[2]]

e·lec·tro·de·pos·it (i lek/trō di poz/it), *Physical Chem.* —*n.* 1. a deposit, usually of metal, produced by electrolysis. —*v.t.* 2. to deposit by electrolysis. [electro- + deposit] —**e·lec·tro·dep·o·si·tion** (i lek/trō-dep/ə zish/ən, -dē/pə-), *n.*

e·lec·tro·di·ag·no·sis (i lek/trō dī/əg nō/sis), *n.*, *pl.* **-ses** (-sēz). *Med.* diagnosis by the observation of the changes in electric irritability that occur as a result of a disease, as recorded by an electroencephalogram or the like. [electro- + diagnosis] —**e·lec·tro·di·ag·nos·tic** (i lek/trō dī/əg nos/tik), *adj.* —**e·lec/tro·di/ag·nos/ti·cal·ly,** *adv.*

e·lec·tro·di·al·y·sis (i lek/trō dī al/i sis), *n.*, *pl.* **-ses** (-sēz/). *Physical Chem.* dialysis in which electrodes of opposite charge are placed on either side of a membrane to accelerate diffusion. [electro- + dialysis] —**e·lec·tro·di·a·lit·ic** (i lek/trō dī/ə lit/ik), *adj.* —**e·lec/tro·di/a·lit/i·cal·ly,** *adv.*

elec/tro·dis/charge machin/ing (i lek/trō dis/chärj), a technique for shaping the surfaces of a metal object by immersing in a dielectric liquid the object and a tool which emits an electric discharge of high current density and short duration.

e·lec·tro·dis·so·lu·tion (i lek/trō dis/ə lōō/shən), *n.* *Elect.* the dissolving of a substance from an electrode by electrolysis. [electro- + dissolution]

e·lec·tro·dy·nam·ic (i lek/trō dī nam/ik), *adj.* 1. pertaining to the force of electricity in motion. 2. pertaining to electrodynamics. Also, **e·lec/tro·dy·nam/i·cal.** [electro- + dynamic]

e·lec·tro·dy·nam·ics (i lek/trō dī nam/iks), *n.* (*construed as sing.*) the branch of physics that deals with the interactions of electric, magnetic, and mechanical phenomena. [electro- + dynamics]

e·lec·tro·dy·nom·e·ter (i lek/trō dī/nə mom/i-tər), *n.* an instrument that uses the interactions between the magnetic fields produced by the currents in two coils or sets of coils to measure current, voltage, or power. [electro- + dynometer]

e·lec·tro·en·ceph·a·lo·gram (i lek/trō en sef/ə lə-gram/), *n.* a graphic record produced by an electroencephalograph. Also called **EEG, E.E.G.** [electro- + encephalogram]

e·lec·tro·en·ceph·a·lo·graph (i lek/trō en sef/ə lə-graf/, -gräf/), *n.* *Med.* an instrument for measuring and recording the electric activity of the brain. [electro- + encephalograph] —**e·lec·tro·en·ceph·a·lo·graph·ic** (i lek/trō en sef/ə lə graf/ik), **e·lec/tro·en·ceph/a·lo·graph/i·cal,** *adj.* —**e·lec/tro·en·ceph/a·lo·graph/i·cal·ly,** *adv.* —**e·lec·tro·en·ceph·a·log·ra·phy** (i lek/trō en sef/ə log/rə fē), *n.*

e·lec·tro·ex·trac·tion (i lek/trō ik strak/shən), *n.* the recovery of metal from metallic salts by means of electrolysis. Also called **electrowinning.** [electro- + extraction]

e·lec·tro·form (i lek/trə fôrm/), *v.t.* to form (an object) by the electrodeposition of a metal upon a mold, often a wax mold. [electro- + form]

e·lec·tro·form·ing (i lek/trō fôr/ming), *n.* the act or process of forming a metallic object by electroplating a removable mandrel or matrix. [electro- + forming]

e·lec·tro·graph (i lek/trə graf/, -gräf/), *n.* 1. a curve or plot automatically traced by the action of an electric device, as an electrometer or an electrically-controlled pen. 2. an apparatus for engraving metal plates on cylinders used in printing. 3. an apparatus for electrically transmitting pictures. 4. a picture produced by such a device. [electro- + -graph] —**e·lec·tro·graph·ic** (i lek/trō graf/ik), *adj.* —**e·lec·trog·ra·phy** (i lek trog/rə fē, ē/lek-), *n.*

e·lec·tro·he·mo·sta·sis (i lek/trō hi mos/tə sis, -hē/mə stā/sis, -hem/ə-), *n.* *Med.* hemostasis by means of an electric device, as an electrocautery. [electro- + hemostasis]

e·lec·tro·jet (i lek/trə jet/), *n.* a current of ions existing in the upper atmosphere, moving with respect to the surface of the earth, and causing various auroral phenomena. [electro- + jet[1]]

e·lec·tro·ki·net·ics (i lek/trō ki net/iks, -kī-), *n.* (*construed as sing.*) the branch of physics that deals with electricity in motion. [electro- + kinetics] —**e·lec/tro·ki·net/ic,** *adj.*

e·lec·tro·less plat/ing (i lek/trō lis), a technique of plating metal by chemical rather than electrical means, in which the piece to be plated is immersed in a reducing agent which, when catalyzed by certain materials, changes metal ions to metal which forms a deposit on the piece. [electro- + -less]

e·lec·tro·lier (i lek/trə lēr/), *n.* a chandelier for electric lamps. [electro- + (chande)lier]

e·lec·trol·o·gist (i lek trol′ə jist), *n.* a person skilled in the use of electrolysis for removing moles, warts, or excess hair. [ELECTRO(LYSIS) + -LOG(Y) + -IST]

e·lec·tro·lu·mi·nes·cence (i lek′trō lo͞o′mə nes′əns), *n.* luminescence produced by the activation of a dielectric phosphor by an alternating current. [ELECTRO- + LUMINESCENCE] —**e·lec′tro·lu′mi·nes′cent,** *adj.*

e·lec·tro·lyse (i lek′trə līz′), *v.t.*, **-lysed, -lys·ing.** *Chiefly Brit.* electrolyze. —**e·lec′tro·ly·sa′tion,** *n.* —**e·lec′tro·lys′er,** *n.*

e·lec·trol·y·sis (i lek trol′i sis, ē′lek-), *n.* **1.** the passage of an electric current through an electrolyte with subsequent migration of positively and negatively charged ions to the negative and positive electrodes. **2.** the destruction of tumors, hair roots, etc., by an electric current. [ELECTRO- + -LYSIS]

e·lec·tro·lyte (i lek′trə līt′), *n.* **1.** Also called **electrolytic conductor.** a conducting medium in which the flow of current is accompanied by the movement of matter in the form of ions. **2.** *Physical Chem.* any substance that dissociates into ions when dissolved in a suitable medium or melted and thus forms a conducto of electricity. [ELECTRO- + -LYTE]

e·lec·tro·lyt·ic (i lek′trə lit′ik), *adj.* **1.** pertaining to or derived by electrolysis. **2.** pertaining to an electrolyte. Also, **e·lec′tro·lyt′i·cal.** [ELECTRO- + -LYTIC] —**e·lec′tro·lyt′i·cal·ly,** *adv.*

elec′trolyt′ic cell′. See under **cell** (def. 8).

elec′trolyt′ic conduc′tor, *Elect.* electrolyte (def. 1).

electrolyt′ic dissocia′tion, *Physical Chem.* the separation of the molecule of an electrolyte into its constituent atoms.

electrolyt′ic interrupt′er, *Elect.* a current interrupter consisting of a cell with two electrodes which is immersed in an electrolyte such that the passage of current through the cell causes bubbles to form in the electrolyte, the bubbles breaking the circuit.

electrolyt′ic machin′ing, removal of metal from a piece by electrolysis.

electrolyt′ic protec′tion. See **cathodic protection.**

e·lec·tro·lyze (i lek′trə līz′), *v.t.*, **-lyzed, -lyz·ing.** *Physical Chem.* to decompose by electrolysis. Also, *esp. Brit.*, **electrolyse.** [ELECTRO- + -LYZE] —**e·lec′tro·ly·za′tion,** *n.* —**e·lec′tro·lyz′er,** *n.*

e·lec·tro·mag·net (i lek′trō mag′nit), *n.* a device consisting of an iron or steel core that is magnetized by electric current in a coil which surrounds it. [ELECTRO- + MAGNET]

e·lec·tro·mag·net·ic (i lek′trō mag net′ik), *adj.* **1.** of or pertaining to an electromagnet. **2.** pertaining to electromagnetism. [ELECTRO- + MAGNETIC]

elec′tromagnet′ic induc′tion, *Elect.* the induction of an electromotive force by the motion of a conductor across a magnetic field or by a change in magnetic flux in a magnetic field.

Electromagnet A, DC power source or battery; B, Core; C, Coil carrying current; D, Armature; E, Load

electromagnet′ic radia′tion, *Physics.* radiation consisting of electromagnetic waves, including radio waves, light, x-ray, and gamma rays.

e·lec·tro·mag·net·ics (i lek′trō mag net′iks), *n.* (*construed as sing.*) electromagnetism (def. 2). [ELECTROMAGNET + -ICS]

elec′tromagnet′ic spec′trum, the entire spectrum, considered as a continuum, of all kinds of electric and magnetic radiation, from gamma rays having a wavelength of .001 angstrom to long waves having a wavelength of more than 1,000,000 kilometers and including the visible spectrum.

elec′tromagnet′ic tape′. See **magnetic tape.**

elec′tromagnet′ic u′nit, a unit, as an abampere, in the system of units derived from the magnetic effects of an electric current. *Abbr.:* emu, EMU

elec′tromagnet′ic wave′, *Physics.* a wave produced by the acceleration of an electric charge and propagated by the periodic variation of intensities of, usually, perpendicular electric and magnetic fields. Also called **electric wave.**

e·lec·tro·mag·net·ism (i lek′trō mag′ni tiz′əm), *n.* **1.** the phenomena associated with the relations between electric current and magnetism. **2.** Also, **electromagnetics.** the science that deals with these phenomena. [ELECTROMAGNET + -ISM] —**e·lec′tro·mag′ne·tist,** *n.*

e·lec·tro·me·chan·i·cal (i lek′trō mə kan′i kəl), *adj.* of or pertaining to mechanical devices or systems electrically actuated, as by a solenoid. [ELECTRO- + MECHANICAL]

e·lec·tro·met·al·lur·gy (i lek′trō met′ᵊlûr′jē, -mə tal′ər jē), *n.* the branch of metallurgy dealing with the processing of metals by means of electricity. [ELECTRO- + METALLURGY] —**e·lec′tro·met′al·lur′gi·cal,** *adj.* —**e·lec′tro·met′al·lur′gist,** *n.*

e·lec·tro·me·te·or (i lek′trō mē′tē ər), *n.* any visible or audible manifestation of atmospheric electricity, as lightning or thunder. [ELECTRO- + METEOR]

e·lec·trom·e·ter (i lek trom′i tər, ē′lek-), *n.* a calibrated device for determining a potential difference by measuring the electrostatic force between two charged bodies with the given potential difference. [ELECTRO- + -METER] —**e·lec·tro·met·ric** (i lek′trə me′trik), **e·lec′tro·met′ri·cal,** *adj.* —**e·lec′tro·met′ri·cal·ly,** *adv.* —**e·lec·trom′e·try,** *n.*

e·lec·tro·mo·tive (i lek′trə mō′tiv), *adj.* pertaining to, producing, or tending to produce a flow of electricity. [ELECTRO- + MOTIVE]

elec′tromo′tive force′, *Elect.* the energy available for conversion from nonelectric to electric form, or vice versa, per unit of charge passing through the source of the energy; the potential difference between the terminals of a source of electrical energy: expressed in volts. *Abbr.:* emf *Symbol:* E

e·lec·tro·mo·tor (i lek′trə mō′tər), *n.* an electric motor. [ELECTRO- + MOTOR]

e·lec·tro·my·o·gram (i lek′trə mī′ə gram′), *n.* *Med.* a graphic record of the electric currents associated with muscular action. [ELECTRO- + MYOGRAM]

e·lec·tro·my·og·ra·phy (i lek′trō mī og′rə fē), *n.* *Med.* the production of electromyograms. [ELECTRO- + MYOGRAPHY] —**e·lec·tro·my·o·graph·ic** (i lek′trō mī′ə graf′ik), *adj.* —**e·lec′tro·my′o·graph′i·cal·ly,** *adv.*

e·lec·tron (i lek′tron), *n.* **1.** Also called **negatron.** *Physics, Chem.* an elementary particle that is a fundamental constituent of matter, having a negative charge of 1.602×10^{-19} coulombs, a mass of 9.108×10^{-31} kilograms, and spin of ½, and existing independently or as the component outside the nucleus of an atom. **2.** *Elect.* a unit of charge equal to the charge on one electron. [< Gk *ēlektron* amber. Cf. ELECTRIC]

e·lec·tro·nar·co·sis (i lek′trō när kō′sis), *n.* *Psychiatry.* shock therapy in which a slight electric current is sent into the brain to induce unconsciousness. [ELECTRO- + NARCOSIS]

elec′tron cam′era, *Electronics.* an apparatus that converts an optical image into a corresponding electric current by electronic means without the intervention of mechanical scanning.

e·lec·tro·neg·a·tive (i lek′trō neg′ə tiv), *adj.* *Physical Chem.* **1.** containing negative electricity; tending to migrate to the positive pole in electrolysis. **2.** assuming negative potential when in contact with a dissimilar substance. **3.** nonmetallic. [ELECTRO- + NEGATIVE] —**e·lec′tro·neg′a·tiv′i·ty,** *n.*

e·lec·tro·neu·tral (i lek′trō no͞o′tral, -nyo͞o′-), *adj.* *Elect.* neutral (def. 7). [ELECTRO- + NEUTRAL] —**e·lec′tro·neu·tral′i·ty,** *n.*

elec′tron gun′, *Television.* the cathode in a cathode ray tube which emits electrons, and the surrounding electrostatic or electromagnetic apparatus which controls and focuses the electron stream.

e·lec·tron·ic (i lek tron′ik, ē′lek-), *adj.* **1.** of or pertaining to electronics or to devices, circuits, or systems developed through electronics. **2.** of or pertaining to electrons or to an electron. **3.** (of a musical instrument) using electric or electronic means to produce or modify the sound. [ELECTRON + -IC] —**e·lec·tron′i·cal·ly,** *adv.*

electron′ic Bohr′ mag′neton, *Physics.* See **Bohr magneton.**

electron′ic brain′, an electronic computer.

electron′ic da′ta proc′essing, the use of electronic computers in the processing of information. *Abbr.:* EDP Cf. **automatic data processing, integrated data processing.**

electron′ic fix′, *Navig.* a fix established with electronic equipment.

electron′ic mu′sic, electronically produced sounds recorded on tape, sometimes modified or distorted, and finally arranged into sequences and combinations by the composer. Cf. **musique concrète.**

e·lec·tron·ics (i lek tron′iks, ē′lek-), *n.* (*construed as sing.*) the science dealing with the development and application of devices and systems involving the flow of electrons in a vacuum, in gaseous media, and in semiconductors. [see ELECTRONIC, -ICS]

electron′ic scan′ning. See **electrical scanning** (def. 2).

electron′ic tube′. See **electron tube.**

elec′tron lens′, a combination of static or varying electric and magnetic fields, used to focus streams of electrons in a manner similar to that of an optical lens.

elec′tron mi′croscope, a microscope of extremely high power that uses beams of electrons focused by magnetic lenses instead of rays of light, the magnified image being formed on a fluorescent screen or recorded on a photographic plate. Its magnification is substantially greater than that of any optical microscope.

elec′tron mul′tiplier, *Electronics.* a vacuum tube containing a number of dynodes that serve to amplify the flow of electrons from the cathode by means of secondary emission.

elec′tron op′tics, the study and use of the physical and optical properties of beams of electrons under the influence of electric or magnetic fields.

e·lec′tron-ray tube′ (i lek′tron rā′), *Electronics.* a small cathode ray tube having a fluorescent screen on which the pattern varies with the voltage applied to the grid: used chiefly in radio receivers to indicate accuracy of tuning. Also called **electric eye.**

elec′tron tel′escope, a telescope that can be used without visible light, in which an infrared image of a distant object is focused on the photosensitive cathode of an image converter tube.

elec′tron tube′, an electronic device that consists, typically, of a sealed glass bulb containing two or more electrodes: used to generate, amplify, and rectify electric oscillations and alternating currents. Cf. **gas tube; vacuum tube.**

e·lec·tron-volt (i lek′tron vōlt′), *n.* *Physics.* a unit of energy, equal to the energy acquired by an electron accelerating through a potential difference of one volt and equivalent to 1.602×10^{-19} joules. *Abbr.:* EV, ev Also, **elec′tron volt′.**

e·lec·tro·or·gan′ic chem′istry (i lek′trō ôr gan′ik), the branch of chemistry dealing with the electrochemistry of organic compounds.

e·lec·tro·os·mo·sis (i lek′trō oz mō′sis, -os-), *n.* *Physical Chem.* the motion of a liquid through a membrane under the influence of an applied electric field. Also, **e·lec′tro·os·mo′sis.** —**e·lec·tro·os·mot·ic, e·lec·tro·os·mot·ic** (i lek′trō oz mot′ik, -os-), *adj.* —**e·lec′tro·os·mot′i·cal·ly, e·lec′tro·os·mot′i·cal·ly,** *adv.*

e·lec·tro·phil·ic (i lek′trə fil′ik), *adj.* *Chem.* of or pertaining to electron acceptance in covalent bonding (opposed to *nucleophilic*). [ELECTRO(N) + -PHILIC] —**e·lec′tro·phil′i·cal·ly,** *adv.*

e·lec·tro·phone (i lek′trə fōn′), *n.* any musical instrument, as a theremin, in which sound is produced by an oscillating electric current. [ELECTRO- + -PHONE] —**e·lec·tro·phon·ic** (i lek′trə fon′ik), *adj.* —**e·lec′tro·phon′i·cal·ly,** *adv.*

e·lec·tro·pho·re·sis (i lek′trō fə rē′sis), *n.* *Physical Chem.* the motion of colloidal particles suspended in a fluid medium, due to the influence of an electric field on the medium. Also called **cataphoresis.** [ELECTRO- + Gk *phórēsis* a being borne; see -PHORE, -SIS] —**e·lec·tro·pho·ret·ic** (i lek′trō fə ret′ik), *adj.*

e·lec·troph·o·rus (i lek trof′ər əs, ē′lek-), *n.*, *pl.* **-o·ri** (-ə rī′). an instrument for generating static electricity by means of induction. [ELECTRO- + *-phorus,* Latinization of -PHORE]

e·lec·tro·pho·tog·ra·phy (i lek′trō fə tog′rə fē), *n.* photography using electric rather than chemical processes to transfer an image onto paper, as in xerography. [ELECTRO- + PHOTOGRAPHY] —**e·lec·tro·pho·to·graph·ic** (i lek′trə fō′tə graf′ik), *adj.*

e·lec·tro·phys·i·ol·o·gy (i lek′trō fiz′ē ol′ə jē), *n.* the branch of physiology dealing with the electric phenomena associated with the body and its functions. [ELECTRO- + PHYSIOLOGY] —**e·lec·tro·phys·i·o·log·i·cal** (i lek′trō fiz′ē ə loj′i kəl), **e·lec′tro·phys′i·o·log′ic,** *adj.* —**e·lec′tro·phys′i·o·log′i·cal·ly,** *adv.* —**e·lec′tro·phys′i·ol′o·gist,** *n.*

e·lec·tro·plaque (i lek′trə plak′), *n.* (in certain fishes) one of a number of plates forming an electric organ, consisting of modified muscle tissue having an electric charge. Also, **e·lec·tro·plax** (i lek′trə plaks′). [ELECTRO- + PLAQUE]

e·lec·tro·plate (i lek′trə plāt′), *v.*, **-plat·ed, -plat·ing,** *n.* —*v.t.* **1.** to plate or coat with a metal by electrolysis. —*n.* **2.** electroplated articles or ware. [ELECTRO- + PLATE[1]] —**e·lec′tro·plat′er,** *n.*

e·lec·tro·pol·ish (i lek′trō pol′ish), *v.t.* to give a smooth surface to (metal) by dissolving projecting irregularities at the anode of an electrolytic cell. [ELECTRO- + POLISH]

e·lec·tro·pos·i·tive (i lek′trə poz′i tiv), *adj.* *Physical Chem.* **1.** containing positive electricity; tending to migrate to the negative pole in electrolysis. **2.** assuming positive potential when in contact with a dissimilar substance. **3.** basic, as an element or group. [ELECTRO- + POSITIVE]

e·lec·tro·re·duc·tion (i lek′trō ri duk′shən), *n.* the process in which electrons are added to a substance near the cathode of an electrolytic cell. [ELECTRO- + REDUCTION]

e·lec·tro·re·fin·ing (i lek′trō ri fī′ning), *n.* the process for refining a metal in an electrolytic cell, in which the impure metal is used as the anode and the refined metal is deposited on the cathode. [ELECTRO- + REFINING]

e·lec·tro·scope (i lek′trə skōp′), *n.* a device for detecting the presence and sign of electricity by electrostatic attraction and repulsion, often between two pieces of gold leaf enclosed in a glass-walled chamber. [ELECTRO- + -SCOPE] —**e·lec·tro·scop·ic** (i lek′trə skop′ik), *adj.*

e·lec·tro·sen·si·tive (i lek′trə sen′si tiv), *adj.* sensitive to electric current. [ELECTRO- + SENSITIVE]

e·lec·tro·shock (i lek′trə shok′), *n.* *Psychiatry.* shock therapy administered by means of electric currents. [ELECTRO- + SHOCK[1]]

e·lec·tro·stat·ic (i lek′trə stat′ik), *adj.* *Elect.* of or pertaining to static electricity. [ELECTRO- + STATIC] —**e·lec′tro·stat′i·cal·ly,** *adv.*

elec′trostat′ic gen′erator, *Physics, Elect.* See **Van de Graaff generator.**

elec′trostat′ic induc′tion, *Elect.* the electrification of a conductor when placed near a charged body.

electrostat′ic precip′itator, a device for removing small particles of smoke, dust, oil, mist, etc., from air by passing the air first through an electrically charged screen which gives a charge to the particles, then between two charged plates where the particles are attracted to one surface.

e·lec·tro·stat·ics (i lek′trə stat′iks), *n.* (*construed as sing.*) the branch of physics dealing with electric phenomena not associated with electricity in motion. [ELECTRO- + STATICS]

elec′trostat′ic u′nit, *Elect.* a unit, as a statampere, in the system of electric units derived from the force of repulsion between two static charges. *Abbr.:* esu, ESU

e·lec·tro·stric·tion (i lek′trə strik′shən), *n.* *Physics.* elastic deformation produced by an electric field, independent of the polarity of the field. [ELECTRO- + STRICTION] —**e·lec·tro·stric·tive,** *adj.*

e·lec·tro·sur·ger·y (i lek′trō sûr′jə rē), *n.* the use in surgery of an electric instrument, as an acusector, or of an electric current, as in electrocoagulation; surgical diathermy. [ELECTRO- + SURGERY] —**e·lec·tro·sur·gi·cal** (i lek′trō sûr′ji kəl), *adj.* —**e·lec′tro·sur′gi·cal·ly,** *adv.*

e·lec·tro·syn·the·sis (i lek′trō sin′thi sis), *n.* *Chem.* synthesis effected by electrolytic oxidation or reduction. [ELECTRO- + SYNTHESIS] —**e·lec·tro·syn·thet·ic** (i lek′trō sin thet′ik), *adj.* —**e·lec′tro·syn·thet′i·cal·ly,** *adv.*

e·lec·tro·tax·is (i lek′trō tak′sis), *n.* *Biol.* galvanotaxis. [ELECTRO- + -TAXIS] —**e·lec·tro·tac·tic** (i lek′trō tak′tik), *adj.*

e·lec·tro·tech·nics (i lek′trō tek′niks), *n.* (*construed as sing.*) the study or science of practical and industrial applications of electricity. Also, **e·lec·tro·tech·nol·o·gy** (i lek′trō tek nol′ə jē). [ELECTRO- + TECHNICS] —**e·lec′tro·tech′nic, e·lec′tro·tech′ni·cal,** *adj.* —**e·lec·tro·tech·ni·cian** (i lek′trō tek nish′ən), *n.*

e·lec·tro·ther·a·peu·tics (i lek′trō ther′ə pyo͞o′tiks), *n.* (*construed as sing.*) therapeutics based on the curative effects of electricity. [ELECTRO- + THERAPEUTICS] —**e·lec′tro·ther′a·peu′tic, e·lec′tro·ther′a·peu′ti·cal,** *adj.*

e·lec·tro·ther·a·pist (i lek′trō ther′ə pist), *n.* a person who specializes in electrotherapeutics. Also, **e·lec·tro·ther·a·peu·tist** (i lek′trō ther′ə pyo͞o′tist). [ELECTRO- + THERAPIST]

e·lec·tro·ther·a·py (i lek′trō ther′ə pē), *n.* treatment of diseases by means of electricity; electrotherapeutics. [ELECTRO- + THERAPY]

e·lec·tro·ther·mal (i lek′trə thûr′məl), *adj.* pertaining to both electricity and heat, esp. to the production of heat by electric current. Also, **e·lec′tro·ther′mic.** [ELECTRO- + THERMAL] —**e·lec′tro·ther′mal·ly,** *adv.*

e·lec·tro·ther·mics (i lek′trō thûr′miks), *n.* (*construed as sing.*) the science dealing with the interchange of electric and heat energy. [ELECTRO- + THERM- + -ICS]

e·lec·trot·o·nus (i lek trot′ənəs, ē′lek-), *n. Physiol.* the altered state of a nerve during the passage of an electric current through it. [< NL; see ELECTRO-, TONUS] —**e·lec·tro·ton·ic** (i lek′trə ton′ik), *adj.*

e·lec·tro·tro·pism (i lek′trə trō′piz əm; i lek trot′rə piz′əm, ē′lek-), *n. Biol.* galvanotropism. [ELECTRO- + -TROPISM] —**e·lec·tro·trop·ic** (i lek′trō trop′ik), *adj.*

e·lec·tro·type (i lek′trə tīp′), *n., v.,* **-typed, -typ·ing.** —*n.* **1.** a facsimile, for use in printing, of a block of type, an engraving, or the like, consisting of a thin copper or nickel shell deposited by electrolytic action in a wax, lead, or plastic mold of the original and backed with lead alloy. **2.** electrotypy. —*v.t.* **3.** to make an electrotype or electrotypes of. [ELECTRO- + TYPE] —**e·lec′tro·typ′er,** *n.*

e·lec·tro·typ·y (i lek′trə tī′pē), *n.* the process of making electrotypes. Also called **galvanoplasty.** [ELECTROTYPE + -Y³] —**e·lec·tro·typ·ic** (i lek′trō tip′ik), *adj.* —**e·lec·tro·typ·ist** (i lek′trō tī′pist), *n.*

e·lec·tro·va·lence (i lek′trō vā′ləns), *n. Chem.* **1.** Also called **polar valence.** the valence of an ion, equal to the number of positive or negative charges acquired by an atom through a loss or gain of electrons. **2.** Also called **elec′trova′lent bond′, ionic bond.** the bond formed between two ions through the transfer of electrons. Also, **e·lec′tro·va′len·cy.** [ELECTRO(N) + VALENCE] —**e·lec′tro·va′lent,** *adj.* —**e·lec′tro·va′lent·ly,** *adv.*

e·lec·tro·win·ning (i lek′trō win′ing), *n.* electroextraction. [ELECTRO- + WINNING]

e·lec·trum (i lek′trəm), *n.* **1.** an amber-colored alloy of gold and silver used in ancient times. **2.** an alloy composed of about 50 percent copper, 30 percent nickel, and 20 percent zinc. **3.** German silver; nickel silver. [< L < Gk *ēlektron* amber, alloy of gold and silver]

E·lec·try·on (i lek′trē ən), *n. Class. Myth.* a son of Perseus and Andromeda who became king of Mycenae: he was the grandfather of Hercules.

e·lec·tu·ar·y (i lek′cho͞o er′ē), *n., pl.* **-ar·ies.** *Pharm., Vet. Med.* a pasty mass comprised of a medicine, usually in powder form, mixed in a palatable medium, as syrup, honey, or other sweet substance: used esp. for animals, and administered by application to the teeth, tongue, or gums. [ME *electuarie* < LL *ēlect(u)ārium,* equiv. to *ēlectu(um)* (< Gk *ēkleikton* electuary, n. use of neut. of *ekleiktós,* verbid of *ekleíchein* to lick out) + *-ārium* -ARY]

el·ee·mos·y·nar·y (el′ə mos′ə ner′ē, -moz′-, el′ē ə-), *adj.* **1.** of or pertaining to alms, charity, or charitable donations; charitable. **2.** derived from or provided by charity. **3.** dependent on or supported by charity: *an eleemosynary educational institution.* [< ML *eleēmosynārius,* equiv. to L *eleēmosyn(a)* (< Gk *eleēmosýnē* mercy; see ALMS) + *-ārius* -ARY]

el·e·gance (el′ə gəns), *n.* **1.** elegant quality: *elegance of dress.* **2.** something elegant; a refinement. [< MF < L *ēlegantia* choiceness. See ELEGANT, -ANCE]

el·e·gan·cy (el′ə gən sē), *n., pl.* **-cies.** elegance. [< L *ēlegantia.* See ELEGANT, -ANCY]

el·e·gant (el′ə gənt), *adj.* **1.** tastefully fine or luxurious in dress, style, design, etc.: *elegant furnishings.* **2.** gracefully refined and dignified, as in tastes, habits, literary style, etc.: *an elegant young gentleman; an elegant prosodist.* **3.** nice, choice, or pleasingly superior in quality or kind, as a contrivance, preparation, or process. **4.** excellent; fine; superior: *an absolutely elegant wine.* [late ME < L *ēlegant-* (s. of *ēlegāns*) tasteful, choice, equiv. to *ēleg-* (akin to *ēlig-* select; see ELECT) + *-ant-* -ANT; orig. prp. of lost v.] —**el′e·gant·ly,** *adv.*
—**Syn. 1.** See **fine. 2.** polished, courtly. —**Ant. 1.** ordinary. **2.** common.

el·e·gi·ac (el′ə jī′ək, -ak, i lē′jē ak′), *adj.* Also, **el′e·gi′a·cal. 1.** *Class. Pros.* noting a distich the first line of which is a dactylic hexameter and the second a pentameter, or a verse differing from the hexameter by suppression of the arsis or metrically unaccented part of the third and the sixth foot. **2.** used in, suitable for, or resembling an elegy. **3.** expressing sorrow or lamentation: *elegiac strains.* —*n.* **4.** an elegiac or distich verse. **5.** a poem or poems in such distichs or verses. [< L *elegīacus* < Gk *elegeiakós.* See ELEGY, -AC]

elegi′ac pentam′eter, *Class. Pros.* pentameter (def. 2).

el·e·gise (el′i jīz′), *v.t., v.i.,* **-gised, -gis·ing.** *Chiefly Brit.* elegize.

el·e·gist (el′i jist), *n.* the author of an elegy. [ELEG(Y) + -IST]

e·le·git (i lē′jit), *n. Law.* a writ of execution against a judgment debtor's goods, property, or land, held by the judgment creditor until payment of the debt, as from rents on the land. [< L: he has chosen, perf. 3rd pers. sing. ind. of *ēligere;* so called from wording of writ]

el·e·gize (el′i jīz′), *v.,* **-gized, -giz·ing.** —*v.t.* **1.** to lament in or as if in an elegy. —*v.i.* **2.** to compose an elegy. Also, *esp. Brit.,* **elegise.** [ELEG(Y) + -IZE]

el·e·gy (el′i jē), *n., pl.* **-gies. 1.** a mournful, melancholy, or plaintive poem, esp. a funeral song or a lament for the dead. **2.** poetry or a poem written in elegiac meter. **3.** a sad or mournful musical composition. [< L *elegī(a)* < Gk *elegeía,* orig. neut. pl. of *elegeíos* elegiac, equiv. to *éleg(os)* a lament + *-eios* adj. suffix]

El′egy Writ′ten in a Coun′try Church′yard, a poem (1750) by Thomas Gray.

e·lek·tra (i lek′trə), *n.* an electronic navigational system establishing approximate position through coincidence in amplitude of two radio signals. [special use of Gk *ēlektra,* pl. of *ēlektron.* See ELECTRON]

elem., 1. element. **2.** elementary. **3.** elements.

el·e·ment (el′ə mənt), *n.* **1.** a component or constituent of a whole or into which a whole may be resolved by analysis: *Letters are the elements out of which all our words are formed.* **2.** one of the substances, usually earth, water, air, and fire, formerly regarded as constituting the material universe. **3.** the natural habitat of something: *Water is the element of fish.* **4.** the sphere of activity, environment, etc., regarded as naturally suited to any person or thing: *to be in one's element.* **5. elements, a.** atmospheric agencies or forces: *a ruddy complexion from exposure to the elements.* **b.** the rudimentary principles of an art, science, etc.: *the elements of grammar.* **c.** the bread and wine of the Eucharistic service. **6.** *Chem.* one of a class of substances, of which 103 are now recognized, that cannot be separated into simpler substances by chemical means. See table on next page. **7.** *Math.* **a.** an infinitesimal part of a given quantity, similar in nature to it. **b.** an entity that satisfies all the conditions of belonging to a given set. **8.** *Geom.* one of the points, lines, planes, or other geometrical forms, of which a figure is composed. **9.** *Astron.* any of the data required to define the precise nature of an orbit and to determine the position of a planet in the orbit at any given time. **10.** *Elect.* an electric device with terminals for connection to other electrical devices. **11.** *Radio.* one of the electrodes in a vacuum tube. **12.** *Gram.* any word, part of a word, or group of words that recurs in various contexts in a language with relatively constant meaning. [ME < L *element(um)* first principle, rudiment]
—**Syn. 1.** ELEMENT, COMPONENT, CONSTITUENT, INGREDIENT refer to the units which build up substances and compounds or mixtures. ELEMENT denotes a fundamental, ultimate part: *the elements of matter, of a discussion.* COMPONENT and CONSTITUENT denote that which goes into the making of a compound, COMPONENT suggesting one of a number of parts, and CONSTITUENT an active and necessary participation: *iron and carbon as components of steel; hydrogen and oxygen the constituents of water.* INGREDIENT denotes something essential or nonessential which enters into a mixture or compound: *the ingredients of a cake.* **4.** medium, milieu.

el·e·men·tal (el′ə men′tᵊl), *adj.* **1.** of the nature of an ultimate constituent; simple; uncompounded. **2.** pertaining to rudiments or first principles. **3.** starkly simple, primitive, or basic: *a spare, elemental prose style; hate, lust, and other elemental emotions.* **4.** of, pertaining to, or of the nature of the four elements or of any one of them. **5.** pertaining to the agencies, forces, or phenomena of physical nature: *elemental gods.* **6.** comparable to the great forces of nature, as in power or magnitude: *elemental grandeur.* **7.** pertaining to chemical elements. [< ML *elementāl(is).* See ELEMENT, -AL¹] —**el′e·men′tal·ly,** *adv.*

el′emental ar′ea, *Television.* a rectangular area on a television screen equal in height to the spacing of scanning lines and in width to the distance traversed by the scanning spot during the shortest possible time required for change from dark to full brilliance.

el·e·men·ta·ry (el′ə men′tə rē, -trē), *adj.* **1.** pertaining to or dealing with elements, rudiments, or first principles: *elementary education; an elementary grammar.* **2.** of or pertaining to an elementary school: *elementary teachers.* **3.** of the nature of an ultimate constituent; simple or uncompounded. **4.** pertaining to the four elements or to the great forces of nature; elemental. **5.** (of a function) expressible by the operations of addition, subtraction, multiplication, division, or taking powers and roots applied a finite number of times each. **6.** *Chem.* of or noting one or more elements. [ME *elementar(i)e* < L *elementāri(us).* See ELEMENT, -ARY] —**el·e·men·ta·ri·ly** (el′ə men ter′ə lē), *adv.* —**el′e·men′ta·ri·ness,** *n.*
—**Syn. 1.** ELEMENTARY, PRIMARY, RUDIMENTARY refer to what is basic and fundamental. ELEMENTARY refers to the introductory, simple, easy facts, steps, or parts of a subject which must necessarily be learned first in order to understand succeeding ones: *elementary facts about geography; elementary arithmetic.* PRIMARY may mean much the same as ELEMENTARY; however, it usually emphasizes the idea of what comes first even more than that of simplicity: *the primary grades in school.* RUDIMENTARY applies to what is undeveloped or imperfect: *a rudimentary form of government.*

el′emen′tary par′ticle, *Physics.* any of several entities that are less complex than an atom and are the constituents of all matter, all once thought to be irreducible, but many now regarded as compounds of others. All such entities can be classified as either bosons or fermions. Also called **fundamental particle, particle.**

el′emen′tary proc′ess, *Physical Chem.* a chemical process complete in one step, characterized by the simultaneous interaction of all the atoms of two or more molecules.

elemen′tary school′, the lowest school giving formal instruction, teaching the rudiments of learning, and extending variously from six to eight years. Also called **primary school.**

el·e·mi (el′ə mē), *n., pl.* **-mis.** any of various fragrant resins from certain trees, esp. *Canarium commune,* used chiefly in the manufacture of varnishes, lacquers, ointments, and in perfumery. Also called **gum elemi.** [short for *gum elemi* < NL *gummi elimī;* cf. Ar *al lāmi* the elemi]

el·e·mong (el′ə mông′), *n. Australian.* hielamon.

El·e·na (el′ə nə, ə lā′nə; *It.* e le′nä), *n.* a girl's given name, form of **Helen.** Also, **Alain, Alayne, Elaine.**

e·len·chus (i leng′kəs), *n., pl.* **-chi** (-kī, -kē). **1.** a logical refutation; an argument that refutes another argument by proving the contrary of its conclusion. **2.** a false refutation; a sophistical argument. [< L < Gk *élenchos* refutation] —**e·lenc·tic** (i lengk′tik), *adj.*

El·e·nor (el′ə nər, -nôr′), *n.* a girl's given name, form of **Helen.** Also, **Eleanor, Eleanora, El′e·nore, Eleonora, Eleonore, Elinor.**

El·e·o·no·ra (el′ē ə nōr′ə, -nôr′ə), *n.* a girl's given name, form of **Helen.** Also, **Eleanor, Eleanora, Elenor, Elenore, El·e·o·nore** (el′ē ə nōr′, -nôr′), **Elinor.**

el·e·op·tene (el′ē op′tēn), *n. Chem.* the liquid part of a volatile oil (opposed to *stearoptene*). Also, **elaeoptene.** [< Gk *élaio(n)* oil + *ptēn(os)* winged, akin to *pétesthai* to fly]

el·e·phant (el′ə fənt), *n., pl.* **-phants,** (*esp. collectively*) **-phant. 1.** any of several large, five-toed mammals, with the nose and upper lip elongated into a prehensile trunk, of the family *Elephantidae,* of the genera *Loxodonta,* of Africa, having large, flapping ears and tusks of ivory in both males and females, and *Elephas,* of India and neighboring regions, having comparatively small ears and tusks in the males only. **2.** a representation of this animal, used in the U.S. since 1874 as the emblem of the Republican party. **3.** See **white elephant. 4.** *Chiefly Brit.* a size of drawing or writing paper, 23 × 28 inches. Cf. **double elephant.** [ME < L *elephant(us)* < Gk *elephant-* (s. of *eléphās*) elephant; r. ME olifaunt < AF] —**el′e·phan·toid′,** *adj.*

African elephant, *Loxodonta africana* (11 ft. high at shoulder; tusks 6 to 8 ft.)

el·e·phan·ta (el′ə fan′tə), *n.* a strong wind from the south or southeast blowing during September and October on the Malabar coast, accompanied by thundersqualls and heavy rain. [< Pg *elefante* < L *elephantus* the elephant being the symbol of the Hindu 13th lunar mansion, when such storms occur]

Indian elephant, *Elephas maximus* (9 ft. high at shoulder; tusks 4 to 5 ft.)

el′ephant bird′, any of several huge, extinct, flightless birds of the genus *Aepyornis,* of Madagascar, reaching a height of about 9 feet.

El′ephant Butte′, a dam and irrigation reservoir in SW New Mexico, on the Rio Grande. Dam, 309 ft. high; reservoir, 40 mi. long.

el′ephant fish′, any of several chimaeroid fishes of the family *Callorhynchidae,* found in deep waters of the Southern Hemisphere, having a long, flexible snout.

el′ephant gun′, a gun of very large caliber, as .410 or greater, used in killing elephants or other big game.

el·e·phan·ti·a·sis (el′ə fən tī′ə sis, -fan-), *n.* **1.** *Pathol.* a chronic disease resulting from lymphatic obstruction, characterized by enormous enlargement of the parts affected, esp. of the legs and scrotum, and usually caused by a filarial infection. **2.** any unfortunate or uncalled-for growth or development: *elephantiasis of the juvenile crime rate.* [< L < Gk *elephantíasis,* equiv. to *elephant-* ELEPHANT + *-iasis* -IASIS] —**el·e·phan·ti·as·ic** (el′ə fan′tē as′ik, -fən tī′ə sik′), *adj.*

el·e·phan·tine (el′ə fan′tin, -tīn, -tēn), *adj.* **1.** pertaining to or resembling an elephant. **2.** huge; ponderous; clumsy: *elephantine movements; elephantine humor.* [< L *elephantin(us)* < Gk *elephántinos.* See ELEPHANT, -INE¹]

el·e·phant's (el′ə fənts), *adj. Chiefly Brit. Slang.* drunk. [short for ELEPHANT'S TRUNK]

el′ephant seal′, either of two seals of the genus *Mirounga,* found along the Pacific coast of North America or in the Antarctic Ocean and adjacent waters, having a curved proboscis resembling an elephant's trunk. Also called **sea elephant.**

el·e·phant's-ear (el′ə fənts ēr′), *n.* the taro.

el·e·phant's-foot (el′ə fənts fo͝ot′), *n., pl.* **-foots.** any climbing vine of the genus *Testudinaria,* of southern Africa, as *T. Elephantipes,* having a massive, edible, yamlike tuber. Also called **Hottentot's bread, tortoise plant.**

el′ephant shrew′, any of several African insectivores of the family *Macroscelididae,* having long hind legs and a long, sensitive snout.

el′ephant's trunk′, *Chiefly Brit. Slang.* drunk. [rhyming slang]

el′ephant's trunk′ snake′, a wart snake, *Acrochordus javanicus,* having a stout body that resembles the trunk of an elephant.

eleu·in (lo͞o′in), *interj. Fox Hunting.* (a cry uttered repeatedly by a huntsman to encourage the hounds.)

El·eu·sin·i·a (el′yo͞o sin′ē ə), *n.* (*sometimes construed as pl.*) either of two festivals, the principal features of which were the Eleusinian mysteries, held at Eleusis and Athens in ancient times and later imitated in other cities of ancient Greece.

El·eu·sin·i·an (el′yo͞o sin′ē ən), *adj.* **1.** of or pertaining to Eleusis or to the Eleusinian mysteries. —*n.* **2.** a native or inhabitant of Eleusis. [< L *Eleusīni(us)* of Eleusis + -AN]

Eleusin′ian mys′teries, the mysteries, celebrated annually at Eleusis and Athens in ancient times, in memory of the abduction and return of Persephone and in honor of Demeter and Bacchus.

E·leu·sis (i lo͞o′sis), *n.* a city in ancient Greece, in Attica.

E·leu·ther·a (ə lo͞o′thər ə), *n.* an island in the central Bahamas. 5386 (est. 1955); 164 sq. mi.

El·eu·the·ri·us (el′yo͞o thēr′ē əs), *n.* **1. Saint,** pope A.D. 175–189. **2.** *Class. Myth.* an epithet of Zeus, meaning "god of freedom."

el·e·vate (el′ə vāt′), *v.,* **-vat·ed, -vat·ing,** *adj.* —*v.t.* **1.** to move or raise to a higher place or position; lift up. **2.** to raise to a higher state, rank, or office; exalt; promote: *an archbishop elevated to cardinal.* **3.** to raise to a higher intellectual or spiritual level: *to elevate the mind.* **4.** to raise the spirits; put in high spirits. **5.** to raise (the voice) in pitch or volume. —*adj.* **6.** *Archaic.* raised; elevated. [< L *ēlevāt(us)* lightened, lifted up (ptp. of *ēlevāre*), equiv. to *ē-* E- + *lev-* light + *-ātus* -ATE¹] —**el′e·vat′ing·ly,** *adv.*
—**Syn. 1.** lift, hoist. **2.** promote, advance, dignify. ELEVATE, ENHANCE, EXALT, HEIGHTEN mean to raise or make higher in some respect. TO ELEVATE is to raise something up to a relatively higher level, position, or state: *to elevate the living standards of a group.* TO ENHANCE is to add to the attractions or desirability of something: *Landscaping enhances the beauty of the grounds. Paved streets enhance the value of real estate.* TO EXALT is to raise very high in rank, character, estimation, mood, etc.: *A king is exalted above his*

PERIODIC TABLE OF THE ELEMENTS

Some Representative Radioactive Isotopes

Ac 227(22y)β^-,α
Ag 110(24s)β^-,γ; 111(7.5d) β^-,γ
Am 241(470y)α,γ,e^-; 242(100y)β^-,K,α,γ; 243(8000y)α,γ
As 76(26.7h)β^-,γ; 77(39h)β^-,γ
At 210(8.3h)K,α,γ; 211(7.5h),Kα,γ
Au 198(2.69d)β^-,γ
Ba 131(12d)K,γ; 133(7.5y)K,γ,e^-
Bi 210(5d)β^-,α
Bk 245(4.9d)K,α,γ; 249(290d)β^-,α,SF
Br 82(36h)β^-,γ
C 14(5600y)β^-
Ca 41(1×10[5]y)K; 45(160d)β^-; 47(4.7d)β^-,γ
Cd 115(43d)β^-,γ
Ce 141(32d)β^-,γ; 143(33h)β^-,γ; 144(285d)β^-,γ
Cf 246(35h)α,γ,SF; 249(500y)α,γ,SF; 251(700y) γ
Cl 36(3×10[5]y)β^-
Cm 243(35y),α,γ; 245(11000y),α,γ; 247(1y)
Co 58(71d),K,β^+, γ; 60(5.27y)β^-,γ
Cr 51(27d),K,γ
Cs 134(2.2y)β^-,γ; 135(3×10[6]y)β^-; 137(30y)β^-,γ
Cu 64(12.8h)K,β^-,β^+,γ
Es 253(20d)α,γ,SF; 254(1y)α,SF
Eu 154(16y)β^-,γ; 155(1.7y)β^-,γ
Fe 55(2.9y)K; 59(45d)β^-,γ
Fm 255(20h)α
Fr 223(22m)β^-,γ,α
Ga 72(14.1h),β^-, γ
Gd 153(236d)K,γ,e^-; 159(18h)β^-,γ
Ge 71(11d)K
H 3(12.3y)β^-
Hf 181(45d)β^-,γ,e^-
Hg 197(65h)K,γ,e^-; 203(47d)β^-,γ,e^-
Ho 166(27.3h)β^-,γ
I 129(10[7]y)β^+,γ,e; 131(8.05d)β^-,γ
In 114(50d)γ
Ir 192(74.4d)β^-,γ
K 40(10[9]y)β^+,K,γ; 42(12.4h),β^-, γ
La 140(40.2h)β^-,γ
Lu 176(10[10]y)β^-,K,γ; 177(6.8d)β^-,γ
Md 256(30m)K,SF
Mo 99(67h)β^-,γ
Na 22(2.6y)β^+,K,γ; 24(15h)β^-,γ
Nd 147(11.1d)β^-,γ
Ni 63(125y)β^-; 59(8×10[4]y),K
Np 237(2.2×10[6]y)α,γ; 239(2.33d)β^-,γ
Os 191(15d)β^-,γ,e^-
P 32(14.2d)β^-
Pa 231(34000y)α,γ
Pb 210(19.4y)β^-,γ,e^-; 202(10[5]y)L
Pd 103(17d)K,γ
Pm 147(2.6y)β^-; 145(25y)K,L,α
Po 210(138.4d)α,γ; 209(100y)α,K,γ
Pr 143(13.8d)β^-
Pt 197(18h)β^-,γ
Pu 242(3.8×10[5]y)α,SF; 241(13y)β^-,α,γ; 239(24300y)α,γ,SF
Ra 226(1620y)α,γ
Rb 86(18.6h)β^-,γ
Re 188(16.7h)β^-,γ; 186(3.7d)β^-,γ
Rn 222(3.82d)α
Ru 103(40d)β^-,γ; 97(2.9d),K,γ,e^-
S 35(87d)β^-
Sb 122(2.8d)β^-,K,β^+,γ; 124(60d)β^-,γ
S 46(84d)β^-,γ
Se 75(121d)K,γ
Sm 153(47h)β^-,γ; 145(340d)K,γ
Sn 113(119d)K,L,γ,e^-
Sr 90(28y)β^-; 89(51d)β^-,γ; 85(64d)K,γ
Ta 182(115d)β^-,γ
Tb 160(73d)β^-,γ
Tc 99(2×10[5]y)β^-; 97(10[5]y)K
Te 127(9.3h)β^-
Th 232(1.4×10[10]y)α,γ,SF; 228(1.91y)β^-
Tl 204(3.56y)β^-,K
Tm 170(127d)β^-,γ,e^-
U 238(4.5×10[9]y)α,γ,SF; 234(2.5×10[5]y)α,γ,SF; 235(7.1×10[8]y)α,γ,SF; 233(1.6×10[5]y)α,γ
W 185(73d)β^-,γ
Y 90(64h)β^-,e^-
Yb 175(4.2d)β^-,γ; 169(31d)K,γ,e^-
Zn 65(245d)K,β^+,γ
Zr 95(65d)β^-,γ,e^-; 93(9×10[5]y)β^-,γ

Half lives are in parentheses where s, m, h, d, and y stand for seconds, minutes, hours, days, and years respectively. The symbols describing the mode of decay and resulting radiation are defined as follows:

α	alpha particle	L	L-electron capture
β^-	beta particle	SF	spontaneous fission
β^+	positron	γ	gamma ray
K	K-electron capture	e^-	internal electron conversion

PERIOD

Period	GROUP IA	IIA	IIIB	IVB	VB	VIB	VIIB	VIII	VIII	VIII	IB	IIB	IIIA	IVA	VA	VIA	VIIA	NOBLE GASES
1	1 **H** -252.7 -259.2 0.071 1.00797 Hydrogen																	2 **He** -268.9 -269.7 0.126 4.0026 Helium
2	3 **Li** 1330 108.5 0.53 6.939 Lithium	4 **Be** 2770 1277 1.85 9.0122 Beryllium											5 **B** - (2030) 2.34 10.811 Boron	6 **C** 4830 3727g 2.26 12.0111 Carbon	7 **N** -195.8 -210 0.81 14.0067 Nitrogen	8 **O** -183 -218.8 1.14 15.9994 Oxygen	9 **F** -188.2 -219.6 1.11 18.9984 Fluorine	10 **Ne** -246 -248.6 1.20 20.183 Neon
3	11 **Na** 892 97.8 0.97 22.9898 Sodium	12 **Mg** 1107 650 1.74 24.312 Magnesium											13 **Al** 2450 660 2.70 26.9815 Aluminum	14 **Si** 2680 1410 2.33 28.086 Silicon	15 **P** 280w 44.2w 1.82w 30.9738 Phosphorus	16 **S** 444.6 119.0 2.07 32.064 Sulfur	17 **Cl** -34.7 -101.0 1.56 35.453 Chlorine	18 **Ar** -185.8 -189.4 1.40 39.948 Argon
4	19 **K** 760 63.7 0.86 39.102 Potassium	20 **Ca** 1440 838 1.55 40.08 Calcium	21 **Sc** 2730 1539 3.0 44.956 Scandium	22 **Ti** 3260 1668 4.51 47.90 Titanium	23 **V** 3450 1900 6.1 50.942 Vanadium	24 **Cr** 2665 1875 7.19 51.996 Chromium	25 **Mn** 2150 1245 7.43 54.938 Manganese	26 **Fe** 3000 1536 7.86 55.847 Iron	27 **Co** 2900 1495 8.9 58.933 Cobalt	28 **Ni** 2730 1453 8.9 58.71 Nickel	29 **Cu** 2595 1083 8.96 63.54 Copper	30 **Zn** 906 419.5 7.14 65.37 Zinc	31 **Ga** 2237 29.8 5.91 69.72 Gallium	32 **Ge** 2830 937.4 5.32 72.59 Germanium	33 **As** 613 817 5.72 74.922 Arsenic	34 **Se** 685 217 4.79 78.96 Selenium	35 **Br** 58 -7.2 3.12 79.909 Bromine	36 **Kr** -152 -157.3 2.6 83.80 Krypton
5	37 **Rb** 688 38.9 1.53 85.47 Rubidium	38 **Sr** 1380 768 2.6 87.62 Strontium	39 **Y** 2927 1509 4.47 88.905 Yttrium	40 **Zr** 3580 1852 6.49 91.22 Zirconium	41 **Nb** 3300 2415 8.4 92.906 Niobium	42 **Mo** 5560 2610 10.2 95.94 Molybdenum	43 **Tc** - 2200 11.5 (99) Technetium	44 **Ru** 4900 2500 12.2 101.07 Ruthenium	45 **Rh** 4500 1966 12.4 102.905 Rhodium	46 **Pd** 3980 1552 12.0 106.4 Palladium	47 **Ag** 2210 960.8 10.5 107.870 Silver	48 **Cd** 765 320.9 8.65 112.40 Cadmium	49 **In** 2000 156.2 7.31 114.82 Indium	50 **Sn** 2270 231.9 7.30 118.69 Tin	51 **Sb** 1380 630.5 6.62 121.75 Antimony	52 **Te** 989.8 449.5 6.24 127.60 Tellurium	53 **I** 183 113.7 4.94 126.904 Iodine	54 **Xe** -108.0 -111.9 3.06 131.30 Xenon
6	55 **Cs** 690 28.7 1.90 132.905 Cesium	56 **Ba** 1640 714 3.5 137.34 Barium	57 **La** 3470 920 6.17 138.91 Lanthanum	72 **Hf** 5400 2222 13.1 178.49 Hafnium	73 **Ta** 5425 2996 16.6 180.948 Tantalum	74 **W** 5930 3410 19.3 183.85 Tungsten	75 **Re** 5900 3180 21.0 186.2 Rhenium	76 **Os** 5500 2700 22.6 190.2 Osmium	77 **Ir** 5300 2454 22.5 192.2 Iridium	78 **Pt** 4530 1769 21.4 195.09 Platinum	79 **Au** 2970 1063 19.3 196.967 Gold	80 **Hg** 357 -38.4 13.6 200.59 Mercury	81 **Tl** 1457 303 11.85 204.37 Thallium	82 **Pb** 1725 327.4 11.4 207.19 Lead	83 **Bi** 1560 271.3 9.8 208.980 Bismuth	84 **Po** - 254 (9.2) (210) Polonium	85 **At** - (302) - (210) Astatine	86 **Rn** (-61.8) (-71) - (222) Radon
7	87 **Fr** - (27) - (223) Francium	88 **Ra** - 700 5.0 (226) Radium	89 **Ac** - 1050 - (227) Actinium															

Period														
6	58 **Ce** 3468 795 6.67 140.12 Cerium	59 **Pr** 3127 935 6.77 140.907 Praseodymium	60 **Nd** 3027 1024 7.00 144.24 Neodymium	61 **Pm** - (1027) - (147) Promethium	62 **Sm** 1900 1072 7.54 150.35 Samarium	63 **Eu** 1439 826 5.26 151.96 Europium	64 **Gd** 3000 1312 7.89 157.25 Gadolinium	65 **Tb** 2800 1356 8.27 158.924 Terbium	66 **Dy** 2600 1407 8.54 162.50 Dysprosium	67 **Ho** 2600 1461 8.80 164.930 Holmium	68 **Er** 2900 1497 9.05 167.26 Erbium	69 **Tm** 1727 1545 9.33 168.934 Thulium	70 **Yb** 1427 824 6.98 173.04 Ytterbium	71 **Lu** 3327 1652 9.84 174.97 Lutetium
7	90 **Th** 3850 1750 11.7 232.038 Thorium	91 **Pa** - (1230) 15.4 (231) Protactinum	92 **U** 3818 1132 19.07 238.04 Uranium	93 **Np** - 637 19.5 (237) Neptunium	94 **Pu** 3235 640 - (242) Plutonium	95 **Am** - - 11.7 (243) Americium	96 **Cm** - - - (247) Curium	97 **Bk** - - - (247) Berkelium	98 **Cf** - - - (251) Californium	99 **Es** - - - (254) Einsteinium	100 **Fm** - - - (253) Fermium	101 **Md** - - - (256) Mendelevium	102 **No** - - - (254) Nobelium	103 **Lw** - - - (257) Lawrencium

KEY

30 **Zn** — ATOMIC NUMBER: 30; BOILING POINT, °C: 906; MELTING POINT, °C: 419.5; DENSITY (g/ml) (3): 7.14; SYMBOL (1): Zn; ATOMIC WEIGHT (2): 65.37; NAME: Zinc; CRYSTAL STRUCTURE (4)

NOTES: (1) Symbols in outline represent synthetically prepared elements.

(2) Based on carbon 12. ( ) indicates most stable or best-known isotope.

(3) Values for gaseous elements are for liquids at the boiling point.

(4) Cubic, face centered; cubic, body centered; diamond; cubic; hexagonal; rhombohedral; tetragonal; orthorhombic; monoclinic.

subjects. To HEIGHTEN is to increase the strength or intensity: *to heighten one's powers of concentration.*

el·e·vat·ed (el′ə vā′tid), *adj.* **1.** raised up, esp. above the ground: *an elevated platform.* **2.** exalted or noble: *elevated thoughts.* **3.** elated; joyful. —*n.* **4.** an elevated railway system. [ELEVATE + -ED[2]]

el′evated rail′road, a railway system operating on an elevated structure, as over streets. Also, **el.**

el·e·va·tion (el′ə vā′shən), *n.* **1.** the height to which something is elevated: *The elevation of the tower is 80 feet.* **2.** the altitude of a place above sea level or ground level. **3.** an elevated place, thing, or part; an eminence. **4.** loftiness; grandeur or dignity; nobleness: *elevation of mind.* **5.** the act of elevating, or the state of being elevated. **6.** *Archit.* a drawing or design which represents an object or structure as being projected geometrically on a vertical plane parallel to one of its sides. **7.** *Survey.* **a.** the angle between the line from an observer or instrument to an object above him or it and a horizontal line. **b.** the distance above a datum level. **8.** the ability of a dancer to stay in the air while executing a step. **9. the Elevation,** *Rom. Cath. Ch.* the lifting by the celebrant of the Eucharistic elements immediately after consecration, for adoration by the communicants. [< L *ēlevātiōn-* (s. of *ēlevātiō*), equiv. to *ēlevāt(us)* (see ELEVATE) + *-iōn-* -ION; r. ME *elevacioun* < AF] —**Syn. 1.** See **height. 3.** height; hill; mountain; plateau. **4.** exaltation. —**Ant. 1.** depth. **3.** depression.

el·e·va·tor (el′ə vā′tər), *n.* **1.** one who or that which elevates or raises. **2.** a moving platform or cage for conveying goods, persons, etc., from one level to another, as in a building. **3.** any of various mechanical devices for raising objects or materials. **4.** a building in which grain is stored and handled by means of mechanical elevator and conveyor devices. **5.** *Aeron.* a hinged horizontal surface on an airplane or the like, used to control the longitudinal inclination and usually placed at the tail end of the fuselage. **6.** See **Elevator shoe.** [< LL; see ELEVATE, -OR[2]]

El′evator shoe′, *Trademark.* a shoe with a thick insole designed to increase the wearer's height.

e·lev·en (i lev′ən), *n.* **1.** a cardinal number, ten plus one. **2.** a symbol for this number, as 11 or XI. **3.** a set of this many persons or things, as a football team. —*adj.* **4.** amounting to eleven in number. [ME *elleven(e)*, OE *ellefne, endleofan;* c. OHG *einlif* (G *elf*), Icel *ellifu*, Goth *ainlib-*, lit., one remaining (after counting 10). See ONE, LEAVE[1]]

e·lev·ens·es (i lev′ən ziz), *n.pl. Brit.* a mid-morning snack, usually taken around eleven o'clock. Also, **e·lev′ens.** [alter. of ELEVEN (o'clock)]

e·lev·enth (i lev′ənth), *adj.* **1.** next after the tenth; being the ordinal number for 11. **2.** being one of 11 equal parts. —*n.* **3.** an eleventh part, esp. of one (1/11). **4.** the eleventh member of a series. [ME *enleventh, enlefte*, OE *endlyfta* (akin to OFris *andlofta*, OS *ellifto*). See ELEVEN, -TH[2]]

elev′enth hour′, the last possible moment for doing something: *to change plans at the eleventh hour.*

el·e·von (el′ə von′), *n. Aeron.* a control surface functioning both as an elevator and as an aileron. [ELEV(ATOR + AILER)ON]

elf (elf), *n., pl.* **elves** (elvz). **1.** one of a class of imaginary beings, esp. from mountainous regions, with magical powers, given to capricious interference in human affairs, and usually imagined to be a diminutive being in human form; sprite; fairy. **2.** a dwarf or small person, esp. a child. **3.** a mischievous person, esp. a child. [ME, back formation from *elven*, OE *elfen* nymph (i.e., female elf), var. of *ælfen;* see ELFIN] —**elf′-like′,** *adj.* —**Syn. 1.** See **fairy.**

Elf, extremely low frequency. Also, **elf**

El Fai·yum (el′ fī yōōm′), Faiyum (def. 2). Also, **El′ Fa·yum′.**

El Fa·sher (el fash′ər), a city in W Sudan. 26,161 (1956).

El Fer·rol (el feʀ ʀôl′), a seaport in NW Spain: naval arsenal and dockyard. 67,881 (1950). Also called **Ferrol.**

elf·in (el′fin), *adj.* **1.** of or like elves. **2.** small and charmingly spritely, merry, or mischievous. —*n.* **3.** an elf. [alter. of ME *elven* elf, OE *elfen, ælfen* nymph, equiv. to *ælf* elf + *-en* fem. suffix (c. G *-in*); *ælf* c. G *Alp* nightmare, puck, Icel *alfr* elf, L *albus* white]

elf·in·wood (el′fin wŏŏd′), *n.* Krummholz. [ELFIN + WOOD[1]]

elf·ish (el′fish), *adj.* elflike; elfin; small and mischievous. Also, **elvish.** [alter. of ME; see ELVISH] —**elf′ish·ly,** *adv.* —**elf′ish·ness,** *n.* —**Syn.** prankish, impish.

elf·land (elf′land′), *n.* the imaginary realm or world of elves; fairyland. [ELF + LAND]

elf·lock (elf′lok′), *n.* a tangled lock of hair. [ELF + LOCK[2]]

El Fos·tat (el′ fŏŏ stat′), al-Fustat. Also, **el′-Fus·tat′.**

elf′ owl′, a small, insectivorous owl, *Micrathene whitneyi*, of the southwestern U.S. and Mexico.

El·ga (el′gə), *n.* a girl's given name.

El·gan (el′gən), *n.* a boy's given name.

El·gar (el′gər, -gär), *n.* **Sir Edward,** 1857–1934, English composer.

El Ge·nei·na (el′ jŏŏ nā′nə, ge-), a city in W Sudan. 11,817 (1956). Also called **Geneina.**

El·ge·ni·a (el jē′nē ə), *n.* a girl's given name.

El·ger (el′gər), *n.* a walled plain in the third quadrant of the face of the moon: about 17 miles in diameter.

El·gin (el′jin *for 1, 4;* el′gin *for 2, 3*), *n.* **1.** a city in NE Illinois. 49,447 (1960). **2.** former name of **Moray. 3.** a town in central Texas. 3511 (1960). **4.** a boy's given name.

El′gin mar′bles (el′gin, -jin), Greek sculpture of the 5th century B.C., originally on the Parthenon in Athens, and supposedly sculptured under the direction of Phidias: presently in the British Museum in London. [after Thomas Bruce, 7th Earl of *Elgin* (1766–1841), who arranged for the collection to be brought from Athens to the British Museum]

El Gi·za (el gē′zə), a city in N United Arab Republic, near Cairo: the ancient Egyptian pyramids and the Sphinx are located nearby. 276,200 (est. 1962). Also, **El Gi′zeh.** Also called **Giza, Gizeh.**

El Go·lé·a (el gō lā′ə), a city in central Algeria. 7452 (1954).

El·gon (el′gon), *n.* an extinct volcano in E Africa, on the boundary between Uganda and Kenya. 14,176 ft.

El Gre·co (el grek′ō; *Sp.* el gʀe′kō), ("*the Greek*") (*Domenikos Theotocopoulos*), 1541–1614, Spanish painter, born in Crete.

El Ha·sa (el hä′sə), Hasa.

el·hi (el′hī), *adj.* elementary and high-school: *the elhi textbook market.* [EL(EMENTARY) + HI(GH SCHOOL)]

E·li (ē′lī), *n.* **1.** Also, *Douay Bible,* **Heli.** a Hebrew judge and priest. I Sam. 1–3. **2.** Also, **El·ie** (el′ē), **Ely.** a boy's given name.

E·li·a (ē′lē ə), *n.* the pen name of Charles Lamb.

E·li·as (i lī′əs), *n.* **1.** *Douay Bible.* Elijah (def. 1). **2.** a boy's given name.

e·lic·it (i lis′it), *v.t.* to draw or bring out or forth; educe; evoke: *to elicit the truth; to elicit a response with a question.* [< L *ēlicit(us)* drawn out (ptp. of *ēlicere*), equiv. to *ē-* E- + *lici-* draw, lure + *-tus* ptp. suffix] —**e·lic′it·a·ble,** *adj.* —**e·lic′i·ta′tion,** *n.* —**e·lic′i·tor,** *n.*

E·li·cius (ē lish′ē əs), *n.* an ancient Roman epithet of Jupiter.

e·lide (i līd′), *v.t.,* **e·lid·ed, e·lid·ing. 1.** to omit (a vowel, consonant, or syllable) in pronunciation. **2.** to suppress; omit; ignore. **3.** *Law.* to annul or quash. [< L *ēlīd(ere)* (to) strike out, equiv. to *ē-* E- + *-līdere*, var. of *laedere* to wound] —**e·lid′i·ble,** *adj.*

el·i·gi·bil·i·ty (el′i jə bil′i tē), *n.* the quality or state of being eligible, esp. legal qualification for election or appointment. [*eligibil-* (see ELIGIBLE) + -ITY]

el·i·gi·ble (el′i jə bəl), *adj.* **1.** fit or proper to be chosen; worthy of choice; desirable: *to marry an eligible bachelor.* **2.** legally qualified to be elected or appointed to office: *eligible for the presidency.* —*n.* **3.** a person or thing that is eligible: *Among the eligibles, only a few are running for office.* [< LL *ēligibil(is)*, equiv. to L *ē-* E- + *ligi-* select + *-bilis* -BLE] —**el′i·gi·bly,** *adv.*

el′igible pa′per, *Banking.* notes, bills, and acceptances qualifying for rediscount by a Federal Reserve Bank.

El·i·hu (el′ə hyōō′, i lī′hyōō), *n.* **1.** a young man who entered into discourse with Job. Job. 32–37. **2.** a boy's given name. [< Heb: my God is he]

E·li·jah (i lī′jə), *n.* **1.** Also, *Douay Bible,* **Elias.** a Hebrew prophet of the 9th century B.C. I Kings 17; II Kings 2. **2.** a boy's given name. [< Heb: my God is Yahweh]

Eli′jah Muham′mad, (*Elijah Poole*) born 1897, U.S. religious leader of the Black Muslims since 1934.

Eli′jah's chair′, the chair customarily set apart in honor of the prophet Elijah at the Jewish rite of circumcision.

Eli′jah's cup′, the cup of wine customarily set apart in honor of the prophet Elijah at the Jewish Seder meal.

e·lim·i·nate (i lim′ə nāt′), *v.t.,* **-nat·ed, -nat·ing. 1.** to remove or get rid of, esp. as being incorrect, offensive, not up to standard, or in some other way undesirable: *to eliminate the marks made by erasing; to eliminate competitors in a contest.* **2.** to omit, esp. as being unimportant or irrelevant: *In paraphrasing my formal report, I have eliminated all statistical tables, which are of interest only to the specialist.* **3.** *Physiol.* to void or expel from an organism. **4.** *Math.* to remove (a quantity) from an equation by elimination. [< L *ēlīmināt(us)* turned out of doors (ptp. of *ēlīmināre*), equiv. to *ē-* E- + *līmen* threshold + *-ātus* -ATE[1]] —**e·lim·i·na·bil·i·ty** (i lim′ə nə bil′i tē), *n.* —**e·lim′i·na·ble,** *adj.* —**e·lim′i·nant,** *n.* —**e·lim′i·na′tive,** *adj.* —**Syn. 1.** reject. See **exclude.** —**Ant. 2.** include.

e·lim·i·na·tion (i lim′ə nā′shən), *n.* **1.** the act of eliminating. **2.** the state of being eliminated. **3.** *Math.* the process of solving a system of linear equations by a procedure in which variables are successively removed. **4.** *Sports.* a game, bout, or match in a tournament in which an individual or team is eliminated from the competition after one defeat. [ELIMINATE + -ION]

e·lim·i·na·tor (i lim′ə nā′tər), *n.* **1.** one who or that which eliminates. **2.** Also called **battery eliminator.** a device that operates from a power line to supply current and voltage to a circuit designed to be operated by a battery. [ELIMINATE + -OR[2]] —**e·lim·i·na·to·ry** (i-lim′ə nə tōr′ē, -tôr′ē), *adj.*

e·lin·guate (i ling′gwāt), *v.t.,* **-guat·ed, -guat·ing.** *Obs.* to subject to elinguation. [< L *ēlinguāt(us)*, ptp. of *ēlinguāre* to deprive of the tongue. See E-, LINGUAL, -ATE[1]]

e·lin·gua·tion (ē′ling gwā′shən), *n. Obs.* the punishment of cutting out the tongue of one who has committed a crime. [< L *ēlinguātiōn-* (s. of *ēlinguātiō*), equiv. to *ēlinguāt(us)* (see ELINGUATE) + *-iōn-* -ION]

E link, a bracket on a binnacle holding a mass of soft iron in a certain position to correct compass deviation.

El·i·nor (el′ə nər, -nôr′), *n.* a girl's given name, form of **Helen.** Also, **Eleanor, Eleanora, Elenor, Elenore, Eleonora, Eleonore.**

El·in·var (el′in vär′), *n. Trademark.* an alloy of iron, nickel, chromium, and other constituents, resistant to rust and magnetization and having a low rate of thermal expansion.

El·i·ot (el′ē ət, el′yət), *n.* **1. Charles William,** 1834–1926, U.S. educator: president of Harvard University 1869–1909. **2. George** (*Mary Ann Evans*), 1819–80, English novelist. **3. John** ("*the Apostle of the Indians*"), 1604–90, American colonial missionary. **4. Sir John,** 1592–1632, British statesman. **5. T(homas) S(tearns)** (stûrnz), 1888–1964, British poet and critic, born in the U.S.: Nobel prize 1948. **6.** Also, **Elliot, Elliott.** a boy's given name, form of **Elias.**

El·i·phaz (el′ə faz′), *n.* **1.** a son of Esau and Adah. Gen. 36:2–4. **2.** a friend of Job. Job 2:11.

E·lis (ē′lis), *n.* **1.** an ancient country in W Greece, in the Peloponnesus: site of the ancient Olympic Games. **2.** the capital of this country.

E·lis·a (i lis′ə, e lē′sə), *n.* a girl's given name, form of **Elizabeth.** Also, **E·li·sia** (i lish′ə), **Elissa.**

E·lis·a·beth (i liz′ə bəth), *n.* **1.** the mother of John the Baptist. Luke 1:5–25. **2.** a girl's given name. Also, **Elizabeth.**

E·lis·a·beth·ville (i liz′ə bəth vil′), *n.* former name of **Lubumbashi.**

E·li·sa·vet·grad (*Russ.* e lē zä vet′gʀät), *n.* former name of **Kirovograd.**

E·li·sa·vet·pol (*Russ.* e lē zä vet′pol y[ə]), *n.* former name of **Kirovabad.**

E·lise (i lēs′), *n.* a girl's given name, form of **Elizabeth.** Also, **Elyse.**

E·li·sha (i lī′shə), *n.* **1.** Also, *Douay Bible,* **El·i·se·us** (el′i sē′əs). a Hebrew prophet of the 9th century B.C., the successor of Elijah. II Kings 3–9. **2.** a boy's given name. [< Heb: God has saved]

e·li·sion (i lizh′ən), *n.* **1.** the omission of a vowel, consonant, or syllable in pronunciation. **2.** (in verse) the omission of a vowel at the end of one word when the next word begins with a vowel, as *th'orient.* [< L *ēlīsiōn-* (s. of *ēlīsiō*) a striking out, equiv. to *ēlīs(us)* (ptp. of *ēlīdere;* see ELIDE) + *-iōn-* -ION]

e·li·sor (i lī′zər), *n. Law.* a person appointed by a court to perform the duties of a sheriff or coroner who is disqualified from acting in a certain case. Also, **eslisor.** [ME *elisour* < AF, equiv. to *elis-* (var. s. of *elire* to choose < L *ēligere*) + *-our* -OR[2]]

E·lis·sa (i lis′ə), *n.* **1.** Phoenician name of **Dido. 2.** a girl's given name, form of **Elizabeth.** Also, **Elisa, Elisia.**

e·lite (i lēt′, ā lēt′), *n.* **1.** (*often construed as pl.*) the choice or best of anything considered collectively, as of a group or class of persons: *The elite of New York society was present.* **2.** (*construed as pl.*) persons of the highest class: *Only the elite were there.* **3.** a group of persons exercising the major share of authority or influence within a larger organization: *the power elite of a major political party.* **4.** a type, approximately 10-point, widely used in typewriters and having 12 characters to the inch. Cf. **pica**[1]. —*adj.* **5.** representing the most choice or select; best: *an elite group of authors.* [< F *élite*, OF *e(s)lite* < ML *ēlecta* choice, alter. of L *ēlectus* choice, n. use of ptp.; see ELECT]

Elite′ Guard′, the Schutzstaffel.

e·lit·ism (i lē′tiz əm, ā lē′-), *n.* **1.** practice of or belief in rule by an elite. **2.** consciousness of or pride in belonging to a select or favored group. [ELITE + -ISM] —**e·lit′ist,** *n.*

elix., (in prescriptions) elixir.

e·lix·ir (i lik′sər), *n.* **1.** *Pharm.* a sweetened, aromatic solution of alcohol and water containing, or used as a vehicle for, medicinal substances. **2.** an alchemic preparation formerly believed to be capable of transmitting base metals into gold or of prolonging life. **3.** the quintessence or absolute embodiment of anything. **4.** a panacea; cure-all; sovereign remedy. [ME < ML < Ar *al iksīr* alchemical preparation < LGk *xērion* drying powder (for wounds), equiv. to Gk *xēr(ós)* dry + *-ion*, neut. of *-ios* adj. suffix]

Eliz., Elizabethan.

E·li·za (i lī′zə), *n.* a girl's given name, form of **Elizabeth.**

E·liz·a·beth (i liz′ə bəth), **1.** *Douay Bible.* Elisabeth. **2.** (*Pauline Elizabeth Ottilie Luise, Princess of Wied*) ("*Carmen Sylva*") 1843–1916, queen of Rumania 1881–1914, and author. **3.** (*Elizaveta Petrovna*) 1709–62, empress of Russia 1741–62 (daughter of Peter the Great). **4. Saint,** 1207–31, Hungarian princess and religious mystic. **5.** a city in NE New Jersey. 107,698 (1960). **6.** a town in SW Pennsylvania. 2597 (1960). **7.** Also, **Elisabeth.** a girl's given name.

Elizabeth I, (*Elizabeth Tudor*) 1533–1603, queen of England 1558–1603 (successor of Mary I; daughter of Henry VIII and Anne Boleyn).

Elizabeth II, (*Elizabeth Alexandra Mary Windsor*) born 1926, queen of Great Britain since 1952 (daughter of George VI).

Elizabethan court cupboard

E·liz·a·be·than (i liz′ə bē′thən, -beth′ən), *adj.* **1.** of or pertaining to Elizabeth I, queen of England, or to her times: *Elizabethan drama; Elizabethan music.* **2.** noting or pertaining to an English Renaissance style of architecture of the reign of Elizabeth I characterized by fantastic sculptured or molded ornament of German or Flemish origin, symmetrical layouts, and an emphasis on domestic architecture. Cf. **Jacobean** (def. 2). —*n.* **3.** a person who lived in England during the Elizabethan period, esp. a poet or dramatist. [ELIZABETH + -AN]

Eliz′abeth Cit′y, a city in NE North Carolina. 14,062 (1960).

E·liz·a·beth·town (i liz′ə bəth toun′), *n.* **1.** a town in central Kentucky. 9641 (1960). **2.** a town in central Pennsylvania. 6780 (1960).

elk (elk), *n., pl.* **elks,** (*esp. collectively*) **elk** for 1, 2. **1.** the largest living deer, *Alces alces*, of Europe and Asia, resembling but smaller than the North American moose, having large, palmate antlers. **2.** Also called **wapiti.** a large, North American deer, *Cervus canadensis*, the male of which has large, spreading antlers. **3.** a pliable leather used for sport shoes, made originally of elk hide but now of calfskin or cowhide tanned and smoked to resemble elk hide. **4.** (*cap.*) a member of a fraternal organization (**Benev′olent and Protec′tive Or′der of Elks′**) that supports or contributes to various charitable causes. [ME; OE *eolc*, appar. equiv. to *eol(a)* elk + *k-* suffix, r. OE *eolh;* c. G *Elch* (OHG *el(a)ho*), L *alcēs*, Gk *álkē*]

Elk, *Cervus canadensis* (5 ft. high at shoulder; horns 5 ft.; length 8 ft.)

El·ka·nah (el kā′nə, -kä′-), *n.* a girl's given name.

Elk′ Cit′y, a town in W Oklahoma. 8196 (1960).

elk′ clo′ver, a perennial herb, *Aralia californica*, that is found from British Columbia to California, has greenish or whitish flowers in umbels and berrylike fruit, and is grown as an ornamental.

El Ke·rak (al kor′ok), Kerak.

elk-grass (elk′gras′, -gräs′), *n.* an herb, *Xerophyllum tenax,* that is found from British Columbia to California and has leaves nearly two feet long and white flowers with violet-colored stamens in racemes nearly 20 inches long. Also called **fire-lily.**

Elk′ Grove′ Vil′lage, a town in NE Illinois. 6608 (1960).

Elk·hart (elk′härt, el′kärt), *n.* a city in N Indiana. 40,274 (1960).

Elk·horn (elk′hôrn′), *n.* a town in SE Wisconsin. 3586 (1960).

elk·hound (elk′hound′), *n.* See **Norwegian elkhound.** [ELK + HOUND[1]]

El·kin (el′kin), *n.* a town in N North Carolina. 2868 (1960).

El·kins (el′kinz), *n.* a town in E West Virginia. 8307 (1960).

El·ko (el′kō), *n.* a town in NE Nevada. 6298 (1960).

Elk·ton (elk′tən), *n.* a town in NE Maryland. 5989 (1960).

ell[1] (el), *n.* an extension usually at right angles to one end of a building. Also, **el.** [ME *ele* transept, lit., wing, old form of AISLE]

ell[2] (el), *n.* a measure of length, now little used, varying in different countries: in England equal to 45 inches. [ME, OE *eln;* c. Icel *eln,* OHG *elina,* Goth *aleina,* L *ulna,* Gk *ōlénē.* See ELBOW]

ell[3] (el), *n.* elbow (def. 5). Also, **el.** [by shortening; also partly from the shape of the letter L]

El·la (el′ə), *n.* a girl's given name.

El·la·mae (el′ə mā′), *n.* a girl's given name. Also, **El′la·may′.**

El·las (e läs′), *n.* Modern Greek name of **Greece.**

Ell·dridge (el′drij), *n.* a boy's given name. Also, **Eldridge.**

El·len (el′ən), *n.* a girl's given name, form of **Helen.** Also, **El′lin.**

El·lens·burg (el′ənz bûrg′), *n.* a town in central Washington. 8625 (1960).

El·len·ville (el′ən vil′), *n.* a town in SE New York. 5003 (1960).

El·ler·y (el′ə rē), *n.* a boy's given name.

Elles′mere Is′land (elz′mēr), an island in the Arctic Ocean, NW of Greenland: a part of Canada. 76,600 sq. mi.

El·li (el′ē), *n. Scand. Myth.* an old woman, a personification of old age, who defeated Thor in a wrestling match. [< Icel *elli,* lit., old age. Cf. ELD]

El′lice Is′lands (el′is), a group of islands in the central Pacific, S of the equator: a part of the British colony of Gilbert and Ellice Islands. 16½ sq. mi. Also called **Lagoon Islands.**

El·ling·ton (el′ing tən), *n.* **Edward Kennedy** ("*Duke*"), born 1899, U.S. jazz pianist, composer, arranger, and conductor.

El·lin·wood (el′in wŏŏd′), *n.* a town in central Kansas. 2729 (1960).

El·li·ot (el′ē ət, el′yət), *n.* **1. Herb(ert James),** born 1938, Australian athlete. **2.** Also, **Eliot, El′li·ott.** a boy's given name.

El′liott eye′, *Naut.* an eye formed at the end of a cable or hawser by dividing the strands and introducing a thimble. Also, **El′liot eye′.** [special use of surname]

el·lipse (i lips′), *n. Geom.* a plane curve such that the sums of the distances of each point in its periphery from two fixed points, the foci, are equal. It is a conic section formed by the intersection of a right circular cone by a plane which cuts obliquely the axis and the opposite sides of the cone. Equation: $\frac{x^2}{a^2} + \frac{y^2}{b^2} = 1$. See diag. under **conic section.** [back formation from earlier ELLIPSIS (or its pl.)]

Ellipse
AB, CD, axes of ellipse; F,G, Foci; FM+MG=GN+NF, M and N being arbitrary points on the ellipse

el·lip·sis (i lip′sis), *n., pl.* **-ses** (-sēz). **1.** *Gram.* **a.** the omission from a sentence of a word or words that would complete or clarify the construction. **b.** the deletion of an element or morpheme from a construction with which the deleted construction is syntactically equivalent. **2.** *Print.* a mark or marks as ——, . . ., * * *, to indicate an omission or suppression of letters or words. [< L *ellīpsis* < Gk *élleipsis* an omission, equiv. to *el-* (var. of *en-* EN-[2]) + *leip-* (s. of *leípein* to leave) + *-sis* -SIS]

el·lip·so·graph (i lip′sə graf′, -gräf′), *n.* an instrument for drawing ellipses, as a trammel. Also, **elliptograph.** [ELLIPSE + -O- + -GRAPH]

el·lip·soid (i lip′soid), *n.* **1.** *Geom.* a solid figure all plane sections of which are ellipses or circles. Equation: $\frac{x^2}{a^2} + \frac{y^2}{b^2} + \frac{z^2}{c^2} = 1$. —*adj.* **2.** ellipsoidal. [ELLIPSE + -OID]

Ellipsoid

el·lip·soi·dal (i lip soid′ᵊl, el′ip-), *adj.* pertaining to or having the form of an ellipsoid. [ELLIPSOID + -AL[1]]

el·lip·ti·cal (i lip′ti kəl), *adj.* **1.** pertaining to or having the form of an ellipse. **2.** pertaining to or marked by grammatical ellipsis. **3.** (of speech or writing) expressed with extreme or excessive economy; relieved of irrelevant matter: *to converse in short, elliptical sentences.* **4.** (of a style of speaking or writing) tending to be ambiguous, cryptic, or obscure in its use of ellipsis: *an elliptical prose that is difficult to translate.* Also, **el·lip′tic.** [< Gk *elleiptik(ós)* defective (see ELLIPSIS, -TIC) + -AL[1]] —**el·lip′ti·cal·ness,** *n.*

ellip′tical light′, *Optics.* light that has been elliptically polarized.

el·lip·ti·cal·ly (i lip′tik lē), *adv.* **1.** in the form of an ellipse. **2.** in an elliptical manner; by an ellipse. **3.** with great economy of words or expression; concisely: *to speak elliptically.* **4.** without sufficient transition or a logical connection between thoughts, ideas, or expressions; ambiguously or cryptically: *to jump elliptically from general principles to specific conclusions.* [ELLIPTICAL + -LY]

ellip′tical polariza′tion, *Optics.* polarization in which the vector representing the instantaneous intensity of the electric field describes an elliptical helix in the direction of propagation. Cf. **circular polarization.** —**ellip′tically po′larized.**

ellip′tic func′tion, *Math.* one of a class of transcendental functions related to elliptic integrals and analogous to trigonometric functions.

ellip′tic geom′etry. See **Riemannian geometry.**

ellip′tic in′tegral, *Math.* a definite integral that is not expressible by means of elementary functions.

el·lip·tic·i·ty (i lip tis′i tē, el′ip-), *n.* the degree of divergence of an ellipse from a circle. [*elliptic-* (see ELLIPTICAL) + -ITY]

ellip′tic spring′, a spring formed from two leaf springs having their convex sides outward.

ellip′tic veloc′ity, *Rocketry.* the velocity of an object in an elliptic orbit.

el·lip·to·graph (i lip′tə graf′, -gräf′), *n.* ellipsograph.

El·lis (el′is), *n.* **1. Alexander John** (*Alexander John Sharpe*), 1814–90, English phonetician and mathematician. **2. (Henry) Have·lock** (hav′lok), 1859–1939, English psychologist and writer. **3.** a boy's given name, form of **Elias.**

El′lis Is′land, an island in upper New York Bay: a former U.S. immigrant examination station.

El·li·son (el′i sən), *n.* **Ralph (Waldo),** born 1914, U.S. novelist, essayist, and lecturer.

El·lis·ville (el′is vil′), *n.* **1.** a town in SE Mississippi. 4592 (1960). **2.** a town in E Missouri. 2732 (1960).

El·lo·ra (e lôr′ə, e lôr′ə), *n.* a village in S central India: important Hindu archaeological site. Also, **Elura.**

Ells·worth (elz′wûrth), *n.* **1. Lincoln,** 1880–1951, U.S. polar explorer. **2. Oliver,** 1745–1807, U.S. jurist and statesman: Chief Justice of the U.S. 1796–1800. **3.** a town in S Maine. 4444 (1960). **4.** a boy's given name.

elm (elm), *n.* **1.** any tree of the genus *Ulmus,* as *U. procera* (**English elm**), characterized by the gradually spreading columnar manner of growth of its branches. Cf. **American elm. 2.** the wood of such a tree. [ME, OE; c. OHG *elm;* akin to Icel *almr,* L *ulmus*]

El·man (el′mən), *n.* **Mi·scha** (mē′shə), 1891–1967, U.S. violinist, born in Russia.

El Man·su·ra (el′ man sŏŏr′ə), a city in the NE United Arab Republic, in the Nile delta: scene of the defeat of the Crusaders 1250 and the capture of Louis IX by the Mamelukes. 172,600 (est. 1962). Also called **Mansura.**

elm′ bark′ bee′tle, either of two bark beetles, *Scolytus multistriatus* or *Hylurgopinus rufipes,* of eastern North America, which are vectors of Dutch elm disease.

elm′ blight′. See **Dutch elm disease.**

El·mer (el′mər), *n.* a boy's given name.

Elm′ Grove′, a town in SE Wisconsin. 4994 (1960).

Elm·hurst (elm′hûrst), *n.* a city in NE Illinois, W of Chicago. 36,691 (1960).

El·mi·ra (el mī′rə), *n.* a city in S central New York. 46,517 (1960).

Elmi′ra Heights′, a town in S New York. 5157 (1960).

Elmi′ra Southeast′, a town in S New York. 6698 (1960).

El Mis·ti (el mēs′tē), a volcano in S Peru, in the Andes. 19,200 ft. Also called **Misti.**

elm′ leaf′ bee′tle, a chrysomelid beetle, *Galerucella luteola,* of eastern North America, that feeds on the foliage of elm.

El·mont (el′mont), *n.* a town on W Long Island, in SE New York. 30,138 (1960).

El Mon·te (el mon′tē), **1.** a city in SW California, near Los Angeles. 13,163 (1960). **2.** a town in W California. 4186 (1960).

Elms·ford (elmz′fərd), *n.* a town in SE New York. 3795 (1960).

Elm′wood Place′ (elm′wŏŏd′), a town in SW Ohio. 3813 (1960).

elm·y (el′mē), *adj.,* **elm·i·er, elm·i·est.** abounding in or consisting of elms. [ELM + -Y[1]]

El O·beid (el ō bād′), a city in the central Sudan: Egyptian army defeated by the Mahdi 1883. 52,372 (1956). Also, **Obeid.**

el·o·cu·tion (el′ə kyōō′shən), *n.* **1.** a person's manner of speaking or reading in public: *The actor's elocution is impeccable.* **2.** *Speech.* the study and practice of oral delivery, including the control of both voice and gesture. [< L *ēlocūtiōn-* (s. of *ēlocūtiō*) a speaking out, equiv. to *ē-* E- + *locūtiōn-* LOCUTION] —**el·o·cu·tion·ar·y** (el′ə kyōō′shə ner′ē), *adj.* —**el′o·cu′tion·ist,** *n.* —**Syn. 2.** oratory, declamation.

E·lo·him (e′lō him′, e lō′him; *Heb.* e lō hēm′; *in liturgical use* e lō kēm′), *n.* God, esp. as used in the Hebrew text of the Old Testament. [< Heb, pl. of *elōh* God] —**El·o·him·ic** (el′ō him′ik), *adj.* —**E·lo′·hism,** *n.*

E·lo·hist (e lō′hist), *n.* a writer of one of the major sources of the Hexateuch, in which God is characteristically referred to as *Elohim* rather than *Yahweh.* Cf. **Yahwist.** [< Heb *elōh* God + -IST] —**El′o·his′tic,** *adj.*

e·loign (i loin′), *v.t.* to remove (oneself) to a distance. Also, **e·loin′.** [late ME *e(s)loi(g)ne* < AF *e(s)loigner* to go or take far, equiv. to *es-* EX-[1] + *loigner,* deriv. of *loing* < L *longē* afar, equiv. to *long(us)* distant (see LONG[1]) + *-ē* adv. suffix] —**e·loign′er, e·loin′er,** *n.* —**e·loign′·ment, e·loin′ment,** *n.*

El·o·i·sa to Ab·e·lard (el′ō ē′zə tōō ab′ə lärd′), a poem (1717) by Alexander Pope.

El·o·ise (el′ə wēz′, el′ə wēz′), *n.* a girl's given name.

e·lon·gate (i lông′gāt, i long′-, ē′lông gāt′, ē′long-), *v.,* **-gat·ed, -gat·ing,** *adj.* —*v.t.* **1.** to draw out to greater length; lengthen; extend. —*v.i.* **2.** to increase in length. —*adj.* **3.** extended; lengthened; elongated. [< LL *ēlongāt(us)* (ptp. of *ēlongāre*) lengthened out, equiv. to *ē-* E- + *long(us)* LONG[1] + *-ātus* -ATE[1]] —**e·lon·ga·tive** (ē′lông gā′tiv, ē′long-), *adj.* —**Ant. 1.** shorten.

e·lon·ga·tion (i lông gā′shən, i long-, ē′lông-, ē′long-), *n.* **1.** the act of elongating, or the state of being elongated. **2.** something that is elongated, or an elongated part. **3.** *Astron.* the angular distance, measured from the earth, between a planet or the moon and the sun or between a satellite and the planet about which it revolves. [ME < LL *ēlongātiōn-* (s. of *ēlongātiō*), equiv. to *ēlongāt(us)* (see ELONGATE) + *-iōn-* -ION]

e·lope (i lōp′), *v.i.,* **e·loped, e·lop·ing. 1.** to run off secretly to be married, usually without the consent or knowledge of one's parents. **2.** to run away with a lover. **3.** to abscond or escape. [ME **alopen* to run away (whence AF *aloper*). See A-[3], LOPE] —**e·lope′·ment,** *n.* —**e·lop′er,** *n.*

el·o·quence (el′ə kwəns), *n.* **1.** the action, practice, or art of using language with fluency, power, and aptness. **2.** eloquent language or discourse: *a flow of eloquence.* [ME < MF < L *ēloquentia.* See ELOQUENT, -ENCE]

el·o·quent (el′ə kwənt), *adj.* **1.** having or exercising the power of fluent, forceful, and appropriate speech: *an eloquent orator.* **2.** characterized by forceful and appropriate expression: *an eloquent speech.* **3.** movingly expressive: *looks eloquent of disgust.* [ME < L *ēloquent-* (s. of *ēloquēns,* prp. of *ēloquī*) speaking out, eloquent, equiv. to *ē-* E- + *loqu-* speak + *-ent-* -ENT] —**el′o·quent·ly,** *adv.* —**el′o·quent·ness,** *n.*

El Oued (el wed′), a city in E Algeria. 13,000 (1954).

E·loy (ē′loi), *n.* a town in S Arizona. 4899 (1960).

El·o·yse (el′ō ēz′, el′ō ēz′), *n.* a girl's given name. Also, **Eloise.**

El Pas·o (el pas′ō), a city in W Texas, on the Rio Grande. 276,687 (1960).

El Pa·so de Ro·bles (el pas′ō dā rō′blās; *Sp.* el pä′sô ᵺe rô′vles), a town in SW California. 6677 (1960). Also called **Paso Robles.**

El·pe·nor (el pē′nôr), *n.* (in the *Odyssey*) a companion of Odysseus who was killed when he fell off the roof of Circe's palace.

El Pen·sa·dor Me·xi·ca·no (*Sp.* el pen′sä ᵺôr′ me hē kä′nô), pen name of José Joaquín Fernández de Lizardi.

El·ri·ca (el rē′kə), *n.* a girl's given name.

El Ri·o (el rē′ō), a town in S California. 6966 (1960).

el·ritch (el′rich), *adj.* eldritch.

El·roy (el′roi), *n.* a boy's given name.

El·sa (el′sə), *n.* **1.** a town in S Texas. 3847 (1960). **2.** a girl's given name, form of **Elizabeth.**

El Sal·va·dor (el sal′və dôr′; *Sp.* el säl′vä ᵺôr′), a republic in NW Central America. 2,824,198 (1964); 13,176 sq. mi. *Cap.:* San Salvador. Also called **Salvador.**

Els·don (elz′dən), *n.* a boy's given name.

else (els), *adj.* **1.** other than the persons or things mentioned or implied: *What else could I have done?* **2.** in addition to the persons or things mentioned or implied: *Who else was there?* **3.** other or in addition (used in the possessive following an indefinite pronoun): *someone else's money.* —*adv.* **4.** if not (usually prec. by *or*): *It's a macaw, or else I don't know birds.* **5.** in some other way; otherwise: *How else could I have acted?* **6.** at some other place or time: *Where else might I find this book?* **7. or else,** or suffer the consequences: *Do what I say, or else.* [ME, OE *elles* (c. OHG *elles*), equiv. to *ell-* other (c. Goth *aljis,* L *alius,* Gk *állos*) + *-es* 's[1]]

—**Usage.** The possessive forms of SOMEBODY ELSE, EVERYBODY ELSE, etc., are *somebody else's, everybody else's,* the forms *somebody's else, everybody's else* being considered nonstandard in present-day English. One exception is the possessive for WHO ELSE, which is occasionally formed as *whose else* when a noun does not immediately follow: *Is this book yours? Whose else could it be? No, it's somebody else's.*

El Se·gun·do (el sə gun′dō, -gŏŏn′-), a city in SW California, near Los Angeles. 14,219 (1960).

El·se·ne (el′sə nə), *n.* Flemish name of **Ixelles.**

El·se·vier (el′zə vēr′, -vər), *n., adj.* Elzevir.

else·where (els′hwâr′, -wâr′), *adv.* somewhere else; in or to some other place: *You will have to look elsewhere for an answer.* [ME *elleswher,* OE *elles hwǣr.* See ELSE, WHERE]

else·whith·er (els′hwiᵺ′ər, -wiᵺ′-, els hwiᵺ′-, -wiᵺ′-), *adv.* in another direction; toward a different place or goal: *His thoughts had drifted elsewhither.* [ME *elleswhider,* OE *elleshwider.* See ELSE, WHITHER]

El·sie (el′sē), *n.* **1.** a girl's given name, form of **Elizabeth. 2.** a boy's given name.

El·si·nore (el′sə nôr′, -nōr′), *n.* Helsingør.

Els·mere (elz′mēr), *n.* **1.** a town in N Delaware. 7319 (1960). **2.** a town in N Kentucky. 4607 (1960).

El Som·bre·ro de Tres Pi·cos (*Sp.* el sôm brе′rô ᵺe tres pē′kôs). See **Three-cornered Hat, The.**

El·speth (el′speth, -spəth), *n.* a girl's given name, form of **Elizabeth.**

ELSSE COTAR (el′sē kō′tär), *Electronics.* a passive range-safety radar tracking system for missiles, in which data transmitted by a transponder on the missile are received and correlated by a sky screen on the ground. [*el(ectronic) s(ky) s(creen) e(quipment); c(orrelated) o(rientation) t(racking) a(nd) r(ange system)*]

El·ton (el′tᵊn), *n.* a boy's given name. Also, **Alton.**

el·u·ant (el′yōō ənt), *n.* a liquid used for elution. [< L *elu(ere)* (to) wash out + -ANT]

el·u·ate (el′yōō it, -āt′), *n.* a liquid solution resulting from elution. [< L *elu(ere)* (equiv. to *ē-* E- + *luere* to wash, akin to *lavāre;* see LAVE[1]) + -ATE[1]]

e·lu·ci·date (i lōō′si dāt′), *v.t.,* **-dat·ed, -dat·ing.** to make lucid or clear; throw light upon; explain: *an explanation that elucidated his recent strange behavior.* [< LL *ēlūcidāt(us)* (ptp. of *ēlūcidāre*) enlightened, equiv. to *ē-* E- + *lūcid(us)* LUCID + *-ātus* -ATE[1]] —**e·lu′ci·da′·tion,** *n.* —**e·lu′ci·da′tive,** *adj.* —**e·lu′ci·da′tor,** *n.* —**Syn.** explicate, clarify. See **explain.**

e·lude (i lōōd′), *v.t.,* **e·lud·ed, e·lud·ing. 1.** to avoid or escape by speed, cleverness, trickery, etc.: *to elude pursuers.* **2.** to slip away from; evade: *The answer eludes me.* **3.** *Obs.* to baffle or puzzle. [< L *ēlūde(re)* (to) deceive, evade, equiv. to *ē-* E- + *lūdere* to play, deceive] —**e·lud′er,** *n.* —**Syn. 1.** shun, dodge. See **escape.** —**Ant. 1.** pursue.

E·lul (el′ŏŏl; *Heb.* e lōōl′), *n.* the twelfth month of the Jewish calendar. Cf. **Jewish calendar.**

E·lu·ra (e lŏŏr′ə), *n.* Ellora.

e·lu·sion (i lōō′zhən), *n.* the act of eluding; evasion; clever escape. [< LL *ēlūsiōn-* (s. of *ēlūsiō*) deception, evasion, equiv. to *ēlūs(us),* ptp. of *ēlūdere* to ELUDE (*ē-* E- + *lūd-* play + *-tus* ptp. suffix) + *-iōn-* -ION]

e·lu·sive (i lōō′siv), *adj.* **1.** eluding clear perception or complete mental grasp; hard to express or define: *an elusive concept.* **2.** cleverly or skillfully evasive: *a fish* too elusive to catch. Also, **e·lu·so·ry** (i lo͞o′sə rē). [ELUS(ION) + -IVE] —**e·lu′sive·ly,** *adv.* —**e·lu′sive·ness,** *n.*

e·lute (ē lo͞ot′, i lo͞ot′), *v.t.,* **e·lut·ed, e·lut·ing.** *Physical. Chem.* to remove by dissolving, as adsorbed material from an adsorbent. [< L *ēlūt(us)* (ptp. of *ēluere*) washed out, equiv. to *ē-* E- + *lū-* (var. of *lau-*) LAVE + *-tus* ptp. suffix] —**e·lu′tion,** *n.*

e·lu·tri·ate (i lo͞o′trē āt′), *v.t.,* **-at·ed, -at·ing. 1.** to purify by washing and straining or decanting. **2.** to separate the light and heavy particles of by washing. [< L *ēlutriāt(us)* (ptp. of *ēlutriāre*) washed out, equiv. to *ē-* E- + *lutri-* wash (< ?) + *-ātus* -ATE[1]] —**e·lu′tri·a′tion,** *n.*

e·lu·tri·a·tor (i lo͞o′trē ā′tər), *n.* a machine for separating particles of mineral by elutriation. [ELUTRIATE + -OR[2]]

e·lu·vi·al (i lo͞o′vē əl, -vyəl), *adj.* of or pertaining to eluviation or eluvium. [< NL; see ELUVIUM, -AL[1]]

e·lu·vi·ate (i lo͞o′vē āt′), *v.i.,* **-at·ed, -at·ing.** to undergo eluviation. [ELUVI(UM) + -ATE[1]]

e·lu·vi·a·tion (i lo͞o′vē ā′shən), *n.* the movement through the soil of materials brought into suspension or dissolved by the action of water. [ELUVIATE + -ION]

e·lu·vi·um (i lo͞o′vē əm), *n., pl.* **-vi·a** (-vē ə). *Geol.* a deposit of soil, dust, etc., formed from the decomposition of rock and found in its place of origin. [< NL, equiv. to *ē-* E- in privative or negative sense + (AL)LUVIUM]

El·va (el′və), *n.* a girl's given name.

el·ver (el′vər), *n.* a young eel, esp. one that is migrating up a stream from the ocean. [var. of *elfare,* lit., eel-journey. See EEL, FARE][1]

El·ver·da (el vûr′də), *n.* a girl's given name.

elves (elvz), *n.* pl. of **elf.**

El·vin (el′vin), *n.* a boy's given name. Also, **Elwin, Elwyn.**

El·vine (el vēn′), *n.* a girl's given name. Also, **El·vi·na** (el vē′nə).

El·vi·ra (el vīr′ə, -vēr′ə), *n.* a girl's given name.

El·vis (el′vis), *n.* a boy's given name, form of **Elwin.**

elv·ish (el′vish), *adj.* elfish. [ME; see ELF, -ISH[1]] —**elv′ish·ly,** *adv.*

El·vi·ta (el vē′tə), *n.* a girl's given name.

El·win (el′win), *n.* a boy's given name. Also, **Elvin, El′wyn.**

E·ly (ē′lē *for 1–4;* ē′lī *for 5*), *n.* **1. Isle of,** an administrative county in E England: formerly part of Cambridgeshire. 89,112 (1961); 375 sq. mi. *Co. seat:* March. **2.** a town in this county: medieval cathedral. 9815 (1961). **3.** a town in NE Minnesota. 5438 (1960). **4.** a town in E Nevada. 4018 (1960). **5.** Also, **Eli, Elie.** a boy's given name.

El·y·ot (el′ē ət, el′yət), *n.* **Sir Thomas,** c1490–1546, English scholar and diplomat.

E·lyr·i·a (i lēr′ē ə), *n.* a city in N Ohio. 43,782 (1960).

E·lyse (i lēs′), *n.* a girl's given name, form of **Elizabeth.** Also, **Elise.**

É·ly·sée (ā lē zā′), *n.* a palace in Paris: the official residence of the president of France.

E·ly·sia (i lish′ə), *n.* a girl's given name.

E·ly·sian (i lizh′ən, i lē′zhən), *adj.* **1.** of, pertaining to, or resembling Elysium. **2.** blissful; delightful. [ELYSI(UM) + -AN]

E·ly·si·um (i lizh′ē əm, i lē′zhē-, i liz′-, i lē′zē-, i lizh′əm), *n.* **1.** Also called **Ely′sian Fields′.** *Class. Myth.* the abode of the blessed after death. **2.** any similarly conceived abode or state of the dead. **3.** any place or state of perfect happiness. **4.** an area in the northern hemisphere of Mars, appearing as a light region when viewed telescopically from the earth. [< L < Gk *ēlýsion (pedíon)* blest (plain)]

E·ly·tis (e lē′tis), *n.* **Odysseus** (*Odysseus Alepoudelis*), born 1911, Greek poet: Nobel prize 1979.

el·y·tra (el′i trə), *n.* pl. of **elytron.**

el·y·troid (el′i troid′), *adj.* resembling an elytron. [ELYTR(ON) + -OID]

el·y·tron (el′i tron′), *n., pl.* **-tra** (-trə). one of the pair of hardened forewings of certain insects, as beetles, forming a protective covering for the posterior or flight wings. Also called **wing case, wing cover.** See diag. under **coleopteron.** [< NL < Gk *élytron* a covering] —**el·y·trous** (el′i trəs), *adj.*

el·y·trum (el′i trəm), *n., pl.* **-tra** (-trə). *Obs.* elytron. [Latinized var. of ELYTRON]

El·ze·vir (el′zə vēr′, -vər), *n.* **1. Louis,** c1540–1617, Dutch printer: founder of a printing firm at Leyden (1591?) that was operated by his descendants through the 18th century. **2.** a book produced by this printing house. **3.** a style of printing type with firm hairlines and stubby serifs. —*adj.* **4.** of or pertaining to the Elzevir family or the books it published. **5.** indicating the type originated by this family. Also, **Elsevier, El′ze·vier′.** —**El′ze·vir′i·an,** *adj.*

em (em), *n., pl.* **ems,** *adj.* —*n.* **1.** the letter M, m. **2.** Also called **mut, mutton.** *Print.* **a.** the square of any size of type used as the unit of measurement for matter printed in that type size. **b.** (originally) the portion of a line of type occupied by the letter M in type of the same size. **3.** See **em pica.** —*adj.* **4.** *Print.* having the area of an em quad or the length of an em dash.

'em (əm), *pron. Informal.* them: *Put 'em down there.* [ME *hem,* OE *heom,* dat. pl. of HE[1]]

em-[1], var. of **en-**[1] before *b, p,* and sometimes *m: embalm.* Cf. **im-**[1].

em-[2], var. of **en-**[2] before *b, m, p, ph: embolism, emphasis.*

EM, enlisted man; enlisted men.

Em., *Physical Chem.* emanation (def. 3).

E.M., 1. Earl Marshal. **2.** electromotive. **3.** Engineer of Mines.

e·ma·ci·ate (i mā′shē āt′), *v.t.,* **-at·ed, -at·ing.** to make lean by a gradual wasting away of flesh. [< L *ēmaciāt(us),* wasted away, equiv. to *ē-* E- + *maciātus,* ptp. of *maciāre* to produce leanness (*maci(ēs)* leanness + *-ātus* -ATE[1])]

e·ma·ci·at·ed (i mā′shē ā′tid), *adj.* marked by emaciation. [EMACIATE + -ED[2]]

e·ma·ci·a·tion (i mā′shē ā′shən, -sē-), *n.* **1.** abnormal thinness caused by lack of nutrition or by disease. **2.** the process of emaciating. [< L *ēmaciāt(us)* (see EMACIATE) + -ION]

em·a·gram (em′ə gram′), *n. Meteorol.* a thermodynamic chart indicating temperature as the abscissa on a linear scale and pressure as the ordinate on a logarithmic scale. [EM + (DI)AGRAM]

é·mail en plein (ā mī′ än plăn′; *Fr.* ā mȧ′y äɴ plaɴ′), enamel produced by the basse-taille technique [< F: lit., enamel in full]

é·mail om·brant (ā mī′ ôm bränt′; *Fr.* ā mȧ′y ôɴ bʀäɴ′), a technique of ceramic decoration in which a transparent glaze is laid over an intaglio design to produce an illusion of depth. [< F: lit., a shading enamel]

em·a·nant (em′ə nənt), *adj.* emanating or issuing from or as if from a source: *strains of music emanant from the room above.* [< L *ēmānant-* (s. of *ēmānāns* outflowing, prp. of *ēmānāre*), equiv. to *ē-* E- + *mān-* flow + *-ant-* -ANT]

em·a·nate (em′ə nāt′), *v.,* **-nat·ed, -nat·ing.** —*v.i.* **1.** to flow out, issue, or proceed, as from a source or origin; come forth; originate. —*v.t.* **2.** to send forth; emit. [< L *ēmānāt(us)* having flowed out (ptp. of *ēmānāre*), equiv. to *ē-* E- + *mān-* flow + *-ātus* -ATE[1]] —**em′a·na′tor,** *n.* —**em·a·na·to·ry** (em′ə nə tôr′ē, -tōr′ē), *adj.*
—**Syn. 1.** arise, spring, flow. See **emerge.**

em·a·na·tion (em′ə nā′shən), *n.* **1.** the act or an instance of emanating. **2.** something that emanates or is emanated. **3.** *Physical Chem.* a gaseous product of radioactive disintegration including radon, thoron, and actinon. [< LL *ēmānātiōn-* (s. of *ēmānātiō*), equiv. to *ēmānāt(us)* (see EMANATE) + *-iōn-* -ION] —**em′a·na′tion·al,** *adj.*

em·a·na·tive (em′ə nā′tiv), *adj.* **1.** tending to emanate; emanating. **2.** of or pertaining to emanation. [EMANAT(ION) + -IVE] —**em′a·na′tive·ly,** *adv.*

e·man·ci·pate (i man′sə pāt′), *v.t.,* **-pat·ed, -pat·ing. 1.** to free from restraint, influence, or the like. **2.** to free (a slave) from bondage. **3.** *Roman and Civil Law.* to terminate paternal control over. [< L *ēmancipāt(us)* (ptp. of *ēmancipāre*) freed from control, equiv. to *ē-* E- + *man(us)* hand + *cip-* (var. s. of *capere* to seize) + *-ātus* -ATE[1]] —**e·man′ci·pa′tive,** *adj.*
—**Syn. 1, 2.** See **release.**

e·man·ci·pat·ed (i man′sə pā′tid), *adj.* **1.** freed, as from slavery, bondage, or the like. **2.** not constrained or restricted by custom, tradition, superstition, etc.; uninhibited: *living the uninhibited life of an emancipated woman.* [EMANCIPATE + -ED[2]]

e·man·ci·pa·tion (i man′sə pā′shən), *n.* **1.** the act of emancipating. **2.** the state or fact of being emancipated. [< L *ēmancipātiōn-* (s. of *ēmancipātiō*), equiv. to *ēmancipāt(us)* (see EMANCIPATE) + *-iōn-* -ION]

e·man·ci·pa·tion·ist (i man′sə pā′shə nist), *n.* a person who advocates emancipation, esp. an advocate of the freeing of human beings from slavery. [EMANCIPATION + -IST]

Emancipa′tion Proclama′tion, *U.S. Hist.* the proclamation issued by President Lincoln on January 1, 1863, freeing the slaves in those territories still in rebellion against the Union.

e·man·ci·pa·tor (i man′sə pā′tər), *n.* a person who emancipates. [< LL; see EMANCIPATE, -OR[2]] —**e·man·ci·pa·to·ry** (i man′sə pə tôr′ē, -tōr′ē), *adj.*

e·man·ci·pist (i man′sə pist), *n. Australian.* (formerly) a person who was sent to Australia in penal servitude, served his term, and became a settler. [EMANCIP(ATE) + -IST]

E·man·u·el (i man′yo͞o əl), *n.* a boy's given name. Also, **Immanuel.**

e·mar·gi·nate (i mär′jə nāt′), *adj.* **1.** notched at the margin. **2.** *Bot.* notched at the apex, as a petal or leaf. Also, **e·mar′gi·nat′ed.** [< L *ēmargināt(us)* deprived of its edge, equiv. to *ē-* E- + *margin-* (see MARGIN) + *-ātus* -ATE[1]] —**e·mar′gi·nate′ly,** *adv.* —**e·mar′gi·na′tion,** *n.*

Emarginate leaves

e·mas·cu·late (*v.* i mas′kyə lāt′; *adj.* i mas′kyə lit, -lāt′), *v.,* **-lat·ed, -lat·ing,** *adj.* —*v.t.* **1.** to castrate. **2.** to deprive of strength or vigor; weaken; render effeminate. —*adj.* **3.** emasculated; effeminate. [< L *ēmasculāt(us)* (ptp. of *ēmasculāre*), equiv. to *ē-* E- + *mās* male + *-cul(us)* adj. suffix + *-ātus* -ATE[1]] —**e·mas′cu·la′tion,** *n.* —**e·mas′cu·la′tive,** *adj.* —**e·mas′cu·la′tor,** *n.* —**e·mas·cu·la·to·ry** (i mas′kyə lə tôr′ē, -tōr′ē), *adj.*

E·ma·thi·on (i mā′thē on′), *n. Class. Myth.* a son of Tithonus and Eos.

É·maux et Ca·mées (*Fr.* ā mō′ ā kȧ mā′), a collection of poems (1852) by Théophile Gautier.

em·ba·cle (em bä′kəl, -bak′əl), *n.* an accumulation of broken ice in a river. Cf. **debacle** (def. 2). [F, equiv. to *em-* EM-[1] + *(dé)bâcle* DEBACLE]

em·balm (em bäm′), *v.t.* **1.** to treat (a dead body) so as to preserve it, as with chemicals, drugs, balsams, etc. **2.** to preserve from oblivion; keep in memory. **3.** to cause to remain unchanged; prevent the development of: *great ideas embalmed forever in musty libraries.* **4.** to impart a balmy fragrance to: *lilacs embalming the evening air.* [ME *embalme(n), enbaume(n)* < MF *embamer, embaumer,* OF *emba(u)smer,* equiv. to *em-* EM-[1] + *ba(u)sme* BALM] —**em·balm′er,** *n.* —**em·balm′ment,** *n.*

em·bank (em baŋk′), *v.t.* to enclose, confine, or protect with a bank, mound, dike, or the like. [EM-[1] + BANK[1]]

em·bank·ment (em baŋk′mənt), *n.* **1.** a bank, mound, dike, or the like, raised to hold back water, carry a roadway, etc. **2.** the act of embanking. [EMBANK + -MENT]

em·bar (em bär′), *v.t.,* **-barred, -bar·ring. 1.** to stop or hinder, as by a bar. **2.** to enclose within bars; imprison. [late ME *embarre(n)* < MF *embarrer,* equiv. to *em-* EM-[1] + *barrer* to bar]

em·bar·ca·tion (em′bär kā′shən), *n.* embarkation.

em·bar·go (em bär′gō), *n., pl.* **-goes,** *v.,* **-goed, -go·ing.** —*n.* **1.** an order of a government prohibiting the movement of merchant vessels from or into its ports. **2.** an injunction from a government commerce agency to refuse freight for shipment, in case of congestion, insufficient facilities, etc. **3.** any restriction imposed upon commerce by law. **4.** a restraint or hindrance; prohibition. —*v.t.* **5.** to impose an embargo on. [< Sp, deriv. of *embargar* to hinder, embarrass < VL **imbarricāre,* equiv. to *im-* IM-[1] + *-barricāre* (LL *barr(a)* BAR[1] + *-icāre* causative suffix)]

em·bark (em bärk′), *v.t.* **1.** to put or receive on board a ship. **2.** to involve (someone) in an enterprise. **3.** to venture or invest (something) in an enterprise. —*v.i.* **4.** to board a ship, as for a voyage. **5.** to engage in an enterprise, business, etc. [< MF *embarqu(er)* < OPr *embarcar,* equiv. to *em-* EM-[1] + *barc(a)* BARK[3] + *-ar* inf. suffix]

em·bar·ka·tion (em′bär kā′shən), *n.* the act, process, or an instance of embarking. Also, **embarcation.** [< F *embarcation.* See EMBARK, -ATION]

embarka′tion deck′, *Naut.* any deck from which passengers and crew enter lifeboats in an emergency.

Embarka′tion for Cyth′era, The, a painting (1717) by Antoine Watteau. Also called **A Pilgrimage to the Island of Cythera.**

em·bark·ment (em bärk′mənt), *n.* an embarkation. [EMBARK + -MENT]

em·bar·rass (em bar′əs), *v.t.* **1.** to make uncomfortably self-conscious; cause confusion and shame to; disconcert; abash: *His bad manners embarrassed her.* **2.** to make difficult or intricate, as a question or problem; complicate. **3.** to put obstacles or difficulties in the way of; impede: *The motion was advanced in order to embarrass the progress of the bill.* **4.** to beset with financial difficulties; burden with debt: *The incline of sales embarrassed the company.* —*v.i.* **5.** to become disconcerted, abashed, or confused: *She embarrasses easily.* [< F *embarrass(er)* < Sp *embarazar* < Pg *embaraçar,* equiv. to *em-* EM-[1] + *baraç(a)* noose + *-ar* inf. suffix] —**em·bar′rassed·ly** (em bar′əst lē, -ə sid lē), *adv.* —**em·bar′rass·ing·ly,** *adv.*
—**Syn. 1.** discompose, discomfit, chagrin. See **confuse. 3.** hamper, hinder.

em·bar·rass·ment (em bar′əs mənt), *n.* **1.** the state of being embarrassed; disconcertment; abashment. **2.** the act or an instance of embarrassing. **3.** something that embarrasses. **4.** excessive amount; overabundance: *an embarrassment of riches.* [< F *embarrassement.* See EMBARRASS, -MENT]
—**Syn. 1.** discomposure, confusion, perplexity. See **shame.**

em·bas·sa·dor (em bas′ə dər), *n.* ambassador.

em·bas·sage (em′bə sij), *n. Archaic.* embassy. [var. of *ambassage* < OF *ambasse* (< L *ambactia* office; see EMBASSY) + -AGE]

em·bas·sy (em′bə sē), *n., pl.* **-sies. 1.** a body of persons entrusted with a mission to a sovereign or government; an ambassador and his staff. **2.** the official headquarters of an ambassador. **3.** the function or office of an ambassador. **4.** a mission headed by an ambassador. [var. of *ambassy* < MF *ambassee* < VL **ambactiāta,* equiv. to L *ambacti(a)* office (< Gallic L *ambact(us)* vassal, servant, equiv. to *amb-* AMBI- + *-act(us)* mover ACTOR + *-ia* -Y[3]) + *-āta* fem. suffix]

em·bat·tle[1] (em bat′əl), *v.t.,* **-tled, -tling. 1.** to arrange in order of battle; prepare for battle; arm. **2.** to fortify (a town, camp, etc.). [ME *embataile(n)* < MF *embataillier.* See EM-[1], BATTLE[1]]

em·bat·tle[2] (em bat′əl), *v.t.,* **-tled, -tling.** to furnish with battlements. [ME *embataile(n).* See EM-[1], BATTLE[2]]

em·bat·tled (em bat′əld), *adj. Heraldry.* noting a charge, as an ordinary or a partition line having a series of square indentations suggesting crenelation: *a fess embattled.* [EMBATTLE[2] + -ED[2]]

embat′tled gra′dy (grā′dē), *Heraldry.* See **battled embattled.** [*grady* cut into steps, springing from steps; formed on model of F *-é, -ée* (ptp. ending). See GRADE, -Y[1]]

em·bat·tle·ment (em bat′əl mənt), *n.* battlement. [ME *embatailment.* See EMBATTLE[2], -MENT]

em·bay (em bā′), *v.t.* **1.** to enclose in or as if in a bay; surround or envelop. **2.** to form into a bay. [EM-[1] + BAY[1]]

em·bay·ment (em bā′mənt), *n.* **1.** a bay. **2.** *Phys. Geog.* the process by which a bay is formed. [EMBAY + -MENT]

em·bed (em bed′), *v.t.,* **-bed·ded, -bed·ding. 1.** to fix into a surrounding mass: *to embed stones in cement.* **2.** to lay in or as in a bed. **3.** *Math.* to map a set into another set. Also, **imbed.** [EM-[1] + BED] —**em·bed′ment,** *n.*

em·bed·ding (em bed′ing), *n. Math.* a map from a set into another set. [EMBED + -ING[1]]

em·bel·lish (em bel′ish), *v.t.* **1.** to beautify by or as if by ornamentation; ornament; adorn. **2.** to enhance (a statement or narrative) with fictitious additions. [ME *embelisshe(n)* < MF *embeliss-* (s. of *embelir*), equiv. to *em-* EM-[1] + *bel-* (< L *bellus* pretty) + *-iss* -ISH[2]] —**embel′lish·er,** *n.*
—**Syn. 1.** decorate, garnish, bedeck, embroider. —**Ant. 1.** disfigure.

em·bel·lish·ment (em bel′ish mənt), *n.* **1.** an ornament or decoration. **2.** a fictitious addition, as to a factual statement. **3.** *Music.* **a.** ornament (def. 8). **b.** See **auxiliary tone. 4.** the act of embellishing. **5.** state of being embellished. [EMBELLISH + -MENT]

em·ber (em′bər), *n.* **1.** a small live coal, brand of wood, etc., as in a dying fire. **2. embers,** the smoldering remains of a fire. [ME *eemer, emeri,* OE *ǣmerge, ǣmyrie* (c. Icel *eimyrja,* OHG *eimuria*), equiv. to *ǣm-* (c. Icel *eimr* steam) + *-erge, -yrie,* akin to OE *ys(e)le* ember, L *ūrere* to burn]

Em′ber day′, any of the days in the quarterly three-day period of prayer and fasting (the Wednesday, Friday, and Saturday after the first Sunday in Lent, after Whitsunday, after Sept. 14, and after Dec. 13) observed in the Roman Catholic church and other Western churches. [ME *ymber day,* OE *ymbrendæg*]

em·bez·zle (em bez′əl), *v.t.,* **-zled, -zling.** to appropriate fraudulently to one's own use, as money or property entrusted to one's care. [late ME *embesile(n)* < AF *embeseiller* to destroy, make away with, equiv. to *em-* EM-[1] + *beseiller,* OF *besillier* destroy < ?] —**embez′zle·ment,** *n.* —**em·bez′zler,** *n.*

em·bi·id (em′bē id), *n.* See **web spinner.** [< NL *embiid(ae),* equiv. to *Embi(a)* genus name + *-idae* (see -ID[2])]

em·bi·ot·o·cid (em′bē ot′ə sid), *n.* **1.** any fish of the family *Embiotocidae,* comprising the surfperches. —*adj.* **2.** belonging or pertaining to the family *Embiotocidae.* [< NL *Embiotocidae* name of family, equiv. to *Embiotoc(a)* name of genus (< Gk *émbio(s)* having life + *-toca* < *tókos* offspring) + *-idae* -ID[2]]

em·bit·ter (em bit′ər), *v.t.* **1.** to make bitter or more bitter. **2.** to cause to feel bitter or hostile: *The divorce embittered him against all women.* Also, **imbitter.** [EM-[1] + BITTER] —**em·bit′ter·er,** *n.* —**em·bit′ter·ment,** *n.*

Em·bla (em′blä), *n.* *Scand. Myth.* the first woman, made by the gods from a tree. Cf. **Ask.**

em·blaze[1] (em blāz′), *v.t.*, **-blazed, -blaz·ing.** *Obs.* to emblazon. —**em·blaz′er,** *n.*

em·blaze[2] (em blāz′), *v.t.*, **-blazed, -blaz·ing. 1.** to illuminate, as by a blaze. **2.** to kindle. [EM-[1] + BLAZE[1]] —**em·blaz′er,** *n.*

em·bla·zon (em blā′zən), *v.t.* **1.** to depict, as on an escutcheon in heraldry. **2.** to decorate with brilliant colors. **3.** to proclaim; celebrate or extol. [EM-[1] + BLAZON] —**em·bla′zon·er,** *n.*

em·bla·zon·ment (em blā′zən mənt), *n.* **1.** the act of emblazoning. **2.** something that is emblazoned. [EM-[1] + BLAZONMENT]

em·bla·zon·ry (em blā′zən rē), *n.* **1.** the act or art of emblazoning; heraldic decoration. **2.** brilliant representation or embellishment. [EM-[1] + BLAZONRY]

em·blem (em′bləm), *n.* **1.** an object or its representation, symbolizing a quality, state, class of persons, etc.; symbol. **2.** a sign, design, or figure that identifies or represents something: *the emblem of a school.* **3.** an allegorical picture, often inscribed with a motto supplemental to the visual image with which it forms a single unit of meaning. **4.** *Obs.* an inlaid or tessellated ornament. —*v.t.* **5.** to represent with an emblem. [ME < L *emblēma* inlaid or mosaic work < Gk *émblēma* something put on, equiv. to *em-* EM-[2] + *blêma* something thrown or put, cf. *embállein* to throw in or on] —**Syn. 1.** token, sign, figure, image, device, badge.

em·blem·at·ic (em′blə mat′ik), *adj.* pertaining to, of the nature of, or serving as an emblem; symbolic. Also, **em′blem·at′i·cal.** [< Gk *emblemat-*, s. of *émblēma* (see EMBLEM) + -IC] —**em′blem·at′i·cal·ly,** *adv.* —**em′blem·at′i·cal·ness,** *n.*

em·blem·a·tise (em blem′ə tīz′), *v.t.*, **-tised, -tis·ing.** *Chiefly Brit.* emblematize.

em·blem·a·tist (em blem′ə tist), *n.* a designer, maker, or user of emblems. [*emblemat-* (see EMBLEMATIC) + -IST]

em·blem·a·tize (em blem′ə tīz′), *v.t.*, **-tized, -tiz·ing.** to serve as an emblem of; represent by an emblem. Also, *esp. Brit.*, **emblematise.** [*emblemat-* (see EMBLEMATIC) + -IZE]

em′blem book′, a collection of emblems in book form, often on particular themes.

em·ble·ments (em′blə mənts), *n.pl.* *Law.* the products or profits of land which has been sown or planted. [pl. of *emblement* < AF, MF *emblaement,* equiv. to *emblae(r)* (< ML *imblādāre* to sow with grain, equiv. to *im-* IM-[1] + *blād* grain (F *blé*) < Gmc (cf. MD *blaad,* OE *blǣd*) + *-āre* v. suffix) + *-ment* -MENT]

em·bod·i·ment (em bod′ē mənt), *n.* **1.** the act of embodying. **2.** the state or fact of being embodied. **3.** something in which another thing is embodied; an incarnation. **4.** something embodied. [EMBODY + -MENT]

em·bod·y (em bod′ē), *v.t.*, **-bod·ied, -bod·y·ing. 1.** to provide with a body; incarnate; make corporeal: *to embody a spirit.* **2.** to give a concrete form to; express, personify, or exemplify in concrete form: *to embody an idea in an allegorical painting.* **3.** to collect into or include in a body; organize; incorporate. **4.** to embrace or comprise. [EM-[1] + BODY] —**em·bod′i·er,** *n.*

em·boî·té (*Fr.* äɴ bwa tā′), *n., pl.* **-tés** (-tā′). *Ballet.* a step, performed in series, in which the dancer stands on the toes with legs together and then springs up, swinging one foot out and around to the front of the other. Cf. **déboîté.** [< F: lit., boxed in, ptp. of *emboîter*]

em·bold·en (em bōl′dən), *v.t.* to make bold or bolder; hearten; encourage. [EM-[1] + BOLD + -EN[1]]

em·bo·lec·to·my (em′bə lek′tə mē), *n., pl.* **-mies.** *Surg.* removal of an embolus from an artery that it is obstructing. [EMBOL(US) + -ECTOMY]

em·bol·ic (em bol′ik), *adj.* **1.** *Pathol.* pertaining to an embolus or to embolism. **2.** *Embryol.* of, pertaining to, or resulting from emboly. [EMBOL(US) + -IC]

em·bo·lism (em′bə liz′əm), *n.* **1.** intercalation, as of a day in a year. **2.** a period of time intercalated. **3.** (in a Eucharistic service) the prayer following the final petitions of the Lord's Prayer. **4.** *Pathol.* the occlusion of a blood vessel by an embolus. [< ML *embolism(us)* intercalation < LGk *embolismós,* equiv. to *embol-* (see EMBOLUS) + *-ismos* -ISM] —**em′bo·lis′mic,** *adj.*

em·bo·lite (em′bə līt′), *n.* a mineral, chloride and bromide of silver, used as a minor source of silver. [< Gk *emból(ion)* insertion (see EMBOLUS) + -ITE[1]]

em·bo·lus (em′bə ləs), *n., pl.* **-li** (-lī′). *Pathol.* undissolved material carried by the blood current and impacted in some part of the vascular system, as thrombi or fragments of thrombi, tissue fragments, clumps of bacteria, protozoan parasites, fat globules, gas bubbles, etc. [< L piston < Gk *émbolos* stopper, equiv. to *em-* EM-[2] + *bólos* a throw, akin to *bállein* to throw]

em·bo·ly (em′bə lē), *n., pl.* **-lies.** *Embryol.* the pushing or growth of one part into another, as in the formation of certain gastrulas. [< Gk *embolḗ* a putting into its place, a setting, akin to *embállein* to throw in]

em·bon·point (äɴ bôɴ pwaɴ′), *n.* *French.* excessive plumpness; stoutness. [lit., in good condition]

em·bosk (em bosk′), *v.t.* to hide or conceal (something, oneself, etc.) with or as if with foliage, greenery, or the like: *to embosk oneself within a grape arbor.* [EM-[1] + BOSK]

em·bos·om (em bo͝oz′əm, -bo͞o′zəm), *v.t.* **1.** to enfold, envelop, or enclose. **2.** to take into or hold in the bosom; embrace. **3.** to cherish; foster. Also, **imbosom.** [EM-[1] + BOSOM]

em·boss (em bôs′, -bos′), *v.t.* **1.** to raise or represent (surface designs) in relief. **2.** to cause to bulge out; make protuberant. **3.** *Metalworking.* to raise a design on (a blank) with dies of similar pattern, one the negative of the other. Cf. **coin** (def. 10). **4.** to decorate (a surface) with raised ornament. [ME *embose(n)* < MF *embocer,* equiv. to *em-* EM-[1] + *boce* BOSS[2]] —**em·boss′ment,** *n.*

em·boss·er (em bô′sər, -bos′ər), *n.* **1.** one who or that which embosses. **2.** a machine that embosses or makes surface designs in relief, as on metal, paper, leather, etc. **3.** a person who operates such a machine. [EMBOSS + -ER[1]]

em·bou·chure (äm′bo͞o sho͝or′, äm′bo͞o sho͝or′; *Fr.* äɴ bo͞o shʏʀ′), *n., pl.* **-chures** (-sho͝orz′; *Fr.* -shʏʀ′). **1.** the mouth of a river. **2.** the opening out of a valley into a plain. **3.** *Music.* **a.** the mouthpiece of a wind instrument, esp. when of metal. **b.** the adjustment of a player's mouth to such a mouthpiece. [< F, equiv. to *embouch(er)* (to) put to mouth (*em-* EM- + *bouche* mouth < L *bucca* puffed cheek) + *-ure* -URE]

em·bow (em bō′), *v.t.* *Archaic.* to form into an arch or vault. [ME *embowe(n).* See EM-[1], BOW[2]] —**em·bow′ment,** *n.*

em·bowed (em bōd′), *adj.* **1.** bent; vaulted; arched. **2.** *Heraldry.* **a.** (of a fish) represented in an arched form with the extremities downward: *a dolphin embowed.* **b.** (of a human arm) bent at the elbow. [EMBOW + -ED[2]]

em·bow·el (em bou′əl, -boul′), *v.t.*, **-eled, -el·ing** or (*esp. Brit.*) **-elled, -el·ling. 1.** to disembowel. **2.** *Obs.* enclose, bury deep within. [EM-[1] + BOWEL]

em·bow·er (em bou′ər), *v.t., v.i.* to shelter in or as in a bower; cover or surround with foliage. Also, **imbower.** [EM-[1] + BOWER[1]]

em·brace[1] (em brās′), *v.*, **-braced, -brac·ing,** *n.* —*v.t.* **1.** to take or clasp in the arms; press to the bosom; hug. **2.** to take or receive gladly or eagerly; accept willingly: *to embrace an idea.* **3.** to avail oneself of: *to embrace an opportunity.* **4.** to adopt (a profession, a religion, etc.): *to embrace Buddhism.* **5.** to take in with the eye or the mind. **6.** to encircle; surround; enclose. **7.** to include or contain: *An encyclopedia embraces a great number of subjects.* —*v.i.* **8.** to join in an embrace. —*n.* **9.** the act or an instance of embracing; hug. [ME < OF *embrac(ier),* equiv. to *em-* EM-[1] + *bracier* to embrace, deriv. of *brace* the two arms; see BRACE] —**em·brace′a·ble,** *adj.* —**em·brace′ment,** *n.* —**em·brac′er,** *n.* —**em·brac′ive,** *adj.* —**Syn. 2.** adopt, espouse, welcome. **3.** seize. **7.** cover, embody. See **include.** —**Ant. 7.** exclude.

em·brace[2] (em brās′), *v.t.*, **-braced, -brac·ing.** *Law.* to attempt to influence (a judge or jury) through corrupt means. [late ME < AF *embrac(er)* (-*c*- < EMBRACE[1]), OF *embraser* to instigate (lit., set fire to), equiv. to *em-* EM-[1] + **brase, brese* ember; see BRAISE] —**em·brac′er,** *n.*

em·brace·or (em brā′sər), *n.* *Law.* a person guilty of embracery. [late ME < AF; MF *embraseor* instigator, equiv. to *embrase(r)* (to) EMBRACE[2] + *-eor* -OR[2]]

em·brac·er·y (em brā′sə rē), *n., pl.* **-er·ies.** *Law.* an attempt to influence a judge or jury by corrupt means, as by bribery, threats, or promises. Also, **imbracery.** [ME *embracerie.* See EMBRACE[2], -ERY]

em·branch·ment (em branch′mənt, -bränch′-), *n.* **1.** a branching or ramification. **2.** a branch. [< F *embranchement,* equiv. to *em-* EM-[1] + *branche* BRANCH + *-ment* -MENT]

em·bran·gle (em brang′gəl), *v.t.*, **-gled, -gling.** to confuse; entangle. Also, **imbrangle.** [EM-[1] + *brangle* (b. BRAWL and WRANGLE)] —**em·bran′gle·ment,** *n.*

em·bra·sure (em brā′zhər), *n.* **1.** (in fortification) an opening, as a loophole or crenel, through which missiles may be discharged. **2.** *Archit.* a splayed enlargement of a door or window toward the inner face of a wall. **3.** *Dentistry.* the space between adjacent teeth. [< F, equiv. to obs. *embras(er)* (to) chamfer, widen (*em-* EM-[1] + ?) + *-ure* -URE] —**em·bra′sured,** *adj.*

em·brit·tle (em brit′əl), *v.t., v.i.*, **-tled, -tling.** to make or become brittle. [EM-[1] + BRITTLE]

em·brit·tle·ment (em brit′əl mənt), *n.* the act of becoming brittle, as steel from exposure to certain environments or heat treatments or because of the presence of impurities. [EMBRITTLE + -MENT]

em·bro·cate (em′brō kāt′), *v.t.*, **-cat·ed, -cat·ing.** to moisten and rub with a liniment or lotion. [< ML *embrocāt(us)* (ptp. of *embrocāre*), equiv. to LL *embroch(a)* (< Gk *embrochḗ* infusion, equiv. to *em-* EM-[2] + *brochḗ* a making wet) + *-ātus* -ATE[1]]

em·bro·ca·tion (em′brō kā′shən), *n.* **1.** the act of embrocating a bruised or diseased part of the body. **2.** the liquid used for this; a liniment or lotion. [EMBROCATE + -ION]

em·broi·der (em broi′dər), *v.t.* **1.** to decorate with ornamental needlework. **2.** to produce or form in needlework. **3.** to adorn or embellish rhetorically, esp. with fictitious additions: *He embroidered the story to hold his listeners' interest.* —*v.i.* **4.** to do embroidery. [EM-[1] + BROIDER; r. ME *embrodere(n),* freq. of *embroden* < MF *embro(u)der,* equiv. to *em-* EM-[1] + OF *brosder,* deriv. of *brosd* < EGmc (see BRAD)] —**em·broi′der·er,** *n.*

em·broi·der·ess (em broi′dər is), *n.* a girl or woman who embroiders. [EMBROIDER + -ESS]

em·broi·der·y (em broi′də rē, -drē), *n., pl.* **-der·ies. 1.** the art of working raised and ornamental designs in threads of silk, cotton, gold, silver, or other material, upon any woven fabric, leather, paper, etc., with a needle. **2.** embroidered work or ornamentation. **3.** elaboration or embellishment, as in telling a story. [ME *embrouderie* needlework on cloth < MF *embroud(er)* + ME *-erie* -ERY; *oi* < EMBROIDER]

em·broil (em broil′), *v.t.* **1.** bring into discord or conflict; involve in contention or strife. **2.** to throw into confusion; complicate. [< MF *embrouill(er),* equiv. to *em-* EM-[1] + *brouiller* to BROIL[2]] —**em·broil′er,** *n.* —**em·broil′ment,** *n.*

em·brown (em broun′), *v.t., v.i.* to make or become brown or dark. [EM-[1] + BROWN]

em·brue (em bro͞o′), *v.t.*, **-brued, -bru·ing.** imbrue.

em·brute (em bro͞ot′), *v.t., v.i.*, **-brut·ed, -brut·ing.** imbrute.

embry-, var. of **embryo-** before a vowel.

em·bry·ec·to·my (em′brē ek′tə mē), *n., pl.* **-mies.** *Surg.* removal of an embryo. [EMBRY- + -ECTOMY]

em·bry·o (em′brē ō′), *n., pl.* **-os,** *adj.* —*n.* **1.** an organism in the earlier stages of its development, as before emergence from the egg or before metamorphosis. **2.** the young of a viviparous animal, esp. of a mammal, in the early stages of development within the womb, in man being up to the early part of the third month. Cf. **fetus. 3.** *Bot.* the rudimentary plant usually contained in the seed. **4.** the beginning or rudimentary stage of anything: *He said that the party policy was socialism in embryo.* —*adj.* **5.** embryonic. [< ML *embryon-, embryo* < Gk *émbryon,* n. use of neut. of *émbryos* ingrowing, equiv. to *em-* EM-[2] + *bry-* (s. of *brýein* to swell) + *-os* adj. suffix]

embryo-, a combining form of **embryo:** *embryology.* Also, *esp. before a vowel,* **embry-.**

em·bry·og·e·ny (em′brē oj′ə nē), *n.* the formation and development of the embryo, as a subject of scientific study. Also, **em·bry·o·gen·e·sis** (em′brē ō jen′i sis). [EMBRYO- + -GENY] —**em·bry·o·gen·ic** (em′brē ō jen′ik), **em·bry·o·ge·net·ic** (em′brē ō jə net′ik), *adj.*

em·bry·oid (em′brē oid′), *adj.* of or resembling an embryo. [EMBRY- + -OID]

embryol., embryology.

em·bry·ol·o·gist (em′brē ol′ə jist), *n.* a specialist in embryology. [EMBRYOLOG(Y) + -IST]

em·bry·ol·o·gy (em′brē ol′ə jē), *n., pl.* **-gies. 1.** the science dealing with the formation, development, structure, and functional activities of embryos. **2.** the origin, growth, and development of an embryo: *the embryology of the chick.* [EMBRYO- + -LOGY] —**em·bry·o·log·i·cal** (em′brē ə loj′i kəl), **em′bry·o·log′ic,** *adj.* —**em′bry·o·log′i·cal·ly,** *adv.*

em·bry·on·ic (em′brē on′ik), *adj.* **1.** pertaining to or in the state of an embryo. **2.** rudimentary; undeveloped. Also, **em·bry·o·nal** (em′brē ō′nəl). [*embryon-* (see EMBRYO) + -IC] —**em′bry·on′i·cal·ly,** *adv.*

em′bryo sac′, *Bot.* the megaspore of a seed-bearing plant, being situated within the ovule, giving rise to the endosperm or supposed female prothallium, and forming the egg cell or nucleus from which the embryo plant develops after fertilization of the egg.

em·bry·ot·o·my (em′brē ot′ə mē), *n., pl.* **-mies.** *Surg.* mutilation of a fetus, when natural delivery is impossible, in order to effect its removal. [< F *embryotomie.* See EMBRYO-, -TOMY]

em·bry·o·troph (em′brē ə trof′), *n.* *Embryol.* the liquified material, composed chiefly of secretions from the uterine glands and degenerating uterine tissue, that nourishes a mammalian embryo prior to the formation of the placenta. Also, **em·bry·o·trophe** (em′brē ə trōf′). Cf. **hemotrophe.** [< F, equiv. to *embryo-* EMBRYO- + *-troph* < Gk *trophḗ* nourishment, akin to *tréphein* to feed] —**em·bry·o·troph·ic** (em′brē ə trof′ik), *adj.* —**em·bry·ot·ro·phy** (em′brē o′trə fē), *n.*

em·bry·ul·ci·a (em′brē ul′sē ə), *n.* *Surg.* removal from the uterus, by instrument, of an embryo or fetus. [< NL < Gk *embryoulkía,* equiv. to *embryo-* EMBRYO- + *-olk-* (comb. form of *hélkein* to drag) + *-ia* -IA]

em·bry·ul·cus (em′brē ul′kəs), *n., pl.* **-ul·cus·es, -ul·ci** (-ul′sē, -sī). *Surg.* a hook-shaped instrument for use in embryulcia. [< NL < Gk *embryoulkós.* See EMBRYULCIA]

em·bus (im bus′, em-), *v.i., v.t.*, **-bussed, -bus·sing.** to get into a bus. [EM-[1] + BUS]

em·cee (em′sē′), *n., v.*, **-ceed, -cee·ing.** —*n.* **1.** master of ceremonies. —*v.t.* **2.** to act as master of ceremonies for. —*v.i.* **3.** to act as a master of ceremonies. [from M.C.]

em′ dash′, *Print.* a dash one em long.

Em·den (em′dən), *n.* a seaport in NW West Germany. 46,100 (1963).

eme (ēm), *n.* **1.** *Chiefly Scot.* a friend. **2.** an uncle. [ME *eem(e),* OE *ēam;* c. D *oom,* G (arch.) *Ohm, Oheim;* akin to UNCLE]

-eme, a suffix denoting a basic structural element (of a specified type) in a language: *morpheme.* [< Gk *-ēma* as in *phṓnēma* PHONEME]

e·meer (ə mēr′), *n.* emir.

e·meer·ate (ə mēr′it, -āt), *n.* emirate.

E·mel·da (i mel′də), *n.* a girl's given name.

E·mel·ia (i mēl′yə), *n.* a girl's given name, form of **Emily.**

Em·e·line (em′ə lēn′, -lin′) *n.* a girl's given name. Also, **Em·e·lin** (em′ə lin′), **Em·e·li·na** (em′ə lē′nə, -lī′nə).

e·mend (i mend′), *v.t.* **1.** to edit (a text) by removing errors, flaws, etc. **2.** to free from faults or errors; correct. [ME *emende(n)* < L *ēmendāre* to correct, equiv. to *ē-* E- + *mend(um)* fault + *-āre* v. suffix] —**e·mend′a·ble,** *adj.* —**Syn. 1, 2.** See **amend.**

e·men·date (ē′mən dāt′, i men′dāt), *v.t.*, **-dat·ed, -dat·ing.** to emend (a text). [< L *ēmendāt(us),* ptp. of *ēmendāre.* See EMEND, -ATE[1]] —**e·men·da·tor** (ē′mən dā′tər, em′ən-), *n.*

e·men·da·tion (ē′mən dā′shən, em′ən-), *n.* **1.** a correction. **2.** the act of emending. [< L *ēmendātiōn-* (s. of *ēmendātiō*), equiv. to *ēmendāt(us)* (see EMENDATE) + *-iōn-* -ION] —**e·men′da·to′ry** (i men′də tôr′ē, -tōr′ē), *adj.*

em·er·ald (em′ər əld, em′rəld), *n.* **1.** a rare variety of beryl that is green because of a chromium content and is valued as a gem. **2.** clear, deep green. **3.** *Print. Brit.* a 6½-point type of a size between nonpareil and minion. —*adj.* **4.** having a clear, deep-green color. [ME *emeraude, emeralde* < OF *esmeraude, esmeralde, esmeragde* < L *smaragdus* < Gk *smáragdos;* akin to Skt *marakta* emerald]

Em·er·ald (em′ər əld, em′rəld), *n.* a girl's given name.

em′erald cut′, *Jewelry.* a type of step cut, used esp. on emeralds and diamonds, in which the girdle has the form of a square or rectangle with truncated corners.

Em′erald Isle′, Ireland (def. 1).

em′erald toucanet′. See under **toucanet.**

e·merge (i mûrj′), *v.i.*, **e·merged, e·merg·ing. 1.** to rise or come forth from or as if from water or other liquid. **2.** to come forth into view or notice, as from concealment or obscurity: *a ghost emerging from the grave; a ship emerging from the fog.* **3.** to come up or arise, as a question or difficulty. **4.** to come into existence; develop. **5.** to rise, as from an inferior or unfortunate state or condition. [< L *ēmerge(re)* (to) arise out of, equiv. to *ē-* E- + *mergere* to immerse, sink] —**Syn. 2.** EMERGE, EMANATE, ISSUE mean to come forth from a place or source. EMERGE is used of coming forth from something that envelops or encloses, from a place shut off from view, or from concealment, obscurity, retirement, or the like, into sight and notice: *The sun emerges from behind the clouds.* EMANATE is used esp. of intangible or immaterial things, as light, vapor, ideas, news, etc., spreading or streaming from a source: *Rumors often emanate from irresponsible persons.* ISSUE is most often used of a number of persons, a mass of matter, or a volume of smoke, sound, or the like, coming forth through any outlet or outlets: *The crowd issued from the building.*

e·mer·gence (i mûr′jəns), *n.* **1.** the act or process of emerging. **2.** an outgrowth, as a prickle, on the surface of a plant. 3. *Biol., Philos.* the appearance of new properties in the course of development or evolution that could not have been foreseen in an earlier stage. [EMERGENCY, with -ENCE r. -ENCY]

e·mer·gen·cy (i mûr′jən sē), *n., pl.* **-cies.** a sudden, urgent, usually unforeseen occurrence or occasion requiring immediate action. [< ML *ēmergentia*, equiv. to *ēmerg-* (see EMERGE) + *-entia* -ENCY. See EMERGENT]
—**Syn.** exigency, extremity, pinch, quandary, plight. EMERGENCY, CRISIS, STRAITS refer to situations in which quick action and judgment are necessary, although they may not avert undesirable consequences. An EMERGENCY is a situation demanding immediate action: *A power failure created an emergency in transportation.* A CRISIS is a vital or decisive turning point in a condition or state of affairs, and everything depends on the outcome of it: *Help arrived when affairs had reached a crisis.* STRAIT (usually STRAITS) suggests a pressing situation, often one of need or want, which usually makes necessary some difficult alternative or choice: *The family was in desperate straits for food and clothing.*

emer′gency boat′, *Naut.* See **accident boat.**

emer′gency brake′, a brake set by a hand lever to prevent a motor vehicle from rolling away from a place in which it is halted or parked.

e·mer·gent (i mûr′jənt), *adj.* **1.** emerging; rising from a liquid or other surrounding medium. **2.** coming into view or notice; issuing. **3.** coming into existence, esp. with political independence: *the emergent nations of Africa.* **4.** arising casually or unexpectedly. **5.** calling for immediate action; urgent. **6.** *Biol., Philos.* displaying emergence. —*n.* **7.** *Ecol.* an aquatic plant having its stem, leaves, etc., extending above the surface of the water. [< L *ēmergent-* (s. of *emergēns*) arising out of, prp. of *ēmergere* to EMERGE] —**e·mer′gent·ly,** *adv.* —**e·mer′gent·ness,** *n.*

emer′gent evolu′tion, *Biol., Philos.* the origin of entirely new properties at certain critical stages or levels in the course of evolution, as the origin of multicellular organisms, nervous systems, psychic processes, etc.

e·mer·i·tus (i mer′i təs), *adj., n., pl.* **-ti** (-tī′, -tē′). —*adj.* **1.** retired or honorably discharged from active duty because of age, infirmity, or long service, but retained on the rolls: *a professor emeritus.* —*n.* **2.** an emeritus professor, minister, etc. [< L *ēmeritus* having fully earned (ptp. of *ēmerēre*), equiv. to *ē-* E- + *meri-* earn + *-tus* ptp. suffix]

em·er·ize (em′ə rīz′), *v.t.,* **-ized, -iz·ing.** to finish (fabric) with a cylinder covered with emery in order to make the raised nap even and give luster to the fabric. [EMER(Y) + -IZE]

e·mersed (i mûrst′), *adj.* *Bot.* risen or standing out of water, surrounding leaves, etc. [< L *ēmers(us)* (ptp. of *ēmergere* to EMERGE) + -ED²]

e·mer·sion (i mûr′zhən, -shən), *n.* **1.** Also called **egress.** *Astron.* the emergence of a heavenly body from an eclipse by another body, an occultation, or a transit. Cf. **immersion** (def. 5). **2.** *Archaic.* the act of emerging. [< L *ēmers(us)* (ptp. of *ēmergere* to EMERGE) + -ION]

Em·er·son (em′ər sən), *n.* **1. Ralph Waldo,** 1803–82, U.S. essayist and poet. **2.** a town in NE New Jersey. 6849 (1960). —**Em·er·so·ni·an** (em′ər sō′nē ən), *adj.*

em·er·y (em′ə rē, em′rē), *n.* a granular mineral substance consisting typically of corundum mixed with magnetite or hematite, used powdered, crushed, or consolidated for grinding and polishing. [late ME < MF *emeri* < OF *esmeril* < VL **smēriculum*, equiv. to MGk *smēri* (< Gk *smýris* rubbing powder; akin to SMEAR) + L *-culum* -CULE]

Em·er·y (em′ə rē, em′rē), *n.* a boy's given name. Also, **Emory.**

em′ery board′, a small, stiff strip, as of paper or cardboard, coated with powdered emery, used in manicuring.

em′ery cloth′, emery-coated cloth used as an abrasive.

Em·er·y·ville (em′ə rē vil′, em′rē-), *n.* a town in W California. 2686 (1960).

em′ery wheel′. See **grinding wheel.**

em·e·sis (em′i sis), *n.* *Pathol.* vomiting. [< NL < Gk *émesis* a vomiting, equiv. to *eme-* (s. of *emein* to vomit) + *-sis* -SIS]

E.Met., Engineer of Metallurgy.

e·met·ic (ə met′ik), *adj.* **1.** inducing vomiting, as a medicinal substance. —*n.* **2.** an emetic medicine or agent. [< L *emetic(us)* < Gk *emetikós*, equiv. to *éme-t(os)* vomiting + *-ikos* -IC]

em·e·tine (em′i tēn′, -tin), *n.* *Pharm.* a colorless, crystalline or white, powdery substance, $C_{29}H_{40}N_2O_4$, the active principle of ipecac: used chiefly in the treatment of amoebic dysentery and as an emetic and expectorant. [< Gk *émet(os)* vomiting + -INE²; cf. F *émétine*]

e·meu (ē′myōō), *n.* emu.

é·meute (ā mœt′), *n., pl.* **é·meutes** (ā mœt′). *French.* a riot.

emf, See **electromotive force.** Also, **E.M.F., EMF, e.m.f.**

-emia, *Med.* a suffix referring to the state of the blood: *hyperemia.* Also, **-aemia, -haemia, -hemia.** [< NL < Gk *-(h)aimía* (as in *anaimía* want of blood), equiv. to *haim-* (s. of *haîma*) blood + *-ia* -IA]

e·mic·tion (i mik′shən), *n.* urination. [< LL *ēmict(us)* (ptp. of *ēmingere* to make water), equiv. to *ē-* E- + *mic-* (var. of *mig-* urinate; c. OE *mīgan*, Icel *míga*) + *-t(us)* ptp. suffix + -ION]

em·i·grant (em′ə grənt), *n.* **1.** a person who emigrates, as from his native country. —*adj.* **2.** emigrating. [< L *ēmigrant-* (s. of *ēmigrāns*) moving away (prp. of *ēmigrāre*), equiv. to *ē-* E- + *migrānt-* (*migr-* remove + *-ant-* -ANT)]

em·i·grate (em′ə grāt′), *v.,* **-grat·ed, -grat·ing.** —*v.i.* **1.** to leave one country or region to settle in another; migrate: *to emigrate to Australia.* —*v.t.* **2.** to cause to emigrate: *The revolution emigrated thousands of people.* [< L *ēmigrāt(us)* moved away (ptp. of *ēmigrāre*), equiv. to *ē-* E- + *migrātus* (*migr-* remove + *-ātus* -ATE¹)] —**em′i·gra′tive,** *adj.*
—**Syn. 1.** See **migrate.**

em·i·gra·tion (em′ə grā′shən), *n.* **1.** the act or an instance of emigrating. **2.** a body of emigrants; emigrants collectively: *The emigration settled in large cities.* [< LL *ēmigrātiōn-* (s. of *ēmigrātiō*) removal. See EMIGRATE, -ION] —**em′i·gra′tion·al,** *adj.*

em·i·gra·to·ry (em′ə grə tōr′ē, -tôr′ē), *adj.* migratory. [EMIGRATE + -ORY¹]

é·mi·gré (em′ə grā′; *Fr.* ā mē grā′), *n., pl.* **-grés** (-grāz′; *Fr.* -grā′). **1.** an emigrant, esp. a person who flees from his native land because of political conditions. **2.** a person who fled from France because of opposition to or fear of the revolution that began in 1789. [< F: lit., emigrated, ptp. of *émigrer* < L *ēmigrāre* to EMIGRATE]

E·mil (ē′mil, ā′mil; *Ger.* ā′mēl), *n.* a boy's given name. Also, **É·mile** (ā mēl′).

É·mile (*Fr.* ā mēl′), *n.* a didactic novel (1762) by J. J. Rousseau, dealing principally with the author's theories of education.

E·mi·lia-Ro·ma·gna (e mē′lyä rô mä′nyä), *n.* a region in N Italy. 3,646,507 (1961); 8547 sq. mi.

Em·i·lie (em′ə lē), *n.* a girl's given name. Also, **Emily.**

Em·i·ly (em′ə lē), *n.* a girl's given name. Also, **Emilie.**

Em·i·na (em′ə nə), *n.* a girl's given name.

é·min·cé (*Fr.* ā maɴ sā′), *n.* a dish of leftover meat, sliced thin and warmed in a sauce. [< F: lit., chopped up, ptp. of *émincer*]

em·i·nence (em′ə nəns), *n.* **1.** high station, rank, or repute: *philosophers of eminence.* **2.** a high place or part; a hill or elevation; height. **3.** (*cap.*) a title of honor, applied to cardinals (usually prec. by *His* or *Your*). **4.** *Anat.* an elevation or projection, esp. on a bone. [late ME < MF < L *ēminentia*, equiv. to *ēmin-* (base of *ēminēre* to stand out; see EMINENT) + *-entia* -ENCE]
—**Syn. 1.** conspicuousness, note, fame. **2.** prominence.
—**Ant. 1.** obscurity.

é·mi·nence grise (ā mē näɴs grēz′), *pl.* **é·mi·nences grises** (ā mē näɴs grēz′). *French.* See **gray eminence.**

em·i·nen·cy (em′ə nən sē), *n., pl.* **-cies.** eminence.

em·i·nent (em′ə nənt), *adj.* **1.** high in station, rank, or repute; distinguished: *eminent statesmen.* **2.** conspicuous, signal, or noteworthy: *eminent services; eminent fairness.* **3.** lofty; high: *eminent peaks.* **4.** prominent; projecting; protruding: *an eminent nose.* [ME < L *ēminent-* (s. of *ēminēns*) outstanding (prp. of *ēminēre*), equiv. to *ē-* E- + *min-* project(ion) + *-ent-* -ENT] —**em′i·nent·ly,** *adv.*
—**Syn. 1.** prominent, celebrated, renowned, illustrious, outstanding. See **famous. 2.** noted; notable. —**Ant. 1.** unknown.

em′inent domain′, *Law.* the power of the state to take private property for public use with payment of compensation to the owner.

E·mi·ne·scu (ye′mē ne′skōō), *n.* **Mi·ha·il** (mē′hä ēl′), (*Mihail Iminovici*), 1850–89, Rumanian poet.

e·mir (ə mēr′), *n.* **1.** an Arab chieftain or prince. **2.** a title of honor of the descendants of Muhammad. Also, **emeer.** [< Ar *amīr* commander]

e·mir·ate (ə mēr′it, -āt), *n.* the office or rank of an emir. Also, **emeerate.** [EMIR + -ATE¹]

em·is·sar·y (em′i ser′ē), *n., pl.* **-sar·ies,** *adj.* —*n.* **1.** an agent sent on a mission or errand: *emissaries to negotiate a peace.* **2.** an agent sent on a mission of a secret nature, as a spy. —*adj.* **3.** sent forth, as on a mission. **4.** pertaining to a person acting as a messenger or agent. **5.** *Anat.* sending or coming out, as certain veins that pass through the skull and connect the venous sinuses inside with the veins outside. [< L *ēmissāri(us)* one sent out, equiv. to *ēmiss-* (see EMISSION) + *-ārius* -ARY]

e·mis·sion (i mish′ən), *n.* **1.** the act or an instance of emitting. **2.** something that is emitted; discharge; emanation: *an emission of sound.* **3.** the act or an instance of issuing, as paper money. **4.** *Electronics.* a measure of the number of electrons emitted by the heated filament or cathode of a vacuum tube. **5.** an ejection or discharge of semen or other fluid from the body. **6.** the fluid ejected or discharged. [< L *ēmissiōn-* (s. of *ēmissiō*), equiv. to *ēmiss(us)*, ptp. of *ēmittere* to EMIT (*ē-* E- + *mit-* send + *-tus* ptp. suffix) + *-iōn-* -ION]

emis′sion spec′trum, *Physics.* the spectrum formed by electromagnetic radiations emitted by a given source, characteristic of the source and the type of excitation inducing the radiations.

e·mis·sive (i mis′iv), *adj.* **1.** serving to emit. **2.** pertaining to emission. [EMISS(ION) + -IVE]

em·is·siv·i·ty (em′i siv′i tē), *n.* *Thermodynamics.* the ability of a surface to emit radiant energy compared to that of a black body at the same temperature and with the same area. [EMISSIVE + -ITY]

e·mit (i mit′), *v.t.,* **e·mit·ted, e·mit·ting. 1.** to send forth (liquid, light, heat, sound, particles, etc.); discharge. **2.** to issue, as an order or a decree. **3.** to issue formally for circulation, as paper money. **4.** to utter or voice, as opinions. **5.** to give forth or release (a sound): *an elephant emitting his trumpeting call.* [< L *ēmitte(re)* (to) send forth, equiv. to *ē-* E- + *mittere* to send]
—**Syn. 1.** vent, exhale, exude, expel, eject.

Em·i·tron (em′i tron′), *n.* *Television, Trademark.* a cathode ray tube, similar to an Iconoscope, developed in England.

e·mit·tance (i mit′ᵊns), *n.* *Optics.* the total flux emitted per unit area. Cf. **luminous emittance, radiant emittance.** [EMIT + -ANCE]

e·mit·ter (i mit′ər), *n.* **1.** one who or that which emits. **2.** *Electronics.* an electrode on a transistor from which a flow of electrons or holes enters the region between the electrodes. [EMIT + -ER¹]

Em·lyn (em′lin), *n.* **1.** a girl's given name, form of **Emily. 2.** a boy's given name.

Em·ma (em′ə), *n.* a girl's given name.

Em·ma (em′ə), *n.* a novel (1815) by Jane Austen.

em·mar·ble (i mär′bəl), *v.t.,* **-bled, -bling.** to represent in or adorn with marble; make a marble image of: *a noble hero emmarbled for all posterity.* Also, **enmarble.** [EM-¹ + MARBLE]

Em·man·u·el (i man′yōō əl, *for 1, 2; Fr.* e mᴀ ny el′ *for 3*), *n.* **1.** Jesus Christ, esp. as the Messiah. Matt. 1:23. **2.** Immanuel. **3. Pierre** (pyer), born 1916, French poet.

Em·me·line (em′ə lēn′, -līn′), *n.* a girl's given name, form of **Amelia.** Also, **Em·me·leen, Em·me·lene** (em′ə-lēn′), **Em·me·li·na** (em′ə lē′nə).

Em·men (em′ən), *n.* a city in the NE Netherlands. 69,474 (1962).

em·men·a·gogue (ə men′ə gôg′, -gog′, ə mē′nə-), *Med.* —*n.* **1.** a medicine that promotes the menstrual discharge. —*adj.* **2.** Also, **em·men·a·gog·ic** (ə men′ə-goj′ik, -gog′-, ə mē′nə-). stimulating the menstrual flow. [< Gk *émmēn(a)* menses (see EMMENIA) + -AGOGUE]

em·men·i·a (ə men′ē ə, ə mē′nē ə), *n.* (*construed as sing. or pl.*) *Physiol.* menses. [< NL: neut. pl. of *emménios* monthly, equiv. to *em-* EM-² + *mēn* month (akin to L *mēnsis* month) + *-ios* adj. suffix]

em·men·i·op·a·thy (ə men′ē op′ə thē, -ō′pə-, ə mē′-nē-), *n.* *Pathol.* any disorder of menstruation. [EMMENI(A) + -O- + -PATHY]

Em·men·tha·ler (em′ən tä′lər), *n.* Swiss (def. 4). Also, **Em·men·tal** (em′ən täl′), **Em′men·ta′ler, Em′men·thal′, Em′menthaler cheese′.** [< G, after *Emmenthal* a valley in Switzerland; see -ER¹]

em·mer (em′ər), *n.* a wheat, *Triticum dicoccum*, having a two-grained spikelet, grown as a forage crop in Europe, Asia, and the western U.S. [< G; OHG *amari* spelt]

em·met (em′it), *n.* *Chiefly Dial.* an ant. [ME *emete*, OE *ǣmette* ANT]

Em·met (em′it), *n.* **1. Robert,** 1778–1803, Irish patriot. **2.** Also, **Emmett.** a boy's given name.

em·me·tro·pi·a (em′i trō′pē ə), *n.* *Ophthalm.* the normal refractive condition of the eye, in which the rays of light are accurately focused on the retina. [< NL, equiv. to *emmetr-* (s. of Gk *émmetros* in measure, equiv. to *em-* EM-² + *métron*) + *-opia* -OPIA] —**em′me·trope′,** *n.* —**em·me·trop·ic** (em′i trop′ik), *adj.*

Em·mets·burg (em′its bûrg′), *n.* a town in N Iowa. 3887 (1960).

Em·mett (em′it), *n.* **1.** a town in W Idaho. 3769 (1960). **2.** Also, **Emmet.** a boy's given name.

Em·my (em′ē), *n., pl.* **-mies. 1.** (*sometimes l.c.*) any of several statuettes awarded annually by the Academy of Television Arts and Sciences for excellence in television programming, production, or performance. **2.** Also, **Em′mie.** a girl's given name, form of **Emma.**

Em·my·lou (em′ē lōō′, em′ē lōō′), *n.* a girl's given name.

Em·o·gene (em′ə jēn′), *n.* a girl's given name. Also, **Imogene, Imogen.**

e·mol·lient (i mol′yənt), *adj.* **1.** having the power of softening or relaxing living tissues, as a medicinal substance; soothing, esp. to the skin: *emollient lotions for the face.* —*n.* **2.** *Med.* an emollient medicine or agent. [< L *ēmollient-* (s. of *ēmolliēns*) softening up (prp. of *ēmollīre*), equiv. to *ē-* E- + *molli(s)* soft + *-ent-* -ENT] —**e·mol′lience,** *n.* —**em·ol·li·tion** (im′ə lish′ən), *n.*

e·mol·u·ment (i mol′yə mənt), *n.* profit arising from office or employment; compensation for services; salary or fees: *Tips are an emolument in addition to wages.* [< L *ēmolument(um)* gain, profit (orig. miller's fee), equiv. to *ē-* E- + *molu-* (var. of *moli-*, comb. form of *molere* to grind) + *-mentum* -MENT]
—**Syn.** stipend, honorarium.

Em·o·ry (em′ə rē), *n.* a boy's given name. Also, **Emery.**

Em′ory oak′, a shrubby oak, *Quercus emoryi*, of the southwestern U.S. and Mexico, yielding a hard, heavy wood. [named after W.H. *Emory* (d. 1887), American engineer]

e·mote (i mōt′), *v.i.,* **e·mot·ed, e·mot·ing. 1.** to show or affect emotion: *to emote over the beauties of nature.* **2.** to behave theatrically; act a part, often without talent: *The actress emoted for all she was worth.* [back formation from EMOTION] —**e·mot′er,** *n.*

e·mo·tion (i mō′shən), *n.* **1.** an affective state of consciousness in which joy, sorrow, fear, hate, or the like, is experienced, as distinguished from cognitive and volitional states of consciousness. **2.** any of the feelings of joy, sorrow, fear, hate, love, etc. **3.** any strong agitation of the feelings actuated by experiencing love, hate, fear, etc., and usually accompanied by certain physiological changes, as increased heartbeat, respiration, or the like, and often overt manifestation, as crying, shaking, etc. **4.** an instance of this. **5.** that which causes or effects such a reaction: *the powerful emotion of a great symphony.* [< ML *ēmōtiōn-* (s. of *ēmōtiō*) a moving away, equiv. to L *ēmōt(us)*, ptp. of *ēmovēre* (*ē-* E- + *mō-*, var. of *mov-*, + *-tus* ptp. suffix) + *-iōn-* -ION] —**e·mo′tion·a·ble,** *adj.* —**e·mo′tion·less,** *adj.*
—**Syn. 1.** See **feeling.**

e·mo·tion·al (i mō′shə nᵊl), *adj.* **1.** pertaining to or involving emotion or the emotions. **2.** subject to or easily affected by emotion: *She is an emotional woman, easily upset by any disturbance.* **3.** appealing to the emotions: *an emotional request for contributions.* **4.** showing or revealing very strong emotions: *an emotional scene in a play.* **5.** actuated, effected, or determined by emotion rather than reason: *An emotional decision is almost invariably a wrong decision.* **6.** governed by emotion: *He is in a highly emotional state of mind.* [EMOTION + -AL¹] —**e·mo′tion·al·ly,** *adv.*

e·mo·tion·al·ise (i mō′shə nᵊlīz′), *v.t.,* **-ised, -is·ing.** *Chiefly Brit.* emotionalize.

e·mo·tion·al·ism (i mō′shə nᵊliz′əm), *n.* **1.** excessively emotional character: *the emotionalism of sentimental fiction.* **2.** excessive appeal to the emotions: *the emotionalism of patriotic propaganda.* **3.** a tendency to display or respond with undue emotion, esp. morbid emotion. **4.** unwarranted expression or display of emotion. [EMOTIONAL + -ISM]

e·mo·tion·al·ist (i mō′shə nᵊlist), *n.* **1.** a person who appeals to the emotions, esp. unduly. **2.** a person easily affected by emotion. **3.** a person who bases conduct, or the theory of conduct, upon feelings rather than reason: *a romantic emotionalist.* [EMOTIONAL + -IST] —**e·mo′tion·al·is′tic,** *adj.*

e·mo·tion·al·i·ty (i mō′shə nal′i tē), *n.* emotional state or quality: *the emotionality of the artistic temperament.* [EMOTIONAL + -ITY]

e·mo·tion·al·ize (i mō′shə nᵊlīz′), *v.t.,* **-ized, -iz·ing.** to make emotional; treat as a matter of emotion: *to emotionalize religion.* Also, *esp. Brit.,* **emotionalise.** [EMOTIONAL + -IZE]

e·mo·tive (i mō′tiv), *adj.* **1.** characterized by or pertaining to emotion: *the emotive and rational capacities of man.* **2.** productive of or directed toward the emotions: *Artistic distortion is often an emotive use of form.* [< L ēmōt(us) (see EMOTION) + -IVE] —**e·mo′tive·ly,** *adv.* —**e·mo′tive·ness, e·mo·tiv·i·ty** (ē′mō tiv′i tē), *n.*

emo′tive mean′ing, an emotional connotation, esp. as indicating approval or disapproval, of a word or expression that is used instead of one having a similar denotation but a less affective quality, as "murder" instead of "homicide," "drunk" instead of "inebriated," etc.

Emp., 1. Emperor. 2. Empire. 3. Empress.

emp., (in prescriptions) a plaster. [< L *emplastrum*]

e.m.p., (in prescriptions) after the manner prescribed; as directed. [< L *ex mōdō prescriptō*]

em·pai·stic (em pā′stik), *adj.* (of a decorative object) embossed, inlaid, or stamped. Also, **em·paes·tic** (em pes′tik, -pē′stik), **empestic.** [< Gk *empaistik(ē)* (*téchnē*) the beater's (art), equiv. to *em-* EM-[1] + *paí(ein)* (to) beat, emboss + -(i)*stikē* -ISTIC]

em·pale (em pāl′), *v.t.,* **-paled, -pal·ing.** impale. —**em·pale′ment,** *n.* —**em·pal′er,** *n.*

em·pa·na·da (em′pə nä′də), *n.* *Latin-American Cookery.* a turnover or mold of pastry filled with chopped or ground meat, vegetables, fruit, etc. [< AmerSp, fem. of Sp *empanado* breaded in, equiv. to *em-* EM-[1] + *pan* bread + *-ado* -ATE[1]]

em·pan·el (em pan′əl), *v.t.,* **-eled, -el·ing** or (*esp. Brit.*) **-elled, -el·ling.** impanel.

em·pa·thize (em′pə thīz′), *v.i.,* **-thized, -thiz·ing.** to experience empathy (often fol. by *with*): *His ability to empathize with people sharing his own temperament made him many friends.* [EMPATH(Y) + -IZE]

em·pa·thy (em′pə thē), *n.* *Psychol.* **1.** the intellectual identification with or vicarious experiencing of the feelings, thoughts, or attitudes of another: *Empathy is more enduring and valuable than romantic love.* **2.** the imaginative ascribing to an object, as a natural object or work of art, feelings or attitudes present in oneself: *By means of empathy, a great painting becomes a mirror of the self.* [< Gk *empátheia* affection, equiv. to *em-* EM-[2] + *path-* (var. s. of *páschein* to suffer) + *-eia* -IA; present meaning influenced by G *Einfühlung*] —**em·path·ic** (em path′ik), *adj.* —**em·path′i·cal·ly,** *adv.*

Em·ped·o·cles (em ped′ə klēz′), *n.* c490–c430 B.C., Greek philosopher and statesman.

em·pen·nage (äm′pə näzh′; *Fr.* äN pe NAZH′), *n., pl.* **-nag·es** (-nä′zhiz; *Fr.* -NAZH′). the rear part of an airplane or airship, usually comprising the stabilizer, elevator, vertical fin, and rudder. [< F: lit., feathering, equiv. to *empenn(er)* (to) feather an arrow (*em-* EM-[1] + *penne* feather; see PEN[1]) + *-age* -AGE]

em·per·or (em′pər ər), *n.* **1.** the sovereign or supreme ruler of an empire: *the emperors of Rome.* **2.** a title of sovereignty given to certain monarchs not the heads of empires, to emphasize the sense of the dignity of their kingship: *the Emperor of Japan; the Emperor of Ethiopia.* **3.** *Chiefly Brit.* a size of drawing or writing paper, 48 × 72 inches. [ME *empero(u)r* < OF *empereor* < L *imperātor* leader, equiv. to *imperāt(us)* imposed, ordered, ptp. of *imperāre* (*im-* IM-[1] + *per-,* var. of *par-* set, put + *-ātus* -ATE[1]) + *-or* -OR[2]] —**em′per·or·ship′,** *n.*

Em′peror Jones′, The, a play (1920) by Eugene O'Neill.

Em′peror Justin′ian and His Court′, a mosaic (A.D. 547?) in the choir of the church of San Vitale, Ravenna. Cf. **Empress Theodora and Her Court.**

em′peror pen′guin, the largest of the penguins, *Aptenodytes forsteri,* of the coasts of Antarctica. See illus. under **penguin.**

em·per·y (em′pə rē), *n., pl.* **-per·ies.** **1.** absolute dominion; empire: *The ancient world was under the empery of Rome.* **2.** *Archaic.* the territory of an emperor. [ME *emperie* < AF < L *imperi(um)* mastery, sovereignty, empire, equiv. to *imper(āre)* (to) rule (*im-* IM-[1] + *per-,* var. of *par-* set, put) + *-ium* -Y[3]]

em·pes·tic (em pes′tik, -pē′stik), *adj.* empaistic.

em·pha·sis (em′fə sis), *n., pl.* **-ses** (-sēz′). **1.** stress laid upon, or importance or significance attached to, anything: *The president's statement gave emphasis to the crisis.* **2.** that which is given great stress or importance: *Morality was the emphasis of his speech.* **3.** *Rhet.* **a.** special and significant stress of voice laid on particular words or syllables. **b.** stress laid on particular words, by means of position, repetition, or other indication. **4.** intensity or force of expression, action, etc.: *Determination lent emphasis to his proposals.* **5.** prominence, as of form or outline: *The background detracts from the emphasis of the figure.* **6.** *Electronics.* preemphasis. [< L < Gk *émphasis* indication, equiv. to *em-* EM-[2] + *phásis* PHASIS]

em·pha·sise (em′fə sīz′), *v.t.,* **-sised, -sis·ing.** *Chiefly Brit.* emphasize.

em·pha·size (em′fə sīz′), *v.t.,* **-sized, -siz·ing.** to give emphasis to; lay stress upon; stress: *to emphasize a point; to emphasize the eyes with mascara.* [EMPHAS(IS) + -IZE]

em·phat·ic (em fat′ik), *adj.* **1.** uttered, or to be uttered, with emphasis; strongly expressive. **2.** using emphasis in speech or action. **3.** forceful; insistent: *a big, emphatic man; I must be emphatic about this particular.* **4.** forcibly significant; strongly marked; striking: *the emphatic beauty of sunset.* **5.** clearly or boldly outlined: *It stands, like a great, stone dagger, emphatic against the sky.* **6.** *Phonet.* having a secondary velar articulation, as certain dental consonants in Arabic. —*n.* **7.** an emphatic consonant. [< Gk *emphatik(ós)* indicative, forceful, equiv. to **emphat(ós)* (*em-* EM-[2] + *phatós,* var. of *phantós* visible, equiv. to *phan-,* s. of *phaínesthai* to appear, + *-tos* adj. suffix) + *-ikos* -IC] —**em·phat′i·cal·ly,** *adv.* —**em·phat′i·cal·ness,** *n.*
—**Syn.** **3.** positive, energetic, forcible, pronounced, decided, unequivocal, definite. —**Ant.** **3.** weak.

em·phy·se·ma (em′fi sē′mə, -zē′-), *n.* *Pathol.* abnormal distention of an organ or a part of the body, esp. the lungs, with air or other gas. [< NL < Gk *emphýsēma* inflation, equiv. to *em-* EM-[2] + *physē-* (var. s. of *physân* to blow) + *-ma* n. suffix denoting result of action] —**em·phy·sem·a·tous** (em′fi sem′ə təs, -sē′mə-, -zem′ə-, -zē′mə-), *adj.*

em′ pi′ca, *Print.* about one sixth of an inch, generally used as the unit of measurement in printing.

em·pire (em′pīər; *for 8, 9 also* om pēr′), *n.* **1.** an aggregate of nations or peoples ruled over by an emperor or other powerful sovereign or government: usually a territory of greater extent than a kingdom, as the former British Empire, French Empire, Russian Empire, Byzantine Empire, or Roman Empire. **2.** a government under an emperor. **3.** (*often cap.*) the historical period during which a nation is under such a government: *a history of French decorative arts of the Second Empire.* **4.** supreme power in governing; imperial power; sovereignty: *England has withdrawn from empire.* **5.** supreme control; absolute sway: *to have empire over the minds of men.* **6.** a powerful and important enterprise or holding of large scope that is controlled by a single person, family, or group of associates: *He built an oil empire for himself and his sons.* —*adj.* **7.** (*cap.*) characteristic of or developed during the first French empire, 1804–15. **8.** (*usually cap.*) (of women's attire and coiffures) of the style that prevailed during the first French empire, in clothing being characterized esp. by décolletage and a high waistline, coming just below the bust, from which the skirt hangs straight and loose. **9.** (*cap.*) noting or pertaining to the style of architecture, furnishings, and decoration prevailing in France and imitated to a greater or lesser extent in various other countries, c1800–c1830: characterized by the use of delicate but elaborate ornamentation imitated from Greek and Roman examples or containing classical allusions, as animal forms for the legs of furniture, bas-reliefs of classical figures, motifs of wreaths, torches, caryatids, lyres, urns, etc., and by the occasional use of military and Egyptian motifs and, under the Empire itself, of symbols alluding to Napoleon, as bees or the letter N. [ME < OF < L *imper(ium)*; see EMPERY]
—**Syn.** **4.** dominion, rule, supremacy.

Empire méridienne

Em·pire (em′pīər), *n.* a town in SW Oregon. 3781 (1960).

em′pire build′er, a person who plans or works to extend his dominion or control, as over territory, political or business enterprises, etc.

em′pire build′ing, the plans, activities, achievements, etc., of an empire builder.

Em′pire Day′, **1.** (in Canada) the last school day before Victoria Day, observed with patriotic activities in the schools. **2.** former name of **Commonwealth Day.**

Em′pire State′, the State of New York (used as a nickname).

em·pir·ic (em pir′ik), *n.* **1.** anyone who follows an empirical method. **2.** a quack; charlatan. —*adj.* **3.** empirical. [< L *empīric(us)* < Gk *empeirikós* experienced, equiv. to *em-* EM-[2] + *peir-* (s. of *peirân* to attempt) + *-ikos* -IC]

em·pir·i·cal (em pir′i kəl), *adj.* **1.** derived from or guided by experience or experiment: *to be empirical and practical in confronting reality.* **2.** depending upon experience or observation alone, without using science or theory, esp. as in medicine. **3.** provable or verifiable by experience or experiment. [EMPIRIC + -AL[1]] —**em·pir′i·cal·ly,** *adv.* —**em·pir′i·cal·ness,** *n.*

empir′ical for′mula, *Chem.* a chemical formula indicating the elements of a compound and their relative proportions, as $(CH_2O)_n$. Cf. **molecular formula, structural formula.**

em·pir·i·cism (em pir′i siz′əm), *n.* **1.** empirical method or practice. **2.** *Philos.* the doctrine that all knowledge is derived from experience. **3.** undue reliance upon experience, as in medicine; quackery. **4.** an empirical conclusion. [EMPIRIC + -ISM] —**em·pir′i·cist,** *n., adj.*

Em·pi·rin (em′pə rin, -prin), *n.* *Trademark.* aspirin.

Em′pi·rin Com′pound, *Pharm., Trademark.* a mixture consisting of aspirin, acetophenetidin, and caffeine: used for pain, esp. of headache or neuralgia, and for the symptoms of a cold.

em·pi·rism (em′pə riz′əm), *n.* *Philos.* empiricism (def. 2). [EMPIR(IC) + -ISM] —**em·pi·ris·tic** (em′pə ris′tik), *adj.*

em·place (em plās′), *v.,* **-placed, -plac·ing.** —*v.t.* **1.** to put in place or position: *A statue was emplaced in the square.* —*v.i.* **2.** (of igneous rocks and magmas) to move into a particular position. **3.** (of ore deposits) to develop in a particular place. [back formation from EMPLACEMENT]

em·place·ment (em plās′mənt), *n.* **1.** *Fort.* the space, platform, or the like, for a gun or battery and its accessories. **2.** a putting in place or position; location: *the emplacement of a wall.* **3.** *Geol.* **a.** the intrusion of igneous rocks into a particular position. **b.** the development of an ore deposit in a particular place. [< F, equiv. to obs. *emplac(er)* (to) place (*em-* EM-[1] + *place* PLACE) + *-ment* -MENT]

em·plec·tite (em plek′tīt), *n.* a mineral, copper and bismuth sulfide, occurring in the form of thin gray prisms, found with quartz. [< Gk *émplekt(os)* inwoven (*em-* EM-[2] + *plek-,* s. of *plékein* to plait, + *-tos* ptp. suffix) + -ITE[1]]

em·ploy (em ploi′), *v.t.* **1.** to use the services of (a person or persons); have or keep in one's service: *This factory employs thousands of men.* **2.** to keep busy or at work; engage the attentions of: *He employs himself by reading after work.* **3.** to make use of (an instrument, means, etc.); use; apply: *to employ a hammer to drive a nail.* **4.** to occupy or devote (time, energies, etc.): *I employ my spare time in reading. I employ all my effort in writing well.* —*n.* **5.** employment; service: *to be in someone's employ.* [late ME *employe* < MF *emploie(r)* << L *implicāre* to infold (LL: to engage); see IMPLICATE] —**em·ploy′a·bil′i·ty,** *n.* —**em·ploy′a·ble,** *adj.*
—**Syn.** **1.** engage, hire; retain; occupy, use.

em·ploy·ee (em ploi′ē, em′ploi ē′), *n.* a person working for another person or a business firm for pay. Also, **em·ploy′e, em·ploy′é.** [< F *employé* employed, ptp. of *employer* to EMPLOY]
—**Syn.** worker.

em·ploy·er (em ploi′ər), *n.* a person who employs, esp. for wages: *a fair employer; an inadequate employer of one's time.* [EMPLOY + -ER[1]]

em·ploy·ment (em ploi′mənt), *n.* **1.** the act or an instance of employing. **2.** state of being employed; employ; service: *to begin or terminate employment.* **3.** an occupation by which a person earns a living; work; business. **4.** an activity or the like that occupies a person's time: *She found knitting a comforting employment for her idle hours.* [EMPLOY + -MENT]
—**Syn.** **3.** vocation, calling; job, trade, profession.

employ′ment a′gency, an agency that finds jobs for persons seeking employment or assists employers in finding persons to fill positions that are open. Also called **employ′ment bu′reau.**

employ′ment exchange′, *Brit.* See **Labour Exchange.**

em·poi·son (em poi′zən), *v.t.* **1.** to corrupt: *propaganda designed to empoison the minds of the young.* **2.** to embitter: *Knowledge of his own failure has empoisoned him against all men.* **3.** *Obs.* to poison. [ME *empoysone(n)* < OF *empoisone(r).* See EM-[1], POISON] —**em·poi′son·ment,** *n.*

Em·po·ri·a (em pôr′ē ə, -pōr′-), *n.* **1.** a city in E Kansas. 18,190 (1960). **2.** a town in S Virginia. 5535 (1960).

em·po·ri·um (em pôr′ē əm, -pōr′-), *n., pl.* **-po·ri·ums, po·ri·a** (-pôr′ē ə, -pōr′-). **1.** a place, town, or city of important commerce, esp. a principal center of trade: *New York is one of the world's great emporiums.* **2.** a large store, esp. one selling a great variety of articles and having an air of importance. [< L < Gk *empórion* a market, equiv. to *empor-* (s. of *émporos*) merchant (*em-* EM-[2] + *póros* voyage) + *-ion* n. suffix of place]

Em·po·ri·um (em pôr′ē əm, -pōr′-), *n.* a town in central Pennsylvania. 3397 (1960).

em·pov·er·ish (em pov′ər ish, -pov′rish), *v.t.* *Obs.* impoverish.

em·pow·er (em pou′ər), *v.t.* **1.** to give power or authority to; authorize: *I empowered my agent to make the deal for me.* **2.** to enable or permit: *Long discipline empowers an artist to work with ease.* [EM-[1] + POWER] —**em·pow′er·ment,** *n.*
—**Syn.** **1.** warrant, commission, license, qualify.

em·press (em′pris), *n.* **1.** a female ruler of an empire. **2.** the consort of an emperor. [ME *emperice, emperesse* < OF *emperesse, empereriz* < L *imperātrix,* fem. of *imperātor.* See EMPEROR, -TRIX]

em·presse·ment (äN pres mäN′), *n., pl.* **-ments** (-mäN′). *French.* display of cordiality.

Em′press Theodo′ra and Her Court′, a mosaic (A.D. 547?) in the choir of the church of San Vitale, Ravenna. Cf. **Emperor Justinian and His Court.**

em′press tree′. See **princess tree.**

em·prise (em prīz′), *n.* *Archaic.* **1.** an adventurous enterprise. **2.** knightly daring or prowess. Also, **em·prize′.** [ME < MF, n. use of fem. of *empris* (ptp. of *emprendre* to undertake), equiv. to *em-* EM-[1] + *pris* taken (see PRIZE[1])]

Emp·son (emp′sən), *n.* **William,** born 1906, English critic and poet.

emp·tor (emp′tər, -tôr), *n.* (esp. in legal usage) a person who purchases or contracts to purchase; buyer. [< L, equiv. to *empt(us)* (ptp. of *emere* to buy) + *-or* -OR[2]]

emp·ty (emp′tē), *adj.,* **-ti·er, -ti·est,** *v.,* **-tied, -ty·ing,** *n., pl.* **-ties.** —*adj.* **1.** containing nothing; void of the usual or appropriate contents: *an empty bottle.* **2.** vacant; unoccupied: *an empty house.* **3.** without burden or load: *an empty wagon.* **4.** destitute of people or human activity: *We walked along the empty streets of the city at night.* **5.** destitute of some quality or qualities; devoid (usually fol. by *of*): *Theirs is a life now empty of happiness.* **6.** without force, effect, or significance; hollow; meaningless: *empty compliments; empty pleasures.* **7.** not employed in useful or meaningful activity or work; idle: *empty summer days.* **8.** *Math.* (of a set) null. **9.** hungry: *I'm feeling rather empty—let's have lunch.* **10.** without knowledge or sense; frivolous; foolish: *an empty head.* **11.** completely spent of emotion: *The experience had left him with an empty heart.* —*v.t.* **12.** to make empty; deprive of contents; discharge the contents of: *to empty a bucket.* **13.** to discharge (contents): *to empty the water out of a bucket.* —*v.i.* **14.** to become empty: *The room emptied rapidly after the lecture.* **15.** to discharge contents, as a river: *The river empties into the sea.* —*n.* **16.** something that is empty, as a box, bottle, can, etc.: *Throw the empties into the waste bin.* [ME (with intrusive *-p-*); OE *ǣm(et)tig* (*ǣmett(a)* leisure + *-ig* -Y[1])] —**emp′ti·a·ble,** *adj.* —**emp′ti·er,** *n.* —**emp′ti·ly,** *adv.* —**emp′ti·ness,** *n.*
—**Syn.** **1.** vacuous. EMPTY, VACANT, BLANK, VOID denote absence of content or contents. EMPTY means without appropriate or accustomed contents: *empty barrel; The house is empty* (has no furnishings). VACANT is usually applied to that which is temporarily unoccupied: *vacant chair; vacant* (uninhabited) *house.* BLANK applies to surfaces free from any marks or lacking appropriate markings, openings, etc.: *blank paper; a blank wall.* VOID emphasizes completely unfilled space with vague, unspecified, or no boundaries: *without form and void.* **6.** delusive, vain. **12.** unload, unburden. —**Ant.** **1.** full.

emp·ty-hand·ed (emp′tē han′did), *adj.* **1.** having nothing in the hands; doing no work: *While we were carrying out the luggage, he stood by empty-handed.* **2.** having gained nothing: *to return from a quest empty-handed.*

emp·ty-head·ed (emp′tē hed′id), *adj.* lacking intelligence or knowledge; foolish; brainless: *giggling, empty-headed pupils.* —**emp′ty-head′ed·ness,** *n.*

emp′ty morph′, a morph, as the first *o* in *psychology,* which is considered to have no meaning and is not assigned to any morpheme.

emp′ty word′, (esp. in Chinese grammar) a word that has grammatical meaning rather than lexical meaning; a word or morpheme that functions as a grammatical link or marker, rather than as a contentive. Cf. **full word, function word.**

em·pur·ple (em pûr′pəl), *v.t.,* **-pled, -pling.** to tinge or color with purple. [EM-[1] + PURPLE]

Em·pu·sae (em pyōō′sē), *n.* (*construed as pl.*) *Class. Myth.* a class of man-eating monsters having legs of asses with hoofs of brass.

em·py·e·ma (em′pē ē′mə, -pī-), *n.* *Pathol.* a collection of pus in a body cavity, esp. in the pleural cavity. Also called **pyothorax.** [< LL < Gk *empýēma* abscess, equiv. to *em-* EM-[2] + *pyē-* (var. s. of *pyein* to suppurate, akin to *pýon, pýos* pus) + *-ma* n. suffix denoting result of action] —**em′py·e′mic,** *adj.*

em·pyr·e·al (em pir′ē əl, em′pə rē′əl, -pī-), *adj.* **1.** Also, **empyrean.** pertaining to the highest heaven in the cosmology of the ancients. **2.** pertaining to the sky; celestial: *empyreal blue.* **3.** formed of pure fire or light: *empyreal radiance.* [< LL *empyre(us),* var. of *empyrius* (< Gk *empýrios* fiery, equiv. to *em-* EM-[2] + *pŷr* fire + *-ios* adj. suffix) + -AL[1]]

em·py·re·an (em′pə rē′ən, -pī-, em pir′ē ən), *n.* **1.** the highest heaven, supposed by the ancients to contain the pure element of fire. **2.** the visible heavens; the firmament. —*adj.* **3.** empyreal (def. 1). [< LL *empyre(us)* EMPYREAL + -AN]

em′ quad′, **1.** a square unit of area, one em on each side. **2.** a piece of type consisting of a box one em on each side, as □.

EMR, Electronic Magnetic Resonance.

Ems·worth (emz′wûrth), *n.* a town in SW Pennsylvania. 3341 (1960).

e·mu (ē′myōō), *n.* a large, flightless, ratite bird, *Dromiceius novaehollandiae,* of Australia, resembling the ostrich, but smaller and having a feathered head and neck and rudimentary wings. Also, **emeu.** [alter. of Pg *ema* ostrich (orig. crane)]

Emu
(Height 5 ft.; length 6 ft.)

E.M.U., See **electromagnetic unit.** Also, **EMU**

em·u·late (*v.* em′yə lāt′; *adj.* em′yə lit), *v.,* **-lat·ed, -lat·ing,** *adj.* —*v.t.* **1.** to try to equal or excel; imitate with effort to equal or surpass: *to emulate one's father.* **2.** to rival with some degree of success: *The artists of New York now emulate those of Paris in achievement.* —*adj.* **3.** *Obs.* emulous. [< L *aemulāt(us),* ptp. of *aemulārī* to rival. See EMULOUS, -ATE[1]] —**em′u·la′tive,** *adj.* —**em′u·la′tive·ly,** *adv.* —**em′u·la′tor,** *n.*

em·u·la·tion (em′yə lā′shən), *n.* **1.** effort or desire to equal or excel others. **2.** *Obs.* jealous rivalry. [< L *aemulātiōn-* (s. of *aemulātiō*). See EMULATE, -ION] —**Syn. 1.** competition, rivalry.

em·ul·gens (em′əl jenz′), *n.* (in prescriptions) an emulsifying agent. [< L]

em·u·lous (em′yə ləs), *adj.* **1.** desirous of equaling or excelling; filled with emulation: *boys emulous of their fathers.* **2.** arising from or of the nature of emulation, as actions, attitudes, etc. **3.** *Obs.* jealous; envious. [< L *aemulus* vying with; see -OUS] —**em′u·lous·ly,** *adv.* —**em′u·lous·ness,** *n.*

emuls., (in prescriptions) an emulsion. [< L *ēmulsiō*]

e·mul·si·fy (i mul′sə fī′), *v.t.,* **-fied, -fy·ing.** to make into an emulsion. [< L *ēmuls(us)* (see EMULSION) + -IFY] —**e·mul′si·fi′a·bil′i·ty, e·mul′si·bil′i·ty,** *n.* —**e·mul′si·fi′a·ble, e·mul′si·ble,** *adj.* —**e·mul′si·fi·ca′tion,** *n.* —**e·mul′si·fi′er,** *n.*

e·mul·sion (i mul′shən), *n.* **1.** a liquid preparation of the color and consistency of milk. **2.** *Physical Chem.* any colloidal suspension of a liquid in another liquid. **3.** *Pharm.* a liquid preparation consisting of two completely immiscible liquids, one of which, as minute globules coated by a gum or other mucilaginous substance, is dispersed throughout the other: used as a means of making a medicine palatable. **4.** *Photog.* a composition sensitive to some or all of the actinic rays of light, consisting of one or more of the silver halides suspended in gelatin, applied in a thin layer to one surface of a film or the like. [< NL *ēmulsiōn-* (s. of *ēmulsiō*), equiv. to L *ēmuls(us)* milked out (*ē-* E- + *mulsus,* ptp. of *mulgēre* to milk) + *-iōn-* -ION] —**e·mul′sive,** *adj.*

e·mul·soid (i mul′soid), *n.* **1.** *Physical Chem.* a sol having a liquid disperse phase. Cf. **suspensoid. 2.** (not in scientific use) an emulsion. [< L *ēmuls(us)* (see EMULSION) + -OID] —**e·mul·soi·dal** (i mul soid′ᵊl, ē′mul-), *adj.*

e·munc·to·ry (i mungk′tə rē), *n., pl.* **-ries,** *adj.* —*n.* **1.** a part or organ of the body, as the skin, a kidney, etc., carrying off waste products. —*adj.* **2.** excretory. [< NL *ēmunctōri(um),* equiv. to L *ēmunct(us)* wiped off (*ē-* E- + *munc-,* var. s. of *mungere* to wipe + *-tus* ptp. suffix) + *-ōrium* -ORY[2]]

en (en), *n.* **1.** the letter N, n. **2.** *Print.* half of the width of an em. —*adj.* **3.** *Print.* having the area of an en quad or the length of an en: *en quad; en dash.*

en-[1], **1.** a prefix meaning primarily "in," "into," occurring first in words from French, but now used freely as an English formative with the old concrete force of putting the object into or on something or of bringing the object into a specified condition, often serving to form transitive verbs from nouns or adjectives: *enable; enact; endear; engulf; enshrine; enslave.* **2.** a prefix attached to verbs in order to make them transitive or, if they are already transitive, to give them the transitive sign: *enkindle; entwine; engird; engrave; enshield.* Also, **em-**[1]. Cf. **in-**[2]. [ME < OF < L *in-* IN-[2]]

en-[2], a prefix representing Greek *en-,* corresponding to **en-**[1] and occurring chiefly in combinations already formed in Greek: *energy; enthusiasm.* Also, **em-**[2]. [< Gk (often through L); c. IN-[1], IN-[2]]

-en[1], a suffix formerly used to form transitive and intransitive verbs from adjectives (*fasten; harden; sweeten*), or from nouns (*heighten; lengthen; strengthen*). [ME, OE *-n-* (as in ME *fast-n-e(n),* OE *fæst-n-ian* to make fast, fasten); morphemic now; c. *-n-* of like verbs in other Gmc languages (Icel *fastna*)]

-en[2], a suffix formerly used to form adjectives from nouns: *ashen; golden; oaken.* [ME, OE; c. OHG *-īn,* Goth *-eins,* L *-īnus,* etc.; see -INE[1]]

-en[3], a suffix used to mark the past participle in many strong and some weak verbs: *taken; proven.* [ME, OE; c. G *-en,* Icel *-inn,* etc.]

-en[4], a suffix used in forming the plural of some nouns: *brethren; children; oxen.* [ME; OE *-an,* case ending of n-stem nouns, as in *naman* obl. sing., and nom. and acc. pl. of *nama* name; akin to n-stem forms in other IE languages, as in L *nomen, nomin-* name]

-en[5], a diminutive suffix: *kitten; maiden.* [ME, OE, from neut. of -EN[2]]

E·na (ē′nə), *n.* a girl's given name.

en·a·ble (en ā′bəl), *v.t.,* **-bled, -bling. 1.** to make able; give power, means, or ability to; make competent; authorize: *This document will enable him to pass through the enemy lines unmolested.* **2.** to make possible or easy: *Aeronautics enables us to overcome great distances.* [ME; see EN-[1], ABLE] —**en·a′bler,** *n.*

en·a·bling (en ā′bling), *adj.* (of an act, statute, or the like) empowering a person or corporation to do what he or it would otherwise be incapable of doing. [ENABLE + -ING[2]]

en·act (en akt′), *v.t.* **1.** to make into an act or statute: *They have enacted a new tax law.* **2.** to represent on or as on the stage; act the part of: *to enact Hamlet.* [ME *enacte(n).* See EN-[1], ACT] —**en·act′a·ble,** *adj.* —**en·ac′tor,** *n.*

en·ac·tive (en ak′tiv), *adj.* having power to enact or establish, as a law. [ENACT + -IVE]

en·act·ment (en akt′mənt), *n.* **1.** the act of enacting. **2.** the state or fact of being enacted. **3.** that which is enacted; a law or statute. **4.** a single provision of a law. [ENACT + -MENT]

en·ac·to·ry (en ak′tə rē), *adj.* *Law.* of or pertaining to an enactment which creates new rights and obligations. [ENACT + -ORY[1]]

en·al·la·ge (en al′ə jē), *n.* *Rhet.* the use of one grammatical form in place of another, as the plural for the singular in the editorial use of *we.* [< LL < Gk *enallagḗ* an interchange, equiv. to *en-* EN-[2] + *allag-* (s. of *allássein* to change) + *-ē* n. suffix]

E·na·lus (ēn′ᵊləs), *n.* *Class. Myth.* a youth who leaped into the sea because he was grief-stricken by the impending sacrifice of his love, Phineis: he was carried to safety on the back of a dolphin.

e·nam·el (i nam′əl), *n., v.,* **-eled, -el·ing** or (*esp. Brit.*) **-elled, -el·ling.** —*n.* **1.** a glassy substance, usually opaque, applied by fusion to the surface of metal, pottery, etc., as an ornament or for protection. **2.** enamelware. **3.** any of various enamellike varnishes, paints, etc. **4.** any enamellike surface with a bright luster. **5.** an artistic work executed in enamel. **6.** *Dentistry.* the hard, glossy, calcareous covering of the crown of a tooth, containing only a slight amount of organic substance. See diag. under **tooth. 7.** a cosmetic coating applied to the nails to create a smooth or glossy appearance and usually to color them. —*v.t.* **8.** to inlay or overlay with enamel. **9.** to form an enamellike surface upon: *to enamel cardboard.* **10.** to decorate as with enamel; variegate with colors. [ME *enamele(n)* < AF, MF *enamele(r),* equiv. to *en-* -EN-[1] + *ameler,* contr. of *esmaillier* to enamel, deriv. of *esma(i)l* enamel < ML *smalt(um)* < Gmc; cf. SMELT[1]] —**e·nam′el·er;** *esp. Brit.,* **e·nam′el·ler,** *n.* —**e·nam′el·ist;** *esp. Brit.,* **e·nam′el·list,** *n.* —**e·nam′el·work′,** *n.*

e·nam·el·ing (i nam′ə ling), *n.* **1.** the art, act, or work of a person who enamels. **2.** a decoration or coating of enamel. Also, *esp. Brit.,* **e·nam′el·ling.** [late ME; see ENAMEL, -ING[1]]

e·nam·el·ware (i nam′əl wâr′), *n.* metalware, as cooking utensils, covered with an enamel surface. [ENAMEL + WARE[1]]

en a·mi (äN NA mē′), *French.* as a friend: *to confide in someone en ami.*

en·am·or (en am′ər), *v.t.* to inflame with love; charm; captivate (usually used in the passive and fol. by *of* or sometimes *with*): *to be enamored of a lady; a worthless young woman with whom he became enamored.* Also, *esp. Brit.,* **en·am′our.** [ME *enamoure(n)* < OF *enamoure(r).* See EN-[1], AMOUR] —**en·am′ored·ness;** *esp. Brit.,* **en·am′oured·ness,** *n.* —**Syn.** fascinate, bewitch, enchant.

enantio-, a learned borrowing from Greek meaning "opposite," "opposing," used in the formation of compound words: *enantiomorph.* [< Gk, comb. form of *enantíos.* See EN-[2], ANTI-]

en·an·ti·o·morph (i nan′tē ə môrf′), *n.* *Crystall.* either of two crystals exhibiting enantiomorphism. [ENANTIO- + -MORPH]

en·an·ti·o·mor·phism (i nan′tē ə môr′fiz əm), *n.* *Crystall.* the existence of two chemically identical crystal forms as mirror images of each other. [ENANTIOMORPH + -ISM] —**en·an′ti·o·mor′phic, en·an′ti·o·mor′phous,** *adj.*

en·an·ti·o·sis (i nan′tē ō′sis), *n., pl.* **-ses** (-sēz). *Rhet.* a figure of speech in which what is meant is the opposite of what is said; irony. [< Gk *enantíōsis.* See ENANTIO-, -OSIS]

en·an·ti·ot·ro·py (i nan′tē o′trə pē), *n.* *Crystall.* polymorphism in which one of the polymorphs may revert to the state of the other at a critical temperature and pressure. Cf. **monotropy.** [< Gk *enantiotropía* contrariety of character. See ENANTIO-, -TROPY] —**en·an·ti·o·trop·ic** (i nan′tē ə trop′ik), *adj.*

en·arched (en ärcht′), *adj.* *Heraldry.* arched (def. 3). [obs. *enarch* (ME; see EN-[1], ARCH[1]) + -ED[2]]

E·nar·e·te (i när′i tē′), *n.* *Class. Myth.* the wife of Aeolus.

en·ar·gite (en är′jīt, en′ər jīt′), *n.* a mineral, copper arsenic and sulfide, Cu_3AsS_4, occurring in the form of black orthorhombic crystals having perfect cleavage: an important source of copper. [< Gk *enarg(ḗs)* brilliant (*en-* EN-[2] + *-argēs,* akin to *argós* bright, *árgyros* silver) + -ITE[1]]

en·arme (i närm′, en ärm′), *n.* *Armor.* a loop for securing a shield to the forearm. [< F (obs.), back formation from *enarmer* to equip (a shield) with side straps << L *in-* IN-[2] + *armus* side]

en ar·rière (äN NA RYER′), *French.* backward.

en·ar·thro·sis (en′är thrō′sis), *n., pl.* **-ses** (-sēz). *Anat.* a joint, as at the shoulder, in which a convex end of one bone is socketed in a concavity of another; ball-and-socket joint. [< NL < Gk, equiv. to *en-* EN-[2] + *árthr(on)* joint + *-ōsis* -OSIS] —**en·ar·thro·di·al** (en′är thrō′dē əl), *adj.*

e·nate (ē′nāt), *n.* **1.** a kinsman related on one's mother's side. Cf. **agnate, cognate.** —*adj.* **2.** Also, **e·nat·ic** (ē nat′ik). related on one's mother's side. [< L *ēnāt(us),* ptp. of *ēnāscī* to issue forth, be born]

en a·vant (äN NA väN′), *French.* forward; onward.

en bloc (äN blôk′; *Eng.* en blok′), *French.* as a whole.

en brosse (äN bRôs′), *French.* (of hair) brushed upon top.

enc., **1.** enclosed. **2.** enclosure. **3.** encyclopedia.

en ca·bo·chon (äN KA bô shôN′), *French.* in the form of a cabochon.

en·cae·nia (en sēn′yə, -sē′nē ə), *n.* **1.** (*construed as pl.*) festive ceremonies commemorating the founding of a city or the consecration of a church. **2.** (*often cap.*) (*often construed as sing.*) ceremonies at Oxford University in honor of founders and benefactors. [ME < LL < Gk *enkaínia* consecration festivities, neut. pl. of *enkaínios,* equiv. to *en-* EN-[2] + *-kainios* bound, var. of *kainós* new]

en·cage (en kāj′), *v.t.,* **-caged, -cag·ing.** to confine in or as in a cage; coop up: *to be encaged by inhibitions.* Also, **incage.** [EN-[1] + CAGE]

en·camp (en kamp′), *v.i.* **1.** to settle or lodge in a camp. —*v.t.* **2.** to make into a camp. **3.** to lodge or place in a camp. [EN-[1] + CAMP[1]]

en·camp·ment (en kamp′mənt), *n.* **1.** the act or an instance of encamping; lodgment in a camp. **2.** the place or quarters occupied in camping; camp. [ENCAMP + -MENT]

en·cap·su·late (en kap′sə lāt′), *v.t., v.i.,* **-lat·ed, -lat·ing.** to make, form, or place in or as in a capsule: *to become encapsulated in a protective environment.* [EN-[1] + CAPSULATE] —**en·cap′su·la′tion,** *n.*

en·cap·sule (en kap′səl), *v.t., v.i.,* **-suled, -su·ling.** encapsulate.

en·car·nal·ise (en kär′nᵊlīz′), *v.t.,* **-ised, -is·ing.** *Chiefly Brit.* encarnalize.

en·car·nal·ize (en kär′nᵊlīz′), *v.t.,* **-ized, -iz·ing.** to invest with a worldly or sensual nature or form; make carnal: *the soul encarnalized by the gross body; to encarnalize divinities.* Also, **incarnalize;** *esp. Brit.,* **encarnalise, incarnalise.** [EN-[1] + CARNAL + -IZE]

en·car·pus (en kär′pəs), *n., pl.* **-pi** (-pī). an ornament having draperies, weapons, etc., arranged in the manner of a festoon. [Latinized < Gk *énkarpos* containing fruit (see EN-[2], -CARP); r. *encarpe* Latinized < Gk *énkarpa,* neut. pl. of *énkarpos*]

en car·ré (äN KA Rā′), *French.* (of a bet in roulette) placed at the intersection of four numbers so as to share in any that wins. [lit., squared]

en·case (en kās′), *v.t.,* **-cased, -cas·ing.** to enclose in or as in a case: *We encased the painting in glass to preserve it.* Also, **incase.** [EN-[1] + CASE[2]]

en·case·ment (en kās′mənt), *n.* **1.** the act of encasing. **2.** the state of being encased. **3.** *Biol., Embryol.* the theory that the germs of succeeding generations of a given species are enclosed, one within the other, in the germ cell of one of the parents. **4.** that which encases; case. Also, **incasement.** [ENCASE + -MENT]

en·cas·tré (*Fr.* äN KA stRā′), *adj.* (of a beam) built into masonry or the like at both ends. Also, **en·cas·tered** (en kas′tərd). [< F, ptp. of *encastrer* to fit in, encase << LL *incastrāre* to join, equiv. to L *in-* IN-[2] + *castrāre* to prune, cut off, CASTRATE]

en·caus·tic (en kô′stik), *adj.* **1.** painted with wax colors fixed with heat, or with any process in which colors are burned in. —*n.* **2.** a work of art produced by an encaustic process. [< L *encaustic(us)* < Gk *enkaustikós* for burning in. See EN-[2], CAUSTIC] —**en·caus′ti·cal·ly,** *adv.*

-ence, a noun suffix equivalent to **-ance,** corresponding to the suffix **-ent** in adjectives: *abstinence; continence; dependence; difference.* [ME < OF < L *-entia,* equiv. to *-ent-* -ENT + *-ia* -Y[3]]

en·ceinte[1] (en sānt′; *Fr.* äN SANT′), *adj.* pregnant; with child. [< F, irreg. < L *incient-* (s. of *inciēns*) pregnant; akin to Gk *énkyos,* equiv. to *en-* EN-[2] + *ký(ein)* (to) be great with child]

en·ceinte[2] (en sānt′; *Fr.* äN SANT′), *n., pl.* **-ceintes** (-sänts′; *Fr.* -SANT′). **1.** a wall or enclosure, as of a fortified place. **2.** the place enclosed. [< F: enclosure, also girding fence or rampart < L *incincta,* n. use of fem. of *incinctus* girded in (ptp. of *incingere*), equiv. to *in-* IN-[2] + *cing-* gird + *-tus* ptp. suffix]

En·cel·a·dus (en sel′ə dəs), *n.* **1.** *Class. Myth.* a giant thought to lie buried under Mount Etna, in Sicily. In warring with the gods he had been struck down with a great stone flung at him by Athena. **2.** *Astron.* one of the nine satellites of Saturn.

encephal-, var. of **encephalo-** before a vowel: *encephalic.*

en·ceph·a·lal·gi·a (en sef′ə lal′jē ə), *n.* *Med.* headache. [ENCEPHAL- + -ALGIA]

en·ceph·a·las·the·ni·a (en sef′ə ləs thē′nē ə), *n.* *Pathol.* mental fatigue caused by emotional stress. [ENCEPHAL- + ASTHENIA]

en·ce·phal·ic (en′sə fal′ik), *adj.* of or pertaining to the encephalon or brain. [ENCEPHAL- + -IC]

en·ceph·a·li·tis (en sef′ə lī′tis), *n.* *Pathol.* **1.** inflammation of the substance of the brain. **2.** Also called **encephali′tis le·thar′gi·ca** (li thär′jə kə). a form of this condition, caused by a filterable virus and characterized by apathy and abnormal sleepiness; sleeping sickness. [ENCEPHAL- + -ITIS] —**en·ceph·a·lit·ic** (en sef′ə lit′ik), *adj.*

encephalo-, a learned borrowing from Greek meaning "brain," used in the formation of compound words: *encephalograph.* Also, *esp. before a vowel,* **encephal-.** [< Gk *enképhalo(s).* See ENCEPHALON]

en·ceph·a·lo·gram (en sef′ə lə gram′), *n.* *Med.* an x-ray photograph of the brain. [ENCEPHALO- + -GRAM[1]]

en·ceph·a·lo·graph (en sef′ə lə graf′, -gräf′), *n.* *Med.* **1.** an encephalogram. **2.** an electroencephalograph. [ENCEPHALO- + -GRAPH]

en·ceph·a·log·ra·phy (en sef′ə log′rə fē), *n.* *Med.* the production of encephalograms, following replacement of the cerebrospinal fluid with air or oxygen. [ENCEPHALO- + -GRAPHY] —**en·ceph·a·lo·graph·ic** (en sef′ə lə graf′ik), *adj.* —**en·ceph′a·lo·graph′i·cal·ly,** *adv.*

en·ceph·a·lo·ma (en sef′ə lō′mə), *n., pl.* **-ma·ta** (-mə tə). *Pathol.* **1.** a brain tumor. **2.** hernia of the brain. [ENCEPHAL- + -OMA]

en·ceph·a·lo·ma·la·cia (en sef′ə lō mə lā′shə, -shē ə), *n.* *Pathol.* a degeneration or necrosis of the cerebrum, caused by impairment of the blood supply; softening of the brain. [< NL; see ENCEPHALO-, MALACIA]

en·ceph·a·lo·my·e·li·tis (en sef′ə lō mī′ə lī′tis), *n.* *Pathol.* inflammation of the brain and spinal cord. [ENCEPHALO- + MYELITIS] —**en·ceph·a·lo·my·e·lit·ic** (en sef′ə lō mī′ə lit′ik), *adj.*

en·ceph·a·lon (en sef′ə lon′), *n., pl.* **-la** (-lə). the brain. [< NL, alter. (-*on* for -*os*) of Gk *enképhalos* brain, equiv. to *en-* EN-^{2} + *kephal*(*ḗ*) head + -*os* masc. n. suffix]

en·ceph·a·lop·a·thy (en sef′ə lop′ə thē), *n. Psychiatry.* brain disease. [ENCEPHALO- + -PATHY]

en·ceph·a·lo·sis (en sef′ə lō′sis), *n. Pathol.* any organic disease of the brain. [ENCEPHAL- + -OSIS]

en·ceph·a·lot·o·my (en sef′ə lot′ə mē), *n., pl.* **-mies.** surgical incision or dissection of the brain. [ENCEPHALO- + -TOMY]

en·chain (en chān′), *v.t.* **1.** to fasten with or as with a chain or chains; fetter; restrain: *to be enchained by ignorance and superstition.* **2.** to hold fast, as the attention. [ME *enchaine*(*n*) < OF *enchainer, -chaener.* See EN-^{1}, CHAIN] **—en·chain′ment,** *n.*

en·chaîne·ment (*Fr.* än shen män′), *n., pl.* **-ments** (*Fr.* -män′). *Ballet.* a series of steps constituting a phrase. [< F; see ENCHAIN, -MENT]

en·chant (en chant′, -chänt′), *v.t.* **1.** to subject to magical influence; cast a spell over; bewitch: *fairy-tales about witches who enchant handsome princes and beautiful maidens.* **2.** to impart a magic quality or effect to: *moonlight that enchants the night.* **3.** to delight to a high degree; charm: *Her gaiety and wit have enchanted us all.* [ME *enchante*(*n*) < MF *enchante*(*r*) < L *incantāre* to bespell; see INCANTATION]
—Syn. 3. fascinate; captivate, enrapture, transport, bewitch, attract.

en·chant·er (en chan′tər, -chän′-), *n.* **1.** a person who enchants or delights. **2.** a magician; sorcerer. [ENCHANT + -ER^1; r. ME *enchantour* < AF; OF *enchanteor* < L *incantātor,* equiv. to *incantāt*(*us*) (see INCANTATION) + *-or* -OR^2]

enchant′er's night′shade, any of several herbs of the genus *Circaea,* of cool and temperate regions of the Northern Hemisphere, having white flowers.

en·chant·ing (en chan′ting, -chän′-), *adj.* charming; bewitching: *an enchanting smile.* [ENCHANT + -ING^2] **—en·chant′ing·ly,** *adv.* **—en·chant′ing·ness,** *n.*

en·chant·ment (en chant′mənt, -chänt′-), *n.* **1.** the art, act, or an instance of enchanting. **2.** the state of being enchanted. **3.** that which enchants: *Music is an enchantment that never fails.* [ME *enchantement* < OF < L *incantāment*(*um*). See ENCHANT, -MENT]
—Syn. 1. magic, sorcery, fascination, witchery. **3.** spell, charm.

en·chant·ress (en chan′tris, -chän′-), *n.* **1.** a woman who enchants; sorceress: *the enchantress Circe.* **2.** a fascinating woman: *an enchantress who broke men's hearts.* [ME *enchaunteresse* < MF *enchanteresse.* See ENCHANTER, -ESS]

en·chase (en chās′), *v.t.,* **-chased, -chas·ing. 1.** to place (gems) in an ornamental setting. **2.** to decorate with inlay, embossing, or engraving. [late ME < MF *enchasse*(*r*) to case in, equiv. to *en-* EN-^{1} + *chasse,* var. of *casse* CASE^2] **—en·chas′er,** *n.*

en·chi·la·da (en′chə lä′də, -lad′ə), *n. Mexican Cookery.* a tortilla rolled and filled with a highly seasoned mixture, usually containing meat, and covered with a sauce flavored with chili. [< AmerSp, fem. of Sp *enchilado* spiced with chili (ptp. of *enchilar*), equiv. to *en-* EN-^{1} + *chil*(*e*) CHILI + *-ado* -ATE^1]

en·chi·rid·i·on (en′kī rid′ē ən, -ki-), *n., pl.* **-rid·i·ons, -rid·i·a** (-rid′ē ə). a handbook; manual. [< LL < Gk *encheirídion* handbook, equiv. to *en-* EN-^{2} + *cheír* hand + *-idion* dim. suffix]

en·chon·dro·ma (en′kən drō′mə), *n., pl.* **-mas, -ma·ta** (-mə tə). *Pathol.* a growth of cartilage within the shaft or substance of a bone. [< NL < Gk *en-* EN-^{2} + *chóndr*(*os*) cartilage + *-ōma* -OMA] **—en·chon·drom·a·tous** (en′kən drom′ə təs, -drō′mə-), *adj.*

en·cho·ri·al (en kōr′ē əl, -kôr′-), *n.* (esp. of demotic writing) belonging to or used in a particular country; native; domestic. Also, **en·chor·ic** (en kôr′ik, -kor′-). [< LL *enchori*(*us*) (< Gk *enchṓrios* native, equiv. to *en-* EN-^{2} + *chṓr*(*ā*) country + *-ios* adj. suffix) + -AL^1]

en·ci·na (en sē′nə), *n.* **1.** the live oak, *Quercus virginiana.* **2.** See **California live oak.** [< AmerSp, Sp: holm oak, by syncope, shortening and assimilation < LL *īlicīna* holm oak, orig. fem. of *īlicīnus* pertaining to holm oak, equiv. to L *īlic-* (s. of *īlex*) ILEX + *-īnus* -INE^1] **—en·ci′nal,** *adj.*

En·ci·na (en thē′nä), *n.* **Juan del** (hwän del), 1468?–1529?, Spanish poet, composer, and playwright: among the earliest to use secular in addition to religious themes.

en·cinc·ture (en singk′chər), *v.,* **-tured, -tur·ing,** *n.* **—v.t. 1.** to gird or encompass with or as with a belt or girdle: *A ring of hills encinctures the town.* **—n. 2.** the act, fact, or an instance of encompassing with or as with a belt, girdle, etc.: *An encincture of willows rings the pond.* [EN-^{1} + CINCTURE]

En·ci·ni·tas (en′sə nē′təs), *n.* a town in S California. 2786 (1960).

en·ci·pher (en sī′fər), *v.t.* to convert (a message, communication, etc.) into cipher. [EN-^{1} + CIPHER] **—en·ci′pher·er,** *n.* **—en·ci′pher·ment,** *n.*

en·cir·cle (en sûr′kəl), *v.t.,* **-cled, -cling. 1.** to form a circle round; surround; encompass: *Have our men spread out and encircle the enemy.* **2.** to make a circling movement about; make the circuit of: *Moths encircled the candle.* [ME; see EN-^{1}, CIRCLE] **—en·cir′cle·ment,** *n.*
—Syn. 1. environ, gird, enfold, enclose.

Enc·ke (eng′kē), *n.* a crater in the second quadrant of the face of the moon: about 20 miles in diameter.

encl., 1. enclosed. **2.** enclosure.

en clair (än kler′), *French.* (esp. of diplomatic messages sent by telegraph) in ordinary language; in language that need not be decoded to be understood. [lit., in clear]

en·clasp (en klasp′, -kläsp′), *v.t.* to hold in or as in a clasp or embrace. Also, **inclasp.** [EN-^{1} + CLASP]

en·clave (en′klāv; *Fr.* än klav′), *n., pl.* **-claves** (-klāvz; *Fr.* -klav′). a country, or esp., an outlying portion of a country, entirely or mostly surrounded by the territory of another country. [< F, appar. back formation from *enclaver* < VL **inclāvāre* to lock in, equiv. to L *in-* IN-^{2} + *clāv*(*is*) key + *-āre* v. suffix]

en·clit·ic (en klit′ik), *adj.* **1.** (of a word) closely connected with the preceding word and not having an independent accent or phonological status. **—n. 2.** an enclitic word, as Latin *que* "and" in *arma virumque,* "arms and the man." [< LL *enclitic*(*us*) < Gk *enklitikós,* equiv. to *en-* EN-^{2} + *klit*(*ós*) slope + *-ikos* -IC] **—en·clit′i·cal·ly,** *adv.*

en·close (en klōz′), *v.t.,* **-closed, -clos·ing. 1.** to shut or hem in; close in on all sides: *a valley enclosed by tall mountains.* **2.** to surround, as with a fence or wall: *to enclose land.* **3.** to insert in the same envelope, package, or the like, with the main letter, consignment, etc.: *He enclosed a check.* **4.** to hold or contain: *His letter enclosed a check.* **5.** *Rom. Cath. Ch.* **a.** to restrict to the enclosure of a monastery or convent. **b.** (of a monastery, convent, church, etc.) to establish or fix the boundary of an enclosure. Also, **inclose.** [ME *en-, inclose*(*n*) (to) close in. See IN-^{1}, CLOSE] **—en·clos′a·ble,** *adj.* **—en·clos′er,** *n.*
—Syn. 1. surround, encircle, encompass.

en·clo·sure (en klō′zhər), *n.* **1.** the act or an instance of enclosing. **2.** the state of being enclosed. **3.** the separation and appropriation of land by means of a fence. **4.** a tract of land surrounded by a fence. **5.** that which encloses, as a fence or wall. **6.** that which is enclosed, as a paper sent in a letter. **7.** *Rom. Cath. Ch.* the part of a monastery or convent canonically separated or restricted as the living quarters of the religious, from which a person may leave only with special permission or gain entrance to by special dispensation. Also, **inclosure.** [ENCLOSE + -URE]

enclo′sure act′, *Eng. Hist.* any of the acts of Parliament passed from 1709 to 1869, requiring that private lands be fenced off from common lands.

en·code (en kōd′), *v.t.,* **-cod·ed, -cod·ing.** to convert (a message, information, etc.) into code. [EN-^{1} + CODE] **—en·code′ment,** *n.* **—en·cod′er,** *n.*

en·coi·gnure (en koin′yər, -koin′-, än-; *Fr.* än kô nyr′), *n., pl.* **-coi·gnures** (-kon′yərz, -koin′-; *Fr.* -kô nyr′). *Fr. Furniture.* a low corner cabinet. [< F; see EN-^{1}, COIGN, -URE]

en·col·pi·on (en kōl′pē ən, en kol′pē on′), *n., pl.* **-pi·a** (-pē ə). *Eastern Ch.* a pectoral medallion bearing the image of Christ or the Virgin Mary, worn by bishops. Also, **enkolpion.** Also called **panagia.** [< MGk *enkólpion* < Gk, n. use of neut. of *enkólpios* of the bosom, equiv. to *en-* EN-^{2} + *kólp*(*os*) bosom, lap + *-ios* adj. suffix]

en·co·mi·ast (en kō′mē ast′), *n.* a person who utters or writes an encomium; eulogist. [< Gk *enkōmiast*(*ḗs*), equiv. to *enkṓmi*(*on*) ENCOMIUM + *-astēs* agent n. suffix]

en·co·mi·as·tic (en kō′mē as′tik), *adj.* praising; eulogistic. Also, **en·co′mi·as′ti·cal.** [< Gk *enkōmiastik*(*ós*). See ENCOMIAST, -IC] **—en·co′mi·as′ti·cal·ly,** *adv.*

en·co·mi·en·da (en kō′mē en′də, -kom′ē-; *Sp.* en kô-myen′dä), *n., pl.* **-das** (-dəz; *Sp.* -däs). (formerly in Spanish America) **1.** the system, instituted in 1503, under which a Spanish soldier or colonist was granted a tract of land or a village together with its Indian inhabitants. **2.** the land or village together with its inhabitants. [< Sp: charge, commission, recommendation. See EN-^{1}, COMMEND]

en·co·mi·um (en kō′mē əm), *n., pl.* **-mi·ums, -mi·a** (-mē ə). a formal expression of high praise; eulogy: *An encomium by the president greeted the returning hero.* [< L < Gk *enkṓmion,* equiv. to *en-* EN-^{2} + *kôm*(*os*) a revel + *-ion* -Y^3]
—Syn. commendation, laudation, panegyric.

en·com·pass (en kum′pəs), *v.t.* **1.** to form a circle about; encircle; surround: *The fugitives were encompassed by the police.* **2.** to enclose; envelop: *The folds of a great cloak encompassed her person.* **3.** to include comprehensively: *a work which encompasses the entire range of man's religious belief.* **4.** *Obs.* to outwit. [EN-^{1} + COMPASS] **—en·com′pass·ment,** *n.*

en·co·pre·sis (en′kə prē′sis), *n., pl.* **-ses** (-sēz). *Psychiatry.* involuntary defecation. [< NL < Gk *en-* EN-^{2} + *kópr*(*os*) dung + *-esis,* as in *enuresis*]

en·core (äng′kōr, -kôr, än′-), *interj., n., v.,* **-cored, -cor·ing.** **—interj. 1.** again; once more (used by an audience in calling for a repetition of a song, act, etc., or for an additional number or piece). **—n. 2.** a demand, as by applause, for a repetition of a song, act, etc., or for a performance of a number or piece additional to those on a program, as at the end of a highly applauded concert, recital, etc. **3.** the performance given in response to such a demand: *He chose a Chopin nocturne for his encore.* **—v.t. 4.** to call for a repetition of. **5.** to call for an encore from (a performer). [< F: still, yet, besides < L (*in*) *hanc hōram* until this hour]

en·coun·ter (en koun′tər), *v.t.* **1.** to come upon; meet with, esp. unexpectedly: *Today I encountered an old friend whom I hadn't seen in three years.* **2.** to meet with or contend against (difficulties, opposition, etc.): *We encounter so many problems in our work.* **3.** to meet (a person, military force, etc.) in conflict: *We will encounter the enemy at dawn.* **—v.i. 4.** to meet, esp. in conflict: *We were angry when we encountered, but we parted with smiles.* **—n. 5.** a meeting with a person or thing, esp. casually or unexpectedly: *Our running into each other was merely a chance encounter.* **6.** a meeting of persons or groups that are in conflict or opposition; combat; battle: *Another such encounter and we may lose the war.* **7.** *Obs.* manner of meeting; behavior. [ME *encountre*(*n*) < OF *encontre*(*r*) < LL *incontrāre,* deriv. of *incontrā* facing, equiv. to L *in* in + *contrā*; see COUNTER^3] **—en·coun′ter·er,** *n.*
—Syn. 1–3. confront, face. **6.** conflict, skirmish.

en·cour·age (en kûr′ij, -kur′-), *v.t.,* **-aged, -ag·ing. 1.** to inspire with courage, spirit, or confidence: *His father encouraged him to fight for what he desired.* **2.** to stimulate by assistance, approval, etc.: *One of the chief duties of a teacher is to encourage his students.* [late ME *encorage* < MF *encorag*(*ier*). See EN-^{1}, COURAGE] **—en·cour′ag·er,** *n.* **—en·cour′ag·ing·ly,** *adv.*
—Syn. 1. inspirit, embolden, hearten, reassure, incite. **2.** urge, abet, second; support, aid, help; favor, countenance; foment, promote, advance, foster. **—Ant. 1.** dishearten.

en·cour·age·ment (en kûr′ij mənt, -kur′-), *n.* **1.** the act of encouraging. **2.** the state of being encouraged. **3.** that which encourages: *The praise of those we admire is the greatest encouragement.* [ENCOURAGE + -MENT]
—Ant. 1. disapproval. **2.** depression.

en·crim·son (en krim′zən), *v.t.* to make crimson. [EN-^{1} + CRIMSON]

en·cri·nite (en′krə nīt′), *n.* **1.** a fossil crinoid. **2.** any crinoid. [< NL *encrin*(*us*) (< Gk *en-* EN-^{2} + *krínon* lily) + -ITE^1]

en·croach (en krōch′), *v.i.* **1.** to advance beyond proper limits; make gradual inroads: *A dictatorship of the majority is encroaching on the rights of the individual.* **2.** to trespass upon the property, domain, or rights of another, esp. stealthily or by gradual advances: *Television began to encroach on radio in the late 1940's.* [ME *encroche*(*n*) < OF *encrochie*(*r*) (to) hook in, seize, equiv. to *en-* EN-^{1} + *croc* hook < Gmc; see CROOKED, CROOK] **—en·croach′er,** *n.*
—Syn. 1, 2. See **trespass.**

en·croach·ment (en krōch′mənt), *n.* **1.** the act or an instance of encroaching. **2.** anything taken by encroaching. [ME *encrochement* < AF. See ENCROACH, -MENT]

en·crust (en krust′), *v.t., v.i.* incrust. **—en·crust′ant,** *adj., n.*

en·crus·ta·tion (en′kru stā′shən), *n.* incrustation.

en·crypt (en kript′), *v.t.* to encipher or encode. [EN-^{1} + *-crypt* (abstracted from *cryptic, cryptography,* etc.), modeled on *encode*] **—en·cryp′tion,** *n.*

en·cul·tu·rate (en kul′chə rāt′), *v.t.,* **-rat·ed, -rat·ing.** *Sociol.* to change, modify, or adapt (behavior, ideas, etc.) by enculturation. [? back formation from ENCULTURATION] **—en·cul·tu·ra·tive** (en kul′chə rā′tiv, -chər ə tiv), *adj.*

en·cul·tu·ra·tion (en kul′chə rā′shən), *n.* the process by which a person adapts to a culture and assimilates its values: *an enculturation to European ways.* [EN-^{1} + (AC)CULTURATION]

en·cum·ber (en kum′bər), *v.t.* **1.** to impede or hinder; hamper; retard: *Red tape encumbers all our attempts at action.* **2.** to block up or fill with what is obstructive or superfluous: *a mind encumbered with unnecessary information.* **3.** to burden or weigh down: *She was encumbered with a valise and several packages.* **4.** to burden with obligations, debt, etc. Also, **incumber.** [ME *encombre*(*n*) < MF *encombre*(*r*), equiv. to *en-* EN-^{1} + *combre* barrier < LL *combr*(*us*) < Gallic *comberos* a bringing together; see COM-, BEAR^1] **—en·cum′ber·ing·ly,** *adv.*
—Syn. 4. oppress, overload. **—Ant. 4.** disburden.

en·cum·brance (en kum′brəns), *n.* **1.** that which encumbers; something burdensome, useless, or superfluous; burden; hindrance: *Poverty was a lifelong encumbrance.* **2.** a dependent person, esp. a child. **3.** *Law.* a burden or claim on property, as a mortgage. Also, **incumbrance.** [ME *encombraunce* < MF *encombrance.* See ENCUMBER, -ANCE]

en·cum·branc·er (en kum′brən sər), *n. Law.* a person who holds an encumbrance. [ENCUMBRANCE + -ER^1]

-ency, a noun suffix, equivalent to **-ence:** *consistency; dependency; exigency.* [< L *-entia.* See -ENT, -Y^3]

ency., encyclopedia. Also, **encyc., encycl.**

en·cyc·li·cal (en sik′li kəl, -sī′kli-), *n.* **1.** *Rom. Cath. Ch.* a letter addressed by the pope to all the bishops of the church. **—adj. 2.** (of a letter) intended for wide or general circulation; general. Also, **en·cyc′lic.** [< LL *encyclic*(*us*) (< Gk *enkýklios,* with *-icus* -IC for *-ios,* equiv. to *en-* EN-^{2} + *kýkl*(*os*) circle, CYCLE + *-ios* adj. suffix) + -AL^1]

en·cy·clo·pe·di·a (en sī′klə pē′dē ə), *n.* **1.** a book or set of books containing articles on various topics, usually in alphabetical arrangement, covering all branches of knowledge or, less commonly, all aspects of one subject. **2.** (*cap.*) the French work edited by Diderot and D'Alembert, published in the 18th century, distinguished by its advanced or radical character. Also, **en·cy′clo·pae′di·a.** [< LL *encyclopaedia,* by mistake for Gk *enkýklios paideía* circular (i.e., well-rounded) education. See ENCYCLICAL, PEDI-^{2}]

en·cy·clo·pe·dic (en sī′klə pē′dik), *adj.* **1.** pertaining to or of the nature of an encyclopedia; relating to all branches of knowledge. **2.** comprehending a wide variety of information; comprehensive: *an encyclopedic memory.* Also, **en·cy′clo·pae′dic, en·cy′clo·pe′di·cal, en·cy′clo·pae′di·cal.** [ENCYCLOPED(IA) + -IC] **—en·cy′clo·pe′di·cal·ly, en·cy′clo·pae′di·cal·ly,** *adv.*

en·cy·clo·pe·dism (en sī′klə pē′diz əm), *n.* **1.** encyclopedic learning. **2.** (*often cap.*) the doctrines and influence of the Encyclopedists. Also, **en·cy′clo·pae′dism.** [ENCYCLOPED(IA) + -ISM]

en·cy·clo·pe·dist (en sī′klə pē′dist), *n.* **1.** a compiler of or contributor to an encyclopedia. **2.** (*often cap.*) one of the collaborators on the French Encyclopedia. Also, **en·cy′clo·pae′dist.** [ENCYCLOPED(IA) + -IST]

en·cyst (en sist′), *v.t., v.i. Biol.* to enclose or become enclosed in a cyst. [EN-^{1} + CYST] **—en·cyst′ment, en′cys·ta′tion,** *n.*

end^1 (end), *n.* **1.** the extremity of anything that is longer than it is wide or broad: *the end of a street; the end of a rope.* **2.** a point, line, or limitation that indicates the full extent, degree, etc., of something; limit; bounds: *kindness without end; to walk from end to end of a city.* **3.** a part or place at or adjacent to an extremity: *Put it on the end of the table.* **4.** the furthermost imaginable place or point: *an island at the very end of the world.* **5.** termination; conclusion: *The journey was coming to an end.* **6.** the concluding part: *The end of his speech had to be cut short because of time.* **7.** a purpose or aim: *to gain one's ends.* **8.** the object for which a thing exists: *The happiness of the people is the end of government.* **9.** an issue or result: *What is to be the end of all this bickering?* **10.** termination of existence; death: *He met a horrible end.* **11.** a cause of death, destruction, or ruin: *Another war would be the end of civilization.* **12.** a remnant or fragment: *mill end; ends and trimmings.* **13.** a share or part in something: *He does his end of the job very well.* **14.** *Textiles.* a warp thread running vertically and interlaced with the filling yarn in the woven fabric. **15.** *Football.* **a.** either of the linemen stationed farthest from the center. **b.** the position played by this lineman. **16.** *Archery.* the number of arrows to be shot by a competitor taking his turn in a match. **17.** *Cricket.* a wicket, esp. the one where the batsman is taking his turn. **18.** a unit of a game, as in curling or lawn bowling. **19.** *Kantianism.* any rational being, regarded as worthy to exist for its own sake. **20.** either half of a domino. **21.** *Knots.* the part of a

rope, beyond a knot or the like, that is not used. **22.** *Slang.* **a.** that which finally exhausts one's patience: *That last stupid bungle of his is the end!* **b.** the peak of quality; acme: *That music is the end.* **23. at loose ends, a.** without an occupation; unsettled: *He spent two years wandering about the country at loose ends.* **b.** without definite plans; confused; uncertain: *After their arrival in the strange port, they were at loose ends as to what to do with their time.* **24. at one's wit's end,** at the end of one's ideas or mental resources; perplexed: *I'm at my wit's end with this problem.* Also, **at one's wits' end. 25. end for end,** with the ends in reverse position; inverted: *The cartons were arranged end for end.* **26. end on,** with the end next to or facing: *He backed the truck until it was end on with the loading platform.* **27. end-to-end,** in a position of having an end of one object touching the end of another object: *The pipes were placed end-to-end on the ground.* **28. go off the deep end,** *Informal.* **a.** to go to extremes: *He certainly went off the deep end with that last idea.* **b.** to become violently agitated; lose emotional control: *She goes off the deep end at the mention of his name.* **c.** to commit suicide. **29. keep** or **hold one's end up, a.** to take adequate care of one's own responsibilities: *The work is demanding, but he's holding his end up.* **b.** to defend oneself adequately: *Don't worry, he can hold up his end in any fight.* **30. make both ends meet,** to live within one's means: *With her extravagant tastes, she was incapable of making both ends meet.* Also, **make ends meet. 31. no end,** *Informal.* very much; quite: *They were pleased no end by the warm reception.* **32. on end, a.** having the end down; upright: *to stand a box on end.* **b.** continuously; successively: *They talked for hours on end.* **33. put an end to,** to cause to stop; terminate; finish: *The advent of sound in motion pictures put an end to many a silent star's career.* **34. the ends of the earth,** the most remote regions of the earth; everywhere: *They searched for him to the ends of the earth.* —*v.t.* **35.** to bring to an end or conclusion: *We ended the discussion on a note of optimism.* **36.** to put an end to by force: *This was the battle that ended the war.* **37.** to form the end of: *This passage ends the novel.* **38.** to cause the demise of; kill: *A bullet through the heart ended him.* **39.** to constitute the most outstanding or greatest possible example or instance of (usually used in the infinitive): *You just committed the blunder to end all blunders.* —*v.i.* **40.** to come to an end; terminate; cease: *He ended by settling down.* **41.** to issue or result: *Extravagance ends in want.* **42.** to reach or arrive at a final condition, circumstance, or goal (often fol. by *up*): *to end up in the army; To end as a man, this is the important thing.* [ME, OE *ende;* c. G *Ende,* Icel *endir,* Goth *andeis* end; akin to Skt *ánta* end] —**end′er,** *n.*
—**Syn. 4.** tip, bound, limit, terminus. **5.** END, CLOSE, CONCLUSION, FINISH, OUTCOME refer to the termination of something. END implies a natural termination, completion of an action or process, or attainment of purpose: *the end of a day, of a race; to some good end.* CLOSE implies a planned rounding off of something in process: *the close of a conference.* CONCLUSION suggests a decision or arrangement: *All evidence leads to this conclusion; the conclusion of peace terms.* FINISH emphasizes completion of something begun: *a fight to the finish.* OUTCOME suggests the issue of something which was in doubt: *the outcome of a game.* **6.** finale, peroration. **7.** intent, intention, goal. See **aim. 9.** outcome, consequence. **10.** destruction, extermination, annihilation, ruin. **35.** conclude, complete, close. **40.** close, stop, discontinue. —**Ant. 5.** beginning, start. **35.** begin.

end[2] (end), *v.t. Brit. Dial.* to put wheat, hay, or other grain into a stack or barn. [? var. of *in* to harvest (OE *innian* to lodge, put up). See INN]

end-, var. of **endo-** before a vowel: *endamoeba.*

end., endorsed.

end-all (end′ôl′), *n.* **1.** the end of everything; ultimate conclusion: *Money is the be-all and end-all of his existence.* **2.** that which brings things to such an end or conclusion.

en·dam·age (en dam′ij), *v.t.,* **-aged, -ag·ing.** to damage. [ME; see EN-[1], DAMAGE] —**en·dam′age·ment,** *n.*

en·da·moe·ba (en′də mē′bə), *n., pl.* **-bae** (-bē), **-bas.** any protozoan of the genus *Endamoeba,* a species of which causes dysentery in man. Also, **en′da·me′ba.** [END- + AMOEBA] —**en′da·moe′bic, en′da·me′bic,** *adj.*

end·an·ge·i·tis (en′dan jē ī′tis), *n. Pathol.* an inflammation of the innermost lining of a blood vessel. Also, **end·an·gi·tis** (en′dan jī′tis), **end′an·gi·i′tis, endoangiitis.** [END- + *angeitis;* see ANGI-, -ITIS]

en·dan·ger (en dān′jər), *v.t.* to expose to danger; imperil: *It was foolish to endanger your life in that way.* [late ME; see EN-[1], DANGER] —**en·dan′ger·ment,** *n.*

end·a·or·ti·tis (en′dā ôr tī′tis), *n. Pathol.* an inflammation of the innermost lining of the aorta. Also, **endoaortitis.** [END- + AORT(A) + -ITIS]

en·darch (en′därk), *adj. Bot.* having the protoxylem develop toward the center of the stem or root. [END- + -ARCH] —**en′dar·chy,** *n.*

end′ around′, *Football.* a play on offense in which an end, after running into the backfield, takes a hand-off and attempts to run outside the end of the line opposite his original position.

end·ar·ter·i·tis (en′där tə rī′tis), *n. Pathol.* an inflammation of the innermost lining of an artery. Also, **endoarteritis.** [< NL; see END-, ARTERITIS]

end·ar·te·ri·um (en′där tēr′ē əm), *n., pl.* **-te·ri·a** (-tēr′ē ə). *Anat.* the innermost lining of an artery. [< NL; see END-, ARTERY] —**end′ar·te′ri·al,** *adj.*

en′ dash′, *Print.* a dash one en long.

end-blown (end′blōn′), *adj.* (of a flute) having a mouthpiece at the end of the tube so that the player's breath is directed into the instrument. Cf. **transverse** (def. 3).

end·brain (end′brān′), *n.* the telencephalon. [trans. of TELENCEPHALON]

end′ burn′er. See **restricted propellant.**

en·dear (en dēr′), *v.t.* **1.** to make dear, esteemed, or beloved: *He endeared himself to his mother with his gentle ways.* **2.** *Obs.* to make costly. [EN-[1] + DEAR] —**en·dear′ing·ly,** *adv.*

en·dear·ment (en dēr′mənt), *n.* **1.** the act of endearing. **2.** the state of being endeared. **3.** that which endears; an action or utterance showing affection: *He showers her with endearments; words of endearment.* [ENDEAR + -MENT]

en·deav·or (en dev′ər), *v.i.* **1.** to exert onself to do or effect something; make an effort; strive: *We must constantly endeavor if we are to succeed.* **2.** to attempt; try: *He endeavors to keep things neat about his place.* —*n.* **3.** a strenuous effort; attempt. Also, *esp. Brit.,* **en·deav′our.** [ME *endevere(n).* See EN-[1], DEVOIR] —**en·deav′or·er;** *esp. Brit.,* **en·deav′our·er,** *n.*
—**Syn. 1.** struggle, labor. **1, 2.** See **try. 2.** essay, undertake, seek, aim. **3.** struggle, essay, trial. See **effort.**

En·de·cott (en′də kət, -kot′), *n.* **John,** 1588?–1665, colonial governor of Massachusetts 1644–65, born in England. Also, **Endicott.**

En·de·ïs (en dē′is), *n. Class. Myth.* the second wife of Aeacus.

en·dem·ic (en dem′ik), *adj.* **1.** Also, **en·dem′i·cal.** peculiar to a particular people or locality; indigenous: *endemic folkways; a fever endemic to the tropics.* —*n.* **2.** an endemic disease. [< NL *endēmic(us),* equiv. to Gk *éndēm(os)* endemic (*en-* EN-[2] + *dêm(os)* people + *-os* adj. suffix) + L *-icus* -IC] —**en·dem′i·cal·ly,** *adv.* —**en·de·mism** (en′də miz′əm), **en·de·mic·i·ty** (en′də-mis′i tē), *n.*

En′der·by Land′ (en′dər bē), a part of the coast of Antarctica, E of Queen Maud Land: discovered 1831.

end·er·gon·ic (en′dər gon′ik), *adj. Biochem.* (of a biochemical reaction) requiring energy. Cf. **exergonic.** [END- + Gk *érgon* work + -IC]

en·der·mic (en dûr′mik), *adj.* acting through the skin by absorption, as a medicine. [EN-[1] + -DERM + -IC] —**en·der′mi·cal·ly,** *adv.*

En·ders (en′dərz), *n.* **John Franklin,** born 1897, U.S. bacteriologist: Nobel prize for medicine 1954.

en dés·ha·bil·lé (äɴ dā za bē yā′), *French.* in dishabille or a state of undress.

end′ game′, *Chess.* the final stage of a game, usually following the exchange of queens and the serious reduction of forces, in which the primary objective is to effect checkmate.

end·hand (end′hand′), *n. Cards.* the dealer in a game with three players. Cf. **forehand** (def. 7), **middlehand.** [END[1] + HAND]

En·di·cott (en′də kət; *for 1 also* en′də kot′), *n.* **1. John.** See **Endecott, John. 2.** a city in S New York, on the Susquehanna River. 18,775 (1960).

end·ing (en′diŋ), *n.* **1.** a bringing or coming to an end; termination; close: *The concert marked the ending of the season.* **2.** the final or concluding part; conclusion: *a story with a happy ending.* **3.** death; destruction. **4.** *Gram.* an inflectional morpheme at the end of a word, as *-s* in *cuts.* **5.** (not in technical use) any final word part, as the *-ow* of *widow.* [ME *endyng,* OE *endung.* See END[1], -ING[1]]

en·dive (en′dīv, än′dēv; *Fr.* äɴ dēv′), *n., pl.* **-dives** (-dīvz, -dēvz; *Fr.* -dēv′). **1.** *U.S.* a plant, *Cichorium endivia,* of two main types, one having finely divided, curled leaves and one with broad, fleshy leaves, both used for salads. **2.** chicory (defs. 1, 2). **3.** *Furniture.* an ornamental motif having the form of an arrangement of acanthus or endive leaves. [ME < MF < ML *endīv(ia),* L *intibus, intubus,* etc. < ?]

end′-lap joint′ (end′lap′), a joint in which two timbers meeting at an angle are halved together at their ends.

end·less (end′lis), *adj.* **1.** having or seeming to have no end, limit, or conclusion; boundless; infinite; interminable; incessant: *the endless ages; an endless series of complaints.* **2.** made continuous, as by joining the two ends of a single length: *an endless chain or belt.* [ME *endelees,* OE *endelēas.* See END[1], -LESS] —**end′less·ly,** *adv.* —**end′less·ness,** *n.*
—**Syn. 1.** limitless, illimitable immeasureable, unending, unceasing, continuous, continual, perpetual, everlasting. See **eternal.** —**Ant. 1.** finite.

end′ line′, 1. *Football.* a line at each end of the field parallel to and 10 yards behind the goal line. **2.** *Basketball.* a line at each end of the court that is at right angles to the sidelines.

end·long (end′lông′, -long′), *adv. Archaic.* **1.** lengthwise. **2.** on end. [ME *endelong;* r. OE *andlong* ALONG]

end′ man′, 1. a man at one end of a row or line. **2.** a man at either end of the line of performers of a minstrel troupe, who plays on the bones or tambourine and carries on humorous dialogue with the interlocutor.

end′ mat′ter, *Print.* See **back matter.**

end′ mill′, (in a milling machine) a rotating cutting tool having a cylindrical shank with teeth at the end, used for machining the faces and sides of metal pieces and other objects.

end·most (end′mōst′), *adj.* furthest; most distant; last: *the endmost lands of the earth.* [END[1] + -MOST]

end·note (end′nōt′), *n.* a note, as of explanation, emendation, or the like, added at the end of an article, chapter, etc. [END[1] + NOTE]

endo-, a learned borrowing from Greek meaning "within," used in the formation of compound words: *endocardial.* Also, *esp. before a vowel,* **end-.** [< Gk, comb. form of *éndon* within]

en·do·an·gi·i·tis (en′dō an′jē ī′tis), *n. Pathol.* endangeitis.

en·do·a·or·ti·tis (en′dō ā′ôr tī′tis), *n. Pathol.* endaortitis.

en·do·ar·te·ri·tis (en′dō är′tə rī′tis), *n. Pathol.* endarteritis.

en·do·blast (en′də blast′), *n. Embryol.* **1.** entoderm. **2.** hypoblast (def. 2). [ENDO- + -BLAST] —**en′do·blas′tic,** *adj.*

en·do·car·di·al (en′dō kär′dē əl), *adj.* **1.** situated within the heart; intracardiac. **2.** of or pertaining to the endocardium. [ENDOCARDI(UM) + -AL[1]]

en·do·car·di·tis (en′dō kär dī′tis), *n. Pathol.* inflammation of the endocardium. [< NL; see ENDO-, CARDITIS] —**en·do·car·dit·ic** (en′dō kär dit′ik), *adj.*

en·do·car·di·um (en′dō kär′dē əm), *n., pl.* **-di·a** (-dē ə). *Anat.* the serous membrane that lines the cavities of the heart. [< NL, equiv. to *endo-* ENDO- + *-cardium* < Gk *-kardion,* equiv. to *kard(íā)* heart + *-ion,* neut. of *-ios* adj. suffix]

en·do·carp (en′də kärp′), *n. Bot.* the inner layer of a pericarp, as the stone of certain fruits. See diag. under **pericarp.** [ENDO- + -CARP]

en·do·car·poid (en′dō kär′poid), *adj.* (of a lichen) having the apothecia embedded in the thallus. [< NL *Endocarp(on)* a genus of lichens (see ENDO-, -CARP) + -OID]

en·do·cen·tric (en′dō sen′trik), *adj. Gram.* (of a construction or compound) having the same syntactic function in the sentence as one of its immediate constituents. *Cold water* is an endocentric construction, since it functions as would the noun *water. Greenhouse* is an endocentric compound, since it is a noun as is its head *house.* Cf. **exocentric.** [ENDO- + CENTRIC]

en·do·cra·ni·um (en′dō krā′nē əm), *n., pl.* **-ni·a** (-nē ə). *Anat.* the inner lining membrane of the skull; the dura mater. [< NL; see ENDO-, CRANIUM] —**en′do·cra′ni·al,** *adj.*

en·do·crine (en′də krin, -krīn′, -krēn′), *Anat., Physiol.* —*adj.* Also, **en·do·cri·nal** (en′də krīn′əl), **en′do·crin′ic, endocrinous. 1.** secreting internally: *an endocrine gland.* **2.** of or pertaining to an endocrine gland or its secretion. —*n.* **3.** an internal secretion; hormone. **4.** See **endocrine gland.** [ENDO- + *-crine* < Gk *krī́n(ein)* (to) separate]

en′docrine gland′, any of various glands, as the thyroid, adrenal, and pituitary glands, that secrete certain substances or hormones directly into the blood or lymph; ductless gland.

en·do·cri·nol·o·gy (en′dō krə nol′ə jē, -krī-), *n.* the science dealing with the endocrine glands and their secretions, esp. in relation to their processes or functions. [ENDOCRINE + -O- + -LOGY] —**en·do·crin·o·log·ic** (en′dō krin′əloj′ik), **en′do·crin′o·log′i·cal,** *adj.* —**en′do·cri·nol′o·gist,** *n.*

en·do·cri·nop·a·thy (en′dō krə nop′ə thē, -krī-), *n. Pathol.* any disease resulting from the malfunction of one or more endocrine glands. [ENDOCRINE + -O- + -PATHY] —**en·do·crin·o·path** (en′dō krin′ə path′, -krī′nə-, -krē′-), *n.* —**en′do·crin′o·path′ic,** *adj.*

en·do·crin·o·ther·a·py (en′dō krin′ō ther′ə pē, -krī′nō-), *n.* the treatment of disease by means of hormones from the endocrine glands. [ENDOCRINE + -O- + THERAPY]

en·doc·ri·nous (en dok′rə nəs), *adj.* endocrine. [ENDOCRINE + -OUS]

en·do·derm (en′də dûrm′), *n. Embryol.* entoderm. [ENDO- + -DERM, modeled on F *endoderme*] —**en′do·der′mal, en′do·der′mic,** *adj.*

en·do·der·mis (en′dō dûr′mis), *n. Bot.* a specialized tissue in the roots and stems of vascular plants, composed of a single layer of modified parenchyma cells forming the inner boundary of the cortex. [< NL; see ENDO-, DERMIS]

en·do·don·tics (en′dō don′tiks), *n.* (*construed as sing.*) the branch of dentistry dealing with the cause, diagnosis, prevention, and treatment of diseases of the dental pulp, usually by removal of the nerve and other tissue of the pulp cavity and its replacement with suitable filling material; pulp canal therapy; root canal therapy. Also, **en·do·don·tia** (en′dō don′shə, -shē ə), **en·do·don·tol·o·gy** (en′dō don tol′ə jē). [< NL *endodont(ia)* (see END-, -ODONT, -IA) + -ICS]

en·do·don·tist (en′dō don′tist), *n.* a specialist in endodontics. Also, **en·do·don·tol·o·gist** (en′dō don-tol′ə jist). [ENDODONT(ICS) + -IST]

en·do·don·ti·um (en′dō don′shē əm), *n. Dentistry.* pulp (def. 4). [< NL; see END-, -ODONT, -IUM]

en·do·en·zyme (en′dō en′zīm), *n. Biochem.* an enzyme that functions within a cell. Cf. **exoenzyme.** [ENDO- + ENZYME]

en·do·er·gic (en′dō ûr′jik), *adj. Physical Chem.* of or noting a reaction which is accompanied by an absorption of energy; endothermic (opposed to *exoergic*). [ENDO- + Gk *érg(on)* work + -IC]

end-of-day′ glass′ (end′əv dā′), a glass made of scrap glass melted down at the end of each working day, used for molding decorative articles.

en·dog·a·my (en dog′ə mē), *n.* marriage within a specific tribe or similar social unit. Cf. **exogamy** (def. 1). [ENDO- + -GAMY] —**en·dog′a·mous, en·do·gam·ic** (en′dō gam′ik), *adj.*

en·do·gen (en′də jen′, -jən), *n. Bot.* any plant of the obsolete class *Endogenae,* including the monocotyledons, whose stems were erroneously supposed to grow from within. [ENDO- + -GEN, modeled on F *endogène*]

en·dog·e·nous (en doj′ə nəs), *adj.* **1.** *Biol.* growing or proceeding from within; originating within. **2.** *Physiol., Biochem.* pertaining to the metabolism of nitrogenous elements of cells and tissues. [ENDOGEN + -OUS] —**en·do·ge·nic·i·ty** (en′dō jə nis′i tē), *n.*

en·dog·e·ny (en doj′ə nē), *n. Biol.* development or growth from within. Also, **en·do·gen·e·sis** (en′dō-jen′i sis). [ENDO- + -GENY]

en·do·lith·ic (en′dō lith′ik), *adj.* living embedded in the surface of rocks, as certain lichens. [ENDO- + -LITHIC]

en·do·lymph (en′də limf′), *n. Anat.* the fluid contained within the membranous labyrinth of the ear. [ENDO- + LYMPH] —**en·do·lym·phat·ic** (en′dō lim-fat′ik), *adj.*

en·do·me·tri·o·sis (en′dō mē′trē ō′sis), *n. Pathol.* the presence of uterine lining in other pelvic organs, esp. the ovaries, characterized by cyst formation, adhesions, and menstrual pains. [< NL; see ENDOMETRIUM, -OSIS]

en·do·me·tri·tis (en′dō mi trī′tis), *n. Pathol.* inflammation of the lining of the uterus. [< NL; see ENDOMETRIUM, -ITIS]

en·do·me·tri·um (en′dō mē′trē əm, -də-), *n., pl.* **-tri·a** (-trē ə). *Anat.* the mucous membrane lining the uterus. [ENDO- + NL *-metrium* < Gk *mḗtr(ā)* womb + *-ion* dim. suffix] —**en′do·me′tri·al,** *adj.*

en·do·morph (en′də môrf′), *n.* **1.** a mineral enclosed within another mineral. Cf. **perimorph. 2.** *Psychol.* a person of the endomorphic type. [ENDO- + -MORPH]

en·do·mor·phic (en′də môr′fik), *adj.* **1.** *Mineral.* **a.** occurring in the form of an endomorph. **b.** of or pertaining to endomorphs. **c.** taking place within a rock mass. **2.** *Psychol.* having a heavy body build characterized by the relative prominence of structures developed from the embryonic entoderm (contrasted with *ectomorphic, mesomorphic*). [ENDO- + -MORPHIC] —**en′do·mor′phy,** *n.*

en·do·mor·phism (en′dō môr′fiz əm, -də-), *n.* **1.** *Mineral.* a change brought about within the mass of an intrusive igneous rock. **2.** *Math.* a homomorphism of a set into itself. [ENDOMORPH(IC) + -ISM]

endomor′phism ring′, *Math.* the ring consisting of all endomorphisms of a given Abelian group.

en·do·par·a·site (en′dō par′ə sīt′), *n.* an internal parasite (opposed to *ectoparasite*). [ENDO- + PARASITE] —**en·do·par·a·sit·ic** (en′dō par′ə sit′ik), *adj.*

en·do·pe·rid·i·um (en′dō pi rid′ē əm), *n.* *Bot.* the inner of the two layers into which the peridium is divided. [< NL; see ENDO-, PERIDIUM] —**en′do·pe·rid′i·al,** *adj.*

en·do·pha·sia (en′dō fā′zhə, -zhē ə, -zē ə), *n.* internal speech with no audible vocalization. Cf. **exophasia.** [< It *endofasia.* See ENDO-, -PHASIA]

en·do·phyte (en′də fīt′), *n.* *Bot.* a plant living within another plant, usually as a parasite. [ENDO- + -PHYTE] —**en·do·phyt·ic** (en′də fit′ik), *adj.* —**en′do·phyt′i·cal·ly,** *adv.* —**en·doph·y·tous** (en dof′i təs), *adj.*

en·do·plasm (en′də plaz′əm, -dō-), *n.* *Biol.* the inner portion of the cytoplasm of a cell. Cf. **ectoplasm** (def. 1). [ENDO- + -PLASM] —**en′do·plas′mic,** *adj.*

en·dop·o·dite (en dop′ə dīt′), *n.* *Zool.* the inner or medial branch of a biramous crustacean appendage. Also, **en·do·pod** (en′də pod′). Cf. **exopodite, protopodite.** [ENDO- + *-podite* < Gk *pod-* (s. of *poûs*) foot + -ITE[1]] —**en·dop·o·dit·ic** (en dop′ə dit′ik), *adj.*

en·do·pter·y·gote (en′dō ter′ə gōt′), *adj.* **1.** belonging or pertaining to the division *Endopterygota,* comprising the insects that undergo complete metamorphosis. —*n.* **2.** an insect of the division *Endopterygota.* [< NL *Endopterygot(a)* a group of insects. See ENDO-, PTERYGOTE]

end′ or′gan, *Physiol.* one of several specialized structures found at the peripheral end of sensory or motor nerve fibers.

en·dorse (en dôrs′), *v.,* **-dorsed, -dors·ing,** *n.* —*v.t.* **1.** to approve, support, or sustain: *to endorse a statement.* **2.** to write (something) on the back of a document, paper, etc.: *to endorse instructions; to endorse one's signature.* **3.** to designate oneself as payee of (a check) by signing, usually on the reverse side of the instrument. **4.** to sign one's name on (a commercial document or other instrument). **5.** to make over (a stated amount) to another as payee by one's endorsement. **6.** to acknowledge (payment) by placing one's signature on a bill, draft, etc. —*n.* **7.** *Heraldry.* a narrow pale, about one quarter the usual width and usually repeated several times. Also, **indorse** (for defs. 1–6). [var. (with *en-* for *in-*) of earlier *indorse* < ML *indors(āre)* (to) put on the back, equiv. to L *in-* IN-[2] + *dors(um)* back; r. *endoss,* ME *endosse(n)* < OF *endosse(r),* equiv. to *en-* EN-[1] + *dos* < L *dors(um)*] —**en·dors′a·ble,** *adj.* —**en·dors′er, en·dor′sor,** *n.* —**en·dors′ing·ly,** *adv.*
—**Syn. 1.** sanction, ratify, uphold, sustain, back, second.

en·dorsed (en dôrst′), *adj.* *Heraldry.* **1.** (of a pale) between endorses: *a pale endorsed.* **2.** addorsed. [ENDORSE + -ED[2]]

en·dor·see (en dôr sē′, en′dôr-), *n.* a person to whom a negotiable document is endorsed. Also, **indorsee.** [ENDORSE + -EE]

en·dorse·ment (en dôrs′mənt), *n.* **1.** approval or sanction: *The program for supporting the arts won the government's endorsement.* **2.** the placing of one's signature, instructions, etc., on a document. **3.** the signature, instructions, etc., placed on the reverse of a commercial document, for the purpose of assigning the interest therein to another. **4.** *Insurance.* a clause under which the stated coverage of an insurance policy may be altered. Also, **indorsement.** [ENDORSE + -MENT]

en·do·sarc (en′də särk′), *n.* *Biol.* the endoplasm of a protozoan (opposed to *ectosarc*). [ENDO- + SARC-] —**en′do·sar′cous,** *adj.*

en·do·scope (en′də skōp′), *n.* **1.** a slender, tubular instrument used to examine the interior of a body cavity or hollow viscus. **2.** an optical instrument for distinguishing between natural and cultured pearls by examination of holes drilled into them. [ENDO- + -SCOPE] —**en·do·scop·ic** (en′də skop′ik), *adj.* —**en·dos·co·pist** (en dos′kə pist), *n.* —**en·dos′co·py,** *n.*

en′doscop′ic cam′era, a very small camera that can be inserted through the anus or other body cavity in medical examination.

en·do·skel·e·ton (en′dō skel′i tən), *n.* *Zool.* the internal skeleton or framework of the body of an animal (opposed to *exoskeleton*). [ENDO- + SKELETON] —**en′do·skel′e·tal,** *adj.*

en·dos·mo·sis (en′dos mō′sis, -doz-), *n.* *Physical Chem.* **1.** osmosis from the outside toward the inside. **2.** (in osmosis) the flow of a substance from an area of lesser concentration to one of greater concentration (opposed to *exosmosis*). Also, **en·dos·mos** (en′dos mos′, -doz-). [END- + OSMOSIS] —**en·dos·mot·ic** (en′dos mot′ik, -doz-), *adj.* —**en′dos·mot′i·cal·ly,** *adv.*

en·do·sperm (en′də spûrm′), *n.* *Bot.* nutritive matter in seed-plant ovules, derived from the embryo sac. [ENDO- + SPERM, modeled on F *endosperme*]

en·do·spore (en′də spōr′, -spôr′), *n.* **1.** *Bot.* the inner coat of a spore. **2.** *Bacteriol.* a spore formed within a cell of a rod-shaped organism. [ENDO- + SPORE] —**en·dos·por·ous** (en dos′pər əs, en′dō spōr′-, -spôr′-), *adj.* —**en·dos′por·ous·ly,** *adv.*

en·do·spo·ri·um (en′dō spōr′ē əm, -spôr′-), *n., pl.* **-spo·ri·a** (-spōr′ē ə, -spôr′-). *Bot.* endospore (def. 1). [ENDO- + NL *-sporium* < Gk *spor(á)* seed + *-ion* dim. suffix]

en·dos·te·um (en dos′tē əm), *n., pl.* **-te·a** (-tē ə). *Anat.* the membrane lining the medullary cavity of a bone. [END- + NL *osteum* < Gk *ostéon* bone]

en·dos·to·sis (en′dos stō′sis, -də-), *n.* *Anat.* bone formation beginning in the substance of cartilage. [END- + OSTOSIS]

en·do·the·ci·um (en′dō thē′shē əm, -sē əm), *n., pl.* **-ci·a** (-shē ə, -sē ə). *Bot.* **1.** the lining of the cavity of an anther. **2.** (in mosses) the central mass of cells in the rudimentary capsule, from which the archespore is generally developed. **3.** (in bryophytes) the central mass of cells in the capsule, including the spores and columella. [ENDO- + THECIUM] —**en·do·the·ci·al** (en′dō thē′shē əl, -shəl, -sē əl), *adj.*

endotheli-, a combining form of **endothelium:** *endothelioid.*

en·do·the·li·al (en′dō thē′lē əl), *adj.* pertaining to endothelium. [ENDOTHELI- + -AL[1]]

en·do·the·li·oid (en′dō thē′lē oid′), *adj.* resembling endothelium. [ENDOTHELI- + -OID]

en·do·the·li·o·ma (en′dō thē′lē ō′mə), *n., pl.* **-mas, -ma·ta** (-mə tə). *Pathol.* a tumor originating from the endothelium. [ENDOTHELI- + -OMA]

en·do·the·li·um (en′dō thē′lē əm), *n., pl.* **-li·a** (-lē ə). a type of epithelium composed of a single layer of smooth, thin cells which lines the heart, blood vessels, lymphatics, and serous cavities. [ENDO- + NL *-thelium;* cf. EPITHELIUM]

en·do·ther·mic (en′dō thûr′mik), *adj.* *Chem.* noting or pertaining to a chemical change which is accompanied by an absorption of heat (opposed to *exothermic*). Also, **en·do·ther·mal** (en′dō thûr′məl). [ENDO- + THERM- + -IC] —**en′do·ther′mi·cal·ly,** *adv.* —**en′do·ther′mism,** *n.*

en·do·tox·in (en′dō tok′sin), *n.* *Biochem.* the toxic protoplasm liberated when a microorganism dies and disintegrates, as in *Eberthella typhi,* the causative agent of typhoid fever. Cf. **exotoxin.** [ENDO- + TOXIN] —**en′do·tox′ic,** *adj.*

en·do·tox·oid (en′dō tok′soid), *n.* any toxoid prepared from an endotoxin. [ENDO- + TOXOID]

en·do·troph·ic (en′dō trof′ik), *adj.* (of a mycorrhiza) growing inside the cells of the root. Cf. **ectotrophic.** [ENDO- + -TROPHIC]

en·dow (en dou′), *v.t.* **1.** to provide with a permanent fund or source of income: *to endow a college.* **2.** to furnish, as with some gift, faculty, or quality; equip: *Nature has endowed him with great ability.* **3.** *Archaic.* to provide with dower. [ME *endowe(n)* < OF *endoue(r),* equiv. to *en-* EN-[1] + *douer* < L *dōtāre* to dower, equiv. to *dōt-* (s. of *dōs*) dowry + *-āre* v. suffix] —**en·dow′er,** *n.*
—**Syn. 2.** invest, clothe, endue.

en·dow·ment (en dou′mənt), *n.* **1.** the act of endowing. **2.** the property, funds, etc., with which an institution or person is endowed. **3.** Usually, **endowments.** an attribute of mind or body; a gift of nature. [late ME; see ENDOW, -MENT]
—**Syn. 2.** gift, grant, bequest. **3.** capacity, talent, faculties, ability, capability. —**Ant. 3.** incapacity.

endow′ment insur′ance, life insurance providing for the payment of a stated sum to the insured if he lives beyond the maturity date of the policy, or to a beneficiary if the insured dies before that date.

end′ pa′per, *Bookbinding.* a sheet of paper, often distinctively colored or ornamented, folded to form two leaves, one of which is pasted flat inside either cover of a book, the other forming a flyleaf. Also called **end sheet.**

end·piece (end′pēs′), *n.* a piece that forms, or is at, an end. [END[1] + PIECE]

end′ plate′, *Mining.* one of the shorter members of a set. Cf. **wall plate** (def. 3).

end·play (end′plā′), *Bridge.* —*n.* **1.** any play, usually near the end of a contract, which puts one's opponent into the lead and forces him to lose one or more tricks that he would have won if he were not leading. —*v.t.* **2.** to put into the lead by an endplay. [END[1] + PLAY]

end′ point′, **1.** a final or concluding point. **2.** *Chem.* the point in a titration usually noting the completion of a reaction and marked by a change of some kind, as of the color of an indicator.

end·point (end′point′), *n.* *Math.* the point on each side of an interval marking its extremity on that side. [END[1] + POINT]

end′ prod′uct, the final or resulting product, as of an industry, process of growth, etc.: *Cloth is one of the end products of cotton manufacture. An active mind should be an end product of education.*

en·drin (en′drin), *n.* *Chem.* a white, crystalline, water-insoluble, poisonous, solid isomer of dieldrin, $C_{12}H_8OCl_6$, used as an insecticide. [appar. *en-* or *end-* (< ?) + (DIEL)DRIN]

end′ run′, *Football.* a running play in which the ball-carrier attempts to outflank the defensive end. Also called **end′ sweep′, sweep.**

end·shake (end′shāk′), *n.* *Horol.* the free longitudinal movement of arbors or the like between bearings. [END[1] + SHAKE]

end′ sheet′. See **end paper.**

end-stopped (end′stopt′), *adj.* *Pros.* (of a line of verse) ending at the end of a syntactic unit that is usually followed by a pause in speaking and a punctuation mark in writing.

end′ ta′ble, a small table placed beside a chair or at the end of a sofa.

end-to-end (end′to͞o end′, -tə-), *adj., adv.* end[1] (def. 26).

en·due (en do͞o′, -dyo͞o′), *v.t.,* **-dued, -du·ing. 1.** to invest or endow with some gift, quality, or faculty. **2.** to put on; assume: *Hamlet endued the character of a madman.* **3.** to clothe. Also, **indue.** [ME *endewe(n)* (to) induct, cover < OF *enduire* < L *indūcere* to lead in, cover, INDUCE]

en·dur·a·ble (en do͝or′ə bəl, -dyo͝or′-), *adj.* capable of being endured. [ENDURE + -ABLE] —**en·dur′a·bil′i·ty, en·dur′a·ble·ness,** *n.* —**en·dur′a·bly,** *adv.*
—**Syn.** bearable, tolerable.

en·dur·ance (en do͝or′əns, -dyo͝or′-), *n.* **1.** the fact or power of enduring or bearing anything: *He has amazing physical endurance.* **2.** lasting quality; duration: *His friendships have little endurance.* **3.** something endured, as a hardship; trial. [ENDURE + -ANCE]
—**Syn. 1.** See **patience.**

endur′ance ra′tio. See **fatigue ratio.**

en·dur·ant (en do͝or′ənt, -dyo͝or′-), *adj.* capable of enduring hardship, misfortune, or the like. [ENDURE + -ANT]

en·dure (en do͝or′, -dyo͝or′), *v.,* **-dured, -dur·ing.** —*v.t.* **1.** to hold out against; sustain without impairment or yielding; undergo: *to endure great financial pressures with equanimity.* **2.** to bear without resistance or with patience; tolerate: *I cannot endure to listen to your insults any longer.* **3.** to admit of; allow; bear: *His poetry is such that it will not endure a superficial reading.* —*v.i.* **4.** to continue to exist; last: *These words will endure as long as men live who love freedom.* **5.** to support adverse force or influence of any kind; suffer without yielding; suffer patiently: *Even in the darkest ages man has endured.* **6.** to have or gain continued or lasting acknowledgment or recognition, as of worth, merit, greatness, etc.: *His plays have endured for more than three centuries.* [ME *endure(n)* < OF *endure(r)* < L *indūrāre* to harden, steel, make lasting, equiv. to *in-* IN-[2] + *dūrāre* to last, be or become hard, deriv. of *dūrus* hard] —**en·dur′er,** *n.*
—**Syn. 2.** experience, stand, support, suffer, brook. See **bear. 4.** abide. See **continue.** —**Ant. 1.** fail. **2.** refuse. **4.** fail, die.

en·dur·ing (en do͝or′ing, -dyo͝or′-), *adj.* **1.** lasting; permanent: *a poet of enduring greatness.* **2.** patient; long-suffering. [ENDURE + -ING[2]] —**en·dur′ing·ly,** *adv.* —**en·dur′ing·ness,** *n.*

end′ use′ (yo͞os), the ultimate use for which something is intended or to which it is put.

end·ways (end′wāz′), *adv.* **1.** on end: *We set the table endways in order to fix the legs.* **2.** with the end upward or forward. **3.** toward the ends or end; lengthwise. **4.** end-to-end. Also, **end-wise** (end′wīz′). [END[1] + -WAYS]

En·dym·i·on (en dim′ē ən), *n.* **1.** *Class. Myth.* a young man who was kept immortally youthful and beautiful through eternal sleep; beloved of the goddess Selene, who came to him every night in the cave where he slept. **2.** (*italics.*) a narrative poem (1818) by John Keats. **3.** a crater in the first quadrant of the face of the moon, having a dark floor: about 78 miles in diameter.

end′ zone′, **1.** *Football.* an area at each end of the field between the goal line and the end line. **2.** *Ice Hockey.* an area at each end of the rink between the goal line and the closer of the two blue lines. Cf. **neutral zone.**

-ene, *Chem.* a combining form indicating unsaturated hydrocarbons (*anthracene; benzene*), esp. those of the alkene series (*butylene*). [< Gk *-ēnē,* fem. of *-ēnos,* adj. suffix denoting origin or source]

ENE, east-northeast. Also, **E.N.E.**

en ef·fet (äN nā fe′), *French.* in effect; in fact; in reality.

en·e·ma (en′ə mə), *n.* *Med.* **1.** the injection of a fluid into the rectum. **2.** the fluid injected. [< LL < Gk: injection, equiv. to *en-* EN-[2] + *(h)e-* (s. of *hiénai* to throw) + *-ma* n. suffix]

en·e·my (en′ə mē), *n., pl.* **-mies,** *adj.* —*n.* **1.** a person who feels hatred for or fosters harmful designs against another; an adversary or opponent: *They are enemies now who were our friends.* **2.** an armed foe; an opposing military force: *We attacked the enemy on their home ground.* **3.** a hostile nation or state: *England and France have been enemies.* **4.** a citizen of such a state. **5.** **enemies,** persons, nations, etc., that are hostile to one another: *Let's make up and stop being enemies.* **6.** something harmful or prejudicial: *His unbridled ambition is his worst enemy.* **7.** **the Enemy,** the Devil; Satan. —*adj.* **8.** belonging to a hostile power or to any of its nationals: *enemy property.* **9.** *Obs.* inimical; ill-disposed. [ME *enemi* < OF < L *inimīc(us)* unfriendly, equiv. to *in-* IN-[3] + *amīcus* friendly, friend; see AMICABLE]
—**Syn. 1.** antagonist. ENEMY, FOE refer to a dangerous public or personal adversary. ENEMY emphasizes the idea of hostility: *to overcome the enemy; a bitter enemy.* FOE, a more literary word, may be used interchangeably with enemy, but emphasizes somewhat more the danger to be feared from such a one: *deadly foe; arch foe of mankind (the Devil).* —**Ant. 1.** friend. **2.** ally.

en′emy al′ien, an alien residing in a country at war with the one of which he is a citizen.

En′emy of the Peo′ple, An, a play (1882) by Henrik Ibsen.

E·ne·o·lith·ic (ē′nē ō lith′ik), *adj.* Chalcolithic. Also, **Aeneolithic.**

en·er·get·ic (en′ər jet′ik), *adj.* **1.** possessing or exhibiting energy; forcible; vigorous: *an energetic leader.* **2.** powerful in action or effect; effective: *to take energetic measures against crime.* Also, **en′er·get′i·cal.** [< Gk *energētik(ós),* equiv. to *energē-* (*en-* EN-[2] + *ergē-,* s. of *energein* to be active; see ENERGY) + *-tikos* -TIC] —**en′er·get′i·cal·ly,** *adv.*
—**Syn. 1.** See **active. 2.** effectual, strong, potent. —**Ant. 1.** listless.

en·er·get·ics (en′ər jet′iks), *n.* (*construed as sing.*) the branch of physics that deals with energy. [see ENERGETIC, -ICS] —**en′er·get′i·cist,** *n.* —**en·er·ge·tis·tic** (en′ər ji tis′tik), *adj.*

en·er·gise (en′ər jīz′), *v.t., v.i.,* **-gised, -gis·ing.** *Chiefly Brit.* energize. —**en′er·gis′er,** *n.*

en·er·gism (en′ər jiz′əm), *n.* *Ethics.* the theory that self-realization is the highest good. [< G *Energismus*. See ENERGY, -ISM] —**en′er·gist,** *n., adj.* —**en′er·gis′tic,** *adj.*

en·er·gize (en′ər jīz′), *v.,* **-gized, -giz·ing.** —*v.t.* **1.** to give energy to; rouse into activity: *to energize the spirit with brave words; to energize an electric circuit with current.* —*v.i.* **2.** to be in operation; put forth energy: *To worry is often to energize needlessly.* Also, *esp. Brit.,* **energise.** [ENERG(Y) + -IZE] —**en′er·giz′er,** *n.*

en·er·gu·men (en′ər gyo͞o′mən), *n.* **1.** a person possessed by an evil spirit; demoniac. **2.** a fanatical enthusiast. [< LL *energūmen(os)* possessed of an evil spirit < Gk *energoúmenos* pass. participle of *energein* to be active. See ENERGY]

en·er·gy (en′ər jē), *n., pl.* **-gies. 1.** Often, **energies. a.** the capacity for vigorous activity; available power: *I eat chocolate to get quick energy. My energies are low today.* **b.** a feeling of tension caused or seeming to be caused by an excess of such power: *to work off one's energies at Ping-Pong.* **2.** an adequate or abundant amount of such power: *I seem to have no energy these days.* **3.** an exertion of such power: *She plays tennis with great energy.* **4.** the habit of vigorous activity; vigor as a characteristic: *Foreigners both admire and laugh at American energy.* **5.** the ability to act, lead others, effect, etc., forcefully. **6.** forcefulness of expression: *a writing style of great energy.* **7.** *Physics.* the

capacity to do work; the property of a system which diminishes when the system does work on any other system, by an amount equal to the work so done; potential energy. [< LL *energīa* < Gk *enérgeia* activity, equiv. to *energē-* (s. of *energein* to be active, equiv. to *en-* EN-[2] + *érg(on)* work) + *-ia* -Y[3]]
—Syn. 1a, 2. vigor, force, potency. **4.** zeal, push.

en′ergy lev′el, *Physics.* one of a quantized series of states in which matter may exist, each having constant energy and separated from others in the series by finite quantities of energy. Also called **en′ergy state′.**

en·er·vate (*v.* en′ər vāt′; *adj.* i nûr′vit), *v.,* **-vat·ed, -vat·ing,** *adj.* **—***v.t.* **1.** to deprive of nerve, force, or strength; destroy the vigor of; weaken. **—***adj.* **2.** enervated. [< L *ēnervāt(us)* weakened (ptp. of *ēnervāre*) equiv. to *ē-* E- + *nerv(us)* sinew (see NERVE) + *-ātus* -ATE[1]] **—en′er·va′tion,** *n.* **—en′er·va′tive,** *adj.* **—en′er·va′tor,** *n.*
—Syn. 1. enfeeble, debilitate, sap, exhaust, undermine.

en·er·vat·ed (en′ər vā′tid), *adj.* without vigor, force, or strength; languid. [ENERVATE + -ED[2]]

E·nes·co (e nes′kō), *n.* **Georges** (zhôrzh), 1881–1955, Rumanian violinist, composer, and conductor: teacher of Yehudi Menuhin. Also, **E·nes·cu** (e nes′ko͞o).

en·face (en fās′), *v.t.,* **-faced, -fac·ing. 1.** to write, print, or stamp something on the face of (a note, draft, etc.). **2.** to write, print, or stamp (something) on the face of a note, draft, etc. [EN-[1] + FACE] **—en·face′·ment,** *n.*

en fa·mille (äN FA mē′yə), *French.* in the family: *an intimate,* en famille *dinner.*

en·fant per·du (äN fäN per dʏ′), *pl.* **en·fants per·dus** (äN fäN per dʏ′). *French.* a suicide squad or rear guard of soldiers. [lit., lost child]

En·fants Ter·ri·bles, Les (*Fr.* lā zäN fäN te rε′blə). See **Les Enfants Terribles.**

en·fant ter·ri·ble (äN fäN te rε′blə), *pl.* **en·fants ter·ri·bles** (äN fäN te rε′blə). *French.* **1.** an incorrigible child, as one whose behavior is embarrassing. **2.** a bold or outspoken person who says and does indiscreet or irresponsible things: *Oscar Wilde was the* enfant terrible *of his day.*

en·fee·ble (en fē′bəl), *v.t.,* **-bled, -bling.** to make feeble; weaken: *That bout of pneumonia enfeebled him.* [ME *enfeble(n)* < OF *enfebl(ir).* See EN-[1], FEEBLE] **—en·fee′ble·ment,** *d.* **—en·fee′bler,** *n.*
—Syn. enervate, debilitate.

en·feoff (en fef′, -fēf′), *v.t.* **1.** to invest with a freehold estate in land. **2.** to give as a fief. [ME *enfe(o)ffe(n)* < AF *enfe(o)ffe(r),* equiv. to *en-* EN-[1] + OF *fiefer, fiever,* deriv. of *fief* FIEF] **—en·feoff′ment,** *n.*

en fête (äN fet′; *Eng.* än fet′), *French.* in gala attire.

en·fet·ter (en fet′ər), *v.t.* to bind with or as with fetters. [EN-[1] + FETTER]

En·field (en′fēld′), *n.* **1.** a city in N Middlesex, in SE England, N of London. 109,524 (1961). **2.** a town in N Connecticut. 31,464 (1960). **3.** a town in NE North Carolina. 2978 (1960).

En′field ri′fle, 1. a single-shot, muzzleloading rifle, of .577 caliber, used by the British army in the Crimean War and in limited numbers by both sides in the American Civil War. **2.** a bolt-action, breech-loading, .303-caliber magazine rifle introduced in Britain in 1902. **3.** *Informal.* an American .30-caliber rifle used in World War I by U.S. troops, patterned after the British Enfield rifle. Also called **Enfield.** [named after ENFIELD, England, where it was first made]

en·fi·lade (en′fə lād′, en′fə läd′), *n., v.,* **-lad·ed, -lad·ing. —***n.* **1.** *Mil.* **a.** a position of works, troops, etc., making them subject to a sweeping fire from along the length of a line of troops, a trench, a battery, etc. **b.** the fire thus directed. **2.** *Archit.* **a.** an axial arrangement of doorways connecting a suite of rooms so that a vista is obtained down the whole length of the suite. **b.** an axial arrangement of mirrors on opposite sides of a room so as to give an effect of an infinitely long vista. **—***v.t.* **3.** *Mil.* to attack with an enfilade. [< F, equiv. to *enfil(er)* (to) thread, string (*en-* EN-[1] + *fil* < L *filum* thread) + *-ade* -ADE[1]]

en·fin (äN faN′), *adv. French.* in conclusion; finally. [lit., in (the) end]

en·flame (en flām′), *v.t., v.i.,* **-flamed, -flam·ing.** inflame.

en·fleu·rage (*Fr.* äN flœ RAZH′), *n.* a process of extracting perfumes by exposing inodorous oils or fats to the exhalations of flowers. [< F, equiv. to *enfleur(er)* (to) impregnate with scent of flowers (*en-* EN-[1] + *fleur* FLOWER) + *-age* -AGE]

en·fold (en fōld′), *v.t.* **1.** to wrap up; envelop: *to enfold someone in a cloak.* **2.** to surround as if with folds: *He wished to enfold her in the warmth of his love. What happened is enfolded in mystery.* **3.** to clasp; embrace: *He enfolded her in his arms.* **4.** to form into a fold or folds: *The material of the skirt had been enfolded to form a loose, graceful drape.* Also, **infold.** [EN-[1] + FOLD[1]] **—en·fold′er,** *n.* **—en·fold′ment,** *n.*

en·force (en fōrs′, -fôrs′), *v.t.,* **-forced, -forc·ing. 1.** to put or keep in force; compel obedience to: *to enforce laws or rules.* **2.** to obtain (payment, obedience, etc.) by force or compulsion. **3.** to impose (a course of action) upon a person: *The doctor enforced a strict dietary regimen.* **4.** to support (a demand, claim, etc.) by force: *to enforce one's rights as a citizen.* **5.** to impress or urge (an argument, contention, etc.) forcibly; lay stress upon: *He enforced his argument by adding details.* [ME *enforce(n)* < OF *enforc(ier), enforc(ir)* < LL *infortiāre, infortire,* equiv. to *in-* IN-[2] + *fort(is)* strong; see FORCE] **—en·force′a·bil′i·ty,** *n.* **—en·force′a·ble,** *adj.* **—en·for′ced·ly** (en fōr′sid lē, -fôr′-), *adv.* **—en·forc′er,** *n.* **—en·forc′ive,** *adj.*

en·force·ment (en fōrs′mənt, -fôrs′-), *n.* **1.** the act or process of enforcing. **2.** *Archaic.* that which enforces. [late ME < AF, OF. See ENFORCE, -MENT]

en·fran·chise (en fran′chīz), *v.t.,* **-chised, -chis·ing. 1.** to grant a franchise to; admit to citizenship, esp. to the right of voting. **2.** to endow (a city, constituency, etc.) with municipal or parliamentary rights. **3.** to set free; liberate, as from slavery. Also called **franchise.** [< MF, OF *enfranchiss-* (s. of *enfranchir* to free), equiv. to *en-* EN-[1] + *franch-* free (see FRANK[1]) + *-iss-* -ISH[2]] **—en·fran·chise·ment** (en fran′chiz mənt), *n.* **—en·fran′chis·er,** *n.*

eng (eng), *n.* the symbol, ŋ, that, in the International Phonetic Alphabet and in the pronunciation alphabets of some dictionaries, represents the voiced velar nasal consonant indicated in this dictionary by n͟g, as in the pronunciations of *cling* (klin͟g), and *clink* (klin͟gk). Also called **agma.**

Eng., 1. England. **2.** English.

eng., 1. engine. **2.** engineer. **3.** engineering. **4.** engraved. **5.** engraver. **6.** engraving.

En·ga·dine (eng′gə dēn′), *n.* the valley of the Inn River in E Switzerland: resorts. 60 mi. long.

en·gage (en gāj′), *v.,* **-gaged, -gag·ing. —***v.t.* **1.** to occupy the attention or efforts of (a person or persons): *He engaged her in conversation.* **2.** to secure for aid, employment, use, etc.; hire: *to engage a workman; to engage a room.* **3.** to attract and hold fast: *The novel engaged his attention and interest.* **4.** to attract or please: *His good nature engages everyone.* **5.** to bind, as by pledge, promise, contract, or oath; make liable: *He engaged himself to repay his debt within a month.* **6.** to betroth (usually used in the passive): *They were engaged last week.* **7.** to bring (troops) into conflict; enter into conflict with: *Our army engaged the enemy.* **8.** *Mech.* to cause (gears or the like) to become interlocked; interlock with. **9.** *Archaic.* to entangle or involve. **10.** *Archaic.* to attach or secure. **—***v.i.* **11.** to occupy oneself; become involved: *to engage in business or politics.* **12.** to take employment: *He engaged in his father's business.* **13.** to pledge one's word; assume an obligation: *He was unwilling to engage on such terms.* **14.** to cross weapons; enter into conflict: *The armies engaged early in the morning.* **15.** *Mech.* (of gears or the like) to interlock. [< MF *engag(er),* OF *engagier.* See EN-[1], GAGE[1]] **—en·gag′er,** *n.*
—Ant. 2. discharge. **8.** release.

en·ga·gé (*Fr.* äN GA zhā′), *adj.* having chosen to involve oneself in or commit oneself to something, as opposed to remaining aloof or indifferent. [< F: lit., engaged]

en·gaged (en gājd′), *adj.* **1.** busy or occupied; involved: *deeply engaged scientists.* **2.** under engagement; pledged: *an engaged contractor.* **3.** pledged to be married; betrothed: *an engaged couple.* **4.** entered into conflict with: *desperately engaged armies.* **5.** *Mech.* **a.** interlocked. **b.** (of wheels) in gear with each other. **6.** *Archit.* (of a distinct member) built so as to be truly or seemingly attached in part to the structure before which it stands. [ENGAGE + -ED[2]] **—en·gag·ed·ly** (en gā′jid lē, -gājd′-), *adv.* **—en·gag′ed·ness,** *n.*

engaged′ col′umn, any member, portion of a wall, etc., suggesting a round column built partly into the wall behind it.

en·gage·ment (en gāj′mənt), *n.* **1.** act of engaging; state of being engaged. **2.** a pledge; an obligation or agreement: *All his time seems to be taken up with social engagements.* **3.** betrothal: *They announced their engagement.* **4.** employment, or a period or post of employment: *Her engagement at the nightclub will last five weeks.* **5.** an appointment or arrangement: *a business engagement.* **6.** an encounter, conflict, or battle: *We have had two very costly engagements with the enemy this week alone.* **7.** *Mech.* the act or state of interlocking. **8. engagements,** *Com.* financial obligations. [ENGAGE + -MENT]
—Syn. 2. contract, promise.

engage′ment ring′, a ring, often a diamond solitaire, given by a man to his fiancée at the time of their engagement as a token of troth.

en·gag·ing (en gā′jing), *adj.* winning; attractive; pleasing: *her engaging smile.* [ENGAGE + -ING[2]] **—en·gag′ing·ly,** *adv.* **—en·gag′ing·ness,** *n.*

en garde (än gärd′; *Fr.* äN GARD′), *Fencing.* (used as the call to the fencers by the director of a match to assume the prescribed position preparatory to action.) [< F: on guard]

en·gar·land (en gär′lənd), *v.t.* encircle with a garland. [EN-[1] + GARLAND]

Eng. D., Doctor of Engineering.

Eng·el (eng′gəl), *n.* **Leh·man** (lā′mən), born 1910, U.S. conductor and composer.

En·gel·ber·ta (eng′gəl bûr′tə), *n.* a girl's given name.

En′gel·mann spruce′ (eng′gəl mən), **1.** a spruce, *Picea Engelmanni,* of western North America, yielding a soft, pale-yellow wood. **2.** the soft, light wood of this tree, used in the construction of buildings and in the manufacture of paper, boxes, etc. [named after G. *Engelmann* (1809–84), German-American botanist]

En·gels (eng′əls *for 1;* eng′gels *for 2*), *n.* **1. Frie·drich** (frē′driKH), 1820–95, German socialist writer and manufacturer in England: collaborator with Karl Marx; editor and publisher of Marx's works. **2.** a city in the E Soviet Union in Europe, on the Volga River. 90,000 (1959).

En′gel's law′, the assertion that the percentage of a family's income spent on food decreases as its income increases. [named after Ernst *Engel* (1821–96), German economist]

en·gen·der (en jen′dər), *v.t.* **1.** to produce, cause, or give rise to: *Hatred engenders violence.* **2.** to beget; procreate. **—***v.i.* **3.** to be produced or caused; come into existence: *Conditions for a war were engendering in Europe.* [ME *engendre(n)* < OF *engendre(r)* < L *ingenerāre,* equiv. to *in-* EN-[1] + *generāre* to beget; see GENERATE] **—en·gen′der·er,** *n.* **—en·gen′der·ment,** *n.*
—Syn. 1. beget, occasion, excite, stir up. **1, 2.** create, generate, breed.

En·ghien, d' (däN gaN′), *n.* **Duc** (*Louis Antoine Henry de Bourbon-Condé*), 1772–1804, French prince: executed by Napoleon I.

engin., engineering.

en·gine (en′jən), *n.* **1.** a machine for converting thermal energy into mechanical energy or power to produce force and motion. **2.** a railroad locomotive. **3.** a fire engine. **4.** any mechanical contrivance. **5.** a machine or instrument used in warfare, as a battering ram, catapult, piece of artillery, etc. **6.** *Obs.* an instrument of torture, esp. the rack. [ME *engin* < OF < L *ingen(ium)* nature, innate quality, esp. mental power, hence a clever invention, equiv. to *in-* IN-[2] + *-genium,* equiv. to *gen-* begetting (see KIN) + *-ium* -Y[3]] **—en′gine·less,** *adj.*

en′gine com′pany, a unit of a city's fire department in command of one or more fire-fighting vehicles.

en′gine depart′ment, *Naut.* the department that operates, maintains, and repairs the machinery of a vessel.

en′gine driv′er, *Brit.* an engineer on a locomotive.

en·gi·neer (en′jə nēr′), *n.* **1.** a person versed in the design, construction, and use of engines or machines, or in any of various branches of engineering: *a mechanical engineer; a civil engineer.* **2.** a person who manages an engine or a locomotive. **3.** a member of an army, navy, or air force specially trained in engineering work. **4.** a skillful manager: *a political engineer.* **—***v.t.* **5.** to plan, construct, or manage as an engineer: *He's engineered several big industrial projects.* **6.** to arrange, manage, or carry through by skillful or artful contrivance: *He certainly engineered the election campaign beautifully.* [ENGINE + -EER; r. ME *engyn(e)our* < OF *engigneor* < LL *ingeniātor,* equiv. to *ingeniāt(us),* ptp. of *ingeniāre* to design, devise (L *ingeni(um)* (see ENGINE) + *-ātus* -ATE[1]) + *-or* -OR[2]]

en·gi·neer·ing (en′jə nēr′ing), *n.* **1.** the art or science of making practical application of the knowledge of pure sciences, as physics, chemistry, biology, etc. **2.** the action, work, or profession of an engineer. **3.** skillful or artful contrivance; maneuvering. [ENGINEER + -ING[1]] **—en′gi·neer′ing·ly,** *adv.*

engineer's′ chain′. See under **chain** (def. 8a).

en′gine house′, a building in which a fire engine is stationed.

en·gine·man (en′jən man′, -mən), *n., pl.* **-men** (-men′, -mən). **1.** *Railroads.* one of the crew of a locomotive. **2.** a person who operates or helps to operate an engine or locomotive. [ENGINE + MAN[1]]

en·gine·ry (en′jən rē), *n., pl.* **-ries. 1.** engines collectively; machinery. **2.** engines of war collectively. **3.** skillful or artful contrivance. [ENGINE + -RY]

en′gine turn′ing, ornament having the form of a pattern of circular arcs, engraved by a rose engine.

en·gi·nous (en′jə nəs), *adj. Obs.* clever; crafty. [ME < MF *engigneus* < L *ingeniōs(us)* talented, equiv. to *ingeni(um)* (see ENGINE) + *-ōsus* -OUS, -OSE[1]]

en·gird (en gûrd′), *v.t.,* **-girt** or **-gird·ed, -gird·ing.** to encircle; encompass: *The equator engirds the earth.* [EN-[1] + GIRD[1]]

en·gir·dle (en gûr′dəl), *v.t.,* **-dled, -dling.** to engird. [EN-[1] + GIRDLE]

en·gla·cial (en glā′shəl), *adj. Geol.* **1.** within the ice of a glacier. **2.** believed to have been formerly within the ice of a glacier: *englacial debris.* [EN-[1] + GLACIAL] **—en·gla′cial·ly,** *adv.*

Eng·land (ing′glənd *or, often,* -lənd), *n.* **1.** the largest division of the United Kingdom, occupying, with Scotland and Wales, the island of Great Britain. 43,430,972 (1961); 50,327 sq. mi. *Cap.:* London. Latin, **Anglia. 2.** a town in central Arkansas. 2861 (1960). **3.** *Heraldry.* an escutcheon blazoned as follows: Gules, three lions passant gardant in pale or; Gules, three leopards in pale or.

Eng·land·er (ing′glən dər *or, often,* -lən-), *n.* a native of England. [ENGLAND + -ER[1]]

En·gle (eng′gəl), *n.* **Paul (Hamilton),** born 1908, U.S. poet and educator.

En·gle·wood (eng′gəl wo͝od′), *n.* **1.** a city in central Colorado. 33,398 (1960). **2.** a city in NE New Jersey. 26,057 (1960). **3.** a town in W Florida. 2877 (1960).

En′glewood Cliffs′, a town in NE New Jersey. 2913 (1960).

Eng·lish (ing′glish *or, often,* -lish), *adj.* **1.** of, pertaining to, or characteristic of England or its inhabitants, institutions, etc. **2.** belonging or pertaining to, or spoken or written in, the English language. **—***n.* **3.** the people of England collectively, esp. as distinguished from the Scots, Welsh, and Irish. **4.** the Germanic language of the British Isles, widespread and standard also in the U.S. and most of the British Commonwealth, historically termed Old English (c450–c1150), Middle English (c1150–c1475), and Modern English (after c1475). **5.** (*sometimes l.c.*) *Billiards U.S.* a spinning motion imparted to a ball by being struck off-center by the cue directly or by another ball. **6.** *Print.* a 14-point type of a size between pica and Columbian. **7.** simple, straightforward language: *What does all that jargon mean in English?* **8.** *U.S.* a grade of calendered paper having a smooth matte finish. **—***v.t.* **9.** to translate into English: *to English Euripides.* **10.** to adopt (a foreign word) into English; anglicize. **11.** *Billiards U.S.* to impart English to (a ball). [ME; OE *englisc,* equiv. to *Engle* (pl.) the English (< L *Anglī;* see ANGLES) + *-isc* -ISH[1]]

Eng′lish bond′, a brickwork bond having alternate courses of headers and stretchers. See illus. under **bond.**

Eng′lish Cana′dian, *Chiefly Canadian.* **1.** a Canadian of pure British stock. **2.** an English-speaking Canadian. **3.** of or pertaining to Canadians of British descent.

Eng′lish Chan′nel, an arm of the Atlantic between S England and N France, connected with the North Sea by the Strait of Dover. 350 mi. long; 20–100 mi. wide.

Eng′lish Civ′il War′, the war (1642–46) between the Parliamentarians and the Royalists, sometimes extended to include the events of the period 1646–48.

Eng′lish dai′sy, *Chiefly U.S.* the common European daisy, *Bellis perennis.*

Eng′lish elm′. See under **elm** (def. 1).

Eng·lish·er (ing′gli shər *or, often,* -li-), *n.* **1.** an English citizen or subject. **2.** a person who translates from a foreign language into English. [ENGLISH + -ER[1]]

Eng′lish goose′berry, a spiny shrub, *Ribes Grossularia,* of Eurasia and northern Africa, having greenish flowers in sparse clusters and acid, bristly, green fruit.

Eng′lish hol′ly. See under **holly** (def. 1).

Eng′lish horn′, a large oboe, a fifth lower in pitch than the ordinary oboe, having a pear-shaped bell producing a soft tone. Also called **cor anglais.**

English horn

Eng′lish i′ris, an iris, *Iris xyphioides,* of the Pyrenees Mountains, having two or three deep purple-blue flowers with golden patches.

Eng·lish·ism (iŋ′gli shiz′əm *or, often,* -li-), *n.* **1.** a Briticism. **2.** attachment to what is English. [ENGLISH + -ISM]

Eng′lish i′vy, ivy (def. 1).

Eng′lish lau′rel. See **cherry laurel** (def. 1).

Eng·lish·ly (iŋ′glish lē *or, often,* -lish-), *adv.* in the manner or style of the English people. [ENGLISH + -LY]

Eng′lish Mail′-Coach, The (māl′kōch′), an essay (1849) by Thomas De Quincey.

Eng·lish·man (iŋ′glish mən *or, often,* -lish-), *n., pl.* **-men. 1.** a native or a naturalized citizen of England. **2.** an English ship. [ME; OE *engliscman.* See ENGLISH, MAN1]

Eng′lish muf′fin, a muffin made from yeast dough and baked on a griddle.

Eng·lish·ness (iŋ′glish nis *or, often,* -lish-), *n.* quality of being English. [ENGLISH + -NESS]

Eng′lish Pale′, pale2 (def. 6).

Eng′lish prim′rose. See under **primrose** (def. 1).

Eng′lish red′, a Venetian red pigment and color.

Eng′lish Revolu′tion, the events of 1688–89 by which James II was expelled and the sovereignty conferred on William and Mary. Also called **Glorious Revolution.**

Eng·lish·ry (iŋ′glish rē *or, often,* -lish-), *n.* **1.** the fact of being English, esp. by birth. **2.** a population that is English or of English descent: *the Englishry of Ireland.* [late ME *Englisherie* < AF *Englescherie,* equiv. to ME *Englisch* ENGLISH + AF *-erie* -ERY]

Eng′lish sad′dle, a saddle having a steel cantle and pommel, no horn, full side flaps usually set forward, a well-padded leather seat, and a saddletree or frame designed to conform to the line of the rider's back. See diag. under **saddle.**

Eng′lish sen′nit. See **flat sennit.**

Eng′lish set′ter, one of a breed of medium-sized, long-haired bird dogs having a flat, usually black and white or tan and white coat.

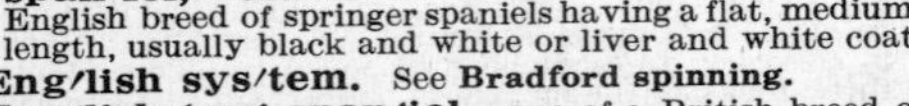

English setter
(2 ft. high at shoulder)

Eng′lish son′net. See **Shakespearean sonnet.**

Eng′lish spar′row. See **house sparrow.**

Eng′lish spring′er span′iel, one of an English breed of springer spaniels having a flat, medium-length, usually black and white or liver and white coat.

Eng′lish sys′tem. See **Bradford spinning.**

Eng′lish toy′ span′iel, one of a British breed of toy spaniels having a long, silky coat, a rounded head, and a short, upturned muzzle.

Eng′lish wal′nut, 1. a walnut tree, *Juglans regia.* **2.** the nut of this tree, widely used in cookery.

Eng·lish·wom·an (iŋ′glish wŏŏm′ən *or, often,* -lish-), *n., pl.* **-wom·en.** a woman who is a native or citizen of England. [ENGLISH + WOMAN]

Eng′lish yew′, a yew, *Taxus baccata,* of Eurasia and northern Africa, grown as an ornamental in the U.S.

en·glut (en glut′), *v.t.,* **-glut·ted, -glut·ting. 1.** to gulp down. **2.** *Archaic.* to fill to satisfaction; satiate. [< MF *englot(ir)* < LL *ingluttire* to swallow, equiv. to L *in-* IN-2 + *gluttire* to swallow; see GLUTTON]

en·gobe (än gōb′), *n. Ceram.* an opaque slip, esp. one forming a foundation for an outer slip or glaze. [< F *engob(er)* (to) coat, equiv. to *en-* EN-1 + *gober* to gulp, take in mouth; see GOB1, GOBBET, GOBBLE]

en·gorge (en gôrj′), *v.t., v.i.,* **-gorged, -gorg·ing. 1.** to swallow greedily; glut or gorge. **2.** *Pathol.* to congest with blood. [< F *engorge(r).* See EN-1, GORGE] —**en·gorge′ment,** *n.*

engr., 1. engineer. **2.** engraved. **3.** engraver. **4.** engraving.

en·graft (en graft′, -gräft′), *v.t.* to insert, as a scion of one tree or plant into another, for propagation: *to engraft a peach on a plum.* Also, **ingraft.** [EN-1 + GRAFT1] —**en′graf·ta′tion, en·graft′ment,** *n.*

en·grail (en grāl′), *v.t.* **1.** to ornament the edge of with curved indentations. **2.** *Minting.* to make dots or curves on the cylindrical edge of (a coin, medal, etc.) so as to form a pattern. [ME *engrele(n)* < MF *engresle(r),* equiv. to *en-* EN-1 + *gresler* to make slender << L *gracil(is)* GRACILE; cf. F *grêle* kind of file, deriv. of *grêler*] —**en·grail′ment,** *n.*

en·grailed (en grāld′), *adj. Heraldry.* **1.** noting an edge of a charge, as an ordinary, consisting of a number of concave curves. **2.** (of a charge, as an ordinary) having such an edge: *a chevron engrailed.* Cf. **invected.** [ME *engrelede.* See ENGRAIL, -ED2]

en·grain (en grān′), *v.t., adj.* ingrain (defs. 1, 2).

en·grained (en grānd′, in′grānd′), *adj.* ingrained. —**en·grain·ed·ly** (en grā′nid lē, -grā′nid-), *adv.*

en·gram (en′gram), *n.* **1.** *Biol.* the durable mark caused by a stimulus upon protoplasm. **2.** *Psychol.* trace1 (def. 8). [EN-2 + -GRAM1] —**en·gram′mic,** *adj.*

en·grave (en grāv′), *v.t.,* **-graved, -grav·ing. 1.** to chase (letters, designs, etc.) on a hard surface, as of metal, stone, or the end grain of wood: *She had the jeweler engrave her name on the back of the watch.* **2.** to print from such a surface. **3.** to mark or ornament with incised letters, designs, etc.: *He engraved the ring in a floral pattern.* **4.** to impress deeply; infix: *That image is engraved on my mind.* [EN-1 + GRAVE3, modeled on F *engraver*] —**en·grav′er,** *n.*

engrav′er's trick′, *Heraldry.* a conventional method of indicating a tincture, as in printing or carving without color. Also called **herald's trick.**

en·grav·ing (en grā′viŋ), *n.* **1.** the act or art of one who or that which engraves. **2.** the art of forming designs by cutting, corrosion by acids, a photographic process, etc., on the surface of metal plates, blocks of wood, or the like, for the purpose of taking off impressions or prints of the design so formed. **3.** the design engraved. **4.** an engraved plate or block. **5.** an impression or print from this. [ENGRAVE + -ING1]

en·gross (en grōs′), *v.t.* **1.** to occupy completely, as the mind or attention; absorb: *Their discussion engrossed his attention. He is engrossed in his work.* **2.** to write or copy in a clear, attractive, large script or in a formal manner, as a public document or record: *to engross a deed.* **3.** to acquire the whole of (a commodity), in order to control the market; monopolize. [ME *engros(s)e(n),* partly < ML *ingross(āre)* (to) thicken, write large and thick (L *in-* IN-2 + *gross(us)* thick); partly < AF, MF *en gros* in quantity, wholesale < L *in* + *grossus;* see GROSS] —**en·gross·ed·ly** (en grō′sid lē, -grōst′-), *adv.* —**en·gross′er,** *n.*

en·gross·ing (en grō′siŋ), *adj.* **1.** fully occupying the mind or attention; absorbing: *I'm reading the most engrossing book.* **2.** having complete control; monopolizing. [ENGROSS + -ING2] —**en·gross′ing·ly,** *adv.* —**en·gross′ing·ness,** *n.*

en·gross·ment (en grōs′mənt), *n.* **1.** the act of engrossing. **2.** the state of being engrossed or absorbed: *to read with engrossment.* **3.** an engrossed copy of a document. [ENGROSS + -MENT]

en·gulf (en gulf′), *v.t.* **1.** to swallow up in or as in a gulf; submerge: *The overflowing river has engulfed many small towns along its banks.* **2.** to plunge or immerse, as into a gulf: *He engulfed himself in his studies.* Also, **ingulf.** [EN-1 + GULF] —**en·gulf′ment,** *n.*

en·hance (en hans′, -häns′), *v.t.,* **-hanced, -hanc·ing. 1.** to raise to a higher degree; intensify; magnify: *The candlelight both softened and enhanced her beauty.* **2.** to raise the value or price of: *Rarity enhances the worth of most collector's items.* [ME *enhaunce(n)* < AF *enhaunce(r),* nasalized var. of OF *enhaucier,* equiv. to *en-* EN-1 + *haucier* to raise, equiv. to *haut* high (< Gmc **hauh* + L *altus*) + v. suffix] —**en·hance′ment,** *n.* —**en·hanc′er,** *n.* —**en·hanc′ive,** *adj.*
—**Syn. 2.** See **elevate.** —**Ant. 1.** diminish. **2.** reduce.

en·hanced (en hanst′, -hänst′), *adj.* **1.** made greater; magnified. **2.** *Heraldry.* (of a charge) higher on an escutcheon than is usual: *a bend enhanced.* [ENHANCE + -ED2]

en·har·mon·ic (en′här mon′ik), *adj. Music.* having the same pitch in the tempered scale but written in different notation, as G sharp and A flat. [< LL *enharmonic(us)* < Gk *enharmónios* (-*icus* r. -*ios*), equiv. to *en-* EN-1 + *harmoní(a)* HARMONY + -*os* adj. suffix] —**en′har·mon′i·cal·ly,** *adv.*

en·heart·en (en här′tən), *v.t.* to inspire or renew courage, hope, fortitude, etc., in: *He was enheartened by the popular acclaim.* [EN-1 + HEARTEN]

E·nid (ē′nid), *n.* **1.** a city in N Oklahoma. 38,859 (1960). **2.** *Arthurian Romance.* the constant and patient wife of Sir Geraint in *The Mabinogion* and in Tennyson's *Idylls of the King.* **3.** a girl's given name.

e·nig·ma (ə nig′mə), *n., pl.* **-mas, -ma·ta** (-mə tə). **1.** a puzzling or inexplicable occurrence or situation: *His disappearance is an enigma that has given rise to much speculation.* **2.** a saying, question, picture, etc., containing a hidden meaning; riddle. **3.** a person of puzzling or contradictory character: *To me he has always been an enigma, one minute completely insensitive, the next moved to tears.* [< L *aenigma* < Gk *aínigma,* equiv. to *ainig-* (var. s. of *ainíssesthai* to speak in riddles, deriv. of *aînos* fable) + *-ma* n. suffix of result]
—**Syn. 1.** problem. See **puzzle.**

enig′ma can′on, *Music.* See **riddle canon.** Also called **en′igmat′ic can′on.**

en·ig·mat·ic (en′ig mat′ik, ē′nig-), *adj.* resembling an enigma; perplexing; mysterious: *We have been unable to unravel the enigmatic circumstances surrounding his death.* Also, **en′ig·mat′i·cal.** [< LL *aenigmatic(us)* < Gk *ainigmatikós,* equiv. to *ainigmat-* (s. of *aínigma*) ENIGMA + *-ikos* -IC] —**en′ig·mat′i·cal·ly,** *adv.*

E·ni·o·peus (i nī′ə pyōōs′), *n.* (in the *Iliad*) a charioteer of Hector who was slain by Diomedes.

en·isle (en īl′), *v.t.,* **-isled, -isl·ing. 1.** to make an island of. **2.** to place on an island. **3.** to isolate. [EN-1 + ISLE]

En·i·we·tok (en′ə wē′tok, ə nē′wi tôk′), *n.* an atoll in the NW Marshall Islands: atomic and hydrogen bomb tests 1947–52.

en·jambe·ment (en jam′mənt, -jamb′-; *Fr.* än zhänb mäN′), *n., pl.* **-ments** (-mənts; *Fr.* -mäN′). enjambment.

en·jamb·ment (en jam′mənt, -jamb′-; *Fr.* än zhänb mäN′), *n., pl.* **-ments** (-mənts; *Fr.* -mäN′). *Pros.* the running on of the thought from one line, couplet, or stanza to the next. [< F *enjambement,* equiv. to *enjamb(er)* (to) stride over, project, encroach (*en-* EN-1 + *jambe* leg; see JAMB1) + *-ment* -MENT] —**en·jambed′,** *adj.*

en·join (en join′), *v.t.* **1.** to direct or order (someone) to do something: *He was enjoined to live austerely.* **2.** to prescribe (a course of action) with authority or emphasis: *The doctor enjoined a strict diet.* **3.** *Law.* to prohibit or restrain by an injunction. [ME *enjoi(g)ne(n)* < OF *enjoind(re)* < L *injungere* to fasten to, bring upon. See IN-2, JOIN] —**en·join′er,** *n.* —**en·join′ment,** *n.*
—**Syn. 1.** charge, bid, command, require. **3.** proscribe, interdict, ban. —**Ant. 3.** encourage.

en·joy (en joi′), *v.t.* **1.** to experience with joy; take pleasure in: *He enjoys good food.* **2.** to have and use with satisfaction; have the benefit of: *He enjoys an excellent income from his trust funds.* **3.** to find or experience pleasure for (oneself): *He seems to enjoy himself at everything he does.* **4.** to undergo (an improvement): *Automobile manufacturers have enjoyed a six-percent rise in sales over the past month.* **5.** to have intercourse with (a woman). [ME *enjoye(n)* (to) make joyful < OF *enjoie(r)* (to) give joy to. See EN-1, JOY] —**en·joy′er,** *n.* —**en·joy′ing·ly,** *adv.*

en·joy·a·ble (en joi′ə bəl), *adj.* giving or capable of giving enjoyment; affording enjoyment: *a very enjoyable film.* [ENJOY + -ABLE] —**en·joy′a·ble·ness,** *n.* —**en·joy′a·bly,** *adv.*
—**Syn.** delightful, pleasant, agreeable, pleasurable.

en·joy·ment (en joi′mənt), *n.* **1.** the act of enjoying. **2.** the possession, use, or occupancy of anything with satisfaction or pleasure: *to have the enjoyment of a large income.* **3.** a particular form or source of pleasure: *Hunting is his greatest enjoyment.* **4.** *Law.* the exercise of a right: *the enjoyment of an estate.* [ENJOY + -MENT]
—**Syn. 2.** delight, delectation, gratification. See **pleasure.**

En·ki (en′kē), *n.* a Sumerian water god and god of wisdom: the counterpart of the Akkadian Ea.

En·ki·du (en′kē dōō), *n.* the servant and friend of Gilgamesh.

en·kin·dle (en kin′dəl), *v.t., v.i.,* **-dled, -dling.** to kindle into flame, ardor, activity, etc. [EN-1 + KINDLE] —**en·kin′dler,** *n.*

en·kol·pi·on (en kōl′pē ən, en kol′pē on′), *n., pl.* **-pi·a** (-pē ə). encolpion.

enl., 1. enlarge. **2.** enlarged. **3.** enlisted.

en·lace (en lās′), *v.t.,* **-laced, -lac·ing. 1.** to bind or encircle with or as with a lace or cord: *Vines enlaced the tree.* **2.** to interlace; intertwine: *to enlace strands of rope.* [ME *enlace(n)* < OF *enlacie(r).* See EN-1, LACE] —**en·lace′ment,** *n.*

en·large (en lärj′), *v.,* **-larged, -larg·ing.** —*v.t.* **1.** to make larger; increase in extent, bulk, or quantity; add to: *They enlarged the house by adding an east wing.* **2.** to increase the capacity or scope of; expand: *We've decided to enlarge the company.* **3.** to make (a photographic print) larger than the negative. —*v.i.* **4.** to grow larger; increase; expand. **5.** to speak or write at large; expatiate: *to enlarge upon a point.* [ME *enlarge(n)* < OF *enlargi(e)(r).* See EN-1, LARGE] —**en·large′a·ble,** *adj.* —**en·larged·ly** (en lärjd′lē, -lär′jid-), *adv.* —**en·lar·ged·ness** (en lär′jid nis, -lärjd′-), *n.* —**en·larg′er,** *n.* —**en·larg′ing·ly,** *adv.*
—**Syn. 1.** extend, magnify, amplify, dilate. See **increase.** —**Ant. 1.** diminish. **2.** contract.

en·large·ment (en lärj′mənt), *n.* **1.** the act of enlarging; increase; expansion; amplification. **2.** anything, as a photograph, that is an enlarged form of something else. **3.** anything that enlarges something else; addition: *The new wing formed a considerable enlargement.* [ENLARGE + -MENT]

en·light·en (en līt′ən), *v.t.* **1.** to give intellectual or spiritual light to; instruct; impart knowledge to: *We hope to enlighten these men in regard to the discoveries made during our research.* **2.** *Archaic.* to shed light upon. [ME *enli(g)htene(n).* See EN-1, LIGHTEN1] —**en·light′ened·ly,** *adv.* —**en·light′ened·ness,** *n.* —**en·light′en·er,** *n.* —**en·light′en·ing·ly,** *adv.*
—**Syn. 1.** illumine, edify, teach, inform.

en·light·en·ment (en līt′ən mənt), *n.* **1.** the act of enlightening. **2.** the state of being enlightened: *to live in spiritual enlightenment.* **3.** (*usually cap.*) *Buddhism, Hinduism.* prajna. **4. the Enlightenment,** a philosophical movement of the 17th and 18th centuries, characterized by belief in the power of human reason and by innovations in political, religious, and educational doctrine. [ENLIGHTEN + -MENT]

En·lil (en′lil), *n.* the king of the Sumerian gods and the god of the air.

en·list (en list′), *v.i.* **1.** to engage for military service by enrolling after mutual agreement. **2.** to enter into some cause, enterprise, etc. —*v.t.* **3.** to engage for military service: *to enlist men for the army.* **4.** to secure (a person, services, etc.) for some cause, enterprise, etc. [EN-1 + LIST1]

enlist′ed man′, any male member of the U.S. armed services who is not a commissioned officer or a warrant officer.

enlist′ed wom′an, any female member of the U.S. armed services who is not a commissioned officer or a warrant officer.

en·list·ee (en lis tē′), *n.* **1.** a person who enlists for military service. Cf. **draftee. 2.** an enlisted man or woman. [ENLIST + -EE]

en·list·er (en lis′tər), *n.* **1.** a person who enlists. **2.** a person who recruits others for military service. **3.** *Archaic.* enlistee. [ENLIST + -ER]

en·list·ment (en list′mənt), *n.* **1.** the period of years for which one engages to serve in the armed forces of one's country. **2.** the act of enlisting. [ENLIST + -MENT]

en·liv·en (en lī′vən), *v.t.* **1.** to make vigorous or active; invigorate: *The wit of Voltaire enlivened his age.* **2.** to make sprightly, gay, or cheerful; brighten: *Flowers enliven any room.* [*enlive* to give life to (EN-1 + LIFE) + -EN1] —**en·liv′en·er,** *n.* —**en·liv′en·ing·ly,** *adv.* —**en·liv′en·ment,** *n.*
—**Syn. 1.** animate, inspirit, vivify, stimulate, quicken. **2.** exhilarate, gladden. See **cheer.** —**Ant. 2.** depress.

en·mar·ble (en mär′bəl), *v.t.,* **-bled, -bling.** emmarble.

en masse (än mas′, en; *Fr.* äN MAS′), in a mass; all together; as a group: *The people cheered en masse.* [< F]

en·mesh (en mesh′), *v.t.* to catch, as in a net; entangle: *He was enmeshed by financial difficulties.* Also, **immesh, inmesh.** [EN-1 + MESH] —**en·mesh′ment,** *n.*

en·mi·ty (en′mi tē), *n., pl.* **-ties.** a feeling or condition of hostility; hatred; ill will; animosity; antagonism. [ME *enemyte* < MF < OF *enemistie* < VL **inimīcitāt-* (s. of **inimīcitās*), equiv. to L *inimīc(us)* ENEMY + *-itāt-* -ITY]

en·ne·ad (en′ē ad′), *n.* **1.** a group of nine persons or things. **2.** *Egyptian Religion.* **a.** (*cap.*) a group of nine related deities, including Osiris, Isis, and Set, whose lineage and functions were arranged and explained by the theologians of Heliopolis. **b.** any group of deities arranged in a similar way, often more or less than nine in number. [< Gk *ennead-* (s. of *enneás*), equiv. to *enné(a)* nine + *-ad-* -AD] —**en′ne·ad′ic,** *adj.*

en·ne·a·gon (en′ē ə gon′), *n.* nonagon. [< Gk *enneágōn(os),* equiv. to *ennéa* nine + *-gōnos* -GON]

en·ne·a·he·dron (en′ē ə hē′drən), *n., pl.* **-dra** (-drə). a solid figure having nine faces. [< Gk *ennéa* nine + -HEDRON] —**en′ne·a·he′dral,** *adj.*

en·ne·a·style (en′ē ə stīl′), *adj.* **1.** *Archit.* having nine columns. **2.** (of a classical temple) having nine columns on one front or on each. Also, **en′ne·a·styl′ar.** [< Gk *ennéa* nine + *-style* < Gk *stŷlos* column]

en·ne·a·sty·los (en′ē ə stī′los), *n.* an enneastyle building, as a classical temple. [< Gk *ennéa* nine + *stŷlos* column]

en·ne·a·syl·lab·ic (en′ē ə si lab′ik), *adj.* consisting of or pertaining to nine syllables. [< Gk *enneasýllab(os)* nine-syllable + -IC]

En·nis (en′is), *n.* **1.** a town in N Texas. 9347 (1960). **2.** a boy's given name.

En·ni·us (en′ē əs), *n.* **Quin·tus** (kwin′təs), 239–169? B.C., Roman poet.

en·no·ble (en nō′bəl), *v.t.,* **-bled, -bling. 1.** to elevate in degree, excellence, or respect; dignify; exalt: *a personality ennobled by true generosity.* **2.** to confer a title of nobility on. [late ME *ennobele(n)* < MF, OF *en-*

nobli(r). See EN-[1], NOBLE] **—en·no′ble·ment,** *n.* **—en·no′bler,** *n.* **—en·no′bling·ly,** *adv.*

En·no·mus (en′ə məs), *n.* (in the *Iliad*) an augur who joined the Trojans in the war against the Greeks.

En·no·sig·ae·us (en′ə sig′ē əs), *n.* *Class. Myth.* an epithet of Poseidon, meaning "earth-shaker."

en·nui (än wē′, än′wē; *Fr.* äɴ nwē′), *n.* a feeling of weariness and discontent resulting from satiety or lack of interest; boredom: *The endless lecture produced an unbearable ennui.* [< F: boredom; OF *enui* displeasure; see ANNOY]

en·nuy·ant (äɴ nwē yäɴ′), *adj. French.* (of a man or things of masculine gender) boring; dull.

en·nuy·ante (äɴ nwē yäɴt′), *adj. French.* (of a woman or things of feminine gender) boring; dull.

en·nuy·é (äɴ nwē yā′), *adj., n., pl.* **-nuy·és** (-nwē yā′). *French.* **—adj. 1.** (of a man) affected with ennui. **—n. 2.** a man affected with ennui.

en·nuy·ée (äɴ nwē yā′), *adj., n., pl.* **-nuy·ées** (-nwē-yā′). *French.* **—adj. 1.** (of a woman) affected with ennui. **—n. 2.** a woman affected with ennui.

E·noch (ē′nək), *n.* **1.** the father of Methuselah. Gen. 5:22. **2.** a son of Cain. Gen. 4:17. **3.** a boy's given name. Also, *Douay Bible,* **Henoch** (for defs. 1, 2).

E′noch Ar′den (är′dən), **1.** (*italics.*) a narrative poem (1864) by Tennyson. **2.** its hero. **3.** any missing person who is eventually presumed dead but is later found to be alive.

e·nol (ē′nōl, ē′nôl, ē′nol), *n. Chem.* an organic compound containing a hydroxyl group attached to a doubly linked carbon atom, as in >C=C(OH)–. [appar. < Gk (*h*)*én* one (neut.) + -OL[1]] **—e·nol·ic** (ē nol′ik), *adj.*

E·no·la (i nō′lə), *n.* a girl's given name.

e·no·late (ēn′ᵊlāt′), *n. Chem.* any metallic derivative of an enol. [ENOL + -ATE[2]]

e·no·lize (ēn′ᵊlīz′), *v.t., v.i.,* **-lized, -liz·ing.** *Chem.* to convert into an enol or enolate. [ENOL + -IZE] **—e′no·liz′a·ble,** *adj.* **—e′no·li·za′tion,** *n.*

e·nol·o·gy (ē nol′ə jē), *n.* oenology.

E·no·ne (i nō′nē), *n.* a girl's given name.

e·norm (ē nôrm′), *adj. Archaic.* enormous; huge; vast. [late ME *enorme* < MF < L *ēnorm(is),* equiv. to *ē-* E- + *norma* NORM]

e·nor·mi·ty (i nôr′mi tē), *n., pl.* **-ties. 1.** outrageous or heinous character; atrociousness: *the enormity of war crimes.* **2.** something outrageous or heinous, as an offense: *The bombing of the defenseless population was an enormity beyond belief.* **3.** greatness of size, scope, extent, or influence; immensity: *The enormity of such an act of generosity is staggering.* [late ME *enormite* < MF < L *ēnormitāt-* (s. of *ēnormitās*). See ENORM, -TY[2]]

e·nor·mous (i nôr′məs), *adj.* **1.** greatly exceeding the common size, extent, etc.; huge; immense: *an enormous fortune.* **2.** outrageous or atrocious: *enormous wickedness; enormous unkindness.* [ENORM + -OUS] **—e·nor′mous·ly,** *adv.* **—e·nor′mous·ness,** *n.*
—Syn. 1. vast, colossal, gigantic, mammoth, prodigious. stupendous. See **huge.**

E·nos (ē′nəs), *n.* **1.** the son of Seth. Gen. 5:6. **2.** a boy's given name.

e·no·sis (e′nô sēs; *Eng.* i nō′sis, ē nō′-), *n.* (*sometimes cap.*) *Greek.* union: used specifically with reference to the movement for securing the political union of Greece and Cyprus. **—e·no′sist,** *n.*

e·nough (i nuf′), *adj.* **1.** adequate for the want or need; sufficient for the purpose or to satisfy desire: *noise enough to wake the dead; I've had enough trouble.* **—n. 2.** an adequate quantity or number; sufficiency. **—adv. 3.** in a quantity or degree that answers a purpose or satisfies a need or desire; sufficiently. **4.** fully or quite: *ready enough.* **5.** tolerably or passably: *He sings well enough.* **—interj. 6.** it or that is sufficient: *Enough! I heard you the first time.* [ME *enogh,* OE *genōh;* c. G *genug,* Goth *ganohs,* Icel *nōgr;* akin to OE *geneah* it suffices, Skt *naśati* (he) reaches]

e·nounce (i nouns′), *v.t.,* **e·nounced, e·nounc·ing. 1.** to announce, declare, or proclaim: *The president enounced his intention to reduce taxes.* **2.** to state definitely, as a proposition. **3.** to utter or pronounce, as words; enunciate. [E- + (AN)NOUNCE, modeled on F *énoncer* < L *ēnuntiāre* to tell; see ENUNCIATE] **—e·nounce′ment,** *n.*

En·o·vid (en ov′id), *n. Pharm., Trademark.* a hormonal compound used in medicine, in varying doses, chiefly for ovulation control, and for adjustment of the menses, severe uterine bleeding, and threatened habitual abortion.

e·now (i nou′; *formerly* i nō′), *adj., adv. Archaic.* enough. [ME *inow,* OE *genōg* (var. of *genōh* ENOUGH); ME *inowe,* OE *genōge,* pl. of *genōg* ENOUGH]

en pa·pil·lote (äɴ pa pē yôt′), *French.* (of food, esp. meat) cooked and served in a wrapping of foil or oiled paper.

en pas·sant (än′ pa sänt′; *Fr.* äɴ pä säɴ′), **1.** (*italics.*) *French.* in passing; by the way. **2.** *Chess.* a method by which a pawn that is moved two squares can be captured by an opponent's pawn covering the square that has been passed.

en·phy·tot·ic (en′fī tot′ik), *adj.* **1.** (of a disease) regularly affecting but not destroying the plants in a given area. **—n. 2.** any enphytotic disease. [EN-[2] + Gk *phyt(ón)* plant + -OTIC]

en·plane (en plān′), *v.i.,* **-planed, -plan·ing.** to enter an airplane: *We enplaned in New York at noon and arrived in Washington an hour later.* [EN-[1] + PLANE[1]]

en plein air (äɴ ple nεʀ′), *French.* in the open air.

en plein jour (äɴ plaɴ zhōōʀ′), *French.* in full daylight; openly.

en prise (än′ prēz′; *Fr.* äɴ pʀēz′), *Chess.* in line for capture; likely to be captured. [< F; see PRIZE[1]]

en′ quad′, *Print.* **1.** a square unit of area, one en on each side. **2.** a piece of type consisting of a box one en on the top and bottom, and type-high on the sides: ▯ *is an en quad.*

en·quire (en kwīᵊr′), *v.t., v.i.,* **-quired, -quir·ing.** inquire.

en·quir·y (en kwīᵊr′ē), *n., pl.* **-quir·ies.** inquiry.

en·rage (en rāj′), *v.t.,* **-raged, -rag·ing.** to put into a rage; infuriate: *His supercilious attitude enraged me.* [< MF *enrage(r).* See EN-[1], RAGE] **—en·rag·ed·ly** (en-rā′jid lē, -rājd′-), *adv.* **—en·rage′ment,** *n.*
—Syn. anger, inflame, madden. ENRAGE, INCENSE, INFURIATE imply stirring to violent anger. To ENRAGE is to provoke a display of wrath: *They enrage him by their deliberate and continual injustice.* To INCENSE is to inflame with indignation or anger: the connotation is serious provocation present or prolonged: *to incense a person by making insulting remarks.* To INFURIATE is to arouse suddenly to fury or fierce and vehement anger: *to infuriate a person by a false accusation.* **—Ant.** appease, pacify.

en rap·port (äɴ ʀa pôʀ′; *Eng.* än′ ra pôr′, -pôr′, rə-), *French.* in sympathy or accord; in agreement; congenial.

en·rapt (en rapt′), *adj.* rapt; transported; enraptured: *His enrapt audience seemed to hang on every word he spoke.* [EN-[1] + RAPT]

en·rap·ture (en rap′chər), *v.t.,* **-tured, -tur·ing.** to move to rapture; delight beyond measure: *We were enraptured by her singing.* [EN-[1] + RAPTURE] **—en·rap′tured·ly,** *adv.*

en·rav·ish (en rav′ish), *v.t.* to enrapture. [EN-[1] + RAVISH]

en·reg·is·ter (en rej′i stər), *v.t.* to register; record. [< MF *enregistre(r).* See EN-[1], REGISTER] **—en·reg′is·tra′tion,** *n.*

En·ri·ca (en rē′kə; *It.* en ʀē′kä), *n.* a girl's given name.

en·rich (en rich′), *v.t.* **1.** to supply with riches, wealth, abundant or valuable possessions, etc.: *Commerce enriches a nation.* **2.** to supply with abundance of anything desirable: *to enrich the mind with knowledge.* **3.** to add greater value or significance to: *Art enriches life.* **4.** to adorn or decorate: *a picture frame enriched with gold.* **5.** to make finer in quality, as by supplying desirable elements or ingredients: *to enrich bread; to enrich soil.* [ME *enriche(n)* < OF *enrichi(r).* See EN-[1], RICH] **—en·rich′er,** *n.* **—en·rich′ing·ly,** *adv.*

en·rich·ment (en rich′mənt), *n.* **1.** the act of enriching. **2.** the state of being enriched. **3.** something that enriches: *the enrichments of education and travel.* [ENRICH + -MENT]

En·ri·co (en rē′kō; *It.* en ʀe′kô), *n.* a boy's given name.

en·robe (en rōb′), *v.t.,* **-robed, -rob·ing.** to dress; attire: *The king was enrobed in velvet.* [EN-[1] + ROBE] **—en·rob′er,** *n.*

en·rol (en rōl′), *v.t., v.i.,* **-rolled, -rol·ling.** enroll.

en·roll (en rōl′), *v.t.* **1.** to write (a name), or insert the name of (a person), in a roll or register; place upon a list: *It took two days to enroll the new students.* **2.** to enlist (oneself). **3.** to put in a record; record: *to enroll the minutes of a meeting; to enroll the great events of history.* **4.** to roll or wrap up: *fruit enrolled in tissue paper.* **5.** *Naut.* to document (a U.S. vessel) by issuing a certificate of enrollment. **—v.i. 6.** to enroll oneself: *He enrolled at Columbia last week.* [ME *enrolle(n)* < OF *enrolle(r).* See EN-[1], ROLL] **—en·roll′er,** *n.*

en·roll·ee (en rō lē′, -rō′lē), *n.* a person who enrolls, or has enrolled, in a class, school, course of study, etc. [ENROLL + -EE]

en·roll·ment (en rōl′mənt), *n.* **1.** the act or process of enrolling; state of being enrolled. **2.** the number of persons enrolled, as for a course or in a school. Also, **en·rol′ment.** [ENROLL + -MENT]

en·root (en rōōt′, -rŏŏt′), *v.t.* **1.** to fix by the root. **2.** to attach or place securely; implant deeply. [EN-[1] + ROOT[1]]

en route (än rōōt′, en; *Fr.* äɴ ʀōōt′), on the way. [< F]

ens (enz), *n., pl.* **en·ti·a** (en′shē ə). *Metaphys.* an existing or real thing; an entity. [< LL, prp. of *esse* to be]

Ens., Ensign.

en·sam·ple (en sam′pəl), *n. Archaic.* example. [ME < MF, var. (*en-* r. *es-*) of *essample* < OF < L *exempl(um)* EXAMPLE]

en·san·guine (en saŋ′gwin), *v.t.,* **-guined, -guin·ing.** to stain or cover with or as with blood: *a flag ensanguined with the blood of battle; a field ensanguined with poppies.* [EN-[1] + SANGUINE]

En·sche·de (en′skhə dā′), *n.* a city in the E Netherlands. 130,256 (1962).

en·sconce (en skons′), *v.t.,* **-sconced, -sconc·ing. 1.** to cover or shelter; hide securely: *He ensconced himself in the closet in order to eavesdrop.* **2.** to settle securely or snugly: *I found him in the library, ensconced in an armchair.* [EN-[1] + SCONCE[2]]

en·scroll (en skrōl′), *v.t.* **1.** to write or inscribe on a scroll. **2.** to commemorate or record in a permanent manner, by or as if by inscribing on parchment. Also, **inscroll.** [EN-[1] + SCROLL]

en·sem·ble (än säm′bəl, -sämb′; *Fr.* äɴ säɴ′blᵊ), *n., pl.* (-bəlz; *Fr.* -blᵊ), *adv.* **—n. 1.** all the parts of a thing taken together, so that each part is considered only in relation to the whole: *to consider the ensemble of one's life, its triumphs and its failures.* **2.** the entire costume of an individual, esp. when all the parts are in harmony: *She was wearing a beautiful ensemble by one of the French designers.* **3.** the general effect, as of a work of art. **4.** *Music.* **a.** the united performance of the full number of singers, musicians, etc. **b.** the group so performing: *a string ensemble.* **5.** a group of supporting entertainers, as actors, dancers, and singers, in a theatrical production. **—adv. 6.** together; all at once; simultaneously: *The crowd gave a rousing cheer ensemble.* [< F: together < L *insimul,* equiv. to *in-* IN-[2] + *simul* together; see SIMULTANEOUS]

En·se·na·da (en′se nä′thä), *n.* a seaport in N Lower California, in NW Mexico. 45,143 (1960).

en·se pe·tit pla·ci·dam sub li·ber·ta·te qui·e·tem (en′se pe′tit plä′ki däm′ sŏŏb lē′beʀ tä′te kwē e′tem; *Eng.* en′sē pē′tit plas′i dam′ sub lib′ər tā′tē kwī ē′tem), *Latin.* by the sword she seeks quiet peace under liberty: motto of Massachusetts.

en·sep·ul·cher (en sep′əl kər), *v.t.* to place in a sepulcher; entomb. Also, *esp. Brit.,* **en·sep′ul·chre.** [EN-[1] + SEPULCHER]

en·sheathe (en shēth′), *v.t.,* **-sheathed, -sheath·ing.** to enclose in or as in a sheath; sheathe. Also, **en·sheath′, insheathe, insheath.** [EN-[1] + SHEATHE]

en·shrine (en shrīn′), *v.t.,* **-shrined, -shrin·ing. 1.** to enclose in or as in a shrine: *His love for her is enshrined forever in his poetry.* **2.** to cherish as sacred: *The memory of our friendship will be enshrined in my heart.* Also, **inshrine.** [EN-[1] + SHRINE] **—en·shrine′ment,** *n.*

en·shroud (en shroud′) *v.t.* to shroud; conceal. [EN-[1] + SHROUD]

en·si·form (en′sə fôrm′), *adj. Biol.* sword-shaped; xiphoid. [< L *ensi(s)* sword + -FORM]

en·sign (en′sīn; *Mil.* en′sən), *n.* **1.** a flag or banner, as a military or naval standard used to indicate nationality. **2.** a badge of office or authority, as heraldic arms. **3.** a sign, token, or emblem: *to wear black as an ensign of mourning.* **4.** *U.S. Navy.* the lowest commissioned officer, ranking next below a lieutenant, junior grade, and equal to a second lieutenant in the Army. **5.** *Brit. Army.* (formerly) an officer who carried the standard or flag of a regiment or company. [ME *ensigne* < OF *enseigne* < L *insignia;* see INSIGNIA] **—en′sign·ship′, en′sign·cy,** *n.*

en′sign staff′, a staff at the stern of a vessel at which the ensign is flown. Also called **poop staff.**

en·si·lage (en′sə lij), *n., v.,* **-laged, -lag·ing. —n. 1.** the preservation of green fodder in a silo or pit. **2.** fodder thus preserved. **—v.t. 3.** ensile. [< F; see ENSILE, -AGE]

en·sile (en sīl′, en′sīl), *v.t.,* **-siled, -sil·ing. 1.** to preserve (green fodder) in a silo. **2.** to make into ensilage. [< F *ensile(r)* < Sp *ensilar,* equiv. to *en-* EN-[1] + *sil(o)* SILO] **—en·si′la·bil′i·ty,** *n.*

en·sky (en skī′), *v.t.,* **-skied** or **-skyed, -sky·ing. 1.** to place in or as in the heavens: *to be enskied by sublime music.* **2.** to raise to or as to the skies: *The birds enskied themselves.* [EN-[1] + SKY]

en·slave (en slāv′), *v.t.,* **-slaved, -slav·ing.** to make a slave of; reduce to slavery: *His alcoholism has completely enslaved him.* [EN-[1] + SLAVE] **—en·slave′ment,** *n.* **—en·slav′er,** *n.*

en·snare (en snâr′), *v.t.,* **-snared, -snar·ing.** to capture in, or involve as in, a snare: *to be ensnared by lies; to ensnare birds.* Also, **insnare.** [EN-[1] + SNARE[1]] **—en·snare′ment,** *n.* **—en·snar′er,** *n.* **—en·snar′ing·ly,** *adv.*
—Syn. entrap, entangle, enmesh. **—Ant.** release.

en so·leil (än sô lā′), *Heraldry.* (of a charge) surrounded by rays, as of the sun: *a white rose en soleil.* [< F: lit., in (the form of the) sun]

En·sor (en′sôr), *n.* **James,** 1860–1949, Belgian painter.

en·sor·cell (en sôr′səl), *v.t.* to bewitch: *The beauty of the moon ensorcelled them.* Also, **en·sor′cel.** [< MF *ensorcele(r)* (to) bewitch, dissimilated var. of *ensorcerer,* OF. See EN-[1], SORCERER] **—en·sor′cell·ment,** *n.*

en·soul (en sōl′), *v.t.* **1.** to endow with a soul. **2.** to place or cherish in the soul: *lines of Shakespeare ensouled by all.* Also, **insoul.** [EN-[1] + SOUL]

en·sphere (en sfēr′), *v.t.,* **-sphered, -spher·ing. 1.** to enclose in or as in a sphere. **2.** to form into a sphere. Also, **insphere.** [EN-[1] + SPHERE]

en·spir·it (en spir′it), *v.t.* inspirit.

ens re·al·is·si·mum (ens ʀe′ä lis′i mŏŏm′; *Eng.* enz′ rē ə lis′ə məm), *Latin.* (in Scholasticism) God, seen as the entity having all attributes of being and perfection in the highest degree. [lit: the most real being]

en·sta·tite (en′stə tīt′), *n. Mineral.* a yellow-green fibrous magnesium silicate, an orthorhombic pyroxene found in norites containing less than five percent ferrous oxide. [< Gk *enstát(ēs)* adversary + -ITE[1]] **—en·sta·tit·ic** (en′stə tit′ik), *adj.*

en·sue (en sōō′), *v.i.,* **-sued, -su·ing. 1.** to follow in order; come afterward, esp. in immediate succession: *As the days ensued, he recovered his strength.* **2.** to follow as a consequence; result: *When those two women meet, a battle of insults ensues.* [ME *ensue(n)* < AF *ensue(r)* (c. OF *ensui(v)re*). See EN-[1], SUE] **—en·su′ing·ly,** *adv.*
—Syn. 1, 2. See **follow. 2.** issue, arise, flow.

en suite (äɴ swēt′), *French.* in succession; in a series or set.

en·sure (en shŏŏr′), *v.t.,* **-sured, -sur·ing. 1.** to secure, or bring surely, as a person: *This letter will ensure you a hearing.* **2.** to make sure or certain: *measures to ensure the success of an undertaking.* **3.** to make secure or safe, as from harm. **4.** insure (defs. 1–3). [ME *ensure(n)* < AF *enseure(r).* See EN-[1], SURE] **—en·sur′er,** *n.*

en·swathe (en swoth′, -swāth′), *v.t.,* **-swathed, -swath·ing.** to swathe. Also, **inswathe.** [EN-[1] + SWATHE] **—en·swathe′ment,** *n.*

-ent, a formal element, equivalent to **-ant,** appearing in nouns and adjectives of Latin origin: *accident; different.* [< L *-ent-* (s. of *-ēns*), prp. of conjugations 2, 3, 4]

en·tab·la·ture (en tab′lə chər), *n. Archit.* **1.** the entire construction of a classical temple or the like between the columns and the eaves, usually composed of an architrave, a frieze, and a cornice. **2.** a decorative imitation of this. [< MF < It *intavolatura,* lit., something tabled, i.e., laid flat, equiv. to *in-* IN-[2] + *tavolat-* (*tavol-* table + *-at-* -ATE[1]) + *-ura* -URE]

en·ta·ble·ment (en tā′bəl mənt), *n.* **1.** the platform above the dado on a pedestal. **2.** *Rare.* an entablature. [< F, equiv. to *entabl(er)* (to) table (see EN-[1], TABLE) + *-ment* -MENT]

en·tail (en tāl′), *v.t.* **1.** to cause or involve by necessity or consequences: *a loss entailing no regret.* **2.** to impose as a burden: *Success entails hard work.* **3.** to limit the passage of (a landed estate) to a specified line of heirs, so that it cannot be alienated, devised, or bequeathed. **4.** to cause (anything) to descend to a fixed series of possessors. **—n. 5.** the act of entailing. **6.** the state of being entailed. **7.** any predetermined order of succession, as to an office. **8.** that which is entailed, as an estate. **9.** the rule of descent settled for an estate. [ME *entaile(n).* See EN-[1], TAIL[2]] **—en·tail′er,** *n.* **—en·tail′ment,** *n.*

en·tan·gle (en taŋ′gəl), *v.t.,* **-gled, -gling. 1.** to make tangled; ensnarl; intertwine: *The cow entangled its horns in the branches.* **2.** to involve in anything like a tangle; ensnare; enmesh: *to be entangled by intrigue.* **3.** to involve in difficulties. **4.** to confuse or perplex. [EN-[1] + TANGLE] **—en·tan′gle·a·ble,** *adj.* **—en·tan′gled·ly,** *adv.* **—en·tan′gled·ness,** *n.* **—en·tan′gler,** *n.* **—en·tan′gling·ly,** *adv.*
—Syn. 3. bewilder, confuse. See **involve.**

en·tan·gle·ment (en taŋ′gəl mənt), *n.* **1.** the act of entangling. **2.** the state of being entangled. **3.** that which entangles; snare; involvement; complication. [ENTANGLE + -MENT]

en·ta·sis (en′tə sis), *n. Archit.* a slight convexity given to a column, tower, etc., to correct an optical illusion or to enhance the effect. [< Gk, equiv. to *enta-* (var. of *entein-,* s. of *enteínein* to stretch tight, equiv. to *en-* EN-[2] + *ta-* (*tein-*) stretch) + *-sis* -SIS]

En·teb·be (en teb′e), *n.* a town in S Uganda, on Lake Victoria. 8500 (est. 1957).

en·tel·e·chy (en tel′ə kē), *n., pl.* **-chies.** **1.** a realization or actuality as opposed to a potentiality. **2.** (in vitalist philosophy) a vital agent or force directing growth and life. [< LL *entelechia* < Gk *entelécheia*, equiv. to *en-* EN-[2] + *tél(os)* goal + *éch(ein)* (to) have + *-eia* -Y[3]] —**en·te·lech·i·al** (en′tə lek′ē əl), *adj.*

en·tel·lus (en tel′əs), *n., pl.* **-lus·es.** hanuman (def. 1). [named after ENTELLUS]

En·tel·lus (en tel′əs), *n.* (in the *Aeneid*) a powerful Sicilian boxer who won a match against Dares.

en·tente (än tänt′; *Fr.* äN täNt′), *n., pl.* **-tentes** (-tänts′; *Fr.* -täNt′). **1.** an arrangement or understanding between nations agreeing to follow a particular policy with regard to affairs of international concern. **2.** an alliance of parties to such an understanding. [< F: understanding, OF: intention, n. use of fem. of *entent*, ptp. of *entendre* to INTEND]

en·tente cor·diale (än tänt′ kôr dyäl′; *Fr.* äN täNt′ kôR dyAl′), a friendly understanding, esp. between two governments. [< F]

en·ter (en′tər), *v.i.* **1.** to come or go in: *May I enter?* **2.** *Theat.* to come upon the stage (used in stage directions as the 3rd person imperative sing. or pl.): *Enter Othello, and Iago at a distance.* **3.** to be admitted into a school, competition, etc.: *He entered for two courses. Some contestants enter as late as a day before the race.* **4.** to make a beginning (often fol. by *on* or *upon*): *We have entered upon a new phase in man's history.* —*v.t.* **5.** to come or go into: *He just entered the theater. The thought never entered my mind.* **6.** to penetrate or pierce: *The bullet entered the flesh.* **7.** to put in or insert: *to enter a wedge.* **8.** to become a member of; join: *to enter a club.* **9.** to cause to be admitted, as into a school, competition, etc.: *to enter a horse in a race.* **10.** to make a beginning of or in, or begin upon; engage or become involved in: *He entered the medical profession.* **11.** to share in; have an intuitive understanding of: *In order to appreciate the novel, one must be able to enter the spirit of the work.* **12.** to make a record of; record or register: *to enter a name on a list.* **13.** *Law.* **a.** to make a formal record of (a fact). **b.** to occupy or to take possession of (lands); make an entrance, entry, ingress in, under claim of a right to possession. **c.** to file an application for (public lands). **14.** to put forward, submit, or register formally: *to enter an objection to a proposed action; to enter a bid for a contract.* **15.** to report (a vessel, cargo, etc.) at the custom house. **16.** **enter into, a.** to participate in; engage in. **b.** to investigate; consider: *We will enter into the question of inherited characteristics at a future time.* **c.** to sympathize with; share in. **d.** to form a constituent part or ingredient of: *There is another factor that enters into the situation.* **e.** to go into a particular state: *to enter into a state of suspended animation.* [ME *entre(n)* < OF *entre(r)* < L *intrāre* to enter, deriv. of L *intrā-* within] —**en′ter·a·ble,** *adj.* —**en′ter·er,** *n.*
—**Ant. 1.** leave. **7.** remove.

enter-, var. of **entero-** before a vowel: *enteritis.*

en·ter·al (en′tər əl), *adj.* enteric. [ENTER- + -AL[1]] —**en′ter·al·ly,** *adv.*

en·ter·al·gia (en′tə ral′jə, -jē ə), *n.* *Pathol.* pain in the intestine; colic. [< NL; see ENTER-, -ALGIA]

en·ter·close (en′tər klōz′), *n.* *Obs.* a passage or screen between two apartments. [ME < OF *entreclos.* See INTER-, CLOSE]

en·ter·ec·to·my (en′tə rek′tə mē), *n., pl.* **-mies.** *Surg.* excision of part of the intestine. [ENTER- + -ECTOMY]

en′tered hound′, *Fox Hunting.* a foxhound that has hunted regularly for one or more seasons.

en·ter·ic (en ter′ik), *adj.* of or pertaining to the enteron; intestinal. [< Gk *enterik(ós).* See ENTER-, -IC]

enter′ic fe′ver, *Pathol.* typhoid (def. 1).

en′tering wedge′, anything that parts, divides, intrudes, etc.

en·ter·i·tis (en′tə rī′tis), *n.* **1.** *Pathol.* inflammation of the intestines. **2.** *Vet. Pathol.* distemper[1] (def. 1c). [< NL; see ENTER-, -ITIS]

entero-, a learned borrowing from Greek meaning "intestine," used in the formation of compound words: *enterology.* Also, *esp. before a vowel,* **enter-.** [< Gk, s. of *énteron* intestine]

en·ter·o·bi·a·sis (en′tə rō bī′ə sis), *n.* *Pathol.* infestation with pinworms. [< NL, equiv. to *enterob(ius)* an intestinal worm (ENTERO- + Gk *bíos* life) + *-iasis* -IASIS]

en·ter·o·co·li·tis (en′tə rō kō lī′tis, -kə-), *n.* *Pathol.* inflammation of the small intestine and the colon. [< NL; see ENTERO-, COLITIS]

en·ter·o·hep·a·ti·tis (en′tə rō hep′ə tī′tis), *n.* *Vet. Med.* blackhead (def. 3). [ENTERO- + HEPATITIS]

en·ter·ol·o·gy (en′tə rol′ə jē), *n.* the branch of medicine dealing with the intestines. [ENTERO- + -LOGY] —**en·ter·o·log·ic** (en′tə rō loj′ik), **en′ter·o·log′i·cal,** *adj.* —**en′te·rol′o·gist,** *n.*

en·ter·on (en′tə ron′), *n., pl.* **-ter·a** (-tər ə). *Anat., Zool.* the alimentary canal; the digestive tract. [< NL < Gk: intestine]

en·ter·op·neust (en′tə rop nōōst′, -nyōōst′), *n.* any invertebrate animal of the class *Enteropneusta,* comprising the acorn worms. [< NL *Enteropneust(a),* equiv. to *entero-* ENTERO- + *-pneusta,* neut. pl. of Gk *pneustós* breathed, verbal of *pnein* to breathe]

en·ter·or·rhex·is (en′tər ə rek′sis), *n.* *Pathol.* rupture of the intestine. [ENTERO- + -RRHEXIS]

en·ter·os·to·my (en′tə ros′tə mē), *n., pl.* **-mies.** *Surg.* the making of an artificial opening into the intestine, which opens onto the abdominal wall, for feeding or drainage. [ENTERO- + -STOMY]

en·ter·o·tox·e·mi·a (en′tə rō tok sē′mē ə), *n.* *Vet. Pathol.* a disease of sheep caused by severe systemic poisoning from bacterial toxins of *Clostridium perfringens* in the intestinal tract. [ENTERO- + TOXEMIA]

en·ter·o·zo·a (en′tər ə zō′ə), *n.pl., sing.* **-zo·on** (-zō′on). (*often cap.*) *Biol.* entozoa. [ENTERO- + -ZOA] —**en′ter·o·zo′an,** *adj., n.*

en·ter·prise (en′tər prīz′), *n.* **1.** a project undertaken or to be undertaken, esp. one that is of some importance or that requires boldness or energy: *To keep the peace is a difficult enterprise.* **2.** a plan for such a project. **3.** participation or engagement in such projects: *Our country was formed by the enterprise of resolute men.* **4.** boldness or readiness in undertaking; adventurous spirit; energy. **5.** a company organized for commercial purposes; business firm. [late ME < MF *entreprise,* n. use of fem. of *entrepris* (ptp. of *entreprendre* to undertake) < L *inter-* INTER- + *prēnsus* grasped, seized, contr. of *prehēnsus,* equiv. to *pre-* PRE- + *hend-* take hold of + *-tus* ptp. suffix] —**en′ter·prise′less,** *adj.*
—**Syn. 1.** plan, undertaking, venture.

En·ter·prise (en′tər prīz′), *n.* a city in S Alabama. 11,410 (1960).

en·ter·pris·er (en′tər prī′zər), *n.* a person who undertakes some enterprise; entrepreneur. [ENTERPRISE + -ER[1]]

en·ter·pris·ing (en′tər prī′zing), *adj.* **1.** ready to undertake projects of importance or difficulty, or untried schemes; energetic in carrying out any undertaking: *Business is in need of enterprising young men.* **2.** characterized by great imagination or initiative: *an enterprising foreign policy.* [ENTERPRISE + -ING[2]] —**en′ter·pris′ing·ly,** *adv.*
—**Syn. 1.** venturous, venturesome, resourceful, adventurous. See **ambitious.** —**Ant. 1.** timid, cautious.

en·ter·tain (en′tər tān′), *v.t.* **1.** to hold the attention of agreeably; divert; amuse. **2.** to treat as a guest; provide food, lodging, etc., for; show hospitality to. **3.** to admit into the mind; consider: *He never entertained such ideas.* **4.** to hold in the mind; harbor; cherish: *She secretly entertained thoughts of revenge.* **5.** *Archaic.* to maintain or keep up. **6.** *Obs.* to give admittance or reception to; receive. —*v.i.* **7.** to exercise hospitality; entertain company; provide entertainment for guests: *She loved to talk, dance, and entertain.* [late ME *entertene* to hold mutually < MF *entreten(ir),* irreg. < LL *intertenēre,* equiv. to *inter-* INTER- + *tenēre* to hold]
—**Syn. 1.** please. See **amuse.** —**Ant. 1.** bore. **2, 6.** exclude. **3.** reject.

en·ter·tain·er (en′tər tā′nər), *n.* **1.** a person who entertains: *She was one of the capital's great entertainers.* **2.** a singer, reciter, or the like, who gives, or takes part in, public entertainments. [ENTERTAIN + -ER[1]]

en·ter·tain·ing (en′tər tā′ning), *adj.* affording entertainment; amusing; diverting: *We spent an entertaining evening at the theater.* [ENTERTAIN + -ING[2]] —**en′ter·tain′ing·ly,** *adv.* —**en′ter·tain′ing·ness,** *n.*

en·ter·tain·ment (en′tər tān′mənt), *n.* **1.** the act of entertaining; agreeable occupation for the mind; diversion; amusement: *Solving the daily crossword puzzle is an entertainment for many.* **2.** something affording diversion or amusement, esp. an exhibition or performance of some kind: *The highlight of the ball was an elaborate entertainment.* **3.** hospitable provision for the wants of guests. **4.** *Obs.* maintenance in service. [ENTERTAIN + -MENT]

en·thal·py (en′thal pē, en thal′-), *n., pl.* **-pies.** *Thermodynamics.* a quantity associated with a thermodynamic system, expressed as the internal energy of a system plus the product of the pressure and volume of the system, having the property that during an isobaric process, the change in the quantity is equal to the heat transferred during the process. *Symbol:* H Also called **heat content, total heat.** [< Gk *enthálp(ein)* (to) warm in (*en-* EN-[2] + *thálpein* to warm) + -Y[3]]

en·thet·ic (en thet′ik), *adj.* introduced from without, as diseases propagated by inoculation. [< Gk *enthetik(ós),* equiv. to *enthet(os)* (verbal of *entithénai* to put in, equiv. to *en-* EN-[2] + *tithénai* to put) + *-ikos* -IC]

en·thral (en thrôl′), *v.t.,* **-thralled, -thral·ling.** enthrall. —**en·thral′ment,** *n.*

en·thrall (en thrôl′), *v.t.* **1.** to captivate; charm: *a performer whose grace, skill, and virtuosity enthrall her audiences.* **2.** to put or hold in thraldom; subjugate: *to be enthralled by illusions and superstitions.* Also, **inthral, inthrall.** [EN-[1] + THRALL] —**en·thrall′er,** *n.* —**en·thrall′ing·ly,** *adv.* —**en·thrall′ment,** *n.*

en·throne (en thrōn′), *v.t.,* **-throned, -thron·ing.** **1.** to place on or as on a throne. **2.** to invest with sovereign or episcopal authority. **3.** to exalt. Also, **inthrone.** [EN-[1] + THRONE]

en·throne·ment (en thrōn′mənt), *n.* **1.** the act of enthroning or enthronizing. **2.** the state or occasion of being enthroned or enthronized. Also, **en·thron′i·za′tion;** *esp. Brit.,* **en·thron′i·sa′tion.** [ENTHRONE + -MENT]

en·thron·ise (en thrō′nīz), *v.t.,* **-ised, -is·ing.** *Chiefly Brit.* enthronize.

en·thron·ize (en thrō′nīz), *v.t.,* **-ized, -iz·ing.** to enthrone. [ME *entronize(n)* < LL *enthroniz(āre),* Latinization of Gk *enthronízein.* See EN-[2], THRONE, -IZE]

en·thuse (en thōōz′), *v.,* **-thused, -thus·ing.** —*v.i.* **1.** to become enthusiastic; show enthusiasm: *All the neighbors enthused over the new baby.* —*v.t.* **2.** to move to enthusiasm. [back formation from ENTHUSIASM]
—**Usage.** Although it is too widely encountered in the speech and writing of reputable teachers and authors to be listed as anything short of standard, ENTHUSE is nonetheless felt by many to be poor style, and in formal writing it would be best to paraphrase it.

en·thu·si·asm (en thōō′zē az′əm), *n.* **1.** absorbing or controlling possession of the mind by any interest or pursuit; lively interest: *He shows marked enthusiasm for his studies.* **2.** an occupation, activity, or pursuit in which such interest is shown: *Hunting is his latest enthusiasm.* **3.** *Archaic.* extravagant religious emotion. [< LL *enthūsiasm(us)* < Gk *enthousiasmós,* equiv. to *enthousí(a)* possession by a god (*énthous,* var. of *éntheos* having a god within, equiv. to *en-* EN-[2] + *-thous, -theos* god-possessing + *-ia* -Y[3]) + *-asmos* (akin to *-ismos* -ISM)]
—**Syn. 1.** eagerness, warmth, fervor, zeal, ardor, passion, devotion. —**Ant. 1.** indifference.

en·thu·si·ast (en thōō′zē ast′), *n.* **1.** a person who is filled with enthusiasm for some principle, pursuit, etc.; a person of ardent zeal: *a sports enthusiast.* **2.** a religious visionary or fanatic. [< Gk *enthousiast(ḗs)* one inspired, equiv. to *enthousi-* (see ENTHUSIASM) + *-astēs,* akin to *-istēs* -IST]
—**Syn. 1.** zealot, devotee, fan.

en·thu·si·as·tic (en thōō′zē as′tik), *adj.* **1.** full of or characterized by enthusiasm; ardent: *He seems very enthusiastic about his role in the play.* **2.** pertaining to or of the nature of enthusiasm. [< Gk *enthousiastik(ós).* See ENTHUSIAST, -IC] —**en·thu′si·as′ti·cal·ly,** *adv.*
—**Syn. 1.** zealous, eager, fervent, passionate, vehement, fervid, impassioned.

en·thy·meme (en′thə mēm′), *n.* *Logic.* a syllogism in which one premise is unexpressed. [< L *enthȳmēma* < Gk, equiv. to *en-* EN-[2] + *thȳm(ós)* spirit, thought + *-ēma* -EME] —**en·thy·me·mat·ic** (en′thə mē mat′ik), *adj.*

en·tice (en tīs′), *v.t.,* **-ticed, -tic·ing.** to draw on by exciting hope or desire; allure; inveigle: *He was enticed by her flirtatious ways. They were enticed westward by dreams of gold.* [ME *entice(n)* < OF *enticie(r)* (to) incite < VL **intitiāre,* equiv. to L *in-* IN-[2] + *titio* firebrand] —**en·tic′ing·ly,** *adv.* —**en·tic′ing·ness,** *n.*
—**Syn.** lure, attract, decoy, tempt. —**Ant.** repel.

en·tice·ment (en tīs′mənt), *n.* **1.** the act or practice of enticing, esp. to evil. **2.** the state of being enticed. **3.** that which entices; allurement. [ME < MF; see ENTICE, -MENT]

en·tire (en tīər′), *adj.* **1.** having all the parts or elements; whole; complete: *He wrote the entire novel in only six weeks.* **2.** not broken, mutilated, or decayed; intact: *We were fortunate to find this relic entire and without fault.* **3.** unimpaired or undiminished: *His entire energies have gone into making the enterprise a success.* **4.** being wholly of one piece; undivided; continuous: *The entire mood of the symphony was joyful.* **5.** *Bot.* without notches or indentations, as leaves. **6.** full or thorough: *He has been given entire freedom of choice in this matter.* **7.** not gelded: *an entire horse.* **8.** *Obs.* wholly of one kind; unmixed or pure. —*n.* **9.** the whole; entirety: *The entire is flawed by poor workmanship.* **10.** an entire horse; stallion. **11.** *Brit.* a kind of malt liquor; porter. [ME *entere* < MF *entier* < L *integrum,* acc. of *integer* whole; see INTEGER] —**en·tire′ness,** *n.*
—**Syn. 1.** See **complete.** —**Ant. 1.** partial. **2.** defective.

entire′ func′tion, *Math.* a function of a complex variable which has a derivative for all finite values of the variable.

en·tire·ly (en tīər′lē), *adv.* **1.** wholly or fully; completely or unreservedly: *I am not entirely satisfied with the results of her test.* **2.** solely or exclusively. [ME; see ENTIRE, -LY]

en·tire·ty (en tīər′tē), *n., pl.* **-ties.** **1.** the state of being entire; completeness: Hamlet *is rarely played in its entirety.* **2.** that which is entire; the whole: *He devoted the entirety of his life to medical research.* [ME *enter(e)te* < MF *entierete* < L *integritāt-* (s. of *integritās*). See INTEGER, -ITY]

en·ti·tle (en tīt′əl), *v.t.,* **-tled, -tling.** **1.** to give (a person or thing) a title, right, or claim to something; furnish with grounds for laying claim: *His station entitled him to certain courtesies rarely accorded others.* **2.** to call by a particular title or name; address: *How does one entitle the queen when speaking directly to her?* **3.** to designate (a person) by an honorary title. Also, **intitle.** [ME *entitle(n)* < AF *entitle(r),* var. of MF *entituler* < LL *intitulāre.* See IN-[2], TITLE] —**en·ti′tle·ment,** *n.*

en·ti·ty (en′ti tē), *n., pl.* **-ties.** **1.** something that has a real existence; thing: *corporeal entities.* **2.** being or existence, esp. when considered as distinct, independent, or self-contained: *He conceived society as composed of particular entities requiring special treatment.* **3.** essential nature: *The entity of justice is universality.* [< ML *entitās,* equiv. to *enti-* (s. of *ēns*) being (prp. of *esse*) + *-tās* -TY[2]] —**en·ti·ta·tive** (en′ti tā′tiv), *adj.* —**en′ti·ta′tive·ly,** *adv.*

ento-, a learned borrowing from Greek meaning "within," used in the formation of compound words: *entoderm.* [comb. form repr. Gk *entós*]

en·to·blast (en′tə blast′), *n.* *Embryol.* **1.** entoderm. **2.** hypoblast (def. 2). [ENTO- + -BLAST] —**en·to·blas·tic** (en′tə blas′tik), *adj.*

en·to·derm (en′tə dûrm′), *n.* *Embryol.* the inner germ layer in the embryo of a metazoan. Also, **endoderm.** [ENTO- + -DERM] —**en·to·der·mal** (en′tō dûr′məl), **en′to·der′mic,** *adj.*

en·toil (en toil′), *v.t.* *Archaic.* to take in toils; ensnare. [EN-[1] + TOIL[2]]

entom., entomology. Also, **entomol.**

en·tomb (en tōōm′), *v.t.* **1.** to place in a tomb; bury; inter. **2.** to serve as a tomb for: *Florentine churches entomb many great men.* Also, **intomb.** [late ME *entoumbe(n)* < MF *entombe(r).* See EN-[1], TOMB] —**en·tomb′ment,** *n.*

entomo-, a learned borrowing from Greek used, with the meaning "insect," in the formation of compound words: *entomology.* Also, *esp. before a vowel,* **entom-.** [comb. form of Gk *éntomos* notched; in neut. pl., insects (verbid of *entémnein* to cut in or up), equiv. to *en-* EN-[2] + *tómos* cut; see -TOMY]

en·to·mog·e·nous (en′tə moj′ə nəs), *adj.* (of a fungus) growing on or in insects. [ENTOMO- + -GENOUS]

en·to·mol·o·gise (en′tə mol′ə jīz′), *v.i.,* **-gised, -gis·ing.** *Chiefly Brit.* entomologize.

en·to·mol·o·gize (en′tə mol′ə jīz′), *v.i.,* **-gized, -giz·ing.** **1.** to study entomology. **2.** to gather entomological specimens. [ENTOMOLOG(Y) + -IZE]

en·to·mol·o·gy (en′tə mol′ə jē), *n., pl.* **-gies.** the branch of zoology dealing with insects. [ENTOMO- + -LOGY] —**en·to·mo·log·i·cal** (en′tə mə loj′i kəl), **en′to·mo·log′ic,** *adj.* —**en′to·mo·log′i·cal·ly,** *adv.* —**en′to·mol′o·gist,** *n.*

en·to·moph·a·gous (en′tə mof′ə gəs), *adj.* feeding on insects; insectivorous. [ENTOMO- + -PHAGOUS]

en·to·moph·i·lous (en′tə mof′ə ləs), *adj.* (of a plant) pollinated by insects. [ENTOMO- + -PHILOUS] —**en′to·moph′i·ly,** *n.*

en·to·mos·tra·can (en′tə mos′trə kən), *adj.* **1.** belonging or pertaining to the *Entomostraca.* —*n.* **2.** any small crustacean of the group *Entomostraca,* including the copepods, ostracods, phyllopods, etc. [< NL *entomostrac(a),* neut. pl. (< Gk *entom-* ENTOM- + *óstraka* shells) + -AN] —**en′to·mos′tra·cous,** *adj.*

en·to·phyte (en′tə fīt′), *n.* *Bot.* endophyte. [ENTO- + -PHYTE] —**en·to·phyt·ic** (en′tə fit′ik), *adj.*

en·top·ic (en top′ik), *adj.* *Anat.* being or occurring in the usual place. [< Gk *éntop(os)* in place (see EN-[2], TOPO-) + -IC]

en·tou·rage (än′tōō räzh′; *Fr.* äN tōō RAzh′), *n.* **1.** attendants, as of a person of rank. **2.** surroundings; environment: *a house with a charming entourage of trees and flowers.* **3.** *Archit.* the landscaping and other nearby environmental features shown on a rendering of a building. [< F, equiv. to *entour(er)* (to) surround (deriv. of *entour* around, equiv. to *en* in + *tour* circuit; see TOUR) + *-age* -AGE]

en·to·zo·a (en′tə zō′ə), *n.pl., sing.* **-zo·on** (-zō′on). (*often cap.*) *Biol.* animals, esp. the intestinal worms, living as parasites within the body of the host. [ENTO- + -ZOA] —**en′to·zo′an,** *adj., n.*

en·to·zo·ic (en′tə zō′ik), *adj. Biol.* living parasitically within an animal. Also, **en′to·zo′al.** [ENTOZO(A) + -IC]

en·tr'acte (än trakt′; *Fr.* äN tRAkt′), *n., pl.* **-tr'actes** (-trakts′; *Fr.* -tRAkt′). **1.** the interval between two consecutive acts of a theatrical or operatic performance. **2.** a performance, as of music or dancing, given during such an interval. **3.** a piece of music or the like for such performance. [< F: between-act, equiv. to *entre* between (< L *inter*) + *acte* ACT]

en·tra·da (en trä′thä), *n., pl.* **-das** (-thäs). *Spanish.* **1.** entry; entrance. **2.** entry into an unexplored territory; exploratory expedition.

en·trails (en′trālz, -trəlz), *n.pl.* **1.** the internal parts of the trunk of an animal body. **2.** the intestines. **3.** the internal parts of anything: *the entrails of a machine.* [ME *entrailles* < MF < ML *intrālia*, deriv. of (by dissimilation and syncope) L *interānea* internals, i.e., entrails]

en·train[1] (en trān′), *v.i.* **1.** to go aboard a train. —*v.t.* **2.** to put aboard a train. [EN-[1] + TRAIN] —**en·train′er,** *n.*

en·train[2] (en trān′), *v.t.* **1.** *Chem.* (of a substance, as a vapor) to carry along (a dissimilar substance, as drops of liquid) during a given process, as evaporation or distillation. **2.** (of a liquid) to trap (bubbles) produced either mechanically through turbulence or chemically through a reaction. **3.** *Meteorol.* to transfer (air) into an organized air current from the surrounding atmosphere (opposed to *detrain*). [< MF *entraine(r)*, equiv. to *en-* EN-[1] + *trainer* to drag, trail; see TRAIN]

en·trance[1] (en′trəns), *n.* **1.** the act of entering, as into a place or upon new duties. **2.** a point or place of entering; an opening or passage for entering, as a doorway. **3.** power or liberty of entering; admission: *People improperly dressed will be refused entrance to the theater.* **4.** *Theat.* the moment, or place in the script, at which an actor comes on the stage. **5.** *Music.* **a.** the point in a musical score at which a particular voice or instrument joins the ensemble. **b.** the way in which this is done: *a sloppy entrance.* **6.** a manner or style of entering a room, group, etc.; way of coming on a scene: *She mimicked Joan's entrance.* **7.** *Naut.* the immersed portion of a hull forward of the middle body (opposed to *run*). [ME *entraunce* < MF *entrance.* See ENTER, -ANCE]

—**Syn. 1, 2.** entry, ingress. **3.** ENTRANCE, ADMITTANCE, ADMISSION refer to the possibility of entering a place or a social group. ENTRANCE may refer to either possibility and carries the least suggestion of permission or supervision: *Entrance is by way of the side door; entrance into a card game.* ADMITTANCE refers more to place and suggests entrance that may be permitted or denied: *to gain admittance to a building; no admittance.* ADMISSION refers more to special groups and suggests entrance by payment, by formal or special permission, privilege, and the like: *admission to a concert, a game, to candidacy, the bar, to society.* —**Ant. 2.** exit.

en·trance[2] (en trans′, -träns′), *v.t.,* **-tranced, -tranc·ing. 1.** to fill with delight or wonder; enrapture. **2.** to put into a trance: *to be hypnotically entranced.* [EN-[1] + TRANCE[1]] —**en·trance′ment,** *n.* —**en·tranc′ing·ly,** *adv.*

en′trance cone′, *Aerodynamics.* the part of a wind tunnel that channels air into the testing chamber.

en′trance pal′let, *Horol.* See **receiving pallet.**

en′trance pu′pil, *Optics.* the image of the aperture viewed from the objective of an optical system limiting the rays that enter the system. Cf. **exit pupil.**

en·trance·way (en′trəns wā′), *n.* an entryway. [ENTRANCE[1] + WAY]

en·trant (en′trənt), *n.* **1.** a person who enters. **2.** a new member, as of an association, a university, etc. **3.** a competitor in a contest. [< F, n. use of *entrant* entering, prp. of *entrer* to ENTER]

en·trap (en trap′), *v.t.,* **-trapped, -trap·ping. 1.** to catch in or as in a trap; ensnare: *The hunters used nets to entrap the lion.* **2.** to bring unawares into difficulty or danger: *He entrapped her in the web of her own lies.* **3.** to draw into contradiction or damaging admission: *He entrapped her into an admission of guilt.* [< MF *entrape(r).* See EN-[1], TRAP[1]] —**en·trap′ment,** *n.* —**en·trap′per,** *n.* —**en·trap′ping·ly,** *adv.*

en·treas·ure (en trezh′ər), *v.t.,* **-ured, -ur·ing.** to lay up in or as in a treasury. [EN-[1] + TREASURE]

en·treat (en trēt′), *v.t.* **1.** to ask (a person) earnestly; beseech; implore; beg: *to entreat the king for mercy.* **2.** to ask earnestly for (something): *He entreated help in his work.* —*v.i.* **3.** to make an earnest request or petition. [ME *entrete(n)* < MF *entraite(r)*, *entraitier.* See EN-[1], TREAT] —**en·treat′ing·ly,** *adv.* —**en·treat′ment,** *n.*

—**Syn. 1.** pray, importune, sue, solicit. See **appeal.**

en·treat·y (en trē′tē), *n., pl.* **-treat·ies.** earnest request or petition; supplication. [ENTREAT + -Y[3]]

—**Syn.** appeal, suit, plea, solicitation.

en·tre·chat (*Fr.* äN tRə shA′), *n., pl.* **-chats** (*Fr.* -shA′). *Ballet.* a jump during which the dancer crosses his feet a number of times while in the air. [< F, alter. of It (*capriola*) *intrecciata* intwined (caper), equiv. to *in-* IN-[2] + *trecci-* TRESS + *-ata* -ATE[1]]

en·tre·côte (*Fr.* äN tRə kōt′), *n., pl.* **-côtes** (*Fr.* -kōt′). a steak sliced from between the ribs of a rib roast cut. [< F < L *inter-* INTER- + *costa* rib]

en·trée (än′trā), *n.* **1.** the act of entering; entrance. **2.** the privilege of entering; access. **3.** a means of obtaining entry: *His friendship with an actor's son was his entrée into the theatrical world.* **4.** *U.S.* any food or sometimes any food other than a roast served as the main course of a meal. **5.** a dish served at dinner before the main course or between the regular courses. **6.** the opening section of a ballet. Also, **en′tree.** [< F, n. use of fem. ptp. of *entrer* to enter; see ENTRY]

en·tre·lac (en′trə lak′), *n. Print.* a decorative border of interlaced garlands and leaves. [< F; akin to *entrelacer* to INTERLACE]

en·tre·mets (än′trə mā′; *Fr.* äN tRə me′), *n., pl.* **-mets** (-māz′; *Fr.* -me′). (*construed as sing. or pl.*) **1.** a dish or dishes served at dinner between the principal courses or with the roast; side dish. **2.** the sweet dishes or dessert course served after the cheese. [< F: lit., between-course; OF *entremes.* See INTER-, MESS]

en·trench (en trench′), *v.t.* **1.** to dig trenches for defensive purposes around (oneself, a military position, etc.). **2.** to place in a position of strength; establish firmly or solidly: *safely entrenched behind undeniable facts.* —*v.i.* **3.** to trench or encroach; trespass; infringe (usually fol. by *on* or *upon*): *to entrench on the domain or rights of another.* **4.** *Archaic.* to verge on; approximate; come within the strict definition of (usually fol. by *on* or *upon*). Also, **intrench.** [EN-[1] + TRENCH]

entrench′ing tool′. See **intrenching tool.**

en·trench·ment (en trench′mənt), *n.* **1.** the act of entrenching. **2.** an entrenched position. **3.** Usually, **entrenchments.** an earth breastwork or ditch for protection against enemy fire. Also, **intrenchment.** [ENTRENCH + -MENT]

en·tre nous (än′trə nōō′; *Fr.* äN tRə nōō′), between ourselves; confidentially. [< F]

en·tre·pôt (än′trə pō′; *Fr.* äN tRə pō′), *n., pl.* **-pôts** (-pōz′; *Fr.* -pō′). **1.** a warehouse. **2.** a commercial center where goods are received for distribution, transshipment, or repackaging. Also, **en′tre·pot′.** [< F, equiv. to *entre* INTER- + *pôt* < L *posit(um)*, n. use of neut. ptp. of *pōnere* to put, place (modeled on *dépôt* DEPOT)]

en·tre·pre·neur (än′trə prə nûr′, -nōōr′; *Fr.* äN tRə pRə nœR′), *n., pl.* **-neurs** (-nûrz′, -nōōrz′; *Fr.* -nœR′). **1.** a person who organizes and manages any enterprise, esp. a business, usually with considerable initiative and risk. **2.** an employer of productive labor; contractor. [< F: lit., one who undertakes (some task), equiv. to *entrepren(dre)* (to) undertake (< L *inter-* INTER- + *prendere* to take, var. of *prehendere*) + *-eur* -OR[2]. See ENTERPRISE] —**en′tre·pre·neur′i·al,** *adj.* —**en′tre·pre·neur′ship,** *n.*

en·tre·pre·neuse (än′trə prə nōōz′; *Fr.* äN tRə pRə nœz′), *n., pl.* **-neus·es** (-nōōz′iz; *Fr.* -nœz′). a female entrepreneur. [< F]

en·tre·sol (en′tər sol′, än′trə-; *Fr.* äN tRə sôl′), *n., pl.* **-sols** (-solz′; *Fr.* -sôl′). *Archit.* a low floor between two higher floors, the lower one usually being a ground floor; mezzanine. [< F: lit., between-floor, equiv. to *entre-* INTER- + *sol* floor < L *sol(um)* ground]

en·tro·py (en′trə pē), *n.* **1.** *Thermodynamics.* a quantity, expressed as a function of the temperature, pressure, and density of a system, that is a measure of the amount of energy unavailable for work during a natural process. For a system undergoing a spontaneous change, this quantity increases. *Symbol:* S **2.** the measure of the frequency with which an event occurs within a system; measure of probability in a closed or isolated system. **3.** degree of sameness or similarity: *increased entropy resulting in disorganization.* **4.** homogeneity, uniformity, or lack of distinction or differentiation: *the tendency of the universe toward entropy.* [EN-[2] + -TROPY]

en·trust (en trust′), *v.t.* **1.** to invest with a trust or responsibility; charge with a specified office or duty involving trust: *We entrusted him with our lives.* **2.** to commit (something) in trust to; confide, as for care, use, or performance: *to entrust a secret, money, powers, or work to another.* Also, **intrust.** [EN-[1] + TRUST] —**en·trust′ment,** *n.*

en·try (en′trē), *n., pl.* **-tries. 1.** the act of entering; entrance: *to be forbidden entry.* **2.** a place of ingress or entrance, esp. an entrance hall or vestibule. **3.** permission or right to enter; access. **4.** the act of entering or recording something in a book, register, list, etc. **5.** the statement, item, etc., so entered or recorded. **6.** a person or thing entered in a contest or competition. **7.** *Law.* act of taking possession of lands or tenements by entering or setting foot on them. **8.** the giving of an account of a ship's cargo at a custom house, to obtain permission to land the goods. **9.** *Bookkeeping.* **a.** See **double entry. b.** See **single entry. 10.** Also called **en′try card′.** *Bridge.* a winning card in one's hand or the hand of one's partner that gives the lead to one hand or the other. [ME *entre(e)* < MF *entree* < L *intrāta* (n. use of fem. of *intrātus*, ptp. of *intrāre* to ENTER), equiv. to *intr-* enter + *-āta* -ATE[1]]

en·try·way (en′trē wā′), *n.* a passage for affording entrance. [ENTRY + WAY]

en·twine (en twīn′), *v.t., v.i.,* **-twined, -twin·ing.** to twine with, about, around, or together. Also, **intwine.** [EN-[1] + TWINE[1]] —**en·twine′ment,** *n.*

en·twist (en twist′), *v.t.* to twist together or about. Also, **intwist.** [EN-[1] + TWIST]

e·nu·cle·ate (*v.* i nōō′klē āt′, i nyōō′-; *adj.* i nōō′klē it, -āt′, i nyōō′-), *v.,* **-at·ed, -at·ing,** *adj.* —*v.t.* **1.** *Biol.* to deprive of the nucleus. **2.** to remove (a kernel, tumor, eyeball, etc.) from its enveloping cover. **3.** *Archaic.* to bring out; disclose; explain. —*adj.* **4.** having no nucleus. [< L *ēnucleāt(us)* (ptp. of *ēnucleāre*), equiv. to *ē-* E- + *nucle(us)* NUCLEUS + *-ātus* -ATE[1]] —**e·nu′cle·a′tion,** *n.* —**e·nu′cle·a′tor,** *n.*

E·nu·gu (ā nōō′gōō), *n.* a city in SE Nigeria. 138,457 (1963).

E·num·claw (ē′nəm klô′), *n.* a town in central Washington. 3269 (1960).

e·nu·mer·a·ble (i nōō′mər ə bəl, i nyōō′-), *adj.* countable (def. 2b). [ENUMER(ATE) + -ABLE] —**e·nu′mer·a·bly,** *adv.*

e·nu·mer·ate (i nōō′mə rāt′, i nyōō′-), *v.t.,* **-at·ed, -at·ing. 1.** to mention separately as if in counting; name one by one; specify, as in a list: *Let me enumerate the several flaws in your hypothesis.* **2.** to ascertain the number of; count. [< L *ēnumerāt(us)* (ptp. of *ēnumerāre*), equiv. to *ē-* E- + *numer(us)* NUMBER + *-ātus* -ATE[1]] —**e·nu·mer·a·tive** (i nōō′mə rā′tiv, -mər ə-, i nyōō′-), *adj.* —**e·nu′mer·a′tor,** *n.*

—**Syn. 1.** recapitulate, recount.

e·nu·mer·a·tion (i nōō′mə rā′shən, i nyōō′-), *n.* **1.** the act of enumerating. **2.** a catalog or list. [< L *ēnumerātiōn-* (s. of *ēnumerātiō*). See ENUMERATE, -ION]

e·nun·ci·ate (i nun′sē āt′, -shē-), *v.,* **-at·ed, -at·ing.** —*v.t.* **1.** to utter or pronounce (words, sentences, etc.), esp. in an articulate or a particular manner: *He enunciates his words distinctly.* **2.** to state or declare definitely, as a theory. **3.** to announce or proclaim: *to enunciate one's intentions.* —*v.i.* **4.** to pronounce words, esp. in an articulate or a particular manner. [< L *ēnuntiāt(us)* (ptp. of *ēnuntiāre*), equiv. to *ē-* E- + *nunti(us)* messenger, message + *-ātus* -ATE[1]] —**e·nun′ci·a·ble,** *adj.* —**e·nun′ci·a·bil′i·ty,** *n.* —**e·nun′ci·a′tive, e·nun′ci·a·to′ry,** *adj.* —**e·nun′ci·a′tive·ly,** *adv.* —**e·nun′ci·a′tor,** *n.*

e·nun·ci·a·tion (i nun′sē ā′shən, -shē-), *n.* **1.** the act or the manner of enunciating. **2.** utterance or pronunciation. **3.** a formal announcement or statement: *the enunciation of a doctrine.* [< L *ēnuntiātiōn-* (s. of *ēnuntiātiō*). See ENUNCIATE, -ION]

en·ure (en yŏŏr′), *v.t., v.i.,* **-ured, -ur·ing.** inure.

en·u·re·sis (en′yə rē′sis), *n. Med.* involuntary discharge of urine; bed-wetting; incontinence. [< NL < Gk *en-* EN-[2] + *ourē-* (s. of *ourein* to urinate) + *-sis* -SIS] —**en·u·ret·ic** (en′yə ret′ik), *adj.*

en·vel·op (en vel′əp), *v.,* **-oped, -op·ing,** *n.* —*v.t.* **1.** to wrap up in or as in a covering: *The long cloak she was wearing enveloped her completely.* **2.** to serve as a wrapping or covering for, as a membrane of an organ, a sheath, etc. **3.** to surround entirely: *Our troops enveloped the enemy.* —*n.* **4.** envelope. [ME *envolupe(n)* < OF *envoluper*, by dissimilation < L *involvere* to wrap up. See INVOLVE] —**en·vel′op·er,** *n.*

—**Syn. 1.** enfold, cover, hide, conceal. **3.** encompass, enclose.

en·ve·lope (en′və lōp′, än′-), *n.* **1.** a flat paper container, as for a letter, thin package, etc., usually having a means of sealing, esp. a gummed flap. **2.** that which envelops; a wrapper, integument, or surrounding cover. **3.** *Bot.* a surrounding or enclosing part, as of leaves. **4.** *Geom.* a curve or surface tangent to each member of a set of curves or surfaces. **5.** *Radio.* (of a modulated carrier wave) a curve connecting the peaks of a graph of the instantaneous value of the electric or magnetic component of the carrier wave as a function of time. **6.** the fabric structure enclosing the gasbag of an aerostat. **7.** the gasbag itself. **8.** *Electronics.* the airtight glass or metal housing of a vacuum tube. Also, **envelop.** [< F *enveloppe*; see ENVELOP]

en′velope chemise′, teddy.

en′velope ta′ble, a table having an envelope top.

en′velope top′, a square top to a table or cabinet having four leaves, in the form of right triangles, folding out to double the area of the top.

en·vel·op·ment (en vel′əp mənt), *n.* **1.** the act of enveloping. **2.** the state of being enveloped. **3.** a wrapping or covering. [ENVELOP + -MENT]

en·ven·om (en ven′əm), *v.t.* **1.** to impregnate with venom; make poisonous. **2.** to embitter. [ME *envenime(n)* < OF *envenime(r).* See EN-[1], VENOM]

En·ver Pa·sha (en veR′ pä shä′), 1881–1922, Turkish soldier and statesman.

en·vi·a·ble (en′vē ə bəl), *adj.* to be envied; worthy of envy; very desirable: *the supposedly enviable lot of the very rich.* [ENVY + -ABLE] —**en′vi·a·ble·ness,** *n.* —**en′vi·a·bly,** *adv.*

en·vi·ous (en′vē əs), *adj.* **1.** full of, feeling, or expressing envy: *envious of a person's success; an envious attack.* **2.** *Obs.* emulous. [ME < AF; OF *envieus* < L *invidiōs(us)* INVIDIOUS] —**en′vi·ous·ly,** *adv.* —**en′vi·ous·ness,** *n.*

en·vi·ron (en vī′rən, -vī′ərn), *v.t.* to form a circle or ring round; surround; envelop: *a house environed by pleasant grounds; to be environed by bad influences.* [ME *enviroune(n)* < OF *environne(r)*, deriv. of *environ* around (*en* in + *viron* a circle)]

en·vi·ron·ment (en vī′rən mənt, -vī′ərn-), *n.* **1.** the aggregate of surrounding things, conditions, or influences, esp. as affecting the existence or development of someone or something. **2.** the act of environing. **3.** the state of being environed. **4.** that which environs. [ENVIRON + -MENT] —**en·vi′ron·men′tal,** *adj.* —**en·vi′ron·men′tal·ly,** *adv.*

en·vi·ron·men·tal·ist (en vī′rən men′tə list), *n.* **1.** an expert on environmental problems. **2.** any person who advocates or works to protect the air, water, animals, plants, and other natural resources from pollution or its effects. [ENVIRONMENTAL + -IST] —**en·vi′ron·men′tal·ism,** *n.*

environmen′tal resist′ance, the limiting effect of environmental conditions on the numerical growth of a population.

en·vi·rons (en vī′rənz, -vī′ərnz, en′vər ənz, -vī ərnz), *n.pl.* surrounding parts or districts, as of a city; outskirts; suburbs. [< F (pl.); r. ME *environ* < OF n.pl. use of ENVIRON]

en·vis·age (en viz′ij), *v.t.,* **-aged, -ag·ing. 1.** to contemplate; visualize: *He envisages an era of even greater scientific discovery and advancement than has been seen in the past.* **2.** *Archaic.* to look in the face of; face. [< F *envisage(r).* See EN-[1], VISAGE] —**en·vis′age·ment,** *n.*

en·vi·sion (en vizh′ən), *v.t.* to picture mentally, esp. some future event or events: *to envision a bright future.* [EN-[1] + VISION]

en·voy[1] (en′voi, än′-), *n.* **1.** a diplomatic agent. **2.** any accredited messenger or representative. **3.** Also called **en′voy extraor′dinary and min′ister plenipoten′tiary.** a diplomatic agent of the second rank, next in dignity after an ambassador. [< F *envoyé* envoy (n. use of ptp. of *envoyer* to send) < LL *inviāt(us)* sent on a journey (lit., way, road), equiv. to *inviā-* be on the road + *-tus* ptp. suffix]

en·voy[2] (en′voi), *n.* a short stanza concluding a poem in certain archaic metrical forms, as a ballade, and serving as a dedication, or a similar postscript to a prose composition. Also, **en′voi.** [ME *envoye* < OF, deriv. of *envoyer* to send; see ENVOY[1]]

en·vy (en′vē), *n., pl.* **-vies,** *v.,* **-vied, -vy·ing.** —*n.* **1.** a feeling of discontent or jealousy, usually with ill will, at seeing another's superiority, advantages, or success. **2.** desire for some advantage possessed by another. **3.** an object of envious feeling: *Her looks made her the envy of her sisters.* **4.** *Obs.* ill will. —*v.t.* **5.** to regard with envy; be envious of: *He envies her the position she has achieved in her profession.* —*v.i.* **6.** *Obs.* to be affected with envy. [ME *envie* < OF < L *invidia*, equiv. to *invid(us)* envious (deriv. of *invidēre* to envy; see INVIDIOUS) + *-ia* -Y[3]] —**en′vi·er,** *n.* —**en′vy·ing·ly,** *adv.*

—**Syn. 1.** jealousy, enviousness, covetousness. **5.** resent. ENVY, BEGRUDGE, COVET refer to one's attitude concerning the possessions or attainments of others. To ENVY is to feel resentful, spiteful, and unhappy because someone else possesses, or has achieved, what one wishes oneself to possess, or to have achieved: *to envy the wealthy, a girl's beauty, an honest man's reputation.* To BEGRUDGE is simply to be unwilling that another should have the possessions, honors, or credit he deserves: *to* *begrudge a man a reward for heroism.* To COVET is to long jealously to possess what someone else possesses: *I covet your silverware.*

en·weave (en wēv′), *v.t.*, **-wove** or **-weaved, -wo·ven** or **-wove** or **-weaved, -weav·ing.** inweave.

en·wind (en wīnd′), *v.t.*, **-wound, -wind·ing.** to wind or coil about; encircle. Also, **inwind.** [EN-[1] + WIND[2]]

en·womb (en wōōm′), *v.t.* to enclose in or as in the womb. [EN-[1] + WOMB]

en·wrap (en rap′), *v.t.*, **-wrapped, -wrap·ping. 1.** to wrap or envelop in something: *fruit enwrapped in leaves.* **2.** to surround or envelop, as in slumber, longing, etc. **3.** to absorb or engross, as in thought. Also, **inwrap.** [ME; see EN-[1], WRAP]

en·wreathe (en rēth′), *v.t.*, **-wreathed, -wreath·ing.** to surround with or as with a wreath. Also, **inwreathe.** [EN-[1] + WREATHE]

en·wrought (en rôt′), *adj.* inwrought.

En·y·a·li·us (en′ē ā′lē əs), *n. Class. Myth.* an epithet of Ares, meaning "slayer of heroes."

E·ny·eus (i nī′yōōs), *n.* (in the *Iliad*) a king of Scyrus.

E·ny·o (i nī′ō), *n.* an ancient Greek war goddess and companion of Ares, identified by the Romans with Bellona.

en·zo·ot·ic (en′zō ot′ik), *adj. Vet. Med.* **1.** (of diseases) prevailing among or afflicting animals in a particular locality. Cf. **endemic.** —*n.* **2.** an enzootic disease. Also, **en′zo·öt′ic.** [EN-[2] + ZO- + -OTIC, modeled on *epizootic*] —**en′zo·ot′i·cal·ly, en′zo·öt′i·cal·ly,** *adv.*

enzoot′ic atax′ia, sway-back (def. 2). Also, **en·zoöt′ic atax′ia.**

en·zy·got·ic (en′zī got′ik, -zi-), *adj.* developed from a single fertilized ovum, as identical twins; monozygotic. [EN-[1] + ZYGOTIC]

en·zy·mat·ic (en′zī mat′ik, -zi-), *adj.* of or pertaining to an enzyme. Also, **en·zy·mic** (en zī′mik, -zim′ik). [ENZYME + -ATIC] —**en′zy·mat′i·cal·ly, en·zy′mi·cal·ly,** *adv.*

en·zyme (en′zīm), *n. Biochem.* any of various complex organic substances, as pepsin, originating from living cells and capable of producing certain chemical changes in organic substances by catalytic action, as in digestion; unorganized ferment. [< MGk *énzym(os)* leavened (Gk *en-* EN-[2] + *zȳm(ē)* leaven + *-os* adj. suffix)]

en·zy·mol·o·gy (en′zī mol′ə jē, -zi-), *n.* the science that deals with the chemistry, biochemistry, and biology of enzymes. [ENZYME + -O- + -LOGY] —**en′zy·mol′o·gist,** *n.*

en·zy·mol·y·sis (en′zī mol′i sis, -zi-), *n. Biochem.* the decomposition of a chemical compound catalyzed by the presence of an enzyme. [ENZYME + -O- + -LYSIS] —**en·zy·mo·lyt·ic** (en′zə mə lit′ik), *adj.*

eo-, a learned borrowing from Greek meaning "early," "primeval," used in the formation of compound words: *Eocene; eohippus.* [< Gk, comb. form of *ēōs* dawn. See EAST, AURORA]

e.o., ex officio.

E·o·cene (ē′ə sēn′), *Geol.* —*adj.* **1.** noting or pertaining to an epoch either of the Tertiary or Paleogene period, occurring from 40,000,000 to 60,000,000 years ago and characterized by the presence of all modern mammals. See table under **era.** —*n.* **2.** the Eocene period or series. [EO- + -CENE]

E·o·gene (ē′ə jēn′), *adj., n. Geol. Obs.* Paleogene.

e·o·hip·pus (ē′ō hip′əs), *n.* a fossil horse of the genus *Eohippus,* from the early Eocene epoch of the western U.S., having four hoofed toes on each forefoot and three on each hind foot. [< NL, equiv. to *eo-* EO- + Gk *híppos* horse]

Eohippus
(9 in. high at shoulder; length 18 in.)

E·o·lan·de (ē′ō lan′də, yō lan′-), *n.* a girl's given name. Also, **Yolande, Yolanda.**

E·o·li·an (ē ō′lē ən), *adj.* **1.** (*l.c.*) *Geol.* noting or pertaining to sand or rock material carried or arranged by the wind. **2.** Aeolian. —*n.* **3.** Aeolian (def. 3).

E·ol·ic (ē ol′ik), *n., adj.* Aeolian. Also, **Aeolic.**

E·o·line (ē′ə lēn′, -līn′), *n.* a girl's given name.

e·o·lith (ē′ə lith), *n.* a chipped flint, shaped probably by natural agencies, thought to have been used as an implement by early man. [EO- + -LITH]

e·o·lith·ic (ē′ə lith′ik), *adj.* of, pertaining to, or characteristic of the earliest stage of human culture, marked chiefly by the use of eoliths. [EOLITH + -IC]

e.o.m., *Chiefly Com.* end of the month.

e·on (ē′ən, ē′on), *n.* **1.** Also, **aeon.** the largest division of geologic time comprising two or more eras. **2.** aeon (def. 1).

e·o·ni·an (ē ō′nē ən), *adj.* aeonian.

e·on·ism (ē′ə niz′əm), *n. Psychiatry.* the adoption of feminine mannerisms, clothing, etc., by a male. [after the Chevalier d'*Éon* (d. 1810), Frenchman who posed as a woman]

e·o no·mi·ne (ē′ō nō′mi ne′; *Eng.* ē′ō nom′i nē), *Latin.* by that name.

E·os (ē′os), *n.* the ancient Greek goddess of the dawn, identified by the Romans with Aurora.

e·o·sin (ē′ə sin), *n. Chem.* **1.** Also called **bromeosin, tetrabromofluorescein.** a red, crystalline, water-insoluble solid, $C_{20}H_8Br_4O_5$, derived from fluorescein by bromination: used chiefly for dyeing silk a rose red color. **2.** any of a variety of eosinlike dyes. Also, **e·o·sine** (ē′ə-sin, -sēn′). [< Gk *ēōs* dawn (see EO-) + -IN[2]] —**e′o·sin′ic,** *adj.* —**e′o·sin·like′,** *adj.*

e·o·sin·o·phil (ē′ə sin′ə fil), *n.* **1.** *Biol.* an eosinophilic cell, tissue, organism, or substance. **2.** *Anat.* a leukocyte having a bean-shaped or lobate nucleus and eosinophilic granules in the cytoplasm. —*adj.* **3.** *Biol.* eosinophilic. Also, **e·o·sin·o·phile** (ē′ə sin′ə fīl′). [EOSIN + -O- + -PHIL(E)]

e·o·sin·o·phil·i·a (ē′ə sin′ə fil′ē ə, -fēl′yə), *n. Med.* the presence of an abnormally increased number of eosinophils in the blood. [< NL; see EOSINOPHIL, -IA]

e·o·sin·o·phil·ic (ē′ə sin′ə fil′ik), *adj. Biol.* having an affinity for eosin and other acid dyes. Also, **e·o·si·noph·i·lous** (ē′ə si nof′ə ləs), **eosinophil.** [EOSINOPHIL + -IC]

Eöt′vös tor′sion bal′ance (ut′vush, et′-), a torsion balance for measuring horizontal gradients of gravity, used in geophysical explorations for determining variations in density of subterranean rock bodies. [named after Roland *Eötvös* (1848–1919), Hungarian physicist]

Eöt′vös u′nit, a unit of measure of horizontal gradients of gravity, equal to one billionth of a gal per horizontal centimeter. [see EÖTVÖS TORSION BALANCE]

-eous, var. of **-ous,** occurring in adjectives borrowed from Latin or (infrequently) derived from Latin nouns: *arboreous.* [< L *-e(us)* adj. suffix + -OUS]

E·o·zo·ic (ē′ə zō′ik), *adj. Geol. Obs.* noting or pertaining to a period of the Precambrian era preceding the Azoic: created when fossils were found in Azoic rock to cover the time preceding the first life. [EO- + ZO- + -IC]

ep-, var. of **epi-** before a vowel or *h: epaxial.*

EP, See **extended play.**

Ep., Epistle.

EPA, Environmental Protection Agency: an independent U.S. federal agency, created in 1970, that establishes and controls rules and standards for protecting the environment and controlling pollution.

e·pact (ē′pakt), *n.* **1.** the difference in days between a solar year and a lunar year. **2.** the age in days of the calendar moon at the beginning of the year starting on January 1. [< LL *epacta* < Gk *epaktḗ,* n. use of fem. of *epaktós* added, equiv. to *ep-* EP- + *ag-* (s. of *ágein* to lead) + *-t-* ptp. suffix + *-os* adj. suffix]

ep·a·go·ge (ep′ə gō′jē), *n. Logic.* induction of a general proposition from particular propositions. [< Gk: a bringing to, argument by induction, equiv. to *ep-* EP- + *agōgḗ* guide, method (deriv. of *ágein* to lead)] —**ep·a·gog·ic** (ep′ə goj′ik), *adj.*

E·pam·i·non·das (i pam′ə non′dəs), *n.* 418?–362 B.C., Theban general and statesman.

ep·a·naph·o·ra (ep′ə naf′ər ə), *n. Rhet.* anaphora (def. 1). [< Gk: referring, reference. See EP-, ANAPHORA]

e·pan·o·dos (i pan′ə dos′), *n. Rhet.* **1.** the repetition of a group of words in reverse order. **2.** the recapitulation of the main ideas of a speech, esp. in the reverse order. **3.** the resumption of the main thread of a speech after a digression. [< Gk: recapitulation, rising, return, equiv. to *ep-* EP- + *an(a)-* ANA- + *(h)odós* way, road, path]

ep·a·nor·tho·sis (ep′ə nôr thō′sis), *n., pl.* **-ses** (-sēz). *Rhet.* the rephrasing of an immediately preceding word or statement for the purpose of intensification, emphasis, or justification, as in "Seems, madam! Nay, it is; I know not 'seems.'" [< Gk: correcting, revision. See EP-, ANA-, ORTHOSIS]

ep·arch (ep′ärk), *n.* **1.** the prefect or governor of an eparchy. **2.** *Gk. Ch.* a bishop or metropolitan of an eparchy. [< Gk *éparch(os)* commander, governor, prefect. See EP-, -ARCH]

ep·ar·chy (ep′är kē), *n., pl.* **-chies. 1.** (in modern Greece) one of the administrative subdivisions of a province. **2.** (in ancient Greece) a province. [< Gk *eparchía* prefecture, province. See EPARCH, -Y[3]] —**ep·ar′chi·al,** *adj.*

é·paule·ment (*Fr.* ā pōl mäN′), *n., pl.* **-ments** (*Fr.* -mäN′). *Ballet.* a position in which the shoulders are at right angles to the direction of the supporting leg, with one shoulder thrust forward and one back. [< F, equiv. to *épaule* (see EPAULET) + *-ment* -MENT]

ep·au·let (ep′ə let′, -lit, ep′ə let′), *n.* an ornamental shoulder piece worn on uniforms, chiefly by army and navy officers. Also, **ep′au·lette′.** [< F *épaulette,* equiv. to *épaule* shoulder (< L *spatula* blade; see SPATULA) + *-ette* -ET]

ep′aulette tree′, a tree, *Pterostyrax hispida,* of China and Japan, having fragrant, white, hanging clusters of flowers from seven to ten inches long.

é·pau·lière (ā′pōl yâr′; *Fr.* ā pō lyer′), *n., pl.* **é·pau·lières** (ā′pōl yârz′; *Fr.* ā pō lyer′). *Armor.* pauldron. [< F, equiv. to *épaule* shoulder + *-ière* agent suffix; see -IER]

ep·ax·i·al (ep ak′sē əl), *adj. Anat.* above or posterior to an axis. [EP- + AXIAL] —**ep·ax′i·al·ly,** *adv.*

é·pée (ā pā′), *n. Fencing.* **1.** a rapier with a three-sided blade and a guard over the tip. **2.** the art or sport of fencing with the épée, points being made by touching any part of the opponent's body with the tip of the weapon. Also, **e·pee′.** [< F: sword < L *spatha* sword < Gk *spáthē* blade. See SPADE[1]]

é·pée·ist (ā pā′ist), *n. Fencing.* a person who fences with an épée. [< F *épéiste.* See ÉPÉE, -IST]

e·pei·ric (i pī′rik), *adj.* extending inland from a continental margin: *an epeiric sea.* [< Gk *ḗpeir(os)* mainland, continent + -IC]

ep·ei·rog·e·ny (ep′ī roj′ə nē), *n. Geol.* vertical or tilting movement of the earth crust, generally affecting broad areas of a continent. Also, **e·pei·ro·gen·e·sis** (i pī′rō jen′i sis), **epirogeny.** [< Gk *ḗpeiro(s)* mainland, continent + -GENY] —**e·pei·ro·gen·ic** (i pī′rō jen′ik), **e·pei·ro·ge·net·ic** (i pī′rō jə net′ik), *adj.*

ep·ei·so·di·on (ep′ī sō′dē on′), *n., pl.* **-di·a** (-dē ə). *Greek.* (in ancient Greek drama) a dramatic interlude or section alternating with the *stasimon,* esp. in tragedy, varying in number from three to six and containing the main action of the drama. Also, **episode.**

ep·en·ceph·a·lon (ep′en sef′ə lon′), *n., pl.* **-lons, -la** (-lə). *Anat.* the hindbrain. [EP- + ENCEPHALON] —**ep·en·ce·phal·ic** (ep′ən sə fal′ik), *adj.*

ep·en·dy·ma (e pen′də mə), *n. Anat.* a membrane lining the canal of the spinal cord and the ventricles of the brain. [< Gk: a covering, garment, equiv. to *ependý(ein)* (to) put on, over (*ep-* EP- + *en-* on + *dýein* to put on) + *-ma* suffix of result] —**ep·en·dy·mal, ep·en·dy·mar·y** (e pen′də mer′ē), *adj.*

ep·en·the·sis (e pen′thi sis), *n., pl.* **-ses** (-sēz′). the insertion of one or more sounds in the middle of a word, as the schwa in the substandard pronunciation (el′əm) of *elm.* [< LL: insertion of a letter < Gk, equiv. to *ep-* EP- + *en-* on + *thésis* placing; see THESIS] —**ep·en·thet·ic** (ep′ən thet′ik), *adj.*

e·pergne (i pûrn′, ā pârn′), *n.* an ornamental piece for the center of a dinner table, often elaborate in design, for holding fruit, flowers, etc. [? < F *épargne* treasury, saving, deriv. of *épargner* to save < Gmc; cf. G *sparen* to save]

E·pe·us (i pē′əs), *n. Class. Myth.* **1.** a son of Panopeus who was noted for his cowardice. With the help of Athena, he built the Trojan Horse. **2.** a son of Endymion who succeeded his father as king in the Peloponnesus.

ep·ex·e·ge·sis (ep ek′si jē′sis), *n., pl.* **-ses** (-sēz). *Rhet.* **1.** the addition of a word or words to explain a preceding word or sentence. **2.** the word or words so added. [< Gk: explanation. See EP-, EXEGESIS]

ep·ex·e·get·ic (ep ek′si jet′ik), *adj.* of, serving as, or like an epexegesis. Also, **ep·ex′e·get′i·cal.** [< Gk *epexēgētik(ós).* See EPEXEGESIS, -TIC] —**ep·ex′e·get′i·cal·ly,** *adv.*

eph-, var. of **epi-** before an aspirate: *ephedrine.*

Eph., Ephesians.

e·phah (ē′fə), *n.* a Hebrew unit of dry measure, equal to about a bushel. Also, **e′pha.** [< Heb]

e·phebe (i fēb′, ef′ēb), *n.* (among the ancient Greeks) a youth just entering upon manhood or just enrolled as a citizen. Also, **ephebos, ephebus.** [< L *ephēb(us)* < Gk *éphēbos,* equiv. to *ep-* EP- + *hḗbē* manhood] —**e·phe′bic,** *adj.*

eph·e·bei·on (ef′ə bī′on), *n., pl.* **-bei·a** (-bī′ə). (in ancient Greek and Roman architecture) a place for gymnastic exercises. [<Gk, equiv. to *éphēb(os)* EPHEBE + *-ion* suffix of place]

eph·e·be·um (ef′ə bē′əm), *n., pl.* **-be·a** (-bē′ə). ephebeion.

e·phe·bos (i fē′bos), *n., pl.* **-boi** (-boi). ephebe.

e·phe·bus (i fē′bəs), *n., pl.* **-bi** (-bī). ephebe.

e·phed·rine (i fed′rin; *Chem.* ef′i drēn′, -drin), *n. Pharm.* a white, crystalline alkaloid, $C_6H_5CHOHCH(CH_3)NHCH_3$, obtained from species of *Ephedra,* or synthesized: used in medicine chiefly for the treatment of asthma, hay fever, and colds. [< NL *Ephedr(a)* name of the genus, L: the plant horsetail < Gk: horsetail, sitting on (*eph-* EPH- + *hédra* seat, chair) + -INE[2]]

e·phem·er·a (i fem′ər ə), *n., pl.* **-er·as, -er·ae** (-ə rē′). **1.** anything short-lived or transitory: *the ephemeras of fashion.* **2.** an ephemerid. [< Gk, neut. pl. of *ephḗmeros,* taken as sing.; see EPHEMERAL]

e·phem·er·al (i fem′ər əl), *adj.* **1.** lasting a very short time; short-lived; transitory: *the ephemeral joys of childhood.* **2.** lasting but one day: *an ephemeral flower.* —*n.* **3.** an ephemeral entity, as certain insects. [< Gk *ephḗmer(os)* short-lived, lasting but a day (*ep-* EP- + *hēmér(a)* day + *-os* adj. suffix) + -AL[1]] —**e·phem′er·al·ly,** *adv.* —**e·phem′er·al·ness,** *n.*
—**Syn. 1.** fleeting, evanescent, transient, momentary, brief. —**Ant. 1.** permanent.

e·phem·er·al·i·ty (i fem′ə ral′i tē), *n., pl.* **-ties** for **2. 1.** the quality or condition of being ephemeral. **2.** something transitory. [EPHEMERAL + -ITY]

e·phem·er·id (i fem′ər id), *n.* an insect of the order *Ephemeroptera,* comprising the mayflies. [< NL *Ephēmerid(ae).* See EPHEMERAL, -ID[2]]

e·phem·er·is (i fem′ər is), *n., pl.* **e·phe·mer·i·des** (ef′ə mer′i dēz′). **1.** a table showing the positions of a heavenly body on a number of dates in a regular sequence. **2.** an astronomical almanac containing such tables. **3.** *Obs.* an almanac or calendar. [< L: day book, diary < Gk: diary, account book, deriv. of *ephḗmeros;* see EPHEMERAL]

ephem′eris sec′ond, *Astron.* the unit of ephemeris time, defined as a precise fraction of the length of the tropical year 1900.

ephem′eris time′, *Astron.* time measured by the orbital movements of the earth, the moon, and the planets.

e·phem·er·on (i fem′ə ron′, -ər ən), *n., pl.* **-er·a** (-ər-ə), **-er·ons.** anything short-lived or ephemeral. [< Gk: short-lived insect, n. use of neut. of *ephḗmeros;* see EPHEMERAL]

Ephes., Ephesians.

E·phe·sian (i fē′zhən), *adj.* **1.** of or pertaining to Ephesus. —*n.* **2.** a native or inhabitant of Ephesus. [< L *Ephesi(us)* (< Gk *Ephésios*) + -AN]

E·phe·sians (i fē′zhənz), *n.* (*construed as sing.*) a book of the New Testament, written by Paul.

Eph·e·sus (ef′i səs), *n.* an ancient city in W Asia Minor, S of Smyrna: famous temple of Artemis, or Diana; early Christian community.

Eph·i·al·tes (ef′ē al′tēz), *n. Class. Myth.* **1.** a son of Poseidon. **2.** one of the Gigantes.

e·phip·pi·um (i fip′ē əm), *n., pl.* **e·phip·pi·a** (i fip′ē ə). *Zool.* a thick shell, consisting of two chitinous plates, which encloses and protects the winter eggs of a cladoceran. [< NL < Gk *ephíppion,* n. use of neut. of *ephíppios* for putting on a horse, equiv. to *epi-* EPI- + *-hippios,* deriv. of *híppos* horse] —**e·phip′pi·al,** *adj.*

eph·od (ef′od, ē′fod), *n. Judaism.* a richly embroidered, apronlike vestment having two shoulder straps and ornamental attachments for securing the breastplate, worn with a waistband by the high priest. Ex. 28:6, 7, 25–28. [ME < ML < Heb *ēphōd,* appar. meaning "idol" in some passages]

eph·or (ef′ôr, ef′ər), *n., pl.* **-ors, -or·i** (-ə rī′). one of a body of magistrates in various ancient Dorian states, esp. at Sparta, where a body of five was annually elected by the people. [< L *ephor(us)* < Gk *éphoros* overseer, guardian, ruler (cf. *ephorân* to look over, equiv. to *ep-* EP- + *horân* to see, look)] —**eph′or·al,** *adj.* —**eph·or·ate** (ef′ə rāt′, -ər it), **eph·or·al·ty** (ef′ər əl-tē), *n.*

Eph·ra·e·mi Sy·ri (ef′ri ē′mī sī′rī), the Greek uncial codex, dating from the early 5th century A.D., that contains portions of the Old and New Testaments. Also called **Ephrae′mi Re·scrip′tus** (ri skrip′təs). Cf. **codex** (def. 2).

E·phra·im (ē′frē əm, ē′frəm), *n.* **1.** the younger son of Joseph. Gen. 41:52. **2.** the tribe of Israel traditionally descended from him. Gen. 48:1. **3.** the Biblical kingdom of the Hebrews in N Palestine, including ten of the twelve tribes. Cf. **Judah** (def. 3). **4.** a boy's given name. [< LL < Gk < Heb *Ephrajim* very fruitful]

E·phra·im·ite (ē′frē ə mīt′), *n.* **1.** a member of the tribe of Ephraim. **2.** an inhabitant of the Northern kingdom of Israel. —*adj.* **3.** Also, **E·phra·i·mit·ic** (ē′-frē ə mit′ik). of or pertaining to the tribe of Ephraim or the Ephraimites. [EPHRAIM + -ITE[1]]

E·phra·ta (ē frā′tə), *n.* **1.** a town in SE Pennsylvania. 7688 (1960). **2.** a town in central Washington. 6548 (1960).

epi-, a prefix occurring in loan words from Greek, where it meant "upon," "on," "over," "near," "at," "before," "after" (*epicedium*); on this model, used in the formation of new compound words (*epicardium*). Also, **ep-, eph-**. [<Gk, comb. form of *epí*, prep. and adv.]

Ep·i·ba·te·ri·us (ep′ə bə tēr′ē əs), *n.* *Class. Myth.* an epithet of Apollo, meaning "seafaring."

ep·i·blast (ep′ə blast′), *n.* *Embryol.* **1.** the ectoderm. **2.** the primordial outer layer of a young embryo before the segregation of the germ layers, capable of becoming the ectoderm and containing cells capable of becoming the mesoderm and entoderm. [EPI- + -BLAST] —**ep′i·blas′tic,** *adj.*

e·pib·o·ly (i pib′ə lē), *n., pl.* **-lies.** *Embryol.* the growth of one part so that it overlies or surrounds another, as in the formation of certain gastrulas. [< Gk *epibolḗ* a throwing on, equiv. to *epi-* EPI- + *bol-* (var. s. of *bállein* to throw) + *-ē* n. suffix] —**ep·i·bol·ic** (ep′ə bol′ik), *adj.*

ep·ic (ep′ik), *adj.* Also, **ep′i·cal. 1.** noting or pertaining to a poetic composition, usually centered upon a hero, in which a series of great achievements or events is narrated continuously and at length in elevated style: *Homer's* Iliad *is an epic poem.* **2.** resembling or suggesting such poetry: *an epic novel on the founding of the country.* **3.** heroic; majestic; impressively great: *the epic events of the war.* **4.** of unusual size or extent: *a crime wave of epic proportions.* —*n.* **5.** an epic poem. **6.** epic poetry. **7.** any composition resembling an epic. **8.** something worthy to form the subject of an epic: *The defense of the Alamo is an American epic.* **9.** (*cap.*) Also called **Old Ionic.** the Greek dialect represented in the *Iliad* and the *Odyssey*, apparently Aeolic modified by Ionic. [< L *epic(us)* < Gk *epikós.* See EPOS, -IC] —**ep′ic·like′,** *adj.*

A, Epicalyx
B, Calyx

ep·i·ca·lyx (ep′ə kā′liks, -kal′iks), *n., pl.* **-ca·lyx·es, -ca·ly·ces** (-kā′li sēz′, -kal′i-). *Bot.* an involucre resembling an outer calyx, as in the mallow. [EPI- + CALYX]

ep·i·can·thus (ep′ə kan′thəs), *n., pl.* **-thi** (-thī, -thē). *Anat.* a fold of skin extending from the eyelid over the inner canthus of the eye, common in members of the Mongolian race. Also called **mongolian fold.** [< NL; see EPI-, CANTHUS] —**ep′i·can′thic,** *adj.*

ep·i·car·di·um (ep′ə kär′dē əm), *n., pl.* **-di·a** (-dē ə). *Anat.* the inner serous layer of the pericardium, lying directly upon the heart. [< NL, equiv. to *epi-* EPI- + *-cardium*, comb. form repr. Gk *kardía* heart] —**ep′i·car′di·al, ep′i·car′di·ac′,** *adj.*

ep·i·carp (ep′ə kärp′), *n.* *Bot.* the outermost layer of a pericarp, as the rind or peel of certain fruits. See diag. under **pericarp.** [EPI- + -CARP]

Ep·i·cas·te (ep′ə kas′tē), *n.* *Homeric Legend.* Jocasta.

ep·i·ce·di·um (ep′i sē′dē əm, -si dī′əm), *n., pl.* **-se·di·a** (-sē′dē ə, -si dī′ə). a funeral song; dirge. [< L < Gk *epikḗdeion*, n. use of neut. of *epikḗdeios* of a funeral, equiv. to *epi-* EPI- + *kēde-* (s. of *kēdos* care, sorrow) + *-ion* neut. n. suffix] —**ep′i·ce′di·al, ep′i·ce′di·an,** *adj.*

ep·i·cene (ep′i sēn′), *adj.* **1.** belonging to, or partaking of the characteristics of, both sexes: *Fashions in clothing are becoming increasingly epicene.* **2.** flaccid; feeble; weak: *an epicene style of writing.* **3.** effeminate; nonmasculine. **4.** (of Greek and Latin nouns) of the same gender class regardless of the sex of the being referred to, as Latin *vulpēs* "fox or vixen" is always grammatically feminine. —*n.* **5.** one who or that which is epicene. [ME < L *epicoen(us)* of both genders < Gk *epíkoinos* common to many, equiv. to *epi-* EPI- + *koinós* common] —**ep′i·cen′ism,** *n.*

ep·i·cen·ter (ep′i sen′tər), *n.* *Geol.* a point, directly above the true center of disturbance, from which the shock waves of an earthquake apparently radiate. Also, *Brit.*, **epicentrum, ep′i·cen′tre.** [< NL *epicentr(um)* < Gk *epíkentros* on the center. See EPI-, CENTER] —**ep′i·cen′tral,** *adj.*

ep·i·cen·trum (ep′i sen′trəm), *n., pl.* **-trums, -tra** (-trə). *Brit.* epicenter.

ep·i·cist (ep′i sist), *n.* a writer of epic poetry. [EPIC + -IST]

e·pi·cle·sis (*Gk.* e pē′klē sēs; *Eng.* ep′ə klē′sis), *n., pl.* **e·pi·cle·ses** (*Gk.* e′pē klē′sēs; *Eng.* ep′ə klē′sēz). *Eastern Ch.* (in a Eucharistic service) an invocation of the Holy Ghost following the prayer of consecration, held to be the moment at which transubstantiation takes place. Also, **epiklesis.** [< Gk *epíklēsis* a name, calling upon, equiv. to *epi-* EPI- + *klēsis* calling, call (*klē-*, var. s. of *kalein* to call + *-sis* -SIS)]

ep′ic machin′ery. See under **machinery** (def. 4).

ep·i·con·dyle (ep′ə kon′dīl, -dəl), *n.* *Anat.* either of the two condyles at the distal end of the humerus. [EPI- + CONDYLE] —**ep·i·con·dyl·i·an** (ep′ə kon dil′ē ən), **ep′i·con·dyl′ic, ep·i·con·dyl·ar** (ep′ə kon′dələr), *adj.*

ep·i·con·ti·nen·tal (ep′i kon′tə nen′təl), *adj.* found or located in or on a continent: *epicontinental minerals; an epicontinental sea.* [EPI- + CONTINENTAL]

ep·i·cot·yl (ep′ə kot′əl, -il), *n.* *Bot.* (in the embryo of a plant) that part of the stem above the cotyledons. See diag. under **cotyledon.** [EPI- + Gk *kotýl(ē)* cup]

e·pic·ri·sis[1] (i pik′ri sis), *n.* a critical study or evaluation. [< Gk *epíkrisis* a judgment (cf. *epikrínein* to judge, equiv. to *epi-* EPI- + *krínein* to judge); see CRISIS]

ep·i·cri·sis[2] (ep′i krī′sis, ep′ē-), *Med.* that which follows a crisis; a secondary crisis. [EPI- + CRISIS]

ep·i·crit·ic (ep′ə krit′ik), *adj.* *Physiol.* noting or pertaining to a discriminating responsiveness to small variations between pain or temperature stimuli (opposed to *protopathic*). [< Gk *epikritik(ós)* determinative. See EPICRISIS[1], -TIC]

ep′ic sim′ile, a simile developed over several lines of verse, esp. one used in an epic poem. Also called **Homeric simile.**

Ep·ic·te·tus (ep′ik tē′təs), *n.* A.D. c60–c120, Greek Stoic philosopher and teacher. —**Ep·ic·te·tian** (ep′ik-tē′shən), *adj.*

ep·i·cure (ep′ə kyŏŏr′), *n.* **1.** a person who cultivates a refined taste, as in food, art, music, etc.; connoisseur. **2.** a person given up to sensual enjoyment. [ME < L *Epicūr(us)* < Gk *Epíkouros* EPICURUS] —**Syn. 1.** gastronome, gourmet, epicurean. **2.** voluptuary, sensualist, gourmand. —**Ant. 1.** ascetic.

ep·i·cu·re·an (ep′ə kyŏŏ rē′ən, -kyŏŏr′ē-), *adj.* **1.** given or adapted to luxury or indulgence in sensual pleasures; of luxurious tastes or habits, esp. in eating and drinking. **2.** fit for an epicure: *epicurean delicacies.* **3.** (*cap.*) of, pertaining to, or characteristic of Epicurus or Epicureanism. —*n.* **4.** a person devoted to the pursuit of pleasure or luxury; epicure. **5.** (*cap.*) a disciple of Epicurus. [ME < L *Epicūre(us)* of Epicurus (< Gk *Epikoúreios*) + -AN]

Ep·i·cu·re·an·ism (ep′ə kyŏŏ rē′ə niz′əm, -kyŏŏr′ē-), *n.* **1.** the philosophical system or doctrine of Epicurus, holding that the external world is a series of fortuitous combinations of atoms and that the highest good is pleasure, interpreted as freedom from disturbance or pain. **2.** (*l.c.*) epicurean indulgence or habits. Also, **Ep·i·cur·ism** (ep′ə kyŏŏ riz′əm, ep′ə kyŏŏr′iz əm). [EPICUREAN + -ISM]

Ep·i·cu·rus (ep′ə kyŏŏr′əs), *n.* 342?–270 B.C., Greek philosopher.

ep·i·cy·cle (ep′i sī′kəl), *n.* **1.** *Astron.* a small circle, the center of which moves around in the circumference of a larger circle: used in Ptolemaic astronomy to account for observed periodic irregularities in planetary motions. **2.** *Math.* a circle that rolls, externally or internally, without slipping, on another circle, generating an epicycloid or hypocycloid. [ME < MF < LL *epicycl(us)* < Gk *epíkyklos.* See EPI-, CYCLE]

ep·i·cy·clic (ep′i sī′klik, -sik′lik), *adj.* of or pertaining to an epicycle. [EPICYCLE + -IC]

ep′icyclic train′, *Mach.* a train of gears or pulleys in which one or more of the axes revolve about a central axis.

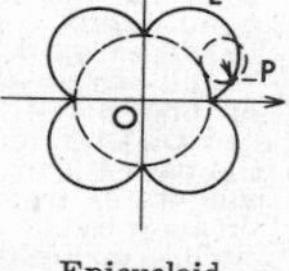

Epicycloid
P, Point tracing epicycloid E on fixed circle

ep·i·cy·cloid (ep′i sī′kloid), *n.* *Geom.* a curve generated by the motion of a point on the circumference of a circle that rolls externally, without slipping, on a fixed circle. Equation: $x = (a + b)\cos\theta - b\cos[(a + b)/b]\theta$, $y = (a + b)\sin\theta - b\sin[(a + b)/b]\theta$. [EPICYCLE + -OID] —**ep′i·cy·cloi′dal,** *adj.*

ep′icycloi′dal gear′, one of the gears of an epicyclic train.

Ep·i·daur·us (ep′i dôr′əs), *n.* an ancient town in S Greece, in Argolis: sanctuary of Asclepius; outdoor theater still in use.

ep·i·deic·tic (ep′i dīk′tik), *adj.* *Rhet.* displaying the oratorical skill of the speaker, as a formal speech of praise or blame. Also, **epidictic.** [< Gk *epideiktik(ós).* See EPI-, DEICTIC]

Ep·i·dem·i·a·rum (ep′i dem′ē är′əm), *n.* **Palus.** See **Palus Epidemiarum.**

ep·i·dem·ic (ep′i dem′ik), *adj.* **1.** Also, **ep′i·dem′i·cal.** affecting at the same time a large number of persons in a locality, and spreading from person to person, as a disease not permanently prevalent there. —*n.* **2.** a temporary prevalence of a disease. **3.** a rapid spread or increase in the prevalence of something: *an epidemic of fads; an epidemic of riots.* [obs. *epidem(y)* (< LL *epidemia* < Gk *epidēmía* staying in one place, among the people, equiv. to *epi-* EPI- + *dêm(os)* people of a district + *-ia* -Y[3]) + -IC] —**ep′i·dem′i·cal·ly,** *adv.* —**ep·i·de·mic·i·ty** (ep′i də mis′i tē), *n.*

epidem′ic encephali′tis, *Pathol.* See **sleeping sickness** (def. 2).

epidem′ic pleurodyn′ia, *Pathol.* pleurodynia (def. 2).

ep·i·de·mi·ol·o·gy (ep′i dē′mē ol′ə jē), *n.* the branch of medicine dealing with epidemic diseases. [EPIDEMI(C) + -O- + -LOGY] —**ep·i·de·mi·o·log·i·cal** (ep′i dē′mē ə loj′i kəl), *adj.* —**ep′i·de′mi·o·log′i·cal·ly,** *adv.* —**ep′i·de′mi·ol′o·gist,** *n.*

ep·i·der·mis (ep′i dûr′mis), *n.* **1.** *Anat.* the outer, nonvascular, nonsensitive layer of the skin, covering the true skin or corium. **2.** *Zool.* the outermost living layer of an animal, usually composed of one or more layers of cells. **3.** *Bot.* a thin layer of cells forming the outer integument of seed plants and ferns. See diag. under **stem.** [< LL: surface skin < Gk: upper skin. See EPI-, DERMA] —**ep′i·der′mal, ep′i·der′mic,** *adj.* —**ep′i·der′mi·cal·ly,** *adv.*

ep·i·der·moid (ep′i dûr′moid), *adj.* resembling epidermis. Also, **ep′i·der·moi′dal.** [EPIDERM(IS) + -OID]

ep·i·di·a·scope (ep′i dī′ə skōp′), *n.* *Optics.* a type of magic lantern that projects the image of an opaque object onto a screen. [EPI- + DIA- + -SCOPE]

ep·i·dic·tic (ep′i dik′tik), *adj.* epideictic.

ep·i·did·y·mis (ep′i did′ə mis), *n., pl.* **-di·dym·i·des** (-di dim′i dēz′). *Anat.* an elongated organ on the posterior surface of a testis which constitutes the convoluted beginning of the vas deferens. [< Gk; see EPI-, DIDYMOUS] —**ep′i·did′y·mal,** *adj.*

ep·i·di·o·rite (ep′i dī′ə rīt′), *n.* *Petrog.* a schistose metamorphic rock resulting from the alteration of augite to hornblende in a gabbro or dolerite. [EPI- + DIORITE]

ep·i·dote (ep′i dōt′), *n.* a mineral, calcium aluminum iron silicate, $Ca_2(Al, Fe)_3Si_3O_{12}(OH)$, occurring in green prismatic crystals. [< F *épidote* < Gk *epídot(os)* given besides, increased (ptp. of *epididónai*), equiv. to *epi-* EPI- + *dotós* given (ptp. of *didónai*)] —**ep·i·dot·ic** (ep′i dot′ik), *adj.*

ep′idote group′, a group of minerals, complex calcium iron aluminum silicates, found in igneous and metamorphic rocks.

ep·i·fo·cal (ep′ə fō′kəl), *adj.* *Geol.* epicentral. [EPI- + FOCAL]

ep·i·gam·ic (ep′ə gam′ik), *adj.* *Zool.* attracting the opposite sex during the mating period, as the colors of certain birds. [< Gk *epígam(os)* marriageable (see EPI-, -GAMOUS) + -IC]

ep·i·gas·tric (ep′ə gas′trik), *adj.* lying upon, distributed over, or pertaining to the epigastrium. [EPIGASTR(IUM) + -IC]

ep·i·gas·tri·um (ep′ə gas′trē əm), *n., pl.* **-tri·a** (-trē ə). *Anat.* the upper and median part of the abdomen, lying over the stomach. [< NL < Gk *epigástrion*, n. use of neut. of *epigástrios* over the stomach. See EPI-, GASTR-, -IUM]

ep·i·ge·al (ep′i jē′əl), *adj.* **1.** *Entomol.* living near the surface of the ground, as on low herbs or on other surface vegetation. **2.** *Bot.* epigeous. Also, **ep′i·ge′an.** [EPIGE(OUS) + -AL[1]]

ep·i·gene (ep′i jēn′), *adj.* *Geol.* formed or originating on the earth's surface (opposed to *hypogene*). [< F *épigène* < Gk *epigen(ḗs)* born after, growing after. See EPI-, -GEN]

E·pi·ge·nes (i pij′ə nēz′), *n.* a crater in the second quadrant of the face of the moon: about 30 miles in diameter.

ep·i·gen·e·sis (ep′i jen′i sis), *n.* **1.** *Biol.* the theory that an embryo develops from the successive differentiation of an originally undifferentiated structure (opposed to *preformation*). **2.** *Geol.* ore deposition subsequent to the original formation of the enclosing country rock. [EPI- + -GENESIS] —**ep′i·gen′e·sist, e·pig·e·nist** (i pij′ə nist), *n.* —**ep·i·ge·net·ic** (ep′i jə net′ik), *adj.* —**ep′i·ge·net′i·cal·ly,** *adv.*

e·pig·e·nous (i pij′ə nəs), *adj.* *Bot.* growing on the surface, esp. the upper surface, as fungi on leaves. [EPI- + -GENOUS]

ep·i·ge·ous (ep′i jē′əs), *adj.* *Bot.* **1.** growing on or close to the ground. **2.** (of cotyledons) lifted above ground in germination. [< Gk *epígei(os)* on, of the world, equiv. to *epi-* EPI- + *-geios* (*gê* earth + *-ios* adj. suffix); see -OUS]

ep·i·glot·tis (ep′ə glot′is), *n., pl.* **-glot·tis·es, -glot·ti·des** (-glot′i dēz′). *Anat.* a thin, valvelike, cartilaginous structure that covers the glottis during swallowing, preventing the entrance of food and drink into the larynx. See diag. under **larynx.** [< Gk; see EPI-, GLOTTIS] —**ep′i·glot′tal, ep′i·glot′tic, ep·i·glot·ti·de·an** (ep′ə glo tid′ē ən), *adj.*

ep·i·gone (ep′ə gōn′), *n.* an undistinguished imitator or follower of an important writer, painter, etc. Also, **ep·i·gon** (ep′ə gon′). [< L *epigon(us)* < Gk *epígonos* (one) born afterwards; in pl., the Epigoni, equiv. to *epi-* EPI- + *-gonos*, akin to *gígnesthai* to be born] —**ep·i·gon·ic** (ep′ə gon′ik), *adj.* —**e·pig·o·nism** (i pig′ə niz′əm, e pig′-, ep′ə gō niz əm, -gon′iz-), *n.*

ep·i·go·nei·on (ep′ə gō nī′ən), *n.* an ancient Greek musical instrument with many strings, thought to resemble a zither. [< Gk; named after *Epigonos*, the inventor]

E·pig·o·ni (i pig′ə nī′), *n.pl., sing.* **-o·nus** (-ə nəs). *Class. Myth.* the sons of the Seven against Thebes. [see EPIGONE]

ep·i·gram (ep′ə gram′), *n.* **1.** any witty, ingenious, or pointed saying tersely expressed. **2.** epigrammatic expression: *Wilde had a genius for epigram.* **3.** a short poem, often satirical, dealing concisely with a single subject and usually ending with a witty or ingenious turn of thought. [ME < L *epigram(ma)* inscription < Gk: inscription, epigram. See EPI-, -GRAM[1]]

ep·i·gram·mat·ic (ep′ə grə mat′ik), *adj.* **1.** of or like an epigram; terse and ingenious in expression. **2.** given to epigrams. [< L *epigrammatic(us)* < Gk *epigrammatikós*, equiv. to *epigrammat-* (s. of *epígramma*) EPIGRAM + *-ikos* -IC] —**ep′i·gram·mat′i·cal·ly,** *adv.*

ep·i·gram·ma·tise (ep′ə gram′ə tīz′), *v.t., v.i.*, **-tised, -tis·ing.** *Chiefly Brit.* epigrammatize.

ep·i·gram·ma·tism (ep′ə gram′ə tiz′əm), *n.* epigrammatic character or style. [< L *epigrammat-* inscription (s. of *epigramma*; see EPIGRAM) + -ISM]

ep·i·gram·ma·tist (ep′ə gram′ə tist), *n.* a maker of epigrams. [< LL *epigrammatist(a)* < Gk *epigrammatistḗs.* See EPIGRAMMATIC, -IST]

ep·i·gram·ma·tize (ep′ə gram′ə tīz′), *v.*, **-tized, -tiz·ing.** —*v.t.* **1.** to express in epigrams. **2.** to make epigrams about (a person or thing). —*v.i.* **3.** to make epigrams. Also, *esp. Brit.*, **epigrammatise.** [< Gk *epigrammatíz(ein).* See EPIGRAMMATIC, -IZE]

ep·i·graph (ep′ə graf′, -gräf′), *n.* **1.** an inscription, esp. on a building, statue, or the like. **2.** an apposite quotation at the beginning of a book, chapter, etc. [< Gk *epigraphḗ* inscription. See EPI-, -GRAPH]

ep·i·graph·ic (ep′ə graf′ik), *adj.* **1.** of or pertaining to epigraphs. **2.** of or pertaining to epigraphy. **3.** of the style characteristic of epigraphs. Also, **ep′i·graph′i·cal.** [EPIGRAPH + -IC] —**ep′i·graph′i·cal·ly,** *adv.*

e·pig·ra·phy (i pig′rə fē), *n.* **1.** the study or science of epigraphs or inscriptions, esp. of ancient inscriptions. **2.** inscriptions collectively. [EPIGRAPH + -Y[3]] —**e·pig′ra·phist, e·pig′ra·pher,** *n.*

Epigynous stamens
S, Stamen; P, Petal;
O, Ovary

e·pig·y·nous (i pij′ə nəs), *adj.* *Bot.* **1.** (of flowers) having all floral parts conjoint and generally divergent from the ovary at or near its summit. **2.** (of stamens, petals, etc.) having the parts so arranged. [EPI- + -GYNOUS]

e·pig·y·num (i pij′ə nəm), *n.* **1.** (in arachnids) the female genital opening. **2.** (in a spider) the chitinous plate that covers this opening. Also, **ep·i·gyne** (ep′i-jīn′). [< NL, equiv. to *epi-* EPI- + *-gynum* < Gk *-gynon*, neut. of *-gynos*; see -GYNOUS]

e·pig·y·ny (i pij′ə nē), *n.* an epigynous condition. [EPIGYN(OUS) + -Y[3]]

e·pi·kle·sis (*Gk.* e pē′klē sēs; *Eng.* ep′i klē′sis), *n., pl.* **e·pi·kle·ses** (*Gk.* e′pē klē′sēs; *Eng.* ep′i klē′sēz). epiclesis.

ep·i·late (ep′ə lāt′), *v.t.*, **-lat·ed, -lat·ing.** *Med.* to remove hair by means of physical, chemical, or radiological agents; depilate. [< F *épil(er)* (< L *ē-* E- + *pil(us)* hair) + -ATE[1]] —**ep′i·la′tion,** *n.* —**ep′i·la′tor,** *n.*

ep·i·lep·sy (ep′ə lep′sē), *n.* *Pathol.* a disorder of the nervous system, usually characterized by fits of convulsions that end with loss of consciousness. Also, **ep′i·lep′si·a.** Cf. **grand mal, petit mal.** [< LL *epilēpsia* < Gk: epileptic seizure (akin to *epilambánein* to get hold of, attack), equiv. to *epi-* EPI- + *-lēp-* take + *-sia* result of]

ep·i·lep·tic (ep′ə lep′tik), *adj.* *Pathol.* **1.** pertaining to or symptomatic of epilepsy. —*n.* **2.** a person affected with epilepsy. [< L *epilēptic(us)* << Gk *epilēptikós*, equiv. to *epi-* EPI- + *-lēp-* take + *-tikos* -TIC] —**ep′i·lep′ti·cal·ly,** *adv.*

ep·i·lep·toid (ep′ə lep′toid), *adj. Pathol.* resembling epilepsy. Also, **ep·i·lep·ti·form** (ep′ə lep′tə fôrm′). [EPILEPT(IC) + -OID]

ep·i·lim·ni·on (ep′ə lim′nē on′, -ən), *n., pl.* **-ni·a** (-nē ə). (in certain lakes) the layer of water above the thermocline. [EPI- + Gk *limnion* small pond, dim. of *límnē* pool, lake] —**ep·i·lim·net·ic** (ep′ə lim net′ik), **ep′i·lim′ni·al,** *adj.*

ep·i·lith·ic (ep′ə lith′ik), *adj.* (of plants) growing on stones. [EPI- + -LITHIC]

e·pil·o·gist (i pil′ə jist), *n.* the writer or speaker of an epilogue. [EPILOGUE + -IST]

ep·i·logue (ep′ə lôg′, -log′), *n., v.,* **-logued, -logu·ing.** —*n.* Also, **ep′i·log′. 1.** a speech, usually in verse, delivered by one of the actors after the conclusion of a play. **2.** the person or persons speaking this. **3.** a concluding part added to a literary work, as a novel. —*v.t.* **4.** to provide with an epilogue: *a later edition of the play, which the author had epilogued.* [ME < L *epilog(us)* < Gk *epílogos* peroration of a speech, equiv. to *epi-* EPI- + *lógos* word]

Ep·i·men·i·des (ep′ə men′i dēz′), *n.* a crater in the third quadrant of the face of the moon: about 18 miles in diameter.

ep·i·mer (ep′ə mər), *n. Chem.* either of a pair of isomeric aldose compounds, esp. of certain sugars, which differ from each other in the positions of the H and OH at the second atom from the end of the carbon chain, as d-glucose and d-mannose. Also, **e·pim·er·ide** (ə pim′ə rīd′). [EPI- + -MER] —**ep·i·mer·ic** (ep′ə-mer′ik), *adj.*

ep·i·mer·ise (ep′ə mə rīz′), *v.t.,* **-ised, -is·ing.** *Chiefly Brit.* epimerize.

ep·i·mer·ize (ep′ə mə rīz′), *v.t.* **-ized, -iz·ing.** to convert into an epimer. Also, *esp. Brit.,* **epimerise.** [EPIMER + -IZE]

Ep·i·me·the·us (ep′ə mē′thē əs, -thōōs), *n. Class. Myth.* a son of Iapetus and brother of Prometheus and Atlas; the husband of Pandora and the father of Pyrrha.

ep·i·mor·phism (ep′ə môr′fiz əm), *n. Math.* a homomorphism from one set onto a second set. [EPI- + -MORPHISM]

ep·i·mor·pho·sis (ep′ə môr′fə sis, -môr fō′-), *n. Zool.* a form of development in segmented animals in which body segmentation is completed before hatching. [EPI- + MORPHOSIS] —**ep′i·mor′phic,** *adj.*

ep·i·my·o·car·di·um (ep′ə mī′ə kär′dē əm), *n. Embryol.* the outer, mesodermal layer of the embryonic heart, which develops into the epicardium and the myocardium. [EPI- + MYOCARDIUM] —**ep′i·my′o·car′di·al,** *adj.*

É·pi·nal (ā pē nal′), *n.* a city in and the capital of Vosges, in NE France. 34,806 (1962).

ep·i·na·os (ep′ə nā′os), *n., pl.* **-na·oi** (-nā′oi). a rear vestibule, as of a classical temple. Also called **opisthodomos, posticum.** Cf. **pronaos.** [EPI- + NAOS]

ep·i·nas·ty (ep′ə nas′tē), *n. Bot.* (esp. of leaves) increased growth on the upper surface of an organ or part, causing it to bend downward. [EPI- + Gk *nast(ós)* pressed close + -Y[3]] —**ep′i·nas′tic,** *adj.*

ep·i·neph·rine (ep′ə nef′rin, -rēn), *n.* **1.** *Biochem.* a hormone, $C_6H_3(OH)_2CHOHCH_2NHCH_3$, produced by the medullary portion of the adrenal glands and causing a rise in blood pressure. **2.** *Pharm.* a commercial form of this substance, extracted from the medullary portion of the adrenal glands of sheep and cattle, or synthesized: used chiefly as a heart stimulant, to constrict the blood vessels, and to relax the bronchi in asthma. Also, **ep′i·neph′rin.** Also called **adrenin, adrenine, suprarenalin.** [EPI- + Gk *nephr(ós)* kidney + -INE[2]]

ep·i·neu·ri·um (ep′ə nŏŏr′ē əm, -nyŏŏr′-), *n., pl.* **-neu·ri·a** (-nŏŏr′ē ə, -nyŏŏr′-). *Anat.* the dense sheath of connective tissue which surrounds the trunk of a nerve. [< NL, equiv. to *epi-* EPI- + Gk *neûron* sinew, tendon; see -IUM] —**ep′i·neu′ri·al,** *adj.*

é·pin·glé (ā paN glā′), *n.* a fabric constructed in plain weave, used in the manufacture of women's dress goods. [< F, special use of *épingle* pin]

E·pi·o·ne (i pī′ə nē′), *n. Class. Myth.* the wife of Asclepius.

ep·i·o·nych·i·um (ep′ē ō nik′ē əm), *n., pl.* **-nych·i·a** (-nik′ē ə). eponychium.

Ep·i·pa·le·o·lith·ic (ep′ə pā′lē ə lith′ik, -pal′ē-), *adj.* of, pertaining to, or characteristic of the human cultures existing at the end of the Paleolithic and the beginnings of the Mesolithic periods of the Stone Age. [EPI- + PALEOLITHIC]

ep·i·pas·tic (ep′ə pas′tik), *Med.* —*adj.* **1.** suitable for use as a dusting powder. —*n.* **2.** an epipastic substance or preparation. [< Gk *epípast(os)* sprinkled over, on (verbid of *epipássein,* equiv. to *epi-* EPI- + *pássein* to sprinkle) + -IC]

ep·i·pet·a·lous (ep′ə pet′ələs), *adj.* (of a flower) having the stamens inserted on the petals. [EPI- + PETALOUS]

Epiph., Epiphany.

Ep·i·pha·ni·a (ep′ə fə nī′ə), *n.* ancient name of **Hama.**

e·piph·a·nise (i pif′ə nīz′), *v.t.,* **-nised, -nis·ing.** *Chiefly Brit.* epiphanize.

e·piph·a·nize (i pif′ə nīz′), *v.t.,* **-nized, -niz·ing.** *Literature.* to describe or represent in an epiphany. [EPIPHANY + -IZE]

E·piph·a·ny (i pif′ə nē), *n., pl.* **-nies. 1.** a Christian festival, observed on January 6, commemorating the manifestation of Christ to the gentiles in the persons of the Magi. **2.** (*l.c.*) an appearance or manifestation, esp. of a deity. **3.** (*l.c.*) *Literature.* **a.** a sudden, intuitive perception of or insight into the reality or essential meaning of something, usually initiated by some simple, homely, or commonplace occurrence or experience. **b.** a literary work or section of a work presenting, usually symbolically, such a moment of revelation and insight. [ME *epiphanie* < eccl. L *epiphania* < LGk *epipháneia,* Gk: apparition, equiv. to *epi-* EPI- + *-phan-* appear (s. of *phaínein*) + *-eia* -Y[3]] —**ep·i·phan·ic** (ep′ə fan′ik), *adj.*

ep·i·phe·nom·e·nal·ism (ep′ē fə nom′i nəliz′əm), *n.* the doctrine that consciousness is merely an epiphenomenon of physiological processes, and that it has no power to affect these processes. [EPI- + PHENOMENALISM] —**ep′i·phe·nom′e·nal·ist,** *n.*

ep·i·phe·nom·e·non (ep′ē fə nom′ə non′, -nən), *n.* **1.** *Pathol.* a secondary or additional symptom or complication arising during the course of a malady. **2.** any secondary phenomenon. [EPI- + PHENOMENON] —**ep′i·phe·nom′e·nal,** *adj.* —**ep′i·phe·nom′e·nal·ly,** *adv.*

ep·i·phloe·dal (ep′ə flēd′əl), *adj. Bot.* growing on bark, as a lichen. Also, **ep′i·phloe′dic.** [EPI- + Gk *phloi(ós)* bark of trees + hiatus-filling *-d-* + -AL[1]]

ep·i·pho·ne·ma (ep′ə fō nē′mə), *n., pl.* **-mas, -mae** (-mē). *Rhet.* a sentence that is an exclamation, a general or striking comment, or a succinct summary of what has previously been said. [< L: exclamation < Gk. See EPI-, PHONEME]

e·piph·o·ra (i pif′ər ə), *n.* **1.** *Pathol.* an overflow of tears due to an excessive secretion or obstruction of the lacrimal ducts. **2.** *Rhet.* epistrophe (def. 1). [< L: an afflux, repetition < Gk: a bringing upon. See EPI-, -PHORE]

ep·i·phragm (ep′ə fram′), *n.* a covering of calcified slime secreted by a land snail during dry weather to cover its shell opening and prevent desiccation. [< Gk *epíphragma* covering, lid, equiv. to *epi-* EPI- + *phrágma* fence] —**ep·i·phrag·mal** (ep′ə frag′məl), *adj.*

ep·i·phy·lax·is (ep′ə fī lak′sis, -fi-), *n. Med.* reinforcement of the defenses of the body against disease. [< NL < Gk *epi-* EPI- + *phýlaxis* a watching, guarding]

ep·i·phyll (ep′ə fil), *n. Bot.* an epiphyte that grows on the surface, esp. the upper surface, of leaves, as a lichen. [EPI- + -PHYLL] —**ep′i·phyl′lous, ep·i·phyl·line** (ep′ə fil′ēn, -in), *adj.*

e·piph·y·sis (i pif′i sis), *n., pl.* **-ses** (-sēz′). *Anat.* **1.** a part or process of a bone separated from the main body of the bone by a layer of cartilage, and subsequently uniting with the bone through further ossification. **2.** See **pineal body.** [< NL < Gk: a growth upon, equiv. to *epi-* EPI- + *phýsis* growth (*phý(ein)* to make grow, bring forth, produce + *-sis* -SIS)] —**ep·i·phys·e·al** (ep′ə fiz′ē əl, i pif′i sē′əl, -zē′-), **ep′i·phys′i·al,** *adj.*

ep·i·phyte (ep′ə fīt′), *n. Bot.* a plant that grows nonparasitically upon another, deriving its nutrients and water from rain, the air, dust, etc.; an air plant or aerophyte. [EPI- + -PHYTE] —**ep·i·phyt·ic** (ep′ə-fit′ik), **ep′i·phyt′i·cal,** *adj.* —**ep′i·phyt′i·cal·ly,** *adv.*

ep·i·phy·tot·ic (ep′ə fī tot′ik), *adj.* **1.** (of a disease) destroying a large number of plants in an area at the same time. —*n.* **2.** the widespread, destructive outbreak of a plant disease. [EPIPHYTE + -OTIC]

ep·i·plex·is (ep′ə plek′sis), *n. Rhet.* a device in which the speaker reproaches his audience in order to arouse, incite, or convince them. [< LL: a reproof < Gk, equiv. to *epi-* EPI- + *plēg-* stroke, blow (akin to *plḗssein* to strike, wound) + *-sis* -SIS]

e·pip·lo·on (i pip′lō on), *n. Anat.* See **greater omentum.** [< Gk] —**ep·i·plo·ic** (ep′ə plō′ik), *adj.*

ep·i·rog·e·ny (ep′ī-roj′ə nē), *n. Geol.* epeirogeny. —**e·pi·ro·gen·ic** (i pī′rə jen′ik), **e·pi·ro·ge·net·ic** (i pī′rō jə net′ik), *adj.*

E·pi·rus (i pī′rəs), *n.* **1.** an ancient district in NW Greece and S Albania. **2.** a modern region in NW Greece. 352,604 (1961); 3573 sq. mi. —**E·pi·rote** (i pī′rōt), **E·pei·rot** (i-pī′rət), *n.*

Epis., 1. Episcopal. **2.** Episcopalian. **3.** Epistle.

Episc., 1. Episcopal. **2.** Episcopalian.

e·pis·co·pa·cy (i pis′kə pə sē), *n., pl.* **-cies. 1.** government of the church by bishops; church government in which there are three distinct orders of ministers, namely bishops, priests or presbyters, and deacons. **2.** the office or incumbency of a bishop. **3.** the order of bishops. [EPISCOPA(TE) + -CY]

e·pis·co·pal (i pis′kə pəl), *adj.* **1.** of or pertaining to a bishop: *episcopal authority.* **2.** based on or recognizing a governing order of bishops: *an episcopal hierarchy.* **3.** (*cap.*) designating the Anglican Church or some branch of it, as the Protestant Episcopal Church. —*n.* **4.** (*cap.*) *Informal.* an Episcopalian. [ME < LL *episcopāl(is).* See BISHOP, -AL[1]] —**e·pis′co·pal·ly, E·pis′co·pal·ly,** *adv.*

E·pis·co·pa·lian (i pis′kə pāl′yən, -pā′lē ən), *adj.* **1.** pertaining or adhering to the Protestant Episcopal Church of the Anglican communion. **2.** (*l.c.*) pertaining or adhering to the episcopal form of church government. —*n.* **3.** a member of an episcopal church. **4.** (*l.c.*) an adherent of the episcopal system of church government. [EPISCOPAL + -IAN] —**E·pis′co·pa′lian·ism,** *n.*

e·pis·co·pal·ism (i pis′kə pə liz′əm), *n.* the theory of church polity according to which the supreme ecclesiastical authority is vested in the episcopal order as a whole, and not in any individual except by delegation. [EPISCOPAL + -ISM]

epis′copal san′dal, campagus.

e·pis·co·pate (i pis′kə pit, -pāt′), *n.* **1.** the office and dignity of a bishop; bishopric. **2.** the order or body of bishops. **3.** the incumbency of a bishop. [< LL *episcopāt(us)* the office of a bishop. See BISHOP, -ATE[1]]

e·pis·co·pise (i pis′kə pīz′), *v.,* **-pised, -pis·ing.** *Chiefly Brit.* —*v.t., v.i.* episcopize.

e·pis·co·pize (i pis′kə pīz′), *v.,* **-pized, -piz·ing.** —*v.t.* **1.** to make a bishop of. **2.** to convert to Episcopalianism. —*v.i.* **3.** to function as a bishop. [EPISCOP(AL) + -IZE]

e·pis·co·tist·er (ə pis′kə tis′tər, e′pis kō tis′tər), *n.* a disk with a sector removed which when rotated in front of a light source allows the periodic passage of flashes of light: used in studying the motion of a body. Also, **e·pis′ko·tist·er.** [< Gk *episkot(ízein)* (to) overshadow (see EPI-, SCOTIA, -IZE) + -IST + -ER[1]]

ep·i·se·meme (ep′i sē′mēm), *n.* the meaning of a tagmeme. [EPI- + SEMEME]

ep·i·sep·a·lous (ep′i sep′ə ləs), *adj.* (of a flower) having the stamens inserted on the sepals. [EPI- + -SEPALOUS]

e·pi·si·ot·o·my (ə pē′zē ot′ə mē, ep′i sī-), *n., pl.* **-mies.** *Obstet., Surg.* incision of the vulva to allow sufficient clearance for birth. [< Gk *epísio(n)* + -TOMY]

ep·i·sode (ep′i sōd′, -zōd′), *n.* **1.** an incident in the course of a series of events, in a person's life or experience, etc. **2.** an incident, scene, etc., within a narrative, usually fully developed and either integrated within the main story or digressing from it. **3.** one of a number of loosely connected, but usually thematically related, scenes or stories comprising a literary work. **4.** epeisodion. **5.** *Music.* an intermediate or digressive passage, esp. in a contrapuntal composition. **6.** *Motion Pictures, Radio, and Television.* any one of the separate productions that constitute a serial. [< Gk *epeisód(ion)* addition, episode, n. use of neut. of *epeisódios* coming in addition, equiv. to *epi-* EPI- + *eísod(os)* entrance (*eis-* into + *hodós* road, way) + *-ios* adj. suffix]
—**Syn. 1.** happening. See **event.**

ep·i·sod·ic (ep′i sod′ik, -zod′-), *adj.* **1.** pertaining to or of the nature of an episode. **2.** divided into separate or tenuously related parts or sections; loosely connected: *an episodic novel.* Also, **ep′i·sod′i·cal.** [EPISODE + -IC] —**ep′i·sod′i·cal·ly,** *adv.*

ep·i·spas·tic (ep′i spas′tik), *adj.* **1.** raising a blister. —*n.* **2.** a blistering agent; vesicatory. [< Gk *epispastik(ós)* adapted, drawing to one's self. See EPI-, SPASTIC]

e·pis·ta·sis (i pis′tə sis), *n., pl.* **-ses** (-sēz′). **1.** *Genetics.* a form of interaction between nonallelic genes in which one combination of such genes has a dominant effect over other combinations. **2.** *Med.* **a.** the stoppage of a secretion or discharge. **b.** a scum that forms on a urine specimen upon standing. [< Gk: stopping, stoppage. See EPI-, STASIS] —**ep·i·stat·ic** (ep′i stat′ik), *adj.*

ep·i·stax·is (ep′i stak′sis), *n. Pathol.* nosebleed. [< Gk: a dripping, equiv. to *epi-* EPI- + *stag-* drop + *-sis* -SIS]

ep·i·ste·mic (ep′i stē′mik, -stem′ik), *adj.* of or pertaining to knowledge or the conditions for acquiring it. [< Gk *epistēmik(ós),* equiv. to *epistḗm(ē)* knowledge + *-ikos* -IC] —**ep·i·ste·me** (ep′i stē′mē), *n.* —**ep′i·ste′mi·cal·ly,** *adv.*

e·pis·te·mol·o·gy (i pis′tə mol′ə jē), *n.* a branch of philosophy that investigates the origin, nature, methods, and limits of human knowledge. [< Gk *epistḗm(ē)* knowledge + -O- + -LOGY] —**e·pis·te·mo·log·i·cal** (i pis′tə mə loj′i kəl), *adj.* —**e·pis′te·mo·log′i·cal·ly,** *adv.* —**e·pis′te·mol′o·gist,** *n.*

ep·i·ster·num (ep′i stûr′nəm), *n., pl.* **-na** (-nə). **1.** *Anat.* the manubrium. **2.** *Entomol.* the anterior portion of a pleuron. [EPI- + STERNUM]

e·pis·tle (i pis′əl), *n.* **1.** a letter, esp. a formal or didactic one; written communication. **2.** (*usually cap.*) one of the apostolic letters in the New Testament. **3.** (*often cap.*) an extract, usually from one of the Epistles of the New Testament, forming part of the Eucharistic service in certain churches. [ME; OE *epistol* < L *epistula, epistola* < Gk *epistolḗ* message, letter, equiv. to *epi-* EPI- + *stol-* (var. s. of *stéllein* to send) + *-ē* n. suffix]

epis′tle side′, the right side of a church, facing the altar. Cf. **gospel side.**

Epistle to Dr. Ar·buth·not (är′bəth not′), a satirical poem (1735) by Alexander Pope.

e·pis·to·lar·y (i pis′tə ler′ē), *adj.* **1.** contained in or carried on by letters: *an epistolary friendship.* **2.** of, pertaining to, or consisting of letters. [ME < L *epistolār(is)* of, belonging to a letter. See EPISTLE, -ARY]

epis′tolary nov′el, a novel written in the form of a series of letters.

e·pis·to·ler (i pis′tə lər), *n.* **1.** Also, **e·pis′to·list.** a writer of an epistle. **2.** the person who reads or chants the epistle in the Eucharistic service. Also, **e·pis·tler** (i pis′lər, i pist′lər). [< L *epistol(a)* EPISTLE + -ER[1]]

ep·i·stol·ic (ep′i stol′ik), *adj.* epistolary. Also, **ep′i·stol′i·cal.** [< L *epistolic(us)* < Gk *epistolikós* suited to a letter. See EPISTLE, -IC]

e·pis·to·lise (i pis′təlīz′), *v.i., v.t.,* **-lised, -lis·ing.** *Chiefly Brit.* epistolize.

e·pis·to·lize (i pis′təlīz′), *v.,* **-lized, -liz·ing.** —*v.i.* **1.** to write a letter. —*v.t.* **2.** to write a letter to (a person). [< L *epistol(a)* EPISTLE + -IZE]

e·pis·to·log·ra·phy (i pis′təlog′rə fē), *n.* the practices and principles of letter writing; art of epistolary composition. [< L *epistol(a)* EPISTLE + -O- + -GRAPHY]

e·pis·tro·phe (i pis′trə fē), *n.* **1.** Also called **epiphora.** *Rhet.* the repetition of a word or words at the end of two or more successive verses, clauses, or sentences, as in "I should do Brutus wrong, and Cassius wrong. . . ." Cf. **anaphora** (def. 1). **2.** *Neoplatonism.* the realization by an intellect of its remoteness from the One. [< NL < Gk; see EPI-, STROPHE]

ep·i·style (ep′i stīl′), *n.* the architrave of a classical temple. [< L *epistȳl(ium)* the cross-beam resting on the column < Gk *epistýlion* cross-beam of architrave (*epi-* EPI- + *stŷl(os)* a column, pillar, post + *-ion,* dim. suffix)] —**ep′i·sty′lar,** *adj.*

ep·i·syl·lo·gism (ep′i sil′ə jiz′əm), *n. Logic.* a syllogism one of the premises of which is the conclusion of a preceding syllogism; any of the syllogisms included in a polysyllogism except the first one. Cf. **polysyllogism.** [< NL *episyllogism(us).* See EPI-, SYLLOGISM]

epit., 1. epitaph. **2.** epitome.

ep·i·taph (ep′i taf′, -täf′), *n.* **1.** a commemorative inscription on a tomb or mortuary monument. **2.** a brief poem or other writing in praise of a deceased person. —*v.t.* **3.** to commemorate (something or someone) in or with an epitaph. [ME *epitaphe* < L *epitaph(ium)* < Gk *epitáphion* over or at a tomb, equiv. to *epi-* EPI- + *táph(os)* tomb + *-ion* n., adj. suffix] —**ep′i·taph′ic** (ep′i taf′ik), *adj.* —**ep′i·taph′ist,** *n.* —**ep′i·taph′less,** *adj.*

e·pit·a·sis (i pit′ə sis), *n.* the part of an ancient drama, following the protasis, in which the main action is developed. Cf. **catastasis, catastrophe** (def. 4), **protasis.** [< Gk: emphasis, increase of intensity, stretching, equiv. to *epi-* EPI- + *-ta-* (var. s. of *teínein* to stretch) + *-sis* -SIS]

ep·i·tax·is (ep′i tak′sis), *n. Crystall.* an oriented overgrowth of crystalline material upon the surface of another crystal of different chemical composition but similar structure. [< NL; see EPI-, -TAXIS] —**ep·i·tax·i·al** (ep′i tak′sē əl), **ep′i·tax′ic,** *adj.*

ep·i·tha·la·mi·on (ep′ə thə lā′mē ən), *n., pl.* **-mi·a** (-mē ə) for 2. **1.** (*cap., italics.*) a nuptial poem (1595) by Edmund Spenser. **2.** a nuptial song or poem; a poem in honor of a bride and bridegroom. [< Gk: nuptial, n. use of neut. of *epithalámios* nuptial. See EPI-, THALAMUS]

ep·i·tha·la·mi·um (ep′ə thə lā′mē əm), *n., pl.* **-mi·ums, -mi·a** (-mē ə). epithalamion. —**ep·i·tha·lam·ic** (ep′ə thə lam′ik), *adj.*

ep·i·thal·a·mus (ep′i thal′ə məs), *n., pl.* **-mi** (-mī′). *Anat.* the dorsal area of the diencephalon containing a habenula and the pineal body. [< NL; see EPI-, THALAMUS]

ep·i·the·ci·um (ep′i thē′shē əm, -sē əm), *n., pl.* **-ci·a** (-shē ə, -sē ə). *Bot.* the surface layer of tissue of the apothecium of lichens and fungi, formed by the union of the tips of the paraphyses over the asci. [< NL; see EPI-, THECIUM] —**ep·i·the·ci·al** (ep′ə thē′shē əl, -shəl), *adj.*

ep·i·the·li·al (ep′ə thē′lē əl), *adj.* of or pertaining to epithelium. [EPITHELI(UM) + -AL[1]]

epithe′lial pearl′, *Pathol.* pearl[1] (def. 7).

ep·i·the·li·oid (ep′ə thē′lē oid′), *adj.* resembling epithelium. [EPITHELI(UM) + -OID]

ep·i·the·li·o·ma (ep′ə thē′lē ō′mə), *n., pl.* **-mas, -ma·ta** (-mə tə). *Pathol.* a cancer or malignant growth consisting chiefly of epithelial cells. [EPITHELI(UM) + -OMA] —**ep·i·the·li·om·a·tous** (ep′ə thē′lē om′ə təs), *adj.*

ep·i·the·li·o·mus·cu·lar (ep′ə thē′lē ō mus′kyə lər), *adj. Zool.* of or pertaining to an epithelial cell of a coelenterate which contains a contractile fibril that acts as a muscle. [EPITHELI(UM) + -O- + MUSCULAR]

ep·i·the·li·um (ep′ə thē′lē əm), *n., pl.* **-li·ums, -li·a** (-lē ə). *Biol.* any tissue which covers a surface, or lines a cavity or the like, and which performs protective, secreting, or other functions, as the epidermis, the lining of blood vessels, etc. [< NL < Gk *epi-* EPI- + *thēl(ē)* teat; see -IUM]

ep·i·the·li·za·tion (ep′ə thē′li zā′shən), *n.* the production of epithelium. [EPITHEL(IUM) + -IZATION]

ep·i·thet (ep′ə thet′), *n.* **1.** any word or phrase applied to a person or thing to describe an actual or attributed quality. "Richard the Lion-Hearted" is an epithet of Richard I. **2.** a characterizing word or phrase firmly associated with a person or thing and often occurring in its place, as "man's best friend" for "dog." **3.** a word, phrase, etc., used invectively as a term of abuse or contempt, to express hostility, or the like: *She hurled vicious epithets at him and fled the room.* [< L *epithet(on)* epithet, adjective < Gk: epithet, something added, equiv. to *epi-* EPI- + *the-* (var. s. of *tithénai* to put) + *-ton* neut. ptp. suffix] —**ep′i·thet′ic, ep′i·thet′i·cal,** *adj.*

e·pit·o·me (i pit′ə mē), *n.* **1.** a summary or condensed account, esp. of a literary work; abstract. **2.** a representative, as of some greater body or quality, that is typical of the whole: *He is the epitome of goodness.* [< L: abridgment (var. of *epitoma*) < Gk: abridgment, surface incision. See EPI-, -TOME] —**ep·i·tom·i·cal** (ep′i tom′i kəl), **ep′i·tom′ic,** *adj.*

e·pit·o·mise (i pit′ə mīz′), *v.t.,* **-mised, -mis·ing.** *Chiefly Brit.* epitomize. —**e·pit′o·mi·sa′tion,** *n.* —**e·pit′o·mis′er,** *n.*

e·pit·o·mist (i pit′ə mist), *n.* a person who makes an epitome. [EPITOM(E) + -IST]

e·pit·o·mize (i pit′ə mīz′), *v.t.,* **-mized, -miz·ing. 1.** to make an epitome of: *to epitomize an argument.* **2.** to contain or represent in small compass; typify: *This meadow epitomizes the beauty of the whole area.* Also, *esp. Brit.,* **epitomise.** [EPITOM(E) + -IZE] —**e·pit′o·mi·za′tion,** *n.* —**e·pit′o·miz′er,** *n.*

e·pi·tra·che·li·on (e′pē trä кнē′lē ôn; *Eng.* ep′i trə kē′lē on′, -kēl′yən), *n., pl.* **-che·li·a** (-кнē′lē ä; *Eng.* -kē′lē ə, -kēl′yə). *Gk. Orth. Ch.* a long, narrow, silk liturgical stole worn by priests and bishops. [< Gk, equiv. to *epi-* EPI- + *trachēl(os)* neck + *-ion,* neut. of *-ios* adj. suffix]

ep·i·xy·lous (ep′i zī′ləs), *adj. Bot.* growing on wood, as certain fungi. [EPI- + XYL- + -OUS]

ep·i·zo·ic (ep′i zō′ik), *adj. Zool.* externally parasitic. [EPIZO(ON) + -IC] —**ep′i·zo′ism,** *n.* —**ep·i·zo·ite** (ep′i zō′it), *n.*

ep·i·zo·on (ep′i zō′on, -ən), *n., pl.* **-zo·a** (-zō′ə). an external parasite; ectozoon. Also, **ep′i·zo′ön.** [< NL; see EPI-, -ZOON]

ep·i·zo·ot·ic (ep′i zō ot′ik), *Vet. Med.* —*adj.* **1.** (of diseases) prevalent temporarily among animals. —*n.* **2.** an epizootic disease. Also, **ep′i·zo·öt′ic.** [EPI- + ZO(O)- + -OTIC] —**ep′i·zo·ot′i·cal·ly, ep′i·zo·öt′i·cal·ly,** *adv.*

epizoot′ic aph′tha (af′thə, ap′thə), *Vet. Pathol.* See **foot-and-mouth disease.**

ep·i·zo·o·ty (ep′i zō′ə tē), *n., pl.* **-ties.** *Pathol.* an epizootic disease. Also, **ep′i·zo′ö·ty.** [EPIZOOT(IC) + -Y[3]]

e plu·ri·bus u·num (e plo͞o′ri bo͝os′ o͞o′no͝om; *Eng.* ē′ plo͝or′ə bəs yo͞o′nəm), *Latin.* one out of many (motto of the U.S.).

ep·och (ep′ək *or, esp. Brit.,* ē′pok), *n.* **1.** a particular period of time marked by distinctive features, events, etc.: *The treaty ushered in an epoch of peace and good will.* **2.** the beginning of a distinctive period in the history of anything: *The splitting of the atom was an epoch in the development of man.* **3.** a point of time distinguished by a particular event or state of affairs; a memorable date: *His coming of age was an epoch in his life.* **4.** *Geol.* any of several divisions of a geological period during which a geological series is formed. Cf. **age** (def. 12). **5.** *Astron.* **a.** an arbitrarily fixed instant of time or date, usually the beginning of a century or half century, used as a reference in giving the elements of a planetary orbit or the like. **b.** the mean longitude of a planet as seen from the sun at such an instant or date. **6.** *Physics.* the displacement from zero at zero time of a body undergoing simple harmonic motion. [< LL *epocha* < Gk *epochḗ* pause, check, fixed time, equiv. to *ep-* EP- + *-och-* (var. s. of *échein* to have) + *-ē* n. suffix]

—Syn. 1. era, date. See **age.**

ep·och·al (ep′ə kəl), *adj.* **1.** of or pertaining to an epoch or epochs. **2.** of the nature of an epoch. **3.** epoch-making. [EPOCH + -AL[1]] —**ep′och·al·ly,** *adv.*

ep·och-mak·ing (ep′ək mā′king), *adj.* opening a new era, as in human history, thought, or knowledge: *an epoch-making discovery.*

ep·ode (ep′ōd), *n.* **1.** *Class. Pros.* a kind of lyric poem, invented by Archilochus, in which a long verse is followed by a short one. **2.** the part of a lyric ode following the strophe and antistrophe and composing with them a triadic unit. [< L *epōd(os)* < Gk *epōidós* an aftersong, singing after. See EP-, ODE]

é·ponge (ā pônzh′; *Fr.* ā pônzh′), *n.* a soft, loosely woven fabric. [< F: lit., SPONGE]

ep·o·nych·i·um (ep′ə nik′ē əm), *n.* **1.** *Embryol.* the modified outer layer of the epidermis that partially covers the fetal fingernails and toenails and that persists after birth as the cuticle. **2.** *Anat.* a thin, cuticular fold extending over the lunula of a nail. Also, **eponychium.** [< NL, equiv. to *ep-* EP- + *onych-* (see ONYX) + *-ium* -IUM]

ep·o·nym (ep′ə nim), *n.* **1.** a person, real or imaginary, from whom something, as a tribe, nation, or place, takes or is said to take its name: *Brut, the supposed grandson of Aeneas, is the eponym of the Britons.* **2.** any ancient official whose name was used to designate his year of office. [back formation from EPONYMOUS] —**ep′o·nym′ic,** *adj.*

ep·on·y·mous (e pon′ə məs), *adj.* giving one's name to a tribe, place, etc.: *Romulus, the eponymous founder of Rome.* [< Gk *epṓnymos* giving name. See EP-, -ONYM, -OUS]

ep·on·y·my (e pon′ə mē), *n.* the derivation of names from eponyms. [< Gk *epōnymía* surname, derived name. See EPONYMOUS, -Y[3]]

ep·o·pee (ep′ə pē′, ep′ə pē′), *n.* **1.** an epic. **2.** epic poetry. Also, **ep·o·poe·ia** (ep′ə pē′ə). [< F *épopée* < Gk *epopoiía,* equiv. to *épo(s)* EPOS + *poi(ein)* (to) make + *-ia* -IA]

ep·os (ep′os), *n.* **1.** an epic. **2.** epic poetry. **3.** a group of poems, transmitted orally, concerned with parts of a common epic theme. **4.** a series of events suitable for treatment in epic poetry. [< L < Gk: speech, tale, song; akin to L *vox* VOICE, Skt *vacas* word, hymn]

ep·ox·y (e pok′sē), *adj., n., pl.* **-ox·ies.** *Chem.* —*adj.* **1.** containing an oxygen atom bound to two already connected, usually carbon, atoms, thus forming a ring, as in ethylene oxide or epoxy ethane, $H_2C(O)CH_2$. —*n.* **2.** Also called **epox′y res′in.** any of a class of substances derived by polymerization from certain viscous liquid or brittle solid epoxy chemicals: used chiefly in adhesives, coatings, electrical insulation, solder mix, and in the casting of tools and dies. [EP- + OXY-[2]]

Ep′ping For′est (ep′ing), a park in E England, NE of London: formerly a royal forest.

ep·si·lon (ep′sə lon′, -lən *or, esp. Brit.,* ep sī′lən), *n.* **1.** the fifth letter of the Greek alphabet (E, ϵ). **2.** the consonant sound represented by this letter. **3.** *Math.* an arbitrarily small quantity, used to indicate that a given quantity is small, or close to zero. [< Gk, equiv. to *è psīlón* bare (simple, i.e., unaspirated)]

ep·si·lon-del·ta (ep′sə lon′del′tə, -lən- *or, esp. Brit.,* ep sī′lən-), *adj. Math.* of or pertaining to a method or proof in calculus involving arbitrarily small numbers.

ep·si·lon-neigh·bor·hood (ep′sə lon′nā′bər ho͝od′, -lən-), *n. Math.* the set of all points whose distance from a given point is less than some specified number *epsilon.*

Ep·som (ep′səm), *n.* a town in SE England, S of London: site of a famous race track **(Ep′som Downs′)** where the annual Derby is held. 71,177 (1961). Official name, **Ep′som and Ew′ell.**

ep·som·ite (ep′sə mīt′), *n. Mineral.* the natural form of Epsom salt, $MgSO_4 \cdot 7H_2O$, found as a crust in caves and lake deposits. [named after EPSOM; see -ITE[1]]

Ep′som salt′, Often, **Epsom salts.** *Chem., Pharm.* hydrated magnesium sulfate, $MgSO_4 \cdot 7H_2O$, occurring as small colorless crystals: used in the dyeing of fabrics, leather tanning, fertilizers, etc., and in medicine chiefly as a cathartic. [named after EPSOM]

Ep·stein (ep′stīn), *n.* **Sir Jacob,** 1880–1959, English sculptor, born in the U.S.

EPT, excess-profits tax.

ep·u·lo (ep′yə lō′; *Lat.* ep′o͝o lō′), *n., pl.* **ep·u·lo·nes** (ep′yə lō′nēz; *Lat.* ep′o͝o lō′nes). (in ancient Rome) a member of a body of priests who performed sacred rites during sacrificial banquets in honor of the gods. [< L: lit., a feaster]

ep·u·ra·tion (ep′yə rā′shən), *n.* a purification or purge, as of government officials considered disloyal or treacherous. [< F, equiv. to *épur(er)* (to) purify (see E-, PURE) + *-ation* -ATION]

Ep′worth League′ (ep′wərth), the Methodist youth organization, founded in 1889 to promote fellowship, worship, Christian service, and the study of the Scriptures.

EQ, educational quotient.

eq., **1.** equal. **2.** equation. **3.** equivalent.

eqpt., equipment.

eq·ua·ble (ek′wə bəl, ē′kwə-), *adj.* **1.** free from variations; uniform, as motion or temperature. **2.** uniform in operation or effect, as laws. **3.** tranquil, even, or not easily disturbed, as the mind. [< L *aequābil(is)* that can be made equal, similar, equiv. to *aequ(us)* equal, even + *-ābilis* -ABLE] —**eq′ua·bil′i·ty, eq′ua·ble·ness,** *n.* —**eq′ua·bly,** *adv.*

—Syn. 1, 3. See **even. 3.** steady, regular, temperate. **—Ant. 1.** variable.

e·qual (ē′kwəl), *adj., n., v.,* **e·qualed, e·qual·ing** *or (esp. Brit.)* **e·qualled, e·qual·ling.** —*adj.* **1.** as great as; the same as (often fol. by *to* or *with*): *The velocity of sound is not equal to that of light.* **2.** like or alike in quantity, degree, value, etc.; of the same rank, ability, merit, etc.: *two students of equal brilliance.* **3.** evenly proportioned or balanced: *an equal mixture; an equal contest.* **4.** uniform in operation or effect: *equal laws.* **5.** adequate or sufficient in quantity or degree: *The supply is equal to the demand.* **6.** having adequate powers, ability, or means: *He was not equal to the task.* **7.** level, as a plain. **8.** *Archaic.* tranquil or undisturbed: *to confront death with an equal mind.* **9.** *Archaic.* impartial or equitable. —*n.* **10.** one who or that which is equal. —*v.t.* **11.** to be or become equal to; match: *So far the rate of production doesn't equal the demand. If A equals B and B equals C, then A equals C.* **12.** to make or do something equal to: *No matter how he tries, he can't equal his brother's achievements.* **13.** *Archaic.* to recompense fully. **14.** *Archaic.* to make equal; equalize. [ME < L *aequāl(is)* equal, like, equiv. to *aequ(us)* even, plain, just + *-ālis* -AL[1]]

—Syn. 2. proportionate, commensurate, coordinate, correspondent. EQUAL, EQUIVALENT, TANTAMOUNT imply a correspondence between two or more things. EQUAL indicates a correspondence in all respects, unless a particular respect (or respects) is stated or implied: *A dime is equal to 10 cents* (that is, in purchasing power, which is implied). EQUIVALENT indicates a correspondence in one or more respects, but not in all: *An egg is said to be the equivalent of a pound of meat* (that is, in nutritive value). TANTAMOUNT, a word of limited application, is used of immaterial things that are equivalent to such an extent as to be practically identical: *The prisoner's refusal to answer was tantamount to an admission of guilt.* **4.** even, uniform, regular, unvarying, invariant. **6.** suited, fitted. **10.** peer, compeer, match, mate, fellow. **—Ant. 2.** different. **5.** disproportionate. **6.** inadequate.

e′qual-ar′e·a projec′tion (ē′kwəl âr′ē ə), *Cartog.* a projection in which regions on the earth's surface that are of equal area are represented as equal.

e·qual·ise (ē′kwə līz′), *v.t.,* **-ised, -is·ing.** *Chiefly Brit.* equalize. —**e′qual·i·sa′tion,** *n.*

e·qual·i·tar·i·an (i kwol′i târ′ē ən), *adj.* **1.** pertaining or adhering to the doctrine of equality among men. —*n.* **2.** a person who adheres to the doctrine of equality among men. [EQUALIT(Y) + -ARIAN] —**e·qual′i·tar′i·an·ism,** *n.*

e·qual·i·ty (i kwol′i tē), *n., pl.* **-ties. 1.** the state of being equal; correspondence in quantity, degree, value, rank, ability, etc. **2.** uniform character, as of motion or surface. [ME < L *aequālitāt-* (s. of *aequālitās*). See EQUAL, -ITY]

Equal′ity State′, Wyoming (used as a nickname).

equaliza′tion fund′. See **stabilization fund.**

e·qual·ize (ē′kwə līz′), *v.t.,* **-ized, -iz·ing. 1.** to make equal: *to equalize tax burdens.* **2.** to make uniform: *to equalize a rate of production.* Also, *esp. Brit.,* **equalise.** [EQUAL + -IZE] —**e′qual·i·za′tion,** *n.*

e·qual·iz·er (ē′kwə lī′zər), *n.* **1.** one who or that which equalizes. **2.** any of various devices or appliances for equalizing strains, pressures, etc. **3.** *Elect.* an electric network of inductance, capacitance, or resistance established between two points in a given network to secure some constant relation, as even attenuation, between the two points. **4.** *Slang.* a weapon, as a pistol, blackjack, or switchblade knife. Also, *esp. Brit.,* **e′qual·is′er.** [EQUALIZE + -ER[1]]

e·qual·ly (ē′kwə lē), *adv.* **1.** in an equal or identical manner: *to treat rich and poor equally.* **2.** to an equal degree or extent: *You are equally matched.* [EQUAL + -LY]

e·qual-sign (ē′kwəl sīn′), *n. Math.* the symbol =, used in a mathematical expression to indicate that the terms it separates are equal.

e′qual tem′perament, *Music.* the division of an octave into 12 equal semitones, as in the tuning of a piano.

E·qua·nil (ē′kwə nil), *n. Pharm., Trademark.* meprobamate.

e·qua·nim·i·ty (ē′kwə nim′i tē, ek′wə-), *n.* mental or emotional stability or composure, esp. under tension or strain; calmness; equilibrium. [< L *aequanimitāt-* (s. of *aequanimitās*), equiv. to *aequ(us)* even, plain, equal + *anim(us)* mind, spirit, feelings + *-itāt-* -ITY]

e·quan·i·mous (i kwan′ə məs), *adj.* having or showing equanimity; even-tempered: *It was difficult to remain equanimous in the face of such impertinence.* [< L *aequanim(is)* (see EQUANIMITY) + -OUS] —**e·quan′i·mous·ly,** *adv.* —**e·quan′i·mous·ness,** *n.*

e·quate (i kwāt′), *v.t.,* **e·quat·ed, e·quat·ing. 1.** to state the equality of or between; put in the form of an equation: *to equate growing prosperity with the physical health of a nation.* **2.** to reduce to an average; make such correction or allowance in as will reduce to a common standard of comparison. **3.** to regard, treat, or represent as equivalent: *We cannot equate the possession of wealth with goodness.* [ME < L *aequāt(us)* made equal (ptp. of *aequāre*), equiv. to *aequ(us)* EQUAL + *-ātus* -ATE[1]] —**e·quat′a·bil′i·ty,** *n.* —**e·quat′a·ble,** *adj.*

e·qua·tion (i kwā′zhən, -shən), *n.* **1.** the act of making equal; equalization: *the symbolic equation of darkness with death.* **2.** equally balanced state; equilibrium. **3.** *Math.* an expression or a proposition, often algebraic, asserting the equality of two quantities, often used in determining a value of an unknown included in one or both quantities. **4.** *Chem.* a symbolic representation showing the kind and amount of the starting materials and products of a reaction. [< L *aequātiōn-* (s. of *aequātiō*) an equalizing. See EQUATE, -ION]

e·qua·tion·al (i kwā′zhə nəl, -shə-), *adj.* **1.** of, using, or involving equations. **2.** *Biol.* pertaining to the second or nonreductional cell division in meiosis, in which each chromosome divides into two equal parts. **3.** *Gram.* (of a sentence or predication) consisting of a subject and a complement with either a copula or no linking verb; nominal: *"Very interesting, those books" is an equational sentence.* [EQUATION + -AL[1]] —**e·qua′tion·al·ly,** *adv.*

equa′tion move′ment, *Horol.* a movement in certain clocks **(equa′tion clock′)** for driving a hand **(equa′tion hand′)** which shows the relation of the mean day of 24 hours to the length of the current solar day.

equa′tion of state′, *Physics.* an equation relating the temperature, pressure, and volume of a given thermodynamic system. Also called **characteristic equation.**

equa′tion of time′, *Astron.* apparent time minus mean solar time, ranging from minus 14 minutes in February to over 16 minutes in November.

e·qua·tor (i kwā′tər), *n.* **1.** the great circle on a sphere or heavenly body whose plane is perpendicular to the axis, equidistant everywhere from the two poles of the sphere or heavenly body. **2.** the great circle of the earth, equidistant from the North Pole and South Pole. **3.** a circle separating a surface into two congruent parts. **4.** See **celestial equator.** [ME < LL *aequātor,* lit., equalizer (of day and night, as when the sun is on the equator). See EQUATE, -OR[2]]

e·qua·to·ri·al (ē′kwə tôr′ē əl, -tōr′-, ek′wə-), *adj.* **1.** of, pertaining to, or near an equator, esp. the equator of the earth. **2.** of, like, or typical of the regions at the earth's equator: *equatorial vegetation; equatorial temperatures.* —*n.* **3.** a telescope mounting having two axes of motion, one parallel to the earth's axis, and one at right angles to it. [EQUATOR + -IAL] —**e′qua·to′ri·al·ly,** *adv.*

E·qua·to/rial Guin/ea, a republic in W equatorial Africa, comprising the mainland province of Rio Muni and the island province of Fernando Po; formerly a Spanish colony. 224,534 (1960); 10,824 sq. mi. *Cap.:* Santa Isabel. Formerly, **Spanish Guinea.**

equato/rial tide/, a semimonthly tide that appears when the moon is over the equator.

equato/rial trough/, the quasi-continuous belt of low atmospheric pressure that lies between the subtropical high-pressure belts of the Northern and Southern hemispheres.

eq·uer·ry (ek/wə rē), *n., pl.* **-ries.** **1.** an officer of a royal or similar household, charged with the care of the horses. **2.** an officer who attends on the British sovereign. [< F *écurie,* OF *escuirie,* equiv. to *escuir* SQUIRE + *-ie* -Y[3]]

e·ques·tri·an (i kwes/trē ən), *adj.* **1.** of or pertaining to horsemen or horsemanship: *equestrian skill.* **2.** mounted on horseback: *equestrian knights.* **3.** of or pertaining to the ancient Roman equites: *the equestrian order.* **4.** representing a person mounted on a horse: *an equestrian statue of Marcus Aurelius.* **5.** pertaining to or composed of knights or mounted warriors: *an equestrian class; an equestrian code of honor.* **—n. 6.** a person who rides horses. [< L *equestri(s)* (cf. *eques* horseman) + -AN] **—e·ques/tri·an·ism,** *n.*

e·ques·tri·enne (i kwes/trē en/), *n.* a female equestrian. [EQUESTRI(AN) + *-enne,* as in *comedienne*]

equi-, a combining form meaning "equal": *equidistant.* [ME < L *aequi-,* comb. form repr. *aequus* equal]

e·qui·an·gu·lar (ē/kwē aŋ/gyə lər), *adj.* having all the angles equal. [EQUI- + ANGULAR] **—e/qui·an/gu·lar/i·ty,** *n.*

equian/gular hyper/bola. See **rectangular hyperbola.**

e·qui·con·tin·u·ous (ē/kwə kən tin/yo͞o əs), *adj. Math.* of or pertaining to a set of functions that have the same domain and such that for any given number, there exists a smaller number having the property that two points whose difference is less than the smaller number have functional values, for all functions in the set, whose difference is less than the larger number. Cf. **continuous** (def. 3). [EQUI- + CONTINUOUS]

e·qui·dis·tance (ē/kwi dis/təns), *n.* equal distance. [EQUI- + DISTANCE]

e·qui·dis·tant (ē/kwi dis/tənt), *adj.* equally distant. [< MF < LL *aequidistant-* (s. of *aequidistāns*). See EQUI-, DISTANT] **—e/qui·dis/tant·ly,** *adv.*

e·qui·form (ē/kwə fôrm/, ek/wə-), *adj.* having the same shape or serving the same purpose. Also, **e/qui·for/mal.** [< LL *aequiform(is).* See EQUI-, -FORM]

e·qui·lat·er·al (ē/kwə lat/ər əl), *adj.* **1.** having all the sides equal. **—n. 2.** a figure having all its sides equal: *an equilateral triangle.* **3.** a side equivalent, or equal, to others. [< LL *aequilaterā-l(is).* See EQUI-, LATERAL] **—e/qui·lat/er·al·ly,** *adv.*

60°

Equilateral triangle

equilat/eral hyper/bola. See **rectangular hyperbola.**

e·quil·i·brant (i kwil/ə brənt), *n. Physics.* a counterbalancing force or system of forces. [< F *équilibrant.* See EQUILIBRIUM, -ANT]

e·quil·i·brate (i kwil/ə brāt/, ē/kwə lī/brāt), *v.,* **-brat·ed, -brat·ing.** **—v.t. 1.** to balance equally; keep in equipoise or equilibrium. **2.** to be in equilibrium with; counterpoise. **—v.i. 3.** to balance. [< LL *aequilībrāt(us),* ptp. of *aequilībrāre* to be in EQUILIBRIUM; see -ATE[1]] **—e·qui·li·bra·tion** (ē/kwə lə brā/shən, i kwil/ə-), *n.* **—e·qui·li·bra·tor** (ē/kwə lī/brā tər, i-kwil/ə brā/-), *n.*

e·quil·i·brist (i kwil/ə brist), *n.* a performer who is skilled at balancing in unusual positions and hazardous movements, as a tightrope walker in a circus. [< F *équilibriste.* See EQUILIBRIUM, -IST] **—e·quil/i·bris/tic,** *adj.*

e·qui·lib·ri·um (ē/kwə lib/rē əm), *n., pl.* **-ri·ums, -ri·a** (-rē ə). **1.** a state of rest or balance due to the equal action of opposing forces. **2.** equal balance between any powers, influences, etc.; equality of effect. **3.** mental or emotional balance; equanimity: *The extremities of the situation caused her to lose her equilibrium.* **4.** *Chem.* the condition existing when a chemical reaction and its reverse reaction proceed at equal rates. [< L *aequilībrium,* equiv. to *aequi-* EQUI- + *lībr(a)* balance + *-ium* -IUM] **—e·quil·i·bra·to·ry** (i kwil/ə brə tôr/ē, -tōr/ē, ē/kwə lib/rə-), *adj.* **—e/qui·lib/ri·ous,** *adj.*

equilib/rium valve/, (in a reciprocating engine) a valve opening a passage from one end of a cylinder to the other to equalize pressure upon both faces of the piston.

e·qui·mo·lec·u·lar (ē/kwə mə lek/yə lər), *adj. Physics, Chem.* containing equal numbers of molecules. [EQUI- + MOLECULAR]

e·quine (ē/kwīn), *adj.* **1.** of or resembling a horse: *a bold, equine face.* **—n. 2.** a horse: *the racing equines.* [< L *equīn(us),* equiv. to *equ(us)* horse + *-īnus* -INE[1]] **—e/quine·ly,** *adv.* **—e·quin/i·ty,** *n.*

e/quine distem/per, *Vet. Pathol.* distemper[1] (def. 1b).

e/quine infec/tious ane/mia, *Vet. Pathol.* See **infectious anemia of horses.**

e·qui·noc·tial (ē/kwə nok/shəl), *adj.* **1.** pertaining to an equinox or the equinoxes, or to the equality of day and night. **2.** pertaining to the celestial equator. **3.** occurring at or about the time of an equinox. **4.** *Bot.* (of a flower) opening regularly at a certain hour. **—n. 5.** See **celestial equator. 6.** See **equinoctial storm.** [ME < L *aequinoctiāl(is)* pertaining to the equinox. See EQUINOX, -AL[1]]

equinoc/tial cir/cle, *Astron.* See **celestial equator.**

equinoc/tial hour/, *Astron.* an hour as measured by a sundial during the vernal equinox, a standard time interval by ancient and medieval astronomers.

equinoc/tial line/. See **celestial equator.**

equinoc/tial point/, either of the two points at which the celestial equator and the ecliptic intersect each other; the position of the sun's center at the equinoxes.

equinoc/tial rains/, rainy seasons that occur, in numerous regions near the equator, near or soon after the times of the equinoxes.

equinoc/tial storm/, a storm of violent winds and rain occurring at or near the time of an equinox and popularly, but erroneously, believed to be physically associated with it. Also called **equinoctial, line gale, line storm.**

equinoc/tial year/, year (def. 4b).

e·qui·nox (ē/kwə noks/, ek/wə-), *n.* **1.** the time when the sun crosses the plane of the earth's equator, making night and day of equal length all over the earth and occurring about March 21 (**vernal equinox**) and September 22 (**autumnal equinox**). **2.** either of the equinoctial points. [ME < ML *equinox(ium)* for L *aequinoctium* the time of equal days and nights (*aequi-* EQUI- + *noct-* (s. of *nox*) NIGHT + *-ium* -IUM)]

e·quip (i kwip/), *v.t.,* **e·quipped, e·quip·ping.** **1.** to furnish or provide with whatever is needed for service or for any undertaking; fit out, as a ship, army, etc.: *He spent several thousand dollars to equip his boat.* **2.** to dress out; array: *He equipped himself in all his finery.* **3.** to furnish with intellectual or emotional needs: *Education and travel have equipped him to deal with all sorts of people.* [< MF *equip(er),* OF *esquiper* to fit out, equip, prob. < Scand; cf. Icel *skipa* to put in order, arrange, man (a ship)] **—e·quip/per,** *n.*
—Syn. 1. outfit, rig. See **furnish.**

eq·ui·page (ek/wə pij), *n.* **1.** a carriage. **2.** a carriage drawn by horses and attended by servants. **3.** outfit, as of a ship, an army, or a soldier; equipment. **4.** a set of small household articles, as of china. **5.** a collection of articles for personal ornament or use. [< MF; see EQUIP, -AGE]

e/qui·par·ti/tion of en/ergy (ē/kwə pär tish/ən, ē/kwə-), *Thermodynamics.* the theorem that the kinetic energy is the same for each degree of freedom in a system in thermal equilibrium. [EQUI- + PARTITION]

e·quip·ment (i kwip/mənt), *n.* **1.** anything used in or provided for equipping. **2.** the act of equipping. **3.** the state of being equipped. **4.** a person's knowledge and skill necessary for a task, occupation, etc.: *He has the necessary equipment for law.* **5.** the rolling stock of a railroad. [EQUIP + -MENT] **—Syn. 1.** apparatus, paraphernalia, gear, accouterment.

e·qui·poise (ē/kwə poiz/, ek/wə-), *n.* **1.** an equal distribution of weight; even balance; equilibrium. **2.** a counterpoise. [EQUI- + POISE[1]]

e/quipoise rud/der, *Naut.* See **balanced rudder.**

e·qui·pol·lent (ē/kwə pol/ənt), *adj.* **1.** equal in power, effect, etc.; equivalent. **2.** *Logic.* (of two propositions, statements, etc.) logically deducible from each other, as "All men are mortal" and "No men are immortal." **—n. 3.** an equivalent. [ME < L *aequipollent-* (s. of *aequipollēns*) of equal value, equiv. to *aequi-* EQUI- + *pollent-* (s. of *pollēns*) able, prp. of *pollere* to be strong] **—e/qui·pol/lence, e/qui·pol/len·cy,** *n.* **—e/qui·pol/lent·ly,** *adv.*

e·qui·pon·der·ance (ē/kwə pon/dər əns), *n.* equality of weight; equipoise. Also, **e/qui·pon/der·an·cy.** [*equiponder(ant)* (< ML *aequiponderant-,* s. of *aequiponderāns,* prp. of *aequiponderāre;* see EQUI-, PONDER, -ANT) + -ANCE] **—e/qui·pon/der·ant,** *adj.*

e·qui·pon·der·ate (ē/kwə pon/də rāt/), *v.t.,* **-at·ed, -at·ing.** to equal or offset in weight, force, importance, etc.; counterbalance. [< ML *aequiponderāt(us),* ptp. of *aequiponderāre.* See EQUI-, PONDER, -ATE[1]] **—e/qui·pon/der·a/tion,** *n.*

e·qui·po·tent (ē/kwə pōt/ᵊnt), *adj.* equal in power, ability, or effect. [EQUI- + POTENT[1]]

e·qui·po·ten·tial (ē/kwə pə ten/shəl), *adj. Physics.* of the same or exhibiting uniform potential at every point: *equipotential surface.* [EQUI- + POTENTIAL] **—e/qui·po·ten/ti·al/i·ty,** *n.*

e·qui·prob·a·bil·ism (ē/kwə prob/ə bə liz/əm), *n. Rom. Cath. Theol.* a theory that in cases of doubt as to the lawfulness or unlawfulness of an action, it is permissible to follow either argument. Cf. **probabilism** (def. 2). [EQUIPROBABLE + -ISM]

e·qui·prob·a·ble (ē/kwə prob/ə bəl), *adj.* equal in probability. [EQUI- + PROBABLE] **—e/qui·prob/a·bil/i·ty,** *n.* **—e/qui·prob/a·bly,** *adv.*

e·qui·ro·tal (ē/kwə rōt/ᵊl), *adj.* having wheels all of the same size or diameter, as a vehicle. [EQUI- + L *rot(a)* wheel + -AL[1]]

eq·ui·se·tum (ek/wi sē/təm), *n., pl.* **-tums, -ta** (-tə). any plant of the genus *Equisetum,* comprising the horsetails or scouring rushes. [< NL; L *equisaetum,* equiv. to *equi-* horse + *saeta* bristle] **—eq/ui·se/tic,** *adj.*

eq·ui·ta·ble (ek/wi tə bəl), *adj.* **1.** characterized by equity or fairness; just and right; fair; reasonable: *equitable treatment of all citizens.* **2.** *Law.* pertaining to or valid in equity, as distinguished from the common law. [EQUIT(Y) + -ABLE] **—eq/ui·ta·ble·ness,** *n.* **—eq/ui·ta·bly,** *adv.*

eq·ui·tant (ek/wi tənt), *adj. Bot.* straddling or overlapping, as leaves whose bases overlap the leaves above or within them. [< L *equitant-* (s. of *equitāns*) riding (prp. of *equitāre*), equiv. to *equit-* (s. of *eques;* see EQUITES) + *-ant-* -ANT]

eq·ui·ta·tion (ek/wi tā/shən), *n.* the act or art of riding on horseback. [< L *equitātiōn-* (s. of *equitātiō*), equiv. to *equitāt(us)* (ptp. of *equitāre* to ride) + *-iōn-* -ION]

eq·ui·tes (ek/wi tēz/), *n., pl. Rom. Hist.* **1.** the mounted military units; cavalry. **2.** members of a specially privileged class derived from the ancient Roman cavalry and having status intermediate between those of senatorial rank and the common people. [< L, pl. of *eques* horseman, deriv. of *equus* horse]

eq·ui·ty (ek/wi tē), *n., pl.* **-ties.** **1.** the quality of being fair or impartial; fairness; impartiality: *the equity of Solomon.* **2.** that which is fair and just. **3.** *Law.* **a.** the application of the dictates of conscience or the principles of natural justice to the settlement of controversies. **b.** a system of jurisprudence or a body of doctrines and rules developed in England and followed in the United States, serving to supplement and remedy the limitations and the inflexibility of the common law. **c.** an equitable right or claim. **d.** an equity of redemption. **4.** the interest of the owner of common stock in a corporation. **5.** (in a margin account) the excess of the market value of the securities over any indebtedness. **6.** (*cap.*) See **Actors' Equity Association.** [ME *equite* < L *aequitās.* See EQUI-, -TY[2]]

eq/uity cap/ital, that portion of the capital of a business provided by the sale of stock.

eq/uity of redemp/tion, **1.** the right of a mortgagor to redeem the property by paying the debt, even after default in payment of the sum owed. **2.** the interest of an owner of land subject to a mortgage.

eq/uity secu/rity, a security, esp. a common stock, representing an ownership rather than a debt claim.

equiv., equivalent.

e·quiv·a·lence (i kwiv/ə ləns *or, esp. for 3,* ē/kwə-vā/ləns), *n.* **1.** the state or fact of being equivalent; equality in value, force, significance, etc.: *the equivalence between time and work.* **2.** an instance of this; an equivalent: *a choice between equivalences.* **3.** *Chem.* the quality of having equal valence. **4.** *Logic, Math.* **a.** the relation between two propositions such that they are either both true or both false. **b.** the relation between two propositions such that each logically implies the other. **—adj. 5.** (of a logical or mathematical relationship) reflexive, symmetrical, and transitive: Also, **equivalency** (for defs. 1, 2). [< MF < ML *aequivalentia,* equiv. to L *aequivalent-* EQUIVALENT + *-ia* -IA; see -ENCE]

equiv/alence class/, *Math.* the set of elements associated by an equivalence relation with a given element of a set.

equiv/alence rela/tion, *Math.* a relation which is reflexive, symmetrical, and transitive, as equality.

e·quiv·a·len·cy (i kwiv/ə lən sē), *n., pl.* **-cies.** equivalence (defs. 1, 2). [< ML *aequivalentia.* See EQUIVALENT, -ENCY]

e·quiv·a·lent (i kwiv/ə lənt *or, esp. for 5,* ē/qwə vā/-lənt), *adj.* **1.** equal in value, measure, force, effect, significance, etc.: *His silence is equivalent to an admission of guilt.* **2.** corresponding in position, function, etc.: *In some ways their prime minister is equivalent to our president.* **3.** *Geom.* having the same extent, as a triangle and a square of equal area. **4.** *Math.* (of two sets) able to be placed in one-to-one correspondence. **5.** *Chem.* having the same capacity to combine or react chemically. **—n. 6.** that which is equivalent. [late ME < LL *aequivalent-* (s. of *aequivalēns*), prp. of *aequivalēre.* See EQUI-, -VALENT] **—e·quiv/a·lent·ly,** *adv.*
—Syn. 1. See **equal.**

equiv/alent weight/, *Chem.* the combining power, esp. in grams (**gram equivalent**), of an element or compound, equivalent to hydrogen as a standard of 1.00797 or oxygen as a standard of 8; the atomic weight divided by the valence.

e·qui·valve (ē/kwə valv/), *adj.* (of a bivalve mollusk) having the valves of the shell equal in shape and size. [EQUI- + VALVE]

e·quiv·o·cal (i kwiv/ə kəl), *adj.* **1.** of uncertain significance; not determined: *an equivocal attitude.* **2.** of doubtful nature or character; questionable; dubious; suspicious: *aliens of equivocal loyalty.* **3.** having different meanings equally possible, as a word or phrase; susceptible of double interpretation; ambiguous: *an equivocal answer.* [ME *equivoc* < L *aequivoc(us)* ambiguous (L *aequi-* EQUI- + *vōc-,* s. of *vōx* VOX + *-us* adj. suffix) + -AL[1]] **—e·quiv/o·cal/i·ty, e·quiv·o·ca·cy** (i kwiv/ə kə sē), *n.* **—e·quiv/o·cal·ly,** *adv.* **—e·quiv/o·cal·ness,** *n.*
—Syn. 3. See **ambiguous.**

e·quiv·o·cate (i kwiv/ə kāt/), *v.i.,* **-cat·ed, -cat·ing.** to use ambiguous or unclear expressions, usually to avoid commitment or in order to mislead; prevaricate or hedge: *When asked directly what was his position, the candidate only equivocated.* [late ME < ML *aequivocāt(us),* ptp. of *aequivocāre.* See EQUIVOCAL, -ATE[1]] **—e·quiv/o·cat/ing·ly,** *adv.* **—e·quiv/o·ca/tor,** *n.*

e·quiv·o·ca·tion (i kwiv/ə kā/shən), *n.* **1.** the use of equivocal or ambiguous expressions, esp. in order to mislead or hedge; prevarication. **2.** an equivocal, ambiguous expression; equivoque: *The speech was marked by elaborate equivocations.* **3.** *Logic.* a fallacy caused by the double meaning of a word. [late ME *equivocacion* < LL *aequivocātiōn-* (s. of *aequivocātiō*). See EQUIVOCATE, -ION]

eq·ui·voque (ek/wə vōk/, ē/kwə-), *n.* **1.** an equivocal term; an ambiguous expression. **2.** a play upon words; pun. **3.** double meaning; ambiguity. Also, **eq/ui·voke/.** [ME *equivoc* adj.; see EQUIVOCAL]

E·quu·le·us (i kwo͞o/lē əs), *n., gen.* **-le·i** (-lē ī/). *Astron.* the Little Horse, a small northern constellation between Delphinus and Aquarius. [< L]

er (ə, ər), *interj.* (used to express or represent a pause, hesitation, uncertainty, etc.).

-er[1], **1.** a suffix used in forming nouns designating persons from the object of their occupation or labor (*hatter; tiler; tinner; moonshiner*), or from their place of origin or abode (*Icelander; southerner; villager*), or designating either persons or things from some special characteristic or circumstance (*six-footer; three-master; teetotaler; fiver; tenner*). **2.** a suffix serving as the regular English formative of agent nouns, being attached to verbs of any origin (*bearer; creeper; employer; harvester; teacher; theorizer*). [OE *-ere;* c. G *-er;* akin to L *-ārius*]

-er[2], a suffix of nouns denoting persons or things concerned or connected with something: *butler; grocer; garner.* [ME < AF *-er,* equiv. to OF *-er, -ier* < L *-ārius, -ārium.* Cf. -ARY]

-er[3], a termination of nouns denoting action or process: *dinner; rejoinder; remainder; trover.* [< F, orig. inf. suffix]

-er[4], a suffix regularly used in forming the comparative degree of adjectives: *harder; smaller.* [OE *-ra, -re;* c. G *-er*]

-er[5], a suffix regularly used in forming the comparative degree of adverbs: *faster.* [OE *-or;* c. OHG *-or,* G *-er*]

-er[6], a formal element appearing in verbs having frequentative meaning: *flicker; flutter; shiver; shudder.* [OE *-r-;* c. G *-(e)r-*]

E.R., **1.** East Riding (Yorkshire). **2.** East River (New York City). **3.** King Edward. [< L *Edwardus Rex*] **4.** Queen Elizabeth. [< L *Elizabeth Regina*]

Er, *Chem.* erbium.

e·ra (ēr/ə, er/ə), *n.* **1.** a period of time marked by distinctive character, events, etc.: *The use of steam for power marked the beginning of an era.* **2.** the period of time to which anything belongs or is to be assigned: *She was born in the era of hansoms and gaslight.* **3.** a system of chronologic notation reckoned from a given date: *The era of the Romans was based upon the time the city* *of Rome was founded.* **4.** a point of time from which succeeding years are numbered, as at the beginning of a system of chronology: *Caesar died many years before our era.* **5.** a date or an event forming the beginning of any distinctive period: *1492 marks an era in world history.* **6.** *Geol.* a major division of geological time composed of a number of periods. [< LL *aera* fixed date, era, epoch (from which time is reckoned), prob. special use of L *aera* counters (pl. of *aes* piece of metal, money, brass); c. Goth *aiz*, OE *ār* ORE, Skt *ayah*] **—Syn. 1.** See **age.**

ERA	YEARS AGO	PERIOD	EPOCH	CHARACTERIZED BY
Archeozoic	5,000,000,000-1,500,000,000			earth's crust formed; unicellular organisms; earliest known life
Proterozoic	1,500,000,000-600,000,000			bacteria, algae, and fungi; primitive multicellular organisms
Paleozoic	600,000,000-500,000,000	Cambrian		marine invertebrates
	500,000,000-440,000,000	Ordovician		conodonts, ostracods, algae, and seaweeds
	440,000,000-400,000,000	Silurian		air-breathing animals
	400,000,000-350,000,000	Devonian		dominance of fishes; advent of amphibians and ammonites
	350,000,000-300,000,000	Mississippian (Carboniferous)		increase of land areas; primitive ammonites; development of winged insects
	300,000,000-270,000,000	Pennsylvanian (Carboniferous)		warm climates; swampy lands; development of large reptiles and insects
	270,000,000-220,000,000	Permian		many reptiles
Mesozoic	220,000,000-180,000,000	Triassic		volcanic activity; marine reptiles, dinosaurs
	180,000,000-135,000,000	Jurassic		dinosaurs, conifers
	135,000,000-70,000,000	Cretaceous		extinction of giant reptiles; advent of modern insects; flowering plants
Cenozoic	70,000,000-60,000,000	Paleogene (Tertiary)	Paleocene	advent of birds, mammals
	60,000,000-40,000,000		Eocene	presence of modern mammals
	40,000,000-25,000,000		Oligocene	sabertoothed cats
	25,000,000-10,000,000	Neogene (Tertiary)	Miocene	grazing mammals
	10,000,000-1,000,000		Pliocene	growth of mountains; increase in size and numbers of mammals; gradual cooling of climate
	1,000,000-10,000	Quaternary	Pleistocene	widespread glacial ice
	10,000-present		Recent	development of man

ERA, **1.** *Baseball.* See **earned run average. 2.** Emergency Relief Administration. **3.** Equal Rights Amendment (to the U.S. Constitution, esp. referring to sexual equality).

era, *Baseball.* See **earned run average.**

e·ra·di·ate (i rā′dē āt′), *v.i., v.t.,* **-at·ed, -at·ing.** to radiate. [E- + RADIATE]

e·ra·di·a·tion (i rā′dē ā′shən), *n.* the act or process of shooting forth rays of light, heat, etc.; radiation. [E- + RADIATION]

e·rad·i·ca·ble (i rad′ə kə bəl), *adj.* capable of being eradicated. [< LL *ērādicābil(is)*, equiv. to L *ērādīc(āre)* (to) ERADICATE + *-ābilis* -ABLE] **—e·rad′i·ca·bly,** *adv.*

e·rad·i·cate (i rad′ə kāt′), *v.t.,* **-cat·ed, -cat·ing. 1.** to remove or destroy utterly; extirpate: *to eradicate an army.* **2.** to erase by rubbing or by means of a chemical solvent: *to eradicate a spot.* **3.** to pull up by the roots: *to eradicate weeds.* [< L *ērādīcāt(us)* rooted out (ptp. of *ērādīcāre*), equiv. to *ē-* E- + *rādīc-* (s. of *rādix*) root + *-ātus* -ATE¹] **—e·rad·i·cant** (i rad′ə kənt), *adj., n.* **—e·rad′i·ca′tion,** *n.* **—e·rad′i·ca′tive,** *adj.* **—e·rad′i·ca′tor,** *n.*
—Syn. 1. obliterate, uproot, exterminate, annihilate. See **abolish.**

e·rad·i·cat·ed (i rad′ə kā′tid), *adj. Heraldry.* (of a tree or other plant) with the roots depicted: *a lily eradicated.* [ERADICATE + -ED²]

E′ra of Good′ Feel′ing, *U.S. Hist.* a period corresponding to the greater part of the administrations of James Monroe, or about 1817 to 1824, during which there was little political strife.

e·rase (i rās′), *v.,* **e·rased, e·ras·ing.** **—***v.t.* **1.** to rub or scrape out, as letters or characters written, engraved, etc.; efface. **2.** to obliterate material recorded on magnetic tape or on wire from a tape recorder or wire recorder by demagnetizing the tape or wire. **3.** *Slang.* to murder: *The gang had to erase him before he informed on them.* **—***v.i.* **4.** to give way to effacement readily or easily. **5.** to obliterate characters, letters, markings, etc., from something. [< L *ērās(us)* (ptp. of *ērādere*), equiv. to *ē-* E- + *rāsus* scraped; see RAZE] **—e·ras′a·bil′i·ty,** *n.* **—e·ras′a·ble,** *adj.*
—Syn. 1. expunge, obliterate. See **cancel. —Ant. 1, 2.** restore.

e·rased (i rāst′), *adj.* **1.** rubbed out; removed; obliterated. **2.** *Heraldry.* (of the head, leg, or forepart of an animal or bird) represented as torn off so as to leave a ragged edge. Cf. **couped.** [ERASE + -ED²]

e·ras·er (i rā′sər), *n.* **1.** an instrument, as a piece of rubber or cloth, for erasing marks made with pen, pencil, chalk, etc. **2.** one who or that which erases. [ERASE + -ER¹]

e·ra·sion (i rā′zhən), *n.* **1.** the act of erasing. **2.** *Surg.* **a.** the scraping away of tissue, esp. of bone. **b.** Also called **arthrectomy.** excision of a joint. [ERASE + -ION]

E·ras·mi·an (i raz′mē ən), *adj.* **1.** of, pertaining to, or like Erasmus. **—***n.* **2.** a follower of Erasmus. [ERASM(US) + -IAN] **—E·ras′mi·an·ism,** *n.*

E·ras·mus (i raz′məs), *n.* **1. Des·i·de·ri·us** (dez′i dēr′ē əs), 1466?–1536, Dutch humanist, scholar, theologian, and writer. **2.** a boy's given name.

E·ras·tian (i ras′chən, -tē ən), *adj.* **1.** of or pertaining to Thomas Erastus or Erastianism. **—***n.* **2.** an advocate of Erastianism. [ERAST(US) + -IAN]

E·ras·tian·ism (i ras′chə niz′əm, -tē ə niz′-), *n.* the doctrine, advocated by Thomas Erastus, of the supremacy of the state over the church in ecclesiastical matters. [ERASTIAN + -ISM]

E·ras·tus (i ras′təs; *Ger.* ä räs′to͝os), *n.* **1. Thom·as** (tom′əs; *Ger.* tō′mäs), 1524–83, a Swiss-German theologian. **2.** a boy's given name.

e·ra·sure (i rā′shər), *n.* **1.** the act or an instance of erasing. **2.** a place where something has been erased: *You can't turn your theme in with so many erasures in it.* [ERASE + -URE]

Er·a·to (er′ə tō′), *n. Class. Myth.* the Muse of love poetry.

Er·a·tos·the·nes (er′ə tos′thə nēz′), *n.* **1.** 276?–195? B.C., Greek mathematician and astronomer at Alexandria. **2.** a walled plain in the second quadrant of the face of the moon: about 38 miles in diameter.

Er·bil (ir′bil), *n.* a town in N Iraq: built on the site of ancient Arbela. 26,086 (1947). Also, **Arbil.**

er·bi·um (ûr′bē əm), *n. Chem.* a rare-earth metallic element, having pink salts. *Symbol:* Er; *at. wt.:* 167.26; *at. no.:* 68. [< NL, named after (*Ytt*)*erb*(*y*), Sweden, where it is found; see -IUM]

Er·cel·doune (ûr′səl doun′), *n.* **Thomas of.** See **Thomas of Erceldoune.**

Er·cil·la (er thē′lyä, -sē′yä), *n.* **A·lon·so de** (ä lôn′sô de), 1533–94, Spanish epic poet; soldier in the conquest of Chile

Erck·mann-Cha·tri·an (erk man′sha trē än′), *n.* joint pen name of **É·mile Erckmann** (ā mēl′), 1822–99, and **A·le·xan·dre Chatrian** (a lek sän′drə), 1826–90, collaborating French novelists and dramatists.

ere (âr), *prep., conj. Poetic.* before. [ME; OE *ǣr*, *ēr* (c. G *ehr*), comp. of *ār* soon, early; c. Goth *air.* See ERST, EARLY]

Er·e·bus (er′ə bəs), *n.* **1.** *Class. Myth.* the darkness under the earth, imagined either as the abode of sinners after death or of all the dead. **2. Mount,** a volcano in Antarctica, on Ross Island. 13,202 ft. [< L < Gk *Érebos*; c. Skt *rājas* darkness, Aram *erek* evening, Goth *riquis* darkness]

E·rech (ē′rek, er′ek), *n.* Biblical name of **Uruk.**

E·re·chim (i ri shēm′), *n.* a city in S Brazil. 29,590 (1960).

E·rech·the·um (i rek′thē əm, er′ək thē′əm), *n.* a temple at Athens, begun c420 B.C., having two Ionic porches and a porch of caryatides: regarded as one of the finest examples of classical architecture.

E·rech·the·us (i rek′thē əs, -thyo͞os), *n. Gk. Legend.* a king of Athens and the father of Procris.

e·rect (i rekt′), *adj.* **1.** upright in position or posture: *to stand or sit erect.* **2.** raised or directed upward: *a dog with ears erect.* **3.** *Bot.* vertical throughout; not spreading or declined: *an erect stem; an erect leaf or ovule.* **4.** *Heraldry.* **a.** (of a charge) represented palewise: *a sword erect.* **b.** (of an animal or part of an animal) represented upright: *a boar's head erect.* **5.** *Optics.* (of an image) having the same position as the object; not inverted. **—***v.t.* **6.** to build; construct; raise: *to erect a house.* **7.** to raise and set in an upright or vertical position: *to erect a telegraph pole.* **8.** *Geom.* to draw or construct (a line or figure) upon a given line, base, or the like. **9.** *Optics.* to change (an inverted image) to the normal position. **10.** to form or create legally (usually fol. by *into*): *to erect a territory into a state.* **11.** to set up or establish, as an institution; found: *He erected the college as a monument to his own name.* **12.** to bring about; cause to come into existence: *to erect barriers to progress.* **13.** *Mach.* to assemble; make ready for use. **—***v.i.* **14.** to become erect; stand up or out. [< L *ērect(us)* raised up (ptp. of *ērigere*), equiv. to *ē-* E- + *reg-* guide, direct (see ROYAL) + *-tus* ptp. suffix] **—e·rect′a·ble,** *adj.* **—e·rect′er,** *n.* **—e·rect′ly,** *adv.* **—e·rect′ness,** *n.*
—Syn. 1. standing, vertical. See **upright. 6.** upraise. **—Ant. 1.** reclining.

e·rec·tile (i rek′tᵊl, -til), *adj.* **1.** capable of being erected or set upright. **2.** *Anat.* capable of being distended with blood and becoming rigid, as tissue. [< F *érectile.* See ERECT, -ILE] **—e·rec·til·i·ty** (i rek til′i tē, ē′rek-), *n.*

erect′ing prism′, *Optics.* See **Dove prism.**

e·rec·tion (i rek′shən), *n.* **1.** the act of erecting. **2.** the state of being erected. **3.** something erected, as a building or other structure. **4.** *Physiol.* a distended and rigid state of an organ or part containing erectile tissue, esp. of the penis or the clitoris. [< LL *ērectiōn-* (s. of *ērectiō*). See ERECT, -ION]

e·rec·tive (i rek′tiv), *adj.* tending to erect. [ERECT + -IVE]

e·rec·tor (i rek′tər), *n.* **1.** one who or that which erects; erecter. **2.** *Anat.* a muscle which erects the body or one of its parts. [ERECT + -OR²]

E region. See **E layer.**

-erel, var. of **-rel.**

ere·long (âr lông′, -long′), *adv. Archaic.* before long; soon. [ERE + LONG¹]

er·e·mite (er′ə mīt′), *n.* a hermit or recluse, esp. one under a religious vow. [< LL *erēmīt(a)* HERMIT] **—er·e·mit·ic** (er′ə mit′ik), **er′e·mit′i·cal, er·e·mit·ish** (er′ə mī′tish), *adj.* **—er′e·mit′ism,** *n.*

er·e·moph·i·lous (er′ə mof′ə ləs), *adj. Zool.* living in a desert. [< NL *eremo-* (see EREMOPHYTE) + -PHILOUS]

er·e·mo·phyte (er′ə mō fīt′, i rē′mə-), *n.* a plant that grows in a desert. [< NL *eremo-* (comb. form repr. Gk *érēmos* solitary, empty; see EREMITE) + -PHYTE]

ere·now (âr nou′), *adv. Archaic.* before this time. [ME *ar now.* See ERE, NOW]

e·rep·sin (i rep′sin), *n. Biochem.* a mixture of proteolytic enzymes, consisting of peptidases and occurring in the intestinal secretions. [< L *ēr(ipere)* (to) take away (*ē-* E- + *rapere* to take) + (P)EPSIN]

E·resh·ki·gal (ā resh′kē′gäl, er′esh kig′əl), *n.* the Sumerian and Akkadian goddess of death; the consort of Nergal. Also, **E·resh·ki·gel** (ā resh′kē′gel, er′esh kig′əl).

er·e·thism (er′ə thiz′əm), *n. Physiol.* an unusual or excessive degree of irritability or stimulation in an organ or tissue. [< F *éréthisme* < Gk *erethism(ós)* irritation, equiv. to *ereth(ízein)* (to) irritate + *-ismos* -ISM] **—er′e·this′mic, er·e·this·tic** (er′ə this′tik), **er′e·thit′ic, e·reth·ic** (ə reth′ik, e reth′-), *adj.*

Er·eu·tha·li·on (er′o͞o thā′lē ən), *n.* (in the *Iliad*) an Arcadian warrior who was killed in a duel with Nestor.

ere·while (âr hwīl′, -wīl′), *adv. Archaic.* a while before; formerly. [ME; see ERE, WHILE]

Er·e·whon (er′ə hwon′, -hwən, -won′, -wən), *n.* a satirical novel (1872) by Samuel Butler.

Er·furt (er′fo͝ort), *n.* a city in and the capital of Thuringia, in central Germany. 220,016.

erg¹ (ûrg), *n. Physics.* the centimeter-gram-second unit of work or energy, equal to the work done by a force of one dyne when its point of application moves through a distance of one centimeter in the direction of the force; 10^{-7} joule. [< Gk *érg(on)* work]

erg² (erg), *n. Geol.* any vast area covered with sand, as parts of the Sahara Desert. [< F; of Hamitic orig.]

erg-, var. of **ergo-**¹ before a vowel: *ergodic.*

Er·ga·ne (ûr′gə nē), *n. Class. Myth.* an epithet of Athena, meaning "worker."

er·gate (ûr′gāt), *n.* a worker ant. [< Gk *ergátē(s)* worker, doer, producer, equiv. to *érg(on)* ERG¹ + *-atēs* agent suffix]

er·ga·tive (ûr′gə tiv), *Gram.* **—***adj.* **1.** noting a case whose distinctive function is to indicate the agent or instrument of an action involving something else. **—***n.* **2.** the ergative case. [< Gk *ergát(es)* worker (see ERGATE) + -IVE]

Er·gi·nus (ər jī′nəs), *n. Class. Myth.* a Minyan king who engaged in frequent struggles with the Thebans.

er·go (ûr′gō, er′gō), *conj., adv.* therefore. [< L]

ergo-¹, a combining form meaning "work": *ergograph.* Also, *esp. before a vowel,* **erg-.** [comb. form repr. Gk *érgon*]

ergo-², a combining of **ergot:** *ergotoxin.* [< F]

er·go·cal·cif·er·ol (ûr′gō kal sif′ə rōl′, -rôl′, -rol′), *n. Biochem.* calciferol. [ERGO-² + CALCIFEROL]

er·god·ic (ûr god′ik), *adj. Math., Statistics.* of or pertaining to the condition that, in an interval of sufficient duration, a system will return to states which are closely similar to previous ones: the assumption of such a condition underlies statistical methods used in modern dynamics and atomic theory. [ERG- + Gk *hod(ós)* way, road + -IC] **—er·go·dic·i·ty** (ûr′gə dis′i tē), *n.*

er·go·graph (ûr′gə graf′, -gräf′), *n.* an instrument that records the amount of work done when a muscle contracts. [ERGO-¹ + -GRAPH] **—er′go·graph′ic** (ûr′gə graf′ik), *adj.*

er·go·met·rine (ûr′gə me′trēn, -trin, -mē′-), *n. Pharm.* ergonovine. [ERGO-² + METR- + -INE²]

er·go·nom·ics (ûr′gə nom′iks), *n.* (*construed as sing. or pl.*) biotechnology. [ERG- + (EC)ONOMICS] **—er′go·nom′ic,** *adj.*

er·go·no·vine (ûr′gə nō′vēn, -vin), *n. Pharm.* a crystalline alkaloid, $C_{19}H_{23}N_3O_2$, obtained from ergot: used chiefly in the form of its maleate in the prevention or treatment of hemorrhage following childbirth or abortion. [ERGO-² + *nov-* (< L *novus* new) + -INE²]

er·gos·ter·ol (ûr gos′tə rōl′, -rôl′, -rol′), *n. Biochem.* a colorless, crystalline, water-insoluble sterol, $C_{28}H_{43}OH$, that occurs in ergot and yeast and that, when irradiated with ultraviolet light, is converted into vitamin D. [ERGO-² + STEROL]

er·got (ûr′gət, -got), *n.* **1.** *Plant Pathol.* **a.** a disease of rye and other cereal grasses, caused by a fungus of the genus *Claviceps*, esp. *C. purpurea*, which replaces the affected grain with a long, hard, hornlike, dark-colored, sclerotial body. **b.** the sclerotial body itself. **2.** *Pharm.* the sclerotium of *C. purpurea*, developed on rye plants: used chiefly to prevent or check postpartum hemorrhage. [< F: lit., a rooster's spur; OF *argos, argoz, argot* spur(s)]

er·got·a·mine (ûr got′ə mēn′, -min), *n. Pharm.* a crystalline, water-soluble polypeptide, $C_{33}H_{35}N_5O_5$, obtained from ergot: used chiefly in the form of its tartrate to stimulate uterine contractions during labor and in the treatment of migraine. [ERGOT + -AMINE]

er·got·in (ûr′gə tin), *n. Pharm.* any of various extracts of ergot used in medicine. Also, **er′got·ine.** [ERGOT + -IN²]

er·got·i·nine (ûr got′ə nēn′, -nin), *n. Pharm.* a white, crystalline, water-soluble alkaloid of ergot, $C_{35}H_{39}N_5O_5$, having no pharmacological effect; the anhydride of ergotoxine. [ERGOTIN + -INE²]

er·got·ism (ûr′gə tiz′əm), *n. Pathol.* a condition caused by eating rye or some other grain that is infected with ergot fungus or by taking an overdose of an ergot medicinal agent: characterized by cramps, spasms, and a form of gangrene. [ERGOT + -ISM]

er·go·tox·ine (ûr′gə tok′sēn, -sin), *n. Pharm.* a white, crystalline, water-insoluble alkaloid obtained from ergot, $C_{35}H_{41}N_5O_6$: used chiefly as a uterine stimulant. [ERGO-² + TOXINE]

Er·go·trate (ûr′gə trāt′), *n. Pharm., Trademark.* ergonovine.

Er·hard (âr′härt; *Ger.* ᴇʀ′härt), *n.* **Lud·wig** (lud′wig; *Ger.* lo͞ot′vɪᴋʜ, lo͞od′-), born 1897, West German economist and government official: chancellor 1963–66.

Er·hardt (âr′härt; *Ger.* ᴇʀ′häʀt), *n.* a boy's given name.

Er·i·boe·a (er′ə bē′ə), *n. Class. Myth.* a wife of Aloeus.

Er·ic (er′ik), *n.* **1.** See **Eric the Red.** **2.** Also, **Erik.** a boy's given name.

Er·i·ca (er′i kə), *n.* a girl's given name. Also, **Erika.**

er·i·ca·ceous (er′ə kā′shəs), *adj.* belonging to the *Ericaceae*, or heath family of plants, which includes the heath, arbutus, azalea, rhododendron, American laurel, etc. [< NL *Ericāce(ae)* (L *erīc(a)* heath, broom (< Gk *ereíkē*) + *-āceae* -ACEAE) + -OUS]

er·i·ce·tic·o·lous (er′ə si tik′ə ləs), *adj.* living or growing in a heath. [< L **ericēt(um)* place where heath grows (deriv. of *erīca* heath; see ERICACEOUS) + -I- + -COLOUS]

Er·ich·tho·ni·us (er′ik thō′nē əs), *n. Class. Myth.* **1.** a legendary king of Athens, a son of Hephaestus and Gaea, sometimes identified with Erechtheus. **2.** a son of Dardanus who succeeded to his father's throne.

er·i·coid (er′ə koid′), *adj.* resembling a heath of the genus *Erica* or of the family *Ericaceae.* [< NL *Eric(a)* (see ERICACEOUS) + -OID]

Er·ic·son (er′ik sən), *n.* **Leif** (lēf; *Icel.* lāv), fl. A.D. c1000, Norse mariner: according to Icelandic saga, discoverer of Vinland (son of Eric the Red). Old Norse, **Eiríkson.** Also, **Ericsson.**

Er·ics·son (er′ik sən), *n.* **1. John,** 1803–89, Swedish engineer and inventor; in the U.S. after 1839. **2.** See **Ericson, Leif.**

Er′ic the Red′, born A.D. c950, Norse mariner: explorer and colonizer of Greenland c985. Also called **Eric.**

E·rid·a·nus (i rid′ənəs), *n., gen.* **-a·ni** (-ənī′). *Astron.* the River, a large southern constellation between Cetus and Orion, containing the bright star Achernar.

E·ri·du (ā′ri do͞o), *n.* an ancient Sumerian and Babylonian city near the Euphrates in S Iraq: center for the worship of Ea; partially excavated.

E·rie (ēr′ē), *n., pl.,* for 3, **E·ries,** (*esp. collectively*) **E·rie.** **1. Lake,** a lake between the NE central United States and SE central Canada: the southernmost lake of the Great Lakes; Commodore Perry's defeat of the British in 1813. 239 mi. long; 9940 sq. mi. **2.** a port in NW Pennsylvania, on Lake Erie. 138,440 (1960). **3.** a member of a tribe of American Indians formerly living along the southern shore of Lake Erie.

E′rie Canal′, a canal in New York between Albany and Buffalo, connecting the Hudson River with Lake Erie: completed in 1825. Cf. **New York State Barge Canal** (def. 2).

E·rig·e·na (e rij′ə nə), *n.* **Jo·han·nes Sco·tus** (jō han′ēz skō′təs, -han′is), A.D. c810–c877, Irish philosopher and theologian.

e·rig·er·on (i rij′ə ron′), *n.* any composite plant of the genus *Erigeron*, having flower heads resembling those of the asters but with narrower and usually more numerous white or purple rays. [< L *ērigeron* the plant groundsel < Gk *ērigérōn*, equiv. to *ēri* early (c. ERE) + *gérōn* (see GERONTO-)]

E·rig·o·ne (i rig′ə nē), *n. Class. Myth.* **1.** the daughter of Icarius who killed herself for grief over the murder of her father. **2.** a daughter of Clytemnestra and Aegisthus who hanged herself when Orestes was acquitted of the murder of her parents.

Er·ik (er′ik), *n.* a boy's given name. Also, **Eric.**

Er·i·ka (er′i kə), *n.* a girl's given name. Also, **Erica.**

Er·i·man·thus (er′ə man′thəs), *n.* Erymanthus.

Er·in (er′in, ēr′in, âr′in), *n. Poetic.* Ireland.

Er·i·na (âr′ə nə), *n.* a girl's given name.

er·i·na·ceous (er′ə nā′shəs), *adj.* of the hedgehog kind or family. [< L *ērināce(us)* hedgehog + -OUS]

e·rin·go (i ring′gō), *n., pl.* **-goes, -gos.** eryngo.

Er·in go bragh (âr′in gō bʀä′, ēr′in, ᴇʀ′in), *Gaelic.* Ireland forever.

E·rin·ys (i rin′is, i rī′nis), *n., pl.* **E·rin·y·es** (i rin′ē ēz′). *Class. Myth.* **1.** any of the Furies. **2.** an epithet of Demeter, meaning "fury."

er·i·o·phyl·lous (er′ē ō fil′əs), *adj. Bot.* having leaves covered with a woolly pubescence. [< Gk *erio-* (comb. form of *érion* wool) + -PHYLLOUS]

E·ris (ēr′is, er′is), *n.* the ancient Greek goddess of discord and sister of Ares. She threw the apple of discord among the guests at the wedding of Peleus and Thetis: identified by the Romans with Discordia.

er·is·tic (e ris′tik), *adj.* **1.** Also, **er·is′ti·cal.** pertaining to controversy or disputation; controversial. —*n.* **2.** a person who engages in disputation; controversialist. **3.** the art of disputation. [< Gk *eristik(ós)*, equiv. to *erist(ós)* (verbid of *erízein*, deriv. of *éris* discord) + *-ikos* -IC] —**er·is′ti·cal·ly,** *adv.*

Er·i·tre·a (er′i trē′ə; *It.* e′ʀē tʀe′ä), *n.* an autonomous province federated with Ethiopia, in NE Africa, on the Red Sea: formerly an Italian colony. 1,422,300 (est. 1962); 47,076 sq. mi. *Cap.:* Asmara. —**Er′i·tre′an,** *adj., n.*

E·ri·van (*Russ.* ᴇʀ′i vän′yᵊ), *n.* a city in and the capital of Armenia, in the S Soviet Union in Europe. 623,000 (1965). Also, **Yerevan.**

erk (ûrk), *n. Brit.* **1.** an aircraftsman, the lowest rank in the Royal Air Force. **2.** *Slang.* a worthless, stupid person; jerk. [by alter. from *airc* (repr. *aircraftsman*)]

Er·lan·der (ᴇʀ′län dəʀ), *n.* **Ta·ge (Fri·tiof)** (tä′gə fʀē′chəf), born 1901, Swedish statesman: prime minister since 1946.

Er·lan·ger (ûr′lang ər), *n.* **Joseph,** 1874–1965, U.S. physiologist: Nobel prize for medicine 1944.

Er·lene (ûr lēn′), *n.* a girl's given name. Also, **Earleen′, Earlene, Earline, Erlina, Er·line.**

Er′len·mey·er flask′ (ûr′lən mī′ər, er′-), a flask having a wide base, narrow neck, and conical form, convenient in laboratory experimentation for swirling liquids by hand. [named after E. *Erlenmeyer* (d. 1909), German chemist]

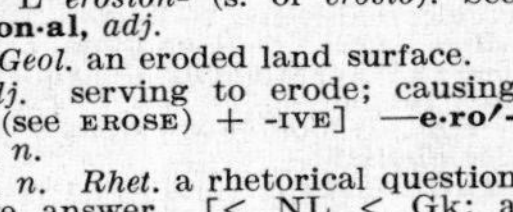

Erlenmeyer flask

Er·li·na (ûr lē′nə), *n.* a girl's given name. Also, **Earleen, Earlene, Earline, Erlene, Er·line′.**

erl·king (ûrl′king′), *n.* (in German and Scandinavian mythology) a spirit or personified natural power that works mischief, esp. to children. [< G *Erlkönig* alder (tree) king, Herder's mistrans. of Dan *ellerkonge*, var. of *elverkonge* king of the elves]

Er·ma (ûr′mə), *n.* a girl's given name, form of **Ermengarde.** Also, **Irma.**

Er·ma·lin·da (ûr′mə lin′də), *n.* a girl's given name.

Er·men·trude (ûr′mən tro͞od′), *n.* a girl's given name.

Er·mi·na (ûr mē′nə), *n.* a girl's given name, form of **Hermione.**

er·mine (ûr′min), *n., pl.* **-mines,** (*esp. collectively*) **-mine,** *adj.* —*n.* **1.** an Old World weasel, *Mustela erminea*, having a white winter coat with black at the tip of the tail. Cf. **stoat.** **2.** *U.S.* any of various weasels having a white winter coat. **3.** the lustrous, white, winter fur of the ermine, often having fur from the animal's black tail tip inserted at intervals for contrast. **4.** the rank, position, or status of a king, peer, or judge, esp. one who, in some parts of the world, wears a robe trimmed with ermine, as on official or state occasions. **5.** *Heraldry.* a fur, consisting of a conventional representation of tails, often with a pattern of dots, sable on argent. —*adj.* **6.** made of, covered, or adorned with ermine. [ME < OF *(h)ermine*, n. use of fem. of *(h)ermin* (masc. adj.) < L *Armen(ius)*, short for *Armenius (mūs)* Armenian (rat)]

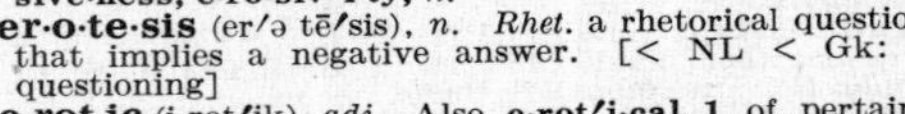

Ermine (Total length 1 ft.; tail 4½ in.)

Er·mine (ûr′min), *n.* a boy's given name.

er·mined (ûr′mind), *adj.* covered or adorned with ermine. [ERMINE + -ED³]

er·mines (ûr′minz), *n. Heraldry.* a fur similar to ermine, but argent on sable.

er·mi·nois (ûr′mi noiz′), *n. Heraldry.* a fur similar to ermine, but sable on or. [< MF *erminois, herminois*, equiv. to OF *ermine* ERMINE + *-ois* adj. suffix]

-ern, an adjective suffix occurring in names of directions: *northern; southern.* [ME, OE *-erne;* c.OHG *-rōni* (as in *nordrōni* northern)]

Er·na (ûr′nə), *n.* a girl's given name.

Er·na·line (ûr′nəlēn′), *n.* a girl's given name, form of **Erna.**

erne (ûrn), *n.* See **sea eagle.** Also, **ern.** [ME *ern, arn*, OE *earn;* c. OHG *arn* (G *Aar*), MLG *arn(e);* akin to Lith *erelis* eagle, Gk *órnis* bird]

Er·nest (ûr′nist), *n.* a boy's given name.

Er·nes·tine (ûr′ni stēn′), *n.* a girl's given name. Also, **Er′nes·tyne′.**

Ernst (ûrnst; *Ger.* ᴇʀnst), *n.* **1. Max** (maks; *Ger.* mäks), born 1891, German painter, in the U.S. since 1941. **2.** a boy's given name, form of **Ernest.**

e·rode (i rōd′), *v.,* **e·rod·ed, e·rod·ing.** —*v.t.* **1.** to eat out or away; destroy by slow consumption: *Constant worry erodes the nerves.* **2.** to form (a channel) by eating or wearing away (used esp. in geology to note the action of all the forces of nature that wear away the earth's surface). —*v.i.* **3.** to become eroded. [< L *ērōd(ere)*, equiv. to *ē-* E- + *rōdere* to gnaw] —**e·rod′i·bil′i·ty, e·rod′a·bil′i·ty,** *n.* —**e·rod′i·ble, e·rod′a·ble, e·ro·si·ble** (i rō′zə bəl), *adj.*

e·rod·ent (i rōd′ənt), *adj.* eroding; erosive: *the erodent power of wind.* [< L *ērōdent-* (s. of *ērōdēns*). See ERODE, -ENT]

e·ro·di·um (i rō′dē əm), *n.* any geraniaceous plant of the genus *Erodium*, comprising the heron's-bills. [< NL < Gk *erōd(iós)* heron; see -IUM]

e·rog·e·nous (i roj′ə nəs), *adj.* **1.** sexually gratifying or sensitive: *the erogenous zones of the body.* **2.** arousing or tending to arouse sexual desire. Also, **er·o·gen·ic** (er′ə jen′ik). [< Gk *érō(s)* EROS + -GENOUS] —**e·rog·e·ne·i·ty** (i roj′ə nē′i tē), *n.*

E·ro′i·ca Sym′phony (e rō′i kə), the third symphony (1804) in E♭, opus 55, by Beethoven.

E·ros (ēr′os, er′os), *n., pl.* **E·ro·tes** (ə rō′tēz). **1.** the ancient Greek god of love, identified by the Romans with Cupid. **2.** a representation of this god. **3.** a winged figure of a child representing love or the power of love. **4.** (*sometimes l.c.*) physical love; sexual desire. Cf. **agape** (def. 2). **5.** *Astron.* an asteroid that approaches to within 14 million miles of the earth once every 44 years. **6.** *Psychiatry.* **a.** the libido. **b.** instincts for self-preservation collectively. **7.** (*sometimes l.c.*) a type of love that seeks fulfillment without injury or violation of some other: *Many contemporary anarchists look to Eros as the solution to modern problems.*

e·rose (i rōs′), *adj.* **1.** uneven, as if gnawed away. **2.** *Bot.* having the margin irregularly incised as if gnawed, as a leaf. [< L *ērōs(us)*, ptp. of *ērōdere.* See ERODE] —**e·rose′ly,** *adv.*

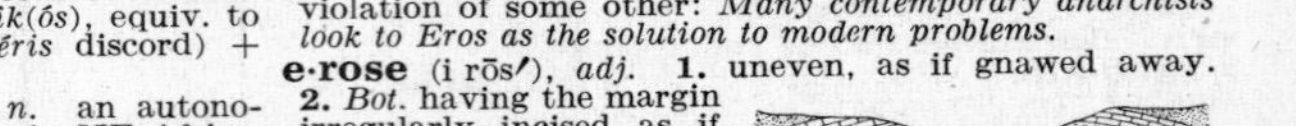

Erosion
Section of stratified rock bent into a low anticline by erosion

e·ro·sion (i rō′zhən), *n.* **1.** the act or state of eroding; state of being eroded. **2.** the process by which the surface of the earth is worn away by the action of water, glaciers, winds, waves, etc. [< L *ērōsiōn-* (s. of *ērōsiō*). See EROSE, -ION] —**e·ro′sion·al,** *adj.*

ero′sion sur′face, *Geol.* an eroded land surface.

e·ro·sive (i rō′siv), *adj.* serving to erode; causing erosion. [< L *ērōs(us)* (see EROSE) + -IVE] —**e·ro′sive·ness, e·ro·siv′i·ty,** *n.*

er·o·te·sis (er′ə tē′sis), *n. Rhet.* a rhetorical question that implies a negative answer. [< NL < Gk: a questioning]

e·rot·ic (i rot′ik), *adj.* Also, **e·rot′i·cal.** **1.** of, pertaining to, or treating of sexual love; amatory. **2.** arousing or satisfying sexual desire. **3.** subject to or marked by strong sexual desires. —*n.* **4.** an erotic poem. **5.** an erotic person. [< Gk *erōtik(ós)* of love, caused by love, given to love, equiv. to *erōt-* (s. of *erōs*) EROS + *-ikos* -IC] —**e·rot′i·cal·ly,** *adj.*

e·rot·i·ca (i rot′i kə), *n.* literature or art dealing with sexual love. [< Gk, neut. pl. of *erōtikós* EROTIC]

e·rot·i·cism (i rot′i siz′əm), *n.* **1.** the sexual or erotic quality or character of something. **2.** the use of sexually arousing or suggestive symbolism, settings, allusions, situations, etc., in art, literature, drama, or the like. **3.** the condition of being sexually aroused or excited. **4.** sexual drive or tendency. **5.** an abnormally persistent sexual drive. Also, **er·o·tism** (er′ə tiz′əm). [EROTIC + -ISM]

eroto-, a combining form denoting sexual desire: *erotomania.* [< Gk, comb. form, equiv. to *erōt-* (s. of *érōs*) love + *-o-* -O-]

e·ro·to·gen·e·sis (i rō′tə jen′i sis, i rot′ə-), *n.* the arousal of erotic impulses. [< NL; see EROTO-, -GENESIS]

e·ro·to·gen·ic (i rō′tə jen′ik, i rot′ə-), *adj.* erogenous. [EROTO- + -GENIC]

e·ro·to·ma·ni·a (i rō′tə mā′nē ə, -mān′yə, i rot′ə-), *n. Psychiatry.* abnormally strong or persistent sexual desire. [EROTO- + -MANIA] —**e·ro·to·ma·ni·ac** (i rō′tə mā′nē ak′, i rot′ə-), *n.*

ERP, See **European Recovery Program.** Also, **E.R.P.**

err (ûr, er), *v.i.* **1.** to go astray in thought or belief; be mistaken; be incorrect. **2.** to go astray morally; sin. **3.** to deviate from the true course, aim, or purpose. [ME *erre(n)* < OF *err(er)* < L *errāre;* akin to Goth *airzjan*, OHG *irrôn*, G *irren*] —**err′a·bil′i·ty,** *n.* —**err′a·ble,** *adj.*

er·ran·cy (ûr′ən sē), *n., pl.* **-cies.** **1.** the state or an instance of erring. **2.** tendency to err. [< L *errantia* a wandering. See ERRANT, -CY]

er·rand (er′ənd), *n.* **1.** a trip to convey a message or execute a commission; a short journey for a specific purpose: *He was sent on an errand to the office.* **2.** a special business entrusted to a messenger; commission: *He won't be back until he has finished his errands.* **3.** the purpose of any trip or journey: *His errand was to deliver the groceries.* [ME *erande*, OE *ǣrende;* c. OHG *ārunti;* cf. OE *ār* messenger, Goth *airus*]

er·rant (er′ənt), *adj.* **1.** journeying or traveling, as a medieval knight in quest of adventure; roving adventurously. **2.** deviating from the regular or proper course; erring. **3.** moving in an aimless or lightly changing manner: *an errant breeze.* [ME *erraunt* < MF *errant*, prp. of *errer* to travel, OF *esrer* < VL *iterāre* to journey; b. MF *errant*, prp. of *errer* to ERR] —**er′rant·ly,** *adv.*

er·rant·ry (er′ən trē), *n., pl.* **-ries.** conduct or performance like that of a knight-errant. [ERRANT + -RY]

er·ra·re hu·ma·num est (ᴇʀ ʀä′ʀe ho͞o mä′no͝om est′; *Eng.* e rār′ē hyo͞o mā′nəm est′), *Latin.* to err is human.

er·ra·ta (i rā′tə, i rä′-), *n.* pl. of **erratum.**

er·rat·ic (i rat′ik), *adj.* **1.** deviating from the proper or usual course in conduct or opinion; eccentric; queer: *He is prone to rather erratic behavior.* **2.** having no certain course; wandering; not fixed: *erratic winds.* **3.** *Geol.* noting or pertaining to a boulder or the like carried by some natural means, as glacial action, from the place of origin to an unusual location. —*n.* **4.** an erratic or eccentric person. **5.** *Geol.* an erratic boulder or the like. [ME < L *errātic(us)*, equiv. to *errāt(us)* (ptp. of *errāre* to ERR) + *-icus* -IC] —**er·rat′i·cal·ly,** *adv.* —**er·rat′i·cism,** *n.*

er·ra·tum (i rā′təm, i rä′-), *n., pl.* **-ta** (-tə). an error in writing or printing. [< L, n. use of *errātum* wandered, erred, strayed (neut. ptp. of *errāre*). See ERR, -ATE¹]

Er·rhe·pho·ri·a (er′ə fôr′ē ə, -fōr′-), *n.* Arrephoria.

er·rhine (er′īn, er′in), *Med.* —*adj.* **1.** designed to be snuffed into the nose. **2.** occasioning discharges from the nose. —*n.* **3.** a medicine to be snuffed up the nostrils to promote sneezing and increased discharges. [< NL *errhin(um)* < Gk *érrīnon*]

err·ing (ûr′ing, er′-), *adj.* **1.** going astray; in error; wrong. **2.** sinning. [ME *errand.* See ERR, -ING²] —**err′ing·ly,** *adv.*

Er·rol (er′əl), *n.* a boy's given name.

erron., 1. erroneous. 2. erroneously.

er·ro·ne·ous (ə rō′nē əs, e rō′-), *adj.* 1. containing error; mistaken; incorrect: *an erroneous answer.* 2. *Archaic.* straying from the right. [ME < L *errōneus* straying, equiv. to *errōn-* (s. of *errō*) wanderer (deriv. of *err-;* see ERR) + *-eus* -EOUS] —**er·ro′ne·ous·ly,** *adv.* —**er·ro′ne·ous·ness,** *n.*
—**Syn. 1.** inaccurate, wrong, untrue, false. —**Ant. 1.** accurate.

er·ror (er′ər), *n.* 1. a deviation from accuracy or correctness; a mistake, as in action, speech, etc.: *His speech contained several grammatical errors.* 2. belief in something untrue; the holding of mistaken opinions. 3. the condition of believing what is not true: *in error about the date.* 4. a moral offense; wrongdoing; sin. 5. *Math.* the difference between the observed or approximately determined value and the true value of a quantity. 6. *Baseball.* a misplay that enables a base runner to reach base safely or advance a base, or a batter to have his turn at bat prolonged, as the dropping of a ball batted in the air, the fumbling of a batted or thrown ball, the throwing of a wild ball, etc., but not including a passed ball or wild pitch. 7. *Philately.* a stamp distinguished by an error or errors in design, engraving, selection of inks, or setting up of the printing apparatus. Cf. **freak**[1] (def. 5), **variety** (def. 8). 8. *Law.* **a.** a mistake in a matter of fact or law in a case tried in a court of record. **b.** See **writ of error.** [ME *errour* < L *errōr-* (s. of *error*), equiv. to *err-* ERR + *-or* -OR[1]] —**er′ror·less,** *adj.*
—**Syn. 1.** blunder, slip, oversight. See **mistake. 4.** fault; transgression, trespass, misdeed.

er′ror of clo′sure, *Survey.* 1. the amount by which a closed traverse fails to satisfy the requirements of a true mathematical figure, as the length of line joining the true and computed position of the same point. 2. the ratio of this linear error to the perimeter of the traverse. 3. (for angles) the amount by which the sum of the observed angles fails to equal the true sum. 4. (in leveling) the amount by which an elevation determined by a series of levels fails to agree with an established elevation. Also called **closing error.**

ers (ûrs, ârs), *n.* ervil. [MF < OPr < LL *ervus,* var. of L *ervum.* See ERVIL]

er·satz (er′zäts, -säts), *adj.* 1. serving as a substitute; synthetic; artificial: *an ersatz meat dish made of eggplant and oatmeal.* —*n.* 2. a substitute; an artificial substance or article used to replace something natural or genuine. [< G *Ersatz* a substitute (deriv. of *ersetzen* to replace)]

Erse (ûrs), *n.* (not in technical use) Gaelic, esp. Scots Gaelic.

Er·skine (ûr′skin), *n.* 1. **John** (*Erskine of Carnock*), 1695–1768, Scottish writer on law. 2. **John,** 1879–1951, U.S. novelist, poet, and essayist. 3. a boy's given name.

erst (ûrst), *adv. Archaic.* before the present time; formerly. [ME *erest,* OE *ǣrest* (c. OHG *ērist,* G *erst*), equiv. to *ǣr* ERE + *-est* -EST[1]]

erst·while (ûrst′hwīl′, -wīl′), *adj.* 1. former; of times past: *erstwhile enemies.* —*adv.* 2. *Archaic.* formerly; erst. [ERST + WHILE]

Er·te·bol·le (er′tə bol′ə, -bul′ə), *adj.* of, pertaining to, or characteristic of an early Neolithic culture of Scandinavia.

er·u·bes·cent (er′o͝o bes′ənt), *adj.* becoming red or reddish; blushing. [< L *ērubēscent-* (s. of *ērubēscēns*), prp. of *ērubēscere.* See E-, RUBESCENT] —**er′u·bes′cence,** *n.*

e·ru·ci·form (i ro͞o′sə fôrm′), *adj.* caterpillarlike. [< L *ērūc(a)* caterpillar + -I- + -FORM]

e·ruct (i rukt′), *v.t., v.i.* 1. to belch forth, as wind from the stomach. 2. to emit or issue violently, as matter from a volcano. [< L *ēruct(āre)* (to) belch, equiv. to *ē-* E- + *ructus* belched, cf. *rūgāre* to belch + *ructāre* to belch]

e·ruc·tate (i ruk′tāt), *v.t., v.i.,* **-tat·ed, -tat·ing.** to eruct. [< L *ēructāt(us)* belched forth, sent forth. See ERUCT, -ATE[1]] —**e·ruc·ta·tion** (i ruk tā′shən, ē′ruk-), *n.* —**e·ruc·ta·tive** (i ruk′tə tiv), *adj.*

er·u·dite (er′yo͝o dīt′, er′o͝o-), *adj.* characterized by erudition; learned or scholarly: *an erudite professor; an erudite commentary.* [ME < L *ērudīt(us),* equiv. to *ērud-* (*ē-* E- + *rud-* unformed, rough, RUDE) + *-ītus* -ITE[2]] —**er′u·dite′ly,** *adv.* —**er′u·dite′ness,** *n.*

er·u·di·tion (er′yo͝o dish′ən, er′o͝o-), *n.* knowledge acquired by study, research, etc.; learning; scholarship: *a man of great erudition.* [ME < L *ērudītiōn-* (s. of *ērudītiō*) an instruction. See ERUDITE, -ION] —**er′u·di′tion·al,** *adj.* —**Syn.** See **learning.**

Er·u·lus (er′yə ləs), *n.* (in the *Aeneid*) a king of Italy whose mother, the goddess Feronia, granted him three lives.

e·rum·pent (i rum′pənt), *adj.* 1. bursting forth. 2. *Bot.* prominent, as if bursting through the epidermis. [< L *ērumpent-* (s. of *ērumpēns*), prp. of *ērumpere,* equiv. to *ē-* E- + *rumpere* to break; see -ENT]

e·rupt (i rupt′), *v.i.* 1. to burst forth, as volcanic matter: *Molten lava and burning debris erupted from the top of the volcano.* 2. (of a volcano, geyser, etc.) to eject matter. 3. to break out of a pent-up state, usually in a sudden and violent manner: *His patience finally gave way, and words of anger erupted from him.* 4. to break out in a skin rash: *Hives erupted all over his face and hands.* 5. (of teeth) to break through surrounding hard and soft tissues and become visible in the mouth. —*v.t.* 6. to cause to burst forth: *He erupted angry words.* 7. (of a volcano, geyser, etc.) to eject (matter). [< L *ērupt(us)* burst forth, broken out (ptp. of *ērumpere*), equiv. to *ē-* E- + *ruptus,* ptp. of *rumpere* to break, RUPTURE] —**e·rupt′i·ble,** *adj.*

e·rup·tion (i rup′shən), *n.* 1. an issuing forth suddenly and violently; outburst; outbreak. 2. *Geol.* the ejection of molten rock, water, etc., as from a volcano, geyser, etc. 3. that which is erupted or ejected, as molten rock, volcanic ash, water, etc. 4. *Pathol.* **a.** the breaking out of a rash or the like. **b.** a rash or exanthema. [ME < L *ēruptiōn-* (s. of *ēruptiō*). See ERUPT, -ION] —**e·rup′tion·al,** *adj.*

e·rup·tive (i rup′tiv), *adj.* 1. bursting forth, or tending to burst forth. 2. pertaining to or of the nature of an eruption. 3. *Geol.* noting a rock formed by the eruption of molten material. 4. *Pathol.* causing or attended with an eruption or rash. —*n.* 5. *Geol.* an eruptive rock. [< F *éruptif.* See ERUPT, -IVE] —**e·rup′tive·ly,** *adv.* —**e·rup·tiv′i·ty, e·rup′tive·ness,** *n.*

E.R.V., English Revised Version.

er·vil (ûr′vil), *n.* a vetch, *Vicia Ervilia,* grown in Europe for forage. Also called **ers.** [< L *ervilia,* akin to *ervum* bitter vetch; prob. of non-IE origin]

Er·vin (ûr′vin), *n.* a boy's given name. Also, **Erwin, Irvin, Irvine, Irving, Irwin.**

Er·vine (ûr′vin), *n.* **St. John Greer** (grēr), born 1883, Irish dramatist and novelist.

Er·win (ûr′win), *n.* 1. a town in NE Tennessee. 3210 (1960). 2. a town in central North Carolina. 3183 (1960). 3. a boy's given name.

Er·win·i·a (ûr win′ē ə), *n. Bacteriol.* a genus of rod-shaped bacteria that are pathogenic for plants. [< NL; named after *Erwin* F. Smith (1854–1927), American pathologist; see -IA]

-ery, a suffix of nouns denoting occupation, business, calling or condition, place or establishment, goods or products, things collectively, qualities, actions, etc.: *archery; bakery; cutlery; fishery; grocery; nunnery; pottery; finery; foolery; prudery; scenery; tracery; trickery; witchery.* [ME < OF *-erie,* equiv. to *-ier* -ER[2] + *-ie* -Y[3]]

Er·y·ci·na (er′i sī′nə), *n. Class. Myth.* an epithet of Aphrodite. [< L *Erycīna;* after *Eryx,* city in Sicily famous for its temple of Aphrodite; see -INE[1]]

Er·y·man′thi·an boar′ (er′ə man′thē ən), *Class. Myth.* a savage boar that plagued Arcadia and was captured by Hercules.

Er·y·man·thus (er′ə man′thəs), *n.* a mountain in S Greece, in the NW Peloponnesus. 7295 ft. Also, **Erimanthus, Er·y·man·thos** (er′i man′thos, -thôs, -thōs). Also called **Olonos.**

e·ryn·go (i ring′gō), *n., pl.* **-goes, -gos.** any of several umbelliferous herbs of the genus *Eryngium,* as the sea holly. Also, **eringo.** [< L *ēryngion* a kind of thistle < Gk, dim. of *ḗryngos* the eryngo]

Er·y·sich·thon (er′i sik′thon), *n. Class. Myth.* a man who cut down a tree sacred to Demeter, in spite of several warnings, and was punished with a hunger that caused him to devour himself.

er·y·sip·e·las (er′i sip′ə ləs, ēr′i-), *n.* 1. *Pathol.* an acute, febrile infectious disease, caused by a specific streptococcus, characterized by diffusely spreading deep-red inflammation of the skin or mucous membranes. 2. Also called **swine erysipelas.** *Vet. Pathol.* a disease of swine, caused by the organism *Erysipelothrix insidiosa,* characterized by urticaria, vegetative endocarditis, arthritis, and sometimes septicemia. [ME *erisipila* < L *erysipelas* < Gk, equiv. to *erysi-* (prob. akin to *erythrós* red) + *-pelas* prob. skin (akin to *pélma* sole of the foot; cf. L *pellis* skin)] —**er·y·si·pel·a·tous** (er′i si pel′ə təs, ēr′-), *adj.*

er·y·sip·e·loid (er′i sip′ə loid′, ēr′i-), *n. Pathol.* a disease of man contracted by contact with the bacillus *Erysipelothrix rhusiopathiae* that causes erysipelas in swine, characterized by a painful local ulcer, generally on one of the hands. [ERISIPEL(AS) + -OID]

er·y·sip·e·lo·thrix (er′i sip′ə lō thriks′, ēr′i-), *n. Bacteriol.* any of several rod-shaped, facultatively anaerobic bacteria of the genus *Erysipelothrix,* often forming long filaments and occurring as parasites on mammals, birds, and fish. [ERYSIPEL(AS) + -O- + -THRIX]

Er·y·the·is (er′ə thē′is), *n. Class. Myth.* one of the Hesperides who transformed herself into an elm tree.

er·y·the·ma (er′ə thē′mə), *n. Pathol.* abnormal redness of the skin due to local congestion, as in inflammation. [< NL < Gk, equiv. to *erythr(ós)* red + *-ēma* n. suffix] —**er·y·the·mat·ic** (er′ə thi mat′ik), **er·y·them·a·tous** (er′ə them′ə təs, -thē′mə-), **er′y·the′mic, er′y·the′mal,** *adj.*

Er·y·thrae·um (er′i thrē′əm), *n.* **Mare.** See **Mare Erythraeum.**

e·ryth·re·de·ma pol·y·neu·rop·a·thy (i rith′ri dē′mə pol′ē no͝o rop′ə thē, -nyo͝o-), *Pathol.* acrodynia. [< NL; see ERYTHRO-, EDEMA; *polyneuropathy,* equiv. to POLY- + NEUROPATHY]

e·ryth·rism (i rith′riz əm), *n.* abnormal redness, as of plumage or hair. [ERYTHR(O)- + -ISM] —**er·y·thris·mal** (er′ə thriz′məl), **er·y·thris·tic** (er′ə thris′tik), *adj.*

e·ryth·rite (i rith′rīt), *n.* 1. a mineral, hydrous cobalt arsenate, $Co_3As_2O_8 \cdot 8H_2O$, occurring as a powdery, usually red incrustation on cobalt minerals; cobalt bloom. 2. erythritol. [ERYTHR(O)- + -ITE[1]]

e·ryth·ri·tol (i rith′ri tōl′, -tôl′, -tol′), *n. Chem., Pharm.* a white, crystalline, water-soluble, sweet-tasting, tetrahydroxyl compound, $CH_2OHCHOHCHOHCH_2OH$, related to the carbohydrates, obtained from certain lichens: used for coronary vasodilatation and in the treatment of hypertension. [ERYTHRITE + -OL[1]]

erythro-, a learned borrowing from Greek meaning "red," used in the formation of compound words: *erythrocyte.* [< Gk *erythró(s)* red, reddish]

e·ryth·ro·blast (i rith′rə blast′), *n. Anat.* a nucleated cell in the bone marrow from which erythrocytes develop. [ERYTHRO- + -BLAST] —**e·ryth′ro·blas′tic,** *adj.*

e·ryth·ro·blas·to·sis (i rith′rō blas stō′sis), *n. Pathol.* 1. the presence of erythroblasts in the blood. 2. Also called **erythroblasto′sis fe·tal′is** (fi tal′is), **erythroblasto′sis ne·o·na·to′rum** (nē′ō nə tôr′əm, -tōr′-). this condition in the fetus or newborn, usually caused by an Rh incompatibility between mother and baby. [ERYTHROBLAST + -OSIS] —**e·ryth·ro·blas·tot·ic** (i rith′rō bla stot′ik), *adj.*

e·ryth·ro·cyte (i rith′rə sīt′), *n. Physiol.* one of the red cells of the blood, which in mammals are enucleate disks concave on both sides, contain hemoglobin, and carry oxygen to the cells and tissues and carbon dioxide back to the respiratory organs. [ERYTHRO- + -CYTE] —**e·ryth·ro·cyt·ic** (i rith′rə sit′ik), *adj.*

e·ryth·ro·cy·tom·e·ter (i rith′rō sī tom′i tər), *n.* an apparatus used for counting red blood cells. [ERYTHROCYTE + -O- + -METER] —**e·ryth′ro·cy·tom′e·try,** *n.*

e·ryth·ro·my·cin (i rith′rō mī′sin), *n.* 1. *Pharm.* an antibiotic, $C_{37}H_{67}NO_{13}$, produced by an actinomycete, *Streptomyces erythraeus:* used chiefly in the treatment of diseases caused by many Gram-positive and some Gram-negative organisms. 2. (*cap.*) a trademark for this antibiotic. [ERYTHRO- + MYC- + -IN[2]]

e·ryth·ro·pho·bi·a (i rith′rə fō′bē ə), *n. Psychiatry.* 1. an abnormal fear of the color red. 2. extreme fear of blushing. [< NL; see ERYTHRO-, -PHOBIA]

e·ryth·ro·phyll (i rith′rə fil′), *n. Biochem.* a substance in vegetation, responsible in the autumn for the red coloration in leaves. [ERYTHRO- + -PHYLL]

e·ryth·ro·poi·e·sis (i rith′rō poi ē′sis), *n.* the production of erythrocytes. [ERYTHRO- + -POIESIS] —**e·ryth·ro·poi·et·ic** (i rith′rō poi et′ik), *adj.*

er·y·throp·sin (er′ə throp′sin), *n. Biochem.* rhodopsin. [ERYTHRO- + (RHODO)PSIN]

Er·yx (er′iks), *n. Class. Myth.* a boxer who challenged Hercules to a match and was killed by him.

Erz′ Moun′tains (ârts), a mountain range in central Europe, on the boundary between Germany and the Czech Republic. Highest peak, Keilberg, 4080 ft. German. **Erz·ge·bir·ge** (erts′gə bēr′gə).

Er·zu·rum (er′zə ro͝om′), *n.* a city in NE Turkey in Asia. 106,301 (1965). Also, **Er′ze·rum′.**

es-. For words with initial **es-,** see also **aes-.**

-es[1], a plural suffix occurring in loan words from Greek: *Hyades.* [< Gk *-es*]

-es[2], var. of **-s**[2] in verbs ending in *s, z, ch, sh,* or post-consonantal *y: passes; buzzes; pitches; dashes; studies.*

-es[3], var. of **-s**[3] in nouns ending in *s, z, ch, sh,* or post-consonantal *y,* and in nouns in *f* with *v* in the plural: *losses; mazes; riches; ashes; babies; sheaves.*

Es, *Chem.* einsteinium.

E.S., Education Specialist.

E·sau (ē′sô), *n.* 1. a son of Isaac and Rebekah, older brother of Jacob, to whom he sold his birthright. Gen. 25:21–25. 2. a boy's given name.

Es·bjerg (es′byer), *n.* a seaport in SW Denmark. 58,225 (1960).

Esc., escudo; escudos.

es·ca·drille (es′kə dril′; *Fr.* es ka drē′yə), *n., pl.* **-drilles** (-drilz′; *Fr.* -drē′yə). 1. a squadron or divisional unit of airplanes: *the Lafayette Escadrille of World War I.* 2. *Obs.* a small naval squadron. [< F: flotilla, MF < Sp *escuadrilla,* dim. of *escuadra* SQUADRON]

es·ca·lade (es′kə lād′), *n., v.,* **-lad·ed, -lad·ing.** —*n.* 1. a scaling or mounting by means of ladders, esp. in an assault upon a fortified place. —*v.t.* 2. to mount, pass, or enter by means of ladders. [< F < It *scalata,* deriv. of *scalare* to SCALE[3]; see -ADE[1]] —**es′ca·lad′er,** *n.*

es·ca·late (es′kə lāt′), *v.t., v.i.,* **-lat·ed, -lat·ing.** 1. to increase in intensity, magnitude, etc.: *to escalate a war.* 2. to raise, lower, rise, or descend on or as if on an escalator. [back formation from ESCALATOR] —**es′ca·la′tion,** *n.*

es·ca·la·tor (es′kə lā′tər), *n.* 1. Also called **moving staircase, moving stairway.** a continuously moving stairway for carrying passengers up or down. 2. a means of rising or descending, increasing or decreasing, etc., esp. by stages: *the social escalator.* [formerly a trademark]

es′calator clause′, a provision in a contract between a labor union and a business organization permitting wage increases or decreases under specified conditions.

es·cal·lop (e skol′əp, e skal′-), *v.t.* 1. to bake (food cut in pieces) in a sauce or other liquid, often with crumbs on top; scallop. 2. to bake (fish, potatoes, etc.) in scallop shells. 3. to bake (as potatoes or fish) in a sauce. —*n.* 4. scallop. 5. *Heraldry.* a representation of a scallop shell: traditionally associated with pilgrimages and crusades. Also, **es·cal′op** (for defs. 1–4). [ME < MF *escalope* shell < Gmc; cf. D *schelp* shell]

Es·ca·na·ba (es′kə nä′bə), *n.* a city in NW Michigan, in the Upper Peninsula. 15,391 (1960).

es·ca·pade (es′kə pād′, es′kə pād′), *n.* 1. a reckless adventure or wild prank, esp. one contrary to usual or proper behavior. 2. an escape from confinement or restraint. [< F < Sp *escapada,* equiv. to *escap(ar)* (to) ESCAPE + *-ada* -ADE[1]]

es·cape (e skāp′), *v.,* **-caped, -cap·ing,** *n.* —*v.i.* 1. to slip or get away, as from confinement or restraint; gain or regain liberty: *to escape from jail.* 2. to slip away from pursuit or peril; avoid capture, punishment, or any threatened evil. 3. to issue from a confining enclosure, as a fluid. 4. to slip away; fade: *The words escaped from memory.* 5. *Bot.* (of an introduced plant) to grow wild. 6. (of a rocket, molecule, etc.) to achieve escape velocity. —*v.t.* 7. to slip away from or elude (pursuers, captors, etc.): *He escaped the police.* 8. to succeed in avoiding (any threatened or possible danger or evil): *He escaped capture.* 9. to elude (one's memory, notice, search, etc.): *I'm afraid her costume escaped my notice.* 10. to fail to be noticed or recollected by (a person): *His reply escapes me.* 11. to slip from or be uttered by (a person, one's lips, etc.) inadvertently, as a remark: *No words of pity or mercy escaped his lips.* —*n.* 12. the act or an instance of escaping. 13. the fact of having escaped. 14. a means of escaping: *We used the tunnel as an escape.* 15. avoidance of reality: *Her illness has become a form of escape for her.* 16. leakage, as of water, gas, etc. 17. *Bot.* a plant originally cultivated, now growing wild. 18. *Physics, Rocketry.* the act of achieving escape velocity. [ME *escape(n)* < ONF *escap(er)* < L *ex-* EX-[1] + *cappa* cloak] —**es·cap′a·ble,** *adj.* —**es·cap·ee′,** *n.* —**es·cape′less,** *adj.* —**es·cap′er,** *n.* —**es·cap′ing·ly,** *adv.*
—**Syn. 1.** flee, abscond, decamp. 7. shun, fly. ESCAPE, ELUDE, EVADE mean to keep free of something. To ESCAPE is to succeed in keeping away from danger, pursuit, observation, etc.: *to escape punishment.* To ELUDE implies slipping through an apparently tight net, thus avoiding, often by a narrow margin, whatever threatens; it implies, also, using vigilance, adroitness, dexterity, or slyness so as to baffle or foil: *A fox managed to elude the hounds.* To EVADE is to turn aside from or go out of reach of a person or thing (at least temporarily), usually by using artifice or stratagem to direct attention elsewhere: *to evade the police.* See **avoid. 12.** flight.

escape′ art′ist, 1. an entertainer expert in getting out of handcuffs, ropes, chains, trunks, or other confining devices. 2. an inmate of a prison who has a reputation for being able to escape confinement.

escape′ mech′anism, *Psychol.* a means of avoiding an unpleasant life situation, as daydreaming.

es·cape·ment (e skāp′mənt), *n.* **1.** *Horol.* the portion of a watch or clock that measures beats and controls the speed of the going train. **2.** a mechanism for regulating the motion of a typewriter carriage, consisting of pawls and a toothed wheel or rack. **3.** a mechanism in a piano which causes a hammer to fall back into rest position immediately after striking a string. **4.** *Archaic.* **a.** an act of escaping. **b.** a way of escape; outlet. [ESCAPE + -MENT (calque of F *échappement*)]

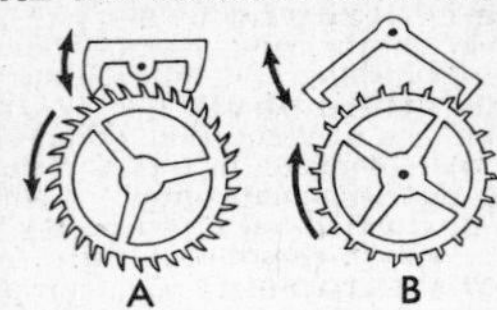

Escapements (def. 1)
A, Anchor escapement
B, Deadbeat escapement

escape′ment er′ror, *Horol.* loss of isochronism in the movement of a pendulum as a result of its relation to the escapement.

escape′ veloc′ity, *Physics, Rocketry.* the minimum speed that an object at a given distance from a gravitating body must have so that it will continue to move away from the body instead of orbiting about it.

es·cape·way (e skāp′wā′), *n.* **1.** a passage designed for the purpose of escape or through that escape is possible. **2.** See **fire escape.** [ESCAPE + WAY]

escape′ wheel′, *Horol.* a toothed wheel for regulating a going train to which it is geared, engaging intermittently with the pallets of a pendulum or balance mechanism in such a way as to cause the mechanism to oscillate rhythmically, and in so doing free the going train for part of each oscillation. Also called **scape wheel.**

es·cap·ism (e skā′piz əm), *n.* the avoidance of reality by absorption of the mind in entertainment or in an imaginative situation, activity, etc.: *His habit of going to the movies is a form of escapism.* [ESCAPE + -ISM] —**es·cap′ist,** *adj., n.*

es·car·got (e skar gō′), *n., pl.* **-gots** (-gō′). *French.* an edible snail.

es·car·go·tière (*Fr.* e skar gô tyer′), *n., pl.* **-tières** (*Fr.* -tyer′). any of the kitchen middens, consisting chiefly of small snail shells, found in parts of N Africa. [< F: lit., snailery]

es·ca·role (es′kə rōl′), *n.* a broad-leaved chicory, used for salads. [< F << VL **ēscāriola,* equiv. to L *ēscāri(us)* (*ēsc(a)* food + *-ārius* -ARY) + *-ola* dim. suffix]

es·carp (e skärp′), *n.* **1.** *Fort.* the inner slope or wall of the ditch surrounding a rampart. See diag. under **bastion.** **2.** any similar steep slope. —*v.t.* **3.** to make into an escarp; give a steep slope to; furnish with escarps. [< F *escarpe,* MF < OIt *scarpa*]

es·carp·ment (e skärp′mənt), *n.* **1.** a long, precipitous, clifflike ridge of land, rock, or the like, commonly formed by faulting or fracturing of the earth's crust. **2.** ground cut into an escarp about a fortification or defensive position. [< F *escarpement.* See ESCARP, -MENT]

es·car·tel·ly (i skär′tᵊlē), *adj.* *Heraldry.* **1.** noting a partition line having a single crenelation. **2.** (of an ordinary) having an edge or edges so formed. Also, **es·car′te·lé, es·car′teled, es·car′te·lée.** [alter. of *escartelé,* ptp. of *escarteler* to break into quarters, equiv. to *es-* (see EX-[1]) + *-cartel(er)* < ML *quartell(us),* dim. of L *quartus* fourth]

Es·caut (es kō′), *n.* French name of **Scheldt.**

-esce, a suffix appearing in verbs borrowed from Latin, where it had an inchoative meaning: *convalesce; putresce.* [< L *-ēscere*]

-escence, a suffix of nouns denoting action or process, change, state, or condition, etc., and corresponding to verbs ending in *-esce* or adjectives ending in *-escent: convalescence; luminescence.* [< L *-ēscentia.* See -ESCE, -ENCE]

-escent, a suffix of adjectives borrowed from Latin, where it had an inchoative force; often corresponding to verbs in *-esce* and nouns in *-escence: convalescent; recrudescent.* [< L, s. of *-ēscēns,* prp. ending]

esch·a·lot (esh′ə lot′, esh′ə lot′), *n.* shallot. [< F, MF *eschalotte,* dim. of *eschaloigne* SCALLION]

es·char[1] (es′kär, -kər), *n.* *Pathol.* a hard crust or scab, as from a burn. [ME *escare* < LL *eschara* < Gk *eschára* hearth, brasier, coals and therefore indication of burning; cf. SCAR[1]]

es·char[2] (es′kär, -kər), *n.* esker.

es·cha·rot·ic (es′kə rot′ik), *Med.* —*adj.* **1.** producing an eschar, as a medicinal substance; caustic. —*n.* **2.** an escharotic agent. [< LL *escharōtic(us)* < Gk *escharōtikós.* See ESCHAR[1], -OTIC]

es·cha·tol·o·gy (es′kə tol′ə jē), *n.* *Theol.* **1.** any system of doctrines concerning last, or final, matters, as death, the judgment, the future state, etc. **2.** the branch of theology dealing with such matters. [< Gk *éschato(s)* last + -LOGY] —**es·cha·to·log·i·cal** (es′kə tᵊloj′i kəl), *adj.* —**es′cha·to·log′i·cal·ly,** *adv.* —**es′cha·tol′o·gist,** *n.*

es·cheat (es chēt′), *Law.* —*n.* **1.** the reverting of property to the state or some agency of the state, or, as in England, to the lord of the fee or to the crown, when there is a failure of persons legally qualified to inherit or to claim. **2.** the right to take property subject to escheat. —*v.i.* **3.** to revert by escheat, as to the crown or the state. —*v.t.* **4.** to make an escheat of; confiscate. [ME *eschete* < OF *eschete, escheoite,* fem. ptp. of *escheoir* < LL **excadēre* to fall to a person's share, equiv. to L *ex-* EX-[1] + *cadere* to fall (VL *cadēre*)] —**es·cheat′a·ble,** *adj.*

es·cheat·age (es chē′tij), *n.* the right of succeeding to an escheat. [ESCHEAT + -AGE]

es·cheat·or (es chē′tər), *n.* an officer in charge of escheats. [ME *eschetour* < AF. See ESCHEAT, -OR[2]]

Esch·e·rich·i·a (esh′ə rik′ē ə), *n.* *Bacteriol.* a genus of rod-shaped, facultatively anaerobic bacteria, certain species of which, as *E. coli,* are found in the large intestine of man and animals and are sometimes pathogenic. [< NL, named after T. *Escherich* (d. 1911), German physician; see -IA]

es·chew (es chōō′), *v.t.* to abstain from; shun; avoid: *to eschew evil.* [ME *eschewe(n)* < OF *eschive(r), escheve(r)* < Gmc; cf. OHG *sciuhen,* G *scheuchen,* SHY[2]] —**es·chew′al,** *adj.* —**es·chew′er,** *n.*

es·co·lar (es′kə lär′), *n., pl.* (*esp. collectively*) **-lar,** (*esp. referring to two or more kinds or species*) **-lars.** a snake mackerel, esp. *Lepidocybium flavobrunneum.* [< Sp: lit., scholar; so called from the spectacle like rings round the eyes]

Es·con·di·do (es′kən dē′dō), *n.* a city in SW California. 16,377 (1960).

es·con·son (i skon′sən), *n.* sconcheon.

Es·co·ri·al (e skōr′ē əl, -skôr′-; *Sp.* es′kô ryäl′), *n.* a building in central Spain, 27 miles NW of Madrid, containing a monastery, palace, church, and mausoleum of the Spanish sovereigns: erected 1563–84. Also, **Escurial.**

es·cort (*n.* es′kôrt; *v.* e skôrt′), *n.* **1.** a body of persons, or a single person, accompanying another or others for protection, guidance, or courtesy: *An escort of servants accompanied the queen.* **2.** an armed guard, as a body of soldiers, ships, etc.: *The president traveled with a large escort of motorcycle police.* **3.** a man or boy who accompanies a woman or girl in public: *He is to be my escort for the dance tonight.* **4.** protection, safeguard, or guidance on a journey: *to travel without escort.* —*v.t.* **5.** to attend or accompany as an escort. [< F < It *scorta,* deriv. of *scorgere* to conduct < LL **excorrigere.* See EX-[1], CORRECT]
—**Syn. 4.** convoy. **5.** conduct, usher, guard, guide. See **accompany.**

es′cort car′rier, *Navy.* a small aircraft carrier used chiefly as an antisubmarine escort for a convoy or task force.

es′cort fight′er, a fighter plane equipped to accompany other planes, esp. bombers, on missions as a protection against air attack.

e·scribe (e skrīb′), *v.t.,* **e·scribed, e·scrib·ing.** *Geom.* to draw a circle outside of a triangle tangent to one side of the triangle and to the extensions of the other two sides. [E- + L *scrīb(ere)* (to) write; see SCRIBE[1]]

es·cri·toire (es′kri twär′), *n.* See **writing desk** (def. 1). [< F, MF < L *scrīptōr(ium).* See SCRIPT, -ORY[2]]

es·crow (es′krō, e skrō′), *n.* *Law.* **1.** a contract, deed, bond, or other written agreement deposited with a third person, by whom it is to be delivered to the grantee or promisee on the fulfillment of some condition. **2. in escrow,** in the keeping of a third person for delivery to a given party upon the fulfillment of some condition. [ME < AF *escro(u)we,* OF *escro(u)e.* See SCROLL]

es·cu·age (es′kyōō ij), *n.* scutage. [< AF, OF, equiv. to *escu* (< L *scūtum* shield) + *-age* -AGE]

Es·cu·de·ro (es′kōō ŧħe′rō), *n.* **Vi·cen·te** (bē then′te), born 1892?, Spanish dancer.

es·cu·do (e skōō′dō; *Port.* es kōō′ŧħō), *n., pl.* **-dos** (-dōz; *Port.* -dōōs; *Sp.* -ŧħōs). **1.** a nickel and bronze coin and monetary unit of Portugal and Portuguese territories, equal to 100 centavos and equivalent to about .035 of a U.S. dollar. *Abbr.:* Esc. **2.** a paper money and monetary unit of Chile, equal to 100 condors or 1000 pesos and equivalent to about .36 of a U.S. dollar. **3.** any of various former gold coins of Spain, Spanish America, and Portugal. **4.** a former silver coin of Spain, discontinued in 1868. [< Sp: shield < L *scūtum*]

Es·cu·la·pi·an (es′kyōō lā′pē ən), *n., adj.* Aesculapian.

es·cu·lent (es′kyə lənt), *adj.* **1.** suitable for use as food; edible. —*n.* **2.** something edible, esp. a vegetable. [< L *ēsculent(us)* edible, full of food, equiv. to *ēsc(a)* food (see ESCAROLE) + *-ulentus* -ULENT]

es·cu·lin (es′kyə lin), *n.* *Chem.* a white, crystalline, slightly water-soluble glucoside, $C_{15}H_{16}O_9$, obtained from the bark of the common horse chestnut: used chiefly in skin preparations as a protective against sunburn. Also, **aesculin.** [< It *esculina* < NL *Aescul(us)* (first part of genus name of species that produces it) + It *-ina* -IN[2]]

Es·cu·ri·al (e skyōōr′ē əl), *n.* Escorial.

es·cutch·eon (e skuch′ən), *n.* **1.** a shield or shieldlike surface on which a coat of arms is depicted. **2.** an ornamental or protective plate around a keyhole, door handle, drawer pull, light switch, etc. **3.** *Naut.* a panel on the stern of a vessel bearing its name and port of registry. **4. blot on one's escutcheon,** a stain on one's reputation; disgrace: *His prison record was a blot on his escutcheon.* [< ONF *escuchon* << L *scūtum* shield] —**es·cutch′eoned,** *adj.*

escutch′eon of pretence′, a small escutcheon bearing the family arms of a heraldic heiress, placed over the center of a larger escutcheon bearing the family arms of her husband.

Esd., Esdras.

Es·dra·e·lon (es′drā ē′lon, -drə-, ez′-), *n.* a plain in N Israel, extending from the Mediterranean near Mt. Carmel to the Jordan River: scene of ancient battles. Also called **Plain of Jezreel.** Cf. **Megiddo.**

Es·dras (ez′drəs), *n.* **1.** either of the first two books of the Apocrypha, I Esdras or II Esdras. **2.** *Douay Bible.* **a.** Ezra (def. 1). **b.** either of two books, I or II Esdras, corresponding to the books of Ezra and Nehemiah, respectively, in the Authorized Version.

Es·dud (is dōōd′), *n.* Ashdod.

-ese, a suffix of nouns and adjectives referring to locality, nationality, language, literary style, etc.: *Bengalese; Chinese; journalese.* [ME < OF *-eis* << L *-ēnsis*]

ESE, east-southeast. Also, **E.S.E.**

E·se·nin (*Russ.* ye se′nin), *n.* **Ser·gey A·le·ksan·dro·vich** (*Russ.* ser gā′ ä′le ksän′dro vich). See **Yesenin, Sergey Aleksandrovich.**

es·er·ine (es′ə rēn′, -rin), *n.* *Chem.* physostigmine. [*eser-* (African name for Calabar bean) + -INE[2]]

Esh·kol (esh′kôl, esh kôl′), *n.* **Le·vi** (lē′vē, lā′vē), (*Levi Shkolnik*), born 1895, Israeli statesman, born in Russia: prime minister since 1963.

Es·i·drix (es′i driks), *n.* *Pharm., Trademark.* hydrochlorothiazide.

-esis, a suffix of Greek origin used to form nouns of action or process: *ecesis.*

Esk., Eskimo.

es·ker (es′kər), *n.* *Geol.* a serpentine ridge of gravelly and sandy drift, believed to have been formed by streams under or in glacial ice. Also, **eschar, es·kar** (es′kär, -kər). [< Ir *eiscir* ridge of mountains]

E·skil·stu·na (es′kil styōō′nä), *n.* a city in SE Sweden, W of Stockholm. 62,429 (1965).

Es·ki·mo (es′kə mō′), *n., pl.* **-mos, -mo,** *adj.* —*n.* **1.** a member of a people, characterized generally by short stature, stocky build, light-brown complexion, and broad, flat facial structure, inhabiting areas of Greenland, northern Canada, Alaska, and northeastern Siberia. **2.** either of two related polysynthetic languages spoken by the Eskimos, esp. the one spoken in all of the Eskimo territory except southern Alaska. —*adj.* **3.** Eskimoan. Also, **Esquimau.** [< Dan *Eskimo,* F *Eskimau* < Algonquian, name applied to tribes farther north] —**Es·ki·moid** (es′kə moid′), *adj.*

Es·ki·mo-Al·e·ut (es′kə mō′ al′ē ōōt′), *n.* **1.** a stock of languages, consisting of Eskimo and Aleut. —*adj.* **2.** of or belonging to Eskimo-Aleut.

Es·ki·mo·an (es′kə mō′ən), *adj.* of or pertaining to the Eskimos or their language. Also, **Es′ki·mau′an.** [ESKIMO + -AN]

Es′kimo cur′lew, a nearly extinct, New World curlew, *Numenius borealis,* that breeds in northern North America.

Es′kimo dog′, **1.** one of a breed of strong, medium-sized dogs having a dense, coarse coat, used in arctic regions for hunting and drawing sleds. **2.** any dog of the arctic regions of North America used for drawing sleds.

Eskimo dog (2 ft. high at shoulder)

Es·ki·mol·o·gy (es′kə mol′ə jē), *n.* the study of Eskimo civilization, language, culture, etc. [ESKIMO + -LOGY] —**Es′ki·mol′o·gist,** *n.*

Es′kimo Pie′, *Trademark.* an oblong portion of ice cream coated with chocolate, skewered on a narrow, thin stick, by which it is held in the hand for eating.

Es·ki·se·hir (es kē′she hēr′), *n.* a city in W Turkey in Asia. 122,755 (1955). Also, **Es·ki′she·hir′.**

Es·lie (es′lē), *n.* a boy's given name.

es·li·sor (ā lē′zôr, -zər), *n.* *Law.* elisor.

Es·me (ez′mē), *n.* a boy's or girl's given name.

Es·me·ral·da (ez′mə ral′də; *Sp.* es′me räl′dä), *n.* a girl's given name.

Es·me·ral·das (es′me räl′däs), *n.* a seaport in NW Ecuador. 20,700 (est. 1959).

Es·mond (ez′mənd), *n.* a boy's given name.

es·ne (ez′nē, -ne), *n.* (in Anglo-Saxon England) a member of the lowest class; laborer. [OE; c. OHG *asni,* Goth *asneis* day laborer, harvester, akin to *asans* harvest]

es·ne·cy (es′ni sē), *n.* *Eng. Law Obs.* the right of the oldest member of a coparcenary to have first choice of share upon division of the inheritance. [< ML *aesnecia,* Latinization of OF *ainsneece, ainsnesse* position of an older brother or sister, deriv. of *ainsne* elder (cf. L *antenātus* (one) born before another)]

eso-, a prefix meaning "inner": *esonarthex.* [< Gk, comb. form repr. *ésō* within]

es·o·nar·thex (es′ō när′theks), *n.* an inner narthex. [ESO- + NARTHEX]

e·soph·a·ge·al (i sof′ə jē′əl, ē′sə faj′ē əl), *adj.* pertaining to the esophagus. Also, **oesophageal.** [ESOPHAG(US) + *-eal,* var. of -IAL]

esoph′age′al speech′, *Speech Pathol.* a technique for producing speech sounds without using the larynx, for people whose larynges are lacking or disabled, by expelling air from the esophagus instead of the trachea and causing it to actuate vocal cavities and articulations.

e·soph·a·gi·tis (i sof′ə jī′tis, ē sof′-), *n.* *Pathol.* inflammation of the esophagus. [< NL; see ESOPHAGUS, -ITIS]

e·soph·a·gus (i sof′ə gəs, ē sof′-), *n., pl.* **-gi** (-jī′). *Anat., Zool.* a tube connecting the mouth or pharynx with the stomach in invertebrate and vertebrate animals; gullet. Also, **oesophagus.** [< LL *oesophagus* < Gk *oisophágos* gullet, lit., channel for eating (*oiso-,* akin to *oísein,* fut. inf. of *phérein* to carry + *-phagos* eating); r. ME *ysophagus* < ML]

es·o·ter·ic (es′ə ter′ik), *adj.* **1.** understood by or meant for only the select few who have special knowledge or interest; recondite: *poetry full of esoteric allusions.* **2.** belonging to the select few. **3.** private; secret; confidential. **4.** (of a philosophical doctrine or the like) intended to be revealed only to the initiates of a group: *the esoteric doctrines of Pythagoras.* [< Gk *esōterik(ós)* inner, equiv. to *esōter(os)* inner + *-ikos* -IC] —**es′o·ter′i·cal·ly,** *adv.* —**es′o·ter′i·cism, es·o·te·rism** (es′ə tə riz′əm), **es′o·ter′y,** *n.* —**es′o·ter′i·cist, es′o·ter′ist,** *n.*

es·o·ter·i·ca (es′ə ter′i kə), *n. pl.* **1.** things understood by or meant for a select few; recondite matters or items. **2.** curiosa. [< NL, n. use of neut. pl. of Gk *esōterikós* ESOTERIC]

es·o·tro·pi·a (es′ə trō′pē ə), *n.* *Ophthalm.* See **convergent squint.** [< NL; see ESO-, -TROPE, -IA]

ESP, extrasensory perception: perception or communication outside of normal sensory activity, as in telepathy and clairvoyance.

esp., especially.

es·pa·da (*Sp.* es pä′ŧħä), *n.* a swordfish. [< Sp: lit., sword < L *spatha.* See SPATULA]

es·pa·drille (es′pə dril′), *n.* a flat sandal, usually with a canvas upper and a rope sole, held on by lacing that ties around the ankle. [< F < Pr *espardilho,* dim. of *espart* ESPARTO]

es·pa·gnole (es′pən yōl′, -pan-; *Fr.* e spa nyôl′), *n.* See **brown sauce.** [< F: lit., Spanish]

es·pa·gno·lette (e span′yə let′, es pan′yə let′), *n.* **1.** (on a French window or the like) a pair of rods, controlled by a knob mechanism, having hooked ends that engage catches in the head and sill of the opening. **2.** *Furniture.* a feature, often a bronze mount, set at the top of a leg and having the form of a female breast. [< F < Pr *espagnouleto,* dim. of *espanhol* Spanish]

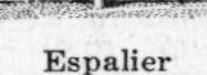
Espalier

es·pal·ier (e spal′yər), *n.* **1.** a trellis or framework on which fruit trees or shrubs are trained to grow flat. **2.** a plant so trained. —*v.t.* **3.** to train on an espalier. **4.** to furnish with an espalier. [< F, MF: trellis < OIt *spalliera,* equiv. to *spall(a)* shoulder, support + *-iera* -IER]

Es·pa·ña (es pä′nyä), *n.* Spanish name of **Spain.**

es·pa·ñol (es pä nyôl′), *n., pl.* **-ño·les** (-nyô′les) for 2, *adj. Spanish.* —*n.* **1.** the Spanish language. **2.** a native or inhabitant of Spain. —*adj.* **3.** of or pertaining to Spain, the Spanish people, or the Spanish language.

es·pan·toon (es′pan to͞on′), *n.* (in Baltimore) a policeman's night stick. [alter. of SPONTOON]

Es·par·te·ro (es′pär te′rō), *n.* **Bal·do·me·ro** (bäl′-dō me′rō), **Count of Lu·cha·na** (lo͞o chä′nä), 1792–1879, Spanish general and statesman.

es·par·to (e spär′tō), *n., pl.* **-tos.** any of several grasses, esp. *Stipa tenacissima,* of S Europe and N Africa, used for making paper, cordage, etc. Also, **espar′to grass′.** [< Sp < L *spartum* < Gk *spárton* rope made of *spártos* kind of rush]

espec., especially.

es·pe·cial (e spesh′əl), *adj.* **1.** special; exceptional; outstanding: *of no especial importance; an especial friend.* **2.** of a particular kind, or peculiar to a particular one: *your especial case.* [ME < MF < L *speciāl(is)* pertaining to a particular kind. See SPECIAL] —**es·pe′cial·ness,** *n.*

es·pe·cial·ly (e spesh′ə lē), *adv.* particularly; exceptionally; markedly: *Be especially watchful.* [late ME; see ESPECIAL, -LY]

—**Syn.** signally, notably; mainly. ESPECIALLY, CHIEFLY, PARTICULARLY, PRINCIPALLY refer to those cases of a class or kind which seem to be significant. ESPECIALLY and PARTICULARLY single out the most prominent case or example (often in order to particularize a general statement): *Winter is especially severe on old people. Corn grows well in the Middle West, particularly in Iowa.* CHIEFLY and PRINCIPALLY imply that the general statement applies to a majority of the cases in question, and have a somewhat comparative force: *Owls fly chiefly at night. Crime occurs principally in large cities.*

es·per·ance (es′pər əns), *n. Obs.* hope. [late ME *esperaunce* < MF *esperance* < LL *spērantia,* equiv. to L *spērant-* (s. of *spērāns*) hoping (prp. of *spērāre* < *spēs* hope) + *-ia* -IA]

Es·pe·ran·to (es′pə rän′tō, -ran′-), *n.* an artificial language invented in 1887 by L. L. Zamenhof (1859–1917), a Russian philologist, and intended for international use. It is based on the commonest words in the most important European languages. [orig. pseudonym of inventor; lit., the hoping one. See ESPERANCE] —**Es′pe·ran′tism,** *n.* —**Es′pe·ran′tist,** *n.*

es·pi·al (e spī′əl), *n.* **1.** the act of spying. **2.** the act of keeping watch; observation. [ME *espiaille* < MF. See ESPY, -AL[2]]

es·piè·gle (e spye′gl[ə]), *adj. French.* roguish; playful.

es·piè·gle·rie (e spye glə rē′), *n., pl.* **-ries** (-rē′). *French.* a roguish or playful trick.

es·pi·o·nage (es′pē ə näzh′, -nij, es′pē ə näzh′), *n.* **1.** the practice of spying on others. **2.** the systematic use of spies by a government to discover the military and political secrets of other nations. [< F *espionnage,* MF *espionage,* equiv. to *espionn(er)* (to) spy (deriv. of *espion* spy < It *spione* < Gmc; akin to G *spähen* to look out) + *-age* -AGE]

Es·pí·ri·to San·to (es pē′rē to͝o sänn′to͝o), a state in E Brazil. 1,188,665 (1960); 15,196 sq. mi. *Cap.:* Vitória.

es·pla·nade (es′plə näd′, -nād′), *n.* any open, level space, esp. one serving for public walks or drives. [< F < Sp *esplanada,* deriv. of *esplanar* < L *explānāre* to level; see -ADE]

es·plees (e splēz′), *n.pl. Law.* the yield from land, as produce or rents. [< AF *esple(t)z* < ML *explēta,* pl. of *explētum* revenue, r. L *explicitum* something unfolded. See EXPLOIT[1]]

es·pous·al (e spou′zəl), *n.* **1.** adoption or advocacy, as of a cause or principle. **2.** Sometimes, **espousals. a.** a marriage ceremony. **b.** an engagement or betrothal celebration. [ME *espousaille* < MF, OF *espousailles* < L *spōnsālia* (n. use of neut. pl. of *spōnsālis*), equiv. to *spōns(us)* SPOUSE + *-ālia* -AL[2]]

es·pouse (e spouz′), *v.t.,* **-poused, -pous·ing. 1.** to make one's own; adopt or embrace, as a cause. **2.** to take in marriage; marry. **3.** *Obs.* to give (a woman) in marriage. [< MF *espous(er)* < L *spōnsāre* to betroth, espouse] —**es·pous′er,** *n.*

es·pres·so (e spres′ō), *n.* a strong coffee prepared by forcing live steam under pressure, or boiling water, through ground dark-roast coffee beans. [< It *(caffè) espresso* pressed (coffee)]

es·prit (e sprē′), *n.* sprightliness of spirit or wit; lively intelligence. [< F < L *spīrit(us)* SPIRIT]

es·prit de corps (e sprē′ də kôr′), a sense of union and of common interests and responsibilities, as developed among a group of persons associated together. [< F]

Es·prit des Lois, L' (*Fr.* le sprē dā lwä′). See **Spirit of Laws, The.**

Es·pron·ce·da (es′prôn the′thä), *n.* **Jo·sé de** (hō se′ the), 1808–42, Spanish poet.

es·py (e spī′), *v.t.,* **-pied, -py·ing.** to see at a distance; catch sight of. [ME *espy(en)* < OF *espi(er)* << Gmc; cf. G *spähen* to spy]

—**Syn.** discern, descry, discover, perceive, make out.

Esq., Esquire.

e·squa·mate (ē skwā′māt), *adj.* having no squamae, or scales; not scaly. [E- + SQUAMATE]

-esque, an adjective suffix indicating style, manner, or distinctive character: *arabesque; Romanesque.* [< F < It *-esco* << Gmc; see -ISH[1]]

Es·qui·line (es′kwə līn′), *n.* one of the seven hills on which ancient Rome was built.

Es·qui·mau (es′kə mō′), *n., pl.* **-maux** (-mō′, -mōz′), *adj.* Eskimo.

es·quire (e skwī[ə]r′, es′kwī[ə]r), *n., v.,* **-quired, -quir·ing.** —*n.* **1.** *(cap.)* an unofficial title of respect, having no precise significance, sometimes placed, esp. in its abbreviated form, after a man's surname in written address: in the U.S., usually applied to lawyers; in Britain, applied to a commoner considered to have gained the social position of a gentleman. *Abbr.:* Esq. **2.** (in the Middle Ages) a squire, or aspirant to knighthood, attendant upon a knight. **3.** a man belonging to the order of English gentry ranking next below a knight. **4.** *Archaic.* squire (def. 1). —*v.t.* **5.** to raise to the rank of esquire. **6.** to address as "Esquire." **7.** to escort or attend in public. [ME *esquier* < MF *escuier* < L *scūtārius* shield-bearer, equiv. to *scūt(um)* (see SCUTAGE) + *-ārius* -ARY]

es·quisse-es·quisse (e skēs′e skēs′), *n. Archit.* a rough sketch, esp. for a major building project, used to work out the general features of the design. [< F: lit., sketch-sketch]

es·rog (es rōg′, es′rōg, -rəg), *n., pl.* **es·ro·gim** (es rō-gēm′, es rō′gim), **es·rogs.** *Judaism.* ethrog.

ess (es), *n.* **1.** the letter S, s. **2.** something shaped like an S: *The road wound among the mountains in great esses.*

-ess, a suffix forming distinctively feminine nouns: *countess; hostess; lioness.* [ME *-esse* < OF < LL *-issa* < Gk]

es·say (*n.* es′ā *for 1;* es′ā, e sā′ *for 2–4; v.* e sā′), *n.* **1.** a short literary composition on a particular theme or subject, usually in prose and generally analytic, speculative, or interpretative. **2.** an effort to perform or accomplish something; attempt: *His essays at friendliness were met with suspicion.* **3.** *Philately.* a design for a proposed stamp differing in any way from the design of the stamp as issued. **4.** *Obs.* a tentative effort; trial; assay. —*v.t.* **5.** to try; attempt. **6.** to put to the test; make trial of. [late ME (v.) < MF *essay(er),* c. AF *assayer* < LL *exagium* a weighing. See EX-[1], AGENT] —**es·say′er,** *n.*

—**Syn. 5.** See **try.**

es·say·ist (es′ā ist), *n.* **1.** a writer of essays. **2.** *Rare.* a person who makes essays or trials. [ESSAY + -IST]

es·say·is·tic (es′ā is′tik), *adj.* **1.** of, pertaining to, or like an essay, esp. in style, format, or organization and often reflecting a more personal approach than a treatise, thesis, or the like. **2.** resembling formal exposition. **3.** expository; discursive; explanatory: *The action of the novel is interrupted by didactic, essayistic interpretations of motive.* [ESSAY + -ISTIC]

Es′say on Crit′icism, An, a didactic poem (1711) by Alexander Pope on critics and criticism.

Es′say on Man′, An, a didactic poem (1733) by Alexander Pope on a deistic theme.

es·se (es′se; *Eng.* es′ē), *n. Latin.* being; existence.

es·se est per·ci·pi (es′se est per′ki pē′; *Eng.* es′ē est pər sip′ē), *Latin.* to be is to be perceived: the basic philosophical principle of Berkeley.

Es·sen (es′ən), *n.* a city in W West Germany: the chief city of the Ruhr River valley; Krupp works. 729,400 (1963).

es·sence (es′əns), *n.* **1.** the basic, real, and unvariable nature of a thing or its significant individual feature or features: *Freedom is the very essence of our democracy.* **2.** a substance obtained from a plant, drug, or the like, by distillation, infusion, etc., and containing its characteristic properties in concentrated form. **3.** an alcoholic solution of an essential oil. **4.** a perfume; scent. **5.** *Philos.* the inward nature, true substance, or constitution of anything, as opposed to what is accidental, phenomenal, illusory, etc. **6.** something that exists, esp. a spiritual or immaterial entity. **7. in essence,** essentially; at bottom (often, despite appearances): *For all his bluster, he is in essence a conformist.* **8. of the essence,** absolutely essential; being the *sine qua non: In chess, cool nerves are of the essence.* [ME *essencia* < ML, for L *essentia.* See ESSE, -ENCE]

es·sence d'o·ri·ent (es′əns dôr′ē ənt, -ent′, dôr′-; *Fr.* e säns dô ryän′), *Jewelry.* a preparation for coating glass beads to make imitation pearls, derived from the scales of fish, esp. of the bleak. [< F: lit., essence of the Orient]

es′sence of ber′gamot, bergamot (def. 2).

es′sence of mir′bane (mûr′bān), *Chem.* nitrobenzene. Also, **es′sence of myr′bane.** [?]

Es·sene (es′ēn, e sēn′), *n. Judaism.* a member of a Palestinian sect, characterized by asceticism, celibacy, and joint holding of property, that flourished from the 2nd century B.C. to the 2nd century A.D. and advocated physical and spiritual purity, piety, and enrichment of the soul. —**Es·se·ni·an** (e sē′nē ən), **Es·sen·ic** (e sen′ik), *adj.*

es·sen·tial (ə sen′shəl), *adj.* **1.** absolutely necessary; indispensable: *Discipline is essential in an army.* **2.** pertaining to or constituting the essence of a thing. **3.** noting or containing an essence of a plant, drug, etc. **4.** being such by its very nature or in the highest sense; natural; spontaneous: *essential happiness; essential poetry.* **5.** *Math.* **a.** (of a singularity of a function of a complex variable) noting that the Laurent series at the point has an infinite number of terms with negative powers. **b.** (of a discontinuity) noting that the function is discontinuous and has no limit at the point. Cf. **removable** (def. 2). —*n.* **6.** a basic, indispensable, or necessary element; chief point: *Concentrate on essentials rather than details.* [ME *essencial* < ML *essenciāl(is)* for L *essentiālis.* See ESSENCE, -AL[1]] —**es·sen′tial·ly,** *adv.* —**es·sen′tial·ness,** *n.*

—**Syn. 1.** fundamental, basic, inherent, intrinsic, vital. See **necessary. 2.** ESSENTIAL, INHERENT, INTRINSIC refer to that which is in the natural composition of a thing. ESSENTIAL suggests that which is in the very essence or constitution of a thing: *Oxygen and hydrogen are essential in water.* INHERENT means inborn or fixed from the beginning as a permanent quality or constituent of a thing: *properties inherent in iron.* INTRINSIC implies belonging to the nature of a thing itself, and comprised within it, without regard to external considerations or accidentally added properties: *the intrinsic value of diamonds.* —**Ant. 2.** accidental, extrinsic.

essen′tial hyperten′sion, *Pathol.* persistent high blood pressure, having no known cause. Also called **hyperpiesia, hyperpiesis.**

es·sen·tial·ism (ə sen′shə liz′əm), *n. Educ.* a doctrine that certain traditional concepts, ideals, and skills are essential to society and should be taught methodically to all students, regardless of individual ability, need, etc. Cf. **progressivism.** [ESSENTIAL + -ISM] —**es·sen′tial·ist,** *n.*

es·sen·ti·al·i·ty (ə sen′shē al′i tē), *n., pl.* **-ties. 1.** the quality of being essential; essential character. **2.** an essential feature, element, or point. [ESSENTIAL + -ITY]

es·sen·tial·ize (ə sen′shə līz′), *v.t.,* **-ized, -iz·ing.** to extract the essence from or express the essence of. [ESSENTIAL + -IZE]

essen′tial oil′, any of a class of volatile oils obtained from plants, possessing the odor and other characteristic properties of the plant, used chiefly in the manufacture of perfumes, flavors, and pharmaceuticals.

es·se quam vi·de·ri (es′se kwäm wi′de rē; *Eng.* es′ē kwam vi dâr′ī), *Latin.* to be rather than to seem: motto of North Carolina.

Es·se·qui·bo (es′ə kwē′bō), *n.* a river flowing from S Guyana N to the Atlantic. ab. 550 mi. long.

Es·sex (es′iks), *n.* **1. 2nd Earl of.** See **Devereux, Robert. 2.** a county in SE England. 2,286,970 (1961); 1528 sq. mi. *Co. seat:* Chelmsford. **3.** a town in N Maryland, near Baltimore. 35,205 (1960).

Es′sex Junc′tion, a town in NW Vermont. 5340 (1960).

Es′sex Jun′to (jun′tō), *U.S. Hist.* **1.** (originally) a group of extreme Federalist party members from Essex county, Massachusetts. **2.** any Federalist.

Es′sex ta′ble, *Carpentry.* a chart tabulating the number of board feet, to the nearest twelfth, contained in pieces of wood one inch thick and of varying standard sizes.

Es·sex·ville (es′iks vil′), *n.* a town in E Michigan. 4590 (1960).

Es·sie (es′ē), *n.* a girl's given name, form of **Esther.**

es·sive (es′iv), *Gram.* —*adj.* **1.** noting a case, as in Finnish, whose distinctive function is to indicate a state of being. —*n.* **2.** the essive case. [< Finn *essivi* < L *ess(e)* (to) be + *-īvus* -IVE]

es·so·nite (es′ə nīt′), *n. Mineral.* a gem variety of grossularite. Also, **hessonite.** [< F < Gk *hḗssōn* less, inferior + *-ītēs* -ITE[1]]

-est[1], a suffix forming the superlative degree of adjectives and adverbs: *warmest; fastest; soonest.* [OE *-est, -ost.* Cf. Gk *-isto-*]

-est[2], a native English suffix formerly used to form the second person singular indicative of verbs: *knowest; sayest; goest.* Also, **-st.** [ME; OE *-est, -ast, -st* 2nd pers. sing. pres. indic. endings of some verbs (*-s* earlier verbal ending + *-t,* by assimilation from *thū* THOU[1]) and 2nd pers. sing. past endings of weak verbs (earlier *-es* + *-t*)]

EST, Eastern Standard Time. Also, **E.S.T., e.s.t.**

est., 1. established. **2.** estate. **3.** estimated. **4.** estuary.

estab., established.

es·tab·lish (e stab′lish), *v.t.* **1.** to found, institute, build, or bring into being on a firm or permanent basis: *to establish a university; The doctor established a good practice in Los Angeles.* **2.** to install or settle in a position, place, business, etc.: *to establish one's son in business.* **3.** to cause to be accepted or recognized: *to establish a custom; He established himself as a leading surgeon.* **4.** to show to be valid or true; prove: *to establish the facts of the matter.* **5.** to enact, appoint, or ordain for permanence, as a law; fix unalterably. **6.** to bring about permanently: *The Romans established order in the countries they subdued.* **7.** to make (a church) a national or state institution. **8.** *Cards.* to obtain control of (a suit) so that one can win all the subsequent tricks in it. [ME *establisse(n)* < MF *establiss-,* extended s. of *establir* < L *stabilīre,* akin to *stabilis* STABLE[2]] —**es·tab′lish·a·ble,** *adj.* —**es·tab′lish·er,** *n.*

—**Syn. 1.** form, organize. See **fix. 4.** verify, substantiate. **5.** decree. —**Ant. 1.** abolish. **4.** disprove.

estab′lished church′, a church that is recognized by law, and often financially supported, as the official church of a nation. Also called **state church.** Cf. **national church.**

estab′lishing shot′, *Motion Pictures, Television.* a camera shot, esp. a long shot, that shows the setting for the action or scene that follows.

es·tab·lish·ment (e stab′lish mənt), *n.* **1.** the act or an instance of establishing. **2.** the state or fact of being established. **3.** something established; a constituted order or system. **4. the Establishment,** the existing power structure in society, a field of endeavor, etc.; institutional authority: *The Establishment believes exploring outer space is worth any tax money spent. Young writers feel that the literary Establishment is unjust.* **5.** a household; place of residence including its furnishings, grounds, etc. **6.** a place of business together with its employees, merchandise, equipment, etc. **7.** a permanent civil, military, or other force or organization. **8.** an institution, as a school, hospital, etc. **9.** the recognition by the state of a church as the state church. **10.** the church so recognized, esp. the Church of England. **11.** *Archaic.* a fixed or settled income. [ESTABLISH + -MENT]

es·tab·lish·men·tar·i·an (e stab′lish mən târ′ē ən), *adj.* **1.** of or pertaining to an established church, esp. the Church of England, or the principle of state religion. —*n.* **2.** a supporter or adherent of the principle of the establishment of a church by state law; an advocate of state religion. [ESTABLISHMENT + -ARIAN] —**es·tab′lish·men·tar′i·an·ism,** *n.*

es·ta·fette (es′tə fet′), *n.* a mounted courier. [< F < It *staffetta,* dim. of *staffa* stirrup < OHG *stapho* step; see -ETTE]

Es·taing, d' (des taN′), **Charles Hec·tor** (sharl ek tôr′), 1729–94, French admiral.

es·ta·min (es′tə min), *n.* a worsted fabric constructed in twill weave with a rough surface. Also, **es·ta·mene** (es′tə mēn′). [< F *estamine* << L *stāminea,* fem. of *stāmineus* made of threads. See STAMEN, -EOUS]

es·ta·mi·net (e stA mē ne′), *n., pl.* **-nets** (-ne′). *French.* a bistro or small cafe.

es·tam·pie (es täm pē′), *n.* a medieval dance and instrumental form, in several repeated sections, associated chiefly with the trouvères. [< F, OF, deriv. of *estampir* to roar, resound < Gmc; see STAMP]

es·tan·cia (e stän′sē ə; *Sp.* es tän′syä), *n., pl.* **-cias** (-sē əz; *Sp.* -syäs). (in Spanish America) a landed estate or a cattle ranch. [< AmerSp, Sp: dwelling]

es·tan·cie·ro (e stän′sē âr′ō; *Sp.* es′tän sye′rō), *n., pl.* **-cie·ros** (-sē âr′ōz; *Sp.* -sye′rôs). a person who owns an estancia; rancher. [< AmerSp; see ESTANCIA, -IER]

es·tate (e stāt′), *n., v.,* **-tat·ed, -tat·ing.** —*n.* **1.** a piece of landed property, esp. one of large extent with an elaborate house on it: *to have an estate in the country.* **2.** *Law.* **a.** property or possessions. **b.** the legal position or status of an owner, considered with respect to his property in land or other things. **c.** the degree or quantity of interest that a person has in land with respect to the nature of the right, its duration, or its relation to the rights of others. **d.** interest, ownership, or property in land or other things. **e.** the property of

a deceased person, a bankrupt, etc., viewed as an aggregate. 3. *Brit.* a housing development. 4. a period or condition of life: *to attain to man's estate.* 5. a major political or social group or class, esp. one once having specific political powers, as the clergy, nobles, and commons in France or the lords spiritual, lords temporal, and commons in England. 6. condition or circumstances with reference to worldly prosperity, estimation, etc.; social status or rank. 7. *Archaic.* pomp or state. 8. *Obs.* high social status or rank. —*v.t.* 9. *Obs.* to establish in or as in an estate. [ME *estat* < MF; c. Pr *estat.* See STATE]
—**Syn. 1.** See **property.**

estate′ a′gent, *Brit.* 1. the steward or manager of a landed estate. 2. a real-estate agent; realtor.

estate′ car′, *Brit.* See **station wagon.** Also called **estate′ wag′gon.**

Estates′ Gen′eral, *French Hist.* the States-General.

estate′ tax′, a tax imposed on a decedent's property, assessed on the gross estate prior to distribution to the heirs.

Es·te (es′te), *n.* a city in NE Italy: medieval fortress; ancient Roman ruins. 15,659 (1961). Ancient, **Ateste.**

es·teem (e stēm′), *v.t.* 1. to regard highly or favorably; regard with respect or admiration: *I esteem him for his honesty.* 2. to consider as of a certain value; regard: *I esteem it worthless.* 3. *Obs.* to set a value on; appraise. —*n.* 4. favorable opinion or judgment; respect or regard: *to hold a person in esteem.* 5. *Archaic.* opinion or judgment; estimation; valuation. [ME *esteme(n),* < MF *estime(r)* < L *aestimāre* to fix the value of]
—**Syn. 1.** honor, revere, respect. See **appreciate.** 4. favor, admiration, honor, reverence, veneration. See **respect.** —**Ant. 1.** disdain.

Es·telle (e stel′, i stel′), *n.* a girl's given name. Also, **Es·tel·la** (e stel′ə, i stel′ə).

es·ter (es′tər), *n. Chem.* a compound produced by the reaction between an acid and an alcohol with the elimination of a molecule of water, as ethyl acetate, $CH_3COOC_2H_5$, or dimethyl sulfate, $(CH_3O)_2SO_2$. [coined by L. Gmelin (1788–1853), German chemist]

Es·ter (es′tər), *n.* a girl's given name. Also, **Esther.**

es·ter·ase (es′tə rās′), *n. Biochem.* any enzyme that hydrolyzes an ester into an alcohol and an acid. [ESTER + -ASE]

es′ter gum′, *Chem.* any of several hard resins produced by the esterification of a natural resin, esp. rosin, with a polyhydric alcohol, chiefly glycerol: used in the manufacture of paints, varnishes, and lacquers.

Es·ter·ha·zy (es′tər hä′zē; *Fr.* e ster A zē′), *n.* **Ma·rie Charles Fer·di·nand Wal·sin** (MA RĒ′ SHARL FER DĒ NÄN′ VAL SAN′), 1847–1923, French army officer, confessed forging evidence that convicted Alfred Dreyfus.

es·ter·i·fy (e ster′ə fī′), *v.t., v.i.,* **-fied, -fy·ing.** *Chem.* to convert into an ester. [ESTER + -IFY] —**es·ter′i·fi′a·ble,** *adj.* —**es·ter′i·fi·ca′tion,** *n.*

Es·tes (es′tis), *n.* a boy's given name.

Es′tes Park′ (es′tiz), a summer resort in N Colorado. 1175 (1960).

Est Est Est (est′ est′ est′), a medium-dry white wine from Montefiascone, Italy. [< L: lit., this is it, this is it, this is it]

Esth., 1. Esther. 2. Esthonia.

Es·ther (es′tər), *n.* 1. the wife of Ahasuerus. 2. a book of the Bible bearing her name. 3. a number of prayers, visions, interpretations of dreams, etc., which are included in the Douay Bible as chapters 10–16. 4. Also, **Ester.** a girl's given name.

Es·ther·ville (es′tər vil′), *n.* a town in N Iowa. 7927 (1960).

es·the·sia (es thē′zhə, -zhē ə, -zē ə), *n.* capacity for sensation or feeling; sensitivity. Also, **aesthesia.** [< Gk *aísthēs(is)* (see ESTHESIS) + -IA]

esthesio-, a combining form meaning "sensation": *esthesiometry.* [comb. form repr. Gk *aísthēsis* ESTHESIS]

es·the·si·om·e·ter (es thē′zē om′i tər), *n. Med.* an instrument for measuring the degree of tactile sensibility. [ESTHESIO- + -METER]

es·the·si·om·e·try (es thē′zē om′i trē), *n. Med.* the process of measuring the degree of tactile sensibility with an esthesiometer. [ESTHESIO- + -METRY]

es·the·sis (es thē′sis), *n.* sensation; feeling. Also, **aesthesis.** [< Gk *aísthēsis* sensation, perception]

es·thete (es′thēt), *n.* aesthete.

es·thet·ic (es thet′ik), *adj.* aesthetic.

es·thet·i·cal (es thet′i kəl), *adj.* aesthetical. —**es·thet′i·cal·ly,** *adv.*

es·the·ti·cian (es′thi tish′ən), *n.* aesthetician.

es·thet·i·cism (es thet′i siz′əm), *n.* aestheticism.

es·thet·ics (es thet′iks), *n.* aesthetics.

Es·tho·ni·a (e stō′nē ə, es thō′-), *n.* Estonia.

Es·tho·ni·an (e stō′nē ən, es thō′-), *adj., n.* Estonian.

Es·tienne (es tyen′), *n.* 1. Also, **Étienne.** a family of French printers, book dealers, and scholars, including esp. **Hen·ri** (ÄN RĒ′), died 1520; his son, **Ro·bert** (RŌ·BER′), 1503?–59; **Henri** (son of Robert), 1531?–98. 2. a French printing firm founded by this family.

es·ti·ma·ble (es′tə mə bəl), *adj.* 1. worthy of esteem; deserving respect or admiration. 2. capable of being estimated. [ME < MF < L *aestimābil(is),* equiv. to *aestim(āre)* (to) ESTEEM + *-ābilis* -ABLE] —**es′ti·ma·ble·ness,** *n.* —**es′ti·ma·bly,** *adv.*
—**Syn. 1.** reputable, respectable, worthy, meritorious, excellent, good. —**Ant. 1.** contemptible.

es·ti·mate (*v.* es′tə māt′; *n.* es′tə mit, -māt′), *v.,* **-mat·ed, -mat·ing,** *n.* —*v.t.* 1. to form an approximate judgment or opinion regarding the value, amount, size, weight, etc., of; calculate approximately: *to estimate the cost of a college education.* 2. to form an opinion of; judge. —*v.i.* 3. to make an estimate. —*n.* 4. an approximate judgment or calculation, as of the value, amount, time, size, weight, etc., of something. 5. a judgment or opinion, as of the qualities of a person or thing. 6. a statement of the approximate charge for work to be done, submitted by a person ready to undertake the work. [< L *aestimāt(us),* ptp. of *aestimāre* to value, estimate; see -ATE[1]] —**es′ti·mat′ing·ly,** *adv.* —**es′ti·ma′tor,** *n.*
—**Syn. 1.** compute, count, reckon, gauge, assess, value, evaluate, appraise. 4. valuation, calculation, appraisal.

es·ti·ma·tion (es′tə mā′shən), *n.* 1. judgment or opinion: *In my estimation the boy is guilty.* 2. esteem; respect. 3. approximate calculation; estimate: *to make an estimation of one's resources.* [ME *estimacioun* < MF < L *aestimātiōn-* (s. of *aestimātiō*). See ESTIMATE, -ION]
—**Syn. 2.** appreciation, regard, honor, veneration.

es·ti·ma·tive (es′tə mā′tiv), *adj.* 1. capable of estimating. 2. pertaining to or based upon estimation; estimated. [ME < ML *aestimātīv(us).* See ESTIMATE, -IVE]

e·stip·u·late (ē stip′yə lit, -lāt′), *adj. Bot.* exstipulate.

es·ti·val (es′tə vəl, e stī′vəl), *adj.* pertaining or appropriate to summer. Also, **aestival.** [ME < LL *aestīvāl(is),* equiv. to L *aestīv(us)* summer + *-ālis* -AL[1]]

es·ti·vate (es′tə vāt′), *v.i.,* **-vat·ed, -vat·ing.** 1. to spend the summer, as at a specific place or in a certain activity. 2. *Zool.* to pass the summer in a torpid condition. Also, **aestivate.** [< L *aestīvāt(us),* ptp. of *aestīvāre* to reside during the summer (akin to *aestīvus* summer); see -ATE[1]] —**es′ti·va′tor,** *n.*

es·ti·va·tion (es′tə vā′shən), *n.* 1. *Zool.* the act of estivating. 2. *Bot.* the arrangement of the parts of a flower in the bud. Also, **aestivation.** [< NL; see ESTIVATE, -ION]

est mo·dus in re·bus (est mō′dŏŏs in RE′bŏŏs; *Eng.* est mō′dəs in rē′bəs), *Latin.* there is a due measure in things. Horace, *Satires* I, 1, 106.

es·toc (e stok′; *Fr.* e stôk′), *n., pl.* **es·tocs** (e stoks′; *Fr.* e stôk′). a thrusting sword of the 13th–17th centuries having a long, narrow blade of rectangular section. [< OF: lit., point (of a sword). See STOCK]

es·to·ca·da (es′tə kä′də), *n.* the thrust of the sword by the matador into the bull in the final stage of a bullfight, designed to kill the bull by passing through the back of the neck near the head and downward into the heart. [< Sp < F *estoqu(ier)* (to) give sword thrusts. See ESTOC, -ADE[1]]

es·toile (e stoil′, e·twäl′), *n. Heraldry.* a star having a number of wavy rays or points, either six or a specified greater number: *an estoile of eight points.* [< MF < L *stella* STAR]

Es·to·ni·a (e stō′nē ə, e ston′yə), *n.* a republic in N Europe, on the Baltic, S of the Gulf of Finland: an independent republic 1918–40; annexed by the Soviet Union 1940; regained independence 1991. 1,573,000; 17,413 sq. mi. *Cap.:* Tallinn. Also, **Esthonia.**

Es·to·ni·an (e stō′nē ən), *adj.* 1. of or pertaining to Estonia or its people. —*n.* 2. one of a Finnish people inhabiting Estonia, Livonia, and other districts of Russia. 3. the Uralic language of Estonia, very closely related to Finnish. Also, **Esthonian.** [ESTONI(A) + -AN]

es·top (e stop′), *v.t.,* **-topped, -top·ping.** 1. *Law.* to hinder or prevent by estoppel. 2. *Archaic.* to stop. [ME < OF *estop(er)* (to) stop up (AF *estopper* legal sense), deriv. of *estoupe* << L *stuppa* tow. Cf. STOP]

es·to per·pe·tu·a (es′tō PER pet′ŏŏ ä′; *Eng.* es′tō pər pech′ŏŏ ə), *Latin.* may she live forever: motto of Idaho.

es·top·page (e stop′ij), *n.* the condition of being estopped. [< F; see ESTOP, -AGE]

es·top·pel (e stop′əl), *n. Law.* a bar or impediment preventing a party from asserting a fact or a claim inconsistent with a position he previously took, either by conduct or words, esp. where a representation has been relied or acted upon by others. [< MF *estoupail* stopper. See ESTOP, -AL[2]]

Es·tour·nelles de Con·stant, d′ (de stŏŏR nel′ də kôN stäN′), **Paul Hen·ri Ben·ja·min Bal·luat** (pôl äN RĒ′ baN zha MAN′ BA lwA′), **Baron Con·stant de Re·becque** (kôN stäN′ də Rə bek′), 1852–1924, French diplomat: Nobel peace prize 1909.

es·to·vers (e stō′vərz), *n.pl. Law.* necessaries allowed by law, as wood and timber to a tenant, alimony to a wife, etc. [ME < AF, n. use of OF *estovoir, estover* to be necessary < L *est opus* there is need]

Es·tra·da Ca·bre·ra (es trä′thä kä vre′rä), **Man·uel** (mä nwel′), 1857–1924, Guatemalan politician: president 1898–1920.

es·trade (e sträd′), *n.* 1. a slightly raised platform in a room or hall. 2. a platform, as for a throne or bed of state. [< F < Sp *estrado* part of a room in which a carpet is spread < L *strātum;* see STRATUM]

es·tra·di·ol (es′trə dī′ôl, -ōl, -ol), *n.* 1. *Biochem.* an estrogenic hormone, $C_{18}H_{24}O_2$, produced by the maturing Graafian follicle, that causes proliferation and thickening of the tissues and blood vessels of the endometrium. 2. *Pharm.* a commercial form of this compound, obtained from the urine of pregnant humans and mares or synthesized and used in the treatment of estrogen deficiency and certain menopausal and postmenopausal conditions. Also, **oestradiol.** [*estra-* (comb. form repr. ESTRIN) + DI-[1] + -OL[1]]

es·tra·gon (es′trə gon′), *n.* tarragon.

es·tral (es′trəl), *adj.* estrous. [ESTR(US) + AL[1]]

es·trange (e strānj′), *v.t.,* **-tranged, -trang·ing.** 1. to turn away in feeling or affection; alienate the affections of: *Their quarrel estranged the two lovers.* 2. to remove to or keep at a distance: *The necessity for traveling in his business has estranged him from his family.* 3. to divert from the original use or possessor. [< MF; OF *estranger;* c. Pg *estranhar,* Sp *estrañar,* It *straniare* < LL *extrāneāre,* L: to treat as a stranger] —**es·trange′ment,** *n.* —**es·trang′er,** *n.*

es·tranged (e strānjd′), *adj.* displaying or evincing a feeling of alienation; alienated. [ESTRANGE + -ED[2]] —**es·trang·ed·ness** (e strān′jid nis, -strānjd′-), *n.*

es·tray (e strā′), *n.* 1. anything that has strayed away. 2. *Law.* a domestic animal, as a horse or a sheep, found wandering or without an owner. —*v.i.* 3. to stray. [ME *astrai* < AF *estray,* deriv. of OF *estraier* to STRAY]

es·treat (e strēt′), *Eng. Law.* —*n.* 1. a true copy or extract of an original writing or record, as of a fine. —*v.t.* 2. to make an estreat of (a fine, levy, etc.) for prosecution. 3. to levy (fines) under an estreat; exact (anything) by way of fine or levy. [ME *estrete* < AF, c. OF *estraite* (ptp. of *extraire*) < L *extracta* (fem. ptp. of *extrahere*); see EXTRACT]

Es·tre·ma·du·ra (es′tRe mä thŏŏ′Rä), *n.* a region in W Spain, formerly a province. Also, **Extremadura.**

es·tril·dine (es′tril dīn′, -din), *adj.* 1. of or pertaining to the subfamily *Estrildinae,* comprising the grass finches, waxbills, mannikins, and other small finches. —*n.* 2. a bird of the subfamily *Estrildinae.* [< NL *Estrildinae*]

es·trin (es′trin), *n. Biochem.* estrone. [< NL; see ESTRUS, -IN[2]]

es·tri·ol (es′trē ōl′, -ôl′, -ol′), *n.* 1. *Biochem.* an estrogenic hormone, $C_{18}H_{21}(OH)_3$, occurring in urine during pregnancy. 2. *Pharm.* a commercial form of this compound, obtained from the urine of human placentae or of pregnant women and used in conditions involving estrogen deficiency. Also, **oestriol.** [ESTR(IN) + TRI- + -OL[1]]

es·tro·gen (es′trə jən), *n. Biochem.* any one of a group of female hormones that induce estrus in immature, spayed mammals. Also, **oestrogen.** [ESTR(US) + -O- + -GEN]

es·tro·gen·ic (es′trə jen′ik), *adj. Biochem.* promoting or producing estrus. [ESTROGEN + -IC] —**es′tro·gen′i·cal·ly,** *adv.*

Es·tron (es′tron), *n. Trademark.* an acetate yarn.

es·trone (es′trōn), *n.* 1. *Biochem.* an estrogenic hormone, $C_{18}H_{22}O_2$, produced by the ovarian follicles and found in pregnancy urine and placental tissue. 2. *Pharm.* a commercial form of this compound, obtained from the urine of pregnant women or synthesized from ergosterol and used in the treatment of estrogen deficiency and certain menopausal and postmenopausal conditions. Also, **estrin, oestrin, oestrone.** Also called **theelin.** [ESTR(IN) + -ONE]

es·trous (es′trəs), *adj.* involving or pertaining to the estrus. Also, **oestrous.** [ESTR(IN) + -OUS]

es′trous cy′cle, *Zool.* a recurrent series of physiological changes in sexual and other organs in female mammals, between rutting periods.

es·trus (es′trəs), *n. Zool.* 1. the period of heat or rut; the period of maximum sexual receptivity of the female. 2. See **estrous cycle.** Also, **es·trum** (es′trəm), **oestrus.** [< L *oestrus* frenzy] —**es·tru·al** (es′trŏŏ əl), *adj.*

es·tu·a·rine (es′chŏŏ ə rīn′, -ər in), *adj.* 1. formed in an estuary. 2. found in estuaries. [ESTUAR(Y) + -INE[1]]

es·tu·ar·y (es′chŏŏ er′ē), *n., pl.* **-ar·ies.** 1. that part of the mouth or lower course of a river in which the river's current meets the sea's tide. 2. an arm or inlet of the sea at the lower end of a river. [< L *aestuāri(um)* channel, creek, inlet, equiv. to *aestu(s)* tide + *-ārium* -ARY] —**es·tu·ar·i·al** (es′chŏŏ âr′ē əl), *adj.*

esu, *Elect.* See **electrostatic unit.** Also, **ESU**

e·su·ri·ent (i sŏŏr′ē ənt), *adj.* hungry; greedy. [< L *ēsurient-* (s. of *ēsuriēns,* prp. of *ēsurīre*) hungering, equiv. to *ēsur-* hunger + *-ent-* -ENT] —**e·su′ri·ence, e·su′ri·en·cy,** *n.* —**e·su′ri·ent·ly,** *adv.*

-et, a noun suffix having properly a diminutive force (now lost in many words): *islet; bullet; midget; owlet; plummet.* Cf. **-ette.** [ME < OF *-et* (masc.), *-ette* (fem.)]

et (et), *conj. Latin.* and.

Et, *Chem.* ethyl.

E.T., Eastern Time.

e.t., 1. eastern time. 2. electrical transcription.

e·ta (ā′tə, ē′tə), *n.* 1. the seventh letter of the Greek alphabet (H, η). 2. the vowel sound represented by this letter.

E·ta (ā′tä), *n., pl.* **E·tas, E·ta.** (in Japan) 1. an outcast class. 2. a member of this class.

Et·a (et′ə), *n.* a girl's given name, form of **Ethel.**

E.T.A., estimated time of arrival. Also, **ETA**

é·ta·gère (ā tA zheR′), *n., pl.* **-gères** (-zheR′). *French.* a series of open shelves for bric-a-brac.

et al. (et al′, äl′, ôl′), 1. and elsewhere. [< L *et alibi*] 2. and others. [< L *et aliī*]

e·ta·lon (āt′əlon′), *n. Optics.* an interferometer consisting of two parallel, lightly silvered, very flat glass plates that reflect approximately half of each ray of light incident upon them and that are separated by a small, fixed distance: used to compare wavelengths and to study the hyperfine structure of atomic spectra. Also called **Fabry-Perot etalon, multiple-beam interferometer.** [< F; MF *estalon* standard, deriv. of OF *estal* place < Gmc; see STALL[1]]

et·a·mine (et′ə mēn′), *n.* a lightweight cotton or worsted fabric constructed in plain weave and loosely woven. [< F; see ESTAMIN]

et·a·oin shrd·lu (et′ə oin′ shûrd′lōō, ē′tē-), the letters produced by running the finger down the first two vertical rows of keys at the left of the keyboard of a Linotype machine, used as a temporary marking slug but sometimes inadvertently cast and printed.

é·tape (ā tap′; *Fr.* ā tAp′), *n., pl.* **é·tapes** (ā taps′; *Fr.* ā tAp′). *Mil.* 1. a place where troops camp after a day's march. 2. a day's march. 3. *Archaic.* supplies issued to troops during a march. [< F; MF *estaple* < MD *stapel* warehouse; see STAPLE[2]]

etc., See **et cetera.**

et cet·er·a (et set′ər ə, se′trə), and others; and so forth; and so on (used to indicate that more of the same sort or class might have been mentioned, but for shortness are omitted). *Abbr.:* etc. [< L]

et·cet·er·a (et set′ər ə, -se′trə), *n., pl.* **-ras.** 1. a number of other things or persons unspecified. 2. **etceteras,** extras or sundries. [n. use of ET CETERA]

etch (ech), *v.t.* 1. to cut, bite, or corrode with an acid or the like; engrave with an acid or the like, as to form a design in furrows which when charged with ink will give an impression on paper. 2. to produce (a design, image, etc.) by this method, as on copper or glass. 3. to outline clearly or sharply; delineate, as a person's features, character, etc. 4. to fix permanently in or implant firmly on the mind; root in the memory: *Our last conversation is etched in my memory.* 5. to cut (a geological feature) into the surface of the earth by means of erosion: *a deep canyon etched into the land by the river's* *rushing waters.* —*v.i.* **6.** to practice the art of etching. —*n.* **7.** *Print.* an acid used for etching. [< D *etsen* < G *ätzen* to etch, orig. cause to eat; c. OE *ettan* to graze; akin to EAT] —**etch′er,** *n.*

etch·ing (ech′ing), *n.* **1.** the act or process of making designs or pictures on a metal plate, glass, etc., by the corrosive action of an acid instead of by a burin. **2.** an impression, as on paper, taken from an etched plate. **3.** the design so produced. **4.** a metal plate bearing such a design. [ETCH + -ING[1]]

etch′ing ground′, ground[1] (def. 9).

E.T.D., estimated time of departure. Also, **ETD**

E·te·o·cles (i tē′ə klēz′), *n.* *Class. Myth.* a son of Oedipus and the brother of Polynices, by whom he was slain. Cf. **Seven against Thebes** (def. 1).

Et·e·o·cre·tan (et′ē ō krēt′ən, ē′tē-), *adj.* noting or pertaining to certain inscriptions found on Crete, written in an early form of the Greek alphabet.

e·ter·nal (i tûr′nəl), *adj.* **1.** lasting forever; without beginning or end; always existing (opposed to *temporal*): *eternal life.* **2.** perpetual; ceaseless; endless: *eternal quarreling; eternal chatter.* **3.** enduring; immutable: *eternal principles.* **4.** *Metaphys.* existing outside of all relations of time; not subject to change. —*n.* **5.** that which is eternal. **6. the Eternal,** God. [ME < LL *aeternāl(is),* equiv. to *aetern(us)* (see ETERNE) + *-ālis* -AL[1]] —**e·ter′nal·ly,** *adv.* —**e·ter·nal·i·ty** (ē′tûr nal′i tē), **e·ter′nal·ness,** *n.*
—**Syn. 1.** permanent, unending. ETERNAL, ENDLESS, EVERLASTING, PERPETUAL imply lasting or going on without ceasing. That which is ETERNAL is, by its nature, without beginning or ending: *God, the eternal Father.* That which is ENDLESS never stops but goes on continually as if in a circle: *an endless succession of years.* That which is EVERLASTING will endure through all future time: *a promise of everlasting life.* PERPETUAL implies continuous renewal as far into the future as one can foresee: *perpetual strife between nations.* **3.** timeless, immortal, deathless, undying, imperishable, indestructible. —**Ant. 1.** transitory. **3.** mutable.

Eter′nal Cit′y, The, the city of Rome, Italy.

e·ter·nal·ise (i tûr′nəlīz′), *v.t.*, **-ised, -is·ing.** *Chiefly Brit.* eternalize.

e·ter·nal·ize (i tûr′nəlīz′), *v.t.*, **-ized, -iz·ing.** to eternize. [ETERNAL + -IZE]

eter′nal ob′ject, (in the philosophy of Whitehead) an essence or potentiality combining in space-time with others to form an occasion; one of innumerable possibilities intersecting with others to form an actual event.

eter′nal recur′rence, recurrence of a given event an infinite number of times: argued by Nietzsche from the existence of a finite number of combinations of factors and of an infinity of time.

e·terne (i tûrn′), *adj.* *Archaic.* eternal. [ME < L < *aeternus,* contr. of *aeviternus,* equiv. to *aev(um)* age + *-i-* -I- + *-ternus* (as in *sempiternus*)]

e·ter·nise (i tûr′nīz), *v.t.*, **-nised, -nis·ing.** *Chiefly Brit.* eternize. —**e·ter′ni·sa′tion,** *n.*

e·ter·ni·ty (i tûr′ni tē), *n., pl.* **-ties. 1.** infinite time; duration without beginning or end. **2.** eternal existence, esp. as contrasted with mortal life: *the eternity of God.* **3.** the state into which the soul passes at a person's death. **4.** an endless or seemingly endless period of time: *We had to wait an eternity for the ship to sail.* **5. eternities,** the truths or realities of life and thought that are regarded as timeless or eternal. [ME *eternite* < L *aeternitās.* See ETERNE, -ITY]

e·ter·nize (i tûr′nīz), *v.t.*, **-nized, -niz·ing. 1.** to make eternal; perpetuate. **2.** to immortalize. Also, *esp. Brit.*, **eternise.** [< ML *ēterniz(āre).* See ETERNE, -IZE] —**e·ter′ni·za′tion,** *n.*

e·te·sian (i tē′zhən), *adj.* (of certain Mediterranean winds) occurring annually. [< L *etēsiae* < Gk *etēsiai (ánemoi)* periodical (winds) + -AN]

eth (eth), *n.* a letter in the form of a crossed *d* (ð or ð), used in Old English writing to represent both voiced and unvoiced *th* and in modern Icelandic and in phonetic alphabets to represent voiced *th.* Also, **edh.**

-eth[1], an ending of the third person singular present indicative of verbs, now occurring only in archaic forms or used in solemn or poetic language: *doeth* or *doth; hopeth; sitteth.* [OE *-eth, -ath, -oth, -th;* akin to L *-t*]

-eth[2], var. of **-th**[2], the ordinal suffix, used when the cardinal number ends in *-y: twentieth; thirtieth.*

Eth., Ethiopa.

eth·al (eth′al, ē′thal), *n.* *Chem.* See **cetyl alcohol.**

E·than (ē′thən), *n.* a boy's given name.

e·than·a·mide (i than′ə mīd′), *n.* *Chem.* acetamide.

eth·ane (eth′ān), *n.* *Chem.* a colorless, odorless, flammable gas, CH_3CH_3, of the methane series, present in natural gas, illuminating gas, and crude petroleum: used chiefly in organic synthesis and as a fuel gas. Also called **bimethyl, dimethyl, ethyl hydride, methyl methane.** [ETH(YL) + -ANE]

eth′ane di·ni′trile (dī nī′tril, -trēl, -tril), *Chem.* cyanogen (def. 1). [DI-[1] + NITRILE]

eth′ane·di·o′ic ac′id (eth′ān dī ō′ik, eth′-), *Chem.* See **oxalic acid.** [ETHANE + DI-[1] + -O- + -IC]

eth·ane·thi·ol (eth′ān thī′ōl, -ôl, -ol), *n.* *Chem.* mercaptan (def. 2). [ETHANE + THIOL]

E′than Frome′ (frōm), a novel (1911) by Edith Wharton.

Eth·a·nim (eth′ə nim; *Heb.* e tä nēm′), *n.* *Chiefly Biblical.* the month of the Jewish calendar equivalent to Tishri. I Kings 8:2. [< Heb]

eth·a·nol (eth′ə nōl′, -nôl′, -nol′), *n.* *Chem.* alcohol (def. 1). [ETHANE + -OL[1]]

eth·chlor·vy·nol (eth klôr′və nōl′, -nôl′, -nol′, -klōr′-), *n.* *Pharm.* a colorless to yellow, pungent, aromatic liquid, C_7H_9ClO, used as a hypnotic and sedative. [formerly trademark]

Eth·el (eth′əl), *n.* a girl's given name. Also, **Ethyl, Ethyle.**

Eth·el·bert (eth′əl bûrt′), *n.* **1.** Ancient, **Ædilberct, Æthelbert.** A.D. 552?–616, king of Kent 560–616. **2.** a boy's given name.

E·thel·da (i thel′də), *n.* a girl's given name, form of **Ethel.**

Eth·e·lee (eth′ə lē′), *n.* a girl's given name.

Eth·e·lene (eth′ə lēn′), *n.* a girl's given name, form of **Ethel.** Also, **Eth·e·line** (eth′ə lēn′, -līn′), **Eth·e·lyn, Eth·e·lynne** (eth′ə lin).

Eth·e·lette (eth′ə let′), *n.* a girl's given name, form of **Ethel.**

Eth·e·lind (eth′ə lind), *n.* a girl's given name. Also, **Ethlyn.**

Eth·e·lin·da (eth′ə lin′də), *n.* a girl's given name.

Eth·el·red II (eth′əl red′), (*"the Unready"*) A.D. 968?–1016, king of the English 978–1016.

eth·ene (eth′ēn), *n.* *Chem.* ethylene (def. 2). [ETH(YL) + -ENE]

e·ther (ē′thər), *n.* **1.** Also called **diethyl ether, diethyl oxide, ethyl ether, ethyl oxide, sulfuric ether.** *Chem., Pharm.* a colorless, highly volatile, flammable liquid, $(C_2H_5)_2O$, having a pleasant aromatic odor and sweet, burning taste, derived from ethyl alcohol by the action of sulfuric acid: used as a solvent and in medicine chiefly as an inhalant anesthetic. **2.** *Chem. Obs.* one of a class of compounds in which two organic groups are attached directly to an oxygen atom, having the general formula, ROR, as ethyl ether. **3.** the upper regions of space; the clear sky; the heavens. **4.** the medium supposed by the ancients to fill the upper regions of space. **5.** *Physics.* a hypothetical substance supposed to occupy all space, postulated to account for the propagation of electromagnetic radiation through space. Cf. **Michelson-Morley experiment.** Also, **aether** (for defs. 3–5). [ME < L *aether* the upper air, pure air, ether < Gk *aithér,* equiv. to *aith-* (s. of *aíthein* to glow, burn; akin to OE *ād* funeral pyre, L *aestus* heat) + *-ēr* -OR[1]]

e·the·re·al (i thēr′ē əl), *adj.* **1.** light, airy, or tenuous: *an ethereal world created through the poetic imagination.* **2.** extremely delicate or refined: *ethereal beauty.* **3.** heavenly or celestial. **4.** of the ether or upper regions of space. **5.** *Chem.* pertaining to, containing, or resembling ethyl ether. Also, **aethereal** (for defs. 1–4). [< L *aethere(us)* (< Gk *aithérios*), equiv. to *aether* ETHER + *-e(us)* adj. suffix + -AL[1]] —**e·the′re·al′i·ty, e·the′re·al·ness,** *n.* —**e·the′re·al·ly,** *adv.* —**e·the′re·ous,** *adj.*

e·the·re·al·ise (i thēr′ē ə līz′), *v.t.*, **-ised, -is·ing.** *Chiefly Brit.* etherealize. Also, **etherialise.** —**e·the′re·al·i·sa′tion,** *n.*

e·the·re·al·ize (i thēr′ē ə līz′), *v.t.*, **-ized, -iz·ing.** to make ethereal. Also, **etherialize.** [ETHEREAL + -IZE] —**e·the′re·al·i·za′tion,** *n.*

Eth·er·ege (eth′ər ij), *n.* **Sir George,** 1635?–91, English dramatist.

E·the·ri·a (i thēr′ē ə), *n.* a genus of fresh-water, bivalve mollusks, of Africa and Madagascar, the shell of which has a pearly, bright-green interior.

e·the·ri·al·ise (i thēr′ē ə līz′), *v.t.*, **-ised, -is·ing.** *Chiefly Brit.* etherealize. —**e·the′ri·al·i·sa′tion,** *n.*

e·the·ri·al·ize (i thēr′ē ə līz′), *v.t.*, **-ized, -iz·ing.** etherealize. —**e·the′ri·al·i·za′tion,** *n.*

e·ther·i·fy (i ther′ə fī′, ē′thər-), *v.t.*, **-fied, -fy·ing.** *Chem.* to convert into an ether. [ETHER + -IFY] —**e·ther′i·fi·ca′tion,** *n.*

e·ther·ize (ē′thə rīz′), *v.t.*, **-ized, -iz·ing.** *Med.* to put under the influence of ether. [ETHER + -IZE] —**e′ther·i·za′tion,** *n.* —**e′ther·iz′er,** *n.*

eth·ic (eth′ik), *n.* **1.** the body of moral principles or values governing or distinctive of a particular culture or group: *the Christian ethic; the tribal ethic of the Zuñi.* **2.** a complex of moral precepts held or rules of conduct followed by an individual: *a personal ethic.* —*adj.* **3.** ethical. [ME *ethic, etic* < L *ēthic(us)* < Gk *ēthikós,* equiv. to *ēth(ós)* ETHOS + *-ikos* -IC]

eth·i·cal (eth′i kəl), *adj.* **1.** pertaining to or dealing with morals or the principles of morality; pertaining to right and wrong in conduct. **2.** in accordance with the rules or standards for right conduct or practice, esp. the standards of a profession: *It is not considered ethical for physicians to advertise.* **3.** (of drugs) sold only upon medical prescription. [ETHIC + -AL[1]] —**eth′i·cal·ly,** *adv.* —**eth′i·cal·ness, eth′i·cal′i·ty,** *n.*
—**Syn. 2.** moral, upright, honest, righteous, virtuous, honorable. —**Ant. 2.** immoral.

eth′ical ni′hilism, *Ethics.* the denial of the existence of any possible bases for the establishment of an ethical or moral philosophy. —**eth′ical ni′hilist.**

eth′ical rel′ativism, *Ethics.* **1.** the view that moral standards and principles are relative to the nature of the particular society in which they exist and admit of no outside criticism or evaluation. **2.** a similar view concerning the moral standards and principles of an individual. —**eth′ical rel′ativist.**

eth·i·cize (eth′i sīz′), *v.t.*, **-cized, -ciz·ing.** to make ethical; treat or regard as ethical. [ETHIC + -IZE]

eth·ics (eth′iks), *n.pl.* **1.** (*construed as sing. or pl.*) a system of moral principles: *the ethics of a culture.* **2.** the rules of conduct recognized in respect to a particular class of human actions or a particular group, culture, etc.: *medical ethics; Christian ethics.* **3.** moral principles, as of an individual: *His ethics forbade betrayal of a confidence.* **4.** (*usually construed as sing.*) that branch of philosophy dealing with values relating to human conduct, with respect to the rightness and wrongness of certain actions and to the goodness and badness of the motives and ends of such actions. Cf. **axiological ethics, deontological ethics.** [ETHIC + -S[3], modeled on Gk *tà ēthiká,* neut. pl.] —**e·thi·cian** (e thish′ən), **eth·i·cist** (eth′i sist), *n.*
—**Syn. 2.** See **moral.**

Eth′ics of the Fa′thers. See **Pirke Aboth.**

e·thin·a·mate (i thin′ə māt′), *n.* *Pharm.* a crystalline, slightly water-soluble powder, $H{\equiv}CC_6H_{10}OOCNH_2$, used as a hypnotic. [formerly trademark]

eth·ine (eth′in), *n.* acetylene. [ETH(YL) + -INE[1]]

E·thi·op (ē′thē op′), *adj., n.* Ethiopian. Also, **E·thi·ope** (ē′thē ōp′). [ME < L *Aethiop(s)* < Gk *Aithíops*]

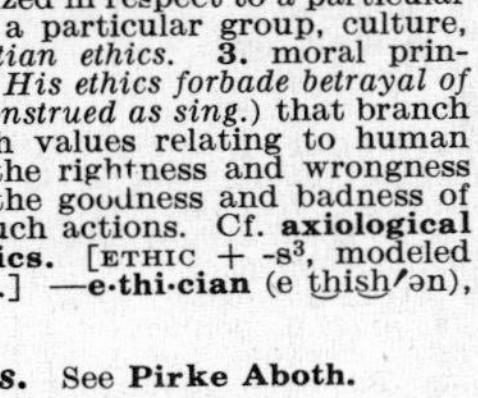

E·thi·o·pi·a (ē′thē ō′pē ə), *n.* **1.** Formerly, **Abyssinia.** a kingdom in E Africa: a part of the former Italian E Africa 1936–41. 21,461,700 (est. 1962); 409,266 sq. mi. Present boundaries include Eritrea. *Cap.:* Addis Ababa. **2.** an ancient region in NE Africa, bordering on Egypt and the Red Sea.

E·thi·o·pi·an (ē′thē ō′pē ən), *adj.* **1.** of or pertaining to Ethiopia or to its inhabitants. **2.** Negro. **3.** belonging to the part of Africa which is south of the equator. **4.** *Zoogeog.* belonging to a geographical division comprising Africa south of the tropic of Cancer, the southern part of the Arabian Peninsula, and Madagascar. —*n.* **5.** a native of Ethiopia. **6.** a member of any of various supposedly dark-skinned peoples regarded by the ancients as coming from a country lying south of Egypt. **7.** a Negro. [ETHIOPI(A) + -AN]

Ethio′pian Church′, the Monophysitic church founded by Frumentius in the 4th century A.D., and resembling the Coptic Church in doctrine, practice, and discipline, but using Ethiopic in its liturgy. Also called **Abyssinian Church.**

E·thi·op·ic (ē′thē op′ik, -ō′pik), *adj.* **1.** Ethiopian. —*n.* **2.** Also called **Geez, Ge'ez.** the Semitic language of ancient Ethiopia, now used only as the liturgical language of the Ethiopian Church. [< L *Aethiopic(us).* See ETHIOP, -IC]

Eth·lyn (eth′lin), *n.* a girl's given name. Also, **Ethelind.**

eth·moid (eth′moid), *Anat.* —*adj.* **1.** Also, **eth·moi′dal.** of or pertaining to a bone at the base of the cranium at the root of the nose, containing numerous perforations for the filaments of the olfactory nerve. —*n.* **2.** the ethmoid bone. [< Gk *ēthmoeidḗs* sievelike; see -OID]

eth·narch (eth′närk), *n.* the ruler of a people, tribe, or nation. [< Gk *ethnárchēs.* See ETHNO-, -ARCH]

eth·nar·chy (eth′när kē), *n., pl.* **-chies.** the government, office, or jurisdiction of an ethnarch. [< Gk *ethnarchía.* See ETHNARCH, -Y[3]]

eth·nic (eth′nik), *adj.* **1.** pertaining to or characteristic of a people, esp. to a speech or culture group. **2.** referring to the origin, classification, characteristics, etc., of such groups. **3.** pertaining to non-Christians. **4.** belonging to or deriving from the cultural, racial, religious, or linguistic traditions of a people or country, esp. a primitive one: *ethnic dances.* Also, **eth′ni·cal.** [ME *ethnik* heathen < LL *ethnic(us)* < Gk *ethnikós.* See ETHNO-, -IC] —**eth′ni·cal·ly,** *adv.* —**eth·nic·i·ty** (eth nis′i tē), *n.*

eth′nic group′, *Sociol.* a group of people of the same race or nationality who share a common and distinctive culture. Also called **ethnos.**

ethno-, a learned borrowing from Greek meaning "race," "culture," "people," used in the formation of compound words: *ethnography.* [< Gk, comb. form of *éthnos*]

eth·no·cen·trism (eth′nō sen′triz əm), *n.* **1.** *Sociol.* the belief in the inherent superiority of one's own group and culture accompanied by a feeling of contempt for other groups and cultures. **2.** a tendency to view alien groups or cultures in terms of one's own. [ETHNO- + CENT(E)R + -ISM] —**eth′no·cen′tric,** *adj.* —**eth′no·cen′tri·cal·ly,** *adv.* —**eth′no·cen·tric′i·ty,** *n.*

eth·noc·ra·cy (eth nok′rə sē), *n.* rule by a particular race or ethnic group. [ETHNO- + -CRACY]

ethnog., ethnography.

eth·nog·e·ny (eth noj′ə nē), *n.* *Anthropol.* a branch of ethnology which studies the origin of distinctive populations or races. [ETHNO- + -GENY] —**eth·no·gen·ic** (eth′nō jen′ik), *adj.* —**eth·nog′e·nist,** *n.*

eth·nog·ra·phy (eth nog′rə fē), *n.* a branch of anthropology dealing with the scientific description of individual cultures. [ETHNO- + -GRAPHY] —**eth·nog′ra·pher,** *n.* —**eth·no·graph·ic** (eth′nə graf′ik), **eth′no·graph′i·cal,** *adj.* —**eth′no·graph′i·cal·ly,** *adv.*

eth·no·his·to·ry (eth′nō his′tə rē), *n.* a branch of anthropology dealing with the development of cultures, esp. through the analysis of archaeological findings. [ETHNO- + HISTORY] —**eth·no·his·to·ri·an** (eth′nō hi stôr′ē ən, -stōr′-), *n.* —**eth·no·his·tor·i·cal** (eth′nō hi stôr′i kəl, -stor′-), **eth′no·his·tor′ic,** *adj.* —**eth′no·his·tor′i·cal·ly,** *adv.*

ethnol., **1.** ethnological. **2.** ethnology.

eth·no·lin·guis·tics (eth′nō ling gwis′tiks), *n.* (*construed as sing.*) the study of language as an aspect or part of culture, esp. the study of the influence of language on culture and of culture on language. [ETHNO- + LINGUISTICS] —**eth′no·lin′guist,** *n.* —**eth′no·lin·guis′tic,** *adj.*

eth·nol·o·gy (eth nol′ə jē), *n.* **1.** a branch of anthropology that analyzes cultures, esp. in regard to their historical development and the similarities and dissimilarities between them. **2.** a branch of anthropology dealing with the origin, distribution, and distinguishing characteristics of the races of mankind. [ETHNO- + -LOGY] —**eth·no·log·i·cal** (eth′nə loj′i kəl), **eth′no·log′ic,** *adj.* —**eth′no·log′i·cal·ly,** *adv.* —**eth·nol′o·gist,** *n.*

eth·no·mu·si·col·o·gy (eth′nō myōō′zi kol′ə jē), *n.* the study of folk and primitive music and of their relationship to the peoples and cultures to which they belong. [ETHNO- + MUSICOLOGY] —**eth·no·mu·si·co·log·i·cal** (eth′nō myōō′zi kə loj′i kəl), *adj.* —**eth′no·mu′si·co·log′i·cal·ly,** *adv.* —**eth′no·mu′si·col′o·gist,** *n.*

eth·nos (eth′nos), *n.* *Sociol.* See **ethnic group.**

et hoc ge·nus om·ne (et hōk′ gen′ōōs ôm′ne; *Eng.* et hok′ jē′nəs om′nē), *Latin.* and all this (or that) sort of thing. Also, **et id genus omne.**

e·thol·o·gy (e thol′ə jē, ē thol′-), *n.* the scientific study of animal behavior, esp. in relation to habitat. [< Gk *ēthología.* See ETHOS, -LOGY] —**eth·o·log·i·cal** (eth′ə loj′i kəl), *adj.* —**eth′o·log′i·cal·ly,** *adv.* —**e·thol′o·gist,** *n.*

e·thos (ē′thos, eth′os), *n.* **1.** *Sociol.* the fundamental character or spirit of a culture; the underlying sentiment that informs the beliefs, customs, or practices of a group or society; dominant assumptions of a people or period: *In the Greek ethos the individual was highly valued.* **2.** the moral element in dramatic literature that determines a man's action rather than his thought or emotion. **3.** the character or disposition of a community, group, person, etc. [< Gk: custom, habit, character]

eth·rog (es′rōg, -rəg; *Heb.* et rôg′, es rōg′), *n., pl.* **eth·rogs,** *Heb.* **eth·ro·gim** (et rō gēm, es rō-). *Juda-*

ism. a citron for use with the lulab during the Sukkoth festival service. Also, **esrog, etrog.** [< Heb *ethrōgh*]

eth·yl (eth′əl), *adj.* **1.** *Chem.* containing the ethyl group, as ethyl ether, $(C_2H_5)_2O$. —*n.* **2.** a type of antiknock fluid, containing tetraethyllead and other ingredients for a more even combustion. [ETH(ER) + -YL]

Eth·yl (eth′əl), *n.* a girl's given name. Also, **Ethel, Ethyle.**

eth′yl ac′etate, *Chem.* a colorless, volatile, flammable liquid, $CH_3COOC_2H_5$, having a fragrant, fruitlike odor: used chiefly as a scent in the manufacture of perfume, flavorings, and confections, and as a solvent for paints, varnishes, and lacquers.

eth′yl ac′etone. See **methyl propyl ketone.**

eth′yl al′cohol, *Chem.* alcohol (def. 1).

eth′yl a·mi·no·ben′zo·ate (ə mē′nō ben′zō āt′, -it, am′ə nō-), *Pharm.* benzocaine. [AMINO- + BENZOATE]

eth·yl·ate (eth′ə lāt′), *v.*, **-at·ed, -at·ing,** *n. Chem.* —*v.t.* **1.** to introduce one or more ethyl groups into (a compound). —*n.* **2.** a metallic derivative of ethyl alcohol, as potassium ethylate, KOC_2H_5. [ETHYL + -ATE[1]] —**eth′yl·a′tion,** *n.*

eth·yl·ben·zene (eth′əl ben′zēn, -ben zēn′), *n. Chem.* a colorless liquid, $C_6H_5C_2H_5$, used chiefly as an intermediate in the manufacture of styrene and as a solvent and diluent for paints and varnishes. [ETHYL + BENZENE]

eth′yl bu′tan·o·ate (byōō′tan ō āt′, byōō tan′-), *Chem.* See **ethyl butyrate.** [BUTANE + -OATE]

eth′yl bu′tyrate, *Chem.* a colorless, volatile, nontoxic liquid having the odor of pineapple, $C_3H_7CO_2C_2H_5$, used chiefly in flavoring extracts, and in the manufacture of perfumes and sprays. Also called **butyric ether, ethyl butanoate.**

eth′yl cap′ro·ate (kap′rō āt′), *Chem.* a colorless to yellow liquid, soluble in alcohol or ether, $C_5H_{11}COOC_2H_5$, used chiefly in artificial fruit essences and organic synthesis. Also, **eth′yl cap′ro·nate** (kap′rō-nāt′). Also called **ethyl hexoate, ethyl hexanoate.** [CAPRO(IC) + -ATE[2]]

eth′yl car′ba·mate (kär′bə māt′, kär bam′āt), *Chem.* urethan (def. 2). [CARBAM(IC) + -ATE[2]]

eth·yl·di·chlo·ro·ar·sine (eth′əl dī klôr′ō är′sēn, -klōr′-), *n. Chem.* a colorless, volatile, poisonous liquid, $C_2H_5AsCl_2$, having an irritating, fruitlike odor: formerly used as a blister gas. [ETHYL + DI-[1] + CHLORO-[2] + ARSINE]

Eth·yle (eth′əl), *n.* a girl's given name. Also, **Ethel, Ethyl.**

eth·yl·e·na·tion (eth′ə lə nā′shən), *n. Chem.* the process of introducing the ethylene group into a compound. [ETHYLENE + -ATION]

eth·yl·ene (eth′ə lēn′), *Chem.* —*adj.* **1.** containing the ethylene group. —*n.* **2.** Also called **elayl, ethene, olefiant gas.** a colorless, flammable gas, $CH_2{=}CH_2$, having a sweet, unpleasant odor and taste, the first member of the ethylene series, usually obtained from petroleum and natural gas: used as an agent to improve the color of citrus fruits, in the synthesis of polyethylene, ethylene dibromide, ethylene oxide, and other organic compounds, and in medicine chiefly as an inhalation anesthetic. [ETHYL + -ENE] —**eth·yl·e·nic** (eth′ə lē′nik, -len′ik), *adj.*

eth′ylene al′cohol, glycol (def. 1).

eth′ylene dibro′mide, *Chem.* a colorless, volatile, sweet smelling, nonflammable liquid, CH_2BrCH_2Br, produced from ethylene by reaction with bromine: used chiefly in gasoline to overcome the undesired effects of lead in antiknock agents, as a solvent, and in organic synthesis. Also called **eth′ylene bro′mide.**

eth′ylene dichlo′ride, *Chem.* a colorless, heavy, oily, toxic liquid, CH_2ClCH_2Cl, having a chloroformlike odor: used in the synthesis of vinyl chloride, and as a solvent for fats, oils, waxes, gums, resins, rubber, etc. Also called **eth′ylene chlo′ride.**

eth′ylene gly′col, *Chem.* glycol (def. 1).

eth′ylene group′, *Chem.* the bivalent group, $-CH_2CH_2-$, derived from ethylene or ethane. Also called **eth′ylene rad′ical.**

eth′ylene ox′ide, *Chem.* a colorless, odorless, gaseous, toxic, ring compound C_2H_4O, usually obtained by the oxidation of ethylene: used chiefly in the synthesis of ethylene glycol.

eth′ylene se′ries, *Chem.* See **alkene series.**

eth′yl e′ther, *Chem.* ether (def. 1).

eth′yl group′, *Chem.* the univalent group, CH_3CH_2-, derived from ethane. Also called **eth′yl rad′ical.**

eth′yl hex′o·ate (hek′sō āt′), *Chem.* See **ethyl caproate.** Also called **eth′yl hex′a·no·ate** (hek′sə-nō āt′). [*hexo(ic acid)* (from HEXANE) + -ATE[2]]

eth′yl hy′dride, *Chem.* ethane.

e·thyl·ic (ə thil′ik), *adj.* of, pertaining to, or characteristic of the ethyl group. [ETHYL + -IC]

e·thyl′i·dene dieth′yl e′ther (ə thil′i dēn′), *Chem.* acetal (def. 1). [ETHYL + -IDE + -ENE]

eth′yl mal′onate, *Chem.* a colorless, water-insoluble liquid, $CH_2(COOC_2H_5)_2$, having a pleasant, aromatic odor: used chiefly as an intermediate in the synthesis of barbiturates. Also called **diethyl malonate.**

eth′yl mercap′tan, *Chem.* mercaptan (def. 2).

eth′yl meth′yl ke′tone, *Chem.* See **methyl ethyl ketone.**

eth′yl ni′trate, *Chem.* a colorless, sweet, water-insoluble, dangerous, powerful, explosive liquid, $C_2H_5ONO_2$, used chiefly in organic synthesis. Also called **nitric ether.**

eth′yl ni′trite, *Chem.* a colorless or yellowish, very volatile, highly aromatic, flammable liquid, C_2H_5ONO, used chiefly in the preparation of organic substances. Also called **nitrous ether.**

eth′yl ni′trite spir′it, *Pharm.* a four percent solution of ethyl nitrite in alcohol, formerly used in medicine as a diaphoretic, diuretic, and antispasmodic. Also called **spirit of nitrous ether, sweet spirit of nitre.**

eth′yl oe·nan′thate (i nan′thāt), *Chem.* a colorless to yellowish, oily, water-insoluble liquid, $CH_3(CH_2)_5COOC_2H_5$, having a fruitlike odor, found naturally in the alcohols of cognac and other wines: synthesized for use chiefly as artificial flavoring in various alcoholic beverages. Also called **oenanthic ester, cognac oil, oenanthic ether.** [OENANTH(IC) + -ATE[2]]

eth′yl ox′ide, *Chem.* ether (def. 1).

eth′yl sul′fide, *Chem.* a colorless, oily, slightly water-soluble liquid, $(C_2H_5)_2S$, having a garliclike odor: used chiefly as a solvent for certain salts and in organic synthesis. Also called **diethyl sulfide, eth·yl·thi·o·e·ther** (eth′əl thī′ō ē′thər), **eth·yl·thi·o·eth·ane** (eth′əl-thī′ō eth′ān).

eth′yl u′rethane, *Chem.* urethan (def. 2). Also, **eth′yl u′rethan.**

eth·yne (eth′in, e thīn′), *n. Chem.* acetylene. [ETH(YL) + -*yne* (var. of -INE[1])]

e·thy·nyl (e thī′nəl), *adj. Chem.* containing the ethynyl group. [ETHYNE + -YL]

e·thy·nyl·a·tion (e thī′nəlā′shən), *n. Chem.* the process of introducing the ethynyl group into a compound. [ETHYNYL (GROUP) + -ATION]

ethy′nyl group′, *Chem.* the univalent group, $HC{\equiv}C-$, derived from acetylene. Also called **ethy′nyl rad′ical.**

et·i·am (et′ē äm′; *Eng.* et′ē am′), *adv. Latin.* also; besides.

-etic, a suffix used in the formation of adjectives: *eidetic.* [< L *-eticus*, Gk *-etikos*, equiv. to *-et-*, a formative occurring in some nouns, + *-ikos* -IC]

et id ge·nus om·ne (et id′ gen′ōōs ōm′ne; *Eng.* et id′ jē′nəs om′nē), *Latin.* See **et hoc genus omne.**

É·tienne (ā tyen′), *n.* Estienne (def. 1).

etio-, a combining form of Greek origin meaning "cause": *etiology.* Also, **aetio-.** [< Gk *aitio-*, comb. form repr. *aitía* cause]

e·ti·o·late (ē′tē ə lāt′), *v.*, **-lat·ed, -lat·ing.** —*v.t.* **1.** to cause (a plant) to whiten by excluding light; bleach: *to etiolate celery.* —*v.i.* **2.** (of plants) to whiten through lack of light. [< F *étiol(er)* (to) make pale (< ?) + -ATE[1]]

e·ti·ol·o·gy (ē′tē ol′ə jē), *n.*, *pl.* **-gies.** **1.** *Pathol.* the study of the causes of diseases. **2.** the cause or origin of a disease. **3.** the study of causation. **4.** any study of causes, causation, or causality, as in philosophy, biology, or physics. Also, **aetiology.** [< L *aetiologia* < Gk *aitiología* determining the cause of something. See ETIO-, -LOGY] —**e·ti·o·log·i·cal** (ē′tē ə loj′i kəl), *adj.* —**e′ti·o·log′i·cal·ly,** *adv.* —**e′ti·ol′o·gist,** *n.*

et·i·quette (et′ə kit, -ket′), *n.* **1.** conventional requirements as to social behavior; proprieties of conduct as established in any class or community or for any occasion. **2.** a prescribed or accepted code of usage in matters of ceremony, as at a court or in official or other formal observances. **3.** the unwritten code of ethical behavior regarding professional practice or action among the members of a profession in their dealings with each other: *It is regarded a breach of medical etiquette for a doctor to steal another physician's patient.* [< F *étiquette*, MF *estiquette* ticket, memorandum, deriv. of *estiqu(i)er* to attach, stick < Gmc. See STICK[2], -ETTE]

—**Syn. 1.** ETIQUETTE, DECORUM, PROPRIETY imply observance of the formal requirements governing behavior in polite society. ETIQUETTE refers to conventional forms and usages: *the rules of etiquette.* DECORUM suggests dignity and a sense of what is becoming or appropriate for a person of good breeding: *a fine sense of decorum.* PROPRIETY (usually plural) implies established conventions of morals and good taste: *She never fails to observe the proprieties.*

et·na (et′nə), *n.* an arrangement once used to heat small amounts of a beverage, liquid food, etc., consisting of a cup fixed to a saucer in which alcohol is burned. [after Mount ETNA, from its shape]

Et·na (et′nə), *n.* **1.** Also, **Aetna. Mount,** an active volcano in E Sicily. 10,758 ft. **2.** a town in SW Pennsylvania. 5519 (1960).

ETO, (in World War II) European Theater of Operations. Also, **E.T.O.**

é·toile (ā twal′), *n.*, *pl.* **é·toiles** (ā twal′). *French.* **1.** a star or something shaped like a star. **2.** See **prima ballerina.**

E·ton (ēt′ən), *n.* a town in S Buckinghamshire, in S England, on the Thames River, W of London: the site of Eton College. 3901 (1961).

E′ton col′lar, a broad, stiff collar, originally of linen, as that worn folded outside an Eton jacket.

E′ton Col′lege, a preparatory school for boys in Eton, England, founded in 1440 by Henry VI.

E·to·ni·an (ē tō′nē ən), *n.* **1.** a person who is or has been a pupil at Eton College. —*adj.* **2.** of or pertaining to Eton College. [ETON + -IAN]

E′ton jack′et, **1.** a boy's short jacket reaching to the waistline, as worn by students at Eton College. **2.** a similar short jacket worn by women.

Eton jacket

Et·o·wah (et′ə wä′), *n.* a town in SE Tennessee. 3223 (1960).

Etr., Etruscan.

É·tran·ger, L' (*Fr.* lā trän zhā′). See **Stranger, The.**

et·rog (es′rōg, -rəg; *Heb.* et rôg′, es rōg′), *n.*, *pl.* **et·rogs,** *Heb.* **et·ro·gim** (et rō gēm′, es rō-). *Judaism.* ethrog.

E·tru·ri·a (i trŏŏr′ē ə), *n.* an ancient country located between the Arno and Tiber rivers, roughly corresponding to modern Tuscany in W Italy.

E·trus·can (i trus′kən), *adj.* **1.** pertaining to Etruria, its inhabitants, civilization, art, or language. —*n.* **2.** an inhabitant of ancient Etruria. **3.** the extinct language of Etruria, not known to be related to any other language despite attempts to connect it with Basque, Sumerian, Elamite, and the languages of the Caucasus. *Abbr.:* Etr. Also called **E·tru·ri·an** (i trŏŏr′ē ən). [< L *Etrusc(us)* of Etruria + -AN]

Etrus′can ware′, a black ceramic ware ornamented in encaustic colors, developed by Josiah Wedgwood.

E·trus·col·o·gy (ē′trə skol′ə jē), *n.* the study of Etruscan antiquities. [ETRUSC(AN) + -O- + -LOGY] —**E′trus·col′o·gist,** *n.*

et seq., *pl.* **et seqq., et sqq.** and the following. [< L *et sequēns*]

et seqq., and those following. Also, **et sqq.** [< L *et sequentēs, et sequentia*]

et sic de si·mi·li·bus (et sēk de si mil′i bōōs′; *Eng.* et sik dē si mil′ə bəs), *Latin.* and thus concerning similar ones.

Et·ta (et′ə), *n.* a girl's given name, form of **Henrietta.**

Et·ta·beth (et′ə bəth, -beth′), *n.* a girl's given name.

Et·tarre (i tär′, e tär′ə), *n. Arthurian Romance.* the vain and heartless lady beloved by Sir Pelleas.

-ette, a noun suffix, the feminine form of *-et*, occurring with the original diminutive force (*cigarette*), as a distinctively feminine ending (*coquette*), in various colloquial or humorous formations (*usherette*), and in trademarks of imitations or substitutes (*Leatherette*). Cf. **-et.** [< F, fem. of *-et* -ET]

Et·trick (et′rik), *n.* a town in central Virginia. 2998 (1960).

et tu, Bru·te (et tōō′ brōō′tā), *Latin.* and thou, Brutus!: alleged dying words of Julius Caesar uttered as his friend Brutus stabbed him.

é·tude (ā′tōōd, ā′tyōōd, ā tōōd′, ā tyōōd′; *Fr.* ā tyd′), *n.*, *pl.* **é·tudes** (ā′tōōdz, ā′tyōōdz, ā tōōdz′, ā tyōōdz′; *Fr.* ā tyd′). *Music.* **1.** a composition, usually instrumental, intended mainly for the practice of some point of technique. **2.** study[1] (def. 12). [< F; see STUDY[1]]

e·tui (ā twē′, et′wē), *n.*, *pl.* **e·tuis.** a small, often decorative case, esp. one for needles, toilet articles, or the like. Also, **e·twee′.** [< F *étui*, OF *estui* holder, back formation from *estuier* to keep < VL *studiāre* to treat with care]

ETV, educational television.

etym., **1.** etymological. **2.** etymology. Also, **etymol.**

et·y·mol·o·gise (et′ə mol′ə jīz′), *v.t.*, *v.i.*, **-gised, -gis·ing.** *Chiefly Brit.* etymologize. —**et′y·mol′o·gis′a·ble,** *adj.*

et·y·mol·o·gize (et′ə mol′ə jīz′), *v.*, **-gized, -giz·ing.** —*v.t.* **1.** to trace the history of (a word). —*v.i.* **2.** to study etymology. **3.** to give or suggest the etymology of words. [< LL *etymologiz(āre)*. See ETYMOLOGY, -IZE] —**et′y·mol′o·giz′a·ble,** *adj.*

et·y·mol·o·gy (et′ə mol′ə jē), *n.*, *pl.* **-gies.** **1.** the study of historical linguistic change, esp. as applied to individual words. **2.** an account of the history of a particular word. **3.** the derivation of a word. [< L *etymologia* < Gk *etymología*, equiv. to *etymológ(os)* studying words (*étymo(s)* true + *lógos* word, reason) + *-ia* -Y[3]] —**et·y·mo·log·i·cal** (et′ə mə loj′i kəl), **et′y·mo·log′ic,** *adj.* —**et′y·mo·log′i·cal·ly,** *adv.* —**et′y·mol′o·gist,** *n.*

et·y·mon (et′ə mon′), *n.*, *pl.* **-mons, -ma** (-mə). the linguistic form from which another form is historically derived, as the Latin *cor* "heart," which is the etymon of English *cordial*, or the Indo-European **k(e)rd-*, which is the etymon of Latin *cor*, Greek *kardía*, Russian *serdtse*, and English *heart.* [< L: the origin of a word < Gk *étymon* the essential meaning of a word seen in its origin (neut. of *étymos* true, actual, real)]

Et·zel (et′səl), *n. Germanic Legend.* Attila: represented in the *Nibelungenlied* as the second husband of Kriemhild after the death of Siegfried. Cf. **Atli.**

eu-, a prefix meaning "good," "well," occurring chiefly in words of Greek origin: *eupepsia.* [< Gk, comb. form of *eûs* good (adj.) or *eû* (neut., used as adv.) well]

Eu, *Chem.* europium.

e.u., *Thermodynamics.* entropy unit. Also, **E.U.**

Eu·aech·me (yōō ēk′mē), *n. Class. Myth.* a daughter of Megareus who married Alcathous.

eu·bac·te·ri·um (yōō′bak tēr′ē əm), *n.*, *pl.* **-te·ri·a** (-tēr′ē ə). *Bacteriol.* any of several spherical or rod-shaped bacteria of the order *Eubacteriales*, characterized by simple, undifferentiated cells with rigid walls; a true bacterium. [EU- + BACTERIUM]

Eu·boe·a (yōō bē′ə), *n.* a Greek island in the W Aegean Sea. 166,097 (1961); 1586 sq. mi. *Cap.:* Chalcis. Also called **Negropont.** Modern Greek, **Evvoia.** —**Eu·boe′an,** *adj.*, *n.* —**Eu·bo·ic** (yōō bō′ik), *adj.*

Eu·bu·le·us (yōō byōō′lē əs), *n. Class. Myth.* a son of Trochilus who helped Demeter find Persephone.

eu·caine (yōō kān′), *n. Pharm.* a white, crystalline solid, $C_{15}H_{21}NO_2$, used chiefly in the form of its hydrochloride as a local anesthetic. Also called **beta-eucaine, betacaine, benzamine.** [EU- + -*caine* (as in COCAINE)]

eu·ca·lyp′tene hydrochlo′ride (yōō′kə lip′tēn), *Pharm.* a yellowish-white, crystalline, water-insoluble solid, $C_{10}H_{16}{\cdot}2HCl$, used chiefly as an antiseptic. Also called **eu·ca·lyp·te·ol** (yōō′kə lip′tē ōl′, -ôl′, -ol′). [EUCALYPT(US) + -ENE]

eu·ca·lyp·tol (yōō′kə lip′tōl, -tôl, -tol), *n. Chem.* cineole. Also, **eu·ca·lyp·tole** (yōō′kə lip′tōl). [EUCALYPT(US) + -OL[2]]

eu·ca·lyp·tus (yōō′kə lip′təs), *n.*, *pl.* **-ti** (-tī), **-tus·es.** any of numerous aromatic, evergreen, myrtaceous trees of the genus *Eucalyptus.* Also, **eu·ca·lypt** (yōō′kə lipt′). [< NL < Gk *eu-* EU- + *kalyptós* covered, wrapped, akin to *kalýptein* to cover] —**eu′ca·lyp′tic,** *adj.*

eu·car·pic (yōō kär′pik), *adj.* (of a fungus) having only part of the thallus converted into fructifications. Also, **eu·car′pous.** Cf. **holocarpic.** [EU- + -CARPIC]

eu·cha·ris (yōō′kə ris), *n.* any of several South American, amaryllidaceous plants of the genus *Eucharis*, certain species of which are cultivated for their large, fragrant, white flowers. [< NL, special use of Gk *eúcharis* gracious, equiv. to *eu-* EU- + *cháris* grace, favor; see CHARISMA]

Eu·cha·rist (yōō′kə rist), *n.* **1.** the sacrament of Holy Communion; the sacrifice of the Mass; the Lord's Supper. **2.** the consecrated elements of the Holy Communion, esp. the bread. **3.** (*l.c.*) the giving of thanks; thanksgiving. [ME *eukarist* < eccl. L *eucharistia* < eccl. Gk *eucharistía* gratefulness, thanksgiving. See EU-, CHARISMA, -IA] —**Eu′cha·ris′tic, Eu′cha·ris′ti·cal,** *adj.* —**Eu′cha·ris′ti·cal·ly,** *adv.*

Eu·che·nor (yōō kē′nôr), *n.* (in the *Iliad*) a son of the soothsayer Polyidus who fought with the Greeks and was slain by Paris.

Eu·chite (yo͞o′kīt), *n.* a member of a mendicant, ascetic sect living chiefly in Syria and Mesopotamia in the 4th–7th centuries A.D., and holding a belief that the demon in each person can be expelled only by ceaseless prayer. Also called **Messalian.**

eu·cho·lo·gi·on (*Gk.* ef′ᴋʜô lô′yē ôn; *Eng.* yo͞o′kə lō′jē on′), *n., pl.* **-gi·a** (*Gk.* -yē ä; *Eng.* -jē ə). *Eastern Ch.* a service book containing liturgies, prayers, and other rites. Also, **euchology.** [< eccl. Gk *euchológion* prayer-book, equiv. to *euch(ḗ)* prayer + *-o-* -O- + *-log-* word + *-ion* n. suffix]

eu·chol·o·gy (yo͞o kol′ə jē), *n., pl.* **-gies.** euchologion.

eu·chre (yo͞o′kər), *n., v.,* **-chred, -chring.** —*n.* **1.** *Cards.* a game played by two, three, or four persons, usually with the 32, but sometimes with the 28 or 24, highest cards in the pack. **2.** an instance of euchring or being euchred. —*v.t.* **3.** to get the better of (an opponent) in a hand at euchre by his failure to win three tricks after having made the trump. **4.** *Informal.* to outwit; get the better of, as by scheming (usually fol. by *out*). [?]

eu·chro·ma·tin (yo͞o krō′mə tin), *n. Genetics.* the part of a chromosome that is not as compact or as stainable as heterochromatin and is believed to contain the genetically active material of the chromosome. [EU- + CHROMATIN] —**eu·chro·mat·ic** (yo͞o′krə mat′ik), *adj.*

eu·chro·mo·some (yo͞o krō′mə sōm′), *n. Genetics.* autosome. [EU- + CHROMOSOME]

Euck·en (oi′kən), *n.* **Ru·dolph Chris·toph** (ro͞o′dôlf kʀis′tôf), 1846–1926, German philosopher: Nobel prize for literature 1908.

eu·clase (yo͞o′klās), *n.* a rare green or blue mineral, beryllium aluminum silicate, $HBeAl(SiO_5)$, occurring in prismatic crystals. [< F < Gk *eu-* EU- + *klásis* a breaking (*kla-* break + *-sis* -SIS)]

Eu·cle·a (yo͞o klē′ə), *n.* a girl's given name.

Eu·clid (yo͞o′klid), *n.* **1.** fl. c300 B.C., Greek geometrician and educator at Alexandria. **2.** See **Euclidean geometry. 3.** a city in NE Ohio, near Cleveland. 62,998 (1960). **4.** a boy's given name.

Eu·clid·e·an (yo͞o klid′ē ən), *adj.* of or pertaining to Euclid, or adopting his postulates. Also, **Eu·clid′i·an.** [< L *Euclīdē(us)* of Euclid (< Gk *Eukleídeios*) + -AN]

Euclid′ean al′gorithm, *Algebra.* a method based on the division algorithm for finding the greatest common divisor of two given integers. Cf. **division algorithm.**

Euclid′ean domain′, *Math.* a commutative integral domain with a multiplicative identity, in which a function having the same properties as the absolute value of real numbers is defined.

Euclid′ean geom′etry, geometry based upon the postulates of Euclid, esp. the postulate that only one line may be drawn through a given point parallel to a given line.

Euclid′ean group′, *Math.* the set of rigid motions that are also affine transformations.

Euclid′ean space′, *Math.* **1.** ordinary three-dimensional space. **2.** any vector space on which a real-valued inner product is defined.

Eu·cli·des (yo͞o′kli dēz′), *n.* a crater in the third quadrant of the face of the moon: about 7 miles in diameter.

eu·crite (yo͞o′krīt), *n. Petrog.* a basic gabbro consisting mainly of bytownite and augite. [< G *Eukrit* < Gk *eúkrit(os)* readily chosen, equiv. to *eu-* EU- + *kritós* separated (ptp. of *krínein*)]

eu·cryp·tite (yo͞o krip′tīt), *n.* a mineral, lithium aluminum silicate, $LiAlSiO_4$, occurring in colorless to white hexagonal crystals: a source of lithium. [EU- + CRYPT(O)- + -ITE[1]]

Euc·te·mon (yo͞ok′tə mon′), *n.* a walled plain in the first quadrant of the face of the moon: about 41 miles in diameter.

eu·de·mon (yo͞o dē′mən), *n.* a good demon or spirit. Also, **eu·dae′mon.** [< Gk *eudaímōn* with a good genius, fortunate, happy, equiv. to *eu-* EU- + *daímōn* destiny, fortune, lot; see DEMON]

eu·de·mo·ni·a (yo͞o′di mō′nē ə), *n.* **1.** happiness. **2.** *Aristotelianism.* happiness as the result of an active life governed by reason. Also, **eu′dae·mo′ni·a.** [< Gk *eudaimonía.* See EUDEMON, -IA]

eu·de·mon·ic (yo͞o′di mon′ik), *adj.* **1.** pertaining or conducive to happiness. **2.** pertaining to eudemonics or eudemonism. Also, **eu′dae·mon′ic.** [< Gk *eudaimonik(ós).* See EUDEMON, -IC]

eu·de·mon·ics (yo͞o′di mon′iks), *n.* (*usually construed as sing.*) **1.** the theory or art of happiness. **2.** the practice of eudemonism. Also, **eu′dae·mon′ics.** [see EUDEMONIC, -ICS]

eu·de·mon·ism (yo͞o dē′mə niz′əm), *n. Ethics.* the doctrine that the basis of moral obligations is to be found in the tendency of right actions to produce happiness. Also, **eu·dae′mon·ism.** [EUDEMON + -ISM] —**eu·de′mon·ist, eu·dae′mon·ist,** *n.* —**eu·de′mon·is′tic, eu·dae′mon·is′tic, eu·de′mon·is′ti·cal, eu·dae′mon·is′ti·cal,** *adj.* —**eu·de′mon·is′ti·cal·ly, eu·dae′mon·is′ti·cal·ly,** *adv.*

eu·di·om·e·ter (yo͞o′dē om′i tər), *n. Chem.* a graduated glass measuring tube for gas analysis. [< Gk *eúdio(s)* clear, mild (lit., well skied, equiv. to *eu-* EU- + *di-,* s. of *Zeus* god of the sky, + *-os* adj. suffix) + -METER] —**eu·di·o·met·ric** (yo͞o′dē ə me′trik), **eu′di·o·met′ri·cal,** *adj.* —**eu′di·o·met′ri·cal·ly,** *adv.*

eu·di·om·e·try (yo͞o′dē om′i trē), *n. Chem.* the measurement and analysis of gases with the eudiometer. [EUDIOMET(E)R + -Y[3]]

Eu·dist (yo͞o′dist), *n. Rom. Cath. Ch.* a member of the "Congregation of Jesus and Mary," founded in 1643 in France, chiefly for educational and missionary work. [< F *eudiste;* after Jean *Eudes* (1601–80), French priest and missionary who founded the order; see -IST]

Eu·do·ra (yo͞o dôr′ə, -dōr′ə), *n.* **1.** a town in SE Arkansas. 3598 (1960). **2.** a girl's given name.

Eu·do·rus (yo͞o dôr′əs, -dōr′-), *n.* (in the *Iliad*) a son of Polymela and Hermes who led the Myrmidons in battle against the Trojans.

Eu·dox·us (yo͞o dok′səs), *n.* a crater in the first quadrant of the face of the moon: about 40 miles in diameter.

Eu·e·mer·us (yo͞o ē′mər əs, -em′ər-), *n.* Euhemerus.

Eu·fau·la (yo͞o fô′lə), *n.* a town in SE Alabama. 8357 (1960).

eu·fla·vine (yo͞o flā′vēn, -vin), *n. Chem.* acriflavine.

Eu·gene (yo͞o jēn′ *or, for 2,* yo͞o′jēn), *n.* **1.** a city in W Oregon. 50,977 (1960). **2.** a boy's given name.

Eu·gène (œ zhen′), *n.* **Prince** (*François Eugène de Savoie-Carignan*), 1663–1736, Austrian general, born in France.

Eugene I. See **Eugenius I.**

Eugene II. See **Eugenius II.**

Eugene III. See **Eugenius III.**

Eugene IV. See **Eugenius IV.**

Eugene′ O·ne′gin (ō nā′gin), **1.** a verse narrative (1823–31) by Alexander Pushkin. **2.** an opera (1879), by Peter Ilych Tschaikovsky, based on Pushkin's narrative.

Eu·ge·ni·a (yo͞o jē′nē ə), *n.* a girl's given name. Also, **Eu·ge·nie** (yo͞o jē′nē).

eu·gen·ic (yo͞o jen′ik), *adj.* **1.** of or bringing about improvement in the type of offspring produced. **2.** having good inherited characteristics. Also, **eu·gen′i·cal.** Cf. **dysgenic.** [< Gk *eugen(ḗs)* well born (see EU-, -GEN) + -IC] —**eu·gen′i·cal·ly,** *adv.*

eu·gen·i·cist (yo͞o jen′i sist), *n.* **1.** a specialist in eugenics. **2.** an advocate of eugenic measures. Also, **eu·ge·nist** (yo͞o′jə nist). [EUGENIC + -IST]

eu·gen·ics (yo͞o jen′iks), *n.* (*construed as sing.*) **1.** the science of improving the qualities of the human race, esp. by the careful selection of parents. **2.** the process of improving offspring. [see EUGENIC, -ICS]

Eu·gé·nie (œ zhā nē′), *n.* **Comtesse de Te·ba** (de te′bä), (*Marie Eugénie de Montijo de Guzmán*), 1826–1920, wife of Napoleon III, born in Spain: Empress of France 1853–71.

Eu·ge·ni·us I (yo͞o jē′nē əs, -jēn′yəs), **Saint,** died A.D. 657, pope 654–657. Also, **Eugene I.**

Eugenius II, died A.D. 827, Italian ecclesiastic: pope 824–827. Also, **Eugene II.**

Eugenius III, (*Bernardo Pignatelli* or *Paganelli*) died 1153, Italian ecclesiastic: pope 1145–53. Also, **Eugene III.**

Eugenius IV, (*Gabriele* or *Gabriel Condolmieri* or *Condulmer*) 1383–1447, Italian ecclesiastic: pope 1431–47. Also, **Eugene IV.**

eu·ge·nol (yo͞o′jə nōl′, -nôl′, -nol′), *n. Chem., Pharm.* a colorless, oily, spicy, aromatic, very slightly water-soluble liquid, $C_{10}H_{12}O_2$, extracted from certain essential oils, as oil of cloves: used chiefly in perfumery and in dentistry as an antiseptic. Also called **eugen′ic ac′id.** [< NL *Eugen(ia)* name of genus of trees (see EUGENIC) + -OL[2]]

Eu·gle·na (yo͞o glē′nə), *n.* a genus of green protozoans having a reddish eyespot and a single flagellum, found in fresh, esp. stagnant water. [< NL < Gk *eu-* EU- + *glḗnē* the pupil, eyeball, socket of a joint]

eu·gon·ic (yo͞o gon′ik), *adj. Bacteriol.* thriving on artificial media, as certain bacteria. Cf. **dysgonic.** [EU- + GON(O)- + -IC]

eu·he·dral (yo͞o hē′drəl), *adj. Petrog.* idiomorphic (def. 1). [EU- + -HEDRAL]

eu·he·mer·ise (yo͞o hē′mə rīz′, -hem′ə-), *v.t., v.i.,* **-ised, -is·ing.** *Chiefly Brit.* euhemerize.

eu·he·mer·ism (yo͞o hē′mə riz′əm, hem′ə-), *n.* **1.** (*often cap.*) the theory of Euhemerus that the mythologies of various gods arose out of the deification of dead heroes. **2.** mythological interpretation which reduces the gods to the level of distinguished men; the derivation of mythology from history. [EUHEMER(US) + -ISM] —**eu·he′mer·ist,** *n.* —**eu·he′mer·is′tic,** *adj.* —**eu·he′mer·is′ti·cal·ly,** *adv.*

eu·he·mer·ize (yo͞o hē′mə rīz′, -hem′ə-), *v.t., v.i.,* **-ized, -iz·ing.** to treat or explain (myths) by euhemerism. Also, *esp. Brit.,* **euhemerise.** [EUHEMER(US) + -IZE]

Eu·he·mer·us (yo͞o hē′mər əs), *n.* fl. c300 B.C., Greek mythographer. Also, **Euemerus, Evemerus.** Cf. **euhemerism.**

Eu·ip·pe (yo͞o ip′ē), *n.* **1.** *Rom. Legend.* a daughter of Daunus who married Diomedes. **2.** *Class. Myth.* a horse that was once a maiden. Cf. **Thea.**

Eu·la (yo͞o′lə), *n.* a girl's given name, form of **Eulalia.** Also, **Ula.**

eu·la·chon (yo͞o′lə kon′), *n.* candlefish. [< Chinook *ulakan*]

Eu·la·lia (yo͞o lāl′yə), *n.* a girl's given name. Also, **Eu·la·lie** (yo͞o lā′lē).

Eu·lee (yo͞o′lē), *n.* a girl's given name.

Eu·ler (oi′lər; *Ger.* oi′lᴀʀ), *n.* **1.** **Le·on·hard** (*Ger.* lā′ôn härt′), 1707–83, Swiss mathematician. **2.** a crater in the second quadrant of the face of the moon: about 19 miles in diameter.

Eu′ler characteris′tic, *Math.* the number of vertices plus the number of faces minus the number of edges of a given polyhedron. [named after L. EULER]

Eu·ler-Chel·pin (oi′lᴀʀ kel′pin), *n.* **Hans Karl Au·gust Si·mon von** (häns kärl ou′go͝ost zē′mōn fən), born 1873, German chemist in Sweden: Nobel prize 1929.

Eu′ler's con′stant, *Math.* the number, equal to .57721, that is $\lim_{n\to\infty}(1 + \frac{1}{2} + \frac{1}{3} + \ldots + {}^{1}/n - \log n)$. [named after L. EULER]

Eu′ler's for′mula, **1.** *Math.* the theorem that $e^{ix} = \cos x + i \sin x$ for every real number x. **2.** *Mech.* a formula for determining the maximum load that can be applied to a given column without causing it to buckle. [named after L. EULER]

Eu′ler's phi′-func·tion (fī′fungk′shən), *Math.* the function that assigns to each integer the number of positive integers less than the given integer and relatively prime to the given integer. Also called **totient.** [named after L. EULER]

Eu·lis (yo͞o′lis), *n.* a boy's given name.

eu·lo·gi·a (yo͞o lō′jē ə; *for 2 also Gk.* ev′lô yē′ä), *n.* **1.** Also called **antidoron, holy bread.** *Eastern Ch.* blessed bread given to the congregation during vespers or at the end of the liturgy. **2.** *Gk. Orth. Ch.* a blessing. [< LL < Gk *eulogía* praise, blessing. See EU-, -LOGY, -IA]

eu·lo·gise (yo͞o′lə jīz′), *v.t.,* **-gised, -gis·ing.** *Chiefly Brit.* eulogize. —**eu′lo·gi·sa′tion,** *n.* —**eu′lo·gis′er,** *n.*

eu·lo·gist (yo͞o′lə jist), *n.* a person who eulogizes. [EULOG(Y) + -IST]

eu·lo·gis·tic (yo͞o′lə jis′tik), *adj.* pertaining to or containing eulogy; laudatory. Also, **eu′lo·gis′ti·cal.** [EULOGIST + -IC] —**eu′lo·gis′ti·cal·ly,** *adv.*

eu·lo·gi·um (yo͞o lō′jē əm), *n., pl.* **-gi·ums, -gi·a** (-jē ə). **1.** a eulogy. **2.** eulogistic language. [< ML, equiv. to L *eu-* EU- + *(ē)logium* inscription on a tombstone]

eu·lo·gize (yo͞o′lə jīz′), *v.t.,* **-gized, -giz·ing.** to praise highly; speak or write a eulogy about. Also, *esp. Brit.,* **eulogise.** [EULOG(Y) + -IZE] —**eu′lo·gi·za′tion,** *n.* —**eu′lo·giz′er,** *n.*

—**Syn.** extol, laud, commend, panegyrize.

eu·lo·gy (yo͞o′lə jē), *n., pl.* **-gies.** **1.** a speech or writing in praise of a person or thing, esp. a set oration in honor of a deceased person. **2.** high praise or commendation. [< LL *eulogia* EULOGIA and ML *eulogium* EULOGIUM]

-eum, a formal element occurring in some Latin scientific names (*peritoneum*), and in the corresponding loan words in English (*petroleum*).

Eu·mae·us (yo͞o mē′əs), *n.* (in the *Odyssey*) the faithful swineherd of Odysseus.

Eu·me·des (yo͞o mē′dēz), *n.* **1.** (in the *Iliad*) a wealthy Trojan herald. **2.** (in the *Aeneid*) the son of Dolon who was a companion of Aeneas.

eu·mel·a·nin (yo͞o mel′ə nin), *n. Biochem.* a pigment containing melanin, found in bird feathers. [EU- + MELANIN]

Eu·me·lus (yo͞o mē′ləs), *n.* **1.** (in the *Iliad*) the commander of the Thessalian forces. He lost a chariot race to Diomedes. **2.** (in the *Aeneid*) a Trojan companion of Aeneas.

Eu·men·i·des (yo͞o men′i dēz′), *n.pl.* **1.** *Class. Myth.* the Furies. **2.** (*italics.*) a tragedy (458 B.C.) by Aeschylus. Cf. **Oresteia.**

Eu·mol·pus (yo͞o mol′pəs), *n. Class. Myth.* **1.** a son of Poseidon and Chione who founded the mysteries at Eleusis. **2.** a flute player who supported the false accusations of Phylonome against Tenes.

Eu·ne·us (yo͞o nē′əs), *n. Class. Myth.* a son of Jason and Hypsipyle.

Eu·nice (yo͞o′nis), *n.* **1.** a town in SE New Mexico. 3531 (1960). **2.** a girl's given name.

Eu·no·mi·a (yo͞o nō′mē ə), *n. Class. Myth.* one of the Horae: the personification of order.

Eu·no·mus (yo͞o′nə məs), *n. Class. Myth.* a youth unintentionally killed by Hercules.

eu·no·my (yo͞o′nə mē), *n. Rare.* good order under good laws and a just constitution. [< Gk *eunomía* good order. See EU-, -NOMY]

eu·nuch (yo͞o′nək), *n.* a castrated man, esp. formerly one employed by Oriental rulers as a harem attendant or palace official. [ME *eunuk* < L *eunūch(us)* < Gk *eunoûchos* eunuch, chamberlain, equiv. to *eun(ḗ)* bed, place of sleeping + *-ouchos* keeping (akin to *échein* to hold)]

eu·nuch·ise (yo͞o′nə kīz′), *v.t.,* **-ised, -is·ing.** *Chiefly Brit.* eunuchize.

eu·nuch·ism (yo͞o′nə kiz′əm), *n.* the state of being a eunuch. Also, **eu·nuch·ry** (yo͞o′nək rē).

eu·nuch·ize (yo͞o′nə kīz′), *v.t.,* **-ized, -iz·ing.** to castrate; emasculate. Also, *esp. Brit.,* **eunuchise.**

eu·nuch·oid (yo͞o′nə koid′), *adj.* **1.** affected with eunuchoidism. —*n.* **2.** a person affected with eunuchoidism. [EUNUCH + -OID]

eu·nuch·oid·ism (yo͞o′nə koi diz′əm), *n. Pathol.* a state characterized by lack of fully developed reproductive organs and the manifestation of certain female sex characteristics, as high voice, lack of facial and body hair, etc., resulting from the absence of a normal production of male sex hormones. [EUNUCHOID + -ISM]

eu·on·y·mus (yo͞o on′ə məs), *n.* any of several shrubs or small trees of the genus *Euonymus,* of northern temperate regions, usually bearing crimson or rose-colored capsules which on opening disclose the seed. Also, **evonymus.** [< L, n. use of Gk *euṓnymos* of good name. See EU-, -ONYM, -OUS]

eu·pa·to·ri·um (yo͞o′pə tôr′ē əm, -tōr′-), *n.* any of numerous composite plants of the genus *Eupatorium,* comprising the bonesets or thoroughworts. [< NL < Gk *eupatórion* hemp agrimony, after *Eupátor* surname of Mithridates, said to have first used it]

eu·pat·rid (yo͞o pa′trid, yo͞o′pə-), *n., pl.* **-pat·ri·dae** (-pa′tri dē′). **1.** one of the hereditary aristocrats of ancient Athens and other states of Greece, who at one time formed the ruling class. **2.** *Rare.* any aristocrat or patrician. [< Gk *eupatríd(ēs),* lit., of a good father, of noble descent, equiv. to *eu-* EU- + *patr-* (s. of *patḗr*) FATHER + *-idēs* -ID[2]]

Eu·pen and Mal·mé·dy (œ pen′; mal mā dē′), a district on the Belgian-German border: ceded to Belgium 1919; reannexed to Germany 1940; now part of Belgium.

eu·pep·sia (yo͞o pep′shə, -sē ə), *n.* good digestion (opposed to *dyspepsia*). Also, **eu·pep·sy** (yo͞o′pep sē). [< NL < Gk *eupepsía* good digestion, equiv. to *eu-* EU- + *péps(is)* digestion + *-ia* -IA] —**eu·pep·tic** (yo͞o pep′tik), *adj.*

Eu·phe·mi·a (yo͞o fē′mē ə), *n.* a girl's given name. Also, **Eu·phe·mie** (yo͞o fē′mē).

eu·phe·mise (yo͞o′fə mīz′), *v.t., v.i.,* **-mised, -mis·ing.** *Chiefly Brit.* euphemize. —**eu′phe·mi·sa′tion,** *n.* —**eu′phe·mis′er,** *n.*

eu·phe·mism (yo͞o′fə miz′əm), *n.* **1.** the substitution of a mild, indirect, or vague expression for one thought to be offensively harsh or blunt. **2.** the expression so substituted: "*To pass away*" *is a euphemism for "to die."* [< Gk *euphēmism(ós)* the use of words of good omen, equiv. to *eu-* EU- + *phḗm(ē)* speaking, fame + *-ismos* -ISM] —**eu′phe·mist,** *n.* —**eu′phe·mis′tic, eu′phe·mis′ti·cal, eu·phe·mi·ous** (yo͞o fē′mē əs), *adj.* —**eu′phe·mis′ti·cal·ly, eu·phe′mi·ous·ly,** *adv.*

eu·phe·mize (yo͞o′fə mīz′), *v.,* **-mized, -miz·ing.** —*v.t.* **1.** to refer to by means of euphemism. —*v.i.* **2.** to employ euphemism. Also, *esp. Brit.,* **euphemise.** [< Gk *euphēmíz(ein)* (to) use words of good omen. See EUPHEMISM, -IZE] —**eu′phe·mi·za′tion,** *n.* —**eu′phe·miz′er,** *n.*

Eu·phe·mus (yo͞o fē′məs), *n. Class. Myth.* a son of Poseidon and Europa who aided the journey of the Argonauts.

eu·pho·ni·a (yo͞o fō′nē ə, -fōn′yə), *n.* any of several small tanagers of the genus *Tanagra,* having a melodious song, most species of which have yellow and glossy black plumage. [< NL; see EUPHONY]

eu·phon·ic (yo͞o fon′ik), *adj.* pertaining to or characterized by euphony. Also, **eu·phon′i·cal.** [EUPHON(Y) + -IC] —**eu·phon′i·cal·ly,** *adv.* —**eu·phon′i·cal·ness,** *n.*

eu·pho·ni·ous (yo͞o fō′nē əs), *adj.* pleasant in sound; agreeable to the ear; characterized by euphony: *a sweet, euphonious voice.* [EUPHONY + -OUS] —**eu·pho′ni·ous·ly,** *adv.* —**eu·pho′ni·ous·ness,** *n.*

eu·pho·nise (yo͞o′fə nīz′), *v.t.,* **-nised, -nis·ing.** *Chiefly Brit.* euphonize.

eu·pho·ni·um (yo͞o fō′nē əm), *n.* a brass musical instrument similar to the baritone tuba but with a wider bore and mellower tone. [EUPH(ONY + HARM)ONIUM]

eu·pho·nize (yo͞o′fə nīz′), *v.t.,* **-nized, -niz·ing.** to make euphonious. Also, *esp. Brit.,* **euphonise.** [EUPHON(Y) + -IZE]

Euphonium

eu·pho·ny (yo͞o′fə nē), *n., pl.* **-nies. 1.** agreeableness of sound; pleasing effect to the ear, esp. a pleasant-sounding or harmonious combination or succession of words: *the majestic euphony of Milton's poetry.* **2.** *Phonet.* harmoniousness or economy of utterance of speech sounds, supposedly resulting from combinatory phonetic change with an effect considered pleasing to the ear. [< LL *euphōnia* < Gk *euphōnía.* See EU-, -PHONY]

eu·phor·bi·a (yo͞o fôr′bē ə), *n.* any plant of the genus *Euphorbia,* comprising the spurges. [ME *euforbia* for L *euphorbea,* an African plant named after *Euphorbos,* a Greek physician]

eu·phor·bi·a·ceous (yo͞o fôr′bē ā′shəs), *adj.* belonging to the *Euphorbiaceae,* or spurge family of plants, comprising the spurges, the cascarilla, castor oil, and cassava plants, etc. [< NL *Euphorbiace(ae)* name of family (see EUPHORBIA, -ACEAE) + -OUS]

Eu·phor·bus (yo͞o fôr′bəs), *n. Class. Myth.* a son of Panthous who fought with the Trojans against the Greeks.

eu·pho·ri·a (yo͞o fōr′ē ə, -fôr′-), *n. Psychol.* a feeling of well-being, esp. an exaggerated one having no basis in truth or reality. [< NL < Gk *euphoría* state of well-being. See EU-, -PHORE, -IA] —**eu·phor·ic** (yo͞o fôr′ik, -for′-), *adj.*

Eu·pho·ri·on (yo͞o fōr′ē ən, -fôr′-), *n. Class. Myth.* a son of Helen and Achilles who fled from the love of Zeus.

eu·phra·sy (yo͞o′frə sē), *n., pl.* **-sies.** the eyebright, *Euphrasia officinalis.* [late ME *eufrasie* < L *euphrasia* < Gk: cheerfulness, gladness (cf. *euphraínein* to cheer, be glad), equiv. to *eu-* EU- + *phra-* (var. of *phrēn* mind, heart) + *-s(is)* -SIS + *-ia* -Y[3]]

Eu·phra·tes (yo͞o frā′tēz), *n.* a river in SW Asia, flowing from E Turkey through Syria and Iraq, joining the Tigris to form the Shatt-al-Arab near the Persian Gulf. 1700 mi. long. —**Eu·phra′te·an,** *adj.*

eu·phroe (yo͞o′frō, -vrō), *n. Naut.* a suspended batten or plate of wood or brass pierced with holes through which the cords of a crowfoot are rove to suspend an awning. Also, **euvrou, uphroe.** [< D: pseudolearned sp. of *juffrouw,* lit., young woman; c. G *Jungfrau*]

Eu·phros·y·ne (yo͞o fros′ə nē′), *n. Class. Myth.* one of the Graces. [< Gk, personification of *euphrosýnē* mirth, merriment]

Eu·phu·es (yo͞o′fyo͞o ēz′), *n.* the main character in John Lyly's works *Euphues, the Anatomy of Wit* (1579), and *Euphues and His England* (1580).

eu·phu·ism (yo͞o′fyo͞o iz′əm), *n.* **1.** an affected style in imitation of that of Lyly, fashionable in England about the end of the 16th century, characterized chiefly by long series of antitheses, frequent similes relating to fabulous natural history, alliteration, etc. Cf. **Euphues. 2.** any similar ornate style of writing or speaking; high-flown, periphrastic language. **3.** an instance of such style or language. [EUPHU(ES) + -ISM] —**eu′phu·ist,** *n.* —**eu′phu·is′tic, eu′phu·is′ti·cal,** *adj.* —**eu′phu·is′ti·cal·ly,** *adv.*

eu·plas·tic (yo͞o plas′tik), *adj. Physiol.* capable of being transformed into organized tissue. [< Gk *eúplast(os)* malleable + -IC. See EU-, PLASTIC]

Eu·plo·tes (yo͞o plō′tēz), *n.* a genus of hypotrichous ciliates occurring in fresh and salt waters. [< NL < Gk *eu-* EU- + *plōt-* (s. of *plōs*) swimmer + *-es* pl. n. suffix] —**eu·plo′tid,** *adj., n.*

eup·ne·a (yo͞op nē′ə), *n. Pathol.* easy or normal breathing (opposed to *dyspnea*). Also, **eup·noe′a.** [< NL *eupnoea* < Gk *eúpnoia* ease of breathing, equiv. to *eu-* EU- + *-pno(os)* breathing + *-ia* -IA] —**eup·ne′ic,** *adj.*

eu·po·tam·ic (yo͞o′pə tam′ik), *adj. Ecol.* (of a plant or animal) living or growing in fresh water. [EU- + POTAMIC]

Eur., 1. Europe. 2. European.

Eur·a·mer·i·can (yo͝or′ə mer′i kən), *adj.* common to Europe and to America. Also, **Euro-American.** [EUR(OPE) + AMERICAN]

Eur·a·sia (yo͝o rā′zhə, -shə), *n.* Europe and Asia considered as a whole. [EUR(OPE) + ASIA]

Eur·a·sian (yo͝o rā′zhən, -shən), *adj.* **1.** of or pertaining to Eurasia. **2.** of mixed European and Asian descent. —*n.* **3.** the offspring of a European and an Asian. [EURASI(A) + -AN]

Eur·at·om (yo͝o rat′əm), *n.* an organization formed in 1957, comprising France, the Netherlands, Belgium, Luxembourg, and the Federal Republic of Germany, for cooperative, coordinated action in developing and marketing their nuclear resources. [EUR(OPE) + ATOM]

Eure (œr), *n.* a department in NW France. 361,904 (1962); 2331 sq. mi. *Cap.:* Evreux.

Eure-et-Loir (œr ā lwar′), *n.* a department in central France. 277,546 (1962); 2293 sq. mi. *Cap.:* Chartres.

eu·re·ka (yo͝o rē′kə), *interj.* **1.** I have found (it) (the reputed exclamation of Archimedes when, after long study, he discovered a method of detecting the amount of alloy mixed with the gold in the crown of the king of Syracuse): motto of California. **2.** (an exclamation of triumph at a discovery.) [< Gk *heúrēka,* 1st person sing. perf. indic. act of *heurískein* to find, discover]

Eu·re·ka (yo͝o rē′kə), *n.* **1.** a city in NW California. 28,137 (1960). **2.** a town in SE Kansas. 4055 (1960). **3.** a town in central Illinois. 2538 (1960).

eu·rhyth·mic (yo͞o rith′mik), *adj.* **1.** characterized by a pleasing rhythm; harmoniously ordered or proportioned. **2.** of or pertaining to eurhythmics. Also, **eurythmic.** [EURHYTHM(Y) + -IC]

eu·rhyth·mics (yo͞o rith′miks), *n.* (*construed as sing. or pl.*) the art of interpreting in bodily movements the rhythm of musical compositions: applied to a method invented by Emile Jaques-Dalcroze, a Swiss composer, aiming to develop the sense of rhythm and symmetry. Also, **eurythmics.** [see EURHYTHMIC, -ICS]

eu·rhyth·my (yo͞o rith′mē), *n.* rhythmical movement or order; harmonious motion or proportion. Also, **eurythmy.** [< L *eurythmia* < Gk *eurhythmía* good proportion, gracefulness. See EU-, RHYTHM, -Y[3]]

Eu·rip·i·des (yo͝o rip′i dēz′), *n.* c480–406? B.C., Greek dramatist. —**Eu·rip′i·de′an,** *adj.*

Eu·rip·pa (yo͝o rip′ə), *n. Class. Myth.* an epithet of Artemis, meaning "delighting in horses."

eu·ri·pus (yo͝o rī′pəs), *n., pl.* **-pi** (-pī). a strait, esp. one in which the flow of water is violent. [< L *eurīpus* < Gk *eúrīpos* (applied esp. to the strait between Euboea and Boeotia, equiv. to *eu-* EU- + *-rīpos* rusher, akin to *ripḗ* rush]

eu·ri·ther·mo·phile (yo͝or′ə thûr′mə fīl′), *n.* a eurythermophic bacterium.

eu·ri·ther·mo·phil·ic (yo͝or′ə thûr′mə fil′ik), *adj.* (of bacteria) capable of growth at temperatures of from below 30° to 60°C. [EURYTHERMOPHILE + -IC]

Eu·ro-A·mer·i·can (yo͝or′ō ə mer′i kən), *adj.* Euramerican.

Eu·roc·ly·don (yo͝o rok′li don′), *n.* a stormy north-east or north-northeast wind. [< Gk *euroklýdōn,* equiv. to *Eûro(s)* EURUS + *klýdōn* wave, surge, cf. *klýzein* to dash against, wash]

Eu·ro·com·mu·nism (yo͝or′ō kom′yə niz′əm), *n.* a form of communism in some West European nations (Spain, France, Italy, etc.) which claimed to be independent of the Communist party of the Soviet Union. [EURO(PE) + COMMUNISM]

Eu·ro·dol·lars (yo͝or′ə dol′ərz), *n.pl.* U.S. dollars deposited in European foreign banks and used as a medium of international credit, esp. to finance trade. [EURO(PE) + DOLLAR + -S[3]]

Eu·ro·mar·ket (yo͝or′ō mär′kit), *n.* See **Common Market.** [EURO(PE) + MARKET]

Eu·ro·mart (yo͝or′ə märt′), *n.* See **Common Market.** [EURO(PE) + MART]

Eu·ro·pa (yo͝o rō′pə), *n.* **1.** Also, **Europe.** *Class. Myth.* a sister of Cadmus who was abducted by Zeus in the form of a bull and taken to Crete, where she bore him Rhadamanthus, Minos, and Sarpedon. **2.** *Astron.* one of the 12 satellites of Jupiter.

Eu·rope (yo͝or′əp, yûr′- *for 1;* yo͝o rō′pē, yə- *for 2*), *n.* **1.** a continent in the W part of the landmass lying between the Atlantic and Pacific oceans, separated from Asia by the Ural Mountains on the E and the Caucasus Mountains and the Black and Caspian seas on the SE. In British usage, *Europe* sometimes contrasts with *England.* 702,300,000 including the Russian Federation; ab. 4,017,000 sq. mi **2.** *Class. Myth.* Europa (def. 1.)

Eu·ro·pe·an (yo͝or′ə pē′ən), *adj.* **1.** of or pertaining to Europe or its inhabitants. **2.** native to or derived from Europe: *traditional European customs; European languages.* —*n.* **3.** a native or inhabitant of Europe. **4.** a person of European descent or connections. [< L *Eurōpae(us)* (see EUROPE, -EOUS) + -AN] —**Eu′ro·pe′an·ly,** *adv.*

Europe′an Atom′ic En′ergy Commu′nity. See **Euratom.**

Europe′an beech′, a beech, *Fagus sylvatica,* of Europe, cultivated in North America in many ornamental varieties.

Eu′ropean bird′ cher′ry. See under **bird cherry** (def. 1).

Europe′an blastomyco′sis, *Pathol.* cryptococcosis.

Europe′an chest′nut. See under **chestnut** (def. 2).

Europe′an Coal′ and Steel′ Commu′nity, the European economic union created in 1952, providing for the pooling of coal, iron, and steel production in Belgium, France, Italy, Luxembourg, the Netherlands, and West Germany.

Europe′an corn′ bor′er. See under **corn borer.**

Europe′an cran′berry. See under **cranberry** (def. 1).

Europe′an Econom′ic Commu′nity, official name of the **Common Market.**

Europe′an el′der, an elder, *Sambucus nigra,* of Europe and Asia, bearing black fruit. Also called **bourtree.**

Europe′an fan′ palm′. See **dwarf fan palm.**

Europe′an fly′ hon′eysuckle, a bushy shrub, *Lonicera Xylosteum,* of Eurasia, having red-tinged, tubular, yellow flowers and red fruit.

Europe′an globe′flower, a hardy, perennial herb, *Trollius europaeus,* of Europe, having lemon-yellow flowers with spoon-shaped petals.

Europe′an gold′enrod, a small, perennial herb, *Solidago Virgaurea,* of Europe, having small, golden-yellow flowerheads on a stalk about five inches tall.

Eu·ro·pe·an·ise (yo͝or′ə pē′ə nīz′), *v.t.,* **-ised, -is·ing.** *Chiefly Brit.* Europeanize. —**Eu′ro·pe′an·i·sa′tion,** *n.*

Eu·ro·pe·an·ism (yo͝or′ə pē′ə niz′əm), *n.* **1.** European characteristics, ideas, methods, sympathies, etc. **2.** a European trait or practice. **3.** belief in or advocacy of the unification of Europe. [EUROPEAN + -ISM]

Eu·ro·pe·an·ize (yo͝or′ə pē′ə nīz′), *v.t.,* **-ized, -iz·ing.** to make European. Also, *esp. Brit.,* **Europeanise.** [EUROPEAN + -IZE] —**Eu′ro·pe′an·i·za′tion,** *n.*

Europe′an larch′, a pine tree, *Larix decidua,* of northern and central Europe, having slender, yellow-gray branchlets and oval cones with downy scales, grown for timber and as an ornamental.

Europe′an lin′den. See under **linden** (def. 1).

Europe′an mal′low. See **vervain mallow.**

Europe′an plan′, *U.S.* a method of conducting a hotel according to which the fixed charge per day covers only lodging and service.

Europe′an rasp′berry, an erect, shrubby plant, *Rubus idaeus,* of Eurasia, having conical or thimble-shaped, red fruit.

Europe′an Recov′ery Pro′gram, a broad plan for aiding the European nations in economic recovery after World War II, first proposed by U.S. Secretary of State George C. Marshall in 1947 and implemented in 1948 under the European Cooperation Administration. *Abbr.:* ERP, E.R.P.

Europe′an spruce′ saw′fly. See under **spruce sawfly.**

Europe′an white′ hel′lebore. See under **hellebore** (def. 2).

eu·ro·pi·um (yo͝o rō′pē əm), *n. Chem.* a rare-earth metallic element whose salts are light pink. *Symbol:* Eu; *at. wt.:* 151.96; *at. no.:* 63. [EUROPE + -IUM]

Eu·ro·tas (yo͝o rō′təs), *n. Class. Myth.* the son of Myles.

Eu·rus (yo͝or′əs), *n.* the ancient Greek personification of the east or southeast wind. Cf. **Volturnus.**

eury-, a combining form meaning "broad," "wide": *eurypterid.* [< Gk, comb. form of *eurýs* wide]

Eu·ry·a·le (yo͝o rī′ə lē′), *n. Class. Myth.* one of the three Gorgons.

Eu·ry·ba·tes (yo͝o rī′bə tēz′), *n.* (in the *Odyssey*) a companion of Odysseus.

Eu·ryb·i·a (yo͝o rib′ē ə), *n. Class. Myth.* a daughter of Pontus and Gaea.

eu·ry·cho·ric (yo͝or′ə kōr′ik, -kôr′-), *adj. Ecol.* (of a plant or animal) widely distributed geographically. Cf. **stenochoric.** [EURY- + Gk *chōr(eîn)* (to) spread + -IC]

Eu·ry·cle·a (yo͝or′ə klē′ə), *n.* (in the *Odyssey*) the nurse of Telemachus who recognized the disguised Odysseus by a scar on his leg. Also, **Eu·ry·cli·a** (yo͝or′ə klī′ə).

Eu·ryd·a·mas (yo͝o rid′ə məs), *n. Class. Myth.* **1.** one of the Argonauts. **2.** (in the *Iliad*) an elderly Trojan diviner.

Eu·ryd·i·ce (yo͝o rid′i sē′), *n. Class. Myth.* the wife of Orpheus.

Eu·ry·ga·ne·ia (yo͝or′ə gä′nē ə, yo͝or′ə gə nī′ə), *n. Class. Myth.* a woman sometimes believed to be the mother, by Oedipus, of Polynices and Eteocles.

eu·ry·ha·line (yo͝or′ə hā′līn, -lin, -hal′īn, -in), *adj. Ecol.* (of a plant or animal) able to live in an environment of widely varying salinity. Cf. **stenohaline.** [EURY- + Gk *hálin(os)* of salt; see HALO-]

Eu·ryl·o·chus (yo͝o ril′ə kəs), *n.* (in the *Odyssey*) a companion of Odysseus on the return from Troy. He reported to Odysseus that Circe had changed Odysseus' men into swine.

Eu·rym·a·chus (yo͝o rim′ə kəs), *n.* (in the *Odyssey*) a deceitful suitor of Penelope.

Eu·rym·e·de (yo͝o rim′i dē′), *n. Class. Myth.* a woman thought to be the mother of Bellerophon.

Eu·rym·e·don (yo͝o rim′i don′), *n. Class. Myth.* an epithet of Perseus, meaning "wide-ruling."

Eu·ryn·o·me (yo͝o rin′ə mē′), *n. Class. Myth.* a goddess, the mother, by Zeus, of the Graces.

eu·ryph·a·gous (yo͝o rif′ə gəs), *adj. Ecol.* (of an animal) able to subsist on a wide variety of foods. Cf. **stenophagous.** [EURY- + -PHAGOUS] —**eu·ry·phage** (yo͝or′ə fāj′), *n.*

eu·ryp·ter·id (yo͝o rip′tə rid), *n.* any aquatic arthropod of the extinct order *Eurypterida,* from the Paleozoic era, somewhat resembling horseshoe crabs. [< NL *Eurypter(idae).* See EURY-, -PTEROUS, -ID[2]]

Eu·ryp·y·lus (yo͝o rip′ə ləs), *n. Class. Myth.* **1.** a son of Poseidon, slain by Hercules. **2.** a nephew of Priam, slain by Neoptolemus in the Trojan War. **3.** a brave Greek warrior who was driven insane by an image of Dionysus that he received as part of the Trojan spoils.

Eu·rys·a·ces (yo͝o ris′ə sēz′), *n. Class. Myth.* the son of Telamonian Ajax and Tecmessa who inherited his father's shield of thick bull's hide.

Eu·rys·the·nes (yo͝o ris′thə nēz′), *n. Class. Myth.* a son of Aristodemus who shared the Spartan throne with his twin brother, Procles.

Eu·rys·the·us (yo͝o ris′thē əs, -tho͞os), *n. Class. Myth.* a king of Mycenae and cousin of Hercules, upon whom he imposed 12 labors. Cf. **labors of Hercules.**

eu·ry·ther·mal (yo͝or′ə thûr′məl), *adj. Ecol.* (of a plant or animal) able to withstand wide variations in temperature. Also, **eu′ry·ther′mic, eu′ry·ther′mous.** Cf. **stenothermal.** [EURY- + THERMAL]

eu·ryth·mic (yo͝o rith′mik), *adj.* eurhythmic. —**eu·ryth′my,** *n.*

eu·ryth·mics (yo͝o rith′miks), *n.* (*construed as sing. or pl.*) eurhythmics.

Eu·ryt·i·on (yo͝o rit′ē on′), *n. Class. Myth.* **1.** a centaur who was killed by Hercules. **2.** (in the *Aeneid*) a companion of Aeneas during the flight from Troy. **3.** an adopted son of Actor accidentally killed by Peleus. **4.** a son of Ares who guarded the cattle of Geryon.

eu·ry·top·ic (yo͝or′ə top′ik), *adj. Ecol.* (of a plant or animal) able to tolerate wide variations in conditions of the environment, as in temperature, humidity, etc. Cf. **stenotopic.** [EURY- + TOP(O)- + -IC] —**eu·ry·to·pic·i·ty** (yo͝or′ē tō pis′i tē), *n.*

Eu·ry·tus (yo͝or′i təs), *n. Class. Myth.* **1.** the son of Melaneus of Thessaly who was a famous archer. **2.** a son of Augeas. **3.** a son of Actor. Cf. **Molionidae. 4.** one of the giants who was killed by Hercules.

-eus, a formal element occurring in Latin scientific names and in the corresponding loan words in English: *nucleus.*

Eu·se·bi·us (yo͞o sē′bē əs), *n.* pope A.D. 309 or 310.

Euse′bius of Caesare′a, (*Pamphili*) A.D. 263?–c340, Christian theologian and historian: Bishop of Caesarea c315–c340.

eu·sol (yo͞o′sōl, -sôl, -sol), *n. Pharm.* an antiseptic solution prepared from chlorinated lime and boric acid, used chiefly in treating wounds. [*E(dinburgh) U(niversity) sol(ution)*]

eu·spo·ran·gi·ate (yo͞o′spō ran′jē āt′, -spô-), *adj. Bot.* having sporangia derived from a group of cells. [EU- + SPORANGI(UM) + -ATE[1]]

Eus·tace (yo͞o′stəs), *n.* a boy's given name.

Eu·sta′chian tube′ (yo͞o stā′shən, -stā′kē ən), *Anat.* a canal extending from the middle ear to the pharynx; auditory canal. See diag. under **ear**[1]. [named after EUSTACHIO; see -AN]

E·u·sta·chio (e′o͞o stä′kyô), *n.* **Bar·to·lom·me·o** (bär′tô lôm me′ô), 1524?–1574, Italian anatomist. Latin, **Eu·sta·chi·us** (yo͞o stā′kē əs).

Eu·sta·cia (yo͞o stā′shə), *n.* a girl's given name.

eu·sta·cy (yo͞o′stə sē), *n., pl.* **-cies.** *Geol.* a worldwide change in sea level, usually caused by the advance or retreat of continental glaciers. [EU- + -*stacy* for STASIS] —**eu·stat·ic** (yo͞o stat′ik), *adj.* —**eu·stat′i·cal·ly,** *adv.*

Eus·tis (yo͞o′stis), *n.* a town in central Florida. 6189 (1960).

eu·style (yo͞o′stīl), *adj.* having an intercolumniation of 2¼ diameters. See illus. under **intercolumniation.** [< Gk *eústȳl(os)* well columned (i.e., with the columns well spaced), equiv. to *eu-* EU- + *stȳl(os)* pillar + *-os* adj. suffix]

Eu·taw (yo͞o′tô), *n.* a town in W Alabama. 2784 (1960).

eu·tax·y (yo͞o′tak sē, yo͞o tak′sē), *n.* good or right order. [< Gk *eutaxía,* equiv. to *eútakt(os)* well arranged (see EU-, TACTIC) + *-ia* -Y[3]]

eu·tec·tic (yo͞o tek′tik), *Physical Chem.* —*adj.* **1.** of greatest fusibility: said of an alloy or mixture whose melting point is lower than that of any other alloy or mixture of the same ingredients. **2.** noting or pertaining to such a mixture or its properties: *a eutectic melting point.* —*n.* **3.** a eutectic substance. [< Gk *eútēkt(os)* easily melted, dissolved (*eu-* EU- + *tēktós* melted) + -IC]

eu·tec·toid (yo͞o tek′toid), *adj.* **1.** resembling a eutectic. —*n.* **2.** a eutectoid alloy. [EUTECT(IC) + -OID]

Eu·ter·pe (yo͞o tûr′pē), *n. Class. Myth.* the Muse of music and lyric poetry. —**Eu·ter′pe·an,** *adj.*

eu·tha·na·sia (yo͞o′thə nā′zhə, -zhē ə, -zē ə), *n.* **1.** Also called **mercy killing.** the act of putting to death painlessly a person suffering from an incurable and painful disease or condition. **2.** painless death. [< NL < Gk *euthanasía* an easy death, equiv. to *eu-* EU- + *thánat(os)* death + *-ia* -Y[3]] —**eu·tha·na·sic** (yo͞o′thə nā′zik), *adj.*

eu·then·ics (yo͞o then′iks), *n.* (*construed as sing.*) a science concerned with bettering the condition of human beings through the improvement of their environment. [< Gk *euthēn(eín)* (to) be well off, prosper + -ICS] —**eu·then′ist,** *n.*

eu·the·ri·an (yo͞o thēr′ē ən), *adj.* **1.** belonging or pertaining to the group *Eutheria,* comprising the placental mammals. —*n.* **2.** a eutherian animal. [< NL *Euthéri(a)* (< Gk *eu-* EU- + *thēría,* pl. of *thēríon* wild beast) + -AN]

eu·ther·mic (yo͞o thûr′mik), *adj.* producing or creating heat or warmth. [EU- + THERM- + -IC]

eu·to·ci·a (yo͞o tō′shē ə, -sē ə), *n. Med.* normal childbirth. [< NL < Gk *eutokía,* equiv. to *eu-* EU- + *tók(os)* a bringing forth, birth + *-ia* -IA]

Eu·to·pi·a (yo͞o tō′pē ə), *n.* a place in which human society, natural conditions, etc., are so ideally perfect that there is complete contentment. [EU- + Gk *tóp(os)* place + -IA]

eu·troph·ic (yo͞o trof′ik), *adj.* **1.** *Med.* pertaining to or being in a condition of eutrophy. **2.** *Ecol.* (of a lake) characterized by an abundant accumulation of nutrients that support a dense growth of plant and animal life, the decay of which depletes the shallow waters of oxygen in summer. [EUTROPH(Y) + -IC] —**eu·troph′i·ca′tion,** *n.*

eu·tro·phy (yo͞o′trə fē), *n.* **1.** *Med.* healthy or adequate nutrition or development. **2.** *Ecol.* the state of being eutrophic. [< Gk *eutrophía.* See EU-, TROPHO-, -Y[3]]

Eu·tych·i·a·nus (yo͞o tik′ē ā′nəs), *n.* **Saint,** died A.D. 283, pope 275–283. Also, **Eu·tych·i·an** (yo͞o tik′ē ən).

eu·vrou (yo͞o′vrō), *n.* euphroe.

eux·e·nite (yo͞ok′sə nīt′), *n.* a rare, brownish-black mineral of complex composition, containing yttrium, columbium, titanium, uranium, etc. [< Gk *eúxen(os)* kind to strangers, hospitable (see EU-, XENO-) + -ITE[1]]

Eux·ine (yo͞ok′sin, -sīn), *adj.* of or pertaining to the Black Sea.

Eux′ine Sea′. See **Black Sea.**

EV, electron-volt. Also, **ev**

E.V., (of the Bible) English Version.

E·va (ē′və), *n.* a girl's given name, form of **Eve.**

EVA, extravehicular activity, as in space flight.

e·vac·u·ant (i vak′yo͞o ənt), *Med.* —*adj.* **1.** evacuating; promoting evacuation, esp. from the bowels. —*n.* **2.** an evacuant medicine or agent. [< L *ēvacuant-* (s. of *ēvacuāns,* prp. of *ēvacuāre*). See EVACUATE, -ANT]

e·vac·u·ate (i vak′yo͞o āt′), *v.,* **-at·ed, -at·ing.** —*v.t.* **1.** to leave empty; vacate. **2.** to remove (persons or things) from a place, as a disaster area, for reasons of safety or protection: *to evacute the inhabitants of towns in the path of a flood.* **3.** to remove residents from (a city, town, area, etc.) for reasons of safety: *to evacuate an area threatened by a forest fire.* **4.** *Mil.* **a.** to remove (troops, wounded soldiers, civilians, etc.) from a place, as a war zone, combat area, etc. **b.** to withdraw from or quit (a town, fort, etc., that has been occupied). **5.** *Physiol.* to discharge or eject as through the excretory passages, esp. from the bowels. **6.** to deprive: *Fear evacuated their minds of reason. Strenuous effort evacuated his body of strength.* **7.** to produce a vacuum in. —*v.i.* **8.** to leave a place because of military or other threats: *They evacuated when the enemy approached the city.* **9.** to void; defecate. [ME < L *ēvacuāt(us)* (ptp. of *ēvacuāre* to empty out, equiv. to *ē-* E- + *vacuāre* to empty); see -ATE[1]]

e·vac·u·a·tion (i vak′yo͞o ā′shən), *n.* **1.** the act or process of evacuating, or the condition of being evacuated; discharge or expulsion, as of contents. **2.** *Physiol.* discharge, as of waste matter through the excretory passages, esp. from the bowels. **3.** that which is evacuated or discharged. **4.** the removal of persons or things from an endangered area. **5.** *Mil.* **a.** clearance by removal of troops, equipment, etc. **b.** the withdrawal or removal of troops, civilians, etc. [late ME *evacuaicoun* < medical L *ēvacuātiōn-* (s. of *ēvacuātiō*). See EVACUATE, -ION] —**e·vac·u·a·tive** (i vak′yo͞o ā′tiv), *adj.*

e·vac·u·a·tor (i vak′yo͞o ā′tər), *n.* **1.** one who or that which evacuates. **2.** *Med.* an instrument for cleansing the bowels or bladder, as in the removal of urinary stones. [EVACUATE + -OR[2]]

e·vac·u·ee (i vak′yo͞o ē′, i vak′yo͞o ē′), *n.* a person who is withdrawn or removed from a place of danger. [< F *évacué,* ptp. of *évacuer* to EVACUATE; see -EE]

e·vade (i vād′), *v.,* **e·vad·ed, e·vad·ing.** —*v.t.* **1.** to escape from by trickery or cleverness: *to evade capture.* **2.** to get around by trickery: *to evade the law; to evade rules.* **3.** to avoid doing or fulfilling: *evade a duty, obligation, etc.* **4.** to avoid answering directly: *to evade a question.* **5.** to elude; escape: *a word that evades definition; The solution evaded him.* —*v.i.* **6.** to practice evasion. **7.** to elude or get away by craft or slyness. [< L *ēvād(ere)* (to) pass over, go out, equiv. to *ē-* E- + *vādere* to go, walk] —**e·vad′a·ble, e·vad′i·ble,** *adj.* —**e·vad′er,** *n.* —**e·vad′ing·ly,** *adv.*
—**Syn. 1.** avoid, shun, dodge. **3.** See **escape. 6.** prevaricate, equivocate, quibble, fence. —**Ant. 1.** face, confront.

E·vad·ne (i vad′nē), *n. Class. Myth.* **1.** the wife of Capaneus who threw herself on his funeral pyre. **2.** a daughter of Pelias, king of Iolcus. Cf. **Amphinome. 3.** a daughter of Poseidon and the nymph Pitana. **4.** a girl's given name.

e·vag·i·nate (i vaj′ə nāt′), *v.t.,* **-nat·ed, -nat·ing.** to turn inside out, or cause to protrude by eversion, as a tubular organ. [< LL *ēvāgīnāt(us)* (ptp. of *ēvāgīnāre*) unsheathed, equiv. to *ē-* E- + *vāgīn(a)* scabbard, sheath (see VAGINA) + *-ātus* -ATE[1]] —**e·vag·i·na·ble** (i vaj′ə nə bəl), *adj.* —**e·vag′i·na′tion,** *n.*

e·val·u·ate (i val′yo͞o āt′), *v.t.,* **-at·ed, -at·ing. 1.** to determine or set the value or amount of; appraise: *to evaluate property; to evaluate an argument.* **2.** *Math.* to ascertain the numerical value of (a function, relation, etc.). [back formation from *evaluation* < F. See E-, VALUATION] —**e·val·u·a·ble** (i val′yo͞o ə bəl), *adj.* —**e·val′u·a′tion,** *n.* —**e·val′u·a′tive,** *adj.* —**e·val′u·a′tor,** *n.*

Ev·an (ev′ən), *n.* a boy's given name, Welsh form of **John.** Also, **Ewan.**

E·van·der (i van′dər), *n. Rom. Legend.* a son of Hermes who, as a Greek settler in Italy, founded a town at the foot of the Palatine Hill in Rome and allied himself with Aeneas upon the latter's arrival.

ev·a·nesce (ev′ə nes′, ev′ə nes′), *v.i.,* **-nesced, -nesc·ing.** to disappear gradually; vanish; fade away. [< L *ēvānēsc(ere)* (to) VANISH] —**ev′a·nes′ci·ble,** *adj.* —**ev′a·nes′cence,** *n.*

ev·a·nes·cent (ev′ə nes′ənt), *adj.* **1.** vanishing; passing away; fleeting. **2.** tending to become imperceptible; scarcely perceptible. [< L *ēvānēscent-* (s. of *ēvānēscēns*) vanishing, disappearing. See EVANESCE, -ENT] —**ev′a·nes′cent·ly,** *adv.*

Evang., Evangelical.

e·van·gel[1] (i van′jəl), *n.* **1.** the good tidings of the redemption of the world through Jesus Christ; the gospel. **2.** (*usually cap.*) any of the four Gospels. **3.** doctrine taken as a guide or regarded as of prime importance. **4.** good news or tidings. [ME < eccl. L *ēvangel(ium)* < Gk *euangélion* good news (see EU-, ANGEL); r. ME *evangile* < MF]

e·van·gel[2] (i van′jəl), *n.* an evangelist. [< LL *evangelus* < Gk *euángelos* (*adj.*) bringing good news. See EVANGEL[1]]

e·van·gel·i·ar·y (ē′van jel′ē er′ē, ev′ən-, -ə rē), *n., pl.* **-ar·ies.** evangelistary.

e·van·gel·i·cal (ē′van jel′i kəl, ev′ən-), *adj.* Also, **e′van·gel′ic. 1.** pertaining to or in keeping with the gospel and its teachings. **2.** belonging to or designating the Christian churches that emphasize the teachings and authority of the Scriptures, esp. of the New Testament, in opposition to the institutional authority of the church itself, and that stress as paramount the tenet that salvation is achieved by personal conversion to faith in the atonement of Christ. **3.** pertaining to certain movements in the Protestant churches in the 18th and 19th centuries that stressed the importance of personal experience of guilt for sin, and of reconciliation to God through Christ. **4.** marked by ardent or zealous enthusiasm for a cause. **5.** evangelistic. —*n.* **6.** an adherent of evangelical doctrines or a person who belongs to an evangelical church or party. [< LL *ēvangelic(us)* (< eccl. Gk *euangelikós;* see EVANGEL[1], -IC) + -AL[1]] —**e′van·gel′i·cal·ly,** *adv.* —**e′van·gel′i·cal·ness, e′van·gel′i·cal′i·ty,** *n.*

e·van·gel·i·cal·ism (ē′van jel′i kə liz′əm, ev′ən-), *n.* **1.** evangelical doctrines or principles. **2.** adherence to evangelical principles or doctrines or to an evangelical church or party. [EVANGELICAL + -ISM]

E·van·ge·line (i van′jə lēn′, -līn′, -lin), *n.* a girl's given name. Also, **E·van·ge·li·na** (i van′jə lē′nə).

E·van·ge·line (i van′jə lin), *n.* a narrative poem (1847) by Longfellow.

e·van·ge·lise (i van′jə līz′), *v.t., v.i.,* **-lised, -lis·ing.** *Chiefly Brit.* evangelize. —**e·van′ge·li·sa′tion,** *n.* —**e·van′ge·lis′er,** *n.*

e·van·ge·lism (i van′jə liz′əm), *n.* **1.** the preaching or promulgation of the gospel; the work of an evangelist. **2.** evangelicalism. **3.** missionary zeal, purpose, or activity. [EVANGEL[2] + -ISM]

e·van·ge·list (i van′jə list), *n.* **1.** a preacher of the gospel. **2.** (*cap.*) any of the writers (Matthew, Mark, Luke, and John) of the four Gospels. **3.** (in the primitive church) a person who first brought the gospel to a city or region. **4.** a revivalist. **5.** an occasional or itinerant preacher. **6.** (*cap.*) *Mormon Ch.* a patriarch. **7.** a person marked by evangelical enthusiasm for or support of any cause; crusader: *an ardent evangelist for the temperance movement.* [ME *evangeliste* < L *evangelist(a)* < Gk *euangelistés.* See EVANGEL[1], -IST]

e·van·ge·lis·ta·ry (i van′jə lis′tə rē), *n., pl.* **-ries.** a book containing passages from the four Gospels to be read at a divine service. Also, **evangeliary.** [< ML *ēvangelistāri(um).* See EVANGELIST, -ARY]

e·van·ge·lis·tic (i van′jə lis′tik), *adj.* **1.** pertaining to evangelists or to preachers of the gospel. **2.** evangelical. **3.** seeking to evangelize; striving to convert sinners. **4.** designed or fitted to evangelize. **5.** (*often cap.*) of or pertaining to the four Evangelists. [EVANGELIST + -IC] —**e·van′ge·lis′ti·cal·ly,** *adv.*

e·van·ge·lize (i van′jə līz′), *v.,* **-lized, -liz·ing.** —*v.t.* **1.** to preach the gospel to. **2.** to convert to Christianity. —*v.i.* **3.** to preach the gospel; act as an evangelist. Also, *esp. Brit.,* **evangelise.** [ME *evangelise(n)* < eccl L *ēvangelizāre* < LGk *euangelízesthai.* See EVANGEL[1], -IZE] —**e·van′ge·li·za′tion,** *n.* —**e·van′ge·liz′er,** *n.*

e·van·ish (i van′ish), *v.i. Poetic.* **1.** to vanish or disappear. **2.** to cease to be. [ME *evanissh(en)* < MF *esvaniss-,* extended s. of *esvanir.* See EX-[1], EVANESCE, VANISH]

Ev·ans (ev′ənz), *n.* **1. Sir Arthur John,** 1851–1941, English archaeologist. **2. Dame Edith,** born 1888, English actress. **3. Herbert Mc·Lean** (mə klān′), born 1882, U.S. embryologist and anatomist. **4. Mary Ann.** See **Eliot, George. 5. Maurice,** born 1901, English actor and producer. **6. Oliver,** 1755–1819, U.S. inventor: constructed the first high-pressure steam engine in the U.S. 1801?. **7. Rob·ley Dung·li·son** (rob′lē dung′gli sən), ("*Fighting Bob*"), 1846–1912, U.S. admiral. **8. Ru·dulph** (ro͞o′dulf), 1878–1960, U.S. sculptor.

Ev·ans·dale (ev′ənz dāl′), *n.* a town in NE Iowa. 5738 (1960).

Ev·an·ston (ev′ən stən), *n.* **1.** a city in NE Illinois, on Lake Michigan, near Chicago. 79,283 (1960). **2.** a town in SW Wyoming. 4901 (1960).

Ev·ans·ville (ev′ənz vil′), *n.* **1.** a city in SW Indiana, on the Ohio River. 141,543 (1960). **2.** a town in S Wisconsin. 2858 (1960).

e·vap·o·ra·ble (i vap′ər ə bəl), *adj.* capable of being evaporated. [EVAPOR(ATE) + -ABLE] —**e·vap′o·ra·bil′i·ty,** *n.*

e·vap·o·rate (i vap′ə rāt′), *v.,* **-rat·ed, -rat·ing.** —*v.i.* **1.** to turn to vapor; pass off in vapor. **2.** to give off moisture. **3.** to disappear; vanish; fade: *As the situation became clear to him, his hopes began to evaporate.* —*v.t.* **4.** to convert into a gaseous state or vapor; drive off or extract in the form of vapor: *The sun evaporated the dew.* **5.** to extract moisture or liquid from, as by heat, so as to make dry or to reduce to a denser state: *to evaporate fruit.* **6.** to cause to disappear or fade; dissipate: *His involvement in the recent government scandal has evaporated any hopes he might have entertained regarding his future political life.* [late ME (ptp.) < L *ēvapōrāt(us)* (ptp. of *ēvapōrāre*) dispersed in vapor, equiv. to *ē-* E- + *vapōr-* VAPOR + *-ātus* -ATE[1]] —**e·vap′o·ra′tor,** *n.*
—**Syn. 1.** vaporize. **3.** evanesce. **5.** EVAPORATE, DEHYDRATE, DRY mean to abstract moisture from. To EVAPORATE is to remove moisture by means of heat, forced ventilation, or the like, and thus to produce condensation or shriveling: *to evaporate milk, sliced apples.* To DEHYDRATE is to remove all vestiges of moisture: *One may dehydrate foods in order to make them easier to preserve and transport.* To DRY may mean to wipe moisture off the surface or to withdraw moisture by natural means, such as exposure to air or heat: *to dry a dish, clothes.*

evap′orated milk′, thick, unsweetened, canned milk made by removing some of the water from whole milk.

e·vap·o·ra·tion (i vap′ə rā′shən), *n.* **1.** the act or process of evaporating. **2.** the state of being evaporated. **3.** *Archaic.* matter or the quantity of matter evaporated or passed off in vapor. [ME *evaporacioun* < L *ēvapōrātiōn-* (s. of *ēvapōrātiō*). See EVAPORATE, -ION] —**e·vap·o·ra·tive** (i vap′ə rā′tiv, -ər ə tiv), *adj.* —**e·vap′o·ra′tive·ly,** *adv.*

evapora′tion pan′, an atmometer consisting of a pan about four feet in diameter and ten inches in depth.

e·vap·o·rim·e·ter (i vap′ə rim′i tər), *n.* atmometer. Also, **e·vap·o·rom·e·ter** (i vap′ə rom′i tər). Also called **evapora′tion gauge′.** [EVAPOR(ATION) + -I- + -METER]

e·vap·o·rite (i vap′ə rīt′), *n. Geol.* any sedimentary rock, as gypsum or rock salt, formed by precipitation from evaporating sea water. [EVAPOR(ATION) + -ITE[1]]

e·vap·o·tran·spi·ra·tion (i vap′ō tran′spə rā′shən), *n. Meteorol.* **1.** the process of transferring moisture from the earth to the atmosphere by evaporation of water and transpiration from plants. **2.** Also called **flyoff, water loss.** the total volume transferred by this process. [EVAPO(RATION) + TRANSPIRATION]

Ev·a·ris·tus (ev′ə ris′təs), *n.* **Saint,** died A.D. 105, pope 97–105.

Ev·arts (ev′ərts), *n.* **William Maxwell,** 1818–1901, U.S. lawyer and statesman.

é·va·sé (ā′vä zā′), *adj.* widened at the top, as a vase, chimney flue, etc. [< F, adj. use of ptp. of *évaser* to widen the mouth of, equiv. to *e-* E- + *vas* VASE]

e·va·sion (i vā′zhən), *n.* **1.** the act or an instance of escaping, avoiding, or shirking something: *evasion of one's duty; his evasion of responsibilities.* **2.** the avoiding of an argument, accusation, question, or the like, as by a subterfuge: *The old political boss was notorious for his practice of evasion.* **3.** a means of evading; subterfuge; an excuse or trick to avoid or get around something: *His polite agreement was an evasion that enabled him to conceal what he really felt.* **4.** physical or mental escape: *They use their house in Maine for summertime evasions from the city and its heat. Her daydreaming is an evasion from the world of reality.* **5.** the act or an instance of violating the tax laws by refusing or failing to pay all or part of one's taxes: *Many gangland bosses have been brought to trial and convicted on a charge of tax evasion.* [late ME < L *ēvāsiōn-* (s. of *ēvāsiō*), equiv. to *ēvās(us)* gone out (ptp. of *ēvādere;* see EVADE) + *-iōn-* -ION] —**e·va′sion·al,** *adj.*
—**Syn. 1.** avoidance, dodging. **2.** prevarication, equivocation, quibbling.

e·va·sive (i vā′siv), *adj.* **1.** tending or seeking to evade; characterized by evasion: *an evasive answer.* **2.** elusive or evanescent. [EVAS(ION) + -IVE] —**e·va′sive·ly,** *adv.* —**e·va′sive·ness,** *n.*

Ev·att (ev′ət), *n.* **Herbert Vere** (vēr), 1894-1966, Australian lawyer and statesman: president of the General Assembly of the United Nations 1948–49.

eve (ēv), *n.* **1.** the evening or the day before a holiday, church festival, or any date or event: *Christmas Eve; the eve of execution.* **2.** the period preceding or leading up to any event, crisis, etc.: *on the eve of a revolution.* **3.** the evening. [ME; var. of EVEN[2]]

Eve (ēv), *n.* **1.** the first woman. Gen. 3:20. **2.** a girl's given name.

e·vec·tion (i vek′shən), *n. Astron.* a periodic irregularity in the moon's motion, caused by the attraction of the sun. [< L *ēvectiōn-* (s. of *ēvectiō*) a going upwards, flight, equiv. to *ēvect(us)* (ptp. of *ēvehere*) carried forth, moved forth + *-iōn-* -ION] —**e·vec′tion·al,** *adj.*

Ev·e·leen (ev′ə lēn′; *Brit.* ēv′lēn), *n.* a girl's given name. Also, **Ev·e·li·na** (ev′ə lī′nə, -lē′nə), **Ev·e·line** (ev′ə lin′, -lēn′), **Evelyn, Evelynne.**

Ev·e·leth (ev′ə leth), *n.* a town in NE Minnesota. 5721 (1960).

Ev·e·lyn (ev′ə lin, ēv′lin), *n.* **1. John,** 1620–1706, English diarist. **2.** Also, **Ev′e·lynne.** a girl's given name. **3.** *Chiefly Brit.* a boy's given name.

E·ve·mer·us (i vē′mər əs, i vem′ər-), *n.* Euhemerus.

e·ven[1] (ē′vən), *adj.* **1.** level; flat; without irregularities; smooth: *an even surface; even country.* **2.** on the same level; in the same plane or line; parallel: *even with the ground.* **3.** free from variations or fluctuations; regular: *even motion.* **4.** uniform in action, character, or quality: *an even color; to hold an even course.* **5.** equal in measure or quantity: *even quantities of two substances.* **6.** divisible by two, as a number (opposed to *odd*). **7.** denoted by such a number: *the even pages of a book.* **8.** exactly expressible in integers, or in tens, hundreds, etc., without fractional parts: *an even mile; an even hundred.* **9.** *Math.* (of a function) having a sign that remains the same when the sign of each independent variable is changed at the same time. **10.** equally balanced or divided; equal: *Check to see if the scales are even.* **11.** leaving no balance of debt on either side; square: *We will not be even until I can repay him for saving my life.* **12.** calm; placid; not easily excited or angered: *an even temper.* **13.** equitable, impartial, or fair: *an even bargain; an even contest.* —*adv.* **14.** evenly: *The road ran even over the fields.* **15.** still; yet (used to emphasize a comparative): *even more suitable.* **16.** (used to suggest that something mentioned as a possibility constitutes an extreme case or an unlikely instance): *The slightest noise, even, disturbs him. Even if he attends, he may not participate.* **17.** just (used to emphasize occurrence, coincidence, or simultaneousness of occurrences): *even now; Even as he lay dying, they argued over his estate.* **18.** fully or quite: *even to death.* **19.** indeed (used as an intensive for stressing identity or truth of something): *He is willing, even eager, to do it.* **20.** *Archaic.* exactly or precisely: *It was even so.* **21. break even,** to have one's profits equal one's losses; neither gain nor lose: *The company barely broke even last year.* **22. get even,** to be revenged; retaliate: *He vowed to get even for the insult.* —*v.t.* **23.** to make even; level; smooth: *to even a board with a plane.* **24.** to place in an even state as to claim or obligation; balance (often fol. by *up*): *to even up accounts.* —*v.i.* **25.** to become even: *The racing odds evened before the race.* [ME; OE *efen;* c. Goth *ibns,* OHG *eban,* ON *jafn* even, equal] —**e′ven·er,** *n.* —**e′ven·ly,** *adv.* —**e′ven·ness,** *n.*
—**Syn. 1.** plane. See **level. 3.** EVEN, EQUABLE, UNIFORM imply a steady sameness. EVEN implies freedom from inequalities or irregularities: *even breathing; an even flow.* EQUABLE suggests the inherent quality of regularity or, in a nonmaterial reference, that of being well-balanced, not easily disturbed, and impartial in judgment: *an equable temperament.* UNIFORM emphasizes sameness and conformity to a standard: *uniform height or practice.* **12.** tranquil, temperate, composed, peaceful. **13.** just. —**Ant. 1.** irregular. **12.** mercurial. **13.** biased.

e·ven[2] (ē′vən), *n.* *Archaic.* evening; eve. [ME; OE *ǣfen;* akin to G *Abend,* OFris *āvond.* See EVENING]

e·ven·fall (ē′vən fôl′), *n.* the beginning of evening. [EVEN[2] + FALL]

e·ven-hand·ed (ē′vən han′did), *adj.* impartial; equitable: *even-handed justice.* —**e′ven-hand′ed·ly,** *adv.* —**e′ven-hand′ed·ness,** *n.*

eve·ning (ēv′ning), *n.* **1.** the latter part of the day and early part of the night. **2.** the period from sunset to bedtime: *He spent the evenings reading.* **3.** *Chiefly Southern and Midland U.S.* the time between noon and sunset, including the afternoon and twilight. **4.** any concluding or declining period: *the evening of life.* **5.** an evening's reception or entertainment: *Her evenings at home were extremely fashionable.* —*adj.* **6.** of or pertaining to evening: *The evening sky shone with stars.* **7.** occurring or seen in the evening: *The evening mist clings to the valleys and hills.* [ME; OE *ǣfnung,* equiv. to *ǣfn-* (s. of *ǣfnian*) draw toward evening + *-ung* n. suffix]
—**Syn. 1.** eventide, dusk, twilight, gloaming, nightfall.

eve′ning cam′pion, a sticky, hairy herb, *Lychnis alba,* of Europe, having night-blooming, fragrant flowers. Also called **white campion.**

eve′ning dress′, formal or semiformal attire for evening wear. Cf. **morning dress.**

eve′ning em′erald, *Jewelry.* peridot: not a true emerald.

eve′ning gown′, a woman's formal dress, usually having a floor-length skirt. Also called **gown.**

eve′ning gros′beak, a North American grosbeak, *Hesperiphona vespertina,* having yellowish, black, and white plumage.

Eve′ning Prayer′, *Anglican Ch.* evensong (def. 1).

eve′ning prim′rose, 1. an onagraceous plant, *Oenothera biennis,* having yellow flowers that open at nightfall. **2.** any of various plants of the same or related genera.

eve·nings (ēv′ningz), *adv.* in or during the evening regularly: *He worked days and played evenings.*

eve′ning school′. See **night school.**

eve′ning star′, 1. a bright planet seen in the west directly after sunset, esp. Venus. **2.** a bulbous herb, *Cooperia drummondi,* of the southwestern U.S., having solitary, fragrant, white, night-blooming flowers, reddish-tinged on the outside. [OE *ǣfensteorra.* See EVEN[2], STAR]

eve′ning stock′, a low herb, *Mathiola bicornis,* of Eurasia, having small, night-blooming, fragrant, purple flowers.

eve′ning watch′, *Naut.* the watch from 4 p.m. until 8 p.m., often adapted in place of the two dog watches.

Eve′ning With Monsieur′ Teste′, An (test), a prose work (1896) by Paul Valéry. French, **La Soirée avec Monsieur Teste.**

e·ven-mind·ed (ē′vən mīn′did), *adj.* not easily ruffled, disturbed, prejudiced, etc.; calm; equable: *an even-minded judge.* —**e′ven-mind′ed·ness,** *n.*

e′ven mon′ey, 1. the equal sum staked by each better. **2.** equal odds in a wager: *It's even money that the home team will win.* —**e′ven-mon′ey,** *adj.*

e′ven permuta′tion, *Math.* a permutation of a set of *n* elements, $x_1, x_2, \ldots x_n$, which leaves the product of all differences of the form $(x_i - x_j)$ where *i* is less than *j*, unchanged. Cf. **odd permutation.**

e·ven·song (ē′vən sông′, -song′), *n.* **1.** (*usually cap.*) Also called **Evening Prayer.** *Anglican Ch.* a form of worship appointed to be said or sung at evening. **2.** vesper (def. 5b). **3.** *Archaic.* evening. [ME; OE *ǣfensang.* See EVEN[2], SONG]

e·ven-ste·ven (ē′vən stē′vən), *adj.* *Informal.* having an equal chance or score; tied. [rhyming compound based on EVEN[1]]

e·vent (i vent′), *n.* **1.** anything that happens or is regarded as happening; an occurrence, esp. one of some importance. **2.** the outcome, issue, or result of anything: *The venture had no successful event.* **3.** *Philos.* something that occurs in a certain place during a particular interval of time. **4.** *Sports.* any of the contests in a program made up of one sport or of a number of sports: *The main event on the boxing card; The broad jump event followed the pole vault event.* **5. at all events,** regardless of what happens; in any case: *At all events, she will take care of you until you are completely recovered.* Also, **in any event. 6. in the event,** if it should happen; in case: *In the event of rain, the party will be held indoors.* [< L *ēvent(us)* occurrence, outcome, equiv. to *ēvent-* (ptp. s. of *ēvenīre* to occur, come out) + *-us* n. suffix (4th decl.)] —**e·vent′less,** *adj.*
—**Syn. 1.** happening, affair, case, circumstance. EVENT, EPISODE, INCIDENT, OCCURRENCE are terms for a happening. An EVENT is usually an important happening, esp. one that comes out of and is connected with previous happenings: *historical events.* An EPISODE is one of a progressive series of happenings, frequently distinct from the main course of events but arising naturally from them and having a continuity and interest of its own: *an episode in one's life.* An INCIDENT is usually a happening that takes place in connection with an event or a series of events of greater importance: *an amusing incident in a play.* An OCCURRENCE is something (usually of an ordinary nature) that happens, having no particular connection with (or causation by) antecedent happenings: *His arrival was an unexpected occurrence.* **2.** consequence.

e·ven-tem·pered (ē′vən tem′pərd), *adj.* not easily ruffled or disturbed; calm: *He is one of the most even-tempered individuals I know.*

e·vent·ful (i vent′fəl), *adj.* **1.** full of events or incidents, esp. of a striking character: *The latter part of the war was an eventful period.* **2.** having important issues or results; momentous. [EVENT + -FUL] —**e·vent′ful·ly,** *adv.* —**e·vent′ful·ness,** *n.*

e·ven·tide (ē′vən tīd′), *n.* evening. [ME; OE *ǣfentīd.* See EVEN[2], TIDE[2]]

e·ven·tra·tion (ē′ven trā′shən), *n.* *Med.* protrusion of the abdominal viscera through an opening in the abdominal wall. [< F, equiv. to *éventr(er)* (to) disembowel (see E-, VENTRAL) + *-ation* -ATION]

eventu-, a combining form meaning "event": *eventuate.* [repr. L *ēventus*]

e·ven·tu·al (i ven′cho͞o əl), *adj.* **1.** happening at some indefinite future time or after a series of occurrences; ultimate: *His mistakes led to his eventual dismissal.* **2.** depending upon uncertain events; contingent. [EVENTU- + -AL[1], modeled of F *éventuel*]

e·ven·tu·al·i·ty (i ven′cho͞o al′i tē), *n., pl.* **-ties. 1.** a contingent event; a possible occurrence or circumstance: *Rain is an eventuality to be reckoned with in planning the picnic.* **2.** the state or fact of being eventual; contingent character. [EVENTUAL + -ITY]

e·ven·tu·al·ly (i ven′cho͞o ə lē), *adv.* **1.** finally; ultimately; at some time: *Eventually we must die.* **2.** *Math.* residually (def. 1). [EVENTUAL + -LY]

e·ven·tu·ate (i ven′cho͞o āt′), *v.i.,* **-at·ed, -at·ing. 1.** to have issue; result. **2.** to be the issue or outcome; come about. [EVENTU- + -ATE[1]] —**e·ven′tu·a′tion,** *n.*

E·ven·tus (i ven′təs), *n.* *Rom. Religion.* See **Bonus Eventus.**

E·ve·nus (i vē′nəs), *n.* *Class. Myth.* a son of Ares and the father of Marpessa.

Eve′ of St. Ag′nes, The, a narrative poem (1819) by John Keats.

ev·er (ev′ər), *adv.* **1.** at all times; always: *He is ever ready to excuse himself.* **2.** continuously: *ever since then.* **3.** at any time: *Did you ever see anything like it?* **4.** in any possible case; by any chance; at all (often used to intensify or emphasize a phrase or an emotional reaction as surprise, impatience, etc.): *How did you ever manage to do it? If the band ever plays again, we will dance.* **5. ever and again,** now and then; from time to time. Also, *Literary,* **ever and anon. 6. ever so,** to a great extent or degree; exceedingly: *He talked for ever so long. They were ever so kind to me.* [ME; OE *ǣfre;* perh. akin to AY[1], and to Goth *aiws* time]
—**Syn. 1.** eternally, perpetually, constantly. See **always.** —**Ant. 1.** never.

Ev·e·rard (ev′ə rärd′), *n.* a boy's given name.

ev·er·bear·ing (ev′ər bâr′ing), *adj.* continuously producing or bringing forth, as a tree, shrub, etc. [EVER + BEARING]

Ev·er·dur (ev′ər do͝or′), *n.* *Trademark.* any of several alloys of copper and silicon with other constituents, esp. manganese, having high resistance to corrosion.

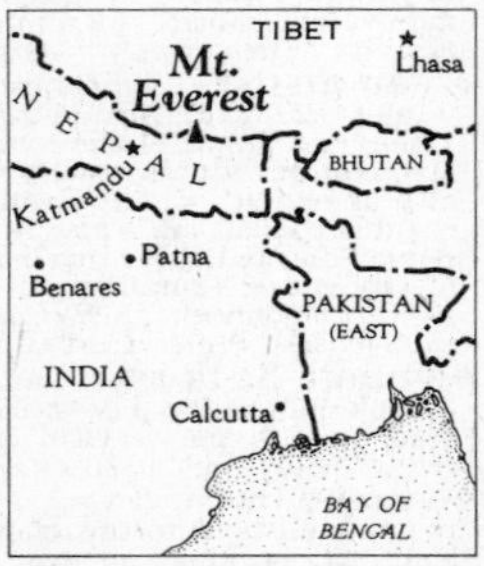

Ev·er·es (ev′ə rēz′, i-vēr′ēz), *n.* *Class. Myth.* the father of Tiresias.

Ev·er·est (ev′ər ist), *n.* **1. Mount,** a mountain in S Asia, on the boundary between Nepal and Tibet, in the Himalayas: the highest mountain in the world. 29,028 ft. **2.** a boy's given name.

Ev·er·ett (ev′ər it, ev′-rit), *n.* **1. Edward,** 1794–1865, U.S. statesman, orator, and writer. **2.** a city in E Massachusetts, near Boston. 43,544 (1960). **3.** a seaport in NW Washington on Puget Sound. 40,304 (1960). **4.** a boy's given name, form of **Everard.**

ev·er·glade (ev′ər glād′), *n.* *Southern U.S.* a tract of low, swampy land characterized by clumps of tall grass and numerous branching waterways. [EVER + GLADE]

ev′erglade palm′, a fan palm, *Paurotis wrighti,* of southern Florida, having prickly leaves and tiny fruit. Also called **saw cabbage palm.**

Ev·er·glades (ev′ər glādz′), *n.* (*construed as pl.*) a swampy and partly forested region in S Florida, mostly S of Lake Okeechobee. Over 5000 sq. mi.

Ev′erglades Na′tional Park′, a national park in the Everglades region of S Florida. 423 sq. mi.

Ev·er·good (ev′ər go͝od′), *n.* **Philip** (*Philip Blashki*), born 1901, U.S. painter.

ev·er·green (ev′ər grēn′), *adj.* **1.** (of trees, shrubs, etc.) having green leaves throughout the entire year, the leaves of the past season not being shed until after the new foliage has been completely formed. —*n.* **2.** an evergreen plant. **3. evergreens,** evergreen twigs or branches used for decoration. [EVER + GREEN]

Ev·er·green (ev′ər grēn′), *n.* a town in S Alabama. 3703 (1960).

ev′ergreen black′berry. See **cutleaf blackberry.**

ev′ergreen grape′, an evergreen vine, *Cissus capensis,* of South Africa, having forked tendrils and red-black fruit.

ev′ergreen magno′lia, a magnolia, *Magnolia grandiflora,* of the southern U.S., having evergreen foliage and fragrant, white flowers, grown as a shade and ornamental tree in the warmer parts of the U.S.: the State tree of Mississippi. Also called **big-leaved magnolia, bull bay, southern magnolia.**

ev′ergreen oak′, any of several oaks, as the holm oak, having evergreen foliage.

Ev′ergreen Park′, a city in NE Illinois, near Chicago. 24,178 (1960).

Ev′ergreen State′, the State of Washington (used as a nickname).

ev·er·last·ing (ev′ər las′ting, -lä′sting), *adj.* **1.** lasting forever; eternal. **2.** lasting or continuing for an indefinitely long time: *the everlasting hills.* **3.** incessant; constantly recurring: *He is plagued by everlasting attacks of influenza.* **4.** wearisome; tedious: *She tired of his everlasting puns.* —*n.* **5.** eternal duration; eternity: *What is the span of one life compared with the everlasting?* **6. the Everlasting,** the Eternal Being; God. **7.** Also, **ev′erlast′ing flow′er.** any of various plants or flowers which retain their shape, color, etc., when dried, as certain asteraceous plants of the genus *Helichrysum,* or various cudweeds of the genus *Gnaphalium.* [ME; see EVER, LASTING] —**ev′er·last′ing·ly,** *adv.* —**ev′er·last′ing·ness,** *n.*
—**Syn. 1.** See **eternal.** —**Ant. 1.** transitory.

ev′erlast′ing pea′, 1. a vinelike, perennial herb, *Lathyrus grandiflorus,* of southern Europe, having showy, fragrant, rose-purple flowers on a long stalk, and pods about three inches long. **2.** Also called **perennial pea.** a related herb, *L. latifolius,* of Europe, having rose-pink flowers and pods from three to five inches long.

ev′erlast′ing thorn′, an evergreen, thorny shrub, *Pyracantha coccinea,* of Eurasia, having hairy flower clusters and bright red fruit.

ev·er·more (ev′ər mōr′, -môr′), *adv.* **1.** always; continually; forever. **2.** at all future times; henceforth. [ME *evermor.* See EVER, MORE]

ev′er-nor′mal gran′ary (ev′ər nôr′məl), *U.S.* surplus agricultural produce purchased and stored by the federal government to equalize farm prices and guard against shortages resulting from crop failures.

e·ver·si·ble (i vûr′sə bəl), *adj.* capable of being everted. [< L *ēvers(us)* (ptp. of *ēvertere;* see EVERT) overturned, overthrown + -IBLE]

e·ver·sion (i vûr′zhən, -shən), *n.* a turning or being turned outward or inside out. [late ME < L *ēversiōn-* (s. of *ēversiō*), equiv. to *ēvers(us)* (see EVERSIBLE) + *-iōn-* -ION]

e·vert (i vûrt′), *v.t.* to turn outward or inside out. [ME < L *ēvert(ere)* (to) overturn, equiv. to *ē-* E- + *vertere* to turn]

e·ver·tor (i vûr′tər), *n.* *Anat.* a muscle which turns a part toward the outside. [EVERT + -OR[2]]

ev·er·y (ev′rē), *adj.* **1.** being one of an aggregate or series taken collectively; each: *We go there every day. Be sure to remember every word he says.* **2.** all possible; the greatest possible degree of: *every prospect of success.* **3. every bit,** *Informal.* in every respect; completely: *This is every bit as good as she says it is.* **4. every now and then,** on occasion; from time to time: *She bakes her own bread every now and then.* **5. every other,** every second; every alternate: *milk deliveries every other day.* **6. every which way,** *Informal.* in all directions; in disorganized fashion: *I brushed against the table, and the cards fell every which way.* [ME *every, everich,* OE *ǣfre ǣlc* EVER, EACH]
—**Syn. 1.** See **each.**

ev·er·y·bod·y (ev′rē bod′ē), *pron.* every person. [EVERY + BODY]

ev·er·y·day (ev′rē dā′), *adj.* **1.** of or pertaining to every day; daily: *an everyday occurrence.* **2.** of or for ordinary days, as contrasted with Sundays or special occasions: *everyday clothes.* **3.** such as is met with every day; ordinary; commonplace: *a placid, everyday scene.* [ME *everydayes.* See EVERY, DAY] —**ev′er·y·day′ness,** *n.*

ev·er·y·how (ev′rē hou′), *adv.* in all ways; in every manner. [EVERY + HOW]

Ev·er·y·man (ev′rē man′), *n.* **1.** (*italics.*) a 15th-century English morality play. **2.** (*usually l.c.*) an ordinary man; the common man. —*pron.* **3.** everybody; everyone. [EVERY + MAN[1]]

Ev′ery Man′ in His Hu′mour, a comedy (1598) by Ben Jonson.

Ev′ery Man′ Out′ of His Hu′mour, a satirical comedy (1599) by Ben Jonson.

ev·er·y·one (ev′rē wun′, -wən), *pron.* every person; everybody. Also, **ev′ery one′.** [ME *everichon.* See EVERY, ONE]

ev·er·y·place (ev′rē plās′), *adv.* everywhere. [EVERY + PLACE]
—**Usage.** See **anyplace.**

ev·er·y·thing (ev′rē thing′), *pron.* **1.** every thing or particular of an aggregate or total; all. **2.** something extremely important: *This news means everything to us.* —*n.* **3.** that which is extremely or most important: *Money is his everything.* [ME; see EVERY, THING[1]]

ev·ery·way (ev′rē wā′), *adv.* in every way; in every direction, manner, or respect: *They tried everyway to find the information.* [EVERY + WAY]

ev·ery·when (ev′rē hwen′, -wen′), *adv.* all the time; always. [EVERY + WHEN]

ev·ery·where (ev′rē hwâr′, -wâr′), *adv.* in every place or part; in all places. [ME *everihwer*, OE *ǣfre* EVER + *gehwǣr* (*ge-* Y- + *hwǣr* WHERE)]

ev·ery·where-dense (ev′rē hwâr′dens′, -wâr′-), *adj.* (of a set in a topological space) dense.

Eve·sham (ēv′shəm, ē′shəm, ē′səm), *n.* a town in SE Worcestershire, in W England: battle 1265. 12,608 (1961).

e·vict (i vikt′), *v.t.* **1.** to expel (a person, esp. a tenant) from land, a building, etc., by legal process. **2.** to recover (property, titles, etc.) by virtue of superior legal title. [ME *evict(en)* < LL *ēvict(us)* having recovered one's property by law, L: overcome, conquered (ptp. of *ēvincere;* see EVINCE), equiv. to *ē-* E- + *vic-* (ptp. s. of *vincere;* see VICTOR) + *-tus* ptp. suffix] —**e·vic′tion,** *n.* —**e·vic′tor,** *n.*

e·vict·ee (i vik tē′, i vik′tē), *n.* a person who has been evicted. [EVICT + -EE]

evic′tion clause′. See **stop clause.**

ev·i·dence (ev′i dəns), *n., v.,* **-denced, -denc·ing.** —*n.* **1.** ground for belief; that which tends to prove or disprove something; proof. **2.** something that makes evident; an indication or sign: *His flushed look was visible evidence of his fever.* **3.** *Law.* data presented to a court or jury in proof of the facts in issue and which may include the testimony of witnesses, records, documents, or objects. **4. in evidence,** plainly visible; conspicuous: *The first signs of spring are in evidence.* **5. turn state's evidence,** (of an accomplice in a crime) to become a witness for the prosecution against the others involved. Also, *esp. Brit.,* **turn queen's** or **king's evidence.** —*v.t.* **6.** to make evident or clear; show clearly; manifest: *He evidenced his approval by promising his full support.* **7.** to support by evidence: *He evidenced his accusation with incriminating letters.* [ME < MF < LL *ēvidentia.* See EVIDENT, -ENCE]
—**Syn. 3.** information, deposition, affidavit. EVIDENCE, EXHIBIT, TESTIMONY, PROOF refer to information furnished in a legal investigation to support a contention. EVIDENCE is any information so given, whether furnished by witnesses or derived from documents or from any other source: *Hearsay evidence is not admitted in a trial.* An EXHIBIT in law is a document or article which is presented in court as evidence: *The signed contract is Exhibit A.* TESTIMONY is usually evidence given by witnesses under oath: *The jury listened carefully to the testimony.* PROOF is evidence that is so complete and convincing as to put a conclusion beyond reasonable doubt: *proof of the innocence of the accused.* **6.** demonstrate.

ev·i·dent (ev′i dənt), *adj.* plain or clear to the sight or understanding: *His frown made it evident to all that he was displeased. It was evident to all that the project was a total failure.* [ME < L *ēvident-* (s. of *ēvidēns,* prp. of *ēvidēre*), equiv. to *ē-* E- + *vident-* (s. of *vidēns*) seeing; see VIDEO, -ENT] —**ev′i·dent·ness,** *n.*
—**Syn.** obvious, manifest, palpable, patent, unmistakable. See **apparent.** —**Ant.** concealed.

ev·i·den·tial (ev′i den′shəl), *adj.* noting, pertaining to, serving as, or based on evidence. [< LL *ēvidenti(a)* (see EVIDENCE) + -AL[1]] —**ev′i·den′tial·ly,** *adv.*

ev·i·den·tia·ry (ev′i den′shə rē), *adj.* **1.** evidential. **2.** *Law.* pertaining to or constituting evidence. [< LL *ēvidenti(a)* EVIDENCE + -ARY]

ev·i·dent·ly (ev′i dənt lē, -dent′-; *for emphasis* ev′i-dent′lē), *adv.* obviously; apparently. [ME; see EVIDENT, -LY]
—**Syn.** See **clearly.**

e·vil (ē′vəl), *adj.* **1.** morally wrong; immoral; wicked: *evil deeds; an evil life.* **2.** harmful; injurious: *evil laws.* **3.** characterized or accompanied by misfortune or suffering; unfortunate; disastrous: *to be fallen on evil days.* **4.** due to actual or imputed bad conduct or character: *an evil reputation.* **5.** marked by anger, irritability, irascibility, etc.: *He is known for his evil disposition.* **6. the evil one,** the devil; Satan. —*n.* **7.** that which is evil; evil quality, intention, or conduct: *to choose the lesser of two evils.* **8.** the force in nature that governs and gives rise to wickedness and sin. **9.** the wicked or immoral part of someone or something: *the evil in his nature has destroyed the good.* **10.** harm; mischief; misfortune: *to wish one evil.* **11.** anything causing injury or harm: *Tobacco is considered by some to be an evil.* **12.** a disease, as king's evil. —*adv.* **13.** in an evil manner; badly; ill: *It went evil with him.* [ME *evel, evil,* OE *yfel;* c. Goth *ubils,* OHG *ubil,* G *übel,* OFris, MD *evel*] —**e′vil·ly,** *adv.* —**e′vil·ness,** *n.*
—**Syn. 1.** sinful, iniquitous, depraved, vicious, corrupt, immoral, base, vile, nefarious. See **bad. 2.** pernicious, destructive. **7.** wickedness, depravity, iniquity, unrighteousness, corruption, baseness. **10.** disaster, calamity, woe, misery, suffering, sorrow. —**Ant. 1.** righteous.

e·vil·do·er (ē′vəl do͞o′ər, ē′vəl do͞o′ər), *n.* a person who does evil or wrong. [ME; see EVIL, DOER] —**e·vil-do·ing** (ē′vəl do͞o′ing, ē′vəl do͞o′ing), *n.*

e′vil eye′, the power, superstitiously attributed to certain persons, of inflicting injury or bad luck by a look. —**e′vil-eyed′,** *adj.*

e·vil-mind·ed (ē′vəl mīn′did), *adj.* **1.** having an evil disposition or harmful, malicious intentions. **2.** disposed to construe words, phrases, etc., in a lascivious, lewd manner; salacious. —**e′vil-mind′ed·ly,** *adv.* —**e′vil-mind′ed·ness,** *n.*

e·vince (i vins′), *v.t.,* **e·vinced, e·vinc·ing. 1.** to show clearly; make evident or manifest; prove. **2.** to reveal the possession of (a quality, trait, etc.). [< L *ēvince(re)* (to) conquer, overcome, carry one's point, equiv. to *ē-* E- + *vincere* to conquer] —**e·vin′ci·ble,** *adj.*
—**Syn. 1.** See **display.**

e·vin·cive (i vin′siv), *adj.* serving to evince; indicative. [EVINCE + -IVE]

Ev·i·pal (ev′ə pal′, -pôl′), *n. Pharm., Trademark.* hexobarbital.

e·vis·cer·ate (i vis′ə rāt′), *v.,* **-at·ed, -at·ing,** *adj.* —*v.t.* **1.** to disembowel: *to eviscerate a chicken.* **2.** to deprive of vital or essential parts: *The censors eviscerated the book to make it inoffensive to the leaders of the party.* —*adj.* **3.** *Surg.* disemboweled, usually after a surgical operation on the abdomen when the wound breaks open as the result of a technical error or poor healing. [< L *ēviscerāt(us)* (ptp. of *ēviscerāre*) deprived of entrails, torn to pieces, equiv. to *ē-* E- + *viscer(a)* VISCERA + *-ātus* -ATE[1]] —**e·vis′cer·a′tion,** *n.* —**e·vis′cer·a′tor,** *n.*

E·vi·ta (e vē′tä), *n.* a girl's given name.

ev·i·ta·ble (ev′i tə bəl), *adj.* that can be avoided. [< L *ēvītābil(is).* See EVITE, -ABLE]

e·vite (i vīt′), *v.t.,* **e·vit·ed, e·vit·ing.** *Archaic.* to avoid; shun. [< L *ēvīt(āre),* equiv. to *ē-* E- + *vītāre* to avoid]

E·vi·us (ē′vē əs), *n. Class. Myth.* Dionysus. [< Gk *Evios,* from the cry *evaí, evoí* associated with Dionysus in lyric passages]

Ev·nis·syen (ev′nis yen), *n. Welsh Legend.* a brother of Bran, Manawyddan, and Brunwen. He killed the son of Matholwych, causing a war between Britain and Ireland.

ev·o·ca·ble (ev′ə kə bəl), *adj.* that may be evoked. [EVOC(ATION) + -ABLE]

ev·o·ca·tion (ev′ə kā′shən), *n.* **1.** the act or an instance of evoking; a calling forth: *the evocation of old memories.* **2.** *Law.* (formerly) an action of a court in summoning a case from another, usually lower, court for purposes of complete review and decision, as on an appeal in which the issue is incidental or procedural and the court of first instance has not yet rendered a decision on its merits; the removal of a case from one court to another. [ME *evocacioun* < L *ēvocātiōn-* (s. of *ēvocātiō*) calling forth, out, equiv. to *ēvocāt(us)* (ptp. of *ēvocāre* to EVOKE) + *-iōn-* -ION]

e·voc·a·tive (i vok′ə tiv, -vō′kə-), *adj.* tending to evoke: *The perfume was evocative of spring.* [< L *ēvocātīv(us),* equiv. to *ēvocāt(us)* (see EVOKE, -ATE[1]) + *-īvus* -IVE] —**e·voc′a·tive·ly,** *adv.* —**e·voc′a·tive·ness,** *n.*

ev·o·ca·tor (ev′ə kā′tər), *n.* **1.** a person who evokes, esp. one who calls up spirits. **2.** *Embryol.* the chemical substance in an organizer that functions as a morphogenetic stimulus. [< L: one who calls to arms, equiv. to *ēvoc(āre)* (to) EVOKE + *-ātor* -ATOR]

e·voke (i vōk′), *v.t.,* **e·voked, e·vok·ing. 1.** to call up or produce (memories, feelings, etc.): *to evoke a memory, a smile, etc.* **2.** to elicit or draw forth: *His comment evoked protests from the shocked listeners.* **3.** to call up; cause to appear; summon: *to evoke a spirit from the dead.* **4.** to produce or suggest through artistry and imagination a vivid impression of reality: *a short passage that manages to evoke the smells, colors, sounds, and shapes of that metropolis.* [< L *ēvoc(āre),* equiv. to *ē-* E- + *voc-* call (see VOX) + *-āre* inf. suffix] —**e·vok′er,** *n.*

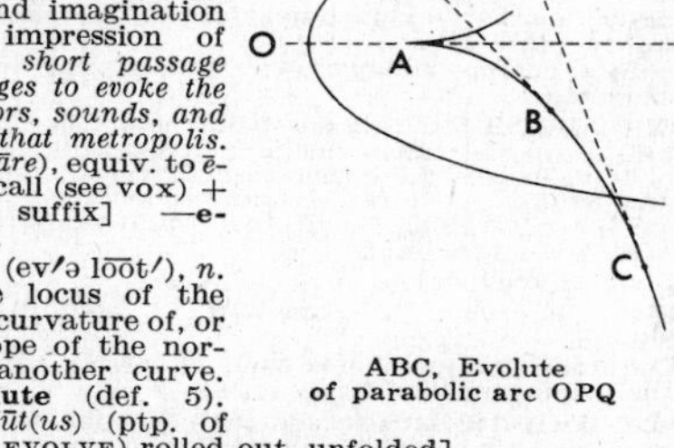

ABC, Evolute of parabolic arc OPQ

ev·o·lute (ev′ə lo͞ot′), *n. Geom.* the locus of the centers of curvature of, or the envelope of the normals to, another curve. Cf. **involute** (def. 5). [< L *ēvolūt(us)* (ptp. of *ēvolvere* to EVOLVE) rolled out, unfolded]

ev·o·lu·tion (ev′ə lo͞o′shən *or, esp. Brit.,* ē′və-), *n.* **1.** any process of formation or growth; development: *the evolution of man; the evolution of the drama; the evolution of the airplane.* **2.** a product of such development; something evolved: *The space program is the evolution of years of research and planning in the fields of aeronautics and nuclear physics.* **3.** *Biol.* the continuous genetic adaptation of organisms or species to the environment by the integrating agencies of selection, hybridization, inbreeding, and mutation. **4.** a motion incomplete in itself, but combining with coordinated motions to produce a single action, as in a machine. **5.** a pattern formed by or as by a series of movements: *the evolutions of a figure skater.* **6.** an evolving or giving off of gas, heat, etc. **7.** *Math. Obsolesc.* the extraction of roots from powers. Cf. **involution** (def. 9b). **8.** *Obs.* **a.** a movement or one of a series of movements of troops, ships, etc., as for disposition in order of battle or in line on parade. **b.** any similar movement, esp. in close order drill. [< L *ēvolūtiōn-* (s. of *ēvolūtiō*) an unrolling, opening, equiv. to *ēvolūt(us)* (see EVOLUTE) + *-iōn-* -ION] —**ev′o·lu′tion·al,** *adj.* —**ev′o·lu′tion·al·ly,** *adv.*

ev·o·lu·tion·ar·y (ev′ə lo͞o′shə ner′ē *or, esp. Brit.,* ē′və-), *adj.* **1.** pertaining to evolution or development; developmental: *the evolutionary origin of species.* **2.** in accordance with the theory of evolution. **3.** pertaining to or performing evolutions. [EVOLUTION + -ARY] —**ev′o·lu′tion·ar′i·ly,** *adv.*

ev·o·lu·tion·ist (ev′ə lo͞o′shə nist *or, esp. Brit.,* ē′və-), *n.* **1.** a person who believes in a doctrine of evolution. —*adj.* Also, **ev′o·lu′tion·is′tic. 2.** of or pertaining to evolution or evolutionists. **3.** believing in or supporting a doctrine of evolution. [EVOLUTION + -IST] —**ev′o·lu′tion·ism,** *n.* —**ev′o·lu′tion·is′ti·c′al·ly,** *adv.*

ev·o·lu·tive (ev′ə lo͞o′tiv *or, esp. Brit.,* ē′və-), *adj.* **1.** of, pertaining to, or promoting evolution; evolutionary: *evolutive conditions; an evolutive process.* **2.** tending to evolve, or toward evolution. [EVOLUT(ION) + -IVE]

e·volve (i volv′), *v.,* **e·volved, e·volv·ing.** —*v.t.* **1.** to develop gradually: *to evolve a scheme; The whole idea evolved from a casual remark.* **2.** *Biol.* to develop by a process of evolution to a more highly organized state or condition: *Man was evolved from an ancestor that was probably arboreal.* **3.** to give off or emit, as odors, vapors, etc. —*v.i.* **4.** to come forth gradually into being; develop; undergo evolution. [< L *ēvolve(re)* (to) unroll, open, unfold, equiv. to *ē-* E- + *volvere* to roll, turn] —**e·volv′a·ble,** *adj.* —**e·volve′ment,** *n.* —**e·volv′er,** *n.*

e·von·y·mus (e von′ə məs), *n.* euonymus.

É·vo·ra (e′vo͝o rə), *n.* a city in central Portugal: Roman ruins; cathedral. 34,145 (1960).

Ev·tu·shen·ko (*Russ.* ef′to͝o shen′ko), *n.* **Ev·ge·nii A·le·xan·dro·vich** (*Russ.* ef ge′ni ä′le ksän′dro vich). See **Yevtushenko, Yevgeny Alexandrovich.**

e·vul·sion (i vul′shən), *n.* the act of plucking or pulling out; forcible extraction. [< L *ēvulsiōn-* (s. of *ēvulsiō*). See E-, CONVULSION]

Ev·va (ev′ə), *n.* a girl's given name, form of **Eve.**

Ev·y·leen (ev′ə lēn′), *n.* a girl's given name.

Ev·voi·a (e′vē ä), *n.* Modern Greek name of **Euboea.**

ev·zone (ev′zōn), *n.* an infantryman belonging to an elite corps in the Greek army. [< NGk, Gk *eúzōn(os)* well girt (i.e., equipped). See EU-, ZONE]

E·wa (ā′wä, ā wä′), *n.* a town on S Oahu, in central Hawaii. 3257 (1960).

E·wald (*Germ.* ā′vält), *n.* a boy's given name.

Ew·an (yo͞o′ən), *n.* a boy's given name, Welsh form of **John.** Also, **Evan.**

ewe (yo͞o; *Dial.* yō), *n.* a female sheep. [ME; OE *ēowu, ēwe;* c. OHG *ou, ouwi,* D *ooi,* L *ovis,* Gk *oís,* Skt *ávi*]

E·we (ā′vā, ā′wā), *n.* a Kwa language of western Africa that is spoken in parts of Togo and Ghana.

ewe′ lamb′, a young female sheep.

Ew·ell (yo͞o′el), *n.* **1. Richard Stod·dert** (stod′ərt), 1817–72, Confederate lieutenant general in the U.S. Civil War. **2.** a boy's given name.

ewe-neck (yo͞o′nek′), *n.* a thin hollow neck, low in front of the shoulder, as of a horse or other animal. —**ewe′-necked′,** *adj.*

ew·er (yo͞o′ər), *n.* **1.** a pitcher with a wide spout. **2.** *Decorative Art.* a vessel having a spout and a handle, esp. a tall, slender vessel with a base. [ME < AF, equiv. to OF *evier* < L *aquārius* vessel for water, equiv. to *aqu(a)* water + *-ārius* -ARY]

Ewer (def. 2)

ew·er·y (yo͞o′ə rē), *n., pl.* **-er·ies.** *Archaic.* **1.** a room for storing ewers, towels, napkins, etc. **2.** a scullery, as in a monastery. [ME; see EWER, -Y[3]]

E·wig·weib·li·che (ā′viKH vīp′li KHə), *n. German.* the eternal feminine.

Ew·ing (yo͞o′ing), *n.* a town in W New Jersey. 26,628 (1960).

ex[1] (eks), *prep.* **1.** *Finance.* without, not including, or without the right to have: *ex interest; ex rights.* **2.** *Com.* free of charges to the purchaser until the time of removal from a specified place or thing: *ex ship; ex warehouse; ex elevator.* **3.** (in U.S. colleges and universities) from, but not graduated with, the class of: *ex '47.* [< L. See EX-[1]]

ex[2] (eks), *n.* the letter X, x.

ex-[1], a prefix meaning "out of," "from," and hence "utterly," "thoroughly," and sometimes imparting a privative or negative force or indicating a former title, status, etc.; freely used as an English formative, occurring before vowels and *c, p, q, s, t: exstipulate; exterritorial; ex-president* (former president); *ex-member; ex-wife.* Also, **e-, ef-.** [< L, comb. form of *ex, ē* (prep.) out of, from, beyond]

ex-[2], var. of **exo-.**

ex-[3], a prefix identical in meaning with **ex-**[1], occurring before vowels in words of Greek origin: *exarch; exegesis.* Also, **ec-.** [< Gk; see EX-[1]]

Ex., Exodus.

ex., **1.** examination. **2.** examined. **3.** example. **4.** except. **5.** exception. **6.** exchange. **7.** excursion. **8.** executed. **9.** executive.

ex·ac·er·bate (ig zas′ər bāt′, ik sas′-), *v.t.,* **-bat·ed, -bat·ing. 1.** to increase the bitterness or violence of (disease, ill feeling, etc.); aggravate. **2.** to embitter the feelings of (a person); irritate; exasperate. [< L *exacerbāt(us)* (ptp. of *exacerbāre*) exasperated, provoked, equiv. to *ex-* EX-[1] + *acerbātus* ACERBATE] —**ex·ac′er·bat′ing·ly,** *adv.* —**ex·ac′er·ba′tion,** *n.*

ex·act (ig zakt′), *adj.* **1.** strictly accurate or correct: *an exact likeness; an exact description.* **2.** precise, as opposed to approximate: *the exact sum; the exact date.* **3.** admitting of no deviation, as laws, discipline, etc.; strict or rigorous. **4.** characterized by or using strict accuracy, precision, etc.: *exact instruments; an exact thinker.* **5.** *Math.* (of a differential equation) noting that the collection of all its terms, equated to zero, is an exact differential. —*v.t.* **6.** to call for, demand, or require: *to exact obedience and respect from one's children.* **7.** to force or compel the payment, yielding, or performance of: *to exact money; to exact tribute from a conquered people.* [late ME *exacte* (v.) < L *exact(us)* (ptp. of *exigere*) driven out, thrust out, equiv. to *ex-* EX-[1] + *ag-* (s. of *agere*) drive + *-tus* ptp. suffix] —**ex·act′a·ble,** *adj.* —**ex·act′er, ex·ac′tor,** *n.* —**ex·act′ness,** *n.*
—**Syn. 3.** rigid, severe, unbending. **4.** methodical, careful, punctilious, demanding, scrupulous. **6.** force, compel. **7.** wring. See **extract.** —**Ant. 1, 2.** imprecise.

exact′ differen′tial, *Math.* an expression that is the total differential of some function.

ex·act·ing (ig zak′ting), *adj.* **1.** unduly severe or rigid in demands or requirements: *an exacting teacher.* **2.** requiring close application or attention: *an exacting task.* **3.** given to or characterized by exaction; extortionate. [EXACT + -ING[2]] —**ex·act′ing·ly,** *adv.* —**ex·act′ing·ness,** *n.*

ex·ac·tion (ig zak′shən), *n.* **1.** the act of exacting; extortion: *the exactions of usury.* **2.** something exacted. [ME *exactioun* < L *exactiōn-* (s. of *exactiō*) a demanding. See EXACT, -ION]

ex·act·i·tude (ig zak′ti to͞od′, -tyo͞od′), *n.* the quality of being exact; exactness; preciseness; accuracy. [< F; see EXACT, -I-, -TUDE]

ex·act·ly (ig zakt′lē), *adv.* **1.** in an exact manner; precisely according to rule, measure, fact, etc.; accurately. **2.** just: *He will do exactly what he wishes.* **3.** quite so; that's right. [EXACT + -LY]

exact′ sci′ence, a science, as chemistry, that deals with specific and objective facts.

ex ae·quo et bo·no (eks ī′kwō et bō′nō; *Eng.* eks ē′kwō et bō′nō), *Latin.* according to what is fair and good.

ex·ag·ger·ate (ig zaj′ə rāt′), *v.,* **-at·ed, -at·ing.** —*v.t.* **1.** to magnify beyond the limits of truth; overstate; represent disproportionately: *to exaggerate one's importance; to exaggerate the difficulties of a situation.* **2.**

to increase or enlarge abnormally: *Those shoes exaggerate the size of her feet.* —*v.i.* **3.** to employ exaggeration, as in speech or writing: *a person who is always exaggerating.* [< L *exaggerāt(us)* (ptp. of *exaggerāre*) heaped up, equiv. to *ex-* EX-[1] + *agger(āre)* (to) heap + *-ātus* -ATE[1]] —**ex·ag′ger·at′ing·ly,** *adv.* —**ex·ag′ger·a′tor,** *n.*
—**Ant. 1.** minimize.

ex·ag·ger·at·ed (ig zaj′ə rā′tid), *adj.* **1.** unduly magnified: *to have an exaggerated opinion of oneself.* **2.** abnormally increased or enlarged. [EXAGGERATE + -ED[2]] —**ex·ag′ger·at′ed·ly,** *adv.*

ex·ag·ger·a·tion (ig zaj′ə rā′shən), *n.* **1.** the act of exaggerating or overstating. **2.** an instance of exaggerating; an overstatement: *His statement concerning the size of his income is a gross exaggeration.* [< L *exaggerātiōn-* (s. of *exaggerātiō*), equiv. to *exaggerāt(us)* (see EXAGGERATE) + *-iōn-* -ION]

ex·ag·ger·a·tive (ig zaj′ə rā′tiv, -ər ə tiv), *adj.* given to or characterized by exaggeration. Also, **ex·ag·ger·a·to·ry** (ig zaj′ər ə tôr′ē, -tōr′ē). [EXAGGERATE + -IVE] —**ex·ag′ger·a′tive·ly,** *adv.*

ex·alt (ig zôlt′), *v.t.* **1.** to elevate in rank, honor, power, character, quality, etc.: *He was exalted to the position of president.* **2.** to praise; extol: *to exalt someone to the skies.* **3.** to stimulate, as the imagination: *The lyrics of Shakespeare exalted the audience.* **4.** to intensify, as a color: *complementary colors exalt each other.* **5.** *Obs.* to elate, as with pride or joy. [late ME *exalte* < L *exaltā(re)* (to) lift up, equiv. to *ex-* EX-[1] + *alt(us)* high + *-āre* inf. ending] —**ex·alt′er,** *n.*
—**Syn. 1.** promote, dignify, raise, ennoble. See **elevate. 2.** glorify. —**Ant. 1.** humble. **2.** depreciate.

ex·al·ta·tion (eg′zôl tā′shən), *n.* **1.** the act of exalting. **2.** the state of being exalted. **3.** elation of mind or feeling, sometimes abnormal or morbid in character; rapture: *mystical exaltation; euphoric exaltation.* **4.** abnormal intensification of the action of an organ. **5.** *Brit. Obs.* a flight of larks. **6.** *Astrol.* the part of the zodiac in which the strongest influence of a planet is exerted. Cf. **descension** (def. 1). **7.** *Chem. Obs.* the process of subliming. [ME *exaltacioun* < L *exaltātiōn-* (s. of *exaltātiō*). See EXALT, -ATION]

ex·alt·ed (ig zôl′tid), *adj.* **1.** elevated, as in rank or character; of high station: *an exalted personage.* **2.** noble or elevated; lofty: *an exalted style of writing.* **3.** rapturously excited. [EXALT + -ED[2]] —**ex·alt′ed·ly,** *adv.* —**ex·alt′ed·ness,** *n.*
—**Syn. 1.** sublime, grand.

ex·am (ig zam′), *n.* *Informal.* an examination, as in school. [short form]

exam., **1.** examination. **2.** examined. **3.** examinee. **4.** examiner.

ex·a·men (ig zā′men), *n.* *Eccles.* an examination, as of conscience. [< L *exāmen* means of weighing, testing, akin to *exigere* to weigh. See EXACT]

ex·am·i·nant (ig zam′ə nənt), *n.* an examiner. [< L *exāminant-* (s. of *exāmināns*, prp. of *exāmināre*) weighing, trying, examining. See EXAMINE, -ANT]

ex·am·i·na·tion (ig zam′ə nā′shən), *n.* **1.** the act of examining; inspection; inquiry; investigation. **2.** the state of being examined. **3.** the act or process of testing pupils, candidates, etc., as by questions. **4.** the test itself; the list of questions asked. **5.** the answers, statements, etc., made by one examined. **6.** *Law.* formal interrogation. [ME *examinacioun* < L *exāminātiōn-* (s. of *exāminātiō*). See EXAMINE, -ATION] —**ex·am′i·na′tion·al,** *adj.*
—**Syn. 1.** observation, inquisition. EXAMINATION, INSPECTION, SCRUTINY refer to a looking at something. An EXAMINATION may mean a careful noting of details or may mean little more than a casual glance over something: *A thorough examination of the plumbing revealed a defective pipe.* An INSPECTION is a formal and official examination: *an inspection of records, a military inspection.* SCRUTINY implies a critical and minutely detailed examination: *The papers seemed to be in good order but they would not stand close scrutiny.* See **investigation.**

ex·am·ine (ig zam′in), *v.t.*, **-ined, -in·ing. 1.** to inspect or scrutinize carefully: *to examine a prospective purchase.* **2.** to inquire into or investigate: *to examine one's motives.* **3.** to test the knowledge, reactions, or qualifications of (a pupil, candidate, etc.), as by questions or assigning tasks. **4.** to subject to legal inquisition; put to question in regard to conduct or to knowledge of facts; interrogate: *to examine a witness or a suspected person.* [ME < MF *examin(er)* < L *exāmināre* to weigh, examine, test, equiv. to *exāmin-* (s. of *exāmen* EXAMEN) + *-āre* inf. ending] —**ex·am′in·a·ble,** *adj.* —**ex·am·i·na·to·ri·al** (ig zam′ə nə tôr′ē əl, -tōr′-), *adj.* —**ex·am′in·er,** *n.* —**ex·am′in·ing·ly,** *adv.*
—**Syn. 1.** search, probe, explore, study. **2.** catechize.

ex·am·i·nee (ig zam′ə nē′), *n.* a person who is examined. [EXAMINE + -EE]

ex·am·ple (ig zam′pəl, -zäm′-), *n.*, *v.*, **-pled, -pling.** —*n.* **1.** one of a number of things, or a part of something, taken to show the character of the whole: *an example of his work.* **2.** a pattern or model, as of something to be imitated or avoided: *to set a good example.* **3.** an instance serving for illustration; specimen: *The case histories gave carefully detailed examples of this disease; an example of a rare butterfly.* **4.** an instance illustrating a rule or method, as a mathematical problem proposed for solution. **5.** an instance, esp. of punishment, serving as a warning to all others; warning: *Public executions were meant to be examples to the populace.* **6.** a precedent; parallel case: *an action without example.* —*v.t.* **7.** *Rare.* to give or be an example of; exemplify (used in the passive). [ME *exa(u)mple* < MF *example* < L *exemplum*, akin to *eximere* to take out (*ex-* EX-[1] + *emere* to buy); r. ME *exemple* < L, as above]
—**Syn. 1.** EXAMPLE, SAMPLE, SPECIMEN refer to an individual phenomenon taken as representative of a type, or to a part representative of the whole. EXAMPLE is used of an object, activity, condition, etc., which is assumed to illustrate a certain principle, law, or standard: *a good example of baroque architecture.* SAMPLE, used mainly in a concrete reference, refers to a small portion of a substance or to a single representative of a group or type which is intended to show what the rest of the substance or the group is like: *a sample of yarn.* SPECIMEN usually suggests that the "sample" chosen is intended to serve a scientific or technical purpose: *a blood specimen; zoological specimens.* **2.** See **ideal. 3.** See **case**[1].

ex·an·i·mate (ig zan′ə mit, -māt′), *adj.* **1.** inanimate or lifeless. **2.** spiritless; disheartened. [< L *exanimā-t(us)* (ptp. of *exanimāre*) deprived of life, equiv. to *ex-* EX-[1] + *anim(a)* life, spirit + *-ātus* -ATE[1]] —**ex·an′i·ma′tion,** *n.*

ex a·ni·mo (eks ä′ni mō′; *Eng.* eks an′ə mō′), *Latin.* from the heart; sincerely.

ex an·te (eks an′tē), based on anticipated changes or activity in an economy (opposed to *ex post*). [< L: lit., from (what might lie) ahead; according to (what lies) ahead]

ex·an·them (eg zan′thəm, ig-, ek-san′-), *n.* *Pathol.* an eruptive disease, esp. one attended with fever, as smallpox or measles. [< LL *exanthēma* < Gk *exánthēma* skin eruption, breaking forth, lit., a bursting into flower, equiv. to *ex-* EX-[3] + *anthe-* (verbid s. of *anthein* to blossom; see ANTHO-) + *-ma* n. suffix] —**ex·an·the·mat·ic** (eg zan′thə mat′ik, ek san′-), **ex·an·them·a·tous** (eg′zan-them′ə təs, ek′san-), *adj.*

ex·an·the·ma (eg′zan thē′mə, ek′san-), *n.*, *pl.* **-the·ma·ta** (-them′ə tə, -thē′mə-), **-the·mas.** exanthem.

ex·a·rate (ek′sə rāt′), *adj.* (of a pupa) having the antennae, legs, and wings free. Cf. **obtect.** [< L *exarāt(us)* plowed up (ptp. of *exarāre*). See EX-[1], ARABLE, -ATE[1]]

Exarate pupa of clover seed chalcid fly, *Bruchophagus gibbus*

ex·arch[1] (ek′särk), *n.* **1.** *Eastern Ch.* **a.** a patriarch's deputy. **b.** a title originally applied to a patriarch but later applied only to a bishop ranking below a patriarch and above a metropolitan. **2.** the ruler of a province in the Byzantine Empire. [< LL *exarch(us)* superintendent < Gk *éxarchos* overseer, leader, equiv. to *ex-* EX-[3] + *-arch-* -ARCH] —**ex·arch′al,** *adj.*

ex·arch[2] (ek′särk), *adj.* *Bot.* having the protoxylem toward the periphery of a stem or root. [EX-[2] + Gk *archḗ* beginning]

ex·ar·chate (ek′sär kāt′, ek sär′kāt), *n.* the office, jurisdiction, or province of an exarch. [< ML *exarchā-t(us)* domain of an exarch. See EXARCH[1], -ATE[1]]

ex·as·per·ate (ig zas′pə rāt′), *v.*, **-at·ed, -at·ing,** *adj.* —*v.t.* **1.** to irritate to a high degree; annoy extremely; infuriate: *He was exasperated by the senseless delays.* **2.** to increase the intensity or violence of (disease, pain, feelings, etc.). —*adj.* **3.** *Bot.* rough; covered with hard, projecting points, as a leaf. [< L *exasperāt(us)* (ptp. of *exasperāre*) made rough, provoked, equiv. to *ex-* EX-[1] + *asper* harsh, rough + *-ātus* -ATE[1]] —**ex·as′per·at′ed·ly,** *adv.* —**ex·as′per·at′er,** *n.* —**ex·as′per·at′ing·ly,** *adv.*
—**Syn. 1.** incense, anger, vex, inflame. See **irritate. 2.** exacerbate.

ex·as·per·a·tion (ig zas′pə rā′shən), *n.* **1.** the act or an instance of exasperating; provocation. **2.** the state of being exasperated; irritation; extreme annoyance: *His exasperation at being interrupted was understandable.* [< L *exasperātiōn-* (s. of *exasperātiō*) roughness, bitterness. See EXASPERATE, -ION]

Exc., Excellency.

exc., **1.** except. **2.** exception. **3.** excudit. **4.** excursion.

Ex·cal·i·bur (ek skal′ə bər), *n.* *Arthurian Romance.* the magic sword of King Arthur.

ex·car·di·na·tion (eks kär′dənā′shən), *n.* the transfer of a cleric from the jurisdiction of one bishop to that of another. [EX-[1] + (IN)CARDINATION]

ex ca·the·dra (eks kə thē′drə, kath′i drə), *Latin.* from the seat of authority; with authority. [lit., from the chair] —**ex′-ca·the′dra,** *adj.*

ex·cau·date (eks kô′dāt), *adj.* *Zool.* tailless; lacking a tail or taillike process. [EX-[1] + CAUDATE]

ex·ca·vate (eks′kə vāt′), *v.t.*, **-vat·ed, -vat·ing. 1.** to make hollow by removing the inner part; make a hole or cavity in; form into a hollow, as by digging: *The ground was excavated for a foundation.* **2.** to make (a hole, tunnel, etc.) by removing material. **3.** to dig or scoop out (earth, sand, etc.). **4.** to expose or lay bare by digging; unearth: *to excavate an ancient city.* [< L *excavāt(us)* (ptp. of *excavāre*) hollowed out, equiv. to *ex-* EX-[1] + *cav-* hollow, CAVE[1] + *-ātus* -ATE[1]]

ex·ca·va·tion (eks′kə vā′shən), *n.* **1.** a hole or cavity made by excavating. **2.** the act of excavating. [< L *excavātiōn-* (s. of *excavātiō*) a hollowing. See EXCAVATE, -ION]
—**Syn. 2.** See **hole.**

ex·ca·va·tor (eks′kə vā′tər), *n.* **1.** one who or that which excavates. **2.** a power-driven machine for digging, moving, or transporting loose gravel, sand, or soil. **3.** a sharp, spoonlike instrument used for scraping out diseased tissue, as in dentistry. [EXCAVATE + -OR[2]]

ex·ceed (ik sēd′), *v.t.* **1.** to go beyond the bounds or limits of: *to exceed one's powers.* **2.** to go beyond in quantity, degree, rate, etc.: *to exceed the speed limit.* **3.** to surpass; be superior to; excel: *His performance exceeded all the others.* —*v.i.* **4.** to be greater, as in quantity or degree. **5.** to surpass others, excel, or be superior. [ME *exceden* < L *excēd(ere)* (to) go out or beyond. See EX-[1], CEDE] —**ex·ceed′a·ble,** *adj.* —**ex·ceed′er,** *n.*
—**Syn. 1.** overstep, transcend. **3.** outdo, outstrip, beat, cap, top.

ex·ceed·ing (ik sē′ding), *adj.* **1.** extraordinary; exceptional. —*adv.* **2.** exceedingly. [EXCEED + -ING[2]]

ex·ceed·ing·ly (ik sē′ding lē), *adv.* to an unusual degree; extremely: *The children were doing exceedingly well at school.* [EXCEEDING + -LY]

ex·cel (ik sel′), *v.*, **-celled, -cel·ling.** —*v.t.* **1.** to surpass; be superior to; outdo: *He excels all other poets of his day.* —*v.i.* **2.** to surpass others or be superior in some respect: *to excel in speed and accuracy.* [late ME *excelle(n)* < L *excell(ere)*, equiv. to *ex-* EX-[1] + **cellere* to rise high, tower]
—**Syn. 1.** outstrip, eclipse, transcend, exceed, top, beat. EXCEL, OUTDO, SURPASS imply being better than others or being superior in achievement. To EXCEL is to be superior to others in some (usually) good or desirable quality, attainment, or performance: *to excel opponents at playing chess.* To OUTDO is to make more successful effort than others: *to outdo competitors in the high jump.* To SURPASS is to go beyond others (who are definitely pointed out), esp. in a contest as to quality or ability: *to surpass one's classmates in knowledge of corporation law.*

ex·cel·lence (ek′sə ləns), *n.* **1.** the fact or state of excelling; superiority; eminence: *his excellence in hockey.* **2.** an excellent quality or feature: *Precision is one of the excellences of the French language.* **3.** (*usually cap.*) excellency (def. 1). [ME < MF < L *excellentia.* See EXCEL, -ENCE]
—**Syn. 1.** preeminence, transcendence, distinction. **2.** merit, virtue. —**Ant. 2.** inferiority.

ex·cel·len·cy (ek′sə lən sē), *n.*, *pl.* **-cies. 1.** (*usually cap.*) Also, **Excellence.** a title of honor given to certain high officials, as governors and ambassadors. **2.** (*usually cap.*) a person so entitled. **3.** excellence. [ME *excellencie* < L *excellentia.* See EXCELLENT, -ENCY]

ex·cel·lent (ek′sə lənt), *adj.* **1.** possessing excellence or superior merit; remarkably good. **2.** *Obs.* extraordinary; superior. [< L *excellent-* (s. of *excellēns*), prp. of *excellere* to EXCEL; see -ENT] —**ex′cel·lent·ly,** *adv.*
—**Syn. 1.** worthy, estimable, choice, fine, first-rate, prime, admirable. —**Ant. 1.** inferior.

ex·cel·si·or (ik sel′sē ər, ek-), *n.* **1.** a kind of fine wood shavings, used for stuffing, packing, etc. **2.** *Print.* a 3-point type of a size smaller than brilliant. [formerly trademark]

ex·cel·si·or (ek sel′si ōr′; *Eng.* ik sel′sē ôr′), *adj.* *Latin.* ever upward: motto of New York State.

Excel′sior Springs′, a town in W Missouri. 6473 (1960).

ex·cen·tric (ik sen′trik), *adj.*, *n.* *Chiefly Brit.* eccentric.

ex·cept[1] (ik sept′), *prep.* **1.** with the exclusion of; excluding; save; but: *They were all there except me.* —*conj.* **2.** only; with the exception (usually fol. by *that*): *parallel cases except that one is younger than the other.* **3.** otherwise than; but (fol. by an adv., phrase, or clause): *well fortified except here.* **4.** *Archaic.* unless. [late ME < L *except(us)* (ptp. of *excipere*) taken out, equiv. to *ex-* EX-[1] + *-ceptus* (comb. form of *captus*, ptp. of *capere* to take)]
—**Syn. 1.** EXCEPT (more rarely EXCEPTING), BUT, SAVE point out something excluded from a general statement. EXCEPT emphasizes the excluding: *Take any number except 12.* BUT merely states the exclusion: *We ate all but one.* SAVE is now mainly found in poetic use: *nothing in sight save sky and sea.*

ex·cept[2] (ik sept′), *v.t.* **1.** to exclude; leave out: *present company excepted.* —*v.i.* **2.** to object (usually fol. by *to* or *against*): *to except to a statement; to except against a witness.* [ME *except(en)* < MF *except(er)* < L *exceptāre*, deriv. of *exceptus* (ptp.); see EXCEPT[1]] —**ex·cept′a·ble,** *adj.*

ex·cept·ing (ik sep′ting), *prep.* **1.** excluding; barring; saving; except: *Excepting the last chapter, the book is finished.* —*conj.* **2.** *Archaic.* except; unless; save. [EXCEPT[2] + -ING[2]]
—**Syn. 1.** See **except**[1].

ex·cep·tion (ik sep′shən), *n.* **1.** the act of excepting or the fact of being excepted. **2.** something excepted; an instance or case not conforming to the general rule. **3.** an adverse criticism, esp. on a particular point; opposition of opinion; objection; demurral: *a statement liable to exception.* **4.** *Law.* **a.** an objection, as to a ruling of the court in the course of a trial. **b.** a notation that an objection is preserved for purposes of appeal: *saving an exception.* **5. take exception, a.** to make an objection; demur: *They took exception to several points in the contract.* **b.** to take offense: *She took exception to what I said about her hat.* [ME *excepcioun* < L *exceptiōn-* (s. of *exceptiō*), equiv. to *except(us)* (see EXCEPT[1]) + *-iōn-* -ION] —**ex·cep′tion·less,** *adj.*

ex·cep·tion·a·ble (ik sep′shə nə bəl), *adj.* liable to exception or objection; objectionable. [EXCEPTION + -ABLE] —**ex·cep′tion·a·ble·ness,** *n.* —**ex·cep′tion·a·bly,** *adv.*

ex·cep·tion·al (ik sep′shə nəl), *adj.* **1.** forming an exception or unusual instance; unusual; extraordinary: *The warm weather was exceptional for January.* **2.** unusually excellent; superior: *an exceptional violinist.* **3.** *Educ.* (of a child) being intellectually gifted or physically or mentally handicapped to an extent that special schooling is required. [EXCEPTION + -AL[1]] —**ex·cep′tion·al′i·ty,** *n.* —**ex·cep′tion·al·ly,** *adv.* —**ex·cep′tion·al·ness,** *n.*
—**Syn. 1.** uncommon, peculiar, singular, rare, strange, unnatural, aberrant, anomalous. See **irregular.** —**Ant. 2.** average.

ex·cep·tive (ik sep′tiv), *adj.* **1.** being or making an exception. **2.** disposed to take exception; objecting. [< LL *exceptīv(us).* See EXCEPT[2], -IVE] —**ex·cep′tive·ly,** *adv.*

ex·cerpt (*n.* ek′sûrpt; *v.* ik sûrpt′), *n.* **1.** a passage taken out of a book, document, film, or the like; extract. —*v.t.* **2.** to take (a passage) from a book, film, or the like; extract. **3.** to take or select passages from (a book, film, or the like); abridge by choosing representative sections. [late ME < L *excerpt(us)* (ptp. of *excerpere*) picked out, plucked out, equiv. to *ex-* EX-[1] + *-cerp-* (comb. form of *carpere* to pluck) + *-tus* ptp. suffix] —**ex·cerpt′er, ex·cerp′tor,** *n.* —**ex·cerpt′i·ble,** *adj.* —**ex·cerp′tion,** *n.*

ex·cerp·ta (ik sûrp′tə), *n.pl.* short selections or pieces of writing, esp. summary statements or parts of a longer work. [< L, n. use of neut. pl. ptp. of *excerpere.* See EXCERPT]

ex·cess (*n.* ik ses′; *adj.* ek′ses, ik ses′), *n.* **1.** the fact of exceeding something else in amount or degree: *His strength is in excess of yours.* **2.** the amount or degree by which one thing exceeds another: *The bill showed an excess of several dollars over what he had planned to spend.* **3.** an extreme or excessive amount or degree; superabundance: *to have an excess of energy.* **4.** a going beyond ordinary or proper limits: *to talk to excess.* **5.** immoderate indulgence; intemperance in eating, drinking, etc. —*adj.* **6.** more than or above what is necessary, usual, or specified; extra: *excess baggage; excess profits.* [ME < L *excess(us)*, n. use of ptp. of *excēdere* to EXCEED]
—**Syn. 3.** overplus, surplus, surplusage, superfluity, redundancy. **5.** dissipation. —**Ant. 3.** lack, deficiency.

ex′cess insur′ance, insurance covering a policyholder only for that portion of losses which exceeds a stated amount.

ex·ces·sive (ik ses′iv), *adj.* exceeding the usual or proper limit or degree; characterized by excess: *excessive charges; excessive indulgence.* [late ME (see EXCESS,

-IVE); r. ME *excessif* < MF] —**ex·ces′sive·ly,** *adv.* —**ex·ces′sive·ness,** *n.*
—**Syn.** immoderate, extravagant, extreme, inordinate, exorbitant, outrageous, unreasonable, disproportionate. —**Ant.** reasonable.

ex′cess-prof′its tax′ (ek′ses prof′its), a tax on the profits of a business enterprise in excess of the average profits for a number of base years, or of a specified rate of return on capital.

ex′cess sound′ pres′sure, *Physics.* See **sound pressure** (def. 1).

exch., 1. exchange. 2. exchequer.

ex·change (iks chānj′), *v.*, **-changed, -chang·ing,** *n.* —*v.t.* **1.** to part with for some equivalent; give up (something) for something else; change for another. **2.** to replace (returned merchandise) with an equivalent or something else: *Most stores will allow the purchaser to exchange goods.* **3.** to give and receive reciprocally; interchange: *to exchange blows; Friends often exchange gifts at Christmas.* **4.** to part with in return for some equivalent; transfer for a recompense; barter: *to exchange goods with foreign countries.* **5.** *Chess.* to capture (an enemy piece) in return for a capture by the opponent generally of pieces of equal value. —*v.i.* **6.** to make an exchange. **7.** to pass or be taken in exchange or as an equivalent. —*n.* **8.** the act, process, or an instance of exchanging: *an exchange of gifts; The contesting nations arranged for an exchange of prisoners.* **9.** that which is given or received in exchange or substitution for something else: *The car was a fair exchange.* **10.** a place for buying and selling commodities, securities, etc., typically open only to members. **11.** a central office or central station: *a telephone exchange.* **12.** the method or system by which debits and credits in different places are settled without the actual transfer of money, by means of bills of exchange representing money values. **13.** the discharge of obligations in different places by the transfer of credits. **14.** the amount or percentage charged for exchanging money, collecting a draft, etc. **15.** the reciprocal transfer of equivalent sums of money, as in the currencies of two different countries. **16.** the giving or receiving of a sum of money in one place for a bill ordering the payment of an equivalent sum in another. **17.** See **rate of exchange. 18.** the amount of the difference in value between two or more currencies, or between the values of the same currency at two or more places. **19.** the checks, drafts, etc., exchanged at a clearing house. **20.** *Chess.* a reciprocal capture of pieces of equivalent value by opponents in a single series of moves. **21.** *Brit.* See **labour exchange.** [late ME *exchaunge,* ME *eschaunge* < AF << LL *excambium.* See EX-[1], CHANGE] —**ex·chang′er,** *n.*
—**Syn. 1.** interchange, commute, barter, trade, swap. **8.** interchange, trade, traffic, business, commerce, barter. **10.** market.

ex·change·a·ble (iks chān′jə bəl), *adj.* capable of being exchanged. [EXCHANGE + -ABLE] —**ex·change′a·bil′i·ty,** *n.* —**ex·change′a·bly,** *adv.*
—**Syn.** EXCHANGEABLE, INTERCHANGEABLE apply to something that may replace something else. That is EXCHANGEABLE which may be taken or sent back to the place at which it was purchased, to be exchanged for money, credit, or other purchases to the amount of the original purchase: *These dishes are exchangeable if you find they are not satisfactory.* INTERCHANGEABLE applies to those things capable of being reciprocally put in each other's place: *Standard parts are interchangeable.*

ex·chang·ee (iks chān jē′, -chān′jē, eks′chān jē′), *n.* a person who takes or has taken part in an exchange, as of students, prisoners, etc. [EXCHANGE + -EE]

exchange′ equaliza′tion fund′. See **stabilization fund.**

exchange′ rate′. See **rate of exchange.**

exchange′ stabiliza′tion fund′. See **stabilization fund.**

ex·cheq·uer (eks′chek ər, iks chek′ər), *n.* **1.** a treasury, as of a state or nation. **2.** (in Great Britain) **a.** (*often cap.*) the governmental department in charge of the public revenues. **b.** (formerly) an office administering the royal revenues and determining all cases affecting them. **c.** (*cap.*) Also called **Court of Exchequer.** an ancient common-law court of civil jurisdiction in which cases affecting the revenues of the crown were tried, now merged in the King's Bench Division of the High Court. **3.** *Informal.* funds; finances. [ME *escheker, eschequier* < AF *escheker, eschekier* (OF *eschequier*) chessboard, counting table. See CHECKER[1]]

ex·cide (ik sīd′), *v.t.*, **-cid·ed, -cid·ing.** to cut out; excise. [< L *excīde(re)* (to) cut out, equiv. to *ex-* EX-[1] + *cīd-* (var. s. of *caedere* to cut)]

ex·cip·i·ent (ik sip′ē ənt), *n.* *Pharm.* a pharmacologically inert, adhesive substance, as honey, syrup, or gum arabic, used to bind the contents of a pill or tablet. [< L *excipient-* (s. of *excipiēns,* prp. of *excipere*) taking out, excepting, taking up, equiv. to *ex-* EX-[1] + *-cip-* (var. of *capere* to take) + *-i-* -I- + *-ent-* -ENT]

ex·ci·ple (ek′sə pəl), *n.* *Bot.* (in certain lichens) the rim or outer covering of the apothecium. Also, **ex·ci·pule** (ek′sə pyo͞ol′), **excipulum.** [see EXCIPLE]

ex·cip·u·lum (ek sip′yə ləm), *n.*, *pl.* **-la** (-lə). *Bot.* exciple. [< NL, special use of ML *excipulum* device for catching fish. See EXCIPIENT, -ULE]

ex·cir·cle (eks′sûr′kəl), *n.* *Geom.* an escribed circle. [EX-[1] + CIRCLE]

ex·cis·a·ble[1] (ik sī′zə bəl), *adj.* subject to excise duty. [EXCISE[1] + -ABLE]

ex·cis·a·ble[2] (ek′sī zə bəl), *adj.* capable of being expunged or cut out. [EXCISE[2] + -ABLE]

ex·cise[1] (*n.* ek′sīz, -sīs; *v.* ik sīz′), *n.*, *v.*, **-cised, -cis·ing.** —*n.* **1.** an inland tax or duty on certain commodities, as spirits, tobacco, etc., levied on their manufacture, sale, or consumption within the country. **2.** a tax levied for a license to carry on certain employments, pursue certain sports, etc. **3.** *Brit.* the branch of the civil service that collects excise taxes. —*v.t.* **4.** to impose an excise on. [appar. < MD *excijs,* var. of *accijs* < ML *accīsa* tax, lit., a cut, n. use of fem. ptp. of L *accīdere* to cut into. See AC-, -CIDE]

ex·cise[2] (ik sīz′), *v.t.*, **-cised, -cis·ing. 1.** to expunge, as a passage or sentence, from a text. **2.** to cut out or off, as a tumor. [< L *excīs(us)* cut out, hewn down, ptp. of *excīdere* to EXCIDE] —**ex·cis′a·ble,** *adj.*

ex·cise·man (ek′sīz mən), *n.*, *pl.* **-men.** *Brit.* an officer who collects excise taxes and enforces excise laws. [EXCISE[1] + MAN[1]]

ex·ci·sion (ek sizh′ən, ik-), *n.* **1.** the act of removal; an excising. **2.** *Surg.* extirpation; resection. **3.** excommunication. [< L *excīsiōn-* (s. of *excīsiō*) a cutting out. See EXCISE[2], -ION]

ex·cit·a·bil·i·ty (ik sī′tə bil′i tē), *n.* **1.** the quality of being excitable. **2.** *Physiol.* irritability. [EXCITABLE + -ITY]

ex·cit·a·ble (ik sī′tə bəl), *adj.* **1.** capable of being excited. **2.** easily excited: *Prima donnas have the reputation of being excitable and temperamental.* [< LL *excitābil(is).* See EXCITE, -ABLE] —**ex·cit′a·ble·ness,** *n.* —**ex·cit′a·bly,** *adv.*
—**Syn. 2.** emotional, passionate, fiery. —**Ant. 2.** placid.

ex·cit·ant (ik sīt′ənt, ek′si tənt), *adj.* **1.** exciting; stimulating. —*n.* **2.** *Physiol.* something that excites; stimulant. [< L *excitant-* (s. of *excitāns*) calling forth, arousing. See EXCITE, -ANT]

ex·ci·ta·tion (ek′sī tā′shən), *n.* **1.** the act of exciting. **2.** the state of being excited. **3.** *Elect.* **a.** the application of voltage to an electric device, as an electron-tube circuit, an antenna, a dynamotor, or the like, often for producing a magnetic field in the device. **b.** the voltage applied. **4.** *Physics.* a process in which a molecule, atom, nucleus, or particle is excited. **5.** Also called **drive.** *Electronics.* the varying voltage applied to the control electrode of a vacuum tube. [ME *excitacioun* < L *excitātiōn-* (s. of *excitātiō*), equiv. to *excitāt(us)* (ptp. of *excitāre;* see EXCITE) + *-iōn-* -ION]

ex·cit·a·tive (ik sī′tə tiv), *adj.* tending to excite. Also, **ex·cit·a·to·ry** (ik sī′tə tôr′ē, -tōr′ē). [< F *excitatif* < L **excitātīv(us).* See EXCITATION, -IVE]

ex·cite (ik sīt′), *v.t.*, **-cit·ed, -cit·ing. 1.** to arouse or stir up the emotions or feelings of: *to excite a person to anger; His actions excite his father's wrath.* **2.** to arouse or stir up (emotions or feelings): *to excite jealousy or hatred.* **3.** to cause; awaken: *to excite interest or curiosity.* **4.** to stir to action; stir up: *to excite a dog by baiting him.* **5.** *Physiol.* to stimulate: *to excite a nerve.* **6.** *Elect.* to supply with electricity for producing electric activity or a magnetic field: *to excite a dynamo.* **7.** *Physics.* to raise (an atom, molecule, etc.) to an excited state. [ME < L *excit(āre),* freq. of *excīere* to set in motion, awaken, instigate, equiv. to *ex-* EX-[1] + *cīere* to set in motion]
—**Syn. 1.** stir, awaken, stimulate, animate, kindle, inflame. **2.** evoke. **4.** disturb, agitate, ruffle. —**Ant. 1.** calm, soothe.

ex·cit·ed (ik sī′tid), *adj.* **1.** stirred emotionally; agitated: *An excited crowd awaited the arrival of the famed statesman.* **2.** stimulated to activity; brisk: *an excited buying and selling of stocks.* [EXCITE + -ED[2]] —**ex·cit′ed·ly,** *adv.* —**ex·cit′ed·ness,** *n.*
—**Syn. 1.** ruffled, discomposed, stormy, perturbed, impassioned. **2.** eager, active, enthusiastic. —**Ant. 1.** calm.

excit′ed state′, *Physics.* any of the energy levels of a physical system, esp. an atom, molecule, etc., which has higher energy than the lowest energy level.

ex·cite·ment (ik sīt′mənt), *n.* **1.** an excited state or condition. **2.** something that excites. [late ME *excitament* < ML **excitāment(um).* See EXCITE, -MENT]
—**Syn. 1.** perturbation, commotion, ado. See **agitation.** —**Ant. 1.** serenity.

ex·cit·er (ik sī′tər), *n.* **1.** one who or that which excites. **2.** *Elect.* an auxiliary generator which supplies energy for the excitation of another electric machine. [ME; see EXCITE, -ER[1]]

excit′er lamp′, a lamp that produces a light which passes through a film sound track and impinges on a photoelective cell causing current fluctuations that actuate a loudspeaker.

ex·cit·ing (ik sī′ting), *adj.* producing excitement; stirring; thrilling: *an exciting account of his trip to Tibet.* [EXCITE + -ING[2]] —**ex·cit′ing·ly,** *adv.*

excit′ing cur′rent, *Elect.* See **field current.**

excito-, a combining form of **excitor** or **exciting:** *excitomotor.*

ex·ci·to·mo·tor (ik sī′tə mō′tər), *adj.* *Physiol.* causing an increase of motor activity: *excitomotor nerves.* Also, **ex·ci·to·mo·to·ry** (ik sī′tə mō′tə rē). [EXCITO- + MOTOR]

ex·ci·tor (ik sī′tər, -tôr), *n.* **1.** *Physiol.* a nerve whose stimulation excites greater action. **2.** *Archaic.* an exciter. [EXCITE + -OR[2]]

excl., 1. exclamation. 2. excluding. 3. exclusive.

ex·claim (ik sklām′), *v.i.* **1.** to cry out or speak suddenly and vehemently, as in surprise, strong emotion, protest, etc. —*v.t.* **2.** to cry out; say loudly or vehemently. [earlier *exclame* < L *exclām(āre)* (to) cry out. See EX-[1], CLAIM] —**ex·claim′er,** *n.*

exclam., 1. exclamation. 2. exclamatory.

ex·cla·ma·tion (ek′sklə mā′shən), *n.* **1.** the act of exclaiming; outcry; loud complaint or protest: *The speech was continually interrupted by rude exclamations.* **2.** an interjection. **3.** *Rhet.* ecphonesis. [ME *exclamacio(u)n* < L *exclāmātiōn-* (s. of *exclāmātiō*) a calling out, equiv. to *exclāmāt(us)* (ptp. of *exclāmāre;* see EXCLAIM) + *-iōn-* -ION] —**ex′cla·ma′tion·al,** *adj.*
—**Syn. 1.** cry, ejaculation, vociferation.

exclama′tion point′, **1.** the sign (!) used in writing after an exclamation. **2.** this mark sometimes used in writing two or more times in succession to indicate intensity of emotion, loudness, etc.: *Long live the Queen!!* **3.** this mark sometimes used without accompanying words in writing direct discourse to indicate a speaker's dumfounded astonishment: *"Rosette just gave birth to quintuplets." "!"* Also called **exclama′tion mark′.**

ex·clam·a·to·ry (ik sklam′ə tôr′ē, -tōr′ē), *adj.* **1.** using, containing, or expressing exclamation. **2.** pertaining to exclamation. [< L *exclāmāt(us)* called out (see EXCLAMATION) + -ORY[1]] —**ex·clam′a·to′ri·ly,** *adv.*

ex·clave (eks′klāv), *n.* a portion of a country geographically separated from the main part by surrounding alien territory: *West Berlin is an exclave of West Germany.* [EX-[1] + *-clave,* modeled on *enclave*]

ex·clo·sure (ik sklō′zhər), *n.* an area protected against any intruders, as by fences. [EX-[1] + *closure,* modeled on *enclosure*]

ex·clude (ik sklo͞od′), *v.t.*, **-clud·ed, -clud·ing. 1.** to shut or keep out; prevent the entrance of. **2.** to shut out from consideration, privilege, etc.: *Employees and their relatives were excluded from participation in the contest.* **3.** to expel and keep out; thrust out; eject: *He was excluded from the club for infractions of the rules.* [ME < L *exclūd(ere)* (to) shut out, cut off, equiv. to *ex-* EX-[1] + *clūd-* (var. s. of *claudere* to close)] —**ex·clud′a·bil′i·ty,** *n.* —**ex·clud′a·ble, ex·clud′i·ble,** *adj.* —**ex·clud′er,** *n.* —**ex·clu·so·ry** (ik sklo͞o′sə rē), *adj.*
—**Syn. 1.** bar, prohibit, except, omit, preclude. **2.** EXCLUDE, DEBAR, ELIMINATE mean to remove from a certain place, or from consideration in a particular situation. To EXCLUDE is to set aside as unwanted, unusable, etc.: *words excluded from polite conversation.* To DEBAR is to prohibit, esp. in a legal sense, from a place or from the enjoyment of privileges, rights, or the like: *to debar all candidates lacking the necessary preparation.* To ELIMINATE is to select and remove, esp. as irrelevant, unnecessary, or undesirable: *to eliminate such objections.* **3.** reject. —**Ant. 1.** include.

ex·clu·sion (ik sklo͞o′zhən), *n.* **1.** the act or an instance of excluding. **2.** the state of being excluded. **3.** *Physiol.* a keeping apart; blocking of an entrance. [late ME < L *exclūsiōn-* (s. of *exclūsiō*), equiv. to *exclūs(us)* shut out (ptp. of *exclūdere;* see EXCLUDE) + *-iōn-* -ION] —**ex·clu·si·ble** (ik sklo͞o′sə bəl), *adj.*

exclu′sion clause′, *Insurance.* a clause in a policy stipulating risks not covered in the policy.

ex·clu·sion·ism (ik sklo͞o′zhə niz′əm), *n.* the principle, policy, or practice of exclusion, as from rights or privileges. [EXCLUSION + -ISM] —**ex·clu′sion·ist, ex·clu′sion·er,** *n.*

exclu′sion prin′ciple, *Physics.* the principle that no two electrons, protons, or neutrons in a given system can be in states characterized by the same set of quantum numbers. Also called **Pauli exclusion principle.**

ex·clu·sive (ik sklo͞o′siv), *adj.* **1.** not admitting of something else; incompatible: *mutually exclusive plans of action.* **2.** excluding from consideration or account (often fol. by *of*): *a profit of ten percent, exclusive of taxes.* **3.** limited to the object or objects designated: *exclusive attention to business.* **4.** shutting out all others from a part or share: *an exclusive right to film the novel.* **5.** in which no others have a share: *exclusive information.* **6.** single or sole: *the exclusive means of communication between two places.* **7.** disposed to resist the admission of outsiders to association, intimacy, etc.: *an exclusive circle of intimate friends.* **8.** admitting only members of a socially restricted or very carefully selected group: *an exclusive club; an exclusive school.* **9.** *Logic.* excluding all except what is specified: *an exclusive proposition.* —*n.* **10.** *Journalism.* a piece of news, or the reporting of a piece of news, obtained by a newspaper or other news organization, along with the privilege of using it first: *The paper promised an exclusive on the Hollywood divorce.* [late ME < ML *exclūsīv(us).* See EXCLUSION, -IVE] —**ex·clu′sive·ly,** *adv.* —**ex·clu′sive·ness, ex·clu·siv·i·ty,** (eks′klo͞o siv′i tē), *n.*
—**Syn. 7.** select, narrow, clannish, snobbish, restrictive, cliquish, selfish, illiberal. —**Ant. 1, 2, 4.** inclusive.

exclu′sive disjunc′tion, *Logic.* See under **disjunction** (def. 2a).

exclu′sive representa′tion, *Labor.* the right of a union, chosen by a majority of the employees in a plant, craft, industry, or department of a shop or business, to represent all the employees in the unit, regardless of whether they are members of the union or not.

ex·clu·siv·ism (ik sklo͞o′sə viz′əm), *n.* the practice of being exclusive. [EXCLUSIVE + -ISM] —**ex·clu′siv·ist,** *n.* —**ex·clu′siv·is′tic,** *adj.*

ex·cog·i·tate (eks koj′i tāt′), *v.t.*, **-tat·ed, -tat·ing. 1.** to think out; devise; invent. **2.** to study intently and carefully in order to grasp or comprehend fully. [< L *excōgitāt(us)* deduced, devised, invented, ptp. of *excōgitāre.* See EX-[1], COGITATE] —**ex·cog·i·ta·ble** (eks koj′i tə bəl), *adj.* —**ex·cog′i·ta′tion,** *n.* —**ex·cog′i·ta′tive,** *adj.* —**ex·cog′i·ta′tor,** *n.*

ex·com·mu·ni·ca·ble (eks′kə myo͞o′nə kə bəl), *adj.* **1.** liable or deserving to be excommunicated, as a person. **2.** punishable by excommunication, as an offense. [EXCOMMUNIC(ATE) + -ABLE]

ex·com·mu·ni·cate (*v.* eks′kə myo͞o′nə kāt′; *n., adj.* eks′kə myo͞o′nə kit, -kāt′), *v.*, **-cat·ed, -cat·ing,** *n.*, *adj.* —*v.t.* **1.** to cut off from communion or membership, esp. from the sacraments and fellowship of the church by ecclesiastical sentence. —*n.* **2.** an excommunicated person. —*adj.* **3.** cut off from communion with the church; excommunicated. [late ME < LL *excommūnicāt(us),* lit., put out of the community (ptp. of *excommūnicāre*), equiv. to *ex-* EX-[1] + *commūn(is)* COMMON, public + *-ic-* (by analogy with *commūnicāre* to COMMUNICATE) + *-ātus* -ATE[1]] —**ex′com·mu′ni·ca′tor,** *n.*

ex·com·mu·ni·ca·tion (eks′kə myo͞o′nə kā′shən), *n.* **1.** the act of excommunicating. **2.** the state of being excommunicated. **3.** the ecclesiastical sentence by which a person is excommunicated. [late ME < LL *excommūnicātiōn-* (s. of *excommūnicātiō*). See EXCOMMUNICATE, -ION]

ex·com·mu·ni·ca·tive (eks′kə myo͞o′nə kā′tiv, -kə-tiv), *adj.* disposed or serving to excommunicate. [EXCOMMUNICATE + -IVE]

ex·com·mu·ni·ca·to·ry (eks′kə myo͞o′nə kə tôr′ē, -tōr′ē), *adj.* relating to or causing excommunication. [EXCOMMUNICATE + -ORY[1]]

ex·co·ri·ate (ik skôr′ē āt′, -skōr′-), *v.t.*, **-at·ed, -at·ing. 1.** to strip off or remove the skin from: *His palms were excoriated by the hard labor of shoveling.* **2.** to denounce or berate severely; flay verbally: *He was excoriated for his mistakes.* [late ME < L *excoriāt(us)* stripped, skinned (ptp. of *excoriāre*). See EX-[1], CORIUM, -ATE[1]]

ex·co·ri·a·tion (ik skôr′ē ā′shən, -skōr′-), *n.* **1.** the act of excoriating. **2.** the state of being excoriated. **3.** an excoriated place on the body. [ME *excoriacioun* < LL *excoriātiōn-* (s. of *excoriātiō*). See EXCORIATE, -ION]

ex·cor·ti·cate (eks kôr′tə kāt′), *v.t.*, **-cat·ed, -cat·ing.** decorticate. [late ME *excorticat* (adj.) < ML *excorticāt(us),* ptp. of *excorticāre* to peel. See EX-[1], CORTEX, -ATE]

ex·cre·ment (ek′skrə mənt), *n.* waste matter discharged from the body, esp. the feces. [< L *excrēment(um),* equiv. to *excrē-* (perf. s. of *excernere* to EXCRETE) + *-mentum* -MENT] —**ex·cre·men·tous** (ek′skrə men′təs) *adj.*

ex·cre·men·ti·tious (ek′skrə men tish′əs), *adj.* of or like excrement. Also, **ex·cre·men·tal** (ek′skrə men′tᵊl). [EXCREMENT + -ITIOUS] —**ex′cre·men·ti′tious·ly, ex′cre·men′tal·ly,** *adv.*

ex·cres·cence (ik skres′əns), *n.* **1.** abnormal growth or increase. **2.** an abnormal outgrowth, usually harmless, on an animal or vegetable body. **3.** a normal outgrowth, such as hair, horns, etc. **4.** any disfiguring addition. [late ME < L *excrēscentia.* See EXCRESCENT, -ENCE]

ex·cres·cen·cy (ik skres′ən sē), *n.* **1.** the act of excreting. **2.** the substance excreted, as sweat or urine or certain plant products. [var. of EXCRESCENCE; see -ENCY]

ex·cres·cent (ik skres′ənt), *adj.* **1.** growing abnormally out of something else; superfluous. **2.** *Phonet.* (of a speech sound) inserted or added as a result of articulatory interaction or impetus, as the *t*-sound in *sense* (sents) or *against* (from Middle English *ageynes*), without grammatical or historical justification; intrusive. [< L *excrēscent-* (s. of *excrēscēns*), prp. of *excrēscere.* See EX-[1], CRESCENT] **—ex·cres′cent·ly,** *adv.*

ex·cre·ta (ik skrē′tə), *n.pl.* excreted matter, as sweat, urine, feces, etc. [< L: things sifted out or separated, neut. pl. of *excrētus;* see EXCRETE] **—ex·cre′tal,** *adj.*

ex·crete (ik skrēt′), *v.t.,* **-cret·ed, -cret·ing.** to separate and eliminate from an organic body; separate and expel from the blood or tissues, as waste or harmful matters. [< L *excrēt(us)* (ptp. of *excernere*) sifted out, separated, equiv. to *ex-* EX-[1] + *crē-* (perf. s. of *cernere* to sift) + *-tus* ptp. suffix] **—ex·cret′er,** *n.* **—ex·cre′tive,** *adj.*

ex·cre·tion[1] (ik skrē′shən), *n.* **1.** act of excreting. **2.** the substance excreted, as sweat or urine, or certain plant products. [< L *excrētiōn-* (s. of *excrētiō*) that which is sifted out. See EXCRETE, -ION]

ex·cre·tion[2] (ik skrē′shən), *n.* **1.** state of being excrescent. **2.** an excrescence. [< LL *excretiōn-* (s. of *excretiō*), equiv. to L *excrēt(us)* (ptp. of *excrescere;* see EX-[1], CRESCENT) + *-iōn-* -ION]

ex·cre·to·ry (ek′skri tōr′ē, -tôr′ē, ik skrē′tə rē), *adj.* pertaining to or concerned in excretion; having the function of excreting: *excretory organs.* [EXCRETE + -ORY[1]]

ex·cru·ci·ate (ik skrōō′shē āt′), *v.t.,* **-at·ed, -at·ing.** **1.** to inflict severe pain upon; torture: *The headache excruciated him.* **2.** to cause mental anguish to; irritate greatly. [< L *excruciāt(us)* tormented greatly, tortured (ptp. of *excruciāre*). See EX-[1], CRUCIATE]

ex·cru·ci·at·ing (ik skrōō′shē ā′ting), *adj.* extremely painful; causing intense suffering; unbearably distressing; torturing: *an excruciating noise; an excruciating worry.* [EXCRUCIATE + -ING[2]] **—ex·cru′ci·at′ing·ly,** *adv.*

ex·cru·ci·a·tion (ik skrōō′shē ā′shən), *n.* **1.** the act of excruciating. **2.** the state of being excruciated. **3.** an instance of this; torture. [< L *excruciātiōn-* (s. of *excruciātiō*). See EXCRUCIATE, -ION]

ex·cu·bi·to·ri·um (ek skyōō′bi tōr′ē əm, -tôr′-), *n., pl.* **-to·ri·a** (-tōr′ē ə, -tôr′-). **1.** (in an ancient Roman city) a night watchman's post or sentry box. **2.** (in a monastery) a room for monks remaining awake during the night. [< L, equiv. to *excubit(us)* (ptp. of *excubāre* to watch, lit., lie out; see EX-[1], INCUBUS) + *-ōrium* -ORY[2]]

excud., excudit.

ex·cu·dit (eks kōō′dit), *Latin.* he printed or engraved (this); she printed or engraved (this). *Abbr.:* exc., excud.

ex·cul·pate (ek′skul pāt′, ik skul′pāt), *v.t.,* **-pat·ed, -pat·ing.** to clear from a charge of guilt or fault; free from blame; vindicate. [< L *exculpāt(us)* freed from blame, equiv. to *ex-* EX-[1] + *culpātus* blamed (ptp. of *culpāre;* see CULPABLE)] **—ex·cul·pa·ble** (ik skul′pə bəl), *adj.* **—ex′cul·pa′tion,** *n.*

ex·cul·pa·to·ry (ik skul′pə tōr′ē, -tôr′ē), *adj.* tending to clear from a charge of fault or guilt. [EXCULPATE + -ORY[1]]

ex·cur·rent (ik skûr′ənt, -skur′-), *adj.* **1.** running out or forth. **2.** *Zool.* giving passage outward; affording exit: *the excurrent canal of certain sponges.* **3.** *Bot.* **a.** having the axis prolonged so as to form an undivided main stem or trunk, as the stem of the spruce. **b.** projecting beyond the apex, as the midrib in certain leaves. [< L *excurrent-* (s. of *excurrēns*) running forth, prp. of *excurrere.* See EX-[1], CURRENT]

ex·cur·sion (ik skûr′zhən, -shən), *n.* **1.** a short journey or trip to some point for a special purpose, with the intention of a prompt return: *a pleasure excursion; a scientific excursion.* **2.** a trip on a train, ship, etc., at a reduced rate: *weekend excursions to seashore or mountain resorts.* **3.** the group of persons making such a journey: *an excursion of tourists.* **4.** deviation or digression: *excursions into futile philosophizing; excursions from the major theme.* **5.** *Physics.* the displacement of a body or a point from a mean position or neutral value, as in an oscillation. **6.** an accidental increase in the power level of a reactor, usually forcing its emergency shutdown. **7.** *Mach.* **a.** the range of stroke of any moving part. **b.** the stroke itself. **8.** *Obs.* a sally or raid. **—*v.i.*** **9.** to go on or take an excursion. **—*adj.*** **10.** of, pertaining to, or intended for use on excursions: *an excursion fare; an excursion bus.* [< L *excursiōn-* (s. of *excursiō*). See EXCURSUS, -ION] **—ex·cur′sion·al, ex·cur′sion·ar′y,** *adj.*

—Syn. 1. EXCURSION, JAUNT, JUNKET, TOUR are trips made primarily for pleasure. An EXCURSION is a short trip, often no more than a day's outing, made usually by a number of persons, as a result of special inducements (low fare, a special event, etc.): *an excursion at reduced rates.* JAUNT is a familiar term for a short, agreeable trip, now esp. by automobile: *Take a little jaunt to the country, over to a cousin's house.* JUNKET, with a still stronger suggestion of pleasure-seeking, is frequently applied to trips made ostensibly on official business, enjoyed at public expense: *the junket of a congressional committee.* A TOUR is a planned trip to celebrated places, to see interesting scenery, etc.: *a tour of Europe.*

ex·cur·sion·ist (ik skûr′zhə nist, -shə-), *n.* a person who goes on an excursion. [EXCURSION + -IST]

excur′sion tick′et, a round-trip ticket at a reduced fare to a resort, special event, etc.

ex·cur·sive (ik skûr′siv), *adj.* **1.** given to making excursions in speech, thought, etc.; wandering; digressive. **2.** of the nature of such excursions; rambling; desultory: *excursive conversation.* [< L *excurs(us)* (see EXCURSUS) + -IVE] **—ex·cur′sive·ly,** *adv.* **—ex·cur′sive·ness,** *n.*

ex·cur·sus (ek skûr′səs), *n., pl.* **-sus·es, -sus.** **1.** a detailed discussion of some point in a book, esp. one added as an appendix. **2.** a digression or incidental excursion, as in a narrative. [< L: a running out, sally, digression (ptp. of *excurrere*). See EX-[1], COURSE]

ex·cur·vate (eks kûr′vāt′, ik skûr′vit), *adj.* excurved. [EX-[1] + CURVE + -ATE[1]]

ex·cur·va·ture (eks kûr′və chər), *n.* the condition of being curved outward or away from the center. Also, **ex·cur·va·tion** (ek′skər vā′shən). [EX-[1] + CURVATURE]

ex·curved (ek′skûrvd), *adj.* curving or curved outward. Also, **excurvate.** [EX-[1] + CURVE + -ED[3]]

ex·cus·a·to·ry (ik skyōō′zə tōr′ē, -tôr′ē), *adj.* serving or intended to excuse. [late ME < ML *excūsātōri(us),* equiv. to LL *excūsātōr-* (s. of *excūsātor,* equiv. to *excūsāt(us),* ptp. of *excūsāre* to EXCUSE + *-or* -OR[2]) + *-ius* adj. suffix; see -ORY[1]]

ex·cuse (*v.* ik skyōōz′; *n.* ik skyōōs′), *v.,* **-cused, -cusing,** *n.* **—*v.t.*** **1.** to regard or judge with indulgence; pardon or forgive; overlook (a fault, error, etc.): *Excuse his bad manners.* **2.** to offer an apology for; apologize for; seek to remove the blame of: *He excused his absence by saying that he was ill.* **3.** to serve as an apology or justification for; justify: *Ignorance of the law excuses no man.* **4.** to release from an obligation or duty: *to be excused from attending a meeting.* **5.** to seek or obtain exemption or release for (oneself): *to excuse oneself from duty.* **6.** to refrain from exacting; remit; dispense with: *to excuse a debt.* **—*n.*** **7.** an explanation offered as a reason for being excused; a plea offered in extenuation of a fault or for release from an obligation, promise, etc.: *His excuse for being late was unacceptable.* **8.** something serving to excuse; a ground or reason for excusing: *Ignorance is no excuse.* **9.** the act of excusing: *He requested a chance to explain in excuse of his conduct.* **10.** a pretext or subterfuge: *He uses his poor health as an excuse for evading all responsibility.* **11.** an inferior or inadequate specimen of something specified: *That coward is barely an excuse for a man. His latest effort is a poor excuse for a novel.* [ME *excuse(n)* < L *excūsāre* to put outside, exonerate, equiv. to *ex-* EX-[1] + *-cūsāre,* deriv. of *causa* CAUSE; r. ME *escuse(n)* < MF *escuser*] **—ex·cus′a·ble,** *adj.* **—ex·cus′a·ble·ness,** *n.* **—ex·cus′a·bly,** *adv.* **—ex·cus′al,** *n.* **—ex·cuse′less,** *adj.* **—ex·cus′er,** *n.* **—ex·cus′ing·ly,** *adv.* **—ex·cus′ive,** *adj.* **—ex·cus′ive·ly,** *adv.*

—Syn. 1. EXCUSE, FORGIVE, PARDON imply being lenient or giving up the wish to punish. EXCUSE means to overlook some (usually) slight offense, because of circumstance, realization that it was unintentional, or the like: *to excuse bad manners.* FORGIVE is applied to excusing more serious offenses; the person wronged not only overlooks the offense but harbors no ill feeling against the offender: *to forgive and forget.* PARDON usually applies to a specific act of lenience or mercy by an official or superior in remitting all or the remainder of the punishment that belongs to a serious offense or crime: *The governor was asked to pardon the condemned criminal.* **3.** extenuate, palliate. **4.** free. **7.** justification. EXCUSE, APOLOGY both imply an explanation of some failure or failing. EXCUSE implies a desire to avoid punishment or rebuke. APOLOGY usually implies acknowledgment that one has been, at least seemingly, in the wrong; it may aim at setting matters right by either alleging extenuating circumstances, or expressing regret for an error. **10.** pretense, evasion, makeshift.

ex·cuss (ik skus′), *v.t. Law.* to take possession of (goods) by legal authority. [< L *excuss(us)* shaken out, driven out, sent forth (ptp. of *excutere*), equiv. to *ex-* EX-[1] + *-cussus,* var. of *quassus* shaken, disturbed, ptp. of *quatere*] **—ex·cus′sion,** *n.*

ex·cus·si·o (ek skush′ē ō′), *n. Civil Law.* the exhausting of every remedy against a principal debtor before proceeding against a surety. [< LL *excussiō.* See EXCUSS, -ION]

ex′ div′idend, *Stock Exchange.* without or not including a previously declared dividend. *Abbr.:* ex div. Cf. **cum dividend.**

Ex. Doc., executive document.

ex·e·at (ek′sē at′), *n.* **1.** permission granted by a bishop to a priest to leave his diocese. **2.** *Brit.* official permission for a student to be absent from a university. [n. use of L *exeat* let (him) go out, 3rd pers. sing. pres. subj. of *exīre* to go out]

exec., **1.** executive. **2.** executor.

ex·e·cra·ble (ek′sə krə bəl), *adj.* **1.** utterly detestable; abominable; abhorrent. **2.** very bad: *an execrable stage performance.* [ME: expressing a curse < L *ex(s)ecrābil(is)* accursed, detestable. See EXECRATE, -ABLE] **—ex′e·cra·ble·ness,** *n.* **—ex′e·cra·bly,** *adv.*

ex·e·crate (ek′sə krāt′), *v.,* **-crat·ed, -crat·ing.** **—*v.t.*** **1.** to detest utterly; abhor; abominate. **2.** to curse; imprecate evil upon; damn; denounce: *He execrated all who opposed him.* **—*v.i.*** **3.** to utter curses. [< L *ex(s)ecrāt(us)* cursed (ptp. of *execrārī*), equiv. to *ex-* EX-[1] + *sacr-* (root of *sacrāre;* see SACRAMENT) + *-ātus* -ATE[1]] **—ex′e·cra′tor,** *n.*

ex·e·cra·tion (ek′sə krā′shən), *n.* **1.** the act of execrating. **2.** a curse or imprecation: *The execrations of the prophet terrified the sinful multitude.* **3.** the object execrated; a thing held in abomination. [ME *execracioun* < L *ex(s)ecrātiōn-* (s. of *exsecrātiō*). See EXECRATE, -ION]

ex·e·cra·tive (ek′sə krā′tiv), *adj.* **1.** pertaining to or characterized by execration. **2.** prone to execrate. [EXECRATE + -IVE] **—ex′e·cra′tive·ly,** *adv.*

ex·e·cra·to·ry (ek′sə krə tōr′ē, -tôr′ē, -krā′tə rē), *adj.* **1.** pertaining to execration. **2.** having the nature of or containing an execration. [EXECRATE + -ORY[1]]

ex·ec·u·tant (ig zek′yə tənt), *n.* **1.** a person who executes or performs, esp. musically. **—*adj.*** **2.** of or pertaining to a performer, esp. a musician. **3.** performing, esp. in public. [< F *exécutant.* See EXECUTE, -ANT]

ex·e·cute (ek′sə kyōōt′), *v.t.,* **-cut·ed, -cut·ing.** **1.** to carry out; accomplish: *to execute a plan or order.* **2.** to perform or do: *to execute a maneuver or gymnastic feat.* **3.** to inflict capital punishment on; put to death according to law. **4.** to produce in accordance with a plan or design: *to execute a statue; a painting executed by an unknown artist of the 16th century.* **5.** to perform or play (a piece of music): *to execute a violin concerto with supreme virtuosity.* **6.** *Law.* **a.** to give effect or force to (a law, decree, judicial sentence, etc.). **b.** to carry out the terms of (a will). **c.** to transact or carry through (a contract, mortgage, etc.) in the manner prescribed by law; complete and give validity to (a legal instrument) by fulfilling the legal requirements, as by signing, sealing, etc. [ME *execute(n),* back formation from EXECUTOR] **—ex′e·cut′a·ble,** *adj.* **—ex′e·cut′er,** *n.*

—Syn. 1. achieve, complete, finish, consummate. **2.** See **perform. 3.** See **kill**[1]. **6a.** enforce, administer.

ex·e·cu·tion (ek′sə kyōō′shən), *n.* **1.** the act or process of executing. **2.** the state or fact of being executed. **3.** the infliction of capital punishment or, formerly, of any legal punishment. **4.** the process of performing a judgment or sentence of a court: *The judge stayed execution of the sentence pending appeal.* **5.** a mode or style of performance; technical skill, as in music: *The pianist's execution of the sonata was consummate.* **6.** effective, usually destructive action, or the result attained by it (usually prec. by *do*): *The grenades did rapid execution.* **7.** *Law.* a judicial writ directing the enforcement of a judgment. [ME *execucioun* < L *execūtiōn-* (s. of *execūtiō*). See EXECUTIVE, -ION] **—ex′e·cu′tion·al,** *adj.*

ex·e·cu·tion·er (ek′sə kyōō′shə nər), *n.* **1.** an official who inflicts capital punishment in pursuance of a legal warrant. **2.** a person who executes an act, will, judgment, etc. [EXECUTION + -ER[1]]

ex·ec·u·tive (ig zek′yə tiv), *n.* **1.** a person or group of persons having administrative or supervisory authority, as in a company. **2.** the person or persons in whom the supreme executive power of a government is vested. **3.** the executive branch of a government. **—*adj.*** **4.** of, for, pertaining to, or suited for carrying out plans, duties, etc.: *executive ability.* **5.** pertaining to or charged with the execution of laws or the administration of public affairs: *executive appointments; executive committees.* **6.** designed for or used by executives: *an executive dining room.* [ME < ML *execūtīv(us),* equiv. to L *execūt(us)* followed up, performed (ptp. of *ex(s)equī;* see EX-[1], SEQUENCE) + *-īvus* -IVE] **—ex·ec′u·tive·ly,** *adv.* **—ex·ec′u·tive·ness,** *n.*

exec′utive agree′ment, *U.S.* an agreement, usually pertaining to administrative matters and less formal than an international treaty, made between chiefs of state without senatorial approval.

exec′utive coun′cil, **1.** a council having the highest executive authority. **2.** a council appointed to give advice to the head of a government.

Exec′utive Man′sion, *U.S.* **1.** the official residence of the governor of a State. **2.** See **White House** (def. 1).

Exec′utive Of′fice of the Pres′ident, *U.S.* a group of federal agencies supervised by directors or staffs that work directly with the President or a presidential assistant.

exec′utive or′der, (*usually cap.*) an order issued by the President of the U.S. to the army, navy, or other part of the executive branch of the Government.

exec′utive ses′sion, *Govt.* a session, generally closed to the public, of a legislative body or its leaders.

ex·ec·u·tor (ig zek′yə tər), *n.* **1.** a person who executes, carries out, or performs some duty, job, assignment, artistic work, etc. **2.** *Law.* a person named by a decedent in his will to carry out the provisions of his will. [ME *executour* < ML *execūtor,* equiv. to L *execūt(us)* (see EXECUTIVE) + *-or* -OR[2]; r. ME *esecutor* < AF *essecutour*] **—ex·ec·u·to·ri·al** (ig zek′yə tōr′ē əl, -tôr′-), *adj.* **—ex·ec′u·tor·ship′,** *n.*

ex·ec·u·to·ry (ig zek′yə tōr′ē, -tôr′ē), *adj.* **1.** executive. **2.** *Law.* to be performed or executed. [ME *executorie* operative, being in effect < LL *ex(s)ecūtōri(us)* executive. See EXECUTOR, -ORY[1]]

ex·ec·u·trix (ig zek′yə triks), *n., pl.* **ex·ec·u·tri·ces** (ig zek′yə trī′sēz), **ex·ec·u·trix·es.** *Law.* a female executor. [ME < L; see EXECUTOR, -TRIX]

ex·ed·ra (ek′si drə, ek sē′-), *n., pl.* **ex·ed·rae** (ek′si-drē′, ek sē′drē). **1.** (in ancient Greece and Rome) a room or covered area open on one side, used as a meeting place. **2.** a permanent outdoor bench, semicircular in plan and having a high back. Also, **exhedra.** [< L: hall furnished with seats < Gk: (covered) walk with seats, equiv. to *ex-* EX-[3] + *hédra* seat, bench] **—ex′e·dral,** *adj.*

ex·e·ge·sis (ek′si jē′sis), *n., pl.* **-ses** (-sēz). critical explanation or interpretation, esp. of Scripture. [< Gk *exḗgēsis* an interpretation, explanation, equiv. to *ex-* EX-[3] + *ēge-* (verbid s. of *hēgéesthai* to guide) + *-sis* -SIS]

ex·e·gete (ek′si jēt′), *n.* a person skilled in exegesis. [< Gk *exēgētḗs* guide, director, interpreter, equiv. to *exēgē-* (see EXEGESIS) + *-tēs* agent suffix]

ex·e·get·ic (ek′si jet′ik), *adj.* pertaining to exegesis; expository. Also, **ex′e·get′i·cal.** [< Gk *exēgētik(ós),* equiv. to *exēgēt(ḗs)* EXEGETE + *-ikos* -IC] **—ex′e·get′i·cal·ly,** *adv.*

ex·e·get·ics (ek′si jet′iks), *n.* (*construed as sing.*) the science of exegesis; exegetical theology. [see EXEGETIC, -ICS]

ex·e·gi mo·nu·men·tum ae·re pe·ren·ni·us (eks-e′gē mō′nōō men′tōōm ī′re pe ren′ē ōōs′; *Eng.* ek-sē′jī mon′yə men′təm ēr′ē pə ren′ē əs), *Latin.* I have made a monument more lasting than bronze.

ex·em·pla (ig zem′plə), *n.* pl. of **exemplum.**

ex·em·plar (ig zem′plər, -plär), *n.* **1.** a model or pattern to be copied or imitated: *Washington is the exemplar of patriotic virtue.* **2.** a typical example or instance. **3.** an original or archetype: *Plato thought nature but a copy of ideal exemplars.* **4.** a copy of a book or text. [ME < L, var. of *exemplāre,* n. use of neut. of *exemplāris* EXEMPLARY; r. ME *exaumplere* < MF *examplaire*]

ex·em·plar·ism (ig zem′plə riz′əm), *n.* **1.** *Theol.* the doctrine that all knowledge is based on the perception of the exemplars of reality which exist in the mind of God. **2.** the doctrine that the death of Christ is of service to man solely as an exemplar of perfect love and self-surrender. [EXEMPLAR + -ISM]

ex·em·pla·ry (ig zem′plə rē, eg′zəm pler′ē), *adj.* **1.** worthy of imitation; commendable: *the exemplary conduct of our war heroes.* **2.** serving as a warning: *an exemplary penalty.* **3.** serving as a model or pattern: *The authoritative and exemplary text of the work is in the Bodleian Library at Oxford University.* **4.** serving as an illustration or specimen; illustrative; typical: *The sentences read are exemplary of the style of the essay as a whole.* **5.** of, pertaining to, or composed of exempla: *the exemplary literature of the medieval period.* [< L *exemplār(is).* See

EXEMPLUM, -ARY] —**ex·em′pla·ri·ly,** *adv.* —**ex·em′pla·ri·ness, ex′em·plar′i·ty,** *n.*

exem′plary dam′ages, *Law.* damages awarded to a plaintiff in excess of due compensation for his injury to punish the defendant for wanton or reckless behavior causing the injury. Also called **punitive damages.** Cf. **compensatory damages.**

ex·em·pli cau·sa (ek sem′plē kou′sä), *Latin.* See **e.c.**

ex·em·pli·fi·ca·tion (ig zem′plə fə kā′shən), *n.* **1.** the act of exemplifying. **2.** that which exemplifies; an illustration or example. **3.** *Law.* an attested copy of a document, under official seal. [late ME < ML *exemplificātiōn-* (s. of *exemplificātiō*) a setting forth, equiv. to *exemplificāt(us)* (ptp. of *exemplificāre* to EXEMPLIFY) + *-iōn-* -ION]

ex·em·pli·fi·ca·tive (ig zem′plə fə kā′tiv), *adj.* serving to exemplify. [EXEMPLIFICAT(ION) + -IVE]

ex·em·pli·fy (ig zem′plə fī′), *v.t.*, **-fied, -fy·ing. 1.** to show or illustrate by example. **2.** to furnish or serve as an example of: *The plays of Wilde exemplify the comedy of manners.* **3.** *Law.* to transcribe or copy; make an attested copy of (a document) under seal. [ME *exemplifie(n)* < MF *exemplifie(r)* < ML *exemplificāre* to copy. See EXEMPLUM, -IFY] —**ex·em′pli·fi′a·ble,** *adj.* —**ex·em′pli·fi′er,** *n.*

ex·em·pli gra·ti·a (ek sem′plē grä′tē ä′; *Eng.* ig zem′plī grā′shē ə), *Latin.* See **e.g.**

ex·em·plum (ig zem′pləm), *n., pl.* **-pla** (-plə). **1.** an anecdote that illustrates or supports a moral point, as in a medieval sermon. **2.** an example. [< LL, L: lit., a pattern, model, copy]

ex·empt (ig zempt′), *v.t.* **1.** to free from an obligation or liability to which others are subject; release: *to exempt someone from military service or from an examination.* —*adj.* **2.** released from, or not subject to, an obligation, liability, etc.: *persons exempt from taxes.* —*n.* **3.** a person who is exempt from, or not subject to, an obligation, duty, etc. **4.** (in Britain) exon. [ME *exempt(en)* < L *exempt(us)* (ptp. of *eximere*) taken out, freed, released, equiv. to *ex-* EX-[1] + *emptus* (ptp. of *emere* to buy, obtain)] —**ex·empt′i·ble,** *adj.*

exempt′ car′rier, a company operating vehicles performing services or carrying goods, as taxicabs or cargo trucks, that are not subject to the regulatory laws of the Interstate Commerce Act.

ex·emp·tion (ig zemp′shən), *n.* **1.** *U.S.* the circumstances of a taxpayer, as age, number of dependents, etc., that allow him to make certain deductions from his taxable income. **2.** the act of exempting. **3.** the state of being exempted; immunity. [late ME < L *exemptiōn-* (s. of *exemptiō*) removal. See EXEMPT, -ION] —**ex·emp′tive,** *adj.*

—**Syn. 3.** exception. EXEMPTION, IMMUNITY, IMPUNITY imply special privilege or freedom from requirements imposed upon others. EXEMPTION implies release or privileged freedom from sharing with others some (usually arbitrarily imposed) duty, tax, etc.: *exemption from military service.* IMMUNITY implies freedom from a penalty or from some natural or common liability, esp. one that is disagreeable or threatening: *immunity from disease.* IMPUNITY (limited mainly to the fixed expression *with impunity*) primarily suggests freedom from punishment: *The police force was so inadequate that crimes could be committed with impunity.* —**Ant. 3.** liability.

ex·en·ter·ate (*v.* ek sen′tə rāt′; *adj.* ek sen′tər it), *v.*, **-at·ed, -at·ing,** *adj.* —*v.t.* **1.** to remove the contents of; disembowel; eviscerate. —*adj.* **2.** *Surg.* eviscerate. [< L *exenterāt(us)* disemboweled, drawn (ptp. of *exenterāre*), equiv. to *ex-* EX-[1] + *enter-* (< Gk *éntera* entrails) + *-ātus* -ATE[1]] —**ex·en′ter·a′tion,** *n.*

ex·e·qua·tur (ek′sə kwā′tər), *n.* **1.** a written recognition of a consul by the government of the state in which he is stationed authorizing him to exercise his powers. **2.** an authorization granted by a secular ruler for the publication of papal bulls or other ecclesiastical enactments to give them binding force. [< L: lit., he may perform, 3rd pers. sing. pres. subj. of *exequī.* See EXEQUY]

ex·e·quy (ek′sə kwē), *n., pl.* **-quies. 1.** Usually, **exequies.** a funeral rite or ceremony; obsequy. **2.** a funeral procession. [ME *exequies* (pl.) < ML, L *exequiae,* lit., train of followers, equiv. to *exequ-* follow to the grave (s. of *exequī,* equiv. to *ex-* EX-[1] + *sequī* to follow) + *-ae* n. pl. suffix] —**ex·e·qui·al** (ek sē′kwē əl), *adj.*

ex·er·cise (ek′sər sīz′), *n., v.*, **-cised, -cis·ing.** —*n.* **1.** bodily or mental exertion, esp. for the sake of training or improvement. **2.** something done or performed as a means of practice or training: *exercises for the piano.* **3.** a putting into action, use, operation, or effect: *the exercise of caution or care; the exercise of will power.* **4.** a written composition, musical piece, or artistic work executed for practice or to illustrate a particular aspect of technique. **5.** a literary, artistic, or musical performance whose intrinsic value is technical rather than aesthetic. **6.** Often, **exercises.** a ceremony: *graduation exercises.* **7.** a religious observance or service. —*v.t.* **8.** to put through exercises, or forms of practice or exertion, designed to train, develop, condition, etc.: *to exercise troops; to exercise a horse.* **9.** to put (faculties, rights, etc.) into action, practice, or use: *to exercise one's strength; to exercise freedom of speech.* **10.** to use or display in one's action or procedure: *to exercise caution, patience, and judgment.* **11.** to make use of (one's privileges, powers, etc.): *to exercise one's constitutional rights.* **12.** to discharge (a function); perform: *to exercise the duties of one's office.* **13.** to have as an effect: *to exercise an influence on someone.* **14.** to worry; make uneasy; annoy: *to be much exercised about one's health.* —*v.i.* **15.** to go through exercises; take bodily exercise. [ME < MF *exercice* < L *exercitium,* equiv. to *exercit(us)* drilled, ptp. of *exercēre* to train (*ex-* EX-[1] + *-ercēre,* comb. form of *arcēre* to restrain) + *-ium* n. suffix] —**ex′er·cis′a·ble,** *adj.*

—**Syn. 1.** activity; calisthenics, gymnastics. **2.** EXERCISE, DRILL, PRACTICE refer to activities undertaken for training in some skill. An EXERCISE may be either physical or mental, and may be more or less irregular in time and varied in kind: *an exercise in arithmetic.* DRILL is disciplined repetition of set exercises, often performed in a group, directed by a leader: *military drill.* PRACTICE is methodical exercise, usually characterized by much repetition, with a view to becoming perfect in some operation or pursuit and to acquiring further skills: *Even great musicians require constant practice.* **3.** employment, application, practice, performance. **7.** ritual. **8.** discipline, drill, school. **10.** employ, apply, exert, practice. **14.** try, trouble. —**Ant. 1.** inaction.

ex·er·cis·er (ek′sər sī′zər), *n.* **1.** one who or that which exercises. **2.** an athletic device or machine employed in exercising. **3.** a groom in a stable responsible for exercising horses. [EXERCISE + -ER[1]]

ex·er·ci·ta·tion (ig zûr′si tā′shən), *n.* **1.** exercise or exertion, as of the faculties or powers of the body or mind: *an exercitation of the imagination.* **2.** practice or training: *exercitations in logical thinking.* **3.** the performance of a religious observance; an act of worship. **4.** a disquisition or discourse performed as a display of skill. [ME *exercitacioun* < L *exercitātiōn-* (s. of *exercitātiō*) exercise, practice, equiv. to *exercitāt(us)* exercised (ptp. of *exercitāre,* freq. of *exercēre;* see EXERCISE) + *-iōn-* -ION]

ex·er·gon·ic (ek′sər gon′ik), *adj.* *Biochem.* (of a biochemical reaction) liberating energy. Cf. **endergonic.** [EX-[2] + Gk *érgon* work + -IC]

ex·ergue (ig zûrg′, ek′sûrg), *n.* the space below the device on a coin or medal, sometimes separated from the field by a line. [< F, appar. < Gk *ex-* EX-[3] + *érg(on)* work] —**ex·ergu·al** (ig zûr′gəl), *adj.*

ex·ert (ig zûrt′), *v.t.* **1.** to put forth, as power; exercise, as ability or influence; put into vigorous action: *to exert every effort.* **2.** to put (oneself) into strenuous, vigorous action or effort. [< L *exert(us)* (ptp. of *exserere*) thrust out, equiv. to *ex-* EX-[1] + *ser-* bind together + *-tus* ptp. suffix] —**ex·er′tive,** *adj.*

ex·er·tion (ig zûr′shən), *n.* **1.** vigorous action or effort: *physical and mental exertion.* **2.** an effort: *a great exertion to help others.* **3.** exercise, as of power or faculties: *His studies required little intellectual exertion on his part.* **4.** an instance of this. [EXERT + -ION]

—**Syn. 1.** endeavor, struggle, attempt, activity, strain. See **effort.**

Ex·e·ter (ek′si tər), *n.* **1.** a city in and the county seat of Devonshire, in SW England: cathedral. 80,215 (1961). **2.** a town in SE New Hampshire. 5896 (1960). **3.** a town in central Pennsylvania. 4747 (1960). **4.** a town in central California. 4264 (1960).

ex·e·unt (ek′sē ənt), *v.i.* (they) go offstage (used as a stage direction, usually preceding the names of the characters): *Exeunt John and Bill.* [< L]

ex·e·unt om·nes (ek′sē ənt om′nēz), they all go out (used as a stage direction). [< L]

ex fa·ci·e (eks fā′shē ē′), *Law.* (of a document) considered on the basis of its face; apparently: *The contract was ex facie satisfactory.* [< L: on the face, from the face]

ex fac·to (eks fäk′tō; *Eng.* eks fak′tō), *Latin.* according to fact; actually.

ex·fo·li·ate (eks fō′lē āt′), *v.*, **-at·ed, -at·ing.** —*v.t.* **1.** to throw off in scales, splinters, etc. **2.** to remove the surface of (a bone, the skin, etc.) in scales or laminae. —*v.i.* **3.** to throw off scales or flakes; peel off in thin fragments: *The bark of some trees exfoliates.* **4.** *Geol.* **a.** to split or swell into a scaly aggregate, as certain minerals when heated. **b.** to separate into rudely concentric layers or sheets, as certain rocks during weathering. **5.** *Surg.* to separate and come off in scales, as scaling skin or any structure separating in flakes. [< LL *exfoliāt(us)* stripped of leaves, ptp. of *exfoliāre.* See EX-[1], FOLIATE] —**ex·fo·li·a·tive** (eks fō′lē ā′tiv, -ə tiv), *adj.*

ex·fo·li·a·tion (eks fō′lē ā′shən), *n.* **1.** the act or state of exfoliating. **2.** the state of being exfoliated. **3.** that which is exfoliated or scaled off. [*exfoliātiōn-* (s. of *exfoliātiō*). See EXFOLIATE, -ION]

ex·hal·ant (eks hā′lənt, ig zā′-), *adj.* **1.** exhaling; emitting. —*n.* **2.** that which exhales, as the ducts of certain mollusks. [< L *exhālant-* (s. of *exhālāns*), prp. of *exhālāre* to EXHALE; see -ANT]

ex·ha·la·tion (eks′hə lā′shən, eg′zə-), *n.* **1.** the act of exhaling. **2.** that which is exhaled; vapor; emanation. [ME *exalacion* < L *exhālātiōn-* (s. of *exhālātiō*). See EXHALE, -ATION]

ex·hale (eks hāl′, ig zāl′), *v.*, **-haled, -hal·ing.** —*v.i.* **1.** to emit breath or vapor. **2.** to pass off as vapor; pass off as an effluence. —*v.t.* **3.** to breathe out; emit (air, vapor, sound, etc.): *to exhale a sigh.* **4.** to give off as vapor: *The engine exhaled steam.* **5.** to draw out as a vapor or effluence; evaporate. [late ME *exale* < L *exhāl(āre),* equiv. to *ex-* EX-[1] + *hālāre* to breathe]

ex·haust (ig zôst′), *v.t.* **1.** to use up or consume completely; expend the whole of: *He exhausted a fortune in speculation.* **2.** to drain of strength or energy, wear out, or fatigue greatly, as a person: *I have exhausted myself working.* **3.** to draw out all that is essential in (a subject, topic, etc.); treat or study thoroughly. **4.** to empty by drawing out the contents: *to exhaust a tank of fuel oil.* **5.** to create a vacuum in. **6.** to draw out or drain off completely. **7.** to deprive wholly of useful or essential properties, possessions, resources, etc. **8.** to deprive of ingredients by the use of solvents, as a drug. **9.** to destroy the fertility of (soil), as by intensive cultivation. —*v.i.* **10.** to pass out or escape, as spent steam from the cylinder of an engine. —*n. Mach.* **11.** the escape of steam or gases from the cylinder of an engine. **12.** the steam or gases ejected. **13.** the parts of an engine through which the exhaust is ejected. [< L *exhaust(us)* emptied out, drained out, ptp. of *exhaurīre*] —**ex·haust′er,** *n.* —**ex·haust′i·bil′i·ty,** *n.* —**ex·haust′i·ble,** *adj.* —**ex·haust′ing·ly,** *adv.*

—**Syn. 1.** waste, squander, spend, dissipate. **2.** tire, enervate, prostrate, debilitate. See **tired**[1]. **4.** void. **12.** fumes, smoke, vapor. —**Ant. 2.** strengthen, invigorate. **4.** fill.

exhaust′ fan′, a fan for ventilating an interior by drawing air from the interior and expelling it outside.

ex·haus·tion (ig zôs′chən, -zôsh′-), *n.* **1.** the act or state of exhausting. **2.** the state of being exhausted. **3.** extreme weakness or fatigue. [< NL *exhaustiōn-* (s. of *exhaustiō*). See EXHAUST, -ION]

—**Syn. 3.** weariness, lassitude.

ex·haus·tive (ig zôs′tiv), *adj.* **1.** exhausting a subject, topic, etc.; comprehensive; thorough: *He published an exhaustive study of Roman ruins.* **2.** tending to exhaust or drain, as of resources or strength: *a protracted, exhaustive siege of illness.* [EXHAUST + -IVE] —**ex·haust′ive·ly,** *adv.* —**ex·haust′ive·ness,** *n.*

ex·haust·less (ig zôst′lis), *adj.* inexhaustible. [EXHAUST + -LESS] —**ex·haust′less·ly,** *adv.* —**ex·haust′less·ness,** *n.*

exhaust′ veloc′ity, *Rocketry.* the velocity, relative to a rocket, at which exhaust gases leave the nozzle of the rocket's engine.

ex·he·dra (ek sē′drə, eks hē′-), *n., pl.* **-drae** (-drē). exedra.

ex·hib·it (ig zib′it), *v.t.* **1.** to offer or expose to view; present for inspection. **2.** to manifest or display: *to exhibit anger; to exhibit interest.* **3.** to place on show: *to exhibit paintings.* **4.** to make manifest; explain. **5.** *Law.* to submit (a document, object, etc.) in evidence in a court of law. **6.** *Med. Obs.* to administer (something) as a remedy. —*v.i.* **7.** to make or give an exhibition; present something to public view. —*n.* **8.** an act or instance of exhibiting; exhibition. **9.** that which is exhibited. **10.** an object or a collection of objects shown in an exhibition, fair, etc. **11.** *Law.* a document or object exhibited in court and referred to and identified in written evidence. [late ME < L *exhibit(us)* held out, shown (ptp. of *exhibēre*), equiv. to *ex-* EX-[1] + *-hib-* (var. s. of *habēre* to have) + *-itus* -ITE[2]] —**ex·hib′it·a·ble,** *adj.* —**ex·hib′i·tor, ex·hib′it·er, ex·hib′it·ant,** *n.*

—**Syn. 1.** show, demonstrate. See **display. 2.** evince, disclose, betray, show, reveal. **8.** showing, show, display, exposition. **9, 11.** See **evidence. 10.** display. —**Ant. 2.** conceal.

ex·hi·bi·tion (ek′sə bish′ən), *n.* **1.** an exhibiting, showing, or presenting to view. **2.** a public display, as of the work of artists or craftsmen, the products of farms or factories, the skills of performers, objects of general interest, etc. **3.** *Chiefly Brit.* an exposition; a large fair of extended duration, as a World's Fair. **4.** an allowance given to a student in an English college, university, or school, usually upon the result of a competitive examination. **5.** *Med. Obs.* administration, as of a remedy. [ME *exhibicion* < LL *exhibitiōn-* (s. of *exhibitiō*) a presenting. See EXHIBIT, -ION]

ex·hi·bi·tion·er (ek′sə bish′ə nər), *n.* a student who receives an exhibition. [EXHIBITION + -ER[1]]

ex·hi·bi·tion·ism (ek′sə bish′ə niz′əm), *n.* **1.** a tendency to display one's abilities or to behave in such a way as to attract attention: *Some actors are notorious for their exhibitionism.* **2.** *Psychiatry.* the attaining of sexual gratification by exhibiting and attracting attention to the genitals. [EXHIBITION + -ISM]

ex·hi·bi·tion·ist (ek′sə bish′ə nist), *n.* **1.** a person who desires to make an exhibition of himself or his powers, personality, etc. **2.** *Psychiatry.* a person affected with the compulsions of exhibitionism. [EXHIBITION + -IST] —**ex′hi·bi′tion·is′tic,** *adj.*

ex·hib·i·tive (ig zib′i tiv), *adj.* serving for exhibition; tending to exhibit. [< NL *exhibitīv(us).* See EXHIBIT, -IVE] —**ex·hib′i·tive·ly,** *adv.*

ex·hib·i·to·ry (ig zib′i tōr′ē, -tôr′ē), *adj.* pertaining to or intended for exhibition or display. [< LL *exhibitōri(us)* relating to showing, displaying. See EXHIBIT, -ORY[1]]

ex·hil·a·rant (ig zil′ər ənt), *adj.* **1.** exhilarating. —*n.* **2.** something that exhilarates. [< L *exhilarant-* (s. of *exhilarāns*) gladdening, cheering, prp. of *exhilarāre.* See EXHILARATE, -ANT]

ex·hil·a·rate (ig zil′ə rāt′), *v.t.*, **-rat·ed, -rat·ing. 1.** to make cheerful or merry. **2.** to enliven; invigorate; stimulate: *The cold weather exhilarated the walkers.* [< L *exhilarāt(us)* greatly gladdened, cheered, ptp. of *exhilarāre,* equiv. to *ex-* EX-[1] + *hilarāre* to cheer (see HILARITY); see -ATE[1]] —**ex·hil′a·rat′ing·ly,** *adv.* —**ex·hil′a·ra′tor,** *n.*

—**Syn. 1.** cheer, gladden. **2.** animate, inspirit, elate. —**Ant. 1.** depress.

ex·hil·a·ra·tion (ig zil′ə rā′shən), *n.* **1.** exhilarated condition or feeling. **2.** the act of exhilarating. [< LL *exhilarātiōn-* (s. of *exhilarātiō*). See EXHILARATE, -ION]

—**Syn. 1.** animation, joyousness, gaiety, jollity, hilarity.

ex·hil·a·ra·tive (ig zil′ə rā′tiv, -ər ə tiv), *adj.* tending to exhilarate. Also, **ex·hil·a·ra·to·ry** (ig zil′ər ə tōr′ē, -tôr′ē). [EXHILARATE + -IVE]

ex·hort (ig zôrt′), *v.t.* **1.** to urge, advise, or caution earnestly; admonish urgently. —*v.i.* **2.** to make exhortation; give admonition. [late ME *ex(h)orte* < L *exhort(ārī)* (to) encourage greatly, equiv. to *ex-* EX-[1] + *hortārī* to urge] —**ex·hort′er,** *n.* —**ex·hort′ing·ly,** *adv.*

ex·hor·ta·tion (eg′zôr tā′shən, ek′sôr-), *n.* **1.** the act or process of exhorting. **2.** an utterance, discourse, or address conveying urgent advice or recommendations. [ME *exhortacion* < L *exhortātiōn-* (s. of *exhortātiō*) a pleading, urging. See EXHORTATIVE, -ION]

—**Syn. 1, 2.** See **advice.**

ex·hor·ta·tive (ig zôr′tə tiv), *adj.* **1.** serving or intended to exhort. **2.** pertaining to exhortation. Also, **ex·hor·ta·to·ry** (ig zôr′tə tōr′ē, -tôr′ē). [late ME < L *exhortātīv(us),* equiv. to *exhortāt(us)* (ptp. of *exhortārī* to EXHORT) + *-īvus* -IVE] —**ex·hor′ta·tive·ly,** *adv.*

ex·hume (ig zōōm′, -zyōōm′, eks hyōōm′), *v.t.*, **-humed, -hum·ing. 1.** to dig (something buried, esp. a dead body) out of the earth; disinter. **2.** to revive or restore after neglect or a period of forgetting; bring to light: *to exhume a literary reputation; to exhume old letters.* [late ME < ML *exhumāre,* equiv. to L *ex-* EX-[1] + *humāre* to inter] —**ex·hu·ma·tion** (eks′hyōō mā′shən), *n.* —**ex·hum′er,** *n.*

ex·i·geant (ek′si jənt; *Fr.* eg zē zhäN′), *adj.* exigent. Also, *referring to a woman,* **ex·i·geante** (ek′si jənt; *Fr.* eg zē zhäNt′). [< F]

ex·i·gen·cy (ek′si jən sē), *n., pl.* **-cies. 1.** exigent state or character; urgency. **2.** Usually, **exigencies.** the need, demand, or requirement intrinsic to a circumstance, condition, etc.: *the exigencies of city life.* **3.** a case or situation wihch demands prompt action or remedy; emergency: *He promised help in any exigency.* Also, **ex′i·gence.** [< ML *exigentia.* See EXIGENT, -ENCY]

ex·i·gent (ek′si jənt), *adj.* **1.** requiring immediate action or aid; urgent; pressing. **2.** requiring a great deal, or more than is reasonable. Also, **exigeant.** [ME < L *exigent-* (s. of *exigēns*) driving out, demanding (prp. of *exigere*), equiv. to *ex-* EX-[1] + *-ig-* drive (var. s. of *agere*) + *-ent-* -ENT] —**ex′i·gent·ly,** *adv.*

ex·i·gi·ble (ek′si jə bəl), *adj.* liable to be exacted; requirable. [< F; see EXIGENT, -IBLE]

ex·ig·u·ous (ig zig′yōō əs, ik sig′-), *adj.* scanty; meager; small; slender: *a merely exiguous income.* [< L *exiguus* scanty in measure or number, small, equiv. to *exig(ere)* (see EXIGENT) + *-u-* (unexplained) + *-us*

-OUS] —**ex·i·gu·i·ty** (ek′sə gyōō′i tē), **ex·ig′u·ous·ness,** *n.* —**ex·ig′u·ous·ly,** *adv.*

ex·i·larch (eg′zə lärk′, ek′sə-), *n.* a hereditary ruler of the Jewish community in Babylonia from about the 2nd century A.D. to the beginning of the 11th century. [EXILE + Gk *arch(ós)* leader]

ex·ile (eg′zīl, ek′sīl), *n., v.,* **-iled, -il·ing.** —*n.* **1.** prolonged separation from one's country or home, as by stress of circumstances: *wartime exile.* **2.** anyone separated from his country or home voluntarily or by stress of circumstances. **3.** expulsion from one's native land by authoritative decree. **4.** the fact or state of such expulsion: *to live in exile.* **5.** a person banished from his native land. **6. the Exile,** the Babylonian captivity of the Jews, 597–538 B.C. —*v.t.* **7.** to separate from country, home, etc.: *Disagreements exiled him from his family.* **8.** to expel or banish (a person) from his country; expatriate. [ME *exil* banishment < L *ex(s)il(ium),* equiv. to *exsul* banished person + *-ium* n. suffix of state or condition] —**ex′il·a·ble,** *adj.* —**ex′il·er,** *n.*

ex·il·ic (eg zil′ik, ek sil′-), *adj.* pertaining to exile, as that of the Jews in Babylon. Also, **ex·il′i·an.** [EXILE + -IC]

ex·im·i·ous (eg zim′ē əs), *adj. Archaic.* distinguished; eminent; excellent. [< L *eximius* select, distinguished, excellent (deriv. of *eximere* to take out, remove), equiv. to *ex-* EX-¹ + *-im-* (var. s. of *emere* to buy, take) + *-ius* -IOUS] —**ex·im′i·ous·ly,** *adv.*

ex·ine (ek′sēn, -sīn), *n. Bot.* the outer coat of a spore, esp. a pollen grain. Also, **extine.** [EX-¹ + -INE¹]

ex int., without interest.

ex·ist (ig zist′), *v.i.* **1.** to have actual being; be. **2.** to have life or animation; live. **3.** to continue to be or live: *Belief in magic still exists.* **4.** to have being in a specified place or under certain conditions; be found; occur: *War exists in many parts of the world.* [< L *ex(s)ist(ere)* (to) exist, appear, emerge, equiv. to *ex-* EX-¹ + *sistere* to stand] —**ex·ist′er,** *n.*

ex·ist·ence (ig zis′təns), *n.* **1.** the state or fact of existing; being. **2.** continuance in being or life; life: *a struggle for existence.* **3.** mode of existing: *They were working for a better existence.* **4.** all that exists: *Existence shows a universal order.* **5.** something that exists; entity; being: *There may be existences in the universe other than ourselves.* [late ME < LL *ex(s)istentia.* See EXIST, -ENCE]

ex·ist·ent (ig zis′tənt), *adj.* **1.** existing; having existence. **2.** now existing. —*n.* **3.** one who or that which exists. [< L *existent-* (s. of *existēns*) appearing, arising, prp. of *existere* to EXIST; see -ENT]

ex·is·ten·tial (eg′zi sten′shəl, ek′si-), *adj.* pertaining to existence. [< LL *existentiāl(is)* relating to existing. See EXISTENCE, -AL¹] —**ex′is·ten′tial·ly,** *adv.*

ex·is·ten·tial·ism (eg′zi sten′shə liz′əm, ek′si-), *n. Philos.* **1.** the doctrine that man forms his essence in the course of the life he chooses to lead. **2.** Also called **philosophical existentialism.** a movement based on this doctrine, emphasizing man's responsibility for making his own nature as well as the importance of personal freedom, personal decision, and personal commitment. [EXISTENTIAL + -ISM] —**ex′is·ten′tial·ist,** *adj., n.* —**ex′is·ten′tial·is′tic,** *adj.* —**ex′is·ten′tial·is′ti·cal·ly,** *adv.*

existen′tial psychol′ogy, 1. psychology limited to the observation and description of existent data as the content of experience. **2.** the psychological theories or doctrines of existentialism, esp. those dealing with man's situation in a universe seen as purposeless or irrational.

existen′tial quan′tifier, *Logic.* a quantifier indicating that the sentential function within its scope is true for at least one value of the variable included in the quantifier. Also called **particular quantifier.** Cf. **universal quantifier.**

ex·it¹ (eg′zit, ek′sit), *n.* **1.** a way or passage out. **2.** a going out or away; departure: *to make one's exit.* **3.** a departure of an actor from the stage as part of the action of a play. **4.** Also, **ex′it card′.** *Bridge.* a card that enables a player to relinquish the lead when having it is a disadvantage. —*v.i.* **5.** to go out; leave. **6.** *Bridge.* to play an exit card. [< L *exit(us),* n. use of ptp. of *exīre* to go out]

ex·it² (eg′zit, ek′sit), *v.i.* (he or she) goes offstage (used as a stage direction, often preceding the name of the character): *Exit Falstaff.* [< L]

ex′it pal′let, *Horol.* See **discharging pallet.**

ex′it pu′pil, *Optics.* the ridge of the entrance pupil of an optical system, indicating the place where the pupil of the eye should be placed to view the object. Also called **eye point.**

ex le·ge (eks le′ge; *Eng.* eks lē′jē), *Latin.* by virtue of law.

ex lib., ex libris.

ex li·bris (eks li′bris, lē′-), *pl.* **-bris** for 2. **1.** from the library of (a phrase inscribed in or on a book before the name of the owner): *Ex libris George Rivers.* **2.** an inscription in or on a book, to indicate the owner; bookplate. [< L: out of the books (of), from the books (of)]

Ex·moor (eks′mŏŏr′), *n.* a moorland in SW England, in Somersetshire and Devonshire: the scene of Blackmore's novel, *Lorna Doone.*

ex mo·re (eks mō′re; *Eng.* eks mōr′ē, môr′ē), *Latin.* according to custom.

ex na·tu·ra re·i (eks nä tōō′rä re′ē), *Latin.* out of the nature of things.

ex ni·hi·lo ni·hil fit (eks ni′hi lō′ ni′hil fit′; *Eng.* eks nī′hi lō′ nī′hil fit′), *Latin.* nothing is created from nothing.

exo-, a learned borrowing from Greek meaning "outside," "outer," "external," used in the formation of compound words: *exocentric.* Also, **ex-**². [< Gk, comb. form of *éxō* outside]

ex·o·bi·ol·o·gy (ek′sō bī ol′ə jē), *n.* the study of life beyond the earth's atmosphere, as on other planets. [EXO- + BIOLOGY] —**ex′o·bi·ol′o·gist,** *n.*

ex·o·carp (ek′sō kärp′), *n. Bot.* epicarp. [EXO- + -CARP]

ex·o·cen·tric (ek′sō sen′trik), *adj. Gram.* not having the same syntactic function in the sentence as any one of its immediate constituents. *In the garden* is an exocentric construction, since it does not function in the same way as the noun *garden.* The noun *bittersweet* is an exocentric compound, since it is a noun but its elements are both adjectives. Cf. **endocentric.** [EXO- + CENTRIC]

ex·o·crine (ek′sə krin, -krīn′, -krēn′), *Anat., Physiol.* —*adj.* **1.** secreting externally. **2.** of or pertaining to an exocrine gland or its secretion. —*n.* **3.** an external secretion. [EXO- + *-crine* < Gk *krī́n(ein)* (to) separate]

ex′ocrine gland′, any of several glands, as the salivary glands, that secretes externally through a duct.

Exod., Exodus.

ex·o·der·mis (ek′sō dûr′mis), *n. Bot.* a temporary, protective layer of cells in some roots, as in certain orchids. [EXO- + DERMIS] —**ex′o·der′mal,** *adj.*

ex·o·don·tics (ek′sə don′tiks), *n.* (*construed as sing.*) the branch of dentistry dealing with the extraction of teeth. Also, **ex·o·don·tia** (ek′sə don′shə, -shē ə). [EX-² + -ODONT- + -ICS]

ex·o·don·tist (ek′sə don′tist), *n.* a specialist in exodontics. [EXODONT(ICS) + -IST]

ex·o·dos (ek′sə dos′), *n., pl.* **-doi** (-doi′). *Greek.* (in ancient Greek drama) the final scene or departure, esp. in tragedy and usually Old Comedy: usually following the last *stasimon.*

ex·o·dus (ek′sə dəs), *n.* **1.** a going out; a departure or emigration, usually of a large number of people: *the summer exodus to the country and shore.* **2. the Exodus,** the departure of the Israelites from Egypt under Moses. **3.** (*cap.*) the second book of the Bible, containing an account of the Exodus. [< L: a going out < Gk *éxodos* a marching out, going out, equiv. to *ex-* EX-³ + *hodós* way]

ex·o·en·zyme (ek′sō en′zīm), *n. Biochem.* an enzyme, as pepsin, that functions outside of the cell producing it. Also called **ectoenzyme.** Cf. **endoenzyme.** [EXO- + ENZYME]

ex·o·er·gic (ek′sō ûr′jik), *adj. Physical Chem.* of or noting a reaction which is accompanied by a liberation of energy; exothermic (opposed to *endoergic*). [EXO- + Gk *érg(on)* work + -IC]

ex off., ex officio.

ex of·fi·ci·o (eks ə fish′ē ō′), by virtue of office or official position. [< L] —**ex′-of·fi′ci·o′,** *adj.*

ex·og·a·my (ek sog′ə mē), *n.* **1.** marriage outside a specific tribe or similar social unit. Cf. **endogamy. 2.** *Biol.* the union of gametes of unrelated parents. [EXO- + -GAMY] —**ex·og·a·mous** (ek sog′ə məs), **ex·o·gam·ic** (ek′sə gam′ik), *adj.*

ex·o·gen (ek′sə jən), *n. Bot.* any plant of the obsolete class *Exogenae,* including the dicotyledons. [< NL *Exogena.* See EXO-, -GEN]

ex·og·e·nous (ek soj′ə nəs), *adj.* **1.** having its origin external; derived externally. **2.** *Bot.* **a.** (of plants, as the dicotyledons) having stems which grow by the addition of an annual layer of wood to the outside beneath the bark. **b.** pertaining to plants having such stems. **c.** belonging to the exogens. **3.** *Physiol., Biochem.* of or noting the metabolic assimilation of proteins or other metabolites, the elimination of nitrogenous catabolites being in direct proportion to the amount of metabolites taken in. [EXOGEN + -OUS] —**ex·og′e·nism,** *n.* —**ex·og′e·nous·ly,** *adv.*

ex·on (ek′son), *n.* (in Britain) one of four yeomen of the guard who act as commanding officers in the absence of higher authority. Also called **exempt.** [earlier *exant* for F *exempt* (attempt to show F pronunciation)]

ex·o·nar·thex (ek′sō när′theks), *n.* a covered walk, vestibule, or narthex situated before a narthex; an outer narthex. [EXO- + NARTHEX]

ex·on·er·ate (ig zon′ə rāt′), *v.t.,* **-at·ed, -at·ing. 1.** to clear, as of a charge; free from blame; exculpate: *He was exonerated from the accusation of cheating.* **2.** to relieve, as from an obligation, duty, or task. [late ME < L *exonerāt(us)* (ptp. of *exonerāre* to unburden, discharge), equiv. to *ex-* EX-¹ + *oner-* (s. of *onus*) a burden + *-ātus* -ATE¹] —**ex·on′er·a′tion,** *n.* —**ex·on′er·a′tive,** *adj.* —**ex·on′er·a′tor,** *n.*
—**Syn. 1.** vindicate. See **absolve. 2.** release, discharge, free. —**Ant. 1.** blame.

ex·o·path·ic (ek′sə path′ik), *adj. Pathol.* noting or pertaining to a disease whose cause is outside the body. [EXO- + -PATHIC]

ex·o·pe·rid·i·um (ek′sō pi rid′ē əm), *n. Bot.* the outer of the two layers into which the peridium is divided. [EXO- + PERIDIUM]

ex·o·pha·sia (ek′sō fā′zhə, -zhē ə), *n.* ordinary, vocalized, audible speech. Cf. **endophasia.** [< NL; see EXO-, -PHASIA]

ex′ophthal′mic goi′ter, *Pathol.* hyperthyroidism characterized by exophthalmos.

ex·oph·thal·mos (ek′sof thal′məs, -mos), *n. Pathol.* protrusion of the eyeball from the orbit, caused by disease, esp. hyperthyroidism, or injury. Also, **ex·oph·thal·mus** (ek′sof thal′məs), **ex·oph·thal·mi·a** (ek′sof thal′mē ə). [< NL < Gk, equiv. to *ex-* EX-³ + *ophthalmós*; see OPHTHALMIC] —**ex′oph·thal′mic,** *adj.*

ex·op·o·dite (ek sop′ə dīt′), *n. Zool.* the outer or lateral branch of a biramous crustacean appendage. Cf. **endopodite, protopodite.** Also, **ex·o·pod** (ek′sə pod′). [EXO- + POD- + -ITE¹] —**ex·op·o·dit·ic** (ek sop′ə dit′ik), *adj.*

ex·o·pter·y·gote (ek′sō ter′ə gōt′), *adj.* **1.** belonging or pertaining to the *Exopterygota,* comprising the insects that undergo incomplete metamorphosis. —*n.* **2.** an insect of the division *Exopterygota.* [< NL *Exopterygot(a),* equiv. to *exo-* EXO- + Gk *pterygōtá,* neut. pl. *pterygōtós* winged]

ex·o·ra·ble (ek′sər ə bəl), *adj.* susceptible of being persuaded or moved by entreaty. [< L *exōrābil(is),* equiv. to *exōr(āre)* (to) prevail upon, move by entreaty (*ex-* EX-¹ + *ōrāre* to pray, beg) + *-ābilis* -ABLE] —**ex′o·ra·bil′i·ty,** *n.*

ex·or·bi·tance (ig zôr′bi təns), *n.* the quality of being exorbitant; excessiveness. Also, **ex·or′bi·tan·cy.** [late ME; see EXORBITANT, -ANCE]

ex·or·bi·tant (ig zôr′bi tənt), *adj.* exceeding the bounds of custom, propriety, or reason, esp. in amount or extent: *to charge an exorbitant price; exorbitant luxury.* [late ME < LL *exorbitant-* (s. of *exorbitāns,* prp. of *exorbitāre* to go out of the track), equiv. to *ex-* EX-¹ + *orbit(a)* wheel track (see ORBIT) + *-ant-* -ANT] —**ex·or′bi·tant·ly,** *adv.*
—**Syn.** inordinate, excessive, extravagant, unreasonable, unconscionable. —**Ant.** fair.

ex·or·cise (ek′sôr sīz′), *v.t.,* **-cised, -cis·ing. 1.** to seek to expel (an evil spirit) by adjuration or religious or solemn ceremonies: *to exorcise a demon.* **2.** to deliver (a person, place, etc.) from evil spirits or malignant influences. Also, **ex′or·cize′.** [late ME < LL *exorciz(āre)* < Gk *exorkízein,* equiv. to *ex-* EX-³ + *horkízein* to cause (someone) to swear an oath] —**ex′or·cise′ment,** *n.* —**ex′or·cis′er,** *n.*

ex·or·cism (ek′sôr siz′əm), *n.* **1.** the act or process of exorcising. **2.** the ceremony or the formula used in exorcising: *An elaborate exorcism was pronounced over the sick man.* [ME *exorcism(us)* < LL < Gk *exorkismós* administration of an oath. See EXORCISE, -ISM] —**ex·or·cis·mal** (ek′sôr siz′məl), **ex·or·ci·so·ry** (ek′sôr′sī zə rē), **ex′or·cis′ti·cal, ex′or·cis′tic,** *adj.*

ex·or·cist (ek′sôr sist), *n.* **1.** a person who practices exorcism. **2.** *Rom. Cath. Ch.* **a.** a member of the second-ranking of the four minor orders. **b.** the order itself. Cf. **acolyte** (def. 2), **lector** (def. 2), **ostiary** (def. 1). [ME < LL *exorcista* < Gk *exorkistḗs.* See EXORCISM, -IST]

ex·or·di·um (ig zôr′dē əm, ik sôr′-), *n., pl.* **-di·ums, -di·a** (-dē ə). **1.** the beginning of anything. **2.** the introductory part of an oration or discourse. [< L, equiv. to *ex-* EX-¹ + *ōrd-* begin (s. of *ōrdīrī*) + *-ium* neut. n. suffix] —**ex·or′di·al,** *adj.*

ex·o·skel·e·ton (ek′sō skel′i tən), *n. Zool.* an external covering or integument, esp. when hard, as the shell of crustaceans, the scales and plates of fishes, etc. (opposed to *endoskeleton*). [EXO- + SKELETON] —**ex′o·skel′e·tal,** *adj.*

ex·os·mo·sis (ek′sos mō′sis, ek′soz-), *n. Physical Chem.* **1.** osmosis from the inside toward the outside. **2.** (in osmosis) the flow of a substance from an area of greater concentration to one of lower concentration (opposed to *endosmosis*). Also, **ex·os·mose** (ek′sos mōs′, -soz-). [EX-² + OSMOSIS] —**ex·os·mot·ic** (ek′sos-mot′ik, -soz-), **ex·os·mic** (ek sos′mik, -soz′-), *adj.*

ex·o·sphere (ek′sō sfēr′), *n.* the highest region of the atmosphere, where the air density is so low that an air molecule, moving rapidly straight upward, is more than 50 percent likely to escape from the atmosphere instead of hitting other molecules. [EXO- + -SPHERE] —**ex·o·spher·i·cal** (ek′sō sfer′i kəl), **ex·o·spher·ic** (ek′sō sfer′ik), *adj.*

ex·o·spore (ek′sə spōr′, -spôr′), *n. Bot.* the outer coat of a spore. [EXO- + SPORE] —**ex·o·spor·al** (ek′sə spōr′əl, -spôr′-, ek sos′pər-), **ex′o·spor′ous,** *adj.*

ex·os·to·sis (ek′so stō′sis, -sə-), *n., pl.* **-ses** (-sēz). *Pathol.* the abnormal formation of a bony growth on a bone or tooth. [< NL < Gk: an outgrowth. See EX-³, OSTOSIS] —**ex′os·tosed′,** *adj.* —**ex·os·tot·ic** (ek′so-stot′ik), *adj.*

ex·o·ter·ic (ek′sə ter′ik), *adj.* **1.** suitable for or communicated to the general public. **2.** not belonging or pertaining to the inner or select circle, as of disciples or intimates. **3.** popular; simple; commonplace: *exoteric notions about what occurs in circles of power.* **4.** pertaining to the outside; exterior; external. [< LL, neut. pl. *exōteric(us)* external < Gk *exōterikós,* equiv. to *exṓter(os)* inclined outward (*exo-* EXO- + *-teros* comp. suffix) + *-ikos* -IC] —**ex′o·ter′i·cal·ly,** *adv.* —**ex′o·ter′i·cism,** *n.*

ex·o·ter·i·ca (ek′sə ter′ə kə), *n.pl.* ideas, principles, writings, or the like, of an exoteric nature. [< LL neut. pl. of *exotericus* EXOTERIC]

ex·o·ther·mic (ek′sō thûr′mik), *adj. Chem.* noting or pertaining to a chemical change that is accompanied by a liberation of heat (opposed to *endothermic*). Also, **ex′o·ther′mal.** [EXO- + THERMIC] —**ex′o·ther′mi·cal·ly, ex′o·ther′mal·ly,** *adv.* —**ex·o·ther·mic·i·ty** (ek′sō thər mis′i tē), *n.*

ex·ot·ic (ig zot′ik), *adj.* **1.** of foreign origin or character; not native; introduced from abroad, but not fully naturalized or acclimatized: *exotic foods; exotic manners; exotic speech.* **2.** striking or unusual in effect or appearance; strange; exciting; glamorous: *the exotic dress of traditional Japan.* **3.** of, pertaining to, or involving strip-teasing: *the exotic clubs where strippers are featured; an exotic dancer.* —*n.* **4.** anything exotic, as a plant. [< L *exōtic(us)* < Gk *exōtikós* foreign. See EXO-, -TIC] —**ex·ot′i·cal·ly,** *adv.* —**ex·ot′ic·ness,** *n.*

exot′ic danc′er, stripper (def. 3).

ex·ot·i·cism (ig zot′i siz′əm), *n.* **1.** tendency to adopt what is exotic. **2.** exotic quality or character. **3.** anything exotic, as a foreign word or idiom. [EXOTIC + -ISM] —**ex·ot′i·cist,** *n.*

ex·o·tox·in (ek′sō tok′sin), *n. Biochem.* a soluble toxin excreted by a microorganism. Cf. **endotoxin.** [EXO- + TOXIN] —**ex′o·tox′ic,** *adj.*

ex·o·tro·pi·a (ek′sə trō′pē ə), *n. Ophthalm.* See **divergent squint.** [EXO- + Gk *-tropia* a turning; see TROPE, -IA]

exp., 1. expenses. **2.** expired. **3.** exponential. **4.** export. **5.** exportation. **6.** exported. **7.** exporter. **8.** express.

ex·pand (ik spand′), *v.t.* **1.** to increase in extent, size, volume, scope, etc.: *Heat expands metal.* **2.** to spread or stretch out; unfold: *A bird expands its wings.* **3.** to express in fuller form or greater detail; develop: *to expand a short story into a novel.* **4.** *Math.* **a.** to write (a mathematical expression) so as to show the products of its factors. Cf. **factor** (def. 12). **b.** to rewrite (a mathematical expression) as a sum, product, etc., of terms of a particular kind: *to expand a function in a power series.* —*v.i.* **5.** to increase or grow in extent, bulk, scope, etc.: *Most metals expand with heat. The mind expands with experience.* **6.** to spread out; unfold; develop: *The buds had not yet expanded.* **7.** to express more fully or in greater detail (usually fol. by *on* or *upon*): *Please ask him to expand on that statement.* [late ME *expande(n)* < L *expande(re)* (to) spread out, equiv. to *ex-* EX-¹ + *pandere* to extend, stretch] —**ex·pand′a·bil′i·ty, ex·pand′i·bil′i·ty,** *n.* —**ex·pand′a·ble, ex·pand′i·ble,** *adj.*
—**Syn. 1.** extend, swell, enlarge, increase. EXPAND, DILATE, DISTEND, INFLATE imply becoming larger and filling more space. TO EXPAND is to spread out, usually in every direction, so as to occupy more space or have more capacity: *to expand one's chest.* TO DILATE is esp. to increase the width or circumference, and applies to space enclosed within confines or to hollow bodies: *to dilate the pupils of the eyes.* TO DISTEND is to stretch, often beyond the point of natural expansion: *to distend an artery.* TO INFLATE is to blow out or swell a hollow body with air or gas: *to inflate a balloon.*

ex·pand·ed (ik span′did), *adj.* **1.** increased in area, bulk, or volume; enlarged: *an expanded version of a story.* **2.** spread out; extended: *the expanded frontiers of the Roman Empire.* **3.** *Print.* (of type) wider in proportion to its height. Cf. **condensed** (def. 4). [late ME; see EXPAND, -ED²] —**ex·pand′ed·ness,** *n.*

expand′ed met′al, sheet metal slotted and stretched to make a stiff network with openings of various patterns, used for lathing, wastebaskets, and various decorative and semistructural applications.

ex·pand·er (ik span′dər), *n.* **1.** one who or that which expands. **2.** *Electronics.* a transducer that produces an output with a range of voltages greater than that of the input signal. Cf. **compressor** (def. 5). [EXPAND + -ER¹]

ex·panse (ik spans′), *n.* **1.** that which is spread out, esp. over a relatively large area: *that great expanse, the sky.* **2.** an uninterrupted space or area; a wide extent of anything: *an expanse of water.* **3.** expansion; extension: *the wide expanse of scientific knowledge.* [< L *expans(um),* n. use of neut. of *expansus,* ptp. of *expandere* to EXPAND]

ex·pan·si·ble (ik span′sə bəl), *adj.* capable of being expanded: *Most metals are expansible.* [< L *expans(us)* (see EXPANSE) + -IBLE] —**ex·pan′si·bil′i·ty,** *n.*

ex·pan·sile (ik span′sil, -sīl), *adj.* **1.** capable of expanding; such as to expand. **2.** pertaining to expansion. [EXPANS(ION) + -ILE]

ex·pan·sion (ik span′shən), *n.* **1.** the act or state of expanding. **2.** the state of being expanded. **3.** the amount or degree of expanding. **4.** an expanded, dilated, or enlarged portion or form of a thing: *The present article is an expansion of one he wrote last year.* **5.** anything spread out; expanse. **6.** *Math.* the development at length of an expression indicated in a contracted form, as $a^2 + 2ab + b^2$ of the expression $(a + b)^2$. **7.** *Mach.* that part of the operation of an engine in which the volume of the working medium increases and its pressure decreases. [< LL *expansiōn-* (s. of *expansiō*) a spreading out. See EXPANSE, -ION] —**ex·pan′sion·al, ex·pan′sion·ar′y,** *adj.*

expan′sion at′tic, an attic space planned to be finished as a living space if necessary at some time.

expan′sion bolt′, *Building Trades.* a bolt inserted into a hole drilled in masonry and mechanically expanded to serve as an anchor for shelves, timbers, etc.

expan′sion cham′ber, *Physics.* See **cloud chamber.**

ex·pan·sion·ism (ik span′shə niz′əm), *n.* a policy of expansion, as of territory or currency: *the colonial expansionism of Europe in the 19th century.* [EXPANSION + -ISM] —**ex·pan′sion·ist,** *n.* —**ex·pan′sion·is′tic,** *adj.*

expan′sion joint′, a joint between two parts of a structure, machine, etc., permitting expansion, as from heat, without structural damage.

expan′sion wave′, a shock wave that expands the medium through which it is transmitted. Cf. **compression wave.**

ex·pan·sive (ik span′siv), *adj.* **1.** tending to expand or capable of expanding. **2.** causing expansion: *the expansive force of heat.* **3.** having a wide range or extent; comprehensive; extensive: *expansive mountain scenery; an expansive treatment of a topic.* **4.** (of a person's character or speech) effusive, unrestrained, free, or open: *Our expansive host welcomed us warmly.* **5.** working by expansion, as an engine. **6.** *Psychiatry.* marked by an abnormal euphoristic state and by delusions of grandeur. [EXPANS(ION) + -IVE] —**ex·pan′sive·ly,** *adv.*

expan′sive bit′, *Carpentry.* an adjustable bit for drilling holes of different sizes. Also, **expan′sion bit′.**

expan′sive classifica′tion, *Library Science.* a system of classifying books and other materials consisting of seven classification schemes, each after the first being progressively further subdivided.

ex·pan·siv·i·ty (ek′span siv′i tē), *n.* *Physics.* See **coefficient of expansion.** [EXPANSIVE + -ITY]

ex par·te (eks pär′tē), from or on one side only, as in a controversy; in the interest of one party. [< L]

ex·pa·ti·ate (ik spā′shē āt′), *v.i.,* **-at·ed, -at·ing. 1.** to enlarge in discourse or writing; be copious in description or discussion: *to expatiate upon a theme.* **2.** to move or wander about intellectually, imaginatively, etc., without restraint. [< L *expatiāt(us)* wandered, digressed, ptp. of *ex(s)patiārī,* equiv. to *ex-* EX-¹ + *spatiārī* to walk about; see -ATE¹] —**ex·pa′ti·a′tion,** *n.* —**ex·pa′ti·a′tor,** *n.*

ex·pa·tri·ate (*v.* eks pā′trē āt′; *adj., n.* eks pā′trē it, -āt′), *v.,* **-at·ed, -at·ing,** *adj., n.* —*v.t.* **1.** to banish (a person) from his native country. **2.** to withdraw (oneself) from residence in one's native country. **3.** to withdraw (oneself) from allegiance to one's country. —*adj.* **4.** expatriated; exiled. —*n.* **5.** an expatriated person: *Many American writers have been expatriates in Paris.* [< LL *expatriāt(us)* banished (ptp. of *expatriāre*), equiv. to *ex-* EX-¹ + *patri(a)* native land + *-ātus* -ATE¹] —**ex·pa′tri·a′tion,** *n.*

ex·pect (ik spekt′), *v.t.* **1.** to look forward to; regard as likely to happen; anticipate the occurrence or the coming of: *I expect to do it. I expect him to come. She expects that they will come.* **2.** to look for with reason or justification: *We expect obedience.* **3.** to suppose or surmise: *I expect that you are tired from the trip.* **4.** to anticipate the birth of (one's child): *Paul and Sylvia expect their second right after Christmas.* —*v.i.* **5.** to be pregnant; be gravid: *The cat is expecting again.* [< L *ex(s)pect(āre)* (to) look out for, await, equiv. to *ex-* EX-¹ + *spectāre* to look at; see SPECTACLE] —**ex·pect′a·ble,** *adj.* —**ex·pect′a·bly,** *adv.* —**ex·pect′er,** *n.* —**ex·pect′ing·ly,** *adv.*

—**Syn. 1.** EXPECT, ANTICIPATE, HOPE, AWAIT all imply looking to some future event. EXPECT implies confidently believing, usually for good reasons, that an event will occur: *to expect a visit from a friend.* ANTICIPATE is to look forward to an event and even to picture it: *to anticipate seeing a play; Do you anticipate trouble?* HOPE implies a wish that an event may take place and an expectation that it will: *to hope for the best.* AWAIT (WAIT FOR) implies being alert and ready, whether for good or evil: *to await news after a cyclone.* —**Usage. 3.** This sense of EXPECT (*I expect you went with them. I expect you want to leave now.*) is encountered in the speech of educated people but seldom in their writing.

ex·pect·an·cy (ik spek′tən sē), *n., pl.* **-cies. 1.** the quality or state of expecting; expectation; anticipatory belief or desire. **2.** the state of being expected. **3.** an object of expectation; something expected. Also, **ex·pec′tance.** [< ML *ex(s)pectantia.* See EXPECTANT, -ANCY]

ex·pect·ant (ik spek′tənt), *adj.* **1.** having expectations; expecting: *an excited, expectant audience.* **2.** in expectation; expected; prospective: *an expectant fortune.* **3.** pregnant; expecting: *an expectant mother.* **4.** characterized by expectations: *a passive, expectant attitude.* —*n.* **5.** a person who expects or who waits in expectation. [ME < L *expectant-* (s. of *expectāns*), prp. of *expectāre* to EXPECT; see -ANT] —**ex·pect′ant·ly,** *adv.*

ex·pec·ta·tion (ek′spek tā′shən), *n.* **1.** the act of expecting. **2.** the state of expecting: *to wait in expectation.* **3.** an expectant mental attitude: *a high pitch of expectation.* **4.** something expected; a thing looked forward to. **5.** Often, **expectations.** a prospect of future good or profit: *to have great expectations.* **6.** the degree of probability of the occurrence of something: *There is little expectation that he will come.* **7.** *Statistics.* See **mathematical expectation. 8.** the state of being expected: *a large sum of money in expectation.* [< L *expectātiōn-* (s. of *expectātiō*) an awaiting, equiv. to *expectāt(us)* (ptp. of *expectāre* to EXPECT) + *-iōn-* -ION]

—**Syn. 2.** expectancy, anticipation, hope, trust.

expecta′tion of life′, the average duration of life beyond any age, of persons who have attained that age, as shown by mortality tables.

Expecta′tion Sun′day, the Sunday before Whitsunday.

Expecta′tion Week′, the ten days between Ascension Day and Whitsunday.

ex·pect·a·tive (ik spek′tə tiv), *adj.* **1.** of or pertaining to expectation. **2.** characterized by expectation. [ME < ML *expectātīv(us).* See EXPECTATION, -IVE]

expect′ed val′ue, *Statistics.* **1.** (of any variate) the expectation of a function equal to the variate itself. **2.** the arithmetic mean of a variable over a finite class.

ex·pec·to·rant (ik spek′tə rənt), *Med.* —*adj.* **1.** promoting the secretion of fluid from the respiratory tract. —*n.* **2.** an expectorant medicine. [< L *expectorant-* (s. of *expectorāns*), prp. of *expectorāre* to EXPECTORATE; see -ANT]

ex·pec·to·rate (ik spek′tə rāt′), *v.,* **-rat·ed, -rat·ing.** —*v.t.* **1.** to eject or expel, as phlegm, from the throat or lungs by coughing or hawking and spitting; spit. —*v.i.* **2.** to spit. [< L *expectorāt(us)* (ptp. of *expectorāre* to expel from the breast), equiv. to *ex-* EX-¹ + *pector-* (s. of *pectus*) breast + *-ātus* -ATE¹] —**ex·pec′to·ra′tor,** *n.*

ex·pec·to·ra·tion (ik spek′tə rā′shən), *n.* **1.** the act of expectorating. **2.** matter that is expectorated. [EXPECTORATE + -ION]

ex pe·de Her·cu·lem (eks ped′e her′kŏŏ lem′; *Eng.* eks pē′dē hûr′kyŏŏ lem′), *Latin.* from a part or sample we may judge the whole. [lit., from the foot (we may know) Hercules]

ex·pe·di·en·cy (ik spē′dē ən sē), *n., pl.* **-cies. 1.** the quality of being expedient; advantageousness; advisability. **2.** a regard for what is politic or advantageous rather than for what is right or just; a sense of self-interest. **3.** something expedient. Also, **ex·pe′di·ence.** [< LL *expedientia.* See EXPEDIENT, -ENCY]

ex·pe·di·ent (ik spē′dē ənt), *adj.* **1.** tending to promote some proposed or desired object; fit or suitable for the purpose; proper under the circumstances: *It is expedient that you go.* **2.** conducive to advantage or interest, as opposed to right. **3.** acting in accordance with expediency. —*n.* **4.** a means to an end: *Aspirin is a useful expedient for dulling minor pain.* **5.** a means devised or employed in an exigency; resource; shift: *Use any expedients you think necessary to get over the obstacles in your way.* [late ME < L *expedient-* (s. of *expediēns*), prp. of *expedīre.* See EXPEDITE, -ENT] —**ex·pe′di·ent·ly,** *adv.*

—**Syn. 1.** advantageous, profitable, advisable, appropriate, desirable. **5.** device, contrivance, resort. —**Ant. 1.** disadvantageous.

ex·pe·di·en·tial (ik spē′dē en′shəl), *adj.* pertaining to or regulated by expediency. [EXPEDIENT + -IAL]

ex·ped·i·tate (ek sped′i tāt′), *v.t.,* **-tat·ed, -tat·ing.** to cut off the pads or claws of (an animal, esp. a dog) in order to inhibit deer chasing. [< ML *expedītāt(us)* (ptp. of *expedītāre*), equiv. to L *ex-* EX-¹ + *pedit-* (s. of *pedes*) afoot + *-ātus* -ATE¹] —**ex·ped′i·ta′tion,** *n.*

ex·pe·dite (ek′spi dīt′), *v.,* **-dit·ed, -dit·ing,** *adj.* —*v.t.* **1.** to speed up the progress of; hasten: *Industrial processes were expedited to meet the demands of consumers.* **2.** to accomplish promptly, as a piece of business; dispatch: *to expedite one's duties.* **3.** to issue or dispatch, as an official document, letter, etc. —*adj.* **4.** *Obs.* ready for action; alert. [< L *expedīt(us)* disengaged, set free (the feet) (ptp. of *expedīre*), equiv. to *ex-* EX-¹ + *ped-* (s. of *pēs*) foot + *-ītus* -ITE²] —**ex′pe·dit′er, ex′pe·di′tor,** *n.*

—**Syn. 1.** quicken, push, accelerate, hurry. —**Ant. 1.** delay.

ex·pe·di·tion (ek′spi dish′ən), *n.* **1.** an excursion, journey, or voyage made for some specific purpose, as of war or exploration. **2.** the body of persons, ships, etc., engaged in such an activity: *a large expedition of scientists and military personnel.* **3.** promptness or speed in accomplishing something: *He worked with great expedition.* [late ME < L *expeditiōn-* (s. of *expeditiō*) a (military) traveling. See EXPEDITE, -ION]

—**Syn. 1.** See **trip. 3.** haste, quickness, dispatch, alacrity.

ex·pe·di·tion·ar·y (ek′spi dish′ə ner′ē), *adj.* pertaining to or composing an expedition: *an expeditionary force.* [EXPEDITION + -ARY]

ex·pe·di·tious (ek′spi dish′əs), *adj.* characterized by promptness; quick: *an expeditious answer to an inquiry.* [EXPED(ITION) + -ITIOUS] —**ex′pe·di′tious·ly,** *adv.* —**ex′pe·di′tious·ness,** *n.*

ex·pel (ik spel′), *v.t.,* **-pelled, -pel·ling. 1.** to drive or force out or away; discharge or eject: *to expel air from the lungs; to expel an invader from a country.* **2.** to cut off from membership or relations: *to expel a student from a college.* [ME *expelle* < L *expell(ere)* (to) drive out, drive away, equiv. to *ex-* EX-¹ + *pellere* to push, drive] —**ex·pel′la·ble,** *adj.*

—**Syn. 2.** oust, dismiss, exile.

ex·pel·lant (ik spel′ənt), *adj.* **1.** expelling, or having the power to expel. —*n.* **2.** an expellant medicine. Also, **ex·pel′lent.** [var. of *expellent* (see -ANT) < L *expellent-* (s. of *expellēns*), prp. of *expellere* to EXPEL; see -ENT]

ex·pel·lee (ek′spe lē′, -spə-, ik spel′ē), *n.* a person who has been expelled, esp. one deported from a native or adopted country and resettled in another, usually one to which he bears an ethnic relation. [EXPEL + -EE]

ex·pel·ler (ik spel′ər), *n.* **1.** one who or that which expels. **2.** a press used to extract oil from corn, soybeans, etc. [EXPEL + -ER¹]

ex·pend (ik spend′), *v.t.* **1.** to use up: *He expended energy, time, and care on his work.* **2.** to pay out; disburse; spend. [late ME < L *expend(ere)* (to) weigh out, lay out, pay. See EX-¹, PEND] —**ex·pend′er,** *n.*

—**Syn. 1.** consume, empty. See **spend.**

ex·pend·a·ble (ik spen′də bəl), *adj.* **1.** capable of being expended. **2.** (of an item of equipment or supply) consumed in use or not reusable. **3.** *Mil.* (of men, equipment, or supplies) capable of being sacrificed in order to accomplish a military objective. —*n.* **4.** Usually, **expendables.** an expendable person or item of equipment or supply, esp. in warfare. [EXPEND + -ABLE] —**ex·pend′a·bil′i·ty,** *n.*

ex·pend·i·ture (ik spen′di chər), *n.* **1.** the act of expending; disbursement; consumption. **2.** that which is expended; expense: *Unnecessary expenditures include those for luxury items.* [< ML *expendit(us)* laid out, paid (var. of *expēnsus,* ptp. of *expendere;* see EXPEND) + -URE]

ex·pense (ik spens′), *n.* **1.** cost or charge. **2.** a cause or occasion of spending: *Owning a car is a great expense.* **3.** the act of expending; expenditure. **4. expenses,** *Com.* **a.** charges incurred in the execution of an undertaking or commission. **b.** money paid as reimbursement for such charges: *to receive a salary and expenses.* **5. at the expense of,** at the sacrifice of; to the detriment of: *quantity at the expense of quality.* [ME < LL *expēnsa,* n. use of fem. of *expēnsus,* ptp. of *expendere* to EXPEND] —**ex·pense′less,** *adj.*

—**Syn. 1.** outlay, expenditure. See **price.**

expense′ account′, an account of expenditures for which an employee will be reimbursed by his employer.

ex·pen·sive (ik spen′siv), *adj.* entailing great expense; very high-priced; costly: *an expensive party.* [EXPENSE + -IVE] —**ex·pen′sive·ly,** *adv.* —**ex·pen′sive·ness,** *n.*

—**Syn.** EXPENSIVE, COSTLY, DEAR, HIGH-PRICED apply to that which is higher in price than the average person's usual purchases. EXPENSIVE is applied to whatever entails considerable expense; it suggests a price more than the average person would normally be able to pay or a price paid by the average person only for something special or especially desirable: *an expensive automobile.* COSTLY implies that the price is a large sum, usually because of the fineness, preciousness, etc., of the object: *a costly jewel.* DEAR is commonly applied in England to that which is selling beyond its usual or just price. In the U.S., HIGH-PRICED is the usual equivalent. —**Ant.** cheap, low-priced.

ex·pe·ri·ence (ik spēr′ē əns), *n., v.,* **-enced, -enc·ing.** —*n.* **1.** a particular instance of personally encountering or undergoing something: *My encountering the bear in the woods was a frightening experience.* **2.** the process or fact of personally observing, encountering, or undergoing something: *business experience.* **3.** the observing, encountering, or undergoing of things generally as they occur in the course of time: *to learn from experience; the range of human experience.* **4.** knowledge or practical wisdom gained from what one has observed, encountered, or undergone: *men of experience.* **5.** *Philos.* the totality of the cognitions given by perception; all that is perceived, understood, and remembered. —*v.t.* **6.** to have experience of; meet with; undergo; feel: *to experience nausea.* **7.** to learn by experience. **8. experience religion,** to undergo a spiritual conversion by which one gains or regains faith in God. [ME < L *experientia,* equiv. to *experient-* (s. of *experiēns,* ptp. of *experīrī* to try, test; see EX-¹, PERIL + *-ia;* see -ENCE] —**ex·pe′ri·ence·a·ble,** *adj.* —**ex·pe′ri·ence·less,** *adj.* —**ex·pe′ri·enc·er,** *n.*

—**Syn. 6.** encounter, know, endure, suffer. EXPERIENCE, UNDERGO refer to encountering situations, conditions, etc., in life, or to having certain sensations or feelings. EXPERIENCE implies being affected by what one meets with (pleasant or unpleasant), so that to a greater or lesser degree one suffers a change: *to experience a change of heart, bitter disappointment.* UNDERGO usually refers to the bearing or enduring of something hard, difficult, disagreeable, or dangerous: *to undergo severe hardships, an operation.*

ex·pe·ri·enced (ik spēr′ē ənst), *adj.* **1.** wise or skillful in a particular field through experience: *an experienced teacher; an experienced general.* **2.** having learned through experience; taught by experience: *experienced in living; experienced through adversity.* **3.** endured; undergone; suffered through: *experienced misfortunes.* [EXPERIENCE + -ED²]

—**Syn. 1.** skilled, expert, practiced, veteran, accomplished, versed, adept, qualified.

expe′rience meet′ing. See **testimony meeting.**

expe′rience ta′ble, *Insurance.* See **mortality table.**

ex·pe·ri·en·tial (ik spēr′ē en′shəl), *adj.* pertaining to or derived from experience. [< ML *experientiāl(is).* See EXPERIENCE, -AL¹] —**ex·pe′ri·en′tial·ly,** *adv.*

ex·pe·ri·en·tial·ism (ik spēr′ē en′shə liz′əm), *n.* *Epistemology.* any doctrine or theory that maintains that personal experience is the only or the principal basis of knowledge. [EXPERIENTIAL + -ISM] —**ex·pe′ri·en′tial·ist,** *n.* —**ex·pe′ri·en′tial·is′tic,** *adj.*

ex·per·i·ment (*n.* ik sper′ə mənt; *v.* ek sper′ə ment′), *n.* **1.** a test, trial, or tentative procedure; an act or operation for the purpose of discovering something unknown or of testing a principle, supposition, etc.: *a chemical experiment; a teaching experiment; an experiment in living.* **2.** the conducting of such operations; experimentation: *a product that is the result of long experiment.* **3.** *Obs.* experience. —*v.i.* **4.** to try or test, esp. in order to find something: *to experiment with drugs in order to find a cure for the common cold.* [ME: proof

< L *experīment(um).* See EXPERIENCE, -MENT] **—ex·per/i·ment/er, ex·per/i·men/tor, ex·per/i·men·ta/tor,** *n.*
—Syn. 1. See **trial. 2.** research, investigation.

ex·per·i·men·tal (ik sper/ə men/tᵊl), *adj.* **1.** pertaining to, derived from, or founded on experiment: *an experimental science.* **2.** based on or derived from experience; empirical: *experimental religion; experimental knowledge.* **3.** of the nature of an experiment; tentative: *It is still in an experimental stage.* **4.** functioning as an experiment or used for experimentation: *an experimental airplane; experimental theater.* [late ME < ML *experīmentāl(is).* See EXPERIMENT, -AL¹] **—ex·per/i·men/tal·ly,** *adv.*

ex·per·i·men·tal·ism (ik sper/ə men/tᵊliz/əm), *n.* **1.** doctrine or practice of relying on experimentation; empiricism. **2.** fondness for experimenting or innovating: *The psychologists' children were raised in an atmosphere of vigorous experimentalism.* [EXPERIMENTAL + -ISM] **—ex·per/i·men/tal·ist,** *n.*

ex·per·i·men·ta·tion (ik sper/ə men tā/shən), *n.* the act, process, practice, or an instance of making experiments. [EXPERIMENT + -ATION] **—ex·per·i·men·ta·tive** (ik sper/ə men/tə tiv), *adj.*

exper/iment sta/tion, an establishment in which experiments in a particular line of research or activity, as agriculture or mining, are systematically carried on.

ex·pert (*n., v.* ek/spûrt; *adj.* ik spûrt/, ek/spûrt), *n.* **1.** a person who has special skill or knowledge in some particular field; specialist; authority: *a language expert; an expert on mining.* **—adj. 2.** possessing special skill or knowledge; trained by practice; skillful or skilled (often fol. by *in* or *at*): *an expert driver; to be expert at driving a car.* **3.** pertaining to, coming from, or characteristic of an expert: *expert work; expert advice.* **—v.t. 4.** to act as an expert for. [ME < L *expert(us),* ptp. of *experīrī* to try, EXPERIENCE] **—ex·pert/ly,** *adv.* **—ex·pert/ness,** *n.*
—Syn. 1. connoisseur, master. **2.** experienced, proficient, dexterous, adroit. See **skillful. —Ant. 1.** novice. **2.** clumsy.

ex·per·tise¹ (ek/spər tēz/), *n.* expert skill or knowledge; expertness; know-how: *business expertise.* [< F: survey, report (made by experts; *ise-* taken to mean -ness. See EXPERT, -ISE²]

ex·pert·ise² (ek/spər tīz/), *v.t., v.i.,* **-ised, -is·ing.** *Chiefly Brit.* expertize.

ex·pert·ism (ek/spər tiz/əm), *n.* expertness or skill, esp. in a specific field. [EXPERT + -ISM]

ex·pert·ize (ek/spər tīz/), *v.t., v.i.,* **-ized, -iz·ing.** to study or investigate as an expert. Also, *esp. Brit.,* expertise. [EXPERT + -IZE]

ex·per·to cre·di·te (eks PER/tō KRE/di te/; *Eng.* ek spûr/tō kred/i tē/), *Latin.* believe in the expert; trust one who has had experience.

ex·pi·a·ble (ek/spē ə bəl), *adj.* capable of being expiated: *an expiable crime.* [< LL *expiābil(is),* equiv. to *expiā(re)* (to) EXPIATE + *-bilis* -BLE]

ex·pi·ate (ek/spē āt/), *v.t.,* **-at·ed, -at·ing.** to atone for; make amends or reparation for: *to expiate one's guilt.* [< L *expiāt(us)* atoned for, made good (ptp. of *expiāre*), equiv. to *ex-* EX-¹ + *piā(re)* (to) propitiate (see PIOUS) + *-tus* ptp. suffix] **—ex/pi·a/tor,** *n.*

ex·pi·a·tion (ek/spē ā/shən), *n.* **1.** the act of expiating. **2.** the means by which atonement or reparation is made. [late ME *expiacion* < L *expiātiōn-* (s. of *expiātiō*) atonement, satisfaction. See EXPIATE, -ION] **—ex/pi·a/tion·al,** *adj.*

ex·pi·a·to·ry (ek/spē ə tôr/ē, -tōr/ē), *adj.* able to make atonement or expiation; offered by way of expiation: *expiatory sacrifices.* [< LL *expiātōri(us),* equiv. to *expiāt(us)* (see EXPIATE) + *-ōrius* -ORY¹]

ex·pi·ra·tion (ek/spə rā/shən), *n.* **1.** a coming to an end; termination; close: *the expiration of a contract.* **2.** the act of expiring, or breathing out; emission of air from the lungs. **3.** *Archaic.* death. [late ME *expiracioun* < L *expīrātiōn-* (s. of *expīrātiō*), equiv. to *expīrāt(us)* (ptp. of *ex(s)pīrāre* to EXPIRE) + *-iōn-* -ION]

ex·pir·a·to·ry (ik spīᵊr/ə tôr/ē, -tōr/ē), *adj.* pertaining to the expiration of air from the lungs. [EXPIRAT(ION) + -ORY¹]

ex·pire (ik spīᵊr/), *v.,* **-pired, -pir·ing. —v.i. 1.** to come to an end; terminate, as a contract, guarantee, etc. **2.** to die out, as a fire. **3.** to emit the last breath; die. **4.** to breathe out. **—v.t. 5.** to breathe out; emit (air) from the lungs. **6.** *Obs.* to give off, emit, or eject. [late ME < L *ex(s)pīr(āre)* (to) breathe out, equiv. to *ex-* EX-¹ + *spīrāre* to breathe] **—ex·pir/er,** *n.* **—ex·pir/ing·ly,** *adv.*

ex·pir·ee (ek/spī rē/, ik spīᵊr/ē), *n.* *Australian.* emancipist. [EXPIRE + -EE]

ex·pi·ry (ik spīᵊr/ē, ek/spə rē), *n., pl.* **-ries. 1.** expiration of breath. **2.** an end or termination, as of life, a contract, etc. [EXPIRE + -Y³]

ex·pis·cate (ek/spi skāt/, ik spis/kāt), *v.t.,* **-cat·ed, -cat·ing.** *Chiefly Scot.* to find out by thorough and detailed investigation; discover through scrupulous examination. [< L *expiscāt(us),* ptp. of *expiscārī* to fish out. See EX-¹, PISCI-, -ATE¹] **—ex/pis·ca/tion,** *n.* **—ex·pis·ca·to·ry** (ek spis/kə tôr/ē, -tōr/ē), *adj.*

ex·plain (ik splān/), *v.t.* **1.** to make plain or clear; render intelligible: *to explain an obscure point.* **2.** to make known in detail: *to explain how to do something; to explain a process.* **3.** to assign a meaning to; interpret: *How can you explain such a silly remark?* **4.** to make clear the cause or reason of; account for: *I cannot explain your untoward behavior.* **—v.i. 5.** to give an explanation. **6. explain away, a.** to dispel (doubts, difficulties, etc.) by explanation: *She explained away the child's fears.* **b.** to diminish or nullify the significance of by explanation: *He couldn't explain away his absence from home at the time the robbery was committed.* [late ME *explane(n)* < L *explān(āre)* (to) smooth out, make intelligible, spread out on flat surface. See EX-¹, PLANE¹] **—ex·plain/a·ble,** *adj.* **—ex·plain/er, ex·pla·na·tor** (ek/splə nā/tər), *n.*
—Syn. 1. explicate. EXPLAIN, ELUCIDATE, EXPOUND, INTERPRET imply making the meaning of something clear or understandable. To EXPLAIN is to make plain, clear, or intelligible something that is not known or understood: *to explain a theory or a problem.* To ELUCIDATE is to throw light on what before was dark and obscure, usually by illustration and commentary and sometimes by elaborate explanation: *They asked him to elucidate his statement.* To EXPOUND is to give a methodical, detailed, scholarly explanation of something, usually Scriptures, doctrines, or philosophy: *to expound the doctrine of free will.* To INTERPRET is to give the meaning of something by paraphrase, by translation, or by an explanation (sometimes involving one's personal opinion and therefore original), which is often of a systematic and detailed nature: *to interpret a poem or a symbol.* **4.** justify. **—Ant. 1.** confuse.

ex·pla·nate (eks/plə nāt/, eks plā/nāt), *adj.* *Bot., Zool.* flattened; spread out. [< L *explānāt(us),* ptp. of *explānāre* to EXPLAIN; see -ATE¹]

ex·pla·na·tion (ek/splə nā/shən), *n.* **1.** the act or process of explaining. **2.** that which explains; a statement made to clarify something and make it understandable; exposition: *the explanation of a poem.* **3.** a meaning or interpretation: *to find an explanation of a mystery.* **4.** a mutual declaration of the meaning of words spoken, actions, motives, etc., with a view to adjusting a misunderstanding or reconciling differences: *After a long, emotional explanation they were friends again.* [ME *explanacioun* < L *explānātiōn-* (s. of *explānātiō*), equiv. to *explānāt(us)* (see EXPLANATE) + *-iōn-* -ION]
—Syn. 1. elucidation, explication, exposition, definition, interpretation, description. **3.** solution, key, answer, account, justification.

ex·plan·a·to·ry (ik splan/ə tôr/ē, -tōr/ē), *adj.* serving to explain: *an explanatory footnote.* Also, **ex·plan/a·tive.** [< LL *explānātōri(us).* See EXPLANATE, -ORY¹] **—ex·plan/a·to/ri·ly, ex·plan/a·tive·ly,** *adv.*

ex·plant (eks plant/, -plänt/), *v.t.* **1.** to take living material from an animal or plant and place it in a culture medium. **—n. 2.** a piece of explanted tissue. [< NL *explant(āre).* See EX-¹, PLANT] **—ex/plan·ta/tion,** *n.*

ex·ple·ment (ek/splə mənt), *n.* *Math.* the quantity by which an angle or an arc falls short of 360° or a circle. [< L *explēment(um)* that which fills up, equiv. to *explē(re)* (to) fill (*ex-* EX-¹ + *plēre* to fill) + *-mentum* -MENT] **—ex·ple·men·tal** (ek/splə men/tᵊl), **ex·ple·men·ta·ry** (ek/splə men/tə rē, -trē), *adj.*

ex/plemen/tary an/gle, *Math.* either of two angles that added together produce an angle of 360°.

ex·ple·tive (ek/splə tiv), *adj.* **1.** Also, **ex·ple·to·ry** (ek/splə tôr/ē, -tōr/ē). added merely to fill out a sentence or line, give emphasis, etc.: *Expletive remarks padded the speech.* **—n. 2.** a syllable, word, or phrase serving to fill out. **3.** an interjectory word or expression, frequently profane; an exclamatory oath: *When angry, father employed the expletives he learned in the army.* **4.** *Gram.* a word considered as regularly filling the syntactic position of another, as *it* in *It is his duty to go,* or *there* in *There is nothing here.* [< LL *explētīv(us)* serving to fill out, equiv. to L *explēt(us)* filled, filled up (ptp. of *explēre;* see EXPLEMENT) + *-īvus* -IVE] **—ex/ple·tive·ly,** *adv.*

ex·pli·ca·ble (ek/spli kə bəl, ik splik/ə bəl), *adj.* capable of being explained. [< L *explicābil(is),* equiv. to *explicā(re)* (to) EXPLICATE + *-bilis* -BLE]

ex·pli·can·dum (ek/splə kan/dəm), *n., pl.* **-da** (-də). a term or statement that is to be explained, as in a philosophical discussion. [< L, neut. of ger. of *explicāre* to EXPLICATE]

ex·pli·cans (ek/splə kanz/), *n., pl.* **-can·ti·a** (-kan/chē ə). the meaning of a term or statement, as in a philosophical discussion. [< L, neut. of prp. of *explicāre* to EXPLICATE]

ex·pli·cate (ek/splə kāt/), *v.t.,* **-cat·ed, -cat·ing. 1.** to develop (a principle, theory, etc.). **2.** to make plain or clear; explain; interpret. [< L *explicāt(us)* unfolded, set forth, ptp. of *explicāre,* equiv. to *ex-* EX-¹ + *plicāre* to fold; see -ATE¹] **—ex/pli·ca/tor,** *n.*

ex·pli·ca·tion (ek/splə kā/shən), *n.* **1.** the act of explicating. **2.** an explanation; interpretation. [< F < L *explicātiōn-* (s. of *explicātiō*). See EXPLICATE, -ION]

ex·pli·ca·tion de texte (ek splē kä syôɴ də tekst/), *pl.* **ex·pli·ca·tions de texte** (ek splē kä syôɴ də tekst/). *French.* an approach to literary criticism involving close examination, analysis, and exposition of the text of a work, and concentrating on language, style, content, and the interrelationships of the parts to the whole in regard to meaning and symbolism. [lit., explanation of text]

ex·pli·ca·tive (ek/splə kā/tiv, ik splik/ə tiv), *adj.* explanatory; interpretive. Also, **ex·pli·ca·to·ry** (ek/splə kə tôr/ē, -tōr/ē). [< L *explicātīv(us).* See EXPLICATE, -IVE] **—ex/pli·ca/tive·ly,** *adv.*

ex·plic·it (ik splis/it), *adj.* **1.** fully and clearly expressed; leaving nothing merely implied; unequivocal: *an explicit statement; an explicit instruction.* **2.** clearly developed or formulated: *explicit knowledge; explicit belief.* **3.** definite and unreserved in expression; outspoken: *He was quite explicit on what he expected us to do for him.* **4.** *Math.* (of a function) having the dependent variable expressed directly in terms of the independent variables, as $y = 3x + 4$. Cf. **implicit** (def. 4). [< L *explicit(us)* unfolded, set forth, var. ptp. of *explicāre.* See EXPLICATE] **—ex·plic/it·ly,** *adv.* **—ex·plic/it·ness,** *n.*
—Syn. 1. express, definite, precise, exact, unambiguous. **3.** open, definite, unabashed. **—Ant. 1.** indefinite, ambiguous.

ex·plode (ik splōd/), *v.,* **-plod·ed, -plod·ing. —v.i. 1.** to expand with force and noise because of rapid chemical change or decomposition, as gunpowder, nitroglycerine, etc. (opposed to *implode*). **2.** to burst, fly into pieces, or break up violently with a loud report, as a boiler from excessive pressure of steam. **3.** to burst forth violently or emotionally, esp. with noise, laughter, violent speech, etc.: *He exploded with rage when contradicted.* **4.** *Phonet.* (of plosives) to terminate the occlusive phase with a plosion. Cf. **implode** (def. 2). **5.** *Golf.* to play an explosion shot on a golf ball. **—v.t. 6.** to cause (gunpowder, a boiler, etc.) to explode. **7.** to cause to be rejected; destroy the repute of; discredit or disprove: *to explode a theory.* **8.** *Phonet.* to end with plosion. **9.** *Golf.* to play an explosion shot on (a golf ball). **10.** *Obs.* to drive (a player, play, etc.) from the stage by loud expressions of disapprobation. [< L *explōd(ere)* (to) drive off by clapping, drive away, equiv. to *ex-* EX-¹ + *plōdere* to clap, beat] **—ex·plod/er,** *n.* **—ex·plo·si·bil·i·ty** (ik splō/zə bil/i tē, -sə-), *n.* **—ex·plo/si·ble,** *adj.*

explod/ed view/, a drawing, photograph, or the like, that shows the individual parts of a mechanism separately but indicates their proper relationship.

A, Exploded view of marine steam engine connecting rod; B, Assembled; 1, Connecting rod; 2, Strap; 3, Brass; 4, Gib; 5, Cotter

ex·plod·ent (ik splōd/ᵊnt), *n.* an explosive. [< L *explōdent-* (s. of *explōdēns*), prp. of *explōdere* to EXPLODE; see -ENT]

ex·ploit¹ (ek/sploit, ik sploit/), *n.* a striking or notable deed; feat; spirited or heroic act: *the exploits of Alexander the Great.* [ME *exploit, espleit* < OF *esploit,* AF *espleit* < L *explicit(um),* n. use of neut. of *explicitus* (ptp.). See EXPLICIT]
—Syn. accomplishment. See **achievement.**

ex·ploit² (ik sploit/), *v.t.* **1.** to utilize, esp. for profit; turn to practical account: *to exploit a business opportunity.* **2.** to use selfishly for one's own ends: *mothers who exploit their beautiful daughters.* **3.** to advance or further through exploitation; promote: *He exploited his new movie through a series of guest appearances and press parties.* [< F *exploit(er),* deriv. of *exploit* (n.); r. late ME *expleite* to achieve < AF *espleiter,* deriv. of *espleit* (n.). See EXPLOIT¹] **—ex·ploit/a·ble,** *adj.* **—ex·ploit/a·tive, ex·ploit·a·to·ry** (ik sploit/ə tôr/ē, -tōr/ē), **ex·ploit/ive,** *adj.*

ex·ploi·ta·tion (ek/sploi tā/shən), *n.* **1.** utilization for profit: *the exploitation of newly discovered oil fields.* **2.** selfish utilization: *He got ahead through the exploitation of his friends.* **3.** the combined, often varied, use of public-relations and advertising techniques to promote a person, movie, product, etc. [< F; see EXPLOIT, -ATION]

ex·ploit·er (ik sploi/tər), *n.* **1.** a person who exploits someone or something. **—v.t. 2.** to exploit. [EXPLOIT + -ER¹]

ex·plo·ra·tion (ek/splə rā/shən), *n.* **1.** the act or an instance of exploring or investigating; examination. **2.** the investigation of unknown regions. [< L *explōrātiōn-* (s. of *explōrātiō*) an examination, equiv. to *explōrāt(us)* searched out, examined (ptp. of *explōrāre* to EXPLORE) + *-iōn-* -ION]

ex·plor·a·to·ry (ik splōr/ə tôr/ē, -splôr/ə tôr/ē), *adj.* **1.** pertaining to or concerned with exploration: *an exploratory operation.* **2.** inclined to make explorations. Also, **ex·plor/a·tive.** [late ME < L *explōrātōri(us).* See EXPLORATION, -ORY¹] **—ex·plor/a·tive·ly,** *adv.*

ex·plore (ik splōr/, -splôr/), *v.,* **-plored, -plor·ing. —v.t. 1.** to traverse or range over (a region, area, etc.) for the purpose of discovery: *to explore the island.* **2.** to look into closely; scrutinize; examine: *Let us explore the possibilities for improvement in this area.* **3.** *Surg.* to investigate into, esp. mechanically, as with a probe. **4.** *Obs.* to search for; search out. **—v.i. 5.** to engage in exploration. [< L *explōr(āre)* (to) search out, examine, equiv. to *ex-* EX-¹ + *plōrāre* to make flow] **—ex·plor/a·ble,** *adj.* **—ex·plor/ing·ly,** *adv.*

ex·plor·er (ik splōr/ər, -splôr/-), *n.* **1.** one who or that which explores. **2.** a person who investigates unknown regions: *the great explorers of the Renaissance.* **3.** any instrument used in exploring or sounding a wound, or a cavity in a tooth, etc. **4.** a boy of 14 years or over who is an active participant in the exploring program sponsored by the Boy Scouts of America. **5.** (*cap.*) *U.S.* one of a series of satellites equipped to study cosmic rays, radiation belts, micrometeorites, gamma radiation, etc. Explorer I was the first successful U.S. satellite. [EXPLORE + -ER¹]

explor/er tent/, a low, wide tent having a ridgepole and affording considerable sleeping space but very little headroom.

ex·plo·sim·e·ter (ek/splō zim/i tər, -sim/-), *n.* a device for measuring the concentration of potentially explosive fumes. [*explosi(bility)* (see EXPLOSIVE, -IBLE, -ITY) + -METER]

ex·plo·sion (ik splō/zhən), *n.* **1.** the act or an instance of exploding; a violent expansion or bursting with noise, as of gunpowder or a boiler (opposed to *implosion*). **2.** the noise itself: *The explosion woke them.* **3.** a violent outburst, as of laughter, anger, etc. **4.** a sudden, rapid, or great increase: *a population explosion.* **5.** the burning of the mixture of fuel and air in an internal-combustion engine. **6.** *Phonet.* plosion. [< L *explōsiōn-* (s. of *explōsiō*), equiv. to *explōs(us)* driven off by clapping (ptp. of *explōdere* to EXPLODE) + *-iōn-* -ION]

explo/sion shot/, *Golf.* a shot for playing a golf ball out of a sand trap in which the club is swung down into the sand just under and behind the ball.

ex·plo·sive (ik splō/siv), *adj.* **1.** tending or serving to explode: *Nitroglycerin is an explosive substance.* **2.** pertaining to or of the nature of an explosion: *explosive violence.* **3.** *Phonet.* plosive. **—n. 4.** an explosive agent or substance, as dynamite. **5.** *Phonet.* plosive. [EXPLOS(ION) + -IVE] **—ex·plo/sive·ly,** *adv.* **—ex·plo/sive·ness,** *n.*

explosive D, dunnite.

explo/sive riv/et, a rivet for driving into an inaccessible area, containing an explosive charge detonated after driving to expand the shank on the far side of the hole.

ex·po·nent (ik spō/nənt *or, esp. for 3,* ek/spō nənt), *n.* **1.** one who or that which expounds or explains; an interpreter: *an exponent of modern theory in the arts.* **2.** one who or that which is a representative, advocate, type, or symbol of something: *Lincoln is an exponent of American democracy.* **3.** *Algebra.* a symbol placed above and after another symbol to denote the power to which the latter is to be raised, as *n* in the expression x^n. [< L *expōnent-* (s. of *expōnēns*), prp. of *expōnere* to EXPOUND; see -ENT]

ex·po·nen·tial (ek/spō nen/shəl), *adj.* **1.** of or pertaining to an exponent or exponents. **2.** *Math.* **a.** of or pertaining to the constant *e.* **b.** (of an equation) having one or more unknown variables in one or more exponents. —*n.* **3.** *Math.* the constant *e* raised to the power equal to a given expression, as e^{3x}, which is the exponential of 3*x*. [EXPONENT + -IAL] —**ex′po·nen′tial·ly,** *adv.*

exponen′tial horn′, a loudspeaker horn with a cross-sectional area varying as a constant raised to an exponent proportional to the distance from the vertex.

ex·po·ni·ble (ik spō′nə bəl), *Logic.* —*adj.* **1.** (of a proposition) requiring an expanded and revised statement to remove some obscurity. —*n.* **2.** an exponible proposition. [< ML *expōnibil(is).* See EXPOUND, -IBLE]

ex·port (*v.* ik spōrt′, -spôrt′, ek′spōrt, -spôrt; *n., adj.* ek′spōrt, -spôrt), *v.t.* **1.** to send (commodities) to other countries or places for sale, exchange, etc. —*n.* **2.** the act of exporting; exportation: *the export of coffee.* **3.** that which is exported; an article exported: *Coffee is a major export of Colombia.* —*adj.* **4.** of or pertaining to exportation of goods or to exportable goods. [< L *export(āre)* (to) carry out, bear away, equiv. to *ex-* EX-[1] + *portāre* to carry, bear] —**ex·port′a·ble,** *adj.* —**ex·port′er,** *n.*

ex·por·ta·tion (ek′spōr tā′shən, -spôr-), *n.* **1.** the act of exporting; the sending of commodities out of a country, typically in trade. **2.** something exported. [< L *exportātiōn-* (s. of *exportātiō*), equiv. to *exportāt(us)* (ptp. of *exportāre* to EXPORT) + *-iōn-* -ION]

Ex′port-Im′port Bank′ (ek′spōrt im′pōrt, ek′spôrt im′pôrt), *U.S.* a federal bank, established in 1934, which is authorized, in the interest of promoting foreign trade, to make loans to foreign governments and commercial enterprises, with the provision that such funds be used only to purchase U.S. goods.

ex·pos·al (ik spō′zəl), *n.* an exposure. [EXPOSE + -AL[2]]

ex·pose (ik spōz′), *v.t.,* **-posed, -pos·ing.** **1.** to lay open to danger, attack, harm, etc.: *to expose soldiers to gunfire; to expose one's character to attack.* **2.** to lay open to something specified: *to expose oneself to the influence of good company.* **3.** to uncover or bare to the air, cold, etc.: *to expose one's head to the rain.* **4.** to present to view; exhibit; display: *The vender exposed his wares.* **5.** to make known, disclose, or reveal (intentions, secrets, etc.): *He exposed the secret she had confided to him.* **6.** to reveal or unmask (a crime, fraud, impostor, etc.). **7.** to hold up to public reprehension or ridicule (fault, folly, a fool, etc.). **8.** to desert in an unsheltered or open place; abandon, as a child. **9.** to subject, as to the action of something: *to expose a photographic plate to light.* [ME *expose(n)* < OF *expose(r),* equiv. to *ex-* EX-[1] + *poser* to put (see POSE[1]); but assoc. with deriv. of L *expōnere* to set forth, EXPOUND] —**ex·pos′a·ble,** *adj.* —**ex·pos′er,** *n.*
—**Syn. 1.** subject (to), endanger, imperil, jeopardize. **5.** uncover, unveil, betray. —**Ant. 2.** protect (from). **5.** conceal.

ex·po·sé (ek′spō zā′), *n.* an exposure or revelation, as of something discreditable: *Certain cheap magazines make a fortune out of sensational exposés.* [< F, n. use of ptp. of *exposer* to EXPOSE]

ex·posed (ik spōzd′), *adj.* **1.** left or being without shelter or protection: *The house stood on a windy, exposed plot of ground.* **2.** laid open to view; unconcealed: *an exposed king of spades.* **3.** susceptible to attack; vulnerable. [EXPOSE + -ED[2]] —**ex·pos·ed·ness** (ik spō′zid nis), *n.*

ex·po·si·tion (ek′spə zish′ən), *n.* **1.** an exhibition or show, as of the products of art and manufacture: *an art exposition; an automobile exposition.* **2.** the act of expounding, setting forth, or explaining: *the exposition of a point of view.* **3.** a detailed statement or explanation; explanatory treatise: *The students prepared expositions on familiar essay themes.* **4.** the act of presenting to view; display: *The singer gave a splendid exposition of vocal talent.* **5.** exposure (def. 7). **6.** the state of being exposed; exposure. **7.** *Music.* the first section of a fugue or a sonata form, in which the principal themes normally are introduced. [ME *exposicioun* < L *expositiōn-* (s. of *expositiō*), equiv. to *exposit(us)* (see EXPOSE) + *-iōn-* -ION] —**ex·po·si′tion·al,** *adj.*
—**Syn. 1.** exhibit, demonstration, display, presentation. **3.** elucidation, commentary; critique, interpretation, exegesis, explication.

ex·pos·i·tor (ik spoz′i tər), *n.* a person who expounds or gives an exposition. [ME < L *expositōr-* (s. of *expositor*), equiv. to *exposit(us)* (see EXPOSE) + *-ōr* -OR[2]] —**ex·pos·i·to·ri·al** (ik spoz′i tōr′ē əl, -tôr′-), *adj.* —**ex·pos′i·to′ri·al·ly,** *adv.*

ex·pos·i·to·ry (ik spoz′i tōr′ē, -tôr′ē), *adj.* of the nature of exposition; serving to expound, set forth, or explain: *an expository essay.* Also, **ex·pos′i·tive.** [< ML *expositōri(us).* See EXPOSITOR, -ORY[1]] —**ex·pos′i·to′ri·ly, ex·pos′i·tive·ly,** *adv.*

ex post (eks pōst′), based on analysis of the past performance of any economy (opposed to *ex ante*). [< L: from (what lies) behind, according to (what lies) behind]

ex post fac·to (eks′ pōst′ fak′tō), from or by subsequent action; subsequently; retrospectively. [< L: from a thing done afterward, from what is done afterward]

ex′ post′ fac′to law′, a law passed after an occurrence which, if applied to the facts of this occurrence, would alter the legal situation.

ex·pos·tu·late (ik spos′chə lāt′), *v.i.,* **-lat·ed, -lat·ing.** to reason earnestly with a person against something he intends to do or has done; remonstrate: *His father expostulated with him about the evils of gambling.* [< L *expostulāt(us)* demanded urgently, required (ptp. of *expostulāre*). See EX-[1], POSTULATE] —**ex·pos′tu·lat′ing·ly,** *adv.* —**ex·pos′tu·la′tor,** *n.*

ex·pos·tu·la·tion (ik spos′chə lā′shən), *n.* **1.** the act of expostulating; remonstrance; earnest and kindly protest: *In spite of my expostulations, he insisted on driving me home.* **2.** an expostulatory remark or address. [< L *expostulātiōn-* (s. of *expostulātiō*) complaint. See EXPOSTULATE, -ION]

ex·pos·tu·la·to·ry (ik spos′chə lə tōr′ē, -tôr′ē), *adj.* expostulating; conveying expostulation. Also, **ex·pos·tu·la·tive.** (ik spos′chə lā′tiv). [EXPOSTULATE + -ORY[1]]

ex·po·sure (ik spō′zhər), *n.* **1.** the act of exposing. **2.** disclosure, as of something private or secret: *the exposure of their invasion plans.* **3.** the act or an instance of revealing or unmasking, as an impostor, crime, fraud, etc.: *the exposure of graft and corruption.* **4.** presentation to view, esp. in an open or public manner: *His exposure of his anger shocked the company.* **5.** a laying open or subjecting to the action or influence of something: *exposure to the weather; The exposure of his theories to ridicule destroyed his self-confidence.* **6.** *Photog.* **a.** the act of presenting a film or the like to the actinic rays of light. **b.** each of the areas exposed on a film. **7.** a putting out without shelter or protection, as of a child; abandonment. **8.** the state of being exposed. **9.** situation with regard to sunlight or wind; aspect: *a southern exposure.* **10.** something exposed, as to view; an exposed surface: *exposures of rock.* [EXPOSE + -URE]
—**Syn. 2.** divulgement, revelation, exposé. **4.** display. —**Ant. 1.** concealment.

expo′sure in′dex, *Photog.* a figure indicating the proper exposure for a film of a certain speed in a certain light.

expo′sure me′ter, *Photog.* an instrument for measuring the intensity of light in a certain place or upon a certain object, having an adjustable scale for determining the optimum relations of shutter speeds and stops at each intensity. Also called **light meter.**

ex·pound (ik spound′), *v.t.* **1.** to set forth or state in detail: *to expound theories.* **2.** to explain; interpret. [ME *expoune(n), expounde(n)* < OF *espondre* < L *expōnere* to put out, set forth, explain, equiv. to *ex-* EX-[1] + *pōnere* to put] —**ex·pound′er,** *n.*
—**Syn. 2.** See **explain.**

ex-pres·i·dent (eks′prez′i dənt), *n.* a former president.

ex·press (ik spres′), *v.t.* **1.** to put (thought) into words: *to express an idea clearly.* **2.** to show, manifest, or reveal: *to express one's satisfaction.* **3.** to set forth the opinions, feelings, etc., of (oneself), as in speaking, writing, or painting: *He can express himself eloquently.* **4.** to represent by a symbol, character, figure, or formula: *to express water as H_2O; to express unknown quantities algebraically.* **5.** *U.S.* to send express: *to express a package or merchandise.* **6.** to press or squeeze out: *to express the juice of grapes.* **7.** to exude or emit (a liquid, odor, etc.), as if under pressure: *The roses expressed a sweet perfume.* —*adj.* **8.** clearly indicated; distinctly stated; definite; explicit; plain: *He defied my express command.* **9.** special; definite: *We have an express purpose in being here.* **10.** duly or exactly formed or represented: *an express image.* **11.** pertaining to an express: *an express agency.* **12.** specially direct or fast, as a train, highway, etc.: *An express bus passed the local bus.* —*n.* **13.** an express train, bus, elevator, etc. **14.** a system or method of sending freight, parcels, money, etc., that is faster and safer, but more expensive, than ordinary freight service: *We agree to send the package by express.* **15.** a company engaged in this business. **16.** *Brit.* a messenger or a message specially sent. **17.** that which is sent by express. —*adv.* **18.** by express: *to travel express.* **19.** *Obs.* expressly. [ME *expresse(n)* < L *express(us)* (ptp. of *exprimere*). See EX-[1], PRESS[1]] —**ex·press′er, ex·pres′sor,** *n.* —**ex·press′i·ble, ex·press′a·ble,** *adj.* —**ex·press′less,** *adj.*
—**Syn. 1.** utter, declare, word, state, formulate. **2.** indicate, represent. **4.** indicate, designate, signify, denote. **8.** obvious, unambiguous. **9.** particular, singular. **10.** faithful, exact, accurate, precise. **12.** swift, rapid, nonstop. **14.** courier. —**Ant. 2.** conceal.

ex·press·age (ik spres′ij), *n.* **1.** the business of transmitting parcels, money, etc., by express. **2.** the charge for such transmission. [EXPRESS + -AGE]

express′ boil′er, a marine water-tube boiler designed for the rapid generation of steam.

express′ deliv′ery, *Brit.* See **special delivery.**

expressed′ al′mond oil′. See **almond oil** (def. 1).

ex·pres·sion (ik spresh′ən), *n.* **1.** the act of expressing or setting forth in words: *the expression of opinions.* **2.** a particular word, phrase, or form of words: *archaic expressions.* **3.** the manner or form in which a thing is expressed in words; wording; phrasing: *delicacy of expression.* **4.** power of expressing in words: *joy beyond expression.* **5.** indication of feeling, spirit, character, etc., as on the face, in the voice, or in artistic execution: *the lyric expression embodied in his poetry.* **6.** a look or intonation expressing personal reaction, feeling, etc.: *a shocked expression.* **7.** the quality or power of expressing attitude, emotion, etc.: *a face that lacks expression; to read with expression.* **8.** the act of expressing or representing, as by symbols. **9.** *Math.* a symbol or a combination of symbols representing a value, relation, or the like. **10.** *Ling.* the stylistic characteristics of an utterance (opposed to *meaning*). **11.** *Ling.* the system of verbal utterances specific to a language (opposed to *content*). **12.** the act of expressing or pressing out. [ME < L *expressiōn-* (s. of *expressiō*) a pressing out. See EXPRESS, -ION] —**ex·pres′sion·al,** *adj.* —**ex·pres′sion·less,** *adj.* —**ex·pres′sion·less·ly,** *adv.*
—**Syn. 1.** utterance, declaration, assertion, statement. **2.** term, idiom. **3.** language, diction, phraseology. **5.** manifestation, sign. **6.** aspect, air, countenance, mien, tone.

Ex·pres·sion·ism (ik spresh′ə niz′əm), *n.* **1.** *Fine Arts.* **a.** (*usually l.c.*) a manner of painting, drawing, sculpting, etc., in which forms derived from nature are distorted or exaggerated and colors are intensified for emotive or expressive purposes. **b.** a style of art developed in the 20th century, characterized chiefly by heavy, often black lines that define forms, sharply contrasting, often vivid colors, and subjective or symbolic treatment of thematic material. **c.** *German,* **Ex·pres·si·o·nis·mus** (eks pres′ē ō nis′mo͝os). modern art, esp. the experimental or nonacademic styles of contemporary art. **2.** (*often l.c.*) *Theat.* a style of playwriting and stage presentation stressing the emotional content of a play, the subjective reactions of the characters, symbolic or abstract representations of reality, and nonnaturalistic techniques of scenic design. **3.** *Literature.* a technique of distorting objects and events in order to represent them as they are perceived by a character in a literary work. **4.** (*usually l.c.*) a phase in the development of early 20th-century music marked by the use of atonality and complex, unconventional rhythm, melody, and form, intended to express the composer's psychological and emotional life. [< G *Expressionism(us).* See EXPRESSION, -ISM] —**Ex·pres′sion·ist,** *n., adj.* —**Ex·pres′sion·is′tic,** *adj.* —**Ex·pres′sion·is′ti·cal·ly,** *adv.*

ex·pres·sive (ik spres′iv), *adj.* **1.** serving to express; indicative of power to express: *a look expressive of gratitude.* **2.** full of expression; meaningful: *an expressive shrug.* **3.** of, pertaining to, or concerned with expression: *Dance is a highly expressive art.* **4.** *Sociol.* (of a crowd or group) engaging in nonpurposeful activity of an expressive and often rhythmic nature, as weeping, dancing, shouting, etc. Cf. **active** (def. 14), **orgiastic** (def. 2). [ME < MF; see EXPRESS, -IVE] —**ex·pres′sive·ly,** *adv.* —**ex·pres′sive·ness,** *n.*
—**Syn. 1.** EXPRESSIVE, MEANING, SIGNIFICANT, SUGGESTIVE imply the conveying of a thought, indicating an attitude of mind, or the like, by words or otherwise. EXPRESSIVE suggests conveying, or being capable of conveying a thought, intention, emotion, etc., in an effective or vivid manner: *an expressive shrug.* MEANING and SIGNIFICANT imply an underlying and unexpressed thought whose existence is plainly shown although its precise nature is left to conjecture. MEANING implies a more secret and intimate understanding between the persons involved: *Meaning looks passed between them.* SIGNIFICANT suggests calling the attention of a person or persons to a happening which is important in some way to them or to others: *On hearing this statement, he gave the officers a significant glance.* SUGGESTIVE implies an indirect or covert conveying of a meaning, sometimes mentally stimulating, sometimes verging on impropriety or indecency: *a suggestive story or remark.* —**Ant. 1.** expressionless.

ex·pres·siv·i·ty (ek′spre siv′i tē), *n.* **1.** *Genetics.* the degree to which a particular gene produces its effect in an organism. Cf. **penetrance. 2.** the quality or state of being expressive. [< G *Expressivität.* See EXPRESSIVE, -ITY]

express′ let′ter, *Brit.* a special-delivery letter.

ex·press·ly (ik spres′lē), *adv.* **1.** in an express manner; explicitly: *I asked him expressly to stop talking.* **2.** for the express purpose; specially: *I came expressly to see you.* [ME *expressli.* See EXPRESS, -LY]

ex·press·man (ik spres′mən), *n., pl.* **-men. 1.** a man engaged in the express business. **2.** a man who makes collections or deliveries for an express company. [EXPRESS + MAN[1]]

express′ ri′fle, a rifle designed for firing at game at short range.

express′ wag′on, 1. a wagon for carrying or delivering goods sent by express. **2.** a low, rectangular, shallow wagon having a long handle for pulling, used by children at play.

ex·press·way (ik spres′wā′), *n.* a highway especially planned for high-speed traffic, usually having few if any intersections, limited points of access or exit, and a divider between opposite directions of traffic. [EXPRESS + WAY]

ex·pro·pri·ate (eks prō′prē āt′), *v.t.,* **-at·ed, -at·ing. 1.** to take possession of, esp. for public use by the right of eminent domain, thus divesting the title of the private owner: *The estate expropriated the land for a recreation area.* **2.** to dispossess (a person) of ownership: *The revolutionary government expropriated the landowners from their estates.* **3.** to take (something) from another's possession for one's own use: *He expropriated my ideas for his own article.* [< ML *expropriāt(us)* separated from one's own (ptp. of *expropriāre*), equiv. to *ex-* EX-[1] + *propri(āre)* (to) appropriate (deriv. of *proprius* PROPER) + *-ātus* -ATE[1]] —**ex·pro·pri·a·ble** (eks prō′prē ə bəl), *adj.* —**ex·pro′pri·a′tion,** *n.* —**ex·pro′pri·a′tor,** *n.*

ex·pugn·a·ble (ek spyo͞o′nə bəl, -spug′nə-), *adj.* able to be overcome, conquered, defeated, etc. [< L *expugnābil(is),* equiv. to *expugnā(re)* (to) take by storm (*ex-* EX-[1] + *pugnāre* to fight) + *-bilis* -BLE]

ex·pul·sion (ik spul′shən), *n.* **1.** the act of driving out or expelling: *expulsion of air; expulsion from a club.* **2.** the state of being expelled: *The prisoner's expulsion from society embittered him further.* [late ME < L *expulsiōn-* (s. of *expulsiō*), equiv. to *expuls(us)* driven out (ptp. of *expellere* to EXPEL) + *-iōn-* -ION]

ex·pul·sive (ik spul′siv), *adj.* tending or serving to expel. [ME < MF *expulsive* (fem.) < ML *expulsīv(us).* See EXPULSION, -IVE]

ex·punc·tion (ik spungk′shən), *n.* the act of expunging; erasure. [< L *expunctiōn-* (s. of *expunctiō*) a blotting out, equiv. to *expunct(us)* blotted out (ptp. of *expungere* to EXPUNGE) + *-iōn-* -ION]

ex·punge (ik spunj′), *v.t.,* **-punged, -pung·ing. 1.** to strike or blot out; erase; obliterate. **2.** to efface; wipe out or destroy. [< L *expung(ere)* (to) blot out, erase, equiv. to *ex-* EX-[1] + *pungere* to prick] —**ex·pung′er,** *n.*

ex·pur·gate (ek′spər gāt′, ik spûr′gāt), *v.t.,* **-gat·ed, -gat·ing. 1.** to amend by removing offensive or objectionable matter: *to expurgate a book.* **2.** to purge or cleanse of moral offensiveness. [< L *expurgāt(us),* ptp. of *expurgāre* to clean out. See EX-[1], PURGE, -ATE[1]] —**ex′pur·ga′tion,** *n.* —**ex′pur·ga′tor,** *n.*

ex·pur·ga·to·ri·al (ik spûr′gə tōr′ē əl, -tôr′-), *adj.* pertaining to an expurgator or to expurgation. [EXPURGATOR(Y) + -IAL]

ex·pur·ga·to·ry (ik spûr′gə tōr′ē, -tôr′ē), *adj.* **1.** serving to expurgate. **2.** of or pertaining to expurgation. [EXPURGATE + -ORY[1]]

ex·qui·site (ek′skwi zit, ik skwiz′it), *adj.* **1.** of special beauty or charm, or rare and appealing excellence, as a face, a flower, coloring, music, poetry, etc. **2.** extraordinarily fine or admirable; consummate: *the exquisite weather of June.* **3.** intense, acute, or keen, as pleasure, pain, etc. **4.** keenly or delicately sensitive or responsive: *an exquisite ear for music; an exquisite sensibility.* **5.** of rare excellence of production or execution, as works of art or workmanship: *the exquisite statues of the Renaissance.* **6.** of peculiar refinement or elegance, as taste, manners, etc., or persons. **7.** *Obs.* carefully sought out, chosen, ascertained, devised, etc. —*n.* **8.** a person, esp. a man, who is excessively concerned about his clothes, grooming, etc.; dandy; coxcomb. [late ME < L *exquīsīt(us)* sought after (ptp. of *exquīrere*). See EX-[1], QUEST, -ITE[2]] —**ex′qui·site·ly,** *adv.* —**ex′qui·site·ness,** *n.*
—**Syn. 1.** dainty, beautiful, elegant, rare. See **delicate. 2.** perfect, matchless. See **fine**[1]. **3.** poignant. **5.** select, choice, precious. **6.** discriminating. —**Ant. 1.** gross. **2.** ordinary. **3.** dull.

exr., executor.

ex′ rights′, *Stock Exchange.* without having the right to subscribe to new issues of stock, the rights being retained by the seller of the stock. Also, **ex′-rights′.**

ex·san·gui·nate (eks sang′gwə nāt′), *v.,* **-nat·ed, -nat·ing.** —*v.t.* **1.** to drain of blood; make bloodless. —*v.i.* **2.** to bleed to death. [< LL *exsanguināt(us)* bloodless, deprived of blood (ptp. of *exsanguināre*), equiv. to L *ex-* EX-[1] + *sanguin-* (s. of *sanguis* blood; see SANGUINE) + *-ātus* -ATE[1]] —**ex·san′gui·na′tion,** *n.*

ex·san·guine (eks sang′gwin), *adj.* anemic; bloodless. [< L *exsangu(is)* bloodless (see EX-[1], SANGUINE) + -INE[1]] —**ex′san·guin′i·ty,** *n.*

ex·scind (ek sind′), *v.t.* to cut out or off. [< L *exscind(ere)* (to) destroy, tear away, equiv. to *ex-* EX-[1] + *scindere* to cut, tear; see SCISSION]

exsec, exsecant.

ex·se·cant (eks′sē′kənt, -kant), *n.* *Trig.* the secant of a given angle or arc minus one: $\text{exsec}\,\theta = \sec\theta - 1$. *Abbr.:* exsec [EX-[1] + SECANT]

ex·sect (ek sekt′), *v.t.* to cut out. [< L *exsect(us)* cut out, cut away, ptp. of *ex(s)ecāre*, equiv. to *ex-* EX-[1] + *secāre* to cut; see SECT] —**ex·sec·tile** (ek sek′tᵊl, -tīl, -til), *adj.* —**ex·sec′tion,** *n.*

ex·sert (ek sûrt′), *v.t.* **1.** to thrust out. —*adj.* **2.** thrust out; exserted. [< L *exsert(us)* stretched out, put forth, var. of *exertus*; see EXERT] —**ex·ser′tion,** *n.*

ex·sert·ed (eks sûr′tid), *adj.* *Biol.* projecting beyond the surrounding parts, as a stamen. [EXSERT + -ED[2]]

ex·ser·tile (eks sûr′tᵊl, -til), *adj.* *Biol.* capable of being exserted or protruded. [< F *exertile*. See EXSERT, -ILE]

ex·ser·vice·man (eks′sûr′vis man′), *n., pl.* **-men.** *Chiefly Brit.* a person who has served in one of the armed services, esp. during wartime; veteran.

ex·sic·cate (ek′sə kāt′), *v.,* **-cat·ed, -cat·ing.** —*v.t.* **1.** to dry or remove the moisture from, as a substance. **2.** to dry up, as moisture. —*v.i.* **3.** to dry up. [late ME < L *exsiccāt(us)* dried up ptp. of *exsiccāre*, equiv. to *ex-* EX-[1] + *siccāre* to dry, make dry; see -ATE[1]] —**ex′sic·ca′tion,** *n.* —**ex′sic·ca′tive,** *adj.* —**ex′sic·ca′tor,** *n.*

ex·so·lu·tion (eks′sə lo͞o′shən), *n.* the process of exsolving. [< L *exsolūtiōn-* (s. of *exsolūtiō*). See EX-[1], SOLUTION]

ex·solve (eks solv′), *v.i.,* **-solved, -solv·ing.** (of two minerals in solid solution) to separate from one another at a critical point in temperature. [< L *exsolve(re)*. See EX-[1], SOLVE]

ex·stip·u·late (eks stip′yo͝o lit, -lāt′), *adj.* *Bot.* having no stipules. Also, **estipulate.** [EX-[1] + STIPULE + -ATE[1]]

ex′ store′, *Com.* with shipping costs from the store or warehouse to be paid by the buyer or consignee.

ex·suf·fli·cate (ik suf′li kit, -kāt′), *adj.* *Obs.* overblown. [arbitrary formation from *exsufflate* to blow out, away < L *exsufflāt(us)* (ptp. of *exsufflāre*). See EX-[1], SUFFLATE]

ext., **1.** extension. **2.** external. **3.** extinct. **4.** extra. **5.** extract.

ex·tant (ek′stənt, ik stant′), *adj.* **1.** in existence; still existing; not destroyed or lost: *three extant copies of the book.* **2.** *Archaic.* standing out; protruding. [< L *ex(s)tant-* (s. of *ex(s)tāns*) standing out, prp. of *exstāre*, equiv. to *ex-* EX-[1] + *stāre* to stand]

Ex·ta·sie, The (ek′stə sē), a poem (1590–1600?) by John Donne, published in 1633. Also, **The Ecstasie, The Ecstasy.**

ex·tem·po·ral (ik stem′pər əl), *adj.* *Archaic.* extemporaneous; extempore. [< L *extemporāl(is)* on the spur of the moment. See EXTEMPORE, -AL[1]] —**ex·tem′po·ral·ly,** *adv.*

ex·tem·po·ra·ne·ous (ik stem′pə rā′nē əs), *adj.* **1.** done, spoken, performed, etc., without special advance preparation; impromptu: *an extemporaneous speech.* **2.** previously planned but delivered with the help of few or no notes: *extemporaneous lectures.* **3.** speaking or performing with little or no advance preparation: *extemporaneous actors.* **4.** made for the occasion, as a shelter. [< LL *extemporāneus* on the spur of the moment. See EXTEMPORE, -ANEOUS] —**ex·tem′po·ra′ne·ous·ly,** *adv.* —**ex·tem′po·ra′ne·ous·ness, ex·tem·po·ra·ne·i·ty** (ik stem′pə rə nē′i tē), *n.*
—**Syn. 1.** EXTEMPORANEOUS (EXTEMPORARY, EXTEMPORE), IMPROMPTU, IMPROVISED are used of (artistic) expression given without preparation or based on only partial preparation. EXTEMPORANEOUS, although often used interchangeably with IMPROMPTU, is applied esp. to an unmemorized speech given from an outline or notes: *an extemporaneous discussion.* IMPROMPTU is applied to a speech (poem, song, etc.) delivered without preparation, and at a moment's notice: *Called upon without warning, she nevertheless gave an excellent impromptu speech.* IMPROVISED is applied to that which is composed (recited, sung, acted) on a particular occasion, and is made up, at least in part, as one goes along: *an improvised piano accompaniment.* —**Ant. 1.** memorized.

ex·tem·po·rar·y (ik stem′pə rer′ē), *adj.* **1.** extemporaneous; extempore. **2.** *Obs.* sudden; unexpected. [EXTEMPOR(E) + -ARY] —**ex·tem·po·rar·i·ly** (ik stem′pə râr′ə lē), *adv.* —**ex·tem′po·rar′i·ness,** *n.*
—**Syn. 1.** See **extemporaneous.**

ex·tem·po·re (ik stem′pə rē), *adv.* **1.** on the spur of the moment; without premeditation or preparation; offhand: *Questions were asked extempore from the floor.* **2.** without notes: *to speak extempore.* **3.** (of musical performance) by improvisation. —*adj.* **4.** extemporaneous; impromptu. [< L: lit., out of the time, at the moment, equiv. to *ex-* EX-[1] + *tempore* the time (abl. sing. of *tempus*)]
—**Syn. 4.** See **extemporaneous.**

ex·tem·po·rise (ik stem′pə rīz′), *v.i., v.t.,* **-rised, -ris·ing.** *Chiefly Brit.* extemporize. —**ex·tem′po·ri·sa′tion,** *n.* —**ex·tem′po·ris′er,** *n.*

ex·tem·po·rize (ik stem′pə rīz′), *v.,* **-rized, -riz·ing.** —*v.i.* **1.** to speak extemporaneously: *He can extemporize on any of a number of subjects.* **2.** to sing, or play on an instrument, composing the music as one proceeds; improvise. **3.** to do or manage something in a makeshift way. —*v.t.* **4.** to make or devise extempore. **5.** *Music.* to compose offhand; improvise. [EXTEMPOR(E) + -IZE] —**ex·tem′po·ri·za′tion,** *n.* —**ex·tem′po·riz′er,** *n.*

ex·tend (ik stend′), *v.t.* **1.** to stretch out; draw out to the full length: *He extended the measuring tape as far as it would go.* **2.** to stretch, draw, or arrange in a given direction, or so as to reach a particular point, as a cord, wall, line of troops, etc. **3.** to stretch forth or hold out, as the arm or hand. **4.** to place at full length, esp. horizontally, as the body, limbs, etc. **5.** to increase the length or duration of; lengthen; prolong: *to extend a visit for another week.* **6.** to stretch out in various or all directions; expand; spread out in area: *A huge tent was extended over the field to house the spectators.* **7.** to enlarge the scope of, or make more comprehensive, as operations or influence: *The European powers extended their authority in Asia.* **8.** to hold forth as an offer or grant; offer; grant; give: *to extend aid to needy scholars.* **9.** *Finance.* to postpone (the payment of a debt) beyond the time originally agreed upon. **10.** *Bookkeeping.* to transfer (figures) from one column to another. **11.** *Law.* **a.** *Brit.* to assess or value. **b.** to make a seizure or levy upon, as land, by a writ of extent. **12.** *Manège.* to bring (a horse) into an extended attitude. **13.** *Obs.* to take by seizure. **14.** *Obs.* to exaggerate. —*v.i.* **15.** to be or become extended; stretch out in length, duration, or various or all directions. **16.** to reach, as to a particular point. **17.** to increase in length, area, scope, etc. **18.** *Manège.* (of a horse) to come into an extended attitude. [ME *extend(en)* < L *extend(ere)* (to) stretch out. See EX-[1], TEND[1]] —**ex·tend′i·ble, ex·tend′a·ble,** *adj.* —**ex·tend′i·bil′i·ty, ex·tend′a·bil′i·ty,** *n.*
—**Syn. 5.** continue. See **lengthen. 6.** spread, enlarge; widen, dilate. **8.** bestow, impart. —**Ant. 1.** shorten, contract.

ex·tend·ed (ik sten′did), *adj.* **1.** stretched out: *extended wires.* **2.** continued or prolonged: *extended efforts.* **3.** spread out: *extended flags fluttering in the breeze.* **4.** widespread or extensive; having extension or spatial magnitude: *extended treatment of a subject; extended frontiers.* **5.** outstretched: *extended arms; extended wings.* **6.** *Print.* expanded. **7.** *Manège.* **a.** (of a moving horse) noting an elongated pose in which the legs reach out from the body, the chin is out from the chest, etc. Cf. **collected** (def. 3a). **b.** (of the gait of a horse) characterized by long, low, usually fast strides. Cf. **collected** (def. 3b). [EXTEND + -ED[2]] —**ex·tend′ed·ly,** *adv.* —**ex·tend′ed·ness,** *n.*

extend′ed com′plex plane′, *Math.* the complex plane with a point at infinity added.

extend′ed cov′erage, an endorsement to a fire-insurance policy, covering losses resulting from such perils as windstorms, boiler explosions, and riots.

extend′ed fam′ily, *Anthropol.* a special group consisting of a family nucleus and various near relatives.

extend′ed or′der, 1. an irregular formation of troops to suit the tactical requirements and the terrain. **2.** See **open order.**

extend′ed play′, a phonograph record of 45 r.p.m. that plays a longer time than the standard 45 r.p.m. record. *Abbr.:* EP

extend′ed real′ num′ber sys′tem, *Math.* the set of all real numbers with the points plus infinity and minus infinity added.

extend′ed term′ insur′ance, life insurance in which a policyholder ceases to pay the premiums but keeps the full amount of the policy in force for as long as the cash value will permit.

ex·tend·er (ik sten′dər), *n.* any inert chemical substance added to paint chiefly to increase its volume. [EXTEND + -ER[1]]

ex·ten·si·ble (ik sten′sə bəl), *adj.* capable of being extended. [EXTENS(ION) + -IBLE] —**ex·ten′si·bil′i·ty, ex·ten′si·ble·ness,** *n.*

ex·ten·sile (ik sten′səl, -sīl), *adj.* *Chiefly Zool., Anat.* capable of being extended; adapted for stretching out; extensible; protrusible. [EXTENS(ION) + -ILE]

ex·ten·sim·e·ter (ek′sten sim′i tər), *n.* extensometer.

ex·ten·sion (ik sten′shən), *n.* **1.** the act, state, or an instance of extending. **2.** the state of being extended. **3.** that by which something is extended; prolongation: *a four-room extension to a house; a two-hour extension of a dance.* **4.** something extended; an extended object: *a table with drop-leaf extensions.* **5.** range of extending; degree of extensiveness; extent: *the extension of man's knowledge.* **6.** a telephone that operates on the same line as another; an additional telephone: *He has a telephone in the bedroom and an extension in the kitchen.* **7.** *Com.* a written engagement on the part of a creditor, allowing a debtor further time to pay a debt. **8.** *Physics.* that property of a body by which it occupies space. **9.** *Anat.* **a.** the act of straightening a limb. **b.** the position which a limb assumes when it is straightened. **10.** *Surg.* the act of pulling the broken or dislocated part of a limb in a direction from the trunk, in order to bring the ends of the bone into their natural situation. **11.** Also called **extent.** *Logic.* the class of things to which a term is applicable, as "the class of such beings as Plato and Alexander" to which the term "man" is applicable. Cf. **intension** (def. 5). **12.** *Math.* a function having a domain that includes the domain of a given function and that has the same value as the given function at each point in the domain of the given function. Cf. **Tietze's extension theorem. 13.** *Manège.* the act of bringing or coming into an extended attitude. [late ME < LL *extensiōn-* (s. of *extensiō*). See EXTENSIVE, -ION] —**ex·ten′sion·al′i·ty, ex·ten′sion·al·ism,** *n.* —**ex·ten′sion·al,** *adj.* —**ex·ten′sion·al·ly,** *adv.* —**ex·ten′sion·less,** *adj.*
—**Syn. 1.** stretching, expansion, enlargement, increase, dilation. **3.** lengthening, protraction, continuation; delay. **5.** limit. —**Ant. 1.** contraction.

exten′sion bolt′, a bolt fitted into a mortise in a door or the like, sliding into a socket in the head or the sill and having a head projecting from the surface of the door.

exten′sion cours′es, (in many universities and colleges) a program for persons not regularly enrolled as students, frequently provided through evening classes or classes in off-campus centers, or by correspondence. Cf. **university extension.**

exten′sion field′, *Math.* a field which contains a given field as a subfield.

exten′sion lad′der, a ladder having two or more sections joined by a sliding mechanism which allows the ladder to be extended to the total length.

exten′sion rule′, a folding rule having a sliding part equal in length to one section so as to permit exact measurement of internal dimensions.

ex·ten·si·ty (ik sten′si tē), *n.* **1.** the quality of having extension. **2.** *Psychol.* the attribute of sensation from which the perception of extension is developed. [< L *extens(us)* (see EXTENSIVE) + -ITY]

ex·ten·sive (ik sten′siv), *adj.* **1.** of great extent; wide; broad: *an extensive area.* **2.** covering or extending over a great area: *extensive travels.* **3.** far-reaching; comprehensive; thorough: *extensive knowledge; extensive inquiries.* **4.** lengthy: *a novel with an extensive preface; an extensive journey.* **5.** great in amount, number, or degree: *an extensive fortune; He wants to have extensive political influence.* **6.** of or having extension: *Space is extensive; time, durational.* **7.** noting or pertaining to a system of agriculture involving the use or cultivation of large areas of land with a minimum of labor and expense (opposed to *intensive*). [late ME < LL *extensīv(us)*, equiv. to L *extens(us)* (ptp. of *extendere* to EXTEND) + *-īvus* -IVE] —**ex·ten′sive·ly,** *adv.* —**ex·ten′sive·ness, ex·ten·siv·i·ty** (ek′sten siv′i tē, ik-), *n.*
—**Syn. 1.** extended, large, spacious, ample, vast. **3.** inclusive. —**Ant. 1, 3.** limited, narrow. confined; **3.** parochial.

ex·ten·som·e·ter (ek′sten som′i tər), *n.* *Mach.* an instrument for measuring minute degrees of expansion, contraction, or deformation. Also, **extensimeter.** [EXTENS(ION) + -O- + -METER]

ex·ten·sor (ik sten′sər, -sôr), *n.* *Anat.* a muscle that serves to extend or straighten a part of the body. [< NL, equiv. to L *extens(us)* (see EXTENSIVE) + *-or* -OR[2]]

ex·tent (ik stent′), *n.* **1.** the space or degree to which a thing extends; length, area, volume, or scope: *the extent of his lands; to be right to a certain extent.* **2.** something extended; an extended space; a particular length, area, or volume; something having extension: *the limitless extent of the skies.* **3.** *U.S. Law.* a writ, or a levy, by which a creditor has his debtor's lands valued and transferred to himself, absolutely or for a term of years. **4.** *Eng. Law.* **a.** Also called **writ of extent.** a writ to recover debts of record due to the crown, under which land, property, etc., may be seized. **b.** a seizure made under such a writ. **5.** *Archaic.* assessment or valuation, as of land. **6.** *Logic.* extension (def. 11). [ME *extente* assessment < ML *extenta*, n. use of fem. of L *extentus*, ptp. of *extendere* to EXTEND]
—**Syn. 1.** magnitude, measure, amount, scope, compass, range, expanse, stretch, reach, length, area. See **size.**

ex·ten·u·ate (ik sten′yo͞o āt′), *v.t.,* **-at·ed, -at·ing.** **1.** to represent (a fault, offense, etc.) as less serious: *to extenuate a crime.* **2.** to serve to make (a fault, offense, etc.) seem less serious: *a new development that extenuates the circumstances.* **3.** to underestimate, underrate, or make light of: *Do not extenuate the difficulties we are in.* **4.** *Archaic.* **a.** to make thin, lean, or emaciated. **b.** to reduce the consistency or density of. [late ME (adj.) < L *extenuāt(us)*, ptp. of *extenuāre*, equiv. to *ex-* EX-[1] + *tenuāre* to make thin or small; see -ATE[1]] —**ex·ten′u·at′ing,** *adj.* —**ex·ten′u·at′ing·ly,** *adv.* —**ex·ten′u·a′tive,** *adj.* —**ex·ten′u·a′tor,** *n.*

ex·ten·u·a·tion (ik sten′yo͞o ā′shən), *n.* **1.** the act of extenuating. **2.** the state of being extenuated. **3.** that which extenuates; a partial excuse: *The youth of the defendant served as an extenuation.* [late ME *extenuacioun* < L *extenuātiōn-* (s. of *extenuātiō*). See EXTENUATE, -ION]

ex·ten·u·a·to·ry (ik sten′yo͞o ə tôr′ē, -tōr′ē), *adj.* tending to extenuate; characterized by extenuation; extenuating. [< LL *extenuātōri(us)*. See EXTENUATE, -ORY[1]]

ex·te·ri·or (ik stēr′ē ər), *adj.* **1.** outer; being on the outer side: *the exterior surface; exterior decorations.* **2.** intended or suitable for outdoor use: *exterior paint; exterior plywood.* **3.** situated or being outside; pertaining to or connected with what is outside: *the exterior territories of a country.* —*n.* **4.** the outer surface or part; outside. **5.** outward form or appearance: *She has a pleasant exterior, but inside she is tormented.* **6. exteriors,** the externals: *He could see through the exteriors of any situation.* **7.** *Math.* the collection of points not contained in the closure of a given set. [< L, comp. of *exter* or *exterus* on the outside, outward. See EX-[1]] —**ex·te′ri·or·ly,** *adv.*
—**Syn. 1.** outward, outside, external, superficial. **3.** outlying, extraneous, foreign; extrinsic. **4.** face. **5.** mien, aspect, face. —**Ant. 1, 4.** interior.

exte′rior an′gle, *Geom.* **1.** an angle formed outside parallel lines by a third line that intersects them. See diag. under **interior angle. 2.** an angle formed outside a polygon by one side and an extension of an adjacent side; the supplement of an interior angle of the polygon.

exte′rior ballis′tics, a branch of ballistics dealing with the motion of projectiles after they leave the muzzle of the firing weapon.

ex·te·ri·or·ise (ik stēr′ē ə rīz′), *v.t.,* **-ised, -is·ing.** *Chiefly Brit.* exteriorize. —**ex·te′ri·or·i·sa′tion,** *n.*

ex·te·ri·or·ize (ik stēr′ē ə rīz′), *v.t.,* **-ized, -iz·ing.** **1.** to make exterior; externalize. **2.** *Surg.* to expose (an internal structure) temporarily outside the body, for observation, surgery, or experimentation. [EXTERIOR + -IZE] —**ex·te′ri·or·i·za′tion,** *n.*

ex·ter·mi·nate (ik stûr′mə nāt′), *v.t.,* **-nat·ed, -nat·ing.** to get rid of by destroying; destroy totally; extirpate: *to exterminate an enemy; to exterminate insects.* [< L *extermināt(us)*, ptp. of *extermināre* to EXTERMINE; see -ATE[1]] —**ex·ter·mi·na·ble** (ik stûr′mə nə bəl), *adj.* —**ex·ter′mi·na′tion,** *n.* —**ex·ter′mi·na′tor,** *n.*
—**Syn.** eradicate, abolish, annihilate, eliminate.

ex·ter·mi·na·to·ry (ik stûr′mə nə tôr′ē, -tōr′ē), *adj.* serving or tending to exterminate. Also, **ex·ter·mi·na·tive** (ik stûr′mə nā′tiv). [EXTERMINATE + -ORY[1]]

ex·ter·mine (ik stûr′min), *v.t.,* **-mined, -min·ing.** *Obs.* to exterminate. [late ME < L *extermin(āre)* (to) drive beyond the boundaries. See EX-[1], TERMINATE]

ex·tern (ek′stûrn, ik stûrn′), *n.* **1.** a person connected with an institution but not residing in it, as a doctor or student. **2.** a nun of a strictly enclosed order, as the Carmelites, who resides inside the convent but outside its enclosure and who chiefly goes on outside errands. —*adj.* **3.** *Archaic.* external; outer. [< L *extern(us)*, deriv. of *exter, exterus.* See EXTERIOR]

ex·ter·nal (ik stûr′nᵊl), *adj.* **1.** of or pertaining to the outside or outer part; outer: *an external surface.* **2.** *Med.* to be applied to the outside of a body, as a remedy: *for external use only.* **3.** situated or being outside of something; acting or coming from without: *external influences.* **4.** pertaining to the outward or visible appearance or show: *external acts of worship.* **5.** pertaining to or concerned with what is outside or foreign: *external commerce.* **6.** *Zool., Anat.* on the side farthest away from the body, from the median line, or from the center of a radially symmetrical form. **7.** *Metaphys.* of or pertaining to the world of things, considered as independent of the perceiving mind: *external world.* —*n.* **8.** the outside; outer surface; exterior. **9.**

that which is external. **10. externals,** external features, circumstances, etc.; outward appearance; superficialities: *The externals of a religion attract the shallow and the simple-minded.* [late ME; see EXTERN, -AL[1]] **—ex·ter′nal·ly,** *adv.*

exter′nal au′ditory mea′tus, *Anat.* the canal extending from the opening in the external ear to the tympanic membrane. See diag. under **ear.**

ex·ter·nal-com·bus·tion (ik stûr′nᵊl kəm bus′chən), *adj.* noting or pertaining to an engine, as a steam engine, in which fuel ignition takes place outside the cylinder, turbine, or the like, in which heat energy is transformed into mechanical force.

exter′nal ear′, the outer portion of the ear, consisting of the auricle and the canal extending to the tympanic membrane. Cf. **ear**[1] (def. 1). See diag. under **ear.**

exter′nal hem′orrhoid, *Pathol.* See under **hemorrhoid.**

exter′nal il′iac ar′tery, *Anat.* See **iliac artery** (def. 2).

ex·ter·nal·i·sa·tion (ik stûr′nᵊli zā′shən), *n. Chiefly Brit.* externalization.

ex·ter·nal·ise (ik stûr′nᵊlīz′), *v.t.,* **-ised, -is·ing.** *Chiefly Brit.* externalize.

ex·ter·nal·ism (ik stûr′nᵊliz′əm), *n.* attention or devotion to externals; excessive attention to externals, esp. in religion. [EXTERNAL + -ISM] **—ex·ter′nal·ist,** *n.*

ex·ter·nal·i·ty (ek′stər nal′i tē), *n., pl.* **-ties. 1.** the state or quality of being external. **2.** something external; an outward feature. **3.** excessive attention to externals. [EXTERNAL + -ITY]

ex·ter·nal·i·za·tion (ik stûr′nᵊli zā′shən), *n.* **1.** the act or process of externalizing. **2.** the quality or state of being externalized. **3.** that which is externalized. Also, *esp. Brit.,* **externalisation.** [EXTERNALIZE + -ATION]

ex·ter·nal·ize (ik stûr′nᵊlīz′), *v.t.,* **-ized, -iz·ing. 1.** to make external; embody in an outward form: *Metaphors externalize the relational capacity of the imagination.* **2.** to regard as consisting of externals. **3.** to regard or treat as being caused by externals; attribute to external causes: *to externalize one's difficulties.* **4.** to direct (the personality) outward in social relationships. Also, *esp. Brit.,* **externalise.** [EXTERNAL + -IZE]

exter′nal jug′ular vein′. See under **jugular** (def. 1b).

exter′nal rela′tion, *Philos.* a relation between any two entities such that if they had not been in this relation to each other, the nature of each would not necessarily have been different. Cf. **internal relation.**

ex·ter·o·cep·tive (ek′stər ə sep′tiv), *adj. Physiol.* pertaining to exteroceptors, the stimuli acting upon them, or the nerve impulses initiated by them. [*extero-* (comb. form of L *exterus* EXTERIOR) + (RE)CEPTIVE]

ex·ter·o·cep·tor (ek′stər ə sep′tər), *n. Physiol.* a receptor responding to stimuli originating from outside the body. [*extero-* (see EXTEROCEPTIVE) + (RE)CEPTOR]

ex·ter·ri·to·ri·al (eks′ter i tôr′ē əl, -tōr′-), *adj.* exterritorial. [EX-[1] + TERRITORIAL] **—ex·ter′ri·to′ri·al′i·ty,** *n.* **—ex·ter·ri·to′ri·al·ly,** *adv.*

ex·tinct (ik stingkt′), *adj.* **1.** not existing now; that has ended or died out: *an extinct species of fish.* **2.** no longer in use; obsolete: *an extinct custom.* **3.** extinguished; quenched; not burning. **4.** having ceased eruption; no longer active: *an extinct volcano.* [late ME < L *ex(s)tinct(us)* put out, quenched, ptp. of *ex(s)tinguere* to EXTINGUISH]
—Syn. 1. gone, vanished. See **dead. 2.** archaic. **3, 4.** out.

ex·tinc·tion (ik stingk′shən), *n.* **1.** the act of extinguishing. **2.** the fact or condition of being extinguished or extinct. **3.** suppression; abolition; annihilation: *the extinction of an army; the extinction of hopes.* **4.** *Biol.* the act or process of becoming extinct; a coming to an end or dying out: *the extinction of a species.* **5.** *Psychol.* the reduction or loss of a conditioned response as a result of the absence or withdrawal of reinforcement. [late ME *extinccio(u)n* < L *ex(s)tinctiōn-* (s. of *ex(s)tinctiō*). See EXTINCT, -ION]

extinc′tion me′ter, *Photog.* an exposure meter indicating the intensity of light by the invisibility or extreme faintness of one of a series of figures on a ground glass or sheet of celluloid of varying thickness.

ex·tinc·tive (ik stingk′tiv), *adj.* tending or serving to extinguish. [EXTINCT + -IVE]

ex·tine (ek′stēn, -stin), *n. Bot.* exine. [< L *ext(imus)* most outward + -INE[1]]

ex·tin·guish (ik sting′gwish), *v.t.* **1.** to put out (a fire, light, etc.); put out the flame of (something burning or lighted): *to extinguish a candle.* **2.** to put an end to or bring to an end; wipe out of existence; annihilate: *to extinguish hope.* **3.** to obscure or eclipse, as by superior brilliancy: *Her beauty extinguished that of all other women.* **4.** *Law.* to discharge (a debt), as by payment. [< L *ex(s)tingu(ere)* (*ex-* EX-[1] + *stinguere* to quench) + -ISH[2]] **—ex·tin′guish·a·ble,** *adj.* **—ex·tin′guish·ment,** *n.*

ex·tin·guish·er (ik sting′gwi shər), *n.* **1.** one who or that which extinguishes. **2.** any of various portable apparatuses for extinguishing fire: *a chemical extinguisher.* [EXTINGUISH + -ER[1]]

ex·tir·pate (ek′stər pāt′, ik stûr′pāt), *v.t.,* **-pat·ed, -pat·ing. 1.** to remove utterly; destroy totally; exterminate; do away with. **2.** to pull up by or as if by the roots; root up: *to extirpate a bad habit; to extirpate an unwanted hair.* [< L *ex(s)tirpāt(us)* plucked up by the stem (ptp. of *ex(s)tirpāre*), equiv. to *ex-* EX-[1] + *stirp-* (s. of *stirps*) stem + *-ātus* -ATE[1]] **—ex′tir·pa′tion,** *n.* **—ex′tir·pa′tive,** *adj.* **—ex′tir·pa′tor,** *n.*

ex·tol (ik stōl′, -stol′), *v.t.,* **-tolled, -tol·ling.** to praise highly; laud; eulogize: *to extol the beauty of Naples.* Also, **ex·toll′.** [late ME *extolle(n)* < L *extoll(ere)* (to) lift up, raise, equiv. to *ex-* EX-[1] + *tollere* to lift, raise up] **—ex·tol′ler,** *n.* **—ex·tol′ling·ly,** *adv.* **—ex·tol′ment, ex·toll′ment,** *n.*
—Syn. commend, glorify, exalt, celebrate. **—Ant.** disparage.

ex·tor·sive (ik stôr′siv), *adj. Law.* serving or tending to extort: *extorsive measures.* [< L *extors(us)* (ptp. of *extorquere;* see EXTORT) + -IVE] **—ex·tor′sive·ly,** *adv.*

ex·tort (ik stôrt′), *v.t.* **1.** *Law.* **a.** to wrest or wring (money, information, etc.) from a person by violence, intimidation, or abuse of authority; obtain by force, torture, threat, or the like. **b.** to take illegally under color of office. **2.** to compel (something) of a person or thing: *Her charm and vivacity extorted their admiration.* [late ME (adj.) < L *extort(us),* ptp. of *extorquēre,* equiv. to *ex-* EX-[1] + *torquēre* to twist] **—ex·tort′er,** *n.* **—ex·tor′tive,** *adj.*
—Syn. 1. See **extract.**

ex·tor·tion (ik stôr′shən), *n.* **1.** the act or an instance of extorting. **2.** *Law.* the crime of obtaining money or some other thing of value under color of office, when none or not so much is due, or before it is due. **3.** oppressive or illegal exaction, as of excessive price or interest: *the extortions of usurers.* **4.** anything extorted. [ME *extorcion* < L *extortiōn-* (s. of *extortiō*). See EXTORT, -ION]
—Syn. 1, 4. blackmail.

ex·tor·tion·ar·y (ik stôr′shə ner′ē), *adj.* characterized by or given to extortion. [EXTORTION + -ARY]

ex·tor·tion·ate (ik stôr′shə nit), *adj.* **1.** exorbitant; grossly excessive: *extortionate prices.* **2.** characterized by extortion, as persons: *extortionate moneylenders.* [EXTORTION + -ATE[1]] **—ex·tor′tion·ate·ly,** *adv.*

ex·tor·tion·er (ik stôr′shə nər), *n.* a person who practices extortion. Also, **ex·tor′tion·ist.** [ME *extorciouner.* See EXTORTION, -ER[1]]

ex·tra (ek′strə), *adj.* **1.** beyond or more than what is usual, expected, or necessary; additional: *an extra edition of a newspaper; an extra price.* **2.** larger or better than what is usual: *an extra binding.* **—n. 3.** something extra or additional: *the little amenities and extras that make life pleasant.* **4.** an additional expense. **5.** an edition of a newspaper other than the regular edition or editions. **6.** something of superior quality: *The Italian sports car was an extra.* **7.** *Motion Pictures.* a person hired by the day to play a minor part as a member of a mob or crowd. **8.** an additional worker: *The company hired several extras in order to finish the work on time.* **9.** Usually, **extras.** *Cricket.* a score or run not made from the bat, as a bye or a wide. **—adv. 10.** in excess of the usual or specified amount: *an extra high price.* **11.** beyond the ordinary degree; unusually; uncommonly: *done extra well; extra large.* [? by shortening of EXTRAORDINARY]

extra-, a prefix meaning "outside," "beyond," freely used as an English formative: *extrajudicial; extraterritorial; extra-atmospheric.* Also, **extro-.** [< L, comb. form of *extrā* (adv. and prep.) outside (of), without]

ex·tra-at·mos·pher·ic (ek′strə at′məs fer′ik), *adj.* outside the earth's atmosphere.

ex′tra-base′ hit′ (ek′strə bās′), *Baseball.* a base hit that enables a batter to reach more than one base safely, as a two-base hit, three-base hit, or home run.

ex·tra·bold (ek′strə bōld′), *Print.* **—n. 1.** unusually heavy boldface type. **—adj. 2.** in extrabold. [EXTRA- + BOLD]

ex·tra·ca·non·i·cal (ek′strə kə non′i kəl), *adj. Eccles.* not included in the canon of Scripture. [EXTRA- + CANONICAL]

ex·tra·cap·su·lar (ek′strə kap′sə lər), *adj.* outside a capsule or capsular thing. [EXTRA- + CAPSULAR]

ex·tra·cel·lu·lar (ek′strə sel′yə lər), *adj. Biol.* outside a cell or cells. [EXTRA- + CELLULAR] **—ex′tra·cel′lu·lar·ly,** *adv.*

ex·tra-con·densed (ek′strə kən denst′), *adj. Print.* (of type) narrower than condensed type in proportion to its height.

ex′tra cov′er, *Cricket.* **1.** the position of a fielder between mid off and cover point. **2.** the fielder occupying this position. Also, **ex′tra cov′er point′.**

ex·tract (*v.* ik strakt′; *n.* ek′strakt), *v.t.* **1.** to get, pull, or draw out, usually with special effort or force: *to extract a tooth.* **2.** to deduce (a doctrine, principle, interpretation, etc.): *He extracted a completely personal meaning from what was said.* **3.** to derive or obtain (pleasure, comfort, etc.) from a particular source: *He extracted satisfaction from the success of his sons.* **4.** to take or copy out (matter), as from a book. **5.** to make excerpts from (a book, pamphlet, etc.). **6.** to extort (information, money, etc.): *to extract a secret from someone.* **7.** to separate or obtain (a juice, ingredient, principle, etc.) from a mixture by pressure, distillation, treatment with solvents, or the like. **8.** *Math.* to determine (the root of a quantity). **—n. 9.** something extracted. **10.** a passage taken from a book, article, etc.; excerpt; quotation. **11.** a solution or preparation containing the active principles of a drug, plant juice, or the like; concentrated solution: *vanilla extract.* **12.** a solid, viscid, or liquid substance extracted from a plant, drug, or the like: *beef extract.* [late ME < L *extract(us)* (ptp. of *extrahere*). See EX-[1], TRACT[1]] **—ex·tract′a·bil′i·ty, ex·tract′i·bil′i·ty,** *n.* **—ex·tract′a·ble, ex·tract′i·ble,** *adj.*
—Syn. 1. pry out. **6.** evoke, educe, draw out, elicit. EXTRACT, EXACT, EXTORT, WREST imply using force to remove something. To EXTRACT is to draw forth something as by pulling, importuning, or the like: *to extract a confession by using third-degree methods.* To EXACT is to impose a penalty, or to obtain by force or authority, something to which one lays claim: *to exact payment, obedience.* To EXTORT is usually to wring something by intimidation or threats from an unwilling person: *to extort money by threats of blackmail.* To WREST is to take by force or violence in spite of active resistance: *The courageous minority wrested the power from their oppressors.* **7.** withdraw, distill. **10.** citation, selection. **11.** decoction, distillation.

ex·tract·ant (ik strak′tənt), *n. Chem.* the substance extracted. [EXTRACT + -ANT]

ex·trac·tion (ik strak′shən), *n.* **1.** the act or an instance of extracting. **2.** the state or fact of being extracted: *In its extraction from the text the statement makes little sense.* **3.** descent or lineage: *to be of foreign extraction.* **4.** something extracted; extract. [late ME *extraccioun* < ML *extractiōn-* (s. of *extractiō*). See EXTRACT, -ION]

ex·trac·tive (ik strak′tiv), *adj.* **1.** tending or serving to extract or based upon extraction: *the coal, oil, copper, and other extractive industries.* **2.** capable of being extracted. **3.** of or of the nature of an extract. **—n. 4.** something extracted. [EXTRACT + -IVE]

ex·trac·tor (ik strak′tər), *n.* **1.** one who or that which extracts. **2.** (in a firearm or cannon) the mechanism that, after firing, pulls an empty or unfired cartridge or shell case out of the chamber and brings it into place for action by the ejector. **3.** a centrifuge for spinning wet laundry so as to remove excess water. **4.** *Med., Dentistry.* an instrument for drawing out, extracting, or pulling. [EXTRACT + -OR[2]]

ex′tract print′ing. See **discharge printing.**

ex·tra·cur·ric·u·lar (ek′strə kə rik′yə lər), *adj.* **1.** outside the regular curriculum: *extracurricular reading.* **2.** of or pertaining to school activities exclusive of the regular academic course, as sports, singing in a glee club, etc. [EXTRA- + CURRICULAR]

ex·tra·dit·a·ble (ek′strə dī′tə bəl, ek′strə dī′-), *adj.* **1.** capable of being extradited; subject to extradition: *an extraditable person.* **2.** capable of incurring extradition: *an extraditable offense.* [EXTRADITE + -ABLE]

ex·tra·dite (ek′strə dīt′), *v.t.,* **-dit·ed, -dit·ing. 1.** to give up (a fugitive or prisoner) to another nation or authority. **2.** to obtain the extradition of. [back formation from EXTRADITION]

ex·tra·di·tion (ek′strə dish′ən), *n.* the surrender of a fugitive from justice or a prisoner by one state or authority to another. [< F; see EX-[1], TRADITION]

ex′tra div′idend. See **special dividend.**

ex·tra·dos (ek′strə dos′, -dōs′, ek strā′dos, -dōs), *n., pl.* **-dos** (-dōz′, -dōz), **-dos·es.** *Archit.* the exterior curve or surface of an arch or vault. Also called **back.** Cf. **intrados.** See diag. under **arch.** [< F, equiv. to *extra-* EXTRA- + *dos* back (< L *dorsum* DORSUM)]

ex·tra·dosed (ek strā′dost), *adj.* (of an arch) having a curved intrados the form of which is repeated by the extrados. [EXTRADOS + -ED[3]]

ex·tra·em·bry·on·ic (ek′strə em′brē on′ik), *adj.* situated outside the body of the embryo; developed in connection with the embryo but not as a structural part of it. Also, **ex′tra·em′bry·on′al.** [EXTRA- + EMBRYONIC]

ex·tra·flo·ral (ek′strə flôr′əl, -flōr′-), *adj. Bot.* situated outside the flower, as a nectary. [EXTRA- + FLORAL]

ex·tra·ga·lac·tic (ek′strə gə lak′tik), *adj.* outside the Milky Way system: *an extragalactic nebula.* [EXTRA- + GALACTIC]

extragalac′tic neb′ula, *Astron.* nebula (def. 1c).

ex·tra·ju·di·cial (ek′strə jōō dish′əl), *adj.* **1.** outside of judicial proceedings; beyond the action or authority of a court. **2.** beyond, outside, or against the usual procedure of justice; legally unwarranted: *an extrajudicial penalty.* [EXTRA- + JUDICIAL] **—ex′tra·ju·di′cial·ly,** *adv.*

ex·tra·le·gal (ek′strə lē′gəl), *adj.* being beyond the province or authority of law. [EXTRA- + LEGAL] **—ex′tra·le′gal·ly,** *adv.*

ex·tra·mar·i·tal (ek′strə mar′i tᵊl), *adj.* pertaining to sexual relations with someone other than one's spouse. [EXTRA- + MARITAL]

ex·tra·met·ri·cal (ek′strə me′tri kəl), *adj. Pros.* containing one or more syllables in addition to those required by the meter: *an extrametrical line.* [EXTRA- + METRICAL]

ex·tra·mun·dane (ek′strə mun′dān, -mun dān′), *adj.* beyond our world or the material universe. [< LL *extrāmundān(us)* beyond the world. See EXTRA-, MUNDANE]

ex·tra·mu·ral (ek′strə myŏŏr′əl), *adj.* **1.** involving representatives of more than one school: *extramural athletics.* **2.** outside the walls or boundaries, as of a city or town or a university: *extramural teaching; an extramural church.* Cf. **intramural** (defs. 1, 2). [EXTRA- + MURAL] **—ex′tra·mu′ral·ly,** *adv.*

ex·tra·ne·ous (ik strā′nē əs), *adj.* **1.** introduced or coming from without; not belonging or proper to a thing; external; foreign. **2.** not pertinent; irrelevant: *an extraneous remark; extraneous decoration.* [< L *extrāneus* external, foreign, equiv. to *extr(a)-* EXTRA- + *-āneus* -ANEOUS] **—ex·tra′ne·ous·ly,** *adv.* **—ex·tra′ne·ous·ness,** *n.*
—Syn. 1. extrinsic, adventitious, alien. **2.** inappropriate, nonessential, superfluous. **—Ant. 1.** intrinsic. **2.** pertinent.

ex·tra·nu·cle·ar (ek′strə nōō′klē ər, -nyōō′-), *adj.* pertaining to or affecting the parts of a cell outside the nucleus. [EXTRA- + NUCLEAR]

ex·traor·di·nar·y (ik strôr′dᵊner′ē, ek′strə ôr′dᵊner′ē), *adj.* **1.** beyond what is usual, ordinary, regular, or established: *extraordinary powers given to the President in wartime; unexpected extraordinary costs.* **2.** exceptional in character, amount, extent, degree, etc.; noteworthy; remarkable: *extraordinary weather; extraordinary speed; an extraordinary man.* **3.** (of an official, employee, etc.) outside of or additional to the ordinary staff; having a special, often temporary task or responsibility: *an extraordinary delegate to the Vatican.* [late ME *extraordinarie* < L *extrāordinārī(us)* beyond what is ordinary. See EXTRA-, ORDINARY] **—ex·traor·di·nar·i·ly** (ik strôr′dᵊnâr′ə lē, ek′strə ôr′-), *adv.* **—ex·traor′di·nar′i·ness,** *n.*
—Syn. 1. inordinate. **2.** uncommon, singular, rare, phenomenal, special, signal, egregious. **—Ant. 1, 2.** common, usual.

extraor′dinary ju′bilee. See under **jubilee**[1] (def. 5b).

extraor′dinary ray′, *Optics, Crystall.* the part of a doubly-refracted ray that has changed speed and vibrations in the principal plane of the crystal.

extraor′dinary wave′, *Radio.* (of the two waves into which a radio wave is divided in the ionosphere under the influence of the earth's magnetic field) the wave with characteristics more different from those that the undivided wave would have exhibited in the absence of the magnetic field. Also called **X-wave.** Cf. **ordinary wave.**

ex·tra·phys·i·cal (ek′strə fiz′i kəl), *adj.* outside the physical; not subject to physical laws. [EXTRA- + PHYSICAL]

ex·trap·o·late (ik strap′ə lāt′, ek′strə pə-), *v.,* **-lat·ed, -lat·ing. —v.t. 1.** *Statistics.* to estimate the value of a variable outside its tabulated or observed range. **2.** to infer (that which is not known) from that which is known; conjecture. **—v.i. 3.** to perform extrapolation. [EXTRA- + (INTER)POLATE] **—ex·trap′o·la′tion,** *n.* **—ex·trap′o·la′tive, ex·trap·o·la·to·ry** (ik strap′ə lə tôr′ē, -tōr′ē), *adj.* **—ex·trap′o·la′tor,** *n.*

ex·tra·pro·fes·sion·al (ek′strə prə fesh′ə nəl), *adj.* outside ordinary limits of professional interest or duty. [EXTRA- + PROFESSIONAL]

ex·tra·pu·ni·tive (ek′strə pyo͞o′ni tiv), *adj. Psychol.* (in frustrating situations) directing one's hostility outward toward persons or objects in the environment. Cf. **impunitive, intropunitive.** [EXTRA- + PUNITIVE]

ex·tra·sen·so·ri·al (ek′strə sen sôr′ē əl, -sōr′-), *adj.* extrasensory. [EXTRA- + SENSORIAL]

ex·tra·sen·so·ry (ek′strə sen′sə rē), *adj.* outside of normal sense perception. [EXTRA- + SENSORY]

ex′trasen′sory percep′tion. See **ESP.**

ex·tra·sys·to·le (ek′strə sis′tə lē), *n. Pathol.* a premature contraction of the heart, resulting in momentary interruption of the normal heartbeat. Also called **premature beat, premature contraction.** [< NL; see EXTRA-, SYSTOLE] —**ex·tra·sys·tol·ic** (ek′strə sis-tol′ik), *adj.*

ex·tra·ter·res·tri·al (ek′strə tə res′trē əl), *adj.* outside, or originating outside, the limits of the earth. [EXTRA- + TERRESTRIAL]

ex·tra·ter·ri·to·ri·al (ek′strə ter′i tôr′ē əl, -tōr′-), *adj.* **1.** beyond local territorial jurisdiction, as the status of persons resident in a country but not subject to its laws. **2.** pertaining to such persons. Also, **exterritorial.** [EXTRA- + TERRITORIAL] —**ex′tra·ter′ri·to′ri·al·ly,** *adv.*

ex·tra·ter·ri·to·ri·al·i·ty (ek′strə ter′i tôr′ē al′i tē, -tōr′-), *n.* the possession or exercise of political rights by a foreign power within a state having its own government. Also, **exterritoriality.** [EXTRA- + TERRITORIALITY]

ex′tra·trop′i·cal cy′clone (ek′strə trop′i kəl, ek′-), any large-scale, cyclonic storm that is not a tropical cyclone, esp. the common frontal cyclone of the middle and high latitudes. Cf. **tropical cyclone.** [EXTRA- + TROPICAL]

ex·tra·u·ter·ine (ek′strə yo͞o′tər in, -tə rīn′), *adj.* being or developing outside the uterus. [EXTRA- + UTERINE]

ex′trau′terine preg′nancy, *Med.* See **ectopic pregnancy.**

ex·trav·a·gance (ik strav′ə gəns), *n.* **1.** excessive expenditure or outlay of money. **2.** an instance of this: *That mink-lined hat is an inexcusable extravagance.* **3.** unrestrained or fantastic excess, as of actions, opinions, etc.: *The mother loved her children with extravagance.* **4.** an extravagant action, notion, etc.: *the extravagances one commits in moments of stress.* [< F, MF; see EXTRAVAGANT, -ANCE] —**Syn. 3.** lavishness, profusion. —**Ant. 1.** frugality.

ex·trav·a·gan·cy (ik strav′ə gən sē), *n., pl.* **-cies.** extravagance. [EXTRAVAG(ANT) + -ANCY]

ex·trav·a·gant (ik strav′ə gənt), *adj.* **1.** spending much more than is necessary or wise; wasteful: *an extravagant wife.* **2.** excessively high: *extravagant expenses; extravagant prices.* **3.** exceeding the bounds of reason, as actions, demands, opinions, passions, etc. **4.** going beyond what is deserved or justifiable: *the extravagant praise of her new novel.* **5.** *Obs.* wandering beyond bounds. [ME < ML *extrāvagant-* (s. of *extrāvagāns*), prp. of *extrāvagārī*, equiv. to *extrā-* EXTRA- + *vagārī* to wander] —**ex·trav′a·gant·ly,** *adv.* —**ex·trav′a·gant·ness,** *n.* —**Syn. 1.** imprudent, lavish, spendthrift, prodigal. **2.** immoderate, excessive, inordinate. **3.** unreasonable, unrestrained, fantastic, wild, absurd, preposterous. —**Ant. 1.** prudent, thrifty. **2.** moderate. **3.** reasonable.

ex·trav·a·gan·za (ik strav′ə gan′zə), *n.* a musical or dramatic composition or production, as comic opera or musical comedy, marked by a loose structure, a frivolous theme, and elaborate costuming and staging. [alter. of It *(e)stravaganza* extravagance]

ex·trav·a·gate (ik strav′ə gāt′), *v.i.,* **-gat·ed, -gat·ing.** *Archaic.* **1.** to wander beyond bounds; stray; roam at will. **2.** to go beyond the bounds of propriety or reason. [< ML *extrāvagāt(us)* strayed, wandered away from, ptp. of *extrāvagārī*. See EXTRAVAGANT, -ATE¹]

ex·tra·vag·i·nal (ek′strə vaj′ə nəl), *adj. Bot.* developing outside the sheath, as the young shoots of certain grasses. [EXTRA- + VAGINAL]

ex·trav·a·sate (ik strav′ə sāt′), *v.,* **-sat·ed, -sat·ing,** *n.* —*v.t.* **1.** *Pathol.* to force out from the proper vessels, as blood, esp. so as to diffuse through the surrounding tissues. **2.** *Geol.* to pour forth, as lava, from a subterranean source in a molten state. —*v.i.* **3.** *Pathol.* to be extravasated, as blood. **4.** *Geol.* to pour forth lava or the like. —*n.* **5.** *Pathol.* the extravasated material; extravasation. [EXTRA- + VAS + -ATE¹]

ex·trav·a·sa·tion (ik strav′ə sā′shən), *n.* **1.** the act of extravasating. **2.** the matter extravasated. [EXTRAVASATE + -ION]

ex·tra·vas·cu·lar (ek′strə vas′kyə lər), *adj. Anat.* situated outside of a blood vessel or vessels. [EXTRA- + VASCULAR]

ex·tra·ve·hic·u·lar (ek′strə vē hik′yə lər), *adj.* of, pertaining to, or being an activity performed by an astronaut outside his space vehicle during a space flight. [EXTRA- + VEHICULAR]

ex·tra·ver·sion (ek′strə vûr′zhən, -shən; ek′strə-vûr′-), *n. Psychol.* extroversion (def. 2). —**ex′tra·ver′sive, ex′tra·ver′tive,** *adj.* —**ex′tra·ver′sive·ly, ex′tra·ver′tive·ly,** *adv.*

ex·tra·vert (ek′strə vûrt′), *n., adj., v.t. Psychol.* extrovert. —**ex′tra·vert′ish,** *adj.*

Ex·tre·ma·du·ra (*Sp.* es′tre mä tho͞o′rä), *n.* Estremadura.

ex·tre·mal (ik strē′məl), *adj. Math.* of or pertaining to an extremum or the calculation of extrema: *an extremal problem.* [EXTREM(UM) + -AL¹]

ex·treme (ik strēm′), *adj.,* **-trem·er, -trem·est,** *n.* —*adj.* **1.** of a character or kind farthest removed from the ordinary or average: *an extreme case; extreme measures.* **2.** utmost or exceedingly great in degree: *extreme joy.* **3.** farthest from the center or middle; outermost; endmost: *the extreme limits of a town.* **4.** farthest, utmost, or very far in any direction: *an object at the extreme point of vision.* **5.** going to the utmost lengths, or exceeding the bounds of moderation: *extreme fashions.* **6.** going to the utmost or very great lengths in action, habit, opinion, etc.: *an extreme socialist.* **7.** last or final: *extreme hopes.* —*n.* **8.** the utmost or highest degree, or a very high degree: *showy in the extreme; cautious to an extreme.* **9.** one of two things as remote or different from each other as possible: *the extremes of joy and grief.* **10.** the furthest or utmost length; an excessive length, beyond the ordinary or average: *to go to extremes in dress.* **11.** an extreme act, measure, condition, etc.: *the extreme of poverty; The proposed legislation was an extreme.* **12.** *Math.* **a.** the first or the last term, as of a proportion or series. **b.** a relative maximum or relative minimum value of a function in a given region. **13.** *Logic.* the subject or the predicate of the conclusion of a syllogism; either of two terms which are separated in the premises and brought together in the conclusion. **14.** *Archaic.* the utmost point, or extremity, of something. [late ME < L *extrēm(us)*, superl. of *exterus* outward. See EXTERIOR] —**ex·treme′ness,** *n.* —**Syn. 2.** greatest, highest; superlative. **3.** ultimate, last, uttermost, remotest. **6.** extravagant, immoderate, excessive, fanatical, uncompromising, unreasonable. See **radical.** —**Ant. 6.** moderate.

extreme′ clip′per, *Naut.* a clipper of the mid-19th century built for speed rather than capacity and having a narrow hull with a sharp entrance and a large sail area.

ex·treme·ly (ik strēm′lē), *adv.* in an extreme degree; very; exceedingly: *extremely cold.* [EXTREME + -LY]

extreme′ly high′ fre′quency, *Radio.* any frequency between 30,000 and 300,000 megacycles per second. *Abbr.:* EHF

extreme′ unc′tion, *Rom. Cath. Ch.* a sacrament consisting of anointment with oil and the recitation of prayer, administered by a priest to a person in danger of dying.

ex·trem·ism (ik strē′miz əm), *n.* a tendency or disposition to go to extremes or an instance of going to extremes, esp. in political matters: *Leftist extremism; the extremism of the Nazis.* [EXTREME + -ISM]

ex·trem·ist (ik strē′mist), *n.* **1.** a person who goes to extremes, esp. in political matters. **2.** a supporter of extreme doctrines or practices. —*adj.* **3.** belonging or pertaining to extremists. [EXTREME + -IST]

ex·trem·i·ty (ik strem′i tē), *n., pl.* **-ties.** **1.** the extreme or terminal point, limit, or part of something. **2.** a limb of the body. **3.** Usually, **extremities.** the end part of a limb, as a hand or foot: *to experience cold in one's extremities.* **4.** Sometimes, **extremities.** a condition, or circumstance, of extreme need, distress, etc.: *to suffer the extremities of being poor.* **5.** the utmost or any extreme degree: *the extremity of joy.* **6.** an extreme or extraordinary measure, act, etc.: *to go to any extremity to feed the children.* **7.** extreme nature or character: *the extremity of his views on foreign trade.* **8.** *Archaic.* a person's last moment before death. [ME < L *extrēmitās.* See EXTREME, -ITY] —**Syn. 1.** end, termination; verge; border, boundary.

ex·tre·mum (ik strē′məm), *n., pl.* **-ma** (-mə). *Math.* a maximum or minimum value of a function in a specified neighborhood. [< NL, n. use of neut. of L *extrēmus* EXTREME]

ex·tri·ca·ble (ek′strə kə bəl, ik strik′ə bəl), *adj.* capable of being extricated. [< L *extric(āre)* (see EXTRICATE) + -ABLE]

ex·tri·cate (ek′strə kāt′), *v.t.,* **-cat·ed, -cat·ing.** **1.** to free or release from entanglement; disengage: *to extricate someone from a difficult situation.* **2.** to liberate (gas) from combination, as in a chemical process. [< L *extricāt(us)* (ptp. of *extricāre*), equiv. to *ex-* EX-¹ + *tric(ae)* perplexities + *-ātus* -ATE¹] —**ex′tri·ca′tion,** *n.*

ex·trin·sic (ik strin′sik), *adj.* **1.** not essential or inherent; not a basic part or quality of: *facts that are extrinsic to the matter under discussion.* **2.** being outside of a thing; outward or external; operating or coming from without: *extrinsic influences.* **3.** *Anat.* (of certain muscles, nerves, etc.) originating outside the anatomical limits of a part. Also, **ex·trin′si·cal.** [< LL *extrinsec(us)* outward, adj. use of L *extrinsecus* (adv.) on the outward side, equiv. to *extrin-* (deriv. of *exter* outward) + *secus* beside (deriv. of *sequī* to follow)] —**ex·trin′si·cal·ly,** *adv.*

extro-, var. of **extra-** (used to contrast with **intro-**): *extrovert.*

ex·trorse (ek strôrs′), *adj. Bot.* turned or facing outward, as anthers which open toward the perianth. [< LL *extrors(us)* in outward direction, equiv. to *extr(a)-* EXTRA- + *(vo)rsus* (adv.) turned] —**ex·trorse′ly,** *adv.*

ex·tro·spec·tion (ek′strə spek′shən), *n.* the consideration and observation of things external to the self; examination and study of externals. [EXTRO- + (INTRO)SPECTION)] —**ex′tro·spec′tive,** *adj.*

ex·tro·ver·sion (ek′strō vûr′zhən, -shən, ek′strō-vûr′-, -strə-), *n.* **1.** *Pathol.* a turning inside out, as of the eyelids or of the bladder. **2.** Also, **extraversion.** *Psychol.* **a.** the act of directing one's interest outward or to things outside the self. **b.** the state of being concerned primarily with things outside the self, with the external environment rather than with one's own thoughts and feelings. Cf. **introversion** (def. 4). [EXTRO- + L *versiōn-* (s. of *versiō*) a turning] —**ex′tro·ver′sive, ex′tro·ver′tive,** *adj.* —**ex′tro·ver′sive·ly, ex′tro·ver′tive·ly,** *adv.*

ex·tro·vert (ek′strō vûrt′, -strə-), *Psychol.* —*n.* **1.** a person characterized by extroversion; a person concerned primarily with the physical and social environment (opposed to *introvert*). —*adj.* **2.** marked by extroversion. —*v.t.* **3.** to direct (the mind, one's interest, etc.) outward or to things outside the self. Also, **extravert.** [EXTRO- + L *vert(ere)* (to) turn] —**ex′tro·vert′ish,** *adj.*

ex·trude (ik stro͞od′), *v.,* **-trud·ed, -trud·ing.** —*v.t.* **1.** to thrust out; force or press out; expel: *to extrude molten rock; to extrude a criminal from society.* **2.** to form (metal, plastic, etc.) with a desired cross section by forcing it through a die. —*v.i.* **3.** to protrude. **4.** to be extruded: *This metal extrudes easily.* [< L *extrūd(ere)* (to) thrust out, drive out, equiv. to *ex-* EX-¹ + *trūdere* to thrust, push] —**ex·trud′er,** *n.* —**ex·tru·si·ble** (ik stro͞o′sə bəl), *adj.*

ex·tru·sile (ik stro͞o′sil), *adj.* able to be thrust out or extruded. [*extrus(ion)* (< ML *extrūsiōn-*, s. of *extrūsiō*, equiv. to L *extrūs(us)*, ptp. of *extrūdere* to EXTRUDE, + *-iōn-* -ION) + -ILE]

ex·tru·sion (ik stro͞o′zhən), *n.* **1.** the act of extruding, or the state of being extruded. **2.** something that is extruded. [< ML *extrūsiōn-* (s. of *extrūsiō*), equiv. to L *extrūs(us)* (ptp. of *extrūdere* to EXTRUDE) + *-iōn-* -ION]

ex·tru·sive (ik stro͞o′siv), *adj.* **1.** tending to extrude. **2.** pertaining to extrusion. **3.** *Geol.* (of rocks) having been forced out in a molten or plastic condition at the surface of the earth. [*extrus(ion)* (see EXTRUSILE) + -IVE]

ex·u·ber·ance (ig zo͞o′bər əns), *n.* **1.** Also, **ex·u′ber·an·cy.** the state of being exuberant. **2.** an instance of this: *His pranks are youthful exuberances.* [< L *exūberantia.* See EXUBERANT, -ANCE] —**Syn. 1.** superabundance, excess, copiousness, profusion, luxuriance, lavishness, superfluity, overflow. —**Ant. 1.** scarcity.

ex·u·ber·ant (ig zo͞o′bər ənt), *adj.* **1.** lavish; effusively and almost uninhibitedly enthusiastic: *an exuberant welcome for the hero.* **2.** extremely good; overflowing; plentiful: *exuberant health.* **3.** enjoying extremely good health and happiness **4.** profuse in growth or production; luxuriant; superabundant: *exuberant vegetation.* [late ME < L *exūberant-* (s. of *exūberāns*), prp. of *exūberāre*, equiv. to *ex-* EX-¹ + *ūberāre* to be fruitful (deriv. of *ūber* fertile); see -ANT] —**ex·u′ber·ant·ly,** *adv.* —**Syn. 4.** copious, rank. —**Ant. 4.** sparse.

ex·u·ber·ate (ig zo͞o′bə rāt′), *v.i.,* **-at·ed, -at·ing.** to be exuberant; superabound; overflow. [late ME < L *exūberāt(us).* See EXUBERANT, -ATE¹]

ex·u·date (eks′yo͝o dāt′, ek′sə-, eg′zə-), *n.* a substance exuded; exudation. [EXUDE + -ATE¹]

ex·u·da·tion (eks′yo͝o dā′shən, ek′sə-, eg′zə-), *n.* **1.** the act of exuding. **2.** that which is exuded. **3.** a discharge of certain elements of the blood into the tissues. [< LL *ex(s)ūdātiōn-* (s. of *ex(s)ūdātiō*), equiv. to *ex(s)ūdāt(us)* (ptp. of *ex(s)ūdāre* to EXUDE) + *-iōn-* -ION] —**ex·u·da·tive** (ig zo͞o′də tiv, ik so͞o′-), *adj.*

ex·ude (ig zo͞od′, ik so͞od′), *v.,* **-ud·ed, -ud·ing.** —*v.i.* **1.** to come out gradually in drops, as sweat, through pores or small openings; ooze out. —*v.t.* **2.** to send out, as sweat; emit through pores or small openings. [< L *ex(s)ūd(āre)*, equiv. to *ex-* EX-¹ + *sūdāre* to sweat]

ex·ult (ig zult′), *v.i.* **1.** to show or feel a lively or triumphant joy; rejoice exceedingly; be highly elated or jubilant: *They exulted over their victory.* **2.** *Obs.* to leap, esp. for joy. [< L *ex(s)ult(āre)* (to) leap up, equiv. to *ex-* EX-¹ + *-sultāre* (comb. form of *saltāre* to leap)] —**ex·ult′ing·ly,** *adv.*

ex·ult·ant (ig zul′tᵊnt), *adj.* exulting; highly elated; jubilant; triumphant. [< L *ex(s)ultant-* (s. of *ex(s)ultāns*), prp. of *exultāre* to EXULT; see -ANT] —**ex·ult′ant·ly,** *adv.*

ex·ul·ta·tion (eg′zul tā′shən, ek′sul-), *n.* the act of exulting; lively or triumphant joy, as over success or victory. Also, **ex·ult·an·cy** (ig zul′tᵊn sē), **ex·ult′ance.** [late ME < L *ex(s)ultātiōn-* (s. of *ex(s)ultātiō*), equiv. to *ex(s)ultāt(us)* (ptp. of *ex(s)ultāre* to EXULT) + *-iōn-* -ION]

Ex·ul·tet (ig zo͞ol′tet), *n. Rom. Cath. Ch.* a hymn of praise sung by the deacon at the blessing of the paschal candle. [after the first word of L hymn, *exultet* may exult]

ex·urb (ek′sərb, eg′zərb), *n.* a small community beyond the suburbs of a city. [EX-¹ + (SUB)URB]

ex·ur·ban·ite (eks ûr′bə nīt′), *n.* a person who has moved from a city to an exurb but typically continues to earn his living in the city. [EX-¹ + (SUB)URBANITE]

ex·ur·bi·a (eks ûr′bē ə), *n.* a generalized area comprising the exurbs. [EX-¹ + (SUB)URBIA]

ex·u·vi·ae (ig zo͞o′vē ē′, ik so͞o′-), *n.pl.* the cast skins, shells, or other coverings of animals. [< L, deriv. of *exuere* to remove, strip off, divest oneself of, equiv. to *ex-* EX-¹ + *-uere* to put on] —**ex·u′vi·al,** *adj.*

ex·u·vi·ate (ig zo͞o′vē āt′, ik so͞o′-), *v.i., v.t.,* **-at·ed, -at·ing.** to cast off or shed (exuviae); molt. [EXUVI(AE) + -ATE¹] —**ex·u′vi·a′tion,** *n.*

ex vo·to (eks wō′tō; *Eng.* eks vō′tō), *Latin.* from, or in pursuance of, a vow.

-ey¹, var. of **-y¹** esp. after *y: clayey.*

-ey², var. of **-y²** esp. after *y.*

e·ya·let (ā′yä let′), *n.* vilayet. [< Turk *eyālet* < Ar *iyālat*]

ey·as (ī′əs), *n.* **1.** a nestling. **2.** *Falconry.* a young falcon taken from the nest for training. Also, *esp. Brit.,* **ey′ass.** [ME, var. of *nyas, nias* (*a nyas* taken as *an eyas*) < MF *niais* nestling, deriv. of L *nīdus* nest]

Eyck (īk), *n.* **Hu·bert van** (hyo͞o′bərt van; *Du.* hy′ bert vän), or **Huy·brecht van** (*Du.* hoi′brekht vän), 1366–1426, and his brother **Jan van** (*Du.* yän vän) (*Jan van Brugge*), 1385?–1440: Flemish painters.

eye (ī), *n., pl.* **eyes,** (*Archaic*) **ey·en** or **eyne;** *v.,* **eyed, ey·ing** or **eye·ing.** —*n.* **1.** the organ of sight, in vertebrates typically one of a pair of spherical bodies contained in an orbit of the skull and in man appearing externally as a dense, white, curved membrane, or sclera, surrounding a circular, colored portion, or iris, that is covered by a clear, curved membrane, or cornea, and in the center of which is an opening, or pupil, through which light passes to the retina. **2.** the aggregate of structures situated within or near the orbit which assist, support, or protect the eye. **3.** this organ with respect to the color of the iris: *blue eyes.* **4.** the region surrounding the eye: *a black eye; puffy eyes.* **5.** sight; vision: *a keen eye; a sharp eye.* **6.** power of seeing; appreciative or discriminating visual perception: *the eye of an artist.* **7.** look, glance, or gaze: *to cast one's eye on a thing.* **8.** an attentive look, close observation, or watch: *The prisoners are under the eye of the guards.* **9.** regard, respect, view, aim, or intention: *to have an eye to one's own advantage.* **10.** manner or way of looking at a

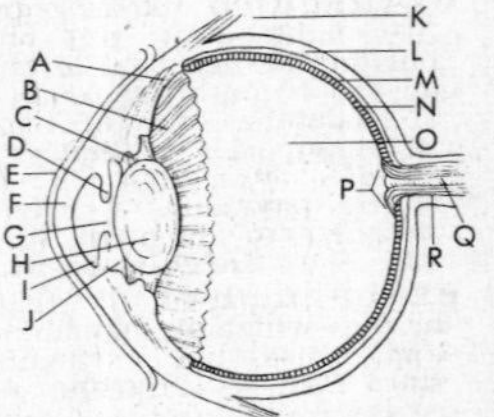

Eye (Human)
A, Ciliary muscle; B, Ciliary processes; C, Suspensory ligament; D, Iris; E, Conjunctiva; F, Cornea; G, Pupil; H, Crystalline lens; I, Anterior chamber; J, Posterior chamber; K, Ocular muscles; L, Sclera; M, Choroid coat; N, Retina; O, Vitreous humor; P, Blind spot; Q, Optic nerve; R, Retinal artery

thing; estimation; opinion: *In my eyes you are wrong; in the eyes of the law.* **11.** a center of light, intelligence, influence, etc. **12.** something resembling or suggesting the eye in appearance, shape, etc., as the opening in the lens of a camera, a peephole, a buttonhole, etc. **13.** the bud of a potato, Jerusalem artichoke, etc. **14.** the central spot of a target; bull's-eye. **15.** one of the round spots on the tail feathers of a peacock. **16.** the hole in a needle. **17.** a hole made in a thing for the insertion of some object, as the handle of a tool: *the eye of an ax.* **18.** a metal or other ring through which something, as a rope or rod, is passed. **19.** the loop into which a hook is inserted. **20.** *Building Trades.* a ring on the end of a tension member, as an eye bar or eye bolt, for connection with another member. **21.** a hole formed during the maturation of cheese, esp. Emmenthaler or Gruyère. **22.** a loop worked at the end of a rope. **23.** *Meteorol.* the approximately circular region of relatively light winds and fair weather found at the center of a severe tropical cyclone. **24. eyes,** *Naut.* the extreme forward part of the upper deck at the bow of a vessel. **25.** *Naut.* the precise direction from which a wind is blowing. **26. an eye for an eye,** repayment in kind, as revenge for an injustice. **27. be all eyes,** to give all one's attention to; look intently at: *When the hungry dog saw the bone he was all eyes.* **28. catch someone's eye,** to draw or attract someone's attention: *The bright red dress caught her eye. He finally caught the waiter's eye.* **29. give someone the eye,** *Slang.* to look fixedly at, esp. with obvious admiration; ogle: *She ignored the men who were giving her the eye.* **30. have an eye for,** to have the ability to appreciate distinctions; be discerning or perceptive: *She has an eye for antique furniture.* **31. have eyes only for, a.** to want no other person or thing but: *She was always surrounded by admirers, but she had eyes only for Harry.* **b.** to see, or view, or desire to see only: *In Amsterdam, I had eyes only for the Rembrandts.* Also, **only have eyes for. 32. in a pig's eye,** *Slang.* absolutely not; never: *In a pig's eye I will!* **33. keep an eye on,** to watch over attentively: *Please keep an eye on my plants in my absence.* **34. keep an eye out for,** to be vigilant; watch for: *The announcer told his listeners to keep an eye out for the wanted criminal.* **35. keep one's eyes open,** to be especially alert or observant: *Keep your eyes open or we'll miss the turnoff.* **36. lay, clap, or set eyes on,** *Informal.* to catch sight of; see: *They had never laid eyes on such a big car before.* **37. make eyes at,** to gaze flirtatiously or amorously at: *The students gathered in the town square to make eyes at the pretty girls.* **38. my eye!** *Informal.* (a mild exclamation of contradiction or surprise): *He says he wasn't told about this? My eye!* **39. open one's eyes,** to bring someone to a realization of the truth or of something previously unknown: *A trip through Asia opened his eyes to the conditions under which millions had to live.* **40. pipe one's eye,** to weep. **41. run one's eye over,** to glance briefly at; examine hastily: *I ran my eye over the samples.* **42. see eye to eye,** to have exactly the same opinion; agree: *They have never been able to see eye to eye on politics.* **43. see with half an eye,** to see or realize immediately or with ease: *Anyone can see with half an eye that the plan is doomed to fail.* **44. shut one's eyes,** to refuse to see or consider; disregard: *We can no longer shut our eyes to the gravity of the situation.* **45. sight for sore eyes,** a welcome sight; a pleasant surprise: *After our many days in the desert, the wretched village was a sight for sore eyes.* **46. with an eye to,** with an object or advantage in mind: *She looked at furniture displays with an eye to decorating her own apartment.* **47. with one's eyes open,** aware of the inherent or potential risks: *She signed the papers with her eyes open.* —*v.t.* **48.** to fix the eyes upon; view: *to eye a pretty girl.* **49.** to observe or watch narrowly: *She eyed the two strangers with suspicion.* **50.** to make an eye in: *to eye a needle.* —*v.i.* **51.** *Obs.* to appear to the eye. [ME *eie, ie,* OE *ēge,* var. of *ēage;* c. G *Auge;* akin to L *oculus,* Skt *akṣi*] —**eye′a·ble,** *adj.* —**eye′like′,** *adj.* —**ey′er,** *n.*

eye′ appeal′, *Informal.* the quality of appealing to the eye; attractiveness; beauty.

eye·ball (ī′bôl′), *n.* the ball or globe of the eye. [EYE + BALL[1]]

eye′ bank′, a place for the storage of corneas which have been removed from people who died recently for transplanting to the eyes of those suffering from corneal defects.

eye·bar (ī′bär′), *n.* *Civ. Eng.* a tension member, used esp. in bridge and roof trusses, having the form of a metal bar enlarged at each end to include an eye. [EYE + -BAR]

eye′ bath′, eyecup.

eye·beam (ī′bēm′), *n.* a beam or glance of the eye. [EYE + BEAM]

eye·bolt (ī′bōlt′), *n.* a bolt or screw having an eye or opening formed at one end. [EYE + BOLT[1]]

eye·bright (ī′brīt′), *n.* **1.** any of various scrophulariaceous herbs of the genus *Euphrasia,* as *E. officinalis* of Europe, formerly used for treating diseases of the eye. **2.** the scarlet pimpernel. See under **pimpernel.** [EYE + BRIGHT]

eye·brow (ī′brou′), *n.* **1.** the arch or ridge forming the upper part of the orbit of the eye. **2.** the fringe of hair growing on this arch or ridge. **3.** a dormer having a roof which is an upwardly curved continuation of the main roof plane. **4.** *Print., Journ.* kicker (def. 7). **5.** Also called **brow, watershed.** *Naut.* a curved molding protecting a port from falling or dripping water. [EYE + BROW]

Eyebrow (def. 3)

eye′brow pen′cil, a pencil for shading eyebrows.

eye′ catch′er, *Informal.* something intended to attract the eye: *Her dress was a real eye catcher.*

eye-catch·ing (ī′kach′ing), *adj.* *Informal.* attracting the eye.

eye·cup (ī′kup′), *n.* a device for applying lotions to the eye, consisting of a cup or glass with a rim shaped to fit snugly about the orbit of the eye. Also called **eye bath.** [EYE + CUP]

eyed (īd), *adj.* **1.** having an eye or eyes: *an eyed needle; an eyed potato.* **2.** having eyelike spots. [ME; see EYE, -ED[3]]

eye′ di′alect, the literary use of misspellings that are intended to convey a speaker's lack of education or his use of humorously dialectal pronunciations but that are actually no more than respellings of standard pronunciations, as *wimmin* for "women," *wuz* for "was," and *peepul* for "people."

eye·drop·per (ī′drop′ər), *n.* a dropper, esp. one for eyedrops. [EYE + DROPPER]

eye′ drops′, *Med.* drops for use in the eyes.

eye-fill·ing (ī′fil′ing), *adj.* *Informal.* attractive to the eye; providing an eyeful.

eye·ful (ī′fo͝ol′), *n., pl.* **-fuls. 1.** an amount of foreign matter thrown, blown, etc., into the eye: *an eyeful of dust.* **2.** as much as one can or wants to see: *The tourists got an eyeful of slum life.* **3.** *Informal.* a very beautiful woman. [EYE + -FUL]

eye·glass (ī′glas′, ī′gläs′), *n.* **1. eyeglasses.** Also called **glasses.** a device to aid defective vision or to protect the eyes from light, dust, and the like, consisting usually of two glass lenses set in a frame which rests on the nose and is held in place by pieces passing over or around the ears. Cf. **goggle** (def. 1), **pince-nez, spectacle** (def. 3). **2.** a single lens used to aid vision, esp. one worn or carried on the person; monocle. **3.** eyepiece. **4.** an eyecup. [EYE + GLASS]

eye·ground (ī′ground′), *n.* the fundus of the eye as seen through an ophthalmoscope, examined chiefly to determine changes in the blood vessels. [EYE + GROUND[1]]

eye·hole (ī′hōl′), *n.* **1.** See **eye socket. 2.** a hole to look through, as in a mask or a curtain. **3.** a circular opening for the insertion of a pin, hook, rope, etc.; eye. [EYE + HOLE]

eye·lash (ī′lash′), *n.* **1.** one of the short, thick, curved hairs growing as a fringe on the edge of an eyelid. **2.** the fringe of hairs itself. [EYE + LASH[1]]

eye′ lens′, *Optics.* the lens of an eyepiece closest to the eye.

eye·less (ī′lis), *adj.* **1.** lacking eyes: *eyeless fish that evolved in the dark.* **2.** lacking sight; blind. [EYE + -LESS]

eye·let (ī′lit), *n., v.,* **-let·ed** or **-let·ted, -let·ing** or **-let·ting.** —*n.* **1.** a small hole, usually round and finished along the edge, as in cloth or leather for the passage of a lace or cord or as in embroidery for ornamental effect. **2.** a metal ring for lining a small hole; grommet. **3.** an eyehole in a wall, mask, etc. **4.** Also, **oillet, oyelet, oylet.** (in medieval architecture) a small aperture in a wall used as a window or loophole. **5.** a small eye. —*v.t.* **6.** to make (an eyelet) in. **7.** to insert metal eyelets in. [ME *oilet* < OF *oillet,* equiv. to *oill* (< L *oculus;* see OCULAR) + *-et* -ET; influenced by EYE]

eye·let·eer (ī′li tēr′), *n.* a small, pointed instrument for making eyelet holes. [EYELET + -EER]

eye·lid (ī′lid′), *n.* **1.** the movable lid of skin which serves to cover and uncover the eyeball. **2.** *Aerodynamics.* either of two devices near the exhaust nozzle of a jet engine which vary the size of the nozzle opening to control thrust. [ME; see EYE, LID]

eye-mind·ed (ī′mīn′did), *adj.* disposed to perceive one's environment in visual terms and to recall sights more vividly than sounds, smells, etc. Cf. **ear-minded, motor-minded.** —**eye′-mind′ed·ness,** *n.*

ey·en (ī′ən), *n.* *Archaic.* pl. of **eye.**

eye·o·pen·er (ī′ō′pə nər), *n.* **1.** an experience or disclosure that startles one into a fresh realization: *Her behavior at the party was a real eyeopener.* **2.** a drink of liquor taken early in the day and intended to wake a person up fully. [EYE + OPENER]

eye-o·pen·ing (ī′ō′pə ning), *adj.* *U.S.* serving as an eyeopener; enlightening: *An eye-opening investigation of government corruption.*

eye·piece (ī′pēs′), *n.* the lens or combination of lenses in an optical instrument through which the eye views the image formed by the objective lens or lenses; ocular. See diag. under **microscope.** [EYE + PIECE]

eye·pit (ī′pit′), *n.* an eye socket. [EYE + PIT[1]]

eye′ point′, *Optics.* See **exit pupil.**

eye-pop·per (ī′pop′ər), *n.* *Slang.* something that causes astonishment or excitement.

eye-pop·ping (ī′pop′ing), *adj.* *Slang.* astonishing or thrilling.

eye′ rhyme′. See **sight rhyme.**

eye·serv·ant (ī′sûr′vənt), *n.* a servant or other employee who does his work only when watched by his employer. Also, **eye′serv′er.** [EYE + SERVANT]

eye·serv·ice (ī′sûr′vis), *n.* **1.** work or service done only when the employer is watching. **2.** homage paid with the eyes; admiring looks. [EYE + SERVICE]

eye·shade (ī′shād′), *n.* a visor worn on the head or forehead to shield the eyes from overhead light. [EYE + SHADE]

eye′ shad′ow, a cosmetic coloring material applied to the eyelids.

eye·shot (ī′shot′), *n.* **1.** range of vision; view: *The ship passed out of eyeshot.* **2.** *Archaic.* a glance. [EYE + SHOT[1]]

eye·sight (ī′sīt′), *n.* **1.** the power or faculty of seeing. **2.** the action or fact of seeing. **3.** the range of the eye: *to come within eyesight.* [ME; see EYE, SIGHT]

eyes′ left′, *Mil.* (at ceremonies) the command to turn the head and eyes to the left in salute.

eye′ sock′et, the socket or orbit of the eye.

eye·some (ī′səm), *adj.* pleasant to look at: *She was an eyesome creature.* [EYE + -SOME[1]]

eye·sore (ī′sōr′, ī′sôr′), *n.* something unpleasant to look at: *The broken window was an eyesore to the neighbors.* [EYE + SORE]

eye′ splice′, a splice made in a rope by turning back one end and interweaving it with the main body of the rope so as to form a loop. See illus. under **splice.**

eye·spot (ī′spot′), *n.* **1.** a sensory organ of lower animals, having a light-perceiving function. **2.** an eyelike spot, as on the tail of a peacock; eye. **3.** *Plant Pathol.* a disease of plants, characterized by elliptical lesions on the leaves and stems, rotting, and stunting of growth, caused by any of several fungi. [EYE + SPOT]

eyes′ right′, *Mil.* (at ceremonies) the command to turn the head and eyes to the right in salute.

eye·stalk (ī′stôk′), *n.* *Zool.* the stalk or peduncle upon which the eye is borne in lobsters, shrimps, etc. [EYE + STALK[1]]

eye·stone (ī′stōn′), *n.* a small calcareous body, flat on one side and convex on the other, passed between the eye and the eyelid to bring out cinders or other foreign matter. [EYE + STONE]

eye·strain (ī′strān′), *n.* a sensation of discomfort produced in the eyes by their excessive or faulty use: *to have eyestrain from reading fine print.* [EYE + STRAIN]

eye·strings (ī′stringz′), *n.pl.* *Obs.* the muscles, nerves, or tendons of the eye. [EYE + STRING + -S[3]]

eye·tooth (ī′to͞oth′), *n., pl.* **-teeth** (-tēth′). **1.** *Dentistry.* a canine tooth of the upper jaw: so named from its position under the eye. **2. cut one's eyeteeth, a.** to gain sophistication or experience; become worldly-wise. **b.** Also, **cut one's eyeteeth on.** to be initiated or gain one's first experience in a career, hobby, skill, etc.: *She cut her eyeteeth on television and went on to become a movie star.* **3. give one's eyeteeth,** to give something one considers very precious, usually in exchange for an object or situation one desires: *She would give her eyeteeth for that job.* [EYE + TOOTH]

eye·wash (ī′wosh′, ī′wôsh′), *n.* **1.** Also called **collyrium.** *Pharm.* a solution applied locally to the eye for irrigation or administering medication; eye lotion. **2.** *Slang.* nonsense; bunk: *Don't listen to that eyewash about his success in Europe.* [EYE + WASH]

eye·wa·ter (ī′wô′tər, ī′wot′ər), *n.* *Archaic.* **1.** a tear. **2.** a lotion for the eyes. [EYE + WATER]

eye·wink (ī′wingk′), *n.* **1.** a wink of the eye. **2.** *Obs.* a look or glance. [EYE + WINK]

eye·wink·er (ī′wing′kər), *n.* **1.** an eyelash. **2.** anything that enters or irritates the eye and causes blinking. [EYEWINK + -ER[1]]

eye·wit·ness (*n.* ī′wit′nis, ī′wit′nis; *v.* ī′wit′nis), *n.* **1.** a person who actually sees some act, occurrence, or thing and can give a firsthand account of it: *There were two eyewitnesses to the murder.* —*v.t.* **2.** to view with one's own eyes: *to eyewitness a murder.* [EYE + WITNESS]

eye′ worm′, a filarial worm, *Loa loa,* of west and central Africa, that is parasitic in the subcutaneous tissue of man, often migrating into the eye region.

eyne (īn), *n.* *Archaic.* pl. of **eye.**

ey·ot (ī′ət, āt), *n.* *Brit. Dial.* ait.

ey·ra (âr′ə, ī′rə), *n.* a jaguarundi. [< AmerSp < Tupi *eira*(*ra*)]

eyre (âr), *n.* **1.** a journey in a circuit. **2.** *Old Eng. Law.* **a.** the circuit made by judges **(justices in eyre)** commissioned to hold court in different counties. As developed after 1176 the eyres occasioned extensive royal inquests into county affairs. They were replaced in the late 13th century by itinerant judges with more narrowly defined powers. **b.** a court held by justices in eyre. [ME *eyre* < AF; OF *erre,* deriv. of *errer* to journey; see ERR]

Eyre (âr), *n.* **Lake,** a shallow salt lake in S South Australia. 3430 sq. mi.

Eyre′ Penin′sula, a peninsula in S Australia, E of the Great Australian Bight. Also, **Eyre's′ Penin′sula** (ârz).

ey·rie (âr′ē, ēr′ē), *n.* aerie. Also, **ey′ry.**

ey·rir (ā′rēr), *n., pl.* **au·rar** (oi′rär). an aluminum bronze coin of Iceland, the 100th part of a krona, equivalent to about .00023 of a U.S. dollar. [< OIcel < ON: ounce, unit of money; c. Sw *öre* < L *aureus* golden]

Eysk (āsk), *n.* Yeisk.

Ez., Ezra. Also, **Ezr.**

Ez·e·chi·as (ez′ə kī′əs), *n.* *Douay Bible.* Hezekiah.

Ezek., Ezekiel.

E·ze·ki·el (i zē′kē əl), *n.* **1.** a Major Prophet of the 6th century B.C. **2.** a book of the Bible bearing his name. **3. Moses Jacob,** 1844–1917, U.S. sculptor, in Rome. **4.** a boy's given name. Also, *Douay Bible,* **E·ze·chi·el** (i zē′kē əl) (for defs. 1, 2).

Ezr., Ezra.

Ez·ra (ez′rə), *n.* **1.** Also, *Douay Bible,* **Esdras.** a Jewish scribe and prophet of the 5th century B.C., who with Nehemiah led the revival of Judaism in Palestine. **2.** Also, *Douay Bible,* **I Esdras.** a book of the Bible bearing his name. **3.** a boy's given name.

Ez·zard (ez′ərd), *n.* a boy's given name.

F

F, f (ef), *n., pl.* **F's** or **Fs, f's** or **fs.** **1.** the sixth letter of the English alphabet, a consonant. **2.** any spoken sound represented by the letter *F* or *f*, as in *fat, differ, huff,* etc. **3.** something having the shape of an F. **4.** a written or printed representation of the letter *F* or *f*. **5.** a device, as a printer's type, for reproducing the letter *F* or *f*.

F, **1.** Fahrenheit. **2.** *Elect.* farad. **3.** fermi. **4.** *Math.* field. **5.** *Genetics.* filial. **6.** firm. **7.** French. **8.** *Math.* function (of).

F, **1.** the sixth in order or in a series. **2.** *Music.* **a.** the fourth tone in the scale of C major or the sixth tone in the relative minor scale, A minor. **b.** a string, key, or pipe tuned to this tone. **c.** a written or printed note representing this tone. **d.** (in the fixed system of solmization) the fourth tone of the scale of C major, called *fa.* **e.** the tonality having F as the tonic note. **3.** (*sometimes l.c.*) the medieval Roman numeral for 40. Cf. **Roman numerals.** **4.** *Chem.* fluorine. **5.** *Physics.* **a.** force. **b.** F-state.

f, **1.** (in some grading systems) failing. **2.** *Elect.* farad. **3.** firm. **4.** *Photog.* See **f number.** **5.** *Music.* forte.

f, **1.** *Optics.* See **focal length.** **2.** *Physics.* **a.** force. **b.** frequency.

F-, *U.S. Mil.* (in designations of aircraft) fighter: *F-105.*

F., **1.** Fahrenheit. **2.** February. **3.** Fellow. **4.** forint. **5.** franc; francs. **6.** France. **7.** French. **8.** Friday.

f., **1.** (in prescriptions) make. [< L *fac*] **2.** *Elect.* farad. **3.** farthing. **4.** father. **5.** fathom. **6.** feet. **7.** female. **8.** feminine. **9.** (in prescriptions) let them be made. [< L *fiant*] **10.** (in prescriptions) fiat. **11.** filly. **12.** fine. **13.** fluid (ounce). **14.** folio. **15.** following. **16.** foot. **17.** form. **18.** formed of. **19.** franc. **20.** from. **21.** *Math.* function (of). **22.** (in the Netherlands) gulden; guldens. [< D *florin*]

f/, *Photog.* See **f number.** Also, **f/, f, f:**

F_1 layer (ef′ wun′). See under **F layer.**

F_2 layer (ef′ to͞o′). See under **F layer.**

fa (fä), *n. Music.* **1.** the syllable used for the fourth tone of a diatonic scale. **2.** (in the fixed system of solmization) the tone F. Cf. **sol-fa** (def. 1). [ME; see GAMUT]

FA, *Mil.* Field Artillery.

fā (fä), *n.* the 20th letter of the Arabic alphabet. [< Ar]

FAA, **1.** *U.S. Govt.* Federal Aviation Agency: the division of the Department of Transportation that inspects and rates civilian aircraft and airmen and enforces the rules of air safety. **2.** Federal Alcohol Administration.

F.A.A.A.S., **1.** Fellow of the American Academy of Arts and Sciences. **2.** Fellow of the American Association for the Advancement of Science.

fa·ba·ceous (fə bā′shəs), *adj.* belonging to the *Fabaceae,* or bean family of plants, sometimes included in the *Leguminosae,* including many herbs, shrubs, and trees, as the bean, pea, lentil, furze, broom, locust, etc., which bear seeds in pods or legumes. [< L *fabāceus* of, consisting of beans, equiv. to *fab(a)* a bean + *-āceus* -ACEOUS]

Fa·bens (fā′bənz), *n.* a town in W Texas. 3134 (1960).

Fa·ber·gé (fab′ər zhā′ *for 1;* fab′ər jā′, -zhā′; *Fr.* fa ber zhā′ *for 2*), *n.* **1.** **(Peter) Carl Gus·ta·vo·vich** (kärl gə stä′və vich), 1846–1920, Russian goldsmith and jeweler. **2.** fine gold and enamel ware made in St. Petersburg, Russia, in the late 19th and early 20th centuries, much of it for the Russian court.

Fa·bi·an (fā′bē ən), *adj.* **1.** seeking victory by delay and harassment rather than by a decisive battle as in the manner of Fabius Maximus: *Fabian policy.* **2.** of or pertaining to the Fabian Society. —*n.* **3.** a member of or sympathizer with the Fabian Society. [< L *Fabiān(us).* See FABIUS, -AN]

Fa·bi·an (fā′bē ən, fāb′yən), *n.* **1.** **Saint,** died A.D. 250, pope 236–250. **2.** a boy's given name.

Fa′bian Soci′ety, a socialist organization founded in England in 1884, favoring the gradual spread of socialism by peaceful means.

Fa·bi·us Max·i·mus (fā′bē əs mak′sə məs), (*Quintus Fabius Maximus Verrucosus*) (*Cunctator*) 275–203 B.C., Roman statesman and general: harassed Hannibal's army without risking a pitched battle.

fa·ble (fā′bəl), *n., v.,* **-bled, -bling.** —*n.* **1.** a short tale to teach a moral, often with animals or inanimate objects as characters; apologue: *the fable of the tortoise and the hare; Aesop's fables.* **2.** a story not founded on fact: *This biography is largely a self-promoting fable.* **3.** a story about supernatural or extraordinary persons or incidents; legend: *the fables of gods and heroes.* **4.** legends or myths collectively: *the heroes of Greek fable.* **5.** an untruth; falsehood: *This boast of a cure is a medical fable.* **6.** *Archaic.* the plot of an epic, a dramatic poem, or a play. **7.** *Archaic.* idle talk: *old wives' fables.* —*v.i.* **8.** to tell or write fables. **9.** to speak falsely; lie: *to fable about one's past.* —*v.t.* **10.** to describe as if actually so; talk about as if true: *She is fabled to be the daughter of a king.* [ME, var. of *fabel, fabul* < L *fābula* a story, tale, equiv. to *fā(rī)* (to) speak + *-bula* suffix of means or result] —**fa′bler,** *n.*
—**Syn. 1.** parable, allegory. See **legend. 3.** myth. **5.** lie, fib, fiction, invention, fabrication. —**Ant. 2, 5.** truth.

fa·bled (fā′bəld), *adj.* **1.** celebrated in fables: *a fabled goddess of the wood.* **2.** having no real existence; fictitious: *a fabled chest of gold.* [FABLE + -ED[3]]

Fa·bles (*Fr.* fä′blᵊ; *Eng.* fā′bəlz), *n.* twelve books of fables in verse (1668–94) by Jean de La Fontaine.

fab·li·au (fab′lē ō′; *Fr.* fa blē ō′), *n., pl.* **fab·li·aux** (fab′lē ōz′; *Fr.* fa blē ō′). one of the short metrical tales of the medieval French poets, usually ribald and humorous. [< F, irreg. dim. of *fable* FABLE]

Fa·bre (fä′bər; *Fr.* fa′brᵊ), *n.* **Jean Hen·ri** (zhäN äN rē′), 1823–1915, French entomologist and popular writer on insect life.

Fa·bri·a·no (*It.* fä brē ä′nô), *n.* **Gen·ti·le da** (*It.* jen tē′le dä). See **Gentile da Fabriano.**

fab·ric (fab′rik), *n.* **1.** a cloth made by weaving, knitting, or felting fibers: *woolen fabrics.* **2.** the texture of the woven, knitted, or felted material: *cloth of a soft, pliant fabric.* **3.** framework; structure: *the fabric of society.* **4.** a building; edifice. **5.** the method of construction. **6.** the act of constructing, esp. of a church building. **7.** the maintenance of such a building. **8.** *Petrog.* the spatial arrangement and orientation of the constituents of a rock. [late ME *fabrike* < L *fabrica* piece of skilled work, workshop. See FORGE[1]]

fab·ri·cant (fab′rə kənt), *n.* a maker or manufacturer. [< L *fabricant-* (s. of *fabricāns*) making, prp. of *fabricāre.* See FABRICATE, -ANT]

fab·ri·cate (fab′rə kāt′), *v.t.,* **-cat·ed, -cat·ing.** **1.** to make by art and labor; construct: *The finest craftsmen fabricated this clock.* **2.** to make by assembling standard parts or sections: *to fabricate a house.* **3.** to devise or invent (a legend, lie, etc.). **4.** to fake; forge (a document, signature, etc.). [< L *fabricāt(us)* made, ptp. of *fabricāre.* See FABRIC, -ATE[1]] —**fab′ri·ca′tive,** *adj.* —**fab′ri·ca′tor,** *n.*
—**Syn. 1.** build. See **manufacture. 2.** erect. —**Ant. 1.** destroy.

fab·ri·ca·tion (fab′rə kā′shən), *n.* **1.** the act or process of fabricating; manufacture. **2.** something fabricated, esp. an untruthful statement: *His story of his whereabouts on that night is a fabrication.* [ME *fabricacioun* < L *fabricātiōn-* (s. of *fabricātiō*). See FABRICATE, -ION]
—**Syn. 2.** See **fiction.**

Fa·bri·cius (fä brē′syo͝os *for 1;* fa brish′ē əs, -brish′əs, fə- *for 2*), *n.* **1.** **Jo·han Chris·tian** (yō hän′ kris′tyän), 1743–1808, Danish entomologist. **2.** a crater in the fourth quadrant of the face of the moon: about 55 miles in diameter.

Fab·ri·koid (fab′rə koid′), *n. Trademark.* a waterproof fabric having a cloth foundation and a pyroxylin surface: used as a substitute for leather, cloth, etc.

Fa·bri·ti·us (fä brē′tsē o͞os), *n.* **Ca·rel** (kä′rəl), 1624–54. Dutch painter: pupil of Rembrandt.

Fab·ron (fab′rən), *n.* a boy's given name.

Fa·bry′-Pe·rot′ e′talon (fa brē′pə rō′), *Optics.* etalon. [named after Charles *Fabry* (1867–1945), and A. *Perot,* French physicists]

Fabry′-Perot′ interferom′eter, *Optics.* an etalon in which the plate separation is continuously adjustable. [see FABRY-PEROT ETALON]

fab·u·list (fab′yə list), *n.* **1.** a person who invents or relates fables. **2.** a liar. [< MF *fabuliste,* equiv. to *fabul-* (< L *fābula* FABLE) + *-iste* -IST]

fab·u·lous (fab′yə ləs), *adj.* **1.** almost unbelievable; incredible. **2.** exceptionally good or unusual; marvelous; superb: *a fabulous bargain; fabulous jewels.* **3.** told about in fables; purely imaginary: *the fabulous exploits of Hercules.* **4.** known about only through myths or legends. [< L *fābulōs(us),* equiv. to *fābul(a)* FABLE + *-ōsus* -OUS] —**fab′u·lous·ly,** *adv.* —**fab′u·lous·ness,** *n.*
—**Syn. 1.** amazing, astonishing, astounding. **3.** fabled, fictitious, invented, fictional. —**Ant. 1.** usual. **3.** actual, historical.

fab·ur·den (fab′ər dᵊn), *n. Music.* fauxbourdon. [late ME *faburdon.* See FA, BURDEN[2]]

fac., **1.** facsimile. **2.** factor. **3.** factory.

fac (fäk), *v. imperative. Latin.* make.

Façade (def. 1)

fa·çade (fə säd′, fa-; *Fr.* fa sad′), *n., pl.* **-çades** (-sädz′; *Fr.* -sad′). **1.** *Archit.* the front of a building, esp. an imposing or decorative one. **2.** a superficial appearance or illusion of something: *They maintained a façade of wealth.* Also, **fa·cade′.** [< F < It *facciata,* equiv. to *facci(a)* FACE + *-ata* -ADE[1]]

face (fās), *n., v.,* **faced, fac·ing.** —*n.* **1.** the front part of the head, from the forehead to the chin. **2.** a look or expression on this part: *a sad face.* **3.** an expression or look that indicates ridicule, disgust, etc.; grimace: *The child put on a face when it was told to go to bed.* **4.** cosmetics; make-up: *It took her an hour to put on her face.* **5.** *Informal.* boldness; impudence: *to have the face to ask a rude question.* **6.** outward appearance: *These are just old problems with new faces. The future presented a fair face to the fortunate youth.* **7.** outward show or pretense, esp. as a means of preserving one's dignity when under stress or of concealing a detrimental fact, condition, etc.: *Though shamed beyond words, he managed to show a bold face.* **8.** good reputation; dignity; prestige: *They hushed up the family scandal to preserve face.* **9.** the amount specified in a bill or note, exclusive of interest. **10.** the manifest sense or express terms, as of a document. **11.** the geographic characteristics or general appearance (of a land surface). **12.** the surface: *face of the earth.* **13.** the side, or part of a side, upon which the use of a thing depends: *the face of a watch; the face of a playing card.* **14.** the most important or most frequently seen side; front: *the face of a building.* **15.** the acting, striking, or working surface of an implement, tool, etc. **16.** *Geom.* any one of the bounding surfaces of a solid figure: *a cube has six faces.* **17.** *Mining.* the front or end of a drift or excavation, where the material is being or was last mined. **18.** *Print.* **a.** the working surface of a type, of a plate, etc. See diag. under **type. b.** Also called **typeface.** any design of type, including a full range of characters, as letters, numbers, and marks of punctuation, in all sizes: *Caslon is one of the most popular faces.* **c.** Also called **typeface.** the general style or appearance of type: *broad or narrow face.* **19.** *Naut., Aeron.* the rear or after side of a propeller blade (opposed to *back*). **20.** *Fort.* either of the two outer sides that form the salient angle of a bastion or the like. See diag. under **bastion. 21.** *Crystall.* any of the outer plane surfaces of a crystal. **22.** *Electronics.* faceplate (def. 2). **23.** *Archaic.* sight;

presence: *to flee from the face of the enemy.* **24. face to face, a.** facing one another; opposite: *We sat face to face at the table.* **b.** in contact with; near: *face to face with death.* **c.** in conflict with; to a critical point. **25. fly in the face of.** See **fly**[1] (def. 20). **26. in the face of, a.** in spite of; notwithstanding: *She persevered in the face of many obstacles.* **b.** when confronted with: *They were steadfast in the face of disaster.* **27. lose face,** to suffer embarrassment, humiliation, or disgrace: *It was impossible to retreat without losing face.* **28. make a face,** to scowl, as in distaste or contempt; contort one's face: *When he discovered that he wasn't going along, the child made a face.* **29. on the face of,** to outward appearances; superficially; seemingly: *On the face of it, there was no hope for a comeback.* **30. put on a bold face,** to give the appearance of confidence or assurance: *Everyone knew that he had been fired, even though he put on a bold face.* Also, **put a bold face on. 31. save face,** to avoid disgrace or humiliation: *She tried to save face by saying that she'd been ill and couldn't remember what she'd promised.* **32. set one's face against,** to disapprove strongly of; oppose: *The mother set her face against her daughter's engagement.* **33. show one's face,** to make an appearance; be seen: *I would be ashamed to show my face in such an outlandish outfit.* **34. to one's face,** in one's presence; brazenly; directly: *Tell him to his face that he's a liar!*
—*v.t.* 35. to look toward or in the direction of: *to face the light.* **36.** to have the front toward or permit a view of: *The building faces 19th street. The bedroom faces the park.* **37.** to confront directly: *to be faced with a problem; to face the future confidently.* **38.** to confront courageously, boldly, or impudently (usually fol. by *down* or *out*): *He could always face down his detractors. We must face out this ugly situation.* **39.** to oppose or to meet defiantly: *to face fearful odds. Army faces Navy in today's football game.* **40.** to cover or partly cover with a different material in front: *They faced the old wooden house with brick.* **41.** to finish the edge of a garment with facing. **42.** to turn the face of (a playing card) upwards. **43.** to dress or smooth the surface of (a stone or the like). **44.** to cause (soldiers) to turn to the right, left, or in the opposite direction. **45.** *Ice Hockey.* (of a referee) to put (the puck) in play by dropping it between two opposing players each having his stick on the ice and facing the goal of the opponent.
—*v.i.* 46. to turn or be turned (often fol. by *to* or *toward*): *She faced toward the sea.* **47.** to be placed with the front in a certain direction (often fol. by *on, to,* or *toward*): *The house faces on the street. The barn faces south.* **48.** to turn to the right, left, or in the opposite direction: *Left face!* **49.** *Ice Hockey.* to face the puck (often fol. by *off*). **50. face up to, a.** to acknowledge; admit: *to face up to the facts.* **b.** to meet courageously; confront: *He refused to face up to his problems.* [ME < OF < VL **facia,* r. L *faciēs* FACIES] **—face′a·ble,** *adj.*
—Syn. 1. features. FACE, COUNTENANCE, VISAGE refer to the front of the (usually human) head. The FACE is the combination of the features: *a face with broad cheekbones.* COUNTENANCE, a more formal word, denotes the face as it is affected by or reveals the state of mind, and hence often signifies the look or expression on the face: *an expressive countenance.* VISAGE, still more formal, refers to the face as seen in a certain aspect, esp. as revealing seriousness or severity: *a stern visage.* **2.** appearance, aspect, mien. **7.** exterior. **14.** façade. **40.** veneer.

face′ bow′ (bō), *Dentistry.* a device for determining the relationship of the maxillae to the mandibular joint.

face′ brick′, 1. a brick for facing a wall. **2.** a quantity of such bricks. **3.** a variety of such bricks.

face′ card′, the king, queen, or jack of playing cards.

face-cen·tered (fās′sen′tərd), *adj. Crystall.* (of a crystal structure) having lattice points on the faces of the unit cells. Cf. **body-centered.**

face′ gear′, *Mach.* a disklike gear having teeth cut on the face more or less radially and engaging with a spur or helical pinion the axis of which is at right angles to it.

face′ ham′mer, a hammer for the rough dressing of stones, having one flat face and one blunt-edged face.

face-hard·en (fās′här′dᵊn), *v.t.* to harden the surface of (metal), as by chilling or casehardening.

face·less (fās′lis), *adj.* **1.** without a face: *a faceless apparition.* **2.** lacking personal distinction or identity: *a faceless mob.* **3.** unable to be identified; concealing one's identity: *a faceless kidnapper.* [FACE + -LESS]

face-lift (fās′lift′), *n.* **1.** See **face lifting. —*v.t.* 2.** to perform a face lifting upon.

face′ lift′ing, plastic surgery on the face for elevating sagging tissues and eliminating wrinkles and other signs of age.

face′ mold′, a drawing or templet for forming a molded member, esp. the wreath of a stair.

face-off (fās′ôf′, -of′), *n. Ice Hockey.* the act of facing the puck, as at the start of a game or period. [n. use of v. phrase *face off*]

face·plate (fās′plāt′), *n.* **1.** (on a lathe) a perforated plate, mounted on the live spindle, to which the work is attached. **2.** Also called **face.** *Electronics.* the glass front of a cathode ray tube upon which the image is displayed, and having its inner surface coated with fluorescent material that glows when excited by a beam of electrons. [FACE + PLATE[1]]

face′ pow′der, a cosmetic powder used esp. by women, actors, etc., to give a mat finish to the face.

fac·er (fā′sər), *n.* **1.** one who or that which faces. **2.** *Informal.* a blow in the face. **3.** *Brit. Informal.* an unexpected major difficulty, dilemma, or defeat. [FACE + -ER[1]]

face-sav·ing (fās′sā′ving), *adj.* **1.** serving to save one's prestige or dignity. **—*n.* 2.** any act that saves one's prestige or dignity.

fac·et (fas′it), *n., v.,* **-et·ed, -et·ing** or (*esp. Brit.*) **-et·ted, -et·ting. —*n.* 1.** one of the small, polished plane surfaces of a cut gem. **2.** a similar surface cut on a fragment of rock by the action of water, windblown sand, etc. **3.** aspect; phase: *They carefully examined every facet of the argument.* **4.** *Archit.* any of the faces of a column cut in a polygonal form. **5.** *Zool.* one of the corneal lenses of a compound arthropod eye. **—*v.t.* 6.** to cut facets on. [< F *facette* little face. See FACE, -ET]

fa·cete (fə sēt′), *adj. Archaic.* facetious; witty. [< L *facēt(us),* courteous, elegant, witty] **—fa·cete′ly,** *adv.* **—fa·cete′ness,** *n.*

fa·ce·ti·ae (fə sē′shē ē′), *n.* (*construed as pl.*) **1.** amusing or witty remarks or writings. **2.** coarsely witty books, stories, etc. [< L, pl. of *facētia* something witty. See FACETE, -IA]

fa·ce·tious (fə sē′shəs), *adj.* **1.** not meant to be taken seriously or literally. **2.** amusing; humorous: *a facetious remark.* **3.** characterized by a lack of serious intent; concerned with that which is nonessential, amusing, or frivolous: *a facetious person.* [FACETE + -IOUS; see FACETIAE] **—fa·ce′tious·ly,** *adv.* **—fa·ce′tious·ness,** *n.*
—Syn. 2. comical, funny, droll, jocular. See **humorous.**

face-to-face (fās′tə fās′), *adv.* **1.** in a position with the fronts or faces turned toward each other, esp. when close together: *The two buildings stood face-to-face on the walkway.* **2.** in a way involving close contact or direct opposition: *to fight out an issue face-to-face.* **—*adj.* 3.** with the fronts or faces toward each other, esp. when close together. **4.** involving close contact or direct opposition: *a face-to-face confrontation of an adversary.*

face′ tow′el, a small towel for the face.

face′ val′ue, 1. the value printed on the face of a stock, bond, or other financial instrument or document. **2.** apparent value: *Do not accept promises at face value.*

face′ wall′. See **breast wall.**

fa·cial (fā′shəl), *adj.* **1.** of the face: *facial expression.* **2.** for the face: *a facial cream.* **—*n.* 3.** a massage or other treatment to beautify the face. [< ML *faciāl(is).* See FACE, -AL[1]] **—fa′cial·ly,** *adv.*

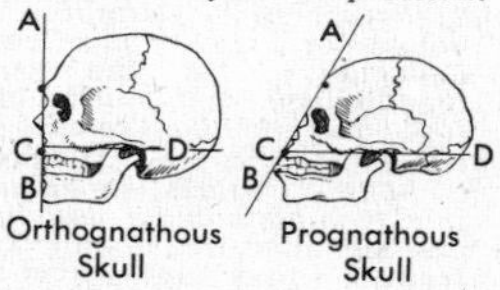

A A C D B C D B
Orthognathous Skull   Prognathous Skull
ACD, Facial angle; AB, Axis of face; CD, Axis of skull

fa′cial an′gle, *Craniom.* the angle formed by a line from nasion to prosthion at its intersection with the plane of the Frankfurt horizontal.

fa′cial in′dex, *Craniom.* the ratio of the breadth of a face to its height.

fa′cial nerve′, *Anat.* either one of the seventh pair of cranial nerves, consisting of motor fibers that innervate the stylohyoid, the posterior belly of the digastric, the muscles of the face and ear, the lacrimal, submaxillary, and sublingual glands, sensory fibers that conduct impulses from the anterior two-thirds of the tongue, the soft palate, the pharynx, and the external auditory meatus to the brain.

fa′cial neural′gia, *Pathol.* See **tic douloureux.**

fa·ci·end (fā′shē end′), *n. Math., Obs.* operand. [< L *faciend(um)* thing done (ger. of *facere*), equiv. to *faci-* (s. of *facere*) + *-endum* ger. suffix]

-facient, a learned borrowing from Latin meaning "that makes or causes (something)," used in the formation of compound words: *febrifacient.* [< L *facient-* (s. of *faciēns,* prp. of *facere*) making, equiv. to *faci-* (s. of *facere*) + *-ent-* -ENT]

fa·ci·es (fā′shē ēz′), *n., pl.* **fa·ci·es. 1.** general appearance, as of an animal or vegetable group. **2.** *Geol.* the composite nature of sedimentary deposits reflecting the conditions and environment of their origin. **3.** *Med.* a facial expression characteristic of a disease or pathological condition. [ME < L: form, figure, appearance, face, akin to *facere* to make]

fac·ile (fas′il or, *esp. Brit.,* -īl), *adj.* **1.** moving, acting, working, proceeding, etc., with ease: *facile fingers; a facile mind.* **2.** easily done, performed, used, etc.: *a facile victory; a facile method.* **3.** easy or unconstrained, as manners or persons; affable, agreeable, or complaisant; easily influenced: *Facile people are pleasant to be with, but one tires of their shallowness.* [late ME < L *facil(is)* that can be done, easy, equiv. to *fac(ere)* (to) do, make + *-ilis* -ILE] **—fac′ile·ly,** *adv.* **—fac′ile·ness,** *n.*
—Syn. 1. smooth, flowing, fluent; glib, superficial. **3.** bland, suave; urbane.

fa·ci·le prin·ceps (fä′ki le′ priŋ′keps; *Eng.* fas′ə lē prin′seps), *Latin.* easily the first or best.

fa·ci·lis de·scen·sus A·ver·no (fä′ki lis des ken′-sōōs ä wer′nō; *Eng.* fas′ə lis di sen′səs ə vûr′nō), *Latin.* (the) descent to hell is easy; it is easy to take the downward path. Vergil, *Aeneid,* 6:126.

fa·cil·i·tate (fə sil′i tāt′), *v.t.,* **-tat·ed, -tat·ing. 1.** to make easier or less difficult; help forward (an action, a process, etc.): *Careful planning facilitates any kind of work.* **2.** to assist the progress of (a person). [FACILIT(Y) + -ATE[1]] **—fa·cil′i·ta′tive,** *adj.* **—fa·cil′i·ta′tor,** *n.*

fa·cil·i·ta·tion (fə sil′i tā′shən), *n.* **1.** the act or process of facilitating. **2.** *Physiol.* the lowering of resistance in a neural pathway to an impulse, resulting from previous or simultaneous stimulation. [FACILITATE + -ION]

fa·cil·i·ty (fə sil′i tē), *n., pl.* **-ties. 1.** something designed, built, installed, etc., to serve a specific function affording a convenience or service: *transportation facilities. This town needs more educational facilities.* **2.** the quality of being easily or conveniently done or performed. **3.** something that permits the easier performance of an action, course of conduct, etc.: *to provide someone with every facility for accomplishing a task.* **4.** freedom from difficulty; ease: *facility of understanding.* **5.** readiness or ease due to skill, aptitude, or practice; dexterity: *to compose with great facility.* **6.** an easy-flowing manner: *facility of style.* **7.** ready compliance: *Her facility in cooperating made her an excellent employee.* [late ME *facilite* < L *facilitās.* See FACILE, -ITY]

fac·ing (fā′siŋ), *n.* **1.** a covering in front, for ornament, protection, etc., as an outer layer of stone different from that of the rest of a wall. **2.** a lining applied to the edge of a garment for ornament or strengthening, as a cuff or as material turned inward for a hem. **3. facings,** coverings of a different color applied on the collar, cuffs, or other parts of a military coat. **4.** *Mil.* the act of turning to face in a given direction in response to a command. [FACE + -ING[1]]

fac′ing ham′mer, a hammer for dressing stone or concrete, having a row of teeth at each end of its head at right angles to the direction of the handle.

fac′ing tool′, a lathe tool for smoothing a plane surface at right angles to the axis of rotation.

fa·cin·o·rous (fə sin′ər əs), *adj. Archaic.* atrociously wicked. [< L *facinorōs(us)* criminal, atrocious, equiv. to *facinor-* (s. of *facinus* bad deed, akin to *facere* to do) + *-ōsus* -OUS]

fa·con·ne (fas′ə nā′, fas′ə nā′), *adj.* **1.** (of a fabric) having a small and elaborate pattern. **—*n.* 2.** a fabric having a faconne pattern or motif. **3.** the small and elaborate pattern on a faconne fabric. [< F *façonné,* ptp. of *façonner* to work, FASHION; see -EE]

facsim., facsimile.

fac·sim·i·le (fak sim′ə lē), *n., v.,* **-led, -le·ing. —*n.* 1.** an exact copy, as of a book, painting, manuscript, etc. **2.** a method of transmitting drawings, printed material, or the like, by means of radio or telegraph. **3.** dropout (def. 5). **—*v.t.* 4.** to reproduce in facsimile; make a facsimile of. [earlier *fac simile* make the like, equiv. to L *fac* (impv. of *facere*) + *simile,* n. use of neut. of *similis* like; see SIMILE]
—Syn. 1. replica, reproduction. **1, 4.** duplicate.

facsim′ile tel′egraph, a telegraphic device permitting the transmitting of black-and-white pictures, drawings, and printed material for reproduction at a distant place.

fact (fakt), *n.* **1.** that which actually exists; reality; truth: *Your fears have no basis in fact.* **2.** something known to exist or to have happened: *Space travel is now a fact.* **3.** a truth known by actual experience or observation; that which is known to be true: *Scientists gather facts to combat idle conjectures and superstitions.* **4.** something said to be true or supposed to have happened: *The facts given by the witness are highly questionable.* **5.** *Law.* Often, **facts.** an actual or alleged event or circumstance, as distinguished from its legal effect or consequence. Cf. **question of fact, question of law. 6. after the fact,** *Law.* after the commission of a crime: *an accessory after the fact.* **7. before the fact,** *Law.* prior to the commission of a crime: *an accessory before the fact.* **8. in fact,** really; indeed: *In fact, it was a wonder that anyone came at all.* [< L *fact(um)* something done, deed, n. use of neut. of *factus* done, ptp. of *facere* to do] **—fact′ful,** *adj.*

fact-find·ing (fakt′fīn′diŋ), *adj.* **1.** engaged in determining facts: *a fact-finding committee.* **—*n.* 2.** determination of facts: *The fact-finding was obstructed by unwilling witnesses.*

Fac·tice (fak′tis), *Trademark. n.* a rubberlike substance produced by vulcanizing vegetable oils with sulfur or sulfur chloride.

fac·tion (fak′shən), *n.* **1.** a group or clique within a larger group, party, government, organization, or the like: *a faction in favor of big business.* **2.** party strife and intrigue; dissention: *an era of faction and treason.* [< L *factiōn-* (s. of *factiō*) a doing, company, equiv. to *fact(us)* done (see FACT) + *-iōn-* -ION]

fac·tion·al (fak′shə nᵊl), *adj.* **1.** of a faction or factions. **2.** self-interested; partisan: *Factional interests had obstructed justice.* [FACTION + -AL[1]] **—fac′tion·al·ism,** *n.* **—fac′tion·al·ist,** *n.*

fac·tious (fak′shəs), *adj.* **1.** given to faction; dissentious: *A factious nobility undermined the state.* **2.** pertaining to or proceeding from faction: *factious quarrels.* [< L *factiōs(us)* fond of doing, busy, of a company or party, equiv. to *facti-* (see FACTION) + *-ōsus* -OUS] **—fac′tious·ly,** *adv.* **—fac′tious·ness,** *n.*

fac·ti·tious (fak tish′əs), *adj.* **1.** artificial; contrived; not spontaneous or natural: *factitious laughter; factitious enthusiasm.* **2.** made; manufactured: *a decoration of factitious flowers and leaves.* [< L *factītius,* var. of *factīcius* made by art, artificial. See FACT, -ITIOUS] **—fac·ti′tious·ly,** *adv.* **—fac·ti′tious·ness,** *n.*
—Syn. 1. forced, feigned, engineered. **—Ant. 1.** genuine, sincere.

fac·ti·tive (fak′ti tiv), *adj. Gram.* noting or pertaining to verbs that express the idea of making or rendering in a certain way and that take a direct object and an additional word or group of words indicating the result of the process, as *made* in *They made him king.* [< NL *factitīv(us),* equiv to *factit-* (s. of L *factitāre* to do often, practice, declare (someone) to be) + *-īvus* -IVE] **fac′ti·tive·ly,** *adv.*

fact′ of life′, 1. any aspect of human existence or of a human situation that must be confronted or regarded as unalterable or presently existing: *Old age is a fact of life. War is a fact of life in our times.* **2. facts of life,** the facts concerning sex, reproduction, and birth: *to teach children the facts of life.*

fac·tor (fak′tər), *n.* **1.** one of the elements contributing to a particular result or situation: *Unknown factors frustrate our desire to make exact predictions.* **2.** *Math.* one of two or more numbers, algebraic expressions, or the like, which when multiplied together produce a given product; a divisor: *6 and 3 are factors of 18.* **3.** *Biol.* a gene, allele, or determiner for hereditary characters. **4.** *Biochem.* any of certain substances necessary to a biochemical or physiological process, esp. those whose exact nature and function are unknown. **5.** *Com.* a business organization that lends money on accounts receivable or buys and collects accounts receivable. **6.** an agent; a person who acts or transacts business for another. **7.** *Chiefly Brit.* an agent or salesman entrusted with the possession of goods for sale; an agent or merchant earning a commission by selling goods belonging to others. **8.** a person who or business organization that provides money for another's new business venture; one who finances another's business. **9.** *U.S. Law.* (in some States) a person charged as a garnishee. **10.** See **factor of production. 11.** *Scot.* the steward or bailiff of an estate. **—*v.t.* 12.** *Math.* to express (a mathematical quantity) as a product of two or more quantities of like kind, as $30 = 2 \cdot 3 \cdot 5$, or $x^2 - y^2 = (x + y)(x - y)$. Cf. **expand** (def. 4a). [late ME *facto(u)r* < L *factor* a maker, doer, performer. See FACT, -OR[2]] **—fac′tor·a·bil′i·ty,** *n.* **—fac′tor·a·ble,** *adj.* **—fac′tor·ship′,** *n.*

fac·tor·age (fak′tər ij), *n.* **1.** the action or business of a factor. **2.** the allowance or commission paid to a factor. [FACTOR + -AGE]

fac′tor anal′ysis, *Statistics.* the use of one of several methods for reducing a set of variables to a lesser number of new variables each of which is a function of one or more of the original variables.

fac′tor group′, *Math.* See **quotient group.**

fac·to·ri·al (fak tōr′ē əl, -tôr′-), *n.* **1.** *Math.* the product of a given positive integer multiplied by all lesser positive integers. *Symbol: n!,* ⌊n where *n* is the given integer. —*adj.* **2.** *Math.* of or pertaining to factors or factorials. **3.** of or pertaining to a factor or a factory. [FACTOR + -IAL] —**fac·to′ri·al·ly,** *adv.*

facto′rial stop′ sys′tem, *Photog.* See **F-stop system.**

fac·tor·ing (fak′tər ing), *n.* **1.** *Com.* the business of purchasing and collecting accounts receivable or of advancing cash on the basis of accounts receivable. **2.** the act or process of separating an equation, formula, cryptogram, etc., into its component parts. [FACTOR + -ING[1]]

fac·tor·ize (fak′tə rīz′), *v.t.,* **-ized, -iz·ing. 1.** *Math.* to resolve into factors. **2.** *Law.* garnishee (def. 1). [FACTOR + -IZE] —**fac′tor·i·za′tion,** *n.*

fac′tor of adhe′sion, *Railroads.* the ratio of the force that can be exerted on driving wheels with full traction to the weight on the driving wheels, usually expressed as a percentage. Also called **adhesion, adhesive factor.**

fac′tor of produc′tion, any instrument, agent, etc., employed in the production of goods and services.

fac′tor of safe′ty, the ratio of the maximum stress that a structural part or other piece of material can withstand to the maximum stress estimated for it in the use for which it is designed. Also called **safety factor.**

fac·to·ry (fak′tə rē), *n., pl.* **-ries. 1.** a building or group of buildings with facilities for the manufacture of goods. **2.** *Informal.* any place producing a uniform product, without concern for individuality: *They call it an art school, but it's just a painting factory.* **3.** (formerly) an establishment for factors and merchants carrying on business in a foreign country. [< ML *factōria.* See FACTOR, -Y[3]] —**fac′to·ry·like′,** *adj.*
—**Syn. 1.** manufactory, mill, workshop, plant.

fac′tory ship′, a whaling ship equipped to process the killed whales and to transport the oil and by-products.

fac·to·tum (fak tō′təm), *n.* a person employed to do all kinds of work, as the chief servant of a household. [< ML, equiv. to L *fac* make, do (impv. of *facere*) + *tōtum,* neut. of *tōtus* all]

fac·tu·al (fak′cho͞o əl), *adj.* **1.** of or pertaining to facts; concerning facts: *factual accuracy.* **2.** based on or restricted to facts: *a factual statement.* [FACT + (ACT)UAL] —**fac′tu·al·ly,** *adv.* —**fac′tu·al′i·ty, fac′tu·al·ness,** *n.*

fac·tu·al·ism (fak′cho͞o ə liz′əm), *n.* emphasis on, devotion to, or extensive reliance upon facts: *the factualism of scientific experiment.* [FACTUAL + -ISM] —**fac′tu·al·ist,** *n.* —**fac′tu·al·is′tic,** *adj.*

fac·ture (fak′chər), *n.* **1.** the act, process, or manner of making anything; construction. **2.** the thing made. [late ME < L *factūra* the making (of something). See FACT, -URE]

fac·u·la (fak′yə lə), *n., pl.* **-lae** (-lē′). *Astron.* an irregular, unusually bright patch on the sun's surface. [< L: little torch, equiv. to *fac-* (s. of *fax*) torch + *-ula* -ULE] —**fac′u·lar,** *adj.*

fac·ul·ta·tive (fak′əl tā′tiv), *adj.* **1.** conferring a faculty, privilege, permission, or the power of doing or not doing something: *a facultative enactment.* **2.** left to one's option or choice; optional: *The last questions in the examination were facultative.* **3.** that may or may not take place; that may or may not assume a specified character. **4.** *Biol.* having the capacity to live under more than one specific set of environmental conditions, as an animal or plant that can lead either a parasitic or a nonparasitic life (opposed to *obligate*). **5.** of or pertaining to the faculties. [< NL *facultātīv(us).* See FACULTY, -IVE] —**fac′ul·ta′tive·ly,** *adv.*

fac·ul·ty (fak′əl tē), *n., pl.* **-ties. 1.** an ability, natural or acquired, for a particular kind of action: *a faculty for making friends easily.* **2.** one of the powers of the mind, as memory, reason, speech, etc.: *Though very old, he is in full possession of all his faculties.* **3.** an inherent capability of the body: *the faculties of sight and hearing.* **4.** *U.S.* exceptional ability or aptitude: *a president with a faculty for management.* **5.** *Educ.* **a.** one of the departments of learning, as theology, medicine, or law, in a university. **b.** the teaching body, sometimes with the students, in any of these departments. **c.** the entire teaching and administrative force of a university, college, or school. **6.** the members of a learned profession: *the medical faculty.* **7.** a power or privilege conferred by the state, a superior, etc.: *The police had the faculty to suppress the demonstrators.* **8.** *Eccles.* a dispensation, license, or authorization. [ME *faculte* < MF < L *facultāt-* (s. of *facultās*) feasibility, means, equiv. to *facul* easily (see FACILE) + *-tāt-* -TY[2]]
—**Syn. 1.** capacity, aptitude, knack. See **ability.**

fad (fad), *n.* a temporary fashion, manner of conduct, etc., esp. one followed enthusiastically by a group: *The fad of wearing white neckties swept the campus.* [n. use of dial. *fad* to look after things, busy oneself with trifles, back formation from obs. *faddle* to play with, fondle. See FIDDLE] —**fad′like′,** *adj.*
—**Syn.** craze, vogue.

fad·dish (fad′ish), *adj.* **1.** like a fad. **2.** given to fads: *a faddish, sophisticated crowd.* [FAD + -ISH[1]] —**fad′dish·ness,** *n.*

fad·dist (fad′ist), *n.* a person who has a fad or is given to fads, as one who seeks and adheres briefly to a passing variety of unusual diets, beliefs, etc. [FAD + -IST] —**fad′dism,** *n.*

fad·dy (fad′ē), *adj.,* **-di·er, -di·est.** faddish. [FAD + -Y[1]]

fade (fād), *v.,* **fad·ed, fad·ing.** —*v.i.* **1.** to lose brightness or vividness of color. **2.** to become dim, as light, or lose brightness of illumination. **3.** to lose freshness, vigor, strength, or health: *The flower faded.* **4.** to disappear or die gradually (often fol. by *away* or *out*): *His anger faded away.* **5.** *Motion Pictures, Television.* **a.** to appear gradually, esp. by becoming lighter (usually fol. by *in*). **b.** to disappear gradually, esp. by becoming darker (usually fol. by *out*). **6.** *Broadcasting, Recording.* **a.** to increase gradually in volume of sound, as in recording or broadcasting music, dialogue, etc. (usually fol. by *in*). **b.** to decrease gradually in volume of sound (usually fol. by *out*). **7.** *Football.* (of an offensive back) to move back toward his goal line, usually with the intent to pass, after receiving the snapback from center or a hand-off or lateral pass behind the line of scrimmage. —*v.t.* **8.** to cause to fade: *Sunshine faded the tapestry.* **9.** (in dice throwing) to make a wager against (the caster). **10.** *Motion Pictures, Television.* **a.** to cause (a scene) to appear gradually (usually fol. by *in*). **b.** to cause (a scene) to disappear gradually (usually fol. by *out*). **11.** *Broadcasting, Recording.* to cause a gradual increase or decrease in the volume of sound (usually fol. by *in* or *out*). [ME *fade(n),* deriv. of *fade* pale, dull < OF < VL **fatid(us),* r. L *fatuus* FATUOUS] —**fad′a·ble,** *adj.* —**fad′ed·ly,** *adv.* —**fad′ed·ness,** *n.*
—**Syn. 1.** blanch, bleach, pale. **3.** wither, droop, languish, decline, decay. **4.** See **disappear.** —**Ant. 3.** flourish.

fade (fad), *adj. French.* insipid; tasteless; dull.

fade-in (fād′in′), *n.* **1.** *Motion Pictures, Television.* a gradual increase in the visibility of a scene. **2.** *Broadcasting, Recording.* a gradual increase in the volume of sound, esp. of recorded or broadcast music, dialogue, or the like, usually starting from complete inaudibility. [n. use of v. phrase *fade in*]

fade·less (fād′lis), *adj.* not fading or diminishing; unfading: *the fadeless glory of a nation's heroes.* [FADE + -LESS] —**fade′less·ly,** *adv.*

Fade·om·e·ter (fā dom′i tər), *n. Trademark.* an apparatus using an arc lamp that emits light similar in spectrum to sunlight for testing the effects of light on a given substance, as on a dyed textile or the like.

fade-out (fād′out′), *n.* **1.** *Motion Pictures, Television.* a gradual decrease in the visibility of a scene. **2.** *Broadcasting, Recording.* a gradual decrease in the volume of sound, esp. of recorded or broadcast music, dialogue, or the like, usually ending in complete inaudibility. **3.** a disappearance, esp. a gradual one: *the fade-out of a brilliant career.* [n. use of v. phrase *fade out*]

fad·er (fā′dər), *n.* **1.** one who or that which fades. **2.** *Motion Pictures, Broadcasting, Recording.* a multiple-unit volume control used in changing gradually from one signal source to another, decreasing the volume from the first audio or visual source while increasing the volume from the second. [FADE + -ER[1]]

Fa·de·yev (fä dye′yəf), *n.* **A·le·ksan·dr A·le·ksan·dro·vich** (ä′le ksän′dər ä′le ksän′dro vich), 1901–56, Russian novelist. Also, **Fa·de′ev.**

fadge (faj), *v.i.,* **fadged, fadg·ing.** *Brit. Dial.* **1.** to fit; suit; agree. **2.** to succeed; thrive. [akin to OE *gefæg* acceptable. See FAY[2], FUDGE[3]]

Fad·i·man (fad′ə mən), *n.* **Clifton,** born 1904, U.S. writer and critic.

FAdm, Fleet Admiral.

fa·do (fä′do͝o; *Eng.* fä′dō), *n.* a Portuguese popular song or dance, typically accompanied on the guitar. [< Pg < L *fātum* FATE]

Fae (fā), *n.* a girl's given name. Also, **Fay, Faye.**

fae·ces (fē′sēz), *n.pl.* feces. —**fae·cal** (fē′kəl), *adj.*

fa·e·na (fä ā′nə), *n.* **1.** the final third of a bullfight in which the matador uses a muleta and the sword in making the final series of passes preparatory to the kill. **2.** *Informal.* a bullfight. [< Sp: lit., task < obs. Catalan < L *facienda* (neut. pl.). See FACIEND]

Fa·en·za (fä en′zə; *It.* fä en′tsä), *n.* a city in N Italy, SE of Bologna. 51,269 (1961).

fa·er·ie (fā′ə rē, fâr′ē), *n.* **1.** the imaginary land of the fairies. **2.** *Archaic.* a fairy. —*adj.* **3.** fairy. Also, **fa′ër·ie, faery, faëry.** [var. of FAIRY]

Fa′erie Queene′, The (kwēn), a chivalric romance in verse (1590–96), by Edmund Spenser, containing an intricate allegory.

Faer′oe Is′lands (fâr′ō), a group of 21 islands in the N Atlantic between Great Britain and Iceland, belonging to Denmark but having extensive home rule. 34,596 (1960); 540 sq. mi. *Cap.:* Torshaven. Also, **Faroe Islands.** Also called **Faer′oes.** Danish, **Faer·ö·er·ne** (fɛʀ œ′ʀ nə).

Faer·o·ese (fâr′ō ēs′, -ēz′), *n., pl.* **-ese,** *adj.* —*n.* **1.** a native or inhabitant of the Faeroe Islands. **2.** the North Germanic language spoken there. —*adj.* **3.** of or pertaining to the Faeroe Islands, the people, or their language. Also, **faroese.**

fa·er·y (fā′ə rē, fâr′ē), *n., pl.* **fa·er·ies,** *adj.* faerie. Also, **fa′ër·y.**

Faf·nir (fäv′nir, fôv′-), *n. Scand. Myth.* a dragon, a son of Hreidmar and the brother of Otter and Regin: he killed Hreidmar for the cursed treasure of Andvari and was killed in turn by Sigurd at the instigation of Regin.

fag[1] (fag), *v.,* **fagged, fag·ging,** *n.* —*v.t.* **1.** to tire by labor; exhaust (often fol. by *out*): *The long climb fagged us out.* **2.** *Brit.* to require (a younger public-school pupil) to do menial chores. —*v.i.* **3.** *Chiefly Brit.* to work until wearied; work hard: *to fag away at French.* **4.** *Brit. Informal.* to do menial chores for an older public-school pupil. **5.** *Naut.* to fray or unlay the end of (a rope). —*n.* **6.** *Slang.* a cigarette. **7.** a fag end, as of cloth. **8.** *Chiefly Brit.* drudgery; toil. **9.** *Brit. Informal.* a younger pupil in a British public school required to perform certain menial tasks for, and submit to the hazing of, an older pupil. **10.** a drudge. [late ME *fagge* a loose end, broken thread (in cloth)]

fag[2] (fag), *n. Slang.* a male homosexual. [short for FAGGOT[2]]

fa·ga·ceous (fə gā′shəs), *adj.* belonging to the *Fagaceae,* or beech family of trees and shrubs, which includes the beech, chestnut, oak, etc. [< NL *Fāgāce(ae)* name of the family (L *fāg(us)* beech + *-āceae* -ACEAE) + -OUS]

fag′ end′, 1. the last part or very end of something: *The fag end of the rope was frayed and needed repair. We stayed till the fag end of the party.* **2.** the unfinished end of a piece of cloth; remnant: *The hat was made from a fag end of velvet.*

Fag·gi (fä′jē; *It.* fäd′jē), *n.* **Al·fe·o** (al fā′ō; *It.* äl fe′ō), born 1885, U.S. sculptor, born in Italy.

fag·got[1] (fag′ət), *n. Brit.* fagot.

fag·got[2] (fag′ət), *n.* fag[2]. [?]

Fa·gin (fā′gin), *n.* (in Dickens' *Oliver Twist*) a villainous old man who employs young boys as thieves.

fag·ot (fag′ət), *n.* **1.** a bundle of sticks, twigs, or branches bound together and used as fuel, a fascine, etc. **2.** a bundle; bunch. **3.** a bundle of pieces of iron or steel to be welded or rolled together. **4.** See **bouquet garni.** —*v.t.* **5.** to bind or make into a fagot. **6.** to ornament with fagoting. Also, *Brit.,* **faggot.** [ME < MF; cf. Gk *phákelos* fagot] —**fag′ot·er,** *n.*

fag·ot·ing (fag′ə ting), *n.* **1.** an openwork decoration of fabric in which thread is drawn in crisscross stitches across an open seam. **2.** Also called **kidding.** fagots or fascines used as a revetment for riverbanks or the like. Also, *Brit.,* **fag′got·ing.** [FAGOT + -ING[1]]

Fagoting

fahl·band (fäl′band′; *Ger.* fäl′bänt′), *n. Mining.* a belt or zone of rock impregnated with metallic sulfides. [< G, equiv. to *fahl* pale-colored + *Band* ribbon, stripe]

Fahne′stock clip′ (fän′stok′), *Elect.* a type of terminal using a spring that clamps readily onto a connecting wire. [named after J. F. *Fahnestock* (1859–1924)]

Fahr., Fahrenheit (thermometer). Also, **Fah.**

Fahr·en·heit (far′ən hīt′; *Ger.* fär′ən hīt′), *n.* **1. Ga·bri·el Da·ni·el** (*Ger.* gä′bʀē el′ dä′nē el′), 1686–1736, German physicist, devised a temperature scale and introduced the use of mercury in thermometers. —*adj.* **2.** noting, pertaining to, or measured according to a temperature scale (**Fahr′enheit scale′**) in which 32° represents the ice point and 212° the steam point. *Abbr.:* F See illus. under **thermometer.**

fa·ïence (fī äns′, fā-; *Fr.* fa yäns′), *n.* glazed earthenware or pottery, esp. a fine variety with highly colored designs. Also, **fa·ience′.** [< F, orig. pottery of *Faenza,* city in northern Italy]

fail (fāl), *v.i.* **1.** to fall short of success or achievement in something expected, attempted, desired, or approved: *The experiment failed.* **2.** to receive less than the passing grade or mark in an examination, class, or course of study: *He failed in history.* **3.** to be or become deficient or lacking; fall short; be insufficient or absent: *Our supplies failed.* **4.** to dwindle, pass, or die away: *The flowers failed for lack of rain.* **5.** to lose strength or vigor; become weaker: *His health failed after the operation.* **6.** to become unable to meet or pay debts or business obligations; become insolvent or bankrupt. **7.** (of a building member, structure, machine part, etc.) to break, bend, crush, or be otherwise destroyed or made useless because of an excessive load. **8.** to stop functioning or operating: *The electricity failed during the storm.* —*v.t.* **9.** to be unsuccessful in the performance or completion of: *He failed to do his duty.* **10.** to prove of no use or help to, as some expected or usual resource: *His friends failed him. Words failed him.* **11.** to receive less than a passing grade or mark in: *He failed history.* **12.** to declare (a person) unsuccessful in a test, course of study, etc.; give less than a passing grade to: *The professor failed him in history.* **13. fail safe,** to furnish a mechanism for safety in the event an error, power failure, etc., occurs. —*n.* **14.** *Obs.* failure as to performance, occurrence, etc. **15. without fail,** with certainty; positively: *I will visit you tomorrow without fail.* [ME *faile(n)* < OF *faill(ir)* < VL *fallire,* r. L *fallere* to disappoint, deceive]
—**Syn. 5.** decline, fade, sink, wane. **10.** desert, forsake, disappoint. —**Ant. 1.** succeed. **5.** improve. **10.** support.

fail·ing (fā′ling), *n.* **1.** the act or state of one who or that which fails; failure: *His failing is due to general incompetence.* **2.** a defect; shortcoming; weakness: *His lack of generosity is a grave failing.* —*prep.* **3.** in the absence or default of: *Failing payment, we shall sue.* [ME; see FAIL, -ING[1]] —**fail′ing·ly,** *adv.* —**fail′ing·ness,** *n.*
—**Syn. 2.** deficiency, frailty, imperfection, flaw. See **fault.** —**Ant. 2.** strength.

faille (fīl, fāl; *Fr.* fa′yə), *n.* a soft, transversely ribbed fabric of silk, rayon, or lightweight taffeta. [< F]

fail-safe (fāl′sāf′), *adj.* **1.** *Electronics.* pertaining to or noting a mechanism built into a system, as in an early warning system or a nuclear reactor, for insuring safety should the system fail to operate properly. **2.** equipped with a secondary system that insures continued operation even if the primary system fails. **3.** (*sometimes cap.*) of, pertaining to, or designating a system of coded military controls in which bombers dispatched to a prearranged point as part of a standard operating procedure cannot advance farther without direct orders from a designated authority and cannot have the nuclear warheads they carry armed until they have passed their prearranged point. —*n.* **4.** (*sometimes cap.*) the point beyond which the bombers cannot go without specific instruction; the fail-safe point. [adj., n. use of v. phrase *fail safe*]

fail·ure (fāl′yər), *n.* **1.** the act or an instance of failing or proving unsuccessful; lack of success: *His effort ended in failure. The campaign was a failure.* **2.** nonperformance of something due, required, or expected: *a failure to do what one has promised; a failure to appear.* **3.** an insufficiency; a subnormal quantity or quality: *the failure of crops.* **4.** deterioration or decay, esp. of vigor, strength, etc.: *The failure of his health made retirement necessary.* **5.** a condition of being bankrupt by reason of insolvency. **6.** a becoming insolvent or bankrupt: *the failure of a bank.* **7.** one who or that which proves unsuccessful: *He is a failure in his career. The cake is a failure.* [FAIL + -URE; r. *failer* a (de)fault < AF (n. use of inf.), c. F *faillir*]
—**Syn. 2.** neglect, omission, dereliction. **4.** decline.

fain (fān), *Archaic.* —*adv.* **1.** gladly; willingly: *He fain would accept.* —*adj.* **2.** content; willing: *They were fain to go.* **3.** constrained; obliged: *He was fain to obey his Lord.* **4.** glad; pleased. **5.** desirous; eager. [ME; OE *fæg(e)n;* c. Icel *feginn* happy; akin to FAIR[1], FAY[2]]

fai·naigue (fə nāg′), *v.,* **-naigued, -nai·guing.** —*v.i.* **1.** *Brit. Dial.* to shirk; evade work or responsibility. **2.** to renege at cards. **3.** *Informal.* to cheat; finagle. —*v.t.* **4.** *Informal.* to deceive, cheat, or trick someone. [var. of *fenege,* alter. of RENEGE] —**fai·nai′guer,** *n.*

fai·né·ant (fā′nē ənt; *Fr.* fe nā än′), *adj., n., pl.* **-ants** (-ənts; *Fr.* -än′). —*adj.* **1.** doing nothing; idle; indolent. —*n.* **2.** an idler. [< F, earlier *fait-nient,* lit., he does nothing, pseudo-etymological alter. of *faignant* idler,

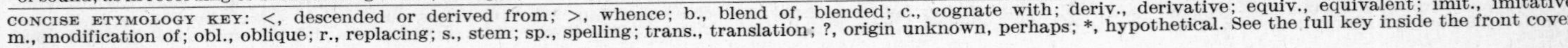
CONCISE ETYMOLOGY KEY: <, descended or derived from; >, whence; b., blend of, blended; c., cognate with; deriv., derivative; equiv., equivalent; imit., imitative; m., modification of; obl., oblique; r., replacing; s., stem; sp., spelling; trans., translation; ?, origin unknown, perhaps; *, hypothetical. See the full key inside the front cover.

n. use of prp. of *se faindre* to shirk. See FEIGN, FAINT] —**fai·ne·ance** (fā′nē əns), **fai′ne·an·cy**, *n.*

faint (fānt), *adj.* **1.** lacking brightness, vividness, clearness, loudness, strength, etc.: *a faint light; faint color; a faint sound.* **2.** feeble or slight: *faint resistance; faint praise; faint resemblance; a faint idea.* **3.** feeling weak, dizzy, or exhausted; about to lose consciousness: *faint with hunger.* **4.** lacking courage; cowardly; timorous: *Faint heart never won fair maid.* **5.** *Law.* unfounded: *a faint action.* —*v.i.* **6.** to lose consciousness temporarily. **7.** *Archaic.* **a.** to lose brightness. **b.** to grow weak; lose spirit or courage. —*n.* **8.** temporary loss of consciousness; a swoon: *to fall into a faint.* [ME < OF, ptp. of *faindre*, var. of *feindre* to FEIGN] —**faint′er**, *n.* —**faint′ing·ly**, *adv.* —**faint′ish**, *adj.* —**faint′ish·ness**, *n.* —**faint′ly**, *adv.* —**faint′ness**, *n.*
—**Syn. 1.** indistinct, ill-defined, dim, faded, dull. **2.** faltering, irresolute, weak. **3.** languid. **4.** pusillanimous, fearful, timid, dastardly. **6.** pass out, black out.

faint·heart (fānt′härt′), *n.* a fainthearted person; coward. [back formation from FAINTHEARTED]

faint·heart·ed (fānt′här′tid), *adj.* lacking courage; cowardly; timorous. [late ME *feynt hertyd.* See FAINT, HEARTED] —**faint′heart′ed·ly**, *adv.* —**faint′heart′ed·ness**, *n.*

faints (fānts), *n.pl.* the impure spirit produced in the first and last stages of the distillation of whiskey. Also, **feints.** Cf. **foreshots.** [n. use (in pl.) of FAINT (adj.)]

fair[1] (fâr), *adj.* **1.** free from bias, dishonesty, or injustice: *a fair decision; a fair judge.* **2.** legitimately sought, pursued, done, given, etc.; proper under the rules: *a fair fight.* **3.** moderately large; ample: *a fair income.* **4.** neither excellent nor poor; moderately good: *fair health.* **5.** marked by favoring conditions; likely; promising: *in a fair way to succeed.* **6.** *Meteorol.* **a.** (of the sky) bright; sunny; cloudless to half-cloudy. **b.** (of the weather) fine; with no aspect of rain, snow, or hail; not stormy. **7.** *Naut.* (of a wind or tide) tending to aid the progress of a vessel. **8.** unobstructed; not blocked up: *The way was fair for our advance.* **9.** without irregularity or unevenness: *a fair surface.* **10.** free from blemish, imperfection, or anything that impairs the appearance, quality, or character: *Her fair reputation was ruined by gossip.* **11.** clear; easy to read: *fair handwriting.* **12.** of a light hue; not dark: *fair skin.* **13.** pleasing in appearance; attractive: *a fair young maiden.* **14.** seemingly good or sincere but not really so: *The lover beguiled his mistress with fair speeches.* **15.** courteous; civil: *fair words.* **16. fair to middling,** *U.S. Informal.* only tolerably good; so-so. —*adv.* **17.** in a fair manner: *He doesn't play fair.* **18.** straight; directly, as in aiming or hitting: *He threw the ball fair to the goal.* **19.** favorably; auspiciously. **20.** *Brit., Australian.* entirely; completely; quite: *It happened so quickly that it fair took my breath away.* **21. bid fair,** to seem likely: *This entry bids fair to win first prize.* **22. fair and square,** *Informal.* **a.** honestly; justly; straightforwardly: *He won the race fair and square.* **b.** honest; just; straightforward: *He was admired for being fair and square in all his dealings.* —*n.* **23.** *Archaic.* that which is fair. **24.** *Archaic.* **a.** a woman. **b.** a beloved woman. —*v.t.* **25.** *Shipbuilding.* **a.** to draw and adjust (the lines of a hull being designed) to produce regular surfaces of the correct form. **b.** to adjust the form of (a frame or templet) in accordance with a design, or cause it to conform to the general form of a hull. **c.** to restore (a bent plate or structural member) to its original form. **d.** to align (the frames of a vessel under construction) in their proper positions. **26.** to bring (rivet holes in connecting structural members) into perfect alignment. **27.** *Obs.* to make fair. —*v.i.* **28.** *Dial.* (of the weather) to clear. [ME; OE *fæger*; c. OS, OHG *fagar*, Icel *fagr*, Goth *fagrs*] —**fair′ness**, *n.*
—**Syn. 1.** unbiased, equitable, just, honest. FAIR, IMPARTIAL, DISINTERESTED, UNPREJUDICED refer to lack of bias in opinions, judgments, etc. FAIR implies the treating of all sides alike, justly and equitably: *a fair compromise.* IMPARTIAL, like FAIR, implies showing no more favor to one side than another, but suggests particularly a judicial consideration of a case: *an impartial judge.* DISINTERESTED implies a fairness arising particularly from lack of desire to obtain a selfish advantage: *The motives of her guardian were entirely disinterested.* UNPREJUDICED means not influenced or swayed by bias, or by prejudice caused by irrelevant considerations: *an unprejudiced decision.* **4.** passable, tolerable, average, middling. **8.** open, clear, unencumbered. **10.** clean, spotless, pure, untarnished, unsullied, unstained. **11.** legible, distinct. **12.** blond, pale. **13.** pretty, comely, lovely. **15.** polite, gracious.

fair[2] (fâr), *n.* **1.** a competitive exhibition of farm products, livestock, etc., in the U.S. often combined with carnivallike entertainment and held annually by a county or state. **2.** *Chiefly Brit.* a periodic gathering of buyers and sellers in an appointed place. **3.** an exhibition and sale of articles to raise money, often for some charitable purpose. [ME *feire* < OF < LL *fēria* holiday (ML: market), in L only pl.; akin to FEAST]

fair′ ball′, *Baseball.* a batted ball that both lands and settles within the foul lines in the infield or that first lands within the four lines of the outfield or would if it were not caught or deflected.

Fair·banks (fâr′baŋks′), *n.* **1. Charles Warren,** 1852–1918, political leader: vice president of the U.S. 1905–09. **2. Douglas,** 1883–1939, U.S. motion picture actor. **3.** a town in central Alaska, on the Tanana River. 13,311 (1960).

fair′bod·y draft′ (fâr′bod′ē), *Naval Archit.* See **molded draft.**

Fair·born (fâr′bôrn′), *n.* a city in W Ohio, near Dayton. 19,453 (1960).

Fair·bur·y (fâr′ber′ē, -bə rē), *n.* **1.** a town in SE Nebraska. 5572 (1960). **2.** a town in central Illinois. 2937 (1960).

fair′ catch′, *Football.* a catch of a kicked ball in which the receiver signals that he will not advance the ball and therefore may not be interfered with or tackled.

fair′ cop′y, 1. a copy of a document made after final correction. **2.** the condition of such a copy. **3.** an exact copy.

Fair′ Deal′, the principles of the liberal wing of the Democratic party under the leadership of President Harry S Truman, consisting largely of a continuation and development of the principles of the New Deal. Cf. **Great Society, New Deal, New Frontier.** —**Fair′ Deal′er.**

fair′ employ′ment, the employment of persons on the basis of their capabilities only, without regard to race, sex, national origin, or religion.

Fair·fax (fâr′faks), *n.* **1. Thomas** (*3rd Baron Fairfax of Cameron*), 1612–71, British general: commander in chief of the parliamentary army 1645–50. **2. Thomas** (*6th Baron Fairfax of Cameron*), 1692–1782, English colonist in Virginia. **3.** a town in NE Virginia. 13,585 (1960). **4.** a town in W California. 5813 (1960). **5.** a town in E Alabama. 3107 (1960). **6.** a boy's given name.

Fair·field (fâr′fēld′), *n.* **1.** a town in SW Connecticut. 46,183 (1960). **2.** a city in central Alabama. 15,816 (1960). **3.** a town in central Ohio. 9734 (1960). **4.** a town in SE Iowa. 8054 (1960). **5.** a town in SE Illinois. 6362 (1960). **6.** a town in S Maine. 3766 (1960).

fair′ game′, a legitimate or likely object of attack, mockery, etc.: *With his fat, round face, the politician was fair game for the cartoonists.*

fair′ green′, *Golf Obs.* fairway (def. 2).

fair·ground (fâr′ground′), *n.* Often, **fairgrounds.** a place where fairs, horse races, etc., are held, in the U.S. usually an area set aside by a city, county, or state for an annual fair and often containing exhibition buildings. [FAIR[2] + GROUND[1]]

fair-haired (fâr′hârd′), *adj.* **1.** having light-colored hair. **2. fair-haired boy,** *Informal.* **a.** a youth or man favored by a superior: *The supervisor's fair-haired boy got another raise.* **b.** a youth or man who works hard or tries to impress a superior: *He's the fair-haired boy at the office and volunteers for all the extra work.* [FAIR[1] + HAIR + -ED[3]]

Fair′ Ha′ven, a town in E New Jersey. 5678 (1960).

Fair·hope (fâr′hōp′), *n.* a town in SW Alabama. 4858 (1960).

fair′ hous′ing, *U.S.* See **open housing.**

fair·i·ly (fâr′ə lē), *adv.* in a manner suggestive of fairies; delicately. [FAIRY + -LY]

fair·ing[1] (fâr′iŋ), *n.* *Aeron.* a structure on the exterior of an aircraft, for reducing drag. [FAIR[1] + -ING[1]]

fair·ing[2] (fâr′iŋ), *n.* *Archaic.* a gift, esp. one given at or bought at a fair. [FAIR[2] + -ING[1]]

fair·ish (fâr′ish), *adj.* **1.** moderately good, large, or well: *a fairish income; fairish health.* **2.** moderately light in color: *a fairish complexion.* [FAIR[1] + -ISH[1]]

Fair′ Lawn′, a city in NE New Jersey. 36,421 (1960).

fair·lead (fâr′lēd′), *n.* **1.** a pulley, thimble, etc., used to guide a rope forming part of the rigging of a ship, crane, etc., in such a way as to prevent chafing. **2.** *Mach.* (on power shovels or cranes) a swiveling mounting for sheaves, over which cables pass. **3.** *Naut.* a horizontal batten pierced with holes through which the lines of running rigging are rove in order to lead them to their proper places on a pin rail. Also, **fair′lead′er.** [FAIR[1] + LEAD[1]]

Fair·leigh (fâr′lē), *n.* a boy's given name. Also, **Fairley, Farley.**

Fair·ley (fâr′lē), *n.* a boy's given name. Also, **Fairleigh, Farley.**

fair′ list′. See **white list.**

fair·ly (fâr′lē), *adv.* **1.** in a fair manner; justly; impartially. **2.** moderately; tolerably: *a fairly heavy rain.* **3.** actually; completely: *The wheels fairly spun.* **4.** properly; legitimately: *a claim fairly made.* **5.** clearly; distinctly: *fairly seen.* **6.** *Obs.* softly. **7.** *Obs.* courteously. [late ME; see FAIR[1], -LY]

fair-mind·ed (fâr′mīn′did), *adj.* characterized by fair judgment; impartial; unprejudiced: *a wise and fair-minded judge.* —**fair′-mind′ed·ness**, *n.*

Fair·mont (fâr′mont), *n.* **1.** a city in W West Virginia. 27,477 (1960). **2.** a town in S Minnesota. 9745 (1960).

Fair′mont Cit′y, a town in SW Illinois. 2688 (1960).

Fair·mount (fâr′mount′), *n.* a town in central Indiana. 3080 (1960).

Fair′ Oaks′, 1. Also called **Seven Pines.** a locality in E Virginia, near Richmond: battle 1862. **2.** a town in central Georgia. 7969 (1960).

Fair′ Plain′, a town in SW Michigan. 7998 (1960).

fair′ play′, just and honorable treatment, action, or conduct: *The campaign was notably lacking in fair play.*

Fair·port (fâr′pōrt′, -pôrt′), *n.* **1.** a town in W New York. 5507 (1960). **2.** a town in NE Ohio. 4267 (1960).

fair′ sex′, women collectively: *The fair sex is traditionally thought to be fickle.*

fair-spo·ken (fâr′spō′kən), *adj.* speaking or spoken in a courteous, civil, or plausible manner; smooth-spoken. —**fair′-spo′ken·ness**, *n.*

fair′ trade′, trade carried on under a fair-trade agreement.

fair-trade (fâr′trād′), *v.*, **-trad·ed, -trad·ing,** *adj.* —*v.t.* **1.** to sell (a commodity) under a fair-trade agreement. —*adj.* **2.** subject to or resulting from a fair-trade agreement: *fair-trade items; fair-trade prices.* —**fair′-trad′er**, *n.*

fair′-trade′ agree′ment, *U.S.* an agreement or contract between a manufacturer and a retailer to sell a branded or trademarked product at no less than a specific price.

fair′-trade′ law′, *U.S.* a State or federal law authorizing fair-trade agreements.

Fair·view (fâr′vyo͞o′), *n.* **1.** a town in NE New Jersey. 9399 (1960). **2.** a town in SE New York. 8626 (1960). **3.** a town in S Washington. 2758 (1960).

fair·wa·ter (fâr′wô′tər, -wot′ər), *n.* *Naut.* **1.** an assemblage of plating or a casting for improving the flow of water past an area or feature of a hull. **2.** See **fairwater cap.** [FAIR[1] + WATER]

fair′water cap′, *Naut.* a threaded, convex, conical cap covering the end of a propeller shaft and acting as a fairwater. Also called **fair′water cone′.**

fair′water sleeve′, *Naut.* a conical casing around the projecting end of a propeller shaft, serving as a fairwater.

fair·way (fâr′wā′), *n.* **1.** an unobstructed passage, way, or area. **2.** *Golf.* **a.** the part of the course where the grass is cut short between the tees and the putting greens, exclusive of the rough, trees, and hazards. **b.** the mowed part of any hole between the tee and the green. **3.** *Naut.* **a.** the navigable portion of a river, harbor, or other enclosed body of water. **b.** the channel customarily navigated by vessels in such a body of water. [FAIR[1] + WAY]

Fair·way (fâr′wā′), *n.* a town in E Kansas. 5398 (1960).

fair-weath·er (fâr′weth′ər), *adj.* **1.** for fair weather only. **2.** weakening or failing in time of trouble: *His fair-weather friends left him when he lost his money.*

Fair·weath·er (fâr′weth′ər), *n.* **Mount,** a mountain in SE Alaska. 15,292 ft.

fair′-weather cu′mulus. See **cumulus humilis.**

fair·y (fâr′ē), *n., pl.* **fair·ies,** *adj.* —*n.* **1.** one of a class of imaginary supernatural beings, generally conceived as having a diminutive human form, possessing magical powers, and intervening with them in human affairs. **2.** *Slang.* a male homosexual. —*adj.* **3.** of or pertaining to fairies: *fairy magic.* **4.** of the nature of a fairy; fairylike. **5.** See **fairy green.** [ME *faierie* < OF: fairyland. See FAY[1], -ERY] —**fair′y·like′**, *adj.*
—**Syn. 1.** fay, pixy, leprechaun, nix, nixie. FAIRY, BROWNIE, ELF, SPRITE are terms for imaginary beings usually less than human size, thought to be helpful or harmful to mankind. FAIRY is the most general name for such beings: *a good fairy as a godmother; misadventures caused by an evil fairy.* A BROWNIE is a good-natured tiny man who appears usually at night to do household tasks: *Perhaps the brownies will come and mow the lawn tonight.* ELF suggests a young, mischievous or roguish fairy: *That child is a perfect little elf.* SPRITE suggests a fairy of pleasing appearance, older than an elf, to be admired for ease and lightness of movement; it may, however, be impish or even hostile: *a dainty sprite.*

fair′y blue′bird, any of several fruit-eating, passerine birds of the genus *Irena*, of the East Indies, the males of which are black below and chiefly purple-blue above.

fair′y fan′, an herb, *Eucharidium breweri*, of California, having fragrant, fan-shaped, deep pink flowers.

fair′y glove′. See **purple foxglove.**

fair′y green′, a medium yellow-green color. Also called **fairy.**

fair·y·hood (fâr′ē ho͝od′), *n.* **1.** a fairy state or nature: *the fairyhood of Puck.* **2.** fairies collectively. [FAIRY + -HOOD]

fair·y·ism (fâr′ē iz′əm), *n.* **1.** fairylike quality. **2.** belief in fairies. [FAIRY + -ISM]

fair′y lamp′, a lamp using a candle as the source of illumination, usually constructed of glass or ceramic material, set on a metal base, and having a fabric shade.

fair·y·land (fâr′ē land′), *n.* **1.** the imaginary realm of the fairies. **2.** any enchantingly beautiful region: *The country is a fairyland in spring.* [FAIRY + LAND]

fair′y lil′y, 1. a bulbous herb, *Cooperia pedunculata*, of Texas, having solitary, fragrant, white, night-blooming flowers, reddish on the outside. **2.** See **atamasco lily.**

fair′y prim′rose, a tender, perennial herb, *Primula malacoides*, of China, having hairy leaves and small, pink or lilac-colored flowers.

fair′y ring′, a circle formed on the grass in a field by the growth of certain fungi, formerly supposed to be caused by fairies in their dances.

fair′y tale′, 1. a story, usually for children, about elves, hobgoblins, dragons, fairies, or other magical creatures. **2.** an incredible or misleading statement, account, or belief: *The reports of men from Mars are fairy tales.* Also called **fair′y sto′ry.**

fair′y tern′, a small, pure white tern, *Gygis alba*, of tropical islands of both hemispheres.

Fai·sal (fī′səl), *n.* (*Faisal Abdel Aziz al Saud al Faisal*) born 1904, king of Saudi Arabia since 1964 (son of ibn-Saud and brother of Saud).

Faisal I, 1885–1933, king of Syria 1920; king of Iraq 1921–33. Also, **Feisal I, Feisul I.**

Faisal II, 1935–58, king of Iraq 1939–58 (grandson of Faisal I). Also, **Feisal II.**

fait ac·com·pli (fe tA kôN plē′), *pl.* ***faits ac·com·plis*** (fe zA kôN plē′). *French.* an accomplished fact; a thing already done: *The enemy's defeat was a* fait accompli *long before the formal surrender.*

faites vos jeux (fet′ vō zhœ′), *French.* (esp. in roulette) place your bets.

faith (fāth), *n.* **1.** confidence or trust in a person or thing: *faith in another's ability.* **2.** belief which is not based on proof: *He had faith that the hypothesis would be substantiated by fact.* **3.** belief in God or in the doctrines or teachings of religion: *old pilgrims, strong in their faith.* **4.** belief in anything, as a code of ethics, standards of merit, etc.: *to be of the same faith with someone in all matters.* **5.** a system of religious belief: *the Christian faith; the Jewish faith.* **6.** the obligation of loyalty or fidelity to a person, promise, engagement, etc.: *Failure to appear would be breaking faith.* **7.** the observance of this obligation; fidelity to one's promise, oath, allegiance, etc.: *to act in good faith.* **8.** *Christian Theol.* the trust in God and in His promises as made through Christ and the Scriptures by which man is justified or saved. **9. in faith,** in truth; indeed: *In faith, he is a fine lad.* [ME *feith* < AF *feid* < L *fid(e)-*, s. of *fidēs* trust, akin to *fīdere* to trust. See CONFIDE]
—**Syn. 5.** doctrine, tenet, creed, dogma, persuasion, religion. —**Ant. 1, 2.** distrust.

Faith (fāth), *n.* a girl's given name.

faith′ cure′, 1. a method of attempting to cure disease by prayer and religious faith. **2.** a cure thus effected.

faith·ful (fāth′fəl), *adj.* **1.** strict or thorough in the performance of duty: *a faithful worker.* **2.** true to one's word, promises, vows, etc. **3.** steady in allegiance or affection; loyal. **4.** reliable, trusted, or believed. **5.** adhering or true to fact or an original: *a faithful account; a faithful copy.* **6.** *Obs.* full of faith; believing. —*n.* **7.** the body of loyal members of any party or group. **8. the faithful,** the believers, esp. members of a Christian church or adherents of Islam. [ME *feithful.* See FAITH, -FUL] —**faith′ful·ly**, *adv.* —**faith′ful·ness**, *n.*
—**Syn. 1, 3.** true, devoted, staunch. **3.** FAITHFUL, CONSTANT, LOYAL imply qualities of stability, dependability, and devotion. FAITHFUL implies long-continued and steadfast fidelity to whatever one is bound to by a pledge, duty, or obligation: *a faithful friend.* CONSTANT suggests firmness and steadfastness in attachment: *a constant affection.* LOYAL implies unswerving allegiance to a person, organization, cause, or idea: *loyal to one's associates, one's country.* **5.** accurate, precise, exact.

faith′ heal′er, a person who claims ability to heal the sick by prayer and religious faith.

faith′ heal′ing, 1. healing effected through faith in God. 2. a method employing faith in the hope of receiving such healing.

faith·less (fāth′lis), *adj.* 1. not adhering to allegiance, promises, vows, or duty. 2. not trustworthy; unreliable. 3. without trust or belief. 4. without religious faith. 5. (among Christians) without Christian faith. [ME *faithles.* See FAITH, -LESS] —**faith′less·ly,** *adv.* —**faith′less·ness,** *n.*
—**Syn.** 1. false, inconstant, fickle; disloyal, perfidious, treacherous.

fai·tour (fā′tər), *n. Archaic.* impostor; fake. [ME < AF: impostor, c. OF *faitor* perpetrator, lit., doer, maker < L *factor.* See FACTOR]

Fai·yum (fī yo͞om′), *n.* 1. a province in the E central Arab Republic: many archaeological remains. 763,650 (1957); 691 sq. mi. 2. Also called **El Faiyum, El Fayum.** a city in and the capital of this province, SW of Cairo. 89,448 (est. 1957). —*adj.* 3. pertaining to or designating a style of portrait painting developed in Egypt under Roman rule, examples of which have been found principally in Faiyum dating from the 2nd and 3rd centuries A.D., characterized chiefly by the frontality of the head, the modeling of form, and emphasis on the eyes. Also, **Fayum.**

Faiz·a·bad (fī′zä bäd′), *n.* Fyzabad.

fake[1] (fāk), *v.*, **faked, fak·ing,** *n., adj.* —*v.t.* 1. prepare or make (something specious, deceptive, or fraudulent): *to fake a report showing nonexistent profits.* 2. to conceal the defects of or make appear more attractive, interesting, valuable, etc., usually in order to deceive: *The story was faked a bit to make it more sensational.* 3. to pretend; simulate: *to fake illness.* 4. *Slang.* to act or behave extemporaneously or by improvising: *I don't know the job, but I can fake it.* 5. *Jazz.* a. to improvise: *to fake an accompaniment.* b. to play (music) without reading from a score. —*v.i.* 6. to fake something; pretend. —*n.* 7. anything made to appear otherwise than it actually is; counterfeit: *This necklace is a fake.* 8. a person who fakes; faker: *The doctor with the reputed cure for cancer proved to be a fake.* 9. a spurious report or story. —*adj.* 10. designed to deceive or cheat; not real; counterfeit. [orig. vagrants' slang: to do for, rob, kill (someone), shape (something); ? var. of obs. *feak, feague* to beat, akin to D *veeg* a slap, *vegen* to sweep, wipe]
—**Syn.** 8. fraud, impostor, quack, charlatan, deceiver.

fake[2] (fāk), *n., v.,* **faked, fak·ing.** *Naut.* —*n.* 1. any complete turn of a rope that has been faked down. 2. any of the various ways in which a rope may be faked down. —*v.t.* 3. to lay (a rope) in a coil or series of long loops so that it will run freely without fouling or kinking (often fol. by *down*). Also, **flake.** [late ME *fake(n)*]

fake′ book′, *Jazz.* a book containing the melodies or the basic harmonic progressions for various songs.

fa·keer (fə kēr′), *n.* fakir.

fake·ment (fāk′mənt), *n. Informal.* something that is faked. [FAKE[1] + -MENT]

fak·er (fā′kər), *n. Informal.* 1. a person who fakes. 2. a petty swindler. 3. a peddler or street vendor of articles of dubious value. [FAKE[1] + -ER[1]]

fak·er·y (fā′kə rē), *n., pl.* **-er·ies.** the practice or result of faking. [FAKE[1] + -ERY]

fa·kir (fə kēr′, fā′kər), *n.* 1. a Muslim or Hindu religious ascetic or mendicant monk. 2. a member of any Islamic religious order. Also, **fakeer.** [< Ar *faqīr* poor]

fa·la (fä lä′), *n.* 1. a text or refrain in old songs. 2. a type of part song or madrigal popular in the 16th and 17th centuries. Also, **fal la.** [special use of *fa la,* meaningless sound sequence found in old popular refrains]

Fa·lange (fā′lanj; *Sp.* fä län′he), *n.* the fascist party in power in Spain since the Civil War of 1936–39. [see PHALANX]

Fa·lan·gist (fə lan′jist), *n.* a member of the Falange. [FALANGE + -IST]

Fa·la·sha (fä lä′shə), *n., pl.* **-shas,** (*esp. collectively*) **-sha.** a member of an Ethiopian people who speak a Hamitic language and who practice a modified form of Judaism.

fal·ba·la (fal′bə lə), *n.* a furbelow or puckered flounce for decorating dresses in the 17th century. Also, **fal·be·lo** (fal′bə lō′). [< F < It. See FURBELOW]

fal·cate (fal′kāt), *adj.* hooked; curved like a scythe or sickle; falciform. [< L *falcāt(us)* sickle-shaped, equiv. to *falc-* (s. of *falx*) sickle + *-ātus* -ATE[1]]

fal·chion (fôl′chən, -shən), *n.* 1. a broad, short sword having a convex edge curving sharply to the point. 2. *Archaic.* any sword. [< It *falcione,* equiv. to *falce* sickle (see FALX) + *-one* aug. suffix; r. ME *fauchoun* < OF]

fal·cial (fal′shəl, -chəl, fôl′-), *adj. Anat.* of or pertaining to a falx. [< NL; see FALX, -IAL]

fal·ci·form (fal′sə fôrm′), *adj.* sickle-shaped; falcate. [< L *falci-* (s. of *falx*) sickle + -FORM]

fal·con (fôl′kən, fal′-, fô′kən), *n.* 1. any of several diurnal birds of prey of the family *Falconidae,* esp. of the genus *Falco,* having long, pointed wings and a notched bill. Cf. **gyrfalcon, peregrine falcon.** 2. *Falconry.* a. the female gyrfalcon. b. the female peregrine. c. any bird of prey trained for use in falconry. Cf. **tercel.** 3. an old kind of cannon. [< LL *falcōn-* (s. of *falcō*) hawk (akin to *falx* sickle); r. ME *faucon* < OF] —**fal·co·nine** (fôl′kə-nīn′, -nin, fal′-, fô′-), *adj.* —**fal′co·noid′,** *adj.*

Peregrine falcon, *Falco peregrinus* (Length 18 in.)

fal·con·er (fôl′kə nər, fal′-, fô′kən-), *n.* 1. a person who hunts with falcons; one who follows the sport of hawking. 2. a person who trains hawks for hunting. [FALCON + -ER[2]; r. ME *falkenar* (< ML *falcōnārius*), *fauconer* < AF, c. OF *fauconier*]

Fal·con·er (fôl′kə nər), *n.* a town in W New York. 3343 (1960).

fal·co·net[1] (fôl′kə net′, fal′-, fô′kə-), *n.* any of several small Asian falcons, esp. of the genus *Microhierax.* [FALCON + -ET]

fal·co·net[2] (fôl′kə net′, fal′-, fô′kə-), *n.* an antique form of light cannon. [< It *falconett(o).* See FALCON, -ET]

fal·con-gen·tle (fôl′kən jen′tᵊl, fal′-, fô′kən-), *n.* 1. the female of the peregrine falcon. 2. any female falcon. [trans. of F *faucon gentil;* r. ME *gentil fauco(u)n, facon jent,* etc.]

Fal′con Heights′, a town in E Minnesota. 5927 (1960).

fal·con·i·form (fôl kō′nə fôrm′, fal-, fô kō′-, fôl′kə-nə-, fal′-, fô′kə-), *adj.* of, pertaining to, or belonging to the order *Falconiformes,* comprising the vultures, hawks, eagles, ospreys, falcons, caracaras, etc. [FALCON + -I- + -FORM]

fal·con·ry (fôl′kən rē, fal′-, fô′kən-), *n.* 1. the sport of hunting with falcons or hawks; hawking. 2. the art of training hawks to hunt. [FALCON + -RY, modeled on F *fauconnerie*]

fal·da (fol′də), *n.* a white silk vestment extending from the waist to the ground, worn over the cassock by the pope on solemn occasions. [< It]

Fal·da (fôl′də), *n.* a girl's given name.

fal·de·ral (fal′də ral′), *n.* 1. meaningless syllables forming the refrain of various old songs. 2. mere nonsense; foolish talk or ideas. 3. a trifle; gimcrack; gewgaw. Also, **fal·de·rol** (fal′də rol′), **folderol.**

fald·stool (fôld′sto͞ol′), *n.* 1. a chair or seat, originally one capable of being folded, used by a bishop or other prelate when officiating in his own church away from the throne or in a church not his own. 2. a movable folding stool or desk at which worshipers kneel during certain acts of devotion. 3. such a stool placed at the south side of the altar, at which the kings or queens of England kneel at their coronation. 4. a desk at which the litany is said or sung. [OE *fealdestōl* folding chair; c. OHG *faltistuol.* See FOLD[1], STOOL]

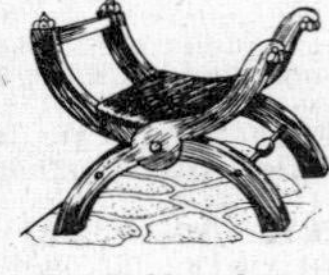

Faldstool

Fa·ler·ni·an (fə lûr′nē ən), *adj.* (esp. of a wine celebrated by Horace) of, coming from, or made in a district of Campania, Italy. [< L (*ager*) *Falern(us)* Falernian (field) + -IAN]

Fa·ler·num (fə lûr′nəm), *n. Trademark.* a white syrup made in the West Indies and the U.S. from cane sugar, with lime, almond, ginger, and other spices added, used to flavor mixed drinks.

Fal·fur·ri·as (fal fo͝or′ē əs), *n.* a town in S Texas. 6515 (1960).

Fa·lie·ri (*It.* fä lye′rē), *n.* **Ma·ri·no** (*It.* mä rē′nô), 1278?–1355, Venetian army commander: doge of Venice 1354–55. Also, **Fa·lie′ro** (*It.* fä lye′rô).

Fal·ken·hayn (fäl′kən hīn′), *n.* **E·rich von** (ā′rikh fən), 1861–1922, German general of World War I.

Fal·kirk (fôl′kûrk), *n.* a city in central Scotland, W of Edinburgh: Scots defeated by the English under Wallace 1298. 37,000 (1956).

Falk′land Is′lands (fôk′lənd), a group of about 200 islands in the S Atlantic, ab. 300 mi. E of the Strait of Magellan: a British crown colony; Germans defeated by British in naval battle 1914. 2253 (1957); with dependencies 3630 (1953); 4618 sq. mi. *Cap.:* Stanley. Spanish, **Islas Malvinas.**

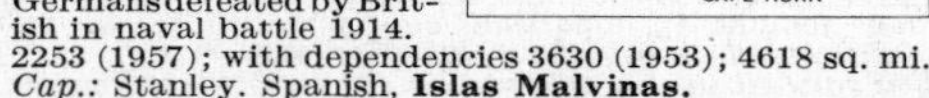

Falk·ner (fôk′nər), *n.* 1. **William.** See **Faulkner, William.** 2. Also, **Faulkner.** a boy's given name.

fall (fôl), *v.,* **fell, fall·en, fall·ing,** *n.* —*v.i.* 1. to descend under the force of gravity, as to a lower place through loss or lack of support. 2. to come or drop down suddenly to a lower position, esp. to leave a standing or erect position suddenly, whether voluntarily or not: *to fall on one's knees.* 3. to become of a lower level, degree, amount, quality, value, number, etc.; to become less or lower; decline: *The temperature fell ten degrees. Stock prices fell to a new low.* 4. to subside or abate. 5. to hang down; extend downward: *Her hair falls to her shoulders.* 6. to become lowered or directed downward, as the eyes: *Her eyes fell before his steady gaze.* 7. to succumb to temptation, esp. to become unchaste or to lose one's innocence. 8. to lose status, position, dignity, character, etc. 9. to succumb to attack: *The city fell to the enemy.* 10. to be overthrown, as a government. 11. to drop down wounded or dead, esp. to be slain: *to fall in battle.* 12. to pass into some physical, mental, or emotional condition: *to fall asleep; to fall in love.* 13. to envelop or come as if by dropping, as stillness, night, etc. 14. to issue forth: *Witty remarks fall easily from his lips.* 15. to come by lot or chance: *Their choice fell upon him.* 16. to come by chance into a particular position: *to fall among thieves.* 17. to come to pass, occur, or become at a certain time: *Christmas falls on a Monday this year. The rent falls due the first of every month.* 18. to have its proper place: *The accent falls on the last syllable.* 19. to come by right: *The inheritance fell to the only living relative.* 20. to be naturally divisible (usually fol. by *into*): *The story fell into two distinct parts.* 21. to lose animation; appear disappointed, as the face. 22. to slope or extend in a downward direction: *The field falls gently to the stream.* 23. to be directed, as light, sight, etc., on something: *His eyes fell upon the forgotten jewelry.* 24. to collapse; topple: *The old tower fell under its own weight.* —*v.t.* 25. to fell (a tree, animal, etc.). 26. **fall away,** a. to withdraw support or allegiance: *The candidate's supporters fell away when he advocated racial discrimination.* b. to become lean or thin; diminish; decline. c. to forsake one's faith, cause, or principles: *Many fell away because they were afraid of reprisals.* 27. **fall back,** to give way; recede; retreat: *The relentless shelling forced the enemy to fall back.* 28. **fall back on** or **upon,** a. Also, **fall back to.** to retreat to: *They fell back on their entrenchments. The troops fell back to their original position.* b. to have recourse to; rely on: *They had no savings to fall back on.* 29. **fall behind,** a. to lag, in pace or progress: *We are falling behind in our work. Fatigued, some of the marchers fell behind.* b. to fail to pay (a debt, obligation, etc.) at the appointed time: *She fell behind in her tax payments, and the property was confiscated.* 30. **fall down,** *Informal.* to perform disappointingly; to disappoint; fail: *He was doing well on the exam until he fell down on the last essay question.* 31. **fall for,** *Slang.* a. to be deceived by: *Imagine falling for such a story!* b. to fall in love with: *He's not at all the type you would expect her to fall for.* 32. **fall foul** or **afoul of.** See **foul** (def. 20). 33. **fall in,** a. to fall to pieces toward the interior; sink inward. b. to take one's place in the ranks, as a soldier. c. Also, **fall in with,** to become acquainted with, esp. by chance: *We fell in with an interesting chap from Beirut.* 34. **fall off,** a. to separate from; withdraw. b. to deteriorate; decline: *Business falls off in the summer.* c. to decrease in number, amount, or intensity; diminish: *The tourists fall off when summer is over.* d. *Naut.* to deviate from the heading; fall to leeward. 35. **fall on** or **upon,** a. to assault; attack: *The enemy fell on them suddenly from the rear.* b. to be the obligation of: *It has fallen on me to support the family.* c. to experience; encounter: *Once well-to-do, they had fallen on hard times.* d. to chance upon; come upon: *I fell upon the idea while looking through a magazine.* 36. **fall on one's feet.** See **land** (def. 24). 37. **fall out,** a. to quarrel; disagree: *We fell out over who was to wash the dishes.* b. to happen; occur: *It fell out that we met by chance weeks later.* c. to leave one's place in the ranks, as a soldier: *They were ordered to fall out when the parade ended.* 38. **fall** or **come short.** See **short** (def. 29). 39. **fall through,** to come to nothing; fail of realization: *After all his efforts the deal fell through.* 40. **fall to,** a. to apply oneself; begin: *to fall to work.* b. to begin to eat: *They fell to and soon finished off the entire turkey.* 41. **fall under,** a. to be the concern or responsibility of. b. to be classified as; be included within: *That case falls under the heading of errors of judgment.*
—*n.* 42. the act or an instance of falling or dropping from a higher to a lower place or position. 43. that which falls or drops: *a fall of rain; a fall of leaves.* 44. *Chiefly U.S.* autumn. 45. a becoming less; a lowering or decline; a sinking to a lower level: *a gradual fall in reputation.* 46. the distance through which anything falls: *It is a long fall to the ground from this height.* 47. Usually, **falls.** a cataract or waterfall: *He went over the falls in a barrel.* 48. downward slope or declivity: *the gentle rise and fall of the meadow.* 49. a falling from an erect position, as to the ground: *to have a bad fall.* 50. a hanging down: *a fall of long hair.* 51. a succumbing to temptation; lapse into sin. 52. **the Fall,** (*sometimes l.c.*) *Theol.* the lapse of mankind into a state of natural or innate sinfulness through the sin of Adam and Eve. 53. *Slang.* an arrest by the police. 54. surrender or capture, as of a city. 55. proper place: *the fall of an accent on a syllable.* 56. *Wrestling.* a. the act or an instance of holding or forcing an opponent's shoulders against the mat for a specified length of time. b. a match or division of a match. 57. an opaque veil hanging loose from the back of a hat. 58. See **falling band.** 59. a decorative cascade of lace, ruffles, or the like. 60. *Mach., Naut.* the part of the rope of a tackle to which the power is applied in hoisting. 61. *Hunting.* a deadfall. 62. the long soft hair that hangs over the forehead and eyes of certain terriers. 63. *Armor.* a pivoted peak projecting over the face opening of a burgonet. 64. *Obs.* a fall front on a desk or the like. 65. **ride for a fall,** to risk or be destined for disaster, embarrassment, a loss of pride or status, etc.: *He is very proud, but he is riding for a fall.* [ME *falle(n),* OE *feallan;* c. G *fallen,* Icel *falla;* akin to Lith *pùlti* to fall]

Fall, The, a novel (1957) by Albert Camus. French, **La Chute.**

fal la (fäl lä′), fa-la.

Fal·la (fä′yə; *Sp.* fä′lyä), *n.* **Ma·nuel de** (mä nwel′ de), 1876–1946, Spanish composer.

fal·la·cious (fə lā′shəs), *adj.* 1. deceptive; misleading: *fallacious testimony.* 2. containing a fallacy; logically unsound: *fallacious arguments.* 3. disappointing; delusive: *a fallacious peace.* [< LL *fallāciōs(us)* deceitful, deceptive. See FALLACY, -OUS] —**fal·la′cious·ly,** *adv.* —**fal·la′cious·ness,** *n.*

fal·la·cy (fal′ə sē), *n., pl.* **-cies.** 1. a deceptive, misleading, or false notion, belief, etc.: *That the world is flat was at one time a popular fallacy.* 2. a misleading or unsound argument. 3. deceptive, misleading, or false nature; erroneousness: *the fallacy of our trust in such methods was soon apparent.* 4. *Logic.* any of various types of erroneous reasoning that render arguments logically unsound. 5. *Obs.* deception. [< L *fallāci(a)* a trick, deceit, equiv. to *fallāc-* (s. of *fallax*) deceitful, fallacious + *-ia* -Y[3]; r. ME *fallace* < MF]

fal·lal (fal lal′), *n.* a bit of finery; a showy article of dress. Also, **fal-lal.** [? syncopated var. of FALDERAL] —**fal·lal′ish·ly, fal-lal′ishly,** *adv.*

fal·lal·er·y (fal lal′ə rē), *n.* fallals collectively; finery. Also, **fal-lal′er·y.** [FALLAL + -ERY]

Fall·brook (fôl′bro͝ok′), *n.* a town in S California. 4814 (1960).

fall′ dan′de·lion, a small, scapose, European herb, *Leontodon autumnalis,* naturalized in the U.S., having yellow flowers.

fall·en (fô′lən), *v.* 1. pp. of **fall.** —*adj.* 2. having dropped or come down from a higher place, from an upright position, or from a higher level, degree, amount, quality, value, number, etc. 3. on the ground; prostrate; down flat: *Exhausted, the racers lay fallen by the road.* 4. degraded or immoral. 5. (of a woman) having lost one's chastity. 6. overthrown, destroyed, or conquered: *a fallen city.* 7. dead: *The fallen troops still lay on the battlefield.*

fall·er (fô′lər), *n.* 1. one who or that which falls. 2. any of various devices that operate by falling. 3. *Textiles.* a device, for cleaning, straightening, and separating fibers during combing of worsted stock, consisting of a series of metal pins set into a rectangular bar or rod. [late ME; see FALL, -ER[1]]

fall·fish (fôl′fish′), *n., pl.* **-fish·es,** (*esp. collectively*) **-fish.** a large minnow, *Semotilus corporalis,* found in the eastern U.S. [FALL + FISH]

fall′ front′, a part of a desk front, hinged at the lower end and opening out to provide a writing surface. Also called **drop front.**

CONCISE ETYMOLOGY KEY: <, descended or derived from; >, whence; b., blend of, blended; c., cognate with; deriv., derivative; equiv., equivalent; imit., imitative; m., modification of; obl., oblique; r., replacing; s., stem; sp., spelling; trans., translation; ?, origin unknown, perhaps; *, hypothetical. See the full key inside the front cover.

fall′ guy′, *U.S. Slang.* **1.** an easy victim. **2.** a scapegoat.

fal·li·bi·lism (fal′ə bə liz′əm), *n. Philos.* the doctrine that no statement can be accepted as true beyond all possible doubt. [FALLIBLE + -ISM] —**fal′li·bi·list,** *n., adj.*

fal·li·ble (fal′ə bəl), *adj.* **1.** (of persons) liable to be deceived or mistaken; liable to err. **2.** liable to be erroneous or false: *fallible information.* [< ML *fallibil(is),* equiv. to L *fall(ī)* (pass. of *fallere* to deceive) + *-ibilis* -IBLE] —**fal′li·bil′i·ty, fal′li·ble·ness,** *n.* —**fal′li·bly,** *adv.*

fall′ing-ball′ clock′ (fô′ling bôl′), a gravity clock having the form of a suspended ball, the numerals being on a horizontal band rotating above an ornamental pointer.

fall′ing band′, a large, flat collar, usually trimmed with lace, worn by men in the 17th century. Also called **fall.**

fall′ing diph′thong, *Phonet.* a diphthong in which the first of the two apparent vocalic elements is of greater stress or sonority and the second is of lesser stress or sonority, as in (ī), (ou), (oi), etc. Cf. **rising diphthong.**

fall′ing door′. See **flap door** (def. 1).

fall′ing home′, *Naut.* See **tumble home.**

fall·ing-out (fô′ling out′), *n., pl.* **fall·ings-out, fall·ing-outs.** a quarrel or estrangement among persons formerly in close association with one another. [n. use of v. phrase *fall out*]

fall′ing rhythm′, *Pros.* a rhythmic pattern created by the succession of metrical feet each of which is composed of one accented syllable followed by one or more unaccented syllables.

fall′ing sick′ness, epilepsy.

fall′ing star′, an incandescent meteor; a shooting star.

fall′ line′, **1.** an imaginary line, marked by waterfalls and rapids, where rivers descend abruptly from an upland to a lowland. **2.** (*caps.*) the imaginary line between the Piedmont and the coastal plain. **3.** *Skiing.* the path of natural descent from one point on a slope to another.

fall-off (fôl′ôf′, -of′), *n.* a decline in quantity, vigor, etc.: *Industry suffers a fall-off in times of depression.* [n. use of v. phrase *fall off*]

Fall′ of the House′ of Ush′er, The, a short story (1839), by Edgar Allan Poe.

Fal·lon (fal′ən), *n.* a town in W Nevada. 2734 (1960).

Fal·lo′pi·an tube′ (fə lō′pē ən), (*sometimes l.c.*) *Anat., Zool.* either of a pair of slender tubes leading from the body cavity to the uterus, which transports ova from the ovary to the uterus; the oviduct of mammals. [named after Gabriello *Fallopio* (d. 1562), Italian anatomist; see -IAN]

fall·out (fôl′out′), *n.* **1.** the settling to the ground of airborne particles of radioactive dust, soot, and other materials that result from a nuclear explosion. **2.** the particles themselves. Also, **fall′-out′.** Also called **radioactive fallout.** [n. use of v. phrase *fall out*]

fal·low[1] (fal′ō), *adj.* **1.** (of land) plowed and left unseeded for a season or more; uncultivated. —*n.* **2.** land that has undergone plowing and harrowing and has been left unseeded for one or more growing seasons. **3.** the plowing and harrowing of land that is to be left unseeded for a growing season. —*v.t.* **4.** to make (land) fallow for agricultural purposes. [ME *falwe,* OE *fealga* fallow land, pl. of *fealh;* akin to FELLOE] —**fal′low·ness,** *n.*

fal·low[2] (fal′ō), *adj.* pale-yellow; light-brown; dun. [ME *fal(o)we,* OE *fealu;* c. G *falb*]

fal′low deer′, a Eurasian deer, *Dama dama,* with a fallow or yellowish coat.

Fallow deer (3 ft. high at shoulder; antlers to 2½ ft.; length 5 ft.)

Fall′ Pip′pin, **1.** an American variety of yellow apple that ripens in the autumn. **2.** the tree bearing this fruit.

Fall′ Riv′er, a seaport in SE Massachusetts, on an arm of Narragansett Bay. 99,942 (1960).

Fall′ Riv′er Leg′end, a ballet (1948) by Morton Gould.

Falls (fôlz), *n.* a town in NE Pennsylvania, on the Susquehanna River. 29,082 (1960).

Falls′ Cit′y, a town in SE Nebraska. 5598 (1960).

fall′ web′worm. See under **webworm.**

fall′ wind′ (wind), *Meteorol.* a strong, cold, downhill wind. Cf. **gravity wind, foehn.**

Fal·mouth (fal′məth), *n.* **1.** a seaport in SW Cornwall, in SW England. 15,427 (1961). **2.** a town in SE Massachusetts. 3308 (1960). **3.** a town in N Kentucky. 2568 (1960).

false (fôls), *adj.,* **fals·er, fals·est,** *adv.* —*adj.* **1.** not true or correct; erroneous: *a false statement.* **2.** uttering or declaring what is untrue: *a false witness.* **3.** not faithful or loyal; treacherous: *a false friend.* **4.** tending to deceive or mislead; deceptive: *a false impression.* **5.** not genuine; counterfeit; fake: *a false signature; a false diamond.* **6.** based on mistaken, erroneous, or inconsistent impressions, ideas, or facts: *false pride.* **7.** used as a substitute or supplement, esp. temporarily: *false supports for a bridge.* **8.** *Biol.* having a superficial resemblance to something that properly bears the name: *the false acacia.* **9.** not properly, accurately, or honestly made, done, or adjusted: *a false balance.* **10.** inaccurate in pitch, as a musical note. —*adv.* **11.** dishonestly; faithlessly; treacherously: *Did he speak false against me?* **12. play someone false,** to betray someone; be treacherous or faithless: *He would play his own brother false if there was some profit in it.* [ME, OE *fals* < L *fals(us)* feigned, false, orig. ptp. of *fallere* to deceive] —**false′ly,** *adv.* —**false′ness,** *n.*

—**Syn. 1.** mistaken, incorrect, wrong, untrue. **2.** untruthful, lying, mendacious. **3.** insincere, hypocritical, disingenuous, disloyal, unfaithful, inconstant, recreant, perfidious, traitorous. **4.** misleading, fallacious. **5.** artificial, spurious, bogus, forged. FALSE, SHAM, COUNTERFEIT agree in referring to something that is not genuine. FALSE is used mainly of imitations of concrete objects; it often implies an intent to deceive: *false teeth; false hair.* SHAM is rarely used of concrete objects and has nearly always the suggestion of intent to deceive: *sham title; sham tears.* COUNTERFEIT always has the implication of cheating; it is used particularly of spurious imitation of coins, paper money, etc.

false′ aca′cia. See **black locust.**

false′ alarm′, **1.** a false report of fire to a fire department. **2.** something that excites unfounded alarm or expectation: *Rumors of an impending transit strike proved to be a false alarm.*

false′ al′oe, any of several plants of the genus *Agave,* esp. *A. Virginica,* of the southeastern U.S., having fragrant, greenish-yellow flowers. Also called **rattlesnake master.**

false′ arrest′, *Law.* arrest or detention of a person contrary to or unauthorized by law.

false′ beech′drops. See under **pinesap.**

false′ bot′tom, a horizontal partition above the actual bottom of a box, trunk, etc., esp. one forming a secret compartment.

false′ bread′-fruit (bred′fro͞ot′), ceriman.

false′ buck′thorn, a spiny, sapotaceous shrub or small tree, *Bumelia lanuginosa,* of the southern U.S., yielding a hard, light-brown wood.

false′ card′, *Chiefly Bridge.* a card played with a view to giving an opponent a mistaken idea of the quality or length of one's holding in the suit led.

false-card (fôls′kärd′), *v.i. Chiefly Bridge.* to play a false card.

false′ cast′, *Angling.* a throw of the line in fly casting in which the line, leader, and fly are prevented from hitting the water.

false′ cheek′, *Foundry.* a part of a flask lying within and overlapping adjacent edges of the cope and the drag.

false′ cir′rus. See **cirrus spissatus.**

false′ dawn′, zodiacal light occurring before sunrise.

False′ Decre′tals, the Pseudo-Isidorian documents.

false′ face′, a mask that covers the entire face, esp. one meant to be grotesque or humorous.

false′ fox′glove, any scrophulariaceous plant of the genus *Gerardia* of North America, related to the foxglove.

false′ front′, **1.** a façade falsifying the size, finish, or importance of a building, esp. one having a humble purpose or cheap construction. **2.** any deceptive appearance: *He hid his timidity behind a false front of aggressiveness.*

false′ gold′enrod. See under **goldenrod** (def. 2).

false-heart·ed (fôls′här′tid), *adj.* having a false or treacherous heart; deceitful; perfidious. —**false′-heart′ed·ly,** *adv.* —**false′-heart′ed·ness,** *n.*

false′ hel′lebore, hellebore (def. 2).

false·hood (fôls′ho͝od), *n.* **1.** a false statement; lie. **2.** lack of conformity to truth or fact: *the falsehood of superstitions.* **3.** something false; an untrue idea, belief, etc.: *The Nazis propagated the falsehood of racial superiority.* **4.** the act of lying or making false statements. **5.** *Obs.* deception. [ME *falshede.* See FALSE, -HOOD]

—**Syn. 1.** distortion, fabrication, fiction. FALSEHOOD, FIB, LIE, UNTRUTH refer to something untrue or incorrect. A FALSEHOOD is a statement that distorts or suppresses the truth, in order to deceive: *to tell a falsehood about one's ancestry in order to gain acceptance.* A FIB denotes a trivial falsehood, and is often used to characterize that which is not strictly true: *a polite fib.* A LIE is a vicious falsehood: *to tell a lie about one's neighbor.* An UNTRUTH is an incorrect statement, either intentionally misleading (less harsh, however, than falsehood or lie) or arising from misunderstanding or ignorance: *I'm afraid you are telling an untruth.* **4.** untruthfulness, inveracity, mendacity. —**Ant. 1.** truth.

false′ hori′zon, a line or plane that simulates the horizon, used in altitude measuring devices or the like.

false′ impris′onment, *Law.* the unlawful restraint of a person from exercising his right to freedom of movement.

false′ ip′ecac. See **bowman's root.**

false′ Jeru′salem cher′ry, a low shrub, *Solanum Capsicastrum,* of Brazil, having grayish foliage and globe-shaped, scarlet or yellow fruit.

false′ keel′, *Naut.* **1.** an extension to the keel of a vessel, made to offer lateral resistance to the water and thus to reduce leeway. **2.** shoe (def. 20a).

false′ la′bor, *Obstet.* painful contractions of the uterus prior to actual labor, usually occurring at irregular intervals. Also called **false′ pains′.**

false′ lil′y of the val′ley, a liliaceous herb, *Maianthemum canadense,* of eastern North America, resembling the lily of the valley.

false′ loose′strife, any of several onograceous herbs of the genus *Ludwigia,* found in swampy or aquatic habitats and having yellow flowers.

false′ mil′dew. See **downy mildew** (def. 1).

false′ net′tle, any of several urticaceous trees, shrubs, or herbs of the genus *Boehmeria,* having green flowers without petals and no stinging hairs.

false′ pile′, *Building Trades.* a pile attached to the head of another pile to permit further driving.

false′ pretens′es, *Law.* **1.** a deliberate misrepresentation of facts as a means to obtain title to money or property. **2.** the use of such misrepresentation.

false′ prosce′nium, *Theat.* a frame for the stage opening that is situated within the proscenium arch.

false′ raft′er, an extension to a rafter for supporting the roofing over the eaves; a tail or lookout.

false′ rela′tion, *Music.* See **cross relation.**

false′ rib′, *Anat.* any of the lower five ribs on either side of the body which are not directly attached to the sternum.

false′ ridge′pole, (on a roof) a board laid over the ridgepole to form a cresting or the foundation of a cresting.

false′ shade′ line′, (in architectural shades and shadows) an imaginary line upon a surface dividing an area of shade from an area of shadow.

false′ Solomon's-seal′, any of several liliaceous herbs of the genus *Smilacina,* having racemes or clusters of greenish-white flowers.

false′ step′, **1.** a stumble. **2.** an unwise act.

false′ sun′flower, a sneezeweed, *Helenium autumnale,* of the eastern U.S. Also called **yellow star.**

false′ teeth′, a denture, esp. a pair of removable full dentures of both jaws.

false′ to′paz, citrine (def. 2).

fal·set·to (fôl set′ō), *n., pl.* **-tos,** *adj., adv.* —*n.* **1.** an unnaturally or artificially high-pitched voice or register, esp. in a man: *He spoke in falsetto to imitate his wife.* **2.** a person, esp. a man, who sings with such a voice. —*adj.* **3.** of, noting, or having the quality and compass of such a voice. **4.** singing in a falsetto —*adv.* **5.** in a falsetto: *to speak falsetto.* [< It, equiv. to *fals(o)* (< L *falsus* FALSE) + *-etto* -ET]

false′ vam′pire, any of several large carnivorous bats of the families *Megadermatidae* and *Phyllostomatidae,* of Africa, Asia, and Australia, erroneously reputed to suck the blood of animals and man.

false′ vo′cal cords′, *Anat.* either one of the upper pair of vocal cords, not concerned with vocal production. Cf. **true vocal cords, vocal cords.**

false·work (fôls′wûrk′), *n.* framework for supporting a structure under construction which is not yet capable of supporting itself. [FALSE + WORK]

fals·ie (fôl′sē), *n. Informal.* either of a pair of rubber or fabric cups worn inside a brassiere to give the breasts a larger or more shapely appearance. [FALSE + -IE]

fal·si·fy (fôl′sə fī′), *v.,* **-fied, -fy·ing.** —*v.t.* **1.** to make false or incorrect, esp. so as to deceive: *to falsify income-tax reports.* **2.** to alter fraudulently. **3.** to represent falsely; misrepresent: *He falsified the history of his family to conceal his humble origins.* **4.** to show or prove to be false; disprove: *to falsify a theory.* —*v.i.* **5.** to make false statements. [late ME *falsifie(n)* < MF *falsifi(er)* < LL *falsificāre.* See FALSE, -IFY] —**fal′si·fi′a·bil′i·ty,** *n.* —**fal′si·fi′a·ble,** *adj.* —**fal·si·fi·ca·tion** (fôl′sə fə kā′shən), *n.* —**fal′si·fi′er,** *n.*

fal·si·ty (fôl′si tē), *n., pl.* **-ties.** **1.** the quality or condition of being false; incorrectness; untruthfulness; treachery. **2.** something false; falsehood. [ME *falsete* < OF < LL *falsitās.* See FALSE, -ITY]

Fal·staff (fôl′staf, -stäf), *n.* **1. Sir John,** the jovial, fat knight of brazen assurance and few scruples in Shakespeare's *Henry IV,* Parts 1 and 2, and *The Merry Wives of Windsor.* **2.** (*italics.*) an opera (1893) by Giuseppe Verdi, with a libretto by Arrigo Boito based on the Shakespearean character.

Fal·staff·i·an (fôl staf′ē ən), *adj.* of, pertaining to, or having the qualities of Falstaff, esp. his robust, bawdy humor, good-natured rascality, and brazen braggadocio: *Falstaffian wit.* [FALSTAFF + -IAN]

Fal·ster (fäl′stər), *n.* an island in SE Denmark. 46,662 (1960); 198 sq. mi.

falt·boat (fält′bōt′), *n.* a small boat having a collapsible wooden frame covered with canvas. Also, **foldboat.** [< G *Faltboot* folding-boat. See FOLD[1], BOAT]

fal·ter (fôl′tər), *v.i.* **1.** to hesitate or waver in action, purpose, etc.; give way: *Her courage did not falter at the prospect of hardship.* **2.** to speak hesitatingly or brokenly. **3.** to move unsteadily; stumble: *The old man faltered on the stairs.* —*v.t.* **4.** to utter hesitatingly or brokenly: *to falter an apology.* —*n.* **5.** the act of faltering; an unsteadiness of gait, voice, action, etc. **6.** a faltering sound. [ME *faltre(n)* < Scand; cf. Icel *faltrast* to be uncertain] —**fal′ter·er,** *n.* —**fal′ter·ing·ly,** *adv.*

—**Syn. 1.** vacillate. **2.** stammer, stutter.

falx (falks, fôlks), *n., pl.* **fal·ces** (fal′sēz, fôl′-). *Anat.* a structure shaped like a sickle, as a fold of dura mater separating the cerebral hemispheres. [< NL, L: sickle] —**fal·cial** (fal′shəl, fôl′-), *adj.*

fam., **1.** familiar. **2.** family.

F.A.M., Free and Accepted Masons. Also, **F. & A.M.**

fa·ma·cide (fā′mə sīd′), *n. Law.* a person who destroys another's reputation; a defamer or slanderer. [< L *fāma* FAME + -CIDE]

Fa·ma·gu·sta (fä mə go͞o′stə), *n.* a seaport on the E coast of Cyprus, on an inlet of the Mediterranean: castle; large cathedral (now a mosque). 277,650 (est. 1957).

fa·ma·ti·nite (fam′ə tē′nīt, fä′mə-), *n.* a rare mineral, copper antimony sulfide, Cu_3SbS_4, occurring in reddish-gray crystals. [named after *Famatina* Mountains, Argentina; see -ITE[1]]

fame (fām), *n., v.,* **famed, fam·ing.** —*n.* **1.** widespread reputation, esp. of a favorable character; renown; public eminence: *the literary fame of Tennyson; to seek fame as a discoverer.* **2.** reputation; common estimation or opinion generally held of a person or thing. —*v.t.* **3.** to have or spread the renown of; to be or make famous: *French cooking is famed throughout the world.* [ME < L *fāma* talk, public opinion, repute, akin to *fārī* to speak] —**fame′less,** *adj.*

—**Syn. 1.** repute. notoriety, celebrity, honor, glory. —**Ant. 1.** obscurity; ignominy.

famed (fāmd), *adj.* very well known; famous. [FAME + -ED[3]]

Fa·meuse (fə myo͞oz′), *n.* **1.** an American variety of red apple that ripens in early winter. **2.** the tree bearing this fruit. [< F, fem. of *fameux* FAMOUS]

fa·mil·ial (fə mil′yəl, -mil′ē əl), *adj.* **1.** of, pertaining to, or characteristic of a family: *familial ties.* **2.** appearing in individuals by heredity: *a familial disease.* [< F; see FAMILY, -AL[1]]

fa·mil·iar (fə mil′yər), *adj.* **1.** commonly or generally known or seen: *a familiar sight.* **2.** well-acquainted; thoroughly conversant: *to be familiar with a subject.* **3.** informal; easy; unceremonious; unconstrained: *to write in a familiar style.* **4.** closely intimate: *a familiar friend; to be on familiar terms.* **5.** unduly intimate; taking liberties; presuming: *The duchess disliked familiar servants.* **6.** domesticated; tame. **7.** of or pertaining to a family or household. —*n.* **8.** a familiar friend or associate. **9.** See **familiar spirit.** **10.** *Rom. Cath. Ch.* **a.** an officer of the Inquisition, employed to arrest accused or suspected persons. **b.** a person who belongs to the household of the pope or of a bishop, rendering

domestic though not menial service. [ME < L *familiā-r(is)* of a household (see FAMILY, -AR[1]); r. ME *familier* < MF] —**fa·mil′iar·ly,** *adv.* —**fa·mil′iar·ness,** *n.*
—**Syn. 1.** common, well-known, frequent. **3.** free. **4.** close, friendly. FAMILIAR, CONFIDENTIAL, INTIMATE suggest a long association between persons. FAMILIAR means well acquainted with another person: *a familiar friend.* CONFIDENTIAL suggests a sense of mutual trust which extends to the sharing of confidences and secrets: *a confidential advisor.* INTIMATE suggests close acquaintance or connection, often based on interest, sympathy, or affection: *intimate and affectionate letters.* **5.** free, forward, intrusive, bold, presumptuous. —**Ant. 1.** strange. **2.** unacquainted. **5.** respectful, cautious, circumspect, prudent.

fa·mil·iar·ise (fə mil′yə rīz′), *v.t., v.i.,* **-ised, -is·ing.** *Chiefly Brit.* familiarize. —**fa·mil′iar·i·sa′tion,** *n.* —**fa·mil′iar·is′er,** *n.* —**fa·mil′iar·is′ing·ly,** *adv.*

fa·mil·i·ar·i·ty (fə mil′ē ar′i tē), *n., pl.* **-ties. 1.** thorough knowledge of a thing, subject, etc. **2.** the state of being familiar; friendly relationship; close acquaintance; intimacy. **3.** an absence of ceremony and formality; informality. **4.** undue intimacy; freedom of behavior justified only by the closest relationship. **5.** Often, **familiarities.** an instance or manifestation of such freedom, as in action or speech. **6.** a sexual liberty or impropriety. [ME *familiarite* < OF < L *familiāritāt-* (s. of *familiāritās*) intimacy. See FAMILIAR, -ITY]
—**Syn. 3.** unconstraint. **4.** liberty, freedom, license.
—**Ant. 1.** ignorance. **3.** constraint. **4.** reserve.

fa·mil·iar·ize (fə mil′yə rīz′), *v.,* **-ized, -iz·ing.** —*v.t.* **1.** to make (a person) well acquainted or conversant with something. **2.** to make (something) well-known; bring into common knowledge or use. **3.** *Archaic.* to make familiar; establish (a person) in friendly intimacy. —*v.i.* **4.** *Archaic.* to associate in a familiar way. Also, *esp. Brit.,* **familiarise.** [FAMILIAR + -IZE] —**fa·mil′iar·i·za′tion,** *n.* —**fa·mil′iar·iz′er,** *n.*

famil′iar spir′it, a supernatural spirit or demon supposed to attend on or serve a person.

fam·i·lism (fam′ə liz′əm), *n. Sociol.* the subordination of the personal interests and prerogatives of an individual to the values and demands of the family: *Familism characterized the patriarchal family.* [FAMIL(Y) + -ISM] —**fam′i·list,** *n.* —**fam′i·lis′tic,** *adj.*

fam·i·ly (fam′ə lē, fam′lē), *n., pl.* **-lies,** *adj.* —*n.* **1.** parents and their children, whether dwelling together or not. **2.** the children of one person or one couple collectively: *My wife and I want a large family.* **3.** the spouse and children of one person: *I'm taking my family on vacation next week.* **4.** any group of persons closely related by blood, as parents, children, uncles, aunts, and cousins: *She married into a socially prominent family.* **5.** all those persons considered as descendants of a common progenitor: *The Tudor family reigned long.* **6.** *Chiefly Brit.* approved lineage, esp. noble, titled, famous, or wealthy ancestry: *young men of family.* **7.** a group of persons who form a household under one head, including parents, children, servants, etc. **8.** the staff, or body of assistants, of an official: *the office family.* **9.** a group of related things or people: *the family of romantic poets; the halogen family of elements.* **10.** *Biol.* the usual major subdivision of an order or suborder in the classification of plants and animals, usually consisting of several genera. **11.** *Ling.* the largest category into which languages related by common origin can be classified with certainty: *Indo-European, Sino-Tibetan, and Malayo-Polynesian are the most widely spoken families of languages.* Cf. **stock** (def. 13), **subfamily** (def. 2). **12.** *Math.* **a.** a given class of solutions of the same basic equation, differing from one another only by the different values assigned to the constants in the equation. **b.** a class of functions or the like defined by an expression containing a parameter. **c.** a set. —*adj.* **13.** of, pertaining to, or characteristic of a family: *a family trait.* **14.** belonging to or used by a family: *a family automobile; a family room.* **15. in a** or **the family way,** expecting a child; pregnant: *She told her husband that she was in a family way.* [ME *familie* < L *familia* a household, family servants, equiv. to *famul(us)* servant + *-ia* -Y[3]] —**fam′i·ly·ish,** *adj.*

fam′ily Bi′ble, a large Bible usually having pages for recording the marriages, births, and deaths in a family.

fam′ily cir′cle, 1. the closely related members of a family as a group: *a scandal known only within the family circle.* **2.** a section in a theater, opera house, etc., containing inexpensive seats, as the topmost gallery.

fam′ily court′. See **court of domestic relations.**

fam′ily doc′tor, the general practitioner customarily consulted by a family. Also called **fam′ily physi′cian.**

fam′ily man′, 1. a man who has a family. **2.** a man inclined to lead a domestic life: *Americans want their leaders to be family men.*

fam′ily name′, 1. the hereditary surname of a family. **2.** a given name frequently used in a family.

fam′ily of curves′, *Math.* a collection of curves whose equations differ only by values assigned a parameter or parameters.

fam′ily plan′, a special rate, esp. of air passenger carriers, under which the head of a household purchasing a full-fare ticket may take his wife and children at reduced fares on certain days. Also called **family fare, family-fare plan.**

fam′ily plan′ning, 1. the concept or a program of limiting the size of families through the spacing or prevention of pregnancies, esp. for economic reasons. Cf. **planned parenthood. 2.** (loosely) birth control.

fam′ily skel′eton, skeleton (def. 9).

fam′ily style′, (of a meal) with the serving platters on the table so that all present can serve themselves.

fam′ily tree′, a genealogical chart showing the ancestry, descent, and relationship of all members of a family. Also called **genealogical tree.**

fam′ily way′, family (def. 15).

fam·ine (fam′in), *n.* **1.** extreme and general scarcity of food. **2.** any extreme and general scarcity: *We are suffering from a famine of devoted workers in our cause.* **3.** extreme hunger; starvation. [ME < MF < VL **famina,* equiv. to L *fam(ēs)* hunger + *-īna* -INE[2]]

fam·ish (fam′ish), *v.t., v.i. Archaic.* **1.** to suffer or cause to suffer extreme hunger; starve. **2.** to starve to death. [late ME *famisshe,* equiv. to *fam(en)* (to) starve (< MF *afamer* < VL **affamāre,* equiv. to L *af-* AF- + *famēs* hunger) + *-isshe* -ISH[2]]

fam·ished (fam′isht), *adj.* very hungry: *to be famished after a hike; famished, homeless multitudes.* [late ME; see FAMISH, -ED[2]] —**Syn.** See **hungry.**

fa·mous (fā′məs), *adj.* **1.** having a widespread reputation; renowned; celebrated: *a famous victory; a famous emperor.* **2.** *Informal.* first-rate; excellent: *The singer gave a famous performance.* **3.** *Obs.* notorious (used pejoratively). [ME < L *fāmōs(us).* See FAME, -OUS] —**fa′mous·ly,** *adv.* —**fa′mous·ness,** *n.*
—**Syn. 1.** famed, notable, illustrious. FAMOUS, CELEBRATED, EMINENT, DISTINGUISHED refer to someone or something widely and favorably known. FAMOUS is the general word: *a famous lighthouse.* CELEBRATED originally referred to something commemorated, but now usually refers to someone or something widely known for conspicuous merit, services, etc.: *a celebrated writer.* EMINENT implies high standing among one's contemporaries, esp. in one's own profession or craft: *an eminent physician.* DISTINGUISHED adds to eminent the idea of honors conferred more or less publicly: *a distinguished scientist.* —**Ant. 1.** unknown, obscure.

fam·u·lus (fam′yə ləs), *n., pl.* **-li** (-lī′). a servant or attendant, esp. of a scholar or a magician. [< L: house-slave]

fan[1] (fan), *n., v.,* **fanned, fan·ning.** —*n.* **1.** any device for causing a current of air by the movement of a broad surface or a number of such surfaces. **2.** an implement of feathers, leaves, paper, cloth, etc., often in the shape of a long triangle or of a semicircle, for waving lightly in the hand to create a cooling current of air about a person: *We sat on the veranda, cooling ourselves with palm-leaf fans.* **3.** anything resembling such an implement, as the tail of a bird. **4.** any of various devices consisting essentially of a series of radiating vanes or blades attached to and revolving with a central hublike portion to produce a current of air: *ceiling fan; wall fan.* **5.** a series of revolving blades supplying air for winnowing or cleaning grain. **6.** *Horol.* fly[1] (def. 33). —*v.t.* **7.** to move or agitate (the air) with or as with a fan. **8.** to cause air to blow upon, as from a fan; cool or refresh with or as with a fan: *He fanned his face with a newspaper.* **9.** to stir to activity with or as with a fan: *to fan a flame; to fan emotions.* **10.** (of a breeze, current of air, etc.) to blow upon, as if driven by a fan: *A cool breeze fanned the shore.* **11.** to spread out like a fan: *The dealer fanned the cards.* **12.** *Agric.* to winnow, esp. by an artificial current of air. **13.** *Baseball.* (of a pitcher) to strike out (a batter). —*v.i.* **14.** to strike, swing, or brush lightly at something. **15.** to spread out like a fan (often fol. by *out*): *The forest fire fanned out in all directions.* **16.** *Baseball.* (of a batter) to strike out, usually by swinging at and missing the pitch charged as the third strike. [ME, OE *fann* < L *vann(us)* winnowing fan] —**fan′like′,** *adj.* —**fan′ner,** *n.*

fan[2] (fan), *n.* an enthusiastic devotee or follower: *a baseball fan; a movie fan.* [short for FANATIC]

fa·na (fə nä′), *n. Islam.* the ecstatic union of the Sufi with the Divine. [< Ar *fanā'* annihilation]

fa·na·ka·lo (fä′nä kä′lō), *n.* a lingua franca based on English, Afrikaans, Xhosa, and Zulu, spoken in the mines in South Africa. Also, **Fa·na·ga·lo** (fä′nä gä′lō).

fa·nat·ic (fə nat′ik), *n.* **1.** a person with an extreme and uncritical enthusiasm or zeal, as in religion, politics, etc. —*adj.* **2.** fanatical. [< L *fānātic(us)* pertaining to a temple, inspired, frantic, equiv. to *fān(um)* temple + *-āticus,* equiv. to *-ātus* -ATE[1] + *-icus* -IC]
—**Syn. 1.** enthusiast, zealot, bigot.

fa·nat·i·cal (fə nat′i kəl), *adj.* actuated or characterized by an extreme, uncritical enthusiasm or zeal, as in religion, politics, etc. Also, **fanatic.** [FANATIC + -AL[1]] —**fa·nat′i·cal·ly,** *adv.* —**fa·nat′i·cal·ness,** *n.*
—**Syn.** enthusiastic, zealous, frenzied, rabid. See **intolerant, radical.**

fa·nat·i·cise (fə nat′i sīz′), *v.t., v.i.,* **-cised, -cis·ing.** *Chiefly Brit.* fanaticize.

fa·nat·i·cism (fə nat′i siz′əm), *n.* fanatical character, spirit, or conduct. [FANATIC + -ISM]

fa·nat·i·cize (fə nat′i sīz′), *v.,* **-cized, -ciz·ing.** —*v.t.* **1.** to make fanatical. —*v.i.* **2.** to act with or show fanaticism. Also, *esp. Brit.,* **fanaticise.** [FANATIC + -IZE]

fan·back (fan′bak′), *adj.* **1.** (of a chair) having a fan-shaped back. **2.** (of a Windsor chair or the like) having a back of vertical spindles fanning out from seat to upper rail. [FAN[1] + BACK[1]]

Fan·chette (fan chet′), *n.* a girl's given name.

Fan·cia (fan′shə), *n.* a girl's given name.

fan·cied (fan′sēd), *adj.* **1.** unreal; imaginary: *to be upset by fancied grievances.* **2.** desired or favored; favorite: *a fancied horse.* [FANCY + -ED[2]]

fan·ci·er (fan′sē ər), *n.* **1.** a person having a liking for or interest in something; enthusiast: *a fancier of sports cars.* **2.** a person who breeds animals, plants, etc., esp. in order to improve the strain: *a horse fancier.* **3.** a person under the influence of his fancy. [FANCY + -ER[1]]

fan·ci·ful (fan′si fəl), *adj.* **1.** exhibiting fancy; capricious or whimsical in appearance: *a fanciful design of butterflies and flowers.* **2.** suggested by fancy; imaginary; unreal: *fanciful lands of romance.* **3.** led by fancy rather than by reason and experience; whimsical: *a fanciful mind.* [FANCY + -FUL] —**fan′ci·ful·ly,** *adv.* —**fan′ci·ful·ness,** *n.* —**Syn. 2.** visionary, baseless, illusory. **3.** unpredictable, curious, queer, peculiar, odd.

fan·ci·less (fan′si lis), *adj.* without fancy or imagination. [FANCY + -LESS]

Fan·ciul·la del West, La (*It.* lä fän chōōl′lä del west′). See **Girl of the Golden West, The.**

fan′ club′, a club, often of teen-age girls, enthusiastically devoted to a movie star or other celebrity.

fan·cy (fan′sē), *n., pl.* **-cies,** *adj.,* **-ci·er, -ci·est,** *v.,* **-cied, -cy·ing,** *interj.* —*n.* **1.** imagination or inclination, esp. as exercised in a capricious manner. **2.** the artistic ability of creating unreal or whimsical imagery, decorative detail, etc., as in poetry or drawing. **3.** a mental image or conception: *He had happy fancies of marrying a pretty girl.* **4.** an idea or opinion with little foundation; hallucination: *Her belief that she is superior is a mere fancy.* **5.** a caprice; whim; vagary: *It was her fancy to fly to Paris occasionally for dinner.* **6.** capricious preference; inclination; a liking: *to take a fancy to walking barefoot in the streets.* **7.** critical judgment; taste. **8.** the breeding of animals to develop points of beauty or excellence. **9.** people deeply interested in a sport, art, etc. **10.** *Obs.* love. —*adj.* **11.** made, designed, grown, adapted, etc., to please the taste or fancy; of superfine quality or exceptional appeal: *fancy goods; fancy fruits.* **12.** ornamental; decorative; not plain: *a cake with a fancy icing.* **13.** depending on imagination or caprice; whimsical; irregular: *a fancy conception of time.* **14.** bred to develop points of beauty or excellence, as an animal. —*v.t.* **15.** to form a conception of; picture to oneself: *Fancy living with that ogre all your life!* **16.** to believe without being absolutely sure or certain: *I fancy you are my new neighbor.* **17.** to take a liking to; like. **18.** to breed to develop a special type of animal. —*interj.* **19.** (used as an exclamation of mild surprise.) [ME *fan(t)sy,* syncopated var. of *fantasie* FANTASY] —**fan′ci·ness,** *n.*
—**Syn. 2.** FANCY, FANTASY, IMAGINATION refer to qualities in literature or other artistic composition. The creations of FANCY are casual, whimsical, and often amusing, being at once less profound and less moving or inspiring than those of imagination: *letting one's fancy play freely on a subject; an impish fancy.* FANTASY now usually suggests an unrestrained or extravagant fancy, often resulting in caprice: *The use of fantasy in art creates interesting results.* The term and concept of creative IMAGINATION are less than two hundred years old; previously only the *reproductive* aspect had been recognized, hardly to be distinguished from memory. "Creative imagination" suggests that the memories of actual sights and experiences may so blend in the mind of the writer or artist as to produce something that has never existed before—often a hitherto unperceived vision of reality: *to use imagination in portraying character and action.* **3.** thought, notion, impression, idea. **5.** quirk, humor, crotchet. **11.** fine, elegant, choice. **12.** decorated, ornate. **15.** envision, conceive, imagine.

fan′cy Dan′ (dan), **1.** a fop; dandy. **2.** a person, esp. a boxer or other athlete, who seeks to impress others by elaborate, pretentious, or showy display.

fan′cy dive′, any of the series of specified dives executed in fancy diving, as the jackknife or gainer.

fan′cy div′ing, diving competition from a springboard into water, the contestants being judged chiefly by their grace and control in executing a specified series of dives in a prescribed manner. —**fan′cy div′er.**

fan′cy dress′, a costume for a ball, masquerade, etc., chosen to please the fancy, usually a costume characteristic of a particular period or place, class of persons, or historical or fictitious character.

fan′cy dress′ ball′, a ball at which fancy dress is worn. Also called **fan′cy ball′.**

Fan′cy Free′, a ballet (1944) by Leonard Bernstein.

fan·cy-free (fan′sē frē′), *adj.* free from any influence, esp. that of love.

fan′cy gera′nium. See **show geranium.**

fan′cy man′, 1. a woman's lover. **2.** a pimp.

fan′cy wom′an, 1. an immoral woman, esp. a man's mistress. **2.** a prostitute. Also, **fan′cy la′dy.**

fan·cy·work (fan′sē wûrk′), *n.* ornamental needlework. [FANCY + WORK]

fan′ dance′, a provocative solo dance performed by a nude or nearly nude woman using a fan or fans for covering and provocation.

fan′ danc′er, a female performer, as in a cabaret, who dances the fan dance. Cf. **bubble dancer.**

fan·dan·go (fan dang′gō), *n., pl.* **-gos. 1.** a lively Spanish or Spanish-American dance in triple time, performed by a man and woman playing castanets. **2.** a piece of music for such a dance or one having its rhythm. **3.** (esp. in the southwest U.S.) a ball or dance. [< Sp < ?]

fan′ del′ta, a partially submerged alluvial fan which has merged with a delta.

fane (fān), *n. Archaic.* **1.** a temple. **2.** a church. [ME < L *fān(um)* temple, sanctuary]

fa·ne·ga (fə nā′gə; *Sp.* fä ne′gä), *n., pl.* **-gas** (-gəz; *Sp.* -gäs). **1.** a unit of dry measure in Spanish-speaking countries, equal in Spain to 1.58 U.S. bushels. **2.** a Mexican unit of land measure, equal to 8.81 acres. [< Sp < Ar *faniqah* big bag]

fa·ne·ga·da (fä′ne gä′thä), *n., pl.* **-das** (-thäs). a unit of land measure in Spanish-speaking countries varying from 1¼ to 1¾ acres. [< Sp; see FANEGA, -ADE[1]]

Fan·euil (fan′əl, -yəl), *n.* **Peter,** 1700–43, American merchant: builder of Faneuil Hall.

Fan′euil Hall′, a market house and public hall in Boston, Massachusetts, called "the Cradle of Liberty" because it was used as a meeting place by American patriots immediately before the Revolutionary War.

Fan·fa·ni (fän fä′nē), *n.* **A·min·to·re** (ä′mēn tô′re), born 1908, Italian statesman: premier 1958–63.

fan·fare (fan′fâr), *n.* **1.** a flourish or short air played on trumpets or the like. **2.** an ostentatious display or flourish. **3.** *Informal.* publicity or advertising. [< F, back formation from *fanfarer* to blow a fanfare, deriv. of *fanfaron* FANFARON]

fan·fa·ron (fan′fə ron′), *n.* **1.** a braggart. **2.** a fanfare. [< F < Sp *fanfarrón* braggart < Ar *farfār* talkative]

fan·fa·ron·ade (fan′fə rə nād′), *n.* bragging; bravado; bluster. [< F *fanfaronnade* < Sp *fanfarronada.* See FANFARON, -ADE[1]]

fan′ Fink′ truss′, *Engineering, Building Trades.* a Fink truss having two or more struts meeting at a common foot in each half of the truss.

fan·fish (fan′fish′), *n., pl.* **-fish·es,** (*esp. collectively*) **-fish.** a pelagic fish, *Pteraclis velifera,* having greatly expanded dorsal and anal fins. [FAN[1] + FISH]

fan·fold (fan′fōld′), *n.* **1.** a pad or tablet of invoices, bills, blank sheets, etc., interleaved with carbon paper for making a copy or copies of the writing or typing on the uppermost leaf. —*adj.* **2.** (of a pad or tablet of invoices, bills, blank sheets, etc.) made up in such a form. [FAN[1] + FOLD[1]]

F, Fangs (of rattlesnake)

fang[1] (fang), *n.* **1.** one of the long, sharp, hollow or grooved teeth of a venomous snake by which poison is injected. **2.** a canine tooth. **3.** a tooth resembling a dog's. **4.** the root of a tooth. **5.** one of the chelicerae of a spider. **6.** a pointed, tapering part of a thing. **7.** *Mach.* the tang of a tool. [ME, OE: something caught; c. G *Fang* capture, booty, Icel *fang* a grasp, hold. See FANG[2]] —**fanged** (fangd), *adj.* —**fang′less,** *adj.* —**fang′like′,** *adj.*

fang[2] (fang), *v.t. Brit. Dial.* to seize; grab. [ME *fange(n)* (to) seize, catch; c. OS *fangan,* G *fangen,* Vernerian var. of proto-Gmc **fanhan-,* whence OE *fōn,* c. OS, OHG, Goth *fāhan,* Icel *fā;* akin to OE *gefangian* to fasten]

fan·gle (fang′gəl), *n.* a fashion: *new fangles of dress.* [abstracted from NEWFANGLED] —**fan′gled,** *adj.*

fan·go (fang′gō), *n. Med.* clay or mud, esp. a clay obtained from certain hot springs in Battaglio, Italy, used as a hot application in the treatment of certain diseases. [< It: mud, ? < Gmc; cf. OE *fūht* damp, Skt *pañkas* mire. See FEN[1]]

fan·ion (fan′yən), *n.* a small flag, originally carried by military brigades, used by soldiers and surveyors as a positional marker. [< F, deriv. of *fanon* FANON]

fan·jet (fan′jet′), *n.* **1.** Also called **turbofan.** a jet engine having a large impeller that takes in air only part of which is used for the combustion of fuel, the remainder being mixed with the combustion products to form a low-velocity exhaust jet. **2.** an airplane having one or more of such engines. Also, **fan′ jet′.** [FAN[1] + JET[1]]

fan·leaf (fan′lēf′), *n. Plant Pathol.* a disease of grapevines, characterized by the deformation of leaves into a fanlike shape, caused by a virus transmitted in grafting. [FAN[1] + LEAF]

fan·light (fan′līt′), *n.* a transom window, esp. one having the form of a semicircle or of half an ellipse. [FAN[1] + LIGHT[1]]

fan′ magazine′, a magazine containing information and gossip about celebrities in some field of sports or entertainment, as baseball, motion pictures, etc.

fan′ mail′, mail sent to a celebrity by his admirers.

Fan·nie (fan′ē), *n.* a girl's given name, form of **Frances.** Also, **Fanny.**

fan′ning mill′, *Agric.* a machine for winnowing grain by the action of riddles and sieves and an air blast.

fan·ny (fan′ē), *n., pl.* **-nies.** *Informal.* the buttocks. [? alter. of FANCY vulva (obs. euphemism)]

Fan·ny (fan′ē), *n.* a girl's given name. Also, **Fannie.**

Fan·ny (fan′ē, fä′nē; *Fr.* FA nē′), *n.* a play (1931) by Marcel Pagnol.

Fan′ny May′ (fan′ē), a nickname for the Federal National Mortgage Association. [from *FNMA*]

Fa·no (fä′nō), *n.* a town in central Italy, on the Adriatic: cathedral; Roman ruins. 41,033 (1961). Ancient, **Fanum Fortunae.**

fan·on (fan′ən), *n. Eccles.* **1.** a maniple. **2.** Also called **orale.** a striped scarflike vestment worn by the pope over the alb when celebrating solemn Pontifical Mass. [ME *fano(u)n,* priest's maniple < ML *fanōn-* (s. of *fanō*) < OHG; c. VANE]

fan′ palm′, **1.** a palm having fan-shaped leaves, as the talipot. **2.** See **Chinese fan palm.**

fan′ roof′, a vaulted roof having fan tracery.

fan·tail (fan′tāl′), *n.* **1.** a tail, end, or part shaped like a fan. **2.** one of a breed of domestic pigeons, having a fan-shaped tail. **3.** any of various small birds having fanlike tails, as the Old World flycatchers of the genus *Rhipidura* and the American wood warblers of the genus *Euthlypis.* **4.** an artificially bred variety of goldfish with double anal and caudal fins. **5.** a North American, fresh-water fish, *Poecilichthys flabellaris,* of the perch family. **6.** *Building Trades, Archit.* a structure or structural member having a number of radiating parts, as an arch centering. **7.** *U.S. Naut.* **a.** the part of a rounded stern extending abaft the aftermost perpendicular; a rounded counter. **b.** the area within this. —*adj.* **8.** *Cookery.* (of shrimp) shelled, split almost through, and flattened slightly before cooking. [FAN[1] + TAIL[1]] —**fan′-tailed′,** *adj.*

Fantail (def. 2)

fan′tail stern′, *Naut.* a type of stern having a counter **(fan′tail coun′ter)** that projects well aft of the sternpost and is composed of two sloping surfaces that are faired into the afterbody of the hull at their forward ends. Also called **counter stern.**

fan-tan (fan′tan′), *n.* **1.** Also, **fan′ tan′.** Also called **parliament, sevens.** *Cards.* a game in which the players play their sevens and other cards forming sequences in the same suits as their sevens, the winner being the player who first gets rid of his cards. **2.** a Chinese gambling game in which a pile of coins, counters, or objects is placed under a bowl and bets are made on what the remainder will be after they have been counted off in fours. [< Chin *fan t'an* repeated divisions]

fan·ta·sia (fan tā′zhə, -zhē ə, fan′tə zē′ə), *n.* **1.** *Music.* **a.** a composition in fanciful or irregular form or style. **b.** a potpourri of well-known airs arranged with interludes and florid decorations. **2.** fantasy (def. 9). [< It; see FANTASY]

fan·ta·sist (fan′tə sist, -zist; fan tā′zhist), *n.* a person who writes or composes fantasies or fantasias. [FANTAS(Y) + -IST]

fan·ta·size (fan′tə sīz′), *v.,* **-sized, -siz·ing.** —*v.i.* **1.** to conceive fanciful or extravagant notions, ideas, suppositions, or the like (often fol. by *about*): *to fantasize about the ideal husband.* —*v.t.* **2.** to create in one's fancy, daydreams, or the like; imagine: *to fantasize a trip through space.* Also, **phantasize.** [FANTAS(Y) + -IZE]

fan·tasm (fan′taz əm), *n.* phantasm.

fan·tas·ma·go·ri·a (fan taz′mə gôr′ē ə, -gōr′-), *n.* phantasmagoria. —**fan·tas′ma·go′ric,** *adj.* —**fan·tas′ma·go′ri·cal·ly,** *adv.*

fan·tast (fan′tast), *n.* a visionary. Also, **phantast.** [< G, var. of *Phantast* < Gk *phantast(ḗs)* boaster; mod. sense by assoc. with FANTASTIC]

fan·tas·tic (fan tas′tik), *adj.* **1.** conceived or appearing as if conceived by an unrestrained imagination; grotesque; eccentric; odd: *fantastic rock formations; fantastic designs.* **2.** fanciful or capricious, as persons or their ideas, actions, etc.: *We never know what that fantastic creature will say next.* **3.** imaginary or groundless; not real or based on reality: *fantastic fears.* **4.** extravagantly fanciful; irrational. **5.** incredibly great or extreme; exorbitant: *to spend fantastic sums of money.* **6.** highly unrealistic or impractical: *a fantastic scheme to make a million dollars betting on horse races.* **7.** *Informal.* extraordinarily good: *a fantastic musical.* Also, **fan·tas′ti·cal.** [ME *fantastik* pertaining to imagination < ML *fantastic(us),* var. of LL *phantasticus* < Gk *phantastikós* able to present or show (to the mind), equiv. to *phantáz(ein)* (to) make visible + *-tikos* -TIC] —**fan·tas′ti·cal·ly,** *adv.* —**fan·tas′ti·cal·ness, fan·tas′ti·cal′i·ty,** *n.*

fan·ta·sy (fan′tə sē, -zē), *n., pl.* **-sies,** *v.,* **-sied, -sy·ing.** **1.** imagination, esp. when extravagant and unrestrained. **2.** the forming of grotesque mental images: *She was powerless to control her fantasy of death.* **3.** a mental image, esp. when grotesque: *a nightmare fantasy.* **4.** *Psychol.* an imaginative sequence fulfilling a psychological need; daydream. **5.** a hallucination. **6.** a supposition based on no solid foundation; visionary idea: *dreams of Utopias and similar fantasies.* **7.** caprice; whim. **8.** an ingenious or fanciful thought, design, or invention. **9.** Also, **fantasia.** *Literature.* an imaginative or fanciful work, esp. one dealing with supernatural or unnatural events or characters: *The stories of Poe are fantasies of horror.* **10.** *Music.* fantasia (def. 1). —*v.t., v.i.* **11.** to form mental images; imagine; fantasize. **12.** *Rare.* to write or play fantasias. Also, **phantasy.** [ME *fantasie* imaginative faculty, mental image < L *phantasia* < Gk *phantasía* an idea, notion, image, lit., a making visible, equiv. to *phantas-* (see FANTASTIC) + *-ia* -Y[3]] —**Syn. 1.** See **fancy.**

Fan·ta·sy (fan′tə sē), *n.* a girl's given name.

Fan·ti (fan′tē, fän′-), *n.* a dialect that is spoken and written in Ghana, belongs to the Kwa group of languages, and is mutually intelligible with Twi.

fan·tigue (fan tēg′), *n. Brit. Dial.* an overwrought state or condition. Also, **fan·teeg′.** [earlier *fantique,* alter. of FRANTIC]

Fan·tin-La·tour (fän tan lä to͞or′), *n.* **(Ig·nace) Hen·ri (Jo·seph Thé·o·dore)** (ē nyas′ äN rē′ zhô zef′ tā ô dôr′), 1836–1904, French painter.

fan·toc·ci·ni (fan′tə chē′nē), *n. pl.* **1.** puppets operated by concealed wires or strings. **2.** dramatic representations in which such puppets are used. [< It: marionettes, pl. of *fantoccino* little doll, dim. of *fantoccio,* equiv. to *fant(e)* boy (< L *infante-,* s. of *infans* INFANT) + *-occio* aug. suffix]

fan·tom (fan′təm), *n., adj.* phantom.

fan′ trac′ery, *Archit.* the tracery on the surface of a fan vault.

fan′ truss′, *Engineering, Building Trades.* a truss having two or more struts supported at their feet by a common suspension member from which they diverge.

Fa·num For·tu·nae (fā′nəm fôr tyo͞o′nē), ancient name of **Fano.**

fan′ vault′, a vault composed of a number of concave conoidal surfaces, usually four, springing from the corners of the vaulting compartment and touching or intersecting at the top, often decorated with ribs, usually found in English architecture in the late 15th and early 16th centuries. See illus. under **vault**[1].

fan′ vault′ing, a system of fan vaults.

fan·weed (fan′wēd′), *n.* the penny-cress, *Thlaspi alpestre.* [FAN[1] + WEED[1]]

fan′ win′dow, *Archit.* a window having a fanlike form with radiating sash bars, used esp. as a fanlight.

fan·wise (fan′wīz′), *adv.* spread out like an open fan: *to hold cards fanwise.* [FAN[1] + -WISE]

fan′ worm′. See **feather-duster worm.**

fan·wort (fan′wûrt′), *n.* any aquatic plant of the genus *Cabomba,* having white flowers and submerged and floating leaves. [FAN[1] + WORT[2]]

FAO, See **Food and Agricultural Organization.**

fa·qir (fə kēr′, fā′kər), *n.* fakir. Also, **fa·quir′.**

far (fär), *adv., adj.,* **far·ther** or **fur·ther, far·thest** or **fur·thest.** —*adv.* **1.** at or to a great distance; a long way off; at or to a remote point: *We sailed far ahead of the fleet.* **2.** to or at a remote or advanced time: *We talked far into the night.* **3.** at or to a great, advanced, or definite point of progress, or degree: *Having come this far, we might as well continue.* **4. as far as,** to the degree or extent that: *It is an excellent piece of work, as far as I can tell.* **5. by far, a.** by a great deal; very much: *too expensive by far.* **b.** plainly; obviously: *This melon is by far the ripest of the lot.* **6. far and away,** by far; undoubtedly: *She is far and away the prettiest girl in the class.* **7. far and wide,** to great lengths; over great distances: *He traveled far and wide in search of his missing son.* Also, **far and near, near and far. 8. far be it from me,** I do not wish or dare (to interrupt, criticize, etc.): *Far be it from me to complain, but it's getting stuffy in here.* **9. far out,** *Slang.* **a.** unconventional; offbeat: *I would say that his sense of humor is far out.* **b.** radical; extreme: *political opinions that are far out.* **c.** recondite or esoteric: *an interest in art that was considered far out.* **10. go far, a.** to attain success: *With so much talent he should go far.* **b.** to have a great effect toward; help: *The new evidence will go far toward proving the defendant's guilt.* **11. how far,** to what distance, extent, or degree: *She didn't know how far they had gone in the mathematics text. How far do you think they can be trusted?* **12. in so far as,** to the extent that: *In so far as one seeks the good, so will he find it. So far as I'm concerned, forget the whole thing.* Also, **insofar as, so far as. 13. so far, a.** up to now: *So far, I've had no reply to my request.* **b.** up to a certain point or extent: *We were able to plan only so far because of various factors beyond our control.* **14. so far so good,** no difficulty up to the present: *The work is difficult, but so far so good.* —*adj.* **15.** being at a great distance; remote in time or place: *a far country; the far future.* **16.** extending to a great distance: *the far frontiers of empire.* **17.** more distant of the two: *the far side.* **18. a far cry from,** greatly different from: *His present large fortune is a far cry from his former poverty.* **19. few and far between.** See **few** (def. 2). [ME *far, fer,* OE *feorr;* c. OHG *ferr,* Icel *fjar,* Goth *fairra;* akin to G *fern* far, L *porro* far off, long ago, forwards, etc.] —**far′ness,** *n.*

far·ad (far′əd, -ad), *n. Elect.* the meter-kilogram-second unit of capacitance, equivalent to one coulomb per volt and equal to the capacitance of a capacitor in which one coulomb is transferred from one of the conductors of the capacitor to the other, per volt of potential difference between the conductors. *Abbr.:* F, f [named after M. FARADAY]

Far·a·day (far′ə dē, -dā′), *n.* **1. Michael,** 1791–1867, English physicist and chemist: discoverer of electromagnetic induction. **2.** a unit of electricity used in electrolysis, equal to 96,500 coulombs. **3.** a walled plain in the fourth quadrant of the face of the moon: about 42 miles in diameter.

Far′aday dark′ space′, *Physics.* the dark region between the negative glow and the positive column in a vacuum tube occurring when the pressure is low. [named after M. FARADAY]

Far′aday effect′, the rotation of the plane of polarization of plane polarized light as the light passes through certain isotropic media in the direction of a strong magnetic field in which the medium is placed. Also called **magnetic rotation.** [after M. FARADAY]

fa·rad·ic (fə rad′ik), *adj. Elect.* of or pertaining to a discontinuous, asymmetric, alternating current from the secondary winding of an induction coil. [< F *faradique.* See FARAD, -IC]

far·a·dise (far′ə dīz′), *v.t.,* **-dised, -dis·ing.** *Chiefly Brit.* faradize. —**far′a·di·sa′tion,** *n.* —**far′a·dis′er,** *n.*

far·a·dism (far′ə diz′əm), *n. Med.* the use of faradic current for therapeutic purposes. [< F *faradisme.* See FARAD, -ISM]

far·a·dize (far′ə dīz′), *v.t.,* **-dized, -diz·ing.** *Med.* to stimulate or treat (muscles or nerves) with induced alternating electric current (distinguished from *galvanize*). Also, *esp. Brit.,* **faradise.** [< F *faradis(er).* See FARAD, -IZE] —**far′a·di·za′tion,** *n.* —**far′a·diz′er,** *n.*

far·ad·me·ter (far′əd mē′tər), *n. Elect.* an instrument for measuring electric capacitance. [FARAD + -METER]

far·and (fär′ənd), *adj. Chiefly Scot.* farrand.

far·an·dole (far′ən dōl′; *Fr.* FA räN dôl′), *n., pl.* **-doles** (-dōlz′; *Fr.* -dôl′). **1.** a lively dance, of Provençal origin, in which all the dancers join hands and execute various figures. **2.** the music for this dance. [< F < Pr *farandoulo* (akin to Sp *farándula* traveling troupe of comedians) < ?]

far·a·way (fär′ə wā′), *adj.* **1.** distant; remote: *faraway lands.* **2.** abstracted or dreamy, as a look. [FAR + AWAY] —**far′a·way′ness,** *n.*

farce (färs), *n., v.,* **farced, farc·ing.** —*n.* **1.** a light, humorous play in which the plot depends upon a skillfully exploited situation rather than upon the development of character. **2.** humor of the type displayed in such works. **3.** foolish show; mockery; a ridiculous sham. **4.** *Cookery.* forcemeat. —*v.t.* **5.** to season (a speech or composition), esp. with witty material. **6.** *Obs.* to stuff; cram. [ME *fars* stuffing < MF *farce* < LL **farsa,* n. use of fem. of *farsus* stuffed, r. L *fartus,* ptp. of *farcīre* to stuff] —**Syn. 3.** burlesque, travesty.

farce·meat (färs′mēt′), *n. Cookery.* forcemeat.

far·cet·ta (fär set′ə), *n. Theat.* a short farce. [FARCE + It *-etta* -ETTE]

far·ceur (FAR sœr′), *n., pl.* **-ceurs** (-sœr′). *French.* **1.** a writer of farces. **2.** an actor who plays in farces. **3.** a joker or wag.

far·ceuse (FAR sœz′), *n., pl.* **-ceus·es** (-sœz′). *French.* an actress who plays in farces; a female *farceur.*

far·ci (fär sē′; *Fr.* FAR sē′), *adj. Cookery.* stuffed. [< F, ptp. of *farcir* to stuff < L *farcīre*]

far·ci·cal (fär′si kəl), *adj.* **1.** pertaining to or of the nature of farce. **2.** resembling farce; ludicrous; absurd. [FARCE + -ICAL] —**far′ci·cal′i·ty, far′ci·cal·ness,** *n.* —**far′ci·cal·ly,** *adv.* —**Syn. 2.** ridiculous, preposterous.

far·cy (fär′sē), *n., pl.* **-cies.** *Vet. Pathol.* a form of the disease glanders chiefly affecting the superficial lymphatics and the skin of horses and mules. [late ME *farsy,* var. of *farsin* < MF *farcin* < LL *farcīmin(um)* glanders]

far′cy bud′, *Vet. Pathol.* an ulcerated swelling, produced in farcy. Also called **far′cy but′ton.**

fard (färd), *Archaic.* —*n.* **1.** facial cosmetics. —*v.t.* **2.** to apply cosmetics to (the face). [< MF; OF *farde* < Gmc; cf. OS *frataha,* OE *frætwe* adornments]

far·del (fär′dᵊl), *n. Archaic.* a bundle; burden. [ME < MF, OF, equiv. to *farde* bundle (< Ar *fardah* load) + *-el* < L *-ella* dim. suffix]

far·del-bound (fär′dᵊl bound′), *adj. Vet. Pathol.* (of ruminants) having the food impacted in the third compartment of the stomach; costive; constipated.

fare (fâr), *n., v.,* **fared, far·ing.** —*n.* **1.** the price of conveyance or passage. **2.** a person or persons who pay to be conveyed in a vehicle; paying passenger. **3.** a person who hires a public vehicle and its driver. **4.** food; diet: *To thrive on good fare.* **5.** something offered to the public, for entertainment, enjoyment, consumption, etc.: *theater fare; literary fare.* **6.** *Archaic.* state of things. —*v.i.* **7.** to eat; dine: *They fared sumptuously.* **8.** to experience good or bad fortune, treatment, etc.; get on: *He fared well in his profession.* **9.** to go; turn out; happen (used impersonally): *It fared ill with him.* **10.** *Archaic.* to go; travel. [ME *fare(n),* OE *faran;* c. G *fahren,* Icel *fara,* Goth *faran*] —**far′er,** *n.* —**Syn. 4.** See **food.**

Far′ East′, a collective term indicating the countries of E Asia, including China, Japan, Korea, and sometimes adjacent areas. —**Far′ East′ern.**

Far′ East′ern Re′gion, former name of **Khabarovsk.**

fare-thee-well (fâr′thē wel′), *n.* **1.** a state of perfection: *The meal was done to a fare-thee-well.* **2.** the maximum effect; fullest measure or extent: *an actress who plays each scene to a fare-thee-well.* Also, **fare-you-well** (fâr′yo͞o wel′), **fare-ye-well** (fâr′yē wel′).

fare·well (fâr′wel′), *interj.* **1.** may you fare well (used by or to one departing, esp. on an extensive trip or for an extensive length of time). —*n.* **2.** an expression of good wishes at parting: *They made their farewells and left.* **3.** leave-taking; departure: *a fond farewell.* **4.** a party given to a person who is about to embark on a long journey, retire, leave an organization, etc. —*adj.* **5.** parting; final: *a farewell performance.* [ME *farwel.* See FARE, WELL[1]]

Fare·well (fâr′wel′), *n.* **Cape,** a cape in S Greenland: most southerly point of Greenland.

Fare′well to Arms′, A, a novel (1929) by Ernest Hemingway.

fare·well-to-spring (fâr′wel tə spring′), *n.* a slender, showy herb, *Godetia amoena,* of western central North America, having satiny, lilac-crimson or reddish-pink flowers and roundish fruit.

Fa′rey se′quence (fâr′ē), *Math.* the increasing sequence of fractions in which numerator and denominator have no common divisor and in which the denominator is less than or equal to a given positive integer *p:* For *p* = 4, the Farey sequence of order 4 is 0/1, 1/4, 1/3, 1/2, 2/3, 3/4, 1/1.

far-famed (fär′fāmd′), *adj.* widely known; famous.

far·fel (fär′fəl), *n., pl.* **-fel.** *Jewish Cookery.* a solid foodstuff in the form of small pellets or crumbs: *matzo farfel; noodle farfel.* [< Yiddish < MHG *varvelen* noodles]

far-fetched (fär′fecht′), *adj.* improbable; not naturally pertinent; being only remotely connected; forced; strained: *He brought in a far-fetched example in an effort to prove his point.* Also, **far′fetched′.** —**far′-fetched′ness, far′fetched′ness,** *n.*

far-flung (fär′flung′), *adj.* **1.** extending over a great distance. **2.** widely disbursed or distributed.

far-forth (fär′fōrth′, -fôrth′), *adv.* to a great distance or degree. [ME *ferforth.* See FAR, FORTH] —**far′-forth′ly,** *adv.*

Far′ from the Mad′ding Crowd′, a novel (1879) by Thomas Hardy.

Far·go (fär′gō), *n.* a city in SE North Dakota. 46,662 (1960).

far-gone (fär′gôn′, -gon′), *adj.* **1.** remote. **2.** approaching the end, as of life, duration, usefulness, etc.: *He was too far-gone to save. The sleeve is too far-gone to mend.*

Far·i·bault (fâr′ə bō′), *n.* a city in SE Minnesota. 16,926 (1960).

fa·ri·na (fə rē′nə), *n.* **1.** flour or meal made from cereal grains and cooked as cereal, used in puddings, soups, etc. **2.** *Chiefly Brit.* starch, esp. potato starch. **3.** *Brit.* pollen. [< L, equiv. to *fār* spelt + *-īna,* fem. of *-īnus* -INE[1]]

far·i·na·ceous (far′ə nā′shəs), *adj.* **1.** consisting or made of flour or meal, as food. **2.** containing or yielding starch, as seeds; starchy. **3.** mealy in appearance or nature. [< L *farīnāceus.* See FARINA, -ACEOUS]

far·i·nose (far′ə nōs′), *adj.* **1.** yielding farina. **2.** resembling farina; farinaceous. **3.** covered with a mealy powder. [< LL *farīnōs(us)* mealy. See FARINA, -OSE[1]] —**far′i·nose′ly,** *adv.*

far·kle·ber·ry (fär′kəl ber′ē, -bə rē), *n., pl.* **-ries.** a shrub or small tree, *Vaccinium (Batodendron) arboreum,* of the southern U.S., bearing a black, many-seeded berry. [*farkle* (< ?) + BERRY]

farl (färl), *n.* a thin, circular cake of flour or oatmeal. Also, **farle.** [contr. of *fardel* (late ME, repr. OE *fēortha dǣl* fourth part)]

Far·ley (fär′lē), *n.* **1. James A(loysius),** 1888–1976, U.S. political leader. **2.** Also, **Fairleigh, Fairley.** a boy's given name.

farm (färm), *n.* **1.** a tract of land, usually with a house, barn, etc., on which crops and often livestock are raised for livelihood. **2.** land or water devoted to the raising of animals, fish, etc.: *a pig farm; an oyster farm.* **3.** the system, method, or act of collecting revenue by letting out a territory in districts. **4.** a country or district let out for the collection of revenue. **5.** a fixed amount accepted from a person in lieu of taxes or the like which he is authorized to collect. **6.** *Eng. Hist.* **a.** the rent or income from leased property. **b.** the condition of being leased at a fixed rent; a lease; possession under lease. **7.** Also called **farm team, farm′ club′.** *Chiefly Baseball.* a team in a minor league that is owned by or affiliated with a team in a major league, for use in training or keeping players until ready or needed. **8.** *Obs.* a fixed yearly amount payable in the form of rent, taxes, or the like. —*v.t.* **9.** to cultivate (land). **10.** to take the proceeds or profits of (a tax, undertaking, etc.) on paying a fixed sum. **11.** to let or lease (taxes, revenues, an enterprise, etc.) to another for a fixed sum or a percentage (often fol. by *out*). **12.** to let or lease the labor or services of (a person) for hire. **13.** to contract for the maintenance of (a person, institution, etc.): *a county that farms its poor.* **14.** *Chiefly Baseball.* to assign (a player) to a farm (usually fol. by *out*). —*v.i.* **15.** to cultivate the soil; operate a farm. [ME *ferme* lease, rented land, rent < OF < VL **ferma,* deriv. of L *firmāre* to make firm, confirm. See FIRM[1]] —**farm′a·ble,** *adj.*

farm′ belt′, 1. an area or region used principally for farming. **2.** (*cap.*) the central states of the midwestern U.S.

farm′ bloc′, *U.S.* a number of members of Congress united to further the interests of agriculture.

Farm′ Bu′reau. See **American Farm Bureau Federation.**

farm·er (fär′mər), *n.* **1.** a person who farms; one who operates a farm or cultivates land. **2.** a person who undertakes some service, as the care of children or the poor, at a fixed price. **3.** a person who undertakes the collection of taxes, duties, etc., paying a fixed sum for the privilege of retaining them. **4.** *Cards.* **a.** a variety of twenty-one played with a 45-card pack, the object being to obtain cards having a total worth of 16. **b.** the dealer in this game. [ME *fermer* < AF, c. OF *fermier* renter. See FARM, -ER[2]] —**farm′er·like′,** *adj.*

Far·mer (fär′mər), *n.* **1. Fannie (Mer·ritt)** (mer′it), 1857–1915, U.S. authority on cooking. **2. James (Leonard),** born 1920, U.S. civil rights leader.

farm′er cheese′, a pressed cheese made from whole milk or partly skimmed milk, similar in texture to dry cottage cheese, and usually cut in rectangular shapes.

farm·er·ette (fär′mə ret′), *n.* *Informal.* a girl or woman working on a farm. [FARMER + -ETTE]

farm·er-gen·er·al (fär′mər jen′ər əl), *n., pl.* **farm·ers-gen·er·al.** (in France, under the old monarchy) a member of a company of capitalists that farmed certain taxes. [trans. of F *fermier-général*] —**far′mer-gen′er·al·ship′,** *n.*

farm′er in the dell′, a game, accompanied by a song with several verses, in which one person, designated as the farmer, occupies the center of a circle of persons and is joined in the circle by other players designated as wife, child, nurse, cat, rat, and cheese, these then leaving the circle in order except for the one designated as cheese, who is left standing alone in the circle at the end.

Farm′er-La′bor par′ty (fär′mər lā′bər), **1.** a political party in Minnesota, founded in 1920 and merged with the Democratic party in 1944. **2.** a political party founded in Chicago in 1919 and dissolved in 1924.

farm′ers coop′erative, an organization of farmers for marketing their products or buying supplies.

Far′mer's reduc′er (fär′mərz), *Photog.* a solution of ferricyanide and hypo for reducing density and increasing contrast in a negative. [named after E. H. *Farmer* (d. 1944), English photographer]

Farm·ers·ville (fär′mərz vil), *n.* a town in central California. 3101 (1960).

Farm·er·ville (fär′mər vil), *n.* a town in N Louisiana. 2727 (1960).

farm·er·y (fär′mə rē), *n., pl.* **-er·ies.** *Chiefly Brit.* the buildings, yards, etc., of a farm. [FARM + -ERY]

farm′ hand′, a person who works on a farm, esp. a hired worker; a hired hand.

farm·house (färm′hous′), *n., pl.* **-hous·es** (-hou′ziz). a house on a farm, esp. the chief dwelling. [FARM + HOUSE]

farm·ing (fär′ming), *n.* **1.** the business of operating a farm. **2.** the practice of letting or leasing taxes, revenue, etc., for collection. [FARM + -ING[1]]

Farm·ing·dale (fär′ming dāl′), *n.* a town on W Long Island, in SE New York. 6128 (1960).

Farm·ing·ton (fär′ming tən), *n.* **1.** a city in NW New Mexico. 23,786 (1960). **2.** a town in SE Michigan. 6881 (1960). **3.** a town in E Missouri. 5618 (1960). **4.** a town in central Illinois. 2831 (1960). **5.** a town in central Maine. 2749 (1960).

farm·land (färm′land′), *n.* land under cultivation or capable of being cultivated: *to protect valuable farmland from erosion.* [FARM + LAND]

farm·stead (färm′sted′), *n.* a farm together with its buildings. [FARM + STEAD]

farm′ team′, *Chiefly Baseball.* farm (def. 7).

Farm·ville (färm′vil), *n.* **1.** a town in central Virginia. 4293 (1960). **2.** a town in E North Carolina. 3997 (1960).

farm·yard (färm′yärd′), *n.* a yard or enclosure surrounded by or connected with farm buildings. [FARM + YARD[2]]

Far·ne·se (fär ne′ze), *n.* **A·les·san·dro** (ä′les sän′drô), **Duke of Parma,** 1545–92, Italian general, statesman, and diplomat.

far·ne·sol (fär′ni sōl′, -sôl′, -sol′), *n.* *Chem.* a colorless, unsaturated, liquid alcohol, $C_{15}H_{26}O$, having a slight floral odor, extracted from the flowers of the acacia, cassia oil, or the like: used in perfumery. [< NL *(Acacia) farnes(iana)* Farnese Acacia (named after Cardinal O. *Farnese,* 17th-century Italian) + -OL[1]]

Farns·worth (färnz′wûrth′), *n.* **Phi·lo Taylor** (fī′lō), 1906–71, U.S. physicist and inventor: pioneer in the field of television.

far·o (fâr′ō), *n.* *Cards.* a gambling game in which players place bets on a special board or layout, betting on each series of two cards as they are drawn from a box containing the dealer's or banker's pack. [sp. var. of *Pharaoh,* c. It *Faraone,* F *Pharaon,* name given to game. See PHARAOH]

Fa·ro (fä′rŏŏ), *n.* a seaport in S Portugal. 22,085 (1950).

Far′oe Is′lands (fâr′ō). See **Faeroe Islands.**

Far·o·ese (fâr′ō ēz′, -ēs′), *n., pl.* **-ese,** *adj.* Faeroese. [FAEROE (ISLANDS) + -ESE]

far-off (fär′ôf′, -of′), *adj.* distant; remote in space or time: *to visit far-off places; to dream of far-off times.* —**far′-off′ness,** *n.*

fa·rouche (fA rōōsh′), *adj.* *French.* **1.** fierce. **2.** sullenly unsociable or shy, as from lack of cultivation: *farouche, neglected children.*

Fa·rouk I (fä rōōk′). See **Faruk I.**

far-out (fär′out′), *adj. Slang.* **1.** unconventional; offbeat. **2.** radical; extreme. **3.** recondite or esoteric.

far-point (fär′point′), *n.* *Ophthalm.* the point farthest from the eye at which an object is clearly focused on the retina when accommodation of the eye is completely relaxed. Cf. **near-point.**

Far·quhar (fär′kwər, -kwär, -kər), *n.* **George,** 1678–1707, English playwright, born in Ireland.

Farr (fär), *n.* a boy's given name.

far·rag·i·nous (fə raj′ə nəs), *adj.* heterogeneous; mixed: *a farraginous collection of random ideas.* [< L *farrāgin-* (s. of *farrāgō*) mixed fodder (see FARRAGO) + -OUS]

far·ra·go (fə rä′gō, -rā′-), *n., pl.* **-goes.** a confused mixture; hodgepodge; medley: *a farrago of doubts, fears, hopes, and wishes.* [< L: lit., mixed fodder, mash, equiv. to *farr-* (s. of *fār*) spelt, grits + *-āgō* suffix noting kind or nature]

Far·ra·gut (far′ə gət), *n.* **David Glasgow,** 1801–70, U.S. admiral: won the battles of New Orleans and Mobile Bay for the Union in the U.S. Civil War.

far·rand (far′ənd), *adj.* *Chiefly Scot. and North Eng.* having a specific mien; of a specific appearance, nature, or temperament. Also, **farand.** [ME (north) *farand,* prp. of *faren* to seem. See FARE] —**far′rand·ly,** *adv.*

Far·rar (fə rär′), *n.* **Geraldine** (*Mrs. Lou Tellegen*), 1882–1967, U.S. operatic soprano.

far-reach·ing (fär′rē′ching), *adj.* extending far in influence, effect, etc.: *the far-reaching effect of his speech.* —**far′-reach′ing·ly,** *adv.* —**far′-reach′ing·ness,** *n.*

Far·rell (far′əl), *n.* **1. James T(homas),** 1904–79, U.S. novelist. **2.** Also, **Far′rel.** a boy's given name.

far·ri·er (far′ē ər), *n.* *Chiefly Brit.* **1.** a blacksmith. **2.** a veterinarian; a person who doctors farm animals, esp. horses. [var. of *ferrier* < MF, OF < L *ferrār(ius)* smith (see FERRUM, -ARY); r. late ME *fer(r)our* < AF, c. OF *ferreor* < L **ferrātor*]

far·ri·er·y (far′ē ə rē), *n., pl.* **-er·ies.** the art or the establishment of a farrier. [FARRIER + -RY]

far·row[1] (far′ō), *n.* **1.** a litter of pigs. —*v.t.* **2.** (of swine) to bring forth (young). —*v.i.* **3.** to produce a litter of pigs. [ME *farwen* to give birth to a litter of pigs, deriv. of OE *fearh* pig; c. L *porcus;* akin to G *Ferkel* young pig]

far·row[2] (far′ō), *adj.* (of a cow) not pregnant. [late ME *ferow;* akin to Flem *verwe-* (in *verwekoe* barren cow), OE *fearr* ox]

Fars (färs), *n.* a former province in SW Iran.

far·see·ing (fär′sē′ing), *adj.* **1.** having foresight; sagacious; discerning. **2.** able to see objects distinctly at a great distance: *Hawks are far-seeing birds.* —**far′-see′ing·ness,** *n.* —**far′se′er,** *n.*

Far·si (fär′sē), *n.* an Indo-European, Iranian language, the principal language of Iran, written in the Arabic alphabet; Persian.

far·sight·ed (fär′sī′tid, -sī′tid), *adj.* **1.** seeing objects at a distance more clearly than those near at hand; hypermetropic. **2.** seeing to a great distance. **3.** wise, as in foreseeing future developments: *a farsighted statesman.* —**far′sight′ed·ly,** *adv.* —**far′sight′ed·ness,** *n.*

fart (färt), *Slang* (*vulgar*). —*n.* **1.** a flatus expelled through the anus. —*v.i.* **2.** to expel a flatus through the anus. [ME *ferte(n), farte(n)* (v.), *fert, fart* (n.); c. Gk *pérdein* (v.), *pordḗ* (n.)]

far·ther (fär′thər), *adv., compar. of* **far** *with* **farthest** *as superl.* **1.** at or to a greater distance: *He went farther down the road.* **2.** at or to a more advanced point: *They are going no farther in their studies.* **3.** at or to a greater degree or extent: *The application of the law was extended farther.* **4.** *Nonstandard.* further (def. 3). —*adj., compar. of* **far** *with* **farthest** *as superl.* **5.** more distant or remote: *the farther side of the mountain.* **6.** extending or tending to a greater distance: *He made a still farther trip.* **7.** *Nonstandard.* further (def. 6). [ME *ferther;* orig. var. of FURTHER]

Far′ther In′dia, Indochina.

far·ther·most (fär′thər mōst′, -məst), *adj.* most distant or remote; farthest. [FARTHER + -MOST]

far·thest (fär′thist), *adj., superl. of* **far** *with* **farther** *as compar.* **1.** most distant or remote. **2.** most extended; longest. —*adv., superl. of* **far** *with* **farther** *as compar.* **3.** at or to the greatest distance. **4.** at or to the most advanced point. **5.** at or to the greatest degree or extent. [ME *ferthest;* orig. var. of FURTHEST]

far·thing (fär′thing), *n.* **1.** a former bronze coin of Great Britain, equal to one fourth of a British penny: withdrawn in 1961. **2.** something of very small value: *I don't care a farthing for your opinion.* [ME *ferthing,* OE *fēorthing.* See FOURTH, -ING[1]]

far·thin·gale (fär′thing gāl′), *n.* a hoop skirt or framework for expanding a woman's skirt, worn in the 16th and 17th centuries. [earlier *verdyngale* < MF *verdugale,* alter. of OSp *verdugado,* equiv. to *verdug(o)* tree-shoot, rod (lit., something green) + *-ado* -ADE[1]; so called from rod used to extend skirt]

Farthingale (Elizabethan period)

far′thingale chair′, an English chair of c1600 having no arms, a straight, low back, and a high seat.

Fa·ruk I (fä rōōk′), 1920–65, king of Egypt from 1936 until his abdication in 1952. Also, **Farouk.**

Far′ West′, the area of the U.S west of the Great Plains. —**Far′ West′ern.**

FAS, Foreign Agricultural Service.

F.A.S., *Com.* free alongside ship: without charge to the buyer for goods delivered alongside ship. Also, **f.a.s.**

fas·ces (fas′ēz), *n.* (*usually construed as sing.*) a bundle of rods containing an ax with the blade projecting, borne before Roman magistrates as an emblem of official power. [< L, pl. of *fascis* bundle, pack]

Fasces

fas·ci·a (fash′ē ə), *n., pl.* **fas·ci·ae** (fash′ē ē′). **1.** a band or fillet, as for binding the hair. **2.** *Surg.* a bandage. **3.** *Archit.* **a.** any relatively broad, flat, horizontal surface, as the outer edge of a cornice, a stringcourse, etc. See diag. under **column. b.** any of a number of horizontal bands, usually three in number, each projecting beyond the one below to form the architrave in the Ionic, Corinthian, and Composite orders. **4.** *Anat., Zool.* **a.** a band or sheath of connective tissue investing, supporting, or binding together internal organs or parts of the body. **b.** tissue of this kind. **5.** *Zool., Bot.* a distinctly marked band of color, as on an insect, plant, etc. [< L: band, bandage; akin to FASCES] —**fas′ci·al,** *adj.*

fas·ci·ate (fash′ē āt′), *adj.* **1.** bound with a band, fillet, or bandage. **2.** *Bot.* compressed into a band or bundle, as stems grown together. **3.** *Zool.* **a.** composed of bundles. **b.** bound together in a bundle. **c.** marked with a band or bands. Also, **fas′ci·at′ed.** [FASCI(A) + -ATE[1]] —**fas′ci·ate′ly,** *adv.*

fas·ci·a·tion (fash′ē ā′shən), *n.* **1.** the act of binding up or bandaging. **2.** the process of becoming fasciate. **3.** the resulting state. **4.** an abnormality in a plant, in which a stem enlarges into a flat, ribbonlike shape resembling several stems fused together. [FASCIATE + -ION]

fas·ci·cle (fas′i kəl), *n.* **1.** a small bundle, tight cluster, or the like. **2.** a section of a book being published in installments, usually bound together later. **3.** *Bot.* a close cluster, as of flowers or leaves. **4.** *Anat.* a small bundle of fibers within a nerve or the central nervous system. [late ME < L *fascicul(us),* dim. of *fascis.* See FASCES, -CLE]

fas·cic·u·lar (fə sik′yə lər), *adj.* pertaining to or forming a fascicle; fasciculate. [FASCICUL(US) + -AR[1]]

fas·cic·u·late (fə sik′yə lit, -lāt′), *adj.* arranged in a fascicle or fascicles. Also, **fas·cic′u·lat′ed.** [FASCICUL(US) + -ATE[1]] —**fas·cic·u·late·ly** (fə sik′yə lit lē), *adv.*

fas·cic·u·la·tion (fə sik′yə lā′shən), *n.* a fascicular condition. [FASCICULATE + -ION]

fas·ci·cule (fas′ə kyōōl′), *n.* a fascicle, esp. of a book. [var. of FASCICULUS and FASCICLE; see -CULE]

fas·cic·u·lus (fə sik′yə ləs), *n., pl.* **-li** (-lī′). **1.** a fascicle, as of nerve or muscle fibers. **2.** a fascicle of a book. [< L; see FASCICLE]

fas·ci·nate (fas′ə nāt′), *v.,* **-nat·ed, -nat·ing.** —*v.t.* **1.** to attract and hold spellbound by a unique power, personal charm, unusual nature, or some other special quality: *a vivacity that fascinated the audience.* **2.** to allure; arouse the interest or curiosity of. **3.** to transfix or deprive of the power of resistance, as through terror: *The sight of the snake fascinated the rabbit.* **4.** *Obs.* to bewitch. **5.** *Obs.* to cast under a spell by a look. —*v.i.* **6.** to capture the interest or hold the attention. [< L *fascināt(us)* bewitched (ptp. of *fascināre*), equiv. to *fascin(um)* the evil eye + *-ātus* -ATE[1]] —**fas′ci·nat′ed·ly,** *adv.* —**fas′ci·na′tive,** *adj.*
—**Ant. 1.** repel.

fas·ci·nat·ing (fas′ə nā′ting), *adj.* bewitching; enchanting; charming; captivating: *a fascinating poem;*

fascinating jewelry. [FASCINATE + -ING[2]] **—fas′ci·nat′ing·ly,** *adv.*

fas·ci·na·tion (fas′ə nā′shən), *n.* **1.** the act of fascinating. **2.** the state or an instance of being fascinated: *They watched in fascination.* **3.** a fascinating quality; powerful attraction; charm: *the fascination of foreign travel.* **4.** *Cards.* a form of solitaire. [< L *fascinātiōn-* (s. of *fascinātiō*) a bewitching. See FASCINATE, -ION]

fas·ci·na·tor (fas′ə nā′tər), *n.* **1.** one who or that which fascinates. **2.** a scarf of crochet work, lace, or the like, narrowing toward the ends, worn as a head covering by women. [< L; see FASCINATE, -OR[2]]

fas·cine (fa sēn′, fə-), *n.* *Fort.* a long bundle of sticks bound together, used in building earthworks and batteries and in strengthening ramparts. [< F < L *fascīn(a)* bundle of sticks. See FASCES, -INE[1]]

fas·ci·o·li·a·sis (fə sē′ə lī′ə sis, -sī′-), *n.* *Vet. Pathol.* liver-rot. [< NL *Fasciol(a)* (L: small bandage) + -IASIS]

fas·cism (fash′iz əm), *n.* **1.** (*sometimes cap.*) a governmental system led by a dictator having complete power, forcibly suppressing opposition and criticism, regimenting all industry, commerce, etc., and emphasizing an aggressive nationalism and often racism. **2.** (*sometimes cap.*) the philosophy, principles, or methods of fascism. **3.** (*cap.*) a fascist movement, esp. the one established by Mussolini in Italy from 1922–43. [< It *fascism(o),* equiv. to *fasc(io)* bundle, political group (see FASCES) + *-ismo* -ISM]

fas·cist (fash′ist), *n.* **1.** anyone who believes in or sympathizes with fascism. **2.** (*often cap.*) a member of a fascist movement or party, esp. in Italy. **3.** anyone who is dictatorial. **—***adj.* **4.** Also, **fa·scis·tic** (fə shis′tik). of or like fascism or fascists. [< It *fascist(a),* equiv. to *fasc(io)* (see FASCISM) + *-ista* -IST] **—fa·scis′ti·cal·ly,** *adv.*

Fa·scis·ta (fə shis′tə; *It.* fä shē′stä), *n., pl.* **Fa·scis·ti** (fə shis′tē; *It.* fä shē′stē). a member of the Fascist movement in Italy. [< It: FASCIST]

fash (fash), *n., v.t., v.i.* *Scot.* trouble; worry. [< MF *fascher* < LL **fastīdiāre* to disgust, equiv. to L *fastīdi(um)* disgust + *-āre* inf. suffix]

fash·ion (fash′ən), *n.* **1.** a prevailing custom or style of dress, etiquette, procedure, etc.: *the latest fashion in hats.* **2.** conventional usage in dress, manners, etc., esp. of polite society, or conformity to it: *the dictates of fashion; to be out of fashion.* **3.** fashionable people collectively: *a new dance that pleases the fashion.* **4.** manner; way; mode: *in a warlike fashion.* **5.** the make or form of anything: *He liked the fashion of the simple, sturdy furniture.* **6.** a kind; sort: *All fashions of people make up the world.* **7.** *Obs.* workmanship. **8.** *Obs.* act or process of making. **9. after** or **in a fashion,** in some manner or other; in a makeshift, unskillful, or unsatisfactory way: *He's an artist after a fashion.* **—***v.t.* **10.** to give a particular shape or form to; make: *Primitive man fashioned tools from stones.* **11.** to accommodate; adapt: *doctrines fashioned to the varying hour.* **12.** *Shipbuilding.* to bend (a plate) without preheating it. **13.** *Obs.* to contrive; manage. [ME *facioun* shape, manner < OF *faceon* < L *factiōn-* (s. of *factiō*) a doing, company. See FACTION] **—fash′ion·less,** *adj.*

—Syn. 1. mode; fad, rage, craze. FASHION, STYLE, VOGUE imply popularity or widespread acceptance of manners, customs, dress, etc. FASHION is that which characterizes or distinguishes the habits, manners, dress, etc., of a period or group: *the fashions of the 18th century.* STYLE is sometimes the equivalent of FASHION, but also denotes conformance to a prevalent standard: *to be in style; a chair in the Queen Anne style.* VOGUE suggests the temporary popularity of certain fashions: *this year's vogue in popular music.* **5.** shape, cut, pattern, figure. **10.** frame, construct, mold. **11.** suit, fit.

fash·ion·a·ble (fash′ə nə bəl), *adj.* **1.** observant of or conforming to the fashion: *a fashionable young woman.* **2.** of, characteristic of, or patronized by the world of fashion: *a fashionable shop.* **—***n.* **3.** a fashionable person: *a chic new place catering to the young fashionables.* [FASHION + -ABLE] **—fash′ion·a·ble·ness, fash′ion·a·bil′i·ty,** *n.* **—fash′ion·a·bly,** *adv.*

fash·ion·er (fash′ə nər), *n.* **1.** a person who fashions, forms, or gives shape to anything. **2.** *Obs.* a tailor or modiste. [FASHION + -ER[1]]

fash·ion·mon·ger (fash′ən mung′gər, -mong′-), *n.* a person who studies, follows, and helps popularize the current fashion. [FASHION + MONGER]

fash′ion plate′, **1.** a picture showing the prevailing or new fashion in clothes. **2.** a person who consistently wears the latest style in dress.

fash′ion plate′ stem′, *Shipbuilding.* a stem built up of plates bent to shape without preheating and reinforced with occasional horizontal plates. Also called **platted stem, soft nose stem.**

Fa·sho·da (fə shō′də), *n.* a village in the SE Sudan, on the White Nile: conflict of British and French colonial interests 1898 **(Fasho′da In′cident).** Modern name, **Kodok.**

fast[1] (fast, fäst), *adj.* **1.** moving or able to move, operate, function, or take effect quickly; quick; swift; rapid: *a fast horse; a fast pain reliever; a fast thinker.* **2.** done in comparatively little time; taking a comparatively short time: *a fast race; fast work.* **3.** (of time) **a.** indicating a time in advance of the correct time, as of a clock. **b.** noting or according to daylight saving time. **4.** adapted to, allowing, productive of, or imparting rapid movement: *a hull with fast lines; one of the fastest pitchers in baseball.* **5.** characterized by unrestrained conduct or lack of moral conventions, esp. in sexual relations; dissipated; wild: *They consider her fast, if not downright promiscuous.* **6.** characterized by extreme energy or activity, esp. in the pursuit of pleasure: *leading a fast life with the bohemian crowd.* **7.** resistant: *acid-fast.* **8.** firmly fixed in place; not easily moved; securely attached. **9.** held or caught firmly, so as to be unable to escape or be extricated: *an animal fast in a trap.* **10.** firmly tied, as a knot. **11.** closed and made secure, as a door, gate, shutter, etc. **12.** such as to hold securely: *to lay fast hold on a thing.* **13.** firm in adherence; loyal; devoted: *fast friends.* **14.** permanent, lasting, or unchangeable: *a fast color; a hard and fast rule.* **15.** deep or sound, as sleep. **16.** *Photog.* **a.** (of a lens) able to transmit a relatively large amount of light in a relatively short time. **b.** (of a film) requiring a relatively short exposure time to attain a given density. **17.** *Horse Racing.* **a.** (of a track condition) completely dry. **b.** (of a track surface) very hard. **18. pull a fast one,** *Slang.* to play an unfair trick; practice deceit: *He tried to pull a fast one on us, but we outsmarted him.* **—***adv.* **19.** tightly; firmly: *to hold fast.* **20.** soundly: *fast asleep.* **21.** quickly, swiftly, or rapidly. **22.** in quick succession: *Events followed fast upon one another to the crisis.* **23.** in a wild or dissipated way. **24.** ahead of the correct or announced time. **25.** *Archaic.* close; near: *fast by.* **26. play fast and loose.** See **play** (def. 62). **—***n.* **27.** a fastening for a door, window, or the like. [ME; OE *fæst;* c. D *vast,* Icel *fastr* firm, G *fest;* akin to FAST[2]]

—Syn. 1, 2. fleet, speedy. See **quick. 6.** dissipated, dissolute, profligate, immoral; wild, prodigal. **8.** secure, tight, immovable, firm. **9.** inextricable. **13.** faithful, steadfast. **14.** enduring. **15.** profound. **19.** securely, fixedly, tenaciously. **23.** recklessly, wildly, prodigally. **—Ant. 1, 2.** slow. **6.** restrained. **8.** loose.

fast[2] (fast, fäst), *v.i.* **1.** to abstain from all food. **2.** to eat only sparingly or of certain kinds of food, esp. as a religious observance. **—***n.* **3.** an abstinence from food, or a limiting of one's food, esp. when voluntary and as a religious observance; fasting. **4.** a day or period of fasting. [ME *faste(n),* OE *fæstan;* c. G *fasten,* Goth *fastan,* Icel *fasta*]

fast[3] (fast, fäst), *n.* a chain or rope for mooring a vessel. [ME *fest* < Scand; cf. Icel *festr* mooring rope; akin to FAST[1]]

Fast (fast, fäst), *n.* **Howard (Melvin),** born 1914, U.S. novelist.

fast·back (fast′bak′, fäst′-), *n.* **1.** a form of back for an automobile body consisting of a single, unbroken convex curve from the top to the level of the rear bumper. **2.** a car having such a back. [FAST[1] + BACK[1]]

fast′ break′, **1.** *Basketball.* a play or method of play that brings the ball from one end of the court to the other quickly, usually by one or two quick passes in an attempt by the offensive team to score before the defensive team can get into position. **2.** a fast start, as in a race.

fast-break·ing (fast′brā′king, fäst′-), *adj.* (of a news story) occurring suddenly as a series of events in rapid succession.

fast′ day′, a day on which fasting is observed, esp. such a day appointed by some ecclesiastical or civil authority: *Good Friday is a fast day for Roman Catholics.* [ME]

fas·ten (fas′ən, fä′sən), *v.t.* **1.** to attach firmly or securely in place; fix securely to something else. **2.** to make secure, as an article of dress with buttons, clasps, etc., or a door with a lock, bolt, etc. **3.** to enclose securely, as a person or an animal (usually fol. by *in*): *to fasten a monkey in a cage.* **4.** to attach by any connecting agency: *to fasten a nickname on someone.* **5.** to direct (the eyes, thoughts, etc.) intently: *to fasten one's eyes on a speaker.* **—***v.i.* **6.** to become fast, fixed, or firm. **7.** to close firmly or securely; lock: *This clasp won't fasten.* **8.** to take a firm hold; seize (usually fol. by *on* or *upon*): *to fasten on an idea.* **9.** to focus attention; concentrate (usually fol. by *on* or *upon*): *His gaze fastened on the jewels.* [ME *fasten(en),* OE *fæstnian;* c. Icel *fastna* to betroth; akin to FAST[1]]

—Syn. 2. attach, connect, link, hook, clasp, clinch, rivet, clamp, bind, tie, tether. **—Ant. 1, 2.** loosen, loose.

fas·ten·er (fas′ə nər, fä′sə-), *n.* **1.** any of various devices for fastening. **2.** any of various devices, as a snap, hook and eye, etc., for holding together two objects or parts sometimes required to be separate, as two edges or flaps of a piece of clothing. **3.** a workman who fastens things together. [FASTEN + -ER[1]]

fas·ten·ing (fas′ə ning, fä′sə-), *n.* something that fastens, as a lock or clasp. [ME; see FASTEN, -ING[1]]

fast′ freight′ line′, *Railroads.* a route over which shipments are hauled in turn by two or more carriers operating on coordinated schedules.

fast′ groove′, the spiral groove at the end of a disk recording, cut at a greater pitch than the groove of the sound track, through which the needle rides after the end of the sound track. Also called **fast spiral.**

fas·tid·i·ous (fa stid′ē əs), *adj.* **1.** hard to please; excessively critical or demanding: *a fastidious taste in literature.* **2.** requiring or characterized by excessive care or delicacy. [< L *fastīdiōs(us)* squeamish, equiv. to *fastīdi(um)* disgust (*fast(us)* disdain + *-tīdium* for *taedium* TEDIUM) + *-ōsus* -OUS] **—fas·tid′i·ous·ly,** *adv.* **—fas·tid′i·ous·ness,** *n.*

—Syn. 1. See **particular.**

fas·tig·i·ate (fa stij′ē it, -āt′), *adj.* **1.** rising to a pointed top. **2.** *Zool.* joined together in a tapering adhering group. **3.** *Bot.* **a.** erect and parallel, as branches. **b.** having such branches. Also, **fas·tig′i·at′ed.** [FASTIGI(UM) + -ATE[1]]

fas·tig·i·um (fa stij′ē əm), *n., pl.* **-i·ums, -i·a** (-ē ə). *Med.* the highest point of a fever or disease; the period of greatest development of an infection. [< L]

fast-mov·ing (fast′mōō′ving, fäst′-), *adj.* **1.** moving or capable of moving at high speed. **2.** (of a novel, play, or the like) having sustained action and interest with events following one another rapidly.

fast·ness (fast′nis, fäst′-), *n.* **1.** a secure or fortified place; stronghold: *a mountain fastness.* **2.** the state of being fixed or firm: *the fastness of democratic institutions.* **3.** the state of being rapid. [ME; OE *fæstnes.* See FAST[1], -NESS]

Fast′ of Es′ther, *Judaism.* See **Taanith Esther.**

Fast′ of Ged·a·li′ah (ged′ə lī′ə, gə dal′yə), *Judaism.* See **Tzom Gedaliah.**

fast′ one′, *Informal.* **1.** a shrewd action, esp. when unscrupulous or dishonest; an unfair trick, deceitful practice, dishonest dealing, etc. **2.** a very funny joke, esp. a lewd one.

fast′ spi′ral. See **fast groove.**

fast-talk (fast′tôk′, fäst′-), *v.t.* *Informal.* to persuade with facile argument, usually with the intention to deceive or to overwhelm rational objections: *The salesman tried to fast-talk me into buying a suit I didn't want.*

fas·tu·ous (fas′chōō əs), *adj.* **1.** haughty; arrogant. **2.** showy; ostentatious. [< L *fastuōs(us),* equiv. to *fastu(s)* haughtiness, arrogance + *-ōsus* -OUS] **—fas′tu·ous·ly,** *adv.*

fast′ work′er, *Informal.* **1.** a person who is quick and shrewd in gaining personal advantage: *A fast worker, he soon knew everyone who had any pull.* **2.** a person who charms or fast-talks members of the opposite sex easily.

fat (fat), *adj.,* **fat·ter, fat·test,** *n., v.,* **fat·ted, fat·ting.** **—***adj.* **1.** having too much flabby tissue; chubby; corpulent; obese: *a fat woman.* **2.** plump; well-fed: *a good, fat chicken.* **3.** consisting of or containing fat; greasy; oily: *fat gravy; fat meat.* **4.** abounding in a particular element: *Fat pine is rich in resin.* **5.** (of paint) having more oil than pigment. Cf. **lean** (def. 4). **6.** (of coal) highly bituminous; rich in volatile hydrocarbons. **7.** *Ceram.* long (def. 16). **8.** fertile, as land: *Everything grows in this fat soil.* **9.** profitable, as an office: *a fat job on the city commission.* **10.** affording good opportunities, esp. for gain: *a fat business contract.* **11.** wealthy; prosperous; rich: *He grew fat on dishonest profits.* **12.** thick; big, broad, or extended: *a fat sheaf of bills.* **13.** plentiful: *a fat supply of food.* **14.** plentifully supplied; abundant: *a fat larder; a fat feast.* **15.** dull; stupid: *fat clumsiness of manner.* **16. a fat chance,** *Slang.* a very slight chance: *A fat chance he has of winning the title!* **17. a fat lot,** *Slang.* little or not at all: *A fat lot they care about anyone else's troubles!* **—***n.* **18.** any of several white or yellowish greasy substances that form the chief part of adipose tissue of animals and also occur in plants. When pure, fats are colorless, odorless, and tasteless. They are either solid or liquid esters of glycerol with fatty acids and are therefore composed of carbon, hydrogen, and oxygen. Fats are insoluble in water or cold alcohol, but soluble in ether, chloroform, or benzene: used in the manufacture of soap, paints, and other protective coatings, and in cooking. **19.** animal tissue containing much of this substance: *to have rolls of fat around one's waist.* **20.** the richest or best part of anything. **21.** the condition of being obese; corpulence: *In his later years, he inclined to fat.* **22.** especially profitable or advantageous work. **23.** superfluity; an overabundance or excess. **24.** action or lines in a dramatic part which permit an actor to display his abilities. **25.** Also, **phat.** Also called **lift.** *Typesetting.* matter that can be composed easily and profitably, esp. from standing type, illustrations, or the like: *fat work.* Cf. **lean**[2] (def. 6). **26. chew the fat.** See **chew** (def. 9). **27. the fat is in the fire, a.** an irrevocable action or chain of events has been started: *Now that they have been given an ultimatum the fat is in the fire.* **b.** the decision, whether good or bad, has been made. **c.** the crisis is imminent. **28. the fat of the land,** the best or richest of anything obtainable: *to live on the fat of the land.* **—***v.t., v.i.* **29.** to make or become fat. [ME; OE *fǣtt,* orig. ptp. of *fǣtan* to cram, load, adorn; c. Goth *fētjan* to adorn; akin to VAT] **—fat′less,** *adj.* **—fat′like′,** *adj.*

—Syn. 1. portly, adipose, pudgy. See **stout. 3.** unctuous, fatty. **8.** rich, fruitful, productive. **9.** lucrative, remunerative. **13.** copious, abundant. **15.** sluggish. **—Ant. 1.** thin. **3.** lean. **8.** sterile. **15.** clever.

fa·tal (fāt′əl), *adj.* **1.** causing or capable of causing death: *a fatal accident; a fatal dose of poison.* **2.** causing destruction, misfortune, ruin, or failure: *The withdrawal of funds was fatal to the project.* **3.** decisively important; fateful: *The fatal day finally arrived.* **4.** influencing or concerned with fate: *The fatal sisters spun their thread.* **5.** proceeding from or decreed by fate; inevitable: *a fatal series of events.* **6.** *Obs.* doomed. **7.** *Obs.* prophetic. [late ME < L *fātāl(is)* of fate. See FATE, -AL[1]] **—fa′tal·ness,** *n.*

—Syn. 1. FATAL, DEADLY, LETHAL, MORTAL apply to something which has caused or is capable of causing death. FATAL may refer to either the future or the past; in either case, it emphasizes inevitability and the inescapable—the disastrous, whether death or dire misfortune: *The accident was fatal. Such a mistake would be fatal.* DEADLY looks to the future, and suggests that which is likely to cause death (though not inevitably so): *a deadly poison, disease.* Like DEADLY, LETHAL looks to the future but, like many other words of Latin origin, suggests a more technical usage: *a lethal dose; a gas that is lethal.* MORTAL looks to the past and refers to death which has actually occurred: *He received a mortal wound. The disease proved to be mortal.* **5.** predestined, foreordained. **—Ant. 1.** lifegiving.

fa·tal·ism (fāt′əliz′əm), *n.* **1.** *Philos.* the doctrine that all events are subject to fate or inevitable predetermination. **2.** the acceptance of all things and events as inevitable; submission to fate: *Her fatalism helped her to face death with stoic calm.* [FATAL + -ISM] **—fa′tal·ist,** *n.* **—fa′tal·is′tic,** *adj.* **—fa′tal·is′ti·cal·ly,** *adv.*

fa·tal·i·ty (fā tal′i tē, fə-), *n., pl.* **-ties. 1.** a disaster resulting in death. **2.** a death resulting from such an occurrence: *a rise in highway fatalities.* **3.** the quality of causing death or disaster; deadliness; a fatal influence. **4.** a calamity, misfortune, or failure. **5.** predetermined liability to disaster, misfortune, etc.: *a fatality for saying the wrong thing.* **6.** the quality of being predetermined by or subject to fate: *There is a fatality in human affairs that leads to destruction.* **7.** the fate or destiny of a person or thing: *Death is the ultimate fatality of all men.* **8.** a fixed, unalterably predetermined course of things: *to resign oneself to the fatality of life.* [< LL *fātālitās.* See FATAL, -ITY]

fa·tal·ly (fāt′əlē), *adv.* **1.** in a manner leading to death or disaster: *The ships collided fatally.* **2.** by a decree of fate or destiny; by inevitable predetermination. [late ME; see FATAL, -LY]

Fa·ta Mor·ga·na (*It.* fä′tä môr gä′nä), **1.** a mirage, esp. one of the kind seen in the Strait of Messina. **2.** See **Morgan le Fay.** [< It, trans. of MORGAN LE FAY]

fat·back (fat′bak′), *n.* **1.** the fat and fat meat from the upper part of a side of pork, usually cured by salt. **2.** a menhaden. **3.** the bluefish, *Pomatomus saltatrix.* **4.** a mullet. [FAT + BACK[1]]

fat′ cat′, *U.S. Slang.* **1.** a wealthy person from whom large political campaign contributions are expected. **2.** an important, influential, or famous person. **3.** a person who gains certain privileges because of wealth: *Only the fat cats got invitations to the opening performance.*

fat′ cell′, *Anat.* a cell in connective tissue in which fat is stored.

fate (fāt), *n., v.,* **fat·ed, fat·ing.** —*n.* **1.** that which unavoidably befalls one; fortune; lot: *It is always his fate to be left behind.* **2.** divine agency by which the order of things is prescribed: *Fate decreed that they should all die.* **3.** that which is inevitably predetermined; destiny: *Death is man's fate.* **4.** a prophetic declaration of what must be: *The oracle pronounced their fate.* **5.** death, destruction, or ruin. **6. Fates,** *Class. Myth.* the three goddesses of destiny, known to the Greeks as the Moerae and to the Romans as the Parcae. —*v.t.* **7.** to predetermine, as by the decree of fate; destine (used in the passive): *He was fated to be always left behind.* [ME < L *fāt(um)* utterance, oracle, destiny, orig. neut. of *fātus,* ptp. of *fārī* to speak]
—**Syn. 1.** karma, kismet; chance, luck. FATE, DESTINY, DOOM refer to the idea of a fortune, usually adverse, which is predetermined and inescapable. The three words are frequently interchangeable. FATE stresses the irrationality and impersonal character of events: *It was Napoleon's fate to be exiled.* The word is often lightly used, however: *It was my fate to meet him that very afternoon.* DESTINY emphasizes the idea of an unalterable course of events, and is often used of a propitious fortune: *He became a man of destiny. It was his destiny to save his nation.* DOOM esp. applies to the final ending, always unhappy or terrible, brought about by destiny or fate: *He met his doom bravely.* **7.** foreordain, preordain.

fat·ed (fā′tid), *adj.* subject to, guided by, or predetermined by fate; destined or doomed. [FATE + -ED[3]]

fate·ful (fāt′fəl), *adj.* **1.** involving momentous consequences; decisively important: *a fateful meeting between the prime minister and the president.* **2.** fatal, deadly, or disastrous. **3.** controlled by irresistible destiny. **4.** prophetic; ominous. [FATE + -FUL] —**fate′ful·ly,** *adv.* —**fate′ful·ness,** *n.*
—**Syn. 4.** portentous, inauspicious, threatening, unpropitious.

fat-faced (fat′fāst′), *adj.* having a plump or fleshy face.

fath, fathom (def. 1).

fat·head (fat′hed′), *n.* **1.** *Informal.* a stupid person; fool. **2.** sheephead. **3.** See **fathead minnow.** [FAT + HEAD]

fat′head min′now, a North American cyprinid fish, *Pimephales promelas,* having an enlarged, soft head. Also called **fathead.**

fa·ther (fä′thər), *n.* **1.** a male parent. **2.** any male ancestor, esp. the founder of a race, family, or line. **3.** (loosely) a father-in-law, stepfather, or adoptive father. **4.** any man who exercises paternal care over another; a fatherly protector or provider: *a father to the poor.* **5.** a priest. **6.** a title of respect for an old man. **7.** *Chiefly Brit.* the oldest member of a society, profession, etc. Cf. **dean**[1] (def. 3). **8.** one of the leading men in a city, town, etc.: *a scandal involving several of the city fathers.* **9.** a person who has originated or established something: *the father of modern psychology; the founding fathers.* **10.** a precursor, prototype, or early form: *The horseless carriage was the father of the modern automobile.* **11.** (*cap.*) *Theol.* the Supreme Being and Creator; God. **12. the Father,** the first person of the Trinity. **13.** Also called **church father.** *Ch. Hist.* any of the chief early Christian writers, whose works are the main sources for the history, doctrines, and observances of the church in the early ages. **14.** *Eccles.* **a.** (*often cap.*) a title of reverence, as for church dignitaries, officers of monasteries, monks, confessors, and esp. priests. **b.** a person bearing this title. **15. fathers,** *Rom. Hist.* See **conscript fathers.** —*v.t.* **16.** to beget. **17.** to originate; be the author of. **18.** to act as a father toward. **19.** to acknowledge oneself the father of. **20.** to assume as one's own; take the responsibility of. **21.** to charge with the begetting of. [ME *fader,* OE *fæder;* c. G *Vater,* L *pater,* Gk *patḗr,* Skt *pitar,* Ir *athair,* Aram *hayr*] —**fa′ther-like′,** *adj.*

Father, The, a play (1887) by Strindberg.

Fa′ther Christ′mas, *Brit.* See **Santa Claus.**

fa′ther confes′sor, *Eccles.* confessor (def. 2).

fa′ther fig′ure, a man embodying or seeming to embody the qualities of an idealized conception of the male parent, eliciting from others the emotional responses that a child typically has toward his father. Also called **father image.**

fa·ther·hood (fä′thər ho͝od′), *n.* **1.** the state of being a father. **2.** fathers collectively. **3.** the qualities or spirit of a father. [late ME *faderhode;* r. ME *faderheed.* See FATHER, -HOOD]

Fa′ther Hu′go's rose′. See **Hugo rose.**

fa′ther im′age. See **father figure.**

fa·ther-in-law (fä′thər in lô′), *n., pl.* **fa·thers-in-law. 1.** the father of one's husband or wife. **2.** *Brit. Informal.* a stepfather. [ME; see FATHER, IN, LAW[1]]

fa·ther·land (fä′thər land′), *n.* **1.** one's native country. **2.** the land of one's ancestors. [FATHER + LAND]

fa·ther·less (fä′thər lis), *adj.* **1.** without a living father: *a fatherless boy.* **2.** without a known or legally responsible father. [ME *faderles,* OE *fæderlēas.* See FATHER, -LESS]

fa·ther·ly (fä′thər lē), *adj.* **1.** of, like, or befitting a father. **2.** *Archaic.* in the manner of a father. [ME *faderly,* OE *fæderlic.* See FATHER, -LY] —**fa′ther·li·ness,** *n.*
—**Syn. 1.** FATHERLY, PATERNAL refer to the relationship of a male parent to his children. FATHERLY has emotional connotations: it always suggests a kind, protective, tender, or forbearing attitude: *fatherly advice.* PATERNAL may suggest a kindly, more proprietary attitude: *paternal interest;* but it may also be used objectively, as a legal and official term: *his paternal grandmother; paternal estate.*

Fa′thers and Sons′, a novel (1862) by Turgenev. Also called **Fa′thers and Chil′dren.**

Fa′ther's Day′, *U.S.* a day, usually the third Sunday in June, set aside in honor of fathers.

Fa′ther Time′, the personification of time as an old man, usually having a beard and carrying a scythe.

fath·o·gram (fath′ə gram′), *n.* the record made by a sonic depth finder. [FATHO(METER) + -GRAM[1]]

fath·om (fath′əm), *n., pl.* **fath·oms,** (*esp. collectively*) **fath·om,** *v.* —*n.* **1.** a unit of length equal to six feet: used chiefly in nautical and mining measurements. *Abbr.:* fath —*v.t.* **2.** to measure the depth of by means of a sounding line; sound. **3.** to penetrate to the bottom of; understand thoroughly: *to fathom someone's motives.* [ME *fathme,* OE *fæthm* span of outstretched arms; c. G *Faden* six-foot measure, Icel *fathmr;* akin to PATENT] —**fath′om·a·ble,** *adj.* —**fath′om·er,** *n.*

fa·thom·e·ter (fa thom′i tər), *n.* See **sonic depth finder.** [FATHO(M) + -METER]

fath·om·less (fath′əm lis), *adj.* **1.** impossible to measure the depth of; bottomless. **2.** impossible to understand: *fathomless motives.* [FATHOM + -LESS] —**fath′om·less·ly,** *adv.* —**fath′om·less·ness,** *n.*

fa·tid·ic (fā tid′ik, fə-), *adj.* of or pertaining to prophecy; prophetic. Also, **fa·tid′i·cal.** [< L *fātidic(us),* equiv. to *fāti-* (comb. form of *fātum* FATE) + *-dic-* (var. s. of *dīcere* to say) + *-us* adj. suffix] —**fa·tid′i·cal·ly,** *adv.*

fat·i·ga·ble (fat′ə gə bəl), *adj.* easily fatigued or tired. [< L *fatīgābil(is),* equiv. to *fatīgā(re)* (to) tire + *-bilis* -BLE] —**fat′i·ga·ble·ness, fat′i·ga·bil′i·ty,** *n.*

fat·i·gate (fat′i gāt′), *adj., v.,* **-gat·ed, -gat·ing.** *Obs.* —*adj.* **1.** fatigued; tired. —*v.t.* **2.** to tire; fatigue. [< L *fatīgāt(us)* tired, wearied (ptp. of *fatīgāre*). See FATIGUE, -ATE[1]] —**fat′i·ga′tion,** *n.*

fa·tigue (fə tēg′), *n., v.,* **-tigued, -ti·guing.** —*n.* **1.** weariness from bodily or mental exertion. **2.** a cause of weariness; labor; exertion: *the fatigue of driving for many hours.* **3.** *Physiol.* temporary diminution of the irritability or functioning of organs, tissues, or cells after excessive exertion or stimulation. **4.** *Mech.* the weakening or breakdown of material subjected to stress, esp. a repeated series of stresses. **5.** Also called **fatigue′ duty′.** *Mil.* **a.** labor of a generally nonmilitary kind done by soldiers, such as cleaning up an area, digging drainage ditches, or raking up leaves. **b.** the state of being engaged in such labor: *on fatigue.* **6. fatigues,** *Mil.* See **fatigue clothes.** —*v.t.* **7.** to weary with bodily or mental exertion; exhaust the strength of: *Endless chatter fatigues me.* [< F *fatigue* (n.), *fatiguer* (v.), < L *fatīgāre* to tire] —**fa·tigue′less,** *adj.*
—**Syn. 7.** tire, debilitate, enervate.

fatigue′ clothes′, a soldier's uniform for fatigue duty. Also called **fatigues.**

fa·tigued (fə tēgd′), *adj.* tired; wearied. [FATIGUE + -ED[2]]
—**Syn.** See **tired**[1].

fatigue′ life′, the number of applications of a given stress to which a sample of metal can be subjected before failing.

fatigue′ lim′it, the maximum stress to which a material can be subjected without failing.

fatigue′ par′ty, a group of soldiers on fatigue.

fatigue′ ra′tio, the ratio between the fatigue limit and the tensile strength of a material. Also called **endurance ratio.**

Fa·ti·ha (fä′tē hä′), *n.* *Islam.* the first chapter of the Koran, recited at the beginning of every rak'ah. [< Ar *fātiḥah* exordium]

Fá·ti·ma (fä′ti mə), *n.* a village in central Portugal, N of Lisbon: Roman Catholic shrine.

Fat·i·ma (fat′i mə, fä′tē mä′), *n.* **1.** A.D. 606?–632, daughter of Muhammad. **2.** the seventh and last wife of Bluebeard, popularly a symbol for feminine curiosity. **3.** a girl's given name.

Fat·i·mid (fat′ə mid), *n.* **1.** any caliph of the North African dynasty, 909–1171, claiming descent from Fatima and Ali. **2.** any descendant of Fatima and Ali. Also, **Fat·i·mite** (fat′ə mīt′).

fat·ling (fat′ling), *n.* a young animal, as a calf or a lamb, fattened for slaughter. [FAT + -LING[1]]

fat·ly (fat′lē), *adv.* **1.** in the manner of a fat person: *to walk fatly.* **2.** clumsily, heavily, or ponderously. **3.** richly: *a fatly endowed foundation.* [FAT + -LY]

Fat·ma (fat′mə, fät′mä), *n.* a girl's given name, form of **Fatima.**

fat·ness (fat′nis), *n.* **1.** the state or condition of being fat; corpulence. **2.** richness; fertility: *the fatness of the land.* [ME *fatnesse,* OE *fætnes.* See FAT, -NESS]

fats (fats), *n.* **1.** (*cap.*) (*construed as sing.*) *Informal.* (used as an epithet for a fat boy or man): *Yes, Fats is coming this evening.* **2.** (*construed as pl.*) cattle fattened and ready for market. [pl. of FAT]

Fat·shan (fät′shän′), *n.* Nanhai.

fat·so (fat′sō), *n., pl.* **-sos, -soes.** a fat person (often used as an abusive or facetious term of address). [? alter. of phrase *so fat*]

fat-sol·u·ble (fat′sol′yə bəl), *adj.* *Chem.* soluble in oils or fats.

fat·ten (fat′ən), *v.t.* **1.** to make fat. **2.** to feed for slaughter. **3.** to enrich: *to fatten the soil; to fatten one's pocketbook.* **4.** *Cards.* **a.** *Poker.* to increase the number of chips in (a pot). **b.** *Pinochle.* to play a card that scores high on (a trick) expected to be taken by a partner. —*v.i.* **5.** to grow fat. [FAT + -EN[1]] —**fat′ten·a·ble,** *adj.* —**fat′ten·er,** *n.*

fat·ti ma·schi·i, pa·ro·le fe·mi·ne (fät′tē mä′skē ē′ pä rô′le fe′mē ne), *Italian.* deeds (are) manly, words womanish: a motto of Maryland.

fat·tish (fat′ish), *adj.* somewhat fat. [ME; see FAT, -ISH[1]] —**fat′tish·ness,** *n.*

fat·ty (fat′ē), *adj.,* **-ti·er, -ti·est. 1.** consisting of, containing, or resembling fat: *fatty tissue.* **2.** *Pathol.* characterized by overproduction or excessive accumulation of fat. [ME; see FAT, -Y[1]] —**fat′ti·ly,** *adv.* —**fat′ti·ness,** *n.*

fat′ty ac′id, *Chem.* any of a class of aliphatic acids, esp. one such as palmitic, stearic, oleic, or the like, present as glycerides in animal and vegetable fats and oils.

fat′ty degenera′tion, *Pathol.* deterioration of the cells of the body, accompanied by the formation of fat globules within the diseased cells.

fat′ty oil′. See **fixed oil.**

fat′ty tu′mor, *Pathol.* lipoma.

fa·tu·i·tous (fə to͞o′i təs, -tyo͞o′-), *adj.* foolish; complacently stupid. [FATUIT(Y) + -OUS] —**fa·tu′i·tous·ness,** *n.*

fa·tu·i·ty (fə to͞o′i tē, -tyo͞o′-), *n., pl.* **-ties. 1.** foolishness; complacent stupidity. **2.** something foolish, as a fatuous remark. [< L *fatuitās.* See FATUOUS, -ITY]

fat·u·ous (fach′o͞o əs), *adj.* **1.** foolish or inane, esp. in an unconscious, complacent manner; silly. **2.** unreal; illusory. [< L *fatuus* silly, lit., gaping, akin to *fatiscere* to gape] —**fat′u·ous·ly,** *adv.* —**fat′u·ous·ness,** *n.*
—**Syn. 1.** dense, dull, dimwitted. See **foolish.**

fat·wa (fut′wä), *n.* *Islam.* a theological decision given by a mufti. [< Urdu < Ar]

fat-wit·ted (fat′wit′id), *adj.* stupid; dull-witted.

fau·bourg (fō′bo͝or, -bo͝org; *Fr.* fō bo͞or′), *n., pl.* **-bourgs** (-bo͝orz, -bo͝orgz; *Fr.* -bo͞or′). a part of a city outside, or once outside, the walls; suburb. [late ME *faubourgh* < MF *fau(x)bourg,* folk-etymological var. of *forsbourg* < L *foris* outside + G *Burg* town]

Fau·bus (fô′bəs), *n.* **Or·val** (ôr′vəl), born 1910, U.S. politician.

fau·cal (fô′kəl), *adj.* **1.** pertaining to the fauces or opening of the throat. **2.** *Phonet.* **a.** pharyngeal. **b.** exploded into the epipharynx, as the release of the *t*-sound of *catnip,* the *d*-sound of *madness,* etc. [FAUC(ES) + -AL[1]]

fau·ces (fô′sēz), *n., pl.* **-ces. 1.** *Anat.* the cavity at the back of the mouth, leading into the pharynx. **2.** a vestibule of an ancient Roman house. [late ME < L] —**fau·cial** (fô′shəl), *adj.*

fau·cet (fô′sit), *n.* any device for controlling the flow of liquid from a pipe or the like by opening or closing an orifice; tap; cock. [late ME < MF *fausset* vent-peg, equiv. to *fauss(er)* (to) force in (< LL *falsāre* to falsify) + *-et* -ET]

fau·chard (fō shär′; *Fr.* fō shar′), *n., pl.* **-chards** (-shärz′; *Fr.* -shar′). a shafted weapon having a knifelike blade with a convex cutting edge and a beak on the back for catching the blades of other weapons. [< F; OF *fauchart,* var. of *fausart,* equiv. to *faus* scythe (< L *falx* sickle) + *-art* -ART]

faugh (pf; *spelling pron.* fô), *interj.* (used to express disgust.) Also, **foh.**

fauld (fôld), *n.* *Armor.* a piece below the breastplate, composed of lames and corresponding to the culet in back. See diag. under **armor.** [var. of FOLD[1]]

Faulk·ner (fôk′nər), *n.* **1. William,** 1897–1962, U.S. novelist, short-story writer, and critic: Nobel prize 1949. **2.** a boy's given name. Also, **Falkner.**

fault (fôlt), *n.* **1.** a defect or imperfection; flaw; failing: *a fault in a glass; a fault in one's character.* **2.** an error or mistake: *a fault in addition.* **3.** a misdeed or transgression: *to confess one's fault.* **4.** responsibility for failure or a wrongful act: *It is my fault that we have not finished.* **5.** *Geol., Mining.* a break in the continuity of a body of rock or of a vein, with dislocation along the plane of fracture. **6.** *Elect.* a partial or total local failure in the insulation or continuity of a conductor or in the functioning of an electric system. **7.** *Sports.* (in tennis, handball, etc.) **a.** a ball which when served does not land in the proper section of an opponent's court. **b.** a failure to serve the ball in the proper manner or from within a prescribed area. **8.** *Manège.* (of a horse jumping in a show) any of a number of improper executions in negotiating a jump, as a tick, knockdown, refusal, or run-out. **9.** *Hunting.* a break in the line of scent; a losing of the scent; a check. **10.** *Obs.* lack; want. **11. at fault, a.** Also, **in fault.** open to censure; blameworthy: *to be at fault for a mistake.* **b.** in a dilemma; puzzled: *to be at fault as to where to go.* **c.** (of hounds) unable to find the scent. **12. find fault,** to seek and make known defects or flaws; complain; criticize: *He constantly found fault with her cooking.* **13. to a fault,** to an extreme degree; excessively: *She was generous to a fault.* —*v.i.* **14.** *Geol.* to undergo a fault or faults. **15.** to commit a fault; blunder; err. —*v.t.* **16.** *Geol.* to cause a fault in. **17.** to find fault with, blame, or censure. [ME *faute* < MF < LL **fallita,* n. use of fem. of **fallitus,* r. L *falsus,* ptp. of *fallere* to be wrong]

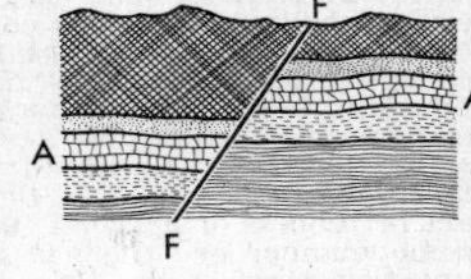

Fault (def. 5)
Section of strata displaced by a fault; A and A′, formerly continuous mass of rock; F, Fault line

—**Syn. 1.** blemish; frailty, shortcoming. FAULT, FAILING, FOIBLE, WEAKNESS, VICE imply shortcomings or imperfections in a person. FAULT is the common word used to refer to any of the average shortcomings of a person; when it is used, condemnation is not necessarily implied: *Of his many faults the greatest is vanity.* FOIBLE, FAILING, WEAKNESS all tend to excuse the person referred to. Of these FOIBLE is the mildest, suggesting a weak point that is slight and often amusing, manifesting itself in eccentricity rather than in wrongdoing: *the foibles of artists.* WEAKNESS suggests that the person in question is unable to control a particular impulse, and gives way to self-indulgence: *a weakness for pretty women.* FAILING is closely akin to FAULT, except that it is particularly applied to humanity at large, suggesting common, often venial, shortcomings: *Procrastination and making excuses are common failings.* VICE (which may also apply to a sin in itself, apart from a person: *the vice of gambling*) is the strongest term, and designates a habit that is truly detrimental or evil.

fault·find·er (fôlt′fīn′dər), *n.* a person who finds fault; one who complains or objects, esp. in a petty way. [FAULT + FINDER]

fault·find·ing (fôlt′fīn′ding), *n.* **1.** the act of pointing out faults, esp. faults of a petty nature; carping: *Even works of genius are not beyond the faultfinding of some critics.* —*adj.* **2.** given to finding fault; disposed to complain or object; captious. [FAULT + FINDING]
—**Syn. 2.** critical, censorious, caviling.

fault·less (fôlt′lis), *adj.* without fault or defect; perfect: *faultless skin; a faultless performance.* [ME *fautles.* See FAULT, -LESS] —**fault′less·ly,** *adv.* —**fault′less·ness,** *n.*

fault′ plane′, *Geol.* the plane of fracture in a fault.

fault·y (fôl′tē), *adj.,* **fault·i·er, fault·i·est. 1.** having faults or defects: *faulty workmanship.* **2.** of the nature of a fault; morally blamable. **3.** *Obs.* culpable; at fault. [ME *fauty.* See FAULT, -Y[1]] —**fault′i·ly,** *adv.* —**fault′i·ness,** *n.*
—**Syn. 1.** defective, imperfect, wrong, incomplete. **2.** blameworthy, reprehensible, censurable. —**Ant. 1.** perfect. **2.** blameless.

faun (fôn), *n.* *Class. Myth.* one of a class of rural deities represented as men with the ears, horns, tail, and later also the hind legs of a goat. [ME, back formation from *Faunes* (pl.) < L *Faunī*. See FAUNUS] —**faun′like′**, *adj.*

fau·na (fô′nə), *n., pl.* **-nas, -nae** (-nē). **1.** the animals of a given region or period considered as a whole. **2.** a treatise on the animals of a given region or period. **3.** (*cap.*) *Rom. Religion.* See **Bona Dea.** [< NL, special use of L *Fauna*, name of sister of FAUNUS] —**fau′nal,** *adj.* —**fau′nal·ly,** *adv.*

faun·tle·roy (fônt′lə roi′, fänt′-), *adj.* noting or pertaining to a suit of children's clothing composed of a short jacket, knee-length pants, frilled shirt, wide collar, and a large loose bow. [after the hero of the novel *Little Lord Fauntleroy* by Frances Hodgson Burnett]

Fau·nus (fô′nəs), *n.* an ancient Italian woodland deity, later identified with Pan, believed by the Romans to be the consort, father, or brother of Bona Dea.

Fau·ré (fō rā′), *n.* **Ga·bri·el Ur·bain** (ga brē el′ o͞or baN′), 1845–1924, French composer, organist, and teacher.

Faust (foust), *n.* **1. Jo·hann** (yō′hän), c1480–c1538, German magician, alchemist, and astrologer. **2.** the chief character of a medieval legend: represented as selling his soul to the devil in exchange for knowledge and power. **3.** (*italics*) a tragedy by Goethe (Part 1, 1808; Part 2, 1832). **4.** (*italics*) an opera (1859) by Charles Gounod.

Faus·ti·an (fou′stē ən), *adj.* **1.** of, pertaining to, or characteristic of Faust: *a Faustian novel.* **2.** characterized by spiritual dissatisfaction; sacrificing spiritual values for power, curiosity, or material gain. [FAUST + -IAN]

Fau·sti·na (fou stē′nə, fô-; *It.* fou stē′nä), *n.* a girl's given name. Also, **Faustine.**

Fau·stine (fou stēn′, fô-; *Fr.* fō stēn′; *Ger.* fou stē′nə), *n.* a girl's given name. Also, **Faustina.**

Fau·sto (fou′stō; *It.* fou′stô), *n.* a boy's given name.

Faus·tu·lus (fô′styə ləs), *n.* *Rom. Legend.* the shepherd or herdsman who raised the abandoned Romulus and Remus.

Faus·tus (fou′stəs, fô′-), *n.* See **Doctor Faustus.**

faute de mieux (fōt də myœ′), *French.* for lack of something better.

fau·teuil (fō′til; *Fr.* fō tœ′yᵊ), *n., pl.* **-teuils** (-tilz; *Fr.* -tœ′yᵊ). **1.** *Fr. Furniture.* an upholstered armchair, esp. one with open sides. Cf. **bergère. 2.** *Brit.* stall[1] (def. 6). [< F; OF *faudestuel* < Gmc; see FALDSTOOL]

Fauve (fōv), *n.* **1.** (*sometimes l.c.*) one of a group of French artists of the early 20th century whose works are characterized chiefly by the use of vivid colors in immediate juxtaposition, contours usually in marked contrast to the color of the area defined, and representational images not described by local color. —*adj.* **2.** (*often l.c.*) of, pertaining to, or derived from the Fauves or the style or use of color characteristic of them. [< F: wild beast, n. use of *fauve* wild, lit., tawny < Gmc; see FALLOW[2]] —**Fauv′ism,** *n.* —**Fauv′ist,** *n.*

faux·bour·don (fō′bər don′; *Fr.* fō bo͞or dôN′), *n.* **1.** *Music.* a 15th-century compositional technique employing three voices, the upper and lower voices progressing an octave or a sixth apart while the middle voice extemporaneously doubles the upper part at a fourth below. **2.** the use of progressions of parallel sixth chords. [Gallicized var. of FABURDEN]

Faux-Mon·nay·eurs, Les (*Fr.* lā fō mô ne yœr′). See **Counterfeiters, The.**

faux pas (fō pä′), *pl.* **faux pas** (fō päz′; *Fr.* fō pä′). a slip or blunder in manners or conduct; a mistake in etiquette or propriety; a social blunder or indiscretion. [< F: false step]
—**Syn.** error; indiscretion, impropriety.

fa·vel·la (fə vel′ə), *n., pl.* **-vel·lae** (-vel′ē). (in certain red algae) a cystocarp covered by a gelatinous envelope. [< NL, equiv. to L *fav(us)* honeycomb + *-ella* dim. suffix]

fa·vel·lid·i·um (fav′ə lid′ē əm), *n., pl.* **-lid·i·a** (-lid′ē ə). (in certain red algae) a cystocarp wholly or partially immersed in a frond. [< NL; see FAVELLA, -IDIUM]

fa·ve·o·late (fə vē′ə lāt′), *adj.* honeycombed; alveolate; pitted. [FAVEOL(US) + -ATE[1]]

fa·ve·o·lus (fā vē′ə ləs), *n., pl.* **-li** (-lī′). a small pit or cavity resembling a cell of a honeycomb; alveola. [< NL, equiv. to L *fav(us)* honeycomb + *(alv)eolus* little cavity; see ALVEOLAR]

Fa·vil·la (fə vil′ə), *n.* a girl's given name.

fa·vism (fä′viz əm), *n.* *Pathol.* acute hemolytic anemia caused by ingestion or inhalation of the pollen of the bean *Vicia faba.* [< It *favism(o)*, equiv. to *fav(a)* bean + *-ismo* -ISM]

Fa·vo·la d'Or·fe·o, La (*It.* lä fä′vô lä dôr fe′ô), an opera (1607) by Claudio Monteverdi.

Fa·vo·ni·a (fə vō′nē ə), *n.* a girl's given name.

fa·vo·ni·an (fə vō′nē ən), *adj.* **1.** of or pertaining to the west wind. **2.** mild, favorable, or propitious. [< L *Favōniān(us).* See FAVONIUS, -AN]

Fa·vo·ni·us (fə vō′nē əs), *n.* the ancient Roman personification of the west wind. Cf. **Zephyrus.**

fa·vor (fā′vər), *n.* **1.** a kind act; something done or granted out of good will, rather than from justice or for remuneration: *to ask a favor.* **2.** friendly regard or disposition; good will: *to win the favor of the king.* **3.** the state of being approved or held in regard: *to be in favor at court; styles that are now out of favor.* **4.** excessive kindness; unfair partiality: *to treat some with favor and neglect others.* **5.** a gift bestowed as a token of good will, kind regard, love, etc., as formerly upon a knight by his lady. **6.** a ribbon, badge, etc., worn in evidence of good will or loyalty, as by an adherent of a political party. **7.** a small gift or decorative or festive item, as a noisemaker, paper hat, etc., often distributed to guests at a party. **8.** a letter, esp. a commercial one. **9.** Usually, **favors.** consent to sexual intimacy. **10. find favor,** to gain the favor of; be liked: *The play found favor with the opening-night audience.* **11. in favor of, a.** on the side of; in support of: *to be in favor of reduced taxation.* **b.** to the advantage of. **c.** (of a check, draft, etc.) payable to: *Make out your checks in favor of the corporation.* **12. in one's favor,** to one's credit; as an advantage: *All the comments were in your favor.* —*v.t.* **13.** to regard with favor: *to favor an enterprise.* **14.** to prefer; treat with partiality: *The father favored his younger son.* **15.** to show favor to; oblige: *The king favored him with an audience.* **16.** to be favorable to; facilitate: *The wind favored their journey.* **17.** to deal with gently: *to favor a lame leg.* **18.** to aid or support: *He favored his party's cause with ample funds.* **19.** *Informal.* to resemble: *to favor one's father.* Also, *esp. Brit.,* **favour.** [ME *favo(u)r* < MF < L *favōr-* (s. of *favor*) goodwill, equiv. to *fav(ēre)* (to) befriend + *-ōr* -OR[2]] —**fa′vor·er,** *n.* —**fa′vor·ing·ly,** *adv.* —**fa′vor·less,** *adj.*
—**Syn. 2.** FAVOR, GOOD WILL imply a kindly regard or friendly disposition shown by an individual or group. FAVOR may be merely an attitude of mind: *to look with favor on a proposal.* GOOD WILL is more active and leads often to outward manifestations of friendly approval: *By frequent applause the audience showed its good will toward the speaker.* **5.** present. **13.** approve, countenance, allow. **14.** encourage, patronize. **18.** help, assist.

fa·vor·a·ble (fā′vər ə bəl), *adj.* **1.** providing aid, advantage, or convenience; advantageous: *a favorable position.* **2.** manifesting favor; inclined to aid or approve: *a favorable report.* **3.** creating or winning favor; pleasing: *to make a favorable impression.* **4.** (of an answer) granting what is desired. **5.** promising well: *The signs are favorable for a new start.* Also, *esp. Brit.,* **favourable.** [ME < MF < L *favōrābil(is).* See FAVOR, -ABLE] —**fa′vor·a·ble·ness,** *n.* —**fa′vor·a·bly,** *adv.*
—**Syn. 1.** helpful, useful, profitable, suitable, comfortable, appropriate; good. **2.** benign, friendly, well-disposed. **5.** propitious, auspicious, benign.

fa·vored (fā′vərd), *adj.* **1.** regarded or treated with preference or partiality: *Her beauty made her the favored child.* **2.** enjoying special advantages: *to be born into the favored classes.* **3.** of specified appearance (usually used in combination): *ill-favored.* Also, *esp. Brit.,* **favoured.** [ME *favo(u)red.* See FAVOR, -ED[2]]

fa·vor·ite (fā′vər it), *n.* **1.** a person or thing regarded with special favor or preference: *That song is an old favorite of mine.* **2.** *Sports.* a competitor considered likely to win. **3.** a person or thing popular with the public. **4.** a person treated with special or undue favor by a king, official, etc.: *favorites at the court.* —*adj.* **5.** regarded with particular favor or preference: *a favorite child.* Also, *esp. Brit.,* **favourite.** [< It *favorit(o),* ptp. of *favorire* to favor. See FAVOR, -ITE[2]]

fa′vorite son′, *U.S. Politics.* (at a national political convention) a candidate nominated for office by delegates from his own State.

fa·vor·it·ism (fā′vər i tiz′əm), *n.* **1.** the favoring of one person or group over others having equal claims: *The parents showed favoritism toward their youngest child.* **2.** the state of being a favorite. Also, *esp. Brit.,* **favouritism.** [FAVORITE + -ISM]

fav·o·site (fav′ə sīt′), *n.* any of numerous corals of the extinct genus *Favosites,* most common during the Silurian and Devonian periods, having polygonal cells with rows of pores in the walls. [back formation from NL *favosītēs,* equiv. to L *fav(us)* honeycomb + *-ōs(us)* -OSE[1] + Gk *-ītēs* -ITE[1]]

fa·vour (fā′vər), *n., v.t.* *Chiefly Brit.* favor. —**fa′vour·er,** *n.* —**fa′vour·ing·ly,** *adv.* —**fa′vour·less,** *adj.*

fa·vour·a·ble (fā′vər ə bəl), *adj.* *Chiefly Brit.* favorable. —**fa′vour·a·ble·ness,** *n.* —**fa′vour·a·bly,** *adv.*

fa·voured (fā′vərd), *adj.* *Chiefly Brit.* favored.

fa·vour·ite (fā′vər it), *n., adj.* *Chiefly Brit.* favorite.

fa·vour·it·ism (fā′vər i tiz′əm), *n.* *Chiefly Brit.* favoritism.

Fa·vrile′ Glass′ (fəv rēl′), *Trademark.* an iridescent art glass, introduced by Tiffany c1890 and used by him for blown vases, flower holders, etc. Also called **Tiffany glass.**

fa·vus (fā′vəs), *n., pl.* **fa·vus·es** for 1, **fa·vi** (fā′vī) for 2. **1.** *Pathol.* a skin disease, esp. of the scalp, characterized by dry incrustations due to the fungus *Achorion schonleinii.* **2.** a hexagonal paving tile or stone. [< NL, special use of L *favus* honeycomb]

Fawkes (fôks), *n.* **Guy,** 1570–1606, English conspirator: leader in the Gunpowder plot 1605.

fawn[1] (fôn), *n.* **1.** a young deer. **2.** a buck or doe of the first year. **3.** a light yellowish-brown color. —*adj.* **4.** light yellowish-brown. —*v.i.* **5.** (of deer) to bring forth young. [ME *fawn, foun* < MF *faon, foun, feon* << VL **fetōn-,* s. of **feto* offspring, var. of L *fētus* FETUS] —**fawn′like′,** *adj.*

fawn[2] (fôn), *v.i.* **1.** to seek notice or favor by servile demeanor: *The courtiers fawned over the king.* **2.** (esp. of dogs) to show fondness by wagging the tail, licking one's hand, etc. [ME *fawne(n),* OE *fagnian,* var. of *fægnian* to rejoice, make glad, deriv. of *fægen* happy; see FAIN] —**fawn′er,** *n.* —**fawn′ing·ly,** *adv.* —**fawn′ing·ness,** *n.*

Fawn of Virginia deer, *Odocoileus virginianus*

Fawn (fôn), *n.* a girl's given name.

fawn′ lil′y, an herb, *Erythronium californicum,* of California, having brown- or white-mottled leaves and cream-white flowers.

fax (faks), *n.* **1.** a method or device for electronically transmitting printed material, drawings, etc., as by telephone, for reproduction at a different place; facsimile. **2.** the material thus transmitted. —*v.t.* **3.** to transmit (material) by this method. [shortening and resp. of FACSIMILE]

fay[1] (fā), *n.* a fairy. [ME *faie, fei* < MF *feie, fee* << L *Fāta* FATE]

fay[2] (fā), *v.t., v.i.* to fit, esp. together closely, as timbers in shipbuilding. [ME *feie(n)* (to) put together, join, OE *fēgan* (akin to *gefōg* joint); c. G *fügen*]

fay[3] (fā), *n.* *Archaic.* faith. [ME *fai, fei* < AF, var. of *feid* FAITH]

fay[4] (fā), *n.* *Slang.* ofay.

Fay (fā), *n.* a girl's given name. Also, **Fae, Faye.**

Fa·yal (fä yäl′), *n.* an island in the Azores, in the N Atlantic. 23,923 (1950); 66 sq. mi.

fay·al·ite (fā′ə līt′, fī ä′līt), *n.* *Mineral.* the iron end member of the olivine group, Fe_2SiO_4: very rare in nature. [named after FAYAL; see -ITE[1]]

Fay·anne (fā an′), *n.* a girl's given name.

Faye (fā), *n.* **1.** Also, **Fae, Fay.** a girl's given name. **2.** a walled plain in the fourth quadrant of the face of the moon: about 26 miles in diameter.

Fay·et·ta (fā et′ə), *n.* a girl's given name. Also, **Fayette.**

Fay·ette (fā et′, fā′et, -it *for 1, 2;* fā et′ *for 3*), *n.* **1.** a town in NW Alabama. 4227 (1960). **2.** a town in central Missouri. 3294 (1960). **3.** Also, **Fayetta.** a girl's given name.

Fay·ette·ville (fā′it vil′), *n.* **1.** a city in S North Carolina. 47,106 (1960). **2.** a city in NW Arkansas. 20,274 (1960). **3.** a town in S Tennessee. 6804 (1960). **4.** a town in central New York. 4311 (1960).

Fay′etteville North′, a town in central North Carolina. 3071 (1960).

Fayme (fām), *n.* a girl's given name.

Fa·yum (fī yo͞om′), *n., adj.* Faiyum.

faze (fāz), *v.t.,* **fazed, faz·ing.** *Informal.* to cause to be disconcerted; daunt: *The worst insults cannot faze him.* [var. of FEEZE]

fa·zen·da (fə zen′də; *Port.* fä zen′dä), *n., pl.* **-das** (-dəz; *Port.* -däs). (in Brazil) a plantation. [< Pg < L *facienda* things to be done; cf. HACIENDA]

f.b., **1.** *Sports.* fullback. **2.** freight bill.

F.B.A., Fellow of the British Academy.

FBI, *U.S. Govt.* Federal Bureau of Investigation: the federal agency charged with investigations for the Attorney General and with safeguarding national security.

FC, foot-candle.

f.c., **1.** *Baseball.* fielder's choice. **2.** *Print.* follow copy.

FCA, Farm Credit Administration.

FCC, *U.S. Govt.* Federal Communications Commission: a board, consisting of seven members, charged with regulating interstate broadcasting and communication by wire, radio, and television.

FCIC, Federal Crop Insurance Corporation.

F clef, *Music.* See **bass clef.**

fcp., foolscap.

fcs., francs.

F.D., **1.** Fidei Defensor. **2.** fire department. **3.** focal distance.

FDA, Food and Drug Administration.

FDIC, See **Federal Deposit Insurance Corporation.**

F-dis·play (ef′di splā′), *n.* *Electronics.* F-scope.

FDR, Franklin Delano Roosevelt.

Fe, *Chem.* iron. [< L *ferrum*]

fe., fecit.

feal (fēl), *adj.* *Archaic.* faithful; loyal. [< MF, OF, var. of *feil* (with change of suffix) < L *fidēl(is)* faithful. See FIDELITY]

Fea·la (fē′lə), *n.* a girl's given name.

fe·al·ty (fē′əl tē), *n., pl.* **-ties. 1.** *Hist.* **a.** fidelity to a lord. **b.** the obligation or the engagement to be faithful to a lord, usually sworn to by a vassal. **2.** fidelity; faithfulness. [< MF *fealte* (see FEAL, -TY[2]); r. ME *fe(a)ute* < MF, earlier *feelte* < L *fidēlitāt-* (s. of *fidēlitās*) FIDELITY]
—**Syn. 2.** loyalty, devotion.

fear (fēr), *n.* **1.** a distressing emotion aroused by impending pain, danger, evil, etc., whether real or imagined; the feeling or condition of being afraid. **2.** a specific instance of such a feeling: *a fear of heights.* **3.** anxiety; solicitude: *a fear for someone's safety.* **4.** reverential awe, esp. toward God. **5.** that which causes a feeling of being afraid; that of which one is afraid: *Cancer is a common fear.* **6. for fear of,** in order to avoid or prevent: *He hesitated to tell her the truth for fear of offending her.* —*v.t.* **7.** to regard with fear; be afraid of. **8.** to have reverential awe of. **9.** *Archaic.* to be afraid (used reflexively). **10.** *Archaic.* to frighten. —*v.i.* **11.** to have fear; be afraid. [ME *fere,* OE *fǣr* sudden attack or danger; c. OS *fār* ambush, D *gevaar,* G *Gefahr* danger, Icel *fār* disaster]
—**Syn. 1.** apprehension, consternation, dismay, terror, fright, panic, horror, trepidation. FEAR, ALARM, DREAD all imply a painful emotion experienced when one is confronted by threatening danger or evil. ALARM implies an agitation of the feelings caused by awakening to imminent danger; it names a feeling of fright or panic: *He started up in alarm.* FEAR and DREAD usually refer more to a condition or state than to an event. FEAR is often applied to an attitude toward something which, when experienced, will cause the sensation of fright: *fear of falling.* DREAD suggests an attitude of anticipating something, usually a particular event, which, when experienced, will be disagreeable rather than frightening: *She lives in dread of losing her money.* The same is often true of FEAR, when used in a negative statement: *She has no fear she'll lose her money.* **3.** concern. **7.** apprehend, dread. —**Ant. 1.** bravery. **3.** indifference.

Fear (fēr), *n.* **1.** a river in SE North Carolina. 202 mi. long. **2. Cape,** a cape at the mouth of this river.

fear·ful (fēr′fəl), *adj.* **1.** causing, or apt to cause, fear: *a fearful apparition.* **2.** feeling fear, dread, apprehension, or solicitude: *fearful for his life; fearful lest he commit suicide.* **3.** full of awe or reverence: *fearful of the Lord.* **4.** showing or caused by fear: *fearful behavior.* **5.** extreme in size, intensity, or badness: *a fearful head cold; fearful poverty.* [ME *ferful.* See FEAR, -FUL] —**fear′ful·ly,** *adv.* —**fear′ful·ness,** *n.*
—**Syn. 2.** afraid, timid, timorous, apprehensive, uneasy, distrustful; solicitous, anxious, concerned, worried.

fear·less (fēr′lis), *adj.* without fear; bold or brave. [ME *fereles.* See FEAR, -LESS] —**fear′less·ly,** *adv.* —**fear′less·ness,** *n.*
—**Syn.** intrepid, dauntless, undaunted. See **brave.**
—**Ant.** cowardly.

fear·nought (fēr′nôt′), *n.* **1.** a stout woolen cloth for overcoats. **2.** an outer garment of this cloth. Also, **fear′naught′.** [FEAR + NOUGHT]

fear·some (fēr′səm), *adj.* **1.** causing fear or awe: *a fearsome noise; a fearsome self-confidence.* **2.** afraid; timid. [FEAR + -SOME[1]] —**fear′some·ly,** *adv.* —**fear′some·ness,** *n.*

fea·sance (fē′zəns), *n.* *Law.* the doing or performing of an act, as of a condition or duty. [< AF *fesa(u)nce,* c. F *faisance,* equiv. to *fais-* (var. s. of *faire* < L *facere* to do) + *-ance* -ANCE]

fea·si·ble (fē′zə bəl), *adj.* **1.** capable of being done, effected, or accomplished: *a feasible plan.* **2.** suitable: *a road feasible for travel.* **3.** probable; likely: *a feasible theory.* [late ME *feseable* (< AF), *faisible* (< MF), equiv. to *fes-, fais-* (var. s. of *faire* < L *facere* to do) + *-ible* -IBLE] —**fea·si·bil·i·ty** (fē′zə bil′i tē), **fea′si·ble·ness,** *n.* —**fea′si·bly,** *adv.*
—**Syn. 1.** workable, practicable. See **possible. 2.** suited, usable. —**Ant. 1.** impracticable.

feast (fēst), *n.* **1.** a periodical celebration or time of celebration, usually of a religious nature, commemorating an event, person, etc.: *Every year, in September, the townspeople have a feast in honor of their patron saint.* **2.** a sumptuous entertainment or meal for many guests: *a wedding feast.* **3.** any rich or abundant meal: *The steak dinner was a feast.* **4.** something highly agreeable: *The Rembrandt exhibition was a feast for the eyes.* —*v.i.* **5.** to have or partake of a feast; eat sumptuously. **6.** to dwell with gratification or delight, as on a picture, a view, etc. —*v.t.* **7.** to provide or entertain with a feast. **8.** to gratify; delight: *to feast one's eyes on the Grand Canyon.* [ME *feste* < OF < L *fēsta*, neut. pl. (taken as fem. sing. n.) of *fēstus* festal, gladsome, equiv. to *fēs-* (akin to FAIR[2]) + *-tus* adj. suffix] —**feast′er,** *n.* —**feast′less,** *adj.*
—**Syn. 2.** FEAST, BANQUET imply large social events, with an abundance of food. A FEAST is a meal with a plenteous supply of food and drink for a large company: *to provide a feast for all company employees.* A BANQUET is an elaborate feast for a formal and ceremonious occasion: *the main speaker at a banquet.*

feast′ day′, a day, esp. a church holiday, for feasting and rejoicing.

feast·ful (fēst′fəl), *adj.* festive; joyful. [ME *festful.* See FEAST, -FUL] —**feast′ful·ly,** *adv.*

Feast′ of Booths′, Sukkoth.

Feast′ of Dedica′tion, Hanukkah. Also called **Feast′ of Lights′.**

Feast′ of Fools′, 1. (in ancient Rome) a special celebration held on February 17th for those people who had not participated with their curia in the Fornacalia. Latin, **Stultorum feriae. 2.** (esp. in France) a mock-reigious celebration in the Middle Ages, held on or about January 1. Also called **Festival of Fools.**

Feast′ of Lan′terns, Bon.

Feast′ of Lots′, Purim.

Feast′ of Or′thodoxy, *Eastern Ch.* a solemn festival held on the first Sunday of Lent (**Orthodoxy Sunday**) commemorating the restoration of the use of icons in the church (A.D. 842) and the triumph over all heresies.

Feast′ of Tab′ernacles, Sukkoth.

Feast′ of Weeks′, Shabuoth.

feast-or-fam·ine (fēst′ər fam′in), *adj.* noting any undertaking, trade, etc., attended by extreme high and low degrees of prosperity or volume of business: *artists who lead a feast-or-famine life.*

feat[1] (fēt), *n.* **1.** a noteworthy or extraordinary act or achievement, usually displaying boldness, skill, etc.: *Arranging the treaty was a diplomatic feat.* **2.** *Obs.* a specialized skill; profession. [ME *fet* (< AF), *fait* (< MF) < L *fact(ūm)* FACT]
—**Syn. 1.** accomplishment. See **achievement.**

feat[2] (fēt), *adj.* *Brit. Dial.* **1.** apt; skillful; dexterous. **2.** suitable. **3.** neat. [late ME < MF *fait* made (to fit) < L *fact(us)*, ptp. of *facere* to make, do]

feath·er (feth′ər), *n.* **1.** one of the horny structures forming the principal covering of birds, consisting typically of a hard, tubular portion attached to the body and tapering into a thinner, stemlike portion bearing a series of slender, barbed processes that interlock to form a flat structure on each side. **2.** condition, as of health, spirits, etc.: *The boss was in good feather till lunch.* **3.** kind; character; species: *two boys of the same feather.* **4.** something like a feather, as a tuft or fringe of hair. **5.** *Carpentry.* **a.** a spline for joining the grooved edges of two boards. **b.** tongue (def. 16). **6.** *Masonry.* See under **plug and feathers. 7.** a featherlike flaw, esp. in a precious stone. **8.** *Archery.* a feather or feathers attached to the nock of an arrow to direct its flight. **9.** something very light, weak, or small: *Your worry is a mere feather.* **10.** *Rowing.* the act of feathering. **11.** *Mach.* See **feather key. 12.** *Archaic.* attire. **13.** *Obs.* plumage. **14. a feather in one's cap,** a praiseworthy accomplishment; distinction; honor: *Being chosen class president is a feather in his cap.* **15. birds of a feather.** See **bird** (def. 8). **16. cut a feather,** *Naut.* (of a vessel) to proceed with speed. **17. in fine** or **high feather,** in good form, humor, or health: *feeling in fine feather.* **18. smooth one's ruffled** or **rumpled feathers,** to regain one's composure; become calm: *After the argument, she retreated to the bedroom to smooth her ruffled feathers.* —*v.t.* **19.** to provide with feathers, as an arrow. **20.** to clothe or cover with or as with feathers. **21.** *Rowing.* to turn (an oar) after a stroke so that the blade becomes nearly horizontal, and hold it thus as it is moved back into position for the next stroke. **22.** *Aeron.* **a.** to change the blade angle of (a propeller) so that the chords of the blades are approximately parallel to the line of flight. **b.** to cause the propeller of (an engine) to rotate in this manner. —*v.i.* **23.** to grow feathers. **24.** to be or become feathery in appearance. **25.** to move like feathers. **26.** *Rowing.* to feather an oar. **27. feather one's nest,** to take advantage of the opportunities to enrich oneself; look after one's own interests: *The mayor had used his term of office to feather his nest.* [ME, OE *fether*; c. D *veder*, G *Feder*, Icel *fjöthr*; akin to Gk *pterón*, Skt *pátram* wing, feather] —**feath′er·less,** *adj.* —**feath′er·less·ness,** *n.* —**feath′er·like′,** *adj.*

Feather
A, Rachis
B, Vane
C, Calamus
D, Down

feath·er·back (feth′ər bak′), *n.* any of several fresh-water fishes of the family *Notopteridae*, found in Asia and western Africa, having a small, feathery dorsal fin and a very long anal fin extending from close behind the head to the tip of the tail. [FEATHER + BACK[1]]

feath′er band′ing, *Furniture.* decorative banding of veneer or inlay having the grain laid diagonally to the grain of the principal surface.

feath′er bed′, a quilt or sack stuffed with feathers and used as a mattress. [ME *fether bed*]

feath·er·bed·ding (feth′ər bed′ing), *n.* **1.** the practice of requiring an employer to hire unnecessary employees or to limit production according to a union rule or safety statute. **2.** an instance of this: *Featherbedding forced the railroads to employ firemen on diesel locomotives.* [FEATHER + BEDDING]

feath·er·bone (feth′ər bōn′), *n.* a substitute for whalebone, made from the quills of domestic fowls. [FEATHER + BONE[1]]

feath·er·brain (feth′ər brān′), *n.* a foolish or giddy person; scatterbrain. [FEATHER + BRAIN] —**feath′er-brained′,** *adj.*

feath·er·cut (feth′ər kut′), *n.* a woman's hair style in which the hair is cut in short and uneven lengths and formed into small curls with featherlike tips. [FEATHER + CUT]

feath′er dust′er, a brush for dusting that is composed of a bundle of large feathers attached to a short handle.

feath′er-dust·er worm′ (feth′ər dus′tər), any of numerous, tube-dwelling polychaete worms of the families *Sabellidae* and *Serpulidae*, having a crown of feathery tentacles used in feeding and respiration. Also called **fan worm, feather worm.**

feath·ered (feth′ərd), *adj.* **1.** clothed, covered, or provided with feathers, as a bird, arrow, etc. **2.** winged; swift: *feathered feet.* **3.** (of a veneer) cut to show a figure resembling a plume. [FEATHER + -ED[3]]

feath·er·edge (feth′ər ej′), *n.* **1.** an edge which thins out like a feather. **2.** the thinner edge of a wedge-shaped board or plank. **3.** a tool for giving a smooth, even finish to plasterwork at corners. **4.** (in silver work) a band of closely-spaced oblique lines engraved along an edge of a piece. [FEATHER + EDGE] —**feath′er·edged′,** *adj.*

feath·er-fleece (feth′ər flēs′), *n.* a bulbous, perennial herb, *Stenanthium gramineum*, of the southeastern U.S., having numerous, greenish-white flowers in pyramidal clusters.

feath·er·foil (feth′ər foil′), *n.* any of several aquatic herbs of the genus *Hottonia*, of Eurasia and North America, having white or whitish flowers. [FEATHER + FOIL[2]]

feath′er gera′nium, an herb, *Chenopodium Botrys*, of Eurasia and Africa, having clusters of inconspicuous flowers and an unpleasant odor. Also called **Jerusalem oak.**

feath′er grass′, any American grass of the genus *Stipa.*

feath·er·head (feth′ər hed′), *n.* **1.** a foolish or giddy person; featherbrain; scatterbrain. **2.** a weak or disorganized mind. [FEATHER + HEAD] —**feath′er-head′ed,** *adj.*

feath·er·ing (feth′ər ing), *n.* *Music.* a very light and delicate use of the violin bow. [FEATHER + -ING[1]]

feath′er joint′, *Joinery.* a joint between two members, as boards butted edge-to-edge, in which a feather or spline is glued into grooves cut in the butting faces.

feath′er key′, *Mach.* a rectangular key connecting the keyways of a shaft and a hub of a gear, pulley, etc., fastened in one keyway and free to slide in the other, so that the hub can drive or be driven by the shaft at various positions along it. Also called **feather, spline.**

feath·er·light (feth′ər līt′), *adj.* extremely light; light as a feather. [FEATHER + LIGHT[2]]

feath′er mer′chant, *Slang.* a person who avoids responsibility and effort; loafer; slacker.

feath′er palm′, any palm having large pinnate or bipinnate leaves, as the date palm or royal palm.

feath′er shot′, *Metall.* fine bean shot.

feath′er star′, a free-swimming crinoid.

feath·er·stitch (feth′ər stich′), *n.* **1.** an embroidery stitch producing work in which a succession of branches extend alternately on each side of a central stem. —*v.t.* **2.** to ornament by featherstitch. [FEATHER + STITCH[1]]

feath′er-tail glid′er (feth′ər tāl′). See **pygmy glider.**

feath′er tract′, pteryla.

feath·er-veined (feth′ər vānd′), *adj.* *Bot.* (of a leaf) having a series of veins branching from each side of the midrib toward the margin, pinnately veined.

feath·er·weight (feth′ər wāt′), *n.* **1.** a boxer or other contestant intermediate in weight between a bantamweight and a lightweight, esp. a professional boxer weighing up to 126 pounds. **2.** an insignificant person or thing: *a great painter among featherweights.* —*adj.* **3.** belonging to the class of featherweights, esp. in boxing: *featherweight contenders.* **4.** trifling; slight. [FEATHER + WEIGHT]

feath′er worm′. See **feather-duster worm.**

feath·er·y (feth′ə rē), *adj.* **1.** clothed or covered with feathers; feathered. **2.** resembling feathers; light; airy; unsubstantial: *feathery clouds; feathery dust.* [FEATHER + -Y[1]] —**feath′er·i·ness,** *n.*

feat·ly (fēt′lē), *adv.* **1.** in a feat manner; fitly. **2.** skillfully; nimbly. **3.** neatly; elegantly. [ME *fetly.* See FEAT[2], -LY] —**feat′li·ness,** *n.*

fea·ture (fē′chər), *n., v.,* **-tured, -tur·ing.** —*n.* **1.** any part of the face, as the nose, chin, etc.: *prominent features.* **2. features,** the face; countenance: *to compose one's features for the photographers.* **3.** the form or cast of the face: *delicate of feature.* **4.** a prominent or conspicuous part or characteristic: *Religious doubt is a feature of our age.* **5.** something offered as a special attraction: *A sale on cameras was the feature of the day.* **6.** the main motion picture in a movie program: *What time is the feature?* **7.** a column, cartoon, etc., appearing regularly in a newspaper or magazine. **8.** See **feature story. 9.** *Archaic.* make, form, or shape. —*v.t.* **10.** to be a feature or distinctive mark of: *Industrial expansion featured the last century.* **11.** to make a feature of; give prominence to: *to feature a story or picture in a newspaper.* **12.** to delineate the main characteristics of; depict; outline. **13.** *Informal.* to conceive of; imagine: *He couldn't quite feature himself as a bon vivant.* **14.** *Chiefly Dial.* to resemble in features; favor. [ME *feture* < AF, c. MF *faiture* < L *factūra* a making. See FACT, -URE]
—**Syn. 4.** FEATURE, CHARACTERISTIC, PECULIARITY refer to a distinctive trait of an individual, or of a class. FEATURE suggests an outstanding or marked property which attracts attention: *Complete harmony was a feature of the convention.* CHARACTERISTIC means a distinguishing mark or quality (or one of such) always associated in one's mind with a particular person or thing: *Defiance is one of his characteristics.* PECULIARITY means that distinct or unusual characteristic which marks off an individual in the class to which he or it belongs: *The arrangement of the petals is a peculiarity of pansies.*

fea·tured (fē′chərd), *adj.* **1.** made a feature of; given prominence to: *a featured article; a featured actor.* **2.** having features or a certain kind of features (usually used in combination): *a well-featured face.* **3.** *Obs.* formed; fashioned. [ME *fetured.* See FEATURE, -ED[3]]

fea·ture-length (fē′chər length′), *adj.* of full length; long enough to be made a feature of: *a feature-length story; a feature-length film.*

fea·ture·less (fē′chər lis), *adj.* without distinctive features; uninteresting: *a featureless landscape.* [FEATURE + -LESS]

fea′ture sto′ry, 1. a newspaper or magazine article or report of a person, event, an aspect of a major event, or the like, often having an emotional, personal, or humorous slant and written in an individual style. Cf. **follow-up** (def. 3b), **hard news, news story. 2.** the main or most prominent story in a magazine. Also called **feature.**

fea·tur·ette (fē′chə ret′), *n.* a short feature, esp. a documentary or educational film on a movie program with the main feature. [FEATURE + -ETTE]

fea·tur·ish (fē′chər ish), *adj.* **1.** *Journalism.* (of copy, page make-up, etc.) similar to a feature story or feature in style, attention-getting characteristics, or other respects: *featurish obituaries.* **2.** using or containing feature stories or features: *Through the years the newspaper's front page has become more and more featurish.* [FEATURE + -ISH[1]]

feaze[1] (fēz), *v.t., v.i.,* **feazed, feaz·ing.** *Naut.* to unlay the end of a rope. [akin to D *vezelen* to fray, MD *veze* frayed edge, OE *fæs* fringe]

feaze[2] (fēz, fāz), *n., v.t.,* **feazed, feaz·ing.** feeze.

feaz·ing (fē′zing), *n.* Often, **feazings.** an unraveled portion at the end of a rope. [FEAZE[1] + -ING[1]]

FEB, Fair Employment Board.

Feb., February.

Fe·be (fē′bē), *n.* a girl's given name. Also, **Phoebe.**

febri-, a learned borrowing from Latin meaning "fever," used in the formation of compound words: *febriferous.* [comb. form repr. L *febris* FEVER]

fe·bric·i·ty (fi bris′i tē), *n.* the state of being feverish. [< ML *febricitās*, equiv. to L **febric(us)* feverish (see FEBRI-, -IC) + *-itās* -ITY]

fe·bric·u·la (fi brik′yə lə), *n.* a slight and short fever, especially when of obscure causation. [< L; see FEBRI-, -CULE]

feb·ri·fa·cient (feb′rə fā′shənt), *adj.* **1.** producing fever. —*n.* **2.** something that produces fever. [FEBRI- + -FACIENT]

fe·brif·er·ous (fi brif′ər əs), *adj.* producing fever. [FEBRI- + -FEROUS]

fe·brif·ic (fi brif′ik), *adj.* producing or marked by fever. [FEBRI- + -FIC]

fe·brif·u·gal (fi brif′yə gəl, feb′rə fyo͞o′gəl), *adj.* of or like a febrifuge. [< medical L *febrifug(us)* driving fevers away (*febri-* FEBRI- + *-fugus* putting to flight; see -FUGE) + -AL[1]]

feb·ri·fuge (feb′rə fyo͞oj′), *adj.* **1.** serving to dispel or reduce fever, as a medicine. —*n.* **2.** a febrifuge medicine or agent. **3.** a cooling drink. [< F < LL *febrifugia* plant good for curing fever. See FEBRI-, -FUGE]

fe·brile (fē′brəl, feb′rəl *or, esp. Brit.,* fē′brīl), *adj.* pertaining to or marked by fever; feverish. [< medical L *febrīl(is).* See FEVER, -ILE] —**fe·bril·i·ty** (fi bril′i tē), *n.*

feb·ris (feb′ris), *n., pl.* **-res** (-rēz). (in prescriptions) fever. [< L]

Feb·ru·ar·y (feb′ro͞o er′ē, feb′yo͞o er′ē), *n., pl.* **-ar·ies.** the second month of the year, ordinarily containing 28 days but containing 29 days in leap years. [ME; OE *Februarius* < L, short for *Februārius mēnsis* expiatory month, named after *Februa* expiation period, pl. of *februum* purgation; see -ARY]

Feb′ruary Revolu′tion. See **Russian Revolution** (def. 1).

fec., fecit.

fe·cal (fē′kəl), *adj.* of, pertaining to, or being feces. [FEC(ES) + -AL[1]]

fe·ces (fē′sēz), *n., pl.* **1.** waste matter discharged from the intestines through the anus; excrement. **2.** dregs; sediment. Also, **faeces.** [late ME < L *faecēs* grounds, dregs, sediment (pl. of *faex*)]

Fech·ner (fekH′nər), *n.* **Gus·tave The·o·dor** (go͝os′täf tā′ō dōr′), 1801–87, German physicist, psychologist, and philosopher.

fe·cit (fā′kit; *Eng.* fē′sit), *v.* *Latin.* he made (it); she made (it): formerly used on works of art after the name of the artist. *Abbr.:* fe., fec.

feck (fek), *n.* *Scot. and North Eng.* **1.** effect; efficacy; value. **2.** amount; number; quantity. **3.** the larger part; majority. [late ME *fek*, var. of *fect*, for EFFECT]

feck·et (fek′it), *n.* *Scot.* a man's suit vest. [?]

feck·less (fek′lis), *adj.* **1.** ineffective; incompetent; feeble: *feckless attempts to repair the plumbing.* **2.** without worth, spirit, or value; indifferent; lazy: *a feckless young man who never assumed responsibilities.* [FECK + -LESS] —**feck′less·ly,** *adv.* —**feck′less·ness,** *n.*

feck·ly (fek′lē), *adv.* *Scot. and North Eng.* almost; for the most part. [FECK + -LY]

fec·u·la (fek′yə lə), *n., pl.* **-lae** (-lē′). **1.** fecal matter, esp. of insects. **2.** dregs or foul or muddy matter. [< L *faecula* burnt tartar, the crust of wine, equiv. to *faec-* (s. of *faex*; see FECES) + *-ula* -ULE]

fec·u·lent (fek′yə lənt), *adj.* full of dregs or fecal matter; foul, turbid, or muddy. [late ME < L *faeculent(us)* full of dregs. See FECES, -ULENT] —**fec′u·lence,** *n.*

fe·cund (fē′kund, -kənd, fek′und, -ənd), *adj.* **1.** producing or capable of producing offspring, or fruit, vegetation, etc., in abundance; prolific; fruitful: *fecund parents; fecund farmland.* **2.** very productive or creative intellectually: *the fecund years of the Italian Renaissance.* [late ME < L *fēcund(us)*, equiv. to *fē-* (see FETUS) + *-cundus* adj. suffix; r. late ME *fecounde* < AF]
—**Syn. 1.** teeming, fertile.

fe·cun·date (fē′kən dāt′, fek′ən-), *v.t.*, **-dat·ed, -dat·ing.** **1.** to make prolific or fruitful. **2.** *Biol.* to impregnate. [< L *fēcundāt(us)* made fruitful, fertilized (ptp. of *fēcundāre*). See FECUND, -ATE[1]] —**fe′cun·da′tion,** *n.* —**fe′cun·da′tor,** *n.* —**fe·cun·da·to·ry** (fi kun′də tōr′ē, -tôr′ē), *adj.*

Fe·cun·di·ta·tis (fā ko͝on′di tä′tis, fē-), *n.* **Mare.** See **Mare Fecunditatis.**

fe·cun·di·ty (fi kun′di tē), *n.* **1.** the quality of being fecund; capacity, esp. in female animals, of producing young in great numbers. **2.** fruitfulness or fertility, as of the earth. **3.** the capacity of abundant production: *fecundity of imagination.* [< L *fēcunditās* fruitfulness, fertility. See FECUND, -ITY]

fed (fed), *v.* **1.** pt. and pp. of **feed.** **2. fed up,** *Informal.* impatient; disgusted; bored: *They were fed up with the same old routine. After several unsuccessful attempts he got fed up trying.*

Fed., Federal.

fed·dan (fə dän′, -dan′), *n., pl.* **-dan, -dans.** an Egyptian unit of area equivalent to 1.038 acres. [< Ar *faddān,* lit., yoke of oxen]

fed·e·li·ni (fed′ᵊlē′nē), *n.* an extremely fine, strandlike pasta, resembling but thinner than vermicelli.

fed·er·a·cy (fed′ər ə sē), *n., pl.* **-cies.** a confederacy. [by aphesis]

fed·er·al (fed′ər əl), *adj.* **1.** of or pertaining to a compact or a league, esp. a league between nations or states. **2.** *Govt.* **a.** pertaining to or of the nature of a union of states under a central government distinct from the individual governments of the separate states: *the federal government of the U.S.* **b.** favoring a strong central government in such a union. **c.** of, pertaining to, or noting such a central government: *federal offices.* **3.** (*cap.*) *U.S. Hist.* **a.** of or pertaining to the Federalists or to the Federalist party. **b.** (in the Civil War) pertaining to or supporting the Union government. **c.** relating to or adhering to the support of the Constitution. **4.** (*cap.*) pertaining to or designating the styles of the arts and crafts current in the U.S. from c1790–c1830. —*n.* **5.** an advocate of federation or federalism. **6.** (*cap.*) *U.S. Hist.* **a.** a Federalist. **b.** an adherent of the Union government during the Civil War; Unionist. **c.** a soldier in the Federal army. [earlier *foederal* < L *foeder-* (nom. *foedus*) league + -AL[1]] —**fed′er·al·ly,** *adv.* —**fed′er·al·ness,** *n.*

Fed′eral Avia′tion A′gency. See **FAA.**

Fed′eral Bu′reau of Investiga′tion. See **FBI.**

Fed′eral Cap′ital Ter′ritory, former name of **Australian Capital Territory.**

Fed′eral Communica′tions Commis′sion. See FCC.

Fed′eral Constitu′tion. See **Constitution of the United States.**

Fed′eral Depos′it Insur′ance Corpora′tion, *U.S.* a public corporation, established in 1933, which insures, up to a specified amount, all demand deposits of member banks. *Abbr.:* FDIC

Fed′eral Dis′trict, a district in which the national government of a country is located, esp. one in Latin America. Spanish, **Distrito Federal.**

fed·er·al·ese (fed′ər ə lēz′, -lēs′), *n.* (*often cap.*) *Facetious.* awkward or pretentious prose said to characterize the publications of U.S. federal bureaus. [FEDERAL + -ESE]

fed·er·al·ise (fed′ər ə līz′), *v.t.*, **-ised, -is·ing.** *Chiefly Brit.* federalize. —**fed′er·al·i·sa′tion,** *n.*

fed·er·al·ism (fed′ər ə liz′əm), *n.* **1.** the federal principle of government. **2.** (*cap.*) *U.S. Hist.* the principles of the Federalist party. [FEDERAL + -ISM]

fed·er·al·ist (fed′ər ə list), *n.* **1.** an advocate of federalism. **2.** (*cap.*) *U.S. Hist.* a member or supporter of the Federalist party. —*adj.* **3.** Also, **fed′er·al·is′tic.** of federalism or the Federalists. [FEDERAL + -IST]

Fed′eralist, The, a series of 85 essays (1787–88) by Alexander Hamilton, James Madison, and John Jay, written in support of the Constitution.

Fed′eralist par′ty, *U.S. Hist.* **1.** a political group that favored the adoption by the States of the Constitution. **2.** a political party in early U.S. history advocating a strong central government. Also, **Fed′eral par′ty.**

fed·er·al·ize (fed′ər ə līz′), *v.t.*, **-ized, -iz·ing.** **1.** to bring under the control of a federal government: *to federalize the National Guard.* **2.** to bring together in a federal union, as different states. Also, *esp. Brit.,* **federalise.** [FEDERAL + -IZE] —**fed′er·al·i·za′tion,** *n.*

Fed′eral Land′ Bank′, a U.S. federal bank for making long-term loans to farmers.

Fed′eral Pow′er Commis′sion. See **FPC.**

Fed′eral Reg′ister, *U.S.* a bulletin, published daily by the federal government containing the schedule of hearings before Congressional and federal agency committees, together with orders, proclamations, etc., released by the executive branch of the government.

Fed′eral Repub′lic of Cameroon′, official name of **Cameroon.**

Fed′eral Repub′lic of Ger′many, **1.** official name of **Germany.** **2.** (formerly) official name of **West Germany.**

Fed′eral Reserve′ Bank′. See under **Federal Reserve System.**

Fed′eral Reserve′ Board′. See under **Federal Reserve System.**

Fed′eral Reserve′ dis′trict, the district served by a certain Federal Reserve Bank.

Fed′eral Reserve′ note′, a form of paper money issued by a Federal Reserve Bank.

Fed′eral Reserve′ Sys′tem, *U.S.* a federal banking system that is under the control of a central board of governors **(Federal Reserve Board)** with a central bank **(Federal Reserve Bank)** in each of 12 districts and that has wide powers in controlling credit and the flow of money as well as in performing other functions, as regulating and supervising its member banks.

Fed′eral Trade′ Commis′sion. See **FTC.**

fed·er·ate (*v.* fed′ə rāt′; *adj.* fed′ər it), *v.*, **-at·ed, -at·ing,** *adj.* —*v.t., v.i.* **1.** to unite in a league or federation. **2.** to organize on a federal basis. —*adj.* **3.** federated; allied. [< L *foederāt(us)* leagued together, allied, equiv. to *foeder-* (nom. s. *foedus*) league + *-ātus* -ATE[1]]

Fed′erated Ma′lay States′, a former federation of four native states in British Malaya: Negri Sembilan, Pahang, Perak, and Selangor.

fed·er·a·tion (fed′ə rā′shən), *n.* **1.** the act of federating or uniting in a league. **2.** the formation of a political unity, with a central government, by a number of separate states, each of which retains control of its own internal affairs. **3.** a league or confederacy. **4.** a federated body formed by a number of states, societies, unions, etc., each retaining control of its own internal affairs. [< LL *foederātiōn-* (s. of *foederātiō*) a leaguing. See FEDERATE, -ION]

Federa′tion of Rhode′sia and Nya′saland. See **Rhodesia and Nyasaland, Federation of.**

Federa′tion of the West′ In′dies. See **West Indies** (def. 2).

fed·er·a·tive (fed′ə rā′tiv, fed′ər ə tiv), *adj.* **1.** pertaining to or of the nature of a federation. **2.** inclined to federate. [FEDERATE + -IVE] —**fed·er·a·tive·ly** (fed′ə rā′tiv lē, -ər ə tiv-), *adv.*

Fe·din (fe′dyin), *n.* **Kon·stan·tin A·le·ksan·dro·vich** (kon stän tēn′ ä′le ksän′dro vich), born 1892, Russian novelist and short-story writer.

fe·do·ra (fi dōr′ə, -dôr′ə), *n.* a soft felt hat with a curled brim, worn with the crown creased lengthwise. [said to be named after *Fédora,* play by Victorien Sardou (1831–1908)]

Fe·do·ra (fi dōr′ə, -dôr′ə), *n.* a girl's given name.

Fed. Res. Bd., Federal Reserve Board.

Fed. Res. Bk., Federal Reserve Bank.

fee (fē), *n., v.,* **feed, fee·ing.** —*n.* **1.** a charge or payment for services: *a doctor's fee.* **2.** a sum paid or charged for a privilege: *an admission fee.* **3.** a gratuity; tip. **4.** a charge allowed by law for the service of a public officer. **5.** *Law.* **a.** an estate of inheritance in land, either absolute and without limitation to any particular class of heirs **(fee simple)** or limited to a particular class of heirs **(fee tail).** **b.** an inheritable estate in land held of a feudal lord on condition of the performing of certain services. **c.** a territory held in fee. —*v.t.* **6.** to give a fee to. **7.** *Chiefly Scot.* to hire; employ. [ME < AF, c. OF *fie,* var. of *fief* FIEF. See FEUDAL] —**fee′less,** *adj.*
—**Syn. 1.** stipend, salary, emolument; honorarium.

fee·ble (fē′bəl), *adj.*, **-bler, -blest.** **1.** physically weak, as from age, sickness, etc. **2.** weak intellectually or morally: *a feeble mind.* **3.** lacking in volume, loudness, brightness, distinctness, etc.: *a feeble voice; feeble light.* **4.** lacking in force, strength, or effectiveness: *feeble resistance; feeble arguments.* [ME *feble* < OF, var. of *fleible* (by dissimilation) < L *flēbil(is)* lamentable, equiv. to *flē(re)* (to) weep + *-bilis* -BLE] —**fee′ble·ness,** *n.* —**fee′blish,** *adj.* —**fee′bly,** *adv.*
—**Syn. 1.** infirm, frail, sickly, enervated, debilitated. See **weak.** **3.** faint, dim. **4.** feckless, ineffective. —**Ant. 1–4.** strong.

fee·ble-mind·ed (fē′bəl mīn′did), *adj.* **1.** lacking the normal mental powers: *congenitally feeble-minded children.* **2.** stupid; dull-witted: *feeble-minded remarks.* **3.** lacking firmness of mind: *to be feeble-minded in a crisis.* —**fee′ble-mind′ed·ly,** *adv.* —**fee′ble-mind′ed·ness,** *n.*

fee·ble-voiced (fē′bəl voist′), *adj.* having a weak, indistinct voice: *a feeble-voiced old man.*

feed (fēd), *v.*, **fed, feed·ing,** *n.* —*v.t.* **1.** to give food to; supply with nourishment: *to feed a child.* **2.** to yield or serve as food for: *This land has fed 10 generations.* **3.** to provide as food. **4.** to furnish for consumption. **5.** to satisfy; minister to; gratify: *Poetry feeds the imagination.* **6.** to supply for maintenance or operation, as to a machine: *to feed paper into a press.* **7.** to provide with the necessary materials for development, maintenance, or operation: *to feed a press with paper.* **8.** to use (land) as pasture. **9.** *Theat. Informal.* **a.** to supply (an actor, esp. a comedian) with lines or action, the responses to which are expected to elicit laughter. **b.** to provide cues to (an actor). **c.** *Chiefly Brit.* to prompt: *Stand in the wings and feed them their lines.* —*v.i.* **10.** to take food; eat: *cows feeding in a meadow; to feed well.* **11.** to be nourished or gratified; subsist: *to feed on grass; to feed on thoughts of revenge.* **12. chain feed,** to pass (work) successively into a machine in such a manner that each new piece is held in place by or connected to the one before. —*n.* **13.** food, esp. for farm animals, as cattle, horses, chickens, etc. **14.** an allowance, portion, or supply of such food. **15.** *Informal.* a meal, esp. a lavish one. **16.** the act of feeding. **17.** the act or process of feeding a furnace, machine, etc. **18.** the material, or the amount of it, so fed or supplied. **19.** a feeding mechanism. **20.** *Elect.* feeder (def. 10). **21.** *Theat. Informal.* **a.** a line spoken by one actor, the response to which by another actor is expected to cause laughter. **b.** an actor, esp. a straight man, who provides such lines. **22. off one's feed,** *Slang.* **a.** reluctant to eat; without appetite. **b.** dejected; sad. **c.** unwell; ill: *He's been off his feed ever since the office party.* [ME *fede(n),* OE *fēdan;* c. Goth *fodjan,* OS *fōdian.* See FOOD] —**feed′a·ble,** *adj.*
—**Syn. 1, 2.** nourish, sustain. **13.** FEED, FODDER, FORAGE, PROVENDER mean food for animals. FEED is the general word: *pig feed; chicken feed.* FODDER is esp. applied to dry or green feed, as opposed to pasturage, fed to horses, cattle, etc.: *fodder for winter feeding; Cornstalks are good fodder.* FORAGE is food which an animal obtains (usually grass, leaves, etc.) by searching about for it: *Lost cattle can usually live on forage.* PROVENDER denotes dry feed, such as hay, oats, or corn: *a supply of provender in the haymow and corn cribs.* —**Ant. 1, 2.** starve.

feed·back (fēd′bak′), *n.* **1.** *Electronics.* the returning of some of the energy of the plate circuit of a vacuum tube to the grid circuits, either to oppose the input **(inverse feedback)** or to aid the input **(regenerative feedback).** **2.** continuous, automatic furnishing of data concerning the output of a machine to an automatic control device so that errors may be corrected. **3.** input of a signal into a microphone from the output of the same system, usually causing a high-pitched whistling noise. **4.** *Psychol.* knowledge of the results of any behavior, considered as influencing or modifying further performance by the organism. **5.** *Computer Technol.* the returning of part of the output of a system to be reintroduced as input, esp. for purposes of correction or control. [n. use of v. phrase *feed back*]

feed′ bag′, **1.** Also called **nose bag.** a bag for feeding horses, placed before the mouth and fastened around the head with straps. **2. put on the feed bag,** *Slang.* to have a meal; eat: *When his friends put on the feed bag they finish everything in sight.* Also, **feed′bag′.**

feed·box (fēd′boks′), *n.* **1.** a box for animal feed. **2.** a casing for the feeding mechanism of a machine. [FEED + BOX[1]]

feed·er (fē′dər), *n.* **1.** one who or that which supplies food or feeds something. **2.** a bin or boxlike device from which farm animals may eat, esp. such a device designed to allow a number of chickens to feed simultaneously or to release a specific amount of feed at regular intervals. **3.** one who or that which takes food or nourishment. **4.** a livestock animal that is fed an enriched diet to fatten it for market. Cf. **stocker** (def. 2). **5.** a person or device that feeds a machine, printing press, etc. **6.** a tributary stream. **7.** a branch railroad. **8.** See **feeder line.** **9.** See **feeder road.** **10.** Also, **feed.** *Elect.* a conductor, or group of conductors, connecting primary equipment in an electric power system. **11.** *Brit.* a baby's bib. **12.** *Theat. Slang.* See **straight man.** [ME; see FEED, -ER[1]]

feed′er line′, a branch of a main transportation line, esp. an airline.

feed′er road′, a secondary road used to bring traffic to a major road.

feed·ing (fē′ding), *n.* **1.** the act of one who or that which feeds. **2.** an instance of eating or of taking or being given nourishment. **3.** grazing land. [ME *feding,* OE *fēding.* See FEED, -ING[1]]

feed′ing cup′. See **spout cup.**

feed·stuff (fēd′stuf′), *n.* a substance used for feed. Also, **feed·ing·stuff** (fē′ding stuf′). [FEED + STUFF]

feed·wa·ter (fēd′wô′tər), *n.* water to be supplied to a boiler from a tank or condenser for conversion into steam. Also, **feed′ wa′ter.** [FEED + WATER]

feel (fēl), *v.*, **felt, feel·ing,** *n.* —*v.t.* **1.** to perceive or examine by touch. **2.** to have a sensation of (something), other than by sight, hearing, taste, or smell: *to feel a toothache.* **3.** to find or pursue (one's way) by touching, groping, or cautious moves. **4.** to be or become conscious of. **5.** to be emotionally affected by: *to feel one's disgrace keenly.* **6.** to experience the effects of: *The whole region felt the storm.* **7.** to have a particular sensation or impression of (often used reflexively and usually fol. by an adjunct or complement): *to feel oneself slighted.* **8.** to have a general or thorough conviction of. —*v.i.* **9.** to have perception by touch or by any nerves of sensation other than those of sight, hearing, taste, and smell. **10.** to make examination by touch; grope. **11.** to have mental sensations or emotions. **12.** to be aware of being: *to feel happy; to feel angry.* **13.** to have sympathy or compassion (usually fol. by *with* or *for*). **14.** to have a sensation of being: *to feel warm.* **15.** to make itself perceived or apparent; seem: *How does it feel to be rich?* **16. feel like,** *Informal.* to have a desire for; be favorably disposed to: *I don't feel like going out tonight. Do you feel like a movie?* **17. feel like oneself,** to be in one's usual frame of mind or state of health: *She hasn't been feeling like herself since the accident.* Also, **feel oneself.** **18. feel out,** *Informal.* to attempt to ascertain (the nature of a situation, someone's attitude, etc.) by indirect or subtle means: *Why not feel out the other neighbors' opinions before you make a complaint.* **19. feel up to,** *Informal.* to feel or be able to; be capable of: *He didn't feel up to going to the theater so soon after his recent illness.* —*n.* **20.** a quality of an object that is perceived by feeling or touching: *the soft feel of cotton.* **21.** a sensation of something felt; a vague mental impression or feeling: *a feel of winter; a feel of sadness in the air.* **22.** the sense of touch: *soft to the feel.* **23.** native ability or inborn knowledge: *to have a feel for what is right.* **24.** *Informal.* the act or an instance of touching with the hand or fingers. [ME *fele(n),* OE *fēlan;* c. OS *fōlian,* G *fühlen;* akin to Icel *falma* to grope. See FUMBLE]

feel·er (fē′lər), *n.* **1.** one who or that which feels. **2.** a proposal, remark, hint, etc., designed to bring out the opinions or purposes of others: *Interested in an accord, both labor and management were putting out feelers.* **3.** *Zool.* an organ of touch, as an antenna or a tentacle. **4.** Also called **feel′er gauge′.** a gauge having several blades of known thickness, used for measuring clearances. **5.** (on a medallion lathe or the like) the pointer that follows the contours of a master or matrix to control the position of the cutter. **6.** *Naut.* **a.** a device for indicating that the lead of a mechanical sounding device has come to the bottom. **b.** *Obs.* a combination of weather conditions suggesting that a gale is about to occur. [FEEL + -ER[1]]

feel·ing (fē′ling), *n.* **1.** the function or the power of perceiving by touch; physical sensation not connected with sight, hearing, taste, or smell. **2.** a particular sensation of this kind: *a feeling of warmth; a feeling of pain.* **3.** *Psychol.* consciousness taken as a state in itself and independent of any reference in a specific thought or perception. **4.** a consciousness or vague awareness: *a feeling of inferiority.* **5.** an emotion or emotional perception or attitude: *a feeling of joy; a feeling of sorrow.* **6.** capacity for emotion, esp. compassion: *to have great feeling for the sufferings of others.* **7.** a sentiment; opinion: *The general feeling was in favor of the proposal.* **8. feelings,** sensibilities; susceptibilities: *to hurt one's feelings.* **9.** fine emotional endowment. **10.** (in music, art, etc.) **a.** emotion or sympathetic perception revealed by an artist in his work: *a poem without feeling.* **b.** the general impression conveyed by a work: *a landscape painting with a spacious feeling.* **c.** sympathetic appreciation, as of music: *to play with feeling.* —*adj.* **11.** sensitive; sentient. **12.** readily affected by emotion; sympathetic: *a feeling heart.* **13.** indicating or characterized by emotion: *a feeling reply to the charge.* [ME; see FEEL, -ING[1], -ING[2]] —**feel′ing·ly,** *adv.* —**feel′ing·ness,** *n.*
—**Syn. 5.** FEELING, EMOTION, PASSION, SENTIMENT refer to pleasurable or painful sensations experienced when one is stirred to sympathy, anger, fear, love, grief, etc. FEELING is a general term for a subjective point of view as well as for specific sensations: *to be guided by feeling rather than by facts; a feeling of sadness, of rejoicing.* EMOTION is applied to an intensified feeling: *agitated by emotion.* PASSION is strong or violent emotion, often so overpowering that it masters the mind or judgment: *stirred to a passion of anger.* SENTIMENT is a mixture of thought and feeling, esp. refined or tender feeling: *Recollections are often colored by sentiment.* **6.** sympathy, empathy, tenderness, sensitivity, sentiment. **11.** emotional, tender. **13.** impassioned, passionate. —**Ant. 5, 6.** apathy. **12.** cold.

feel·ing·ful (fē′ling fəl), *adj.* expressive of strong feeling: *a feelingful expression of joy.* [FEELING + -FUL]

feel·ing·less (fē′ling lis), *adj.* without normal ability to feel. [FEELING + -LESS] —**feel′ing·less·ly,** *adv.*

fee′ sim′ple. See under **fee** (def. 5a). [< AF]

fee·split·ter (fē′split′ər), *n.* a doctor engaged in fee-splitting.

fee·split·ting (fē′split′ing), *n.* the practice of dividing a fee for professional services between two doctors, as between a specialist and the referring doctor, without the knowledge of the patient.

feet (fēt), *n.* **1.** a pl. of **foot. 2. on one's feet, a.** in a standing position. **b.** in an independent or secure position: *The loan helped him get on his feet again.* **c.** in a restored or recovered state; able to continue: *Psychoanalysis helped her get back on her feet after her breakdown.* **3. sit at the feet of,** to attend upon as a disciple or follower: *American writers and painters no longer sit at the feet of Europeans.* **4. stand on one's own feet, a.** to be self-supporting. **b.** to be independent: *Overprotective parents do not prepare their children to stand on their own feet.* **5. sweep one off one's feet,** to impress or overwhelm by ability, enthusiasm, or charm: *The gaiety of the occasion swept them off their feet.* —**feet′less,** *adj.*

fee′ tail′. See under **fee** (def. 5a). [< AF]

feet·first (fēt′fûrst′), *adv.* **1.** with the feet foremost. **2.** *Slang.* as on a stretcher or in a coffin; dead. [FEET + FIRST]

feet′ of clay′, 1. a weakness or hidden flaw in the character of a greatly admired or respected person: *He was further disillusioned to find that all the heroes of his youth had feet of clay.* **2.** any unexpected or critical fault: *In the first days of the invasion, the defending army gave the appearance of having feet of clay.*

feeze (fēz, fāz), *n., v.,* **feezed, feez·ing.** —*n.* **1.** *Dial.* a state of vexation or worry. **2.** *Chiefly Dial.* a violent rush or impact. —*v.t.* **3.** *Dial.* to faze. **4.** *Obs.* to beat; flog. Also, **feaze.** [ME *fese(n)*; akin to OE *fȳsan* to drive away, put to flight]

feign (fān), *v.t.* **1.** to represent fictitiously; put on an appearance of: *to feign sickness.* **2.** to invent fictitiously or deceptively, as a story or an excuse. **3.** to imitate deceptively: *to feign another's voice.* —*v.i.* **4.** to make believe; pretend: *She feigns to be ill.* [ME *fei(g)ne(n)* < OF *feign-,* present s. of *feindre* < L *fingere* to shape, invent, feign] —**feign′er,** *n.* —**feign′ing·ly,** *adv.*
—**Syn. 1.** simulate, affect. **2.** concoct, devise, fabricate, counterfeit. **4.** See **pretend.**

feigned (fānd), *adj.* **1.** pretended; sham; counterfeit: *feigned enthusiasm.* **2.** assumed: *a feigned name.* **3.** disguised: *a feigned voice.* **4.** fictitiously invented. [ME; see FEIGN, -ED[2]] —**feign·ed·ly** (fā′nid lē), *adv.* —**feign′ed·ness,** *n.*

Fein·ing·er (fī′ning ər), *n.* **1. An·dre·as (Bernhard Lyonel)** (an drā′əs, än-), born 1906, U.S. photographer, born in France. **2.** his father, **Lyonel (Charles Adrian),** 1871–1956, U.S. painter.

feint (fānt), *n.* **1.** a movement made in order to deceive an adversary; an attack aimed at one place or point merely as a distraction from the real place or point of attack: *military feints; the feints of a skilled fencer.* **2.** a feigned or assumed appearance: *His air of approval was a feint to conceal his real motives.* —*v.i.* **3.** to make a feint. [< F *feinte,* n. use of fem. of *feint* pretended, ptp. of *feindre* to FEIGN]
—**Syn. 1, 3.** maneuver.

feints (fānts), *n.pl.* faints.

feir·ie (fēr′ē), *adj.* *Scot.* healthy; strong. [late ME (Scot) *fery,* equiv. to *fer* (OE *fēre* able-bodied, fit, deriv. of *fōr* journey; see FARE) + -Y[1]]

Fei·sal I (fī′səl). See **Faisal I.** Also, **Fei′sul I.**

Feisal II. See **Faisal II.**

feist (fīst), *n.* *U.S. Dial.* a small mongrel dog, esp. one that is ill-tempered; cur; mutt. Also, **fice, fist.** [short for *feisting cur;* ME, OE *fīsting* breaking wind; akin to MD *vijsten,* Icel *fīsa* to break wind]

feist·y (fī′stē), *adj.* ill-tempered. [FEIST + Y[1]]

Fel·da (fel′də), *n.* a girl's given name.

feld·spar (feld′spär′, fel′-), *n.* any of a group of minerals, principally aluminosilicates of potassium, sodium, and calcium, characterized by two cleavages at nearly right angles: one of the most important constituents of igneous rocks. Also, *esp. Brit.,* **felspar.** [*feld-* (< G: field) + SPAR[3]; r. *feldspath* < G (*Feld* field + *Spath* spar)]

feld·spath·ic (feld′spath ik, fel′-), *adj.* *Mineral.* of, pertaining to, or containing feldspar. Also, **feld′spath·ose′;** *esp. Brit.,* **felspathic, felspathose.** [< G *Feldspath* (see FELDSPAR) + -IC]

feld·spath·oid (feld′spa thoid′, fel′-), *Mineral.* —*adj.* **1.** Also, **feld′spath·oi′dal.** of or pertaining to a group of minerals similar in chemical composition to certain feldspars except for a lower silica content. —*n.* **2.** a mineral of this group. [< G *Feldspath* (see FIELD-SPAR) + -OID]

Fe·lice (fə lēs′), *n.* a girl's given name, form of **Felicia.**

Fe·li·cia (fə lish′ə, -lish′ē ə, -lē′shə, -lis′ē ə), *n.* a girl's given name.

Fe·li·ci·an·a (fə lish′ē an′ə), *n.* a girl's given name, form of **Felicia.**

Fe·li·ci·dad (fe lē′thē thäth′, -sē-), *n.* a girl's given name, Spanish form of **Felicia.**

fe·li·cif·ic (fē′li sif′ik), *adj.* causing or tending to cause happiness. [< LL *fēlīcific(us),* equiv. to *fēlīci-* (s. of *fēlix*) happy + *-ficus* -FIC]

fe·lic·i·tate (fi lis′i tāt′), *v.,* **-tat·ed, -tat·ing,** *adj.* —*v.t.* **1.** to compliment upon a happy event; congratulate. **2.** *Archaic.* to make happy. —*adj.* **3.** *Obs.* made happy. [< LL *fēlīcitāt(us)* made happy (ptp. of *fēlīcitāre*). See FELICITY, -ATE[1]] —**fe·lic′i·ta′tor,** *n.*

fe·lic·i·ta·tion (fi lis′i tā′shən), *n.* an expression of good wishes; congratulation. [FELICITATE + -ION]

fe·lic·i·tous (fi lis′i təs), *adj.* **1.** well-suited for the occasion, as an action, manner, or expression; apt; appropriate: *The chairman's felicitous anecdote set everyone at ease.* **2.** having a special ability for suitable manner or expression, as a person. [FELICIT(Y) + -OUS] —**fe·lic′i·tous·ly,** *adv.* —**fe·lic′i·tous·ness,** *n.*
—**Syn. 1.** fit, suited, apropos, germane, meet, befitting.

fe·lic·i·ty (fi lis′i tē), *n., pl.* **-ties. 1.** the state of being happy, esp. in a high degree: *marital felicity.* **2.** an instance of this. **3.** a source of happiness. **4.** a skillful faculty: *felicity of expression.* **5.** an instance or display of this: *the many felicities of the poem.* **6.** *Archaic.* good fortune. [ME *felicite* < L *fēlīcitās,* equiv. to *fēlīci-* (s. of *fēlix*) happy + *-tās* -TY[2]]
—**Syn. 1.** See **happiness.**

Fe·lic·i·ty (fi lis′i tē), *n.* a girl's given name, form of **Felicia.** Also, **Fe·lic·i·ta** (fi lis′i tə).

fe·lid (fē′lid), *n.* an animal of the cat family, *Felidae.* [< NL *Fēlid(ae)* name of the family, equiv. to L *fēl-* (s. of *fēlēs*) cat + *-idae* -ID[2]]

fe·line (fē′līn), *adj.* **1.** belonging or pertaining to the cat family, *Felidae,* which includes, besides the domestic cat, the lions, tigers, leopards, lynxes, jaguars, etc. **2.** catlike; characteristic of animals of the cat family: *feline softness of step.* **3.** sly, stealthy, or treacherous: *She betrayed her lover with feline cruelty.* —*n.* **4.** an animal of the cat family. [< L *fēlīn(us),* equiv. to *fēl(ēs)* cat + *-īnus* -INE[1]] —**fe′line·ly,** *adv.* —**fe′line·ness, fe·lin·i·ty** (fi lin′i tē), *n.*

fe′line distem′per, *Vet. Pathol.* distemper[1] (def. 1c). Also called **fe′line agranulocyto′sis, fe′line enteri′tis, fe′line infec′tious enteri′tis, fe′line panleucope′nia, fe′line panleukope′nia.**

Fe·li·pa (fə lē′pə, -lip′ə; *Sp.* fe lē′pä), *n.* a girl's given name. Also, **Fe·lip·pe** (fə lip′ə), **Fi·lip·pa** (fə lip′ə; *It.* fē lēp′pä).

Fe·li·pe (fe lē′pe), *n.* **Le·ón (Ca·mi·no)** (le ôn′ kä mē′nô), born 1884, Spanish poet, in South America after 1939.

Fe·lix (fē′liks), *n.* a boy's given name.

Felix I, Saint, died A.D. 274, pope 269–274.

Felix III, Saint, died A.D. 492, pope 483–492.

Felix IV, Saint, died A.D. 530, pope 526–530.

fell[1] (fel), *v.* pt. of **fall.**

fell[2] (fel), *v.t.* **1.** to cause to fall; knock, strike, shoot, or cut down: *to fell a moose; to fell a tree.* **2.** *Sewing.* to finish (a seam) by sewing the edge down flat. —*n.* **3.** *Lumbering.* the amount of timber cut down in one season. **4.** *Sewing.* a seam finished by felling. [ME *felle(n),* OE *fellan,* causative of *feallan* to FALL; c. Goth *falljan* to cause to fall]

fell[3] (fel), *adj.* **1.** fierce; cruel; dreadful. **2.** destructive; deadly: *fell poison; fell disease.* [ME *fel* < OF, nom. of *felon* wicked. See FELON] —**fell′ness,** *n.*

fell[4] (fel), *n.* the skin or hide of an animal; pelt. [ME, OE; c. D *vel,* G *Fell,* Icel *-fjall* (in *berfjall* bear-skin), Goth *-fill* (in *thrutsfill* scab-skin, leprosy); akin to L *pellis* skin, hide]

fell[5] (fel), *n.* *Scot. and North Eng.* an upland pasture, moor, or thicket; a highland plateau. [ME < Scand; cf. Icel *fjall* mountain, akin to G *Fels(en)* rock, cliff]

fell·a·ble (fel′ə bəl), *adj.* capable of being or fit to be felled. [FELL[2] + -ABLE]

fel·lah (fel′ə), *n., pl.* **fel·lahs,** *Ar.* **fel·la·hin, fel·la·heen** (fel′ə hēn′). a native peasant or laborer in Egypt, Syria, etc. [< Ar: peasant]

fel·la·ti·o (fə lā′shē ō′, fe-), *n.* oral stimulation of the penis, esp. to orgasm. Also, **fel·la·tion** (fə lā′shən, fe-). [< NL *fellātiōn-* (s. of *fellātiō*), equiv. to L *fellāt(us),* *fēlāt(us)* (ptp. of *fellāre, fēlāre* to suck) + *-iōn-* -ION]

fell·er[1] (fel′ər), *n.* *Dial.* fellow. [FELLOW + hiatus-filling *r;* orig. found only before a word beginning with a vowel]

fell·er[2] (fel′ər), *n.* **1.** one who or that which fells. **2.** *Sewing.* one who or that which fells a seam. [ME *fellere.* See FELL[2], -ER[1]]

Fel·ler (fel′ər), *n.* **Robert William Andrew** (*Bob*), born 1918, U.S. baseball player.

Fel·li·ni (fə lē′nē; *It.* fel lē′nē), *n.* **Fe·de·ri·co** (*It.* fe′de rē′kô), born 1920, Italian motion-picture director and writer.

fell·mon·ger (fel′mung′gər, -mong′-), *n.* a dealer in skins or hides of animals, esp. sheepskins. [FELL[4] + MONGER] —**fell′mon′ger·ing, fell′mon′ger·y,** *n.*

fel·loe (fel′ō), *n.* the circular rim, or a part of the rim of a wheel, into which the outer ends of the spokes are inserted. Also, **felly.** [ME *felwe,* OE *felg(e);* c. G *Felge*]

fel·low (fel′ō), *n.* **1.** a man or boy: *a fine, old fellow; a nice, little fellow.* **2.** *Informal.* beau; suitor: *Mary had her fellow over to meet her folks.* **3.** *Informal.* person; one: *They don't treat a fellow very well here.* **4.** a person of small worth or no esteem. **5.** a companion; comrade; associate: *They have been fellows since childhood.* **6.** a person belonging to the same class; equal; peer: *The doctor conferred with his fellows.* **7.** one of a pair; mate; match: *a shoe without its fellow.* **8.** *Educ.* **a.** a graduate student of a university or college to whom an allowance is granted for special study. **b.** *Brit.* an incorporated member of a college, entitled to certain privileges. **c.** a member of the corporation or board of trustees of certain universities or colleges. **9.** a member of any of certain learned societies: *a fellow of the British Academy.* **10.** *Obs.* a partner. —*v.t.* **11.** to make or represent as equal with another. **12.** *Archaic.* to produce a fellow to; match. —*adj.* **13.** belonging to the same class or group; united by the same occupation, interests, etc.; being in the same condition: *fellow students; fellow sufferers.* [ME *felowe, felawe,* late OE *fēolaga* < Scand; cf. Icel *fēlagi* partner, lit., business associate, equiv. to *fē* money, property (c. OE *feoh,* G *Vieh*) + *-lagi* bedfellow, comrade; akin to LAIR[1], LIE[2]]

fel′low crea′ture, a kindred creature, esp. a fellow human being: *He was ashamed of his fellow creatures for their miserable inhumanity.*

fel′low feel′ing, 1. sympathetic feeling; sympathy: *to have fellow feeling for the unfortunate.* **2.** a sense of joint interest: *to act out of fellow feeling to support one's country.*

fel·low·man (fel′ō man′), *n., pl.* **-men.** another member of the human race, esp. a kindred human being: *Don't deny full recognition to your fellow-men.* Also, **fel′low·man′.**

fel′low serv′ant, (under the fellow servant rule) an employee working with another employee for the same employer.

fel′low serv′ant rule′, the common-law rule that the employer is not liable to an employee for injuries resulting from the negligence of a fellow employee.

fel·low·ship (fel′ō ship′), *n., v.,* **-shiped, -ship·ing** or (*esp. Brit.*) **-shipped, -ship·ping.** —*n.* **1.** the condition or relation of being a fellow: *the fellowship of mankind.* **2.** friendly relationship; companionship: *the fellowship of father and son.* **3.** community of interest, feeling, etc. **4.** communion, as between members of the same church. **5.** friendliness. **6.** an association of persons having similar tastes, interests, etc. **7.** a company, guild, or corporation. **8.** *Educ.* **a.** the body of fellows in a college or university. **b.** the position or emoluments of a fellow of a college or university, or the sum of money he receives. **c.** a foundation for the maintenance of a fellow in a college or university. —*v.t.* **9.** *Chiefly U.S.* to admit to fellowship, esp. religious fellowship. —*v.i.* **10.** *Chiefly U.S.* to join in fellowship, esp. religious fellowship. [ME *felaweship.* See FELLOW, -SHIP]

fel′low trav′eler, 1. a nonmember who supports or sympathizes with a political party, esp. the Communist party. **2.** anyone who, although not a member, supports or sympathizes with some organization, movement, or the like.

fel·ly[1] (fel′ē), *n., pl.* **-lies.** felloe. [ME *felien* (pl.), var. of *felwe* FELLOE]

fel·ly[2] (fel′ē), *adv.* *Archaic.* in a fell manner; fiercely; ruthlessly. [ME *felliche.* See FELL[3], -LY]

fe·lo-de-se (fē′lō di sē′, fel′ō-), *n., pl.* **fe·lo·nes-de-se** (fel′ō nēz′di sē′), or **fe·los-de-se** (fē′lōz di sē′, fel′ōz-). **1.** a person who commits suicide or commits an unlawful malicious act resulting in his own death. **2.** the act of suicide. [< AL, equiv. to *felo* a felon + *dē* in respect to, of + *sē* oneself]

fel·on[1] (fel′ən), *n.* **1.** *Law.* a person who has committed a felony. **2.** *Obs.* a wicked person. —*adj.* **3.** *Archaic.* wicked; malicious; treacherous. [ME *fel(o)un* wicked < AF, c. OF *felon* (obl.), ML *fellōn-,* s. of *fellō* treacherous (adj.), traitor, wicked person (n.); ? orig. same word as FELON[2]]

fel·on[2] (fel′ən), *n.* *Pathol.* an acute and painful inflammation of the deeper tissues of a finger or toe, usually near the nail: a form of whitlow. [late ME *felo(u)n* < ML *fellōn-* (s. of *fellō*) scrofulous tumor, deriv. of L *fel* gall, venom]

fe·lo·ni·ous (fə lō′nē əs), *adj.* **1.** *Law.* pertaining to, of the nature of, or involving a felony: *felonious homicide; felonious intent.* **2.** *Archaic.* wicked; base; villainous. [FELONY + -OUS; r. ME *felonous*]
—**fe·lo′ni·ous·ly,** *adv.* —**fe·lo′ni·ous·ness,** *n.*

fel·on·ry (fel′ən rē), *n.* **1.** the whole body or class of felons. **2.** the convict population of a penal colony. [FELON + -RY]

fel·o·ny (fel′ə nē), *n., pl.* **-nies.** *Law.* **1.** any of various offenses, as murder, burglary, etc., of graver character than those called misdemeanors, esp. those commonly punished in the U.S. by imprisonment for more than a year. **2.** *Early Eng. Law.* any crime punishable by loss of life or member and forfeiture of goods and chattels. [ME *felonie* < OF: wickedness. See FELON[1], -Y[3]]

fel′ony mur′der, a murder committed in conjunction with an independent felony, as robbery.

fel·sic (fel′sik), *adj.* *Geol.* (of rocks) consisting chiefly of feldspars, feldspathoids, quartz, and other light-colored minerals. Cf. **mafic.** [FEL(DSPAR) + S(ILICA) + -IC]

fel·site (fel′sīt), *n.* a dense, fine-grained, igneous rock consisting typically of feldspar and quartz, both of which may appear as phenocrysts. [FELS(PAR) + -ITE[1]]
—**fel·sit·ic** (fel sit′ik), *adj.*

fel·spar (fel′spär′), *n.* *Chiefly Brit.* feldspar. [< G *Fels* rock + SPAR[3], by false etymological analysis]

fel·spath·ic (fel spath′ik), *adj.* *Chiefly Brit.* feldspathic. Also, **fel′spath·ose′.**

felt[1] (felt), *v.* pt. and pp. of **feel.**

felt[2] (felt), *n.* **1.** a nonwoven fabric of wool, fur, or hair, matted together by heat, moisture, and great pressure. **2.** any article made of this material, as a hat. **3.** any matted fabric or material, as a mat of asbestos fibers, rags, old paper, etc., used for insulation and in construction. —*adj.* **4.** pertaining to or made of felt. —*v.t.* **5.** to make into felt; mat or press together. **6.** to cover with or as with felt. —*v.i.* **7.** to become matted together. [ME, OE; c. G *Filz;* see FILTER]

felt·ing (fel′ting), *n.* **1.** felted material, either woven or felt fabric. **2.** the act or process of making felt. **3.** the materials of which felt is made. [FELT[2] + -ING[1]]

felt′ side′, the right side of a sheet of paper; the side against the felt rollers during manufacture. Cf. **wire side.**

fe·luc·ca (fə luk′ə), *n.* **1.** a sailing vessel, lateen-rigged on two masts, used in the Mediterranean Sea and along the Spanish and Portuguese coasts. **2.** a small fishing boat, lateen-rigged on one mast having a sharp forward rake and setting a single jib on a spike bowsprit, formerly used in the San Francisco Bay area by fishermen of Italian, Portuguese, and Greek descent. [earlier *falluca* < Sp *faluca* < Ar *fulūk,* pl. of *fulk* ship]

Felucca (def. 1)

fem., 1. female. **2.** feminine.

fe·male (fē′māl), *n.* **1.** a human being of the sex which becomes pregnant and gives birth to young; a woman or girl. **2.** any animal of corresponding sex which bears living young or produces eggs: *the females of a species.* **3.** *Bot.* a pistillate plant. —*adj.* **4.** belonging to the sex which bears young or produces eggs. **5.** of, pertaining to, or characteristic of this sex; feminine: *female suffrage; female charm.* **6.** *Bot.* **a.** designating or pertaining to a plant or its reproductive structure which produces or contains elements that need fertilization. **b.** (of seed plants) pistillate. **7.** *Mach.* noting a part, thread, etc., into which a corresponding male part fits. **8.** *Obs.* womanish; weakly. [ME, var. (by assoc. with *male*) of *femelle* < ML *fēmella* female, L: little woman, dim. of *fēmina;* see FEME] —**fe′male·ness,** *n.*
—**Syn. 1.** See **woman. 5.** FEMALE, EFFEMINATE,

FEMININE refer to attributes of women. FEMALE, referring to anything not male, is the scientific word, and was once the general word, to designate one of the two sexes: *female organs in a plant or animal; a female seminary.* EFFEMINATE is applied reproachfully or contemptuously to qualities which, although natural in women, are seldom applied to women and are unmanly and weak when possessed by men: *effeminate gestures; an effeminate voice.* FEMININE, corresponding to masculine, applies to the attributes particularly appropriate to women, esp. the softer and more delicate qualities. The word is seldom used merely to denote sex, and, if applied to men, suggests the delicacy and weakness of women: *a feminine figure, point of view, features.* —**Ant. 5.** male, masculine.

fe′male imper′sonator, a male performer who dresses as and impersonates women.

fe′male suf′frage. See **woman suffrage.**

feme (fem), *n. Law.* a woman or wife. [< AF << L *fēmina* woman; akin to FETUS, FECUND]

feme′ cov′ert (kuv′ərt), *pl.* **femes covert.** *Law.* a married woman. [< AF: covered (protected) woman]

fem·er·ell (fem′ər əl, -ə rel′), *n.* lantern (def. 5d). [late ME, var. of *fumerell* < MF *fumeril*, alter. of *fumerole* < LL *fūmāriol(um)* vent, equiv. to L *fūmāri(um)* smoke chamber (see FUME, -ARY) + *-olum*, neut. of *-olus* dim. suffix]

feme′ sole′ (sōl), *pl.* **femes sole.** *Law.* **1.** an unmarried woman, whether spinster, widow, or divorcée. **2.** a married woman who is independent of her husband with respect to property. [< AF]

feme′-sole′ trad′er (fem′sōl′), *Law.* a married woman who is entitled to carry on business on her own account and responsibility, independently of her husband. Also called **feme′-sole′ mer′chant.**

fem·i·cide (fem′i sīd′), *n.* **1.** the act of killing a woman. **2.** a person who kills a woman. [FEME + -I- + -CIDE]

fem·i·na·cy (fem′ə nə sē), *n., pl.* **-cies.** feminine nature. [< L *fēmin(a)* + -ACY]

fem·i·ne·i·ty (fem′ə nē′i tē), *n.* feminine nature; womanliness. [< L *fēmine(us)* of a woman (*fēmin(a)* woman + *-eus* -EOUS) + -ITY]

fem·i·nie (fem′ə nē), *n.* women collectively. [ME < MF, OF, equiv. to *femin-* (< L *fēmina*) woman + *-ie* -Y[3]]

fem·i·nine (fem′ə nin), *adj.* **1.** pertaining to a woman or girl: *feminine beauty; feminine dress.* **2.** like a woman; weak; gentle: *feminine delicacy.* **3.** effeminate; womanish: *a man with a feminine walk.* **4.** belonging to the female sex; female: *feminine staff members.* **5.** *Gram.* noting or pertaining to that one of the three genders of Latin, Greek, German, etc., or one of the two genders of French, Spanish, Hebrew, etc., having among its members most nouns referring to females, as well as other nouns, as Latin *stella* "star," or German *Zeit* "time." —*n. Gram.* **6.** the feminine gender. **7.** a noun or other element in or marking that gender. [late ME < L *fēminīna*, fem. of *fēminīnus*, equiv. to *fēmin(a)* woman + *-īnus* -INE[1]] —**fem′i·nine·ly,** *adv.* —**fem′i·nine·ness,** *n.*
—**Syn. 2.** See **female.**

fem′inine ca′dence, *Music.* a cadence in which the final chord falls on a weak beat.

fem′inine caesu′ra, *Pros.* a caesura occurring immediately after an unstressed or short syllable.

fem′inine end′ing, **1.** *Pros.* an unaccented syllable at the close of a line of poetry, often one which is added to the metrical pattern as an extra syllable. **2.** *Gram.* a termination or final syllable marking a feminine word: In Latin *-ā* is a feminine ending for the ablative case in the singular.

fem′inine rhyme′, *Pros.* a rhyme either of two syllables of which the second is unstressed (**double rhyme**), as in *motion, notion,* or of three syllables of which the second and third are unstressed (**triple rhyme**), as in *fortunate, importunate.*

fem·i·nin·i·ty (fem′ə nin′i tē), *n.* **1.** the quality of being feminine; womanliness: *She kept her femininity even in greasy overalls.* **2.** women collectively: *the femininity of the Middle Ages.* **3.** effeminacy. Also, **fe·min·i·ty** (fi min′i tē). [ME *femininite.* See FEMININE, -ITY]

fem·i·nise (fem′ə nīz′), *v.t., v.i.,* **-nised, -nis·ing.** *Chiefly Brit.* feminize. —**fem′i·ni·sa′tion,** *n.*

fem·i·nism (fem′ə niz′əm), *n.* **1.** the doctrine advocating social and political rights of women equal to those of men. **2.** (*sometimes cap.*) an organized movement for the attainment of such rights for women. **3.** feminine character. [< L *fēmin(a)* woman + -ISM] —**fem′i·nist,** *n.* —**fem′i·nis′tic,** *adj.*

fem·i·nize (fem′ə nīz′), *v.t., v.i.,* **-nized, -niz·ing.** to make or become feminine: *a nation feminized by luxury and sloth; a boy feminized by his mother.* Also, *esp. Brit.,* **feminise.** [< L *fēmin(a)* woman + -IZE] —**fem′i·ni·za′tion,** *n.*

femme (fam; *Eng.* fem), *n., pl.* ***femmes*** (fam; *Eng.* femz). *French.* **1.** a woman. **2.** a wife.

femme de cham·bre (fam də shäɴ′brᵊ), *pl.* ***femmes de cham·bre*** (fam də shäɴ′brᵊ). *French.* **1.** a lady's maid. **2.** a chambermaid. Also called **fille de chambre.** [lit., woman of (the) bedroom]

femme fa·tale (fam fa tal′; *Eng.* fem′ fə tal′, -täl′), *pl.* ***femmes fa·tales*** (fam fa tal′; *Eng.* fem fə talz′, -tälz′). *French.* an irresistibly attractive woman, esp. one who leads men into difficult, dangerous, or disastrous situations; siren. [lit., fatal woman]

fem·o·ral (fem′ər əl), *adj.* of, pertaining to, or situated near the thigh or femur. [< L *femor-* (s. of *femur*) thigh + -AL[1]]

fem′oral ar′tery, *Anat.* the main artery of the thigh, supplying blood to the leg.

fe·mur (fē′mər), *n., pl.* **fe·murs, fem·o·ra** (fem′ər ə). **1.** *Anat., Zool.* a bone in the lower limb, extending from the pelvis to the knee, in man the longest, largest, and strongest bone in the body; thighbone. See diag. under **skeleton. 2.** *Zool.* a corresponding bone in a horse or other quadruped extending from the pelvis to the stifle. **3.** *Entomol.* the third segment of the leg of an insect (counting from the base), situated between the trochanter and the tibia. See diag. under **coxa.** [< L: the thigh]

fen[1] (fen), *n.* **1.** *Brit.* low land covered wholly or partially with water; boggy land; a marsh. **2. the Fens,** a marshy region W and S of The Wash, in E England. [ME, OE; c. Icel *fen* quagmire, Goth *fani* mud, D *ven,* G *Fenn* fen, bog]

fen[2] (fen), *n., pl.* **fen.** an aluminum coin of China, the 10th part of a chiao or the 100th part of a jên-min-piao, equivalent to about .004 of a U.S. dollar. [< Chin *fēn*]

fe·na·gle (fi nā′gəl), *v.t., v.i.,* **-gled, -gling.** finagle. —**fe·na′gler,** *n.*

fence (fens), *n., v.,* **fenced, fenc·ing.** —*n.* **1.** a barrier enclosing or bordering a field, yard, etc., usually made of posts and wire or wood, used to prevent entrance, to confine, or to mark a boundary. **2.** the act, practice, art, or sport of fencing. **3.** skill in argument, repartee, etc. **4.** a person who receives and disposes of stolen goods. **5.** the place of business of such a person. **6.** *Mach.* a guard or guide, as for regulating the movements of a tool or work. **7.** *Carpentry.* a slotted guide used esp. with a framing square to lay out cuts on rafters and staircase strings. **8.** *Archaic.* a means of defense; a bulwark. **9. mend one's fences,** to strengthen or reestablish one's position by conciliation or negotiation: *One could tell by his superficially deferential manner that he was trying to mend his fences.* **10. on the fence,** *U.S. Informal.* uncommitted; neutral; undecided: *The new nations are still on the fence.* —*v.t.* **11.** to enclose by some barrier, establishing exclusive right to possession: *to fence a farm.* **12.** to separate by or as by a fence or fences (often fol. by *in, off, out,* etc.): *to fence off a corner of one's yard; to fence out unwholesome influences.* **13.** *Naut.* to reinforce (an opening in a sail or the like) by sewing a grommet or the like around it. **14.** to defend; protect; guard: *The president was fenced by bodyguards wherever he went.* **15.** *Archaic.* to ward off; keep out. —*v.i.* **16.** to practice the art or sport of fencing. **17.** to parry arguments; strive to evade giving direct answers; hedge: *The mayor fenced when asked if he would run again.* **18.** (of a horse) to leap over a fence. **19.** *Obs.* to raise a defense. [late ME *fens,* aph. for *defens* DEFENSE] —**fence′like′,** *adj.*

fence′ liz′ard, a spiny lizard, *Sceloperus undulatus,* of the eastern U.S., often found on fences, rocks, logs, etc. See illus. under **lizard.**

fence-off (fens′ôf′, -of′), *n. Fencing.* a match between individual contestants or teams for settling a tie. [n. use of v. phrase *fence off*]

fenc·er (fen′sər), *n.* **1.** a person who fences. **2.** a person who practices the art of fencing with a sword, foil, etc. **3.** a horse trained to jump barriers, as for show or sport. **4.** *Australian.* a person who builds or repairs fences. [FENCE + -ER[1]]

fence-sit·ter (fens′sit′ər), *n.* a person who remains neutral in a controversy. —**fence′-sit′ting,** *n.*

fen·ci·ble (fen′sə bəl), *n.* **1.** *Archaic.* a soldier enlisted for defensive service in his own country only. —*adj.* **2.** *Scot.* capable of being defended or of making defense. [late ME *fensable,* aph. var. of *defensable* DEFENSIBLE]

fenc·ing (fen′siŋ), *n.* **1.** the art, practice, or sport in which an épée, foil, or saber is used for defense and attack. **2.** a parrying of arguments; evasion of direct answers: *political fencing on important issues.* **3.** an enclosure or railing. **4.** fences collectively. **5.** material for fences. [late ME *fensing* safeguarding, maintenance. See FENCE, -ING[1]]

fend (fend), *v.t.* **1.** to ward off (often fol. by *off*): *to fend off blows.* **2.** *Archaic.* to defend. —*v.i.* **3.** to resist or make defense: *to fend against poverty.* **4.** to parry; fence. **5.** to shift; provide: *to fend for oneself.* [ME *fende(n),* aph. var. of *defenden* to DEFEND]

fend·er (fen′dər), *n.* **1.** one who or that which wards something off. **2.** the pressed and formed sheet-metal part mounted over the road wheels of an automobile, bicycle, etc., to reduce the splashing of mud, water, and the like. **3.** a device on the front of a locomotive, streetcar, or the like, for clearing the track of obstructions. **4.** a mudguard or splashboard on a horse-drawn vehicle. **5.** *Naut.* a piece of timber, bundle of rope, or the like, hung over the side of a vessel to lessen shock or prevent chafing, as between the vessel and a dock or another vessel. **6.** a low metal guard before an open fireplace, to keep back falling coals. [ME *fendour,* aph. var. of *defendour* DEFENDER]

fend·ered (fen′dərd), *adj.* provided or protected with fenders or a fender: *The ship must be well fendered before approaching the dock.* [FENDER + -ED[3]]

fend′er pile′, a pile, usually one of a group, set beside ferry slips, wharves, etc., to guide approaching vessels and driven so as to yield slightly when struck in order to lessen the shock of contact. Also called **pile fender.**

fend′er wall′, a dwarf wall supporting a raised hearth.

Fe·nel·la (fə nel′ə), *n.* a girl's given name. Also, **Finella.**

Fé·ne·lon (fā nᵊlôɴ′), *n.* **Fran·çois de Sa·li·gnac de La Mothe** (fräɴ swa′ də sa lē nyak′ də la môt′), 1651–1715, French theologian and writer.

fen·er·a·tion (fen′ə rā′shən), *n. Law.* the lending of money on interest; usury. [< L *faenerātiōn-* (s. of *faenerātiō*), equiv. to *faenerāt(us)* (ptp. of *faenerārī* to lend on interest) + *-iōn-* -ION]

fen·es·tel·la (fen′i stel′ə), *n., pl.* **-es·tel·lae** (-i stel′ē). *Archit.* **1.** a small window or windowlike opening. **2.** a small windowlike niche in the wall on the south side of an altar, containing the piscina and frequently also the credence. [< L, dim. of *fenestra* window; see FENESTRA]

fe·nes·tra (fi nes′trə), *n., pl.* **-trae** (-trē). **1.** *Anat., Zool.* a small opening or perforation, as in a bone. **2.** *Entomol.* a transparent spot in an otherwise opaque surface, as in the wings of certain butterflies and moths. **3.** *Archit.* a windowlike opening. [< NL, special use of L *fenestra* window, hole (in a wall)] —**fe·nes′tral,** *adj.*

fe·nes·trat·ed (fi nes′trā tid, fen′i strā′tid), *adj.* *Archit.* having windows; windowed; characterized by windows. Also, **fe·nes′trate.** [< L *fenestrāt(us)* furnished with windows (see FENESTRA, -ATE[1]) + -ED[2]]

fen·es·tra·tion (fen′i strā′shən), *n.* **1.** *Archit.* the design and disposition of windows and other exterior openings of a building. **2.** *Furniture.* an ornamental motif having the form of a blind arcade or arch, as in medieval cabinetwork. **3.** *Med., Surg.* **a.** a perforation in a structure. **b.** an operation to effect such an opening. **c.** Also called **fenestra′tion opera′tion, Lempert operation, Lempert's operation.** the creation of an artificial opening into the labyrinth of the ear to restore hearing loss from otosclerosis. [< L *fenestrāt(us)* (see FENESTRATED) + -ION]

Feng·kieh (fuŋ′jye′), *n.* a city in central China, on the Yangtze River. ab. 250,000. Also called **Kweichow.**

Feng·tien (fuŋ′tyen′), *n.* **1.** Mukden. **2.** former name of **Liaoning.**

Fe·ni·an (fē′nē ən, fēn′yən), *n.* **1.** a member of an Irish revolutionary organization founded in New York in 1858, which worked for the establishment of an independent Irish republic. **2.** *Irish Hist.* a member of any of several bands of Scots and Picts fighting the Romans along Hadrian's Wall in Britain. **3.** (in late Irish legends) a member of a roving band of warriors, the center of numerous legends comparable to those of King Arthur and the Round Table. —**Fe′ni·an·ism,** *n.*

Fe′nian cy′cle, the cycle of legends describing and glorifying the bravery, battles, and wandering life of the Irish Fenians of the 2nd and 3rd centuries.

fen·land (fen′land′, -lənd), *n.* a low area of marshy ground. [FEN[1] + LAND]

fen·man (fen′mən), *n., pl.* **-men.** *Brit.* a dweller in the Fens of England. [FEN[1] + MAN[1]]

fen·nec (fen′ek), *n.* a small, pale yellowish-brown fox, *Vulpes zerda,* of northern Africa, having large, pointed ears. [< Ar *fenek*]

fen·nel (fen′ᵊl), *n.* **1.** an umbelliferous plant, *Foeniculum vulgare,* having yellow flowers. **2.** Also, **fen′nel seed′.** the aromatic fruits of this plant, used in cookery and medicine. **3.** any of various more or less similar plants, as *Ferula communis* (**giant fennel**), a tall, ornamental, apiaceous herb. [ME *fenel,* OE *fenol,* var. of *finu(g)l* < VL **fenucl(um),* r. L *fēniculum,* equiv. to *fēni-* (comb. form of *fēnum* hay) + *-culum* -CLE]

fen·nel·flow·er (fen′ᵊl flou′ər), *n.* **1.** any of the ranunculaceous herbs of the genus *Nigella,* esp. *N. sativa,* whose seeds are used in the East as a condiment and medicine. **2.** the flower of this plant. [FENNEL + FLOWER]

fen·ny (fen′ē), *adj.* **1.** marshy; boggy. **2.** inhabiting or growing in fens. [ME; OE *fennig.* See FEN[1], -Y[1]]

Fen·rir (fen′rir), *n. Scand. Myth.* a wolflike monster, a son of Loki and Angerboda, chained by Gleipnir and so restrained for the present, but destined to be released at Ragnarok to eat Odin and to be killed by Vidar. Also called **Fen·ris-wolf** (fen′ris wŏŏlf′).

Fen·ton (fen′tᵊn), *n.* a town in central Michigan. 6142 (1960).

fen·u·greek (fen′yŏŏ grēk′), *n.* a plant, *Trigonella Foenum-Graecum,* indigenous to western Asia, but extensively cultivated elsewhere, chiefly for forage and for its mucilaginous seeds, which are used in medicine. [ME *fenugrek,* OE *fenogrēcum* < L *fēnu(m) Graecum,* lit., Greek hay. See FENNEL]

Fen·wick (fen′wik), *n.* a boy's given name.

feod (fyōōd), *n. Obs.* feud[2]. —**feo′dal,** *adj.* —**feo·dal′i·ty,** *n.*

feo·da·ry (fyōō′də rē), *n., pl.* **-ries.** **1.** a feudal vassal. **2.** *Obs.* a confederate or accomplice. [ME *feodarie* < ML *feodāri(us).* See FEUD[2], -ARY]

Fe·o·dor (fē′ə dôr′; *Russ.* fe ô′dor), *n.* a boy's given name, form of **Theodore.** Also, **Fyodor.**

Fe·o·do·ra (fē′ə dōr′ə, -dôr′ə), *n.* a girl's given name, form of **Fedora.**

feoff (fef, fēf), *v.t.* to invest with a fief or fee; enfeoff. [ME *feoffe(n)* < AF *feoffe(r)* (c. OF *fiefer*), deriv. of *feoff* FIEF] —**feof′for, feoff′er,** *n.*

feoff·ee (fef′ē, fē fē′), *n.* a person invested with a fief. [late ME *feoffe* < AF, ptp. of *feoffer* to FEOFF; see -EE] —**feoff·ee′ship,** *n.*

Fe·o·sol (fē′ə sol′), *n. Pharm., Trademark.* See **ferrous sulfate.**

FEPC, Fair Employment Practices Committee.

fer (fûr; *unstressed* fər), *prep., conj. Eye Dialect.* for.

-fer, a noun suffix borrowed from Latin, meaning "bearing": *conifer.* Cf. **-ferous.** [< L, orig. adj. suffix, akin to *ferre* to bear]

FERA, Federal Emergency Relief Administration.

fe·ra·cious (fə rā′shəs), *adj.* fruitful; productive. [FERACI(TY) + -OUS]

fe·rac·i·ty (fə ras′i tē), *n. Rare.* fruitfulness; productivity. [late ME *feracite* < L *ferācitās* fruitfulness, equiv. to *ferāci-* (s. of *ferax*) fruitful + *-tās* -TY[2]]

fe·rae na·tu·rae (fē′rē nə tŏŏr′ē, -tyŏŏr′ē), *Law.* (of animals) wild or undomesticated (distinguished from *domitae naturae*). [< L: lit., of a wild nature]

fe·ral[1] (fēr′əl, fer′-), *adj.* **1.** existing in a natural state, as animals or plants; not domesticated or cultivated; wild. **2.** having reverted to the wild state, as from domestication. **3.** of or characteristic of wild animals; ferocious; brutal. [< ML *(ferālis),* equiv. to L *fer(a)* wild beast + *-ālis* -AL[1]]

fe·ral[2] (fēr′əl), *adj.* **1.** causing death; fatal. **2.** funereal; gloomy. [< L *ferāl(is)* of the dead, orig. of the bier on which the body was borne to the grave. See BIER, -AL[1]]

fer·bam (fûr′bam), *n. Chem.* a black, fluffy, water-insoluble powder, $[(CH_3)_2NCSS]_3Fe$, used chiefly as a fungicide for protecting certain farm crops. Also called **ferric dimethyldithiocarbamate.** [FER(RIC DIMETHYL-DITHIOCAR)BAM(ATE)]

Fer·ber (fûr′bər), *n.* **Edna,** 1887–1968, U.S. novelist, short-story writer, and playwright.

fer·ber·ite (fûr′bə rīt′), *n.* a mineral, ferrous tungstate, $FeWO_4$, in the wolframite group: a source of tungsten. [named after R. *Ferber,* 19th-century German mineralogist; see -ITE[1]]

Ferd (fûrd), *n.* a boy's given name, form of **Ferdinand.**

fer-de-lance (fer′dᵊlans′, -dᵊläns′), *n.* a large pit viper, *Trimeresurus atrox,* of tropical America. [< F: lit., iron part (i.e., head) of a lance]

Fer·di·nand (fûr′dᵊnand′), *n.* a boy's given name.

Fer·di·nand I (fûr′dᵊnand′; *Ger.* fer′di nänt′), *n.* **1.** 1503–64, king of Bohemia and Hungary 1526–64; emperor of the Holy Roman Empire 1558–64 (brother of Emperor Charles V). **2.** (*Maximilian Karl Leopold Maria*) 1861–1948, king of Bulgaria 1908–18. **3.** Spanish, **Fernando I.** ("*Ferdinand the Great*") died 1065, king of Castile 1033–65, king of Navarre and Leon 1037–65; emperor of Spain 1056–65.

Ferdinand II, 1. 1578–1637, king of Bohemia 1617–19, 1620–37; king of Hungary 1619?–37; emperor of the Holy Roman Empire 1620–37. 2. ("*the Catholic*") 1452–1516, founder of the Spanish monarchy 1506: king of Sicily 1468–1516, king of Aragon 1479–1516; as Ferdinand III, king of Naples 1504–16; as King Ferdinand V, joint sovereign of Castile 1474–1504.

Ferdinand III. See **Ferdinand II** (def. 2).

Ferdinand V. See **Ferdinand II** (def. 2).

Fer·di·nan·da (fûr′dənan′də), *n.* a girl's given name.

Fer·dus (fer′dəs), *n.* Firdausi.

fere (fēr), *n. Obs.* a companion; mate. [ME; OE (*ge*)*fēra*, deriv. of *fēran* to go; akin to FARE, FEIRIE]

fer·e·to·ry (fer′i tōr′ē, -tôr′ē), *n., pl.* **-ries.** 1. a shrine, usually portable, designed to hold the relics of saints. 2. (formerly) a room or chapel, as in a church, cathedral, etc., where shrines were kept. [late ME < ML *feretrāri*(*us*) (with loss of *r* by dissimilation), equiv. to L *feretr*(*um*) bier (< Gk *phéretron*) + *-ārius* -ARY; r. ME *fertre* < AF < L *feretr*(*um*)]

Fer·gus (fûr′gəs), *n.* 1. *Irish Legend.* one of the great warrior kings of Ulster: he lost his throne to Conchobar and became a tutor to Cuchulainn. 2. a boy's given name.

Fer·gu·son (fûr′gə sən), *n.* 1. a city in E Missouri, near St. Louis. 22,149 (1960). 2. a boy's given name.

fer·gu·son·ite (fûr′gə sə nīt′), *n.* a rare mineral, yttrium columbate and tantalate, found in pegmatite. [named after R. *Ferguson*, 19th-century Scottish physician; see -ITE[1]]

fe·ri·a (fēr′ē ə), *n., pl.* **fe·ri·ae** (fēr′ē ē′), **fe·ri·as.** 1. any of the religious holidays of ancient Rome. 2. *Eccles.* a weekday on which no feast is celebrated. [< LL: day of the week (e.g. *secunda fēria* second day, Monday); in L only pl. *fēriae* holidays; see FAIR[2]]

fe·ria (fe′ʀyä; *Eng.* fer′ē ə), *n., pl.* **fe·rias** (fe′ʀyäs; *Eng.* fer′ē əz). *Spanish.* a usually local festival or fair in Spain or Spanish America, usually held in honor of a patron saint.

fe·ri·al (fēr′ē əl), *adj.* 1. pertaining to a holiday. 2. *Eccles.* pertaining to a feria. [< ML *fēriāl*(*is*). See FERIA, -AL[1]]

fe·rine (fēr′īn, -in), *adj.* feral. [< L *ferīn*(*us*), equiv. to *fer*(*a*) a wild animal (n. use of fem. of *ferus* wild) + *-īnus* -INE[1]]

Fe·rin·gi (fə ring′gē), *n. Usually Disparaging.* (in India) 1. a European or a person of European descent. 2. a Portuguese born in India. Also, **Fe·rin′ghee.** [<< Pers *Farangī*, in Ar *Faranjī*, lit., Frank]

fer·i·ty (fer′i tē), *n.* 1. a wild, untamed, or uncultivated state. 2. savagery; ferocity. [< L *feritās*, equiv. to *fer*(*us*) wild, untamed + *-itās* -ITY]

Fer·man·agh (fər man′ə), *n.* a county in SW Northern Ireland. 51,531 (1961); 653 sq. mi. *Co. seat:* Enniskillen.

Fer·mat (fer mᴀ′; *Eng.* fer mä′), *n.* 1. **Pierre de** (pyer də), 1601–65, French mathematician. 2. a crater in the fourth quadrant of the face of the moon: about 25 miles in diameter.

fer·ma·ta (fer mä′tə; *It.* feʀ mä′tä), *n., pl.* **-tas,** *It.* **-te** (-te). *Music.* 1. the sustaining of a note, chord, or rest for a duration longer than the indicated time value, with the length of the extension at the performer's discretion. 2. a symbol 𝄐 placed over a note, chord, or rest indicating a fermata. [< It: stop, pause, n. use of fem. of ptp. of *fermare* to stop < L *firmāre* to make firm. See FIRM[1], -ATE[1]]

Fer·mat's′ last′ the′orem (fer mäz′), *Math.* an unproved theorem that the equation $x^n + y^n = z^n$ has no solution for *x, y, z* nonzero integers when *n* is greater than 2. [named after P. de FERMAT]

Fermat's′ prin′ciple, *Optics.* the law that the path taken by a ray of light in going from one point to another point will be the path that requires the least time. Also called **Fermat's′ prin′ciple of least′ time′.** [named after P. de FERMAT]

Fermat's′ the′orem, *Math.* the theorem that an integer raised to a prime power leaves the same remainder as the integer itself when divided by the prime. [named after P. de FERMAT]

fer·ment (*n.* fûr′ment; *v.* fər ment′), *n.* 1. Also called **organized ferment.** any of a group of living organisms, as yeasts, molds, certain bacteria, etc., that cause fermentation. 2. Also called **unorganized ferment.** an enzyme. 3. fermentation. 4. agitation; unrest; excitement; commotion; tumult: *The new painters worked in a creative ferment. The capital lived in a political ferment.* —*v.t.* 5. to act upon as a ferment. 6. *Biochem.* to cause to undergo fermentation. 7. to inflame; foment: *to ferment prejudiced crowds to riot.* 8. to cause agitation or excitement in: *Reading fermented his active imagination.* —*v.i.* 9. to be fermented; undergo fermentation. 10. to seethe with agitation or excitement. [late ME < L *ferment*(*um*) yeast (n.), *ferment*(*āre*) (to) cause to rise (v.); akin to BARM, L *fervēre* to boil] —**fer·ment′a·bil′i·ty,** *n.* —**fer·ment′a·ble,** *adj.*

fer·men·ta·tion (fûr′men tā′shən), *n.* 1. the act or process of fermenting. 2. *Biochem.* a change brought about by a ferment, as yeast enzymes, which convert grape sugar into ethyl alcohol. 3. agitation; excitement. [ME *fermentacioun* < LL *fermentātiōn-* (s. of *fermentātiō*), equiv. to L *fermentāt*(*us*) fermented (see FERMENT, -ATE[1]) + *-iōn-* -ION]

fermenta′tion al′cohol, alcohol (def. 1).

fer·ment·a·tive (fər men′tə tiv), *adj.* 1. tending to produce or undergo fermentation. 2. pertaining to or of the nature of fermentation. [obs. *fermentate* to cause to ferment (< L *fermentāt*(*us*); see FERMENT, -ATE[1]) + -IVE] —**fer·ment′a·tive·ly,** *adv.* —**fer·ment′a·tive·ness** *n.*

ferme or·née (feʀm ôʀ nā′), *pl.* **fermes or·nées** (feʀm zôʀ nā′). *French.* the residence of a gentleman farmer that has been given a picturesque architectural treatment. [lit., decorated farm]

fer·mi (fûr′mē; *It.* feʀ′mē), *n.* a unit of length, 10^{-13} cm. *Abbr.:* F [named after E. FERMI]

Fer·mi (fûr′mē; *It.* feʀ′mē), *n.* **En·ri·co** (en rē′kō; *It.* en ʀe′kô), 1901–54, Italian physicist, in the U.S. after 1939: Nobel prize 1938.

Fer′mi-Di·rac′ statis′tics (fûr′mē də rak′), *Physics.* quantum statistics defining the possible arrangements of particles in a given system in terms of the exclusion principle. [named after E. FERMI and A. M. DIRAC]

fer·mi·on (fûr′mē on′), *n. Physics.* any of several elementary particles, as a proton or neutron, having half-integral spin and obeying the exclusion principle and Fermi-Dirac statistics. Cf. **boson.** [FERMI + (MES)ON[1]]

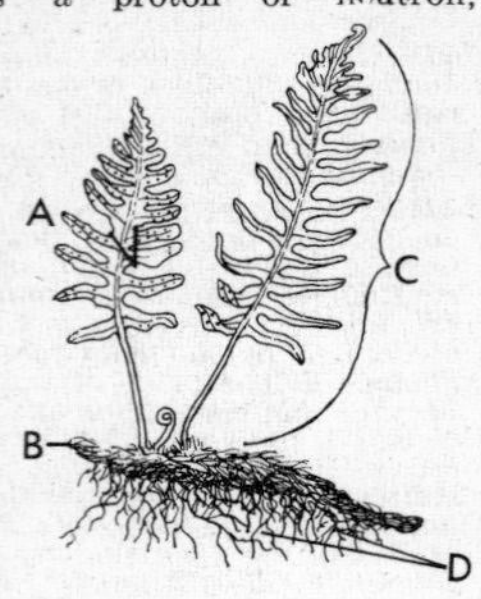

Fern
Mature sporophyte of *Polypodium virginianum*
A, Sori; B, Rhizome (stem); C, Leaf; D, Roots

fer·mi·um (fûr′mē əm), *n. Chem.* a synthetic, radioactive element. *Symbol:* Fm; *at. no.:* 100. [named after E. FERMI; see -IUM]

fern (fûrn), *n. Bot.* any of the pteridophytes of the order *Filicales*, distinguished from other pteridophytes in having few leaves, large in proportion to the stems, and bearing sporangia on the undersurface or margin. [ME *ferne*, OE *fearn;* c. G *Farn* fern, Skt *parṇá* feather] —**fern′less,** *adj.* —**fern′like′,** *adj.*

Fern (fûrn), *n.* a girl's given name.

Fer·nan·da (fûr nan′də; *Sp.* feʀ nän′dä), *n.* a girl's given name, form of **Ferdinanda.**

Fer·nan·del (fûr′nan del′; *Fr.* feʀ näɴ del′), *n.* (*Fernand Joseph Désiré Contandin*) born 1903, French actor.

Fer·nan·dez (fer nan′dez; *Sp.* feʀ nän′deth), *n.* **Juan** (hwän, wän; *Span.* hwän), 1536?–1602?, Spanish navigator: explorer in South America and the Pacific.

Fer·nán·dez de Li·zar·di (feʀ nän′des de lē sär′dē), **Jo·sé Joa·quín** (hô se′ hwä kēn′), ("*El Pensador Mexicano*"), 1776–1827, Mexican journalist and novelist.

Fer·nan·di′na Beach′ (fûr′nən dē′nə), a town in NE Florida. 7276 (1960).

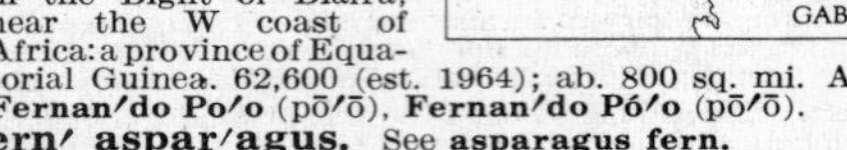

Fer·nan·do de No·ro·nha (feʀ nänn′dōō də nô ʀô′nyə), *n.* an island in the S Atlantic, ab. 125 mi. E of easternmost tip of Brazil: a Brazilian penal colony. 10 sq. mi.

Fer·nan·do Po (fər nan′dō pō′), an island in the Bight of Biafra, near the W coast of Africa: a province of Equatorial Guinea. 62,600 (est. 1964); ab. 800 sq. mi. Also, **Fernan′do Po′o** (pō′ō), **Fernan′do Pó′o** (pō′ō).

fern′ aspar′agus. See **asparagus fern.**

Fer·na·ta (fûr nā′tə, -nä′tə), *n.* a girl's given name, form of **Fern.**

fern·brake (fûrn′brāk′), *n.* a thicket or dense growth of ferns. [FERN + BRAKE[2]]

Fern·dale (fûrn′dāl′), *n.* 1. a city in SE Michigan, near Detroit. 31,347 (1960). 2. a town in central Pennsylvania. 2717 (1960).

Fer·ne·li·us (fûr nā′lē əs), *n.* a walled plain in the fourth quadrant of the face of the moon: about 40 miles in diameter.

fern·er·y (fûr′nə rē), *n., pl.* **-er·ies.** 1. a place or a glass case in which ferns are grown for ornament. 2. a collection of ferns in a garden or a potted display. [FERN + -ERY]

Fern′ Hill′, a poem (1943) by Dylan Thomas.

fern′ seed′, the spores of ferns, formerly supposed to have the power to make persons invisible.

fern·y (fûr′nē), *adj.,* **fern·i·er, fern·i·est.** 1. pertaining to, consisting of, or like ferns: *ferny leaves.* 2. abounding in or overgrown with ferns: *ferny undergrowth.* [FERN + -Y[1]]

fe·ro·cious (fə rō′shəs), *adj.* 1. savagely fierce, as a wild beast, person, action, aspect, etc.; violently cruel. 2. extreme or intense: *a ferocious thirst.* [FEROCI(TY) + -OUS] —**fe·ro′cious·ly,** *adv.* —**fe·ro′cious·ness,** *n.* —**Syn.** 1. rapacious. See **fierce.** —**Ant.** 1. mild, tame.

fe·roc·i·ty (fə ros′i tē), *n.* a ferocious quality or state; savage fierceness. [< L *ferōcitās*, equiv. to *ferōci-* (s. of *ferox*) daring, headstrong + *-tās* -TY[2]]

-ferous, a suffix meaning "bearing," "producing," "yielding," "containing," "conveying," used to form adjectives from stems in **-fer:** *coniferous; pestiferous.* [ME; see -FER, -OUS]

Fer·ra·ra (fə rär′ə; *It.* feʀ ʀä′ʀä), *n.* a city in N Italy, near the Po River: medieval university and cathedral. 151,145 (1961).

fer·rate (fer′āt), *n. Chem.* a salt of the hypothetical ferric acid, H_2FeO_4. [< L *ferr*(*um*) iron + -ATE[2]]

Fer′rel's law′ (fer′əlz), the law that wind is deflected to the right in the Northern Hemisphere and to the left in the Southern Hemisphere, derived from the application of the Coriolis effect to air masses. [named after W. *Ferrel* (d. 1891), American meteorologist]

fer·re·ous (fer′ē əs), *adj.* of, resembling, or containing iron: *a ferreous alloy.* [< L *ferreus*, equiv. to *ferr*(*um*) iron + *-eus* -EOUS]

Fer·re·ro (feʀ ʀe′ʀô), *n.* **Gu·gliel·mo** (gōō lyel′mô), 1871–1942, Italian historian and sociologist.

fer·ret[1] (fer′it), *n.* 1. a domesticated, red-eyed, albinic variety of the polecat, used in Europe for driving rabbits and rats from their burrows. 2. See **black-footed ferret.** —*v.t.* 3. to drive out by or as by means of a ferret (often fol. by *out*): *to ferret rabbits from their burrows; to ferret out enemies.* 4. to hunt with ferrets. 5. to hunt over with ferrets: *to ferret a field.* 6. to search out or bring to light (often fol. by *out*): *to ferret out the facts.* 7. to harry, worry, or torment: *His problems ferreted him day and night.* —*v.i.* 8. to search about. [ME, var. of *furet* < MF << VL **furitt*(*us*), equiv. to *fur* thief (< L) + *-ittus* -ET] —**fer′ret·er,** *n.* —**fer′ret·y,** *adj.*

Black-footed ferret, *Mustela nigripes* (Total length 2 ft.; tail 6 in.)

fer·ret[2] (fer′it), *n.* a narrow tape or ribbon, as of silk or cotton, used for binding, trimming, etc. [alter. of It *fioretto* floss silk, lit., little flower, equiv. to *fior*(*e*) (< L *flōrem;* see FLOWER) + *-etto* -ET]

fer′ret badg′er, any of several small carnivores of the genus *Helictis*, of southern and eastern Asia.

ferri-, 1. a learned borrowing from Latin meaning "iron," used in the formation of compound words: *ferriferous.* 2. *Chem.* a combining form of **ferric,** indicating iron, esp. in the trivalent state: *ferricyanide.* Also, **ferro-.** [< L, comb. form of *ferrum* iron]

fer·ri·age (fer′ē ij), *n.* 1. conveyance or transportation by a ferryboat. 2. the fare or price charged for ferrying. [FERRY + -AGE]

fer·ric (fer′ik), *adj. Chem.* of or containing iron, esp. in the trivalent state. [< L *ferr*(*um*) iron + -IC]

fer′ric ammo′nium ox′alate, *Chem.* a green, crystalline, water-soluble, synthetically-produced powder, $(NH_4)_3Fe(C_2O_4)_3{\cdot}3H_2O$, used chiefly in the manufacture of blueprint paper. Also called **ammonioferric oxalate, iron ammonium oxalate.**

fer′ric chlo′ride, *Chem.* a compound which in its anhydrous form, $FeCl_3$, occurs as a black-brown, water-soluble solid, and which in its hydrated form, $FeCl_3{\cdot}xH_2O$, occurs in orange-yellow, deliquescent crystals: used chiefly in engraving, for deodorizing sewage, as a mordant, and in medicine as an astringent and styptic. Also called **iron trichloride, iron perchloride.**

fer′ric di·meth′yl·di·thi·o·car′ba·mate (dī-meth′əl dī thī′ō kär′bə māt′, -kär bam′āt), *Chem.* ferbam. [DI-[1] + METHYL + DI-[1] + THIO- + CARBAMATE]

fer′ric ox′ide, *Chem.* a dark-red, crystalline, water-insoluble solid, Fe_2O_3, occurring naturally, as hematite and rust, or synthesized: used chiefly as a pigment, as a mordant, and in the manufacture of polishing compounds.

fer′ric so′dium ox′alate, *Chem.* an emerald-green, crystalline, extremely water-soluble salt, $Na_3Fe(C_2O_4)_3{\cdot}4\frac{1}{2}H_2O$, used in photography and blueprinting. Also called **iron sodium oxalate.**

fer′ri·cy·an′ic ac′id (fer′ī sī an′ik, fer′ē-), *Chem.* a brown, crystalline, unstable, water-soluble solid, $H_3Fe(CN)_6$, obtained by the interaction of a ferricyanide and an acid. [FERRI- + CYANIC]

fer·ri·cy·a·nide (fer′ī sī′ə nīd′, fer′ē-), *n. Chem.* a salt of ferricyanic acid, as potassium ferricyanide, $K_3Fe(CN)_6$. [FERRI- + CYANIDE]

Fer·ri·day (fer′i dā′), *n.* a town in central Louisiana. 4563 (1960).

fer·rif·er·ous (fə rif′ər əs), *adj.* producing or yielding iron: *ferriferous rock.* [FERRI- + -FEROUS]

fer·ri·he·mo·glo·bin (fer′ī hē′mə glō′bin, -hem′ə-, fer′ē-), *n. Biochem.* methemoglobin. [FERRI- + HEMOGLOBIN]

Fer·ris (fer′is), *n.* a boy's given name.

Fer′ris wheel′ (fer′is), an amusement ride consisting of a large upright wheel rotating on a permanent stand and having seats suspended freely around its rim so that they remain horizontal as they revolve in a vertical axis. [named after G. W. G. *Ferris* (d. 1896), American engineer]

fer·rite (fer′īt), *n.* 1. *Chem.* a compound, as $NaFeO_2$, formed when ferric oxide is combined with a more basic metallic oxide. 2. *Metall.* the pure iron constituent of ferrous metals, as distinguished from the iron carbides. 3. *Petrog.* any of various reddish-brown, indeterminable mineral substances, probably iron compounds, frequently observed in the microscopic examination of certain igneous rocks. [< L *ferr*(*um*) iron + -ITE[1]]

fer·ri·tin (fer′i tᵊn), *n. Biochem.* an amber-colored, crystalline protein, found in the liver, spleen, and bone marrow, that consists of apoferritin combined with a ferric hydroxide-ferric phosphate complex, and that serves to store iron for use in metabolism. [FERRITE + -IN[2]]

ferro-, a combining form meaning "iron": *ferroconcrete.* In chemical terminology, the meanings of **ferri-** and **ferro-** are specialized to correspond to *ferric* and *ferrous.* Also, **ferri-.** [repr. L *ferrum* iron]

fer·ro·al·loy (fer′ō al′oi, -ə loi′), *n.* an alloy of iron with some other material, used as an alloy of steel. [FERRO- + ALLOY]

fer·ro·a·lu·mi·num (fer′ō ə lōō′mə nəm), *n.* a ferroalloy containing up to 80 percent aluminum. [FERRO- + ALUMINUM]

fer·ro·cal·cite (fer′ō kal′sīt), *n. Mineral.* calcite containing ferrous carbonate, $FeCO_3$. [FERRO- + CALCITE]

fer·ro·cene (fer′ə sēn′), *n. Chem.* 1. Also called **dicyclopentadienyliron.** an orange, crystalline, water-insoluble coordination compound, $(C_5H_5)_2Fe$, having a camphorlike odor: used chiefly as an antiknock agent for gasoline and as a catalyst. 2. Also called **dicyclopentadienyl metal.** any of a class of analogous compounds containing a metal. [FERRO- + C(YCLOPENTAD)IEN]

fer·ro·ce·ri·um (fer′ō sēr′ē əm), *n.* an alloy of 65 percent misch metal and 35 percent iron. [< NL; see FERRO-, CERIUM]

fer·ro·chro·mi·um (fer′ō krō′mē əm), *n.* a ferroalloy containing up to 70 percent chromium. Also, **fer·ro·chrome** (fer′ə krōm′). [FERRO- + CHROMIUM]

fer·ro·con·crete (fer′ō kon′krēt, -kon krēt′), *n.* See **reinforced concrete.** [FERRO- + CONCRETE]

fer′ro·cy·an′ic ac′id (fer′ō sī an′ik), *Chem.* a white, crystalline, unstable, water-soluble solid, $H_4Fe(CN)_6$, obtained by the interaction of a ferrocyanide and an acid. [FERRO- + CYANIC]

fer·ro·cy·a·nide (fer′ō sī′ə nīd′, -nid), *n. Chem.* a salt of ferrocyanic acid, as potassium ferrocyanide, $K_4Fe(CN)_6$. [FERRO- + CYANIDE]

fer·ro·e·lec·tric (fer′ō i lek′trik), *Physics.* —*adj.* 1. pertaining to a substance that possesses spontaneous electric polarization such that the polarization can be reversed by an electric field. —*n.* 2. a ferroelectric substance. [FERRO- + ELECTRIC; coined on analogy with *ferromagnetic*] —**fer′ro·e·lec′tri·cal·ly,** *adv.* —**fer′ro·e·lec·tric′i·ty,** *n.*

Fer·rol (*Sp.* feʀ rôl′), *n.* See **El Ferrol.**

fer·ro·mag·ne·sian (fer/ō mag nē/zhən, -shən), *Mineral.* —*adj.* **1.** (of minerals and rocks) containing iron and magnesium. —*n.* **2.** an iron-magnesium mineral. [FERRO- + MAGNESIAN]

fer·ro·mag·net (fer/ō mag/nit), *n. Physics.* a ferromagnetic substance. [FERRO- + MAGNET]

fer·ro·mag·net·ic (fer/ō mag net/ik), *adj. Physics.* noting or pertaining to a substance, as iron, that below a certain temperature, the Curie point, can possess a magnetization in the absence of an external magnetic field; noting or pertaining to a substance in which the magnetic moments of the atoms have the same direction. Cf. **antiferromagnetic, diamagnetic, paramagnetic.** [FERRO- + MAGNETIC] —**fer·ro·mag·ne·tism** (fer/ō mag/ni tiz/əm), *n.*

fer·ro·man·ga·nese (fer/ō mang/gə nēs/, -nēz/), *n.* a ferroalloy containing up to 90 percent manganese. [FERRO- + MANGANESE]

fer·rom·e·ter (fə rom/i tər), *n. Physics.* a device for determining the magnetic permeability and the hysteresis of ferromagnetic materials, as of iron and steel. [FERRO- + -METER]

fer·ro·mo·lyb·de·num (fer/ō mə lib/də nəm, -mol/ib dē/nəm), *n.* a ferroalloy containing up to 60 percent molybdenum. [FERRO- + MOLYBDENUM]

fer·ro·nick·el (fer/ō nik/əl), *n.* an alloy of iron with nickel, not considered a ferroalloy. [FERRO- + NICKEL]

fer·ro·sil·i·con (fer/ō sil/ə kən), *n.* a ferroalloy containing up to 95 percent silicon. [FERRO- + SILICON]

fer·ro·ti·ta·ni·um (fer/ō tī tā/nē əm, -ti-), *n.* a ferroalloy containing up to 45 percent titanium. [FERRO- + TITANIUM]

fer·ro·tung·sten (fer/ō tung/stən), *n.* a ferroalloy containing up to 80 percent tungsten. [FERRO- + TUNGSTEN]

fer·ro·type (fer/ə tīp/), *v.*, **-typed, -typ·ing,** *n. Photog.* —*v.t.* **1.** to put a glossy surface on (a print) by pressing it while wet on a metal sheet (**ferrotype tin**). —*n.* **2.** a positive photograph made on a sensitized sheet of enameled iron or tin; tintype. **3.** the process of making such photographs. [FERRO- + -TYPE]

fer·rous (fer/əs), *adj. Chem.* of or containing iron, esp. in the bivalent state. [< L *ferr(um)* iron + -OUS]

fer/rous sul/fate, *Chem., Pharm.* a bluish-green, crystalline, saline-tasting, water-soluble heptahydrated solid, $FeSO_4 \cdot 7H_2O$, used chiefly in the manufacture of other iron salts, in water purification, fertilizer, inks, pigments, tanning, photography, and in medicine in the treatment of anemia. Also called **copperas, green copperas, green vitriol, iron vitriol, iron sulfate.**

fer·ro·va·na·di·um (fer/ō və nā/dē əm), *n.* a ferroalloy containing up to 55 percent vanadium. [FERRO- + VANADIUM]

fer·ro·zir·co·ni·um (fer/ō zər kō/nē əm), *n.* a ferroalloy containing up to 40 percent zirconium. [FERRO- + ZIRCONIUM]

fer·ru·gi·nous (fə ro͞o/jə nəs), *adj.* **1.** iron-bearing: *ferruginous clays.* **2.** of the color of iron rust. [< L *ferrūginus* rust-colored, equiv. to *ferrūgin-* (s. of *ferrūgō* iron-rust, deriv. of *ferrum* iron) + *-us* -OUS]

fer·rule (fer/əl, -o͞ol), *n.*, *v.*, **-ruled, -rul·ing.** —*n.* **1.** a ring or cap, usually of metal, put around the end of a post, cane, etc., for strength or protection. **2.** a short metal sleeve for strengthening a tool handle at the end holding the tool. **3.** a bushing or adapter holding the end of a tube and inserted into a hole in a plate in order to make a tight fit, used in boilers, condensers, etc. **4.** a short ring for reinforcing or decreasing the interior diameter of the end of a tube. **5.** a short plumbing fitting, covered at its outer end and calked or otherwise fixed to a branch from a pipe so that it can be removed to give access to the interior of the pipe. **6.** *Angling.* **a.** either of two fittings on the end of a section of a sectional fishing rod, one fitting serving as a plug and the other as a socket for fastening the sections together. **b.** one of two or more small rings spaced along the top of a casting rod to hold and guide the line. —*v.t.* **7.** to furnish with a ferrule. Also, **ferule.** [< L *ferr(um)* iron + -ULE; r. late ME *virole* < MF (c. ML *virola*) < L *viriola,* equiv. to *viri(a)* bracelet + *-ola* dim. suffix]

fer·ry (fer/ē), *n.*, *pl.* **-ries,** *v.*, **-ried, -ry·ing.** —*n.* **1.** a commercial service with terminals and boats for transporting persons, automobiles, etc., across a comparatively small body of water. **2.** a ferryboat. **3.** a service for flying airplanes over a particular route, esp. the delivery of airplanes to an overseas purchaser or base of operations. **4.** the legal right to ferry passengers, baggage, etc., and to charge tolls for the service. —*v.t.* **5.** to carry or convey over water in a boat or plane. —*v.i.* **6.** to pass over water in a boat or by ferry. [ME *ferie(n),* OE *ferian* to carry; c. Icel *ferja,* Goth *farjan;* akin to FARE]

fer·ry·boat (fer/ē bōt/), *n.* a boat used to transport passengers, vehicles, etc., across a river or the like. [late ME *feryboot.* See FERRY, BOAT]

fer·ry·man (fer/ē mən), *n.*, *pl.* **-men.** a man who owns or operates a ferry. [late ME *feryman.* See FERRY, MAN[1]]

fer/ry rack/, a structure of fenders and piles for guiding a ferryboat into its proper position in a slip.

Fer·rys·burg (fer/ēz bûrg/), *n.* a town in SW Michigan. 2590 (1960).

fer·tile (fûr/tᵊl *or, esp. Brit.,* -tīl), *adj.* **1.** bearing, producing, or capable of producing vegetation, crops, etc., abundantly: *fertile soil.* **2.** bearing or capable of bearing offspring: *a thoroughbred horse, overage but still fertile.* **3.** abundantly productive: *a fertile imagination.* **4.** producing an abundance (usually fol. by *of* or *in*): *a land fertile of wheat.* **5.** conducive to productiveness: *fertile showers.* **6.** *Biol.* **a.** fertilized, as an egg or ovum; fecundated. **b.** capable of growth or development, as seeds or eggs. **7.** *Bot.* **a.** capable of producing sexual reproductive structures. **b.** capable of causing fertilization, as an anther with fully developed pollen. **c.** having spore-bearing organs, as a frond. **8.** *Physics.* (of an element or substance) convertible into a fissionable material. **9.** *Obs.* produced in abundance. [late ME < L *fertilis* fruitful, akin to *ferre* to BEAR[1]; see -ILE] —**fer/tile·ly,** *adv.* —**fer/tile·ness,** *n.*
—**Syn. 1-3.** fecund, teeming. See **productive.** —**Ant. 1-3.** sterile.

Fer/tile Cres/cent, **1.** an agricultural region extending from the Levant to Iraq. **2.** an area in the Middle and Near East: formerly fertile, now partly desert.

fer·ti·lise (fûr/tᵊlīz/), *v.t.*, **-lised, -lis·ing.** *Chiefly Brit.* fertilize. —**fer/ti·lis/a·bil/i·ty,** *n.* —**fer/ti·lis/a·ble,** *adj.* —**fer/ti·li·sa/tion,** *n.* —**fer/ti·li·sa/tion·al,** *adj.*

fer·ti·lis·er (fûr/tᵊlī/zər), *n. Chiefly Brit.* fertilizer.

fer·til·i·ty (fər til/i tē), *n.* **1.** the state or quality of being fertile. **2.** *Biol.* the ability to produce offspring; power of reproduction: *the amazing fertility of rabbits.* **3.** (of soil) the capacity to supply nutrients in proper amounts for plant growth when other factors are favorable. [late ME *fertilite* < L *fertilitās.* See FERTILE, -ITY]

Fer·til·i·ty (fər til/i tē), *n.* **Sea of.** See **Mare Fecunditatis.**

fertil/ity cult/, **1.** a religious cult devoted to the enhancement of the fertility of persons, plants, or animals, by means of rituals often associated with a particular deity. **2.** the body of members of such a cult.

fer·ti·li·za·tion (fûr/tᵊli zā/shən), *n.* **1.** the act or process or an instance of fertilizing. **2.** the state of being fertilized. **3.** *Biol.* **a.** the union of male and female gametic nuclei. **b.** fecundation or impregnation of animals or plants. **4.** the enrichment of soil, as for the production of crops. Also, *esp. Brit.,* **fertilisation.** [FERTILIZE + -ATION] —**fer/ti·li·za/tion·al,** *adj.*

fer·ti·lize (fûr/tᵊlīz/), *v.t.*, **-lized, -liz·ing.** **1.** *Biol.* **a.** to render (the female germ cell or gamete) capable of development by union with the male germ cell or gamete. **b.** to fecundate or impregnate (an animal or plant). **2.** to make fertile; enrich: *to fertilize farm land.* **3.** to make productive. Also, *esp. Brit.,* **fertilise.** [FERTILE + -IZE] —**fer/ti·liz/a·bil/i·ty,** *n.* —**fer/ti·liz/a·ble,** *adj.*

fer·ti·liz·er (fûr/tᵊlī/zər), *n.* **1.** any substance used to fertilize the soil, esp. a commercial or chemical manure. **2.** one who or that which fertilizes an animal or plant: *Bees are fertilizers of flowers.* Also, *esp. Brit.,* **fertiliser.** [FERTILIZE + -ER[1]]

fer·til·i·zin (fər til/i zin), *n. Biochem.* an ovum-produced colloidal substance that causes adhesion of sperm to the ovum. [FERTILIZE + -IN[2]]

fer·u·la (fer/o͝o lə, fer/yo͝o-), *n.*, *pl.* **-las, -lae** (-lē/). **1.** *Bot.* any umbelliferous plant of the genus *Ferula,* chiefly of the Mediterranean region and central Asia, generally tall and coarse with dissected leaves, many of the Asian species yielding strongly scented, medicinal gum resins. **2.** ferule (def. 1). [special uses of L *ferula* giant fennel (NL, plant meaning only)]

fer·u·la·ceous (fer/o͝o lā/shəs, fer/yo͝o-), *adj.* pertaining to reeds or canes; having a stalklike reed: *ferulaceous plants.* [< NL *ferulāceus.* See FERULA, -ACEOUS]

fer·ule[1] (fer/əl, -o͞ol), *n.*, *v.*, **-uled, -ul·ing.** —*n.* **1.** Also, **ferula.** a rod, cane, or flat piece of wood for punishing children, esp. by striking them on the hand. —*v.t.* **2.** to punish with a ferule. [< L *ferula* schoolmaster's rod (lit., stalk of giant fennel); r. OE *ferele* < L *ferula*]

fer·ule[2] (fer/əl, -o͞ol), *n.*, *v.t.*, **-uled, -ul·ing.** ferrule.

ferv., (in prescriptions) boiling. [< L *fervens*]

fer·ven·cy (fûr/vən sē), *n.* warmth or intensity of feeling; ardor; zeal; fervor. [late ME < LL *ferventia* (see FERVENT, -ENCY); r. *fervence* < MF < L *ferventia*]

fer·vent (fûr/vənt), *adj.* **1.** having or showing great warmth or intensity of spirit, feeling, enthusiasm, etc.; ardent: *a fervent admirer; a fervent plea.* **2.** hot; burning; glowing. [ME < L *fervent-* (s. of *fervēns*) prp. of *fervēre* to boil; see -ENT] —**fer/vent·ly,** *adv.* —**fer/vent·ness,** *n.*
—**Syn. 1.** fervid, fiery, burning, warm, heated, inflamed; eager, earnest, zealous, vehement, impassioned, passionate. —**Ant. 1.** apathetic.

fer·vid (fûr/vid), *adj.* **1.** heated or vehement in spirit, enthusiasm, etc.: *a fervid orator.* **2.** burning; glowing; hot. [< L *fervid(us)* boiling. See FERVENT, -ID[4]] —**fer·vid/i·ty,** *n.* —**fer/vid·ly,** *adv.* —**fer/vid·ness,** *n.*
—**Syn. 1.** fervent.

Fer·vi·dor (fûr/vi dôr/; *Fr.* fer vē dôr/), *n.* Thermidor. [< F, appar. b. *ferv(eur)* FERVOR and *(therm)idor* THERMIDOR]

fer·vor (fûr/vər), *n.* **1.** great warmth and earnestness of feeling: *to speak with great fervor.* **2.** intense heat. Also, *esp. Brit.,* **fer/vour.** [late ME < L: heat (see FERVENT, -OR[1]); r. ME *fervour* < AF < L *fervōr-,* s. of *fervor*]
—**Syn. 1.** ardor, intensity, eagerness, enthusiasm, passion, zeal. —**Ant. 1.** apathy.

Fes·cen·nine (fes/ə nīn/, -nin), *adj.* scurrilous; licentious; obscene: *Fescennine mockery.* [< L *Fescennīn(us)* of, belonging to Fescennia, a town in Etruria noted for jesting and scurrilous verse; see -INE[1]]

fes·cue (fes/kyo͞o), *n.* **1.** Also called **fes/cue grass/.** any grass of the genus *Festuca,* some species of which are cultivated for pasture or lawns. **2.** a straw, slender twig, etc., used to point out the letters in teaching children to read. [ME *festu* < MF << VL *festucum* stalk, r. L *festūca*]

fess (fes), *n. Heraldry.* **1.** an ordinary in the form of a broad horizontal band across the middle of an escutcheon. **2. in fess,** (designating two or more charges) side by side at the center of an escutcheon. **3. per fess,** horizontally, at the center of an escutcheon: *an escutcheon party per fess.* Also, **fesse.** [late ME *fesse* < AF << L *fascia* FASCIA]

Fes·sen·den (fes/ən dən), *n.* **William Pitt,** 1806–69, U.S. statesman.

fess/ point/, *Heraldry.* the central point of an escutcheon. Also called **heart point.**

fess·wise (fes/wīz/), *adj. Heraldry.* placed horizontally across an escutcheon in the manner of a fess. [FESS + -WISE]

-fest, a combining form denoting a festive occasion, esp. one involving a contest: *songfest.* [< G *Fest,* MHG *vest* < L *festum.* See FEAST]

fes·ta (fes/tə), *n.* a feast, festival, or holiday. [< It < L: holiday]

fes·tal (fes/tᵊl), *adj.* pertaining to or befitting a feast, festival, or gala occasion. [late ME < L *fēst(um)* FEAST + -AL[1]] —**fes/tal·ly,** *adv.*

fes·ter (fes/tər), *v.i.* **1.** to form pus; to generate purulent matter; suppurate. **2.** to cause ulceration, as a foreign body in the flesh. **3.** to putrefy or rot. **4.** to rankle, as a feeling of resentment. —*v.t.* **5.** to cause to fester or rankle: *Malice festered his spirit.* —*n.* **6.** an ulcer; a rankling sore. **7.** a small, purulent, superficial sore. [ME < MF *festre* < L *fistula* ulcer (lit., pipe, tube)]

fes·ti·na len·te (fes tē/nä len/te; *Eng.* fe stī/nə len/tē), *Latin.* make haste slowly.

fes·ti·nate (*v.* fes/tə nāt/; *adj.* fes/tə nāt/, -nit), *v.*, **-nat·ed, -nat·ing,** *adj. Obs.* —*v.t., v.i.* **1.** to hurry; hasten. —*adj.* **2.** hurried. [< L *festīnāt(us)* hurried, ptp. of *festīnāre;* see -ATE[1]] —**fes/ti·nate/ly,** *adv.*

fes·ti·na·tion (fes/tə nā/shən), *n. Pathol.* a gait marked by an involuntary hurrying in walking, observed in certain nerve diseases. [< L *festīnātiōn-* (s. of *festīnātiō*) a hastening. See FESTINATE, -ION]

fes·ti·val (fes/tə vəl), *n.* **1.** a day or time of religious or other celebration, marked by feasting, ceremonies, or other observances: *the festival of Christmas; a Roman festival.* **2.** a periodic commemoration, anniversary, or celebration. **3.** a period or program of festive activities, cultural events, or entertainment: *a music festival.* **4.** gaiety; merrymaking. —*adj.* **5.** of, pertaining to, or befitting a feast or holiday; festal: *a festival atmosphere of unrestrained joy.* [ME < eccl. L *fēstivālis* (*diēs*) holy (day). See FESTIVE, -AL[1]]

Fes/tival of Fools/. See **Feast of Fools.**

fes·tive (fes/tiv), *adj.* **1.** pertaining to or suitable for a feast or festival: *festive decorations; a festive meal.* **2.** joyous; merry. [< L *fēstīv(us)* merry, equiv. to *fēst(us)* festal + *-īvus* -IVE] —**fes/tive·ly,** *adv.* —**fes/tive·ness,** *n.*

fes·tiv·i·ty (fe stiv/i tē), *n.*, *pl.* **-ties.** **1.** a festive celebration or occasion. **2. festivities,** festive events or activities: *the festivities of Christmas.* **3.** festive character or quality; gaiety. [ME *festivite* < L *fēstīvitās.* See FESTIVE, -ITY]

fes·toon (fe sto͞on/), *n.* **1.** a string or chain of flowers, foliage, ribbon, etc., suspended in a curve between two points. **2.** a decorative representation of this, as in architectural work or on pottery. **3.** a fabric suspended, draped, and bound at intervals to form graceful loops or scalloped folds. **4.** *Dentistry.* the garlandlike area of the gums surrounding the necks of the teeth. —*v.t.* **5.** to adorn with or as with festoons: *to festoon a hall.* **6.** to form into festoons: *to festoon flowers and leaves.* **7.** *Dentistry.* to reproduce natural gum patterns around the teeth of a denture. **8.** to connect by festoons. [< F *feston* < It *festone* decoration for a feast, deriv. of *festa* FESTA]

Festoon

festoon/ cloud/, mamma[2] (def. 2).

fes·toon·er·y (fe sto͞o/nə rē), *n.* **1.** a decoration of festoons. **2.** festoons collectively. [FESTOON + -ERY]

Fest·schrift (fest/shrift/), *n.*, *pl.* **-schrift·en** (-shrif/tən), **-schrifts.** a volume of articles, essays, etc., contributed by many authors in honor of a colleague, usually published on the occasion of retirement, an important anniversary, or the like. [< G *Fest* feast, festival + *Schrift* a writing]

Fest·ung Eu·ro·pa (fes/to͝ong oi rō/pä), *German.* fortress Europe: that part of continental Europe once dominated by Nazi troops and regarded by them as impregnable.

Fes·tus (fes/təs), *n.* a town in E Missouri. 7021 (1960).

fet (fet), *v.t.*, **fet, fet·ting.** *Brit. Dial.* to fetch. [ME *fetten,* var. of *feten,* OE *fetian,* akin to *-fat* (in *sīthfat* journey), G *fassen* to grasp]

F.E.T., Federal Excise Tax.

fe·tal (fēt/ᵊl), *adj. Embryol.* of, pertaining to, or having the character of a fetus. Also, **foetal.** [FET(US) + -AL[1]]

fe·ta·tion (fē tā/shən), *n. Embryol.* pregnancy; gestation. Also, **foetation.** [FET(US) + -ATION]

fetch[1] (fech), *v.t.* **1.** to go and bring back; return with; get: *to go up a hill to fetch a pail of water.* **2.** to cause to come; bring: *to fetch a doctor.* **3.** to sell for or bring (a price, financial return, etc.): *The horse fetched $50 more than it cost.* **4.** *Informal.* to charm; captivate: *Her beauty fetched the coldest hearts.* **5.** to take (a breath). **6.** to utter (a sigh, groan, etc.). **7.** to deal or deliver (a stroke, blow, etc.). **8.** to perform or execute (a movement, step, leap, etc.). **9.** *Chiefly Naut. or Dial.* to reach; arrive at: *to fetch port.* **10.** *Hunting.* (of a dog) to retrieve (game). —*v.i.* **11.** to go and bring things. **12.** *Chiefly Naut.* to move or maneuver. **13.** *Hunting.* to retrieve game (often used as a command to a dog). **14.** to go by an indirect route; circle (often fol. by *around* or *about*): *We fetched around through the outer suburbs.* **15. fetch about,** *Naut.* (of a sailing vessel) to come onto a new tack. **16. fetch and carry,** to perform menial tasks: *She had been hired as a governess but was forced by her employer to fetch and carry.* **17. fetch away** or **way,** *Naut.* (of an object on board ship) to leave its proper position because of the motion of the vessel in a seaway. **18. fetch headway,** *Naut.* to begin to move ahead or to move ahead more rapidly. **19. fetch sternway,** *Naut.* to begin to move astern or to move astern more rapidly. **20. fetch up, a.** to end; stop. **b.** *Dial.* to raise (children); bring up: *She had to fetch up her younger sisters.* **c.** *Naut.* (of a vessel) to come to a halt, as by lowering an anchor or running aground; bring up. —*n.* **21.** the act of fetching. **22.** the distance of fetching: *a long fetch.* **23.** an area where ocean waves are being generated by the wind. **24.** the reach or stretch of a thing. **25.** the uninterrupted distance traveled by a wind or an ocean wave. **26.** a trick; dodge. [ME *fecchen,* OE *fecc(e)an,* var. of *fetian* FET] —**fetch/er,** *n.*
—**Syn. 1.** See **bring.**

fetch[2] (fech), *n.* the ghost of a living person, often supposed to appear as an omen of that person's death; wraith. [? short for *fetch-life* one sent to fetch the soul of a dying person]

fetch·ing (fech/ing), *adj. Informal.* charming; captivating. [FETCH + -ING[2]] —**fetch/ing·ly,** *adv.*

fete (fāt; *Fr.* fet), *n.*, *pl.* **fetes** (fāts; *Fr.* fet), *v.*, **fet·ed, fet·ing.** —*n.* **1.** a religious feast or festival: *a fete lasting several days in honor of a saint.* **2.** a festal day; holiday:

The Fourth of July is a great American fete. 3. a festive celebration or entertainment: *The ball was the greatest fete of the season.* —*v.t.* 4. to entertain at or honor with a fete: *to fete a visiting celebrity.* Also, **fête.** [< F, earlier *feste* FEAST]

fête cham·pê·tre (fet shäɴ pe′trᵊ), *pl.* **fêtes cham·pê·tres** (fet shäɴ pe′trᵊ). *French.* an outdoor festival or a garden party.

fete′ day′, a festival day.

fête ga·lante (fet gA länt′), *pl.* **fêtes ga·lantes** (fet gA länt′). *French.* a representation, in art, of elegantly dressed groups at play in a rural or parklike setting: a category of subject matter chiefly associated with Antoine Watteau.

fet·e·ri·ta (fet′ə rē′tə), *n.* a grain sorghum cultivated for grain and forage. [< Ar (Sudan dial.)]

fe·tial (fē′shəl), *adj., n., pl.* **fe·ti·a·les** (fē′shē ā′lēz). —*adj.* 1. pertaining to fetiales. 2. concerned with declarations of war and treaties of peace: *fetial law.* 3. heraldic. —*n.* 4. (in ancient Rome) one of a college of priests who acted as heralds and representatives of the people in disputes with foreign nations and in the declaration of war and the ratification of peace. [back formation from L *fētiālēs* college of priests]

fet·ich (fet′ish, fē′tish), *n.* fetish. —**fet′ich-like′,** *adj.*

fet·ich·ism (fet′i shiz′əm, fē′ti-), *n.* fetishism. —**fet′ich·ist,** *n.* —**fet′ich·is′tic,** *adj.*

fe·ti·cide (fē′ti sīd′), *n.* the act of destroying a fetus or causing an abortion. Also, **foeticide.** [*feti-* (comb. form of FETUS) + -CIDE] —**fe′ti·cid′al,** *adj.*

fet·id (fet′id, fē′tid), *adj.* having an offensive odor; stinking: *a close, fetid apartment.* Also, **foetid.** [< L *fētid(us),* equiv. to *fēt-* (root of *fētēre* to stink) + *-idus* -ID[4]] —**fet′id·ly,** *adv.* —**fet′id·ness, fe·tid′i·ty,** *n.* —**Syn.** malodorous, smelly, noisome.

fe·tip·a·rous (fē tip′ər əs), *adj.* (of a marsupial) bearing young before they are fully developed. Also, **foetiparous.** [*feti-* (comb. form of FETUS) + -PAROUS]

fet·ish (fet′ish, fē′tish), *n.* 1. an object regarded with awe as being the embodiment or habitation of a potent spirit or as having magical potency. 2. any object, idea, etc., eliciting unquestioning reverence, respect, or devotion: *to make a fetish of high grades.* 3. *Psychol.* any object, part of the body, etc., that, although not of a sexual nature, causes an erotic response or fixation. Also, **fetich.** [earlier *fateish* < Pg *feitiço* charm, sorcery (n.), artificial (adj.) < L *facticius* FACTITIOUS; r. *fatisso, fetisso* < Pg, as above] —**fet′ish-like′,** *adj.* —**Syn.** 1. talisman, amulet.

fet·ish·ism (fet′i shiz′əm, fē′ti-), *n.* 1. belief in or use of fetishes. 2. *Psychiatry.* the compulsive use of some object or part of the body as a stimulus in the course of attaining sexual gratification, as a shoe, a lock of hair, underclothes, etc. 3. blind devotion: *a fetishism of sacrifice to one's children.* Also, **fetichism.** [FETISH + -ISM] —**fet′ish·is′tic,** *adj.*

fet·ish·ist (fet′i shist, fē′ti-), *n.* a person who uses fetishes. Also, **fetichist.** [FETISH + -IST]

fet·lock (fet′lok′), *n.* 1. the projection of the leg of a horse behind the joint between the cannon bone and great pastern bone, bearing a tuft of hair. See diag. under **horse.** 2. the tuft of hair itself. 3. Also called **fet′lock joint′.** the joint at this point. Also called **fetterlock.** [ME *fitlok* (c. SwissG *Fisloch*), equiv. to *fitl-* (< ?) + *-ok* -OCK]

fe·tor (fē′tər), *n.* any strong offensive smell; stench. Also, **foetor.** [< L, equiv. to *fēt-* (root of *fētēre* to stink) + *-or* -OR[1]]

fet·ter (fet′ər), *n.* 1. a chain or shackle placed on the feet. 2. Usually, **fetters.** anything that confines or restrains: *Totalitarianism puts fetters upon the imagination.* —*v.t.* 3. to put fetters upon. 4. to confine; restrain. [ME, OE *feter;* c. OHG *fezzera,* Icel *fjǫturr;* akin to FOOT] —**fet′ter·er,** *n.*

fet′ter bone′, the great pastern bone of a horse. See under **pastern** (def. 2).

fet·ter·bush (fet′ər bo͝osh′), *n.* 1. an evergreen, ericaceous shrub, *Lyonia lucida,* of the southern U.S., having fragrant, white, flowers. 2. a similar shrub, *Pieris floribunda,* having white, campanulate flowers. 3. any of several heathlike shrubs of the southern U.S. [FETTER + BUSH[1]; so called because it impedes walkers]

fet·ter·less (fet′ər lis), *adj.* without fetters; unfettered. [FETTER + -LESS]

fet·ter·lock (fet′ər lok′), *n.* fetlock. [FETTER + LOCK[1], by confusion with *fetterlock* padlock]

fet·tle (fet′əl), *n., v.,* **-tled, -tling.** —*n.* 1. state; condition: *in fine fettle.* —*v.t.* 2. *Ceram.* to remove mold marks from (a cast piece). 3. *Foundry.* to remove sand from (a casting). 4. *Metall.* to repair the hearth of (an open-hearth furnace). [ME *fetle* to shape, prepare, back formation from *fetled,* OE **fetelede* girded up, equiv. to *fetel* belt + *-ede* -ED[2]]

fet·tling (fet′ling), *n. Metall.* the material with which the hearth of a puddling furnace is lined, usually a dolomite or refractory mixture. [FETTLE + -ING[1]]

fet·tu·ci·ni (fet′ə chē′nē; *It.* fet′to͞o chē′nē), *n.* (*construed as sing. or pl.*) pasta in the form of narrow strips. Also, **fet·tu·ci·ne** (fet′to͞o chē′ne). [< It]

fe·tus (fē′təs), *n., pl.* **-tus·es.** *Embryol.* (used chiefly of viviparous mammals) the young of an animal in the womb or egg, esp. in the later stages of development when the body structures are in the recognizable form of its kind, in man being from the latter part of the third month until birth. Cf. **embryo** (def. 2). Also, **foetus.** [< L: offspring, equiv. to **fē-* breed (see FEME) + *-tus* n. suffix of result]

feu (fyo͞o), *Scots Law.* —*n.* 1. the renting of land by a vassal in exchange for military service, grain, or money. 2. land so held. —*v.t.* 3. to grant (land) on feu. [late ME (Scot) *few* < MF *fieu* FIEF]

feu·age (fyo͞o′ij), *n. Old Eng. Law.* fumage. [< MF, equiv. to *feu* fire (< L *focus* fireplace) + *-age* -AGE]

feu·ar (fyo͞o′ər), *n. Scots Law.* a person who holds land on feu. [FEU + -AR[2]]

Feucht·wang·er (foiKHt′väng′ər), *n.* **Li·on** (lē′ōn), 1884–1958, German novelist and dramatist.

feud[1] (fyo͞od), *n.* 1. a bitter, continuous hostility, esp. between two families, clans, etc., often lasting for many years or generations. 2. a quarrel or contention: *a feud between labor and management.* —*v.i.* 3. to engage in a feud. [var. of *fead* (*a* being misread as *u*), ME *fede* < MF *fe(i)de* < OHG *fēhida;* c. OE *fǣhth* enmity. See FOE] —**Syn.** 2. argument, difference. See **quarrel.**

feud[2] (fyo͞od), *n.* fee (def. 5). [< ML *feud(um),* var. of *feodum.* See FEE]

feu·dal[1] (fyo͞od′əl), *adj.* 1. of, pertaining to, or of the nature of a fief or fee: *a feudal estate.* 2. of or pertaining to the holding of land in a fief or fee. 3. of, pertaining to, or like the feudal system, its social and economic structure, etc.: *feudal law.* 4. of or pertaining to the Middle Ages. [< ML *feudāl(is).* See FEUD[2], -AL[1]] —**feu′dal·ly,** *adv.*

feu·dal[2] (fyo͞od′əl), *adj.* of or pertaining to a feud. [FEUD[1] + -AL[1]]

feu′dal inves′titure, (in the feudal system) the public grant of land by the lord to the tenant.

feu·dal·ise (fyo͞od′əlīz′), *v.t.,* **-ised, -is·ing.** *Chiefly Brit.* feudalize. —**feu′dal·i·sa′tion,** *n.*

feu·dal·ism (fyo͞od′əliz′əm), *n.* the feudal system, or its principles and practices. [FEUDAL[1] + -ISM] —**feu′dal·ist,** *n.* —**feu′dal·is′tic,** *adj.*

feu·dal·i·ty (fyo͞o dal′i tē), *n., pl.* **-ties.** 1. the state or quality of being feudal. 2. the principles and practices of feudalism. 3. a fief or fee. [FEUDAL[1] + -ITY; r. *feodality* < F *féodalité*]

feu·dal·ize (fyo͞od′əlīz′), *v.t.,* **-ized, -iz·ing.** to make feudal; bring under the feudal system. Also, *esp. Brit.,* **feudalise.** [FEUDAL[1] + -IZE] —**feu′dal·i·za′tion,** *n.*

feu′dal sys′tem, the social and economic system in Europe during the Middle Ages, based on the holding of lands in fief or fee and on the resulting relations between lord and vassal.

feu d'ar·ti·fice (fœ dAR tē fēs′), *pl.* **feux d'ar·ti·fice** (fœ dAR tē fēs′). *French.* a firework or a display of fireworks. [lit., fire of contrivance]

feu·da·to·ry (fyo͞o′də tôr′ē, -tōr′ē), *n., pl.* **-ries,** *adj.* —*n.* 1. a person who holds his lands by feudal tenure; a feudal vassal. 2. a fief or fee. —*adj.* 3. (of a kingdom or state) under the overlordship of another sovereign or state. 4. (of a feudal estate) holding or held by feudal tenure. [< ML *feudātor* fief-holder + -Y[1]. See FEUD[2], -ATE[1], -OR[2]]

feu de joie (fœdᵊ zhwä′), *pl.* **feux de joie** (fœdᵊ zhwä′). *French.* 1. a public bonfire, as in celebration of an event. 2. a firing of guns in rapid succession, as along a line of troops, to mark a victory, celebrate an event, etc. [lit., fire of joy]

feud·ist[1] (fyo͞o′dist), *n.* a person who participates in a feud. [FEUD[1] + -IST]

feud·ist[2] (fyo͞o′dist), *n.* a writer or authority on feudal law. [FEUD[2] + -IST]

Feuil·lant (fœ yäɴ′), *n. Fr. Hist.* a member of a club or party of moderate constitutional monarchists, formed in 1791 and suppressed in 1792. [named after their meeting place, the convent of Notre Dame des *Feuillants*]

Feuil·lée (foi yā′), *n.* a crater in the second quadrant of the face of the moon: about 7 miles in diameter.

feuil·le·ton (foi′i tᵊn; *Fr.* fœyᵊ tôɴ′), *n., pl.* **-tons** (-tᵊnz; *Fr.* -tôɴ′). 1. a part of a newspaper (usually the bottom of one or more pages, marked off by a rule) devoted to light literature, fiction, criticism, etc. 2. an item printed in the feuilleton. [< F, equiv. to *feuillet* little leaf (*feuille* (< L *folium* leaf) + *-et* -ET) + *-on* n. suffix] —**feuil·le·ton·ism** (fœ′yi tə niz′əm), *n.* —**feuil′le·ton·ist,** *n.* —**feuil′le·ton·is′tic,** *adj.*

fe·ver (fē′vər), *n.* 1. an abnormal condition of the body, characterized by undue rise of temperature, quickening of the pulse, and disturbance of various body functions. 2. an abnormal rise of body temperature. 3. the number of degrees of such a temperature above the normal. 4. any of a group of diseases in which high temperature is a prominent symptom: *scarlet fever.* 5. intense nervous excitement: *The audience was in a fever of anticipation.* —*v.t.* 6. to affect with or as with fever: *The excitement fevered him.* [ME; OE *fefer* < L *febr-* (s. of *febris*) fever] —**fe′ver·less,** *adj.*

fe′ver blis′ter. See **fever sore.**

fe·ver·few (fē′vər fyo͞o′), *n.* a perennial composite plant, *Chrysanthemum Parthenium,* bearing small white flowers formerly used as a febrifuge. [late ME < AF **feverfue* (r. early ME *fever fugie,* OE *feferfuge*) < LL *febrifug(ia).* See FEBRIFUGE]

fe′ver heat′, 1. the heat of fever; body heat exceeding 98.6°F. 2. feverish excitement.

fe·ver·ish (fē′vər ish), *adj.* 1. excited, restless, or uncontrolled, as if from fever. 2. having fever, esp. a slight degree of fever. 3. pertaining to, of the nature of, or resembling fever: *a feverish disease; a feverish excitement.* 4. infested with fever, as a region. 5. having a tendency to produce fever. [ME *feverisch.* See FEVER, -ISH[1]] —**fe′ver·ish·ly,** *adv.* —**fe′ver·ish·ness,** *n.*

fe·ver·ous (fē′vər əs), *adj.* feverish. [ME; see FEVER, -OUS] —**fe′ver·ous·ly,** *adv.*

fe′ver pitch′, a high degree of excitement, as of a gathering of people: *The announcement of victory brought the crowd to fever pitch.*

fe·ver·root (fē′vər ro͞ot′, -ro͝ot′), *n.* See **horse gentian.** [FEVER + ROOT[1]]

fe′ver sore′, a vesicular eruption on the face, often accompanying a cold or febrile condition; herpes simplex. Also called **fever blister.**

fe′ver ther′apy, *Med.* therapy by means of an artificially induced fever.

fe′ver tree′, 1. any of several trees which produce or are believed to produce a febrifuge, as the blue gum, which is believed to prevent malaria. 2. a small rubiaceous tree, *Pinckneya pubens,* of the southeastern U.S., having a bark used as a tonic and febrifuge.

fe′ver twig′, the bittersweet, *Celastrus scandens.*

fe·ver·weed (fē′vər wēd′), *n.* any plant of the genus *Eryngium,* esp. *E. foetidum,* of the West Indies, or *E. campestre,* of Europe. [FEVER + WEED[1]]

fe·ver·wort (fē′vər wûrt′), *n.* 1. See **horse gentian.** 2. the thoroughwort or boneset. [FEVER + WORT[2]]

Fé·vri·er (fā vrē ā′), *n.* **Hen·ri** (äɴ rē′), born 1875, French composer.

few (fyo͞o), *adj.* 1. not many but more than one: *Few artists live luxuriously.* 2. **few and far between,** at widely separated intervals; infrequent: *In Nevada the towns are few and far between.* —*n.* 3. (*construed as pl.*) a small number or amount: *Send me a few.* 4. **quite a few,** *Informal.* a fairly large number; many: *There were quite a few interesting things to do.* 5. **the few,** a special, limited number; the minority: *That music appeals to the few. Yachts are for the few.* —*pron.* 6. (*construed as pl.*) a small number of persons or things. [ME *fewe,* OE *fēawe;* c. Goth *fawai;* akin to L *paucus* few, *paulus* little, *pauper* poor, *puer* boy, Gk *paûros* little, few]

few·er (fyo͞o′ər), *adj.* 1. of a smaller number: *fewer words and more action.* —*pron.* 2. (*construed as pl.*) a smaller number: *Fewer have come than we anticipated.* [ME *fewere,* OE **fēawran.* See FEW, -ER[4]]

—**Usage.** 1. FEWER, LESS are sometimes confused because both imply a comparison with something larger (in number or in amount). FEWER is used with plural nouns or pronouns and applies only to number: *Fewer street cars are running now than ten years ago.* LESS is used in various ways. It is used with singular nouns and pronouns and is commonly applied to material in bulk, in reference to amount: *There was less gasoline in the tank than we had thought. There is less of it than we need.* It is also used frequently with abstractions, esp. where the idea of amount is figuratively present: *less courage; less wealth.* LESS applies where such attributes as value, degree, etc., (but not size or number) are concerned: *A nickel is less than a dime* (in value). *A corporal is less than a sergeant* (in rank).

few·ness (fyo͞o′nis), *n.* the state of being few or small in quantity; paucity: *The magazine failed because of the fewness of subscribers.* [ME *fewenesse,* OE *fēawnes.* See FEW, -NESS]

few·ter·er (fyo͞o′tər ər), *n. Obs.* a person employed to take care of hounds, as greyhounds. [late ME < AF *veutrier,* equiv. to *veutre* greyhound (var. of *veltre* < LL *vertragus* < Gaulish) + *-ier* -ER[2]]

-fex, a learned borrowing from Latin, where it meant "maker," used in the formation of compound words: *spinifex.* [< L, equiv. to *fec-* (var. s. of *facere* to make) + *-s* nom. sing. ending. See -FIC]

fey (fā), *adj.* 1. *Brit. Dial.* doomed; fated to die. 2. *Chiefly Scot.* appearing to be under a spell; marked by an apprehension of death, calamity, or evil. 3. supernatural; unreal; enchanted: *elves, fairies, and other fey creatures.* 4. being in unnaturally high spirits, as were formerly thought to precede death. [ME; OE *fǣge* doomed to die; c. Icel *feigr* doomed, G *feig* cowardly]

Feyn·man (fīn′mən), *n.* **Richard Phillips,** born 1918, U.S. physicist: Nobel prize 1965.

fez (fez), *n., pl.* **fez·zes.** a felt cap, usually of a red color, having the shape of a truncated cone, and ornamented with a long black tassel, formerly the national headdress of the Turks. [< Turk *fes,* after *Fes* FEZ] —**fezzed,** *adj.* —**fez′zy,** *adj.*

Fez (Turkish)

Fez (fez), *n.* a city in N Morocco: formerly one of the traditional capitals of the sultanate in the former French zone. 216,133 (1960)

Fez·zan (fez zän′), *n.* a province in SW Libya: a portion of the Sahara with numerous oases. 47,000 (est. 1956); ab. 252,509 sq. mi. *Chief town:* Murzuq.

ff., 1. folios. 2. (and the) following (pages, verses, etc.). 3. *Music.* fortissimo.

FFA, See **Future Farmers of America.**

F.F.A., free from alongside (ship). Also, **f.f.a.**

FFC, 1. Foreign Funds Control. 2. free from chlorine.

F.F.I., 1. French Forces of the Interior. 2. free from infection.

F.F.V., First Families of Virginia.

f.g., *Basketball, Football.* field goal; field goals.

fgn., foreign.

F.G.S.A., Fellow of the Geological Society of America.

FHA, 1. Farmers' Home Administration. 2. Federal Housing Administration.

FHLBA, Federal Home Loan Bank Administration.

f-hole (ef′hōl′), *n.* either of two *f*-shaped holes in the body of a violin, cello, or similar stringed instrument.

fi (fē), *n. Music.* the solmization syllable used for the semitone between the fourth and fifth degrees of a scale.

F.I., Falkland Islands.

fi·a·cre (fē ä′kər, -äk′; *Fr.* fyA′krᵊ), *n., pl.* **-a·cres** (-ä′kərz, -äks′; *Fr.* -krᵊ). a hackney coach. [< F; after the Hotel de St. Fiacre in Paris, where such carriages were first for hire]

fi·an·cé (fē′än sā′, fē än′sā; *Fr.* fyäɴ sā′), *n., pl.* **-cés** (-sāz′, -sāz; *Fr.* -sā′). a man engaged to be married; a man to whom a girl or woman is engaged: *He is the fiancé of Miss Jones. She introduced us to her fiancé.* [< F: betrothed, ptp. of *fiancer,* OF *fiancier,* deriv. of *fiance* a promise, equiv. to *fi(er)* (to) trust (<< L *fīdere*) + *-ance* -ANCE]

fi·an·cée (fē′än sā′, fē än′sā; *Fr.* fyäɴ sā′), *n., pl.* **-cées** (-sāz′, -sāz; *Fr.* -sā′). a girl or woman engaged to be married; a girl or woman to whom a man is engaged: *She is the fiancée of Mr. Phelps. I'd like you to meet John's fiancée.* [< F; fem. of FIANCÉ]

fi·an·chet·to (fē′ən ket′ō, -chet′ō), *n., pl.* **-chet·ti** (-ket′ē, -chet′ē), *v. Chess.* —*n.* 1. the development of a bishop, in an opening move, by advancing one or two pawns so as to permit movement along the bishop's diagonal. —*v.i., v.t.* 2. to set up or develop as a fianchetto. [< It; see FLANK, -ET]

Fi·an·na (fē′ə nə), *n.pl. Irish Hist.* the Fenians.

Fi′anna Fail′ (foil, fīl), a political party in Ireland, organized in 1927 by Eamon De Valera, which was one of the leading parties in the establishment of the Irish republic. [< Ir: Fenians of (the) sod]

fi·ar (fē′ər), *n. Scots Law.* the owner of land in fee simple. [earlier *fear.* See FEE, -AR[2]]

fi·as·co (fē as′kō), *n., pl.* **-cos, -coes.** 1. a complete and ignominious failure. 2. a round-bottomed glass flask for wine, esp. Chianti, fitted with a woven, protective raffia basket that also enables the bottle to stand upright. [< It: lit., bottle, failure (fig.) < Gmc; see FLASK]

fi·at (fī′ət, -at), *n.* 1. an authoritative decree, sanction, or order: *papal fiats.* 2. a formula containing the word *fiat,* by which a person in authority gave his sanction. 3. an arbitrary decree or pronouncement, esp. by a person or group of persons having absolute authority to enforce it: *The king ruled by fiat.* [< L: let it be done, 3rd sing. pres. subj. of *fierī* to become]

fi·at jus·ti·ti·a, ru·at cae·lum (fē′ät yōōs tē′tē ä′ rōō′ät kī′lōōm; *Eng.* fī′at jus tish′ē ə rōō′at sē′ləm), *Latin.* let there be justice, though the heavens fall.

fi·at lux (fē′ät lōōks′; *Eng.* fī′at luks′), *Latin.* let there be light.

fi′at mon′ey, *U.S.* paper currency made legal tender by a fiat of the government, but not based on or convertible into coin.

fib[1] (fib), *n., v.,* **fibbed, fib·bing.** —*n.* **1.** a trivial lie; minor falsehood. —*v.i.* **2.** to tell a fib. [short for *fibble-fable* nonsense, gradational compound based on FABLE] —**fib′ber,** *n.*
—**Syn. 1.** See **falsehood.**

fib[2] (fib), *v.t.,* **fibbed, fib·bing.** *Brit.* to strike; beat. [?]

fi·ber (fī′bər), *n.* **1.** a fine threadlike piece, as of cotton, jute, or asbestos. **2.** a slender filament: *a fiber of platinum.* **3.** filaments collectively. **4.** matter or material composed of filaments: *a plastic fiber.* **5.** something resembling a filament. **6.** an essential character, nature, or strength: *people of strong moral fiber.* **7.** *Bot.* **a.** filamentous matter from the bast tissue or other parts of plants, used for industrial purposes. **b.** a slender, threadlike root of a plant. **c.** a slender, tapered cell which, with like cells, serves to strengthen tissue. **8.** *Anat., Zool.* a slender, threadlike element or cell, as of nerve, muscle, or connective tissue. **9.** *Chem.* See **vulcanized fiber. 10.** *Nutrition.* the wholly or partially indigestible parts of plants, as cellulose and pectin, that stimulate peristalsis in the intestine; bulk or roughage. Also, **fibre.** [ME *fibre* < L *fibra* filament] —**fi′ber·less,** *adj.*

fi·ber·board (fī′bər bōrd′, -bôrd′), *n.* **1.** a building material made of wood or other plant fibers compressed and cemented into rigid sheets. **2.** a sheet of this.

fi′ber bun′dle, *Optics.* a flexible bundle of optical glass that transmits images.

fi·bered (fī′bərd), *adj.* (of plaster) having an admixture of hair or fiber. [FIBER + -ED[3]]

Fi·ber·glas (fī′bər glas′, -gläs′), *n.* *Trademark.* fiberglass.

fi·ber·glass (fī′bər glas′, -gläs′), *n.* a material consisting of extremely fine filaments of glass which are combined in yarn and woven into fabrics, used in masses as a thermal and acoustical insulator, or embedded in various resins to make boat hulls, fishing rods, and the like. Also, **fi′ber glass′.** [FIBER + GLASS]

fi′ber op′tics, the branch of optics dealing with the transmission of images by bundles of fine, transparent fibers.

fi·ber·scope (fī′bər skōp′), *n.* *Optics.* an optical instrument consisting of a fiber bundle with an objective lens at one end and an eyepiece at the other, for viewing objects not accessible to direct viewing.

Fi·bi·ger (fē′bə gər; *Dan.* fē′bē gəʀ), *n.* **Jo·han·nes An·dre·as Grib** (yō hä′nis än dʀe′äs gʀēb), 1867–1928, Danish pathologist: Nobel prize for medicine 1926.

Fi·bo·nac′ci num′bers (fē′bō nä′chē), *Math.* the unending sequence 1, 1, 2, 3, 5, 8, 13, 21, 34, . . . where each term is defined as the sum of its two predecessors. Also called **Fibonac′ci se′quence.**

fibr-, var. of **fibro-** before a vowel: *fibrin.*

fi·bra·tus (fī brā′təs), *adj.* *Meteorol.* (of a cloud) hairlike or striated in composition. [< L: fibered, hairlike, equiv. to *fibr(a)* FIBER + *-ātus* -ATE[1]]

fi·bre (fī′bər), *n.* fiber. —**fi′bre·less,** *adj.*

fi·bri·form (fī′brə fôrm′, fib′rə-), *adj.* of the form of a fiber or fibers. [FIBR- + -I- + -FORM]

fi·bril (fī′brəl, fib′rəl), *n.* **1.** a small or fine fiber or filament. **2.** *Bot.* one of the delicate hairs on the young roots of some plants. **3.** *Anat.* an extracellular threadlike structure or filament. [< NL *fibril(la),* equiv. to L *fibr(a)* fiber + *-illa* dim. suffix]

fi·bril·la (fī bril′ə, fi-), *n., pl.* **-bril·lae** (-bril′ē). a fibril.

fi·bril·lar (fī′brə lər, fib′rə-), *adj.* of, pertaining to, or of the nature of fibrils. [FIBRILL(A) + -AR[1]]

fi·bril·la·tion (fī′brə lā′shən, fib′rə-), *n.* **1.** the formation of fibrils. **2.** *Pathol.* uncontrolled twitching or quivering of muscular fibrils. [FIBRILL(A) + -ATION]

fi·bril·li·form (fī bril′ə fôrm′, fi-), *adj.* of the form of a fibril. [FIBRILL(A) + -I- + -FORM]

fi·bril·lose (fī′brə lōs′, fib′rə-), *adj.* composed of or furnished with fibrils. [FIBRILL(A) + -OSE[1]]

fi·brin (fī′brin), *n.* **1.** *Biochem.* a white, tough, strongly elastic, fibrous protein, formed in the coagulation of blood. **2.** *Bot.* a substance like fibrin found in some plants; gluten. [FIBR- + -IN[2]]

fibrino-, a combining form of **fibrin:** *fibrinolysis.*

fi·brin·o·gen (fī brin′ə jən), *n.* *Biochem.* a globulin occurring in blood and yielding fibrin in the coagulation of blood. [FIBRINO- + -GEN]

fi·brin·o·gen·ic (fī′brə nō jen′ik), *adj.* *Physiol.* producing fibrin. Also, **fi·bri·nog·e·nous** (fī′brə noj′ə nəs). [FIBRINO- + GENIC] —**fi′brin·o·gen′i·cal·ly,** *adv.*

fi·brin·o·kin·ase (fī′brə nō kī′nās, -kin′ās), *n.* *Biochem.* an enzyme, found in bacteria, that serves to convert plasminogen to plasmin. [FIBRINO- + KINASE]

fi·bri·nol·y·sin (fī′brə nol′i sin), *n.* **1.** Also called **plasmin.** *Biochem.* a proteolytic enzyme, formed in the blood from plasminogen, that causes the breakdown of the fibrin in blood clots. **2.** Also called **streptokinase.** *Pharm.* an enzyme, obtained from hemolytic streptococci and used with streptodornase chiefly for the breakdown of blood clots and of fibrinous and purulent matter resulting from injury or infection, as in certain cases of thrombosis.

fi·bri·nol·y·sis (fī′brə nol′i sis), *n., pl.* **-ses** (-sēz′). *Biochem.* the disintegration or dissolution of fibrin, esp. by enzymatic action. [FIBRINO- + -LYSIS] —**fi·bri·no·lyt·ic** (fī′brə nō lit′ik, fī brin′ᵊlit′-), *adj.*

fi·brin·ous (fī′brə nəs), *adj.* containing, composed of, or of the nature of fibrin. [FIBRIN + -OUS]

fibro-, a learned borrowing from Latin meaning "fiber," used in the formation of compound words: *fibrolite.* Also, *esp. before a vowel,* **fibr-.** [comb. form repr. L *fibra* FIBER]

fi·bro·blast (fī′brə blast′), *n.* *Anat.* a cell that contributes to the formation of connective tissue fibers. [FIBRO- + -BLAST] —**fi′bro·blas′tic,** *adj.*

fi·bro·car·ti·lage (fī′brō kär′tᵊlij, -kärt′lij), *n.* *Anat., Zool.* **1.** a type of cartilage having a large number of fibers. **2.** a part or structure composed of such cartilage. [FIBRO- + CARTILAGE] —**fi·bro·car·ti·lag·i·nous** (fī′brō kär′tᵊlaj′ə nəs), *adj.*

fi·broid (fī′broid), *adj.* **1.** resembling fiber or fibrous tissue. **2.** composed of fibers, as a tumor. —*n.* **3.** *Pathol.* a tumor largely composed of smooth muscle. [FIBR- + -OID]

fi·bro·in (fī′brō in), *n.* *Biochem.* an indigestible protein, a principal component of spider webs and silk. [FIBRO- + -IN[2], modeled on F *fibroïne*]

fi·bro·lite (fī′brə līt′), *n.* *Mineral.* sillimanite. [FIBRO- + -LITE]

fi·bro·ma (fī brō′mə), *n., pl.* **-ma·ta** (-mə tə), **-mas.** *Pathol.* a tumor consisting essentially of fibrous tissue. [FIBR- + -OMA] —**fi·brom·a·tous** (fī brom′ə təs), *adj.*

fi·bro·pla·sia (fī′brə plā′zhə, -zhē ə, -zē ə), *n.* *Med.* the formation of fibrous tissue. [< NL; see FIBRO-, -PLASIA] —**fi·bro·plas·tic** (fī′brō plas′tik), *adj.*

fi·bro·sis (fī brō′sis), *n.* *Pathol.* the development in an organ of excess fibrous connective tissue. [FIBR- + -OSIS] —**fi·brot·ic** (fī brot′ik), *adj.*

fi·brous (fī′brəs), *adj.* containing, consisting of, or resembling fibers. [FIBR- + -OUS] —**fi′brous·ly,** *adv.* —**fi′brous·ness,** *n.*

fi·bro·vas·cu·lar (fī′brō vas′kyə lər), *adj.* *Bot.* composed of fibrous and conductive tissue: *a fibrovascular bundle.* [FIBRO- + VASCULAR]

fib·ster (fib′stər), *n.* *Archaic.* a person who tells fibs. [FIB[1] + -STER]

fib·u·la (fib′yə lə), *n., pl.* **-lae** (-lē′), **-las. 1.** *Anat.* the outer and thinner of the two bones of the leg, extending from the knee to the ankle. See diag. under **skeleton. 2.** *Zool.* a corresponding bone, often rudimentary or ankylosed with the tibia, of the leg or hind limb of an animal. **3.** *Archaeol.* a clasp or brooch, often ornamented. [< L: fastener; akin to FIX; see -ULE] —**fib′u·lar,** *adj.*

-fic, a suffix meaning "making," "producing," "causing," appearing in adjectives borrowed from Latin: *frigorific; honorific; pacific; prolific.* [< L *-fic(us)* making, producing, equiv. to *-fic-* (var. s. of *facere* to make) + *-us* adj. suffix; in some words r. *-fique* < MF < L *-fic(us)*]

F.I.C.A., Federal Insurance Contributions Act.

-fication, a suffix of nouns of action or state corresponding to verbs ending in *-fy: deification; pacification.* [< L *-ficātiōn-* (s. of *-ficātiō*) a making, equiv. to *-ficā(re)* -FY + *-tiōn-* -TION; in some words r. ME *-ficacioun* < AF]

fice (fīs), *n.* feist.

Fich·te (fiᴋʜ′tə), *n.* **Jo·hann Gott·lieb** (yō′hän gôt′lēp), 1762–1814, German philosopher.

Fich·te·an (fik′tē ən, fiᴋʜ′-), *adj.* **1.** of, pertaining to, or resembling the philosophy of Fichte. —*n.* **2.** an adherent or advocate of the philosophy of Fichte. [FICHTE + -AN] —**Fich′te·an·ism,** *n.*

fich·u (fish′ōō; *Fr.* fē shʏ′), *n., pl.* **fich·us** (fish′ōōz; *Fr.* fē shʏ′). a women's kerchief of muslin, lace, or the like, generally triangular in shape, for wearing about the neck with the ends drawn together or crossed on the breast. [< F: small shawl, orig. piece (of cloth) insecurely held in place, n. use of *fichu* (adj.) poorly done, equiv. to *fich(er)* (to) thrust in (< VL **figicare,* r. L *figere*) + *(fout)u,* ptp. of *foutre* to thrust in]

fick·le (fik′əl), *adj.* **1.** likely to or characterized by change, esp. due to caprice, irresolution, or instability; casually changeable: *fickle weather.* **2.** not constant or loyal in affections. [ME *fikel,* OE *ficol* deceitful, akin to *fācen* treachery, *fician* to deceive, *gefic* deception] —**fick′le·ness,** *n.*
—**Syn. 1.** unstable, unsteady, changeable, variable, capricious, fitful. **2.** inconstant.

fick·le-mind·ed (fik′əl mīn′did), *adj.* (of a person) prone to change; inconstant.

fi·co (fē′kō), *n., pl.* **-coes. 1.** *Archaic.* the merest trifle. **2.** *Obs.* fig[1] (def. 5). [< It *fico, fica* FIG[1]]

fict., fiction.

fic·tile (fik′tᵊl; *Brit.* fik′tīl), *adj.* **1.** capable of being molded; plastic. **2.** molded into form by art. **3.** made of earth, clay, etc., by a potter. **4.** of or pertaining to pottery. **5.** easily led, as a person or a mob; tractable. [< L *fictil(is)* earthen (lit., moldable), equiv. to *fict(us)* shaped (ptp. of *fingere*) + *-ilis* -ILE]

fic·tion (fik′shən), *n.* **1.** the class of literature comprising works of imaginative narration, esp. in prose form. **2.** works of this class, as novels or short stories: *detective fiction.* **3.** something feigned, invented, or imagined; a made-up story: *We've all heard the fiction of her being in delicate health.* **4.** the act of feigning, inventing, or imagining. **5.** an imaginary thing or event, postulated for the purposes of argument or explanation. **6.** *Law.* an allegation that a fact exists which is known not to exist, made by authority of law to bring a case within the operation of a rule of law. [< L *fictiōn-* (s. of *fictiō*) a shaping, hence a feigning, fiction, equiv. to *fict(us)* molded (ptp. of *fingere*) + *-iōn-* -ION]
—**Syn. 3.** fable, fantasy. FICTION, FABRICATION, FIGMENT suggest a story which is without basis in reality. FICTION suggests a story invented and fashioned either to entertain or to deceive: *clever fiction; pure fiction.* FABRICATION applies particularly to a false but carefully invented statement or series of statements, in which some truth is sometimes interwoven, the whole usually intended to deceive: *fabrications to lure speculators.* FIGMENT applies to a tale, idea, or statement often made up to explain, justify, or glorify oneself: *His rich uncle was a figment of his imagination.* —**Ant. 3.** fact.

fic·tion·al (fik′shə nᵊl), *adj.* of, pertaining to, or of the nature of fiction: *fictional characters.* [FICTION + -AL[1]] —**fic′tion·al·ly,** *adv.*

fic·tion·al·ize (fik′shə nᵊlīz′), *v.t.,* **-ized, -iz·ing.** to make into fiction; give a somewhat imaginative or fictional version of: *to fictionalize a biography.* Also, **fictionize.** [FICTIONAL + -IZE] —**fic′tion·al·i·za′tion,** *n.*

fic·tion·eer (fik′shə nēr′), *n.* a prolific writer of fiction. [FICTION + -EER]

fic·tion·eer·ing (fik′shə nēr′ing), *n.* the writing of fiction, esp. in quantity and without particular regard for quality. [FICTIONEER + -ING[1]]

fic·tion·ise (fik′shə nīz′), *v.t.,* **-ised, -is·ing.** *Chiefly Brit.* fictionize. —**fic′tion·i·sa′tion,** *n.*

fic·tion·ist (fik′shə nist), *n.* a writer of fiction; a novelist or short-story writer. [FICTION + -IST]

fic·tion·ize (fik′shə nīz′), *v.t.,* **-ized, -iz·ing.** to fictionalize. Also, *esp. Brit.,* **fictionise.** [FICTION + -IZE] —**fic′tion·i·za′tion,** *n.*

fic·ti·tious (fik tish′əs), *adj.* **1.** created, taken, or assumed as a convention or by hypothesis; false; not genuine: *fictitious names.* **2.** of, pertaining to or consisting of fiction; imaginatively produced or set forth; created by the imagination: *a fictitious hero.* [< L *ficticius* artificial, equiv. to *fict(us)* shaped, feigned (see FICTION) + *-icius* -ITIOUS] —**fic·ti′tious·ly,** *adv.* —**fic·ti′tious·ness,** *n.*
—**Syn. 1.** spurious, forged, feigned, simulated, fake. **2.** fictional.

ficti′tious per′son, *Law.* a legal entity or artificial person, as a corporation.

fic·tive (fik′tiv), *adj.* **1.** fictitious; imaginary. **2.** pertaining to the creation of fiction: *fictive inventiveness.* [FICT(ION) + -IVE] —**fic′tive·ly,** *adv.*

fid (fid), *n.* *Naut.* **1.** a stout bar of wood or metal lying across the trestletrees of a lower spar of a mast and passing through a hole **(fid hole)** or mortise in the heel of an upper spar so as to support the upper spar. **2.** a stout bar used to hold a running bowsprit in its extended position. **3.** any of various tapered wooden or metal pins for parting the strands at some point in a rope or for forming and stretching grommets and cringle strops. **4.** a bar or pin used as a key or toggle. [?]

-fid, a suffix meaning "divided," "lobed," occurring in adjectives borrowed from Latin (*bifid*); on this model, used in the formation of compound words (*pinnatifid*). [< L *-fid(us)* divided, equiv. to *-fid-* (var. s. of *findere* to split) + *-us* adj. suffix]

fid., fiduciary.

fid·dle (fid′ᵊl), *n., v.,* **-dled, -dling.** —*n.* **1.** a musical instrument of the viol family. **2.** *Informal.* violin. **3.** *Naut.* a small ledge or barrier raised in heavy weather to keep dishes, utensils, etc., from sliding along or off a table, and pots and other objects from sliding off a stove. **4. fit as a fiddle,** in perfect health; very fit: *The doctor told him he was fit as a fiddle.* Also, **as fit as a fiddle. 5. play second fiddle.** See **second fiddle.** —*v.i.* **6.** *Informal.* to play on the fiddle. **7.** to make trifling or fussing movements with the hands (often fol. by *with*): *fiddling with his cuffs.* **8.** to trifle, waste time, etc. (often fol. by *around*): *Stop fiddling around and get to work.* **9.** *Bookbinding.* to bind together (sections or leaves of a book) by threading a cord through holes cut lengthwise into the back. —*v.t.* **10.** *Informal.* to play (a tune) on a fiddle. **11.** to trifle or waste (usually used with *away*): *to fiddle time away.* [ME, OE *fithele* (c. G *Fiedel,* D *vedel*) < LL *vitula,* akin to L *vitulārī* to rejoice]

fid′dle back′, a chair having a solid splat similar in form to that of a fiddle.

fid·dle·back (fid′ᵊl bak′), *n.* **1.** something shaped like a fiddle. —*adj.* **2.** resembling the back or outline of a violin. **3.** (of a veneer figure) having close, fine, dark stripes. [FIDDLE + BACK[1]]

fid′dle block′, *Naut.* a block having a larger and a smaller sheave edge to edge.

fid′dle bow′ (bō *for 1, 2;* bou *for 3*), **1.** a bow strung with horsehair with which the strings of the violin or a similar instrument are set in vibration. **2.** a bow for driving the arbor of a small lathe, as one used by watchmakers. **3.** *Naut.* See **clipper bow.**

fid′dle brace′ back′, a back for a Windsor chair whose top rail is braced by two spindles rising from a narrow tailpiece at the rear of the seat.

fid·dle-de-dee (fid′ᵊl di dē′), *interj., n.* nonsense. Also, **fid′dle·de·dee′, fid′dle·dee·dee′.** [FIDDLE + *-de-* (redupl. prefix) + (TWEEDLE)DEE in obs. sense of fiddler]

fid·dle-fad·dle (fid′ᵊl fad′ᵊl), *n., v.,* **-dled, -dling.** *Informal.* —*n.* **1.** nonsense. **2.** something trivial. —*v.i.* **3.** to fuss with trifles. [gradational compound based on FIDDLE] —**fid′dle-fad′dler,** *n.*

fid·dle·head (fid′ᵊl hed′), *n.* *Naut.* a billethead having a form similar to the volute carved at the upper end of a fiddle. [FIDDLE + HEAD]

fid·dle·neck (fid′ᵊl nek′), *n.* an annual herb, *Phacelia tanacetifolia,* of California, having hairy leaves and curved spikes of small blue flowers. [FIDDLE + NECK; from the shape of the racemes]

fid′dle pat′tern, a pattern of spoon or fork having a handle narrowing abruptly from a broad, flat upper part, and terminating with a pronounced shoulder above the bowl or tines.

fid·dler (fid′lər), *n.* **1.** a person who plays the fiddle. **2.** *Informal.* a violinist. **3.** a person who trifles: *He's a fiddler and can't ever get down to business.* [ME, OE *fithelere;* c. D *vedelaar,* G *Fiedler.* See FIDDLE, -ER[1]]

Fiddler crab, *Uca pugilator* (Shell width about 1 in.)

fid′dler crab′, any small, burrowing crab of the genus *Uca,* the male of which has one greatly enlarged claw.

fid·dler·fish (fid′lər fish′), *n., pl.* (*esp. collectively*) **-fish,** (*esp. referring to two or more kinds or species*) **-fish·es.** any of several guitarfishes, esp. *Trygonorhina fasciata,* found in Australia. [FIDDLER + FISH]

fid′dler's green′, a paradise to which sailors are thought to go after death.

fid·dle·stick (fid′ᵊl stik′), *n.* **1.** a fiddle bow. **2.** a mere nothing: *I don't care a fiddlestick for what they say.* [late ME *fidillstyk.* See FIDDLE, STICK[1]]

fid·dle·sticks (fid′ᵊl stiks′), *interj.* nonsense. [short for *fiddlestick's end,* i.e., the most worthless part of a worthless weapon]

fid·dle·wood (fid′ᵊl wŏŏd′), *n.* **1.** the heavy, hard, durable wood of various West Indian and other trees. **2.** any of these trees, esp. species of the genera *Citharexylum* and *Vitex.* [FIDDLE + WOOD[1]]

fid·dling (fid′ling), *adj.* trifling; trivial: *a fiddling sum of money.* [FIDDLE + -ING[2]]

fi·de·i·com·mis·sar·y (fī/dē ī kom/i ser/ē), *n., pl.* **-sar·ies,** *adj. Civil Law.* —*n.* **1.** the recipient of a fideicommissum. —*adj.* **2.** of, pertaining to, or resembling a fideicommissum. [< LL *fideī commissārī(us),* equiv. to *fideī commiss(um)* a FIDEICOMMISSUM + *-ārius* -ARY]

fi·de·i·com·mis·sum (fī/dē ī kə mis/əm), *n., pl.* **-mis·sa** (-mis/ə). *Civil Law.* a request by a decedent that his heir or legatee convey a specified part of the estate to another person, or permit another person to enjoy such a part. [< LL *fideī commissum* entrusted to faith, equiv. to *fideī,* dat. sing. of *fidēs* FAITH + *commissum,* ptp. of *committere* to COMMIT]

Fi·de·i De·fen·sor (fē/de ē/ de fen/sōr; *Eng.* fī/dē ī/ di fen/sôr), *Latin.* Defender of the Faith: one of the titles of English sovereigns.

Fi·del (fi del/; *Sp.* fē thel/), *n.* a boy's given name.

Fi·del·a (fi del/ə), *n.* a girl's given name, form of **Fidelia.**

Fi·de·lia (fi dēl/yə), *n.* a girl's given name.

Fi·de·lio (fi dāl/yō), *n.* an opera (1805) by Ludwig van Beethoven.

fi·del·i·ty (fi del/i tē, fī-), *n., pl.* **-ties. 1.** strict observance of promises, duties, etc: *a servant's fidelity.* **2.** loyalty: *fidelity to one's country.* **3.** conjugal faithfulness. **4.** adherence to fact or detail. **5.** accuracy; exactness: *The speech was transcribed with great fidelity.* **6.** *Radio.* the ability of a transmitter or receiver to produce radio waves or sound which reproduce its input accurately. [late ME *fidelite* < L *fidēlitās,* equiv. to *fidēli-* (s. of *fidēlis* loyal, equiv. to *fidē(s)* FAITH + *-lis* adj. suffix) + *-tās* -TY[2]]
—Syn. 2. See **loyalty. 5.** precision. **—Ant. 2.** disloyalty.

Fi·des (fī/dēz), *n.* the ancient Roman personification of good faith.

fidge (fij), *v.i.,* **fidged, fidg·ing,** *n. Scot.* fidget. [var. of *fitch* to move back and forth; c. Icel *fikjast* to be eager, MSw *fikja* to be restless; akin to FICKLE]

fidg·et (fij/it), *v.i.* **1.** to move about restlessly, nervously, or impatiently. —*v.t.* **2.** to cause to fidget; make uneasy. —*n.* **3.** Often, **fidgets.** the condition or an instance of being nervously restless, uneasy, or impatient. **4.** Also, **fidg/et·er.** a person who fidgets. [FIDGE + -ET (< ?)] **—fidg/et·ing·ly,** *adv.*

fidg·et·y (fij/i tē), *adj.* **1.** restless; impatient; uneasy. **2.** nervously and excessively fussy. [FIDGET + -Y[1]]

fid·ley (fid/lē), *n., pl.* **-leys.** *Naut.* an open area situated above boilers or machinery. [?]

Fi·do (fī/dō), *n. U.S.* a familiar name for a dog.

FIDO (fī/dō), *n. Aeron.* a system for evaporating the fog above airfield runways by the heat from burners. [*f(og) i(nvestigation) d(ispersal) o(perations)*]

fi·du·cial (fi dōō/shəl, -dyōō/-), *adj.* **1.** *Physics.* accepted as a fixed basis of reference or comparison: *a fiducial point.* **2.** based on or having trust: *fiducial dependence upon God.* [< LL *fīdūciāl(is),* equiv. to *fīdūci(a)* trust (akin to *fīdere* to trust) + *-ālis* -AL[1]] **—fi·du/cial·ly,** *adv.*

fi·du·ci·ar·y (fi dōō/shē er/ē, -dyōō/-), *n., pl.* **-ar·ies,** *adj.* —*n.* **1.** *Law.* a person to whom property or power is entrusted for the benefit of another. —*adj.* **2.** *Law.* of or pertaining to the relation between a fiduciary and his principal: *a fiduciary capacity; a fiduciary duty.* **3.** depending on public confidence for value or currency, as fiat money. **4.** *Obs.* like or based on trust or reliance. [< L *fīdūciāri(us)* of something held in trust, equiv. to *fīdūci(a)* trust + *-ārius* -ARY] **—fi·du/ci·ar/i·ly,** *adv.*

fidu/ciary bond/, a bond filed by a fiduciary administering an estate as surety.

fi·dus A·cha·tes (fē/dōōs ä kä/tes; *Eng.* fī/dəs ə kā/tēz), *Latin.* **1.** faithful Achates. **2.** a devoted, trustworthy friend.

fie (fī), *interj.* **1.** (used to express mild disgust, disapprobation, annoyance, etc.) **2.** (used to express the humorous pretense of being shocked.) [ME *fi* < MF < L; cf. Icel *fȳ,* L *phy*]

Fied·ler (fēd/lər), *n.* **Arthur,** 1894–1979, U.S. symphony conductor.

fief (fēf), *n.* **1.** a fee or feud, or estate in land held of a feudal lord; a tenure of land subject to feudal obligations. **2.** a territory held in fee. [< F, var. of OF *fieu, fie,* c. AF *fe* FEE < Gmc; cf. OHG *fihu,* OE *feoh* cattle, property; akin to L *pecū* flock of sheep, *pecus* cattle, *pecūnia* wealth]

field (fēld), *n.* **1.** a piece of open or cleared ground, esp. one suitable for pasture or tillage. **2.** *Sports.* **a.** a piece of ground devoted to sports or contests. **b.** sports played on such a piece of ground, collectively. **c.** all the contestants or numbers grouped together as one in betting: *to bet on the field in a horse race.* **d.** the players on the playing ground in football: *to dodge through a broken field.* **3.** *Fox Hunting.* the group of participants in a hunt, exclusive of the master of foxhounds and his staff. **4.** *Baseball.* **a.** the team in the field, as opposed to the one at bat. **b.** the outfield. **5.** *Mil.* **a.** the scene or area of active military operations. **b.** a battleground. **c.** a battle. **d.** *Informal* (in the U.S. Army) the locations of the parts of the army not in Washington, D.C.: *out in the field.* **6.** an expanse of anything: *a field of ice.* **7.** any region characterized by a particular feature, product, mineral, mining activity, etc.: *a gold field.* **8.** (in building and road construction, etc.) a job location remote from regular workshop facilities, offices, or the like. **9.** the surface of a canvas, shield, etc., on which something is portrayed: *a gold star on a field of blue.* **10.** (in a flag) the ground of each division. **11.** *Heraldry.* the whole area of an escutcheon, covered with a tincture or tinctures, and able to be parted per fess, per pale, per bend, per chevron, or per saltire, or to be tierced, and to bear charges. **12.** a sphere of activity, interest, etc., esp. within a particular business or profession: *the field of teaching; the field of Shakespearean scholarship.* **13.** the area or region drawn on or serviced by a business or profession; outlying areas, where business, selling, mining, etc., is actually carried on in contrast to a home or branch office: *our representatives in the field.* **14.** Also called **field of force.** *Physics.* a region of space under the influence of some agent, as electricity or magnetism. **15.** Also called **field of view.** *Optics.* the entire angular expanse visible through an optical instrument at a given time. **16.** *Elect.* the structure in a dynamo designed to establish magnetic lines of force in an armature. **17.** *Math.* a number system that has the same properties relative to the operations of addition, subtraction, multiplication, and division as the number system of all real numbers; a commutative division ring. **18.** *Numis.* the blank area of a coin, other than that of the exergue. **19.** *Psychol.* the total complex of interdependent factors within which a psychological event occurs and is perceived as occurring. **20.** *Photog.* the area of a subject that is taken in by a lens at a particular diaphragm opening. **21.** *Television.* a percentage, number, or fraction of the scanning lines, distributed over a frame, the image being transmitted so that each field is covered before proceeding to the next. In the U.S. the frame is divided into two fields, one of all the odd scanning lines and the other of all the even scanning lines, each field being traversed in $^{1}/_{60}$ second. Cf. **frame** (def. 18). **22.** *Computer Technol.* **a.** a set of one or more characters, not necessarily part of the same machine word, considered as a single unit of information. **b.** Also called **card field.** (in a punch card) any number of columns regularly used for recording the same information. **23.** *Obs.* open country. **24. in the field, a.** in actual use or in a situation simulating actual use or application; away from a laboratory, workshop, or the like; practicably: *The machine was tested for six months in the field.* **b.** in contact with a prime source of basic data: *The archaeologist was in the field gathering evidence on the Sumerians. The anthropologist is working in the field in Nigeria.* **c.** within a given profession: *The public knows little of him, but in the field he's known as a fine mathematician.* **25. keep the field,** to remain in competition or in battle; continue to contend: *The troops kept the field under heavy fire.* **26. out in left field.** See **left field** (def. 2). **27. play the field,** *Informal.* to vary one's activities, esp. to date a number of members of the opposite sex rather than only one: *He wanted to play the field for a few years before settling down.* **28. take the field, a.** to begin to play, as in football, baseball, etc.; go into action. **b.** to go into battle: *They took the field at dawn.*
—*v.t. Baseball, Cricket.* **29.** to catch or pick up (the ball) in play: *The shortstop fielded the grounder and threw to first for the out.* **30.** to place (a player, group of players, or a team) in the field to play.
—*v.i. Baseball, Cricket.* **31.** to act as a fielder; field the ball. **32.** to take to the field.
—*adj.* **33.** *Sports.* **a.** of, taking place, or competed for on the field and not on the track, as the discus throw, shot put, etc. **b.** of or pertaining to field events. **34.** *Mil.* of or pertaining to campaign and active combat service as distinguished from service in rear areas or at headquarters: *a field soldier.* **35.** of or pertaining to a field. **36.** grown or cultivated in a field. **37.** working as a farm laborer in a field: *a field hand.* **38.** working as a salesman, engineer, representative, etc., in the field: *an insurance company's field agents.* [ME, OE *feld;* c. G *Feld*]

Field (fēld), *n.* **1. Cyrus West,** 1819–92, U.S. financier: projector of the first Atlantic cable. **2. David Dudley, Jr.,** 1805–94, U.S. jurist (brother of Cyrus West and Stephen Johnson Field). **3. Eugene,** 1850–95, U.S. poet and journalist. **4. Marshall,** 1834–1906, U.S. merchant and philanthropist. **5. Stephen Johnson,** 1816–99, U.S. jurist: associate justice of the U.S. Supreme Court 1863–97 (brother of Cyrus West and David Dudley Field).

field/ ar/mor, armor made primarily for combat purposes, rather than for tournaments or parades.

field/ ar/my, army (def. 2).

field/ ar/row, an arrow for use in hunting.

field/ artil/lery, *Mil.* **1.** artillery mobile enough to accompany troops in the field. **2.** (*caps.*) (from 1907 to 1950) a branch and combat arm of the U.S. Army, troops of which were armed with various types of mobile cannon and supporting equipment: now part of the Artillery.

field/ bag/, *Mil.* See **musette bag.**

field/ bat/tery, *Mil.* a battery of field guns.

field/ bed/, a small bed having an arched tester on short posts.

field/ cap/tain, *Chiefly Football.* a player taking active part in a game who is authorized to make decisions for his team, esp. in regard to planning plays, deciding whether to accept penalties called by an official against the opponents, etc.

field/ chick/weed. See **starry grasswort.**

field/ corn/, feed corn grown for stock.

field/ crick/et. See under **cricket**[1] (def. 1).

field/ cur/rent, *Elect.* the current in a field winding. Also called **exciting current.**

field/ day/, 1. a day devoted to outdoor sport or athletic contests. **2.** an outdoor gathering; outing; picnic. **3.** a day for military exercises and display. **4.** an occasion or opportunity for unrestricted activity, amusement, etc.: *The children had a field day with their new skateboards.*

field/ed pan/el (fēl/did), *Archit., Furniture.* **1.** a panel having its surface raised above that of surrounding woodwork. **2.** a panel subdivided into smaller panels.

field/ emis/sion, *Physics.* the removal of electrons from a metallic conductor by a strong electric field.

field·er (fēl/dər), *n.* **1.** *Baseball, Cricket.* a player who fields the ball. **2.** *Baseball.* any of the players of the infield or the outfield, esp. an outfielder. [FIELD + -ER[1]]

field/er's choice/, *Baseball.* a fielder's attempt to put out a base runner rather than a batter when a play at first base would put out the batter.

field/ event/, an event in a track meet that involves throwing a weight or jumping and is not performed on the running track, as the shot put, pole vault, broad jump, or javelin throw.

field/ ex/ercise, a military exercise in which mock warfare is staged between one force more or less fully equipped and manned and another force, either hypothetical or represented only by token troops and equipment.

field·fare (fēld/fâr/), *n.* a European thrush, *Turdus pilaris,* having reddish-brown plumage with an ashy head and a blackish tail. [ME *feldefare* (with two *f's* by alliterative assimilation), OE *feldeware* field-dweller. See FIELD, WARE[2]]

field/ glass/. See **field glasses.**

field/ glass/es, a compact, easily portable binocular telescope for use out-of-doors.

field/ goal/, 1. *Football.* a three-point goal made by place-kicking or drop-kicking the ball between the opponent's goal posts above the crossbar. **2.** *Basketball.* a goal made while the ball is in play.

field/ guide/, a guide to examples of some class of beings or things, as birds or plants, which is adapted for use where such beings or things are to be observed.

field/ gun/, *Mil.* a cannon mounted on a carriage for service in the field.

field/ hand/, a person who works in the fields of a farm or plantation.

field/ hock/ey, a game played on a rectangular field, having a netted goal at each end, in which two teams of 11 players each compete in driving a small leather-covered ball into the other's goal, each player being equipped with a stick having a curved end or blade that is flat on one side and rounded on the other.

field/ hos/pital, *Mil.* an organization of medical personnel with medical equipment for establishing a temporary hospital at isolated posts or in the field to support ground troops in combat.

field/ house/, 1. a building housing the dressing facilities, storage spaces, etc., used in connection with an athletic field. **2.** a building sheltering an area used for athletic events, as track events.

Field·ing (fēl/ding), *n.* **Henry,** 1707–54, English novelist, dramatist, and essayist.

field/ing av/erage, *Baseball.* a measure of the fielding ability of a player, obtained by dividing the number of put-outs and assists by the number of put-outs, assists, and errors and carrying out the result to three decimal places. A player with 10 errors in 600 chances has a fielding average of .984.

field/ inten/sity, *Physics.* See **field strength.**

field/ jack/et, a jacket for wear by soldiers in the field.

field/ kitch/en, *Mil.* **1.** the portable cooking equipment used by troops in the field. **2.** the place where such equipment is used.

field/ lark/, *U.S. Dial.* See **meadow lark.**

field/ lark/spur, an herb, *Delphinium Consolida,* of Europe, having sparse clusters of blue or violet-colored flowers and smooth fruit. Also called **knight's-spur.**

field/ lens/, *Optics.* the lens in an eyepiece that is furthest from the eye and that deviates rays toward the center of the eye lens.

field/ line/, *Physics.* See **line of force.**

field/ mag/net, a magnet for producing a magnetic field.

field/ mar/shal, an officer of the highest military rank in the British and certain other armies, and of the second highest rank in the French army.

field/ mas/ter, *Fox Hunting.* the honorary member of a hunt staff who is responsible for the conduct of the field.

field/ mint/. See **corn mint.**

field/ mouse/, any of various short-tailed mice or moles inhabiting fields and meadows.

field/ mush/room. See under **mushroom** (def. 2).

field/ mu/sic, *Mil.* **1.** musicians, esp. buglers, drummers, and fifers, who play various calls and music for marching in the absence of a band. **2.** the music they play.

field/ of/ficer, *Mil.* an officer holding a field grade.

field/ of force/, *Physics.* field (def. 14).

field/ of hon/or, the scene of a battle or duel.

field/ of quo/tients, *Math.* a field whose elements are pairs of elements of a given commutative integral domain such that the second element of each pair is not zero. The field of rational numbers is the field of quotients of the integral domain of integers. Also called **field of frac/tions.**

field/ of view/, *Optics.* field (def. 15).

field/ of vi/sion, the entire view encompassed by the eye when it is trained in any particular direction. Also called **visual field.**

field/ pen/ny-cress, the penny-cress, *Thlaspi alpestre.*

field·piece (fēld/pēs/), *n. Mil.* a field gun. [FIELD + PIECE]

field/ ra/tion, *U.S. Army.* ration issued only in actual articles, not in money, and authorized for troops in the field.

Fields (fēldz), *n.* **W. C.,** (*William Claude Dukenfield*), 1880–1946, U.S. actor.

field/ sca/bious. See under **scabious**[2] (def. 1).

field/ serv/ice, any service carried on in the field rather than at some central location.

fields·man (fēldz/mən), *n., pl.* **-men.** *Brit.* a fielder in cricket. [FIELD + -'S[1] + MAN[1]]

Fields/ of Mourn/ing, (in the *Aeneid*) a place in the underworld inhabited by the shades of lovers who had committed suicide.

field/ span/iel, one of a British breed of spaniels having a flat or slightly waved, usually black coat, used for hunting and retrieving game.

field/ spar/row, a common North American finch, *Spizella pusilla,* found in brushy pasture lands.

field·stone (fēld/stōn/), *n.* undressed stone as found in fields, esp. when used for building purposes. [FIELD + STONE]

field/ stop/, *Optics.* the aperture that limits the field of view of a lens or system of lenses.

field/ strength/, *Physics.* the vector sum of all forces exerted by a field on a unit mass, unit charge, unit magnetic pole, etc., at a given point within the field. Also called **field intensity.**

field-strip (fēld/strip/), *v.t.,* **-stripped** or (*Rare*) **-stript, -strip·ping.** *Mil.* **1.** to take apart (a weapon) for cleaning, lubrication, and repair, or for inspection. **2.** to roll up the paper and scatter the tobacco of (a cigarette butt): *Field-strip all cigarette butts to keep the area neat.*

field′ the′ory, *Physics.* a detailed mathematical description of the distribution and movement of matter under the influence of one or more fields.

field′ tri′al, a competition among sporting dogs under natural conditions in the field in which the animals are judged on the basis of excellence of performance in hunting.

field′ trip′, **1.** a trip by students to gain first-hand knowledge away from the classroom, as to a museum, factory, geological area, a region where certain plants and animals may be found, etc. **2.** a trip by a scholar or researcher to gather data at first hand, as to a geological, archaeological, anthropological, or other site.

field′ wind′ing (wīn′ding), *Elect.* the electrically conducting circuit, usually a number of coils wound on individual poles and connected in series, which produces the magnetic field in a motor or generator.

field′ work′, work done in the field, as research, exploration, surveying, etc.: *archaeological field work.* —**field′work′er,** *n.*

field·work (fēld′wûrk′), *n.* *Fort.* a temporary fortification constructed in the field. [FIELD + WORK]

fiend (fēnd), *n.* **1.** Satan; the devil. **2.** any evil spirit. **3.** a diabolically cruel or wicked person. **4.** *Informal.* a person or thing that causes mischief or annoyance: *Those children are little fiends.* **5.** *Informal.* a person who is hopelessly addicted to some pernicious habit: *an opium fiend.* **6.** *Informal.* a person who is excessively interested in some game, sport, etc.; fan; buff: *a bridge fiend.* [ME *feend,* OE *fēond;* c. G *Feind,* Icel *fjandr,* Goth *fijands* foe, orig. prp. of *fijan* to hate] —**fiend′like′,** *adj.*

fiend·ish (fēn′dish), *adj.* diabolically cruel and wicked. [FIEND + -ISH[1]] —**fiend′ish·ly,** *adv.* —**fiend′ish·ness,** *n.*

fiend·ly (fēnd′lē), *adj.,* **-li·er, -li·est.** *Archaic.* of, pertaining to, or befitting a fiend; diabolical. [ME *fendli(ch),* OE *fēondlic.* See FIEND, -LY]

fierce (fērs), *adj.,* **fierc·er, fierc·est.** **1.** menacingly wild, savage, or hostile: *fierce animals; a fierce look.* **2.** violent in force, intensity, etc.: *fierce winds.* **3.** furiously eager or intense: *fierce competition.* **4.** *Informal.* extremely bad or severe: *a fierce cold.* [ME *fiers* < OF < L *ferus* wild, fierce] —**fierce′ly,** *adv.* —**fierce′ness,** *n.*
—**Syn. 1.** untamed, cruel, fell, brutal; barbarous, bloodthirsty, murderous; furious, passionate, turbulent, impetuous. FIERCE, FEROCIOUS, TRUCULENT suggest vehemence and violence of manner and conduct. FIERCE suggests violence of temper, manner, or action: *fierce in repelling a foe.* FEROCIOUS implies fierceness or cruelty, esp. of a bloodthirsty kind, in disposition or action: *a ferocious glare; ferocious brutality toward helpless refugees.* TRUCULENT suggests an intimidating or bullying fierceness of manner or conduct: *His truculent attitude kept them terrified and submissive.* —**Ant. 1.** tame, mild.

fierc·en (fēr′sən), *v.i.* to become fierce or to increase in fierceness. [FIERCE + -EN[2]]

fi·e·ri fa·ci·as (fī′ə rī fā′shē as′), *Law.* a writ commanding a sheriff to levy and sell as much of a debtor's property as is necessary to satisfy a creditor's claim against him. [< L: lit., have it made, equiv. to *fierī* to be made + *faciās* cause, 2nd sing. pres. subj. of *facere* to bring about]

fier·y (fīər′ē, fī′ə rē), *adj.,* **fier·i·er, fier·i·est.** **1.** consisting of, attended with, characterized by, or containing fire: *a volcano's fiery discharge.* **2.** intensely hot: *fiery desert sands.* **3.** like or suggestive of fire: *a fiery heat; a fiery red.* **4.** flashing or glowing, as the eye. **5.** intensely ardent, impetuous, or passionate: *fiery courage; a fiery speech.* **6.** easily angered or provoked: *a fiery temper.* **7.** flammable, as gas in a mine. **8.** containing flammable gas, as a mine. **9.** inflamed, as a tumor or sore. **10.** causing a burning sensation, as certain liquors or condiments. [ME *fi(e)ry.* See FIRE, -Y[1]] —**fier′i·ly,** *adv.* —**fier′i·ness,** *n.*
—**Syn. 3.** flaming, glowing, burning. **5.** fervent, vehement, spirited, impassioned. —**Ant. 2, 3, 5.** cool, cold. **5.** dispassionate.

fier′y cross′, a burning cross, the emblem of several organizations, notably the Ku Klux Klan.

Fie·so·le (*It.* fye′zō le), *n.* **1. Gio·van·ni da** (*It.* jō-vän′nē dä). See **Angelico, Fra.** **2.** a town in central Italy, near Florence: Etruscan and ancient Roman ruins; 12,481 (1961).

fi·es·ta (fē es′tə; *Sp.* fyes′tä), *n., pl.* **-tas** (-təz; *Sp.* -täs). **1.** (in Spain and Latin America) a festive religious celebration of a saint's day. **2.** any festival or festive celebration. [< Sp < L *fēsta;* see FEAST]

fies·ta de to·ros (fyes′tä the tô′rôs; *Eng.* fē es′tə dā tôr′ōs, tôr′-), *pl.* **fies·tas de to·ros** (fyes′täs the tô′rôs; *Eng.* fē es′təz dā tôr′ōs, tôr′-). *Spanish.* bullfight; corrida. Also called **fiesta taurina.**

fies′ta flow′er, an annual herb, *Nemophila aurita,* of central California, having violet flowers.

fies·ta tau·ri·na (fyes′tä tou-rē′nä), *pl.* **fies·tas tau·ri·nas** (fyes′täs tou rē′näs). *Spanish.* See **fiesta de toros.**

fife (fīf), *n., v.,* **fifed, fif·ing.** —*n.* **1.** a high-pitched transverse flute used commonly in military and marching musical groups: *a fife and drum corps.* —*v.i., v.t.* **2.** to play on a fife. [< G *Pfeife* PIPE[1]] —**fif′er,** *n.*

Fife

Fife (fīf), *n.* a county in E Scotland. 316,700 (est. 1956); 505 sq. mi. *Cap.:* Cupar. Also called **Fife·shire** (fīf′shēr, -shər).

fife′ rail′, *Naut.* a rail surrounding or in way of the mast of a sailing vessel for use in holding the pins to which some of the running rigging is belayed. Cf. **pin rail.**

Fi·fi (fē′fē), *n.* a girl's given name, form of **Josephine.** Also, **Fi·fine** (fē fēn′).

FIFO (fī′fō). See **first-in, first-out.**

fif·teen (fif′tēn′), *n.* **1.** a cardinal number, ten plus five. **2.** a symbol for this number, as 15 or XV. **3.** a set of this many persons or things. —*adj.* **4.** amounting to 15 in number. [ME, OE *fiftēne.* See FIVE, -TEEN]

fif·teenth (fif′tēnth′), *adj.* **1.** next after the fourteenth; being the ordinal number for 15. **2.** being one of 15 equal parts. —*n.* **3.** a fifteenth part, esp. of one (1/15). **4.** the fifteenth member of a series. **5.** *Music.* the interval of two octaves. [ME *fiftenthe* (see FIFTEEN, -TH[2]); r. ME *fiftethe,* OE *fīftēotha*]

fifth (fifth), *adj.* **1.** next after the fourth; being the ordinal number for five. **2.** being one of five equal parts. —*n.* **3.** a fifth part, esp. of one (⅕). **4.** the fifth member of a series. **5.** a fifth part of a gallon of liquor or spirits; 4/5 of a quart. **6.** *Music.* **a.** a tone on the fifth degree from another tone (counted as the first). **b.** the interval between such tones. **c.** the harmonic combination of such tones. [earlier *fift,* ME *fifte,* OE *fīfta; -th* by analogy with FOURTH, etc.] —**fifth′ly,** *adv.*

Fifth′ Amend′ment, an amendment to the Constitution of the U.S., providing chiefly that no person be required to testify against himself in a criminal case and that no person be subjected to a second trial for an offense for which he has been duly tried previously.

fifth′ col′umn, **1.** a group of people who, although residing in a country, act traitorously and subversively out of a secret sympathy with an enemy. **2.** (originally) Franco sympathizers in Madrid during the Spanish Civil War: so called in allusion to a statement in 1936 that the insurgents had four columns marching on Madrid and a fifth column of sympathizers in the city ready to rise and betray it. —**fifth′ col′umnist.**

fifth′ mon′archy, the fifth and final monarchy following the Assyrian, Persian, Greek (under Alexander the Great), and Roman monarchies, supposed to have been prophesied in Dan. 2.

Fifth′ Mon′archy Men′, *Eng. Hist.* (during the Commonwealth in the 17th century) a militant sect of Puritans who identified the fifth monarchy with the millennial reign of Christ and who believed they should help to inaugurate that reign by force.

fifth′ posi′tion, *Ballet.* a position similar to the first position, but with the left foot in front, the heel and toe of the left foot adjacent to the toe and heel of the right foot. See illus. under **first position.**

Fifth′ Repub′lic, the republic established in France in 1958, the successor of the Fourth Republic.

fifth′ wheel′, **1.** a horizontal ring or segment of a ring, consisting of two bands which slide on each other, placed above the front axle of a carriage and designed to support the forepart of the body while allowing it to turn freely in a horizontal plane. **2.** an extra wheel for a four-wheeled vehicle. **3.** a superfluous or unwanted person or thing: *They enjoy making any outsider feel like a fifth wheel.*

fif·ti·eth (fif′tē ith), *adj.* **1.** next after the forty-ninth; being the ordinal number for 50. **2.** being one of 50 equal parts. —*n.* **3.** a fiftieth part, esp. of one (1/50). **4.** the fiftieth member of a series. [ME *fiftithe,* OE *fīftigotha.* See FIFTY, -TH[2]]

fif·ty (fif′tē), *n., pl.* **-ties,** *adj.* —*n.* **1.** a cardinal number, ten times five. **2.** a symbol for this number, as 50 or L. **3.** a set of this many persons or things. **4. fifties, a.** the numbers 50 through 59, esp. the 50th through the 59th years of a lifetime or of a given or implied century. **b.** the part of a series which falls between 50 and 60, as in computation of age, time, temperature, etc.: *It's going to be in the fifties again today.* —*adj.* **5.** amounting to 50 in number. [ME; OE *fīftig.* See FIVE, -TY[1]]

fif·ty-eight (fif′tē āt′), *n.* **1.** a cardinal number, 50 plus 8. **2.** a symbol for this number, as 58 or LVIII. **3.** a set of this many persons or things. —*adj.* **4.** amounting to 58 in number.

fif·ty-eighth (fif′tē ātth′), *adj.* **1.** next after the fifty-seventh; being the ordinal number for 58. **2.** being one of 58 equal parts. —*n.* **3.** a fifty-eighth part, esp. of one (1/58). **4.** the fifty-eighth member of a series.

fif·ty-fifth (fif′tē fifth′), *adj.* **1.** next after the fifty-fourth; being the ordinal number for 55. **2.** being one of 55 equal parts. —*n.* **3.** a fifty-fifth part, esp. of one (1/55). **4.** the fifty-fifth member of a series.

fif·ty-fif·ty (fif′tē fif′tē), *adv., adj.* *Informal.* with equality of shares, as of profits, expenses, etc.; sharing equally in profits, payment, responsibility, etc.: *They went fifty-fifty on the dinner.*

fif·ty-first (fif′tē fûrst′), *adj.* **1.** next after the fiftieth; being the ordinal number for 51. **2.** being one of 51 equal parts. —*n.* **3.** a fifty-first part, esp. of one (1/51). **4.** the fifty-first member of a series.

fif·ty-five (fif′tē fīv′), *n.* **1.** a cardinal number, 50 plus 5. **2.** a symbol for this number, as 55 or LV. **3.** a set of this many persons or things. —*adj.* **4.** amounting to 55 in number.

fif·ty-four (fif′tē fôr′, -fōr′), *n.* **1.** a cardinal number, 50 plus 4. **2.** a symbol for this number, as 54 or LIV. **3.** a set of this many persons or things. —*adj.* **4.** amounting to 54 in number.

fif·ty-fourth (fif′tē fôrth′, -fōrth′), *adj.* **1.** next after the fifty-third; being the ordinal number for 54. **2.** being one of 54 equal parts. —*n.* **3.** a fifty-fourth part, esp. of one (1/54). **4.** the fifty-fourth member of a series.

fif·ty-nine (fif′tē nīn′), *n.* **1.** a cardinal number, 50 plus 9. **2.** a symbol for this number, as 59 or LIX. **3.** a set of this many persons or things. —*adj.* **4.** amounting to 59 in number.

fif·ty-ninth (fif′tē nīnth′), *adj.* **1.** next after the fifty-eighth; being the ordinal number for 59. **2.** being one of 59 equal parts. —*n.* **3.** a fifty-ninth part, esp. of one (1/59). **4.** the fifty-ninth member of a series.

fif·ty-one (fif′tē wun′), *n.* **1.** a cardinal number, 50 plus 1. **2.** a symbol for this number, as 51 or LI. **3.** a set of this many persons or things. —*adj.* **4.** amounting to 51 in number.

fif·ty·pen·ny (fif′tē pen′ē), *adj.* noting a nail 5½ inches long. *Abbr.:* 50d [FIFTY + -PENNY]

fif·ty-sec·ond (fif′tē sek′ənd), *adj.* **1.** next after the fifty-first; being the ordinal number for 52. **2.** being one of 52 equal parts. —*n.* **3.** a fifty-second part, esp. of one (1/52). **4.** the fifty-second member of a series.

fif·ty-sev·en (fif′tē sev′ən), *n.* **1.** a cardinal number, 50 plus 7. **2.** a symbol for this number, as 57 or LVII. **3.** a set of this many persons or things. —*adj.* **4.** amounting to 57 in number.

fif·ty-sev·enth (fif′tē sev′ənth), *adj.* **1.** next after the fifty-sixth; being the ordinal number for 57. **2.** being one of 57 equal parts. —*n.* **3.** a fifty-seventh part, esp. of one (1/57). **4.** the fifty-seventh member of a series.

fif·ty-six (fif′tē siks′), *n.* **1.** a cardinal number, 50 plus 6. **2.** a symbol for this number, as 56 or LVI. **3.** a set of this many persons or things. —*adj.* **4.** amounting to 56 in number.

fif·ty-sixth (fif′tē siksth′), *adj.* **1.** next after the fifty-fifth; being the ordinal number for 56. **2.** being one of 56 equal parts. —*n.* **3.** a fifty-sixth part, esp. of one (1/56). **4.** the fifty-sixth member of a series.

fif·ty-third (fif′tē thûrd′), *adj.* **1.** next after the fifty-second; being the ordinal number for 53. **2.** being one of 53 equal parts. —*n.* **3.** a fifty-third part, esp. of one (1/53). **4.** the fifty-third member of a series.

fif·ty-three (fif′tē thrē′), *n.* **1.** a cardinal number, 50 plus 3. **2.** a symbol for this number, as 53 or LIII. **3.** a set of this many persons or things. —*adj.* **4.** amounting to 53 in number.

fif·ty-two (fif′tē tōō′), *n.* **1.** a cardinal number, 50 plus 2. **2.** a symbol for this number, as 52 or LII. **3.** a set of this many persons or things. —*adj.* **4.** amounting to 52 in number.

fig[1] (fig), *n.* **1.** any moraceous tree or shrub of the genus *Ficus,* esp. a small tree, *F. Carica,* native to southwestern Asia, bearing a turbinate or pear-shaped fruit which is eaten fresh or preserved or dried. **2.** the fruit of such a tree or shrub, or of any related species. **3.** any of various plants having a fruit somewhat resembling this. **4.** a contemptibly trifling or worthless amount; the least bit: *His help wasn't worth a fig.* **5.** a gesture of contempt. [ME *fige* < OF < OPr *figa* < LL **fica,* r. L *fīcus;* but note OE *fefigo* condyloma]

fig[2] (fig), *v.,* **figged, fig·ging,** *n.* *Informal.* —*v.t.* **1.** to dress or array (usually fol. by *out*). **2.** to furbish (usually fol. by *up*). —*n.* **3.** dress or array: *to appear at a party in full fig.* **4.** condition: *to feel in fine fig.* [earlier *feague* to liven, whip up < G *fegen* to furbish, sweep, clean; akin to FAIR[1]]

fig., **1.** figurative. **2.** figuratively. **3.** figure; figures.

fig·eat·er (fig′ē′tər), *n.* See **green June beetle.** [FIG[1] + EATER]

fig·gy (fig′ē), *adj.,* **-gi·er, -gi·est.** containing figs: *a figgy cake.* [FIG[1] + -Y[1]]

fight (fīt), *n., v.,* **fought, fight·ing.** —*n.* **1.** a battle or combat. **2.** any contest or struggle: *a fight for recovery from an illness.* **3.** an angry argument or disagreement: *She starts a fight every time she phones me.* **4.** *Boxing.* a bout or contest. **5.** ability or inclination to fight: *There was no fight left in him.* **6.** *Obs.* a bulkhead or screen for protecting the personnel of a warship during a battle. —*v.i.* **7.** to engage in battle or in single combat; attempt to defend oneself against or to defeat, subdue, or destroy an adversary. **8.** to contend in any manner; strive vigorously for or against something: *He fought bravely against despair.* —*v.t.* **9.** to contend with in battle or combat; war against: *England fought Germany.* **10.** to contend with or against in any manner: *to fight despair; to fight the passage of a bill.* **11.** to carry on (a battle, duel, etc.). **12.** to maintain (a cause, quarrel, etc.) by fighting or contending. **13.** to make (one's way) by fighting or striving. **14.** to cause or set (a boxer, dog, etc.) to fight. **15.** to manage or maneuver (troops, ships, guns, planes, etc.) in battle. **16. fight it out,** to fight until a decision is reached: *Let them fight it out among themselves.* **17. fight shy of.** See **shy**[1] (def. 9). **18. fight with windmills.** See **tilt**[1] (def. 9). [ME; OE *fe(o)htan;* c. G *fechten;* akin to L *pugnāre* to fight] —**fight′a·ble,** *adj.* —**fight′ing·ly,** *adv.*
—**Syn. 1, 2.** encounter, engagement, affray, fray, action, skirmish; melee, scuffle, tussle, row, riot. FIGHT, COMBAT, CONFLICT, CONTEST denote a struggle of some kind. FIGHT connotes a hand-to-hand struggle for supremacy, literally or in a figurative sense. COMBAT suggests an armed encounter, to settle a dispute. CONFLICT implies a bodily, mental, or moral struggle caused by opposing views, beliefs, etc. CONTEST applies to either a friendly or a hostile struggle for a definite prize or aim. **7.** conflict, struggle. **8.** contest, struggle.

fight·er (fī′tər), *n.* **1.** *Boxing.* a boxer. **2.** *Mil.* an aircraft designed to seek out and destroy enemy aircraft in the air and to protect bomber aircraft. **3.** a person who fights, struggles, resists, etc. **4.** a person with the will, courage, determination, ability, or disposition to fight, struggle, resist, etc. **5.** an animal, as a dog, trained to fight or having the disposition to fight. [ME; OE *fēohtere.* See FIGHT, -ER[1]]

fight·er-bomb·er (fī′tər bom′ər), *n.* *Mil.* an aircraft that combines the functions of a fighter and a bomber.

fight·er-in·ter·cep·tor (fī′tər in′tər sep′tər), *n.* *Mil.* a fighter plane used for the defense of a region against air attack, esp. by attacking bombers.

fight′ing chair′, a chair fastened to the deck at the stern of a seagoing fishing boat for use by an angler in attempting to land a fish hooked on his line.

fight′ing chance′, a possibility of success following a struggle: *The doctor gave him a fighting chance to survive.*

fight′ing cock′, a gamecock.

fight′ing fish′, any of several brightly colored labyrinth fishes of the genus *Betta,* found in SE Asia. Also called **betta.** Cf. **Siamese fighting fish.**

Siamese fighting fish, *Betta splendens* (Length 2½ in.)

Fight′ing French′, (in World War II) the French movement, organized in London under the leadership of General Charles de Gaulle, that repudiated the 1940 armistice with the Nazis and the government established at Vichy and fought for the liberation of France and the restoration of the republic.

fight′ing top′, a protected structure on a mast of a warship, used as a platform for small weapons and for observation.

fig′ leaf′, **1.** the leaf of a fig tree. **2.** a representation of a fig leaf, as in stone or bronze, used as an ornament in architecture, to cover the genitalia on a male statue, etc. **3.** something intended to conceal what may be considered indecorous or questionable: *to approach the facts of life with the fig leaves of roundabout expressions.*

fig′ mar′i·gold, any of various herbs of the genus *Mesembryanthemum*, having showy, white, yellow, or pink flowers.

fig·ment (fig′mənt), *n.* **1.** a mere product of mental invention; a fantastic notion: *The shrieks in the attic were just a figment of his imagination.* **2.** a feigned, invented, or imagined story, theory, etc.: *biographical and historical figments.* [late ME < L *figment(um)* something made or feigned, equiv. to *fig-* (root of *fingere* to mold, feign) + *-mentum* -MENT]
—**Syn. 2.** See **fiction.**

Fi·gue·res (fē ge′res), *n.* **Jo·sé** (hō se′), born 1908?, Costa Rican businessman and politician: president 1953–58.

fig·ur·al (fig′yər əl), *adj.* consisting of figures, esp. human or animal figures: *the figural representations contained in ancient wall paintings.* [ME < LL *figūrāl(is),* equiv. to L *figūr(a)* FIGURE + *-ālis* -AL[1]] —**fig′ur·al·ly,** *adv.*

fig·u·rant (fig′yŏŏ rant′; *Fr.* fē gʏ räɴ′), *n., pl.* **-rants** (-rants′; *Fr.* -räɴ′). a ballet dancer who dances only with others in groups or figures. [< F, n. use of prp. of *figurer* to FIGURE, appear in; see -ANT]

fig·ur·ate (fig′yər it), *adj.* **1.** of a certain determinate figure or shape. **2.** *Music.* characterized by the use of passing notes or other embellishments; florid. [< L *figūrāt(us)* formed, shaped, ptp. of *figūrāre.* See FIGURE, -ATE[1]] —**fig′ur·ate·ly,** *adv.*

fig′urate num′ber, *Math.* a number having the property that the same number of equally spaced dots can be arranged in the shape of a regular geometrical figure.

fig·u·ra·tion (fig′yə rā′shən), *n.* **1.** the act of shaping into a particular figure. **2.** the resulting figure or shape: *emblematic figurations of the sun and the moon.* **3.** the act of representing figuratively. **4.** a figurative representation: *allegorical figurations.* **5.** the act of marking or adorning with a design. **6.** *Music.* **a.** the employment of passing notes or other embellishments. **b.** the figuring of a bass part. [late ME *figuracioun* < L *figūrātiōn-* (s. of *figūrātiō*) a shaping. See FIGURATE, -ION]

fig·ur·a·tive (fig′yər ə tiv), *adj.* **1.** of the nature of or involving a figure of speech, esp. a metaphor; metaphorical; not literal: *a figurative expression.* **2.** metaphorically so called: *This remark was a figurative boomerang.* **3.** abounding in or fond of figures of speech: *Elizabethan poetry is highly figurative.* **4.** representing by means of a figure or likeness, as in drawing or sculpture. **5.** representing by a figure or emblem; emblematic. [late ME < LL *figūrātīv(us)* (see FIGURATE, -IVE); r. ME *figuratif* < MF] —**fig′ur·a·tive·ly,** *adv.* —**fig′ur·a·tive·ness,** *n.*

fig·ure (fig′yər; *Brit.* fig′ər), *n., v.,* **-ured, -ur·ing.** —*n.* **1.** a written symbol other than a letter. **2.** a numerical symbol, esp. an Arabic numeral. **3.** an amount or value expressed in numbers. **4. figures,** the use of numbers in calculating; arithmetic: *to be poor at figures.* **5.** form or shape, as determined by outlines or exterior surfaces: *to be round, square, or cubical in figure.* **6.** the bodily form or frame: *a slender or graceful figure.* **7.** an individual bodily form or a person with reference to form or appearance: *A tall figure stood in the doorway.* **8.** a person as he appears or is presented publicly: *a controversial political figure.* **9.** a character or personage, esp. one of distinction: *a figure in society.* **10.** the appearance or impression made by a person or sometimes a thing: *to make quite a figure in financial circles; to present a wretched figure of poverty.* **11.** a representation, pictorial or sculptured, of something esp. of the human form: *The frieze was bordered with the figures of men and animals.* **12.** an emblem, type, or symbol: *The dove is a figure of peace.* **13.** *Rhet.* a figure of speech. **14.** a device or pattern, as in cloth: *draperies with an embossed silk figure.* **15.** a movement, pattern, or series of movements in skating. **16.** a distinct movement or division of a dance. **17.** *Music.* a short succession of musical notes, either as melody or as a group of chords, which produces a single complete and distinct impression. **18.** *Geom.* a combination of geometric elements disposed in a particular form or shape: *The circle, square, and polygon are plane figures. The sphere, cube, and polyhedron are solid figures.* **19.** *Logic.* any of the forms of a syllogism with respect to the relative position of the middle term. **20.** *Optics.* the precise curve required on the surface of an optical element, esp. the mirror or correcting plate of a reflecting telescope. **21.** *Obs.* a phantasm or illusion. **22. cut a figure.** See **cut** (defs. 39, 41b). —*v.t.* **23.** to compute or calculate (often fol. by *up*): *to figure up a total.* **24.** to express in figures. **25.** to mark or adorn with a design or pattern. **26.** to portray by speech or action. **27.** to represent or express by a figure of speech. **28.** to represent by a pictorial or sculptured figure, a diagram, or the like; picture or depict; trace (an outline, silhouette, etc.). **29.** *Informal.* to conclude, judge, reason, or think about. **30.** *Music.* **a.** to embellish with passing notes or other decorations. **b.** to write figures above or below (a bass part) to indicate accompanying chords. —*v.i.* **31.** to compute or work with numerical figures. **32.** to be or appear, esp. in a conspicuous or prominent way: *His name figures importantly in my report.* **33.** (of a situation, act, request, etc.) to be logical, expected, or reasonable: *He quit the job when he didn't get a raise—it figured.* **34. figure on,** *Informal.* **a.** to count or rely on. **b.** to take into consideration; plan on: *You had better figure on running into heavy traffic leaving the city.* **35. figure out,** *U.S. Informal.* **a.** to calculate; compute. **b.** to understand; solve: *We couldn't figure out where all the money had gone.* [ME < L *figūra* shape, trope, equiv. to *fig-* (root of *fingere* to shape) + *-ūra* -URE] —**fig′ur·a·ble,** *adj.* —**fig′ure·less,** *adj.* —**fig′ur·er,** *n.*
—**Syn. 2.** number, cipher. **3.** sum, total; price. **5.** See **form. 8.** personality. **23.** reckon. **31.** cipher.

fig·ured (fig′yərd), *adj.* **1.** formed or shaped: *figured stones.* **2.** represented by a pictorial or sculptured figure: *The god is figured as part man, part beast.* **3.** ornamented with a device or pattern: *figured silk; figured wallpaper.* **4.** *Music.* **a.** florid. **b.** having the accompanying chords indicated by figures. **5.** figurative, as language. [ME, ptp. of *figuren* to FIGURE; see -ED[2]] —**fig·ured·ly** (fig′yərd lē, -yər id-), *adv.*

fig′ured bass′ (bās), *Music.* a bass part in which the notes have numbers under them indicating the chords to be played.

fig′ured glass′, plate or sheet glass having a pattern rolled onto one side of the surface.

fig′ure eight′, **1.** a representation in outline of the number eight as traced on ice in figure skating. **2.** See **figure of eight** (def. 1).

fig·ure-ground (fig′yər ground′), *n.* *Psychol.* a property of perception in which a field is divisible into chiefly two reciprocally influencing parts of varying distinctness and articulation, each dependent upon the focus of attention for clarity.

fig·ure·head (fig′yər hed′), *n.* **1.** a person who is head of a group, company, etc., in title but actually has no real authority or responsibility: *Most modern kings are figureheads.* **2.** *Naut.* a carved full-length figure or bust placed at the upper end of a cutwater or stem, esp. beneath a bowsprit. [FIGURE + HEAD]

fig′ure of eight′, **1.** Also, **figure eight.** a figure or form composed of two loops formed by a continuous line crossing itself, as in the figure 8. **2.** Also called **Flemish knot, German knot.** a knot made by forming a bight on the standing part of a rope, turning the end once around the standing part, and passing it through the bight. See illus. under **knot.**

fig′ure of speech′, *Rhet.* any expressive use of language, as a metaphor, simile, personification, antithesis, etc., in which words are used in other than their literal sense, or in other than their ordinary locutions, in order to suggest a picture or image or for other special effect. Cf. **trope** (def. 1).

fig′ure skate′, a shoe skate used in figure skating, esp. one having a blade shorter than that of a racing skate, usually not extending beyond the toe or heel, and with notches or sawteeth on the forward edge of the blade. Cf. **racing skate.** —**fig′ure-skat′er,** *n.*

fig′ure skat′ing, **1.** ice skating in which the skater traces on ice in a prescribed manner representations in outline of selected patterns. **2.** similar skating on roller skates, in which the skaters are judged chiefly on their grace and control since the representations of the patterns executed are not discernible.

fig·u·rine (fig′yə rēn′), *n.* a small ornamental figure of pottery, metalwork, etc.; statuette. [< F < It *figurina,* equiv. to *figur(a)* FIGURE + *-ina* -INE[1] (here dim.)]

fig′ wasp′, a chalcid wasp, *Blastophaga psenes,* introduced into the U.S. from Europe, that pollinates figs, usually of the Smyrna variety.

fig·wort (fig′wûrt′), *n.* **1.** any of numerous, usually coarse, herbs of the genus *Scrophularia.* **2.** any scrophulariaceous plant. [FIG[1] + WORT[2]]

Fi·ji (fē′jē), *n.* **1.** a British colony in the S Pacific, N of New Zealand, comprised of the Fiji Islands and an independent group to the NW. 345,737 (1956); 7040 sq. mi. *Cap.:* Suva. **2.** a native of the Fiji Islands. —**Fi·ji·an** (fē′jē ən, fi jē′ən), *adj., n.*

CORAL SEA
NEW HEBRIDES
NEW CALEDONIA
Fiji Islands
AUSTRALIA
PACIFIC OCEAN
TASMAN SEA
NEW ZEALAND

Fi′ji Is′lands, a group of islands in the S Pacific constituting most of the colony of Fiji.

fike (fīk), *n., v.,* **fiked, fik·ing.** *Scot. and North Eng.* —*n.* **1.** that which causes one to fidget, esp. an itch. **2.** anxiety; fuss; bother. —*v.i.* **3.** to fidget; move restlessly. —*v.t.* **4.** to trouble or bother someone. [< Scand; cf. Icel *fīkjast* to be eager, MSw *fīkja* to be restless. See FIDGE]

fikh (fik), *n.* *Islam.* fiqh.

fil (fil), *n.* fils[2].

fi·la·ceous (fi lā′shəs), *adj.* *Rare.* consisting of threads or threadlike parts; filamentous. [< L *fīl(um)* a thread + -ACEOUS]

fil·a·gree (fil′ə grē′), *n., adj., v.t.,* **-greed, -gree·ing.** filigree.

fil·a·ment (fil′ə mənt), *n.* **1.** a very fine thread or threadlike structure; a fiber or fibril: *filaments of gold.* **2.** a single fibril of natural or synthetic textile fiber, of indefinite length, sometimes several miles long. **3.** *Bot.* **a.** the stalklike portion of a stamen, supporting the anther. See diag. under **flower. b.** a long slender cell or series of attached cells, as in some algae, fungi, etc. **4.** *Ornith.* the barb of a down feather. **5.** (in a light bulb or other incandescent lamp) the threadlike conductor, often of tungsten, in the bulb which is heated to incandescence by the passage of current. **6.** *Electronics.* the heating element (sometimes also acting as a cathode) of a vacuum tube, resembling the filament in an incandescent electric lamp. [< NL *fīlāment(um),* equiv. to ML *fīlā(re)* (to) wind thread, spin (see FILE[1]) + *-mentum* -MENT] —**fil′a·ment·ed,** *adj.*

fil·a·men·ta·ry (fil′ə men′tə rē), *adj.* pertaining to or of the nature of a filament or filaments. [FILAMENT + -ARY]

fil·a·men·tous (fil′ə men′təs), *adj.* **1.** composed of or containing filaments. **2.** resembling a filament. **3.** bearing filaments. **4.** pertaining to filaments. [FILAMENT + -OUS]

fi·lar (fī′lər), *adj.* **1.** of or pertaining to a thread or threads. **2.** having threads or the like. [< L *fīl(um)* a thread + -AR[1]]

fi·lar·i·a (fi lâr′ē ə), *n., pl.* **-lar·i·ae** (-lâr′ē ē′). any slender, threadlike, nematode worm of the family *Filariidae* and related families, parasitic when adult in the blood or tissues of vertebrates, and developing as a larva in certain bloodsucking arthropods. [< NL, equiv. to L *fīl(um)* thread + *-āria* -ARIA]

fi·lar·i·al (fi lâr′ē əl), *adj.* **1.** belonging to the genus *Filaria* and allied genera of the family *Filariidae.* **2.** *Pathol.* pertaining to or noting infection by filariae: *filarial disease.* [FILARI(A) + -AL[1]]

fil·a·ri·a·sis (fil′ə rī′ə sis), *n.* *Pathol.* the presence of filarial worms in the blood and lymph channels, lymph glands, and other tissues. [< NL; see FILARIA, -ASIS]

fi·lar·i·id (fi lâr′ē id), *adj.* **1.** of or pertaining to filariae. —*n.* **2.** a filaria. [FILARI(A) + -ID[2]]

fi·lasse (fi las′), *n.* any of various vegetable fibers, other than cotton, processed for manufacture into yarn. [< F; OF *filace* < VL **filacea,* equiv. to L *fīl(um)* thread + *-acea,* fem. of *-aceus;* see -ACEOUS]

fi·late (fī′lāt), *adj.* *Zool.* threadlike. [< L *fīl(um)* a thread + -ATE[1]]

fil·a·ture (fil′ə chər), *n.* **1.** the act of forming into threads. **2.** a reel for drawing off silk from cocoons. **3.** the reeling of silk from cocoons. **4.** an establishment for reeling silk. [< F < ML *fīlātūra* the spinning art, equiv. to *fīlāt(us)* spun (ptp. of *fīlāre;* see FILAMENT) + *-ūra* -URE]

fil·bert (fil′bərt), *n.* **1.** the thick-shelled, edible nut of certain cultivated varieties of hazel, esp. of *Corylus Avellana,* of Europe. **2.** a tree or shrub bearing such nuts. [ME, short for *filbert nut,* so called because ripe by Aug. 22 (St. Philbert's day)]

filch (filch), *v.t.* to steal (esp. something of small value); pilfer: *to filch ashtrays from fancy restaurants.* [ME *filche(n)* to attack (in a body), take as booty, OE *fylcian* to marshal (troops), draw (soldiers) up in battle array, deriv. of *gefylce* band of men; akin to FOLK] —**filch′er,** *n.* —**filch′ing·ly,** *adv.*
—**Syn.** purloin, take.

file[1] (fīl), *n., v.,* **filed, fil·ing.** —*n.* **1.** a folder, cabinet, or other container in which papers, letters, etc., are arranged in convenient order. **2.** a collection of papers, records, etc., arranged in convenient order: *to make a file for a new account.* **3.** a string or wire on which papers are strung for preservation and reference. **4.** a line of persons or things arranged one behind another (distinguished from *rank*). **5.** *Mil.* **a.** a man in front of or behind another in a military formation. **b.** one step on a promotion list. **6.** one of the vertical lines of squares on a chessboard. **7.** a list or roll. **8. on file,** arrange in order for convenient reference; in a file: *The names are on file in the office.* —*v.t.* **9.** to place in a file. **10.** to arrange (papers, records, etc.) in convenient order for preservation or reference. **11.** *Journalism.* **a.** to arrange (copy) in the proper order for transmittal by wire. **b.** to transmit (copy), as by wire or telephone: *He filed copy from Ankara all through the war.* —*v.i.* **12.** to march in a file or line, one after another, as soldiers: *The parade filed past endlessly.* **13.** to make application: *to file for a civil-service job.* [late ME *file(n)* < MF *file(r)* (to) string documents on a thread or wire, OF: to wind or spin thread < ML *filare,* deriv. of L *fīlum* thread, string] —**fil′er,** *n.*

file[2] (fīl), *n., v.,* **filed, fil·ing.** —*n.* **1.** a long, narrow tool of steel or other metal having a series of ridges or points on its surfaces for reducing or smoothing surfaces of metal, wood, etc. **2.** a small, similar tool for trimming and cleaning fingernails; nail file. **3.** *Brit. Slang.* a cunning, shrewd, or artful person. —*v.t.* **4.** to reduce, smooth, cut, or remove with or as with a file. [ME; OE *fīl, fēol;* c.G *Feile;* akin to Gk *pikrós* sharp] —**fil′er,** *n.*

file[3] (fīl), *v.t.,* **filed, fil·ing.** *Archaic.* to defile; corrupt. [ME; OE *fȳlan* to befoul, defile, deriv. of *fūl* FOUL]

fi·lé (fi lā′), *n.* (esp. in creole cookery) the pulverized leaves of sassafras, used as a thickener in soups, gumbos, etc. [< LaF, n. use of ptp. of *filer* to twist; see FILE[1]]

file′ band′, an endless steel band to which straight lengths of steel files are attached, used on a band mill or band saw.

file′ bot′tom, *Naut.* a hull bottom characterized by straight floors with much deadrise ending in hard bilges.

file′ clerk′, an office employee whose principal work is the filing of papers, records, etc.

file·fish (fīl′fish′), *n., pl.* (*esp. collectively*) **-fish,** (*esp. referring to two or more kinds or species*) **-fish·es. 1.** any of several marine fishes of the family *Monacanthidae,* having a leathery skin covered with small, hard scales. **2.** a triggerfish. [FILE[2] + FISH]

file′ sig′nal, a small tab attached temporarily to a filed folder or card as an indication of its contents or nature.

fi·let (fi lā′, fil′ā; *Fr.* fē le′), *n., pl.* **fi·lets** (fi lāz′, fil′āz; *Fr.* fē le′), *v.t.* fillet (defs. 1, 10).

filet′ lace′, a square mesh net or lace, originally knotted by hand but now copied by machine. [< F *filet* net (OF *file* something spun, ptp. of *filer;* see FILE[1]) + *-et* -ET]

fi·let mi·gnon (fi lā′ min yon′, min′yon; *Fr.* fē le mē nyôɴ′), *pl.* **fi·lets mi·gnons** (fi lā′ min yonz′, min′yonz; *Fr.* fē le mē nyôɴ′). a small, tender round of steak cut from the thick end of a beef tenderloin. [< F: dainty fillet]

fil·i·al (fil′ē əl), *adj.* **1.** of, pertaining to, or befitting a son or daughter: *filial obedience.* **2.** noting or having the relation of a child to a parent. **3.** *Genetics.* pertaining to the sequence of generations following the parental generation, each generation being designated by an F followed by a subscript number indicating its place in the sequence. [ME < LL *fīliāl(is),* equiv. to L *fīli(us)* son + *-ālis* -AL[1]] —**fil′i·al·ly,** *adv.* —**fil′i·al·ness,** *n.*

fil·i·ate (fil′ē āt′), *v.t.,* **-at·ed, -at·ing. 1.** *Law.* to determine judicially the paternity of, as a bastard child. Cf. **affiliate** (def. 5). **2.** *Archaic.* affiliate. [< ML *fīliāt(us)* like the father (said of a son), equiv. to L *fīli(us)* son + *-ātus* -ATE[1]]

fil·i·a·tion (fil′ē ā′shən), *n.* **1.** the fact of being the child of a certain parent. **2.** descent as if from a parent; derivation. **3.** *Law.* the judicial determination of the paternity of a child, esp. of a bastard. **4.** the relation of one thing to another from which it is derived. **5.** the act of filiating. **6.** the state of being filiated. **7.** an affiliated branch, as of a society. [late ME *filiacion* < ML *fīliātiōn-* (s. of *fīliātiō*). See FILIATE, -ION]

fil·i·beg (fil′ə beg′), *n.* the kilt or plaited skirt worn by Scottish Highlanders. Also, **philibeg.** [< ScotGael, equiv. to *feile* kilt + *beag* little]

fil·i·bus·ter (fil′ə bus′tər), *n.* **1.** *U.S.* **a.** the use of irregular or obstructive tactics by a member of a minority in a legislative assembly to prevent the adoption of a measure generally favored or to force a decision almost unanimously disliked. **b.** an exceptionally long speech, as one lasting for a day or days, or a series of such speeches to accomplish this purpose. **c.** a member of a minority in a legislature who makes such a speech. **2.** an irregular military adventurer; freebooter or buccaneer. **3.** a person who engages in an unauthorized military expedition into a foreign country to foment or support a revolution. —*v.i.* **4.** *U.S.* to impede legislation by irregular or obstructive tactics, esp. by making long speeches. **5.** to act as a freebooter, buccaneer, or irregular military adventurer. —*v.t.* **6.** *U.S.* to impede (legislation) by irregular or obstructive tactics, esp. by making long speeches. [< Sp *filibustero* < F *flibustier,* var. of *fribustier* < FREEBOOTER] —**fil′i·bus′ter·er,** *n.* —**fil′i·bus′ter·ism,** *n.* —**fil′i·bus′ter·ous,** *adj.*

fil·i·cide (fil′i sīd′), *n.* **1.** a person who kills his son or daughter: *Ancient myth contains numerous examples of filicide.* **2.** the act of killing one's son or daughter. [< L *fīli(us)* son (*fīli(a)* daughter) + -CIDE] —**fil′i·cid′al,** *adj.*

fil·i·form (fil′ə fôrm′, fī′lə-), *adj.* threadlike; filamentous. [< L *fīl(um)* a thread + -I- + -FORM]

fil·i·grain (fil′ə grān′), *n.* *Archaic.* filigree. Also, **fil′i·grane′.** [< F *filigrane* watermark, filigree < It *filigrana* < ML *fīli(um)*, var. of *fīlum* water current (L: thread) + *grāna* graining, L, pl. of *grānum* GRAIN]

fil·i·gree (fil′ə grē′), *n., adj., v.,* **-greed, -gree·ing.** —*n.* **1.** ornamental work of fine wires, esp. lacy jewelers' work of scrolls and arabesques. **2.** anything very delicate or fanciful: *a filigree of frost.* —*adj.* **3.** composed of or resembling filigree. —*v.t.* **4.** to adorn with or form into filigree. Also, **filagree, fillagree.** [earlier *filigreen*, var. of FILIGRAIN]

fil·i·greed (fil′ə grēd′), *adj.* having filigree decorations. [FILIGREE + -ED²]

fil·ings (fī′liṅgz), *n.* particles removed by a file. [FILE² + -ING¹ + -S³]

fil·i·o·que (fil′ē ō′kwē), *n.* *Latin.* and the Son: in the Niceno-Constantinopolitan Creed, the phrase added by the Western Church: *"qui ex Patria Filioque procedit"* (Who proceeded from the Father and Son).

Fil·i·pi·no (fil′ə pē′nō), *n., pl.* **-nos,** *adj.* —*n.* **1.** a native of the Philippines, esp. a member of a Christianized native tribe. —*adj.* **2.** Philippine. [< Sp, derived from (*las Islas*) *Filipinas* PHILIPPINE (islands)]

fil·is·ter (fil′i stər), *n.* fillister.

fill (fil), *v.t.* **1.** to make full; put as much as can be held into: *to fill a jar with water.* **2.** to occupy to the full capacity: *Water filled the basin. The crowd filled the hall.* **3.** to supply to an extreme degree or plentifully: *to fill a house with furniture; to fill the heart with joy.* **4.** to feed fully; satiate: *The roast beef filled the diners.* **5.** to put into a receptacle: *to fill sand into a pail.* **6.** to be plentiful throughout: *Fish filled the rivers.* **7.** to extend throughout; pervade completely: *The odor filled the room.* **8.** to furnish (a vacancy or office) with an occupant or incumbent. **9.** to occupy and perform the duties of (a vacancy, position, post, etc.). **10.** to execute (a business order). **11.** to supply (a blank space) with written matter, decorative work, etc. **12.** to meet satisfactorily, as requirements: *This book fills a great need.* **13.** to make up or compound (a medical prescription). **14.** to stop up or close (a cavity, hole, etc.): *to fill a tooth.* **15.** *Naut.* **a.** to distend (a sail) by pressure of the wind so as to impart headway to a vessel. **b.** to brace (a yard) so that the sail will catch the wind on its after side. **16.** to adulterate: *filled soaps.* **17.** *Building Trades.* to build up the level of (an area) with earth, stones, etc. —*v.i.* **18.** to become full: *The hall filled rapidly. Her eyes filled with tears.* **19.** to increase in atmospheric pressure: *a filling cyclone.* **20.** to become distended, as sails with the wind. **21.** to fill a cup or other receptacle; pour out drink, as into a cup. **22. fill and stand on,** *Naut.* (of a sailing vessel) to proceed on a tack after being hove to or halted facing the wind; fill away. **23. fill away,** *Naut.* **a.** to fall off the wind and proceed on a board. **b.** to brace the yards, so that sails which have been aback will stand full. **24. fill in, a.** to supply missing or desired information: *Fill in the facts of your business experience.* **b.** to complete by adding detail, as a design or drawing: *to fill in a sketch with shadow.* **c.** to substitute for: *to fill in for a colleague who is ill.* **d.** to fill with some material: *to fill in a crack with putty.* **e.** *Slang.* to supply (someone) with information: *Please fill me in on the news.* **25. fill out, a.** to complete (a document, list, etc.) by supplying missing or desired information. **b.** to become larger, fuller, or rounder, as the figure: *The children have begun to fill out since I saw them last.* **26. fill the bill.** See **bill**¹ (def. 12). **27. fill up, a.** to fill completely: *to fill up a glass.* **b.** to become completely filled: *The river bed filled up in the wake of the steady rains.* —*n.* **28.** a full supply; enough to satisfy want or desire: *to eat one's fill.* **29.** an amount of something sufficient for filling; charge. **30.** *Building Trades.* a quantity of earth, stones, etc., for building up the level of an area of ground. **31.** the feed and water in the digestive tract of a livestock animal, esp. that consumed before marketing. [ME *fille(n)*, OE *fyllan;* c. G *füllen*, Goth *fulljan* to make full; see FULL¹] —**fill′a·ble,** *adj.*

fil·la·gree (fil′ə grē′), *n., adj., v.t.,* **-greed, -greeing.** filigree.

fill′ cap′, a cap screwed down over the hole through which a fuel tank is filled.

fille (fē′yə), *n., pl.* **filles** (fē′yə). *French.* **1.** a daughter. **2.** a girl. **3.** an unmarried woman; spinster. **4.** a prostitute. Cf. **jeune fille.**

fille de cham·bre (fē′yə də shäN′brə), *pl.* **filles de cham·bre** (fē′yə də shäN′brə). *French.* See **femme de chambre.**

fille de joie (fē′yə də zhwä′), *pl.* **filles de joie** (fē′yə də zhwä′). *French.* a prostitute. [lit., pleasure's girl]

filled′ gold′, a composition consisting of gold plating welded to and rolled with a backing of brass or other base metal, at least 1/20 of the total weight being that of the gold. Also called **rolled gold.** Cf. **gold-filled.**

fille d'hon·neur (fē′yə dô nœr′), *pl.* **filles d'honneur** (fē′yə dô nœr′). *French.* (in a wedding party) maid of honor.

filled′ milk′, milk containing a substitute for the butterfat.

fill·er (fil′ər), *n.* **1.** one who or that which fills: *a filler for pies; a filler of orders.* **2.** a thing or substance used to fill a gap, cavity, or the like. **3.** a substance used to fill cracks, pores, etc., in a surface before painting or varnishing. **4.** material placed between the insole and the exterior sole of a shoe. **5.** a form of wood or other material placed in a shoe to maintain its shape while on display, as in a store window. **6.** a liquid, paste, or the like used to coat a surface or to give solidity, bulk, etc., to a substance, as paper, a chemical powder, etc. **7.** the tobacco forming the body of a cigar, as distinguished from the wrapper. **8.** *Journalism.* material, considered of secondary importance, used to fill out a column or page. **9.** *Building Trades.* a plate, slab, block, etc., inserted between two parallel members to connect them. **10.** an implement used in filling, as a funnel. [FILL + -ER¹]

fil·lér (fē′lâr, fil′âr), *n., pl.* **-lér.** a money of account of Hungary, the 100th part of a forint, equivalent to about .0004 of a U.S. dollar. Also, **fil′ler.** [< Hung]

fil·let (fil′it; *usually* fi lā′ *for 1, 10*), *n.* **1.** *Cookery.* **a.** a boneless cut or slice of meat or fish, esp. the beef tenderloin. **b.** a piece of veal or other meat boned, rolled, and tied, for roasting. **2.** a narrow band of ribbon or the like worn around the head, usually as an ornament; headband. **3.** any narrow strip, as wood or metal. **4.** a strip of any material used for binding. **5.** *Bookbinding.* **a.** a decorative line impressed on a book's cover, usually at the top and bottom of the back. **b.** a rolling tool for impressing such lines. **6. a.** Also called **list.** a narrow flat molding or area, raised or sunk between larger moldings or areas. **b.** a narrow portion of the surface of a column left between adjoining flutes. **7.** *Anat.* a band of nerve fibers; lemniscus. **8.** a raised rim or ridge, as a ring on the muzzle of a gun. **9.** *Foundry.* a concave strip forming a rounded interior angle in a pattern. —*v.t.* **10.** *Cookery.* **a.** to cut or prepare (meat or fish) as a fillet. **b.** to cut fillets from. **11.** to bind or adorn with or as with a fillet. **12.** *Mach.* to round off (an interior angle) with a fillet. Also, **filet** (for defs. 1, 10). [ME *filet* < MF, equiv. to *fil* thread + *-et* -ET]

fil′let cross′ (fil′it), *Heraldry.* a very narrow cross used to unify separate coats of arms, borne quarterly, into a new, single coat of arms.

fil·let·ing (fil′i tiṅg), *n.* *Building Trades.* material, as mortar, used as a substitute for flashing. [FILLET + -ING¹]

fil′let weld′ (fil′it), a weld with a triangular cross section joining two surfaces that meet in an interior right angle.

fill-in (fil′in′), *n.* **1.** one who or that which fills in, as a substitute, replacement, insertion, etc.: *She was a fill-in for workers on vacation.* **2.** a brief, informative summary; a run-down: *They gave him a fill-in on what had happened while he was away.* [n. use of v. phrase *fill in*]

fill·ing (fil′iṅg), *n.* **1.** that which is put in to fill something: *the filling of a pie.* **2.** *Dentistry.* a substance in plastic form, as cement, amalgam, gold foil, or the like, used to close a cavity in a tooth. **3.** the act of one who or that which fills; a making or becoming full. **4.** Also called **pick, weft, woof.** *Textiles.* yarn carried by the shuttle and interlacing at right angles with the warp in woven cloth. See diag. under **weave.** [ME; see FILL, -ING¹] —**fill′ing·ly,** *adv.* —**fill′ing·ness,** *n.*

fill′ing knit′ting. See **weft knitting.**

fill′ing sta′tion, a retail business place where services and gasoline, oil, and other supplies for automobiles are available, esp. such a place with a gasoline pump or pumps for supplying cars with gasoline.

fil·lip (fil′əp), *v.t.* **1.** to strike with the nail of a finger snapped from the end of the thumb. **2.** to tap or strike smartly. **3.** to drive by or as by a fillip: *Hope for a future success filliped him when he was weary.* —*v.i.* **4.** to make a fillip with the fingers. —*n.* **5.** the act or an instance of filliping; a smart tap or stroke. **6.** anything that tends to rouse, excite, or revive; a stimulus: *Praise is an excellent fillip for waning ambition.* [late ME *philippe* to make a signal or sound with thumb and right forefinger; appar. special use of name *Philip.* See FLIP]

fil·li·peen (fil′ə pēn′), *n.* philopena.

fil·lis·ter (fil′i stər), *n.* *Carpentry.* **1.** a rabbet or groove, as one on a window sash to hold the glass and putty. **2.** Also called **fil′lister plane′.** a plane for cutting rabbets or grooves. Also, **filister.** [?]

fil′lister head′, a cylindrical screw head. See illus. under **screw.**

Fill·more (fil′mōr, -môr), *n.* **1. Mil·lard** (mil′ərd), 1800–74, 13th president of the United States 1850–53. **2.** a town in S California. 4808 (1960).

fil·ly (fil′ē), *n., pl.* **-lies. 1.** a young female horse. **2.** *Informal.* a girl: *a lively young filly in a calico dress.* [late ME *fyly* < Scand; cf. Icel *fylja* female FOAL]

film (film), *n.* **1.** a thin layer or coating: *a film of grease on a plate.* **2.** a thin sheet of any material: *a film of ice.* **3.** *Photog.* **a.** a cellulose nitrate or cellulose acetate composition made in thin sheets or strips and coated with a sensitive emulsion for taking photographs. **b.** a strip or roll of this. **c.** the coating of emulsion on such a sheet or strip or on a photographic plate. **4.** *Motion Pictures.* **a.** the film strip containing the photographs exhibited in a motion-picture machine. **b.** See **motion picture. 5. films, a.** motion pictures collectively. **b.** the motion-picture industry, or its productions, operations, etc. **c.** motion pictures, as a genre of art or entertainment: *experimental films.* **6.** a thin skin or membrane. **7.** a delicate web of filaments or fine threads. **8.** a thin haze, blur, or mist. —*v.t.* **9.** to cover with a film, thin skin, or pellicle: *filmed eyes.* **10.** *Motion Pictures.* **a.** to photograph with a motion-picture camera. **b.** to reproduce in the form of motion pictures: *to film a novel.* —*v.i.* **11.** to become covered by a film: *The water filmed over with ice.* **12.** *Motion Pictures.* **a.** to be reproduced in a motion picture, esp. in a specified manner: *This story films easily.* **b.** to direct, make, or otherwise engage in the production of motion pictures. [ME *filme*, OE *filmen* membrane; akin to FELL⁴] —**film′like′,** *adj.*

film·a·ble (fil′mə bəl), *adj.* noting or pertaining to a story or to literary work readily adaptable to motion-picture form. [FILM + -ABLE]

film′ clip′, *Television.* a strip of motion picture film used in a telecast, esp. as supplementary material in a live program.

film·dom (film′dəm), *n.* the realm of motion pictures; the motion-picture industry or its personnel: *a famous star of filmdom.* [FILM + -DOM]

film′ gate′, a movable part of a motion-picture camera, printer, or projector, for holding the film against the aperture plate. Also called **film window.**

film·go·er (film′gō′ər), *n.* a person who attends motion picture performances: *a movie without appeal for the average filmgoer.* [FILM + GOER]

film·ing (fil′miṅg), *n.* the act or period of photographing, esp. of a motion picture. [FILM + -ING¹]

film·land (film′land′), *n.* filmdom. [FILM + LAND]

film′ li′brary, *Library Science.* an organized collection of photographs, motion pictures, and other films for private or public use, including reproductions of printed materials on film, slides, motion-picture reels, etc.

film′ mak′er, 1. a producer or director of motion pictures, esp. one having direct involvement in all phases of production: *the leading young film makers of France.* **2.** a person who makes film, esp. for use in photography.

film′ pack′, *Photog.* a number of sheets of film arranged one over the other and connected so that they can be exposed successively.

film′ record′er, a photographic device for producing a sound strip on a motion-picture film.

film·strip (film′strip′), *n.* a length of film containing a series of transparencies for projection on a screen. Also called **slidefilm.** [FILM + STRIP²]

film′ win′dow. See **film gate.**

film·y (fil′mē), *adj.,* **film·i·er, film·i·est.** of the nature of, resembling, or covered with a film: *a gown of a filmy material.* [FILM + -Y¹] —**film′i·ly,** *adv.* —**film′i·ness,** *n.*

Fil·o·me·na (fil′ə mē′nə), *n.* a girl's given name.

fil·o·plume (fil′ə plōōm′, fī′lə-), *n.* *Ornith.* a specialized, hairlike feather having a slender shaft with few or no barbs. [< NL *filoplūma*, equiv. to L *fīl(um)* a thread + *-o-* -O- + *pluma* PLUME]

fi·lose (fī′lōs), *adj.* **1.** threadlike. **2.** ending in a threadlike process. [< L *fīl(um)* a thread + -OSE¹]

fi·lo·sus (fi lō′səs), *adj.* *Meteorol.* fibratus. [< NL, equiv. to L *fīl(um)* thread + *-ōsus* -OSE¹]

fils (fils), *n., pl.* **fils. 1.** a bronze coin of Iraq and Jordan, the thousandth part of a dinar, equivalent to about .0028 of a U.S. dollar. **2.** a cupronickel coin of Kuwait, the thousandth part of a dinar or the hundredth part of a dirhem, equivalent to about .0028 of a U.S. dollar. Also, **fil.** [< Ar]

fils (fēs), *n., pl.* **fils.** *French.* son: sometimes used after a name with the meaning of *Jr.*, as in *Dumas fils.* Cf. **père.**

filt., (in prescriptions) filter. [< L *filtra*]

fil·ter (fil′tər), *n.* **1.** any substance, as cloth, paper, porous porcelain, or a layer of charcoal or sand through which liquid is passed to remove suspended impurities or to recover solids. **2.** any device, as a tank, tube, etc., containing such a substance for filtering. **3.** any of various analogous devices, as for removing dust from air or impurities from tobacco smoke, or for eliminating certain kinds of light rays. **4.** *Informal.* a filter-tipped cigarette. **5.** *Photog.* a screen of dyed gelatin or glass for controlling the rendering of color or for diminishing the intensity of light. **6.** *Physics.* a device that selectively damps oscillations of certain frequencies while not affecting oscillations of other frequencies. **7.** *Math.* a collection of subsets of a topological space, having the properties that the intersection of two subsets in the collection is a subset in the collection and that any set containing a subset in the collection is in the collection. —*v.t.* **8.** to remove by the action of a filter. **9.** to act as a filter for. **10.** to pass through or as through a filter: *The thick leaves filtered the sunlight.* —*v.i.* **11.** to pass through or as through a filter: *Enemy agents managed to filter into the embattled country.* —*adj.* **12.** *Informal.* filter-tipped: *a filter cigarette.* [late ME *filtre* < ML *filtr(um)* felt, piece of felt used to strain liquids < Gmc; see FELT²] —**fil′ter·er,** *n.*

fil·ter·a·ble (fil′tər ə bəl), *adj.* **1.** capable of being filtered. **2.** *Bacteriol.* capable of passing through bacteria-retaining filters: *a filterable virus.* Also, **filtrable.** [FILTER + -ABLE] —**fil′ter·a·bil′i·ty, fil′ter·a·ble·ness,** *n.*

fil′ter bed′, a pond or tank having a false bottom covered with sand and serving to filter river or pond waters.

fil′ter fac′tor, *Photog.* a number indicating the increased exposure that a particular film should receive when a photograph is taken through a particular filter: it is based on the spectral composition of the light, the color sensitivity of the film, and the reflection characteristics of the subject.

fil′ter pa′per, porous paper used in filtering.

fil′ter tip′, 1. a mouthpiece for a cigarette or cigar having a means of filtering the smoke. **2.** a cigarette or cigar having such a mouthpiece. —**fil′ter-tipped′,** *adj.*

filth (filth), *n.* **1.** foul matter; offensive or disgusting dirt or refuse: *the filth loosed into our rivers.* **2.** foul condition: *to live in filth.* **3.** moral impurity, corruption, or obscenity. **4.** vulgar or obscene language. [ME; OE *fȳlth.* See FOUL, -TH¹]

filth′ disease′, a disease resulting from insanitation or from the pollution of soil or of water.

filth·y (fil′thē), *adj.,* **filth·i·er, filth·i·est. 1.** foul with, characterized by, or having the nature of filth; disgustingly or completely dirty. **2.** vile; obscene: *filthy language.* **3.** contemptibly offensive, vile, or objectionable: *to treat one's friends in a filthy manner.* **4.** *Slang.* having an abundance of; abundantly supplied; abounding (often fol. by *with*): *They're filthy with money.* [ME; see FILTH, -Y¹] —**filth′i·ly,** *adv.* —**filth′i·ness,** *n.*

—**Syn. 1.** unclean, defiled. See **dirty. 2.** dirty, pornographic.

filth′y lu′cre, 1. *Disparaging.* money: *to lose one's health for the sake of filthy lucre.* **2.** *Obs.* money acquired by shameful means.

fil·tra·ble (fil′trə bəl), *adj.* filterable. —**fil′tra·bil′i·ty,** *n.*

fil·trate (fil′trāt), *v.,* **-trat·ed, -trat·ing,** *n.* —*v.t., v.i.* **1.** to filter. —*n.* **2.** liquid which has been passed through a filter. [< ML *filtrāt(us)* filtered, ptp. of *filtrāre.* See FILTER, -ATE¹] —**fil′trat·a·ble,** *adj.* —**fil·tra′tion,** *n.*

fil·tre (fēl′trə), *adj.* *French.* filtered. Cf. **café filtre.**

fi·lum (fī′ləm), *n., pl.* **-la** (-lə). a threadlike structure, object, or part; filament. [< L: a thread, filament, fiber]

fim·ble (fim′bəl), *n.* the male or staminate plant of hemp, which is harvested before the female or pistillate plant. [late ME *femaille (hempe)* FEMALE (hemp)]

fim·bri·a (fim′brē ə), *n., pl.* **-bri·ae** (-brē ē′). Often, **fimbriae.** *Bot., Zool.* a fringe or fringed border. [< NL, L: border, edge, fringe] —**fim′bri·al,** *adj.*

fim·bri·ate (*adj.* fim′brē it, -āt′; *v.* fim′brē āt′), *adj., v.,* **-at·ed, -at·ing.** —*adj.* **1.** Also, **fim′bri·at′ed.** *Bot., Zool.* having a border of hairs or filiform processes. —*v.t.* 2. *Heraldry.* to line (an ordinary) with a thin border of a different tincture, as to maintain the alternation of metals with colors. [< L *fimbriāt(us)* fringed. See FIMBRIA, -ATE[1]]

fim·bri·a·tion (fim′brē ā′shən), *n.* *Bot., Zool.* 1. fimbriate or fringed condition. 2. a fringe or fringelike part. [< ML *fimbriātiōn-* (s. of *fimbriātiō*). See FIMBRIATE, -ION]

Fimbriate petals

fim·bril·late (fim bril′it, -āt), *adj.* *Bot., Zool.* bordered by or having a small or fine fringe. [< NL *fimbrill(a)* little fringe (see FIMBRIA) + -ATE[1]]

fin (fin), *n., v.,* **finned, fin·ning.** —*n.* 1. a membranous, winglike or paddlelike organ attached to any of various parts of the body of fishes and certain other aquatic animals, used for propulsion, steering, or balancing. 2. *Naut.* **a.** a horizontal, adjustable, winglike appendage to the underwater portion of a hull, as one for controlling the dive of a submarine or for damping the roll of a surface vessel. **b.** See **fin keel.** 3. *Aeron.* any of certain small, subsidiary structures on an aircraft, usually placed parallel to the plane of symmetry. 4. any of a number of standing ridges on an ordinarily hot object, as a radiator, a cylinder of an internal-combustion engine, etc., intended to maximize heat transfer to the surrounding air by exposing a large surface area. 5. any part, as of a mechanism, resembling a fin. 6. *Metall.* a ridge of metal squeezed through the opening between two rolls, dies, or halves of a mold in which a piece is being formed under pressure; flash. 7. *Slang.* the arm or hand. 8. *Slang.* a five-dollar bill: *Slip the head waiter a fin if you want a good table.* 9. Usually, **fins.** flipper (def. 2). —*v.t.* 10. to cut off the fins from (a fish); carve or cut up, as a chub. —*v.i.* 11. to move the fins; lash the water with the fins, as a whale when dying. [ME, OE *finn;* c. D *vin,* LG *finne;* akin to Sw *fena*] —**fin′less,** *adj.* —**fin′like′,** *adj.*

Fin., 1. Finland. 2. Finnish.

fin., financial.

fin·a·ble (fī′nə bəl), *adj.* subject to a fine. Also, **fineable.** [FINE[2] + -ABLE] —**fin′a·ble·ness,** *n.*

fi·na·gle (fi nā′gəl), *v.,* **-gled, -gling.** *Informal.* —*v.i.* 1. to practice deception or fraud. —*v.t.* 2. to trick or cheat (a person) (often fol. by *out of*): *He finagled the backers out of a fortune.* 3. to get or achieve (something) by guile or trickery: *to finagle a seat on the stock exchange.* 4. to wangle: *to finagle free tickets.* Also, **fenagle.** [*finaig-* (var. of FAINAIGUE) + -LE] —**fi·na′gler,** *n.*

fi·nal (fīn′əl), *adj.* 1. pertaining to or coming at the end; last in place, order, or time: *the final session of the year.* 2. ultimate: *The final goal is world peace.* 3. conclusive or decisive: *a final decision.* 4. *Law.* **a.** precluding further controversy on the questions passed upon: *The judicial determination of the Supreme Court is final.* **b.** determining completely the rights of the parties, so that no further decision upon the merits of the issues is necessary: *a final judgment or decree.* 5. constituting the end or purpose: *a final result.* 6. pertaining to or expressing the end or purpose: *a final clause.* 7. *Phonet.* occurring at the end of a word or syllable, as the *t* in *bit* and *bite.* —*n.* 8. that which is last; that which forms an end or termination. 9. Often, **finals. a.** the last and decisive game, match, contest, or round in a series, as in sports. **b.** the last, usually comprehensive, examination in a course of study. 10. the last edition of a newspaper published on any day. 11. *Music.* Also, **finalis.** the tonic note of a church mode. [ME < L *fīnāl(is),* equiv. to *fīn(is)* end + *-ālis* -AL[1]]
—**Syn.** 1. See **last**[1]. —**Ant.** 1. first.

fi′nal cause′, *Aristotelianism.* See under **cause** (def. 8b).

fi·na·le (fi nal′ē, -nä′lē), *n.* 1. *Music.* the last piece, division, or movement of a concert, opera, or composition. 2. the concluding part of any performance, course of proceedings, etc. [< It, n. use of *finale* (adj.) < L *fīnālis* FINAL]

fi·na·lis (fi nä′lis), *n., pl.* **-les** (-lās). final (def. 11).

fi·nal·ism (fīn′əliz′əm), *n.* the doctrine or belief that all events are determined by final causes. [FINAL + -ISM]

fi·nal·ist (fīn′əlist), *n.* a person who is entitled to take part in the final trial or round, as of an athletic contest. [FINAL + -IST]

fi·nal·i·ty (fī nal′i tē), *n., pl.* **-ties** for 2. 1. state, quality, or fact of being final; conclusiveness or decisiveness. 2. something that is final; a final act, utterance, etc. [FINAL + -ITY]

fi·na·lize (fīn′əlīz′), *v.,* **-lized, -liz·ing.** —*v.t.* 1. to put into final form; complete all the administrative details of. —*v.i.* 2. to complete an agreement; conclude negotiations: *We should finalize by the end of the week.* [FINAL + -IZE] —**fi′na·li·za′tion,** *n.*
—**Usage.** Although FINALIZE is regarded by many as a recent, bureaucratic coinage, the word has been current in both American and British English for at least 40 years, and it appears in all kinds of writing, usually in formal contexts.

fi·nal·ly (fīn′əlē), *adv.* 1. at the final point or moment; in the end. 2. in a final manner; conclusively or decisively. [ME; see FINAL, -LY]

fi·nance (fi nans′, fī′nans), *n., v.,* **-nanced, -nanc·ing.** —*n.* 1. the management of public revenues; the conduct or transaction of money matters generally, esp. those affecting the public, as in the fields of banking and investment. 2. **finances,** the pecuniary resources, as of a government, company, organization, or individual; revenue. —*v.t.* 3. to supply with means of payment; provide capital for; obtain or furnish credit for. 4. to manage financially. —*v.i.* 5. to conduct financial operations; manage finances. [late ME *finaunce* < MF *finance,* equiv. to *fin(er)* (to) end, settle, pay (see FINE[2]) + *-ance* -ANCE]

finance′ bill′, *Govt.* a bill or act of a legislature to obtain funds for the public treasury.

finance′ com′pany, an institution engaged in such specialized forms of financing as purchasing accounts receivable, extending credit to retailers and manufacturers, discounting installment contracts, and granting loans with goods as security.

fi·nan·cial (fi nan′shəl, fī-), *adj.* 1. pertaining to monetary receipts and expenditures; pertaining or relating to money matters; pecuniary: *financial operations.* 2. of or pertaining to those commonly engaged in dealing with money and credit. [FINANCE + -IAL] —**fi·nan′cial·ly,** *adv.*
—**Syn.** 1. FINANCIAL, FISCAL, MONETARY, PECUNIARY refer to matters concerned with money. FINANCIAL usually refers to money matters or transactions of some size or importance: *a financial wizard.* FISCAL is used esp. in connection with government funds, or those of any organization: *the end of the fiscal year.* MONETARY relates especially to money as such: *a monetary system or standard.* PECUNIARY refers to money as used in making ordinary payments: *a pecuniary obligation or reward.*

fin·an·cier (fin′ən sēr′, fī′nən-; *Brit.* fi nan′sē ər), *n.* 1. a person who is skilled or who is engaged in financial operations, whether public, corporate, or individual. —*v.t.* 2. to finance. —*v.i.* 3. to act as a financier. [< F; see FINANCE, -IER]

Financier, The, a novel (1912) by Theodore Dreiser.

fi·nan·cière (*Fr.* fē nän syer′), *adj.* 1. (of a stew, sauce, etc.) prepared or garnished with quenelles, forcemeat, sweetbreads, truffles, olives, diced cockscombs, and mushrooms: *vol-au-vent financière.* —*n.* 2. Also, **sauce financière.** a sauce made with Madeira wine and an essence of truffles. [< F, short for adv. phrase *à la financière* in the manner of a financier. Cf. À LA MODE]

Finback, *Balaenoptera physalus* (Length 60 to 70 ft.)

fin·back (fin′bak′), *n.* any whalebone whale of the genus *Balaenoptera,* having a prominent dorsal fin, esp. *B. physalus,* of Atlantic and Pacific coasts; rorqual. Also, **fin′back whale′.** [FIN + BACK[1]]

fin·ca (fiŋ′kə; *Sp.* fēŋ′kä), *n., pl.* **-cas** (-kəz; *Sp.* -käs). an agricultural property in a Spanish-speaking country, esp. a plantation in tropical Spanish America. [< Sp: farm, deriv. of *fincar* to remain < VL **figicāre;* cf. L *fīgere* to fasten]

finch (finch), *n.* 1. any of numerous small passerine birds of the family *Fringillidae,* including the buntings, sparrows, crossbills, linnets, grosbeaks, etc., most of which have a short, conical bill adapted for eating seeds. 2. any of various nonfringilline birds, esp. the weaverbirds of the family *Ploceidae.* [ME; OE *finc;* c. D *vink,* G *Fink;* akin to Gk *spíngos* finch]

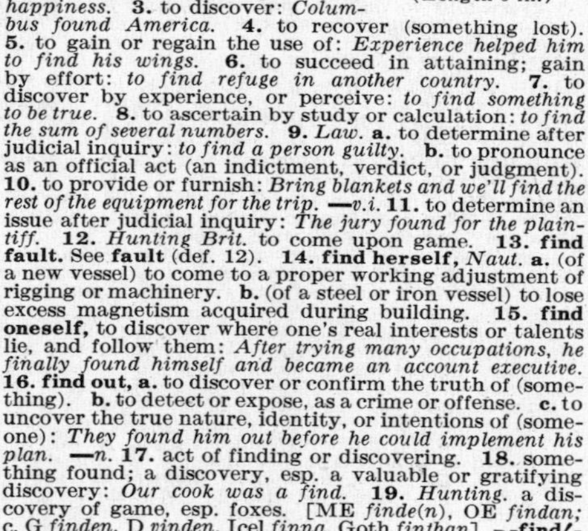

Purple finch, *Carpodacus purpureus* (Length 6 in.)

find (fīnd), *v.,* **found, find·ing,** *n.* —*v.t.* 1. to come upon by chance; meet with: *He found a nickel in the street.* 2. to learn, attain, or obtain by search or effort: *After years of misery, he managed to find happiness.* 3. to discover: *Columbus found America.* 4. to recover (something lost). 5. to gain or regain the use of: *Experience helped him to find his wings.* 6. to succeed in attaining; gain by effort: *to find refuge in another country.* 7. to discover by experience, or perceive: *to find something to be true.* 8. to ascertain by study or calculation: *to find the sum of several numbers.* 9. *Law.* **a.** to determine after judicial inquiry: *to find a person guilty.* **b.** to pronounce as an official act (an indictment, verdict, or judgment). 10. to provide or furnish: *Bring blankets and we'll find the rest of the equipment for the trip.* —*v.i.* 11. to determine an issue after judicial inquiry: *The jury found for the plaintiff.* 12. *Hunting Brit.* to come upon game. 13. **find fault.** See **fault** (def. 12). 14. **find herself,** *Naut.* **a.** (of a new vessel) to come to a proper working adjustment of rigging or machinery. **b.** (of a steel or iron vessel) to lose excess magnetism acquired during building. 15. **find oneself,** to discover where one's real interests or talents lie, and follow them: *After trying many occupations, he finally found himself and became an account executive.* 16. **find out, a.** to discover or confirm the truth of (something). **b.** to detect or expose, as a crime or offense. **c.** to uncover the true nature, identity, or intentions of (someone): *They found him out before he could implement his plan.* —*n.* 17. act of finding or discovering. 18. something found; a discovery, esp. a valuable or gratifying discovery: *Our cook was a find.* 19. *Hunting.* a discovery of game, esp. foxes. [ME *finde(n),* OE *findan;* c. G *finden,* D *vinden,* Icel *finna,* Goth *finthan*] —**find′a·ble,** *adj.*

find·er (fīn′dər), *n.* 1. one who or that which finds. 2. Also called **viewfinder.** *Photog.* a camera part or attachment enabling a photographer to determine what will be included in the picture. 3. *Astron.* a small, wide-angled telescope attached to a larger one for locating the object to be studied by the large telescope. [ME *findere.* See FIND, -ER[1]]

fin de siè·cle (faN də sye′klə), *French.* 1. end of the century. 2. a period relatively free from social and moral traditions or conventions. 3. (toward the close of the 19th century) **a.** modern; up-to-date. **b.** decadent.

find·ing (fīn′diŋ), *n.* 1. act of one who or that which finds; discovery. 2. that which is found or ascertained. 3. *Law.* a decision or verdict after judicial inquiry. 4. **findings,** tools, materials, etc., used by artisans. [ME, OE; see FIND, -ING[1]]

Find·lay (fin′lē, find′-), *n.* a city in NW Ohio. 30,344 (1960).

fine[1] (fīn), *adj.,* **fin·er, fin·est,** *adv., v.,* **fined, fin·ing,** *n.* —*adj.* 1. of superior or best quality; of high or highest grade: *fine wine.* 2. free from imperfections or impurities. 3. choice, excellent, or admirable: *a fine painting.* 4. consisting of minute particles: *fine sand; a fine purée.* 5. very thin or slender: *fine thread.* 6. keen or sharp, as a tool: *Is the knife fine enough to carve well?* 7. delicate in texture: *fine cotton lawn.* 8. delicately fashioned: *fine tracery.* 9. highly skilled or accomplished: *a fine musician.* 10. trained down to the proper degree, as an athlete. 11. characterized by or affecting refinement or elegance: *a fine lady.* 12. polished or refined: *fine manners.* 13. affectedly ornate or elegant: *a style that is much too fine for the average reader.* 14. delicate or subtle: *a fine distinction.* 15. showy or smart; smartly dressed. 16. good-looking or handsome: *a fine young man.* 17. (of an alloy of precious metal) containing a large or specified amount of pure metal: *Sterling silver is 92.5 percent fine.* —*adv.* 18. *Informal.* in an excellent manner; very well: *He did fine. She cooks fine.* 19. finely: *She writes so fine I can hardly read it.* 20. *Billiards, Pool.* in such a way that the driven ball barely touches the object ball in passing. 21. *Naut.* as close as possible to the wind: *sailing fine.* 22. **cut fine,** to calculate precisely, esp. without allowing for possible error or accident: *You may be able to park in that space, but it will be cutting it fine.* —*v.i.* 23. to become fine or finer. 24. to become less, as in size or proportions; reduce; diminish (often fol. by *down*): *to fine down before getting into last winter's clothes.* —*v.t.* 25. to make fine or finer, esp. by refining or pulverizing. 26. to reduce the size or proportions of (often used with *down* or *away*): *to fine down the ornamentation on a building; to fine away superfluous matter in a design.* 27. to clarify (wines or spirits) by filtration. —*n.* 28. **fines,** crushed ore sufficiently fine to pass through a given screen. Cf. **short** (def. 27). [ME *fin* < OF *fin* < L *fīn(is)* end, utmost limit, highest point]
—**Syn.** 1. superior; finished, consummate, perfect; select. FINE, CHOICE, ELEGANT, EXQUISITE are terms of praise with reference to quality. FINE is a general term: *a fine horse, person, book.* CHOICE implies a discriminating selection of the object in question: *a choice piece of steak.* ELEGANT suggests a refined and graceful superiority as is generally associated with luxury and a cultivated taste: *elegant furnishings.* EXQUISITE suggests an admirable delicacy, finish, or perfection: *an exquisite piece of lace.* 4. powdered, pulverized. 6. acute. —**Ant.** 1. inferior.

fine[2] (fīn), *n., v.,* **fined, fin·ing.** —*n.* 1. a sum of money exacted as a penalty for an offense or dereliction; mulct: *a parking fine.* 2. *Law.* a fee paid by a feudal tenant to the landlord, as on the renewal of tenure. 3. *Eng. Law* a conveyance of land through decree of a court, based upon a simulated lawsuit. 4. *Archaic.* a penalty of any kind. 5. **in fine, a.** in short; briefly. **b.** in conclusion; finally: *It was, in fine, a fitting end to the story.* —*v.t.* 6. to subject to a fine or pecuniary penalty; punish by a fine: *The judge fined him and released him on parole.* [ME *fin* < OF < L *fīn(is)* end, ML: settlement, payment]

fi·ne[3] (fē′nā), *n.* *Music.* 1. the end of a repeated section, whether *da capo* or *dal segno.* 2. the end of a composition that is comprised of several movements. [< It < L *fīnis* end]

fine[4] (fēn), *n.* commonplace brandy of France, usually of an unidentified origin. [short for *fine de la maison* bar brandy. Cf. FINE CHAMPAGNE]

fine·a·ble (fī′nə bəl), *adj.* finable. —**fine′a·ble·ness,** *n.*

fine′ art′, visual art as primarily subject to aesthetic criteria or judgments of beauty and meaningfulness, specifically, painting, sculpture, drawing, watercolor, graphics, and architecture. Cf. **commercial art.**

Fine Cham·pagne (*Fr.* fēn shäN paN′yə), a high-quality cognac distilled from grapes grown in the Grande Champagne or Petite Champagne vineyards of France. [< F]

fine-cut (fīn′kut′), *adj.* cut into very thin strips (contrasted with *rough-cut*): *fine-cut tobacco.*

fine-draw (fīn′drô′), *v.t.,* **-drew, -drawn, -draw·ing.** 1. *Sewing.* to sew together so finely that the joining is not noticeable. 2. to draw out to extreme fineness, tenuity, or subtlety. —**fine′-draw′er,** *n.*

fine-drawn (fīn′drôn′), *adj.* drawn out to extreme fineness or thinness: *a fine-drawn wire; fine-drawn distinctions; an interesting face with fine-drawn features.*

Fi·neen (fə nēn′), *n.* a girl's given name.

fine-grain (fīn′grān′), *adj.* *Photog.* 1. (of an image) having an inconspicuous or invisible grain. 2. (of a developer or emulsion) permitting the grain of an image to be inconspicuous or invisible.

fine-grained (fīn′grānd′), *adj.* 1. being of fine grain or texture, as certain types of wood, leather, etc. 2. *Photog.* fine-grain.

Fi·nel·la (fə nel′ə), *n.* a girl's given name. Also, **Fenella.**

fine·ly (fīn′lē), *adv.* 1. in a fine manner; excellently; elegantly; delicately; minutely; nicely; subtly. 2. in fine particles or pieces: *finely chopped onions.* [ME *fineliche.* See FINE[1], -LY]

fine′ nail′, a short steel finishing nail from 1 to 1½ inches long. Cf. **threepenny** (def. 3b).

fine·ness (fīn′nis), *n.* 1. state or quality of being fine. 2. the proportion of pure precious metal in an alloy, often expressed in parts per thousand. [late ME; see FINE[1], -NESS]

fine′ness ra′tio, 1. *Aeron.* the ratio of the length of a streamlined body, as a rocket or airplane hull, to its maximum diameter. 2. See **aspect ratio** (def. 4a).

fine′ print′, the detailed wording of a contract, lease, insurance policy, or the like, often in type smaller than the main body of the document and including restrictions or qualifications that could be considered disadvantageous or undesirable: *Make sure you read the fine print before signing.* Also called **small print.**

fin·er (fī′nər), *adj.* *Math.* of or pertaining to a topology or a topological space whose open sets include all the open sets of a second specified topology on the space. Cf. **coarser.** [special use of comp. of FINE[1]]

fin·er·y[1] (fī′nə rē), *n.* 1. fine or showy dress, ornaments, etc. 2. *Obs.* smartness or elegance. [FINE[1] + -ERY]

fin·er·y[2] (fī′nə rē), *n., pl.* **-er·ies.** *Metalworking.* a hearth for converting cast iron into wrought iron; refinery. [< MF *finerie.* See FINE[1], -ERY]

fines herbes (fēn′ erbz′, ûrbz′; *Fr.* fēn zerb′), *Cookery.* a combination of finely chopped herbs for flavoring soups, sauces, omelets, etc. [< F: fine herbs]

fine·spun (fīn′spun′), *adj.* 1. spun or drawn out to a fine thread. 2. highly or excessively refined or subtle. Also, **fine′-spun′.** [FINE[1] + SPUN]

fi·nesse (fi nes′), *n., v.,* **-nessed, -ness·ing.** —*n.* 1. extreme delicacy or subtlety in action, performance, skill, discrimination, etc. 2. skill in handling a difficult or highly sensitive situation; adroit and artful management. 3. a trick, artifice, or stratagem. 4. *Bridge, Whist.* an attempt to win a trick with a card while holding a higher card not in sequence with it, in the hope that the card or cards between will not be played. —*v.i.* 5. to use finesse or artifice. **6.** to make a finesse at cards. —*v.t.* **7.** to bring about by finesse or artifice. **8.** to make a finesse with (a card). **9.** to force the playing of (a card) by a finesse. [late ME: degree of excellence or purity < MF < LL **fīnitia*. See FINE[1], -ICE]

fi·nes·tra (fi nes′trə), *n.* an aperture, esp. a ventilator in the wall of a tomb. [< It: window]

fine′ struc′ture, *Physics.* a group of lines that are observed in the spectra of certain elements, as hydrogen, and that are caused by various couplings of the azimuthal quantum number and the angular momentum quantum number. Cf. **hyperfine structure.**

fine′-tooth comb′ (fīn′to͞oth′), **1.** a comb having narrow, closely set teeth. **2. go over** or **through with a fine-tooth comb,** to examine in close detail; search thoroughly: *The police went over the apartment with a fine-tooth comb.* Also, **fine′-toothed comb′** (fīn′to͞otht′, -to͞othd′).

fin·foot (fin′fo͝ot′), *n., pl.* **-foots.** any of several aquatic birds of the family *Heliornithidae,* of South America, Asia, and Africa, related to the rails and coots and characterized by lobate toes. Also called **sun grebe.** [FIN + FOOT]

fin-foot·ed (fin′fo͝ot′id), *adj. Ornith.* **1.** web-footed. **2.** having feet whose toes are separately furnished with flaps, as the finfoots and coots.

Fin′gal's Cave′ (fiŋ′gəlz), **1.** a cave on the island of Staffa, in the Hebrides, Scotland. 227 ft. long; 42 ft. wide. **2.** (*italics.*) an overture, op. 26, composed in 1832 by Felix Mendelssohn.

fin·ger (fiŋ′gər), *n.* **1.** any of the terminal members of the hand, esp. one other than the thumb. **2.** a part of a glove made to receive a finger. **3.** the breadth of a finger as a unit of measurement; digit. **4.** the length of a finger: approximately 4½ inches. **5.** *Slang.* an informer; spy. **6.** something like a finger in form, use, or purpose: *the finger on the speedometer.* **7.** any of various projecting parts of machines. **8. burn one's fingers,** to suffer injury or loss by meddling or by acting rashly: *If you get involved in the controversy, you may burn your fingers.* **9. have a finger in the pie, a.** to have an interest or share in. **b.** to meddle in. **10. keep one's fingers crossed,** to wish for good luck or success, as in a specific endeavor: *Keep your fingers crossed that I get the job.* **11. lay** or **put one's finger on, a.** to indicate exactly; remember: *I know the name, but I can't put my finger on it.* **b.** to discover; locate: *I haven't been able to lay my finger on the book you requested.* **12. not lift a finger,** to make no attempt; do nothing: *The house was falling into ruin, but he wouldn't lift a finger to repair it.* **13. put the finger on,** *Slang.* **a.** to inform against or identify (a criminal) to the authorities. **b.** to designate a victim, as of murder or other crime. **14. slip through one's fingers,** to elude one, as an opportunity not taken; escape: *She let the chance of a lifetime slip through her fingers.* **15. snap one's fingers (at),** to exhibit disdain or contempt (for): *She snaps her fingers at the local gossip.* **16. twist around one's little finger,** to exert one's influence easily or successfully upon: *He has a remarkable talent for twisting people around his little finger.* —*v.t.* **17.** to touch with the fingers; handle; toy or meddle with. **18.** to touch with the fingers so as to mar or spoil: *Please don't finger the vegetables.* **19.** to pilfer; filch. **20.** *Music.* **a.** to play on (an instrument) with the fingers. **b.** to perform or mark (a passage of music) with a certain fingering. **21.** *Informal.* to point out or identify, esp. to the police. —*v.i.* **22.** to touch or handle something with the fingers. **23.** *Music.* **a.** to have its keys arranged for playing with the fingers, as a piano, clarinet, etc. **b.** to use the fingers in playing. [ME, OE; c. G *Finger,* D *vinger,* Icel *fingr,* Goth *figgrs*] —**fin′ger·er,** *n.* —**fin′ger·less,** *adj.*

fin′ger board′, **1.** (of a violin, cello, etc.) the strip of wood on the neck against which the strings are stopped by the fingers. **2.** keyboard.

fin′ger bowl′, a small bowl to hold water for rinsing the fingers at table.

fin·ger·breadth (fiŋ′gər bredth′, -bretth′), *n.* the breadth of a finger: approximately ¾ inch. [FINGER + BREADTH]

fin·gered (fiŋ′gərd), *adj.* **1.** having fingers of a specified kind or number (usually used in combination): *a light-fingered pickpocket.* **2.** spoiled or marred by handling, as merchandise. **3.** *Zool., Bot.* digitate. **4.** (of a musical score) marked to show which fingers should be used in playing the notes. [FINGER + -ED[3]]

fin·ger·flow·er (fiŋ′gər flou′ər), *n.* See **purple foxglove.** [FINGER + FLOWER]

fin′ger gate′, *Foundry.* any of a number of small runners radiating from a single gate to distribute metal in several parts of the mold cavity.

fin′ger hole′, **1.** one of a set of holes for the finger on the rotating dial of a telephone. **2.** one of two holes or more on a bowling ball for holding the ball. **3.** one of a series of holes on a wind instrument for changing pitch by being opened or closed.

fin·ger·ing (fiŋ′gər iŋ), *n.* **1.** act of one who fingers. **2.** *Music.* **a.** the action or method of using the fingers in playing on an instrument. **b.** the indication of the way the fingers are to be used in performing a piece of music. [late ME; see FINGER, -ING[1]]

Fin′ger Lakes′, a group of elongated glacial lakes in central and W New York: resort region.

fin·ger·ling (fiŋ′gər liŋ), *n.* **1.** a young or small fish, esp. a very small salmon or trout. **2.** something very small. [late ME: finger stall. See FINGER, -LING[1]]

fin′ger man′, *Slang.* a person who points out someone to be murdered, robbed, etc.

fin′ger mark′, a mark, esp. a smudge or stain, made by a finger. Also, **fin′ger-mark′.**

fin·ger-marked (fiŋ′gər märkt′), *adj.* smudged or marked from handling.

fin·ger·nail (fiŋ′gər nāl′), *n.* **1.** the nail at the end of a finger. **2.** *Print. Slang.* a parenthesis. [ME; see FINGER, NAIL]

fin′ger paint′, a jellylike paint, used chiefly by children in painting, usually with their fingers.

fin·ger-paint (fiŋ′gər pānt′), *v.t., v.i.* to paint by using finger paints on damp or wet paper.

fin′ger paint′ing, **1.** the use of finger paints to produce a painting. **2.** a painting produced with finger paints.

fin′ger post′, a post with one or more directional signs, each usually terminating in a pointed finger or hand.

fin·ger·print (fiŋ′gər print′), *n.* **1.** an impression of the markings of the inner surface of the last joint of the thumb or other finger. **2.** such an impression made with ink for purposes of identification. —*v.t.* **3.** to take the fingerprints of. [FINGER + PRINT]

fin′ger read′ing, the reading of Braille by means of the fingers.

fin·ger·stall (fiŋ′gər stôl′), *n.* a covering used to protect a finger. [late ME *fyngyr stalle.* See FINGER, STALL[1]]

fin·ger·tip (fiŋ′gər tip′), *n.* **1.** the tip of a finger. **2.** a covering used to protect the end joint of a finger. —*adj.* **3.** extending to the fingertips, as a coat, veil, etc.: *a fingertip jacket.* **4. at one's fingertips, a.** close at hand; easily available. **b.** at one's command or disposal, as recall of factual information: *He has the answer at his fingertips.* **5. to one's fingertips,** thoroughly; perfectly: *She was a lady to her fingertips.* [FINGER + TIP[1]]

fin′ger wave′, *Hairdressing.* a wave set by impressing the fingers into hair dampened by lotion or water, rather than by using a heated curling iron or the like.

fin·ger·y (fiŋ′gə rē), *adj.* placed or arranged in such a way as to suggest fingers. [FINGER + -Y[1]]

fin·i·al (fin′ē əl, fī′nē-), *n.* **1.** *Archit.* a relatively small, ornamental, terminal feature at the top of a gable, pinnacle, etc. **2.** an ornamental termination to the top of a piece of furniture, or the like, or of one part of such a piece. **3.** *Typography.* a curve terminating the main stroke of the characters in some italic fonts. [late ME, deriv. of L *fīnis* end; see -AL[1]] —**fin′i·aled,** *adj.*

fin·i·cal (fin′i kəl), *adj.* **1.** finicky. **2.** *Archaic.* (of things) overelaborate; containing too much unimportant detail. [FINE[1] + -ICAL] —**fin′i·cal·ness, fin′i·cal′i·ty,** *n.* —**fin′i·cal·ly,** *adv.*

fin·ick (fin′ik), *v.i.* **1.** to affect extreme daintiness or refinement. **2.** to trifle or dawdle. Also, **finnick.** [back formation from FINICAL]

fin·ick·y (fin′ə kē), *adj.* excessively particular or fastidious; difficult to please; fussy. Also, **finnicky, fin·i·king** (fin′ə kiŋ), **fin·ick·in** (fin′ə kin). [FINICK + -Y[1]]

fin·ing (fī′niŋ), *n.* **1.** the process by which fused glass is freed of undissolved gases. **2.** the process of clarifying or filtering a wine or spirit. [FINE[1] + -ING[1]]

fin·is (fin′is, fē nē′, fī′nis), *n.* end; conclusion. [< L]

fi·nis co·ro·nat o·pus (fē′nis kō rō′nät ō′po͝os; *Eng.* fin′is kō rō′nat ō′pəs, kô-), *Latin.* the end crowns the work.

fin·ish (fin′ish), *v.t.* **1.** to bring (something) to an end or to completion; complete: *to finish reading a novel.* **2.** to come to the end of (a course, period of time, etc.): *to finish school.* **3.** to use completely (often fol. by *up* or *off*): *to finish up a can of paint; to finish off the rest of the milk.* **4.** to overcome completely; destroy or kill (often fol. by *off*): *This spray will finish off the cockroaches.* **5.** to complete and perfect in detail; put the final touches on (sometimes fol. by *up*): *He decided to finish his plan more carefully. She finished up a painting.* **6.** to put a finish on (wood, metal, etc.): *We finished the desk in antique red lacquer.* **7.** to perfect (a person) in education, accomplishments, social graces, etc. —*v.i.* **8.** to come to an end: *The course finishes in January.* **9.** to complete a course, project, etc. (sometimes fol. by *up*): *I finished before he did. It was nine o'clock when we finished up.* **10.** *Obs.* to die. —*n.* **11.** the end or conclusion; the last stage. **12.** the end of a hunt, race, etc.: *a close finish.* **13.** a decisive ending: *a fight to the finish.* **14.** the quality of being finished or completed with smoothness, elegance, etc.: *to admire the finish of one's writing.* **15.** educational or social polish: *They hoped that two years of college would give her some finish.* **16.** the manner in which an object is perfected or finished in its preparation, or an effect imparted in finishing. **17.** the surface coating or texture of wood, metal, etc.: *He put a satinlike finish on the table.* **18.** something used or serving to finish, complete, or perfect a thing. **19.** woodwork or the like, esp. in the interior of a building, not essential to the structure but used for purposes of ornament, neatness, etc.: *a finish of black walnut.* **20.** a final coat of plaster or paint. **21.** a material for application in finishing. [ME *finisshe(n)* < MF *finiss-,* long s. of *finir* < L *fīnīre* to end. See FINE[1]] —**fin′ish·er,** *n.*
—**Syn. 1.** terminate, conclude, close. **3.** consume. **5.** consummate, polish. **11.** termination. See **end**[1]. **14.** polish, refinement. —**Ant. 1.** begin.

fin·ished (fin′isht), *adj.* **1.** ended or completed. **2.** completed or perfected in all details, as a product: *to pack and ship finished items.* **3.** polished to the highest degree of excellence: *a dazzling and finished piece of writing.* **4.** highly accomplished: *a finished violinist.* **5.** condemned, doomed, or in the process of extinction: *The finished aristocracy managed to survive the revolution.* [FINISH + -ED[2]]
—**Syn. 1, 2.** consummated. **3.** refined, elegant. **4.** talented, skilled, gifted; proficient, qualified, practiced, experienced, trained.

fin′isher card′, (in manufacturing fibers) the last card in the carding process, for converting stock into roving. Cf. **breaker card, intermediate card.**

fin′ishing nail′, a nail having a small globular head, much slenderer than a common nail of the same length: used for finish work, being driven to slightly beneath the surface and covered with putty or the like. See illus. under **nail.** Cf. **casing nail.**

fin′ishing school′, a private school, usually at the high-school or junior-college level, at which young women are given special preparation for their lives in polite society.

Fin·is·tère (fin′i stâr′; *Fr.* fē nē sterʀ′), *n.* a department in W France. 749,558 (1962); 2714 sq. mi. *Cap.:* Quimper.

Fin·is·terre (fin′i stâr′; *Sp.* fē′nes teʀ′ʀe), *n.* **Cape,** a headland in NW Spain: the westernmost point of Spain.

fi·nite (fī′nīt), *adj.* **1.** having bounds or limits; not too great or too small to be measurable. **2.** *Math.* **a.** (of a set of elements) capable of being completely counted. **b.** not infinite or infinitesimal. **c.** not zero. **3.** subject to limitations or conditions, as of space, time, circumstances, or the laws of nature: *man's finite existence on earth.* —*n.* **4.** that which is finite. [< L *fīnīt(us)* limited, ptp. of *fīnīre.* See FINE[1], -ITE[2]] —**fi′nite·ly,** *adv.* —**fi′nite·ness,** *n.*

fi·nite-di·men·sion·al (fī′nīt di men′shə nəl), *adj. Math.* (of a vector space) having a basis consisting of a finite number of elements.

fi′nite in′tersection prop′erty, *Math.* the property of a collection of nonempty sets in which the intersections of all possible finite numbers of the sets each contain at least one element.

fi′nitely ad′ditive func′tion, *Math.* a set function that upon operating on the union of a finite number of disjoint sets gives the same result as the sum of the functional values of each set. Cf. **countably additive function.**

fi′nite verb′, a verb form which distinguishes person, number, and tense, and also mood or aspect, as *opens* in *She opens the door.*

fin·i·tude (fin′i to͞od′, -tyo͞od′, fī′ni-), *n.* state or quality of being finite. [FINI(TE) + -TUDE]

fink (fiŋk), *Slang.* —*n.* **1.** a strikebreaker. **2.** a labor spy. **3.** an informer; stool pigeon. **4.** a contemptible or thoroughly unattractive person. —*v.i.* **5.** to inform to the police; squeal. **6.** to act as a strikebreaker; scab. **7. fink out, a.** to withdraw from or refuse to support a project, activity, scheme, etc.: *He said he'd lend me his motorcycle, but he finked out.* **b.** to become untrustworthy. [< G slang (? < Yiddish): orig., student who does not belong to a club; lit., a FINCH]

fin′ keel′, *Naut.* a finlike projection extending downward from the keel of a sailboat, serving to prevent lateral motion and acting as additional ballast.

Fink′ truss′ (fiŋk), **1.** a truss, now used esp. in the structures of sloping roofs, having the form of an inverted king-post truss supporting other and smaller similar trusses. **2.** a structure, as of a sloping roof, formed from two or more such trusses. See illus. under **truss.** Also called **French truss.**

Fin·land (fin′lənd), *n.* **1.** Finnish, **Suomi.** a republic in N Europe: formerly a province of the Russian Empire. 4,600,000 (1963); 130,119 sq. mi. *Cap.:* Helsinki. **2. Gulf of,** an arm of the Baltic, S of Finland.

Fin·land·er (fin′lən dər), *n.* an inhabitant of Finland, esp. a native Finn who normally speaks Swedish. [FINLAND + -ER[1]]

Fin·land·i·a (fin lan′dē ə), *n.* symphonic poem, op. 26, composed in 1899 by Jean Sibelius.

Fin·lay (fin′lā), *n.* **Car·los Juan** (kär′lōs wän), 1833–1915, U.S. physician, born in Cuba.

fin·let (fin′lit), *n.* a small, detached ray of a fin in certain fishes, as mackerels. [FIN + -LET]

Fin·let·ter (fin′let′ər), *n.* **Thomas Knight,** born 1893, U.S. lawyer and diplomat.

Fin·ley (fin′lē), *n.* a boy's given name.

fin·mark (fin′märk′), *n.* the markka of Finland. Also, **finnmark.** [< Sw; see FINN, MARK[2]]

Finn (fin), *n.* **1.** an inhabitant or native of Finland. **2.** any native speaker of Finnish, as in America or Russia. **3.** a native speaker of any Finnic language. [OE *Finnas* (pl.)]

Finn (fin), *n.* **1.** Also, **Fionn.** *Irish Legend.* a king of the Tuatha De Danann and the father of Ossian: the subject of many legends. **2.** a boy's given name.

Finn., Finnish. Also, **Finn**

fin·nan had·die (fin′ən had′ē), smoked haddock. Also, **fin′nan had′dock.** [lit., haddock of *Findhorn,* fishing port in Scotland]

finned (find), *adj.* having a fin or fins. [ME *finnede.* See FIN, -ED[3]]

Fin′ne·gans Wake′ (fin′ə ginz), a novel (1922–39) by James Joyce.

Fin·ney (fin′ē), *n.* **Charles Gran·di·son** (gran′di sən), 1792–1875, U.S. clergyman and educator.

Finn·ic (fin′ik), *adj.* **1.** of or belonging to a branch of the Uralic language family that includes esp. Finnish, Estonian, and Lapp. —*n.* **2.** the Finnic branch of Uralic. Also, **Finnish.** [FINN + -IC]

fin·nick (fin′ik), *v.i.* finick.

fin·nick·y (fin′i kē), *adj.* finicky.

Finn·ish (fin′ish), *n.* **1.** the principal language of Finland, a Uralic language related closely to Estonian and remotely to Hungarian. **2.** Finnic. —*adj.* **3.** of or pertaining to Finland or its inhabitants. **4.** Finnic. [FINN + -ISH[1]]

finn·mark (fin′märk′), *n.* finmark.

Finno-, a combining form repr. **Finnish:** *Finno-Ugric.* [FINN + -O-]

Fin′no-Rus′so War′ (fin′ō rus′ō), the war (1939–40) between Finland and the Soviet Union.

Fin·no-U·gri·an (fin′ō o͞o′grē ən, -yo͞o′-), *adj.* **1.** pertaining to the Finns and the Ugrians. **2.** Finno-Ugric. —*n.* **3.** Finno-Ugric.

Fin·no-U·gric (fin′ō o͞o′grik, -yo͞o′-), *n.* **1.** a subfamily of Uralic languages of eastern Europe and western Siberia, including esp. Finnish, Estonian, Lapp, Hungarian, and several languages spoken in the Ural mountains. —*adj.* **2.** of or pertaining to these languages. Also, **Finno-Ugrian.**

fin·ny (fin′ē), *adj.,* **-ni·er, -ni·est.** **1.** pertaining to or abounding in fish. **2.** having fins; finned. **3.** finlike. [FIN + -Y[1]]

fi·no (fē′nō; *Sp.* fē′nô), *n.* a pale, very dry sherry of Spain. [< Sp: lit., FINE[1]]

fi·no·chi·o (fi nō′kē ō′), *n., pl.* **-chi·os.** See **Florence fennel.**

Fin·sen (fin′sən), *n.* **Niels Ry·berg** (nēls ʀʏ′beʀ), 1860–1904, Danish physician: Nobel prize 1903.

fin·spot (fin′spot′), *n.* any clinid fish of the genus *Paraclinus,* having an eyelike spot on the dorsal fin, as *P. integripinnis,* of California. [FIN + SPOT]

Fin·ster·aar·horn (fin′stər är′hôrn), *n.* a mountain in S central Switzerland: highest peak of the Bernese Alps, 14,026 ft.

fin′ whale′, finback.

Fi·o·na (fē ō′nə), *n.* a girl's given name.

Fionn (fin), *n.* *Irish Legend.* Finn (def. 1). Also called **Fionn′ Mac·Cumal′** (mə ko͞ol′).

fiord (fyōrd, fyôrd; *Norw.* fyōʀ, fyo͞oʀ), *n.* fjord.

Fi·o·rel·lo (fē′ə rel′ō; *It.* fyô rel′lô), *n.* a boy's given name.

fi·o·rin (fī′ər in, fē′-), *n.* redtop. [alter. of Ir *fiorthān*]

fio·ri·tu·ra (fē ôr′i to͝or′ə, -ōr′-; *It.* fyô′rē to͞o′rä), *n., pl.* **-tu·re** (-to͝or′ā; *It.* -to͞o′re). *Music.* the ornamentation of a melody, often extemporized by the performer, as in Italian opera during the 18th century. [< It, equiv. to *fiori(re)* (to) FLOWER + *-ura* -URE]

fip′pen·ny bit′ (fip′ə nē, fip′nē), *U.S.* the Spanish half real, the value of which was about six cents. Also called **fip′penny piece′.** [assimilated var. of *fivepenny bit*]

fip·ple (fip′əl), *n.* *Music.* a plug stopping the upper end of a pipe, as a recorder or a whistle, and having a narrow slit through which the player blows. [? special use of dial. *fipple* loose lower lip, pouting lip; cf. Icel *flipi* lower lip of a horse, Norw *flipe* flap, lappet. See FLIP[1], FLAP, FLABBY]

fip′ple flute′, *Music.* a recorder or other flutelike instrument equipped with a fipple. Cf. **recorder** (def. 5).

fiqh (fik), *n.* *Islam.* jurisprudence based on theology: the legal foundation of religious, political, and civil life. Also, **fikh.** [< Ar]

fir (fûr), *n.* **1.** any coniferous tree of the genus *Abies*, characterized by its pyramidal habit of growth. **2.** the wood of such a tree. [ME *firre*, OE *fyrh*; c. OS *furie;* akin to OE *furh-* (in *fuhrwudu* pine), Icel *fura* fir, L *quercus* oak]

Fir·bolg (fēr′bul əg), *n., pl.* **-bolgs,** (*esp. collectively*) **-bolg.** *Irish Legend.* any member of a pre-Celtic race from Greece who were first defeated by the Fomorians and ousted by the Tuatha De Danann.

Fir·crest (fûr′krest′), *n.* a town in central Washington. 3565 (1960).

Fir·dau·si (fēr dou′sē), *n.* (*Abul Qasim Mansu* or *Hasan*) 932–1020, Persian poet. Also, **Ferdus, Firdou·si, Fir·du·si** (fər do͞o′sē).

fire (fīər), *n., v.,* **fired, fir·ing.** —*n.* **1.** state, process, or instance of combustion in which fuel or other material is ignited and combined with oxygen, giving off light, heat, and flame. **2.** a burning mass of material, as on a hearth or in a furnace. **3.** the destructive burning of a building, town, forest, etc.; conflagration. **4.** heat used for cooking, esp. the lighted burner of a stove: *Put the kettle on the fire.* **5.** a composition or device for producing a conflagration or a fiery display: *Greek fire.* **6.** flashing light; luminous appearance. **7.** brilliance, as of a gem. **8.** burning passion; ardor; enthusiasm. **9.** liveliness of imagination. **10.** fever or inflammation. **11.** severe trial or trouble. **12.** exposure to fire as a means of torture or ordeal. **13.** strength, as of an alcoholic beverage. **14.** a spark or sparks. **15.** the discharge of firearms: *to open fire.* **16.** the effect of firing military weapons: *to pour fire upon the enemy.* **17.** *Archaic.* lightning or a thunderbolt. **18.** *Poetic.* a luminous object, as a star: *heavenly fires.* **19. between two fires,** under physical or verbal attack from both or several sides simultaneously: *The senator is between two fires because of his stand on the bill.* **20. catch fire,** to become ignited; burn: *The sofa caught fire from a lighted cigarette.* Also, **catch on fire. 21. fight fire with fire,** to employ the same tactics used by one's opponent in order to combat him; return like for like. **22. go through fire and water,** to brave any danger or endure any trial: *He said he would go through fire and water to win her hand.* **23. hang fire, a.** to be delayed in exploding, or fail to explode. **b.** to be undecided, postponed, or delayed: *The new project is hanging fire because of concerted opposition.* **24. miss fire, a.** to fail to explode or discharge, as a firearm. **b.** to fail to produce the desired effect; be unsuccessful: *He repeated the joke, but it missed fire the second time.* **25. on fire, a.** ignited; burning; afire. **b.** eager; ardent; zealous: *They were on fire to prove themselves in competition.* **26. play with fire,** to trifle with a serious or dangerous matter: *He didn't realize that insulting the border guards was playing with fire.* **27. set fire to, a.** to cause to burn; ignite. **b.** to excite; arouse; inflame: *The painting set fire to the composer's imagination.* Also, **set on fire. 28. take fire, a.** to become ignited; burn. **b.** to become inspired with enthusiasm or zeal: *Everyone who heard him speak immediately took fire.* **29. under fire, a.** under attack, esp. by military forces. **b.** under censure or criticism: *The school administration is under fire for its policies.* —*v.t.* **30.** to set on fire. **31.** to supply with fuel; attend to the fire of: *They fired the boiler.* **32.** to expose to the action of fire; subject to heat. **33.** to apply heat to in a kiln for baking or glazing; burn. **34.** to heat very slowly for the purpose of drying, as tea. **35.** to inflame, as with passion; fill with ardor. **36.** to inspire. **37.** to light or cause to glow as if on fire. **38.** to discharge (a gun). **39.** to project (a bullet or the like) by or as if by discharging from a gun. **40.** to subject to explosion or explosive force, as a mine. **41.** to hurl; throw: *to fire a stone through a window.* **42.** to dismiss from a job. **43.** *Vet. Med.* to apply a heated iron to (the skin) in order to create a local inflammation of the superficial structures, thus favorably affecting deeper inflammatory processes. **44.** *Archaic.* to drive out or away by, or as by, fire. —*v.i.* **45.** to take fire; be kindled. **46.** to glow as if on fire. **47.** to become inflamed with passion; become excited. **48.** to shoot, as a gun. **49.** to discharge a gun: *to fire at a fleeing enemy.* **50.** to hurl a projectile. **51.** *Music.* to ring the bells of a chime all at once. **52.** (of plant leaves) to turn yellow or brown before the plant matures. **53.** (of an internal-combustion engine) to cause ignition of the air-fuel mixture in a cylinder or cylinders. **54. fire away,** *Informal.* to begin to talk and continue without slackening, as to ask a series of questions: *The reporters fired away at the President.* [ME; OE *fyr;* c. Icel *fūrr*, G *Feuer*, Gk *pŷr* (see PYRO-)]

fire′ alarm′, **1.** a signal that a fire has started. **2.** a bell, siren, horn, etc., that provides such a signal.

Fire′ and Ice′, a poem (1920) by Robert Frost.

fire′ ant′, any of several omnivorous ants, as *Solenopsis geminata* of tropical America, having a sting which produces a burning sensation.

fire′ appara′tus, equipment for extinguishing destructive fires.

fire′ ar′ea, any area of a building in which a fire, on breaking out, would be confined by fire-resistant construction.

fire·arm (fīər′ärm′), *n.* a small arms weapon from which a projectile is fired by gunpowder. [FIRE + ARM[2]] —**fire′armed′,** *adj.*

fire·back (fīər′bak′), *n.* **1.** a piece, lining the rear of a fireplace, usually of cast iron. **2.** the rear of a fireplace. [FIRE + BACK[1]]

fire·ball (fīər′bôl′), *n.* **1.** a ball filled with explosive or combustible material, used as a projectile to injure the enemy by explosion or to set fire to their works. **2.** a ball of fire, as the sun. **3.** a luminous meteor, sometimes exploding. **4.** lightning having the appearance of a globe of fire. **5.** the highly luminous central portion of a nuclear explosion. **6.** *Informal.* an unusually energetic or ambitious worker. [FIRE + BALL[1]]

fire′ balloon′, a montgolfier.

fire·base (fīər′ bās′), *n.* *Mil.* an artillery base, esp. one set up quickly to support advancing troops or to forestall enemy advances.

fire′ bay′, *Fort.* a short section of a fire trench, set forward from the rest and forming a baylike indention.

fire′ bee′tle, any of numerous click beetles of the genus *Pyrophorus*, of tropical America, having luminous reddish or greenish spots on the body.

fire·bird (fīər′bûrd′), *n.* *U.S. Dial.* any of several small birds having bright red or orange plumage, esp. the Baltimore oriole. [FIRE + BIRD]

Fire·bird, The (fīər′bûrd′), a ballet (1910) by Stravinsky.

fire′ blight′, *Plant Pathol.* a disease of pears, apples, quinces, etc., characterized by blossom, twig, and fruit blight and stem cankers, caused by a bacterium, *Erwinia amylovora.* [from the burnt look of the foliage]

fire·board (fīər′bōrd′, -bôrd′), *n.* a board used to close a fireplace. [FIRE + BOARD]

fire·boat (fīər′bōt′), *n.* a powered vessel fitted for fire fighting. [FIRE + BOAT]

fire′ boss′, *Mining.* a person who inspects a mine for the presence of noxious gases, dangerous roofs, and other hazards. Also called **gasman, mine examiner;** *Brit.,* **fireman.**

fire·box (fīər′boks′), *n.* **1.** the box or chamber containing the fire of a steam boiler, furnace, etc. **2.** the furnace of a locomotive, where coal, oil, or other fuel is burned to generate steam. **3.** a box or panel with a device for notifying the fire station of an outbreak of fire. **4.** *Obs.* a tinderbox. [FIRE + BOX[1]]

fire·brand (fīər′brand′), *n.* **1.** a piece of burning wood or other material. **2.** one who or that which kindles strife, inflames the passions, etc. **3.** an extremely energetic or impassioned person. [ME; see FIRE, BRAND]

fire·brat (fīər′brat′), *n.* a bristletail, *Thermobia domestica*, that lives in areas around furnaces, boilers, steampipes, etc. [FIRE + BRAT]

fire·break (fīər′brāk′), *n.* *U.S.* a strip of ploughed or cleared land made to check the spread of a prairie or forest fire. [FIRE + BREAK]

fire·brick (fīər′brik′), *n.* a brick made of fire clay. [FIRE + BRICK]

fire′ brigade′, **1.** a body of fire fighters, esp. as formed temporarily or called upon to assist a fire department in an emergency. **2.** a small fire department privately employed by an institution. **3.** *Brit.* a fire department; hook-and-ladder company.

fire·bug (fīər′bug′), *n.* *Informal.* arsonist; pyromaniac. [FIRE + BUG[1]]

fire′ cher′ry. See **pin cherry.**

fire′ clay′, a refractory clay used for making crucibles, firebricks, etc.

fire′ com′pany, **1.** a company of firemen. **2.** a fire-insurance company.

fire′ control′, *Mil.* technical and sometimes automatic supervision of artillery or naval gunfire on a target, as for range, elevation, etc.

fire·crack·er (fīər′krak′ər), *n.* a paper or cardboard cylinder filled with an explosive and having a fuse that can be discharged to make a noise. [FIRE + CRACKER]

fire·crest (fīər′krest′), *n.* a European kinglet, *Regulus ignicapillus*, having a bright, brownish-gold patch on the top of the head. [FIRE + CREST]

fire-cure (fīər′kyo͝or′), *v.t.,* **-cured, -cur·ing.** to cure (tobacco) by means of open fires, the smoke and flame imparting a creosotic flavor.

fire′ cut′, an inward and upward diagonal cut, given to the end of a wooden joist so that if the joist burns through, the end will fall free without dislodging masonry above it.

fire·damp (fīər′damp′), *n.* **1.** a combustible gas consisting chiefly of methane, formed esp. in coal mines, and dangerously explosive when mixed with certain proportions of atmospheric air. **2.** the explosive mixture itself. [FIRE + DAMP]

fire′ depart′ment, **1.** the department of a municipal government charged with the prevention and extinguishing of fire. **2.** the men in this department.

fire′ direc′tion, *Mil.* tactical deployment of fire power, esp. of artillery fire.

fire·dog (fīər′dôg′, -dog′), *n.* an andiron. [FIRE + DOG]

fire′ door′, a door through which a boiler or furnace is fired or through which the fire is inspected.

fire·drake (fīər′drāk′), *n.* a mythical fiery dragon. [ME *fyrdrake*, OE *fȳrdraca.* See FIRE, DRAKE[2]]

fire′ drill′, **1.** a practice drill for a company of firemen, the crew of a ship, etc., to train them in their duties in case of fire. **2.** a drill for pupils in a school, employees in a factory, etc., to train them in the manner of exit to be followed in case of fire.

fire-eat·er (fīər′ē′tər), *n.* **1.** a juggler who pretends to eat fire. **2.** an easily provoked, belligerent person. **3.** *U.S. Hist. Informal.* an extreme advocate of slavery, before the Civil War. —**fire′-eat′ing,** *adj., n.*

fire′ en′gine, a motor truck equipped for fire fighting, now usually having a motor-driven pump for shooting water or chemical solutions at high pressure.

fire′ escape′, an apparatus or structure used to escape from a burning building, as a metal stairway down an outside wall.

fire′ extin′guisher, a portable apparatus, usually containing chemicals, for putting out a fire.

fire·fang (fīər′fang′), *v.i.* (esp. of stored grain) to become dry or scorched due to the heat produced by the decomposition of organic matter. [FIRE + FANG[2]]

fire′ fight′er, a person who fights destructive fires; fireman. —**fire′ fight′ing.**

fire·flaught (fīər′flôt′; *Scot.* fīər′fläkht′), *n.* *Scot.* lightning. [ME *fyre flawcht*, equiv. to *fyre* FIRE + Scot *flawcht* flash, akin to FLAKE[1]]

fire·fly (fīər′flī′), *n., pl.* **-flies.** any of several soft-bodied, nocturnal beetles of the family *Lampyridae*, having light-producing organs at the rear of the abdomen. Also called **glowfly, lightningbug.** Cf. **glowworm.** [FIRE + FLY[2]]

Firefly, *Photuris pennsylvanica* A, Adult; B, Larva (Length ½ in.)

fire′ gild′ing, a process of gilding metalwork in which the metal base is coated with an amalgam of gold and mercury, the latter subsequently being driven off by heat. Also called **amalgam gilding.**

fire·guard (fīər′gärd′), *n.* a protective framework of wire in front of a fireplace. [FIRE + GUARD]

fire′ hat′, a helmet worn by a fireman as a defense against falling materials from burning structures.

fire·horse (fīər′hôrs′), *n.* (formerly) a horse used to pull a fire engine. [FIRE + HORSE]

fire·house (fīər′hous′), *n., pl.* **-hous·es** (-hou′ziz). See **fire station.** [FIRE + HOUSE]

fire′ insur′ance, insurance covering loss or damage caused by fire.

fire′ i′rons, the implements used for tending a fireplace, as tongs, poker, etc. [ME *fire-yren*]

fire·less (fīər′lis), *adj.* lacking fire; without a fire. [late ME *fuyrles.* See FIRE, -LESS]

fire′less cook′er, an insulated container which seals in heat for a long enough time to cook food.

fire·light (fīər′līt′), *n.* the light from a fire, as on a hearth. [ME *firlight*, OE *fȳrlēoht.* See FIRE, LIGHT[1]]

fire-lil·y (fīər′lil′ē), *n., pl.* **-lil·ies.** elk-grass.

fire·lock (fīər′lok′), *n.* **1.** a gun having a lock in which the priming is ignited by sparks struck from flint and steel, as the flintlock musket. **2.** *Archaic.* a soldier armed with such a gun. [FIRE + LOCK[1]]

fire·man (fīər′mən), *n., pl.* **-men. 1.** a man employed to extinguish or prevent fires. **2.** a man employed to tend fires; stoker. **3.** *Railroads.* **a.** a man employed to fire and lubricate a steam locomotive. **b.** a man employed to assist the engineer of a diesel or electric locomotive. **4.** *U.S. Navy.* an enlisted man assigned to the care and operation of a ship's machinery. **5.** *Brit. Mining.* See **fire boss. 6.** *Baseball Slang.* See **relief pitcher.** [FIRE + MAN[1]]

fire′ mar′shal, **1.** an official heading a bureau for the prevention or investigation of fires. **2.** a person who has charge of the fire-prevention equipment and personnel of an industrial plant.

fire-new (fīər′no͞o′, -nyo͞o′), *adj.* brand-new.

Fi·ren·ze (fē ren′dze), *n.* Italian name of **Florence.**

fire′ o′pal, a red, Mexican opal, often with a color play.

fire′ pink′, a caryophyllaceous plant, *Silene virginica*, having brilliant scarlet flowers. Also called **Indian pink.**

fire·place (fīər′plās′), *n.* **1.** the part of a chimney which opens into a room and in which fuel is burned; hearth. **2.** any open structure, usually of masonry, for containing fire, as at a camp site. [FIRE + PLACE]

fire-plow (fīər′plou′), *n.* a stick that is rubbed in a wooden groove to produce sparks for igniting a fire.

fire·plug (fīər′plug′), *n.* a hydrant for use in case of fire. [FIRE + PLUG]

fire′ point′, *Chem.* the lowest temperature at which a volatile liquid, after its vapors have been ignited, will give off vapors at a rate sufficient to sustain combustion.

fire-pol·ish (fīər′pol′ish), *v.t.* *Glassmaking.* to smooth (glass) by reheating to remove tool marks or other imperfections in the surface.

fire′ pol′ishing, *Glassmaking.* the finishing of a glass vessel by reheating.

fire′ pot′, that part of a household furnace in which the fire is made.

fire′ pow′er, *Mil.* **1.** the ability to deliver fire. **2.** the amount of fire delivered by a unit or weapon. Also, **fire′pow′er.**

fire·proof (fīər′pro͞of′), *adj.* **1.** resistant to destruction by fire; totally or almost totally unburnable; incombustible. —*v.t.* **2.** to make fireproof. [FIRE + -PROOF]

fire·proof·ing (fīər′pro͞o′fing), *n.* **1.** act or process of rendering fireproof. **2.** material for use in making anything fireproof. [FIREPROOF + -ING[1]]

fir·er (fīər′ər), *n.* **1.** a person who fires, sets on fire, treats with fire or heat, discharges a firearm, etc. **2.** a firearm of a specified type of firing (usually used in combination): *a single-firer; a rapid-firer.* [FIRE + -ER[1]]

fire-rais·ing (fīər′rā′zing), *n.* *Brit.* arson. —**fire′-rais′er,** *n.*

fire′ red′, **1.** a strong reddish-orange color. **2.** Also called **fire′ red′ ton′er.** a brilliant reddish-orange dye.

fire′ resist′ance, the amount of resistance of a material or construction to fire.

fire-re·sist·ant (fīər′ri zis′tənt), *adj.* noting construction meeting standard requirements when exposed to fire of a certain heat for a certain length of time.

fire-re·tard·ant (fīər′ri tär′dənt), *adj.* able to slow or check the spread of destructive fire: *The law required apartment buildings to be of fire-retardant construction.*

fire′ room′, *Naut.* a chamber in which the boilers of a steam vessel are fired. Also called **stokehold, stokehole.**

fire′ sale′, a special sale of merchandise supposedly injured by fire.

fire′ screen′, a metal screen placed in front of a fireplace for protection.

fire′ set′ting, *Mining.* a method of shattering rock by building a fire against it so as to cause it to split as a result of uneven internal stresses.

fire′ ship′, a vessel loaded with combustibles and explosives, ignited, and set adrift to destroy an enemy's ships or constructions.

fire·side (fīər′sīd′), *n.* **1.** Also called **hearthside.** the space about a fire or hearth. **2.** home. **3.** home or family life. —*adj.* **4.** informal and neighborly in manner: *the President's fireside chat over television.* [FIRE + SIDE[1]]

fire′ sta′tion, a building in which fire-fighting apparatus and often firemen are housed; firehouse.

fire′ step′, *Fort.* a board or narrow ledge about a foot above the bottom of a fire trench, for men to stand on when firing, observing enemy movements, etc.

fire·stone (fīər′stōn′), *n.* a fire-resisting stone, esp. a kind of sandstone used in fireplaces, furnaces, etc. [late ME *fyyrstone,* OE *fȳrstān.* See FIRE, STONE]

Fire·stone (fīər′stōn′), *n.* **Harvey Samuel,** 1868–1938, U.S. industrialist and rubber manufacturer.

fire·stop (fīər′stop′), *n.* any object built into a building frame to block a concealed hollow space through which a fire might pass from one part of the building to another. [FIRE + STOP]

fire′ storm′, an atmospherical phenomenon, caused by a large fire, in which the rising column of air above the fire draws in strong winds often accompanied by rain.

fire′ support′, support given by artillery and airplanes to advancing infantry and armored vehicles.

fire′ thorn′, any of several evergreen, thorny, rosaceous shrubs of the genus *Pyracantha,* of Asia, many species of which are cultivated for the foliage and ornamental fruits.

fire′ tow′er, a tower, as on a mountain, from which a watch for fires is kept.

fire·trap (fīər′trap′), *n.* **1.** a building which, because of its age, material, structure, or the like, is especially dangerous in case of fire. **2.** (in a building) any arrangement of structural, flooring, and finish members creating concealed passages through which fire can spread to other parts of the building. [FIRE + TRAP[1]]

fire′ trench′, *Fort.* a trench from which men can fire rifles and other small arms and in which they are relatively well protected.

fire′-tube boil′er (fīər′to͞ob′, -tyo͞ob′), any boiler for generating steam by passing hot gases and other combustible products through tubes **(fire′ tubes′)** immersed in water to a chimney or uptake. Cf. **water-tube boiler.**

fire′ wall′, **1.** a wall made of fireproof material to prevent the spread of a fire from one part of a building to another. **2.** *Aeron.* a fireproof wall for isolating the engine compartment from the rest of an aircraft.

fire·ward·en (fīər′wôr′dən), *n.* a person having authority in the prevention or extinguishing of fires, as in towns or camps. [FIRE + WARDEN[1]]

fire·wa·ter (fīər′wô′tər, -wot′ər), *n.* *Informal.* alcoholic drink; liquor. [FIRE + WATER]

fire′ weath′er, weather conducive to the outbreak and spread of forest fires, characterized by low humidity, high winds, etc.

fire·weed (fīər′wēd′), *n.* any of various plants appearing in recently burned clearings or districts, as the willow herb, *Epilobium angustifolium,* or the composite weed, *Erechtites hieracifolia,* of North America. [FIRE + WEED[1]]

fire·wood (fīər′wo͝od′), *n.* wood for fuel. [ME *ferwode.* See FIRE, WOOD[1]]

fire·work (fīər′wûrk′), *n.* **1.** Often, **fireworks.** a combustible or explosive device for producing a striking display of light or a loud noise, often also used in signaling at night. **2. fireworks, a.** a pyrotechnic display. **b.** a display of violent temper, esp. between two persons. [FIRE + WORK]

fire·worm (fīər′wûrm′), *n.* **1.** the larva of any of several moths, as *Rhopobota naevana* **(black-headed fireworm),** which feeds on the leaves of cranberries and causes them to wither. **2.** glowworm. [FIRE + WORM]

fir·ing (fīər′ing), *n.* **1.** act of one who or that which fires. **2.** material for a fire; fuel. **3.** the act of baking ceramics or glass. [FIRE + -ING[1]]

fir′ing bat′tery, *Mil.* the part of a battery actually at the firing position when the battery is prepared for action.

fir′ing da′ta, *Mil.* precise calculations in set formula by which cannon, rockets, or the like, are aimed and fired.

fir′ing glass′, a drinking glass of the 18th century having a conical, rounded body on a thick stem and a heavy spreading foot. Also called **hammering glass.**

fir′ing line′, *Mil.* **1.** the positions at which troops are stationed to fire upon the enemy or targets. **2.** the troops firing from this line. **3.** the forefront of any action or activity.

fir′ing or′der, the order in which the cylinders of an internal-combustion engine fire.

fir′ing pin′, *Ordn.* a plunger that strikes the primer in the firing mechanism of a firearm or cannon and thus ignites the propelling charge of a projectile.

fir′ing squad′, **1.** a military detachment assigned to execute a condemned person. **2.** such a detachment assigned to fire a salute at the burial of a person being honored.

fir′ing step′, *Theat. Brit.* a platform in the flies for storing slack rope.

fir·kin (fûr′kin), *n.* **1.** a British unit of capacity usually equal to a quarter of a barrel. **2.** a small wooden vessel or tub for butter, lard, etc. [ME *ferdkyn, firdekyn,* equiv. to *ferde* (var. of *ferthe* FOURTH) + *-kin* -KIN]

firm[1] (fûrm), *adj.* **1.** not soft or yielding when pressed: comparatively solid, hard, stiff, or rigid: *firm ground; firm texture.* **2.** securely fixed in place. **3.** steady; not shaking or trembling: *a firm hand or voice.* **4.** not likely to change; fixed; settled; unalterable: *a firm belief; a firm decree.* **5.** steadfast or unwavering, as persons or principles. **6.** indicating firmness or determination: *a firm expression.* **7.** not fluctuating or falling much, as prices, values, etc.: *The stock market was firm today.* —*v.t., v.i.* **8.** to make or become firm (sometimes fol. by *up*): *to firm up prices.* —*adv.* **9.** firmly: *He stood firm.* [< L *firm(us)*; r. ME *ferm* < MF < L *firm(us)*] —**firm′ly,** *adv.* —**firm′ness,** *n.*

—**Syn. 1.** FIRM, HARD, SOLID, STIFF are applied to substances that tend to retain their form unaltered in spite of pressure or force. FIRM often implies that something has been brought from a more yielding state to a fixed or elastic one: *An increased amount of pectin makes jellies firm.* HARD is applied to substances so resistant that it is difficult to make any impression upon their surface or to penetrate their interior: *as hard as a stone.* SOLID is applied to substances that without external support retain their form and resist pressure: *Water in the form of ice is solid.* It sometimes denotes the opposite of hollow: *a solid block of marble.* STIFF implies rigidity that resists a bending force: *as stiff as a poker.* **2.** fast, stable, immovable. **4.** established, confirmed. **5.** determined, immovable, resolute, staunch, reliable. —**Ant. 1.** yielding, soft.

firm[2] (fûrm), *n.* **1.** a partnership or unincorporated association of two or more persons for carrying on a business. **2.** the name or title under which associated parties transact business: *the firm of Smith & Jones.* [< Sp *firma* signature (hence, legal name of a partnership, etc.) back formation from *firmar* to sign < L *firmāre* to strengthen, confirm, deriv. of *firmus* FIRM[1]] —**Syn. 1.** company, business, concern, house.

fir·ma·ment (fûr′mə mənt), *n.* the vault of heaven; sky. [ME < LL *firmāment(um)* sky, L: support, prop, stay, equiv. to *firmā(re)* (to) strengthen, support (see FIRM[2]) + *-mentum* -MENT] —**fir·ma·men·tal** (fûr′mə men′təl), *adj.*

fir·man (fûr′mən, fər män′), *n., pl.* **-mans.** an edict or administrative order issued by or in the name of a Middle Eastern sovereign (formerly by an Ottoman Turkish sultan). [< Turk *ferman* < Pers]

fir′mer chis′el (fûr′mər), *Carpentry.* a narrow-bladed chisel for paring and mortising, driven by hand pressure or with a mallet. [*firmer* < F *fermoir,* b. *formoir* that which forms (deriv. of *former* to form < L *formāre*) and *fermer* to make firm (< L *firmāre*)]

fir′mer gouge′, a narrow-bladed gouge similar in manner of use to a firmer chisel.

Fir·mi·cus (fûr′mə kəs), *n.* a crater in the first quadrant of the face of the moon, having a dark floor: about 35 miles in diameter.

firn (firn), *n.* névé. [< G (Swiss), n. use of *firn* last year's, old; c. OE *fyrn* former, ancient, Goth *fairneis;* akin to Icel *forn* ancient. See BEFORE]

firn·i·fi·ca·tion (fir′nə fə kā′shən), *n.* the process by which snow changes into névé. [FIRN + -I- + -FICATION]

fir·ry (fûr′ē), *adj.* **1.** of or pertaining to the fir. **2.** made of fir. **3.** abounding in firs. [FIR + -Y[1]]

first (fûrst), *adj.* **1.** being before all others with respect to time, order, rank, importance, etc., used as the ordinal number of *one.* **2.** *Music.* highest or chief among several voices or instruments of the same class: *first alto; first horn.* **3.** *Auto.* low (def. 28). **4. first thing,** before anything else; at once; promptly: *I'll call you first thing when I arrive.* —*adv.* **5.** before all others or anything else in time, order, rank, etc. **6.** before some other thing, event, etc.: *If you're going, phone first.* **7.** for the first time: *He first visited New York in 1930.* **8.** in preference to something else; rather; sooner: *I'd die first.* **9.** in the first place; firstly. **10. first and last,** everything considered; altogether; all in all: *First and last, it is important to know oneself.* **11. first off,** *Informal.* at the outset; immediately: *He wanted to know first off why he hadn't been notified.* **12. first or last,** at one time or another; sooner or later: *He'll get what he deserves first or last.* —*n.* **13.** that which is first in time, order, rank, etc. **14.** the beginning. **15.** the first part; first member of a series. **16.** *Music.* **a.** the voice or instrument that takes the highest or chief part in its class, especially in an orchestra or chorus. **b.** a leader of a part or group of performers. **17.** *Auto.* first gear; low gear: *She shifted into first and drove off.* **18.** the first place in a race or other competition. **19.** *Baseball.* See **first base. 20.** *Brit. Univ.* **a.** first-class honors. Cf. **class** (def. 6). **b.** a person who has won such honors. **21.** Usually, **firsts.** *Com.* a product or goods of the first or highest quality. Cf. **second**[1] (def. 23), **third** (def. 12). [ME; OE *fyr(e)st* (see FORE[1], -EST); c. G *Fürst* prince, lit., he who is first in rank] —**first′ness,** *adj.*

first′ aid′, emergency aid or treatment given to someone injured, suddenly ill, etc., before regular medical services can be obtained. —**first′-aid′,** *adj.* —**first′-aid′er,** *n.*

first′ ax′iom of countabil′ity, *Math.* See under **axiom of countability.**

First′ Bal′kan War′. See **Balkan War** (def. 1).

first′ base′, **1.** *Baseball.* **a.** the first in counterclockwise order of the bases from home plate. **b.** the position of the player covering the area of the infield near first base. **2. get to first base,** *Informal.* to be initially successful in striving toward a goal: *His suggestions for labor-saving techniques never got to first base.*

first′ base′man, *Baseball.* the player whose position is first base.

first-born (fûrst′bôrn′), *adj.* **1.** first in the order of birth; eldest. —*n.* **2.** a first-born child. **3.** a first result or product. [ME; see FIRST, BORN]

First-born, The (fûrst′bôrn′), a religious verse play (1946) by Christopher Fry.

first′ cat′egory, *Math.* the property of a set that can be expressed as the union of a countable number of nowhere-dense sets. Cf. **Baire category theorem, second category.**

first′ cause′, **1.** a cause which does not depend upon any other: *God is the first cause.* **2.** any prime mover.

first′-cause′ ar′gument (fûrst′kôz′), *Philos.* an argument for the existence of God, asserting the necessity of an uncaused cause of all subsequent series of causes, on the assumption that an infinite regress is impossible. Cf. **cosmological argument.**

First′ Cham′ber. See under **States-General** (def. 1).

first-chop (fûrst′chop′), *adj.* (esp. in Anglo-Indian use) being of the highest quality or grade; first-class: *a really first-chop new play.* [FIRST + CHOP[4]]

first′ class′, **1.** the best, finest, or highest class, grade, or rank. **2.** the most expensive and most luxurious class of accommodation on trains, ships, airplanes, etc. **3.** (in the U.S. postal system) the class of mail consisting of letters, postal cards, or the like, together with all mailable matter sealed against inspection, and for which the highest postal rate is charged in view of the special handling services provided, as free forwarding, return to sender, etc. **4.** *Brit. Univ.* the group receiving the highest distinction in an honors course.

first-class (fûrst′klas′, -kläs′), *adj.* **1.** of the highest or best class or quality. **2.** best-equipped and most expensive: *a first-class railroad car.* **3.** given or entitled to preferred treatment, handling, etc.: *first-class mail.* —*adv.* **4.** by first-class conveyance: *to travel first-class.*

first′ cous′in, cousin (def. 1).

First′ day′, (among Quakers) Sunday.

first′-day cov′er (fûrst′dā′, -dā′), *Philately.* a cover marked so as to indicate that it was mailed on the first day of issue of the stamp it bears and from one of the cities at which the stamp was issued on that day.

first′-de·gree′ burn′ (fûrst′di grē′), *Pathol.* See under **burn**[1] (def. 39).

first′ deriv′ative, *Math.* the derivative of a function: *Velocity is the first derivative of distance with respect to time.* Cf. **second derivative.**

first′ derived′ curve′, *Math.* See **derived curve.**

first′ divi′sion, *Sports.* the half of a league comprising the teams having the best records at a particular time, esp. the five teams having the best records in either of the two major leagues of baseball (opposed to *second division*).

first′ edi′tion, **1.** the whole number of copies of a literary work printed first, from the same type, and issued together. **2.** an individual copy from this number. **3.** the first printing of a newspaper for a given date.

First′ Em′pire, the empire (1804–14) established in France by Napoleon Bonaparte.

first′ estate′, the first of the three estates: the clergy in France; the Lords Spiritual in England. Cf. **estate** (def. 5).

first′ fam′ily, a family having the highest or one of the highest social ranks in a given place. **2.** (*often caps.*) *U.S.* the family of the president or the family of the governor of a State. **3.** a family descended from a colonist or early settler in a country, region, etc.: *one of the first families of Virginia.*

first′ floor′, **1.** (in the U.S.) the ground floor of a building. **2.** (in foreign countries, and sometimes in the U.S.) the floor above the ground floor of a building.

first-foot (fûrst′fo͝ot′), *Scot.* —*n.* Also, **first′-foot′er.** **1.** the first person to cross the threshold of a house on New Year's Day. **2.** the first person met after starting out on the day of an important occasion. —*v.t.* **3.** to enter (a house) first on New Year's Day. —*v.i.* **4.** to be the first to enter a house on New Year's Day.

first′ fruits′, **1.** the earliest fruit of the season. **2.** the first product or result of anything. [ME; see FIRST, FRUIT]

first-gen·er·a·tion (fûrst′jen′ə rā′shən), *adj.* noting a U.S. citizen either born as a foreigner and naturalized or born as a native American of parents born as foreigners.

first·hand (fûrst′hand′), *adv.* **1.** from the first or original source: *We heard the news of the accident firsthand from a witness.* —*adj.* **2.** of or pertaining to the first or original source. **3.** direct from the original source: *firsthand knowledge of the riot.* Also, **first′-hand′.** [FIRST + HAND]

first-in, first-out (fûrst′in′, fûrst′out′), an inventory plan which assumes that items purchased first will be sold first and that by valuing inventory items at the price of the most recent purchases, inventory values will be comparable to any rise in prices. *Abbr.:* FIFO Cf. **last-in, first-out.**

first′ inten′tion, *Logic.* See under **intention** (def. 5).

First′ Interna′tional, a socialistic organization (1864–76) formed to unite and promote the interests of workers throughout the world. Cf. **international** (def. 6).

first′ la′dy, **1.** (*often caps.*) *U.S.* the wife of the President of the U.S. or of the governor of a State. **2.** the wife of the head of any country: *the first lady of Brazil.* **3.** the foremost woman in any art, profession, or the like: *first lady of the American theater.*

first′ law′ of mo′tion, *Physics.* See under **law of motion.**

first′ law′ of thermodynam′ics. See under **law of thermodynamics** (def. 1).

first′ lieuten′ant, *Mil.* an officer ranking next above second lieutenant and next below a captain.

first-line (fûrst′līn′), *adj.* **1.** available for immediate service, esp. combat service: *first-line troops.* **2.** of prime importance or quality.

first·ling (fûrst′ling), *n.* **1.** the first of its kind to be produced or to appear. **2.** first offspring. **3.** a first product or result. [FIRST + -LING[1]]

First′ Lord′, *Brit.* the head of a board commissioned to perform the duties of a high office of state: *First Lord of the Admiralty.*

first·ly (fûrst′lē), *adv.* in the first place; first. [FIRST + -LY]

first′ main′ track′, *Railroads.* a main-line track from one terminal to another.

first′ mate′, the officer of a merchant vessel next in command beneath the captain. Also called **chief mate, chief officer, first officer, mate.**

first′ mort′gage, a mortgage having priority over other mortgages on property. —**first′-mort′gage,** *adj.*

first′ mo′tion, *Rocketry.* the initial movement of a missile from the launch pad.

first′ name′. See **given name.**

first-name (fûrst′nām′), *adj.* of or pertaining to one's first, or Christian, name; familiar; intimate: *They were on a first-name basis soon after meeting.*

first-night·er (fûrst′nī′tər), *n.* a person who habitually attends the theater, opera, etc., on opening night.

first′ offend′er, a person convicted of an offense of law for the first time.

first′ of′ficer, **1.** See **first mate. 2.** copilot.

first′ pa′pers, *U.S.* the first documents of record in the naturalization of an alien. Cf. **second papers, citizenship papers.**

first′ per′son, 1. *Gram.* the person used by a speaker in statements referring to himself, as *I* and *we* in English. 2. a form in the first person.

A, First position; B, Second position; C, Third position; D, Fourth position; E, Fifth position

first′ posi′tion, *Ballet.* a position of the feet in which the heels are back to back and the toes point out to the sides.
first′ post′. See under **post**[2] (def. 7).
first′ prin′ciple, any axiom, law, or abstraction assumed and regarded as representing the highest possible degree of generalization.
first′ quar′ter, *Astron.* the instant, approximately one week after a new moon, when one half of the moon's disk is illuminated by the sun. See diag. under **moon.**
first-rate (fûrst′rāt′), *adj.* 1. of the first rate or class. 2. excellent. —*adv.* 3. *Nonstandard.* very well.
First′ Read′er, *Christian Science.* the elected official of a church or society who conducts the services and meetings and reads from the writings of Mary Baker Eddy and the Scriptures. Cf. **Second Reader.**
First′ Reich′, the Holy Roman Empire until its dissolution in 1806. Cf. **Reich.**
First′ Repub′lic, the republic established in France in 1792 and replaced by the First Empire in 1804.
first-run (fûrst′run′), *adj.* of, pertaining to, or offering the first showing of a motion picture in a locality.
first′ ser′geant, *U.S. Army.* the senior noncommissioned officer of a company, squadron, etc., responsible for personnel and administration.
first′ speed′, *Brit.* low or first gear on an automobile.
first-string (fûrst′string′), *adj.* 1. among the foremost in importance or respect: *the first-string critics.* 2. composed of regular members, participants, etc. (distinguished from *substitute*): *the first-string team.*
first′ wa′ter, 1. the highest degree of fineness in a diamond or other precious stone. Cf. **water** (def. 13). 2. the finest quality; highest rank.
First′ World′ War′. See **World War I.**
firth (fûrth), *n.* *Chiefly Scot.* a long, narrow indentation of the seacoast. Also, **frith.** [< Scand; cf. Icel *firth-*, s. of *fjörthr,* FJORD]
fisc (fisk), *n.* a royal or state treasury; exchequer. [ME *fisc(us)* < L: treasury, lit., basket, bag]
fis·cal (fis′kəl), *adj.* 1. of or pertaining to the public treasury or revenues. 2. pertaining to financial matters in general. —*n.* 3. (in some countries) a prosecuting attorney. 4. *Philately.* a revenue stamp. [< L *fiscāl(is).* See FISC, -AL[1]] —**fis′cal·ly,** *adv.*
—**Syn.** 1. See **financial.**
fis′cal a′gent, a person or organization serving as another's financial agent.
fis′cal year′, any yearly period at the end of which a firm, government, etc., determines its financial condition without regard to the calendar year.
Fisch·er (fish′ər), *n.* 1. **Edwin,** 1886–1960, Swiss pianist. 2. **E·mil** (ā′mil), 1852–1919, German chemist: Nobel prize 1902. 3. **Hans** (häns), 1881–1945, German chemist: Nobel prize 1930. 4. **Robert James** (*Bobby*), born 1943, U.S. chess player.
Fisch′er-Tropsch′ proc′ess (fish′ər trōpsh′, -tropsh′), *Chem.* any of several processes for producing hydrocarbons and their derivatives by the interaction, under high temperature and pressure, of a mixture of carbon monoxide and hydrogen in the presence of a catalyst. [named after F. *Fischer* (d. 1948), and H. *Tropsch* (d. 1935), German chemists]
Fisch·er von Er·lach (fish′ər fən er′läkh), **Jo·hann Bern·hard** (yō′hän bern′härt), 1656–1723, Austrian architect.

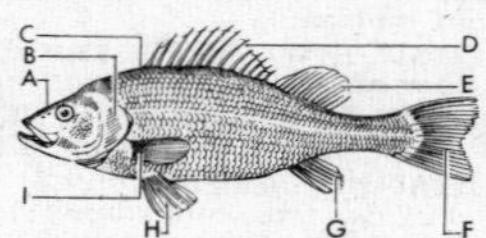

Fish (External features of yellow perch)
A, External nares; B, Operculum; C, Lateral line; D, Spinous dorsal fin; E, Soft dorsal fin; F, Caudal fin; G, Anal fin; H, Pelvic fin; I, Pectoral fin

fish (fish), *n., pl.* (*esp. collectively*) **fish,** (*esp. referring to two or more kinds or species*) **fish·es,** *v.* —*n.* 1. any of various cold-blooded, completely aquatic vertebrates, having gills, commonly fins, and typically an elongated body usually covered with scales. 2. any of various other aquatic animals. 3. the flesh of fishes used as food. 4. **Fishes,** *Astron., Astrol.* the constellation or sign of Pisces. 5. *Informal.* a person: *an odd fish; a poor fish.* 6. a long strip of wood, iron, etc., used to strengthen a mast, joint, etc. 7. *Informal.* any drilling equipment accidentally dropped or left in an oil well. 8. *Cards Slang.* an incompetent player whose incompetence can be exploited. 9. *Slang.* a dollar: *He sold the car for a neat 500 fish.* 10. **cry stinking fish,** to disparage one's own efforts, business, associates, etc., thus bringing discredit upon oneself. 11. **drink like a fish,** to drink to excess: *Nobody invites him out because he drinks like a fish.* 12. **fish out of water,** a person out of his proper or accustomed environment: *He felt like a fish out of water in an academic atmosphere.* 13. **neither fish nor fowl,** having no specific character or conviction; neither one nor the other. Also **neither fish, flesh, (fowl), nor good red herring; neither fish nor fowl nor good red herring.** 14. **other fish to fry,** other matters requiring attention: *When it was time to act, they had other fish to fry.* —*v.t.* 15. to catch or attempt to catch (any species of fish or the like). 16. to try to catch fish in (a stream, lake, etc.): *Let's fish the creek.* 17. to draw as by fishing (often fol. by *up* or *out*): *He fished a coin out of his pocket for the boy.* 18. to search through as by fishing. 19. *Naut.* **a.** to raise the flukes of (an anchor), after catting or raising to the hawsehole, in order to secure it to the deck or side of a vessel. **b.** to reinforce (a mast or other spar) by fastening a spar, batten, metal bar, or the like, lengthwise over a weak place. —*v.i.* 20. to catch or attempt to catch fish, as by angling or drawing a net. 21. to search for or attempt to catch onto something under water, in mud, etc., by the use of a dredge, rake, hook, or the like. 22. to seek to obtain something indirectly or by artifice: *to fish for compliments; to fish for information.* 23. **fish in troubled waters,** to take advantage of troubled or uncertain conditions for personal profit. 24. **fish or cut bait,** to choose a definite course of action, esp. to decide whether to participate in or retreat from an activity. 25. **fish out,** to deplete (a lake, stream, etc.) of fish by fishing. [ME; OE *fisc;* c. D *vis,* G *Fisch,* Icel *fiskr,* Goth *fisks;* akin to L *piscis,* Ir *iasc*] —**fish′a·ble,** *adj.* —**fish′less,** *adj.*
Fish (fish), *n.* **Hamilton,** 1808–93, U.S. statesman: Secretary of State 1869–77.
fish′ and chips′, *Chiefly Brit.* fried fish fillets and French fried potatoes.
fish′ ball′, a small fried cake of shredded fish mixed with mashed potato.
fish-bel·lied (fish′bel′ēd), *adj.* *Building Trades, Mach.* (of a beam or rail) having a convex underside.
fish·bolt (fish′bōlt′), *n.* a bolt for securing a fishplate or fishplates. [FISH + BOLT[1]]
fish′bone this′tle, (fish′bōn′), a thistle, *Cirsium diacantha,* of Syria, having purple flowers. [FISH + BONE[1]]
fish·bowl (fish′bōl′), *n.* a glass bowl for goldfish, snails, etc. Also, **fish′ bowl′.** [FISH + BOWL[1]]
fish′ cake′, a fried ball or cake of shredded fish, esp. salt codfish, and mashed potato. Also called **fish ball.**
fish′ crow′, a crow, *Corvus ossifragus,* of the Atlantic and Gulf coasts of North America, that feeds on fish, mollusks, etc.
fish′ doc′tor, a scaleless, brightly colored eelpout, *Gymnelis viridis,* found in Arctic waters.
fish·er (fish′ər), *n.* 1. a fisherman. 2. any animal that catches fish for food. 3. a dark-brown or blackish, somewhat foxlike marten, *Martes pennanti,* of northern North America. 4. its fur. [ME *fisscher,* OE *fiscere.* See FISH, -ER[1]]

Fisher, *Martes pennanti* (Total length 3 ft.; tail 14 in.)

Fish·er (fish′ər), *n.* 1. **Andrew,** 1862–1928, Australian statesman, born in Scotland: prime minister 1908–09, 1910–13, 1914–15. 2. **Dorothy Can·field** (kan′fēld′), (*Dorothea Frances Canfield Fisher*), 1879–1958, U.S. novelist. 3. **Irving,** 1867–1947, U.S. political economist. 4. **John Arbuthnot, 1st Baron Fisher of Kil·ver·stone** (kil′vər stən), 1841–1920, British admiral.
Fish′er King′, *Arthurian Romance.* (in the story of Percival) the custodian of the Grail.
fish·er·man (fish′ər mən), *n., pl.* **-men.** 1. a person engaged in fishing, whether for profit or pleasure. 2. a ship employed in fishing. [late ME *fissherman*]
fish′erman's bend′, a knot made by taking a round turn on the object to which the rope is to be fastened, passing the end of the rope around the standing part and under the round turn, and securing the end. Also called **anchor bend, anchor knot.** See illus. under **knot.**
fish′erman's reef′, *Naut.* the reduction of the effective sail area of the mainsail of a fore-and-aft-rigged boat by allowing it to luff rather than by reefing it.
fish′erman's ring′, *Rom. Cath. Ch.* the signet ring worn by the pope.
fish′erman's stay′sail, a large, quadrilateral staysail in a schooner, set between the foremast and mainmast and above the main staysail.
fish·er·y (fish′ə rē), *n., pl.* **-er·ies.** 1. the occupation or industry of catching fish or taking other products of the sea or streams from the water. 2. a place where such an industry is regularly carried on. 3. a fishing establishment. 4. *Law.* the right to fish in certain waters. [FISH + -ERY]
fish·eye (fish′ī′), *n., pl.* **-eyes.** 1. (in plasterwork) a surface defect having the form of a spot. 2. an unfriendly or suspicious look: *The doorman gave the unshaven stranger the fisheye.* Also, **fish′ eye′.** [FISH + EYE]
fish′eye lens′, *Photog.* a hemispherical plano-convex lens for photographing in a full 180° in all directions in front of the camera, creating a circular image having an increasing amount of distortion from the center to the periphery.
fish′ flour′, powdered fish, high in protein, used as an ingredient in foods.
fish′ fork′, a small fork having usually three tines, used for eating fish at table.
fish′ fry′, 1. a picnic or dinner at which fish are fried. 2. fried fish.
fish′ gera′nium, a geranium, *Pelargonium hortorum,* having a fishlike odor, showy red, salmon, or white flowers, and roundish leaves with scalloped edges.
fish·gig (fish′gig′), *n.* a spearlike implement with barbed prongs for spearing fish in the water. Also called **fizgig.** [var. (by assoc. with FISH) of *fisgig* < Sp *fisg(a)* harpoon + *-ig* (< ?)]
fish′ hawk′, osprey (def. 1).
fish·hook (fish′ho͝ok′), *n.* a hook used in fishing. [ME *fischhook.* See FISH, HOOK]
fish′hook cac′tus, 1. a ball-like cactus, *Ancistrocactus scheeri,* found in Texas, New Mexico, and Mexico, having whitish spines and greenish-yellow flowers. 2. a bisnaga cactus, *Ferocactus wislizeni.*

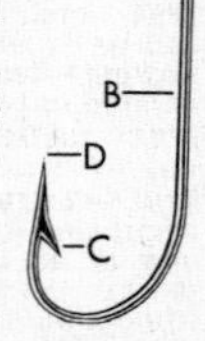

Fishhook
A, Eye
B, Shank
C, Barb
D, Point

fish·ing (fish′ing), *n.* 1. the act of catching fish. 2. the technique, occupation, or diversion of catching fish. 3. a place or facility for catching fish. [ME *fisshing.* See FISH, -ING[1]]
fish′ing banks′, a relatively shallow area of the sea in which fish are usually abundant.
fish′ing expedi′tion, *Informal.* 1. a legal proceeding mainly for the purpose of interrogating an adversary, or of examining his property and documents, in order to gain useful information. 2. an official investigation carried on without reference to any clearly defined plan or purpose or to standards of propriety, in the hope of discovering useful information.
fish′ing ground′, a part of a body of water where the fishing is usually good.
fish′ing pole′, a long, slender rod of wood or other material with a line and hook fastened to one end for use in catching fish. Also called **fish pole.**
fish′ing rod′, a long, slender, cylindrical, flexible rod usually made of bamboo, steel, or fiberglass, for use with a reel and line in catching fish. Cf. **fly rod.**
fish′ing smack′, any of various fore-and-aft-rigged fishing vessels of rather large size, often containing a well to keep the catch alive.
fish′ing tack′le, the rod, line, hooks, and other equipment used in fishing.
fish′ joint′, a joint between two members, as beams or rails, butted together and joined by fishplates.
fish′ knife′, a small knife with a spatulalike blade, used with one's fork in cutting fish at table. [ME *fishknif*]
fish′ lad′der, a series of ascending pools constructed to enable salmon or other fish to swim upstream around or over a dam.
fish′ lead′ (led), *Naut.* a sounding lead left overboard when not in use.
fish·line (fish′līn′), *n.* a line used in fishing. [FISH + LINE[1]]
fish′ louse′, any of numerous small crustaceans, esp. certain copepods, parasitic on the skin and gills of fish.
fish′ meal′, dried fish that has been ground, used as fertilizer or as an ingredient in foods.
fish·mon·ger (fish′mung′gər, -mong′-), *n.* *Chiefly Brit.* a dealer in fish, esp. for eating. [ME *fysshmongere.* See FISH, MONGER]
fish·mouth (fish′mouth′), *v.i.* alligator (def. 6). [v. use of n. phrase *fish mouth*]
fish·net (fish′net′), *n.* a net for catching fish. [ME, OE *fiscnett.* See FISH, NET[1]]
fish·plate (fish′plāt′), *n.* a metal or wooden plate or slab, bolted to each of two members that have been butted or lapped together. [*fish* alter. of F *fiche* fastening, deriv. of *ficher* to fasten, fix (see FICHU) + PLATE[1]]

Fishplates
A, Railroad fishplate or joint bar; B, Fishplates binding two timbers butted together

fish′ pole′. See **fishing pole.**
fish·pound (fish′pound′), *n.* *U.S.* a submerged net used by commercial fishermen for capturing fish. [FISH + POUND[3]]
fish′skin disease′ (fish′skin′), *Pathol.* ichthyosis. [FISH + SKIN]
fish′ slice′, 1. a broad-bladed kitchen implement with a long handle, for turning fish in frying. 2. *Chiefly Brit.* a broad-bladed implement for serving fish at table.
fish′ stick′, an oblong piece of fried fish.
fish′ sto′ry, *Informal.* an exaggerated or incredible story: *It was just another one of his fish stories.*
fish′ tack′le, *Naut.* a tackle for fishing an anchor.
fish·tail (fish′tāl′), *Informal.* —*v.i.* 1. to swerve or skid from side to side, esp. of the rear wheels, as a car. 2. to slow an airplane by causing its tail to move rapidly from side to side. —*n.* 3. such a maneuver. 4. a gas burner having two jets crossing each other so as to produce a flame resembling a fish's tail. 5. a device having a long, narrow slot at the top, placed over a gas jet, as of a Bunsen burner, to give a thin, fanlike flame. 6. *Jewelry.* a setting consisting of four prominent triangular corner prongs to hold the stone. [late ME *fissh taill.* See FISH, TAIL[1]]
fish′ ward′en, a public official who enforces game laws relating to fish.
fish·wife (fish′wīf′), *n., pl.* **-wives.** 1. a woman who sells fish. 2. a coarse-mannered, vulgar-tongued woman. [ME *fisshwyf.* See FISH, WIFE]
fish·worm (fish′wûrm′), *n.* an earthworm. [FISH + WORM]
fish·y (fish′ē), *adj.,* **fish·i·er, fish·i·est.** 1. like a fish in shape, smell, taste, or the like. 2. consisting of fish. 3. abounding in fish. 4. *Informal.* improbable, as a story. 5. *Informal.* of questionable character: *The sudden knockout was fishy.* 6. dull and expressionless: *fishy eyes.* [FISH + -Y[1]] —**fish′i·ly,** *adv.* —**fish′i·ness,** *n.*
fish·y·back (fish′ē bak′), *n.* 1. fishybacking. —*adj.* 2. of, pertaining to, or resembling fishybacking. [*fishie* little fish (i.e., barge) + BACK[1]; cf. PIGGYBACK]
fish·y·back·ing (fish′ē bak′ing), *n.* the transporting of loaded truck trailers by barge, ferry, or similar vessel. [FISHYBACK + -ING[1]]
Fiske (fisk), *n.* 1. **John** (*Edmund Fisk Green; John Fisk*), 1842–1901, U.S. philosopher and historian. 2. **Mrs.** (*Marie Augusta Davey*) ("*Minnie Maddern*"), 1865–1932, U.S. actress. 3. a boy's given name.
fissi-, a learned borrowing from Latin meaning "cleft," used in the formation of compound words: *fissiparous.* [< L, comb. form of *fissus* cloven, *fissum* fissure, special uses of ptp. of *findere* to split]
fis·sile (fis′əl), *adj.* 1. capable of being split or divided; cleavable. 2. fissionable. [< L *fissil(is),* equiv. to *fiss(us)* (see FISSI-) + *-ilis* -ILE]
fis·sion (fish′ən), *n.* 1. act of cleaving or splitting into parts. 2. *Biol.* the division of an organism into new organisms as a process of reproduction. 3. Also called **nuclear fission.** *Physics.* the splitting of the nucleus of an atom into nuclei of lighter atoms, accompanied by the release of energy. Cf. **fusion** (def. 4). [< L *fissiōn-* (s. of *fissiō*) a splitting, dividing, equiv. to *fiss(us)* divided (see FISSI-) + *-iōn-* -ION]

fis·sion·a·ble (fish′ə nə bəl), *adj.* *Physics.* capable of, or possessing a nucleus or nuclei capable of, undergoing fission: *a fissionable nucleus; fissionable material.* Also called **fissile.** [FISSION + -ABLE] —**fis′sion·a·bil′i·ty,** *n.*

fis′sion bomb′. See **atomic bomb.**

fis·sip·a·rous (fi sip′ər əs), *adj.* reproducing by fission. [FISSI- + -PAROUS] —**fis·sip′a·rous·ly,** *adv.* —**fis·sip′a·rous·ness,** *n.*

fis·si·ros·tral (fis′ə ros′trəl), *adj.* *Ornith.* **1.** having a broad, deeply cleft beak or bill, as the swallows and goatsuckers. **2.** (of the bill) deeply cleft. [FISSI- + ROSTRAL]

Fissirostral bill of goatsucker, *Caprimulgus europaeus*

fis·sure (fish′ər), *n.*, *v.*, **-sured, -sur·ing.** —*n.* **1.** a narrow opening produced by cleavage or separation of parts; cleft. **2.** cleavage (def. 1). **3.** *Anat.* a natural division or groove in an organ, as in the brain. —*v.t.* **4.** to make fissures in; cleave; split. —*v.i.* **5.** to open in fissures; become split. [late ME < medical L *fissūra,* equiv. to *fiss(us)* divided (see FISSI-) + *-ūra* -URE] —**fis′sur·al,** *adj.* —**fis′sure·less,** *adj.*

fis′sure of Ro·lan′do (rō lan′dō, -län′-). See **central sulcus.** [named after L. *Rolando* (d.1831), Italian anatomist]

fis′sure of Syl′vi·us (sil′vē əs), *Anat.* See **lateral fissure.** [named after Franciscus *Sylvius* (Latinization of Franz de la Boë, d.1672), German anatomist]

fist[1] (fist), *n.* **1.** the hand closed tightly, with the fingers doubled into the palm. **2.** *Informal.* the hand. **3.** *Informal.* a person's handwriting. **4.** *Print.* index (def. 7). —*v.t.* **5.** to make (one's hand) into a fist. **6.** to grasp in the fist. [ME; OE *fȳst;* c. G *Faust* fist; ? orig. meaning five (fingers) as one, i.e., clenched. See FIVE]

fist[2] (fist), *n.* feist.

fist·fight (fist′fīt′), *n.* a fight with bare fists. [FIST[1] + FIGHT]

fist·ful (fist′fo͝ol), *n., pl.* **-fuls.** a handful: *a fistful of pennies.* [FIST[1] + -FUL]

fist·i·an·a (fis′tē an′ə, -ä′nə), *n.* *Informal.* the sport or world of boxing: *one of fistiana's most colorful characters.* [FISTI(CUFF) + -ANA]

fist·ic (fis′tik), *adj.* of boxing; pugilistic: *fistic heroes.* [FIST[1] + -IC]

fist·i·cuff (fis′tə kuf′), *n.* **1.** a cuff or blow with the fist. **2. fisticuffs,** combat with the fists. —*v.t., v.i.* **3.** to strike or fight with the fists. [earlier *fisty cuff.* See FIST[1], -Y[1], CUFF[2]] —**fist′i·cuff′er,** *n.*

fist·note (fist′nōt′), *n.* a printed note, as in a piece of text, distinguished by the figure of a fist with a pointing index finger. [FIST[1] + NOTE]

fis·tu·la (fis′cho͞o lə), *n., pl.* **-las, -lae** (-lē′). **1.** *Pathol.* a narrow passage or duct formed by disease or injury, as one leading from an abscess to a free surface, or from one cavity to another. **2.** *Surg.* an opening made into a hollow organ, as the bladder or eyeball, for drainage. **3.** *Vet. Pathol.* any of various suppurative inflammations, as in the withers of a horse (**fistulous withers**), characterized by the formation of passages or sinuses through the tissues and to the surface of the skin. **4.** *Obs.* a pipe, as a flute. [ME < L: pipe, tube, reed, ulcer]

fis·tu·lize (fis′cho͞o līz′), *v.*, **-lized, -liz·ing.** —*v.i.* **1.** *Pathol.* to form a fistula. —*v.t.* **2.** *Surg.* to make a fistula. [FISTUL(A) + -IZE] —**fis′tu·li·za′tion,** *n.*

fis·tu·lous (fis′cho͞o ləs), *adj.* **1.** *Pathol.* pertaining to or resembling a fistula. **2.** tubelike; tubular. **3.** containing tubes or tubelike parts. Also, **fis′tu·lar, fis·tu·late** (fis′cho͞o lit). [< L *fistulōs(us).* See FISTULA, -OUS]

fis′tulous with′ers. See under **fistula** (def. 3).

fit[1] (fit), *adj.*, **fit·ter, fit·test,** *v.*, **fit** or **fit·ted, fit·ting,** *n.* —*adj.* **1.** adapted or suited: *meat that is fit to be eaten.* **2.** proper or becoming: *fit behavior.* **3.** qualified or competent, as for an office or function: *a fit candidate.* **4.** worthy or deserving: *This paper is not fit for presentation.* **5.** prepared or ready: *crops fit for gathering.* **6.** in good physical condition, as an athlete, a race horse, military troops, etc. **7.** in good health. **8. fit to be tied,** *Informal.* very annoyed or angry: *He was fit to be tied when I told him I'd wrecked the car.* **9. fit to kill,** *Informal.* to the limit; exceedingly: *She was dressed up fit to kill.* —*v.t.* **10.** to be adapted to or suitable for (a purpose, object, occasion, etc.). **11.** to be proper or becoming for. **12.** to be of the right size or shape for: *The dress fitted her perfectly.* **13.** to adjust or make conform to something: *to fit a ring to the finger.* **14.** to make qualified or competent: *qualities that fit one for leadership.* **15.** to prepare: *This school fits students for college.* **16.** to put with precise placement or adjustment: *He fitted the picture into the frame.* **17.** to provide; furnish; equip: *to fit a door with a new handle.* —*v.i.* **18.** to be suitable or proper. **19.** to be of the right size or shape, as a garment for the wearer, or any object or part for a thing to which it is applied: *The shoes fit yesterday.* **20. fit out** or **up,** to furnish with clothing, furniture, or other requisites; supply; equip: *to fit out an expedition.* —*n.* **21.** the manner in which a thing fits: *a perfect fit.* **22.** something that fits: *The coat is a poor fit.* **23.** the process or a process of fitting. [ME; akin to MD *vitten* to befit] —**fit′ness,** *n.* —**fit′ta·ble,** *adj.*

—**Syn. 1.** suitable, appropriate, apt, corresponding, meet, applicable, apropos. **2.** fitting, befitting.

fit[2] (fit), *n.* **1.** a sudden, acute attack or manifestation of a disease: *a fit of epilepsy.* **2.** an onset, spell, or period of emotion, feeling, inclination, activity, etc.: *a fit of great energy; a fit of anger; a fit of weeping.* **3. by fits and starts,** at irregular intervals; intermittently: *This radio works by fits and starts.* Also, **by fits, in fits and starts. 4. throw a fit,** *Slang.* to become extremely excited or angry: *Your father will throw a fit when he hears what you have done.* [ME; OE *fitt* round of fighting. See FIT[3]]

fit[3] (fit), *n.* *Archaic.* **1.** a song, ballad, or story. **2.** a division of a song, ballad, or story. [ME; OE *fitt* round of singing, canto, song, speech]

fitch (fich), *n.* **1.** the European polecat, *Mustela putorius.* **2.** its fur: *Yellow fitch is often dyed to imitate other furs.* Also, **fitch·et** (fich′it), **fitch·ew** (fich′o͞o). [late ME *fiche* < MD *vitsche* polecat, named from its stench; akin to dial. G *fietschen* to stink]

Fitch (fich), *n.* **1. John,** 1743–98, U.S. inventor: pioneer in development of the steamboat. **2. (William) Clyde,** 1865–1909, U.S. playwright.

Fitch·burg (fich′bûrg), *n.* a city in N Massachusetts. 43,021 (1960).

fitch·er (fich′ər), *v.i.* (of the flutes of a drill) to clog from accumulation of the matter being drilled. [?]

fitch·y (fich′ē), *adj.* *Heraldry.* (of a cross) having the lowermost arm, or other arms as specified, terminating in a point: *a cross-crosslet fitchy.* Also, **fitch·ée** (fich′ē, fi chā′). [< MF *fiche,* ptp. of *ficher* to fix. See FICHU]

fitch′y at the foot′, *Heraldry.* (of a cross) having its normal form but having an additional pointed termination below the foot: *a cross paty fitchy at the foot.*

fit·ful (fit′fəl), *adj.* coming, appearing, acting, etc., in fits or by spells; recurring irregularly. [FIT[2] + -FUL] —**fit′ful·ly,** *adv.* —**fit′ful·ness,** *n.*

fit·ly (fit′lē), *adv.* **1.** in a fit manner. **2.** at a fit time. [FIT[1] + -LY]

fit·ment (fit′mənt), *n.* **1.** equipment; furnishing. **2. fitments,** fittings: *the fitments of a ship.* [FIT[1] + -MENT]

fit·ted (fit′id), *adj.* made so as to follow closely the contours of a form or shape: *fitted clothes; fitted sheets.* [FIT[1] + -ED[2]] —**fit′ted·ness,** *n.*

fit·ten (fit′ən), *adj.* *Dial.* fit; suitable. [FIT[1] + -EN[3]]

fit·ter (fit′ər), *n.* **1.** one who or that which fits. **2.** a person who fits garments. **3.** a worker who fits together or adjusts the parts of machinery. **4.** a person who supplies and fixes fittings or fixtures. **5.** a person who furnishes or equips with whatever is necessary for some purpose. [FIT[1] + -ER[1]]

fit·ting (fit′ing), *adj.* **1.** suitable or appropriate; proper or becoming. —*n.* **2.** act of one who or that which fits. **3.** act or instance of trying on clothes that are being made or altered to determine proper fit. **4.** anything provided as equipment, parts, supply, etc. **5.** Usually, **fittings.** furniture, furnishings, fixtures, etc., as of an apartment, automobile, etc. [FIT[1] + -ING[2], -ING[1]] —**fit′ting·ly,** *adv.* —**fit′ting·ness,** *n.*

—**Syn. 1.** fit, meet, right, decorous, seemly.

Fitz (fits), *n.* a boy's given name.

Fitz·ger·ald (fits jer′əld), *n.* **1. F(rancis) Scott (Key),** 1896–1940, U.S. novelist and short-story writer. **2. Ella,** born 1918, U.S. jazz singer. **3.** a town in central Georgia. 8781 (1960). **4.** a boy's given name.

Fitz·Ger·ald (fits jer′əld), *n.* **Edward,** 1809–83, English poet: translator of drama and poetry, esp. of Omar Khayyám.

FitzGer′ald contrac′tion, *Physics.* the hypothesis, postulated independently by both FitzGerald and Lorentz to explain the results of the Michelson-Morley experiment and later corroborated by Einstein's special theory of relativity, that a moving body exhibits a deformation in the direction of motion, the deformation being negligible for speeds considerably less than the speed of light. Also called **Fitz·Ger′ald-Lo′rentz contrac′tion** (fits jer′əld lôr′ents, -lôr′-), **Lorentz-FitzGerald contraction.** [named after G.F. *FitzGerald* (1851–1901), Irish physicist]

Fitz·hugh (fits hyo͞o′), *n.* a boy's given name.

Fitz·roy (fits roi′), *n.* **Augustus Henry, 3rd Duke of Graf·ton** (graf′tən, gräf′-), 1735–1811, British statesman: prime minister 1768–70.

Fitz·sim·mons (fit sim′ənz, fits-), *n.* **Robert Prometheus,** 1862–1917, English boxer: world heavyweight champion 1897–99.

Fiu·me (fyo͞o′me), *n.* former name of **Rijeka.**

five (fīv), *n.* **1.** a cardinal number, four plus one. **2.** a symbol for this number, as 5 or V. **3.** a set of this many persons or things. **4.** a playing card, die face, or half of a domino face with five pips. **5. take five,** *Informal.* to rest from what one is doing, esp. for five minutes. —*adj.* **6.** amounting to five in number. [ME; OE *fīf;* c. D *vijf,* G *fünf,* Icel *fimm,* Goth *fimf,* L *quinque,* Gk *pénte,* Skt *pañcha*]

five-and-ten (fīv′ən ten′), *n.* **1.** Also called **five′-and-ten′-cent store′** (fīv′ən ten′sent′), **five′-and-dime′** (fīv′ən dīm′), **dime store, ten-cent store.** a store offering a wide assortment of inexpensive items, formerly costing five or ten cents, for personal and household use. —*adj.* **2.** of, pertaining to, or characteristic of a five-and-ten.

five-by-five (fīv′bī fīv′), *adj.* *Slang.* short and fat.

Five′ Civ′ilized Na′tions, the collective name for the Cherokee, Creek, Choctaw, Chickasaw, and Seminole tribes of Indians who settled in the Indian Territory from 1830 to 1840. Also called **Five′ Civ′ilized Tribes′.**

Five′-El′ements School′ (fīv′el′ə mənts). See **Yin-Yang School.**

five-fin·ger (fīv′fing′gər), *n.* **1.** any of certain species of potentilla having leaves of five leaflets, as *Potentilla canadensis.* **2.** See **bird's-foot trefoil. 3.** the oxlip. **4.** See **Virginia creeper.**

five·fold (fīv′fōld′), *adj.* **1.** comprising five parts or members. **2.** five times as great or as much. —*adv.* **3.** in fivefold measure. [ME *fiffold,* OE *fīffeald.* See FIVE, -FOLD]

five-gait·ed (fīv′gā′tid), *adj.* *Manège.* noting an American saddle horse that has been trained to execute the rack and slow-gait in addition to the walk, trot, and canter, and that is used chiefly for showing. Cf. **three-gaited.**

five′ hun′dred, *Cards.* a variety of euchre in which a joker and widow are included, the object being to score 500 points first.

five′ hun′dred rum′my, *Cards.* a variety of rummy in which the winner is the first player to score 500 points. Also called **pinochle rummy.**

five-leg·ged (fīv′leg′id, -legd′), *adj.* *Informal.* (of a schooner) having five masts.

Five′ Na′tions, a confederacy of Iroquoian Indians: the Mohawks, Oneidas, Onondagas, Cayugas, and Senecas, and, after the 18th century, the Tuscarora.

five·pen·ny (fīv′pen′ē), *adj.* **1.** noting a nail 1¾ inches long. *Abbr.:* 5d **2.** worth five pence. [FIVE + -PENNY]

five′ percent′er (pər sen′tər), a person who aids companies in obtaining government contracts for a fee of five percent.

fiv·er (fī′vər), *n.* *Slang.* **1.** a five-dollar bill. **2.** *Brit.* a five-pound note. [FIVE + -ER[1]]

fives (fīvz), *n.* (*construed as sing.*) *Brit.* a game resembling handball, played on a court having a front wall and two side walls. [FIVE + -S[3]]

five′ sens′es, sense (def. 2).

five-spot (fīv′spot′), *n.* **1.** a playing card or the upward face of a die bearing five pips; a domino one half of which bears five pips. **2.** *Slang.* a five-dollar bill. **3.** a low, annual herb, *Nemophila maculata,* of western and central California, having lyre-shaped leaves and bell-shaped, white flowers with a purple spot at the base of each petal.

five-star (fīv′stär′), *adj.* **1.** having five stars to indicate rank or quality: *a five-star general; a five-star brandy.* **2.** of the highest quality, as a literary or dramatic work.

Five′ Towns′. See **the Potteries.**

five W's, who, what, when, where, and why: along with *how,* the essential questions about the subject of a news story that the lead is traditionally expected to answer.

Five′-Year Plan′ (fīv′yēr′), (*sometimes l.c.*) any plan for national economic or industrial development specifying goals to be reached within a period of five years, esp. such a plan, as in the Soviet Union and China, designed to bring about a rapid increase in industrial capacity, the development of natural resources, etc., by central planning and intensive utilization of capital goods and manpower.

fix (fiks), *v.*, **fixed** or **fixt, fix·ing,** *n.* —*v.t.* **1.** to make fast, firm, or stable. **2.** to place definitely and more or less permanently: *to fix a circus poster to a barn.* **3.** to settle definitely; determine: *to fix a price.* **4.** to direct (the eyes, the attention, etc.) steadily: *His eyes were fixed on the distant ship.* **5.** to attract and hold (the eye, the attention, etc.). **6.** to make set or rigid. **7.** to put into permanent form. **8.** to put or place (responsibility, blame, etc.) on a person. **9.** to assign or refer to a definite place, time, etc. **10.** to repair; mend. **11.** to put in order or in good condition; adjust or arrange. **12.** to provide or supply with (something needed or wanted): *How are you fixed for money?* **13.** *Informal.* to arrange matters with, or with respect to, esp. privately or dishonestly, so as to secure favorable action: *to fix a jury or a game.* **14.** to get (a meal); prepare (food): *What time shall I fix supper?* **15.** *Informal.* to put in a condition or position to make no further trouble. **16.** *Informal.* to get even with; get revenge upon. **17.** *Informal.* to castrate or spay (an animal, esp. a pet). **18.** *Chem.* **a.** to make stable in consistence or condition; reduce from fluidity or volatility to a more permanent state. **b.** to convert atmospheric nitrogen into a useful compound, as a nitrate fertilizer. **19.** *Photog.* to render (an image) permanent by removing the light-sensitive silver halides. **20.** *Microscopy.* to kill, make rigid, and preserve for microscopic study. —*v.i.* **21.** to become fixed. **22.** to become set; assume a rigid or solid form. **23.** to become stable or permanent. **24.** to settle down. **25.** *Dial.* to prepare; plan (usually fol. by an infinitive): *I was just fixing to call you. We're fixing to go to Colorado this summer.* **26. fix on** or **upon,** to decide on; determine: *We won't be able to fix on a location for the banquet until we know the number of guests.* **27. fix up,** *U.S. Informal.* **a.** to arrange for: *to fix up a date.* **b.** to provide with; furnish. **c.** to repair; renew. **d.** to smooth over; solve: *They weren't able to fix up their differences.* —*n.* **28.** *Informal.* a position from which it is difficult to escape; predicament. **29.** *Navig.* a charted position of a vessel or aircraft, determined by two or more bearings taken on landmarks, heavenly bodies, etc. **30.** the determining of the position of a ship, plane, etc., by mathematical, electronic, or other means: *The navigator took a fix on the sun and steered the ship due north.* **31.** *Slang.* **a.** an injection of heroin or other narcotic. **b.** the narcotic or amount of narcotic injected. [late ME *fixe(n)* < ML *fixā(re),* deriv. of L *fixus* fixed, ptp. of *fīgere* to fasten] —**fix′a·ble,** *adj.* —**fix′er,** *n.*

—**Syn. 1, 2.** fasten, secure, stabilize. FIX, ESTABLISH imply making firm or permanent. To FIX is to fasten in position securely or to make more or less permanent against change, esp. something already existing: *to fix a bayonet on a gun; fix a principle in one's mind.* To ESTABLISH is to make firm or permanent something (usually newly) originated, created, or ordained: *to establish a business, a claim to property.* **2.** set, plant, implant. **3.** establish, define. **11.** repair, mend, correct, amend. **28.** dilemma, plight, quandary.

—**Usage. 10.** In the sense of *repair,* FIX appears to have been used first in America, but there is evidence for its use in England as early as the beginning of the 19th century. Hence, no formal stigma attaches to such use, and those who persist in objecting to it for reasons of style are groundlessly prejudiced.

fix·ate (fik′sāt), *v.*, **-at·ed, -at·ing.** —*v.t.* **1.** to fix; make stable or stationary. —*v.i.* **2.** to become fixed. **3.** *Psychoanal.* to develop a fixation; suffer an arrest in one's emotional or sexual development. [< L *fix(us)* fixed, firm (see FIX) + -ATE[1]]

fix·a·tion (fik sā′shən), *n.* **1.** act of fixing; state of being fixed. **2.** *Chem.* **a.** reduction from a volatile or fluid to a stable or solid form. **b.** the process of converting atmospheric nitrogen into a useful compound, as a nitrate fertilizer. **3.** *Psychoanal.* a partial arrest of emotional and instinctual development at an early point in life, due to a severe traumatic experience or an overwhelming gratification. [ME *fixacion* < ML *fixātiōn-* (s. of *fixātiō*) a reduction to a fixed state. See FIX, -ATION]

fix·a·tive (fik′sə tiv), *adj.* **1.** serving to fix; making fixed or permanent. —*n.* Also, **fix·a·tif** (fik′sə tiv, -tēf′). **2.** a fixative substance, as a gummy liquid sprayed on a drawing to prevent blurring, or a solution for killing, hardening, and preserving material for microscopic study. **3.** a substance that retards evaporation, as in the manufacture of perfume. [FIX + -ATIVE]

fixed (fikst), *adj.* **1.** fastened, attached, or placed so as to be firm and not readily movable; firmly implanted; stationary; rigid. **2.** rendered stable or permanent, as color. **3.** set or intent upon something; steadily directed: *a fixed stare.* **4.** definitely and permanently placed: *fixed buoy; a fixed line of defense.* **5.** definite;

not fluctuating or varying: *a fixed purpose; a fixed time; fixed prices.* **6.** coming each year on the same calendar date: *Christmas is a fixed holiday, but Easter is not.* **7.** put in order. **8.** *Informal.* arranged with, or arranged, privately or dishonestly: *The fight was fixed.* **9.** *Chem.* **a.** (of an element) taken into a compound from its free state. **b.** nonvolatile, or not easily volatilized: *a fixed oil.* **10.** *Math.* (of a point) mapped to itself by a given function. Cf. **Brouwer fixed-point theorem.** [FIX + -ED²] —**fix·ed·ly** (fik′sid lē), *adv.* —**fix′ed·ness,** *n.*

fixed′ and flash′ing light′, *Navig.* a beacon having a steady light with intermittent flashes of a brighter light or one of a different color.

fixed′ as′set, any long-term asset, as a building, tract of land, or patent. Also called **capital asset.**

fixed′ cap′ital, capital goods, as machinery and tools, that are relatively durable and can be used repeatedly in the production of goods. Cf. **circulating capital.**

fixed′ charge′, **1.** an expense which cannot be modified. **2.** a periodic obligation, as taxes, interest on bonds, etc. **3. fixed charges,** such charges as depreciation, rent, interest, etc., arising out of the maintenance of fixed assets.

fixed′ cost′, a cost that does not vary with a change in the volume of business.

fixed′-do′ sys′tem (fikst′dō′), *Music.* a system of solmization in which the syllable *do* is always C, regardless of the key. Cf. **movable-do system.**

fixed′-fo′cus cam′era (fikst′fō′kəs), *Optics.* a camera with an unadjustable focal length and with a relatively large depth of field.

fixed′ ide′a, **1.** a persistent or obsessing idea, often delusional, from which a person cannot escape. **2.** *Psychiatry.* a delusional idea which dominates the mind in certain forms of insanity.

fixed-in·come (fikst′in′kum), *adj.* noting a person or thing gaining or yielding a more or less uniform rate of income.

fixed′ invest′ment trust′. See **unit trust.**

fixed′ liabil′ity, a liability, as a mortgage or debenture, which will not mature for a relatively long time, usually a year.

fixed′ oil′, *Chem.* a natural vegetable or animal oil that is nonvolatile, as lard oil, linseed oil, etc. Also called **fatty oil.**

fixed′ price′, a price established by a seller, by agreement or by authority, as the price to be charged invariably.

fixed′ sat′ellite, *Rocketry.* an earth satellite having a west-to-east equatorial orbit of 24 hours duration, which keeps the satellite over a particular point on the earth's surface.

fixed′ star′, *Astron.* any of the stars which apparently always retain the same position in respect to one another.

fixed′ trust′. See **unit trust.**

fix·ing (fik′sing), *n.* **1.** act of one who or that which fixes. **2.** Also, **fix·in's** (fik′sinz), **fix·ings** (fik′singz, -sinz). appropriate accompaniments; trimmings: *turkey with all the fixings.* [late ME; see FIX, -ING¹]

fix·i·ty (fik′si tē), *n., pl.* **-ties** for 2. **1.** state or quality of being fixed; stability; permanence. **2.** something fixed, stable, or permanent. [< NL *fixitās.* See FIX, -ITY]

fixt (fikst), *v.* a pt. and pp. of **fix.**

fix·ture (fiks′chər), *n.* **1.** something securely, and usually permanently, attached or appended, as to a house, apartment building, etc.: *the sink and other kitchen fixtures.* **2.** a person or thing long established in the same place or position. **3.** *Mach.* **a.** any of various devices for holding work in a machine tool, esp. one for machining in a straight line, as in a planer or milling machine. **b.** any of various devices for holding parts in certain positions during welding, assembly, etc. **4.** *Law.* a movable chattel, as a machine or heating plant, which, by reason of annexation to real property and adaptation to continuing use in connection with the realty, is considered a part of the realty. **5.** *Fox Hunting.* one of a series of meets scheduled by a hunt to take place at a time and location listed on a card (**fix′ture card′**) which is sent, usually once a month, to each member of a hunt. **6.** act of fixing. **7.** *Brit.* **a.** the date set for a sporting contest. **b.** the contest itself. **c.** a social or community event, as a festival, fair, etc. [var. of FIXURE, with *-t-* from MIXTURE] —**fix′ture·less,** *adj.*

fix·ure (fik′shər), *n. Archaic.* steadfastness; firmness. [< LL *fixūra.* See FIX, -URE]

Fi·zeau (fē zō′), *n.* **Ar·mande Hip·po·lyte Louis** (AR mäNd′ ē pô lēt′ lwē), 1819–96, French physicist.

fiz·gig (fiz′gig′), *n.* **1.** a frivolous, giddy, restless woman or girl. **2.** a kind of firework that makes a loud hissing sound. **3.** a kind of whirling toy that makes a whizzing noise. **4.** fishgig. [earlier *fisgig,* equiv. to *fis* (late ME *fise* term of abuse; akin to Icel *fīsa* to break wind) + *gig* (ME *gigge* girl; see GIGGLE)]

fizz (fiz), *v.i.* **1.** to make a hissing or sputtering sound; effervesce. —*n.* **2.** a hissing sound; effervescence. **3.** *U.S.* **a.** soda water or other effervescent water. **b.** an iced mixed drink made of liquor, lemon juice, sugar, and soda: *gin fizz.* **4.** *Brit. Informal.* champagne. [back formation from FIZZLE] —**fizz′er,** *n.*

fiz·zle (fiz′əl), *v.,* **-zled, -zling,** *n.* —*v.i.* **1.** to make a hissing or sputtering sound, esp. one that dies out weakly. **2.** *Informal.* to fail ignominiously after a good start (often fol. by *out*): *The reform movement fizzled out because of poor leadership.* —*n.* **3.** a fizzling, hissing, or sputtering **4.** *Informal.* a fiasco; a failure. [earlier *fysel* to break wind, freq of **fise* < Scand; cf. Icel *fīsa* to break wind, akin to FEIST]

fizz·wa·ter (fiz′wô′tər, -wot′ər), *n.* effervescent water; soda water. [FIZZ + WATER]

fizz·y (fiz′ē), *adj.,* **fizz·i·er, fizz·i·est.** bubbly; fizzing. [FIZZ + -Y¹]

fjeld (fyeld; *Norw.* fyel), *n.* a rocky, barren plateau of the Scandinavian peninsula. [< Norw; see FELL⁵]

fjord (fyôrd, fyōrd; *Norw.* fyōōR, fyōR), *n.* **1.** a long, narrow arm of the sea bordered by steep cliffs: usually formed by glacial erosion. **2.** (in Scandinavia) a bay. Also, **fiord.** [< Norw; see FIRTH]

Fl., **1.** Flanders. **2.** Flemish.

fl., **1.** florin. **2.** flourished. [< L *floruit*] **3.** fluid.

Fla., Florida.

flab·ber·gast (flab′ər gast′), *v.t. Informal.* to overcome with surprise and bewilderment; astound. [var. of *flabagast* (FLABB(Y) + AGHAST)]
—**Syn.** amaze, astonish, stagger, nonplus, confound; perplex, confuse, mystify.

flab·by (flab′ē), *adj.,* **-bi·er, -bi·est.** **1.** hanging loosely or limply, as flesh, muscles, etc.; flaccid. **2.** having such flesh. **3.** lacking firmness or determination, as character, persons, principles, utterances, etc.; feeble; weak. [alter. of late ME *flabband* (said of webs), equiv. to *flabb-* (< ?) + *-and* prp. ending; see -Y¹] —**flab′bi·ly,** *adv.* —**flab′bi·ness,** *n.*

fla·bel·late (flə bel′it, -āt), *adj. Bot., Zool.* fan-shaped. Also, **fla·bel·li·form** (flə bel′ə fôrm′). [< L *flābell(um)* small fan + -ATE¹]

flabelli-, a combining form of **flabellum:** *flabelliform.*

fla·bel·lum (flə bel′əm), *n., pl.* **-bel·la** (-bel′ə). **1.** a fan, esp. one used in religious ceremonies. **2.** a fan-shaped part. [< L: small fan, dim. of *flābra* breezes, equiv. to *flā(re)* (to) blow + *-bra,* pl. of *-brum* n. suffix of means]

flac·cid (flak′sid), *adj.* soft and limp; not firm; flabby: *flaccid limbs.* [< L *flaccid(us)* flabby, equiv. to *flacc(us)* flabby + *-idus* -ID⁴] —**flac·cid′i·ty, flac′cid·ness,** *n.* —**flac′cid·ly,** *adv.*

flack¹ (flak), *n. Slang.* **1.** See **press agent.** **2.** publicity. [?]

flack² (flak), *n.* flak. [< G; see FLAK]

flac·on (flak′ən; *Fr.* fla kôN′), *n., pl.* **flac·ons** (flak′ənz; *Fr.* fla kôN′). a small bottle or flask with a stopper. Cf. **flagon.** [< F; see FLAGON]

flag¹ (flag), *n., v.,* **flagged, flag·ging.** —*n.* **1.** a piece of cloth, varying in size, shape, color, and design, usually attached at one edge to a staff or cord, and used as the symbol of a nation, state, or organization, as a means of signaling, etc.; ensign; standard; banner; pennant. **2.** *Ornith.* the tuft of long feathers on the legs of falcons and most other hawks; the lengthened feathers on the crus or tibia. **3.** *Hunting.* the tail of a deer or of a setter dog. **4.** *Journalism.* **a.** the nameplate of a newspaper. **b.** masthead (def. 2). **c.** the name of a newspaper as printed on the editorial page. **5.** *Print.* a strip, as of cardboard, projecting from a column of type warning the printer of a change to be made. **6.** *Music.* hook (def. 10). **7.** *Motion Pictures, Television.* a small gobo. **8. strike the flag, a.** to relinquish command, as of a ship. **b.** to submit or surrender: *His financial situation is growing more precarious, but he's not ready to strike the flag.* Also, **strike one's flag.** —*v.t.* **9.** to place a flag or flags over or on; decorate with flags. **10.** to signal or warn (a person, automobile, etc.) with, or as with, a flag (sometimes fol. by *down*): *to flag a taxi; to flag down a passing car.* **11.** to communicate (information) by or as by a flag: *to flag a message to a nearby ship.* **12.** to decoy, as game, by waving a flag or the like to excite attention or curiosity. [? b. FLAP (n.) and FAG¹ (n.) in obs. sense flap] —**flag′ger,** *n.* —**flag′less,** *adj.*

flag² (flag), *n.* **1.** any of various plants with long, sword-shaped leaves, as the sweet flag. **2.** See **blue flag.** **3.** the long, slender leaf of such a plant or of a cereal. [ME *flagge*]

flag³ (flag), *v.i.,* **flagged, flag·ging.** **1.** to hang loosely or limply; droop. **2.** to fall off in vigor, energy, activity, interest, etc.: *Public enthusiasm flagged when the team kept losing.* [? b. of FLAP (v.) and FAG¹ (v.) in obs. sense droop. See FLAG¹]

flag⁴ (flag), *n., v.,* **flagged, flag·ging.** —*n.* **1.** flagstone. **2. flags,** Also, **flagging.** a walk, terrace, etc., paved with such slabs. —*v.t.* **3.** to pave with flagstones. [late ME *flagge* piece of sod, OE *flæcg* poultice, plaster; akin to Icel *flaga* slab] —**flag′ger,** *n.* —**flag′less,** *adj.*

flag′ day′, (*sometimes cap.*) *Brit.* See **tag day.**

Flag′ Day′, June 14, the anniversary of the day (June 14, 1777) when Congress adopted the Stars and Stripes as the national emblem of the United States.

fla·gel·la (flə jel′ə), *n.* pl. of **flagellum.**

flag·el·lant (flaj′ə lənt, flə jel′ənt), *n.* **1.** a person who flagellates. **2.** a person who flagellates or scourges himself for religious discipline. **3.** (*often cap.*) one of a medieval European sect of fanatics who practiced scourging in public. —*adj.* **4.** flagellating. **5.** severely criticizing: *a flagellant attack on the opposition party.* [< L *flagellant-* (s. of *flagellāns*) whipping, prp. of *flagellāre.* See FLAGELLUM, -ANT] —**flag′el·lant·ism,** *n.*

Flag·el·la·ta (flaj′ə lā′tə), *n.* *Mastigophora.* [< NL, special use of neut. pl. of L *flagellātus* FLAGELLATE]

flag·el·late (*v.* flaj′ə lāt′; *adj., n.* flaj′ə lit, -lāt′), *v.,* **-lat·ed, -lat·ing,** *adj., n.* —*v.t.* **1.** to whip; scourge; flog; lash. —*adj.* **2.** Also, **flag′el·lat′ed.** *Biol.* having flagella. **3.** *Bot.* producing filiform runners or runnerlike branches, as the strawberry. **4.** pertaining to or caused by flagellates. —*n.* **5.** any protozoan of the class *Mastigophora* (*Flagellata*), having one or more flagella. [< L *flagellāt(us)* whipped, ptp. of *flagellāre.* See FLAGELLUM, -ATE¹] —**flag′el·la′tion,** *n.* —**flag′el·la′tor,** *n.* —**flag·el·la·to·ry** (flaj′ə lə tôr′ē, -tōr′ē), *adj.*

F

Flagellate, Genus *Euglena* F, Flagellum

fla·gel·li·form (flə jel′ə fôrm′), *adj. Biol.* long, slender, and flexible, like the lash of a whip. [< L *flagell(um)* a whip, scourge + -I- + -FORM]

fla·gel·lum (flə jel′əm), *n., pl.* **-gel·la** (-jel′ə), **-gel·lums.** **1.** *Biol.* a long, lashlike appendage serving as an organ of locomotion in certain reproductive bodies, bacteria, protozoa, etc. **2.** *Bot.* a runner. **3.** Also called **clavola.** *Entomol.* (in an antenna) the whiplike portion above the basal joints. **4.** a whip or lash. [< L: a little whip, dim. of *flagrum* a whip, scourge]

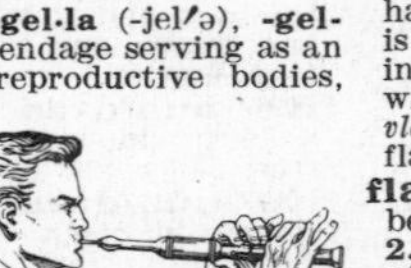
Flageolet

flag·eo·let (flaj′ə let′, -lā′), *n.* **1.** a small end-blown flute with four finger holes in front and two in the rear. **2.** any fipple flute. [< F, sp. var. of OF *flajolet,* equiv. to *flajol* flute (< VL **flabeolum,* deriv. of L *flāre* to blow) + *-et* -ET]

fla·geo·let (fla zhō le′), *n. French.* a green baby lima bean.

flag·fish (flag′fish′), *n., pl.* (*esp. collectively*) **-fish,** (*esp. referring to two or more kinds or species*) **-fish·es.** **1.** Also called **American flagfish.** a cyprinodont fish, *Jordanella floridae,* found in the swamps and streams of Florida, blue-brown above with red stripes on its whitish sides, often kept in aquariums. **2.** any of several other brightly colored fishes. [FLAG¹ + FISH]

Flagg (flag), *n.* **James Montgomery,** 1877–1960, U.S. painter and illustrator.

flag·ging¹ (flag′ing), *adj.* **1.** weak, fatigued, or drooping. **2.** showing a loss of energy, determination, etc.; weakening; failing: *We made an effort to bolster his flagging spirits.* [FLAG³ + -ING²] —**flag′ging·ly,** *adv.*

flag·ging² (flag′ing), *n.* **1.** flagstones collectively. **2.** a pavement of flagstones; flags. [FLAG⁴ + -ING¹]

flag′ging i′ron, (in coopering) a forklike tool for holding open a joint of a barrel being calked.

flag·gy¹ (flag′ē), *adj.,* **-gi·er, -gi·est.** flagging; drooping; limp. [FLAG³ + -Y¹]

flag·gy² (flag′ē), *adj.* consisting of or resembling flags or flagstone; laminate. [FLAG⁴ + -Y¹]

flag·gy³ (flag′ē), *adj.* abounding in, consisting of, or resembling flag plants. [ME *flaggi.* See FLAG², -Y¹]

fla·gi·tious (flə jish′əs), *adj.* **1.** shamefully wicked, as persons, actions, times, etc. **2.** heinous or flagrant, as a crime or crimes; infamous. [ME *flagicious* < L *flāgitiōs(us),* equiv. to *flāgiti(um)* shame, scandal + *-ōsus* -OUS] —**fla·gi′tious·ly,** *adv.* —**fla·gi′tious·ness,** *n.*
—**Syn. 1.** profligate, corrupt, depraved, dissolute, villainous. **2.** nefarious, vicious, iniquitous, atrocious.

flag·man (flag′mən), *n., pl.* **-men.** **1.** a person who has charge of or carries a flag. **2.** a person who signals with a flag or lantern, as at a railroad crossing. [FLAG¹ + MAN¹]

flag′ of conven′ience, the national flag of a nation with which merchant ships owned by persons of other nations are registered in order to effect a saving on taxes, wages, etc.

flag′ of′ficer, **1.** a naval officer above the rank of captain, as a fleet admiral, admiral, vice-admiral, rear admiral, or commodore, who is entitled to display a flag indicating his rank. **2.** (formerly) an officer in command of a fleet, squadron, or group of ships.

flag′ of truce′, *Mil.* a white flag displayed as an invitation to the enemy to confer, or carried as a sign of peaceful intention by one sent to deal with the enemy.

flag·on (flag′ən), *n.* **1.** a large bottle for wine, liquors, etc. **2.** a container for holding liquids, as for use at table, esp. one with a handle, a spout, and usually a cover. [late ME, var. of *flakon* < MF *fla(s)con* < LL *flascōn-* (s. of *flascō*) FLASK]

flag·pole (flag′pōl′), *n.* a staff or pole on which a flag is displayed. Also called **flagstaff.** [FLAG¹ + POLE¹]

flag′ rank′, naval rank above that of captain.

fla·grant (flā′grənt), *adj.* **1.** outrageously glaring, noticeable, or evident: *a flagrant error.* **2.** notorious; scandalous: *a flagrant crime; a flagrant offender.* **3.** *Archaic.* blazing, burning, or glowing. [late ME < L *flagrant-* (s. of *flagrāns*) burning, prp. of *flagrāre;* see -ANT] —**fla′gran·cy, fla′grance, fla′grant·ness,** *n.* —**fla′grant·ly,** *adv.*
—**Syn. 2.** disgraceful, shocking.

fla·gran·te de·lic·to (flə gran′tē di lik′tō), *Law.* while the crime is, or was, being committed. [< L: lit., while the crime is blazing]

flag′ salute′, a salute, made between a vessel and another vessel or the shore, in which the ensigns of both are lowered and raised.

flag′ seat′, *Furniture.* a seat woven from reeds, rushes, or iris leaves.

flag·ship (flag′ship′), *n.* **1.** a ship bearing the flag officer or the commander of a fleet, squadron, or the like, and displaying his flag. **2.** the main vessel of a shipping line. **3.** any of the best or largest ships or airplanes operated by a passenger line. [FLAG¹ + SHIP]

flag′ smut′, *Plant Pathol.* a disease of cereals and other grasses, characterized by stripes of black spores on the affected leaves and stems which later dry up and become shredded, caused by several smut fungi of the genus *Urocystis.*

Flag·stad (flag′stad; *Norw.* fläg′stä), *n.* **Kir·sten Ma·rie** (kûr′stən mə rē′; *Norw.* KHish′tən mä Rē′ə, KHir′stən), 1895–1962, Norwegian operatic soprano.

flag·staff (flag′staf′, -stäf′), *n., pl.* **-staves, -staffs.** flagpole. [FLAG¹ + STAFF¹]

Flag·staff (flag′staf′, -stäf′), *n.* a city in central Arizona. 18,214 (1960). ab. 6900 ft. high.

flag′ sta′tion, a railroad station where trains stop only when a flag or other signal is displayed or when passengers are to be discharged. Also called **flag′ stop′.**

flag·stone (flag′stōn′), *n.* **1.** Also called **flag.** a flat stone slab used esp. for paving. **2. flagstones,** a walk, terrace, etc., paved with flagging. **3.** rock, as sandstone or shale, suitable for splitting into flagstones. [FLAG⁴ + STONE]

flag-wav·ing (flag′wā′ving), *n.* an ostentatiously emotional display of patriotism or factionalism.

Fla·her·ty (flä′ər tē, flä′-), *n.* **Robert Joseph,** 1884–1951, U.S. pioneer in the production of documentary motion pictures.

flail (flāl), *n.* **1.** an instrument for threshing grain by hand, consisting of a staff or handle to one end of which is attached a freely swinging stick or bar. **2.** a similar instrument used as a weapon of war. —*v.t.* **3.** to strike with or as if with a flail. [ME *fleil,* OE **flegel;* c. D *vlegel,* G *Flegel* < WGmc **flagil-* < LL *flagell(um)* flail, L: whip, scourge. See FLAGELLUM]

flair (flâr), *n.* **1.** a natural talent, aptitude, or ability; bent; knack: *a flair for dressing smartly at little cost.* **2.** smartness of style, manner, etc.: *Their window display has absolutely no flair at all.* **3.** keen perception or discernment. **4.** *Hunting.* scent; sense of smell. [< F, OF: scent, back formation from *flairier* to reek << LL *flagrāre,* dissimilated var. of L *frāgrāre.* See FRAGRANT]

flak (flak), *n.* antiaircraft fire, esp. as experienced by the crews of combat airplanes at which the fire is directed. Also, **flack.** [< G *Fl(ieger)-a(bwehr)-k(anone)* antiaircraft gun, equiv. to *Flieger* aircraft (lit., flyer) + *Abwehr* defense + *Kanone* cannon]

flake[1] (flāk), *n.*, *v.*, **flaked, flak·ing.** —*n.* **1.** a small, flat, thin piece, esp. one that has been or become detached from a larger piece or mass: *flakes of old paint.* **2.** any small piece or mass: *a flake of cloud.* **3.** a stratum or layer. —*v.i.* **4.** to peel off or separate in flakes. **5.** to fall in flakes, as snow. —*v.t.* **6.** to remove in flakes. **7.** to break flakes or chips from; break into flakes: *to flake fish.* **8.** to cover with or as with flakes. **9.** to form into flakes. [ME; akin to OE *flac-* in *flacor* flying (said of arrows), Icel *flakka* to rove, wander, MD *vlacken* to flutter] —**flake′less,** *adj.* —**flak′er,** *n.*

flake[2] (flāk), *n.* a frame, as for drying fish. [ME *flake, fleke* < Scand; cf. Icel *flaki, fleki* hurdle]

flake[3] (flāk), *n.*, *v.*, **flaked, flak·ing.** *Naut.* —*n.* **1.** fake[2] (defs. 1, 2). —*v.t.* **2.** fake[2]. **3.** to lower (a fore-and-aft sail) so as to drape the sail equally on both sides over its boom. [var. of FAKE[2]]

flake·board (flāk′bōrd′, -bôrd′), *n.* a form of particle board. [FLAKE[1] + BOARD]

flake·let (flāk′lit), *n.* a small flake, as of snow. [FLAKE[1] + -LET]

flake′ out′, *Slang.* to fall asleep, esp. from complete exhaustion; take a nap: *After the picnic the kids flaked out as soon as they got in the car.*

flake′ white′. See **lead white.**

flak′ jack′et, *U.S. Air Force.* an armored garment made of steel plates covered by a padded fabric, designed to protect vital parts of the body from shrapnel. Also called **flak′ vest′.**

flak′ ship′, a ship equipped with antiaircraft guns.

flak′ suit′, *U.S. Air Force.* a suit of two or more padded armored garments designed to protect the body from shrapnel.

flak′ train′, a railroad train equipped with antiaircraft guns.

flak·y (flā′kē), *adj.*, **flak·i·er, flak·i·est. 1.** of or like flakes. **2.** lying or cleaving off in flakes or layers. [FLAKE[1] + -Y[1]] —**flak′i·ly,** *adv.* —**flak′i·ness,** *n.*

flam[1] (flam), *n.*, *v.*, **flammed, flam·ming.** *Informal.* —*n.* **1.** a falsehood. **2.** a deception or trick. —*v.t.*, *v.i.* **3.** to deceive; delude; cheat. [short for FLIM-FLAM]

flam[2] (flam), *n.* a drumbeat consisting of two notes in quick succession, with the accent on the second. [imit.]

flam[3] (flam), *n.* *Naut.* the flare of the bow of a vessel, esp. the upper part approaching most nearly the horizontal. [appar alter. of dial. *flan* to widen outwards < ? Cf. FLANGE]

flam·bé (flām bā′; *Fr.* flȧN bā′), *adj.* **1.** Also, **flam·béed** (flām bād′). (of food) served in flaming liquor, esp. brandy: *crêpes suzettes flambé.* **2.** *Ceram.* **a.** (of a glaze) dense and streaked with contrasting colors, usually red and blue. **b.** (of a ceramic object) covered with a flambé glaze. [< F, ptp. of *flamber* to flame. See FLAMBEAU]

flam·beau (flam′bō), *n.*, *pl.* **-beaux** (-bōz), **-beaus. 1.** a flaming torch. **2.** a torch for use at night in illuminations, processions, etc. **3.** a large, decorated candlestick, as of bronze. **4.** an ornament having the form of a flaming torch. [< F: torch, irreg. deriv. of OF *flambe* FLAME]

flambé′ glaze′, (in Chinese ceramics) a variegated glaze produced by controlled irregularities of firing.

flam·boy·ant (flam boi′ənt), *adj.* **1.** strikingly bold or brilliant; showy: *flamboyant colors.* **2.** conspicuously dashing and colorful: *the flamboyant idol of international society.* **3.** florid; ornate; elaborately styled: *flamboyant speeches.* **4.** *Archit.* **a.** having the form of an ogee, as a bar of tracery. **b.** noting or pertaining to French Gothic architecture of the late 15th and early and middle 16th centuries, characterized by the use of flamboyant tracery, intricacy of détailing, virtuosity of workmanship, and loss of overall coherence. —*n.* **5.** See **royal poinciana.** [< F, prp. of *flamboyer* to flame, flair, deriv. of OF *flambe* FLAME; see -ANT] —**flam·boy′ance, flam·boy′an·cy,** *n.* —**flam·boy′ant·ly,** *adv.*

flame (flām), *n.*, *v.*, **flamed, flam·ing.** —*n.* **1.** burning gas or vapor, as from wood, coal, etc., which is undergoing combustion; a portion of ignited gas or vapor. **2.** Often, **flames.** state or condition of blazing combustion: *to burst into flames.* **3.** any flamelike condition; glow; inflamed condition. **4.** brilliant light; scintillating luster. **5.** bright coloring; a streak or patch of color. **6.** See **flame color. 7.** intense ardor, zeal, or passion. **8.** *Informal.* an object of the passion of love; sweetheart: *He's taking out his new flame tonight.* —*v.i.* **9.** to burn with a flame or flames; burst into flames; blaze. **10.** to glow like flame; shine brilliantly; flash. **11.** to burn as with flame, as passion; break into open anger, indignation, etc. (often fol. by *out* or *up*). —*v.t.* **12.** to subject to the action of flame or fire. [ME *flaume* < AF, var. of *flaumbe,* c. OF *flambe,* earlier *flamble* < L *flammula,* dim. of *flamma* flame; see -ULE] —**flam′er,** *n.* —**flame′less,** *adj.* —**flame′like′,** *adj.*
—**Syn. 1.** fire. FLAME, BLAZE, CONFLAGRATION refer to the light and heat given off by combustion. FLAME is the common word, referring to a combustion of any size: *the light of a match flame.* BLAZE usually denotes a quick, hot, bright, and comparatively large flame: *The fire burst into a blaze.* CONFLAGRATION refers to destructive flames which spread over a considerable area: *A conflagration destroyed Chicago.* **7.** fervor, warmth, enthusiasm. **9.** flare.

flame′ azal′ea, an azalea, *Azalea calendulacea,* of the eastern U.S., having yellow, orange, or scarlet flowers.

flame′ cell′, *Zool.* one of the hollow cells terminating the branches of the excretory tubules of certain lower invertebrates, containing a tuft of continuously moving cilia.

flame′ col′or, bright reddish-orange. Also called **flame.** —**flame′-col′ored,** *adj.*

flame·fish (flām′fish′), *n.*, *pl.* **-fish·es,** (*esp. collectively*) **-fish.** a cardinalfish, *Apogon maculatus,* found along the Atlantic coast from Florida to Brazil. [FLAME + FISH]

flame′-fu′sion proc′ess (flām′fyōō′zhən). See **Verneuil process.**

flame·hold·er (flām′hōl′dər), *n.* *Aeron.* a device in certain jet engines to facilitate the efficient mixing of fuel and air and prevent flame-outs. Also, **flame′ hold′er.** [FLAME + HOLDER]

fla·men (flā′mən, -men), *n.*, *pl.* **fla·mens, fla·mi·nes** (flam′ə nēz′). (in ancient Rome) a priest devoted to the service of one deity. [< L (? earlier **flădmen*; akin to OE *blōtan* to sacrifice); r. ME *flamin* < L *flāmin-* (s. of *flāmen*)]

fla·men·co (flä meng′kō), *adj.*, *n.*, *pl.* **-cos.** —*adj.* **1.** of or like a gypsy, esp. like the music and dances of the Andalusian gypsies: *flamenco rhythms.* —*n.* **2.** a style of dancing, characteristic of the Andalusian gypsies, that is strongly rhythmic and involves vigorous actions, such as clapping the hands and stamping the feet. **3.** *Music.* **a.** a style of instrumental or vocal music originating in southern Spain and typically of an intensely rhythmic, improvisatory character. **b.** music in this style performed by itself or as an accompaniment to flamenco dancing. [< Sp: gypsy like, orig. Fleming. See FLAMINGO]

flame-of-the-woods (flām′əv thə wōōdz′), *n.*, *pl.* **flames-of-the-woods.** an evergreen shrub, *Ixora coccinea,* of the East Indies, having red flowers in dense clusters. Also called **jungle geranium.**

flame-out (flām′out′), *n.* the failure of a jet engine due to an interruption of the fuel supply or to faulty combustion. Also, **flame′out′.** Also called **blowout.** [n. use of v. phrase *flame out*]

flame·proof (flām′prōōf′), *adj.* resisting the effect of flames; not readily ignited or burned by flames. [FLAME + -PROOF]

flame′ stitch′, an ornamental stitch, used on bedspreads, upholstery fabrics, and the like, producing rows of ogees in various colors.

Flame stitch

flame·throw·er (flām′thrō′ər), *n.* *Mil.* a weapon, either mounted or portable, that squirts ignited incendiary fuel for some distance. [FLAME + THROWER]

flame-tree (flām′trē′), *n.* a tree, *Brachychiton acerifolium,* of Australia, having brilliant scarlet flowers and smooth, black fruit, grown as an ornamental.

Flamingo, *Phoenicopterus ruber* (Height 5 ft.; length 4 ft.)

flam·ing (flā′ming), *adj.* **1.** emitting flames; blazing; fiery. **2.** like a flame in brilliance, heat, or shape. **3.** intensely ardent or passionate: *flaming youth.* [ME *flammande.* See FLAME, -ING[2]] —**flam′ing·ly,** *adv.*

fla·min·go (flə ming′gō), *n.*, *pl.* **-gos, -goes.** any of several aquatic birds of the family *Phoenicopteridae,* having very long legs and neck, webbed feet, a bill bent downward at the tip, and pinkish to scarlet plumage. [< Pg *flamengo* (c. Sp *flamenco*), lit., Fleming < MD *Vlaming;* name assoc. with *flama* flame and so with bird from its color]

fla·min·go-flow·er (flə ming′gō flou′ər), *n.* a plant, *Anthurium scherzerianum,* of Central America, having wide, leathery, green leaves and red, yellow, white, or rose-colored flowers, grown as an ornamental.

Fla·min′i·an Way′ (flə min′ē ən), an ancient Roman road extending N from Rome to what is now Rimini. 215 mi. long.

Fla·min·i·us (flə min′ē əs), *n.* **Ga·ius** (gā′əs), died 217 B.C., Roman statesman and general who was defeated by Hannibal.

flam·ma·ble (flam′ə bəl), *adj.* easily set on fire; combustible; inflammable. [< L *flammā(re)* (to) set on fire + -BLE] —**flam′ma·bil′i·ty,** *n.*

Flam·ma·rion (flȧ mȧ ryôN′ *for 1;* flə mâr′ē on *for 2*), *n.* **1. (Ni·co·las) Ca·mille** (nē kô lä′ kȧ mē′yə), 1842–1925, French astronomer and author. **2.** a walled plain in the third quadrant of the face of the moon: about 50 miles in diameter.

Flam·steed (flam′stēd), *n.* **1. John,** 1646–1719, English astronomer. **2.** a crater in the third quadrant of the face of the moon: about 9 miles in diameter.

flam·y (flā′mē), *adj.*, **flam·i·er, flam·i·est.** of or like flame. [FLAME + -Y[1]]

flan (flan, flän; *for 1 also Fr.* flȧN; *for 2 also Sp.* flän), *n.*, *pl.* **flans** (flanz, flänz; *for 1 also Fr.* flȧN); *Sp.* **fla·nes** (flä′nes) for 2. **1.** an open, tartlike pastry, the shell of which is baked in a bottomless band of metal (**flan ring**) on a baking sheet, removed from the ring and filled with custard, cream, fruit, etc. **2.** (in Spanish cookery) a sweetened egg custard. **3.** a piece of metal shaped ready to form a coin, but not yet stamped by the die. **4.** the metal of which a coin is made, as distinct from its design. [< F; OF *flaon* < LL *fladōn-,* s. of *fladō* < OHG: flat cake, G *Fladen*]

Flan·a·gan (flan′ə gən), *n.* **Edward Joseph** ("*Father Flanagan*"), 1886–1948, U.S. Roman Catholic priest, born in Ireland: founder of *Boys Town.*

flanch (flanch), *n.* *Heraldry.* a charge, usually one of a pair, formed by an inwardly curved arc extending from the upper corner of one side of an escutcheon to the base of the same side. Also, **flanche, flaunch, flaunche.** [? < MF *flanche.* See FLANK]

flan·chard (flang′kərd), *n.* *Armor.* a piece for the middle of one side of a horse, between the peytral and the crupper. Also, **flan′card.** [late ME *flancard* < MF. See FLANK, -ARD]

Flan·ders (flan′dərz), *n.* a medieval country in W Europe, extending along the North Sea from the Strait of Dover to the Schledt River: the corresponding modern regions include the provinces of East Flanders and West Flanders in W Belgium, and the adjacent parts of N France and SW Netherlands.

flâ·ne·rie (flänə rē′), *n.* *French.* idleness; dawdling.

flâ·neur (flä nœr′), *n.*, *pl.* **-neurs** (-nœr′). *French.* idler; dawdler; loafer.

flange (flanj), *n.*, *v.*, **flanged, flang·ing.** —*n.* **1.** a projecting rim, collar, or ring on a shaft, pipe, machine housing, etc., cast or formed to give additional strength, stiffness, or supporting area, or to provide a place for the attachment of other objects. **2.** a broad ridge or pair of ridges projecting from the edge of a rolled metal shape generally at right angles, in order to strengthen or stiffen it. **3.** a ring or collar, usually provided with holes for bolts, and screwed or welded over the end of a tube or pipe to permit other objects to be attached to it. **4.** (in plumbing) a plate or flat ring bolted to the flange at the end of a length of pipe to close the end or to connect it with the flange of another such length: *blind flange; spectacle flange.* —*v.i.* **5.** to project like, or take the form of, a flange. [late ME *flaunche* side charge (on shield face) < MF *flanche,* fem. of *flanc* FLANK] —**flange′less,** *adj.* —**flang′er,** *n.*

Flanges
A, Flanges on consecting pipe ends; B, Flanges on I beam; C, Flange on foot of rail

flange′ plate′, *Building Trades.* See **cover plate.**

flange·way (flanj′wā′), *n.* *Railroads.* an opening, parallel to a rail, made through platforms, pavements, track structures, etc., to permit passage of wheel flanges. [FLANGE + WAY]

flank (flangk), *n.* **1.** the side of an animal or a man between the ribs and hip. **2.** the thin piece of flesh constituting this part. **3.** a slice of meat from the flank. **4.** the side of anything, as of a building. **5.** *Mil., Navy.* the extreme right or left side of an army or fleet, or a subdivision of an army or fleet. **6.** *Fort.* **a.** the right or left side of a work or fortification. **b.** the part of a bastion that extends from the curtain to the face and protects the curtain and the opposite face. See diag. under **bastion. 7.** *Mach.* (on a screw thread or the like) either of the two vertical inclined surfaces between the crest and the root. —*v.t.* **8.** to stand or be placed or posted at the flank or side of. **9.** to defend or guard at the flank. **10.** to pass around or turn the flank of. —*v.i.* **11.** to occupy a position at the flank or side. **12.** to present the flank or side. [ME; OE *flanc* < ML *flanc(us)* side < Gmc; cf. OHG *hlanca* loin]

flank·er (flang′kər), *n.* **1.** one who or that which flanks. **2.** *Mil.* one of a body of soldiers employed on the flank of an army to guard a line of march. **3.** *Fort.* a fortification projecting so as to defend another work or to command the flank of an assailing body. **4.** *Football.* **a.** an offensive end who lines up some distance outside of a tackle. **b.** Also called **flank′er back′.** an offensive back who lines up outside of an end. [FLANK + -ER[1]]

flank′ speed′, the full speed of a ship.

flan·nel (flan′əl), *n.*, *v.*, **-neled, -nel·ing** or (*esp. Brit.*), **-nelled, -nel·ling.** —*n.* **1.** a warm, soft, napped fabric of wool or cotton or blends of wool and cotton, wool and rayon, or of cotton warp with wool filling. **2. flannels, a.** an outer garment, esp. trousers, made of flannel. **b.** woolen undergarments. —*v.t.* **3.** to cover or clothe with flannel. **4.** to rub with flannel. [ME *flaunneol,* dissimilated var. of *flanyn* garment for penitents < Welsh; cf. Welsh *gwlanen* a flannel, equiv. to *gwlân* wool (akin to L *lāna*) + *-en* piece]

flan·nel·board (flan′əl bōrd′, -bôrd′), *n.* a flannel-covered surface to which other flannel pieces, as letters of the alphabet, numbers, etc., adhere merely by contact, used mainly in elementary schools as an audio-visual aid. [FLANNEL + BOARD]

flan′nel cake′, *Chiefly Dial.* griddlecake; pancake.

flan·nel·et (flan′əlet′), *n.* a cotton fabric, plain or printed, napped on one side. Also, **flan′nel·ette′.** [FLANNEL + -ET]

flan·nel·leaf (flan′əl lēf′), *n.*, *pl.* **-leaves.** mullein (def. 1). [FLANNEL + LEAF]

flan·nel·ly (flan′əlē), *adj.* **1.** made of or resembling flannel. **2.** thick or blurred, as speech. [FLANNEL + -Y[1]]

flan·nel·mouth (flan′əl mouth′), *n.*, *pl.* **-mouths** (-mouthz′). *Disparaging.* **1.** a person whose speech is thick, as due to a brogue. **2.** a person whose speech is smoothly deceptive. [FLANNEL + MOUTH]

flan·nel·mouthed (flan′əl mouthd′, -moutht′), *adj.* *Disparaging.* **1.** talking thickly, as with a brogue. **2.** characterized by deceptive or shifty speech. [FLANNEL + MOUTH + -ED[3]]

flan′nelmouth suck′er, *Ichthyol.* a sucker, *Catostomus latipinnis,* found in the Colorado River region.

flan′nel plant′, the mullein, *Verbascum Thapsus.*

flan·ning (flan′ing), *n.* (in masonry) the splay of a sconcheon. [dial. *flan* to splay + -ING[1]]

flan′ ring′. See under **flan** (def. 1).

flap (flap), *v.*, **flapped, flap·ping,** *n.* —*v.i.* **1.** to swing or sway about loosely, esp. with noise: *A loose shutter flapped outside the window.* **2.** to move up and down, as wings; flap the wings, or make similar movements. **3.** to strike a blow with something broad and flexible. —*v.t.* **4.** to move (wings, arms, etc.) up and down. **5.** to cause to swing or sway loosely, esp. with noise. **6.** to strike with something broad and flexible. **7.** *Informal.* to toss, fold, shut, etc., smartly, roughly, or noisily. **8.** *Phonetics.* to pronounce (a sound) with articulation resembling that of a flap: *The British often flap their r's.* —*n.* **9.** a flapping motion. **10.** the noise produced by something that flaps. **11.** a blow given with something broad and flexible. **12.** something broad and flexible, or flat and thin, that hangs loosely, attached at one side only. **13.** one leaf of a folding door, shutter, or the like. **14. a.** Also called **backflap hinge, flap′ hinge′,** a hinge having a strap or plate for screwing to the face of a door, shutter, or the like. **b.** one leaf of a hinge. **15.** *Surg.* a portion of skin or flesh that is partially separated from the body and may subsequently be transposed by grafting. **16.** *Aeron.* a movable surface used for increasing the lift or drag of an airplane. **17.** one of the two ends of a book jacket that are folded around the covers. **18.** *Slang.* **a.** a state of nervous excitement. **b.** an emergency situation. **19.**

Phonet. **a.** a rapid flip of the tongue tip against the upper teeth or alveolar ridge, as in the *r*-sound in a common British pronunciation of *very*, or the *t*-sound in the common American pronunciation of *water*. **b.** a trill. **c.** a flipping out of the lower lip from a position of pressure against the upper teeth so as to produce an audible pop, as in emphatic utterances containing *f*-sounds or *v*-sounds. [ME *flappe* a blow, slap, *flappe(n)* (to) hit, slap; cf. D *flap, flappen*] —**flap′less,** *adj.*

flap·doo·dle (flap′do͞od′əl), *n. Informal.* nonsense; bosh. [?]

flap′ door′, **1.** Also called **falling door.** a door hinged at the bottom so as to fall downward and outward. **2.** a door placed horizontally or on a shallow incline, as an exterior cellar door.

flap·drag·on (flap′drag′ən), *n.* **1.** an old game in which the players snatch raisins, plums, etc., out of burning brandy, and eat them. **2.** the object so caught and eaten. [FLAP + DRAGON]

flap·er·on (flap′ə ron′), *n. Aeron.* a control surface functioning both as a flap and as an aileron. [FLAP + (AIL)ERON]

flap·jack (flap′jak′), *n.* griddlecake. [FLAP + JACK[1]]

flap·per (flap′ər), *n.* **1.** something broad and flat for striking with, or for making a noise by striking. **2.** a broad, flat, hinged or hanging piece; flap. **3.** a young bird just learning to fly. **4.** a young woman, esp. one who, during the decade following World War I, behaved in a manner free from traditional social or moral restraints. **5.** *Slang.* the hand. [FLAP + -ER[1]] —**flap′per·dom,** *n.* —**flap′per·ish,** *adj.* —**flap′per·ism,** *n.*

flap·py (flap′ē), *adj.,* **-pi·er, -pi·est.** slack or loose, so as to flap readily. [FLAP + -Y[1]]

flaps (flaps), *n.* (*construed as sing.*) *Vet. Pathol.* swelling of the lips of a horse. [FLAP (n.) + -S[3]]

flap′ valve′. See **clack valve.**

flare (flâr), *v.,* **flared, flar·ing,** *n.* —*v.i.* **1.** to burn with an unsteady, swaying flame, as a torch or candle in the wind. **2.** to blaze with a sudden burst of flame (often fol. by *up*): *The fire flared up as the paper caught on.* **3.** to start up or burst out in sudden, fierce activity, passion, etc. (sometimes fol. by *up* or *out*): *His anger flared when his motives were questioned.* **4.** to shine or glow. **5.** to spread gradually outward, as the end of a trumpet, the bottom of a wide skirt, the sides of a ship, etc. —*v.t.* **6.** to cause (a candle, torch, etc.) to burn with a swaying flame. **7.** to display conspicuously or ostentatiously. **8.** to signal by flares of fire or light. **9.** to cause (something) to spread gradually outward in form. **10.** *Metall.* to heat (a high-zinc brass) to such a high temperature that the zinc vapors begin to burn. **11. flare out** or **up,** *Informal.* to vent one's anger; become suddenly enraged: *He flared out at us for no apparent reason. She flares up easily.* —*n.* **12.** a flaring or swaying flame or light, as of torches in the wind. **13.** a sudden blaze or burst of flame. **14.** a bright blaze of fire or light used as a signal, a means of illumination or guidance, etc. **15.** a device or substance used to produce such a blaze of fire or light. **16.** a sudden burst, as of zeal or of temper. **17.** a gradual spread outward in form; outward curvature: *the flare of a skirt.* **18.** something that spreads out. **19.** *Optics.* unwanted light reaching the image plane of an optical instrument, resulting from extraneous reflections, scattering by lenses, and the like. **20.** *Photog.* a fogged appearance given to an image by reflection within a camera lens or within the camera itself. [orig. meaning: spread out, said of hair, a ship's sides, etc.; cf. OE *flǣre* either of the spreading sides at the end of the nose]
—**Syn. 1.** flame. **13.** flash.

flare·back (flâr′bak′), *n.* **1.** a blast of flame that sometimes issues from the breech of a large gun or cannon when it is opened after firing. **2.** a brief, unexpected recurrence: *a flareback of winter in May.* [n. use of v. phrase *flare back*]

flare-up (flâr′up′), *n.* **1.** a sudden flaring up of flame or light. **2.** a sudden outburst of anger. **3.** a sudden outbreak of violence, disease, or other condition thought to be quelled, checked, or inactive. [n. use of v. phrase *flare up*]

flar·ing (flâr′ing), *adj.* **1.** blazing; flaming. **2.** glaringly bright or showy. **3.** spreading gradually outward in form: *a flaring skirt.* [FLARE + -ING[2]]. —**flar′ing·ly,** *adv.*

flash (flash), *n.* **1.** a brief, sudden burst of bright light: *a flash of lightning.* **2.** a sudden, brief outburst or display of joy, wit, etc. **3.** a very brief moment; instant: *I'll be back in a flash.* **4.** flashlight (def. 1). **5.** ostentatious display; gaudy showiness. **6.** Also called **news flash.** *Journalism.* a brief dispatch sent by a wire service, usually transmitting preliminary news of an important story or development. Cf. **bulletin** (def. 2). **7.** *Photog.* **a.** bright artificial light thrown briefly upon a subject during an exposure. **b.** See **flash lamp. 8.** the sudden flame or intense heat produced by a bomb or other explosive device. **9.** a device as a lock or sluice, for confining and releasing water to send a boat down a shallow stream. **10.** *Metall.* **a.** a ridge of metal left on a casting by a seam between parts of the mold. **b.** a ridge formed at the edge of a forging or weld where excess metal has been squeezed out. **11.** *Poker.* a hand containing all five suits in a game played with a five-suit pack. **12.** *Archaic.* an artificially induced rush of water for sending a boat down a shallow stream. **13.** *Obs.* the cant or jargon of thieves, vagabonds, etc. **14. flash in the pan, a.** a brief, intense effort that produces no significant result. **b.** a person who makes such an effort; one who enjoys short-lived success: *She was a flash in the pan who had one hit record and then disappeared from show business.*
—*v.i.* **15.** to break forth into sudden flame or light, esp. transiently or intermittently: *a buoy flashing in the distance.* **16.** to speak or behave with sudden anger, outrage, or the like (often fol. by *out*): *I couldn't help flashing out at such a stupid remark. He flashed crimson with rage at her rudeness.* **17.** to gleam. **18.** to burst suddenly into view or perception: *The answer flashed into his mind.* **19.** to move like a flash. **20.** to break into sudden action. **21.** *Archaic.* to make a flash or sudden display. **22.** *Archaic.* to dash or splash, as the sea or waves.
—*v.t.* **23.** to emit or send forth (fire or light) in sudden flashes. **24.** to cause to flash, as powder by ignition or a sword by waving. **25.** to change (water) instantly into steam by causing it to strike a hot surface. **26.** to send forth like a flash. **27.** to communicate instantaneously, as by telegraph. **28.** *Informal.* to make an ostentatious display of: *He's forever flashing a large roll of bills.* **29.** to increase the flow of water in (a river, channel, etc.). **30.** *Glassmaking.* **a.** to coat (plain glass or a glass object) with a layer of colored, opalescent, or white glass. **b.** to apply (such a layer). **c.** to color or make (glass) opaque by reheating. **31.** *Building Trades.* to protect with flashing. **32.** to reduce the permanent magnetism of (a vessel) by wrapping a cable horizontally around the vessel and energizing the cable. **33.** *Cards.* to expose (a card) in the process of dealing. **34.** *Archaic.* to dash or splash (water).
—*adj.* **35.** showy or ostentatious. **36.** counterfeit or sham. **37.** of or belonging to sporting men; sporty. **38.** belonging to or connected with thieves, vagabonds, etc., or their cant or jargon. **39.** sudden and brief: *a flash storm.* **40.** caused by or used as protection against flash: *a number of flash injuries; to wear flash clothing.* [ME *flasshe(n)* (to) sprinkle; ? b. FLY[1] and WASH] —**flash′er,** *n.* —**flash′ing·ly,** *adv.*
—**Syn. 1.** flare, gleam, glare. **3.** twinkling, wink. **17.** scintillate. FLASH, GLANCE, GLINT, GLITTER mean to send forth a sudden gleam (or gleams) of bright light. To FLASH is to send forth light with a sudden, transient brilliancy: *A shooting star flashed briefly.* To GLANCE is to emit a brilliant flash of light as a reflection from a smooth surface: *Sunlight glanced from the glass windshield.* GLINT suggests a hard bright gleam of reflected light as from something polished or burnished: *Light glints from silver or from burnished copper.* To GLITTER is to reflect intermittent flashes of light from a hard surface: *Ice glitters in the moonlight.* **35.** flashy, gaudy, tawdry, pretentious, superficial. **36.** false, fake.

flash·back (flash′bak′), *n.* a scene representing an earlier event inserted into a current situation depicted in a novel, motion picture, play, etc. [n. use of v. phrase *flash back*]

flash·board (flash′bōrd′, -bôrd′), *n. Civ. Eng.* a board, or one of a series of boards, as on a milldam, used to increase the depth of the impounded water. [FLASH + BOARD]

flash′ bulb′, *Photog.* **1.** a glass bulb, filled with oxygen and aluminum or zirconium wire or foil, which, when ignited electrically, burns with a brilliant flash to provide momentary illumination of a subject. **2.** Also called **flashtube, flash tube.** an electronic flash lamp consisting of a glass or quartz tube filled with xenon or krypton and having an electrode at each end. Also, **flash′bulb′.**

flash′ burn′, a burn produced by brief exposure to intense, radiant heat, as from an explosion.

flash′ card′, a card having words, numerals, or pictures on it, designed for gaining a rapid response from pupils when held up briefly by a teacher, used esp. in reading, arithmetic, or vocabulary drills.

flash·cube (flash′kyo͞ob′), *n. Photog.* a cube, for attaching to a camera, that contains a flash bulb in each vertical side and rotates automatically for taking four pictures in rapid succession. [FLASH + CUBE[1]]

flash′ flood′, a sudden and destructive rush of water down a narrow gully or over a sloping surface: caused by heavy rainfall. —**Syn.** See **flood.**

flash′ gun′, *Photog.* a device that simultaneously discharges a flash bulb and operates a camera shutter.

flash·ing (flash′ing), *n.* **1.** *Building Trades.* pieces of sheet metal or the like used to cover and protect certain joints and angles, as where a roof comes in contact with a wall or chimney. **2.** act of creating an artificial flood in a conduit or stream, as in a sewer for cleansing it. [FLASH + -ING[1]]

flash′ing point′, *Physical Chem.* See **flash point.**

flash′ lamp′, *Photog.* a lamp for providing momentary illumination for the subject of a photograph. Also, **flash′lamp′.**

flash·light (flash′līt′), *n.* **1.** a small, portable electric lamp powered by dry batteries or a tiny generator. **2.** a flash of light, or a light that flashes. **3.** any source of artificial light as used in flash photography. [FLASH + LIGHT[1]]

flash-lock (flash′lok′), *n.* stanch[1] (def. 5).

flash·o·ver (flash′ō′vər), *Elect.* —*n.* **1.** a disruptive discharge around or over the surface of a solid or liquid insulator. —*v.i.* **2.** to establish a flashover. [orig. n. use of v. phrase *flash over*]

flash′ photog′raphy, photography using a momentary flash of artificial light as a source of illumination. Also called **photoflash photography.**

flash′ pic′ture, a photograph made with a flash lamp or flashcube.

flash′ point′, *Physical Chem.* the lowest temperature at which a liquid in a specified apparatus will give off sufficient vapor to ignite momentarily on application of a flame. Also, **flashing point.**

flash·tube (flash′to͞ob′, -tyo͞ob′), *n. Photog.* See **flash bulb** (def. 2). Also, **flash′ tube′.** [FLASH + TUBE]

flash·y (flash′ē), *adj.,* **flash·i·er, flash·i·est. 1.** sparkling or brilliant, esp. in a superficial way or for the moment: *a flashy performance.* **2.** pretentiously smart; showy; gaudy: *flashy clothes.* **3.** *Archaic.* flashing with light. [FLASH + -Y[1]] —**flash′i·ly,** *adv.* —**flash′i·ness,** *n.*
—**Syn. 2.** See **gaudy**[1].

flask[1] (flask, fläsk), *n.* **1.** a bottle-shaped container made of glass, metal, etc.: *a flask of brandy.* **2.** an iron container for shipping mercury, holding a standard commercial unit of 76 pounds. **3.** *Foundry.* a container into which sand is rammed around a pattern to form a mold. [ME; OE *flasce, flaxe;* cf. FLAGON]

flask[2] (flask, fläsk), *n. Ordn.* **1.** the armored plates making up the sides of a gun-carriage trail. **2.** *Obs.* the bed of a gun carriage. [< dial. F *flasque* cheek of a gun carriage < LL *flasca* FLASK[1]]

flask·et (flas′kit, fläs′kit), *n.* **1.** a small flask. **2.** a long, shallow basket. [ME *flaskett* < OF *flasquet,* dim. of *flasque* FLASK[1]]

flat[1] (flat), *adj.,* **flat·ter, flat·test,** *n., v.,* **flat·ted, flat·ting,** *adv.* —*adj.* **1.** horizontally level: *a flat roof.* **2.** level, even, or without inequalities of surface, as land, table tops, etc. **3.** having a surface that is without marked projections or depressions: *a broad, flat face.* **4.** lying horizontally and at full length, as a person: *He was flat on the canvas after the knockdown.* **5.** lying wholly on or against something: *The ladder stood flat against a wall.* **6.** thrown down, laid low, or level with the ground, as fallen trees or buildings. **7.** having a generally level shape or appearance; not deep or thick: *a flat plate.* **8.** (of the heel of a shoe) low and broad. **9.** spread out, as an unrolled map, the open hand, etc. **10.** deflated; collapsed: *a flat tire.* **11.** without qualification; absolute, downright, or positive: *a flat denial.* **12.** without modification or variation: *a flat price; a flat rate.* **13.** *Informal.* lacking money; broke: *I'd lend you the dollar but I'm absolutely flat myself.* **14.** without vitality or animation; lifeless; dull: *flat writing.* **15.** having lost its flavor, sharpness, or life, as wine, food, etc.; stale. **16.** (of a beverage) having lost its effervescence: *flat beer.* **17.** without flavor; not spiced: *flat cooking.* **18.** prosaic, banal, or insipid: *a flat style.* **19.** pointless, as a remark, joke, etc. **20.** commercially dull, as trade or the market. **21.** *Painting.* **a.** not having the illusion of volume or depth. **b.** lacking gradations of tone or color: *flat background.* **c.** without gloss; mat. **22.** not clear, sharp, or ringing, as sound, a voice, etc. **23.** lacking resonance and variation in pitch; monotonous: *a flat delivery of the speech.* **24.** *Music.* **a.** (of a tone) lowered a half step in pitch: *B flat.* **b.** below an intended pitch, as a note; too low (opposed to *sharp*). **25.** *Gram.* derived without change in form, as English *to brush* from the noun *brush* and adverbs which do not add *-ly* to the adjective form as *fast, cheap, slow,* etc. **26.** *Phonet.* lenis; voiced. **27.** *Naut.* (of a sail) **a.** cut with little or no fullness. **b.** trimmed as nearly fore-and-aft as possible, for sailing to windward. **28. flat a,** the *a*-sound (a) of *glad, bat,* or *act.* **29. flat aft,** *Naut.* so that fore-and-aft sails present as flat a surface as possible, as in sailing close to the wind: *Haul the sheets flat aft!* **30. flat on one's back,** confined to bed because of illness or other physical disorder: *He's been flat on his back for two weeks now with that virus.*
—*n.* **31.** something flat. **32.** Often, **flats.** a shoe, esp. a woman's shoe, with a flat heel or no heel. **33.** a flat surface, side, or part of anything: *the flat of a blade; He struck her with the flat of his hand.* **34.** flat or level ground; a flat area: *salt flats.* **35.** a marsh, shoal, or shallow. **36.** *Music.* **a.** (in musical notation) the character ♭, which when attached to a note or to a staff degree lowers its significance one chromatic half step. **b.** a tone one chromatic half step below another: *The flat of B is B flat.* **c.** (on keyboard instruments, with reference to any given note) the key next below or to the left. **37.** *Theat.* a piece of scenery consisting of a wooden frame, usually rectangular, covered with lightweight board or fabric. **38.** a broad, thin book, chiefly for children: *a juvenile flat.* **39.** *Informal.* a deflated automobile tire. **40.** *Archit.* a flat roof or deck. **41.** Also called **platform.** *Naut.* **a.** a partial deck between two full decks. **b.** a low, flat barge or lighter. **42.** *Shipbuilding.* **a.** a broad, flat piece of iron or steel for overlapping and joining two plates at their edges. **b.** a straight timber in a frame or other assembly of generally curved timbers. **43.** an iron or steel bar of rectangular section. **44.** *Textiles.* one of a series of laths covered with card clothing, used in conjunction with the cylinder in carding. **45.** *Photog.* **a.** a device for holding a negative or positive flat for reproduction by photoengraving. **b.** one or more negatives or positives in position to be reproduced. **46.** *Hort.* a shallow box used for rooting seeds and cuttings. **47.** *Football.* the area of the field immediately inside of or outside of an offensive end, close behind or at the line of scrimmage. **48. flats,** *Informal.* flat races between horses. Cf. **flat race.**
—*v.t.* **49.** to make flat. **50.** *Music.* to lower (a pitch), esp. one half step.
—*v.i.* **51.** to become flat. **52. flat in,** *Naut.* to pull the clew of (a fore-and-aft sail) as nearly amidships as possible; flatten in.
—*adv.* **53.** in a flat position; horizontally; levelly. **54.** in a flat manner; positively; absolutely. **55.** completely; utterly: *flat broke.* **56.** exactly; precisely: *He raced around the track in two minutes flat.* **57.** *Music.* below the true pitch: *to sing flat.* **58.** *Finance.* without interest. **59. fall flat,** to fail to produce the desired effect; fail completely: *Their attempts at photography fell flat.* [ME < Scand; cf. Icel *flat(r),* Sw *flat;* akin to OE *flet* floor. See FLAT[2]] —**flat′ly,** *adv.* —**flat′ness,** *n.*
—**Syn. 1.** plane. See **level. 4.** low, supine, prostrate, prone. **11.** outright, peremptory, categorical. **14.** boring, spiritless, prosaic. **17.** vapid, unsavory. —**Ant. 1, 4.** upright, vertical. **14.** spirited. **17.** savory.

flat[2] (flat), *n.* **1.** an apartment or suite of rooms on one floor, forming a residence, as for a family. **2.** *Brit.* a floor or story of a building. [var. of obs. *flet,* OE: floor, house, hall; akin to FLAT[1]]

flat′ arch′, an arch having a more or less flat intrados and extrados with voussoirs radiating from a center below the arch. See illus. under **arch.** Also called **jack arch.**

flat′ back′, **1.** a book spine presenting a completely flat surface. **2.** a book bound with such a spine.

flat′-bed cyl′inder press′ (flat′bed′), a printing press in which a flat bed holding the printing form moves against a revolving cylinder which carries the paper.

flat′-bed press′. See **cylinder press.**

flat·boat (flat′bōt′), *n.* a large, flat-bottomed boat for use in shallow water, esp. on rivers. [FLAT[1] + BOAT]

flat-bot·tomed (flat′bot′əmd), *adj.* (of boats) having a flat bottom.

flat·bread (flat′bred′), *n.* a thin, waferlike rye bread baked esp. in Scandinavian countries. Also, **flat·brod** (flat′brōd). [trans. of Norw *flatbröd*]

flat′ bug′, any of numerous flattened hemipterous insects of the family *Aradidae* that live under bark and feed on fungi. Also called **fungus bug.**

flat·car (flat′kär′), *n. U.S.* a railroad car consisting of a platform without sides or top. [FLAT[1] + CAR[1]]

flat·fish (flat′fish′), *n., pl.* (*esp. collectively*) **-fish,** (*esp. referring to two or more kinds or species*) **-fish·es.** any fish of the order *Heterosomata* (*Pleuronectiformes*), including the halibut, sole, flounder, etc., having a greatly compressed body, with both eyes on the upper side in the adult, and swimming on one side. [FLAT[1] + FISH]

flat·foot (flat′fo͝ot′ *or, for 1,* -fo͝ot′), *n., pl.* **-feet** for 1, **-foots** for 2. **1.** *Pathol.* **a.** a condition in which the arch of the foot is flattened so that the entire sole rests upon the ground. **b.** a foot with such an arch. **2.** *Slang.* a policeman. [FLAT[1] + FOOT]

flat·foot·ed (flat′fo͝ot′id), *adj.* **1.** having flatfeet. **2.** *Informal.* taking or showing an uncompromising stand in a matter; firm and explicit. **3. catch one flatfooted,** *Informal.* to catch one off his guard; surprise: *The amount of the check caught us flatfooted.* [FLATFOOT + -ED[3]] —**flat′-foot′ed·ly,** *adv.* —**flat′-foot′ed·ness,** *n.*

flat-grained (flat′grānd′), *adj.* (of sawed lumber) having the annual rings at an angle of less than 45° with the broader surfaces. Cf. **edge-grained.**

flat-hat (flat′hat′), *v.i.,* **-hat·ted, -hat·ting.** *Informal.* to fly an airplane unnecessarily low. —**flat′-hat′ter,** *n.*

flat·head (flat′hed′), *n., pl.* (*esp. collectively*) **-head,** (*esp. referring to two or more kinds or species*) **-heads.** any of several scorpaenoid fishes of the family *Platycephalidae,* found chiefly in the Indo-Pacific region, where they are used for food. [FLAT[1] + HEAD, so called from physical appearance]

Flat·head (flat′hed′), *n.* **1.** a member of a tribe of Salishan Indians of northwest Montana. **2.** a Chinook Indian. [so called from their supposed practice of flattening their children's heads]

flat′head cat′fish, a yellow and brown catfish, *Pylodictus olivaris,* common in the central U.S., having a flattened head and a projecting lower jaw. Also called **goujon, mudcat.**

flat′head·ed ap′ple tree′ bor′er (flat′hed′id). See **apple tree borer** (def. 1).

flat′headed bor′er, the larva of a metallic wood-boring beetle, having an expanded and flattened anterior end. Also called **hammerhead.**

flat·i·ron (flat′ī′ərn), *n.* **1.** an iron with a flat bottom, heated for use in pressing clothes, cloth, etc. **2.** *Geol.* a triangular-shaped hogback that resembles a flatiron resting on its base. [FLAT[1] + IRON]

flat′-joint′ point′ing (flat′joint′), *Masonry.* pointing having flush joints of common mortar.

flat-knit (flat′nit′), *adj.* (of a fabric) made by flat knitting. Cf. **circular-knit.**

flat′ knit′ting, a knitting process in which the yarn is knitted horizontally on needles set in a straight line. Cf. **circular knitting.**

flat′ knot′. See **reef knot.**

flat·ling (flat′ling), *adv.* Also, **flat′lings.** *Brit. Dial.* **1.** in a flat position; with the flat side, as of a sword. **2.** flatly or positively. —*adj.* **3.** *Obs.* dealt with the flat side. [ME; see FLAT[1], -LING[2]]

flat′ palm′, a feather palm, *Howea forsteriana,* of Lord Howe Island, having flat, plumy leaves about ten feet long.

flat′ pass′, *Football.* a forward pass describing little or no arc in flight and thrown toward a sideline into or to the far side of a flat.

flat′ race′, *Track, Horse Racing.* a race run on a level track having no hurdles, water jumps, hedges, or the like to hinder the speed of the entrants.

Flat′ Riv′er, a town in E Missouri. 4515 (1960).

Flat′ Rock′, a town in SE Michigan. 4696 (1960).

flat′ roof′, a watertight roof sloping only enough to permit drainage.

flat-saw (flat′sô′), *v.t.,* **-sawed, -sawed** or **-sawn, -saw·ing.** plain-saw.

flat′ sen′nit, a rope made of three or more yarns or strands plaited together. Also called **common sennit, English sennit.**

flat′ sil′ver, flatware (def. 1).

flat′ sour′, **1.** fermentation occurring in canned foods after sealing. **2.** canned food so fermented. —**flat′-sour′,** *adj.*

flat·ten (flat′ən), *v.t.* **1.** to make flat. **2.** *Boxing Slang.* to knock out (an opponent). —*v.i.* **3.** to become flat. **4. flatten in,** *Naut.* to pull the clew of (a fore-and-aft sail) as nearly amidships as possible; flat in. **5. flatten out,** *Aeron.* to fly into a horizontal position, as after a dive. [FLAT[1] + -EN[1]] —**flat′ten·er,** *n.*

flat·ter[1] (flat′ər), *v.t.* **1.** to try to please by complimentary speech or attention. **2.** to compliment insincerely. **3.** to praise effusively or excessively: *She flatters his ego by constantly praising his books.* **4.** to represent favorably; gratify by falsification: *The portrait flatters her.* **5.** to show to advantage: *The black dress flattered her figure.* **6.** to play upon the vanity or susceptibilities of; cajole, wheedle, or beguile: *They flattered him into contributing heavily to the foundation.* **7.** to please or gratify by compliments or attentions: *They flattered the young man with an invitation to the White House.* **8.** to feel satisfaction with (oneself) esp. with reference to an accomplishment, act, or occasion: *He flattered himself that the dinner had gone well.* **9.** to beguile with hope; encourage prematurely, falsely, etc. —*v.i.* **10.** to use flattery. [ME *flat(t)er(en)* (to) float, flutter, fawn upon, OE *floterian* to float, flutter; for sense development, cf. FLICKER[1], Icel *flathra;* not connected with F *flatter* to flatter] —**flat′ter·a·ble,** *adj.* —**flat′ter·er,** *n.* —**flat′ter·ing·ly,** *adv.*

flat·ter[2] (flat′ər), *n.* **1.** one who or that which makes something flat. **2.** a flat-faced blacksmith's tool, laid on a forging and struck with a hammer to smooth the surface of the forging. **3.** a drawplate with a flat orifice for drawing flat metal strips, as for watch springs. [FLAT[1] + -ER[1]]

flat·ter·y (flat′ə rē), *n., pl.* **-ter·ies.** **1.** act of flattering. **2.** a flattering compliment or speech; excessive, insincere praise. [ME *flaterie* < MF, equiv. to *flat(er)* to flatter + *-erie* -ERY. Cf. FLATTER[1]]

flat·tie (flat′ē), *n.* *Naut.* a sharpie having raking masts. [FLAT[1] + -IE]

flat·ting (flat′ing), *n.* the act of one who or that which makes flat, as in the manufacture of sheet metal, flat paint, etc. [FLAT[1] + -ING[1]]

flat′ tire′, a pneumatic tire that has lost all or most of its air through leakage, puncture, or the like.

flat·tish (flat′ish), *adj.* somewhat flat. [FLAT[1] + -ISH[1]]

flat·top (flat′top′), *n.* *U.S. Navy Informal.* an aircraft carrier. Also, **flat′-top′.** [FLAT[1] + TOP[1]]

flat·u·lent (flach′ə lənt), *adj.* **1.** generating gas in the alimentary canal, as food. **2.** attended with, caused by, or suffering from, such an accumulation of gas. **3.** having unsupported pretentions; inflated and empty; pompous; turgid: *a flatulent style.* [< NL *flātulent(us);* see FLATUS, -ULENT] —**flat′u·lence, flat′u·len·cy,** *n.* —**flat′u·lent·ly,** *adv.*

fla·tus (flā′təs), *n., pl.* **-tus·es.** an accumulation of gas in the stomach, intestines, or other body cavity. [< L: a blowing, breathing, breath, deriv. (4th decl.) of *flātus,* ptp. of *flāre* to blow]

flat·ware (flat′wâr′), *n.* **1.** silver utensils, knives, forks, etc. **2.** dishes or containers for the table, or for other use, that are more or less flat, as plates, saucers, etc. (distinguished from *hollowware*). [FLAT[1] + WARE[1]]

flat′ wash′, flatwork.

flat·wise (flat′wīz′), *adv.* with the flat side, rather than the edge, foremost or in contact. Also, **flat·ways** (flat′wāz′). [FLAT[1] + -WISE]

flat·woods (flat′wo͝odz′), *n.* (*construed as pl.*) a woodland in a low-lying region having little drainage. [FLAT[1] + WOODS]

Flat·woods (flat′wo͝odz′), *n.* a town in NE Kentucky. 3741 (1960).

flat·work (flat′wûrk′), *n.* articles of linen, clothing, etc., which are ordinarily ironed mechanically rather than by hand. Also called **flat wash.** [FLAT[1] + WORK]

flat·worm (flat′wûrm′), *n.* a platyhelminth. [FLAT[1] + WORM]

Flau·bert (flō bâr′; *Fr.* flō beʀ′), *n.* **Gus·tave** (gys tav′), 1821–80, French novelist.

flaunch (flônch), *n.* *Heraldry.* flanch. Also, **flaunche.**

flaunched (flôncht), *adj.* *Heraldry.* **1.** (of an escutcheon) having flaunches. **2.** noting an escutcheon bearing specified differenced arms on flaunches, the field being plain. [FLAUNCH + -ED[3]]

flaunt (flônt), *v.i.* **1.** to parade or display oneself conspicuously or boldly. **2.** to wave conspicuously in the air. —*v.t.* **3.** to parade or display ostentatiously: *to flaunt one's wealth.* **4.** *Nonstandard.* to ignore or treat with disdain: *He was expelled for flaunting military regulations.* —*n.* **5.** act of flaunting. **6.** *Obs.* something flaunted. [< Scand; cf. Norw *flanta* to gad about, deriv. of *flana* to roam; akin to Gk *plánē* roaming (see PLANET)] —**flaunt′er,** *n.* —**flaunt′ing·ly,** *adv.*

—**Syn. 3.** flourish.

—**Usage. 4.** This sense of FLAUNT stems from its confusion with FLOUT, and, although this confusion is quite common in the speech, if not the writing, of educated people, it is nonetheless regarded as nonstandard usage.

flaunt·y (flôn′tē), *adj.,* **flaunt·i·er, flaunt·i·est.** **1.** (of persons) given to display; inclined to be ostentatious, showy, or vain. **2.** (of things) gaudy; flashy; ostentatious. [FLAUNT + -Y[1]] —**flaunt′i·ly,** *adv.* —**flaunt′i·ness,** *n.*

flau·tist (flô′tist, flou′-), *n.* flutist. [< It *flautist(a),* equiv. to *flaut(o)* flute + *-ista* -IST]

flav-, var. of **flavo-** before a vowel: *flavin.*

flav., (in prescriptions) yellow. [< L *flāvus*]

fla·ves·cent (flə ves′ənt), *adj.* turning yellow; yellowish. [< L *flāvescent-,* s. of *flāvescēns,* prp. of *flāvescere* to become yellow. See FLAV-, -ESCE, -ENT]

Fla·vi·a (flā′vē ə), *n.* a girl's given name.

fla·vin (flā′vin), *n.* *Chem.* **1.** a complex heterocyclic ketone which is common to the nonprotein part of several important yellow enzymes, the flavoproteins. **2.** quercetin. Also, **flavine.** [FLAV- + -IN[2]]

-flavin, *Chem.* a combining form indicating any of a number of natural derivatives of flavin: *riboflavin.*

fla·vine (flā′vin, -vēn), *n.* *Chem.* **1.** See **acriflavine hydrochloride. 2.** flavin.

flavo-, a learned borrowing from Latin meaning "yellow," used in the formation of compound words (*flavopurpurin*); in some chemical terms, specialized in meaning to indicate **flavin** (*flavoprotein*). Also, *esp. before a vowel,* **flav-.** [comb. form repr. L *flāvus*]

fla·vo·bac·te·ri·um (flā′vō bak tēr′ē əm), *n., pl.* **-te·ri·a** (-tēr′ē ə). *Bacteriol.* any of several rod-shaped, aerobic to facultatively anaerobic bacteria of the genus *Flavobacterium,* found in soil and water. [< NL; see FLAVO-, BACTERIUM]

fla·vone (flā′vōn), *n.* *Chem.* **1.** a colorless, crystalline, water-insoluble compound, $C_{15}H_{10}O_2$, the parent substance of a group of naturally occurring derivatives some of which have been used as yellow dyes. **2.** any derivative of this compound. [FLAV- + -ONE]

fla·vo·nol (flā′və nōl′, -nôl′, -nol′), *n.* *Chem.* **1.** the 3-hydroxy derivative of flavone, $C_{15}H_9O_2(OH)$, many of whose derivatives, as quercetin, are naturally occurring yellow dyes. **2.** any derivative of this compound. [FLAVONE + -OL[1]]

fla·vo·pro·tein (flā′vō prō′tēn, -tē ən), *n.* *Biochem.* an enzyme, containing riboflavin and linked chemically with a protein, active in the oxidation of foods in animal cells. [FLAVO- + PROTEIN]

fla·vo·pur·pu·rin (flā′vō pûr′pyə rin), *n.* *Chem.* a yellow, crystalline anthraquinone dye, $C_{14}H_5O_2(OH)_3$, isomeric with purpurin, used in dyeing. [FLAVO- + PURPURIN]

fla·vor (flā′vər), *n.* **1.** taste, esp. the distinctive taste of something as it is experienced in the mouth. **2.** a substance or extract that provides a particular flavor. **3.** the characteristic quality of a thing: *He captured the flavor of the experience in his book.* **4.** a particular quality noticeable in a thing: *language with a strong nautical flavor.* **5.** *Archaic.* smell, odor, or aroma. —*v.t.* **6.** to give flavor to (something). Also, *esp. Brit.,* **flavour.** [ME < MF *fla(o)ur* < LL **flātor* stench, breath, alter. of L *flatus* a blowing, breathing, equiv. to *flāt-* (ptp. s. of *flāre* to blow) + *-us* n. suffix (4th decl.); see -OR[1]] —**fla′vor·less,** *adj.*

—**Syn. 1.** See **taste. 2.** seasoning. **3.** essence, spirit.

fla·vor·ful (flā′vər fəl), *adj.* full of flavor; tasty. Also, *esp. Brit.,* **flavourful.** [FLAVOR + -FUL] —**fla′vor·ful·ly,** *adv.*

fla·vor·ing (flā′vər ing), *n.* something that gives flavor; a substance or preparation used to give a particular flavor to food or drink. Also, *esp. Brit.,* **flavouring.** [FLAVOR + -ING[1]]

fla·vor·ous (flā′vər əs), *adj.* **1.** full of flavor. **2.** pleasant to the taste or smell. [FLAVOR + -OUS]

fla·vor·some (flā′vər səm), *adj.* **1.** of a full, rich, pleasant flavor; tasty. **2.** having or giving a particular flavor: *writing that is interspersed with flavorsome accounts of local customs.* Also, *esp. Brit.,* **flavoursome.** [FLAVOR + -SOME[1]]

fla·vor·y (flā′və rē), *adj.* rich in flavor, as a tea. Also, *esp. Brit.,* **flavoury.** [FLAVOR + -Y[1]]

fla·vour (flā′vər), *n.* *Chiefly Brit.* flavor. —**fla′vour·less,** *adj.*

fla·vour·ful (flā′vər fəl), *adj.* *Chiefly Brit.* flavorful. —**fla′vour·ful·ly,** *adv.*

fla·vour·ing (flā′vər ing), *n.* *Chiefly Brit.* flavoring.

fla·vour·some (flā′vər səm), *adj.* *Chiefly Brit.* flavorsome.

fla·vour·y (flā′və rē), *adj.* *Chiefly Brit.* flavory.

flaw[1] (flô), *n.* **1.** a feature that mars the perfection of something; defect; fault: *beauty without flaw; There were several flaws in our plan.* **2.** a defect impairing legal soundness or validity: *There's a flaw in our new lease.* **3.** a crack, break, breach, or rent. —*v.t.* **4.** to produce a flaw in. —*v.i.* **5.** to contract a flaw; become cracked or defective. [ME *flaw(e), flage* < Scand; akin to Icel *flaga* thin layer of earth, Dan *flage,* Sw *flaga* sliver, chip, OE *flēan* to FLAY] —**flaw′less,** *adj.* —**flaw′less·ly,** *adv.* —**flaw′less·ness,** *n.*

—**Syn. 1.** imperfection, blot, spot. See **defect. 3.** fissure, rift.

flaw[2] (flô), *n.* **1.** Also called **windflaw.** a sudden, usually brief windstorm or gust of wind. **2.** a short spell of rough weather. **3.** *Obs.* a burst of feeling, fury, etc. [< Scand; cf. Icel *flaga* sudden onset, Norw *flaga* gust; MLG *vlage*]

flawed (flôd), *adj.* characterized by flaws; having imperfections: *a flawed gem; a seriously flawed character.* [FLAW[1] + -ED[3]] —**flawed′ness,** *n.*

flaw·y (flô′ē), *adj.,* **flaw·i·er, flaw·i·est.** characterized by gusts, as wind. [FLAW[2] + -Y[1]]

flax (flaks), *n.* **1.** any plant of the genus *Linum,* esp. *L. usitatissimum,* a slender, erect, annual plant having narrow, lance-shaped leaves and blue flowers, cultivated for its fiber and seeds. **2.** the fiber of this plant, manufactured into linen yarn for thread or woven fabrics. **3.** any of various plants resembling flax. [ME; OE *fleax;* c. D, LG *vlas,* G *Flachs*]

flax·en (flak′sən), *adj.* **1.** made of flax. **2.** pertaining to flax. **3.** resembling flax. **4.** of the pale yellowish color of dressed flax. Also, **flax′y.** [FLAX + -EN[2]]

flax′ lil′y. See **New Zealand flax.**

Flax·man (flaks′mən), *n.* **John,** 1755–1826, English sculptor and draftsman.

flax·seed (flaks′sēd′), *n.* the seed of flax, yielding linseed oil; linseed. [FLAX + SEED]

flay (flā), *v.t.* **1.** to strip off the skin or outer covering of. **2.** to criticize or rebuke with scathing severity. **3.** to deprive or strip of money or property; fleece. [ME *fle(n),* OE *flēan;* c. MD *vlaen,* Icel *flā*] —**flay′er,** *n.*

F layer, the highest of the radio-reflective, ionospheric layers, consisting of two parts, the lower part (**F_1 layer**) being detectable in the daytime only, the higher (**F_2 layer**) being constant and constituting the ionospheric layer most favorable for long-range radio communication.

F.L.B., Federal Land Bank.

fld., **1.** field. **2.** fluid.

fl dr, fluid dram; fluid drams.

fldxt., (in prescriptions) fluidextract. [< L *fluidextractum*]

flea (flē), *n.* **1.** any of numerous small, wingless bloodsucking insects of the order *Siphonaptera,* parasitic upon mammals and birds, and noted for their ability to leap. **2.** any of various small beetles and crustaceans which leap like a flea, or swim in a jumpy manner, as the water flea and beach flea. **3. flea in one's ear,** a disconcerting rebuke or rebuff; a broad hint: *The next time he shows his face around here he'll get a flea in his ear.* [ME *fle,* OE *flēah, flēa;* c. G *Floh;* akin to FLEE]

Dog flea, *Ctenocephalides canis* (Length 1/8 in.)

flea·bag (flē′bag′), *n.* *Slang.* **1.** a bed. **2.** a sleeping bag. **3.** a cheap, run-down hotel or rooming house. **4.** any shabby or low-grade public establishment. **5.** a dog, esp. one that is flea-ridden. **6.** a worthless racehorse. [FLEA + BAG]

flea·bane (flē′bān′), *n.* any of various composite plants, as *Pulicaria dysenterica,* of Europe, or *Erigeron philadelphicus,* of the U.S., reputed to destroy or drive away fleas. [FLEA + BANE]

flea′ bee′tle, any of several leaf beetles of the genera *Haltica, Epitrix,* etc., with the rear legs adapted for jumping, which infest and feed on a wide variety of plants.

flea·bite (flē′bīt′), *n.* **1.** the bite of a flea. **2.** the red spot caused by it. **3.** any petty annoyance or irritation, as a trifling wound. [late ME *flee byte.* See FLEA, BITE]

flea-bit·ten (flē′bit′ən), *adj.* **1.** bitten by a flea or fleas. **2.** (of a horse) having a light-colored coat with small reddish spots or streaks.

fleam (flēm), *n.* **1.** *Surg.* a kind of lancet, as for opening veins. **2.** the beveled leading edge of a sawtooth. [ME *fleme, fleom* < MF *flieme* << LL *phlebotom(um).* See PHLEBOTOMY]

flea′ mar′ket, an open-air market, esp. in one of the larger cities of Europe, where old or used articles are sold.

flea·wort (flē′wûrt′), *n.* **1.** a rough-leaved composite herb, *Inula Conyza,* of Europe. **2.** a European plantain, *Plantago Psyllium,* whose seeds resemble fleas and are used in medicine. [ME *flewort,* OE *flēawyrt.* See FLEA, WORT[2]]

flèche (flāsh; *Fr.* flesh), *n., pl.* **flè·ches** (flā′shiz; *Fr.* flesh). **1.** *Archit.* a steeple or spire, esp. one in the Gothic style, emerging from the ridge of a roof. **2.** *Fort.* a fieldwork consisting of two faces forming a salient angle and having an open gorge. **3.** *Fencing.* a method of attack with the saber or épée in which the attacker leaves from his rear foot and advances rapidly toward the opponent. [< F: lit., arrow, prob. < Gmc. Cf. FLY¹]

flèches d'amour (flesh dȧ-mōōr′), *French.* See **love arrows.**

flé·chette (flā shet′), *n., pl.* **flé·chettes** (flā shets′; *Fr.* flā shet′). *Mil.* a steel dart thrown from an airplane, used chiefly in World War I in personnel strafing. [< F; see FLECHE, -ETTE]

fleck (flek), *n.* **1.** a spot or mark on the skin, as a freckle. **2.** a spot or small patch of color, light, etc.: *the dapple mare with flecks of gray.* **3.** a speck; a small bit: *a fleck of dirt.* —*v.t.* **4.** to mark with a fleck or flecks; spot; dapple. [< Scand; c. OIcel *flekk(r)* spot, streak, Sw *fläck,* OHG *flec* (G *Fleck*); akin to OIcel *flekka* to soil, MLG, MD *vlecken*] —**fleck′y,** *adj.*

fleck·less (flek′lis), *adj.* having no flecks or spots. [FLECK + -LESS] —**fleck′less·ly,** *adv.*

flec·tion (flek′shən), *n.* **1.** act of bending. **2.** state of being bent. **3.** a bend; bent part. **4.** *Anat.* flexion. **5.** *Gram.* inflection (def. 2). Also, *esp. Brit.,* **flexion** (for defs. 1–3). [< L *flexiōn-* (s. of *flexiō*) a bending, turning. See FLEX, -ION] —**flec′tion·al,** *adj.* —**flec′tion·less,** *adj.*

Flèche

fled (fled), *v.* pt. and pp. of **flee.**

Fle·da (flē′də), *n.* a girl's given name. Also, **Fleta.**

Fle·der·maus, Die (*Ger.* dē flā′dər mous′), an opera (1874) by Johann Strauss, Jr.

fledge (flej), *v.,* **fledged, fledg·ing,** *adj.* —*v.t.* **1.** to bring up (a young bird) until it is able to fly. **2.** to furnish with or as if with feathers or plumage. **3.** to provide (an arrow) with feathers. —*v.i.* **4.** (of a young bird) to acquire the feathers necessary for flight. —*adj.* **5.** *Archaic.* (of young birds) able to fly. [ME *flegge,* OE *-flycge* (see UNFLEDGED); c. OHG *flucki,* MLG *vlügge* (G *flügge*). See FLY¹] —**fledge′less,** *adj.*

fledged (flejd), *adj.* **1.** having the plumage or feathers necessary for flight. **2.** having the characteristics of maturity. [FLEDGE + -ED²]

fledg·ling (flej′ling), *n.* **1.** a young bird just fledged. **2.** an inexperienced person. Also, *esp. Brit.,* **fledge′ling.** [FLEDGE + -LING¹]

fledg·y (flej′ē), *adj.,* **fledg·i·er, fledg·i·est.** feathered or feathery. [FLEDGE + -Y¹]

flee (flē), *v.,* **fled, flee·ing.** —*v.i.* **1.** to run away, as from danger, pursuers, etc.; take flight. **2.** to move swiftly; fly; speed. —*v.t.* **3.** to run away from (a place, person, etc.): *They fled the town because of the plague.* [ME *flee(n),* OE *flēon;* c. OHG *flichan* (G *fliehen*), Goth *thliuhan;* cf. OE *flēogan* to FLY¹]

fleece (flēs), *n., v.,* **fleeced, fleec·ing.** —*n.* **1.** the coat of wool that covers a sheep or a similar animal. **2.** the amount of wool shorn at one time. **3.** something resembling a fleece: *a fleece of clouds in a blue sky.* **4.** a fabric with a soft, silky pile, used for warmth, as for lining garments. **5.** the soft nap or pile of such a fabric. —*v.t.* **6.** to remove the fleece of (a sheep). **7.** to deprive of money or belongings by fraud, hoax, or the like; swindle: *He fleeced the stranger of several dollars. It was a good place to get fleeced.* **8.** to overspread, as with a fleece; fleck with fleecelike masses: *a host of clouds fleecing the summer sky.* [ME *flees,* OE *flēos, flȳs;* c. MD *vlies,* MHG *vlius,* G *Vlies*] —**fleece′a·ble,** *adj.* —**fleece′less,** *adj.* —**fleece′like′,** *adj.* —**fleec′er,** *n.*

fleece-vine (flēs′vīn′), *n.* See **silver-lace vine.**

fleec·y (flē′sē), *adj.,* **fleec·i·er, fleec·i·est.** covered with, consisting of, or resembling a fleece or wool. [FLEECE + -Y¹] —**fleec′i·ly,** *adv.* —**fleec′i·ness,** *n.*

fleer¹ (flēr), *v.i.* **1.** to grin or laugh coarsely or mockingly. —*v.t.* **2.** to mock or deride. —*n.* **3.** a fleering look; a jeer or gibe. [ME *fler(ien)* < Scand; cf. Norw *flire* a grin] —**fleer′ing·ly,** *adv.*

fle·er² (flē′ər), *n.* a person who flees. [ME; see FLEE, -ER¹]

fleet¹ (flēt), *n.* **1.** the largest organized unit of naval ships grouped for tactical or other purposes. **2.** the largest organization of warships under the command of a single officer. **3.** a number of naval vessels, or vessels carrying armed men. **4.** a large group of ships, airplanes, trucks, etc., operated by a single company or under the same ownership: *He owns a fleet of cabs.* **5.** a large group of airplanes, automobiles, etc., moving or operating together. [ME *flete,* OE *flēot,* flowing water, ship, deriv. of *flēotan* to float]

fleet² (flēt), *adj.* **1.** swift; rapid: *to be fleet of foot; a fleet horse.* —*v.i.* **2.** to move swiftly; fly. **3.** *Naut.* to change position; shift. **4.** *Archaic.* to glide away like a stream. **5.** *Archaic.* to fade; vanish. **6.** *Obs.* to float; drift. **7.** *Obs.* to swim. —*v.t.* **8.** to cause (time) to pass lightly or swiftly. **9.** *Naut.* **a.** to move or change the position of. **b.** to separate the blocks of (a tackle). **c.** to lay (a rope) along a deck. **d.** to extend (a messenger) from a capstan or winch to a hawser to which it is to be bent for hauling in. [ME *flete(n)* (to) be fleet, OE *flēotan* to FLOAT] —**fleet′ly,** *adv.* —**fleet′ness,** *n.*
—**Syn. 8.** speed, hasten; beguile.

fleet³ (flēt), *n.* *Brit. Dial.* **1.** an arm of the sea; inlet. **2.** a creek; stream; water course. **3. the Fleet,** a former prison in London, long used for debtors. [ME *flete,* OE *flēot* flowing water; c. G *Fliess* brook]

fleet′ ad′miral, *U.S. Navy.* the highest ranking naval officer, ranking next above admiral.

fleet-foot·ed (flēt′fo͝ot′id), *adj.* able to run fast.

fleet·ing (flē′ting), *adj.* passing swiftly; vanishing quickly; transient; transitory. [ME; see FLEET², -ING²] —**fleet′ing·ly,** *n.* —**fleet′ing·ness,** *n.*
—**Syn.** passing, flitting, flying, brief, fugitive.

Fleet′ Street′, a street in central London, England: location of many newspaper offices; often used figuratively to mean the entire British newspaper world.

Fleet·wood (flēt′wo͝od′), *n.* a town in central Pennsylvania. 2647 (1960).

Flem., Flemish. Also, **Flem**

Flem·ing (flem′ing), *n.* **1.** a native of Flanders. **2.** a Flemish-speaking Belgian. [ME < MD *Vlaming;* cf. OIcel *flǣming,* OHG *Flaming,* ML *Flamingus,* Sp *flamenco* FLAMENCO]

Flem·ing (flem′ing), *n.* **1. Sir Alexander,** 1881–1955, Scottish bacteriologist and physician: codiscoverer of penicillin 1929; Nobel prize for medicine 1945. **2. Ian (Lancaster),** 1908–1964, British writer of suspense novels.

Flem·ing·ton (flem′ing tən), *n.* a town in W New Jersey. 3232 (1960).

Flem′ing valve′, *Electronics Obs.* a diode. [named after Sir John Ambrose *Fleming* (1849–1945), English inventor and electrical engineer]

Flem·ish (flem′ish), *adj.* **1.** of or pertaining to Flanders, its people, or their language. **2.** pertaining to or designating the style of art, esp. painting, as developed principally in Flanders and northern France during the 15th century, chiefly characterized by sharply delineated forms, naturalistic proportions, clear, usually cool colors, and the use of perspective. —*n.* **3.** the people of Flanders collectively; the Flemings. **4.** one of the official languages of Belgium, a Germanic dialect mutually intelligible with Dutch. —*v.t.* **5.** (*sometimes l.c.*) *Naut.* to fake down (rope) in a Flemish coil. *Abbr.:* Flem., Flem [ME < coastal D dial. var. of MD *Vlamisch* (D *Vlaamsch*), equiv. to *Vlam-* (see FLEMING) + *-isch* -ISH¹]

Flem′ish bond′, a brickwork bond having alternate stretchers and headers in each course, each header being centered above and below a stretcher. See illus. under **bond.**

Flem′ish coil′, *Naut.* a fake in the form of a flat, closely wound spiral. Also called **Flem′ish fake′.**

Flem′ish horse′, a short footrope attached to a yard on a sailing vessel.

Flem′ish knot′. See **figure of eight** (def. 2).

Flem′ish scroll′, a scroll, as on a chair leg, having the form of two intersecting and oppositely curved C-scrolls.

Flemish scroll

flense (flens), *v.t.,* **flensed, flens·ing.** **1.** to strip the blubber or the skin from (a whale, seal, etc.). **2.** to strip off (blubber or skin). Also, **flench** (flench), **flinch.** [< D *flense(n)*] —**flens′er,** *n.*

flesh (flesh), *n.* **1.** the soft substance of an animal or human body, consisting of muscle and fat. **2.** muscular and fatty tissue. **3.** this substance or tissue in animals, viewed as an article of food, usually excluding fish and sometimes fowl; meat. **4.** fatness; weight: *to put on flesh.* **5.** the body, esp. as distinguished from the spirit or soul: *The flesh is weak.* **6.** man's physical or animal nature, as distinguished from his moral or spiritual nature: *the needs of the flesh.* **7.** mankind. **8.** living creatures generally. **9.** one's family, relatives, or kindred. **10.** *Bot.* the soft pulpy portion of a fruit, vegetable, etc., as distinguished from the core, skin, shell, etc. **11.** the surface of the human body, esp. with respect to its color or outward appearance: *A person with tender flesh should not expose it to direct sunlight.* **12.** See **flesh color. 13. in the flesh,** present before one's eyes; in person: *Her screen idol looked quite different in the flesh.* **14. pound of flesh,** something due to someone which strict justice demands, but which could be paid only by disregarding considerations of charity. —*v.t.* **15.** to plunge (a weapon) into the flesh. **16.** *Hunting.* to feed (a hound or hawk) with flesh in order to make it more eager for the chase. Cf. **blood** (def. 21). **17.** to incite and accustom (persons) to bloodshed or battle by an initial experience. **18.** to inflame the ardor or passions of by a taste of indulgence. **19.** to feed full with flesh or fleshly enjoyments; surfeit; glut. **20.** to overlay or cover (a skeleton or skeletal frame) with flesh or with a fleshlike substance. **21.** to give dimension, substance, or reality to (often fol. by *out*): *The playwright fleshed out his characters.* **22.** to remove adhering flesh from (hides), in leather manufacture. [ME *flesc,* OE *flǣsc;* c. OFris *flēsk,* OHG *fleisk* (G *Fleisch*), OIcel *flesk* bacon] —**flesh′less,** *adj.*

flesh′ and blood′, **1.** offspring or relatives: *one's own flesh and blood.* **2.** the human body or nature: *more than flesh and blood can endure.* [ME *flesh and blod*]

flesh′ col′or, the color of a white person's skin; yellowish pink; pinkish cream. —**flesh′-col′ored,** *adj.*

flesh·er (flesh′ər), *n.* **1.** a person who fleshes hides. **2.** a tool for fleshing hides. [ME *fleshour.* See FLESH, -ER¹]

flesh′ fly′, any of several dipterous insects of the family *Sarcophagidae* that deposit their eggs or larvae in carrion or in the flesh of living animals.

flesh·hook (flesh′ho͝ok′), *n.* **1.** a hook for use in lifting meat, as from a pot. **2.** a hook to hang meat on. [ME; see FLESH, HOOK]

flesh·ings (flesh′ingz), *n.* (*construed as pl.*) flesh-colored tights. [FLESH + -ING¹ + -S³]

flesh·ly (flesh′lē), *adj.,* **-li·er, -li·est.** **1.** of or pertaining to the flesh or body; bodily, corporeal, or physical. **2.** carnal; sensual. **3.** worldly, rather than spiritual. **4.** having a sensuous quality: *the fleshly poetry of the 17th century.* **5.** *Obs.* having much flesh; fleshy. [ME; OE *flǣsclic.* See FLESH, -LY] —**flesh′li·ly,** *adv.* —**flesh′li·ness,** *n.*

flesh·pot (flesh′pot′), *n.* **1.** a pot or vessel containing flesh or meat. **2.** a place offering luxurious and unrestrained pleasure or amusement: *the fleshpots of Las Vegas.* **3. fleshpots,** luxurious and unrestrained living. [FLESH + POT¹]

flesh′ wound′ (wo͞ond), a wound which does not extend beyond the flesh; a slight or superficial wound.

flesh·y (flesh′ē), *adj.,* **flesh·i·er, flesh·i·est.** **1.** having much flesh; plump; fat. **2.** consisting of or resembling flesh. **3.** *Bot.* consisting of fleshlike substance; pulpy, as a fruit; thick and tender, as a leaf. [ME; see FLESH, -Y¹] —**flesh′i·ness,** *n.*

Fle·ta (flē′tə), *n.* a girl's given name. Also, **Fleda.**

fletch (flech), *v.t.* to provide (an arrow) with a feather. [back formation from FLETCHER]

fletch·er (flech′ər), *n.* a person who makes arrows. [ME *fleccher* < OF *flechier.* See FLECHE, -ER²]

Fletch·er (flech′ər), *n.* **1. John,** 1579–1625, English dramatist: collaborated with Francis Beaumont 1606?–16; with Philip Massinger 1613–25. **2. John Gould,** 1886–1950, U.S. poet. **3.** a boy's given name.

Fletch·er·ise (flech′ə rīz′), *v.i., v.t.,* **-ised, -is·ing.** *Chiefly Brit.* Fletcherize.

Fletch·er·ism (flech′ə riz′əm), *n.* the practice of chewing food until it is reduced to a finely divided, liquefied mass: advocated by Horace Fletcher, 1849–1919, U.S. nutritionist. [*Fletcher* + -ISM]

Fletch·er·ize (flech′ə rīz′), *v.i., v.t.,* **-ized, -iz·ing.** to chew (food) slowly and thoroughly. Also, *esp. Brit.,* **Fletcherise.** [FLETCHER(ISM) + -IZE]

Flett′ner control′ (flet′nər), servocontrol (def. 3). [named after A. *Flettner* (b. 1885), German engineer and inventor]

Fleur (flûr, flo͝or; *Fr.* flœr), *n.* a girl's given name.

fleur-de-lis (flûr′dᵊlē′, -lēs′, flo͝or′-; *Fr.* flœr də lē′), *n., pl.* **fleurs-de-lis** (flûr′dᵊlēz′, flo͝or′-; *Fr.* flœr də lē′). **1.** a heraldic device somewhat resembling three petals or floral segments of an iris tied by an encircling band. **2.** the distinctive bearing of the royal family of France. **3.** the iris flower or plant. Also, **fleur-de-lys** (for defs. 1, 2). [< F; r. ME *flourdelis* < AF *flour de lis,* lit., lily flower]

Fleurs-de-lis shown on royal arms of France, before 1376

fleur-de-lys (flûr′dᵊlē′, -lēs′, flo͝or′-; *Fr.* flœr də lēs′), *n., pl.* **fleurs-de-lys** (flûr′dᵊlēz′, flo͝or′-; *Fr.* flœr də lēs′). fleur-de-lis (defs. 1, 2).

fleu·rette (flo͞o ret′, flo͝o-), *n.* an ornament formed like a small conventionalized flower. [< F: lit., little flower]

Fleu·rette (flo͞o ret′, flo͝o-; *Fr.* flœ ret′), *n.* a girl's given name.

fleu·ron (flûr′on, flo͝or′-), *n.* **1.** a floral motif, as one used as a terminal point or in a decorative series on an object. **2.** *Print.* flower (def. 6). [< F; MF *floron,* equiv. to *flor* FLOWER + *-on* n. suffix]

Fleurs du Mal, Les (*Fr.* lā flœr dү mal′). See **Flowers of Evil.**

fleu·ry (flûr′ē, flo͝or′ē), *adj.* *Heraldry.* **1.** terminating in fleurs-de-lis: *a cross fleury; a fess fleury.* **2.** ornamented with fleurs-de-lis. Also, **flory.** [late ME *flourre* < MF *fleure,* deriv. of *fleur* FLOWER; see -EE]

Fleu·ry (flœ rē′), *n.* **1. An·dré Her·cule de** (äɴ drā′ er kүl′ də), 1653–1743, French cardinal and statesman. **2. Claude** (klōd), 1640–1723, French ecclesiastical historian.

flew¹ (flo͞o), *v.* a pt. of **fly¹.**

flew² (flo͞o), *n.* flue³.

flews (flo͞oz), *n.pl.* the large, pendulous sides of the upper lip of certain dogs, as bloodhounds. See diag. under **dog.** [?]

flex (fleks), *v.t., v.i.* **1.** to bend, as a part of the body: *He flexed his arms to show off his muscles.* —*n.* **2.** act of flexing. **3.** *Brit.* **a.** any flexible, insulated electric cord; an electric cord or extension cord. **b.** *Slang.* an elastic band, as a garter. **4.** *Math.* an inflection point. [< L *flex(us)* bent, turned, curved, ptp. of *flectere* to bend, turn]

flexed (flekst), *adj.* *Heraldry.* (of a human leg) depicted as bent at the knee: *a human leg flexed.* [FLEX + -ED²]

flex·i·ble (flek′sə bəl), *adj.* **1.** capable of being bent; easily bent: *a flexible willow wand.* **2.** susceptible of modification or adaptation; adaptable: *a flexible system; a flexible schedule; a flexible mind.* **3.** willing or disposed to yield; pliable: *a flexible personality.* [ME < L *flexibil(is)* pliant, easily bent. See FLEX, -IBLE] —**flex′i·bil′i·ty, flex′i·ble·ness,** *n.* —**flex′i·bly,** *adv.*
—**Syn. 1.** pliable, elastic, supple. FLEXIBLE, LIMBER, PLIANT refer to that which bends easily. FLEXIBLE refers to that which is capable of being bent and adds sometimes the idea of compressibility or expansibility: *a flexible piece of rubber hose.* LIMBER is esp. applied to the body to refer to ease of movement; it resembles FLEXIBLE except that there is an idea of even greater ease in bending: *a young and limber dancer.* PLIANT stresses an inherent quality or tendency to bend which does not require force or pressure from the outside; it may mean merely adaptable or may have a derogatory sense: *a pliant character.* **2.** tractable, compliant. —**Ant. 1.** stiff. **2.** rigid.

flex·ile (flek′sil *or, esp. Brit.,* -sīl), *adj.* flexible; pliant; tractable; adaptable. [< L *flexil(is)* pliant, pliable. See FLEX, -ILE] —**flex·il′i·ty,** *n.*

flex·ion (flek′shən), *n.* **1.** *Anat.* **a.** the act of bending a limb. **b.** the position which a limb assumes when it is bent. **2.** *Chiefly Brit.* flection (defs. 1–3). [< L *flexiōn-* (s. of *flexiō*) a bending, turning. See FLEX, -ION] —**flex′ion·al,** *adj.* —**flex′ion·less,** *adj.*

flex·i·time (flek′si tīm′), *n.* a work arrangement under which employees are individually allowed to choose, within limits, their own working hours. Also, **flex′time′.** [FLEXI(BLE) + TIME]

Flex·ner (fleks′nər), *n.* **1. Abraham,** 1866–1959, U.S. educator. **2.** his brother **Simon,** 1863–1946, U.S. pathologist and bacteriologist.

Flex·og·ra·phy (flek sog′rə fē), *n.* *Print., Trademark.* a letterpress printing technique employing rubber or plastic plates and fairly fluid inks. —**flex·o·graph·ic** (flek′sə graf′ik), *adj.*

flex·or (flek′sər), *n.* *Anat.* a muscle which serves to flex or bend a part of the body. [< NL; see FLEX, -OR²]

flex′ point′, *Math.* See **inflection point.**

flex·u·os·i·ty (flek′sho͞o os′i tē), *n.* quality or condition of being flexuous. [< LL *flexuōsitās.* See FLEXUOUS, -ITY]

flex·u·ous (flek′sho͞o əs), *adj.* full of bends or curves; winding; sinuous. Also, **flex·u·ose** (flek′sho͞o ōs′). [< L *flexuōs(us)* full of turns, winding, crooked, equiv. to *flexu(s)* (see FLEX) + *-ōsus* -OUS] —**flex′u·ous·ly, flex′u·ose′ly,** *adv.* —**flex′u·ous·ness, flex′u·ose′ness,** *n.*

flex·ure (flek′shər), *n.* **1.** act of flexing or bending. **2.** state of being flexed or bent. **3.** the part bent; bend; fold. [< L *flexūra* a bending, turning, winding. See FLEX, -URE] —**flex′ur·al,** *adj.*

fley (flā), *v.,* **fleyed, fley·ing.** *Chiefly Scot.* to frighten; terrify. [ME *flaie(n), fleie(n),* OE *-flīgan* (in *ā-flȳgan*); c. OIcel *fleygia* to make to fly. Cf. FLY[1] —**fley·ed·ly** (flā′id lē), *adv.* —**fley′ed·ness,** *n.*

flib·ber·ti·gib·bet (flib′ər tē jib′it), *n.* **1.** a chattering or flighty, light-headed person, usually a woman. **2.** *Archaic.* a gossip. [ME *flepergebet, flipergebet;* appar. imit.]

flic·flac (flik′flak′), *n.* a step in dancing in which the feet strike rapidly together. [< F; imit.]

flicht·er (flikн′tər), *v.i. Scot.* **1.** (of birds) to fly feebly; flutter. **2.** to tremble; quiver. Also, **flighter.** [*flicht* FLIGHT + -ER[6]]

flick[1] (flik), *n.* **1.** a sudden light blow or stroke, as with a whip or the finger: *She gave the horse a flick with her riding crop.* **2.** the sound made by such a blow or stroke. **3.** a light and rapid movement: *a flick of the wrist.* **4.** something thrown off with or as with a jerk: *a flick of mud.* —*v.t.* **5.** to strike lightly with a whip, the finger, etc. **6.** to remove with such a stroke: *to flick dust from one's coat; to flick away a crumb.* **7.** to move (something) with a sudden stroke or jerk. —*v.i.* **8.** to move with a jerk or jerks. **9.** to flutter. [late ME *flykke;* appar. imit.]

flick[2] (flik), *n. Slang.* a motion picture. Also, **flicker.** [back formation from FLICKER[1]]

flick·er[1] (flik′ər), *v.i.* **1.** to burn unsteadily; shine with a wavering light: *The candle flickered in the wind and went out.* **2.** to wave to and fro; vibrate; quiver: *The long grasses flickered in the wind.* **3.** to flutter. —*v.t.* **4.** to cause to flicker. —*n.* **5.** an unsteady flame or light. **6.** a flickering; flickering movement. **7.** a brief occurrence or appearance: *a flicker of hope.* **8.** Often, **flickers.** *Slang.* flick[2]. **9.** *Ophthalm.* the visual sensation of flickering that occurs when the interval between intermittent flashes of light is too long to permit fusion. [ME *flikere(n),* OE *flicorian* to flutter; c. D *flikkeren*] —**flick′er·ing·ly,** *adv.* —**flick′er·y,** *adj.*
—**Syn. 1.** flare, flash, gleam, shimmer.

flick·er[2] (flik′ər), *n.* any of several American woodpeckers of the genus *Colaptes,* having the underside of the wings and tail brightly marked with yellow or red. [imit.]

flick·er·tail (flik′ər tāl′), *n.* See **Richardson ground squirrel.** [FLICKER[1] + TAIL[1]]

flied (flīd), *v.* a pt. and pp. of **fly**[1].

fli·er (flī′ər), *n.* **1.** something that flies, as a bird or insect. **2.** an aviator. **3.** one who or that which moves with great speed. **4.** some part of a machine having a rapid motion. **5.** *Informal.* a flying jump or leap: *He took a flier off the bridge.* **6.** *Informal.* a financial venture outside of one's ordinary business: *Our little flier in uranium stocks was a disaster.* **7.** *Archit.* one of the steps in a straight flight. Cf. **winder** (def. 2). **8.** *U.S.* a small handbill. **9.** a silvery-green sunfish, *Centrarchus macropterus,* found from Virginia to Florida and through the lower Mississippi valley. Also, **flyer.** [ME; see FLY[1], -ER[1]]

flight[1] (flīt), *n.* **1.** act, manner, or power of flying. **2.** the distance covered or the course taken by a flying object: *a 500-mile flight; the flight of the ball.* **3.** a number of beings or things flying or passing through the air together: *a flight of swallows.* **4.** a trip by an airplane, glider, etc. **5.** a scheduled trip on an airline: *a 5 o'clock flight.* **6.** the basic tactical unit of military air forces, consisting of two or more aircraft. **7.** act, principles, or technique of flying an airplane: *flight training.* **8.** a journey into or through outer space, as of a rocket. **9.** swift movement, transition, or progression: *the flight of time.* **10.** a soaring above or transcending ordinary bounds: *a flight of fancy.* **11.** *Archit.* **a.** a series of steps between any landing and the next. **b.** a series of steps, and sometimes of landings, between any floor and the next. **12.** *Archery.* **a.** a light arrow for long-distance shooting. **b.** the distance such an arrow travels when shot. —*v.i.* **13.** (of wild fowls) to fly in flights. [ME; OE *flyht;* c. D *vlucht;* akin to FLY[1]] —**flight′less,** *adj.*
—**Syn. 3.** flock.

flight[2] (flīt), *n.* **1.** act of fleeing; hasty departure. **2.** **put to flight,** to force to flee; rout: *She succeeded in putting the intruder to flight.* **3.** **take flight,** to retreat; flee: *The wild animals took flight before the onrushing fire.* Also, **take to flight.** [ME; c. G *Flucht;* akin to FLEE]

flight′ ar′row, *Archery.* **1.** an arrow having a conical or pyramidal head without barbs. **2.** any long and light arrow; a shaft or arrow for the longbow, as distinguished from the bolt.

flight′ control′, **1.** the direction of airplane movements, esp. take-offs and landings, by messages from the ground. **2.** the system by which this direction is done. **3.** the office from which this direction is done. **4.** the system by which the pilot of an airplane controls the movement of the airplane.

flight′ deck′, **1.** *Navy.* the upper deck of an aircraft carrier, constructed and equipped for the landing and take-off of aircraft. **2.** *Aeron.* (in certain aircraft) an elevated compartment containing the instruments and controls used by the pilot, copilot, and flight engineer to operate the aircraft.

flight·er (flikн′tər), *v.i. Scot.* flichter.

flight′ feath′er, *Ornith.* one of those large, stiff feathers of the wing and tail of a bird which are essential to flight.

flight′ forma′tion, an arrangement of two or more airplanes flying together in a group, usually in an agreed pattern.

flight′ in′dicator, *Aeron.* See **artificial horizon** (def. 3).

flight′ in′strument, *Aeron.* any instrument used to indicate the altitude, attitude, airspeed, drift, or direction of an aircraft.

flight′ lead′er, a pilot who leads a flight of military airplanes.

flight·less (flīt′lis), *adj.* incapable of flying: *flightless birds such as the moa, rhea, and dodo.* [FLIGHT[1] + -LESS]

flight′ nurse′, a nurse in the U.S. Air Force who tends patients being moved by air.

flight′ of′ficer, an officer of the U.S. Army Air Force in World War II, having a rank equivalent to that of a warrant officer junior grade.

flight′ path′, the locus of the center of gravity of a moving airplane.

flight′ pay′, a pay supplement allowed by the U.S. Air Force to certain crewmen who attain a certain minimum flight time per month.

flight′ shoot′ing, *Archery.* competitive shooting for distance only.

flight′ strip′, *Aeron.* **1.** a strip of cleared land used as an emergency runway for aircraft. **2.** runway. **3.** a series of continuous aerial reconnaissance photographs.

flight′ sur′geon, a medical officer in the U.S. Air Force who is qualified to attend to the medical needs of airmen.

flight-test (flīt′test′), *v.t.* to test (an airplane or the like) in flight.

flight·y (flī′tē), *adj.,* **flight·i·er, flight·i·est.** **1.** given to flights of fancy; capricious; frivolous. **2.** slightly delirious; light-headed; mildly crazy. **3.** irresponsible: *She's too flighty to take care of young children.* **4.** *Archaic.* swift or fleet. [FLIGHT[1] + -Y[1]] —**flight′i·ly,** *adv.* —**flight′i·ness,** *n.*
—**Syn. 1.** mercurial, undependable, irresponsible.

flim·flam (flim′flam′), *n., v.,* **-flammed, -flam·ming.** *Informal.* —*n.* **1.** a piece of nonsense; twaddle; bosh. **2.** a trick or deception; humbug. —*v.t.* **3.** to trick; delude; humbug; cheat: *A fortune-teller flim-flammed her out of her savings.* [cf. Icel *flimska* mockery] —**flim′flam′mer,** *n.*

flim·sy (flim′zē), *adj.,* **-si·er, -si·est,** *n., pl.* **-sies.** —*adj.* **1.** without material strength or solidity: *a flimsy material; a flimsy structure.* **2.** weak; inadequate; not effective or convincing: *a flimsy excuse or argument.* —*n.* **3.** a thin kind of paper, esp. for use in making several copies at a time of an article, telegraphic dispatch, or the like, as in newspaper work. **4.** a copy of a report or dispatch on such paper. [? metathetic var. of FILMY modeled on *tipsy, limpsy*] —**flim′si·ly,** *adv.* —**flim′si·ness,** *n.*
—**Syn. 1.** shoddy, weak, unstable, unsteady. **2.** unconvincing, lame, vague. —**Ant. 1.** sturdy.

flinch[1] (flinch), *v.i.* **1.** to draw back or shrink from what is dangerous, difficult, or unpleasant. **2.** to shrink under pain; wince. **3.** *Croquet.* to let the foot slip from the ball in the act of croqueting. —*v.t.* **4.** to draw back or withdraw from. —*n.* **5.** act of flinching. **6.** *Cards.* a game in which the cards are accumulated on the table. [? nasalized var. of dial. *flitch* to flit, shift one's position] —**flinch′er,** *n.* —**flinch′ing·ly,** *adv.*
—**Syn. 1.** recoil, withdraw, blench.

flinch[2] (flinch), *v.t.* flense.

flin·ders (flin′dərz), *n.pl.* splinters; small pieces or fragments. [late ME *flendris,* ? < Scand; cf. Norw *flindra* splinter; perh. akin to FLINT]

Flin′ders bar′ (flin′dərz), *Navig.* a bar of soft iron, mounted vertically beneath a compass to compensate for vertical magnetic currents. See diag. under **binnacle.** [named after Matthew *Flinders* (d.1814), English mariner]

Flin′ders Range′, a mountain range in S Australia. Highest peak, St. Mary Peak, 3900 ft.

Flin Flon (flin′ flon′), a city in NW Manitoba, in central Canada. 11,104 (1961).

fling (fling), *v.,* **flung, fling·ing,** *n.* —*v.t.* **1.** to throw, cast, or hurl with force or violence: *to fling the first stone.* **2.** to move (oneself) violently with impatience, contempt, or the like: *She flung herself angrily from the room.* **3.** to put suddenly or violently: *to fling someone into jail.* **4.** to project or speak sharply, curtly, or forcefully: *He flung his answer at the questioner.* **5.** to involve (oneself) vigorously in an undertaking. **6.** to move, do, or say (something) quickly: *to fling a greeting in passing.* **7.** to send forth suddenly and rapidly: *to fling fresh troops into a battle.* **8.** to throw aside or off. **9.** to throw to the ground, as in wrestling or horseback riding. —*v.i.* **10.** to move with haste or violence; rush; dash. **11.** to fly into violent and irregular motions, as a horse; throw the body about, as a person. **12.** to speak harshly or abusively (usually fol. by *out*): *He flung out disgustedly against the whole human race.* —*n.* **13.** act of flinging. **14.** a short period of unrestrained indulgence of one's impulses: *He had his fling before he was drafted.* **15.** a severe or contemptuous remark or gibe. **16.** Also called **Highland fling.** a lively Scottish dance characterized by flinging movements of the arms and legs. **17.** **take a fling at,** to make an attack upon or attempt at something: *She often takes a fling at my taste in neckties. He took a fling at playwriting.* [ME; cf. Sw *flänga* to fly, race]

fling·er (fling′ər), *n.* **1.** one who or that which flings. **2.** Also called **slinger, thrower.** a device, mounted on a rotating shaft, for throwing lubricant onto a bearing or for keeping grit out of a bearing by centrifugal force. [FLING + -ER[1]]

flint (flint), *n.* **1.** a hard kind of stone, a form of silica resembling chalcedony but more opaque, less pure, and less lustrous. **2.** a piece of this, esp. as used for striking fire. **3.** something very hard or unyielding. —*v.t.* **4.** to furnish with flint. [ME, OE; c. MD *vlint,* Dan *flint;* cf. PLINTH] —**flint′like′,** *adj.*

Flint (flint), *n.* **1.** **Austin,** 1812–86, U.S. physician: founder of Bellevue and Buffalo medical colleges. **2.** his son **Austin,** 1836–1915, U.S. physiologist and physician. **3.** a city in SE Michigan. 196,940 (1960). **4.** Flintshire.

flint′ corn′, a variety of corn, *Zea Mays indurata,* having very hard-skinned kernels not subject to shrinkage.

flint′ glass′, *Optics.* an optical glass of high dispersion and relatively high index of refraction, composed of alkalis, lead oxide, and silica, with or without other bases.

flint·head (flint′hed′), *n.* the wood ibis, *Mycteria americana.* [FLINT + HEAD]

flint·lock (flint′lok′), *n.* **1.** a gunlock in which a piece of flint striking against steel produces sparks that ignite the priming. **2.** a firearm with such a lock. [FLINT + LOCK[1]]

Flintlock fowling piece
A, Steel struck by flint; B, Powder pan; C, Touchhole; D, Flint; E, Cock

Flint·shire (flint′shēr, -shər), *n.* a county in NE Wales. 149,888 (1961); 256 sq. mi. *Co. seat:* Mold. Also called **Flint.**

flint·y (flin′tē), *adj.,* **flint·i·er, flint·i·est.** **1.** composed of, containing, or resembling flint, esp. in hardness. **2.** unyielding; unmerciful; cruel; obdurate: *his flinty heart.* [FLINT + -Y[1]] —**flint′i·ly,** *adv.* —**flint′i·ness,** *n.*

flip[1] (flip), *v.,* **flipped, flip·ping,** *n.* —*v.t.* **1.** to toss or put in motion with a sudden impulse as a snap of a finger and thumb, esp. as to cause to turn over in the air: *to flip a coin.* **2.** to move (something) suddenly or jerkily: *He flipped the extra nails to the side.* **3.** to turn over, esp. with a short rapid gesture: *He flipped the cards as he spoke.* —*v.i.* **4.** to make a flicking movement; strike at something smartly or sharply; snap. **5.** to move oneself with or as with flippers: *The seals flipped along the beach.* **6.** to move with a jerk or jerks. **7.** *Slang.* to react to something in an excited, astonished, or delighted manner: *He really flipped over his new girl friend.* —*n.* **8.** an instance of flipping; a smart tap or strike. **9.** a sudden jerk. **10.** a somersault, esp. one performed in the air: *a back flip off the diving board.* **11.** *Cards.* a variety of seven-card stud in which each player receives his first four cards face down and selects two of them to expose before receiving his next card. [prob. imit.; see FILLIP]

flip[2] (flip), *n.* a mixed drink made with liquor or wine, sugar, and egg, topped with powdered nutmeg and served hot or cold. [? n. use of FLIP[1], so called from tossing or flipping of ingredients in preparation]

flip[3] (flip), *adj.,* **flip·per, flip·pest.** *Informal.* smart; pert; flippant. [adj. use of FLIP[1]]

flip-flop (flip′flop′), *n., adv., v.,* **-flopped, -flop·ping.** —*n.* **1.** Also called **flip′-flop cir′cuit.** *Electronics.* an electronic circuit having two stable conditions, each one corresponding to one of two alternative input signals. **2.** any of several similar devices having two alternative states, the change of state being caused by some input signal or by some change of input. **3.** a backward somersault. **4.** the sound and motion of something flapping, as a wind-blown shutter; a banging to and fro. **5.** (in advertising) a display or presentation, usually on an easel, consisting of a series of pages hinged at the top and flipped over in sequence. —*adv.* **6.** with repeated sounds and motions, as of something flapping: *The shutters went flip-flop against the window.* —*v.i.* **7.** to execute a backward somersault. **8.** to flap; bang to and fro: *The door flip-flopped in the high wind.* Also, **flip-flap** (flip′flap′) (for defs. 3, 4, 6).

flip·pant (flip′ənt), *adj.* **1.** frivolously shallow, disrespectful, or lacking in seriousness; characterized by levity: *The audience was shocked by his flippant remarks about patriotism.* **2.** *Chiefly Dial.* nimble, limber, or pliant. **3.** *Obs.* glib; voluble. [? FLIP[3] + -ANT; cf. Icel *fleipa* to babble, Sw *flipa* to cry] —**flip′pan·cy, flip′pant·ness,** *n.* —**flip′pant·ly,** *adv.*
—**Syn. 1.** saucy, impertinent, impudent.

flip·per (flip′ər), *n.* **1.** a broad, flat limb, as of a seal, whale, etc., especially adapted for swimming. **2.** Usually, **flippers.** Also called **fin.** one of a pair of paddlelike devices, usually of rubber, worn on the feet as an aid in swimming. **3.** *Theat.* a narrow flat hinged or attached at right angles to a larger flat. **4.** *Slang.* the hand. [FLIP[1] + -ER[1]]

flip′ side′, *Slang.* the reverse and, sometimes, less important side of a phonograph record.

flip-top (flip′top′), *adj.* having a hinged upper portion which can be pulled outward or upward to increase the top surface or to reveal an enclosed area underneath: *a flip-top box.*

flirt (flûrt), *v.i.* **1.** to court triflingly or act amorously without serious intentions; play at love; coquet. **2.** to trifle or toy, as with an idea: *She flirted with the notion of buying a wig.* **3.** to move with a jerk or jerks; dart about: *butterflies flirting from flower to flower.* —*v.t.* **4.** to give a sudden or brisk motion to; wave smartly, as a fan. **5.** to throw or propel with a toss or jerk; fling suddenly. —*n.* **6.** Also, **flirt′er.** a person who is given to flirting: *an accomplished flirt.* **7.** a quick throw or toss; sudden jerk or darting motion. [imit.] —**flirt′ing·ly,** *adv.*
—**Syn. 1.** tease. **1, 2.** dally. **6.** minx, coquette, tease.

flir·ta·tion (flûr tā′shən), *n.* **1.** act or practice of flirting; coquetry. **2.** a love affair which is not serious. [FLIRT + -ATION] —**flir·ta′tion·al,** *adj.* —**flir·ta′tion·less,** *adj.*

flir·ta·tious (flûr tā′shəs), *adj.* **1.** given or inclined to flirtation. **2.** pertaining to flirtation. Also, **flirt′y.** [FLIRTAT(ION) + -IOUS] —**flir·ta′tious·ly,** *adv.* —**flir·ta′tious·ness,** *n.*

flit (flit), *v.,* **flit·ted, flit·ting,** *n.* —*v.i.* **1.** to move lightly and swiftly; fly, dart, or skim along: *bees flitting from flower to flower.* **2.** to flutter, as a bird. **3.** to pass away quickly, as time: *hours flitting by.* **4.** *Chiefly Scot. and North Eng.* **a.** to depart or die. **b.** to change one's residence. —*v.t.* **5.** *Archaic.* to remove; transfer; oust or dispossess. —*n.* **6.** a light, swift movement; flutter. **7.** *Scot. and North Eng.* a change of residence; instance of moving to a new address. **8.** *Slang.* a male homosexual. [ME *flitte(n)* < Scand; c. Icel *flytja* to carry, convey, Sw *flytta.* See FLEET[2]]
—**Syn. 1.** See **fly**[1].

flitch (flich), *n.* **1.** the side of a hog (or, formerly, some other animal) salted and cured: *a flitch of bacon.* **2.** a steak cut from a halibut. **3.** *Carpentry.* **a.** a piece, as a board, forming part of a flitch beam. **b.** a thin piece of wood, as a veneer. **c.** a bundle of veneers, arranged as cut from the log. **d.** a log about to be cut into veneers. **e.** cant[2] (def. 8). —*v.t.* **4.** to cut into flitches. **5.** *Carpentry.* to assemble (boards or the like) into a laminated construction. [ME *flicche,* OE *flicca;* c. MLG *vlicke,* Icel *flikki*]

flitch′ beam′, *Carpentry.* a beam composed of planks bolted together side by side and often reinforced with a plate of iron or steel. Also called **flitch′ gird′er, sandwich beam, sandwich girder.**

flitch·plate (flich′plāt′), *n.* an iron or steel plate for reinforcing a flitch beam. [FLITCH + PLATE[1]]

flite (flīt), *v.,* **flit·ed, flit·ing,** *n. Scot. and North Eng.* —*v.i.* **1.** to dispute; wrangle; scold; jeer. —*n.* **2.** a dispute or wrangle; scolding. Also, **flyte.** [ME *flitte(n),* OE *flītā(n)* to strive, contend; akin to MHG *vlīzen* (G *Fleiss* industry), OS *flītan*]

flit·ing (flī′ting), *n.* **1.** contention. **2.** war of words, in versified dialogue. [ME; see FLITE, -ING[1]]

flit·ter[1] (flit′ər), *v.i., v.t.* to flutter. [FLIT + -ER[6]]

flit·ter[2] (flit′ər), *n.* one who or that which flits. [FLIT + -ER[1]]

flit·ter[3] (flit′ər), *n.* fine metallic fragments, esp. as used for ornamentation. [< G]

flit·ter·mouse (flit′ər mous′), *n., pl.* **-mice.** *Archaic.* bat[2] (def. 1). [FLITTER[1] + MOUSE; calque of G *Fledermaus*]

flit·ting (flit′ing), *adj.* moving lightly and swiftly; passing quickly; fluttering. [ME; see FLIT, -ING[2]] —**flit′ting·ly,** *adv.*

fliv·ver (fliv′ər), *n.* **1.** *Facetious.* an automobile. **2.** *Slang.* something of unsatisfactory quality or inferior grade. [?]

F.L.N., an organization of Algerian nationalists. [< F *Front de Libération Nationale*]

Flo (flō), *n.* a girl's given name, form of **Florence.**

float (flōt), *v.i.* **1.** to rest or remain on the surface of a liquid; be buoyant: *Does this soap float?* **2.** to move gently on the surface of a liquid; drift along: *The canoe floated downstream.* **3.** to rest or move in a liquid, the air, etc.: *a balloon floating on high.* **4.** to move lightly and gracefully: *She floated down the stairs.* **5.** to move or hover before the eyes or in the mind: *Romantic visions floated before his eyes.* **6.** to pass from one person to another: *A nasty rumor about him is floating around town.* **7.** to be free from attachment. **8.** to move or drift about: *to float from place to place.* **9.** to be uninvolved: *floating through life.* **10.** to vacillate (often fol. by *between*). **11.** to be launched or floated, as a company, scheme, etc. **12.** *Com.* to be in circulation, as an acceptance; be awaiting maturity —*v.t.* **13.** to cause to float. **14.** to cover with water; flood; irrigate. **15.** to make smooth with a float, as the surface of plaster. **16.** to cover (a surface) with a liquid: *They floated the surface of the stone with water before grinding.* **17.** to launch (a company, scheme, etc.); set going. **18.** to sell on the stock market, as an issue of stocks or bonds. **19.** to make smooth or level, as the surface of plaster. **20.** *Theat.* to lay down (a flat), usually by bracing the bottom edge of the frame with the foot and allowing the rest to fall slowly to the floor. —*n.* **21.** something that floats, as a raft. **22.** something for buoying up. **23.** an inflated bag to sustain a person in water; life preserver. **24.** *Plumbing, Mach.* (in certain types of apparatus, cisterns, etc.) a device, as a hollow ball, which through its buoyancy automatically regulates the level, supply, or outlet of a liquid. **25.** *Naut.* a floating platform attached to a wharf, a bank, or the like, and used as a landing. **26.** *Aeron.* a hollow, boatlike structure under the wing or fuselage of an airplane, keeping it afloat in water. **27.** *Angling.* a piece of cork or other material for supporting a baited line in the water and indicating by its movements when a fish bites. **28.** *Zool.* an inflated organ that supports an animal in the water. **29.** Also called **float·board** (flōt′bōrd′, -bôrd′). paddle[1] (def. 6). **30.** *Geol.* loose fragments of rock, ore, etc., that have been moved from one place to another by the action of wind, water, etc. **31.** a vehicle bearing a display, usually an elaborate tableau, in a parade or procession: *The beauty queen will ride a float in the big parade.* **32.** a low-bodied dray for transporting heavy goods. **33.** *Building Trades.* **a.** a flat tool for spreading and smoothing plaster or stucco. **b.** a tool for polishing marble. **34.** a single-cut file of moderate smoothness. **35.** the loose yarn on the back of cloth due to a figure weave or brocading. **36.** *Banking.* uncollected checks and commercial paper in process of transfer from bank to bank. **37.** *Mining.* **a.** ore that has been washed downhill from an orebody and is found lying on the surface of the ground. **b.** any mineral in suspension in water. **38.** Usually, **floats.** *Theat. Brit.* footlights. [ME *flote(n)*, OE *flotian;* c. OIcel *flota*, MD *vloten*. See FLEET[2]]

float·a·ble (flō′tə bəl), *adj.* **1.** capable of floating; that can be floated. **2.** that can be floated on, as a river. [FLOAT + -ABLE] —**float′a·bil′i·ty,** *n.*

float·age (flō′tij), *n.* flotage.

float·a·tion (flō tā′shən), *n.* *Chiefly Brit.* flotation.

float′ bridge′, a bridge, as from a pier to a boat, floating at one end and hinged at the other to permit loading and unloading at any level of water.

float′ cham′ber, *Navig.* a float for a compass card.

float·er (flō′tər), *n.* **1.** one who or that which floats. **2.** *Informal.* a person who is continually changing his place of abode, employment, etc. **3.** *U.S.* **a.** a voter not attached to any party, esp. one whose vote may be purchased. **b.** a person who fraudulently votes, usually for pay, in different places in the same election. **4.** Also called **floating policy.** *Insurance.* a policy in which property that is frequently moved from one place to another is insured against theft, damage, etc. **5.** *Slang.* a police order to leave town. [FLOAT + -ER[1]]

float-feed (flōt′fēd′), *adj.* *Mach.* equipped with a float to control the feed.

float·ing (flō′ting), *adj.* **1.** being buoyed up on water or other liquid: *a floating bridge.* **2.** having little or no attachment. **3.** *Pathol.* away from its proper position, esp. in a downward direction: *a floating kidney.* **4.** not fixed or settled in a definite place or state: *a floating population.* **5.** *Finance.* **a.** in circulation or use, or not permanently invested, as capital. **b.** composed of sums due within a short time: *a floating debt.* **6.** *Mach.* **a.** having a soft suspension greatly reducing vibrations between the suspended part and its support. **b.** working smoothly. [FLOAT + -ING[2]] —**float′ing·ly,** *adv.*

Float′ing Cloud′, The. See **Drifting Cloud, The.**

float′ing dock′, a submersible, floating structure used as a dry dock, having a floor that is submerged, slipped under a floating vessel, and raised so as to raise the vessel entirely out of the water. Also called **float′ing dry′ dock′.**

float′ing founda′tion, a foundation used in yielding soil, having for its footing a raft tending to displace a weight greater than that of the building.

float′ing gang′, *Railroads U.S.* a group of workmen who service or repair the track but are not assigned to a particular section. Cf. **section gang.**

float′ing heart′, **1.** any of certain perennial aquatic herbs of the genus *Nymphoides*, esp. *N. lacunosum*, having floating, more or less heart-shaped leaves. **2.** a floating, aquatic plant, *Nymphoides cordatum*, of North America, having somewhat oval or round leaves that are purple beneath and white flowers.

float′ing inspec′tor, a factory inspector who examines production work by spot check, either in accordance with requirements or at his discretion.

float′ing is′land, **1.** a dessert consisting of boiled custard with portions of meringue, whipped cream, or whipped egg whites and sometimes jelly floating upon it or around it. **2.** a floating islandlike mass of earth and partly decayed vegetation held together by interlacing roots, as on a lake: usually formed by the accumulation of plant litter; sometimes artificially built on wooden platforms, as in the Orient.

float′ing parti′tion, *Carpentry.* a partition running parallel to and between two joists and resting on blocking between them.

float′ing pol′icy, **1.** (in marine insurance) a policy that provides protection of a broad nature for shipments of merchandise and that is valid continuously until canceled. **2.** floater (def. 4).

float′ing rib′, *Anat.* one member of the two lowest pairs of ribs, which are attached neither to the sternum nor to the cartilages of other ribs.

float′ing screed′, screed (def. 3).

float′ing stage′, *Theat.* **1.** a motor-operated platform or stage which can be raised and moved to a place offstage. **2.** an aquatic stage, as in the ancient Roman theater. **3.** a showboat.

float′ing stock′, stock not held for permanent investment and hence available for speculation; stock held by brokers and speculators rather than investors.

float′ing supply′, the aggregate supply of ready-to-market goods or securities.

float′ing vote′, *U.S.* the voters collectively who are not permanently attached to any political organization, and whose votes therefore cannot be counted upon by party managers.

float·man (flōt′mən), *n., pl.* **-men.** a person in charge of a car float. [FLOAT + MAN[1]]

float·plane (flōt′plān′), *n.* *Aeron.* a seaplane having landing gear consisting of one or more floats. Also, **float′ plane′.** Cf. **flying boat.** [FLOAT + PLANE[1]]

float·stone (flōt′stōn′), *n.* a stone for rubbing bricks to be gauged. Also called **rubbing stone.** [FLOAT + STONE]

float′ switch′, an electric switch controlled by a conductor floating in a liquid.

float′ valve′, a valve admitting or discharging a liquid to or from a tank and regulated by a float on the surface of the liquid within the tank to maintain a nearly constant height of liquid.

float·y (flō′tē), *adj.,* **float·i·er, float·i·est.** **1.** able to float; buoyant. **2.** (of a boat) drawing little water. [ME *floty*. See FLOAT, -Y[1]]

floc (flok), *n.* a tuftlike mass, as in a chemical precipitate. Also, **flock.** [< L *flocc(us)* FLOCCUS]

floc·cil·la·tion (flok′sə lā′shən), *n.* *Pathol.* a delirious picking of the bedclothes by the patient, as in certain fevers. Also called **carphology.** [< L **floccill(us)*, equiv. to *flocc(us)* FLOCCUS + *-ill(us)* dim. suffix + -ATION]

floc·cose (flok′ōs), *adj.* **1.** *Bot.* consisting of or bearing woolly tufts or long soft hairs. **2.** flocculent. [< LL *floccōs(us)* full of tufts of wool. See FLOCCUS, -OSE[1]]

floc·cu·lant (flok′yə lənt), *n.* a chemical for producing flocculation of suspended particles, as to improve the plasticity of clay for ceramic purposes. [FLOCCULE + -ANT]

floc·cu·late (flok′yə lāt′), *v.,* **-lat·ed, -lat·ing.** —*v.t.* **1.** to form into flocculent masses. —*v.i.* **2.** to form flocculent masses, as a cloud, a chemical precipitate, etc.; form aggregated or compound masses of particles. [FLOCCUL(US) + -ATE[1]] —**floc·cu·la·ble** (flok′yə lə bəl), *adj.* —**floc′cu·la′tion,** *n.* —**floc′cu·la′tor,** *n.*

floc·cule (flok′yōōl), *n.* **1.** something resembling a small flock or tuft of wool. **2.** a bit of flocculent matter, as in a liquid. [< NL *floccul(us)*. See FLOCCUS, -ULE]

floc·cu·lent (flok′yə lənt), *adj.* **1.** like a clump or tuft of wool. **2.** covered with a soft, woolly substance. **3.** consisting of or containing loose woolly masses. **4.** flaky. [FLOCC(US) + -ULENT] —**floc′cu·lence, floc′cu·len·cy,** *n.* —**floc′cu·lent·ly,** *adv.*

floc′culent precip′itate, *Chem.* a woolly-looking precipitate, as aluminum hydroxide formed by the addition of ammonia to an aluminum-salt solution.

floc·cu·lus (flok′yə ləs), *n., pl.* **-li** (-lī′). **1.** floccule. **2.** *Astron.* one of the bright or dark patches on the sun's surface, visible in a spectroheliogram. [< NL; see FLOCCULE]

floc·cus (flok′əs), *n., pl.* **floc·ci** (flok′sī), *adj.* —*n.* **1.** a small tuft of woolly hairs. —*adj.* **2.** *Meteorol.* (of a cloud) having elements in the form of small, rounded tufts. [< L: tuft of wool]

flock[1] (flok), *n.* **1.** a number of animals of one kind, esp. sheep, goats, or birds, that keep or feed together or are herded together. **2.** a crowd; large number of people. **3.** (in New Testament and ecclesiastical use) **a.** the Christian church in relation to Christ. **b.** a single congregation in relation to its pastor. **4.** *Archaic.* a band or company of persons. —*v.i.* **5.** to gather or go in a flock, company, or crowd. [ME; OE *floc;* c. Icel *flokkr*] —**flock′less,** *adj.*

—**Syn. 1, 2.** bevy, covey, flight, gaggle; brood, hatch, litter; shoal, school, swarm, group, company. FLOCK, DROVE, HERD, PACK refer to a company of animals, often under the care or guidance of someone. FLOCK is the popular term, which applies to groups of animals, esp. of sheep or goats, and companies of birds: *This lamb is the choicest of the flock. A flock of wild geese flew overhead.* DROVE is esp. applied to a number of oxen, sheep, or swine when driven in a group: *A drove of oxen was taken to market. A large drove of swine filled the roadway.* HERD is usually applied to large animals such as cattle, originally meaning those under the charge of someone; but by extension, to other animals feeding or driven together: *a buffalo herd; a herd of elephants.* PACK applies to a number of animals kept together or keeping together for offense or defense: *a pack of hounds kept for hunting; a pack of wolves.* As applied to groups of people, DROVE, HERD, and PACK carry a contemptuous implication.

flock[2] (flok), *n.* **1.** a lock or tuft of wool, hair, cotton, etc. **2.** (*sometimes construed as pl.*) wool refuse, shearings of cloth, old cloth torn to pieces, or the like, for upholstering furniture, stuffing mattresses, etc. **3.** (*sometimes construed as pl.*) finely powdered wool, cloth, etc., for decorating wallpaper, covering phonograph turntables, etc. **4.** floc. —*v.t.* **5.** to stuff with flock, as a mattress. **6.** to cover or coat with flock, as wallpaper, phonograph turntables, etc. [ME *flok* < OF *floc* < L *flocc(us)* FLOC. Cf. OHG *floccho*]

flock·bed (flok′bed′), *n.* a bed with a mattress stuffed with wool refuse, shearings of cloth, or the like. [FLOCK[2] + BED]

flock′ dot′, a pattern of dots or figures which are not woven but attached to cloth with adhesive.

flock′ pa′per, a wallpaper treated with flock to emphasize a design or effect.

flock·y (flok′ē), *adj.,* **flock·i·er, flock·i·est.** like or characterized by flocks or tufts; flocculent. [FLOCK[2] + -Y[1]]

Flod·den (flod′ən), *n.* a hill in NE England, in Northumberland county: the invading Scots were disastrously defeated here by the English, 1513.

floe (flō), *n.* **1.** Also called **ice floe.** a sheet of floating ice, chiefly on the surface of the sea, smaller than an ice field. **2.** a detached floating portion of such a sheet. [? < Norw *flo* layer (cf. Icel *flō* layer, level); c. OE *flōh* piece, flagstone; cf. FLAW[1]]

floe·berg (flō′bərg), *n.* a mass of ice floes resembling an iceberg. [FLOE + BERG; modeled on *iceberg*]

flog (flog, flôg), *v.t.,* **flogged, flog·ging.** **1.** to beat hard with a whip, stick, etc.; whip; castigate; chastise; scourge. **2.** *Brit. Informal.* to sell, esp. aggressively or vigorously. [? b. FLAY and *jog*, var. of JAG[1] to prick, slash; but cf. FLAGELLATE] —**flog′ga·ble,** *adj.* —**flog′ger,** *n.*

—**Syn. 1.** thrash, lash, belabor.

flog·ging (flog′ing, flô′ging), *n.* punishment by beating or whipping. [FLOG + -ING[1]] —**flog′ging·ly,** *adv.*

Flo·is (flō′is), *n.* a girl's given name.

flong (flong, flông), *n.* *Print.* the material of which a stereotype mold is made. [alter. of F *flan* FLAN]

flood (flud), *n.* **1.** a great flowing or overflowing of water, esp. over land not usually submerged. **2. the Flood,** the universal deluge recorded as having occurred in the days of Noah. Gen. 7. **3.** any great outpouring or stream: *a flood of words, tears, light, lava, etc.* **4.** the flowing in of the tide (opposed to *ebb*). **5.** *Informal.* a floodlight. **6.** *Archaic.* a large body of water. —*v.t.* **7.** to overflow in or cover with a flood; fill to overflowing: *Don't flood the bathtub.* **8.** to cover, as with a flood. **9.** to overwhelm with an abundance of something. **10.** to floodlight. —*v.i.* **11.** to flow or pour in, or as in, a flood. **12.** to rise in a flood; overflow. **13.** *Pathol.* **a.** to suffer uterine hemorrhage, esp. in connection with childbirth. **b.** to have an excessive menstrual flow. [ME *flod*, OE *flōd;* c. Goth *flōd(us)*, OHG *fluot* (G *Flut*)] —**flood′a·ble,** *adj.* —**flood′er,** *n.* —**flood′less,** *adj.* —**flood′like′,** *adj.*

—**Syn. 1.** FLOOD, FLASH FLOOD, DELUGE, FRESHET, INUNDATION refer to the overflowing of normally dry areas, often after heavy rains. FLOOD is usually applied to the overflow of a great body of water, as, for example, a river, although it may refer to any water which overflows an area: *a flood along the river; a flood in a basement.* A FLASH FLOOD is one which comes so suddenly that no preparation can be made against it; it is usually destructive, but begins almost at once to subside: *a flash flood caused by a downpour.* DELUGE suggests a great downpouring of water, sometimes with destruction: *The rain came down in a deluge.* FRESHET suggests a small, quick overflow such as that caused by heavy rains: *a freshet in an abandoned watercourse.* INUNDATION, a literary word, suggests the covering of a great area of land by water: *the inundation of thousands of acres.* **8, 9.** inundate, deluge.

flood′able length′, *Naval Archit.* the maximum portion of a hull that can be flooded without sinking the hull below the margin line.

flood′ an′chor, *Naut.* an anchor holding a vessel in place at the flood of a tide (opposed to *ebb anchor*).

flood′ control′, *Civ. Eng.* the act or technique of controlling river flow with dams, dikes, artificial channels, etc., so as to minimize the occurrence of floods.

flood·ed (flud′id), *adj.* covered or inundated, as with water, gas, oil, etc. [FLOOD + -ED[2]]

flood·gate (flud′gāt′), *n.* **1.** *Civ. Eng.* a gate designed to regulate the flow of water. **2.** anything serving to control the indiscriminate flow or passage of something. [ME; see FLOOD, GATE]

flood′ insur′ance, insurance covering loss or damage to property arising from a flood, flood tide, or the like.

flood′ lamp′, a floodlight.

flood·light (flud′līt′), *n., v.,* **-light·ed** or **-lit, -light·ing.** —*n.* **1.** an artificial light so directed or diffused as to give a comparatively uniform illumination over a rather large given area. **2.** a floodlight lamp or projector. —*v.t.* **3.** to illuminate with a floodlight. [FLOOD + LIGHT[1]]

flood′light projec′tor, a powerful lamp having a reflector curved to produce a floodlight.

flood′ plain′, *Phys. Geog.* a nearly flat plain along the course of a stream that is naturally subject to flooding.

flood′ tide′, the inflow of the tide; rising tide.

flood·wa·ter (flud′wô′tər, -wot′ər), *n.* the water that overflows as the result of a flood. [FLOOD + WATER]

floor (flōr, flôr), *n.* **1.** that part of a room or the like which forms its lower enclosing surface and upon which one walks. **2.** a continuous, supporting surface extending horizontally throughout a building, having a number of rooms, apartments, or the like, and constituting one level or stage in the structure; story. **3.** a level, supporting surface in any structure: *the floor of a bridge; the elevator floor.* **4.** one of two or more layers of material composing a floor: *rough floor; finish floor.* **5.** a platform or prepared level area for a particular use: *a threshing floor.* **6.** the flat bottom of any more or less hollow place: *the floor of a tunnel.* **7.** a more or less flat extent of surface: *the floor of the ocean; a valley floor.* **8.** the part of a legislative chamber, auditorium, etc., where the members or spectators sit, and from which they speak. **9.** the right of one member to speak from such a place in preference to other members: *to get the floor; The Senator from Alaska has the floor.* **10.** the main part of a stock or commodity exchange or the like, as distinguished from the galleries, platform, etc. **11.** *Mining.* **a.** the bottom of a horizontal passageway. **b.** an underlying stratum, as of ore, usually flat. **12.** *Naut.* **a.** the bottom of a hull. **b.** any of a number of deep, transverse framing members at the bottom of a steel or iron hull, either situated above the lowest portions of the frames or connected at their outer ends to the bottoms of the frames: generally interrupted by and joined to any vertical keel or keelsons, which are usually continuous members. **c.** the lowermost member of a frame in a wooden vessel, generally built side by side with another of different length, the two being butted to the first and second futtocks of the frame. **13.** the bottom, base, or minimum charged or paid: *The government avoided establishing a price or wage floor.* **14. mop** or **wipe the floor with,** *Slang.* to overwhelm completely; defeat: *He expected to mop the floor with his opponents.* **15. take the floor,** to arise for the purpose of addressing a meeting: *The chairman permitted an opponent of the proposed amendment to take the floor.* —*v.t.* **16.** to cover or furnish with a floor. **17.** to bring down to the floor or ground; knock down: *He floored his opponent with a wicked right.* **18.** to overwhelm; defeat. **19.** *Informal.* to confound; nonplus: *He was floored by the problem.* [ME *flor,* OE *flōr;* c. OIcel *flōr(r),* MLG *vlōr,* MHG *vluor* (G *Flur*)] —**floor′less,** *adj.*

floor·age (flōr′ij, flôr′-), *n.* floor space. [FLOOR + -AGE]

floor·board (flōr′bōrd′, flôr′bôrd′), *n.* any of the boards composing a floor. [FLOOR + BOARD]

floor′ bro′ker, a member of a stock or commodity exchange who executes orders on the floor of the exchange for other brokers. Cf. **floor trader.**

floor·cloth (flōr′klôth′, -kloth′, flôr′-), *n., pl.* **-cloths** (-klôthz′, -klothz′, -klôths′, -kloths′). **1.** a cloth for washing or wiping floors. **2.** a piece of cloth or the like, as crash, drugget, linoleum, etc., used with or without a carpet for covering a floor. **3.** See **ground cloth.** [FLOOR + CLOTH]

floor·er (flōr′ər, flôr′-), *n.* **1.** a person who lays floors. **2.** a person, blow, etc., that knocks someone or something to the floor. **3.** *Informal.* something that beats, overwhelms, or confounds. [FLOOR + -ER[1]]

floor·ing (flōr′ing, flôr′-), *n.* **1.** a floor. **2.** floors collectively. **3.** materials for making floors.

floor′ing brad′, a brad having a very small head, made in lengths from two to four inches.

floor′ing saw′, *Carpentry.* a saw having a curved edge.

floor′ lamp′, a tall lamp designed to stand on the floor.

floor′ lead′er, *U.S. Govt.* the party member in either the Senate or the House of Representatives who directs the activities of his party on the floor.

floor·man (flōr′mən, flôr′-), *n., pl.* **-men.** a floorwalker. [FLOOR + MAN[1]]

floor′ man′ager, 1. a person assigned to direct the proceedings on the floor of an assembly, as at a political convention. **2.** the stage manager of a television program.

floor′ mod′el, 1. an appliance, piece of furniture, or the like, on exhibition in a store. **2.** a form of radio, television set, or other furnishing or appliance intended to stand on the floor rather than on a table; console. **3.** See **floor sample.**

floor′ plan′, a plan of one floor or level of a building, looking downward.

floor′ pock′et, *Theat.* a stage pocket set into the floor of the stage.

floor′ sam′ple, an appliance, piece of furniture, etc., which has been used in a store for display, usually sold at a reduced price.

floor′ show′, an entertainment given in a night club or cabaret, usually consisting of a series of singing, dancing, and, often, comic acts.

floor′ trad′er, a member of a stock or commodity exchange who executes orders on the floor of the exchange for his own account. Cf. **floor broker.**

floor·walk·er (flōr′wô′kər, flôr′-), *n.* a person employed in a store to direct customers, supervise salespeople, etc. [FLOOR + WALKER]

floo·zy (flōō′zē), *n., pl.* **-zies.** *Slang.* a gaudily dressed, dissipated, and usually immoral woman, esp. a seedy prostitute. Also, **floo′zie.** [?]

flop (flop), *v.,* **flopped, flop·ping,** *n.* —*v.i.* **1.** to fall or plump down suddenly, esp. with noise; drop or turn with a sudden bump or thud (sometimes fol. by *down*): *The puppy flopped down on the couch.* **2.** to change suddenly, as from one side or party to another (often fol. by *over*). **3.** *Informal.* to yield or break down suddenly; fail: *The play flopped dismally.* **4.** to flap, as in the wind. —*v.t.* **5.** to drop, throw, etc., with a sudden bump or thud: *He flopped his books on a chair.* **6.** to flap clumsily and heavily, as wings. **7.** to invert (the negative of a photograph) so that the right and left sides are transposed. —*n.* **8.** act of flopping. **9.** the sound of flopping; a thud. **10.** *Informal.* a failure: *The new comedy was the worst flop of the season.* [var. of FLAP] —**flop′per,** *n.*

flop-eared (flop′ērd′), *adj.* having long, drooping ears, as a hound.

flop′ forg′ing, *Metalworking.* forging of both sides of a piece from the same die, the sides being identical.

flop·house (flop′hous′), *n., pl.* **-hous·es** (-hou′ziz). a cheap, rundown hotel, usually for men only. [FLOP + HOUSE]

flop·o·ver (flop′ō′vər), *n.* *Television.* a continuous, vertical movement of the picture, caused by interference in reception or by improper tuning. [n. use of v. phrase *flop over*]

flop·py (flop′ē), *adj.,* **-pi·er, -pi·est.** tending to flop. [FLOP + -Y[1]] —**flop′pi·ly,** *adv.* —**flop′pi·ness,** *n.*

flop′py disk′, *Computer Technol.* a thin, round, flexible disk with magnetic surfaces, for storing and retrieving data. Also called **diskette, floppy.**

flor-, var. of **flori-:** *florist.*

flor., flourished. [< L *floruit*]

flo·ra (flōr′ə, flôr′ə), *n., pl.* **flo·ras, flo·rae** (flōr′ē, flôr′ē) for 2. **1.** the plants of a particular region or period, listed by species and considered as a whole. **2.** a work systematically describing such plants. **3.** plants, as distinguished from fauna. [< L, deriv. of *flōr-* (s. of *flōs*) FLOWER]

Flo·ra (flōr′ə, flôr′ə), *n.* **1.** a town in central Illinois. 5331 (1960). **2.** the Roman goddess of flowers. **3.** a girl's given name.

flo·ral (flōr′əl, flôr′-), *adj.* **1.** pertaining to or consisting of flowers: *floral decoration.* **2.** (*cap.*) of or pertaining to the goddess Flora. [< L *flōrāl(is)* pertaining to *Flōra.* See FLORA, -AL[1]] —**flo′ral·ly,** *adv.*

Flor·al·a (flō ral′ə, flo-), *n.* a town in S Alabama. 3011 (1960).

flo′ral clock′, a large outdoor clock with a dial formed of a bed of flowers of various colors, a pair of horizontally rotating hands, and a clock mechanism concealed in the earth beneath the flower bed.

flo′ral em′blem, a flower or plant serving as the emblem of a city, state, etc.

flo′ral en′velope, *Bot.* the calyx and corolla of a flower.

Flo·ra·li·a (flō rā′lē ə, -rāl′yə, flô-), *n.* (*sometimes construed as pl.*) an annual festival held in ancient Rome in honor of Flora. [< L, special use of neut. pl. of *flōrālis.* See FLORAL]

Flo′ral Park′, 1. a city on W Long Island, in SE New York. 17,499 (1960). **2.** a town in SW Montana. 4079 (1960).

Flo·ré·al (flō RĀ AL′), *n.* (in the French Revolutionary calendar) the eighth month of the year, extending from April 20 to May 19. [< F < L *flōre(us)* of flowers (*flōr-,* s. of *flōs* flower + *-eus* adj. suffix) + F *-al* -AL[1]]

flo·re·at·ed (flōr′ē ā′tid, flôr′-), *adj.* floriated.

Flor·ence (flôr′əns, flor′-), *n.* **1.** a city in central Italy, on the Arno River: capital of the former grand duchy of Tuscany. 438,138 (1961). Italian, **Firenze. 2.** a city in NW Alabama, on the Tennessee River. 31,649 (1960). **3.** a city in E South Carolina. 24,722 (1960). **4.** a town in N Kentucky. 5837 (1960). **5.** a town in W New Jersey. 4215 (1960). **6.** a town in central Colorado. 2821 (1960). **7.** Also, **Flor′ance.** a girl's given name.

Flor′ence fen′nel, a variety of fennel, *Foeniculum vulgare dulce,* having enlarged leaf bases which are blanched and used esp. as an ingredient in salads. Also called **finochio.**

Flor′ence flask′, *Chem.* a round bottle having a flat bottom and long neck, for use in laboratory experimentation.

Florence flask

Flo·ren·ci·ta (flôr′ən sē′tə, flor′-), *n.* a girl's given name, form of **Florence.**

Flo·ren·da (flō ren′də, flô-), *n.* a girl's given name, form of **Florence.**

Flor·en·tine (flôr′ən tēn′, -tīn′, flor′-), *adj.* **1.** of or pertaining to Florence, Italy: *the Florentine poets of the 14th century.* **2.** pertaining to or designating the style of art developed in Florence during the late 13th to the 15th centuries. **3.** (of food) served or prepared with spinach: *eggs Florentine.* —*n.* **4.** a native or inhabitant of Florence. **5.** (*often l.c.*) a cooky made with orange peel and almond and coated with chocolate. [< L *Flōrentīn(us)* pertaining to *Flōrent(ia)* FLORENCE + *-īnus* -INE[1]]

flo·res (flōr′ēz, flôr′-), *n.* (*construed as pl.*) *Chem.* flower (def. 12). [< L, pl. of *flōs* FLOWER]

Flo·res (*Sp.* flô′res *for 1, 2; Port.* flô′rish *for 3*), *n.* **1. Juan Jo·sé** (hwän hô se′), 1800–64, Ecuadorian general and statesman: president 1830–35, 1839–45. **2.** one of the Lesser Sunda Islands in Indonesia, separated from Celebes by the Flores Sea. 194,203 with adjacent islands (est. 1961); 7753 sq. mi. **3.** the westernmost island of the Azores, in the N Atlantic. 7832 (1950); 55 sq. mi.

flo·res·cence (flō res′əns, flô-, flə-), *n.* act, state, or period of flowering; bloom. [< NL *flōrēscentia,* equiv. to L *flōrēscent-* (s. of *flōrēscēns,* prp. of *flōrēscere*) beginning to flower or blossom, equiv. to *flōr-* FLOR- + *-ēscentia* -ESCENCE] —**flo·res′cent,** *adj.*

Flo′res Sea′ (flōr′is, -ēz, flôr′-), a sea between Celebes and the Lesser Sunda Islands in Indonesia. ab. 180 mi. wide.

flo·ret (flōr′it, flôr′-), *n.* **1.** a small flower. **2.** *Bot.* one of the closely clustered small flowers that make up the flower head of a composite flower, as the daisy. **3.** Also, **flo·rette** (flō ret′, flô-). spun silk obtained from floss. **4.** *Print.* flower (def. 6). [ME *flouret* < OF *florete,* dim. of *flor* FLOWER; see -ET]

flo·ret·ty (flō ret′ē, flô-), *adj.* *Heraldry.* **1.** noting a charge, as an ordinary, or a partition line having fleurs-de-lis as an additional ornament: *a fess dancetty floretty at the points.* **2.** semé-de-lys. **3.** (of a cross) having a fleur-de-lis sprouting from each of the couped ends or from a knop on each end. Cf. **fleury.** [ME *flourte, flortee, florette* < MF *flourete* ornamented with flowery designs. See FLORET, -Y[1]]

Flo·rey (flōr′ē, flôr′ē), *n.* **Sir Howard Walter,** 1898–1968, Australian pathologist in England: Nobel prize for medicine 1945.

Flor·ham Park′ (flôr′əm), a town in N New Jersey. 7222 (1960).

flori-, a learned borrowing from Latin meaning "flower," used in the formation of compound words: *floriferous.* Also, **flor-.** [< L, comb. form, equiv. to *flōr-* (s. of *flōs*) flower + *-i-* -I-]

Flo·ri·a (flōr′ē ə, flôr′-), *n.* a girl's given name, form of **Flora.**

Flo·ria·no (flōō RYä′nōō), *n.* a city in NE Brazil. 16,063 (1960).

Flo·ri·a·nóp·o·lis (flōr′ē ə nop′ə lis, flôr′-; *Port.* flô′Ryə nô′pōō lēs′), *n.* a seaport in and the capital of Santa Catarina state, on an island off the S coast of Brazil. 78,068 (1961). Formerly, **Desterro.**

flo·ri·at·ed (flōr′ē ā′tid, flôr′-), *adj.* made of or decorated with floral ornamentation: *floriated design; floriated china.* Also, **floreated.** [FLORI- + -ATE[1] + -ED[2]]

flo·ri·bun·da (flōr′ə bun′də, flôr′-), *n.* any of a class of roses characterized by a long blooming period and the production of large flowers often in thick clusters. [< NL, n. use of fem. of *flōribundus* flowering freely, equiv. to *flōri-* FLORI- + *-bundus* adj. suffix]

flo·ri·can (flōr′ə kən, flôr′-), *n.* any of various smaller species of bustards. [?]

flo·ri·cul·ture (flōr′ə kul′chər, flôr′-), *n.* the cultivation of flowers or flowering plants, esp. under glass. [FLORI- + CULTURE] —**flo′ri·cul′tur·al,** *adj.* —**flo′ri·cul′tur·al·ly,** *adv.* —**flo′ri·cul′tur·ist,** *n.*

flor·id (flôr′id, flor′-), *adj.* **1.** reddish, ruddy, or rosy: *a florid complexion.* **2.** flowery; excessively ornate; showy: *The late Victorians relished florid writing.* **3.** *Obs.* abounding in or consisting of flowers. [< L *flōrid(us).* See FLOR, -ID[4]] —**flo·rid·i·ty** (flō rid′i tē, flə-), **flor′id·ness,** *n.* —**flor′id·ly,** *adv.*

—**Syn. 2.** adorned, embellished, decorated, sumptuous. —**Ant. 1.** pale. **2.** plain, simple, unaffected.

Flor·i·da (flôr′i də, flor′-), *n.* a State in the SE United States between the Atlantic and the Gulf of Mexico. 4,951,560 (1960); 58,560 sq. mi. *Cap.:* Tallahassee.

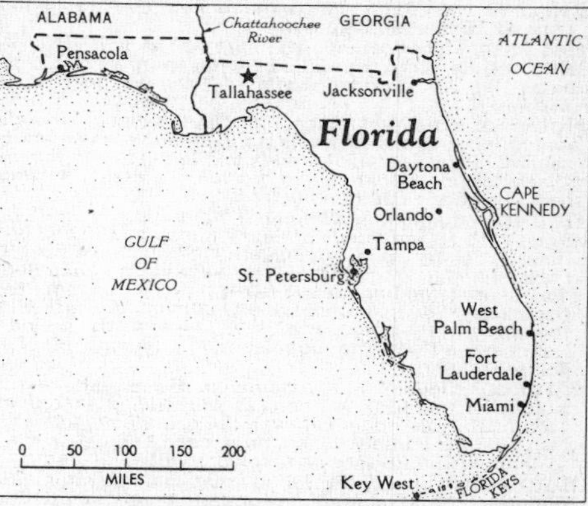

Flor′ida cat's′-claw, cat's-claw.

Flor′ida Cit′y, a town in S Florida. 4114 (1960).

Flor′ida Cur′rent, the part of the Gulf Stream which extends from the Florida Strait to Cape Hatteras.

Flor′ida Keys′, a chain of small islands and reefs off the coast of S Florida. ab. 225 mi. long.

Flor′ida moss′. See **Spanish moss.**

Flor′ida Strait′, a strait between Florida, Cuba, and the Bahamas, connecting the Gulf of Mexico and the Atlantic.

Flor′ida vel′vet bean′, a tropical vine, *Stizolobium deeringianum,* having showy, purple flowers in drooping clusters and black-hairy pods, grown as an ornamental.

Flor·ie (flôr′ē, flor′ē), *n.* a girl's given name, form of **Florence.** Also, **Florrie, Florry, Flory.**

flo·rif·er·ous (flō rif′ər əs, flô-), *adj.* flower-bearing. [< L *flōrifer* (see FLORI-, -FER) + -OUS] —**flo·rif′er·ous·ly,** *adv.* —**flo·rif′er·ous·ness,** *n.*

flor·in (flôr′in, flor′-), *n.* **1.** a cupronickel coin of Great Britain, equal to two shillings or the tenth part of a pound: first issued in 1849 as a silver coin. **2.** the gulden of the Netherlands. **3.** a former gold coin of Florence, first issued in 1252 and widely imitated. **4.** a former gold coin of England, first issued under Edward III. **5.** a former gold coin of Austria, first issued in the middle of the 14th century. [ME < MF < OIt *fiorin(o)* Florentine coin stamped with a lily, deriv. of *fiore* flower < L *flōr-* FLOR-]

Flo·ri·na (flō rē′nə, flô-), *n.* a girl's given name. Also, **Florine.**

Flo·rine (flō rēn′, flô-), *n.* a girl's given name. Also, **Florina.**

Flo·ri·o (flōr′ē ō′, flôr′-), *n.* **John,** 1553?–1625, English lexicographer and translator.

Flo·ris (flōr′is, flôr′-, flor′-), *n.* a girl's given name.

Flor·is·sant (flôr′i sənt), *n.* a city in E Missouri, near St. Louis. 38,166 (1960).

flo·rist (flôr′ist, flōr′-, flor′-), *n.* a retailer of flowers, ornamental plants, etc. [FLOR- + -IST]

flo·ris·tic (flō ris′tik, flô-), *adj.* pertaining to flowers or a flora. [FLOR- + -ISTIC] —**flo·ris′ti·cal·ly,** *adv.*

-florous, a learned borrowing from Latin meaning "-flowered," "having flowers," used in the formation of adjectives: *uniflorous.* [< L *-flōrus* flowered, bloomed. See FLORI-, -OUS]

Flor·rie (flôr′ē, flor′ē), *n.* a girl's given name, form of **Florence.** Also, **Florie, Flor′ry, Flor′y.**

flo·ru·it (flō′rōō it; *Eng.* flôr′yōō it, flōr′-, flor′-), *n.* *Latin.* he (or she) flourished: used to indicate the period during which a person flourished, esp. when the exact birth and death dates are unknown.

flo·ry (flōr′ē, flôr′ē), *adj.* *Heraldry.* fleury.

flo′ry coun′ter-flo′ry (koun′tər flōr′ē, -flôr′ē), *Heraldry.* (of a narrow charge) ornamented with fleurs-de-lis such that the heads project alternately from one side or the other: *a tressure flory counter-flory.*

flos fer·ri (flôs′ fer′ī, flos), *Mineral.* a coralloid variety of aragonite. [< L: lit., flower of iron]

floss (flôs, flos), *n.* **1.** the cottony fiber yielded by the silk-cotton tree. **2.** silk filaments with little or no twist, used in weaving as brocade or in embroidery. **3.** any silky, filamentous matter, as the silk of corn. Also called **floss′ silk′.** [< Scand; cf. Icel *flos* shag of velvet] —**floss′er,** *n.*

floss′ hole′, *Metall.* a hole in a puddling furnace for the removal of ash or slag. [*floss* < G *Flosz* in same sense]

Flos·sie (flô′sē, flos′ē), *n.* a girl's given name, form of **Florence.**

Floss·moor (flôs′môr, flos′-), *n.* a town in NE Illinois. 4624 (1960).

floss′-silk tree′ (flôs′silk′, flos′-), a spiny tree, *Chorisia speciosa,* of Brazil, having solitary, pink, purple, or white flowers appearing in early winter, grown as an ornamental.

floss·y (flô′sē, flos′ē), *adj.,* **floss·i·er, floss·i·est. 1.** made of or resembling floss; downy. **2.** *Slang.* showily stylish; fancy. [FLOSS + -Y[1]]

flo·tage (flō′tij), *n.* **1.** act of floating. **2.** state of floating. **3.** floating power; buoyancy. **4.** anything that floats; flotsam. **5.** the ships, refuse, etc., afloat on a river. **6.** the part of a ship above the water line. Also, **floatage.** [FLOAT + -AGE; cf. F *flottage*]

flo·ta·tion (flō tā′shən), *n.* **1.** act or state of floating. **2.** the floating or launching of a commercial venture, loan, etc. **3.** *Metall.* a process for separating the different crystalline phases in a mass of powdered ore based on their tendency to sink in, or float on, a given liquid. 4. the science of floating bodies. Also, *esp. Brit.*, **floatation.** [FLOAT + -ATION; cf. F *flottaison* (see FLOTSAM)]

flo·til·la (flō til′ə), *n.* 1. a group of small naval vessels, esp. a naval unit containing two or more squadrons. 2. a small fleet. [< Sp, dim. of *flota* fleet < F *flotte* < OE *flota*]

Flo·tow (flō′tō), *n.* **Frie·drich von** (frē′drIKH fən), 1812–83, German composer.

flot·sam (flot′səm), *n.* the part of the wreckage of a ship and its cargo found floating on the water. Cf. **jetsam.** [< AF *floteson*, deriv. of *floter* to float < OE *flot(ian)*]

flot′sam and jet′sam, 1. the wreckage of a ship and its cargo found either floating upon the sea or washed ashore. 2. useless trifles; odds and ends: *the flotsam and jetsam that tourists bring back from their travels.* 3. penniless vagrants, drifters, and tramps.

flounce[1] (flouns), *v.*, **flounced, flounc·ing,** *n.* —*v.i.* 1. to go with an impatient or angry movement of the body (usually fol. by *away, off, out,* etc.): *She flounced out of the room in a rage.* 2. to throw the body about, as in floundering or struggling; twist; turn; jerk. 3. to move self-consciously and in a conspicuous manner: *She was flouncing around in her new mink stole.* —*n.* 4. the action of flouncing; a flouncing movement. [< Scand; cf. Norw *flunsa* to hurry]

flounce[2] (flouns), *n.*, *v.*, **flounced, flounc·ing.** —*n.* 1. a strip of material, wider than a ruffle, gathered and attached at one edge and with the other edge left hanging: used for trimming, esp. on women's skirts. —*v.t.* 2. to trim with a flounce or flounces. [alter. of FROUNCE]

flounc·ing (floun′sing), *n.* 1. material used in making flounces. 2. trimming consisting of a flounce. [FLOUNCE[2] + -ING[1]]

floun·der[1] (floun′dər), *v.i.* 1. to struggle with stumbling or plunging movements (usually fol. by *about, along, on, through,* etc.): *He saw the child floundering about in the water.* 2. to struggle clumsily or helplessly in embarrassment or confusion: *He floundered about helplessly on the first day of his new job.* —*n.* 3. action of floundering; a floundering movement. [? b. FLOUNCE[1] and FOUNDER[2]] —**floun′der·ing·ly,** *adv.*

Winter flounder, *Pseudopleuronectes americanus* (Length to 1½ ft.)

floun·der[2] (floun′dər), *n.*, *pl.* (*esp. collectively*) **-der,** (*esp. referring to two or more kinds or species*) **-ders.** 1. a European, marine flatfish, *Platichthys flesus*, used for food. 2. any of numerous similar or closely related non-European flatfishes. 3. any flatfish other than soles. [ME < AF *floundre* < Scand; cf. Norw *flundra*]

flour (flour, flou′ər), *n.* 1. the finely ground meal of grain, esp. the finer meal separated by bolting. 2. the finely ground and bolted meal of wheat. 3. any finely ground, powdery foodstuff, as of dehydrated potatoes, fish, or bananas. 4. any fine, soft powder: *flour of emery.* —*v.t.* 5. to make (grain or the like) into flour; grind and bolt. 6. *Cookery.* to sprinkle or dredge with flour. —*v.i.* 7. (of mercury) to refuse to amalgamate with another metal because of some impurity of the metal; lie on the surface of the metal in the form of minute globules. 8. chalk (def. 9). [ME; special use of FLOWER. Cf. F *fleur de farine* the flower or finest part of the meal] —**flour′less,** *adj.*

flour′ bee′tle, any of several brown darkling beetles, esp. of the genus *Tribolium*, that infest, breed in, feed on, and often pollute flour, stored grain, and other stored produce.

flour·ish (flûr′ish, flur′-), *v.i.* 1. to be in a vigorous state; thrive: *a period in which art flourished.* 2. to be in its or in one's prime; be at the height of fame, excellence, influence, etc. 3. to be successful; prosper. 4. to grow luxuriantly, or thrive in growth, as a plant: *The African violet flourished.* 5. to make strokes or flourishes with a brandished weapon or the like: *The drunken warrior flourished and flailed about wildly.* 6. to make an ostentatious display. 7. to add embellishments and ornamental lines to writing, letters, etc. 8. to speak or write in flowery or pretentious language. 9. *Music.* a. to play a showy passage. b. to play in a showy manner. c. to sound a trumpet call or fanfare. —*v.t.* 10. to brandish or wave (a sword, stick, one's limbs, etc.) about in the air. 11. to parade, flaunt, or display ostentatiously: *to flourish one's wealth.* 12. to decorate or embellish (writing, a page of script, etc.) with sweeping or fanciful curves or lines. 13. to adorn with decorative designs, color, etc. —*n.* 14. a brandishing or waving, as of a sword, stick, or the like. 15. an ostentatious display. 16. a decoration or embellishment in writing: *He added a few flourishes to his signature.* 17. *Rhet.* a parade of fine language; an expression used merely for effect. 18. *Music.* a. an elaborate passage or addition largely for display. b. a trumpet call or fanfare. 19. *Rare.* the condition of flourishing or thriving: *in full flourish.* 20. *Obs.* state of flowering. [ME *florisshe(n)* < MF *floriss-*, long s. of *florir* < < L *flōrēre* to bloom. See FLOWER] —**flour′ish·er,** *n.*
—**Syn.** 1. grow, increase. See **succeed.** 6. flaunt. 12, 13. ornament. 16. ornament, adornment. —**Ant.** 1. fade, decline, fail.

flour·ish·ing (flûr′i shing, flur′-), *adj.* growing vigorously; thriving; prosperous. [ME; see FLOURISH, -ING[2]] —**flour′ish·ing·ly,** *adv.*

flour′ mill′, a mill for grinding grain into flour.

flour·y (flour′ē, flou′ə rē), *adj.* 1. of, pertaining to, or resembling flour. 2. white with flour. [FLOUR + -Y[1]]

flout (flout), *v.t.* 1. to treat with disdain, scorn, or contempt; scoff at; mock: *to flout the rules of propriety.* —*v.i.* 2. to show disdain, scorn, or contempt; scoff, mock, or gibe (often fol. by *at*). —*n.* 3. a disdainful, scornful, or contemptuous remark, act, etc.; mocking insult; gibe. [ME *floute(n)* (to) play the FLUTE; cf. D *fluiten* to play the flute, jeer] —**flout′er,** *n.* —**flout′ing·ly,** *adv.*
—**Usage.** See **flaunt.**

flow (flō), *v.i.* 1. to move along in a stream, as water or other liquid: *The river flowed slowly to the sea.* 2. to circulate, as the blood. 3. to stream or well forth. 4. to issue or proceed from a source: *Orders flowed regularly from the central office.* 5. to menstruate. 6. to come or go as in a stream, as persons or things: *A constant stream of humanity flowed by.* 7. to proceed continuously and smoothly, as thought, speech, etc. 8. to fall or hang loosely at full length, as hair: *Her hair flowed over her shoulders.* 9. to overflow or abound with something: *The tavern flowed with wine.* 10. to rise and advance, as the tide (opposed to *ebb*). —*v.t.* 11. to cause or permit to flow: *to flow paint on a wall before brushing.* 12. to cover with water or other liquid; flood. —*n.* 13. act of flowing. 14. movement in or as in a stream; any continuous movement, as of thought, speech, trade, etc. 15. the rate of flowing. 16. the volume of fluid that flows through a passage of any given section in a unit of time: *Oil flow of the well was 500 barrels a day.* 17. that which flows; a stream. 18. *Scot.* a. a coastal channel or small inlet. b. a wetland. 19. an outpouring or discharge of something, as in a stream: *The doctor stopped the flow of blood.* 20. menstruation. 21. an overflowing. 22. the rise of the tide (opposed to *ebb*). 23. *Mach.* progressive distortion of a metal object under continuous service at high temperature. 24. *Physics.* the transference of energy: *heat flow.* [ME *flowe(n)*, OE *flōwan*; c. MLG *vlōien*, Icel *flōa*] —**flow′a·ble,** *adj.*
—**Syn.** 1. FLOW, GUSH, SPOUT, SPURT refer to certain of the movements characteristic of fluids. FLOW is the general term: *Water flows. A stream of blood flows.* To GUSH is to rush forth copiously from a cavity, in as large a volume as can issue therefrom, as the result of some strong impelling force: *The water will gush out if the main breaks.* SPOUT and SPURT both imply the ejecting of a liquid from a cavity by some internal impetus given to it. SPOUT implies a rather steady, possibly well-defined, jet or stream, not necessarily of long duration but always of considerable force: *A whale spouts.* SPURT implies a forcible, possibly sudden, spasmodic, or intermittent issue or jet: *The liquid spurted out suddenly when the bottle cap was pushed in. Juice is likely to spurt from oranges or grapefruit.* SPOUT applies only to liquids; the other terms apply also to gases. 7. run. 9. teem. 17. current. 17, 19, 21. flood.

flow·age (flō′ij), *n.* 1. act of flowing; flow. 2. state of being flooded. 3. flowing or overflowing water, or other liquid. 4. *Mech.* gradual internal motion or deformation. [FLOW + -AGE]

flow′ brec′cia, breccia of which the ground mass and fragments are from the same lava flow.

flow′ chart′, 1. Also called **flow sheet.** a detailed diagram or chart of the operations and equipment through which material passes, as in a manufacturing process. 2. *Computer Technol.* a graphic representation, more detailed than a flow diagram, of a sequence of operations in a computer program.

flow′ cleav′age, *Geol.* cleavage resulting from the parallel alignment of the mineral constituents of a rock when in a plastic condition.

flow′ di′agram, *Computer Technol.* a schematic representation, less detailed than a flow chart, of a sequence of subroutines, indicating the general flow of information for solving a problem by a computer.

flow·er (flou′ər), *n.* 1. the blossom of a plant. 2. *Bot.* a. that part of a seed plant comprising the reproductive organs and their envelopes if any, esp. when such envelopes are more or less conspicuous in form and color. b. an analogous reproductive structure in other plants, as the mosses. 3. a plant considered with reference to its blossom or cultivated for its floral beauty. 4. state of efflorescence or bloom: *Peonies were in flower.* 5. an ornament representing a flower. 6. Also called **fleuron, floret.** *Print.* an ornamental piece of type, esp. a stylized floral design, often used in a line to decorate chapter headings, page borders, bindings, etc. 7. any ornament or adornment. 8. See **figure of speech.** 9. the finest or most flourishing state or period, as of life or beauty: *Poetic drama was in flower in Elizabethan England.* 10. the best or finest member or part of a number, body, or whole: *the flower of American youth.* 11. the finest or choicest product or example. 12. **flowers,** (construed as sing.) *Chem.* a substance in the form of a fine powder, esp. as obtained by sublimation: *flowers of sulfur.* —*v.i.* 13. to produce flowers, as a plant; blossom; come to full bloom. 14. to come out into full development; mature: *Ideas flower under favorable conditions.* —*v.t.* 15. to cover or deck with flowers. 16. to decorate with a floral design. [ME *flour* flower, best of anything < OF *flor, flour, flur* < L *flōr-* (s. of *flōs*). Cf. BLOSSOM]

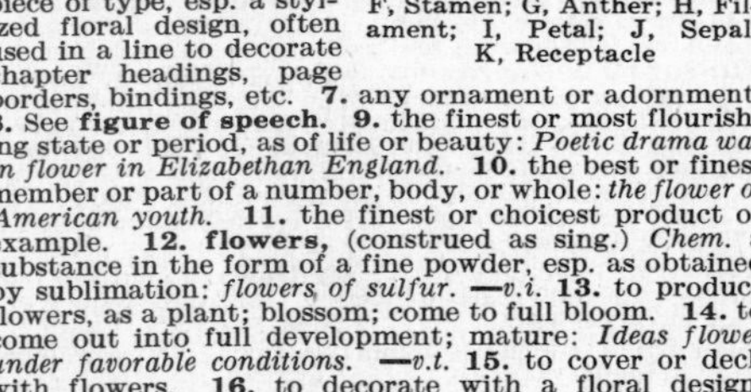

Flower
A, Pistil; B, Stigma; C, Style; D, Ovule; E, Ovary; F, Stamen; G, Anther; H, Filament; I, Petal; J, Sepal; K, Receptacle

Flow·er (flou′ər), *n.* a girl's given name.

flow·er·age (flou′ər ij), *n.* 1. flowers collectively. 2. floral ornament or decoration. 3. the process or state of flowering. [FLOWER + -AGE]

flow′er bee′tle, 1. any of numerous, usually brightly colored beetles, as of the families *Malachiidae* and *Dasytidae*, that live on flowers and are predaceous on other insects. 2. any of certain scarabaeid beetles of the subfamily *Cetoniinae* that feed on pollen.

flow′er box′, a usually rectangular box used for growing decorative plants in or around the home, often attached outside a window.

flow′er bud′. See under **bud**[1] (def. 1a).

flow′er bug′, any of several hemipterous insects of the family *Anthocoridae* that live on flowers and are predaceous on aphids and other small insects.

flow·er-de-luce (flou′ər də lōōs′), *n.* the iris flower or plant. [Anglicization of F *fleur de lis*]

flow·ered (flou′ərd), *adj.* 1. having flowers. 2. decorated with flowers or a floral pattern: *a flowered-print dress.* [ME; see FLOWER, -ED[3]]

flow·er·er (flou′ər ər), *n.* a plant that flowers at a specific time or in a certain manner. [FLOWER + -ER[1]]

flow·er·et (flou′ər it), *n.* a small flower; floret. [var. of FLORET]

flow′er fence′. See **Barbados pride.** (def. 1).

flow′er fly′. See **syrphid fly.**

flow′er girl′, 1. a young girl at a wedding ceremony who precedes the bride and carries or scatters flowers in her path. 2. *Brit.* a woman of any age who sells flowers in the street.

flow′er head′, *Bot.* an inflorescence consisting of a dense cluster of sessile florets; capitulum.

Flow′er Hill′, a town on NW Long Island, in SE New York. 4594 (1960).

flow·er·ing (flou′ər ing), *adj.* bearing flowers. [ME; see FLOWER, -ING[2]]

flow′ering cur′rant, 1. See **golden currant.** 2. a shrub, *Ribes sanguineum*, of northwestern North America, having showy, sticky, red flowers and bluish-black fruit.

flow′ering dog′wood, a North American tree, *Cornus florida*, having small greenish flowers in the spring, surrounded by white or pink bracts that resemble petals: the state flower and the state tree of Virginia. Also called **boxwood.**

flow′ering flax′, an annual herb, *Linum grandiflorum*, of northern Africa, having red or pink flowers.

Flow′ering Ju′das, a collection of short stories (1930) by Katherine Anne Porter.

flow′ering ma′ple, any malvaceous shrub of the genus *Abutilon*, having large, bright-colored flowers.

flow′ering moss′, widow's-cross.

flow′ering plant′, a plant that produces flowers, fruit, and seeds; angiosperm.

flow′ering quince′, any rosaceous shrub of the genus *Chaenomeles*, of E Asia, having showy, waxy flowers and a quincelike fruit, grown as an ornamental in the U.S.

flow′ering rasp′berry, a showy, perennial shrub, *Rubus odoratus*, of eastern North America, having purplish or rose-purple flowers and inedible, dry, red fruit.

flow′ering spurge′, a hardy, perennial herb, *Euphorbia corollata*, of eastern North America, having clustered flowers with showy, white appendages, grown as an ornamental. Also called **milk purslane.**

flow′ering tobac′co, any solanaceous plant of the genus *Nicotiana*, as *N. alata* and *N. sylvestris*, having clusters of fragrant flowers, grown as an ornamental.

flow′ering win′tergreen, gaywings.

flow·er·less (flou′ər lis), *adj.* 1. having no flowers. 2. *Bot.* having no true seeds; cryptogamic. [FLOWER + -LESS] —**flow′er·less·ness,** *n.*

flow·er·let (flou′ər lit), *n.* a small flower; floret. [FLOWER + -LET]

flow·er·like (flou′ər līk′), *adj.* resembling or in the shape of a flower; delicate; graceful. [FLOWER + -LIKE]

flow·er-of-Jove (flou′ər əv jōv′), *n.*, *pl.* **flow·ers-of-Jove.** a white-woolly, perennial herb, *Lychnis Flos-Jovis* having red or purple flowers in dense clusters. [trans. of NL *Flōs-Jovis*]

flow·er·peck·er (flou′ər pek′ər), *n.* any of numerous small, arboreal, usually brightly colored oscine birds of the family *Dicaeidae*, of southeastern Asia and Australia. [FLOWER + PECKER]

flow·er·pot (flou′ər pot′), *n.* a container, usually a clay pot, in which to grow plants. [FLOWER + POT[1]]

Flow′ers of E′vil, a collection of poems (1857) by Charles Baudelaire. French, **Les Fleurs du Mal.**

flow′ers of sul′fur, *Pharm.* sublimed sulfur in the form of a fine yellow powder, used in medicine chiefly to kill parasites and fungi and to treat certain skin diseases.

flow′ers of zinc′. See **zinc oxide.**

flow·er·y (flou′ə rē), *adj.* 1. covered with or having many flowers. 2. decorated with floral designs. 3. full of highly ornate language, elaborate figures of speech, etc.: *a flowery style of oratory.* 4. resembling a flower, esp. in fragrance: *a Rhine wine with a flowery aroma.* [ME; see FLOWER, -Y[1]] —**flow′er·i·ly,** *adv.* —**flow′er·i·ness,** *n.*
—**Syn.** 3. florid, showy, elaborate.

flow·ing (flō′ing), *adj.* 1. moving in or as in a stream: *flowing water.* 2. proceeding smoothly or easily; facile: *flowing language.* 3. long, smooth, graceful, and without sudden interruption or change of direction: *flowing lines; flowing gestures.* 4. falling or hanging loosely at full length: *flowing hair.* 5. abounding; having in excess: *a land flowing with milk and honey.* [ME *flowynge*, OE *flōende.* See FLOW, -ING[2]] —**flow′ing·ly,** *adv.* —**flow′ing·ness,** *n.*

flown[1] (flōn), *v.* a pp. of **fly**[1].

flown[2] (flōn), *adj.* 1. decorated with colors that have been fluidly blended: *flown ceramic ware.* 2. *Archaic.* filled to excess. [ME *flōwen*; ptp. of FLOW]

flow′ sheet′. See **flow chart** (def. 1).

Floy (floi), *n.* 1. a boy's given name, form of **Floyd.** 2. a girl's given name, form of **Florence.**

Floyce (flois), *n.* a girl's given name.

Floyd (floid), *n.* a boy's given name, form of **Lloyd.**

Floyd·a·da (floi dā′də), *n.* a town in NW Texas. 3769 (1960).

fl oz, fluid ounce; fluid ounces.

flu (flōō), *n.* influenza. [shortened form]

flub (flub), *v.*, **flubbed, flub·bing,** *n.* *Informal.* —*v.t., v.i.* 1. to perform poorly; blunder; bungle: *He flubbed the last shot and lost the match.* —*n.* 2. a blunder. [?]

flub·dub (flub′dub′), *n.* *Informal.* pretentious nonsense or show; airs. [?]

fluc·tu·ant (fluk′chōō ənt), *adj.* 1. fluctuating; varying; unstable. 2. undulating; moving, or seeming to move, in waves. 3. *Med.* having a soft, semiliquid center, as a boil or abscess ripe for lancing. [< L *fluctuant-* (s. of *fluctuāns*) undulating, moving to and fro (prp. of *fluctuāre*). See FLUCTUATE, -ANT]

fluc·tu·ate (fluk′chōō āt′), *v.*, **-at·ed, -at·ing.** —*v.i.* 1. to change continually from one position, condition, etc., to another; move back and forth; vary irregularly; be undecided or unstable; vacillate: *He fluctuated between elation and depression.* 2. to move in waves or like waves. —*v.t.* 3. to cause to fluctuate. [< L *fluctuāt(us)* undulated, ptp. of *fluctuāre* to flow. See FLUX, -ATE[1]]
—**Syn.** 1. See **waver.** 2. undulate, oscillate.

fluc·tu·a·tion (fluk′chōō ā′shən), *n.* 1. continual change from one course, position, condition, etc., to another; alternating variation; vacillation; wavering; instability. 2. wavelike motion; undulation. 3. *Genetics.* a body variation due to environmental factors and not inherited. [< L *fluctuātiōn-* (s. of *fluctuātiō*) a fluctuation, wavering. See FLUCTUATE, -ION]

flue[1] (flōō), *n.* 1. a passage or duct for smoke in a chimney. 2. any duct or passage for air, gas, or the like. 3. a tube, esp. a large one, in a fire-tube boiler. 4. *Music.*

a. See **flue pipe.** b. Also called **windway.** a narrow slit in the upper end of a pipe through which the air current is directed. [earlier *flew,* ? repr. OE *flēwsa* a flowing, the form *flews* being taken as pl.]

flue[2] (flo͞o), *n.* downy matter; fluff. [? OE *flug-* (in *flugol* swift, fleeting); akin to FLY[1]. Cf. LG *flug*]

flue[3] (flo͞o), *n.* a fishing net. Also, **flew.** [ME *flowe;* cf. MD *vluwe* fishing net]

flue[4] (flo͞o), *n.* 1. *Ornith. Rare.* a barb of a feather. 2. *Naut.* fluke[1] (defs. 1, 2). [? cf. Sw *fly*] —**flued,** *adj.*

flue[5] (flo͞o), *v.i.,* **flued, flu·ing.** (of the reveals of a window, the sides of a fireplace, etc.) to splay. [special use of dial. *flue* shallow (ME *flew*)]

flue-cure (flo͞o′kyo͝or′), *v.t.,* **-cured, -cur·ing.** to dry or cure by warm air that has been passed through flues.

flu·ent (flo͞o′ənt), *adj.* 1. indicating facility in or command of something: *He spoke fluent French.* 2. able to speak or write smoothly, easily, or readily: *a fluent speaker.* 3. easy; graceful: *fluent motion; fluent curves.* 4. flowing, as a stream. 5. capable of flowing, or fluid, as liquids or gases. 6. easily changed or adapted; pliant. [< L *fluent-* (s. of *fluēns*) flowing, prp. of *fluere;* see -ENT] —**flu′en·cy, flu′ent·ness,** *n.* —**flu′ent·ly,** *adv.*
—**Syn.** 1. FLUENT, GLIB, VOLUBLE may refer to a flow of words. FLUENT suggests an easy and ready flow and is usually a term of commendation: *a fluent and interesting speech.* GLIB implies an excessive fluency divorced from sincerity or profundity; it often suggests talking smoothly and hurriedly to cover up or deceive, not giving the hearer a chance to stop and think; it may also imply a plausible, prepared, and well-rehearsed lie: *He had a glib answer for everything.* VOLUBLE implies the overcopious, and often rapid flow of words, characteristic of a person who loves to talk and will spare his audience no details: *She overwhelmed him with her voluble answer.* —**Ant.** 1. terse, curt.

flue′ pipe′, *Music.* a pipe, esp. an organ pipe, having a flue.

flue′ stop′, a rank of flue pipes in an organ.

fluff (fluf), *n.* 1. light, downy particles, as of cotton. 2. a soft, light, downy mass: *a fluff of summer clouds.* 3. a light, frivolous thing; trifle: *That novel was a bit of fluff.* 4. *Informal.* an error or blunder, esp. one made by a performer in the delivery of his lines. —*v.t.* 5. to make into fluff; shake or puff out (feathers, hair, etc.) into a fluffy mass. 6. *Informal.* to make a mistake in: *The leading man fluffed his lines.* —*v.i.* 7. to become fluffy; move, float, or settle down like fluff. 8. *Informal.* to make a mistake, esp. in the delivery of lines by a performer; blunder. [? b. FLUE[2] and PUFF] —**fluff′er,** *n.*

fluff·y (fluf′ē), *adj.,* **fluff·i·er, fluff·i·est.** 1. of, resembling, or covered with fluff. 2. light or airy: *a fluffy cake.* 3. having little or no intellectual weight; frivolous: *a fluffy play; fluffy thinking.* [FLUFF + -Y[1]] —**fluff′i·ly,** *adv.* —**fluff′i·ness,** *n.*

Flü·gel·horn (flo͞o′gəl hôrn′; *Ger.* flʏ′gəl hôrn′), *n.* a brass wind instrument with three valves, usually pitched in B flat and used esp. in military bands. [< G, equiv. to *Flügel* wing + *Horn* horn]

flu·gel·man (flo͞o′gəl mən), *n., pl.* **-men.** fugleman.

flu·id (flo͞o′id), *n.* 1. a substance, as a liquid or gas, that is capable of flowing and that changes its shape at a steady rate when acted upon by a force tending to change its shape. —*adj.* 2. pertaining to a substance that easily changes its shape; capable of flowing. 3. consisting of or pertaining to fluids. 4. changing readily; shifting; not fixed, stable, or rigid: *the fluid movement of urban populations.* [< L *fluid(us),* equiv. to *flu(ere)* (to) flow + *-idus* -ID[4]] —**flu·id′ic, flu′id·al,** *adj.* —**flu·id′i·ty, flu′id·ness,** *n.* —**flu′id·ly, flu′id·al·ly,** *adv.*

flu′id cou′pling, an apparatus in which a fluid, usually oil, transmits torque from one shaft to another, producing an equal torque in the other shaft. Also called **hydraulic coupling.** Cf. **hydraulic torque converter.**

flu′id dram′, the eighth part of a fluid ounce. *Abbr.:* fl dr, f ʒ Also, **fluid′ drachm′.**

flu′id drive′, *Auto.* a power coupling for permitting a smooth start in any gear, consisting of two vaned rotors in a sealed casing filled with oil, such that one rotor, driven by the engine, moves the oil to drive the other rotor, which, in turn, drives the transmission.

flu·id·ex·tract (flo͞o′id ek′strakt), *n. Pharm.* a liquid preparation, containing alcohol as a solvent or as a preservative, that contains in each cubic centimeter the medicinal activity of one gram of the crude drug in powdered form. [FLUID + EXTRACT]

flu·id·ics (flo͞o id′iks), *n.* (*construed as sing.*) the technology dealing with the use of a flowing liquid or gas in various devices, esp. controls, to perform functions usually performed by an electric current in electronic devices. [FLUID + -ICS] —**flu·id′ic,** *adj.*

flu·id·ise (flo͞o′i dīz′), *v.t.,* **-ised, -is·ing.** *Chiefly Brit.* fluidize. —**flu′id·i·sa′tion,** *n.* —**flu′id·is′er,** *n.*

flu·id·ize (flo͞o′i dīz′), *v.t.,* **-ized, -iz·ing.** 1. to make (something) fluid. 2. *Chem.* to suspend or transport (finely divided particles) in a stream of gas or air. Also, *esp. Brit.,* **fluidise.** [FLUID + -IZE] —**flu′id·i·za′tion,** *n.* —**flu′id·iz′er,** *n.*

flu′id mechan′ics, an applied science dealing with the basic principles of gaseous and liquid matter.

flu′id ounce′, a measure of capacity equal to 1/16 pint or 1.8047 cubic inches in the U.S., and to 1/20 of an imperial pint, or 1.7339 cubic inches in Great Britain. *Abbr.:* fl oz, f ℥

flu′id pres′sure, *Physics, Mech.* the pressure exerted by a fluid, directly proportional to the specific gravity at any point and to the height of the fluid above the point.

fluke[1] (flo͞ok), *n.* 1. the part of an anchor that catches in the ground, esp. the flat triangular piece at the end of each arm. See diag. under **anchor.** 2. a barb, or the barbed head, of a harpoon, spear, arrow, or the like. 3. either half of the triangular tail of a whale. [? special use of FLUKE[3]] —**fluke′less,** *adj.*

fluke[2] (flo͞ok), *n., v.,* **fluked, fluk·ing.** —*n.* 1. an accidental advantage; stroke of good luck: *He was lucky enough to get the job by a fluke.* 2. an accidentally successful stroke, as in billiards. —*v.t.* 3. *Informal.* to gain by a chance. [?; cf. dial. *fluke* a guess]

fluke[3] (flo͞ok), *n.* 1. any of several American flounders of the genus *Paralichthys,* esp. *P. dentatus,* found in the Atlantic Ocean. 2. any of various other flatfishes. 3. a trematode. [ME *flok(e), fluke,* OE *flōc;* c. OIcel *flōki;* cf. OHG *flah* flat (G *flach*)] —**fluke′less,** *adj.*

fluk·ey (flo͞o′kē), *adj.,* **fluk·i·er, fluk·i·est.** fluky.

fluk·y (flo͞o′kē), *adj.,* **fluk·i·er, fluk·i·est.** 1. *Informal.* obtained by chance rather than skill. 2. uncertain, as a wind. [FLUKE[2] + -Y[1]] —**fluk′i·ness,** *n.*

flume (flo͞om), *n., v.,* **flumed, flum·ing.** —*n.* 1. a deep narrow defile containing a mountain stream or torrent. 2. an artificial channel or trough for conducting water, as one used for the transportation of logs, fish, or the like. —*v.t.* 3. to transport (logs, fish, etc.) in a flume. 4. to divert (a stream) by a flume. [ME *flum* < OF << L *flūmen* stream]

flum·mer·y (flum′ə rē), *n., pl.* **-mer·ies.** 1. oatmeal or flour boiled with water until thick. 2. a type of fruit custard or blancmange, usually thickened with cornstarch. 3. any of various dishes made of flour, milk, eggs, sugar, etc. 4. foolish humbug; empty compliment. [alter. of Welsh *llymru*]

flum·mox (flum′əks), *v.t. Informal.* to bewilder; confuse. [?]

flump (flump), *Informal.* —*v.i., v.t.* 1. to plump down suddenly or heavily; flop. —*n.* 2. act or sound of flumping. [imit.]

flung (flung), *v.* pt. and pp. of **fling.**

flunk (flungk), *Informal.* —*v.i.* 1. to fail, as a student in a recitation or examination. 2. to give up; back out; surrender: *It was a regiment that never flunked, even in the fiercest battle.* 3. to fail and be unable to continue in, as school or the like (usually fol. by *out*): *He flunked out of flight training and was sent back to the infantry.* —*v.t.* 4. to fail to get a passing mark in: *to flunk math.* 5. to give a failing grade to; remove (a student) as unqualified from a school, course, etc. —*n.* 6. a failure, as in a course or examination. [? akin to FLINCH[1], FUNK[1]]

flun·key (flung′kē), *n., pl.* **-keys.** flunky. —**flun′key·ism,** *n.*

flun·ky (flung′kē), *n., pl.* **-kies.** 1. *Contemptuous.* a male servant in livery; lackey. 2. a servile follower; toady. 3. an assistant who does menial work. Also, **flunkey.** [? alter. of FLANKER] —**flun′ky·ism,** *n.*

fluo-, var. of **fluoro-:** *fluoboric.*

flu·o·bo·rate (flo͞o′ə bôr′āt, -it, -bōr′-), *n. Chem.* a salt of fluoboric acid. [FLUO- + BORATE]

flu·o·bo·ric (flo͞o′ə bôr′ik, -bōr′-), *adj. Chem.* containing the univalent group BF_4^-. [FLUO- + BORIC]

flu′obo′ric ac′id, *Chem.* a clear, colorless liquid, HBF_4, that ionizes abundantly in solution, used chiefly in the synthesis of fluoborates.

flu·o·phos·phate (flo͞o′ə fos′fāt), *n. Chem.* fluorophosphate.

flu′ophosphor′ic ac′id (flo͞o′ō fos fôr′ik, -for′-, flo͞o′-), *Chem.* See **fluorophosphoric acid.**

flu·or (flo͞o′ôr, -ər), *n. Mineral.* fluorite. [< L *fluor* a flowing; so called from its use as a flux]

fluor-, var. of **fluoro-** before a vowel: *fluorene; fluoric.*

flu·o·rene (flo͞o′ə rēn′, -rin, flo͝or′ēn, -in, flôr′-, flōr′-), *n. Chem.* a white, crystalline, water-insoluble solid, $C_{13}H_{10}$, used chiefly in the manufacture of resins and dyes. [< F; see FLUOR-, -ENE]

flu·o·resce (flo͞o′ə res′, flo͝o res′, flō-, flô-), *v.i.,* **-resced, -resc·ing.** to exhibit the phenomenon of fluorescence. [back formation from FLUORESCENCE]

flu·o·res·ce·in (flo͞o′ə res′ē in, flo͝o res′-, flō-, flô-), *n. Chem.* an orange-red, crystalline, water-insoluble solid, $C_{20}H_{12}O_5$, that in alkaline solutions produces an orange color and an intense green fluorescence: used to trace subterranean waters and in dyes. Also, **flu′o·res′ce·ine.** Also called **resorcinolphthalein.** [FLUORESCE + -IN[2]]

flu·o·res·cence (flo͞o′ə res′əns, flo͝o res′-, flō-, flô-), *n. Physics, Chem.* 1. the emission of radiation, esp. of visible light, by a substance during exposure to external radiation, as light or x-rays. Cf. **phosphorescence** (def. 1). 2. the property possessed by a substance capable of such emission. 3. the radiation so produced. [FLUOR- + -ESCENCE]

flu·o·res·cent (flo͞o′ə res′ənt, flo͝o res′-, flō-, flô-), *adj.* possessing the property of fluorescence; exhibiting fluorescence. [FLUOR- + -ESCENT]

fluores′cent lamp′, a tubular electric discharge lamp in which light is produced by the fluorescence of phosphors coating the inside of the tube.

flu·or·ic (flo͞o ôr′ik, -or′-), *adj.* 1. *Chem.* pertaining to or obtained from fluorine. 2. *Mineral.* of, pertaining to, or derived from fluorite. [< F *fluorique.* See FLUOR-, -IC]

fluor·i·date (flo͝or′i dāt′, flôr′-, flōr′-), *v.t.,* **-dat·ed, -dat·ing.** to introduce a fluoride into. [back formation from FLUORIDATION]

fluor·i·da·tion (flo͝or′i dā′shən, flôr′-, flōr′-), *n.* the addition of fluorides to the public water supply to reduce the incidence of tooth decay. [FLUORIDE + -ATION]

flu·o·ride (flo͞o′ə rīd′, flo͝or′id, flôr′-, flōr′-), *n. Chem.* 1. a salt of hydrofluoric acid consisting of two elements, one of which is fluorine, as sodium fluoride, NaF. 2. a compound containing fluorine, as methyl fluoride, CH_3F. [FLUOR- + -IDE]

fluor·i·dise (flo͝or′i dīz′, flôr′-, flōr′-), *v.t.,* **-dised, -dis·ing.** *Brit.* fluoridize. —**fluor′i·di·sa′tion,** *n.*

fluor·i·dize (flo͝or′i dīz′, flôr′-, flōr′-), *v.t.,* **-dized, -diz·ing.** to treat, impregnate, or affect with a fluoride. Also, *esp. Brit.,* **fluoridise.** [FLUORIDE + -IZE] —**fluor′i·di·za′tion,** *n.*

flu·o·rim·e·ter (flo͞o′ə rim′i tər, flo͝o rim′-, flō-, flô-), *n.* fluorometer.

fluor·i·nate (flo͝or′ə nāt′, flôr′-, flōr′-), *v.t.,* **-nat·ed, -nat·ing.** *Chem.* to treat or combine with fluorine. [FLUORINE + -ATE[1]] —**fluor′i·na′tion,** *n.*

flu·o·rine (flo͞o′ə rēn′, -rin, flo͝or′ēn, -in, flôr′-, flōr′-), *n. Chem.* the most reactive nonmetallic element, a pale-yellow, corrosive, toxic gas that occurs combined, esp. in fluorite, cryolite, phosphate rock, and other minerals. *Symbol:* F; *at. wt.:* 18.9984; *at. no.:* 9. [FLUOR- + -INE[1]]

flu′orine dat′ing, a method of determining the relative age of fossil bones found in the same excavation by comparing their fluorine content.

flu·o·rite (flo͞o′ə rīt′, flo͝or′īt, flôr′-, flōr′-), *n.* a common mineral, calcium fluoride, CaF_2, occurring in green, blue, purple, yellow, or colorless crystals, usually in cubes: the principal source of fluorine, used also as a flux in metallurgy and for ornament. Also called **fluor, fluorspar, fluor spar.** [< It; see FLUOR-, -ITE[1]]

fluoro-, 1. a combining form indicating the presence of fluorine: *fluorocarbon.* 2. a combining form of **fluorescence:** *fluoroscopy.* Also, **fluo-, fluor-.** [< NL; see FLUOR, -O-]

flu·o·ro·car·bon (flo͞o′ə rō kär′bən, flo͝or′ō-, flôr′-, flōr′-), *n. Chem.* any of a class of compounds produced by substituting fluorine for hydrogen in a hydrocarbon, and characterized by great chemical stability: used chiefly as a lubricant, fire extinguishing agent, and in industrial applications in which resistance to heat, radioactivity, or the like, is essential. [FLUORO- + CARBON]

flu·o·rom·e·ter (flo͞o′ə rom′i tər, flo͝o rom′, flō-, flô-), *n.* an instrument for measuring fluorescence, often as a means of determining the nature of the substance emitting the fluorescence. Also, **fluorimeter.** [FLUORO- + -METER] —**flu·o·ro·met·ric** (flo͞o′ər ə me′trik, flo͝or′ə-, flôr′ə-, flōr′ə-), *adj.* —**flu′o·rom′e·try,** *n.*

flu·o·ro·phos·phate (flo͞o′ə rō fos′fāt, flo͝or′ō-, flôr′-, flōr′-), *n. Chem.* a salt or ester of a fluorophosphoric acid. Also, **fluophosphate.** [FLUORO- + PHOSPHATE]

flu′o·ro·phos·phor′ic ac′id (flo͞o′ə rō fos fôr′ik, -for′-, flo͝or′ō-, flôr′-, flōr′-, flo͞o′ə rō-, flo͝or′ō-, flôr′-, flōr′-), *Chem.* any of three acids containing fluorine and phosphorus, HPF_6, HPO_2F_2, or H_2PO_3F. Also, **fluophosphoric acid.** [FLUORO- + PHOSPHORIC]

fluor·o·scope (flo͝or′ə skōp′, flôr′-, flōr′-, flo͞o′ər ə-), *n.* a tube or box fitted with a screen coated with a fluorescent substance, used for viewing objects by means of x-ray or other radiation. [FLUORO- + -SCOPE]

fluor·o·scop·ic (flo͝or′ə skop′ik, flôr′-, flōr′-, flo͞o′ər ə-), *adj.* of or pertaining to the fluoroscope or fluoroscopy. [FLUOROSCOPE + -IC] —**fluor′o·scop′i·cal·ly,** *adv.*

fluor·os·co·py (flo͝o ros′kə pē, flō-, flô-, flo͞o′ə ros′-), *n.* the use of or examination by means of a fluoroscope. [FLUORO- + -SCOPY]

fluo·ro·sis (flo͝o rō′sis, flō-, flô-, flo͞o′ə rō′-), *n. Pathol.* poisoning by fluorides. [FLUOR- + -OSIS]

flu·or·spar (flo͞o′ôr spär′, -ər-), *n. Mineral.* fluorite. Also, **flu′or spar′.** [FLUOR- + SPAR[3]]

flu·o·sil·i·cate (flo͞o′ə sil′ə kit, -kāt′), *n. Chem.* a salt of fluosilicic acid. [FLUO- + SILICATE]

flu′o·si·lic′ic ac′id (flo͞o′ō si lis′ik, flo͞o′-), *Chem.* an unstable acid, H_2SiF_6, known only in its colorless, poisonous, fuming aqueous solution or in the form of its salts: used chiefly as a wood preservative, a disinfectant, and as a hardening agent in the manufacture of ceramic ware, cement, and concrete. [FLUO- + SILICIC]

flur·ried (flûr′ēd, flur′-), *adj.* confused; flustered; agitated or excited. [FLURRY + -ED[2]]

flur·ry (flûr′ē, flur′ē), *n., pl.* **-ries,** *v.,* **-ried, -ry·ing.** —*n.* 1. a shower of snow. 2. sudden commotion, excitement, or confusion; nervous hurry: *There was a flurry of activity before the guests arrived.* 3. *Stock Exchange.* a brief agitation in prices. 4. *Rare.* a sudden gust of wind. —*v.t.* 5. to put (a person) into a flurry; confuse; fluster. [b. FLUTTER and HURRY] —**flur′ried·ly,** *adv.*
—**Syn.** 2. upset, pother, stir, to-do, fuss, fluster, ado.

flush[1] (flush), *n.* 1. a blush; rosy glow: *There was a flush of embarrassment on his face.* 2. a rushing or overspreading flow, as of water. 3. a sudden rise of emotion or excitement: *the first flush of success; a flush of anger.* 4. glowing freshness or vigor: *the flush of youth.* 5. the hot stage of a fever. —*v.t.* 6. to redden; cause to blush or glow. 7. to flood with water, as for cleansing purposes: *They flushed the wall with water and then scrubbed it down.* 8. to wash out (a sewer, toilet, etc.) by a sudden rush of water. 9. *Metall.* a. to remove slag from (a blast furnace). b. to spray (a coke oven) to cool the gases generated and wash away the ammonia and tars distilled. 10. to animate or excite; inflame. —*v.i.* 11. to blush; redden. 12. to flow with a rush; flow and spread suddenly. [b. FLASH and GUSH; in some senses, further blended with BLUSH] —**flush′er,** *n.* —**flush′ing·ly,** *adv.*

flush[2] (flush), *adj.* 1. even or level, as with a surface; forming one plane: *The bottom of the window is flush with the floor.* 2. having direct contact; being right next to; immediately adjacent; contiguous: *The table was flush against the wall.* 3. well-supplied, as with money; affluent; prosperous: *He was feeling flush on payday.* 4. abundant or plentiful, as money. 5. having a ruddy or reddish color; blushing. 6. full of vigor; lusty. 7. full to overflowing. 8. *Naut.* noting a continuous weather deck that has no superstructure but may have deckhouses, companions, etc. Cf. **flush-deck vessel.** 9. *Print.* even or level with the right or left margins of the type page; without an indention. —*adv.* 10. on the same level; in a straight line; without a change of plane: *to be made flush with the top of the table.* 11. in direct contact; squarely: *It was set flush against the edge.* —*v.t.* 12. to make flush or even. 13. to improve the nutrition of (a ewe) to bring on optimum physiological conditions for breeding. —*v.i.* 14. to send out shoots, as plants in spring. —*n.* 15. a fresh growth, as of shoots and leaves. [? special uses of FLUSH[1]] —**flush′ness,** *n.*

flush[3] (flush), *Hunting.* —*v.t.* 1. to rouse and cause to start up or fly off: *to flush a woodcock.* —*v.i.* 2. to fly out or start up suddenly. —*n.* 3. a flushed bird, or flock of birds. [ME *flussh* < ?]

flush[4] (flush), *Cards.* —*adj.* 1. consisting entirely of cards of one suit: *a flush hand.* —*n.* 2. a hand or set of cards all of one suit. Cf. **royal flush, straight flush.** 3. *Pinochle.* a meld of ace, king, queen, jack, and ten of the trump suit. Cf. **marriage** (def. 6), **royal marriage.** [cf. F (obs.) *flus,* var. of *flux* flow, flush (cf. phrase *run* of cards) < L *flux(us)* FLUX]

flush-decked (flush′dekt′), *adj. Naut.* having a weather deck flush with the hull.

flush′-deck ves′sel (flush′dek′), *Naut.* a vessel having no shelter deck, poop, forecastle, or other superstructure of any kind above the freeboard deck, but sometimes having deckhouses, companions, etc. Also, **flush′-decked′ ves′sel.**

flush′ girt′, *Carpentry.* a girt running parallel to joists and at the same level. Also called **raised girt.** Cf. **drop girt.**

Flush·ing (flush′ing), *n.* 1. a seaport on Walcheren Island, in the SW Netherlands. 28,856 (1964). Dutch, **Vlissingen.** 2. a town in central Michigan. 3761 (1960).

flus·ter (flus′tər), *v.t.* 1. to put into a state of nervous, agitated confusion: *His constant criticism flustered her.* 2. to excite and confuse with drink. —*v.i.* 3. to become nervously and agitatedly confused. —*n.* 4. nervous excitement; confusion; flurry. [ME *flostre(n);* cf. Icel *flaustr* to hurry, bustle and cf. BLUSTER]
—**Syn.** 1. upset, bewilder, disconcert, disturb. 4. turmoil, agitation, upset, bewilderment, distraction.

flus·ter·ate (flus′tə rāt′), *v.t.,* **-at·ed, -at·ing.** *Informal.* flustrate. —**flus′ter·a′tion,** *n.*

flus·trate (flus′trāt), *v.t.*, **-trat·ed, -trat·ing.** *Informal.* to fluster. [FLUST(E)R + -ATE[1], modeled on *frustrate*] —**flus·tra′tion,** *n.*

flus·trat·ed (flus′trā tid) *adj.*, *Informal.* flustered; agitated. Also, **flus′ter·at′ed.** [FLUSTRATE + -ED[2]]

flute (flo͞ot), *n.*, *v.*, **flut·ed, flut·ing.** —*n.* **1.** a musical wind instrument consisting of a tube with a series of fingerholes or keys, in which the wind is directed against a sharp edge, either directly, as in the modern transverse flute, or through a flue, as in the recorder. **2.** an organ stop with wide flue pipes, having a flutelike tone. **3.** *Archit., Furniture.* a channel, groove, or furrow, as on the shaft of a column. **4.** any groove or furrow, as in a woman's ruffle, on a pie crust, on the stem of a glass, etc. **5.** one of the helical grooves of a twist drill. **6.** a slender, footed wineglass of the 17th century, having a tall, conical bowl with a large, spherical knop. —*v.i.* **7.** to produce flutelike sounds. **8.** to play on a flute. **9.** (of a metal strip or sheet) to kink or break in bending. —*v.t.* **10.** to utter in flutelike tones. **11.** to form longitudinal flutes or furrows in: *to flute a piecrust.* [ME *floute* < MF *flaüte, flahute, fleüte* < OPr *flaüt* (perh. alter. of *flaujol, flauja*) < VL* *flabeol(um).* See FLAGEOLET, LUTE] —**flute′like′,** *adj.*

Flute

flut·ed (flo͞o′tid), *adj.* **1.** fine, clear, and mellow; flutelike: *fluted notes.* **2.** having flutes, grooves, ruffles, or the like: *a fluted column; fluted material.* [FLUTE + -ED[3]]

flut·er (flo͞o′tər), *n.* **1.** a person who makes flutings. **2.** *Archaic.* a flutist. [ME *flouter, floutour* < OF *fleuteur, flauteor,* equiv. to *flaut(er)* (to) play the flute + *-eur, -eor* -ER[1]]

flut·ey (flo͞o′tē), *adj.*, **flut·i·er, flut·i·est.** fluty.

flut·ing (flo͞o′ting), *n.* **1.** the act of playing on the flute. **2.** the sound made by such playing; a flutelike sound. **3.** anything having ornamental grooves, as a Greek column. **4.** act of making such grooves or fluted work. **5.** a groove, furrow, or flute, or a number of these. [FLUTE + -ING[1]]

flut′ing i′ron, an iron that is specially shaped for pressing material into a fluted form.

flut·ist (flo͞o′tist), *n.* a flute player. Also, **flautist.** [FLUTE + -IST; see FLAUTIST]

flut·ter (flut′ər), *v.i.* **1.** to wave, flap, or toss about in the air, as a flag: *Banners fluttered in the breeze.* **2.** (of birds) to flap the wings, or fly with flapping movements. **3.** to move in quick, irregular motions; vibrate: *Her eyelids fluttered as she awoke.* **4.** to beat rapidly and irregularly, as the heart. **5.** to be tremulous or agitated. **6.** to go with irregular motions or aimless course: *to flutter back and forth.* —*v.t.* **7.** to cause to flutter; vibrate; agitate. **8.** to throw into a state of nervous or tremulous excitement; cause mental agitation; confuse. —*n.* **9.** a fluttering movement: *She made little nervous flutters with her hands.* **10.** a state of nervous excitement or mental agitation: *a flutter of anticipation.* **11.** sensation; stir: *to cause a flutter.* **12.** *Swimming.* See **flutter kick. 13.** a rapid variation in pitch fidelity resulting from fluctuations in the speed of a recording. [ME *flotere(n),* OE *floterian,* freq. of *flotian* to FLOAT] —**flut′ter·er,** *n.* —**flut′ter·ing·ly,** *adv.*
—**Syn. 2.** See **fly**[1].

flut·ter·board (flut′ər bōrd′, -bôrd′), *n.* a kickboard. [FLUTTER + BOARD]

flut′ter kick′, *Swimming.* a kick in which the legs make rapid alternate up-and-down movements while the knees remain rigid, as in the crawl.

flut′ter wheel′, a water wheel at the bottom of a chute, turned by the falling water.

flut·ter·y (flut′ə rē), *adj.* fluttering; apt to flutter. [FLUTTER + -Y[1]]

flut·y (flo͞o′tē), *adj.*, **flut·i·er, flut·i·est.** flutelike, as in tone. Also, **flutey.** [FLUTE + -Y[1]]

flu·vi·al (flo͞o′vē əl), *adj.* **1.** of or pertaining to a river: *fluvial contour.* **2.** produced by or found in a river: *fluvial plants.* [< L *fluviāl(is),* equiv. to *fluvi(us)* river (deriv. of *fluere* to flow) + *-ālis* -AL[1]]

flu·vi·a·tile (flo͞o′vē ə til, -tīl′), *adj.* pertaining or peculiar to rivers; found in or near rivers. [< L *fluviātil(is),* equiv. to *fluvi-* (see FLUVIAL) + *-ātil(is)* assoc. suffix]

flu·vi·o·ma·rine (flo͞o′vē ō mə rēn′), *adj.* of or formed by the combined action of river and sea. [< L *fluvi-* river (see FLUVIAL) + -O- + MARINE]

flux (fluks), *n.* **1.** a flowing or flow. **2.** the flowing in of the tide. **3.** continuous change, passage, or movement: *His political views are in flux.* **4.** lack of certainty, purpose, or direction; instability: *The nation was in a state of flux after the revolution.* **5.** *Pathol.* **a.** an abnormal or morbid discharge of liquid matter from the bowels, as a bloody flux. **b.** dysentery. **6.** *Physics.* **a.** the rate of flow of fluid, particles, or energy. **b.** a quantity expressing the strength of a field of force in a given area. **7.** *Chem., Metall.* **a.** a substance used to refine metals by combining with impurities to form a molten mixture that can be readily removed. **b.** a substance used to remove oxides from and prevent further oxidation of fused metal, as in soldering or hot-dip coating. **c.** (in the refining of scrap or other metal) a salt or mixture of salts which combines with nonmetallic impurities, causing them to float or coagulate. **8.** fusion. —*v.t.* **9.** to melt; make fluid. **10.** to fuse by the use of flux. **11.** *Obs.* to purge. —*v.i.* **12.** to flow. [ME < L *flux(us)* a flowing, n. use of ptp. of *fluere* to flow]

flux′ den′sity, *Physics.* the magnetic, radiant, or electric flux per unit of cross-sectional area.

flux′ gate′, an instrument, often used in gyrocompasses, for indicating the field strength of an external magnetic field, as that of the earth, producing an electric signal that has a magnitude of the field and a phase indicating the direction of the field. Also called **flux′ valve′.**

flux·graph (fluks′graf′, -gräf′), *n.* an instrument for detecting and recording the magnetic field about a coil. [FLUX + -GRAPH]

flux·ion (fluk′shən), *n.* **1.** act of flowing; a flow or flux. **2.** *Math. Obs.* the derivative relative to the time. [< MF < L *fluxiōn-* (s. of *fluxiō*) a flowing. See FLUX, -ION] —**flux′ion·al, flux′ion·ar·y,** *adj.* —**flux′ion·al·ly,** *adv.*

flux′ link′age, *Elect.* the product of the magnetic flux and the number of turns in a given coil.

flux·me·ter (fluks′mē′tər), *n.* *Physics.* an instrument for measuring magnetic flux, consisting essentially of a ballistic galvanometer. [FLUX + -METER]

fluyt (flīt), *n.* a small 17th-century merchant ship of northern Europe, having a rounded stern, a flat bottom, and three masts. [var. of *flute* a flyboat < D *fluit* FLUTE]

fly[1] (flī), *v.*, **flew** or, for 11, 18, **flied, flown; fly·ing;** *n.*, *pl.* **flies.** —*v.i.* **1.** to move through the air on wings, as a bird. **2.** to be carried through the air by the wind or any other force or agency: *bits of paper flying about.* **3.** to float or flutter in the air: *hair flying in the wind; flags flying in the breeze.* **4.** to travel through the air in an aircraft or as an aircraft does. **5.** to move suddenly and quickly; start unexpectedly and rapidly: *He flew from the room.* **6.** to change rapidly and unexpectedly from one state or position to another: *to fly apart; to fly into a rage; The door flew open.* **7.** to flee: *They were forced to fly when the government changed.* **8.** to travel through outer space in a satellite or rocket, or as a rocket does. **9.** to move or pass swiftly: *The train flew down the track. How time flies!* **10.** to attack by flying, as a hawk does (usually fol. by *at*). **11.** *Baseball.* **a.** to bat a fly ball: *He flied into right field.* **b.** to fly out. —*v.t.* **12.** to make (something) float or move through the air: *to fly a kite.* **13.** to operate (an aircraft, spaceship, or the like). **14.** to hoist aloft, as for display, signaling, etc.: *to fly a flag.* **15.** to operate an aircraft over (a particular route): *to fly the Pacific.* **16.** to transport or convey (something) by air: *We will fly the merchandise to Boston.* **17.** to escape from (something): *to fly someone's wrath.* **18.** *Theat.* **a.** to hang (scenery) above a stage by means of rigging supported by the gridiron. **b.** to raise (scenery) from the stage or acting area into the flies. **19. fly at** or **into,** to attack or lash out at, either verbally or physically: *He flew at us for being ten minutes late.* **20. fly in the face of,** to act in defiance of (authority, custom, etc.): *He flew in the face of family tradition and became a career soldier instead of a lawyer.* **21. fly off the handle.** See **handle** (def. 7). **22. fly out,** *Baseball, Softball.* to be put out by hitting a fly ball that is caught by a player of the opposing team. **23. go fly a kite!** *Slang.* go away! beat it! **24. let fly, a.** to hurl or propel (a weapon, missile, etc.). **b.** to give free rein to an emotion: *She let fly with a veritable deluge of tears.* —*n.* **25.** a strip of material sewn along one edge of a garment opening for concealing buttons or other fasteners. **26.** a flap forming the door of a tent. **27.** Also called **tent fly.** a piece of canvas extending over the ridgepole of a tent and forming an outer roof. **28.** act of flying; a flight. **29.** the course of a flying object, as a ball. **30.** *Baseball.* See **fly ball. 31.** *Brit.* a light, covered, public carriage drawn by one horse; hansom; hackney coach. **32.** *Mach.* a horizontal arm, weighted at each end, that pivots about the screw of a press so that when the screw is lowered the momentum of the fly will increase the force of the press. **33.** Also called **fan.** *Horol.* a regulating device for chime and striking mechanisms, consisting of an arrangement of vanes on a revolving axis. **34.** *Print.* **a.** (in some presses) the apparatus for removing the printed sheets to the delivery table. **b.** Also called **flyboy.** (formerly) a printer's devil employed to remove printed sheets from a press. **35.** (on a flag) **a.** the horizontal dimension of a flag as flown from a vertical staff. **b.** the edge of a flag parallel to that running next to the staff. Cf. **hoist** (def. 8). **36. flies.** Also called **fly loft.** *Theat.* the space above the stage, used chiefly for storing scenery and equipment. **37.** *Naut.* a propellerlike device streamed to rotate and transfer information on speed to a mechanical log. **38. on the fly, a.** during flight; before reaching the ground: *to catch a baseball on the fly.* **b.** hurriedly; without pausing: *We had dinner on the fly.* [ME *flīe(n),* OE *flēogan;* c. OHG *fliogan,* G *fliegen,* OIcel *fljuga*] —**fly′a·bil′i·ty,** *n.* —**fly′a·ble,** *adj.*
—**Syn. 1.** FLY, FLIT, FLUTTER, HOVER, SOAR refer to moving through the air as on wings. FLY is the general term: *Birds fly. Airplanes fly.* To FLIT is to make short rapid flights from place to place: *A bird flits from tree to tree.* To FLUTTER is to agitate the wings tremulously, either without flying or in flying only short distances: *A young bird flutters out of a nest and in again.* To HOVER is to linger in the air, or to move over or about something within a narrow area or space: *hovering clouds; a hummingbird hovering over a blossom.* To SOAR is to (start to) fly upward to a great height usually with little advance in any other direction, or else to (continue to) fly at a lofty height without visible movement of the wings: *Above our heads an eagle was soaring.* **9.** pass, glide, slip, elapse.

fly[2] (flī), *n.*, *pl.* **flies. 1.** Also called **true fly.** any of numerous two-winged insects of the order *Diptera,* esp. of the family *Muscidae,* as the common housefly. **2.** any of various winged insects, as the mayfly or firefly. **3.** *Angling.* a fishhook dressed with hair, feathers, silk, tinsel, etc., so as to resemble an insect or small fish, for use as a lure or bait. **4.** (*cap.*) *Astron.* the constellation Musca. **5. fly in the ointment,** a circumstance, esp. a trifling inconvenience, that detracts from the enjoyment or usefulness of something: *The only fly in the ointment on our vacation was the cool weather.* **6. no flies on,** *Slang.* (of a person) unlikely to be fooled; alert; sharp: *He's an uneducated farm boy, but there ain't no flies on him.* [ME *flīe,* OE *flēoge, flyge;* akin to MD *vliege* (D *vlieg*), OHG *flioga* (G *Fliege*)] —**fly′less,** *adj.*

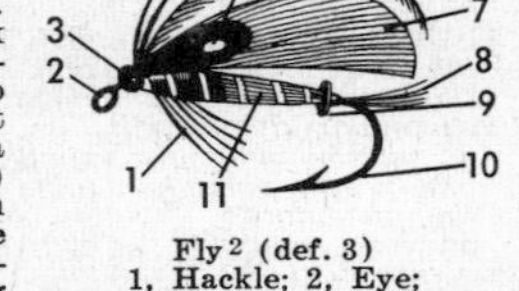

Fly[2] (def. 3)
1, Hackle; 2, Eye; 3, Head; 4, Horns; 5, Cheek; 6, Topping; 7, Wing; 8, Tail; 9, Butt; 10, Hook; 11, Body

fly[3] (flī), *adj.* *Brit. Slang.* **1.** knowing; sharp; smart; nimble-minded. **2.** agile; nimble. [? special use of FLY[1]]

fly′ ag′aric, a very poisonous mushroom, *Amanita muscaria,* yielding a substance that is toxic to flies.

fly′ ash′, 1. fine particles of ash of a solid fuel carried out of the flue of a furnace with the waste gases produced during combustion. **2.** such ash recovered from the waste gases, used chiefly as a reinforcing agent in the manufacture of bricks, concrete, etc.

fly·a·way (flī′ə wā′), *adj.* **1.** fluttering or streaming in the wind; windblown. **2.** flighty; frivolous; giddy. [adj. use of v. phrase *fly away*]

fly·back (flī′bak′), *n.* *Electronics.* **1.** the return to its starting point of the electron beam in a cathode ray tube, as after the completion of a line in a television picture or of a trace in an oscilloscope. **2.** the shorter element of a sawtooth wave. [n. use of v. phrase *fly back*]

fly′ ball′, *Baseball.* a ball that is batted up into the air. Also called **fly.** Cf. **ground ball.**

fly·belt (flī′belt′), *n.* an area having a large number of tsetse flies. [FLY[2] + BELT]

fly′ block′, *Mach., Naut.* **1.** (in a Spanish burton or the like) a block, supported by a runner, through which the hauling part of the fall is rove. **2.** any block that shifts with the movement of its tackle.

fly·blow (flī′blō′), *v.*, **-blew, -blown, -blow·ing,** *n.* —*v.t.* **1.** to deposit eggs or larvae on (meat or other food). —*n.* **2.** the egg or young larva of a blowfly, deposited on meat or other food. [back formation from FLYBLOWN]

fly·blown (flī′blōn′), *adj.* **1.** covered with flyblows: *flyblown meat.* **2.** spoiled; tainted; contaminated. [FLY[2] + BLOWN[1]]

fly·boat (flī′bōt′), *n.* a small, fast boat. [< D *vlieboot,* equiv. to *vlie* channel + *boot* boat]

fly′ book′, *Angling.* a booklike case for artificial flies.

fly·boy (flī′boi′), *n.* **1.** *Print.* fly[1] (def. 34b). **2.** *U.S. Air Force Slang.* a member of an aircrew, esp. a pilot. **3.** *Slang.* any member of the U.S. Air Force. [FLY[1] + BOY]

fly-by-night (flī′bī nīt′), *adj.* **1.** not reliable or responsible, esp. in business: *a fly-by-night operation.* **2.** not lasting; brief; impermanent; transitory: *a fly-by-night theater.* —*n.* **3.** one who or that which is unreliable, esp. a debtor who evades, or attempts to evade, his creditors. **4.** a person regarded as a poor credit risk.

fly′ cast′ing, *Angling.* act or technique of casting with an artificial fly as the lure, the rod used being longer and more flexible than that used in bait casting.

fly·catch·er (flī′kach′ər), *n.* **1.** any of numerous Old World birds of the family *Muscicapidae,* that feed on insects captured in the air. **2.** Also called **tyrant flycatcher.** any of numerous similar American birds of the family *Tyrannidae.* [FLY[2] + CATCHER]

fly·er (flī′ər), *n.* **1.** *Textiles.* **a.** a rotating device that adds twist to the slubbing or roving and winds the stock onto a spindle or bobbin in a uniform manner. **b.** a similar device for adding twist to yarn. **2.** flier. [late ME; see FLY[1], -ER[1]]

fly-fish (flī′fish′), *v.i.* *Angling.* to fish with artificial flies as bait.

fly′ front′, a flap of material down one side of the front opening of a garment to conceal buttons, fasteners, or the like, as on a coat or dress.

fly′ gal′lery, *Theat.* a narrow platform at the side of a stage from which ropes are manipulated to raise or lower scenery, battens, etc. Also called **fly′ floor′.**

fly·ing (flī′ing), *adj.* **1.** that flies; making flight or passing through the air: *a flying insect; an unidentified flying object.* **2.** floating, fluttering, waving, hanging, or moving freely in the air: *flying banners; flying hair.* **3.** extending through the air. **4.** moving swiftly. **5.** made while moving swiftly: *a flying leap.* **6.** hasty; brief; fleeting or transitory: *a flying visit; a flying remark.* **7.** designed or organized for swiftness: *The police flying squad sped to the scene.* **8.** fleeing, running away, or taking flight: *They pursued the flying enemy.* **9.** *Naut.* (of a sail) having none of its edges bent to spars or stays. —*n.* **10.** act of moving through the air on wings; flight. —*adv.* **11.** *Naut.* without being bent to a yard, stay, or the like: *a sail set flying.* [ME (n.), OE *flēogende* (n.). See FLY[1], -ING[2], -ING[1]]

fly′ing boat′, an aircraft whose main body consists of a single hull or boat. Cf. **floatplane.**

fly′ing bomb′. See **robot bomb.**

fly′ing bond′, a brickwork bond having random, widely spaced headers. Also called **Yorkshire bond.**

fly′ing box′car, *Informal.* a large airplane designed to carry cargo.

fly′ing bridge′, *Naut.* an open platform, esp. one on top of a pilothouse, having duplicate controls, usually including a steering wheel, engine room telegraphs, and other instruments, as well as the standard compass of the vessel. Also called **monkey bridge, navigating bridge.**

fly′ing but′tress, *Archit.* a segmental arch transmitting an outward and downward thrust to a solid buttress which through its inertia transforms the thrust into a vertical one. See illus. under **buttress.**

fly′ing cir′cus, 1. a squadron of airplanes operating together, esp. any of several squadrons of famous World War I aviators. **2.** a carnival troupe, or the like, offering exhibitions of stunt flying at fairs, circuses, etc.

fly′ing col′ors, victory; triumph; success: *The debating team came off with flying colors.*

fly′ing col′umn, *Mil.* (formerly) a force of troops equipped and organized to move swiftly and independently of a principal unit to which it is attached.

fly′ing doc′tor, *Australian.* a doctor listed with local authorities as willing to be flown to remote areas to give emergency medical care.

fly′ing drag′on, any of several arboreal lizards of the genus *Draco,* having an extensible membrane along each side by means of which it makes long, gliding leaps. Also called **flying lizard.**

Fly′ing Dutch′man, 1. a legendary Dutch ghost ship supposed to be seen at sea, esp. near the Cape of Good Hope. **2.** the captain of this ship, supposed to have been condemned to sail the sea, beating against the wind, till the Day of Judgment. **3.** (*italics*) **The**, an opera (1841) by Richard Wagner.

fly′ing field′, *Aeron.* a small landing field with short runways and facilities for servicing airplanes on a lesser scale than an airport.

fly·ing·fish (flī′ing fish′), *n., pl.* (*esp. collectively*) **-fish**, (*esp. referring to two or more kinds or species*) **-fish·es.** **1.** any of several fishes of the family *Exocoetidae*, having stiff and greatly enlarged pectoral fins enabling it to glide considerable distances through the air after leaping from the water. **2.** (*cap.*) *Astron.* the constellation Volans. [FLYING + FISH]

Flyingfish *Cypseturus californicus* (Length 1½ ft.)

fly′ing for′tress, a heavy bomber with four radial piston engines, widely used over Europe and the Mediterranean by the U.S. Army Air Force in World War II. *Symbol:* B-17.

fly′ing fox′, **1.** any large fruit-eating bat of the family *Pteropodidae*, esp. of the genus *Pteropus*, as *P. edulis*, of Old World tropical regions, having a foxlike head. **2.** *Australian.* an aerial conveyor belt or suspended carrier operating on cables, often used to convey ore, dirt, or the like, over rivers and gorges in mining or construction operations.

fly′ing frog′, an East Indian frog, *Rhacophorus nigrapalmtus*, having broadly webbed feet enabling it to make long, gliding leaps.

fly′ing gang′way, *Naut.* See **monkey bridge** (def. 2).

fly′ing gur′nard, any of several marine fishes of the family *Dactylopteridae*, esp. *Dactylopterus volitans*, having greatly enlarged, colorful pectoral fins, thought to be capable of gliding short distances through the air. Also called **butterflyfish, flying robin.**

fly′ing jib′, *Naut.* the outer or outermost of two or more jibs, set well above the jib boom. See diag. under **ship.**

fly′ing jib′ boom′, *Naut.* an extension on a jib boom, to which a flying jib is fastened.

fly′ing kite′, *Naut.* **1.** any of various sails set above the royals or skysails in light weather; jolly jumper. **2.** any of various light upper staysails, studdingsails, or jibs. **3.** (in yachting) any of various racing sails, as spinnakers or balloon jibs. Also called **kite.**

fly′ing le′mur, either of two lemurlike mammals, *Cynocephalus temminckii*, of southeastern Asia and the East Indies, or *C. volans*, of the Philippines, having broad folds of skin on both sides of the body to aid in gliding from tree to tree.

fly′ing liz′ard. See **flying dragon.**

fly′ing machine′, a contrivance which sustains itself in and propels itself through the air; an airplane or the like.

fly′ing mare′, *Wrestling.* a method of attack in which a wrestler grasps the wrist of his opponent, turns in the opposite direction, and throws him over his shoulder and down.

fly′ing moor′, *Naut.* the act of mooring a vessel between two anchors, the first dropped while the vessel has way on.

fly′ing mouse′. See **pygmy glider.**

fly′ing night′ingale, *Naut.* the standing rigging extending from the end of the flying jib boom to the lower end of the martingale.

Flying phalanger genus *Petaurus* (Total length to 2½ ft; tail 16 in.)

fly′ing phalan′ger, any of various small phalangers of Australia and New Guinea, having a parachutelike fold of skin on each side of the body to give gliding assistance in leaping.

fly′ing rob′in. See **flying gurnard.**

fly′ing sau′cer, any of various disk-shaped objects allegedly seen flying at high speeds and altitudes, often with extreme changes in speed and direction, and generally presumed to be from outer space.

fly′ing shear′, *Metalworking.* (in a continuous rolling mill) a shear that moves with the piece being cut.

fly′ing sky′sail, *Naut.* a skysail set on a yard having neither lifts nor braces and furled on the royal yard.

fly′ing spot′, *Television.* the moving spot of light that scans a scene being televised.

fly′ing squad′, a trained, mobile group of policemen, businessmen, labor officials, or the like, capable of performing specialized tasks whenever or wherever sent, often for use in emergencies: *The group was a flying squad of executives sent to investigate foreign markets. The police sent a flying squad to disperse the rioters.*

fly′ing squir′rel, a squirrellike animal, esp. of the genus *Glaucomys*, as *G. volans* of the eastern U.S., with folds of skin connecting the fore and hind legs, enabling it to take long gliding leaps.

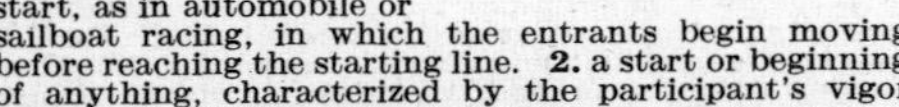

Flying squirrel, *Glaucomys volans* (Total length 1 ft.; tail 4 in.)

fly′ing start′, **1.** a start, as in automobile or sailboat racing, in which the entrants begin moving before reaching the starting line. **2.** a start or beginning of anything, characterized by the participant's vigor and enthusiasm and sometimes by a certain advantage over competitors: *She's off to a flying start in her new job as furniture buyer.*

fly′ing tack′le, *Football.* a tackle made by hurling one's body through the air at the player carrying the ball.

fly′ing wing′, *Aeron.* an airplane whose wings form almost all the airframe, with the fuselage almost or entirely within the wing structure.

fly·leaf (flī′lēf′), *n., pl.* **-leaves.** a blank leaf in the front or the back of a book. [FLY³ + LEAF]

fly′ line′, *Angling.* a line designed for use in fly-fishing.

fly′ loft′, *Theat.* fly¹ (def. 36).

fly·man (flī′mən), *n., pl.* **-men.** *Theat.* a stagehand, esp. one who operates the apparatus in the flies. [FLY¹ + MAN¹]

fly′ net′, a net or fringe to protect a horse from flies.

fly-off (flī′ôf′, -of′), *n.* *Meteorol.* evapotranspiration (def. 2). [n. use of v. phrase *fly off*]

fly·o·ver (flī′ō′vər), *n.* **1.** a formation of aircraft in flight for observation from the ground, esp. a prearranged, low-altitude flight over a public gathering. **2.** a flight over a simulated target by a bomber or bombing planes. **3.** *Brit.* an overhead crossing, esp. a highway overpass. [n. use of v. phrase *fly over*]

fly·pa·per (flī′pā′pər), *n.* paper designed to destroy flies by poisoning them or catching them on its sticky surface. [FLY² + PAPER]

fly′ rail′, **1.** *Furniture.* a horizontally swinging bracket for supporting a drop leaf. **2.** Also called **fly′-rail′, working rail.** *Theat.* the upper row of pins or cleats on a pin rail, used for tying off or fastening lines of scenery to be flied.

Fly′ Riv′er (flī), a river in New Guinea, flowing SE from the central part to the Gulf of Papua. ab. 800 mi. long.

fly′ rod′, a light, extremely flexible fishing rod specially designed for use in fly-fishing.

fly′ sheet′, a sheet of instructions or information; handbill.

fly·speck (flī′spek′), *n.* **1.** a speck or tiny stain from the excrement of a fly. **2.** a minute spot. **3.** *Plant Pathol.* a disease of pome fruits, characterized by small, raised, dark spots on the fruit, caused by a fungus, *Leptothyrium pomi.* —*v.t.* **4.** to mark with flyspecks. [FLY² + SPECK]

fly′ swat′ter, a device for killing flies, mosquitoes, and other insects, usually a square sheet of wire mesh attached to a long handle and variously ornamented.

flyte (flīt), *v.i.*, **flyt·ed, flyt·ing,** *n.* *Scot. and North Eng.* flite.

fly·trap (flī′trap′), *n.* **1.** any of various plants which entrap insects, esp. Venus's-flytrap. **2.** a trap for flies. [FLY² + TRAP¹]

fly-up (flī′up′), *n.* a formal ceremony at which a girl leaves her Brownie troop, receives a pair of embroidered wings for her uniform, and becomes a member of an intermediate Girl Scout troop. [n. use of v. phrase *fly up*]

fly·way (flī′wā′), *n.* a specific air route taken by birds during migration between breeding and wintering areas. [FLY¹ + WAY]

fly·weight (flī′wāt′), *n.* a boxer or other contestant of the lightest competitive class, esp. a professional boxer weighing up to 112 pounds. [FLY² + WEIGHT]

fly·wheel (flī′hwēl′, -wēl′), *n.* *Mach.* a heavy disk or wheel rotating on a shaft so that its momentum gives almost uniform rotational speed to the shaft and to all connected machinery. [FLY¹ + WHEEL]

FM, See **frequency modulation.** Also, **F.M.**

Fm, *Chem.* fermium.

fm., **1.** fathom. **2.** from.

f.m., (in prescriptions) make a mixture. [< L *fīat mistūra*]

FMB, Federal Maritime Board.

FMCS, Federal Mediation and Conciliation Service.

FM cyclotron, *Physics.* synchrocyclotron.

F. Mk., Finnish mark; markka. Also, **FMk**

fn, footnote.

FNMA, Federal National Mortgage Association.

f number, *Optics, Photog.* a number corresponding to the ratio of the focal length to the diameter of a lens system, esp. a camera lens, written following the symbol *f*, a smaller number indicating a larger lens diameter for a specific focal length and hence a smaller time of exposure. In *f*/1.4, 1.4 is the f number and signifies that the focal length of the lens is 1.4 times as great as the diameter. *Abbr.:* *f*/, *f*, f, f: Also called **focal ratio, speed, stop number.** Cf. **relative aperture.**

Fo (fō), *n.* *Chinese.* Buddha (def. 1).

fo., folio.

F.O., **1.** field officer. **2.** foreign office.

foal (fōl), *n.* **1.** a young horse, mule, or other related animal, esp. one that is not yet one year of age. —*v.t., v.i.* **2.** to give birth to (a colt or filly). [ME *fole*, OE *fola;* c. OHG *folo* (G *Fohlen*); akin to L *pullu(s)* young animal, Gk *pôlos* foal]

foam (fōm), *n.* **1.** a collection of minute bubbles formed on the surface of a liquid by agitation, fermentation, etc.: *foam on a glass of beer.* **2.** the froth of perspiration formed on the skin of a horse or other animal from great exertion. **3.** froth formed in the mouth, as in epilepsy and rabies. **4.** (in fire fighting) **a.** a substance which, on being discharged from a fire extinguisher into a burning liquid, smothers the flames by forming a layer of minute, stable, heat-resistant bubbles on the surface of the liquid. **b.** the layer of bubbles so formed. —*v.i.* **5.** to form or gather foam; emit foam; froth. —*v.t.* **6.** to cause to foam. **7. foam at the mouth,** to be extremely or uncontrollably angry: *He was just about foaming at the mouth when the children wouldn't obey him.* [ME *fom*, OE *fām;* c. G *Feim*] —**foam′ing·ly,** *adv.* —**foam′less,** *adj.* —**foam′like′,** *adj.*

foam·flow·er (fōm′flou′ər), *n.* a North American, saxifragaceous herb, *Tiarella cordifolia*, bearing white flowers in the spring. [FOAM + FLOWER]

foam′ glass′, cellular glass made by fusing powdered glass with carbon particles or other gas-generating material, used chiefly for industrial purposes.

Foam′ing Sea′. See **Mare Spumans.**

foam′ rub′ber, a light, spongy rubber, used for mattresses, cushions, etc.

foam·y (fō′mē), *adj.*, **foam·i·er, foam·i·est.** **1.** covered with or full of foam. **2.** consisting of foam. **3.** resembling foam. **4.** pertaining to foam. [ME *fomy*, OE *fāmig.* See FOAM, -Y¹] —**foam′i·ly,** *adv.* —**foam′i·ness,** *n.*

fob¹ (fob), *n.* **1.** a watch pocket just below the waistline in trousers or breeches. Cf. **watch pocket. 2.** a short chain or ribbon with a medallion or similar ornament, attached to a watch and worn hanging from a pocket. [? cf. HG (dial.) *fuppe* pocket, *fuppen* to pocket stealthily]

fob² (fob), *v.t.*, **fobbed, fob·bing.** **1.** *Archaic.* to cheat; deceive. **2. fob off, a.** to cheat someone by substituting something spurious or inferior; palm off (often fol. by *on*): *He tried to fob off an inferior brand on us.* **b.** to put (someone) off by deception or trickery: *She fobbed us off with false promises.* [ME *fobbe(n)*; c. G *foppen* to delude; cf. FOB¹]

f.o.b., *Com.* free on board: without charge to the buyer for goods placed on board a carrier at the point of shipment: *automobiles shipped f.o.b. Detroit.* Also, **F.O.B.**

fo·cal (fō′kəl), *adj.* of or pertaining to a focus. [< NL *focāl(is).* See FOCUS, -AL¹] —**fo′cal·ly,** *adv.*

fo′cal infec′tion, *Pathol., Dentistry.* an infection in which the bacteria are localized in some region, as the tissue around a tooth or a tonsil, from which they may spread to some other organ or structure of the body.

fo·cal·ise (fō′kə līz′), *v.t.*, **-ised, -is·ing.** *Chiefly Brit.* focalize. —**fo′cal·i·sa′tion,** *n.*

fo·cal·ize (fō′kə līz′), *v.t.*, **-ized, -iz·ing.** focus. [FOCAL + -IZE] —**fo′cal·i·za′tion,** *n.*

fo′cal length′, *Optics.* **1.** the distance from a focal point of a lens or mirror to the corresponding principal plane. *Symbol:* f **2.** the distance between an object lens and its corresponding focal plane in a telescope. Also called **fo′cal dis′tance.**

fo′cal plane′, *Optics.* **1.** a plane through a focal point and normal to the axis of a lens, mirror, or other optical system. Cf. **principal plane. 2.** the transverse plane in a telescope where the real image of a distant view is in focus.

fo′cal-plane shut′ter (fō′kəl plān′), *Photog.* a camera shutter situated directly in front of the film. Cf. **curtain shutter.**

fo′cal point′, **1.** the central or principal point of focus. **2.** the point at which disparate elements converge; center of activity or attention: *The focal point of our discussion was the need for action.* **3.** *Optics.* either of two points on the axis of a mirror, lens, or other optical system, one point being such that rays diverging from it are deviated parallel to the axis upon refraction or reflection by the system and the other point being such that rays parallel to the axis of the system converge to the point upon refraction or reflection by the system. Also called **principal focus.**

fo′cal ra′tio, *Optics, Photog.* See **f number.**

Foch (fosh; *Fr.* fôsh), *n.* **Fer·di·nand** (fer dē näN′), 1851–1929, French marshal.

fo·ci (fō′sī), *n.* a pl. of **focus.**

fo·com·e·ter (fō kom′i tər), *n.* *Optics.* an instrument for measuring the focal length of a lens or other optical system. [FOC(US) + -O- + -METER]

fo′c's′le (fōk′səl), *n.* *Naut.* forecastle. Also, **fo′c'sle.**

fo·cus (fō′kəs), *n., pl.* **-cus·es, -ci** (-sī), *v.*, **-cused, -cus·ing** or (*esp. Brit.*) **-cussed, -cus·sing.** —*n.* **1.** *Physics.* a point at which rays of light, heat, or other radiation, meet after being refracted or reflected. **2.** *Optics.* **a.** the focal point of a lens. **b.** the focal length of a lens. **c.** the clear and sharply defined condition of an image. **d.** the position of a viewed object or the adjustment of an optical device necessary to produce a clear image: *in focus; out of focus.* **3.** a central point, as of attraction, attention, or activity. **4.** *Geom.* one of the points from which the distances to any point of a given curve are in a linear relation. See diag. under **parabola. 5.** the starting place of an earthquake. **6.** *Pathol.* the primary center from which a disease develops or in which it localizes. —*v.t.* **7.** to bring to a focus or into focus: *to focus the lens of a camera.* **8.** to concentrate: *to focus one's thoughts.* —*v.i.* **9.** to become focused. [< L: fireplace, hearth] —**fo′cus·a·ble,** *adj.* —**fo′cus·er,** *n.*

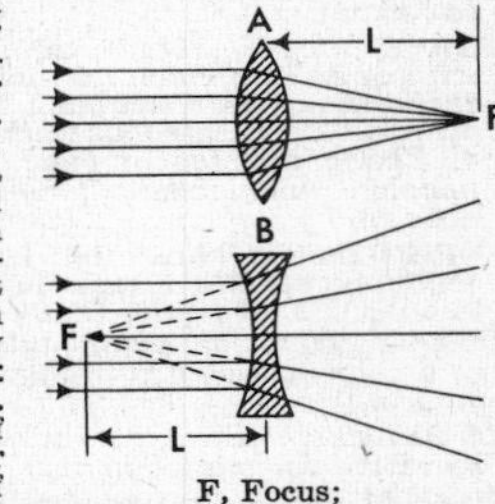

F, Focus; L, Focal distance; A, convex lens; B, Concave lens

fo′cusing cloth′, an opaque cloth surrounding the ground glass of a camera so as to shield the eyes of the photographer from light that would otherwise prevent him from seeing the image in the ground glass.

fod·der¹ (fod′ər), *n.* **1.** coarse food for livestock, composed of entire plants, including leaves, stalks, and grain, of such forages as corn and sorghum. **2.** people considered as readily available and of little value: *cannon fodder.* —*v.t.* **3.** to feed with or as with fodder. [ME; OE *fodder, fōdor;* c. G *Futter;* akin to FOOD] —**Syn. 1.** See **feed.**

fod·der² (fod′ər), *v.t.* *Naut.* fother.

fodg·el (foj′əl), *adj.* *Scot.* fat; stout; plump. [*fodge* (var. of FADGE) a short, fat person + *-el* adj. suffix]

foe (fō), *n.* **1.** a person who feels enmity, hatred, or malice toward another; enemy: *a bitter foe.* **2.** an enemy in war; hostile army. **3.** a person belonging to a hostile army or nation. **4.** an opponent in a game or contest; adversary: *a political foe.* **5.** a person who is opposed in feeling, principle, etc., to something: *a foe to progress.* **6.** a thing that is harmful to or destructive of something: *Sloth is the foe of health.* [ME *foo*, OE *fāh* hostile, *gefāh* enemy; c. OHG *gifēh* at war. See FEUD¹] —**Syn. 1, 3-5.** opponent, adversary, antagonist. —**Ant. 1-3.** friend.

F.O.E., Fraternal Order of Eagles.

Foe·cun·di·ta·tis (fā ko͝on′di tä′tis, fē-), *n.* **Mare.** See **Mare Fecunditatis.**
foehn (fān; *Ger.* fœn), *n.* a warm, dry wind descending a mountain, as on the north side of the Alps. Also, **föhn.** [< G *Föhn* < Romansh *favugn* < L *Favōn(ius)*]
foe·man (fō′mən), *n., pl.* **-men.** *Literary.* an enemy in war. [ME *foman,* OE *fāhman.* See FOE, MAN[1]]
Foerst′ner bit′ (fŏrst′nər). See **Forstner bit.**
foe·ta·tion (fē tā′shən), *n.* fetation.
foe·ti·cide (fē′ti sīd′), *n.* feticide. —**foe′ti·cid′al,** *adj.*
foet·id (fet′id, fē′tid), *adj.* fetid.
foe·tip·a·rous (fē tip′ər əs), *adj.* fetiparous.
foe·tor (fē′tər), *n.* fetor.
foe·tus (fē′təs), *n., pl.* **-tus·es.** fetus. —**foe′tal,** *adj.*
fog[1] (fog, fôg), *n., v.,* **fogged, fog·ging.** —*n.* **1.** a cloudlike mass or layer of minute water droplets or ice crystals near the surface of the earth, appreciably reducing visibility. Cf. **ice fog, mist, smog. 2.** any darkened state of the atmosphere, or the diffused substance which causes it. **3.** a state of mental confusion or obscurity; daze; stupor; vagueness: *The survivors were in a fog for days after the catastrophe.* **4.** *Photog.* a hazy effect on a developed negative or positive, caused by light other than that forming the image, by improper handling during development, or by the use of excessively old film. **5.** *Phys. Chem.* a mixture consisting of liquid particles dispersed in a gaseous medium. —*v.t.* **6.** to envelop with or as with fog: *The warm room fogged his glasses.* **7.** *Photog.* to produce fog on (a negative or positive). **8.** to confuse or obscure: *The debate did little else but fog the issue.* **9.** to bewilder or perplex: *to fog the mind.* —*v.i.* **10.** to become enveloped or obscured with or as with fog. **11.** *Photog.* (of a negative or positive) to become affected by fog. **12.** *Brit.* to place fog signals along a railway line. [back formation from FOGGY. See FOG[2]] —**fog′less,** *adj.*
—**Syn. 1.** See **cloud. 3.** obfuscation. **8.** becloud, obfuscate, dim, blur, darken. **9.** daze, befuddle, muddle, mystify. —**Ant. 3.** clarity. **8.** clarify. **10.** clear.
fog[2] (fog, fôg), *n.* **1.** a second growth of grass, as after mowing. **2.** long grass left standing in fields during the winter. [ME *fogge, fog* < Scand; cf. Norw *fogg* long grass on damp ground, obs. E *foggy* marshy]
Fo·gar·ty (fō′gər tē), *n.* **Anne,** born 1919, U.S. fashion designer.
fog′ bank′, a stratum of fog as seen from a distance.
fog′ bell′, a bell used as a fog signal.
fog·bound (fog′bound′, fôg′-), *adj.* *Naut.* unable to navigate because of heavy fog. [FOG[1] + -BOUND[1]]
fog·bow (fog′bō′, fôg′-), *n.* a bow, arc, or circle of white or yellowish hue seen in or against a bank of fog; a rainbow formed by fog droplets. Also called **mistbow, seadog, white rainbow.** [FOG[1] + (RAIN)BOW]
fog·dog (fog′dôg′, -dog′, fôg′-), *n.* a bright spot sometimes seen in a fog bank. [FOG[1] + DOG]
fog′ drip′, water falling to the ground from trees, esp. conifers, which have collected the moisture from fog.
fo·gey (fō′gē), *n., pl.* **-geys.** fogy.
fog′ for′est, the thick forest growth at fairly high elevations on tropical mountains, where there is a prevalence of clouds, high humidity, and mild temperature.
fog·gage (fog′ij, fô′gij), *n.* *Chiefly Scot.* fog[2]. [< legal L *fogāg(ium).* See FOG[2], -AGE]
Fog·gia (fôd′jä), *n.* a city in SE Italy. 117,485 (1961).
fog′ gong′, a gong used as a fog signal.
fog′ gun′, a gun, fired at regular intervals, used as a fog signal.
fog·gy (fog′ē, fô′gē), *adj.,* **-gi·er, -gi·est. 1.** thick with or having much fog; misty: *a foggy valley; a foggy spring day.* **2.** resembling fog; dim; obscure: *a foggy mirror.* **3.** confused or unclear; vague: *foggy thinking.* **4.** *Photog.* affected by fog. [FOG[2] + -Y[1]; orig. meaning marshy, thick, murky] —**fog′gi·ly,** *adv.* —**fog′gi·ness,** *n.*
fog·horn (fog′hôrn′, fôg′-), *n.* **1.** a deep, loud horn for sounding warning signals in foggy weather, as to ships. **2.** a deep, loud voice. [FOG[1] + HORN]
fog′ light′, an automobile headlight throwing light of a color intended to diminish the effect of fog, dust, etc., in the air.
fo·gram (fō′grəm), *n.* an old-fashioned or overly conservative person; fogy. Also, **fo′grum.** [?]
fog′ sig′nal, any of various types of signal used as a warning by vessels navigating in fog or mist.
fo·gy (fō′gē), *n., pl.* **-gies.** an excessively conservative or old-fashioned person, esp. one who is dull (usually prec. by *old*): *The board of directors were old fogies still living in the 19th century.* Also, **fogey.** [?] —**fo′gy·ish,** *adj.* —**fo′gy·ism,** *n.*
foh (fô), *interj.* faugh.
föhn (fān; *Ger.* fœn), *n.* foehn.
foi·ble (foi′bəl), *n.* **1.** a minor weakness or failing of character; slight flaw or defect: *the foibles of an age; an all-too-human foible.* **2.** the weaker part of a sword blade, between the middle and the point (opposed to *forte*). [< F, obs. form of *faible* FEEBLE]
—**Syn. 1.** frailty, quirk, crotchet, eccentricity, peculiarity. See **fault.** —**Ant. 1.** strength.
foie gras (fwä grä′; *Fr.* fwȧ grȧ′), the liver of specially fattened geese or ducks, used as a table delicacy, esp. in the form of a paste (**pâté de foie gras**). [< F: lit., fat liver]
foil[1] (foil), *v.t.* **1.** to prevent the success of; frustrate; balk: *Loyal troops foiled his attempt to overthrow the government.* **2.** to defeat; repulse; check: *Curses, foiled again!* —*n.* **3.** *Archaic.* a defeat; check; repulse. [ME *foile(n),* aberrant adaptation of OF *fuler* to trample, full (cloth). See FULL[2]] —**foil′a·ble,** *adj.*
—**Syn. 1.** thwart; impede, hamper.
foil[2] (foil), *n.* **1.** metal in the form of very thin sheets: *aluminum foil.* **2.** the metallic backing applied to glass to form a mirror. **3.** a thin layer of metal placed under a gem in a closed setting to improve its color or brilliancy. **4.** a person or thing that makes another seem better by contrast: *The straight man was an able foil to the comic.* **5.** *Archit.* an arc or a rounded space between cusps, as in the tracery of a window or other ornamentation. **6.** an airfoil or hydrofoil. —*v.t.* **7.** to cover or back with foil. **8.** to set off by contrast. [ME *foille, foil* < OF *fuelle, fueille, foille* (< L *folia* leaves), *fuel fueil, fol* (< L *folium* leaf, blade)]
foil[3] (foil), *n.* *Fencing.* **1.** a flexible four-sided rapier having a blunt point. **2. foils,** the art or practice of fencing with this weapon, points being made by touching the trunk of the opponent's body with the tip of the weapon. [?]
foiled (foild), *adj.* *Archit.* ornamented with foils, as a gable, spandrel, or balustrade. [FOIL[2] + -ED[3]]
foils·man (foilz′mən), *n., pl.* **-men.** *Fencing.* a person who fences with a foil. [FOIL[3] + -'S[1] + MAN[1]]
foin (foin), *Archaic.* —*n.* **1.** a thrust with a weapon. —*v.i.* **2.** to thrust with a weapon; lunge. [ME (v.), appar. < OF *foine* fish spear < L *fuscina*]
Fo·ism (fō′iz əm), *n.* Chinese Buddhism. [Fo + -ISM] —**Fo′ist,** *n.*
foi·son (foi′zən), *n.* *Archaic.* **1.** abundance; plenty. **2.** abundant harvest. [ME *foisoun* < MF *foison* < L *fūsiōn-* (s. of *fūsiō*). See FUSION]
foist (foist), *v.t.* **1.** to force upon or impose fraudulently or unjustifiably (usually fol. by *on* or *upon*): *to foist inferior merchandise on a customer.* **2.** to bring, put, or introduce surreptitiously or fraudulently (usually fol. by *in* or *into*): *to foist subversive ideas into a book.* [< D (dial.) *vuist(en)* (to) take in the hand, MD *vūsten,* deriv. of *vūst* fist]
Fo·kine (fō kēn′; *Fr.* fô kēn′; *Russ.* fô′kin), *n.* **Mi·chel Mi·khay·lo·vich** (mi shel′ mi hī′lə vich), 1880–1942, Russian choreographer and ballet dancer, in the U.S. after 1925.
Fok·ker (fok′ər; *Du.* fok′ər), *n.* **1. An·tho·ny Her·man Ge·rard** (än tō′nə her′män gā′rärt), 1890–1939, Dutch airplane designer and builder. **2.** an aircraft designed or built by Fokker, esp. as used by Germany in World War I.
fol., 1. folio. **2.** (in prescriptions) a leaf. [< L *folium*] **3.** followed. **4.** following.
fol·a·cin (fol′ə sin), *n.* *Biochem.* See **folic acid.** [FOL(IC) AC(ID) + -IN[2]]
Fol·croft (fol′krôft, -kroft), *n.* a town in SE Pennsylvania. 7013 (1960).
fold[1] (fōld), *v.t.* **1.** to bend (cloth, paper, etc.) over upon itself. **2.** to bring into a compact form by bending and laying parts together (often fol. by *up*): *to fold up a map; to fold one's legs under oneself.* **3.** to bring (the arms, hands, etc.) together in an intertwined or crossed manner; clasp; cross: *He folded his arms on his chest.* **4.** to bend or wind (usually fol. by *about, round,* etc.): *to fold one's arms about a person's neck.* **5.** to bring (the wings) close to the body, as a bird on alighting. **6.** to enclose; wrap; envelop: *to fold something in paper.* **7.** to clasp or embrace; enfold: *to fold someone in one's arms.* **8.** *Cookery.* to mix in or add, as beaten egg whites to a batter, by gently turning one part over another with a spatula, spoon, or the like (usually fol. by *in*): *Gently fold in the eggs.* **9.** to enclose, enwrap. **10.** *Cards.* to place (one's cards) face down so as to withdraw from the play. —*v.i.* **11.** to be folded or be capable of folding: *The doors fold back.* **12.** *Cards.* to place one's cards face down so as to withdraw from the play. **13.** (of a theatrical production) to end or close, esp. through lack of patronage: *The show will fold after Saturday night's performance.* **14. fold up,** *Informal.* **a.** to break down; collapse: *He folded up when the prosecutor discredited his story.* **b.** to fail, esp. to go out of business: *The dress shop on our corner just folded up.* —*n.* **15.** a part that is folded; pleat; layer: *to wrap something in folds of cloth.* **16.** a crease made by folding: *He cut the paper along the fold.* **17.** a hollow made by folding: *to carry something in the fold of one's dress.* **18.** a hollow place in undulating ground: *a fold of the mountains.* **19.** *Geol.* a portion of strata which is folded or bent, as an anticline or syncline, or which connects two horizontal or parallel portions of strata of different levels (as a monocline). **20.** *Journalism.* **a.** the line formed along the horizontal center of a standard-sized newspaper when it is folded after printing. **b.** a rough-and-ready dividing line, esp. on the front page and other principal pages, between stories of primary and lesser importance. **21.** a coil of a serpent, string, etc. **22.** act of folding or doubling over. **23.** *Anat.* a margin or ridge formed by the folding of a membrane or other flat body part; plica. [ME *folde(n),* OE *faldan;* r. OE *fealdan,* c. G *falten*] —**fold′a·ble,** *adj.*
fold[2] (fōld), *n.* **1.** an enclosure for sheep or, occasionally, other domestic animals. **2.** the sheep contained in it. **3.** a flock of sheep. **4.** a church or the members of a church: *He preached to the fold.* **5.** a group sharing common beliefs, values, etc.: *He rejoined the fold after his youthful escapade.* —*v.t.* **6.** to confine (sheep or other domestic animals) in a fold. [ME *fold, fald,* OE *fald, falod;* akin to OS *faled* pen, enclosure, MLG *vālt* pen, enclosure, manure heap, MD *vaelt, vaelde*]
-fold, a native English suffix meaning "of so many parts," or denoting multiplication by the number indicated by the stem or word to which the suffix is attached: *twofold; manifold.* [ME; OE *-fald* r. OE *-feald,* c. G *-falt,* Goth *-falþs;* akin to Gk *-paltos* (as in *dipaltos* double), L *-plex*]
fold·a·way (fōld′ə wā′), *adj.* designed to be folded out of the way when not in use: *a foldaway bed.* [adj. use of v. phrase *fold away*]
fold·boat (fōld′bōt′), *n.* faltboat.
fold·er (fōl′dər), *n.* **1.** one who or that which folds. **2.** a printed sheet, usually folded into a number of separate pages or leaves, as a circular or timetable. **3.** a folded sheet of light cardboard used to cover or hold papers, letters, etc. [FOLD[1] + -ER[1]]
fol·de·rol (fol′də rol′), *n.* falderal.
fold′ing doors′, a door with hinged sections that can be folded flat against one another when opened.
fold′ing fin′, *Rocketry.* a fin attached by hinges to a rocket or missile, which lies flat until after take-off.
Fo·ley (fō′lē), *n.* a town in SW Alabama. 2889 (1960).
fo·li·a (fō′lē ə), *n.* pl. of **folium.**
fo·li·a·ceous (fō′lē ā′shəs), *adj.* **1.** of, like, or of the nature of a plant leaf; leaflike. **2.** bearing leaves or leaflike parts. **3.** pertaining to or consisting of leaves. **4.** consisting of leaflike plates or laminae; foliated. [< L *foliāceus* leafy, like a leaf. See FOLIUM, -ACEOUS] —**fo′li·a′ceous·ness,** *n.*
fo·li·age (fō′lē ij), *n.* **1.** the leaves of a plant, collectively; leafage. **2.** leaves in general. **3.** the representation of leaves, flowers, and branches in painting, architectural ornament, etc. [ME *foilage* < MF *fueillage, foillage,* deriv. of *feuille* leaf; influenced by L *folium.* See FOIL[2], -AGE] —**fo′li·aged,** *adj.*
fo·li·ar (fō′lē ər), *adj.* of, pertaining to, or having the nature of a leaf or leaves. [< NL *foliār(is).* See FOLIUM, -AR[1]]
fo·li·ate (*adj.* fō′lē it, -āt′; *v.* fō′lē āt′), *adj., v.,* **-at·ed, -at·ing.** —*adj.* **1.** covered with or having leaves. **2.** like a leaf, as in shape. **3.** Also, **foliated.** *Archit.* **a.** ornamented with or composed of foils: *foliate tracery.* **b.** ornamented with representations of foliage: *a foliate capital.* —*v.i.* **4.** to put forth leaves. **5.** to split into thin leaflike layers or laminae. —*v.t.* **6.** to shape like a leaf or leaves. **7.** to decorate with foils or foliage. **8.** to form into thin sheets. **9.** to spread over with a thin metallic backing. **10.** to number leaves, as distinguished from pages, of (a book). [< L *foliāt(us)* leafy. See FOLIUM, -ATE[1]]
fo·li·at·ed (fō′lē ā′tid), *adj.* **1.** shaped like a leaf or leaves: *foliated ornaments.* **2.** *Crystall.* consisting of thin and separable laminae. **3.** *Archit.* foliate (def. 3). [FOLIATE + -ED[2]]
fo′liated joint′, a joint between the rabbeted and overlapping edges of two boards, forming a continuous surface on each side.
fo·li·a·tion (fō′lē ā′shən), *n.* **1.** the act or process of putting forth leaves. **2.** state of being in leaf. **3.** *Bot.* **a.** the arrangement of leaves within a bud. **b.** the arrangement of leaves on a plant. **4.** leaves or foliage. **5.** the consecutive numbering of the leaves, as distinguished from pages, of a manuscript or book. **6.** the total number of such leaves. **7.** *Geol.* the splitting up or the arrangement of certain rocks or certain kinds of rocks in leaflike layers. **8.** ornamentation with foliage, or an arrangement of foliage. **9.** *Archit.* **a.** ornamentation with foils. **b.** ornamentation with representations of foliage. **10.** formation into thin sheets. **11.** the application of foil to glass to make a mirror. [FOLIATE + -ION]
fo·li·a·ture (fō′lē ə chər), *n.* a cluster of leaves; foliage. [< LL *foliātūra* foliage. See FOLIATE, -URE]
fo·lic (fō′lik, fol′ik), *adj.* *Chem.* of or derived from folic acid. [< L *foli(um)* FOLIUM + -IC]
fo′lic ac′id, *Biochem.* a synthetic form of one of the B-complex vitamins, considered to be esp. effective in treating certain forms of anemia. Also called **folacin, PGA, pteroylglutamic acid, pteroylmonoglutamic acid, vitamin Bc, vitamin M.**
fo·lie (fô lē′), *n., pl.* **-lies** (-lē′). *French.* madness; insanity.
fo·lie à deux (fo lē′ ə do͞o′; *Fr.* fô lē ȧ dœ′), *pl.* **fo·lies à deux** (fo lēz′ ə do͞o′; *Fr.* fô lē zȧ dœ′). *Psychiatry.* the sharing of delusional ideas by two people who are closely associated. [< F]
fo·li·co·lous (fō′lē ik′ə ləs), *adj.* **1.** growing on leaves, as certain liverworts. **2.** parasitic on leaves, as certain fungi. [< L *folii* (pl.) (see FOLIUM) + -COLOUS]
fo·li·if·er·ous (fō′lē if′ər əs), *adj.* *Bot.* bearing leaves or leaflike structures. [< L *folii* (pl.) (see FOLIUM) + -FEROUS]
fo·lin′ic ac′id (fō lin′ik), *Biochem., Pharm.* a crystalline, slightly water-soluble solid, $C_{20}H_{23}N_7O_7$, produced by fermentation or derived from folic acid, used in medicine in the treatment of certain anemias. Also called **citrovorum factor.** [FOL(IC) + -IN[2] + -IC]
fo·li·o (fō′lē ō′), *n., pl.* **-li·os,** *adj., v.,* **-li·oed, -li·o·ing.** —*n.* **1.** a sheet of paper folded once to make two leaves (four pages) of a book. **2.** a volume having pages of the largest size, esp. one more than 30 centimeters in height. **3.** a leaf of a manuscript or book numbered only on the front side. **4.** *Print.* **a.** (in a book) the number of each page. **b.** (in a newspaper) the number of each page together with the date and the name of the newspaper. **5.** *Bookkeeping.* a page of an account book or a left-hand page and a right-hand page facing each other and having the same serial number. **6.** *Law.* a certain number of words, in the U.S. generally 100, taken as a unit for computing the length of a document. —*adj.* **7.** pertaining to or having the format of a folio: *a folio volume.* —*v.t.* **8.** to number each leaf or page of. **9.** *Law.* to mark each folio in (a pleading or the like) with the proper number. [< L *foliō* (orig. in phrase *in foliō* in a leaf, sheet), abl. of *folium* FOLIUM]
fo·li·o·late (fō′lē ə lāt′), *adj.* *Bot.* pertaining to or consisting of leaflets (often used in combination, as *bifoliolate*). [< LL **foliolāt(us).* See FOLIOLE, -ATE[1]]
fo·li·ole (fō′lē ōl′), *n.* *Bot.* **1.** a leaflet, as of a compound leaf. **2.** a small leaflike organ or appendage. [< F < LL *foliol(um),* dim. of *folium* leaf]
fo·li·ose (fō′lē ōs′), *adj.* *Bot.* leafy. Also, **fo·li·ous** (fō′lē əs). [< L *foliōs(us).* See FOLIUM, -OSE[1]]
fo·li·ot (fō′lē ət), *n.* See under **verge escapement.** [ME: foolish matter < OF: watch spring, ? deriv. of *folier* to play the fool]
-folious, an adjectival suffix meaning "having leaves (of a specified number or type)": *unifolious.* [comb. form repr. < L *foliōsus* leafy]
fo·li·o ver·so (fō′lē ō′ wer′sō; *Eng.* fō′lē ō′ vûr′sō), *Latin.* the back of the page.
fo·li·um (fō′lē əm), *n., pl.* **-li·a** (-lē ə). **1.** a thin leaflike stratum or layer; a lamella. **2.** *Geom.* a loop; part of a curve terminated at both ends by the same node. Equation: $x^3 + y^3 = 3axy$. [< L: lit., a leaf]

Folium (of Descartes)

folk (fōk), *n., adj.* —*n.* **1.** Usually, **folks.** (*construed as pl.*) people in general: *Folks say there wasn't much rain last summer.* **2.** Often, **folks.** (*construed as pl.*) people of a specified class or group: *town folk; poor folks.* **3.** (*construed as pl.*) people as the carriers of culture, esp. as representing the composite of social mores, customs, forms of behavior, etc., in a society: *The folk are the bearers of oral tradition.* **4. folks,** *Informal.* **a.** members of one's family; relatives: *All his folks come from France.* **b.** one's parents: *Will your folks let you go?* **5.** *Archaic.* a people or tribe. **6. just folks,** *Informal.* (of persons) simple, unaffected, unsophisticated, or open-hearted people: *He enjoyed visiting his grandparents because they were just folks.* —*adj.* **7.** originating among the common people: *folk belief.* **8.** having unknown origins and reflecting the traditional forms of a society: *folk culture; folk art.* [ME; OE *folc;* c. OS, OIcel *folk,* OHG *folk* (G *Volk*)] **—folk′ish,** *adj.* **—folk′ish·ness,** *n.*

folk′ dance′, **1.** a dance which originated among, and has been transmitted through, the common people. Cf. **court dance. 2.** a piece of music for such a dance.

Folke·stone (fōk′stən), *n.* a seaport in E Kent, in SE England, on the Strait of Dover. 44,129 (1961).

Fol·ke·ting (fōl′kə tiŋ′), *n.* **1.** the unicameral parliament of Denmark. **2.** *Hist.* the lower house of the Rigsdag. Also, **Fol·ke·thing** (fōl′kə tiŋ′). [< Dan; see FOLK, THING[2]]

folk′ etymol′ogy, modification, often pseudo-learned, of a linguistic form according either to a falsely assumed etymology, as *Welsh rarebit* from *Welsh rabbit,* or to a historically irrelevant analogy, as *bridegroom* from *bridegome.*

folk·lore (fōk′lōr′, -lôr′), *n.* **1.** the traditional beliefs, legends, customs, etc., of a people; lore of a people. **2.** the study of such lore. [FOLK + LORE] **—folk′lor′ic,** *adj.* **—folk′lor′ist,** *n.* **—folk′lor·is′tic,** *adj.*

folk·moot (fōk′mo͞ot′), *n.* (formerly, in England) a general assembly of the people of a shire, town, etc. Also, **folk·mote, folk·mot** (fōk′mōt′). [ME; OE *folcmōt* folk meeting. See FOLK, MOOT[1]]

folk′ mu′sic, music, usually of simple character and anonymous authorship, handed down by oral tradition and characteristic chiefly of rural communities.

folk·right (fōk′rīt′), *n.* a law or right of the people as opposed to that of the privileged classes. [OE *folcriht.* See FOLK, RIGHT]

folk-rock (fōk′rok′), *n.* **1.** a style of music combining characteristics of rock-′n′-roll and folk music. **—***adj.* **2.** of or pertaining to this style of music. [FOLK + ROCK[2]]

folk·say (fōk′sā′), *n.* an informal verbal expression, as a proverb, idiom, or exclamation, characteristic of a relatively unsophisticated group of people, as *Was I ever!* instead of *I certainly was!* [FOLK + SAY]

folk′ sing′er, a singer who specializes in folk songs and usually provides his own accompaniment, typically on guitar.

folk′ sing′ing, the practice of singing folk songs, esp. by a group of people.

folk′ soci′ety, *Sociol.* an often small, homogeneous, and isolated community or society functioning chiefly through primary contacts and strongly attached to its traditional ways of living.

folk′ song′, **1.** a song originating among the people of a country or area, passed by oral tradition from one singer or generation to the next, often existing in several versions, and marked generally by simple, modal melody and stanzaic, narrative verse. **2.** a song of similar character written by a known composer.

folk·sy (fōk′sē), *adj.,* **-si·er, -si·est. 1.** sociable; neighborly; casual; familiar; unceremonious: *The Senator adopted a folksy style just before election.* **2.** belonging to the common people, esp. in regard to a conscious use of mannerisms, speech patterns, attitudes, etc.: *folksy humor; folksy story.* [FOLKS + -Y[1]] **—folk′si·ness,** *n.*

folk′ tale′, a tale or legend originating and traditional among a people or folk, esp. one forming part of an oral tradition. Also called **folk′ sto′ry.**

folk·ways (fōk′wāz′), *n.pl. Sociol.* the ways of living and acting in a human group, built up without conscious design but serving as compelling guides of conduct. [FOLK + WAYS]

foll., following.

Fol·lans·bee (fol′ənz bē′), *n.* a town in N West Virginia. 4052 (1960).

Folle de Chail·lot, La (*Fr.* LA fôl də shA yō′). See **Madwoman of Chaillott, The.**

fol·li·cle (fol′ə kəl), *n.* **1.** *Bot.* a dry one-celled seed vessel consisting of a single carpel, and dehiscent only by the ventral suture, as the fruit of milkweed. **2.** *Anat.* a small cavity, sac, or gland. [< L *follicul(us)* small bag, shell, pod. See FOLLIS, -CLE]

Follicle of milkweed

fol′li·cle-stim·u·lat·ing hor′mone (fol′ə kəl stim′yə lā′tiŋ), *Biochem.* See **FSH.**

fol·lic·u·lar (fə lik′yə lər), *adj.* **1.** pertaining to, consisting of, or resembling a follicle or follicles; provided with follicles. **2.** *Pathol.* affecting or originating in a follicle or follicles. Also, **fol·lic·u·late** (fə lik′yə lit, -lāt′), **fol·lic′u·lat′ed.** [< L *follicul(us)* (see FOLLICLE) + -AR[1]]

fol·lic·u·lin (fə lik′yə lin), *n. Biochem.* estrone. [< L *follicul(us)* (see FOLLICLE) + -IN[2]]

fol·lic·u·li·tis (fə lik′yə lī′tis), *n. Pathol.* inflammation of hair follicles. [< L *follicul(us)* (see FOLLICLE) + -ITIS]

fol·lis (fol′is), *n., pl.* **fol·les** (fol′ēz). **1.** a unit in the ancient Roman money of account. **2.** a silver-plated copper coin of ancient Rome, first issued by Diocletian. **3.** a copper coin of the Eastern Roman Empire, A.D. c500. [< L: lit., bag, bellows]

fol·low (fol′ō), *v.t.* **1.** to come after in sequence, order of time, etc.; succeed: *The speech follows the dinner.* **2.** to go or come after; move behind in the same direction: *Drive ahead, and I'll follow you.* **3.** to accept as a guide or leader; accept the authority of or give allegiance to: *The Germans followed Hitler.* **4.** to conform to, comply with, or act in accordance with; obey: *to follow orders; to follow someone's advice.* **5.** to imitate or copy; use as an exemplar: *She followed the fashions slavishly.* **6.** to move forward along (a road, path, etc.): *Follow this road for a mile.* **7.** to come after as a result or consequence; result from: *Reprisals often follow victory.* **8.** to go after or along with (a person) as companion. **9.** to go in pursuit of: *to follow an enemy.* **10.** to try for or attain to: *to follow an ideal.* **11.** to engage in or be concerned with as a pursuit: *He followed the sea as his true calling.* **12.** to watch the movements, progress, or course of: *to follow a bird in flight.* **13.** to watch the development of or keep up with: *to follow the news.* **14.** to keep up with and understand (an argument, story, etc.): *Do you follow me?* **—***v.i.* **15.** to come next after something else in sequence, order of time, etc. **16.** to happen or occur after something else; come next as an event: *After the defeat great disorders followed.* **17.** to attend or serve. **18.** to go or come after a person or thing in motion: *Go on ahead, and I'll follow.* **19.** to result as an effect; occur as a consequence: *It follows then that he must be innocent.* **20. follow out,** to carry to a conclusion; execute: *They followed out their orders to the letter.* **21. follow suit.** See **suit** (def. 12). **22. follow through, a.** to carry out fully, as a stroke of a club in golf, a racket in tennis, etc. **b.** to proceed in an endeavor and pursue it to completion: *It was a brilliant idea, but no one had the imagination to follow through with it. She always followed through on her plans.* **23. follow up, a.** to pursue closely and tenaciously. **b.** to increase the effect of by further action. **c.** to pursue to a solution or conclusion: *The reporter followed up the activities of the mob until he had enough information to write an exposé.* **—***n.* **24.** act of following. **25.** *Billiards, Pool.* See **follow shot** (def. 1). **26.** follow-up (def. 3). [ME *folwe(n),* OE *folgian;* c. OS *folgon,* OHG *folgēn, folgōn* (G *folgen*)] **—fol′low·a·ble,** *adj.*

—Syn. 3. obey. **4.** heed, observe. **8.** accompany, attend. **9.** pursue, chase; trail, track, trace. **19.** arise, proceed. FOLLOW, ENSUE, RESULT, SUCCEED imply coming after something else, in a natural sequence. FOLLOW is the general word: *We must wait to see what follows. A detailed account follows.* ENSUE implies a logical sequence, what might be expected normally to come after a given act, cause, etc., and indicates some duration: *When the power lines were cut, a paralysis of transportation ensued.* RESULT emphasizes the connection between a cause or event and its effect, consequence, or outcome: *The accident resulted in injuries to those involved.* SUCCEED implies coming after in time, particularly coming into a title, office, etc.: *In England the oldest son succeeds to his father's title.* **—Ant. 1.** precede. **2, 3.** lead. **4.** disregard. **9.** flee.

fol′low board′, *Foundry.* (in a flask) a board at the top of the drag, following the outline of the pattern.

fol·low·er (fol′ō ər), *n.* **1.** one who or that which follows. **2.** a person who follows another in regard to his ideas or belief; disciple or adherent. **3.** a person who imitates, copies, or takes as an exemplar: *He was little more than a follower of current modes.* **4.** an attendant, servant, or retainer: *He and his followers remained at the inn.* **5.** *Brit. Informal.* a boy friend or suitor, esp. of a maidservant. **6.** *Mach.* a part receiving motion from or following the movements of another part, esp. a cam. **7.** *Engineering, Building Trades.* a concrete form attached to the head of a timber pile to permit casting of a concrete cap or pier. [ME *folwer,* OE *folgere.* See FOLLOW, -ER[1]]

—Syn. 2. pupil. FOLLOWER, ADHERENT, PARTISAN refer to one who demonstrates allegiance to a person, a doctrine, a cause, and the like. FOLLOWER often has an implication of personal relationship or of slavish acquiescence. ADHERENT, a more formal word, has also implications of more active championship of a person or a point of view. PARTISAN, ordinarily meaning a person prejudiced and unreasoning in adherence to a party, during World War II took on the meaning of a member of certain groups in occupied countries of Europe, who carried on underground resistance to the Nazis. **4.** supporter. **—Ant. 2.** leader, teacher; enemy, foe.

fol·low·ing (fol′ō iŋ), *n.* **1.** a body of followers, attendants, adherents, etc. **2.** the body of admirers, attendants, patrons, etc., of someone or something: *That television show has a large following.* **3. the following,** that which comes immediately after, as pages, lines, etc.: *See the following for an explanation of this theory.* **—***adj.* **4.** that follows or moves in the same direction: *a following wind.* **5.** that comes after or next in order or time; ensuing: *the following day.* **6.** that is now to follow; now to be mentioned, described, related, or the like: *Check the following report for details.* [ME *folwing.* See FOLLOW, -ING[1], -ING[2]]

fol′low shot′, **1.** *Billiards, Pool.* a stroke that causes the cue ball to roll forward after striking the object ball. Cf. **draw shot. 2.** *Motion Pictures, Television.* a traveling shot made as the camera moves along with the subject: *a follow shot of the buffalo stampede, taken from a low-flying helicopter.*

fol′low the lead′er, a child's game in which players, one behind the other, follow a leader and must repeat or follow everything he does.

fol·low-through (fol′ō thro͞o′, -thro͞o′), *n.* **1.** the completion of a motion, as in the stroke of a tennis racket. **2.** the portion of such a motion after the ball has been hit. **3.** the execution of a plan, project, scheme, or the like. [n. use of v. phrase *follow through*]

fol·low-up (fol′ō up′), *n.* **1.** the act of following up. **2.** a letter or circular sent to a person to increase the effectiveness of a previous one, as in advertising. **3.** Also called **follow.** *Journalism.* **a.** a news story providing additional information on a story or article previously published. **b.** Also called **sidebar, supplementary story.** a minor news story used to supplement a related story of major importance. Cf. **feature story** (def. 1), **human-interest story, shirttail. —***adj.* **4.** following an earlier action: *a follow-up phone call; follow-up contact.* **5.** (of business letters, circulars, etc.) sent to a prospective customer to obtain an additional order or renew a previous offer. **6.** of or pertaining to action that follows an initial treatment, course of study, etc.: *follow-up schooling; follow-up care in mental illnesses; a follow-up survey.* [n., adj. use of v. phrase *follow up*]

fol·ly (fol′ē), *n., pl.* **-lies. 1.** state or quality of being foolish; lack of understanding or sense. **2.** a foolish action, practice, idea, etc.; absurdity: *the folly of performing without a rehearsal.* **3.** a costly and foolish undertaking; unwise investment or expenditure. **4.** *Archit.* a whimsical or extravagant structure, either useless or having an appearance completely unrelated to its purpose, built to serve as a conversation piece, lend interest to a view, commemorate a person or event, symbolize a religious, political, or philosophical attitude, etc.: built esp. in England in the 18th century. **5. follies,** a theatrical revue. **6.** *Obs.* wickedness; wantonness. [ME *folie* < OF, deriv. of *fol, fou* foolish, mad. See FOOL[1]]

Fol·som (fōl′səm), *n.* a town in central California. 3925 (1960).

Fol·som (fōl′səm), *adj.* of or pertaining to a prehistoric people who inhabited an extensive part of the North American continent east of the Rocky Mountains, probably during the late Pleistocene: distinguished chiefly by a thin, finely made flint blade having the shape of a leaf: *Folsom culture.* [after *Folsom,* New Mexico, one of the settlements]

Fol′som man′, a member of a prehistoric people who inhabited part of what is now the U.S. and Canada; an individual of the Folsom culture.

Fol′som point′, a carefully carved flint point for a projectile, as a spear, used by Folsom man in hunting.

Fo·mal·haut (fō′məl hôt′, -mə lō′), *n. Astron.* a star of the first magnitude and the brightest star in the constellation Piscis Austrinus. Also called **Al′pha Pis′cis Austri′ni.** [< Ar *fam al-khūt* mouth of a fish; so called from its position in the constellation]

fo·ment (fō ment′), *v.t.* **1.** to instigate or foster (discord, rebellion, etc.); promote the growth or development of: *to foment trouble; to foment dissatisfaction.* **2.** to apply warm water or medicated liquid, cloths dipped in such liquid, or the like, to (the surface of the body). [ME *foment(en)* < L *fōmentāre,* deriv. of *fōmentum* a warm application, poultice, contr. of **fōrimentum,* equiv. to *fov(ēre)* (to) keep warm + *-mentum* -MENT] **—fo·ment′er,** *n.*

—Syn. 1. incite, provoke, arouse, inflame, excite, stir up; encourage, stimulate.

fo·men·ta·tion (fō′men tā′shən), *n.* **1.** instigation; encouragement of discord, rebellion, etc. **2.** the application of warm liquid, ointments, etc., to the surface of the body. **3.** the liquid, ointments, etc., so applied. [< LL *fōmentātiōn-* (s. of *fōmentātiō*), equiv. to *fōmentāt(us)* (ptp. of *fōmentāre* to FOMENT) + *-iōn-* -ION]

fo·mes (fō′mēz), *n., pl.* **fom·i·tes** (fom′i tēz′, fō′mi-). Usually, **fomites.** *Med.* any agent, as clothing or bedding, that is capable of absorbing and transmitting the infecting organism of a disease. [< L: kindling wood, tinder, akin to *fovēre* to keep warm. See FOMENT]

Fo·mor·i·an (fō môr′ē ən), *n. Irish Legend.* one of a race of pirates or sea-demons who raided and pillaged Ireland but were finally defeated: sometimes associated with the hostile powers of nature. Also, **Fo·mor** (fō′môr).

fond[1] (fond), *adj.* **1.** having a liking for (usually fol. by *of*): *to be fond of animals.* **2.** loving; affectionate: *to give someone a fond look.* **3.** excessively tender; overindulgent; doting: *a fond parent.* **4.** cherished with strong or unreasoning feeling: *to nourish fond hopes of becoming president.* **5.** *Chiefly Dial.* foolish or silly. **6.** *Archaic.* foolishly credulous or trusting. [ME *fond, fonned* (ptp. of *fonnen* to be foolish), deriv. of *fon, fonne* a fool]

—Syn. 2. cherishing. **5.** infatuated. **6.** gullible.

fond[2] (fond; *Fr.* fôN), *n., pl.* **fonds** (fondz; *Fr.* fôN). **1.** a background or groundwork, esp. of lace. **2.** *Obs.* fund; stock. [< F; see FUND]

Fon·da (fon′də), *n.* a girl's given name.

fon·dant (fon′dənt; *Fr.* fôN däN′), *n.* **1.** a thick, creamy sugar paste, the basis of many candies. **2.** a candy made of this paste. [< F: lit., melting, prp. of *fondre* to melt, FOUND[3]]

Fond du Lac (fon′ də lak′, jo͝o lak′), a city in E Wisconsin, on Lake Winnebago. 32,719 (1960).

fon·dle (fon′dəl), *v.,* **-dled, -dling. —***v.t.* **1.** to handle or touch lovingly, affectionately, or tenderly; caress: *to fondle a precious object; to fondle a child.* **2.** *Obs.* to treat with fond indulgence. **—***v.i.* **3.** to show fondness, as by manner, words, or caresses. [*fond* (v.) (see FOND[1]) + -LE] **—fon′dler,** *n.* **—fon′dling·ly,** *adv.*

—Syn. 1. cuddle, snuggle, pet, pat, stroke.

fond·ly (fond′lē), *adv.* **1.** in a fond manner; lovingly or affectionately: *He looked fondly at his child.* **2.** with complacent credulity: *They fondly believed the war would come to a favorable end.* [ME; see FOND[1], -LY]

fond·ness (fond′nis), *n.* **1.** state or quality of being fond. **2.** tenderness or affection. **3.** doting affection. **4.** a liking or weakness for something: *He has a fondness for sweets.* **5.** *Archaic.* complacent credulity. [ME; see FOND[1], -NESS]

fon·du (fon do͞o′, fon′do͞o *for 1; Fr.* fôN dY′ *for 1, 2*), *adj., n., pl.* **-dus** (*Fr.* -dY′) *for 2.* **—***adj.* **1.** fondue (def. 3). **—***n.* **2.** *Ballet.* a slow bending of the supporting leg. [< F, ptp. of *fondre* to melt, FOUND[3]]

fon·due (fon do͞o′, fon′do͞o; *Fr.* fôN dY′), *n., pl.* **-dues** (*Fr.* -dY′), *adj. Cookery.* **—***n.* **1.** a saucelike dish of Swiss origin, made with melted cheese and seasonings, together with dry white wine, and sometimes eggs and butter, usually flavored with kirsch and served as a hot dip for pieces of bread. **2.** a baked soufflélike dish usually containing cracker crumbs or bread crumbs. **—***adj.* **3.** Also, **fondu.** melted. [< F; fem. of FONDU]

Fons (fönz), *n.* the ancient Roman god of springs.

fons et o·ri·go (fōns′ et ō Rē′gō; *Eng.* fonz et ō rī′gō), *Latin.* source and origin.

font[1] (font), *n.* **1.** a receptacle, usually of stone, as in a baptistery or church, containing the water used in baptism. **2.** a receptacle for holy water; stoup. **3.** the reservoir for oil in a lamp. **4.** *Archaic.* a fountain. [ME; OE *font, fant* < L *font-* (s. of *fons*) baptismal font, spring, fountain]

font[2] (font), *n. Print.* a complete assortment of type of one style and size. Also, *Brit.,* **fount.** [< MF *fonte* < VL **funditus* a pouring, molding, casting, L, ptp. of *fundere.* See FOUND[3]]

Font[1] (def. 1)

Fon·taine (fon tān′, -ten′), *n.* a boy's given name.

Fon·taine·bleau (fon′tin blō′; *Fr.* fôN ten blō′), *n.* a town in N France, SE of Paris: famous palace, long a favorite residence of French kings; extensive forest. 22,704 (1962).

Fon′tainebleau School′, a group of artists, many of them Italian and Flemish, who worked on the decorations of the palace of Fontainebleau in the 16th century.

font·al (fon′təl), *adj.* **1.** pertaining to or coming from a fountain or spring. **2.** pertaining to or being the source of something: *fontal concepts.* **3.** of or pertaining to a font, as of baptism. [< ML *fontāl(is).* See FONT[1], -AL[1]]

Fon·tan·a (fon tan′ə), *n.* a crater in the third quadrant of the face of the moon: about 30 miles in diameter.

fon·ta·nel (fon′tənel′), *n.* **1.** *Anat.* one of the spaces, covered by membrane, between the bones of the fetal or young skull. **2.** *Pathol. Obs.* an opening for the discharge of pus. Also, **fon′ta·nelle′.** [ME *fontinel* < MF *fontanele* little spring, dim. of *fontaine* FOUNTAIN]

fon·tange (fôN tänzh′), *n., pl.* **-tanges** (-tänzh′). Often, **fontanges.** commode (def. 4). [< F, named after Marie Angélique de Scorraille de Roussilles, Duchess of *Fontanges* (1661–81), mistress of Louis XIV]

Fon·tanne (fon tan′), *n.* **Lynn,** 1887–1983, U.S. actress, born in England (wife of Alfred Lunt).

Fon·te·nelle (fon′tᵊnəl′), *n.* a crater in the second quadrant of the face of the moon: about 23 miles in diameter.

Fon·teyn (fon tān′), *n.* **Dame Mar·got** (mär′gō), (*Margaret Hookham*), born 1919, English ballerina.

Foo·chow (fo͞o′chou′; *Chin.* fo͞o′jō′), *n.* a seaport in and the capital of Fukien, in SE China, opposite Taiwan. 616,000 (est. 1957). Also called **Minhow.**

food (fo͞od), *n.* **1.** any nourishing substance that is eaten or otherwise taken into the body to sustain life, provide energy, promote growth, etc. **2.** more or less solid nourishment, as distinguished from liquids. **3.** a particular kind of solid nourishment: *a breakfast food.* **4.** whatever supplies nourishment to organisms: *plant food; dog food.* **5.** anything serving for consumption or use: *food for thought.* [ME *fode,* OE *fōda;* cf. OE *fēdan,* Goth *fōdjan* to FEED; cf. FODDER[1], FOSTER] —**food′less,** *adj.* —**food′less·ness,** *n.*

—**Syn. 1.** nutrition, aliment, bread, sustenance, victuals; meat, viands; diet, regimen, menu. FOOD, FARE, PROVISIONS, RATION(S) refer to nutriment for any organism, whether of man, animal, or plant. FOOD is the general word: *Breakfast foods have become very popular. Many animals prefer grass as food.* FARE refers to the whole range of foods which may nourish person or animal: *an extensive bill of fare; The fare of some animals is limited in range.* PROVISIONS is applied to a store or stock of necessary things, esp. food, prepared beforehand: *provisions for a journey.* RATION implies an allotment or allowance of provisions: *a daily ration for each man of a company.* RATIONS often mean food in general: *to be on short rations.*

Food′ and Agricul′tural Organiza′tion, the agency of the United Nations that institutes and administers programs, esp. in underdeveloped countries, for improving farming methods and increasing food production. *Abbr.:* FAO

food′ chain′, *Ecol.* a series of organisms interrelated in their feeding habits, the smallest being fed upon by a larger one, which in turn feeds a still larger one, etc.

food′ fish′, any fish used for food by man.

food-gath·er·ing (fo͞od′gath′ər iŋ), *adj.* (of a primitive people) procuring food by hunting or fishing or the gathering of seeds, berries, or roots, rather than by agricultural means.

food′ of the gods′, asafetida.

food·stuff (fo͞od′stuf′), *n.* a substance or material used as food. [FOOD + STUFF]

food′ web′, *Ecol.* a series of organisms related by predator-prey activities; a series of interrelated food chains. Also called **food′ cy′cle.**

food′ poi′soning, **1.** an acute gastrointestinal condition characterized by headache, fever, chills, abdominal and muscular pain, nausea, diarrhea, and prostration, caused by foods that are naturally toxic, as poisonous mushrooms, by vegetable foods that are chemically contaminated, as by insecticides, or by bacteria or their toxins, esp. of the genus salmonella. Cf. **ptomaine.** **2.** (erroneously) ptomaine poisoning.

food′ proc′essor, an electric appliance for slicing, chopping, or mixing food at high speeds.

foo·fa·raw (fo͞o′fə rô′), *n. Informal.* **1.** a fuss or disturbance about very little. **2.** an excessive amount of decoration or ornamentation, as on a piece of clothing, a building, etc. [?]

fool[1] (fo͞ol), *n.* **1.** a silly or stupid person; one who lacks sense. **2.** a professional jester, formerly kept by a person of rank for amusement: *the court fool.* **3.** a person who has been imposed on by others and made to appear silly or stupid: *to make a fool of someone.* **4.** a weak-minded or idiotic person. **5.** an ardent enthusiast who cannot resist an opportunity to indulge his enthusiasm (usually prec. by a present participle): *The musicians were a bunch of playing fools who went on until morning.* **6. be nobody's fool,** to be wise or shrewd: *You think you can kid him, but I warn you he's nobody's fool.* —*v.t.* **7.** to trick, deceive, or impose on: *They tried to fool him.* —*v.i.* **8.** to act like a fool; joke; play. **9.** to jest; pretend; make believe: *I was only fooling.* **10. fool around, a.** to putter aimlessly; waste time: *She fooled around all through school. They fool around too much with minor details.* **b.** to trifle, philander, or waste time: *to fool around with a girl who's much too young.* **11. fool away,** to spend foolishly, as time or money; squander: *to fool away the entire afternoon.* **12. fool with,** to handle or play with idly or carelessly: *to be hurt while fooling with a loaded gun.* [ME *fol, fool* < OF *fol* < L *foll(is)* bellows, bag]

—**Syn. 1.** simpleton, dolt, dunce, blockhead, numskull, ignoramus, dunderhead, ninny, nincompoop, booby, saphead, sap. **2.** zany, clown. **4.** moron, imbecile, idiot. **7.** delude, hoodwink, cheat, gull, hoax, cozen.

fool[2] (fo͞ol), *n. British Cookery.* a dish made of fruit, scalded or stewed, crushed and mixed with cream or the like: *gooseberry fool.* [prob. special use of FOOL[1]]

fool·er·y (fo͞o′lə rē), *n., pl.* **-er·ies.** **1.** foolish action or conduct. **2.** a foolish action, performance, or thing. [FOOL[1] + -ERY]

fool·fish (fo͞ol′fish′), *n., pl.* **-fish·es,** (*esp. collectively*) **-fish.** filefish (def. 1). [FOOL[1] + FISH]

fool·har·dy (fo͞ol′här′dē), *adj.,* **-di·er, -di·est.** bold without judgment; foolishly rash or venturesome; reckless. [ME *folhardy* < OF *fol hardi.* See FOOL[1], HARDY] —**fool′har′di·ly,** *adv.* —**fool′har′di·ness,** *n.*

fool′ hen′, *U.S.* any of various grouses, as the spruce grouse, which can be killed easily because of their relative tameness.

fool·ish (fo͞o′lish), *adj.* **1.** lacking forethought or caution. **2.** resulting from or showing a lack of sense; ill-considered; unwise: *a foolish action, speech, etc.* **3.** trifling, insignificant, or paltry. [ME *folish, foolish.* See FOOL[1], -ISH[1]] —**fool′ish·ly,** *adv.* —**fool′ish·ness,** *n.*

—**Syn. 1.** senseless, vacant, vapid, simple, witless. FOOLISH, FATUOUS, SILLY, INANE, STUPID, ASININE imply weakness of intellect and lack of judgment. FOOLISH implies lack of common sense or good judgment or, sometimes, weakness of mind: *a foolish decision; The child seems foolish.* FATUOUS implies being not only foolish, dull, and vacant in mind, but complacent and highly self-satisfied as well: *fatuous and self-important; fatuous answers.* SILLY denotes extreme and conspicuous foolishness; it may also refer to pointlessness of jokes, remarks, etc.: *silly and senseless behavior; a perfectly silly statement.* INANE applies to silliness that is notably lacking in content, sense, or point: *inane questions that leave one no reply.* STUPID implies natural slowness or dullness of intellect, or, sometimes, a benumbed or dazed state of mind; it is also used to mean foolish or silly: *well-meaning but stupid; rendered stupid by a blow; It is stupid to do such a thing.* ASININE originally meant like an ass; it applies to witlessly stupid conversation or conduct and suggests a lack of social grace or perception: *He failed to notice the reaction to his asinine remarks.* **2.** imprudent, unreasonable, foolhardy, irrational; thoughtless, nonsensical, ridiculous, absurd, pointless, preposterous. —**Ant. 1, 2.** wise, intelligent.

fool′ish guil′lemot, *Brit.* the common murre, *Uria aalge.*

fool·proof (fo͞ol′pro͞of′), *adj.* **1.** involving no risk or harm, even when tampered with. **2.** never-failing: *a foolproof method.* [FOOL[1] + -PROOF]

fools·cap (fo͞olz′kap′), *n.* **1.** *Chiefly Brit.* a size of drawing or printing paper, 13½ × 17 inches. *Abbr.:* cap., fcp. **2.** See **fool's cap** (def. 1). **3.** Also called **fools′cap octa′vo.** a size of book, about 4¼ × 6¾ inches, untrimmed. **4.** Also called **fools′cap quar′to.** *Chiefly Brit.* a size of book, about 6¾ × 8½ inches untrimmed. [so called from the watermark of a fool's cap formerly used on such paper]

fool's′ cap′, **1.** a traditional jester's cap or hood, often multicolored and usually having several drooping peaks from which bells are hung. **2.** See **dunce cap.**

fool's′ er′rand, an absurd, pointless, or useless errand.

fool's′ gold′, iron or copper pyrites, sometimes mistaken for gold.

fool's′ par′adise, enjoyment based on false beliefs or hopes; a state of illusory happiness.

fool's-pars·ley (fo͞olz′pärs′lē), *n.* an Old World fetid, poisonous umbelliferous herb, *Aethusa Cynapium,* resembling parsley.

foot (fo͝ot), *n., pl.* **feet** or, often for 20, **foots;** *v.* —*n.* **1.** (in vertebrates) the terminal part of the leg, below the ankle joint, on which the body stands and moves. **2.** (in invertebrates) any part similar in position or function. **3.** such a part considered as the organ of locomotion. **4.** a unit of length derived from the length of the human foot. In English-speaking countries it is divided into 12 inches and equal to 30.48 centimeters. **5.** infantry. **6.** walking or running motion; pace: *swift of foot.* **7.** quality or character of movement or motion; tread; step. **8.** any part or thing resembling a foot, as in function, placement, shape, etc. **9.** *Furniture.* **a.** a shaped or ornamented feature terminating a leg at its lower part. **b.** any of several short legs supporting a central shaft, as of a pedestal table. **10.** a rim, flange, or flaring part, often distinctively treated, serving as a base for a table furnishing or utensil, as a glass, teapot, candlestick, etc. **11.** the part of a stocking, sock, etc., covering the foot. **12.** the lowest part, or bottom, as of a hill, ladder, page, etc. **13.** a supporting part; base: *The stem of a goblet is attached to the foot.* **14.** the part of anything opposite the top or head: *He marched at the foot of the column.* **15.** the end of a bed, grave, etc., toward which the feet are placed: *Put the blanket at the foot of the bed.* **16.** *Print.* the part of the type body which forms the sides of the groove, at the base. See diag. under **type.** **17.** the last, as of a series. **18.** that which is written at the bottom, as the total of an account. **19.** *Pros.* a group of syllables constituting a metrical unit of a verse. **20.** Usually, **foots. a.** sediment or dregs. **b.** footlights. **21.** a rim on the bottom of a glass or ceramic object. **22.** *Naut.* the lower edge of a sail. **23. get off on the right** or **wrong foot,** to begin favorably or unfavorably: *He got off on the wrong foot with a tactless remark about his audience.* **24. fall** or **land on one's feet,** to be successful in spite of unfavorable circumstances: *After he was fired, he fell on his feet and found a better job.* **25. feet first, a.** with one's feet going before: *We plunged into the river feet first.* **b.** Also, **feet foremost.** dead: *They took him out of the ring feet first.* **26. have one foot in the grave.** See **grave**[1] (def. 5). **27. on foot, a.** by walking or running, rather than by riding. **b.** in progress or operation; afoot: *The new building program is finally on foot.* **28. put one's best foot forward, a.** to attempt to make as good an impression as possible. **b.** to proceed with all possible haste; hurry. **29. put one's foot down,** to take a firm stand; be decisive or determined: *Now is the time to put your foot down.* **30. put one's foot in it** or **into it,** *Informal.* to make an embarrassing blunder. Also, **put one's foot in one's mouth.** **31. put** or **set someone on his feet,** to restore someone to his former condition, position, etc.: *A few weeks of rest should put her on her feet again.* **32. set foot on** or **in,** to go on or into; enter (used in negative constructions): *Never set foot on our property again!* —*v.i.* **33.** to walk; go on foot (often fol. by *it*): *If we're going to get there on time, we'll have to foot it.* **34.** to move the feet rhythmically, as to music or in dance (often fol. by *it*). **35.** (of vessels) to move forward; cover distance: *to foot briskly across the open water.* —*v.t.* **36.** to set foot on; walk or dance on. **37.** to traverse on or as if on foot. **38.** to make or attach a foot to: *to foot a stocking.* **39.** *Informal.* to pay or settle, as a bill: *Can you afford to foot the bill?* **40.** to seize with talons, as a hawk. **41.** to establish. **42.** *Obs.* to kick, esp. to kick away. **43. foot up, a.** to total or accumulate, as an account or bill. **b.** to add, as a column of figures, and set the sum at the foot: *The waiter footed up our bill.* [ME; OE *fōt;* c. G *Fuss;* akin to L *pēs,* Gk *poûs*]

-foot, a combining form of **foot** used with numerals to form compound adjectives: *ten-foot; two-foot.*

foot·age (fo͝ot′ij), *n.* **1.** length or extent in feet: *the footage of lumber.* **2.** *Mining.* **a.** payment by the running foot of work done. **b.** the amount so paid. **3.** a motion-picture scene or scenes: *newsreel footage; jungle footage.* [FOOT + -AGE]

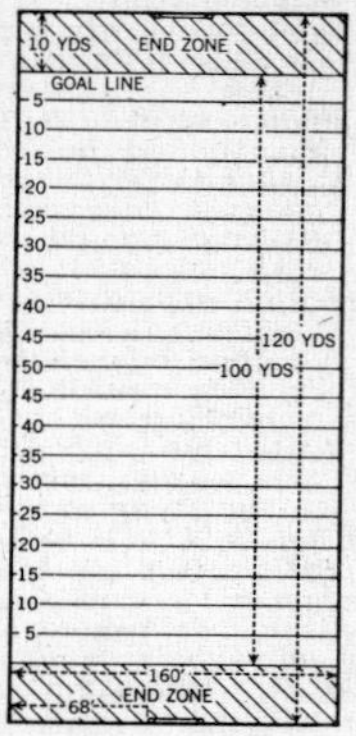

foot′-and-mouth′ disease′ (fo͝ot′ᵊn mouth′), *Vet. Pathol.* an acute, contagious, febrile disease of cattle, hogs, sheep, and other hoofed animals, characterized by vesicular eruptions in the mouth and about the hoofs, teats, and udder. Also called **aphthous fever, epizootic aphtha, hoof-and-mouth disease.**

foot·ball (fo͝ot′bôl′), *n.* **1.** a game in which two opposing teams of 11 players each defend goals at opposite ends of a field having goal posts at each end, with points being scored chiefly by carrying the ball across the opponent's goal line and by place-kicking or drop-kicking the ball over the crossbar between the opponent's goal posts. Cf. **conversion** (def. 13), **field goal, safety** (def. 6), **touchdown.** **2.** the ball used in this game, an inflated oval with a bladder contained in a casing usually made of leather. **3.** *Brit.* Rugby (def. 3). **4.** *Brit.* soccer. **5.** any person or thing treated roughly, casually, etc.: *They're making a political football of this issue.* [late ME *fut ball.* See FOOT, BALL[1]]

Football field (Intercollegiate)

foot·bind·ing (fo͝ot′bīn′diŋ), *n.* (formerly in China) act or practice of tightly binding the feet of infant girls to keep the feet as small as possible.

foot·board (fo͝ot′bōrd′, -bôrd′), *n.* **1.** a board or small platform on which to support the foot or feet. **2.** an upright piece across the foot of a bedstead. **3.** a treadle. [FOOT + BOARD]

foot·boy (fo͝ot′boi′), *n.* a boy in livery employed as a servant; page. [FOOT + BOY, modeled on *footman*]

foot′ brake′, a brake that is operated by pressure on a foot pedal.

foot·bridge (fo͝ot′brij′), *n.* a bridge intended for pedestrians only. [ME *fotbrigge.* See FOOT, BRIDGE[1]]

foot-can·dle (fo͝ot′kan′dᵊl), *n. Optics.* a unit of illuminance or illumination, equivalent to the illumination produced by a source of one candle at a distance of one foot and equal to one lumen incident per square foot. *Abbr.:* FC Also, **foot′ can′dle.**

foot·cloth (fo͝ot′klôth′, -kloth′), *n., pl.* **-cloths** (-klôthz′, -klothz′, -klôths′, -kloths′). **1.** a carpet or rug. **2.** a richly ornamented caparison for a horse, hanging to the ground. [FOOT + CLOTH]

foot′ drop′, *Pathol.* extension of the foot caused by paralysis of the flexor muscles of the leg. Also called **foot′ dan′gle.**

Foote (fo͝ot), *n.* **1. Andrew Hull,** 1806–63, U.S. naval officer. **2. Arthur William,** 1853–1937, U.S. composer and organist.

foot·ed (fo͝ot′id), *adj.* having a foot or feet (often used in combination): *a four-footed animal.* [late ME; see FOOT, -ED[3]]

foot·er (fo͝ot′ər), *n.* **1.** a person who walks; walker; pedestrian. **2.** *Brit. Informal.* **a.** See **Rugby football.** **b.** soccer. [FOOT + -ER[1]]

foot·fall (fo͝ot′fôl′), *n.* **1.** a footstep. **2.** the sound of footsteps: *She heard a footfall on the stairs.* [FOOT + FALL]

foot′ fault′, *Tennis.* a fault consisting in the failure of the server to keep both feet behind the base line until the ball is hit or to keep at least one foot on the ground while hitting the ball.

foot·fault (fo͝ot′fôlt′), *v.i. Tennis.* to commit a foot fault. [v. use of FOOT FAULT]

foot·gear (fo͝ot′gēr′), *n.* covering for the feet, as shoes, boots, etc. [FOOT + GEAR]

Foot′ Guards′, (in Britain) an infantry unit forming part of the ceremonial guard of the monarch. Cf. **Coldstream Guards, household troops.**

foot·hill (fo͝ot′hil′), *n.* a low hill at the base of a mountain or mountain range. [FOOT + HILL]

foot·hold (fo͝ot′hōld′), *n.* **1.** a hold or support for the feet; a place where a person may stand or tread securely. **2.** a secure position, esp. a firm basis for further progress or development: *They gained a foothold in the new markets before beginning their campaign.* [FOOT + HOLD[1]]

foot·ie (fo͝ot′ē), *n. Informal.* footsie (def. 1).

foot·ing (fo͝ot′iŋ), *n.* **1.** a secure and established position; foothold. **2.** the basis or foundation on which anything is established. **3.** a place or support for the feet; surface to stand on. **4.** the act of one who moves on foot, as in walking or dancing. **5.** a firm placing of the feet; stability: *He regained his footing.* **6.** *Building Trades, Civ. Eng.* the part of a foundation bearing directly upon the earth. **7.** position or status assigned to a person, group, etc., in estimation or treatment. **8.** mutual standing; reciprocal relation: *to be on a friendly footing with someone.* **9.** entrance into a new position or relationship: *to gain a footing in society.* **10.** a fee demanded from a person upon his entrance into a trade, society, etc. **11.** act of adding a foot to something, as to a stocking. **12.** that which is added as a foot. **13.** act of adding up a column of figures. **14.** the total of such a column. [ME; see FOOT, -ING[1]]

foot′ing piece′, *Building Trades.* one of a series of horizontal transverse timbers supporting a platform of a staging.

foot′ i′ron, *Theat.* a metal bar, usually L-shaped, for securing pieces of scenery to the stage floor.

foot-lam·bert (fo͝ot′lam′bərt), *n. Optics.* a unit of luminance or photometric brightness, equal to the luminance of a surface emitting a luminous flux of one lumen per square foot, the luminance of a perfectly reflecting surface receiving an illumination of one foot-candle. *Abbr.:* ft-L

foo·tle (fo͞ot′ᵊl), *v.,* **-tled, -tling,** *n.* —*v.i.* **1.** to act or talk in a foolish or silly way. —*n.* **2.** nonsense; foolishness; silliness. [? cf. FOOTY]

foot·less (fŏŏt′lis), *adj.* **1.** lacking a foot or feet. **2.** having no support or basis; unsubstantial. **3.** *Informal.* awkward, helpless, or inefficient. [ME; see FOOT, -LESS]

foot′ lev′el, a foot rule, hinged in the middle, having a spirit level in one section and a graduated arc from which the angle made by the two sections can be read.

foot·light (fŏŏt′līt′), *n.* **1.** Usually, **footlights.** *Theat.* the lights at the front of a stage that are nearly on a level with the feet of the performers. **2. the footlights,** the stage; acting profession. [FOOT + LIGHT[1]]

foot′ line′, **1.** *Print.* a line at the bottom of a page of type, esp. a black line or a line containing the folio. **2.** *Curling.* See **foot score.**

foot·ling (fŏŏt′ling), *adj.* *Informal.* foolish; silly; trifling: *Don't bother everyone with your ridiculous, footling remarks.* [FOOTLE + -ING[2]]

foot·lock·er (fŏŏt′lok′ər), *n.* a small trunk, esp. for containing the personal effects of a soldier and kept at the foot of his bed. [FOOT + LOCKER]

foot-loose (fŏŏt′lo͞os′), *adj.* free to go or travel about; not confined by responsibilities.

foot·mak·er (fŏŏt′mā′kər), *n.* a glassworker who blows and shapes the foot and often the stem on a goblet. [FOOT + MAKER]

foot·man (fŏŏt′mən), *n., pl.* **-men. 1.** a liveried servant who attends the door or carriage, waits on table, etc. **2.** a metal stand before a fire, to keep something hot. **3.** *Rare.* an infantryman. [ME *fotman.* See FOOT, MAN[1]]

foot·mark (fŏŏt′märk′), *n.* a footprint. [FOOT + MARK[1]]

foot′men's gal′lery, the rearmost section of seats in the balcony of an English theater, esp. in the late 17th and early 18th centuries.

foot·note (fŏŏt′nōt′), *n., v.,* **-not·ed, -not·ing.** —*n.* **1.** an explanatory or documenting note or comment at the bottom of a page, referring to a specific part of the text on the page. **2.** a minor or tangential comment added to a main statement. —*v.t.* **3.** to add footnotes to (a text); annotate: *His next step is to footnote his dissertation.* [FOOT + NOTE]

foot·pace (fŏŏt′pās′), *n.* **1.** walking pace. **2.** a raised portion of a floor; platform. **3.** a landing or resting place at the end of a short flight of steps. [FOOT + PACE[1]]

foot·pad (fŏŏt′pad′), *n.* a highwayman or robber who goes on foot. [FOOT + PAD[2]]

foot·path (fŏŏt′path′, -päth′), *n., pl.* **-paths** (-pathz′, -päthz′, -paths′, -päths′). **1.** a path for pedestrians. **2.** *Brit.* footway (def. 2). [FOOT + PATH]

foot·plate (fŏŏt′plāt′), *n.* *Carpentry.* a plate running beneath and supporting a row of studs; mudsill. [FOOT + PLATE[1]]

foot-pound (fŏŏt′pound′), *n.* *Physics.* a foot-pound-second unit of work or energy, equal to the work done by a force of one pound when its point of application moves through a distance of one foot in the direction of the force. *Abbr.:* ft-lb

foot-pound·al (fŏŏt′poun′dᵊl), *n.* *Physics.* a foot-pound-second unit of work or energy equal to the work done by a force of one poundal when its point of application moves through a distance of one foot in the direction of the force. *Abbr.:* ft-pdl

foot-pound-sec·ond (fŏŏt′pound′sek′ənd), *adj.* of or pertaining to the system of units in which the foot, pound, and second are the principal units of length, mass and time. *Abbr.:* fps, f.p.s.

foot·print (fŏŏt′print′), *n.* **1.** a mark left by the shod or unshod foot, as in earth, sand, etc. **2.** an impression of the sole of a person's foot, esp. one taken for purposes of identification. [FOOT + PRINT]

foot′ rail′, *Furniture.* a stretcher connecting the front legs of a piece.

foot·rest (fŏŏt′rest′), *n.* a support for a person's feet, as an attachment to a barber's chair or a dentist's chair. [FOOT + REST[1]]

foot·rope (fŏŏt′rōp′), *n.* *Naut.* **1.** the portion of the boltrope to which the lower edge of a sail is sewn. **2.** a rope suspended a few feet beneath a yard, bowsprit, jib boom, or spanker boom to give a footing for men handling sails. [FOOT + ROPE]

foot′ rot′, *Vet. Pathol.* an infection of the feet of sheep, causing inflammatory changes of the toes and lameness. Also called **fouls, stinkyfoot.**

foot′ rule′, a ruler one foot in length.

foot′ score′, *Curling.* a line at each end of the rink that is at right angles to its length. Also called **foot line.**

foot·scrap·er (fŏŏt′skrā′pər), *n.* a metal bar, set in a small frame and attached to a doorstep, used in cleaning the bottoms of the shoes before entering a house. [FOOT + SCRAPER]

foot·sie (fŏŏt′sē), *n.* **1.** Sometimes, **footsies.** Also, **footie.** *Informal.* the act of flirting or sharing a surreptitious intimacy. **2. play footsie with, a.** to flirt with (someone); be slyly or furtively intimate with. **b.** to curry favor with; seek advantage from, esp. by discreet or stealthy means: *He's been playing footsie with Amalgamated Doorknobs, hoping to get a vice-presidency.* [childish dim. of FOOT]

foot′ sol′dier, an infantryman.

foot·sore (fŏŏt′sōr′, -sôr′), *adj.* having sore or tender feet, as from much walking. [FOOT + SORE] —**foot′sore′ness,** *n.*

foot·stalk (fŏŏt′stôk′), *n.* *Bot., Zool.* a pedicel; peduncle. [FOOT + STALK[1]]

foot·stall (fŏŏt′stôl′), *n.* **1.** the stirrup of a woman's sidesaddle. **2.** *Archit.* a pedestal, plinth, or base, as of a statue, column, or pier. [FOOT + STALL[1]]

foot·step (fŏŏt′step′), *n.* **1.** the setting down of a foot, or the sound so produced; footfall; tread. **2.** the distance covered by a step in walking; pace. **3.** a footprint. **4.** a step by which to ascend or descend. **5. follow in someone's footsteps,** to succeed or imitate another person. [ME *foote steppe.* See FOOT, STEP]

foot·stone (fŏŏt′stōn′), *n.* **1.** a stone placed at the foot of a grave. **2.** Also called **skew table.** *Masonry.* a kneeler at the foot of a gable. [FOOT + STONE. Cf. HEADSTONE]

foot·stool (fŏŏt′sto͞ol′), *n.* a low stool upon which to rest one's feet. [FOOT + STOOL]

foot-ton (fŏŏt′tun′), *n.* *Physics.* a foot-pound-second unit of work or energy, equivalent to 2240 foot-pounds and equal to the energy expended in raising a ton of 2240 pounds a distance of one foot against the force of gravity.

foot·wall (fŏŏt′wôl′), *n.* **1.** *Mining.* the top of the rock stratum underlying a vein or bed of ore. Cf. **hanging wall** (def. 1). **2.** *Geol.* a mass of rock lying beneath a fault plane. [FOOT + WALL]

foot′ warm′er, any of various devices, esp. other than items of footwear, for keeping one's feet warm.

foot·way (fŏŏt′wā′), *n.* **1.** a way or path for pedestrians. **2.** Also called **footpath.** *Brit.* a sidewalk. [ME *fotewey.* See FOOT, WAY]

foot·wear (fŏŏt′wâr′), *n.* articles to be worn on the feet, as shoes, slippers, boots, etc. [FOOT + WEAR]

foot·work (fŏŏt′wûrk′), *n.* **1.** the use of the feet, as in tennis, boxing, etc. **2.** travel by foot from one place to another, as in gathering facts, fulfilling an assignment or obligation, etc.; legwork: *The project entailed a great deal of footwork.* **3.** the act or process of maneuvering, esp. in a skillful manner: *It took a bit of fancy footwork to avoid the issue.* [FOOT + WORK]

foot·worn (fŏŏt′wōrn′, -wôrn′), *adj.* **1.** worn by the feet: *a footworn pavement.* **2.** footsore. [FOOT + WORN]

foo·ty (fo͞o′tē), *adj.,* **-ti·er, -ti·est.** *Chiefly Dial.* poor; worthless; paltry. [var. of *foughty* musty, OE *fūht* moist, damp (c.G *feucht*); see -Y[1]]

foo·zle (fo͞o′zəl), *v.,* **-zled, -zling,** *n.* —*v.t., v.i.* **1.** to bungle; play clumsily: *to foozle a stroke in golf; to foozle on the last hole.* —*n.* **2.** act of foozling, esp. a bad stroke in golf. [? < dial. G *fuseln* to work badly, clumsily, hurriedly]

fop (fop), *n.* a man who is excessively vain and concerned about his manners and appearance. [ME *foppe,* *fop;* akin to FOB[2]]

fop·per·y (fop′ə rē), *n., pl.* **-per·ies. 1.** the clothes, manners, actions, etc., of a fop. **2.** something foppish. [FOP + -ERY]

fop·pish (fop′ish), *adj.* resembling or befitting a fop; excessively refined and fastidious in taste and manner. [FOP + -ISH[1]] —**fop′pish·ly,** *adv.* —**fop′pish·ness,** *n.*

for (fôr; *unstressed* fər), *prep.* **1.** with the object or purpose of: *to run for exercise.* **2.** intended to belong to, or be used in connection with: *equipment for the army; a closet for dishes.* **3.** suiting the purposes or needs of: *medicine for the aged.* **4.** in order to obtain, gain, or acquire: *a suit for alimony; to work for wages.* **5.** (used to express a wish, as of something to be experienced or obtained): *O, for a cold drink!* **6.** sensitive or responsive to: *an eye for beauty; an ear for music.* **7.** desirous of: *a longing for something; a taste for fancy clothes.* **8.** in consideration of, or in return for: *three for a dollar; to be thanked for one's efforts.* **9.** appropriate or adapted to: *a subject for speculation; clothes for winter.* **10.** with regard or respect to: *pressed for time; too warm for April.* **11.** during the continuance of: *for a long time.* **12.** in favor of; on the side of: *to be for honest government.* **13.** in place of; instead of: *a substitute for butter.* **14.** in the interest of, or on behalf of: *to act for a client.* **15.** in exchange for; as an offset to: *blow for blow; money for goods.* **16.** in punishment of: *payment for the crime.* **17.** in honor of: *to give a dinner for a person.* **18.** with the purpose of reaching: *to start for London.* **19.** contributive to: *for the advantage of everybody.* **20.** in order to save: *to flee for one's life.* **21.** in order to become: *to go for a soldier.* **22.** in assignment or attribution to: *an appointment for the afternoon; That's for you to decide.* **23.** such as to allow of or to require: *too many for separate mention.* **24.** such as results in: *his reason for going.* **25.** as affecting the interests or circumstances of: *bad for one's health.* **26.** in proportion or with reference to: *He is tall for his age.* **27.** in the character of; as being: *to know a thing for a fact.* **28.** by reason of; because of: *to shout for joy; a city famed for its beauty.* **29.** in spite of: *He's a decent guy for all that.* **30.** to the extent or amount of: *to walk for a mile.* **31.** (used to introduce an infinitive phrase equivalent to a construction with a relative clause): *It's time for me to go.* **32. for it,** *Brit.* See **in** (def. 21). —*conj.* **33.** seeing that; since. **34.** because. [ME, OE; c. OS *for;* akin to FORE[1], L *per* through, Gk *prō* before, ahead]

for-, a prefix meaning "away," "off," " to the uttermost," "extremely," "wrongly," or imparting a negative or privative force, occurring in verbs and nouns formed from verbs of Old or Middle English origin, many of which are now obsolete or archaic: *forbid; forbear; forswear; forbearance.* [ME, OE; cf. G *ver-,* Gk *peri-,* L *per-*]

For., Forester.

for., **1.** foreign. **2.** forester. **3.** forestry.

F.O.R., free on rails. Also, **f.o.r.**

for·age (fôr′ij, for′-), *n., v.,* **-aged, -ag·ing.** —*n.* **1.** food for horses or cattle; fodder; provender. **2.** the seeking or obtaining of such food. **3.** act of searching for provisions of any kind. **4.** a raid. —*v.i.* **5.** to wander or go in search of supplies. **6.** to search about; seek; rummage; hunt: *He went foraging in the attic for old mementos.* **7.** to make a raid. —*v.t.* **8.** to collect forage from; strip of supplies; plunder: *to forage the countryside.* **9.** to supply with forage. **10.** to obtain by foraging. [ME < OF *fourrage,* deriv. of *fuerre* FODDER[1] (< Gmc)] —**for′ag·er,** *n.*
—**Syn. 1.** See **feed.**

for′age cap′, *Mil.* (formerly) a small, low, undress military cap.

for′aging ant′, any of several ants, as army ants, that forage as part of a large group.

For·a·ker (fôr′ə kər, for′-), *n.* **Mount,** a mountain in central Alaska, in the Alaska Range, near Mt. McKinley. 17,280 ft.

for·am (fôr′əm), *n.* a foraminifer. [by shortening]

fo·ra·men (fō rā′mən, fô-, fə-), *n., pl.* **-ram·i·na** (-ram′ə nə). an opening, orifice, or short passage, as in a bone or in the integument of the ovule of a plant. [< L: hole, opening, equiv. to *forā(re)* (to) bore, pierce + *-men* resultative n. suffix] —**fo·ram·i·nal** (fə ram′ənᵊl), *adj.*

fora′men mag′num (mag′nəm), the large hole in the occipital bone forming the passage from the cranial cavity to the spinal canal. [< NL: lit., great hole]

fora′men o·va′le (ō val′ē, ō vā′lē, ō vä′-), *Anat.* a fetal opening in the septum between the atria of the heart, through which blood is diverted from the right atrium to the left atrium. [< NL: lit., oval hole]

fo·ram·i·nate (fō ram′ə nit, fô-, fə-), *adj.* full of holes or foramina. Also, **fo·ram′i·nous.** [< LL *forāmināt(us)* bored, pierced, equiv. to *forāmin-* (s. of *forāmen*) FORAMEN + *-ātus* -ATE[1]] —**fo·ram′i·na′tion,** *n.*

for·a·min·i·fer (fôr′ə min′ə fər, for′-), *n.* any chiefly marine rhizopod of the order *Foraminifera,* typically having a calcareous shell perforated by small holes or pores. [< L *forāmin-* (s. of *forāmen*) FORAMEN + -I- + -FER] —**fo·ram·i·nif·er·al** (fō ram′ə nif′ər əl, fô-, fə-), **fo·ram′i·nif′er·ous,** *adj.*

for·as·much (fôr′əz much′, fər-), *conj.* in view of the fact that; seeing that; since (usually fol. by *as*). [ME; see FOR, AS[1], MUCH]

for·ay (fôr′ā, for′ā), *n.* **1.** a quick raid, usually for the purpose of taking plunder: *Vikings made a foray on the port.* **2.** a quick, sudden attack: *The defenders made a foray outside the walls.* —*v.i.* **3.** to make a raid; forage; pillage. —*v.t.* **4.** to ravage in search of plunder. [ME *forraie(n);* back formation from FORAYER]

for·ay·er (fôr′ā ər, for′-), *n.* a marauder. [ME *forreier* < OF, deriv. of *forrier* forager. See FORAGE, -ER[1]]

forb (fôrb), *n.* any herb that is not a grass or grasslike. [< Gk *phorbḗ* food, fodder, deriv. of *phérbein* to feed; akin to OE *beorgan, birgan* to taste, eat, OIcel *bergja* to taste]

for·bade (fər bad′, -bād′, fôr-), *v.* a pt. of **forbid.** Also, **for·bad′.**

for·bear[1] (fôr bâr′), *v.,* **-bore, -borne, -bear·ing.** —*v.t.* **1.** to refrain or abstain from; desist from. **2.** to keep back; withhold. **3.** *Archaic.* to endure. —*v.i.* **4.** to refrain; hold back. **5.** to be patient or self-controlled when subject to annoyance or provocation. [ME *forbere(n),* OE *forberan.* See FOR-, BEAR[1]] —**for·bear′er,** *n.* —**for·bear′ing·ly,** *adv.*
—**Syn. 1.** forgo, sacrifice, renounce.

for·bear[2] (fôr′bâr′), *n.* forebear.

for·bear·ance (fôr bâr′əns), *n.* **1.** act of forbearing; a refraining from something. **2.** forbearing conduct or quality; patient endurance; leniency. **3.** an abstaining from the enforcement of a right. **4.** a creditor's giving of indulgence after the day originally fixed for payment. [FORBEAR[1] + -ANCE]
—**Syn. 1.** abstinence. **2.** tolerance, toleration, sufferance; indulgence.

Forbes (fôrbz), *n.* **1. Esther,** 1894?–1967, U.S. novelist. **2. George William,** 1869–1947, New Zealand statesman: prime minister 1930–35.

Forbes-Rob·ert·son (fôrbz′rob′ərt sən), *n.* **Sir Johnston,** 1853–1937, English actor and theatrical manager.

for·bid (fər bid′, fôr-), *v.t.,* **-bade** or **-bad, -bid·den** or **-bid, -bid·ding. 1.** to command (a person) not to do something, have something, etc., or not to enter some place: *to forbid him entry to the house.* **2.** to prohibit (something); place an interdiction against: *to forbid the use of lipstick; to forbid smoking.* **3.** to hinder or prevent; make impossible. **4.** to exclude; bar: *Burlesque is forbidden in New York City.* [ME *forbede(n),* OE *forbēodan.* See FOR-, BID[1]] —**for·bid′der,** *n.*
—**Syn. 1, 2.** interdict. FORBID, INHIBIT, PROHIBIT, TABOO indicate a command to refrain from some action. FORBID, a common and familiar word, usually denotes a direct or personal command of this sort: *I forbid you to go. It was useless to forbid children to play in the park.* INHIBIT, besides indicating ecclesiastical prohibition, implies a checking or hindering of impulses by the mind: *to inhibit one's desires.* PROHIBIT, a formal or legal word, means usually to forbid by official edict, enactment, or the like: *to prohibit the sale of liquor.* TABOO, primarily associated with primitive superstition, means to prohibit by common disapproval and by social custom: *to taboo a subject in polite conversation.* **3.** preclude, stop, obviate, deter. —**Ant. 1.** permit.

for·bid·dance (fər bid′ᵊns, fôr-), *n.* **1.** act of forbidding. **2.** state of being forbidden. [FORBID + -ANCE]

for·bid·den (fər bid′ᵊn, fôr-), *v.* **1.** a pp. of **forbid.** —*adj.* **2.** not allowed; prohibited: *The forbidden apple was offered by Eve.* **3.** *Physics.* involving a change in quantum numbers that is not permitted by the selection rules: *forbidden transition.* —**for·bid′den·ly,** *adv.* —**for·bid′den·ness,** *n.*

Forbid′den Cit′y, a walled section of Peking, built in the 15th century, containing the imperial palace and other buildings of the Chinese Empire.

forbid′den fruit′, **1.** the fruit of the tree of knowledge of good and evil, tasted by Adam and Eve against God's prohibition. Gen. 2:17; 3:3. **2.** any unlawful pleasure, esp. illicit sexual indulgence. **3.** (*cap.*) *Trademark.* an orange-colored liqueur made in the U.S. and consisting of brandy and the fruit of the shaddock tree. **4.** shaddock (def. 1).

for·bid·ding (fər bid′ing, fôr-), *adj.* **1.** grim; unfriendly; hostile; sinister: *a forbidding countenance.* **2.** dangerous; threatening: *forbidding clouds; forbidding cliffs.* [FORBID + -ING[2]] —**for·bid′ding·ly,** *adv.* —**for·bid′ding·ness,** *n.*

for·bore (fôr bōr′, -bôr′), *v.* pt. of **forbear**[1].

for·borne (fôr bōrn′, -bôrn′), *v.* pp. of **forbear**[1].

for·by (fôr bī′), *prep., adv.* *Chiefly Scot.* **1.** close by; near. **2.** besides. Also, **for·bye′.** [ME; see FOR-, BY]

force (fōrs, fôrs), *n., v.,* **forced, forc·ing.** —*n.* **1.** strength; energy; power; intensity: *a personality of great force.* **2.** efficacious power; power to influence, affect, or control: *the force of circumstances; a force for law and order.* **3.** physical power or strength possessed by a living being: *He used all his force in opening the window.* **4.** strength or power exerted upon an object; physical coercion; violence: *to use force to open the window; to use force on a person.* **5.** *Law.* violence offered to persons or things, as the use of force in breaking into a house. **6.** persuasive power; power to convince: *They felt the force of his arguments.* **7.** mental or moral strength: *the force of one's mind, intellect, or will.* **8.** might, as of a ruler or realm; strength for war. **9.** Often, **forces.** a large body of armed men; army. **10.** any body of persons combined for joint action: *a police force; an office force.* **11.** intensity or strength of effect: *the force of her acting; the force of his writing.* **12.** *Physics.* **a.** an influence on a body or system, producing or tending to produce a change in movement or in shape or other effects. **b.** the intensity of such an influence. *Symbol:* F, f **13.** any

influence or agency analogous to physical force: *social forces.* **14.** binding power, as of an agreement. **15.** value; significance; meaning. **16.** Also called **force play.** *Baseball.* a situation, as with the bases full, in which, on a fair ground ball, a base runner must leave the base he occupies and attempt to reach the next base. **17.** *Billiards.* a stroke in which the cue ball is forcibly struck directly below the center in such a manner as to cause it to stop abruptly, bound back, or roll off to one side after hitting the object ball. **18. in force, a.** in operation; effective; enforced; valid: *This rule is no longer in force.* **b.** in large numbers; at full strength: *They attacked in force.*
—*v.t.* **19.** to compel, constrain, or oblige (oneself or someone) to do something: *to force a suspect to confess.* **20.** to drive or propel against resistance: *He forced his way through the crowd. They forced air into his lungs.* **21.** to bring about or effect by force; bring about of necessity or as a necessary result: *to force a passage; to force a smile.* **22.** to put or impose (something or someone) forcibly on or upon a person: *to force something on someone's attention; She forced herself upon them.* **23.** to compel by force; overcome the resistance of: *to force acceptance of something.* **24.** to obtain or draw forth by or as if by force; extort: *to force a confession.* **25.** to overpower; enter or take by force: *They forced the town after a long siege.* **26.** to break open (a door, lock, etc.). **27.** to cause (plants, fruits, etc.) to grow or mature at an increased rate by artificial means. **28.** to press, urge, or exert (an animal, person, etc.) to violent effort or to the utmost. **29.** to use force upon. **30.** *Baseball.* **a.** to cause (a base runner) to be retired by obliging him, as by a ground ball, to advance to a base in order to make room for another runner or the batter. **b.** to cause (a base runner or run) to score, as by walking a batter with the bases full (often fol. by *in*). **31.** *Cards.* **a.** to compel (a player) to trump by leading a suit of which he has no cards. **b.** to compel a player to play (a particular card). **c.** to compel (a player) to play so as to make known the strength of the hand. **32.** *Photog.* **a.** to develop (a print or negative) for longer than usual in order to increase density or bring out details. **b.** to bring out underexposed parts of (a print or negative) by adding alkali to the developer. **33.** *Archaic.* to give force to; strengthen; reinforce. **34.** *Obs.* to enforce (a law).
—*v.i.* **35.** to make one's way by force. [ME < MF < VL *fortia*, deriv. of L *fortis* strong] —**force′a·ble,** *adj.* —**force′less,** *adj.* —**forc′er,** *n.* —**forc′ing·ly,** *adv.*
—**Syn. 1.** vigor. See **strength. 4.** compulsion, constraint. **6.** efficacy, effectiveness, cogency, potency, validity, conviction. **19.** coerce. **20.** impel. **25.** overcome; violate, ravish, rape. —**Ant. 1.** weakness. **6.** impotence.

forced (fōrst, fôrst), *adj.* **1.** enforced or compulsory: *forced labor.* **2.** strained, unnatural, or affected: *a forced smile.* **3.** subjected to force. **4.** emergency: *a forced landing of an airplane.* [FORCE + -ED[2]] —**forc·ed·ly** (fōr′sid lē, fôr′-), *adv.* —**forc′ed·ness,** *n.*

forced′ cod′ing. See **minimum access programming.**

forced′ land′ing, an airplane landing which a pilot is forced to make because of an emergency beyond his control.

forced′ march′, *Mil.* any march that is longer than troops are accustomed to and maintained at a faster pace than usual, generally undertaken for a particular objective under emergency conditions.

forced′ sale′, *Law.* a sale held as a result of a judicial order.

force′ feed′, lubrication under pressure, as from a pump, used esp. in internal-combustion engines.

force-feed (fōrs′fēd′, fôrs′-), *v.t.*, **-fed, -feed·ing. 1.** to compel to take food through the use or threat of force: *They force-fed their kids and made a mess of their gastronomic habits.* **2.** to compel to absorb or accept: *The government force-fed the country on war propaganda in the hopes of drumming up support for their policy.*

force′ fit′, *Mach.* See **press fit.**

force·ful (fōrs′fəl, fôrs′-), *adj.* **1.** full of force; powerful; vigorous; effective: *a forceful plea for peace.* **2.** acting or driven with force. [FORCE + -FUL] —**force′ful·ly,** *adv.* —**force′ful·ness,** *n.*
—**Syn. 1.** cogent, telling.

force ma·jeure (*Fr.* fôrs MA zhœr′), *pl.* **forces majeures** (*Fr.* fôrs MA zhœr′). *Law.* an unexpected and disruptive event which may operate to excuse a party from a contract. [< F: lit., superior force]

force·meat (fōrs′mēt′, fôrs′-), *n.* *Cookery.* a mixture of finely chopped and seasoned foods, usually containing egg white, meat or fish, etc., used as a stuffing or served alone. Also, **farcemeat.** [*force*, var. of obs. *farce* stuffing + MEAT]

force-out (fōrs′out′, fôrs′-), *n.* *Baseball.* **1.** a put-out of a base runner at the base that he was forced to run to by a following base runner: *a force-out at second.* **2.** a put-out of the batter at first base. [n. use of v. phrase *force out*]

force′ play′, *Baseball.* a play in which a base runner in a force is put out at the base that he was attempting to reach: *to hit into a force play.*

for·ceps (fôr′səps, -seps), *n.*, *pl.* **-ceps, -ci·pes** (-sə pēz′). **1.** an instrument, as pincers or tongs, for seizing and holding objects, as in surgical operations. **2.** *Anat., Zool.* a part or process that resembles a forceps. [< L: pair of tongs, pincers, fire tongs, equiv. to *for-* (s. of *formus*) warm, hot + *-cep-* (s. of *capere* to take) + *-s* nom. sing. suffix] —**for′ceps·like′,** *adj.* —**for·cip·i·al** (fôr sip′ē əl), *adj.*

force′ pump′, a pump that delivers a liquid under pressure, so as to eject it forcibly (distinguished from *lift pump*).

forc·er[1] (fōr′sər, fôr′-), *n.* one who or that which forces. [FORCE + -ER[1]]

forc·er[2] (fōr′sər, fôr′-), *n.* *Obs.* a coffer or chest. [ME < OF]

for·ci·ble (fōr′sə bəl, fôr′-), *adj.* **1.** effected by force: *forcible entry into a house.* **2.** having force; producing a powerful effect; effective. **3.** convincing, as reasoning: *a forcible theory.* **4.** characterized by the use of force or violence. [ME < MF; see FORCE, -IBLE] —**for′ci·ble·ness, for′ci·bil′i·ty,** *n.* —**for′ci·bly,** *adv.*

for·ci·pate (fôr′sə pāt′, fôr′-), *adj.* having the shape of or resembling a forceps. [< L *forcip-* (s. of *forceps*) FORCEPS + -ATE[1]]

for·ci·pres·sure (fôr′sə presh′ər, fôr′-), *n.* *Surg.* a method for preventing hemorrhage by compressing bleeding arteries with forceps. [< L *forcip-* (s. of *forceps*) FORCEPS + PRESSURE]

ford (fōrd, fôrd), *n.* **1.** a place where a river or other body of water is shallow enough to be crossed by wading. —*v.t.* **2.** to cross (a river, stream, etc.) by a ford. [ME, OE; c. OFris *forda*, G *Furt;* akin to OIcel *fjörthr*, FARE, PORT[1]] —**ford′a·ble,** *adj.*

Ford (fōrd, fôrd), *n.* **1. Ford Mad·ox** (mad′əks), (*Ford Madox Hueffer*), 1873–1939, English novelist, poet, critic, and editor. **2. Gerald R.,** born 1913, 38th president of the U.S. 1974–76. **3. Guy Stanton,** 1873–1963, U.S. historian, educator, and editor. **4. Henry,** 1863–1947, U.S. automobile manufacturer. **5. John,** 1586?–c1640, English playwright. **6. John** (*Sean O'Feeney*), 1895–1973, U.S. motion-picture director. **7.** a boy's given name.

Ford′ Cit′y, 1. a town in central Pennsylvania. 5440 (1960). **2.** a town in central California. 3926 (1960).

Ford·ize (fōr′dīz, fôr′-), *v.t.*, **-ized, -iz·ing. 1.** to mass-produce (standardized units) on an assembly-line basis. **2.** to standardize (people, production methods, etc.) in order to or as if in order to increase efficiency in mass production. [Henry FORD + -IZE]

ford·less (fōrd′lis, fōrd′-), *adj.* **1.** having no ford. **2.** that cannot be crossed on foot: *a fordless stream.* [FORD + -LESS]

for·do (fôr do͞o′), *v.t.*, **-did, -done, -do·ing.** *Archaic.* **1.** to do away with; kill; destroy. **2.** to ruin; undo. Also, **foredo.** [ME *fordo(n)*, OE *fordōn* (see FORE-, DO[1]); c. D *verdoen*, OHG *fartuon*]

for·done (fôr dun′), *adj.* exhausted with fatigue. Also, **foredone.** [ptp. of FORDO]

For·dyce (fôr′dīs), *n.* a town in central Arkansas. 3890 (1960).

fore[1] (fōr, fôr), *adj.* **1.** situated at or toward the front, as compared with something else. **2.** first in place, time, order, rank, etc.; forward; earlier. **3.** *Naut.* **a.** of or pertaining to a foremast. **b.** noting a sail, yard, boom, etc., or any rigging belonging to a fore lower mast or to some upper mast of a foremast. **c.** noting any stay running aft and upward to the head of a fore lower mast or to some specified upper mast of a foremast: *fore topmast stay.* **d.** situated at or toward the bow of a vessel; forward. —*adv.* **4.** *Naut.* at or toward the bow. **5.** *Archaic.* before. **6.** *Dial.* forward. **7. fore and aft,** *Naut.* in, at, or to both ends of a ship. —*n.* **8.** the forepart of anything; front. **9. the fore,** *Naut.* the foremast. **10. to the fore, a.** into a conspicuous place or position; to the front. **b.** at hand; ready; available. **c.** still alive. —*prep., conj.* **11.** Also, **'fore.** *Dial.* before. [special use of FORE-, detached from words like *forepart, forefather*, etc.]

fore[2] (fōr, fôr), *interj.* *Golf.* (used as a cry of warning to persons on a course who are in danger of being struck by the ball.) [prob. aph. var. of BEFORE]

fore-, a native English prefix meaning "before" (in space, time, condition, etc.), "front," "superior," etc.: *forehead; forecastle; forecast; foretell; foreman.* [comb. form repr. ME, OE *for(e)*]

fore-and-aft (fōr′ənd aft′, -äft′, fôr′-), *Naut.* —*adj.* **1.** located along or parallel to a line from the stem to the stern. —*adv.* **2.** fore[1] (def. 7).

fore-and-af·ter (fōr′ənd af′tər, äf′-, fôr′-), *n.* *Naut.* **1.** a fore-and-aft-rigged vessel. **2.** a beam running fore and aft across a hatchway to support hatch covers laid athwart the hatchway. **3.** a vessel having a sharp stern; a double ender. **4.** deerstalker (def. 2). [FORE-AND-AFT + -ER[1]]

fore′-and-aft′ rig′, *Naut.* a rig in which the principal sails are fore-and-aft. —**fore′-and-aft′-rigged′,** *adj.*

fore′-and-aft′ sail′, *Naut.* any of various sails, as jib-headed sails, gaff sails, lugsails, lateen sails, spritsails, staysails, and jibs, that do not set on yards and whose normal position, when not trimmed, is in a fore-and-aft direction amidships.

fore′-and-aft′ schoon′er, *Naut.* a schooner rigged entirely with fore-and-aft sails.

fore·arm[1] (fōr′ärm′, fôr′-), *n.* **1.** the part of the arm or upper limb between the elbow and the wrist. **2.** the part of the foreleg between the elbow and the knee in certain quadrupeds. See diag. under **horse.** [FORE- + ARM[1]]

fore·arm[2] (fōr ärm′, fôr-), *v.t.* to arm beforehand. [FORE- + ARM[2]]

fore·bear (fōr′bâr′, fôr′-), *n.* Usually, **forebears.** ancestors; forefathers. Also, **forbear.** [ME (Scot), equiv. to *fore-* FORE- + *-bear* being, var. of *beer;* see BE, -ER[1]]

fore·bode (fōr bōd′, fôr-), *v.*, **-bod·ed, -bod·ing.** —*v.t.* **1.** to foretell or predict; portend; be an omen of; indicate beforehand: *clouds that forebode a storm.* **2.** to have a strong inner certainty of (a future misfortune, evil, catastrophe, etc.); have a presentiment of. —*v.i.* **3.** to prophesy. **4.** to have a presentiment. [FORE- + BODE] —**fore·bod′er,** *n.*
—**Syn. 1.** foreshadow, presage, forecast, augur.

fore·bod·ing (fōr bō′ding, fôr-), *n.* **1.** a prediction; portent. **2.** a strong inner certainty of a future misfortune, evil, etc.; presentiment. —*adj.* **3.** that forebodes, esp. evil. [ME *forbodyng* (n.). See FOREBODE, -ING[1], -ING[2]] —**fore·bod′ing·ly,** *adv.* —**fore·bod′ing·ness,** *n.*

fore·bod·y (fōr′bod′ē, fôr′-), *n.*, *pl.* **-bod·ies.** *Naut.* the part of a ship's hull forward of the middle body. [FORE- + BODY]

fore·brain (fōr′brān′, fôr′-), *n.* *Anat.* **1.** the prosencephalon, being the anterior of the three primary divisions of the brain in the embryo of a vertebrate or the part of the adult brain derived from this tissue including the diencephalon and telencephalon. **2.** the telencephalon. [FORE- + BRAIN]

fore·cad·die (fōr′kad′ē, fôr′-), *n.* *Golf.* a caddie positioned on the course at a distance from the tee or a given lie, to locate balls after they are hit. [FORE- + CADDIE]

fore·cast (fōr′kast′, -käst′, fôr′-), *v.*, **-cast** or **-cast·ed, -cast·ing,** *n.* —*v.t.* **1.** to form an opinion beforehand; predict. **2.** to make a prediction of: *to forecast the weather.* **3.** to serve as a forecast of; foreshadow. **4.** to contrive or plan beforehand; prearrange. —*v.i.* **5.** to conjecture beforehand; make a forecast. **6.** to plan or arrange beforehand. —*n.* **7.** a conjecture as to something in the future. **8.** a prediction, esp. as to the weather. **9.** the act, practice, or faculty of forecasting. **10.** *Archaic.* foresight in planning. [ME *fore cast.* See FORE-, CAST[1]] —**fore′cast′er,** *n.*
—**Syn. 1.** foretell, anticipate. See **predict. 4.** project. **5, 7.** guess, estimate. **10.** prevision, forethought, prescience.

Forecastle (def. 1)

fore·cas·tle (fōk′səl, fōr′kas′əl, -käs′əl, fôr′-), *n.* *Naut.* **1.** a superstructure at or immediately aft of the bow of a vessel, used as a shelter for stores, machinery, etc., or as quarters for seamen. **2.** any seamen's quarters located in the forward part of a vessel, as a deckhouse. **3.** the forward part of the weather deck of a vessel, esp. that part forward of the foremast. Also, **fo'c's'le, fo'c'sle.** [ME *forcastel.* See FORE-, CASTLE]

fore′castle deck′, *Naut.* a partial weather deck on top of a forecastle superstructure; topgallant forecastle.

fore′castle head′, *Naut.* **1.** the extreme fore part of a forecastle superstructure. **2.** the extreme fore part of the main weather deck of a vessel that has no forecastle superstructure.

fore-check (fōr′chek′, fôr′-), *v.i.* *Ice Hockey.* to obstruct or impede the movement or progress of an attacking opponent while he is in his own defensive zone. Cf. **back-check, check** (def. 14).

fore·choir (fōr′kwīər′, fôr′-), *n.* antechoir. [FORE- + CHOIR]

fore·cit·ed (fōr′sī′tid, fôr′-), *adj.* previously cited. [FORE- + CITED]

fore·close (fōr klōz′, fôr-), *v.*, **-closed, -clos·ing.** —*v.t.* **1.** *Law.* **a.** to deprive (a mortgagor or pledgor) of the right to redeem his property, esp. on failure to make payment on a mortgage when due, ownership of property then passing to mortgagee. **b.** to take away the right to redeem (a mortgage or pledge). **2.** to shut out; exclude; bar. **3.** to hinder or prevent, as from doing something. **4.** to establish an exclusive claim to. **5.** to close, settle, or answer beforehand. —*v.i.* **6.** to foreclose a mortgage or pledge. [ME *foreclose(n)* < OF *forclos*, ptp. of *forclore* to exclude, equiv. to *for-* out + *clore* to shut (< L *claudere*)] —**fore·clos′a·ble,** *adj.*

fore·clo·sure (fōr klō′zhər, fôr-), *n.* *Law.* the act of foreclosing a mortgage or pledge. [FORECLOSE + -URE]

fore·con·scious (fōr′kon′shəs, fôr′-), *n.* *Psychol.* the preconscious. [FORE- + CONSCIOUS]

fore·course (fōr′kōrs′, fôr′kôrs′), *n.* the lowermost sail on a square-rigged foremast; a square foresail. See diag. under **ship.** [FORE- + COURSE]

fore·court (fōr′kōrt′, fôr′kôrt′), *n.* **1.** a courtyard before the entrance to a building or group of buildings. **2.** *Tennis.* the part of either half of a tennis court that lies between the net and the line that marks the inbounds limit of a service. Cf. **backcourt** (def. 2). [FORE- + COURT]

fore·date (fōr dāt′, fôr-), *v.t.*, **-dat·ed, -dat·ing.** to antedate. [FORE- + DATE[1]]

fore·deck (fōr′dek′, fôr′-), *n.* *Naut.* the fore part of a weather deck, esp. between a bridge house or superstructure and a forecastle superstructure. [FORE- + DECK[1]]

fore·do (fōr do͞o′, fôr-), *v.t.*, **-did, -done, -do·ing.** fordo.

fore·done (fōr dun′, fôr-), *adj.* fordone.

fore·doom (*v.* fōr do͞om′, fôr-; *n.* fōr′do͞om′, fôr′-), *v.t.* **1.** to doom beforehand. —*n.* **2.** *Archaic.* a doom ordained beforehand. [FORE- + DOOM]

fore′ edge′, the front outer edge of a book, opposite the bound edge.

fore′-edge paint′ing (fōr′ej′, fôr′-), a technique of painting a picture on the fore edge of a book in such a manner that when the pages are slightly fanned the picture is revealed.

fore·fa·ther (fōr′fä′thər, fôr′-), *n.* an ancestor. [ME *forefader.* See FORE-, FATHER] —**fore′fa′ther·ly,** *adj.*

Fore′fathers' Day′, the anniversary of the day (December 21, 1620, in Old Style December 11) on which the Pilgrims landed at Plymouth, Massachusetts. Owing to an error in changing the date from the Old Style to the New, it is generally observed on December 22.

fore·feel (*v.* fōr fēl′, fôr-; *n.* fōr′fēl′, fôr′-), *v.*, **-felt, -feel·ing,** *n.* —*v.t.* **1.** to feel or perceive beforehand; have a presentiment of. —*n.* **2.** a feeling beforehand. [FORE- + FEEL]

fore·fend (fōr fend′, fôr-), *v.t.* forfend.

fore·fin·ger (fōr′fing′gər, fôr′-), *n.* the first finger next to the thumb. Also called **index finger.** [late ME *forefyngure.* See FORE-, FINGER]

fore·foot (fōr′fo͝ot′, fôr′-), *n.*, *pl.* **-feet. 1.** *Zool.* one of the front feet of a quadruped, an insect, etc. **2.** *Naut.* **a.** the point at which the stem of a hull joins the keel; the forward end of a keel. **b.** a curved member at this point in a wooden hull. [late ME *forfot, forefote.* See FORE-, FOOT]

fore·front (fōr′frunt′, fôr′-), *n.* the foremost part or place. [late ME *forfrount, forefrount.* See FORE-, FRONT]

fore·gath·er (fōr gath′ər, fôr-), *v.i.* forgather.

fore·gift (fōr′gift′, fôr′-), *n.* *Brit.* an advance payment or premium paid by a tenant on taking or renewing a lease. [FORE- + GIFT]

fore·glimpse (fōr′glimps′, fôr′-), *n.* a revelation or glimpse of the future. [FORE- + GLIMPSE]

fore·go[1] (fōr gō′, fôr-), *v.t., v.i.* **-went, -gone, -go·ing.** to go before; precede. [ME *forgon, forgan*, OE *foregān.* See FORE-, GO[1]] —**fore·go′er,** *n.*

fore·go[2] (fōr gō′, fôr-), *v.t.*, **-went, -gone, -go·ing.** forgo. —**fore·go′er,** *n.*

fore·go·ing (fōr gō′ing, fôr-), *adj.* going before; preceding: *The foregoing paragraph presents the problem.* [late ME; see FOREGO[1], -ING[2]]
—**Syn.** precedent, previous, prior, earlier, former, antecedent, anterior.

fore·gone (fōr gôn′, -gon′, fôr-; fōr′gôn′, -gon′, fôr′-), *adj.* that has gone before; previous; past. [FORE- + GONE] —**fore·gone′ness,** *n.*

fore′gone′ conclu′sion, 1. an inevitable conclusion or result. 2. a conclusion, opinion, or decision formed in advance of proper consideration of evidence, arguments, etc.

fore·ground (fōr′ground′, fôr′-), *n.* the ground or parts situated, or represented as situated, in the front; the nearer portion of a scene (opposed to *background*). [FORE- + GROUND[1]]

fore·gut (fōr′gut′, fôr′-), *n.* *Embryol., Zool.* the upper part of the embryonic alimentary canal from which the pharynx, esophagus, stomach, and part of the duodenum develop. Cf. **hindgut, midgut.** [FORE- + GUT]

fore·hand (fōr′hand′, fôr′-), *adj.* 1. (in tennis, squash, etc.) of, pertaining to, or noting a stroke made from the same side of the body as that of the hand holding the racket, paddle, etc. Cf. **backhand** (def. 5). 2. being in front or ahead. 3. foremost or leading. 4. done beforehand; given or made in advance, as a payment. —*n.* 5. (in tennis, squash, etc.) a forehand stroke. 6. the part of a horse which is in front of the rider. 7. *Cards.* the player on the dealer's left, in a game with three players. Cf. **endhand, middlehand.** 8. *Archaic.* a superior or advantageous position. —*adv.* 9. (in tennis, squash, etc.) made, or struck, forehand; with a forehand stroke. [FORE- + HAND]

fore·hand·ed (fōr′han′did, fôr′-), *adj.* 1. forehand (def. 1). 2. capable of dealing or coping with unexpected problems: *A good military officer must be forehanded.* 3. providing for the future; prudent; thrifty. 4. in easy circumstances; well-to-do. —*adv.* 5. forehand (def. 9). [FOREHAND + -ED[3]] —**fore′hand′ed·ly,** *adv.* —**fore′hand′ed·ness,** *n.*

fore·head (fôr′id, for′-; fôr′hed′, for′-), *n.* 1. the part of the face above the eyes; brow. 2. the fore or front part of anything. [ME *forehe(v)ed,* OE *forhēafod.* See FORE-, HEAD]

fore·hearth (fōr′härth′, fôr′-), *n.* (in a blast furnace or cupola) a reservoir for iron or slag, accessible through a door at hearth level. [FORE- + HEARTH]

for·eign (fôr′in, for′-), *adj.* 1. of, pertaining to, or derived from another country or nation; not native. 2. of or pertaining to contact or dealings with other countries; connected with foreign affairs: *foreign policy.* 3. external to one's own country or nation: *a foreign country.* 4. carried on abroad, or with other countries: *foreign trade.* 5. belonging to or coming from another district, province, etc. 6. located outside a specific district, province, etc. 7. *Law.* outside the legal jurisdiction of a State of the U.S.; alien. 8. belonging to or proceeding from other persons or things: *a statement supported by foreign testimony.* 9. not belonging to the place or body where found: *foreign matter in a watch movement.* 10. not related to or connected with the thing under consideration: *foreign to our discussion.* 11. alien in character; irrelevant or inappropriate; remote. 12. strange or unfamiliar. —*adv.* 13. **go foreign,** *Naut.* a. to ship as a seaman on a vessel trading with a foreign country. b. to go to places outside one's own or its own territorial waters: *a ship going foreign.* 14. **sell foreign,** *Naut.* to sell (a vessel) to foreign owners. [ME *forein* < OF *forain, forein* < VL *forān(us), deriv. of L *forās* outside] —**for′eign·ly,** *adv.* —**for′eign·ness,** *n.*
—**Syn.** 1, 3. alien. 4. international. 10. irrelevant, extraneous, outside.

for′eign affairs′, international relations; activities of a nation arising from its dealings with other nations.

for′eign aid′, government assistance, usually on a large scale, from a great power to a war-devastated or underdeveloped nation, consisting of economic, technical, or military aid, given primarily in the form of monetary or material grants or financial loans, for purposes of relief and rehabilitation, for economic stabilization, or for mutual defense. Also called **aid.** —**for′eign-aid′,** *adj.*

for′eign bill′, a bill of exchange drawn on a payer in one country by a maker in another. Cf. **inland bill.**

for·eign-born (fôr′in bôrn′, for′-), *adj.* born in a country other than that in which one resides.

for′eign correspond′ent, a correspondent, as for a periodical, assigned to send back articles and news dispatches from a foreign country for publication.

for·eign·er (fôr′ə nər, for′-), *n.* 1. a person not native to or naturalized in the country or jurisdiction under consideration; alien. 2. a thing produced in or brought from a foreign country. 3. *Naut.* a foreign vessel. [ME *foreiner.* See FOREIGN, -ER[1]]
—**Syn.** 1. outlander. See **stranger.**

for′eign exchange′, 1. commercial paper drawn on a person or corporation in a foreign nation. 2. the process of balancing accounts in commercial transactions between businessmen of different nations.

for·eign-flag (fôr′in flag′, for′-), *adj.* 1. (of a vessel or aircraft) having a registry under a nationality other than one's own: *rivalry between U.S.-flag freighters and foreign-flag ships.* 2. *U.S.* (esp. of a ship) owned by a national of one country and registered under the maritime laws of another country: *Some foreign-flag vessels are actually owned by American shipping companies.*

for·eign·ism (fôr′ə niz′əm, for′-), *n.* 1. a foreign custom, mannerism, etc. 2. any trait, deviating from accepted speech standards, derived from a foreign language. 3. imitation of anything foreign. 4. a foreign quality. [FOREIGN + -ISM]

for′eign le′gion, 1. a military unit consisting of foreign volunteers in the service of a state. 2. (*caps.*) a former military body in the French army, consisting of men of all nationalities assigned to military operations and duties outside France.

for′eign min′ister, (in countries other than the U.S.) a cabinet minister who conducts and supervises foreign and diplomatic relations with other states. Also, *esp. Brit.,* **foreign secretary.** Cf. **secretary of state** (def. 1). —**for′eign min′istry.**

for′eign mis′sion, 1. mission (def. 6). 2. mission (def. 3).

for′eign of′fice, the department of a government that handles foreign affairs: *the French foreign office.*

for′eign rela′tions, 1. the dealings and relationships between states or nations. 2. the field of foreign affairs: *an expert in foreign relations.* 3. the quality or character of foreign affairs as a consequence of foreign policy: *a deterioration in their foreign relations; improved foreign relations.*

for′eign sec′retary, *Chiefly Brit.* See **foreign minister.**

for′eign serv′ice, (*often cap.*) a division of the U.S. Department of State or of a foreign office that maintains diplomatic and consular posts and personnel in other countries.

fore·judge[1] (fōr juj′, fôr-), *v.t.,* **-judged, -judg·ing.** to judge beforehand; prejudge. [FORE- + JUDGE] —**fore·judg′er,** *n.*

fore·judge[2] (fōr juj′, fôr-), *v.t.,* **-judged, -judg·ing.** forjudge.

fore·know (fōr nō′, fôr-), *v.t.,* **-knew, -known, -know·ing.** to know beforehand. [late ME *foreknowe(n).* See FORE-, KNOW] —**fore·know′a·ble,** *adj.* —**fore·know′er,** *n.* —**fore·know′ing·ly,** *adv.*
—**Syn.** foresee, divine, discern, anticipate.

fore·knowl·edge (fōr′nol′ij, fôr′-, fōr nol′ij, fôr-), *n.* knowledge of a thing before it exists or happens; prescience: *Did you have any foreknowledge of the scheme?* [FORE- + KNOWLEDGE]

for·el (fôr′əl, for′-), *n.* 1. a slipcase for a book. 2. parchment of poor quality, used in its natural color for making book covers. Also, **forrel.** [ME *forel* case, sheath < OF *forrel, fourrel,* dim. of *fuerre* sheath. See FUR]

fore·la·dy (fōr′lā′dē, fôr′-), *n., pl.* **-dies.** a forewoman. [FORE- + LADY]

fore·land (fōr′land′, fôr′-), *n.* 1. a cape, headland, or promontory. 2. land or territory lying in front. [ME *forlonde.* See FORE-, LAND]

fore·leg (fōr′leg′, fôr′-), *n.* one of the front legs of a quadruped, an insect, etc. [late ME *forlegge.* See FORE-, LEG]

fore·limb (fōr′lim′, fôr′-), *n.* a front limb of an animal. [FORE- + LIMB]

fore·lock[1] (fōr′lok′, fôr′-), *n.* 1. the lock of hair that grows from the fore part of the head. 2. (of a horse) a tuft of hair above or on the forehead. See diag. under **horse.** 3. **take time by the forelock.** See **time** (def. 51). [FORE- + LOCK[2]]

fore·lock[2] (fōr′lok′, fôr′-), *n.* 1. a pin or flat wedge passed through a hole near the end of a threadless bolt to fasten parts together. —*v.t.* 2. to fasten by means of a forelock. [FORE- + LOCK[1]]

fore·man (fōr′mən, fôr′-), *n., pl.* **-men.** 1. a man in charge of a particular department, group of workmen, etc., as in a factory or the like. 2. the chairman and spokesman of a jury. [ME *forman* leader. See FORE-, MAN[1]] —**fore′man·ship′,** *n.*

fore·mast (fōr′mast′, -mäst′, fôr′-; *Naut.* fōr′məst, fôr′-), *n.* *Naut.* the mast nearest the bow in all vessels having two or more masts. [FORE- + MAST[1]]

fore·most (fōr′mōst′, -məst, fôr′-), *adj., adv.* first in place, order, rank, etc. [FORE[1] + -MOST; r. ME, OE *formest,* equiv. to *form(a)* first, var. of *fruma* (cf. L *prīmus*) + *-est* -EST]
—**Syn.** primary, prime, chief, principal, paramount.

fore·name (fōr′nām′, fôr′-), *n.* a name that precedes the family name or surname; first name. [FORE- + NAME]

fore·named (fōr′nāmd′, fôr′-), *adj.* named before; mentioned before in the same writing or discourse; aforementioned. [FORE- + NAMED]

fore·noon (*n.* fōr′no͞on′, fôr′-; *adj.* fōr′no͞on′, fôr′-), *n.* 1. the period of daylight before noon. 2. the latter part of the morning. —*adj.* 3. of or pertaining to the forenoon. [FORE- + NOON]

fore′noon watch′, *Naut.* the watch from 8 A.M. until noon.

fo·ren·sic (fə ren′sik), *adj.* 1. pertaining to, connected with, or used in courts of law or public discussion and debate. 2. adapted or suited to argumentation; rhetorical. —*n.* 3. **forensics,** (*construed as sing. or pl.*) the art or study of argumentation and formal debate. [< L *forēns(is)* of, belonging to the forum, public, equiv. to *for(um)* FORUM + *-ēns-* of, belonging to + -IC] —**fo·ren·si·cal·i·ty** (fə ren′si kal′i tē), *n.* —**fo·ren′si·cal·ly,** *adv.*

foren′sic chem′istry, the application of facts concerning chemistry to questions of civil and criminal law. Also called **legal chemistry.**

foren′sic med′icine, the application of medical knowledge to questions of civil and criminal law, esp. in court proceedings. Also called **foren′sic jurispru′dence, legal medicine, medical jurisprudence.**

foren′sic psychi′atry, the use of psychiatric knowledge and techniques in questions of law, as in determining legal insanity.

fore·or·dain (fōr′ôr dān′, fôr′-), *v.t.* 1. to ordain or appoint beforehand. 2. to predestine; predetermine. [late ME *forordein(en).* See FORE-, ORDAIN] —**fore′or·dain′ment,** *n.*

fore·or·di·nate (fōr ôr′dᵊnāt′, fôr-), *v.t.,* **-nat·ed, -nat·ing.** foreordain. [back formation from FOREORDINATION]

fore·or·di·na·tion (fōr′ôr dᵊnā′shən, fôr′-), *n.* 1. previous ordination or appointment. 2. predestination. [FORE- + ORDINATION]

fore·part (fōr′pärt′, fôr′-), *n.* the fore, front, or early part. [ME *forpart.* See FORE-, PART]

fore·passed (fōr past′, -päst′, fôr-), *adj.* already in the past; bygone. Also, **fore·past′.** [FORE- + PASSED]

fore·paw (fōr′pô′, fôr′-), *n.* the paw of a foreleg. [FORE- + PAW]

fore·peak (fōr′pēk′, fôr′-), *n.* *Naut.* the extreme forward part of the interior of a hull (opposed to *afterpeak*). [FORE- + PEAK[1]]

fore′ plane′, *Carpentry.* a plane, intermediate in size between a jack plane and a jointer plane, used for preliminary smoothing.

fore·play (fōr′plā′, fôr′-), *n.* sexual stimulation of a person of the opposite sex, intended as a prelude to sexual intercourse. [FORE- + PLAY]

fore·pleas·ure (fōr′plezh′ər, fôr′-), *n.* the aggregate of pleasurable sensations that lead to a heightened physical or emotional response, as of those aroused in sexual intercourse that lead to an orgasm. [FORE- + PLEASURE]

fore·pole (*n.* fōr′pōl′, fôr′-; *v.* fōr pōl′, fôr-), *n., v.,* **-poled, -pol·ing.** *Mining.* —*n.* 1. Also called **spile, spill.** one of a number of boards or timbers driven forward on top of a set to protect miners lengthening a tunnel from falling debris. —*v.t.* 2. to reinforce (the end of an excavated tunnel) with forepoles. [FORE- + POLE[1]]

fore·quar·ter (fōr′kwôr′tər, fôr′-), *n.* the forward end of half of a carcass, as of beef, lamb, etc. [FORE- + QUARTER]

fore·rake (fōr′rāk′, fôr′-), *n.* *Naut.* a forward rake, as of a stem or mast. [FORE- + RAKE[3]]

fore·reach (fōr rēch′, fôr-), *v.i.* 1. to gain, as one ship on another. 2. to maintain headway, as when coming about or drifting after taking in sail or stopping engines. —*v.t.* 3. to gain upon; overhaul and pass. [FORE- + REACH]

fore·run (fōr run′, fôr-), *v.t.,* **-ran, -run, -run·ning.** 1. to run in front of; come before; precede. 2. to be the precursor or harbinger of; prefigure. 3. to anticipate or foretell. 4. *Archaic.* to forestall. 5. *Obs.* to outrun or outstrip. [OE *forarn* to run on in front. See FORE-, RUN]

fore·run·ner (fōr′run′ər, fôr′-, fōr run′ər, fôr-), *n.* 1. predecessor; ancestor; forebear; precursor. 2. an omen, sign, or symptom of something to follow; portent: *a forerunner of summer.* 3. one who goes or is sent in advance to announce the coming of someone or something that follows; herald; harbinger. 4. **the Forerunner,** John the Baptist. [ME *forrenner.* See FORE-, RUNNER]

fore·sad·dle (fōr′sad′ᵊl, fôr′-), *n.* the forepart of a saddle of veal, mutton, venison, etc. [FORE- + SADDLE]

fore·said (fōr′sed′, fôr′-), *adj.* aforementioned; aforesaid. [ME *forsaid,* OE *foresǣd.* See FORE-, SAID]

fore·sail (fōr′sāl′, fôr′-; *Naut.* fōr′səl, fôr′-), *n.* *Naut.* 1. the lowermost sail on a foremast. See diag. under **ship.** 2. the staysail or jib, set immediately forward of the mainmast of a sloop, cutter, knockabout, yawl, ketch, or dandy. [FORE- + SAIL]

fore·see (fōr sē′, fôr-), *v.,* **-saw, -seen, -see·ing.** —*v.t.* 1. to have prescience of; foreknow. 2. to see beforehand. —*v.i.* 3. to exercise foresight. [ME; OE *foresēon.* See FORE-, SEE[1]] —**fore·see′a·bil′i·ty,** *n.* —**fore·see′a·ble,** *adj.* —**fore·se′er,** *n.*
—**Syn.** 1. divine, discern. See **predict.**

fore·shad·ow (fōr shad′ō, fôr-), *v.t.* to show or indicate beforehand; prefigure. [FORE- + SHADOW] —**fore·shad′ow·er,** *n.*

fore·shank (fōr′shangk′, fôr′-), *n.* 1. shin[1] (def. 2). 2. See under **shank** (def. 4). [FORE- + SHANK]

fore·sheet (fōr′shēt′, fôr′-), *n.* *Naut.* 1. the sheet of a headsail. 2. **foresheets,** (*construed as pl.*) the space, in an open boat, in front of the foremost rower's seat. Also called **headsheet.** [FORE- + SHEET]

fore·shore (fōr′shōr′, fôr′shôr′), *n.* 1. the ground between the water's edge and cultivated land; land along the edge of a body of water. 2. the part of the shore between the high-water mark and low-water mark. [FORE- + SHORE[1]]

fore·short·en (fōr shōr′tᵊn, fôr-), *v.t.* 1. *Fine Arts.* to reduce or distort (those forms of a represented object that are not parallel to the picture plane) in order to convey the illusion of three-dimensional space as perceived by the human eye: often done according to the rules of perspective. 2. to abridge, reduce, or contract; make shorter. [FORE- + SHORTEN]

fore·shots (fōr′shots′, fôr′-), *n.pl.* the weak spirits that come over in the initial phase in distilling whiskey. Cf. **faints.** [FORE- + SHOT[1] + -S[3]]

fore·show (fōr shō′, fôr-), *v.t.,* **-showed, -shown, -show·ing.** to show beforehand; foretell; foreshadow. [ME *forescewe(n),* OE *foresċēawian.* See FORE-, SHOW]

fore·side (fōr′sīd′, fôr′-), *n.* 1. the front side or part. 2. the upper side. 3. *U.S.* a stretch of land along the edge of the sea. [ME; see FORE-, SIDE[1]]

fore·sight (fōr′sīt′, fôr′-), *n.* 1. care or provision for the future; provident care; prudence. 2. the act or power of foreseeing; prevision; prescience. 3. act of looking forward. 4. knowledge or insight gained by or as by looking forward; a view of the future. 5. *Survey.* a. a sight or reading taken on a forward point. b. (in leveling) a rod reading on a point the elevation of which is to be determined. 6. a sight on the muzzle of a gun. [ME *forsight.* See FORE-, SIGHT] —**fore′sight′ed,** *adj.* —**fore′sight′ed·ness,** *n.*
—**Syn.** 1. See **prudence.** 4. foreknowledge.

fore·skin (fōr′skin′, fôr′-), *n.* the prepuce of the penis. [FORE- + SKIN]

fore·sleeve (fōr′slēv′, fôr′-), *n.* 1. the part of the sleeve covering the forearm. 2. a detachable sleeve or part of a sleeve, often having an ornamental function. [ME; see FORE-, SLEEVE]

fore·speak (fōr spēk′, fôr-), *v.t.,* **-spoke** or (*Archaic*) **-spake; -spo·ken** or (*Archaic*) **-spoke; -speak·ing.** 1. to predict; foretell. 2. to speak for, or claim, in advance. [ME *forespeke(n).* See FORE-, SPEAK]

fore·spent (fōr spent′, fôr-), *adj.* *Archaic.* forspent.

for·est (fôr′ist, for′-), *n.* 1. a large tract of land covered with trees and underbrush; extensive wooded area. 2. the trees alone: *to cut down a forest.* 3. *Eng. Law.* a tract of wooded grounds and pastures, generally belonging to the sovereign and set apart for game. 4. a large number of things; a thick cluster. —*v.t.* 5. to cover with trees; convert into a forest. [ME < OF < VL *forest(is)* an unenclosed wood (as opposed to a park), deriv. of L *foris* outside. See FOREIGN] —**for′est·al, fo·res·tial** (fə res′chəl), *adj.* —**for′est·less,** *adj.* —**for′est·like′,** *adj.*
—**Syn.** 1. FOREST, GROVE, WOOD refer to an area covered with trees. A FOREST is an extensive area, preserving some or all of its primitive wildness and usually having game or wild animals in it: *Sherwood Forest; the Black Forest.* A GROVE is a group or cluster of trees, usually not very large in area and cleared of underbrush. It is usually tended or cultivated: *a shady grove; a grove of pines; an orange grove: a walnut grove.* WOODS (A WOOD) is a smaller tract of land than a forest and resembles one, although less wild in character and generally closer to civilization: *lost in the woods; a wood covering several acres.*

For·est (fôr′ist, for′-), *n.* 1. a town in central Mississippi. 3917 (1960). 2. Also, **Forrest.** a boy's given name.

For′est A′cres, a town in central South Carolina. 3842 (1960).

fore·staff (fōr′staf′, -stäf′, fôr′-), *n., pl.* **-staves, -staffs.** cross-staff. [FORE- + STAFF[1]]

CONCISE PRONUNCIATION KEY: act, āble, dâre, ärt; ebb, ēqual; if, īce; hot, ōver, ôrder, oil, bo͝ok, o͞oze, out; up, ûrge; chief; sing; shoe; thin, that; zh as in *measure.* ə = *a* as in *alone, e* as in *system, i* as in *easily, o* as in *gallop, u* as in *circus;* ᵊ as in *button* (butᵊn), *fire* (fīᵊr), *cradle* (krādᵊl). See the full key inside the front cover.

fore·stage (fōr′stāj′, fôr′-), *n.* the part of a stage in front of the proscenium or the closed curtain, as the apron or an extension of it. [FORE- + STAGE]

fore·stall (fōr stôl′, fôr-), *v.t.* **1.** to prevent, hinder, or thwart by action in advance; take measures concerning or dealing with (a thing) in advance. **2.** to deal with, meet, or realize in advance of the natural or proper time; be beforehand with or get ahead of (a person, situation, etc.) in action. **3.** to buy up (goods) in advance, in order to increase the price when resold. **4.** to prevent sales at (a fair, market, etc.) by buying up or diverting goods. [ME *forstalle*, deriv. of OE *foresteall* intervention (to defeat justice), waylaying. See FORE-, STALL[2]] —**fore·stall′er,** *n.* —**fore·stall′ment, fore·stal′ment,** *n.*
—**Syn. 1.** preclude, obviate, intercept, obstruct. **1, 2.** anticipate.

for·est·a·tion (fôr′i stā′shən, for′-), *n.* the planting of forests. [FOREST + -ATION]

fore·stay (fōr′stā′, fôr′-), *n. Naut.* **1.** a stay leading aft and upward from the stem or knightheads of a vessel to the head of the fore lower mast; the lowermost stay of a foremast. **2.** a stay leading aft and upwards toward the mainmast of a sloop, knockabout, cutter, ketch, yawl, or dandy. [ME *forstay*. See FORE-, STAY[3]]

fore·stay·sail (fōr′stā′sāl′, fôr′-; *Naut.* fōr′stā′səl, fôr′-), *n. Naut.* a triangular sail set on a forestay; the innermost headsail of a vessel. See diag. under **ship.** [FORESTAY + SAIL]

For′est Cit′y, 1. a town in SW North Carolina. 6556 (1960). **2.** a town in N Iowa. 2930 (1960). **3.** a town in NE Pennsylvania. 2651 (1960).

for·est·er (fôr′i stər, for′-), *n.* **1.** one who is expert in forestry. **2.** an officer having responsibility for the maintenance of a forest. **3.** *Zool.* an animal of the forest. **4.** a large, gray kangaroo, *Macropus canguru.* **5.** any of several moths of the family *Agaristidae*, typically black with two yellowish or whitish spots on each wing. [ME < OF *forestier.* See FOREST, -ER[2]]

For·est·er (fôr′i stər, for′-), *n.* **C(ecil) S(cott),** 1899–1966, English novelist and journalist.

For′est Grove′, a town in NW Oregon. 5628 (1960).

For′est Heights′, a town in central Maryland. 3524 (1960).

For′est Hill′, a town in N Texas. 3221 (1960).

For′est Hills′, 1. a town in SW Pennsylvania. 8796 (1960). **2.** a residential area in New York City, on W Long Island, in SE New York: international tennis tournaments.

fore·stick (fōr′stik′, fôr′-), *n.* the front log in a wood fire, as in a fireplace. [FORE- + STICK[1]]

For′est Ne′gro, a native African, esp. from the tropical rain forests of West Africa, having Negroid features that are developed to a pronounced degree.

For′est of Dean′, a royal forest in Gloucestershire, in W England. ab. 184 sq. mi.

For′est Park′, a town in NE Illinois; a suburb of Chicago. 14,451 (1960).

for′est reserve′, *U.S.* an area of forest set aside by the government as a reserve.

for·est·ry (fôr′i strē, for′-), *n.* **1.** the science of planting and taking care of forests. **2.** the process of establishing and managing forests; forestation. **3.** forest land. [< MF *foresterie.* See FOREST, -RY]

fore·taste (*n.* fōr′tāst′, fôr′-; *v.* fōr tāst′, fôr-), *n., v.,* **-tast·ed, -tast·ing.** —*n.* **1.** a slight and partial experience, knowledge, or awareness of something to come in the future; anticipation. —*v.t.* **2.** to have some advance experience, knowledge, etc., of (something to come). [ME *fortaste.* See FORE-, TASTE]

fore·tell (fōr tel′, fôr-), *v.,* **-told, -tell·ing.** —*v.t.* **1.** to tell of beforehand; predict or prophesy. **2.** (of things) to foreshadow. —*v.i.* **3.** to utter a prediction or a prophecy. [ME *fortell.* See FORE-, TELL[1]] —**fore·tell′er,** *n.*
—**Syn. 1.** forecast, augur. **2.** foreshow, presage, forebode.

fore·thought (fōr′thôt′, fôr′-), *n.* **1.** thoughtful provision beforehand; provident care; prudence. **2.** a thinking of something beforehand; previous consideration; anticipation. [ME *for-thoght.* See FORE-, THOUGHT[1]]
—**Syn. 1.** See **prudence.**

fore·thought·ful (fōr thôt′fəl, fôr-), *adj.* full of or having forethought; provident. [FORETHOUGHT + -FUL] —**fore·thought′ful·ly,** *adv.* —**fore·thought′ful·ness,** *n.*

fore·time (fōr′tīm′, fôr′-), *n.* former or past time; the past. [FORE- + TIME]

fore·to·ken (*n.* fōr′tō′kən, fôr′-; *v.* fōr tō′kən, fôr-), *n.* **1.** a sign or token of a future event; a forewarning. —*v.t.* **2.** to foreshadow. [ME *fortokne,* OE *foretācn.* See FORE-, TOKEN]

fore·tooth (fōr′tōōth′, fôr′-), *n., pl.* **-teeth.** a tooth in the front of the mouth; incisor. [FORE- + TOOTH]

fore·top (fōr′top′, fôr′-; *for 1 also Naut.* fōr′təp, fôr′-), *n.* **1.** *Naut.* a platform at the head of a fore lower mast. **2.** the forelock of an animal, esp. a horse. **4.** *Obs.* a human forelock, or a lock of hair on the front of a wig. [ME *fortop.* See FORE-, TOP[1]]

fore-top·gal·lant (fōr′top gal′ənt, fôr′-; *Naut.* fōr′tə gal′ənt, fôr′-), *adj. Naut.* noting a sail, yard, rigging, etc., belonging to a fore-topgallant mast.

fore-top·gal′lant mast′, *Naut.* the spar or section of a spar forming the topgallant portion of a foremast.

fore-top·mast (fōr′top′mast′, -mäst′, fôr′-; *Naut.* fōr′top′məst, fôr′-), *n. Naut.* the spar or section of a pole mast serving as the topmast of a foremast.

fore-top·sail (fōr′top′sāl′, fôr′-; *Naut.* fōr′top′səl, fôr′-), *n. Naut.* a topsail set on a foremast.

for·ev·er (fôr ev′ər, fər-), *adv.* **1.** eternally; without ever ending: *to last forever.* **2.** continually; incessantly: *He's forever complaining.* **3. forever and a day,** eternally; always: *They pledged to love forever and a day.* Also, *Literary,* **forever and aye.** [orig. phrase *for ever*]

for·ev·er·more (fôr ev′ər mōr′, -môr′, fər-), *adv.* for ever hereafter. [FOR + EVERMORE]

fore·warn (fōr wôrn′, fôr-), *v.t.* to warn beforehand or in advance. [ME *forwarn(en).* See FORE-, WARN] —**fore·warn′ing·ly,** *adv.*
—**Syn. 1.** caution, admonish.

fore·went (fōr went′, fôr-), *v.* pt. of **forego.**

fore·wing (fōr′wing′, fôr′-), *n.* either of the anterior and usually smaller parts of the wings of an insect having four wings. [FORE- + WING]

fore·wom·an (fōr′wŏŏm′ən, fôr′-), *n., pl.* **-wom·en. 1.** a woman in charge of a particular department, group of workers, etc., as in a factory. **2.** the chairlady and spokesman of a jury. [FORE- + WOMAN]

fore·word (fōr′wûrd′, -wərd, fôr′-), *n.* a preface or introductory statement in a book, magazine article, etc. Cf. **afterword.** [FORE- + WORD]
—**Syn.** See **introduction.**

fore·worn (fōr wōrn′, fôr wôrn′), *adj. Archaic.* forworn.

fore·yard (fōr′yärd′, fôr′-), *n. Naut.* **1.** a yard on the lower mast of a square-rigged foremast, used to support the foresail. **2.** a yard forming the lowest spar of the foremast of a topsail schooner, used to hold out the clews of the topsail or lower topsails. **3.** a yard forming the main lower mast of a ketch or yawl, used to support a square course. [FORE- + YARD[2]]

For·far (fôr′fər, -fär), *n.* **1.** a town in and the county seat of Angus, in E Scotland. 10,252 (1961). **2.** former name of **Angus.**

for·feit (fôr′fit), *n.* **1.** a fine; penalty. **2.** act of forfeiting; forfeiture. **3.** something to which the right is lost as a result of committing a crime or misdeed, neglecting a duty, violating a contract, etc. **4.** an article deposited in a game because of a mistake and redeemable by a fine or penalty. **5. forfeits,** (*construed as sing.*) any game in which such articles are taken from the players. —*v.t.* **6.** to lose as a forfeit. **7.** to lose, or become liable to lose, in consequence of crime, fault, breach of engagement, etc. —*adj.* **8.** lost by forfeiture. [ME *forfet* < OF (ptp. of *forfaire* to commit crime, to lose possession or right through a criminal act) < ML *foris factum* penalty, ptp. of *foris facere* to transgress, equiv. to *foris* outside, wrongly + *facere* to make, do] —**for′feit·a·ble,** *adj.* —**for′feit·er,** *n.*

for·fei·ture (fôr′fi chər), *n.* **1.** act of forfeiting. **2.** that which is forfeited; a fine or mulct. [ME *forfeiture, forfeture* < OF. See FORFEIT, -URE]

for·fend (fôr fend′), *v.t.* **1.** to defend, secure, or protect. **2.** *Archaic.* to fend off, avert, or prevent. Also, **forefend.** [ME *forfend(en).* See FOR-, FEND]

for·fi·cate (fôr′fə kit, -kāt′), *adj.* deeply forked, as the tail of certain birds. [< L *forfic-* (s. of *forfex*) pair of shears (*for(us)* a passage + *-fic-* -FIC) + -ATE[1]]

for·gat (fər gat′), *v. Archaic.* a pt. of **forget.**

for·gath·er (fôr gath′ər), *v.i.* **1.** to gather together; convene; assemble. **2.** to encounter or meet, esp. by accident. **3.** to associate or fraternize (usually fol. by *with*). Also, **foregather.** [FOR- + GATHER]

for·gave (fər gāv′), *v.* pt. of **forgive.**

forge[1] (fōrj, fôrj), *n., v.,* **forged, forg·ing.** —*n.* **1.** the special fireplace, hearth, or furnace in which metal is heated before shaping. **2.** the workshop of a blacksmith; smithy. —*v.t.* **3.** to form by heating and hammering; beat into shape. **4.** to form or make in any way. **5.** to invent (a fictitious story, a lie, etc.). **6.** to imitate (handwriting, a signature, etc.) fraudulently; fabricate by false imitation. —*v.i.* **7.** to commit forgery. **8.** to work at a forge. **9.** (of a horse at a trot) to strike the forefeet with the shoes of the hind feet. [ME *forge(n)* < MF *forg(ier)* < L *fabricāre* to fabricate; see FABRIC] —**forge′a·ble,** *adj.* —**forg′er,** *n.*
—**Syn. 4.** shape, fabricate, manufacture, fashion, mold.

forge[2] (fōrj, fôrj), *v.i.,* **forged, forg·ing.** to move ahead or progress slowly, with difficulty, or by mere momentum (usually fol. by *ahead*): *to forge through dense underbrush; to forge ahead with one's routine work.* [?]

for·ger·y (fōr′jə rē, fôr′-), *n., pl.* **-ger·ies. 1.** *Law.* the false making or alteration of a writing by which the legal rights or obligations of another person are apparently affected; simulated signing of another person's name to any such writing whether or not it is also the forger's name. **2.** the production of a spurious work which is claimed to be genuine, as a coin, a painting, etc. **3.** something, as a coin, a work of art, a writing, etc., produced by forgery. **4.** act of fabricating or producing falsely. **5.** *Archaic.* fictitious invention; deception or artifice. [FORGE[1] + -ERY]

for·get (fər get′), *v.,* **-got** or (*Archaic*) **-gat; -got·ten** or **-got; -get·ting.** —*v.t.* **1.** to cease to remember; fail to remember; be unable to recall. **2.** to omit or neglect unintentionally (usually fol. by an infinitive): *I forgot to shut the window before leaving.* **3.** to leave behind unintentionally; neglect to take: *to forget one's keys.* **4.** to omit mentioning; leave unnoticed. **5.** to fail to think of; take no note of. **6.** to neglect willfully; disregard or slight. —*v.i.* **7.** to cease or omit to think of something. **8. forget oneself,** to say or do something improper or unbefitting one's rank, position, or character. [FOR- + GET; r. ME *foryete(n),* OE *forg(i)etan;* c. OS *fargetan,* OHG *firgezzan*] —**for·get′ta·ble,** *adj.* —**for·get′ter,** *n.*
—**Syn. 3, 4.** overlook.

for·get·ful (fər get′fəl), *adj.* **1.** apt to forget; that forgets: *a forgetful person.* **2.** heedless or neglectful (often fol. by *of*): *to be forgetful of others.* **3.** *Archaic.* causing to forget. [ME; see FORGET, -FUL] —**for·get′ful·ly,** *adv.* —**for·get′ful·ness,** *n.*
—**Syn. 1.** absent-minded.

for·ge·tive (fōr′ji tiv, fôr′-), *adj. Archaic.* inventive; creative. [? b. FORGE[1] and CREATIVE]

for·get-me-not (fər get′mē not′), *n.* **1.** a small, Old World, boraginaceous plant, *Myosotis palustris,* having a light-blue flower commonly regarded as an emblem of constancy and friendship. **2.** any of several other plants of the same genus. **3.** any of various similar plants. [trans. of MF *ne m'oubliez mye*]

for·get·ter·y (fər get′ə rē), *n.* a faculty or facility for forgetting; faulty memory: *a witness with a very convenient forgettery.* [FORGET + -ERY]

forge′ weld′ing, the welding of pieces of hot metal with pressure or blows.

forg·ing (fōr′jing, fôr′-), *n.* something forged; a piece of forged work in metal. [ME; see FORGE[1], -ING[1]]

for·give (fər giv′), *v.,* **-gave, -giv·en, -giv·ing.** —*v.t.* **1.** to grant free pardon for or remission of (an offense, debt, etc.); absolve. **2.** to give up all claim on account of; remit (a debt, obligation, etc.). **3.** to grant free pardon to (a person). **4.** to cease to feel resentment against: *to forgive one's enemies.* —*v.i.* **5.** to pardon an offense or an offender. [FOR- + GIVE; r. ME *foryive(n),* OE *forgiefan*] —**for·giv′a·ble,** *adj.* —**for·giv′er,** *n.*
—**Syn. 1.** See **excuse. 3.** absolve, acquit. —**Ant. 1, 3.** blame.

for·give·ness (fər giv′nis), *n.* **1.** act of forgiving; state of being forgiven. **2.** disposition or willingness to forgive. [ME *forgifenesse,* OE *forgifennys.* See FORGIVE, -NESS]

for·giv·ing (fər giv′ing), *adj.* that forgives; disposed to forgive; indicating forgiveness: *a forgiving soul; a forgiving smile.* [FORGIVE + -ING[2]] —**for·giv′ing·ly,** *adv.* —**for·giv′ing·ness,** *n.*

for·go (fôr gō′), *v.t.,* **-went, -gone, -go·ing. 1.** to abstain or refrain from; do without; give up, renounce, or resign. **2.** *Archaic.* to neglect or overlook. **3.** *Archaic.* to quit or leave. **4.** *Obs.* to go or pass by. Also, **forego.** [ME *forgo(n),* OE *forgān.* See FOR-, GO[1]] —**for·go′er,** *n.*
—**Syn. 1.** forbear, sacrifice, forsake.

for·got (fər got′), *v.* a pt. and pp. of **forget.**

for·got·ten (fər got′ən), *v.* a pp. of **forget.**

for·int (fôr′int), *n.* an aluminum coin and monetary unit of Hungary, equal to 100 fillér and equivalent to about .04 of a U.S. dollar. *Abbr.:* F., Ft. [< Hung < It *fiorino.* See FLORIN]

for·judge (fôr juj′), *v.t.,* **-judged, -judg·ing.** *Law.* to exclude, expel, dispossess or deprive by a judgment. Also, **forejudge.** [ME *forjuge(n)* < OF *forjugie(r),* equiv. to *for-* out + *jugier* to JUDGE] —**for·judg′ment,** *n.*

fork (fôrk), *n.* **1.** an instrument having two or more prongs or tines, for holding, lifting, etc., as any of various agricultural tools or, esp., an implement for handling food at table or in cooking. **2.** something resembling or suggesting this in form. **3.** See **tuning fork. 4.** *Mach.* yoke[1] (def. 6). **5.** a division into branches. **6.** the point or part at which a thing, as a river or a road, divides into branches. **7.** each of the branches into which a thing divides. **8.** *Horol.* (in a lever escapement) the forked end of the lever engaging with the ruby pin. **9.** *Chiefly U.S.* a principal tributary of a river. **10.** *Obs.* the barbed head of an arrow. —*v.t.* **11.** to pierce, raise, pitch, dig, etc., with a fork. **12.** to make into the form of a fork. **13.** *Chess.* to maneuver so as to place (two opponent's pieces) under simultaneous attack by the same piece. —*v.i.* **14.** to divide into branches: *Turn left where the road forks.* **15. fork over** or **out** or **up,** *Informal.* to hand over; deliver; pay: *He was angry at having to fork over so much money for such simple repairs.* [ME *forke,* OE *forca* < L *furca* fork, gallows, yoke] —**fork′less,** *adj.* —**fork′like′,** *adj.*

forked (fôrkt, fôr′kid), *adj.* **1.** having a fork or forklike branches. **2.** zigzag, as lightning. **3.** expressing duality, insincerity, or lies: *He speaks with a forked tongue.* Also, **forky.** [ME; see FORK, -ED[3]] —**fork·ed·ly** (fôr′kid lē), *adv.* —**fork′ed·ness,** *n.*

forked′ chain′, *Chem.* See **branched chain.**

fork′-lift truck′ (fôrk′lift′), an electric vehicle having two parallel horizontal arms for lifting and carrying a loaded pallet.

fork′ lunch′eon, 1. See **déjeuner à la fourchette. 2.** *Brit.* a buffet luncheon.

fork·y (fôr′kē), *adj.,* **fork·i·er, fork·i·est.** forked. [FORK + -Y[1]] —**fork′i·ness,** *n.*

for·la·na (fôr lä′nə; *It.* fôr lä′nä), *n., pl.* **-ne** (-nā; *It.* -ne), **-nas.** an old Italian dance in triple meter, resembling the gigue. Also, **furlana.** [< It, fem. of *forlano, furlano,* var. of *friulano* FRIULIAN]

For·lì (fôr lē′), *n.* a city in N Italy, SE of Bologna. 91,146 (1961).

for·lorn (fôr lôrn′), *adj.* **1.** desolate or dreary; unhappy or miserable, as in feeling, condition, or appearance. **2.** abandoned, deserted, or forsaken (sometimes fol. by *of*). **3.** hopeless; despairing. **4.** bereft; destitute (usually fol. by *of*). [ME *foreloren* (ptp. of *forlesen* to lose completely), OE *forloren* (ptp. of *forlēosan*); c. OHG *firliosan* (G *verlieren*), Goth *fraliusan.* See FOR-, LORN] —**for·lorn′ly,** *adv.* —**for·lorn′ness,** *n.*
—**Syn. 1.** pitiful, pitiable, helpless, woebegone, comfortless. **2.** alone, lost, solitary. See **desolate. 4.** deprived. —**Ant. 1.** happy. **2.** accompanied.

forlorn′ hope′, 1. a vain hope; an undertaking almost certain to fail. **2.** a perilous or desperate enterprise. **3.** *Obs.* a group of soldiers assigned to perform some unusually perilous service. [< D, folk-etymological alter. of *verloren hoop,* lit., lost troop]

form (fôrm), *n.* **1.** external appearance of a clearly defined area, as distinguished from color or material; configuration. **2.** the shape of a thing or person. **3.** a body, esp. that of a human being. **4.** a dummy having the same measurements as a human body, used for fitting or displaying clothing: *a dressmaker's form.* **5.** something that gives or determines shape; a mold. **6.** a particular condition, character, or mode in which something appears: *water in the form of ice; a denunciation in the form of a letter.* **7.** the manner or style of arranging and coordinating parts for a pleasing or effective result, as in literary or musical composition: *a unique form for the novel.* **8.** *Fine Arts.* **a.** the organization, placement, or relationship of basic elements, as lines and colors in a painting or volumes and voids in a sculpture, so as to produce a coherent image; the formal structure of a work of art. **b.** three-dimensional quality or volume, as of a represented object or anatomical part. **c.** an object, person, or part of the human body or the appearance of any of these, esp. as seen in nature: *His work is characterized by the radical distortion of the human form.* **9.** any assemblage of things of a similar kind constituting a component of a group, especially of a zoological group. **10.** *Crystall.* the combination of all the like faces possible on a crystal of given symmetry. **11.** due or proper shape; orderly arrangement of parts; good order. **12.** *Philos.* **a.** the structure, pattern, organization, or essential nature of anything. **b.** structure or pattern as distinguished from matter. **c.** (*cap.*) *Platonism.* idea (def. 7c). **d.** *Aristotelianism.* that which places a thing in its particular species or kind. **13.** *Logic.* the abstract relations of terms in a proposition, and of propositions to one another. **14.** a set, prescribed, or customary order or method of doing something. **15.** a set order of words, as for use in religious ritual or in a legal document: *a form for initiating new members.* **16.** a document with blank spaces to be filled in with particulars before it is executed: *a tax form.* **17.** a typical document to be used as a guide in framing others for like cases: *a form for a deed.* **18.** a conventional method of procedure or behavior: *Most of society's forms are rooted in common sense and mutual consideration.* **19.** a formality or ceremony, often with implication of absence of real meaning: *to go through the outward forms of a religious wedding.* **20.** procedure according to a set order or method. **21.** formality; ceremony; conformity to the usages of society: *the elaborate forms prevalent in the*

courts of Renaissance kings. **22.** procedure or conduct, as judged by social standards: *Such behavior is very bad form. Good form demands that we go.* **23.** manner or method of performing something; technique: *His playing is perceptive but lacks form.* **24.** physical condition or fitness, as for performing: *a tennis player in peak form.* **25.** *Gram.* **a.** a word, part of a word, or group of words forming a construction that recurs in various contexts in a language with relatively constant meaning. **b.** a particular shape of such a form that occurs in more than one shape. In *I'm, 'm* is a form of *am.* **c.** a word with a particular inflectional ending or other modification. *Goes* is a form of *go.* **26.** *Ling.* the shape or pattern of a word or other construction (distinguished from *substance*). **27.** *Building Trades.* temporary boarding or sheeting of plywood or metal for giving a desired shape to poured concrete, rammed earth, etc. **28.** a grade or class of pupils in a British secondary school. **29.** a grade or class in certain U.S. private schools. **30.** *Brit.* a bench or long seat. **31.** Also, *Brit.,* **forme.** *Print.* an assemblage of types, leads, etc., secured in a chase to print from.
—*v.t.* **32.** to construct or frame. **33.** to make or produce. **34.** to serve to make up; serve as; compose; constitute: *The remaining members will form the program committee.* **35.** to place in order; arrange; organize. **36.** to frame (ideas, opinions, etc.) in the mind. **37.** to contract (habits, friendships, etc.). **38.** to give form or shape to; shape; fashion: *He forms the clay and fires it with absolute mastery.* **39.** to give a particular form or shape to; fashion in a particular manner: *She formed the dough into squares.* **40.** to mold by discipline or instructions: *The sergeant's job was to form boys into men.* **41.** *Gram.* to stand in relation to (a particular derivative or other form) by virtue of the absence or presence of an affix or other grammatical element or change. **42.** *Mil.* to draw up in lines or in formation.
—*v.i.* **43.** to take or assume form. **44.** to be formed or produced: *Ice began to form on the window.* **45.** to take a particular form or arrangement: *The ice formed in patches across the window.* [ME *forme* < OF < L *forma* form, figure, model, mold, sort, ML: seat] —**form′a·bil′i·ty,** *n.* —**form′a·ble,** *adj.* —**form′a·bly,** *adv.*
—**Syn. 1.** mold, appearance, cast, cut. FORM, FIGURE, OUTLINE, SHAPE refer to an appearance which can be recognized. FORM, FIGURE, and SHAPE are often used to mean an area clearly defined by contour without regard for other identifying qualities, as color or material. OUTLINE refers to the line that delimits a form, figure, or shape: *the outline of a hill.* SHAPE usually refers to a flat area of definite outline; even when used with reference to the human body it connotes a silhouette of a particular character. In contrast, FORM often includes a sense of mass or volume. FIGURE always refers to a concrete object, but FORM and SHAPE may also be applied to abstractions: *the figure of a man; the form of a cow; the shape or form of the future.* FORM is applied to physical objects, mental images, methods of procedure, etc.; it is a more inclusive term than either SHAPE or FIGURE: *the form of a cross, of a ceremony, of a poem.* **4.** model, pattern, jig. **9.** sort, kind, order, type. **14.** ceremony, ritual, formula, formality, rule, convention. **16.** blank. **19, 20.** system, mode, practice, formula. **32.** model, fabricate, mold, forge, cast, outline. **33.** create. **35.** systematize, dispose. **40.** teach, educate, train. —**Ant. 1.** substance.

-form, a suffix of Latin origin meaning "having the form of": *cruciform.* [< L *-formis*]

for·mal[1] (fôr′məl), *adj.* **1.** being in accordance with the usual requirements, customs, etc.; conventional: *to pay one's formal respects.* **2.** marked by form or ceremony: *a formal occasion.* **3.** observant of conventional requirements of behavior, procedure, etc., as persons; ceremonious. **4.** excessively ceremonious: *a manner that was formal and austere.* **5.** being a matter of form only; perfunctory: *We expected more than just formal courtesy.* **6.** made or done in accordance with procedures that ensure validity: *a formal authorization.* **7.** of, pertaining to, or emphasizing the organization or composition of the constituent elements in a work of art perceived separately from its subject matter: *a formal approach to painting; the formal structure of a poem.* **8.** being in accordance with prescribed or customary forms: *a formal siege.* **9.** *Theat.* (of a stage setting) generalized and simplified in design, esp. of architectural elements, and serving as a permanent set for a play irrespective of changes in location. **10.** acquired in school; academic: *He had little formal training in sociology.* **11.** extremely symmetrical: *a formal garden.* **12.** of, reflecting, or noting a usage of language in which syntax, pronunciation, etc., adhere to traditional standards of correctness and usage is characterized by the absence of casual, contracted, and colloquial forms: *The paper was written in formal English. Modern writers tend to eschew an overly formal prose style.* **13.** *Philos.* **a.** pertaining to form. **b.** *Aristotelianism.* not material; essential. **14.** pertaining to the form, shape, or mode of a thing, esp. as distinguished from the substance: *formal writing, bereft of all personality.* **15.** being such merely in appearance or name; nominal: *a formal head of the government having no actual powers.* **16.** *Math.* **a.** (of a proof) in strict logical form with a justification for every step. **b.** (of a calculation) correct in form; made with strict justification for every step. —*n.* **17.** a social event, as a dance or ball, that requires evening dress. **18.** See **evening dress.** —*adv.* **19.** *Informal.* in formal attire: *We're supposed to go formal.* [ME *formal, formel* < L *formāl(is).* See FORM, -AL[1]] —**for′mal·ness,** *n.*
—**Syn. 2.** FORMAL, ACADEMIC, CONVENTIONAL may have either favorable or unfavorable implications. FORMAL may mean in proper form, or may imply excessive emphasis on empty form. In the favorable sense, ACADEMIC applies to scholars or higher institutions of learning; it may, however imply slavish conformance to mere rules, or to belief in impractical theories. CONVENTIONAL, in a favorable sense, applies to desirable conformity with accepted conventions or customs; but it more often is applied to arbitrary, forced, or meaningless conformity. **3.** conforming, conformist, conventional. **4.** stiff, prim, punctilious. **6.** official.

for·mal[2] (fôr′mal), *n.* *Chem.* methylal. [from FORMALDEHYDE]

for′mal cause′ (fôr′məl), *Aristotelianism.* See under **cause** (def. 8b). [ME]

form·al·de·hyde (fôr mal′də hīd′, fər-), *n.* *Chem.* a colorless, toxic, water-soluble gas, HCHO, having a suffocating odor, usually derived from methyl alcohol by oxidation; used chiefly in aqueous solution, as a disinfectant and preservative, and in the manufacture of various resins and plastics. Also called **methanal.** Cf. **formalin.** [FORM(IC) + ALDEHYDE; modeled on G *Formaldehyd*]

for·ma·lin (fôr′mə lin), *n.* *Chem.* a clear, colorless, aqueous solution of 40 percent formaldehyde. Also called **formol.** [formerly trademark]

for·mal·ise (fôr′mə līz′), *v.t., v.i.,* **-ised, -is·ing.** *Chiefly Brit.* formalize. —**for′mal·i·sa′tion,** *n.* —**for′mal·is′er,** *n.*

for·mal·ism (fôr′mə liz′əm), *n.* **1.** strict adherence to, or observance of, prescribed or traditional forms. **2.** *Relig.* excessive attachment to external forms and observances. **3.** *Ethics.* the doctrine that acts are in themselves right or wrong regardless of consequences. [FORMAL[1] + -ISM] —**for′mal·ist,** *n.* —**for′mal·is′tic,** *adj.*

for·mal·i·ty (fôr mal′i tē), *n., pl.* **-ties. 1.** condition or quality of being formal; accordance with required or traditional rules, procedures, etc.; conventionality. **2.** rigorously methodical character. **3.** excessive adherence to established rules, procedures, etc.; rigidity. **4.** observance of form or ceremony. **5.** marked or excessive ceremoniousness. **6.** an established order or method of proceeding: *the formalities of judicial process.* **7.** a formal act or observance. **8.** something done merely for form's sake; a requirement of custom or etiquette: *the formality of a thank-you note.* [< L *formālitās.* See FORMAL[1], -ITY]
—**Syn. 7.** rite, ritual, ceremony.

for·mal·ize (fôr′mə līz′), *v.,* **-ized, -iz·ing.** —*v.t.* **1.** to make formal, esp. for the sake of official or authorized acceptance: *to formalize an understanding by drawing up a legal contract.* **2.** to give a definite form or shape to. **3.** to state or restate (the rules or implied rules of a grammar or the like) in symbolic form. —*v.i.* **4.** to be formal; act with formality: *She doesn't formalize when she's among friends.* Also, *esp. Brit.,* **formalise.** [FORMAL[1] + -IZE] —**for′mal·i·za′tion,** *n.* —**for′mal·iz′er,** *n.*

for′mal log′ic, the branch of logic concerned exclusively with the principles of deductive reasoning and with the form rather than the content of propositions.

for·mal·ly (fôr′mə lē), *adv.* **1.** in a formal manner: *The store was formally opened on Tuesday.* **2.** as regards form; in form: *It may be formally correct, but it is substantively wrong.* [FORMAL[1] + -LY]

for·mant (fôr′mənt), *n.* **1.** *Music.* the range and number of partials present in a tone of a specific instrument, representing its timbre. **2.** *Acoustic Phonetics.* one of the regions of concentration of energy, prominent on a sound spectrogram, which collectively constitute the frequency spectrum of a speech sound. The relative positioning of the first and second formants, whether periodic or aperiodic, as of the *o* of *hope* at approximately 500 and 900 cycles per second, is usually sufficient to distinguish a sound from all others. [< L *formant-* (s. of *formāns*), prp. of *formāre* to FORM; see -ANT]

for·mat (fôr′mat), *n., v.,* **-mat·ed** or **-mat·ted, -mat·ing** or **-mat·ting.** —*n.* **1.** the shape and size of a book as determined by the number of times the original sheet has been folded to form the leaves. Cf. **duodecimo, folio** (def. 2), **octavo, quarto. 2.** the general physical appearance of a book, magazine, or newspaper, such as the type face, binding, quality of paper, margins, etc. **3.** the organization, plan, style, or type of something: *They tailored their script to a half-hour format. The format of the show allowed for topical and controversial gags.* **4.** *Computer Technol.* the organization or disposition of symbols on a magnetic tape, punch card, or the like, in accordance with the input requirements of a computer, card-sort machine, etc. —*v.t.* **5.** *Computer Technol.* to adapt (the organization or disposition of coded information) on a magnetic tape, punch card, or the like, to conform to the input requirements of a computer, card-sort machine, etc. [< F < L (*liber*) *formāt(us)* (a book) formed (in a certain way)]

for·mate (fôr′māt), *n.* *Chem.* a salt or ester of formic acid. [FORM(IC) + -ATE[2]]

for·ma·tion (fôr mā′shən), *n.* **1.** act or process of forming; state of being formed. **2.** the manner in which a thing is formed; disposition of parts; formal structure or arrangement. **3.** *Mil.* **a.** a particular disposition of troops, as in columns, squares, etc. **b.** any required assembling of the soldiers of a unit. **4.** something formed: *the formation of rust on metal.* **5.** *Geol.* **a.** a body of rocks classed as a unit for geologic mapping. **b.** the process of depositing rock or mineral of a particular composition or origin. [ME *formacioun* < L *formātiōn-* (s. of *formātiō*), equiv. to *formāt(us)* (see FORM, -ATE[1]) + *-iōn-* -ION] —**for·ma′tion·al,** *adj.*

form·a·tive (fôr′mə tiv), *adj.* **1.** giving form or shape; forming; shaping; fashioning; molding: *a formative process in manufacturing.* **2.** pertaining to formation or development: *a child's most formative years.* **3.** *Biol.* **a.** capable of developing new cells or tissue by cell division and differentiation: *formative tissue.* **b.** concerned with the formation of an embryo, organ, or the like. **4.** *Gram.* pertaining to a formative. —*n.* **5.** *Gram.* a derivational affix, particularly one that determines the part of speech of the derived word, as *-ness,* in *loudness, hardness,* etc. [< MF *formatif.* See FORMATION, -IVE] —**form′a·tive·ly,** *adv.* —**form′a·tive·ness,** *n.*

form′ative el′ement, *Gram.* **1.** a morpheme that serves as an affix, not as a base, or root, in word formation. **2.** any noninflectional morpheme, whether base or affix.

form·board (fôrm′bōrd′, -bôrd′), *n.* a board or slab serving as a form for poured concrete. [FORM + BOARD]

form′ class′, *Gram.* a class of words or forms in a given language that have one or more grammatical features in common, as, in Latin, all masculine nouns in the nominative singular, all masculine singular nouns, all masculine nouns, or all nouns.

form′ drag′, *Physics.* the portion of the resisting force encountered by a body moving through a fluid that is due to the irregularity of shape of the body, reducible to a minimum by streamlining.

forme (fôrm), *n.* *Brit.* form (def. 31). [< F]

for·mée (fôr mā′), *adj.* paty. [< F, fem. ptp. of *former* to FORM]

for·mer[1] (fôr′mər), *adj.* **1.** preceding in time; prior or earlier: *during a former stage in the proceedings.* **2.** past, long past, or ancient: *in former times.* **3.** preceding in order; being the first of two: *Our former process was too costly.* **4.** being the first mentioned of two (distinguished from *latter*): *The former suggestion was preferred to the latter.* **5.** having once, or previously, been; erstwhile: *a former president.* [ME, equiv. to *forme* (OE *forma* first) + *-er* -ER[4] Cf. FOREMOST]
—**Syn. 3.** foregoing, antecedent. **5.** past, ex-.

form·er[2] (fôr′mər), *n.* one who or that which forms or serves to form. [ME *fourmer.* See FORM, -ER[1]]

for·mer·et (fôr′mə ret′), *n.* *Archit.* (in a ribbed vault) a rib along a wall or within an arcade. [< F, deriv. of *forme* FORM]

for·mer·ly (fôr′mər lē), *adv.* **1.** in time past; in an earlier period or age; previously: *a custom formerly observed.* **2.** *Obs.* in time just past; just now. [FORMER[1] + -LY]

form·fit·ting (fôrm′fit′ing), *adj.* designed to fit snugly around a given shape; close-fitting: *a formfitting blouse.* [FORM + FITTING]

form′ ge′nus, *Biol.* an artificial taxonomic category including species grouped together on the basis of morphological resemblance.

for·mic (fôr′mik), *adj.* **1.** of or pertaining to ants. **2.** *Chem.* of or derived from formic acid. [irreg. < L *formīca* ant. Cf. F *formique*]

For·mi·ca (fôr mī′kə), *n.* *Trademark.* a thermosetting plastic, usually used in transparent or printed sheets as a chemical-proof and heat-proof covering for furniture, wall-panels, etc.

for′mic ac′id, *Chem., Pharm.* a colorless, irritating, fuming, water-soluble liquid, HCOOH, originally obtained from ants, now manufactured synthetically; used in dyeing and tanning and in medicine chiefly as a counterirritant and astringent.

for′mic al′dehyde, *Chem.* formaldehyde.

for·mi·car·i·um (fôr′mə kâr′ē əm), *n., pl.* **-car·i·a** (-kâr′ē ə). formicary.

for·mi·car·y (fôr′mə ker′ē), *n., pl.* **-car·ies.** an ant nest. [< ML *formīcāri(um)* ant hill, n. use of neut. of **formīcāri(us)* of, pertaining to ants. See FORMIC, -ARY]

for·mi·da·ble (fôr′mi də bəl), *adj.* **1.** feared or dreaded, esp. in encounters or dealings: *a formidable opponent in business.* **2.** of discouraging or awesome strength, size, difficulty, etc.; intimidating: *a formidable precipice blocking the way.* **3.** arousing feelings of awe or admiration because of grandeur; vastly superior; great; exceptional: *He has a formidable knowledge of history.* **4.** of great strength; forceful; powerful: *formidable opposition to the proposal.* [< F < L *formīdābil(is)* causing fear, equiv. to *formīd-* (s. of *formīdāre* to fear) + *-ābilis* -ABLE] —**for′mi·da·ble·ness, for′mi·da·bil′i·ty,** *n.* —**for′mi·da·bly,** *adv.*
—**Syn. 1.** dreadful, appalling, threatening, menacing, fearful, terrible, frightful, horrible. —**Ant. 1.** pleasant.

form·less (fôrm′lis), *adj.* lacking a definite or regular form or shape; shapeless. [FORM + -LESS] —**form′less·ly,** *adv.* —**form′less·ness,** *n.*

form′ let′ter, a letter, usually printed or typed, which can be sent to any number of readers, occasionally personalized by inserting the name and address of each recipient in the salutation.

form′ mas′ter, the teacher in charge of a grade of pupils, esp. in the British school system.

form′ nail′. See **scaffold nail.**

for·mol (fôr′mōl, -mōl), *n.* *Chem.* formalin. [formerly trademark]

For·mo·sa (fôr mō′sə), *n.* Taiwan.

Formo′sa Strait′, an arm of the Pacific between China and Taiwan, connecting the East and South China seas. Also called **Taiwan Strait.**

For·mo·sus (fôr mō′səs), *n.* A.D. c816–896, Italian ecclesiastic: pope 891–896.

form′ spe′cies, *Biol.* one of the species comprising a form genus.

form′ stop′, (in poured-concrete construction) a board placed across a form to retain concrete until it sets.

for·mu·la (fôr′myə lə), *n., pl.* **-las, -lae** (-lē′), *adj.* —*n.* **1.** a set form of words, as for stating or declaring something definitely or authoritatively, for indicating procedure to be followed, or for prescribed use on some ceremonial occasion. **2.** any fixed or conventional method for doing something: *His mystery stories were written according to the current formula for such bits of fiction.* **3.** *Math.* a rule or principle frequently expressed in algebraic symbols. **4.** *Chem.* an expression of the constituents of a compound by symbols and figures. Cf. **empirical formula, molecular formula, structural formula. 5.** a recipe or prescription: *a new formula for currant wine.* **6.** a lukewarm mixture of milk and other ingredients, usually sugar and water, in prescribed proportions for feeding a baby. **7.** a formal statement of religious doctrine. —*adj.* **8.** made or executed according to a formula; formulaic; formulary: *a formula painting; formula literature; a formula vow.* [< L: small pattern, form, rule, method. See FORM, -ULE]

for·mu·la·ic (fôr′myə lā′ik), *adj.* **1.** made according to a formula; composed of formulas: *a formulaic plot.* **2.** being or constituting a formula: *formulaic instructions.* [FORMULA + -IC] —**for′mu·la′i·cal·ly,** *adv.*

for·mu·lar·ise (fôr′myə lə rīz′), *v.t.,* **-ised, -is·ing.** *Chiefly Brit.* formularize. —**for′mu·lar·i·sa′tion,** *n.* —**for′mu·lar·is′er,** *n.*

for·mu·lar·ize (fôr′myə lə rīz′), *v.t.,* **-ized, -iz·ing.** formulate. [FORMULAR(Y) + -IZE] —**for′mu·lar·i·za′tion,** *n.* —**for′mu·lar·iz′er,** *n.*

for·mu·lar·y (fôr′myə ler′ē), *n., pl.* **-lar·ies,** *adj.* —*n.* **1.** a collection or system of formulas. **2.** a set form of words; formula. **3.** *Pharm.* a book listing pharmaceutical substances and formulas for making medicinal preparations. **4.** *Eccles.* a book containing prescribed forms used in the service of a church. —*adj.* **5.** of or pertaining to a formula or formulas: *the formulary aspect of a science.* **6.** of the nature of a formula: *He dispenses easy, formulary solutions to our problems.* [< LL *formulāri(us).* See FORMULA, -ARY]

for·mu·late (fôr′myə lāt′), *v.t.,* **-lat·ed, -lat·ing. 1.** to express in precise form; state definitely or systematically: *He finds it extremely difficult to formulate his new theory.* **2.** to devise or develop, as a method, system, etc. **3.** to reduce to or express in a formula. [FORMUL(A)

+ -ATE[1]] —**for/mu·la·ble** (fôr/myə lə bəl), *adj.* —**for/-mu·la/tion,** *n.* —**for/mu·la/tor,** *n.*

for·mu·lise (fôr/myə līz/), *v.t.,* **-lised, -lis·ing.** *Chiefly Brit.* formulize. —**for/mu·li·sa/tion,** *n.* —**for/mu-lis/er,** *n.*

for·mu·lism (fôr/myə liz/əm), *n.* **1.** adherence to or reliance on formulas: *the trite formulism of his ideas.* **2.** a system of formulas. [FORMUL(A) + -ISM] —**for/-mu·list,** *n.* —**for/mu·lis/tic,** *adj.*

for·mu·lize (fôr/myə līz/), *v.t.,* **-lized, -liz·ing.** formulate. Also, *esp. Brit.,* **formulise.** [FORMUL(A) + -IZE] —**for/mu·li·za/tion,** *n.* —**for/mu·liz/er,** *n.*

form·work (fôrm/wûrk/), *n.* the assemblage of boards, bolts, etc., composing a form for poured-concrete or rammed-earth construction. [FORM + WORK]

for·myl (fôr/mil), *adj. Chem.* containing the formyl group. [FORM(IC) + -YL]

for·myl·ate (fôr/mə lāt/), *v.t.,* **-at·ed, -at·ing.** *Chem.* to introduce the formyl group into (an organic compound). [FORMYL + -ATE[1]] —**for/myl·a/tion,** *n.*

for/myl group/, *Chem., Biochem.* the univalent group, O=CH–, derived from formic acid. Also, **for/myl rad/ical.**

For·na·ca·li·a (fôr/nə kā/lē ə, -kāl/yə), *n.* (*sometimes construed as pl.*) an ancient Roman corn festival in honor of Fornax, held in February on specific days for the curiae. Cf. **Feast of Fools** (def. 1).

For·nax (fôr/naks), *n., gen.* **For·nac·is** (fôr nas/is, -nā/-sis). **1.** the Furnace, a small southern constellation south of Cetus and Eridanus. **2.** the ancient Roman goddess of baking in whose honor the Fornacalia was held. [< L: lit., furnace, kiln, oven]

for·nent (fər nent/), *Dial.* —*prep.* **1.** in front of; opposite to; facing. —*adj.* **2.** opposite; facing. **3.** *Chiefly Dial.* up against; close to: *the fence is fornent the house.* Also, **for·ninst** (fər ninst/, -ninst/), **for·nenst** (fər nenst/, -nenst/). [FORE[1] + (A)NENT]

For·ney (fôr/nē, fôr/-), *n., pl.* **-neys.** a steam locomotive having no front truck, four driving wheels, and a four-wheeled rear truck. [named after J. H. *Forney* (1829–1902), American engineer]

for·ni·cate[1] (fôr/nə kāt/), *v.i.,* **-cat·ed, -cat·ing.** to commit fornication. [< LL *fornicāt(us)* (ptp. of *fornicārī*), equiv. to L *fornic-* (s. of *fornix*) arch, vault, basement, brothel + *-ātus* -ATE[1]] —**for/ni·ca/tor,** *n.*

for·ni·cate[2] (fôr/nə kit, -kāt/), *adj. Biol.* arched or vaulted in form. Also, **for/ni·cat/ed.** [< L *fornicāt(us)*, equiv. to *fornic-* (see FORNICATE[1]) + *-ātus* -ATE[1]]

for·ni·ca·tion (fôr/nə kā/shən), *n.* **1.** voluntary sexual intercourse between two unmarried persons or two persons not married to each other. **2.** *Bible.* **a.** adultery. **b.** idolatry. [ME *fornicacioun* < LL *fornicātiōn-* (s. of *fornicātiō*). See FORNICATE[1], -ION] —**for·ni·ca·to·ry** (fôr/nə kə tôr/ē, -tōr/ē), *adj.*

for·ni·ca·trix (fôr/nə kā/triks), *n., pl.* **-ca·tri·ces** (-kə trī/sēz). a woman who commits fornication. [< LL; fem. of FORNICATOR; see -TRIX]

for·nic·i·form (fôr nis/ə fôrm/), *adj.* having the form of a vault. [< L *fornic-* (s. of *fornix*) vault + -I- + -FORM]

for·nix (fôr/niks), *n., pl.* **-ni·ces** (-ni sēz/). *Anat.* any of various arched or vaulted structures, as an arching fibrous formation in the brain. [< L: vault, arch] —**for/ni·cal,** *adj.*

for·rel (fôr/əl, for/-), *n.* forel.

For·rest (fôr/ist, for/-), *n.* **1. Edwin,** 1806–72, U.S. actor. **2. John, 1st Baron,** 1847–1918, Australian explorer and statesman. **3. Nathan Bedford,** 1821–77, Confederate cavalry general in the U.S. Civil War. **4.** Also, **Forest.** a boy's given name.

For·res·tal (fôr/ist[ə]l, for/-), *n.* **James Vincent,** 1892–1949, U.S. financier, Secretary of Defense 1947–49.

for·rit (fôʀ/it, foʀ/-) *adj., adv. Scot.* forward.

for·sake (fôr sāk/), *v.t.,* **-sook, -sak·en, -sak·ing.** **1.** to quit or leave entirely; desert: *He has forsaken his country for an uninhabited island.* **2.** to give up or renounce (a habit, way of life, etc.): *to forsake his wicked ways.* [ME *forsake(n)* (to) deny, reject, OE *forsacan,* equiv. to *for-* FOR- + *sacan* to dispute] —**for·sak/er,** *n.*
—**Syn. 1.** See **desert**[2]. **2.** forswear, relinquish, forgo, drop.

for·sak·en (fôr sā/kən), *v.* **1.** pp. of **forsake.** —*adj.* **2.** deserted; abandoned; forlorn: *an old, forsaken farmhouse on the edge of the desert.* —**for·sak/en·ly,** *adv.* —**for·sak/en·ness,** *n.*

For·se·ti (fôr/se tē/), *n. Scand. Myth.* the god of justice, the son of Balder and Nanna. Also, **For·se·te** (fôr/se-tā/).

for·sook (fôr sŏŏk/), *v.* a pt. of **forsake.**

for·sooth (fôr sōōth/), *adv. Archaic.* (now used in derision or to express disbelief) in truth; in fact; indeed. [ME *forsothe,* OE *forsōth.* See FOR, SOOTH]

for·spent (fôr spent/), *adj. Archaic.* worn out, as from exertion; having one's energy completely spent; exhausted. Also, **forespent.** [ptp. of ME *forspend(en),* OE *forspendan.* See FOR-, SPEND]

Forss·man (fôrs/män, -mən, fôrs/-; *Ger.* fôʀs/män), *n.* **Wer·ner** (*Ger.* veʀ/nəʀ), born 1904, German surgeon: Nobel prize 1956.

For·ster (fôr/stər), *n.* **E(dward) M(organ),** born 1879, English novelist.

for·ster·ite (fôr/stə rīt/), *n. Mineral.* the magnesium end member, Mg_2SiO_4, of the olivine group. [named after J. R. *Forster* (1729–98), German naturalist; see -ITE[1]]

Forst/ner bit/ (fôrst/nər), *Carpentry.* a bit for drilling blind holes, guided from the rim rather than from the center to permit it to enter the wood at an oblique angle. Also, **Foerstner bit.**

for·swear (fôr swâr/), *v.,* **-swore, -sworn, -swear·ing.** —*v.t.* **1.** to reject or renounce upon oath or with protestations: *to forswear an injurious habit.* **2.** to deny vehemently or upon oath: *He forswore his own son at the trial.* **3.** to perjure (oneself): *He didn't seem to realize he was forswearing himself.* —*v.i.* **4.** to swear falsely; commit perjury. [ME *forswere(n),* OE *forswerian.* See FOR-, SWEAR] —**for·swear/er,** *n.*
—**Syn. 1.** abjure, relinquish, forgo, forsake, abandon.

for·sworn (fôr swōrn/, -swôrn/), *v.* **1.** pp. of **forswear.** —*adj.* **2.** perjured. —**for·sworn/ness,** *n.*

For/syte Sa/ga, The (fôr/sīt), a series of novels by John Galsworthy, including *The Man of Property, In Chancery, To Let,* and two shorter works, *Indian Summer of a Forsyte* and *Awakening.*

For·syth (fôr sīth/, fər-, fôr/sīth), *n.* a town in central Georgia. 3697 (1960).

for·syth·i·a (fôr sith/ē ə, -sī/thē ə, fər-), *n.* any oleaceous shrub of the genus *Forsythia,* native to China and southeastern Europe, species of which are much cultivated for their showy yellow flowers, appearing in early spring before the leaves. [named after William *Forsyth* (1737–1804), English horticulturist; see -IA]

fort (fōrt, fôrt), *n.* **1.** a strong or fortified place occupied by troops and usually surrounded by walls, ditches, and other defensive works; a fortress; fortification. **2.** (in North America) a trading post. **3. hold the fort, a.** to defend one's position against attack or criticism. **b.** to maintain the existing state of affairs. [< MF, n. use of adj. *fort* strong < L *fort(is)*]

fort., **1.** fortification. **2.** fortified.

For·ta·le·za (fôr/t[ə]lā/zə; *Port.* fôʀ/tə le/zə), *n.* a seaport in NE Brazil. 470,778 (1960). Also called **Ceará.**

for·ta·lice (fôr/t[ə]lis), *n.* **1.** a small fort; an outwork. **2.** *Obs.* a fortress. [ME < ML *fortalitia, fortalitium,* deriv. of L *fortis* strong. See FORTRESS]

For·tas (fôr/təs), *n.* **Abe,** born 1910, U.S. lawyer, government official, and jurist: associate justice of the U.S. Supreme Court since 1965.

Fort/ At/kinson, a town in S Wisconsin. 7908 (1960).

Fort/ Boi/se, a fort formerly near Boise, in SW Idaho: an important post on the Oregon Trail.

Fort/ Bragg/, a town in NW California. 4433 (1960).

Fort/ Cas/per, a fort in central Wyoming, near Casper: an important post on the Oregon Trail.

Fort-Dau·phin (fôrt/dō/fin, fôrt/-; *Fr.* fôʀ dō faɴ/), *n.* a seaport in SE Madagascar. 11,847 (1960).

Fort/ Dear/born, a former U.S. fort on the site of Chicago, 1803–37.

Fort-de-France (fôʀ də fʀäɴs/), *n.* a seaport in and the capital of Martinique, in the French West Indies. 60,648 (1954).

Fort/ Dodge/, a city in central Iowa, on the Des Moines River. 28,399 (1960).

Fort/ Don/elson, a Confederate fort in NW Tennessee, on the Cumberland River: captured by Union forces in 1862.

Fort/ Duquesne/, a French fort that stood on the site of Pittsburgh, Pennsylvania: captured in 1758 by the British in the French and Indian War.

forte[1] (fōrt, fôrt), *n.* **1.** a strong point, as of a person; that in which one excels: *I don't know what her forte is, but it's not cooking.* **2.** the stronger part of a sword blade, between the middle and the hilt (opposed to *foible*). [earlier *fort* < MF. See FORT]

for·te[2] (fôr/tā; *It.* fôʀ/te), *Music.* —*adj.* **1.** (a direction) loud; with force (opposed to *piano*). —*adv.* **2.** (a direction) loudly. —*n.* **3.** a passage that is loud and forcible, or is intended to be so. [< It < L *fortis* strong]

Fort/ Ed/ward, a town in E New York. 3737 (1960).

for·te-pi·a·no (fôr/tā pē ä/nō; *It.* fôʀ/te pyä/nô), *adj., adv. Music.* loud and immediately soft.

for·tes for·tu·na ju·vat (fôʀ/tes fôʀ tōō/nä yōō/-wät; *Eng.* fôr/tēz fôr tōō/nə jōō/vat, -tyōō/-), *Latin.* fortune favors the brave.

Fort/ Fair/field, a town in NE Maine. 3082 (1960).

forth (fôrth, fōrth), *adv.* **1.** forward; onward or outward in place or space: *to come forth; step forth; go forth.* **2.** onward in time, in order, or in a series: *from that day forth.* **3.** out, as from concealment or inaction; into view or consideration: *The author's true point comes forth midway through the book.* **4.** away, as from a place or country; abroad: *to journey forth.* —*prep.* **5.** *Archaic.* out of; forth from. [ME, OE; c. G *fort;* akin to FURTHER]

Forth (fōrth, fôrth), *n.* **Firth of,** an arm of the North Sea, in SE Scotland: the estuary of the Forth River. 48 mi. long.

forth·com·ing (fōrth/kum/ing, fôrth/-), *adj.* **1.** coming forth, or about to come forth; about to appear; approaching in time: *a poster about the forthcoming election.* **2.** ready or available when required or expected: *He assured us that payment in full would be forthcoming.* —*n.* **3.** a coming forth; appearance. [FORTH + COMING] —**forth/com/ing·ness,** *n.*

Fort/ Hen/ry, a Confederate fort in NW Tennessee, on the Tennessee River: captured by Union forces in 1862.

For the Time/ Be/ing, (*A Christmas Oratorio*) a work in verse (1944) by W. H. Auden.

forth·right (*adj., n.* fōrth/rīt/, fôrth/-; *adv.* fōrth/rīt/, fôrth/-, fōrth/rīt/, fôrth/rīt/), *adj.* **1.** going straight to the point; outspoken: *It's sometimes difficult to be forthright and not give offense.* **2.** proceeding in a straight course; direct; straightforward: *a forthright glance.* —*adv.* Also, **forth/right/ly.** **3.** straight or directly forward; in a direct or straightforward manner: *He sent the arrow forthright toward the target. He told us forthright just what his objections were.* **4.** straightway; at once; immediately: *He saw forthright that such an action was folly.* —*n.* **5.** *Archaic.* a straight course or path. [ME; OE *forthrihte.* See FORTH, RIGHT] —**forth/right/ness,** *n.*

forth·with (fōrth/with/, -with/, fôrth/-), *adv.* immediately; at once; without delay: *Any member guilty of such conduct will be suspended forthwith.* [ME; see FORTH, WITH]

for·ti·eth (fôr/tē ith), *adj.* **1.** next after the thirty-ninth; being the ordinal number for 40. **2.** being one of 40 equal parts. —*n.* **3.** a fortieth part, esp. of one (1/40). **4.** the fortieth member of a series. [ME *fourtithe,* OE *fēowertigotha.* See FORTY, -ETH]

for·ti·fi·ca·tion (fôr/tə fə kā/shən), *n.* **1.** act of fortifying or strengthening. **2.** that which fortifies or protects. **3.** art or science of constructing defensive military works. **4.** Often, **fortifications.** military works constructed for the purpose of strengthening a position; a fort: *Supposedly impregnable, the fortifications were quickly overrun.* **5.** strengthening, as by the addition of or by intensification with another ingredient: *the fortification of wine with alcohol.* [late ME < LL *fortificātiōn-* (s. of *fortificātiō*), equiv. to *fortificāt(us)* fortified (see FORTIFY, -ATE[1]) + *-iōn-* -ION]
—**Syn. 4.** fortress, citadel, stronghold, bulwark, fastness.

fortifica/tion ag/ate, an agate, used as a gem, having polygonal banding such that it suggests the plan of a bastion.

for/tified wine/, a wine, as port, sherry, or the like, to which brandy has been added in order to arrest fermentation or to increase the alcoholic content to between 16 and 23 percent.

for·ti·fy (fôr/tə fī/), *v.,* **-fied, -fy·ing.** —*v.t.* **1.** to strengthen against attack; surround with defenses; provide with defensive military works; protect with fortifications. **2.** to furnish with a means of resisting force or standing strain, wear, etc.: *to fortify cotton with nylon.* **3.** to make strong; impart strength or vigor to, as the body: *to fortify oneself against fatigue or illness.* **4.** to increase the effectiveness of (something), as by additional ingredients: *to fortify a diet with vitamins; to fortify a lotion with lanolin.* **5.** to strengthen mentally or morally: *to be fortified by self-confidence.* **6.** to confirm or corroborate: *He marshaled the facts to fortify his accusation.* **7.** to add alcohol to (wines or the like). —*v.i.* **8.** to set up defensive works; erect fortifications. [ME *fortifie(n)* < MF *fortifie(r)* < LL *fortificāre,* equiv. to L *forti(s)* strong + *-ficāre* -FY] —**for/ti·fi/a·ble,** *adj.* —**for/ti·fi/er,** *n.* —**for/ti·fy/ing·ly,** *adv.*

For/tin barom/eter (fôr/tan; *Fr.* fôʀ taɴ/), an adjustable cistern barometer, the most common of those employing mercury. [named after J. *Fortin* (1750–1831), French physicist who invented it]

for·tis (fôr/tis), *adj., n., pl.* **-tes** (-tēz). *Phonet.* —*adj.* **1.** pronounced with considerable muscular tension and breath pressure, resulting in a strong fricative or explosive sound. In stressed position (*p, t, k, ch, f, th, s, sh*) and sometimes (*h*) are fortis as compared with (*b, d, g, j, v, th, z,* and *zh*) which are lenis. Cf. **lenis.** —*n.* **2.** a fortis consonant. [< L: strong, powerful, firm]

for·tis·si·mo (fôr tis/ə mō/; *It.* fôʀ tēs/sē mô/), *Music.* —*adj.* **1.** (a direction) very loud. —*adv.* **2.** (a direction) very loudly. [< It; superl. of FORTE[2]]

for·ti·tude (fôr/ti tōōd/, -tyōōd/), *n.* patient courage under affliction, privation, or temptation; moral strength or endurance: *Never once did her fortitude waver during that long illness.* [< L *fortitūdō* strength, firmness, courage, equiv. to *forti(s)* strong + *-tūdō* -TUDE]
—**Syn.** See **patience.**

for·ti·tu·di·nous (fôr/ti tōōd/[ə]nəs, -tyōōd/-), *adj.* having fortitude; marked by bravery or courage. [< L *fortitūdin-* (s. of *fortitūdō*) FORTITUDE + -OUS]

Fort/ Jef/ferson, a national monument in Dry Tortugas, Florida: a federal prison 1863–73; now a marine museum.

Fort/ Kear/ney, a former fort in S Nebraska, near Kearney: an important post on the Oregon Trail.

Fort/ Kent/, a town in N Maine. 2787 (1960).

Fort/ Knox/, a military reservation in N Kentucky, SSW of Louisville: location of U.S. federal gold depository since 1936.

Fort-La·my (*Fr.* fôʀ lᴀ mē/), *n.* a city in and the capital of Chad, in the SW part. 30,600 (est. 1955).

Fort/ Lar/amie, a former U.S. fort in SE Wyoming: important post on the Oregon Trail.

Fort/ Lau/der·dale (lô/dər dāl/), a city in SE Florida: seashore resort. 83,648 (1960).

Fort/ Lee/, a city in NE New Jersey. 21,815 (1960).

Fort/ Mad/ison, a city in SE Iowa, on the Mississippi. 15,247 (1960).

Fort/ McHen/ry, a fort in N Maryland, at the entrance to Baltimore harbor: during its bombardment by the British in 1814, Francis Scott Key wrote *The Star-Spangled Banner.*

Fort/ Meade/, a town in central Florida. 4014 (1960).

Fort/ Meigs/, a former fort in NW Ohio: unsuccessfully attacked by the British in 1813.

Fort/ Mill/, a town in N South Carolina. 3315 (1960).

Fort/ Mims/, a stockade in SW Alabama, near the junction of the Alabama and Tombigbee rivers: Indian massacre, 1813.

Fort/ Monroe/, a fort at the entrance to Hampton Roads, in SE Virginia.

Fort/ Mor/gan, a town in NE Colorado. 7379 (1960).

Fort/ Moul/trie (mōōl/trē), a fort in the harbor of Charleston, South Carolina: played an important role in the bombardment of Fort Sumter and in Confederate defense during the Civil War.

Fort/ My/ers, a city on the W coast of Florida. 22,523 (1960).

fort·night (fôrt/nīt/, -nit), *n.* the space of fourteen nights and days; two weeks. [ME *fourtenight,* contr. of OE *fēowertēne niht.* See FOURTEEN, NIGHT]

fort·night·ly (fôrt/nīt/lē), *adj., adv., n., pl.* **-lies.** —*adj.* **1.** occurring or appearing once a fortnight. —*adv.* **2.** once a fortnight. —*n.* **3.** a periodical issued every two weeks. [FORTNIGHT + -LY]

Fort/ Or/ange, a former Dutch fort on the site of Albany, New York.

Fort/ Payne/, a town in NE Alabama. 7029 (1960).

Fort/ Peck/ (pek), a dam on the Missouri River in NE Montana.

Fort/ Pick/ens, a fort in NW Florida, at the entrance to Pensacola Bay: occupied by Union forces throughout the Civil War.

Fort/ Pierce/, a city on the E coast of Florida. 25,256 (1960).

Fort/ Pierre/ (pēr), a town in central South Dakota. 2649 (1960).

Fort/ Plain/, a town in central New York. 2809 (1960).

Fort/ Pulas/ki, a fort in E Georgia, at the mouth of the Savannah River: captured by Union forces in 1862; now a national monument.

FORTRAN (fôr/tran), *n. Computer Technol.* a coding system using mathematical notation for programming scientific problems to be solved by a computer. [*for(mula) tran(slation)*]

for·tress (fôr/tris), *n.* **1.** a large fortified place; a fort or group of forts, often including a town. **2.** any place of security. —*v.t.* **3.** to furnish with or defend by a fortress: *They fortressed the town against the anticipated flood.* [ME *forteresse* < OF. See FORT, -ESS]

Fort′ Scott′, a town in SE Kansas. 9410 (1960).

Fort′ Smith′, a city in W Arkansas, on the Arkansas River. 52,991 (1960).

Fort′ Stock′ton (stok′tən), a town in W Texas. 6373 (1960).

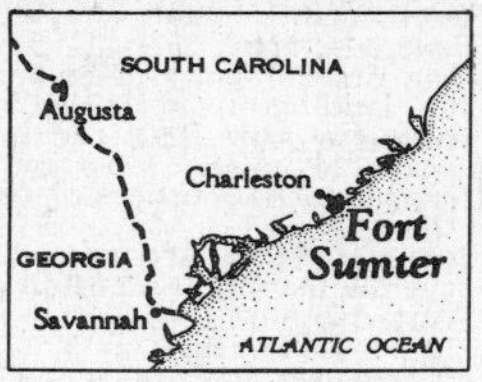

Fort′ Sum′ter, a fort in SE South Carolina, in the harbor of Charleston: its bombardment by the Confederates opened the Civil War on April 12, 1861.

for·tu·i·tism (fôr to͞o′i tiz′əm, -tyo͞o′-), *n.* *Philos.* the doctrine or belief that adaptations in nature come about by chance, not by design. [FORTUIT(OUS) + -ISM] —**for·tu′i·tist,** *n., adj.*

for·tu·i·tous (fôr to͞o′i təs, -tyo͞o′-), *adj.* **1.** happening or produced by chance; accidental: *a fortuitous encounter.* **2.** lucky; fortunate: *a series of fortuitous circumstances that advanced her career.* [< L *fortuit(us),* irreg. deriv. of *forte* by chance (abl. of *fors* chance) + -OUS] —**for·tu′i·tous·ly,** *adv.* —**for·tu′i·tous·ness,** *n.*
—**Syn. 1.** incidental. See **accidental.** —**Ant. 1.** intentional.

for·tu·i·ty (fôr to͞o′i tē, -tyo͞o′-), *n., pl.* **-ties. 1.** state or fact of being fortuitous; fortuitous character. **2.** accident or chance. **3.** an accidental occurrence. [FORTUIT(OUS) + -Y³]

For·tu·na (fôr to͞o′nə, -tyo͞o′-), *n.* **1.** the ancient Roman goddess of Fortune, identified with the Greek goddess Tyche. **2.** a town in NW California. 3523 (1960). **3.** a girl's given name.

for·tu·nate (fôr′chə nit), *adj.* **1.** having good fortune; receiving good from uncertain or unexpected sources; lucky. **2.** bringing or indicating good fortune; resulting favorably; auspicious: *fortunate circumstances.* [ME *fortunat* < L *fortūnāt(us)* made prosperous or happy (ptp. of *fortūnāre*). See FORTUNE, -ATE¹] —**for′tu·nate·ly,** *adv.* —**for′tu·nate·ness,** *n.*
—**Syn. 1.** advantageous, successful, prosperous. FORTUNATE, HAPPY, LUCKY refer to persons who enjoy, or events which produce, good fortune. FORTUNATE implies that the success is obtained by the operation of favorable circumstances more than by direct effort; it is usually applied to grave or large matters (esp. those happening in the ordinary course of things): *fortunate in one's choice of a wife; a fortunate investment.* HAPPY emphasizes a pleasant ending or something which happens by chance at just the right moment: *By a happy accident I received the package on time.* LUCKY, a more colloquial word, is applied to situations of minor import that turn out well by chance: *lucky at cards; my lucky day.* **2.** propitious, favorable.

for·tune (fôr′chən), *n., v.,* **-tuned, -tun·ing.** —*n.* **1.** position in life as determined by wealth: *to make one's fortune; a man of fortune.* **2.** amount or stock of wealth: *to lose one's fortune in bad investments.* **3.** great wealth; ample stock of wealth: *to be worth a fortune.* **4.** chance; luck. **5.** Often, **fortunes.** that which happens or is to happen to a person in his life or in some particular incident. **6.** lot; destiny: *whatever my fortune may be.* **7.** (*cap.*) chance personified, commonly regarded as a goddess distributing arbitrarily or capriciously the lots of life: *Perhaps Dame Fortune will smile on our venture.* **8.** good luck; success; prosperity: *a family blessed by fortune.* **9.** *Archaic.* a woman of wealth; an heiress. **10. tell someone's fortune,** to profess to inform someone of future events in his own life; foretell. —*v.t.* **11.** *Archaic.* to endow (someone or something) with a fortune. —*v.i.* **12.** *Archaic.* to chance or happen; come by chance. [ME < OF < L *fortūna* chance, luck, fortune, deriv. of *fort-* (s. of *fors*) chance] —**for′tune·less,** *adj.*

For·tune (fôr′chən), *n.* a girl's given name.

for′tune cook′y, a thin wafer folded several times, containing a fortune, maxim, or the like, printed on a slip of paper: often served as a dessert in Chinese restaurants.

for′tune hunt′er, a person who hopes to gain wealth, esp. through marriage. —**for′tune-hunt′ing,** *adj., n.*

for·tune·tell·er (fôr′chən tel′ər), *n.* a person who professes to predict the future. [FORTUNE + TELLER¹]

for·tune·tell·ing (fôr′chən tel′ing), *n.* the act or practice of predicting the future. [FORTUNE + TELL + -ING¹]

Fort′ Val′ley, a town in central Georgia. 8310 (1960).

Fort′ Wayne′, a city in NE Indiana. 161,776 (1960).

Fort′ Wil′liam, a port in S Ontario, in S Canada, on Lake Superior. 45,214 (1961).

Fort′ Worth′, a city in N Texas. 385,141.

for·ty (fôr′tē), *n., pl.* **-ties,** *adj.* —*n.* **1.** a cardinal number, ten times four. **2.** a symbol for this number, as 40 or XL or XXXX. **3.** a set of this many persons or things. **4. forties,** the numbers 40 through 49, esp. the 40th through the 49th years of a lifetime or of a given or implied century. —*adj.* **5.** amounting to 40 in number. [ME *fourti,* OE *fēowertig* (c. OFris *fiuwertich,* OHG *fiorzug,* G *vierzig*). See FOUR, -TY¹]

For′ty Days′ of Mu′sa Dagh′, The (mo͞o′sä däg′), a novel (1933) by Franz Werfel.

for·ty-eight (fôr′tē āt′), *n.* **1.** a cardinal number, 40 plus 8. **2.** a symbol for this number, as 48 or XLVIII. **3.** a set of this many persons or things. —*adj.* **4.** amounting to 48 in number.

for·ty-eighth (fôr′tē ātth′), *adj.* **1.** next after the forty-seventh; being the ordinal number for 48. **2.** being one of 48 equal parts. —*n.* **3.** a forty-eighth part, esp. of one (1/48). **4.** the forty-eighth member of a series.

Forty-Eight, The, the 48 preludes and fugues contained in J. S. Bach's *Well-Tempered Clavier.*

for·ty-eight·mo (fôr′tē āt′mō), *n., pl.* **-mos** for 2, *adj.* —*n.* **1.** a book size of about 2½ × 4 inches, determined by printing on sheets folded to form 48 leaves or 96 pages. *Abbr.:* 48mo, 48° **2.** a book of this size. —*adj.* **3.** in forty-eightmo.

for·ty-fifth (fôr′tē fifth′), *adj.* **1.** next after the forty-fourth; being the ordinal number for 45. **2.** being one of 45 equal parts. —*n.* **3.** a forty-fifth part, esp. of one (1/45). **4.** the forty-fifth member of a series.

for·ty-first (fôr′tē fûrst′), *adj.* **1.** next after the fortieth; being the ordinal number for 41. **2.** being one of 41 equal parts. —*n.* **3.** a forty-first part, esp. of one (1/41). **4.** the forty-first member of a series.

for·ty-five (fôr′tē fīv′), *n.* **1.** a cardinal number, 40 plus 5. **2.** a symbol for this number, as 45 or XLV. **3.** a set of this many persons or things. —*adj.* **4.** amounting to 45 in number.

For′ty Fort′, a town in central Pennsylvania. 6431 (1960).

for·ty-four (fôr′tē fôr′, -fōr′), *n.* **1.** a cardinal number, 40 plus 4. **2.** a symbol for this number, as 44 or XLIV. **3.** a set of this many persons or things. —*adj.* **4.** amounting to 44 in number.

for·ty-fourth (fôr′tē fôrth′, -fōrth′), *adj.* **1.** next after the forty-third; being the ordinal number for 44. **2.** being one of 44 equal parts. —*n.* **3.** a forty-fourth part, esp. of one (1/44). **4.** the forty-fourth member of a series.

for·ty·ish (fôr′tē ish), *adj.* **1.** approaching or around the age of 40 years. **2.** around the number 40 or a quantity of 40. [FORTY + -ISH¹]

for·ty-nine (fôr′tē nīn′), *n.* **1.** a cardinal number, 40 plus 9. **2.** a symbol for this number, as 49 or XLIX. **3.** a set of this many persons or things. —*adj.* **4.** amounting to 49 in number.

for·ty-nin·er (fôr′tē nī′nər), *n.* a person who went to California in 1849 during the gold rush.

for·ty-ninth (fôr′tē nīnth′), *adj.* **1.** next after the forty-eighth; being the ordinal number for 49. **2.** being one of 49 equal parts. —*n.* **3.** a forty-ninth part, esp. of one (1/49). **4.** the forty-ninth member of a series.

for·ty-one (fôr′tē wun′), *n.* **1.** a cardinal number, 40 plus 1. **2.** a symbol for this number, as 41 or XLI. **3.** a set of this many persons or things. —*adj.* **4.** amounting to 41 in number.

for·ty·pen·ny (fôr′tē pen′ē), *adj.* noting a nail five inches long. *Abbr.:* 40d [FORTY + -PENNY]

for·ty-sec·ond (fôr′tē sek′ənd), *adj.* **1.** next after the forty-first; being the ordinal number for 42. **2.** being one of 42 equal parts. —*n.* **3.** a forty-second part, esp. of one (1/42). **4.** the forty-second member of a series.

42nd Parallel, The, a novel (1930) by John Dos Passos. Cf. **U.S.A.** (def. 4).

for·ty-sev·en (fôr′tē sev′ən), *n.* **1.** a cardinal number, 40 plus 7. **2.** a symbol for this number, as 47 or XLVII. **3.** a set of this many persons or things. —*adj.* **4.** amounting to 47 in number.

for·ty-sev·enth (fôr′tē sev′ənth), *adj.* **1.** next after the forty-sixth; being the ordinal number for 47. **2.** being one of 47 equal parts. —*n.* **3.** a forty-seventh part, esp. of one (1/47). **4.** the forty-seventh member of a series.

for·ty-six (fôr′tē siks′), *n.* **1.** a cardinal number, 40 plus 6. **2.** a symbol for this number, as 46 or XLVI. **3.** a set of this many persons or things. —*adj.* **4.** amounting to 46 in number.

for·ty-sixth (fôr′tē siksth′), *adj.* **1.** next after the forty-fifth; being the ordinal number for 46. **2.** being one of 46 equal parts. —*n.* **3.** a forty-sixth part, esp. of one (1/46). **4.** the forty-sixth member of a series.

For′ty Thieves′, The, one of the tales of the *Arabian Nights' Entertainments,* often called *Ali Baba and the Forty Thieves.* Cf. **Ali Baba.**

for·ty-third (fôr′tē thûrd′), *adj.* **1.** next after the forty-second; being the ordinal number for 43. **2.** being one of 43 equal parts. —*n.* **3.** a forty-third part, esp. of one (1/43). **4.** the forty-third member of a series.

for·ty-three (fôr′tē thrē′), *n.* **1.** a cardinal number, 40 plus 3. **2.** a symbol for this number, as 43 or XLIII. **3.** a set of this many persons or things. —*adj.* **4.** amounting to 43 in number.

for·ty-two (fôr′tē to͞o′), *n.* **1.** a cardinal number, 40 plus 2. **2.** a symbol for this number, as 42 or XLII. **3.** a set of this many persons or things. —*adj.* **4.** amounting to 42 in number.

for′ty winks′, *Informal.* a short nap: *to take forty winks.*

fo·rum (fôr′əm, fōr′əm), *n., pl.* **fo·rums, fo·ra** (fôr′ə, fōr′ə). **1.** the market place or public square of an ancient Roman city, the center of judicial and business affairs and a place of assembly for the people. **2.** a court or tribunal: *the forum of public opinion.* **3.** an assembly for the discussion of questions of public interest. **4. the Forum,** the forum in the ancient city of Rome. [< L: an outside space, market place, public place, akin to *foris, foras* outside, *foris, fores* door]

for·ward (fôr′wərd), *adv.* Also, **forwards. 1.** toward or at a place, point, or time in advance; onward; ahead: *to move forward; from this day forward; to look forward.* **2.** toward the front: *Let's move forward so we can hear better.* **3.** out; forth; into view or consideration: *to come forward; to bring forward.* **4.** toward the bow or front of a vessel or aircraft. —*adj.* **5.** directed toward a point in advance; moving ahead; onward: *a forward motion.* **6.** being in a condition of advancement; well-advanced: *It was quite forward in the season when we finished our planting.* **7.** ready, prompt, or eager. **8.** presumptuous, impertinent, or excessively bold: *a rude, forward child that has never been punished.* **9.** situated in the front or forepart: *the forward part of the ship.* **10.** lying ahead or to the front: *Take the forward path.* **11.** of or pertaining to the future: *forward buying.* **12.** radical or extreme, as persons or opinions: *the forward trend in certain liberal thought.* —*n.* **13.** *Sports.* **a.** a player stationed in advance of others on his team. **b.** *Football.* a lineman. **c.** *Basketball.* either of two players stationed in the forecourt. —*v.t.* **14.** to send forward; transmit, esp. to a new address: *to forward a letter.* **15.** to advance or help onward; hasten; promote: *The training will help to forward your career.* **16.** *Bookbinding.* to prepare (a book) for the finisher. Cf. **forwarding** (def. 1). [ME; OE *for(e)weard.* See FORE¹, -WARD] —**for′ward·ly,** *adv.*
—**Syn. 1.** FORWARD, ONWARD both indicate a direction toward the front or a movement in a frontward direction. FORWARD applies to any movement toward what is or is conceived to be the front or a goal: *to face forward; to move forward in the aisles.* ONWARD applies to any movement in continuance of a course: *to march onward toward a goal.* **7.** willing, earnest, zealous. **8.** assuming, impudent. See **bold. 11.** early, preliminary, future, premature. **12.** unconventional, progressive. **15.** further, foster. —**Ant. 5.** backward.

for′ward deliv′ery, *Com.* delivery at a future date.

for·ward·er (fôr′wər dər), *n.* **1.** a person who forwards or sends forward. **2.** See **freight forwarder.** [FORWARD + -ER¹]

for′ward exchange′, a foreign bill purchased at a stipulated price and payable at a future date.

for·ward·ing (fôr′wər ding), *n.* **1.** *Bookbinding.* a stage in which sections of a book are stitched, fitted with a back, pasted, etc., before being placed in the completed cover. **2.** *Engraving.* the process of starting a copper plate by etching and of finishing with a graver. [FORWARD + -ING¹]

for′warding a′gent. See **freight forwarder.**

for·ward-look·ing (fôr′wərd lo͝ok′ing), *adj.* planned in view of the future; not limited by present considerations; progressive.

for·ward·ness (fôr′wərd nis), *n.* **1.** overreadiness to push oneself forward; presumption; boldness; lack of due modesty: *His forwardness makes him insufferable.* **2.** cheerful readiness; promptness; eagerness: *We appreciate your forwardness in helping the committee.* **3.** condition of being forward or in advance. [FORWARD + -NESS]

for′ward pass′, *Football.* a pass in which the ball is thrown toward the opponent's goal.

for′ward quota′tion, *Com.* the price quoted on a forward delivery.

for·wards (fôr′wərdz), *adv.* forward. [FORWARD + -S¹]

for·went (fôr went′), *v.* pt. of **forgo.**

For Whom′ the Bell′ Tolls′, a novel (1940) by Ernest Hemingway.

for·why (fôr hwī′, -wī′), *Archaic.* —*adv.* **1.** why; wherefore. —*conj.* **2.** because. [ME; OE *for hwī.* See FOR, WHY]

for·worn (fôr wôrn′, -wōrn′), *adj. Archaic.* worn-out; exhausted. Also, **foreworn.** [ptp. of obs. *forwear,* ME *forwere(n).* See FOR-, WEAR]

for·zan·do (fôrt sän′dō; *It.* fôr tsän′dô), *adj., adv. Music.* sforzando.

F.O.S., 1. free on station. **2.** free on steamer. Also, **f.o.s.**

Fos·dick (foz′dik), *n.* **Henry Emerson,** born 1878, U.S. preacher and author.

Fosh·an (fush′än′), *n.* Nanhai.

Foss (fos), *n.* **Lu·kas** (lo͞o′kəs), born 1922, U.S. pianist, conductor, and composer; born in Germany.

fos·sa (fos′ə), *n., pl.* **fos·sae** (fos′ē). *Anat.* a pit, cavity, or depression as in a bone. [< L: ditch, trench, fosse, short for *fossa (terra)* dug or dug out (earth), n. use of fem. of *fossus,* ptp. of *fodere* to dig]

fos·sar·i·an (fo sâr′ē ən, fō-), *n.* fossor. [< LL *fossāri(us)* (see FOSSA, -ARY) + -AN]

fosse (fos, fôs), *n.* **1.** a moat or defensive ditch in a fortification, usually filled with water. **2.** any ditch, trench, or canal. Also, **foss.** [ME < MF < L *fossa* FOSSA]

fos·sette (fo set′, fô-), *n.* **1.** a small hollow or depression, as in a bivalve shell; a dimple. **2.** *Pathol.* a small, deep corneal ulcer. [< F: dimple, small cavity. See FOSSE, -ETTE]

fos·sick (fos′ik), *Australian.* —*v.i.* **1.** *Mining.* to undermine another's digging; search for waste gold in relinquished workings, washing places, etc. **2.** to search for any object by which to make gain: *to fossick for clients.* —*v.t.* **3.** to hunt; seek; ferret out. [cf. dial. *fossick* troublesome person, *fussick* to bustle about, appar. FUSS + *-ick,* var. of -OCK] —**fos′sick·er,** *n.*

fos·sil (fos′əl), *n.* **1.** any remains, impression, or trace of an animal or plant of a former geological age, as a skeleton, footprint, etc. **2.** *Informal.* an outdated or old-fashioned person or thing. **3.** *Obs.* anything dug out of the earth. —*adj.* **4.** of the nature of a fossil: *fossil insects.* **5.** dug out of the earth; obtained by digging: *fossil fuel.* **6.** belonging to a past epoch or discarded system; fossilized; antiquated: *a fossil approach to teaching.* [< L *fossil(is)* dug up (cf. *fodere* to dig); r. earlier *fossile* < F] —**fos′sil·like′,** *adj.*

fos′sil gum′, any gum, found chiefly in the earth, that was yielded by a now fossilized tree.

fos·sil·if·er·ous (fos′ə lif′ər əs), *adj.* bearing or containing fossils, as rocks or strata. [FOSSIL + -I- + -FEROUS]

fos·sil·ise (fos′ə līz′), *v.t., v.i.,* **-ised, -is·ing.** *Chiefly Brit.* fossilize. —**fos′sil·is′a·ble,** *adj.* —**fos′sil·i·sa′tion,** *n.*

fos·sil·ize (fos′ə līz′), *v.,* **-ized, -iz·ing.** —*v.t.* **1.** *Geol.* to convert into a fossil; replace organic substances with mineral in the remains of an organism. **2.** to change as if into mere lifeless remains or traces of the past. **3.** to make rigidly antiquated, as persons, ideas, etc.: *Time has fossilized such methods.* —*v.i.* **4.** to become a fossil: *The plant fossilized in comparatively recent geological time.* [FOSSIL + -IZE] —**fos′sil·iz′a·ble,** *adj.* —**fos′sil·i·za′tion,** *n.*

fos′sil tur′quoise. See **bone turquoise.**

fos·sor (fos′ər), *n.* (in the early Christian church) a minor clergyman employed as a gravedigger. Also called **fossarian.** [< L: digger (LL: gravedigger)]

fos·so·ri·al (fo sôr′ē əl, -sōr′-), *adj. Zool.* **1.** digging or burrowing. **2.** adapted for digging, as the hands, feet, and skeleton of moles, armadillos, and aardvarks. [< LL *fossōri(us)* adapted to digging (equiv. to L *fossor* (see FOSSOR) + *-ius* adj. suffix) + -AL¹]

fos·su·la (fos′yə lə), *n., pl.* **-lae** (-lē′). *Anat.* a small fossa. [< L: a little ditch. See FOSSA, -ULE]

fos·ter (fô′stər, fos′tər), *v.t.* **1.** to promote the growth or development of; further; encourage: *to foster community development.* **2.** to bring up or rear, as a foster child. **3.** to care for or cherish. **4.** *Brit.* to place (a child) in a foster home. **5.** *Obs.* to feed or nourish. —*n.* **6.** *Obs.* See **foster parent.** [ME; OE *fōstor* nourishment, *fōstrian* to nourish; c. OIcel *fōstr;* akin to FOOD] —**fos′ter·er,** *n.* —**fos′ter·ing·ly,** *adv.*
—**Syn. 1.** favor, forward, advance; foment, instigate. **2.** nurse, nourish, sustain, support, maintain. **3.** See **cherish.** —**Ant. 1.** discourage.

Fos·ter (fô′stər, fos′tər), *n.* **1. Stephen (Collins),** 1826–64, U.S. song writer. **2. William Z(eb·u·lon)** (zeb′yə lən), 1881–1961, U.S. labor organizer: leader in the Communist party. **3.** a boy's given name.

fos·ter·age (fô′stər ij, fos′tər-), *n.* **1.** act of fostering or rearing another's child as one's own. **2.** condition of being a foster child. **3.** act of promoting or encouraging: *The board will undertake the fosterage of our new project.* [FOSTER + -AGE]

fos′ter broth′er, a boy brought up with another child of different parents. [OE *fōster brōthor*]

fos′ter care′, supervision of foster children, as orphans or delinquents, in a public institution or private home.

fos′ter child′, a child raised by someone not its own mother or father. [ME *fostercild*]

fos′ter daugh′ter, a girl raised like one's own daughter, though not such by birth.

fos′ter fa′ther, one who takes the place of a father in raising a child. [ME *forster fader*, OE *fōsterfæder*]

fos′ter home′, a household in which a child is raised by someone other than its own mother or father.

fos·ter·ling (fô′stər ling, fos′tər-), *n.* See **foster child.** [ME *fosterling*, OE *fōstorling*. See FOSTER, -LING[1]]

fos′ter moth′er, **1.** a woman who takes the place of the mother in raising a child. **2.** a nurse. [ME *foster moder*, OE *fōstormōdor*]

fos′ter par′ent, a foster father or foster mother.

fos′ter sis′ter, a girl brought up with another child of different parents.

fos′ter son′, a boy raised like one's own son, though not such by birth. [late ME *foster sone*]

Fos·to·ri·a (fô stōr′ē ə, -stôr′-, fo-), *n.* a city in N Ohio. 15,732 (1960).

fos·tress (fô′stris, fos′tris), *n.* a woman who fosters. [FOST(E)R(ER) + -ESS]

foth·er (foth′ər), *Naut. Archaic.* —*v.t.* **1.** to fill (a sail, tarpaulin, etc.) with oakum, old rope yarns, etc., and place over a leak in a ship's hull. —*v.i.* **2.** to stop a leak in a hull in this way. —*n.* **3.** the material used. Also, **fodder.** [? < LG *fodern* to line, deriv. of *föder* lining, c. G (*Unter-*) *futter* lining]

Foth·er·in·ghay (foth′ə ring gā′), *n.* a village in NE Northamptonshire, in E England, near Peterborough: Mary, Queen of Scots, imprisoned here and executed 1587.

fou (fo͞o), *adj. Scot.* drunk. [ME (Scot) *fow* FULL]

Fou·cault (fo͞o kō′ *for 1;* fo͞o′kôlt *for 2*), *n.* **1. Jean Ber·nard Lé·on** (zhäN ber nar′ lā ôN′). 1819–68, French physicist. **2.** a crater in the second quadrant of the face of the moon: about 10 miles in diameter.

Fou′cault pen′dulum, *Astron.* a pendulum that demonstrates the rotation of the earth by exhibiting an apparent change in its plane of oscillation. [named after J.B.L. FOUCAULT]

Fouc·quet (*Fr.* fo͞o ke′), *n.* Fouquet.

fou·droy·ant (fo͞o droi′ənt; *Fr.* fo͞o drwa yäN′), *adj.* **1.** striking as with lightning; sudden and overwhelming in effect; stunning; dazzling. **2.** *Pathol.* (of disease) beginning in a sudden and severe form. [< F, prp. of *foudroyer* to strike with lightning, deriv. of *foudre* lightning < L *fulgur*]

fouet·té (fwe tā′), *n., pl.* **-tés** (-tāz′; *Fr.* -tā′). *Ballet.* a whipping movement of the free leg, often executed during a turn. [< F, ptp. of *fouetter* to whip]

fought (fôt), *v.* pt. and pp. of **fight.**

fought·en (fôt′ən), *adj. Archaic.* that has been the scene of fighting: *a foughten field.* [archaic ptp. of FIGHT]

Fou·ji·ta (fo͞o′jē tä′), *n.* **Tsu·gou·ha·ru** (tso͞o′go͞o-hä′ro͞o), born 1886, Japanese painter, living in France.

foul (foul), *adj.* **1.** grossly offensive to the senses; disgustingly loathsome; noisome: *a foul smell.* **2.** charged with or characterized by offensive or noisome matter: *foul air; foul stagnant water.* **3.** filthy or dirty, as places, receptacles, clothes, etc. **4.** muddy, as a road. **5.** clogged or obstructed with foreign matter: *a foul gas jet.* **6.** unfavorable or stormy: *foul weather.* **7.** contrary, violent, or unfavorable, as the wind. **8.** grossly offensive in a moral sense. **9.** abominable, wicked, or vile, as deeds, crime, slander, etc.: *a foul assassination.* **10.** scurrilous, profane, or obscene: *foul language.* **11.** contrary to the rules or established usages, as of a sport or game; unfair: *a foul blow.* **12.** *Baseball.* pertaining to a foul ball or a foul line. **13.** limited in freedom of movement by obstruction, entanglement, etc.: *a foul anchor.* **14.** abounding in errors or in marks of correction, as a printer's proof, manuscript, or the like. **15.** *Naut.* **a.** (of the underwater portion of a hull) encrusted and impeded with barnacles, seaweed, etc. **b.** (of a mooring place) involving inconveniences and dangers, as of colliding with vessels or other objects when swinging with the tide. **c.** (of the bottom of a body of water) affording a poor hold for an anchor. **16.** *Dial.* not fair; ugly or unattractive. **17.** *Obs.* disfigured.
—*adv.* **18.** in a foul manner; vilely; unfairly. **19.** *Baseball.* into foul territory; so as to be foul: *It looked like a homer when he hit it, but it went foul.* **20. fall foul** or **afoul of, a.** to collide with, as ships. **b.** to come into conflict with; quarrel. **c.** to make an attack; assault. **21. run foul of,** to come into collision or controversy with: *to run foul of the press.*
—*n.* **22.** that which is foul. **23.** a collision or entanglement: *a foul between two racing sculls.* **24.** a violation of the rules of a sport or game: *The referee called it a foul.* **25.** *Baseball.* See **foul ball.**
—*v.t.* **26.** to make foul; defile; soul. **27.** to clog or obstruct, as a chimney or the bore of a gun: *Soot had fouled the chimney.* **28.** to collide with. **29.** to cause to become entangled or caught, as a rope. **30.** to defile; dishonor; disgrace: *His reputation had been fouled by unfounded accusations.* **31.** *Naut.* (of barnacles, seaweed, etc.) to cling to a hull so as to encumber it. **32.** to hit (a pitch) foul (often fol. by *off* or *away*): *He fouled off two curves before being struck out on a fast ball.*
—*v.i.* **33.** to become foul. **34.** *Naut.* to come into collision, as two boats. **35.** to become entangled or clogged: *The rope fouled.* **36.** *Sports.* to make a foul play; give a foul blow. **37.** *Baseball.* to hit a foul ball. **38. foul out,** to be put out by hitting a foul ball caught on the fly by a player on the opposing team. **39. foul up,** *Slang.* to cause confusion or disorder; bungle; spoil. [ME *ful, foul*, OE *fūl*; c. Goth *ful(s)*, Icel *fūl(l)*, OHG *fūl*; akin to L *pūs* pus, *pūtere* to stink, Gk *pýon* pus] —**foul′ly,** *adv.*
—**Syn. 1.** repulsive, repellent. **2.** fetid, putrid, stinking. **3.** unclean, polluted, sullied, soiled, stained, tainted, impure. See **dirty. 6.** rainy, tempestuous. **7.** adverse. **9.** base, shameful, infamous. **10.** smutty, vulgar, coarse, low. **26.** sully, stain, dirty, besmirch, taint, pollute. **30.** shame. —**Ant. 1.** pleasant. **3, 26.** clean. **5, 6.** clear. **6, 7, 11, 12, 15, 16.** fair. **9.** pure.

foul′ an′chor, an emblem of an old-fashioned anchor, with a stock, having a slack length of cable wound over its stock or one of its flukes. Also, **fouled′ an′chor.**

Foul anchor

fou·lard (fo͞o lärd′, fə-), *n.* a soft, lightweight silk, rayon, or cotton of plain or twill weave with printed design, for neckties, trimmings, etc. [< F < ?]

foul′ ball′, *Baseball.* **1.** a batted ground ball that is hit and played outside the foul lines, or that passes outside the foul lines at first or third base, or that is played outside the foul line between home and first or third base regardless of where hit. **2.** a batted fly ball played or landing outside the foul lines.

foul·brood (foul′bro͝od′), *n.* any of several bacterial diseases of honeybee larvae, characterized by the putrefying of body tissues. [FOUL + BROOD]

fouled-up (fould′up′), *adj. Informal.* confused; chaotic; disorganized: *When things get this fouled-up, it's time to quit.* [adj. use of v. phrase *foul up*]

foul′ line′, **1.** *Baseball.* either of the two lines connecting home plate with first and third base respectively, or their continuations to the end of the outfield. **2.** Also called **free throw line.** *Basketball.* a line on the court 15 feet from the backboard, from which foul shots are made. **3.** *Bowling.* a line on an alley at right angles to the gutters and 60 feet from the center of the spot for the head pin that marks the limit of a fair delivery of the ball.

foul·mart (fo͞o′mərt, -märt′), *n.* foumart.

foul-mouthed (foul′mouthd′, -moutht′), *adj.* using obscene, profane, or scurrilous language; given to filthy or abusive speech. [FOUL + MOUTH + -ED[3]]

foul·ness (foul′nis), *n.* **1.** state or quality of being foul: *The foulness of the accusation incensed us all.* **2.** that which is foul; foul matter; filth. **3.** wickedness: *Someday his foulness will be the end of him.* [ME; OE *fūlnes.* See FOUL, -NESS]

foul′ play′, **1.** any treacherous or unfair dealing, esp. one that involves murder: *We feared that he had met with foul play.* **2.** unfair conduct in a game.

foul′ pole′, *Baseball.* either of two poles, one on each foul line, being the vertical continuation of the outfield fence or wall, used to aid the umpire in determining whether a fly ball hit near the foul line is a fair or foul ball.

fouls (foulz), *n.* (*construed as sing.*) *Vet. Pathol.* See **foot rot.** [FOUL + -S[3]]

foul′ shot′, *Basketball.* **1.** a throw from the foul line, given a player after a foul has been called against an opponent. **2.** a score of one point made on this throw. Also called **free throw.**

foul′ tip′, *Baseball.* a pitched ball that glances off the bat into foul territory, usually near the catcher, ruled a strike if the catcher catches it before it hits the ground, otherwise ruled an ordinary foul ball.

foul-up (foul′up′), *n. Informal.* **1.** a condition of confusion or disorder brought on by inefficiency, stupidity, etc. **2.** failure of a mechanical part to operate correctly. [n. use of v. phrase *foul up*]

fou·mart (fo͞o′mərt, -märt′), *n.* the European polecat. Also, **foulmart.** [ME *fulmard*, OE **fūlmeard.* See FOUL, MARTEN]

found[1] (found), *v.* **1.** pt. and pp. of **find.** —*adj.* **2.** *Brit.* provided or furnished without additional charge, as to a tenant; included within the price, rent, etc., paid (often used postpositively): *Room to let, laundry found.* —*n.* **3.** *Brit.* that which is provided or furnished without charge, esp. meals given a domestic: *Maid wanted, good salary and found.*

found[2] (found), *v.t.* **1.** to set up or establish on a firm basis or for enduring existence: *to found a dynasty.* **2.** to lay the lowest part of, fix, or build (a structure) on a firm base or ground: *a house founded on the solid hillside, above the erosive water.* **3.** to base or ground (usually fol. by *on* or *upon*): *a story founded on fact.* **4.** to provide a basis or ground for. —*v.i.* **5.** to be founded or based (usually fol. by *on* or *upon*). **6.** to base one's opinion (usually fol. by *on* or *upon*). [ME *found(en)* < OF *fond(er)* < L *fundāre*, deriv. of *fundus* bottom, foundation]

found[3] (found), *v.t.* **1.** to melt and pour (metal, glass, etc.) into a mold. **2.** to form or make (an article) of molten material in a mold; cast. [ME *fond(en)* < MF *fondre* to melt, cast < L *fundere* to pour, melt, cast] —**found′er,** *n.*

foun·da·tion (foun dā′shən), *n.* **1.** that on which something is founded. **2.** the basis or groundwork of anything: *the moral foundation of both society and religion.* **3.** the natural or prepared ground or base on which some structure rests: *The blast shook the foundation of every building.* **4.** the lowest division of a building, wall, or the like, usually of masonry and partly or wholly below the surface of the ground. **5.** act of founding, setting up, establishing, etc.: *a policy in effect since the foundation.* **6.** state of being founded. **7.** a donation or legacy for the support of an institution; an endowment: *to solicit foundations from alumni.* **8.** an endowed institution: *a private foundation for study abroad.* **9.** a cosmetic, as a cream or liquid, used as a base for facial make-up. **10.** See **foundation garment. 11.** *Solitaire.* a card of given denomination on which other cards are to be added according to denomination or suit. [ME *foundacioun* < L *fundātiōn-* (s. of *fundātiō*), equiv. to *fundāt(us)* (ptp. of *fundāre*; see FOUND[2]) + *-iōn-* -ION] —**foun·da′tion·al,** *adj.* —**foun·da′tion·al·ly,** *adv.* —**foun·da′tion·ar′y,** *adj.*
—**Syn. 3.** See **base**[1]. **3, 4.** footing. **5, 6.** establishment, settlement. —**Ant. 3, 4.** superstructure.

Founda′tion Day′, a legal holiday in Australia, the first Monday after January 25, to commemorate the landing of the British in 1788.

founda′tion gar′ment, an undergarment, as a girdle or corset, worn by women to support or give shape to the contours of the body. Also called **foundation.**

founda′tion stone′, **1.** any of the stones composing the foundation of a building. **2.** a cornerstone.

found·er[1] (foun′dər), *n.* one who founds or establishes. [ME; see FOUND[2], -ER[1]]

found·er[2] (foun′dər), *v.i.* **1.** (of a ship, boat, etc.) to fill with water and sink. **2.** to fall or sink down, as buildings, ground, etc.: *Built on a former lake bed, the building has foundered nearly 10 feet.* **3.** to suffer wreck; fail utterly: *The project foundered because public support was lacking.* **4.** to stumble, break down, or go lame, as a horse: *His mount foundered on the rocky path.* **5.** to become ill from overeating: *A pet may founder if fed improperly.* **6.** *Vet. Pathol.* (of a horse) to suffer from laminitis. —*v.t.* **7.** to cause to founder: *Rough seas had foundered the ship in mid-ocean.* **8.** *Vet. Pathol.* to cause (a horse) to break down, go lame, or suffer from laminitis. —*n.* **9.** *Vet. Pathol.* laminitis. [ME *foundre(n)* < MF *fondr(er)* (to) plunge to the bottom, submerge < L *fund(us)* bottom. See FOUND[2]]

found·er[3] (foun′dər), *n.* a person who founds or casts metal, glass, etc. [ME; see FOUND[3], -ER[1]]

foun·der·ous (foun′dər əs), *adj.* miry; swampy. [FOUNDER[2] + -OUS]

foun′ders' shares′, *Finance.* shares of stock given, at least nominally, for consideration to the organizers or original subscribers of a corporation, sometimes carrying special voting privileges, but likely to receive dividends after other classes of stock.

found′ers' type′, *Print. Brit.* See **foundry type.**

found·ling (found′ling), *n.* an infant found abandoned; a child without a parent or guardian. [ME *found(e)ling.* See FOUND[1], -LING[1]]

found′ling hos′pital, an institutional home for foundlings.

found′ ob′ject, a natural or manufactured object that is perceived as being aesthetically satisfying and exhibited as such. Cf. **ready-made** (def. 4).

foun·drous (foun′drəs), *adj.* founderous.

found·ry (foun′drē), *n., pl.* **-ries. 1.** an establishment for producing castings in molten metal. **2.** the act or process of founding metal. **3.** the category of metal objects made by founding; castings. **4.** *Obs.* the casting of metals. [< F *fonderie.* See FOUND[3], -ERY]

found′ry proof′, *Print.* a proof pulled for a final checking before printing plates are made.

found′ry type′, *Print.* type cast in individual characters for setting by hand. Also, *Brit.*, **founders' type.**

fount[1] (fount), *n.* **1.** a spring of water; fountain. **2.** a source or origin: *a fount of inspiration to his audiences.* [short for FOUNTAIN]

fount[2] (fount, font), *n. Print. Brit.* font[2].

Fount (fount), *n.* a boy's given name.

foun·tain (foun′tən), *n.* **1.** a spring or source of water; the source or head of a stream. **2.** the source or origin of anything. **3.** a jet or stream of water (or other liquid) made by mechanical means to spout or rise from an opening or structure, as to afford water for use, or to cool the air, or to serve for ornament. **4.** a structure for discharging such a jet or a number of jets, often an elaborate or artistic work with basins, sculptures, etc. **5.** See **drinking fountain. 6.** See **soda fountain. 7.** a reservoir for a liquid to be supplied gradually or continuously, as in a fountain pen. **8.** *Heraldry.* a roundel barry-wavy, argent and azure. [late ME *fontayne* < OF *fontaine* < LL *fontāna*, n. use of fem. of *fontānus* of a spring, equiv. to *font-* (s. of *fons*) spring + *-ānus* -AN] —**foun′tained,** *adj.* —**foun′tain·less,** *adj.* —**foun′tain·like′,** *adj.*

foun′tain grass′, a perennial grass, *Pennisetum ruppeli*, of Abyssinia, having bristly spikes, often rose-purple, grown as an ornamental.

foun·tain·head (foun′tən hed′), *n.* **1.** a fountain or spring from which a stream flows; the head or source of a stream. **2.** a chief source of anything: *a fountainhead of information.* [FOUNTAIN + HEAD]

Fountainhead, The, a novel (1943) by Ayn Rand.

Foun′tain Hill′, a town in E Pennsylvania. 5428 (1960).

Foun′tain of Youth′, a mythical spring, sought in the Bahamas and Florida by Ponce de León, Narváez, DeSoto, and others. Indians of Central America believed that it was to the north, and that its waters would cure ills and renew youth.

foun′tain pen′, a pen with a reservoir that provides a continuous supply of ink to the point.

foun′tain plant′, **1.** Also called **coral plant.** a shrubby, branching plant, *Russelia equisetiformis*, of Mexico, having showy, red flowers. **2.** Joseph's-coat.

Fou·qué (fo͞o kā′), *n.* **Frie·drich Hein·rich Karl, Baron de la Motte-** (frē′driKH hīn′riKH kärl, də lä mōt′), 1777–1843, German romanticist: poet and novelist.

Fou·quet (*Fr.* fo͞o ke′), *n.* **1. Jean** or **Je·han** (zhäN), c1420–c80, French painter. **2. Ni·co·las** (nē kō lä′), (*Marquis de Belle-Isle*), 1615–80, French statesman. Also, **Foucquet.**

Fou·quier-Tin·ville (fo͞o kyā taN vēl′), *n.* **Antoine Quen·tin** (äN twaN′ käN taN′), 1747?–95, French revolutionist: prosecutor during the Reign of Terror.

four (fōr, fôr), *n.* **1.** a cardinal number, three plus one. **2.** a symbol of this number, 4 or IV or IIII. **3.** a set of this many persons or things. **4.** a playing card, die face, or half of a domino face with four pips. **5. on all fours.** See **all fours** (def. 3). —*adj.* **6.** amounting to four in number. [ME *four, fower*, OE *fēower*; c. OHG *fior* (G *vier*), Goth *fidwor*; akin to L *quattuor*, Gk *téttares*]

four-a-cat (fôr′ə kat′, fôr′-), *n.* See **four old cat.**

four·bag·ger (fôr′bag′ər, fôr′-), *n. Baseball Slang.* See **home run.** [FOUR + BAGGER]

four′-ball′ match′ (fôr′bôl′, -bôl′, fôr′-), *Golf.* a match, scored by holes, between two pairs of players, in which the four players tee off and each player alternates with his partner in hitting the pair's ball having the better lie off the tee.

four′ bits′, *Slang.* fifty cents. —**four′-bit′,** *adj.*

four·ché (fo͝or shā′), *adj. Heraldry.* forked or divided into two at the extremity or in extremities: *a lion's tail fourché; a cross fourché.* Also, **four·chée′.** [< F; see FORK, -EE]

four·chette (fo͝or shet′), *n.* **1.** *Anat.* the fold of skin which forms the posterior margin of the vulva. **2.** *Ornith.* furcula; wishbone. **3.** *Zool.* the frog of an animal's foot. **4.** a strip of leather or fabric joining the front and back sections of a glove finger. **5.** *Chiefly Bridge.* a tenace. [< F, dim. of *fourche.* See FORK]

four′-col′or prob′lem (fôr′kul′ər, fôr′-), *Math.* an unproved theorem that any geographic map can be colored using only four colors so that no connected countries with a common boundary are colored the same color.

four′-col·or proc′ess (fôr′kul′ər, fôr′-), *Print.* a process for reproducing colored illustrations in a close approximation to their original hues by photographing the artwork successively through magenta, cyan, yellow, and color-absorbing filters to produce four plates that are printed successively with yellow, red, blue, and black inks.

Four′ Cor′ners, a town in NW Oregon. 4743 (1960).

four-cy·cle (fôr′sī′kəl, fôr′-), *adj.* noting or pertaining to an internal-combustion engine in which a complete cycle in each cylinder requires four strokes, one to draw in air or an air-fuel mixture, one to compress it, one to ignite it and do work, and one to scavenge the cylinder. Cf. **two-cycle.**

four-di·men·sion·al (fôr′di men′shə nəl, fôr′-), *adj. Math.* of a space having points, or a set having elements, which require four coordinates for their unique determination.

Four·drin·i·er (fo͝or drin′ē ər), *n.* an automatic machine for manufacturing paper. [named after Henry and Sealy *Fourdrinier,* 19th-century English papermakers]

four-eyed (fôr′īd′, fôr′-), *adj.* **1.** having or seeming to have four eyes. **2.** *Often Disparaging.* wearing eyeglasses.

four′-eyed fish′, any of several surface-swimming cyprinodont fishes of the genus *Anableps,* found in brackish waters of Central America, having each eye divided, with the upper half adapted for seeing in air and the lower half adapted for seeing in water.

four′-eyed opos′sum, a small opossum, *Philander opossum,* found from Mexico to Brazil, having a white spot above each eye.

four-eyes (fôr′īz′, fôr′-), *n., pl.* **-eyes. 1.** See **four-eyed fish. 2.** *Usually Disparaging.* a person who wears eyeglasses (often used as a term of address).

4-F (fôr′ef′, fôr′-), *n.* **1.** a U.S. Selective Service classification designating a person considered physically, psychologically, or morally unfit for military duty. **2.** a person so classified.

four′ flush′, *Poker.* **1.** four cards of a possible flush, which, with one card of a different suit, make up a hand. **2.** an imperfect flush.

four-flush (fôr′flush′, fôr′-), *v.i. Informal.* to act as a fourflusher.

four·flush·er (fôr′flush′ər, fôr′-), *n. Informal.* a person who makes pretensions that he cannot or does not bear out. [FOUR FLUSH + -ER[1]]

four·fold (fôr′fōld′, fôr′-), *adj.* **1.** comprising four parts or members. **2.** four times as great or as much. —*adv.* **3.** in fourfold measure. [ME *foure fald,* OE *feowerfealdum.* See FOUR, -FOLD]

four′fold block′, a block having four pulleys or sheaves.

four′fold pur′chase, a tackle that is composed of a rope passed through two fourfold blocks in such a way as to provide mechanical power in the ratio of 1 to 5 or 1 to 4, depending on whether hauling is done on the running or the standing block and without considering friction.

four-foot·ed (fôr′fo͝ot′id, fôr′-), *adj.* having four feet. [ME *four foted*]

four′-footed but′terfly. See **brush-footed butterfly.**

four′ free′doms, freedom of speech and worship and freedom from want and fear, being the objectives of U.S. foreign policy as stated by President Roosevelt in a message to Congress on January 6, 1941.

four·gon (fo͞or gôn′), *n., pl.* **-gons** (-gôn′). *French.* a long covered wagon for carrying baggage, goods, military supplies, etc.; a van or tumbril.

four-hand·ed (fôr′han′did, fôr′-), *adj.* **1.** involving four hands or players, as a game at cards: *Bridge is usually a four-handed game.* **2.** intended for four hands, as a piece of music for the piano. **3.** having four hands, or four feet adapted for use as hands; quadrumanous.

Four′-H′ Club′ (fôr′āch′, fôr′-), an organization sponsored by the U.S. Department of Agriculture, established chiefly to instruct young people of rural communities in modern farming methods. Also, **4-H Club.** [so called from the aim of the organization to improve head, heart, hands, and health] —**4-H,** *adj.* —**4-H′er,** *n.*

Four′ Horse′men of the Apoc′alypse, four riders on white, red, black, and pale horses symbolizing pestilence, war, famine, and death, respectively. Also called **Four′ Horse′men.**

Four′ Horse′men of the Apoc′alypse, The, a novel (1918) by Vicente Blasco Ibáñez.

Four′ Hun′dred, *U.S.* the exclusive social set of a city: *New York's Four Hundred can generally be counted on for good copy.* Also, **400.**

four-hun·dred-day′ clock′ (fôr′hun′drəd dā′, fôr′-), a clock that needs to be wound once a year, having the works exposed under a glass dome and utilizing a torsion pendulum.

Fou·rier (fo͝or′ē ā′, -ē ər; *for 1, 2 also Fr.* fo͞o ryā′), *n.* **1. Fran·çois Ma·rie Charles** (fräN swa′ ma rē′ sharl), 1772–1837, French socialist, writer, and reformer. **2. Jean Bap·tiste Jo·seph** (zhäN ba tēst′ zhō zef′), 1768–1830, French mathematician and physicist. **3.** a crater in the third quadrant of the face of the moon: about 36 miles in diameter.

Fou′rier anal′ysis, *Physics, Math.* the expression of any periodic function as a sum of sine and cosine functions, as in an electromagnetic wave function. Cf. **Fourier series.** [named after J.B.J. FOURIER]

Fou·ri·er·ism (fo͝or′ē ə riz′əm), *n.* the social system proposed by François Marie Charles Fourier, under which society was to be organized into phalanxes or associations, each large enough for all industrial and social requirements. [< F *fouriérisme.* See FOURIER, -ISM] —**Fou′ri·er·ist, Fou·ri·er·ite** (fo͝or′ē ə rīt′), *n.* —**Fou′ri·er·is′tic,** *adj.*

Fou′rier se′ries, *Math.* an infinite series that involves linear combinations of sines and cosines and approximates a given function on a specified domain. [see FOURIER ANALYSIS]

Fou′rier trans′form, *Math.* a function, $f(x)$, obtained from a given function, $g(x)$, by the formula $f(x) = \int_{-\infty}^{\infty} \frac{g(t)e^{ixt}dt}{\sqrt{2\pi}}$. [see FOURIER ANALYSIS]

four-in-hand (fôr′in hand′, fôr′-), *n.* **1.** a long necktie to be tied in a slipknot with the ends left hanging. **2.** a vehicle drawn by four horses and driven by one person. **3.** a team of four horses. —*adj.* **4.** of or pertaining to a four-in-hand.

four′-leaf clo′ver (fôr′lēf′, fôr′-), a clover leaf having four leaflets instead of the usual three; said to bring good luck.

four-leg·ged (fôr′leg′id, -legd′, fôr′-), *adj. Informal.* (of a schooner) having four masts.

four′-let·ter word′ (fôr′let′ər, fôr′-), any of a number of short words, usually of four letters, considered to be offensive or vulgar because of reference to excrement or sex.

four-mast·ed (fôr′mas′tid, -mä′stid, fôr′-), *adj. Naut.* carrying four masts.

four′-masted brig′, *U.S. Naut.* See **jackass bark** (def. 2).

Four·nier (fo͝or′nē ā′, fo͝or′nē ā′; *Fr.* fo͞or nyā′), *n.* **A·lain** (a laN′), (*Henri Fournier*), 1886–1914, French novelist.

Four′ No′ble Truths′, the doctrines of Buddha: all life is suffering, the cause of suffering is ignorant desire, this desire can be destroyed, the means to this is the Eightfold Path.

four-o'clock (fôr′ə klok′, fôr′-), *n.* **1.** a common nyctaginaceous garden plant, *Mirabilis Jalapa,* having red, white, yellow, or variegated flowers which open late in the afternoon. **2.** a similar red-flowered plant, *M. laevis,* common in California. **3.** any plant of the same genus.

four′ of a kind′, *Poker.* a set of four cards of the same denominations.

four old cat (fôr′ ə kat′, fôr′), *Games.* three old cat played with four batters. Also, **four′ o'cat′, four-a-cat.**

four′-part har′mony (fôr′pärt′, fôr′-), *Music.* harmony in which each chord has four tones, creating, in sum, four melodic lines.

four·pence (fôr′pəns, fôr′-), *n. Brit.* **1.** a sum of money of the value of four English pennies, or about eight U.S. cents. **2.** a silver coin of this value. [FOUR + PENCE]

four·pen·ny (fôr′pen′ē, -pə nē, fôr′-), *adj.* **1.** *Carpentry.* **a.** noting a nail $1\frac{1}{2}$ inches long. **b.** noting certain fine nails $1\frac{3}{8}$ inches long. *Abbr.:* 4d **2.** *Brit.* of the amount or value of fourpence. [FOUR + -PENNY]

four·post·er (fôr′pō′stər, fôr′-), *n.* **1.** a bed with four corner posts, as for supporting curtains, a canopy, etc. **2.** a four-masted sailing vessel. [FOUR + POST[1] + -ER[1]]

Four′ Quartets′, a cycle of four poems (1943) by T. S. Eliot, consisting of *East Coker, Burnt Norton, The Dry Salvages,* and *Little Gidding.*

four′ ques′tions, *Judaism.* the four questions about the significance of the Seder service, traditionally asked by the youngest boy at the table and answered by the reading of the Haggadah by the eldest male.

four·ra·gère (fo͝or′ə zhâr′; *Fr.* fo͞o ra zher′), *n., pl.* **-gères** (-zhârz′; *Fr.* -zher′). (in French and U.S. military use) **1.** an ornament of cord worn on the shoulder. **2.** such a cord awarded as an honorary decoration, as to members of a regiment or other unit that has received a requisite number of citations. [< F]

four′-rowed bar′ley (fôr′rōd′, fôr′-), a class of barley having, in each spike, six rows of grain, with two pairs of rows overlapping.

Four′ Saints′ in Three′ Acts′, an opera (1934) by Virgil Thomson.

four·score (fôr′skôr′, fôr′skôr′), *adj.* four times twenty; eighty. [ME; see FOUR, SCORE]

four·some (fôr′səm, fôr′-), *n.* **1.** *Golf.* **a.** a match between two pairs of players, each of whom plays his own ball. **b.** Also called **Scotch foursome.** a match between two pairs of players, in which each pair plays one ball and partners stroke alternately. **2.** a company or set of four; two couples; a quartet: *to make up a foursome for bridge.* —*adj.* **3.** consisting of four persons, things, etc.; performed by or requiring four persons. [FOUR + -SOME[2]]

four-spot (fôr′spot′, fôr′-), *n.* a playing card or the upward face of a die bearing four pips; a domino, one half of which bears four pips.

four·square (fôr′skwâr′, fôr′-), *adj.* **1.** consisting of four corners and four right angles; square: *a solid, foursquare building.* **2.** firm; steady; unswerving: *He maintained a foursquare position in the controversy.* **3.** forthright; frank; blunt: *a foursquare presentation of the company's financial condition.* —*adv.* **4.** without equivocation; frankly; forthrightly. —*n.* **5.** a square. [ME *fouresquare.* See FOUR, SQUARE] —**four′square′ly,** *adv.* —**four′square′ness,** *n.*

four-strip·er (fôr′strī′pər, fôr′-), *n.* a captain in the U.S. Navy.

four·teen (fôr′tēn′, fôr′-), *n.* **1.** a cardinal number, ten plus four. **2.** a symbol for this number, as 14 or XIV. **3.** a set of this many persons or things. —*adj.* **4.** amounting to 14 in number. [ME *fourtene,* OE *fēowertēne.* See FOUR, -TEEN]

four·teen·er (fôr′tē′nər, fôr′-), *n. Pros.* a line, esp. an iambic line, consisting of fourteen syllables. [FOURTEEN + -ER[1]]

Four′teen Points′, The, a statement of the war aims of the Allies, made by President Wilson on January 8, 1918.

four·teenth (fôr′tēnth′, fôr′-), *adj.* **1.** next after the thirteenth; being the ordinal number for 14. **2.** being one of 14 equal parts. —*n.* **3.** a fourteenth part, esp. of one ($\frac{1}{14}$). **4.** the fourteenth member of a series. [ME *fourtenthe,* OE *fēowertēotha.* See FOURTEEN, -TH[2]]

Four′ Tem′peraments, The, a ballet (1944) by Paul Hindemith.

fourth (fôrth, fôrth), *adj.* **1.** next after the third; being the ordinal number for four. **2.** being one of four equal parts. —*n.* **3.** a fourth part, esp. of one (¼). **4.** the fourth member of a series. **5.** *Music.* **a.** a tone on the fourth degree from a given tone (counted as the first). **b.** the interval between such tones. **c.** the harmonic combination of such tones. **6.** (*cap.*) Independence Day; the Fourth of July (usually prec. by *the*). [ME *fourthe,* OE *fēowertha.* See FOUR, -TH[2]]

fourth′ class′, (in the U.S. postal system) the class of mail consisting of merchandise exceeding 16 ounces, and all first, second, or third class matter not under 8 ounces or sealed against inspection.

fourth-class (fôrth′klas′, -kläs′, fôrth′-), *adj.* **1.** of, pertaining to, or designated as a class next below third, as for mailing, shipping, etc. —*adv.* **2.** as fourth-class matter; by fourth-class mail: *Send it fourth-class.*

fourth′ dimen′sion, the dimension of time, required in addition to three spatial dimensions, to locate a point in space-time. —**fourth′-di·men′sion·al,** *adj.*

fourth′ estate′, (*often caps.*) **1.** a group other than the usual powers, as the three estates of France, that wields influence in the politics of a country. **2.** the journalistic profession or its members; the press.

Fourth′ Interna′tional, a loose federation of small groups of radical socialists formed in 1936 under the leadership of Leon Trotsky and hostile to the Soviet Union. Cf. **international** (def. 6).

fourth·ly (fôrth′lē, fôrth′-), *adv.* in the fourth place: *Fourthly, there is the matter of tardiness.* [FOURTH + -LY]

Fourth′ of July′. See **Independence Day.**

fourth′ posi′tion, *Ballet.* a position in which the feet are at right angles to the direction of the body, the toes pointing out, with the left foot forward and the right foot back. See illus. under **first position.**

Fourth′ Repub′lic, the republic established in France in 1945 and replaced by the Fifth Republic in 1958.

fourth′ wall′, *Theat.* the imaginary wall of a box set, represented by the space framed by the proscenium.

four-way (fôr′wā′, fôr′-), *adj.* **1.** providing access or passage in four directions: *a four-way entrance; a four-way pipe connection.* **2.** exerting influence or benefit in four different ways: *a four-way blessing; a four-way remedy.* **3.** made up of four participants: *a four-way discussion.*

four-wheel (fôr′hwēl′, -wēl′, fôr′-), *adj.* **1.** having four wheels. **2.** functioning on or by four wheels: *a jeep with four-wheel drive.* Also, **four′-wheeled′.**

four-wheel·er (fôr′hwē′lər, -wē′-, fôr′-), *n.* a four-wheeled vehicle, esp. a hackney carriage.

fou·ter (fo͞o′tər), *n. Archaic.* that which has no value (used in expressions of contempt): *A fouter for the world, say I!* Also, **fou·tra** (fo͞o′trə), **fou′tre.** [< MF *foutre* to copulate with, copulate < L *futuere*]

fo·ve·a (fō′vē ə), *n., pl.* **-ve·ae** (-vē ē′). *Biol.* a small pit or depression in a bone or other structure. [< L: small pit] —**fo′ve·al,** *adj.*

fo′vea cen·tra′lis (sen trā′lis), *Anat.* a small pit or depression at the back of the retina forming the point of sharpest vision. [< NL: central fovea]

fo·ve·ate (fō′vē it, -āt′), *adj. Biol.* having foveae; pitted. Also, **fo′ve·at′ed.** [FOVE(A) + -ATE[1]]

fo·ve·o·la (fō vē′ə lə), *n., pl.* **-lae** (-lē′). *Biol.* a small fovea; a very small pit or depression. [< NL; dim. of FOVEA] —**fo·ve′o·lar,** *adj.*

fo·ve·o·late (fō′vē ə lit, -lāt′), *adj. Biol.* having foveolae, or very small pits. Also, **fo′ve·o·lat′ed.** [FOVEOL(A) + -ATE[1]]

fo·ve·ole (fō′vē ōl′), *n.* a foveola. Also, **fo·ve·o·let** (fō′vē ə let′, fō vē′ə lit).

fowl (foul), *n., pl.* **fowls,** (*esp. collectively*) **fowl,** *v.* —*n.* **1.** the domestic or barnyard hen or rooster; a chicken. Cf. **domestic fowl. 2.** any of several other usually gallinaceous birds that are barnyard, domesticated, or wild, as the duck, turkey, or pheasant. **3.** (in market and household use) a full-grown domestic fowl for food purposes, as distinguished from a chicken or young fowl. **4.** the flesh or meat of a domestic fowl. **5.** any bird (used chiefly in combination): *waterfowl; wild fowl.* —*v.i.* **6.** to hunt or take wild fowl. [ME *foul,* OE *fugol, fugel;* c. OS *fugal,* Goth *fugl(s),* OHG *fogal* (G *Vogel*)]

fowl′ chol′era, *Vet. Pathol.* a specific, acute, diarrheal disease of fowls, esp. chickens, caused by a bacterium, *Pasteurella multocida.* Cf. **hemorrhagic septicemia.**

fowl·er (fou′lər), *n.* a hunter of fowls. [ME *foweler,* OE *fughelere.* See FOWL, -ER[1]]

Fow·ler (fou′lər), *n.* **1. Henry H(am·ill)** (ham′əl), born 1908, U.S. lawyer and government official: Secretary of the Treasury 1965–68. **2. Henry Watson,** 1858–1933, English lexicographer.

Fow′ler flap′, *Aeron.* a flap normally forming a part of the trailing edge of an airplane wing, capable of being moved backward and rotated downward in order to increase lift through increased camber and wing area. [named after Harlan D. *Fowler,* 20th-century American aeronautical engineer]

Fow′ler's toad′, a toad, *Bufo woodhousei fowleri,* of the U.S. chiefly east of the Mississippi, having a light streak down the middle of the back. [named after S. P. *Fowler* (d.1888), American naturalist]

Fow·liang (fo͞o′lyäng′, fō′-), *n.* a city in NE Kiangsi, in E China: known for manufacture of fine porcelain. 87,000 (1948). Formerly, **Kingtehchen.**

fowl·ing (fou′ling), *n.* the practice or sport of shooting or snaring birds. [ME *foulynge.* See FOWL, -ING¹]

fowl′ing piece′, a shotgun for shooting wild fowl.

fowl′ leuko′sis, *Vet. Pathol.* leukosis.

fowl′ pox′, *Vet. Pathol.* a virus disease of chickens and other birds characterized by warty excrescences on the comb and wattles, and often by diphtherialike changes in the mucous membranes of the head. Also, **fowl′pox′.** Also called **avian diphtheria, avian pox, contagious epithelioma, sore head.**

fowl′ spirocheto′sis, *Vet. Pathol.* a specific, infectious, usually fatal blood disease of chickens caused by a spirochete, *Borrelia anserina.* Also called **avian spirochetosis.**

fowl′ ty′phoid, *Vet. Pathol.* a septicemic disease of fowl, esp. chickens, caused by the organism *Salmonella gallinarum* and marked by fever, loss of appetite, thirst, anemic pallor of the skin of the head, and prostration.

fox (foks), *n., pl.* **fox·es,** (*esp. collectively*) **fox,** *v.* —*n.* **1.** any of several carnivores of the dog family, esp. those of the genus *Vulpes,* smaller than wolves, having a pointed muzzle, erect ears, and a long, bushy tail. **2.** the fur of this animal. **3.** a cunning or crafty person. **4.** *Naut.* a length of small stuff made by hand by twisting a yarn against its lay or by twisting two or more yarns together. **5.** (*cap.*) a member of a tribe of North American Algonquian Indians, formerly in Wisconsin, later merged with the Sac tribe. **6.** (*cap.*) the Algonquian language of the Fox, Sac, and Kickapoo Indians. **7.** *Bible.* a scavenger, perhaps the jackal. Psalms 63:10; Lam. 5:18. **8.** a word formerly used in communications to represent the letter F. —*v.t.* **9.** *Informal.* to deceive or trick. **10.** to repair or make (a shoe) with leather or other material applied so as to cover or form part of the upper front. **11.** *Obs.* to intoxicate or befuddle. —*v.i.* **12.** to act cunningly or craftily. **13.** (of book leaves, prints, etc.) to become foxed. [ME, OE; c. OS *vohs,* MLG *vos,* OHG *fuhs* (G *Fuchs*). See VIXEN] —**fox′like′,** *adj.*

Red fox, *Vulpes fulva* (16 in. high at shoulder; total length 4 ft.; tail 1½ ft.)

Fox (foks), *n.* **1. Charles James,** 1749–1806, British orator and statesman. **2. George,** 1624–91, English religious leader and writer: founder of the Society of Friends. **3. John.** See **Foxe, John. 4. John William, Jr.,** 1863–1919, U.S. novelist. **5. Sir William,** 1812–93, New Zealand statesman, born in England: prime minister 1856, 1861–62, 1869–72, 1873.

fox·ber·ry (foks′ber′ē, -bə rē), *n., pl.* **-ries.** the cowberry, *Vaccinium Vitis-Idaea.* [FOX + BERRY]

fox′ bolt′, an anchor bolt secured by a foxtail wedge forced into its end as it is screwed into a blind hole.

Fox·bor·ough (foks′bûr′ō, -bur′ō), *n.* a town in E Massachusetts. 3169 (1960).

fox′ brush′, the tail of a fox.

Fox′ Chap′el, a town in SW Pennsylvania. 3302 (1960).

Foxe (foks), *n.* **John,** 1516–87, English martyrologist.

foxed (fokst), *adj.* **1.** deceived; tricked. **2.** stained or spotted a yellowish brown, as by age: *a dog-eared and foxed volume of romantic poetry.* [FOX + -ED²]

fox-fire (foks′fīᵊr′), *n. U.S.* **1.** organic luminescence, esp. from certain fungi on decaying wood. **2.** any of various fungi causing luminescence in decaying wood.

fox′ gera′nium. See **herb Robert.**

fox·glove (foks′gluv′), *n.* any scrophulariaceous plant of the genus *Digitalis,* esp. *D. purpurea,* of Europe, having drooping, tubular, purple or white flowers, and leaves that are used as digitalis in medicine. [ME *foxes glove,* OE *foxes glōfa.* See FOX, GLOVE]

fox′glove beard′tongue, a perennial herb, *Pentstemon Digitalis,* found throughout the U.S. and southern Canada east of the Rocky Mountains, having white, bearded flowers.

fox′ grape′, **1.** a grape, *Vitis Labrusca,* of the northern U.S., from which numerous cultivated varieties have been developed. **2.** the usually purplish-black, tart or sweet, musky fruit of this vine. **3.** a vine, *Vitis Labrusca,* of the eastern U.S., bearing musky, thick-skinned, purplish-black, edible fruit.

Foxglove, *Digitalis purpurea*

fox·hole (foks′hōl′), *n.* a small pit, usually for one or two men, used for cover in a battle area. [FOX + HOLE]

fox·hound (foks′hound′), *n.* one of any of several breeds of medium-sized hounds trained to hunt foxes and having a black-and-tan, black, tan, and white, or tan and white coat. [FOX + HOUND¹]

fox′ hunt′ing, a sport in which mounted hunters follow hounds in pursuit of a fox. —**fox′ hunt′er.**

Foxhound (23 in. high at shoulder)

fox·ing (fok′sing), *n.* **1.** material used to cover the upper portion of a shoe. **2.** discoloration, as of book leaves, prints, etc. [FOX + -ING¹]

Fox′ Lake′, a town in NE Illinois. 3700 (1960).

Fox′ Point′, a town in SE Wisconsin. 7315 (1960).

fox′ spar′row, a North American sparrow, *Passerella iliaca,* having a bright rufous tail and streaked breast.

fox′ squir′rel, any of several North American arboreal squirrels varying in color and remarkable for large size.

fox·tail (foks′tāl′), *n.* **1.** the tail of a fox. **2.** any of various grasses having soft, brushlike spikes of flowers. [ME; see FOX, TAIL¹]

fox′tail mil′let, an annual grass, *Setaria italica,* of numerous varieties, introduced into the U.S. from Europe and Asia, and grown chiefly for use as hay.

fox′tail saw′. See **dovetail saw.**

fox′tail wedge′, a wedge in the split end of a tenon, bolt, or the like, for spreading and securing it when driven into a blind mortise or hole. Also called **fox′ wedge′.**

fox′ ter′rier, one of either of two English breeds of small terriers having either a long, wiry coat or a short, flat coat, formerly used for driving foxes from their holes.

Fox terrier (15 in. high at shoulder)

fox′ trot′, **1.** a social dance, in quadruple meter, performed by couples, characterized by various combinations of short, quick steps. **2.** a pace, as of a horse, consisting of a series of short steps, as in slackening from a trot to a walk.

fox-trot (foks′trot′), *v.i.,* **-trot·ted, -trot·ting.** to dance a fox trot.

Fox·trot (foks′trot′), *n.* a word used in communications to represent the letter F. [special use of FOX TROT]

fox·y (fok′sē), *adj.,* **fox·i·er, fox·i·est. 1.** foxlike; cunning or crafty; clever. **2.** discolored or foxed: *pages of a book that had become foxy.* **3.** yellowish- or reddish-brown, as of the color of the common red fox. **4.** (of wines) having the pronounced flavor natural to native American grape varieties, as that of fox grapes or of Concord or Catawba grapes. **5.** *Archaic.* (esp. of a painting) having excessively warm tones; containing too much red. [FOX + -Y¹] —**fox′i·ly,** *adv.* —**fox′i·ness,** *n.* —**Syn. 1.** wily, tricky, sly, artful.

foy (foi), *n. Scot.* **1.** a feast, gift, etc., given by or to a person about to start on a journey. **2.** a feast held on some special occasion, as at the end of the harvest. [< D *fooi, foye, voye,* ?< F *voie* way, journey]

foy·er (foi′ər, foi′ā; *Fr.* fwa yā′), *n., pl.* **-ers** (-ərz, -āz; *Fr.* -yā′). **1.** the lobby of a theater or hotel. **2.** a vestibule or entrance hall in a house. [< F: fireplace, hearth (orig. a room to which theater audiences went for warmth between the acts) < Romanic *focār(ium),* deriv. of L *focus* hearth; see ARY]

fo·zy (fō′zē, foz′ē), *adj.,* **-zi·er, -zi·est.** *Chiefly Scot.* **1.** spongy; loose-textured. **2.** (of a vegetable or fruit) overripe. **3.** (of a person) fat; flabby. **4.** *Informal.* dull-witted; stupid; fat-headed. [cf. D *voos* spongy, LG *fussig*] —**fo′zi·ness,** *n.*

fp, *Music.* forte-piano.

F.P., foot-pound.

f.p., 1. fireplug. **2.** foot-pound. **3.** *Music.* forte-piano. **4.** freezing point. **5.** fully paid.

FPC, *U.S. Govt.* Federal Power Commission: a board of five members established chiefly to regulate the natural gas and electric power industries engaged in interstate commerce.

FPHA, Federal Public Housing Authority.

fpm, feet per minute. Also, **ft/min**

FPO, 1. field post office. **2.** fleet post office.

fps, feet per second. Also, **ft/sec**

f.p.s., 1. feet per second. **2.** foot-pound-second. **3.** frames per second.

fpsps, feet per second per second. Also, **ft/s²**

FR, freight release.

Fr, *Chem.* francium.

Fr., 1. Father. **2.** *pl.* **Fr., Frs.** franc. **3.** frater¹. **4.** French. **5.** Friar. **6.** Friday.

fr., 1. fragment. **2.** *pl.* **fr., frs.** franc. **3.** from.

Fra (frä), *n. Rom. Cath. Ch.* a title of address for a friar or brother. [< It, shortened form of *frate* brother]

fra·cas (frā′kəs; *Brit.* frak′ä), *n.* a disorderly noise, disturbance, or fight; uproar. [< F < It *fracass(o),* deriv. of *fracassare* to smash, equiv. to *fra-* (< L *infrā* among) completely + *cassare* (<< L *quassāre* to shake)]

Fra·cas·to·ri·us (frä′ka stôr′ē əs, -stōr′-), *n.* a walled plain in the fourth quadrant of the face of the moon: about 60 miles in diameter.

Frack·ville (frak′vil), *n.* a town in central Pennsylvania. 5654 (1960).

frac·ta·ble (frak′tə bəl), *n. Archit.* (on a gable wall) a coping concealing the slopes of the roof, esp. one having an ornamental silhouette. [obs. *fract* broken, cracked (see FRACTURE) + -ABLE]

frac·tion (frak′shən), *n.* **1.** *Math.* **a.** a number usually expressed in the form a/b, where a is any real number and b is any real number different from 0, equal to the quotient of a divided by b; the ratio between any two numbers. **b.** a ratio of algebraic quantities similarly expressed. **2.** a part as distinct from the whole of anything; a portion or section: *The meeting started with a fraction of us present.* **3.** a very small part of anything; minute portion: *Only a fraction of the regiment came back.* **4.** a very small amount; a little bit: *It was only a fraction away from completion.* **5.** a piece broken off; fragment or bit. **6.** act of breaking. **7.** *Eccles.* (in a Eucharistic service) the breaking of the Host. —*v.t.* **8.** to divide or break into fractions. [ME *fraccioun* < LL *frāctiōn-* (s. of *frāctiō*) a breaking (in pieces), equiv. to L *frāct(us)* (see FRACTO-) + *-iōn-* -ION] —**Syn. 2, 5.** See **part.**

frac·tion·al (frak′shə nᵊl), *adj.* **1.** pertaining to fractions; comprising a part or the parts of a unit; constituting a fraction: *fractional numbers.* **2.** comparatively small; inconsiderable or insignificant: *The profit on the deal was fractional.* **3.** *Chem.* of or noting a process, as distillation, crystallization, or oxidation, by which the component substances of a mixture are separated according to differences in certain of their properties, as boiling point, critical temperature, solubility, etc. Also, **frac·tion·ar·y** (frak′shə ner′ē). [FRACTION + -AL¹] —**frac′tion·al·ly,** *adv.*

frac′tional cur′rency, coins or paper money of a smaller denomination than the basic monetary unit.

frac′tional distilla′tion, the separation of volatile components of different boiling points in a mixture by the gradual increase of temperature and the separate collection of each component.

frac·tion·ate (frak′shə nāt′), *v.t.,* **-at·ed, -at·ing. 1.** to separate or divide into component parts, fragments, divisions, etc. **2.** to separate (a mixture) into its ingredients or into portions having different properties, as by distillation or crystallization; cause to undergo fractional distillation, crystallization, or the like. **3.** to obtain by such a process. [FRACTION + -ATE¹] —**frac′tion·a′tion,** *n.*

frac·tion·a·tor (frak′shə nā′tər), *n.* an apparatus for fractional distillation. [FRACTIONATE + -OR²]

frac·tion·ise (frak′shə nīz′), *v.t., v.i.,* **-ised, -is·ing.** *Chiefly Brit.* fractionize. —**frac′tion·i·sa′tion,** *n.*

frac·tion·ize (frak′shə nīz′), *v.t., v.i.,* **-ized, -iz·ing.** to divide into fractions. [FRACTION + -IZE] —**frac′tion·i·za′tion,** *n.*

frac·tious (frak′shəs), *adj.* **1.** peevish; irritable; quarrelsome: *an incorrigibly fractious young man.* **2.** refractory or unruly: *a fractious animal that would not submit to the harness.* [FRACTI(ON) + -OUS] —**frac′tious·ly,** *adv.* —**frac′tious·ness,** *n.*
—**Syn. 1.** testy, captious, petulant, snappish, pettish, waspish, touchy. **2.** stubborn, difficult. —**Ant. 1.** temperate. **2.** tractable.

fracto-, a learned borrowing from Latin meaning "broken," used in the formation of compound words: *fractostratus.* [comb. form repr. L *fractus* (ptp. of *frangere* to break)]

frac·to·cu·mu·lus (frak′tō kyo͞o′myə ləs), *n., pl.* **-lus.** *Meteorol.* See **cumulus fractus.** [FRACTO- + CUMULUS]

frac·to·stra·tus (frak′tō strā′təs), *n., pl.* **-tus.** *Meteorol.* See **stratus fractus.** [FRACTO- + STRATUS]

frac·ture (frak′chər), *n., v.,* **-tured, -tur·ing.** —*n.* **1.** the breaking of a bone, cartilage, or the like, or the resulting condition. Cf. **comminuted fracture, complete fracture, compound fracture, greenstick fracture, simple fracture. 2.** the characteristic manner of breaking: *a material of unpredictable fracture.* **3.** the characteristic appearance of a broken surface, as of a mineral. **4.** act of breaking; state of being broken. **5.** a break, breach, or split. —*v.t.* **6.** to break or crack. **7.** to cause or to suffer a fracture in (a bone, etc.). —*v.i.* **8.** to become fractured; break: *a mineral that does not fracture easily.* [late ME < MF < L *frāctūra* a breach, cleft, fracture, equiv. to *frāct(us)* (see FRACTO-) + *-ūra* -URE] —**frac′tur·a·ble,** *adj.* —**frac′tur·al,** *adj.*

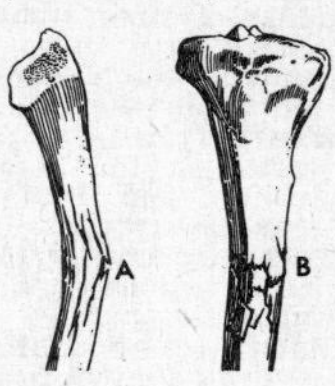

Fractures
A, Greenstick
B, Comminuted

frac·tus (frak′təs), *adj. Meteorol.* (of a cloud) containing small, individual elements that have a ragged appearance. [< L: broken. See FRACTO-]

frae (frā), *prep., adv. Scot.* from. [ME (north) *fra, frae* < ON *frā* FROM]

frae·nu·lum (frē′nyə ləm), *n., pl.* **-la** (-lə). frenulum.

frae·num (frē′nəm), *n., pl.* **-na** (-nə). frenum.

Fra Fi·lip·po Lip·pi (frä fi lip′ō lip′ē; *It.* frä fē lēp′pô lēp′pē). See **Lippi, Fra Filippo.**

frag (frag), *v.t.,* **fragged, frag·ging.** *U.S. Army & Marine Corps Slang.* to injure or assault (esp. one's unpopular or overzealous superior) with a fragmentation grenade. [by shortening] —**frag′ging,** *n.*

frag·ile (fraj′əl; *Brit.* fraj′īl), *adj.* **1.** easily broken, shattered, or damaged; delicate; brittle; frail. **2.** lacking in substance or force; flimsy: *a fragile excuse.* [< L *fragil(is),* equiv. to *frag-* (s. of *frangere* to break) + *-ilis* -ILE] —**frag′ile·ly,** *adv.* —**fra·gil·i·ty** (frə jil′i tē), **frag′ile·ness,** *n.*
—**Syn. 1.** See **frail¹.**

frag·ment (frag′mənt), *n.* **1.** a part broken off or detached: *scattered fragments of rock.* **2.** a portion that is unfinished or incomplete: *Fragments of his latest novel were penciled in odd places.* **3.** an odd piece, bit, or scrap. —*v.i.* **4.** to disintegrate; collapse or break into fragments: *The chair fragmented under his weight.* —*v.t.* **5.** to break (something) into pieces or fragments; cause to disintegrate: *The vase was fragmented in shipment. Outside influences soon fragmented the culture.* **6.** to divide into fragments; disunify. [ME < L *fragment(um)* a broken piece, remnant, equiv. to *frag-* (s. of *frangere* to break) + *-mentum* -MENT]
—**Syn. 1–3.** See **part.**

frag·men·tal (frag men′tᵊl), *adj.* **1.** fragmentary. **2.** *Geol.* clastic. [FRAGMENT + -AL¹] —**frag·men′tal·ly,** *adv.*

frag·men·tar·y (frag′mən ter′ē), *adj.* consisting of or reduced to fragments; broken; disconnected; incomplete: *fragmentary evidence; fragmentary remains.* [FRAGMENT + -ARY] —**frag′men·tar′i·ly,** *adv.* —**frag′men·tar′i·ness,** *n.*

frag·men·ta·tion (frag′mən tā′shən), *n.* **1.** act or process of fragmenting; state of being fragmented. **2.** the disintegration, collapse, or breakdown of norms of thought, behavior, or social relationship. **3.** the pieces of an exploded fragmentation bomb or grenade. [FRAGMENT + -ATION]

fragmenta′tion bomb′, a bomb designed to break into many small, high-velocity fragments when detonated.

fragmenta′tion grenade′, a grenade with a heavy metal casing that shatters, on exploding, into fragments that travel at high speed and with great force.

frag·ment·ed (frag′mən tid), *adj.* **1.** reduced to fragments. **2.** existing or functioning as though broken into separate parts; disorganized; disunified: *a fragmented personality; a fragmented society.* [FRAGMENT + -ED³]

frag·ment·ise (frag′mən tīz′), *v.t.,* **-ised, -is·ing.** *Chiefly Brit.* fragmentize. —**frag′ment·i·sa′tion,** *n.*

frag·ment·ize (frag′mən tīz′), *v.t.,* **-ized, -iz·ing.** to break (something) into fragments. [FRAGMENT + -IZE] —**frag′ment·i·za′tion,** *n.*

frag·men·tized (frag′mən tīzd′), *adj.* fragmented. [FRAGMENTIZE + -ED²]

Fra·go·nard (fra gô nar′), *n.* **Jean Ho·no·ré** (zhäN ô nô rā′), 1732–1806, French painter.

fra·grance (frā′grəns), *n.* quality of being fragrant; a sweet or pleasing scent. [< MF < LL *frāgrantia.* See FRAGRANT, -ANCE]
—**Syn.** See **perfume.**

fra·gran·cy (frā′grən sē), *n., pl.* **-cies.** fragrance.

fra·grant (frā′grənt), *adj.* **1.** having a pleasant odor; sweet-smelling; sweet-scented: *a fragrant rose.* **2.** delightful; pleasant: *fragrant memories.* [< L *frāgrant-* (s. of *frāgrāns*), prp. of *frāgāre* to smell sweet] —**fra′grant·ly,** *adv.* —**fra′grant·ness,** *n.*
—**Syn. 1.** perfumed, odorous, redolent, aromatic. —**Ant. 1.** malodorous, noisome.

fra′grant su′mac, a sprawling shrub, *Rhus aromatica,* of eastern North America, having aromatic foliage and greenish-yellow flowers in small spikes.

frail[1] (frāl), *adj.* **1.** weak; not robust; having delicate health: *He's still frail after his long illness.* **2.** easily broken or destroyed; fragile. **3.** morally weak; easily tempted. [ME *frail(e), frel(e)* < OF < L *fragil(is)* FRAGILE] —**frail′ly,** *adv.* —**frail′ness,** *n.*
—**Syn. 1, 2,** feeble; breakable, frangible. FRAIL, BRITTLE, FRAGILE imply a delicacy or weakness of substance or construction. FRAIL applies particularly to health, and immaterial things: *a frail constitution; frail hopes.* BRITTLE implies a hard outside finish of material that snaps or breaks to pieces easily: *brittle as glass.* FRAGILE implies that the object must be handled carefully to avoid breakage or damage: *fragile bric-a-brac.* —**Ant. 1, 2.** sturdy.

frail[2] (frāl), *n.* **1.** a flexible basket made of rushes, used esp. for dried fruits, as dates, figs, or raisins. **2.** a certain quantity of raisins, about 75 pounds, contained in such a basket. [ME *frayel, fraelle* < OF *frayel* < ?]

frai·le·ro (frī lâr′ō; *Sp.* frī le′rō), *n., pl.* **-le·ros** (-lâr′ōz; *Sp.* -le′rōs). *Sp. Furniture.* an armchair of the Renaissance, having a leather seat and a leather back stretched between plain wooden members and having a broad front stretcher. Also called **friar's chair.** [< Sp: lit., of, belonging to a friar, deriv. of *fraile* friar]

frail·ty (frāl′tē), *n., pl.* **-ties** for 3. **1.** quality or state of being frail. **2.** moral weakness; liability to yield to temptation: *a pretty face that tempts one's frailty.* **3.** a fault resulting from moral weakness: *frailties of the human flesh.* [ME *frailte, frelete* < OF *frailete* < L *fragilitāt-* (s. of *fragilitās*). See FRAIL[1], -ITY]
—**Syn. 1.** delicacy, weakness, fragility. **2.** susceptibility, suggestibility. **3.** flaw, defect.

fraise (frāz), *n.* **1.** *Fort.* a defense consisting of pointed stakes projecting from the ramparts in a horizontal or an inclined position. **2.** a ruff worn around the neck in the 16th century. **3.** *Horol.* a cutter for correcting inaccuracies in the teeth of a wheel. [< F, deriv. of *fraiser* to frizzle, curl < Pr *frezar* << Gmc; cf. OE *frīs* curled]

Frak·tur (fräk to͞or′), *n. Print.* German text, a style of type. [< G < L *fractūra* action of breaking (in reference to the curlicues that broke up the continuous line of a word). See FRACTURE]

Fra Lip·po Lip·pi (frä lip′ō lip′ē), a dramatic monologue (1855) by Robert Browning.

fram·be·sia (fram bē′zhə), *n. Pathol.* yaws. Also, **fram·boe′sia.** [< NL, Latinization of F *framboise.* See FRAMBOISE]

fram·boise (*Fr.* fräN bwaz′), *n.* a raspberry brandy, from Alsace. [< F: raspberry < Romanic *frambosia,* contr. of *frāga ambrosia* ambrosia strawberry]

Fra Mau·ro (frä′ mär′ō, mô′rō), a walled plain in the third quadrant of the face of the moon: about 50 miles in diameter.

frame (frām), *n., v.,* **framed, fram·ing.** —*n.* **1.** an open border or case for enclosing a picture, mirror, etc. **2.** a rigid structure formed of relatively slender pieces, joined so as to surround sizeable empty spaces or nonstructural panels, and generally used as a major support in building or engineering works, machinery, furniture, etc. **3.** a body, esp. a human body, with reference to its size or build: *a man of unusually large frame.* **4.** a structure for admitting or enclosing something: *a window frame.* **5.** lines to enclose or set off printed matter in a newspaper, magazine, or the like; a box. **6** Usually, **frames.** the framework for a pair of eyeglasses. **7.** any of various machines operating on or within a framework. **8.** a machine or part of a machine used in textile production: *drawing frame; spinning frame; harness frame.* **9.** a particular state, as of the mind: *an unhappy frame of mind.* **10.** form, constitution, or structure in general; system; order. **11.** *Naut.* **a.** any of a number of transverse, riblike members for supporting and stiffening the shell of each side of a hull, rising either from the centerline of the bottom or from the outer ends of the floors. **b.** any of a number of longitudinal members running between web frames to support and stiffen the shell plating of a metal hull. **12.** *Baseball Slang.* an inning. **13.** *Bowling.* **a.** one of the 10 divisions of a game. **b.** one of the squares on the scorecard, in which the score for a given frame is recorded. **14.** *Pool.* rack[1] (def. 3). **15.** *Motion Pictures.* one of the successive small pictures on a strip of film. **16.** *Computer Technol.* a unit of equipment of a computer: *main frame; tape frame; card frame.* **17.** *Television.* a single traversal by the electron beam of all the scanning lines on a television screen. In the U.S. this is a total of 525 lines traversed in $^{1}/_{30}$ second. Cf. **field** (def. 21). **18.** *Print.* the workbench of a compositor, consisting of a cabinet, cupboards, bins, and drawers, and having flat and sloping work surfaces on top. **19.** *Bookbinding.* an ornamental border, like a picture frame, stamped on the front cover of a book. **20.** *Slang.* a frame-up. **21. in frame,** *Shipbuilding.* (of a hull) with all frames erected and ready for planking or plating.
—*v.t.* **22.** to form or make, as by fitting and uniting parts together; construct. **23.** to contrive, devise, or compose, as a plan, law, poem, etc.: *to frame a new constitution.* **24.** to conceive or imagine, as an idea. **25.** to give utterance to: *Astonished, I attempted to frame adequate words of protest.* **26.** to form or seem to form (speech) with the lips, as if enunciating carefully. **27.** to fashion or shape: *to frame a bust from marble.* **28.** to shape or adapt to a particular purpose: *to frame a reading list for ninth graders.* **29.** *Informal.* to contrive or prearrange fraudulently or falsely, as in a scheme, race, etc. **30.** *Informal.* to incriminate (an innocent person) through the use of false evidence, information, etc. **31.** to provide with or put into a frame, as a picture: *The artist will frame the painting if we buy it.* **32.** to adjust (film) in a motion-picture projector so as to secure exact correspondence of the outlines of the frame and aperture. **33.** *Obs.* to direct, as one's steps.
—*v.i.* **34.** *Archaic.* to betake oneself; resort. **35.** *Archaic.* to prepare, attempt, give promise, or manage to do something. [ME *framen,* OE *framian* to avail, profit; c. OIcel *frama* to further, OHG *(gi)framōn* to do] —**fram′a·ble, frame′a·ble,** *adj.* —**fram′a·ble·ness, frame′a·ble·ness,** *n.* —**frame′less,** *adj.* —**fram′er,** *n.*

frame′ house′, *U.S.* a house constructed with a skeleton frame of timber, as the ordinary wooden house.

frame′ line′, a horizontal line separating consecutive frames on a strip of film.

frame′ of ref′erence, *pl.* **frames of reference. 1.** a structure of concepts, values, customs, views, etc., by means of which an individual or group perceives or evaluates data, communicates ideas, and regulates behavior. **2.** Also called **reference frame.** *Physics.* a framework that is used for the observation and mathematical description of physical phenomena and the formulation of physical laws, usually consisting of an observer, a coordinate system, and a clock or clocks assigning times at positions with respect to the coordinate system.

frame-up (frām′up′), *n. Informal.* **1.** a conspiracy against an innocent person, esp. when it results in his arrest or conviction. **2.** act of framing someone. [n. use of v. phrase *frame up*]

frame·work (frām′wûrk′), *n.* **1.** a frame or structure composed of parts fitted and joined together. **2.** a skeletal structure designed to support or enclose something: *a framework for the grape arbor; the framework of a play.* **3.** frames collectively: *a related framework for all his compositions; an art dealer who specializes in framework.* **4.** work done in, on, or with a frame. [FRAME + WORK]

fram·ing (frā′ming), *n.* **1.** act, process, or manner of constructing anything. **2.** act of providing with a frame. **3.** framed work; a frame or a system of frames. [late ME; see FRAME, -ING[1]]

fram′ing chis′el, a woodworking chisel for heavy work and deep cuts, often having a handle reinforced to receive blows from a metal hammer head. Also called **mortise chisel.**

Fram·ing·ham (frā′ming ham′), *n.* a town in E Massachusetts. 44,526 (1960).

fram′ing square′, *Carpentry.* a steel square having on its faces various tables and scales useful to the carpenter, as a rafter table, brace table, etc.

fram′ing ta′ble, *Carpentry.* See **rafter table.**

Fran (fran), *n.* **1.** a boy's given name, form of **Francis. 2.** a girl's given name, form of **Frances.**

franc (frangk; *Fr.* fräN), *n., pl.* **francs** (frangks; *Fr.* fräN). **1.** an aluminum or nickel coin and monetary unit of France, equal to 100 centimes and equivalent to about .20 of a U.S. dollar: value established in 1960 at 100 of the then existing francs. *Abbr.:* F., f., Fr. **2.** any of the monetary units of various other nations and territories, as Algeria, Belgium, Liechtenstein, Luxembourg, Martinique, Senegal, Switzerland, and Tahiti, equal to 100 centimes. **3.** the fractional currency unit of Morocco, the 100th part of the dirham, equivalent to about .002 of a U.S. dollar. **4.** a former silver coin of France, first issued under Henry III. [ME *frank* < OF *franc,* so called because the coin was first inscribed with the name of the king as *Rex Francōrum* King of the Franks]

Fran·çaix (fräN se′), *n.* **Jean** (zhäN), born 1912, French composer.

France (frans, fräns; *Fr.* fräNs), *n.* **1. A·na·tole** (a na tôl′), (*Jacques Anatole Thibault*), 1844–1924, French novelist and essayist: Nobel prize 1921. **2.** a republic in W Europe. 53,000,000; 212,736 sq. mi. *Cap.:* Paris. **3.** *Heraldry.* fleurs-de-lis or upon azure: *a bordure of France; a label of France.*

France′ An′cient, *Heraldry.* an escutcheon blazoned as follows: Azure, semé-de-lys or.

France′ Mod′ern, *Heraldry.* an escutcheon blazoned as follows: Azure, three fleurs-de-lis or.

Fran·ces (fran′sis), *n.* a girl's given name.

Fran·ces·ca (fran ches′kə, frän-; *It.* fRän che′skä), *n.* **1. Pie·ro del·la** (pē âr′ō del′ə; *It.* pye′Rō del′lä), (*Piero dei Franceschi*), c1420–92, Italian painter. **2.** Also, **Fran·cis·ca** (fran sis′kə). a girl's given name, form of **Frances.**

Fran·ces·cat·ti (frän′chi skä′tē), *n.* **Zi·no** (zē′nō), born 1905, French violinist.

Franche-Com·té (fräNsh kôN tā′), *n.* a former province in E France: once a part of Burgundy.

fran·chise (fran′chīz), *n., v.,* **-chised, -chis·ing.** —*n.* **1.** the right to vote: *to guarantee the franchise of every citizen.* **2.** a privilege of a public nature conferred on an individual or body of individuals by a governmental grant: *a franchise for a street railway.* **3.** permission granted by a manufacturer to a distributor or retailer to sell his products. **4.** the territory to which such permission extends. **5.** a privilege arising from the grant of a sovereign or government, or from prescription, which presupposes a grant. **6.** *Archaic.* a legal immunity or exemption from a particular burden, exaction, or the like. **7.** *Obs.* freedom, esp. from imprisonment, servitude, or moral restraint. —*v.t.* **8.** to grant (an individual, a company, etc.) a franchise: *The corporation has just franchised our local dealer.* **9.** enfranchise. [ME < OF, deriv. of *franc* free. See FRANK[1]] —**fran·chise·ment** (fran′chiz mənt), *n.*

fran′chise clause′, (esp. in marine-insurance policy) a clause stipulating that the insured will be responsible for any loss not in excess of a stated amount, and the insurance company will be liable for full payment of the loss equaling or exceeding the amount up to the insured amount. Cf. **deductible clause.**

fran·chis·er (fran′chī zər), *n.* a distributor or retailer who holds a franchise. [FRANCHISE + -ER[1]]

Fran·chot (fran′chət), *n.* a boy's given name, form of **Francis.**

Fran·cie (fran′sē), *n.* a girl's given name, form of **Frances.** Also, **Francy.**

Fran·cine (fran sēn′), *n.* a girl's given name, form of **Frances.** Also, **Francyne.**

Fran·cis (fran′sis), *n.* a boy's given name.

Francis I, 1. 1494–1547, king of France 1515–47. **2.** 1768–1835, first emperor of Austria 1804–35; as Francis II, last emperor of the Holy Roman Empire 1792–1806.

Francis II. See **Francis I** (def. 2).

Fran·cis·can (fran sis′kən), *adj.* **1.** of or pertaining to St. Francis or the Franciscans. —*n.* **2.** a member of the mendicant order founded by St. Francis in the 13th century. [< ML *Francisc(us)* St. Francis of Assisi + -AN]

Francis′can night′shade, lady-of-the-night.

Fran·cis·co (fran sis′kō; *Sp.* fRän thēs′kō, -sēs′-), *n.* a boy's given name.

Fran′cis Fer′dinand, 1863–1914, archduke of Austria: heir apparent to the thrones of Austria and Hungary whose assassination precipitated the outbreak of World War I (nephew of Francis Joseph I). German, **Franz Ferdinand.**

Fran′cis Jo′seph I, 1830–1916, emperor of Austria 1848–1916; king of Hungary 1867–1916. German, **Franz Josef.**

Fran′cis of Assi′si, Saint (*Giovanni Francesco Bernardone*), 1182?–1226, Italian friar: founder of the Franciscan order.

Fran′cis of Pa′u·la (pä′o͞o lä), **Saint,** 1416–1507, Italian monk: founder of order of Minims.

Fran′cis of Sales′ (sālz; *Fr.* sAl), **Saint,** 1567–1622, French ecclesiastic and writer on theology: bishop of Geneva 1602–22.

Fran′cis Xa′vier, Saint. See **Xavier, Saint Francis.**

fran·ci·um (fran′sē əm), *n. Chem.* a radioactive element of the alkali metal group. *Symbol:* Fr; *at. no.:* 87. [named after FRANCE where first identified; see -IUM]

Franck (frängk; *Fr.* fRäNk), *n.* **1. Cé·sar (Au·guste)** (sā zAR′ ō gyst′), 1822–90, French composer, born in Belgium. **2. James,** 1882–1964, U.S. physicist, born in Germany: Nobel prize 1925.

Fran·co (frang′kō; *Sp.* fRäng′kō), *n.* **Fran·cis·co** (fran sis′kō; *Sp.* fRän thēs′kō), (*Francisco Paulino Hermenegildo Teódulo Franco-Bahamonde*) ("*El Caudillo*"), 1892–1975, Spanish military leader and dictator: chief of state 1939–47; regent of the kingdom of Spain 1947–75. —**Fran′co·ism,** *n.* —**Fran′co·ist,** *n.*

Franco-, a combining form of **French** or **France:** *Francophile; Franco-Prussian.* [comb. form repr. ML *Francus* a Frank, a Frenchman]

Fran′co-Bel′gian sys′tem (frang′kō bel′jən). See **French system.**

Fran·çois′ Vase′ (fran swä′; *Fr.* fRäN swA′), a Greek krater (c570 B.C.) signed by Ergotimos, potter, and Kleitias, painter.

fran·co·lin (frang′kə lin), *n.* any of numerous Old World gallinaceous birds of the genus *Francolinus* and allied genera. [< F < It *francolino* < ?]

Fran·co·ni·a (frang kō′nē ə, -nyə, fran-), *n.* a medieval duchy in Germany, largely in the valley of the Main River.

Fran·co·ni·an (frang kō′nē ən, -nyən, fran-), *n.* **1.** a part of West Germanic, consisting of Frankish and the dialects descended from Frankish. —*adj.* **2.** of, pertaining to, or characteristic of Franconia. **3.** of or pertaining to Franconian. [FRANCONI(A) + -AN]

Fran·co·phile (frang′kə fīl′), *adj.* **1.** friendly to or having a strong liking for France or the French. —*n.* **2.** a person who is friendly to or has a strong liking for France or the French. Also, **Fran·co·phil** (frang′kə fil). [FRANCO- + -PHILE] —**Fran·co·phil·i·a** (frang′kə fil′ē ə, -fēl′yə), *n.*

Fran·co·phobe (frang′kə fōb′), *adj.* **1.** fearing or hating France. —*n.* **2.** one who fears or hates France. [FRANCO- + -PHOBE] —**Fran′co·pho′bi·a,** *n.*

Fran·co-Pro·ven·çal (frang′kō prō′vən säl′), *n.* a Romance dialect group of W Switzerland and neighboring parts of France that represents a fusion of Provençal and northern French.

Fran′co-Prus′sian War′ (frang′kō prush′ən), the war between France and Prussia, 1870–71.

franc-ti·reur (fräN tē Rœr′), *n., pl.* **francs-ti·reurs** (fräN tē Rœr′). *French.* a sharpshooter in the French army.

Fran·cy (fran′sē), *n.* a girl's given name, form of **Frances.** Also, **Francie.**

Fran·cyne (fran sēn′), *n.* a girl's given name, form of **Frances.** Also, **Francine.**

fran·gi·ble (fran′jə bəl), *adj.* capable of being broken; breakable: *Most frangible toys are not suitable for young children.* [ME < OF, deriv. of L *frangere* to break; see -IBLE] —**fran′gi·bil′i·ty, fran′gi·ble·ness,** *n.*
—**Syn.** fragile, frail.

fran′gible boost′er, *Rocketry.* a booster or other rocket having a casing composed of easily fragmented material so that there will be no large pieces to cause a hazard should the rocket have to be destroyed in flight.

fran·gi·pane (fran′jə pān′), *n.* **1.** a kind of pastry cake, filled with cream, almonds, and sugar. **2.** frangipani. [< F; said to be named after *Frangipani* the inventor]

fran·gi·pan·i (fran′jə pan′ē, -pä′nē), *n., pl.* **-pan·is, -pan·i. 1.** a perfume prepared from or imitating the odor of the flower of an apocynaceous tree or shrub, *Plumeria rubra,* of tropical America. **2.** the tree or shrub itself. [see FRANGIPANE]

Fran·glais (fräN glē′), *n. French.* English words and expressions, esp. of American origin, that have become current in French. [b. F *français* and *anglais*]

frank[1] (frangk), *adj.* **1.** open or unreserved in speech; candid or outspoken; sincere: *His criticism of my work was frank but absolutely fair.* **2.** without inhibition or subterfuge; direct; undisguised: *a frank appeal to base motives.* **3.** *Archaic.* liberal or generous. **4.** *Obs.* free. —*n.* **5.** a signature or mark affixed by special privilege to a letter, package, or the like, to ensure its transmission free of charge, as by mail. **6.** the privilege of franking letters, packages, etc. **7.** a franked letter, package, etc. —*v.t.* **8.** to mark (a letter, package, etc.) for transmission free of the usual charge, by virtue of official or special privilege; send free of charge, as mail. **9.** to convey (a person) free of charge. **10.** to enable to pass or go freely: *to frank a visitor through customs.* **11.** to facilitate the comings and goings of (a person), esp. in society:

A sizable inheritance will frank you faster than anything else. **12.** to secure exemption for. **13.** *Carpentry.* to assemble (millwork, as sash bars) with a miter joint through the moldings and a butt joint or mortise-and-tenon joint for the rest. [ME < OF *franc* < LL *franc(us)* free, orig. FRANK] —**frank′a·ble,** *adj.* —**frank′er,** *n.*
—**Syn. 1.** unrestrained, free, bold, uninhibited. FRANK, CANDID, OPEN, OUTSPOKEN imply a freedom and boldness in speaking. FRANK is applied to one unreserved in expressing the truth and to his real opinions and sentiments: *a frank analysis of a personal problem.* CANDID suggests that one is sincere and truthful or impartial and fair in judgment, sometimes unpleasantly so: *a candid expression of opinion.* OPEN implies a lack of reserve or of concealment: *open antagonism.* OUTSPOKEN applies to one who expresses himself freely, even when this is inappropriate: *an outspoken and unnecessary show of disapproval.* —**Ant. 1.** restrained.

frank² (frangk), *n. Informal.* frankfurter. [by shortening]

Frank (frangk), *n.* **1.** a member of a group of ancient Germanic peoples dwelling in the regions of the Rhine, one division of whom, the Salians, conquered Gaul about A.D. 500, founded an extensive kingdom, and gave origin to the name *France.* **2.** (in the Levant) any native or inhabitant of western Europe. [ME *Franke,* OE *Franca* (c. OHG *Franko*); usually said to be from the name of the national weapon; cf. OE *franka* spear, javelin]

Frank (frangk, frängk; *Russ., Ger.* fʀängk), *n.* **1. Il·ya M.** (ēl yä′), born 1908, Russian physicist: Nobel prize 1958. **2. Le·on·hard** (lā′ôn härt), 1882–1961, German novelist. **3.** a boy's given name.

Frank., Frankish.

Frank·en·stein (frang′kən stīn′), *n.* **1.** a person who creates a monster or a destructive agency that he cannot control or that brings about his own ruin. **2.** Also called **Frank′enstein mon′ster.** the monster or destructive agency itself. [after the monster created by Baron *Frankenstein,* character in *Frankenstein,* novel (1818) by Mary Shelley]

Frank·fort (frangk′fərt), *n.* **1.** a city in and the capital of Kentucky, in the N part. 18,365 (1960). **2.** a city in central Indiana. 15,302 (1960). **3.** a town in central New York. 3872 (1960). **4.** See **Frankfort on the Main.**

frank·fort·er (frangk′fər tər), *n.* frankfurter. Also, **frank′fort.**

Frank′fort on the Main′ (mān), a city in central West Germany, on the Main River. 694,200 (1963). Also called **Frankfort.** German, **Frank·furt am Main** (fʀängk′fŏŏʀt äm mīn′), **Frank′furt.**

Frank′fort on the O′der (ō′dər), a city in E East Germany, on the Oder River. 57,200 (est. 1959). German, **Frank·furt an der O·der** (fʀängk′fŏŏʀt än dəʀ ō′dəʀ), **Frank′furt.**

frank·furt·er (frangk′fər tər), *n.* a small, cooked and smoked sausage, usually of beef and pork, manufactured with or without casing and often linked. Also, **frankfort, frankforter, frank′furt.** [< G: Frankfort sausage]

Frank·furt·er (frangk′fər tər), *n.* **Felix,** 1882–1965, U.S. jurist born in Austria: associate justice of the U.S. Supreme Court 1939–62.

Frank′furt horizon′tal (frangk′fərt), **1.** *Craniom.* the plane established when right and left poria and left orbitale are in the same horizontal plane. **2.** *Cephalom.* the plane established when right and left tragia and left orbitale are in the same horizontal plane. [named after *Frankfort* on the Main]

Frank·ie (frang′kē), *n.* **1.** a boy's given name, form of **Francis** or **Franklin. 2.** a girl's given name, form of **Frances.** Also, **Franky.**

frank·in·cense (frang′kin sens′), *n.* an aromatic gum resin from various Asian and African trees of the genus *Boswellia,* esp. *B. Carteri,* used chiefly for burning as incense in regular or ceremonial practices, in perfumery, and in pharmaceutical and fumigating preparations. Also called **gum thus, olibanum.** [ME *fraunk encense.* See FRANK¹, INCENSE¹]

Frank·ish (frang′kish), *adj.* **1.** of or pertaining to the Franks. —*n.* **2.** the West Germanic language of the ancient Franks; Old Franconian. Cf. **Frank** (def. 1). [FRANK + -ISH¹]

frank·lin (frangk′lin), *n. Eng. Hist.* (in the 14th and 15th centuries) a freeholder who was not of noble birth. [ME *fra(u)nkelin* < AF *fraunclein,* equiv. to *fraunc* free, FRANK¹ + *-lein* -LING¹; formed on model of OF *chamberlain* CHAMBERLAIN]

Frank·lin (frangk′lin), *n.* **1. Benjamin,** 1706–90, American statesman, diplomat, author, scientist, and inventor. **2. Sir John,** 1786–1847, English Arctic explorer. **3.** a district in extreme N Canada, in the Northwest Territories, including the Boothia and Melville peninsulas, Baffin Island and other Arctic islands. 549,253 sq. mi. **4.** a town in central Pennsylvania. 9586 (1960). **5.** a town in central Indiana. 9453 (1960). **6.** a town in S Louisiana. 8673 (1960). **7.** a town in SW Ohio. 7917 (1960). **8.** a town in SE Virginia. 7264 (1960). **9.** a town in SE Idaho. 7222 (1960). **10.** a town in central Tennessee. 6977 (1960). **11.** a town in central New Hampshire. 6742 (1960). **12.** a town in S Massachusetts. 6391 (1960). **13.** a town in S Kentucky. 5319 (1960). **14.** a town in NW New Jersey. 3264 (1960). **15.** a crater in the first quadrant of the face of the moon: about 34 miles in diameter. **16.** a boy's given name.

frank·lin·ite (frangk′li nīt′), *n.* a mineral of the spinel group, an oxide of zinc, manganese, and iron, occurring in black octahedral crystals or in masses: an ore of zinc. [named after FRANKLIN, New Jersey where it is found; see -ITE¹]

Frank′lin Lakes′, a town in NE New Jersey. 3316 (1960).

Frank′lin Park′, a city in NE Illinois, near Chicago. 18,322 (1960).

Frank′lin's gull′, a black-headed, North American gull, *Larus pipixcan,* feeding chiefly on insects. [named after Sir John FRANKLIN]

Frank′lin Square′, a town on W Long Island, in SE New York. 32,483 (1960).

Frank′lin stove′, 1. a cast-iron stove having the general form of a fireplace with enclosed top, bottom, side, and back, the front being completely open or able to be closed by doors. **2.** any of various fireplaces having a cast-iron top, back, and sides, with some provision for circulating air behind them in order to provide heat. [named after Benjamin FRANKLIN who designed it]

Franklin stove (def. 1)

Frank·lin·ton (frangk′lin tən), *n.* a town in SE Louisiana. 3141 (1960).

frank·ly (frangk′lē), *adv.* in a frank manner; freely; openly; unreservedly; candidly; plainly: *He presented his arguments frankly and objectively.* [FRANK¹ + -LY]

frank·ness (frangk′nis), *n.* plainness of speech; candor; openness. [FRANK¹ + -NESS]

Fran·ko (frän′ko), *n.* **I·van** (i vän′), 1856–1916, Ukrainian writer.

frank·pledge (frangk′plej′), *n. Old Eng. Law.* **1.** a system of dividing a community into tithings or groups of 10 men, each member of which was responsible for the conduct of the other members of his group and for the assurance that a member charged with a breach of the law would be produced at court. **2.** a member of a tithing. **3.** the tithing itself. [ME *fra(u)nkplegge* < AF *fraunc-plege.* See FRANK¹, PLEDGE]

Frank·y (frang′kē), *n.* **1.** a boy's given name, form of **Francis** or **Franklin. 2.** a girl's given name, form of **Frances.** Also, **Frankie.**

Fran·nie (fran′ē), *n.* a girl's given name, form of **Frances.** Also, **Fran′ny.**

fran·tic (fran′tik), *adj.* **1.** wild with excitement, passion, fear, pain, etc.; frenzied. **2.** *Archaic.* insane; mad. [ME *frantik, frenetik* < OF *frenetique* < L *phrenēticus* delirious < Gk *phrenētikós.* See FRENZY, -TIC] —**fran′ti·cal·ly, fran′tic·ly,** *adv.* —**fran′tic·ness,** *n.*

Franz (franz; *Ger.* fʀänts), *n.* **1.** a walled plain in the first quadrant of the face of the moon: about 16 miles in diameter. **2.** a boy's given name, German form of **Frank.**

Franz Fer·di·nand (franz fûr′dᵊnand′; *Ger.* fʀänts feʀ′di nänt′). See **Francis Ferdinand.**

Franz Jo·sef (frants jō′səf; *Ger.* fʀänts yō′zef). See **Francis Joseph I.**

Franz′ Jo′sef Land′ (land; *Ger.* länt), an archipelago in the Arctic Ocean, E of Spitzbergen and N of Novaya Zemlya: belongs to the Soviet Union. Also called **Fridtjof Nansen Land.**

Franz Jo·seph II (yō′zef), born 1906, prince of Liechtenstein since 1938.

frap (frap), *v.t.,* **trapped, frap·ping.** *Naut.* to bind or wrap tightly with ropes or chains. [ME *frap(p)e(n)* < OF *frape(r)* (to) strike, beat, prob. < Gmc (cf. OIcel *hrapa* to hurl, hurry)]

frap·pé (fra pā′; *Fr.* fʀa pā′), *n., pl.* **-pés** (-pāz′; *Fr.* -pā′), *adj.* —*n.* **1.** *U.S.* a fruit juice mixture frozen to a mush, to be served as an appetizer or relish. **2.** an after-dinner drink consisting of a liqueur, as crème de menthe, poured over cracked or shaved ice. **3.** Also, **frappe** (frap). (esp. in the northeastern U.S.) See **milk shake. 4.** *Ballet.* a beating of the toe of the working foot against the ankle of the supporting foot. —*adj.* **5.** chilled; iced; frozen. [< F: iced, beaten, ptp. of *frapper* to ice, strike]

Fras·ca·ti (ʀä skä′tē), *n.* a fruity white wine from Rome. [after *Frascati,* city in Central Italy]

Fra·ser (frā′zər), *n.* **1. James Earle,** 1876–1953, U.S. sculptor. **2. John Malcolm,** born 1930, Australian political leader: prime minister since 1975. **3. Peter,** 1884–1950, New Zealand statesman, born in Scotland: prime minister 1940–49. **4.** a river in SW Canada, flowing S through British Columbia to the Pacific. 695 mi. long. **5.** a town in SE Michigan. 7027 (1960). **6.** Also, **Frazer.** a boy's given name.

frat (frat), *n. Slang.* fraternity (def. 1). [by shortening]

fratch (frach), *Brit. Dial.* —*v.t.* **1.** to disagree; quarrel. —*n.* **2.** a quarrel; argument; dispute. [ME *fracche(n)* (to) creak < ?] —**fratch′er,** *n.*

fratch·ing (frach′ing), *n. Brit. Dial.* a quarrel; disagreement; argument. [FRATCH + -ING¹]

fra·ter¹ (frā′tər), *n.* a brother, as in a religious or fraternal order; comrade. [< L: BROTHER]

fra·ter² (frā′tər), *n. Ecc. Hist. Obs.* the refectory of a religious house. Also, **fratry.** [ME *frater, freitour* < OF *fraitur,* short for *refreitor* < ML *rĕfectōr(ium)* REFECTORY]

fra·ter·nal (frə tûr′nᵊl), *adj.* **1.** of or befitting a brother or brothers; brotherly. **2.** of or being a society of men associated in brotherly union, as for mutual aid or benefit: *fraternal order; fraternal association.* [< L *frātern(us)* (see FRATER¹) + -AL¹] —**fra·ter′nal·ism,** *n.* —**fra·ter′nal·ly,** *adv.*

frater′nal insur′ance, insurance underwritten by a fraternal society, under either a legal reserve plan or an assessment plan.

frater′nal soci′ety, a club or other association, usually of men, having a limited membership and devoted to professional, religious, charitable, or social activities.

frater′nal twin′, one of a pair of twins of the same or different sexes, not necessarily resembling one another, that develop from two fertilized ova. Cf. **identical twin.**

frat·er·nise (frat′ər nīz′), *v.i., v.t.,* **-nised, -nis·ing.** *Chiefly Brit.* fraternize. —**frat′er·ni·sa′tion,** *n.* —**frat′er·nis′er,** *n.*

fra·ter·ni·ty (frə tûr′ni tē), *n., pl.* **-ties. 1.** *U.S.* a local or national organization of male students, primarily for social purposes, with secret initiation and rites and a name composed of two or three letters of the Greek alphabet. **2.** a group of persons associated by or as by ties of brotherhood. **3.** any group or class of persons having common purposes, interests, etc.: *the medical fraternity.* **4.** an organization of laymen for religious or charitable purposes. **5.** the quality of being brotherly; brotherhood: *liberty, equality, and fraternity.* **6.** the relation of a brother or between brothers. [ME *fraternite* < L *frāternitās.* See FRATERNAL, -ITY]

frater′nity house′, a house occupied by a college or university fraternity.

frat·er·nize (frat′ər nīz′), *v.,* **-nized, -niz·ing.** —*v.i.* **1.** to associate in a fraternal or friendly way. **2.** to associate cordially or intimately with enemy troops, natives of a conquered country, etc. —*v.t.* **3.** *Rare.* to bring into fraternal association or sympathy. Also, *esp. Brit.,* **fraternise.** [< F *fraternis(er)* < ML *frāternizāre.* See FRATERNAL, -IZE] —**frat′er·ni·za′tion,** *n.* —**frat′er·niz′er,** *n.*

Fra·tres Ar·va·les (*Lat.* frä′tʀes äʀ′vä les; *Eng.* frā′trēz är vā′lēz). See **Arval Brothers.**

frat·ri·cide (fra′tri sīd′, frā′-), *n.* **1.** a person who kills his own brother. **2.** act of killing one's own brother. [ME < MF < L *frātricīd(a), -um,* equiv. to *frātri-* (s. of *frāter*) brother + *-cīda, -um* -CIDE] —**frat′ri·cid′al,** *adj.*

fra·try (frā′trē), *n., pl.* **-tries.** frater².

Frau (frou; *Eng.* frou), *n., pl.* **Frau·en** (frou′ən), *Eng.* **Fraus** (frouz). *German.* a married woman; a wife; a lady (often used as a term of address).

fraud (frôd), *n.* **1.** deceit, trickery, sharp practice, or breach of confidence, used to gain some unfair or dishonest advantage. **2.** a particular instance of such deceit or trickery: *mail fraud; election frauds.* **3.** any deception, trickery, or humbug: *That book is a fraud and a waste of time.* **4.** a person who makes deceitful pretenses; impostor. [ME *fraude* < OF < L *fraud-* (s. of *fraus*) deceit, injury] —**fraud′ful,** *adj.* —**fraud′ful·ly,** *adv.*
—**Syn. 1.** See **deceit. 3.** wile, hoax.

fraud·u·lent (frô′jə lənt), *adj.* **1.** given to or using fraud, as a person; cheating; dishonest. **2.** characterized by, involving, or proceeding from fraud, as actions, enterprise, methods, gains, etc.: *a fraudulent scheme to evade taxes.* [ME < L *fraudulent(us).* See FRAUD, -ULENT] —**fraud′u·len·cy,** *n.* —**fraud′u·lent·ly,** *adv.*

Frau·en·feld (*Ger.* fʀou′ən felt), *n.* a town in and the capital of Thurgau, in N Switzerland. 14,702 (1960).

Frau·en·lie·be und Le·ben (*Ger.* fʀou′ən lē′bə ŏŏnt lā′bən), a song cycle (1840) by Robert Schumann consisting of eight songs set to poems by Adelbert von Chamiso.

fraught (frôt), *adj.* **1.** involving; full of; accompanied by (usually fol. by *with*): *an undertaking fraught with danger.* **2.** *Archaic.* filled or laden (with): *ships fraught with precious wares.* —*n.* **3.** *Scot.* a load; cargo; freight (of a ship). [ME < MD or MLG *vracht* freight money, FREIGHT; cf. OHG *frēht* earnings, OE *ǣht* possession]

Fräu·lein (froi′līn; *Eng.* froi′līn or, *often,* frô′-, frou′-), *n., pl.* **Fräu·lein,** *Eng.* **Fräu·leins.** *German.* an unmarried woman; a young lady (often used as a term of address).

Fraun·ho·fer (froun′hō′fər, frou′ən hof′ər; *for 1 also Ger.* fʀoun′hō′fəʀ), *n.* **1. Jo·seph von** (jō′zəf von, -səf; *Ger.* yō′zef fən), 1787–1826, German optician and physicist. **2.** a crater in the fourth quadrant of the face of the moon: about 30 miles in diameter.

Fraun′hofer lines′, the dark lines of the solar spectrum. [named after J. von FRAUNHOFER]

Frau oh·ne Schat·ten, Die (*Ger.* dē fʀou′ ō′nə shät′ᵊn), an opera (1919) by Richard Strauss.

Fra·va·shi (frə vä′shē), *n. Zoroastrianism.* the soul of a dead ancestor. [< Avestan]

frax·i·nel·la (frak′sə nel′ə), *n.* dittany (def. 3). [< NL, equiv. to L *frāxin(us)* ash tree + *-ella* fem. dim. suffix]

fray¹ (frā), *n.* **1.** a noisy quarrel; brawl; fight, skirmish, or battle. **2.** *Archaic.* fright. —*v.t.* **3.** *Archaic.* to frighten. —*v.i.* **4.** *Archaic.* to fight; brawl. [ME *frai;* aph. var. of AFFRAY]

fray² (frā), *v.t.* **1.** to wear (cloth, rope, etc.) to loose, raveled threads or fibers at the edge or end; cause to ravel out. **2.** to wear by rubbing (sometimes fol. by *through*). **3.** to cause strain on (something); upset; discompose: *The argument frayed their nerves.* **4.** to rub. —*v.i.* **5.** to become frayed, as cloth, etc; ravel out: *My sweater frayed at the elbows.* **6.** to rub against something: *tall grass fraying against my knees.* —*n.* **7.** a frayed part, as in cloth: *frays at the toes of well worn sneakers.* [ME *fraie(n)* < OF *fray(er), frei(ier)* (to) rub < L *fricāre.* See FRICTION]

fraze (frāz), *v.t.,* **frazed, fraz·ing.** to reduce the diameter of (a gear). [var. of FRAISE]

Fra·zer (frā′zər), *n.* **1. Sir James George,** 1854–1941, Scottish anthropologist: writer of socio-anthropological studies. **2.** Also, **Fraser.** a boy's given name.

fra·zil (frā′zəl, fraz′əl, frə zēl′, -zil′), *n. Geol.* ice crystals formed in turbulent water. [< CanF *frasil, frazil, fraisil,* F *fraisil* coal cinders, OF *faisil*]

fraz·zle (fraz′əl), *v.,* **-zled, -zling,** *n. Informal.* —*v.i., v.t.* **1.** to fray; wear to threads or shreds. **2.** to weary; tire out: *Those six eight-year-olds frazzled me.* —*n.* **3.** state of being frazzled or worn-out. **4.** a remnant; shred. [b. FRAY² + *fazzle,* ME *fasel(in)* (to) unravel, c. G *faseln*]

fraz·zled (fraz′əld), *adj. Informal.* worn out; fatigued: *a late party that left us frazzled.* [FRAZZLE + -ED²]

FRB, 1. Federal Reserve Bank. **2.** Federal Reserve Board. Also, **F.R.B.**

FRC, Federal Radio Commission.

F.R.C.P., Fellow of the Royal College of Physicians.

F.R.C.S., Fellow of the Royal College of Surgeons.

freak¹ (frēk), *n.* **1.** a sudden and apparently causeless change or turn of events, the mind, etc.; an apparently capricious notion, occurrence, etc.: *That kind of sudden storm is a freak.* **2.** any abnormal product or curiously unusual object; anomaly; aberration: *a freak of the modern sensibility.* **3.** a person or animal on exhibition as an example of some strange deviation from nature; monster. **4.** *Numis.* an imperfect coin, undetected at the mint and put into circulation. **5.** *Philately.* a stamp differing from others of the same printing because of creases, dirty engraving plates, etc. Cf. **error** (def. 7), **variety** (def. 8). **6.** *Archaic.* capriciousness; whimsicality. —*adj.* **7.** unusual; odd; irregular: *a freak condition; a freak circumstance.* [? akin to OE *frīcian* to dance]
—**Syn. 2.** vagary, quirk, crotchet.

freak² (frēk), *v.t.* **1.** to fleck, streak, or variegate: *great splashes of color freaking the sky.* —*n.* **2.** a fleck or streak of color. [? v. use of FREAK¹; appar. coined by Milton]

freak·ish (frē′kish), *adj.* **1.** given to or full of freaks; whimsical; capricious: *freakish behavior.* **2.** resembling a freak; queer; odd; grotesque: *freakish appearance.* [FREAK¹ + -ISH¹] —**freak′ish·ly,** *adv.* —**freak′ish·ness,** *n.*

freak′ of na′ture, 1. a person or animal that is born or grows with abnormal physical features. **2.** an unusual, unexpected natural phenomenon.

freak′ out′, *Slang.* **1.** to react with wild excitement, as when under the influence of a hallucinogenic drug. **2.** to lose one's sanity, composure, or mental stability.

freak-out (frēk′out′), *n. Slang.* a period or event characterized by wild excitement or loss of sanity. Also, **freak′out′.**

freak′ show′, an exhibition of physical freaks.

freak·y (frē′kē), *adj.,* **freak·i·er, freak·i·est.** freakish. [FREAK¹ + -Y¹] —**freak′i·ly,** *adv.* —**freak′i·ness,** *n.*

Fré·chet (*Fr.* frā shε′), *n.* **Re·né Mau·rice** (rə nā′ mō rēs′), born 1878, French mathematician.

Fré·chette (*Fr.* frā shet′), *n.* **Louis Ho·no·ré** (*Fr.* lwē ô nô rā′), 1839–1908, Canadian poet and journalist.

freck·le (frek′əl), *n., v.,* **-led, -ling.** —*n.* **1.** a small, brownish spot on the skin, usually caused by exposure to sunlight. **2.** any small spot or discoloration: *freckles of paint spattered on the floor.* —*v.t.* **3.** to cover with freckles; produce freckles on. —*v.i.* **4.** to become freckled. [b. obs. *frecken* freckle (ME *frekne* < Scand; cf. Icel *freknur,* pl.) and SPECKLE (n.)]

freck·le-faced (frek′əl fāst′), *adj.* having a face conspicuously covered with freckles.

freck·ly (frek′lē), *adj.,* **-li·er, -li·est.** full of freckles. [FRECKLE + -Y¹]

Fred (fred), *n.* a boy's given name, form of **Frederick.**

Fre·da (frē′də), *n.* a girl's given name. Also, **Frieda.**

Fred·die (fred′ē), *n.* **1.** a boy's given name, form of **Frederick. 2.** a girl's given name, form of **Freda.** Also, **Fred′dy.**

Fred·e·ri·ca (fred′ə rē′kə, fre drē′-), *n.* a girl's given name. Also, **Frederika.**

Fred·er·ick (fred′rik, -ər ik), *n.* **1.** a city in central Maryland. 21,744 (1960). **2.** a town in SW Oklahoma. 5879 (1960). **3.** Also, **Fred′er·ic, Fredric, Fredrich, Friedrich.** a boy's given name.

Frederick I, 1. ("*Frederick Barbarossa*") 1123?–90, king of Germany 1152–90; king of Italy 1152–90: emperor of the Holy Roman Empire 1152–90. **2.** 1194–1250, king of Sicily 1198–1212: as Frederick II, king of Germany and emperor of the Holy Roman Empire 1215–50. **3.** 1657–1713, king of Prussia 1701–13 (son of Frederick William the Great Elector).

Frederick II, 1. See **Frederick I** (def. 2). **2.** ("*Frederick the Great*") 1712–86, king of Prussia 1740–86 (son of Frederick William I).

Frederick III, ("*the Wise*") 1463–1525, elector of Saxony 1486–1525: protector of Martin Luther.

Frederick IX, born 1899, king of Denmark since 1947 (son of Christian X).

Fred·e·ri·ka (fred′ə rē′kə, fre drē′-), *n.* a girl's given name. Also, **Frederica.**

Fred′erick Bar·ba·ros′sa (bär′bə ros′ə). See **Frederick I** (def. 1).

Fred·er·icks·burg (fred′riks bûrg′), *n.* **1.** a city in NE Virginia, on the Rappahannock River: scene of a Confederate victory 1862. 13,639 (1960). **2.** a town in central Texas. 4629 (1960).

Fred′erick the Great′. See **Frederick II** (def. 2).

Fred·er·ick·town (fred′rik toun′, fred′ər ik-), *n.* a town in SE Missouri. 3484 (1960).

Fred′erick Wil′liam, 1. ("*the Great Elector*") 1620–88, elector of Brandenburg who increased the power and importance of Prussia. **2.** 1882–1951, German general: crown prince of Germany 1888–1918 (son of William II of Germany).

Frederick William I, 1688–1740, king of Prussia 1713–40.

Frederick William II, 1744–97, king of Prussia 1786–97.

Frederick William III, 1770–1840, king of Prussia 1797–1840.

Frederick William IV, 1795–1861, king of Prussia 1840–61 (brother of William I of Prussia).

Fred·er·ic·ton (fred′ər ik tən), *n.* a city in and the capital of New Brunswick, in SE Canada, on the St. John River. 19,683 (1961).

Fre·de·riks·berg (fre′thə rēks barkh′), *n.* a city in E Denmark: a part of Copenhagen. 114,285 (1960).

Fre·do·nia (fri dōn′yə), *n.* **1.** a town in W New York. 8477 (1960). **2.** a town in SE Kansas. 3233 (1960).

Fred·ric (fred′rik), *n.* a boy's given name. Also, **Frederic, Frederick, Fred′rich, Friedrich.**

free (frē), *adj.,* **fre·er, fre·est,** *adv., v.,* **freed, free·ing.** —*adj.* **1.** enjoying personal rights or liberty, as one not in slavery: *a land of free men.* **2.** pertaining to or reserved for those who enjoy personal liberty: *They were thankful to be living on free soil.* **3.** existing under, characterized by, or possessing civil and political liberties that are, as a rule, constitutionally guaranteed by representative government: *the free nations of the world.* **4.** enjoying political independence, as a people or country not under foreign rule. **5.** exempt from external authority, interference, restriction, etc., as a person, the will, thought, choice, action, etc.; independent; unfettered. **6.** able to do something at will; at liberty: *free to choose.* **7.** not subject to special regulations, restrictions, duties, etc.: *The ship was given free passage.* **8.** not literal, as a translation, adaptation, or the like. **9.** not subject to rules, set forms, etc.: *the free song of a bird; free skating.* **10.** clear of obstructions or obstacles, as a road, corridor, etc.: *The highway is now free of fallen rock.* **11.** not occupied or in use: *I'll try to call her again if the line is free.* **12.** exempt or released from something specified that controls, restrains, burdens, etc. (usually fol. by *from* or *of*): *free from worry; free of taxes.* **13.** having immunity or being safe (usually fol. by *from*): *free from criticism.* **14.** uncombined chemically: *free oxygen.* **15.** that may be used by or is open to all : *a free market.* **16.** engaged in by all present; general: *a free fight.* **17.** unimpeded, as motion or movement; easy, firm, or swift. **18.** loose; not held fast; unattached: *the free end of a rope; to get one's arm free.* **19.** not joined to or in contact with something else: *The free end of the cantilever sagged.* **20.** acting without self-restraint or reserve: *to be too free with one's tongue.* **21.** frank and open; unconstrained, unceremonious, or familiar. **22.** unrestrained by decency; loose or licentious: *We were appalled at her free behavior.* **23.** ready in giving; liberal; lavish: *to be free with one's advice.* **24.** given readily or in profusion; unstinted. **25.** given without consideration of a return, as a gift. **26.** provided without, or not subject to, a charge or payment: *free schools; a free sample.* **27.** at liberty to enter and enjoy at will (usually fol. by *of*): *to be free of a friend's house.* **28.** easily worked, as stone, land, etc. **29.** *Naut.* (of a wind) nearly on the quarter, so that a sailing vessel may sail free. **30.** *Phonet.* (of a vowel) situated in an open syllable (opposed to *checked*). **31.** traveling without power; under no force except that of gravity or inertia: *free flight.* **32.** *Math.* (of a vector) having specified magnitude and direction but no specified initial point. Cf. **bound¹** (def. 8). **33. free and clear,** *Law.* without any encumbrance, as a lien or mortgage: *They owned their house free and clear.* **34. free and easy, a.** unrestrained; casual; informal. **b.** excessively or inappropriately casual; presumptuous. **35. set free,** to release; liberate; free: *The prisoners were at last set free.* **36. with a free hand,** generously; freely; openhandedly: *He entertains visitors with a free hand.* —*adv.* **37.** in a free manner; freely. **38.** without cost or charge. **39.** *Naut.* away from the wind so that the vessel need not be close-hauled: *running free.* **40. make free with, a.** to use as one's own; help oneself to: *If you make free with their liquor, you won't be invited again.* **b.** to treat with too much familiarity; take liberties with. —*v.t.* **41.** to make free; set at liberty; release from bondage, imprisonment, or restraint. **42.** to exempt or deliver (usually fol. by *from*). **43.** to relieve or rid (usually fol. by *of*): *to free oneself of responsibility.* **44.** to disengage (usually fol. by *from* or *of*). [ME *fre,* OE *frēo;* c. Goth *frei(s),* OHG *frī* (G *frei*), D *vrij,* Skt *priyá-* dear. See FRIEND, FRIDAY]

free′ a′gent, 1. one who is self-determining and is not responsible for his actions to any authority. **2.** a professional athlete who has been released by the team to which he was under contract and is free to sign a contract with another team.

free′ air′, 1. See **free atmosphere. 2.** air not affected by local conditions.

free′ along′side ship′. See **F.A.S.** Also called **free′ along′side ves′sel.**

Free′ and Accept′ed Ma′sons. See under **Freemason** (def. 1).

free′ ascent′, *Rocketry.* the upward traveling or path of a rocket carried by its own inertia after its engine has stopped operating.

free-as·so·ci·ate (frē′ə sō′shē āt′, -sē-), *v.i.,* **-at·ed, -at·ing.** to engage in free association.

free′ associa′tion, *Psychoanal.* the uncensored expression of the ideas, impressions, etc., passing through the mind of the analysand, used to facilitate access to the unconscious processes.

free′ at′mosphere, the part of the atmosphere that lies above the frictional influence of the earth's surface. Also called **free air.**

free′ balloon′, a balloon, often equipped to carry passengers, that drifts with air currents and whose ascent and descent are controlled by the release of ballast and buoyant gas. —**free′ balloon′ing.**

free·base (frē′bās′), *v.,* **-based, basing.** —*v.t.* **1.** to purify (cocaine) with ether. —*v.i.* **2.** to use freebased cocaine. [FREE + BASE¹] —**free′bas′er,** *n.*

free′ bid′, *Bridge.* a bid made in response to a partner's bid when responding is not required by convention or is not necessary to keep the auction open.

free-blown (frē′blōn′), *adj.* (of glass) blown and shaped manually and without the use of a mold. Cf. **blown-molded, offhand** (def. 5).

free·board (frē′bōrd′, -bôrd′), *n. Naut.* **1.** the distance between the level of the water and the upper surface of the freeboard deck amidships at the side of a hull: regulated by the agencies of various countries according to the construction of the hull, the type of cargo carried, the area of the world in which it sails, the type of water, and the season of the year. Cf. **load line. 2.** (on a cargo vessel) the distance between the uppermost deck considered fully watertight and the official load line. **3.** the portion of the side of a hull that is above the water. [FREE + BOARD; trans. of F *franc bord*]

free′board deck′, *Naut.* (on a cargo vessel) the uppermost deck officially considered to be watertight: used as the level from which the Plimsoll marks are measured.

free′board length′, *Naut.* the length of a vessel, measured on the summer load line from the fore side of the stem to some part of the stern, usually the after side of the rudderpost.

free·boot (frē′bōōt′), *v.i.* to act as a freebooter. [back formation from FREEBOOTER]

free·boot·er (frē′bōō′tər), *n.* a person who goes about in search of plunder; a pirate or buccaneer. [Anglicization of D *vrijbuiter,* equiv. to *vrij* free + *buit* BOOTY + *-er* -ER¹]

free·boot·y (frē′bōō′tē), *n. Obs.* plunder; loot; spoil. [FREEBOOT(ER + BOOT)Y]

free-bored (frē′bōrd′, -bôrd′), *adj.* (of a rifle) having a bore that is not rifled within a short distance of the breech, so that a fired cartridge travels about one-half inch before being engaged by the lands, thus reducing initial high pressures.

free·born (frē′bôrn′), *adj.* **1.** born free, rather than in slavery, bondage, or vassalage. **2.** pertaining to or befitting persons born free. [ME *freborn, freeborn.* See FREE, BORN]

free′ church′, 1. (*sometimes cap.*) a church free from state control. Cf. **established church.. 2.** (*sometimes cap.*) a dissenting or nonconforming church. **3.** (*cap.*) Also, **Free Kirk.** (in Scotland) the church established by those who left the Church of Scotland in 1843.

free′ church′man, 1. (*sometimes cap.*) a member of a free church. **2.** (*cap.*) a member of the Free Church of Scotland.

free′ cit′y, a city having an independent government and forming a sovereign state by itself.

free′ coin′age, the unrestricted coinage of bullion, or of a specified metal, as silver, into money for any person bringing it to the mint, either with or without charge for minting.

free′ compan′ion, a member of a band of mercenary soldiers of the Middle Ages.

free′ com′pany, a band of free companions.

free′ deliv′ery, *U.S.* the delivery of mail without charge.

free′ div′ing, *Chiefly Brit.* See **skin diving.**

freed·man (frēd′mən), *n., pl.* **-men.** a man who has been freed from slavery. [FREED + MAN¹]

free·dom (frē′dəm), *n.* **1.** state of being at liberty rather than in confinement or under physical restraint: *He won his freedom after a retrial.* **2.** exemption from external control, interference, regulation, etc. **3.** power of determining one's or its own action: *freedom of choice.* **4.** *Philos.* the power to make one's own choices or decisions without constraint from within or without; autonomy; self-determination. **5.** civil liberty, as opposed to subjection to an arbitrary or despotic government. **6.** political or national independence. **7.** a particular immunity or privilege enjoyed, as by a city or corporation: *freedom to levy taxes.* **8.** personal liberty, as opposed to bondage or slavery: *a former slave who bought his freedom.* **9.** absence of or release from ties, obligations, etc. **10.** exemption or immunity: *freedom from taxation.* **11.** exemption from the presence of anything specified (usually fol. by *from*): *freedom from fear.* **12.** ease or facility of movement or action: *to enjoy the freedom of living in the country.* **13.** frankness of manner or speech. **14.** absence of ceremony or reserve. **15.** a liberty taken. **16.** the right of enjoying all the privileges or special rights of citizenship, membership, etc., in a community or the like. **17.** the right of frequenting, enjoying, or using at will: *to have the freedom of a friend's library.* [ME *fredom,* OE *frēodōm.* See FREE, -DOM]

—**Syn. 1.** FREEDOM, INDEPENDENCE, LIBERTY refer to an absence of undue restrictions and an opportunity to exercise one's right and powers. FREEDOM emphasizes the opportunity given for the exercise of one's rights, powers, desires, or the like: *freedom of speech or conscience; freedom of movement.* INDEPENDENCE implies not only lack of restrictions but also the ability to stand alone, unsustained by anything else: *Independence of thought promotes invention and discovery.* LIBERTY, though most often interchanged with FREEDOM, is also used to imply undue exercise of freedom: *He took liberties with the text.* **3.** franchise. **13.** openness, ingenuousness. **15.** license. **17.** run. —**Ant. 1–3.** restraint. **5, 6, 8.** oppression.

Free·dom (frē′dəm), *n.* **1.** a town in W California. 4206 (1960). **2.** a town in W Pennsylvania. 2895 (1960).

free′dom fight′er, a fighter for freedom, esp. one who battles against established forces of tyranny.

free′dom of speech′, the right of people to express their opinions publicly without governmental interference, subject to the laws against libel, incitement to violence or rebellion, etc. Also called **free speech.**

free′dom of the cit′y, 1. nominal citizenship in a city, conferred as an honor upon celebrated visitors. **2.** (formerly) official citizenship in a city, conferred upon distinguished nonresidents.

free′dom of the press′, the right to publish newspapers, magazines, and other printed matter without governmental restriction and subject only to the laws of libel, obscenity, sedition, etc.

free′dom of the seas′, *Internat. Law.* the doctrine that ships of neutral countries may sail anywhere on the high seas without interference by warring powers.

free′dom ride′, a bus trip made to parts of the southern U.S. by persons engaging in efforts to integrate racially segregated facilities. Also, **Free′dom Ride′.**

free′dom rid′er, a person who participates in a freedom ride. Also, **Free′dom Rid′er.**

freed·wom·an (frēd′wŏŏm′ən), *n., pl.* **-wom·en.** a woman who has been freed from slavery. [FREED + WOMAN]

free′ en′ergy, *Thermodynamics.* a quantity related to the work obtainable from or the work put into a system during certain reversible processes. Cf. **Gibbs free energy, Helmholtz free energy.**

free′ en′terprise, 1. an economic and political doctrine holding that a capitalist economy can regulate itself in a freely competitive market through the relationship of supply and demand with a minimum of governmental intervention and regulation. **2.** the practice of free enterprise in an economy: "*We no longer have free enterprise in this country,*" *cried the P.R. man when his company lost the antitrust suit.*

free′ en′thalpy, *Thermodynamics.* See **Gibbs free energy.**

free′ expan′sion, *Thermodynamics.* the expansion of a gas into an evacuated space without the transfer of heat or the performance of work.

free′ fall′, 1. the hypothetical fall of a body such that the only force acting upon it is that of gravity. **2.** the part of a parachute jump that precedes the opening of the parachute.

free-float·ing (frē′flō′ting), *adj.* **1.** (of people) independent; uncommitted, as to a doctrine, political party, etc. **2.** (of an emotional state) lacking a specific cause or object; generalized: *free-floating hostility.* **3.** capable of relatively free movement.

free-for-all (frē′fər ôl′), *n.* a fight, argument, contest, etc., open to everyone and usually without rules.

free′ form′, 1. *Ling.* a linguistic form that can occur by itself, as *fire, book, run,* etc. Cf. **bound form. 2.** a shape having an irregular contour, chiefly used in nonrepresentational art and industrial design.

free-form (frē′fôrm′), *adj.* characterized by free form: *a free-form chair; free-form bowl; free-form sculpture.*

Free′ French′. See **Fighting French.**

free′ gold′, 1. *U.S.* treasury gold, including the legal reserve, not restricted to the redemption of gold certificates or other specific uses. **2.** *Mining.* gold found in a pure state in nature, as in placer mining.

free′ goods′, **1.** imported goods that are not subject to duty. **2.** goods having utilitarian value, as air and water, but available in such great quantities as to have no cost.

free′ hand′, unrestricted freedom or authority: *They gave the decorator a free hand in doing their apartment over.*

free·hand (frē′hand′), *adj., adv.* by hand without guiding instruments, measurements, or other aids: *a freehand map; to do a drawing freehand.* [FREE + HAND]

free-hand·ed (frē′han′did), *adj.* **1.** open-handed; generous; liberal. **2.** freehand. —*adv.* **3.** freehand. —**free′-hand′ed·ly,** *adv.* —**free′-hand′ed·ness,** *n.*

free-heart·ed (frē′här′tid), *adj.* light-hearted; spontaneous; frank; generous. [ME *free herted.* See FREE, -HEARTED]

free·hold (frē′hōld′), *Law.* —*n.* **1.** a form of tenure by which an estate is held in fee simple, fee tail, or for life. **2.** an estate in land, inherited or held for life. —*adj.* **3.** pertaining to, of the nature of, or held by freehold. [ME *frehold* (see FREE, HOLD[1]); trans. of AF *franc tenement* (see FRANK[1], TENEMENT)]

Free·hold (frē′hōld′), *n.* a town in E New Jersey: battle of Monmouth courthouse 1778. 9140 (1960). Formerly, **Monmouth.**

free·hold·er (frē′hōl′dər), *n.* the owner of a freehold. [ME *freholder* (see FREE, HOLDER); trans. of AF *fraunc tenaunt* (see FRANK[1], TENANT)]

free′ house′, *Brit.* a tavern that, having no contract with a particular brewery, serves several brands of beer, ale, etc.

free′ing port′, *Naut.* an opening in the bottom of a bulwark, for rapid drainage of a weather deck in heavy seas; scupper.

Free′ Kirk′. See **free church** (def. 3). —**Free′ Kirk′er.**

free′ lance′, **1.** a person who works as a writer, designer, performer, etc., but not on a regular salary basis for any one employer, organization, or the like. **2.** a person who contends in a cause, or in a succession of various causes, as he chooses, without personal attachment or allegiance. **3.** a mercenary soldier or military adventurer of the Middle Ages, often of knightly rank, who offered his services to any state, party, or cause.

free-lance (frē′lans′, -läns′), *v.,* **-lanced, -lanc·ing,** *adj., adv.* —*v.i.* **1.** to act or work as a free lance: *I understand he's free-lancing now.* —*adj.* **2.** of or pertaining to a free lance or his work: *a free-lance writer.* —*adv.* **3.** in the manner of a free lance: *She works free-lance.* —**free′-lanc′er,** *n.*

Free·land (frē′lənd), *n.* **1.** a town in central Pennsylvania. 5068 (1960). **2.** a boy's given name.

free′ list′, *Commerce U.S.* a list or register of articles that may be brought into a country duty-free.

free′ liv′er, a person who follows a way of life in which he freely indulges his appetites, desires, etc.

free-liv·ing (frē′liv′ing), *adj.* **1.** following a way of life in which one freely indulges his appetites, desires, etc. **2.** *Biol.* noting an organism that is neither parasitic, symbiotic, nor sessile.

free·load·er (frē′lō′dər), *n.* *Informal.* one who imposes on others for free food, entertainment, etc. [FREE + LOADER] —**free′load′ing,** *n.*

free′ love′, the doctrine or practice of having sexual relations without legal marriage or any continuing obligation.

free′ lunch′, food formerly provided without charge in some bars and saloons to attract customers.

free·ly (frē′lē), *adv.* in a free manner. [ME *freliche,* OE *frēolīce.* See FREE, -LY]

free-ma·chin·ing (frē′mə shē′ning), *adj.* **1.** (of certain metals) readily machinable at high speeds with low force. **2.** noting a class of steels having quantities of certain additives, as sulfur, lead, etc., to make them readily machinable.

free·man (frē′mən), *n., pl.* **-men.** **1.** a man who is free; a man who enjoys personal, civil, or political liberty. **2.** a person who enjoys or is entitled to citizenship, franchise, or other special privilege: *a freeman of a city.* [ME *freman,* OE *frēoman.* See FREE, MAN[1]]

Free·man (frē′mən), *n.* **1. Douglas Sou·thall** (sou′thôl), 1886–1953, U.S. journalist and biographer. **2. Edward Augustus,** 1823–92, English historian. **3. Mary E(leanor Wilkins),** 1862–1930, U.S. novelist and short-story writer. **4.** a boy's given name.

free·mar·tin (frē′mär′tən), *n.* a usually sterile female calf that is born as a twin with a male. [?]

Free·ma·son (frē′mā′sən, frē′mā′-), *n.* **1.** a member of a widely distributed secret order (**Free and Accepted Masons**), having for its object mutual assistance and the promotion of brotherly love among its members. **2.** (*l.c.*) *Hist.* **a.** one of a class of skilled stoneworkers of the Middle Ages, possessing secret signs and passwords. **b.** a member of a society composed of such workers, with honorary members (**accepted masons**) who were not connected with the building trades. [ME *fremason.* See FREE, MASON] —**free·ma·son·ic** (frē′mə-son′ik), *adj.*

free·ma·son·ry (frē′mā′sən rē), *n.* **1.** secret or tacit brotherhood; instinctive sympathy: *the freemasonry of those who hunger for knowledge.* **2.** (*cap.*) the principles, practices, and institutions of Freemasons. [ME *fremasonry.* See FREEMASON, -RY]

free·ness (frē′nis), *n.* state or quality of being free. [ME *frenesse.* See FREE, -NESS]

free′ on board′. See **f.o.b.**

free′ perspec′tive, exaggeration of perspectival devices to increase the illusion of depth, used esp. in stage-set painting and construction.

free′ port′, **1.** a port open under equal conditions to all traders. **2.** a part or all of a port not included in customs territory so as to expedite transshipment of what is not to be imported.

Free·port (frē′pōrt′, -pôrt′), *n.* **1.** a village on SW Long Island, in SE New York. 34,419 (1960). **2.** a city in NW Illinois. 26,628 (1960).

free′ press′, a body of publications, as books, newspapers, etc., not controlled or restricted, esp. by government censorship in political or ideological matters: *The country lacked a free press.*

fre·er[1] (frē′ər), *n.* one who or that which frees. [FREE + -ER[1]]

fre·er[2] (frē′ər), *adj.* comparative of **free.**

Freer (frēr), *n.* a town in S Texas. 2724 (1960).

free′ rad′ical, *Chem.* an atom or compound in which there is an unpaired electron, as H· or ·CH_3; a group or radical.

free′ reach′, *Naut.* a course sailed by a sailing vessel having the wind on the quarter.

free′ reach′ing, *Naut.* sailing on a free reach.

free′ rid′er, a non-union worker who enjoys the benefits of union activities. Also, **free′-rid′er.**

free·si·a (frē′zhē ə, -zē ə, -zhə), *n.* any iridaceous plant of the genus *Freesia,* native to South Africa, having fragrant, white, yellow, or sometimes rose-colored, tubular flowers. [< NL; named after E.M. *Fries* (1794–1878), Swedish botanist; see -IA]

free′ sil′ver, *Econ.* the free coinage of silver, esp. at a fixed ratio with gold. —**free′-sil′ver,** *adj.*

free′ soc′age, land held by a tenant who rendered certain honorable and nonservile duties to his feudal lord. Also called **free and common socage.** Cf. **villein socage.**

free-soil (frē′soil′), *adj.* *U.S. Hist.* **1.** pertaining to or opposing the extension of slavery in the Territories. **2.** pertaining to or characteristic of the Free Soil party. —**free′-soil′ism,** *n.*

Free-Soil·er (frē′soi′lər), *n.* a member of the Free Soil party or a supporter of its principles. [FREE SOIL (PARTY) + -ER[1]]

Free′ Soil′ par′ty, *U.S.* a former political party (1848–56) that opposed the extension of slavery in the Territories.

free′ speech′. See **freedom of speech.**

free-spo·ken (frē′spō′kən), *adj.* given to speaking freely or without reserve; outspoken. —**free′-spo′ken·ly,** *adv.* —**free′-spo′ken·ness,** *n.*

fre·est (frē′ist), *adj.* superlative of **free.**

free·stand·ing (frē′stan′ding), *adj.* (of sculpture or architectural elements) unattached to a supporting unit or background. Also, **free′-stand′ing.** [FREE + STANDING]

Free′ State′, **1.** *U.S.* (before the Civil War) a State in which slavery was prohibited. **2.** See **Irish Free State.**

Free′ Stat′er (stā′tər), **1.** a native or inhabitant of a Free State. **2.** a person of European descent who is a native or resident of the Orange Free State. [FREE STATE + -ER[1]]

free·stone (frē′stōn′), *n.* **1.** any stone, as sandstone, which can be freely worked or quarried, esp. one which cuts well in all directions without splitting. **2.** a freestone fruit, esp. a peach or plum. —*adj.* **3.** having a stone from which the pulp is easily separated, as certain peaches and plums. [ME *freston* (see FREE, STONE); trans. of OF *franche piere;* see FRANK[1]]

Free′stone State′ (frē′stōn′), Connecticut (used as a nickname).

free·style (frē′stīl′), *n.* *Swimming.* a race in which the stroke to be used is not specified, the competitors being free to use any stroke they choose. [FREE + STYLE]

free-swim·mer (frē′swim′ər), *n.* *Zool.* an animal, as a fish, that swims about freely.

free-swim·ming (frē′swim′ing), *adj.* *Zool.* (of aquatic animals) not fixed or attached; capable of swimming about freely.

Free′ Ter′ritory of Trieste′. See **Trieste, Free Territory of.**

free·think·er (frē′thing′kər), *n.* one who forms his opinions independently of authority or tradition, esp. in matters concerning religion. [FREE + THINKER] —**free′think′ing,** *adj., n.*
—**Syn.** skeptic, agnostic; atheist.

free′ thought′, thought unrestrained by deference to authority, esp. in matters of religion.

free′ throw′, *Basketball.* See **foul shot.**

free′ throw′ line′, *Basketball.* See **foul line** (def. 2).

Free·town (frē′toun′), *n.* a seaport in and the capital of Sierra Leone, in W Africa. 127,917 (1963).

free′ trade′, **1.** trade between different countries, free from governmental restrictions or duties. **2.** international trade free from protective duties and subject only to such tariffs as are needed for revenue. **3.** the system, principles, or maintenance of such trade. **4.** *Obs.* smuggling. —**free′-trade′,** *adj.*

free·trad·er (frē′trā′dər), *n.* **1.** a person who advocates free trade. **2.** *Obs.* a smuggler. Also, **free′ trad′er.** [FREE TRADE + -ER[1]]

free′ var′iable, *Logic.* (in functional calculus) a variable occurring in a sentential function and not within the scope of any quantifier containing it. Cf. **bound variable.**

free′ varia′tion, *Ling.* a relation between the members of a pair of phones, phonemes, morphs, or other linguistic entities such that either of the two may occur in the same position with no change in the meaning of the utterance: In the first syllable of "economics," "e" and "ē" are in free variation. Cf. **complementary distribution.**

free′ verse′, *Pros.* verse that does not follow a fixed metrical pattern. —**free-ver·si·fi·er** (frē′vûr′sə fī′ər), *n.*

free·way (frē′wā′), *n.* an express highway, usually having traffic routed on and off cloverleaves. [FREE + WAY]

free·wheel (frē′hwēl′, -wēl′), *n.* **1.** an overrunning clutch device in connection with the transmission gearbox of a motor vehicle that automatically disengages the drive shaft whenever it tends to rotate more rapidly than the shaft driving it. **2.** a form of rear bicycle wheel that has a device freeing it from the driving mechanism, as when the pedals are stopped in coasting. —*v.i.* **3.** (of a vehicle or its operator) to coast with the wheels disengaged from the driving mechanism. **4.** to move or function freely, independently, unconcernedly, or the like (often fol. by *about, through, around,* etc.): *The boys freewheeled around the country after graduation.* [FREE + WHEEL]

free·wheel·er (frē′hwē′lər, -wē′-), *n.* a vehicle that can freewheel. [FREEWHEEL + -ER[1]]

free·wheel·ing (frē′hwē′ling, -wē′-), *adj.* **1.** operating in the manner of a freewheel. **2.** (of a person) moving about freely, independently, or irresponsibly. **3.** (of words, remarks, actions, etc.) not governed or influenced by rules, responsibilities, or the like: *Loose, freewheeling charges were traded during the argument.* [FREEWHEEL + -ING[2]]

free′ will′, **1.** free choice; voluntary decision. **2.** *Philos.* the doctrine that the conduct of human beings expresses personal choice and is not simply determined by physical or divine forces.

free·will (frē′wil′), *adj.* **1.** made or done freely or of one's own accord; voluntary. **2.** of or pertaining to the metaphysical doctrine of the freedom of the will: *the freewill controversy.* [ME *fre wil.* See FREE, WILL[2]]

free′will of′fering, a voluntary religious contribution made in addition to what is expected or required.

freeze (frēz), *v.,* **froze, fro·zen, freez·ing,** *n.* —*v.i.* **1.** to become hardened into ice or into a solid body; to change from the liquid to the solid state by loss of heat. **2.** to become hard or rigid because of loss of heat, as objects containing moisture: *The washing froze soon after being hung on the line.* **3.** to become obstructed by the formation of ice, as pipes: *Water pipes in poorly heated buildings often freeze in winter.* **4.** to become fixed to something by or as by the action of frost. **5.** (of a screw, nail, or the like) to become rigidly fixed in place, as from rust, dirt, etc. **6.** to be of the degree of cold at which water freezes: *It is freezing tonight.* **7.** to suffer the effects of intense cold; have the sensation of extreme cold: *We sat there freezing until the heat came on.* **8.** to die of frost or cold. **9.** to lose warmth of feeling; be chilled with fear, shock, etc.: *My heart froze when she told me the news.* **10.** to stop suddenly; halt: *Fear made him freeze in his tracks.* **11.** to become immobilized through fear, shock, etc.: *When he got in front of the audience he froze. A good driver doesn't freeze in an emergency.* —*v.t.* **12.** to congeal; harden into ice; change from a fluid to a solid form by loss of heat. **13.** to form ice on the surface of (a river, pond, etc.). **14.** to obstruct or close (a pipe or the like) by the formation of ice: *The storm had frozen the hydrant.* **15.** to fix fast with ice: *a sled frozen to a sidewalk.* **16.** to harden or stiffen by cold, as objects containing moisture. **17.** to quick-freeze. **18.** to subject (something) to freezing temperature; place (something) in a freezer or in the freezing compartment of a refrigerator. **19.** to cause to suffer the effects of intense cold; produce the sensation of extreme cold in. **20.** to kill by frost or cold: *A late snow froze the buds.* **21.** to cause to lose warmth as if by cold; chill with fear; dampen the enthusiasm of. **22.** to cause (a person or animal) to become fixed through fright, alarm, shock, etc.: *Terror froze him to the steering wheel.* **23.** *Finance Informal.* to render impossible of liquidation or collection: *Bank loans are frozen in business depressions.* **24.** to fix (rents, prices, etc.) at a specific amount, usually by government order. **25.** *Surg.* to render part of the body insensitive to pain or slower in its function by artificial means. **26.** *Canasta.* to play a wild card on (the discard pile) so as to make it frozen. **27. freeze on** or **onto,** *Informal.* to adhere closely to; hold on; seize. **28. freeze out,** *U.S. Informal.* to exclude or compel to withdraw from some position of influence or advantage by cold treatment or severe competition. **29. freeze over,** to coat or become coated with ice: *The lake freezes over for several months each year.* —*n.* **30.** act of freezing; state of being frozen. **31.** *Meteorol.* a widespread occurrence of temperatures below 32°F, persisting at least several days: *A freeze is expected in the coastal areas.* **32.** a frost. **33.** a legislative action, esp. in time of national emergency, to control prices, rents, production, etc.: *The government will put a freeze on new construction.* [ME *fresen,* OE *frēosan;* c. MLG *vrēsen,* OIcel *frjōsa,* OHG *friosan* (G *frieren*)] —**freez′a·ble,** *adj.*

freeze-dry (frēz′drī′), *v.t.,* **-dried, -dry·ing.** *Chem.* to subject to freeze-drying.

freeze-dry·ing (frēz′drī′ing), *n.* *Chem.* a process for drying heat-sensitive substances, as blood plasma, antibiotics, and the like, by freezing the substance and then subliming the ice or other frozen solvent in a high vacuum and at a low temperature.

freez·er (frē′zər), *n.* **1.** one who or that which freezes or chills. **2.** a machine containing cold brine, ice, etc., for making ice cream, sherbet, or the like. **3.** a refrigerator or cabinet held at or below 0°C. [FREEZE + -ER[1]]

freez′er burn′, light-colored spots that appear on frozen food, caused by loss of surface moisture due to faulty packaging or improper freezing methods.

freez·ing (frē′zing), *adj.* **1.** (of temperatures) approaching, at, or below the freezing mark. **2.** extremely or uncomfortably cold: *We were both freezing and welcomed the hot cocoa.* **3.** beginning to freeze; partially frozen. [FREEZE + -ING[2]] —**freez′ing·ly,** *adv.*

freez′ing driz′zle, drizzle that falls as a liquid but freezes into glaze or rime upon contact with solid objects.

freez′ing point′, *Physical Chem.* the temperature at which a liquid freezes: *The freezing point of water is 32°F, 0°C.*

freez′ing rain′, rain which, falling as a liquid, freezes into glaze upon contact with solid objects.

free′ zone′, a free port area.

F region, the ionospheric region in which the F layer forms.

Frei (frā), *n.* **E·duar·do** (e dwär′thō), born 1911, Chilean statesman: president since 1964.

Frei·a (frā′ə), *n.* Freya.

Frei·burg (frī′bo͝orkh′), *n.* **1.** a city in SW Baden-Wurttemberg, in SW West Germany. 150,400 (1963). **2.** German name of **Fribourg.**

freight (frāt), *n.* **1.** the ordinary conveyance or means of transport of goods provided by common carriers, (distinguished from *express*): *Shipping by freight is usually less expensive.* **2.** the charges, fee, or compensation paid for such transportation: *We pay the freight.* **3.** *U.S. and Canada.* cargo or lading carried for pay either by water, land, or air. **4.** *U.S. Informal.* cost: *The freight on that new model was more than I could carry.* **5.** (esp. in Britain) the cargo, or any part of the cargo, of a vessel; merchandise transported by water. **6.** *Chiefly Brit.* transportation of goods by water. **7.**

See **freight train.** —*v.t.* **8.** to load; burden: *a story heavily freighted with private meaning.* **9.** to load with goods or merchandise for transportation: *It took all night to freight the ship.* **10.** to transport as freight; send by freight. [ME *freyght* < MD or MLG *vrecht*, var. of *vracht*. See FRAUGHT] —**freight′less,** *adj.*
—**Syn. 2.** freightage, haulage. **3.** load. FREIGHT, CARGO, SHIPMENT refer to goods being transported from place to place. FREIGHT is the general term for goods transported from one place to another by any means: *to send freight from New York to New Orleans.* CARGO is the term generally used for goods carried by ship or plane: *to send a cargo to Europe.* SHIPMENT is a quantity of goods destined for a particular place, no matter how sent: *a shipment of potatoes.* **8.** charge.

freight·age (frā′tij), *n.* **1.** the transportation of goods. **2.** the price for this. **3.** freight, cargo, or lading. [FREIGHT + -AGE]

freight′ a′gent, a representative of a common carrier who manages the freight business in his local district.

freight′ car′, *Railroads.* any car for carrying freight.

freight′ en′gine, a locomotive for pulling freight trains, designed for high drawbar pull rather than high speed.

freight·er (frā′tər), *n.* **1.** a vessel used mainly for carrying cargo. **2.** a person whose occupation it is to receive and forward freight. **3.** a person for whom freight is transported; a shipper. [FREIGHT + -ER[1]]

freight′ for′warder, a person or firm that arranges to pick up or deliver goods on instructions of a shipper or a consignee from or to a point by various necessary conveyances and common carriers. Also called **forwarder, forwarding agent.**

freight′ house′, *U.S.* a depot or storage place for freight.

freight′ ton′, ton[1] (def. 2).

freight′ train′, a train of freight cars.

Frei·schütz, Der (*Ger.* der frī′shyts), an opera (1821) by Carl Maria von Weber.

Fre′ki and Ge′ri (fre′kē), *Scand. Myth.* the two wolves of Odin, who received all food offered the god, except mead.

Fre·ling·huy·sen (frē′ling hī′zən), *n.* **Frederick Theodore,** 1817–85, U.S. statesman.

Fre·man·tle (frē′man′tᵊl), *n.* a seaport in SW Australia, near Perth. 21,980 (1961).

fremd (fremd, frāmd), *adj. Scot.* **1.** foreign; strange. **2.** unfriendly. [ME *frem(e)d*, OE *frem(e)de*; c. Goth *framathei(s)* foreign, OHG *fremidi*, G *fremd*. See FROM] —**fremd′ly,** *adv.* —**fremd′ness,** *n.*

frem·i·tus (frem′i təs), *n., pl.* **-tus.** *Pathol.* palpable vibration, as of the walls of the chest. [< L: a roaring, murmuring, n. use of ptp. of *fremere*]

Fre·mont (frē′mont), *n.* **1.** a city in W California, near San Francisco Bay. 43,790 (1960). **2.** a city in E Nebraska, on the Platte River, near Omaha. 19,698 (1960). **3.** a city in N Ohio. 17,573 (1960). **4.** a town in central Michigan. 3384 (1960). **5.** a boy's given name.

Fré·mont (frē′mont), *n.* **John Charles,** 1813–90, U.S. general and explorer: first Republican presidential candidate, 1856.

fre·nate (frē′nāt), *adj.* having a frenum or frenulum. [< NL *frēnāt(us)*, special use of L *frēnātus* furnished with a bridle. See FRENUM, -ATE[1]]

French (french), *adj.* **1.** of, pertaining to, or characteristic of France, its inhabitants, or their language, culture, etc.: *French cooking.* —*n.* **2.** the people of France and their direct descendants. **3.** a Romance language of the analytic type, spoken in France, parts of Belgium and Switzerland, and in areas colonized after 1500 by France. It is widely used as an international language for diplomacy, scholarship, and science. —*v.t.* **4.** (*often l.c.*) to prepare (food) according to a French method. **5.** (*often l.c.*) to cut (snap beans) into slivers or thin strips before cooking. **6.** (*often l.c.*) to trim the meat from the end of (a rib chop); prepare a french chop for cooking. **7.** (*often l.c.*) to prepare (meat) for cooking by slicing it into strips and pounding. **8.** *Slang.* to short-sheet (a bed). [ME *Frensh, French*, OE *Frenc(i)sc.* See FRANK, -ISH[1]] —**French′ly,** *adv.* —**French′ness,** *n.*

French (french), *n.* **1. Alice** (*Octave Thanet*), 1850–1934, U.S. novelist and short story writer. **2. Daniel Chester,** 1850–1931, U.S. sculptor. **3. Sir John Den·ton Pink·stone** (den′tᵊn pingk′stōn, -stən), **1st Earl of Ypres,** 1852–1925, English field marshal in World War I.

French′ Acad′emy, an association of 40 scholars and men of letters, established in 1635 by Cardinal Richelieu and devoted chiefly to preserving the purity of the French language and establishing standards of proper usage. French, **Académie Française.**

French′ and In′dian War′, the war in America in which France and its Indian allies opposed England 1754–60; treaty signed in 1763.

French′ arch′, an arch similar to a flat arch, but having voussoirs inclined to the same angle on each side of the center.

French′ bean′, **1.** *Chiefly Brit.* the pod of the bean, as a green bean, wax bean, etc., used as a vegetable; string bean. **2.** *Brit.* kidney bean.

French′ bread′, a yeast-raised bread made of dough containing water and distinguished by its thick, well-browned crust, usually made in long, slender loaves with tapered ends.

French′ bull′dog, one of a French breed of small, bat-eared dogs having a large, square head, a short tail, and a short, sleek coat.

French′ Cameroons′, Cameroun (def. 2).

French′ Cana′dian, **1.** a descendant of the early French colonists of Canada. **2.** the language of the French Canadians. **3.** one of a Canadian breed of small, dark-brown dairy cattle, raised chiefly in Quebec.

French′ chalk′, a talc for marking lines on fabrics.

French′ chop′, a rib chop, usually of lamb, with the meat trimmed from the end of the bone.

French′ Commu′nity, a federation of France, its overseas departments and territories, and former French territories that chose to maintain association after becoming independent republics: formed 1958; includes the republics of France, Cameroun, Central Africa, Chad, Republic of Congo, Dahomey, Gabon, Ivory Coast, Malagasy Republic, Mali, Mauritania, Niger, Senegal, Togo, and Upper Volta.

French′ Con′go, former name of the Republic of Congo.

French′ cuff′, a cuff formed by folding back a wide band at the end of a sleeve, usually fastened by a cuff link. Cf. **barrel cuff.**

French′ curve′, a flat drafting instrument consisting of several scroll-like curves enabling a draftsman to draw curves of varying radii.

French curve and line drawn through three points

French′ door′, a door having glass panes throughout or nearly throughout its length. Also called **casement door.**

French′ drain′, a drainage trench filled to ground level with fragments of brick, rock, etc.

French′ dress′ing, (*often l.c.*) salad dressing prepared from oil, vinegar, and seasonings.

French′ en′dive, a variety of chicory the leaves of which are blanched and used for salads. Also called **witloof, witloof chicory.**

French′ Equato′rial Af′rica, a former federation of French territories in central Africa, including Chad, Gabon, Middle Congo, and Ubangi-Shari: each became autonomous in 1958.

French′ fake′, *Naut.* a fake in which the rope is laid down in a series of lengths side-by-side and perpendicular to the direction in which the rope is hauled. Cf. **long fake.**

French′ flat′, *Theat. Brit.* a flat that can be raised to or hung from the flies, and that contains practicable doors, windows, etc.

French′ foot′, *Furniture.* **1.** Also called **knurl toe, scroll foot, whorl foot.** a foot of the mid-18th century having the form of a scroll, continuing the leg downward and outward, supported by a shoe. **2.** a bracket foot comprising a downward and outward continuation of the adjoining surfaces of the piece, the corner of the foot being a concave outward curve and the inner edges being a pair of ogee curves continuing the lines of the bottom rails downward.

French′ fried′ pota′toes, thin strips of potatoes, deep-fried. Also called **French′ fries′.**

French′ Gui·an′a (gē an′ə, gē ä′nə), an overseas department of France, on the NE coast of South America: formerly a French colony. 31,000 (est. 1960); 35,135 sq. mi. *Cap.:* Cayenne. See map under **Guiana.** —**French′ Guianese′, French′ Guian′an.**

French′ Guin′ea, former name of **Guinea.**

French′ harp′, *Chiefly Dial.* harmonica (def. 1).

French′ heel′, a high, curved heel, characterized by a heel breast curving into a shank, used on women's shoes. Cf. **Spanish heel.** —**French′-heeled′,** *adj.*

French′ hon′eysuckle, a bushy, perennial herb, *Hedysarum Coronarium*, of Europe, having hairy leaflets and deep red, fragrant flowers. Also called **sulla clover.**

French′ horn′, a musical brass wind instrument with a long, coiled tube having a conical bore and a flaring bell. See illus. under **horn.**

French′ ice′ cream′, a kind of ice cream characterized by a high content of eggs and cream.

French·i·fy (fren′chə fī′), *v.t.,* **-fied, -fy·ing.** *Informal.* (*often l.c.*) to make (something or someone) resemble the French, as in manners, customs, dress, etc.: *to Frenchify the spelling of one's name.* [FRENCH + -IFY] —**French′i·fi·ca′tion,** *n.*

French′ In′dia, the five small former French territories in India, including Chandernagor, Karikal, Pondicherry, and Yanaon on the E coast, and Mahé on the W coast.

French′ In′dochi′na, an area in SE Asia, formerly a French colonial federation including Cochin-China, the protectorates of Annam, Cambodia, Tonkin, and Laos, and the leased territory of Kwangchowan: now comprising the three independent states of Vietnam, Cambodia, and Laos. *Cap.:* Hanoi. Cf. **Indochina.**

French′ kid′, kidskin tanned by an alum or vegetable process and finished in a manner originally employed by the French.

French′ kiss′. See **soul kiss.**

French-kiss (french′kis′), *v.t., v.i.* to soul-kiss.

French′ leave′, a departure without ceremony, permission, or notice: *Taking French leave, he tricked his creditors.*

French′ lug′, *Naut.* See **balance lug.**

French·man (french′mən), *n., pl.* **-men.** **1.** a native or inhabitant of the French nation, esp. a male. **2.** a French ship. **3.** *Masonry.* a tool for trimming mortar joints. [ME *Frenshman*, OE *Francisc man.* See FRENCH, MAN[1]]

French′ mar′igold, an annual herb, *Tagetes patula*, of Mexico, having yellow flowers with red markings.

French′ Moroc′co. See under **Morocco** (def. 1).

French′ mul′berry, a shrub, *Callicarpa americana*, of the south-central U.S. and the West Indies, having violet-colored fruit and variously colored flowers.

French′ net′tle. See **red dead nettle.**

French′ Ocean′ia, former name of **French Polynesia.**

French′ pan′cake, a thin, light pancake, usually served with a sweet or savory filling.

French′ pas′try, fine, rich, or fancy pastry, esp. made from puff paste and filled with cream or fruit preparations.

French′ pitch′, *Music.* See **diapason normal pitch.**

French′ pol′ish, a furniture finish, consisting of shellac dissolved in spirits.

French-pol·ish (french′pol′ish), *v.t.* to finish (a piece of furniture) with French polish.

French′ Polyne′sia, a French overseas territory in the S Pacific, including the Society Islands, Marquesas Islands, and other scattered island groups. 84,550 (1962); 1544 sq. mi. *Cap.:* Papeete. Formerly, **French Oceania.**

French′ pox′, syphilis.

French′ Revolu′tion, *Fr. Hist.* the revolution that began in 1789, overthrew the absolute monarchy of the Bourbons and the system of aristocratic privileges, and ended with Napoleon's overthrow of the Directory and seizure of power in 1799.

French′ Revolu′tionary cal′endar. See **Revolutionary calendar.**

French′ roll′, a coiffure for women in which the hair is combed back from the face and arranged in a vertical roll on the back of the head.

French′ roof′, a mansard roof the sides of which are nearly perpendicular.

French′ rose′. See **Provence rose.**

French′ seam′, *Sewing.* a seam in which the raw edges of the cloth are completely covered by sewing them together, first on the right side, then on the wrong.

French′ Soma′liland, former name of the **Afars and Issas Territory.**

French′ Sudan′, former name of Republic of Mali.

French′ sys′tem, a method of spinning in which fibers of extremely short-staple wool are not twisted before being spun. Also called **continental system, Franco-Belgian system.** Cf. **Bradford spinning.**

French′ tab′, *Theat. Chiefly Brit.* See **draw tab.**

French′ tam′arisk. See **salt cedar.**

French′ tel′ephone, a telephone with the receiver and transmitter at the ends of a handle; a handset.

French′ toast′, bread dipped in a batter of egg and milk and sautéed until brown, usually served sprinkled with sugar and cinnamon, molasses, or syrup.

French′ truss′. See **Fink truss.**

French′ twist′. See **French roll.**

French′ Un′ion, a former association of France and its overseas territories, colonies, and protectorates as constituted in 1946: superseded by the French Community in 1958.

French·weed (french′wēd′), *n.* the penny-cress, *Thlaspi alpestre.* [FRENCH + WEED[1]]

French′ West′ Af′rica, a former French federation in W Africa, including Dahomey, French Guinea, French Sudan, Ivory Coast, Mauritania, Niger, Senegal Dakar, and Upper Volta.

French′ West′ In′dies, the French islands in the Lesser Antilles of the West Indies, including Martinique and Guadaloupe and its dependencies: administered as two overseas departments. 575,285 (1961); 1114 sq. mi.

French′ win′dow, a window extending to the floor, closed by French doors and usually usable as an entrance or exit.

French·wom·an (french′wo͝om′ən), *n., pl.* **-wom·en.** a female native or inhabitant of the French nation. [FRENCH + WOMAN]

French·y (fren′chē), *adj.,* **French·i·er, French·i·est.** characteristic or suggestive of the French. [FRENCH + -Y[1]] —**French′i·ly,** *adv.* —**French′i·ness,** *n.*

French·y (fren′chē), *n., pl.* **French·ies.** *Slang.* a Frenchman. [FRENCH + -Y[2]]

Fre·neau (fri nō′), *n.* **Philip,** 1752–1832, U.S. poet and editor.

Fre·net′ for′mula (fre nā′), *Math.* one of a set of formulas for finding the curvature and torsion of a plane or space curve in terms of vectors tangent or normal to the curve.

fre·net·ic (frə net′ik), *adj.* frantic; frenzied. Also, **fre·net′i·cal, phrenetic, phrenetical.** [ME; see FRANTIC] —**fre·net′i·cal·ly,** *adv.*

fren·u·lum (fren′yə ləm), *n., pl.* **-la** (-lə). **1.** *Anat., Zool.* a small frenum. **2.** *Entomol.* a strong spine or group of bristles on the hind wing of many lepidopterous insects, projecting beneath the forewing and serving to hold the two wings together in flight. Also, **fraenulum.** [< NL; see FRENUM, -ULE] —**fren′u·lar,** *adj.*

fre·num (frē′nəm), *n., pl.* **-na** (-nə). *Anat., Zool.* a fold of membrane which checks or restrains the motion of a part, as the fold on the underside of the tongue. Also, **fraenum.** [< NL, L *frēnum, frænum* bridle]

fren·zied (fren′zēd), *adj.* wildly excited or enthusiastic; frantic. Also, **phrensied.** [FRENZY + -ED[3]] —**fren′zied·ly,** *adv.*

fren·zy (fren′zē), *n., pl.* **-zies,** *v.,* **-zied, -zy·ing.** —*n.* **1.** violent mental agitation; wild excitement or enthusiasm. **2.** a fit or spell of violent mental excitement; a paroxysm characteristic of or resulting from a mania: *He is subject to these frenzies several times a year.* —*v.t.* **3.** to drive to frenzy; make frantic: *She was frenzied by fear each time he left her alone in the house.* Also, **phrensy.** [ME *frenesie* < OF < LL *phrenēsis* < LGk, r. Gk *phrenītis*] —**fren′zi·ly,** *adv.*
—**Syn. 2.** madness, insanity, lunacy, aberration; rage, fury, raving. —**Ant. 1.** calm. **2.** sanity.

Fre·on (frē′on), *n. Chem., Trademark.* any of a class of fluorinated hydrocarbons used chiefly as a refrigerant, as the colorless and odorless gas dichlorodifluoromethane.

freq., **1.** frequent. **2.** frequentative. **3.** frequently.

fre·quen·cy (frē′kwən sē), *n., pl.* **-cies.** **1.** Also, **fre′quence.** state or fact of being frequent; frequent occurrence: *We are alarmed by the frequency of fires in the neighborhood.* **2.** rate of recurrence: *The doctor has increased the frequency of his visits.* **3.** *Physics.* **a.** the number of periods or regularly occurring events of any given kind in unit of time, usually in one second. **b.** the number of cycles or completed alternations per unit time of a wave or oscillation. *Symbol:* f **4.** *Math.* the number of times a value recurs in a unit change of the independent variable of a given function. **5.** *Statistics.* the number of items occurring in a given category. Cf. **relative frequency** (def. 2). [< L *frequentia* assembly, multitude, crowd. See FREQUENT, -CY]

fre′quency distribu′tion, *Statistics.* the correspondence of a set of frequencies with the set of categories, intervals, or values into which a population is classified.

fre′quency modula′tion, *Electronics.* **1.** a method of impressing a signal on a radio carrier wave by varying its frequency (distinguished from *amplitude modulation*). **2.** a system of radio broadcasting using such a method. *Abbr.:* FM

fre′quency swing′, *Radio.* (in frequency modulation) the difference between the maximum and minimum values of instantaneous frequency in a signal.

fre·quent (*adj.* frē′kwənt; *v.* fri kwent′, frē′kwənt), *adj.* **1.** happening or occurring at short intervals: *to make frequent trips to a place.* **2.** constant, habitual, or regular: *a frequent guest.* **3.** located at short distances apart: *a coast with frequent lighthouses.* —*v.t.* **4.** to visit often; go often to; be often in: *to frequent the art galleries.* [late ME < L *frequent-* (s. of *frequēns*) crowded] —**fre·quent′a·ble,** *adj.* —**fre·quent′er,** *n.* —**fre′quent·ness,** *n.*
—**Syn. 4.** haunt.

fre·quen·ta·tion (frē′kwən tā′shən), *n.* the practice of frequenting; habit of visiting often. [< F *fréquentation* < L *frequentātiōn-* (s. of *frequentātiō*). See FREQUENT, -ATION]

fre·quen·ta·tive (fri kwen′tə tiv), *Gram.* —*adj.* **1.** noting or pertaining to a verb aspect expressing repetition of an action. —*n.* **2.** the frequentative aspect. **3.** a verb in the frequentative aspect, as *wrestle* from *wrest.* [< L *frequentātīv(us)* denoting repetition of an act. See FREQUENT, -ATE[1], -IVE]

fre·quent·ly (frē′kwənt lē), *adv.* **1.** often; many times; at short intervals. **2.** *Math.* so that corresponding to each element in the directed set of a net there is a second element in the directed set in relation to the first element which has the property that the element of the net corresponding to the second element is in some given set. [FREQUENT + -LY]
—**Syn. 1.** repeatedly. See **often.**

frère (frer), *n., pl.* **frères** (frer). *French.* **1.** brother; fellow member of an organization. **2.** friar; monk.

fres·co (fres′kō), *n., pl.* **-coes, -cos,** *v.,* **-coed, -co·ing.** —*n.* **1.** Also called **buon fresco, true fresco.** the art or technique of painting on a moist, lime plaster surface with colors ground in water or a limewater mixture. Cf. **fresco secco. 2.** a picture or design so painted. —*v.t.* **3.** to paint in fresco. [< It: cool, FRESH (< Gmc)] —**fres′co·er,** *n.*

Fres·co·bal·di (fres kō bäl′dē), *n.* **Gi·ro·la·mo** (jē rô′lä mô), 1583–1643, Italian organist and composer.

fres′co sec′co, the technique of painting in water colors on dry plaster. Also called **dry fresco, secco.** Cf. **fresco** (def. 1). [< It: lit., dry fresco]

fresh (fresh), *adj.* **1.** newly made or obtained: *fresh footprints; lettuce fresh from the garden.* **2.** newly arrived; just come: *fresh from school; fresh from the beauty parlor.* **3.** new; not previously known, met with, etc.; novel: *to uncover fresh facts; to seek fresh experiences.* **4.** additional or further: *fresh supplies.* **5.** not salt, as water. **6.** retaining the original properties unimpaired; not deteriorated: *Are you sure the milk is still fresh?* **7.** not frozen or canned; not preserved by pickling, salting, drying, etc.: *fresh meat; fresh vegetables.* **8.** not fatigued; brisk; vigorous: *She was still fresh after that long walk.* **9.** not faded, worn, obliterated, etc.: *fresh paint; fresh appearance.* **10.** looking youthful and healthy: *a fresh beauty that we all admired.* **11.** pure, cool, or refreshing, as air. **12.** *Meteorol.* (of wind) moderately strong or brisk. **13.** inexperienced; green; callow: *A shipment of fresh recruits arrived at the training camp.* **14.** *Informal.* forward or presumptuous. **15.** (of a cow) having recently given birth to a calf. —*n.* **16.** the fresh part or time. **17.** a freshet. —*v.t., v.i.* **18.** to make or become fresh. —*adv.* **19.** newly; recently; just now: *He is fresh out of ideas. The eggs are fresh laid.* [ME; OE *fersc;* c. OFris *fersk,* OHG *frisc* (G *frisch*), ON *fersk(r)*] —**fresh′ly,** *adv.* —**fresh′ness,** *n.*
—**Syn. 1.** recent. See **new. 10.** robust, well, hearty. **11.** invigorating, sweet, unadulterated. **13.** artless, untrained, raw, uncultivated, unskilled. —**Ant. 1.** old. **6.** stale, contaminated. **13.** skilled.

fresh′ breeze′, *Meteorol.* (on the Beaufort scale) a wind of 19–24 miles per hour. Cf. **breeze**[1] (def. 2).

fresh·en (fresh′ən), *v.t.* **1.** to make fresh; refresh, revive, or renew: *We need a good rain to freshen the flowers.* **2.** to remove saltiness from. **3.** *Naut.* to preserve (a rope in use) from prolonged friction or concentrated stress on any one part, as by paying it out slightly. —*v.i.* **4.** to become or grow fresh: *The flowers freshened after the rain.* **5.** to make oneself fresh, as by washing, changing clothes, etc. (usually fol. by *up*): *After the long trip we all wanted to freshen up.* [FRESH + -EN[1]] —**fresh′en·er,** *n.*

fresh·er (fresh′ər), *n. Brit. Slang.* freshman. [FRESH + -ER[1]]

fresh·et (fresh′it), *n.* **1.** a sudden rise in the level of a stream, or a flood, due to heavy rains or the rapid melting of snow and ice. **2.** a fresh-water stream flowing into the sea. [dim. of FRESH used as n.]
—**Syn. 1.** See **flood.**

fresh′ gale′, *Meteorol.* (on the Beaufort scale) a wind of 39–46 miles per hour. Cf. **gale**[1] (def. 2).

fresh·man (fresh′mən), *n., pl.* **-men,** *adj.* —*n.* **1.** a student in the first year of the course at a university, college, or school. **2.** a novice. —*adj.* **3.** of, pertaining to, or characteristic of a freshman: *to outgrow one's freshman attitudes.* **4.** lacking seniority or experience; junior: *freshman senator.* **5.** required of or suitable for freshmen: *freshman courses.* **6.** initial; first: *This is my freshman year with the company.* [FRESH + MAN[1]] —**fresh′man·ship′,** *n.*

fresh·man·ic (fresh man′ik), *adj.* of, pertaining to, or characteristic of a freshman: *freshmanic enthusiasm.* [FRESHMAN + -IC]

fresh′man week′, a week at the beginning of the school year with a program planned to orient entering students, esp. at a college.

fresh′ wa′ter, 1. water that does not contain a large amount of salt. **2.** inland water, as ponds, lakes, streams, etc., that is not salt.

fresh-wa·ter (fresh′wô′tər, -wot′ər), *adj.* **1.** of or living in water that is fresh or not salt: *fresh-water fish.* **2.** accustomed to fresh water only, and not to the sea. **3.** *U.S.* small or little known: *a fresh-water college.* **4.** *Obs.* untrained or of little experience.

fresh′-water drum′, *Ichthyol.* an edible drum, *Aplodinotus grunniens,* of the fresh waters of North and Central America, sometimes reaching a weight of 60 pounds.

fresh′wa·ter stay′ (fresh′wô′tər, -wot′ər), *U.S. Naut.* See **triatic stay** (def. 1).

Fres·nel (frā nel′, frə-; *Fr.* frā nel′), *n.* a unit of frequency, equal to 10^{12} cycles per second. [named after A. J. FRESNEL (1788–1827), French physicist]

Fresnel′ lens′, a large lens with a surface composed of many small lenses arranged to produce a short focal length, used in searchlights, spotlights, etc.

Fresnel′ mir′rors, *Optics.* two plane mirrors joined together at an angle of slightly less than 180° so that an incident light beam will be reflected in somewhat different directions by the two, each producing interference fringes in the region receiving reflected light from both mirrors. Also called **Fresnel′ dou′ble mir′ror.**

Fres·no (frez′nō), *n.* a city in central California. 133,929 (1960).

fress (fres), *v.i.* to eat, esp. large quantities; gourmandize. [< G *fress(en)* (to) devour; see FRET[1]]

fress·er (fres′ər), *n.* a person who eats, esp. often and in large amounts; gourmandizer. [FRESS + -ER[1]]

fret[1] (fret), *v.,* **fret·ted, fret·ting,** *n.* —*v.i.* **1.** to feel or express worry, annoyance, discontentment, or the like: *Fretting about the situation isn't going to help.* **2.** to cause corrosion; gnaw into something: *acids that fret at the strongest metals.* **3.** to make a way by gnawing, corrosion, wearing away, etc.: *The river frets at its banks until a new channel is formed.* **4.** to become eaten, worn, or corroded (often fol. by *away*): *Limestone slowly frets away under pounding by the wind and rain.* **5.** to move in agitation or commotion, as water: *water fretting over the stones of a brook.* —*v.t.* **6.** to torment; irritate, annoy, or vex: *The uncertainty continued to fret him. You mustn't fret yourself about that.* **7.** to wear away or consume by gnawing, friction, rust, corrosives, etc.: *the ocean fretting its shores.* **8.** to form or make by wearing away a substance: *The river had fretted an underground passage.* **9.** to agitate (water): *Strong winds were fretting the channel.* —*n.* **10.** an irritated state of mind; annoyance; vexation. **11.** erosion; corrosion; gnawing. **12.** a worn or eroded place. [ME *frete(n),* OE *fretan* to eat up, consume; c. OS *fretan,* Goth *fra-itan,* OHG *frezzan* (G *fressen*)]
—**Syn. 1.** fume, rage. **6.** worry, harass, goad, tease. **7.** erode, gnaw, corrode, abrade, grind, rub, rust. **10.** harassment, agitation, worry, irritation.

fret[2] (fret), *n., v.,* **fret·ted, fret·ting.** —*n.* **1.** an interlaced, angular design; fretwork. **2.** an angular design of bands within a border. **3.** *Heraldry.* a charge composed of two diagonal strips interlacing with and crossing at the center of a mascle. **4.** a piece of decoratively pierced work placed in a clock case to deaden the sound of the mechanism. —*v.t.* **5.** to ornament with a fret or fretwork. [ME *frette* < ?; cf. MF *frete* trellis-work, OE *fretwian,* var. of *frætwian* to adorn] —**fret′less,** *adj.*

Fret[2] (def. 2)

fret[3] (fret), *n., v.,* **fret·ted, fret·ting.** —*n.* **1.** any of the ridges of wood, metal, or string, set across the finger board of a lute or similar instrument, which help the fingers to stop the strings at the correct points. —*v.t.* **2.** to provide with frets. [?] —**fret′less,** *adj.*

fret·ful (fret′fəl), *adj.* disposed to fret; irritable or peevish. Also, **fret·some** (fret′səm). [FRET[1] + -FUL] —**fret′ful·ly,** *adv.* —**fret′ful·ness,** *n.*
—**Syn.** petulant, querulous, impatient, pettish, testy. —**Ant.** calm.

fret′ saw′, a long, narrow-bladed saw used to cut ornamental work from thin wood.

Fret saw

fret·ted (fret′id), *adj.* ornamented or provided with frets: *a fretted molding.* [FRET[2] + -ED[3]]

fret·ty[1] (fret′ē), *adj.,* **-ti·er, -ti·est.** fretful; peevish. [FRET[1] + -Y[1]]

fret·ty[2] (fret′ē), *adj. Heraldry.* covered with crisscrossed and interlacing diagonal strips: *argent, fretty sable.* [< MF *frette,* deriv. of *frete* trellis-work. See FRET[2], -EE]

fret·work (fret′wûrk′), *n.* **1.** ornamental work consisting of interlacing parts, esp. work in which the design is formed by perforation. **2.** any pattern of dark and light, such as that of perforated fretwork. [FRET[2] + WORK]

Freud (froid; *Ger.* froit), *n.* **Sig·mund** (sig′mənd; *Ger.* zēkh′mŏŏnt), 1856–1939, Austrian neurologist: founder of psychoanalysis.

Freud·i·an (froi′dē ən), *adj.* **1.** of or pertaining to Sigmund Freud or his doctrines, esp. with respect to the causes and treatment of neurotic and psychopathic states, the interpretation of dreams, etc. —*n.* **2.** a person, esp. a psychoanalyst, who adheres to the basic doctrines of Freud. [FREUD + -IAN] —**Freud′i·an·ism,** *n.*

Frey (frā), *n. Scand. Myth.* the god of peace, prosperity, and marriage: one of the Vanir, originally brought to Asgard as a hostage. Also, **Freyr** (frâr).

Frey·a (frā′ə, frā′ä), *n. Teutonic Myth.* the goddess of love, beauty, and fecundity, and leader of the Valkyries: one of the Vanir; confused in Germany with Frigg. Also **Freia, Frey·ja** (frā′yä), **Fri, Fria.**

Frey·re (frā′rə), *n.* **Gil·ber·to** (gil ber′tŏŏ), born 1900, Brazilian sociologist and anthropologist.

Frey·tag (frī′täkh), *n.* **Gus·tav** (gŏŏs′täf), 1816–95, German novelist, playwright, and journalist.

F.R.G.S., Fellow of the Royal Geographical Society.

Fri (frē), *n. Teutonic Myth.* **1.** Freya. **2.** Frigg. Also, **Fri·a** (frē′ə).

Fri., Friday.

fri·a·ble (frī′ə bəl), *adj.* easily crumbled or reduced to powder; crumbly: *friable rock.* [< L *friābil(is),* equiv. to *fri-* (s. of *friāre* to rub, crumble) + *-ābilis* -ABLE] —**fri′a·bil′i·ty, fri′a·ble·ness,** *n.*
—**Syn.** fragile, frangible.

fri·ar (frī′ər), *n.* **1.** *Rom. Cath. Ch.* a member of a religious order, esp. the mendicant orders of Franciscans, Dominicans, Carmelites, and Augustinians. **2.** *Print.* a blank or light area on a printed page caused by uneven inking of the plate or type. Cf. **monk** (def. 2). [ME *frier, frere* brother < OF *frere* < L *frāter* BROTHER]
—**Syn. 1.** See **monk.**

fri·ar·bird (frī′ər bûrd′), *n.* any of various Australasian honey eaters, esp. of the genus *Philemon.* [FRIAR + BIRD; so called from its tonsured head]

Fri′ar Mi′nor, *pl.* **Friars Minor.** *Rom. Cath. Ch.* a friar belonging to the branch of the Franciscan order that follows literally the rule of St. Francis. Cf. **capuchin** (def. 4), **Friar Minor Conventual.**

Fri′ar Mi′nor Cap′uchin, *pl.* **Friars Minor Capuchin.** *Rom. Cath. Ch.* capuchin (def. 4).

Fri′ar Mi′nor Conven′tual, *pl.* **Friars Minor Conventual.** *Rom. Cath. Ch.* a friar belonging to a branch of the Franciscan order that separated from the Observants in the 15th century, and that observes a modification of the rule of St. Francis. Also called **Conventual.** Cf. **Friar Minor, capuchin.**

Fri′ar Preach′er, *pl.* **Friars Preachers.** a Dominican friar.

fri′ar's chair′, frailero.

fri′ar's lan′tern. See **ignis fatuus.** (def. 1).

Fri′ar Tuck′ (tuk), the jolly, pugnacious friar who was a member of Robin Hood's band.

fri·ar·y (frī′ə rē), *n., pl.* **-ar·ies. 1.** a monastery of friars, esp. those of a mendicant order. **2.** a brotherhood of friars. [alter. of earlier *frary* friary, brotherhood FRIAR + -Y[3]; r. ME *fra(i)rie* < MF, alter. of ML *frātria.* See FRATER, -IA]

frib·ble (frib′əl), *v.,* **-bled, -bling,** *n., adj.* —*v.i.* **1.** to act in a foolish or frivolous manner; to trifle. —*v.t.* **2.** to waste foolishly (often fol. by *away*): *He fribbled away one opportunity after another.* —*n.* **3.** a trifler. **4.** anything trifling or frivolous. **5.** frivolousness. —*adj.* **6.** frivolous; foolish; trifling. [? alter. of FRIVOL] —**frib′bler,** *n.*

Fri·bourg (*Fr.* frē bōōr′), *n.* **1.** a canton in W Switzerland. 159,194 (1960); 644 sq. mi. **2.** a town in and the capital of this canton. 32,583 (1960). German, **Freiburg.**

fric·an·deau (frik′ən dō′, frik′ən dō′), *n., pl.* **-deaus, -deaux** (-dōz′, -dōz′). a loin of veal, larded and braised, or roasted. Also, **fricando.** [< F, MF, appar. akin to FRICASSEE]

fric·an·do (frik′ən dō′, frik′ən dō′), *n., pl.* **-does.** fricandeau.

fric·as·see (frik′ə sē′), *n., v.,* **-seed, -see·ing.** —*n.* **1.** meat, esp. chicken or veal, browned lightly, stewed, and served in a white sauce made with its own stock. —*v.t.* **2.** to prepare as a fricassee. [< MF, n. use of fem. ptp. of *fricasser* to fricassee, cf. *frire* to FRY]

fri·ca·tion (fri kā′shən), *n. Phonet.* an audible, constrained rush of air accompanying and characteristic of certain speech sounds, as fricatives, affricates, and initial stops. [< L *fricātiōn-* (s. of *fricātiō*), equiv. to *fricāt(us)* rubbed (ptp. of *fricāre;* see FRICTION) + *-iōn-* -ION]

fric·a·tive (frik′ə tiv), *Phonet.* —*adj.* **1.** (of a speech sound) produced with frication; spirantal; spirant. —*n.* **2.** Also called **spirant.** a fricative consonant. [FRICAT(ION) + -IVE]

Frick (frik), *n.* **Henry Clay,** 1849–1919, U.S. industrialist and philanthropist.

fric·tion (frik′shən), *n.* **1.** *Mech., Physics.* the resistance of a surface to the relative motion, as sliding or rolling, of a body moving along a given surface. **2.** the rubbing of the surface of one body against that of another. **3.** dissension or conflict between persons, nations, etc., because of differing ideas, wishes, etc. [< L *frictiōn-* (s. of *frictiō*) a rubbing, equiv. to *frict(us)* (ptp. of *fricāre*) + *-iōn-* -ION] —**fric′tion·less,** *n.* —**fric′tion·less·ly,** *adv.*

fric·tion·al (frik′shə nəl), *adj.* **1.** of, pertaining to, or of the nature of friction. **2.** moved, worked, or produced by friction. [FRICTION + -AL[1]] —**fric′tion·al·ly,** *adv.*

fric′tion clutch′, *Mach.* a clutch in which one part turns another by friction between them.

fric′tion drive′, *Auto. Obs.* a power transmission system utilizing a set of friction gears so arranged that varying their positions relative to one another gives a wide range of speed ratios.

fric′tion gear′ing, wheels or disks transmitting power by means of frictional contact.

fric′tion head′, (in a hydraulic system) the part of a head of water or of another liquid that represents the energy that the system dissipates through friction with the sides of conduits or channels and through heating from turbulent flow.

fric′tion lay′er. See **surface boundary layer.**

fric′tion match′, a kind of match tipped with a compound that ignites by friction.

fric′tion pile′, *Engineering, Building Trades.* a pile depending on the friction of surrounding earth for support. Cf. **point-bearing pile.**

fric′tion saw′, a saw that cuts by melting the material adjacent to it through frictional heat.

fric·tion-saw (frik′shən sô′), *v.t.,* **-sawed, -sawed** or **-sawn, -saw·ing.** to cut with a friction saw.

fric′tion tape′, a cloth adhesive tape used esp. to insulate electrical conductors.

Fri·day (frī′dē, -dā), *n.* the sixth day of the week, following Thursday. [ME; OE *Frīgedæg* Freya's day, equiv. to *Frīge* (gen. sing. of *Frēo*) + *dæg* day; *Frēo* is identical with OE adj. *frēo* free]

Fri·days (frī′dēz, -dāz), *adv.* on Fridays: *The cleaning woman always comes Fridays.*

fridge (frij), *n. Chiefly Brit. Informal.* a refrigerator. [by shortening and alter.]

Frid·ley (frid′lē), *n.* a city in SE Minnesota, near Minneapolis. 15,173 (1960).

Fridt′jof Nan′sen Land′ (frit′yôf nän′sən, nan′-). See **Franz Josef Land.**

fried (frīd), *adj.* **1.** cooked in fat. **2.** *Slang.* drunk; intoxicated; inebriated. —*v.* **3.** pt. and pp. of **fry**[1].

Fried (frēd; *Ger.* frēt), *n.* **Al·fred Her·mann** (al′frid hûr′mən; *Ger.* äl′frāt her′män), 1864–1921, Austrian writer and journalist: Nobel peace prize 1911.

Frie·da (frē′də), *n.* a girl's given name. Also, **Freda.**

fried·cake (frīd′kāk′), *n.* a doughnut or other small cake cooked in deep fat. [FRIED + CAKE]

Frie·del′-Crafts′ reac′tion (frē del′krafts′, -kräfts′), *Chem.* a reaction for the synthesis of hydrocarbons and ketones by the alkylation or acylation of an aromatic compound in the presence of a catalyst, typically anhydrous aluminum chloride.

Fried′län·der's bacil′lus (frēd′len dərz, lən-), pneumobacillus. Also called **Fried′länder's pneumo·bacil′lus.** [named after Carl *Friedländer* (d. 1887), German pathologist]

Frie·drich (frē′drik; *Ger.* frē′drikh), *n.* a boy's given name. Also, **Frederic, Frederick, Fredric, Fredrich.**

friend (frend), *n.* **1.** a person attached to another by feelings of affection or personal regard. **2.** a person who gives assistance; a patron or supporter: *a list of friends of the Boston Symphony.* **3.** one who is on good terms with another; one not hostile: *to identify oneself as friend or foe; a cat and dog who are not friends.* **4.** a member of the same nation, party, etc. **5.** (*cap.*) a member of the Society of Friends; a Quaker. **6. make friends with,** to enter into friendly relations with; become a friend to. —*v.t.* **7.** *Rare.* to befriend. [ME *friend, frend,* OE *frēond* friend, lover, relative (c. OS *friund,* OHG *friunt* (G *Freund*), Goth *frijōnd(s)*), orig. prp. of *frēogan,* c. Goth *frijōn* to love] —**friend′less,** *adj.* —**friend′less·ness,** *n.*
—**Syn. 1.** comrade, chum, crony, confidant. See **acquaintance. 2.** backer, advocate. **4.** ally, associate, confrère, compatriot. —**Ant. 1, 4.** enemy, foe.

friend′ at court′, a friend in a position of influence or power who may advance one's interests, esp. a helpful person who is close to someone in authority.

friend·ed (fren′did), *adj.* *Archaic.* provided with or accompanied by friends. [late ME frended. See FRIEND, -ED[2]]

friend·ly (frend′lē), *adj.,* **-li·er, -li·est,** *adv.* —*adj.* **1.** characteristic of or befitting a friend; showing friendship: *a friendly greeting.* **2.** like a friend; kind; helpful: *a little friendly advice.* **3.** favorably disposed; inclined to approve, help, or support: *a friendly bank.* **4.** not hostile or at variance; amicable: *a friendly warship; friendly natives.* —*adv.* **5.** in a friendly manner; like a friend. [ME *frendly,* OE *frēondlīc.* See FRIEND, -LY] —**friend′li·ly,** *adv.* —**friend′li·ness,** *n.*
—**Syn. 1.** companionable, neighborly. **2.** kindly, amiable, cordial, genial, affectionate, kind-hearted. **3.** benevolent, well-disposed, helpful, favorable; advantageous, propitious. —**Ant. 3.** antagonistic.

Friend′ly Is′lands, Tonga.

friend′ of the court′, *Law.* See **amicus curiae.**

friend·ship (frend′ship), *n.* **1.** friendly feeling or disposition: *to value a person's friendship.* **2.** state of being a friend; association as friends: *The two countries professed friendship.* **3.** a friendly relation or intimacy. [ME; OE *frēondscipe.* See FRIEND, -SHIP]

Friend′ship sloop′, a sloop used along the New England coast for fishing and lobstering, having a hull with a centerboard and pronounced forward sheer with a clipper bow. [after *Friendship,* Maine, where they are built]

fri·er (frī′ər), *n.* fryer.

fries (frīz), *n.* **1.** pl. of **fry**[1]. —*v.* **2.** 3rd pers. sing. pres. indic. of **fry**[1].

Frie·sian (frē′zhən), *adj., n.* **1.** Frisian. **2.** *Chiefly Brit.* Holstein (def. 1).

Fries·land (frēz′lənd; *Du.* frēs′länt′), *n.* a province in the N Netherlands. 487,061 (1962); 1431 sq. mi. *Cap.:* Leeuwarden. Also, *esp. Brit.,* **Frisian.**

frieze[1] (frēz), *n.* **1.** *Archit.* **a.** the part of a classical entablature between the architrave and the cornice, usually decorated with sculpture in low relief: omitted in some examples. **b.** any decorative band on an outside wall, broader than a stringcourse and bearing lettering, sculpture, etc. **2.** any decorative band at the top or beneath the cornice of an interior wall, a piece of furniture, etc. **3.** *Furniture.* skirt (def. 6b). [ME *frise frese* < OF *frise* ? < ML *phrygium, frigium, frisium* embroidered cloth, embroidery, L *Phrygium,* neut. of *Phrygius* Phrygian]

frieze[2] (frēz), *n.* a heavy, napped woolen cloth for coats. [ME *frise* < OF; see FRIEZE[1]]

frieze′ board′, *Carpentry.* a board nailed to a wall above the siding and immediately below the projecting members of a cornice in the manner of a frieze.

friez·ing (frē′zing), *n.* carved or painted work formerly decorating the upper parts of the hulls of vessels, esp. in the 16th and 17th centuries. [FRIEZE[1] + -ING[1]]

frig (frig), *v.t.,* **frigged, frig·ging.** *Slang (vulgar).* to have coitus with (a woman). [prob. special use of dial. *frig* to rub, late ME *friggen*]

frig·ate (frig′it), *n.* a fast naval vessel of the late 18th and early 19th centuries, generally having a lofty ship rig and heavily armed on one or two decks. [< F *frégate* < It *fregata*]

frig′ate bird′, any of several rapacious, totipalmate sea birds of the genus *Fregata,* noted for their powers of flight. Also called **man-o'-war bird.**

frig′ate mack′erel, a scombroid fish, *Auxis thazard,* found in tropical marine water, having dark, oily flesh that is sometimes used as food.

Frigg (frig), *n.* *Teutonic Myth.* the wife of Odin and goddess of the clouds, the sky, and conjugal love: one of the Aesir; confused in Germany with Freya. Also, **Frig·ga** (frig′ə), **Fri, Frija.**

frig·ger (frig′ər), *n.* a novelty or ornament made of glass. [?]

frig·ging (frig′in, -ing), *adj.* *Slang.* damned. [FRIG + -ING[2]]

fright (frīt), *n.* **1.** sudden and extreme fear; a sudden terror. **2.** a person or thing of shocking, grotesque, or ridiculous appearance. —*v.t.* **3.** to frighten. [ME; OE *frytu, fyrhto;* akin to G *Furcht*]
—**Syn. 1.** dismay, consternation, alarm. See **terror.** —**Ant. 1.** bravery.

fright·en (frīt′ᵊn), *v.t.* **1.** to throw into a fright; terrify; scare. **2.** to drive (usually fol. by *away, off,* etc.) by scaring: *to frighten away pigeons from the roof.* [FRIGHT + -EN[1]] —**fright′en·a·ble,** *adj.* —**fright′en·er,** *n.* —**fright′en·ing·ly,** *adv.*
—**Syn. 1.** shock, startle, dismay, intimidate. FRIGHTEN, ALARM, SCARE, TERRIFY, TERRORIZE, APPALL all mean to arouse fear in people or animals. TO FRIGHTEN is to shock with sudden, startling, but usually short-lived fear, especially that arising from the apprehension of physical harm: *to frighten someone by a sudden noise.* To ALARM is to arouse the feelings through the realization of some imminent or unexpected danger: *to alarm someone by a scream.* To SCARE is to frighten into a loss of poise or dignity: *A child often makes a game of scaring people by suddenly popping out of peculiar places.* To TERRIFY is to strike with violent, overwhelming, or paralyzing fear: *to terrify a city by lawless acts.* To TERRORIZE is to terrify in a general, continued, systematic manner, either wantonly or in order to gain control: *His marauding armies terrorized the countryside.* To APPALL is to overcome or confound by dread, dismay, shock, or horror: *The suffering caused by the earthquake appalled him.*

fright·ened (frīt′ᵊnd), *adj.* **1.** thrown into a fright; afraid; scared: *a frightened child cowering in the corner.* **2.** afraid; fearful (usually fol. by *of*): *She has always been frightened of the dark.* [FRIGHTEN + -ED[2]] —**fright′ened·ly,** *adv.*
—**Syn. 2.** See **afraid.**

fright·ful (frīt′fəl), *adj.* **1.** such as to cause fright; dreadful, terrible, or alarming: *A frightful explosion rocked the harbor.* **2.** horrible, shocking, or revolting: *The storm did frightful damage to the town.* **3.** *Informal.* unpleasant; disagreeable: *We had a frightful time.* **4.** *Informal.* very great: *That actor is very funny and a frightful ham.* [ME; see FRIGHT, -FUL] —**fright′ful·ly,** *adv.* —**fright′ful·ness,** *n.*
—**Syn. 1.** fearful, awful. **2.** hideous, dread, horrid, ghastly; gruesome. —**Ant. 1, 2.** delightful.

frig·id (frij′id), *adj.* **1.** very cold in temperature: *a frigid climate.* **2.** without warmth of feeling; without ardor or enthusiasm: *a frigid reaction to the proposal.* **3.** stiff or formal: *a welcome that was polite but frigid.* **4.** (of a woman) **a.** indifferent or hostile to sexual intercourse. **b.** unresponsive to sexual advances or stimuli. **c.** not able to have an orgasm in sexual intercourse. **5.** unemotional or unimaginative; lacking passion, sympathy, or sensitivity: *a correct, but frigid presentation.* [< L *frīgid(us),* equiv. to *frīg(us)* coldness (akin to Gk *rhīgos;* see RIGID) + *-idus* -ID[4]] —**fri·gid′i·ty, frig′id·ness,** *n.* —**frig′id·ly,** *adv.*

Frig·id·aire (frij′i dâr′), *n.* *Trademark.* an electric refrigerator.

frig·i·dar·i·um (frij′i dâr′ē əm), *n., pl.* **-dar·i·a** (-dâr′ē ə). (in an ancient Roman bath) a room having a bath of unheated water. [< L; see FRIGID, -ARIUM]

frig·i·do·re·cep·tor (frij′i dō ri sep′tər), *n.* *Physiol., Biol.* a receptor stimulated by cold. [FRIGID + -O- + RECEPTOR]

Frig′id Zone′, either of two regions, one between the Arctic Circle and the North Pole, or one between the Antarctic Circle and the South Pole.

frig·o·rif·ic (frig′ə rif′ik), *adj.* causing or producing cold. [< L *frīgorific(us)* cooling, equiv. to *frīgor-* (s. of *frīgus*) cold + *-i-* -I- + *-ficus* -FIC]

Fri·go·ris (fri gōr′is, -gôr′-), *n.* **Mare.** See **Mare Frigoris.**

Fri·ja (frē′yä), *n.* Frigg.

fri·jol (frē′hōl; *Sp.* frē hôl′), *n., pl.* **fri·jo·les** (frē′hōlz, frē hō′lēz; *Sp.* frē hô′les). any bean of the genus *Phaseolus,* esp. the kidney bean, the seeds of which are used for food in Mexico, in the southwestern U.S., etc. Also, **fri·jo·le** (frē hō′lē). [< Sp, earlier *fresol, fesol* << L *faesol(us), phaseolus,* dim. of *phasēlus* < Gk *phásēlos* a kind of bean]

frill (fril), *n.* **1.** a trimming, as a strip of cloth or lace, gathered at one edge and left loose at the other; a ruffle. **2.** something resembling such a trimming, as the fringe of hair on the chest of some dogs. **3.** affectation of manner, style, etc. **4.** something that is superfluous and bothersome. **5.** *Photog.* wrinkling or loosening of an emulsion at the edges, usually due to excessively high temperature during developing. —*v.t.* **6.** to trim or ornament with a frill or frills. **7.** to form into a frill. —*v.i.* **8.** *Photog.* (of an emulsion) to become wrinkled or loose. [? < Flem *frul* frill (of a collar), *frullen* to have frills] —**frill′er,** *n.* —**frill′y,** *adj.*

frill·ing (fril′ing), *n.* frilled edging. [FRILL + -ING[1]]

Fri·maire (frē mer′), *n.* (in the French Revolutionary calendar) the third month of the year, extending from November 21 to December 20. [< F, equiv. to *frim(as)* hoarfrost, deriv. of OF *frim* (< Gmc; cf. OE *hrīm* RIME[2]) + *-aire* -ARY]

Friml (frim′əl), *n.* **Rudolf,** 1881–1972, U.S. composer and pianist, born in Austria.

fringe (frinj), *n., v.,* **fringed, fring·ing.** —*n.* **1.** a decorative border of thread, cord, or the like, usually hanging loosely from a raveled edge or separate strip. **2.** anything resembling or suggesting this: *a fringe of grass running past a tennis court.* **3.** something regarded as belonging to or as being pertinent to something else without being fully typical of, or essential to it: *the lunatic fringe of a strong political party.* **4.** *Optics.* one of the alternate light and dark bands produced by diffraction or interference. —*v.t.* **5.** to furnish with or as with a fringe. **6.** to serve as a fringe for, or to be arranged around or along so as to suggest a fringe: *armed guards fringing the building.* [ME *frenge* < OF (*frange*) < LL *frimbia* (L *fimbria*) border, fringe] —**fringe′less,** *adj.* —**fringe′like′,** *adj.*

fringe-bell (frinj′bel′), *n.* See **fringed galax.**

fringe′ ben′efit, a benefit, as free life or health insurance, received by an employee in addition to his regular pay.

fringed′ ga′lax, a low, tufted plant, *Schizocodon soldanelloides,* of Japan, having roundish, leathery leaves and nodding, deep rose-colored flowers, shading to white at the edges. Also called **fringe-bell.**

fringed′ gen′tian, a gentian, *Gentiana crinita,* of eastern North America, having a blue, fringed corolla.

fringed′ or′chis, any of several American orchids of the genus *Habenaria,* having a cut, fringed lip.

fringe·head (frinj′hed′), *n.* any of several clinid fishes of the genus *Neoclinus,* having a row of fleshy processes on the head, as *N. blanchardi* (**sarcastic fringehead**), found off the coast of California. [FRINGE + HEAD]

fringe′-toed liz′ard (frinj′tōd′), an iguanid lizard, *Uma notata,* of sandy deserts of the western U.S. and Mexico, having a wedge-shaped snout and toes fringed with long, pointed scales.

fringe′ tree′, an oleaceous shrub or small tree, *Chionanthus virginicus,* of the southern U.S., bearing panicles of white flowers with long, narrow petals. Also called **old-man's-beard.**

frin·gil·lid (frin jil′id), *adj.* **1.** Also, **frin·gil·line** (frin jil′īn, -in) belonging or pertaining to the family *Fringillidae,* comprising the finches and related birds. —*n.* **2.** a fringillid bird. [< NL *Fringillid(ae)* name of family, equiv. to L *fringill(a)* chaffinch + *-idae* -ID[2]]

fring′ing reef′, a coral reef close to and along the land.

frip·per·y (frip′ə rē), *n., pl.* **-per·ies.** **1.** finery in dress, esp. when showy, gaudy, or the like. **2.** empty display; ostentation. **3.** gewgaws; trifles. [< F *friperie,* OF *freperie,* equiv. to *frepe* rag + *-erie* -ERY]

Fris., Frisian.

Fris·bee (friz′bē), *n.* *Trademark.* a plastic disc that can be spun through the air in various catching games. [from pie tins of the Frisbie Pie Co., Bridgeport, CT, formerly used in catching games]

Frisch (frish; *Ger.* frish), *n.* **1. Karl von** (kärl von; *Ger.* kärl fən), born 1886, Austrian zoologist. **2. Ot·to Ro·bert** (ot′ō rob′ərt; *Ger.* ôt′ō rō′bərt), born 1904, Austrian physicist.

Frisch·es Haff (frish′is häf′), a lagoon in N Poland. 52 mi. long; 4–12 mi. wide.

Fris·co (fris′kō), *n.* *Informal.* San Francisco. [by shortening]

fri·sé (fri zā′), *n.* a rug or upholstery fabric having the pile in uncut loops or in a combination of cut and uncut loops. [< F: curly]

fri·sette (fri zet′), *n.* a fringe of curled or frizzed hair, esp. artificial, worn on the forehead by women. Also, **frizette.** [< F: little curl, deriv. of *friser* to curl]

fri·seur (frē zœr′), *n., pl.* **-seurs** (-zœr′). *French.* a hairdresser.

Fri·sian (frizh′ən, frē′zhən), *adj.* **1.** of or pertaining to Friesland, its inhabitants, or their language. —*n.* **2.** a native or inhabitant of Friesland. **3.** the Germanic language most closely related to English, spoken in Friesland and nearby islands. **4.** *Chiefly Brit.* **a.** Friesland. **b.** Holstein (def. 1). Also, **Friesian.** [< L *Frisī* the people of a Germanic tribe + -AN]

Fri′sian carv′ing, (in Pennsylvania Dutch furniture) geometrical incised carving.

Fri′sian Is′lands, a chain of islands in the North Sea, extending along the coasts of the Netherlands, West Germany, and Denmark: includes groups belonging to the Netherlands (**West′ Fri′sians**) and to West Germany (**East′ Fri′sians**) and a group divided between West Germany and Denmark (**North′ Fri′sians**).

frisk (frisk), *v.i.* **1.** to dance, leap, skip, or gambol, as in frolic: *The dogs and children frisked about on the lawn.* —*v.t.* **2.** to search (a person) for concealed weapons, contraband goods, etc., by feeling his clothing. **3.** *Slang.* to steal something from (someone) in this way. —*n.* **4.** a leap, skip, or caper. **5.** a frolic or gambol. [orig. adj. < OF *frisque* < Gmc; cf. G *frisch* lively, FRESH] —**frisk′er,** *n.* —**frisk′ing·ly,** *adv.*

fris·ket (fris′kit), *n.* **1.** a mask of thin paper laid over an illustration to shield certain areas when retouching artwork with an airbrush. **2.** *Print.* a mask of strong paper set in a rectangular frame attached to the tympan of certain presses and cut so as to prevent accidental soiling or printing by furniture or the chase. [< F *frisquette.* See FRISK, -ET]

frisk·y (fris′kē), *adj.,* **frisk·i·er, frisk·i·est.** lively; frolicsome; playful. [FRISK + -Y[1]] —**frisk′i·ly,** *adv.* —**frisk′i·ness,** *n.*

frit (frit), *n., v.,* **frit·ted, frit·ting.** —*n.* **1.** *Ceram.* **a.** a fused or partially fused material used as a basis for glazes or enamels. **b.** the composition from which artificial soft porcelain is made. **2.** fused or calcined material prepared as part of the batch in glassmaking. —*v.t.* **3.** to fuse (materials) in making frit. Also, **fritt.** [< It *fritta,* fem. ptp. of *friggere* to fry < L *frīgere*]

frit′ fly′, a minute fly, *Oscinella frit,* found chiefly in Europe, the larvae of which are serious pests of wheat and other cereals. [*frit* < ?]

frith (frith), *n.* firth.

frith·stool (frith′stōōl′), *n.* (in Anglo-Saxon England) a seat in a church, placed near the altar, for persons who claimed the right of sanctuary. [OE *frithstōl,* equiv. to *frith* peace, security (akin to OIcel *frithr,* Goth *Fritha(reiks)* Frederick; see FRIEND) + *stōl* STOOL]

frit·il·lar·i·a (frit′ᵊlâr′ē ə), *n.* any liliaceous plant of the genus *Fritillaria,* comprising bulbous herbs having drooping, bell-shaped flowers. [< NL, name of genus, equiv. to L *fritill(us)* dice box + *-āria* -ARY]

frit·il·lar·y (frit′ᵊler′ē), *n., pl.* **-lar·ies.** any of several orange-brown nymphalid butterflies, usually marked with black lines and dots and with silvery spots on the undersides of the wings. [< NL; see FRITILLARIA]

frit·ter[1] (frit′ər), *v.t.* **1.** to disperse or squander piecemeal; waste little by little (usually fol. by *away*): *to fritter away one's money; to fritter away an afternoon.* **2.** to break or tear into small pieces or shreds. —*v.i.* **3.** to dwindle, shrink, degenerate, etc. (often fol. by *away*): *to watch one's fortune fritter away.* **4.** to separate or break into fragments: *a plastic material having a tendency to fritter.* —*n.* **5.** a small piece, fragment, or shred. [earlier *fitter,* deriv. of *fit* part] —**frit′ter·er,** *n.*

frit·ter[2] (frit′ər), *n.* a small cake of batter, sometimes containing fruit, clams, or some other ingredient, fried in deep fat or sautéed. [ME *friture, frytour* < OF *friture* << L *frict(us)* (ptp. of *frīgere* to FRY) + OF *-ure* -URE]

fritz (frits), *n.* **on the fritz,** *Slang.* not operating; in need of repair: *The television set is on the fritz.* [?]

Fritz (frits), *n.* **1.** *Slang.* a German, esp. a German soldier. **2.** a boy's given name. [< G; common nickname for *Friederich*]

Fri·u·li·an (frē ōō′lē ən), *n.* a Rhaeto-Romanic dialect spoken by about half a million people of the plains of extreme NE Italy. [*Friuli* region of Italy + -AN]

Fri·u·li-Ve·ne·zia Giu·lia (frē ōō′lē ve ne′tsyä jōō′lyä), a region in NE Italy: formerly part of Venezia Giulia, most of which was ceded to Yugoslavia. 1,205,222 (1961); 2947 sq. mi.

friv·ol (friv′əl), *v.,* **-oled, -ol·ing** or (*esp. Brit.*) **-olled, -ol·ling.** *Informal.* —*v.i.* **1.** to behave frivolously; trifle: *Now, now, don't frivol with the girls.* —*v.t.* **2.** to spend frivolously (usually fol. by *away*): *to frivol away* one's time. [back formation from FRIVOLOUS] —**friv′ol·er**; esp. Brit., **friv′ol·ler**, n.

fri·vol·i·ty (fri vol′i tē), n., pl. **-ties** for 2. **1.** quality or state of being frivolous: *the frivolity of Mardi gras.* **2.** a frivolous act or thing: *It was a frivolity he had a hard time living down.* [< F *frivolité*. See FRIVOLOUS, -ITY]

friv·o·lous (friv′ə ləs), adj. **1.** of little or no weight, worth, or importance; not worthy of serious notice: *a frivolous suggestion.* **2.** characterized by lack of seriousness or sense: *frivolous conduct.* **3.** (of a person) given to trifling or undue levity: *a frivolous, empty-headed girl.* [ME < L *frīvol(us)* silly, trifling; see -OUS] —**friv′o·lous·ly**, adv. —**friv′o·lous·ness**, n.
—**Syn. 1.** light, trifling, petty, paltry, trivial, flimsy. **3.** idle, silly, foolish, childish, puerile. —**Ant. 1.** weighty. **3.** serious.

friz (friz), v., **frizzed, friz·zing**, n., pl. **friz·zes**. —v.t., v.i. **1.** to form into small, crisp curls or little tufts. —n. **2.** state of being frizzed. **3.** something frizzed; frizzed hair. Also, **frizz.** [back formation from FRIZZLE[1]] —**friz′er**, n.

fri·zette (fri zet′), n. frisette.

frizz[1] (friz), v.i., v.t. frizzle[2]. —**frizz′er**, n.

frizz[2] (friz), v.i., v.t., n. friz. —**frizz′er**, n.

friz·zle[1] (friz′əl), v., **-zled, -zling**, n. —v.t., v.i. **1.** to friz. —n. **2.** a short, crisp curl. [? cf. OE *fris* curled, OFris *frēsle* lock of hair] —**friz′zler**, n.

friz·zle[2] (friz′əl), v., **-zled, -zling.** —v.i. **1.** to make a sizzling or sputtering noise in frying or the like: *the sound of bacon frizzling on the stove.* —v.t. **2.** to make (food) crisp by frying. [b. FRY and FRIZZLE[1]]

friz·zly (friz′lē), adj., **-zli·er, -zli·est.** frizzy. [FRIZZLE[1] + -Y[1]]

friz·zy (friz′ē), adj., **-zi·er, -zi·est.** formed into small, tight curls, as hair; frizzed. Also, **frizzly.** [FRIZZ[1] + -Y[1]] —**friz′zi·ly**, adv. —**friz′zi·ness**, n.

fro (frō), adv. **1.** *Obs.* from; back. **2. to and fro,** alternating from one place to another; back and forth: *The trees were swaying to and fro in the wind.* [ME *frō, frā* < Scand; cf. OIcel *frā*; akin to OE *fram* FROM]

Fro·bish·er (frō′bi shər, frob′i-), n. **Sir Martin,** 1535?–94, English navigator and explorer.

frock (frok), n. **1.** a gown or dress worn by a woman. **2.** a loose outer garment worn by peasants and workmen; smock. **3.** a coarse outer garment with large sleeves, worn by monks. **4.** See **frock coat.** —v.t. **5.** to provide with, or clothe in, a frock. **6.** to invest with priestly or clerical office. [ME *froke* < OF *froc* < ?] —**frock′less**, adj.

frock′ coat′, a man's close-fitting coat, usually double-breasted, extending approximately to the knees.

Fro·di·na (frō dē′nə), n. a girl's given name. Also, **Fro·dine** (frō dēn′).

froe (frō), n. *Chiefly U.S.* frow.

Froe·bel (frœ′bəl), n. **Frie·drich** (frē′drikh), 1782–1852, German educational reformer: founder of the kindergarten system. —**Froe·bel·i·an** (frə bē′lē ən, -bēl′yən, frā-), adj.

frog[1] (frog, frôg), n., v., **frogged, frog·ging.** —n. **1.** any of numerous tailless amphibians of the order *Anura* that have long hind legs adapted for jumping, esp. the smooth-skinned species that live in a damp or aquatic habitat. **2.** a slight hoarseness caused by mucus on the vocal cords: *a frog in the throat.* **3.** (*cap.*) *Disparaging.* a Frenchman. **4.** a small holder made of heavy material, placed in a bowl or vase to hold flower stems in position. **5.** a recessed panel on the bed of a brick or the like. **6.** a sheath suspended from a belt and supporting a scabbard. —v.i. **7.** to catch or search for frogs. [ME *frogge*, OE *frogga, frocga*; cf. ME *frosh*, OIcel *frosk(r)*, OHG *frosk* (G *Frosch*)] —**frog′like′**, adj.

Frog 1, *Rana catesbeiana* (Length to 8 in.)

frog[2] (frog, frôg), n. **1.** an ornamental fastening for the front of a coat, consisting of a button and a loop through which it passes. **2.** *Railroads.* a device at the intersection of two tracks to permit the wheels and flanges on one track to cross or branch from the other. [? < Pg *froco* < L *floccus* FLOCK[2]]

frog[3] (frog, frôg), n. *Zool.* a triangular mass of elastic, horny substance in the middle of the sole of the foot of a horse or related animal. [special use of FROG[1]]

Frog 2 (def. 1)

frog·bit (frog′bit′, frôg′-), n. frog's-bit.

frog·eye (frog′ī′, frôg′ī′), n., pl. **-eyes** for 1. *Plant Pathol.* **1.** a small, diseased, whitish leaf spot with a narrow darker border, produced by certain fungi. **2.** a disease so characterized. [FROG[1] + EYE] —**frog′-eyed′**, adj.

frog·fish (frog′fish′, frôg′-), n., pl., (*esp. collectively*) **-fish,** (*esp. referring to two or more kinds or species*) **-fish·es.** **1.** any of several tropical marine fishes of the family *Antennariidae*, having a wide, froglike mouth and broad, limblike pectoral fins. **2.** angler (def. 2). [FROG[1] + FISH]

frog·gy (frog′ē, frô′gē), adj., **-gi·er, -gi·est.** **1.** of or characteristic of a frog. **2.** abounding in frogs. [FROG[1] + -Y[1]]

frog·hop·per (frog′hop′ər, frôg′-), n. any of numerous leaping, homopterous insects of the family *Cercopidae*, which in the immature stages live in a spittlelike secretion on plants. Also called **spittle bug, spittle insect.** [FROG[1] + HOPPER]

frog′ kick′, *Swimming.* a type of kick in which the legs are bent at the knees, extended outward, and then brought together forcefully.

frog′ lil′y, a yellow water lily.

frog·man (frog′man′, -mən, frôg′-), n., pl. **-men** (-men′, -mən). a swimmer specially equipped with air tanks, wet suit, diving mask, etc., for underwater demolition, salvage, scientific exploration, etc. [FROG[1] + MAN[1]]

frog·mouth (frog′mouth′, frôg′-), n., pl. **-mouths** (-mouthz′). any of several Australian and Oriental birds of the family *Podargidae*, related to the goatsuckers, having a broad, flattened, froglike mouth. [FROG[1] + MOUTH]

Frogs, The, a comedy (405 B.C.) by Aristophanes.

frog's-bit (frogz′bit′, frôgz′-), n. **1.** an aquatic, floating plant, *Hydrocharis Morsus-ranae*, of Europe and Asia, having thick roundish, spongy leaves. **2.** an aquatic, floating plant, *Limnobium Spongia*, of tropical America, having oblong, cordate, or ovate leaves. Also, **frogbit.**

frog′ spit′, any of several filamentous, fresh-water green algae forming floating masses. Also, **frog′ spit′tle.**

Froh·man (frō′mən), n. **Charles,** 1860–1915, U.S. theatrical producer.

Frois·sart (froi′särt; *Fr.* FRWA SAR′), n. **Jean** (zhäN), 1333?–c1400, French chronicler.

frol·ic (frol′ik), n., v., **-icked, -ick·ing,** adj. —n. **1.** merry play; gay prank; gaiety; fun. **2.** a merrymaking or party. —v.i. **3.** to gambol merrily; to play in a frisky, light-spirited manner; have fun; play merry pranks: *The children were frolicking in the snow.* —adj. **4.** *Archaic.* gay; merry; full of fun. [< D *vrolijk* joyful (c. G *fröhlich*), equiv. to *vro* glad + *-lijk* -like] —**frol′ick·er**, n.
—**Syn. 3.** sport, romp, revel.

frol·ic·ly (frol′ik lē), adv. *Obs.* in a frolicsome manner. Also, **frol′ick·ly.** [FROLIC + -LY]

frol·ic·some (frol′ik səm), adj. merrily playful; full of fun. [FROLIC + -SOME[1]] —**frol′ic·some·ly**, adv. —**frol′ic·some·ness**, n.

from (frum, from; *unstressed* frəm), prep. **1.** (used to specify a starting point in spatial movement): *a train running west from New York City.* **2.** (used to specify a starting point in an expression of limits): *The number of stores will be increased from 25 to a total of 30.* **3.** (used to express removal or separation, as in space, time, order, etc.): *two miles from shore; 30 minutes from now; from one page to the next.* **4.** (used to express discrimination or distinction): *to be excluded from membership; to differ from one's father.* **5.** (used to indicate source or origin): *to come from the Midwest; to take a pencil from one's pocket.* **6.** (used to indicate agent or instrumentality): *death from starvation.* **7.** (used to indicate cause or reason): *From the evidence, he must be guilty.* [ME; OE, var. of *fram* from (prep.), forward (adv.); c. Goth *fram*, Icel *frā* (see FRO), *fram* (adv.)]

Fro·ma (frō′mə), n. a girl's given name.

fro·mage (frô mazh′), n. *French.* cheese.

Fro·men·tin (frô mäN taN′), n. **Eu·gène** (œ zhen′), 1820–76, French painter, critic, and author.

fro·men·ty (frō′mən tē), n. *Brit. Dial.* frumenty.

From Here′ to Eter′nity, a novel (1951) by James Jones.

Fromm (from), n. **Er·ich** (er′ik), 1900–80, U.S. psychoanalyst and author, born in Germany.

Fro·na (frō′nə), n. a girl's given name. Also, **Fronia, Fronya.**

frond (frond), n. *Bot.* **1.** an often large, finely divided leaf, esp. as applied to the ferns and certain palms. **2.** a leaflike expansion not differentiated into stem and foliage, as in lichens. [< L *frond-* (s. of *frōns*) branch, bough, foliage] —**frond′ed**, adj. —**frond′less**, adj.

Fron·da (fron′də), n. a girl's given name. Also, **Fronde** (frond).

Fronde (FRÔND; *Eng.* frŏnd, frond), n. **1.** the unsuccessful series of rebellions (1648–53) of the parliament of Paris (**Fronde′ of the Par′lement**) and members of the nobility (**Fronde′ of the Princ′es**) against the court party led by Cardinal Mazarin during the minority of Louis XIV. The rebellions resulted in the humiliation of the nobles and the strengthening of monarchical authority. **2.** the groups that waged the rebellions. [< F: lit., sling]

fron·des·cence (fron des′əns), n. **1.** the process or period of putting forth leaves, as a tree, plant, or the like. **2.** leafage; foliage. [< NL *frondēscentia*, deriv. of L *frondēscent-* (s. of *frondēscēns*) becoming leafy (prp. of *frondēscere*), freq. of *frondēre* to have leaves. See FROND, -ESCENSE] —**fron·des′cent**, adj.

Fron·di·zi (fron dē′zē; *Sp.* FRÔN dē′sē), n. **Ar·tu·ro** (är to͝or′ō; *Sp.* är to͞o′Rô), born 1908, Argentine lawyer and political leader: president of Argentina 1958–62.

Fron·ya (frōn′yə), n. a girl's given name. Also, **Frona, Fron′ia.**

frons (fronz), n., pl. **fron·tes** (fron′tēz). the upper anterior portion of the head of an insect, above or behind the clypeus. [< L *frōns* forehead, FRONT]

front (frunt), n. **1.** the foremost part or surface of anything. **2.** the part or side of anything, as a house, which seems to look or to be directed forward: *She was dusting in the front of the house.* **3.** any side or face, as of a house. **4.** a façade, considered with respect to its architectural treatment or material: *a false front; a cast-iron front.* **5.** a property line along a street or the like: *the entire block front; a fifty-foot front.* **6.** a place or position directly before anything, in front of a person, etc.: *We decided to plant trees in the front.* **7.** *Mil.* **a.** the foremost line or part of an army. **b.** a line of battle. **c.** the place where combat operations are carried on. **8.** land facing a road, river, etc. **9.** *Brit.* a promenade along a seashore. **10.** *Informal.* a distinguished person listed as an official of an organization, for the sake of prestige, and who is usually inactive. **11.** *Informal.* someone or something that serves as a cover or disguise for another activity, esp. one of a disreputable nature; a blind: *The store was a front for foreign agents.* **12.** *Informal.* outward impression of rank, position, or wealth. **13.** bearing or demeanor in confronting anything: *a calm front.* **14.** haughtiness; self-importance: *That clerk has the most outrageous front.* **15.** the forehead, or the entire face: *the statue's gracefully chiseled front.* **16.** a coalition or movement to achieve a particular end, usually political: *people's front.* **17.** something attached or worn at the breast, as a shirt front, dicky, etc.: *to wear a contrasting front; to spill gravy down one's front.* **18.** *Meteorol.* a discontinuous surface separating two dissimilar air masses. **19.** *Theat.* **a.** the auditorium. **b.** the business offices of a theater. **c.** the front of the stage; downstage. **20. in front,** in a forward place or position: *Sit down, you in front!* **21. in front of, a.** ahead of: *to walk in front of a moving crowd.* **b.** outside the entrance of: *to wait in front of a house.* **c.** in the presence of: *to behave badly in front of company.* **22. out front, a.** outside the entrance: *He's waiting out front.* **b.** ahead of competitors: *This advertising campaign ought to put our business 'way out front.* **c.** *Theat.* in the audience or auditorium. —adj. **23.** of or pertaining to the front: *The front view of the dress was disappointing.* **24.** situated in or at the front: *front yard; front seats.* **25.** *Phonet.* (of a speech sound) articulated with the tongue blade relatively far forward in the mouth, as the sounds of *lay.* —v.t. **26.** to have the front toward; face: *Our house fronts the lake.* **27.** to meet face to face; confront: *to front life's problems without flinching.* **28.** to face in opposition, hostility, or defiance. **29.** to furnish or supply a front to: *They decided to front the building with sandstone.* **30.** to serve as a front to: *Imported marble will front the building. A long, sloping lawn fronted their house.* **31.** to lead (a jazz or dance band). —v.i. **32.** to have or turn the front in some specified direction: *Our house fronts on the lake.* **33.** to serve as a cover or disguise for another activity, esp. something of a disreputable nature: *The shop fronts for a narcotics ring.* —interj. **34.** (used to call or command someone to come, look, etc., to the front, as in an order to troops on parade or in calling a hotel bellboy to the front desk): *Front and center, on the double! Eyes, front!* [ME *frount, front* < L *front-* (s. of *frōns*) forehead, brow, front]

front·ad (frun′tad), adv. *Anat., Zool.* toward the front. [FRONT + *-ad* (< L *ad* toward)]

front·age (frun′tij), n. **1.** the front of a building or lot. **2.** the lineal extent of this front: *a frontage of 200 feet.* **3.** the direction it faces: *My house has an ocean frontage.* **4.** land abutting on a river, street, etc.: *He was willing to pay the higher cost of a lake frontage.* **5.** the space lying between a building and the street, a body of water, etc.: *He complained that the new sidewalk would decrease his frontage.* [FRONT + -AGE]

fron·tal (frun′tᵊl), adj. **1.** of, in, or at the front: *a frontal attack.* **2.** *Anat.* of, pertaining to, or situated near the forehead or the frontal bone. **3.** *Meteorol.* of or pertaining to the division between dissimilar air masses: *frontal zone; frontal surface.* **4.** *Fine Arts.* **a.** exhibiting frontality. **b.** parallel to the surface in the pictorial arts or seen from the front view in sculpture: *the frontal plane.* —n. **5.** *Eccles.* a movable cover or hanging for the front of an altar. **6.** frontlet (def. 3). **7.** *Anat.* any of several parts in the frontal region, esp. the frontal bone. [< LL *frontāl(is)* (NL, in anatomy sense); r. ME *frountel* < OF *frontel.* See FRONT, -AL[1]] —**fron′tal·ly**, adv.

fron′tal bone′, *Anat.* a broad membrane bone of the skull, forming the forehead and the upper portion of each orbit. See diag. under **skull.**

fron′tal cy′clone, any extratropical cyclone associated with a front: the most common cyclonic storm.

fron′tal gy′rus, *Anat.* any of several convolutions on the outer surface of the frontal lobe of the cerebrum. Also, **fron′tal convolu′tion.**

fron·tal·i·ty (frun tal′i tē, fron-), n. *Fine Arts.* **1.** the representation of the front view of figures or objects in a work of art. **2.** the organization of planes parallel to the picture plane in the pictorial arts, or the composition of volumes entirely from the front view in sculpture. [FRONTAL + -ITY]

fron′tal lobe′, *Anat.* the anterior part of each cerebral hemisphere, in front of the central sulcus.

front′ bench′, *Brit.* (in the House of Commons) either of two seats near the Speaker, on which the leaders of the major parties sit. Cf. **back bench.**

front′ door′, **1.** the main entrance to a house or other building, usually facing a street. **2.** anything offering the best or most convenient approach to a place, situation, objective, etc.

Fron·te·nac (fron′tᵊnak′; *for 1 also Fr.* FRÔNᵗᵊ NAK′), n. **1. Louis de Bu·ade de** (lwē də BY ad′ də), c1620–98, French governor of Canada 1672–82, 1689–98. **2.** a town in E Missouri. 3089 (1960).

front′ foot′, *U.S.* a foot measured along the front of a lot.

fron·tier (frun tēr′), n. **1.** the part of a country that borders another country; boundary; border. **2.** *U.S.* land that forms the furthest extent of a country's settled or inhabited regions. **3.** Often, **frontiers. a.** the limit of knowledge or the most advanced achievement in a particular field: *the frontiers of historical research; to advance the frontiers of nuclear science.* **b.** an outer limit in a field of endeavor, esp. one in which the opportunities for research and development have not been exploited: *the frontiers of space exploration.* **4.** *Math.* boundary (def. 2). —adj. **5.** of, pertaining to, or located on the frontier: *frontier justice; a frontier town.* [ME *frounter* < OF *frontier*, equiv. to *front* (in the sense of opposite side; see FRONT) + *-ier* -IER] —**fron·tier′less**, adj. —**fron·tier′like′**, adj.

fron·tiers·man (frun tērz′mən), n., pl. **-men.** *U.S.* a man who lives on the frontier, esp. in sparsely settled regions under somewhat primitive conditions. [FRONTIERS + MAN[1]]

fron·tis (frun′tis), n. the front wall of a cancha or jai alai court. Cf. **rebote** (def. 1). [< Sp, appar. alter. of *frente* front]

fron·tis·piece (frun′tis pēs′, fron′-), n. **1.** an illustrated leaf preceding the title page of a book. **2.** *Archit.* a façade, or a part or feature of a façade, rendered especially important by ornamentation. [alter. (conformed to PIECE) of earlier *frontispice* < F < ML *frontispic(ium)*, equiv. to L *fronti-* FRONT + *-spicium* (comb. form repr. *specere* to look at)]

front·lash (frunt′lash′), n. an action or opinion opposing a backlash, countermovement, or the like. [FRONT + LASH, modeled on *backlash*]

front·less (frunt′lis), adj. *Archaic.* shameless; unblushing. [FRONT + -LESS] —**front′less·ly**, adv. —**front′less·ness**, n.

front·let (frunt′lit), n. **1.** the forehead of an animal. **2.** *Ornith.* the forehead when marked by a different color or texture of the plumage. **3.** Also, **frontal.** a decorative band, ribbon, or the like, worn across the forehead: *The princess wore a richly bejeweled frontlet.* **4.** *Judaism.* the phylactery worn on the forehead. [ME *frontlet* < OF, dim of *frontel* FRONTAL]

front′ mat′ter, *Print. U.S.* all matter in a book that precedes the text proper. Cf. **back matter.**

front′ mon′ey, 1. payment advanced to a commission agent. 2. Also called **advance fee.** money furnished by a company to a financier under a promise to procure funds for it.

fronto-, a learned borrowing from Latin used to refer to the frontal bone or lobe (*frontoparietal*) or, in meteorological terms, to a frontal zone (*frontogenesis*). [comb. form repr. L *front-* (s. of *frōns*) forehead, front]

front′ of′fice, the executive or administrative office of a firm.

fron·to·gen·e·sis (frun′tə jen′i sis), *n. Meteorol.* the formation or increase of a front or frontal zone. Cf. **frontolysis.** [FRONTO- + -GENESIS]

fron·tol·y·sis (frun tol′i sis), *n. Meteorol.* the dissipation or decrease of a front or frontal zone. Cf. **frontogenesis.** [FRONTO- + -LYSIS]

fron·ton (fron′ton, fron ton′), *n.* a building in which jai alai is played, containing the cancha or court and sometimes having facilities for betting. [< Sp *frontón,* irreg. aug. of *frente* forehead, FRONT]

fron·to·pa·ri·e·tal (frun′tō pə rī′i tᵊl), *adj. Anat.* 1. of or pertaining to the frontal and parietal bones of the cranium. 2. of or pertaining to the frontal and parietal lobes of a cerebral hemisphere. [FRONTO- + PARIETAL]

front-page (frunt′pāj′), *adj., v.,* **-paged, -pag·ing.** —*adj.* 1. of consequence; worth putting on the first page of a newspaper. —*v.t.* 2. to run (copy) or carry (a news report) on the front page, esp. of a newspaper: *Let's front-page this story.*

Front′ Range′, a mountain range extending from central Colorado to S Wyoming: part of the Rocky Mountains. Highest peak, Grays Peak, 14,274 ft.

front-rank (frunt′rangk′), *adj.* among the best or most important; foremost.

front′ room′, a room at the front of a house, esp. a parlor.

Front′ Roy′al, a town in N Virginia. 7949 (1960).

front′ run′ner, 1. *Sports.* a. an entrant in a race, as in horse racing or track, characterized typically by superior performance only when ahead of the field. b. *Track.* an entrant in a race who breaks to the front immediately and establishes the pace for the field. 2. one who leads in any competition: *a front runner in automobile manufacturing.*

front′ scene′, *Theat.* 1. a scene or act played downstage, usually in front of an olio, drop scene, or the like. 2. a set or drop placed downstage.

front·stall (frunt′stôl′), *n. Armor.* chanfron. [FRONT + STALL¹]

front·ward (frunt′wərd), *adv.* in a direction toward the front. Also, **front′wards.** [FRONT + -WARD]

front′ win′dow. See **cottage window.**

frore (frōr, frôr), *adj.* frozen; frosty. [ME *frore(n);* ptp. of FREEZE]

frosh¹ (frosh), *n., pl.* **frosh.** *Informal.* a college freshman. [by alter. and shortening]

frosh² (frosh), *n. Brit. Dial.* a frog. Also, **frosk** (frosk). [ME *frosk, frosh,* OE *forsc, frox* FROG¹]

frost (frôst, frost), *n.* 1. state or condition of the temperature which causes the freezing of water. 2. Also called **hoarfrost.** a covering of minute ice needles, formed from the atmosphere at night upon the ground and exposed objects when they have cooled by radiation below the dew point, and when the dew point is below the freezing point. 3. the act or process of freezing. 4. coldness of manner or temperament: *We noticed a slight frost in his greeting.* 5. *Informal.* a coolness between persons. 6. *Informal.* something that meets with unlooked-for coldness or lack of enthusiasm, as a theatrical performance, party, etc. 7. **degree of frost,** *Brit.* the degree of temperature Fahrenheit below the freezing point: *10 degrees of frost is equivalent to 22°F.* —*v.t.* 8. to cover with frost. 9. to give a frostlike surface to (glass, metal, etc.). 10. to ice (cookies, a cake, etc.). 11. to kill or injure by frost: *a freezing rain that badly frosted the plants.* —*v.i.* 12. to freeze or become covered with frost (often fol. by *up* or *over*): *I think the water pipes have frosted up. The windshield has frosted over.* 13. (of varnish, paint, etc.) to dry with a film resembling frost. [ME, OE *frost, forst;* c. OS, OHG, OIcel, G *frost;* akin to FREEZE] —**frost′less,** *adj.* —**frost′like′,** *adj.*

Frost (frôst, frost), *n.* **Robert (Lee),** 1874–1963, U.S. poet.

frost·bite (frôst′bīt′, frost′-), *n., v.,* **-bit, -bit·ten, -bit·ing.** —*n.* 1. the inflamed, gangrenous effect of excessive exposure to extreme cold. —*v.t.* 2. to injure by frost or extreme cold. [FROST + BITE]

frost·bit·er (frôst′bī′tər, frost′-), *n. Informal.* 1. a person who sails or races an iceboat. 2. an iceboat. [FROSTBITE + -ER¹]

frost·bit·ing (frôst′bī′ting, frost′-), *n. Informal.* iceboating. [FROSTBITE + -ING¹]

frost·bit·ten (frôst′bit′ᵊn, frost′-), *adj.* 1. injured by frost or extreme cold. —*v.* 2. pp. of **frostbite.**

Frost·burg (frôst′bûrg, frost′-), *n.* a town in W Maryland. 6722 (1960).

frost·ed (frô′stid, fros′tid), *adj.* 1. covered with or having frost. 2. frostbitten. 3. coated with frosting or icing, as a cake. 4. made frostlike in appearance, as certain opaque glass: *a frosted door; a frosted light bulb.* 5. quick-frozen. 6. made with ice cream, as a confection, beverage, or the like: *frosted malted.* —*n.* 7. a thick beverage, usually made with milk, flavoring syrup, and ice cream whipped together. [FROST + -ED²]

frost′ feath′ers. See **ice feathers.**

frost·fish (frôst′fish′, frost′-), *n., pl. (esp. collectively)* **-fish,** *(esp. referring to two or more kinds or species)* **-fish·es.** 1. either of two North American fishes, the tomcod of the Atlantic Ocean or the round whitefish, that appear when frost sets in. 2. scabbardfish. [FROST + FISH]

frost·flow·er (frôst′flou′ər, frost′-), *n.* 1. a liliaceous plant, *Milla biflora,* of the southwestern U.S. and Mexico. 2. its waxy-white, starlike flower. 3. any aster. [FROST + FLOWER]

frost′ flow′ers. See **ice flowers** (def. 2).

frost′ grape′. See **riverbank grape.**

frost′ heave′, *Geol.* an uplift in soil caused by the freezing of internal moisture.

frost·ing (frô′sting, fros′ting), *n.* 1. a sweet mixture, cooked or uncooked, for coating or filling cakes, cookies, and the like; icing. 2. a lusterless finish, as of metal or glass. 3. a material used for decorative work, as signs, displays, etc., made from coarse flakes of powdered glass. [FROST + -ING¹]

frost′ line′, 1. the maximum depth at which soil is frozen. 2. the lower limit of permafrost. Cf. **permafrost table.**

frost′ mist′. See **ice crystals.**

frost′ point′, the temperature of the air at which hoarfrost begins to form.

Frost·proof (frôst′pro͞of′, frost′-), *n.* a town in central Florida. 2664 (1960).

frost′ smoke′, *Meteorol.* 1. Also called **barber.** an ice fog caused by extremely cold air flowing over a body of comparatively warm water, esp. in polar regions. 2. See **steam fog.**

frost′ snow′. See **ice crystals.**

frost·work (frôst′wûrk′, frost′-), *n.* 1. the delicate tracery formed by frost, esp. on glass. 2. similar ornamentation, as on metal or glass. [FROST + WORK]

frost·y (frô′stē, fros′tē), *adj.,* **frost·i·er, frost·i·est.** 1. attended with or producing frost; freezing; very cold: *frosty weather.* 2. consisting of or covered with a frost: *frosty designs on the windows; an avenue of frosty trees.* 3. lacking warmth of feeling: *Their frosty greeting puzzled us.* 4. resembling frost; white or gray, as hair: *a wedding dress of frosty satin; frosty curls.* 5. of or characteristic of old age: *a frosty brow.* [ME; see FROST, -Y¹] —**frost′i·ly,** *adv.* —**frost′i·ness,** *n.* —**frost′less,** *adj.*

froth (frôth, froth), *n.* 1. an aggregation of bubbles, as on a fermented or agitated liquid, at the mouth of a hard-driven horse, etc.; foam; spume. 2. a foam of saliva or fluid resulting from disease. 3. something unsubstantial or evanescent, as idle talk; trivial ideas: *The play was a charming bit of froth.* —*v.t.* 4. to cover with froth: *giant waves frothing the sand.* 5. to cause to foam: *to froth egg whites with a whisk.* 6. to emit like froth: *a demagogue frothing his hate.* —*v.i.* 7. to give out froth; foam: *frothing at the mouth; giant breakers heaving and frothing.* [ME *frothe,* ? < Scand; cf. Icel *frodha, fraudh* foam; akin to OE *āfrēothan* to foam] —**froth′er,** *n.*

froth·y (frô′thē, froth′ē), *adj.,* **froth·i·er, froth·i·est.** 1. of, like, or having froth; foamy. 2. unsubstantial; trifling; shallow. [FROTH + -Y¹] —**froth′i·ly,** *adv.* —**froth′i·ness,** *n.*

frot·tage (frô täzh′), *n.* 1. a technique in the visual arts of obtaining textural effects or images by rubbing lead, chalk, charcoal, etc., over paper laid on a granular or relieflike surface. Cf. **rubbing** (def. 2). 2. a work of art containing shapes and textures produced by frottage. 3. *Psychol.* the practice of getting sexual stimulation and satisfaction by rubbing against something, esp. another person. [< F, equiv. to *frott(er)* (to) rub + *-age* -AGE]

frot·teur (frô tûr′), *n.* a person who practices frottage. [< F, equiv. to *frott(er)* (to) rub + *-eur;* see -OR²]

frot·to·la (frôt′ᵊlə, frot′-; *It.* fʀôt′tô lä′), *n., pl.* **frot·to·le** (frôt′ᵊlā′, frot′-; *It.* fʀôt′tô le′). a homophonic, strophic song of 15th- and 16th-century Italy. [< It, OIt, deriv. of *frotta* crowd, var. of *fiotta* < Gmc]

Froude (fro͞od), *n.* **James Anthony,** 1818–94, English historian.

frou-frou (fro͞o′fro͞o′), *n.* 1. a rustling, particularly the rustling of silk, as in a woman's dress. 2. elaborate decoration, as frills, ribbons, ruffles, etc., esp. on women's clothing. [< F; imit.]

frounce (frouns), *n., v.,* **frounced, frounc·ing.** —*n.* 1. *Archaic.* affectation; empty show. —*v.t. Obs.* 2. to curl the hair of. 3. to pleat. —*v.i.* 4. *Obs.* to frown. [ME *fro(u)nce(n)* (v.) < OF *fronc(ier),* deriv. of *fronc* a wrinkle, fold < Gmc; cf. Icel *hrukka,* WRINKLE, G *Runzel* wrinkle]

frous·y (frou′zē), *adj.,* **frous·i·er, frous·i·est.** frowsy.

frouz·y (frou′zē), *adj.,* **frouz·i·er, frouz·i·est.** frowzy.

frow (frō), *n. U.S.* a cleaving tool having a wedge-shaped blade, with a handle set at right angles to it. Also, **froe.** [special use of FROW(ARD) (turned away from)]

fro·ward (frō′wərd, frō′ərd), *adj.* perverse; willfully contrary; refractory; not easily managed: *to be worried about one's froward, intractable daughter.* [ME *froward, fraward.* See FRO-, -WARD] —**fro′ward·ly,** *adv.* —**fro′ward·ness,** *n.*
—**Syn.** obstinate, willful, disobedient, fractious, wayward, unmanageable, difficult. —**Ant.** docile, tractable.

frown (froun), *v.i.* 1. to contract the brow, as in displeasure or deep thought; scowl. 2. to look displeased; have an angry look. 3. to look disapprovingly (usually fol. by *on* or *upon*): *to frown upon a scheme.* —*v.t.* 4. to express by a frown: *to frown one's displeasure.* 5. to force or shame with a disapproving frown: *to frown someone into silence; He rose to jeer, but I frowned him down.* —*n.* 6. a frowning look; scowl. 7. any expression or show of disapproval: *a tax bill that received Congressional frowns.* [ME *froune(n)* < OF *froign(ier),* deriv. of *froigne* surly expression < Celt] —**frown′er,** *n.* —**frown′ing·ly,** *adv.*
—**Syn.** 1. glower, lower, gloom.

frowst (froust), *v.i. Brit.* to sit or sprawl indoors in a lazy mood; lounge. [?]

frowst·y (frou′stē), *adj.* **frowst·i·er, frowst·i·est.** *Brit. Informal.* musty; ill-smelling. [? dial. var. of FROWZY] —**frowst′i·ly,** *adv.* —**frowst′i·ness,** *n.*

frows·y (frou′zē), *adj.,* **frows·i·er, frows·i·est.** frowzy. Also, **frousy.** —**frows′i·ly,** *adv.* —**frows′i·ness,** *n.*

frowz·y (frou′zē), *adj.,* **frowz·i·er, frowz·i·est.** 1. dirty and untidy; slovenly. 2. ill-smelling; musty. Also, **frouzy.** [?] —**frowz′i·ly,** *adv.* —**frowz′i·ness,** *n.*

froze (frōz), *v.* pt. of **freeze.**

fro·zen (frō′zən), *v.* 1. pp. of **freeze.** —*adj.* 2. congealed by cold; covered with ice, as a stream. 3. frigid; very cold. 4. injured or killed by frost or cold. 5. obstructed by ice, as pipes. 6. chilly or cold in manner; unfeeling: *a frozen stare.* 7. quick-frozen. 8. (of food) chilled or refrigerated: *frozen custard.* 9. in a form that is not readily convertible into cash: *frozen assets.* 10. *Canasta.* (of the discard pile) unable to be picked up by a player unless he can match the top card of the pile with a natural pair in his hand. Cf. **freeze** (def. 26). —**fro′zen·ly,** *adv.* —**fro′zen·ness,** *n.*

fro′zen dai′quiri, a cocktail consisting of rum, lime juice, and sugar, vigorously beaten together with finely crushed ice and served with a straw.

fro′zen fog′. See **ice fog.**

fro′zen pud′ding, a frozen or chilled dessert mixture of rich custard, nuts or candied fruit, and sometimes liquor.

FRS, Federal Reserve System.

Frs., Frisian.

frs., francs.

F.R.S., Fellow of the Royal Society.

F.R.S.L., Fellow of the Royal Society of Literature.

F.R.S.S., Fellow of the Royal Statistical Society.

frt., freight.

fruct-, var. of **fructi-** before a vowel: *fructose.*

fruct·ed (fruk′tid, fro͝ok′-), *adj. Heraldry.* (of a tree or other plant) represented as bearing fruit, seeds, or the like: *an apple tree vert fructed gules.* [< L *frūct(us)* (see FRUCTI-) + -ED³]

fructi-, a learned borrowing from Latin meaning "fruit," used in the formation of compound words: *fructiferous.* Also, *esp. before a vowel,* **fruct-.** [< L, comb. form of *frūctus* FRUIT]

Fruc·ti·dor (fʀʏk tē dôr′), *n.* (in the French Revolutionary calendar) the 12th month of the year, extending from August 18 to September 16. [< F < L *frūcti-* FRUCTI- + Gk *dôr(on)* gift]

fruc·tif·er·ous (fruk tif′ər əs, fro͝ok′-), *adj.* fruit-bearing; producing fruit. [< L *frūctiferus.* See FRUCTI-, -FER, -OUS] —**fruc·tif′er·ous·ly,** *adv.*

fruc·ti·fi·ca·tion (fruk′tə fə kā′shən, fro͝ok′-), *n.* 1. act of fructifying; the fruiting of a plant. 2. the fruit of a plant. 3. the organs of fruiting. [< LL *frūctificātiōn-* (s. of *frūctificātiō*) a bearing of fruit, equiv. to L *frūctificāt(us)* (ptp. of *frūctificāre;* see FRUCTIFY) + *-iōn* -ION]

fruc·ti·fi·ca·tive (fruk′tə fə kā′tiv, fro͝ok′-), *adj.* having the ability to yield or produce fruit. [FRUCTIFICAT(ION) + -IVE]

fruc·ti·fi·er (fruk′tə fī′ər, fro͝ok′-), *n.* one who or that which fructifies: *Fructifiers were added to enrich the dirt.* [FRUCTIFY + -ER¹]

fruc·ti·fy (fruk′tə fī′, fro͝ok′-), *v.,* **-fied, -fy·ing.** —*v.i.* 1. to bear fruit; become fruitful: *With careful tending, the soil will fructify.* —*v.t.* 2. to make fruitful or productive; fertilize: *warm spring rains fructifying the earth.* [ME *fructifie(n)* < OF *fructifi(er)* < L *frūctificāre.* See FRUCTI-, -FY]

fruc·to·san (fruk′tə san′, fro͝ok′-), *n. Biochem.* any of the class of hexosans, as inulin and the like, that yield fructose upon hydrolysis. [FRUCTOSE + -AN]

fruc·tose (fruk′tōs, fro͝ok′-), *n. Chem., Pharm.* a yellowish to white, crystalline, water-soluble, levorotatory ketose sugar, $C_6H_{12}O_6$, sweeter than sucrose, occurring in invert sugar, honey, and a great many fruits: used in foodstuffs and in medicine chiefly in solution as an intravenous nutrient. Also called **levulose, fruit sugar.** [FRUCT- + -OSE²]

fruc·to·side (fruk′tə sīd′, fro͝ok′-), *n. Biochem.* a glycoside that yields fructose upon hydrolysis. [FRUCTOSE + -IDE]

fruc·tu·ous (fruk′cho͞o əs), *adj.* productive; fertile; profitable: *a fructuous region, rich in natural resources.* [ME < L *frūctuōs(us),* deriv. of *frūctus* fruit; see -OUS] —**fruc′tu·ous·ly,** *adv.* —**fruc′tu·ous·ness,** *n.*

frug (fro͞og), *n., v.,* **frugged, frug·ging.** —*n.* 1. a dance deriving from the twist. —*v.i.* 2. to dance the frug.

fru·gal (fro͞o′gəl), *adj.* 1. economical in use or expenditure; prudently saving or sparing. 2. entailing little expense; requiring few resources; meager; scanty: *a frugal meal.* [< L *frūgāl(is)* economical, equiv. to *frūg(ī)* (indeclinable adj., orig. dat. of *frūx* produce, fruit) + *-ālis* -AL¹] —**fru·gal·i·ty** (fro͞o gal′i tē), **fru′gal·ness,** *n.* —**fru′gal·ly,** *adv.*
—**Syn.** 1. self-denying, thrifty, chary, provident, careful; parsimonious, penurious, stingy. See **economical.** —**Ant.** 1. lavish, wasteful.

fru·giv·o·rous (fro͞o jiv′ər əs), *adj.* fruit-eating, as certain bats. [< L *frūgi* (see FRUGAL) + -VOROUS]

fruit (fro͞ot), *n., pl.* **fruits,** *(esp. collectively)* **fruit,** *v.* —*n.* 1. any product of vegetable growth useful to men or animals. 2. *Bot.* a. the developed ovary of a seed plant with its contents and accessory parts, as the pea pod, nut, tomato, pineapple, etc. b. the edible part of a plant developed from a flower, with any accessory tissues, as the peach, mulberry, banana, etc. c. the spores and accessory organs of a cryptogam. 3. anything produced or accruing; product, result, or effect; return or profit: *the fruits of one's labors.* 4. *Slang.* a male homosexual. —*v.i., v.t.* 5. to bear or cause to bear fruit: *a tree that fruits in late summer; careful pruning which sometimes fruits a tree.* [ME < OF < L *frūct(us)* enjoyment, proceeds, fruit (n. use of ptp. of *frui* to enjoy)] —**fruit′like′,** *adj.*

fruit·age (fro͞o′tij), *n.* 1. the bearing of fruit: *soil additives to hasten the fruitage.* 2. fruits collectively. 3. product or result: *This year's fruitage was of better quality.* [< MF *fruit(er)* (to) bear fruit + *-age* -AGE]

fruit·ar·i·an (fro͞o târ′ē ən), *n.* a person whose diet consists chiefly of fruit. [FRUIT + -ARIAN]

fruit′ cake′, a rich cake containing raisins, nuts, citron, etc.

fruit′ cup′, an assortment of fruits served in a glass or a cup as an appetizer or dessert.

fruit′ dot′, a sorus.

fruit·ed (fro͞o′tid), *adj.* 1. having or bearing fruit. 2. with fruit added. [FRUIT + -ED³]

fruit·er (fro͞o′tər), *n.* 1. a cargo vessel carrying fruit. 2. a person who grows fruit. [late ME; see FRUIT, -ER¹]

fruit·er·er (fro͞o′tər ər), *n. Chiefly Brit.* a dealer in fruit. [ME; extended form of FRUITER]

fruit·er·y (fro͞o′tə rē), *n., pl.* **-er·ies.** *Archaic.* fruit. [FRUIT + -ERY]

fruit′ fly′, 1. any of numerous small dipterous insects of the family *Trypetidae,* the larvae of which feed on the fruit of several plants, as *Ceratitis capitata* **(Mediterranean fruit fly),** which attacks citrus. 2. See **vinegar fly.**

fruit·ful (fro͞ot′fəl), *adj.* **1.** abounding in fruit, as trees or other plants; bearing fruit abundantly. **2.** producing an abundant growth, as of fruit: *fruitful soil; fruitful rain.* **3.** productive of good results; profitable: *fruitful investigations.* [ME; see FRUIT, -FUL] —**fruit′ful·ly,** *adv.* —**fruit′ful·ness,** *n.*
—**Syn. 2, 3.** See **productive.** —**Ant. 3.** barren.

fruit′ing bod′y, *Bot.* an organ that produces spores; fructification.

fru·i·tion (fro͞o ish′ən), *n.* **1.** attainment of anything desired; realization of good results: *After much labor he finally brought his idea to full fruition.* **2.** enjoyment, as of something attained or realized. **3.** state of bearing fruit. [ME *fruicioun* < LL *fruitiōn-* (s. of *fruitiō*) enjoyment, equiv. to L *fruit(us)* (var. of *frūctus;* see FRUIT) + *-iōn-* -ION]
—**Syn. 1.** consummation, accomplishment, fulfillment, achievement, completion, perfection, result.

fru·i·tive[1] (fro͞o′i tiv), *adj.* able to produce fruit or fruition; fruitful. [FRUIT(ION) + -IVE]

fru·i·tive[2] (fro͞o′i tiv), *adj.* able to enjoy or to produce enjoyment. [< ML *fruitīv(us).* See FRUIT, -IVE]

fruit′ jar′, a glass jar for preserving fruit or vegetables, usually holding one pint or one quart and having an airtight cap. Cf. **Mason jar.**

fruit′ knife′, a small knife, usually having a distinctive handle and a stainless steel blade with a sharp or serrated edge, used at table for paring and cutting fruit.

fruit·less (fro͞ot′lis), *adj.* **1.** useless; unproductive; without results or success: *a fruitless search for the missing treasure.* **2.** without fruit; barren. [ME; see FRUIT, -LESS] —**fruit′less·ly,** *adv.* —**fruit′less·ness,** *n.*
—**Syn. 1.** ineffective, abortive, unprofitable, bootless, futile, unavailing, idle. **2.** sterile, unfruitful. —**Ant. 1.** useful, profitable. **2.** abundant, fertile.

fruit′ ranch′, *Western U.S.* a farm where fruit is the main produce.

fruit′ sug′ar, *Chem.* fructose.

fruit′ tree′, a tree bearing edible fruit.

fruit·wood (fro͞ot′wo͝od′), *n.* any of various woods from fruit-bearing trees, used for cabinetmaking and the like. [FRUIT + WOOD[1]]

fruit·y (fro͞o′tē), *adj.,* **fruit·i·er, fruit·i·est. 1.** resembling fruit; having the taste or flavor of fruit. **2.** rich in flavor; pungent. **3.** excessively sweet or mellifluous; cloying; syrupy: *a specialist in fruity prose; to read poetry in a fruity voice.* **4.** *Slang.* insane; crazy. **5.** *Slang.* homosexual. [FRUIT + -Y[1]] —**fruit′i·ness,** *n.*

fru·men·ta·ceous (fro͞o′mən tā′shəs), *adj.* of the nature of or resembling wheat or other grain. [< LL *frūmentāceus* of corn or grain, equiv. to L *frūment(um)* grain + *-āceus* -ACEOUS]

Fru·men·ti·us (fro͞o men′shē əs), *n.* **Saint,** A.D. c300–c380, founder of the Ethiopian Church.

fru·men·ty (fro͞o′mən tē), *n. Brit. Dial.* a dish of hulled wheat boiled in milk and seasoned with sugar, cinnamon, and raisins. Also, **fromenty, furmenty, furmety.** [ME *frumentee* < OF, equiv. to *frument* grain (< L *frūmentum*) + *-ee* -Y[3]]

frump (frump), *n.* a woman who is dowdy, drab, and unattractive. [?]

frump·ish (frum′pish), *adj.* (of a woman) dowdy and unattractive. [FRUMP + -ISH[1]] —**frump′ish·ly,** *adv.* —**frump′ish·ness,** *n.*

frump·y (frum′pē), *adj.,* **frump·i·er, frump·i·est.** frumpish. [FRUMP + -Y[1]] —**frump′i·ly,** *adv.* —**frump′i·ness,** *n.*

Frun·ze (fro͞on′zə; *Russ.* fro͞on′zyə), *n.* a former name (1926–91) of **Bishkek.**

frus·trate (frus′trāt), *v.,* **-trat·ed, -trat·ing,** *adj.* —*v.t.* **1.** to make (plans, efforts, etc.) worthless or of no avail; defeat; baffle; nullify: *The student's indifference frustrated the teacher's efforts to help him.* **2.** to disappoint or thwart (a person): *a woman whom life had frustrated.* —*v.i.* **3.** to become frustrated: *His trouble is that he frustrates much too easily.* —*adj.* **4.** *Archaic.* frustrated. [ME *frustrate(n)* < L *frustrāt(us)* (ptp. of *frustrārī*), equiv. to *frustr(ā)* in vain + *-ātus* -ATE[1]] —**frus′trat·er,** *n.* —**frus·tra·tive** (frus′trā-tiv, -trə-), *adj.*
—**Syn. 1.** balk, foil, circumvent, disconcert, check. See **thwart.**
—**Ant. 1.** encourage, foster.

frus·trat·ed (frus′trā tid), *adj.* disappointed; thwarted: *a preacher who was a frustrated actor; a frustrated boycott.* [FRUSTRATE + -ED[2]]

frus·tra·tion (fru strā′shən), *n.* **1.** act of frustrating; state of being frustrated: *to aim at the frustration of another's efforts.* **2.** an instance of being frustrated: *to experience a series of frustrations before completing a project.* [ME *frustracioun* < L *frustrātiōn-* (s. of *frustrātiō*) deception, disappointment. See FRUSTRATE, -ION]

frus·tule (frus′cho͞ol), *n. Bot.* the siliceous cell wall of a diatom. [< F < LL *frustul(um),* dim. of *frustum* FRUSTUM]

frus·tu·lum (frus′tə ləm, -chə-), *n., pl.* **-la** (-lə). *Rom. Cath. Ch.* a small breakfast permitted on fast days. [< L; see FRUSTULE]

frus·tum (frus′təm), *n., pl.* **-tums, -ta** (-tə). **1.** *Geom.* **a.** the part of a conical solid left after cutting off a top portion with a plane parallel to the base. **b.** the part of a solid, as a cone or pyramid, between two usually parallel cutting planes. **2.** *Archit.* **a.** a truncated column. **b.** one drum of a column. **c.** one course of a pier, formed of a single stone. [< L: piece, bit; prob. akin to OIr *brūid* he breaks, OE *brȳsan* to crush]

F

F, Frustum of a cone

fru·tes·cent (fro͞o tes′ənt), *adj. Bot.* tending to be shrublike; shrubby. [< L *frut(ex)* shrub, bush + -ESCENT] —**fru·tes′cence,** *n.*

fru·ti·cose (fro͞o′tə kōs′), *adj. Bot.* having the form of a shrub; shrublike. [< L *fruticōs(us)* full of shrubs, bushy, equiv. to *frutic-* (s. of *frutex*) shrub + *-ōsus* -OSE[1]]

fry[1] (frī), *v.,* **fried, fry·ing,** *n., pl.* **fries.** —*v.t.* **1.** to cook with fat, oil, etc., usually over direct heat. **2.** *Slang.* to execute by electrocution in an electric chair. —*v.i.* **3.** to undergo cooking in fat. **4.** *Slang.* to die by electrocution in an electric chair. —*n.* **5.** a dish of something fried. **6.** an occasion at which the chief food is fried, frequently outdoors: *a fish fry.* [ME *frie(n)* < OF *fri(re)* < L *frīgere* to fry]

fry[2] (frī), *n., pl.* **fry. 1.** the young of fishes. **2.** the young of various other animals, as frogs. **3.** *Informal.* people; individuals, esp. children: *games that are fun for the small fry.* [ME *frie, fry* seed, descendant, perh. < Scand; cf. Icel *frjō,* Sw *frö,* Goth *fraiw* seed]

Fry (frī), *n.* **Christopher,** born 1907, English playwright.

fry·er (frī′ər), *n.* **1.** one who or that which fries. **2.** something, as a young chicken, for frying. Also, **frier.** [FRY[1] + -ER[1]]

fry′ing pan′, 1. a shallow, long-handled pan in which food is fried. **2. out of the frying pan into the fire,** free of one predicament but immediately involved in another more difficult one. Also, **fry-pan, fry·pan** (frī′pan′). Also called **skillet.** [ME *fryinge panne*]

f.s., foot-second.

FSA, Farm Security Agency.

F-scope (ef′skōp′), *n. Electronics.* a radarscope on which the target reflection is in the center when the antenna is beamed directly on target and on which vertical and horizontal changes in target position are reflected as vertical and horizontal displacements of the target reflection on the scope. Also called **F-display.**

FSH, *Biochem.* a hormone, produced by the anterior lobe of the pituitary gland, that regulates the development of the Graafian follicle in the female and stimulates the production of spermatozoa in the male. Also called **follicle-stimulating hormone.**

FSR, Field Service Regulations.

F-state (ef′stāt′), *n. Physics.* the energy state of an electron in an atom having an orbital angular momentum of three units: so called because the associated spectral lines of alkali spectra were originally considered fundamental in that the frequencies are the smallest for any energy state. *Symbol:* F

f′-stop sys′tem (ef′stop′), *Photog.* a system of lens openings calibrated according to f numbers. Also called **factorial stop system.** Cf. **T-stop system.**

Ft., forint; forints.

ft., 1. feet. **2.** (in prescriptions) **a.** let it be made. [< L *fīat*] **b.** let them be made. [< L *fiant*] **3.** foot; feet. **4.** fort. **5.** fortification.

FTC, *U.S. Govt.* Federal Trade Commission: a board, consisting of five members, charged with investigating and enjoining illegal practices in interstate trade, as price-fixing, fraudulent advertising, etc.

fth., fathom. Also, **fthm.**

ft-L, foot-lambert.

ft-lb, foot-pound.

ft-pdl, foot-poundal.

Fu·ad I (fo͞o äd′), (*Ahmed Fuad Pasha*) 1868–1936, king of Egypt 1922–36.

fu·age (fyo͞o′ij), *n. Old Eng. Law.* fumage.

fub (fub), *v.t.,* **fubbed, fub·bing.** fob[2].

fub·sy (fub′zē), *adj.,* **-si·er, -si·est.** *Brit. Dial.* short and stout. [obs. *fubs* chubby person + -Y[1]]

fu·chi (fo͞o chē′), *n., pl.* **-chi.** an ornamental band above the tsuba on the hilt of a Japanese sword or knife, usually decorated to match the kashira. [< Jap]

fuch·sia (fyo͞o′shə), *n.* **1.** any onagraceous plant of the genus *Fuchsia,* which includes many varieties cultivated for their handsome drooping flowers. **2.** Also called **California fuchsia.** a herbaceous shrub, *Zauschneria californica,* having large crimson flowers. **3.** a bright, purplish-red color. —*adj.* **4.** of the color fuchsia: *a fuchsia dress.* [< NL; named after Leonhard *Fuchs* (1501–66), German botanist; see -IA]

fuch·sin (fo͞ok′sin), *n.* a greenish, water-soluble, solid, coal-tar derivative, obtained by the oxidation of a mixture of aniline and the toluidines, that forms deep-red solutions: used chiefly as a dye. Also, **fuchsine** (fo͞ok′sin, -sēn). Also called **basic fuchsin, basic fuchsine, basic magenta, magenta.** [FUCHS(IA) + -IN[2]]

fuchs·ite (fyo͞ok′sīt, fo͞ok′-), *n.* a mineral, a bright green variety of muscovite having chromium in place of some of the aluminum. [< G *Fuchsit;* named after J. N. von *Fuchs,* 19th-century German geologist; see -ITE[1]]

fu·coid (fyo͞o′koid), *adj.* **1.** resembling or related to seaweeds of the genus *Fucus.* —*n.* **2.** a fucoid seaweed. [FUC(US) + -OID]

fu·cus (fyo͞o′kəs), *n., pl.* **-ci** (-sī), **-cus·es.** any olive-brown seaweed or alga of the genus *Fucus,* having branching fronds and often air bladders. [< L < Gk *phŷkos* orchil, red color, rock lichen, rouge]

fud·dle (fud′əl), *v.,* **-dled, -dling,** *n.* —*v.t.* **1.** to intoxicate. **2.** to muddle or confuse: *a jumble of sounds to fuddle the senses.* —*v.i.* **3.** to tipple. —*n.* **4.** a confused state; muddle; jumble: *to be in a fuddle over personal problems; a fuddle of dirty clothes.* [?]

fud′dling cup′, an English earthenware drinking vessel of the 17th and 18th centuries, having the form of a cluster of three or more cups communicating at their bottoms in such a way that the entire vessel can be drained from any of them.

fud′dling glass′. See **coaching glass.**

fud·dy-dud·dy (fud′ē dud′ē, -dud′ē), *n., pl.* **-dud·dies,** *adj. Informal.* —*n.* **1.** a person who is stuffy, old-fashioned, and conservative. **2.** a person who is fussy or picayune about details; fuss-budget. —*adj.* **3.** resisting change; conservative. **4.** fussy; picayune. [?]

fudge[1] (fuj), *n.* a kind of candy composed of sugar, butter, milk, chocolate, or the like. [?]

fudge[2] (fuj), *n., v.,* **fudged, fudg·ing.** —*n.* **1.** *Usually Contemptuous.* nonsense or foolishness (often used interjectionally). —*v.i.* **2.** to talk nonsense. [?]

fudge[3] (fuj), *n., v.,* **fudged, fudg·ing.** —*n.* **1.** a small stereotype or a few lines of specially prepared type, bearing a newspaper bulletin, for replacing a detachable part of a page plate without the need to replate the entire page. **2.** the bulletin thus printed, often in color. **3.** a machine or attachment for printing such a bulletin. —*v.t.* **4.** to avoid coming to grips with (a subject, issue, etc.); evade; dodge: *to fudge a direct question.* —*v.i.* **5.** to cheat or welsh (often fol. by *on*): *to fudge on an exam; to fudge on one's campaign promises.* [var. of FADGE]

Fu·e·gi·an (fyo͞o ē′jē ən, fwā′jē-), *adj.* **1.** of or belonging to Tierra del Fuego or its indigenous Indians. —*n.* **2.** a native or inhabitant of Tierra del Fuego. [(TIERRA DEL) FUEG(O) + -IAN]

Fueh·rer (fyo͝or′ər), *n.* Führer.

fu·el (fyo͞o′əl), *n., v.,* **-eled, -el·ing** or (*esp. Brit.*) **-elled, -el·ling.** —*n.* **1.** combustible matter used to maintain fire, as coal, wood, oil, etc. **2.** that which gives nourishment or incentive: *Our discussion provided him with fuel for the debate.* —*v.t.* **3.** to supply with fuel. —*v.i.* **4.** to obtain or replenish fuel. [ME *fuel(le), feuel* < OF *feuaile* < LL *focālia,* neut. pl. of *focālis* of the hearth, fuel. See FOCUS, -AL[1]] —**fu′el·er, fu′el·ler,** *n.*

fu′el cell′, a device that produces a continuous electric current directly from the oxidation of a fuel, as that of hydrogen by oxygen.

fu′el injec′tion, the spraying of liquid fuel into the cylinders or combustion chambers of an engine.

fu′el oil′, an oil used for fuel, esp. one used as a substitute for coal, as crude petroleum.

Fuer·tes (fyo͝or′tēz, -tēs, fyo͞o′ər-), *n.* **Louis Agassiz** (ag′ə sē), 1874–1927, U.S. painter and naturalist.

fug (fug), *n.* **1.** *Chiefly Brit.* stale air, esp. the humid, warm, ill-smelling air of a crowded room, kitchen, etc. **2.** *Scot.* fog. [var. of FOG[1]]

fu·ga·cious (fyo͞o gā′shəs), *adj.* **1.** *Bot.* falling or fading early. **2.** fleeting; transitory: *a sensational story with but a fugacious claim on the public's attention.* [< L *fugāci-* (s. of *fugāx*) apt to flee, fleet, equiv. to *fug(ere)* (to) flee + *-i-* -I- + -OUS] —**fu·ga′cious·ly,** *adv.* —**fu·ga′cious·ness, fu·gac·i·ty** (fyo͞o gas′i tē), *n.*

fu·gal (fyo͞o′gəl), *adj. Music.* of or pertaining to a fugue, or composed in the style of a fugue. [FUGUE + -AL[1]] —**fu′gal·ly,** *adv.*

fu·gate (fyo͞o′gāt), *n. Music.* a piece composed in fugue style but not according to strict rules. [FUGUE + -ATE[1]]

fu·ga·to (fo͞o gä′tō, fyo͞o-; *It.* fo͞o gä′tô), *n., pl.* **-tos.** *Music.* a section of a composition that is in fugal style but does not constitute a real fugue. [< It; see FUGUE, -ATE[1]]

-fuge, a noun suffix indicating something which puts to flight: *vermifuge.* [comb. form repr. L *-fugia,* deriv. of *fugāre* to put to flight]

Fug·ger (fo͝og′ər), *n.* **Ja·kob II** (yä′kôp), ("*the Rich*"), 1459–1525, German financier, a member of the German family of bankers and merchants of the 14th to 17th centuries.

fu·ghet·ta (fo͞o get′ə, fyo͞o-; *It.* fo͞o get′tä), *n., pl.* **-tas;** *It.* **-te** (-te). *Music.* a short fugue. [< It, dim. of *fuga,* FUGUE]

fu·gi·tive (fyo͞o′ji tiv), *n.* **1.** a person who is fleeing, as from prosecution, intolerable circumstances, etc.; a runaway: *a fugitive from the law; a fugitive from the slums.* —*adj.* **2.** having taken flight, or run away: *a fugitive slave.* **3.** fleeting; transitory: *fugitive thoughts that could not be formulated.* **4.** *Fine Arts.* changing color as a result of exposure to light and chemical substances present in the atmosphere, in other pigments, or in the medium. **5.** dealing with subjects of passing interest, as writings; ephemeral: *fugitive essays.* **6.** wandering, roving, or vagabond: *a fugitive carnival.* [< L *fugitīv(us)* fleeing, equiv. to *fugit(us)* (ptp. of *fugere* to flee) + *-īvus* -IVE; r. ME *fugitif* < OF] —**fu′gi·tive·ly,** *adv.* —**fu′gi·tive·ness, fu′gi·tiv′i·ty,** *n.*
—**Syn. 3.** transient, passing, flitting, flying, brief, temporary. **5.** momentary, evanescent, trivial, light. **6.** straying, roaming. —**Ant. 3, 4.** permanent. **5.** lasting.

fu·gle (fyo͞o′gəl), *v.i.,* **-gled, -gling.** *Informal.* **1.** to act as a guide or model. **2.** to signal, or motion as if signaling. [back formation from FUGLEMAN]

fu·gle·man (fyo͞o′gəl mən), *n., pl.* **-men. 1.** (formerly) a well-drilled soldier placed in front of a military company as a model or guide for others. **2.** a person who heads a group, company, political party, etc.; a leader or manager. [< G *Flügelmann,* lit., flank man]

fu·gu (fo͞o′go͞o), *n.* any of several species of puffer fish eaten as a delicacy, esp. in Japan, after the removal of the skin and certain organs which contain a deadly poison. [< Jap]

fugue (fyo͞og), *n.* **1.** *Music.* a polyphonic composition based upon one, two, or more themes, which are enunciated by several voices or parts in turn, subjected to contrapuntal treatment, and gradually built up into a complex form having somewhat distinct divisions or stages of development and a marked climax at the end. **2.** *Psychiatry.* a period during which a patient suffers from loss of memory, often begins a new life, and, upon recovery, remembers nothing of the amnesic period. [< F < It *fuga* < L: flight] —**fugue′like′,** *adj.*

Füh·rer (fʏ′rər; *Eng.* fyo͝or′ər), *n. German.* **1.** leader. **2. der Führer** (dər), the leader, applied to Adolf Hitler. Also, **Fuehrer.**

Fu-hsi (fo͞o′shē′), *n. Chinese Legend.* a sage who taught mankind to hunt, fish, and cook.

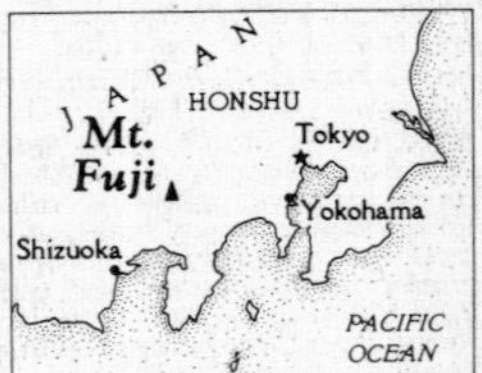

Fu·ji (fo͞o′jē), *n.* an extinct volcano in central Japan, on Honshu island: highest mountain in Japan. 12,395 ft. Also called **Fu·ji·ya·ma** (fo͞o′jē yä′mə; *Jap.* fo͞o′jē-yä′mä), **Fu·ji-san** (fo͞o′jē-sän′).

Fu·ji·wa·ra (fo͞o′jē wä′rä), *n.* a member of a powerful family in Japan, A.D. 866–1160, that often provided regents exercising power in the name of the emperor.

Fu·kien (fo͞o′kyen′), *n.* a province in SE China, opposite Taiwan. 14,650,000 (est. 1957); 45,845 sq. mi. *Cap.:* Foochow.

Fu·ku·o·ka (fo͞o′ko͞o ô′kä), *n.* a city on N Kyushu, in SW Japan. 771,679 (est. 1964).

Ful (fo͞ol), *n., pl.* **Fuls,** (*esp. collectively*) **Ful.** Fulani (def. 2).

-ful, a suffix meaning "full of," "characterized by" (*shameful; beautiful; careful; thoughtful*); "tending to," "able to" (*wakeful; harmful*); "as much as will fill" (*spoonful*). [ME, OE *-full, -ful,* repr. *full, ful* FULL[1]]

Fu·la (fo͞o′lə, fo͝ol′ə), *n., pl.* **-las,** (*esp. collectively*) **-la.** Fulani.

Fu·lah (fo͞o′lä), *n., pl.* **-lahs,** (*esp. collectively*) **-lah.** Fulani (def. 1).

Fu·la·ni (fo͞o′lä nē, fo͞o lä′-), *n., pl.* **-nis,** (*esp. collectively*) **-ni.** **1.** Also, **Fulah.** a member of a pastoral and nomadic people of mixed Negroid and Mediterranean stock, scattered through the Sudan from Senegal eastward. **2.** Also, **Ful.** the language of the Fulani, a Niger-Congo language closely related to Wolof. Also, **Fula.**

Ful·bright (fo͝ol′brīt′), *n.* **1. James William,** born 1905, U.S. politician. **2.** *Informal.* a grant awarded under the provisions of the Fulbright Act.

Ful′bright Act′, an act of Congress (1946) by which funds derived chiefly from the sale of U.S. surplus property abroad are made available to U.S. citizens for study, research, etc., in foreign countries as well as to foreigners to engage in similar activities in the U.S. [named after J. W. FULBRIGHT]

ful·crum (fo͝ol′krəm, ful′-), *n., pl.* **-crums, -cra** (-krə), *v.* —*n.* **1.** the support, or point of rest, on which a lever turns in moving a body. **2.** any prop or support. **3.** *Zool.* any of various structures in an animal serving as a hinge or support. —*v.t.* **4.** to fit with a fulcrum; put a fulcrum on. **5.** to make into a fulcrum. [< L: bedpost, equiv. to *fulc(īre)* (to) prop up, support + *-rum* neut. suffix]

ful·fil (fo͝ol fil′), *v.t.,* **-filled, -fil·ling.** fulfill.

ful·fill (fo͝ol fil′), *v.t.* **1.** to carry out, or bring to realization, as a prophecy, promise, etc. **2.** to perform or do, as duty; obey or follow, as commands. **3.** to satisfy (requirements, obligations, etc.): *a book that fulfills a long-felt need.* **4.** to bring to an end; finish or complete, as a period of time: *He felt that life was over when one had fulfilled his threescore years and ten.* **5.** to develop the full potential of (usually used reflexively): *She realized that she could never fulfill herself in such work.* Also, **fulfil.** [ME *fulfille(n),* OE *fulfyllan.* See FULL[1], FILL] —**ful·fill′er,** *n.*
—**Syn. 1.** accomplish, achieve, complete, realize. **2.** execute, discharge, observe. **3.** meet, answer, fill, comply with. **4.** end, terminate, conclude.

ful·fill·ment (fo͝ol fil′mənt), *n.* **1.** act or state of fulfilling: *to witness the fulfillment of a dream; to achieve fulfillment of one's hopes.* **2.** state or quality of being fulfilled; completion; realization: *a vague plan that had no hope of fulfillment; to seek fulfillment elsewhere.* Also, **ful·fil′ment.** [FULFILL + -MENT]

ful·gent (ful′jənt), *adj.* shining brightly; dazzling; resplendent: *fulgent patterns of sunlight.* [ME < L *fulgent-* (s. of *fulgēns,* prp. of *fulgēre*), equiv. to *fulg-* flash + *-ent-* -ENT] —**ful′gent·ly,** *adv.* —**ful′gent·ness,** *n.*

ful·gid (ful′jid), *adj.* glittering; shining. [< L *fulgid(us)* flashing, shining, equiv. to *fulg-* (see FULGENT) + *-idus* -ID[4]]

ful·gor (ful′gər), *n.* *Archaic.* a brilliant light; resplendence. Also, **ful′gour.** [< L: lightning, a flash, gleam, equiv. to *fulg-* (see FULGENT) + *-or* -OR[2]] —**ful′gor·ous, ful′gour·ous,** *adj.*

ful·gu·rant (ful′gyər ənt), *adj.* flashing like lightning. [< L *fulgurant-* (s. of *fulgurāns,* prp. of *fulgurāre*), equiv. to *fulgur-* (see FULGURATE) + *-ant-* -ANT]

ful·gu·rate (ful′gyə rāt′), *v.,* **-rat·ed, -rat·ing.** —*v.i.* **1.** to flash or dart like lightning. —*v.t.* **2.** *Med.* to destroy (esp. an abnormal growth) by electricity. [< L *fulgurāt(us)* (ptp. of *fulgurāre* to flash, glitter, lighten), equiv. to *fulgur-* (s. of *fulgor*) lightning + *-ātus* -ATE[1]] —**ful′gu·ra′tion,** *n.*

ful·gu·rat·ing (ful′gyə rā′ting), *adj.* *Med.* (of pains) sharp and piercing, like lightning. [FULGURATE + -ING[2]]

ful·gu·rite (ful′gyə rīt′), *n.* a tubelike formation in sand or rock, caused by lightning. [< L *fulgur-* (see FULGURATE) + -ITE[1]]

ful·gu·rous (ful′gyər əs), *adj.* characteristic of or resembling lightning: *the fulgurous cracking of a whip.* [< L *fulgur-* (see FULGURATE) + -OUS]

ful·ham (fo͝ol′əm), *n.* a die loaded at one corner either to favor a throw of 4, 5, or 6 (**high fulham**) or to favor a throw of 1, 2, or 3 (**low fulham**). Also, **fullam, fullom.** [?]

fu·lig·i·nous (fyo͞o lij′ə nəs), *adj.* **1.** sooty; smoky: *the fuliginous air hanging over an industrial city.* **2.** of the color of soot, as dark gray, dull brown, black, etc. [< L *fūlīginōs(us)* full of soot, equiv. to *fūlīgin-* (s. of *fūlīgō*) soot + *-ōsus* -OUS] —**fu·lig′i·nous·ly,** *adv.* —**fu·lig′i·nous·ness,** *n.*

full[1] (fo͝ol), *adj.* **1.** filled; containing all that can be held; filled to utmost capacity: *a full cup.* **2.** complete; entire; maximum: *a full supply of food for a three-day hike.* **3.** of the maximum size, amount, extent, volume, etc.: *a full load of five tons; to receive full pay.* **4.** (of garments, drapery, etc.) wide, ample, or having ample folds. **5.** abundant; well-supplied: *a yard full of litter; a cabinet full of medicine.* **6.** filled or rounded out, as in form: *a full bust.* **7.** engrossed; occupied: *She was full of her own anxieties.* **8.** of the same parents: *full brothers.* **9.** *Music.* ample and complete in volume or richness of sound. **10.** (of wines) having considerable body. **11.** *Baseball.* **a.** (of the count on a batter) amounting to three balls and two strikes: *He hit a slider for a homer on a full count.* **b.** having base runners at first, second, and third bases; loaded. **12. full and by,** *Naut.* so as to be close-hauled: *sailing full and by.* —*adv.* **13.** exactly or directly: *The blow struck him full in the face.* **14.** very: *You know full well what I mean.* **15.** *Archaic.* fully, completely, or entirely; quite; at least: *The blow knocked him full around. It happened full 30 years ago.* —*v.t.* **16.** *Sewing.* **a.** to make full, as by gathering or pleating. **b.** to bring (the cloth) on one side of a seam to a little greater fullness than on the other by gathering or tucking very slightly. —*v.i.* **17.** (of the moon) to become full. —*n.* **18.** the highest or fullest state, condition, or degree: *The moon is at the full.* **19. in full, a.** to or for the full or required amount. **b.** without abridgment: *The book was reprinted in full.* **20. to the full,** to the greatest extent; thoroughly: *They enjoyed themselves to the full.* [ME, OE *full ful;* c. Goth *full(s),* OIcel *full(r),* OHG *fol(l)* (G *voll*), L *plēnus,* Gk *plḗrēs*] —**full′ness,** *n.* —**ful′ly,** *adv.*

full[2] (fo͝ol), *v.t.* **1.** to cleanse and thicken (cloth) by special processes in manufacture. —*v.i.* **2.** (of cloth) to become compacted or felted. [ME *fulle(n);* back formation from FULLER[1]]

ful·lam (fo͝ol′əm), *n.* fulham.

full·back (fo͝ol′bak′), *n.* *Football.* **1.** a back who typically lines up between two halfbacks and farthest from the line of scrimmage. **2.** the position played by this back. **3.** (in soccer, Rugby, field hockey) a player stationed near his own goal to carry out chiefly defensive duties. [FULL[1] + BACK[1]]

full′ bind′ing, a complete binding of a volume in any one material, generally leather. —**full-bound** (fo͝ol′bound′), *adj.*

full′ blood′, **1.** a person or animal of unmixed ancestry; one descended of a pure breed. Cf. **purebred. 2.** relationship through both parents.

full-blood·ed (fo͝ol′blud′id), *adj.* **1.** of unmixed ancestry; thoroughbred: *a full-blooded Cherokee.* **2.** vigorous; virile; hearty: *full-blooded enjoyment.* —**full′-blood′ed·ness,** *n.*

full-blown (fo͝ol′blōn′), *adj.* **1.** in full bloom: *a full-blown rose.* **2.** completely developed: *a full-blown panic; an idea expanded into a full-blown novel.*

full-bod·ied (fo͝ol′bod′ēd), *adj.* of full strength, flavor, richness, etc.: *full-bodied wine; full-bodied writing.*

full′ bri′dle, a bridle with a bridoon and a curb, each controlled by a separate pair of reins.

full′ cous′in, cousin (def. 1).

full-cut (fo͝ol′kut′), *adj.* *Jewelry.* (of a brilliant) cut with 58 facets, including the table and culet.

full′ den′ture. See under **denture.**

full′ dress′, **1.** a ceremonial style of dress. **2.** the formal attire customarily worn in the evening, usually consisting of black tailcoats and white bow ties for men, and floor-length dresses for women. —**full′-dress′,** *adj.*

full·er[1] (fo͝ol′ər), *n.* a person who fulls cloth. [ME; OE *fullere* < L *full(ō)* fuller; see -ER[1]]

full·er[2] (fo͝ol′ər), *n.* **1.** a half-round hammer used for grooving and spreading iron. **2.** *Metalworking.* a tool or part of a die for reducing the sectional area of a piece of work. —*v.t.* **3.** to reduce the sectional area of (a piece of metal) with a fuller or fullers. **4.** to calk (riveted joints). **5.** a groove running along the flat of a sword blade. [orig. n. appar. FULL[1] in sense to make full, close compact + -ER[1]]

Ful·ler (fo͝ol′ər), *n.* **1. George,** 1822–84, U.S. painter. **2. Melville Wes·ton** (wes′tən), 1833–1910, Chief Justice of the U.S. 1888–1910. **3. R(ichard) Buck·minster,** born 1895, U.S. engineer, designer, and architect. **4. (Sarah) Margaret** (*Marchioness Ossoli*), 1810–50, U.S. author and literary critic. **5. Thomas,** 1608–61, English clergyman and historian.

Ful′ler rose′ bee′tle, a beetle, *Pantomorus godmani,* that feeds on the leaves of roses as well as on those of citrus and other fruit trees. [? named after A. S. Fuller (d. 1896), American horticulturist]

ful′ler's earth′, an absorbent clay, used esp. for removing grease from fabrics, in fulling, as a filter, and as a dusting powder.

ful′ler's tea′sel, the teasel, *Dipsacus fullonum.*

Ful·ler·ton (fo͝ol′ər tən), *n.* a city in SW California, SE of Los Angeles. 56,180 (1960).

full-faced (fo͝ol′fāst′), *adj.* **1.** having a plump or round face. **2.** facing squarely toward the spectator or in a given direction. **3.** *Print.* (of type) bold-faced. —**full′face′,** *n., adv.*

full-fash·ioned (fo͝ol′fash′ənd), *adj.* knitted to conform to the shape of a body part, as of the foot or leg: *full-fashioned hosiery; a full-fashioned sweater.*

full-fledged (fo͝ol′flejd′), *adj.* **1.** fully developed. **2.** of full rank or standing: *a full-fledged professor.*

full′ frame′, *Carpentry.* See **braced frame.**

full′ gain′er, *Diving.* a dive in which the diver takes off facing forward and performs a backward somersault, entering the water feet first and facing away from the springboard.

full-grown (fo͝ol′grōn′), *adj.* fully grown; mature.

full′ house′, *Poker.* a hand consisting of three of a kind and a pair, as three queens and two tens. Also called **full′ hand′.**

full-length (fo͝ol′lengkth′, -length′), *adj.* **1.** of customary length; not abridged or skimpy: *a full-length movie; full-length stockings.* **2.** having, showing, or accommodating the full length or height of the human body: *a full-length sofa; a full-length mirror.*

full-limbed (fo͝ol′limd′), *adj.* having a normal complement of limbs: *a full-limbed tree.*

full′ lin′ear group′, *Math.* the group of all nonsingular linear transformations mapping a finite-dimensional vector space into itself.

full′ moon′, **1.** the moon when the whole of its disk is illuminated, occurring when in opposition to the sun. **2.** the phase of the moon at this time. See diag. under **moon.** [ME *ful moyne,* OE *fulles monan*]

full′-moon ma′ple (fo͝ol′mo͞on′, -mo͞on′). See **Japanese maple.**

full-mouthed (fo͝ol′mouthd′), *adj.* **1.** (of cattle, sheep, etc.) having a complete set of teeth. **2.** noisy; loud. —**full′-mouth′ed·ly,** *adv.*

full′ nel′son, a hold in which a wrestler, from behind his opponent, passes each arm under the corresponding arm of the opponent and locks the arms at the fingers or wrists on the back of the opponent's neck. Cf. **nelson.**

full′ness of time′, the proper or destined time.

ful·lom (fo͝ol′əm), *n.* fulham.

full′ pow′ered, *Naut.* (of a vessel) relying on engines for propulsion without assistance from sails.

full′ profes′sor, professor (def. 5).

full′ rhyme′, *Pros.* rhyme in which the stressed vowels and all following consonants and vowels are identical, but the consonants preceding the rhyming vowels are different, as in *chain, brain; marry, tarry.* Also called **perfect rhyme, rime suffisante.**

full-rigged (fo͝ol′rigd′), *adj.* **1.** *Naut.* (of a sailing vessel) rigged as a ship; square-rigged on all of three or more masts. **2.** having all equipment.

full′ sail′, **1.** all the sails of a vessel. **2.** with all sails set: *The ship was moving ahead full sail.* **3.** rapidly; forcefully: *He proceeded full sail to make sure there would be time for certain legislation.* —**full′-sailed′,** *adj.*

full-scale (fo͝ol′skāl′), *adj.* **1.** having the exact size or proportions of the original: *a full-scale replica.* **2.** using all possible means, facilities, etc.; complete: *The factory will commence full-scale operation next month.*

full′-scant′ling ves′sel (fo͝ol′skant′ling), *Naut.* a cargo vessel considered sufficiently strong and watertight in all cargo spaces to have the legal maximum draft. Cf. **scantling-draft vessel.**

full′ sen′tence, *Gram.* any sentence the form of which exemplifies the most frequently used structural pattern of a particular language, as, in English, any sentence that contains at least one phrase consisting of a subject and a predicate; a sentence from which elliptical sentences may be derived by grammatical transformations.

full′ speed′, **1.** the maximum speed. **2.** *Naut.* the speed normally maintained on a passage. **3.** at maximum speed: *to move full speed ahead.*

full′ stop′, period (def. 16).

full′ swing′, full capacity; greatest activity: *For the first time in years the factory was in full swing. The meeting was in full swing when we arrived.*

full-term (fo͝ol′tûrm′), *adj.* *Obstet.* of or noting the entire duration of normal pregnancy.

full′ tilt′, at the full potential, speed, energy, forcefulness, etc.: *The motor was running full tilt. The factory is now going full tilt.*

full′ time′, the number of hours in a period, as a day, week, or month, considered customary for pursuing an activity, esp. working at a job: *The factory now operates on full time. He works there full time.* Cf. **part time.**

full-time (fo͝ol′tīm′), *adj.* working or operating the customary number of hours in each day, week, or month: *a full-time housekeeper; full-time production.* Cf. **part-time.**

full-to-full (fo͝ol′tə fo͝ol′), *adj.* *Naut.* from one tack with sails filled to the other tack with sails filled: *The schooner could tack full-to-full in 25 seconds.*

full′ trail′er, a trailer supported entirely by its own wheels. Cf. **semitrailer.**

full′-turn stair′ (fo͝ol′tûrn′), a staircase requiring a full turn at each landing for continued ascent or descent.

full′ twist′, *Fancy Diving.* a dive made by a complete rotation of the body on its vertical axis. Cf. **half twist** (def. 1).

full′-wave rec′tifier (fo͝ol′wāv′), *Elect.* a rectifier that transmits both halves of a cycle of alternating current as a direct current. Cf. **half-wave rectifier.**

full′ word′, (esp. in Chinese grammar) a word that has lexical meaning rather than grammatical meaning; a word or morpheme that functions grammatically as a contentive. Cf. **empty word.**

ful·mar (fo͝ol′mər), *n.* any of certain oceanic birds of the petrel family, esp. *Fulmarus glacialis,* a gull-like arctic species. [orig. Hebrides dial. < Scand; cf. Icel *fūll* foul + *mār* gull (with reference to its stench)]

ful·mi·nant (ful′mə nənt), *adj.* **1.** occurring suddenly and with great intensity or severity; fulminating. **2.** *Pathol.* developing or progressing suddenly: *fulminant plague.* [< L *fulminant-* (s. of *fulmināns*), prp. of *fulmināre.* See FULMINATE, -ANT]

ful·mi·nate (ful′mə nāt′), *v.,* **-nat·ed, -nat·ing,** *n.* —*v.i.* **1.** to explode with a loud noise; detonate. **2.** to issue denunciations or the like (usually fol. by *against*): *The minister fulminated against legalized vice.* —*v.t.* **3.** to cause to explode. **4.** to issue or pronounce with vehement denunciation, condemnation, or the like. —*n.* **5.** *Chem.* one of a group of unstable, explosive compounds derived from fulminic acid, esp. the mercury salt of fulminic acid which is a powerful detonating agent. [late ME *fulminate(n)* < L *fulmināt(us)* (ptp. of *fulmināre*) thundered, equiv. to *fulmin-* (s. of *fulmen*) thunderbolt, lightning + *-ātus* -ATE[1]] —**ful′mi·na′tor,** *n.* —**ful·mi·na·to·ry** (ful′mə nə tôr′ē, -tōr′ē), *adj.*

ful′minating com′pound, *Chem.* a fulminate.

ful′minating pow′der, *Chem.* **1.** powder that explodes by percussion. **2.** a fulminate.

ful·mi·na·tion (ful′mə nā′shən), *n.* **1.** a violent denunciation or censure: *a sermon that was one long fulmination.* **2.** violent explosion. [< L *fulminātiōn-* (s. of *fulminātiō*) a thundering, fuming. See FULMINATE, -ION]

ful·mine (ful′min), *v.t., v.i.* **-mined, -min·ing.** *Archaic.* to fulminate. [< L *fulmin(āre)*]

ful·min·ic (ful min′ik), *adj.* **1.** highly explosive; unstable. **2.** *Chem.* of or derived from fulminic acid. [< L *fulmin-* (s. of *fulmen*) lightning]

fulmin′ic ac′id, *Chem.* an unstable acid, HONC, isomeric with cyanic acid, and known only in the form of its salts.

ful·mi·nous (ful′mə nəs), *adj.* of, pertaining to, or resembling thunder and lightning: *a fulminous attack on the opposition.* [< L *fulmin(e)us* of, belonging to lightning, equiv. to *fulmin-* (s. of *fulmen*) lightning + *-(e)us* -OUS]

ful·ness (fo͝ol′nis), *n.* fullness.

ful·some (fo͝ol′səm, ful′-), *adj.* **1.** offensive to good taste, esp. as being excessive; gross: *fulsome language; fulsome praise; fulsome ostentation.* **2.** disgusting; sickening; repulsive: *a table heaped with fulsome mounds of greasy foods.* [ME *fulsom.* See FULL[1], -SOME[1]] —**ful′some·ly,** *adv.* —**ful′some·ness,** *n.*

Ful·ton (fo͝ol′tᵊn), *n.* **1. Robert,** 1765–1815, U.S. engineer and inventor: builder of the first profitable steamboat. **2.** a town in NW Illinois. 3387 (1960). **3.** a town in SW Kentucky. 3265 (1960). **4.** a boy's given name.

Ful·vi·a (ful′vē ə, fo͝ol′-; *It.* fo͝ol′vyä), *n.* a girl's given name.

ful·vous (ful′vəs), *adj.* tawny; dull yellowish-gray or yellowish-brown. [< L *fulvus* deep yellow, tawny, reddish-yellow]

ful′vous tree′ duck′. See under **tree duck.**

fu·mage (fyo͞o′mij), *n.* *Old Eng. Law.* a tax payable to the king for each hearth in every house owned by one not exempt from church taxes and poor taxes. Also, **feuage, fuage.** [< ML *fūmāg(ium).* See FUME, -AGE]

fu·mar·ic (fyo͞o mar′ik), *adj.* *Chem.* of or derived from fumaric acid. [< NL *Fumār(ia)* name of genus (LL: fumitory; see -ARIA) + -IC]

fumar′ic ac′id, *Chem.* a colorless, odorless, crystalline, slightly water-soluble solid, HOOCCH=CHCOOH, isomeric with maleic acid, occurring in many plants and essential to animal and vegetable respiration; used in the making of synthetic resins and as a replacement for tartaric acid in beverages and baking powders. Also called **boletic acid, lichenic acid.**

fu·ma·role (fyo͞o′mə rōl′), *n.* a hole, in or near a volcano, from which vapor rises. [< F *fumerolle* < LL *fūmāriōl(um),* dim. of L *fūmārium* smoke chamber, equiv. to *fūm(us)* smoke + *-ārium* -ARY] **—fu·ma·rol·ic** (fyo͞o′mə rol′ik), *adj.*

fu·ma·to·ri·um (fyo͞o′mə tōr′ē əm, -tôr′-), *n., pl.* **-to·ri·a** (-tōr′ē ə, -tôr′-). *Rare.* an airtight structure in which plants are fumigated to destroy fungi or insects. [< NL, equiv. to L *fūmāt(us)* smoked (ptp. of *fūmāre;* see FUME, -ATE[1]) + *-ōrium* -ORIUM]

fum·ble (fum′bəl), *v.,* **-bled, -bling,** *n.* **—*v.i.* 1.** to feel or grope about clumsily: *She fumbled for the doorknob.* **2.** *Sports.* to fumble the ball. **3.** *Football.* to drop the ball after gaining or having possession of it. **—*v.t.* 4.** to make, handle, etc., clumsily or inefficiently: *to fumble an attempt; He fumbled his way through the crowded room. I fumbled the papers, looking for the letter.* **5.** *Sports.* to fail to catch and hold (a ball). **6.** *Football.* to lose (a ball) through a fumble. **—*n.* 7.** act of fumbling: *We completed the difficult experiment without a fumble.* **8.** *Football.* act or instance of failing to catch a snap from center or a lateral pass. [cf. Sw *fumla* to grope] **—fum′bler,** *n.* **—fum′bling·ly,** *adv.* **—fum′bling·ness,** *n.*

fume (fyo͞om), *n., v.,* **fumed, fum·ing. —*n.* 1.** Often, **fumes.** any smokelike or vaporous exhalation from matter or substances, esp. of an odorous or harmful nature: *the fumes of tobacco; noxious fumes of carbon monoxide.* **2.** an irritable or angry mood: *He has been in a fume ever since the contract fell through.* **—*v.t.* 3.** to emit or exhale, as fumes, vapor, or the like: *giant stacks fuming their sooty smoke.* **4.** to treat with or expose to fumes. **—*v.i.* 5.** to rise, or pass off, as fumes: *smoke fuming from an ash tray.* **6.** to emit fumes: *The leaky pipe fumed alarmingly.* **7.** to show fretful irritation or anger: *She loves to fume at waiters.* [ME < OF *fum* < L *fūm(us)* smoke, steam, fume] **—fum′er,** *n.* **—fume′less,** *adj.* **—fume′like′,** *adj.* **—fum′ing·ly,** *adv.*
—Syn. 2. rage, fury, agitation, storm. **7.** chafe, fret, rage, rave, bluster.

fu·mé (fʏ mā′), *adj. French.* smoked.

fumed (fyo͞omd), *adj.* darkened or colored by exposure to ammonia fumes, as oak and other wood. [FUME + -ED[2]]

fumed′ oak′, oak exposed to fumes of ammonia to give it a dark, aged appearance.

fu·met (fyo͞o′mit), *n.* a stock made by simmering fish, chicken, game, etc., in water, wine, or in both, often boiled down to concentrate the flavor and used as a flavoring. Also, **fu·mette** (fyo͞o met′). [< F: fumes, odor of wine or meat, deriv. of MF *fumer* to smoke, expose to fumes]

fu·meuse (*Fr.* fʏ mœz′), *n., pl.* **-meuses** (*Fr.* -mœz′). *Fr. Furniture.* a chair of the 18th century, having a crest rail incorporating a place for pipes and tobacco. [< F: lit., smoker (fem. of *fumeur*)]

fu·mi·gant (fyo͞o′mi gənt), *n.* any volatile or volatilizable chemical compound used as a disinfectant or pesticide. [< L *fūmigant-* (s. of *fūmigāns,* prp. of *fūmigāre*), equiv. to *fūmig-* (see FUMIGATE) + *-ant-* -ANT]

fu·mi·gate (fyo͞o′mə gāt′), *v.t.,* **-gat·ed, -gat·ing.** to expose to smoke or fumes, as in disinfecting. [< L *fūmigāt(us)* (ptp. of *fūmigāre*) smoked, fumigated, equiv. to *fūmig-* FUME + *-ātus* -ATE[1]] **—fu′mi·ga′tion,** *n.* **—fu·mi·ga·to·ry** (fyo͞o′mə gə tōr′ē, -tôr′ē, -gā′tə-rē), *adj.*

fu·mi·ga·tor (fyo͞o′mə gā′tər), *n.* **1.** one who or that which fumigates. **2.** a structure in which plants are fumigated to destroy insects. [FUMIGATE + -OR[2]]

fum′ing ni′tric ac′id, *Chem.* a colorless, yellowish, or brownish fuming corrosive liquid, usually prepared from nitric acid by the addition of excess nitrogen dioxide; used in organic synthesis for nitration, and as an oxidizer in liquid propellants for rockets.

fum′ing sulfu′ric ac′id, *Chem.* See **pyrosulfuric acid.**

fu·mi·to·ry (fyo͞o′mi tōr′ē, -tôr′ē), *n., pl.* **-ries.** any plant of the genus *Fumaria,* of the family *Fumariaceae,* esp. a delicate herb, *F. officinalis,* having finely dissected leaves and racemes of purplish flowers. [alter. of earlier *fumiterre,* ME *fumetere* < MF < ML *fumus terrae,* lit., smoke of the earth]

fu·mu·lus (fyo͞o′myə ləs), *n., pl.* **-lus.** (formerly) a very thin, almost transparent veil of clouds; a layer of haze. [< NL; see FUME, -ULE]

fum·y (fyo͞o′mē), *adj.,* **fum·i·er, fum·i·est.** emitting or full of fumes; fumelike. [FUME + -Y[1]]

fun (fun), *n., v.,* **funned, fun·ning,** *adj.* **—*n.* 1.** that which provides mirth or amusement; enjoyment; playfulness: *A picnic would be fun. She's full of fun.* **2. for** or **in fun,** as a joke; not seriously; playfully: *His insults were only in fun.* **3. like fun,** *Informal.* certainly not; of doubtful truth: *He told us that he finished the exam in an hour. Like fun he did!* **4. make fun of,** to make the object of ridicule; deride: *The youngsters made fun of their teacher.* **—*v.i.* 5.** *Informal.* to make fun; joke; kid. **—*adj.* 6.** *Informal.* of or pertaining to fun, esp. to social fun: *a fun thing to do; really a fun person.* **7.** *Informal.* whimsical; flamboyant: *The fashions that she wears are definitely on the fun side and fairly squeak for attention.* [? dial. var. of obs. *fon* to befool. See FOND[1]]
—Syn. 1. merriment, pleasure, play, gaiety, frolic, revel.
—Ant. 1. misery, melancholy.

fu·nam·bu·list (fyo͞o nam′byə list), *n.* a tightrope walker. [< L *fūnambul(us)* ropedancer + -IST] **—fu·nam′bu·lism,** *n.*

Fun·chal (*Port.* fo͞oN shäl′), *n.* a seaport in and the capital of the Madeira Islands, on SE Madeira: winter resort. 63,044 (1960).

func·tion (fuŋk′shən), *n.* **1.** the kind of action or activity proper to a person, thing, or institution. **2.** any ceremonious public or social gathering or occasion. **3.** a factor related to or dependent upon other factors: *Price is a function of supply and demand.* **4.** *Math.* **a.** Also called **correspondence, map, mapping, transformation.** a relation between two sets in which one element of the second set is assigned to each element of the first set, as the expression $y = x^2$; operator. **b.** a relation between two sets in which one or more elements of the second set are assigned to each element of the first set, as $x^2 + y^2 = 1$ which assigns to each real number x between −1 and 1 the two values $\sqrt{1-x^2}$ and $\sqrt{1-x^2}$. **c.** a set of ordered pairs in which none of the first elements of the pairs appears twice. **5.** *Geom.* **a.** a formula expressing a relation between the angles of a triangle and its sides, as sine, cosine, etc. **b.** See **hyperbolic function. 6.** *Gram.* **a.** the grammatical role a linguistic form has or the position it occupies in a particular construction. **b.** the grammatical roles or the positions of a linguistic form or form class collectively. **—*v.i.* 7.** to perform a specified action or activity; act; carry out normal activity or processes; work; operate: *The battery doesn't function. He rarely functions before noon.* **8.** to have or exercise a function; serve: *In earlier English the present tense often functioned as a future. This orange crate can function as a chair.* [< L *functiōn-* (s. of *functiō*) a performance, execution, equiv. to *funct(us)* (ptp. of *fungī*) performed, executed + *-iōn-* -ION] **—func′tion·less,** *adj.*

func·tion·al (fuŋk′shə nəl), *adj.* **1.** of or pertaining to a function or functions: *functional difficulties in the administration.* **2.** having or serving a utilitarian purpose; capable of serving the purpose for which it was designed: *functional architecture; a chair that is functional as well as decorative.* **3.** Also, **func′tion·al·is′tic.** (of a building or furnishing) constructed or made according to the principles of functionalism or primarily as a direct fulfillment of a material need. **4.** capable of operating or functioning: *When will the ventilating system be functional again?* **5.** pertaining to an algebraical operation: *a functional symbol.* **6.** *Psychol.* without a known organic cause or structural change: *functional disorder.* Cf. **organic** (def. 5). **—*n.* 7.** *Math.* a function that has a domain whose elements are functions, sets, or the like and that assumes numerical values. [FUNCTION + -AL[1]] **—func′tion·al·ly,** *adv.*

func′tional anal′ysis, *Math.* the branch of mathematics that deals with the theory of vector spaces and linear functionals.

func′tional cal′culus, the branch of symbolic logic that includes the sentential calculus and that deals with sentential functions and quantifiers and with logical relations between propositions containing quantifiers. Also called **predicate calculus.**

func′tional disease′, *Pathol.* a disease in which there is an abnormal change in the function of an organ, but no structural alteration in the tissues involved (opposed to *organic disease*).

func′tional group′, *Chem.* a group of atoms that causes the characteristic behavior of the class of compounds in which the group occurs, as the hydroxyl group in alcohols.

func′tional illit′erate, a person whose ability to read or write is inadequate for the needs of his job, the demands of a situation, or the like: *the high number of functional illiterates rejected by draft boards.*

func·tion·al·ism (fuŋk′shə nəliz′əm), *n.* **1.** (*usually cap.*) *Chiefly Archit., Furniture.* **a.** a design movement evolved from several previous movements or schools in Europe in the early 20th century, advocating the design of buildings, furnishings, etc., as direct fulfillments of material requirements, as for shelter, repose, the serving of food, etc., with the construction, materials, and purpose clearly expressed or at least not denied, and with aesthetic effect derived chiefly from proportions and finish, purely decorative effects being excluded or greatly subordinated. **b.** the doctrines and practices associated with this movement. **2.** *Psychol.* the doctrine that emphasizes the adaptiveness of the mental or behavioral processes. [FUNCTIONAL + -ISM]

func·tion·al·ist (fuŋk′shə nəlist), *n.* **1.** a person who advocates, or works according to, the principles of functionalism. **—*adj.* 2.** of or pertaining to functionalism. **3.** built or made according to the principles of Functionalism by one associated with the movement. Also, **Functionalist.** [FUNCTIONAL + -IST]

func′tional representa′tion, *Govt.* representation in a governing body on the basis of social class or occupation.

func′tional yield′, *Ling.* the relative frequency of occurrence of words that are differentiated in one and the same position by only one distinctive feature. In English, the opposition of voiced and voiceless *th* has a low functional yield, being used only to distinguish such pairs as *ether* and *either,* or *wreath* and *wreathe.* Also called **func′tional load′.**

func·tion·ar·y (fuŋk′shə ner′ē), *n., pl.* **-ar·ies.** a person who functions in a specified capacity, esp. in government service; an official: *civil servants, diplomats, bureaucrats, and other functionaries.* [FUNCTION + -ARY, modeled on F *fonctionnaire*]

func′tion space′, *Math.* a linear space, the elements of which are functions.

func′tion word′, a word, as a pronoun or preposition, that is used in a language as a substitute for another or as a marker of syntactic relationship; a member of a small, closed form class whose membership is relatively fixed. Cf. **empty word, full word.**

func·tor (fuŋk′tər), *n.* that which functions. [FUNCT(ION) + -OR[2]]

fund (fund), *n.* **1.** a stock of money or pecuniary resources, as for some purpose: *a fund for his education; a retirement fund.* **2.** a store or stock of something immaterial or material: *a fund of knowledge; a fund of jewels.* **3. funds,** money in hand; pecuniary resources: *to be momentarily without funds.* **—*v.t.* 4.** to provide a fund to pay the interest or principal of (a debt). **5.** to convert (general outstanding debts) into a more or less permanent debt, represented by interest-bearing bonds. [< L *fund(us)* bottom, estate; r. FOND[2] in most of its meanings]

fun·da·ment (fun′də mənt), *n.* **1.** the physical characteristics of a geographical region, as land forms, drainage, climate, soils, etc. **2.** the buttocks. [< L *fundāment(um)* foundation; r. ME *fondement* < OF. See FUND, -MENT]

fun·da·men·tal (fun′də men′təl), *adj.* **1.** serving as, or being an essential part of, a foundation or basis; basic; underlying: *fundamental principles; the fundamental structure.* **2.** of, pertaining to, or affecting the foundation or basis: *a fundamental revision.* **3.** being an original or primary source: *a fundamental idea.* **4.** *Music.* (of a chord) having its root as its lowest note. **—*n.* 5.** a basic principle, rule, law, or the like, which serves as the groundwork of a system; essential part: *to master the fundamentals of a trade.* **6.** Also called **fun′damen′tal note′, fun′damen′tal tone′.** *Music.* **a.** the root of a chord. **b.** the generator of a series of harmonics. **7.** *Physics.* the component of lowest frequency in a composite wave. [ME < NL *fundāmentāl(is)* of, belonging to a foundation. See FUNDAMENT, -AL[1]] **—fun·da·men·tal·i·ty** (fun′də men tal′i tē), *n.* **—fun′da·men′tal·ness,** *n.* **—fun′da·men′tal·ly,** *adv.*
—Syn. 1. indispensable, essential, necessary, elementary, first, primary, chief, principal, main, central. **3.** first. **—Ant. 1.** secondary, superfluous; last; least.

fundamen′tal bass′ (bās), *Music.* a bass consisting of the roots of the chords employed.

fun′damen′tal fre′quency, *Physics.* **1.** the lowest frequency at which a medium will freely oscillate. **2.** the frequency of the fundamental.

fun·da·men·tal·ism (fun′də men′təliz′əm), *n.* **1.** (*sometimes cap.*) a movement in American Protestantism that arose in the early part of the 20th century in reaction to modernism and that stresses the inerrancy of the Bible not only in matters of faith and morals but also as a literal historical record, holding as essential to Christian faith belief in such doctrines as the virgin birth, physical resurrection, atonement by the sacrificial death of Christ, and the Second Coming. **2.** the beliefs held by those in this movement. [FUNDAMENTAL + -ISM] **—fun′da·men′tal·ist,** *n., adj.*

fun′damen′tal par′ticle. See **elementary particle.**

fun′damen′tal se′quence, *Math.* an infinite sequence, $x_1, x_2, . . .,$ whose terms are points in E_k, in which there exists a point y such that $\lim_{n\to\infty} X_n = y$ if and only if for every $\epsilon>0$, there exists a number N such that $i>N$ and $j>N$ implies $|x_i - x_j|<\epsilon$. Also called **Cauchy sequence.** Cf. **complete** (def. 9b).

fun′damen′tal the′orem of al′gebra, *Math.* the theorem that every polynomial equation with degree greater than zero and having complex number coefficients has at least one root which is a complex number.

fun′damen′tal the′orem of arith′metic, *Math.* the theorem that every integer can be written uniquely as 1 or −1 times a product of positive prime integers. Also called **unique factorization theorem.**

fun′damen′tal the′orem of cal′culus, *Math.* one of several theorems of calculus, esp. the theorem that the definite integral of a derivative is the difference of two values of the original function.

fun′damen′tal u′nit, *Physics.* one of the units of mass, length, and time taken as a basis for a system of units.

fund′ed debt′, a debt, as in the form of bonds, having a long period of maturity.

fun·dus (fun′dəs), *n., pl.* **-di** (-dī). *Anat.* the base of an organ, or the part opposite to or remote from an aperture. [< L: lit., the bottom] **—fun′dic,** *adj.*

Fun·dy (fun′dē), *n.* **Bay of,** an inlet of the Atlantic in SE Canada, between New Brunswick and Nova Scotia, having swift tidal currents.

Fü·nen (fʏ′nən), *n.* German name of **Fyn.**

fu·ner·al (fyo͞o′nər əl), *n.* **1.** the ceremonies for a dead person prior to burial or cremation; obsequies. **2.** a funeral procession. **3. be one's funeral,** *Informal.* to end unhappily for one; to have unpleasant consequences for one: *Let him worry—it's his funeral!* [ME < ML *fūnerāl(ia),* neut. pl. n. use of adj.]
—*adj.* 4. of or pertaining to a funeral: *funeral services; funeral expenses.* [ME < ML *fūnerāl(is),* equiv. to L *fūn(us)* funeral, death + *-ālis* -AL[1]]

fu′neral direc′tor, a mortician; undertaker.

fu′neral home′, an establishment specifically intended as a place where the body of the deceased may repose before the funeral and where those who knew the deceased may pay him their last respects. Also called **fu′neral chap′el, fu′neral church′, fu′neral par′lor, fu′neral res′idence, mortuary.**

fu·ner·ar·y (fyo͞o′nə rer′ē), *adj.* of or pertaining to a funeral or burial: *a funerary urn.* [< LL *fūnerāri(us)* of, relating to a funeral. See FUNERAL, -ARY]

fu·ne·re·al (fyo͞o nēr′ē əl), *adj.* **1.** of or pertaining to a funeral. **2.** mournful; gloomy; dismal: *a funereal aloofness that was quite chilling.* [< L *fūnere(us)* of, belonging to a FUNERAL + AL[1]] **—fu·ne′re·al·ly,** *adv.*

fu·nest (fyo͞o nest′), *adj.* boding or causing evil or death; sinister; fatal; disastrous. [< F *funeste* < L *fūnest(us),* deriv. of *fūnus* funeral, death]

fun′ fair′, *Chiefly Brit.* an amusement park.

fun·fest (fun′fest′), *n.* a party or other gathering for fun and entertainment. [FUN + -FEST]

Fünf·kir·chen (fʏnf′kēr′ḵən), *n.* German name of **Pécs.**

fun·gal (fuŋ′gəl), *adj.* **1.** fungous. **—*n.* 2.** a fungus. [< NL *fungāl(is).* See FUNGUS, -AL[1]]

fun·gi (fun′jī), *n.* a pl. of **fungus.**

fungi-, a combining form of **fungus:** *fungicide.*

fun·gi·ble (fun′jə bəl), *Law.* **—*adj.* 1.** (esp. of goods) being of such nature or kind as to be freely exchangeable or replaceable, in whole or in part, for another of like nature or kind. **—*n.* 2.** a fungible thing, as money or grain. [< ML *fungibil(is),* equiv. to L *fungī* to perform the office of + *-bilis* -BLE] **—fun′gi·bil′i·ty,** *n.*

fun·gi·cide (fun′ji sīd′), *n.* an agent, such as a spray or dust, used for destroying fungi. [FUNGI- + -CIDE] **—fun′gi·cid′al,** *adj.* **—fun′gi·cid′al·ly,** *adv.*

fun·gi·form (fun′jə fôrm′), *adj.* having the form of a fungus or mushroom. [FUNGI- + -FORM]

Fun′gi Im·per·fec′ti (im′pər fek′tī), a class of fungi for which a sexual reproduction stage does not exist or has not yet been identified. [< NL: lit., imperfect fungi]

fun·gi·stat (fun′ji stat′), *n.* a fungistatic agent or preparation. [FUNGI- + -STAT]

fun·gi·stat·ic (fun′ji stat′ik), *adj.* (of a substance or preparation) inhibiting the growth of a fungus. [FUNGI- + STATIC] **—fun′gi·stat′i·cal·ly,** *adv.*

fun·gi·tox·ic (fun′ji tok′sik), *adj.* toxic to fungi. [FUNGI- + TOXIC] **—fun·gi·tox·ic·i·ty** (fun′ji tok sis′i tē, fuŋ′gi-), *n.*

fun·giv·or·ous (fən jiv′ər əs), *adj.* feeding on fungi, as certain insects. [FUNGI- + -VOROUS]

fun·go (fuŋ′gō), *n., pl.* **-goes.** *Baseball.* **1.** (in practice sessions) a ball tossed into the air by the batter himself and struck as it comes down. **2.** a batted ball, esp. a fly ball, hit in this manner. **3.** Also called **fun′go bat′,** a bat used in hitting fungoes, being lighter, longer, and narrower than an ordinary baseball bat. [?]

fun·goid (fuŋg′goid), *adj.* **1.** resembling a fungus; of the nature of a fungus. **2.** *Pathol.* characterized by funguslike growths. [FUNG(US) + -OID]

fun·gos·i·ty (fuŋg gos′i tē), *n., pl.* **-ties** for 2. **1.** the condition of being fungous. **2.** a fungous excrescence. [< L *fungōs(us)* FUNGOUS + -ITY]

fun·gous (fuŋg′gəs), *adj.* **1.** of, pertaining to, or caused by fungi; fungal. **2.** of the nature of or resembling a fungus. [ME < L *fungōs(us)* full of holes, spongy. See FUNGUS, -OUS]

fun·gus (fuŋg′gəs), *n., pl.* **fun·gi** (fun′jī), **fun·gus·es,** *adj.* —*n.* **1.** any of numerous thallophytes of the division *fungi,* comprising the mushrooms, molds, mildews, rusts, smuts, etc., characterized chiefly by absence of chlorophyll and by subsisting upon dead or living organic matter. **2.** *Pathol.* a spongy, abnormal growth, as proud flesh formed in a wound. —*adj.* **3.** fungous. [< L; cf. Gk *spóngos, sphóngos* sponge] —**fun·gic** (fun′jik), *adj.* —**fun′gus·like′,** *adj.*

fun′gus bug′. See **flat bug.**

fun′gus gnat′, any of several mosquitolike insects of the family *Mycetophilidae,* the larvae of which feed on fungi or decaying vegetation.

fun′ house′, (in an amusement park) a building which is specially constructed and has devices for surprising and amusing patrons as they walk along a passage.

fu·ni·cle (fyōō′nə kəl), *n. Bot.* the stalk of an ovule or seed. [< L *fūnicul(us).* See FUNICULUS, -CLE]

fu·nic·u·lar (fyōō nik′yə lər), *adj.* **1.** of or pertaining to a rope or cord, or its tension. **2.** worked by a rope or the like. —*n.* **3.** See **funicular railway.** [< L *fūnicul(us)* (see FUNICULUS) + -AR¹]

funic′ular rail′way, a short, very steep railway having two parallel sets of tracks, upon each of which is a car or train raised or lowered upon a cable that also raises or lowers the other car or train in such a way that the two are approximately counterbalanced.

fu·nic·u·late (fyōō nik′yə lit, -lāt′), *adj. Bot.* having a funicle. [FUNICUL(US) + -ATE¹]

fu·nic·u·lus (fyōō nik′yə ləs), *n., pl.* **-li** (-lī′). **1.** *Anat.* a conducting cord such as a nerve cord, umbilical cord, etc. **2.** *Bot.* a funicle. **3.** *Entomol.* (in certain insects) the portion of the antenna between the basal segments and the club. [< L: small rope, cord, equiv. to *fūni(s)* rope, line + *-culus* -CULE]

funk¹ (fuŋgk), *Informal.* —*n.* **1.** cowering fear; state of fright or terror. **2.** a dejected mood: *He's been in a funk ever since she walked out on him.* —*v.t.* **3.** to be afraid of. **4.** to frighten. **5.** to shrink from; try to shirk. —*v.i.* **6.** to shrink or quail in fear. [? < early Flem *fonck* disturbance] —**funk′er,** *n.*

funk² (fuŋgk), *n. Jazz.* an earthy, blues-based quality characteristic of some modern jazz. [special use of FUNK¹]

funked (fuŋgkt), *adj. Southern U.S.* (of tobacco) rotten; moldy. [*funk* punk (n.) (ME *fonk;* c. D *vonk,* G *Funke*) + -ED³]

fun·ki·a (fuŋg′kē ə, fōōŋg′-), *n.* See **plantain lily.** [< NL; named after C. H. Funck (d. 1839), German botanist; see -IA]

funk·y¹ (fuŋg′kē), *adj.,* **funk·i·er, funk·i·est.** *Informal.* overcome with fear; terrified. [FUNK¹ + -Y¹]

funk·y² (fuŋg′kē), *adj.,* **funk·i·er, funk·i·est.** *Jazz.* having an earthy, blues-based quality or character. [FUNK² + -Y¹]

funk·y³ (fuŋg′kē), *adj.* **funk·i·er, funk·i·est.** *Slang.* evil-smelling; foul. [*funk* stench (akin to ONF *funkier* < LL **fūmicāre;* see FUME) + -Y¹]

fun·nel (fun′ᵊl), *n., v.,* **-neled, -nel·ing** or (*esp. Brit.*) **-nelled, -nel·ling.** —*n.* **1.** a cone-shaped utensil with a tube at the apex, for conducting liquid or other substance through a small opening, as into a bottle, jug, or the like. **2.** a smokestack, esp. of a steamship or a locomotive. **3.** a flue, tube, or shaft, as for ventilation. —*v.t.* **4.** to concentrate, channel, or focus: *They funneled all income into research projects.* [late ME *fonel,* < MF **founel* < OPr *fonilh* < LL **fundibul(um),* aph. var. of L *infundibulum,* deriv. of *infundere* to pour in] —**fun′nel·like′,** *adj.*

fun′nel cloud′, tuba (def. 4).

fun·nel·form (fun′ᵊl fôrm′), *adj.* shaped like a funnel, as the corolla of the morning-glory; infundibuliform. [FUNNEL + -FORM]

fun·ny¹ (fun′ē), *adj.,* **-ni·er, -ni·est,** *n., pl.* **-nies.** —*adj.* **1.** providing fun; amusing; comical: *a funny remark; a funny person.* **2.** attempting to amuse; facetious: *Did you really mean that or were you just being funny?* **3.** warranting suspicion; deceitful; underhanded: *We thought there was something funny about those extra charges.* **4.** insolent; sassy: *Don't get funny with me, young man!* **5.** *Informal.* curious; strange; peculiar; odd: *Her speech has a funny twang.* —*n.* **6.** *Informal.* a funny remark or story; a joke: *to make a funny.* **7. funnies,** *U.S.* **a.** comic strips. **b.** Also called **funny paper.** the section of a newspaper reserved for comic strips, word games, etc. [FUN + -Y¹] —**fun′ni·ly,** *adv.* —**fun′ni·ness,** *n.*

—**Syn. 1.** diverting, comic, farcical, absurd, ridiculous, incongruous, droll, witty, facetious, humorous. FUNNY, LAUGHABLE, LUDICROUS refer to that which excites laughter. FUNNY and LAUGHABLE are both applied to that which provokes laughter or deserves to be laughed at; FUNNY is a colloquial term loosely applied and in popular use is commonly interchangeable with the other terms: *a funny story, scene, joke; a laughable incident, mistake.* That which is LUDICROUS excites laughter by its incongruity and foolish absurdity: *The monkey's attempts to imitate the woman were ludicrous.* —**Ant. 1.** solemn, sad, melancholy.

fun·ny² (fun′ē), *n., pl.* **-nies.** a shell or light skiff rowed by one person with sculls. [perh. special use of FUNNY¹]

fun′ny bone′, **1.** the part of the elbow where the ulnar nerve passes by the internal condyle of the humerus, which when struck causes a peculiar, tingling sensation in the arm and hand; crazy bone. **2.** a good sense of humor.

fun′ny busi′ness, *Slang.* improper or unethical conduct, as deception, trickery, etc.: *He won't stand for any funny business here.*

fun·ny·man (fun′ē man′), *n., pl.* **-men.** a comedian or humorist. [FUNNY¹ + MAN¹]

fun′ny pa′per, funny (def. 7b).

fun·ster (fun′stər), *n.* a person who intentionally creates fun, as by jokes, slapstick, humor, etc., esp. a reveler or comedian. [FUN + -STER]

Fun·ston (fun′stən), *n.* **Frederick,** 1865–1917, U.S. general.

Fu′quay Springs′ (fōō′kwā), a town in central North Carolina. 3389 (1960).

fur (fûr), *n., adj., v.,* **furred, fur·ring.** —*n.* **1.** *Zool.* the fine, soft, thick, hairy coating of the skin of a mammal. **2.** the skin of certain animals, as the sable, ermine, beaver, etc., covered with such a coat, used for lining, trimming, or making garments. **3.** Often, **furs.** a garment made of fur. **4.** any coating resembling or suggesting fur, as diseased matter on the tongue. **5.** *Heraldry.* any conventional representation of a fur, as ermine, vair, potent, or their variations. **6. make the fur fly, a.** to cause a scene or disturbance, esp. of a violent nature; make trouble: *When the kids got mad they really made the fur fly.* **b.** to do things quickly: *She was late and made the fur fly in her rush to get out.* **7. the fur fly, a.** the way things were torn apart, thrown around, wrecked, battered, etc.: *You should've seen the fur fly when she got mad.* **b.** things get accomplished quickly, hurriedly, violently, etc.: *Boy, did the fur fly when she worked.* —*adj.* **8.** of or pertaining to fur, animal skins, dressed pelts, etc.: *fur rug; fur trader.* —*v.t.* **9.** to line, face, or trim, with fur, as a garment. **10.** *Building Trades.* to apply furring to (a wall, ceiling, etc.). **11.** to clothe (a person) with fur. **12.** to coat with foul or deposited matter. [ME *furre* < MF *fourr(er)* (to) line a garment, OF *forrer,* orig. to encase, deriv. of *fuerre* sheath < Gmc; akin to OE *fōdder* case, sheath, Icel *fōthr,* Gk *pōma*] —**fur′less,** *adj.*

fur., furlong; furlongs.

fu·ran (fyŏŏr′an, fyŏŏ ran′), *n. Chem.* a colorless, liquid, unsaturated, five-membered heterocyclic compound, C_4H_4O, obtained from furfural: used chiefly in organic synthesis. Also called **furfuran.** [aph. form of FURFURAN]

fur·be·low (fûr′bə lō′), *n.* **1.** a festooned flounce, as on a woman's gown. **2.** any bit of showy trimming or finery. —*v.t.* **3.** to ornament with or as with furbelows: *to furbelow an old dress.* [var. of FALBALA]

fur·bish (fûr′bish), *v.t.* to restore to freshness of appearance or condition (often fol. by *up*): *to furbish up a run-down neighborhood; to furbish up one's command of a foreign language.* [ME *furbish(en)* < MF *forbiss-,* long s. of *forbir* to polish, clean < Gmc; cf. OHG *furban*] —**fur′bish·er,** *n.*

fur·cate (*adj.* fûr′kāt, -kit; *v.* fûr′kāt), *adj., v.,* **-cat·ed, -cat·ing.** —*adj.* **1.** forked; branching. —*v.i.* **2.** to form a fork; divide into branches. [< ML *furcāt(us)* cloven. See FORK, -ATE¹] —**fur·ca·tion** (fər kā′shən), *n.*

fur·cu·la (fûr′kyə lə), *n., pl.* **-lae** (-lē′). **1.** *Ornith.* the forked clavicular bone of a bird; wishbone. **2.** *Entomol.* the ventral, forked appendage on the abdomen of a springtail that is used in springing. [< L: a forked prop. See FORK, -ULE] —**fur′cu·lar,** *adj.*

fur·cu·lum (fûr′kyə ləm), *n., pl.* **-la** (-lə). furcula. [< NL]

fur′ farm′, a farm on which animals are raised for their pelts.

fur′ farm′ing, the raising of animals for their pelts.

fur·fur (fûr′fər), *n., pl.* **fur·fur·es** (fûr′fyə rēz′). **1.** the formation of flakelike particles on the surface of the skin, as of dandruff. **2. furfures,** these particles. [< L: bran, scurf, scales on the skin]

fur·fu·ra·ceous (fûr′fyə rā′shəs), *adj.* **1.** resembling bran; branlike. **2.** scaly; scurfy. [< LL *furfurāceus.* See FURFUR, -ACEOUS] —**fur′fu·ra′ceous·ly,** *adv.*

fur·fur·al (fûr′fə ral′, -fyə-), *n. Chem.* a colorless, oily liquid, C_4H_3OCHO, having an aromatic odor, obtained from bran, sugar, wood, corncobs, or the like by distillation: used chiefly in the manufacture of plastics and as a solvent in the refining of lubricating oils. Also called **fur·fur·al·de·hyde** (fûr′fə ral′də hīd′, -fyə-), **pyromucic aldehyde.** [FURFUR + -AL³]

fur·fur·an (fûr′fə ran′), *n. Chem.* furan. [FURFUR + -AN]

fur·fu·rol (fûr′fər əl, -fyər-), *n.* (erroneously) furfural. Also, **fur·fu·role** (fûr′fə rōl′, -fyə-).

Fu·ri·ae (fyŏŏr′ē ē′), *n.pl. Rom. Myth.* fury (def. 3).

fu·ri·ant (fyŏŏr′ē änt′, fyŏŏr′ē änt′), *n.* **1.** a quick Bohemian dance in triple meter with shifting accents. **2.** the music for this dance. [< Czech < L *furiant-* (s. of *furiāns*). See FURY, -ANT]

fu·ri·bund (fyŏŏr′ə bund′), *adj.* furious; frenzied; raging. [< L *furibund(us)* raging, furious, angry, equiv. to *furi-* FURY + *-bundus* adj. suffix]

fu·ri·ous (fyŏŏr′ē əs), *adj.* **1.** full of fury, violent passion, or rage: *He was furious about the accident.* **2.** intensely violent, as wind, storms, etc. **3.** of unrestrained energy, speed, etc.: *His furious activity put us all to shame.* [ME < L *furiōs(us).* See FURY, -OUS] —**fu′ri·ous·ly,** *adv.* —**fu′ri·ous·ness,** *n.*

furl (fûrl), *v.t.* **1.** to gather into a compact roll and bind securely, as a sail against a spar or a flag against its staff. —*v.i.* **2.** to become furled. **3. furl in a body,** *Naut.* to furl (a square sail) with loose canvas gathered at the mast, so as to make a harbor furl. **4. furl in the bunt,** *Naut.* to furl (a square sail) by gathering canvas upward, so as to load the yard equally at all points. —*n.* **5.** act of furling. **6.** something furled, as a roll. [cf. F *ferler,* OF *ferlier,* equiv. to *fer* firm (< L *fir(mus)*) + *lier* to bind (< L *ligāre*)] —**furl′a·ble,** *adj.* —**furl′er,** *n.*

furl., furlough.

fur·la·na (fŏŏr lä′nə; *It.* fōōr lä′nä), *n., pl.* **-nas,** *It.* **-ne** (-ne). forlana.

fur·long (fûr′lôŋg, -loŋg), *n.* a unit of distance, equal to 220 yards or ⅛ mile. *Abbr.:* fur. [ME; OE *furlang* length of a furrow. See FURROW, LONG¹]

fur·lough (fûr′lō), *Mil.* —*n.* **1.** vacation granted to an enlisted man: in the U.S. Army, one month per year. **2.** a temporary or permanent dismissal of a railroad worker because of insufficient work for him or her to do; layoff. —*v.t.* **3.** to grant a furlough to. **4.** to lay off (a railroad worker). [var. of earlier *furloff* < D *verlof;* cf. G *Verlaub* leave, permission; current pronunciation by assoc. with *dough, though*]

fur·men·ty (fûr′mən tē), *n. Brit. Dial.* frumenty. Also, **fur·me·ty** (fûr′mi tē).

fur·mint (fŏŏr′mint), *n.* **1.** a variety of grape from which Tokay is made. **2.** the vine bearing this grape, grown in northeastern Hungary. [< Hung]

fur·nace (fûr′nis), *n., v.,* **-naced, -nac·ing.** —*n.* **1.** a structure or apparatus in which heat may be generated, as for heating houses, smelting ores, producing steam, etc. **2.** a place characterized by intense heat: *The volcano was a seething furnace.* **3.** (*cap.*) *Astron.* the constellation Fornax. —*v.t.* **4.** *Metall.* to heat (a piece) in a furnace, as to soften it for bending. [ME *furneis, furnais* < OF *fornais, fournais* < L *fornac-* (s. of *fornax* kiln, oven), akin to *formus* warm] —**fur′nace·like′,** *adj.*

Fur·ner·i·us (fûr nâr′ē əs), *n.* a walled plain in the fourth quadrant of the face of the moon: about 80 miles in diameter.

Fur·ness (fûr′nis), *n.* **Horace Howard,** 1833–1912, and his son **Horace Howard,** 1865–1930, U.S. Shakespearean scholars and editors.

fur·nish (fûr′nish), *v.t.* **1.** to provide or supply (often fol. by *with*): *The delay furnished me with the time I needed.* **2.** to fit out (a house, room, etc.) with necessary appliances, esp. furniture. [ME *furnissh(en)* < OF *furniss-,* long s. of *furnir* to accomplish, furnish < Gmc; cf. OHG *frumjan* to provide] —**fur′nish·er,** *n.*

—**Syn. 1.** purvey, cater. **1, 2.** rig, outfit, deck out. FURNISH, APPOINT, EQUIP all refer to providing something necessary. FURNISH emphasizes the idea of providing necessary or customary services or appliances in living quarters: *to furnish board; a room meagerly furnished with a bed, desk, and a wooden chair.* APPOINT (now found only in WELL-APPOINTED) means to furnish completely with all requisites or accessories or in an elegant style: *a well-appointed house.* EQUIP means to supply with necessary materials or apparatus for some service, action, or undertaking; it emphasizes preparation: *to equip a vessel, a soldier.*

fur·nish·ing (fûr′ni shiŋg), *n.* **1.** that with which anything is furnished. **2. furnishings, a.** fittings, appliances, articles of furniture, etc., for a house or room. **b.** accessories of dress: *men's furnishings.* [FURNISH + -ING¹]

furnit., furniture.

fur·ni·ture (fûr′nə chər), *n.* **1.** the movable articles, as tables, chairs, bedsteads, desks, cabinets, etc., required for use or ornament in a house, office, or the like. **2.** fittings, apparatus, or necessary accessories for something. **3.** Also called **bearer, dead metal.** *Print.* pieces of wood or metal, less than type high, set in and about pages of type to fill them out and hold the type in place in a chase. [< F *fourniture,* deriv. of *fournir* to FURNISH] —**fur′ni·ture·less,** *adj.*

Fur·ni·vall (fûr′nə vəl), *n.* **Frederick James,** 1825–1910, English philologist and editor.

fu·ror (fyŏŏr′ôr), *n.* **1.** a general outburst of enthusiasm, excitement, controversy, or the like. **2.** a prevailing mania or craze. **3.** fury; rage; madness. Also, *esp. Brit.,* **fu′rore** (defs. 1, 2). [< L: a raging; r. late ME *fureur* < MF]

—**Syn. 1, 3.** frenzy.

furred (fûrd), *adj.* **1.** having fur. **2.** made with or of fur, as garments. **3.** clad in fur or furs, as persons: *elegantly furred in a floor-length chinchilla.* **4.** coated with diseased matter, as the tongue. [ME; see FUR, -ED³]

fur·ri·er¹ (fûr′ē ər), *n.* a person who buys and sells furs, or one who makes, repairs, or cleans furs and fur garments; a fur dealer or fur dresser. [ME *furrer* < AF (OF *forrer, fourrer* to line with fur; see FUR) + *-er* -ER²]

fur·ri·er² (fûr′ē ər), *adj.* comparative of **furry.**

fur·ri·er·y (fûr′ē ə rē), *n., pl.* **-er·ies.** **1.** the business, trade, or craftsmanship of a furrier. **2.** *Archaic.* furs in general. [FURRI(ER)¹ + -ERY]

fur·ring (fûr′iŋg), *n.* **1.** act of lining, trimming, or clothing with fur: *Furring this coat will take several weeks* **2.** the fur used: *What kind of furring would you like?* **3.** the formation of a coating of matter on something, as on the tongue: *A heavy furring could mean a high fever.* **4.** *Building Trades.* **a.** the attaching of strips of wood or the like (**fur′ring strips′**) to a wall or other surface, as to provide an even support for lath or to provide an air space between the wall and plasterwork. **b.** material used for this purpose. [ME; see FUR, -ING¹]

fur·row (fûr′ō, fur′ō), *n.* **1.** a narrow groove made in the ground, esp. by a plow. **2.** a narrow, trenchlike depression in any surface: *the furrows of a wrinkled face.* —*v.t.* **3.** to make a furrow or furrows in. **4.** to make wrinkles in (the face): *to furrow one's brow.* —*v.i.* **5.** to make a furrow or furrows; become furrowed: *His brow furrowed in deep thought.* [ME *forwe, furgh,* OE *furh;* c. OFris *furch,* OHG *fur(u)h* (G *Furche*), L *porca* ridge between furrows] —**fur′row·er,** *n.* —**fur′row·less,** *adj.* —**fur′row·like′,** *adj.* —**fur′row·y,** *adj.*

fur·ry (fûr′ē), *adj.,* **fur·ri·er, fur·ri·est.** **1.** consisting of or resembling fur: *a deep, furry rug in front of the fireplace; the furry undergrowth of the forest.* **2.** covered with fur; wearing fur: *The animal's furry coat is heavier in winter than in summer.* **3.** obstructed or coated as if with fur: *a furry voice; a furry tongue.* [FUR + -Y¹] —**fur′ri·ly,** *adv.* —**fur′ri·ness,** *n.*

fur′ seal′, any of several eared seals, as *Callorhinus alascanus,* having a plush underfur used in making coats, trimmings, etc.

Fürth (fʏʀt), *n.* a city in S West Germany, near Nuremberg. 98,300 (1963).

fur·ther (fûr′thər), *compar. adv. and adj. of* **far** *with superl.* **fur·thest,** *v.* —*adv.* **1.** at or to a greater distance; farther: *I'm too tired to go further.* **2.** at or to a more advanced point; to a greater extent: *Let's not discuss it further.* **3.** in addition; moreover: *Further, he should be here any minute.* —*adj.* **4.** more distant or remote; farther: *The map shows it to be further than I thought.* **5.** more extended: *Does this mean a further delay?* **6.** additional; more: *Further meetings seem pointless.* —*v.t.* **7.** to help forward (a work, undertaking, cause, etc.); promote; advance; forward: *You can always count on him to further his own interests.* [ME *furthere,* OE *furthra;* c. G *vordere* more advanced] —**fur′ther·er,** *n.*

fur·ther·ance (fûr′thər əns), *n.* act of furthering; promotion; advancement. [late ME *fortheraunce.* See FURTHER, -ANCE]

fur·ther·more (fûr′thər mōr′, -môr′), *adv.* moreover; besides; in addition: *Furthermore, he left orders not to be disturbed.* [ME; see FURTHER, MORE]

fur·ther·most (fûr′thər mōst′), *adj.* most distant: *Their house is furthermost on the right.* [ME; see FURTHER, -MOST]

fur·thest (fûr′thist), *adj., adv. superl. of* **far** *with* **further** *as compar.* farthest.

fur·tive (fûr′tiv), *adj.* **1.** taken, done, used, etc., by stealth; secret: *a furtive glance.* **2.** sly; shifty: *a furtive manner.* [< L *furtīv(us),* equiv. to *furt(um)* theft (cf. *fūr* thief) + *-īv(us)* -IVE] —**fur′tive·ly,** *adv.* —**fur′tive·ness,** *n.*
—**Syn. 1.** surreptitious, clandestine, covert. **2.** underhand, cunning, foxy.

Furt·wäng·ler (fōōrt′veng′lər), *n.* **Wil·helm** (vil′-helm), 1886–1954, German orchestral conductor.

fu·run·cle (fyōōr′ung kəl), *n. Pathol.* boil². [< L *fūrunculus*) petty thief, boil, equiv. to *fūr* thief (see FURTIVE) + *-unc(o)-* dim. suffix + *-ulus* -ULE] —**fu·run·cu·lar** (fyōō rung′kyə lər), **fu·run′cu·lous,** *adj.*

fu·run·cu·lo·sis (fyōō rung′kyə lō′sis), *n. Pathol.* the condition characterized by the presence of furuncles. [< L *furuncul(us)* (see FURUNCLE) + -OSIS]

fu·ry (fyōōr′ē), *n., pl.* **-ries. 1.** unrestrained or violent anger, rage, passion, or the like: *The gods unleashed their fury on the offending mortal.* **2.** violence; vehemence; fierceness: *the fury of a hurricane; a fury of creative energy.* **3. Furies,** *Class. Myth.* female divinities: the daughters of Gaea who punished crimes at the instigation of the victims; known to the Greeks as the Erinyes or Eumenides and to the Romans as the Furiae or Dirae. Originally there were an indefinite number, but were later restricted to Alecto, Megaera, and Tisiphone. **4.** a fierce and violent person, esp. a woman: *He found himself married to a jealous fury.* **5. like fury,** *Informal.* violently; intensely: *It rained like fury.* [ME < L *furia* rage, equiv. to *fur(ere)* (to) be angry, rage + *-ia* -Y²]
—**Syn. 1.** furor, frenzy, ire, wrath. See **anger. 2.** turbulence, impetuosity. **4.** shrew, virago, termagant, vixen, hag. —**Ant. 1.** calm, serenity.

furze (fûrz), *n.* any leguminous plant of the genus *Ulex,* esp. *U. europaeus,* a low, much-branched, spiny shrub having yellow flowers, common on waste lands in Europe. Also called, *esp. Brit.,* **gorse, whin.** [ME *furse, firse,* OE *fyr(e)s;* akin to Russ *pyrej,* Gk *pȳrós* corn, Lith *pūrai* autumn-sown wheat]

Furze, *Ulex europaeus*

furz·y (fûr′zē), *adj.* **furz·i·er, furz·i·est.** *Brit.* **1.** of or pertaining to furze. **2.** overgrown with furze. [FURZE + -Y¹]

fu·sain (fyōō zān′, fyōō′zān; *Fr.* fʏ zaN′), *n., pl.* **-sains** (-zānz′, -zānz; *Fr.* -zaN′) for 2. **1.** a fine charcoal used in drawing, made from the wood of the spindle tree. **2.** a drawing made with this charcoal. **3.** the charcoallike layers in a coal bed, probably formed by natural fires. [< F: spindle tree, charcoal made from its wood < VL **fūsāgin-* (s. of *fūsāgō*), deriv. of L *fūsus* spindle]

Fu·san (fōō′sän′), *n.* former name of **Pusan.**

fu·sar·i·um wilt′ (fyōō zâr′ē əm), *Plant Pathol.* a disease of plants, characterized by damping-off, wilting, and a brown dry rot, caused by any of several fungi of the genus *Fusarium.* [*fusarium* < NL, equiv. to L *fūs(us)* spindle + *-ārium* -ARIUM]

fu·sa·role (fyōō′sə rōl′), *n.* a molding of convex section cut to resemble beads or the like. [< F *fusarolle, fusarole* < OIt *fusarola,* deriv. of *fuso* < L *fusus* spindle]

fus·cous (fus′kəs), *adj.* of brownish-gray or dusky color. [< L *fusc(us)* dark, tawny, dusky + -OUS]

fuse¹ (fyōōz), *n., v.,* **fused, fus·ing.** —*n.* **1.** *Elect.* a protective device, used in an electric circuit, containing a piece of metal that melts under heat produced by an excess current in the circuit, thereby breaking the circuit. **2.** a tube, cord, or the like, filled or saturated with combustible matter, for igniting an explosive. **3.** fuze (def. 1). —*v.i.* **4.** *Chiefly Brit.* to overload an electric circuit, burning out the fuse; blow a fuse. —*v.t.* **5.** fuze (def. 3). [< It *fuso* < L *fūsus* spindle] —**fuse′less,** *adj.* —**fuse′like′,** *adj.*

fuse² (fyōōz), *v.,* **fused, fus·ing.** —*v.t.* **1.** to combine or blend by melting together; melt. **2.** to unite or blend into a whole, as if by melting together: *The author skillfully fuses these fragments into a cohesive whole.* —*v.i.* **3.** to become liquid under the action of heat; melt: *At a relatively low temperature the metal will fuse.* **4.** to become united or blended, as if by melting together: *the excitement created when taste fuses with virtuosity.* [< L *fūsus* melted, poured, cast, ptp. of *fundere*]
—**Syn. 1.** See **melt. 2, 4.** amalgamate, liquefy, dissolve, merge. **4.** coalesce. —**Ant. 1, 3.** solidify. **2, 4.** separate.

Fu·se (fōō′sä), *n.* a city on SW Honshu, in S Japan, SE of Osaka. 256,593 (est. 1964).

fused′ quartz′, glass made entirely from quartz: a form of silica glass.

fused′ sil′ica. See **silica glass.**

fu·see (fyōō zē′), *n.* **1.** a wooden match having a large head and ignited by friction. **2.** a red flare light, used on a railroad as a warning signal to approaching trains. **3.** *Horol.* a spirally grooved, conical pulley and chain arrangement for counteracting the diminishing power of the uncoiling mainspring. **4.** a fuse. Also, **fuzee.** [< F *fusée* spindleful, deriv. of OF *fus* spindle. See FUSE¹]

fu·se·lage (fyōō′sə lij, fyōō′sə läzh′, -zə-), *n. Aeron.* the complete central structure to which the wing, tail surfaces, and engines are attached on an airplane. [< F, equiv. to *fusel(é)* spindle-shaped (deriv. of *fuseau* spindle; see FUSEE) + *-age* -AGE]

Fu·se·li (fyōō′zə lē), *n.* **(John) Henry** (*Johann Heinrich Füssli*), 1741–1825, English painter, illustrator, and essayist; born in Switzerland.

fuse′ link′, *Elect.* the element, made of fusible wire or cast from fusible metal, that carries the current in a fuse.

fu′sel oil′ (fyōō′zəl, -səl), a mixture consisting chiefly of amyl alcohols obtained as a by-product in the fermentation of grains. [< G *Fusel* bad liquor]

fuse·tron (fyōōz′tron), *n. Elect.* a type of fuse that allows an overcurrent for a short period of time before it opens a circuit. [FUSE¹ + -TRON]

Fu·shih (fōō′shē′), *n.* Yenan.

fu·si·bil·i·ty (fyōō′zə bil′i tē), *n.* **1.** quality of being fusible, or convertible from a solid to a liquid state by heat. **2.** the degree to which a substance is fusible. [< F *fusibilité.* See FUSIBLE, -ITY]

fu·si·ble (fyōō′zə bəl), *adj.* capable of being fused or melted. [ME < ML *fūsibil(is).* See FUSE², -IBLE] —**fu′si·ble·ness,** *n.* —**fu′si·bly,** *adv.*

fu′sible met′al, *Metall.* any of various alloys, as one of bismuth, lead, and tin, which melt at comparatively low temperatures, and hence can be used for making various safety devices. Also called **fu′sible al′loy.**

fu·si·form (fyōō′zə fôrm′), *adj.* spindle-shaped; rounded and tapering from the middle toward each end, as some roots. [< L *fūs(us)* spindle + -I- + -FORM]

fu·sil¹ (fyōō′zəl, -sil), *n.* a light flintlock musket. [< F: musket, OF *fuisil, foisil* steel for striking fire < VL **focīl(is),* deriv. of L *focus* fire. See FOCUS]

fu·sil² (fyōō′zəl, -sil), *adj.* **1.** formed by melting or casting; fused; founded. **2.** *Archaic.* capable of being melted; fusible. **3.** *Archaic.* melted; molten. Also, **fu·sile** (fyōō′zəl, -sil, -sīl). [ME < L *fūsil(is)* molten, fluid. See FUSE², -ILE]

fu·sil³ (fyōō′zəl, -sil), *n. Heraldry.* a narrow, elongated lozenge. [< MF, OF *fu(i)sel* < VL **fūsell(us),* dim. of L *fūsus* spindle]

fu·sil·ier (fyōō′zə lēr′), *n.* **1.** a term used in the names of certain British regiments. **2.** (formerly) a soldier armed with a fusil. Also, **fu′si·leer′.** [< F; see FUSIL¹, -IER]

fu·sil·lade (fyōō′sə lād′, -läd′, -zə-), *n., v.,* **-lad·ed, -lad·ing.** —*n.* **1.** a simultaneous or continuous discharge of firearms. **2.** a general discharge or outpouring of anything: *a fusillade of questions.* —*v.t.* **3.** to attack or shoot by a fusillade. [< F, equiv. to *fusill(er)* (to) shoot (see FUSIL¹) + *-ade* -ADE¹]

fu·si·ly (fyōō′zə lē), *adj. Heraldry.* (of an escutcheon) divided into fusils of two alternating tinctures: *fusilly or and azure.* [ME *fusile.* See FUSIL³, -Y¹]

fu·sion (fyōō′zhən), *n.* **1.** act or process of fusing; state of being fused. **2.** that which is fused; the result of fusing: *A theatrical production is the fusion of many talents.* **3.** *Politics.* **a.** a coalition of parties or factions. **b.** (*cap*) the political party resulting from such a coalition. **4.** Also called **nuclear fusion.** *Physics.* a thermonuclear reaction in which nuclei of light atoms join to form nuclei of heavier atoms, as the combination of deuterium atoms to form helium atoms. Cf. **fission** (def. 3). **5.** *Ophthalm.* **a.** Also called **binocular fusion.** the correct blending of the images of both eyes. **b.** the perception of rapid, intermittent flashes of light as a continuous beam. [< L *fūsiōn-* (s. of *fūsiō*) a pouring out, melting. See FUSE², -ION]

fu′sion bomb′. See **hydrogen bomb.**

fu·sion·ism (fyōō′zhə niz′əm), *n. Politics.* the principle, policy, or practice of fusion. [FUSION + -ISM] —**fu′sion·ist,** *n., adj.*

fu·so·bac·te·ri·um (fyōō′zō bak tēr′ē əm), *n., pl.* **-te·ri·a** (-tēr′ē ə). *Bacteriol.* any of several fusiform, rod-shaped, anaerobic bacteria of the genus *Fusobacterium,* certain species of which are pathogenic for man. [< NL, equiv. to *fuso-* (comb. form repr. L *fūsus* spindle) + *bacterium* BACTERIUM]

fuss (fus), *n.* **1.** an excessive display of anxious attention or activity; needless or useless bustle: *Remember that she expects you to make a fuss over her.* **2.** an argument or noisy dispute: *They had a fuss about who should wash dishes.* —*v.i.* **3.** to make a fuss; make much ado about trifles: *She fusses so over details.* —*v.t.* **4.** to disturb, esp. with trifles; annoy; bother. [?] —**fuss′er,** *n.*
—**Syn. 1.** pother, to-do, stir, commotion. **4.** pester. —**Ant. 1.** inactivity.

fuss′ and feath′ers, elaborate or pretentious display; ostentation: *the fuss and feathers of a society wedding.*

fuss·budg·et (fus′buj′it), *n.* a fussy or needlessly fault-finding person. Also called **fuss·pot** (fus′pot′). [FUSS + BUDGET] —**fuss′budg′et·y,** *adj.*

fuss·y (fus′ē), *adj.,* **fuss·i·er, fuss·i·est. 1.** excessively busy with trifles; anxious or particular about petty details. **2.** (of clothes, decoration, etc.) elaborately made, trimmed, or decorated: *She wears such fussy dresses. All the bric-a-brac gave the room a fussy, cluttered look.* **3.** full of details, esp. in excess: *His writing is so fussy I lose the thread of the story.* [FUSS + -Y¹] —**fuss′i·ly,** *adv.* —**fuss′i·ness,** *n.*

fus·ta·nel·la (fus′tə nel′ə, fōō′stə-), *n.* a short stiff skirt, usually pleated, made of white cotton or linen, worn by men in some parts of the Balkans. Also, **fustinella.** [< It < NGk *phoustánella,* dim. of *phoustáni* woman's dress < It *fustagno* FUSTIAN]

fus·tet (fu stet′), *n.* **1.** the smoke tree, *Cotinus Coggygria.* **2.** Also called **young fustic.** the dyewood of this tree. [< F < Pr < Sp *fustete,* by assoc. with *fuste* stick. See FUSTIC]

fus·tian (fus′chən), *n.* **1.** a stout fabric of cotton and flax. **2.** a fabric of stout twilled cotton or of cotton and low-quality wool, with a short nap or pile. **3.** inflated or turgid language in writing or speaking; bombast; rant; claptrap: *Fustian can't disguise the author's meager plot.* —*adj.* **4.** made of fustian: *a fustian coat; fustian bed linen.* **5.** pompous or bombastic, as language: *fustian melodrama.* **6.** worthless; cheap: *fustian knaves and dupes.* [ME < OF *fustaigne* < LL *fustān(eum)* (deriv. of L *fūstis* cudgel), trans. of Gk *xýlinon,* deriv. of *xýlon* wood]

fus·tic (fus′tik), *n.* **1.** the wood of a large, moraceous tree, *Chlorophora tinctoria,* of tropical America, yielding a light-yellow dye. **2.** the tree itself. **3.** the dye. **4.** any of several other dyewoods. Also called **old fustic** (for defs. 1–3). [< F *fustoc* < Sp < Ar *fustuq;* akin to Gk *pistákē* pistachio tree]

fus·ti·gate (fus′tə gāt′), *v.t.,* **-gat·ed, -gat·ing. 1.** to cudgel; beat; punish severely. **2.** to criticize harshly; castigate: *a new satire that fustigates bureaucratic shillyshallying.* [< L *fūstigāt(us)* cudgeled to death (ptp. of *fūstigāre;* see -ATE¹), deriv. of *fūstis* cudgel] —**fus′ti·ga′tion,** *n.* —**fus′ti·ga′tor,** *n.* —**fus·ti·ga·to·ry** (fus′tə gə tōr′ē, -tôr′ē), *adj.*

fus·ti·nel·la (fus′tə nel′ə, fōō′stə-), *n.* fustanella.

fus·ty (fus′tē), *adj.,* **-ti·er, -ti·est. 1.** moldy; musty; having a stale smell; stuffy: *fusty rooms that were in need of a good airing.* **2.** old-fashioned or out-of-date, as architecture, furnishings, etc.: *They still live in that fusty, gingerbread house.* **3.** stubbornly conservative or old-fashioned; fogyish: *a charming, but fusty, old gentleman who still wore a wing collar.* [*fust* (n.) < OF: wine cask, log (< L *fūstis* cudgel) + -Y¹] —**fus′ti·ly,** *adv.* —**fus′ti·ness,** *n.*
—**Syn. 1.** close, stale, smelly, oppressive, malodorous.

fu·su·la (fyōō′zə lə), *n., pl.* **-lae** (-lē′), **-las.** (in the spinneret of a spider) the terminal tube of a silk gland. [< NL; see FUSE¹, -ULE]

fu·su·ma (fyōō′sə mä′), *n.* a sliding door in a Japanese house, esp. one serving as a room partition. [< Jap]

fut., future.

Fu·ta·ba·tei (fōō tä′bä tā′), *n.* **Shi·mei** (shē mā′), (*Tatsunosuke Hasegawa*), 1864–1909, Japanese author.

fu·thorc (fōō′thôrk), *n.* the runic alphabet. Also, **fu′thork, fu·tharc, fu·thark** (fōō′thärk). [so called from first six letters of OE and Scand runic alphabet: *f, uth, o, r, k* (modeled on ALPHABET)]

fu·tile (fyōōt′əl, fyōō′til; *Brit.* fyōō′tīl), *adj.* **1.** incapable of producing any result; ineffective; useless; not successful: *Attempting to force-feed the sick horse is a futile effort.* **2.** trifling; frivolous; unimportant: *a head stuffed with silly, futile ideas.* [< L *fūt(t)il(is)* that which flows easily, is vain, worthless, equiv. to *fūt-* (akin to *fundere* to pour, melt) + *-ilis* -ILE] —**fu′tile·ly,** *adv.* —**fu′tile·ness,** *n.*
—**Syn. 1.** ineffectual, unavailing, vain, idle, profitless, unprofitable, bootless. See **useless. 2.** trivial, nugatory. —**Ant. 1.** effectual.

fu·til·i·tar·i·an (fyōō til′i târ′ē ən), *adj.* **1.** believing that human hopes are vain, and human strivings unjustified. —*n.* **2.** a person who holds this belief. [FUTILE + (UTIL)ITARIAN] —**fu·til′i·tar′i·an·ism,** *n.*

fu·til·i·ty (fyōō til′i tē), *n., pl.* **-ties. 1.** quality of being futile; ineffectiveness; uselessness. **2.** trifle; frivolity; unimportance: *the large collection of futilities that make up her thinking.* **3.** a futile act or event: *a long series of futilities preceded the rebel's defeat.* [< L *fūtilitāt-* (s. of *fūtilitās*). See FUTILE, -ITY]

fut·tock (fut′ək), *n. Naut.* any of a number of timbers forming the lower, more curved portion of a frame in a wooden hull, generally secured side by side with another futtock placed somewhat farther above or below, so that the two are butted against similarly disposed pairs of floors, other futtocks, or top timbers in a series of broken joints. [perh. alter. of *foothook*]

fut′tock band′, *Naut.* a metal band around a lower mast somewhat below the top, for holding the lower ends of the futtock shrouds. Also called **fut′tock hoop′, fut′tock wye′** (wī), **spider band.**

fut′tock plate′, *Naut.* any of several chain plates at the rim of the top of a lower mast, connected at their lower ends to futtock shrouds and at their upper ends to topmast shrouds. Also called **fut′tock chain′.**

fut′tock shroud′, *Naut.* any of several metal rods secured at their lower ends to a futtock band and at their upper ends to futtock plates.

fu·tu·ram·a (fyōō′chə ram′ə, -rä′mə), *n.* **1.** an exhibition or display that attempts to depict certain elements of life in the future. **2.** a comprehensive projection of the future. [after *Futurama* (b. FUTURE and PANORAMA), name of an exhibit at the New York World's Fair (1939)] —**fu·tu·ram·ic** (fyōō′chə ram′ik), *adj.*

fu·ture (fyōō′chər), *n.* **1.** time that is to be or come hereafter. **2.** that which will exist or happen in future time: *The future is rooted in the past.* **3.** a future condition, esp. of success or failure: *Some people believe a gypsy can tell you your future.* **4.** *Gram.* **a.** the future tense. **b.** another future formation or construction. **c.** a form in the future, as *He will come.* **5.** Usually, **futures.** speculative purchases or sales of commodities for future receipt or delivery. —*adj.* **6.** that is to be or come hereafter: *future events; on some future day.* **7.** pertaining to or connected with time to come: *one's future prospects; future plans.* **8.** *Gram.* noting or pertaining to a tense or other verb formation or construction that refers to events or states in time to come. [ME *futur* < L *fūtūr(us)* about to be (fut. participle of *esse* to be)]

Fu′ture Farm′er, a member of the Future Farmers of America.

Fu′ture Farm′ers of Amer′ica, a national organization of farm boys studying vocational agriculture in high school. *Abbr.:* FFA

fu·ture·less (fyōō′chər lis), *adj.* without a future; having no prospect of future betterment or prosperity: *He disintegrated into a futureless bum.* [FUTURE + -LESS]

fu′ture life′, afterlife (def. 2).

fu′ture per′fect, *Gram.* **1.** perfect with respect to a temporal point of reference in time to come; completed with respect to a time in the future, esp. when incomplete with respect to the present. **2.** noting or pertaining to a tense or other verb formation or construction with such reference. **3.** the future perfect tense. **4.** another verb formation or construction with future perfect meaning. **5.** a form in the future perfect, as *He will have come.*

Fu·tur·ism (fyōō′chə riz′əm), *n.* **1.** (*sometimes l.c.*) a style of the fine arts developed originally by a group of Italian artists about 1910 in which forms derived chiefly from Cubism were used to represent rapid movement and dynamic motion. **2.** (*usually l.c.*) a style of art, literature, music, etc., and a theory of art and life in which violence, power, speed, mechanization or machines, and hostility to the past or to traditional forms of expression were advocated or portrayed. [< It *futurism(o).* See FUTURE, -ISM]

Fu·tur·ist (fyōō′chər ist), *n.* **1.** a follower of Futurism, esp. an artist or writer. **2.** (*l.c.*) *Theol.* a person who maintains that the prophecies in the Apocalypse will be fulfilled in the future. Cf. **presentist, preterist.** [< It *futurist(a).* See FUTURE, -IST]

fu·tur·is·tic (fyōō′chə ris′tik), *adj.* **1.** of or pertaining to the future: *a futuristic advance in automation.* **2.**

(*usually cap.*) of or pertaining to Futurism: *the Futuristic rejection of traditional forms.* [FUTURE + -ISTIC] —**fu′tur·is′ti·cal·ly,** *adv.*

fu·tu·ri·ty (fyo͞o to͝or′i tē, -tyo͝or′-, -cho͝or′-), *n., pl.* **-ties. 1.** future time: *Such discussion is better left to futurity.* **2.** succeeding generations; posterity: *What will futurity say about this?* **3.** the after life: *the promise of eternal rest in futurity.* **4.** a future state or condition; a future event, possibility, or prospect: *We are concerned about the futurity of unsubsidized opera. His tactfulness remains more of a futurity than a reality.* **5.** quality of being future: *the futurity of man's travel among the stars.* **6.** See **futurity race.** [FUTURE + -ITY]

futu′rity race′, *Horse Racing.* a race, usually for two-year-olds, in which the entrants are selected long before the race is run, sometimes before the birth of the foal.

fuze (fyo͞oz), *n., v.,* **fuzed, fuz·ing.** —*n.* **1.** a mechanical or electronic device to detonate an explosive charge, esp. as contained in an artillery shell, a missile, projectile, or the like. **2.** fuse[1] (def. 2). —*v.t.* **3.** Also, **fuse.** to attach a fuze or fuzes to (a bomb, mine, etc.). [var. of FUSE[1]]

fu·zee (fyo͞o zē′), *n.* fusee.

fuzz (fuz), *n., pl.* **fuzz, fuzz·es** for 3a, *v.* —*n.* **1.** loose, light, fibrous or fluffy matter. **2.** a mass or coating of such matter: *Be sure to wash the fuzz off the peach before you eat it.* **3.** *U.S. Slang.* **a.** a policeman or detective. **b.** the police; policemen collectively. —*v.t.* **4. fuzz up,** to make unclear; confuse; bungle: *He fuzzed up the plot line with a lot of emotional nonsense.* [cf. D *voos* spongy]

fuzz·ball (fuz′bôl′), *n.* a puffball. [FUZZ + BALL[1]]

fuzz·y (fuz′ē), *adj.,* **fuzz·i·er, fuzz·i·est. 1.** of the nature of or resembling fuzz: *a soft, fuzzy material.* **2.** covered with fuzz: *a plant with broad, fuzzy leaves.* **3.** indistinct; blurred: *A fuzzy photograph usually means you jiggled the camera.* **4.** muddleheaded; incoherent, often as a result of intoxication: *a fuzzy thinker; to become fuzzy after one drink.* [FUZZ + -Y[1]] —**fuzz′i·ly,** *adv.* —**fuzz′i·ness,** *n.*

fuzz·y-head·ed (fuz′ē hed′id), *adj.* **1.** not given to clear thinking; foolish. **2.** giddy; light-headed.

f.v., on the back of the page. [< L *folio verso*]

f value. See **f number.**

f.w., fresh water.

FWA, Federal Works Agency.

fwd., forward.

-fy, a verbal suffix meaning "to make," "cause to be," "render" (*simplify; beautify*); "to become," "be made" (*liquefy*). The suffix was introduced into English in loan words from Old French (*deify*), but is also used in the formation of new words, usually on a Latin root (*reify*). [< OF *-fier* << L *-ficāre* to do, make]

FYI, *Chiefly Mil.* for your information.

fyke (fīk), *n.* *U.S.* a bag-shaped fish trap. [< D *fuik,* MD *vūke;* c. OFris *fūcke*]

fyl·fot (fil′fot), *n.* a swastika. [? var. of *fill-foot* foot filler]

Fyn (fyn), *n.* an island in S Denmark. 376,872 (1960); 1149 sq. mi. German, **Fünen.**

Fy·o·dor (fē′ə dôr′; *Russ.* fyô′dor), *n.* a boy's given name, form of **Theodore.** Also, **Feodor.**

fyrd (fûrd), *n.* **1.** the militia in Anglo-Saxon England. **2.** the duty to serve in this militia. [OE *fyrd, fierd,* akin to *faran* to go, FARE]

fytte (fit), *n.* fit[3].

Fyz·a·bad (fī′zä bäd′), *n.* a city in SE Uttar Pradesh, in N India. 83,717 (1961). Also, **Faizabad.**

F.Z.S., Fellow of the Zoological Society, London. Also, **F.Z.S.L.**

G

G, g (jē), *n., pl.* **G's** or **Gs, g's** or **gs.** **1.** the seventh letter of the English alphabet, a consonant. **2.** any spoken sound represented by the letter *G* or *g*, as in *get, garage, sing,* etc. **3.** something having the shape of a G. **4.** a written or printed representation of the letter *G* or *g*. **5.** a device, as a printer's type, for reproducing the letter G or g.

G, **1.** *Elect.* gauss. **2.** *Psychol.* general intelligence. **3.** German. **4.** good.

G, *pl.* **Gs** or **G's.** *Slang.* the sum of one thousand dollars. [abbr. for GRAND]

G, **1.** the seventh in order or in a series. **2.** *Music.* **a.** the fifth tone in the scale of C major or the seventh tone in the relative minor scale, A minor. **b.** a string, key, or pipe tuned to this tone. **c.** a written or printed note representing this tone. **d.** (in the fixed system of solmization) the fifth tone of the scale of C major, called *sol.* **e.** the tonality having G as the tonic note. **3.** (*sometimes l.c.*) the medieval Roman numeral for 400. Cf. **Roman numerals.** **4.** *Physics.* See **constant of gravitation.** **5.** *Elect.* conductance.

g, **1.** *Psychol.* general intelligence. **2.** good. **3.** *Metrics.* gram; grams. **4.** *Physics.* gravity.

g, *Physics.* See **acceleration of gravity.**

G., **1.** German. **2.** gourde; gourdes. **3.** (specific) gravity. **4.** Gulf.

g., **1.** gauge. **2.** gender. **3.** general. **4.** generally. **5.** genitive. **6.** going back to. **7.** gold. **8.** grain; grains. **9.** gram; grams. **10.** *Football.* guard. **11.** *Brit.* guinea. **12.** gun.

Ga (gä), *n.* a Kwa language of Ghana, spoken in Accra and vicinity.

Ga, *Chem.* gallium.

Ga., Georgia.

G.A., **1.** General Agent. **2.** General Assembly. **3.** General Average.

g.a., general average. Also, **G/A**

gab[1] (gab), *v.,* **gabbed, gab·bing,** *n.* *Informal.* —*v.i.* **1.** to talk idly; chatter. [ME *gabbe(n)* < ON; c. Icel *gabba*] —*n.* **2.** idle talk; chatter. [ME *gab(be)* < ON; c. Icel *gabb*] —**gab′ber,** *n.*

gab[2] (gab), *n.* *Mach.* a hook or fork which engages temporarily with a moving rod or lever. [prob. < Flem *gabbe* notch, gash]

gab[3] (gab), *n.* *Scot. Slang.* gob[3].

Gab·a·on (gab′ā ən), *n.* *Douay Bible.* Gibeon.

Gab·a·on·ite (gab′ā ə nīt′), *n.* *Douay Bible.* Gibeonite.

Ga·bar (gä′bər), *n.* an Iranian Zoroastrian. Also, **Gheber.** [< Pers < Ar *kāfir;* see KAFFIR]

gab·ar·dine (gab′ər dēn′, gab′ər dēn′), *n.* **1.** Also, **gaberdine.** firm, woven fabric of worsted, cotton, or spun rayon, with a twill weave. **2.** gaberdine (def. 1). [var. of GABERDINE]

Gab·bai (gä bī′), *n., pl.* **Gab·ba·im** (gä bä ēm′; *Eng.* gä bī′im), *Eng.* **gab·bais.** *Hebrew.* **1.** a minor official of a synagogue, having limited ceremonial or administrative functions. **2.** (formerly) a government official charged with collecting taxes. [lit., treasurer]

gab·bard (gab′ərd), *n.* a small sailing vessel or barge formerly used in Scotland. Also, **gab·bart** (gab′ərt). [< MF *gabarre* < OPr *gabarra;* akin to Catalan, Sp, Pg *gabarra*]

gab·ble (gab′əl), *v.,* **-bled, -bling,** *n.* —*v.i.* **1.** to speak or converse rapidly and unintelligibly; jabber. **2.** (of hens, geese, etc.) to cackle. —*v.t.* **3.** to utter rapidly and unintelligibly. —*n.* **4.** rapid, unintelligible talk; meaningless sounds. [GAB[1] + -LE] —**gab′bler,** *n.*

gab·bro (gab′rō), *n., pl.* **-bros.** *Petrog.* a granular igneous rock composed essentially of labradorite and augite. [< It; akin to L *glaber* smooth] —**gab·bro·ic** (gə brō′ik), **gab′bro·it′ic,** *adj.* —**gab·broid** (gab′roid), *adj.*

gab·by (gab′ē), *adj.* **-bi·er, -bi·est.** talkative; loquacious. [GAB[1] + -Y[1]]

Gab·by (gab′ē), *n.* **1.** a boy's given name, form of **Gabriel.** **2.** a girl's given name, form of **Gabriella.**

Gabe (gāb), *n.* a boy's given name, form of **Gabriel.**

ga·belle (gə bel′), *n.* **1.** a tax; an excise. **2.** *Fr. Hist.* a tax on salt, abolished in 1790. [< F < L *gabell(a),* cf. *gablum, gabulum* a tax, import] —**ga·belled′,** *adj.*

gab·er·dine (gab′ər dēn′, gab′ər dēn′), *n.* **1.** Also, **gabardine.** a long, loose coat or frock for men, worn in the Middle Ages, esp. by Jews. **2.** gabardine (def. 1). [< MF *gauvardine, gallevardine,* ? < MHG *wallevart* pilgrimage; cf. Sp *gabardina*]

gab·er·lun·zie (gab′ər lun′zē; *Scot.* gä′bər lo͞on′yē), *n.* *Scot.* a wandering beggar, esp. a mendicant or beadsman. Also, **ga·ber·loon·ie** (gä′bər lo͞on′yē). [?]

Ga·be·ro·nes (gä′bə rō′nes, gab′ə-), *n.* a town in and the capital of Botswana, in the SE part. ab. 5000.

Ga·bès (gä′bes), *n.* **Gulf of,** a gulf of the Mediterranean on the E coast of Tunisia.

gab·fest (gab′fest′), *n.* *U.S. Informal.* a gathering at which there is a great deal of conversation. [GAB[1] + -FEST]

ga·bi·on (gā′bē ən), *n.* **1.** a cylinder of wickerwork filled with earth, used as a military defense. **2.** a cylinder filled with stones and sunk in water, used in laying the foundations of a dam or jetty. [< MF: rough, two-handled basket < It *gabbione,* aug. of *gabbia* cage < L *cavea* cavity, cage]

ga·bi·on·ade (gā′bē ə nād′), *n.* **1.** a work formed of or with gabions. **2.** a row of gabions sunk in a stream to control the current. [< MF; see GABION, -ADE[1]]

ga·ble (gā′bəl), *n.* *Archit.* **1.** an area of the front of a building enclosed by or masking the end of a roof that slopes downward at an angle from a central ridge, as a double-pitched roof or gambrel roof. **2.** a decorative member suggesting a gable, used esp. in Gothic architecture. **3.** Also called **ga′ble wall′.** a wall bearing a gable. [ME < ON (cf. OIcel *gafl*), OF (< Gmc); cf. OE *gafol, geafel* a fork] —**ga′ble·like′,** *adj.*

Gable (def. 1)

Ga·ble (gā′bəl), *n.* **1. (William) Clark,** 1901–60, U.S. motion-picture actor. **2.** a boy's given name.

ga·bled (gā′bəld), *adj.* **1.** provided with a gable or gables: *a gabled house.* **2.** built with a gable or gables.

ga′ble end′, an end wall bearing a gable. —**ga′ble-end′ed,** *adj.*

ga′ble roof′, a roof sloping downward in two parts at an angle from a central ridge, so as to leave a gable at each end. —**ga′ble-roofed′,** *adj.*

ga·blet (gā′blit), *n.* a miniature gable, esp. as an ornament. [< AF; see GABLE, -ET]

ga′ble win′dow, a window in or under a gable. —**ga′ble-win′dowed,** *adj.*

Ga·bo (gä′bə, -bō), *n.* **Naum** (noum), (*Naum Pevsner*), born 1890, U.S. sculptor, born in Russia (brother of Antoine Pevsner).

Ga·bon (gᴀ bôɴ′), *n.* **1.** Official name, **Gab′onese Repub′lic.** a republic in SW Africa: formerly a member of French Equatorial Africa; an independent member of the French Community. 454,000 (est. 1964); 102,290 sq. mi. *Cap.:* Libreville. **2.** an estuary in W Gabon. ab. 40 mi. long. Also, **Gabun.**

Gab·o·nese (gab′ə nēz′, -nēs′, gä′bə-), *adj., n., pl.* **-nese.** —*adj.* **1.** of or pertaining to Gabon, its inhabitants, or their language. —*n.* **2.** an inhabitant or native of Gabon. [GABON + -ESE]

ga·boon (gə bo͞on′, ga-, gä-), *n.* **1.** Also called **gaboon′ mahog′any.** the soft, reddish-brown wood of an African tree, *Aucoumea klaineana,* used for making furniture. **2.** the tree itself. Also called **okoume.** [var. of GABON]

Ga·bo·riau (gᴀ bô ʀyō′), *n.* **É·mile** (ā mēl′), 1835–73, French author of detective stories.

Ga·bri·el (gā′brē əl), *n.* **1.** one of the archangels, appearing usually as a divine messenger. Dan. 8:16, 9:21; Luke, 1:19, 26. **2.** a boy's given name. [< Heb: perh. meaning "God is strong"]

Ga·bri·el (gᴀ bʀē el′), *n.* **Jacques Ange** (zhäk äɴzh), 1698–1782, French architect.

Ga·bri·e·li (gä′bʀē e′lē), *n.* **1. An·dre·a** (än dʀe′ä), 1510–86, Italian organist and composer. **2.** his nephew, **Gio·van·ni** (jô vän′nē), 1557–1612, Italian organist and composer. Also, **Ga·bri·el·li** (gä′bʀē el′lē).

Ga·bri·el·la (gā′brē el′ə, gab′rē-), *n.* a girl's given name. Also, **Ga′bri·el′a, Gabrielle.**

Ga·bri·elle (gā′brē el′, gab′rē-; *Fr.* gᴀ bʀē el′), *n.* a girl's given name. Also, **Gabriella, Gabriela.**

Ga·bri·lo·witsch (gä′bri luv′ich; *Russ.* gä′bʀi lô′vich), *n.* **Os·sip** (ô′sip), 1878–1936, Russian pianist and conductor, in America.

Ga·bun (gə bo͞on′), *n.* Gabon.

ga·by (gā′bē), *n., pl.* **-bies.** *Brit. Slang.* a fool. [?]

Ga·by (gab′ē), *n.* a girl's given name, form of **Gabriella.**

G/A con., *Insurance.* general average contribution.

gad[1] (gad), *v.,* **gad·ded, gad·ding,** *n.* —*v.i.* **1.** to move restlessly or aimlessly from one place to another: *to gad about.* —*n.* **2.** the act of gadding. [ME *gadd(en),* ? back formation from *gadeling* GADLING, in the sense of a wanderer or vagabond; see GATHER] —**gad′der,** *n.* —**gad′ding·ly,** *adv.*

gad[2] (gad), *n., v.,* **gad·ded, gad·ding.** —*n.* **1.** a goad for driving cattle. **2.** a pointed mining tool for breaking up rock, coal, etc. —*v.t.* **3.** to break up or loosen with a mining gad. [ME < Scand; cf. Icel *gaddr* spike; c. Goth *gazds*]

Gad (gad), *interj.* *Informal.* (a euphemistic form of *God,* used as a mild oath.) Also, **gad.**

Gad (gad), *n.* **1.** a son of Zilpah. Gen. 30:11. **2.** one of the twelve tribes of Israel. **3.** a Hebrew prophet and chronicler of the court of David. II Sam. 24:11–19.

gad·a·bout (gad′ə bout′), *n.* a person who moves restlessly or aimlessly about, esp. for curiosity or gossip. [n. use of v. phrase *gad about*]

gad·di (gud′ē), *n.* *Anglo-Indian.* **1.** a hassock. **2.** a throne. **3.** the status of a ruler. Also, **ga′di.** [< Hindi *gaddī*]

Gad·di (gäd′dē), *n.* **Tad·de·o** (täd de′ô), 1300–66, Italian painter and architect.

G/A dep., *Insurance.* general average deposit.

gad·fly (gad′flī′), *n., pl.* **-flies.** **1.** any of various flies, as a stable fly or warble fly, that bite or annoy domestic animals. **2.** a person who repeatedly and persistently annoys others with schemes, ideas, demands, requests, etc. [GAD[2] + FLY[2]]

gadg·et (gaj′it), *n.* a mechanical contrivance or device; any ingenious article. [< ?; cf. F *gâchette* the catch of a lock, sear of a gunlock] —**gadg·et·y** (gaj′i tē), *adj.*

gadg·e·teer (gaj′i tēr′), *n.* one who invents or is particularly fond of using gadgets. [GADGET + -EER]

gadg·et·ry (gaj′i trē), *n.* mechanical or electronic contrivances; gadgets: *the gadgetry of the well-equipped modern kitchen.* [GADGET + -RY]

Ga·dhel·ic (gə del′ik), *adj., n.* Goidelic.

ga·did (gā′did), *adj.* **1.** belonging or pertaining to the cod family, *Gadidae.* —*n.* **2.** a gadid fish. Also, **gadoid.** [< NL *gad(us)* cod (< Gk *gádos* a kind of fish) + -ID[2]]

Gad·ite (gad′īt), *n.* a member of the tribe of Gad. [GAD + -ITE[1]]

gad·ling (gad′ling), *n.* *Armor.* any of a number of embossed or pointed lames covering the finger joints of a gauntlet. [ME; see GAD[2], -LING[1]]

ga·doid (gā′doid), *adj., n.* gadid. [< NL *gad(us)* (see GADID) + -OID]

gad·o·lin·ite (gad′əli nīt′), *n.* a silicate ore from which the rare-earth metals gadolinium, holmium, and rhenium are extracted. [named after J. *Gadolin* (1760–1852), Finnish chemist; see -ITE[1]]

gad·o·lin·i·um (gad′əlin′ē əm), *n. Chem.* a rare-earth metallic element. *Symbol:* Gd; *at. wt.:* 157.25; *at. no.:* 64. [named after J. *Gadolin;* see -IUM] —**gad′o·lin′ic,** *adj.*

ga·droon (gə dro͞on′), *n.* **1.** *Archit.* an elaborately carved or indented convex molding. **2.** a decorative series of curved, inverted flutings, or of convex and concave flutings, as on silversmith's work. Also, **godroon.** [< F *godron,* OF *goderon* < ?] —**ga·drooned′,** *adj.* —**ga·droon′age,** *n.*

ga·droon·ing (gə dro͞o′ning), *n.* ornamentation with gadroons. [GADROON + -ING[1]]

Gads·bod·i·kins (gadz′bod′ə kinz), *interj. Archaic.* (used as a mild oath.) Also, **Odsbodikins, Ods bodkins.** [GAD + -'S[1] + *bodikin* (BODY + -KIN) + -S[1]]

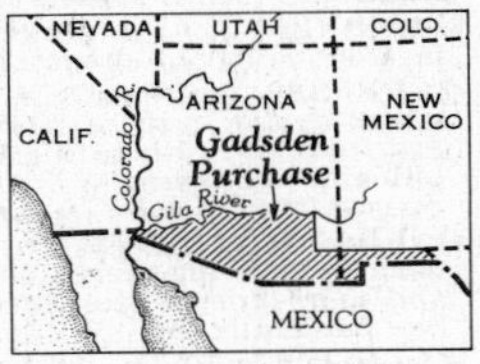

Gads·den (gadz′dən), *n.* **1. James,** 1788–1858, U.S. railroad promoter and diplomat. **2.** a city in NE Alabama. 58,088 (1960).

Gads′den Pur′chase, a tract of 45,535 square miles, now contained in New Mexico and Arizona, purchased for $10,000,000 from Mexico in 1853, the treaty being negotiated by James Gadsden.

Gads·woons (gadz′wo͞onz′), *interj. Archaic.* (used as a mild oath.) [dial. var. of *God's Wounds;* see GAD]

gad·wall (gad′wôl′), *n., pl.* **-walls,** (*esp. collectively*) **-wall.** a grayish-brown wild duck, *Anas strepera,* found in temperate parts of the Northern Hemisphere. [?]

Gad·zooks (gad′zo͞oks′), *interj. Archaic.* (used as a mild oath.) Also, **Odzooks, Odzookers.** [prob. var. of *God's wounds;* see GAD]

Gae·a (jē′ə), *n.* the ancient Greek goddess of the earth, mother of Uranus, Pontus, and the mountains; also mother, with Uranus, of the Titans, Cyclopes, and Hecatonchires; mother of various other beings, including the Erinyes. Also, **Gaia, Ge.** [< Gk *gaîa* earth]

Gaek·war (gīk′wär), *n.* the title of the ruler of the former Indian native state of Baroda. Also, **Gaikwar.** [< Marathi: lit., cowherd]

Gael (gāl), *n.* **1.** a Scottish Celt or Highlander. **2.** a Gaelic-speaking Celt. [< ScotGael *Gaidheal;* akin to OIr *Gaidel, Goidel*]

Gael, Gaelic (def. 1). Also, **Gael.**

Gael·ic (gā′lik), *n.* **1.** a Celtic language that includes the speech of ancient Ireland and the dialects that have developed from it, esp. those usually known as Irish, Manx, and Scots Gaelic. Gaelic constitutes the Goidelic subbranch of Celtic. *Abbr.:* Gael —*adj.* **2.** of or in Gaelic. **3.** of or pertaining to the Gaels or their language. [GAEL + -IC (repr. ScotGael *Gaidhlig,* deriv. of *Gaidheal* GAEL)]

gaff[1] (gaf), *n.* **1.** an iron hook with a handle for landing large fish. **2.** a metal spur for a gamecock. **3.** the spur on a climbing iron, esp. as used by linemen. **4.** *Naut.* a spar rising aft from a mast to support the head of a quadrilateral fore-and-aft sail **(gaff sail):** formed either as a permanently fixed spar **(standing gaff)** or as one secured to the mast by hoops and hoisted with the sail **(hoisting gaff). 5. stand the gaff,** *U.S. Slang.* to weather hardship or strain; endure patiently: *Parents spoil their children outrageously and then wonder why, later on, they can't stand the gaff.* —*v.t.* **6.** to hook or land (a fish) with a gaff. **7.** *Slang.* to cheat; fleece. [< F *gaffe* < Pr *gaf* boat hook]

gaff[2] (gaf), *Brit. Slang.* —*n.* **1.** a place of cheap entertainment or amusement, as a music hall, street fair, or the like. —*v.i.* **2.** to gamble, esp. to indulge in petty gambling, as to toss coins. [?]

gaffe (gaf), *n.* a social blunder; faux pas. [< F *gaffe* blunder, GAFF[1]]

gaf·fer (gaf′ər), *n.* **1.** an old fellow, esp. an elderly rustic. **2.** *Brit.* **a.** a foreman or overseer, esp. the boss of a gang of physical laborers. **b.** *Slang.* father. **3.** *Glassmaking.* a master glassblower responsible for shaping glassware. [contr. of GODFATHER]

gaff′ sail′, *Naut.* See under **gaff**[1] (def. 4). Also called **gaff′-head·ed sail′** (gaf′hed′id).

gaff′ topgal′lant sail′, *Naut.* a jib-headed fore-and-aft sail set above the upper gaff of a spanker mast having a quadrilateral gaff topsail.

gaff′ top′sail, *Naut.* **1.** a jib-headed fore-and-aft sail set above a gaff. **2.** Also called **upper spanker.** a quadrilateral fore-and-aft sail set above the spanker of a bark, between the gaff of the spanker and an upper gaff.

gaff-top′sail cat′fish (gaf′top′sāl′), a sea catfish, *Bagre marinus,* found along the Atlantic and Gulf coasts of the U.S., having the spine of the dorsal fin greatly prolonged and flattened. Also called **sloop rig.**

gag[1] (gag), *v.,* **gagged, gag·ging,** *n.* —*v.t.* **1.** to stop up the mouth of (a person) by putting something in it, thus preventing speech, shouts, etc. **2.** to restrain by force or authority from freedom of speech. **3.** to fasten open the jaws of, as in surgical operations. **4.** to cause to retch or choke. **5.** *Metalworking.* to straighten or bend (a bar, rail, etc.) with a gag. —*v.i.* **6.** to retch or choke. —*n.* **7.** something put into a person's mouth to prevent speech, shouting, etc. **8.** any violent or arbitrary suppression of freedom of speech. **9.** a surgical instrument for holding the jaws open. **10.** *Metalworking.* a shaped block of steel used with a press to straighten or bend a bar, rail, etc. [ME *gagg(en)* (to) suffocate; perh. imit. of the sound made in choking]

gag[2] (gag), *v.,* **gagged, gag·ging,** *n. Informal.* —*v.t.* **1.** to introduce interpolations into (an actor's stage part) (usually fol. by *up*). —*v.i.* **2.** to introduce interpolations or gags in acting. **3.** to play on another's credulity, as by telling false stories. —*n.* **4.** a joke. **5.** an interpolation introduced by an actor into his part. **6.** any contrived piece of wordplay or horseplay. [? special use of GAG[1]; cf. Icel *gagg* yelp]

gag[3] (gag), *n., pl.* (*esp. collectively*) **gag,** (*esp. referring to two or more kinds or species*) **gags. 1.** a serranid game fish, *Mycteroperca microlepsis,* found along the southeastern coast of the U.S. **2.** any of several related fishes. [?]

Gág (gäg), *n.* **Wanda,** 1893–1946, U.S. painter, illustrator, and writer of children's books.

ga·ga (gä′gä′), *adj.* excessively and foolishly enthusiastic: *She goes gaga over the new fashions.* [< F; imit.]

Ga·ga·rin (gä gär′in, gə-; *Russ.* gä gä′rin), *n.* **Yu·ri A·le·kse·ye·vich** (yo͞or′ē; *Russ.* yo͞o′ri ä′le kse′yəvich), 1934–68, Russian astronaut: first human being to make orbital space flight (1961).

gage[1] (gāj), *n., v.,* **gaged, gag·ing.** —*n.* **1.** something, as a glove, thrown down in token of challenge to combat. **2.** a challenge. **3.** a pledge or pawn; security. —*v.t.* **4.** *Archaic.* to pledge, stake, or wager. [ME < MF < Gmc; see WAGE]

gage[2] (gāj), *n., v.t.,* **gaged, gag·ing.** *Chiefly Technical.* gauge. —**gag′er,** *n.*

gage[3] (gāj), *n.* any of several varieties of the plum, *Prunus domestica.* [shortened form of GREENGAGE]

Gage (gāj), *n.* **Thomas,** 1721–87, British general in America 1763–76.

gag·ger[1] (gag′ər), *n.* **1.** one who or that which gags. **2.** an L-shaped rod for reinforcing sand in a foundry mold. [GAG[1] + -ER[1]]

gag·ger[2] (gag′ər), *n.* a person who writes or tells gags. [GAG[2] + -ER[1]]

gag·gle (gag′əl), *v.,* **-gled, -gling,** *n.* —*v.i.* **1.** to cackle. —*n.* **2.** a flock of geese. **3.** a cackle. [imit.]

gag′ law′, 1. any law restricting freedom of the press, free speech, or the right of petition. **2.** See **gag rule.**

gag·man (gag′man′), *n., pl.* **-men.** one who writes comic material for public performers. Also called **gagster.** [GAG[2] + MAN[1]]

gag·root (gag′ro͞ot′, -ro͝ot′), *n.* See **Indian tobacco.** [GAG[1] + ROOT[1]]

gag′ rule′, any rule restricting open discussion or debate concerning a given issue, esp. in a deliberative body.

gag·ster (gag′stər), *n.* **1.** gagman. **2.** *Slang.* one who invents jokes or humorous remarks; joker; comic. [GAG[2] + -STER]

Ga·han·na (gə han′ə), *n.* a town in central Ohio. 2717 (1960).

gahn·ite (gä′nīt), *n.* a dark-green to black mineral of the spinel group, zinc aluminate, $ZnAl_2O_4$. [named after J. G. *Gahn* (1745–1818), Swedish chemist; see -ITE[1]]

Gai·a (gā′ə), *n. Gk. Myth.* Gaea.

gai·e·ty (gā′i tē), *n., pl.* **-ties. 1.** the state of being gay or cheerful; gay spirits. **2.** Often, **gaieties.** merrymaking or festivity: *the gaieties of the New Year season.* **3.** showiness; finery: *gaiety of dress.* Also, **gayety.** [< F *gaieté,* equiv. to *gai* GAY + *-té* -TY[2]]
—**Syn. 1.** merriment, mirth, glee, jollity, joyousness, liveliness, sportiveness, hilarity, vivacity, cheerfulness, joviality. **3.** brilliance, glitter, flashiness, gaudiness. —**Ant. 1.** sadness.

Gaik·war (gīk′wär), *n.* Gaekwar.

Gail (gāl), *n.* a boy's or girl's given name. Also, **Gale, Gayle.**

gail·lard (gal′yərd), *n., adj.* galliard.

Gail·lard′ Cut′ (gil yärd′, gā′lärd), an artificial cutting in the Panama Canal Zone, NW of the city of Panama: excavated for the Panama Canal. 8 mi. long. Formerly, **Culebra Cut.** [named after Col. D. DuB. *Gaillard* (1859–1913), U.S. Army engineer]

gail·lar·di·a (gā lär′dē ə), *n.* any herb of the genus *Gaillardia,* comprising the blanket-flowers. [< NL, named after *Gaillard* de Charentonneau, 18th-century French botanical amateur; see -IA]

gai·ly (gā′lē), *adv.* **1.** with merriment; merrily; cheerfully. **2.** with showiness; showily. Also, **gayly.** [ME; see GAY, -LY]

gain[1] (gān), *v.t.* **1.** to get (something desired), esp. as a result of one's efforts: *to gain possession of an object; to gain permission to enter a country.* **2.** to win; get in competition: *to gain the prize.* **3.** to win (someone) to one's own side or point of view; persuade (often fol. by *over*): *They gained him over early in the contest.* **4.** to acquire as an increase or addition: *to gain weight; to gain speed.* **5.** to obtain as a profit: *He gained ten dollars by this deal.* **6.** to reach by effort; get to; arrive at: *to gain one's destination.* —*v.i.* **7.** to improve; make progress; advance: *to gain in health after an illness.* **8.** to get nearer, as in pursuit (usually fol. by *on* or *upon*): *Our horse was gaining on the favorite at the far turn.* **9.** to draw away from or farther ahead of one's fellow contestants in a race, one's pursuers, etc. (usually fol. by *on* or *upon*). **10. gain time,** to arrange a postponement or delay for a particular purpose, esp. by roundabout means. —*n.* **11.** profit; advantage. **12. gains,** profits; winnings. **13.** an increase or advance. **14.** the act of gaining; acquisition. **15.** an increase in the volume of sound from a radio, phonograph, etc. **16.** the volume control of a radio, phonograph, amplifier, etc. [late ME (n.) < MF, contr. of OF *gaaing,* back formation from *gaaignier* to till, earn, win < Gmc; cf. OHG *weidanōn* to hunt, forage for food] —**gain′a·ble,** *adj.*
—**Syn. 1.** procure, get. GAIN, ATTAIN, EARN, WIN imply obtaining a reward or something advantageous. GAIN carries the least suggestion of method or of effort expended. ATTAIN emphasizes the reaching of a goal. EARN emphasizes the exertions and labor expended which deserve reward. WIN emphasizes attainment in spite of competition or opposition. **6.** attain. **13.** addition, increment, acquisition. —**Ant. 1.** lose.

gain[2] (gān), *Carpentry.* —*n.* **1.** a notch, dado, or mortise cut into a piece of wood, as to receive another piece or to house a flap of a hinge. **2.** tusk (def. 4). **3.** a short or to rabbet, for receiving a flap of a butt hinge. —*v.t.* **4.** to make a gain or gains in. **5.** to fasten or support by means of a gain. [? akin to obs. *gane,* OE (north) *gan(ian)* (to) yawn, open]

gaine (gān), *n.* a small quadrilateral pillar or pilaster tapering inward from top to bottom, as that forming the lower part of a herm. [< F: lit., sheath; see VAGINA]

gain·er (gā′nər), *n.* **1.** one who or that which gains. **2.** See **full gainer.** [GAIN[1] + -ER[1]]

Gaines (gānz), *n.* **Edmund Pendleton,** 1777–1849, U.S. general.

Gaines·ville (gānz′vil), *n.* **1.** a city in N Florida. 27,701 (1960). **2.** a city in N Georgia. 16,523 (1960).

gain·ful (gān′fəl), *adj.* profitable; lucrative: *gainful employment.* [GAIN[1] + -FUL] —**gain′ful·ly,** *adv.* —**gain′ful·ness,** *n.*

gain·less (gān′lis), *adj.* unprofitable; profitless; unavailing. [GAIN[1] + -LESS] —**gain′less·ness,** *n.*

gain·ly (gān′lē), *adj. Chiefly Dial.* agile; handsome. [*gain,* obs. adj. (see AGAIN) + -LY] —**gain′li·ness,** *n.*

gain·say (gān′sā′), *v.,* **-said, -say·ing,** *n.* —*v.t.* **1.** to deny. **2.** to speak or act against. —*n.* **3.** the act or possibility of gainsaying; contradiction; denial: *Beyond gainsay it is a genuine Rembrandt.* [ME *gainsaie(n)* again, say[1]] —**gain′say′er,** *n.*
—**Syn. 2.** dispute, controvert, contradict.

Gains·bor·ough (gānz′bûr′ō, -bur′ō; *Brit.* gānz′bər ə), *n.* **Thomas,** 1727–88, English painter.

'gainst (genst *or, esp. Brit.,* gānst), *prep., conj.* against. Also, **gainst.**

Gai·ser·ic (gī′zə rik), *n.* Genseric.

gait (gāt), *n.* **1.** a manner of walking, stepping, or running. **2.** any of the manners in which a horse moves, as a walk, trot, canter, gallop, single-foot, etc. —*v.t.* **3.** to teach a specified gait or gaits to (a horse). [Scot, ME sp. var. of GATE[1] in various senses]

gait·ed (gā′tid), *adj.* having a specified gait (usually used in combination): *slow-gaited; heavy-gaited oxen.* [GAIT + -ED[3]]

gait·er (gā′tər), *n.* **1.** a covering of cloth or leather for the ankle and instep and sometimes also the lower leg, worn over the shoe or boot. Cf. **upper** (def. 8). **2.** a cloth or leather shoe with elastic insertions at the sides. [< F *guêtre,* MF *guiestre, guestre,* perh. < Frankish **wrist* ankle; see WRIST] —**gai′ter·less,** *adj.*

Gai·thers·burg (gā′thərz bûrg′), *n.* a town in central Maryland. 3847 (1960).

Gait·skell (gāt′skəl), *n.* **Hugh Todd Nay·lor** (tod nā′lər), 1906–63, English economist and statesman: Labour party leader 1955–63.

Ga·ius (gā′əs), *n.* **1.** Also, **Caius.** A.D. c110–c180, Roman jurist and writer: esp. on civil law. **2.** Caius (def. 1).

gal[1] (gal), *n. Informal.* a girl or woman. [orig. vulgar or dial. pronunciation]

gal[2] (gal), *n.* a centimeter-gram-second unit of acceleration, equal to one centimeter per second per second. [named after GALILEO]

gal, gallon; gallons.

Gal., Galatians.

ga·la (gā′lə, gal′ə; *esp. Brit.* gä′lə), *adj.* **1.** festive; festal; showy: *His birthday parties were always gala occasions.* —*n.* **2.** a celebration; festive occasion; special entertainment: *a gala featuring opera stars in their most famous scenes.* **3.** festal pomp or dress. [< F < It < OF; see GALLANT]

galact-, var. of **galacto-** before a vowel: *galactagogue.*

ga·lac·ta·gogue (gə lak′tə gôg′, -gog′), *adj.* **1.** increasing the amount of milk collected, either with or without increasing the amount secreted. —*n.* **2.** a galactagogue agent or medicine. [GALACT- + -AGOGUE]

ga·lac·tan (gə lak′tən, -tan), *n. Biochem.* any of the class of hexosans, as agar, that yield galactose upon hydrolysis. Also, **galactosan.** [GALACT- + -AN]

ga·lac·tic (gə lak′tik), *adj.* **1.** *Astron.* pertaining to a galaxy or to the Milky Way. **2.** *Physiol.* pertaining to or stimulating the secretion of milk. [< Gk *galaktik(ós)* milky. See GALACT-, -IC]

galac′tic cir′cle, *Astron.* See **galactic equator.**

galac′tic coor′dinates, *Astron.* a system of coordinates utilizing galactic latitude and galactic longitude to define the position of a celestial body with reference to the Milky Way.

galac′tic equa′tor, *Astron.* the great circle on the celestial sphere that is equidistant from the galactic poles, being inclined approximately 62° to the celestial equator and lying about one degree north of the center line of the Milky Way. Also called **galactic circle.**

galac′tic lat′itude, *Astron.* the angular distance from the galactic equator of a point on the celestial sphere.

galac′tic lon′gitude, *Astron.* the arc on the galactic equator measured eastward from the direction of the galactic equator in Scarpius to the foot of the great circle passing through the galactic poles and a given point on the celestial sphere.

galac′tic plane′, *Astron.* the plane of the galactic equator.

galac′tic poles′, *Astron.* the two opposite points on the celestial sphere that are farthest north and south of the Milky Way.

ga·lac·tin (gə lak′tin), *n. Biochem.* luteotropin. [GALACT- + -IN[2]]

ga·lac·tite (gə lak′tīt), *n.* a rare mineral, a variety of natrolite occurring in colorless, pointed crystals. [< MF < L *galactīt(ēs)* < Gk *galaktítēs* (*líthos*) (stone) that makes water milky. See GALACT-, -ITE[1]]

galacto-, a learned borrowing from Greek meaning "milk," used in the formation of compound words: *galactopoietic.* Also, *esp. before a vowel,* **galact-.** [< Gk *galakto-,* comb. form of *galakt-,* s. of *gála* milk]

ga·lac·toid (gə lak′toid), *adj.* resembling milk; milky. [GALACT- + -OID]

gal·ac·tom·e·ter (gal′ək tom′i tər), *n.* a lactometer. [GALACTO- + -METER] —**gal′ac·tom′e·try,** *n.*

ga·lac·to·phore (gə lak′tə fôr′, -fōr′), *n. Anat.* a galactophorous duct. [GALACTO- + -PHORE]

gal·ac·toph·or·ous (gal′ək tof′ər əs), *adj. Anat.* bearing milk; lactiferous. [< Gk *galaktophóros.* See GALACTO-, -PHOROUS]

ga·lac·to·poi·et·ic (gə lak′tə poi et′ik), *adj.* **1.** increasing the secretion of milk. —*n.* **2.** a galactopoietic agent or medicine. [GALACTO- + -POIETIC] —**ga·lac·to·poi·e·sis** (gə lak′tə poi ē′sis), *n.*

ga·lac·to·san (gə lak′tə san′, -sən), *n.* galactan. [GALACTOSE + -AN]

ga·lac·to·scope (gə lak′tə skōp′), *n.* a lactoscope. [GALACTO- + -SCOPE]

ga·lac·tose (gə lak′tōs), *n. Chem.* a white, crystalline, water-soluble hexose sugar, $C_6H_{12}O_6$, obtained in its dextrorotatory form from milk sugar by hydrolysis, and in its levorotatory form from mucilages. [GALACT- + -OSE[2]]

ga·lah (gə lä′), *n.* an Australian cockatoo, *Kakatoe roseicapilla,* having rose-colored underparts. [< native Austral name]

Gal·a·had (gal′ə had′), *n.* **1. Sir,** *Arthurian Romance.* the noblest and purest knight of the Round Table, son of Lancelot and Elaine: fated to retrieve the Holy Grail. **2.** a man characterized by uncompromising devotion to the highest ideals. **3.** a boy's given name.

ga·lan·gal (gə lang′gəl), *n.* the aromatic, medicinal rhizome of certain plants of the ginger family, esp. *Alpine officinarum,* of China and the East Indies. [var. of GALINGALE]

gal·an·tine (gal′ən tēn′, gal′ən tēn′), *n.* a dish of boned meat or fish, stuffed with forcemeat, cooked in gelatin stock, pressed, and served cold with aspic or its own jelly. Also, **galatine.** [ME < OF *galentine, gala(n)tine* fish sauce < ML *galatina,* prob. equiv. to *gelāt(us)* (ptp. of *gelāre* to freeze, congeal) + *-ina* -INE[2]]

ga·lan′ty show′ (gə lan′tē), (in 19th-century England) a shadow play in pantomime. [? < It *galanti* (pl.) < MF *galant.* See GALLANT]

Ga·lá′pa·gos Is′lands (gə lä′pə gōs′; *Sp.* gä lä′pä gôs′), an archipelago on the equator in the Pacific, ab. 600 mi. W of and belonging to Ecuador: many unique species of animal life. 1817 (est. 1959); 3029 sq. mi. Also called **Colón Archipelago.** Spanish, **Archipiélago de Colón.**

Ga·la·ta (gä′lä tä), *n.* **1.** the chief commercial section of Istanbul, Turkey. **2.** *Class. Myth.* the ancestress of the Gallic race by her union with Hercules.

gal·a·te·a (gal′ə tē′ə), *n.* a strong cotton fabric, plain or striped, for clothing. [named after the 19th-century British man-of-war H.M.S. *Galatea;* the fabric was once used for children's sailor suits]

Gal·a·te·a (gal′ə tē′ə), *n.* *Class. Myth.* **1.** a sea nymph courted in vain by Polyphemus, who killed her sweetheart, Acis, in jealousy. **2.** a maiden who had been an ivory statue carved by Pygmalion and who was brought to life by Aphrodite in response to the prayers of the sculptor, who had fallen in love with his work. **3.** a girl's given name.

Ga·la·tia (gə lā′shə, -shē ə), *n.* an ancient country in central Asia Minor: later a Roman province; site of early Christian community.

Ga·la·tians (gə lā′shənz), *n.* (*construed as sing.*) a book in the New Testament, written to the Christians in Galatia. [GALATI(A) + -AN + -S[3]]

gal·a·tine (gal′ə tēn′, gal′ə tēn′), *n.* galantine.

Ga·latz (gä′läts), *n.* a port in E Rumania, on the Danube River. 101,878 (est. 1959). Also, **Ga·la·ti** (gä läts′, -lä′tsē).

gal·a·vant (gal′ə vant′), *v.i.* gallivant.

ga·lax (gā′laks), *n.* an evergreen herb, *Galax aphylla,* of the southeastern U.S., having small white flowers. [< NL < Gk *gála* milk + L *-x* n. suffix]

Ga·lax (gā′laks), *n.* a town in SW Virginia. 5254 (1960).

gal·ax·y (gal′ək sē), *n., pl.* **-ax·ies.** **1.** *Astron.* **a.** a large system of stars held together by mutual gravitation and isolated from similar systems by vast regions of space. **b.** (*usually cap.*) See **Milky Way.** **2.** any large and brilliant assemblage of persons or things. [ME *galaxie, galaxias* < ML *galaxia,* var. of L *galaxias* milk-stone, Milky Way < Gk; see GALACT-]

Gal·ba (gal′bə), *n.* **Ser·vi·us Sul·pi·cius** (sûr′vē əs sul pish′əs), 5? B.C.–A.D. 69, Roman emperor A.D. 68–69.

gal·ba·num (gal′bə nəm), *n.* a gum resin with a peculiar, disagreeable odor, obtained from certain Asian plants of the apiaceous genus *Ferula,* used in medicine and the arts. [ME < L; c. Gk *chalbánē,* Heb *chelbenāh*]

Gal·braith (gal′brāth), *n.* **J(ohn) Kenneth,** born 1908, U.S. economist and diplomat, born in Canada.

Gal·cha (gal′chä), *n., pl.* **-chas,** (*esp. collectively*) **-cha.** a member of an Iranian people inhabiting the Pamirs. —**Gal′chic,** *adj.*

gale[1] (gāl), *n.* **1.** a strong wind. **2.** a wind of 32–63 miles per hour. **3.** a noisy outburst: *a gale of laughter.* **4.** *Archaic.* a gentle breeze. [? < Dan *gal* furious or Norw *geil* (< G *geil* rank, exuberant); c. OE *gāl* gay, wanton]

gale[2] (gāl), *n.* See **sweet gale.** [ME *gail,* OE *gagel;* c. G *Gagel*]

gale[3] (gāl), *n.* *Brit.* a periodic payment of rent. [? contr. of GAVEL; cf. GAVELKIND]

Gale (gāl), *n.* **1. Zo·na** (zō′nə), 1874–1938, U.S. novelist, short-story writer, playwright, and poet. **2.** Also, **Gail, Gayle.** a boy's or girl's given name.

ga·le·a (gā′lē ə), *n., pl.* **-le·ae** (-lē ē′). **1.** *Bot.* any part of the calyx or corolla in the form of a helmet, as the upper lip of the corolla of the monkshood. **2.** *Anat.* any of several helmet-shaped structures. **3.** a type of bandage for the head. [< L: helmet]

gal·e·as (gal′ē as′, -ē əs), *n.* *Naut.* **1.** Also, **galeass.** a sailing vessel used for trading and fishing along the Baltic and Norwegian coasts, generally ketch-rigged, sometimes with a square foresail set flying. **2.** galleass. [var. of GALLEASS]

gal·e·ass (gal′ē as′, -ē əs), *n.* *Naut.* **1.** galeas (def. 1). **2.** galleass.

ga·le·ate (gā′lē āt′), *adj.* *Bot.* having a galea. Also, **ga′le·at′ed.** [< L *galeāt(us)* covered with a helmet (ptp. of *galeāre*), equiv. to *gale(a)* helmet + *-ātus* -ATE[1]]

ga·lee·ny (gə lē′nē), *n., pl.* **-nies.** *Brit. Dial.* a guinea fowl. [< Sp *gallin(a)* (*morisca*), lit., Moorish hen < L *gallina* hen (*gall(us)* cock + *-ina* -INE[1]) + -Y[2]]

ga·le·i·form (gə lē′ə fôrm′), *adj.* helmet-shaped; resembling a galea. [< L *gale-* (s. of *galea*) helmet + -I- + -FORM]

Ga·len (gā′lən), *n.* **1.** Latin, **Ga·le·nus** (gə lē′nəs). **Claudius,** A.D. c130–c200, Greek physician and writer on medicine. **2.** any physician.

ga·le·na (gə lē′nə), *n.* a common, heavy mineral, lead sulfide, PbS, occurring in lead-gray crystals, usually cubes, and cleavable masses: the principal ore of lead. Also called **galenite.** [< L: lead ore]

Ga·le·na (gə lē′nə), *n.* **1.** a town in NW Illinois. 4410 (1960). **2.** a town in SE Kansas. 3827 (1960).

ga·len·ic (gə len′ik, -lē′nik), *adj.* of, pertaining to, or containing galena. [GALEN(A) + -IC]

Ga·len·ic (gā len′ik, gə-), *adj.* **1.** of or pertaining to Galen, his principles, or his methods. **2.** (*usually l.c.*) of or pertaining to galenicals or Galenic pharmacy. [GALEN + -IC]

ga·len·i·cal (gā len′ə kəl, gə-), *n.* *Pharm.* **1.** an herb or other vegetable drug, distinguished from a mineral or chemical drug. **2.** a crude drug, tincture, or decoction, distinguished from a preparation that has been refined. —*adj.* **3.** galenic. **4.** (*cap.*) Galenic (def. 1). **5.** Galenic (def. 2). [GALENIC + -AL[1]]

Galen′ic phar′macy, the art or practice of preparing and dispensing galenicals.

Ga·len·ism (gā′lə niz′əm), *n.* the medical system or principles of Galen. [GALEN + -ISM] —**Ga′len·ist,** *n.*

ga·le·nite (gə lē′nīt), *n.* galena. [< G *Galenit* < L *galen(a)* GALENA + G *-it* -ITE[1]]

Gales·burg (gālz′bûrg), *n.* a city in NW Illinois. 37,243 (1960).

gal·et (gal′it), *n., v.t.* gallet.

Ga·le·us (gā′lē əs), *n.* *Class. Myth.* a lizard who was the son of Apollo.

gal′ Fri′day. See **girl Friday.**

Gal·gal (gal′gal), *n.* *Douay Bible.* Gilgal.

Ga·li·bi (gä lē′bē), *n., pl.* **-bis,** (*esp. collectively*) **-bi.** a member of an Indian people of French Guiana. [< Carib; see CANNIBAL]

Ga·li·ci·a (gə lish′ē ə, -lish′ə; *for 2 also Sp.* gä lē′thyä), *n.* **1.** a former crown land of Austria, included in S Poland after World War I, and now partly in the Soviet Union. ab. 30,500 sq. mi. **2.** a maritime region in NW Spain: a former kingdom, and later a province. 11,256 sq. mi. —**Ga·li′cian,** *adj., n.*

Gal·i·le·an (gal′ə lē′ən), *adj.* **1.** of or pertaining to Galilee. —*n.* **2.** a native or inhabitant of Galilee. **3.** *Rare.* a Christian. **4. the Galilean,** Jesus. [< L *Galilae(a)* GALILEE + -AN]

Gal·i·le·an (gal′ə lē′ən), *adj.* of or pertaining to Galileo, his theories, or his discoveries. [GALILE(O) + -AN]

Gal′ile′an sat′ellites, *Astron.* the four largest and brightest satellites of Jupiter: Io, Europa, Ganymede, and Callisto, discovered by Galileo in 1610.

Gal′ile′an tel′escope, a refracting telescope that forms an erect image, consisting of an objective of relatively long focal length that causes light rays to converge and an eyepiece of short focal length that causes them to diverge.

Galile′an transforma′tion, *Physics.* one of a series of equations in classical mechanics that relate position and time in two frames of reference that are moving uniformly with respect to each other. Cf. **Lorentz transformation.**

gal·i·lee (gal′ə lē′), *n.* a porch or vestibule, often on the ground floor of a tower, at the entrance of some English churches. [< ML *galilaea* porch of a church, L *Galilaea* GALILEE; perh. alluding to Galilee as an outlying portion of the Holy Land]

Gal·i·lee (gal′ə lē′), *n.* **1.** an ancient Roman province in what is now N Israel. **2. Sea of.** Also called **Sea of Tiberias.** a lake in NE Israel through which the Jordan River flows. 14 mi. long; 682 ft. below sea level.

Gal·i·le·o (gal′ə lē′ō, -lā′ō; *It.* gä′lē le′ô), *n.* (*Galileo Galilei*) 1564–1642, Italian physicist and astronomer.

gal·i·ma·ti·as (gal′ə mā′shē əs, -mat′ē əs), *n.* confused or unintelligible talk; gibberish. [< F < ?; perh. a student coinage, ending in Gk *amathía* ignorance]

gal·in·gale (gal′in gāl′), *n.* any sedge of the genus *Cyperus,* esp. *C. longus,* of England, having aromatic roots. [ME *galingale* < MF *galingal, garingal* < Ar *khalanjān*]

Ga·lin·thi·as (gə lin′thē əs), *n.* *Class. Myth.* a handmaid of Alcmene.

gal·i·ot (gal′ē ət), *n.* **1.** a small galley propelled by both sails and oars. **2.** a small, ketchlike sailing vessel used for trade along the coast of Germany and nearby countries. Also, **galliot.** [ME *galiote* < MF < ML *galeota,* dim. of *galea* GALLEY]

gal·i·pot (gal′ə pot′), *n.* a type of turpentine exuded on the stems of certain species of pine. Also, **gallipot.** [< F *galipot, galipo,*? < OF *garipot* a species of pine tree]

gall[1] (gôl), *n.* **1.** something bitter or severe. **2.** bitterness of spirit; rancor. **3.** bile, esp. that of the ox. **4.** impudence; effrontery. **5. gall and wormwood,** bitterness of spirit; deep resentment. [ME; OE *galla;* r. OE *gealla;* c. G *Galle;* akin to L *fel,* Gk *cholḗ* gall, bile]

gall[2] (gôl), *v.t.* **1.** to make sore by rubbing; chafe severely: *The saddle galled the horse's back.* **2.** to vex; irritate: *Discourtesy galls me.* —*v.i.* **3.** to be or become chafed. **4.** *Mach.* (of either of two engaging metal parts) to lose metal to the other because of heat or molecular attraction resulting from friction. **5.** *Metall.* (of a die or compact in powder metallurgy) to lose surface material through adhesion to the die. —*n.* **6.** a sore on the skin, esp. of a horse, due to rubbing; excoriation. **7.** something vexing or irritating. **8.** a state of irritation. [ME *galle,* (n.), *gallen* (v.) gall, sore < LL *galla* tumor, L: gall-nut, oak-apple]

gall[3] (gôl), *n.* any abnormal vegetable growth or excrescence on plants, caused by various agents, as insects, nematodes, fungi, bacteria, viruses, chemicals, and mechanical injuries. [ME *galle* < MF < L *galla* gall-nut. See GALL[2]]

Gal·la (gal′ə), *n., pl.* **-las,** (*esp. collectively*) **-la.** **1.** a member of a nomadic, pastoral people of Ethiopia and Kenya. **2.** the language of the Galla, a Cushitic language of the Afro-Asian family.

gal·lant (*adj.* gal′ənt *for 1–3;* gə lant′, -länt′, gal′ənt *for 4, 5; n.* gə lant′, -länt′, gal′ənt; *v.* gə lant′, -länt′), *adj.* **1.** brave, high-spirited, or chivalrous: *a gallant knight.* **2.** stately; grand: *a gallant pageant.* **3.** gay or showy, as in dress; magnificent. **4.** polite and attentive to women; courtly. **5.** amorous; amatory. —*n.* **6.** a brave, high-spirited, or chivalrous man. **7.** a gay and dashing man. **8.** a man particularly attentive to women. **9.** a suitor or lover. **10.** a paramour. —*v.t.* **11.** to court or act as a lover of (a woman). **12.** to escort (a woman). —*v.i.* **13.** to attend or pay court as a gallant. [ME *gala(u)nt* < OF *galant,* prp. of *galer* to amuse oneself, make merry, perh. < Gmc; cf. OHG *wallan,* OE *weallan* to seethe, rage] —**gal′lant·ly,** *adv.* —**gal′lant·ness,** *n.*
—**Syn. 1.** valorous, courageous, heroic, bold, daring, intrepid. See **brave. 4.** chivalrous, courteous. —**Ant. 1.** cowardly. **4.** impolite.

gal·lant·ry (gal′ən trē), *n., pl.* **-ries.** **1.** dashing courage; heroic bravery. **2.** gallant or courtly attention to women. **3.** a gallant act, action, or speech. [< MF *galanterie,* equiv. to OF *galant* (see GALLANT) + *-erie* -RY]
—**Syn. 1.** bravery, valor, heroism. **2.** chivalry, courtliness. —**Ant. 1.** cowardice. **2.** rudeness.

gal·late (gal′āt, gô′lāt), *n.* *Chem.* a salt or ester of gallic acid. [GALL[3] + -ATE[1]]

Gal·la·tin (gal′ə tin), *n.* **1. Albert,** 1761–1849, U.S. statesman: Secretary of the Treasury 1801–13. **2.** a town in N Tennessee. 7901 (1960).

Gal·lau·det (gal′ə det′), *n.* **Thomas Hopkins,** 1787–1851, U.S. educator and writer.

gall·ber·ry (gôl′ber′ē, -bə rē), *n., pl.* **-ries.** the inkberry, *Ilex glabra,* or its berry. [GALL[3] + BERRY]

gall′ blad′der, *Anat.* a vesicle attached to the under surface of the right lobe of the liver, which stores and concentrates the bile.

Galle (gäl), *n.* a seaport in SW Ceylon. 55,874 (1953).

Gal·le (gä′lə), *n.* a crater in the first quadrant of the face of the moon: about 13 miles in diameter.

gal·le·ass (gal′ē as′), *n.* *Naut.* a fighting galley, lateen-rigged on three masts, used in the Mediterranean Sea from the 15th to the 18th centuries. Also, **galeas, galeass, galliass.** [< OF *galleasse, galiace* < OIt *galeazza,* aug. of *galea* GALLEY]

Gal·le·gos (gä ye′gôs), *n.* **1. Ró·mu·lo** (rô′mo͞o lô′), born 1884, Venezuelan educator, statesman, novelist, and short-story writer: president of Venezuela 1948. **2.** See **Río Gallegos.**

gal·le·on (gal′ē ən, gal′yən), *n.* a large sailing vessel of the 15th to the 19th centuries used as a fighting or merchant ship, square-rigged on the foremast and mainmast and generally lateen-rigged on one or two after masts. [< Sp *galeón,* aug. of *galea* GALLEY]

Galleon

gal·ler·y (gal′ə rē, gal′rē), *n., pl.* **-ler·ies.** **1.** a long covered area, narrow and open at one or both sides, used esp. as a walk or corridor. **2.** a long porch or portico; veranda. **3.** a long, relatively narrow room, esp. one for public use. **4.** a corridor, esp. one having architectural importance through its scale or decorative treatment. **5.** a raised, balconylike platform or passageway running along the exterior wall of a building inside or outside. **6.** a raised area, often having a stepped or sloping floor, constructed in a theater, church, or other public building to accommodate spectators, exhibits, etc. **7.** the uppermost of such areas in a theater, usually containing the cheapest seats. **8.** the occupants of such an area in a theater. **9.** the general public, esp. when regarded as having popular or uncultivated tastes. **10.** *Theat.* a narrow, raised platform located beyond the acting area, used by stagehands or technicians to stand on when working. **11.** any group of spectators or observers, as at a golf match, a Congressional session, etc. **12.** a room, series of rooms, or building devoted to the exhibition and often the sale of works of art. **13.** a collection of art for exhibition. **14.** a large room or building used for photography, target practice, or other special purposes. **15.** *Naut.* a projecting balcony or structure on the quarter or stern of a vessel. Cf. **quarter gallery, stern gallery.** **16.** *Furniture.* an ornamental railing or cresting surrounding the top of a table, stand, desk, etc. **17.** *Mining.* a level or drift. **18.** a small tunnel in a dam, mine, or rock, for various purposes, as inspection or drainage. **19.** *Jewelry.* a bezel stamped as a continuous strip. **20.** *Obs.* a passageway made by an animal. **21.** *Fort. Obs.* an underground or covered passage to another part of a fortified position. **22. play to the gallery,** to attempt to appeal to the popular taste, as opposed to a more refined or esoteric taste: *Motion pictures, though still playing mainly to the gallery, have taken their place as a significant art form.* [ME < OF *galerie* < ML *galeria* (? alter. of *galilea, galilaea;* see GALILEE)] —**gal′ler·ied,** *adj.* —**gal′ler·y·like′,** *adj.*

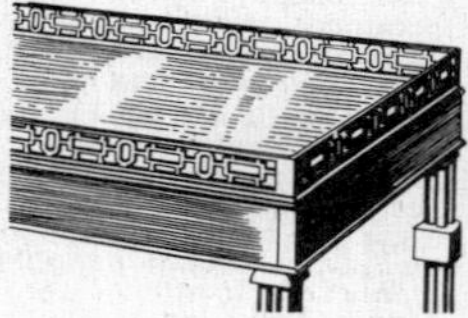

Gallery (def. 16)

gal·ler·y·ite (gal′ə rē it′), *n.* a spectator in a theater gallery. [GALLERY + -ITE[1]]

gal·let (gal′it), *n.* **1.** spall (def. 1). —*v.t.* **2.** *Masonry.* to fill (a mortar joint) with gallets; garret. Also, **galet.** [< F *galet* pebble; OF, dim. of *gall;* cf. OIr *gall* stone pillar]

gal·let·ing (gal′i ting), *n.* *Masonry.* a number of spalls for filling mortar joints. [GALET + -ING[1]]

gal·ley (gal′ē), *n., pl.* **-leys.** **1.** *Naut.* **a.** a seagoing vessel propelled mainly by oars, sometimes with the aid of sails. **b.** a long rowboat, as one used as a ship's boat by a warship or one used for dragging a seine. **c.** a kitchen aboard a vessel. **d.** (formerly, in the U.S. Navy) a shoal-draft vessel, variously rigged, relying mainly on its sails but able to be rowed by sweeps. **2.** *Print.* **a.** a long, narrow tray, usually of metal, for holding type which has been set. **b.** See **galley proof. c.** a rough unit of measurement for type composition (about 22 inches). [ME *galei(e)* < OF *galee, galie,* ? < OPr *galea* < LGk *galéa, galaía*] **—gal′ley·like′,** *adj.*

Galley

gal′ley proof′, *Print.* proof from type on a galley.
gal′ley slave′, **1.** a person condemned to work at an oar on a galley. **2.** an overworked person; drudge: *Factory workers are no longer mere galley slaves.*
gal·ley-west (gal′ē west′), *adv. U.S. Informal.* unquestionably out of action; into unconsciousness: *He knocked his opponent galley-west.* [alter. of Brit. dial. *collywest*]
gall·fly (gôl′flī′), *n., pl.* **-flies.** any of various insects that deposit their eggs in plants, causing the formation of galls. [GALL[3] + FLY[2]]
gall′ gnat′. See **gall midge.**
Gal·li·a (gal′ē ä), *n.* Latin name of **Gaul.**
gal·liard (gal′yərd), *n.* **1.** a spirited dance for two dancers in triple rhythm, common in the 16th and 17th centuries. **—***adj.* **2.** *Archaic.* lively or gay. Also, **gaillard.** [ME *gaillard* < OF *gaillard, gaillart* < ?] **—gal′liard·ly,** *adv.*
gal·liard·ise (gal′yər dēz′, -dīz′), *n. Archaic.* **1.** merrymaking; revelry. **2.** an instance of merriment; revel. [< F; OF *gaillard* (see GALLIARD) + *-ise* n. suffix]
gal·li·ass (gal′ē as′), *n.* galleass.
gal·lic[1] (gal′ik), *adj. Chem.* of or containing gallium, esp. in the trivalent state. [GALL(IUM) + -IC]
gal·lic[2] (gal′ik, gô′lik), *adj.* pertaining to or derived from plant galls: *gallic acid.* [GALL[3] + -IC]
Gal·lic (gal′ik), *adj.* **1.** pertaining to the Gauls or Gaul. **2.** pertaining to the French or France. [< L *Gallic(us),* equiv. to *Gall(us)* a GAUL + *-icus* -IC] **—Gal′li·cal·ly,** *adv.*
gal′lic ac′id, *Chem.* a white or yellowish, crystalline, sparingly water-soluble solid, $C_6H_2(OH)_3COOH$, obtained from nutgalls, used chiefly in tanning and in ink dyes. [< F *acide gallique*]
Gal·li·can (gal′i kən), *adj.* **1.** Gallic; French. **2.** *Eccles.* **a.** of or pertaining to the Roman Catholic Church in France. **b.** of or pertaining to a school or party of French Roman Catholics, before 1870, advocating restricting papal authority in favor of the authority of general councils, the bishops, and temporal rulers. [< L *Gallicān(us)* belonging to Gallia, Gallican, equiv. to *Gallic-* GALLIC + *-ānus* -AN]
Gal·li·can·ism (gal′i kə niz′əm), *n.* the body of doctrines, chiefly associated with the Gallican church, advocating the restriction of papal authority in certain matters. Cf. **ultramontanism.** [< F; see GALLICAN, -ISM]
Gal′lican lib′erties, the liberties enjoyed by the Gallican church in being largely under the control of local spiritual and temporal authorities.
Gal·li·ce (gal′i sē), *adv.* in French. [< ML: in Gallic, equiv. to L *Gallic(us)* GALLIC + *-e* adv. suffix]
Gal·li·cise (gal′i sīz′), *v.t., v.i.,* **-cised, -cis·ing.** *Chiefly Brit.* Gallicize. **—Gal′li·ci·sa′tion,** *n.* **—Gal′li·cis′er,** *n.*
Gal·li·cism (gal′i siz′əm), *n.* **1.** a French linguistic peculiarity. **2.** a French idiom or expression used in another language, as *Je ne sais quoi* when used in English. Also, **gal′li·cism.** [< F *gallicisme.* See GALLIC, -ISM]
Gal·li·cize (gal′i sīz′), *v.t., v.i.,* **-cized, -ciz·ing.** to make or become French in language, character, etc. Also, **gal′li·cize′;** *esp. Brit.,* **Gallicise.** [< L *Gallic(us)* GALLIC + -IZE] **—Gal′li·ci·za′tion,** *n.* **—Gal′li·ciz′er,** *n.*
Gal·li·co (gal′ə kō′), *n.* **Paul William,** born 1897, U.S. journalist and short-story writer.
Gal·li-Cur·ci (gal′i kûr′chē; *It.* gäl′lē ko͞or′chē), *n.* **A·me·li·ta** (ä′me lē′tä), 1889–1964, Italian soprano in the U.S.
Gal·li·e·nus (gal′ē ē′nəs), *n.* (*Publius Licinius Egnatius*) died A.D. 268, emperor of Rome 253–268 (son of Valerian).
gal·li·gas·kins (gal′ə gas′kinz), *n.* (*construed as pl.*) **1.** loose hose or breeches worn in the 16th and 17th centuries. **2.** loose breeches in general. **3.** leggings or gaiters of leather. [appar. alter. of F *garguesque,* metathetic var. of *greguesque* < It *grechesa,* abstracted from *alla grechesa* in the Greek manner]
gal·li·mau·fry (gal′ə mô′frē), *n., pl.* **-fries. 1.** a hodgepodge; jumble; confused medley. **2.** a ragout or hash. [< MF *galimafree* < ?]
gal·li·na·cean (gal′ə nā′shən), *n.* a gallinaceous bird. [< NL *Gallināce(ae)* name of a group (fem. pl. of L *gallināceus* (adj.) GALLINACEOUS) + -AN]
gal·li·na·ceous (gal′ə nā′shəs), *adj.* **1.** pertaining to or resembling the domestic fowls. **2.** belonging or pertaining to the order *Galliformes,* comprising the grouse, pheasants, turkeys, partridges, domestic fowls, etc. [< L *gallināceus* pertaining to poultry, equiv. to *gallīn(a)* hen (deriv. of *gallus* cock) + *-aceus* -ACEOUS]
Gal·li·nas (gä yē′näs), *n.* **Pun·ta** (po͞on′tä), a cape in NE Colombia: northernmost point of South America.

gall·ing (gô′liṅg), *adj.* that galls; chafing; irritating; exasperating. [GALL[2] + -ING[2]] **—gall′ing·ly,** *adv.* **—gall′ing·ness,** *n.*
gal·li·nip·per (gal′ə nip′ər), *n. Informal.* any of various insects that sting or bite, esp. a large American mosquito, *Psorophora ciliata.* [?]
gal·li·nule (gal′ə no͞ol′, -nyo͞ol′), *n.* any of several aquatic birds of the family *Rallidae,* having elongated, webless toes. [< NL *Gallinul-* (s. of *Gallīnula*) name of the genus, LL *gallīnula* chicken, equiv. to L *gallīn(a)* hen + *-ula* -ULE]
gal·li·ot (gal′ē ət), *n.* galiot.
Gal·lip·o·li Penin′sula (gə lip′ə lē), a peninsula in European Turkey, between the Dardanelles and the Aegean Sea. 60 mi. long.

BULGARIA
BLACK SEA
TURKEY (EUROPE)
Istanbul
GREECE
SEA OF MARMARA
AEGEAN SEA
Gallipoli Peninsula
TURKEY (ASIA)

Gal·li·po·lis (gal′ə pə lēs′), *n.* a town in S Ohio. 8775 (1960).
gal·li·pot[1] (gal′ə pot′), *n.* a small glazed pot used by apothecaries for medicines, confections, or the like. [ME *galy pott.* See GALLEY, POT[1]]
gal·li·pot[2] (gal′ə pot′), *n.* galipot.
Gal·li·tzin (gə lit′sən), *n.* a town in central Pennsylvania. 2783 (1960).
gal·li·um (gal′ē əm), *n. Chem.* a rare, steel-gray, trivalent metallic element used in high temperature thermometers because of its high boiling point (1983°C) and low melting point (30°C). *Symbol:* Ga; *at. wt.:* 69.72; *at. no.:* 31; *sp. gr.:* 5.91 at 20°C. [< NL < L *gall(us)* cock (trans. of F *coq,* from *Lecoq* de Boisbaudran, 19th-century French chemist) + *-ium* -IUM]
gal·li·vant (gal′ə vant′), *v.i.* **1.** to gad about gaily or frivolously. **2.** to act as a gallant. Also, **galavant.** [? fanciful alter. of GALLANT] **—gal′li·vant′er,** *n.*
gal·li·wasp (gal′ə wosp′), *n.* any of several New World lizards of the genera *Celustus* and *Diploglossus,* esp. *C. occiduus,* of Jamaica, which grows to a length of 22 inches. [?]
gall′ midge′, any of several dipterous insects of the family *Cecidomyiidae,* the larvae of which form characteristic galls on plants. Also called **gall gnat.**
gall·nut (gôl′nut′), *n.* a nutlike gall on plants. [GALL[3] + NUT]
Gallo-, a combining form of **Gallic:** *Gallo-Romance.* [< L, comb. form of *Gallus* a Gaul]
gal·lo·glass (gal′ō glas′, -gläs′), *n. Irish Hist.* a follower and supporter of or a soldier owing allegiance to an Irish chief. Also, **gallowglass.** [< IrGael *gallōglāch,* equiv. to *gall* a stranger, foreigner + *ōglach* a youth, soldier, servant, deriv. of OIr *ōac, ōc* young]
gal·lon (gal′ən), *n.* a common unit of capacity in English-speaking countries, equal to four quarts, the U.S. standard gallon being equal to 231 cubic inches (3.7853 liters), and the British imperial gallon to 277.42 cubic inches (4.546 liters). *Abbr.:* gal [ME *galo(u)n, gallon* < OF *galon,* ML *galōna* << Gallic *galla* vessel, bowl]
gal·lon·age (gal′ə nij), *n.* **1.** the number of gallons of something used. **2.** the rate at which gallons of something are used. [GALLON + -AGE]
gal·loon (gə lo͞on′), *n.* a braid or trimming of worsted, silk or rayon tinsel, gold or silver, etc. [< MF *galon,* OF *galonn(er)* (to) adorn one's head with ribbons, deriv. of *gale* GALA] **—gal·looned′,** *adj.*
gal·loot (gə lo͞ot′), *n.* galoot.
gal·lop (gal′əp), *v.i.* **1.** to ride a horse at a gallop; ride at full speed: *They galloped off to meet their friends.* **2.** to run rapidly by leaps, as a horse; go at a gallop. **3.** to go fast, race, or hurry, as a person, time, etc. **—***v.t.* **4.** to cause (a horse or other animal) to gallop. **—***n.* **5.** a fast gait of the horse or other quadruped in which, in the course of each stride, all four feet are off the ground at once. **6.** a run or ride at this gait. **7.** a rapid rate of going, or a period of going rapidly. [ME *galop(en)* (v.) < OF *galop, galop(er)* < ?] **—gal′lop·er,** *n.*
gal·lo·pade (gal′ə pād′), *n.* galop. Also, **galopade.** [< F *galopade,* equiv. to *galop(er)* (to) GALLOP + *-ade* -ADE[1]]
gal·lop·ing (gal′ə piṅg), *adj.* **1.** at a gallop; moving quickly. **2.** moving rapidly to some conclusion, as a disease: *galloping pneumonia.* **3.** growing rapidly. [GALLOP + -ING[2]]
gal′loping dan′druff, *U.S. Slang.* fleas or ticks in the hair.
gal′loping dom′inoes, *U.S. Slang.* dice, esp. as used in the game of craps.
gal′lop rhythm′, *Pathol.* an abnormal heart rhythm characterized by three clear sounds in each beat, resembling the sound of a horse's gallop.
Gallo-Rom., Gallo-Romance.
Gal·lo-Ro·mance (gal′ō rō mans′), *n.* the vernacular language, a development from Latin, spoken in France from about A.D. 600–900.
gal·lous (gal′əs), *adj. Chem.* containing bivalent gallium. [GALL(IUM) + -OUS]
Gal·lo·way (gal′ə wā′), *n.* **1.** a region in SW Scotland, comprising the counties of Wigtown and Kircudbright. **2.** one of a Scottish breed of beef cattle having a coat of curly, black hair. **3.** one of a Scottish breed of small, strong horses.
gal·low·glass (gal′ō glas′, -gläs′), *n. Irish Hist.* galloglass.
gal·lows (gal′ōz, -əz), *n., pl.* **-lows·es, -lows. 1.** a wooden frame, consisting of a cross beam on two uprights, on which condemned persons are executed by hanging. **2.** a similar structure from which something is suspended. **3.** execution by hanging: *a crime deserving of the gallows.* **4.** Also called **gallows bitts.** *Naut.* a support on the deck of a vessel, generally one of two or more, consisting of a crosspiece on two uprights, for spars, boats, etc. [ME *galwes,* OE *g(e)algan,* pl. of *g(e)alga* gallows; c. G *Galgen*]
gal′lows bird′, *Informal.* one who deserves to be hanged.
gal′lows bitts′, *Naut.* gallows (def. 4).
gal′lows frame′, *Mining.* headframe.
gal′lows hu′mor, ghoulish or macabre humor.

gal′lows tree′, a gallows. Also, **gal′low tree′.** [ME *galwe tree,* OE *galgtrēow,* equiv. to *galga* GALLOWS + *trēow* TREE]
gall·stone (gôl′stōn′), *n. Pathol.* a calculus, or stone, formed in the gall bladder or bile passages. Also called **biliary calculus.** [GALL[1] + STONE]
Gal·lup (gal′əp), *n.* **1. George Horace,** born 1901, U.S. statistician. **2.** a city in W New Mexico. 14,089 (1960).
Gal′lup poll′, a representative sampling of public opinion or public awareness concerning a certain issue. [after G. H. GALLUP]
gal·lus (gal′əs), *n., pl.* **-lus·es.** *Chiefly Dial.* a pair of suspenders for trousers. Often, **galluses.** [var. of GALLOWS] **—gal′lused,** *adj.*
Gal·lus (gal′əs), *n. Class. Myth.* a priest of Cybele who established the practice of having eunuchs serve the goddess.
Gal·lus (gal′əs), *n.* **Sulpicius.** See **Sulpicius Gallus.**
gall′ wasp′, any of several hymenopterous insects of the family *Cynipidae,* the larvae of which form characteristic galls on plants.
gal′ly tile′ (gal′ē), a tin-glazed earthenware tile of the 17th and 18th centuries, used for pavements and wall decorations. [var. of GALLEY]
Ga·lo·fa·lo (*It.* gä lô′fä lô), *n.* modern name of **Charybdis.** Also, **Garofaro.**
Ga·lois′ field′ (gal wä′; *Fr.* ga lwa′), *Math.* a field with a finite number of elements. [named after Évariste *Galois* (1811–32), French mathematician]
Galois′ the′ory, *Math.* the branch of mathematics that deals with the application of the theory of finite groups to the solution of algebraic equations. [named after Évariste *Galois;* see GALOIS FIELD]
ga·loot (gə lo͞ot′), *n. Slang.* an awkward, silly person. Also, **galloot.** [?]
gal·op (gal′əp), *n.* **1.** a lively round dance in duple time. **2.** a piece of music for, or in the rhythm of, this dance. Also called **gallopade, gal′o·pade′.** [< F *galop;* see GALLOP]
ga·lore (gə lōr′, -lôr′), *adv.* **1.** in abundance; in plentiful amounts: *food and drink galore.* **—***n.* **2.** *Obs.* abundance. [< Ir *go leōr* (Gael *gu leòr, leòir*), equiv. to *go* to + *leōr* sufficiency (< OIr *lour*); see LUCRE]
ga·losh (gə losh′), *n.* a high overshoe. Also, **ga·loshe′, golosh.** [< F *galoche,* prob. < L *gallicula* Gallic (sandle)]
ga·lou·bet (gal′o͝o bā′; *Fr.* ga lo͞o be′), *n.* a recorder with a narrow bore and three finger holes that is played with one hand while the other hand plays a small drum. [< F < Pr]
gals., gallons.
Gals·wor·thy (gôlz′wûr′thē, galz′-), *n.* **John,** 1867–1933, English novelist, dramatist, and short-story writer: Nobel prize 1932.
Galt (gôlt), *n.* a boy's given name.
Gal·ton (gôl′tən), *n.* **Sir Francis,** 1822–1911, English scientist and writer. **—Gal·to·ni·an** (gôl tō′nē ən), *adj.*
ga·lumph (gə lumf′), *v.i. Informal.* to move along heavily and clumsily. [phonesthemic invention of Lewis Carroll, perh. b. GALLOP and TRIUMPHANT]
Ga·lup·pi (gä lo͞op′pē), *n.* **Bal·das·sa·re** (bäl′däs-sä′re), ("*Il Buranello*"), 1706–85, Italian composer, esp. of comic operas.
Ga·luth (gä lo͞ot′, gô′ləs), *n.* (*sometimes l.c.*) *Hebrew.* the forced exile of Jews, esp. from countries where they were most persecuted. [lit., exile]
Gal·va (gal′və), *n.* **1.** a town in NW Illinois. 3060 (1960). **2.** a boy's given name.
Gal·va·ni (gäl vä′nē), *n.* **Lu·i·gi** (lo͞o ē′jē), 1737–98, an Italian physiologist whose experiments led to the discovery that electricity may result from chemical action.
gal·van·ic (gal van′ik), *adj.* **1.** pertaining to or produced by galvanism; producing or caused by an electric current. **2.** affecting or affected as if by galvanism; startling; shocking: *the galvanic effect of his speech.* [< F *galvanique,* named after Luigi GALVANI; see -IC] **—gal·van′i·cal·ly,** *adv.*
galvan′ic bat′tery, *Elect.* See **voltaic battery.**
galvan′ic cell′, *Elect.* an electrolytic cell capable of producing electric energy by electrochemical action.
galvan′ic pile′. See **voltaic pile.**
gal·va·nise (gal′və nīz′), *v.t.,* **-nised, -nis·ing.** *Chiefly Brit.* galvanize. **—gal′va·ni·sa′tion,** *n.* **—gal′va·nis′er,** *n.*
gal·va·nism (gal′və niz′əm), *n.* **1.** *Elect.* electricity, esp. as produced by chemical action. **2.** *Med.* the therapeutic application of electricity to the body. [< F *galvanisme,* named after Luigi GALVANI; see -ISM]
gal·va·nize (gal′və nīz′), *v.t.,* **-nized, -niz·ing. 1.** to stimulate by or as by a galvanic current. **2.** *Med.* to stimulate or treat (muscles or nerves) with induced alternating current (distinguished from *faradize*). **3.** to startle into sudden activity. **4.** to coat (metal, esp. iron or steel) with zinc. Also, *esp. Brit.,* **galvanise.** [< F *galvanis(er),* named after Luigi GALVANI; see -IZE] **—gal′va·ni·za′tion,** *n.* **—gal′va·niz′er,** *n.*
gal′vanized i′ron, iron coated with zinc to prevent rust.
galvano-, a combining form representing **galvanic, galvanism:** *galvanometer.*
gal·va·no·cau·ter·y (gal′və nō kô′tə rē, gal van′-ō-), *n., pl.* **-ter·ies.** *Med.* **1.** a cautery heated by a galvanic current. **2.** cauterization by means of such a cautery. [GALVANO- + CAUTERY]
gal·va·nom·e·ter (gal′və nom′i tər), *n.* an instrument for detecting the existence and determining the strength of small electric currents. [GALVANO- + -METER]
gal·va·nom·e·try (gal′və nom′i trē), *n.* the method or process of determining the strength of electric currents. [GALVANO- + -METRY] **—gal·va·no·met·ric** (gal′və nō me′trik, gal van′ə-), **gal′va·no·met′ri·cal,** *adj.* **—gal′va·no·met′ri·cal·ly,** *adv.*
gal·va·no·plas·tic (gal′və nō plas′tik, gal van′ō-), *adj. Obs.* pertaining to reproduction by electrotypy. [GALVANO- + -PLASTIC] **—gal′van·o·plas′ti·cal·ly,** *adv.*
gal·va·no·plas·tics (gal′və nō plas′tiks, gal van′ō-), *n.* (*construed as sing.*) *Obs.* galvanoplasty. [GALVANO- + -PLASTIC; see -ICS]
gal·va·no·plas·ty (gal′və nō plas′tē, gal van′ō-), *n. Obs.* electrotypy. [GALVANO- + -PLASTY]

gal·va·no·scope (gal′və nə skōp′, gal van′ə-), *n.* an instrument for detecting the existence and determining the direction of an electric current. [GALVANO- + -SCOPE] —**gal·va·no·scop·ic** (gal′və nō skop′ik, gal-van′ō-), *adj.* —**gal·va·nos·co·py** (gal′və nos′kə pē), *n.*

gal·va·no·tax·is (gal′və nō tak′sis, gal van′ō-), *n.* movement of an organism or any of its parts in a particular direction in response to an electric current; electrotaxis. [< NL; see GALVANO-, TAXIS] —**gal·va·no·tac·tic** (gal′və nō tak′tik, gal van′ō-), *adj.*

gal·va·no·ther·my (gal′və nō thûr′mē, gal van′ō-), *n. Med.* the production of heat by electric current. [GALVANO- + -THERMY]

gal·va·not·ro·pism (gal′və no′trə piz′əm), *n.* the growth or movement of an organism or any of its parts toward or away from an electric current; electrotropism. [GALVANO- + -TROPISM] —**gal·va·no·trop·ic** (gal′və-nō trop′ik, gal van′ō-), *adj.*

Gal·ves·ton (gal′vi stən), *n.* a seaport in SE Texas, on an island at the mouth of Galveston Bay. 67,175 (1960).

Gal′veston Bay′, an inlet of the Gulf of Mexico.

Gal′veston plan′. See **commission plan.**

Gal·way (gôl′wā), *n.* **1.** a county in S Connaught, in W Republic of Ireland. 149,887 (1961); 2293 sq. mi. **2.** its county seat: a seaport in the W part. 22,028 (1961).

gal·ways (gôl′wāz), *n.pl. Slang.* whiskers extending from ear to ear and following the chin line. Also, **Gal′-ways.** [? special use of GALWAY]

Gal·we·gian (gal wē′jən), *adj.* **1.** of or pertaining to the region of Galloway, Scotland. —*n.* **2.** a native or inhabitant of Galloway. [irreg. < ML *Galwedi(a)* GAL-LOWAY + -AN]

gal·yak (gal′yak), *n.* a sleek, flat fur made from lambskin or from the pelt of a young goat. Also, **gal′yac.** [< native name in the Uzbek S.S.R.]

gam[1] (gam), *n., v.,* **gammed, gam·ming.** —*n.* **1.** a herd or school of whales. **2.** *U.S. Dial.* a social meeting, visit, or the like, as between vessels at sea. —*v.i.* **3.** (of whales) to assemble into a herd or school. **4.** *Naut.* (of the officers and crews of two whaling vessels) to visit or converse with one another for social purposes. **5.** *U.S. Dial.* to participate in a gam or social visit. —*v.t.* **6.** to have a gam with: *We gammed the New Bedford bark for nearly an hour.* [? dial. var. of GAME[1]]

gam[2] (gam), *n. Slang.* a person's leg, esp. an attractive female leg. [prob. dial. var. of F *gambe* leg; see GAMB]

gam-, var. of **gamo-** before a vowel: *gamone.*

Ga·ma (gam′ə; *Port.* gä′mə), *n.* **Vas·co da** (vas′kō də; *Port.* väsh′kōō də), c1460–1524, Portuguese navigator and discoverer of the sea route from Portugal around the continent of Africa to India.

ga′ma grass′ (gä′mə), an ornamental, reedlike grass, *Tripsacum dactyloides:* one of the largest grasses in the U.S., growing from four to seven feet high. [var. of GRAMA GRASS]

Ga·ma·li·el (gə mā′lē əl, -māl′yəl), *n.* **1.** ("*the Elder*" or "*Gamaliel I*"), died A.D. 50?, the teacher of Paul (Acts 22:3); the grandson of Hillel. **2.** his grandson ("*the Younger*" or "*Gamaliel II*"), died A.D. 115?, leader of the Jews after the destruction of Jerusalem, A.D. 70. **3.** a boy's given name.

gamb (gamb, gam), *n.* the leg of a heraldic animal. Also, **gambe.** [< OF *gambe;* alter. of *jambe* leg; see JAMB]

gam·ba·do[1] (gam bā′dō), *n., pl.* **-dos, -does. 1.** either of a pair of large protective boots or gaiters fixed to a saddle instead of stirrups. **2.** any long gaiter or legging. [< It *gamb(a)* leg + *-ado* -ADE[1]]

gam·ba·do[2] (gam bā′dō), *n., pl.* **-dos, -does. 1.** a spring or leap by a horse. **2.** a caper or antic. Also, **gam-bade** (gam bād′, -bäd′). [m. F *gambade* a leap or spring; see GAMBOL]

Gam·bart (gam′bärt), *n.* a walled plain in the second quadrant of the face of the moon; about 17 miles in diameter.

gam·be·son (gam′bi sən), *n. Armor.* a quilted garment worn above or below mail in the Middle Ages; acton. [ME *ga(u)mbeson* a military tunic < OF *gambison, gambeison,* prob. < Gmc]

Gam·bet·ta (gam bet′ə; *Fr.* gän be tA′), *n.* **Lé·on** (lā ôN′), 1838–82, French statesman.

Gam·bi (gam′bē), *n.* a girl's given name, form of **Gamble.**

Gam·bi·a (gam′bē ə), *n.* **1.** a river in W Africa, flowing W to the Atlantic. 500 mi. long. **2. The,** a republic extending inland along both sides of this river: formerly a British crown colony and protectorate; gained independence 1965; member of the British Commonwealth of Nations. 290,000 (est. 1959); 4003 sq. mi. *Cap.:* Bathurst.

gam·bier (gam′bēr), *n.* an astringent extract obtained from the leaves and young shoots of a tropical Asian rubiaceous shrub, *Uncaria gambir,* used in medicine, dyeing, tanning, etc. [< Malay *gambir* the name of the plant]

Gam′bier Is′lands (gam′bēr), a group of islands in French Polynesia, belonging to the Tuamotu Archipelago. ab. 2000; 12 sq. mi.

gam·bit (gam′bit), *n.* **1.** *Chess.* an opening in which the player seeks by sacrificing a pawn or piece to obtain some advantage. **2.** any maneuver by which one seeks to gain an advantage. [< F < Sp *gambit(o)* or It *gambett(o)* (akin to OF *gambet, jambet*), equiv. to *gamb(a)* leg + *-etta* -ET]

gam·ble (gam′bəl), *v.,* **-bled, -bling,** *n.* —*v.i.* **1.** to play at any game of chance for stakes. **2.** to stake or risk money, or anything of value, on the outcome of something involving chance: *to gamble on the result of a race.* —*v.t.* **3.** to lose or squander by betting (usually fol. by *away*): *He gambled all his hard-earned money away in one night.* **4.** to make (a wager): *I'm gambling that you'll like the way we do things.* —*n.* **5.** any matter or thing involving risk or hazardous uncertainty. **6.** a venture in a game of chance for stakes, esp. for high stakes. [ME *gamenen* to play (OE *gamenian*), with substitution of -LE for *-en;* see GAME[1]] —**gam′bler,** *n.*

Gam·ble (gam′bəl), *n.* a girl's given name.

gam′bling house′, a place used for gambling, esp. for a large number of betting games, as a gambling resort.

gam·boge (gam bōj′, -bōōzh′), *n.* **1.** Also, **cambogia.** a gum resin from various trees of the genus *Garcinia,* esp. *G. Hanburyi,* of Cambodia, Siam, etc., used as a yellow pigment and as a cathartic. **2.** yellow or yellow-orange. [< NL *gambog-* (s. of *gambogium*), var. of *cambog-,* after CAMBODIA] —**gam·bo′gi·an,** *adj.*

gam·boised (gam′boizd), *adj.* (of gambesons, cuisses, etc.) heavily quilted. [< MF *gamboise,* deriv. of *gambeison.* See GAMBESON, -ED[3]]

gam·bol (gam′bəl), *v.,* **-boled, -bol·ing** or (*esp. Brit.*) **-bolled, -bol·ling,** *n.* —*v.i.* **1.** to skip about, as in dancing or playing; frolic. —*n.* **2.** a skipping or frisking about; frolic. [earlier *gambold, gambald, gamba(u)de* < MF *gambade;* see GAMBADE]
—**Syn. 1.** spring, caper, frisk, romp.

gam·brel (gam′brəl), *n.* **1.** the hock of an animal, esp. of a horse. **2.** Also called **gam′brel stick′.** a wood or metal device for suspending a slaughtered animal. [< ONF *gamberel,* akin to F *jambier* legging, *jambe* leg]

gam′brel roof′, a gable roof, each side of which has a shallower slope above a steeper one. Cf. **mansard** (def. 1). See illus. under **roof.** —**gam′brel-roofed′,** *adj.*

Gam·bri·nus (gam brī′nəs), *n.* a mythical Flemish king, the reputed inventor of beer.

gam·bu·sia (gam byōō′zhə, -zhē ə, -zē ə), *n. Ichthyol.* any of several livebearers of the genus *Gambusia* that feed on aquatic insect larvae and are used to control mosquitoes. [< NL, m. CubanSp *gambusino*]

game[1] (gām), *n., adj.,* **gam·er, gam·est,** *v.,* **gamed, gam·ing.** —*n.* **1.** an amusement or pastime: *children's games.* **2.** the material or equipment used in playing certain games: *a store selling toys and games.* **3.** a competitive activity involving skill, chance, or endurance on the part of two or more persons who play according to a set of rules, usually for their own amusement or for that of spectators. **4.** a single occasion of such an activity, or a definite portion of one: *the final game of the season; a rubber of three games at bridge.* **5.** the number of points required to win a game. **6.** the score at a particular stage in a game: *With five minutes to play, the game was 7 to 0.* **7.** a particular manner or style of playing a game: *His game of chess is improving.* **8.** anything resembling a game, as in requiring skill, endurance, etc.: *the game of diplomacy.* **9.** a trick or strategy: *to see through someone's game.* **10.** fun; sport of any kind; joke: *That's about enough of your games.* **11.** wild animals, including birds and fishes, such as are hunted or taken for sport or profit. **12.** the flesh of such wild animals or other game, used as food: *a dish of game.* **13.** any object of pursuit, attack, abuse, etc.: *The new boy at school seemed to be fair game for practical jokers.* **14.** *Informal.* a business or profession: *He's in the real-estate game.* **15.** fighting spirit; pluck. **16. make game of,** to make fun of; ridicule: *Only boors make game of the weak and defenseless.* **17. play the game,** *Informal.* **a.** to act or play in accordance with the rules. **b.** to act honorably or justly: *We naïvely assumed that our allies would continue to play the game.* —*adj.* **18.** pertaining to or composed of animals hunted or taken as game or to their flesh. **19.** having the fighting spirit of a gamecock; plucky: *a game sportsman.* **20.** *Informal.* having the required spirit or will (often fol. by *for* or an infinitive). **21. die game, a.** to die after a brave struggle. **b.** to remain steadfast or in good spirits at the moment of defeat: *He knew that as a candidate he didn't have a chance in the world, but he campaigned anyway and died game.* —*v.i.* **22.** to play games of chance for stakes; gamble. —*v.t.* **23.** to squander in gaming (usually fol. by *away*). [ME *game(n),* OE *gamen;* c. OHG *gaman* glee] —**game′-less,** *adj.* —**game′like′,** *adj.* —**game′ly,** *adv.* —**game′ness,** *n.*
—**Syn. 3.** sport, contest, competition. **9.** scheme, artifice, stratagem, plan, plot, venture. **13.** prey, quarry. **19.** brave, bold, intrepid, dauntless, fearless.

game[2] (gām), *adj. Informal.* lame: *a game leg.* [?]

game·bag (gām′bag′), *n.* a bag, usually of leather or canvas, for carrying game, esp. birds, killed by a hunter. [GAME[1] + BAG]

game′ bird′, any bird hunted chiefly for sport, as a quail or pheasant, esp. such a bird that is protected by game laws.

game·cock (gām′kok′), *n.* a rooster of a fighting breed, or one bred and trained for fighting. [GAME[1] + COCK[1]]

game′ fish′, an edible fish capable of affording sport to the angler in its capture.

game′ fowl′, a domestic fowl of a breed much used for fighting.

game·keep·er (gām′kē′pər), *n. Chiefly Brit.* a person employed, as on an estate or game preserve, to prevent poaching and provide a natural environment conducive to the propagation of game, as by thinning brush, scattering food after a snowstorm, and the like. [GAME[1] + KEEPER] —**game′keep′ing,** *n.*

gam·e·lan (gam′ə lan′, -lən), *n.* a type of orchestra characteristic of southeast Asia, consisting of bowed stringed instruments, flutes, and a great variety of percussion instruments, and performing music that is heterophonic and rhythmically highly complex. [< Javanese: percussion instrument]

game′ law′, a law enacted for the preservation of game, as by restricting the number and kinds of game that may be taken and by designating periods of the year when specified game may be taken.

game′ of chance′, a game in which the outcome is determined by chance rather than by skill, as roulette.

game′ of skill′, a game in which the outcome is determined by skill rather than by chance, as chess.

game′ point′, (in tennis, squash, handball, etc.) the point that if won by the scorer would enable him or his side to win the game.

game′ room′, a room used for recreation, esp. for table games.

games·man·ship (gāmz′mən ship′), *n.* the use of methods, esp. in a sports contest, which are dubious or seemingly improper but which are not strictly illegal. [GAME[1] + 's[1] + MAN[1] + -SHIP]

games′ mas′ter, *Brit.* a physical-education teacher or school athletic director. Also, *referring to a woman,* **games′ mis′tress.**

game·some (gām′səm), *adj.* playful; frolicsome; gay. [ME; see GAME[1], -SOME[1]] —**game′some·ly,** *adv.* —**game′some·ness,** *n.*

game·ster (gām′stər), *n.* a person who gambles habitually; gambler. [GAME[1] + -STER]

gamet-, var. of **gameto-** before a vowel: *gametangium.*

gam·e·tan·gi·um (gam′i tan′jē əm), *n., pl.* **-gi·a** (-jē ə). *Bot.* an organ or body producing gametes. [< NL; see GAMET-, ANGIO-, -IUM]

gam·ete (gam′ēt, gə mēt′), *n. Biol.* a mature sexual reproductive cell, as a sperm or egg, which unites with another cell to form a new organism. [< NL *gamet(a)* < Gk *gamet-* (s. of *gametḗ* wife, *gamétēs* husband), deriv. of *gamein* to marry] —**ga·met·ic** (gə met′ik), **ga·me·tal** (gə mēt′əl), *adj.* —**ga·met′i·cal·ly,** *adv.*

game′ the′ory, a mathematical theory that deals with strategies for maximizing gains and minimizing losses within prescribed constraints, as the rules of a card game: widely applied in the solution of various decision-making problems, as those of military strategy and business policy. Also called **theory of games.**

gameto-, a combining form representing **gamete:** *gametophore.* Also, *esp. before a vowel,* **gamet-.** [< NL *gamet(a)* GAMETE + *-o-* -O-]

ga·me·to·cyte (gə mē′tə sīt′), *n. Biol.* a cell that produces gametes. [GAMETO- + -CYTE]

gam·e·to·gen·e·sis (gam′i tō jen′i sis), *n. Biol.* the development of gametes. [GAMETO- + -GENESIS] —**gam′-e·to·gen′ic, gam·e·tog·e·nous** (gam′i toj′ə nəs), *adj.*

ga·me·to·phore (gə mē′tə fōr′, -fôr′), *n. Bot.* a part or structure producing gametes. [GAMETO- + -PHORE] —**ga·me·to·phor·ic** (gə mē′tə fōr′ik, -for′-), *adj.*

ga·me·to·phyte (gə mē′tə fīt′), *n. Bot.* the sexual form of a plant in the alternation of generations (opposed to *sporophyte*). [GAMETO- + -PHYTE] —**gam·e·to·phyt·ic** (gam′i tə fit′ik), *adj.*

game′ war′den, a public official who enforces game laws.

gam·ic (gam′ik), *adj. Biol.* sexual (def. 3). [< Gk *gamik(ós)* bridal, of marriage, equiv. to *gám(os)* marriage, wedding + *-ikos* -IC]

gam·in (gam′in; *Fr.* gA maN′), *n., pl.* **gam·ins** (gam′-inz; *Fr.* gA maN′). a neglected boy left to run about the streets; street urchin. [< F]

gam·ine (gam′ēn, -in, ga mēn′; *Fr.* gA mēn′), *n., pl.* **gam·ines** (gam′ēnz, -inz, ga mēnz′; *Fr.* gA mēn′). **1.** a tomboy; hoyden. **2.** a diminutive girl, esp. one who is pert, impudent, or playfully mischievous. [< F; fem. of GAMIN]

gam·ing (gā′ming), *n.* gambling. [GAME[1] + -ING[1]]

gam′ing ta′ble, a table used for gambling, esp. one designed with a game board and slots for chips.

gam·ma (gam′ə), *n.* **1.** the third letter of the Greek alphabet (γ, Γ). **2.** the consonant sound represented by this letter. **3.** the third of any series, as in mathematics, biology, etc. **4.** (*cap.*) *Astron.* a star that is usually the third brightest of a constellation: *The third brightest star in the Southern Cross is Gamma Crucis.* **5.** a unit of weight equal to one microgram. **6.** *Physics.* a unit of magnetic field strength, equal to 10^{-5} oersted. **7.** *Photog.* a measure of the degree of development of a negative or print. **8.** an analogous numerical indication of the degree of contrast between light and dark in the reproduction of an image in television. **9.** *Chiefly Brit.* a grade showing that a student is in the lowest or third of three scholastic sections in his class. Cf. **alpha** (def. 6), **beta** (def. 5). [< Gk *gámma*]

gam·ma·di·on (gə mā′dē ən), *n., pl.* **-di·a** (-dē ə). an ornamental figure consisting of combinations of the Greek capital gamma, esp. in the form of a swastika or fylfot, or of a voided Greek cross. [< LGk *gammádion* little gamma (sp. var. of *gammátion*), equiv. to *gámma* GAMMA + *-d-* connective + *-ion* dim. suffix]

gam′ma func′tion, *Math.* the function of x defined by the improper integral, $\int_0^\infty t^{x-1}e^{-u}du$ and which equals $(x-1)!$ when x is a positive integer.

gam′ma glob′ulin, *Biochem.* a protein component of blood plasma, containing antibodies effective against certain microorganisms, as those of measles, infectious hepatitis, and poliomyelitis.

gam′ma i′ron, austenite (def. 2).

gam′ma ray′, *Physics.* a high-frequency, penetrating radiation emitted from the nucleus of a radioactive atom and lowering the energy level of the nucleus.

gam·mer (gam′ər), *n. Brit.* an old woman. [contr. of GODMOTHER; cf. GAFFER]

Gam·mex·ane (gam ek′sān), *n. Trademark.* lindane.

gam·mon[1] (gam′ən), *n.* **1.** the game of backgammon. **2.** *Backgammon.* a victory in which the winner throws off all his men before his opponent throws off any. —*v.t.* **3.** *Backgammon.* to win a gammon over. [? special use of ME *gamen* GAME[1]]

gam·mon[2] (gam′ən), *n.* **1.** a smoked or cured ham. **2.** the lower end of a side of bacon. [< OF *gambon* ham (F *jambon*), deriv. of *gambe;* see JAMB]

gam·mon[3] (gam′ən), *Brit. Informal.* —*n.* **1.** deceitful nonsense; bosh. —*v.i.* **2.** to talk gammon. **3.** to make pretense. —*v.t.* **4.** to humbug. [perh. special use of GAMMON[1]] —**gam′mon·er,** *n.*

gam·mon[4] (gam′ən), *v.t. Naut.* to fasten (a bowsprit) to the stem of a ship. [? akin to GAMMON[2], alluding to the tying up of a ham]

gam·mon·ing (gam′ə ning), *n. Naut.* a lashing that fastens a bowsprit to the stem of a ship. [GAMMON[4] + -ING[1]]

gamo-, a learned borrowing from Greek meaning "united," used in the formation of compound words: *gamopetalous.* Also, *esp. before a vowel,* **gam-.** [comb. form repr. Gk *gámos* marriage]

gam·o·gen·e·sis (gam′ə jen′i sis), *n. Biol.* sexual reproduction. [GAMO- + -GENESIS] —**gam·o·ge·net·ic** (gam′ō jə net′ik), **gam′o·ge·net′i·cal,** *adj.* —**gam′o·ge·net′i·cal·ly,** *adv.*

gam·one (gam′ōn), *n. Biochem.* any of various hormonelike substances, thought to be produced by ova or spermatozoa, that affect the gamete of the opposite sex during fertilization. [GAM- + -ONE]

gam·o·pet·al·ous (gam′ə pet′əl əs), *adj. Bot.* having the petals united. [< NL; see GAMO-, PETALOUS]

gam·o·phyl·lous (gam′ə fil′əs), *adj. Bot.* having leaves united by their edges. [GAMO- + -PHYLLOUS]

gam·o·sep·al·ous (gam′ə sep′ə ləs), *adj. Bot.* having the sepals united. [GAMO- + -SEPALOUS]

Gamopetalous flower

-gamous, a combination of **gamo-** and **-ous** as final element of compound adjectives: *polygamous.* [comb. form repr. Gk *-gamos* marrying]

gamp (gamp), *n.* *Brit. Facetious.* an umbrella. [after the umbrella of Mrs. Sarah *Gamp* in Dickens' *Martin Chuzzlewit*]

gam·ut (gam′ət), *n.* **1.** the entire scale or range: *the gamut of dramatic emotion from grief to gaiety.* **2.** *Music.* **a.** the whole series of recognized musical notes. **b.** the major scale. [< ML; contr. of *gamma ut,* equiv. to *gamma,* used to represent the first or lowest tone (G) in the medieval scale + *ut* (later *do*); the notes of the scale being named from a Latin hymn to St. John: *Ut* queant laxis *re*sonare fibris. *Mi*ra gestorum *fa*muli tuorum, *Sol*ve polluti *la*bi reatum, Sancte Iohannes]

gam·y (gā′mē), *adj.,* **gam·i·er, gam·i·est.** **1.** having the flavor of game, esp. game kept uncooked until slightly tainted, as preferred by connoisseurs: *The meat had a gamy flavor.* **2.** plucky; spirited. [GAME[1] + -Y[1]] —**gam′i·ly,** *adv.* —**gam′i·ness,** *n.*

-gamy, a combination of **gamo-** and **-y**[3] as final element of compounds: *polygamy.* [comb. form repr. Gk *-gamia* act of marrying]

gan (gan), *v.* pt. of **gin**[3].

Gand (gäɴ), *n.* French name of **Ghent.**

Gan·da (gan′də, gän′-), *n.* Luganda.

gan·der (gan′dər), *n.* **1.** the male of the goose. Cf. **goose** (def. 2). **2.** *U.S. Slang.* a look; glance: *Take a gander.* [ME; OE *gan(d)ra;* c. MLG *ganre,* D *gander;* akin to GOOSE, G *Gans*]

Gan·der (gan′dər), *n.* an airport in NE Newfoundland, on the great circle route between New York and northern Europe: fuel stop for some transatlantic airplanes.

Gan·dha·ra (gun där′ə), *n.* **1.** an ancient region in NW India and E Afghanistan. —*adj.* **2.** Also, **Gan·dha·ran** (gun där′ən). of or pertaining to Gandhara, its inhabitants, or its art.

Gan·dhar·va (gun där′və), *n.* *Hindu Myth.* any of a group of supernatural beings variously represented, latterly as celestial musicians.

Gan·dhi (gän′dē, gan′-), *n.* **1. In·di·ra** (in dēr′ə), born 1917, Indian political leader: prime minister 1966–77 and since 1980 (daughter of Jawaharlal Nehru). **2. Mo·han·das Kar·am·chand** (mō′hən däs′ kur′əm-chund′), (*Mahatma Gandhi*), 1869–1948, Hindu religious leader, nationalist, and social reformer.

Gan·dhi·an (gän′dē ən, gan′-), *adj.* of or pertaining to Mohandas Gandhi or to Gandhiism. [GANDHI + -AN]

Gan′dhi cap′, a white cap, pointed in front and back and having a wide band, worn by men in India.

Gan·dhi·ism (gän′dē iz′əm, gan′-), *n.* the principles associated with Mohandas Gandhi, esp. his principles of noncooperation and passive resistance in gaining political and social reforms. Also, **Gan·dhism** (gän′-diz əm, gan′-). Cf. **Satyagraha.** [GANDHI + -ISM] —**Gan′dhi·ist, Gan·dhist** (gän′dist, gan′-), *n.*

gan′dy danc′er (gan′dē), *Railroad Slang.* a person who maintains or lays track. [?]

Gand·zha (*Russ.* gänd′zhä), *n.* former name of **Kirovabad.**

ga·nef (gä′nəf), *n.* *Slang.* **1.** a thief or petty crook. **2.** a person who is unscrupulously opportunistic, esp. in pursuit of career ambitions or profit. Also, **ga′nev, ganof, gonif, gonoph.** [< Yiddish < Heb *gannābh*]

Ga·ne·sha (gə nä′shə), *n.* the Hindu god of wisdom.

gang[1] (gang), *n.* **1.** a group or band: *A gang of boys gathered around the winning pitcher.* **2.** a group of youngsters or youths who associate closely, often exclusively, for social reasons. **3.** a group of persons working together; squad; shift: *a gang of laborers.* **4.** a group of persons associated for some criminal or other antisocial purpose: *a gang of thieves.* **5.** a set of tools, oars, etc., arranged to work together or simultaneously. —*v.t.* **6.** to arrange in gangs; form into a gang. **7.** *Informal.* to attack in a gang. —*v.i.* **8.** *Informal.* to form or act as a gang: *Cutthroats who gang together hang together.* **9.** *Brit. Dial.* to walk; go. **10. gang up on,** *Informal.* (of a number of persons) to unite in opposition of (a person); combine against: *The bigger boys ganged up on the smaller ones in the schoolyard.* [ME *gong(e), gang(en),* OE *gongan, gangan;* c. OHG *gangan*] —**Syn. 1.** company, crowd, crew; party, set, clique, coterie. **3.** team.

gang[2] (gang), *n.* gangue.

gang·board (gang′bōrd′, -bôrd′), *n.* *Naut.* a raised walk on a sailing ship, crossing the waist and connecting the forecastle directly with the quarter deck. [GANG[1] + BOARD]

gang′ cul′tivator, a cultivator having several shares or shovels mounted to be operated as a gang.

gang′ drill′, a drilling machine having a number of separately driven vertical spindles in a row, used for drilling holes in a piece successively. Cf. **multiple drill.**

gang·er (gang′ər), *n.* a foreman of a gang of laborers. [GANG[1] + -ER[1]]

Gan·ges (gan′jēz), *n.* a river flowing SE from the Himalayas in N India into the Bay of Bengal: sacred to the Hindus. 1550 mi. long. —**Gan·get·ic** (gan jet′ik), *adj.*

gang′ hook′, *Angling.* a hook with several points, made by joining the shanks of two or three hooks.

gang·land (gang′land′, -lənd), *n.* the criminal underworld. [GANG[1] + LAND]

gangli-, a combining form of **ganglion:** *gangliate.*

gan·gli·a (gang′glē ə), *n.* pl. of **ganglion.**

gan·gli·ate (gang′glē āt′, -it), *adj.* having ganglia. Also, **gan′gli·at′ed.** [GANGLI- + -ATE[1]]

gan·gli·form (gang′glə fôrm′), *adj.* having the form of a ganglion. [GANGLI- + -FORM]

gan·gling (gang′gling), *adj.* awkwardly tall and spindly; lank and loosely built. Also, **gangly.** [akin to obs. *gangrel* gangling person; cf. GANG[1]]

gan·gli·oid (gang′glē oid′), *adj.* resembling a ganglion. [GANGLI- + -OID]

gan·gli·on (gang′glē ən), *n., pl.* **-gli·a** (-glē ə), **-gli·ons.** **1.** *Anat.* a gray mass of nerve tissue existing outside the brain and spinal cord. **2.** *Pathol.* a cyst or enlargement in connection with the sheath of a tendon, usually at the wrist. **3.** a center of intellectual or industrial force, activity, etc. [< LL: a type of swelling < Gk *gánglion* a tumor under the skin, on or near a tendon] —**gan′gli·al, gan′gli·ar,** *adj.*

gan·gli·on·ate (gang′glē ə nāt′, -nit), *adj.* gangliate. Also, **gan′gli·on·at′ed.** [GANGLION + -ATE[1]]

gan·gli·on·ec·to·my (gang′glē ə nek′tə mē), *n., pl.* **-mies.** *Surg.* the excision of a ganglion. [GANGLION + -ECTOMY]

gan·gli·on·ic (gang′glē on′ik), *adj.* *Anat.* of, pertaining to, or consisting of ganglia. [GANGLION + -IC]

gan′glion′ic block′ing a′gent, *Med.* a drug, as hexamethonium chloride, used to prevent the transmission of nerve impulses at the ganglia.

gan·gli·o·side (gang′glē ə sīd′), *n.* *Biochem.* any of the class of glycolipids, found chiefly in nerve ganglia, that upon hydrolysis yield sphingosine, neuraminic acid, a fatty acid, and a monosaccharide. [GANGLI- + -OSE[2] + -IDE]

gan·gly (gang′glē), *adj.,* **-gli·er, -gli·est.** gangling.

gang·plank (gang′plangk′), *n.* a flat plank or small, portable, bridgelike structure for use by persons boarding or leaving a vessel at a pier. Also called **brow, gangway.** [GANG[1] + PLANK]

gang′ plow′, a combination of two or more plows in one frame.

gang′ punch′, *Computer Technol.* **1.** to punch (identical information) in a group of punch cards. **2.** to punch (a group of punch cards) with identical information.

gan·grel (gang′grəl, -rəl), *n.* *Brit. Dial.* **1.** a lanky, loose-jointed person. **2.** a wandering beggar; vagabond. [GANG[1] + -REL; cf. GANGLING]

gan·grene (gang′grēn, gang grēn′), *n., v.,* **-grened, -gren·ing.** *Pathol.* —*n.* **1.** the dying or death of soft tissue on part of the body, as from the interruption of circulation; mortification. —*v.t., v.i.* **2.** to affect or become affected with gangrene. [< MF *gangrene* (earlier *cancrene*) < L *gangraena* < Gk *gángraina* an eating sore] —**gan·gre·nous** (gang′grə nəs), *adj.*

gang′ saw′, a saw having several parallel blades for making simultaneous cuts. —**gang′ saw′yer.**

gang·ster (gang′stər), *n.* a member of a gang of criminals, esp. a racketeer. [GANG[1] + -STER]

gang′ switch′, *Elect.* a collection of switches connected to separate circuits and operating simultaneously.

gang′ tool′, any of various machine tools having a number of cutters acting simultaneously on different surfaces or successively on the same surface.

gangue (gang), *n.* the stony or earthy minerals occurring with the metallic ore in a vein or deposit. Also, **gang.** Also called **matrix.** [< F < G *Gang;* see GANG[1]]

gang·way (*n.* gang′wā′; *interj.* gang′wā′), *n.* **1.** a passageway. **2.** *Naut.* **a.** an opening in the railing or bulwark of a vessel, as that into which a gangplank fits. **b.** gangplank. **c.** an area of the weather deck of a vessel, between the side and a deckhouse. **3.** *Railroads.* **a.** the space between the cab of a steam locomotive and its tender. **b.** the side entrance of a diesel or electric locomotive. **4.** *Brit.* **a.** an aisle in a theater, restaurant, etc. **b.** an aisle in the House of Commons separating the more influential members of the political parties from the younger, less influential members. **c.** a runway in a theater. **5.** a temporary path of planks, as at a building site. **6.** *Mining.* a main passage or level. **7.** Also called **logway.** the ramp up which logs are moved into a sawmill. —*interj.* **8.** clear the way! [OE *gangweg.* See GANG[1], WAY] —**gang′wayed′,** *adj.*

gang′way board′, *Naut.* either of two boards, often decoratively carved, that line the opening cut in a high bulwark to provide a gangway.

gang′way lad′der, *Naut.* **1.** See **accommodation ladder.** **2.** any ladder from a pier or the like to a gangplank.

gan·is·ter (gan′i stər), *n.* **1.** a highly refractory, siliceous rock used to line furnaces. **2.** a synthetic product similar to this rock, made by mixing ground quartz with a bonding material. [?]

gan·net (gan′it), *n.* any of several large, web-footed, pelagic birds of the family *Sulidae,* having a long, pointed bill and wings and a wedge-shaped tail. [ME; OE *ganot;* akin to D *gent* GANDER]

gan·o·blast (gan′ə blast′), *n.* *Anat.* an ameloblast. [< NL *gano-* (comb. form) < Gk *gános* sheen, brightness + -BLAST]

ga·nof (gä′nəf), *n.* ganef.

gan·oid (gan′oid), *adj.* **1.** belonging or pertaining to the *Ganoidei,* a group of fishes that are now mostly extinct, many species of which have hard, smooth scales. **2.** (of the scale of a fish) having a smooth, shiny surface of ganoin or a similar substance. —*n.* **3.** a ganoid fish. [< F *ganoïde* < Gk *gán(os)* brightness + *-oïde* -OID]

gan·o·in (gan′ō in), *n.* *Ichthyol.* a hard, shiny, enamellike substance secreted by the corium, composing the outer layer of the scales of certainfishes. Also, **gan′o·ine.** [GANO(ID) + -IN[2]]

ga·no·sis (gə nō′sis), *n., pl.* **-ses** (-sēz). *Gk. and Rom. Antiq.* the process of polishing marble statues. [< Gk *gánōsis,* equiv. to *gan(oûn)* (to) make bright, polish (deriv. of *gános* sheen, brightness) + *-ōsis* -OSIS]

Ganse·voort (ganz′vōrt, -vôrt), *n.* **Peter,** 1749–1812, U.S. general: soldier in the American Revolutionary War.

gan·te·lope (gan′tᵊlōp′), *n.* *Archaic.* gauntlet[2]. [var. of GANTLOPE]

gant·let[1] (gant′lit, gônt′-), *n.* **1.** *Railroads.* a track construction used in narrow places, in which two parallel tracks converge so that their inner rails cross, run parallel, and diverge again, so that a train remains on its own track at all times. **2.** gauntlet[2] (defs. 1, 2, 4). —*v.t.* **3.** *Railroads.* to form or lay down as a gantlet: *to gantlet tracks.* Also, **gauntlet.** [var. of GANTLOPE]

Gantlet (def. 1)

gant·let[2] (gant′lit, gônt′-), *n.* gauntlet[1]. —**gant′let·ed,** *adj.*

gant·line (gant′līn′), *n.* *Naut.* a rope rove through a single block hung from a mast, funnel, etc., as a means of hoisting workmen, tools, staging, flags, or the like. Also called **girthline, girtline.** [var. of GIRTLINE]

gant·lope (gant′lōp), *n.* *Archaic.* gauntlet[2]. [< Sw *gatlopp,* lit., lane run, equiv. to *gat(a)* way, lane + *lopp* a running course]

Gan·tri·sin (gan′tri sin), *n.* *Pharm., Trademark.* sulfisoxazole.

gan·try (gan′trē), *n., pl.* **-tries.** **1.** a framework spanning a railroad track or tracks for displaying signals. **2.** any of various spanning frameworks, as a bridgelike portion of certain cranes. **3.** *Rocketry.* a frame consisting of scaffolds on various levels used to erect vertically launched missiles. **4.** a frame for supporting a barrel or cask. Also, **gauntry.** [? < OF *gantier* wooden stand, frame, var. of *chantier* < ML *cantārius* < L *canthērius* < Gk *kanthḗlios* pack-ass]

Ga·nym·e·da (gə nim′i də), *n.* *Class. Myth.* Hebe (def. 1).

Gan·y·mede (gan′ə mēd′), *n.* **1.** Also, **Gan·y·me·des** (gan′ə mē′dēz). *Class. Myth.* a Trojan youth who was abducted and taken to Olympus, where he was made the cupbearer of the gods and became immortal. **2.** *Astron.* one of the 12 satellites of Jupiter. **3.** (*usually l.c.*) a young waiter who serves liquors.

Ga·o (gä′ō, gou), *n.* a city in E Mali. ab. 10,000.

GAO, General Accounting Office.

gaol (jāl), *n., v.t.* *Brit.* jail. —**gaol′er,** *n.*

gaol·bird (jāl′bûrd′), *n.* *Brit. Informal.* jailbird.

Ga·on (gä′ōn, gä ōn′), *n., pl.* **Ge·o·nim** (gə ō′nim, gā ō nēm′), **Ga·ons.** **1.** a title of honor for the directors of the Jewish academies at Sura and Pumbedita in Babylonia, used from the end of the 6th century A.D. to about the beginning of the 11th century. **2.** an eminent Jewish scholar noted for his wisdom and for his knowledge of the Talmud: *the Gaon of Vilna.* [< Heb: lit., majesty] —**Ga·on·ic** (gā on′ik), *adj.*

gap (gap), *n., v.,* **gapped, gap·ping.** —*n.* **1.** a break or opening, as in a fence, wall, military line, or the like; breach: *We found a gap in the enemy's line of fortifications.* **2.** an empty space or interval; hiatus: *a momentary gap in a siren's wailing; a gap in his memory.* **3.** a wide divergence or difference; disparity: *the gap between expenses and income; the gap between ideals and actions.* **4.** a deep, sloping ravine or cleft cutting a mountain ridge. **5.** a mountain pass: *the Cumberland Gap.* **6.** *Aeron.* the distance between one supporting surface of an airplane and another above or below it. —*v.t.* **7.** to make a gap, opening, or breach in. [ME < Scand; cf. OIcel *gap* chasm] —**gap′less,** *adj.*

gape (gāp, gap), *v.,* **gaped, gap·ing,** *n.* —*v.i.* **1.** to stare with open mouth, as in wonder. **2.** to open the mouth wide involuntarily, as the result of hunger, sleepiness, or absorbed attention. **3.** to open as a gap; split or become open wide. —*n.* **4.** a wide opening; gap; breach. **5.** the act of gaping. **6.** a stare, as in astonishment or with the mouth wide open. **7.** a yawn. **8.** *Zool.* the width of the open mouth. [ME < Scand; cf. OIcel *gapa* to open the mouth wide; cf. G *gaffen*] —**gap′er,** *n.* —**gap′ing·ly,** *adv.* —**Syn. 1.** See **gaze. 2, 3.** yawn.

gapes (gāps, gaps), *n.* (*construed as sing.*) **1.** *Vet. Pathol.* a disease of poultry and other birds, attended with frequent gaping, due to infestation of the trachea and bronchi with gapeworms. **2.** a fit of yawning. [special use of GAPE] —**gap′y,** *adj.*

gape·seed (gāp′sēd′, gap′-), *n.* *Brit. Dial.* **1.** a daydream or reverie. **2.** an idealistic, impossible, or unreal plan or goal. **3.** a person who gapes or stares in wonder, esp. a rustic or unworldly person who is easily awed. **4.** something that is gaped at; anything unusual or remarkable. **5. seek gapeseed,** *Brit. Dial.* **a.** to daydream; to go woolgathering. **b.** to plan, strive, or wish for impossible or unreal goals. Also, **plant gapeseed, reap gapeseed, sow gapeseed.** [GAPE + SEED]

gape·worm (gāp′wûrm′, gap′-), *n.* a nematode worm, *Syngamus trachea,* that causes gapes. [GAPE + WORM]

gap·o·sis (gap ō′sis), *n.* *Informal.* **1.** a noticeable gap or series of gaps between buttoned buttons or closed snaps on a garment when worn, as when the fabric is stretched out of shape around the fasteners. **2.** the condition of having such gaps: *The only ways to get rid of gaposis are to buy a zipper or to lose weight.* [GAP + -OSIS]

gapped′ scale′, *Music.* a scale formed by the omission of certain tones from a more complete musical scale.

gap-toothed (gap′tōōtht′, -tōōthd′), *adj.* having a gap between two teeth. Also, **gat-toothed.**

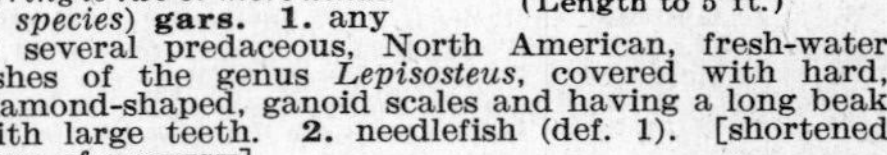

Gar, *Lepisosteus osseus* (Length to 5 ft.)

gar[1] (gär), *n., pl.* (*esp. collectively*) **gar,** (*esp. referring to two or more kinds or species*) **gars.** **1.** any of several predaceous, North American, fresh-water fishes of the genus *Lepisosteus,* covered with hard, diamond-shaped, ganoid scales and having a long beak with large teeth. **2.** needlefish (def. 1). [shortened form of GARFISH]

gar[2] (gär), *v.t.,* **garred, gar·ring.** **1.** *Chiefly Scot.* to compel or force (someone) to do something. **2.** *Scot. and North Eng. Obs.* to do, perform, or cause. [ME *ger(en), garr(en), gair(e)* < Scand; cf. Icel *göra, görva, gera;* akin to OE *gearwian* to prepare]

Gar (gär), *n.* a boy's given name.

G.A.R., Grand Army of the Republic.

ga·rage (gə räzh′, -räj′ *or, esp. Brit.,* gar′ij, -äzh), *n., v.,* **-raged, -rag·ing.** —*n.* **1.** a building or place for sheltering, cleaning, or repairing motor vehicles. —*v.t.* **2.** to put or keep in a garage: *He garages his car near the railroad station.* [< F, equiv. to *gar(er)* (to) shelter (< Gmc) + *-age* -AGE]

Gar·a·mas (gar′ə məs), *n.* *Class. Myth.* Amphithemis.

Gar·a·mond (gar′ə mond′), *n.* a printing type designed in 1540 by Claude Garamond, French type founder.

Gar′and ri′fle (gar′ənd, gə rand′), a semiautomatic, gas-operated, clip-fed rifle having a caliber of

.30 inch and weighing 8.56 pounds: the standard rifle of the U.S. Army in World War II and the Korean War. Also called **M-1.** See illus. under **rifle.** [named after John C. Garand (b. 1888), American who designed it]

garb[1] (gärb), *n.* **1.** a fashion or mode of dress, esp. of a distinctive, uniform kind: *in the garb of a monk.* **2.** wearing apparel; clothes. **3.** outward semblance or form. —*v.t.* **4.** to dress; clothe. [< MF *garbe* graceful outline < OIt *garb(o)* grace < Gmc; cf. OHG *garawen,* OE *gearwian* to prepare, adorn (see GAR[2]), GEAR] —**garb′less,** *adj.*
—**Syn. 1.** style, cut. **2.** clothing, dress, costume, attire, garments, raiment. **4.** attire, array.

garb[2] (gärb), *n. Heraldry.* a sheaf of grain, usually wheat. [ME < ONF *garbe* < Gmc; cf. G *Garbe* sheaf, OHG *garba* (lit., what is grasped). See GRAB[1]]

gar·bage (gär′bij), *n.* **1.** discarded animal and vegetable matter from a kitchen; refuse. **2.** anything that is contemptibly worthless, inferior, or vile: *the garbage that occasionally passes as art.* **3.** *Slang.* worthless talk; lies; foolishness. **4.** *Slang.* any unnecessary item added to something else, as for appearance only; garnish: *I'll have an Old Fashioned, but leave out the cherry and the slice of orange and all that garbage.* **5.** useless man-made satellites or parts of rockets floating in outer space, as satellites that are no longer transmitting information to earth or rocket boosters jettisoned in flight. [ME; prob. < AF *garbelage* removal of refuse. See GARB[2], -AGE]

gar′bage can′, a container for the disposal of waste matter, esp. kitchen refuse. Cf. **trash can.**

gar·ban·zo (gär ban′zō, -bän′-; *Sp.* gäʀ vän′thô, -sô), *n., pl.* **-zos** (-zōz; *Sp.* -thôs, -sôs). chickpea (def. 1). [< Sp, alter. of OSp *arvanço;* perh. akin to L *ervum* (see ERVIL)]

gar·ble (gär′bəl), *v.,* **-bled, -bling,** *n.* —*v.t.* **1.** to make unfair or misleading selections from or arrangement of (fact, statements, writings, etc.); distort: *to garble a quotation.* **2.** to confuse innocently or ignorantly; jumble: *to garble instructions.* **3.** *Archaic.* to take out the best of. —*n.* **4.** the act or process of garbling. **5.** an instance of garbling; a garbled phrase, literary passage, etc. [late ME *garbel* < OIt *garbell(are)* (to) sift < Ar *gharbala* < LL *cribellāre,* deriv. of *cribellum* small sieve] —**gar′ble·a·ble,** *adj.* —**gar′bler,** *n.*

Gar·bo (gär′bō), *n.* **Greta,** born 1906, U.S. actress, born in Sweden.

gar·board (gär′bōrd′, -bôrd′), *n. Naut.* a plank or plate forming part of a garboard strake. [< D *gaarboord*]

gar′board strake′, *Naut.* the first strake on each side of a keel. Also called **ground strake, sand strake.**

gar·boil (gär′boil), *n. Archaic.* confusion. [< MF *garbouil* < OIt *garbuglio*]

Gar·cí·a Lor·ca (gäʀ sē′ä lôʀ′kä), **Fe·de·ri·co** (fe′the ʀē′kô), 1899–1936, Spanish poet and dramatist.

Gar·cí·a Mo·re·no (gäʀ sē′ä mô ʀe′nô), **Ga·bri·el** (gä′vʀe el′), 1821–75, Ecuadorian journalist and political leader: president of Ecuador 1861–65; 1869–75.

Gar·ci·a y I·ñi·guez (gäʀ sē′ä ē ē′nye ges), **Ca·lix·to** (kä lēs′tō), 1839?–98, Cuban lawyer, soldier, and revolutionist.

Gar·ci·la·so de la Ve·ga (gäʀ′se lä′sô the lä be′gä, gäʀ′the-), ("*el Inca*") 1539?–1616, Peruvian historian and author in Spain.

gar·çon (gaʀ sôɴ′), *n., pl.* **-çons** (-sôɴ′). *French.* **1.** (usually in direct address) a waiter in a restaurant. **2.** a boy or a young unmarried man. **3.** a male employee or servant.

gar·çon d'hon·neur (gaʀ sôɴ dô nœʀ′), *pl.* **gar·çons d'hon·neur** (gaʀ sôɴ dô nœʀ′). *French.* the best man at a wedding.

Gard (gaʀ), *n.* a department in S France. 435,482 (1962); 2271 sq. mi. *Cap.:* Nîmes.

Gar·da (gär′də), *n.* **1. Lake,** a lake in N Italy: the largest lake in Italy. 35 mi. long; 143 sq. mi. **2.** a girl's given name.

gar·dant (gär′dᵊnt), *adj.* guardant.

gard·brace (gärd′brās′), *n. Armor.* a supplementary plate fitting over and reinforcing a pauldron. [ME < F *garde-bras.* See GUARD, BRACE]

garde à che·val (gaʀd a shə val′), *pl.* **gardes à che·val** (gaʀd zash ə val′). *French.* a mounted guard.

garde du corps (gaʀd dʏ kôʀ′), *pl.* **gardes du corps** (gaʀd dʏ kôʀ′). *French.* a bodyguard.

garde-feu (gaʀd fœ′), *n., pl.* **garde-feu, garde-feux** (gaʀd fœ′). *French.* See **fire screen.**

garde-man·ger (gaʀd män zhā′), *n., pl.* **garde-man·ger.** *French.* **1.** a cool room used for storing foods and for preparing certain dishes, esp. cold buffet dishes. **2.** a chef or cook who supervises the preparation of cold dishes. [lit., that (which) keeps food]

gar·den (gär′dᵊn), *n.* **1.** a plot of ground, usually near a house, where flowers, vegetables, or herbs are cultivated. **2.** a piece of ground or other space commonly with ornamental plants, trees, etc., used as a park or other public recreation area, as an arboretum. **3.** a fertile and delightful spot or region. **4.** *Brit.* yard[2] (def. 1). —*adj.* **5.** pertaining to, produced in, or suitable for cultivating in a garden: *fresh garden vegetables.* **6. lead one up the garden path,** *Informal.* to mislead; delude: *He couldn't see that she was leading him up the garden path because he might be useful.* —*v.i.* **7.** to lay out or cultivate a garden. —*v.t.* **8.** to cultivate as a garden. [ME *gardin* < OF *gardin, jardin* < Gmc; cf. OHG *gartin-,* G *Garten,* YARD[2]] —**gar′den·a·ble,** *adj.* —**gar′den-less,** *adj.* —**gar′den-like′,** *adj.*

Gar·den (gär′dᵊn), *n.* **Mary,** 1877–1967, U.S. soprano.

Gar·de·na (gär dē′nə), *n.* a city in SW California, near Los Angeles. 35,943 (1960).

gar′den balm′, the lemon balm. See under **balm** (def. 5).

gar′den but′tercup, a buttercup, esp. *Ranunculus aconitifolius,* having white or yellow, often double flowers, cultivated in gardens.

Gar′den Cit′y, 1. a city in SE Michigan, near Detroit. 38,017 (1960). **2.** a city on W Long Island, in SE New York. 23,948 (1960). **3.** a city in W Kansas. 11,811 (1960). **4.** a town in SE Georgia. 5451 (1960).

gar′den cress′, a peppergrass, *Lepidium sativum,* used as a salad vegetable.

Gar·den·dale (gär′dᵊn dāl′), *n.* a town in central Alabama. 4712 (1960).

gar·den·er (gärd′nər), *n.* **1.** a person who is employed to cultivate or care for a garden, lawn, etc. **2.** any person who cultivates or is skillful in cultivating gardens. [ME < ONF *gardinier* (OF *jardinier*). See GARDEN, -ER[2]]

gar′den fly′ hon′eysuckle. See **Tartarian honeysuckle.**

Gar′den Grove′, a city in SW California. 84,238 (1960).

gar′den he′liotrope, the valerian, *Valeriana officinalis.*

gar·de·nia (gär dē′nyə, -nē ə), *n.* **1.** any evergreen, rubiaceous tree or shrub of the genus *Gardenia,* native to the warmer parts of the Eastern Hemisphere, cultivated for their fragrant, waxlike, white flowers. **2.** the flower of any of these plants. [named after Dr. Alexander *Garden* (1730–91), American physician; see -IA]

Gar·de·nia (gär dē′nyə, -nē ə), *n.* a girl's given name.

gar·den·ing (gärd′ning), *n.* **1.** the act of cultivating a garden. **2.** the work or art of a gardener. [GARDEN + -ING[1]]

gar′den mint′, spearmint.

Gar′den of E′den, Eden.

gar′den par′ty, a party given out of doors in a garden or yard.

gar′den phlox′, an herb, *Phlox paniculata,* of the eastern U.S., having variously colored flowers in large, spreading clusters. Also called **perennial phlox.**

gar′den portulac′a. See **rose moss.**

gar′den rock′et. See **dame's rocket.**

Gar′den State′, New Jersey (used as a nickname).

gar′den verbe′na, a trailing perennial herb, *Verbena hortensis,* having fragrant pink, red, yellow, or white flowers.

gar′den-wall bond′ (gär′dən wôl′), a brickwork bond having a header and two or more stretchers alternating in each course.

gar′den war′bler, any of various small birds esteemed in Italy as a table delicacy, as the warblers of the family *Sylviidae,* esp. *Sylvia hortensis.*

gar′den web′worm. See under **webworm.**

garde·robe (gärd′rōb′), *n.* **1.** a wardrobe or its contents. **2.** a private room, as a bedchamber. **3.** (in medieval architecture) a latrine. [< F: lit., that (which) keeps clothing]

gar·dez la foi (gaʀ dā la fwä′), *French.* keep the faith.

Gar·di·ner (gärd′nər, gär′di nər), *n.* **1. Samuel Raw·son** (rô′sən), 1829–1902, English historian. **2. Stephen,** 1483–1555, English statesman. **3.** a town in S Maine. 6897 (1960).

Gard·ner (gärd′nər), *n.* **1. Erle Stanley** (ûrl), born 1889, U.S. writer of detective stories. **2. John W(illiam),** born 1912, U.S. government official: Secretary of Health, Education, and Welfare 1965–68. **3.** a city in N Massachusetts. 19,038 (1960). **4.** a boy's given name.

gar·dy·loo (gär′dē lo͞o′), *interj.* (a cry formerly used in Scotland to warn pedestrians when slops were about to be thrown from an upstairs window.) [Anglicized form of F *gare (de) l'eau* beware of the water]

gare (gâr), *n.* low-grade wool fibers from the legs of sheep. [< AF, var. of OF *gard, jart*]

gare·fowl (gâr′foul′), *n., pl.* **-fowls,** (*esp. collectively*) **-fowl.** *Rare.* the great auk. [< Scand; cf. Icel *geir-fugl, geir-fálki* GYRFALCON]

Gar·eth (gar′ith), *n.* **1.** *Arthurian Romance.* nephew of King Arthur. **2.** Also, **Garth.** a boy's given name.

Gar·ey (gâr′ē, gar′ē), *n.* a boy's given name. Also, **Gari, Gary, Garry.**

Gar·field (gär′fēld′), *n.* **1. James Abram,** 1831–81, 20th president of the United States, 1881. **2.** a city in NE New Jersey. 29,253 (1960). **3.** a boy's given name.

Gar′field Heights′, a city in NE Ohio, near Cleveland. 38,455 (1960).

gar·fish (gär′fish′), *n., pl.* (*esp. collectively*) **-fish,** (*esp. referring to two or more kinds or species*) **-fish·es.** gar. [ME; cf. OE *gār* spear]

garg., (in prescriptions) a gargle. [< L *gargarisma*]

gar·ga·ney (gär′gə nē), *n., pl.* **-neys.** a small Old World duck, *Anas querquedula.* [m. It *garganello,* deriv. of *garg-* throat]

Gar·gan·tu·a (gär gan′cho͞o ə), *n.* **1.** an amiable giant and king, noted for his enormous capacity for food and drink, in Rabelais' *Gargantua* and *Pantagruel.* **2.** (*italics.*) a satirical novel (1534) by Rabelais. Cf. **Pantagruel.**

gar·gan·tu·an (gär gan′cho͞o ən), *adj.* gigantic; enormous; prodigious. [GARGANTU(A) + -AN]

Gar·ga·phi·a (gär gā′fē ə), *n.* **Vale of,** *Class. Myth.* the place where Actaeon was torn apart by his hounds.

gar·get (gär′git), *n.* **1.** *Vet. Pathol.* inflammation of the udder of a cow; bovine mastitis. **2.** the pokeweed. [ME *garget, gargat* throat < MF *gargate* throat; perh. orig. a disease of the throat] —**gar′get·y,** *adj.*

gar·gle (gär′gəl), *v.,* **-gled, -gling,** *n.* —*v.t.* **1.** to wash or rinse (the throat or mouth) with a liquid held in the throat and kept in motion by a stream of air from the lungs. **2.** to utter with a gargling sound. —*v.i.* **3.** to gargle the throat or mouth. —*n.* **4.** any liquid used for gargling. [< F *gargouill(er)* (to) gargle, rattle the throat, deriv. of *gargouille* throat; perh. imit.] —**gar′gler,** *n.*

gar·goyle (gär′goil), *n.* **1.** a grotesquely carved figure of a human or animal. **2.** a spout, terminating in a grotesque representation of a human or animal figure with open mouth, projecting from the gutter of a building for throwing rain water clear of a building. [ME *gargulye* < OF *gargouille, gargoule,* appar. the same word as *gargouille* throat; see GARGLE] —**gar′goyled,** *adj.*

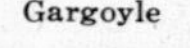
Gargoyle

gar·goyl·ism (gär′goi liz′əm), *n. Pathol.* a congenital abnormality characterized chiefly by grotesque deformities of the head, trunk, and limbs, dwarfism, mental retardation, and enlargement of the liver and spleen. [GARGOYLE + -ISM]

Gar·i (gâr′ē, gar′ē), *n.* a boy's given name. Also, **Garey, Gary, Garry.**

gar·i·bal·di (gar′ə bôl′dē), *n.* **1.** a loose blouse worn by women and children in the mid-19th century, made in imitation of the red shirts worn by the soldiers of Garibaldi. **2.** a brilliant orange damselfish, *Hypsypops rubicundus,* found off the rocky coasts of southern California.

Gar·i·bal·di (gar′ə bôl′dē; *It.* gä′ʀē bäl′dē), *n.* **Giu·sep·pe** (jə sep′ē; *It.* jo͞o zep′pe), 1807–82, Italian patriot and general. —**Gar′i·bal′di·an,** *adj., n.*

Gar·i·fa·li·a (gar′ə fā′lē ə, -fāl′yə), *n.* a girl's given name.

GARIOA, Government and Relief in Occupied Areas.

gar·ish (gâr′ish, gar′-), *adj.* **1.** crudely or tastelessly colorful, showy, or elaborate, as clothes, decoration, etc. **2.** excessively ornate or elaborate, as buildings, writings, etc. **3.** dressed in or ornamented with bright colors. **4.** excessively bright; glaring. [earlier *gaurish,* equiv. to obs. *gaure* to stare (ME *gauren*) + -ISH[1]] —**gar′ish·ly,** *adv.* —**gar′ish·ness,** *n.*
—**Syn. 1.** loud, tawdry. See **gaudy. 2.** overdecorated.

gar·land (gär′lənd), *n.* **1.** a wreath or festoon of flowers, leaves, or other material, worn for ornament or as an honor or hung on something as a decoration. **2.** a representation of such a wreath or festoon. **3.** a collection of short literary pieces, as poems and ballads; literary miscellany. **4.** *Naut.* a band, collar, or grommet, as of rope. **5.** *Mining.* a channel cut or built within the lining of a shaft as a collection place for seepage. —*v.t.* **6.** to crown with a garland; deck with garlands. [ME *ger(e)lande, garlande* < OF < ?] —**gar′land·less,** *adj.* —**gar′land·like′,** *adj.*

Gar·land (gär′lənd), *n.* **1. Ham·lin** (ham′lin), 1860–1940, U.S. novelist, short-story writer, and poet. **2. Judy** (*Frances Gumm*), born 1922, U.S. singer and actress. **3.** a city in NE Texas, near Dallas. 38,501 (1960). **4.** a boy's or girl's given name.

gar′land crab′ apple′. See **American crab.**

gar′land lark′spur, a perennial herb, *Delphinium cheilanthum,* of eastern Asia, having showy, blue flowers.

gar·lic (gär′lik), *n.* **1.** a hardy liliaceous plant, *Allium sativum,* whose strong-scented, pungent bulb is used in cookery and medicine. **2.** any of various other plants of the genus *Allium.* **3.** the bulb of such a plant or the flesh of the bulb as used in any form for cooking, as a toe of such a bulb, a powdered quantity of it, etc. **4.** the flavor or smell of this bulb. —*adj.* **5.** cooked, flavored, or seasoned with garlic: *garlic bread; garlic salt.* **6.** of or pertaining to garlic. [ME *garlec,* OE *gārlēac* (*gar* spear (c. G *Ger*) + *lēac* LEEK)]

gar·lick·y (gär′lə kē), *adj.* **1.** like or containing garlic. **2.** tasting or smelling of garlic: *a garlicky sauce; garlicky breath.* [GARLIC + -Y[1] (spelled with *-ck-* to convey velar sound)]

Garm (gärm), *n. Scand. Myth.* the watchdog of Hel in Niflheim. Also, **Garmr** (gär′mər).

gar·ment (gär′mənt), *n.* **1.** any article of clothing: *dresses, suits, and other garments.* **2.** an outer covering or outward appearance. —*v.t.* **3.** to clothe or cover. [ME *garnement* < OF *garniment,* equiv. to *garn(ir)* (to) GARNISH + *-ment* -MENT] —**gar′ment·less,** *adj.*

Gar′ment Cen′ter, an area in the borough of Manhattan, in New York City, including portions of Seventh Avenue and Broadway between 34th and 40th Streets and the streets intersecting them, that contains many factories, showrooms, etc., related to the manufacture and wholesale distribution of women's clothing. Also called **Gar′ment Dis′trict, Seventh Avenue.**

gar·ner (gär′nər), *v.t.* **1.** to gather or deposit in or as if in a granary or other storage place. **2.** to get; acquire: *He gradually garnered a national reputation as a financial expert.* **3.** to gather, collect, or hoard. —*n.* **4.** a granary or grain bin. **5.** a store of anything. [ME *garner, gerner* < OF *gernier, grenier* < L *grānārium* GRANARY]

Gar·ner (gär′nər), *n.* **1. John Nance** (nans), 1868–1967, vice-president of the U.S. 1933–41. **2.** a town in central North Carolina. 3451 (1960).

gar·net[1] (gär′nit), *n.* **1.** any of a group of hard, vitreous minerals, silicates of calcium, magnesium, iron, or manganese with aluminum or iron, varying in color: a deep-red transparent variety is used as a gem and as an abrasive. **2.** a deep red color. [ME *garnet, gernate* < OF *gernate, grenade* < L *grānāt(um)* granular; cf. POMEGRANATE] —**gar′net-like′,** *adj.*

gar·net[2] (gär′nit), *n. Naut.* a tackle having two single blocks; gun tackle. [< ?; cf. D *garnaat, karnaat*]

Gar·net (gär′nit), *n.* a boy's given name.

gar′net hinge′, cross-garnet. [ME *garnette,* ? < ONF *carne* hinge < L *cardin-* (s. of *cardō*)]

gar′net jade′. See **Transvaal jade.**

gar′net pa′per, an abrasive paper coated with pulverized garnet.

gar·nett (gär net′), *v.t.* **1.** *Textiles.* to reduce (waste material) to its fibrous state for reuse in textile manufacturing. —*n.* **2.** a machine used in garnetting. [after the surname *Garnett*] —**gar·nett′er,** *n.*

Gar·nett (gär′nit, *also, for 1,* gär net′), *n.* **1. Constance Black,** 1862–1946, English translator from Russian. **2.** a town in E Kansas. 3034 (1960).

gar·ni (gaʀ nē′), *adj. French.* garnished.

gar·ni·er·ite (gär′nē ə rīt′), *n.* a mineral, hydrous nickel magnesium silicate, occurring in earthy, green masses: an important ore of nickel. [named after Jules *Garnier* (d. 1904), French geologist; see -ITE[1]]

gar·nish (gär′nish), *v.t.* **1.** to provide or supply with something ornamental; adorn; decorate. **2.** to provide (a food) with something that adds flavor, decorative color, etc.): *to garnish boiled potatoes with chopped parsley.* **3.** *Law.* **a.** to summon in, so as to take part in litigation already pending between others. **b.** to attach (as money due, property belonging to a debtor, etc.) while it is in the hands of a third person, by warning the latter not to pay it over or surrender it; garnishee. —*n.* **4.** something placed around or on a food or in a beverage to add flavor, decorative color, etc. **5.** adornment or decoration. **6.** *Slang.* a fee demanded of a new worker or convict by his boss, warden, or fellow workers or prisoners. [ME *garnish(en)* < OF

garniss- (extended s. of *garnir, guarnir* to furnish < Gmc); cf. WARN] —**gar′nish·a·ble,** *adj.* —**gar′nish·er,** *n.*
—**Syn. 1.** embellish, ornament, beautify, trim, bedeck, bedizen, set off, enhance. **5.** ornament; garniture.

gar′nish bolt′, *Shipbuilding.* a bolt having a decorative head.

gar·nish·ee (gär′ni shē′), *v.,* **-nish·eed, -nish·ee·ing,** *n. Law.* —*v.t.* **1.** to attach (money or property) by garnishment. **2.** to serve (a person) with a garnishment. —*n.* **3.** a person served with a garnishment. [GARNISH + -EE]

gar·nish·ment (gär′nish mənt), *n.* **1.** adornment or decoration. **2.** *Law.* **a.** a summons to appear in litigation pending between others. **b.** a warning served on a person, at the suit of a creditor plaintiff, to hold, subject to the court's direction, money or property of the defendant in his possession. [GARNISH + -MENT]

gar·ni·ture (gär′ni chər), *n.* **1.** something that garnishes; decoration; adornment. **2.** *Armor.* a set of plate armor having pieces of exchange for all purposes. [< F, equiv. to MF *garni(r)* (to) GARNISH + *-ture* n. suffix; see -URE]

gar·ni·ture de che·mi·née (gär′ni chər də shem′ə nā′; *Fr.* GAR nē TYR′ də shə mē nā′), *pl.* **gar·ni·tures de che·mi·née** (gär′ni chərz də shem′ə nā′; *Fr.* GAR nē TYR′ də shə mē nā′). a set of five vases, two open and three covered, used as a mantel ornament in the 17th century. [< F: ornamentation for the mantelpiece; see GARNITURE, CHIMNEY]

Ga·ro·fa·lo (*It.* gä rô′fä lô), *n.* Galofalo.

Ga·ronne (GA rôn′), *n.* a river in SW France, flowing NW from the Pyrenees to the Gironde River. 350 mi. long.

ga·rote (gə rōt′, -rot′), *n., v.t.,* **-rot·ed, -rot·ing.** garrote. —**ga·rot′er,** *n.*

ga·rotte (gə rot′, -rōt′), *n., v.t.,* **-rot·ted, -rot·ting.** garrote. —**ga·rot′ter,** *n.*

gar·pike (gär′pīk′), *n.* a gar. [formed after GARFISH]

gar·ret[1] (gar′it), *n.* attic (def. 1). [ME *garite* watchtower < OF *garite, guerite* watchtower, deriv. of *garir, guarir* to defend, protect; see GARRISON] —**gar′ret·ed,** *adj.*

gar·ret[2] (gar′it), *v.t.* gallet (def. 2).

gar·ret·eer (gar′i tēr′), *n. Archaic.* one who lives in a garret, esp. an impoverished author, artist, or musician. [GARRET[1] + -EER]

Gar·rett (gar′it), *n.* **1.** a town in NE Indiana. 4364 (1960). **2.** a boy's given name, form of **Gerald.**

Gar·rick (gar′ik), *n.* **David,** 1717–79, English actor and theatrical manager.

gar·ri·son (gar′i sən), *n.* **1.** a body of troops stationed in a fortified place. **2.** the place where such troops are stationed. **3.** any military post, esp. a permanent one. —*v.t.* **4.** to provide (a fort, town, etc.) with a garrison. **5.** to occupy (a fort, post, station, etc.) with troops. **6.** to put (troops) on duty in a fort, post, station, etc. [ME *garisoun* protection, stronghold < OF *garison, gareison* defense, provision, deriv. of *garir, guerir* to defend < OHG *warjan* to defend]

Gar·ri·son (gar′i sən), *n.* **William Lloyd,** 1805–79, U.S. leader in the abolition movement.

gar′rison cap′. See **overseas cap.**

Gar′rison fin′ish, the finish of a race, esp. a horse race, in which the winner comes from behind to win at the last moment. [prob. named after Snapper *Garrison,* 19th-century American jockey who often won in this fashion]

gar·rot (gar′ət), *n. Dial.* goldeneye (def. 1). [< F]

gar·rote (gə rōt′, -rot′), *n., v.,* **-rot·ed, -rot·ing.** —*n.* **1.** a method of capital punishment of Spanish origin in which an iron collar is tightened around a condemned man's neck until death occurs by strangulation or by injury to the spinal column at the base of the brain. **2.** the collarlike instrument used for this method of execution. **3.** strangulation or throttling, esp. in the course of a robbery. **4.** an instrument, usually a cord or wire with handles attached at the ends, used for strangling a victim. —*v.t.* **5.** to execute by the garrote. **6.** to strangle or throttle, esp. in the course of a robbery. Also, **garote, garotte, garrotte.** [< Sp *garrote* or F *garrot* packing-stick < ?] —**gar·rot′er,** *n.*

gar·rotte (gə rot′, -rōt′), *n., v.t.,* **-rot·ted, -rot·ting.** garrote. —**gar·rot′ter,** *n.*

gar·ru·li·ty (gə rōō′li tē), *n.* the quality of being garrulous; talkativeness; loquacity. [< F *garrulité* < L *garrulitāt-* (s. of *garrulitās*). See GARRULOUS, -ITY]

gar·ru·lous (gar′ə ləs, gar′yə-), *adj.* **1.** excessively talkative in a rambling, roundabout manner, esp. about trivial matters. **2.** wordy or diffuse: *a garrulous and boring speech.* [< L *garrulus* talkative, garrulous, equiv. to *garr(īre)* (to) chatter + *-ulus* -ULOUS] —**gar′ru·lous·ly,** *adv.* —**gar′ru·lous·ness,** *n.*
—**Syn. 1.** prating, babbling. See **talkative. 2.** verbose, prolix.

Gar·ry (gâr′ē, gar′ē), *n.* a boy's given name. Also, **Garey, Gari, Gary.**

Gar·son (gär′sən), *n.* a boy's given name.

Gart (gärt), *n.* a boy's given name, form of **Garrett.**

gar·ter (gär′tər), *n.* **1.** Also called, *Brit.,* **sock suspender, suspender.** an article of clothing for holding up a stocking or sock, usually an elastic band around the leg or an elastic strap hanging from a girdle or other undergarment. **2.** a similar band worn to hold up a shirt sleeve. **3.** a leather strap for passing through a loop at the back of a boot and buckling around the leg to keep the boot from slipping. **4.** *Brit.* **a.** the badge of the Order of the Garter. **b.** membership in the Order. **c.** (*cap.*) the Order itself. **d.** (*usually cap.*) a member of the Order. —*v.t.* **4.** to fasten with a garter. [ME < ONF *gartier,* deriv. of *garet* the bend of the knee < Celt *garra* leg] —**gar′ter·less,** *adj.*

gar′ter belt′, a wide belt of cloth or elastic, having supporters suspended from it, worn by women to hold up stockings.

gar′ter snake′, any of numerous harmless snakes of the genus *Thamnophis,* common in North and Central America, often having three light, longitudinal stripes on the back.

garth (gärth), *n.* **1.** Also called **cloister garth.** an open courtyard enclosed by a cloister. **2.** *Archaic.* a yard or garden. [ME < Scand; cf. OIcel *gardh(r)* YARD[2]]

Garth (gärth), *n.* a boy's given name. Also, **Gareth.**

Garth·rod (gärth′rəd), *n.* a boy's given name.

Gärt·ner (gärt′nər), *n.* a walled plain in the first quadrant of the face of the moon: about 63 miles in diameter.

ga·rú·a (gə rōō′ə; *Sp.* gä rōō′ä), *n.* a thick fog or drizzle on the Pacific coast of South America. Also called **camanchaca.** [< AmerSp]

gar·vey (gär′vē), *n., pl.* **-veys.** a scowlike open boat, variously propelled, used by oyster and clam fishermen in Delaware Bay and off the coasts of Delaware and New Jersey. [prob. from a proper name]

Gar·vin (gär′vin), *n.* a boy's given name.

Gar·wood (gär′wŏŏd′), *n.* a town in NE New Jersey. 5426 (1960).

Gar·y (gâr′ē, gar′ē), *n.* **1. Elbert Henry,** 1846–1927, U.S. financier and lawyer. **2.** a port in NW Indiana, on Lake Michigan. 178,320 (1960). **3.** Also, **Garey, Gari, Garry.** a boy's given name.

gas (gas), *n., pl.* **gas·es,** *v.,* **gassed, gas·sing.** —*n.* **1.** *Physics.* a substance possessing perfect molecular mobility and the property of indefinite expansion, as opposed to a solid or liquid. **2.** any such fluid or mixture of fluids other than air. **3.** any such fluid used as an anesthetic: *Did the dentist give you gas for your extraction?* **4.** any such combustible fluid used as fuel: *Light the gas in the oven.* **5.** *U.S. Informal.* **a.** gasoline. **b.** the accelerator of an automobile or other vehicle: *Take your foot off the gas.* **6.** *Coal Mining.* an explosive mixture of firedamp with air. **7.** an aeriform fluid or a mistlike assemblage of fine particles suspended in air, used in warfare to asphyxiate, poison, or stupefy an enemy. **8.** *Slang.* empty talk. **9.** *Slang.* **a.** one who or that which is very entertaining, pleasing, or successful: *The party was an absolute gas, and we loved it.* **b.** one who or that which affects one strongly. **10. step on the gas,** *Slang.* to increase the speed of one's movement or activity; hurry: *We'd better step on the gas or we'll be late for the concert.* —*v.t.* **11.** to supply with gas. **12.** to overcome, poison, or asphyxiate with gas or fumes. **13.** to singe (yarns or fabrics) with a gas flame to remove superfluous fibers. **14.** to treat or impregnate with gas. **15.** *Slang.* to talk nonsense or falsehood to. **16.** *Slang.* to amuse or affect strongly: *Her weird clothes really gas me.* —*v.i.* **17.** to give off gas, as a storage battery being charged. **18.** *Slang.* to indulge in idle, empty talk. **19. gas up,** to fill the gasoline tank of an automobile or truck. [coined by J. B. van Helmont (1577–1644), Flemish chemist; suggested by Gk *cháos* atmosphere] —**gas′less,** *adj.*

gas′ attack′, a military attack in which an asphyxiating or poisonous gas is spread over an enemy, as by spraying a gas from airplanes or by bombardment with gas shells.

gas′ bacil′lus, any of several pathogenic bacilli, esp. of the genus *Clostridium,* that produce gas in infected tissue.

gas·bag (gas′bag′), *n.* **1.** a bag for holding gas, as in a balloon or dirigible. **2.** *Slang.* a talkative, boastful person; windbag. [GAS + BAG]

gas′ black′, the soot of a natural gas flame, used in paints; fine carbon.

gas′ blad′der. See **air bladder** (def. 2).

gas′ burn′er, 1. the tip, jet, or endpiece of a gas fixture, from which the gas issues, as on a stove. **2.** a stove or the like that burns gas as a fuel.

gas′ cap′, *Astron.* the compressed, heated gas immediately in front of a falling meteor.

gas′ cham′ber, a room used for the execution of prisoners by means of a poisonous gas.

Gas′ Cit′y, a town in central Indiana. 4469 (1960).

gas′ coal′, a soft coal suitable for the production of gas.

Gas·cogne (GA skôn′yᵊ), *n.* French name of **Gascony.**

Gas·coigne (gas′koin), *n.* **George,** 1525?–77, English poet.

Gas·con (gas′kən), *n.* **1.** a native of Gascony, France, the inhabitants of which were noted for their boastfulness. **2.** (*l.c.*) a boaster or braggart. —*adj.* **3.** pertaining to Gascony and its people. **4.** (*l.c.*) boastful; bragging. [ME *gascoun* < OF; akin to L *Vascōnes* Vascones (Basque)]

Gas·con (gas′kən), *n.* a boy's given name.

gas·con·ade (gas′kə nād′), *n., v.,* **-ad·ed, -ad·ing.** —*n.* **1.** extravagant boasting; boastful talk. —*v.i.* **2.** to boast extravagantly; bluster. [< F *gasconnade* deriv. of *gasconner* to boast, chatter. See GASCON, -ADE[1]] —**gas′con·ad′er,** *n.*

AUVERGNE
BAY OF BISCAY
Bordeaux
GUIENNE
Gascony
Toulouse
LANGUEDOC
MEDIT. SEA
SPAIN

gas′ con′stant, *Physics.* See **universal gas constant.**

Gas·co·ny (gas′kə nē), *n.* a former province in SW France. French, **Gascogne.**

Gas·coyne-Ce·cil (gas′koin ses′əl), *n.* **Robert Arthur Tal·bot** (tôl′bət), **3rd Marquis of Salisbury,** 1830–1903, British statesman: prime minister 1885–86, 1886–92, 1895–1902.

gas·e·lier (gas′ə lēr′), *n.* gasolier.

gas′ en′gine, an internal-combustion engine driven by a mixture of air and gas.

gas·e·ous (gas′ē əs, gash′əs), *adj.* **1.** pertaining to or having the characteristics of gas. **2.** existing in the state of a gas; not solid or liquid. **3.** *Informal.* lacking firmness or solidity; uncertain; not definite. [GAS + -EOUS] —**gas′e·ous·ness, gas·e·i·ty** (ga sē′i tē), *n.*

gas′ field′, a district yielding natural gas.

gas-fired (gas′fīᵊrd′), *adj.* using a gas for fuel.

gas′ fit′ter, a person who installs gas pipes and apparatus in buildings.

gas′ fit′ting, 1. the work or business of a gas fitter. **2. gas fittings,** fittings for the use of illuminating gas.

gas′ fix′ture, a permanent fixture attached to a gas pipe in the ceiling or wall of a room, as a more or less ornamental pipe without or with branches, bearing a burner or burners with regulating devices for a gaslight.

gas′ fo′cusing, *Electronics.* (in a cathode ray tube) a method of concentrating an electron beam by ionizing the gas within it.

gas′ fur′nace, 1. a furnace using gas as a fuel. **2.** a furnace for distilling gas from a solid fuel, as coal.

gas′ gan′grene, *Pathol.* a gangrenous infection developing in wounds, esp. deep wounds with closed spaces, caused by bacteria that form gases in the subcutaneous tissues.

gash[1] (gash), *n.* **1.** a long, deep wound or cut; slash. —*v.t.* **2.** to make a long, deep cut in; slash. [alter. of ME *garsen* < OF *gars(er), jars(ier)* (F *gercer*) (to) scarify, wound < VL *charissāre* < Gk *charáss(ein)* (to) scratch, notch]

gash[2] (gash), *Chiefly Scot.* —*n.* **1.** an insolent or disrespectful remark. —*adj.* **2.** talkative; loquacious. [?]

gash[3] (gash), *adj.* **1.** wise, sagacious. **2.** having a wise or dignified appearance. **3.** neat; well-groomed. [?]

gash[4] (gash), *adj. Scot. Archaic.* dreary or gloomy in appearance. [?]

gas′ hel′met, *Mil.* a type of gas mask.

gas·hold·er (gas′hōl′dər), *n.* a container for holding gas, esp. a large, cylindrical or spherical storage tank. [GAS + HOLDER]

gas·i·form (gas′ə fôrm′), *adj.* having the form of gas; gaseous. [GAS + -I- + -FORM]

gas·i·fy (gas′ə fī′), *v.t., v.i.,* **-fied, -fy·ing.** to convert into or become a gas. [GAS + -IFY] —**gas′i·fi′a·ble,** *adj.* —**gas′i·fi·ca′tion,** *n.* —**gas′i·fi′er,** *n.*

gas′ jet′, 1. a gas burner on a gas fixture. **2.** a flame of illuminating gas.

Gas·kell (gas′kəl), *n.* **Mrs.** (*Elizabeth Cleghorn Stevenson Gaskell*), 1810–65, English novelist.

gas·ket (gas′kit), *n.* **1.** a rubber, metal, or rope ring, for packing a piston or placing around a joint to make it watertight. **2.** Also, **gassit.** *Naut.* any of a number of light lines for securing a furled sail to a boom, gaff, or yard. [< ?; perh. < F *garcette* a plait of rope]

gas·kin[1] (gas′kin), *n.* **1.** the part of the hind leg of a horse or other hoofed quadruped between the stifle and the hock. See diag. under **horse. 2. gaskins,** *Obs.* hose or breeches; galligaskins. [perh. shortened form of GALLIGASKINS]

gas·kin[2] (gas′kin), *n.* a gasket. Also, **gas·king** (gas′king). [by alter.]

gas′ law′, *Physics.* See **ideal gas law.**

gas·light (gas′līt′), *n.* **1.** light produced by the combustion of illuminating gas. **2.** a gas burner or gas jet for producing this kind of light. [GAS + LIGHT[1]] —**gas′light′ed,** *adj.*

gas′ liq′uor, *Chem.* See **ammonia liquor.**

gas·lit (gas′lit′), *adj.* **1.** having illumination provided by burning gas: *gaslit streets.* **2.** characterized by the widespread use of the gaslight: *the gaslit era.* [GAS + LIT]

gas′ log′, a gas burner in a fireplace, made to resemble a log.

gas′ main′, a large pipe for conducting and distributing gas to lesser pipes or ducts, esp. such a pipe carrying and distributing household gas beneath the streets of a town or city.

gas·man (gas′man′), *n., pl.* **-men. 1.** a man who works for a company that sells or distributes household gas, esp. a man who goes from building to building reading gas meters to determine what charge is to be billed. **2.** See **gas fitter. 3.** *Mining.* See **fire boss.** [GAS + MAN[1]]

Gas mask

gas′ man′tle, mantle (def. 4).

gas′ mask′, a masklike device containing or attached to a component that filters the air inhaled by the wearer through charcoal and chemicals, for protecting the face and lungs against noxious gases and fumes, as in warfare or in certain industrial processes.

gas′ me′ter, an apparatus for measuring and recording the amount of gas produced or consumed, esp. such an apparatus metering the amount of household gas piped into a dwelling.

gas·o·gene (gas′ə jēn′), *n.* gazogene.

gas·o·hol (gas′ə hôl′, -hol′), *n.* a mixture of 90% unleaded gasoline and 10% anhydrous ethyl alcohol, used esp. as an automobile fuel. [GAS(OLINE + ALC)OHOL]

gas·o·lier (gas′ə lēr′), *n.* a chandelier furnished with gaslights. Also, **gaselier.** [GAS + -O- + (CHANDE)LIER]

gas·o·line (gas′ə lēn′, gas′ə lēn′), *n.* a volatile, flammable liquid mixture of hydrocarbons, obtained from petroleum, and used as fuel for internal-combustion engines, as a solvent, etc. Also, **gas′o·lene′.** [GAS + -OL[2] + -INE[2]] —**gas′o·line′less,** *adj.* —**gas·o·lin·ic** (gas′ə lē′nik, -lin′ik), *adj.*

gas·om·e·ter (gas om′i tər), *n.* **1.** an apparatus for measuring and storing gas in a laboratory. **2.** *Brit.* a large tank or cylindrical reservoir of gas, as at a gasworks, to be piped to homes, factories, etc. [< F *gazomètre.* See GAS, -O-, -METER]

gas·om·e·try (gas om′i trē), *n. Chem.* the measurement of gases. [GAS + -O- + -METRY] —**gas·o·met·ric** (gas′ə me′trik), **gas′o·met′ri·cal,** *adj.* —**gas′o·met′ri·cal·ly,** *adv.*

gasp (gasp, gäsp), *n.* **1.** a sudden, short breath; a convulsive effort to breathe. **2.** a short, convulsive utterance: *the words came out in gasps.* **3. at one's last gasp,** at the point of death: *At his last gasp he confessed to the murder.* —*v.i.* **4.** to catch the breath or struggle for breath with one's mouth open; breathe convulsively. **5.** to long with breathless eagerness; desire; crave (usually fol. by *for* or *after*). —*v.t.* **6.** to utter with gasps (often fol. by *out, forth, away,* etc.): *She gasped out the words.* **7.** to breathe or emit with gasps (often fol. by *away*). [ME *gasp(en),* prob. OE **gāspen,* equiv. to OIcel *geispa;* akin to GAPE] —**gasp′ing·ly,** *adv.*
—**Syn. 4.** puff blow. See **pant.**

Gas·par (gas′pər; *Port.* gəsh pär′, gäs-; *Sp.* gäs-pär′; *Fr.* GA SPAR′), *n.* a boy's given name, form of **Caspar.**

Gas·pé′ Penin′sula (gas pā′; *Fr.* GA spā′), a peninsula in SE Canada, in Quebec province, between New Brunswick and the St. Lawrence River.

gas·per (gas′pər, gä′spər), *n. Brit. Slang.* a cigarette, esp. a cheap one. [GASP + -ER[1]]

gas·per·eau (gas′pə rō′), *n., pl.* **-eaus,** (*esp. collectively*) **-eau.** *Canadian.* alewife[1]. [< CanF: a kind of herring]

gas·per·gou (gas′pər go͞o′), *n., pl.* **-gous,** (*esp. collectively*) **-gou.** See **fresh-water drum.** [< LaF *casburgot,* F *casse-burgot,* equiv. to *cass(er)* (to) break + *burgeau* a kind of shellfish]

Gas·pe·ri (*It.* gäs′pe rē), *n.* **Al·ci·de De** (*It.* äl che′de de). See **De Gasperi, Alcide.**

gas-plant (gas′plant′, -plänt′), *n.* dittany (def. 3).

gas′ pli′ers, (in plumbing) pliers for handling pipes of small diameter, having jaws with concave, serrated faces.

gas′ range′, a cooking stove that uses gas as fuel.

Gas·sen·di (ga sän dē′ *for 1;* gə sen′dē *for 2*), *n.* **1. Pierre** (pyer), 1592–1655, French philosopher and scientist. **2.** a walled plain in the third quadrant of the face of the moon: about 55 miles in diameter.

gas·ser (gas′ər), *n.* **1.** one who or that which gasses. **2.** a well or boring yielding natural gas. **3.** *Slang.* something that is extraordinarily pleasing or successful, esp. a very funny joke. [GAS + -ER[1]]

Gas·ser (gas′ər), *n.* **Herbert Spencer,** 1888–1963, U.S. physiologist: Nobel prize for medicine 1944.

gas′ shell′, *Mil.* an explosive shell containing a liquid or other material that is converted into an asphyxiating or poisonous gas or vapor when the shell bursts.

gas·sing (gas′ing), *n.* **1.** the act of one who or that which gasses. **2.** an affecting, overcoming, or poisoning with gas or fumes. **3.** the evolution of gases during electrolysis. **4.** a process by which something is gassed, as in fumigation. [GAS + -ING[1]]

gas·sit (gas′it), *n.* *Naut.* gasket (def. 2).

gas′ sta′tion, a place that sells gasoline, oil, tires, etc., and provides other services for motor vehicles; filling station. Also called **service station.**

gas·sy (gas′ē), *adj.,* **-si·er, -si·est. 1.** full of or containing gas. **2.** resembling gas. **3.** flatulent. [GAS + -Y[1]] **—gas′si·ness,** *n.*

gas′ tank′, **1.** a tank for storing gas or gasoline. **2.** a tank containing the gasoline supply in a car, truck, or other gasoline-engine vehicle.

gas·ter (gas′tər), *n.* (in ants and other hymenopterous insects) the part of the abdomen behind the petiole. [< Gk *gastḗr* paunch, belly]

Gas·ter·o·chei·res (gas′tə rō kī′rēz), *n.pl.* *Class. Myth.* seven Cyclopes who accompanied Proteus from Lycia.

gas·ter·o·pod (gas′tər ə pod′), *n., adj.* gastropod.

gast·haus (gäst′hous′), *n., pl.* **-haus·es** (-hou′ziz), **-häus·er** (-hoi′zər). a German inn or tavern. [< G: lit., guesthouse]

gas′ thermom′eter, a device for measuring temperature by observing the change in either pressure or volume of an enclosed gas.

gas·tight (gas′tīt′), *adj.* **1.** not penetrable by a gas. **2.** not admitting a given gas under a given pressure. [GAS + TIGHT] **—gas′tight′ness,** *n.*

Gas·ton (gas′tən; *Fr.* GA stôN′), *n.* a boy's given name.

Gas·to·ni·a (ga stō′nē ə), *n.* a city in S North Carolina, W of Charlotte. 37,276 (1960).

gastr-, var. of **gastro-** before a vowel: *gastrectomy.*

gas·tral·gi·a (ga stral′jē ə, -jə), *n.* *Pathol.* **1.** neuralgia of the stomach. **2.** any stomach pain. [< NL; see GASTR-, -ALGIA] **—gas·tral′gic,** *adj., n.*

gas·trec·ta·sia (gas′trek tā′zhə, -zē ə, -shə, -sē ə), *Med.* dilatation of the stomach. Also, **gas·trec·ta·sis** (gas′trek tā′sis). [GASTR- + NL *ectasia;* see ECTASIS, -IA]

gas·trec·to·my (ga strek′tə mē), *n., pl.* **-mies.** *Surg.* partial or total excision of the stomach. [GASTR- + -ECTOMY]

gas·tric (gas′trik), *adj.* pertaining to the stomach. [GASTR- + -IC]

gas′tric juice′, *Biochem.* the digestive fluid, containing pepsin and other enzymes, secreted by the glands of the stomach.

gas′tric lav′age, *Med.* the washing out of the stomach; lavage.

gas′tric ul′cer, *Pathol.* an erosion of the stomach's inner wall caused in part by the corrosive action of the gastric juice on the mucous membrane. Cf. **peptic ulcer.**

gas·trin (gas′trin), *n.* *Biochem.* a hormone that stimulates the secretion of gastric juice. [GASTR- + -IN[2]]

gas·tri·tis (ga strī′tis), *n.* *Pathol.* inflammation of the stomach, esp. of its mucous membrane. [< NL; see GASTR-, -ITIS] **—gas·trit·ic** (ga strit′ik), *adj.*

gastro-, a learned borrowing from Greek meaning "stomach," used in the formation of compound words: *gastrology.* Also, *esp. before a vowel,* **gastr-.** [< Gk, comb. form of *gastḗr*]

gas·troc·ne·mi·us (gas′trok nē′mē əs, gas′trə nē′-), *n., pl.* **-mi·i** (-mē ī′). *Anat.* the largest muscle in the calf of the leg, the action of which extends the foot, raises the heel, and assists in bending the knee. [< NL < Gk *gastroknēm(ía)* calf of the leg + L *-ius* n. suffix] **—gas′troc·ne′mi·al, gas′troc·ne′mi·an,** *adj.*

gas·tro·col·ic (gas′trō kol′ik), *adj.* *Anat.* of, pertaining to, or involving the stomach and colon. [GASTRO- + COLIC]

gastrocol′ic omen′tum. See **greater omentum.**

gas·tro·der·mis (gas′trō dûr′mis), *n.* *Zool.* the inner cell layer of the body of a coelenterate. [GASTRO- + DERMIS] **—gas′tro·der′mal,** *adj.*

gas·tro·du·o·de·nos·to·my (gas′trō do͞o′ə dᵊnos′tə mē, -dyo͞o′-), *n., pl.* **-mies.** *Surg.* See under **gastroenterostomy.** [GASTRO- + DUODENO- + -STOMY]

gas·tro·en·ter·i·tis (gas′trō en′tə rī′tis), *n.* *Pathol.* inflammation of the stomach and intestines. [GASTROENTER(O)- + -ITIS] **—gas·tro·en·ter·it·ic** (gas′trō en′tə rit′ik), *adj.*

gastroentero-, a combining form of **gastro-** and **entero-:** *gastroenterostomy.*

gas·tro·en·ter·ol·o·gy (gas′trō en′tə rol′ə jē), *n.* the study of the structure and diseases of digestive organs. [GASTROENTERO- + -LOGY] **—gas·tro·en·ter·o·log·ic** (gas′trō en′tər ə loj′ik), **gas′tro·en′ter·o·log′i·cal,** *adj.* **—gas′tro·en′ter·ol′o·gist,** *n.*

gas·tro·en·ter·os·to·my (gas′trō en′tə ros′tə mē), *n., pl.* **-mies.** *Surg.* the making of a new passage between the stomach and the duodenum **(gastroduodenostomy)** or, esp., the jejunum **(gastrojejunostomy).** [GASTROENTERO- + -STOMY]

gas·tro·he·pat·ic (gas′trō hi pat′ik), *adj.* *Anat.* of, pertaining to, or involving the stomach and the liver. [GASTRO- + HEPATIC]

gas′trohepat′ic omen′tum. See **lesser omentum.**

gas·tro·in·tes·ti·nal (gas′trō in tes′tə nᵊl), *adj.* *Anat.* of, pertaining to, or affecting the stomach and intestines. [GASTRO- + INTESTINAL]

gas·tro·je·ju·nos·to·my (gas′trō ji jo͞o nos′tə mē), *n., pl.* **-mies.** *Surg.* See under **gastroenterostomy.** [GASTRO- + JEJUNOSTOMY]

gas·tro·lith (gas′trə lith), *n.* *Pathol.* a calculous concretion in the stomach. [GASTRO- + -LITH]

gas·trol·o·gy (ga strol′ə jē), *n.* the study of the structure, functions, and diseases of the stomach. [GASTRO- + -LOGY] **—gas·tro·log·i·cal·ly** (gas′trə loj′ik lē), *adv.* **—gas·trol′o·gist,** *n.*

gas·tro·nome (gas′trə nōm′), *n.* a gourmet; epicure. Also, **gas·tron·o·mer** (ga stron′ə mər), **gas·tron′o·mist.** [< F, back formation from *gastronomie* GASTRONOMY]

gas·tron·o·my (ga stron′ə mē), *n.* **1.** the art or science of good eating. **2.** a style or custom of cooking or eating. [< F *gastronomie* < Gk *gastronomía.* See GASTRO-, -NOMY] **—gas·tro·nom·ic** (gas′trə nom′ik), **gas′tro·nom′i·cal,** *adj.* **—gas′tro·nom′i·cal·ly,** *adv.*

gas·tro·pod (gas′trə pod′), *n.* **1.** any mollusk of the class *Gastropoda,* comprising the snails. **—***adj.* **2.** Also, **gas·trop·o·dous** (ga strop′ə dəs). belonging or pertaining to the *Gastropoda.* Also, **gasteropod.** [< NL *Gast(e)ropod(a)* a class of mollusk(s). See GASTRO-, -POD]

Gas·trop·o·da (ga strop′ə də), *n.* the class comprising the snails, whelks, slugs, etc. [< NL: GASTROPOD]

gas·tros·chi·sis (ga stros′ki sis), *n.* *Pathol.* a congenital malformation in which the ventral abdomen wall does not close. [< NL, equiv. to *gastro-* GASTRO- + Gk *schísis* split (*schíz(ein)* (to) split + *-sis* -SIS)]

gas·tro·scope (gas′trə skōp′), *n.* *Med.* an instrument for inspecting the interior of the stomach. [GASTRO- + -SCOPE] **—gas·tro·scop·ic** (gas′trə skop′ik), *adj.*

gas·tros·co·py (ga stros′kə pē), *n., pl.* **-pies.** *Med.* the examination with a gastroscope to detect disease. [GASTRO- + -SCOPY]

gas·tros·to·my (ga stros′tə mē), *n., pl.* **-mies.** *Surg.* the operation of cutting into the stomach and leaving a more or less permanent opening for feeding or drainage. [GASTRO- + -STOMY]

gas·trot·o·my (ga strot′ə mē), *n., pl.* **-mies.** *Surg.* the operation of cutting into the stomach. [GASTRO- + -TOMY] **—gas·tro·tom·ic** (gas′trə tom′ik), *adj.*

gas·tro·trich (gas′trə trik), *n.* any of the microscopic, multicellular animals of the class or phylum *Gastrotricha,* found in fresh or salt water, characterized by bands of cilia on the ventral side of the body. [< NL, equiv. to *gastro-* GASTRO- + Gk *trich-* (s. of *thríx*) hair]

gas·tro·vas·cu·lar (gas′trō vas′kyə lər), *adj.* *Zool.* serving for digestion and circulation, as a cavity. [GASTRO- + VASCULAR]

gas·tru·la (gas′tro͝o lə), *n., pl.* **-las, -lae** (-lē′). *Embryol.* a metazoan embryo in an early state of germ layer formation following the blastula stage, consisting of a cuplike body of two layers of cells, the ectoderm and endoderm, enclosing a central cavity or archenteron that opens to the outside by the blastopore. [< NL; see GASTRO-, -ULE] **—gas′tru·lar,** *adj.*

gas·tru·late (gas′tro͝o lāt′), *v.i.,* **-lat·ed, -lat·ing.** *Embryol.* to undergo gastrulation. [GASTRUL(A) + -ATE[1]]

gas·tru·la·tion (gas′tro͝o lā′shən), *n.* *Embryol.* **1.** the formation of a gastrula. **2.** any process, as invagination, by which a blastula or other form of embryo is converted into a gastrula. [GASTRULATE + -ION]

gas′ tube′, an electron tube the envelope of which contains a highly rarefied gas.

gas′ tur′bine, a turbine utilizing the gaseous products of combustion.

gas′ well′, a well from which natural gas is obtained.

gas·works (gas′wûrks′), *n., pl.* **-works.** (*construed as sing.*) a plant where heating and illuminating gas is manufactured and piped to homes and buildings. Also called **gashouse.** [GAS + WORKS]

gat[1] (gat), *v.* *Archaic.* pt. of **get.**

gat[2] (gat), *n.* *Slang.* a pistol or revolver. [abbr. of GATLING GUN]

gat[3] (gat), *n.* a passage or channel that extends inland from a shore through shoals, cliffs, etc. [< Scand; cf. OIcel *gat* lane, pathway]

ga·ta (gä′tə), *n.* the nurse shark, *Ginglymostoma cirratum.* [< AmerSp, Sp: cat < LL *catta* CAT[1]]

gate[1] (gāt), *n., v.,* **gat·ed, gat·ing.** **—***n.* **1.** a movable barrier, usually doorlike, closing an opening in a fence, wall, or other enclosure. **2.** an opening permitting passage through an enclosure. **3.** a tower, architectural setting, etc., for defending or adorning such an opening or for providing a monumental entrance to a street, park, etc. **4.** any means of access or entrance. **5.** a mountain pass. **6.** any movable barrier, as at a road or railroad crossing. **7.** a sliding barrier for regulating the passage of water, steam, or the like, as in a dam, pipe, etc.; valve. **8.** *Skiing.* **a.** an obstacle in a slalom race, consisting of two upright poles anchored in the snow a certain distance apart. **b.** the opening between these poles, through which a competitor in a slalom race must ski. **9.** the number of persons who pay for admission to an athletic contest, a performance, an exhibition, etc. **10.** the total receipts from such admissions. **11.** a sash or frame for a saw or gang of saws. **12.** *Foundry.* **a.** Also called **ingate.** a channel or opening in a mold through which molten metal is poured into the mold cavity. **b.** the waste metal left in such a channel after hardening. **13.** *Electronics.* **a.** a signal that makes an electronic circuit operative or inoperative either for a certain time interval or until another such signal is received. **b.** a circuit with one output that is activated only by certain combinations of two or more inputs. **14. get the gate,** *Slang.* to be rejected, sent away, or dismissed. **15. give (someone) the gate,** *Slang.* **a.** to reject a person, as one's fiancé, lover, friend, etc. **b.** to dismiss from one's employ: *They gave him the gate because he was caught stealing.* **—***v.t.* **16.** (at British universities) to punish by restricting (a student) within the college gates. **17.** *Electronics.* **a.** to control the operation of (an electronic device) by means of a gate. **b.** to select the parts of (a wave signal) that are within a certain range of amplitude or within certain time intervals. **—***v.i.* **18.** *Foundry.* to make or use a gate. [ME *gat, gate,* OE *geat* (pl. *gatu*); c. LG, D *gat* hole, breach; cf. GATE[2]] **—gate′less,** *adj.* **—gate′like′,** *adj.*

gate[2] (gāt), *n.* **1.** *Archaic.* a path; way. **2.** *Dial.* habitual manner or way of acting. [ME < ON *gata* path; perh. akin to OE *geat* GATE[1]; cf. GAT[3]]

ga·teau (gä tō′), *n., pl.* **-teaux** (-tōz′). a cake, esp. a small one, frosted and decorated with fruit, nuts, etc. [< F *gâteau* cake, OF *gastel* < Gmc]

gate-crash·er (gāt′krash′ər), *n.* a person who attends or enters a social function without an invitation or a commercial entertainment without a ticket.

gat·ed (gā′tid), *adj.* (of patterns in a foundry mold) linked by gates. [GATE[1] + -ED[3]]

gate·fold (gāt′fōld′), *n.* *Print.* a page, larger than the trim size of a book or periodical, folded one or more times so as not to extend beyond the edges. [GATE[1] + FOLD[1]]

gate′ hinge′, a flap hinge having its knuckle supported by a lug from each leaf.

gate·house (gāt′hous′), *n., pl.* **-hous·es** (-hou′ziz). **1.** a house at or over a gate, used as a keeper's quarters, fortification, etc. **2.** a house or structure at the gate of a dam, reservoir, etc., with equipment or controls for regulating the flow of water. [ME; see GATE[1], HOUSE]

gate·keep·er (gāt′kē′pər), *n.* a person in charge of a gate, usually to identify, count, supervise, etc., the traffic or flow through it. [GATE[1] + KEEPER]

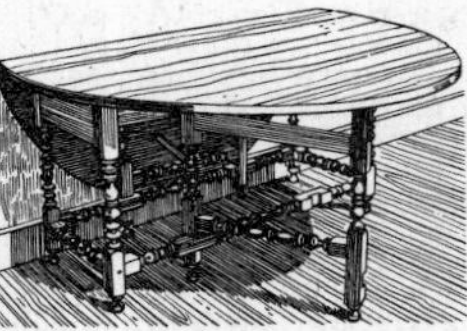
Gate-leg table (18th century)

gate′ leg′, *Furniture.* a leg attached to a hinged frame that can be swung out to support a drop leaf. Cf. **swing leg.**

gate′-leg ta′ble (gāt′leg′), a table having drop leaves supported by gate legs. Also, **gate′-legged′ ta′ble.**

gate·man (gāt′mən, -man′), *n., pl.* **-men** (-mən, -men′). a gatekeeper. [GATE[1] + MAN[1]]

gate·post (gāt′pōst′), *n.* the vertical post on which a gate is suspended by hinges, or the post against which the gate is closed. [GATE[1] + POST[1]]

ga·ter (gā′tər), *U.S. Dial.* alligator. Also, **'ga′ter, gator.** [shortened form]

Gates (gāts), *n.* **1. Horatio,** 1728–1806, American Revolutionary general, born in England. **2.** a boy's given name.

Gates·head (gāts′hed′), *n.* a seaport in N Durham, in NE England, on the Tyne River opposite Newcastle. 103,232 (1961).

gate′ shear′. See **guillotine shears.**

Gates·ville (gāts′vil), *n.* a town in central Texas. 4626 (1960).

gate′ valve′, a valve with its opening closed by a sliding disk.

gate·way (gāt′wā′), *n.* **1.** a passage or entrance that may be closed by a gate. **2.** a structure for enclosing such an opening or entrance. **3.** any passage by or point at which a region may be entered: *New York soon became a gateway to America.* [GATE[1] + WAY]

Gath (gath), *n.* a Philistine city. I Sam. 6:17; Chron. 18:1. Also, *Douay Bible,* **Geth.**

Ga·tha (gä′tə, -tä), *n.* *Zoroastrianism.* one of several groups of hymns **(the Gathas)** forming the oldest part of the Avesta. [< Avestan *gāthā-;* c. Skt *gāthā* song]

gath·er (gath′ər), *v.t.* **1.** to bring together into one group, collection, or place. **2.** to bring together or assemble from various places, sources, or people; collect gradually: *The college is gathering a faculty from all over the country.* **3.** to learn or conclude from observation; infer; deduce: *I gather that he is the real leader.* **4.** to pick or harvest (any crop or natural yield) from its place of growth or formation: *to gather fruit; to gather flowers.* **5.** to pick up piece by piece: *Gather your toys from the floor.* **6.** to serve as a center of attention for; attract: *That tabletop gathers a great deal of dust. A good football game always gathers a crowd.* **7.** to collect; make a collection of. **8.** to wrap or draw around or close to someone or something: *He gathered his scarf around his neck and went out into the cold. She gathered the crying child in her arms.* **9.** to take by selection from among other things; sort out; cull. **10.** to assemble or collect (one's energies or oneself) as for an effort (often fol. by *up*): *He gathered up his strength for the hard job.* **11.** to contract (the brow) into wrinkles. **12.** to draw (cloth) up on a thread in fine folds or puckers by means of even stitches. **13.** *Bookbinding.* to assemble (the printed sections of a book) in proper sequence for binding. **14.** to increase (speed, momentum, etc.), as a moving vehicle. **15.** *Naut.* to gain (way) from a dead stop or extremely slow speed. **16.** *Metalworking.* to increase the sectional area of (stock) by any of various operations. **17.** *Glassmaking.* to accumulate or collect (molten glass) at the end of a tube for blowing, shaping, etc. **—***v.i.* **18.** to come together around a central point; assemble: *Let's gather round the fire and sing a few songs.* **19.** to collect or accumulate: *Clouds were gathering in the northeast.* **20.** to grow, as by accretion; increase. **21.** to become contracted into wrinkles, folds, creases, etc., as the brow or as cloth. **22.** to come to a head, as a sore in suppurating. **23. be gathered to one's fathers,** to die: *Alone and sick, she prayed to be gathered to her fathers.* **—***n.* **24.** a drawing together; contraction. **25.** Often, **gathers.** a fold or pucker, as in gathered cloth. **26.** the act or an instance of gathering. **27.** an amount or number gathered, as during a harvest. **28.** *Glassmaking.* a mass of molten glass attached to the end of a punty. [ME *gader(en),* OE *gaderian,* deriv. of *geador* together, akin to *gæd* fellowship; cf. TOGETHER, GOOD] **—gath′er·a·ble,** *adj.* **—gath′er·er,** *n.*

—Syn. 2. accumulate, amass, garner, hoard. GATHER, ASSEMBLE, COLLECT, MUSTER, MARSHAL imply bringing or drawing together. GATHER expresses the general idea usually with no implication of arrangement: *to gather seashells.* ASSEMBLE is used of objects or facts brought together preparatory to arranging them: *to assemble data for a report.* COLLECT implies purposeful accumulation to form an ordered whole: *to collect evidence.* MUSTER, primarily a military term, suggests thoroughness in the process of collection: *to muster all one's resources.* MARSHAL, another term primarily military, suggests rigorously ordered, purposeful arrangement: *to marshal facts for effective presentation.* **3.** assume, understand. **4.** pluck, crop, reap, glean, garner. **19.** accrete. **—Ant. 1, 18.** separate, disperse.

gath·er·ing (gath′ər ing), *n.* **1.** the act of one who or that which gathers. **2.** something that is gathered together. **3.** an assembly or meeting. **4.** an assemblage of people; crowd. **5.** a collection, assemblage, or compilation of anything. **6.** a gather or a series of gathers in cloth. **7.** an inflamed and suppurating swelling. **8.** (in a flue, duct, or the like) a tapered section forming a transition between two sections, one of which has a greater area than the other. **9.** *Bookbinding.* a section in a book, usually a sheet cut into several leaves. [ME *gaderinge,* OE *gaderunge.* See GATHER, -ING[1]]
—Syn. 3. assemblage. **4.** congregation, concourse, company, throng. **7.** boil, abscess, carbuncle.

Ga·thic (gä′tik), *n.* **1.** an ancient Iranian language of the Indo-European family; the language in which the Gathas were written. Cf. **Avestan.** **—***adj.* **2.** of, pertaining to, or expressed in this language. **3.** of or pertaining to the Gathas. [GATH(A) + -IC]

Gat′ling gun′ (gat′ling), an early type of machine gun consisting of a revolving cluster of barrels around a central axis, each barrel being automatically loaded and fired during every revolution of the cluster. [named after R. J. *Gatling* (1818–1903), American inventor]

ga·tor (gā′tər), *n.* gater.

GATT, See **General Agreement on Tariffs and Trade.**

Gat·ta·me·la·ta (gä′tə mə lä′tə; *It.* gät′tä me lä′tä), an equestrian portrait in bronze (1445–50) by Donatello of Erasmo da Narni, known as Gattamelata (1370?–1443), condottiere and commander of the Venetian armies on the Italian mainland.

gat-toothed (gat′to͞otht′, -to͞othd′), *adj.* gap-toothed.

Ga·tun (gä to͞on′), *n.* **1.** a town in the N Canal Zone of Panama. 692 (1960). **2.** a large dam near this town. 1½ mi. long.

Gatun′ Lake′, an artificial lake in the Canal Zone, forming part of the Panama Canal: created by the Gatun dam. 164 sq. mi. See map under **Panama Canal.**

gaub′ line′ (gôb), *Naut.* See **martingale backrope.** [*gaub* < Hindi *gāb*]

gauche (gōsh), *adj.* lacking social grace, sensitivity, or acuteness; awkward; crude; tactless: *Her reply was typically gauche.* [< F: awkward, left, MF, deriv. of *gauchir* to turn, veer < Gmc] **—gauche′ly,** *adv.* **—gauche′ness,** *n.*

gau·che·rie (gō′shə rē′; *Fr.* gōsh[ə] rē′), *n., pl.* **-ries** (-rēz′; *Fr.* -rē′). **1.** lack of social grace, sensitivity, or acuteness; awkwardness; crudeness; tactlessness. **2.** an act, movement, etc., that is socially graceless, awkward, or tactless: *She committed the gaucherie of dunking the cake in the coffee.* [< F; see GAUCHE, -ERY]

gau·cho (gou′chō; *Sp.* gou′chô), *n., pl.* **-chos** (-chōz; *Sp.* -chôs). a native cowboy of the South American pampas, usually of mixed Spanish and Indian ancestry. [< AmerSp < Arawak *cachu* comrade]

gaud (gôd), *n.* **1.** a showy ornament. **2.** Usually, **gauds.** showy display or ceremony. [ME, perh. < AF, n. use of *gaudir* to rejoice < L *gaudēre* to enjoy]

gau·de·a·mus (gô′dē ā′məs; *Lat.* gou′dä ä′mo͝os), *n., pl.* **-mus·es.** a revel, esp. of college students. [< L: lit., let us rejoice]

Gau·de·a·mus i·gi·tur (gou′dä ä′mo͝os ig′i to͝or′), *Latin.* Let us therefore be joyful.

gaud·er·y (gô′də rē), *n., pl.* **-er·ies.** **1.** ostentatious show. **2.** finery; gawdy or showy things: *a fashionable woman and her gaudery.* [GAUD + -ERY]

Gau·de′te Sun′day (gou dā′tā), the third Sunday in Advent, so called from the first word of the introit. Also called **Gau·de′te.**

Gau·di·bert (gô′də bûrt′), *n.* a walled plain in the third quadrant of the face of the moon: about 19 miles in diameter.

Gau·dí i Cor·net (gou dē′ ē kôr′net), **An·to·ni** (än tô′nē), 1852–1926, Spanish architect and designer.

gaud·y[1] (gô′dē), *adj.,* **gaud·i·er, gaud·i·est.** **1.** brilliantly or excessively showy. **2.** showy without taste; flashy. **3.** ostentatiously ornamented; garish. [orig. attributive use of GAUDY[2] large bead of rosary, feast; later taken as a deriv. of GAUD] **—gaud′i·ly,** *adv.* **—gaud′i·ness,** *n.*
—Syn. 2. tawdry, loud; conspicuous, obvious. GAUDY, FLASHY, GARISH, SHOWY agree in the idea of conspicuousness and, often, bad taste. That which is GAUDY challenges the eye, as by brilliant colors or evident cost, and is not in good taste: *a gaudy hat.* FLASHY suggests insistent and vulgar display, in rather a sporty manner: *a flashy necktie.* GARISH suggests a glaring brightness, or crude vividness of color, and too much ornamentation: *garish decorations.* SHOWY applies to that which is strikingly conspicuous, but not necessarily offensive to good taste: *a garden of showy flowers; a showy dress.* **—Ant. 2.** modest, sober.

gaud·y[2] (gô′dē), *n., pl.* **gaud·ies.** *Brit.* a festival or celebration, esp. an annual college feast. [ME < L *gaudi(um)* joy, delight]

gauf·fer (gô′fər, gof′ər), *n., v.t.* goffer.

gauf·fer·ing (gô′fər ing, gof′ər-), *n.* goffering.

Gau·ga·me·la (gô′gə mē′lə), *n.* an ancient village in Assyria, E of Nineveh: Alexander the Great defeated Darius III here 331 B.C. The battle is often mistakenly called "battle of Arbela."

gauge (gāj), *v.,* **gauged, gaug·ing,** *n.* **—***v.t.* **1.** to appraise, estimate, or judge. **2.** to determine the exact dimensions, capacity, quantity, or force of; measure. **3.** to make conformable to a standard. **4.** to mark or measure off; delineate. **5.** to prepare or mix (plaster) with a definite proportion of plaster of Paris and mortar. **6.** to chip or rub (bricks or stones) to a uniform size or shape. **—***n.* **7.** a standard of measure or measurement: *a narrow gauge railroad.* **8.** a standard dimension, size, or quantity. **9.** any device or instrument for measuring, registering measurements, or testing something, esp. for measuring a dimension, quantity, or mechanical accuracy: *pressure gauge; marking gauge.* **10.** a means of estimating or judging; criterion; test. **11.** extent; scope; capacity: *trying to determine the gauge of his own strength.* **12.** *Ordn.* a unit of measure of the internal diameter of a shotgun barrel, determined by the number of spherical lead bullets of a diameter equal to that of the bore that are required to make one pound: *a twelve-gauge shotgun.* **13.** *Railroads.* the distance between the inner edges of the heads of the rails in a track, usually 4 feet 8½ inches **(standard gauge),** but sometimes more **(broad gauge)** and sometimes less **(narrow gauge).** **14.** the distance between a pair of wheels on an axle. **15.** the thickness or diameter of various, usually thin, objects, as the thickness of sheet metal or the diameter of a wire or screw. **16.** the fineness of a knitted fabric as expressed in loops per every 1½ inch: *15 denier, 60 gauge stockings.* **17.** *Naut.* the position of one vessel as being to the windward **(weather gauge)** or to the leeward **(lee gauge)** of another vessel on an approximately parallel course. **18.** *Building Trades.* the portion of the length of a slate, tile, etc., left exposed when laid in place. **19.** the amount of plaster of Paris mixed with mortar or common plaster to hasten the set. Also, *esp. in technical use,* **gage.** [ME < ONF (F *jauge*) < ? Gmc] **—gauge′a·ble,** *adj.* **—gauge′a·bly,** *adv.*

gauge′ board′. See **pitch board.**

gauge′ pile′, *Building Trades.* a pile driven according to survey as a reference point for other piling. Also, **gauged′ pile′.**

gaug·er (gā′jər), *n.* **1.** one who or that which gauges. **2.** a worker or inspector who checks the dimensions or quality of machined work. **3.** an exciseman, customs official, or the like. Also, *esp. in technical use,* **gager.** [ME < AF *gaugeour.* See GAUGE, -OR[2]]

Gau·guin (gō gaN′), *n.* **(Eu·gène Hen·ri) Paul** (œ zhen′ äN rē′ pôl), 1848–1903, French painter.

Gau·ha·ti (gou hä′tē), *n.* a city in W Assam, in E India. 100,700 (1961).

Gaul (gôl), *n.* **1.** an ancient region in W Europe, including the modern areas of N Italy, France, Belgium, and the S Netherlands: consisted of two main divisions, that part S of the Alps **(Cisalpine Gaul)** and that part N of the Alps **(Transalpine Gaul).** **2.** Latin, **Gallia.** a province of the ancient Roman Empire, including the territory corresponding to modern France, Belgium, the S Netherlands, Switzerland, the part of Germany W of the Rhine, S Britain, Spain, and Portugal. **3.** an inhabitant of the ancient region of Gaul. **4.** a Frenchman.

Gau·lei·ter (gou′lī′tər), *n.* the leader or chief official of a political district under Nazi control. [< G, equiv. to *Gau* region + *Leiter* director]

Gaul·ish (gô′lish), *n.* **1.** the extinct, Celtic language of ancient Gaul. **—***adj.* **2.** of or pertaining to ancient Gaul, its inhabitants, or their language. [GAUL + -ISH[1]]

Gaull·ism (gō′liz əm, gô′-), *n.* **1.** a political movement in France led by Charles de Gaulle. **2.** the principles and policies of the Gaullists. [Charles (DE) GAULLE + -ISM]

Gaull·ist (gō′list, gô′-), *n.* **1.** a supporter of the political principles of Charles de Gaulle. **2.** a Frenchman who supported the French resistance movement against the Nazi occupation in World War II. [< F *Gaulliste.* See Charles DE GAULLE, -IST]

gaul·the·ri·a (gôl thēr′ē ə), *n.* any of several aromatic, evergreen, ericaceous shrubs of the genus *Gaultheria,* as the wintergreen. [< NL; named after Jean-François *Gaultier* (d. 1756), Canadian physician and botanist; see -IA]

gaulthe′ria oil′, wintergreen (def. 2).

gaunt (gônt), *adj.* **1.** extremely thin and bony; emaciated; haggard and drawn, as from great hunger, weariness, torture, etc. **2.** bleak, desolate, or grim, as places or things: *a gaunt, windswept landscape.* [ME, prob. < OF *gaunet, jaunet* yellowish, deriv. of *gaune, jaune* yellow < L *galbin(us)* greenish-yellow] **—gaunt′ly,** *adv.* **—gaunt′ness,** *n.*
—Syn. 1. lean, spare, scrawny, lank, angular, raw-boned. See **thin.** **—Ant. 1.** stout.

Gaunt (gônt, gänt), *n.* **John of.** See **John of Gaunt.**

gaunt·let[1] (gônt′lit, gänt′-), *n.* **1.** a medieval glove, as of mail or plate, to protect the hand. **2.** a glove with an extended cuff for the wrist. **3.** the cuff itself. **4. take up** or **throw down the gauntlet, a.** to accept (or extend) a challenge to fight: *He was always willing to take up the gauntlet for a good cause.* **b.** to show one's defiance. Also, **take up** or **throw down the glove.** [ME *gantelet* < MF, dim. of *gant* glove < Gmc; c. OIcel *vǫttr*] **—gaunt′let·ed,** *adj.*

Gauntlet (17th century)

gaunt·let[2] (gônt′lit, gänt′-), *n.* **1.** a former punishment, chiefly military, in which the offender was made to run between two rows of men who struck at him with switches or weapons as he passed. **2.** the two rows of men administering this punishment. **3.** an attack from two or all sides. **4.** trying conditions; an ordeal. **5.** gantlet[1] (def. 1, 3). **6. run the gauntlet,** to suffer severe criticism or tribulation. Also, **gantlet** (for defs. 1, 2, 4). [alter. of GANTLOPE]

gaun·try (gôn′trē), *n., pl.* **-tries.** gantry.

gaur (gour, gou′ər), *n., pl.* **gaurs,** *(esp. collectively)* **gaur.** a massive wild ox, *Bibos frontalis gaurus,* of southeastern Asia and the Malay Archipelago, growing to a height of six feet at the shoulder. [< Hindi < Skt *gaur(a)*]

Gau·ri·cus (gou rē′kəs), *n.* a walled plain in the third quadrant of the face of the moon: about 40 miles in diameter.

gauss (gous), *n.* **1.** *Elect.* the centimeter-gram-second unit of magnetic induction, equal to the magnetic induction of a magnetic field in which one abcoulomb of charge, moving with a component of velocity perpendicular to the field and equal to one centimeter per second, is acted on by a force of one dyne; 1 maxwell per square centimeter or 10^{-4} weber per square meter. *Abbr.:* G **2.** *Obs.* oersted (def. 1). [named after K. F. GAUSS]

Gauss (gous), *n.* **1. Karl Frie·drich** (kärl frē′drikh), 1777–1855, German mathematician and astronomer. **2.** a walled plain in the first quadrant of the face of the moon: about 110 miles in diameter. **—Gauss·i·an,** *adj.*

Gauss′ian curve′, *Statistics.* See **normal curve.**

Gauss′ian distribu′tion, *Statistics.* See **normal distribution.**

Gauss′ian domain′, *Math.* See **unique factorization domain.**

Gauss′ian im′age, *Optics.* the point in an optical system with spherical aberration at which the paraxial rays meet. Also called **Gauss′ian im′age point′.**

Gauss′ian in′teger, *Math.* a complex number of the form *a* + *bi* where *a* and *b* are integers.

Gauss′ law′, *Physics.* the principle that the total electric flux of a closed surface in an electric field is equal to 4π times the electric charge inside the surface. Also, **Gauss′′ law′, Gauss′′s law′.** [named after K. F. GAUSS]

Gauss′′ lem′ma, *Math.* the theorem that the product of primitive polynomials is a primitive polynomial. [named after K. F. GAUSS]

gauss·me·ter (gous′mē′tər), *n.* a magnetometer for measuring the intensity of a magnetic field, calibrated in gauss. [GAUSS + -METER]

Gauss′ plane′, *Math.* See **Argand diagram.** [named after K. F. GAUSS]

Gau·ta·ma (gô′tə mə, gou′-), *n.* Buddha (def. 1). Also, **Gotama.** Also called **Gau′tama Bud′dha.**

Gau·tier (gō tyā′), *n.* **Thé·o·phile** (tā ô fēl′), 1811–72, French poet, novelist, and critic of art and literature.

gauze (gôz), *n.* **1.** any thin transparent fabric made from any fiber in a plain or leno weave. **2.** a surgical dressing of loosely woven cotton. **3.** any material made of an open, meshlike weave, as of wire. **4.** a thin haze. [< F *gaze* < ?] **—gauze′like′,** *adj.*

gauze′ weave′, leno (def. 1).

gauz·y (gô′zē), *adj.,* **gauz·i·er, gauz·i·est.** like gauze; transparently thin and light. [GAUZE + -Y[1]] **—gauz′i·ly,** *adv.* **—gauz′i·ness,** *n.*

ga·vage (gə väzh′; *Fr.* GA VAZH′), *n.* forced feeding, as of poultry or human beings, as by a flexible tube and a force pump. [< F, equiv. to *gav(er)* (to) stuff (OF (dial.) *gave* gullet, throat) + *-age* -AGE]

gave (gāv), *v.* pt. of **give.**

gav·el[1] (gav′əl), *n.* **1.** a small mallet used by a judge, the presiding officer of a meeting, etc., for signaling for attention or order. **2.** *Masonry.* kevel. [?]

gav·el[2] (gav′əl), *n.* feudal rent or tribute. [ME *govel,* OE *gafol,* akin to *giefan* to give; cf. GABELLE]

gav·el·kind (gav′əl kīnd′), *n.* *Eng. Law.* **1.** (originally) a tenure of land in which the tenant was liable for a rental in money or produce rather than for labor or military service. **2.** a customary system of land tenure, whose chief feature was equal division of land among the heirs of the holder. **3.** the land so held. [ME *gavelkinde, gavlikind,* OE *gafel* GAVEL[2] + *(ge)cynd* KIND[2]]

gav·e·lock (gav′ə lok′), *n.* *Brit. Dial.* a crowbar. [ME *gaveloc,* OE *gafeluc* < ?]

Gavial (Length 20 ft.)

ga·vi·al (gā′vē əl), *n.* a large crocodilian, *Gavialis gangeticus,* of India and Pakistan, having elongated jaws. [< F < Hindi *ghariyāl*] **—ga′vi·al·oid′,** *adj.*

Gav·in (gav′in), *n.* a boy's given name, form of **Gawain.**

Gäv·le (yäv′le), *n.* a seaport in E Sweden. 59,686.

ga·votte (gə vot′), *n.* **1.** an old French dance in moderately quick quadruple meter. **2.** a piece of music for, or in the rhythm of, this dance, often forming one of the movements in the classical suite, usually following the saraband. Also, **ga·vot′.** [< F < Pr *gavot(o)* dance of the Gavots (Alpine mountaineers), fem. of *gavot* hillbilly < pre-Rom *gav-* mountain stream]

gaw (gô), *n.* *Chiefly Scot.* a narrow, trenchlike depression, esp. a furrow in the earth or a worn or thin area in cloth. [?]

G.A.W., guaranteed annual wage.

Ga·wain (gä′win, gô′-), *n.* **1.** *Arthurian Romance.* one of the knights of the Round Table: a nephew of King Arthur. **2.** a boy's given name.

gawk (gôk), *n.* **1.** an awkward, foolish person. **—***v.i.* **2.** to stare stupidly; gape: *The onlookers gawked at arriving celebrities.* [appar. repr. OE word meaning fool, equiv. to *ga(gol)* foolish + *-oc* -OCK; used attributively in *gawk hand, gallock hand* left hand]

gawk·y (gô′kē), *adj.,* **gawk·i·er, gawk·i·est.** awkward; ungainly; clumsy. Also, **gawk·ish** (gô′kish). [GAWK + -Y[1]] **—gawk′i·ly, gawk′ish·ly,** *adv.* **—gawk′i·ness, gawk′ish·ness,** *n.*

Gaw·ra (*Turk.* gou rä′), *n.* See **Tepe Gawra.**

gaw·sy (gô′sē), *adj.* *Scot. and North Eng.* **1.** (of people) well-dressed and of cheerful appearance. **2.** (of things) large and handsome. Also, **gaw′sie.** [var. of GAUDY[1]]

gay (gā), *adj.* **1.** having or showing a joyous mood: *gay spirits; gay music.* **2.** bright or showy: *gay colors; gay ornaments.* **3.** given to or abounding in social or other pleasures: *a gay social season.* **4.** licentious; dissipated; wanton: *a gay old bachelor who is a tireless womanizer.* **5.** homosexual. **—***n.* **6.** a homosexual person, esp. a male. [ME *gai* < OF < Gmc; cf. OHG *gâhi* fast, sudden] **—gay′ness,** *n.*
—Syn. 1. gleeful, jovial, glad, joyous, happy, cheerful, sprightly, blithe, airy, light-hearted; lively, vivacious, frolicsome, sportive, hilarious. GAY, JOLLY, JOYFUL, MERRY describe a happy or light-hearted mood. GAY suggests a lightness of heart or liveliness of mood that is openly manifested: *when hearts were young and gay.* JOLLY indicates a good-humored, natural, expansive gaiety of mood or disposition: *a jolly crowd at a party.* JOYFUL suggests gladness, happiness, rejoicing: *joyful over the good news.* MERRY is often interchangeable with gay: *a merry disposition; a merry party;* it suggests, even more than the latter, convivial animated enjoyment. **2.** brilliant. **—Ant. 1.** unhappy, miserable.

Gay (gā), *n.* **1. John,** 1685–1732, English poet and dramatist. **2.** a girl's given name.

Ga·ya (gə′yə, gī′ə, gə yä′), *n.* a city in central Bihar, in NE India: Hindu center of pilgrimage. 151,100 (1961).

Ga′ya Mar′e·tan (mar′i tan′), *n.* Gayomart.

ga·yal (gə yäl′), *n., pl.* **-yals,** (*esp. collectively*) **-yal.** an ox, *Bibos frontalis,* of southeastern Asia and the Malay Archipelago, sometimes considered to be a domesticated breed of the gaur. Also called **mithan.** [< Bengali *gayāl*]

ga·ya·tri (gä′yə trē′), *n.* *Hinduism.* a Vedic mantra, recited daily by Brahmans, expressing hope for enlightenment. [< Skt *gāyatrī,* deriv. of *gāyatra* song, hymn]

gay·e·ty (gā′i tē), *n., pl.* **-ties.** gaiety.

gay-feath·er (gā′feth′ər), *n.* **1.** Also called **blue blazing star, rattlesnake master.** a weedy, perennial herb, *Liatris scariosa,* found in the U.S. from Pennsylvania to South Carolina, having bluish-purple flower heads. **2.** Also called **devil's-bit, prairie pine.** a related herb, *L. spicata,* of eastern North America, having a very leafy stem and rose-purple flowers.

Gayle (gāl), *n.* a boy's or girl's given name. Also, **Gail, Gale.**

Gay·lord (gā′lôrd′), *n.* **1.** a town in N Michigan. 2568 (1960). **2.** a boy's given name.

Gay-Lus·sac (gā′lə sak′; *Fr.* gä lʏ sak′), *n.* **1. Joseph Lou·is** (jō′zəf lo͞o′ē, -səf; *Fr.* zhô zef′ lwē), 1778–1850, French chemist and physicist. **2.** a crater in the second quadrant of the face of the moon: about 15 miles in diameter.

Gay-Lussac's′ law′, *Thermodynamics.* the principle that, for relatively low pressures, the density of an ideal gas at constant pressure varies inversely with the absolute temperature of the gas. Also called **Charles' law.** Cf. **Boyle's law.** [named after J. L. GAY-LUSSAC]

gay·lus·site (gā′lə sīt′), *n.* a rare mineral, hydrated carbonate of sodium and calcium. [named after J. L. GAY-LUSSAC; see -ITE[1]]

gay·ly (gā′lē), *adv.* gaily.

Gay·nor (gā′nər), *n.* a girl's given name.

Ga·yo·mart (gä yō′märt), *n.* *Zoroastrianism.* the first Aryan and the sixth creation of Ahura Mazda. Also called **Gaya Maretan.**

Gay-Pay-Oo (gā′pā′o͞o′; *Russ.* ge′pe′o͞o′), *n.* See **G.P.U.**

gay′ pow′er, the organized influence exerted by homosexuals as a group, esp. to ensure equal rights in employment, housing, etc.

gay·wings (gā′wingz′), *n., pl.* **-wings.** the fringed milkwort, *Polygala paucifolia,* whose aerial flowers have paired, large, usually pink-purple petals. Also called **flowering wintergreen.** [GAY + WING + -S[3]]

gaz., 1. gazette. **2.** gazetteer.

Ga·za (gä′zə, gaz′ə, gā′zə), *n.* a seaport adjacent to SW Israel; occupied by Israel since 1967: ancient trade-route center. 37,820 (est. 1952).

ga·za·bo (gə zā′bō), *n., pl.* **-bos.** *Slang.* a fellow; man; boy. Also, **gazebo.** [?]

Ga′za Strip′, a coastal area on the W Mediterranean, formerly in the Palestine mandate; administered by Egypt, 1949–67; occupied by Israel since 1967.

gaze (gāz), *v.,* **gazed, gaz·ing,** *n.* —*v.i.* **1.** to look steadily and intently, as with great curiosity, interest, wonder, etc. —*n.* **2.** a steady or intent look. **3. at gaze,** *Heraldry.* (of a deer or deerlike animal) represented as seen from the side with the head looking toward the spectator: *a stag at gaze.* [ME *gase(n)* < ON; cf. Norw, Sw (dial.) *gasa* to gape, stare] —**gaze′less,** *adj.* —**gaz′er,** *n.* —**gaz′ing·ly,** *adv.*

—**Syn. 1.** GAZE, STARE, GAPE suggest looking fixedly at something. To GAZE is to look steadily and intently at something, esp. at that which excites admiration, curiosity, or interest: *to gaze at scenery, at a scientific experiment.* To STARE is to gaze with eyes wide open, as from surprise, wonder, alarm, stupidity, or impertinence: *to stare unbelievingly or rudely.* GAPE is a word with uncomplimentary connotations; it suggests openmouthed, often ignorant or rustic wonderment or curiosity: *to gape at a tall building, at a circus parade.*

ga·ze·bo[1] (gə zē′bō, -zā′-), *n., pl.* **-bos, -boes.** a structure, as a pavilion or summerhouse, built on a site affording an enjoyable view. [?]

ga·ze·bo[2] (gə zā′bō, -zē′-), *n., pl.* **-bos.** gazabo.

gaze·hound (gāz′hound′), *n.* a dog that hunts by sight rather than by scent. [GAZE + HOUND[1]]

Ga·zel·la (gə zel′ə), *n.* a girl's given name.

ga·zelle (gə zel′), *n., pl.* **-zelles,** (*esp. collectively*) **-zelle.** any of various small antelopes of the genus *Gazella* and allied genera, noted for graceful movements and lustrous eyes. [< F; OF *gazel* < Ar *ghazāla*] —**ga·zelle′like′,** *adj.*

Gazelle, *Gazella subgutturosa* (2½ ft. high at shoulder; horns 14 in.; length 4 ft.)

ga·zelle-boy (gə zel′boi′), *n.* a boy assumed to have been reared by or among gazelles.

gazelle′ hound′, Saluki.

ga·zette (gə zet′), *n., v.,* **-zet·ted, -zet·ting.** —*n.* **1.** a newspaper (used chiefly in the names of newspapers): *The Phoenix Gazette.* **2.** *Chiefly Brit.* an official government journal containing lists of government appointments and promotions, bankruptcies, etc. —*v.t.* **3.** *Chiefly Brit.* to publish, announce, or list in an official government journal. [< F < It *gazzetta,* var. of Venetian *gazeta,* orig. a coin (the price of the paper), dim. of *gaza* magpie]

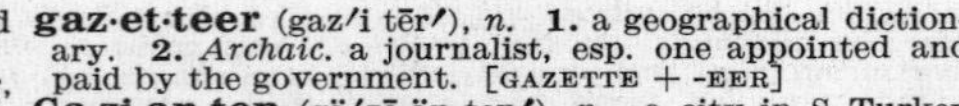

gaz·et·teer (gaz′i tēr′), *n.* **1.** a geographical dictionary. **2.** *Archaic.* a journalist, esp. one appointed and paid by the government. [GAZETTE + -EER]

Ga·zi·an·tep (gä′zē än tep′), *n.* a city in S Turkey in Asia. 97,144 (1955). Formerly, **Aintab.**

gaz·o·gene (gaz′ə jēn′), *n.* an apparatus for impregnating a liquid with a gas, esp. carbon dioxide. [< F *gazogène.* See GAS, -O-, -GEN]

gaz·pa·cho (gəz pä′chō; *Sp.* gäth pä′chô, gäs-), *n.* *Spanish Cookery.* a thick soup made of cucumbers, tomatoes, onions, bread, oil, and vinegar, all mashed together and strained, flavored with garlic, and served cold. [< Sp]

G.B., Great Britain.

Gba·ri (gə bär′ē), *n., pl.* **-ris,** (*esp. collectively*) **-ri.** Gwari.

G.B.E., Knight Grand Cross of the British Empire or Dame Grand Cross of the British Empire.

Gc, 1. gigacycle; gigacycles. **2.** gigacycles per second.

GCA, *Aeron.* See **ground controlled approach.**

g-cal, gram calorie; gram calories.

G.C.B., Grand Cross of the Bath.

G.C.D., greatest common divisor. Also, **g.c.d.**

G.C.F., greatest common factor. Also, **g.c.f.**

GCI, *Mil.* ground controlled interception.

G clef, *Music.* See **treble clef.**

G.C.M., greatest common measure. Also, **g.c.m.**

GCR, *Mil.* ground controlled radar.

Gc/s, gigacycles per second.

G.C.T., Greenwich Civil Time.

Gd, *Chem.* gadolinium.

gd., guard.

G.D., 1. Grand Duchess. **2.** Grand Duke.

Gdansk (gdīnsk; *Eng.* gə dänsk′, -dansk′), *n.* Polish name of **Danzig.**

Gde., gourde.

gds., goods.

Gdy·nia (gə din′ē ə; *Pol.* gdi′nyä), *n.* a seaport in N Poland, on the Bay of Danzig. 137,400 (est. 1957).

Ge (jē, gē), *n.* Gaea.

Ge, *Chem.* germanium.

g.e., (in bookbinding) gilt edges.

gean (gēn), *n.* See **heart cherry.** [< MF *guigne* < ?]

ge·an·ti·cli·nal (jē′an ti klīn′əl), *Geol.* —*adj.* **1.** of or pertaining to an anticlinal fold extending over a relatively large part of the earth's surface. —*n.* **2.** a geanticlinal fold. [< Gk *gê* earth + ANTICLINAL]

ge·an·ti·cline (jē an′ti klīn′), *n.* *Geol.* a geanticlinal fold. [< Gk *gê* earth + ANTICLINE]

gear (gēr), *n.* **1.** *Mach.* **a.** a part, as a disk, wheel, or section of a shaft, having cut teeth of such form, size, and spacing that they mesh with teeth of identical form, size, and spacing in another part to transmit or receive force and motion. **b.** an assembly of such parts. **c.** the state of such parts in being connected or meshed with each other: *in gear; out of gear.* **d.** of several possible arrangements of such parts in a mechanism, as an automobile transmission, for affording different relations of torque and speed between the driving and the driven machinery, or for permitting the driven machinery to run in either direction: *first gear; reverse gear.* **e.** a mechanism or group of parts performing one function or serving one purpose in a complex machine: *steering gear.* **2.** implements, tools, or apparatus, esp. as used for a particular occupation or activity; paraphernalia: *fishing gear.* **3.** a harness, esp. of horses. **4.** *Naut.* **a.** the lines, tackles, etc., of a particular sail or spar. **b.** the personal tools, clothing, and other possessions of a sailor. **5.** portable items of personal property, including clothing; possessions: *The campers keep all their gear in footlockers.* **6.** armor or arms. **7. in** or **into high gear,** in or into a state of utmost speed, activity, or efficiency: *The defense effort moved into high gear.* —*v.t.* **8.** to provide with or connect by gearing. **9.** to provide with gear; supply; fit; harness. **10.** to prepare, adjust, or adapt to a particular situation, person, etc., in order to bring about satisfactory results: *The producers geared their output to seasonal demands.* —*v.i.* **11.** to fit exactly, as one part of gearing into another; come into or be in gear. [ME *gere* < ON; cf. OIcel *gervi, gørvi;* akin to OE *gearwe* equipment] —**gear′less,** *adj.*

gear·box (gēr′boks′), *n.* **1.** a shield or housing for gears. **2.** a transmission, as in an automobile. Also, **gear′ box′.** [GEAR + BOX[1]]

gear·ing (gēr′ing), *n.* *Mach.* **1.** an assembly of parts, esp. a train of gears, for transmitting and modifying motion and torque in a machine. **2.** the act or process of equipping with gears. **3.** the method of installation of such gears. [GEAR + -ING[1]]

gear′ pump′. See **lobular pump.**

gear′ ra′tio, *Mach.* **1.** the ratio of the rotational speeds of the first and final gears in a train of gears or of any two meshing gears. **2.** the ratio of the diameters of the pitch surfaces of any two meshing gears or of the numbers of their teeth.

gear·shift (gēr′shift′), *n.* a device, as a lever, for selecting or engaging and disengaging gears for a power-transmission system, esp. in a motor vehicle. Also called, *Brit.,* **gear′ lev′er.** [GEAR + SHIFT]

gear·wheel (gēr′hwēl′, -wēl′), *n.* a wheel having teeth or cogs that engage with those of another wheel or part; cogwheel. Also, **gear′ wheel′.** [GEAR + WHEEL]

Geb (geb), *n.* *Egyptian Religion.* the god of the earth and the father of Osiris and Isis. Also, **Keb.**

geb., born. [< G *geboren*]

Ge·ber (jē′bər *for 1;* gā′bər *for 2*), *n.* **1.** (*Jabir ibn Hayyan*) 8th-century A.D. Arab alchemist. Also, **Jabir. 2.** a crater in the fourth quadrant of the face of the moon: about 25 miles in diameter.

Ge·brauchs·mu·sik (*Ger.* gə brouкнs′mo͞o zēk′), *n.* music written in a deliberately simple style for performance by small amateur groups. [< G, equiv. to *Gebrauch* use + *Musik* music]

geck (gek), *n.* *Chiefly Scot.* **1.** a contemptible person. **2.** a gesture or expression of scorn, esp. toward a fool or dupe; mockery. —*v.t.* **3.** *Scot. and North Eng.* to mock; deride. [< LG]

geck·o (gek′ō), *n., pl.* **geck·os, geck·oes.** any of numerous harmless, typically nocturnal lizards of the family *Gekkonidae,* many of which have an adhesive pad at the tip of each digit and produce a loud call, found chiefly in the tropics. [< Malay *gēkoq;* imit.]

ged (ged), *n., pl.* (*esp. collectively*) **ged,** (*esp. referring to two or more kinds or species*) **geds.** *Scot. and North Eng.* any fish of the pike family. Also, **gedd.** [< Scand; cf. OIcel *gedda* spike, goad; cf. GAD[2]]

Ged·a·li·ah (ged′ə lī′ə), *n.* the governor of Judah after its conquest by Babylon. II Kings 25:22–26. Also, *Douay Bible,* **Godolias.**

gedd (ged), *n., pl.* (*esp. collectively*) **gedd,** (*esp. referring to two or more kinds or species*) **gedds.** *Scot. and North Eng.* ged.

Ged·des (ged′ēz), *n.* **1. Norman Bel** (bel), 1893–1958, U.S. industrial and stage designer and architect. **2. Sir Patrick,** 1854–1932, Scottish biologist, sociologist, and town planner.

Ge·di·ke (*Russ.* ge′di ke), *n.* **Alexander.** See **Goedicke, Alexander.**

gee[1] (jē), *interj., v.,* **geed, gee·ing.** —*interj.* **1.** (a word of command to a horse or other draft animal directing it to turn to the right.) **2. gee up,** (a word of command to a horse or other draft animal directing it to go faster.) —*v.i.* **3.** to turn to the right. —*v.t.* **4.** to turn (something) to the right. **5.** to evade. [?]

gee[2] (jē), *interj.* *Informal.* (used to express surprise, enthusiasm, or simple emphasis): *Gee, that's great! Gee, I can't remember the book's title.* [euphemism for JESUS]

gee[3] (jē), *v.i.,* **geed, gee·ing.** *Informal.* to agree; get along. [?]

gee[4] (jē), *n.* a radio navigational system by which a fix can be obtained by comparing the pulse repetition rates of high-frequency ground waves from two separate stations. [?]

geek (gēk), *n.* *Slang.* **1.** a carnival performer who performs sensationally morbid or disgusting acts, as biting off the head of a live chicken. **2.** person; fellow: *He's a perfectly pleasant old geek.* [prob. var. of GECK]

Gee·long (ji lông′), *n.* a seaport in SE Australia, SW of Melbourne. 88,160 with suburbs (est. 1959).

Geel′vink Bay′ (*Du.* кнāl′vingk), a bay on the NW coast of New Guinea.

geese (gēs), *n.* a pl. of **goose.**

geest (gēst), *n.* *Geol.* an old alluvial deposit or group of old deposits. [< LG: dry or sandy soil]

Ge·ez (gē ez′, gā-), *n.* Ethiopic (def. 2). Also, **Ge'ez′.**

gee·zer (gē′zər), *n.* *Slang.* an odd character. [var. of GUISER, repr. dial. pronunciation]

ge·füll′te fish′ (gə fil′tə), *Jewish Cookery.* a forcemeat of boneless fish, esp. whitefish, carp, or pike, blended with eggs, matzo meal, and seasoning, shaped into balls or sticks and simmered in a vegetable broth, and usually served chilled. Also, **ge·fill′te fish′, ge·fil′te fish′, ge·ful′te fish′.** [< Yiddish; also *kafilte fish* < G *gefüllte Fische* stuffed fish]

ge·gen·i·on (gā′gən ī′ən, -ī′on), *n.* *Physical Chem.* counter-ion. [< G *gegen* against + ION]

ge·gen·schein (gā′gən shīn′), *n.* *Astron.* a faint, elliptical patch of light in the night sky that appears opposite the sun, being a reflection of sunlight by meteoric material in space. Also called **counterglow.** Cf. **zodiacal light.** [< G: counterglow]

Ge·hen·na (gi hen′ə), *n.* **1.** the valley of Hinnom, near Jerusalem, where propitiatory sacrifices were made to Moloch. II Kings 23:10. **2.** hell (def. 1). **3.** any place of extreme torment or suffering. [< LL < Gk *Géenna* < Heb *Gē-Hinnōm* hell, short for *gē ben Hinnōm,* lit., valley of the son of Hinnom]

geh·len·ite (gā′lə nīt′), *n.* a mineral, aluminum calcium silicate, occurring in prismatic crystals varying in color from gray-green to brown. [named after A. F. *Gehlen* (1775–1815), German chemist; see -ITE[1]]

ge·hock·te le·ber (gə hok′tə lā′bər), *Jewish Cookery.* chopped (usually chicken or goose) liver. [< Yiddish]

Geh·rig (ger′ig), *n.* **Henry Louis** ("**Lou**"), 1903–41, U.S. baseball player.

Gei·ger (gī′gər), *n.* **Hans** (häns), 1882–1947, German physicist.

Gei′ger count′er, an instrument for detecting ionizing radiations, consisting of a gas-filled tube in which electric-current pulses are produced when the gas is ionized by radiation, and of a device to register these pulses: used chiefly to measure radioactivity. Also called **Gei′ger-Mül′ler count′er, GM counter.** [named after H. GEIGER]

Gei′ger-Mül′ler thresh′old (gī′gər myo͞o′lər, -mul′ər), *Physics.* the minimum voltage applied to an ionization chamber, as in a Geiger counter, at which the charge collected per count is independent of the nature of the ionizing event producing the count. Also called **Gei′ger thresh′old.** [named after H. GEIGER and W. *Müller,* 20th-century German physicist]

Gei′ger-Mül′ler tube′, *Physics.* a tube functioning as an ionization chamber within a Geiger counter. Also called **Gei′ger tube′.** [see GEIGER-MÜLLER THRESHOLD]

Gei·kie (gē′kē), *n.* **Sir Archibald,** 1835–1924, Scottish geologist.

Gei·sel (gī′zəl), *n.* **Theodor Seuss** (so͞os), ("*Dr. Seuss*"), born 1904, U.S. humorist, illustrator, and author of children's books.

gei·sha (gā′shə, gē′-), *n., pl.* **-sha, -shas.** a Japanese girl trained as a professional singer, dancer, and companion for men. [< Jap]

gei·son (gī′son, -sən, gī′-), *n., pl.* **-sa** (-sä, -sə). *Archit.* **1.** the projection of a cornice from a wall or colonnade. **2.** the material forming a cornice. **3.** the flat area formed before the tympanum of a pediment by a cornice. [< Gk *geîson, geîsson* cornice]

Geiss′ler tube′ (gīs′lər), a sealed glass tube with platinum connections at the ends, containing rarefied gas made luminous by an electrical discharge. [named after H. *Geissler* (1814–79), German inventor]

Geist (gīst), *n.* *German.* spirit; mind.

Geis·town (gīs′toun′), *n.* a town in central Pennsylvania. 3186 (1960).

gei·to·nog·a·my (gīt′ənog′ə mē), *n.* *Bot.* pollination of a flower by pollen from another flower on the same plant. Cf. **xenogamy.** [< Gk *geitono-* (s. of *geítōn*) neighbor + -GAMY] —**gei′to·nog′a·mous,** *adj.*

gel (jel), *n., v.,* **gelled, gel·ling.** —*n.* **1.** *Physical Chem.* a semirigid colloidal dispersion of a solid with a liquid or gas, as jelly, glue, etc. 2. *Theat.* gelatin (def. 5). —*v.i.* 3. to form or become a gel. [back formation from GELATIN]

ge·län·de·läu·fer (gə len′də loi′fər), *n.* *Skiing.* a participant in cross-country skiing. [< G, equiv. to *Gelände* countryside + *Läufer* runner]

ge·län·de·sprung (gə len′də sprŏŏng′; *Ger.* gə len′-də shprŏŏng′), *n.* *Skiing.* a jump, usually over an obstacle, in which the skier plants both poles in the snow in advance of the skis, bends close to the ground, and propels himself chiefly by the use of the poles. Also called **ge·län′de jump′** (gə len′də). [< G, equiv. to *Gelände* countryside + *Sprung* jump]

Ge·la·nor (jə lā′nôr), *n.* *Class. Myth.* a king of Argos who peacefully yielded his throne to Danaus.

Ge·la·sia (jə lā′shə, -shē ə), *n.* a girl's given name.

Ge·la·si·us I (jə lā′shē əs, -zhē-, -zē-), **Saint,** died A.D. 496, pope 492–496.

Gelasius II, (*Giovanni de Gaeta*) died 1119, Italian ecclesiastic: pope 1118–19.

ge·lat·i·fi·ca·tion (jə lat′ə fə kā′shən), *n.* the process of gelatinizing. [GELAT(IN) + -I- + -FICATION]

gel·a·tin (jel′ə tin, -ə tən), *n.* 1. a brittle, nearly transparent, faintly yellow, odorless, and almost tasteless glutinous substance obtained by boiling in water the ligaments, bones, skin, etc., of animals, and forming the basis of jellies, glues, and the like. 2. any of various similar substances, as vegetable gelatin. 3. a preparation or product in which such an animal or vegetable substance is the essential constituent. 4. an edible jelly made of this substance. 5. Also called **gel′atin slide′.** *Theat.* a thin sheet made of translucent gelatin colored with an aniline dye, placed over stage lights, and used as a color medium in lighting effects. Also, **gel′a·tine.** [< F *gélatine* < ML *gelātin(a)*, equiv. to L *gelāt(us)* frozen, thickened, ptp. of *gelāre* (*gel-* freeze + *-ātus* -ATE[1]) + *-ina* -IN[2]]

ge·lat·i·nate (jə lat′ənāt′), *v.t., v.i.,* **-nat·ed, -nat·ing.** gelatinize. [GELATIN + -ATE[1]] —**ge·lat′i·na′tion,** *n.*

ge·lat·i·nise (jə lat′əniz′, jel′ə tənīz′), *v.t., v.i.,* **-nised, -nis·ing.** *Chiefly Brit.* gelatinize. —**ge·lat′i·ni·sa′tion,** *n.* —**ge·lat′i·nis′er,** *n.*

ge·lat·i·nize (jə lat′ənīz′, jel′ə tənīz′), *v.,* **-nized, -niz·ing.** —*v.t.* 1. to make gelatinous. 2. to coat with gelatin, as paper. —*v.i.* 3. to become gelatinous. Also, **gelatinate.** [GELATIN + -IZE] —**ge·lat′i·ni·za′tion,** *n.* —**ge·lat′i·niz′er,** *n.*

ge·lat·i·noid (jə lat′ənoid′), *adj.* 1. resembling gelatin; gelatinous. —*n.* 2. a gelatinoid substance. [GELATIN + -OID]

ge·lat·i·nous (jə lat′ənəs), *adj.* 1. having the nature of or resembling jelly, esp. in consistency; jellylike. 2. pertaining to, containing, or consisting of gelatin. [GELATIN + -OUS] —**ge·lat′i·nous·ly,** *adv.* —**ge·lat′i·nous·ness, gel·a·tin·i·ty** (jel′ə tin′i tē), *n.*

ge·la·tion[1] (je lā′shən, jə-), *n.* solidification by cold; freezing. [< L *gelātiōn-* (s. of *gelātiō*) a freezing, equiv. to *gelāt(us)* (see GELATIN) + *-iōn-* -ION]

ge·la·tion[2] (je lā′shən, jə-), *n.* *Physical Chem.* the process of gelling. [GEL + -ATION]

geld[1] (geld), *v.t.,* **geld·ed** or **gelt, geld·ing.** to castrate (an animal, esp. a horse). [ME *geld(en)* < Scand; cf. OIcel *gelda*] —**geld′er,** *n.*

geld[2] (geld), *n.* *Eng. Hist.* 1. a payment; tax. 2. a tax paid to the crown by landholders under the Anglo-Saxon and Norman kings. [< ML *geld(um)* payment, tribute < Gmc; cf. OE *geld,* G *Geld*]

Gel·der·land (gel′dər land′; *Du.* кнel′dər länt′), *n.* a province in the E Netherlands. 1,339,682 (1962); 1965 sq. mi. *Cap.:* Arnhem. Also called **Guelders.**

geld·ing (gel′ding), *n.* 1. a castrated male horse. 2. a eunuch. [ME < Scand; cf. Icel *gelding(r).* See GELD[1], -ING[1]]

ge·lech·i·id (jə lek′ē id), *n.* 1. any of numerous small moths of the family *Gelechiidae,* including many crop pests, as the Angoumois grain moth, potato tuberworm, etc. —*adj.* 2. belonging or pertaining to the family *Gelechiidae.* [< NL *Gelechiid(ae)* name of the family, equiv. to *Gelechi(a)* name of the genus (< Gk *gēlech(ēs)* sleeping on earth) + *-idae* -ID[2]]

Ge·lée (zhə lā′), *n.* **Claude** (klōd). See **Lorrain, Claude.**

Ge·lene (jə lēn′), *n.* a girl's given name.

Ge·lett (jə let′), *n.* a boy's given name, form of **Gilbert.** Also, **Gillett, Gillette.**

gel·id (jel′id), *adj.* very cold; icy. [< L *gelid(us)* icy cold, equiv. to *gel(um)* frost, cold + *-idus* -ID[4]] —**ge·lid·i·ty** (jə lid′i tē), **gel′id·ness,** *n.* —**gel′id·ly,** *adv.*

gel′ min′eral, a colloidal mineral.

Ge·lo·nus (jə lō′nəs), *n.* *Class. Myth.* a son of Hercules.

gel·se·mi·um (jel sē′mē əm), *n., pl.* **-mi·ums, -mi·a** (-mē ə). *Pharm.* the dried rhizome and roots of yellow jasmine formerly used, in the form of its crude powder, tincture, or fluid extract, as a sedative. [< NL < It *gelsom(ino)* jasmine + L *-ium* -IUM]

Gel·sen·kir·chen (gel′zən kir′кнən), *n.* a city in W West Germany, in the Ruhr valley. 380,600 (1963).

gelt[1] (gelt), *v.* a pt. and pp. of **geld**[1].

gelt[2] (gelt), *n.* *Slang.* money. [< Yiddish < MHG *geld* money; akin to YIELD]

Ge·lug·pa (ge′lŏŏg′pä′), *n.* *Lamaism.* See **Yellow Hats.**

gem (jem), *n., v.,* **gemmed, gem·ming,** *adj.* —*n.* 1. a cut and polished precious stone or pearl fine enough for use in jewelry. 2. something likened to or prized as such a stone because of its beauty or worth: *His painting was the gem of the collection.* 3. a person held in great esteem or affection. 4. muffin (def. 1). 5. *Print. Brit.* a 4-point type of a size between brilliant and diamond. —*v.t.* 6. to adorn with or as with gems; begem. —*adj.* 7. *Jewelry.* noting perfection or very high quality: *gem color; a gem ruby.* [ME *gemme* < OF < L *gemma* bud, jewel] —**gem′less,** *adj.* —**gem′like′,** *adj.*

Ge·ma·ra (gə mär′ə, -môr′ə; *Heb.* gə mä rä′), *n.* 1. the section of the Talmud consisting essentially of commentary on the Mishnah. 2. the Talmud. —**Ge·ma′ric,** *adj.* —**Ge·ma′rist,** *n.*

ge·mein·schaft (*Ger.* gə mīn′shäft′), *n., pl.* **-schaf·ten** (*Ger.* -shäf′tən). (*often cap.*) 1. an association of individuals having sentiments, tastes, and attitudes in common; fellowship. 2. *Sociol.* a society or group characterized chiefly by a strong sense of common identity, close personal relationships, and an attachment to traditional and sentimental concerns. Cf. **Gesellschaft.** [< G: community, equiv. to *gemein* common + *-schaft* -SHIP]

gem·el (jem′əl), *n.* 1. Also called **gem′el bar′.** *Heraldry.* See **bar gemel.** 2. *Obs.* a hinge. —*adj.* 3. gemeled. [ME < OF < L *gemell(us),* dim. of *geminus* twin]

gem′el bot′tle, a bottle consisting of two flasks set side by side with the necks curving in opposite directions.

gem·eled (jem′əld), *adj.* (of two architectural members) coupled: *gemeled arches.* Also, **gemel.** [GEMEL + -ED[3]]

gem·i·nate (*v.* jem′ə nāt′; *adj.* jem′ə nit, -nāt′), *v.,* **-nat·ed, -nat·ing,** *adj.* —*v.t., v.i.* 1. to make or become doubled or paired. —*adj.* 2. Also, **gem′i·nat′ed.** twin; combined or arranged in pairs; coupled. [< L *gemināt(us)* doubled (ptp. of *gemināre*), equiv. to *gemin-* double + *-ātus* -ATE[1]] —**gem′i·nate·ly,** *adv.*

gem·i·na·tion (jem′ə nā′shən), *n.* 1. a doubling; duplication; repetition. 2. *Phonet.* the doubling of an originally single consonantal sound. 3. *Rhet.* the immediate repetition of a word, phrase, etc., for rhetorical effect. [< L *geminātiōn-* (s. of *geminātiō*), equiv. to *gemināt(us)* (see GEMINATE) + *-iōn-* -ION]

Gem·i·ni (jem′ə nī′, -nē, jim′-), *n.pl., gen.* **Gem·i·no·rum** (jem′ə nōr′əm, -nôr′-, jim′-) for 1. 1. *Astron.* the Twins, a zodiacal constellation between Taurus and Cancer containing the bright stars Castor and Pollux. 2. *Astrol.* the third sign of the zodiac. See illus. under **zodiac.** 3. *U.S.* a two-man spacecraft designed for orbital rendezvous. [< L *gemini,* pl. of *geminus*]

Ge·mi·nia·ni (je′mē nyä′nē), *n.* **Fran·ces·co** (frän-ches′kô), c1680–1762, Italian violinist and composer.

gem·i·ni·flo·rous (jem′ə nē flōr′əs, -flôr′-), *adj.* *Bot.* having flowers arranged in pairs. [< L *gemin(us)* twin + -I- + -FLOROUS]

Gem·i·nus (jem′ə nəs), *n.* a crater in the first quadrant of the face of the moon: about 55 miles in diameter.

gem′ jade′. See **imperial jade.**

gem·ma (jem′ə), *n., pl.* **gem·mae** (jem′ē). 1. *Bot.* a cell or cluster of cells, or a leaflike or budlike body, which separates from the parent plant and forms a new plant, as in mosses, liverworts, etc. 2. *Zool., Bot.* a bud. [< L: bud, GEM]

Gem·ma (jem′ə), *n.* a girl's given name.

gem·ma·ceous (je mā′shəs), *adj.* of, pertaining to, or resembling gemmae. [GEMM(A) + -ACEOUS]

Gem·ma Fri·si·us (jem′ə frē′zē əs), a walled plain in the fourth quadrant of the face of the moon: about 80 miles in diameter.

gem·mate (jem′āt), *adj., v.,* **-mat·ed, -mat·ing.** *Bot., Zool.* —*adj.* 1. having buds; increasing by budding. —*v.i.* 2. to put forth buds; increase by budding. [< L *gemmāt(us)* budded, adorned with gems. See GEMMA, -ATE[1]]

gem·ma·tion (je mā′shən), *n.* *Biol.* the process of reproduction by gemmae. [< F *gemmation.* See GEMMATE, -ION]

gem·mif·er·ous (je mif′ər əs), *adj.* bearing buds or gemmae; gemmiparous. [GEMM(A) + -I- + -FEROUS]

gem·mi·form (jem′ə fôrm′), *adj.* *Biol.* shaped like a bud. [GEMM(A) + -I- + -FORM]

gem·mip·a·ra (je mip′ər ə), *n.pl.* gemmiparous animals, as hydra. Also, **gem·mip·a·res** (je mip′ə rēz′). [GEMM(A) + -I- + NL *-para,* deriv. of L *parere* to bear]

gem·mip·a·rous (je mip′ər əs), *adj.* producing or reproducing by buds or gemmae. [< NL *gemmiparus.* See GEMMA, -PAROUS] —**gem·mi·par·i·ty** (jem′i par′i tē), *n.*

gem·mu·la·tion (jem′yə lā′shən), *n.* *Biol.* gemmation. [GEMMULE + -ATION]

gem·mule (jem′yōōl), *n.* 1. *Bot.* gemma. 2. *Zool.* an asexually produced mass of cells that will develop into an animal. 3. *Biol.* one of the hypothetical living units conceived by Darwin in the theory of pangenesis as the bearers of the hereditary attributes. [< F < L *gemmul(a).* See GEMMA, -ULE]

gem·mu·lif·er·ous (jem′yə lif′ər əs), *adj.* *Zool.* producing or reproducing by gemmules. [GEMMULE + -I- + -FEROUS]

gem·my (jem′ē), *adj.,* **-mi·er, -mi·est.** 1. having gems; set with gems. 2. like a gem, esp. in being bright, glittering, or sparkling. [GEM + -Y[1]] —**gem′mi·ly,** *adv.* —**gem′mi·ness,** *n.*

gem·ol·o·gy (je mol′ə jē), *n.* the science dealing with natural and artificial gemstones. Also, **gem·mol′o·gy.** [GEM + -O- + -LOGY] —**gem·o·log·i·cal, gem·mo·log·i·cal** (jem′ə loj′i kəl), *adj.* —**gem·ol′o·gist, gem·mol′o·gist,** *n.*

ge·mot (gə mōt′), *n.* (in Anglo-Saxon England) a legislative or judicial assembly. Also, **ge·mote′.** [OE *gemōt,* equiv. to *ge-* collective prefix + *mōt* meeting; see MOOT]

gem·pyl·id (jem pil′id), *n.* 1. any of several fishes of the family *Gempylidae,* comprising the snake mackerels. —*adj.* 2. belonging or pertaining to the family *Gempylidae.* [< NL *Gempylid(ae)* name of the family, equiv. to *Gempyl(us)* name of the genus (< Gk *gempýlos* a kind of fish) + *-idae* -ID[2]]

Gemsbok (4½ ft. high at shoulder; horns 3 to 4 ft.)

gems (gems), *n., pl.* **gems·es** (gem′siz). chamois (def. 1). Also, **gemse.** [< G; OHG *gamiza* < LL *camoc-* (s. of *camox*)]

gems·bok (gemz′bok′), *n., pl.* **-boks,** (*esp. collectively*) **-bok.** a large antelope, *Oryx gazella,* of southern Africa, having long, straight horns and a long, tufted tail. Also, **gemsbuck.** [< SAfrD < G *Gemsbock* male chamois. See GEMS, BUCK[1]]

gems·buck (gemz′buk′), *n., pl.* **-bucks,** (*esp. collectively*) **-buck.** gemsbok.

gem·stone (jem′stōn′), *n.* a precious stone suitable for cutting and polishing as a gem or gems. [ME *gimstone,* OE *gimstān.* See GEM, STONE]

ge·müt·lich (gə myt′liкн), *adj.* *German.* congenial; agreeable. Also, **ge·muet′lich.** [lit., feelingly]

Ge·müt·lich·keit (gə myt′liкн kīt′), *n.* *German.* congeniality; agreeableness. Also, **Ge·muet′lich·keit′.** [lit., feeling]

gen (jen), *n.* *Brit. Slang.* general information. [by shortening]

Gen (jen), *n.* a girl's given name, form of **Genevieve.**

-gen, a learned borrowing from Greek meaning "production (of)," used in the formation of compound words: *endogen; hydrogen.* [< F *-gène* << Gk *-gen(ēs)* born, produced; akin to L *genus,* KIN]

Gen., 1. *Mil.* General. 2. Genesis. 3. Geneva.

gen., 1. gender. 2. general. 3. genitive. 4. genus.

ge·na (jē′nə, gen′ə), *n., pl.* **ge·nae** (jē′nē, gen′ē). *Zool., Anat.* the cheek or side region of the head. [< L: cheek; c. Gk *gényś* jaw, and CHIN] —**ge′nal,** *adj.*

ge·nappe (jə nap′, zhə-), *v.t.,* **-napped, -nap·ping.** to singe (worsted yarn) in order to remove loose or protruding fibers. [after *Genappe,* Belgium, where the yarn was originally manufactured]

genappe′ yarn′, a worsted yarn that has been genapped and made smooth and lustrous.

gen·darme (zhän′därm; *Fr.* zhäN darm′), *n., pl.* **-darmes** (-därmz; *Fr.* -darm′). 1. a policeman in any of several European countries, esp. a French policeman. 2. a soldier, esp. in France, serving in an army group acting as armed policemen with authority over civilians. 3. (formerly) a cavalryman in charge of a French cavalry squad. 4. *Geol.* a towering formation of rock, usually on a ridge. [< F, back formation from *gens d'armes,* alter. of *gent d'armes* men at arms]

gen·dar·me·rie (zhän där′mə rē; *Fr.* zhäN dar mə-rē′), *n.* gendarmes collectively; a body of gendarmes. Also, **gen·darm′er·y.** [< F; see GENDARME, -ERY]

gen·der[1] (jen′dər), *n.* 1. *Gram.* **a.** (in many languages) a set of classes that together include all nouns, membership in a particular class being shown by the form of the noun itself or by the form or choice of words that modify, replace, or otherwise refer to the noun, as, in English, the choice of *he* to replace *the man,* of *she* to replace *the woman,* of *it* to replace *the table,* of *it* or *she* to replace *the ship.* The number of genders in different languages varies from two to more than twenty; often the classification correlates in part with sex or animateness. The most familiar sets of genders are of three classes (as masculine, feminine, and neuter in Latin and German) or of two (as common and neuter in Dutch, or masculine and feminine in French and Spanish). **b.** one class of such a set. **c.** such classes or sets collectively or in general. **d.** membership of a word or grammatical form, or an inflectional form showing membership, in such a class. 2. sex: *She always minced her words when referring to persons of the feminine gender.* 3. *Archaic.* kind, sort, or class. [ME < MF *gendre, genre* < L *gener-* (s. of *genus*) kind, sort]

gen·der[2] (jen′dər), *v.t., v.i.* *Archaic.* to engender. [ME *gendre(n), gender(en)* < MF *gendr(er)* < L *generāre* to beget, deriv. of *gener-* GENDER[1]]

gene (jēn), *n.* *Genetics.* the unit of heredity transmitted in the chromosome and that, partially through interaction with other genes, controls the development of hereditary character. [< Gk *geneā́,* *gén(os)* race, stock, descent; c. L *genus, gener-*]

Gene (jēn), *n.* a boy's given name, form of **Eugene.**

geneal., genealogy.

ge′nealog′ical tree′. See **family tree.**

ge·ne·al·o·gy (jē′nē ol′ə jē, -al′-, jen′ē-), *n., pl.* **-gies.** 1. a record or account of the ancestry and descent of a person, family, group, etc. 2. the study of family ancestries and histories. 3. descent from an original form or progenitor; lineage; ancestry. [ME *genealogie* < MF < LL *geneālogia* < Gk *geneālogía* pedigree, equiv. to *geneā́* race (see GENE) + *-logia* -LOGY] —**ge·ne·a·log·i·cal** (jē′nē ə loj′i kəl, jen′ē-), **ge′ne·a·log′ic,** *adj.* —**ge′ne·a·log′i·cal·ly,** *adv.* —**ge′ne·al′o·gist,** *n.*
—**Syn.** 1. See **pedigree.**

gen·e·arch (jen′ē ärk′), *n.* a chief of a family or tribe. [< Gk *geneárch(ēs)* founder of a family, equiv. to *gene(ā́)* race (see GENE) + *árchēs* -ARCH]

Ge·nei·na (jŏŏ nā′nə, ge-), *n.* See **El Geneina.**

gen·er·a (jen′ər ə), *n.* a pl. of **genus.**

gen·er·a·ble (jen′ər ə bəl), *adj.* capable of being generated or produced. [< L *generābil(is)* creative, productive, equiv. to *gener(āre)* to beget, produce (see GENDER[2]) + *-ābilis* -ABLE] —**gen′er·a·bil′i·ty, gen′er·a·ble·ness,** *n.*

gen·er·al (jen′ər əl), *adj.* 1. of or pertaining to all persons or things belonging to a group or category: *a general meeting of the employees of a firm.* 2. of, pertaining to, or true of such persons or things in the main, with possible exceptions; common to most; prevalent or usual: *the general will of the people.* 3. not limited to one class, field, product, service, etc.; miscellaneous: *the general public; general science.* 4. dealing with all or the overall, universal aspects of the subject under consideration, esp. without attempting to consider or deal with details or specific aspects: *general instructions; a general description.* 5. not specific or definite: *I could give them only a general idea of what was going on.* 6. *Med.* (of anesthesia or an anesthetic) causing loss of consciousness and abolishing sensitivity to pain throughout the body. 7. having extended command or superior or chief rank: *a general chairman.* —*n.* 8. *Mil.* **a.** *U.S. Army and Air Force.* an officer ranking above a lieutenant general and below a general of the army or general of the air force. **b.** *U.S. Army.* an officer of any of the five highest ranks: a brigadier general, major general, lieutenant general, general, or general of the army. **c.** *U.S. Marines.* an officer holding the highest rank in the corps. **d.** (in numerous foreign armies) an officer in the second or third highest rank, as one ranking immediately below a field marshal in the British army. 9. *Eccles.* the chief official of a religious order. 10. a statement or principle involving or applicable to the whole. 11. *Archaic.* the general public. 12. **in general, a.** with respect to the whole class referred to; as a whole: *He likes people in general.* **b.** as a rule; usually: *In general, the bus is here by 9 a.m.* [ME < L *generāl(is),* equiv. to *gener-* (s. of *genus*) GENUS + *-ālis* -AL[1]] —**gen′er·al·ness,** *n.*
—**Syn.** 1, 2. customary, prevailing, regular, ordinary; catholic. GENERAL, COMMON, POPULAR, UNIVERSAL agree in the idea of being nonexclusive and widespread. GENERAL means belonging to, or prevailing throughout, a whole class or body collectively, irrespective of individuals: *a general belief.* COMMON means shared by all,

and belonging to one as much as another: *a common interest; common fund;* but use of this sense is frequently avoided because of ambiguity of sense. **9.** POPULAR means belonging to, adapted for, or favored by the people or the public generally, rather than by a particular (esp. a superior) class: *the popular conception; a popular candidate.* UNIVERSAL means found everywhere, and with no exceptions: *a universal longing.* **5.** ill-defined, inexact, imprecise. **—Ant. 1.** special, limited. **5.** definite.

gen′eral adapta′tion syn′drome, *Physiol.* the pattern and sequence of responses of the body to stress, involving an alarm reaction, a stage of resistance or adaptation, and a stage of exhaustion in which the adaptation can no longer be maintained.

Gen′eral Agree′ment on Tar′iffs and Trade′, an international organization formed in 1948 to establish common rules governing tariffs and to eliminate restrictive trade practices. *Abbr.:* GATT

Gen′eral Amer′ican Speech′, a pronunciation of American English showing few regional peculiarities: *Most U.S. radio and television announcers use General American Speech.*

Gen′eral Assem′bly, 1. the legislature in some States of the United States. **2.** the main deliberative body of the United Nations, composed of delegations from member nations.

gen′eral confes′sion, 1. confession of sins made in common by an entire congregation, esp. as part of a public prayer. **2.** a confession of sins committed over a long period of time.

Gen′eral Court′, 1. (in colonial New England) any of various local assemblies having both legislative and judicial powers. **2.** the State legislature of Massachusetts or New Hampshire.

gen′eral court′-martial, a court-martial having the authority to try any offense against military law and to impose a sentence of dishonorable discharge or of death when provided by law.

gen·er·al·cy (jen′ər əl sē), *n.* the office or tenure of a general. [GENERAL + -CY]

gen′eral deliv′ery, 1. a postal service that permits the delivery of mail to a specific post office where it is held for collection by an addressee when direct delivery is not possible or desirable. **2.** the postal department that handles such mail.

gen′eral dis′charge, *U.S. Mil.* **1.** a discharge from military service, by administrative action, of a person who has served honorably but who has not met all the conditions of an honorable discharge. **2.** a certificate of such a discharge.

gen′eral elec′tion, 1. *U.S.* **a.** a regularly scheduled local, State, or national election in which voters may choose from among candidates nominated in a primary or write in a name not listed on the regular ballot or voting machine. Cf. **primary** (def. 13). **b.** a State or national election, as opposed to a local election. **2.** *Brit.* an election, which must be held at any time within five years of the last election, in which constituents elect members of the House of Commons. Cf. **by-election.**

gen′eral head′quarters, *U.S. Army.* the headquarters of the commanding officer of a large military force. *Abbr.:* GHQ, G.H.Q.

gen·er·al·is·si·mo (jen′ər ə lis′ə mō′), *n., pl.* **-mos. 1.** (in certain foreign armies) the supreme commander of several armies acting together. **2.** (in China and U.S.S.R.) the supreme commander of all the forces of the country. [< It, superl. of *generale* GENERAL]

gen·er·al·ist (jen′ər ə list), *n.* a person whose knowledge, aptitudes, and skills are applied to a variety of different fields, as opposed to a specialist. [GENERAL + -IST]

gen·er·al·i·ty (jen′ə ral′i tē), *n., pl.* **-ties. 1.** an indefinite, unspecific, or undetailed statement: *to speak in generalities about human rights.* **2.** a general principle, rule, or law. **3.** the greater part or majority: *the generality of people.* **4.** the state or quality of being general. [late ME *generalite* < L *generālitās.* See GENERAL, -ITY]

gen·er·al·i·za·tion (jen′ər ə li zā′shən), *n.* **1.** the act or process of generalizing. **2.** a result of this process; a general statement, idea, or principle. **3.** *Logic.* **a.** a proposition asserting something to be true either of all members of a certain class or of an indefinite part of that class. **b.** the process of obtaining such propositions. **4.** *Psychol.* **a.** Also called **stimulus generalization.** the act or process of responding to a stimulus similar to but distinct from the conditioned stimulus. **b.** Also called **response generalization.** the act or process of making a different but similar response to the same stimulus. **c.** Also called **mediated generalization.** the act or process of responding to a stimulus not physically similar to the conditioned stimulus and not previously encountered in conditioning. **d.** the act or process of perceiving similarity or relation between different stimuli, as between words, colors, sounds, lights, concepts, feelings, etc.; the formation of a general notion. Also, *esp. Brit.,* **gen′er·al·i·sa′tion.** [GENERALIZE + -ATION]

gen·er·al·ize (jen′ər ə līz′), *v.,* **-ized, -iz·ing.** **—*v.t.* 1.** to give a general rather than a specific or special character or form to. **2.** to infer (a general principle, trend, etc.) from facts, statistics, or the like. **3.** to infer or form (a principle, opinion, conclusion, etc.) from only a few facts, examples, or the like. **4.** to make general; bring into general use or knowledge. **—*v.i.* 5.** to form general notions. **6.** to deal, think, or speak in generalities. **7.** to make general inferences. Also, *esp. Brit.,* **gen′er·al·ise′.** [GENERAL + -IZE] **—gen′er·al·iz′a·ble,** *adj.* **—gen′er·al·iz′er,** *n.*

gen′eralized coor′dinates, *Physics.* the least number of coordinates needed to specify the state of a given system.

gen′eral linguis′tics, the study of language in general rather than of a particular language or group of languages.

gen·er·al·ly (jen′ər ə lē), *adv.* **1.** with respect to the larger part; for the most part: *a generally accurate interpretation of the facts.* **2.** usually; commonly; ordinarily: *He generally comes home at noon.* **3.** without reference to or disregarding particular persons, things, situations, etc., which may be an exception: *generally speaking.* [ME; see GENERAL, -LY]
—Syn. 2. See **often. —Ant. 2.** seldom.

gen′eral of′ficer, *Mil.* an officer ranking above colonel.

gen′eral of the air′ force′, the highest ranking officer in the U.S. Air Force.

gen′eral of the ar′mies, *U.S. Army.* a special rank held by John J. Pershing, equivalent to general of the army.

gen′eral of the ar′my, *U.S. Army.* the highest ranking military officer; the next rank above general. Cf. **fleet admiral.**

gen′eral or′ders, *Mil.* **1.** a set of permanent orders from a headquarters establishing policy for a command or announcing official acts. **2.** a set of permanent orders governing the duties and behavior of sentries on routine guard duty. Cf. **special order.**

gen′eral paral′ysis, *Pathol.* a syphilitic brain disorder characterized by chronic inflammation and degeneration of cerebral tissue resulting in mental and physical deterioration. Also called **gen′eral pare′sis.**

gen′eral part′ner, a partner whose liability for his firm's debts is without limitation. Cf. **special partner.**

gen′eral part′nership, a partnership in which each of the partners is fully liable for the firm's debts. Cf. **limited partnership.**

Gen′eral Post′al Un′ion. See **Universal Postal Union.** *Abbr.:* GPU

gen′eral post′ of′fice, (in the U.S. postal system) the main post office of a city, county, etc., that also has branch post offices. *Abbr.:* GPO

gen′eral practi′tioner, a medical practitioner who does not specialize in a particular branch of medicine or limit his practice to a specific class of diseases.

gen′eral preces′sion, *Astron.* the precession that results from both lunisolar precession and planetary precession; precession of the equinoxes.

gen·er·al-pur·pose (jen′ər əl pûr′pəs), *adj.* useful in many ways; not limited in use or function: *a good general-purpose dictionary.*

gen′eral rule′, *Law.* See under **rule** (def. 9).

gen′eral seman′tics, an educational discipline concerning the relationship between symbols and behavior. Also called **semantics.**

gen′eral ses′sions, *U.S.* a court of general jurisdiction in criminal cases in some States.

gen·er·al·ship (jen′ər əl ship′), *n.* **1.** skill as commander of a large military force or unit. **2.** management or tactics. **3.** the rank or functions of a general. [GENERAL + -SHIP]

gen′eral solu′tion, *Math.* a solution to a differential equation, containing arbitrary, unevaluated constants. Cf. **particular solution.**

gen′eral staff′, *Mil.* a group of officers who are without command and whose duty is to assist high commanders in planning and carrying out orders in peace and war.

gen′eral store′, a store, usually in a rural area, that sells a wide variety of merchandise, as clothing, food, hardware, etc.

gen′eral strike′, a mass strike in all or many trades and industries in a section or in all parts of a country.

gen′eral the′ory of relativ′ity, *Physics.* See under **relativity** (def. 2).

gen·er·ate (jen′ə rāt′), *v.t.,* **-at·ed, -at·ing. 1.** to bring into existence; cause to be. **2.** to reproduce; procreate. **3.** to produce by a chemical process. **4.** to create by a vital or natural process. **5.** to create and distribute vitally and profusely: *He generates ideas that we all should consider. A good diplomat generates good will.* **6.** *Math.* **a.** to trace (a figure) by the motion of another: *A point generates a line.* **b.** to act as base for all the elements of a given set: *The number 2 generates the set 2,4,8,16.* [ME < L *generāt(us)* produced, ptp. of *generāre* to beget; see GENUS]

gen·er·a·tion (jen′ə rā′shən), *n.* **1.** the entire body of individuals born and living at about the same time: *the postwar generation.* **2.** the term of years, roughly 30 among human beings, accepted as the average period between the birth of parents and the birth of their offspring. **3.** a single step in natural descent, as of human beings, animals, or plants. **4.** a group of individuals, most of whom are the same approximate age, having similar ideas, problems, attitudes, etc. Cf. **beat generation, Lost Generation. 5.** a group of individuals having equal status at the same time: *Chaplin belonged to the generation of silent-screen stars.* **6.** a form, type, class, etc., of objects existing at the same time and having many similarities or developed from a common model or ancestor: *Detroit's generation of cars with tailfins.* **7.** the offspring of a certain parent or couple, considered as a step in natural descent. **8.** the act or process of generating; procreation. **9.** the state of being generated. **10.** production by natural or artificial processes; evolution, as of heat or sound. **11.** *Biol.* a form or phase of a plant or animal with reference to its manner of reproduction. **12.** *Math.* the production of a geometrical figure by the motion of another figure. **13.** *Physics.* one of the successive sets of nuclei produced in a chain reaction. [ME *generacioun* < MF < L *generātiōn-* (s. of *generātiō*). See GENERATE, -ION]

gen·er·a·tive (jen′ə rā′tiv, -ər ə tiv), *adj.* **1.** pertaining to the production of offspring. **2.** capable of producing. [ME < MF *generatif,* LL *generātīv(us).* See GENERATE, -IVE] **—gen′er·a′tive·ly,** *adv.* **—gen′er·a′tive·ness,** *n.*

gen′erative gram′mar, *Ling.* **1.** any theory of grammar that considers language as consisting of an indefinitely large number of sentences all of which may be specified or generated by the application of a set of rules. **2.** a set of such rules.

gen·er·a·tor (jen′ə rā′tər), *n.* **1.** one who or that which generates. **2.** a machine that converts one form of energy into another, esp. mechanical energy into electrical energy, as a dynamo, or electrical energy into sound, as an acoustic generator. **3.** *Chem.* an apparatus for producing a gas or vapor. [< L *generātor* producer, equiv. to *generāt(us)* (see GENERATE) + *-or* -OR[2]]

gen·er·a·trix (jen′ə rā′triks), *n., pl.* **gen·er·a·tri·ces** (jen′ər ə trī′sēz). *Math.* an element generating a figure. [< L *generātrīx* she who brings forth. See GENERATE, -TRIX]

ge·ner·ic (jə ner′ik), *adj.* **1.** of, pertaining to, or noting a genus, esp. in biology. **2.** of, applicable to, or referring to all the members of a genus, class, group, or kind; general. **3.** not protected by trademark registration: *"Cola" and "cleanser" are generic words.* Also, **ge·ner′i·cal.** [< L *gener-* (see GENDER[1]) + -IC] **—ge·ner′i·cal·ly,** *adv.* **—ge·ner′i·cal·ness,** *n.*
—Syn. 2. common; scientific.

gen·er·os·i·ty (jen′ə ros′i tē), *n., pl.* **-ties. 1.** readiness or liberality in giving. **2.** freedom from meanness or smallness of mind or character. **3.** a generous act: *We thanked him for his many generosities.* **4.** largeness or fullness; amplitude. [ME *generosite* < L *generōsitāt-* (s. of *generōsitās*), equiv. to *generōs(us)* GENEROUS + *-itāt-* -ITY]
—Syn. 1. munificence, bountifulness. **2.** nobleness, magnanimity. **—Ant. 1.** stinginess. **2.** pettiness.

gen·er·ous (jen′ər əs), *adj.* **1.** liberal in giving; munificent; bountiful; unselfish: *a generous patron of the arts; a generous gift.* **2.** free from meanness or smallness of mind or character; magnanimous. **3.** large; abundant; ample: *a generous portion of pie.* **4.** rich or strong in flavor: *a generous wine.* **5.** fertile; prolific: *generous soil.* [ME < OF < L *generōs(us),* equiv. to *gener-* (see GENDER[2]) + *-ōsus* -OUS] **—gen′er·ous·ly,** *adv.* **—gen′er·ous·ness,** *n.*
—Syn. 1. open-handed, free, unstinting. **2.** high-minded, noble, big. **3.** plentiful, copious. **5.** fruitful. **—Ant. 1.** selfish. **2.** mean. **3.** meager. **5.** barren.

Gen·e·see (jen′i sē′), *n.* a river flowing N from N Pennsylvania through W New York into Lake Ontario. 144 mi. long.

Gen·e·se·o (jen′i sē′ō), *n.* **1.** a town in NW Illinois. 5169 (1960). **2.** a town in central New York. 3284 (1960).

ge·nes·ic (ji nes′ik, -nē′sik), *adj.* pertaining to genesis or reproduction; genetic. [GENES(IS) + -IC]

gen·e·sis (jen′i sis), *n., pl.* **-ses** (-sēz′). an origin, creation, or beginning. [< L: generation, birth < Gk *génesis* origin, source]

Gen·e·sis (jen′i sis), *n.* the first book of the Bible, dealing with the Creation. **—Ge·ne·si·ac** (ji nē′sē ak′), **Gen·e·si·a·cal** (jen′ə sī′ə kəl), **Gen′e·sit′ic,** *adj.*

-genesis, a combining form of **genesis:** *parthenogenesis.*

gene-splic·ing (jēn′splī′siṅg), *n. Biochem.* See **recombinant DNA.**

gen·et[1] (jen′it, ji net′), *n.* **1.** any small, Old World carnivore of the genus *Genetta,* esp. *G. genetta,* related to the civets but not having a scent pouch. **2.** the fur of such an animal. Also, **ge·nette′.** [ME < OF *genette* < Ar *jarnait*]

Genet, *Genetta genetta* (Total length 3 ft.; tail 18 in.)

gen·et[2] (jen′it), *n.* jennet.

Ge·nêt (zhə nā′; *Fr.* zhə ne′), *n.* **1. Ed·mond Charles É·dou·ard** (ed môN′ sharl ā dwar′), ("*Citizen Genêt*"), 1763–1834, French minister to the U.S. in 1793. **2. Jean** (zhäN), born 1910, French playwright and novelist.

ge·neth·li·ac (ji neth′lē ak′), *adj. Astrol.* of or pertaining to birthdays or to the position of the stars at one's birth. [< L *genethliac(us)* < Gk *genethliakós,* equiv. to *genéthli(os)* pertaining to one's birth (deriv. of *genéthlē* birth) + *-akos* -AC] **—ge·neth·li·a·cal·ly** (jen′eth lī′ik lē, -ith-), *adj.*

ge·neth·li·al·o·gy (ji neth′lē ol′ə jē, -al′-), *n. Astrol.* the science of calculating positions of the heavenly bodies on nativities or birthdays. [< Gk *genethlialogía* casting of destinies, equiv. to *genéthlia* (pl. of *genéthlē* birth) + *-logia* -LOGY] **—ge·neth·li·a·log·ic** (ji neth′lē ə loj′ik), **ge·neth′li·a·log′i·cal,** *adj.*

ge·net·ic (jə net′ik), *adj.* **1.** *Biol.* pertaining or according to genetics. **2.** of, pertaining to, or produced by genes; genic. **3.** of, pertaining to, or influenced by geneses or origins. Also, **ge·net′i·cal.** [GENE(SIS) + -TIC] **—ge·net′i·cal·ly,** *adv.*

-genetic, a suffix of adjectives corresponding to nouns with stems ending in **-genesis:** *parthenogenetic.*

genet′ic engineer′ing, *Biochem.* the techniques by which genetic material can be altered by recombinant DNA so as to change or improve the hereditary properties of microorganisms, animals, plants, etc. **—genet′ic engineer′.**

genet′ic fal′lacy, *Logic.* the fallacy of confusing questions of validity and logical order with questions of origin and temporal order.

ge·net·i·cist (jə net′i sist), *n.* a specialist in genetics. [GENETIC + -IST]

genet′ic meth′od, the explanation or evaluation of a thing or event in terms of its origin and development.

ge·net·ics (jə net′iks), *n. pl.* (*construed as sing.*) **1.** *Biol.* the science of heredity, dealing with resemblances and differences of related organisms resulting from the interaction of their genes and the environment. **2.** the genetic properties and phenomena of an organism. [see GENETIC, -ICS]

Gen·e·trix (jen′i triks), *n.* an ancient Roman epithet of Venus, meaning "mother."

Gé·né·trix (*Fr.* zhā nā treks′), *n.* Genitrix.

ge·ne·va (jə nē′və), *n.* See **Hollands.** [< D *genever* < OF *genevre* < L *jūniper(us)* JUNIPER]

Ge·ne·va (jə nē′və), *n.* **1.** a city in and the capital of the canton of Geneva, in SW Switzerland, on the Lake of Geneva: seat of the League of Nations 1920–46. 176,183 (1960). **2.** a canton in SW Switzerland. 259,234 (1960); 109 sq. mi. **3. Lake of.** Also called **Lake Leman.** a lake between SW Switzerland and France. 45 mi. long; 225 sq. mi. **4.** a city in central New York. 17,286 (1960). **5.** a town in NE Illinois. 7646 (1960). **6.** a town in NE Ohio. 5677 (1960). **7.** a town in SE Alabama. 3840 (1960). **8.** Also, **Genevra, Ginevra.** a girl's given name. French, **Genève** (for defs. 1–3).

Gene′va bands′, two bands or pendent stripes made usually of white lawn and worn at the throat as part of clerical garb, originally by the Swiss Calvinist clergy. Also called **bands.**

Gene′va Conven′tion, *Mil.* an international agreement, first made in Geneva, Switzerland in 1864 and followed by the U.S., Great Britain, and many other nations, establishing rules for the humane treatment of prisoners of war and of the sick, the wounded, and the dead in battle.

Gene′va cross′, a red Greek cross on a white background, displayed to distinguish ambulances, hospitals, and persons belonging to the Red Cross Society.

Gene′va gown′, a loose, large-sleeved, black preaching gown worn by Protestant clergymen: so named from its use by the Genevan Calvinist clergy.

Ge·ne·van (jə nē′vən), *adj.* **1.** of or pertaining to Geneva. **2.** Calvinistic. —*n.* **3.** a native or inhabitant of Geneva. **4.** a Calvinist. [GENEV(A) + -AN]

Gene′va no′menclature, *Chem.* an internationally accepted system for naming organic carbon compounds.

Ge·nève (zhə nev′), *n.* French name of **Geneva.**

Gen·e·vese (jen′ə vēz′), *adj., n., pl.* **-vese.** Genevan.

Gen·e·vieve (jen′ə vēv′), *n.* **1. Saint,** A.D. 422–512, French nun: patron saint of Paris. **2.** a girl's given name. Also, **Gene·viève** (*Fr.* zhə nᵊvyev′).

Ge·nev·ra (jə nev′rə), *n.* a girl's given name, form of **Geneviève.**

Gen·ghis Khan (jeng′gis kän′), 1162–1227, Mongol conqueror of most of Asia and of E Europe to the Dnieper River. Also, **Jenghis Khan, Jenghiz Khan.**

Ge·ni·a (jē′nē ə), *n.* a girl's given name, form of **Eugenia.**

gen·ial[1] (jēn′yəl, jē′nē əl), *adj.* **1.** sympathetically cheerful; cordial: *a genial disposition; a genial host.* **2.** favorable for life, growth, or comfort; pleasantly warm; comfortably mild: *the genial climate of Hawaii.* **3.** characterized by genius. [< L *geniāl(is)* festive, jovial, pleasant, equiv. to *geni(us)* tutelar deity, the spirit of social enjoyment + *-ālis* -AL[1]] —**gen′ial·ly,** *adv.* —**gen′ial·ness,** *n.*
—**Syn. 1.** friendly, hearty, pleasant, agreeable, kindly, well-disposed. —**Ant. 1.** sullen, cool.

ge·ni·al[2] (jə nī′əl), *adj.* *Anat., Zool.* of or pertaining to the chin. [< Gk *génei(on)* chin, equiv. to *gén(us)* under jaw (c. L *gena*) + -AL[1]]

ge·ni·al·i·ty (jē′nē al′i tē), *n.* the quality of being genial; sympathetic cheerfulness or kindliness. [< LL *geniālitāt-* (s. of *geniālitās*). See GENIAL[1], -ITY]

gen·ic (jen′ik), *adj.* *Biol.* of, pertaining to, resembling, or arising from a gene or genes. [GENE + -IC]

-genic, an adjective suffix meaning "producing," "pertaining to a gene or genes," often corresponding to nouns with stems ending in **-gen** or **-geny:** *cyanogenic.*

ge·nic·u·late (jə nik′yə lit, -lāt′), *adj.* *Biol.* **1.** having kneelike joints or bends. **2.** bent at a joint like a knee. [< L *geniculāt(us)* knotted, equiv. to *genicul(um)* (*gen(u)* knee + *-culum* -CULE) + *-ātus* -ATE[1]] —**ge·nic′u·late·ly,** *adv.*

ge·nic·u·la·tion (jə nik′yə lā′shən), *n.* **1.** the state of being geniculate. **2.** a geniculate formation. [< LL *geniculātiōn-* (s. of *geniculātiō*) a kneeling < L *geniculāt(us)* (see GENICULATE) + *-iōn-* -ION]

ge·nie (jē′nē), *n.* *Islamic Myth.* jinn. [< F *génie* < L *geni(us)* tutelary genius]

ge·ni·i (jē′nē ī′), *n.* a pl. of **genius.**

ge·nip (gə nip′), *n.* **1.** Also, **ginep.** a genipap. **2.** *Bot.* **a.** a tropical American tree, *Melicocca bijuga,* bearing a yellow, sweet, edible fruit. **b.** the fruit itself. [shortened form of GENIPAP]

gen·i·pap (jen′ə pap′), *n.* **1.** the edible fruit of a tropical American rubiaceous tree, *Genipa americana,* used for preserves or in making beverages. **2.** the tree itself. [< Pg *genipap(o)* < Tupi]

ge·nis·ta (jə nis′tə), *n.* an evergreen broom, *Cytisus canariensis,* of the Canary Islands, having fragrant yellow flowers, cultivated in greenhouses. [< L: the broom-plant (sp. var. of *genesta*)]

genit., genitive.

gen·i·tal (jen′i tᵊl), *adj.* **1.** of, pertaining to, or noting generation or the sexual organs. **2.** *Psychoanal.* **a.** of or pertaining to the final stage of libidinal development, in which full gratification, as love or happiness, is found in the sexual partner. **b.** of or pertaining to the centering of sexual impulses and excitation on the genitalia. [ME < OF < L *genitāl-* (deriv. of *genit(us)* ptp. of *gignere* to beget) + *-āl-* -AL[1]]

gen·i·ta·lia (jen′i tā′lē ə, -tāl′yə), *n.pl.* *Anat.* the organs of reproduction, esp. the external organs. [< L; see GENITAL, -IA] —**gen·i·tal·ic** (jen′i tal′ik), **gen·i·tal·i·al** (jen′i tā′lē əl), *adj.*

gen·i·tals (jen′i tᵊlz), *n.pl.* genitalia. [n. use of GENITAL]

gen·i·tive (jen′i tiv), *Gram.* —*adj.* **1.** (in certain inflected languages) noting a case used primarily to indicate that a noun is a modifier of another noun, often to express possession, measure, origin, characteristic, etc., as *John's* hat, *man's* fate, *week's* vacation, *duty's* call. **2.** noting an affix or other element characteristic of this case, or a word containing such an element. **3.** similar to such a case form in function or meaning. —*n.* **4.** the genitive case. **5.** a word in the genitive case. **6.** a construction noting this case. Cf. **possessive.** [ME < L *genetīv(us),* equiv. to *genit(um)* (supine of *gignere* to beget) + *-īvus* -IVE] —**gen·i·ti·val** (jen′i tī′vəl), *adj.* —**gen′i·ti′val·ly,** *adv.*

genito-, a combining form of **genital:** *genitourinary.*

gen·i·tor (jen′i tər), *n.* a parent, esp. a father. [ME < L; cf. Gk *genétēs;* akin to L *genus* birth]

gen·i·to·u·ri·nar·y (jen′i tō yŏŏr′ə ner′ē), *adj.* *Anat., Physiol.* of or pertaining to the genital and urinary organs; urogenital. [GENITO- + URINARY]

Gen·i·trix (jen′i triks), *n.* a novel (1924) by François Mauriac. French, **Génétrix.**

gen·i·ture (jen′i chər), *n.* **1.** *Obs.* birth; generation. **2.** *Astrol.* nativity. [< L *genitūr-* (s. of *genitūra*). See GENITAL, -URE]

gen·ius (jēn′yəs), *n., pl.* **gen·ius·es** for 2, 3, 8, **gen·i·i** (jē′nē ī′) for 6, 7, 9. **1.** an exceptional natural capacity of intellect, especially as shown in creative and original work in art, music, etc. **2.** a person having such capacity. **3.** a person having extraordinarily high intelligence, esp. one with an I.Q. of 140 or above. **4.** natural ability or capacity; strong inclination: *a special genius for pediatric medicine.* **5.** distinctive character or spirit, as of a nation, period, language, etc. **6.** the guardian spirit of a place, institution, etc. **7.** either of two mutually opposed spirits, one good and the other evil, supposed to attend a person throughout his life. **8.** a person who strongly influences for good or ill the character, conduct, or destiny of a person, place, or thing: *Rasputin, the evil genius of Russian politics.* **9.** Usually **genii.** any demon or spirit, esp. a jinn. [< L: tutelary deity or genius of a person; cf. GENUS]
—**Syn. 4.** gift, talent, aptitude, faculty.

ge·ni·us lo·ci (gen′i ŏŏs′ lō′kē; *Eng.* jē′nē əs lō′sī), *Latin.* **1.** guardian of a place. **2.** the peculiar character of a place with reference to the impression that it makes on the mind.

Genl., General.

Gen·na·ro (jə när′ō; *It.* jen nä′rô), *n.* **San** (san; *It.* sän), Januarius.

Ge·no (jē′nō), *n.* a boy's given name.

gen·o·a (jen′ō ə), *n.* (*sometimes cap.*) *Naut.* a large jib for cruising and racing yachts, overlapping the mainsail. Also called **gen′oa jib′, Gen′oa jib′, reaching jib.** [after GENOA]

Gen·o·a (jen′ō ə), *n.* a seaport in NW Italy, S of Milan. 775,106 (1961). Italian, **Genova.**

gen′oa fore′sail. See **reaching foresail.** Also, **Gen′oa fore′sail.**

gen·o·cide (jen′ə sīd′), *n.* the deliberate and systematic extermination of a national or racial group. [< Gk *géno(s)* race + -CIDE] —**gen′o·cid′al,** *adj.*

Gen·o·ese (jen′ō ēz′, -ēs′), *adj., n., pl.* **-ese.** —*adj.* **1.** of, pertaining to, or characteristic of Genoa or its inhabitants. —*n.* **2.** a native or inhabitant of Genoa. Also, **Genovese.** [GENO(A) + -ESE]

Ge·nol·la (jə nol′ə), *n.* a girl's given name.

ge·nome (jē′nōm), *n.* *Genetics.* a haploid set of chromosomes. Also, **ge·nom** (jē′nom). [< G *Genom,* equiv. to *Gen* GENE + (*Chromos*)*om* CHROMOSOME] —**ge·no·mic** (jə nō′mik, -nom′ik), *adj.*

gen·o·type (jen′ə tīp′), *n.* *Genetics.* **1.** the genetic constitution of an organism or group of organisms. **2.** a group or class sharing a specific genetic constitution. **3.** the sum total of genes transmitted from parent to offspring. Cf. **phenotype.** [< Gk *géno(s)* origin, race + -TYPE] —**gen·o·typ·ic** (jen′ə tip′ik), **gen′o·typ′i·cal,** *adj.* —**gen′o·typ′i·cal·ly,** *adv.*

ge·nouil·lère (zhə nōō yer′), *n., pl.* **ge·nouil·lères** (zhə nōō yer′). *Armor.* poleyn. [ME *genulere* < MF, OF *genouil* knee (< VL **genuclum,* dim. of L *genu*) + *-iere,* fem. of *-ier* -IER]

-genous, a suffix of adjectives corresponding to nouns with stems in **-gen:** *hydrogenous.* [-GEN + -OUS]

Ge·no·va (je′nô vä′), *n.* Italian name of **Genoa.**

Gen·o·vese (jen′ə vēz′, -vēs′), *adj., n., pl.* **-vese.** Genoese.

Gen·o·ve·va (jen′ə vē′və), *n.* a girl's given name, form of **Genevieve.**

gen·re (zhän′rə; *Fr.* zhäN′rᵊ), *n., pl.* **-res** (-rəz; *Fr.* -rᵊ), *adj.* —*n.* **1.** genus; kind; sort; style. **2.** a class or category of artistic endeavor having a particular form, content, technique, or the like: *the difficult genre of epic poetry; the twelve-tone genre of musical composition.* **3.** *Fine Arts.* **a.** paintings in which scenes of everyday life form the subject matter. **b.** a realistic style of painting using such subject matter. —*adj.* **4.** *Fine Arts.* of or pertaining to genre. [< F: kind, sort; see GENDER[1]]

gen·ro (gen′rō′), *n.pl.* (*often cap.*) the elder statesmen of Japan. [< Jap: lit., old men]

gens (jenz), *n., pl.* **gen·tes** (jen′tēz). **1.** a group of families in ancient Rome claiming descent from a common ancestor and united by a common name and common ancestral religious rites. **2.** *Anthropol.* a group tracing common descent in the male line; clan. [< L *gēns* race, people; cf. *genus* nation]

Gen·san (gen′sän′), *n.* Japanese name of **Wŏnsan.**

gen·seng (jen′seng′), *n.* ginseng.

Gen·ser·ic (jen′sər ik, gen′-), *n.* A.D. c390–477, king of the Vandals, conqueror in northern Africa and Italy. Also, **Gaiseric.**

gent[1] (jent), *n.* **1.** *Informal.* gentleman (defs. 1, 2). **2. gents,** *Slang.* See **men's room.** [by shortening]

gent[2] (jent), *adj.* *Obs.* **1.** of high birth; well-bred. **2.** elegant; graceful. [ME < OF < L *genit(um)* begotten, born]

Gent (KHent), *n.* Flemish name of **Ghent.**

Gent., gentleman or gentlemen. Also, **gent.**

gen·teel (jen tēl′), *adj.* **1.** belonging or suited to polite society. **2.** well-bred or refined; polite; elegant; stylish. **3.** affectedly or pretentiously polite, delicate, etc. [< F *gentil;* see GENTLE] —**gen·teel′ly,** *adv.* —**gen·teel′ness,** *n.*

gen·teel·ism (jen tē′liz əm), *n.* a word or phrase used in place of another, supposedly less genteel term: *"Limb" is a genteelism for "leg."* [GENTEEL + -ISM]

gen·tian (jen′shən), *n.* **1.** any of several plants of the genus *Gentiana,* having usually blue, or sometimes yellow, white, or red flowers, esp. the fringed gentian of North America, or *G. lutea,* of Europe. **2.** any of various plants resembling the gentian. **3.** the root of *G. lutea,* or a preparation of it, used as a tonic. [ME *gencian* < L *gentiana;* said to be named after *Gentius,* an Illyrian king]

gen·ti·a·na·ceous (jen′shē ə nā′shəs), *adj.* belonging to the *Gentianaceae,* or gentian family of plants. [< NL *gentianace(ae)* the family of plants, equiv. to L *gentian(a)* GENTIAN + *-aceae;* see -ACEOUS]

gen·tian·el·la (jen′shə nel′ə, -shē ə nel′-), *n.* any of several alpine gentians, esp. *Gentiana acaulis,* having showy blue flowers, grown in gardens. [< NL, dim. of L *gentiana* GENTIAN]

gen′ti·an′ic ac′id (jen′shē an′ik, jen′-), *Pharm.* gentisin. Also called **gen·tian·in** (jen′shə nin), **gen·ti·in** (jen′tē in).

gen′tian vi′olet, a dye derived from rosaniline, used in chemistry as an indicator and in medicine as a fungicide, bactericide, anthelmintic, and in the treatment of burns. Also called **crystal violet, methylrosaniline chloride.**

gen·til (zhäN tē′), *adj.* *French.* kind; gentle; noble.

gen·tile (jen′tīl), *adj.* **1.** of or pertaining to any people not Jewish. **2.** Christian, as distinguished from Jewish. **3.** *Mormonism.* neither Mormon nor Jewish. **4.** heathen or pagan. **5.** (of a linguistic expression) expressing nationality or local origins. **6.** of or pertaining to a tribe, clan, people, nation, etc. —*n.* **7.** a person who is not Jewish, esp. a Christian. **8.** (among Mormons) a person who is not a Mormon. **9.** a heathen or pagan. Also, **Gen′tile.** [ME < L *gentīl(is),* equiv. to *gent-* nation + *-īlis* -ILE]

gen·ti·lesse (jen′tᵊles′), *n.* *Archaic.* the quality of being gentle. [ME < MF *gentillesse,* equiv. to *gentil* (see GENTEEL, GENTLE) + *-esse* n. suffix]

gen·til·ism (jen′tᵊliz′əm), *n.* the quality of being a gentile, esp. heathenism; paganism. [GENTILE + -ISM]

gen·til·i·ty (jen til′i tē), *n.* **1.** superior refinement or elegance, whether actual or affected. **2.** the condition of having gentle birth or of belonging to the gentry. **3.** persons of gentle birth; gentry. [ME < OF *gentilite* < L *gentīlitāt-* (s. of *gentīlitās*), equiv. to *gentīl(is)* (see GENTLE) + *-itāt-* -ITY]

gen·ti·sate (jen′ti sāt′), *n.* *Chem.* a salt or ester of gentisic acid. [GENTIS(IC) + -ATE[2]]

gen·tis′ic ac′id (jen tis′ik, -tiz′-), *Pharm.* a crystalline, water-soluble compound, $(HO)_2C_6H_3COOH$, used chiefly in the form of its sodium salt as an analgesic and diaphoretic. [GENTI(AN) + *-s* connective + -IC]

gen·ti·sin (jen′ti sin), *n.* *Biochem.* a yellow, crystalline, slightly water-soluble compound, $C_{14}H_{10}O_5$, obtained from gentian root. [< NL *Genti(ana)* (see GENTIAN) + *-sin* (as in *pepsin*)] Also called **gentianic acid, gentianin, gentiin.**

gen·tle (jen′tᵊl), *adj.,* **-tler, -tlest,** *v.,* **-tled, -tling.** —*adj.* **1.** kindly; amiable: *a gentle manner.* **2.** mild; not severe, rough, or violent: *a gentle wind; a gentle tap on the shoulder.* **3.** moderate: *gentle heat.* **4.** gradual: *a gentle slope.* **5.** of good birth or family; wellborn. **6.** characteristic of good birth; honorable; respectable: *a gentle upbringing.* **7.** easily handled or managed; tractable: *a gentle animal.* **8.** soft or low: *a gentle sound.* **9.** polite; refined: *Consider, gentle reader, my terrible predicament at this juncture.* **10.** entitled to a coat of arms; armigerous. **11.** *Archaic.* noble; chivalrous: *a gentle knight.* —*v.t.* **12.** to tame; render tractable. **13.** to mollify; calm; pacify. **14.** to make gentle. **15.** to stroke; soothe by petting. **16.** *Obs.* to ennoble; dignify. [ME *gentle, gentil(e)* < OF *gentil* highborn, noble < L *gentīl(is)* belonging to the same family, equiv. to *gent-* (s. of *gēns*) family, race + *-īlis* -LE] —**gen′tleness,** *n.* —**gen′tly,** *adv.*
—**Syn. 1.** clement, peaceful, pacific, soothing; tender, humane, lenient, merciful. GENTLE, MEEK, MILD refer to an absence of bad temper or belligerence. GENTLE has reference esp. to disposition and behavior, and often suggests a deliberate or voluntary kindness or forbearance in dealing with others: *a gentle pat; gentle with children.* MEEK implies a submissive spirit, and may even indicate undue submission in the face of insult or injustice: *meek and even servile or weak.* MILD suggests absence of harshness or severity, rather because of natural character or temperament than conscious choice: *a mild rebuke; a mild manner.* **3.** temperate. **5.** noble. **7.** manageable, docile, tame, quiet. **9.** courteous; polished. —**Ant. 1.** harsh, cruel. **2.** violent, sudden. **7.** wild, unruly.

gen′tle breeze′, *Meteorol.* (on the Beaufort scale) a wind of 8–12 miles per hour.

gen′tle craft′, **1.** Also called **gen′tle art′.** the sport of angling or fishing (usually prec. by *the*). **2.** *Obs.* shoemaking (usually prec. by *the*).

gen·tle·folk (jen′tᵊl fōk′), *n.* (*construed as pl.*) persons of good family and breeding. Also, **gen′tle·folks′.** [GENTLE + FOLK]

gen·tle·hood (jen′tᵊl hŏŏd′), *n.* the status of a person entitled to a coat of arms. [GENTLE + -HOOD]

gen·tle·man (jen′tᵊl mən), *n., pl.* **-men. 1.** a man of good breeding, education, and manners. **2.** (used as a polite term or form of address) any man: *Gentlemen, please come this way.* **3.** a civilized, educated, sensitive, or well-mannered man: *Are you going to be a gentleman and hold the door open for her?* **4.** a male personal servant, esp. of a man of social position; valet. **5.** a male attendant upon a king, queen, or other royal person, who is himself of high birth or rank. **6.** a man of good social standing, as a noble or an armigerous commoner. **7.** a man with an independent income who does not work for a living. **8.** a male member of the U.S. Senate or House of Representatives: *The chair recognizes the gentleman from Massachusetts.* **9.** *Hist.* a man who is above the rank of yeoman. [ME; see GENTLE, MAN[1]] —**gen′tle·man·like′,** *adj.*

gen·tle·man-at-arms (jen′tᵊl mən at ärmz′), *n., pl.* **gen·tle·men-at-arms.** (in England) one of a guard of 40 gentlemen with their officers who attend the sovereign on state occasions.

gen·tle·man-com·mon·er (jen′tᵊl mən kom′ə nər), *n., pl.* **gen·tle·men-com·mon·ers.** (formerly) a member of a class of commoners enjoying special privileges at Oxford University.

gen·tle·man-farm·er (jen′tᵊl mən fär′mər), *n., pl.* **gen·tle·men-farm·ers. 1.** a man whose wealth or income from other sources permits him to farm for pleasure rather than for profit. **2.** a man whose income from his farm has freed him from the necessity of physical labor.

gen·tle·man·ly (jen′tᵊl mən lē), *adj.* like, befitting, or characteristic of a gentleman. [GENTLEMAN + -LY] —**gen′tle·man·li·ness,** *n.*

gen′tleman of the road′, **1.** a highwayman. **2.** *U.S.* a tramp or hobo.

gen·tle·man-pen·sion·er (jen′tᵊl mən pen′shə nər), *n., pl.* **gen·tle·men-pen·sion·ers.** (formerly) a gentleman-at-arms.

gen′tleman's gen′tleman, a valet.

Gen′tleman Ush′er of the Black′ Rod′. See **Black Rod** (def. 1).

gen′tlemen's agree′ment, **1.** an agreement that, although unenforceable at law, is binding as a matter of personal honor. **2.** an unwritten agreement by a socially prominent clique, private club, etc., to discriminate against or refuse to accept members of religious, racial, or national minority groups. Also, **gen′tleman's agree′ment.**

gen′tle sex′, women in general: *a member of the gentle sex.*

gen·tle-voiced (jen′tᵊl voist′), *adj.* having a gentle voice: *a demure, gentle-voiced young lady.*

gen·tle·wom·an (jen′tᵊl wŏŏm′ən), *n., pl.* **-wom·en. 1.** a woman of good family or breeding; a lady. **2.** a woman who attends upon a lady of rank. **3.** a female member of the U.S. Senate or House of Representatives: *The chair recognizes the gentlewoman from Maine.* [ME; see GENTLE, WOMAN] —**gen′tle·wom′an·ly,** *adv.*

Gen·too (jen′to͞o), *n., pl.* **-toos,** *adj. Archaic.* —*n.* **1.** a Hindu. **2.** any of the non-European languages of the Hindus, esp. Telugu. —*adj.* **3.** of or relating to the Gentoos. [< Pg *gentio* GENTILE]

gen′too pen′guin (jen′to͞o), a penguin, *Pygoscelis papua,* of small Antarctic islands.

gen·tri·fi·ca·tion (jen′trə fi kā′shən), *n.* the buying and renovation of houses in deteriorated urban neighborhoods, esp. by middle-income professionals, thus improving property values but often displacing low-income families.

gen·try (jen′trē), *n.* **1.** wellborn and well-bred people. **2.** (in England) the class under the nobility. **3.** an aristocracy. **4.** nonnobles entitled to a coat of arms, esp. those owning large tracts of land. **5.** (*construed as pl.*) *Informal.* people, esp. considered as a specific group, class, or kind: *The polo crowd doesn't go there, but these hockey gentry do.* **6.** the state or condition of being a gentleman. [ME < OF *genterie.* See GENTILE, GENTLE]

gen·ty (jen′tē), *adj. Scot.* genteel; graceful. [< F *gentil;* see GENTEEL, GENTLE]

ge·nu (jē′no͞o, -nyo͞o, jen′o͞o, -yo͞o), *n., pl.* **ge·nu·a** (jen′o͞o ə, -nyo͞o ə). *Anat., Zool.* **1.** the knee. **2.** a kneelike part or bend. [< L; c. Gk *gónu* KNEE] —**ge′nu·al,** *adj.*

gen·u·flect (jen′yo͝o flekt′), *v.i.* **1.** to bend the knee or knees in reverence or worship. **2.** to express a servile attitude. [< ML *genūflect(ere)* (to) bend the knee, equiv. to L *genū* knee + *flectere* to bend] —**gen′u·flec′tor,** *n.*

gen·u·flec·tion (jen′yo͝o flek′shən), *n.* an act of bending the knee or knees in reverence or worship. Also, *esp. Brit.,* **gen′u·flex′ion.** [< ML *genūflexiōn-* (s. of *genūflexiō*). See GENUFLECT, -ION]

gen·u·ine (jen′yo͞o in), *adj.* **1.** possessing the purported character, quality, or origin; not counterfeit; authentic; real: *genuine sympathy; a genuine antique.* **2.** properly so called: *a genuine case of smallpox.* **3.** free from pretense, affectation, or hypocrisy; sincere: *a genuine person.* **4.** proceeding from the original stock; pure in breed: *a genuine Celtic people.* [< L *genuīn(us)* innate, natural, equiv. to *genu-* (as in *ingenuus* native) + *-īnus* -INE[1]] —**gen′u·ine·ly,** *adv.* —**gen′u·ine·ness,** *n.*

gen·u·pec·tor·al (jen′yo͞o pek′tər əl), *adj.* pertaining to the knees and chest. [GENU + PECTORAL]

ge·nus (jē′nəs), *n., pl.* **gen·e·ra** (jen′ər ə), **ge·nus·es.** **1.** a kind; sort; class. **2.** *Biol.* the usual major subdivision of a family or subfamily in the classification of plants and animals, usually consisting of more than one species. **3.** *Logic.* a class or group of individuals, or of species of individuals. [< L: race, stock, kind, gender; c. Gk *génos.* See GENS, GENDER[1]]

-geny, a learned borrowing from Greek meaning "origin," used in the formation of compound words: *phylogeny.* [< Gk *-geneia.* See -GEN, -Y[3]]

geo-, a learned borrowing from Greek meaning "the earth," used in the formation of compound words: *geochemistry.* [< Gk *geō-,* comb. form of *gê* the earth]

Geo., George.

ge·o·cen·tric (jē′ō sen′trik), *adj.* **1.** *Astron.* viewed or measured from the center of the earth: *the geocentric position of the moon.* **2.** having or representing the earth as a center: *a geocentric theory of the universe.* **3.** using the earth or earthly life as the only basis of evaluation. [GEO- + CENTRIC] —**ge′o·cen′tri·cal·ly,** *adv.*

ge′ocen′tric par′allax. See under **parallax** (def. 2).

ge·o·chem·is·try (jē′ō kem′i strē), *n.* the science dealing with the chemical changes in and the composition of the earth's crust. [GEO- + CHEMISTRY] —**ge·o·chem·i·cal** (jē′ō kem′i kəl), *adj.* —**ge′o·chem′ist,** *n.*

ge·o·chro·nol·o·gy (jē′ō krə nol′ə jē), *n.* the chronology of the earth based on geological data. [GEO- + CHRONOLOGY] —**ge·o·chron·o·log·ic** (jē′ō kron′əloj′ik), **ge′o·chron′o·log′i·cal,** *adj.* —**ge′o·chro·nol′o·gist,** *n.*

geod., **1.** geodesy. **2.** geodetic.

ge·ode (jē′ōd), *n.* **1.** *Geol.* a hollow concretionary or nodular stone often lined with crystals. **2.** the hollow or cavity of this. **3.** any similar formation. [< F *géode* < L *geōd(ēs)* < Gk *geṓdēs* earthlike. See GEO-, -ODE[1]] —**ge·od·ic** (jē od′ik), **ge·od·al** (jē ōd′əl), *adj.*

ge·o·des·ic (jē′ə des′ik, -dē′sik), *adj.* **1.** Also, **ge′o·des′i·cal.** pertaining to the geometry of curved surfaces, in which geodesic lines take the place of the straight lines of plane geometry. —*n.* **2.** See **geodesic line.** [< F *géodésique.* See GEODESY, -IC]

ge′odes′ic dome′, a light, domelike structure developed by R. Buckminster Fuller to combine the structurally desirable properties of the tetrahedron and the sphere. Its form varies according to size, materials, and purpose, but consists essentially of a grid of compression or tension members lying upon or parallel to great circles running in three directions in any given area, the typical form being the projection upon a sphere of an icosahedron, the triangular faces of which are filled with a symmetrical triangular, hexagonal, or quadrangular grid.

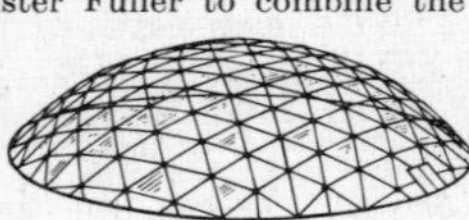
Geodesic dome

ge′odes′ic line′, *Math.* the shortest line lying on a given surface and connecting two given points.

ge·od·e·sy (jē od′i sē), *n.* the branch of applied mathematics that deals with the measurement of the shape and area of large tracts of country, the exact position of geographical points, and the curvature, shape, and dimensions of the earth. Also, **ge·o·det·ics** (jē′ə det′iks). [< F *géodésie* < Gk *geōdaisía,* equiv. to *geō-* GEO- + *daíein* to divide] —**ge·od′e·sist,** *n.*

ge·o·det·ic (jē′ə det′ik), *adj.* **1.** pertaining to geodesy. **2.** geodesic. Also, **ge′o·det′i·cal.** [irreg. from GEODESY; see -IC] —**ge′o·det′i·cal·ly,** *adv.*

ge′odet′ic sur′vey, a land area survey in which the curvature of the surface of the earth is taken into account.

ge·o·dy·nam·ics (jē′ō dī nam′iks), *n.* the science dealing with dynamic processes or forces within the earth. [GEO- + DYNAMICS] —**ge′o·dy·nam′ic, ge′o·dy·nam′i·cal,** *adj.* —**ge·o·dy·nam·i·cist** (jē′ō dī nam′i sist), *n.*

Geof·frey (jef′rē), *n.* a boy's given name. Also, **Jeffrey.**

Geof′frey of Mon′mouth, 1100?–1154, English chronicler.

geog., **1.** geographer. **2.** geographic; geographical. **3.** geography.

ge·og·no·sy (jē og′nə sē), *n.* the branch of geology that deals with the constituent parts of the earth, its envelope of air and water, its crust, and the condition of its interior. [< F *géognosie,* equiv. to *géo-* GEO- + Gk *gnôsis* knowledge] —**ge·og·nos·tic** (jē′og nos′tik), **ge′og·nos′ti·cal,** *adj.* —**ge′og·nos′ti·cal·ly,** *adv.*

ge·og·ra·pher (jē og′rə fər), *n.* a person who specializes in geographical research, deliniation, and study. [< LL *geōgraph(us)* (< Gk *geōgráphos,* equiv. to *geō-* GEO- + *gráphos* a writer) + -ER[1]]

ge·o·graph·i·cal (jē′ə graf′i kəl), *adj.* **1.** of or pertaining to geography. **2.** of or pertaining to the natural features, population, industries, etc., of a region or regions. Also, **ge′o·graph′ic.** [< LL *geōgraphic(us)* (< Gk *geōgraphikós;* see GEO-, -GRAPH) + *-ikos* -IC) + -AL[2]] —**ge′o·graph′i·cal·ly,** *adv.*

ge′ograph′ical mile′, mile (def. 1b).

geograph′ic deter′minism, *Sociol.* a doctrine that regards geographical conditions as the determining or molding agency of group life.

geograph′ic envi′ronment, *Sociol.* the entire natural surroundings of man, independent of but underlying and conditioning his activity.

ge′ograph′ic range′, *Navig.* the distance at which a certain light, as that of a lighthouse, is visible to the eye at a given elevation, assuming that the weather is clear and that the light is sufficiently powerful to be visible from any point at which it appears above the horizon. Cf. **luminous range.**

ge·og·ra·phy (jē og′rə fē), *n., pl.* **-phies.** **1.** the science dealing with the areal differentiation of the earth's surface, as shown in the character, arrangement, and interrelations over the world of such elements as climate, elevation, soil, vegetation, population, land use, industries, or states, and of the unit areas formed by the complex of these individual elements. **2.** the study of this science. **3.** a book dealing with this science or study, as a textbook. **4.** the topographical features of a region, usually of the earth, sometimes of the planets. **5.** a word game in which each player in rotation must say aloud a geographic place name beginning with the last letter of the place name mentioned by the preceding player. [< LL *geōgraphia* < Gk *geōgraphía* earth-description. See GEO-, -GRAPHY]

ge·oid (jē′oid), *n.* **1.** an imaginary surface that coincides with the mean sea level in the ocean and its extension through the continents. **2.** the geometric figure formed by this surface, an ellipsoid flattened at the poles. [< Gk *geoeid(ḗs).* See GEO-, -OID] —**ge·oi′dal,** *adj.*

ge·o·i·so·therm (jē′ō ī′sə thûrm′), *n.* isogeotherm.

geol., **1.** geologic; geological. **2.** geologist. **3.** geology.

Geol.E., geological engineer.

ge·o·log·ic (jē′ə loj′ik), *adj.* of or pertaining to geology. Also, **ge′o·log′i·cal.** [GEOLOG(Y) + -IC] —**ge′o·log′i·cal·ly,** *adv.*

ge′olog′ic time′, the succession of eras, periods, and epochs as considered in historical geology.

ge·ol·o·gist (jē ol′ə jist), *n.* a person who specializes in geologic research and study. [GEOLOG(Y) + -IST]

ge·ol·o·gize (jē ol′ə jīz′), *v.,* **-gized, -giz·ing.** —*v.i.* **1.** to study geology. —*v.t.* **2.** to examine geologically. Also, *esp. Brit.,* **ge·ol′o·gise′.** [GEOLOG(Y) + -IZE]

ge·ol·o·gy (jē ol′ə jē), *n., pl.* **-gies.** **1.** the science that deals with the physical history of the earth, the rocks of which it is composed, and the physical changes which the earth has undergone or is undergoing. **2.** the study of this science. **3.** the geologic features and processes occurring in a given region on the earth or on a celestial body: *the geology of Mars; the geology of eastern Kentucky.* [< LL *geōlogia* science of earthly things, earth science. See GEO-, -LOGY]

geom., **1.** geometric; geometrical. **2.** geometry.

ge·o·mag·net·ic (jē′ō mag net′ik), *adj.* of or pertaining to terrestrial magnetism. [GEO- + MAGNETIC] —**ge·o·mag·ne·ti·cian** (jē′ō mag′ni tish′ən), **ge′o·mag′ne·tist,** *n.*

ge·o·man·cer (jē′ə man′sər), *n.* a person versed in or practicing geomancy. [ME; see GEOMANCY, -ER[1]]

ge·o·man·cy (jē′ə man′sē), *n.* divination by means of a figure made by a handful of earth thrown down at random or by figures or lines formed by a number of dots made at random. [ME < OF *geomancie* << LGk *geōmanteía.* See GEO-, -MANCY] —**ge′o·man′tic, ge′o·man′ti·cal,** *adj.* —**ge′o·man′ti·cal·ly,** *adv.*

ge·o·med·i·cine (jē′ō med′i sən *or, esp. Brit.,* -med′sin), *n.* the branch of medicine dealing with the effect of geography on disease. [GEO- + MEDICINE] —**ge·o·med·i·cal** (jē′ō med′i kəl), *adj.*

ge·om·e·ter (jē om′i tər), *n.* **1.** geometrician. **2.** a geometrid moth or larva. [ME < L *geōmetra* < Gk *geōmétra* land measurer; see GEOMETRY]

ge·o·met·ric (jē′ə me′trik), *adj.* **1.** of or pertaining to geometry or to the principles of geometry. **2.** resembling or employing the simple rectilinear or curvilinear lines or figures used in geometry. **3.** of or pertaining to painting, sculpture, or ornamentation of predominantly geometric characteristics. **4.** (*often cap.*) *Fine Arts.* **a.** pertaining to or designating a style of vase painting developed in Greece between the 10th and 8th centuries B.C., characterized chiefly by rectilinear or curvilinear shapes in abstract and human figuration, often arranged in tiers or panels around the vase. **b.** designating a style of Greek sculpture of approximately the same period, exemplified chiefly in small figurines or reliefs having a schematic and generalized treatment of the human form. Also, **ge′o·met′ri·cal.** [< L *geōmetric(us)* < Gk *geōmetr(ēs)* geometer. See GEO-, METRIC[2]] —**ge′o·met′ri·cal·ly,** *adv.*

geomet′rical lathe′. See **rose engine.**

geomet′rical op′tics, the branch of optics dealing with light as rays, esp. in the study of the effects of lenses and mirrors on light beams and of their combination in optical instruments.

geomet′rical pace′, a pace of five feet, representing the distance between the places at which the same foot rests on the ground in walking. Also called **great pace.**

geomet′rical stair′, a winding or angled stair having no newels.

ge·om·e·tri·cian (jē om′i trish′ən, jē′ə mi-), *n.* a person skilled in geometry. [GEOMETRIC + -IAN]

ge′omet′ric mean′, *Math.* the mean of *n* positive numbers obtained by taking the *n*th root of the product of the numbers: *The geometric mean of 6 and 24 is 12.*

geomet′ric progres′sion, *Math.* a sequence of terms in which the ratio between any two successive terms is the same, as the progression 1, 3, 9, 27, 81 or 144, 12, 1, 1/12, 1/144. Also called **geometric series.**

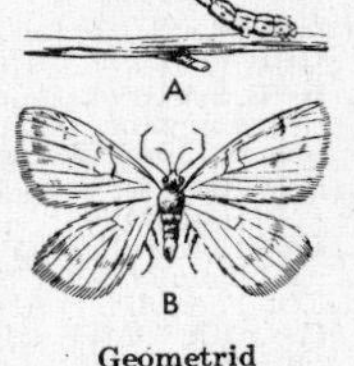
Geometrid
Fall cankerworm, *Alsophila pometaria*
A, Larva; B, Adult male

ge′omet′ric ra′tio, *Math.* the ratio of consecutive terms in a geometric progression.

ge′omet′ric se′ries, *Math.* **1.** an infinite series of the form, $c + cx + cx^2 + cx^3 + \ldots$, where c and x are real numbers. **2.** See **geometric progression.**

ge·om·e·trid (jē om′i trid), *adj.* **1.** belonging or pertaining to the family *Geometridae,* comprising slender-bodied, broad-winged moths, the larvae of which are called measuring worms. —*n.* **2.** a geometrid moth. [< NL *Geōmetrid(ae)* name of genus of moths, equiv. to L *geōmetr(es)* GEOMETER + *-idae* -ID[2]]

ge·om·e·trise (jē om′i trīz′), *v.i., v.t.,* **-trised, -tris·ing.** *Chiefly Brit.* geometrize.

ge·om·e·trize (jē om′i trīz′), *v.,* **-trized, -triz·ing.** —*v.i.* **1.** to work by geometric methods. —*v.t.* **2.** to put into geometric form. [GEOMETR(Y) + -IZE]

ge·om·e·try (jē om′i trē), *n.* **1.** the branch of mathematics that deals with the deduction of the properties, measurement, and relationships of points, lines, angles, and figures in space from their defining conditions by means of certain assumed properties of space. **2.** any specific system of this that operates in accordance with a specific set of assumptions: *Euclidean geometry.* **3.** the study of this branch of mathematics. **4.** a book on this study, esp. a textbook. **5.** the shape or form of a surface or solid. **6.** a design or arrangement of objects in simple rectilinear or curvalinear form. [ME < L *geōmetria* < Gk *geōmetría.* See GEO-, -METRY]

ge·o·mor·phic (jē′ə môr′fik), *adj.* **1.** of or pertaining to the figure of the earth or the forms of its surface. **2.** resembling the earth in form. [GEO- + -MORPHIC]

ge·o·mor·phol·o·gy (jē′ə môr fol′ə jē), *n.* the study of the characteristics, origin, and development of land forms. [GEO- + MORPHOLOGY] —**ge·o·mor·pho·log·i·cal** (jē′ə môr′fə loj′i kəl), **ge′o·mor′pho·log′ic,** *adj.* —**ge′o·mor·phol′o·gist,** *n.*

ge·o·nav·i·ga·tion (jē′ō nav′ə gā′shən), *n.* navigation by means of observations of terrestrial objects. [GEO- + NAVIGATION]

Ge·o·nim (gā ō′nim, gā ō nēm′), *n. Hebrew.* a pl. of **Gaon.** —**Ge·on·ic** (gā on′ik), *adj.*

ge·oph·a·gy (jē of′ə jē), *n.* the practice of eating earthy matter, esp. clay or chalk. Also, **ge·o·pha·gi·a** (jē′ə fā′jə, -jē ə), **ge·oph·a·gism** (jē of′ə jiz′əm). [< Gk **geōphagia* the eating of earth. See GEO-, -PHAGY] —**ge·oph′a·gist,** *n.* —**ge·oph·a·gous** (jē of′ə gəs), *adj.*

ge·oph·i·lous (jē of′ə ləs), *adj. Bot., Zool.* terrestrial, as certain snails, or any plant fruiting underground. [< NL *Geophil(us)* name of genus (see GEO-, -PHILE) + -OUS]

ge·o·phys·ics (jē′ō fiz′iks), *n.* (*construed as sing.*) the physics or the science dealing with the physics of the earth, including oceanography, seismology, volcanology, magnetism, etc. [GEO- + PHYSICS] —**ge′o·phys′i·cal,** *adj.* —**ge′o·phys′i·cal·ly,** *adv.* —**ge′o·phys′i·cist,** *n.*

ge·o·phyte (jē′ə fīt′), *n. Bot.* a plant with underground buds. [GEO- + -PHYTE] —**ge·o·phyt·ic** (jē′ə-fit′ik), *adj.*

ge·o·pol·i·tics (jē′ō pol′i tiks), *n.* (*construed as sing.*) **1.** the study or the application of the influence of political and economic geography on the politics, national power, foreign policy, etc., of a state. **2.** the combination of geographic and political factors influencing or delineating a country or region. **3.** a national policy based on the interrelation of politics and geography. **4.** a Nazi doctrine that a combination of political, geographic, historical, racial, and economic factors showed Germany's right to expand its borders and control various strategic land masses and natural resources. [trans. of G *Geopolitik.* See GEO-, POLITICS] —**ge′o·pol′i·tic, ge·o·po·lit·i·cal** (jē′ō pə lit′i kəl), *adj.* —**ge′o·po·lit′i·cal·ly,** *adv.* —**ge·o·pol·i·ti·cian** (jē′ō pol′i tish′ən), **ge′o·pol′i·tist,** *n.*

ge·o·pon·ic (jē′ə pon′ik), *adj.* of or pertaining to tillage or agriculture; agricultural. [< Gk *geōponik(ós)* pertaining to husbandry, equiv. to *geōpón(os)* husbandman (*geō-* GEO- + *pon-* work, toil, cf. *pénesthai* to labor) + *-ikos* -IC]

ge·o·pon·ics (jē′ə pon′iks), *n.* (*construed as sing.*) the art or science of agriculture. [see GEOPONIC, -ICS]

ge·o·po·ten·tial (jē′ō pə ten′shəl), *n. Physics.* the difference between the potential energy of a mass at a given altitude and the potential energy of an identical mass at sea level, equivalent to the energy required to move the mass from sea level to the given altitude. [GEO- + POTENTIAL]

ge·o·ram·a (jē′ə ram′ə, -rä′mə), *n.* a large hollow globe on the inside of which is depicted a map of the earth's surface, to be viewed by a spectator within the globe. [GEO- + (PANO)RAMA]

Geor·die (jôr′dē), *n. Scot. and North Eng.* **1.** the sum of 21 shillings. **2.** (formerly) a guinea. [after the figure of St. George on these coins]

Geor·die (jôr′dē), *n. Scot. and North Eng.* **1.** a miner. **2.** a collier vessel whose home port is on the river Tyne, in Northumberland. [special use of *Geordie,* dim. of *George*]

Geor·die (jôr′dē), *n. Scot. and North England.* a miner's safety lamp. [after George STEPHENSON who invented it]

Geor·gann (jôr jan′), *n.* a girl's given name.

George (jôrj), *n.* **1.** a figure of St. George killing the dragon, esp. one forming part of the insignia of the Order of the Garter. **2.** *Brit. Slang.* any coin bearing the image of St. George. **3.** a word formerly used in communications to represent the letter G. **4.** *Brit. Slang.* an automatic pilot on an airplane.

George (jôrj; *for 4 also Ger.* gā ôr′gə), *n.* **1. David Lloyd.** See **Lloyd George, David. 2. Henry,** 1839–97, U.S. economist: advocate of a single tax. **3. Saint,** died A.D. 303?, Christian martyr: patron saint of England. **4. Ste·fan An·ton** (shte′fän än′tōn), 1868–1933, German poet. **5. Lake,** a lake in E New York. 36 mi. long. **6.** a boy's given name.

George I, **1.** 1660–1727, king of England 1714–27. **2.** 1845–1913, king of Greece 1863–1913.

George II, **1.** 1683–1760, king of England 1727–60 (son of George I). **2.** 1890–1947, king of Greece 1922–23 and 1935–47.

George III, 1738–1820, king of England 1760–1820 (grandson of George II).

George IV, 1762–1830, king of England 1820–30 (son of George III).

George V, 1865–1936, king of England 1910–36 (son of Edward VII).

George VI, 1895–1952, king of England 1936–1952 (second son of George V; brother of Edward VIII).

Geor·gene (jôr jēn′), *n.* a girl's given name, form of **Georgia.**

Geor′ges Bank′ (jôr′jiz), a bank extending generally NE from Nantucket: fishing grounds. 150 mi. long.

Geor·ges·man (jôr′jiz mən), *n., pl.* **-men.** a vessel used in fishing in the area of Georges Bank.

George′ Town′, a seaport in and the capital of the state of Penang, in NW Malaysia. 234,903 (1957). Also, **Georgetown.** Also called **Penang.**

George·town (jôrj′toun′), *n.* **1.** See **George Town. 2.** a seaport in and the capital of Guyana, at the mouth of the Essequibo. 72,991 (1960). **3.** a residential section in the District of Columbia. **4.** a town in N Kentucky. 6986 (1960). **5.** a town in central Texas. 5218 (1960). **6.** a town in E Illinois. 3544 (1960). **7.** a town in SW Ohio. 2674 (1960).

Geor·gette (jôr jet′), *n.* a sheer silk or rayon crepe of dull texture. Also called **Georgette′ crepe′.** [formerly trademark]

Geor·gette (jôr jet′, jôr′jet), *n.* a girl's given name, form of **Georgia.**

Geor·gia (jôr′jə), *n.* **1.** a State in the SE United States. 5,464,265; 58,876 sq. mi. *Cap.:* Atlanta. *Abbr.:* GA (for use with zip code), Ga. **2.** Also called **Geor′gian Repub′lic.** a republic in Transcaucasia, bordering on the Black Sea, N of Turkey and Armenia: an independent kingdom for ab. 2000 years. 5,167,000; 26,872 sq. mi. *Cap.:* Tbilisi. **3. Strait of,** an inlet of the Pacific in SW Canada between Vancouver Island and the mainland. 150 mi. long. **2.** a girl's given name: *George* + feminine ending *-a.*

Geor·gian (jôr′jən), *adj.* **1.** of or pertaining to the period of British history from the accession of George I in 1714 to the death of George IV in 1830, or the four kings named George who reigned successively during this period. **2.** of or pertaining to the period of the reign of George V (1910–36) or to George V himself. **3.** of or pertaining to the State of Georgia in the U.S. **4.** of or pertaining to Georgia in the Soviet Union. **5.** of, noting, or designating the styles of architecture, arts, and crafts current in England esp. from 1714–1811. Cf. **Regency** (def. 6). —*n.* **6.** a person, esp. a writer, of either of the Georgian periods in England. **7.** the styles or character of either of the Georgian periods. **8.** a native or inhabitant of the State of Georgia in the U.S. **9.** a native or inhabitant of Georgia in the Soviet Union. **10.** the most important South Caucasian language, written in a distinctive script derived from the Aramaic alphabet. [GEORGE or GEORGI(A) + -AN]

Geor·gi·an·a (jôr′jē an′ə), *n.* a girl's given name.

Geor′gian Bay′, the NE part of Lake Huron, in Ontario, Canada. 6000 sq. mi.

Geor′gia pine′. See **longleaf pine.**

geor·gic (jôr′jik), *adj.* **1.** agricultural. —*n.* **2.** a poem on an agricultural theme. [< L *geōrgic(us)* < Gk *geōrgikós,* equiv. to *geōrg(ós)* husbandman (*gē* GEO- + *érgon* work) + *-ikos* -IC]
—Syn. 1, 2. bucolic.

Geor·gics, The (jôr′jiks), a didactic poem (39–29 B.C.) by Vergil.

Geor·gi·na (jôr jē′nə), *n.* a girl's given name. Also, **Geor·gine** (jôr jēn′).

ge·o·stat·ic (jē′ə stat′ik), *adj.* **1.** of or pertaining to pressure exerted by earth or a similar substance. **2.** (of a construction) resistant to such pressure. [GEO- + STATIC]

ge·o·stroph·ic (jē′ə strō′fik), *adj.* of or pertaining to the balance between the Coriolis force and the horizontal pressure force in the atmosphere. [GEO- + STROPHIC]

ge′ostroph′ic wind′, *Meteorol.* a wind whose velocity and direction are mathematically defined by the balanced relationship of the pressure gradient force and the Coriolis force: conceived as blowing parallel to isobars. Cf. **gradient wind.**

ge·o·syn·cli·nal (jē′ō sin klīn′əl), *Geol.* —*adj.* **1.** pertaining to a synclinal fold that involves a relatively large part of the earth's surface. —*n.* **2.** a geosyncline. [GEO- + SYNCLINAL]

ge·o·syn·cline (jē′ō sin′klīn), *n.* *Geol.* a portion of the earth's crust subjected to downward warping during a large fraction of geologic time; a geosynclinal fold. [GEO- + SYNCLINE]

ge·o·tax·is (jē′ō tak′sis), *n.* *Biol.* oriented movement of a motile organism toward or away from a gravitational force. [GEO- + -TAXIS] —**ge·o·tac·tic** (jē′ō tak′tik), *adj.* —**ge′o·tac′ti·cal·ly,** *adv.*

ge·o·tec·ton·ic (jē′ō tek ton′ik), *adj.* of or pertaining to the structure of the earth's crust or to the arrangement and form of its constituents. [GEO- + TECTONIC]

geotecton′ic geol′ogy. See **structural geology.**

ge·o·ther·mal (jē′ō thûr′məl), *adj.* of or pertaining to the internal heat of the earth. Also, **ge′o·ther′mic.** [GEO- + THERMAL]

ge·o·trop·ic (jē′ō trop′ik), *adj.* *Biol.* of, pertaining to, or exhibiting geotropism. [GEO- + -TROPIC] —**ge′o·trop′i·cal·ly,** *adv.*

ge·ot·ro·pism (jē o′trə piz′əm), *n.* *Biol.* oriented movement or growth with respect to the force of gravity. [GEO- + -TROPISM]

Ger., **1.** German. **2.** Germany.

ger., **1.** gerund. **2.** gerundive.

Ge·ra (gā′rä), *n.* a city in S East Germany. 99,250 (1960).

ge·rah (gē′rə), *n.* a Hebrew weight and coin, equal to ¹⁄₂₀ of a shekel. [< Heb < Akkadian *girū*]

Ge·raint (ji rānt′), *n.* *Arthurian Romance.* one of the knights of the Round Table, husband of Enid.

Ger·ald (jer′əld), *n.* a boy's given name.

Ge·ral·da (jə ral′də), *n.* a girl's given name.

Ger·al·dine (jer′əl dēn′), *n.* a girl's given name.

Ger·ald·ton (jer′əld tən, -al-), *n.* a seaport in W Australia. 10,894 (1961).

ge·ra·ni·a·ceous (ji rā′nē ā′shəs), *adj.* belonging to the *Geraniaceae,* or geranium family of plants. [< NL *Geraniāce(ae)* (see GERANIUM, -ACEAE) + -OUS]

ge·ra·ni·al (ji rā′nē əl), *n.* citral a. See under **citral.** [GERANI(UM) + -AL³]

ge·ra·ni·um (ji rā′nē əm), *n.* **1.** any of several plants of the genus *Geranium,* comprising the crane's-bills. **2.** Also called **stork's-bill.** any of several plants of the allied genus *Pelargonium,* of southern Africa, having showy flowers or fragrant leaves, cultivated in gardens, greenhouses, etc. **3.** a flower of this plant. **4.** a vivid red color. [< L: the plant, stork's bill (sp. var. of *geranion*) < Gk *gerānion* crane's bill, geranium, deriv. of *géranos* crane; c. L *grūs*]

Ge·ra·ni·um (ji rā′nē əm), *n.* a girl's given name.

Ge·rar (gē′rär), *n.* an ancient city in Palestine, near the Mediterranean; now an archaeological site in Israel.

Ge·rard (jə rärd′), *n.* **1.** Also, **Gé·rard′.** a boy's given name, form of **Gerald. 2.** a walled plain in the second quadrant of the face of the moon, in the libration area: about 50 miles in diameter.

Gé·rard (zhā rär′), *n.* **Comte É·tienne Mau·rice** (kôNt ā tyen′ mo rēs′), 1773–1852, French marshal under Napoleon.

ger·a·tol·o·gy (jer′ə tol′ə jē), *n.* the study of the decline of life, as in old age or in animals approaching extinction. [< Gk *gērat-* (s. of *gēras*) old age + -o- + -LOGY] —**ger·a·to·log·ic** (jer′ə tᵊloj′ik), **ger·a·tol·o·gous** (jer′ə tol′ə gəs), *adj.*

ger·bil (jûr′bil), *n.* any of numerous burrowing rodents of the genus *Gerbillus* and related genera, of Asia, Africa, and southern Russia, having long hind legs used for jumping. Also, **ger′bille.** [< F *gerbille* < NL *gerbill(us),* dim. of *gerbo* JERBOA]

Gerd (gûrd), *n.* a boy's given name.

Ger·da (gûr′də, gâr′-), *n.* **1.** Also, **Gerd** (gûrd, gârd). *Scand. Myth.* the daughter of a giant and the consort of Frey, who wooed her through his servant Skirnir. **2.** a girl's given name.

Ger·die (gûr′dē), *n.* a girl's given name, form of **Gerda.** Also, **Ger′dye.**

ge·re·fa (ye rā′vä), *Eng. Hist.* an administrative officer under the Anglo-Saxon kings. [OE *gerēfa;* see REEVE¹]

ge·rent (jēr′ənt), *n.* a ruler or manager. [< L *gerent-* (s. of *gerēns*) bearing, conducting, managing, equiv. to *ger-* bear + *-ent-* -ENT]

ger·e·nuk (ger′ə nŏŏk′, gə ren′ek), *n.* a reddish-brown antelope, *Litocranius walleri,* of eastern Africa, having a long, slender neck. [< Somali *garanug*]

ger·fal·con (jûr′fôl′kən, -fô′-), *n.* gyrfalcon.

Ge·ri (gâr′ē), *n.* *Scand. Myth.* See **Freki and Geri.**

ger·i·at·ric (jer′ē a′trik), *adj.* of or pertaining to geriatrics or aged persons. [< Gk *gér(ōn)* old man + -IATRIC]

ger·i·at·rics (jer′ē a′triks), *n.* (*construed as sing.*) **1.** the medical science dealing with the diseases, debilities, and care of aged persons. **2.** the study of the physical process and problems of aging; gerontology. [see GERIATRIC, -ICS] —**ger·i·a·tri·cian** (jer′ē ə trish′ən), **ger′i·at′rist,** *n.*

Gé·ri·cault (zhā rē kō′), *n.* **(Jean Louis An·dré) Thé·o·dore** (zhäN lwē äN drā′ tā ô dôr′), 1791–1824, French painter.

Ge·ring (gēr′ing), *n.* a town in W Nebraska. 4585 (1960).

Ger·la·chov·ka (ger′lä кнôf′kä), *n.* a mountain in N Slovakia: highest peak of the Carpathian Mountains. 8737 ft.

germ (jûrm), *n.* **1.** a microorganism, esp. when disease-producing; microbe. **2.** something that serves as a source or initial stage for subsequent development: *the germ of an idea.* **3.** *Embryol.* **a.** a bud, offshoot, or seed. **b.** the rudiment of a living organism; an embryo in its early stages. **4.** *Biol.* the initial stage in development or evolution, as a germ cell or ancestral form. —*adj.* **5.** *Pathol.* of, pertaining to, or caused by disease-producing germs. [< F *germe* < L *germen* seed] —**germ′less,** *adj.* —**germ′like′,** *adj.*

Ger·maine (jər mān′; *Fr.* zher men′), *n.* a girl's given name. Also, **Ger·main′.**

ger·man (jûr′mən), *adj.* **1.** having the same father and mother, as a full brother or sister (usually used in combination): *a brother-german.* **2.** born of the brother or sister of one's father or mother, as a first cousin. (usually used in combination): *a cousin-german.* **3.** *Archaic.* germane. [ME *germain* < OF < L *germān(us)* one who is of the same blood]

Ger·man (jûr′mən), *adj.* **1.** of or pertaining to Germany, its inhabitants, or their language. —*n.* **2.** a native or inhabitant of Germany. **3.** a descendant of a native of Germany. **4.** Also called **High German.** a moderately inflecting Indo-European language that is based on a High German dialect, is official in Germany, Austria, and Switzerland, and is also widely used as an international language for scholarship and science. **5.** *Ling.* any variety of West Germanic speech native to Germany, Austria, or Switzerland. **6.** (*usually l.c.*) an elaborate social dance resembling a cotillion. **7.** (*l.c.*) a party at which only this dance is danced. [< L *Germān(us)* German; c. Gk *Germanoí* (pl.)]

Ger′man Af′rica, the former German colonies in Africa, comprising German East Africa, German Southwest Africa, Cameroons, and Togoland.

Ger′man Bap′tist Breth′ren. See **Church of the Brethren.**

Ger′man cam′omile. See under **camomile** (def. 2). Also called **sweet false camomile.**

Ger′man catch′fly, a perennial herb, *Lychnis Viscaria,* of Eurasia, having a sticky-hairy stem beneath the red or purple flowers.

Ger′man cock′roach, a yellowish-brown cockroach, *Blatta germanica,* brought into the U.S. from Europe. Also called **Croton bug.**

Ger′man Democrat′ic Repub′lic, official name of **East Germany.**

ger·man·der (jər man′dər), *n.* **1.** any of several labiate herbs or shrubs of the genus *Teucrium,* as *T. Chamaedrys,* of Europe, and *T. canadense,* of America. **2.** Also called **german′der speed′well.** a speedwell, *Veronica Chamaedrys,* having blue flowers. [ME < ML *germandr(e)a* < LGk *chamandryā*]

ger·mane (jər mān′), *adj.* **1.** closely or significantly related; relevant; pertinent: *a fact germane to his question.* **2.** *Obs.* closely related. [var. of GERMAN] —**ger·mane′ly,** *adv.* —**ger·mane′ness,** *n.*
—Syn. 1. related, applicable, apposite, appropriate, fitting, apt, suited.

Ger′man East′ Af′rica, a former German territory in E Africa: the area now comprised of Tanganyika and the independent republics of Rwanda and Burundi.

ger·man·ic (jər man′ik), *adj.* *Chem.* of or containing germanium, esp. in the tetravalent state. [GERMAN(IUM) + -IC]

Ger·man·ic (jər man′ik), *adj.* **1.** of or pertaining to the Teutons or their languages. **2.** German. **3.** of, pertaining to, or noting the Germanic branch of languages. —*n.* **4.** a branch of the Indo-European family of languages including German, Dutch, English, the Scandinavian languages, Afrikaans, Flemish, Frisian, and the extinct Gothic language. See diag. under **language. 5.** an ancient Indo-European language, the immediate linguistic ancestor of the Germanic languages. [< L *Germānic(us).* See GERMAN, -IC] —**Ger·man′i·cal·ly,** *adv.*

Ger·man′i·cus Cae′sar (jər man′ə kəs), 15 B.C.–A.D. 19, Roman general.

Ger·man·ise (jûr′mə nīz′), *v.t., v.i.,* **-ised, -is·ing.** *Chiefly Brit.* Germanize. —**Ger′man·i·sa′tion,** *n.* —**Ger′man·is′er,** *n.*

Ger·man·ism (jûr′mə niz′əm), *n.* **1.** a German characteristic, usage, or idiom. **2.** a German characteristic, custom, manner, mode of thought, action, etc. **3.** extreme partiality for or attachment to Germany, Germans, or German customs, manners, etc. [GERMAN + -ISM]

Ger·man·ist (jûr′mə nist), *n.* a specialist in the study of German culture, literature, or linguistics. [< G < L *Germān(ia)* GERMANY; see -IST]

ger·ma·ni·um (jər mā′nē əm), *n.* *Chem.* a scarce, metallic, grayish-white element, normally tetravalent, used chiefly in transistors. *Symbol:* Ge; *at. wt.:* 72.59; *at. no.:* 32; *sp. gr.:* 5.36 at 20°C. [GERMAN(Y) + -IUM]

Ger′man i′vy, a tender, herbaceous perennial, *Senecio mikanioides,* of South Africa, having fleshy leaves and yellow flowers.

Ger·man·ize (jûr′mə nīz′), *v.t., v.i.,* **-ized, -iz·ing. 1.** to make or become German in character, sentiment, etc. **2.** *Archaic.* to translate into German. Also, *esp. Brit.,* **Germanise.** [GERMAN + -IZE] —**Ger′man·i·za′tion,** *n.* —**Ger′man·iz′er,** *n.*

Ger′man knot′. See **figure of eight** (def. 2).

Ger′man la′pis, *Jewelry.* jasper stained blue in imitation of lapis lazuli. Also called **blue onyx.**

Ger′man mea′sles, *Pathol.* a contagious virus disease, usually milder than measles, characterized by fever, a sore throat, and a rash resembling that of scarlet fever. Also called **rubella.**

Germano-, a combining form of **German:** *Germanophile.* [< NL, equiv. to ML *Germān(us)* German + *-o-* -o-]

Ger′man O′cean, former name of the **North Sea.**

Ger·man·o·phile (jər man′ə fīl′), *n.* one who is friendly toward or admires or studies Germany or German culture. [GERMANO- + -PHILE]

Ger·man·o·phobe (jər man′ə fōb′), *n.* a person who hates or fears Germany, Germans, or German culture, ideas, etc. [GERMANO- + -PHOBE] —**Ger·man′o·pho′bi·a,** *n.*

ger·man·ous (jər man′əs), *adj.* *Chem.* containing bivalent germanium. [GERMAN(IUM) + -OUS]

Ger′man shep′herd, one of a breed of large shepherd dogs having a coat ranging in color from gray to brindled, black-and-tan, or black, used esp. in police work and as a guide for the blind. Also called **Ger′man shep′herd dog′, Ger′man police′ dog′.**

Ger′man sid′ing, *Carpentry.* drop siding having concave upper edges with corresponding rabbets in the lower edges.

Ger′man sil′ver, any of various alloys of copper, zinc, and nickel; usually white and used for utensils, drawing instruments, etc.; nickel silver.

Ger′man South′west Af′rica, former name of **South-West Africa.**

Ger·man·town (jûr′mən toun′), *n.* **1.** the NW part of Philadelphia, Pa.: American defeat by British 1777. **2.** a town in W Ohio. 3399 (1960). **3.** *Informal.* any

U.S. city neighborhood heavily populated with persons of German descent.

Ger·ma·ny (jûr′mə nē), *n.* a republic in central Europe: after World War II divided into four zones, British, French, U.S., and Soviet, and in 1949 into East Germany and West Germany; East and West Germany were reunited in 1990. 78,420,000; 137,852 sq. mi. *Cap.:* Berlin. Official name, **Federal Republic of Germany.** German, **Deutschland.** Formerly, **Deutsches Reich.** Cf. **East Germany, West Germany.**

germ′ cell′, *Biol.* the sexual reproductive cell at any stage from the primordial cell to the mature gamete.

ger·men (jûr′mən), *n., pl.* **-mens, -mi·na** (-mə nə). *Archaic.* a germ. [< L: offshoot, sprout, bud]

germ·free (jûrm′frē′, -frē′), *adj.* **1.** free from germs: *a germfree laboratory.* **2.** (of experimental animals) born and raised under sterile conditions. [GERM + FREE]

ger·mi·cide (jûr′mi sīd′), *n.* an agent for killing germs or microorganisms. [GERM + -I- + -CIDE] —**ger′mi·cid′al,** *adj.*

ger·mi·nal (jûr′mə nəl), *adj.* **1.** of or pertaining to a germ or germs. **2.** of the nature of a germ or germ cell. **3.** being in the earliest stage of development: *germinal ideas.* [< NL *germināl(is),* equiv. to L *germin-* (s. of *germen*) offshoot + *-ālis* -AL[1]] —**ger′mi·nal·ly,** *adv.*

Ger·mi·nal (jûr′mə nəl; *Fr.* zher mē nal′), *n.* **1.** (in the French Revolutionary calendar) the seventh month of the year, extending from March 21 to April 19. **2.** (*italics*) a novel (1884) by Émile Zola. [< F < L *germin-;* see GERMINAL]

ger′minal disk′, *Embryol.* blastodisk.

ger′minal ves′icle, *Embryol. Obs.* the large, vesicular nucleus of an ovum before the polar bodies are formed.

ger·mi·nant (jûr′mə nənt), *adj.* germinating. [< L *germinant-* (s. of *germināns,* prp. of *germināre*), equiv. to *germin-* (see GERMINAL) + *-ant-* -ANT] —**ger′mi·nance, ger′mi·nan·cy,** *n.*

ger·mi·nate (jûr′mə nāt′), *v.,* **-nat·ed, -nat·ing.** —*v.i.* **1.** to begin to grow or develop. **2.** *Bot.* **a.** to develop into a plant or individual, as a seed, spore, bulb, or the like. **b.** to sprout; put forth shoots. **3.** to come into existence; begin. —*v.t.* **4.** to cause to develop; produce. **5.** to create; cause to come into existence. [< L *germināt(us)* germinated (ptp. of *germināre* to sprout forth, bud), equiv. to *germin-* (see GERMINAL) + *-ātus* -ATE[1]] —**ger·mi·na·ble** (jûr′mə nə bəl), *adj.* —**ger′mi·na′tion,** *n.* —**ger′mi·na′tor,** *n.*

ger·mi·na·tive (jûr′mə nā′tiv, -mə nə tiv), *adj.* capable of germinating, developing, or creating; of or pertaining to germination. [GERMINATE + -IVE] —**ger′mi·na′tive·ly,** *adv.*

Ger·mis·ton (jûr′mi stən), *n.* a city in S Transvaal, in the NE Republic of South Africa. 204,605 (1960).

germ′ lay′er, one of the three primary embryonic cell layers. Cf. **ectoderm, entoderm, mesoderm.**

germ′ plasm′, the protoplasm of the germ cells containing the units of heredity, the chromosomes and genes.

germ·proof (jûrm′pro͞of′), *adj.* not vulnerable to the action or penetration of germs. [GERM + -PROOF]

germ′ the′ory, **1.** *Pathol.* the theory that infection, diseases are due to the agency of germs or microorganisms. **2.** *Biol.* biogenesis.

ger·o·don·tics (jer′ə don′tiks), *n.* (*construed as sing.*) the branch of dentistry dealing with aging and aged persons. Also, **ger·o·don·tia** (jer′ə don′shə, -shē ə). Also called **ger·o·don·tol·o·gy** (jer′ō don tol′ə jē). [< Gk *gêr(as)* old age + -ODONT + -ICS] —**ger′o·don′tic,** *adj.*

Gé·rôme (zhā rōm′), *n.* **Jean Lé·on** (zhän lā ôn′), 1824–1904, French painter and sculptor.

Ge·ron·i·mo (jə ron′ə mō′), *n.* **1.** (*Goyathlay*), 1829–1909, American Apache Indian chief. —*interj.* **2.** (a battle cry used by paratroopers on jumping from a plane.)

ger·on·tine (jə ron′tēn, -tin), *n. Biochem.* spermine.

geronto-, a learned borrowing from Greek used, with the meaning "old age," in the formation of compound words: *gerontology.* Also, *esp. before a vowel,* **geront-.** [< Gk, comb. form repr. *geront-,* s. of *gérōn* old man]

ger·on·toc·ra·cy (jer′ən tok′rə sē), *n., pl.* **-cies.** **1.** government by a council of elders. **2.** a governing body consisting of old men. [GERONTO- + -CRACY]

ge·ron·to·ge·ous (jə ron′tə jē′əs), *adj.* belonging to the Old World. [GERONTO- + GE(O)- + -OUS]

ger·on·tol·o·gy (jer′ən tol′ə jē), *n.* the branch of science that deals with aging and the special problems of aged persons. [GERONTO- + -LOGY] —**ger′on·tol′o·gist,** *n.*

-gerous, a combining form meaning "bearing," "producing," used in the formation of compound words: *setigerous.* [< L *-ger* bearing + -OUS]

Ge·rou·si·a (ji ro͞o′zhē ə, -zhə), *n. Gk. Hist.* the senate or council of elders in certain Dorian cities, esp. Sparta. Also, **Gerusia.**

Ger·ry (ger′ē), *n.* **1. El·bridge** (el′brij), 1744–1814, U.S. politician: vice-president 1813–14. Cf. **gerrymander.** **2.** Also, **Ger′ri.** a girl's given name, form of **Geraldine.**

ger·ry·man·der (jer′i man′dər), *v.t.* **1.** *U.S. Politics.* to subject (a State, county, etc.) to a gerrymander. **2.** to manipulate unfairly. —*n.* **3.** *U.S. Politics.* the dividing of a State, county, etc., into election districts so as to give one political party a majority in many districts while concentrating the voting strength of the other party into as few a number of districts as possible. [after Elbridge *Gerry* (governor of Massachusetts, whose party redistricted the state in 1812) + (*sala*)*mander,* from the fancied resemblance of the map of Essex County, Mass., to this animal, after the redistricting] —**ger′ry·man′der·er,** *n.*

Gers (zher), *n.* a department in SW France. 182,264 (1962); 2429 sq. mi. *Cap.:* Auch.

gers·dorff·ite (gerz′dôr fīt′, gers′-), *n.* a mineral, sulfide-arsenide of nickel, NiAsS, occurring in metallic, light-gray cubes. [< G, named after von *Gersdorff,* the name of a 19th-century family of mine owners in Austria; see -ITE[1]]

Ger·shom (gûr′shəm), *n.* the elder son of Moses and Zipporah. Ex. 18:3. Also, *Douay Bible,* **Ger·sam** (gûr′səm).

Gersh·win (gûrsh′win), *n.* **George,** 1898–1937, U.S. composer.

Gert (gûrt), *n.* a girl's given name, form of **Gertrude.**

Ger·tie (gûr′tē), *n.* a girl's given name, form of **Gertrude.** Also, **Gerty.**

ger·trude (gûr′tro͞od), *n.* a slip or underdress for infants. [special use of GERTRUDE]

Ger·trude (gûr′tro͞od), *n.* a girl's given name.

ger·und (jer′ənd), *n. Gram.* **1.** (in certain languages, as Latin) a form regularly derived from a verb and functioning as a noun, having in Latin all case forms but the nominative, as Latin *dicendī* gen., *dicendō,* dat., abl., etc., "saying." **2.** the English *-ing* form of a verb when functioning as a noun, as *writing* in *Writing is easy.* **3.** a form similar to the Latin gerund in meaning or function. [< LL *gerund(ium),* L *gerund(um)* that which is to be carried on (sp. var. of *gerendum,* neut. ger. of *gerere* to bear, carry on)] —**ge·run·di·al** (jə run′dē əl), *adj.* —**ge·run′di·al·ly,** *adv.*

ger·un·dive (jə run′div), *n.* **1.** (in Latin) the future passive participle, similar to the gerund in formation, as *dicendum* in *Haec dicendum est,* "This must be said." —*adj.* **2.** resembling a gerund. [< LL *gerundīv(us).* See GERUND, -IVE] —**ger·un·di·val** (jer′ən dī′vəl), *adj.* —**ge·run′dive·ly,** *adv.*

Ge·ru·sa·lem·me Li·be·ra·ta (*It.* je ro͞o′zä lem′me lē′be rä′tä). See **Jerusalem Delivered.**

Ge·ru·si·a (ji ro͞o′zhē ə, -zhə), *n. Gk. Hist.* Gerousia.

ger·vais (zher vā′; *Fr.* zher ve′), *n.* an unsalted French cream cheese made from whole milk and cream. [named after Jules *Gervais,* 20th-century cheese manufacturer]

Ge·ry·on (jēr′ē ən, ger′ē-), *n. Class. Myth.* a monster who possessed a large herd of red cattle, the abduction of which was the 10th labor of Hercules. Also, **Ge·ry·on·es** (ji rī′ō nēz′).

Ger·ze·an (ger′zē ən, gûr′-), *adj.* of or pertaining to the predynastic, aeneolithic culture of Upper Egypt, characterized by an emphasis on agriculture and fishing and the use of foreign artifacts and materials.

Ge·sell (gə zel′), *n.* **Arnold Lucius,** 1880–1961, U.S. psychologist.

ge·sell·schaft (*Ger.* gə zel′shäft′), *n., pl.* **-schaf·ten** (*Ger.* -shäf′tən). (*often cap.*) **1.** an association of individuals for common goals, as for entertainment, intellectual, or cultural purposes or for business reasons, etc. **2.** *Sociol.* a society or group characterized chiefly by formal organization, impersonal relations, the absence of generally held or binding norms, a detachment from traditional and sentimental concerns, and often tending to be rationalistic and secular in outlook. Cf. **Gemeinschaft.** [< G, equiv. to *Geselle* companion + *-schaft* -SHIP]

ge·sith (ye sēth′), *n. Eng. Hist.* an attendant or companion of an Anglo-Saxon king; thane. [OE *gesīth;* c. OS *gisīdh,* OHG *gisind,* G *Gesinde* servant; akin to OE *sīth* journey, errand]

Ges·sen (ges′ən), *n. Douay Bible.* Goshen (def. 1).

ges·so (jes′ō), *n.* **1.** gypsum or plaster of Paris prepared with glue for use as a surface for painting. **2.** any plasterlike preparation to prepare a surface for painting, gilding, etc. **3.** a prepared surface of plaster or plasterlike material for painting, gilding, etc. [< It < L *gyps(um)* GYPSUM]

gest[1] (jest), *n. Archaic.* **1.** a metrical romance or history. **2.** a story or tale. **3.** a deed or exploit. Also, **geste.** [ME < OF *geste* action, exploit < L *gesta* exploits, neut. pl. ptp. of *gerere* to carry on, perform (war, etc.)]

gest[2] (jest), *n.* **1.** deportment; conduct. **2.** gesture. Also, **geste.** [< F *geste* < L *gestus* gesture, bearing, ptp. of *gerere* to bear, deport (oneself)]

gest[3] (jest), *n. Obs.* **1.** any of the stages in a journey. **2.** the route of a journey. [var. of *gist,* ME *giste* < OF; see GIST]

ge·stalt (gə shtält′), *n., pl.* **-stalts, -stal·ten** (-shtäl′tən). (*sometimes cap.*) *Psychol.* **1.** a unified whole; a configuration, pattern, or organized field having specific properties that cannot be derived from the summation of its component parts. **2.** an instance or example of such a unified whole. [< G: figure, form, structure]

Gestalt′ psychol′ogy, (*sometimes l.c.*) the theory or doctrine that physiological or psychological phenomena do not occur through the summation of individual elements, as reflexes or sensations, but through gestalts functioning separately or interrelatedly. Also called **configurationism.**

Ge·sta·po (gə stä′pō; *Ger.* gə shtä′pō), *n.* the German state secret police during the Nazi regime, organized in 1933 and notorious for its brutal methods and operations. [< G *Ge(heime) Sta(ats) Po(lizei)*]

Ges·ta Ro·ma·no·rum (jes′tə rō′mə nōr′əm, -nôr′-), a popular collection of stories in Latin, compiled in the late 13th century.

ges·tate (jes′tāt), *v.,* **-tat·ed, -tat·ing.** —*v.t.* **1.** to carry in the womb during the period from conception to delivery. **2.** to think of and develop (an idea, opinion, etc.) slowly in the mind. —*v.i.* **3.** to experience the process of gestating offspring. **4.** to develop slowly. [< L *gestāt(us)* carried (ptp. of *gerere*), equiv. to *gest-* carry + *-ātus* -ATE[1]]

ges·ta·tion (je stā′shən), *n.* the process, state, or period of gestating. [< L *gestātiōn-* (s. of *gestātiō*), equiv. to *gestāt(us)* (see GESTATE) + *-iōn-* -ION] —**ges·ta′tion·al, ges·ta·tive** (jes′tə tiv, je stā′-), *adj.*

geste[1] (jest), *n.* gest[1].

geste[2] (jest), *n.* gest[2].

ges·tic (jes′tik), *adj.* pertaining to bodily motions, esp. in dancing. Also, **ges′ti·cal.** [GEST[2] + -IC]

ges·tic·u·lar (je stik′yə lər), *adj.* pertaining to or characterized by gesticulation: *The comedian's gesticular proficiency was an added asset.* [< LL *gesticul(us)* (see GESTICULATE) + -AR[1]]

ges·tic·u·late (je stik′yə lāt′), *v.,* **-lat·ed, -lat·ing.** —*v.i.* **1.** to make or use gestures, esp. in an animated or excited manner with or instead of speech. —*v.t.* **2.** to express by gesturing. [< L *gesticulāt(us)* having made mimic gestures (ptp. of *gesticulārī*), equiv. to *gesticul(us)* gesture (*gest(us)* GEST[2] + *-culus* -CULE) + *-ātus* -ATE[1]] —**ges·tic′u·la′tor,** *n.*

ges·tic·u·la·tion (je stik′yə lā′shən), *n.* the act of gesticulating; an animated or excited gesture. [< L *gesticulātiōn-* (s. of *gesticulātiō*). See GESTICULATE, -ION]

ges·tic·u·la·tive (je stik′yə lā′tiv, -yə lə tiv), *adj.* tending toward or marked by gesticulation. [GESTICULATE + -IVE] —**ges·tic′u·la′tive·ly,** *adv.*

ges·tic·u·la·to·ry (je stik′yə lə tōr′ē, -tôr′ē), *adj.* consisting in or characterized by gesticulation. [GESTICULATE + -ORY[1]]

ges·tion (jes′chən), *n. Archaic.* conduct; management. [< L *gestiōn-* (s. of *gestiō*), equiv. to *gest-* (see GEST[2]) + *-iōn-* -ION]

ges·ture (jes′chər, jesh′-), *n., v.,* **-tured, -tur·ing.** —*n.* **1.** a movement of the body, head, arms, hands, or face that is expressive of an idea, opinion, emotion, etc.: *the gestures of an orator; a gesture of anger.* **2.** any action or proceeding intended for effect or as a formality; demonstration: *a gesture of friendship.* —*v.i.* **3.** to make or use a gesture or gestures. —*v.t.* **4.** to express by a gesture or gestures. [ME < ML *gestūra* mode of action, manner, bearing. See GEST[2], -URE] —**ges′tur·al,** *adj.* —**ges′ture·less,** *adj.* —**ges′tur·er,** *n.*

Ge·su·al·do (je′zo͞o äl′dō), *n.* **Don Car·lo** (dôn kär′lô), **Prince of Ve·no·sa** (ve nô′sä), c1560–1613, Italian composer and lutanist.

ge·sund·heit (gə zo͝ont′hīt), *interj.* (used to wish good health, as a toast, or esp. to a person who has just sneezed.) [< G: lit., health-hood]

get (get), *v.,* **got** or (Archaic) **gat; got** or **got·ten; get·ting;** *n.* —*v.t.* **1.** to receive or come to have possession, use, or enjoyment of: *to get a birthday present; to get a pension.* **2.** to obtain or acquire; cause to be in one's possession or available for one's use or enjoyment: *to get a good price after bargaining; to get oil by drilling; to get information.* **3.** to take hold of and bring (something) for one's own or for another's purposes; fetch: *Would you get something from the refrigerator for me?* **4.** to cause or cause to become, to do, to move, etc., as specified: *to get one's hair cut; to get a man drunk; to get a fire to burn; to get a dog out of a room.* **5.** to communicate or establish communication with over a distance; reach: *You can always get me by telephone.* **6.** to hear: *I didn't get your last name.* **7.** to acquire a mental grasp or command of; learn: *to get a lesson.* **8.** to capture; seize: *Get him before he escapes!* **9.** to punish with; mete out as a punishment or sentence: *to get 20 years in jail.* **10.** to prevail on; influence or persuade: *We'll get him to go with us.* **11.** to prepare; make ready: *to get dinner.* **12.** (esp. of animals) to beget. **13.** to affect emotionally: *Her tears got me.* **14.** to hit, strike, or wound: *The bullet got him in the leg.* **15.** *Informal.* to kill. **16.** to take vengeance on: *I'll get you yet!* **17.** to suffer from or be subjected to or afflicted with: *Have you got a cold?* **18.** *Slang.* to puzzle; irritate: *Her silly remarks get me.* **19.** *Informal.* to understand; comprehend: *I don't get the joke. This report may be crystal-clear to a scientist, but I don't get it.* —*v.i.* **20.** to come to a specified place; arrive; reach: *to get home late.* **21.** *Informal.* to succeed, become enabled or be permitted: *You get to go to the movies twice a week.* **22.** to become or to cause oneself to become as specified; reach a certain condition: *to get tired in the afternoon; to get promoted.* **23.** to succeed in coming, going, or surviving (usually fol. by *away, in, into, out, over, through,* etc.): *I don't get into town very often. Can he get through another bad winter?* **24.** to earn money; gain. **25.** *Informal.* to leave promptly; scram: *He told us to get.* **26.** to start or enter upon the action of (fol. by a present participle expressing action): *to get moving; Get rolling.* **27. get about, a.** to move about; be active: *He gets about with difficulty since his illness.* **b.** to become known; spread: *It was supposed to be a secret, but somehow it got about.* **c.** to be socially active: *She's been getting about much more since her family moved to the city.* Also, **get around. 28. get across, a.** to make or become understandable: *to get a lesson across to students.* **b.** to be convincing about: *The fire chief got across forcefully the fact that turning in a false alarm is a serious offense.* **29. get ahead,** to be successful, as in business, society, etc.: *He got ahead by sheer determination.* **30. get ahead of,** to surpass; outdo: *He refused to let anyone get ahead of him in business.* **31. get along, a.** to go away; leave. **b.** See **get on. 32. get around, a.** to circumvent; outwit. **b.** to ingratiate oneself with (someone) through flattery or cajolery. **c.** to travel from place to place; circulate: *I don't get around much any more.* **d.** See *get about.* Also, **get round. 33. get at, a.** to reach; touch: *to stretch in order to get at a top shelf.* **b.** to hint at or imply; intimate: *What are you getting at?* **c.** to discover; determine: *to get at the root of a problem.* **d.** *Informal.* to influence by surreptitious means; bribe: *The gangsters couldn't get at the mayor.* **34. get away, a.** to escape; flee: *He tried to get away, but the crowd was too dense.* **b.** to start out; leave: *The race horses got away from the starting gate.* **35. get away with,** to accomplish with impunity; avoid punishment: *Some who lie and cheat always seem to get away with it.* **36. get back, a.** to come back; return: *When will you get back?* **b.** to recover; regain: *He got back his investment with interest.* **c.** to be revenged: *She waited for a chance to get back at her accuser.* **37. get by, a.** to succeed in going past: *to get by a police barricade.* **b.** to manage to exist, survive, continue in business, etc., in spite of difficulties. **c.** to evade the notice of: *He doesn't let much get by him.* **38. get down, a.** to bring or come down; descend: *She climbed the tree but then couldn't get down again.* **b.** to concentrate; attend: *to get down to the matter at hand.* **c.** to depress; discourage; fatigue: *Nothing gets me down so much as a common cold.* **d.** to swallow: *The pill was so large that he couldn't get it down.* **39. get even.** See **even**[1] (def. 22). **40. get going, a.** to begin; act: *They wanted to get going on the construction of the house.* **b.** to increase one's speed; make haste: *If we don't get going we'll never arrive in time.* **41. get in, a.** to go into a place; enter: *He forgot his key and couldn't get in.* **b.** to arrive; come: *They both got in on the same train.* **c.** to become associated with: *He got in with a bad crowd.* **d.** to be chosen, as for office, membership, etc.: *His friends made sure that he got in as secretary of the club.* **e.** to become implicated in: *By embezzling money to pay his gambling debts quickly he was getting in further and further.* **42. get it,** *Informal.* **a.** to be punished or reprimanded: *You'll get it for breaking that vase!* **b.** to understand something: *This is just between us, get it?* **43.**

get off, a. to escape the consequences of or punishment for one's actions. **b.** to help (someone) escape punishment: *A good lawyer might get you off.* **c.** to begin a journey; leave: *He got off on the noon train.* **d.** to leave (a train, plane, etc.); dismount from (a horse); alight. **e.** to tell (a joke); express (an opinion). **f.** *Slang.* to have the effrontery: *Where does he get off telling me how to behave?* **44. get on, a.** to make progress; proceed; advance. **b.** to have sufficient means to manage, survive or fare. **c.** to be on good terms; agree: *She simply can't get on with her mother-in-law.* **d.** to advance in age: *He is getting on in years.* **45. get out, a.** to leave (often fol. by *of*): *Get out of here! We had to get out of the bus at Graz.* **b.** to become publicly known: *We mustn't let this story get out.* **c.** to withdraw or retire (often fol. by *of*): *He decided to get out of the dry goods business.* **d.** to produce or complete: *Let's get this work out!* **46. get over, a.** to recover from: *to get over an illness.* **b.** See **get across. 47. get round.** See **get** (def. 32). **48. get there,** to reach one's goal; succeed: *You'll never get there if you don't try.* **49. get through, a.** to succeed, as in meeting or reaching (usually fol. by *to*): *The messenger wasn't able to get through to our cabin in the woods.* **b.** to complete; finish: *How he ever got through college is a mystery.* **c.** to make oneself understood: *One simply cannot get through to her.* **50. get to, a.** to get into communication with; contact: *It was too late by the time he got to the authorities.* **b.** *Informal.* to make an impression on; affect: *This music really gets to you.* **51. get together, a.** to accumulate; gather: *to get together a portfolio of stocks.* **b.** to congregate; meet: *The alumnae chapter gets together twice a year.* **c.** to come to an accord; agree: *They simply couldn't get together on matters of policy.* **52. get up, a.** to sit up or stand; arise. **b.** to rise from bed. **c.** to ascend or mount. **d.** to prepare; arrange; organize: *to get up an exhibit.* **e.** to acquire a knowledge of. **f.** (to a horse) go! go ahead! go faster! **g.** to launder or clean: *to get up the wash.* **h.** *Informal.* to dress, as in a costume or disguise: *She got herself up as a peasant girl.* **i.** *Informal.* to produce in a specified style, as a book: *It was got up in brown leather with gold endpapers.* **j.** to stimulate; rouse: *to get up one's courage.* **53. has** or **have got, a.** (used in place of "has" or "have," fol. by a direct object and often after a contraction or in a question): *She's got a new hat. Have you got the tickets?* **b.** (used in place of "has" or "have" to emphasize a statement or, esp. after a contraction, to indicate obligation or necessity): *I have got a car. He's got to get to a doctor right away.* —*n.* **54.** an offspring or the total of the offspring, esp. of a male animal: *the get of a stallion.* **55.** a return of a ball, as in tennis, that would normally have resulted in a point for the opponent. **56.** *Brit. Slang.* **a.** something earned, as salary, profits, etc.: *What's your week's get?* **b.** an illegitimate child; bastard. [ME *get(en)* < Scand; cf. OIcel *geta;* c. OE *g(i)etan* (ME *yeten*), G *-gessen,* in *vergessen* to forget] —**get′ta·ble, get′a·ble,** *adj.*

—**Syn. 1, 2.** GET, OBTAIN, ACQUIRE, PROCURE, SECURE imply gaining possession of something. GET may apply to coming into possession in any manner, and either voluntarily or not. OBTAIN suggests putting forth effort to gain possession, and ACQUIRE stresses the possessing after an (often prolonged) effort. PROCURE suggests the method of obtaining as that of search or choice. SECURE, considered in bad taste as a would-be-elegant substitute for GET, is, however, when used with discrimination, a perfectly proper word. It suggests making possession sure and safe, after obtaining something by competition or the like. **2.** win, gain. **7.** apprehend, grasp. **10.** induce, dispose. **12.** engender.

get (get), *n., pl.* **gi·tim** (gē tēm′). *Hebrew.* **1.** a legal document, executed by a rabbi or Jewish court of law, dissolving the marriage bond between husband and wife. **2.** a divorce granted in accordance with Jewish law.

get·at·a·ble (get at′ə bəl), *adj.* capable of being attained or got; accessible. [adj. use of v. phrase *get at;* see -ABLE] —**get′at′a·bil′i·ty, get′at′a·ble·ness,** *n.*

get·a·way (get′ə wā′), *n.* **1.** a getting away; an escape. **2.** the start of a race: *a fast getaway.* [n. use of v. phrase *get away*]

Geth (geth), *n. Douay Bible.* Gath.

Geth·sem·a·ne (geth sem′ə nē), *n.* **1.** a garden east of Jerusalem, near the brook of Kedron: scene of Jesus' agony and betrayal. Matt. 26:36. **2.** (*l.c.*) a scene or occasion of suffering; calvary. —**Geth·se·man·ic, geth·se·man·ic** (geth′sə man′ik), *adj.*

Gethsem′ane cheese′. See **Trappist cheese.**

get-out (get′out′), *n.* **1.** *Commerce.* the break-even point. **2.** *Chiefly Brit.* a method or maneuver used to escape a difficult or embarrassing situation: *The scoundrel has used that get-out once too often.* [n. use of v. phrase *get out*]

get·ter (get′ər), *n.* **1.** one who or that which gets. **2.** any substance introduced into a partial vacuum, as the interior of a vacuum tube or an incandescent lamp, to combine chemically with the residual gas in order to increase the vacuum. **3.** *Chiefly Canadian.* poisoned bait used to exterminate wolves, gophers, and other pests from farm areas. [ME; see GET, -ER[1]]

get·ter·ing (get′ər ing), *n.* the removal of residual gas from a partial vacuum by use of a getter. [GETTER + -ING[1]]

get-to·geth·er (get′tə geth′ər), *n.* an informal and usually small social gathering. [n. use of v. phrase *get together*]

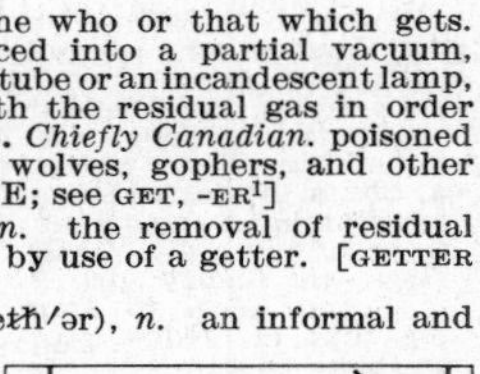

get-tough (get′tuf′), *adj.* characterized by new firmness, determination, aggressiveness, or severity, esp. when confronted with a difficult situation: *Let's try a get-tough policy with those crooks!*

Get·tys·burg (get′iz bûrg′), *n.* a borough in S Pennsylvania: Confederate forces defeated in a crucial battle of the Civil War fought near here on July 1–3, 1863; national cemetery and military park. 7960 (1960).

Get′tysburg Address′, the short speech made by President Lincoln on November 19, 1863, at the dedication of the national cemetery at Gettysburg, Pennsylvania.

get·up (get′up′), *n. Informal.* **1.** format; style: *the getup of a new cookbook.* **2.** costume; outfit: *Everyone will stare at you if you wear that getup.* Also, **get′-up′.** [n. use of v. phrase *get up*]

get′ up′ and go′, energy, drive, and enthusiasm: *With his get up and go he ought to be a success as a salesman.*

Geu·lincx (*Flem.* gœ′lingks), *n.* **Arnold,** 1624?–69, Belgian philosopher.

ge·um (jē′əm), *n.* any plant of the genus *Geum,* comprising the avens. [< NL: a plant genus, L: the herb bennet, avens]

GeV, gigaelectron volt. Also, **Gev**

Ge·vaert (*Fr.* gā vart′), *n.* **Fran·çois Au·guste** (*Fr.* frän swa′ ō gyst′), 1828–1908, Belgian musicologist, educator, and composer.

gew·gaw (gyōō′gô, gōō′-), *n.* **1.** something gaudy and useless; trinket; bauble. —*adj.* **2.** showy, but without value. [gradational compound based on GAU(DY)[1]] —**gew′gawed,** *adj.*

gey (gā), *Scot.* —*adj.* **1.** considerable; fair; tolerable. —*adv.* **2.** considerably; very. [var. of GAY]

gey·ser (gī′zər, -sər *for 1;* gē′zər *for 2*), *n.* **1.** a hot spring that intermittently sends up fountainlike jets of water and steam into the air. **2.** *Brit. Informal.* a hot-water heater. [< Icel *Geysir* gusher, name of a hot spring in Iceland, deriv. of *geysa* to gush] —**gey′ser·al, gey′ser·ic,** *adj.*

gey′ser ba′sin, an area containing a group of geysers.

gey·ser·ite (gī′zə rīt′, -sə-), *n.* a variety of opaline silica deposited about the orifices of geysers and hot springs. [GEYSER + -ITE[1]]

Ge·zer (gē′zər), *n.* an ancient Canaanite town, NW of Jerusalem.

Ge·zi·ra (jə zēr′ə), *n.* a province in central Sudan, between the Blue Nile and the White Nile. 2,069,646 (1956); 54,880 sq. mi. *Cap.:* Wad Medani.

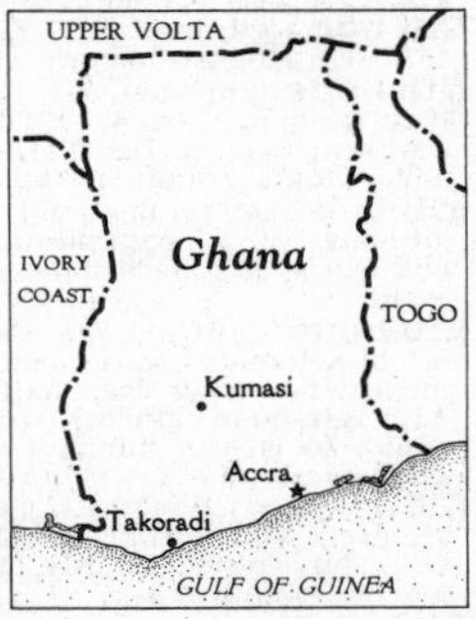

G.F.T.U., General Federation of Trade Unions.

GG, gamma globulin.

ggr, great gross.

GHA, *Navigation.* Greenwich hour angle.

ghain (ʀän), *n.* the 19th letter of the Arabic alphabet. [< Ar]

Gha·na (gä′nə, gan′ə), *n.* a republic in West Africa comprising the former colonies of the Gold Coast and Ashanti, the protectorate of the Northern Territories, and the U.N. trusteeship of British Togoland: member of the British Commonwealth of Nations since 1957. 7,340,000 (est. 1963); 91,843 sq. mi. *Cap.:* Accra. —**Gha·na·ian, Gha·ni·an** (gä′nē ən, gan′ē-), *n., adj.*

Ghar·da·ïa (gär dä′yə), *n.* a city in N Algeria. 14,046 (1954).

ghar·ry (gar′ē), *n., pl.* **-ries.** a horse-drawn cab or carriage used in India. Also, **ghar′ri.** [< Hindi *gārī*]

ghast (gast, gäst), *adj. Archaic.* ghastly. [shortened form]

ghast·ful (gast′fəl, gäst′-), *adj. Obs.* frightful. [ME *gast* spirit (see GHASTLY) + -FUL] —**ghast′ful·ly,** *adv.* —**ghast′ful·ness,** *n.*

ghast·ly (gast′lē, gäst′-), *adj.,* **-li·er, -li·est,** *adv.* —*adj.* **1.** shockingly frightful or dreadful; horrible: *a ghastly murder.* **2.** resembling a ghost, esp. in being very pale: *a ghastly look to his face.* **3.** terrible; very bad: *a ghastly error.* —*adv.* Also, **ghast′li·ly, ghast′i·ly. 4.** in a ghastly manner; horribly; terribly. **5.** with a deathlike quality. [ME *gastly,* OE *gāstlic* spiritual; see GHOSTLY] —**ghast′li·ness,** *n.*

—**Syn. 1.** hideous, grisly, gruesome, grim, dismal. **2.** deathlike, pallid, cadaverous.

ghat (gôt), *n.* (in India) **1.** a passage or stairway descending to a river. **2.** a mountain pass. **3.** a mountain range or escarpment. Also, **ghaut.** [< Hindi *ghāṭ* < Skt *ghaṭṭa*]

Ghats (gôts), *n.* (*construed as sing.*) **1.** See **Eastern Ghats. 2.** See **Western Ghats.**

gha·zal (gə zal′), *n. Pros.* a Persian lyric poem consisting of from 6 to 26 lines in monorhyme. [< Ar]

gha·zi (gä′zē), *n., pl.* **-zis. 1.** a Muslim soldier, esp. one fighting against non-Muslims. **2.** (*cap.*) a title given in Turkey to a victorious sultan, general, etc. [< Ar *ghāzī*]

Ghaz·za·li (ga zä′lē), *n.* **Al-** (al), 1058–1111, Arab philosopher. Also, **Gha·za′li.** Also called **Al-Gazel, Al-Ghazeli.**

Ghe·ber (gā′bər, gē′bər), *n.* Gabar.

ghee (gē), *n.* (in the East Indies) a kind of liquid butter made from the milk of cows and buffaloes and clarified by boiling. [< Hindi *ghī;* akin to Skt *ghr* to sprinkle]

Ghel·de·rode (*Fr.* gel də rōd′), *n.* **Mi·chel de** (*Fr.* mē shel′ də). See **de Ghelderode, Michel.**

Ghent (gent), *n.* a port in NW Belgium, at the confluence of the Scheldt and Lys rivers: treaty 1814. 155,152 (est. 1964). French, **Gand.** Flemish, **Gent.**

Ghent′ azal′ea, any of a group of azaleas, *Azalea gandavensis,* derived by hybridizing American and Old World species.

Gheor·ghiu-Dej (gyôr′gyōō dezh′), *n.* **Gheor·ghe** (gyôr′ge), 1901–65, Rumanian statesman: premier 1952–55; president of the state council 1961–65.

gher·kin (gûr′kin), *n.* **1.** the small, immature fruit of a variety of cucumber, used in pickling. **2.** Also called **bur gherkin, West Indian gherkin.** the small, spiny fruit of a cucurbitaceous vine, *Cucumis Anguria,* of the West Indies, the southern U.S., etc., used in pickling. **3.** the plant yielding this fruit. **4.** a pickle, esp. one made from this fruit. [< D *gurken,* pl. of *gurk* (G *Gurke*) < Slav; cf. Pol *ogórek,* Czech *okurka* << Pers]

ghet·to (get′ō), *n., pl.* **-tos, -toes. 1.** a section of a city in which, in former times in most European countries, all Jews were required to live. **2.** a section predominantly inhabited by Jews. **3.** *U.S.* a section of a city, esp. a thickly populated slum area, inhabited predominantly by Negroes, Puerto Ricans, or any other minority group, often as a result of social or economic restrictions. [< It, perh. abbr. of *borghetto,* dim. of *borgo* settlement outside the city wall]

Ghib·el·line (gib′ə lin, -lēn′), *n.* **1.** a member of the imperial and aristocratic party of medieval Italy, opposed to the Guelphs. —*adj.* **2.** of or pertaining to the Ghibellines. [< It *Ghibellin(o)* < MHG **wībeling-* (G *Waiblingen*) a Hohenstaufen estate in Germany] —**Ghib′el·lin·ism,** *n.*

Ghi·ber·ti (gē ber′tē), *n.* **Lo·ren·zo** (lô ren′tsô), 1378–1455, Florentine sculptor, goldsmith, and painter.

Ghior·des (gyôr′dəs, gôr′-), *n.* a Turkish rug characterized by an uneven pile produced by the Ghiordes knot. [after *Gördes,* (*Ghiordes*), town in Turkey]

Ghior′des knot′, a hand-tied knot, used in rug weaving, in which the parallel ends of looped yarn alternate with two threads of warp, producing an uneven pile effect. Also called **Turkish knot.** Cf. **Sehna knot.**

Ghir·lan·da·io (gēr′län dä′yô), *n.* (*Domenico di Tommaso Curradi di Doffo Bigordi*) 1449–94, Italian painter. Also, **Ghir·lan·da·jo** (gēr′län dä′yô).

ghost (gōst), *n.* **1.** the soul of a dead person, a disembodied spirit imagined as wandering among or haunting living persons. **2.** a mere shadow or semblance; a trace: *He's a ghost of his former self.* **3.** a remote possibility: *He hasn't a ghost of a chance.* **4.** (*sometimes cap.*) a spiritual being. **5.** the principle of life; soul; spirit. **6.** *Informal.* See **ghost writer. 7.** *Television.* a pale, double image, appearing on a screen as a white shadow, caused by poor or double reception or by a defect in the receiver. **8.** an oral word game in which each player in rotation adds a letter to those supplied by preceding players, the object being to avoid ending a word. **9.** *Optics.* a series of false spectral lines produced by a diffraction grating with unevenly spaced lines. **10.** *Metalworking.* a streak appearing on a freshly machined piece of steel containing impurities. **11.** an erythrocyte having no hemoglobin. **12. give up the ghost,** to die: *The doctors thought she would recover, but she gave up the ghost last night.* —*v.t.* **13.** to ghostwrite (a book, speech, etc.) **14.** to haunt. **15.** *Engraving.* to lighten the background of (a photograph) before engraving. —*v.i.* **16.** to ghostwrite. **17.** (of a sailing vessel) to move when there is no perceptible wind. [ME *goost,* OE *gāst;* c. G *Geist* spirit] —**ghost′i·ly,** *adv.* —**ghost′like′,** *adj.*

—**Syn. 1.** apparition, phantom, phantasm, wraith, revenant; shade, spook. GHOST, SPECTER, SPIRIT all refer to the disembodied soul of a person. A GHOST is the soul or spirit of a deceased person, which appears or otherwise makes its presence known to man: *the ghost of a drowned child.* A SPECTER is a ghost or apparition of more or less weird, unearthly, or terrifying aspect: *a frightening specter.* SPIRIT is often interchangeable with GHOST but may mean a supernatural being, usually with an indication of good or malign intent toward man: *the spirit of a friend; an evil spirit.*

ghost′ crab′, a whitish crab, *Ocypode albicans,* found on sandy beaches from the eastern coast of the U.S. to Brazil.

ghost′ dance′, a ritual dance intended to establish communion with the dead, esp. such a dance as performed by various messianic western American Indian cults in the late 19th century.

ghost·dom (gōst′dəm), *n.* the world of ghosts. [GHOST + -DOM]

ghost·fish (gōst′fish′), *n., pl.* **-fish·es,** (*esp. collectively*) **-fish.** wrymouth. [GHOST + FISH]

ghost·ly (gōst′lē), *adj.,* **-li·er, -li·est. 1.** of, characteristic of, or resembling a ghost; spectral. **2.** *Literary.* spiritual. [ME; OE *gāstlic.* See GHOST, -LY] —**ghost′li·ness,** *n.*

ghost′ moth′, swift (def. 8).

Ghosts (gōsts), *n.* a play (1881) by Henrik Ibsen.

ghost′ shrimp′, a shrimplike crustacean of the genus *Callianassa,* of the Pacific coast of North America, having a pinkish, transparent body.

ghost′ town′, a town permanently abandoned by its inhabitants, because of its business decline, a natural catastrophe, or, esp. in the western U.S., because a nearby mine which drew its inhabitants has been worked out.

ghost-weed (gōst′wēd′), *n.* snow-on-the-mountain.

ghost′ word′, a word that has come into existence by error rather than by normal linguistic transmission, as through the mistaken reading of a manuscript, a scribal error, or a misprint.

ghost·write (gōst′rīt′), *v.t., v.i.,* **-wrote, -writ·ten, writ·ing.** to write as a ghost writer. [back formation from GHOST WRITER]

ghost′ writ′er, one who writes speeches, books, articles, etc., for another person who is named as or presumed to be the author. Also, **ghost′-writ′er.**

ghoul (gōōl), *n.* **1.** an evil demon, originally of Oriental legend, supposed to feed on human beings, and especially to rob graves, prey on corpses, etc. **2.** a grave robber. **3.** a person who revels in what is revolting. [< Ar *ghūl,* akin to *ghāla* to seize] —**ghoul′ish,** *adj.* —**ghoul′ish·ly,** *adv.* —**ghoul′ish·ness,** *n.*

G.H.Q., *Mil.* general headquarters. Also, **GHQ**

ghyll (gil), *n. Brit. Dial.* gill[3].

GHz, gigahertz.

GI (jē′ī′), *n., pl.* **GI's** or **GIs,** *adj., v.,* **GI'd, GI'ing.** —*n.* **1.** a member or former member of the U.S. Army, esp. an enlisted man. —*adj.* **2.** rigidly adhering to military regulations and practices: *a platoon leader who tried to be more GI than anyone else.* **3.** of a standardized style or type issued by the U.S. Army: *GI shoes; GI blankets.* **4.** conforming to the regulations or practices of the U.S. Army: *Every recruit must get a GI haircut.* **5.** of, pertaining to, or characteristic of a U.S. enlisted man: *a GI complaint.* —*v.t.* **6.** to clean in preparation for inspection: *They spent Friday night GI'ing the barracks.* —*v.i.* **7.** to follow military regulations and customs closely: *You'd better learn to GI if you want to be promoted.* Also, **G.I.** [orig. abbr. of *galvanized iron,* used in U.S. Army bookkeeping in entering articles (e.g., trash cans) made of it; later extended to all articles issued and finally to soldiers themselves]

Gi, gilbert; gilberts.

gi., gill; gills.

G.I., **1.** galvanized iron. **2.** gastrointestinal. **3.** general issue. **4.** government issue. Also, **GI, g.i.**

Gia·co·met·ti (jä′kə met′ē; *It.* jä′kô met′tē), *n.* **Al·ber·to** (*It.* äl beʀ′tô), 1901–66, Swiss sculptor and painter.

Gian·ni Schic·chi (*It.* jän′nē skē′kē), a one-act opera (1918) by Giacomo Puccini.

gi·ant (jī′ənt), *n.* **1.** an imaginary being of human form but superhuman size, strength, etc. **2.** a person or thing of unusually great size, power, importance, etc.: *an intellectual giant.* **3.** (*often cap.*) *Class. Myth.* any of the Gigantes. **4.** *Mining.* monitor (def. 8). —*adj.* **5.** unusually large, great, or strong; gigantic; huge. **6.** great or eminent above others. [ME *geant* < OF; r. OE *gigant* < L *gigant-* (s. of *gigās*) < Gk] —**gi′ant-like′,** *adj.*

gi′ant ar′rowhead, a perennial, South American, aquatic herb, *Sagittaria montevidensis,* naturalized in the southern U.S., having arrow-shaped leaves and brownish-spotted, white flowers nearly two inches wide.

gi′ant cane′. See under **cane** (def. 5).

gi′ant crab′, a Japanese spider crab, *Macrocheira kaempferi,* that lives in deep waters and sometimes measures 11 feet across from claw to claw.

gi′ant dai′sy, a perennial plant, *Chrysanthemum uglinosum,* of Europe, having solitary, daisylike flowers about 2½ inches wide.

gi·ant·ess (jī′ən tis), *n.* **1.** a female giant. **2.** any very large woman. [ME *geauntesse* < OF. See GIANT, -ESS]

gi′ant fen′nel. See under **fennel** (def. 3).

gi′ant ful′mar. See **giant petrel.**

gi′ant gar′lic, **1.** a large herb, *Allium giganteum,* of Asia, having lilac-colored flowers in dense clusters, grown as an ornamental. **2.** rocambole.

gi′ant granadil′la. See under **granadilla** (def. 1).

gi′ant hol′ly fern′, a hardy, evergreen fern, *Polystichum munitum,* of western North America.

gi′ant hor′net. See under **hornet.**

gi·ant·ism (jī′ən tiz′əm), *n.* **1.** *Pathol.* gigantism. **2.** the state or quality of being a giant. [GIANT + -ISM]

gi′ant lil′y, a plant, *Furcraea gigantea,* of Brazil, having fleshy leaves, grown as an ornamental and as a source of hemp. Also called **cabuya, Mauritius hemp.**

gi′ant liz′ard. See **Komodo dragon.**

gi′ant or′der, *Archit.* See **colossal order.**

gi′ant pan′da, panda (def. 2).

gi′ant pars′nip. See **cow parsnip.**

gi′ant pet′rel, a large, white or brownish petrel, *Macronectes giganteus,* of the Antarctic Ocean and adjacent seas. Also called **giant fulmar.**

gi′ant pow′der, dynamite composed of nitroglycerin and kieselguhr.

gi′ant rag′weed. See under **ragweed** (def. 1).

gi′ant reed′, a stout grass, *Arundo Donax,* of southern Europe, having woody stems and a spirelike flower cluster often two feet long. Also called **Italian reed.**

Gi′ants' Cause′way, a large body of basalt, unusual in displaying perfect columnar jointing, exposed on a promontory on the coast of Northern Ireland.

gi′ant sea′ bass′, a very large serranoid game fish, *Stereolepsis gigas,* found off the coast of California.

gi′ant sequoi′a. See **big tree.**

gi′ant silk′worm moth′, any silkworm moth of the family *Saturniidae.*

gi′ant sla′lom, *Skiing.* a slalom race in which the course has more gates and is longer and steeper than that in a regular slalom.

gi′ant snow′drop, a bulbous herb, *Galanthus elwesi,* of Asia Minor, having bluish-green leaves and white flowers with the inner segments green.

gi′ant star′, *Astron.* a star having a diameter of from 10 to 100 times that of the sun, as Arcturus or Aldebaran. Cf. **supergiant star.**

gi′ant steps′, **1.** a children's game in which a leader calls upon individual players to advance toward him in a given number and variety of steps, the object being for one person to tag the leader and for all of them to run back to the starting line without being caught by the leader. If one is caught, he becomes the leader. **2. giant step,** the longest step that a player is capable of making in this game. Cf. **baby step, umbrella step.**

gi′ant sun′flower, a hardy, perennial herb, *Helianthus giganteus,* of eastern North America, growing nearly twelve feet high and having stiff, hairy stems, hairy leaves, and yellow flower heads nearly three inches wide. Also called **Indian potato, tall sunflower, wild sunflower.**

gi′ant tor′toise, any of several large tortoises of the genus *Testudo,* of the Galápagos Islands and islands near Madagascar.

gi′ant wa′ter bug′. See under **water bug.**

giaour (jour), *n.* *Turkish.* an unbeliever; a non-Muslim, esp. a Christian. [< Turk *giaur* < Pers *gaur,* var. of *gabr*]

Gi·ar·di·a (jē är′dē ə, jär′-), *n.* a genus of flagellates that are parasitic in the intestines of vertebrates. [named after Alfred M. *Giard* (d. 1908), French biologist; see -IA]

Gi·auque (jē ōk′), *n.* **William Francis,** born 1895, U.S. chemist: Nobel prize 1949.

gib[1] (gib), *n., v.,* **gibbed, gib·bing.** —*n.* **1.** a hooked prolongation that develops during the spawning season on the lower jaw of a male salmon or trout. **2.** *Mach.* **a.** a thin, wedgelike strip of metal for controlling the area in which a moving part, as the table of a milling machine, slides. **b.** a keylike part having a head at each end, used with a matching cotter as a fastening. **3.** (in carpentry or ironwork) a heavy metal strap for fastening two members together. —*v.t.* **4.** to fasten (parts) together by means of a gib. [?]

gib[2] (gib), *n.* **1.** a cat, esp. a male cat. **2.** a castrated cat. [ME *gib(be),* short for *Gilbert* proper name]

Gib., Gibraltar.

gibbed (gibd), *adj.* *Vet. Med.* (of a cat) castrated. [GIB[2] + -ED[2]]

gib·ber[1] (jib′ər, gib′-), *v.i.* **1.** to speak inarticulately. **2.** to speak foolishly; chatter. —*n.* **2.** a gibbering utterance. [? freq. of *gib* (obs.) to caterwaul (see GIB[2]); sense and pronunciation influenced by assoc. with JABBER]

gib·ber[2] (gib′ər), *n.* *Australian.* a small, usually rounded stone. [< native Austral]

gib·be·rel′lic ac′id (jib′ə rel′ik), *Biochem.* a metabolite, $C_{18}H_{21}O_4COOH$, of the fungus *Gibberella fujikuroa,* a stimulator of plant growth. [< NL *Gibberell(a)* genus name (dim. of L *gibber* hump) + -IC]

gib·ber·ish (jib′ər ish, gib′-), *n.* **1.** meaningless or unintelligible talk or writing. **2.** talk or writing containing many obscure, pretentious, or technical words. [GIBBER[1] + -ISH[1], modeled on *English*]

gib·bet (jib′it), *n., v.,* **-bet·ed, -bet·ing.** —*n.* **1.** a gallows with a projecting arm at the top, from which the bodies of criminals were formerly hung in chains and left suspended after execution. —*v.t.* **2.** to hang on a gibbet. **3.** to put to death by hanging on a gibbet. **4.** to hold up to public scorn. [ME < OF *gibet* (earlier, staff or cudgel), dim. of *gibe* staff, club]

gib·bon (gib′ən), *n.* any of several small, slender, long-armed arboreal anthropoid apes of the genus *Hylobates,* of the East Indies and southern Asia. [< F, appar. from a dialect of India]

Gibbon, Genus *Hylobates* (Height 2 ft.)

Gib·bon (gib′ən), *n.* **Edward,** 1737–94, English historian.

Gib·bons (gib′ənz), *n.* **1. Grin·ling** (grin′ling), 1648–1720, English wood carver and sculptor, born in the Netherlands. **2. Orlando,** 1583–1625, English organist and composer.

gib·bos·i·ty (gi bos′i tē), *n.* **1.** the state of being gibbous. **2.** a protuberance or swelling. [ME < MF *gibbosite* < ML *gibbōsitāt-* (s. of *gibbōsitās*). See GIBBOUS, -ITY]

gib·bous (gib′əs), *adj.* **1.** humpbacked. **2.** *Astron.* (of a heavenly body) convex at both edges, as the moon when more than half full. See diag. under **moon.** Also, **gib·bose** (gib′ōs). [ME < L *gibbōs(us)* humped, equiv. to *gibb(a)* hump + *-ōsus* -OUS] —**gib′bous·ly, gib′bose·ly,** *adv.* —**gib′bous·ness, gib′bose·ness,** *n.*

Gibbs (gibz), *n.* **1. James,** 1682–1754, Scottish architect and author. **2. Josiah Willard,** 1839–1903, U.S. physicist. **3. Sir Philip,** 1877–1962, English journalist and writer.

Gibbs′ free′ en′ergy, *Thermodynamics.* the quantity expressed as the enthalpy of a system minus the product of the absolute temperature and the entropy of the system: a decrease in the quantity being equal to the maximum amount of work obtainable from the system during a reversible change at constant temperature. Also called **free enthalpy, Gibbs′ func′tion, thermodynamics potential.** Cf. **Helmholtz free energy.** [named after Josiah Willard GIBBS]

gibbs·ite (gib′zīt), *n.* a mineral, hydrated aluminum oxide, $Al_2O_3 \cdot 3H_2O$, occurring in whitish or grayish crystals and masses: an important constituent of bauxite ore. [named after George *Gibbs* (d. 1833), American mineralogist; see -ITE[1]]

Gibbs·town (gibz′toun′), *n.* a town in SW New Jersey. 2820 (1960).

Gib·by (gib′ē), *n.* a boy's given name, form of **Gilbert.**

gibe[1] (jīb), *v.,* **gibed, gib·ing,** *n.* —*v.i.* **1.** to utter mocking words; jeer. —*v.t.* **2.** to taunt; deride; jeer. —*n.* **3.** a taunting or sarcastic remark. Also, **jibe.** [? < MF *gib(er)* (to) handle roughly, shake, deriv. of *gibe* staff, billhook] —**gib′er,** *n.* —**gib′ing·ly,** *adv.*
—**Syn. 1.** mock, sneer, gird. **2.** ridicule, twit, fleer. **3.** sneer, scoff, jeer.

gibe[2] (jīb), *v.i., v.t.,* **gibed, gib·ing,** *n.* jibe[1].

Gib·e·on (gib′ē ən), *n.* a town in ancient Palestine, NW of Jerusalem. Josh. 9:3. Also, *Douay Bible,* **Gabaon.**

Gib·e·on·ite (gib′ē ə nīt′), *n.* one of the inhabitants of Gibeon, who were condemned by Joshua to be hewers of wood and drawers of water for the Israelites. Josh. 9. Also, *Douay Bible,* **Gabaonite.** [GIBEON + -ITE[1]]

gib·let (jib′lit), *n.* Usually, **giblets.** the heart, liver, gizzard, neck, wing, leg ends, and the like, of a fowl, often cooked separately. [ME < OF *gibelet* a stew of game; cf. F *gibelotte* rabbit stew]

Gi·bral·tar (ji brôl′tər), *n.* **1.** a British crown colony comprising a fortress and seaport located on a narrow promontory near the S tip of Spain. 25,721 (est. 1959); 1⅞ sq. mi. **2. Rock of. a.** Ancient, **Calpe.** a long, precipitous mountain nearly coextensive with this colony: one of the Pillars of Hercules. 1396 ft. high; 2½ mi. long. **b.** *Informal.* any person who or thing that has strength and endurance that can be relied on. **3. Strait of,** a strait between Europe and Africa at the Atlantic entrance to the Mediterranean. 8½–23 mi. wide. **4.** any impregnable fortress or stronghold.

Gib·ran (ji brän′), *n.* **Kah·lil** (kä lēl′), 1883–1931, Lebanese mystic, poet, dramatist, and artist; in the U.S. after 1910.

Gib·son (gib′sən), *n.* a dry martini cocktail garnished with a pearl onion. [after the surname *Gibson*]

Gib·son (gib′sən), *n.* **1. Althea,** born 1927, U.S. tennis player. **2. Charles Dana** (dā′nə), 1867–1944, U.S. artist and illustrator. **3.** a boy's given name.

Gib·son·burg (gib′sən bûrg′), *n.* a town in N Ohio. 2540 (1960).

Gib′son Cit′y, a town in central Illinois. 3453 (1960).

Gib′son Des′ert, a desert in W central Australia: scrub; salt marshes. ab. 85,000 sq. mi.

Gib′son girl′, **1.** the idealized American girl of the 1890's as represented in the illustrations of Charles Dana Gibson. **2.** a portable, hand-operated radio transmitter shaped like a rectangular box with a narrow waist, used by pilots downed at sea to signal their location.

gi·bus (jī′bəs), *n., pl.* **-bus·es.** See **opera hat.** Also called **gi′bus hat′.** [named after *Gibus,* 19th-century Frenchman, its inventor]

gid (gid), *n.* *Vet. Pathol.* a disease of cattle and esp. of sheep in which the brain or spinal cord is infested with larvae of the dog tapeworm, *Multiceps multiceps,* producing staggers. Also called **sturdy.** Cf. **water-brain.** [back formation from GIDDY]

Gid·dings (gid′ingz), *n.* a town in central Texas. 2821 (1960).

gid·dy (gid′ē), *adj.,* **-di·er, -di·est,** *v.,* **-died, -dy·ing.** —*adj.* **1.** frivolous and lighthearted; impulsive; flighty: *a giddy mind; a giddy girl.* **2.** *Pathol.* affected with vertigo; dizzy. **3.** attended with or causing dizziness: *a giddy climb.* —*v.t., v.i.* **4.** to make or become giddy. [ME *gidy,* OE *gidig* mad, deriv. of *god* GOD; orig. sense of divine frenzy] —**gid′di·ly,** *adv.* —**gid′di·ness,** *n.*
—**Syn. 1.** unstable, volatile, fickle, inconstant, vacillating. **2.** light-headed, vertiginous. —**Ant. 1.** steady, stable.

Gide (zhēd), *n.* **An·dré (Paul Guil·laume)** (äN dʀā′ pōl gē yōm′), 1869–1951, French novelist, essayist, poet, and critic: Nobel prize 1947.

Gid·e·on (gid′ē ən), *n.* **1.** Also called **Jerubbal.** a judge of Israel and conqueror of the Midianites. Judges 6–8. **2.** a boy's given name.

Gid′eon Soci′ety, an interdenominational society of laymen organized in 1899 to place Bibles in hotel rooms.

gie (gē), *v.i., v.t.,* **gied, gied** or **gien** (gēn), **gie·ing.** *Chiefly Scot.* give.

Giel·gud (gil′go͝od, gēl′-), *n.* **Sir (Arthur) John,** born 1904, English actor and director.

gier-ea·gle (jēr′ē′gəl), *n.* a bird, probably the Egyptian vulture, regarded as unclean. Lev. 11:18; Deut. 14:17. [*gier* (< G *Geier* vulture) + EAGLE]

Gie·se·king (gē′zə king, -sə-), *n.* **Wal·ter (Wil·helm)** (wôl′tər wil′helm; *Ger.* väl′təʀ vil′helm), 1895–1956, German pianist and composer.

Gif·ford (gif′ərd), *n.* **1.** a town in E Florida. 3509 (1960). **2.** a boy's given name.

gift (gift), *n.* **1.** something given voluntarily without charge; present. **2.** the act of giving. **3.** the power or right of giving: *Job offers are a politician's gift.* **4.** a special ability or capacity; natural endowment; talent: *the gift of saying the right thing at the right time.* —*v.t.* **5.** to present with as a gift; bestow gifts upon; endow with. [ME < Scand; cf. Icel *gift*; c. OE *gift* (ME *yift*) marriage gift; akin to GIVE] —**gift′less,** *adj.*
—**Syn. 1.** donation, contribution, offering, benefaction, endowment, bounty, boon, largess, alms, gratuity, tip, premium, allowance, subsidy, bequest, legacy, inheritance, dowry. See **present**[2]. **4.** faculty, aptitude, capability, bent, forte, genius, turn, knack.

gift′ certif′icate, a certificate entitling the bearer to select merchandise of a specified cash value from a store without cost to him, usually presented as a gift.

gift·ed (gif′tid), *adj.* **1.** having great special talent or ability: *the debut of a gifted artist.* **2.** having exceptionally high intelligence: *gifted children.* [GIFT + -ED[3]] —**gift′ed·ly,** *adv.* —**gift′ed·ness,** *n.*

gift′ of gab′, *Informal.* an aptitude for speaking glibly, fluently, or persuasively: *His gift of gab has rescued him from many a scrape.* Also, **gift′ of the gab′.**

gift′ of tongues′. See **speaking in tongues.**

gift′ tax′, a tax imposed on the transfer of money or property from one person during his lifetime to another by gift, payable by the donor.

gift-wrap (gift′rap′), *v.,* **-wrapped** or **-wrapt, -wrap·ping,** *n.* —*v.t.* **1.** to wrap (something), as a package, with decorative paper, ribbon, etc., for presentation as a gift. —*n.* **2.** giftwrapping. —**gift′-wrap′per,** *n.*

gift·wrap·ping (gift′rap′ing), *n.* decorative paper, ribbon, etc., for wrapping objects to be presented as gifts: *Have you any giftwrapping for this package?* [GIFT + WRAPPING]

Gi·fu (gē′fo͞o′), *n.* a city on S Honshu, in central Japan. 345,999 (est. 1964).

gig[1] (gig), *n., v.,* **gigged, gig·ging.** —*n.* **1.** *Naut.* a light boat rowed with four, six, or eight long oars. **2.** a light, two-wheeled one-horse carriage. **3.** something that whirls. **4.** *Obs.* a toy for whirling or spinning; a top. —*v.i.* **5.** to ride in a gig. [ME *gigge, gig* flighty girl, ? < Scand; akin to Dan *gig* top; cf. Norw *giga* to shake about]

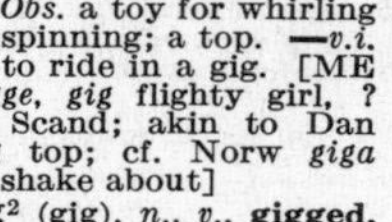

Gig[1] (def. 2)

gig[2] (gig), *n., v.,* **gigged, gig·ging.** —*n.* **1.** a device, commonly four hooks secured back to back, for dragging through a school of fish to hook them through the body. **2.** a spearlike device with a long, thick handle, used for spearing fish and frogs. **3.** Also called **gig mill.** a roller containing teasels, used for raising nap on a fabric. —*v.t.* **4.** to catch or spear (a fish or frog) with a gig. **5.** to raise the nap on (a fabric). —*v.i.* **6.** to catch fish or frogs with a gig. [shortened from *fizgig* < Sp *fisga* harpoon]

gig[3] (gig), *n., v.,* **gigged, gig·ging.** —*n.* **1.** an official report of a minor infraction of regulations, as in school, the army, etc.; a demerit. **2.** a punishment for a minor infraction of rules. —*v.t.* **3.** to give a gig to or punish with a gig. [?]

gig[4] (gig), *n. Jazz.* a single professional engagement, usually of short duration. [?]

giga-, a learned borrowing from Greek where it meant "giant," used with the meaning "billion" in the formation of compound words: *gigameter.* [< Gk *gigā(s)* giant]

gi·ga·cy·cle (jī′gə sī′kəl, jig′ə-), *n.* one billion cycles. *Abbr.:* Gc [GIGA- + CYCLE]

gi′ga·e·lec′tron volt′ (jī′gə i lek′tron, jig′ə-, jī′-, jig′ə-), one billion electron volts. *Abbr.:* GeV, Gev [GIGA- + ELECTRON]

gi·ga·hertz (jī′gə hûrts′, jig′ə-), *n.* one billion hertz. *Abbr.:* GHz [GIGA- + HERTZ]

gi·ga·me·ter (jī′gə mē′tər, jig′ə-), *n. Metric System.* a unit of distance equal to 1,000,000 kilometers or 621,370 miles. *Abbr.:* Gm [GIGA- + METER[1]]

gi·gan·te·an (jī′gan tē′ən, jī gan′tē ən), *adj.* gigantic. [< L *gigante(us)* of giants (*gigant-* GIANT + *-eus* adj. suffix) + -AN]

Gi·gan·tes (ji gan′tēz), *n.pl. Class. Myth.* beings with the heads of men and the bodies of serpents, who were born to Gaea when she was impregnated with the blood of the mutilated Uranus: the Gigantes attacked the gods but were defeated with the help of Hercules. [< L < Gk (pl.): giants]

gi·gan·tesque (jī′gan tesk′), *adj.* of a huge or gigantic size; of or suited to a giant. [< F < It *gigantesc(o)*, equiv. to *gigant(e)* GIANT + *-esco* -ESQUE]

gi·gan·tic (jī gan′tik), *adj.* **1.** very large; huge. **2.** of, like, or befitting a giant. [< L *gigant-* GIANT + -IC] —**gi·gan′ti·cal·ly,** *adv.* —**gi·gan′tic·ness,** *n.*

—**Syn. 1.** enormous, immense, prodigious, herculean, cyclopean, titanic. GIGANTIC, COLOSSAL, MAMMOTH, MONSTROUS are used of whatever is physically or metaphorically of great magnitude. GIGANTIC refers to the size of a giant, or to size or scope befitting a giant: *a gigantic stalk of corn.* COLOSSAL refers to the size of a colossus, to anything huge or vast as befitting a hero or god: *a colossal victory.* MAMMOTH refers to the size of the animal of that name and is used esp. of anything large and heavy: *a mammoth battleship.* MONSTROUS means strikingly unusual or out of the normal in some way, as in size: *a monstrous blunder.* —**Ant. 1.** tiny.

gi·gan·tism (ji gan′tiz əm, jī′gan tiz′əm), *n. Pathol.* abnormally great development in size or stature of the whole body or of parts of the body, most often due to dysfunction of the pituitary gland. [< L *gigant-* GIANT + -ISM]

gi·gan·to·ma·chi·a (jī gan′tə mā′kē ə), *n.* **1.** a war of giants, esp. the war of the giants of Greek mythology against the Olympian gods. **2.** a representation of this, as in sculpture. [< L < Gk; see GIANT, -O-, -MACHY]

Gi·gan·to·pi·the·cus (jī gan′tō pi thē′kəs, -pith′ə-kəs), *n.* a genus of extinct Pleistocene apes of southern China, characterized by large jaws and teeth. [< NL < Gk *gigant-* (s. of *gigās*) giant + *-o-* -O- + *píthēkos* ape]

gi·ga·sec·ond (jī′gə sek′ənd, jig′ə-), *n.* one billion seconds. *Abbr.:* Gs [GIGA- + SECOND[2]]

gi·ga·ton (jī′gə tun′, jig′ə-), *n.* one billion tons. *Abbr.:* GT [GIGA- + TON[1]]

gi·ga·watt (jī′gə wot′, jig′ə-), *n.* one billion watts. *Abbr.:* GW, Gw [GIGA- + WATT]

gig·gle (gig′əl), *v.,* **-gled, -gling,** *n.* —*v.i.* **1.** to laugh in a silly, undignified way, esp. with short, repeated gasps and titters, as from juvenile or ill-concealed amusement, nervous embarrassment, etc. —*n.* **2.** a silly, spasmodic laugh; titter. [imit.; cf. D *giggelen*, G *gickeln*] —**gig′gler,** *n.*

—**Syn. 1, 2.** snicker, snigger.

gig·gly (gig′lē), *adj.,* **-gli·er, -gli·est.** inclined to giggle. [GIGGLE + -Y[1]]

gig·let (gig′lit), *n.* **1.** a giddy, playful girl. **2.** *Obs.* a lascivious woman. Also, **gig′lot.** [ME *gig(e)lot.* See GIG[1], -LET]

Gi·gli (jē′lyē), *n.* **Be·nia·mi·no** (be′nyä mē′nô), 1890–1957, Italian operatic tenor.

gig′ mill′, gig[2] (def. 3).

gig·o·lo (jig′ə lō′, zhig′-), *n., pl.* **-los. 1.** a man living off the earnings or gifts of a woman, esp. a younger man supported by an older woman in return for his sexual attentions and companionship. **2.** a male professional dancing partner or escort. [< F, masc. of *gigole* female dancer, deriv. of MF *giguer* to dance. See JIG[2]]

gig·ot (jig′ət), *n.* **1.** a leg-of-mutton sleeve. **2.** a leg of lamb or mutton. [< MF, appar. dim. of *gigue* fiddle (< Gmc); so called (facetiously) in allusion to its shape]

gigs·man (gigz′mən), *n., pl.* **-men.** *Naut.* a seaman assigned to a gig. [GIG[1] + 'S[1] + MAN[1]]

gigue (zhēg), *n.* **1.** *Dance.* jig (def. 1). **2.** *Music.* a jig, often forming the concluding movement in the classical suite. [< F < It *giga*, orig., a fiddle or lute < Gmc; cf. G *Geige*]

GI Joe, *Informal.* an enlisted soldier in the U.S. Army, esp. in WW II.

Gi·jon (gē hôn′; *Sp.* hē hôn′), *n.* a seaport in NW Spain, on the Bay of Biscay. 116,676 (est. 1956).

Gil (gil), *n.* a boy's given name, form of **Gilbert.**

Gi·la (hē′lə), *n.* a river flowing W from SW Mexico across S Arizona to the Colorado River. 630 mi. long.

Gila monster
(Length to 20 in.)

Gi′la mon′ster, a large, venomous lizard, *Heloderma suspectum*, of northwestern Mexico and the southwestern U.S., having the skin studded with yellow or orange and black beadlike tubercles. [after the GILA]

Gi′la wood′pecker, a dull-colored woodpecker, *Centrus unropygialis*, of the southwestern United States and Mexico. [after the GILA]

gil·bert (gil′bərt), *n. Elect.* the centimeter-gram-second unit of magnetomotive force, equal to .7958 ampere turns. *Abbr.:* Gi [named after William *Gilbert* (1540–1603), English scientist]

Gil·bert (gil′bərt), *n.* **1. Cass,** 1859–1934, U.S. architect. **2. Sir Humphrey,** 1539?–83, English soldier, navigator, and colonizer in America. **3. Sir William Schwenck** (shwengk), 1836–1919, English dramatist and poet: collaborator with Sir Arthur Sullivan. **4.** a town in NE Minnesota. 2591 (1960). **5.** a boy's given name.

Gil·ber·ta (gil bûr′tə), *n.* a girl's given name.

Gil′bert and El′lice Is′lands (el′is), a British colony comprised of the Gilbert Islands, the Ellice Islands, and other widely scattered islands in the central Pacific. 45,000 (est. 1959); 203 sq. mi. *Cap.:* Ocean Island.

Gil·berte (*Fr.* zhēl bert′), *n.* a girl's given name.

Gil·ber·ti·an (gil bûr′tē ən), *adj.* of, pertaining to, or characteristic of the style or humor of Sir William S. Gilbert. [GILBERT + -IAN]

Gil·ber·tine (gil′bər tēn′), *n.* a girl's given name. Also, **Gil·ber·ti·na** (gil′bər tē′nə).

Gil′bert Is′lands, a group of islands in the central Pacific, on the equator: part of the British colony of Gilbert and Ellice Islands. 166 sq. mi.

Gil Blas (*Fr.* zhēl blä′), (*Gil Blas de Santillane*) a picaresque novel (1715–35) by Le Sage.

gild[1] (gild), *v.t.,* **gild·ed** or **gilt, gild·ing. 1.** to coat with gold, gold leaf, or a gold-colored substance. **2.** to give a bright, pleasing, or specious aspect to. **3.** *Obs.* to make red, as with blood. [ME *gild(en)*, OE *gyldan;* deriv. of GOLD] —**gild′a·ble,** *adj.*

gild[2] (gild), *n.* guild.

Gil·da (gil′də), *n.* a girl's given name.

gild·ed (gil′did), *adj.* **1.** covered or highlighted with gold or something of a golden color. **2.** having a pleasing, fine, or showy appearance or exterior which covers or conceals something of little worth; superficially attractive. [ME; OE *gegyld.* See GILD[1], -ED[2]]

Gild′ed Age′, the period in the U.S. from about 1870 to 1898, characterized by a greatly expanding economy and the emergence of plutocratic influences in government and in the social structure.

gild·er[1] (gil′dər), *n.* one who or that which gilds. [GILD[1] + -ER[1]]

gil·der[2] (gil′dər), *n.* gulden (defs. 1, 2).

gild·hall (gild′hôl′), *n.* guildhall.

gild·ing (gil′ding), *n.* **1.** the application of gilt. **2.** the gold leaf or other material with which something is gilded. **3.** the golden surface produced. **4.** any deceptive coating or aspect used to give a pleasing, fine, or showy appearance. [late ME; see GILD[1], -ING[1]]

gilds·man (gildz′mən), *n., pl.* **-men.** guildsman.

Gil·e·ad (gil′ē əd), *n.* **1.** an ancient district of Palestine, E of the Jordan River, in present Jordan. **2. Mount,** a mountain in NW Jordan. 3596 ft.

Gil·e·ad·ite (gil′ē ə dīt′), *n.* **1.** a member of a branch of the Israelite tribe descended from Manasseh. **2.** an inhabitant of ancient Gilead. [GILEAD + -ITE[1]]

Gi·lels (gē′lels, gi lelz′), *n.* **E·mil G(ri·gor·ye·vich)** (e mēl′ gri gôr′yə vich), born 1916, Russian pianist.

Giles (jīlz), *n.* **1. Saint,** 8th century A.D., Athenian hermit in France. **2.** a boy's given name.

gil·gai (gil′gī), *n. Australian.* **1.** a small gully or ditch. **2.** a small pond or pool of water. Also, **gil′gie.** [< native Austral]

Gil·gal (gil′gal), *n.* the name of several places in ancient Palestine, esp. a site near Jericho where the Israelites encamped after crossing the Jordan. Josh. 4:19–24. Also, *Douay Bible,* **Galgal.**

Gil·ga·mesh (gil′gə mesh′), *n.* a legendary Sumerian king, the hero of Sumerian and Babylonian epics.

gil·gul (gil′go͝ol; *Heb.* gil go͞ol′), *n., pl.* **gil·gu·lim** (gil-go͝ol′im; *Heb.* gil go͞o lēm′). *Jewish Folklore.* a dybbuk. [< Yiddish, short for *gilgul haneshomas* transmigration of souls < Heb *galal* to roll, turn over]

gil·guy (gil′gī′), *n. Naut.* **1.** a rope used as a temporary guy. **2.** any device or object not specifically named; gadget. [?]

gill[1] (gil), *n.* **1.** an aquatic respiratory organ for obtaining oxygen dissolved in the water, usually feathery, platelike, or filamentous. **2.** one of the radiating vertical plates on the underside of the cap of an agaric; lamella. **3.** See **ground ivy.** —*v.t.* **4.** to catch (fish) by the gills in a gill net. **5.** to gut or clean (fish). [ME *gile* < Scand; cf. Sw *gäl*, Dan *gælle*] —**gill′-less,** *adj.* —**gill′-like′,** *adj.*

gill[2] (jil), *n.* a unit of liquid measure equal to ¼ pint. [ME *gille* < OF: vat, tub < LL *gillo* wine vessel, *gella* wine measure]

gill[3] (gil), *n. Brit. Dial.* **1.** a deep rocky cleft or wooded ravine forming the course of a stream. **2.** a stream; brook; rivulet. Also, **ghyll.** [ME *gille* < ON *gil*]

gill[4] (jil), *n.* **1.** a girl; sweetheart. **2.** *Obs.* a girl or wench. [ME; special use of short form of GILLIAN]

gill[5] (gil), *Textiles.* —*n.* **1.** a faller used in the combing process, generally for only the highest-quality fibers. —*v.t.* **2.** to comb (fibers) with a gill. [? special use of GILL[1]]

Gill (gil *for 1;* jil *for 2*), *n.* **1.** a boy's given name. **2.** a girl's given name.

gill′ arch′ (gil). See **branchial arch.**

gill′ bar′ (gil). See **branchial arch** (def. 1).

gill′ book′ (gil). See **book gill.**

gill′ box′ (gil), *Textiles.* a machine having a number of gills, used in combing.

gill′ cleft′ (gil). See **branchial cleft.**

Gil·les·pie (gə les′pē), *n.* **1. John Birks** (bûrks), ("*Dizzy*"), born 1917, U.S. jazz trumpeter and composer. **2.** a town in SW Illinois. 3569 (1960).

Gil·lett (ji let′), *n.* **1. Frederick Huntington,** 1851–1935, U.S. political leader: Speaker of the House 1919–25. **2.** Also, **Gelett, Gillette.** a boy's given name, form of **Gilbert.**

Gil·lette (ji let′), *n.* **1. William (Hooker),** 1855–1937, U.S. actor and dramatist. **2.** a town in NE Wyoming. 3580 (1960). **3.** Also, **Gelett, Gillett.** a boy's given name, form of **Gilbert.**

gill′ fil′ament (gil), one of the threadlike processes forming the respiratory surface of a gill.

gill′ fun′gus (gil), an agaricaceous fungus; mushroom.

Gil·li·an (jil′ē ən, -yən), *n.* a girl's given name, form of **Juliana.**

gil·lie (gil′ē), *n. Scot.* **1.** a sportsman's attendant, esp. a hunting or fishing guide. **2.** a male attendant or personal servant to a Highland chieftain. Also, **gilly.** [< Gael *gille* lad, servant]

gill·ing (gil′ing), *n. Textiles.* the process of attenuating worsted fibers and making them parallel by using a gill box while combing. [GILL[5] + -ING[1]]

gill′ net′ (gil), a curtainlike net, suspended vertically in the water, with meshes of such a size as to catch by the gills a fish that has thrust its head through.

gill-net·ter (gil′net′ər), *n.* **1.** a person who uses a gill net in fishing. **2.** a boat used in fishing with a gill net.

gill-o·ver-the-ground (gil′ō′vər thə ground′, -ground′), *n.* See **ground ivy.**

gill′ rak′er (gil), (in fish) one of a series of stiff projections along the inner margins of the branchial arches that prevent food particles from passing through the branchial clefts.

gill′ slit′ (gil). See **branchial cleft.**

gil·ly[1] (gil′ē), *n., pl.* **-lies.** *Scot.* gillie.

gil·ly[2] (gil′ē), *n., pl.* **-lies,** *v.,* **-lied, -ly·ing.** —*n.* **1.** a truck or wagon, esp. one used to transport the equipment of a circus or carnival. —*v.t., v.i.* **2.** to carry or be carried on a gilly. [*gill* (dial.) < ? + -Y[2]]

gil·ly·flow·er (jil′ē flou′ər), *n.* **1.** any of various flowers, as the stock, *Matthiola incana.* **2.** *Archaic or Dial.* the clove pink. Also, **gil′li·flow′er.** [ME *gilofre, geraflour* < OF *gilofre, girofle* < L *caryophyll(um)* < Gk *karyóphyllon* clove (*káryo(n)* nut + *phýllon* leaf)]

Gil·man (gil′mən), *n.* **1. Arthur,** 1837–1909, U.S. educator. **2. Daniel Coit** (koit), 1831–1908, U.S. educator.

Gil·mer (gil′mər), *n.* a town in NE Texas. 4312 (1960).

Gi·lo·lo (jī lō′lō, ji-), *n.* Halmahera.

Gil·roy (gil′roi), *n.* a town in W California. 7348 (1960).

Gil·son (zhēl sôn′), *n.* **É·tienne Hen·ry** (ā tyen′ äN rē′), born 1884, French historian, esp. of medieval Christian philosophy.

gil·son·ite (gil′sə nīt′), *n.* an extremely pure asphalt particularly valuable for the manufacture of paints and varnishes, the chief deposits being in Utah. Also called **uintaite, uintahite.** [formerly trademark]

gilt[1] (gilt), *v.* **1.** a pt. and pp. of **gild**[1]. —*adj.* **2.** gilded. **3.** gold in color; golden. —*n.* **4.** the gold or other material applied in gilding; gilding.

gilt[2] (gilt), *n.* a young female swine, esp. one that has not produced a litter. [ME *gilt(e)* < Scand; cf. OIcel *gylta gilt(r)*]

gilt-edged (gilt′ejd′), *adj.* **1.** having the edge or edges gilded: *gilt-edged paper.* **2.** of the highest or best quality, kind, etc.: *gilt-edged securities.* Also, **gilt′-edge′.**

gilt·head (gilt′hed′), *n.* any of several marine fishes having gold markings, as a sparid, *Sparus auratus,* found in the Mediterranean Sea. [GILT[1] + HEAD]

gim·bals (jim′bəlz, gim′-), *n.* (*construed as sing.*) Sometimes, **gimbal.** a contrivance, consisting of a ring or base on an axis, which permits an object, as a ship's compass, mounted in or on it to tilt freely in any direction, in effect, suspending the object so that it will remain horizontal even when its support is tipped. Also called **gim′bal ring′.** [alter. of GEMEL]

gim·blet (gim′blit), *v.t. Naut.* gimlet (def. 4).

gim·crack (jim′krak′), *n.* **1.** a showy, useless trifle; gewgaw. —*adj.* **2.** showy but useless. [ME *gib(e)crake;* cf. ME *gibben* to waver (< OF *giber* to shake)]

gim·crack·er·y (jim′krak′ə rē), *n.* **1.** worthless or useless trifles, ornaments, trinkets, etc. **2.** obvious or contrived effects, esp. in art, music, literature, etc. [GIMCRACK + -ERY]

gim·el (gim′əl), *n.* **1.** the third letter of the Hebrew alphabet. **2.** the consonant sound represented by this letter. **3.** *Music.* gymel. [< Heb *gīmel*, lit., camel]

gim·let (gim′lit), *n.* **1.** a small tool for boring holes, consisting of a shaft with a pointed screw at one end and a cross handle at the other. **2.** a cocktail made with gin or vodka, sweetened lime juice, and sometimes soda water. —*v.t.* **3.** to pierce with or as with a gimlet. **4.** Also, **gimblet.** *Naut.* to rotate (a suspended anchor) to a desired position. —*adj.* **5.** able to penetrate or bore through. [ME < OF *guimbelet* < Gmc; cf. MD *wimmel* WIMBLE] —**gim′let·y,** *adj.*

Gimlet

gim′let eye′, **1.** a sharp or piercing glance. **2.** an eye that gives or can give a sharp or piercing look. —**gim′let-eyed′,** *adj.*

gim·mal (gim′əl, jim′əl), *n.* any of various joints for transmitting motion between rotating parts, as in a timepiece. [alter. of GEMEL]

gim·mick (gim′ik), *n.* **1.** *U.S. Slang.* any tricky device or means. **2.** *Informal.* a device by which a magician or carnival pitchman works a trick. **3.** *Electronics Informal.* a capacitor formed by intertwining two insulated wires. [?] —**gim′mick·y,** *adj.*

gim·mick·ry (gim′ik rē), *n.* **1.** the use or proliferation of gimmicks. **2.** an abundance of gimmicks. Also, **gim·mick·ery** (gim′ik rē, -ik ə rē). [GIMMICK + -RY]

gimp[1] (gimp), *n.* **1.** a flat trimming of silk, wool, or other cord, sometimes stiffened with wire, for garments, curtains, etc. **2.** a coarse thread, usually glazed, employed in lacemaking to outline designs. [appar. < D *gimp* < ?]

gimp[2] (gimp), *n. Dial.* spirit, vigor, or ambition. [?]

gimp[3] (gimp), *n. Slang.* **1.** a cripple. **2.** a limp. [?] —**gimp′y,** *adj.*

gimp[4] (jimp), *adj. Scot. and North Eng.* jimp.

gin[1] (jin), *n.* **1.** an alcoholic liquor obtained by distilling grain mash with juniper berries. **2.** an alcoholic liquor similar to this, made by redistilling spirits with flavoring agents, esp. juniper berries, orange peel, angelica root, etc. [shortened from GENEVA]

gin[2] (jin), *n., v.,* **ginned, gin·ning.** —*n.* **1.** See **cotton gin. 2.** a trap or snare for game. **3.** a stationary prime mover having a drive shaft rotated by horizontal beams pulled by horses walking in a circle. —*v.t.* **4.** to clear (cotton) of seeds with a gin. **5.** to snare (game). [ME *gyn*, aph. var. of OF *engin* ENGINE] —**gin′ner,** *n.*

gin[3] (gin), *v.i., v.t.,* **gan, gun, gin·ning.** *Archaic.* to begin. [ME *ginne(n)*, OE *ginnan*, aph. var. of *onginnan, beginnen* to BEGIN]

gin[4] (jin), *n., v.,* **ginned, gin·ning.** —*n. Cards.* **1.** Also called **gin rummy.** a variety of rummy for two players, in which a player with 10 or fewer points in unmatched cards can end a game by laying down his hand. **2.** the winning of such a game by laying down a full set of matched cards, earning the winner a bonus of 20 or 25 points. —*v.i.* **3.** to win a game in gin by laying down a hand in which all ten cards are included in sets. [? special use of GIN[1]]

gin[5] (gin), *conj. Chiefly Scot.* if; whether. [prob. var. of *iffen* if then]

gin[6] (jin), *n. Australian Informal.* **1.** a female aborigine. **2.** an aboriginal wife. Also, **jin.** [< native Austral]

Gi·na (jē′nə; *It.* jē′nä), *n.* a girl's given name.

gin′ and ton′ic (jin), a tall drink made with gin and quinine water, usually garnished with a slice of lime or lemon.

gin′ block′ (jin), *Mach.* a block having a large sheave in an open metal frame, used esp. to support a cargo whip.

gi·nep (kə nep′, gə-), *n.* genip.

Gi·nev·ra (ji nev′rə), *n.* a girl's given name, form of **Guinevere.**

gin·gal (jin′gôl), *n.* jingal. Also, **gin′gall.**

gin·ge·li (jin′jə lē), *n., pl.* **-lis.** gingili.

gin·gel·ly (jin′jə lē), *n., pl.* **-lies.** gingili.

gin·ger (jin′jər), *n.* **1.** the pungent, spicy rhizome of any of the reedlike plants of the genus *Zingiber*, esp. of *Z. officinale*, used in cookery and medicine. **2.** any of these plants, native to the East Indies but now cultivated in most tropical countries. **3.** a yellowish or reddish brown. **4.** *Chiefly Brit.* a person with red or sandy hair. **5.** *Informal.* piquancy; animation: *plenty of ginger in their performance of the dance.* —*v.t.* **6.** to treat or flavor with ginger. **7.** *Informal.* to impart spiciness or piquancy to; make lively (usually fol. by *up*): *gingering up a talk with a few jokes.* —*adj.* **8.** flavored or made with ginger. [ME *ginger, gingivere* < OF *gingivre* < LL *gingiber* for L *zingiberi* < Gk *zingíberis*]

Gin·ger (jin′jər), *n.* a girl's given name, form of **Virginia** or **Regina.**

gin′ger ale′, a carbonated soft drink flavored with ginger extract.

gin′ger beer′, a soft drink similar to ginger ale but containing more ginger flavor.

gin·ger·bread (jin′jər bred′), *n.* **1.** a type of cake flavored with ginger and molasses. **2.** a rolled cooky similarly flavored, often cut in fanciful shapes, and sometimes frosted. **3.** elaborate, gaudy, or superfluous ornamentation: *a series of gables embellished with gingerbread.* —*adj.* **4.** heavily, gaudily, and superfluously ornamented: *a gingerbread style of architecture.* [ME *gingebreed* (influenced by *breed* bread), var. of *gingebrad, -brat* ginger paste < OF *gingembras, -brat* preserved ginger < ML **gingi(m)brāt(um)* a medicinal preparation (neut. ptp.), deriv. of L *gingeber* GINGER]

gin′gerbread palm′. See **doom palm.**

gin′gerbread tree′, a tree, *Parinarium macrophyllum*, of western Africa, bearing a large, edible, farinaceous fruit (**gin′gerbread plum′**).

gin′ger group′, *Chiefly Brit.* the most active group within an organization, as a political party.

gin′ger jar′, a Chinese ceramic jar having a wide mouth, a globular body, and a dome-shaped cover.

gin·ger·ly (jin′jər lē), *adv.* **1.** with extreme care or caution; warily. **2.** *Obs.* mincingly; daintily. —*adj.* **3.** cautious, careful, or wary. [perh. < MF *gensor, genzor* delicate, pretty, positive use of compar. of *gent* GENTLE] —**gin′ger·li·ness,** *n.*

gin′ger nut′, *Chiefly Brit.* a gingersnap.

gin·ger·snap (jin′jər snap′), *n.* a small, brittle cooky flavored with ginger and molasses. [GINGER + SNAP]

gin·ger·y (jin′jə rē), *adj.* **1.** gingerlike; pungent; spicy. **2.** of the color of ginger. [GINGER + -Y[1]]

ging·ham (ging′əm), *n.* yarn-dyed, plain-weave cotton fabric, usually striped or checked. [< F *guingan* << Malay *ginggang*, lit., striped]

gin·gi·li (jin′jə lē), *n., pl.* **-lis.** **1.** the sesame plant. **2.** the oil of this plant. Also, **gingeli, gingelly.** [< Hindi *jinjalī* << Ar *juljulān*]

gin·gi·val (jin jī′vəl, jin′jə vəl), *adj.* **1.** of or pertaining to the gums. **2.** *Phonet.* alveolar. [< L *gingīv(a)* gum + -AL[1]]

gin·gi·vi·tis (jin′jə vī′tis), *n. Pathol.* inflammation of the gums. [< L *gingīv(a)* gum + -ITIS]

gin·gly·moid (jing′glə moid′, ging′-), *adj.* of, pertaining to, or resembling a ginglymus. [GINGLYM(US) + -OID]

gin·gly·mus (jing′glə məs, ging′-), *n., pl.* **-mi** (-mī′). *Anat.* a joint in which movement is limited to one plane. Also called **hinge joint.** [< NL < Gk *gínglymos* hinge]

gink (gingk), *n. Slang.* a man, esp. one who is unpleasant or insignificant. [?]

gink·go (ging′kō, jing′kō-), *n., pl.* **-goes.** a large, ornamental, gymnospermous tree, *Ginkgo biloba*, native to China, having fan-shaped leaves, fleshy fruit, and edible nuts. Also, **ging′ko.** Also called **maidenhair-tree.** [< Jap *ginkyo*, equiv. to *gin* silver + *kyo* apricot]

gin′ mill′ (jin), *Slang.* a bar or saloon, esp. a cheap or disreputable one.

ginned (jind), *adj. Slang.* drunk; intoxicated; inebriated. [GIN[1] + -ED[3]]

gin·ner·y (jin′ə rē), *n., pl.* **-ner·ies.** a mill for ginning cotton. [GIN[2] + -ERY]

Gin·nun·ga·gap (gin′o͞ong gä gäp′), *n. Scand. Myth.* a primordial void, filled with mists, existing between Niflheim and Muspelheim.

Gin·ny (jin′ē), *n.* a girl's given name, form of **Ginger (Virginia)** or **Genevieve.**

Gi·no (jē′nō; *It.* jē′nô), *n.* a boy's given name.

gin′ rick′ey (jin), a rickey made with gin.

gin′ rum′my, *Cards.* gin[4] (def. 1).

gin·seng (jin′seng), *n.* **1.** either of two araliaceous plants, *Panax Ginseng (Schinseng)*, of China, Korea, etc., or *P. quinquefolium*, of North America, having an aromatic root used in medicine by the Chinese. **2.** the root itself. **3.** a preparation made from it. Also, **genseng.** [< Chin (Mandarin) *jên shên*, equiv. to *jên* man + *shên* of obscure meaning]

Gin·za (gin′zə), *n.* **the,** a street in Tokyo, Japan, famous for its nightclubs, bars, and the like.

Ginz·berg (ginz′bərg), *n.* **Ash·er** (ash′ər), (*Achad Ha-Am, Ahad Ha-am*), 1856–1927, Hebrew philosophical writer and editor, born in Russia: advocate of cultural Zionism.

gin·zo (gin′zō), *n., pl.* **-zoes.** *Disparaging.* an Italian. [? alter. of GUINEA]

Gio·con·da, La (lä′ jō kon′də; *It.* lä′ jô kôn′dä), **1.** See **Mona Lisa.** **2.** an opera (1876) by Amilcare Ponchielli.

gio·co·so (jə kō′sō; *It.* jô kô′sô), *adj., adv. Music.* merry, playful. [< It: playful < L *jocōs(us)* JOCOSE]

Gio·no (jô nō′), *n.* **Jean** (zhäN), 1895–1970, French novelist.

Gior·da·no (jôr dä′nô), *n.* **1. Lu·ca** (lo͞o′kä), ("*Luca Fapresto*"), 1632–1705, Italian painter. **2. Um·ber·to** (o͞om ber′tô), 1867–1948, Italian composer of operas.

Gior·gio·ne (jôr jô′ne), *n.* (*Giorgione de Castelfranco, Giorgio Barbarelli*) 1478?–1511, Italian painter.

Giot·to (jot′ō; *It.* jôt′tô), *n.* (*Giotto di Bondone*) 1266?–1337, Florentine painter, sculptor, and architect.

Gio·van·na (*It.* jô vän′nä), *n.* a girl's given name.

Gio·van′ni Ar·nol·fi′ni and His Bride′ (jō vä′nē är′nôl fē′nē, jē ə-), a painting (1434) by Jan van Eyck. Also, **Arnolfini and His Bride.**

gip (jip), *v.t.,* **gipped, gip·ping,** *n. U.S. Slang.* gyp[1]. —**gip′per,** *n.*

gi·pon (ji pon′, jip′on), *n.* jupon.

Gip·sy (jip′sē), *n., pl.* **-sies,** *adj. Chiefly Brit.* Gypsy. Also, **gip′sy.** —**gip′sy·dom,** *n.* —**gip′sy·esque′, gip′sy·ish, gip′sy·like′, gip·se′ian,** *adj.* —**gip′sy·hood′,** *n.* —**gip′sy·ism,** *n.*

gip′sy cap′stan, *Naut.* See **gypsy capstan.**

gi·raffe (jə raf′ *or, esp. Brit.,* -räf′), *n.* **1.** a tall, long-necked, spotted ruminant, *Giraffa camelopardalis*, of Africa: the tallest living quadruped animal. **2.** (*cap.*) *Astron.* the constellation Camelopardalis. [< F *girafe* < Ar *zarāfah*, prob. of Afr orig.]

Giraffe
(Height 18 ft.)

gir·an·dole (jir′ən dōl′), *n.* **1.** a rotating and radiating firework. **2.** *Fort.* a group of connected mines. **3.** an ornate bracket for candelabra or the like, sometimes with a reflecting mirror at the back of the shelf. **4.** a pendant, as an earring, consisting of a piece of jewelry surrounded by smaller pendants or jewels. Also, **gi·ran·do·la** (ji ran′dᵊ lə). [< F < It *girandol(a)*, deriv. of *girare* to turn in a circle < L *gȳrāre*, deriv. of *gȳrus* a circle < Gk *gŷros*]

Gi·rard (jə rärd′), *n.* **Stephen,** 1750–1831, American merchant, banker, and philanthropist.

Gi·rard·ville (jə rärd′vil), *n.* a town in central Pennsylvania. 2958 (1960).

gir·a·sol (jir′ə sôl′, -sōl′, -sol′), *n.* **1.** an opal that reflects light in a bright luminous glow. **2.** See **Jerusalem artichoke.** —*adj.* **3.** (of a stone) translucent and bluish-white with reddish reflections under strong light; opalescent. Also, **gir·a·sole** (jir′ə sōl′), **girosol.** [< It, equiv. to *gira(re)* (to) turn (see GIRANDOLE) + *sole* the sun]

Gi·raud (zhē rō′), *n.* **Hen·ri Ho·no·ré** (äN rē′ ô nô rā′), 1879–1949, French general.

Gi·rau·doux (zhēr′ō do͞o′; *Fr.* zhē rō do͞o′), *n.* **Jean** (zhäN), 1882–1944, French novelist, playwright, and diplomat.

gird[1] (gûrd), *v.t.,* **gird·ed** or **girt, gird·ing.** **1.** to encircle or bind with a belt or band. **2.** to surround; hem in. **3.** to prepare (oneself) for action: *He girded himself for the trial ahead.* **4.** to provide, equip, or invest, as with power, strength, etc. [ME *gird(en)*, OE *gyrdan*; c. G *gürten*] —**gird′ing·ly,** *adv.*

gird[2] (gûrd), *v.i.* **1.** to gibe; jeer (usually fol. by *at*). —*v.t.* **2.** *Obs.* to gibe or jeer at; taunt. —*n.* **3.** *Archaic.* a gibe. [ME *gyrd* a stroke, blow, hence a cutting remark, deriv. of *girden* to strike, smite < ?] —**gird′ing·ly,** *adv.*

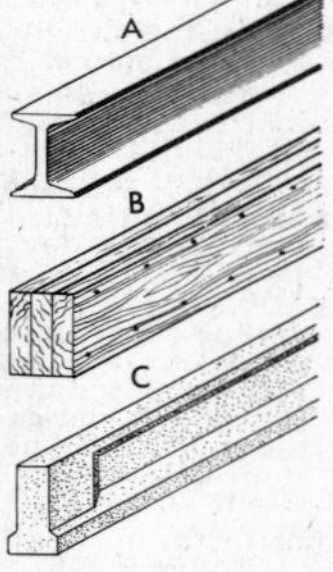

gird·er (gûr′dər), *n.* **1.** a large beam, as of steel, reinforced concrete, or timber, for supporting masonry, joists, purlins, etc. **2.** a principal beam of wood, steel, etc., supporting the ends of joists. [GIRD[1] + -ER[1]] —**gird′er·less,** *adj.*

Girders
A, Steel; B, Wood;
C, Prestressed
concrete

gird·er·ing (gûr′dər ing), *n. Engineering, Building Trades.* a method of concentrating isolated building loads, as from piers or columns, upon a relatively small area of ground by means of beams connecting the piers or columns and resting upon a grillage so distributed as to balance and support the loads. [GIRDER + -ING[1]]

gir·dle (gûr′dᵊl), *n., v.,* **-dled, -dling.** —*n.* **1.** a lightweight undergarment, worn esp. by women, often boned or partly or entirely of elastic, for supporting and giving a slimmer appearance to the abdomen, hips, and buttocks. **2.** a belt, cord, sash, or the like, worn about the waist. **3.** anything that encircles, confines, or limits. **4.** *Jewelry.* the edge or narrow band between the upper and lower facets of a gem. **5.** *Anat.* the bony framework that unites the upper or lower extremities to the axial skeleton. **6.** *Archit.* an ornamental band, esp. one surrounding the shaft of a column. **7.** a ring made about a tree trunk, branch, etc., by removing a band of bark. —*v.t.* **8.** to encircle with a belt; gird. **9.** to encompass; enclose; encircle. **10.** to move around (something or someone) in a circle. **11.** to cut away the bark in a ring around (a tree, branch, etc.). **12.** *Jewelry.* round (def. 54). [ME; OE *gyrdel*, deriv. of *girdan* to GIRD[1]] —**gir′dle·like′,** *adj.* —**gir′dling·ly,** *adv.*

gir·dler (gûrd′lər), *n.* **1.** one who or that which girdles. **2.** any of several insects, as a beetle, *Oncideres cingulata* (**twig girdler**), that cut a groove around the bark of a twig, stem, etc. **3.** a person who makes girdles. [late ME; see GIRDLE, -ER[1]]

gir′dle-tailed liz′ard (gûr′dᵊl tāld′), any of several African lizards of the family *Cordylidae*, having a spiny tail that can be curled across the soft belly for protection.

Gir·gen·ti (*It.* jēr jen′tē), *n.* former name of **Agrigento.**

girl (gûrl), *n.* **1.** a female child or young person. **2.** a young unmarried woman. **3.** a female servant or employee. **4.** a man's or boy's sweetheart. **5.** *Informal.* a woman. **6.** *Informal.* a daughter: *My wife and I have two girls.* [ME *gurle, girle* child, young person, OE *gyrl-* (in *gyrlgyden* virgin goddess); cf. LG *göre* young person]

girl′ Fri′day, **1.** a woman who acts as a secretary or general assistant in a business office or to an executive. **2.** a female office worker with a wide variety of secretarial and clerical duties, esp. in a small office. Also, **gal Friday.** [modeled on MAN FRIDAY]

girl′ friend′, **1.** a female friend. **2.** the girl for whom a boy or man feels a particular attraction and affection; sweetheart.

girl′ guide′, a member of a British organization of girls (**Girl′ Guides′**) founded in England by Lord Robert S. S. Baden-Powell and his sister Lady Agnes as a sister organization of the Girl Scouts.

girl·hood (gûrl′ho͝od), *n.* **1.** the state or time of being a girl. **2.** girls collectively: *the nation's girlhood.* [GIRL + -HOOD]

girl·ie (gûr′lē), *adj.* featuring nude or scantily clad young women: *Without the comedians, burlesque is just a girlie show; girlie magazines.* Also, **girly.** [GIRL + -IE]

girl·ish (gûr′lish), *adj.* of, like, or befitting a girl or girlhood: *girlish laughter.* [GIRL + ISH[1]] —**girl′ish·ly,** *adv.* —**girl′ish·ness,** *n.*

girl-o (gûrl′ō), *n., pl.* **girl-os.** *Australian Informal.* a girl or young woman. [GIRL + *-o* suffix of appurtenance]

Girl′ of the Gold′en West′, The, an opera (1910) by Giacomo Puccini. Italian, **La Fanciulla del West.**

girl′ scout′, a member of an organization of girls (**Girl′ Scouts′**) founded in the U.S. in 1912 by Juliette Low to develop health, citizenship, character, and homemaking ability.

girl·y (gûr′lē), *adj.* girlie.

girn[1] (gûrn), *v.i., v.t., n. Scot.* grin[1].

girn[2] (gûrn), *n., v.t. Scot.* grin[2].

gi·ro (jī′rō), *n., pl.* **-ros.** autogiro. [by shortening]

Gi·ronde (jə rond′; *Fr.* zhē rôNd′), *n.* **1.** an estuary in SW France, formed by the junction of the Garonne and Dordogne rivers. 45 mi. long. **2.** a department in SW France. 935,448 (1962); 4141 sq. mi. *Cap.:* Bordeaux. **3. the Gironde,** the party of the Girondists.

Gi·ron·dist (jə ron′dist), *n.* **1.** *Fr. Hist.* a member of a political party of moderate republicans (1791–93) whose leaders were deputies from the department of Gironde. —*adj.* **2.** of or pertaining to the Girondists. [< F *Girondiste.* See GIRONDE, -IST] —**Gi·ron′dism,** *n.*

gir·o·sol (jir′ə sôl′, -sōl′, -sol′), *n.* girasol.

gi·rou·ette (zhē ro͞o et′), *n., pl.* **-ettes** (-et′). *French* a weathercock.

girt[1] (gûrt), *v.* **1.** a pt. and pp. of **gird**[1]. —*adj.* **2** *Naut.* (of a vessel) so tightly moored as not to swing with the wind or current.

girt[2] (gûrt), *v.t.* gird[1] (def. 1).

girt[3] (gûrt), *n., v.t.* girth[1].

girt[4] (gûrt), *n.* **1.** *Carpentry.* **a.** a timber or plate connecting the corner posts of an exterior wooden frame, as a braced frame, at a floor above the ground floor. **b.** a heavy beam, as for supporting the ends of rafters. **2.** *Print.* (in certain hand presses) one of a pair of leather straps having one end fastened to the bed and the other to the rounce, for drawing the bed under the platen. [alter. of GIRTH[1]]

girth[1] (gûrth), *n.* **1.** the measure around anything; circumference. **2.** a band that passes underneath a horse or other animal to hold a saddle in place, esp. one having a buckle at each end for fastening to straps running from under the flaps of the saddle. **3.** a band or girdle. —*v.t.* **4.** to bind or fasten with a girth. **5.** to girdle; encircle. Also, **girt.** [ME *girth, gerth* < Scand; cf. Icel *gjördh* girdle, hoop; akin to GIRD[1]]

girth[2] (gûrth), *n.* **1.** *Scot.* a place of protection or asylum. **2.** *Obs.* grith. [var. of GRITH]

girth·line (gûrth′līn′), *n. Naut.* gantline. [var. of GIRTLINE]

Gir·tin (gûr′tin), *n.* **Thomas,** 1775–1802, English painter.

girt·line (gûrt′līn′), *n. Naut.* gantline. [GIRT[1] + LINE[1]]

gi·sant (*Fr.* zhē zäN′), *n., pl.* **-sants** (*Fr.* -zäN′). a sculptured representation of a dead person in a recumbent position, usually as part of a sepulchral monument. [< F, n. use of prp. of *gésir* to lie < L *jacēre*; see -ANT]

gi·sarme (gi zärm′), *n.* guisarme.

Gis·borne (giz′bərn), *n.* a seaport on E North Island, in N New Zealand. 20,900 (est. 1959).

Gis·card d'Estaing (zhē skar de staN′), **Va·lé·ry** (va lā rē′), born 1926, French political leader: president 1974–81.

Gi·selle (ji zel′; *Fr.* zhē zel′), *n.* a girl's given name, form of **Elizabeth.** Also, **Gisele.**

Gish (gish), *n.* **Dorothy,** 1898–1968, and her sister **Lillian,** born 1896, U.S. actresses.

gis·mo (giz′mō), *n., pl.* **-mos.** *Informal.* a gadget; a thing. Also, **gizmo.** [?]

Gis·sing (gis′ing), *n.* **George (Robert),** 1857–1903, English novelist.

gist (jist), *n.* **1.** the main or essential part of a matter: *What was the gist of his speech?* **2.** the ground of a legal action. [ME *giste* < OF, 3rd pers. pres. indic. of *gésir* to lie, *gésir en* to consist in, depend on < L *jacēre* to lie]

git (git), *v. Dial.* get.

G.I. tag, *Informal.* See **identification tag.**

Gi·ta·na (ji tä′nə; *Sp.* hē tä′nä), *n.* a girl's given name.

gi·tim (gē tēm′), *n. Hebrew.* pl. of **get.**

git·tern (git′ərn), *n.* cittern.

Giu·ba (jo͞o′bä), *n.* Italian name of **Juba.**

Giu·ki (gyo͞o′kē), *n.* (in the *Volsunga Saga*) a king, the father of Gudrun and Gunnar and the husband of Grimhild. Also, **Gjuki.**

Giu·kung (gyo͞o′ko͞ong), *n.* (in the *Volsunga Saga*) any member of the family of Giuki. Also, **Gjukung.**

Giu·lio Ro·ma·no (jo͞ol′yō rô mä′nô), (*Giulio Pippi de' Giannuzzi*) 1492?–1546, Italian painter and architect.

Giu·sep·pe (jo͞o zep′ē; *It.* jo͞o zep′pe), *n.* a boy's given name, Italian form of **Joseph.**

give (giv), *v.*, **gave, giv·en, giv·ing,** *n.* —*v.t.* **1.** to present voluntarily and without expecting compensation; bestow: *to give a birthday present.* **2.** to place in someone's care: *If you give me your bag, sir, I'll put it in your room.* **3.** to hand to someone: *Give me a match.* **4.** to pay or transfer possession to another in exchange for something: *They gave five dollars for the pictures. What will you give for my car?* **5.** to grant (permission, opportunity, etc.) to someone: *Give me a chance.* **6.** to set forth or show; present; offer: *He gave no reason for his lateness.* **7.** to assign or admit as a basis of calculation or reasoning (usually used passively): *These facts being given, the argument makes sense.* **8.** to furnish, provide, or proffer: *to give evidence; He gave her his arm when they crossed the street.* **9.** to produce, yield, or afford: *to give good results; 9 × 8 gives 72; The hen gave 6 eggs a week.* **10.** to make, do, or perform: *to give a start; to give a lurch.* **11.** to put forth, emit, or utter; issue: *to give a cry; to give a command.* **12.** to impart or communicate: *to give advice; to give a cold to someone.* **13.** to deal or administer: *to give a blow to someone; to give medicine to a patient.* **14.** to relinquish or surrender: *to give one's life for a cause.* **15.** to perform publicly: *to give a play; to give a concert.* **16.** to cause; be responsible for (usually fol. by an infinitive): *They gave me to understand that you would be there.* **17.** to care about something to the value or extent of (something fanciful): *I don't give a hoot about culture.* **18.** to present to an audience, as an entertainer, speaker, act, etc.: *Ladies and gentlemen, I give you the Governor of New York.* **19.** to be connected with, as by a telephone operator: *Give me 235-7522.* **20.** to bestow (the object of one's choice) upon, as if by providence: *If this is gracious urban living, give me ungracious country living every time.* **21.** to propose as the subject of a toast: *Ladies and gentlemen, I give you our country.* **22.** to provide as an entertainment or social function: *to give a dinner for 20 guests.* **23.** to convey or transmit: *Give Aunt Betty my love.* **24.** to assign or allot: *Give every man a full ration of biscuits. They gave him the name of "Joseph."* **25.** to attribute or ascribe: *to give the Devil his due.* **26.** to cause or occasion: *She gives me a pain in the neck.* **27.** to apply fully or freely: *He gives his free time to golf.* **28.** to award by verdict or after consideration: *A decision was given for the defendant.* **29.** to inflict as a punishment; punish by; give a sentence of: *The judge gave him five years.* **30.** to pledge, offer as a pledge, or execute and deliver: *He gave her his promise. Can you give bond?* **31.** to make pregnant, or get, with: *He gave her two children in the first five years of marriage.* **32.** to bear, or be delivered of (fol. by an indirect object): *She gave him a beautiful baby boy.* —*v.i.* **33.** to make a gift or gifts; contribute: *to give to the Red Cross.* **34.** to afford a view or passage; to face, open, or lead (usually fol. by *on, onto,* etc.): *The window gives on the sea. This door gives onto the hallway.* **35.** to yield somewhat, as to influence or force; compromise: *We can't negotiate until each side is willing to give on some points.* **36.** to yield somewhat when subjected to weight, force, pressure, etc.: *A horsehair mattress doesn't give much.* **37.** to collapse; break down; fall apart; fail: *At the height of the storm the bridge gave. The antique chair gave when she sat on it.* **38.** *Informal.* to divulge information: *Okay now, give! What happened?* **39.** to be warm and open in relationships with other persons: *a withdrawn person who doesn't know how to give.* **40. give and take, a.** to compromise in order to cooperate: *A willingness to give and take is important for success in marriage.* **b.** to exchange ideas: *an informal meeting in which there would be opportunities to give and take.* **41. give away, a.** to give as a present; bestow. **b.** to present (the bride) to the bridegroom in a marriage ceremony. **c.** to expose or betray (a person). **d.** to reveal (a confidence or secret, hidden motives, true feelings, etc.): *That remark gives away his real opinion on the matter.* **42. give back,** to return (something), as to its owner; restore: *You haven't given back the books you borrowed from me.* **43. give battle.** See **battle**[1] (def. 5). **44. give birth to.** See **birth** (def. 8). **45. give ground,** to yield before superior force, as of arms or of reasoning. **46. give in, a.** to acknowledge defeat; yield. **b.** to hand in; deliver: *Please give in your timecards.* **47. give it to,** *Informal.* to reprimand or punish: *His father gave it to him for breaking another window.* **48. give of,** to devote or contribute generously of: *to give of oneself; to give of one's abundance.* **49. give off,** to put forth; emit: *The gardenia gives off a very strong fragrance.* **50. give out, a.** to send out; emit. **b.** to make public; announce. **c.** to distribute; issue. **d.** to become exhausted. **e.** to become used up; fail: *The fuel gave out before the plane could reach the airfield.* **f.** to do or express something, esp. unrestrainedly or easily: *to give out with a song.* **51. give over, a.** to put into the care of; transfer: *She gave over all her property to her son.* **b.** to put an end to; stop: *They will never give over their impossible dreams.* **c.** to indulge in without restraint: *She gave herself over to tears.* **d.** to devote to a specified activity: *The day was given over to relaxing in the sun.* **52. give rise to.** See **rise** (def. 53). **53. give up, a.** to abandon hope; despair. **b.** to desist from; renounce: *to give up smoking.* **c.** to surrender; relinquish. **d.** to devote (oneself) entirely to: *The students gave themselves up to demonstrations against the new ruling.* **54. give way.** See **way** (def. 27). —*n.* **55.** the quality or state of being resilient; springiness. [ME < Scand (cf. Dan *give*); r. ME *yeven, yiven,* OE *gefan, gi(e)fan;* c. D *geven,* G *geben,* Goth *giban*] —**giv′a·ble,** *adj.* —**giv′er,** *n.*

—**Syn. 1.** offer, vouchsafe, impart, accord, furnish, provide, supply, donate, contribute. GIVE, CONFER, GRANT, PRESENT may mean that something concrete or abstract is bestowed on one person by another. GIVE is the general word: *to give someone a book, permission, etc.* CONFER usually means to give an honor or a favor; it implies courteous and gracious giving: *to confer a degree.* GRANT is limited to the idea of acceding to a request; it may apply to the bestowal of privileges, or the fulfillment of an expressed wish: *to grant a charter, a prayer, permission, etc.* PRESENT, a more formal word than give, usually implies a certain ceremony in the giving: *to present a citation to a regiment.* **14.** cede, yield. **35.** recede, retire. —**Ant. 1.** receive.

give-and-take (giv′ən tāk′), *n.* **1.** the practice of dealing by compromise or mutual concession; cooperation. **2.** good-humored exchange of talk, ideas, etc.

give·a·way (giv′ə wā′), *n.* **1.** a betrayal of a secret, hidden motive, repressed feeling, etc., usually unintentional. **2.** a premium given with various articles, as to promote sales. **3.** an unscrupulous deal, esp. one which benefits some while defrauding others. **4.** a radio or television program on which prizes are given away to contestants in a question-and-answer game. [n. use of v. phrase *give away*]

giv·en (giv′ən), *v.* **1.** pp. of **give.** —*adj.* **2.** stated, fixed, or specified: *at a given time.* **3.** addicted or disposed (often fol. by *to*): *given to making impromptu speeches.* **4.** bestowed as a gift; conferred. **5.** assigned as a basis of calculation, reasoning, etc.: *Given A and B, C follows.* **6.** *Math.* known or independently determined: *a given magnitude.* **7.** (on official documents) executed and delivered as of the date shown.

giv′en name′, the name given to one, as contrasted with an inherited family name; first name; Christian name: *His given name is John.*

Gi·za (gē′zə), *n.* See **El Giza.** Also, **Gi′zeh.**

giz·mo (giz′mō), *n., pl.* **-mos.** gismo.

giz·zard (giz′ərd), *n.* **1.** the muscular portion of the stomach of birds, in which food is ground after leaving the proventriculus; ventriculus. **2.** *Informal.* the innards or viscera collectively, esp. the intestine and stomach. [ME *giser* < OF *giser, gezier* (F *gésier*) < VL **giger(ium);* cf. L *gigeria* the cooked entrails of poultry]

giz′zard shad′, a silvery herring, *Dorosoma cepedianum,* found in the eastern and central U.S., that has a gizzardlike stomach and is used as food by game fishes.

Gjel·le·rup (gel′ə ro͝op), *n.* **Karl** (kärl), 1857–1919, Danish novelist: Nobel prize 1917.

Gju·ki (gyo͞o′kē), *n.* Giuki.

Gju·kung (gyo͞o′ko͝ong), *n.* Giukung.

Gk., Greek. Also, **Gk**

Gl, *Chem.* glucinum.

gl., 1. glass. **2.** gloss.

gla·bel·la (glə bel′ə), *n., pl.* **-bel·lae** (-bel′ē). *Anat.* the flat area of bone between the eyebrows, used as a craniometric point. [< NL, fem. of L *glabellus* smooth, hairless, equiv. to *glab(er)* without hair, smooth + *-ella* dim. suffix] —**gla·bel′lar,** *adj.*

gla·bel·lum (glə bel′əm), *n., pl.* **-bel·la** (-bel′ə). glabella.

Gla·ber (glā′bər; *Fr.* glA beR′), *n.* **Ra·oul** (rä o͞ol′), or **Ru·dolphe** (ro͞o dôlf′), c990–c1050, French ecclesiastic and chronicler.

gla·brate (glā′brāt, -brit), *adj.* **1.** *Zool.* glabrous. **2.** *Bot.* becoming glabrous; somewhat glabrous. [< L *glabrāt(us)* made bare, deprived of hair (ptp. of *glabrāre*), equiv. to *glabr-* without hair, smooth + *-ātus* -ATE[1]]

gla·bres·cent (glə bres′ənt), *adj. Bot.* becoming glabrous. [< L *glabrescent-* (s. of *glabrescēns,* prp. of *glabrescere*), equiv. to *glabr-* smooth + *-escent-* -ESCENT]

gla·brous (glā′brəs), *adj. Zool., Bot.* smooth or bald; having a surface devoid of hair or pubescence. [< L *glabr(um)* (s. of *glaber*) smooth, hairless + -OUS]

gla·cé (gla sā′), *adj., v.,* **-céed, -cé·ing.** —*adj.* **1.** frozen. **2.** frosted or iced, as cake. **3.** candied, as fruits. **4.** finished with a gloss, as kid or silk. —*v.t.* **5.** to make glacé; ice. [< F, ptp. of *glacer* to freeze, deriv. of *glace* ice < L *glac(iēs)*]

gla·cial (glā′shəl), *adj.* **1.** characterized by the presence of ice in extensive masses or glaciers. **2.** resulting from or associated with the action of ice or glaciers: *glacial terrain.* **3.** of or pertaining to glaciers or ice sheets. **4.** bitterly cold; frigid; icy: *a glacial winter wind.* **5.** icily unsympathetic or immovable: *a glacial stare; glacial indifference.* **6.** *Chem.* of, pertaining to, or tending to develop into, icelike crystals: *glacial phosphoric acid.* [< L *glaciāl(is)* icy, equiv. to *glaci(ēs)* ice + *-ālis* -AL[1]] —**gla′cial·ly,** *adv.*

gla′cial ace′tic ac′id, *Chem.* acetic acid of at least 99.5 percent concentration, solidifying at 16.7°C.

gla′cial depos′it, material, as gravel, sand, clay, etc., transported and deposited by a glacier.

gla′cial ep′och, 1. Also called **glacial period.** the geologically recent Pleistocene epoch, during which much of the northern hemisphere was covered by great ice sheets. **2.** any one of the Permian, Carboniferous, Cambrian, or Precambrian glaciations.

gla·cial·ist (glā′shə list), *n.* a person who studies geological phenomena involving the action of ice, esp. of glaciers. [GLACIAL + -IST]

gla′cial meal′, finely ground rock material produced by the action of a glacier on its bed. Also called **rock flour.**

gla′cial milk′, waters of a glacial stream in which particles of light-colored silt are suspended.

gla′cial pe′riod. See **glacial epoch** (def. 1).

gla·ci·ate (glā′shē āt′, -sē-), *v.,* **-at·ed, -at·ing.** —*v.t.* **1.** to cover with ice or glaciers. **2.** to affect by glacial action. —*v.i.* **3.** to become frozen or covered with ice or glaciers. [< L *glaciāt(us)* made into ice (ptp. of *glaciāre*), equiv. to *glaci(ēs)* ice + *-ātus* -ATE[1]] —**gla′ci·a′tion,** *n.*

gla·cier (glā′shər), *n.* an extended mass of ice formed from snow falling and accumulating over the years and moving very slowly, either descending from high mountains, as in valley glaciers, or moving outward from centers of accumulation, as in continental glaciers. [< dial. F, deriv. of OF *glace* < LL *glacia* (alter. of L *glaciēs* ice)] —**gla′ciered,** *adj.*

gla′cier lil′y, a dogtooth violet, *Erythronium grandiflorum,* of western North America, having bright yellow flowers. Also called **snow lily.**

Gla′cier Na′tional Park′, a national park in NW Montana: glaciers; lakes; forest reserve. 1534 sq. mi.

gla′cier ta′ble, a stone slab supported over the surface of a mountain glacier by a column or columns of ice.

gla·ci·ol·o·gy (glā′shē ol′ə jē, -sē-), *n.* the branch of geology that deals with the nature, distribution, and action of glaciers and with their effects on the earth's topography. [GLACI(ER) + -O- + -LOGY] —**gla·ci·o·log·i·cal** (glā′shē ə loj′i kəl, -sē-), **gla′ci·o·log′ic,** *adj.* —**gla′ci·ol′o·gist,** *n.*

gla·cis (glā′sis, glas′is), *n., pl.* **gla·cis** (glā′sēz, -siz, glas′ēz, -iz), **gla·cis·es. 1.** a gentle slope. **2.** *Fort.* a bank of earth in front of the counterscarp or covered way of a fort, having an easy slope toward the field or open country. [< MF; akin to OF *glacier* to slide; cf. L *glaciāre* to make into ice; see GLACÉ]

Glack·ens (glak′ənz), *n.* **William James,** 1870–1938, U.S. painter and illustrator.

glad[1] (glad), *adj.,* **glad·der, glad·dest,** *v.,* **glad·ded, glad·ding.** —*adj.* **1.** feeling joy or pleasure; delighted; pleased: *glad about the good news; glad that you are here.* **2.** attended with or causing joy or pleasure: *a glad occasion; glad tidings.* **3.** characterized by or showing cheerfulness, joy, or pleasure, as looks, utterances, etc. **4.** willing: *I'll be glad to do you a favor.* —*v.t.* **5.** *Archaic.* to make glad. [ME; OE *glæd;* c. Icel *gladhr* bright, glad, D *glad,* G *glatt* smooth; akin to L *glaber* smooth] —**glad′ly,** *adv.* —**glad′ness,** *n.* —**Syn. 1.** elated, gratified, contented. **3.** merry, joyous, joyful, cheerful, happy, cheery. —**Ant. 1, 2, 3.** sad.

glad[2] (glad), *n. Informal.* gladiolus (def. 1). [by shortening]

Glad (glad), *n.* a girl's given name.

Glad·bach-Rheydt (glät′bäkh rīt′), *n.* a former city in W West Germany; now part of Mönchen-Gladbach.

glad·den (glad′ᵊn), *v.t.* **1.** to make glad. —*v.i.* **2.** *Obs.* to be glad. [ME; see GLAD[1], -EN[1]] —**glad′den·er,** *n.* —**Syn. 1.** See **cheer.**

glade (glād), *n.* an open space in a forest. [akin to GLAD[1], in obs. sense "bright"] —**glade′like′,** *adj.*

Glade·wa·ter (glād′wô′tər, -wot′ər), *n.* a town in E Texas. 5742 (1960).

glad′ eye′, *Informal.* a friendly or interested glance, esp. one intended to encourage attentions from someone of the opposite sex: *She gave every man she met the glad eye.*

glad′ hand′, *Informal.* a hearty welcome or enthusiastic reception that is often effusive or hypocritical: *Visiting dignitaries were being given the glad hand.*

glad-hand (glad′hand′), *v.t. Informal.* **1.** to greet warmly. **2.** to greet in an insincerely effusive manner. —**glad′-hand′er,** *n.*

glad·i·ate (glad′ē it, -āt′, glā′dē-), *adj. Bot.* sword-shaped. [< L *gladi(us)* sword + -ATE[1]]

glad·i·a·tor (glad′ē ā′tər), *n.* **1.** (in ancient Rome) a person, often a slave or captive, who was armed with a sword or other weapon and compelled to fight to the death in a public arena against another person or a wild animal, for the entertainment of the spectators. **2.** a person who engages in a fight or controversy. **3.** a prizefighter. [< L *gladiātōr-* (s. of *gladiātor*), equiv. to *gladi(us)* sword + *-ātōr-* -ATOR]

glad·i·a·to·ri·al (glad′ē ə tôr′ē əl, -tōr′-), *adj.* pertaining to gladiators or to their combats. [< L *gladiātōri(us)* (see GLADIATOR) + -AL[1]]

glad·i·o·la (glad′ē ō′lə), *n.* gladiolus. [< L, neut. pl. treated as if fem. sing.] —**glad′i·o′lar,** *adj.*

glad·i·o·lus (glad′ē ō′ləs), *n., pl.* **-lus, -li** (-lī), **-lus·es** for 1; **-li** for 2. **1.** any iridaceous plant of the genus *Gladiolus,* native esp. to Africa, having erect, gladiate leaves and spikes of variously colored flowers. **2.** *Anat.* the middle and largest segment of the sternum. Cf. **manubrium** (def. 2a), **xiphisternum.** [< L: small sword, sword lily, equiv. to *gladi(us)* sword + *-olus* dim. suffix]

gla·di·us (glā′dē əs), *n., pl.* **-di·i** (-dē ī′). a short sword used in ancient Rome by legionaries. [< L]

glad′ rags′, *Slang.* dressy clothes, esp. evening clothes.

Glads·heim (gläts′hām), *n. Scand. Myth.* the golden palace of Odin, of which Valhalla was a part.

glad·some (glad′səm), *adj.* **1.** giving or causing joy; delightful. **2.** glad. [ME; see GLAD[1], -SOME[1]] —**glad′some·ly,** *adv.* —**glad′some·ness,** *n.*

Glad·stone (glad′stōn′, -stən), *n.* **1.** a four-wheeled pleasure carriage with a calash top, two inside seats, and dickey seats. **2.** See **Gladstone bag. 3.** Also called **Gladstone wine, Glad′stone clar′et.** *Brit. Slang.* cheap French wine. [after William GLADSTONE]

Glad·stone (glad′stōn′, -stən), *n.* **1. William Ew·art** (yo͞o′ərt), 1809–98, British statesman: prime minister four times between 1868 and 1894. **2.** a town in NW Michigan, in the Upper Peninsula. 5267 (1960). **3.** a town in NW Oregon. 3854 (1960).

Glad′stone bag′, a small rectangular suitcase hinged to open into two compartments of equal size. [after William GLADSTONE]

Glad′stone wine′, *Brit. Slang.* Gladstone (def. 3). Also called **Glad′stone clar′et.**

Glad·win (glad′win), *n.* a boy's given name.

Glad·ys (glad′is), *n.* a girl's given name.

Glag·o·lit·ic (glag′ə lit′ik), *adj.* **1.** noting or written in an alphabet, probably invented by St. Cyril in about A.D. 865, formerly used in writing Old Church Slavonic and other Slavic languages: almost completely replaced by Cyrillic starting about the 10th century. —*n.* **2.** the Glagolitic alphabet. [< NL *glagolitic(us),* irreg. < Serbo-Croatian *glagolica* < OSlav *glagolŭ* word]

glaik·it (glā′kit), *adj. Scot. and North Eng.* **1.** foolish; senseless. **2.** (of women) giddy; flighty. Also, **glaik′et.** [ME < ?] —**glaik′it·ness, glaik′et·ness,** *n.*

glair (glâr), *n.* **1.** the white of an egg. **2.** a glaze or size made of egg white. **3.** any viscous substance like egg white. —*v.t.* **4.** to coat with glair. Also, **glaire.** [ME *glaire* < OF: white of an egg < VL **clāris;* cf. L *clārus* clear]

glaire (glâr), *n., v.t.,* **glaired, glair·ing.** glair.

glair·y (glâr′ē), *adj.,* **glair·i·er, glair·i·est. 1.** of the nature of glair; viscous. **2.** covered with glair. Also, **glair·e·ous** (glâr′ē əs). [GLAIR + -Y[1]] —**glair′i·ness,** *n.*

Glai·sher (glā′shər), *n.* a walled plain in the first quadrant of the face of the moon: about 10 miles in diameter.

glaive (glāv), *n. Archaic.* a sword or broadsword. [ME < OF *glaive, glai* < L *glad(ius)* sword] —**glaived,** *adj.*

Gla·mor·gan·shire (glə môr′gən shēr′, -shər), *n.* a county in SE Wales. 1,227,828 (1961); 816 sq. mi. *Co. seat:* Cardiff. Also called **Gla·mor′gan.**

glam·or·ize (glam′ə rīz′), *v.t.*, **-ized, -iz·ing. 1.** to make glamorous. **2.** to glorify or romanticize: *Don't glamorize war.* Also, **glamourize.** [GLAMOUR + -IZE] —**glam′or·i·za′tion,** *n.* —**glam′or·iz′er,** *n.*

glam·or·ous (glam′ər əs), *adj.* **1.** full of glamour; charmingly or fascinatingly attractive, especially in a mysterious or magical way. **2.** full of excitement, adventure, and unusual activity so as to arouse envy: *the glamorous job of a foreign correspondent.* Also, **glam′our·ous.** [GLAMOUR + -OUS] —**glam′or·ous·ly, glam′our·ous·ly,** *adv.* —**glam′or·ous·ness, glam′our·ous·ness,** *n.*

glam·our (glam′ər), *n.* **1.** excitement, adventure, and unusual activity such as to arouse envy: *the glamour of being an explorer.* **2.** the quality of fascinating, alluring, or attracting, esp. by a combination of charm and good looks. **3.** magic or enchantment; spell; witchery. Also, **glam′or.** [earlier *glammar,* dissimilated var. of GRAMMAR in sense of occult learning]

glam′our girl′, a girl or woman, esp. a widely known beauty, whose appearance is considered glamorous by popular standards.

glam·our·ize (glam′ə rīz′), *v.t.* glamorize. —**glam′our·i·za′tion,** *n.* —**glam′our·iz′er,** *n.*

glam′our puss′, *Slang.* someone with an unusually attractive face: *"Ooh," she squealed, "he's a real glamour puss!"*

glance[1] (glans, gläns), *v.*, **glanced, glanc·ing,** *n.* —*v.i.* **1.** to look quickly or briefly. **2.** to gleam or flash: *a silver brooch glancing in the sunlight.* **3.** to strike a surface or object obliquely, esp. so as to bounce off at an angle: (often fol. by *off*): *The arrow glanced off his shield.* **4.** to allude briefly to a topic or subject in passing (usually fol. by *at*). —*v.t. Archaic.* **5.** to cast a glance or brief look at; catch a glimpse of. **6.** to cast or reflect, as a gleam. **7.** to throw, hit, kick, shoot, etc. (something) so that it glances off a surface or object. —*n.* **8.** a quick or brief look. **9.** a gleam or flash of light, esp. reflected light. **10.** a deflected movement or course; an oblique rebound. **11.** a passing reference or allusion; insinuation. **12.** *Cricket.* a stroke in which the batsman deflects the ball with the bat, as to leg. [late ME; nasalized var. of ME *glacen* to strike a glancing blow < OF *glac(i)er* to slip, slide < L *glaciāre* to freeze. See GLACÉ] —**glanc′ing·ly,** *adv.*
—**Syn. 2.** glisten, scintillate. See **flash. 3.** reflect, ricochet. **9.** glitter.

glance[2] (glans, gläns), *n. Mining, Mineral.* any of various minerals having a luster that indicates a metallic nature. [< G *Glanz,* brightness, luster]

glance′ pitch′, a pure asphalt found mainly on Trinidad. Also called **manjak, manjack.**

glanc′ing an′gle, *Optics.* the angle between a ray incident on a plane surface and the surface, as of a beam of electrons incident on a crystal; the complement of the angle of incidence.

gland[1] (gland), *n.* **1.** *Anat.* **a.** a cell, group of cells, or organ producing a secretion. **b.** any of various organs or structures resembling the shape but not the function of true glands. **2.** *Bot.* a secreting organ or structure, esp. one on or near a surface. [ME < L *gland(ēs)* (pl. of *glāns* acorn); cf. It *ghianda*] —**gland′less,** *adj.* —**gland′like′,** *adj.*

gland[2] (gland), *n. Mach.* **1.** a sleeve within a stuffing box, fitted over a shaft or valve stem and tightened against compressible packing in such a way as to prevent leakage of fluid while allowing the shaft or stem to move; lantern ring. **2.** See **stuffing box.** [?]

glan·dered (glan′dərd), *adj. Vet. Pathol.* affected with glanders. [GLANDER(S) + -ED[3]]

glan·ders (glan′dərz), *n.* (*construed as sing.*) *Vet. Pathol.* a contagious disease chiefly of horses and mules but communicable to man, caused by the microorganism *Actinobacillus mallei* and characterized by swellings beneath the jaw and a profuse mucous discharge from the nostrils. Cf. **farcy.** [late ME < MF *glandre(s)* swollen glands < L *glandulae* swollen glands, lit., little acorns. See GLAND[1], -ULE] —**glan′der·ous,** *adj.*

glan·du·lar (glan′jə lər), *adj.* **1.** consisting of, containing, or bearing glands. **2.** of, pertaining to, or resembling a gland: *a glandular disorder.* Also, **glandulous.** [GLANDULE + -AR[1]] —**glan′du·lar·ly,** *adv.*

glan′dular fe′ver, *Pathol.* See **infectious mononucleosis.**

glan·dule (glan′jo͞ol), *n. Anat.* a small gland. [< L *glandula.* See GLAND[1], -ULE]

glan·du·lous (glan′jə ləs), *adj.* glandular. [ME *glandelous* < L *glandulōs(us)* full of kernels. See GLANDULE, -OUS] —**glan′du·lous·ness,** *n.*

glans (glanz), *n., pl.* **glan·des** (glan′dēz). *Anat.* the head of the penis or of the clitoris. [< L: acorn, acorn-shaped ball; akin to Gk *bálanos*]

Glan′-Thomp′son prism′ (glan′tomp′sən), *Optics.* a polarizing calcite prism similar to a Nicol prism but with end faces cut perpendicular to the sides so that light enters and leaves the prism normal to the surfaces.

Glan·ville-Hicks (glan′vil hiks′), *n.* **Peggy,** born 1912, U.S. composer and music critic, born in Australia.

glare[1] (glâr), *n., v.,* **glared, glar·ing.** —*n.* **1.** a very harsh, bright, dazzling light. **2.** a fiercely or angrily piercing stare. **3.** dazzling or showy appearance; showiness. —*v.i.* **4.** to shine with or reflect a very harsh, bright, dazzling light. **5.** to stare with a fiercely or angrily piercing look. **6.** *Archaic.* to appear conspicuous; stand out obtrusively. —*v.t.* **7.** to express with a glare: *They glared their anger at each other.* [ME *glare(n);* c. MD, MLG *glaren;* akin to GLASS (cf. OE *glæren* glassy)] —**glare′less,** *adj.*
—**Syn. 1.** flare, glitter, flash. **4.** See **shine. 5.** GLARE, GLOWER, GLOAT all have connotations of emotion which accompany an intense gaze. To GLARE is to look piercingly or angrily: *A tiger glares at its prey.* To GLOWER is to look fiercely and threateningly, as from wrath; it suggests a scowl along with a glare: *to glower at a persistently mischievous child.* To GLOAT meant originally to look with exultation, avaricious or malignant, on something or someone: *a tyrant gloating over the helplessness of his victim.* Today, however, it may simply imply inner exultation.

glare[2] (glâr), *n.* a bright, smooth surface, as of ice. [special use of GLARE[1]]

glare′ ice′, ice having a smooth, glassy surface that reflects sunlight.

glar·ing (glâr′ing), *adj.* **1.** shining with or reflecting a dazzlingly or harshly bright or brilliant light. **2.** excessively showy or bright; garish. **3.** very conspicuous or obvious; flagrant: *several glaring defects.* **4.** staring in a fiercely or angrily piercing manner. [ME: see GLARE[1], -ING[2]] —**glar′ing·ly,** *adv.* —**glar′ing·ness,** *n.*

Gla·rus (glär′əs, -o͞os), *n.* **1.** a canton in E central Switzerland. 40,148 (1960); 264 sq. mi. **2.** a town in and the capital of this canton, E of Lucerne.

glar·y[1] (glâr′ē), *adj.,* **glar·i·er, glar·i·est.** harshly brilliant; glaring. [GLARE[1] + -Y[1]] —**glar′i·ness,** *n.*

glar·y[2] (glâr′ē), *adj.,* **glar·i·er, glar·i·est.** *U.S.* smooth and slippery, as ice. [GLARE[2] + -Y[1]]

Gla·ser (glā′zər), *n.* **Donald A.,** born 1926, U.S. physicist: Nobel prize 1960.

Glas·gow (glas′gō), *n.* **1. Ellen (Anderson Ghol·son)** (gōl′sən), 1874–1945, U.S. novelist. **2.** a seaport in SW Scotland, on the Clyde River: shipyards. 880,617.

glas·nost (gläs′nəst), *n. Russian.* the open and frank discussion of economic and political realities in the Soviet Union. initiated by Mikhail Gorbachev.

Glas·pell (glas′pel), *n.* **Susan,** 1882–1948, U.S. novelist and dramatist.

glass (glas, gläs), *n.* **1.** a hard, brittle, noncrystalline, more or less transparent substance produced by fusion, usually consisting of mutually dissolved silica and silicates that also contain soda and lime, as in the ordinary variety used for windows, bottles, etc. Cf. **crown glass, flint glass. 2.** any artificial or natural substance having similar properties and composition, as fused borax, obsidian, or the like. **3.** something made of such a substance, as a window. **4.** a tumbler or other comparatively tall, handleless drinking container. **5.** a mirror. **6.** a lens, esp. one used as a magnifying glass. **7.** a spyglass. **8.** a barometer. **9. glasses.** See **eyeglass** (def. 1) (usually used with *pair of*). **10.** things made of glass, collectively; glassware: *They used to collect old glass.* **11.** a glassful. —*adj.* **12.** made of glass: *a glass tray.* **13.** furnished or fitted with panes of glass; glazed. —*v.t.* **14.** to fit with panes of glass. **15.** cover with or encase in glass. **16.** to scan with a spyglass or other optical instrument. **17.** *Literary.* to reflect: *Trees glassed themselves in the lake.* [ME *glas,* OE *glæs;* c. D, G *glas*] —**glass′less,** *adj.* —**glass′like′,** *adj.*

Glass (glas, gläs), *n.* **Carter,** 1858–1946, U.S. statesman.

glass′ block′, a translucent-glass building unit for glazing openings or constructing partitions, consisting of a hollow or solid block, usually square on the face, having the outer surfaces treated in any of various ways. Also called **glass′ brick′.**

glass′ blow′ing, the art or process of forming or shaping a mass of molten or heat-softened glass into ware by blowing air into it through a tube. —**glass′ blow′er.**

glass′-cab·in launch′ (glas′kab′in, gläs′-), a passenger-carrying power craft of the early 20th century, operating in sheltered waters and having a large trunk cabin with large windows.

glass′ ceil′ing, an upper limit to professional advancement, esp. as imposed upon women, that is not readily perceived or openly acknowledged.

glass′ cur′tain, a transparent or translucent curtain covering the interior of a window opening.

glass′ cut′ter, 1. a person who cuts glass into specified sizes. **2.** a person who etches designs onto or otherwise decorates the surface of glass. **3.** a tool for cutting glass. —**glass′ cut′ting.**

glass-faced (glas′fāst′, gläs′-), *adj.* having the front or outer surfaces covered with glass.

glass·ful (glas′fo͝ol, gläs′-), *n., pl.* **-fuls.** an amount contained by or sufficient to fill a glass, or tumbler. [OE *glæs full.* See GLASS, -FUL]

glass′ gall′, sandiver.

glass′ harmon′ica, a musical instrument composed of a set of graduated, revolving glass bowls, the rims of which are moistened and set in vibration by friction from the fingertips.

glass·house (glas′hous′, gläs′-), *n., pl.* **-hous·es** (-hou′ziz). **1.** a glassworks. **2.** *Chiefly Brit.* a greenhouse. [GLASS + HOUSE]

glass·ine (gla sēn′), *n.* a glazed, semitransparent paper used for book jackets, for packaging foods, etc.

glass′ jaw′, a person's jaw, esp. that of a boxer, that is exceptionally vulnerable to even a light blow.

glass′ liz′ard, any of several limbless, snakelike lizards of the genus *Ophisaurus,* of the eastern U.S., having an extremely long and fragile tail that is replaced by a new one if broken off.

glass·mak·ing (glas′mā′king, gläs′-), *n.* the art of making glass or glassware. [GLASS + MAKING] —**glass′mak′er,** *n.*

glass·man (glas′mən, gläs′-), *n., pl.* **-men. 1.** a person who makes or sells glass. **2.** a glazier.

Glass′ Menag′erie, The, a play (1945) by Tennessee Williams.

Glass·port (glas′pōrt′, -pôrt′, gläs′-), *n.* a town in SW Pennsylvania. 8418 (1960).

glass′ pox′, *Pathol.* alastrim.

glass′ snake′, 1. (not used technically) a glass lizard. **2.** any of several lizards of Europe and Asia having an extremely fragile tail.

glass′ tank′, a reverberatory furnace in which glass is melted directly under the flames.

glass·ware (glas′wâr′, gläs′-), *n.* articles of glass, esp. glasses for a table setting. [GLASS + WARE[1]]

glass′ wool′, spun glass similar to wool, used for insulation, filters, etc.

glass·work (glas′wûrk′, gläs′-), *n.* **1.** the manufacture of glass and glassware. **2.** the fitting of glass; glazing. **3.** articles of glass collectively; glassware. [GLASS + WORK] —**glass′work′er,** *n.*

glass·works (glas′wûrks′, gläs′-), *n., pl.* **-works.** (*usually construed as sing.*) a factory where glass is made. [GLASS + WORKS]

glass·wort (glas′wûrt′, gläs′-), *n.* **1.** any of several chenopodiaceous herbs of the genus *Salicornia,* having succulent leafless stems, formerly used, when burned to ashes, as a source of soda for glassmaking. **2.** Also called **prickly glasswort.** the saltwort, *Salsola kali.* [GLASS + WORT[2]]

glass·y (glas′ē, glä′sē), *adj.,* **glass·i·er, glass·i·est,** *n., pl.* **-sies.** —*adj.* **1.** resembling glass, as in transparency, smoothness, etc. **2.** having an expressionless, dull stare: *glassy eyes.* **3.** expressionless; dull: *a glassy stare.* **4.** of the nature of glass; vitreous. —*n.* **5.** *Marbles.* a marble used as a shooter. [ME *glasy.* See GLASS, -Y[1]] —**glass′i·ly,** *adv.* —**glass′i·ness,** *n.*

glass·y-eyed (glas′ē īd′, glä′sē-), *adj.* having a dull or uncomprehending expression; staring fixedly.

Glas′ton·bur·y chair′ (glas′tən ber′ē), a folding chair having legs crossed front-to-back and having arms connected to the back and to the front seat rail. [after the abbey of *Glastonbury* in southwest England, site of the original chair]

Glas·we·gian (gla swē′jən, -jē ən), *adj.* **1.** of or characteristic of Glasgow or its inhabitants. —*n.* **2.** a native or inhabitant of Glasgow. [GLAS(GOW) + -*wegian* (abstracted from GALWEGIAN)]

glau·ber·ite (glou′bə rīt′), *n.* a mineral, sodium calcium sulfate, $Na_2Ca(SO_4)_2$, often found as a deposit on the beds of salt lakes. [< F; so called because chemically similar to GLAUBER'S SALT; see -ITE[1]]

Glau′ber's salt′ (glou′bərz), *Chem., Pharm.* the decahydrate form of sodium sulfate, a colorless, crystalline, water-soluble solid, $Na_2SO_4 \cdot 10H_2O$, used chiefly in textile dyeing and as a cathartic. Also, **Glau′ber salt′.** [named after J. R. *Glauber* (1604–68), German chemist]

Glau·ce (glô′sē), *n.* **1.** *Class. Myth.* Creusa (def. 1). **2.** a daughter of Cychreus who married Telamon.

glau·ces·cent (glô ses′ənt), *adj. Bot.* becoming glaucous; somewhat glaucous. [GLAUC- + -ESCENT] —**glau·ces′cence,** *n.*

Glau·cia (glô′shə), *n. Class. Myth.* a daughter of Scamander.

glauco-, a learned borrowing from Greek where it meant "gleaming," "bluish-gray"; used in the formation of technical terms: *glaucophane.* Also, *esp. before a vowel,* **glauc-.** [< Gk *glauko-, glauk-,* comb. form of *glaukós*]

glau·co·dote (glô′kə dōt′), *n.* a mineral, iron and cobalt sulfarsenide, (Co,Fe)AsS, occurring in grayish-white crystals. Also, **glau′co·dot′.** [< G *Glaukodot,* equiv. to *glauko-* GLAUCO- + *-dot* < Gk *dot(ḗr)* giver]

glau·co·ma (glô kō′mə, glou-), *n. Ophthalm.* a disease of the eye characterized by increased pressure within the eyeball and progressive loss of vision. [< Gk *glaúkōma* opacity of the eye lens. See GLAUC-, -OMA] —**glau·co·ma·tous** (glô kō′mə təs, -kom′ə-, glou-), *adj.*

glau·co·nite (glô′kə nīt′), *n.* a greenish micaceous mineral consisting essentially of a hydrous silicate of potassium, aluminum, and iron and occurring in greensand, clays, etc. [< Gk *glaukón,* neut. of *glaukós* (see GLAUCO-) + -ITE[1]] —**glau·co·nit·ic** (glô′kə nit′ik), *adj.*

glau·co·phane (glô′kə fān′), *n.* a sodium-rich monoclinic mineral of the amphibole family, usually metamorphic. [GLAUCO- + -PHANE]

glau·cous (glô′kəs), *adj.* **1.** light bluish green or greenish blue. **2.** *Bot.* covered with a whitish bloom, as a plum. [< L *glaucus* silvery, gray, bluish-green < Gk *glaukós.* See GLAUCO-, -OUS] —**glau′cous·ly,** *adv.*

glau′cous gull′, a large white and pale-gray gull, *Latus hyperboreus,* of arctic regions.

Glau·cus (glô′kəs), *n. Class. Myth.* **1.** a sea god loved by both Scylla and Circe, or, in some versions, by Amphitrite. **2.** a son of Minos who, having suffocated in a jar of honey, was returned to life by a magic herb discovered by a seer. **3.** a Lycian ally of the Trojans who made friends and exchanged armor with Diomedes upon discovering that their grandfathers had been friends.

glave (glāv), *n. Archaic.* glaive.

glaze (glāz), *v.,* **glazed, glaz·ing,** *n.* —*v.t.* **1.** to furnish or fill with sheets of glass: *to glaze a window.* **2.** to give a vitreous surface or coating to (a ceramic or the like), as by the application of a substance or by fusion of the body. **3.** to cover with a smooth, glossy surface or coating. **4.** *Cookery.* to coat (a food) with sugar, a sugar syrup, or some other glossy, edible substance. **5.** *Fine Arts.* to cover (a painted surface or parts of it) with a thin layer of transparent color in order to modify the tone. **6.** to give a glassy surface to, as by polishing. **7.** to give a coating of ice to (frozen food) by dipping in water. **8.** to grind (cutlery blades) in preparation for finishing. —*v.i.* **9.** to become glazed or glassy. **10.** (of a grinding wheel) to lose abrasive quality through polishing of the surface from wear. —*n.* **11.** a smooth, glossy surface or coating. **12.** the substance for producing such a coating. **13.** *Ceram.* **a.** a vitreous layer or coating on a piece of pottery. **b.** the substance of which such a layer or coating is made. **14.** *Fine Arts.* a thin layer of transparent color spread over a painted surface. **15.** a smooth, lustrous surface on certain fabrics, produced by treating the material with a chemical and calendering. **16.** *Cookery.* **a.** a substance used to coat a food, esp. sugar or sugar syrup. **b.** stock cooked down to a thin paste for applying to the surface of meats. **17.** Also called **glaze′ ice′, silver frost, silver thaw, verglas;** *esp. Brit.,* **glazed′ frost′.** a thin coating of ice on terrestrial objects, caused by rain that freezes on impact. Cf. **rime**[2] (def. 1). [ME *glasen,* deriv. of *glas* GLASS] —**glaz′er,** *n.* —**glaz′i·ly,** *adv.* —**glaz′i·ness,** *n.*

glazed (glāzd), *adj.* **1.** having a surface covered with a glaze; lustrous; smooth; glassy. **2.** fitted or set with glass. [GLAZE + -ED[2]]

glaze·ment (glāz′mənt), *n.* a waterproof glaze for a masonry wall. [GLAZE + -MENT]

glaz·er (glā′zər), *n.* **1.** a person who applies a glaze, as to pottery, baked goods, leather, fur, etc. **2.** any mechanical device used to apply a glaze. [ME *glauser.* See GLAZE, -ER[1]]

gla·zier (glā′zhər), *n.* a person who fits windows or the like with glass or panes of glass. [ME *glas(i)er.* See GLAZE, -ER[1]]

gla′zier's point′, a pointed piece of sheet metal, about one inch long, for holding a pane of glass in a sash until the putty has hardened. Also called **sprig.**

gla·zier·y (glā′zhə rē), *n.* the work of a glazier; glasswork. [GLAZIER + -Y[3]]

glaz·ing (glā′zing), *n.* **1.** the act of furnishing or fitting with glass; the business of a glazier. **2.** panes or sheets of glass set or made to be set in frames, as in windows, doors, mirrors, etc. **3.** the act of applying a glaze. **4.** the glassy surface of something glazed. [ME; see GLAZE, -ING[1]]

glaz′ing bar′, *Chiefly Brit.* muntin (def. 1).

glaz′ing bead′, a convex molding nailed against the edge of a pane of glass to hold it in place.

glaz′ing brad′. See **glazier's point.**

Gla·zu·nov (glä zo͞o nôf′), *n.* **A·le·xan·der Kon·stan·ti·no·vitch** (ä′le ksän′dər kon stän tē′no vich), 1865–1936, Russian composer. Also, **Gla·zu·noff′.**

glb, See **greatest lower bound.**

Gld., gulden.

gleam (glēm), *n.* **1.** a flash or beam of light. **2.** a dim or subdued light. **3.** a brief or slight manifestation or occurrence; trace: *a gleam of hope.* —*v.i.* **4.** to send forth a gleam or gleams. **5.** to appear suddenly and clearly like a flash of light. [ME *glem(e),* OE *glǣm;* c. OHG *gleimo* glowworm; akin to OS *glīmo* brightness. See GLIMMER, GLIMPSE] —**gleam′ing·ly,** *adv.* —**gleam′less,** *adj.*

—**Syn. 1.** GLEAM, GLIMMER, BEAM, RAY are terms for a stream of light. GLEAM denotes a not very brilliant, intermittent or nondirectional stream of light. GLIMMER indicates a nondirectional light that is feeble and unsteady: *a faint glimmer of moonlight.* BEAM usually means a directional, and therefore smaller, stream: *the beam from a searchlight.* RAY usually implies a still smaller amount of light than a beam, a single line of light: *a ray through a pinprick in a window shade.* **4.** shine, glimmer, flash, glitter, sparkle, beam.

glean (glēn), *v.t.* **1.** to gather slowly and laboriously, bit by bit. **2.** to gather (grain or the like) after the reapers or regular gatherers. **3.** to learn, discover, or find out. —*v.i.* **4.** to collect or gather anything little by little or slowly. **5.** to gather what is left by reapers. [ME *glen(en)* < OF *glen(er);* c. OPr *glenar, grenar* < LL *glenāre* << Celt] —**glean′a·ble,** *adj.* —**glean′er,** *n.*

glean·ing (glē′ning), *n.* **1.** the act of one who gleans. **2.** Usually, **gleanings.** something that is gleaned. [ME *glenynge.* See GLEAN, -ING[1]]

gle·ba (glē′bə), *n., pl.* **-bae** (-bē). *Bot.* the sporogenous tissue forming the central part of the sporophore in certain fungi, as in puffballs and stinkhorns. [< NL, L: clod; see GLEBE] —**gle′bal,** *adj.*

glebe (glēb), *n.* **1.** *Archaic.* soil; field. **2.** Also called **glebe′ land′.** *Brit.* the cultivable land owned by a parish church or ecclesiastical benefice. [ME < L *glēba, glæba* clod of earth] —**glebe′less,** *adj.*

glebe′ house′, *Brit. Archaic.* a parsonage, esp. one provided for the holder of a benefice.

glede (glēd), *n.* *Brit. Dial.* the common European kite, *Milvus ictinus.* Also, **gled** (gled). [ME; OE *glī(o)da;* c. OIcel *gledha;* akin to GLIDE]

glee[1] (glē), *n.* **1.** openly shown exultant joy; exultation; demonstrative pleasure. **2.** an unaccompanied part song for three or more voices, popular esp. in the 18th century. [ME; OE *glēo;* c. OIcel *glȳ,* akin to GLOW] —**Syn. 1.** merriment, jollity, hilarity, mirth, joviality, gaiety. See **mirth.**

glee[2] (glē), *Scot. and North Eng.* —*v.i.* **1.** to squint or look with one eye. —*n.* **2.** a squint. **3.** an imperfect eye, esp. one with a cast. Also, **gley.** [ME *glie(n)* (*gle(en)* < ? ON; c. OIcel *glyā* to shine]

Glee (glē), *n.* a girl's given name.

glee′ club′, a chorus organized for singing choral music.

gleed (glēd), *n.* *Dial.* a glowing coal. [ME *gleed(e),* OE *glēd;* c. G *Glut,* OIcel *glōdh;* akin to GLOW]

glee·ful (glē′fəl), *adj.* full of glee; merry; exultant. [GLEE[1] + -FUL] —**glee′ful·ly,** *adv.* —**glee′ful·ness,** *n.*

gleek[1] (glēk), *n.* *Archaic.* **1.** a joke, jest, or scoff. **2.** a trick. —*v.i., v.t.* *Obs.* **3.** to gibe; sneer. **4.** to cheat; trick. [?]

gleek[2] (glēk), *n.* an English card game for three persons played with a 44-card pack, popular from the 16th through the 18th century. [< MF *glic,* perh. < MD *ghelic* like, equal (c. D *gelijk,* G *gleich*); akin to OE *gelīc*]

glee·man (glē′mən), *n., pl.* **-men.** *Archaic.* a strolling professional singer; minstrel. [ME; OE *glēoman.* See GLEE[1], MAN[1]]

glee·some (glē′səm), *adj.* gleeful. [GLEE[1] + -SOME[1]] —**glee′some·ly,** *adv.* —**glee′some·ness,** *n.*

gleet (glēt), *n.* **1.** *Pathol.* **a.** a thin, morbid discharge, as from a wound. **b.** persistent or chronic gonorrhea. **2.** Also called **nasal gleet.** *Vet. Pathol.* an inflammation of the air passages of the nose of a horse, producing a thick discharge. **3.** *Scot.* soft mud, esp. around a marsh or bog; slime. [ME *glete* < MF *glete,* OF *glette* < L *glitt(us)* sticky] —**gleet′y,** *adj.*

gleet·y (glē′tē), *adj.,* **gleet·i·er, gleet·i·est.** characteristic of or resembling gleet. [GLEET + -Y[1]]

gleg (gleg), *adj.* *Scot. and North Eng.* **1.** quick or keen, esp. in sensory perception. **2.** (of objects) bright; shiny; sharp. [ME < Scand; cf. OIcel *gløggr;* c. Goth *glaggw(uba)* carefully; akin to GLOW] —**gleg′ly,** *adv.* —**gleg′ness,** *n.*

Gleip·nir (glāp′nir), *n.* *Scand. Myth.* a chain made by mountain spirits and used by the gods to bind Fenrir. [< OIcel, deriv. of *gleipa* sheer]

Glei·witz (glī′vits), *n.* German name of **Gliwice.**

glen (glen), *n.* a small, narrow, secluded valley. [< Gael *gle(a)nn;* c. Welsh *glynn*] —**glen′like′,** *adj.*

Glen (glen), *n.* a boy's or girl's given name. Also, **Glenn, Glyn, Glynis, Glynn, Glynne.**

Glen′cairn cy′cle (glen′kârn), a cycle of three one-act plays by Eugene O'Neill dealing with events in the lives of the seamen of the *S.S. Glencairn,* consisting of *Bound East for Cardiff, The Long Voyage Home,* and *The Moon of the Caribbees.*

Glen·coe (glen′kō), *n.* **1.** a town in NE Illinois, N of Chicago. 10,472 (1960). **2.** a town in central Minnesota. 3216 (1960). **3.** a town in NE Alabama. 2592 (1960).

Glen′ Cove′, a city on NW Long Island, in SE New York. 23,817 (1960).

Glen·da (glen′də), *n.* a girl's given name.

Glen·dale (glen′dāl′), *n.* **1.** a city in SW California, near Los Angeles. 199,422 (1960). **2.** a city in central Arizona, near Phoenix. 15,696 (1960). **3.** a town in SE Wisconsin. 9537 (1960). **4.** a town in E Missouri. 7048 (1960). **5.** a town in SW Ohio. 2823 (1960).

Glen·dive (glen′dīv), *n.* a town in E Montana. 7058 (1960).

Glen·do·ra (glen dôr′ə, -dōr′ə), *n.* **1.** a city in SW California, near Los Angeles. 20,752 (1960). **2.** a girl's given name.

Glen·dow·er (glen dou′ər, glen′dou-ər), *n.* **Owen,** 1359?–1416?, Welsh rebel against Henry IV of England.

glen·gar·ry (glen gar′ē), *n., pl.* **-ries.** a Scotch cap with straight sides, a crease along the top, and sometimes short ribbon streamers at the back, worn by Highlanders as part of military dress. [after *Glengarry,* a valley in Inverness-shire, Scotland]

Glengarry

Glen′ Ly′on, a town in central Pennsylvania. 4173 (1960).

Glenn (glen), *n.* **John (Herschel),** born 1921, U.S. astronaut: first U.S. orbital space flight 1962.

Glenn·ville (glen′vil), *n.* a town in central Georgia. 2791 (1960).

gle·noid (glē′noid), *adj.* *Anat.* **1.** shallow or slightly cupped, as the articular cavities or the scapula and the temporal bone. **2.** pertaining to such a cavity. [< Gk *glēnoeid(ēs),* equiv. to *glēn(ē)* pupil, eyeball + *-oeidēs* -OID]

Glen·ol·den (glen ōl′dən), *n.* a town in SE Pennsylvania. 7249 (1960).

Glen′ Ridge′, a town in NE New Jersey. 8322 (1960).

Glens′ Falls′, a city in E New York, on the Hudson River. 18,580 (1960).

Gle·nus (glē′nəs), *n.* *Class. Myth.* a son of Hercules and Deianira.

Glen·view (glen′vyo͞o′), *n.* a city in NE Illinois, near Chicago. 18,132 (1960).

Glen·wood (glen′wo͝od′), *n.* **1.** a town in SW Iowa. 4783 (1960). **2.** a town in W Minnesota. 2631 (1960).

Glen′wood Springs′, a town in central Colorado. 3637 (1960).

Glen·yss (glen′is), *n.* a girl's given name. Also, **Glen′is, Glen′ice.**

Gles·sa·ri·ae (gle sâ′rē ē′), *n. pl.* *Class. Myth.* the Amber Islands.

gley (glē, glī), *v.i., n.* *Scot. and North Eng.* glee[2].

gli·a (glī′ə, glē′ə), *n.* *Anat.* neuroglia. [< LGk *gliā* glue] —**gli′al,** *adj.*

gli·a·din (glī′ə din, -dən), *n.* *Biochem.* **1.** a prolamin derived from the gluten of grain, as wheat, rye, or the like, used chiefly as a nutrient in high-protein diets. **2.** any prolamin. Also, **gli·a·dine** (glī′ə dēn′, -din). [< It *gliadin(a).* See GLIA, -IN[2]]

glib (glib), *adj.,* **glib·ber, glib·best.** **1.** ready and fluent, often thoughtlessly, superficially, or insincerely so: *a glib talker; glib answers.* **2.** easy or unconstrained, as actions or manners. [cf. obs. *glibbery* slippery; c. D *glibberig*] —**glib′ly,** *adv.* —**glib′ness,** *n.*

—**Syn. 1.** talkative, loquacious; facile, smooth. See **fluent.**

glid·der (glid′ər), *Brit. Dial.* —*v.t.* **1.** to glaze. —*v.i.* **2.** to slide; move in a smooth, gliding manner. [obs. *glidder* (adj., adv.) slippery; akin to GLIDE; cf. OE *gliddrian* to totter]

glid·der·y (glid′ə rē), *adj.* *Brit. Dial.* slippery. [GLIDDER + -Y[1]]

glide (glīd), *v.,* **glid·ed, glid·ing,** *n.* —*v.i.* **1.** to move smoothly and continuously along, as if without effort or resistance, as a flying bird, a boat, a skater, etc. **2.** to pass by gradual or unobservable change (often fol. by *along, away, by,* etc.). **3.** to move quietly or stealthily or without being noticed (usually fol. by *in, out, along,* etc.). **4.** *Aeron.* to move in the air, esp. at an easy angle downward, with less engine power than for level flight, solely by the action of air currents and gravity, or by momentum already acquired. **5.** *Music.* to pass from one note to another without a break. —*v.t.* **6.** to cause to glide. —*n.* **7.** a gliding movement, as in dancing. **8.** a dance marked by such movements. **9.** *Music.* slur (def. 8a). **10.** *Phonet.* **a.** a speech sound having the characteristics of both a consonant and a vowel, esp. *w* in *wore* and *y* in *your,* and, in some analyses, *r* in *road* and *l* in *load;* semivowel. **b.** a transitional sound heard during the articulation linking two phonemically contiguous sounds, as the *y*-sound often heard between the *i* and *e* of *quiet.* **11.** a calm stretch of shallow, smoothly flowing water, as in a river. **12.** the act or an instance of gliding. **13.** *Metall.* slip[1] (def. 41). [ME *glide(n),* OE *glīdan;* c. G *gleiten*] —**glid′ing·ly,** *adv.*

—**Syn. 1.** flow. See **slide.** —**Ant. 1.** stick.

glide′ bomb′, *Mil.* an aerial bomb equipped with airfoils to provide the necessary lift to enable it to glide toward its target when released from an aircraft. Also called **glid′er bomb′.**

glide-bomb (glīd′bom′), *v.t.* to bomb (a target) from a gliding airplane.

glide′ plane′, *Crystall.* a symmetry element of a space group such that a reflection of the lattice with respect to the plane and a translation of the lattice parallel to the plane bring the lattice back to its original position.

glid·er (glī′dər), *n.* **1.** one who or that which glides. **2.** *Aeron.* a motorless, heavier-than-air craft for gliding from a higher to a lower level by the action of gravity or from a lower to a higher level by the action of air currents. **3.** a porch swing made of an upholstered seat suspended from a steel framework by links or springs. [ME; see GLIDE, -ER[1]]

glid′ing joint′, *Anat.* arthrodia.

Glière (glyer), *n.* **Rein·hold Mo·ri·tzo·vich** (rīn′hōlt mô′ri tso vich), 1875–1956, Russian composer.

gliff (glif), *Scot. and North Eng.* —*n.* **1.** a glimpse or glance; a passing look. —*v.i.* **2.** to look quickly; give a glance. —*v.t.* **3.** to frighten; startle. [ME *gliff(en)* (to) glance; ? akin to D *glippen* to slip]

glim (glim), *n.* *Slang.* **1.** a light or lamp. **2.** an eye. **3.** *Scot.* a scrap; a little bit; a small portion. [see GLIMPSE, GLIMMER]

glime (glīm), *n., v.,* **glimed, glim·ing.** —*n.* **1.** *Brit. Dial.* a sly look or glance. —*v.i.* **2.** *Dial.* to glance slyly. [< Scand]

glim·mer (glim′ər), *n.* **1.** a faint or unsteady light; gleam. **2.** a dim perception; inkling. —*v.i.* **3.** to shine faintly or unsteadily; twinkle, shimmer, or flicker. **4.** to appear faintly or dimly. [ME *glimer(en)* (to) gleam; c. G *glimmern;* cf. OE *gleomu* splendor]

—**Syn. 1.** See **gleam.**

glim·mer·ing (glim′ər ing), *n.* **1.** a faint or unsteady light; glimmer. **2.** a faint glimpse; inkling. —*adj.* **3.** shining faintly or unsteadily; shimmering. [ME; see GLIMMER, -ING[1], -ING[2]] —**glim′mer·ing·ly,** *adv.*

glimpse (glimps), *n., v.,* **glimpsed, glimps·ing.** —*n.* **1.** a very brief, passing look, sight, or view. **2.** a momentary or slight appearance. **3.** a vague idea; inkling. **4.** *Archaic.* a gleam, as of light. —*v.t.* **5.** to catch or take a glimpse of. —*v.i.* **6.** to look briefly; glance (usually fol. by *at*). **7.** *Archaic.* to come into view; appear faintly. [ME *glimse(n);* c. MHG *glimsen* to glow; akin to GLIMMER] —**glimps′er,** *n.*

Glin·ka (gling′kə; *Russ.* glēn′kä), *n.* **Mi·kha·il I·va·no·vich** (mi khä ēl′ i vä′no vich), 1803–57, Russian composer.

glint (glint), *n.* **1.** a gleam or glimmer; sparkle; flash. **2.** gleaming brightness; luster. **3.** a brief or slight manifestation or occurrence; inkling; trace. —*v.i.* **4.** to gleam or flash. **5.** to move suddenly; dart. —*v.t.* **6.** to cause to glint; reflect. [ME *glint,* var. of obs. *glent* < Scand; cf. Dan *glente,* Sw *glänta, glinta* to slip, shine]

—**Syn. 4.** See **flash.**

gli·o·ma (glī ō′mə), *n., pl.* **-mas, -ma·ta** (-mə tə). *Pathol.* a tumor of the brain, arising from and consisting of neuroglia. [< NL; see GLIA, -OMA] —**gli·o·ma·tous** (glī ō′mə təs, -om′ə-), *adj.*

glisk (glisk), *Scot.* —*n.* **1.** a glance; look. **2.** a flash of light; gleam; glimmer. [cf. GLISTEN] —**glisk′y,** *adj.*

glis·sade (gli säd′, -sād′), *n., v.,* **-sad·ed, -sad·ing.** —*n.* **1.** a skillful glide over snow or ice in descending a mountain, as on skis or a toboggan. **2.** *Dance.* a sliding or gliding step. —*v.i.* **3.** to perform a glissade. [< F, equiv. to *gliss(er)* (to) slip, slide + *-ade* -ADE[1]] —**glis·sad′er,** *n.*

glis·san·do (gli sän′dō), *adj., n., pl.* **-di** (-dē). *Music.* —*adj.* **1.** performed with a gliding effect by sliding one or more fingers rapidly over the keys of a piano or strings of a harp. —*n.* **2.** a glissando passage. **3.** (in string playing) a slide. [< It: sliding]

glis·ten (glis′ən), *v.i.* **1.** to reflect a sparkling light or a faint intermittent glow; shine lustrously. —*n.* **2.** a glistening; sparkle. [ME *glis(t)nen,* OE *glisnian,* deriv. of *glisian* to GLITTER; see -EN[1]] —**glis′ten·ing·ly,** *adv.*

—**Syn. 1.** glimmer, gleam, glitter. GLISTEN, SHIMMER, SPARKLE refer to different ways in which light is reflected from surfaces. GLISTEN refers to a lustrous light, as from something sleek or wet, or it may refer to myriads of tiny gleams reflected from small surfaces: *Wet fur glistens. Snow glistens in the sunlight.* SHIMMER refers to the changing play of light on a (generally moving) surface, as of water or silk: *Moonbeams shimmer on water. Silk shimmers in a high light.* To SPARKLE is to give off sparks or small ignited particles, or to send forth small but brilliant gleams, sometimes by reflection: *A diamond sparkles with numerous points of light.*

glis·ter (glis′tər), *v.i.* **1.** *Archaic.* to glisten; glitter. **2.** a glistening; glitter. [ME; akin to GLISTEN] —**glis′ter·ing·ly,** *adv.*

glit·ter (glit′ər), *v.i.* **1.** to reflect light with a brilliant, sparkling luster; sparkle with reflected light. **2.** to make a brilliant show. —*n.* **3.** a sparkling reflected light or luster. **4.** showy splendor. **5.** small glittering ornaments. [ME < Scand; cf. OIcel *glitra,* freq. of *glita* to shine; cf. OE *glitenian,* G *gleissen* to shine, glitter] —**glit′ter·ing·ly,** *adv.*

—**Syn. 1.** See **flash. 3.** sparkle.

glit′ter ice′, *Chiefly Canadian.* ice or a sheet of ice formed on a surface by a quickly freezing rain.

glit·ter·y (glit′ə rē), *adj.* glittering; sparkling. [GLITTER + -Y[1]]

Gli·wi·ce (glē vē′tse), *n.* a city in SW Poland. 145,000 (est. 1963). German, **Gleiwitz.**

gloam (glōm), *n.* *Archaic.* twilight; gloaming. [back formation from GLOAMING]

gloam·ing (glō′ming), *n.* *Literary.* twilight; dusk. [ME *gloming,* OE *glōmung,* deriv. of *glōm;* sp. *-oa-* appar. by assoc. with GLOW]

gloat (glōt), *v.i.* **1.** to look at or think about with great or excessive satisfaction: *She gloated over her son's achievements. The opposing team gloated over our bad luck.* —*n.* **2.** an act or feeling of gloating. [< Scand; cf. OIcel *glotta* to grin; c. G *glotzen* to stare] —**gloat′er,** *n.* —**gloat′ing·ly,** *adv.*

—**Syn. 1.** See **glare**[1].

glob (glob), *n.* **1.** a drop or globule of a liquid. **2.** a usually rounded quantity or lump of some plastic or moldable substance: *a little glob of clay; a huge glob of whipped cream.* [perh. GL(OBE + BL)OB]

glob·al (glō′bəl), *adj.* **1.** pertaining to the whole world; world-wide; universal: *the dream of global peace.* **2.** comprehensive. **3.** globular, or globe-shaped. **4.** of, pertaining to, or using a terrestrial or celestial globe: *They discussed the relative advantages of global and cartographic briefings.* [GLOBE + -AL[1]] —**glo′bal·ly,** *adv.*

glo·bate (glō′bāt), *adj.* shaped like a globe. Also, **glo′bat·ed.** [< L *globāt(us)* made into a ball (ptp. of *globāre*). See GLOBE, -ATE[1]]

globe (glōb), *n., v.,* **globed, glob·ing.** —*n.* **1.** the planet earth (usually prec. by *the*). **2.** a planet or other celestial body. **3.** a sphere on which is depicted a map of the earth (**terrestrial globe**) or of the heavens (**celestial globe**). **4.** a spherical body; sphere. **5.** anything more or less spherical, as a lampshade or a glass fishbowl. **6.** *Hist.* a golden ball borne as an emblem of sovereignty; orb. —*v.t.* **7.** to form into a globe. —*v.i.* **8.** to take the form of a globe. [< MF *globe* < L *glob(us)* round body, ball, sphere] —**globe′like′,** *adj.*

—**Syn. 1.** See **earth. 4.** See **ball**[1].

Globe (glōb), *n.* a town in central Arizona. 6217 (1960).

globe·fish (glōb′fish′), *n., pl.* (*esp. collectively*) **-fish,** (*esp. referring to two or more kinds or species*) **-fish·es.** **1.** puffer (def. 2). **2.** See **ocean sunfish.** [GLOBE + FISH]

globe·flow·er (glōb′flou′ər), *n.* **1.** a ranunculaceous plant, *Trollius europaeus,* of Europe, having pale-yellow, globelike flowers. **2.** a related American plant, *T. laxus.* [GLOBE + FLOWER]

globe′ light′ning. See **ball lightning.**

globe′ this′tle, any of several Old World, thistlelike, composite plants of the genus *Echinops,* having dense heads of blue flowers.

globe-trot·ter (glōb′trot′ər), *n.* a person who travels regularly or frequently to countries all over the world. Also, **globe′trot′ter.** —**globe′-trot′ting, globe′trot′ting,** *n., adj.*

globe′ valve′, a valve with a globular body, closed by a disk seating on an opening in an internal wall.

glo·big·er·i·na (glō bij′ə rī′nə), *n., pl.* **-nas, -nae** (-nē). any marine foraminifer of the genus *globigerina,* having a calcareous shell, occurring either near the surface of the sea or in the mud at the bottom. [< NL, equiv. to L *globi-* globe (comb. form of *globus*) + *-ger* carry (deriv. of *gerere* to carry) + *-ina* fem. n. suffix]

globigeri′na ooze′, a calcareous deposit occurring upon ocean beds and consisting mainly of the shells of dead foraminifers, esp. of the globigerina.

glo·bin (glō′bin), *n. Biochem.* the protein component of hemoglobin. [< L *glob(us)* globe, sphere + -IN[2]]

glo·boid (glō′boid), *adj.* **1.** approximately globular. —*n.* **2.** a globoid figure or body. [GLOBE + -OID]

glo·bose (glō′bōs, glō bōs′), *adj.* globelike; globe-shaped. [< L *globōs(us)* round as a ball. See GLOBE, -OSE[1]] —**glo′bose·ly,** *adv.* —**glo·bos·i·ty** (glō bos′i tē), **glo′bose·ness,** *n.*

glob·u·lar (glob′yə lər), *adj.* **1.** globe-shaped; spherical. **2.** composed of or having globules. **3.** pertaining to the whole world; world-wide; global. Also, **glob′u·lous.** [< L *globul(us)* GLOBULE + -AR[1]] —**glob′u·lar′i·ty, glob′u·lar·ness,** *n.* —**glob′u·lar·ly,** *adv.*

glob·ule (glob′yo͞ol), *n.* a small spherical body. [< L *globul(us).* See GLOBE, -ULE]

glob·u·lif·er·ous (glob′yə lif′ər əs), *adj.* containing or producing globules. [GLOBULE + -I- + -FEROUS]

glob·u·lin (glob′yə lin), *n. Biochem.* any of a group of proteins, as myosin, occurring in plant and animal tissue, insoluble in pure water but soluble in dilute salt water, and coagulable by heat. [GLOBULE + -IN[2]]

glo·chid·i·ate (glō kid′ē it, -āt′), *adj. Bot., Zool.* barbed at the tip, as a hair or bristle. [GLOCHIDI(UM) + -ATE[1]]

glo·chid·i·um (glō kid′ē əm), *n., pl.* **-chid·i·a** (-kid′ē ə). **1.** *Bot.* a hair or bristle having a barbed tip. **2.** the larva of a fresh-water clam of the family *Unionidae,* that lives as a temporary parasite in the gills or on other external parts of fishes. [< NL < Gk **glōchídion* little arrow, equiv. to *glōch(ís)* point of an arrow + *-idion* dim. suffix] —**glo·chid′i·al,** *adj.*

glo·chis (glō′kis), *n., pl.* **glo·chi·nes** (glō kī′nēz). *Bot., Zool.* a barbed hair or spine. [< Gk *glōchís* point of an arrow]

glock·en·spiel (glok′ən spēl′, -shpēl′), *n.* **1.** a musical instrument composed of a set of graduated steel bars mounted in a frame and struck with hammers, used esp. in bands. **2.** a small keyboard instrument that produces bell-like sounds. **3.** a set of bells; carillon. [< G, equiv. to *Glocke* bell + *Spiel* play]

Glockenspiel

glom·er·ate (glom′ər it), *adj.* compactly clustered. [< L *glomerāt(us)* wound or formed into a ball (ptp. of *glomerāre*), equiv. to *glomer-* (s. of *glomus*) ball of yarn, clue + *-ātus* -ATE[1]]

glom·er·a·tion (glom′ə rā′shən), *n.* **1.** a glomerate condition; conglomeration. **2.** a glomerate mass. [GLOMERATE + -ION]

glom·er·ule (glom′ə ro͞ol′), *n. Bot.* a cyme condensed into a headlike cluster. [< NL *glomerul(us)* GLOMERULUS]

glo·mer·u·lo·ne·phri·tis (glō mer′yə lō ni frī′tis, glə-), *n. Pathol.* a kidney disease affecting the capillaries of the glomeruli, characterized by albuminuria, edema, and hypertension. [GLOMERUL(US) + -O- + NEPHRITIS]

glo·mer·u·lus (glō mer′yo͝o ləs, -o͝o ləs, glə-), *n., pl.* **-li** (-lī′). *Anat.* **1.** a compact cluster of capillaries. **2.** Also called **Malpighian tuft.** a tuft of convoluted capillaries in a nephron which filters certain substances from the blood and passes a protein-free filtrate into the proximal convoluted tubule. Cf. **Bowman's capsule, Malpighian corpuscle.** [< NL, equiv. to L *glomer-* (s. of *glomus*) ball of yarn, clue + *-ulus* -ULE] —**glo·mer′u·lar,** *adj.*

Glom·ma (glôm′mä), *n.* a river in E Norway, flowing S into the Skagerrak. 375 mi. long.

glo·mus (glō′məs), *n., pl.* **glom·er·a** (glom′ər ə), **glo·mi** (glō′mī). *Anat.* a small globular body. [< NL, L: a ball of yarn]

glon·o·in (glon′ō in), *n. Chem., Pharm.* nitroglycerin. [GL(YCERIN) + O (oxygen) + NO_3 (nitric anhydride) + -IN[2]]

gloom (glo͞om), *n.* **1.** darkness; dimness. **2.** a state of melancholy or depression; low spirits. **3.** a despondent look or expression. —*v.i.* **4.** to appear or become dark, dim, or somber. **5.** to look dismal or dejected; frown. —*v.t.* **6.** to fill with gloom; make gloomy or sad; sadden. **7.** to make dark or somber. [ME *gloum(ben), glomen* to frown, ? OE **glūmian* (akin to early G *glūmen* to make turbid); see GLUM] —**gloom′ful,** *adj.* —**gloom′ful·ly,** *adv.* —**gloom′less,** *adj.*
—**Syn. 1.** shadow, shade, obscurity. **2.** dejection, despondency, sadness. **4.** glower, scowl. —**Ant. 1.** brightness. **2.** cheerfulness.

gloom·ing (glo͞o′ming), *n. Archaic.* gloaming. [GLOOM + -ING[1]]

glooms (glo͞omz), *n.pl.* the blues; melancholy (usually prec. by *the*). [special use of GLOOM]

gloom·y (glo͞o′mē), *adj.,* **gloom·i·er, gloom·i·est. 1.** dark or dim; deeply shaded: *gloomy skies.* **2.** causing gloom; depressing: *a gloomy prospect.* **3.** filled with or showing gloom; melancholy. **4.** hopeless or despairing; pessimistic: *a gloomy view of the future.* [GLOOM + -Y[1]] —**gloom′i·ly,** *adv.* —**gloom′i·ness,** *n.*
—**Syn. 1.** obscure, shadowy, dusky. **2.** dismal, lowering. **3.** dejected, downcast, downhearted, sad, despondent, depressed, glum, dispirited. —**Ant. 3.** happy.

Gloos·cap (glo͞os′kap′), *n.* a divinity or legendary hero among the northeastern Algonquian Indians.

glop (glop), *n. Informal.* **1.** unappetizing food, esp. of a semiliquid consistency. **2.** any messy substance, esp. of a viscous or semiliquid consistency. **3.** sentimentality; mawkishness. [cf. GOOP, GULP]

Glo·ri·a (glôr′ē ə, glōr′-), *n.* **1.** *Liturgy.* **a.** See **Gloria in Excelsis Deo. b.** See **Gloria Patri. c.** the response *Gloria tibi, Domine* "Glory be to Thee, O Lord." **2.** (*l.c.*) a repetition of one of these. **3.** (*l.c.*) a musical setting for one of these. **4.** (*l.c.*) a halo, nimbus, or aureole, or an ornament in imitation of one. **5.** (*l.c.*) a fabric of silk, cotton, nylon, or wool for umbrellas, dresses, etc., often with a filling of cotton warp and yarn of other fiber. **6.** Also, **Glo·ri, Glo·rie, Glo·ry,** (glōr′ē, glôr′ē), a girl's given name. [ME < L: glory, fame]

Glo·ri·a in Ex·cel·sis De·o (glōr′ē ə in ek sel′sis dā′ō, glôr′-), the hymn beginning, in Latin, *Gloria in Excelsis Deo* "Glory in the highest to God," and in the English version, "Glory be to God on high." Also called **great doxology, greater doxology.**

Glo·ri·an·a (glōr′ē an′ə, glôr′-), a girl's given name, form of **Gloria.** Also, **Glo·ri·ane** (glōr′ē an′, glôr′-).

Glo·ri·ann (glōr′ē an′, glôr′-), *n.* a girl's given name.

Glo·ri·a Pa·tri (glōr′ē ə pä′trē, glôr′-), the short hymn "Glory be to the Father, and to the Son, and to the Holy Ghost. As it was in the beginning, is now, and ever shall be, world without end. Amen." Also called **lesser doxology.** [< L]

glo·ri·fi·ca·tion (glōr′ə fə kā′shən, glôr′-), *n.* **1.** the act of glorifying; exaltation to the glory of heaven. **2.** the state of being glorified. **3.** *Informal.* a glorified or more splendid form of something. [ME < LL *glōrificātiōn-* (s. of *glōrificātiō*), equiv. to *glōrific(āre)* (to) GLORIFY + *-ātiōn-* -ATION]

glo·ri·fy (glōr′ə fī′, glôr′-), *v.t.,* **-fied, -fy·ing. 1.** to magnify with praise; extol. **2.** to transform into or treat as more splendid, excellent, etc., than would normally be considered. **3.** to make glorious; invest with glory. **4.** to promote the glory of (God); ascribe glory and praise in adoration to (God). [ME < OF *glorifi(er)* < L *glōrificāre.* See GLORY, -FY] —**glo′ri·fi′a·ble,** *adj.* —**glo′ri·fi′er,** *n.*

glo·ri·ole (glōr′ē ōl′, glôr′-), *n.* a halo, nimbus, or aureole. [< L *glōriola,* equiv. to *glōri(a)* GLORY + *-ola* dim. suffix]

glo·ri·ous (glōr′ē əs, glôr′-), *adj.* **1.** delightful; wonderful; completely enjoyable: *to have a glorious time at the circus.* **2.** conferring glory: *a glorious victory.* **3.** full of glory; entitled to great renown: *England is glorious in her poetry.* **4.** brilliantly beautiful or magnificent; splendid: *the glorious heavens.* **5.** *Archaic.* blissfully drunk. [ME < AF, OF *glorieus* < L *glōriōs(us).* See GLORY, -OUS] —**glo′ri·ous·ly,** *adv.* —**glo′ri·ous·ness,** *n.*
—**Syn. 3.** famous, famed, renowned, illustrious, noted, celebrated, eminent, distinguished. —**Ant. 1.** unpleasant, disgusting. **3.** unknown.

Glo′rious Revolu′tion. See **English Revolution.**

Glo′rious Twelfth′, *Brit.* August 12th, the opening of the grouse-shooting season on the moors of Scotland and Northern England.

glo·ry (glōr′ē, glôr′ē), *n., pl.* **-ries,** *v.,* **-ried, -ry·ing.** —*n.* **1.** exalted praise, honor, or distinction bestowed by common consent: *to win glory on the field of battle.* **2.** something that makes one honored or illustrious; a distinguished ornament; an object of pride: *a sonnet that is one of the glories of English poetry.* **3.** adoring praise or worshipful thanksgiving: *Give glory to God.* **4.** resplendent beauty or magnificence: *the glory of autumn.* **5.** a state of splendor, magnificence, or great prosperity. **6.** a state of absolute happiness; gratification, contentment, etc.: *She was in her glory as president of the club.* **7.** the splendor and bliss of heaven; heaven. **8.** a ring, circle, or surrounding radiance of light represented about the head or the whole figure of a sacred person, as Christ, a saint, etc.; a halo, nimbus, or aureole. **9.** anticorona. **10. go to glory,** to die. —*v.i.* **11.** to exult with triumph; rejoice proudly (usually fol. by *in*): *Their father gloried in their success.* **12.** *Obs.* to boast. —*interj.* **13.** Also, **glo′ry be′.** Glory be to God (used to express surprise, elation, wonder, etc.). [ME < OF *glorie* < L *glōria*] —**glo′ry·ing·ly,** *adv.*
—**Syn. 1.** fame, eminence, renown, celebrity. **4.** brilliance, refulgence, effulgence. —**Ant. 1.** disgrace, obloquy.

glo′ry hole′, 1. *Naut.* **a.** the quarters on a ship that are occupied by the stewards or the firemen. **b.** lazaretto (def. 3). **c.** any locker or enclosed space for loose gear. **2.** *Glassmaking.* an auxiliary furnace for reheating glass that has cooled during offhand blowing. **3.** *Mining.* See **draw hole.**

glo·ry-of-the-snow (glōr′ē əv *th*ə snō′, -snō′, glôr′-), *n., pl.* **-snows.** any of several Old World, liliaceous herbs of the genus *Chionodoxa,* having showy, blue flowers produced early in the spring.

glo·ry-of-the-sun (glōr′ē əv *th*ə sun′, -sun′, glôr′-), *n., pl.* **-suns.** a bulbous herb, *Leucocoryne ixioides,* of Chile, having whitish, blue-tipped flowers.

glo·ry-pea (glōr′ē pē′, glôr′-), *n.* a showy, vinelike plant, *Clianthus dampieri,* of Australia, having a white-hairy stem and clusters of black-splotched, scarlet flowers.

gloss[1] (glos, glôs), *n.* **1.** a superficial luster or shine: *the gloss of satin.* **2.** a false or deceptive appearance, show, etc. —*v.t.* **3.** to put a gloss upon. **4.** to give a false or deceptive appearance to: *to gloss over flaws in the woodwork.* [< Scand; akin to D **gloos* a glowing, MHG *glosen* to glow, shine] —**gloss′er,** *n.* —**gloss′less,** *adj.*
—**Syn. 1.** shine, glaze. See **polish. 2.** front, pretense.

gloss[2] (glos, glôs), *n.* **1.** an explanation, by means of a marginal or interlinear note, of a technical or unusual expression in a manuscript text. **2.** a series of verbal interpretations of a text. **3.** a glossary. **4.** an artfully misleading interpretation. —*v.t.* **5.** to insert glosses on; annotate. **6.** to place (a word) in a gloss. **7.** to give a specious interpretation of; explain away (often fol. by *over*): *In telling the story, she so glossed over her own actions as to make cowardice look like the height of integrity; to gloss over a mistake.* —*v.i.* **8.** to make glosses. [ME *glose* < LL *glosa, glōssa* < Gk *glôssa* tongue, language] —**gloss′er,** *n.* —**gloss′ing·ly,** *adv.*
—**Syn. 1.** comment, annotation. **2.** commentary, critique, exegesis, explication. **5.** explain, interpret, analyze, explicate.

gloss-, var. of **glosso-** before a vowel: *glossectomy.*

gloss., glossary.

glos·sa (glos′ə, glô′sə), *n., pl.* **-sae** (-sē), **-sas. 1.** *Entomol.* one of a pair of median, sometimes fused lobes of the labium of an insect. **2.** *Anat.* the tongue. [< Gk *glôssa* the tongue]

Glos·sa (glô′sə), *n.* **Cape,** a promontory in SW Albania.

glos·sal (glos′əl, glô′səl), *adj.* of or pertaining to the tongue. [GLOSS(A) + -AL[1]]

glos·sa·ry (glos′ə rē, glô′sə-), *n., pl.* **-ries. 1.** a list of terms in a special subject, field, or area of usage, with accompanying definitions. **2.** such a list at the back of a book, explaining or defining difficult or unusual words and expressions used in the text. [ME *glossarye* < L *glossāri(um).* See GLOSS[2], -ARY] —**glos·sar·i·al** (glo sâr′ē əl, glô-), *adj.* —**glos·sar′i·al·ly,** *adv.* —**glos′sa·rist,** *n.*

glos·sa·tor (glo sā′tər, glô-), *n.* **1.** a person who writes glosses; glossarist. **2.** one of the medieval interpreters of the Roman and canon laws. [ME *glosator* < ML *glossātor* commentator, equiv. to *gloss(āre)* (to) explain, interpret (deriv. of L *glossa* obsolete or foreign word, hard word; see GLOSS[2]) + *-ātor* -ATOR] —**glos·sa·to·ri·al** (glos′ə tōr′ē əl, -tôr′-, glô′sə-), *adj.*

glos·sec·to·my (glo sek′tə mē, glô-), *n., pl.* **-mies.** *Surg.* the removal of all or a portion of the tongue. [GLOSS- + -ECTOMY]

glos·se·mat·ics (glos′ə mat′iks, glô′sə-), *n.* (*construed as sing.*) *Ling.* the study of glossemes. [*glossemat-* (comb. form of GLOSSEME) + -ICS] —**glos′se·mat′ic,** *adj.*

glos·seme (glos′ēm, glô′sēm), *n. Ling.* the smallest meaningful unit of linguistic signaling, consisting of a morpheme and a tagmeme. [GLOSS- + -EME] —**glos·se′mic,** *adj.*

glos·si·tis (glo sī′tis, glô-), *n. Pathol.* inflammation of the tongue. [GLOSS- + -ITIS] —**glos·sit·ic** (glo sit′ik, glô-), *adj.*

gloss·me·ter (glos′mē′tər, glôs′-), *n.* a machine for measuring the reflectivity of a surface. [GLOSS[1] + -METER]

glosso-, a learned borrowing from Greek meaning "tongue," used in the formation of compound words: *glossology.* Also, *esp. before a vowel,* **gloss-.** [< Gk (Ionic), comb. form of *glôssa*]

glos·sog·ra·pher (glo sog′rə fər, glô-), *n.* a glossator. [< Gk *glōssográph(os).* See GLOSSO-, -GRAPHER] —**glos·so·graph·i·cal** (glos′ə graf′i kəl, glô′sə-), *adj.* —**glos·sog′ra·phy,** *n.*

glos·so·la·li·a (glos′ō lā′lē ə, glô′sō-), *n.* See **speaking in tongues.** [GLOSSO- + -LALIA] —**glos·so·la·list** (glo sol′ə list, glô-), *n.*

glos·sol·o·gy (glo sol′ə jē, glô-), *n. Archaic.* linguistics. [GLOSSO- + -LOGY] —**glos·so·log·i·cal** (glos′ə loj′i kəl, glô′sə-), *adj.* —**glos·sol′o·gist,** *n.*

glos·so·pha·ryn·ge·al (glos′ō fə rin′jē əl, -jəl, -far′in jē′əl, glô′sō-), *Anat.* —*adj.* **1.** of or pertaining to the tongue and pharynx. —*n.* **2.** See **glossopharyngeal nerve.** [GLOSSO- + PHARYNGEAL]

glos′sopharyn′geal nerve′, *Anat.* either of the eighth pair of cranial nerves, consisting of motor fibers that innervate the muscles of the pharynx, the soft palate, and the parotid glands, and of sensory fibers that conduct impulses to the brain from the pharynx, the middle ear, and the posterior one third of the tongue.

glos·sot·o·my (glo sot′ə mē, glô-), *n., pl.* **-mies.** *Surg.* incision or dissection of the tongue. [GLOSSO- + -TOMY]

gloss·y (glos′ē, glô′sē), *adj.,* **gloss·i·er, gloss·i·est,** *n., pl.* **gloss·ies.** —*adj.* **1.** having a luster or shine; lustrous. **2.** having a false or deceptive appearance or air, esp. of experience or sophistication; specious. **3.** (of paper) having a shiny surface. Cf. **matte**[1], **semimat.** —*n.* **4.** slick[1] (def. 7). **5.** a photograph printed on glossy paper. [GLOSS[1] + -Y[1]] —**gloss′i·ly,** *adv.* —**gloss′i·ness,** *n.*
—**Syn. 1.** shining, polished, glazed; smooth, sleek. —**Ant. 1.** dull.

gloss′y snake′, a harmless colubrid snake, *Arizona elegans,* of the western U.S. and northern Mexico, having smooth, glistening scales.

glost (glost, glôst), *n. Ceram.* glaze or glazed ware. [alter. of GLOSS[1]]

glost-fired (glost′fī′ərd′, glôst′-), *adj.* (of a ceramic object) fired to fix and harden a glaze.

glost′ fir′ing, *Ceram.* a firing in which glaze is fused onto a piece.

-glot, var. of **glotto-** as final element of a compound word: *polyglot.*

glot·tal (glot′əl), *adj.* **1.** of or pertaining to the glottis. **2.** *Phonet.* articulated at the glottis. —*n.* **3.** See **glottal stop.** [GLOTT(IS) + -AL[1]]

glot·tal·ize (glot′əlīz′), *v.t.,* **-ized, -iz·ing.** *Phonet.* to pronounce with glottal coarticulation. [GLOTTAL + -IZE] —**glot′tal·i·za′tion,** *n.*

glot·tal·ized (glot′əlīzd′), *adj. Phonet.* pronounced with glottal coarticulation. [GLOTTALIZE + -ED[2]]

glot′tal stop′, *Phonet.* **1.** a plosive consonant whose occlusion and release are accomplished chiefly at the glottis, as in the Scottish articulation of the *t*-sound of *little, bottle,* etc. **2.** a stop consonant, without release, having glottal occlusion as a secondary articulation, as in *yep* for *yes, nope* for *no.* Also called **glottal.**

glot·tic (glot′ik), *adj.* **1.** pertaining to the glottis; glottal. **2.** *Archaic.* linguistic. [< Gk *glōttik(ós).* See GLOTTIS, -IC]

glot·tis (glot′is), *n., pl.* **glot·tis·es, glot·ti·des** (glot′i dēz′). *Anat.* the opening at the upper part of the larynx, between the vocal cords. [< NL < Gk *glōttís,* var. of *glôtta* (Attic form of *glôssa* tongue)] —**glot·tid·e·an** (glo tid′ē ən, glô-), *adj.*

glotto-, a learned borrowing from Greek meaning "tongue," used in the formation of compound words: *glottology.* Also, **-glot.** [< Gk (Attic) *glōtto-,* comb. form of *glôtta*]

glot·to·chro·nol·o·gy (glot′ō krə nol′ə jē, glot′ə-), *n. Ling.* the branch of lexicostatistics that studies the rate of replacement of vocabulary and attempts to determine what percentage of basic vocabulary two presently distinct but related languages share, using the information thus obtained to estimate how long ago they ceased being a single language. [GLOTTO- + CHRONOLOGY]

glot·tog·o·ny (glə tog′ə nē), *n. Ling.* the study of the putative origin of language. [GLOTTO- + -GONY] —**glot·to·gon·ic** (glot′ō gon′ik), *adj.*

glot·tol·o·gy (glo tol′ə jē), *n. Obs.* linguistics. [GLOTTO- + -LOGY] —**glot·to·log·ic** (glot′ᵊloj′ik), **glot′to·log′i·cal,** *adj.* —**glot·tol′o·gist,** *n.*

Glouces·ter (glos′tər, glô′stər), *n.* **1. Duke of.** See **Humphrey. 2.** a seaport in W Gloucestershire in SW England, on the Severn River. 69,687 (1961). **3.** a seaport in NE Massachusetts. 25,789 (1960). **4.** Gloucestershire.

Glouces′ter Cit′y, a city in W New Jersey, on the Delaware River. 15,511 (1960).

Glouces·ter·shire (glos′tər shēr′, -shər, glô′stər-), *n.* a county in SW England. 1,000,493 (1961); 1255 sq. mi. *Co. seat:* Gloucester. Also called **Gloucester.**

glove (gluv), *n., v.,* **gloved, glov·ing.** —*n.* **1.** a covering for the hand made with a separate sheath for each finger and for the thumb. **2.** See **boxing glove. 3.** See **baseball glove. 4.** gauntlet. **5. hand and glove.** See **hand** (def. 42). **6. handle with kid gloves.** See **kid gloves** (def. 2). **7. take up** or **throw down the glove.** See **gauntlet**[1] (def. 4). —*v.t.* **8.** to cover with or as if with a glove; provide with gloves. **9.** to serve as a glove for. [ME; OE *glōf;* c. OIcel *glōfi*] —**glove′less,** *adj.* —**glove′like′,** *adj.*

glove′ compart′ment, a compartment in the dashboard of an automobile for storing small items.

glove·man (gluv′man′), *n., pl.* **-men.** *Baseball, Cricket.* fielder. [GLOVE + MAN[1]]

glov·er (gluv′ər), *n.* a person who makes or sells gloves. [ME; see GLOVE, -ER[2]]

Glov·er (gluv′ər), *n.* **John,** 1732–97, American general.

Glov·ers·ville (gluv′ərz vil′), *n.* a city in E New York. 21,741 (1960).

glove′ silk′, a warp knit fabric made of silk or nylon, used in the manufacture of gloves and undergarments.

glow (glō), *n.* **1.** a light emitted by or as by a substance heated to luminosity; incandescence. **2.** brightness of color. **3.** a sensation or state of bodily heat. **4.** a warm, ruddy color of the cheeks. **5.** warmth of emotion or passion; ardor. —*v.i.* **6.** to emit bright light and heat without flame; become incandescent. **7.** to shine like something intensely heated. **8.** to exhibit a strong, bright color; be lustrously red or brilliant. **9.** (of the cheeks) to exhibit a healthy, warm, ruddy color. **10.** to become or feel very warm or hot. **11.** to become filled or animated with emotion or elation: *to glow with pride.* [ME *glow(en),* OE *glōwan;* akin to G *glühen,* Icel *glōa*]

glow′ discharge′, *Physics.* the conduction of electricity in a low-pressure gas, producing a diffuse glow.

glow·er (glou′ər), *v.i.* **1.** to look or stare with sullen dislike, discontent, or anger. —*n.* **2.** a look of sullen dislike, discontent, or anger. [ME (Scot) *glowre(n)* (to) glower; akin to MLG *glūren* to be overcast, MD *gloeren* to leer] —**glow′er·ing·ly,** *adv.*
—**Syn. 1.** See **glare**[1].

glow·fly (glō′flī′), *n., pl.* **-flies.** firefly. [GLOW + FLY[2]]

glow·ing (glō′ing), *adj.* **1.** incandescent. **2.** rich and warm in coloring: *glowing colors.* **3.** showing the radiance of health, excitement, etc. **4.** warmly favorable or complimentary: *a glowing account of his behavior in combat.* [ME *glowynge.* See GLOW, -ING[2]] —**glow′ing·ly,** *adv.*

glow′ lamp′, *Electronics.* a vacuum tube containing a gas that is ionized by the electrons, giving a visible glow.

glow·worm (glō′wûrm′), *n.* **1.** the wingless female or larva of the European beetle, *Lampyris noctiluca,* which emits a greenish light. **2.** any of the luminous larvae or wingless, grublike females of certain beetles of the family *Lampyridae.* [GLOW + WORM]

glox·in·i·a (glok sin′ē ə), *n.* any of several horticultural varieties of an herb of the genus *Sinningia,* esp. *S. speciosa,* having large, white, red, or purple, bell-shaped flowers. [named after Benjamin *Gloxin,* 18th-century German physician and botanist; see -IA]

gloze[1] (glōz), *v.,* **glozed, gloz·ing,** *n.* —*v.t.* **1.** to explain away; extenuate; gloss over (usually fol. by *over*). **2.** to palliate with specious talk. —*v.i.* **3.** *Archaic.* to make glosses; comment. —*n.* **4.** *Archaic.* flattery or deceit. **5.** *Obs.* a specious show. [ME < OF *glos(er),* deriv. of *glose* < LL *glosa* GLOSS[2]] —**gloz′ing·ly,** *adv.*

gloze[2] (glōz), *v.t., v.i.,* **glozed, gloz·ing.** to shine; brighten; gleam. [akin to MHG *glosen* to glow; see GLOSS[1]]

glt., gilt.

gluc-, var. of **gluco-** before a vowel: *glucide.*

glu·car′ic ac′id (glōō kar′ik), *Chem.* See **saccharic acid.** [GLUC- + *-aric,* as in *saccharic*]

glu·cide (glōō′sīd), *n. Chem.* any of various organic compounds, esp. the carbohydrates and glycosides, that consist of or contain a carbohydrate. [GLUC- + -IDE] —**glu·cid·ic** (glōō sid′ik), *adj.*

glu·ci·num (glōō sī′nəm), *n.* (esp. in France) *Chem.* beryllium. *Symbol:* Gl Also, **glu·cin·i·um** (glōō sin′ē əm). [< NL < Gk *glyk(ýs)* sweet (from the taste of some of the salts) + *-in-* -IN[2] + L *-um* n. suffix] —**glu·cin·ic** (glōō sin′ik), *adj.*

Gluck (glŏŏk), *n.* **1. Alma** (*Reba Fiersohn, Mme. Efrem Zimbalist*), 1884–1938, U.S. operatic soprano, born in Rumania. **2. Chris·toph Wil·li·bald von** (kris′tôf vil′i bält′ fən), 1714–87, German operatic composer.

gluco-, var. of **glyco-:** *glucoprotein.* Also, *esp. before a vowel,* **gluc-.**

glu·co·gen·e·sis (glōō′kō jen′i sis), *n. Biochem.* the production of glucose by the decomposition of glycogen or from any nonglucose precursor. [< NL; see GLUCO-, -GENESIS] —**glu′co·gen′ic,** *adj.*

glu·co·ne·o·gen·e·sis (glōō′kō nē′ə jen′i sis), *n. Biochem.* glucose formation in animals from a noncarbohydrate source, as proteins, fats, and the like. Also, **glyconeogenesis.** [GLUCO- + NEO- + -GENESIS] —**glu·co·ne·o·gen·ic** (glōō′kō nē′ə jen′ik), **glu·co·ne·o·ge·net·ic** (glōō′kō nē′ō jə net′ik), *adj.*

glu·con′ic ac′id (glōō kon′ik), *Chem.* a colorless, water-soluble acid, $CH_2OH(CHOH)_4COOH$, obtained by the oxidation of glucose, used commercially in a 50-percent solution for cleaning metals. Also, **glyconic acid, glycogenic acid.** Also called **dextronic acid.** [GLUC- + -ONE + -IC]

glu·co·no·ki·nase (glōō′kō nə kī′nās), *n. Biochem.* an enzyme, found in certain microscopic organisms, that serves to catalyze the phosphorylation of gluconic acid. [GLUCON(IC) (ACID) + -O- + *kinase,* irreg. < Gk *kínēsis* motion]

glu·co·pro·tein (glōō′kō prō′tēn, -tē in), *n. Biochem.* glycoprotein.

glu·co·san (glōō′kə san′), *n. Biochem.* any of a number of polysaccharides that yield glucose upon hydrolysis. [GLUCOSE + -AN]

glu·cose (glōō′kōs), *n.* **1.** *Chem.* a sugar, $C_6H_{12}O_6$, having several optically different forms, the common or dextrorotatory form (**dextroglucose** or **d-glucose**) occurring in many fruits, animal tissues and fluids, etc., and having a sweetness about one half that of ordinary sugar. The levorotatory form (**levoglucose** or **l-glucose**) is rare and not naturally occurring. **2.** Also called **starch syrup.** a syrup containing dextrose, maltose, and dextrine, obtained by the incomplete hydrolysis of starch. [< F < Gk *glyk(ýs)* sweet + F *-ose* -OSE[2]] —**glu·cos′ic,** *adj.*

glu·co·side (glōō′kə sīd′), *n. Chem.* any of an extensive group of compounds that yield glucose and some other substance or substances when treated with a dilute acid or decomposed by a ferment or enzyme. Cf. **glycoside.** [GLUCOSE + -IDE] —**glu′co·sid′al, glu·co·sid·ic** (glōō′kə sid′ik), *adj.*

glu·co·sul·fone (glōō′kō sul′fōn), *n. Pharm.* a compound used chiefly in the form of its white, amorphous, water-soluble sodium salt, $SO_2[C_6H_4NH(SO_3Na)C_6H_{12}O_5]_2$, for the treatment of leprosy. [GLUCO- + SULFONE]

glu·cos·u·ri·a (glōō′kōs yŏŏ rē′ə), *n. Pathol.* glycosuria. —**glu′cos·u′ric,** *adj.*

glu′cu·ron′ic ac′id (glōō′kyə ron′ik, glōō′-), *Biochem.* an acid, $CHO(HCOH)_4COOH$, formed by the oxidation of glucose, found combined with other products of metabolism in the blood and urine. Also, **glycuronic acid.** [GLUC- + Gk *oûron* urine + -IC]

glu·cu·ron·ide (glōō kyŏŏr′ə nīd′), *n. Biochem.* a glycoside that yields glucuronic acid upon hydrolysis. Also, **glycuronide.** [GLUCURON(IC ACID) + -IDE]

glue (glōō), *n., v.,* **glued, glu·ing.** —*n.* **1.** a hard, impure, protein gelatin, obtained by boiling skins, hoofs, and other animal substances in water, that when melted or diluted is a strong adhesive. **2.** any of various solutions or preparations of this substance, used as an adhesive. **3.** any of various other solutions or preparations that can be used as adhesives. —*v.t.* **4.** to join or fasten with glue. **5.** to cover or smear (something) with glue (sometimes fol. by *up*): *He carefully glued each page. The children's clothes were all glued up.* **6.** to fix or attach firmly with or as if with glue; make adhere closely: *to glue a model together; The child glued himself to his father's side.* [ME *glu, gleu* < OF *glu* < L *glūt-* (s. of *glūs*); c. Gk *gloiós* gum, anything sticky] —**glue′like′,** *adj.* —**glu′er,** *n.*

glue′ cell′, colloblast.

glue·pot (glōō′pot′), *n.* a double boiler in which glue is melted. [GLUE + POT[1]]

glue·y (glōō′ē), *adj.,* **glu·i·er, glu·i·est. 1.** like glue; viscid; sticky. **2.** full of or smeared with glue. [ME; see GLUE, -Y[1]] —**glu′ey·ness,** *n.*

glum (glum), *adj.,* **glum·mer, glum·mest.** sullenly or silently gloomy; dejected; morose. [var. of GLOOM] —**glum′ly,** *adv.* —**glum′ness,** *n.*
—**Syn.** morose, moody, sulky; cheerless, despondent, melancholy.

glu·ma·ceous (glōō mā′shəs), *adj.* **1.** glumelike. **2.** consisting of or having glumes. [GLUME + -ACEOUS]

glume (glōōm), *n. Bot.* one of the characteristic bracts of the inflorescence of grasses, sedges, etc., esp. one of the pair of bracts at the base of a spikelet. [< L *glūm(a)* hull or husk (of corn), cf. *glūbere* to peel, strip of bark] —**glume′like′,** *adj.*

glump·y (glum′pē), *adj.,* **glump·i·er, glump·i·est.** *Archaic.* gloomy; glum; grumpy. [*glump* sulky person (akin to GLUM) + -Y[1]] —**glump′i·ly,** *adv.* —**glump′i·ness,** *n.*

glunch (glōōnsh, glunsh), *Scot.* —*v.i.* **1.** to frown; give a sullen, glum, or sulky look; grimace. —*n.* **2.** a frown or grimace; a sullen, glum, or sulky look. [? GL(UM) + *clunch,* var. of CLENCH]

glu·on (glōō′on), *n.* an elementary particle that is conjectured to bind quarks together, thus forming most of the observable nuclear particles, such as protons, neutrons, pions, etc. [GLU(E) + ON]

glu·side (glōō′sīd), *n. Chem.* saccharin. [? alter. (by syncope) of GLUCOSIDE]

glut (glut), *v.,* **glut·ted, glut·ting,** *n.* —*v.t.* **1.** to feed or fill to satiety; sate: *to glut the appetite.* **2.** to feed or fill to excess; cloy. **3.** to flood (the market) with a certain article or commodity so that the supply greatly exceeds the demand. **4.** to choke up: *to glut a channel.* —*v.i.* **5.** to eat to satiety or to excess. —*n.* **6.** a full supply. **7.** an excessive supply or amount; surfeit. **8.** an act of glutting or the state of being glutted. [ME *glute,* back formation from *glutum* GLUTTON[1]] —**glut′ting·ly,** *adv.*
—**Syn. 1.** surfeit, stuff, satiate. **5.** gorge, cram. **7.** surplus, excess superabundance.

glu·ta·mate (glōō′tə māt′), *n. Chem.* a salt or ester of glutamic acid. [GLUTAM(IC ACID) + -ATE[2]]

glu·tam′ic ac′id (glōō tam′ik), *Chem.* an amino acid, $HOOCCH_2CH_2CH(NH_2)COOH$, obtained by hydrolysis from wheat gluten and sugar-beet residues, used chiefly in the form of its sodium salt to intensify the flavor of meat or other food. Also, **glu′ta·min′ic ac′id** (glōō′tə min′ik, glōō′-). [GLUT(EN) + AMIC ACID]

glu·ta·mine (glōō′tə mēn′, -min), *n. Chem.* a crystalline amino acid, $HOOCCH(NH_2)CH_2CH_2CONH_2$, related to glutamic acid. [GLUT(EN) + -AMINE]

glu·ta·thi·one (glōō′tə thī′ōn, -thī ōn′), *n. Biochem.* a crystalline, water-soluble peptide of glutamic acid, cysteine, and glycine, $C_{10}H_{17}N_3O_6S$, found in blood and in animal and plant tissues, and important in tissue oxidations and in the activation of some enzymes. [GLUT(AMIC ACID) + THI- + -ONE]

glu·te·al (glōō′tē əl, glōō tē′əl), *adj. Anat.* pertaining to buttock muscles or to the buttocks. [GLUTE(US) + -AL[1]]

glu·te·lin (glōōt′ᵊlin), *n. Biochem.* any of a group of simple proteins of vegetable origin, esp. one from wheat. [? alter. of *glutenin.* See GLUTEN, -IN[2]]

glu·ten (glōōt′ᵊn), *n.* **1.** the tough, viscid, nitrogenous substance remaining when the flour of wheat or other grain is washed to remove the starch. **2.** *Archaic.* glue or a gluey substance. [< L *glūten* glue]

glu′ten bread′, bread made from gluten flour.

glu′ten flour′, wheat flour from which a large part of the starch has been removed, thus increasing the proportion of gluten.

glu·te·nous (glōōt′ᵊnəs), *adj.* **1.** like gluten. **2.** containing gluten, esp. in large amounts. [GLUTEN + -OUS]

glu·teth·i·mide (glōō teth′ə mīd′), *n. Pharm.* a white, crystalline, water-insoluble powder, $C_{13}H_{15}NO_2$, used as a hypnotic and sedative. [GLUTE(N) + THI- + (A)MIDE]

glu·te·us (glōō′tē əs, glōō tē′-), *n., pl.* **-te·i** (-tē ī′, -tē′ī). *Anat.* any of several muscles of the buttocks, esp. the broad, thick, fleshy one nearest the surface (**gluteus maximus**). [< NL < Gk *gloutós* the rump + L *-eus* adj. suffix]

glu′teus max′i·mus (mak′sə məs), *pl.* **glutei maxi·mi** (mak′sə mī′). See under **gluteus.** [< NL: largest gluteus]

glu·tin (glōōt′ᵊn), *n. Biochem.* **1.** a protein obtained from gelatin by hydrolysis. **2.** vegetable casein. [< F *glutine,* equiv. to *glut-* (< L *glūten* glue) + *-ine* -IN[2]]

glu·tin·ant (glōōt′ᵊnənt), *n. Zool.* a nematocyst that discharges a thread covered with a sticky secretion. [< L *glūtinant-* (s. of *glūtināns*), prp. of *glūtināre* to glue. See GLUTEN, -ANT]

glu·ti·nous (glōōt′ᵊnəs), *adj.* of the nature of glue; gluey; viscid; sticky. [ME < L *glūtinōs(us)* gluey, sticky. See GLUTEN, -OUS] —**glu′ti·nous·ly,** *adv.* —**glu′ti·nous·ness, glu·ti·nos·i·ty** (glōōt′ᵊnos′i tē), *n.*

glu·tose (glōō′tōs), *n. Chem.* an ingredient of a syrupy mixture obtained by the action of alkali on levulose or found in the unfermentable reducing portion of cane molasses. [GLU(COSE + FRUC)TOSE]

glut·ton[1] (glut′ᵊn), *n.* **1.** a person who eats excessively. **2.** a person with a remarkably great desire or capacity for something: *He's a glutton for work.* [ME *glutun* < OF *glouton* < L *glutton-* (s. of *gluttō*), var. of *glūtō* glutton, akin to *glūtīre* to gulp down]
—**Syn. 1.** gourmand; gastronome.

glut·ton[2] (glut′ᵊn), *n.* the wolverine, *Gulo luscus,* of Europe. [trans. of G *Vielfrass* for Sw *fjällfräs,* lit., to much devour]

glut·ton·ise (glut′ᵊnīz′), *v.i., v.t.,* **-ised, -is·ing.** *Chiefly Brit.* gluttonize.

glut·ton·ize (glut′ᵊnīz′), *v.,* **-ized, -iz·ing.** *Archaic.* —*v.i.* **1.** to eat like a glutton. —*v.t.* **2.** to feast gluttonously on. [GLUTTON[1] + -IZE]

glut·ton·ous (glut′ᵊnəs), *adj.* **1.** tending to eat excessively; voracious. **2.** greedy; insatiable. [ME; see GLUTTON[1], -OUS] —**glut′ton·ous·ly,** *adv.* —**glut′ton·ous·ness,** *n.*

glut·ton·y (glut′ᵊnē), *n.* excessive eating and drinking. [ME *glotonie, glutonie* < OF *glotonie;* see GLUTTON[1], -Y[3]]

glyc-, var. of **glyco-** before a vowel: *glycemia.*

glyc., (in prescriptions) glycerite. [< L *glyceritum*]

gly·ce·mi·a (glī sē′mē ə), *n. Med.* the presence of glucose in the blood. Also, **gly·cae′mi·a.** [GLYC- + -EMIA] —**gly·ce′mic, gly·cae′mic,** *adj.*

glyc·er·al·de·hyde (glis′ə ral′də hīd′), *n. Biochem.* a white, crystalline, water-soluble solid, $CH_2OHCHOHCHO$, that is an intermediate in carbohydrate metabolism and yields glycerol on reduction. Also called **glycer′ic al′dehyde.** [GLYCER(IN) + ALDEHYDE]

gly·cer·ic (gli ser′ik, glis′ər ik), *adj. Chem.* of or derived from glycerol. [GLYCER(OL) + -IC]

glycer′ic ac′id, *Chem.* a colorless, syrupy liquid, $CH_2OHCHOHCOOH$, obtained by oxidizing glycerol.

glyc·er·ide (glis′ə rīd′, -ər id), *n. Chem.* any of a group of esters obtained from glycerol by the replacement of one, two, or three hydroxyl groups with a fatty acid: the principal constituent of adipose tissue. Cf. **monoglyceride, diglyceride, triglyceride.** [GLYCER(IN) + -IDE]

glyc·er·in (glis′ər in), *n. Chem.* glycerol. Also, **glyc·er·ine** (glis′ər in, -ə rēn′, glis′ə rēn′). [< F *glycérine,* equiv. to *glycer-* (s. of Gk *glykerós* sweet) + *-ine* -IN[2]]

glyc·er·in·ate[1] (glis′ər ə nāt′), *v.t.,* **-at·ed, -at·ing.** to impregnate with glycerin. [GLYCERIN + -ATE[1]]

glyc·er·in·ate[2] (glis′ər ə nāt′), *n. Chem.* any salt of glyceric acid. [GLYCERIN + -ATE[2]]

glyc·er·ite (glis′ə rīt′), *n. Pharm.* a preparation of a medicinal substance dissolved in or mixed with glycerin. [GLYCER(IN) + -ITE[1]]

glyc·er·ol (glis′ə rōl′, -rôl′, -rol′), *n. Chem.* a colorless, odorless, syrupy, sweet liquid, $HOCH_2CHOHCH_2OH$, usually obtained by the saponification of natural fats and oils: used for sweetening and preserving food, in the manufacture of cosmetics, perfumes, inks, and certain glues and cements, as a solvent and automobile antifreeze, and in medicine in suppositories and skin emollients. Also called **glycerin, glycerine.** [GLYCER(IN) + -OL[1]]

glyc·er·ol·y·sis (glis′ə rol′i sis), *n., pl.* **-ses** (-sēz′). *Chem.* chemical decomposition resulting from the interaction of a compound and glycerol. [GLYCEROL + -LYSIS]

glyc·er·yl (glis′ər il), *adj. Chem.* containing the glyceryl group. [GLYCER(IN) + -YL]

glyc′eryl group′, *Chem.* the trivalent group, $-CH_2(CH-)CH_2-$, derived from glycerol. Also called **glyc′eryl rad′ical.**

glyc′eryl mon·o·ac′e·tate (mon′ō as′i tāt′), *Chem.* acetin. [MONO- + ACETATE]

glyc′eryl tri·ni′trate (trī nī′trāt), *Chem.* nitroglycerin. [TRI- + NITRATE]

glyc′eryl tri·o′le·ate (trī ō′lē āt′), *Chem.* olein. [TRI- + OLEATE]

glyc′eryl tri·pal′mi·tate (trī pal′mi tāt′), *Chem.* palmitin. [TRI- + PALMITATE]

gly·cine (glī′sēn, glī sēn′), *n. Chem.* a colorless, crystalline, sweet, water-soluble solid, H_2NCH_2COOH, the simplest amino acid: used chiefly in organic synthesis and biochemical research. Also called **aminoacetic acid, glycocoll.** [GLYC- + -INE[2]]

glyco-, a learned borrowing from Greek where it meant "sweet"; used as a combining form of **glucose** and of various chemical compounds, such as **glycerol, glycogen, glycol,** having initial *glyc-: glycolipid.* Also, **glyc-, gluco-, gluc-.** [comb. form repr. Gk *glykýs* sweet]

gly·co·coll (glī′kə kol′), *n.* *Chem.* glycine. [GLYCO- + *-coll,* ME *-col* < L *-coll(a)* < Gk *-kolla,* comb. form of *kólla* glue]

gly·co·gen (glī′kə jən), *n.* *Biochem.* a white, tasteless polysaccharide, $(C_6H_{10}O_5)n$, molecularly similar to starch, constituting the principal carbohydrate storage material in animals and occurring chiefly in the liver, in muscle, and in fungi and yeasts. Also called **animal starch.** [GLYCO- + -GEN]

gly·co·gen·ase (glī′kə jə nās′), *n.* *Biochem.* a liver enzyme that breaks down glycogen to glucose in the body. [GLYCOGEN + -ASE]

gly·co·gen·e·sis (glī′kə jen′i sis), *n.* *Biochem.* the formation of glycogen from monosaccharides in the body, esp. glucose. Also, **glycogeny.** [GLYCO- + -GENESIS]

gly·co·ge·net·ic (glī′kō jə net′ik), *adj.* *Biochem.* of or pertaining to the formation of sugar in the liver. Also, **gly·cog·e·nous** (glī koj′ə nəs). [GLYCO- + -GENETIC]

gly·co·gen·ic (glī′kə jen′ik), *adj.* *Biochem.* **1.** of or pertaining to glycogen. **2.** glycogenetic. [GLYCOGEN + -IC]

gly′cogen′ic ac′id, *Chem.* See **gluconic acid.**

gly·co·ge·nol·y·sis (glī′kō jə nol′i sis), *n.* *Biochem.* the breakdown of glycogen to glucose in body tissue. [GLYCOGEN + -O- + -LYSIS] —**gly·co·gen·o·lyt·ic** (glī′kō jen′ᵊlit′ik), *adj.*

gly·co·ge·no·sis (glī′kō jə nō′sis), *n.* *Pathol.* a childhood disease characterized by large deposits of glycogen in the heart, liver, and other organs, caused by abnormal metabolism. Also called **gly′cogen disease′.** [GLYCOGEN + -OSIS]

gly·cog·e·ny (glī koj′ə nē), *n.* *Biochem.* glycogenesis. [GLYCO- + -GENY]

gly·col (glī′kōl, -kôl, -kol), *n.* *Chem.* **1.** Also called **ethylene glycol, ethylene alcohol.** a colorless, sweet liquid, CH_2OHCH_2OH, used chiefly as an automobile antifreeze and as a solvent. **2.** any of a group of alcohols containing two hydroxyl groups. [GLYC(ERIN + ALCOH)OL]

gly·col·ic (glī kol′ik), *adj.* *Chem.* pertaining to or derived from glycol. Also, **gly·col′lic.** [GLYCOL + -IC]

glycol′ic ac′id, *Chem.* a colorless, crystalline, water-soluble powder, $CH_2OHCOOH$, used chiefly for textile printing and dyeing and in pesticides. Also, **glycollic acid.** Also called **hydroxyacetic acid.**

gly·co·lip·id (glī′kə lip′id), *n.* *Biochem.* any of the class of lipids comprising the cerebrosides and gangliosides, that upon hydrolysis yields galactose or a similar sugar, a fatty acid, and sphingosine or dihydrosphingosine. [GLYCO- + LIPID]

glycol′lic ac′id, *Chem.* See **glycolic acid.**

gly·col·y·sis (glī kol′i sis), *n.* *Biochem.* the catabolism of carbohydrates, as glucose and glycogen, by enzymes, with the release of energy and the production of lactic or pyruvic acids. [GLYCO- + -LYSIS]

gly·co·lyt·ic (glī′kə lit′ik), *adj.* *Biochem.* of, relating to, or causing glycolysis. [GLYCO- + -LYTIC] —**gly′co·lyt′i·cal·ly,** *adv.*

gly·co·ne·o·gen·e·sis (glī′kō nē′ō jen′i sis), *n.* *Biochem.* gluconeogenesis. [GLYCO- + NEO- + -GENESIS] —**gly·co·ne·o·ge·net·ic** (glī′kō nē′ō jə net′ik), *adj.*

gly·con′ic ac′id (glī kon′ik), *Chem.* See **gluconic acid.**

gly·co·pep·tide (glī′kō pep′tīd), *n.* *Biochem.* glycoprotein. [GLYCO- + PEPTIDE]

gly·co·pex·is (glī′kō pek′sis), *n.* *Physiol.* the storage of glycogen in the liver. Also, **gly·co·pex·i·a** (glī′kō-pek′sē ə). [GLYCO- + Gk *pêxis* coagulation] —**gly′-ko·pex′ic, gly·ko·pec·tic** (glī′kō pek′tik), *adj.*

gly·co·pro·tein (glī′kō prō′tēn, -tē in), *n.* *Biochem.* any of a group of complex proteins containing a carbohydrate combined with a simple protein, as mucin. Also, **glucoprotein.** Also called **glycopeptide.** [GLYCO- + PROTEIN]

gly·co·side (glī′kə sīd′), *n.* *Biochem.* any of the class of compounds that yield a sugar and an aglycon upon hydrolysis. [GLYCOSE + -IDE] —**gly·co·sid·ic** (glī′kə-sid′ik), *adj.*

gly·cos·u·ri·a (glī′kōs yŏŏ rē′ə), *n.* *Pathol.* excretion of glucose in the urine, as in diabetes. Also, **glucosuria.** [GLYCOSE + -URIA] —**gly′cos·u′ric,** *adj.*

gly′cu·ron′ic ac′id (glī′kyə ron′ik, glī′-), *Biochem.* See **glucuronic acid.**

gly·cur·o·nide (glī kyŏŏr′ə nīd′), *n.* *Biochem.* glucuronide. Also, **gly·cur·o·nid** (glī kyŏŏr′ə nid).

Glyn (glin), *n.* **1. Elinor,** 1864–1943, English writer. **2.** Also, **Glen, Glenn, Glyn·is** (glin′is), **Glynn, Glynne.** a boy's or girl's given name.

gly·ox·a·line (glī ok′sə lēn′, -lin), *n.* *Chem.* imidazole. [GLYC(OL) + OXAL(IC) + -INE²]

glyph (glif), *n.* **1.** *Archit.* an ornamental channel or groove. **2.** a sculptured figure or relief carving. **3.** *Archaeol.* a pictograph or hieroglyph. [< Gk *glyph(ḗ)* carving, deriv. of *glýphein* to hollow out] —**glyph′ic,** *adj.*

gly·phog·ra·phy (gli fog′rə fē), *n.* *Print.* a method for making letterpress plates by engraving onto a waxed copper plate, dusting with graphite, and preparing an electrotype. [GLYPH + -O- + -GRAPHY] —**glyph·o·graph** (glif′ə graf′, -gräf′), *n.* —**gly·phog′ra·pher,** *n.* —**glyph·o·graph·ic** (glif′ə graf′ik), *adj.*

glyp·tic (glip′tik), *adj.* **1.** of or pertaining to carving or engraving on gems or the like. —*n.* **2.** act or process of producing glyptic ornaments. [< Gk *glyptik(ós)* of engraving, of stone carving, equiv. to *glypt(ós)* carved (deriv. of *glýphein* to engrave, hollow out) + *-ikos* -IC]

glyp·tics (glip′tiks), *n.* glyptography (def. 2). [see GLYPTIC, -ICS]

glyp·to·dont (glip′tə-dont′), *n.* any edentate mammal of the extinct genus *Glyptodon,* of the Pleistocene epoch, having the body covered by a horny and bony armor. [< Gk *glypt(ós)* carved + -ODONT]

Glyptodont, genus *Glyptodon* (Length about 9 ft.)

glyp·to·graph (glip′tə graf′, -gräf′), *n.* **1.** an engraved or carved design, as on a gem. **2.** an object, as a gem, having such a design. [< Gk *glyptó(s)* carved + -GRAPH]

glyp·tog·ra·phy (glip tog′rə fē), *n.* **1.** the description or study of engraved gems or other stones. **2.** Also called **glyptics.** the art or process of engraving on gems or the like. [< Gk *glyptó(s)* carved + -GRAPHY] —**glyp·tog′ra·pher,** *n.* —**glyp·to·graph·ic** (glip′tə-graf′ik), *adj.*

Gm, gigameter.

gm., gram; grams.

G.M., 1. General Manager. **2.** Grand Marshal. **3.** Grand Master.

G-man (jē′man′), *n., pl.* **G-men.** an agent for the FBI. [prob. repr. *Government man*]

G.M. & S., general, medical, and surgical.

G.m.a.t., Greenwich mean astronomical time.

Gmc., Germanic. Also, **Gmc**

Gm counter. See **Geiger counter.**

GMT, Greenwich Mean Time. Also, **G.M.T.**

G.N., Graduate Nurse.

gnam·ma (nam′ə), *n.* (in W Australia) a hollow in bare rock, narrow at the opening and wider at the bottom, in which water collects. [< native Austral]

gnar (när), *v.i.,* **gnarred, gnar·ring.** to snarl; growl. Also, **gnarr.** [imit; cf. OE *gnyrran,* G *knarren, knirren,* MD *gnerren, gnorren*]

gnarl¹ (närl), *n.* **1.** a knotty protuberance on a tree; knot. —*v.t.* **2.** to twist. [back formation from GNARLED] —**Syn. 2.** contort, distort.

gnarl² (närl), *v.i.* to growl; snarl. [var. of GNAR]

gnarled (närld), *adj.* **1.** (of trees) full of or covered with gnarls; bent; twisted. **2.** having a rugged, weather-beaten appearance: *a gnarled old sea captain.* **3.** crabby; cantankerous. [var. of KNURLED]

gnarl·y (när′lē), *adj.,* **gnarl·i·er, gnarl·i·est.** gnarled. [GNARL¹ + -Y¹] —**gnarl′i·ness,** *n.*

gnash (nash), *v.t.* **1.** to grind or strike (the teeth) together, esp. in rage or pain. **2.** to bite with grinding teeth. —*v.i.* **3.** to gnash the teeth. —*n.* **4.** an act of gnashing. [var. of obs. *gnast* < Scand; cf. OIcel *gnastan* gnashing of teeth] —**gnash′ing·ly,** *adv.*

gnat (nat), *n.* **1.** any of certain small flies, esp. the biting gnats or punkies of the family *Ceratopogonidae,* the midges of the family *Chironomidae,* and the buffalo gnats or black flies of the family *Simuliidae.* **2.** *Brit.* mosquito. **3. strain at a gnat and swallow a camel,** to fuss about trifles while assenting readily in more serious matters. [ME; OE *gnæt(t)*; c. G (dial.) *Gnatze*] —**gnat′like′,** *adj.*

Gnat, *Simulium vittatum* (Length ¼ in.)

gnat·catch·er (nat′kach′ər), *n.* any of several small, American, insectivorous warblers of the genus *Polioptila,* of the family *Sylviidae.* [GNAT + CATCHER]

gnat·eat·er (nat′ē′tər), *n.* any of several small, long-legged, passerine birds of the family *Conopophagidae,* of South America. Also called **ant-pipit.** [GNAT + EATER]

gnath·ic (nath′ik), *adj.* of or pertaining to the jaw. Also, **gnath′al.** [< Gk *gnáth(os)* jaw + -IC]

gnath′ic in′dex, *Craniol.* the ratio of the distance from basion to prosthion to the distance from basion to nasion, expressed in percent of the latter.

gna·thi·on (nā′thē on′, nath′ē-), *n.* *Craniol.* the lowest point on the anterior margin of the lower jaw in the midsagittal plane. [< NL < Gk *gnáth(os)* jaw, mouth + *-ion* dim. suffix]

gna·thon·ic (na thon′ik), *adj.* sycophantic; fawning. [< L *gnathonic(us),* deriv. of *Gnathon-* (s. of *Gnatho*) name of a sycophantic character in the Roman comedy *Eunuchus* by Terence; see -IC] —**gna·thon′i·cal·ly,** *adv.*

-gnathous, a combining form referring to the jaw: *prognathous.* [< Gk *gnáth(os)* jaw + -OUS]

gnat·ty (nat′ē), *adj.,* **-ti·er, -ti·est.** infested with gnats. [GNAT + -Y¹]

gnaw (nô), *v.,* **gnawed, gnawed** or **gnawn, gnaw·ing.** —*v.t.* **1.** to wear away or remove by persistent biting or nibbling. **2.** to form or make by so doing: *to gnaw a hole through the wall.* **3.** to corrode; waste or wear away. **4.** to trouble or torment by constant annoyance, worry, etc.; vex; plague. —*v.i.* **5.** to bite or chew on persistently: *The spaniel gnawed happily on a bone.* **6.** to cause corrosion: *The acid gnaws at the metal.* **7.** to cause an effect resembling corrosion: *The water gnaws at the shoreline. Her mistake gnawed at her conscience.* [ME *gnaw(en),* OE *gnagen*; c. G *nagen,* OIcel *gnāga*] —**gnaw′a·ble,** *adj.* —**gnaw′er,** *n.*

gnaw·ing (nô′ing), *n.* **1.** the act of one who or that which gnaws. **2.** Usually, **gnawings.** persistent, dull pains, as though caused by biting, nibbling, etc.: *the gnawings of hunger.* [ME; see GNAW, -ING¹] —**gnaw′-ing·ly,** *adv.*

gnawn (nôn), *v.* a pp. of **gnaw.**

gneiss (nīs), *n.* a metamorphic rock, generally made up of bands that differ in color and composition, some bands being rich in feldspar and quartz, others rich in hornblende or mica. [< G] —**gneiss′ic,** *adj.*

gneiss·oid (nī′soid), *adj.* resembling gneiss. [GNEISS + -OID]

Gnes·en (gnā′zən), *n.* a city in W central Poland, ENE of Posen: important in the early history of the country; 10th-century cathedral. 45,000 (est. 1963). Polish, **Gniez·no** (gnyez′nô).

gnome¹ (nōm), *n.* one of a legendary species of diminutive beings, usually described as shriveled little old men, that inhabit the interior of the earth and act as guardians of its treasures; troll. [< F < NL *gnom(us)* < ? Gk *gnṓmē* GNOME²] —**gnom′ish,** *adj.* —**Syn.** See **goblin, sylph.**

gnome² (nōm, nō′mē), *n.* a short, pithy expression of a general truth; aphorism. [< Gk *gnṓmē* judgment, opinion, purpose]

gno·mic (nō′mik, nom′ik), *adj.* **1.** like or containing gnomes or aphorisms. **2.** of, pertaining to, or noting a writer of aphorisms, esp. any of certain Greek poets. Also, **gno′mi·cal.** [< Gk *gnōmik(ós).* See GNOME², -IC] —**gno′mi·cal·ly,** *adv.*

gno·mist (nō′mist), *n.* a writer of aphorisms. [GNOME² + -IST]

gno·mol·o·gy (nō mol′ə jē), *n.* **1.** a collection or anthology of gnomes or aphorisms. **2.** gnomic or aphoristic writing. [< Gk *gnōmología.* See GNOME², -LOGY] —**gno·mo·log·ic** (nō′mə loj′ik), **gno′mo·log′i·cal,** *adj.* —**gno·mol′o·gist,** *n.*

gno·mon (nō′mon), *n.* **1.** an early astronomical instrument consisting of a vertical shaft, column, or the like, for determining the altitude of the sun or the latitude of a position by measuring the length of its shadow cast at noon. **2.** the raised part of a sundial that casts the shadow; a style. **3.** *Geom.* the part of a parallelogram that remains after a similar parallelogram has been taken away from one of its corners. [< L: pin of a sundial < Gk: one who knows, inspector]

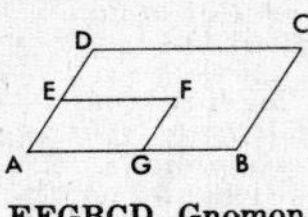

EFGBCD, Gnomon (def. 3)

gno·mon·ic (nō mon′ik), *adj.* **1.** of or pertaining to a gnomon or to a sundial. **2.** of or pertaining to the measurement of time by a gnomon or a sundial. **3.** gnomic. Also, **gno·mon′i·cal.** [< L *gnōmonic(us)* of, belonging to a gnomon < Gk *gnōmonikós.* See GNOMON, -IC]

-gnomy, an element meaning "knowledge," occurring in loan words from Greek and used in combination with other elements of Greek origin: *physiognomy.* [< LL *-gnomia* < Gk *-gnōmía.* See GNOMON, -Y³]

gno·sis (nō′sis), *n.* knowledge of spiritual things; mystical knowledge. [< NL < Gk: a seeking to know, equiv. to *gnō-* know + *-sis* -SIS]

-gnosis, a learned borrowing from Greek meaning "knowledge," used in the formation of compound words: *prognosis.* [< L < Gk *gnōsis*]

Gnos·sus (nos′əs), *n.* Knossos. —**Gnos′si·an,** *adj.*

gnos·tic (nos′tik), *adj.* Also, **gnos′ti·cal. 1.** pertaining to knowledge. **2.** possessing knowledge, esp. esoteric knowledge of spiritual things. **3.** (*cap.*) pertaining to or characteristic of the Gnostics. —*n.* **4.** (*cap.*) a member of any of certain sects among the early Christians who claimed to have superior knowledge of spiritual things, and explained the world as created by powers or agencies arising as emanations from the Godhead. [< LL *Gnostic(ī)* name of the sect < Gk *gnōstikós* pertaining to knowledge, equiv. to *gnōst(ós)* known + *-ikos* -IC] —**gnos′ti·cal·ly,** *adv.*

-gnostic, a combination of **-gnosis** and **-ic,** used to form adjectives from stems ending in **-gnosis:** *prognostic.* [< ML *-gnosticus* < Gk *gnōstikós* pertaining to knowledge]

Gnos·ti·cise (nos′ti sīz′), *v.i., v.t.,* **-cised, -cis·ing.** *Chiefly Brit.* Gnosticize. Also, **gnos′ti·cise′.** —**Gnos′-ti·cis′er,** *n.*

Gnos·ti·cize (nos′ti sīz′), *v.,* **-cized, -ciz·ing.** —*v.i.* **1.** to adopt or maintain Gnostic views. —*v.t.* **2.** to explain on Gnostic principles; give a Gnostic interpretation of or quality to. Also, **gnos′ti·cize′;** *esp. Brit.,* **Gnosticise, gnosticise.** [GNOSTIC + -IZE] —**Gnos′-ti·ciz′er,** *n.*

gno·thi se·au·ton (gnō′thi se ou ton′), *Greek.* know thyself.

gno·to·bi·o·sis (nō′tō bī ō′sis), *n.* *Bacteriol.* an environmental condition in which germfree animals have been inoculated with strains of known microorganisms. [< Gk *gnōtó(s)* known + -O- + -BIOSIS]

gno·to·bi·ote (nō′tō bī′ōt), *n.* *Bacteriol.* a gnotobiotic animal. [< Gk *gnōt(ós)* known + -O- + *-biote,* back formation from BIOTIC]

gno·to·bi·ot·ic (nō′tō-bī ot′ik), *adj.* *Bacteriol.* (of germfree animals) inoculated with microorganisms of a given type. [GNOTOBIOTE + -IC]

GNP, See **gross national product.** Also, **G.N.P.**

gnu (nōō, nyōō), *n., pl.* **gnus,** (*esp. collectively*) **gnu.** any of several African antelopes of the genus *Connochaetes,* having an oxlike head, curved horns, and a long tail. Also called **wildebeest.** [< Kaffir *nqu*]

Gnu, *Connochaetes taurinus* (4 ft. high at shoulder; total length 7 ft.; tail 1½ ft.)

go¹ (gō), *v.,* **went, gone, go·ing,** *n., pl.* **goes,** *interj., adj.* —*v.i.* **1.** to move or proceed, esp. to or from something: *a fishwife going to the market place.* **2.** to leave a place; depart: *People were coming and going all the time.* **3.** to keep or be in motion; function or perform as required: *The engine's going now. Can't you go any faster in your work?* **4.** to become as specified: *to go mad.* **5.** to continue in a certain state or condition; be habitually: *to go in rags.* **6.** to act as specified: *Go warily if he wants to discuss terms.* **7.** to act so as to come into a certain state or condition: *to go into debt; to go to sleep; to go to war.* **8.** to be known: *to go by a false name.* **9.** to reach, extend, or give access to: *This road goes across the mountains. Where does this door go?* **10.** (of time) to pass; elapse: *The time went fast.* **11.** to be applied, allotted, awarded, transferred, etc., to a particular recipient or purpose: *My money goes for food and rent.* **12.** to be sold: *I have a bid of two dollars. Going! Going! Gone!* **13.** to compare or be generally or usually: *This player is short, as pitchers go.* **14.** to conduce or tend: *This only goes to prove the point.* **15.** to result or end; turn out: *How did the game go?* **16.** to belong; have a place: *This book goes on the top shelf.* **17.** (of colors, styles, etc.) to harmonize; be compatible; be suited: *Your blue hat doesn't go with your green gloves.* **18.** to fit around or into; be able to be extended, contained, inserted, etc.: *This belt won't go around my waist. Will all these clothes go in your closet?* **19.** to be or become consumed, spent, finished, etc.: *The cake went fast, but no one finished the pie.* **20.** to be or become discarded, dismissed, put aside, forgotten, etc.: *Those childish jokes of yours have got to go!* **21.** to develop, progress, or proceed, esp. with reference to success or satisfaction: *How is your new job going? The story isn't going very well.* **22.** to pass or circulate, as in transmission or communication: *The rumor has gone around.* **23.** to move or proceed with remarkable speed or energy: *Look at that airplane go!* **24.** to act or operate with sound, as a bell or a gun; make a certain sound: *The gun goes bang.* **25.** to be phrased, written, or composed: *How do the words to that song go?* **26.** to seek or have recourse for a decision, verdict, corroboration, defense, etc.; resort: *to go to court; He always goes to his brother for help.* **27.** to become worn out, weakened, ineffective, etc.: *His eyesight is beginning to go.* **28.** to die: *The old man went peacefully at 3 a.m.* **29.** to fail, break, or give way: *The dike might go any minute.* **30.** to begin; come into action: *Go when you hear the bell.* **31.** to contribute in amount or quantity; be requisite: *Sixteen ounces go to the pound.* **32.** to be or be able to be divided into; be contained as a mathematical element: *Three goes into fifteen five times.* **33.** to contribute to an end result: *the items which go to make up a total.* **34.** to be about, intending, or destined (usually used in the present tense, fol. by an infinitive): *He is going to write.* **35.** to receive approval or be considered acceptable, adequate, or true; succeed: *Anything goes if it is properly presented.* **36.** to be authoritative; be the final word: *This is my house, and what I say goes!* **37.** to subject oneself: *Don't go to any trouble.* **38.** (used in the infinitive as an intensifier to indicate the idea of proceeding or having done something rapidly, impulsively, desperately, or with the expectation of serious consequences): *He finally had to go ask for a raise. He decided to go borrow it.* —*v.t.* **39.** *Informal.* to endure or tolerate: *I can't go his preaching.* **40.** *Informal.* to risk, pay, afford, bet or bid: *I'll go two dollars on number seven. I'll go sixty dollars on a suit, but no more.* **41.** to follow; move or proceed with or according to: *Going my way?* **42.** to share or participate in to the extent of (often fol. by a complementary substantive): *to go partners; to go halves.* **43.** to yield, produce, weigh as a usable amount, or grow to: *These tomatoes will go half a pound each. This field will go 500 bales of cotton.* **44.** to assume the obligation, responsibility, or function of: *His father went bail for him.* **45.** *Informal.* to enjoy, appreciate, desire, or want: *I could go a big steak dinner right now.* **46. go about, a.** *Naut.* to change course by tacking or wearing. **b.** to occupy oneself with; perform: *The shoemaker goes about his work with a smile.* **47. go after,** to attempt to obtain; strive for: *You'll never get what you want if you don't go after it energetically.* **48. go against,** to be in conflict with or opposed to: *It goes against the company's policy to make such an exception.* **49. go ahead,** to proceed without hesitation or delay: *If you want to use the bathroom, go ahead.* **50. go along,** to agree with; concur: *I can't go along with you on that idea.* **51. go and,** to be so thoughtless, unfortunate, or silly as to: *It was going to be a surprise but he went and told her. She had to go and lose her gloves at the theater.* **52. go around, a.** to be often in company (often fol. by *with*): *to go around with a bad crowd.* **b.** to be sufficient for all: *Is there enough food to go around?* **53. go at, a.** to assault; attack: *The dog went at the mailman again.* **b.** to begin or proceed vigorously: *to go at one's work with a will.* **54. go back on.** See **back**[2] (def. 7). **55. go by, a.** to be disregarded or not taken advantage of: *Don't let this chance go by.* **b.** to be guided by or to rely upon: *Don't go by what she says.* **56. go down, a.** to suffer defeat: *to go down fighting.* **b.** to be accepted or believed: *This nonsense goes down as truth with many persons.* **c.** to admit of being consumed: *This food goes down smoothly.* **d.** to be remembered in history or by posterity. **e.** *Brit.* to leave a university, permanently or at the end of a term. **f.** *Bridge.* to fall short of making one's contract. **57. go for, a.** to be used for the purpose of or be a substitute for: *material that goes for silk.* **b.** to make an attempt at; try for: *He is going for the championship.* **c.** to assault: *They went for the stranger with a vengeance.* **d.** to favor; like: *It simply isn't the kind of life you would go for.* **58. go for broke.** See **broke** (def. 6). **59. go in for, a.** to adopt as one's particular interest; approve of; like. **b.** to occupy oneself with; engage in: *Europeans in increasing numbers are going in for camping.* **60. go into, a.** to discuss or investigate: *The author goes into the various influences on Neoclassicism most thoroughly.* **b.** to undertake as one's study or work: *to go into medicine.* **61. go in with,** to join in a partnership or union; combine with: *He asked me to go in with him on the purchase of a boat.* **62. go off, a.** to explode, fire, or perform or begin to function abruptly: *A gun went off in the distance. The alarm clock went off too soon.* **b.** (of what has been expected or planned) to happen: *The interview went off very badly.* **63. go on, a.** to behave; act: *Don't go on like that!* **b.** to continue: *Go on working—don't mind me.* **c.** to talk effusively; chatter: *"Do you go on like that all the time?" he finally managed to say.* **d.** to happen or take place: *What's going on here?* **e.** (used to express disbelief): *Go on, you're kidding me.* **f.** to appear onstage in a theatrical performance: *I can't talk now; I'm going on in five minutes.* **64. go out, a.** to come to an end, esp. to fade in popularity. **b.** to cease or fail to function: *The lights went out during the storm.* **c.** to participate in social activities, on dates, etc.: *She goes out with boys who are older than she is.* **d.** to take part in a strike: *The printers went out yesterday in a contract dispute.* **e.** *Rummy.* to dispose of the last card in one's hand by melding it on the table. **f.** *Cards.* to achieve a point score equal to or above the score necessary to win the game. **65. go over, a.** to read; scan. **b.** to repeat; review. **c.** to be effective or successful: *The proposal really went over very well with the trustees.* **d.** to examine: *The mechanic went over the car but found nothing wrong.* **66. go the whole hog,** to do something thoroughly or consistently: *If you're getting a new amplifier, why don't you go the whole hog and replace everything?* **67. go through, a.** to bear; experience: *The civilian population of Europe went through a great deal during World War II.* **b.** to examine or search carefully: *He went through all of his things but couldn't find the letter.* **c.** to be successful; be accepted: *The proposed appropriation will never go through.* **d.** to use up; spend completely: *He went through his allowance in one day.* **68. go through with,** to persevere with to the end; bring to completion: *It was perhaps the biggest challenge of his life, and he resolved to go through with it.* **69. go to!** *Archaic.* **a.** you don't say! I don't believe you! **b.** let's do it! come on! **70. go together, a.** to be appropriate or harmonious: *The rug and curtains don't go together.* **b.** to keep company; date; court: *They have gone together for two years.* **71. go to it,** *Informal.* to begin vigorously and at once. **72. go under, a.** to be overwhelmed or ruined; fail. **b.** (of a vessel) to founder. **73. go up, a.** to be in the process of construction, as a building. **b.** to increase in cost, value, etc. **c.** to forget, as an actor his lines. **d.** *Brit.* to go to a university at the beginning of a term. **74. go with,** *Informal.* to keep company with; court; date: *He went with her for parts of two semesters.* Also, **go out with. 75. let go, a.** to release one's grasp or hold: *Please let go of my arm.* **b.** to free; release: *The suspects have been let go because of insufficient evidence.* **c.** to cease to employ; dismiss: *Business was slack and many employees were let go.* **d.** to become unrestrained; abandon inhibitions: *She let go and went into a tirade that lasted half an hour.* **e.** to dismiss; forget; discard: *Once he has an idea, he never lets go of it.* **76. let go with,** to express or utter with abandon: *He let go with a sudden yell.* **77. let oneself go,** to free oneself of inhibitions or restraint: *Let yourself go and get mad once in a while.* **78. to go,** *Informal.* (of food) for consumption off the premises where sold: *coffee and doughnuts to go.* —*n.* **79.** the act of going: *the come and go of the seasons.* **80.** energy, spirit, or animation: *a man with a lot of go.* **81.** a try at something; attempt: *to have a go at winning the prize.* **82.** a successful accomplishment: *to make a go of a new business.* **83.** *Informal.* a piece of business at the point of accomplishment; an agreement; deal; bargain: *Thirty dollars? It's a go.* **84.** *Boxing Informal.* a bout: *the main go.* **85.** *Brit. Informal.* the first or preliminary examination at Cambridge University for the degree of A.B. **86. from the word "go,"** from the very start; since the beginning: *He's been against the plan from the word "go."* **87. no go,** *Informal.* futile; useless: *We tried to get there by noon, but it was no go.* **88. on the go,** very busy; active: *Everyone in the city appears to be constantly on the go.* —*interj.* **89.** (in calling the start of a race) start the race; leave the starting line: *On your mark! Get set! Go!* —*adj. U.S.* **90.** ready. **91.** functioning properly: *two minutes before the satellite is to be launched and all systems are go.* [ME *go(n)*, OE *gān*; c. OHG *gēn*, G *gehen*] —**Syn. 1.** walk, run, ride, travel, advance. —**Ant. 1.** stay.

go[2] (gō), *n.* a Japanese game for two persons, played on a board having 361 intersections on which black and white stones or counters are alternately placed, the object being to block off and capture the opponent's stones and control the larger part of the board. Also called **I-go.** [< Jap]

DIU
DAMÃO
Bombay
INDIA
ARABIAN SEA
Gôa

G.O., 1. general office. **2.** general order. Also, **g.o.**

go·a (gō′ə), *n.* a gazelle, *Procapra picticaudata*, of the Tibetan plateau. [< Tibetan *dgoba*]

Gô·a (gō′ə), *n.* a former district in Portuguese India, on the Arabian Sea, ab. 250 mi. S of Bombay: annexed by India December 1961. 551,397 (1950); 1394 sq. mi. *Cap.:* Panjim.

goad (gōd), *n.* **1.** a stick with a pointed or electrically charged end, for driving cattle, oxen, etc.; prod. **2.** anything that pricks, wounds, or urges like such a stick; a stimulus. —*v.t.* **3.** to prick or drive with or as if with, a goad; prod; incite. [ME *gode*, OE *gād*; cf. Langobardic *gaida* spearhead] —**goad′like′,** *adj.* —**Syn. 3.** spur.

goaf (gōf), *n., pl.* **goaves.** *Mining.* **1.** Also, **goaves.** an area of a mine or pit from which all the ore has been removed. **2.** gob[1] (def. 3). [?]

go-a·head (gō′ə hed′), *adj.* **1.** moving forward; advancing. **2.** enterprising: *a go-ahead Yankee peddler.* —*n.* **3.** permission or a signal to proceed: *They got the go-ahead on the construction work.* [n., adj. use of v. phrase *go ahead*]

goal (gōl), *n.* **1.** the result or achievement toward which effort is directed; aim; end. **2.** the terminal point in a race. **3.** a pole or other object by which such a point is marked. **4.** an area, basket, cage or other object or structure toward or into which players of various games attempt to throw, carry, kick, hit, or drive a ball, puck, etc., to score a point or points. **5.** the act of throwing, carrying, kicking, driving, etc., a ball or puck into such an area or object. **6.** the score made by this act. [ME *gol* boundary, limit; cf. OE *gǣlan* to hinder, impede] —**goal′less,** *adj.* —**Syn. 1.** target; purpose, object, objective, intent, intention. **2.** finish.

goal·ie (gō′lē), *n.* a goalkeeper. [GOAL + -IE]

goal·keep·er (gōl′kē′pər), *n.* (in ice hockey, field hockey, lacrosse, soccer, etc.) a player whose chief duty is to prevent the ball or puck from crossing or entering the goal. [GOAL + KEEPER] —**goal′keep′ing,** *n.*

goal′ line′, *Sports.* the line that bounds a goal, esp. the front line.

goal′ post′, either of the two posts supporting a crossbar and forming the goal in certain sports, as football.

goal′-post mast′ (gōl′pōst′), *Naut.* a mast structure used on cargo-carrying vessels, consisting of a pair of short masts **(pair masts),** each with a derrick, set athwartships and connected at the top by a beam sometimes bearing at its center an upper mast for lights or signals.

goal·tend·er (gōl′ten′dər), *n.* a goalkeeper. [GOAL + TENDER[3]]

goal′ tend′ing, *Basketball.* illegally knocking the ball away from the opponents' basket after it has begun its downward arc.

Go′a pow′der, a brownish-yellow, odorless, crystalline powder obtained from the wood or the trunk of the Brazilian tree *Andira araroba*, used as a source of chrysarobin. Also called **araroba.** [after GÔA]

goat (gōt), *n.* **1.** any of numerous agile, hollow-horned ruminants of the genus *Capra*, of the family *Bovidae*, closely related to the sheep, found native in rocky and mountainous regions of the Old World, and widely distributed in domesticated varieties. **2.** any of various related animals, as the Rocky Mountain goat. **3.** *(cap.) Astron., Astrol.* the constellation or sign Capricorn. **4.** *Informal.* scapegoat; victim: *He was always made the goat when someone was needed to take the blame.* **5.** a licentious or lecherous man. **6. get one's goat,** *U.S. Informal.* to anger, annoy, or frustrate a person: *People who get to work late get his goat.* [ME *got*, OE *gāt*; c. G *Geiss*] —**goat′like′,** *adj.*

Goat, *Capra hircus* (2½ ft. high at shoulder; length 4½ ft.)

goat′ an′telope, 1. a goatlike antelope of the genus *Naemorhedus*, as the goral, *N. goral*, or *N. crispus* of Japan. **2.** any antelope of the tribe *Rupicaprini*, a subdivision of the sheep and goat family, and including the chamois, goral, serow, and Rocky Mountain goat.

goat·ee (gō tē′), *n.* a man's beard trimmed to a tuft or point on the chin. [GOAT + -EE, from the resemblance to a goat's tufted chin] —**goat·eed′,** *adj.*

goat·fish (gōt′fish′), *n., pl.* **-fish·es,** *(esp. collectively)* **-fish.** any tropical and subtropical marine fish of the family *Mullidae*, having a pair of long barbels below the mouth. Also called **red mullet.** [GOAT + FISH]

goat′ god′, a deity with the legs and feet of a goat, as Pan or a satyr.

goat·herd (gōt′hûrd′), *n.* a person who tends goats. [ME; OE *gāthyrde*. See GOAT, HERD[2]]

goat·ish (gō′tish), *adj.* **1.** of or like a goat. **2.** lustful; lecherous. [GOAT + -ISH[1]] —**goat′ish·ly,** *adv.* —**goat′ish·ness,** *n.*

goat·pox (gōt′poks′), *n.* *Vet. Pathol.* a virus disease of goats that resembles cowpox and produces lesions inside the thighs and on other hairless skin areas. Also, **goat′ pox′, goat′-pox′.** [GOAT + POX]

goats·beard (gōts′bērd′), *n.* **1.** a composite plant, *Tragopogon pratensis*. **2.** a rosaceous herb, *Aruncus sylvester*, having long, slender spikes of small flowers. [GOAT + -'S[1] + BEARD]

goat·skin (gōt′skin′), *n.* **1.** the skin or hide of a goat. **2.** leather made from it. [ME; see GOAT, SKIN]

goat's-rue (gōts′ro͞o′), *n.* **1.** an American leguminous herb, *Tephrosia virginiana*. **2.** a European leguminous herb, *Galega officinalis*, formerly used in medicine. Also called **catgut, wild sweet pea.**

goat·suck·er (gōt′suk′ər), *n.* **1.** a nocturnal, European bird, *Caprimulgus europaeus*, of the family *Caprimulgidae*, having a short bill and a wide mouth and feeding on insects captured in the air. **2.** any other nocturnal or crepuscular bird of the family *Caprimulgidae*. Also called **nightjar.** [so called because formerly believed to suck the milk of goats; trans. of L *caprimulgus*, itself trans. of Gk *aigothēlas*]

goaves (gōvz), *n.* **1.** pl. of **goaf. 2.** goaf (def. 1).

gob[1] (gob), *n., v.,* **gobbed, gob·bing.** —*n.* **1.** a mass or lump. **2. gobs,** *Informal.* a large quantity: *She must have gobs of money.* **3.** Also called **goaf.** *Mining.* waste or barren material. —*v.t.* **4.** *Mining.* **a.** to fill (a goaf) with waste material. **b.** to put (waste material) into a goaf or pack. [ME *gobbe*, var. of *gob(b)e(t)* GOBBET]

gob[2] (gob), *n.* *Informal.* a seaman in the U.S. Navy. [?]

gob[3] (gob), *n.* *Slang.* the mouth. [? < Gael, Ir *gob* mouth, beak]

gob[4] (gob), *v.i.,* **gobbed, gob·bing,** *n.* *Brit. Dial.* gab[1].

go·bang (gō bäng′), *n.* a Japanese game played on a go board with players alternating and attempting to be first to place five counters in a row. Also, **go·ban** (gō bän′). Also called **go-moku.** [< Jap, equiv. to *go* GO[2] + *bang*, var. of *ban* board]

Go·bat (*Fr.* gô bA′), *n.* **Al·bert** (*Fr.* al beR′), 1843–1914, Swiss lawyer and statesman: Nobel peace prize 1902.

gob·bet (gob′it), *n.* **1.** a fragment or piece, esp. of raw flesh. **2.** a lump or mass. [ME *gobet* < OF: a mouthful, dim. of *gobe*. See GOB[1], -ET]

gob·ble[1] (gob′əl), *v.,* **-bled, -bling.** —*v.t.* **1.** to swallow or eat hastily or hungrily in large pieces; gulp. **2.** *Informal.* to seize upon eagerly (often fol. by *up*): *She gobbled up all the news I told her.* —*v.i.* **3.** to eat hastily. [prob. imit.; formed on GOB[1]] —**Syn. 1.** bolt, devour.

gob·ble[2] (gob′əl), *v.,* **-bled, -bling.** —*v.i.* **1.** to make the characteristic throaty cry of a male turkey. —*n.* **2.** the cry itself. [var. of GABBLE]

gob·ble·de·gook (gob′əl dē go͝ok′), *n.* language characterized by circumlocution and jargon: *the gobbledegook of government reports.* Also, **gob′ble·dy·gook′.** [fanciful formation from GOBBLE[2]]

gob·bler[1] (gob′lər), *n.* a male turkey. [GOBBLE[2] + -ER[1]]

gob·bler[2] (gob′lər), *n.* one who or that which gobbles or consumes voraciously or quickly: *a box of candy for two little gobblers; a gobbler of science fiction.* [GOBBLE[1] + -ER[1]]

Gob·e·lin (gob′ə lin; *Fr.* gô blaN′), *adj.* **1.** made at the tapestry factory of the Gobelins in Paris. **2.** resembling the tapestry made at the Gobelins.

go-be·tween (gō′bi twēn′), *n.* a person who acts as an agent or intermediary between persons or groups; intermediary. [n. use of v. phrase *go between*]

Go·bi (gō′bē), *n.* a desert in E Asia, mostly in Mongolia. ab. 450,000 sq. mi. Chinese, **Shamo.** —**Go′bi·an,** *adj.*

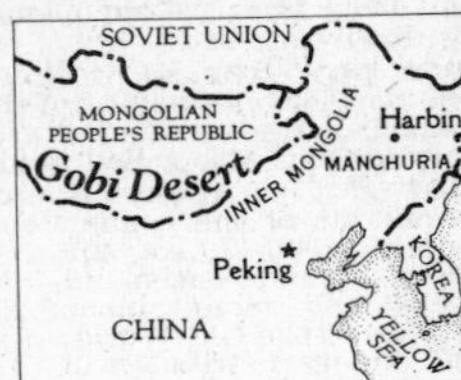

go·bi·oid (gō′bē oid′), *adj.* **1.** of or resembling a goby. —*n.* **2.** a gobioid fish. [< L *gōbi(us)* gudgeon + -OID]

gob·let (gob′lit), *n.* **1.** a drinking glass with a foot and stem. **2.** *Archaic.* a bowl-shaped drinking vessel. [ME *gobelet* < OF, dim. of *gobel* cup << Celt]

gob·lin (gob′lin), *n.* a grotesque sprite or elf that is mischievous or malicious toward people. [ME *gobelin* < MF < MHG *kobold* goblin]

—**Syn.** GOBLIN, GNOME, GREMLIN refer to imaginary beings thought to be malevolent to man. GOBLINS are demons of any size, usually in human or animal forms, which are supposed to assail, afflict, and even torture human beings: "*Be thou a spirit of health or goblin damn'd, . . .*" (Shak. *Hamlet I, iv*). GNOMES are small beings, like ugly little old men, who live in the earth, guarding mines, treasures, etc. They are mysteriously malevolent and terrify human beings by causing dreadful mishaps to occur. GREMLINS are invisible beings who were said by pilots in World War II to cause all sorts of things to go wrong with airplanes.

gob′ line′, *Naut.* See **martingale backrope.**

go·bo (gō′bō), *n., pl.* **-bos, -boes.** *Motion Pictures, Television.* **1.** a screen or mat covered with a dark material for shielding a camera lens from excess light or glare. **2.** a screen or sheet of sound-absorbent material for shielding a microphone from sounds coming from a particular direction. [?]

go·bo·ny (gə bō′nē), *adj. Heraldry.* company. Also, **go·bo·née** (gə bō′nā).

gob′ rope′, *Naut.* See **martingale backrope.**

go-by (gō′bī′), *n. Informal.* a going by without notice; an intentional passing by: *to give one the go-by.* [n. use of v. phrase *go by*]

go·by (gō′bē), *n., pl.* (*esp. collectively*) **-by,** (*esp. referring to two or more kinds or species*) **-bies.** **1.** any small marine or fresh-water fish of the family *Gobiidae,* often having the pelvic fins united to form a suctorial disk. **2.** any fish of the closely related family *Eleotridae,* having the pelvic fins separate. [< L *gōbi(us)* gudgeon (sp. var. of *gōbio* or *cōbius*) < Gk *kōbiós* kind of fish, gudgeon]

go-cart (gō′kärt′), *n.* **1.** a small carriage for young children to ride in; stroller. **2.** a small framework with casters, wheels, etc., in which children learn to walk; walker. **3.** a handcart. **4.** a small, light, low-slung vehicle, consisting of wheels, motor, steering device, and a frame with a seat, for racing or recreation, usually powered by a gasoline motor and capable of speeds upwards of 60 miles an hour.

Go·clen·i·us (gō klen′ē əs), *n.* a crater in the fourth quadrant of the face of the moon: about 32 miles in diameter.

God (god), *n., v.,* **god·ded, god·ding,** *interj.* —*n.* **1.** the one Supreme Being, the creator and ruler of the universe. **2.** the Supreme Being considered with reference to a particular attribute: *the God of battles.* **3.** (*l.c.*) one of several deities, esp. a male deity, presiding over some portion of worldly affairs. **4.** (*often l.c.*) a supreme being according to some particular conception: *the god of pantheism.* **5.** *Christian Science.* the Supreme Being considered with reference to the sum of His attributes. **6.** (*l.c.*) an image of a deity; an idol. **7.** (*l.c.*) any deified person or object. **8.** (*often l.c.*) **Gods,** *Theat.* **a.** the upper balcony in a theater. **b.** the spectators in this part of the balcony. —*v.t.* **9.** (*l.c.*) to regard or treat as a god; deify; idolize. —*interj.* **10.** (used to express disappointment, disbelief, weariness, frustration, annoyance, or the like): *God, there she goes singing off key again!* [ME, OE; c. D *god,* G *Gott,* Icel *godh,* Goth *guth*]

Go·dard (gô dar′), *n.* **Ben·ja·min Louis Paul** (bän zhä män′ lwē pôl), 1849–95, French violinist and composer.

Go·da·va·ri (gō dä′və rē), *n.* a river flowing SE from W India to the Bay of Bengal. 900 mi. long.

God-aw·ful (god′ô′fəl), *adj. Informal.* (*sometimes l.c.*) extremely dreadful or shocking: *What a God-awful thing to say! She looks god-awful in red.*

god·child (god′chīld′), *n., pl.* **-chil·dren.** **1.** a child for whom a godparent serves as sponsor at baptism. **2.** a child of a non-Christian religion for whom a godparent serves as religious sponsor. [ME; see GOD, CHILD]

god·damn (god′dam′), *interj. Informal.* **1.** (used as an exclamation of any strong feeling, esp. of disgust, irritation, etc., and often fol. by *it.*) —*n.* **2.** the utterance of "goddamn" in swearing or for emphasis. **3.** something of negligible value; damn: *not to give a good goddamn.* —*adj.* **4.** damned (def. 2). —*adv.* **5.** damned. —*v.t.* **6.** to curse (someone or something) as being contemptible or worthless; damn. —*v.i.* **7.** to use the word "goddamn"; swear. Also, **god′dam′.** [GOD + DAMN]

god·damned (god′damd′), *adj., superl.* **-damned·est, -damnd·est,** *adv. Informal.* —*adj.* **1.** damned (def. 2). —*adv.* **2.** (esp. in the superlative) most difficult to deal with; extremely complicated or peculiar. **3.** damned. Also, **goddamn, god′dam′.** [GOD + DAMNED]

god·damn·it (god′dam′it), *interj.* (*sometimes cap.*) *Informal.* (used to express anger, perplexity, amazement, etc.) Also, **god′dam′mit.** [GOD + DAMN + IT[1]]

God·dard (god′ərd), *n.* **Robert Hutch·ings** (huch′ingz), 1882–1945, U.S. physicist: pioneer in rocketry.

god·daugh·ter (god′dô′tər), *n.* a female godchild. [ME; OE *goddohtor.* See GOD, DAUGHTER]

god·dess (god′is), *n.* **1.** a female god or deity. **2.** a woman of extraordinary beauty and charm. **3.** a greatly admired or adored woman. [ME; see GOD, -ESS] —**god′dess·hood′, god′dess·ship′,** *n.*

Go·de·froy de Bouil·lon (gôd[ə] frwä′ də bōō yôn′), c1060–1100, French crusader.

Gö·del (gœd′[ə]l), *n.* **Kurt** (kŏŏrt), born 1906, U.S. mathematician and logician, born in Czechoslovakia.

go·den·dag (gō den′däg), *n.* a medieval Flemish club having a spike at the end. [< MFlem *goedendag,* lit., good day, since it dispatched its victims quickly]

Go·des·berg (gō′des berkh′), *n.* a city in W West Germany, SE of Bonn. 66,700 (1963). Official name, **Bad Godesberg.**

go·det (gō det′), *n.* **1.** a triangular piece of fabric, often rounded at the top, inserted in a garment to give fullness. Cf. **gore**[3] (def. 1), **gusset** (def. 1). **2.** a glass or plastic roller for guiding synthetic filaments into the centrifugal box. [orig., drinking cup < MF, equiv. to *god-* (< Gmc; see COD[2]) + *-et* -ET]

go-dev·il (gō′dev′əl), *n.* **1.** a flexible, jointed apparatus forced through a pipe line to free it from obstructions. **2.** a dart dropped into a well to explode a charge of dynamite or nitroglycerin previously placed in a desired position. **3.** *Railroads Slang.* a handcar. **4.** a sled used to drag or carry logs, stone, etc. **5.** Also called **sled cultivator.** a cultivator that rides on wooden runners and is used on listed furrows.

Go·dey (gō′dē), *n.* **Louis An·toine** (an′twän), 1804–78, U.S. publisher: founded the first woman's magazine in the U.S. 1830.

god·fa·ther (god′fä′thər), *n.* **1.** a man who serves as sponsor for a child at baptism. **2.** any male sponsor or guardian. —*v.t.* **3.** to act as godfather to; be sponsor for. [ME *godfader,* OE *godfæder.* See GOD, FATHER]

God-fear·ing (god′fēr′ing), *adj.* **1.** deeply respectful or fearful of God. **2.** (*sometimes l.c.*) pious; devout; deeply religious.

God·for·sak·en (god′fər sā′kən, god′fər sā′-), *adj.* **1.** desolate; remote; deserted: *She wants to move from that Godforsaken place.* **2.** wretched; neglected; pitiable: *She wanted to help the neighborhood's Godforsaken inhabitants.* Also, **god′for·sak′en.** [GOD + FORSAKEN]

God·frey (god′frē), *n.* a boy's given name.

God-giv·en (god′giv′ən), *adj.* **1.** given by, or coming directly from, God: *the God-given laws.* **2.** welcome; propitious; opportune.

God·head (god′hed′), *n.* **1.** the essential being of God; the Supreme Being. **2.** (*l.c.*) godhood or godship. **3.** (*l.c.*) *Rare.* a deity; god or goddess. [ME; see GOD, -HEAD]

god·hood (god′hŏŏd), *n.* divine character or condition; divinity. [ME; OE *godhād.* See GOD, -HOOD]

Go·din (gō′din), *n.* a walled plain in the first quadrant of the face of the moon: about 27 miles in diameter.

Go·di·va (gə dī′və), *n.* **1.** ("*Lady Godiva*") died 1057, wife of Leofric. According to legend, she rode naked through the streets of Coventry, England, to win relief for the people from a burdensome tax. **2.** a girl's given name.

god-king (god′king′, -king′), *n.* a human sovereign believed to be a deity or to have godlike attributes.

god·less (god′lis), *adj.* **1.** having or acknowledging no god or deity; atheistic. **2.** wicked; evil; sinful. [GOD + -LESS] —**god′less·ly,** *adv.* —**god′less·ness,** *n.*

god·like (god′līk′), *adj.* like or befitting God or a god; divine. [GOD + -LIKE] —**god′like′ness,** *n.*

god·ling (god′ling), *n.* a minor god, esp. one whose influence or authority is entirely local. [ME; see GOD, -LING[1]]

god·ly (god′lē), *adj.,* **-li·er, -li·est.** **1.** conforming to the laws and wishes of God; devout; pious. **2.** *Archaic.* coming from God; divine. [ME; OE *godlīc.* See GOD, -LY] —**god′li·ness,** *n.*
—**Syn. 1.** religious, saintly, holy, righteous, good. —**Ant. 1.** wicked, impious.

God·man (god′man′, -man′), *n., pl.* **-men** for 2. **1.** Jesus Christ. **2.** (*l.c.*) one who possesses the combined attributes of a deity and of a human being; demigod.

god·moth·er (god′muth′ər), *n.* **1.** a woman who serves as sponsor for a child at baptism. **2.** any female sponsor or guardian. —*v.t.* **3.** to act as godmother to; sponsor. [ME; OE *godmōdor.* See GOD, MOTHER[1]]

God·o·li·as (god′[ə]lī′əs), *n. Douay Bible.* Gedaliah.

Go·dol·phin (gō dol′fin, gə-), *n.* **Sidney, 1st Earl of,** 1645–1712, English statesman and financier.

go·down (gō doun′), *n.* (in India and other Oriental countries) a warehouse or other storage place. [< Malay *godong,* perh. < Telugu *gidangi,* Tamil *kidangu,* akin to *kiḍu* to lie]

Go·dow·sky (gə dôf′skē, gô-), *n.* **Leopold,** 1870–1938, U.S. composer and pianist, born in Poland.

Go·doy Al·ca·ya·ga (*Sp.* gô thoi′ äl kä yä′gä), *n.* **Lu·ci·la** (*Sp.* lōō sē′lä), real name of Gabriela Mistral.

god·par·ent (god′pâr′ənt, -par′-), *n.* a godfather or godmother. [GOD + PARENT]

go·droon (gō drōōn′), *n.* gadroon.

God's′ a′cre, a cemetery, esp. one adjacent to a church; churchyard. [trans. of G *Gottesacker*]

God's′ coun′try, **1.** an area or region supposed to be favored by God, esp. a naturally beautiful rural area. **2.** one's native region.

god·send (god′send′), *n.* an unexpected thing or event that is particularly welcome and timely, as if sent by God. [earlier *God's send,* var. (by influence of *to send*) of *God's sond* or *sand,* OE *sond, sand* message, service]

god·sent (god′sent′), *adj.* sent by God or as if by God: *a godsent rain.* [GOD + SENT]

god·ship (god′ship), *n.* the rank, character, or condition of a god. [GOD + -SHIP]

god·son (god′sun′), *n.* a male godchild. [ME; OE *godsunu.* See GOD, SON]

God·speed (god′spēd′), *n.* good fortune; success (used as a wish to a person starting on a journey, a new venture, etc.). [ME, in the phrase *God spede* may God prosper (you). See GOD, SPEED]

God's′ pen′ny, *Old Eng. Law.* See **earnest money.**

God's′ plen′ty, an abundant or overabundant quantity.

God's′ Word′, the Bible.

Godt·haab (*Dan.* gôt′hôp′), *n.* a city in and the capital of Greenland, in the SW part. 4876 (1962).

Go·du·nov (god′ənôf′, gŏŏd′-; *Russ.* go dōō nôf′), *n.* **Bo·ris Fe·do·ro·vich** (bo rēs′ fyô′do rô′vich), 1552–1605, regent of Russia 1584–98 and czar 1598–1605.

God·ward (god′wərd), *adv.* **1.** Also, **God′wards.** toward God. —*adj.* **2.** directed toward God. [ME; see GOD, -WARD]

God·win (god′win), *n.* **1.** Also, **God·wi·ne** (god′wi ne). **Earl of the West Saxons,** died 1053, English statesman. **2. Mary Woll·stone·craft** (wŏŏl′stən kraft′, -kräft′), 1759–97, English writer. **3.** her husband **William,** 1756–1836, English political philosopher, novelist, and essayist. **4.** a boy's given name.

God·win Aus·ten (god′win ô′stin). See **K2.**

god·wit (god′wit), *n.* any of several large, New or Old World shore birds of the genus *Limosa,* as *L. haemastica* **(Hudsonian curlew),** of America, having a long bill that curves upward slightly. [? alter. of *good wight*]

Goeb·bels (gœ′bəls), *n.* **Jo·seph Paul** (yō′zef poul), 1897–1945, German propaganda director for the Nazis.

Goe·di·cke (*Ger.* gœ′di kə; *Russ.* ge′di ke), *n.* **A·le·xan·der** (*Ger., Russ.* ä′le ksän′dər), born 1877, Russian pianist and composer. Also, **Gedike.**

go·er (gō′ər), *n.* **1.** one who or that which goes: *We sat in the lobby watching the comers and goers.* **2.** a person who attends frequently or habitually (usually used in combination): *churchgoer; moviegoer.* [ME; see GO[1], -ER[1]]

Goe·ring (gœ′ring), *n.* **Her·mann Wil·helm** (her′män vil′helm). See **Göring, Hermann Wilhelm.**

goes (gōz), *v.* **1.** 3rd pers. sing. pres. ind. of **go.** —*n.* **2.** pl. of **go.**

Goes (gōōs), *n.* **Hu·go van der** (hyōō′gō van dər; *Du.* hy′gō vän dər), c1440–82, Flemish painter.

Goe·thals (gō′thəlz), *n.* **George Washington,** 1858–1928, U.S. major general and engineer: chief engineer of the Panama Canal 1907–14; governor of the Canal Zone 1914–16.

Goe·the (gûr′tə, *Ger.* gœ′tə), *n.* **Jo·hann Wolf·gang von** (yō′hän vôlf′gäng fən), 1749–1832, German poet, dramatist, novelist, and philosopher. —**Goe·the·an, Goe·thi·an** (gûr′tē ən, gœ′-), *adj.*

goe·thite (gō′thīt, gœ′tīt), *n.* a very common mineral, iron hydroxide, FeO(OH), occurring in crystals, but more commonly in yellow or brown earthy masses: an ore of iron. Also, **göthite.** [named after GOETHE; see -ITE[1]]

Goetz (*Ger.* gœts), *n.* **Her·mann** (her′män). See **Götz, Hermann.**

go·fer (gō′fər), *n.* gopher[2].

gof·fer (gof′ər), *n.* **1.** an ornamental plaiting used for frills and borders, as on women's caps. —*v.t.* **2.** to flute (a frill, ruffle, etc.), as with a heated iron. Also, **gauffer.** [< F *gaufre* honeycomb < MD *wāfel*]

gof·fer·ing (gof′ər ing), *n.* a decorative or ornamental frill, ruffle, etc. Also, **gauffering.** [GOFFER + -ING[1]]

Gog (gog), *n.* a chief prince of Meshech and Tubal who came from Magog. Ezek. 38–39.

Gog and Ma·gog (gog′ ən mā′gog), two nations led by Satan in a climactic battle at Armageddon against the kingdom of God. Rev. 20:8.

go-get·ter (gō′get′ər, -get′-), *n. U.S. Informal.* a successfully enterprising, aggressive person. [n. use of v. phrase *go get*] —**go′-get′ting,** *adj.*

gog·gle (gog′əl), *n., v.,* **-gled, -gling,** *adj.* —*n.* **1. goggles,** large spectacles equipped with special lenses, protective rims, etc., to prevent injury to the eyes from strong wind, flying objects, blinding light, etc. **2.** a bulging or wide-open look of the eyes; stare. —*v.i.* **3.** to stare with bulging or wide-open eyes. **4.** (of the eyes) to bulge and be wide open in a stare. **5.** to roll the eyes. **6.** (of the eyes) to roll. **7.** *Informal.* to spearfish. —*v.t.* **8.** to roll (the eyes). —*adj.* **9.** (of the eyes) rolling, bulging, or staring. [ME *gogele(n)* (to) look aside; cf. AGOG]

gog·gle-eye (gog′əl ī′), *n., pl.* **-eyes,** (*esp. collectively*) **-eye.** **1.** See **rock bass.** **2.** Also called **gog′gle-eye scad′.** See **bigeye scad.**

gog·gle-eyed (gog′əl īd′), *adj.* having bulging, wide-open, or rolling eyes, esp. in astonishment or wonderment. —*adv.* **2.** with bulging, wide-open eyes.

gog·gler (gog′lər), *n.* **1.** a person who stares goggle-eyed. **2.** a person who spearfishes. **3.** See **bigeye scad.** [GOGGLE + -ER[1]]

Gogh (gō, gôkh; *Du.* khôkh), *n.* **Vin·cent van** (vin′sənt van; *Du.* vin sent′ vän), 1853–90, Dutch painter.

gog·let (gog′lit), *n.* (esp. in India) a long-necked container, esp. for water, usually of porous earthenware so that its contents are cooled by evaporation. Also, **guglet, gurglet.** [< Pg *gorgoleta* (dim. of *gorja* throat), r. F *gargoulette* (dim. of *gargoule* throat); see GARGLE]

go-go (gō′gō), *n.* See **à gogo.**

go′-go danc′er. See **shindig dancer.**

Go·gol (gō′gəl; *Russ.* gô′gol), *n.* **Ni·ko·lai Va·si·lie·vich** (ni ko lī′ vä sē′lye vich), 1809–52, Russian novelist, short-story writer, and playwright.

goi (goi), *n., pl.* **goy·im, gois.** goy.

Goi·â·ni·a (goi ä′nē ə), *n.* a city in and the capital of Goiás, in central Brazil, SW of Brasília. 133,462 (1960).

Goi·ás (goi äs′), *n.* a state in central Brazil. 1,954,862 (1960); 247,826 sq. mi. *Cap.:* Goiânia.

Goi·del·ic (goi del′ik), *Ling.* —*adj.* **1.** of or belonging to Goidelic; Q-Celtic. —*n.* **2.** Also called **Q-Celtic.** the subbranch of Celtic in which the Proto-Indo-European *kw*-sound remained a velar. Irish and Scots Gaelic belong to Goidelic. Cf. **Brythonic, P-Celtic.** Also, **Gadhelic.** [< OIr *Góidil* a Gael + -IC]

go·ing (gō′ing), *n.* **1.** the act of leaving or departing; departure: *a safe going and quick return.* **2.** the condition of surfaces, as those of roads, for walking or driving: *The going was bad.* **3.** progress; advancement: *good going toward the presidency.* **4.** Usually, **goings.** behavior; conduct; deportment. —*adj.* **5.** moving or working, as machinery. **6.** active, alive, or existing. **7.** continuing to operate or do business, esp. in a successful manner: *a going company.* **8.** current; prevalent; usual: *What is the going price of good farmland in Ohio?* **9.** leaving; departing. **10. going away,** *Sports.* by a wide margin, esp. as established in the late stages of a contest: *The champion won the bout going away.* **11. going on,** nearly; almost: *It's going on four o'clock.* [ME; see GO[1], -ING[1], -ING[2]]

go·ing-o·ver (gō′ing ō′vər), *n., pl.* **go·ings-o·ver** (gō′ingz ō′vər). **1.** an examination or investigation: *The accounts were given a thorough going-over.* **2.** a severe, thorough scolding. **3.** a sound thrashing; beating: *The hoodlums gave him a good going-over when they found him.* [n. use of v. phrase *go over*]

go′ings on′, *Informal.* **1.** conduct or behavior, esp. if open to criticism: *We had never seen such goings on as* *at the last dance.* **2.** happenings; events: *The American newspaper kept her in touch with the goings on back home.* Also, **go′ings-on′.** [n. use of prp. phrase *going on*]

go′ing to Jeru′salem. See **musical chairs.**

go′ing train′, *Horol.* the gear train for moving the hands of a timepiece or giving some other visual indication of the time. Also called **time train.** Cf. **dial train, striking train.**

goi·ter (goi′tər), *n. Pathol.* an enlargement of the thyroid gland, on the front and sides of the neck. Also, **goi′tre.** Cf. **exophthalmic goiter.** [< F *goitre* << L *guttur* throat]

goi·trous (goi′trəs), *adj. Pathol.* pertaining to or affected with goiter. [< F *goitreux.* See GOITER, -OUS]

Go·la (gō′lə), *n.* a girl's given name.

Gol·con·da (gol kon′də), *n.* **1.** a ruined city in S India, near the modern city of Hyderabad: capital of a former Muslim kingdom; famous for its diamond cutting. **2.** (*often l.c.*) a rich mine or other source of great wealth.

gold (gōld), *n.* **1.** a precious yellow metallic element, highly malleable and ductile, and free from liability to rust. *Symbol:* Au; *at. wt.:* 196.967; *at. no.:* 79; *sp. gr.:* 19.3 at 20°C. **2.** a quantity of gold coins: *to pay in gold.* **3.** a monetary standard based on this metal. **4.** money; wealth; riches. **5.** something likened to this metal in brightness, preciousness, superiority, etc.: *a heart of gold.* **6.** a bright, metallic yellow color, sometimes tending toward brown. —*adj.* **7.** consisting of gold. **8.** pertaining to gold. **9.** like gold. **10.** of the color of gold. [ME, OE; c. G *Gold,* Goth *gulth*]

Gol·da (gōl′də), *n.* a girl's given name, form of **Goldie.**

gol·darn (gol′därn′), *n., adj., adv., v.t. Informal.* goddamn (used as a euphemism in expressions of anger, disgust, surprise, etc.): *I don't give a goldarn what you do. The goldarn engine won't start. You're goldarn right I want it! Goldarn it, I told you to stay in the house!* Also, **goldurn.**

gol·darned (gol′därnd′), *adj., superl.* **-darned·est,** *adv. Informal.* goddamned (used as a euphemism in expressions of anger, disgust, surprise, etc.): *The goldarned cat was stuck in the tree. It was the goldarnedest mess I ever did see. No need to be so goldarned snappish.* Also, **goldurned.** [GOLDARN + -ED[3]]

Gold′bach conjec′ture (gōld′bäk), *Math.* an unproved theorem that every even integer greater than 2 can be written as the sum of two prime numbers.

gold′ ba′sis, a gold standard as a basis for prices.

gold′beat·er's skin′ (gōld′bē′tərz), the prepared outside membrane of the large intestine of the ox, used by goldbeaters to lay between the leaves of the metal while they beat it into gold leaf. [GOLD + BEATER + 's[1]]

gold·beat·ing (gōld′bē′ting), *n.* the art or process of beating out gold into gold leaf. Also, **gold′ beat′ing.** [GOLD + BEATING] —**gold′beat′er,** *n.*

gold′ bee′tle, any of several beetles having a golden luster, as a chrysomelid, *Metriona bicolor,* that feeds on morning-glories and roses. Also called **gold-bug** (gōld′bug′).

Gold·berg (gōld′bûrg), *n.* **1. Arthur Joseph,** born 1908, U.S. jurist, statesman, and diplomat: associate justice of the U.S. Supreme Court 1962–65; ambassador to the U.N. 1965–68. **2. Reuben Lucius** (*Rube*), born 1883, U.S. cartoonist.

Gold′berg Varia′tions, a set of 30 variations for harpsichord (1742) written by J. S. Bach for the employer of his pupil Johann Gottlieb Goldberg.

gold′ bond′, a bond payable in gold.

gold-brick (gōld′brik′), *Slang.* —*v.i.* **1.** to shirk; loaf. —*v.t.* **2.** to swindle; cheat. [v. use of n. phrase *gold brick*] —**gold′brick′er,** *n.*

gold·brick (gōld′brik′), *n.* **1.** *Informal.* a brick-shaped mass of gold, or an imitation of it, sold by a swindler who then delivers a spurious substitute. **2.** *Informal.* anything supposed to be valuable but which turns out to be worthless. **3.** *Slang.* a soldier who is assigned to easy duties or who performs his duties without proper effort, responsibility, or care. **4.** *Slang.* a shirker; loafer. [GOLD + BRICK]

gold′ bronze′, an alloy of about 90 percent copper, 5 percent zinc, 3 percent lead, and 2 percent tin.

Gold′ Bug′, The, a short story (1843) by Edgar Allan Poe.

gold′ bul′lion stand′ard, a gold standard in which gold is not coined but may be purchased at a fixed price for foreign exchange.

gold′ certif′icate. See under **certificate** (def. 4b).

gold′ chlo′ride, *Chem.* a chloride of gold, esp. the trichloride, $AuCl_3$, a yellow to red, water-soluble, crystalline solid: used chiefly in photography, gilding ceramic ware and glass, and in the manufacture of purple of Cassius.

Gold′ Coast′, **1.** a former British territory in W Africa; now a part of Ghana. **2.** a wealthy residential area, esp. one along the north shore of Chicago.

gold·crest (gōld′krest′), *n.* a Eurasian kinglet, *Regulus regulus,* having a bright yellow patch on the top of the head. [GOLD + CREST]

gold·cup (gōld′kup′), *n.* a buttercup. [GOLD + CUP]

gold′ dig′ger, **1.** a person who digs or seeks for gold in a gold field. **2.** *Informal.* a woman who associates with or marries a man chiefly to get jewelry, clothes, money, or other valuables from him through gifts or through a divorce settlement.

gold′ dig′ging, **1.** the work of digging for gold. **2. gold diggings,** a region where digging or seeking for gold, esp. by placer mining, is carried on.

gold′ dust′, gold in fine particles.

gold-dust (gōld′dust′), *n.* a perennial, European herb, *Alyssum saxatile,* forming dense mats or clumps and having clusters of golden-yellow flowers and grayish leaves. Also called **basket-of-gold, golden tuft, silver queen.**

gold·en (gōl′dən), *adj.* **1.** of the color of gold; yellow; bright, metallic, or lustrous like gold: *her golden hair.* **2.** made or consisting of gold: *golden earrings.* **3.** exceptionally valuable, advantageous, or excellent: *a golden opportunity.* **4.** having glowing vitality; radiant: *golden youth.* **5.** full of happiness, prosperity, or vigor: *golden hours; a golden era of exploration.* **6.** highly talented and favored; destined for success: *the golden girl of Broadway.* **7.** richly soft and smooth: *a golden voice.* **8.** indicating the 50th event of a series, as a wedding anniversary. **9.** *Slang.* in good circumstances; well off: *If I can raise a hundred dollars more I'll be golden.* [ME; see GOLD, -EN[2]] —**gold′en·ly,** *adv.* —**gold′en·ness,** *n.*

Gold·en (gōl′dən), *n.* a town in central Colorado. 7118 (1960).

gold′en age′, **1.** *Class. Myth.* the first and best of the four ages of man; the age in which man lived in peace and innocence, but which finally yielded to the silver age. **2.** the most flourishing period in the history of a nation, literature, etc. **3.** the period in life after middle age, traditionally characterized by wisdom, contentment, and useful leisure. **4.** (*usually cap.*) a period in Latin literature, 70 B.C.–A.D. 14, in which Cicero, Catullus, Horace, Vergil, Ovid, and others wrote; the first phase of classical Latin. Cf. **silver age** (def. 2).

Gold′en Ass′, The, (*Metamorphoses*) a picaresque novel (A.D. c150–c180) by Apuleius, containing the story of Cupid and Psyche.

gold′en as′ter, any North American, asterlike, composite plant of the genus *Chrysopsis,* having bright, golden-yellow flowers, esp. *C. mariana,* of the eastern U.S.

gold′en bamboo′, an erect, yellow-stemmed grass, *Phyllostachys aurea,* of China and Japan, having leaves that are bluish-gray beneath.

gold′en-band·ed lil′y (gōl′dən ban′did), a Japanese lily, *Lilium auratum,* having white flowers with a yellow band extending the length of each petal and sepal.

gold′en ban′tam corn′, a horticultural variety of sweet corn.

Gold′en Bough′, *Class. Myth.* a branch of mistletoe, sacred to Proserpina, which served Aeneas as a pass to the underworld.

Gold′en Bough′, The, a comparative study in 12 volumes (1890–1915), by Sir James G. Frazer, of the folklore, mythology, and religion of mankind.

Gold′en Bowl′, The, a novel (1904) by Henry James.

gold′en boy′, *Informal.* a man whose talents, circumstances, or ability to gain favor promise great success.

gold′en buck′, a dish consisting of Welsh rabbit topped with a poached egg.

Gold′en Bull′, an edict of Charles IV, emperor of the Holy Roman Empire, issued in 1356 and in force until the extinction of the Empire in 1806, in which the selection of the emperor was entrusted to seven Electors.

gold′en calf′, **1.** a golden idol set up by Aaron. Ex. 32. **2.** either of the two similar idols set up by Jeroboam. I Kings 12:28, 29. **3.** money or material goods: *an age in which the golden calf is idolized.*

gold′en cal′la lil′y, a herb, *Zantedeschia elliottiana,* of South Africa, having white-spotted leaves and trumpet-shaped or funnel-shaped, golden-yellow flowers. Also called **yellow calla lily.**

gold′en chain′, laburnum.

gold′en clem′atis, a woody vine, *Clematis tangutica,* of northeastern Asia, having solitary, yellow flowers and plumed fruit.

gold′en coreop′sis, an herb, *Coreopsis tinctoria,* of the central U.S., having yellow flowers with red-brown centers.

gold′en crown′beard (kroun′bērd′), an annual herb, *Verbesina encelioides,* found from the central U.S. to Mexico, having solitary, golden-yellow flower heads nearly two inches wide. [so called from the bearded appearance of the head]

gold′en-crowned king′let (gōl′dən kround′), a yellowish-green kinglet, *Regulus satrapa,* of North America, having a yellow or orange patch on the top of the head.

gold′en cur′rant, a showy shrub, *Ribes aureum,* of western North America, having fragrant, drooping clusters of yellow flowers that turn reddish and smooth, purplish-brown fruit. Also called **flowering currant.**

Gold·en·dale (gōl′dən dāl′), *n.* a town in S Washington. 2536 (1960).

Gold′en Deli′cious, **1.** an American variety of yellow apple. **2.** the tree bearing this fruit.

gold′en ea′gle, a large eagle, *Aquila chrysaëtos,* of the Northern Hemisphere, having golden-brown feathers on the back of the head and neck. See illus. under **raptorial.**

gold′en ear′drop, an herb, *Dicentra chrysantha,* of California, having bluish-green foliage and large, branched clusters of yellow flowers.

gold·en·eye (gōl′dən ī′), *n., pl.* **-eyes,** (*esp. collectively*) **-eye.** **1.** either of two diving ducks, *Brucephala clangula,* of Eurasia and North America, or *B. islandica* (**Barrow's goldeneye**), of North America, having bright yellow eyes. **2.** Also called **gold′en-eyed fly′.** a lacewing of the family *Chrysopidae.* [GOLDEN + EYE]

gold′en-eyed grass′ (gōl′dən īd′), a perennial herb, *Sisyrinchium californicum,* of the northwestern U.S., having bright yellow flowers with brown markings.

gold′en fizz′, a drink containing egg yolk, gin, lemon juice, sugar, and soda water.

gold′en flax′, a perennial herb, *Linum flavum,* of Europe, having golden-yellow flowers.

Gold′en Fleece′, *Class. Myth.* a fleece of pure gold, kept at Colchis by king Aeëtes from whom it was stolen by Jason and the Argonauts with the help of Aeëtes's daughter, Medea.

Gold′en Gate′, a strait in W California, between San Francisco Bay and the Pacific. 2 mi. wide.

Gold′en Gate′ Bridge′, a bridge connecting N California with San Francisco peninsula. 4200 ft. center span.

gold′en glow′, a tall coneflower, *Rudbeckia laciniata,* having yellow flowers.

gold′en goose′, a legendary goose that laid one golden egg a day and was killed by its impatient owner, who wanted all the gold immediately.

gold′en gram′, the gram, *Phaseolus aureus.*

Gold′en Horde′, the army of Mongol Tartars that overran eastern Europe in the 13th century, established a khanate in Russia, and maintained suzerainty there until the 15th century.

Gold′en Horn′, an inlet of the Bosporus, in European Turkey: forms the inner part of Istanbul.

gold′en ju′bilee. See under **jubilee** (def. 1).

Gold′en Leg′end, **1.** a compilation (1483) by William Caxton, consisting of saints' lives derived from the *Legenda Aurea,* together with homilies and commentaries. **2.** See **Legenda Aurea.**

gold′en loose′strife, a Eurasian, bushy, perennial herb, naturalized in eastern North America, having yellow flowers in leafy clusters. Also called **willow-wort.**

gold′en marguerite′, a garden plant, *Anthemis tinctoria,* of Eurasia, having large, golden-yellow flowers. Also called **oxeye camomile, yellow camomile.**

gold′en mean′, **1.** the perfect moderate course or position that avoids extremes; the happy medium. **2.** See **golden section.**

gold′en mole′, any of several burrowing insectivores of the family *Chrysochloridae,* of southern Africa, whose fur has an iridescent, often golden luster.

gold′en nem′atode, a yellowish nematode, *Heterodera rostochiensis,* that is parasitic on the roots of potatoes, tomatoes, and other solanaceous plants.

gold′en o′riole, an Old World oriole, *Oriolus oriolus,* the male of which is bright yellow with black wings.

gold′en par′achute, a contract or agreement between a company and an executive, guaranteeing severance pay, financial benefits, etc., in the event of job loss.

gold′en pheas′ant, an Asiatic pheasant, *Chrysolophus pictus,* having brilliant scarlet, orange, gold, green, and black plumage.

gold′en plov′er, either of two plovers of the genus *Pluvialis,* having the back marked with golden-yellow spots, *P. apricaria,* of Europe, or *P. dominica,* of America.

gold′en pol′ypody. See **hare's-foot fern.**

gold′en queen′, a hardy, perennial herb, *Trollius ledebouri,* of Siberia, having yellow flowers.

gold′en rag′wort. See under **ragwort.**

gold′en retriev′er, one of an English breed of retrievers having a thick, flat or wavy, golden coat.

gold·en·rod (gōl′dən rod′), *n.* **1.** any composite plant of the genus *Solidago,* most species of which bear numerous small, yellow flowers. **2.** any of various related composite plants, as *Brachychaeta sphacelata* (**false goldenrod**). **3.** a strong to vivid yellow. —*adj.* **4.** of the color goldenrod. [GOLDEN + ROD]

Dwarf goldenrod,
Solidago nemoralis
(Height 2 ft.)

gold′en rose′, *Rom. Cath. Ch.* a gold, bejeweled ornament in the form of a rose or spray of roses, blessed and presented by the pope in recognition of service to the Holy See.

gold′en rule′, a rule of ethical conduct, usually phrased "Do unto others as you would have them do unto you," or, as in Matt. 7:12, "Whatsoever ye would that men should do to you, do ye even so unto them."

gold·en·seal (gōl′dən sēl′), *n.* **1.** a ranunculaceous herb, *Hydrastis canadensis,* having a thick yellow rootstock. **2.** the rhizomes and roots of this plant, formerly much used in medicine. [GOLDEN + SEAL[1]]

A B

Golden section
A is to B as
B is to the
sum of A and B

gold′en sec′tion, *Fine Arts.* a ratio between two portions of a line, or the two dimensions of a plane figure, in which the lesser of the two is to the greater as the greater is to the sum of both: a ratio of approximately 0.616 to 1.000. Also called **golden mean.**

gold′en show′er. See **pudding-pipe tree.**

gold′en spi′der lil′y, a bulbous herb, *Lycoris aurea,* of China, having strap-shaped leaves and funnel-shaped, golden-yellow flowers nearly three inches long.

gold′en star′, a perennial herb, *Chrysopsis mariana,* growing in dry sand in the eastern and southern coastal regions of the U.S., having yellow flowers.

gold′en stars′, a crocuslike, perennial plant, *Bloomeria crocea,* of southern California, having many golden-orange flowers.

Gold′en State′, California (used as a nickname).

gold′en syr′up, *Brit.* treacle (def. 1b).

gold′en this′tle. See **Spanish oyster plant.**

gold′en tuft′, gold-dust.

gold′en war′bler. See **yellow warbler.**

gold′en wat′tle, **1.** a broad-leafed, Australian acacia, *Acacia pycnantha,* having yellow flowers and yielding tanbark and a useful gum. **2.** any similar acacia, esp. *A. longifolia,* of Australia and Tasmania.

gold′en wed′ding, the 50th anniversary of a wedding.

gold′-ex·change′ stand′ard (gōld′iks chānj′), a monetary system in one country in which currency is maintained at a par with that of another country that is on the gold standard.

gold·eye (gōld′ī′), *n., pl.* **-eyes,** (*esp. collectively*) **-eye.** a silvery, herringlike game fish, *Hiodon alosoides,* found in the fresh waters of central North America. [GOLD + EYE]

gold′ fe′ver, greed and excitement caused by a gold rush.

gold′ field′, an area or district where gold is mined.

gold·fields (gōld′fēldz′), *n., pl.* **-fields.** any of several Californian, composite herbs of the genus *Baeria,* having yellow flowers. [GOLD + FIELD + -S[3]]

gold-filled (gōld′fild′), *adj. Jewelry.* composed of a layer of gold backed with a base metal. Cf. **filled gold.**

gold·finch (gōld′finch′), *n.* **1.** a European fringilline songbird, *Carduelis carduelis,* having a crimson face and wings marked with yellow. **2.** any of certain related American finches of the genus *Spinus*, as *S. tristis*, the male of which has yellow body plumage in the summer. [ME; OE *goldfinc*. See GOLD, FINCH]

gold·fin·ny (gōld′fin′ē), *n., pl.* **-nies.** **1.** a brightly colored European wrasse, *Ctenolabrus rupestris*. **2.** any of several related wrasses. [earlier *goldsinny* < ?]

Goldfish, *Carassius auratus* (Length 4 in.)

gold·fish (gōld′fish′), *n., pl.,* (*esp. collectively*) **-fish,** (*esp. referring to two or more kinds or species*) **-fish·es.** **1.** a small, usually yellow or orange fish, *Carassius auratus*, of the carp family, originally found in China, bred in many varieties and often kept in aquariums and pools. **2.** garibaldi (def. 2). [GOLD + FISH]

gold′ foil′, sheets of gold not so thin as gold leaf. —**gold′-foil′,** *adj.*

gold·i·locks (gōl′dē loks′), *n., pl.* **-locks.** **1.** (*construed as sing.*) a person with golden hair. **2.** (*construed as sing. or pl.*) an Old World buttercup, *Ranunculus auricomus*. **3.** (*construed as sing. or pl.*) a European plant, *Linosyris vulgaris*, resembling golden-rod, having small heads of yellow flowers. [obs. *goldy* golden + LOCK[2] + -S[3]]

Gol·ding (gōl′ding), *n.* **1. Louis,** 1895–1958, English novelist and essayist. **2.** a boy's given name.

gold′ leaf′, gold in the form of very thin foil, as for gilding. —**gold′-leaf′,** *adj.*

Gold·mark (gōld′märk′), *n.* **Karl** (kärl), 1830–1915, Hungarian composer.

gold′ mine′, **1.** a mine yielding gold. **2.** a source of great wealth or profit, or any desirable thing. **3.** a copious source or reserve of something required: *a gold mine of information about antiques.*

gold·min·er (gōld′mī′nər), *n.* a person who mines gold or works in a gold mine. [GOLD + MINER]

gold′ min′ing, the act or process of mining gold.

gold′ note′, *U.S.* a bank note payable in gold coin.

gold-of-pleas·ure (gōld′əv plezh′ər), *n.* a brassicaceous herb, *Camelina sativa*, having small yellowish flowers.

Gol·do·ni (gôl dō′nē; *It.* gôl dô′nē), *n.* **Car·lo** (kär′lô), 1707–93, Italian dramatist. —**Gol·do′ni·an,** *adj.*

gold′ or′ange, *Chem.* See **methyl orange.**

Gol·dov·sky (gol dôf′skē; *Russ.* gol dôf′ski), *n.* **Bo·ris** (bôr′is, bōr′-, bor′-; *Russ.* bo res′), born 1908, U.S. conductor, pianist, and opera director; born in Russia.

gold′ plate′, **1.** tableware or containers made of gold. **2.** a plating, esp. electroplating, of gold.

gold-plate (gōld′plāt′), *v.t.,* **-plat·ed, -plat·ing.** to coat (base metal) with gold, esp. by electroplating.

gold′ point′, **1.** the point at which it is equally expensive to buy, sell, export, import, or exchange gold in adjustment of foreign claims or counterclaims. **2.** the melting point of gold, equal to 1036°C and used as a fixed point on the international temperature scale.

gold′ reserve′, that part of the U.S. federal gold supply held by the Treasury in order to maintain the value of governmental promissory notes.

gold′ rush′, a large-scale and hasty emigration of people to a region where gold has been discovered, as to California in 1849.

Golds·bor·o (gōldz′bûr′ō, -bur′ō), *n.* a city in E North Carolina. 28,873 (1960).

Gold·schmidt (gōld′shmit), *n.* a walled plain in the second quadrant of the face of the moon: about 74 miles in diameter.

gold·smith (gōld′smith′), *n.* **1.** a person who makes or sells articles of gold. **2.** (formerly) such a person also acting as a banker, moneylender, etc. [ME, OE. See GOLD, SMITH]

Gold·smith (gōld′smith′), *n.* **Oliver,** 1730?–74, Irish poet, playwright, essayist, and novelist.

gold′smith bee′tle, a brilliant golden scarabaeid beetle, *Cetonia aurata*, of Europe.

gold′ stand′ard, a monetary system with gold of specified weight and fineness as the unit of value.

gold′ star′, a gold-colored star displayed, as on a service flag, to indicate that a member of one's family, organization, or the like, has been killed in war. —**gold′-star′,** *adj.*

gold′ stick′, (in England) **1.** the gilded rod carried on state occasions by certain members of the royal household. **2.** the bearer of it.

gold·stone (gōld′stōn′), *n.* aventurine. [GOLD + STONE]

gold·thread (gōld′thred′), *n.* **1.** a white-flowered ranunculaceous herb, *Coptis trifolia*, having a slender, yellow root. **2.** the root itself, used in medicine. [GOLD + THREAD]

gold′ to′paz, citrine (def. 2).

gol·durn, (gol′dûrn′), *n., adj., adv., v.t. Informal.* goldarn.

gol·durned (gol′dûrnd′), *adj., superl.* **-durned·est,** *adv. Informal.* goldarned.

Gold·was·ser (gōld′vä sər, -wä-, *Ger.* gôlt′vä′sər), *n.* a liqueur flavored with spices, figs, lemons, and herbs, and having minute flakes of gold leaf in suspension. [< G, equiv. to *Gold* GOLD + *Wasser* water]

Gold·wa·ter (gōld′wô′tər, -wot′ər), *n.* **Barry Morris,** born 1909, U.S. politician: Republican candidate for President, 1964.

gold·work (gōld′wûrk′), *n.* work produced by a goldsmith. [GOLD + WORK]

Gold·wyn (gōld′win), *n.* **Samuel** (*Samuel Goldfish*), born 1882, U.S. movie producer, born in Poland.

Gold·wyn·ism (gōld′wi niz′əm), *n.* a phrase or statement involving a humorous and supposedly unintentional misuse of idiom, as "Keep a stiff upper chin," esp. such a statement attributed to Samuel Goldwyn, as "Include me out." [GOLDWYN + -ISM]

go·lem (gō′ləm, -lem), *n.* **1.** *Jewish Folklore.* a man-made figure constructed in the form of a human being and endowed with life. **2.** an automaton. [< Yiddish *goylem* < Heb *gōlem* a shapeless thing]

golf (golf, gôlf; *Brit. also* gof), *n.* **1.** a game in which clubs with wooden or metal heads are used to hit a small, white ball into a number of holes, usually 9 or 18, in succession, situated at various distances over a course having natural or artificial obstacles, the object being to get the ball into each hole in as few strokes as possible. **2.** a word used in communications to represent the letter G. —*v.i.* **3.** to play golf. [ME, ? < Scot] —**golf′er,** *n.*

golf′ bag′, a bag, usually made of canvas, for carrying golf clubs and golf balls.

golf′ ball′, a small, white ball with a tough cover and a resilient core of rubber, used in playing golf.

golf′ club′, **1.** any of various long-handled clubs with wooden or metal heads, for hitting the ball in golf. Cf. **iron** (def. 5), **wood**[1] (def. 8). **2.** an organization of golf players. **3.** *Chiefly Brit.* See **country club.**

golf′ course′, the ground or course over which golf is played. A standard full-scale golf course has 125 to 175 acres, usually with 18 holes varying from 100 to 650 yards in length from tee to cup. Also called **golf′ links′.**

Golfe du Li·on (gôlf dʏ lē ôɴ′), French name of the **Gulf of Lions.**

Golf′ Man′or, a town in SW Ohio. 4648 (1960).

golf′ wid′ow, a woman whose husband frequently leaves her at home while he goes to play golf.

Gol·gi (gôl′jē), *n.* **Ca·mil·lo** (kä mēl′lô), 1843?–1926, Italian physician and histologist: Nobel prize for medicine 1906.

Gol′gi bod′y (gôl′jē), a netlike mass of material in the cytoplasm of animal cells, believed to function in cellular secretion. Also called **Gol′gi apparat′us.**

Gol·go·tha (gol′gə thə), *n.* **1.** Calvary (def. 1). **2.** a place of suffering or sacrifice. **3.** a place of burial. Also, **gol′go·tha** (for defs. 2, 3). [< L (Vulgate) < Gk *golgothā* < Aram *golgothā*, repr. Heb *gulgōleth* skull]

gol·iard (gōl′yərd), *n.* (*sometimes cap.*) one of a class of wandering scholar-poets in Germany, France, and England, chiefly in the 12th and 13th centuries, noted as the authors of satirical Latin verse written in celebration of conviviality, sensual pleasures, etc. [ME < OF *goliart, goliard* drunkard, glutton, equiv. to *gole* throat (F *gueule*) + *-ard* -ARD] —**gol·iar·der·y** (gōl yär′də rē), *n.*

gol·iar·dic (gōl yär′dik), *adj.* of, pertaining to, resembling, or constituting the satirical Latin verse written by the goliards. [GOLIARD + -IC]

Go·li·ath (gə lī′əth), *n.* the giant warrior of the Philistines whom David killed with a stone from a sling. I Sam. 17:48–51.

Goli′ath crane′ a gantry crane for heavy work, as in steel mills. [after GOLIATH]

go·lil·la (gō lil′ə, -lēl′yə), *n.* a collar of lawn or linen, slightly rolled under at the edge and starched to stand out from the neckline, worn in Spain in the 17th century. [< Sp, dim. of *gola* throat]

gol·li·wogg (gol′ē wog′), *n.* (*sometimes cap.*) **1.** a grotesque black doll. **2.** a grotesque person. Also, **gol′li·wog′.** [after the name of a doll in an illustrated series of children's books by Bertha Upton (d. 1912), U.S. writer, and Florence Upton (d. 1922), illustrator]

gol·ly (gol′ē), *interj. Informal.* (used as a mild exclamation expressing surprise, wonder, puzzlement, or the like.) [euphemistic alter. of GOD]

gol·ly·wob·bler (gol′ē wob′lər), *n. Naut.* a very large quadrilateral staysail set between the foremast and mainmast of a schooner. [?]

go·losh (gə losh′), *n.* galosh.

golp (golp), *n. Heraldry.* a roundel purpure. [? < Sp *golpe* a wound]

Golsch·mann (gōlsh′män), *n.* **Vlad·i·mir** (vlad′ə mēr′), born 1893, French orchestra conductor in the U.S.

Goltz (gôlts), *n.* **Baron Kol·mar von der** (kôl′mär fən dər), 1843–1916, German field marshal.

gom·been (gom bēn′), *n. Irish Eng.* usury. [< IrGael *gaimbín*]

gom·been-man (gom bēn′man′), *n., pl.* **-men.** *Irish Eng.* usurer; moneylender.

gom·bo (gum′bō), *n., pl.* **-bos.** gumbo.

gom·broon (gom broon′), *n.* a type of Persian pottery ware. [after *Gombroon*, a town on the Persian Gulf]

Go·mel (gô′mel), *n.* a city in SE Byelorussia, in the W Soviet Union in Europe, on a tributary of the Dnieper. 208,000 (est. 1964).

gom·er·el (gom′ər əl), *n. Scot. and North Eng.* a fool. Also, **gom′er·al, gom′er·il.** [obs. *gome* man (OE *guma*; c. Goth *guma*, L *homō*) + -REL]

Gó·mez (gō′mes), *n.* **Juan Vi·cen·te** (hwän bē sen′te), 1857?–1935, Venezuelan soldier and political leader: commander in chief and dictator of Venezuela 1908–35; president of Venezuela 1908–15, 1922–29, 1931–35.

Gó·mez de la Ser·na (gô′meth de lä ser′nä), *n.* **Ra·món** (rä môn′), ("*Ramón*"), born 1888, Spanish novelist, dramatist, biographer, and critic.

go-mo·ku (gō mō′koo), *n.* gobang. [< Jap]

go·mo·ku-zo·gan (gō mō′koo zō gän′; *Jap.* gô mô′koo zô gän′), *n.* a form of decoration for Japanese metalwork, as sword mounts, consisting of an inlay of fine brass or copper wire in iron. [< Jap, equiv. to *gomoku* variegated (lit., five eyes) + *zogan* inlaid work]

Go·mor·rah (gə môr′ə, -mor′ə), *n.* **1.** Also, *Douay Bible,* **Go·mor′rha.** an ancient city destroyed, with Sodom, because of its wickedness. Gen. 19:24, 25. **2.** any extremely wicked place. —**Go·mor′re·an, Go·mor′rhe·an,** *adj.*

Gom·pers (gom′pərz), *n.* **Samuel,** 1850–1924, U.S. labor leader, born in England: president of the American Federation of Labor 1886–94, 1896–1924.

gom·phi·a·sis (gom fī′ə sis), *n. Dentistry.* looseness of the teeth. [< Gk *gomphí(os)* molar tooth + -ASIS]

gom·pho·sis (gom fō′sis), *n., pl.* **-pho·ses** (-fō′sēz). *Anat.* an immovable articulation in which one bone or part is received in a cavity in another, as a tooth in its socket. [< NL < Gk *gomphṓ(ein)* (to) bolt together, deriv. of *gómphos* bolt, nail; see -OSIS]

Go·mul·ka (gə mool′kə), *n.* **Wla·dy·slaw** (vlä di′släf), born 1905, Polish political leader: First Secretary of the Polish Communist party since 1956.

go·mu·ti (gə moo′tē), *n., pl.* **-tis.** **1.** Also called **gomu′ti palm′.** a sago palm, *Arenga pinnata*, of the East Indies, yielding palm sugar. **2.** a black, horsehairlike fiber obtained from it, used for making cords, ropes, cables, etc. [< Malay *gĕmuti*]

gon-, var. of **gono-** before a vowel: *gonidium.*

-gon, a suffix borrowed from Greek meaning "angled," "angular": *polygon; pentagon.* Cf. **gonio-.** [< Gk *-gōn(on)*, neut. of *-gōnos*]

go·nad (gō′nad, gon′ad), *n. Anat.* a sex gland in which gametes are produced; an ovary or testis. [< NL *gonad-* (s. of *gonas*), equiv. to *gon-* GON- + *-ad* n. suffix] —**go·nad′al, go·na·di·al** (gō nā′dē əl), **go·nad·ic** (gō nad′ik), *adj.*

go·nad·o·trope (gō nad′ə trōp′), *n. Biochem.* a gonadotropic substance. [GONAD + -O- + -TROPE]

go·nad·o·trop·ic (gō nad′ə trop′ik, gon′ə dō-), *adj. Biochem.* pertaining to substances, formed in the hypophysis or the placenta, that affect the activity of the ovary or testis. Also, **go·nad·o·troph·ic** (gō nad′ə trof′ik, gon′ə dō-). [GONAD + -O- + -TROPIC]

go·nad·o·tro·pin (gō nad′ə trō′pin, gon′ə dō-), *n. Biochem.* a gonadotropic substance. Also, **go·nad·o·tro·phin** (gō nad′ə trō′fin, go-, gon′ə dō-). Cf. **chorionic gonadotropin.** [GONADOTROP(IC) + -IN[2]]

Go·na·ïves (*Fr.* gô na ēv′), *n.* **1. Gulf of,** an inlet of the Caribbean Sea, between the two peninsulas of W Haiti. **2.** a seaport in W Haiti. 14,824 (est. 1957).

go·nan·gi·um (gō nan′jē əm), *n., pl.* **-gi·a** (-jē ə), **-gi·ums.** a reproductive polyp of a colonial hydroid, which gives rise asexually to medusa buds. [< NL, equiv. to *gon-* GON- + Gk *angeîon* vessel, reservoir] —**go·nan′gi·al,** *adj.*

Go·nave (*Fr.* gô nav′), *n.* an island in the Gulf of Gonaïves, in W Haiti. 287 sq. mi.

Gon·çal·ves Di·as (gôɴ sôl′vis dē′äs), **An·to·nio** (äɴ tô′nyoo), 1823–64, Brazilian poet.

Gon·cha·rov (gon chä rôf′), *n.* **I·van A·le·xan·dro·vich** (i vän′ ä′le ksän′drо vich), 1812–91, Russian novelist.

Gon·court (gôɴ koor′), *n.* **1. Ed·mond Louis An·toine Huot de** (ed môɴ′ lwē äɴ twan′ ʏ ō′ də), 1822–96, and his brother **Jules Al·fred Huot de** (zhʏl al fred′), 1830–70, French art critics, novelists, and historians: collaborators until the death of Jules. **2. Prix** (prē), an annual award of money made by a French literary society (**Académie Goncourt**) for the best prose work of the year.

Gond (gond), *n.* a member of an aboriginal people of Dravidian stock, in central India and the Deccan.

Gon·dar (gon′dər), *n.* a city in NW Ethiopia, N of Lake Tana: a former capital. 13,500 (est. 1956).

Gon·di (gon′dē), *n.* a Dravidian language, the language of the Gonds.

gon·do·la (gon′dᵊlə), *n.* **1.** a long, narrow, flat-bottomed boat having a tall, ornamental stem and stern and sometimes a small cabin for passengers, rowed by a single oarsman, who stands at the stern, facing forward. **2.** *U.S.* **a.** a double-ended, sloop-rigged vessel of the 18th and 19th centuries. **b.** any of various barges or scows. Cf. **gundalow. c.** *Railroads.* See **gondola car. 3.** a light pleasure rowboat of any sort. **4.** a chair or couch having a gondola back. **5.** the car of a dirigible. **6.** the basket or car suspended beneath a balloon, as for carrying passengers or scientific instruments aloft. [< It (Venetian dial.); cf. It *dondolare* to rock, swing]

Gondola (Venetian)

gon′dola back′, a chair or couch back curving forward and downward to form arms.

gon′dola car′, *U.S.* an open railroad freight car with low sides, for transporting bulk freight and manufactured goods.

gon·do·let·ta (gon′dᵊlet′ə), *n.* a small Venetian gondola. Also, **gon·do·let** (gon′dᵊlet′). [< It; dim. of GONDOLA]

gon·do·lier (gon′dᵊlēr′), *n.* a man who rows or poles a gondola. [< It *gondoliere*. See GONDOLA, -IER]

Gon·do·mar (gôn′dō mär′), *n.* **Die·go Sar·mien·to de A·cu·ña** (dye′gō sär myen′tō de ä koo′nyä), **Count of,** 1567–1626, Spanish diplomat.

Gond·wa·na (gond wä′nə), *n. Geol.* a hypothetical land mass in the Southern Hemisphere which separated near the end of the Paleozoic to form South America, Africa, and Australia. Also called **Gond·wa′na·land′.** Cf. **Laurasia.**

gone (gôn, gon), *v.* **1.** pp. of **go.** —*adj.* **2.** departed; left. **3.** lost or hopeless. **4.** ruined. **5.** that has passed away; dead. **6.** past. **7.** weak and faint: *a gone feeling.* **8.** used up. **9.** pregnant. **10.** *Slang.* exceptionally outstanding. **11. far gone, a.** much advanced; deeply involved. **b.** nearly exhausted; almost worn out. **c.** dying: *The rescue party finally reached the scene of the crash, but most of the survivors were already far gone.* **12. gone on,** *Informal.* infatuated with; in love with: *He is still gone on the girl who jilted him.*

gone′ away′, *Fox Hunting.* the cry uttered by the huntsman as a signal to the field that the hounds are in full cry and the hunt is on.

gone·ness (gôn′nis, gon′-), *n.* a sinking sensation; faintness. [GONE + -NESS]

gon·er (gô′nər, gon′ər), *n. Informal.* a person or thing that is dead, lost, or past recovery. [GONE + -ER[1]]

Gon·er·il (gon′ər il), *n.* (in Shakespeare's *King Lear*) the elder of Lear's two faithless daughters. Cf. **Cordelia, Regan.**

Gone′ With the Wind′ (wind), a novel (1936) by Margaret Mitchell.

gon·fa·lon (gon′fə lən), *n.* **1.** a banner suspended from a crossbar, often with several streamers or tails. **2.** the standard used esp. by the medieval Italian republics. [< It *gonfalone*; cf. Pg *gonfalão*, Sp *confalón*, F *gonfalon* < Gmc; see GONFANON]

gon·fa·lon·ier (gon′fə lə nēr′), *n.* **1.** the bearer of a gonfalon. **2.** a chief magistrate or some other elected official in any of several medieval Italian republics. [< F < It. See GONFALON, -IER]

gon·fa·non (gon′fə nən), *n.* a gonfalon that hangs directly from a pole, esp. from the shaft of a lance just below the lance head. [ME *go(u)nfano(u)n* < OF *gunfanun, gonfanon*, OPr *gonfano* < Gmc; cf. OHG *gund* (OE *gūth*) battle, G *Fahne* flag]

gong (gông, gong), *n.* **1.** a large bronze disk, of Oriental origin, having an upturned rim, sounded by striking with a stick or hammer that has a padded head. **2.** a shallow bell sounded by a hammer operated electrically or mechanically. **3.** (in a clock or watch) a rod or wire, either straight or bent into a spiral, on which the time is struck. —*v.t.* **4.** *Brit.* (of traffic police) to order (a driver) to stop by ringing the gong of a police car. [< Malay; of imit. orig.] —**gong′like′,** *adj.*

gong′ bu′oy, *Naut.* a buoy in which one or more gongs are struck by hammers that swing freely with the motion of the buoy.

Gón·go·ra y Ar·go·te (gông′gô rä′ ē är gô′te), **Lu·is de** (lo͞o ēs′ de), 1561–1627, Spanish poet.

Gon·go·rism (gong′gə riz′əm, gông′-), *n.* imitation of the ornate and intricate style of Góngora y Argote. [< Sp *gongorismo.* See GÓNGORA Y ARGOTE, -ISM] —**Gon′go·rist,** *n.* —**Gon′go·ris′tic,** *adj.*

go·nid·i·um (gə nid′ē əm), *n., pl.* **-nid·i·a** (-nid′ē ə). *Bot.* **1.** (in algae) any one-celled asexual reproductive body, as a tetraspore or zoospore. **2.** an algal cell, or a filament of an alga, growing within the thallus of a lichen. [< NL, equiv. to *gon-* GON- + *-idium* n. suffix] —**go·nid′i·al, go·nid′ic,** *adj.* —**go·nid′i·oid′,** *adj.*

gon·if (gon′əf), *n.* ganef.

gonio-, a learned borrowing from Greek meaning "angle," used in the formation of compound words: *goniometer.* Cf. **-gon.** [< Gk, comb. form of *gōnía*]

go·ni·om·e·ter (gō′nē om′i tər), *n.* an instrument for measuring solid angles, as of crystals. [GONIO- + -METER] —**go·ni·o·met·ric** (gō′nē ə me′trik), **go′ni·o·met′ri·cal,** *adj.* —**go′ni·o·met′ri·cal·ly,** *adv.* —**go′ni·om′e·try,** *n.*

go·ni·on (gō′nē on′), *n., pl.* **-ni·a** (-nē ə). *Craniol.* a point on each side of the lower jaw at the mandibular angle, marked by the intersection of a plane tangent to the lower border of the body and the posterior border of the ascending ramus. [< NL < Gk *gōnía* angle] —**go′ni·al, go′ni·ac′,** *adj.*

go·ni·um (gō′nē əm), *n., pl.* **-ni·a** (-nē ə). *Biol.* the germ cell during the phase marked by mitosis. [< NL; see GON-, -IUM]

-gonium, a combining form of **gonium:** *epigonium.*

gon·na (gô′nə), *Eye Dialect.* going to: *Are ya gonna go?*

gono-, a learned borrowing from Greek meaning "sexual," "reproductive," used in the formation of compound words: *gonophore.* Also, *esp. before a vowel,* **gon-.** [< Gk, comb. form of *gónos, gonḗ* seed, generation, etc.; c. L *genus,* Skt *janas*]

gon·o·coc·cus (gon′ə kok′əs), *n., pl.* **-coc·ci** (-kok′sī). the bacterium *Neisseria gonorrhoeae,* causing gonorrhea. [GONO- + -COCCUS] —**gon′o·coc′cal, gon·o·coc·cic** (gon′ə kok′sik), *adj.* —**gon′o·coc′coid,** *adj.*

gon·o·cyte (gon′ə sīt′), *n.* *Biol.* a germ cell, esp. during the maturation phase; oocyte; spermatocyte. [GONO- + -CYTE]

gon·oph (gon′əf), *n.* ganef.

gon·o·phore (gon′ə fōr′, -fôr′), *n.* **1.** *Zool.* an asexually produced bud in hydrozoans that gives rise to a medusa or its equivalent. **2.** *Bot.* a prolongation of the axis of a flower above the perianth, bearing the stamens and pistil. [GONO- + -PHORE] —**gon·o·phor·ic** (gon′ə fôr′ik, -for′-), **go·noph·o·rous** (gō nof′ər əs), *adj.*

gon·o·po·di·um (gon′ə pō′dē əm), *n., pl.* **-po·di·a** (-pō′dē ə). *Ichthyol.* the modified anal fin of a male poecilid fish, serving as an organ of copulation. [GONO- + -PODIUM] —**gon′o·po′di·al,** *adj.*

gon·or·rhe·a (gon′ə rē′ə), *n.* *Pathol.* a contagious, purulent inflammation of the urethra or the vagina, caused by the gonococcus. Also, *esp. Brit.,* **gon′or·rhoe′a.** [< LL < Gk *gonórrhoia.* See GONO-, -RRHEA] —**gon′or·rhe′al;** *esp. Brit.,* **gon′or·rhoe′al,** *adj.* —**gon′or·rhe′ic;** *esp. Brit.,* **gon′or·rhoe′ic,** *adj.*

gon·o·the·ca (gon′ə thē′kə), *n., pl.* **-cae** (-sē). *Zool.* the part of the perisarc covering a gonangium. [GONO- + THECA] —**gon′o·the′cal,** *adj.*

-gony, an element appearing in loan words from Greek, meaning "production," "genesis," "origination": *theogony; cosmogony.* [< L *-gonia* < Gk *-goneia,* equiv. to *gón(os)* (see GON-) + *-eia* -Y[3]]

go·ny·au·lax (gō′nē ô′laks), *n.* any marine dinoflagellate of the genus *Gonyaulax,* sometimes occurring in great numbers, causing red tide. [< NL < Gk *góny* knee + *aûlax* furrow]

gon·y·camp·sis (gon′ə kamp′sis), *n.* *Pathol.* abnormal curvature of the knee. [< Gk *góny* knee + *kámpsis* bending, curving, equiv. to *kámpt(ein)* (to) bend + *-sis* -SIS]

go·nys (gō′nis), *n.* *Ornith.* the ridge along the ventral side of the lower mandible of a bird's bill. [< NL, prob. m. Gk *génys* cheek, jaw] —**go·nyd·e·al, go·nyd·i·al** (gō nid′ē əl), *adj.*

Gon·zal·es (gən zä′lis *for 1,* gən zal′is *for 2, 3*), *n.* **1. Richard Alonzo** ("*Pancho*"), born 1928, U.S. tennis player. **2.** a town in central Texas. 5829 (1960). **3.** a town in SE Louisiana. 3252 (1960).

goo (go͞o), *n.* *Informal.* a thick or sticky substance: *Wash that goo off your hands.* [? short for BURGOO]

goo·ber (go͞o′bər), *n.* *U.S.* the peanut. Also called **goo′ber pea′.** [< Angolan *nguba*]

Gooch (go͞och), *n.* **George Peabody,** 1873–1968, English historian.

good (go͝od), *adj.,* **bet·ter, best,** *n., interj., adv.* —*adj.* **1.** morally excellent; virtuous; righteous; pious: *a good man.* **2.** satisfactory in quality, quantity, or degree; excellent: *good food; good health; a good supply.* **3.** right; proper; fit: *It is good that you are here. His credentials are good. He is good for nothing.* **4.** well-behaved: *a good child.* **5.** kind, beneficent, or friendly: *to do a good deed.* **6.** honorable or worthy; in good standing: *a good name.* **7.** educated and refined: *She has a good background.* **8.** reliable; safe: *His credit is good.* **9.** genuine; not counterfeit: *They wouldn't give me good bills for the forged ones. You can tell a good quarter by biting on it.* **10.** sound or valid: *good judgment; good reasons.* **11.** reliable; dependable; responsible: *I'll lend him ten dollars because I know he's good for the money.* **12.** healthful; beneficial: *Fresh fruit is good for you.* **13.** not spoiled or tainted; edible; palatable: *The meat was still good after two years of having been frozen in the ice.* **14.** equivalent in value: *Two thousand stamps are good for one coffeepot.* **15.** agreeable; pleasant; genial: *Have a good time.* **16.** attractive: *She has a good figure.* **17.** (of the complexion) smooth; free from blemish. **18.** close; warm: *He's a good friend of mine.* **19.** sufficient or ample: *a good supply.* **20.** fine; upstanding. **21.** advantageous; satisfactory for the purpose: *a good day for fishing.* **22.** competent or skillful; clever: *a good manager; good at arithmetic.* **23.** skillfully or expertly done: *a really good job; a good play.* **24.** deserving; fitting; proper: *Good for you, you've won again!* **25.** remaining available to one: *Don't throw good money after bad.* **26.** comparatively new or of relatively fine quality: *Don't play in the woods, you're wearing good clothes.* **27.** best or most dressy: *He wore his good suit to the office today.* **28.** full: *a good day's journey away; a good two hours from here.* **29.** fairly great: *a good amount.* **30.** free from precipitation or cloudiness: *a good day; good weather.* **31.** (of a return or service in tennis, squash, handball, etc.) landing within the limits of a court or section of a court (opposed to *bad*). **32.** *Horseracing.* (of the surface of a track) drying after a rain so as to be still slightly sticky: *This horse runs best on a good track.* **33.** (of meat, esp. beef) noting or pertaining to the specific grade below "choice," containing more lean muscle and less edible fat than "prime" or "choice." **34.** *Archaic.* an epithet for a ship, town, etc.: *the good ship Syrena.* **35. as good as.** See **as**[1] (def. 12). **36. good full,** *Naut.* (of a sail or sails) well filled, esp. when sailing close to the wind; clean full; rap full. **37. make good, a.** to make recompense for; repay. **b.** to implement an agreement; fulfill. **c.** to be successful. **d.** to substantiate; verify. **e.** to accomplish; execute: *The convicts made good their getaway.* —*n.* **38.** profit; worth; benefit: *What good will that do? We shall work for the common good.* **39.** excellence or merit; kindness: *to do good.* **40.** moral righteousness; virtue (contrasted to *evil*): *to be a power for good.* **41.** advantage; purpose: *That's all to the good. Who's going to get any good out of this?* **42.** (esp. in the grading of U.S. beef) an official grade below that of "choice." **43. goods, a.** possessions, esp. movable effects or personal chattels. **b.** articles of trade; wares; merchandise. **c.** *U.S. Informal.* what has been promised or is expected: *to deliver the goods.* **d.** *U.S. Informal.* the genuine article. **e.** *U.S. Informal.* evidence of guilt, as stolen articles: *to catch someone with the goods.* **f.** *U.S.* cloth or textile material: *Will these goods wash without shrinking?* **g.** *Chiefly Brit.* merchandise sent by land, rather than by water or air. **44. come to no good,** to end in failure or as a failure: *Her jealous relatives said that she would come to no good.* **45. for good,** finally and permanently; forever: *to leave the country for good.* Also, **for good and all. 46. the good, a.** the ideal of goodness or morality. **b.** good things or persons collectively. **47. to the good, a.** generally advantageous. **b.** richer in profit or gain: *When he withdrew from the partnership, he was several thousand dollars to the good.* —*interj.* **48.** (used as an expression of approval or satisfaction.) —*adv.* **49.** *Informal.* well. **50. good and,** *Informal.* very; completely; exceedingly: *This soup is good and hot.* [ME; OE *gōd;* c. D *goed,* G *gut,* OIcel *gothr,* Goth *goths*]

—**Syn. 1.** pure, moral, conscientious, meritorious, worthy, exemplary, upright. **2.** commendable, admirable. **4.** obedient, heedful. **5.** kindly, benevolent, humane, gracious, obliging. **19.** full, adequate. **21.** profitable, useful, serviceable, beneficial. **22.** efficient, proficient, capable, able, ready, suited, suitable, dexterous, expert, adroit, apt. **43.** See **property.** —**Ant.** bad.

—**Usage. 49.** In the speech and writing of educated people, GOOD is rarely encountered as an adverb: *He did well* (not *good*) *on the test. She sees well* (not *good*) *with her new glasses.* Some confusion arises because WELL can be an adjective, too, meaning "healthy," and is the proper word to use after *feel: I feel well* (not *good*) *today.*

Good·a·cre (go͝od′ā′kər), *n.* a crater in the fourth quadrant of the face of the moon: about 30 miles in diameter.

good′ afternoon′, a conventional expression used at meeting or parting in the afternoon.

good′ behav′ior, 1. conduct conformable to law; orderly conduct: *The convict's sentence was reduced for good behavior.* **2.** proper fulfillment of the duties of an office, esp. a public office: *The incumbent could not be discharged during good behavior.*

Good′ Book′, the Bible.

good-by (go͝od′bī′), *interj., n., pl.* **-bys.** —*interj.* **1.** farewell (a conventional expression used at parting). —*n.* **2.** a farewell. [contr. of *God be with you (ye)*]

good-bye (go͝od′bī′), *interj., n., pl.* **-byes.** good-by.

good′ cheer′, 1. cheerful spirits; courage: *to be of good cheer.* **2.** feasting and merrymaking: *to make good cheer.* **3.** good food and drink: *to be fond of good cheer.*

Good′ Con′duct Med′al, *U.S. Mil.* a medal awarded an enlisted man for meritorious behavior during his period of service.

good′ day′, a conventional expression used at meeting or parting during the daytime. [ME *god dai*]

Good′ Earth′, The, a novel (1931) by Pearl S. Buck.

good′ egg′, *Slang.* a person who is pleasant, agreeable, or trustworthy; a good fellow.

good′ eve′ning, a conventional expression used at meeting or parting during the evening.

good′ faith′, accordance with standards of honesty, trust, sincerity, etc. (usually prec. by *in*): *If you act in good faith, he'll have no reason to question your motives.*

good′ fel′low, a friendly and pleasant person.

good-fel·low·ship (go͝od′fel′ō ship′), *n.* a pleasant, convivial spirit; comradeship; geniality.

good-for-noth·ing (go͝od′fər nuth′ing, -nuth′-), *adj.* **1.** worthless. —*n.* **2.** a worthless person.

Good′ Fri′day, the Friday before Easter, a holy day of the Christian church, observed as the anniversary of the Crucifixion of Jesus. [ME]

good-heart·ed (go͝od′här′tid), *adj.* kind; considerate; benevolent. Also, **good′heart′ed.** —**good′-heart′ed·ly, good′heart′ed·ly,** *adv.* —**good′-heart′ed·ness, good′heart′edness,** *n.*

Good′ Hope′, Cape of. See **Cape of Good Hope.**

Good·hue (go͝od′hyo͞o), *n.* **Bertram Gros·ve·nor** (grōv′nər, grō′və-), 1869–1924, U.S. architect.

good′ hu′mor, a cheerful or amiable mood.

good-hu·mored (go͝od′hyo͞o′mərd *or, often,* -yo͞o′-), *adj.* having or showing a pleasant, amiable mood: *a good-humored man; a good-humored remark.* Also, *esp. Brit.,* **good′-hu′moured.** —**good′-hu′mored·ly;** *esp. Brit.,* **good′-hu′moured·ly,** *adv.* —**good′-humored·ness;** *esp. Brit.,* **good′-hu′moured·ness,** *n.*

Good·ing (go͝od′ing), *n.* a town in S Idaho. 2750 (1960).

good·ish (go͝od′ish), *adj.* rather good; fairly good. [GOOD + -ISH[1]]

good′ Joe′, *Informal.* a warm-hearted, goodnatured person.

Good-King-Hen·ry (go͝od′king′hen′rē), *n., pl.* **-ries.** a European, chenopodiaceous weed, *Chenopodium Bonus-Henricus,* naturalized in North America, having spinachlike leaves. Also called **mercury.**

Good·land (go͝od′lənd), *n.* a town in NW Kansas. 4459 (1960).

Good·letts·ville (go͝od′lits vil), *n.* a town in central Tennessee. 3163 (1960).

good′ life′, 1. a life lived according to the moral and religious laws of one's culture. **2.** a life abounding in material comforts and luxuries.

good-look·ing (go͝od′lo͝ok′ing), *adj.* of good or attractive appearance; handsome or beautiful: *a good-looking young man; a good-looking hat.*

good′ looks′, good or attractive personal appearance; handsomeness or beauty.

good·ly (go͝od′lē), *adj.,* **-li·er, -li·est. 1.** of a good quality: *a goodly gift.* **2.** of good or fine appearance. **3.** of good or substantial size, amount, etc.: *a goodly sum.* [ME; OE *gōdlic.* See GOOD, -LY] —**good′li·ness,** *n.*

good·man (go͝od′mən), *n., pl.* **-men.** *Archaic.* **1.** the master of a household; husband. **2.** a title of respect used for those below the rank of gentleman, esp. a farmer or yeoman. [ME; see GOOD, MAN[1]]

Good·man (go͝od′mən), *n.* **Benjamin David** ("*Benny*"), born 1909, U.S. jazz clarinetist and bandleader.

good′ morn′ing, a conventional expression at meeting or parting during the morning.

good′ mor′row, *Archaic.* good morning.

good′ na′ture, pleasant disposition; cheerful nature.

good-na·tured (go͝od′nā′chərd), *adj.* having or showing a pleasant, cheerful disposition or mood: *a warm, good-natured person.* —**good′-na′tured·ly,** *adv.* —**good′-na′tured·ness,** *n.*

—**Syn.** amiable, agreeable, willing, cheerful, equable.

good-neigh·bor (go͝od′nā′bər), *adj.* characterized by friendly political relations and mutual aid between countries.

Good′ Neigh′bor Pol′icy, a diplomatic policy of the U.S., first presented in 1933 by President Roosevelt, for the encouragement of friendly relations and mutual defense by the nations of the Western Hemisphere.

good·ness (go͝od′nis), *n.* **1.** the state or quality of being good. **2.** moral excellence; virtue. **3.** kindly feeling; kindness; generosity. **4.** excellence of quality: *goodness of workmanship.* **5.** the best part of anything; essence; strength. **6.** a euphemism for God: *Thank goodness!* —*interj.* **7.** (used in expressions of surprise, alarm, etc.): *Goodness, you gave me a start! Goodness gracious!* [ME; OE *gōdnes.* See GOOD, -NESS]

—**Syn. 2.** integrity, honesty, uprightness, probity. GOODNESS, MORALITY, VIRTUE refer to qualities of character or conduct that entitle the possessor to approval and esteem. GOODNESS is the simple word for the general quality recognized in character or conduct: *Many could tell of her goodness and kindness.* MORALITY implies conformity to the recognized standards of right conduct: *a citizen of the highest morality.* VIRTUE is a rather formal word, and suggests usually GOODNESS that is consciously or steadily maintained, often in spite of temptations or evil influences: *of unassailable virtue; firm and of unwavering virtue.* **3.** benevolence, benignity, humanity. **4.** worth, value. —**Ant. 1.** badness, evil.

good′ night′, an expression of farewell used in parting at nighttime. [ME *good nyght*]

good-night (go͝od′nīt′), *n.* a farewell or leave-taking.

good′ of′fices, 1. services rendered by a mediator in a dispute. **2.** influence, esp. with a person in a position of power.

good-oh (go͝od′ō), *Brit. Informal.* —*interj.* **1.** good (used as an expression of approval, agreement, or admiration). —*adv.* **2.** all right. **3.** yes. Also, **good′-o.**

Good·rich (go͝od′rich), *n.* **Samuel Gris·wold** (griz′wəld, -wōld, -wôld), ("*Peter Parley*"), 1793–1860, U.S. author and publisher.

good′ Samar′itan, a person who gratuitously gives help or sympathy to those in distress. Luke 10:30–37.

goods′ en′gine, *Brit.* a railway locomotive used to haul a freight train.

Good′ Shep′herd, Jesus Christ. John 10:11–14.

good-sized (go͝od′sīzd′), *adj.* of ample or large size; rather large for its kind: *a good-sized apple.*

good′ speed′, good fortune; success: *to wish someone good speed.*

goods′ train′, *Brit.* See **freight train.**

goods′ wag′on, *Brit.* a heavy railroad freight car, esp. one used in long-distance hauling.

goods′ yard′, *Brit.* a railway freight yard.

good-tem·pered (go͝od′tem′pərd), *adj.* goodnatured; amiable. —**good′-tem′pered·ly,** *adv.* —**good′-tem′pered·ness,** *n.*

good′ use′, (in a language) standard use or usage. Also, **good′ us′age.**

good·wife (go͝od′wīf′), *n., pl.* **-wives** (-wīvz′). **1.** *Chiefly Scot.* the mistress of a household. **2.** *Archaic.* a title of respect for a woman. [ME; see GOOD, WIFE]

good′ will′, 1. friendly disposition; benevolence; favor. **2.** cheerful acquiescence or consent. **3.** *Com.* an intangible, salable asset arising from the reputation of a business and its relations with its customers, distinct from the value of its stock and other tangible assets. Also, **good′will′.**

—**Syn. 1.** kindness. See **favor.**

good·will·y (go͝od′wil′ē), *n., pl.* **-will·ies,** *adj.* *Scot. Obs.* —*n.* **1.** a volunteer. —*adj.* **2.** liberal; generous. **3.** cordial; friendly. Also, **good′will′ie, guidwillie.** [GOOD + WILL[2] + -Y[1]; cf. D *goedwillig,* G *gutwillig*]

Good′win Sands′ (go͝od′win), a line of shoals at the N entrance to the Strait of Dover, off the SE coast of England. 10 mi. long.

good·y[1] (go͝od′ē), *n., pl.* **good·ies,** *interj. Informal.* —*n.* **1.** Usually, **goodies.** something especially attractive or pleasing, esp. sweet food; candy. **2. goodies,** things which cause delight: *A record collector played some goodies for me on his phonograph.* —*interj.* **3.** good (used to express childish delight). [GOOD + -Y[2]]

good·y[2] (go͝od′ē), *adj.* goody-goody. [GOOD + -Y[1]]

good·y[3] (go͝od′ē), *n., pl.* **good·ies. 1.** *Archaic.* a polite term for a woman of humble social standing. **2.** spot (def. 13). [var. of GOODWIFE; cf. HUSSY]

Good·year (go͝od′yēr′), *n.* **Charles,** 1800–60, U.S. inventor: developer of the process of vulcanizing rubber.

good·y-good·y (go͝od′ē go͝od′ē), *adj., n., pl.* **-good·ies.** —*adj.* **1.** Also, **goody.** self-righteously good, often for sentimental reasons; affecting goodness. —*n.* **2.** a goody-goody person. [redupl. of GOODY[2]]

goo·ey (go͞o′ē), *adj.,* **goo·i·er, goo·i·est.** *Informal.* **1.** like or covered with goo; sticky; viscid. **2.** extremely emotional or effusive. [GOO + -Y[1]]

goof (go͞of), *Slang.* —*n.* **1.** a foolish or stupid person. **2.** a mistake or blunder, esp. one due to carelessness. —*v.i.* **3.** to blunder; make an error, misjudgment, etc. **4.** to kill time (often fol. by *off* or *around*): *We just goofed around till train time.* —*v.t.* **5.** to spoil or make a mess of (something); botch; bungle (often fol. by *up*): *You really goofed that one. He goofed up one opportunity after another.* **6. goof off,** *Slang.* to be idle; waste time; evade work: *The employees would goof off whenever the boss wasn't around.* **7. goof up,** *Slang.* to commit a blunder: *I could have won, but I goofed up.* [appar. var. of obs. *goff* dolt < F *goffe* awkward, stupid]

goof·ball (go͞of′bôl′), *n. Slang.* **1.** a pill containing a barbiturate or a tranquilizing drug. **2.** an extremely incompetent or eccentric person. [GOOF + BALL[1]]

goof-off (go͞of′ôf′, -of′), *n. Slang.* a person who habitually shirks responsibility. [n. use of v. phrase *goof off*]

goof-up (go͞of′up′), *n. Slang.* a person who habitually spoils things, gets into trouble, etc., esp. through carelessness or irresponsibility. [n. use of v. phrase *goof up*]

goof·y (go͞o′fē), *adj.,* **goof·i·er, goof·i·est.** *Slang.* ridiculous; silly; wacky; nutty: *a goofy little hat; a fellow who is sort of goofy.* [GOOF + -Y[1]] —**goof′i·ly,** *adv.* —**goof′i·ness,** *n.*

goog (go͝og, go͞og), *n. Australian.* an egg. [?]

goo·gly (go͞o′glē), *n., pl.* **-glies.** *Cricket.* a bowled ball that swerves in one direction and breaks in the other. [?]

goo·gly-eyed (go͞o′glē īd′), *adj.* goggle-eyed.

goo·gol (go͞o′gol), *n.* a number that is equal to 1 followed by 100 zeros and expressed as $10^{10^{10}}$ [fanciful coinage by Edward Kasner (1878–1955), American mathematician]

goo′-goo eyes′ (go͞o′go͞o′), *Informal.* foolishly amorous glances: *They sat there making goo-goo eyes at each other.* [var. of GOGGLE-EYES]

gook (go͝ok, go͞ok), *n. Informal.* **1.** dirt, grime, or sludge. **2.** a viscid liquid or sauce. **3.** *Disparaging and Offensive.* **a.** a foolish person. **b.** a peasant. **c.** an Arab. **d.** anyone who is offensive to others because of stupidity, coarseness, etc. **e.** a member of the yellow race. [phonesthemic; GOO, MUCK]

goon (go͞on), *n.* **1.** *Slang.* a stupid person. **2.** *Informal.* a hired hoodlum or thug used by one side or the other in a labor dispute. **3.** *Informal.* a roughneck. [shortened from dial. *gooney,* var. of obs. *gony* a simpleton (< ?); influenced by the comic-strip character Alice the *Goon* in the series *Thimble Theatre* by E. C. Segar (1894–1938), American cartoonist]

goon·da (go͞on′də), *n. Anglo-Indian.* a rogue or hoodlum. Also, **gunda.** [< Hindi *guṇḍā*]

goo′ney bird′ (go͞o′nē), *Slang.* any of several albatrosses. [prob. from dial. *gooney* idiot; see GOON]

goop (go͞op), *n. Informal.* a bad-mannered or inconsiderate person; clod. [coined in the early 20th century by G. Burgess]

goos·an·der (go͞o san′dər), *n.* **1.** a common merganser, *Mergus merganser,* of Eurasia and North America. **2.** any merganser. [alter. of *gossander;* ? b. GOOSE and BERGANDER]

goose (go͞os), *n., pl.* **geese** for 1–4, 6, 8; **goos·es** for 5, 7; *v.,* **goosed, goos·ing.** —*n.* **1.** any of numerous wild or domesticated, web-footed, swimming birds of the family *Anatidae,* esp. of the genera *Anser* and *Branta,* most of which are larger and have a longer neck and legs than the ducks. **2.** the female of this bird, as distinguished from the male, or gander. **3.** the flesh of a goose, used as food. **4.** a silly or foolish person; simpleton. **5.** a tailor's smoothing iron with a curved handle. **6.** an obsolete board game played with dice and counters in which a player whose cast falls in a square containing the picture of a goose is allowed to advance double the number of his throw. **7.** *Slang.* a poke between the buttocks to startle. **8. cook one's goose,** *Informal.* **a.** to destroy or dampen a person's enthusiasm, hopes, or plans. **b.** to ruin one's chances finally or irrevocably: *His goose was cooked when they found the stolen gems in his pocket.* —*v.t.* **9.** *Slang.* to poke (one) between the buttocks to startle. **10.** *Slang.* to give spurts of fuel to (a motor). [ME *gose, goos,* OE *gōs* (pl. *gēs*); c. G *Gans,* OIcel *gās,* L *anser*] —**goose′like′,** *adj.*

Canada goose, *Branta canadensis* (Length to 3¾ ft.)

goose′ bar′nacle. See under **barnacle**[1] (def. 1).

Goose′ Bay′, an airport on the coast of Labrador, on the great circle route between New York and London: used as a fuel stop by transatlantic airplanes.

goose·ber·ry (go͞os′ber′ē, -bə rē, go͞oz′-), *n., pl.* **-ries. 1.** the small, edible, acid, globular fruit or berry of certain prickly shrubs of the genus *Ribes,* esp. *R. Grossularia.* **2.** the shrub itself. [GOOSE + BERRY]

goose′ egg′, 1. *Slang.* the numeral zero, often used to indicate the failure of a team to score in a game or unit of a game: *a pitchers' duel, with nothing but goose eggs on the scoreboard.* **2.** *Informal.* a lump raised by a blow, esp. on the head.

goose·fish (go͞os′fish′), *n., pl.* **-fish·es,** (*esp. collectively*) **-fish.** angler (def. 2). [GOOSE + FISH]

goose′ flesh′, a rough condition of the skin, resembling that of a plucked goose, induced by cold or fear; horripilation. Also, **goose′flesh′.** Also called **goose pimples, goose′ bumps′, goose skin.**

goose·foot (go͞os′fo͝ot′), *n., pl.* **-foots. 1.** any herb or shrub of the genus *Chenopodium,* having minute, green flowers. **2.** any chenopodiaceous plant. [GOOSE + FOOT]

goose·gog (go͝oz′gog), *n. Brit. Dial.* gooseberry. [GOOSE + *gog* < ?]

goose′ grass′, cleavers.

goose′ grease′, the melted fat of the goose, used in domestic medicine as an ointment.

goose·herd (go͞os′hûrd′), *n.* a person who tends geese. [GOOSE + HERD[2]]

goose·neck (go͞os′nek′), *n.* **1.** a curved object resembling the neck of a goose, often of flexible construction, as in the shaft of a gooseneck lamp, or rigid, as in a boom hook. **2.** *Naut.* a curved piece at the foot of a boom, attached to a mast by a vertical pivot and itself having a horizontal pivot so that the boom can be pointed in a wide angle vertically or horizontally. **3.** *Carpentry.* a vertical continuation of the handrail of a flight of stairs, terminating in a short horizontal part on the top of a newel post. [GOOSE + NECK] —**goose′-necked′,** *adj.*

goose′neck lamp′, a desk lamp having a flexible shaft or stem.

goose′ pim′ples. See **goose flesh.** —**goose′-pim′ply,** *adj.*

goose′ skin′. See **goose flesh.**

goose′ step′, 1. a marching step of the German and other infantries, the legs being swung high and kept straight and stiff. **2.** a military exercise in which the body is balanced on one foot, without advancing, while the other foot is swung forward and back.

goose-step (go͞os′step′), *v.i.,* **-stepped, -step·ping.** to march in a goose step: *Troops goose-stepped past the reviewing stand.* —**goose′-step′per,** *n.*

goose·wing (go͞os′wing′), *n. Naut.* **1.** the weather clew of a square sail, held taut when the lee side of the sail is furled. **2.** either of the triangular areas of a square sail left exposed to the wind when the middle part is lashed to the yard during a gale. **3.** a triangular studdingsail. [GOOSE + WING]

goose·winged (go͞os′wingd′), *adj. Naut.* **1.** (of a square sail) having the lee clew furled while the weather clew is held taut. **2.** (of a fore-and-aft-rigged vessel) having the foresail and mainsail set on opposite sides.

goose′wing jibe′, *Naut.* a jibe made by a boom rather than by the gaff or head of the sail.

Goos·sens (go͞o′sənz), *n.* **Sir Eugene,** 1893–1962, English composer and conductor.

goos·y (go͞o′sē), *adj.* **goos·i·er, goos·i·est. 1.** like a goose; foolish. **2.** *Informal.* ticklish; reacting readily to touch. [GOOSE + -Y[1]]

G.O.P., Grand Old Party (an epithet of the Republican party since 1880).

go·pak (gō′pak), *n.* a folk dance of the Ukraine. [< Russ < Ukrainian *hopak,* deriv. of *hop* (interjection)]

go·pher[1] (gō′fər), *n.* **1.** any of several ground squirrels of the genus *Citellus,* of the prairie regions of North America. **2.** See **pocket gopher. 3.** See **gopher tortoise. 4.** See **gopher snake. 5.** (*cap.*) a native or inhabitant of Minnesota (the **Gopher State**) (used as a nickname). —*v.i.* **6.** *Mining.* **a.** to mine unsystematically. **b.** to enlarge a hole, as in loose soil, with successively larger blasts. [? < F *gaufre* honeycomb, alluding to the burrowing habit of the animal, prob. by folk etymology < AmerInd; cf. earlier *magofer*]

Pocket gopher, *Geomys bursarius* (Total length to 13 in.; tail to 4½ in.)

go·pher[2] (gō′fər), *n. Slang.* a zealously eager person, esp. a salesman. [humorous sp. for *go fer* repr. *go for* (*broke*)]

go′pher ball′, *Baseball Slang.* a pitched ball hit for a home run: *leading the league in gopher balls.*

go·pher·ber·ry (gō′fər ber′ē), *n., pl.* **-ries.** See **bush huckleberry.** [GOPHER[1] + BERRY]

go′pher snake′, 1. a bullsnake, *Pituophis catenifer,* of western North America, that invades burrows to prey on rodents. **2.** See **indigo snake.**

Go′pher State′, Minnesota (used as a nickname).

go′pher tor′toise, any of several North American, burrowing tortoises of the genus *Gopherus,* esp. *G. polyphemus,* of the SE U.S. Also called **go′pher tur′tle.**

go′pher wood′, an unidentified wood used in building Noah's ark. Gen. 6:14. [< Heb *gōpher*]

go·pher·wood (gō′fər wo͝od′), *n.* yellowwood.

gor (gôr), *interj. Brit. Dial.* **1.** (used as a mild oath.) **2.** (used as an exclamation of surprise or disbelief.) Also, **cor.** [alter. of GOD]

go·ral (gôr′əl, gôr′-), *n.* a goat antelope, *Naemorhedus goral,* of the mountainous regions of southeastern Asia, having small horns shorter than the distance between them at their bases. [? << Skt *gaura, gaur*]

Gor·ba·chev (gôr′bə chôf′, -chof′; *Russ.* gor bu chôf′), *n.* **Mi·kha·il S(er·ge·ye·vich)** (mi kīl′ sûr gā′ə vich, mi kāl′; *Russ.* myi khu yēl′ syir gye′yi vyich) born 1931, Soviet political leader: general secretary of the Communist party 1985–91; president of the Soviet Union 1988–91; Nobel peace prize 1990.

gor·bel·ly (gôr′bel′ē), *n., pl.* **-lies.** *Obs.* a protruding belly. [? GORE[1] + BELLY; cf. Sw (dial.) *går-bälg*] —**gor′bel′lied,** *adj.*

gor·bli·mey (gôr blī′mē), *interj. Brit. Slang.* blimey. Also, **gor·bli′my.** Cf. **gor.** [GOR + BLIMEY]

Gor·bo·duc (gôr′bə duk′), *n.* (*The Tragedie of Ferrex and Porrex*) a drama (1561) by Thomas Norton and Thomas Sackville: the earliest English tragedy.

Gor·cha·kov (gor chä kôf′), *n.* **Prince A·le·ksan·dor Mi·khai·lo·vich** (ä′le ksän′dər mi khī′lo vich), 1798–1883, Russian diplomat and statesman.

Gor·di·an (gôr′dē ən), *adj.* **1.** pertaining to Gordius, ancient king of Phrygia, who tied a knot (the **Gor′dian knot**) that, according to prophecy, was to be undone only by the person who was to rule Asia, and that was cut, rather than untied, by Alexander the Great. **2.** resembling the Gordian knot in intricacy. **3. cut the Gordian knot,** to act quickly and decisively in a difficult situation; solve a problem boldly. [< L *Gordi(us)* (< Gk *Górdios* Gordius) + -AN]

Gor·don (gôr′dᵊn), *n.* **1. Charles George** ("*Chinese Gordon*"; "*Gordon Pasha*"), 1833–85, British general: administrator in China and Egypt. **2. Lord George,** 1751–93, English politician. **3. George Hamilton, 4th Earl of Aberdeen,** 1784–1860, British statesman, born in Scotland: prime minister 1852–55. **3.** a boy's given name.

Gor′don set′ter, one of a Scottish breed of medium-sized setters having a black-and-tan coat. [after Alexander, 4th Duke of *Gordon* (1743–1827), Scottish sportsman partly responsible for developing the breed]

gore[1] (gōr, gôr), *n.* blood that is shed, esp. when clotted. [ME; OE *gor* dung, dirt; c. D *goor,* OHG *gor* filth]

gore[2] (gōr, gôr), *v.t.,* **gored, gor·ing.** (of an animal) to pierce with the horns or tusks. [ME *gore(n);* see GORE[3]]

gore[3] (gōr, gôr), *n., v.,* **gored, gor·ing.** —*n.* **1.** a triangular piece of material inserted in a garment, sail, etc., to give it greater width or a desired shape. Cf. **godet** (def. 1), **gusset** (def. 1). **2.** one of the panels, usually tapering or shaped, making up a garment, as a skirt. **3.** a triangular tract of land, esp. one lying between larger divisions. —*v.t.* **4.** to make or furnish with a gore or gores. [ME; OE *gāra* corner (c. G *Gehre* gusset); cf. OE *gār* spear; see GARLIC]

G, Gore

Go·re (gôr′ā, gôr′ā), *n.* a city in W Ethiopia. ab. 10,000.

Gor·en (gôr′ən), *n.* **Charles H.,** born 1901, U.S. authority and writer on contract bridge.

Gor·gas (gôr′gəs), *n.* **William Crawford,** 1854–1920, U.S. physician and epidemiologist: chief sanitary officer of the Panama Canal 1904–13; surgeon general of the U.S. Army 1914–18.

gorge[1] (gôrj), *n., v.,* **gorged, gorg·ing.** —*n.* **1.** a narrow cleft with steep, rocky walls, esp. one through which a stream runs. **2.** a small canyon. **3.** a gluttonous meal. **4.** that which is swallowed; contents of the stomach. **5.** a choking mass. **6.** *Fort.* the rear entrance or part of a bastion or similar outwork. See diag. under **bastion. 7.** Also called **gorge hook.** a primitive type of fishhook consisting of a piece of stone or bone with sharpened ends and a hole or groove in the center for fastening a line. **8.** the throat; gullet. **9. make one's gorge rise,** to evoke violent anger or strong disgust: *The cruelty of war made his gorge rise.* —*v.t.* **10.** to stuff with food (usually used reflexively or passively): *He gorged himself. They were gorged.* **11.** to swallow, esp. greedily. **12.** to choke up (usually used passively). —*v.i.* **13.** to eat greedily. [ME < OF *gorg(er)* (v.), deriv. of *gorge* (n.) throat < VL **gurga,* **garga* < ?] —**gorge′a·ble,** *adj.* —**gorg·ed·ly** (gôr′jid lē), *adv.* —**gorg′er,** *n.*
—**Syn. 1.** defile, ravine, notch, gap. **10.** glut, cram, fill. **11.** devour. **11, 13.** bolt, gulp, gobble. **13.** gormandize.

gorge[2] (gôrj), *n. Heraldry.* gurge (def. 2).

gorged (gôrjd), *adj. Heraldry.* (of a beast) represented wearing something about the neck in the manner of a collar: *a lion gules gorged with a collar or.* [GORGE[1] + -ED[3]]

gorge′ hook′, 1. a fishhook with two barbed prongs; a hook made by fastening two hooks back to back at the shanks. **2.** gorge (def. 7).

gor·geous (gôr′jəs), *adj.* **1.** splendid or sumptuous in appearance, coloring, etc.; magnificent: *a gorgeous gown.* **2.** extremely good, enjoyable, or pleasant: *I had a gorgeous time at the party.* [ME *gorgeouse* < OF *gorgi(as)* fashionable, elegant (< ?); see -OUS] —**gor′geous·ly,** *adv.* —**gor′geous·ness,** *n.*
—**Syn.** rich, superb, grand; brilliant, resplendent, glittering, dazzling. See **magnificent.** —**Ant.** poor, plain.

gor·ger·in (gôr′jər in), *n. Archit.* the neckline portion of a capital of a column, or a feature forming the junction between a shaft and its capital. Also called **necking.** See diag. under **armor.** [< F, deriv. of *gorge* throat; see GORGE[1]]

gor·get (gôr′jit), *n.* **1.** a piece of armor for the throat. **2.** a crescent-shaped ornament worn on a chain around the neck as a badge of rank by officers in the 17th and 18th centuries. **3.** a wimple of the Middle Ages, worn with the ends fastened in the hair. **4.** a patch on the throat of a bird or other animal, distinguished by its color, texture, etc. [ME < OF. See GORGE[1], -ET] —**gor′get·ed,** *adj.*

gorge′ wind′ (wind). See **canyon wind** (def. 2).

Gor·gi·as (gôr′jē əs), *n.* c483–c375 B.C., Greek philosopher.

Gor·gon (gôr′gən), *n.* **1.** *Class. Myth.* any of three sister monsters, Stheno, Euryale, and Medusa, commonly represented as having snakes for hair, wings, brazen claws, and eyes that turned anyone looking into them to stone. Medusa, the only mortal Gorgon, was beheaded by Perseus. **2.** (*l.c.*) a mean, ugly, or repulsive woman. [< L *Gorgōn-* (s. of *Gorgō*) < Gk *Gorgṓ,* special use of *gorgós* fearful, terrible] —**Gor·go·ni·an** (gôr gō′nē ən), *adj.*

gor·go·nei·on (gôr′gə nē′on), *n., pl.* **-nei·a** (-nē′ə). a representation of the head of a Gorgon, esp. that of Medusa. [< Gk, equiv. to *Gorgōn-* GORGON + *-ei* adj. suffix + *-on* neut. nom. sing. suffix]

Gor·go·ni·an (gôr gō′nē ən), *n.* **1.** any of numerous alcyonarian corals of the order *Gorgonacea,* having a usually branching, horny or calcareous skeleton. —*adj.* **2.** belonging or pertaining to the Gorgonacea. [< NL *Gorgoni(a)* name of the genus (L *Gorgōn-* GORGON + *-ia* -IA) + -AN]

gor·gon·ise (gôr′gə nīz′), *v.t.,* **-ised, -is·ing.** *Chiefly Brit.* gorgonize.

gor·gon·ize (gôr′gə nīz′), *v.t.,* **-ized, -iz·ing.** to affect as a Gorgon; hypnotize; petrify. [GORGON + -IZE]

Gor·gon·zo·la (gôr′gən zō′lə), *n.* a strongly flavored, semisoft variety of Italian milk cheese veined with mold. Also called **Gor′gonzo′la cheese′.** [after *Gorgonzola,* Italy, its source]

Gor·goph·o·ne (gôr gof′ə nē), *n. Class. Myth.* the daughter of Perseus and Andromeda, and the wife of Perieres and later of Oebalus. She is sometimes believed to have been the first widow to remarry.

Gor·gyth·i·on (gôr jith′ē on′), *n.* (in the *Iliad*) a son of Priam slain in the Trojan War by Teucer.

gor·hen (gôr′hen′), *n. Brit. Dial.* a female red grouse. [formed on GORCOCK]

go·ril·la (gə ril′ə), *n.* **1.** the largest of the anthropoid apes, *Gorilla gorilla,* terrestrial and vegetarian, of western equatorial Africa and the Kivu highlands. **2.** an ugly, brutish fellow. **3.** *Slang.* a hoodlum or thug, esp. one who threatens or inflicts violence. [< NL < Gk *gorílla(s)* (acc. pl.), prob. of Afr orig.] —**go·ril′la·like′,** *adj.* —**go·ril′li·an, go·ril·line** (gə ril′in, -in), *adj.* —**go·ril′loid,** *adj.*

Gorilla (Standing height 6 ft.)

gor·ing (gôr′ing, gor′-), *n. Naut.* the triangular area along a leech of a square sail, created by the presence of a gore. [GORE[3] + -ING[1]]

Gö·ring (gœ′ring), *n.* **Her·mann Wil·helm** (her′män vil′helm) 1893–1946, German field marshal and Nazi party leader. Also, **Goering.**

Go·ri·zia (gô rē′tsyä), *n.* a city in NE Italy, on the Isonzo River, N of Trieste. 136,989 (1961). German, **Görz.**

Gor·ki (gôr′kē), *n.* **1.** Also, **Gorky. Max·im** (mäk sēm′) (*Aleksvey Maksimovich Pyeshkov*), 1868–1936, Russian novelist, short-story writer, and dramatist. **2.** Formerly, **Nizhni Novgorod.** a city in the RSFSR, in the central Soviet Union in Europe E of Moscow, on the Volga River. 942,000 (1959).

Gor·ky (gôr′kē), *n.* **1. Ar·shile** (är′shēl) (*Vosdanig Adoian*), 1904–48, American painter, born in Armenia. **2. Maxim.** See **Gorki, Maxim.**

Gör·litz (gœr′lits), *n.* a city in SE East Germany, on the Neisse River, at the Polish boundary. 96,147 (est. 1955).

Gor·lov·ka (gor lôf′kä), *n.* a city in the SE Ukraine, in the SW Soviet Union in Europe. 293,000 (1959).

Gor·man (gôr′mən), *n.* a boy's given name.

gor·mand (gôr′mənd), *n.* gourmand. —**gor′mand·ism,** *n.*

gor·mand·ize (gôr′mən dīz′), *v.,* **-ized, -iz·ing,** *n.* —*v.i., v.t.* **1.** to eat like a glutton. —*n.* **2.** epicurean selectivity in choosing one's food and drink. [< F *gourmandise,* equiv. to MF *gourmand* GOURMAND + *-ise* n. suffix later taken as v. suffix -IZE] —**gor′mand·iz′er,** *n.*

gorm·less (gôrm′lis), *adj. Brit. Informal.* witless; senseless; stupid.

Gor′no-Al·tai′ Auton′omous Re′gion (gôr′nō al tī′, -äl-; *Russ.* gôr′nə ul tī′), an autonomous region in the Russian Federation, in the Altai territory bordering China and Mongolia. 192,000; 35,753 sq. mi. *Cap.:* Gorno-Altaisk.

Gor′no-Ba·dakh·shan′ Auton′omous Re′gion (gôr′nō bə däk shän′, -däk shän′; *Russ.* gôr′nə bə dukh shän′), an autonomous region in SE Tadzhikistan (Tajikistan). 161,000; 25,784 sq. mi. *Cap.:* Khorog.

gorse (gôrs), *n. Chiefly Brit.* furze. —**gors′y,** *adj.*

Gor·ton (gôr′tᵊn), *n.* **John Grey,** born 1911, Australian political leader: prime minister since 1968.

Gor·tys (gôr′tis), *n. Class. Myth.* **1.** a son of Rhadamanthys of Crete. **2.** a son of Stymphalus.

gor·y (gôr′ē, gōr′ē), *adj.,* **gor·i·er, gor·i·est. 1.** covered or stained with gore; bloody. **2.** resembling gore. **3.** involving much bloodshed: *a gory battle.* **4.** unpleasant or disagreeable: *to reveal the gory details of a divorce.* [ME; see GORE[1], -Y[1]] —**gor′i·ly,** *adv.* —**gor′i·ness,** *n.*

Görz (gœrts), *n.* German name of **Gorizia.**

Go·sa·la (gō sä′lə), *n.* died c484 B.C., Indian religious leader: founder of the Ajivaka sect.

gosh (gosh), *interj.* an exclamation or mild oath. [euphemistic alter. of GOD]

gos·hawk (gos′hôk′), *n.* any of several powerful, short-winged hawks, as *Accipiter gentilis,* of Europe and America, formerly much used in falconry. [ME *goshauk,* OE *gōshafoc.* See GOOSE, HAWK[1]]

Goshawk, *Accipiter gentilis* (Length 26 in.)

Go·shen (gō′shən), *n.* **1.** Also, *Douay Bible,* **Gessen.** a pastoral region in Lower Egypt, occupied by the Israelites before the Exodus. Gen. 45:10. **2.** a land or place of plenty and comfort. **3.** a town in SE New York. 3906 (1960).

go·shen·ite (gō′shə nīt′), *n.* a colorless beryl, used as a gem. [named after *Goshen,* Massachusetts; see -ITE[1]]

gos·ling (goz′ling), *n.* **1.** a young goose. **2.** a foolish, inexperienced person. [ME *goselyng,* var. (by recomposition) of *geslyng;* ? < Scand; cf. OIcel *gæslingr.* See GOOSE-, -LING[1]]

gos·more (gos′mōr, -môr), *n.* cat's-ear (def. 1). [perh. alter. of GOSSAMER]

gos·pel (gos′pəl), *n.* **1.** the teachings of Jesus and the apostles; the Christian revelation. **2.** glad tidings, esp. concerning salvation and the kingdom of God as announced to the world by Christ. **3.** the story of Christ's life and teachings, esp. as contained in the first four books of the New Testament, namely Matthew, Mark, Luke, or John. **4.** (*usually cap.*) any of these four books. **5.** (*often cap.*) *Eccles.* an extract from one of the four Gospels, forming part of the Eucharistic service in certain churches. **6.** something regarded as true and implicitly believed: *to take his report for gospel.* **7.** a doctrine regarded as of prime importance: *political gospel.* —*adj.* **8.** pertaining to or proclaiming the gospel or its teachings: *gospel hymn; gospel singer; gospel preacher.* **9.** in accordance with the gospel; evangelical. [ME *go(d)spell,* OE *gōdspell* (see GOOD, SPELL[2]); trans. of Gk *eu-angélion*]

gos·pel·er (gos′pə lər), *n. Eccles.* one who reads or sings the Gospel. Also, *esp. Brit.,* **gos′pel·ler.** [ME; OE *gōdspellere.* See GOSPEL, -ER[1]]

gos′pel side′, the left side of a church, facing the altar. Cf. **epistle side.**

gos′pel truth′, an unquestionably true statement, fact, etc.

Gos·plan (gos plän′), *n.* (in the Soviet Union) the official planning organization, which draws up projects embracing trade and industry, agriculture, education, and public health. [< Russ, equiv. to *gos(udar)* national + *plan* PLAN]

gos·po·din (gos po dēn′), *n., pl.* **-po·da** (-po dä′). *Russian.* a title of respect corresponding to *Mr.*

gos·port (gos′pōrt′, -pôrt′), *n.* a flexible speaking tube for communication between separate compartments of an aircraft. [after *Gosport,* England]

Gos·saert (go särt′), *n.* **Jan** (yän). See **Mabuse, Jan.** Also, **Gos·sart′.**

gos·sa·mer (gos′ə mər), *n.* **1.** a fine, filmy cobweb seen on grass or bushes or floating in the air in calm weather, esp. in autumn. **2.** a thread or a web of this substance. **3.** an extremely delicate variety of gauze. **4.** any thin, light fabric. **5.** a thin, waterproof outer garment, esp. for women. —*adj.* **6.** Also, **gos·sa·mer·y** (gos′ə mə rē), **gos′sa·mered.** of or like gossamer; thin and light. [ME *gos(e)somer* (see GOOSE, SUMMER[1]); possibly first used as name for late, mild autumn, a time when goose was a favorite dish (cf. G *Gänsemonat* November), then transferred to the filmy matter also frequent at that time of year]

gos·san (gos′ən, goz′-), *n. Geol.* a rust-colored deposit of mineral matter at the outcrop of a vein or orebody containing iron-bearing materials. Also called **iron hat.** [< Cornish dial., deriv. of *gōs* blood; akin to Welsh *gwaed* blood]

Gosse (gôs, gos), *n.* **Sir Edmond William,** 1849–1929, English poet, biographer, and critic.

gos·sip (gos′əp), *n., v.,* **-siped, -sip·ing.** —*n.* **1.** idle talk or rumor, esp. about the personal or private affairs of others. **2.** light, familiar talk or writing. **3.** Also, **gos′sip·per.** a person, esp. a woman, given to tattling or idle talk. **4.** *Chiefly Brit. Dial.* a godparent. **5.** *Archaic.* a friend, esp. a woman. —*v.i.* **6.** to talk idly, esp. about the affairs of others; go about tattling. —*v.t.* **7.** *Chiefly Brit. Dial.* to stand godparent to. **8.** *Archaic.* to repeat like a gossip. [ME *gossib, godsib(be),* OE *godsibb,* orig. godparent, equiv. to *god* GOD + *sibb* related; see SIB[1]] —**gos′sip·ing·ly,** *adv.*
—**Syn. 1.** small talk, hearsay, palaver, chitchat; (*Slang*) scuttlebutt, rumor. GOSSIP, SCANDAL apply to idle talk and newsmongering about the affairs of others. GOSSIP is light chat or talk: *gossip about the neighbors.* SCANDAL is rumor or general talk that is damaging to reputation; it is usually more or less malicious: *a scandal involving bribes.* **3.** chatterer, talker, gabbler, rumor-monger. **6.** chatter, prattle, prate, palaver.

gos·sip·mon·ger (gos′əp mung′gər, -mong′-), *n.* a person especially addicted to gossiping. [GOSSIP + MONGER]

gos·sip·red (gos′əp red′, -rid), *n.* **1.** (in Ireland) the spiritual relationship between a godchild and his or her godparents. **2.** idle talk by busybodies; gossip. [ME *gossybrede.* See GOSSIP, -RED]

gos·sip·ry (gos′əp rē), *n.* **1.** the practice of gossiping; gossip. **2.** gossips considered collectively: *leader of the neighborhood gossipry.* [GOSSIP + -RY]

gos·sip·y (gos′ə pē), *adj.* **1.** given to or fond of gossip. **2.** full of gossip. [GOSSIP + -Y[1]] —**gos′sip·i·ness,** *n.*

gos·soon (go sōōn′), *n. Irish Eng.* **1.** a boy; lad. **2.** a male servant. [alter. of F *garçon*]

gos·sy·pose (gos′sə pōs′), *n. Chem.* raffinose. [< NL *Gossyp(ium)* name of the genus (L *gossypion* cotton) + -OSE[2]]

got (got), *v.* a pt. and pp. of **get.**
—**Usage.** Some purists object to the form HAVE GOT. The construction *I've got the money* is criticized on the stylistic grounds of being tautological, since *I have the money* has basically the same meaning. Likewise, *You have got to be there on time* can be expressed as *You have to be there on time,* and critics see no rationale for the repetition of the idea of MUST. However, English has many such intensive constructions and, while teachers and others may demand a more elevated style of writing, there is nothing ungrammatical about these usages, especially when used orally.

Go·ta·ma (gō′tə mə, gō′-), *n.* Buddha. Also, **Gautama.** Also called **Go′tama Bud′dha.**

Gö·te·borg (yœ′tə bôr′yᵊ), *n.* a seaport in SW Sweden, on the Kattegat. 416,220 (1965). Also, **Gothenburg.**

Goth (goth), *n.* **1.** one of a Teutonic people who, in the 3rd to 5th centuries, invaded and settled in parts of the Roman Empire. **2.** a rude person; barbarian. [ME *Gothe* < LL *Gothī* (pl.); r. OE *Gotan* (pl.) (*Gota,* sing.); c. Goth *Gut-* (in *Gut-thiuda* Goth-people)]

Goth., Gothic. Also, **Goth, goth.**

Go·tha (gō′tä), *n.* a city in S Thuringia, in SW East Germany. 57,639 (est. 1955).

Goth·am (goth′əm, gō′thəm *for 1;* got′əm, gō′thəm *for 2*), *n.* **1.** a nickname for the city of New York. **2.** an English village, proverbial for the foolishness of its inhabitants. [ME] —**Goth′am·ite′,** *n.*

Goth·en·burg (goth′ən bûrg′; *also, for 1,* got′ᵊn bûrg′), *n.* **1.** Göteborg. **2.** a town in central Nebraska. 3050 (1960).

Goth·ic (goth′ik), *adj.* **1.** noting or pertaining to a style of architecture, originating in France in the middle of the 12th century and existing in the western half of Europe through the middle of the 16th century, characterized by the use of the pointed arch and the ribbed vault, by the use of fine woodwork and stonework, by a progressive lightening of structure, and by the use of such features as flying buttresses, ornamental gables, crockets, foils, etc. **2.** pertaining to or designating the style of painting, sculpture, etc., produced between the 13th and 15th centuries, esp. in northern Europe. **3.** (originally in derogatory use) noting all European art of this period. **4.** of or pertaining to the language of the Teutonic Goths. **5.** of or pertaining to the music, esp. of northern Europe, of the period roughly from 1200 to 1450, including that of the Ars Antiqua, Ars Nova, and the Burgundian school. **6.** pertaining to the Middle Ages; barbarous; rude. **7.** noting or pertaining to a style of literature characterized by a gloomy setting, grotesque or violent events, and an atmosphere of degeneration and decay. **8.** noting or pertaining to the alphabetical script introduced for the writing of Gothic by Ulfilas and derived by him from Greek uncials with the addition of some Latin and some invented letters. —*n.* **9.** the arts and crafts of the Gothic period. **10.** the extinct Germanic language of the Goths, preserved esp. in the 4th-century translation by Ulfilas of the Bible. **11.** *Brit.* See **black letter. 12.** (*l.c.*) *U.S.* a square-cut printing type, without serifs or hairlines. [< LL *Gothic(us)* of, pertaining to the Goths. See GOTH, -IC] —**Goth′i·cal·ly,** *adv.* —**Goth′ic·ness, Goth·ic·i·ty** (go this′i tē), *n.*

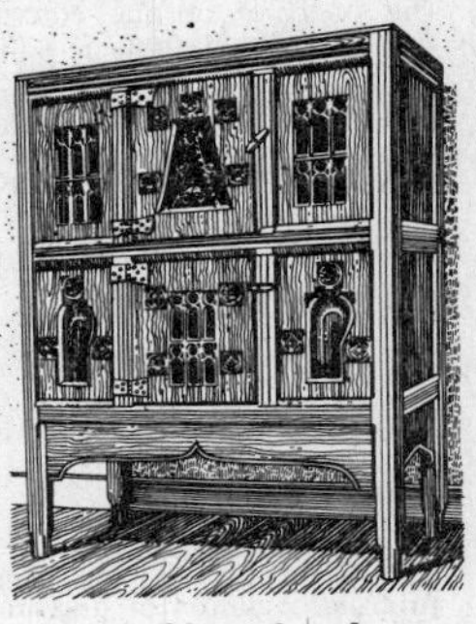

Gothic cupboard (16th century)

Goth′ic arch′, a pointed arch, esp. one having only two centers and equal radii. See illus. under **arch.**

Goth′ic ar′mor, white armor of the 15th century, esp. that characterized by much fluting and ornamentation.

Goth·i·cise (goth′i sīz′), *v.t.,* **-cised, -cis·ing.** *Chiefly Brit.* Gothicize. —**Goth′i·cis′er,** *n.*

Goth·i·cism (goth′i siz′əm), *n.* **1.** conformity or devotion to the Gothic style of architecture, sculpture, painting, etc. **2.** the principles and techniques of the Gothic style. **3.** adherence to aspects of Gothic culture. **4.** (*sometimes l.c.*) barbarism; rudeness. [GOTHIC + -ISM]

Goth·i·cize (goth′i sīz′), *v.t.,* **-cized, -ciz·ing. 1.** to make Gothic, as in style. **2.** to make falsely or deceptively medieval. Also, *esp. Brit.,* **Gothicise.** [GOTHIC + -IZE] —**Goth′i·ciz′er,** *n.*

Goth′ic nov′el, a late 18th-century and early 19th-century style of fiction characterized by historical and picturesque settings, an atmosphere of mystery, gloom, and terror, supernatural or fantastic occurrences, and violent and macabre events.

goth′ic sec′tion, a billet or bar having a rectangular section with slightly bulging sides and rounded corners.

gö·thite (gō′tīt, gœ′-), *n. Mineral.* goethite.

Got·land (got′lənd; *Swed.* gôt′lund, gôl′lund), *n.* an island in the Baltic, forming a province of Sweden. 55,701 (est. 1959); 1212 sq. mi. *Cap.:* Visby. Also, **Gott′land.** —**Got′land·er, Gott′land·er,** *n.*

go-to-meet·ing (gō′tə mē′tᵊn, -mē′ting), *adj.* (of clothes) used for churchgoing and other dressy occasions: *a go-to-meeting suit.*

go·tra (gō′trə), *n.* a Hindu clan tracing its paternal lineage from a common ancestor, usually a saint or sage. [Skt *gotrā*]

got·ten (got′ᵊn), *v.* a pp. of **get.**

Göt·ter·däm·mer·ung (*Ger.* gœt′ər dem′ə rōōng′), *n.* **1.** *German Myth.* the destruction of the gods and of all things in a final battle with evil powers: corresponds to the Scandinavian Ragnarok; Twilight of the Gods. **2.** (*italics.*) one of the music dramas in *The Ring of the Nibelung.* [< G, equiv. to *Götter,* pl. of *Gott* GOD + *Dämmerung* twilight]

Göt·tin·gen (gœt′ing ən), *n.* a city in central West Germany. 82,600 (1963).

Gott·lieb (got′lēb), *n.* **Adolphe,** born 1903, U.S. painter.

Gott mit uns (gôt′ mit ōōnz′), *German.* God is with us; God be with us.

got to (got′ tōō′, tə, got′ə), **1.** am, is, or are required, compelled, or under obligation to (fol. by a stated or implied infinitive); must: *You have simply got to see him.* **2.** need to or needs to (fol. by a stated or implied infinitive); must: *She has got to get her teeth straightened.* **3.** am, is, or are certain to (fol. by a stated or implied infinitive); must: *If he liked the first one, he's got to love this one.*

Gotts·chalk (gots′chôk), *n.* **Louis Mo·reau** (mō rō′, mô-), 1829–69, U.S. pianist and composer.

Gott·wald (gôt′väld), *n.* **Kle·ment** (kle′ment), 1896–1953, Czech Communist leader: prime minister 1946–48; president 1948–53.

Götz (gœts), *n.* **Her·mann** (her′män), 1840–76, German composer. Also, **Goetz.**

gouache (gwäsh, gōō äsh′; *Fr.* gwash), *n., pl.* **gouach·es** (gwä′shiz, gōō ä′shiz; *Fr.* gwash), for 3. **1.** a technique of painting with opaque watercolors prepared with gum. **2.** an opaque color used in painting a gouache. **3.** a work executed in this medium or according to this technique. [< F < It *guazzo* place where there is water << L *aquātiō,* deriv. of *aqua* water]

Gou·da (gou′də, gōō′-; *Du.* khou′dä), *n.* **1.** a city in the W Netherlands, NE of Rotterdam. 43,779 (est. 1962). **2.** Also called **Gou′da cheese′.** a semisoft, cream-colored cheese, made in Holland from whole or partly skimmed milk and usually coated with red wax.

Gou·dy (gou′dē), *n.* **Frederic William,** 1865–1947, U.S. designer of printing types.

gouge (gouj), *n., v.,* **gouged, goug·ing.** —*n.* **1.** a chisel having a partly cylindrical blade with the bevel on either the concave or the convex side. **2.** the act of gouging. **3.** a groove or hole made by gouging. **4.** an extortion or swindle. **5.** *Geol.* **a.** a layer of decomposed rocks or minerals found along the walls of a vein. **b.** fragments of rock that have accumulated between or along the walls of a fault. —*v.t.* **6.** to scoop out or turn with, or as with, a gouge: *to gouge a channel; to gouge holes.* **7.** to dig or force out with, or as with, a gouge: *to gouge out an eye.* **8.** to extort from or swindle. [< F < LL *gulbia;* cf. OPr *goja,* Sp *gubia*] —**goug′er,** *n.*

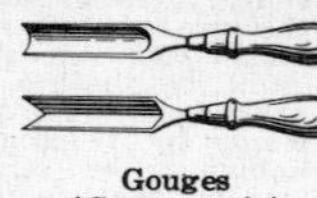
Gouges (Carpenter's)

gou·jon (go͞o′jən), *n., pl.* **-jons,** (*esp. collectively*) **-jon.** See **flathead catfish.** [< LaF, F: GUDGEON[1]]

Gou·jon (go͞o zhôN′), *n.* **Jean** (zhäN), c1510–c1568, French sculptor.

gou·lash (go͞o′läsh, -lash), *n.* **1.** Also called **Hungarian goulash.** a stew of beef, veal, vegetables, etc., with paprika or other seasoning. **2.** a deal in bridge for producing hands of unusual distribution, in which the players arrange their cards of the previous deal by suit and the dealer, after cutting the cards, distributes them without shuffling in three rounds of five, five, and three cards each. [< Hung *gulyas,* short for *gulyas hus* herdsman's meat]

Gould (go͞old), *n.* **1. Glenn Herbert,** born 1932, Canadian pianist and composer. **2. Jay,** 1836–92, U.S. financier. **3. Morton,** born 1913, U.S. composer and pianist. **4.** a walled plain in the third quadrant of the moon: about 24 miles in diameter.

Goulds (go͞oldz), *n.* a town in S Florida. 5121 (1960).

Gou·nod (go͞o′nō; *Fr.* go͞o nō′), *n.* **Charles François** (chärlz fran swä′; *Fr.* sharl fräN swa′), 1818–93, French composer.

gou·ra·mi (go͝or′ə mē), *n., pl.* (*esp. collectively*) **-mi,** (*esp. referring to two or more kinds or species*) **-mis. 1.** a large, air-breathing, nest-building, fresh-water Asiatic fish, *Osphronemus goramy,* used for food. **2.** any of several small, air-breathing, nest-building Asiatic fishes of the genera *Trichogaster, Colisa,* and *Trichopsis,* often kept in aquariums. [< Malay *gurami*]

gourd (gōrd, gôrd, go͝ord), *n.* **1.** the fruit of any of various cucurbitaceous plants, esp. that of *Lagenaria Siceraria* (**bottle gourd**), whose dried shell is used for bottles, sometimes cultivated for ornament. **2.** a plant bearing such a fruit. **3.** a dried and excavated gourd shell used as a bottle, dipper, flask, etc. **4.** a gourd-shaped, small-necked bottle or flask. [ME *gourd(e), courde* < AF (OF *cöorde*) < L *cucurbita*] —**gourd′-like′,** *adj.*

gourd′ cup′, a metal cup of the 16th and 17th centuries, having a gourd-shaped bowl mounted on a stem.

gourde (*Fr.* go͞oRd; *Eng.* go͝ord), *n., pl.* **gourdes** (*Fr.* go͞oRd; *Eng.* go͝ordz). a paper money and monetary unit of Haiti, equal to 100 centimes and equal to about .20 of a U.S. dollar. *Abbr.:* G., Gde. [< F, n. use of fem. of *gourd* dull, slow, heavy < L *gurd(us)* dull, obtuse]

gour·mand (go͝or′mənd; *Fr.* go͞oR mäN′), *n., pl.* **-mands** (-məndz; *Fr.* -mäN′). **1.** a person who is fond of good eating; gourmet; epicure. **2.** a glutton. Also, **gormand.** [ME *gourmaunt* < OF *gormant* a glutton] —**gour′mand·ism,** *n.*

gour·met (go͝or′mā; *Fr.* go͞oR me′), *n., pl.* **-mets** (-māz; *Fr.* -me′). a connoisseur in the delicacies of the table; epicure. [< F; OF *gromet, grommes* valet (esp. of a wine merchant)]
—**Syn.** gastronome; gourmand.

Gour·mont (go͞oR môN′), *n.* **Re·my de** (Rə mē′ də), 1858–1915, French critic and novelist.

Gour·ni·a (go͝or′nē ə), *n.* a village in NE Crete, near the site of an excavated Minoan town and palace.

gout (gout), *n.* **1.** *Pathol.* a constitutional disease characterized by painful inflammation of the joints, chiefly those in the feet and hands, and esp. in the great toe, and by an excess of uric acid in the blood. **2.** a drop, splash, or spot, as of blood. [ME *goute* < OF < L *gutta* a drop (of fluid); in ML, gout in the feet was attributed to drops of a corrupted humor]

goût (go͞o), *n. French.* taste; style; preference.

gout·ish (gou′tish), *adj.* susceptible to gout; gouty. [ME; see GOUT, -ISH[1]]

goutte (go͞ot), *n. Heraldry.* a pear-shaped figure representing a drop of water, of blood, etc. [< F; see GOUT]

gout·té (go͞o tā′), *adj. Heraldry.* semé of gouttes: *goutté gules.* [< AF *gutte* < L *guttāt(us)* GUTTATE]

gout·weed (gout′wēd′), *n.* a European herb, *Aegopodium Podagraria,* having white, umbellate flowers. Also called **bishop's-weed.** [GOUT + WEED[1]]

gout·y (gou′tē), *adj.,* **gout·i·er, gout·i·est. 1.** pertaining to or of the nature of gout. **2.** causing gout. **3.** diseased with or subject to gout. **4.** swollen as if from gout. [ME; see GOUT, -Y[1]] —**gout′i·ly,** *adv.* —**gout′i·ness,** *n.*

gout′y stool′, a footstool of the 18th century, having a top adjustable to a variety of angles.

gou·ver·nante (go͞o veR näNt′), *n., pl.* **-nantes** (-näNt′). *French.* **1.** a female chaperon. **2.** a governess.

Gouv·er·neur (guv′ər no͝or′, -nûr′, go͞o′vər-), *n.* a town in N New York. 4946 (1960).

Gov., governor.

gov., **1.** governor. **2.** government.

gov·ern (guv′ərn), *v.t.* **1.** to rule by right of authority, as a sovereign does: *to govern a nation.* **2.** to exercise a directing or restraining influence over; guide: *the motives governing a decision.* **3.** to hold in check; control: *to govern one's temper.* **4.** to serve as or constitute a law for: *the principles governing a case.* **5.** *Gram.* to be regularly accompanied by or require the use of (a particular form). In *They helped us,* the verb *helped* governs the objective case of the pronoun *we.* **6.** to regulate the speed of (an engine) with a governor. —*v.i.* **7.** to exercise the function of government. **8.** to have predominating influence. [ME *govern(en)* < OF *gouvern(er)* < L *gubernāre* to steer (a ship); c. Gk *kybernân* to steer] —**gov′ern·a·bil′i·ty, gov′ern·a·ble·ness,** *n.* —**gov′ern·a·ble,** *adj.*
—**Syn. 1.** reign. See **rule. 2.** control, sway, influence, check, conduct, supervise, superintend. —**Ant. 1.** obey.

Go·ver·na·dor Va·la·da·res (gô′viR nə dôR′ vä′lə dä′Ris), a city in E Brazil. 20,357 (1960).

gov·ern·ance (guv′ər nəns), *n.* **1.** government; exercise of authority; control. **2.** a method or system of government or management. [ME *governaunce* < OF < ML *gubernantia,* equiv. to L *gubern-* GOVERN + *-antia* -ANCE]

gov·ern·ess (guv′ər nis), *n.* **1.** a woman who is employed to take charge of a child's upbringing, education, etc. **2.** a woman ruler or governor. —*v.t., v.i.* **3.** to act or work as a governess. [ME *govern(er)ess* < OF *gouverneresse,* fem. of *gouverneur* GOVERNOR; see -ESS] —**gov′er·ness·y,** *adj.*

gov·ern·ment (guv′ərn mənt, -ər mənt), *n.* **1.** the political direction and control exercised over the actions of the members, citizens, or inhabitants of communities, societies, and states; direction of the affairs of a state, community, etc.; political administration: *Government is necessary to the existence of society.* **2.** the form or system of rule by which a state, community, etc., is governed: *monarchical government; episcopal government.* **3.** the governing body of persons in a state, community, etc.; administration. **4.** a branch or service of the supreme authority of a state or nation, taken as representing the whole: *to write to the government for information on chicken farming; a dam built by the government.* **5.** (in some parliamentary systems, as that of the United Kingdom) **a.** the particular group of persons forming the cabinet at any given time: *The Prime Minister has formed a new government.* **b.** the parliament along with the cabinet: *The government has fallen.* **6.** direction; control; rule: *the government of one's conduct.* **7.** the district governed; province. **8.** *Gram.* the established usage which requires that one word in a sentence should cause another to be of a particular form. [ME < OF *governement.* See GOVERN, -MENT] —**gov·ern·men·tal** (guv′ərn men′tᵊl), *adj.* —**gov′ern·men′tal·ly,** *adv.*

gov·ern·ment-in-ex·ile (guv′ərn mənt in eg′zīl, -ek′sīl, -ər mənt-), *n.* a government temporarily moved to or formed in a foreign land by exiles who hope to establish that government in their native country after its liberation.

gov′ernment is′sue, (*often cap.*) issued or supplied by the government or one of its agencies.

gov·er·nor (guv′ər nər), *n.* **1.** the executive head of a State in the U.S. **2.** *Chiefly Brit.* a person charged with the direction or control of an institution, society, etc.: *the governors of a bank; the governor of a prison.* **3.** Also called **governor general.** the representative of the crown in a British colony or dependency. **4.** a ruler or chief magistrate appointed to govern a province, town, fort, or the like. **5.** *Mach.* a device for maintaining uniform speed regardless of changes of load, as by regulating the supply of fuel or working fluid. **6.** *Brit. Informal.* **a.** one's father. **b.** one's employer. **c.** *Sometimes Facetious.* any man of superior rank or status. [ME *governour* < OF *governeor, gouverneur* < L *gubernātōr-* (s. of *gubernātor*), equiv. to *gubern-* GOVERN + *-ātōr* -ATOR]

gov′ernor gen′eral, *pl.* **governors general, governor generals. 1.** a governor who has under him subordinate or deputy governors. **2.** *Chiefly Brit.* governor (def. 3). Also, *esp. Brit.,* **gov′er·nor-gen′er·al.** —**gov′er·nor-gen′er·al·ship′,** *n.*

gov·er·nor·ship (guv′ər nər ship′), *n.* the duties, term in office, etc., of a governor. [GOVERNOR + -SHIP]

Gov′ernors Is′land, an island in New York Bay at the S end of the East River: U.S. military post. 2 sq. mi.

Gov′ernor Win′throp desk′, an 18th-century American desk having a slant front. Also called **Winthrop desk.** [after John WINTHROP]

Govt., government. Also, **govt.**

gow·an (gou′ən), *n. Scot., Northern Eng.* any of various yellow or white field flowers, esp. the English daisy. [? var. of obs. *gollan* < Scand; cf. Icel *gullinn* golden] —**gow′aned,** *adj.* —**gow′an·y,** *adj.*

Go·wan·da (gə wän′də), *n.* a town in W New York. 3352 (1960).

gowd (goud), *n. Chiefly Scot.* gold.

Gow·er (gou′ər, gōr, gôr), *n.* **John,** 1325?–1408, English poet.

gowk (gouk, gōk), *n.* **1.** *Brit. Dial.* cuckoo. **2.** a fool or simpleton. [ME *goke* < Scand; cf. OIcel *gaukr;* c. OE *gēac,* G *Gauch*]

gown (goun), *n.* **1.** a woman's dress or robe. **2.** a loose, flowing outer garment in any of various forms, worn by men and women as distinctive of office, profession, or status: *a judge's gown; an academic gown.* **3.** See **evening gown. 4.** the student and teaching body in British university towns (as contrasted to the *town,* or townfolk). —*v.t., v.i.* **5.** to dress in, or put on, a gown. [ME *goune* < OF < LL *gunn(a)* fur or leather garment < Celt]
—**Syn. 1.** frock. See **dress.**

gowns·man (gounz′mən), *n., pl.* **-men.** a man who wears a gown indicating his office, profession, or status. [GOWN + -'S[1] + MAN[1]]

goy (goi), *n., pl.* **goy·im** (goi′im), **goys.** *Often Disparaging.* a non-Jewish person; gentile. Also, **goi.** [< Yiddish < Heb *goi* people, non-Jews] —**goy′ish,** *adj.*

Go·ya (goi′ə; *Sp.* gô′yä), *n.* **Fran·cis·co de** (fran sis′kō də; *Sp.* fRän thēs′kō de), (*Francisco José de Goya y Lucientes*), 1746–1828, Spanish painter.

Go·yen (goi′ən), *n.* **Jan van** (yän vän), 1596–1656, Dutch painter.

G.P., 1. General Practitioner. **2.** Gloria Patri. **3.** Graduate in Pharmacy. **4.** Grand Prix.

gpad, gallons per acre per day.

gpcd, gallons per capita per day.

gpd, gallons per day.

Gp.E., Geophysical Engineer.

gph, gallons per hour. Also, **g.p.h.**

gpm, gallons per minute. Also, **g.p.m.**

GPO, Government Printing Office.

G.P.O., General Post Office.

gps, gallons per second. Also, **g.p.s.**

GPU, General Postal Union. Cf. **Universal Postal Union.**

G.P.U. (gā′pā′o͞o′, jē′pē′yo͞o′), the secret police of the U.S.S.R., 1922–35. Also called **Ogpu, Gay-Pay-Oo.** Cf. **Cheka, MVD, NKVD.** [*G(osudarstvennoe) P(oliticheskoe) U(pravlenie)*]

GQ, General Quarters.

gr, 1. grain; grains. **2.** gross.

Gr., 1. Grecian. **2.** Greece. **3.** Greek.

gr., 1. grade. **2.** grain; grains. **3.** gram; grams. **4.** grammar. **5.** great. **6.** gross. **7.** group.

G.R., King George. [< L *Georgius Rex*]

Graaf′i·an fol′licle (grä′fē ən), (*sometimes l.c.*) one of the small vesicles containing a developing ovum in the ovary of a mammal. [named after Regnier de *Graaf* (d. 1673), Dutch anatomist; see -IAN]

grab[1] (grab), *v.,* **grabbed, grab·bing,** *n.* —*v.t.* **1.** to seize suddenly and eagerly; snatch; clutch: *He grabbed me by the collar.* **2.** to take illegal possession of; seize forcibly or unscrupulously: *to grab land.* —*n.* **3.** a sudden, eager grasp or snatch: *to make a grab at something.* **4.** seizure or acquisition by violent or unscrupulous means. **5.** that which is grabbed. **6.** a mechanical device for gripping objects. **7. up for grabs,** *Informal.* available to anyone willing to expend the energy to get it: *The Republican nomination for mayor was up for grabs.* [c. MD, MLG *grabben,* Sw *grabba*] —**grab′ba·ble,** *adj.* —**grab′ber,** *n.*
—**Syn. 1.** grasp, grip, catch.

grab[2] (grab), *n.* an oriental ship having two or three masts with a square rig. [< Ar *ghurāb* raven]

grab′ bag′, 1. a container or receptacle from which a person at a party or the like draws a gift without knowing what he is getting. **2.** any miscellaneous collection.

grab′ bar′, a bar fixed parallel to a wall to provide a handgrip for a person steadying himself.

grab·ble (grab′əl), *v.i.,* **-bled, -bling. 1.** to feel or search with the hands; grope. **2.** to sprawl; scramble. [GRAB[1] + -LE; cf. D *grabbelen*] —**grab′bler,** *n.*

gra·ben (grä′bən), *n.* a portion of the earth's crust, bounded on at least two sides by faults, that has been moved downward in relation to adjacent portions. Cf. **horst.** [< G: ditch]

grab′ rope′, *Naut.* a rope supported to afford a hold for one approaching a vessel in a boat, walking up a gangplank, working aloft, etc. Also called **grab′ line′.**

Grac·chus (grak′əs), *n.* **1. Ga·ius Sem·pro·ni·us** (gā′əs sem prō′nē əs), 153–121 B.C., and his brother, **Ti·be·ri·us Sempronius** (tī bēr′ē əs), 163–133 B.C., Roman reformers and orators. **2. the Gracchi** (grak′ī), the brothers Gracchus.

grace (grās), *n., v.,* **graced, grac·ing.** —*n.* **1.** elegance or beauty of form, manner, motion, or act. **2.** a pleasing or attractive quality or endowment. **3.** favor or good will. **4.** a manifestation of favor, esp. by a superior: *It was only through the Dean's grace that she wasn't expelled from school.* **5.** mercy; clemency; pardon: *an act of grace.* **6.** favor shown in granting a delay or temporary immunity. **7.** *Law.* an allowance of time to a debtor before suit can be brought against him after his debt has by its terms become payable: *He was given thirty days of grace.* **8.** *Theol.* **a.** the freely given, unmerited favor and love of God. **b.** the influence or spirit of God operating in man to regenerate or strengthen him. **c.** a virtue or excellence of divine origin: *the Christian graces.* **d.** Also called **state of grace.** the condition of being in God's favor. **e.** Also called **state of grace.** the condition of being one of the elect. **9.** moral strength: *the grace to perform a duty.* **10.** a short prayer before or after a meal, in which a blessing is asked and thanks are given. **11.** (*usually cap.*) a formal title used in addressing or mentioning a duke, duchess, or archbishop, and formerly also a sovereign (usually prec. by *your, his,* etc.). **12. Graces,** *Class. Myth.* the goddesses of beauty, daughters of Zeus and Eurynome, worshiped in Greece as the Charities and in Rome as the Gratiae. Athens and Sparta each worshiped two Graces, those of Athens being Auxo (Increase) and Hegemone (Queen), and those of Sparta, Cleta (Sound) and Phaënna (Light); elsewhere, three Graces were worshiped, Aglaia (Brilliance), Euphrosyne (Joy), and Thalia (Bloom). **13.** *Music.* See **grace note. 14. fall from grace, a.** *Theol.* to relapse into sin or disfavor. **b.** to lose favor with someone in power: *Despite his good connections he fell from grace again.* **15. have the grace to,** to be so kind as to: *Would you have the grace to help, please?* **16. in someone's good** or **bad graces,** regarded with favor or disfavor by someone: *It is a wonder that I have managed to stay in her good graces this long.* **17. with bad grace,** reluctantly; grudgingly: *He apologized, but did so with bad grace.* Also, **with a bad grace. 18. with good grace,** willingly; ungrudgingly: *She took on the extra work with good grace.* —*v.t.* **19.** to lend or add grace to; adorn: *Many fine paintings graced the rooms of the house. Numerous trees and flowers grace the landscape.* **20.** to favor or honor: *to grace an occasion with one's presence.* **21.** *Music.* to add grace notes, cadenzas, etc., to. [ME < OF < L *grātia* favor, kindness, esteem, deriv. of *grātus* pleasing] —**grace′like′,** *adj.*
—**Syn. 1.** attractiveness, charm, gracefulness, comeliness, ease, symmetry. **4.** kindness, kindliness, love, benignity; condescension. **5.** lenity, leniency. **19.** embellish, beautify, deck, decorate, ornament; enhance, honor, dignify. —**Ant. 1.** ugliness. **4.** animosity. **5.** harshness. **19.** disfigure.

Grace (grās), *n.* a girl's given name. Also, **Grayce.**

grace-and-fa·vor (grās′ən fā′vər), *adj.* noting a residence owned by a noble or sovereign and bestowed by him upon some person for that person's lifetime.

grace′ cup′, 1. a cup, as of wine, passed round at the end of the meal for the final health or toast. **2.** the drink.

grace·ful (grās′fəl), *adj.* characterized by elegance or beauty of form, manner, movement, or speech; elegant. [ME; see GRACE, -FUL] —**grace′ful·ly,** *adv.* —**grace′ful·ness,** *n.*

grace·less (grās′lis), *adj.* **1.** lacking grace, pleasing elegance, or charm. **2.** without any sense of right or propriety. [ME; see GRACE, -LESS] —**grace′less·ly,** *adv.* —**grace′less·ness,** *n.*

grace′ note′, *Music.* a note not essential to the harmony or melody, added as an embellishment, esp. an appoggiatura.

grace′ pe′riod, *Insurance.* a period, usually of 31 days, permitted a life-insurance policyholder to pay a due premium before the company can declare the policy lapsed or impose penalties.

Gra·cia (grä′shə, -shē ə), *n.* a girl's given name, form of **Grace.** Also, **Gra·cie** (grā′sē).

gra·ci·as (grä′thē äs′, -sē-), *interj. Spanish.* thank you.

grac·ile (gras′il), *adj.* **1.** gracefully slender. **2.** slender; thin. [< L *gracil(is)* slender, slight, thin] —**gra·cil·i·ty** (gra sil′i tē, grə-), **grac′ile·ness,** *n.*

grac·i·lis (gras′ə lis), *n., pl.* **-les** (-lēz′). *Anat.* a muscle in the inner side of the thigh, the action of which assists in drawing the legs toward each other and in bending the knee. [< L: GRACILE]

gra·ci·o·so (grā′shē ō′sō, grā′sē-; *Sp.* grä thyō′sō, -syō′-), *n., pl.* **-sos** (-sōz; *Sp.* -sōs). **1.** a character in Spanish comedy, resembling the English clown. **2.** a low comic character. [< Sp: amiable, gracious, spirited (n. use of adj.) < L *grātiōs(us)* GRACIOUS]

gra·cious (grā′shəs), *adj.* **1.** disposed to show grace or favor; kind; benevolent; courteous. **2.** characterized by good taste, comfort, ease, or luxury: *gracious suburban living; a gracious home.* **3.** indulgent or beneficent in a pleasantly condescending way, esp. to inferiors. **4.** merciful or compassionate: *our gracious king.* **5.** *Obs.* fortunate or happy. —*interj.* **6.** (used as an exclamation of surprise, relief, dismay, etc.) [ME *gracious* < OF < L *grātiōs(us)* amiable, equiv. to *grāti(a)* GRACE + *-ōsus* -OUS] —**gra′cious·ly,** *adv.* —**gra′cious·ness, gra·ci·os·i·ty** (grā′shē os′i tē), *n.*
—**Syn. 1.** benign, friendly, favorable, polite. See **kind**[1]. **4.** tender, clement, mild, gentle. —**Ant. 1.** churlish. **4.** cruel.

grack·le (grak′əl), *n.* **1.** any of several long-tailed American birds of the family *Icteridae,* esp. of the genera *Quiscalus* or *Cassidix,* having usually iridescent black plumage. **2.** any of several Old World birds of the family *Sturnidae,* esp. certain mynas. [< NL *Gracula* name of genus, special use of L *grāculus* jackdaw]

grad[1] (grad), *n. Informal.* a graduate. [by shortening]

grad[2] (grad), *n.* one hundredth of a right angle. Also, **grade.** [< F *grade* degree < L *grad(us)*]

grad., **1.** *Math.* gradient. **2.** graduate. **3.** graduated.

gra·date (grā′dāt), *v.,* **-dat·ed, -dat·ing.** —*v.i.* **1.** to pass by insensible degrees, as one color into another. —*v.t.* **2.** to cause to gradate. **3.** to arrange in grades. [back formation from GRADATION]

gra·da·tim (grā dā′tim), *adv.* (in prescriptions) by degrees; gradually. [< L]

gra·da·tion (grā dā′shən), *n.* **1.** any process or change taking place through a series of stages, by degrees, or in a gradual manner. **2.** a stage, degree, or grade in such a series. **3.** the passing of one tint or shade of color to another, or one surface to another, by very small degrees, as in painting, sculpture, etc. **4.** the act of grading. **5.** ablaut. [< L *gradātiōn-* (s. of *gradātiō*). See GRADE, -ATION] —**gra·da′tion·al,** *adj.* —**gra·da′tion·al·ly,** *adv.*

grade (grād), *n., v.,* **grad·ed, grad·ing.** —*n.* **1.** a degree in a scale, as of rank, advancement, quality, value, intensity, etc.: *the best grade of eggs.* **2.** a class of persons or things of the same relative rank, quality, etc. **3.** a step or stage in a course or process. **4.** a single division of a school classified according to the age or progress of the pupils. American public schools are commonly divided into twelve grades below college. **5.** the pupils in such a division. **6. grades,** elementary school (usually prec. by *the*): *He began teaching first in the grades.* **7.** *U.S.* a number, letter, etc., indicating the relative quality of a student's work in a course, examination, or special assignment; mark. **8.** (of food) a classification or standard based on quality, size, etc.: *grade A eggs.* **9.** inclination with the horizontal of a road, railroad, etc., usually expressed by stating the vertical rise or fall as a percentage of the horizontal distance; slope. **10.** *Building Trades.* the ground level around a building. **11.** an animal resulting from a cross between a parent of common stock and one of a pure breed. **12.** *Math.* grad[2]. **13. at grade, a.** on the same level: *A railroad crosses a highway at grade.* **b.** (of a stream bed) so adjusted to conditions of slope and the volume and speed of water that no gain or loss of sediment takes place. **14. make the grade,** to attain a specific goal; succeed: *It saddened him that his son couldn't make the grade in medical school.* **15. up to grade,** of the desired or required quality: *This shipment is not up to grade.* —*v.t.* **16.** to arrange in a series of grades; class; sort: *a machine that grades two thousand eggs per hour.* **17.** to determine the grade of. **18.** to assign a grade to (a student's work); mark: *I graded forty tests last night.* **19.** to cause to pass by degrees, as from one color or shade to another. **20.** to reduce to a level or to practicable degrees of inclination: *to grade a road.* **21.** to cross (a nondescript animal or a low-grade one) with one of a pure breed. —*v.i.* **22.** to be graded. **23.** to be of a particular grade or quality. **24.** to pass by degrees from one color or shade to another; blend: *See how the various colors grade into one another.* [< F: office < L *grad(us)* step, stage, degree, deriv. of *gradī* to go, step, walk] —**grad′a·ble,** *adj.*

-grade, an element occurring in loan words from Latin, where it meant "step": *retrograde.* [< L *-gradus,* comb. form repr. *gradus* step or *gradī* to walk. See GRADE, GRADIENT]

grade′ cross′ing, an intersection of a railroad track and another track, a road, etc., at the same level.

grade·ly (grād′lē), *Brit. Dial.* —*adj.* **1.** good; commendable; worthy. **2.** complete; thorough. **3.** good-looking; handsome. **4.** healthy; well. **5.** suitable; proper. **6.** real; true. —*adv.* **7.** with care; exactly. **8.** properly; well. **9.** really; truly. [ME *greithly* prompt, good < ON *greithligr,* equiv. to *greith(r)* ready + *-ligr* -LY]

grade·mark (grād′märk′), *n.* **1.** a symbol noting the relative quality of a product, as lumber. —*v.t.* **2.** to mark with a grademark. [GRADE + MARK[1]]

grad·er (grā′dər), *n.* **1.** one who or that which grades. **2.** a pupil of a specified grade at school: *a fourth grader.* **3.** *U.S.* a machine for grading. [GRADE + -ER[1]]

grade′ school′, an elementary school that has its pupils grouped or classified into grades according to their advancement. Also, **grad′ed school′.**

grade′ separa′tion, separation of the levels at which roads, railroads, paths, etc., cross one another in order to prevent conflicting rows of traffic or the possibility of accidents.

gra·di·ent (grā′dē ənt), *n.* **1.** the degree of inclination, or the rate of ascent or descent, in a highway, railroad, etc. **2.** an inclined surface; grade; ramp. **3.** *Physics.* **a.** the rate of change with respect to distance of a variable quantity, as temperature or pressure, in the direction of maximum change. **b.** a curve representing such a rate of change. **4.** *Math.* a differential operator which, operating upon a function of several variables, results in a vector, the coordinates of which are the partial derivatives of the function. *Abbr.:* grad. *Symbol:* ∇ —*adj.* **5.** rising or descending by regular degrees of inclination. **6.** progressing by walking as an animal. **7.** of a type suitable for walking, as the feet of certain birds; gressorial. [< L *gradient-* (s. of *gradiēns* walking, going (prp. of *gradī*), equiv. to *grad-* walk + *-i-* thematic vowel + *-ent-* -ENT]

gra·di·ent·er (grā′dē en′tər), *n. Survey.* an instrument on a transit for measuring angles of inclination in terms of their tangents. [GRADIENT + -ER[1]]

gra′dient wind′ (wind), a wind with a velocity and direction that are mathematically defined by the balanced relationship of the pressure gradient force to the centrifugal force and the Coriolis force: conceived as blowing parallel to isobars. Cf. **geostrophic wind.**

gra·din (grā′din; *Fr.* gra daɴ′), *n., pl.* **-dins** (-dinz; *Fr.* -daɴ′). **1.** one of a series of steps or seats raised one above another. **2.** *Eccles.* a shelf or one of a series of shelves behind and above an altar. Also, **gra·dine** (grə dēn′). [< F: step, ledge of altar < It *gradin(o),* dim. of *grado* GRADE]

grad·u·al (graj′o͞o əl), *adj.* **1.** taking place, changing, moving, etc., by degrees or little by little: *gradual improvement in health.* **2.** rising or descending at an even, moderate inclination: *a gradual slope.* —*n.* **3.** *Eccles.* (*often cap.*) **a.** an antiphon sung between the Epistle and the Gospel in the Eucharistic service. **b.** a book containing the words and music of the parts of the liturgy which are sung by the choir. [ME < ML *graduāl(is)* pertaining to steps, *graduāle* a service sung as the choir stood on the altar steps, equiv. to L *grādu(s)* step, GRADE + *-ālis* -AL[1]] —**grad′u·al·ly,** *adv.* —**grad′u·al·ness,** *n.*
—**Syn. 1.** See **slow. 2.** gentle. —**Ant. 1.** sudden. **2.** precipitous.

grad·u·al·ism (graj′o͞o ə liz′əm) *n.* **1.** the principle or policy of achieving some goal by gradual steps rather than by drastic change. **2.** *Philos.* a theory maintaining that two seemingly conflicting notions are not radically opposed, but are related by others partaking in varying degrees of the character of both. [GRADUAL + -ISM] —**grad′u·al·ist,** *n., adj.* —**grad′u·al·is′tic,** *adj.*

grad·u·ate (*n., adj.* graj′o͞o it, -āt′; *v.* graj′o͞o āt′), *n., adj., v.,* **-at·ed, -at·ing.** —*n.* **1.** a person who has received a degree or diploma on completing a course of study, as in a university, college, or school. **2.** a student who holds the first or bachelor's degree and is studying for an advanced degree. **3.** a cylindrical or tapering graduated container, used for measuring. —*adj.* **4.** of, pertaining to, or involved in academic study beyond the first or bachelor's degree: *the graduate school of business; a graduate student.* **5.** graduated (def. 3). —*v.i.* **6.** to receive a degree or diploma on completing a course of study (often fol. by *from*): *She graduated from Sweet Briar in 1962.* **7.** to pass by degrees; change gradually. —*v.t.* **8.** to confer a degree upon, or to grant a diploma to, at the close of a course of study, as in a university, college, or school: *Cornell graduated eighty students with honors.* **9.** to graduate from: *She graduated college in 1950.* **10.** to arrange in grades or gradations; establish gradation in. **11.** to divide into or mark with degrees or other divisions, as the scale of a thermometer. [< ML *graduāt(us)* (ptp. of *graduāre*), equiv. to *grād(us)* GRADE, step + *-u-* thematic vowel + *-ātus* -ATE[1]] —**grad′u·a′tor,** *n.*

grad·u·at·ed (graj′o͞o ā′tid), *adj.* **1.** characterized by or arranged in degrees, esp. successively, as according to height, depth, difficulty, etc.: *a graduated series of lessons.* **2.** marked with divisions or units of measurement. **3.** (of a bird's tail) having the longest feathers in the center, the others being successively shorter. **4.** (of a tax) increasing along with the taxable base: *a graduated income tax.* [GRADUATE + -ED[2]]

grad′uate nurse′, a person who has graduated from an accredited school of nursing. Also called **trained nurse.**

grad′uate school′, a school, usually a division of a college or university, offering courses leading to degrees more advanced than the bachelor's degree.

grad·u·a·tion (graj′o͞o ā′shən), *n.* **1.** the act of graduating; the state of being graduated. **2.** the ceremony of conferring degrees or diplomas, as at a college or school. **3.** marks or a mark on an instrument or a vessel for indicating degree, quantity, etc. [< ML *graduātiōn-* (s. of *graduātiō*). See GRADUATE, -ION]

gra·dus[1] (grā′dəs), *n., pl.* **-dus·es.** *Music.* a work consisting wholly or in part of exercises of increasing difficulty. [< L: GRADE, step]

gra·dus[2] (grā′dəs), *n., pl.* **-dus·es.** a dictionary of prosody, esp. one that gives word quantities and poetic phrases and that is intended to aid students in the writing of Latin and Greek verse. [after *Gradus ad Parnassum* (a step to Parnassus), Latin title of a dictionary of prosody much used in English public schools during the 18th and 19th centuries]

Gra·dy (grā′dē), *n.* a boy's given name.

Grae·ae (grē′ē), *n.pl. Class. Myth.* three old sea goddesses who had but one eye and one tooth among them and were the protectresses of the Gorgons, their sisters. Also, **Graiae.**

Grae·ci·a Mag·na (grē′shē ə mag′nə). See **Magna Graecia.**

Grae·cise (grē′sīz), *v.t., v.i.,* **-cised, -cis·ing.** *Chiefly Brit.* Graecize.

Grae·cize (grē′sīz), *v.t., v.i.,* **-cized, -ciz·ing.** *Chiefly Brit.* Grecize. Also, **grae′cize.** —**Grae′cism,** *n.*

Graeco-, *Chiefly Brit.* var. of **Greco-.**

Grae·co-Ro·man (grē′kō rō′mən, grek′ō-), *adj., n.* Greco-Roman.

Graeffe′ meth′od (graf′), *Math.* a method, involving the squaring of roots, for approximating the solutions to algebraic equations.

Graf (gräf), *n., pl.* ***Graf·en*** (grä′fən). *German.* a count: a title of nobility in Germany, Austria, and Sweden, equivalent in rank to an English earl.

graf·fi·to (grə fē′tō), *n., pl.* **-ti** (-tē). **1.** *Archaeol.* an ancient drawing or writing scratched on a wall or other surface. **2. graffiti,** words or phrases written on public sidewalks, on the walls of buildings, public restrooms, etc., or the like. [< It, dim. of *graffio* scratch (of a stylus) < L *graphi(um)* < Gk *grāph(ein)* (to) write]

graft[1] (graft, gräft), *n.* **1.** *Hort.* **a.** a bud, shoot, or scion of a plant inserted in a groove, slit, or the like in a stem or stock of another plant in which it continues to grow. **b.** the plant resulting from such an operation; the united stock and scion. **c.** the place where the scion is inserted. **2.** *Surg.* a portion of living tissue surgically transplanted from one part of an individual to another, or from one individual to another, with a view to its adhesion and growth. **3.** the act of grafting. —*v.t.* **4.** to insert (a graft) into a tree or other plant; insert a scion of (one plant) into another plant. **5.** to cause (a plant) to reproduce through grafting. **6.** *Surg.* to transplant (a portion of living tissue) as a graft. **7.** to attach as if by grafting: *an absurdity grafted onto an otherwise coherent body of thought.* **8.** *Naut.* to cover (a rope) with a weaving of rope yarn. —*v.i.* **9.** to insert scions from one plant into another. **10.** to become grafted. [ME *graffe, craffe* < OF *graife, greffe, graffe* stylus < LL *graph(ium)* hunting knife, L: stylus < Gk *grapheîon,* deriv. of *gráphein* to write] —**graft′er,** *n.*

A B C

Grafts
A, Splice;
B, Saddle; C, Cleft

graft[2] (graft, gräft), *n.* **1.** the acquisition of gain or advantage by dishonest, unfair, or sordid means, esp. through the abuse of one's position or influence in politics, business, etc. **2.** a particular instance, method, or means of thus acquiring gain. **3.** the gain or advantage acquired. **4.** *Brit. Slang.* a person's legitimate occupation or work. —*v.t.* **5.** to obtain by graft. —*v.i.* **6.** to practice graft. [? special use of GRAFT[1]] —**graft′er,** *n.*

graft·age (graf′tij, gräf′-), *n.* the art of inserting a part of one plant into another plant in such a way that the two will unite and continue their growth. [GRAFT[1] + -AGE]

graft′ hy′brid, a hybrid plant that is produced by grafting and that exhibits characters of both the stock and the scion.

graft·ing (graf′ting, gräf′-), *n. Surg.* graft[1] (def. 2). [GRAFT[1] + -ING[1]]

Graf·ton (graf′tən, gräf′-), *n.* **1.** a town in NE North Dakota. 5885 (1960). **2.** a town in N West Virginia. 5791 (1960). **3.** a town in E Wisconsin. 3748 (1960).

gra·ger (grä′gər), *n., pl.* ***gra·gers*** (grä′gərz). *Yiddish.* a noise-making device, typically a small container filled with pellets and fitted with a handle, used by children each time Haman's name is said during the traditional reading of the Book of Esther on the Jewish festival of Purim.

gra·ham (grā′əm), *adj.* made of graham flour. [named after S. *Graham* (1794–1851), American reformer in dietetics]

Gra·ham (grā′əm), *n.* **1. Martha,** born 1902?, U.S. dancer and choreographer. **2. Thomas,** 1805–69, Scottish chemist. **3. William Franklin** ("**Billy**"), born 1918, U.S. evangelist. **4.** a town in N Texas. 8505 (1960). **5.** a town in central North Carolina. 7723 (1960). **6.** a boy's given name.

gra′ham crack′er, a semisweet cracker, usually rectangular in shape, made chiefly of whole-wheat flour.

Gra·hame (grā′əm), *n.* **Kenneth,** 1852–1939, Scottish writer, esp. of children's stories.

gra′ham flour′, unbolted wheat flour, containing all of the wheat grain; whole-wheat flour.

gra·ham·ite (grā′ə mīt′), *n. Mineral.* an asphaltite with a pitch-black luster. [named after J. A. and J. L. *Graham,* 19th-century American mineowners; see -ITE[1]]

Gra′ham Land′, **1.** the northern part of the Antarctic Peninsula. **2.** See **Antarctic Peninsula.**

Gra′ham's law′ of diffu′sion, *Physical Chem.* the principle that at a given temperature and pressure the rate of diffusion of a gas is inversely proportional to the square root of its density. [named after T. GRAHAM]

gra′ham wa′fer, *Canadian.* See **digestive biscuit.**

Grai·ae (grā′ē, grī′ē), *n. pl.* Graeae.

Grail (grāl), *n.* (*sometimes l.c.*) a cup or chalice, which according to medieval legend was used by Jesus at the Last Supper, and in which Joseph of Arimathea received the last drops of Jesus' blood at the Cross: often used as a symbol for Christian purity or as the reward for Christian purity. Also called **Holy Grail.** [ME *graiel, graile,* etc. < AF *grahel, grayel,* OF *gräel, grel* < ML *gradāle* platter. See GRADE, -AL[2]]

grain (grān), *n.* **1.** a small, hard seed, esp. the seed of one of the food plants, as wheat, corn, rye, oats, rice, and millet. **2.** the gathered seed of one of the food plants, esp. of cereal plants. **3.** the plants themselves taken collectively, whether standing or gathered. **4.** any small, hard particle, as of sand, gold, pepper, gunpowder, etc. **5.** the smallest unit of weight in most systems, originally determined by the weight of a plump grain of wheat. In the U.S. and British systems, as in avoirdupois, troy, and apothecaries' weights, the grain is identical. In an avoirdupois ounce there are 437.5 grains; in the troy and apothecaries' ounces there are 480 grains. **6.** the smallest possible amount of anything: *a grain of truth.* **7.** the arrangement or direction of fibers in wood, or the pattern resulting from this. **8.** the direction in which the fibers of a piece of dressed wood, as a board, rise to the surface: *You may work with or across the grain, but never against.* **9.** the side of leather from which the hair has been removed. **10.** a stamped pattern that imitates the natural grain of leather: used either on leather to simulate a different type of natural leather, or on coated cloth. **11.** the fibers or yarn in a piece of fabric as differentiated from the fabric itself. **12.** *Textiles.* the direction of threads in relation to the selvage of woven threads. **13.** the lamination or cleavage of stone, coal, etc. **14.** *Metall.* any of the individual crystalline particles forming a metal. **15.** *Jewelry.* a unit of weight equal to 50 milligrams or $^1/_4$ carat, used for pearls and sometimes for diamonds. **16.** the size of constituent particles of any substance; texture: *sugar of fine grain.* **17.** a granular texture or appearance: *a stone of coarse grain.* **18.** a state of crystallization: *boiled to the grain.* **19.** temper or natural character: *two brothers of similar grain.* **20.** *Rocketry.* a unit of solid propellant. **21.** *Obs.* color or hue. **22. against the** or **one's grain,** in opposition to one's temper, inclination, or character: *Shouting always went against her grain.* **23. with a grain of salt,** with reservations; critically: *You should take his promises with a grain of salt.* —*v.t.* **24.** to form into grains; granulate. **25.** to give a granular appearance to. **26.** to paint in imitation of the grain of wood, stone, etc.: *sheet steel grained to resemble oak.* **27.** *Tanning.* **a.** to remove the hair from (skins). **b.** to soften and raise the grain of (leather). [ME *grain, grein* < OF *grain* < L *grān(um)* seed, grain] —**grain′er,** *n.* —**grain′less,** *adj.*

grain′ al′cohol, alcohol (def. 1).

grained (grānd), *adj.* **1.** having, reduced to, consisting of, or bearing grain or grains (usually used in combination): *fine-grained sand; large-grained rye.* **2.** having a granular form, structure, or surface: *wood and other grained materials.* **3.** having an artificially produced granular texture or pattern: *grained kid.* **4.** marked by a particular quality (usually used in combination): *tough-grained journalism.* [GRAIN + -ED³] —**grained′-ness,** *n.*

grain′ el′evator, elevator (def. 4).

grain·field (grān′fēld′), *n.* a field in which grain is grown. [GRAIN + FIELD]

Grain·ger (grān′jər), *n.* **Percy Al·dridge** (ôl′drij), 1882–1961, Australian pianist and composer, in the U.S. after 1915.

grain′ growth′, *Metall.* a tendency of certain grains to grow and absorb others when heated under certain conditions.

grain′ refin′er, *Metall.* any chemical added to a molten metal or alloy to check grain growth.

grains (grānz), *n.* (*often construed as sing.*) an iron instrument with barbed prongs, for spearing or harpooning fish. [earlier *grainse* < Icel *grein* branch, division; cf. Sw *gren*]

grains d'orge (grān′ dôrzh′, dôrzh′), *Armor.* rivet heads, as for mail, formed to resemble seeds. [< F: lit., grains of barley]

grains′ of par′adise, the pungent, peppery seeds of a zingiberaceous plant, *Aframomum Melegueta* (*Granum-Paradisi*), of Africa, used to strengthen cordials and in veterinary medicine. Also called **guinea grains.**

grain′ sor′ghum, any of several varieties of sorghum, as durra or milo, having starchy seeds, grown for fodder in the U.S. and for the grain in the Orient.

grain·y (grā′nē), *adj.*, **grain·i·er, grain·i·est.** **1.** resembling grain; granular. **2.** full of grains or grain. **3.** having a natural or simulated grain, as wood, wallpaper, etc. **4.** *Photog.* (of a negative or positive) having a granular appearance. [GRAIN + -Y¹] —**grain′-i·ness,** *n.*

gral·la·to·ri·al (gral′ə tōr′ē əl, -tôr′-), *adj.* belonging or pertaining to the wading birds, as the snipes, cranes, storks, herons, etc., many species of which have very long legs. [< NL *grallātōri(us)* (L *grallātor* one who walks on stilts, equiv. to *grall(ae)* stilts (cf. *gradus* GRADE) + *-ātor* -ATOR) + -AL]

gram¹ (gram), *n.* a metric unit of mass, equal to 15.432 grains; one thousandth of a kilogram. *Abbr.:* g, g. Also, *esp. Brit.,* **gramme.** [< F *gramme* < LL *gramma* a small weight < Gk *grámma* something drawn, a small weight]

gram² (gram), *n.* **1.** (in the Orient) the chickpea, used as a food for man and cattle. **2.** any of various beans, as *Phaseolus aureus* **(green gram)** and *P. Mungo* **(black gram),** cultivated in India for food. [< Pg *grão* < L *grān(um)* GRAIN]

Gram (gräm), *n.* (in the *Volsunga Saga*) the sword of Sigmund, broken by Odin, repaired by Regin, and used again by Sigurd in killing Fafnir. Cf. **Balmung.**

-gram¹, an element occurring in loan words from Greek, where it meant "written" (*diagram; epigram*); on this model, used in the formation of compound words (*oscillogram*). Cf. **-graph.** [< Gk *-gram(ma),* comb. form of *grámma* something written or drawn; akin to CARVE]

-gram², a combining form of **gram¹:** *kilogram.*

gram., **1.** grammar. **2.** grammarian. **3.** grammatical.

gra′ma grass′ (grä′mə), any grass of the genus *Bouteloua,* of the western and southwestern U.S., as *B. gracilis* **(blue grama).** [< Sp *grama* < L *grāmina,* pl. of *grāmen* grass]

gram·a·rye (gram′ə rē), *n.* occult learning; magic. Also, **gram′a·ry.** [ME *gramary* < OF *gramaire,* lit., GRAMMAR]

gram′ at′om, *Chem.* the quantity of an element whose weight in grams is numerically equal to the atomic weight of the element. Also called **gram′-a·tom′ic weight′.** Cf. **Avogadro's number.**

Gram·bling (gram′bling), *n.* a town in N Louisiana. 3144 (1960).

gram′ cal′orie, calorie (def. 1b). *Abbr.:* g-cal

gram′ equiv′alent, *Chem.* See under **equivalent weight.**

gra·mer·cy (grə mûr′sē), *interj.* **1.** *Archaic.* an exclamation expressing surprise or sudden strong feeling. —*n.* **2.** *Obs.* thanks. [ME *gramerci, grantmerci* < OF *grand merci* great thanks. See GRAND, MERCY]

gram·i·ci·din (gram′i sīd′ən), *n.* *Pharm.* a crystalline, water-insoluble antibiotic obtained from tyrothrycin by extraction, used chiefly in treating local infections caused by Gram-positive organisms. Also called **gramicidin D.** [GRAM-(POSITIVE) + -I- + -CIDE + -IN²]

gra·min·e·ous (grə min′ē əs), *adj.* **1.** grasslike. **2.** pertaining or belonging to the *Gramineae* (or *Poaceae*), or grass family of plants. [< L *grāmineus* pertaining to grass, equiv. to *grāmin-* (s. of *grāmen*) grass + *-eus* -EOUS] —**gra·min′e·ous·ness,** *n.*

gram·i·niv·o·rous (gram′ə niv′ər əs), *adj.* **1.** feeding on seeds or like food. **2.** adapted for feeding on grain, as the jaws, teeth, etc., of gophers and other rodents. [< L *grāmin-* (s. of *grāmen*) grass + -I- + -VOROUS]

gram·ma·logue (gram′ə lôg′, -log′), *n.* a word symbolized by a sign or letter. [< Gk *grámma* letter + -LOGUE]

gram·mar (gram′ər), *n.* **1.** the study of the system underlying the esp. formal features of a language, as the sounds, morphemes, words, or sentences; a theory specifying the manner in which all sentences of a language are constructed. **2.** these features or constructions themselves: *English grammar.* **3.** an account of these features; a set of rules accounting for these constructions: *a grammar of English.* **4.** *Generative Gram.* a device, as a body of rules, whose output is all of the sentences that are permissible in a given language, while excluding all those that are not permissible. **5.** See **prescriptive grammar.** **6.** knowledge or usage of the preferred or prescribed forms in speaking or writing: *She said his grammar was terrible.* **7.** the elements of any science, art, or subject. **8.** a book treating such elements. [ME *gramery* < OF *gramaire* < L *gramatica* < Gk *grammatikḗ* (*téchnē*) GRAMMATICAL (art); see -AR²] —**gram′mar·less,** *adj.*

gram·mar·i·an (grə mâr′ē ən), *n.* **1.** a specialist in the study of grammar. **2.** a person who claims to establish or is reputed to have established standards of usage in a language. [ME *gramarien* < OF *gramairien.* See GRAMMAR, -IAN]

gram′mar school′, **1.** a graded school intermediate between a primary school and a high school. **2.** *Brit.* a secondary school corresponding to an American high school. **3.** (formerly) a secondary school in which Latin and Greek are among the principal subjects taught.

gram·mat·i·cal (grə mat′i kəl), *adj.* **1.** of or pertaining to grammar: *grammatical analysis.* **2.** conforming to standard usage: *grammatical speech.* [< L *grammatic(us)* (< Gk *grammatikós* knowing one's letters, equiv. to *grammat-,* s. of *grámma* letter, + *-ikos* -IC) + -AL¹] —**gram·mat′i·cal·ly,** *adv.* —**gram·mat′i·cal·ness, gram·mat′i·cal′i·ty,** *n.*

grammat′ical gen′der, *Gram.* gender based on arbitrary assignment, without regard to the referent of a noun, as in French *le livre* (masculine) "the book," and German *das Mädchen* (neuter) "the girl." Cf. **natural gender.**

grammat′ical mean′ing, the meaning of an inflectional morpheme or of some other syntactic device, as word order. Cf. **lexical meaning.**

gram·mat·i·cism (grə mat′i siz′əm), *n.* *Rare.* **1.** a point or principle of grammar. **2.** a grammatical definition. [GRAMMATIC(AL) + -ISM]

gramme (gram), *n.* *Chiefly Brit.* gram¹.

gram′ mol′ecule, *Chem.* that quantity of a substance whose weight in grams is numerically equal to the molecular weight of the substance. Also, **gram′-molec′ular weight′.** Cf. **Avogadro's number.** —**gram-mo·lec·u·lar** (gram′mə lek′yə lər), **gram-mo·lar** (gram′mō′lər), *adj.*

Gram-neg·a·tive (gram′neg′ə tiv), *adj.* (*often l.c.*) (of bacteria) not retaining the violet dye when stained by Gram's method.

Gra·mont (GRA môn′), *n.* **Phi·li·bert** (fē lē beʀ′), **Comte de,** 1621–1707, French courtier, soldier, and adventurer. Also, **Gram·mont′.**

Gram·o·phone (gram′ə fōn′), *n.* *Trademark.* a phonograph. —**gram·o·phon·ic** (gram′ə fon′ik), **gram′o·phon′i·cal,** *adj.* —**gram′o·phon′i·cal·ly,** *adv.*

Gram·pi·ans (gram′pē ənz), *n.* **The,** (*construed as pl.*) a range of low mountains in central Scotland, separating the Highlands from the Lowlands. Highest peak, Ben Nevis, 4406 ft. Also called **Gram′pi·an Hills′.**

Gram-pos·i·tive (gram′poz′i tiv), *adj.* (*often l.c.*) (of bacteria) retaining the violet dye when stained by Gram's method.

Grampus, *Grampus griseus* (Length 9 to 13 ft.)

gramps (gramps), *n.* *Informal.* grandfather. [alter. of *gramp,* short for GRANDPA]

gram·pus (gram′pəs), *n., pl.* **-pus·es.** **1.** a cetacean, *Grampus griseus,* of the dolphin family, widely distributed in northern seas. **2.** any of various related cetaceans, as the killer, *Orca orca.* [earlier *grampoys,* var. (by assimilation) of *graundepose* great fish, equiv. to *graunde* GRAND + *pose, poys* < MF *pois, peis* < L *piscem,* acc. of *piscis* fish; r. ME *gra(s)peis* < MF << L *crassum piscem* fat fish (acc.)]

Gram′-Schmidt′ orthogonaliza′tion (gram′-shmit′), *Math.* a process for constructing an orthogonal basis for a Euclidean space, given any basis for the space. [named after Hans C. J. *Gram* (see GRAM'S METHOD) and Bernhardt *Schmidt* (1879–1939), Russian-German optician]

Gram's′ meth′od (gramz), (*sometimes l.c.*) a method of staining and distinguishing bacteria, in which a fixed bacterial smear is stained with crystal violet, treated with Gram's solution, decolorized with alcohol, counterstained with safranine, and washed with water. Cf. **Gram-negative, Gram-positive.** [named after Hans C. J. *Gram* (1853–1938), Danish bacteriologist]

Gram's′ solu′tion, (*sometimes l.c.*) a solution of iodine, potassium iodide, and water, used in staining bacteria. Cf. **Gram's Method.**

gra·na (grā′nə), *n.* (in prescriptions) pl. of **granum.** [< L]

Gra·na·da (grə nä′də; *Sp.* grä nä′thä), *n.* **1.** a medieval kingdom along the Mediterranean coast of S Spain. See map under **Castile.** **2.** a city in S Spain: the capital of this former kingdom and last stronghold of the Moors in Spain; site of the Alhambra. 153,409 (est. 1960).

gran·a·dil·la (gran′ə dil′ə), *n.* **1.** the edible fruit of any of several species of passionflower, esp. *Passiflora edulis* **(purple granadilla)** and *P. quadrangularis* **(giant granadilla).** **2.** any of the plants yielding these fruits. [< Sp *granadilla,* dim. of *granada* pomegranate]

Gra·na·dos (grä nä′thôs), *n.* **En·ri·que** (en rē′ke), (*Enrique Granados Campina*), 1867–1916, Spanish pianist and composer.

gra·na·ry (grā′nə rē, gran′ə-), *n., pl.* **-ries.** **1.** a storehouse or repository for grain, esp. after it has been threshed or husked. **2.** a region that produces great quantities of grain. [< L *grānāri(um),* equiv. to *grān(um)* GRAIN + *-ārium* -ARY]

gra′nary wee′vil, a reddish-brown weevil, *Sitophilus granarius,* that infests, breeds in, and feeds on stored grain.

Gran Ca·na·ria (grän′ kä nä′ʀyä), one of the Canary Islands, in the central part. 303,839 (1950); 650 sq. mi. *Cap.:* Las Palmas. Also, **Grand Canary.**

Gran Cha·co (grän chä′kō), an extensive subtropical region in central South America, in Argentina, Bolivia, and Paraguay. 300,000 sq. mi. Cf. **Chaco** (def. 1).

grand (grand), *adj., n., pl.* **grands** for 13, **grand** for 14. —*adj.* **1.** impressive or imposing in size, appearance, or general effect: *grand mountain scenery.* **2.** stately, majestic, or dignified: *In front of an audience her manner is grand and regal.* **3.** highly ambitious or idealistic: *grand plans gone awry; grand ideas for bettering the human condition.* **4.** magnificent or splendid: *a grand palace; a grand display.* **5.** noble or revered: *a grand old man.* **6.** highest, or very high, in rank or official dignity: *a grand potentate.* **7.** main or principal; chief: *the grand staircase.* **8.** of great importance, distinction, or pretension: *a man used to entertaining grand personages.* **9.** complete or comprehensive: *a grand total.* **10.** pretending to grandeur, as a result of minor success, good fortune, etc.; conceited: *Jane is awfully grand since her husband got promoted.* **11.** first-rate; very good; splendid: *to have a grand time; grand weather; to feel grand.* **12.** *Music.* **a.** written on a large scale or for a large ensemble: *a grand fugue.* **b.** applied to compositions which contain all the regular parts or movements in a complete form. —*n.* **13.** a grand piano. **14.** *Informal.* an amount equal to a thousand dollars: *The cops found most of the loot, but they're still missing about five grand.* [ME *gra(u)nd, gra(u)nt* < OF *grant, grand* < L *grand-* (s. of *grandis*) great, large full-grown] —**grand′ly,** *adv.* —**grand′-ness,** *n.*
—**Syn. 2.** princely, regal, royal, exalted. **4.** great, large, palatial; brilliant, superb, glorious. **9.** inclusive. —**Ant. 1.** insignificant. **2.** base. **3.** small; mean. **7.** minor.

grand-, a prefix used in genealogical terminology meaning "one generation more remote": *grandfather; grandnephew.* [special use of GRAND]

gran·dam (gran′dəm, -dam), *n.* **1.** a grandmother. **2.** an old woman. Also, **gran·dame** (gran′dām, -dəm). [ME *gra(u)ndame* < AF. See GRAND, DAME]

Grand′ Ar′my of the Repub′lic, an organization, founded in 1866, composed of men who served in the U.S. Army and Navy during the Civil War. The last member died in 1956.

grand·aunt (grand′ant′, -änt′), *n.* an aunt of one's father or mother; great-aunt. [GRAND- + AUNT]

Grand′ Baha′ma, an island in the W Bahamas. 4600 (est. 1955); 430 sq. mi.

Grand′ Banks′, an extensive shoal SE of Newfoundland: fishing grounds. 350 mi. long; 40,000 sq. mi. Also, **Grand′ Bank′.**

Grand′ Canal′, **1.** a canal in E China, extending S from Tientsin to Hangchow. 900 mi. long. **2.** a canal in Venice, Italy, forming the main city thoroughfare.

Grand′ Canar′y. See **Gran Canaria.**

Grand′ Can′yon, a gorge of the Colorado River in N Arizona. over 200 mi. long; 1 mi. deep.

Grand′ Can′yon Na′tional Park′, a national park in N Arizona, including part of the Grand Canyon and the area around it. 1009 sq. mi.

grand·child (gran′-chīld′), *n., pl.* **-chil·dren.** a child of one's son or daughter. [GRAND- + CHILD]

grand′ chop′, (in China and India trade) a customs clearance.

grand′ climac′teric. See under **climacteric** (def. 4).

Grand′ Cou′lee (ko͞o′lē), **1.** a dry canyon in central Washington: cut by the Columbia River in the glacial period. 52 mi. long; over 400 ft. deep. **2.** a dam on the Columbia River at the N end of this canyon: the largest concrete dam in the world. 550 ft. high.

grand′ coun′cil fire′, a formal gathering of campfire girls requiring a minimum attendance of three troops.

grand′ coup′, *Bridge, Whist.* the trumping of a trick that could have been taken by the winner's partner.

grand·dad (gran′dad′), *n.* *Informal.* grandfather. [GRAND- + DAD¹]

grand·dad·dy (gran′dad′ē), *n., pl.* **-dies.** *Informal.* grandfather. [GRAND- + DADDY]

grand·daugh·ter (gran′dô′tər), *n.* a daughter of one's son or daughter. [GRAND- + DAUGHTER]

grand′ drag′on, a high-ranking official of the Ku Klux Klan.

grand′ dra′pery, *Theat.* a valance across the proscenium arch, forming part of the decorative frame for the stage.

grand′ duch′ess, **1.** the wife or widow of a grand duke. **2.** a woman who governs a grand duchy in her own right. **3.** a daughter of a czar or of a czar's son.

grand′ duch′y, a territory ruled by a grand duke or grand duchess.

Grand′ Duch′y of Mus′covy, Muscovy (def. 1). Also, **Grand′ Duch′y of Mos′cow.**

grand′ duke′, **1.** the sovereign of a territory called a grand duchy, ranking next below a king. **2.** a son of a czar or of a czar's son. —**grand′-du′cal,** *adj.*

Gran·de (gran′dē, grand; *Sp.* grän′de; *Port.* grännn′də), *n.* **Rio.** See **Rio Grande.**

Grande Char·treuse, La (lA gräɴd shar trœz′), the Carthusian monastery at Grenoble, France: the chief monastery of the Carthusians until 1903.

grande dame (gränd dam′), *pl.* **grandes dames** (gränd dam′). *French.* a great lady; a lady of dignified or aristocratic bearing.

gran·dee (gran dē′), *n.* a man of high social position or eminence, esp. a Spanish or Portuguese nobleman. [< Sp, Pg *grande.* See GRAND, -EE] —**gran·dee′ship,** *n.*

Grande Jatte, La (lä gränd′ zhät′; *Fr.* la gränd zhat′), a painting (1884–86) by Georges Seurat. Also called **Sunday Afternoon on La Grande Jatte.**

grande pas·sion (gränd pä syôn′), *pl.* **grandes pas·sions** (gränd pä syôn′). *French.* See **grand passion.**

Grande′ Prai′rie (grand), a city in W Alberta, in W Canada. 8352 (1961).

gran·deur (gran′jer, -jŏŏr), *n.* **1.** the quantity or state of being impressive or awesome: *the grandeur of the prophets.* **2.** the quality or state of being lofty or elevated in conception or treatment: *the grandeur of a prose style; the architectural grandeur of the Baroque.* **3.** the quality or state of being exalted in some deliberate way: *the grandeur of a royal court.* **4.** an instance of something that is grand: *the grandeurs and miseries of war.* [< F, OF, equiv. to *grand-* GRAND + *-eur* -OR[1]]
—**Syn. 3.** stateliness, majesty, sublimity; pomp, splendor, state.

Grand′ Falls′, a waterfall of the Hamilton River in Labrador. 200 ft. wide; 316 ft. high.

grand·fa·ther (gran′fä′thər, grand′-), *n.* **1.** the father of one's father or mother. **2.** a forefather. **3.** the founder or originator of a family, species, type, etc.; the first of one's or its kind, or the one being longest in existence: *the grandfather of all steam locomotives.* [ME; see GRAND-, FATHER]

grand′father clause′, *U.S. Hist.* a clause in the constitutions of some Southern States after the Civil War, designed to disfranchise Negroes by means of high literacy and property qualifications from which only those voters or their lineal descendants were exempt who had voted before 1867: declared unconstitutional in 1915.

grand·fa·ther·ly (gran′fä′thər lē, grand′-), *adj.* **1.** of, or in the manner of, a grandfather. **2.** indulgent; kindly. [GRANDFATHER + -LY]

grand′father's chair′. See **wing chair.**

grand′father's clock′, a pendulum floor clock having a case as tall as, or taller than, a person; a tall-case clock. Also, **grand′father clock′.**

grand feu (*Fr.* grän fœ′), *Ceram.* **1.** a firing of ceramics at a high temperature. **2.** the category of ceramic colors fired at high temperature. Cf. **petit feu.** [< F: lit., great fire]

grand′ fina′le, the concluding portion of a performance or entertainment, as a musical show, rodeo, etc., usually spectacular and involving most or all of the prior participants.

grand′ fir′, a large fir, *Abies grandis,* of the western coast of North America, yielding a soft wood used for lumber, pulp, and boxes. Also called **lowland white fir, lowland fir.**

Grand′ Forks′, a town in E North Dakota. 34,451 (1960).

Grand·gent (gran′jənt), *n.* **Charles Hall,** 1862–1939, U.S. philologist and essayist.

Grand Gui·gnol (*Fr.* grän gē nyôl′), **1.** a short drama stressing horror and sensationalism. **2.** noting, pertaining to, or resembling such a drama. [after *Le Grand Guignol,* small theater in Paris where such dramas were played]

gran·dil·o·quence (gran dil′ə kwəns), *n.* speech that is lofty in tone, esp. when so to the point of being pompous or bombastic. [< L *grandiloqu(us)* speaking loftily (*grandi(s)* great + *-loquus* speaking) + -ENCE]

gran·dil·o·quent (gran dil′ə kwənt), *adj.* speaking or expressed in a lofty or pompous style; bombastic. [GRANDILOQU(ENCE) + -ENT] —**gran·dil′o·quent·ly,** *adv.*
—**Syn.** turgid, inflated, rhetorical, pretentious. —**Ant.** simple, sincere.

grand′ inquis′itor, (*often cap.*) the presiding officer of a court of inquisition.

gran·di·ose (gran′dē ōs′), *adj.* **1.** grand in an imposing or impressive way. **2.** affectedly grand or stately; pompous. [< F < It *grandioso* < L *grandi(s)* grand + *-ōsus* -OSE[1]] —**gran′di·ose′ly,** *adv.* —**gran·di·os·i·ty** (gran′dē os′i tē), *n.*

gran·di·o·so (gran′dē ō′sō), *adj., adv. Music.* majestic; broad. [< It: GRANDIOSE]

Grand′ Is′land, a city in S Nebraska. 25,742 (1960).

grand je·té (*Fr.* grän zhə tā′), *pl.* **grands je·tés** (*Fr.* grän zhə tā′). *Ballet.* a jump or jeté, preceded by a grand battement or high kick, in which the dancer lands on the opposite leg from that from which he leaps. [< F]

grand′ ju′ror, a person serving on a grand jury. Also called **grand′ ju′ryman.**

grand′ ju′ry, a jury, usually of 12 to 33 persons, designated to inquire into alleged violations of the law in order to ascertain whether the evidence is sufficient to warrant trial by a petty jury. [ME < AF *graund juree*]

Grand′ La′ma, the chief monk and ruler of Tibet: called the Dalai Lama since the middle of the 17th century.

grand′ lar′ceny, *Law.* larceny in which the value of the goods taken is above a certain amount. Cf. **petty larceny.**

Grand′ Ledge′, a town in central Michigan. 5165 (1960).

grand·ma (gran′mä′, grand′-, gram′-, gram′mə), *n.* *Informal.* grandmother. [GRAND- + MA]

grand mal (gran′ mal′; *Fr.* grän mal′), *Pathol.* a form of epilepsy characterized by a sudden loss of consciousness, muscular spasms, clonic convulsions, cyanosis, and frothing at the mouth. Cf. **petit mal.** [< F: (the) great ailment, epilepsy]

grand·mam·ma (grand′mə mä′; gran′mä′mə, grand′-, gram′-), *n.* *Informal.* grandmother. [GRAND- + MAMMA[1]]

Grand′ma Mo′ses. See **Moses, Anna Mary Robertson.**

Grand′ Ma·nan′ (mə nan′), a Canadian island at the entrance to the Bay of Fundy: a part of New Brunswick; summer resort. ab. 3000; 57 sq. mi.

grand′ march′, the opening ceremonies of a formal ball, in which guests promenade into or around the ballroom.

Grand′ Mas′ter, the head of a military order of knighthood, a lodge, fraternal order, or the like.

grand monde (grän môNd′), *French.* the fashionable world; the best society. [lit., great world]

grand·moth·er (gran′muth′ər, grand′-, gram′-), *n.* **1.** the mother of one's father or mother. **2.** an ancestress. [ME; see GRAND-, MOTHER[1]]

grand·moth·er·ly (gran′muth′ər lē, grand′-, gram′-), *adj.* **1.** of or in the manner of a grandmother. **2.** like a grandmother. **3.** overly particular about petty details and unimportant rules. [GRANDMOTHER + -LY] —**grand′moth′er·li·ness,** *n.*

grand′mother's clock′, a pendulum clock similar to a grandfather's clock but shorter. Also, **grand′mother clock′.**

Grand′ Muf′ti, the chief legal authority for Muslims in Jerusalem.

grand·neph·ew (gran′nef′yōō, -nev′yōō, grand′-), *n.* a son of one's nephew or niece. [GRAND- + NEPHEW]

grand·niece (gran′nēs′, grand′-), *n.* a daughter of one's nephew or niece. [GRAND- + NIECE]

grand′ old′ man′, a highly respected, elderly person who is important in a field, as in politics or art, esp. one who has been active for a very long time.

Grand′ Old′ Par′ty. See **G.O.P.**

grand′ op′era, a drama interpreted by music, the text being sung throughout.

grand·pa (gran′pä′, grand′-, gram′-, gram′pə), *n.* *Informal.* grandfather. [GRAND- + PA]

grand·pa·pa (grand′pə pä′; gran′pä′pə, grand′-, gram′-), *n.* *Informal.* grandfather. [GRAND- + PAPA[1]]

grand·par·ent (gran′pâr′ənt, -par′-, grand′-), *n.* a parent of a parent. [GRAND- + PARENT] —**grand·pa·ren·tal** (gran′pə ren′tᵊl, grand′-), *adj.*

grand′ pas′sion, **1.** an intense or overwhelming attraction or love. **2.** the object of such feelings. [trans. of F *grande passion*]

grand′ peniten′tiary. See under **penitentiary** (def. 3).

grand′ pian′o, a piano with a harp-shaped horizontal body.

Grand′ Prai′rie, a city in NE Texas. 30,386 (1960).

Grand Pré (gran′ prā′; *Fr.* grän prā′), a village in central Nova Scotia, on Minas Basin: locale of Longfellow's *Evangeline.*

grand prix (grän prē′), *pl.* **grands prix** (grän prē′). *French.* grand prize; the highest award.

Grand Prix (grän prē′), *pl.* **Grand Prix** (grän prēz′), **Grands Prix** (grän prēz′), **Grand Prixes** (grän prēz′) any of a number of important automobile races over a long, arduous course, usually held annually between drivers of different countries.

grand′ quar′ter, *Heraldry.* a quartered coat of arms, itself one of the quarters of a coat of arms.

Grand′ Rap′ids, **1.** a city in SW Michigan: furniture factories. 177,313 (1960). **2.** a town in central Minnesota. 7265 (1960). **3.** noting or pertaining to mass-produced furniture of generally low quality.

gran·drelle (gran drel′), *n.* (*sometimes cap.*) a two-ply yarn made by twisting together two singles of contrasting color. [?]

Grand′ Riv′er, **1.** former name of the Colorado River above its junction with the Green River in SE Utah. **2.** a river in SW Michigan, flowing W to Lake Michigan. 260 mi. long. **3.** Hamilton (def. 6).

grand-scale (grand′skāl′), *adj.* of large proportion, extent, magnitude, etc.: *The grand-scale efforts of energetic minority members defeated the amendment.*

grand′ ser′jeanty, *Medieval Eng. Law.* serjeanty in which the tenant rendered services of a personal, honorary nature to the king, as carrying his sword or banner. Cf. **petit serjeanty.** [ME *graunte sergaunte* < AF]

grand·sire (grand′sīᵊr′), *n.* **1.** a method of ringing changes on a peal of bells. **2.** *Archaic.* **a.** a grandfather. **b.** a forefather. **c.** an old man. [ME *graunt-sire* < AF. See GRAND-, SIRE]

grand′ slam′, **1.** *Bridge.* the winning of all thirteen tricks of a deal. Cf. **little slam.** **2.** *Baseball.* Also, **grand′-slam′mer.** a home run with three men on base. **3.** *Sports.* the winning of all major championship contests in one season, as in golf or tennis.

grand·son (gran′sun′, grand′-), *n.* a son of one's son or daughter. [GRAND- + SON]

grand′ son′ne·rie (son′ə rē), *Horol.* a system of striking in which the hour is struck along with each quarter. [*sonnerie* < F: a sounding. See SOUND[1], -ERY]

grand·stand (gran′stand′, grand′-), *n., v.,* **-stand·ed, -stand·ing,** *adj.* —*n.* **1.** that part of a seating area of a stadium, racecourse, or the like, consisting of tiers with rows of individual seats. **2.** the people sitting in these seats. —*v.i.* **3.** to conduct oneself or perform showily or ostentatiously in an attempt to impress onlookers: *He doesn't hesitate to grandstand if it makes his point.* —*adj.* **4.** situated in or as if in a grandstand: *grandstand seats.* **5.** having a vantage point resembling that of a grandstand: *From our office windows on the third floor, we had a grandstand view of the parade.* **6.** intended to impress an onlooker or onlookers: *a grandstand catch.* [GRAND + STAND] —**grand′stand′er,** *n.*

grand′stand play′, *Slang.* **1.** an ostentatious play, as in a sport, overemphasized deliberately to elicit applause from spectators. **2.** any action or attempt designed to win approval or to make a strong impression: *She burst into tears upon hearing of his death, but it was only a grandstand play.*

Grand′ Te′ton Na′tional Park′ (tē′ton), a national park in NW Wyoming, including a portion of the Teton Range. 148 sq. mi.

grand′ tour′, an extended tour of Europe, formerly regarded as a necessary part of the education of young British aristocrats.

grand·un·cle (grand′ung′kəl), *n.* an uncle of one's father or mother; a great-uncle. [GRAND- + UNCLE]

grand′ vic′ar, *Rom. Cath. Ch.* the vicar-general of a French diocese.

Grand·view (grand′vyōō′), *n.* **1.** a town in W Missouri. 6027 (1960). **2.** a town in S Washington. 3366 (1960).

Grand′view Heights′, a town in central Ohio. 8270 (1960).

Grand·ville (grand′vil), *n.* a town in SW Michigan. 7975 (1960).

grand′ vizier′, the chief officer of state of various Muslim countries, as in the former Ottoman Empire.

grange (grānj), *n.* **1.** a farm. **2.** *Chiefly Brit.* a country dwelling house with its various farm buildings; dwelling of a yeoman or gentleman farmer. **3.** an outlying farmhouse with barns, sheds, etc., belonging to a feudal manor or a religious establishment, where crops and tithes in kind were stored. **4.** (*cap.*) *U.S.* a lodge or local branch of the "Patrons of Husbandry," an association for promoting the interests of agriculture. **5. the Grange,** the association itself. [ME *gra(u)nge* barn < AF < LL **grānica* (occurs in ML), equiv. to L *grān(um)* GRAIN + *-ica,* fem. of *-icus* -IC]

Grange (grānj), *n.* **Harold** ("*Red*"), born 1903, U.S. football player.

grang·er (grān′jər), *n.* **1.** a farmer. **2.** a farm steward. **3.** (*cap.*) *U.S.* a member of a Grange. [ME *gra(u)nger* farm-bailiff < AF; OF *grangier.* See GRANGE, -ER[2]]

grang·er·ise (grān′jə rīz′), *v.t.,* **-ised, -is·ing.** *Chiefly Brit.* grangerize. —**grang′er·i·sa′tion,** *n.* —**grang′er·is′er,** *n.*

grang·er·ize (grān′jə rīz′), *v.t.,* **-ized, -iz·ing.** **1.** to augment the illustrative content of (a book) by inserting additional prints, drawings, engravings, etc., not included in the original volume. **2.** to mutilate (books) in order to get illustrative material for such a purpose. [after James *Granger* (1723–1776), English clergyman whose *Biographical History of England* (1769) was arranged for such illustration; see -IZE] —**grang′er·ism,** *n.* —**grang′er·i·za′tion,** *n.* —**grang′er·iz′er,** *n.*

Grange·ville (grānj′vil), *n.* a town in central Idaho. 3642 (1960).

Gra·ni (grä′nē), *n.* (in the *Volsunga Saga*) the horse of Sigurd.

grani-, a learned borrowing from Latin meaning "grain," used in the formation of compound words: *granivorous.* [< L, comb. form of *grānum;* akin to CORN[1]]

Gra·ni·cus (grə nī′kəs), *n.* a river in NW Turkey, flowing N to the Sea of Marmara: battle 334 B.C. 45 mi. long.

gra·nif·er·ous (grə nif′ər əs), *adj.* producing or bearing grain. [< L *grānifer* grain-bearing (see GRANI-, -FER) + -OUS]

gran·ite (gran′it), *n.* **1.** a granular igneous rock composed chiefly of orthoclase and albite feldspars and of quartz, usually with one or more other minerals, as mica, hornblende, or augite. **2.** anything compared to this rock in great hardness, firmness, or durability. [< It *granit(o)* grainy. See GRAIN, -ITE[1]] —**gra·nit·ic** (grə nit′ik), *adj.* —**gran′ite·like′,** *adj.*

Gran′ite Cit′y, a city in SW Illinois, near St. Louis, Missouri. 40,073 (1960).

Gran′ite Falls′, **1.** a town in SW Minnesota. 2728 (1960). **2.** a town in central North Carolina. 2644 (1960).

gran′ite pa′per, paper containing fibers of various colors that give it a granitelike appearance.

Gran′ite State′, New Hampshire (used as a nickname).

gran·ite·ware (gran′it wâr′), *n.* **1.** a kind of ironware with a gray, stonelike enamel. **2.** pottery with a speckled appearance like that of granite. **3.** a semivitreous white pottery somewhat harder than earthenware. [GRANITE + WARE[1]]

gran·it·ite (gran′i tīt′), *n.* a granite rich in biotite. [GRANITE + -ITE[1]]

gran·it·i·za·tion (gran′i ti zā′shən), *n.* the process of forming granite. Also called **gran·i·ti·fi·ca·tion** (gran′i tə fə kā′shən). [GRANITIZE + -ATION]

gran·it·ize (gran′i tīz′), *v.t.,* **-ized, -iz·ing.** to subject to granitization. [GRANITE + -IZE]

gran·it·oid (gran′i toid′), *adj.* resembling or having the texture of granite. [GRANITE + -OID]

gra·niv·o·rous (grə niv′ər əs), *adj.* feeding on grain and seeds. [< NL *grānivorus.* See GRANI-, -VOROUS] —**gran·i·vore** (gran′ə vōr′, -vôr′), *n.*

Gran·jon (gran′jən), *n.* *Print.* a style of type originally cut by the French designer Robert Granjon.

gran·ny (gran′ē), *n., pl.* **-nies.** **1.** *Informal.* a grandmother. **2.** an old woman. **3.** a fussy person. **4.** *Southern U.S.* a nurse or midwife. **5.** See **granny knot.** Also, **gran′nie.** [nursery abbr. for GRANDMOTHER; cf. NANNY]

gran′ny knot′, an incorrect version of a square knot in which the bights cross each other in the wrong direction next to the end, so as to produce a knot likely to slip or jam. See illus. under **knot.** Also, **gran′ny's knot′.** [so called in contempt]

grano-, a combining form of **granite:** *granophyre.* [< G, comb. form of *Granit* granite]

Gran·o·lith (gran′ᵊlith), *n.* *Trademark.* a composition stone for pavements, made from crushed granite or the like. —**gran′o·lith′ic,** *adj.*

gran·o·phyre (gran′ə fīᵊr′), *n.* a fine-grained or porphyritic granitic rock with a micrographic intergrowth of the minerals of the groundmass. [GRANO- + -PHYRE] —**gran·o·phy·ric** (gran′ə fir′ik), *adj.*

grant (grant, gränt), *v.t.* **1.** to bestow or confer, esp. by a formal act: *to grant a charter.* **2.** to give or accord: *to grant permission.* **3.** to agree or accede to: *to grant a request.* **4.** to admit or concede; accept for the sake of argument: *I grant that point.* **5.** to transfer or convey, esp. by deed or writing: *to grant property.* —*n.* **6.** that which is granted, as a privilege or right, a sum of money, or a tract of land. **7.** the act of granting. **8.** *Law.* a transfer of property. **9.** a geographical unit in Vermont, Maine, and New Hampshire, originally a grant of land to a person or group of people. [ME *gra(u)nt(en)* < OF *graunt(er),* var. of *crëanter* < L *crēdent-* (s. of *crēdēns,* prp. of *crēdere* to believe) + *-āre* inf. suffix] —**grant′a·ble,** *adj.* —**grant′ed·ly,** *adv.* —**grant′er,** *n.*
—**Syn. 1.** award, vouchsafe. **2.** See **give. 6, 7.** concession, bequest. **7.** conveyance. —**Ant. 1, 2.** receive.

Grant (grant), *n.* **1. Cary** (*Archibald Leach*), born 1904, U.S. actor, born in England. **2. He·ber Jed·e·di·ah** (hē′bər jed′i dī′ə), 1856–1945, U.S. president of the Mormon Church 1918–45. **3. Ulysses S(impson)** (simp′sən), 1822–85, 18th president of the U.S.; Union general in the Civil War. **4.** a boy's given name.

Gran·ta (gran′tə), *n.* Cam (def. 1).

gran·tee (gran tē′, grän-), *n. Law.* a person to whom a grant is made. [ME; see GRANT, -EE]

Granth (grunt), *n.* the sacred scripture of the Sikhs, original text compiled 1604. Also, **Grunth.** Also called **Adigranth, Grant′ Sa′hib** (grunt). [< Hindi < Skt *grantha* a tying together, a book]

grant-in-aid (grant′in ād′), *n., pl.* **grants-in-aid. 1.** a subsidy furnished by a central government to a local one to help finance a public project, as the construction of a highway or school. **2.** something similar to such a subsidy or grant, esp. financial assistance given to an individual or institution for educational purposes.

Grant·land (grant′lənd), *n.* a boy's given name.

gran·tor (gran′tər, grän′-, gran tôr′, grän-), *n. Law.* a person who makes a grant. [< AF; see GRANT, -OR²]

Grants′ Pass′, a city in SW Oregon. 10,118 (1960).

gran·u·lar (gran′yə lər), *adj.* **1.** of the nature of granules. **2.** composed of or bearing granules or grains. **3.** showing a granulated structure. [GRANULE + -AR¹] —**gran·u·lar·i·ty** (gran′yə lar′i tē), *n.* —**gran′u·lar·ly,** *adv.*

gran·u·late (gran′yə lāt′), *v.,* **-lat·ed, -lat·ing.** —*v.t.* **1.** to form into granules or grains. **2.** to raise in granules; make rough on the surface. —*v.i.* **3.** to become granular. **4.** *Pathol.* to form granulation tissue. [GRANULE + -ATE¹] —**gran′u·lat′er, gran′u·la′tor,** *n.* —**gran·u·la·tive** (gran′yə lā′tiv, -lə tiv), *adj.*

gran′ulated sug′ar, a coarsely ground white sugar, widely used as a sweetener.

gran·u·la·tion (gran′yə lā′shən), *n.* **1.** the act or process of granulating. **2.** a granulated condition. **3.** any of the grains of a granulated surface. **4.** *Pathol.* **a.** the formation of granulation tissue, esp. in healing. **b.** See **granulation tissue. 5.** *Astron.* one of the small, short-lived features of the sun's surface which in the aggregate give it a mottled appearance when viewed with a telescope. [GRANULE + -ATION]

granula′tion tis′sue, *Pathol.* tissue formed in ulcers and in early wound healing and repair, composed largely of newly growing capillaries and so called from its irregular surface in open wounds; proud flesh.

gran·ule (gran′yo͞ol), *n.* **1.** a little grain. **2.** a small particle; pellet. **3.** a corpuscle; sporule. [< LL *grānul(um)* small grain. See GRAIN, -ULE]

gran·u·lite (gran′yə līt′), *n. Petrog.* a metamorphic rock composed of granular minerals of uniform size, as quartz, feldspar, or pyroxene, and showing a definite banding. [GRANULE + -ITE¹] —**gran·u·lit·ic** (gran′yə-lit′ik), *adj.*

gran·u·lo·blast (gran′yə lō blast′), *n. Anat.* an immature granulocyte. [GRANULE + -O- + -BLAST] —**gran′u·lo·blas′tic,** *adj.*

gran·u·lo·cyte (gran′yə lō sīt′), *n. Anat.* a leukocyte, the cytoplasm of which contains granules. [GRANULE + -O- + -CYTE] —**gran·u·lo·cyt·ic** (gran′yə lō-sit′ik), *adj.*

gran·u·lo·ma (gran′yə lō′mə), *n., pl.* **-mas, -ma·ta** (-mə tə). *Pathol.* an inflammatory tumor or growth composed of granulation tissue. [GRANULE + -OMA] —**gran·u·lom·a·tous** (gran′yə lom′ə təs), *adj.*

gran·u·lo·ma·to·sis (gran′yə lō mə tō′sis), *n. Pathol.* a condition characterized by a number of granulomas. [< NL *granulomat-* (s. of *granuloma*) GRANULOMA + -OSIS]

gran·u·lose (gran′yə lōs′), *adj.* granular. [GRANULE + -OSE¹]

gra·num (grā′nəm), *n., pl.* **-na** (-nə). (in prescriptions) a grain. [< L]

Gran·ville (gran′vil), *n.* **1. Earl of.** See **Carteret, John. 2.** a town in central Ohio. 2868 (1960). **3.** a town in E New York. 2715 (1960). **4.** a boy's given name.

Gran·ville-Bar·ker (gran′vil bär′kər), *n.* **Harley,** 1877–1946, English dramatist, actor, and critic.

grape (grāp), *n.* **1.** the edible, pulpy, smooth-skinned berry or fruit which grows in clusters on vines of the genus *Vitis,* and from which wine is made. **2.** any vine bearing this fruit. **3.** a dull, dark, purplish-red color. **4. grapes,** (*construed as sing.*) *Vet. Pathol.* **a.** tuberculosis occurring in cattle, characterized by the internal formation of grapelike clusters, esp. in the lungs. **b.** tuberculosis occurring in horses, characterized by grapelike clusters on the fetlocks. **5.** grapeshot. **6. the grape,** wine. [ME < OF, var. of *crape* cluster of fruit or flowers, orig. hook < Gmc; cf. G *Krapf* hook and GRAPPEL, GRAPNEL] —**grape′like′,** *adj.*

grape′ fern′, any of several ferns of the genus *Botrychium,* having grapelike clusters of sporangia.

grape·fruit (grāp′fro͞ot′), *n.* **1.** Also called **pomelo.** a large, roundish, yellow-skinned, edible citrus fruit having a juicy, acid pulp. **2.** the tropical or semitropical, rutaceous tree, *Citrus paradisi,* yielding it. [GRAPE + FRUIT, appar. from the resemblance of its clusters to those of grapes]

grape′fruit league′, *Baseball Informal.* a series of training games played by major-league teams before the opening of the season (so named because they take place in the citrus-growing South, as in Florida).

grape′ hy′acinth, any liliaceous plant of the genus *Muscari,* as *M. botryoides,* having globular, blue flowers resembling tiny grapes.

grape·line (grap′lin), *n. Naut.* grapnel. [alter. of GRAPPLING]

grape′ phylloxe′ra. See under **phylloxera.**

grap·er·y (grā′pə rē), *n., pl.* **-er·ies. 1.** a building where grapes are grown. **2.** a vineyard. [GRAPE + -ERY]

grape·shot (grāp′shot′), *n. Archaic.* a cluster of small cast-iron balls used as a charge for a cannon. [GRAPE + SHOT¹]

Grapes′ of Wrath′, The, a novel (1939) by John Steinbeck.

grape·stone (grāp′stōn′), *n.* the seed of a grape. [GRAPE + STONE]

grape′ sug′ar, dextrose.

grape·vine (grāp′vīn′), *n.* **1.** a vine that bears grapes. **2.** Also called **grape′vine tel′egraph.** a person-to-person method of relaying secret reports which cannot be obtained through regular channels. **3.** an unauthenticated report; rumor. [GRAPE + VINE]

Grape·vine (grāp′vīn′), *n.* a town in N Texas. 2821 (1960).

grap·ey (grā′pē), *adj.,* **grap·i·er, grap·i·est.** grapy.

graph (graf, gräf), *n.* **1.** a diagram representing a system of connections or interrelations among two or more things by a number of distinctive dots, lines, bars, etc. **2.** *Math.* **a.** a series of points, discrete or continuous, as in forming a curve or surface, each of which represents a value of a given function. **b.** Also called **linear graph.** a network of lines connecting points. **3.** a written symbol for an idea, a sound, or a linguistic expression. —*v.t.* **4.** to draw (a curve) as representing a given function. **5.** to represent by means of a graph. [short for *graphic formula;* see GRAPHIC] —**Syn. 1.** See **map.**

Graphs
Line graph (above); Bar graph (below)

graph-, var. of **grapho-** before a vowel: *grapheme.*

-graph, an element, borrowed from Greek, meaning "drawn," "written" (*monograph; lithograph*); specialized in meaning to indicate the instrument rather than the written product of the instrument (*telegraph; phonograph*). [< Gk *-graph(os)* (something) drawn or written, one who draws or writes. See GRAPHO-]

Graph·al·loy (graf′ə loi′), *n. Trademark.* a compound of graphite impregnated with Babbitt metal, bronze, copper, gold, etc., used as a low-friction material.

graph·eme (graf′ēm), *n. Ling.* **1.** a minimal unit of a writing system. **2.** a unit of a writing system consisting of all the written symbols or sequences of written symbols that are used to represent a single phoneme. [GRAPH- + -EME]

gra·phe·mics (gra fē′miks), *n.* (*construed as sing.*) *Ling.* the study of writing systems and of their relation to speech. [GRAPHEME + -ICS]

-grapher, a combination of **-graph** and **-er¹,** used to form agent nouns to stems in **-graph:** *telegrapher.*

graph·ic (graf′ik), *adj.* **1.** giving a clear and effective picture; vivid: *a graphic account of an accident.* **2.** pertaining to the use of diagrams, graphs, mathematical curves, or the like; diagrammatic. **3.** of, pertaining to, or expressed by writing: *graphic symbols.* **4.** written, inscribed, or drawn. **5.** *Geol.* (of a rock) having a texture formed by the intergrowth of certain minerals so as to resemble written characters. **6.** *Math.* pertaining to the determination of values, solution of problems, etc., by direct measurement on diagrams instead of by ordinary calculations. **7.** of or pertaining to the graphic arts. Also, **graph′i·cal.** [< L *graphic(us)* of painting or drawing < Gk *graphikós* able to draw or paint, equiv. to *gráph(ein)* (to) draw, write + *-ikos* -IC] —**graph′i·cal·ly, graph′ic·ly,** *adv.* —**graph′i·cal·ness, graph′ic·ness,** *n.*
—**Syn. 1.** striking, telling; detailed. See **picturesque.**

-graphic, a combination of **-graph** and **-ic,** used to form adjectives to stems in **-graph:** *telegraphic.*

graph′ic ac′cent, *Gram.* **1.** any mark written above a letter, esp. one indicating stress in pronunciation, as in Spanish *rápido.* **2.** any of the written or printed signs used as diacritics to indicate an accent, esp. the acute accent used to mark stress.

graph′ic arts′, 1. Also called **graphics.** the arts or techniques, as engraving, etching, drypoint, woodcut, lithography, and other methods by which copies of an original design are printed from a plate, block, or the like. **2.** the arts of drawing, painting, and printmaking.

graph′ic gran′ite, a pegmatite that has crystals of darkly colored quartz imbedded in microcline in such a manner that they resemble cuneiform writing.

graph·ics (graf′iks), *n.* **1.** (*construed as sing.*) the art of drawing, esp. as used in mathematics, engineering, etc. **2.** (*construed as pl.*) See **graphic arts** (def. 1). **3.** (*construed as sing.*) the science of calculating by diagrams. [see GRAPHIC, -ICS]

graph·ite (graf′īt), *n.* a very common mineral, soft native carbon, occurring in black to dark-gray foliated masses, with metallic luster and greasy feel: used for pencil leads, as a lubricant, for making crucibles and other refractories, etc.; plumbago; black lead. [orig. < G *Graphit* < Gk *gráph(ein)* (to) write, draw + G *-it* -ITE¹] —**gra·phit·ic** (gra fit′ik), *adj.*

graph·i·tize (graf′i tīz′), *v.t.,* **-tized, -tiz·ing. 1.** to convert into graphite. **2.** to cover (the surface of an object) with graphite. [GRAPHITE + -IZE] —**graph′i·ti·za′tion,** *n.*

grapho-, a learned borrowing from Greek meaning "writing," used in the formation of compound words: *graphomotor.* Also, *esp. before a vowel,* **graph-.** Cf. **-graph, -grapher, -graphic, -graphy.** [< Gk, comb. form of *graphḗ;* akin to CARVE]

graph·ol·o·gy (gra fol′ə jē), *n.* the study of handwriting, esp. as regarded as an expression of the writer's character. [GRAPHO- + -LOGY] —**graph·o·log·ic** (graf′ə loj′ik), **graph′o·log′i·cal,** *adj.* —**graph·ol′o·gist,** *n.*

graph·o·mo·tor (graf′ə mō′tər), *adj. Med.* pertaining to the muscular movements in writing. [GRAPHO- + MOTOR]

gra·phon·o·my (gra fon′ə mē), *n.* the scientific study of writing systems. [GRAPHO- + -NOMY]

Graph·o·phone (graf′ə fōn′), *n. Trademark.* a phonograph for recording and reproducing sounds on wax records. —**graph·o·phon·ic** (graf′ə fon′ik), *adj.*

Graph·o·type (graf′ə tīp′), *n. Trademark.* a typewriterlike machine for embossing letters upon thin sheets of metal, as for use in an addressing machine. —**graph·o·typ·ic** (graf′ə tip′ik), *adj.*

graph′ pa′per, paper printed with a pattern of straight or curved lines, used for plotting graphs and curves.

-graphy, a combining form denoting some process or form of drawing, writing, representing, recording, describing, etc., or an art or science concerned with such process: *biography; choreography; geography; orthography; photography.* [< Gk *-graphia.* See -GRAPH, -Y³]

Grapnel (def. 2)

grap·nel (grap′nᵊl), *n.* **1.** a device consisting essentially of one or more hooks or clamps, for grasping or holding something; grapple; grappling iron. **2.** a small anchor with three or more flukes. Also called **grapeline, grap·lin, grap·line** (grap′lin). [ME *grapnel(l),* dim. of OF *grapin,* dim. of *grape* hook, GRAPE]

grap·pa (gräp′pä), *n.* an unaged brandy, originally from Italy, distilled from the pomace of a wine press. [< It: grape stalk < Gmc; see GRAPE]

grap′pi·er cement′ (grap′ē ā′), a by-product of the calcination of hydraulic lime, having similar properties and made from ground, unslaked lumps. [< F *grappier,* deriv. of *grappe* bunch of grapes. See GRAPE, -IER]

grap·ple (grap′əl), *n., v.,* **-pled, -pling.** —*n.* **1.** a hook or an iron instrument by which one thing, as a ship, fastens onto another; grapnel. **2.** a seizing or gripping. **3.** a grip or close hold in wrestling or hand-to-hand fighting. **4.** a close, hand-to-hand fight. —*v.t.* **5.** to seize, hold, or fasten with or as with a grapple. **6.** to seize in a grip, take hold of: *The thug grappled him around the neck.* —*v.i.* **7.** to hold or make fast to something, as with a grapple. **8.** to use a grapple. **9.** to seize another, or each other, in a firm grip, as in wrestling; clinch. **10.** to engage in a struggle or close encounter (usually fol. by *with*): *He was grappling with a boy twice his size.* **11.** to try to overcome or deal (usually fol. by *with*): *to grapple with a problem.* [appar. a freq. of OE *gegrǣppian* to seize; associated with GRAPNEL] —**grap′pler,** *n.*

grap′ple ground′, an anchorage, esp. for small vessels.

grap′ple plant′, the wait-a-bit, *Harpagophytum procumbens.*

grap′ple shot′, *Naut.* a grapnellike projectile fired from a gun and used as a hold for the end of a line in rescue operations or in kedging. Also called **anchor shot.**

grap·pling (grap′ling), *n.* **1.** that by which anything is seized and held. **2.** grapnel. [GRAPPLE + -ING¹]

grap′pling i′ron, a grapnel. Also called **grap′pling hook′.**

grap·to·lite (grap′tə līt′), *n.* any colonial animal of the extinct class *Graptolithina,* most common in the Ordovician and Silurian periods, thought to be related to the pterobranchs. [< Gk *graptó(s)* painted, marked with letters (deriv. of *gráphein* to write) + -LITE] —**grap·to·lit·ic** (grap′tə lit′ik), *adj.*

grap·y (grā′pē), *adj.,* **grap·i·er, grap·i·est. 1.** of, like, or composed of grapes. **2.** tasting of grapes or grape juice: *a grapy wine.* Also, **grapey.** [GRAPE + -Y¹]

Gras·mere (gras′mēr, gräs′-), *n.* **1.** a lake in Westmoreland, in NW England. 1 mi. long. **2.** a village on this lake: Wordsworth's home 1790–1808.

grasp (grasp, gräsp), *v.t.* **1.** to seize and hold by or as by clasping with the fingers. **2.** to seize upon; hold firmly. **3.** to get hold of mentally; comprehend; understand: *I don't grasp your meaning.* —*v.i.* **4.** to make an attempt to seize, or a motion of seizing, something (usually fol. by *at* or *for*): *a drowning man grasping at straws; to grasp for an enemy's wrist.* —*n.* **5.** the act of grasping or gripping, as with the hands or arms: *to make a grasp at something.* **6.** a hold or grip: *to have a firm grasp of a hammer.* **7.** one's arms or hands, in embracing or gripping: *He took her in his grasp.* **8.** one's power of seizing and holding; reach: *to have a thing within one's grasp.* **9.** hold, possession, or mastery: *to wrest power from the grasp of a usurper.* **10.** mental hold or capacity; power to understand. **11.** broad or thorough comprehension: *a good grasp of one's subject.* [ME *grasp(en), graps(en);* c. LG *grapsen;* akin to OE *gegrǣppian* to seize (see GRAPPLE)] —**grasp′a·ble,** *adj.* —**grasp′er,** *n.* —**grasp′less,** *adj.*
—**Syn. 1.** grip, clutch; grab. See **catch. 9.** clutches. **10.** scope, comprehension. GRASP, REACH refer to the power of seizing, either concretely or figuratively. GRASP suggests actually seizing and closing the hand upon something (or, figuratively, thoroughly comprehending something) and therefore refers to something within one's possession or immediate possibility of possession: *a good grasp of a problem; immense mental grasp.* REACH suggests a stretching out of (usually) the hand to touch, strike, or, if possible, seize something; it therefore refers to a potentiality of possession which requires an effort. Figuratively, it implies perhaps a faint conception of something still too far beyond one to be definitely and clearly understood. —**Ant. 1.** release.

grasp·ing (gras′ping, gräs′-), *adj.* **1.** that grasps. **2.** greedy; avaricious. [GRASP + -ING²] —**grasp′ing·ly,** *adv.* —**grasp′ing·ness,** *n.*

grass (gras, gräs), *n.* **1.** any plant of the family *Gramineae,* characterized by jointed stems, sheathing leaves, flower spikelets, and fruit consisting of a seedlike grain or caryopsis. **2.** herbage in general, or the plants on which grazing animals pasture or which are cut and dried as hay. **3.** the grass-covered ground. **4.** pasture: *Half the farm is grass.* **5.** *U.S. Slang.* marijuana. **6. grasses,** stalks or sprays of grass: *filled with dried grasses.* **7.** the season of the new growth of grass. **8. go to grass,** to give up the practice of one's occupation or profession; retire: *Many men lack a sense of purpose after they have gone to grass.* **9. let the grass grow under one's feet,** to become slack in one's efforts: *Our competitors aren't letting the grass grow under their feet, so we have to put our shoulders to the wheel.* —*v.t.* **10.** to cover with grass or turf. **11.** to feed with growing grass; pasture. **12.** to lay (something) on the grass, as for the purpose of bleaching. —*v.i.* **13.** to feed on growing grass; graze. **14.** to produce grass; become covered with grass. [ME *gras,* OE *græs;* c. D, G, Icel, Goth *gras;* akin to GROW, GREEN] —**grass′less,** *adj.* —**grass′like′,** *adj.* —**grass′wards,** *adv.*

grass′ cloth′, a fabric made from tough vegetable fibers. Also called **Canton linen, China grass cloth.**

grass′ court′, an outdoor tennis court having a turf surface, common chiefly in the British Isles. Cf. **clay court, hard court.**

grass·cut·ter (gras′kut′ər, gräs′-), *n.* **1.** a device used to cut grass, as a lawn mower. **2.** *Baseball Slang.* a ground ball that travels with great speed across the infield close to and barely touching the turf. [GRASS + CUTTER]

Grasse (gräs), *n.* **1. Fran·çois Jo·seph Paul** (fräɴ-swȧ′ zhō zef′ pôl), **Count de** (*Marquis de Grasse-Tilly*), 1722–1788, French admiral. **2.** a city in S France, near the Mediterranean: tourist center; perfume industry. 27,226 (1962).

gras·se·rie (gras′ə rē, grä′sə-), *n.* a virus disease of silkworms, characterized by yellowness of the integument and an excessive accumulation of fluid within the body. Also called **jaundice.** [< F, equiv. to *gras* fat (< L *crass(us)* + *-erie* -ERY]

grass′ finch′, **1.** any of several Australian weaverbirds, esp. of the genus *Poëphila.* **2.** *U.S. Dial.* the vesper sparrow.

Grasshopper, *Melanoplus differentialis* (Length 1¼ in.)

grass-green (gras′-grēn′, gräs′-), *adj.* yellowish green.

grass′ hock′ey, *Canadian.* See **field hockey.**

grass·hop·per (gras′-hop′ər, gräs′-), *n.* **1.** any of numerous herbivorous, orthopterous insects, esp. of the families *Acrididae* and *Tettigoniidae,* having the hind legs adapted for leaping and having chewing mouth parts, some species being highly destructive to vegetation. **2.** *Aeron. Informal.* cub (def. 5). [ME; see GRASS, HOPPER]

grass′hopper en′gine, a steam engine having a piston attached to one end of a beam which is hinged to an upright at the other end, the connecting rod being suspended from near the center of the beam.

grass′hopper escape′ment, an early clock escapement, designed to eliminate the necessity of oiling pallets, in which the pallets are offset from the pallet arbor so as to move in arcs as nearly normal as possible to the circumference of the escape wheel.

grass′hopper spar′row, a brown and white North American sparrow, *Ammodramus savannarum,* having a buffy breast.

grass·land (gras′land′, gräs′-), *n.* an area in which the natural vegetation consists largely of perennial grasses, characteristic of subhumid and semiarid climates. [GRASS + LAND]

Grass·man (gräs′mən, -män; *Ger.* gräs′män′), *n.* **Her·mann Gün·ther** (her′män gʏn′tər), 1809–77, German mathematician and linguist.

Grass′man's law′, *Ling.* an observation, made by H. G. Grassman, that when aspirated consonants occurred in successive syllables in Sanskrit and Classical Greek, one, usually the first, was unaspirated, becoming a voiced stop in Sanskrit and a voiceless stop in Greek.

grass-of-Par·nas·sus (gras′əv pär nas′əs, gräs′-), *n.* any plant of the genus *Parnassus,* of marshy areas, having broad, smooth leaves and single, pale flowers.

grass′ par′akeet, any of several Australian parakeets, esp. the budgerigar.

grass′ pink′, **1.** a pink, *Dianthus plumarius,* of Europe and Asia, having fragrant pink, purplish, or white flowers. **2.** an orchid, *Calopogon pulchellus,* having rose or purplish-pink flowers, found in bogs of eastern North America.

grass·plot (gras′plot′, gräs′-), *n.* a plot of ground covered with or reserved for grass. [GRASS + PLOT[2]]

grass·quit (gras′kwit′, gräs′-), *n.* any of several small fringilline birds, esp. of the genus *Tiaris,* of tropical America and the West Indies. [GRASS + *quit,* prob. imit.]

grass′ roots′, (*construed as sing. or pl.*) **1.** the agricultural and rural areas of a country. **2.** the people inhabiting these areas, esp. as a political, social, or economic group. **3.** the common or ordinary people, esp. as contrasted to the leadership or elite of a political party, social organization, etc.; the rank and file. **4.** the origin or basis of something; the basic or primary concept, rule, part, or the like.

grass-roots (gras′ro͞ots′, -ro͝ots′, gräs′-), *adj.* of, pertaining to, or involving the common people, esp. as contrasted to or separable from an elite: *a grass-roots movement for democratic reform.*

grass′ rug′, a rug woven of strong marsh grass and cotton, usually with stenciled designs.

grass′ shears′, special shears for trimming grass that is hard to cut properly with a mower, as around the base of a tree.

grass′ snake′, **1.** Also called **ring snake.** a common, European colubrid snake, *Natrix natrix,* having a collar of bright orange or yellow. **2.** any of several small, slender, harmless colubrid snakes of North America.

grass′ snipe′, *U.S. Dial.* the pectoral sandpiper.

grass′ sor′ghum, any of several varieties of sorghum, as Sudan grass, grown for pasturage and hay.

grass′ sponge′, a large, dark-brown, commercial sponge, *Spongia graminea,* of Florida, the West Indies, and the Gulf of Mexico.

grass′ style′, a style of Japanese calligraphy and *sumi-e* painting, characterized chiefly by free or loose brush strokes.

grass′ ta′ble, *Archit.* See **earth table.**

grass′ tree′, **1.** any Australian, liliaceous plant of the genus *Xanthorrhoea,* having a stout, woody stem bearing a tuft of long grasslike leaves and a dense flower spike. **2.** any of various similar plants of Australasia.

grass′ wid′ow, a woman who is separated, divorced, or lives apart from her husband. [the first element may perh. be used in the sense of "at grass"; cf. D *grasweduwe,* G *Strohwittwe,* lit., straw-widow] —**grass′-wid′ow·hood′,** *n.*

grass′ wid′ower, a man who is separated, divorced, or lives apart from his wife.

grass·y (gras′ē, grä′sē), *adj.,* **grass·i·er, grass·i·est.** **1.** covered with grass. **2.** of, like, or pertaining to grass; grasslike. **3.** of the color of grass: *grassy green.* [GRASS + -Y[1]] —**grass′i·ness,** *n.*

grate[1] (grāt), *n., v.,* **grat·ed, grat·ing.** —*n.* **1.** a frame of metal bars for holding fuel when burning, as in a fireplace or furnace. **2.** a framework of parallel or crossed bars, used as a partition, guard, cover, or the like; grating. **3.** a fireplace. —*v.t.* **4.** to furnish with a grate or grates. [ME < LL *grāt(a)* a grating, var. of *crāta,* deriv. of L *crāt-* (s. of *crātis*) wickerwork, hurdle; cf. CRATE] —**grate′less,** *adj.* —**grate′like′,** *adj.*

grate[2] (grāt), *v.,* **grat·ed, grat·ing.** —*v.i.* **1.** to have an irritating or unpleasant effect on the feelings: *His constant chatter grates on my nerves.* **2.** to make a sound of, or as of, rough scraping; rasp. **3.** to sound harshly; jar: *to grate on the ear.* **4.** to scrape or rub with rough or noisy friction, as one thing on or against another. —*v.t.* **5.** to rub together with a harsh, jarring sound: *to grate the teeth.* **6.** to reduce to small particles by rubbing against a rough surface or a surface with many sharp-edged openings: *to grate a carrot.* **7.** *Archaic.* to wear down or away by rough friction. [ME *grate(n)* < OF *grat(er)* < Gmc; cf. G *kratzen* to scratch] —**grat′er,** *n.*

grate·ful (grāt′fəl), *adj.* **1.** warmly or deeply appreciative of kindness or benefits received; thankful: *I am grateful to you for your kindness.* **2.** expressing or actuated by gratitude: *a grateful letter.* **3.** pleasing to the mind or senses; agreeable or welcome; refreshing: *the grateful sound of rain.* [*grate* pleasing (< L *grātus*) + -FUL] —**grate′ful·ly,** *adv.* —**grate′ful·ness,** *n.*
—**Syn. 1.** obliged, indebted. GRATEFUL, THANKFUL describe an appreciative attitude for what one has received. GRATEFUL indicates a warm or deep appreciation of personal kindness as shown to one: *grateful for favors; grateful to one's neighbors for help in time of trouble.* THANKFUL indicates a disposition to express gratitude by giving thanks, as to a benefactor or to a merciful Providence; there is often a sense of deliverance as well as of appreciation: *thankful that one's life was spared in an accident; thankful for the comfort of one's general situation.* **3.** pleasant, gratifying, satisfying.

Gra·tia (grā′shə, -shē ə), *n.* a girl's given name, form of **Grace.**

Gra·ti·ae (grā′shē ē′), *n.pl.* the ancient Roman name for the Graces.

Gra·ti·an (grā′shē ən, -shən), *n.* (*Flavius Gratianus*) A.D. 359–383, Roman emperor 375–383.

grat·i·cule (grat′ə kyo͞ol′), *n.* **1.** *Navig.* a network of parallels and meridians on a map or chart. **2.** *Optics.* a reticle. [< F < L *crāticula,* dim. of *crātis.* See GRATE[2], -CULE]

grat·i·fi·ca·tion (grat′ə fə kā′shən), *n.* **1.** the state of being gratified; great satisfaction. **2.** something that gratifies; source of pleasure or satisfaction. **3.** the act of gratifying. **4.** *Archaic.* a reward, recompense, or gratuity. [< L *grātificātiōn-* (s. of *grātificātiō*). See GRATIFY, -ATION]

grat·i·fy (grat′ə fī′), *v.t.,* **-fied, -fy·ing.** **1.** to give pleasure to (a person or persons) by satisfying desires or humoring inclinations or feelings. **2.** to satisfy; indulge; humor, as one's desires or appetites. **3.** *Obs.* to reward; remunerate. [ME *gratifi(en)* < L *grātificāre,* equiv. to *grāt(us)* pleasing + *-i-* -I- + *-ficāre* -FY] —**grat′i·fi′a·ble,** *adj.* —**grat·i·fi·ed·ly** (grat′ə fī′id-lē, -fīd′-), *adv.* —**grat′i·fi′er,** *n.*
—**Syn. 1.** See **humor.**

grat·i·fy·ing (grat′ə fī′ing), *adj.* that gratifies; pleasing; satisfying. [GRATIFY + -ING[2]] —**grat′i-fy′ing·ly,** *adv.*
—**Syn.** See **interesting.**

grat·in (grat′ən, grät′-; *Fr.* gra taɴ′), *n.* See **au gratin.** [< F, MF; see GRATE[2]]

grat·i·nate (grat′ənāt′), *v.t.,* **-nat·ed, -nat·ing.** to bake or broil (food) in au gratin style. [GRATIN + -ATE[1]]

grat·ing[1] (grā′ting), *n.* **1.** a fixed frame of bars or the like covering an opening to exclude persons, animals, coarse material, or objects while admitting light, air, or fine material. **2.** *Physics.* See **diffraction grating.** [GRATE[1] + -ING[1]]

grat·ing[2] (grā′ting), *adj.* **1.** irritating or unpleasant to one's feelings. **2.** (of a sound or noise) harsh, discordant, or rasping. [GRATE[2] + -ING[2]] —**grat′ing·ly,** *adv.*

gra·tis (grat′is, grā′tis), *adv.* **1.** without charge or payment; freely: *to provide a service gratis.* —*adj.* **2.** free; gratuitous. [ME < L *grātis* freely, contr. of *grātiīs* with favors, graces (abl. pl. of *grātia* GRACE)]

grat·i·tude (grat′i to͞od′, -tyo͞od′), *n.* the quality or feeling of being grateful or thankful. [ME < ML *grātitūdin-* (s. of *grātitūdō*) thankfulness, equiv. to *grāt(us)* pleasing + *-i-* -I- + *-tūdin-* -TUDE]

Grat·tan (grat′ən), *n.* **Henry,** 1746–1820, Irish statesman and orator.

grat·toir (grä twär′; *Fr.* gra twar′), *n., pl.* **-toirs** (-twärz′; *Fr.* -twar′). *Archaeol.* a chipped-stone implement used for working wood or leather; scraper. [< F, equiv. to *gratt(er)* (to) GRATE[2] + *-oir* -ORY[2]]

gra·tu·i·tous (grə to͞o′i təs, -tyo͞o′-), *adj.* **1.** given, bestowed, or obtained without charge or payment; free. **2.** being without apparent reason, cause, or justification: *a gratuitous insult.* **3.** *Law.* given without receiving any return value. [< L *grātuīt(us)* free, freely given, spontaneous (deriv. of *grātia* favor, grace) + -OUS] —**gra·tu′i·tous·ly,** *adv.* —**gra·tu′i·tous·ness,** *n.*
—**Syn. 2.** unnecessary, superfluous, redundant; causeless, unreasonable, groundless, unprovoked, unjustified, needless.

gratu′itous con′tract, *Law.* a contract for the benefit of only one of the parties, the other party receiving nothing as consideration.

gra·tu·i·ty (grə to͞o′i tē, -tyo͞o′-), *n., pl.* **-ties.** **1.** a gift of money, over and above payment due for service; tip. **2.** that which is given without claim or demand. **3.** *Brit.* **a.** a bonus granted to war veterans by the government. **b.** a bonus given military personnel on discharge or retirement. [< MF *gratuite* < L *grātuīt(us).* See GRATUITOUS, -ITY]

grat·u·lant (grach′ə lənt), *adj.* expressing gratification; congratulatory. [< L *grātulant-* (s. of *grātulāns*), equiv. to *grātul-* express joy (see GRATULATE) + *-ant-* -ANT]

grat·u·late (grach′ə lāt′), *v.,* **-lat·ed, -lat·ing.** *Archaic.* —*v.t.* **1.** to hail with joy; express joy at. **2.** to congratulate. —*v.i.* **3.** to express joy. [< L *grātulātus* having expressed joy (ptp. of *grātulārī*), equiv. to *grātul-* express joy, congratulate, thank (deriv. of *grātus* pleasing) + *-ātus* -ATE[1]] —**grat·u·la·to·ri·ly** (grach′ə lə-tôr′ə lē, -tōr′-), *adv.* —**grat′u·la·to′ry,** *adj.*

grat·u·la·tion (grach′ə lā′shən), *n.* *Archaic.* **1.** a feeling of joy. **2.** the expression of joy. [< L *grātulātiōn-* (s. of *grātulātiō*). See GRATULATE, -ION]

Grau·bün·den (grou′bʏn′dən), *n.* German name of **Grisons.**

grau·pel (grou′pəl), *n.* See **snow pellets.** [< G; dim. of *Graupe* hulled grain]

Grau·stark (grou′stärk, grô′-), *n.* a novel (1901) by George Barr McCutcheon about the romantic and melodramatic adventures of military and courtly figures in the fictional kingdom of Graustark. —**Grau-stark′i·an,** *adj.*

gra·va·men (grə vā′mən), *n., pl.* **-vam·i·na** (-vam′ə-nə). *Law.* **1.** the part of an accusation that weighs most heavily against the accused; the substantial part of a charge or complaint. **2.** a grievance. [< LL: trouble, physical inconvenience, equiv. to L *gravā(re)* (to) load, weigh down (deriv. of *gravis* heavy, burdened) + *-men* n. suffix]

grave[1] (grāv), *n.* **1.** an excavation made in the earth to receive a dead body in burial. **2.** any place of interment; a tomb or sepulcher. **3.** any place that becomes the receptacle of what is dead, lost, or past: *the grave of dead reputations.* **4.** death: *O grave, where is thy victory?* **5. have one foot in the grave,** to be so old or sick that death appears imminent: *It was a shock to see my uncle looking as if he had one foot in the grave.* **6. make (one) turn in one's grave,** to do something to which a specified dead person would have objected bitterly: *This production of* Hamlet *is enough to make Shakespeare turn in his grave.* [ME; OE *græf;* c. G *Grab;* see GRAVE[3]] —**grave′less,** *adj.* —**grave′like′,** *adj.* —**grave′-ward, grave′wards,** *adv., adj.*

grave[2] (grāv; *for 4 also* gräv), *adj.,* **grav·er, grav·est** for 1–3, 5, *n.* —*adj.* **1.** dignified; sedate; serious; earnest; solemn: *a grave person; grave thoughts.* **2.** weighty, momentous, or important: *grave responsibilities.* **3.** threatening a seriously bad outcome or involving serious issues; critical: *a grave situation; a grave illness.* **4.** *Gram.* **a.** unaccented. **b.** spoken on a low or falling pitch. **c.** noting or having a particular accent (`) indicating originally a comparatively low pitch (as in French *père*), distinct syllabic value (as in English *belovèd*), etc. (opposed to *acute*). **5.** (of colors) dull; somber. —*n.* **6.** the grave accent. [< MF < L *grav(is*); akin to Gk *barýs* heavy] —**grave′ly,** *adv.* —**grave′ness,** *n.*
—**Syn. 1.** staid, thoughtful. GRAVE, SOBER, SOLEMN refer to the condition of being serious in demeanor or appearance. GRAVE indicates a weighty dignity, or the character, aspect, demeanor, speech, etc., of one conscious of heavy responsibilities or cares, or of threatening possibilities: *The jury looked grave while studying the evidence.* SOBER (from its original sense of freedom from intoxication, and hence temperate, staid, sedate) has come to indicate absence of levity, gaiety, or mirth, and thus to be akin to serious and grave: *as sober as a judge; a sober expression on one's face.* SOLEMN implies an impressive seriousness and deep earnestness: *The minister's voice was solemn as he announced the text.* —**Ant. 1.** frivolous, gay.

grave[3] (grāv), *v.t.,* **graved, grav·en** or **graved, grav·ing.** **1.** to incise or engrave. **2.** to impress deeply: *graven on the mind.* [ME *grave(n),* OE *grafan;* c. G *graben*] —**grav′er,** *n.*

grave[4] (grāv), *v.t.,* **graved, grav·ing.** *Naut.* to clean and apply a protective composition of tar to (the bottom of a vessel). [? akin to GRAVEL]

gra·ve[5] (grä′vā; *It.* grä′ve), *Music.* —*adj.* **1.** slow; solemn. —*adv.* **2.** slowly; solemnly. [< It *grave* < L *gravis* heavy; see GRAVE[2]]

grave·clothes (grāv′klōz′, -klōthz′), *n.pl.* the clothes in which a body is buried; cerements. [GRAVE[1] + CLOTHES]

grave·dig·ger (grāv′dig′ər), *n.* **1.** a person who earns his living by digging graves. **2.** See **burying beetle.** [GRAVE[1] + DIGGER]

grav·el (grav′əl), *n., v.,* **-eled, -el·ing** or (*esp. Brit.*) **-elled, -el·ling,** *adj.* —*n.* **1.** small stones and pebbles, or a mixture of these with sand. **2.** *Pathol.* **a.** multiple small calculi formed in the kidneys. **b.** the disease characterized by such concretions. —*v.t.* **3.** to cover with gravel. **4.** to bring to a standstill from perplexity; puzzle. **5.** *Informal.* to be a cause of irritation to. **6.** *Obs.* to run (a vessel) aground, as on a beach. —*adj.* **7.** harsh and grating: *a gravel voice.* [ME < OF *gravele,* dim. of *grave* sandy shore < Celt] —**grav′el·ish,** *adj.*

grav·el-blind (grav′əl blīnd′), *adj.* more blind or dim-sighted than sand-blind and less than stone-blind.

grav·el·div·er (grav′əl dī′vər), *n.* any of several eellike fishes of the family *Scytalinidae,* found off the Pacific coast of North America, esp. *Scytalina cerdale,* which burrows among rocks. [GRAVEL + DIVER]

grave·less (grāv′lis), *adj.* **1.** not buried; lacking proper burial. **2.** having no grave. [GRAVE[1] + -LESS]

grav·el·ly (grav′ə lē), *adj.* **1.** of, like, or abounding in gravel. **2.** harsh and grating: *a gravelly voice.* [GRAVEL + -LY]

grav·el·weed (grav′əl wēd′), *n.* a low shrub, *Diervilla lonicera,* of central North America, having small, funnel-shaped, yellow flowers. [GRAVEL + WEED[1]]

grav·en (grā′vən), *v.* **1.** a pp. of **grave**[3]. —*adj.* **2.** deeply impressed; firmly fixed. **3.** carved; sculptured: *a graven idol.* [GRAVE[3] + -EN[3]]

Gra·ven·ha·ge, 's (sᴋнrä′vən hä′ᴋнə), Dutch name of **The Hague.**

grav′en im′age, an idol.

Gra·ven·stein (grä′vən stīn′, grav′ən stēn′), *n.* a large, yellowish-red apple maturing in the autumn. [after *Gravenstein,* a village formerly in Schleswig-Holstein, Germany, now in Denmark]

grav·er (grā′vər), *n.* **1.** any of various tools for chasing, engraving, etc., as a burin. **2.** an engraver. [ME; see GRAVE[3], -ER[1]]

grave·rob·ber (grāv′rob′ər), *n.* **1.** a person who steals valuables from graves and crypts. **2.** (formerly) a person who steals corpses after burial, esp. for dissection. [GRAVE[1] + ROBBER] —**grave′rob′bing,** *n.*

Graves (grāvz), *n.* **Robert (Ran·ke)** (rang′kə), born 1895, English poet, novelist, and critic.

Graves (gräv; *Fr.* GRAV), *n.* a wine-growing district in Gironde department, in SW France. **2.** a dry, red or white table wine produced in this region.

Graves′ disease′, *Pathol.* a disease characterized by an enlarged thyroid, a rapid pulse, and increased basal metabolism due to excessive thyroid secretion; exophthalmic goiter. [named after R. J. *Graves* (1796–1853), Irish physician]

Graves·end (grāvz′end′), *n.* a seaport in NW Kent, in SE England, on the Thames River. 51,388 (1961).

grave·stone (grāv′stōn′), *n.* a stone marking a grave. [ME; see GRAVE[1], STONE]

Gra·vett·i·an (grə vet′ē ən), *adj.* of, pertaining to, or characteristic of an Upper Paleolithic culture of Europe. [after *la Gravette* on the Dordogne, France; see -IAN]

grave·yard (grāv′yärd′), *n.* **1.** cemetery; burial ground. **2.** *Informal.* See **graveyard shift.** [GRAVE[1] + YARD[2]]

grave′yard shift′, *Slang.* **1.** a work shift usually beginning at midnight and continuing through the early morning hours. **2.** those who work this shift. Also called **graveyard watch.**

grave′yard watch′, **1.** See **graveyard shift. 2.** *Naut.* See **middle watch.**

grav·i·cem·ba·lo (grav′i chem′bə lō′, grä′vi-), *n., pl.* **-cem·ba·li** (-chem′bə lē′), **-cem·ba·los.** a harpsichord. [< It, alter. of *clavicembalo* harpsichord (by assoc. with *grave* heavy); see CLAVICEMBALO]

grav·id (grav′id), *adj.* pregnant. [< L *gravid*(*us*), equiv. to *grav*(*is*) burdened, loaded + *-idus* -ID[4]] **—gra·vid·i·ty** (grə vid′i tē), **grav′id·ness,** *n.* **—grav′id·ly,** *adv.*

gra·vim·e·ter (grə vim′i tər), *n.* **1.** an instrument for measuring the specific gravity of a solid or liquid. **2.** Also called **gravity meter.** an instrument for measuring variations in the gravitational field of the earth by detecting differences in weight of an object of constant mass at different points on the earth's surface. [< F *gravimètre*, equiv. to *gravi-* (comb. form of L *gravis* heavy) + *-mètre* -METER]

grav·i·met·ric (grav′ə me′trik), *adj.* of or pertaining to measurement by weight. Also, **grav′i·met′ri·cal.** [*gravi-* (comb. form of L *gravis* heavy) + -METRIC] **—grav′i·met′ri·cal·ly,** *adv.*

gravimet′ric anal′ysis, *Chem.* analysis of materials by weight methods. Cf. **volumetric analysis.**

gra·vim·e·try (grə vim′i trē), *n.* the measurement of weight or density. [*gravi-* (comb. form of L *gravis* heavy) + -METRY]

grav′ing dock′, *Naut.* an excavated shore drydock for the repair and maintenance of vessels, having means by which the entrance from the water can be sealed and the water in the dry dock pumped out after the vessel has entered.

grav′ing piece′, *Naut.* a piece of wood let into a wooden hull to replace decayed wood.

grav·i·tate (grav′i tāt′), *v.i.,* **-tat·ed, -tat·ing. 1.** to move or tend to move under the influence of gravitational force. **2.** to tend toward the lowest level; sink; fall. **3.** to have a natural tendency or be strongly attracted (usually fol. by *to* or *toward*): *Social outcasts gravitate toward one another.* [< NL *gravitāt*(*us*) (ptp. of *gravitāre*). See GRAVITY, -ATE[1]] **—grav′i·tat′er,** *n.*

grav·i·ta·tion (grav′i tā′shən), *n.* **1.** *Physics.* **a.** the force of mutual attraction between all bodies, equal to a constant times the quotient of the product of the masses of the bodies divided by the square of the distance between them. Cf. **constant of gravitation. b.** an act or process caused by this force. **2.** a sinking or falling. **3.** natural tendency toward some point or object of influence: *the gravitation of people toward the suburbs.* [< NL *gravitātiōn-* (s. of *gravitātiō*). See GRAVITATE, -ION] **—grav′i·ta′tion·al,** *adj.* **—grav′i·ta′tion·al·ly,** *adv.*

grav′ita′tional con′stant, *Physics.* See **constant of gravitation.**

grav′ita′tional field′, *Physics.* a region surrounding a mass of such size that gravitational effects caused by the mass can be detected.

grav·i·ta·tive (grav′i tā′tiv), *adj.* **1.** of or pertaining to gravitation. **2.** tending or causing to gravitate. [GRAVITATE + -IVE]

grav·i·ton (grav′i ton′), *n.* *Physics.* the theoretical quantum of gravitation, usually assumed to be an elementary particle that is its own antiparticle and that has zero rest mass and charge and a spin of two. Cf. **photon.** [GRAVIT(Y) + -ON]

grav·i·ty (grav′i tē), *n., pl.* **-ties. 1.** the force of attraction by which terrestrial bodies tend to fall toward the center of the earth. **2.** heaviness or weight. **3.** gravitation in general. **4.** serious or dignified behavior; dignity; solemnity: *to preserve one's gravity.* **5.** serious or critical character: *He seemed to ignore the gravity of his illness.* **6.** lowness in pitch, as of sounds. [< L *gravitāt-* (s. of *gravitās*) heaviness, equiv. to *grav*(*is*) heavy, GRAVE[2] + *-itāt-* -ITY]

grav′ity cell′, *Elect.* a cell containing two electrolytes that have different specific gravities.

grav′ity clock′, a clock driven by its own weight as it descends a rack, cord, incline, etc.

grav′ity dam′, a dam resisting the pressure of impounded water through its own weight.

grav′ity escape′ment, *Horol.* an escapement, used esp. in large outdoor clocks, in which the impulse is given to the pendulum by means of a weight falling through a certain distance.

grav′ity fault′, *Geol.* a fault along an inclined plane in which the upper side or hanging wall appears to have moved downward with respect to the lower side or footwall (opposed to *thrust fault*).

grav′ity feed′, **1.** the supplying of fuel, materials, etc., by force of gravity. **2.** a system or device designed for this purpose.

grav′ity hinge′, a hinge closing automatically by means of gravity.

grav′ity knife′, a switchblade opened by snapping or flicking the wrist downward.

grav′ity me′ter, gravimeter (def. 2).

grav′ity rail′road, a railroad depending partly on the force of gravity for motive power.

grav′ity wind′ (wind), a light wind directed downslope, occurring at night because of the cooling and densification of the air near the ground. Also called **drainage wind.**

gra·vure (grə vyŏŏr′, grā′vyər), *n.* **1.** an intaglio process of photomechanical printing, such as photogravure or rotogravure. **2.** a plate or a print produced by gravure. **3.** the metal or wooden plate used in photogravure. [< F, equiv. to *grav*(*er*) (to) engrave < Gmc (see GRAVE[3]) + *-ure* -URE]

gra·vy (grā′vē), *n., pl.* **-vies. 1.** the fat and juices that drip from cooking meat, often thickened, used as a sauce for meat, potatoes, rice, etc. **2.** *Slang.* **a.** money easily obtained or received unexpectedly. **b.** money illegally or dishonestly acquired, esp. through graft. **3.** something advantageous or of worth that is received or obtained as a benefit beyond what is due or expected. [ME *grave, gravey* < OF *graue*, perh. misreading of *grane* < L *granāt*(*us*) full of grains, deriv. of *grān*(*um*) GRAIN]

gra′vy boat′, a small dish, often boat-shaped, for serving gravy or sauce.

gra′vy train′, *Slang.* a position in which a person or group receives excessive and unjustified advantages with little or no effort: *The top executives got on the gravy train to make a killing before the company went broke.*

gray (grā), *adj.* **1.** of a color between white and black; having a neutral hue; achromatic in color. **2.** dark, dismal, or gloomy: *gray skies.* **3.** having gray hair; grayheaded. **4.** pertaining to old age; mature. **5.** old or ancient. **6.** indeterminate and intermediate in character: *The tax audit concentrated on deductions in the gray area between purely personal and purely business expenses.* **—***n.* **7.** any achromatic color; any color with zero chroma, intermediate between white and black. **8.** something of this color. **9.** gray material or clothing: *to dress in gray.* **10.** an unbleached and undyed condition. **11.** a member of the Confederate army, or the army itself. Cf. **blue** (def. 5). **12.** a horse of a gray color. **13.** a horse that appears white but is not an albino. **—***v.t., v.i.* **14.** to make or become gray. Also, **grey.** [ME; OE *grǣg*; c. G *grau*] **—gray′ly,** *adv.* **—gray′ness,** *n.*

Gray (grā), *n.* **1. A·sa** (ā′sə), 1810–88, U.S. botanist. **2. Thomas,** 1716–71, English poet.

gray·back (grā′bak′), *n.* **1.** any of various animals, as a bird, the knot, *Tringa canutus,* and a whale, *Rhachianectes glaucus,* of the northern Pacific. **2.** *U.S. Informal.* a Confederate soldier. [GRAY + BACK[1]]

gray·beard (grā′bērd′), *n.* **1.** a man whose beard is gray; old man; sage. **2.** bellarmine. Also, **greybeard.** [GRAY + BEARD] **—gray′beard′ed,** *adj.*

gray′ birch′, a birch, *Betula populifolia,* of stony or sandy areas of the eastern U.S., having grayish-white bark.

gray′ bod′y, *Physics.* any body that emits radiation at each wavelength in a constant ratio less than unity to that emitted by a black body at the same temperature.

Grayce (grās), *n.* a girl's given name. Also, **Grace.**

gray′-cheeked thrush′ (grā′chēkt′), a North American thrush, *Hylocichla minima,* having olive upper parts and grayish cheeks.

gray′ dog′wood, a shrub, *Cornus racemosa,* of the eastern U.S., having white fruit and branched clusters of white flowers.

Gray·don (grād′ən), *n.* a boy's given name.

gray′ duck′, any of several ducks in which certain immature or female plumages are predominantly gray, as the gadwall, *Anas strepera,* and the pintail, *A. acuta.*

gray′ em′inence, a person who wields unofficial power, esp. through another person and often surreptitiously or selfishly. French, **éminence grise.** [trans. of F *éminence grise*]

gray·fish (grā′fish′), *n., pl.* **-fish·es,** (*esp. collectively*) **-fish.** a name used in marketing for any of several American sharks, esp. the dogfishes of the genus *Squalus.* [GRAY + FISH]

gray′ fox′, a fox, *Urocyon cinereoargenteus,* found from Central America through the southwestern and eastern U.S., having blackish-gray upper parts and rusty-yellowish feet, legs, and ears.

Gray′ Fri′ar, a Franciscan friar. [ME; so called from the traditional color of the habit]

gray′ gold′enrod. See **dwarf goldenrod.**

gray′ goods′, a woven fabric as it comes from the loom and before it has been submitted to the finishing process. Also called **greige, griege.**

gray′ gum′, any of several Australian eucalyptuses, as *Eucalyptus tereticornis,* having a gray bark.

gray-head·ed (grā′hed′id), *adj.* **1.** having gray hair. **2.** of or pertaining to old age or old men. **3.** old. Also, **grey-headed.**

gray·hound (grā′hound′), *n.* greyhound.

gray′ i′ron, pig iron or cast iron having much of its carbon in the form of graphite and exhibiting a gray fracture.

gray·ish (grā′ish), *adj.* **1.** having a tinge of gray, slightly gray: *The sky was full of dark, grayish clouds.* **2.** similar to gray: *a grayish color; a grayish purple.* Also, **greyish.** [GRAY + -ISH[1]]

Gray′ La′dy, a woman worker in the American Red Cross who serves as a volunteer aide in medical services.

gray·lag (grā′lag′), *n.* a common, gray, wild goose, *Anser anser,* of Europe. Also, **greylag.** [GRAY + LAG[1] (with reference to its habit of remaining longer in England before migrating than other species of the genus)]

gray·ling (grā′ling), *n.* **1.** any fresh-water fish of the genus *Thymallus,* related to the trouts, but having a longer, and higher, brilliantly colored dorsal fin. **2.** any of several grayish or brownish satyr butterflies. [ME; see GRAY, -LING[1]]

gray′ man′ganese ore′, manganite.

gray′ mar′ket, a market operating within the law but exacting excessive prices for scarce goods. Cf. **black market.**

gray′ mat′ter, **1.** *Anat.* nerve tissue, esp. of the brain and spinal cord, which contains fibers and nerve cells and is of a dark reddish-gray color. Cf. **white matter. 2.** *Informal.* one's brains or intellect.

gray′ mold′, **1.** *Plant Pathol.* a disease of plants, characterized by a gray, furry coating on the decaying parts, caused by any of several fungi. **2.** any fungus causing this disease, as *Botrytis cinerea.*

gray′ mul′let, mullet (def. 1).

gray′ or′chis. See **showy orchis.**

gray′ ox′, kouprey.

gray′ par′rot, an ashy gray, African parrot, *Psittacus erithacus,* having a short, red tail, noted esp. for its ability to mimic speech. Also called **African gray.**

gray′ pine′. See **jack pine.**

grays·by (grāz′bē), *n., pl.* **-bies.** a serranid fish, *Petrometopon cruentatum,* found in warm waters of the western Atlantic Ocean, having a reddish-gray body marked with vermilion spots. [?]

gray′ scale′, a scale of achromatic colors having several, usually ten, equal gradations ranging from white to black, used in television and photography.

gray′ sea′ ea′gle, a grayish-brown sea eagle, *Haliaetus albicilla,* of the Old World and Greenland, having a white tail. Also called **white-tailed sea eagle.**

Gray's′ Inn′. See under **Inns of Court** (def. 1).

gray′ skate′, a skate, *Raja batis,* found off the coast of Great Britain.

Grays·lake (grāz′lāk′), *n.* a town in NE Illinois. 3762 (1960).

gray′ snap′per, a snapper, *Lutjanus griseus,* found in the shallow waters of Florida, having a grayish-green body with a brown spot on each scale. Also called **mangrove snapper.**

Gray·son (grā′sən), *n.* **1. David,** pen name of Ray Stannard Baker. **2.** a boy's given name.

gray′ squir′rel, a common, grayish squirrel, *Sciurus carolinensis,* of eastern North America. See illus. under **squirrel.**

Grays·ville (grāz′vil), *n.* a town in central Alabama. 2870 (1960).

gray·wacke (grā′wak′, -wak′ə), *n.* a grit or sandstone, usually dark, containing feldspar, fragments of rock such as slate or schist, various dark minerals, and interstitial clay. Also, **greywacke.** [partly trans., partly adapted from G *Grauwacke*; see WACKE]

gray·weth·er (grā′weth′ər), *n.* sarsen. [GRAY + WETHER]

gray′ whale′, a grayish-black whalebone whale, *Eschrichtius gibbosus,* of the North Pacific, growing to a length of 50 feet.

gray′ wolf′, a wolf, *Canis lupus,* formerly common in Eurasia and North America, having a usually grizzled, blackish or whitish coat.

Graz (gräts), *n.* a city in SE Austria. 237,041 (1961).

graze[1] (grāz), *v.,* **grazed, graz·ing. —***v.i.* **1.** to feed on growing herbage, as do cattle, sheep, etc. **—***v.t.* **2.** to feed on (growing grass). **3.** to put cattle, sheep, etc., to feed on (grass, pasture land, etc.). **4.** to tend (cattle, sheep, etc.) while they are at pasture. [ME *grase*(*n*), OE *grasian,* deriv. of *græs* GRASS] **—graze′a·ble,** *adj.* **—graz′er,** *n.*

graze[2] (grāz), *v.,* **grazed, graz·ing,** *n.* **—***v.t.* **1.** to touch or rub lightly in passing. **2.** to scrape the skin from; abrade: *The bullet just grazed his shoulder.* **—***v.i.* **3.** to touch or rub something lightly, or so as to produce slight abrasion, in passing: *to graze against a rough wall.* **—***n.* **4.** a grazing; a touching or rubbing lightly in passing. **5.** a slight scratch in passing; abrasion. [? special use of GRAZE[1], for the semantic shift cf. F *effleurer,* deriv. of *fleur* flower, in the same meaning] **—graz′er,** *n.* **—graz′ing·ly,** *adv.*

gra·zier (grā′zhər), *n.* *Chiefly Brit.* one who grazes cattle for the market. [late ME *grasier.* See GRAZE[1], -ER[2]]

graz·ing (grā′zing), *n.* pasture land; a pasture. [ME; see GRAZE[1], -ING[1]]

Gr. Br., Great Britain. Also, **Gr. Brit.**

grease (*n.* grēs; *v.* grēs, grēz), *n., v.,* **greased, greas·ing.** **—***n.* **1.** the melted or rendered fat of animals, esp. when in a soft state. **2.** fatty or oily matter in general; lubricant. **3.** Also called **grease′ wool′.** wool, as shorn, before being cleansed of the oily matter. **4.** Also called **grease-heel.** *Vet. Pathol.* inflammation of a horse's skin in the fetlock region, attended with an oily secretion. **—***v.t.* **5.** to put grease on; lubricate: *to grease the axle of a car.* **6.** to smear with grease. **7.** to cause to occur easily; smooth the way; facilitate. **8.** *Informal.* to bribe. **9. grease someone's palm.** See **palm**[1] (def. 11). [ME *grese, grece, greice* < AF *grece, gresse,* OF *craisse* (F *graisse*) < VL **crassia,* equiv. to L *crass*(*us*) fat, thick + *-ia* n. suffix] **—grease′less,** *adj.* **—grease′less·ness,** *n.* **—grease′proof′,** *adj.*

grease·ball (grēs′bôl′), *n.* **1.** *Disparaging.* a person of Italian, Spanish, Greek, or Portuguese descent. **2.** *Slang.* a person having oily skin. [GREASE + BALL[1]]

grease·bush (grēs′bŏŏsh′), *n.* greasewood. [GREASE + BUSH[1]]

grease′ cup′, oilcup.

grease′ gun′, a hand-operated pump for greasing bearings under pressure.

grease-heel (grēs′hēl′), *n.* *Vet. Pathol.* grease (def. 4).

grease′ mon′key, *Slang.* a mechanic, esp. on an automobile or airplane.

grease′ paint′, **1.** an oily mixture of melted tallow or grease and a pigment, used by actors for making up their faces. **2.** theatrical make-up.

greas·er (grē′sər), *n.* **1.** one who or that which greases. **2.** *Disparaging.* a Latin-American, esp. a Mexican. [GREASE + -ER[1]]

grease·wood (grēs′wŏŏd′), *n.* **1.** a chenopodiaceous shrub, *Sarcobatus vermiculatus,* of the alkaline regions of the western U.S., containing a small amount of oil and used for fuel. **2.** any of various similar shrubs. **3.** See **white sage.** Also called **greasebush.** [GREASE + WOOD[1]]

greas·y (grē′sē, -zē), *adj.,* **greas·i·er, greas·i·est. 1.** smeared or soiled with grease. **2.** composed of or containing grease; oily: *greasy food.* **3.** greaselike in appearance or to the touch; slippery. **4.** *Vet. Pathol.* affected with grease. [GREASE + -Y[1]] **—greas′i·ly,** *adv.* **—greas′i·ness,** *n.*

greas′y spoon′, *Slang.* a run-down and rather unsanitary restaurant, esp. one specializing in short-order fried foods.

great (grāt), *adj., adv., n., pl.* **greats,** (*esp. collectively*) **great. —***adj.* **1.** unusually or comparatively large in size or dimensions: *Sixty years ago a great fire destroyed nearly half the city.* **2.** large in number; numerous: *Great hordes of tourists descend on Europe each summer.* **3.** unusual or considerable in degree, power, intensity, etc.: *great pain; the great roar of the jet's engines.* **4.** notable; remarkable; exceptionally outstanding: *a great occasion.* **5.** distinguished; famous: *He is one of the great founding fathers of this country.* **6.** important; highly significant or consequential: *the great issues in American history.* **7.** chief or principal: *the great hall; This was the great work of his middle period.* **8.** of high rank, official position, or social standing: *a great noble.* **9.** of noble or lofty character: *great thoughts; a man great of heart.* **10.** much in use or favor: *"Humor" was a great word with the old physiologists.* **11.** being such in an extreme degree: *great friends; a great oaf; a great talker; a great person for saving money.* **12.** of extraordinary powers; having unusual merit; very admirable: *a great statesman.* **13.** of marked duration or length: *There is a great series of runs just before the final coda. We waited a great while before the guests began to arrive.* **14.** *Informal.* **a.** enthusiastic about some specified activity (usually fol. by *at, for,* or *on*): *He's great on reading poetry aloud.* **b.** skillful; expert (usually fol. by *at* or *on*): *He's great on golf. This author is great on characterization.* **c.** first-rate; very good: *to have a great time; a great gun for duck hunting; a great one for getting into trouble; I'm feeling great.* **15.** *Chiefly Dial.* pregnant. —*adv.* **16.** *Informal.* very well: *Things have been going great for him the last few months.* —*n.* **17.** a person who has achieved importance or distinction in his field: *She is one of the theater's greats. Many of the greats of science were there.* **18.** great persons, collectively: *The Poet's Corner houses the tombs of many of England's literary great.* **19.** (*often cap.*) **greats,** (*construed as sing.*) Also called **great′ go′.** *Brit. Informal.* **a.** the final examination for the bachelor's degree in the classics and mathematics, or *Literae Humaniores,* esp. at Oxford University and usually for honors. **b.** the course of study. **c.** the subject studied. **20.** *Archaic.* the whole; gross. [ME *greet,* OE *grēat;* c. D *groot,* G *gross*] —**great′ness,** *n.*

—**Syn. 1.** immense, enormous, gigantic, huge, vast, grand. GREAT, BIG, LARGE refer to size, extent, and degree. In reference to the size and extent of concrete objects, BIG is the most general and most colloquial word, LARGE is somewhat more formal, and GREAT is highly formal and even poetic, suggesting also that the object is notable or imposing: *a big tree; a large tree; a great oak; a big field; a large field; great plains.* When the reference is to degree or a quality, GREAT is the usual word: *great beauty; great mistake; great surprise;* although BIG sometimes alternates with it in colloquial style: *a big mistake; a big surprise;* LARGE is not used in reference to degree, but may be used in a quantitative reference: *a large number* (*great number*). **4.** noteworthy. **5.** famed, eminent, noted, notable, prominent, celebrated, illustrious, renowned. **6.** weighty, serious, momentous, vital, critical. **7.** main, grand, leading. **9.** elevated, exalted, dignified. —**Ant. 1.** small. **4–6.** insignificant.

Great′ Ab′a·co (ab′ə kō′). See under **Abaco.**

Great′ A′jax, *Gk. Legend.* Ajax (def. 1).

great′ ant′eater. See **ant bear** (def. 1).

great′ ape′, any anthropoid ape, as a gorilla or chimpanzee.

great′ auk′, a large, flightless, extinct auk, *Pinguinus impennis,* formerly found in northern areas of the North Atlantic.

great-aunt (grāt′ant′, -änt′), *n.* a grandaunt.

Great′ Austral′ian Bight′, a wide bay in S Australia.

Great′ Awak′ening, the series of religious revivals among Protestants in the American colonies, esp. in New England, lasting from about 1725 to 1770.

great′ barracu′da, a large barracuda, *Sphyraena barracuda,* found on both sides of the Atlantic Ocean and in the western Pacific Ocean. See illus. under **barracuda.**

Great′ Bar′rier Reef′, a coral reef parallel to the coast of Queensland, in NE Australia. 1250 mi. long. Also called **Barrier Reef.**

Great′ Bar′rington, a town in SW Massachusetts. 2943 (1960).

Great′ Ba′sin, a region in the W United States which has no drainage to the ocean: includes most of Nevada and parts of Utah, California, Oregon, and Idaho. 210,000 sq. mi.

great′ bas′inet, *Armor.* a basinet having a beaver permanently attached.

Great′ Bear′, *Astron.* the constellation Ursa Major.

Great′ Bear′ Lake′, a lake in NW Canada, in the Northwest Territories. 12,000 sq. mi.

Great′ Bend′, a city in central Kansas. 16,670 (1960).

great′ black′-backed gull′ (blak′bakt′). See under **black-backed gull.**

great′ blue′ her′on, a large, American heron, *Ardea herodias,* having bluish-gray plumage. See illus. under **heron.**

great′ blue′ shark′. See **blue shark.**

Great′ Brit′ain, an island of NW Europe, separated from the mainland by the English Channel and the North Sea: since 1707 the name has applied politically to England, Scotland, and Wales. 46,417,600; 88,139 sq. mi. Cf. **United Kingdom.**

great′ bus′tard, a large bustard, *Otis tarda,* of southern and central Europe and western and central Asia, usually weighing about 30 pounds and having a wingspread of about 8 feet.

great′ cal′orie, calorie (def. 1a).

great′ cir′cle, 1. a circle on a sphere such that the plane containing the circle passes through the center of the sphere. Cf. **small circle. 2.** the line of shortest distance between two points on the surface of the earth. —**great′-cir′cle,** *adj.*

great′-cir·cle sail′ing (grāt′sûr′kəl), *Navig.* sailing between two points more or less according to an arc of a great circle, in practice almost always using a series of rhumb lines of different bearings to approximate the arc, whose own bearing changes constantly unless it coincides with a meridian or the equator.

great·coat (grāt′kōt′), *n. Chiefly Brit.* a heavy overcoat. [GREAT + COAT] —**great′coat′ed,** *adj.*

great′ coun′cil, 1. (in Norman England) an assembly composed of the king's tenants in chief that served as the principal council of the realm and replaced the witenagemot. **2.** (formerly in Italy) the municipal council in some towns or cities, as in Venice.

great′ crest′ed grebe′, a large, Old World grebe, *Podiceps cristatus,* having black, earlike tufts of feathers projecting backward from the top of the head. See illus. under **grebe.**

Great′ Dae′dala. See under **Daedala.**

Great′ Dane′, one of a breed of large, powerful, shorthaired dogs ranging in color from fawn to brindle, blue, black, or white with black spots.

Great Dane (32 in. high at shoulder)

Great′ Depres′sion, the economic crisis and period of low business activity in the U.S. and other countries, roughly beginning with the stock-market crash in October, 1929, and continuing through the 1930's.

Great′ Divide′, 1. the continental divide of North America; the Rocky Mountains. **2.** any similar continental divide. **3.** the passage from life to death: *He crossed the Great Divide before his promise as a poet was recognized.* **4.** an important division or difference; crisis.

Great′ Divid′ing Range′, a mountain range extending along the E coast of Australia: vast watershed region. 100 to 200 mi. wide.

Great′ Dog′, *Astron.* the constellation Canis Major.

great′ doxol′ogy. See **Gloria in Excelsis Deo.** Also called **great′er doxol′ogy.**

great·en (grāt′ᵊn), *Chiefly Literary.* —*v.t.* **1.** to make greater; enlarge; increase. —*v.i.* **2.** to become greater. [ME; see GREAT, -EN¹]

Great′ En′trance, *Eastern Ch.* the solemn procession in which the unconsecrated Eucharistic elements are carried from the prothesis through the nave of the church and into the bema. Cf. **Little Entrance.**

Great·er (grā′tər), *adj.* designating a city or country and its adjacent area: *Greater New York; Greater Los Angeles.* [GREAT + -ER⁴]

Great′er Antil′les. See under **Antilles.**

great′er Bai′ram. See under **Bairam.**

Great′er Diony′sia, (in ancient Athens) the feasts comprising one of the festivals of the Dionysia, a celebration of the coming of spring. Also called **City Dionysia.**

great′er Ion′ic. See under **Ionic** (def. 2).

great′er multan′gular bone. See under **multangulum.**

great′er omen′tum, *Anat.* an omentum attached to the stomach and the colon and hanging over the small intestine. Also called **caul, gastrocolic omentum.** Cf. **lesser omentum.**

great′er prai′rie chick′en. See under **prairie chicken** (def. 1).

great′er shear′water, a sooty brown and white shearwater, *Puffinus gravis,* of the eastern coast of North and South America.

Great′er Sun′da Is′lands. See under **Sunda Islands.**

great′er wee′ver. See under **weever.**

great′er yel′lowlegs. See under **yellowlegs.**

great′est com′mon divi′sor, the largest number that is a common divisor of a given set of numbers.

great′est-in′te·ger func′tion (grā′tist in′ti jər), *Math.* the function that assigns to each real number the greatest integer less than or equal to the number. *Symbol:* [*x*]

great′est low′er bound′, *Math.* a lower bound which is greater than or equal to all the lower bounds of a given set: 1 is the greatest lower bound of the set consisting of 1, 2, 3. *Abbr.:* glb. Also called **infimum.** Cf. **bound³** (def. 5), **least upper bound, lower bound, upper bound.**

Great′ Expecta′tions, a novel (1861) by Dickens.

Great′ Falls′, 1. a city in central Montana, on the Missouri River. 55,357 (1960). **2.** a town in N South Carolina. 3030 (1960).

Great′ Gats′by, The (gats′bē), a novel (1925) by F. Scott Fitzgerald.

great′ go′, *Brit. Informal.* great (def. 19).

Great′ God′ Brown′, The, a play (1926) by Eugene O'Neill.

great-grand·aunt (grāt′grand′ant′, -änt′), *n.* an aunt of one's grandfather or grandmother.

great-grand·child (grāt′gran′chīld′), *n., pl.* **-chil·dren.** a grandchild of one's son or daughter.

great-grand·daugh·ter (grāt′gran′dô′tər), *n.* a granddaughter of one's son or daughter.

great-grand·fa·ther (grāt′gran′fä′thər, -grand′-), *n.* a grandfather of one's father or mother.

great-grand·moth·er (grāt′gran′muth′ər, -grand′-, -gram′-), *n.* a grandmother of one's father or mother.

great-grand·neph·ew (grāt′gran′nef′yo͞o, -nev′-yo͞o, -grand′-), *n.* a grandson of one's nephew or niece.

great-grand·niece (grāt′gran′nēs′, -grand′-), *n.* a granddaughter of one's nephew or niece.

great-grand·par·ent (grāt′gran′pâr′ənt, -par′-, -grand′-), *n.* a grandfather or grandmother of one's father or mother.

great-grand·son (grāt′gran′sun′, -grand′-), *n.* a grandson of one's son or daughter.

great-grand·un·cle (grāt′grand′ung′kəl), *n.* an uncle of one's grandfather or grandmother.

great′ gray′ owl′, a large, smoky gray owl, *Strix nebulosa,* of northern North America and western Eurasia.

great′ gross′, a unit of quantity equivalent to 12 gross. *Abbr.:* g gr

great′ guns′, 1. *Informal.* in a relentlessly energetic or successful manner: *The new president has the company going great guns.* **2.** an expression of surprise, astonishment, exasperation, etc.

great-heart·ed (grāt′här′tid), *adj.* **1.** having or showing a generous heart; magnanimous. **2.** high-spirited; courageous; fearless: *great-hearted defense of liberty.* Also, **great′heart′ed.** [ME *grete hartyd*] —**great′-heart′ed·ly, great′heart′ed·ly,** *adv.* —**great′-heart′ed·ness, great′heart′ed·ness,** *n.*

great′ helm′, *Armor.* helm² (def. 2).

great′ horned′ owl′, a large, rapacious, American owl, *Bubo virginianus,* having a prominent, earlike tuft of feathers on each side of the head. See illus. under **owl.**

Great′ I·dae′an Moth′er (ī dē′ən), Cybele.

Great′ Khing′an′ (khing′än′), a mountain range in NE China: highest peak, 5000 ft.

Great′ Lakes′, a series of five lakes between the U.S. and Canada, comprising Lakes Erie, Huron, Michigan, Ontario, and Superior; connected with the Atlantic by the St. Lawrence River.

great′ lau′rel. See **great rhododendron.**

great′ lobel′ia. See **blue lobelia.**

great·ly (grāt′lē), *adv.* **1.** in or to a great degree; much: *greatly improved in health.* **2.** in a great manner. [ME; see GREAT, -LY]

Great′ Mi·am′i, Miami (def. 2).

Great′ Mo′gul, 1. the emperor of the former Mogul empire in India founded in 1626 by Baber. **2.** (*l.c.*) an important or distinguished person.

great′ mul′lein, the mullein, *Verbascum Thapsus.*

Great′ Neck′ Estates′, a town on NW Long Island, in SE New York. 3262 (1960).

Great′ Neck′ Pla′za, a town on NW Long Island, in SE New York. 4948 (1960).

great-neph·ew (grāt′nef′yo͞o, -nev′yo͞o), *n.* a son of one's nephew or niece; grandnephew.

great′ net′tle. See **stinging nettle.**

great-niece (grāt′nēs′), *n.* a daughter of one's nephew or niece; grandniece.

Great′ Ouse′, Ouse (def. 2).

great′ pace′. See **geometrical pace.**

great′ pas′tern bone′. See under **pastern.**

Great′ Plague′, the bubonic plague occurring in London in 1665: killed about 15% of the city's population. Also, **great′ plague′.**

Great′ Plains′, a semiarid region E of the Rocky Mountains, in the U.S. and Canada.

Great′ Pow′er, a nation that has exceptional military and economic strength, and consequently plays a major, often decisive, role in international affairs. —**Great′-Pow′er, great′-pow′er,** *adj.*

great′ pox′, syphilis.

great′ prim′er, *Print.* an 18-point type of a size larger than Columbian, formerly used for Bibles.

Great′ Pyr′enees, one of a breed of large dogs having a heavy, white coat, raised originally in the Pyrenees for herding sheep and as a watchdog.

great′ rag′weed. See under **ragweed** (def. 1).

Great′ Rebel′lion. See **English Civil War.**

great′ rhododen′dron, a tall rhododendron, *Rhododendron maximum,* of the eastern U.S., having pink or white flowers. Also called **great laurel, great′ rose′bay.**

Great′ Rus′sian, 1. a member of the main stock of the Russian people, dwelling chiefly in the northern or central parts of the Soviet Union in Europe. **2.** the Russian language, excluding Ukrainian and Byelorussian.

great′ sal′low. See under **sallow².**

Great′ Salt′ Des′ert, Dasht-i-Kavir.

Great′ Salt′ Lake′, a shallow salt lake in NW Utah. 2300 sq. mi.; 80 mi. long; maximum depth 60 ft.

Great′ Sand′y Des′ert, 1. a desert in NW Australia, ab. 300 mi. long; 500 mi. wide; ab. 160,000 sq. mi. **2.** See **Rub′al Khali.**

Great′ San′hedrin, Sanhedrin (def. 1).

Great′ Schism′, a period of division in the Roman Catholic Church, 1378–1417, over papal succession, during which there were two, or sometimes three, claimants to the papal office.

Great′ Scott′, a euphemistic interjection or oath, usually expressing surprise, amazement, or the like. [*Scott,* alter. of GOD]

great′ seal′, 1. the principal seal of a government or state. **2.** (*caps.*) *Brit.* **a.** the Lord Chancellor, keeper of the principal seal of Great Britain. **b.** his office. [ME *grete Seel*]

great′ sku′a, *Brit.* skua (def. 1).

Great′ Slave′ Lake′, a lake in NW Canada, in the Northwest Territories. 11,172 sq. mi.

Great′ Smok′y Moun′tains, a range of the Appalachian Mountains in North Carolina and Tennessee; most of the range is included in Great Smoky Mountains National Park. 720 sq. mi. Highest peak, Clingman's Dome, 6642 ft. Also called **Smoky Mountains, Great′ Smok′ies.**

Great′ Soci′ety, the goal of the Democratic party under the leadership of President Lyndon B. Johnson upon his election in 1964, chiefly to enact domestic programs to improve education, provide medical care for the aged, and eliminate poverty. Cf. **Fair Deal, New Deal, New Frontier.**

Great′ Spir′it, the chief deity in the religion of many North American Indian tribes.

Great St. Bernard. See **St. Bernard, Great.**

Great′ Sun′day, *Eastern Church.* See **Easter Sunday.** [trans. of LGk *megálē hēméra,* lit., great day]

Great′ Syn′agogue, (according to Jewish tradition) a council of 120 members, established by Ezra, which directed the Jews chiefly in religious matters, c450–c200 B.C., and made significant contributions to the Jewish liturgy and Bible.

great′ tit′, an Old World titmouse, *Parus major,* yellowish-green above with white cheeks.

great′ toe′, *Anat.* See **big toe.**

great′ tu′na. See **bluefin tuna.**

great-un·cle (grāt′ung′kəl), *n.* a granduncle.

great′ unwashed′, the general public; the populace or masses. Also, **Great′ Unwashed′.**

Great′ Victo′ria Des′ert, a desert in SW central Australia. 125,000 sq. mi. Also called **Victoria Desert.**

Great′ Vow′el Shift′, *Ling.* a series of changes in the quality of the long vowels between Middle and Modern English as a result of which all were raised but (ē) and (o͞o), which became the diphthongs (ī) and (ou).

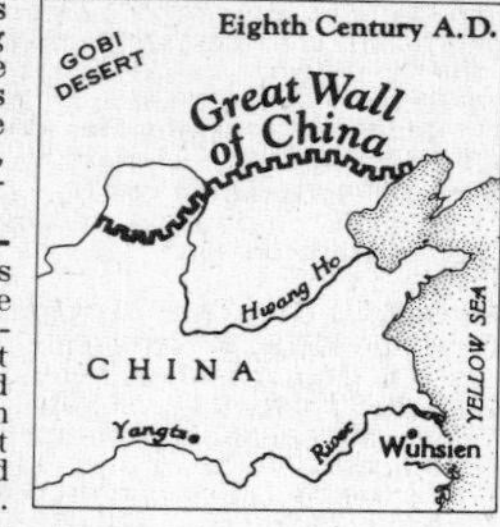

Great′ Wall′ of Chi′na, a system of walls constructed as a defense for China against the nomads of the regions that are now Mongolia and Manchuria: completed in the third century B.C., but later repeatedly modified and rebuilt. 2000 mi. long. Also called **Chinese Wall.**

Great′ War′. See **World War I.**

Great′ Week′, *Eastern Ch.* See **Holy Week.** [trans. of LGk *megálē hebdomás*]

great′ wheel′, *Horol.* the wheel immediately driven by the power source.

Great′ White′ Fa′ther, *Facetious.* **1.** the president of the U.S. **2.** a man who holds a position of great authority.

great′ white′ her′on, 1. a large white heron, *Ardea occidentalis*, of Florida and the Florida Keys. **2.** a large white egret, *Casmerodius albus*, of southeastern Europe, tropical Africa, Asia, New Zealand, and America.

great′ white′ shark′, a large shark, *Carcharodon carcharias*, found in tropical and temperate seas, occasionally attacking man. Also called **man-eater, white shark.**

great′ white′ tril′lium, a trillium, *Trillium grandiflorum*, of the eastern and central U.S., the flowers of which have large white petals that turn rose. Also called **trinity lily.**

Great′ White′ Way′, the theater district along Broadway, near Times Square in New York City.

great′ wil′low herb′. See **willow herb.**

Great′ Yar′mouth (yär′məth), a seaport in E Norfolk, in E England. 52,860 (1961).

great′ year′, *Astron.* See **Platonic year.**

Great′ Zimbab′we. See under **Zimbabwe.**

greave (grēv), *n.* *Armor.* a piece of plate armor for the leg between the knee and the ankle, usually composed of front and back pieces. Also called **jamb, jambart, jambeau.** See diag. under **armor.** [ME *greve(s)* (pl.) < OF < ?] —**greaved,** *adj.*

greaves (grēvz), *n.* (*construed as sing. or pl.*) crackling (def. 3). [< LG *grev(en)*; c. OHG *griubo*, G *Grieben*]

grebe (grēb), *n.* any of several diving birds of the family *Podicepedidae*, related to the loons, but having lobate rather than webbed toes and a rudimentary tail. Cf. **great crested grebe, pied-billed grebe.** [< F *grèbe* < ?]

Great crested grebe, *Podiceps cristatus* (Length 19 in.)

gre·ca·le (grā kä′lā), *n.* gregale.

Gre·cian (grē′shən), *adj.* **1.** Greek. —*n.* **2.** a Greek. **3.** an expert in the Greek language or literature. [< L *Gr(a)eci(a)* GREECE + -AN]

Gre′cian bend′, (esp. in the late 19th century) a posture or walk, often considered fashionable, in which the body is bent forward from the waist.

Gre′cian pro′file, a profile distinguished by the absence of the hollow between the upper ridge of the nose and the forehead, thereby forming a straight line.

Gre·cise (grē′sīz), *v.t., v.i.,* **-cised, -cis·ing.** *Chiefly Brit.* Grecize.

Gre·cism (grē′siz əm), *n.* **1.** the spirit of Greek thought, art, etc. **2.** adoption or imitation of this. **3.** an idiom or peculiarity of Greek. Also, *esp. Brit.,* **Graecism.** [< ML *Graecism(us)*, equiv. to L *Graec(us)* GREEK + *-ismus* -ISM]

Gre·cize (grē′sīz), *v.,* **-cized, -ciz·ing.** —*v.t.* **1.** to impart Greek characteristics to. **2.** to translate into Greek. —*v.i.* **3.** to conform to what is Greek; adopt Greek speech, customs, etc. Also, **gre′cize;** *esp. Brit.,* **Graecize, graecize, Graecise, Grecise.** [< L *graecizāre* (to) imitate the Greeks < Gk *graikízein* (to) adopt a Greek manner; see -IZE]

Gre·co (grek′ō; *Sp., It.* gre′kô), *n.* **1. Jo·sé** (hō zā′; *Sp.* hô se′), born 1918, U.S. dancer and choreographer, born in Italy. **2. El** (el). See **El Greco.**

Greco-, a combining form of **Greek:** *Greco-Roman.* Also, *esp. Brit.,* **Graeco-.** [< L *Graeco-*, comb. form of *Graecus* Greek]

Gre·co-Ro·man (grē′kō rō′mən, grek′ō-), *adj.* **1.** of or having both Greek and Roman characteristics: *the Greco-Roman influence.* **2.** pertaining to or designating a style of the fine arts developed in Rome or the Roman Empire from the middle of the 1st century B.C. to the early 4th century A.D., chiefly characterized by an apparent indebtedness to Greek forms or motifs modified by technological innovation, monumental scale, the combination of symbolic with narrative treatment of subject matter, and an emphasis on the commemorative aspect of a work of art. —*n.* **3.** a style of wrestling in which the contestants are forbidden to trip, tackle, and use holds below the waist. Cf. **catch-as-catch-can** (def. 1). Also, *esp. Brit.,* **Graeco-Roman.**

gree[1] (grē), *n.* *Chiefly Scot.* **1.** superiority, mastery, or victory. **2.** the prize for victory. **3.** *Obs.* a step. [ME *gre* < OF < L *grad(us)* step, GRADE; cf. DEGREE]

gree[2] (grē), *n.* *Archaic.* **1.** favor; good will. **2.** satisfaction, as for an injury. [ME *gre* < OF *gre* (F *gré*) < L *grāt(um)* what is agreeable]

gree[3] (grē), *v.t., v.i.,* **greed, gree·ing.** *Brit. Dial.* agree.

Greece (grēs), *n.* a kingdom in S Europe at the S end of the Balkan Peninsula. 8,350,000 (est. 1961); 50,147 sq. mi. *Cap.:* Athens. Ancient Greek, **Hellas.** Modern Greek, **Ellas.**

greed (grēd), *n.* excessive, inordinate, or rapacious desire, esp. for wealth. [back formation from GREEDY] —**greed′less,** *adj.* —**greed′some,** *adj.*
—**Syn.** avarice, avidity, cupidity, covetousness; voracity, ravenousness, rapacity. GREED, GREEDINESS denote an excessive, extreme desire for something, often more than one's proper share. GREED means avid desire for gain or wealth (unless some other application is indicated) and is definitely uncomplimentary in implications: *His greed drove him to exploit his workers.* GREEDINESS, when unqualified, suggests a craving for food; it may, however, be applied to all avid desires, and need not be always uncomplimentary: *greediness for knowledge, fame, praise.* —**Ant.** generosity.

greed·y (grē′dē), *adj.,* **greed·i·er, greed·i·est. 1.** excessively or inordinately desirous of wealth, profit, etc.; avaricious. **2.** having a strong or great desire for food or drink. **3.** keenly desirous; eager (often fol. by *of*): *greedy of praise.* [ME *gredy*, OE *grēdig*; r. OE *grǣdig*; c. OIcel *grāthugr*, Goth *gredags*] —**greed′i·ly,** *adv.* —**greed′i·ness,** *n.*
—**Syn. 1.** grasping, rapacious, selfish. **2.** ravenous, voracious, gluttonous, insatiable. **3.** covetous, anxious. —**Ant. 1.** generous, unselfish.

gree·gree (grē′grē), *n.* grigri.

Greek (grēk), *adj.* **1.** of or pertaining to Greece, the Greeks, or their language. **2.** pertaining to the Greek Church. **3.** noting or pertaining to the alphabetical script derived from a Semitic form of writing and employing some letters that originally represented consonants for vowel sounds, which was used from about the beginning of the first millennium B.C. for the writing of Greek, and from which the Latin, Cyrillic, and other alphabets were derived. —*n.* **4.** a native inhabitant of Greece. **5.** the language of the ancient Greeks and any of the languages which have developed from it, as Hellenistic Greek, Biblical Greek, the Koine, and Modern Greek. **6.** anything unintelligible, as speech, writing, etc.: *It's Greek to me.* **7.** a member of the Greek Church. **8.** Hellenic (def. 2). **9.** one who belongs to a Greek-letter fraternity or sorority. **10.** *Archaic.* a cheater, esp. one who cheats at cards. [ME; OE *Grēcas* (pl.) < L *Graecī* the Greeks (nom. pl. of *Graecus*) < Gk *Graikoí*, pl. of *Graikós* Greek] —**Greek′dom,** *n.* —**Greek′ish,** *adj.*

Greek′ Anthol′ogy, The, a collection of poetic epigrams in Greek, originally compiled by Meleager, as the *Garland of Meleager* (c90 B.C.), and added to periodically until given its final form by Cephalas in the 10th century. Also called **The Palatine Anthology.**

Greek′ cal′ends, at no time; never: *She will do it on the Greek calends.* Also, **Greek′ Kal′ends.**

Greek′ Cath′olic, 1. a member of the Greek Orthodox Church. **2.** a Uniat belonging to a church observing the Greek rite.

Greek′ Church′. See **Greek Orthodox Church** (def. 1).

Greek′ cross′, a cross consisting of an upright crossed in the middle by a horizontal piece of the same length. See illus. under **cross.**

Greek′ fire′, 1. an incendiary mixture of unknown composition, used in warfare in medieval times by Byzantine Greeks. **2.** any of a group of inflammable mixtures; wildfire.

Greek′ ju′niper, a tree, *Juniperus excelsa*, of southwestern Europe and Asia Minor, having scalelike, bluish-green leaves and purplish-brown fruit.

Greek′-let·ter frater′nity (grēk′let′ər), a fraternity whose name consists usually of two or three Greek letters.

Greek′-letter soror′ity, a sorority whose name consists usually of two or three Greek letters.

Greek′ Or′thodox Church′, 1. that branch of the Orthodox Church constituting the national church of Greece. **2.** See **Orthodox Church** (def. 2).

Greek′ Reviv′al, a style of architecture, furnishings, and decoration prevalent in the United States and in parts of Europe in the first half of the 19th century, characterized by a more or less close imitation of ancient Greek designs and ornamented motifs. —**Greek′ Reviv′alism.** —**Greek′ Reviv′alist.**

Greek′ rite′, the rite of the Greek Orthodox Church and of certain Uniat churches, observed in the Greek language. Also called **Byzantine rite, Constantinopolitan rite.**

Greek′ tor′toise, a small tortoise, *Testudo marginata*, of Greece, having a black shell with yellow markings.

Greek′ vale′rian. See **Jacob's ladder** (def. 1).

Gree·ley (grē′lē), *n.* **1. Horace,** 1811–72, U.S. journalist, editor, and political leader. **2.** a city in N Colorado. 26,314 (1960).

Gree·ly (grē′lē), *n.* **Adolphus Washington,** 1844–1935, U.S. general and arctic explorer.

green (grēn), *adj.* **1.** of the color of growing foliage, between yellow and blue in the spectrum. **2.** covered with herbage or foliage; verdant: *green fields.* **3.** characterized by the presence of verdure. **4.** made of green vegetables, as lettuce, endive, chicory, etc.: *a green salad.* **5.** full of life and vigor; young: *a man ripe in years but green in heart.* **6.** unseasoned; not dried or cured: *green lumber.* **7.** not fully developed or perfected in growth or condition; unripe; not properly aged: *a green berry.* **8.** immature in age or judgment; untrained; inexperienced: *Ranchers usually won't take on a green hand during the round-up.* **9.** simple; gullible; easily fooled. **10.** fresh, recent, or new: *a green wound.* **11.** having a sickly appearance; pale; wan: *green with fear; green with envy.* **12.** freshly killed: *green meat.* **13.** not fired, as bricks or pottery. **14.** (of cement or mortar) freshly set and not completely hardened. **15.** *Foundry.* **a.** (of sand) sufficiently moist to form a compact lining for a mold without further treatment. **b.** (of a casting) as it comes from the mold. **c.** (of a powder, in powder metallurgy) unsintered. —*n.* **16.** a color intermediate in the spectrum between yellow and blue, found in nature as the color of most grasses and leaves while growing, of some fruits while ripening, and of the sea. **17.** green coloring matter, as paint, dye, etc. **18.** green material or clothing: *to be dressed in green.* **19.** grassy land; a plot of grassy ground. **20.** See **putting green. 21.** See **bowling green. 22.** a shooting range for archery. **23.** a piece of grassy ground constituting a town or village common. **24. greens, a.** fresh leaves or branches of trees, shrubs, etc., used for decoration; wreaths. **b.** the leaves and stems of plants, as spinach, lettuce, cabbage, etc., used for food. **c.** a blue-green uniform of the U.S. Army. —*v.i., v.t.* **25.** to become or make green. [ME, OE *grēne*; c. G *grün*; akin to GROW] —**green′age,** *n.* —**green′ly,** *adv.*

Green (grēn), *n.* **1. Henry** (*Henry Vincent Yorke*), born 1905, English novelist. **2. John Richard,** 1837–83, English historian. **3. Julian,** born 1900, U.S. writer. **4. Paul Eliot,** born 1894, U.S. playwright, novelist, and teacher. **5. William,** 1873–1952, U.S. labor leader: president of the A.F.L. 1924–52.

green′ al′ga, any grass-green alga of the class *Chlorophyceae.*

Green·a·way (grēn′ə wā′), *n.* **Kate** (*Catherine*), 1846–1901, English painter and author and illustrator of children's books.

green·back (grēn′bak′), *n.* a United States legal-tender note, usually printed in green on the back, originally issued against the credit of the country and not against gold or silver on deposit. [GREEN + BACK[1]]

Green′back par′ty, *U.S. Hist.* a former political party, organized in 1874, opposed to the retirement or reduction of greenbacks and favoring their increase as the only paper currency. —**Green′back′er,** *n.* —**Green′back′ism,** *n.*

green′ bag′, *Brit.* **1.** a bag or briefcase made of green cloth, formerly used by lawyers for carrying documents. **2.** *Slang.* **a.** the legal profession. **b.** a lawyer. Also, **green′-bag′.**

green′ ball′, a ball-shaped colony of the green alga, *Cladophora trichotoma*, found on the Atlantic and Pacific coasts of North America.

green′-barked aca′cia (grēn′bärkt′), paloverde.

green′ bass′ (bas). See **largemouth bass.**

Green′ Bay′, 1. an arm of Lake Michigan, in NE Wisconsin. 120 mi. long. **2.** a port in E Wisconsin at the S end of this bay. 62,888 (1960).

green belt (grēn′ belt′ *for 1;* grēn′ belt′ *for 2*), **1.** an area of parks or unoccupied ground surrounding a community. **2.** *Judo.* a green belt conferred by a judo association on a player, usually in his second year of training, to be worn with his judo costume. Cf. **black belt** (def. 2), **blue belt, brown belt, white belt.** —**green′-belt′,** *adj.*

Green·belt (grēn′belt′), *n.* a town in central Maryland. 7479 (1960).

Green·berg (grēn′bûrg), *n.* **Henry B.** (*Hank*), born 1911, U.S. baseball player.

green·board (grēn′bōrd′, -bôrd′), *n.* a green chalkboard or blackboard. [GREEN + BOARD]

green′bot′tle fly′ (grēn′bot′əl), any of several metallic green blowflies, as *Phaenicia sericata*. Also called **green′bot′tle.** [GREEN + BOTTLE[1]]

green·bri·er (grēn′brī′ər), *n.* **1.** a climbing, liliaceous plant, *Smilax rotundifolia*, of the eastern U.S., having a prickly stem and thick leaves. **2.** any plant of this genus. [GREEN + BRIER[1]]

Green·cas·tle (grēn′kas′əl, -kä′səl), *n.* **1.** a town in central Indiana. 8506 (1960). **2.** a town in S Pennsylvania. 2988 (1960).

green′ cop′peras. See **ferrous sulfate.**

green′ corn′. See **sweet corn** (def. 2).

Green′ Cove′ Springs′, a town in NE Florida. 4233 (1960).

green′ crab′, a yellowish-green crab, *Carcinides maenas*, found in shallow waters along rocky shores.

Green·dale (grēn′dāl′), *n.* **1.** a town in SE Wisconsin. 6843 (1960). **2.** a town in SE Indiana. 2861 (1960).

green′ drag′on. See under **dragon** (def. 8). Also called **dragonroot.**

Greene (grēn), *n.* **1. Graham,** born 1904, English novelist and journalist. **2. Nathanael,** 1742–86, American Revolutionary general. **3. Robert,** 1558–92, English dramatist and poet.

green′ earth′, a pigment used in painting consisting mainly of iron silicate, characterized chiefly by its variable grayish-green hue, lack of tinting strength, and permanence. Also, **terra verde.**

green·er·y (grē′nə rē), *n., pl.* **-er·ies** for 2. **1.** green foliage or vegetation; verdure. **2.** a place where green plants are grown or kept. [GREEN + -ERY]

green-eyed (grēn′īd′), *adj.* jealous; envious; distrustful.

green′-eyed mon′ster, jealousy: *Othello fell under the sway of the green-eyed monster.*

green′ fee′. See **greens fee.**

Green·field (grēn′fēld′), *n.* **1.** a city in SE Wisconsin, near Milwaukee. 17,636 (1960). **2.** a town in central Indiana. 9049 (1960). **3.** a town in SW Ohio. 5422 (1960).

green·finch (grēn′finch′), *n.* a European finch, *Chloris chloris*, having green and yellow plumage. [GREEN + FINCH]

green′ fin′gers, *Brit. Informal.* See **green thumb.**

green·fish (grēn′fish′), *n., pl.* **-fish·es,** (*esp. collectively*) **-fish.** opaleye. [GREEN + FISH]

green′ flash′, *Astron.* a green coloration of the upper portion of the sun, caused by atmospheric refraction and occasionally seen as the sun rises above or sinks below the horizon.

green·gage (grēn′gāj′), *n.* one of several varieties of light-green plums. [GREEN + *Gage*, after Sir William *Gage*, 18th-century English botanist who introduced it from France c1725]

green′ gland′, *Zool.* one of the pair of excretory organs in each side of the head region of decapod crustaceans, emptying at the base of the antennae.

green′ glass′, glass of low quality, colored green by impurities in the materials from which it is made.

green′ gram′. See under **gram**[2] (def. 2).

green·gro·cer (grēn′grō′sər), *n.* *Chiefly Brit.* a retailer of fresh vegetables and fruit. [GREEN + GROCER]

green·gro·cer·y (grēn′grō′sə rē), *n., pl.* **-cer·ies.** *Chiefly Brit.* **1.** a greengrocer's shop. **2.** the fruits and vegetables stocked and sold in such a shop. [GREEN + GROCERY]

green·head (grēn′hed′), *n.* a male mallard. [GREEN + HEAD]

green·heart (grēn/härt/), *n.* **1.** a South American, lauraceous tree, *Ocotea* (or *Nectandra*) *Rodiaei*, yielding a hard, durable wood often used for wharves and bridges and in shipbuilding, and whose bark yields bebeerine. **2.** any of certain other timber trees of tropical America. **3.** their valuable greenish wood. [GREEN + HEART]

green/ her/on, a small, American heron, *Butorides virescens*, having glossy green wings.

green·horn (grēn/hôrn/), *n.* **1.** a raw, inexperienced person. **2.** a person easily imposed upon. [ME; see GREEN, HORN; orig. applied to cattle with green (i.e., young) horns] —**green/horn/ism,** *n.*

green·house (grēn/hous/), *n., pl.* **-hous·es** (-hou/ziz). a building, usually chiefly of glass, in which the temperature is maintained within a desired range, used for cultivating tender plants or growing plants out of season. [GREEN + HOUSE]

green/house effect/, the effect produced by certain gases, as carbon dioxide, on a planet's atmosphere by raising the equilibrium temperature of the surface of the planet, thus preventing the outward transmission of long-wave radiation from the surface but permitting the inward transmission of short-wave radiation from the sun to the surface.

green·ing (grē/ning), *n.* any variety of apple whose skin is green when ripe. [GREEN + -ING[1]]

green·ish (grē/nish), *adj.* somewhat green; having a tinge of green. [ME: see GREEN, -ISH[1]]

green/ June/ bee/tle, a large, greenish scarabaeid beetle, *Cotinis nitida*, of the southern U.S. Also called **figeater.**

green·keep·er (grēn/kē/pər), *n.* greenskeeper.

Green·land (grēn/lənd, -land/), *n.* a Danish overseas territory located NE of North America: the largest island in the world. 35,499 (1962); ab. 840,000 sq. mi. (over 700,000 sq. mi. ice-capped). —**Green/land·er,** *n.* —**Green/land·ish,** *adj.*

Green/land Sea/, a part of the Arctic Ocean, NE of Greenland and N of Iceland.

Green/land whale/, bowhead.

Green·lawn (grēn/lôn/), *n.* a town on NW Long Island, in SE New York. 5422 (1960).

green/ lead/ ore/ (led), pyromorphite.

green·let (grēn/lit), *n.* a vireo. [GREEN + -LET]

green/ light/, **1.** a green lamp, used as a traffic signal to mean "go." **2.** *Informal.* authorization; approval; permission.

green·ling (grēn/ling), *n.* any spiny-finned fish of the genus *Hexagrammos*, found about rocks and kelp in the North Pacific. [late ME; see GREEN, -LING[1]]

green·mail (grēn/māl/), *n.* the practice of buying a large amount of stock in a company in order to threaten to take over control of the company if the stock is not bought back from the buyer at an inflated price. [GREEN ("money") + (BLACK)MAIL] —**green/mail/er,** *n.*

Green/ Man/sions, a novel (1904) by W. H. Hudson.

green/ manure/, *Agric.* **1.** a crop of growing plants, as clover and other nitrogen-fixing plants, plowed under to enrich the soil. **2.** manure which has not undergone decay.

green/ mint/, spearmint.

green/ mold/. See **blue mold** (def. 1).

green/ mon/key, a monkey, *Cercopithecus aethiops sabaeus*, of West Africa, with a greenish-gray back and yellow tail.

Green/ Moun/tain Boys/, the soldiers from Vermont in the American Revolution, originally organized by Ethan Allen in 1775 to oppose the territorial claims of New York.

Green/ Moun/tains, a mountain range in Vermont: a part of the Appalachian system. Highest peak, Mt. Mansfield, 4393 ft.

Green/ Moun/tain State/, Vermont (used as a nickname).

green·ness (grēn/nis), *n.* **1.** the quality or state of being green. **2.** green vegetation, grass, or the like; verdure or verdancy. **3.** lack of maturity or experience; youthfulness. **4.** the state or quality of being naïve; innocence; gullibility. [ME, OE *grēnnes.* See GREEN, -NESS]

Green·ock (grē/nək, gren/ək), *n.* a seaport in SW Scotland, on the Firth of Clyde. 74,578 (1961).

green·ock·ite (grē/nə kīt/), *n.* a yellow mineral, cadmium sulfide, CdS, associated with zinc ores and used as a source of cadmium. [named after Charles Cathcart, Lord *Greenock* (1807–43), Englishman who discovered it; see -ITE[1]]

green/ on/ion, a young onion with a small bulb, used as a table vegetable, usually raw, esp. in salads; scallion.

green/ o/sier, a shrub, *Cornus rugosa*, of eastern North America, having round leaves, blue fruit, and flat-topped clusters of small, white flowers.

Green·ough (grē/nō), *n.* **Horatio,** 1805–52, U.S. sculptor.

Green/ Pas/tures, The, a play (1930) by Marc Connelly.

green/ pep/per, **1.** the fruit of the bell or sweet pepper, *Capsicum frutescens grossum.* **2.** the mild, unripe fruit of any of the garden peppers, *Capsicum frutescens*, used as a green vegetable.

green/ plov/er, *Brit.* lapwing.

Green·port (grēn/pōrt/, -pôrt/), *n.* a town on NE Long Island, in SE New York. 2608 (1960).

Green/ Riv/er, **1.** a river flowing S from W Wyoming through E Utah to the Colorado River. 730 mi. long. **2.** a town in SW Wyoming. 3497 (1960).

green·room (grēn/ro͞om/, -ro͝om/), *n.* a lounge in a theater, for the use of actors and actresses when they are not required on the stage. [GREEN + ROOM, prob. so called because formerly painted green]

green·sand (grēn/sand/), *n.* a sandstone containing much glauconite, which gives it a greenish hue. [GREEN + SAND]

green/sand proc/ess, a process for casting iron with sand not previously heated.

Greens·bo·ro (grēnz/bûr/ō, -bur/ō), *n.* **1.** a city in N North Carolina. 119,574 (1960). **2.** a town in W Alabama. 3081 (1960). **3.** a town in central Georgia. 2773 (1960).

Greens·burg (grēnz/bûrg), *n.* **1.** a city in SW Pennsylvania. 17,383 (1960). **2.** a town in central Indiana. 6605 (1960).

green/ sea/, *Naut.* a solid mass of water breaking over the bow or bulwark of a vessel.

green/ seg/ment. See **green flash.**

greens/ fee/, a fee for playing on a golf course, payable by guests of a member of a golf club, usually higher in price on weekends than on weekdays. Also, **green fee.**

green·shank (grēn/shangk/), *n.* an Old World shore bird, *Tringa nebularia*, having green legs. [GREEN + SHANK]

green·sick·ness (grēn/sik/nis), *n.* *Pathol.* chlorosis (def. 2). [GREEN + SICKNESS] —**green/sick/,** *adj.*

greens·keep·er (grēnz/kē/pər), *n.* a person charged with the care and maintenance of a golf course. Also, **greenkeeper.** [GREEN + 'S[1] + KEEPER]

green/ snake/, any of several slender, green colubrid snakes of the genus *Opheodrys*, of North America, which feed chiefly on insects.

green/ soap/, a soap made chiefly from potassium hydroxide and linseed oil, used in treating skin diseases.

Green's/ the/orem, *Math.* one of several theorems that connect an integral in *n* dimensional space with one in *n*–1 dimensional space.

green/stick frac/ture (grēn/stik/), an incomplete fracture of a long bone, in which one side is broken and the other side is still intact. See illus. under **fracture.** [GREEN + STICK[1]]

green·stone (grēn/stōn/), *n.* any of various altered basaltic rocks having a dark-green color caused by the presence of chlorite, epidote, etc. [GREEN + STONE]

green/ strength/, **1.** *Foundry.* the tensile strength of green sand. **2.** *Metall.* the tensile strength of an unsintered compact.

green·sward (grēn/swôrd/), *n.* turf green with grass. [GREEN + SWARD] —**green/sward/ed,** *adj.*

green/ tea/, a tea subjected to a heating process without previous special withering and fermenting.

greenth (grēnth), *n.* green growth; verdure. [GREEN + -TH[1]]

green/ thumb/, a conspicuous aptitude for gardening or for growing plants successfully: *Penthouse gardens provide an outlet for the city dweller with a green thumb.*

Green·tree (grēn/trē/), *n.* a town in SW Pennsylvania. 5226 (1960).

green/ tur/tle, a sea turtle, *Chelonia mydas*, common in tropical and subtropical seas, the flesh of which is used for turtle soup.

green/ veg/etables, vegetables the edible parts of which are green in color, as leafy vegetables, peas, broccoli, etc.

green/ ver/diter. See under **verditer.**

Green·ville (grēn/vil), *n.* **1.** a city in NW South Carolina. 66,188 (1960). **2.** a city in W Mississippi, on the Mississippi River. 41,502 (1960). **3.** a city in E North Carolina. 22,860 (1960). **4.** a city in NE Texas. 19,087 (1960). **5.** a town in NW Pennsylvania. 8765 (1960). **6.** a town in central Michigan. 7440 (1960). **7.** a town in S Alabama. 6894 (1960). **8.** a town in central Illinois. 4569 (1960). **9.** a town in W Kentucky. 3198 (1960).

Green/ville North/, a town in W Mississippi. 2516 (1960).

green/ vit/riol. See **ferrous sulfate.**

green/ wat/tle, a tree, *Acacia decurrens*, of California, having golden-yellow flower heads and dark-green leaves. Cf. **black wattle, silver wattle.**

Green·wich (grin/ij, -ich, gren/- *for 1;* gren/ich, grin/-, grēn/wich *for 2*), *n.* **1.** a borough in SE London, England: located on the prime meridian from which geographic longitude is measured; Royal Observatory. 85,585 (1961). **2.** a town in SW Connecticut. 53,793 (1960).

Green/wich hour/ an/gle, *Astron.* hour angle measured from the meridian of Greenwich, England.

Green/wich Time/, the standard of time as designated at the Observatory in Greenwich, England: used in England and as a basis of calculation elsewhere. Also called **Green/wich Mean/ Time/, Green/wich Civ/il Time/.**

Green/wich Vil/lage (gren/ich, grin/-), a section of New York City, in lower Manhattan: frequented by artists, writers, and students.

green/-winged teal/ (grēn/wingd/), either of two small, fresh-water ducks, *Anas carolinensis*, of America, or *A. crecca*, of Europe, having an iridescent green speculum in the wing.

green·wood (grēn/wo͝od/), *n.* a wood or forest when green, as in summer. [ME; see GREEN, WOOD[1]]

Green·wood (grēn/wo͝od/), *n.* **1.** a city in NW Mississippi. 20,436 (1960). **2.** a city in W South Carolina. 16,644 (1960). **3.** a town in central Indiana. 7169 (1960). **4.** a town in E Alabama. 3561 (1960).

green/ wood/pecker, a woodpecker, *Picus viridis*, of Eurasia and northern Africa, having green plumage with a yellow rump and red on the top of the head.

Greer (grēr), *n.* **1.** a town in NW South Carolina. 8967 (1960). **2.** a girl's given name.

greet[1] (grēt), *v.t.* **1.** to address with some form of salutation; welcome. **2.** to meet or receive: *to be greeted by cheering crowds; to greet a proposal with boos and hisses.* **3.** to manifest itself to: *Music greeted his ear as he entered the salon.* —*v.i.* **4.** *Obs.* to give salutations on meeting. [ME *gret(en)*, OE *grētan;* c. G *grüssen*] —**greet/er,** *n.*
—**Syn. 1.** hail, accost.

greet[2] (grēt), *Scot. and North Eng. Archaic.* —*v.i.* **1.** to grieve; lament; cry. —*v.t.* **2.** to lament; bewail. [ME *grete*, OE *grētan*, north var. of *grǣtan;* c. Icel *grāta*, Goth *gretan*]

greet·ing (grē/ting), *n.* **1.** the act or words of one who greets. **2.** a friendly message from someone who is absent: *to bring a greeting from a friend in another country.* **3. greetings,** an expression of friendly or respectful regard: *Send greetings from me to all your family. On the glass was etched, "Greetings from Long Branch, N.J."* [ME *greting.* See GREET[1], -ING[1]] —**greet/ing·less,** *adj.* —**greet/ing·ly,** *adv.*

greet/ing card/, card[1] (def. 5).

Greg (greg), *n.* a boy's given name, form of **Gregory.**

gre·ga·le (grā gä/lā), *n.* a strong northeast wind that blows in the central and western Mediterranean area. Also, **grecale, gré·gal** (grā gäl/), **gre·gau** (grā gou/), **guergal.** [< It *grecale, gregale* < LL *Grecāl(is).* See GREEK, -AL[1]]

greg·a·rine (greg/ə rīn/, -ər in), *n.* **1.** a type of sporozoan parasite that inhabits the digestive and other cavities of various invertebrates and produces cysts filled with spores. —*adj.* **2.** having the characteristics of or pertaining to a gregarine or gregarines. [< NL *Gregarīn(a)* name of type, equiv. to L *gregār(ius)* (see GREGARIOUS) + *-īna* -INE[1]]

gre·gar·i·ous (gri gâr/ē əs), *adj.* **1.** living in flocks or herds, as animals. **2.** *Bot.* growing in open clusters; not matted together. **3.** fond of the company of others; sociable. **4.** pertaining to a flock or crowd. [< L *gregārius* belonging to a flock, equiv. to *greg-* (s. of *grex*) flock + *-ārius* -ARIOUS] —**gre·gar/i·ous·ly,** *adv.* —**gre·gar/i·ous·ness,** *n.*

Gregg (greg), *n.* **John Robert,** 1864–1948, U.S. educator: inventor of a system of shorthand.

gre·go (grē/gō, grā/-), *n., pl.* **-gos.** a short, hooded jacket or cloak of coarse fabric, worn by the Greeks and Levantines. [? < Pg (cf. Sp *griego*, It *greco*) < L *Graecus* GREEK]

Gre·go·ri·an (gri gōr/ē ən, -gôr/-), *adj.* of or pertaining to any of the popes named Gregory, esp. Gregory I or Gregory XIII. [< NL *gregoriān(us)* of, pertaining to Pope Gregory, equiv. to LL *Gregori(us)* + L *-ānus* -AN]

Grego/rian cal/endar, the reformed Julian calendar now in use, according to which the ordinary year consists of 365 days, and a leap year of 366 days occurs in every year whose number is exactly divisible by 4 except centenary years whose numbers are not exactly divisible by 400, as 1700, 1800, and 1900. [named after Pope GREGORY XIII]

Grego/rian chant/, **1.** the plain song or cantus firmus used in the ritual of the Roman Catholic Church. **2.** a melody in this style. [named after Pope GREGORY I] —**Gre·go/ri·an·ist,** *n.*

Grego/rian mode/, *Music.* See **church mode.** [named after Pope GREGORY I]

Grego/rian tel/escope, a telescope similar in nature to the Cassegrainian telescope but less widely used. [named after James GREGORY; see -AN]

Grego/rian wa/ter, *Rom. Cath. Ch.* a mixture of water, salt, ashes, and wine, blessed and sprinkled over the altar in the consecration of a church.

Greg·o·ry (greg/ə rē), *n.* **1. Lady Augusta** (*Isabella Augusta Persse*), 1852–1932, Irish dramatist. **2. Horace,** born 1898, U.S. poet and critic. **3. James,** 1638–75, Scottish mathematician. **4.** a boy's given name.

Gregory I, **Saint** (*"Gregory the Great"*), A.D. c540–604, Italian ecclesiastic: pope 590–604.

Gregory II, **Saint,** died A.D. 731, pope 715–731.

Gregory III, **Saint,** died A.D. 741, pope 731–741.

Gregory IV, died A.D. 844, pope 827–844.

Gregory V, (*Bruno of Carinthia*) died A.D. 999, German ecclesiastic: pope 996–999.

Gregory VI, (*Johannes Gratianus*) died 1048, German ecclesiastic: pope 1045–46.

Gregory VII, **Saint** (*Hildebrand*), c1020–85, Italian ecclesiastic: pope 1073–85.

Gregory VIII, (*Alberto de Mora* or *Alberto di Morra*) died 1187, Italian ecclesiastic: pope 1187.

Gregory IX, (*Ugolino di Segni* or *Ugolino of Anagni*) c1143–1241, Italian ecclesiastic: pope 1227–41.

Gregory X, (*Teobaldo Visconti*) c1210–76, Italian ecclesiastic: pope 1271–76.

Gregory XI, (*Pierre Roger de Beaufort*) 1330–78, French ecclesiastic: pope 1370–78.

Gregory XII, (*Angelo Correr, Corrario,* or *Corraro*) c1327–1417, Italian ecclesiastic: installed as pope in 1406 and resigned office in 1415.

Gregory XIII, (*Ugo Buoncompagni*) 1502–85, Italian ecclesiastic: pope 1572–85, educator and innovator of the modern calendar.

Gregory XIV, (*Niccolò Sfondrati*) 1535–91, Italian ecclesiastic: pope 1590–91.

Gregory XV, (*Alessandro Ludovisi*) 1554–1623, Italian ecclesiastic: pope 1621–23.

Gregory XVI, (*Bartolommeo Alberto Cappellari*) 1765–1846, Italian ecclesiastic: pope 1831–46.

Greg/ory of Nys/sa (nis/ə), **Saint,** A.D. c330–395?, Christian bishop and theologian in Asia Minor (brother of Saint Basil).

Greg/ory of Tours/, **Saint,** A.D. 538?–594, Frankish bishop and historian.

greige (grā, grāzh), *n.* See **gray goods.** [< F *grège* raw (of silk) < It *greggio* GRAY]

grei·sen (grī/zən), *n.* a hydrothermally altered rock of granite texture composed chiefly of quartz and mica, common in the tin mines of Saxony. [< G]

gre·mi·al (grē/mē əl), *n.* *Eccles.* a cloth placed on the lap of the bishop, as during the celebration of Mass or when he confers orders. [< LL *gremiāl(is)* growing in a cluster from a stump, equiv. to L *grem(ium)* lap, bosom + *-ālis* -AL[1]]

grem·lin (grem/lin), *n.* a mischievous invisible being, said by airplane pilots in World War II to cause engine trouble and mechanical difficulties. [?]
—**Syn.** See **goblin.**

Gre·na·da (gri nā/də), *n.* **1.** one of the Windward Islands, in the E West Indies: a member of the West Indies Associated States; formerly a British colony. 91,967 (est. 1964); 133 sq. mi. *Cap.:* St. George's. **2.** a town in central Mississippi. 7914 (1960). —**Gre·na·di·an** (gri nā/dē ən), *adj., n.*

gre·nade (gri nād/), *n.* **1.** a small explosive shell thrown by hand or fired from a rifle. **2.** a glass missile used for scattering chemicals, as in dispersing tear gas or fire-extinguishing substances. [< F < Sp *granad(a)* pomegranate, special use of *granado* having grains < L *grānātus.* See GRAIN, -ATE[1]]

gre·nade′ launch′er, *Mil.* a device attached to the muzzle of a rifle, permitting the firing of rifle grenades.

gren·a·dier (gren′ə dēr′), *n.* **1.** (in the British army) a member of the first regiment of household infantry (**Gren′adier Guards′**). **2.** (formerly) a specially selected foot soldier in certain elite units. **3.** (formerly) a soldier who threw grenades. **4.** Also called **rat-tail.** any of several deep-sea fishes of the family *Macrouridae*, having an elongated, tapering tail. [< F; see GRENADE, -IER] —**gren′a·dier′i·al,** *adj.* —**gren′a·dier′ly,** *adv.* —**gren′a·dier′ship,** *n.*

gren·a·dine[1] (gren′ə dēn′, gren′ə dēn′), *n.* a thin fabric of leno weave in silk, nylon, rayon, or wool. [< F, ? after GRANADA, Spain]

gren·a·dine[2] (gren′ə dēn′, gren′ə dēn′), *n.* a syrup made from pomegranate juice. [< F, dim. of *grenade* pomegranate. See GRENADE, -INE[1]]

Gren·a·dines (gren′ə dēnz′, gren′ə dēnz′), *n.* (*construed as pl.*) a chain of about 600 British islands in the E West Indies in the Windward Islands.

Gren·fell (gren′fel), *n.* **Sir Wilfred Thom·a·son** (tom′ə sən), 1865–1940, English physician and missionary in Labrador and Newfoundland.

Gre·no·ble (grə nō′bəl; *Fr.* grə nô′blᵊ), *n.* a city in and the capital of Isère, in SE France. 162,764 (1962).

Gren·ville (gren′vil), *n.* **1. George,** 1712–70, British statesman: prime minister 1763–65. **2.** Also, **Greyn·ville. Sir Richard,** 1541?–91, British naval commander. **3. William Wyndham, Baron Grenville,** 1759–1834, British statesman: prime minister 1806–07 (son of George Grenville).

Gresh·am (gresh′əm), *n.* **1. Sir Thomas,** 1519?–79, English merchant and financier. **2.** a town in NW Oregon. 3944 (1960).

Gresh′am's law′, *Econ.* the tendency of the inferior of two forms of currency to circulate more freely than, or to the exclusion of, the superior, because of the hoarding of the latter. [named after Sir Thomas GRESHAM]

gres·so·ri·al (gre sōr′ē əl, -sôr′-), *adj.* *Zool.* adapted for walking, as the feet of some birds. [< NL *gressōri(us)* ambulatory (L *gress(us)* walked, stepped, ptp. of *gradī*, + *-ōrius* -ORY[1]) + -AL[1]]

Gret·a (gret′ə), *n.* a girl's given name, form of **Margaret.** Also, **Gret′ta.**

Gret·chen (grech′ən; *Ger.* grāt′shən), *n.* a girl's given name, form of **Margaret.**

Gret·na (gret′nə), *n.* a city in SE Louisiana, near New Orleans. 21,967 (1960).

Gret′na Green′, a village in S Scotland, near the English border, to which many English couples formerly eloped to be married.

Gret′na Green′ mar′riage, *Brit. Informal.* marriage without parental consent; elopement.

Greuze (grœz), *n.* **Jean Bap·tiste** (zhäN ba tēst′), 1725–1805, French painter.

grew (grōō), *v.* pt. of **grow.**

grew·some (grōō′səm), *adj.* gruesome. —**grew′some·ly,** *adv.* —**grew′some·ness,** *n.*

grex (greks), *n.* a numerical system for measuring the size of fibers, filaments, or yarns, based on the weight in grams of 10,000 meters of the fibrous material. [from the expression *gram per x* (ten)]

grey (grā), *adj., n., v.t., v.i.* gray. —**grey′ish,** *adj.* —**grey′ly,** *adv.* —**grey′ness,** *n.*

Grey (grā), *n.* **1. Charles, 2nd Earl,** 1764–1845, British statesman: prime minister 1830–34. **2. Sir Edward** (*Viscount Fallodon*), 1862–1933, British statesman. **3. Sir George,** 1812–98, British statesman and colonial administrator: prime minister of New Zealand 1877–79. **4. Lady Jane** (*Lady Jane Dudley*), 1537–54, descendant of Henry VII of England; executed to eliminate her as a potential rival for the throne. **5. Zane** (zān), 1875–1939, U.S. novelist.

grey·back (grā′bak′), *n.* grayback.

grey·beard (grā′bērd′), *n.* graybeard.

grey-head·ed (grā′hed′id), *adj.* gray-headed.

grey·hen (grā′hen′), *n.* *Brit.* the female of the black grouse. [GREY + HEN]

grey·hound (grā′hound′), *n.* **1.** one of a breed of tall, slender, short-haired dogs, noted for its keen sight and swiftness. **2.** a swift ship, esp. a fast ocean liner. Also, **grayhound.** [ME *greihund, gre-, gri-,* OE *grīghund* < ON *greyhund(r)*; cf. OIcel *grey* bitch; see HOUND[1]]

Greyhound (28 in. high at shoulder)

grey·ish (grā′ish), *adj.* grayish.

grey·lag (grā′lag′), *n.* graylag.

Greyn·ville (grān′vil, gren′-), *n.* **Sir Richard.** See **Grenville, Sir Richard.**

grey′ plov′er, *Brit.* the black-bellied plover.

grey·wacke (grā′wak′, -wak′ə), *n.* graywacke.

grib·ble (grib′əl), *n.* a small, marine isopod crustacean of the genus *Limnoria*, which destroys submerged timber by boring into it. [? akin to GRUB]

grice (grīs), *n.* *Chiefly Scot.* a pig, esp. a young or suckling pig. [ME *gris* < Scand; cf. OIcel *grīs(s)* young pig]

grid (grid), *n.* **1.** a grating of crossed bars; gridiron. **2.** *Elect.* a metallic framework employed in a storage cell or battery for conducting the electric current and supporting the active material. **3.** a system of electrical distribution serving a large area, esp. by means of high-tension lines. **4.** *Electronics.* an electrode in a vacuum tube, usually consisting of parallel wires, a coil of wire, or a screen, for controlling the flow of electrons between the other electrodes. **5.** *Survey.* a basic system of reference lines for a region, consisting of straight lines intersecting at right angles, computed by establishing a system of scale corrections for measured distances. **6.** a network of horizontal and perpendicular lines, uniformly spaced, for locating points on a map, chart, or aerial photograph by means of a system of coordinates. **7.** *Archit.* a rectangular system of coordinates used in locating the principal elements of a plan. **8.** grillage. **9.** *Football.* gridiron (def. 3). [short for GRIDIRON]

grid′ bi′as, *Electronics.* the voltage difference applied between a grid and the cathode of a vacuum tube. Also called **C-bias.**

grid′ capac′itor, *Electronics.* a capacitor connected in series with the grid.

grid′ cir′cuit, *Electronics.* that part of a circuit which contains the cathode and the grid of a vacuum tube.

grid′ cur′rent, *Electronics.* the current which moves within the vacuum tube from the grid to the cathode.

grid·der (grid′ər), *n.* *U.S. Informal.* a football player. [GRID + -ER[1]]

grid·dle (grid′ᵊl), *n., v.,* **-dled, -dling.** —*n.* **1.** a frying pan with a handle and a slightly raised edge, for cooking pancakes, bacon, etc., over direct heat. **2.** any flat, heated surface, esp. on the top of a stove, for cooking food: *a quick breakfast from the drugstore's griddle.* —*v.t.* **3.** to cook on a griddle: *Griddle two eggs and a couple of sausages for me, will you?* [ME *gridel, gredil* < OF *gridil, gredil;* see GRILL[1]]

grid·dle·cake (grid′ᵊl kāk′), *n.* a thin cake of batter cooked on a griddle; flapjack; pancake. [GRIDDLE + CAKE]

gride (grīd), *v.,* **grid·ed, grid·ing,** *n.* —*v.i.* **1.** to grate; grind; scrape harshly; make a grating sound. —*v.t.* **2.** to pierce or cut. —*n.* **3.** a griding or grating sound. [ME; metathetic var. of GIRD[2]]

grid·i·ron (grid′ī′ərn), *n.* **1.** a utensil consisting of parallel metal bars on which to broil meat or other food. **2.** any framework or network resembling a gridiron. **3.** a football field. **4.** a structure above the stage of a theater, from which hung scenery and the like are manipulated. [ME *gridirne, gridir(e), gridere,* var. of *gridel* GRIDDLE; variants in *-irne, -ire,* etc. by folk etymology assoc. with *irne, ire* IRON]

grid′iron pen′dulum, a clock pendulum having, as part of its shaft, an arrangement of brass and steel rods having different coefficients of expansion, such that the pendulum has the same length at any temperature.

grid′i·ron-tailed liz′ard (grid′ī′ərn tāld′). See **zebra-tailed lizard.**

grid′ leak′, *Electronics.* a high-resistance device which permits excessive charges on the grid to leak off or escape.

Grid·ley (grid′lē), *n.* a town in central California. 3343 (1960).

grid·lock (grid′lok′), *n.* **1.** the total paralysis of vehicular traffic in all directions in an urban area because key intersections are blocked by traffic. **2.** (loosely) the blocking of an intersection by vehicular traffic entering the intersection but unable to pass through it. [GRID + LOCK[1]]

grid′ road′, *Canadian.* a municipal road that follows a grid line established by the original survey of the area.

grid′ varia′tion, *Navig.* the angle, at any point on the surface of the earth, between the magnetic and true meridians passing through that point. Also called **grivation.**

grief (grēf), *n.* **1.** keen mental suffering or distress over affliction or loss; sharp sorrow; painful regret. **2.** a cause or occasion of keen distress or sorrow. **3. come to grief,** to suffer disappointment or misfortune; fail: *Their marriage came to grief after only two years.* [ME *gref, grief* < AF *gref;* see GRIEVE] —**grief′less,** *adj.* —**grief′less·ness,** *n.*
—**Syn. 1.** anguish, heartache, woe, misery; sadness, melancholy, moroseness. See **sorrow.** —**Ant. 1.** joy.

grief-strick·en (grēf′strik′ən), *adj.* overwhelmed by grief; afflicted; sorrowful.

Grieg (grēg; *Norw.* grig), *n.* **Ed·vard** (ed′värd; *Norw.* ed′värt), 1843–1907, Norwegian composer.

griege (grā, grāzh), *n.* See **gray goods.** [var. of GREIGE]

grie·shoch (grē′shoKH), *n.* *Scot.* a bed of embers, esp. of a peat or moss fire. [< Gael *griosach* embers]

griev·ance (grē′vəns), *n.* **1.** a wrong, real or fancied, considered as grounds for complaint: *a popular grievance.* **2.** resentment or complaint, or the grounds for complaint, against an unjust act: *to have a grievance against someone.* [ME *greva(u)nce* < OF *grevance.* See GRIEVE, -ANCE]

griev′ance commit′tee, a board of representatives chosen from a labor union or from both labor and management to consider and remedy workers' grievances.

grieve (grēv), *v.,* **grieved, griev·ing.** —*v.i.* **1.** to feel grief; sorrow: *She has grieved over his loss for nearly three years.* —*v.t.* **2.** to distress mentally; cause to feel grief or sorrow: *It grieves me to see you so unhappy.* **3.** *Obs.* to oppress or wrong. [ME *grev(en), griev(en)* < OF *grev(er)* < L *gravāre* to burden, deriv. of *gravis* heavy, GRAVE[2]] —**griev·ed·ly** (grē′vid lē, grēvd′-), *adv.* —**griev′er,** *n.* —**griev′ing·ly,** *adv.*
—**Syn. 1.** lament, weep, bewail, bemoan; suffer. GRIEVE, MOURN imply showing suffering caused by sorrow. GRIEVE is the stronger word, implying deep mental suffering often endured alone and in silence but revealed by one's aspect: *to grieve over the loss (or death) of a friend.* MOURN usually refers to manifesting sorrow outwardly, either with or without sincerity: *to mourn publicly and wear black.* **2.** sadden, pain.

griev·ous (grē′vəs), *adj.* **1.** causing grief or sorrow: *grievous news.* **2.** flagrant; atrocious: *a grievous offense against morality.* **3.** full of or expressing grief; sorrowful: *a grievous cry.* **4.** burdensome or oppressive. **5.** causing great physical suffering: *an arrest for causing grievous bodily harm to someone in a bar.* [ME *grevous* < OF *grevo(u)s.* See GRIEVE, -OUS] —**griev′ous·ly,** *adv.* —**griev′ous·ness,** *n.*
—**Syn. 1.** distressing, sad, sorrowful, painful, regrettable. **2.** deplorable, lamentable, calamitous, heinous, outrageous, flagitious, dreadful, shameful, iniquitous. —**Ant. 1.** delightful.

griff (grif), griffin[2]. [by shortening]

griffe[1] (grif), *n.* *Chiefly Louisiana.* **1.** the offspring of a Negro and a mulatto. **2.** a person of mixed Negro and American Indian blood. **3.** a mulatto, esp. a woman. [< LaF < AmerSp *grifo* curly-haired]

griffe[2] (grif), *n.* *Archit.* an ornament at the base of a column, projecting from the torus toward a corner of the plinth. Also called **spur.** [< F: claw < Gmc]

G

G, Griffe[2]

Grif·fes (grif′əs), *n.* **Charles Tomlinson,** 1884–1920. U.S. composer.

grif·fin[1] (grif′in), *n.* *Class. Myth.* a fabled monster, usually having the head and wings of an eagle and the body of a lion. Also, **griffon, gryphon.** [ME *griffoun* < MF *grifon* < L *grȳph(us)* < Gk *gryp-* (s. of *grýps*) curled, curved, having a hooked nose] —**grif′fin·esque′,** *adj.*

grif·fin[2] (grif′in), *n.* (in India and the East) a newcomer, esp. a white person from a Western country. [?] —**grif′fin·age, grif′fin·hood′, grif′fin·ism,** *n.* —**grif′fin·ish,** *adj.*

Griffin[1]

Grif·fin (grif′in), *n.* **1.** a city in W Georgia. 21,735 (1960). **2.** a boy's given name.

Grif·fith (grif′ith), *n.* **1. D(avid Lewelyn) W(ark)** (wûrk), 1875–1948, U.S. motion-picture producer and director. **2.** a town in NW Indiana. 9483 (1960). **3.** a boy's given name, form of **Griffin.**

grif·fon[1] (grif′ən), *n.* a vulture of the genus *Gyps,* esp. *G. fulvus,* of southern Europe. [< F; see GRIFFIN[1]]

grif·fon[2] (grif′ən), *n.* **1.** any of several varieties of the Brussels griffon differing from each other in coloration or in the texture of the coat. Cf. **Belgian griffon, Brabançon, Brussels griffon. 2.** Also called **wire-haired pointing griffon.** one of a Dutch breed of medium-sized dogs having a coarse, steel-gray or grayish-white coat with chestnut markings, used for pointing and retrieving birds. [< F; akin to GRIFFIN[1]]

grif·fon[3] (grif′ən), *n.* *Class. Myth.* griffin[1].

grift (grift), *Slang.* —*n.* **1.** (*sometimes construed as pl.*) a group of methods for obtaining money falsely through the use of swindles, frauds, dishonest gambling, etc. **2.** money obtained from such practices. —*v.i.* **3.** to profit by the use of grift: *a man known to have grifted for many years.* —*v.t.* **4.** to obtain (money or other profit) by grift. [perh. alter. of GRAFT[2]]

grift·er (grif′tər), *n.* **1.** a person who manages a side show at a circus, fair, etc., esp. a gambling attraction. **2.** *Slang.* a swindler, dishonest gambler, or the like. [GRIFT + -ER[1]]

grig (grig), *n.* *Chiefly Dial.* **1.** a cricket or grasshopper. **2.** a small or young eel. **3.** a lively person. [ME *grig, grege,* perh. < Scand; cf. Sw (dial.) *krik* a little creature, Norw *krek* a crawling creature]

Gri·gnard (grēn yärd′; *Fr.* grē nyAR′), *n.* **(François Au·guste) Vic·tor** (fräN swA′ ō gyst′ vēk tôr′), 1871–1935, French organic chemist: Nobel prize 1912.

Grignard′ reac′tion, *Chem.* the reaction of a Grignard reagent with any of the numerous types of compounds with which it can combine, as alcohols, acids, aldehydes, ketones, or esters: used chiefly in organic synthesis.

Grignard′ rea′gent, *Chem.* any of the group of reagents produced by the interaction of magnesium and an organic halide, usually in the presence of an ether, and having the general formula RMgX, where R is an organic group and X is a halogen: used in the Grignard reaction.

gri·gri[1] (grē′grē), *n., pl.* **-gris.** an African charm, amulet, or fetish. Also, **greegree.** [of Afr orig.]

gri·gri[2] (grē′grē), *n., pl.* **-gris.** grugru (def. 1).

grill[1] (gril), *n.* **1.** a grated utensil for broiling meat, fish, vegetables, etc., over a fire; gridiron. **2.** a dish of grilled meat, fish, etc. **3.** grillroom. **4.** *Philately.* a group of small pyramidal marks, embossed or impressed in parallel rows on certain U.S. and Peruvian stamps of the late 19th century to prevent erasure of cancellation marks. —*v.t.* **5.** to broil on a gridiron or other apparatus over or before a fire. **6.** to torment with heat. **7.** to mark with a series of parallel bars like those of a grill. **8.** *Informal.* to subject to severe and persistent cross-examination or questioning. —*v.i.* **9.** to undergo broiling. [< F *gril* gridiron << L *crāticul(um),* dim. of *crātis* wickerwork, hurdle. See GRILLE] —**grill′er,** *n.*
—**Syn. 5.** barbecue. **6.** torture. **8.** interrogate, probe.

grill[2] (gril), *n.* grille.

gril·lade (gri lād′; *Fr.* grē yAd′), *n., pl.* **gril·lades** (gri lādz′; *Fr.* grē yAd′), *v.,* **-lad·ed, -lad·ing.** —*n.* **1.** a dish or serving of broiled or grilled meat. **2.** the act of grilling. —*v.t.* **3.** *Obs.* to grill or broil (meat). [< F: something grilled, equiv. to OF *grille* GRILL[1] + *-ade* -ADE[1]]

gril·lage (gril′ij), *n.* a framework of crossing beams used for spreading heavy loads over large areas. Also called **grid.** [< F; see GRILLE, -AGE]

grille (gril), *n.* **1.** a grating or openwork barrier, as for a gate, usually of metal and often of decorative design. **2.** an opening, usually covered by grillwork, for admitting air to cool the engine of an automobile or the like; radiator grille. **3.** any of various perforated screens, sheets, etc., used to cover something, as on a radio for protecting the amplifier or in cryptography for coding purposes. **4.** a ticket window covered by a grating. **5.** *Court Tennis.* a square-shaped winning opening on the hazard side of the court. Also, **grill.** Cf. **dedans** (def. 1), **winning gallery.** [< F, OF < LL *graticula, L crāticula (cf. OPr grazilha), dim. of crātis] —**grilled,** *adj.*

Grille

gril·lé (*Fr.* grē yā′), *adj.* **1.** cooked on a grill; broiled. **2.** *Textiles.* having an ornamental bar or grate pattern across the open areas of a lace motif. Also, **gril·lée′.** [< F: grilled; see GRILLE]

Grill·par·zer (gril′pärt′sər), *n.* **Franz** (fränts), 1791–1872, Austrian poet and dramatist.

grill·room (gril′rōōm′, -rŏŏm′), *n.* a room or restaurant where meats or other foods are grilled and served. [GRILL[1] + ROOM]

grill·work (gril′wûrk′), *n.* material so formed as to function as or have the appearance of a grill. [GRILL[1] + WORK]

grilse (grils), *n., pl.* **grils·es,** (*esp. collectively*) **grilse.** a mature, undersized, male salmon returning to fresh water, usually after one year of sea life, to spawn for the first time. [ME *grills, grilles* (pl.) < ?]

grim (grim), *adj.*, **grim·mer, grim·mest.** **1.** stern and admitting of no appeasement or compromise: *grim determination; grim necessity.* **2.** of a sinister or ghastly character; repellent: *a grim joke.* **3.** having a harsh, surly, forbidding, or morbid air: *a grim man but a just one; a grim countenance.* **4.** fierce, savage, or cruel: *War is a grim business.* [ME, OE; c. OS, OHG *grimm,* OIcel *grimmr*] —**grim′ly,** *adv.* —**grim′ness,** *n.*
—**Syn. 1.** harsh, unyielding. **2.** frightful, horrible, dire, appalling, horrid, grisly, gruesome, hideous, dreadful. **3.** severe, stern, hard. **4.** ferocious, ruthless. —**Ant. 1.** lenient. **2.** attractive. **3.** gentle.

grim·ace (grim′əs, gri mās′), *n., v.,* **-maced, -mac·ing.** —*n.* **1.** a facial expression, often ugly or contorted, that indicates disapproval, pain, etc. —*v.i.* **2.** to make grimaces. [< F < Sp *grimazo* panic, fear, deriv. of *grima* fright < Goth] —**grim′ac·er,** *n.* —**grim′ac·ing·ly,** *adv.*

Gri·mal·di (gri mäl′dē, -môl′-), *n.* **1. Joseph,** 1779–1837, English actor, mime, and clown. **2.** a walled plain in the third quadrant of the face of the moon having a dark floor: about 120 miles in diameter.

Gri·mal·di·an (gri mäl′dē ən, -môl′-), *adj.* of, pertaining to, or characteristic of an Upper Paleolithic cultural epoch in northwestern Italy. [after the *Grimaldi* caves, Italy + -AN]

gri·mal·kin (gri mal′kin, -môl′-), *n.* **1.** a cat. **2.** an old female cat. **3.** an ill-tempered old woman. [appar. alter. of GRAY + *malkin,* dim. of *Maud* proper name]

grime (grīm), *n., v.,* **grimed, grim·ing.** —*n.* **1.** dirt or foul matter, esp. lying upon or embedded in a surface. —*v.t.* **2.** to cover with dirt; soil; make very dirty. [appar. special use of OE *grīma* mask to denote layer of dust; cf. Flem *grijm*]

Grimes′ Gold′en (grīmz), an edible yellow apple maturing in late autumn. [named after Thomas P. *Grimes* of West Virginia]

Grimes′ Grave′, any of the pits in Suffolk, England, mined in Neolithic times for flint. [?]

Grim·hild (grim′hild), *n.* (in the *Volsunga Saga*) a sorceress, the wife of Giuki and the mother of Gudrun and Gunnar. She gave Sigurd a potion to make him forget Brynhild so that he would marry Gudrun.

Grimm (grim), *n.* **Ja·kob Lud·wig Karl** (yä′kop lo͞ot′vıкн kärl, lo͞od′-), 1785–1863, and his brother **Wil·helm Karl** (vil′helm), 1786–1859, German philologists and folklorists.

Grimm's′ law′, *Ling.* the statement of the regular pattern of consonant correspondences presumed to represent changes from Proto-Indo-European to Germanic, according to which voiced aspirated stops became voice obstruents, voiced unaspirated stops became unvoiced stops, and unvoiced stops became unvoiced fricatives, first formulated in 1820–22 by Jakob Grimm.

Grim′ Reap′er, reaper (def. 3).

Grims·by (grimz′bē), *n.* a seaport in NE Lincolnshire, in E England at the mouth of the Humber estuary. 96,665 (1961).

grim·y (grī′mē), *adj.,* **grim·i·er, grim·i·est.** covered with grime; dirty. [GRIME + -Y[1]] —**grim′i·ly,** *adv.* —**grim′i·ness,** *n.*

grin[1] (grin), *v.,* **grinned, grin·ning,** *n.* —*v.i.* **1.** to smile broadly, esp. as an indication of pleasure, amusement, or the like. **2.** to draw back the lips so as to show the teeth, as a snarling dog or a person in pain. **3.** to separate or part. **4.** to show or be exposed through an opening, crevice, etc. —*v.t.* **5.** to express or produce by grinning: *The little boy grinned his approval of the treat.* —*n.* **6.** the act of producing a broad smile, or the smile itself. **7.** the act of withdrawing the lips and showing the teeth. [ME *grinn(en), grenn(en),* OE *grennian;* c. OHG *grennan* to mutter] —**grin′ner,** *n.* —**grin′ning·ly,** *adv.*
—**Syn. 1.** See **laugh.**

grin[2] (grin), *n., v.,* **grinned, grin·ning.** —*n.* **1.** *Chiefly Scot.* a snare like a running noose. —*v.t.* **2.** to catch in a nooselike snare. [ME *grin(e),* OE *grin, gryn*]

grind (grīnd), *v.,* **ground** or (*Rare*) **grind·ed; grind·ing;** *n.* —*v.t.* **1.** to wear, smooth, or sharpen by abrasion or friction; whet: *to grind a lens; to grind an ax.* **2.** to reduce to fine particles, as by pounding or crushing; bray, triturate, or pulverize. **3.** to oppress; torment; torture; harass: *to grind the faces of the poor.* **4.** to rub harshly or gratingly; grate together; grit: *to grind one's teeth.* **5.** to operate by turning a crank: *to grind a hand organ.* **6.** to produce by crushing or abrasion: *to grind flour.* —*v.i.* **7.** to perform the operation of reducing to fine particles. **8.** to rub harshly; grate. **9.** to be or become ground. **10.** to be polished or sharpened by friction. **11.** *Informal.* to work or study laboriously (often fol. by *away*): *He was grinding away at his algebra.* **12.** (in a dance) to rotate the hips in a suggestive manner. Cf. **bump** (def. 10). —*n.* **13.** the act of grinding. **14.** a grinding sound. **15.** laborious, usually uninteresting work: *Copying out the footnotes was a scholarly grind.* **16.** *Slang.* a student who studies with unrelieved diligence. **17.** a dance movement in which the hips are rotated in a suggestive manner. Cf. **bump** (def. 21). [ME *grind(en),* OE *grindan;* akin to Goth *grinda-,* L *frendere*] —**grind′a·ble,** *adj.* —**grind′ing·ly,** *adv.*
—**Syn. 2.** crush, powder, comminute, pound. **3.** persecute, plague, afflict, trouble. **4.** abrade.

grin·de·li·a (grin dē′lē ə, -dēl′yə), *n.* **1.** any of the coarse, yellow-flowered asteraceous herbs of the genus *Grindelia.* **2.** the dried leaves and tops of certain species of this plant, used in medicine. [named after D.H. *Grindel* (1777–1836), Russian scientist; see -IA]

grind·er (grīn′dər), *n.* **1.** one who or that which grinds. **2.** a sharpener of tools. **3.** a molar tooth. **4.** See **hero sandwich. 5. grinders,** the teeth. [GRIND + -ER[1]]

grind·er·y (grīn′də rē), *n., pl.* **-er·ies. 1.** a workshop for grinding edge tools. **2.** *Brit.* **a.** a shoemaker's or leatherworker's material and equipment. **b.** a shop where such material and equipment may be purchased. [GRIND + -ERY]

grind′ing wheel′, a wheel composed of abrasive material, used for grinding.

grin·dle (grin′dəl), *n.* bowfin. [< G *Gründel,* dim. of *Grund* ground, bottom]

grind·stone (grīnd′stōn′), *n.* **1.** a rotating solid stone wheel used for sharpening, shaping, etc. **2.** a millstone. [ME; see GRIND, STONE]

grin·go (griŋ′gō), *n., pl.* **-gos.** *Disparaging.* (among Spanish-Americans) a foreigner, esp. one from the U.S. [< Sp: foreigner, special use of *griego* a Greek]

Grin·nell (gri nel′), *n.* a town in SE Iowa. 7367 (1960).

grip (grip), *n., v.,* **gripped** or **gript, grip·ping.** —*n.* **1.** the act of grasping; a seizing and holding fast; firm grasp. **2.** the power of gripping: *He has a strong grip.* **3.** a grasp, hold, or control. **4.** a small suitcase. **5.** mental or intellectual hold: *to have a good grip on a problem.* **6.** competence or firmness in dealing with situations in one's work or personal affairs: *The work is still good, mind you, but the boss is old and is losing his grip.* **7.** a special mode of clasping hands: *Once you are a member of the club, you can use the secret grip.* **8.** something which seizes and holds, as a clutching device on a cable car. **9.** a handle or hilt: *That knife has a very unusual grip.* **10.** a sudden, sharp pain; spasm of pain. **11.** grippe. **12.** *Slang.* **a.** *Theat.* a stagehand, esp. one who works on the stage floor. **b.** *Motion Pictures, Television.* a stagehand in the studio who works for the camera crew, changes the set, etc. **13. come to grips with, a.** to encounter; meet; cope with: *He had never come to grips with such a situation before.* **b.** to deal with directly or firmly: *We couldn't come to grips with the real problem.* —*v.t.* **14.** to grasp or seize firmly; hold fast: *We gripped the sides of the boat as the waves tossed us about.* **15.** to take hold on; hold the interest of: *to grip the mind.* **16.** to attach by a grip or clutch. —*v.i.* **17.** to take firm hold; hold fast. **18.** to take hold on the mind. [ME, OE *gripe* grasp; c. G *Griff,* OE *gripa* handful; see GRIPE] —**grip′less,** *adj.*

gripe (grīp), *v.,* **griped, grip·ing,** *n.* —*v.t.* **1.** to seize and hold firmly; grip; grasp; clutch. **2.** to distress or oppress. **3.** to produce pain in (the bowels) as if by constriction. **4.** *Naut.* to secure (a boat) to a deck or against a pudding boom on davits. —*v.i.* **5.** to grasp or clutch, as a miser. **6.** to suffer pain in the bowels. **7.** *Informal.* to complain naggingly or constantly; grumble. **8.** *Naut.* (of a sailing vessel) to tend to come into the wind; to be ardent. —*n.* **9.** the act of gripping, grasping, or clutching. **10.** a firm hold; clutch. **11.** a grasp; hold; control. **12.** that which grips or clutches; a claw or grip. **13.** *U.S. Informal.* complaint. **14.** *Naut.* **a.** a lashing or chain by which a boat is secured to a deck or in position on davits. **b.** Also called **gripe′ piece′.** a curved timber connecting the stem or cutwater of a wooden hull with the keel. **c.** the exterior angle or curve formed by this piece; forefoot. **d.** the forward end of the dished keel of a metal hull. **15.** a handle, hilt, etc. **16.** Usually, **gripes.** *Pathol.* an intermittent spasmodic pain in the bowels. [ME *grip(en),* OE *grīpan;* c. D *grijpen,* G *griefen;* see GRIP, GROPE] —**grip′er,** *n.* —**gripe′ful,** *adj.* —**grip′ing·ly,** *adv.*

grip·ey (grī′pē), *adj.,* **grip·i·er, grip·i·est.** gripy.

grip·man (grip′mən), *n., pl.* **-men.** a workman on a cable car who operates the grip, which, by grasping or releasing the moving cable, starts or stops the car. [GRIP + MAN[1]]

grippe (grip), *n. Pathol.* influenza. [< F, deriv. of *gripper* to seize suddenly] —**gripp′al,** *adj.* —**grippe′like′,** *adj.*

grip·per (grip′ər), *n.* **1.** one who or that which grips. **2.** a large snap fastener used esp. on children's clothing and on sportswear. **3.** *Print.* (in certain presses) one of a number of fingerlike devices for gripping a sheet and transferring it to or from the printing surface. **4.** *Metalworking.* dog (def. 14). [GRIP + -ER[1]]

grip·ping (grip′iŋ), *adj.* holding the attention or interest; fascinating; enthralling: *a gripping play; a gripping book.* [GRIP + -ING[2]] —**grip′ping·ly,** *adv.* —**grip′ping·ness,** *n.*

grip·ple (grip′əl), *adj. Brit. Dial.* miserly; avaricious. [b. GRIP and GRAPPLE]

grip·py (grip′ē), *adj.,* **-pi·er, -pi·est.** *Informal.* afflicted with the grippe. [GRIPPE + -Y[1]]

grip·sack (grip′sak′), *n.* a traveling bag; grip. [GRIP + SACK[1]]

gript (gript), *v.* a pp. and pt. of **grip.**

grip·y (grī′pē), *adj.,* **grip·i·er, grip·i·est.** resembling or causing gripes. Also, **gripey.** [GRIPE + -Y[1]]

Gri·qua (grē′kwə, grik′wə), *n.* a South African half-breed. [< SAfrD *Griekwa*]

Gris (grēs), *n.* **Juan** (hwän), (*José Vittoriano González*), 1887–1927, Spanish painter in France.

gri·saille (gri zī′, -zāl′; *Fr.* grē zä′yᵊ), *n., pl.* **-sailles** (-zīz′, -zālz′; *Fr.* -zä′yᵊ) for 2. **1.** monochromatic painting in shades of gray. **2.** a work of art, as a painting or stained-glass window, executed in grisaille. [< F: painted in gray monotone, equiv. to *gris* gray + *-aille* n. suffix]

Gri·sel·da (gri zel′də), *n.* **1.** a woman of exemplary meekness and patience. **2.** a girl's given name.

Gri·sel·dis (gri sel′dis, -zel′-), *n.* a girl's given name, form of **Griselda.**

gris·e·ous (gris′ē əs, griz′-), *adj.* gray; pearl-gray. [< ML *griseus* bluish-gray; see -EOUS]

gri·sette (gri zet′), *n.* a French working girl or salesgirl. [< F, equiv. to *gris* gray + *-ette* -ETTE] —**gri·set′tish,** *adj.*

gris·kin (gris′kin), *n. Brit.* **1.** a chop or steak, esp. a pork chop. **2.** *Archaic.* a pork loin, esp. the lean part. [GRICE + -KIN]

gris·ly[1] (griz′lē), *adj.,* **-li·er, -li·est. 1.** causing a shudder or feeling of horror; horrible; gruesome: *a grisly monster.* **2.** formidable; grim: *a grisly countenance.* [ME; OE *grislīc* horrible; c. OHG *grīsenlīh*] —**gris′li·ness,** *n.*

gris·ly[2] (gris′lē), *adj.,* **-li·er, -li·est.** *Obs.* gristly.

gri·son (grī′sən, griz′ən), *n.* a musteline carnivore, *Grison vittata,* of South and Central America, having the upper surface of the body grayish-white and the lower dark-brown. [< F, equiv. to MF *gris* gray + *-on* dim. suffix]

Gri·sons (grē zôɴ′), *n.* a canton in E Switzerland. 147,458 (1960). 2747 sq. mi. *Cap.:* Chur. German, **Graubünden.**

Gris·sel (gris′əl), *n.* a girl's given name, form of **Griselda.** Also, **Grizel, Grizzel, Grizzle.**

grist (grist), *n.* **1.** grain to be ground. **2.** ground grain; meal produced from grinding. **3.** a quantity of grain for grinding at one time; the amount of meal from one grinding. **4.** *Chiefly U.S. Dial.* a quantity or lot. **5. grist to one's mill,** something employed to one's profit or advantage, esp. something seemingly unpromising: *Every delay was so much more grist to his mill.* [ME, OE; akin to OE *grindan* to GRIND] —**grist′er,** *n.*

gris·tle (gris′əl), *n.* cartilage. [ME, OE; c. OFris, MLG *gristal;* akin to OE *grost* cartilage]

gris·tly (gris′lē), *adj.,* **-tli·er, -tli·est.** resembling or containing gristle; cartilaginous. [ME; see GRISTLE, -Y[1]] —**gris·tli·ness** (gris′lē nis), *n.*

grist·mill (grist′mil′), *n.* a mill for grinding grain, esp. the customer's own grain. [GRIST + MILL[1]] —**grist′mill′er,** *n.* —**grist′mill′ing,** *n.*

Gris·wold (griz′wôld, -wəld), *n.* **1. Erwin Nathaniel,** born 1904, U.S. lawyer and educator: dean of Harvard University Law School since 1950. **2.** a boy's given name.

grit (grit), *n., v.,* **grit·ted, grit·ting.** —*n.* **1.** fine, abrasive particles, as those deposited in the form of dust from the air or occurring as impurities in food, water, etc. **2.** firmness of character; indomitable spirit; pluck: *One thing I'll say for him, he has grit.* **3.** a coarse-grained siliceous rock, usually with sharp, angular grains. **4.** sand or other fine grainy particles eaten by fowl to aid in digestion. —*v.t.* **5.** to grate or grind: *to grit the teeth.* —*v.i.* **6.** to make a scratchy or slightly grating sound, as of sand being walked on; grate. [ME *gret, griet, grit,* OE *greōt;* c. G *Griess,* OIcel *grjōt* pebble, boulder; see GRITS] —**grit′less,** *adj.* —**grit′ter,** *n.*
—**Syn. 2.** resolution, fortitude, courage. **3.** sand, gravel.

grith (grith), *n. Chiefly Scot.* protection or asylum for a limited period of time, as under church or crown. [ME, OE < Scand; cf. OIcel *grith* home; in pl.: peace, security]

grits (grits), *n.* (*construed as sing. or pl.*) **1.** grain hulled and coarsely ground. **2.** *Chiefly Southern U.S.* coarsely ground hominy. [ME *gryttes* (pl.), OE *gryt(t);* c. G *Grütze*]

grit·ty (grit′ē), *adj.,* **-ti·er, -ti·est. 1.** consisting of, containing, or resembling grit; sandy. **2.** resolute and courageous; plucky. [GRIT + -Y[1]] —**grit′ti·ly,** *adv.* —**grit′ti·ness,** *n.*

gri·va·tion (gri vā′shən, grī-), *n.* See **grid variation.** [GRI(D) + V(ARI)ATION]

griv·et (griv′it), *n.* a small Abyssinian monkey, *Cercopithecus aethiops,* with a grayish back, gray tail, black face, and dark extremities. [?]

Griz·el (griz′əl), *n.* a girl's given name, form of **Griselda.** Also, **Grissel, Griz′zel, Griz′zle.**

griz·zle[1] (griz′əl), *v.,* **-zled, -zling,** *adj., n.* —*v.i., v.t.* **1.** to become or make gray. —*adj.* **2.** gray; devoid of hue. —*n.* **3.** gray hair. **4.** a gray wig. [ME *grisel* < OF, deriv. of *gris* gray < Gmc; cf. G *greis* gray, hoary]

griz·zle[2] (griz′əl), *v.i.,* **-zled, -zling.** *Brit.* **1.** to complain; whimper; whine. **2.** to sneer; laugh or grin in mockery. [cf. MHG *grisgramen* to gnash one's teeth, G *Griesgram* sourpuss] —**griz′zler,** *n.*

griz·zled (griz′əld), *adj.* **1.** gray-haired. **2.** gray. [GRIZZLE[1] + -ED[3]]

griz·zling (griz′liŋ), *n. Brit.* the act of complaining or whimpering. [GRIZZLE[2] + -ING[1]]

griz·zly (griz′lē), *adj.,* **-zli·er, -zli·est,** *n., pl.* **-zlies.** —*adj.* **1.** somewhat gray; grayish. **2.** gray-haired. —*n.* **3.** See **grizzly bear. 4.** a device for screening ore, consisting of a row of iron or steel bars. [GRIZZLE[1] + -Y[1]]

Grizzly bear
(3 to 3½ ft. high at shoulder; length 6 to 8½ ft.)

griz′zly bear′, a large, ferocious bear, *Ursus horribilis,* of western North America, varying in color from grayish to brownish.

gro., gross (def. 8).

groan (grōn), *n.* **1.** a low, mournful sound uttered in pain or grief: *the groans of dying soldiers.* **2.** a deep, inarticulate sound uttered in derision, disapproval, desire, etc. **3.** a deep grating or creaking sound due to a sudden or continued overburdening, as with a great weight: *We heard the groan of the ropes as the crane lowered the heavy cargo into the ship's hold.* —*v.i.* **4.** to utter a deep, mournful sound expressive of pain or grief; moan. **5.** to make a deep, inarticulate sound expressive of derision, disapproval, or desire. **6.** to make a sound resembling a groan; resound harshly: *The steps of the old house groaned under my weight.* **7.** to be overburdened or overloaded. **8.** to suffer greatly or lamentably: *groaning under an intolerable burden.* —*v.t.* **9.** to utter or salute with groans. [ME *gron(en),* OE *grānian;* c. G *greinen* to whine] —**groan′er,** *n.* —**groan′ing·ly,** *adv.*
—**Syn. 1.** GROAN, MOAN refer to sounds indicating deep suffering. A GROAN is a brief, strong, deep-throated sound emitted involuntarily under pressure of pain or suffering: *The wounded man groaned when they lifted him.* A MOAN is a prolonged, more or less continuous, low, inarticulate sound indicative of suffering, either physical or mental: *She was moaning after the operation. She did not weep but moaned softly.*

groat (grōt), *n.* a silver coin of England, equal to four pennies, issued from 1279 to 1662. [ME *groat* < D: lit., large (coin)]

groats (grōts), *n.* (*construed as sing. or pl.*) **1.** hulled grain, as wheat or oats, broken into fragments. **2.** hulled kernels of oats, buckwheat, or barley. [ME *grotes* (pl.), OE *grot* meal; akin to GRITS]

gro·cer (grō′sər), *n.* a dealer in general supplies for the table, as flour, sugar, coffee, etc., and in other articles of household use. [ME < OF *gross(i)er* wholesale merchant. See GROSS, -ER[2]]

gro·cer·y (grō′sə rē), *n., pl.* **-cer·ies. 1.** *U.S.* a grocer's store. **2.** Usually, **groceries.** food and other commodities sold by a grocer. **3.** the business of a grocer. [ME *grocerie* < OF *grosserie.* See GROSS, -ERY]

gro·cer·y·man (grō′sə rē mən, -man′), *n., pl.* **-men** (-mən, -men′). one who deals in groceries; grocer. [GROCERY + MAN[1]]

Grod·no (grôd′nō), *n.* a city in W Byelorussia, in the W Soviet Union in Europe, on the Niemen River: formerly in Poland. 72,000 (1959).

Groe·nen·dael (gro͞o′nən däl′, grō′-, grā′-, gren′ən-), *n.* a Belgian sheepdog having a long, black coat. [after the village in Belgium where it was bred]

Groete (*Du.* ᴋʜʀo͞o′tə; *Eng.* grōt), *n.* **Ger·hard** (*Du.* ᴋʜā′ʀäʀt; *Eng.* gâr′härt). See **Groote, Gerhard.**

Gro·fé (grō′fā), *n.* **Fer·de** (fûr′dē), born 1892, U.S. composer.

grog (grog), *n.* **1.** a mixture of alcoholic liquor and water. **2.** strong drink. **3.** *Ceram.* fired and crushed clay. [from Old *Grog*, (alluding to his *grogram* cloak) the nickname of Edward Vernon (d. 1757), British admiral, who in 1740 ordered the alcoholic mixture to be served, instead of pure spirits, to sailors.]

grog·ger·y (grog′ə rē), *n., pl.* **-ger·ies.** a slightly disreputable barroom. [ɢʀᴏɢ + -ᴇʀʏ]

grog·gy (grog′ē), *adj.,* **-gi·er, -gi·est.** **1.** *Informal.* **a.** staggering, as from exhaustion or blows: *a boxer groggy from his opponent's hard left jab.* **b.** dazed and weakened, as from lack of sleep: *Late nights always make me groggy the next morning.* **2.** *Archaic.* drunk; intoxicated. [ɢʀᴏɢ + -ʏ[1]] **—grog′gi·ly,** *adv.* **—grog′gi·ness,** *n.*

grog′ lift′er. See **punch lifter.**

grog·ram (grog′rəm), *n.* a coarse fabric of silk, of silk and mohair or wool, or of wool, formerly in use. [< MF *gros grain.* See ɢʀᴏsɢʀᴀɪɴ]

grog·shop (grog′shop′), *n.* *Brit.* a saloon or barroom, esp. a cheap one. [ɢʀᴏɢ + sʜᴏᴘ]

groin (groin), *n.* **1.** *Anat.* the fold or hollow on either side of the body where the thigh joins the abdomen. **2.** *Archit.* the curved line or edge formed by the intersection of two vaults. See illus. under **vault**[1]. **3.** Also, **groyne.** a small jetty extending from a shore to prevent beach erosion. **—*v.t.*** **4.** *Archit.* to form with groins. [earlier *grine*, ME *grinde*; cf. OE *grynde* abyss, akin to *grund* bottom, ɢʀᴏᴜɴᴅ[1]]

groin·ing (groi′ning), *n.* **1.** the intersection of two vaults. **2.** the construction of groined vaults.

Gro·li·er (grō′lē ər; *Fr.* gʀô lyā′), *adj.* *Bookbinding.* pertaining to a decorative design **(Gro′lier design′)** in bookbinding, consisting of bands interlaced in geometric forms. [named after J. Gʀᴏʟɪᴇʀ ᴅᴇ Sᴇʀᴠɪᴇʀᴇs]

Gro·lier de Ser·vières (gʀô lyā′ də sᴇʀ vyᴇʀ′), **Jean** (zhäɴ), 1479–1565, French bibliophile.

gro·ma (grō′mə), *n.* (in ancient Roman surveying) an instrument having a cruciform wooden frame with a plumb line at the end of each arm, used for laying out lines at right angles to existing lines. [< LL *grōma* surveyor's pole, measuring-rod (sp. var. of *grūma*)]

grom·met (grom′it), *n.* **1.** *Mach.* **a.** any of various rings or eyelets of metal or the like. **b.** an insulated washer of rubber or plastic, inserted in a hole in a metal part to prevent grounding of a wire passing through the hole. **2.** *Naut.* **a.** a ring or strop of fiber or wire; becket. **b.** a ring having a thickness of three strands, made by forming a loop of a single strand, then laying the ends around the loop. **c.** a ring of fiber used as a seal or gasket, as under the head of a bolt. **3.** a washer or packing for sealing joints between sections of pipe. **4.** *U.S. Mil.* a stiff ring of rubber or metal inside the top of a service cap, designed to keep the top of the cap stretched flat. Also, **grummet.** [< obs. F *gromette* curb of bridle << L *grum(us)* throat]

grom·well (grom′wəl), *n.* any boraginaceous plant of the genus *Lithospermum*, having varicolored flowers and smooth, stony nutlets. [ME *gromil* < OF < L *grumum (milium)* grain (millet)]

Gro·my·ko (grō mē′kō, grə-; *Russ.* gʀᴏ mē′ko), *n.* **An·drei An·dre·ie·vich** (än dʀā′ än dre′yə vich), born 1909, Russian diplomat.

Gron·chi (grông′kē; *It.* gʀôn′kē), *n.* **Gio·van·ni** (jô vän′nē), born 1887, Italian statesman: president 1955–62.

Gro·ning·en (grō′ning ən; *Du.* ᴋʜʀō′ning ən), *n.* a city in the NE Netherlands. 149,486 (1962).

groom (gro͞om, gro͝om), *n.* **1.** a man or boy in charge of horses or the stable. **2.** a bridegroom. **3.** any of several officers of the English royal household. **4.** *Archaic.* a manservant. **—*v.t.*** **5.** to tend carefully as to person and dress; make neat or tidy. **6.** to tend (horses). **7.** to prepare for a position, election, etc.: *to groom a political candidate.* [ME *grom* boy, groom; appar. akin to ɢʀᴏᴡ] **—groom′er,** *n.* **—groom′ish,** *adj.* **—groom′ish·ly,** *adv.*

groom's′ cake′, a fruit cake in layers of graduated size, served at a wedding.

grooms·man (gro͞omz′mən, gro͝omz′-), *n., pl.* **-men.** a man who attends the bridegroom in a wedding ceremony. [ɢʀᴏᴏᴍ + -'s[1] + ᴍᴀɴ[1]]

Groot (*Du.* ᴋʜʀōt; *Eng.* grōt), *n.* **1. Huig** (*Du.* hoikh) **de** (də) or **van** (vän). See **Grotius, Hugo.** **2. Gerhard.** See **Groote, Gerhard.**

Groote (*Du.* ᴋʜʀō′tə; *Eng.* grōt), *n.* **Ger·hard** (*Du.* ᴋʜā′ʀäʀt; *Eng.* gâr′härt), (*Gerardus Magnus*), 1340–84, Dutch religious reformer, educator, and author: founder of the order of Brethren of the Common Life. Also, **Groot, Groete.**

groove (gro͞ov), *n., v.,* **grooved, groov·ing.** **—*n.*** **1.** a long, narrow cut or indentation occurring in a surface or formed there by some means or agency. **2.** the track or channel of a phonograph record for the needle or stylus. **3.** a fixed routine: *to get into a groove.* **4.** *Print.* the furrow at the bottom of a piece of type. See diag. under **type.** **5. in the groove,** *Slang.* **a.** in perfect functioning order. **b.** in the popular fashion; up-to-date: *If you want to be in the groove this summer, you'll need a bikini.* **—*v.t.*** **6.** to cut a groove in; furrow. **7.** to fix in a groove. [ME *grofe, groof* mining shaft; c. MD *groeve,* D *groef,* G *Grube* pit, ditch; akin to ɢʀᴀᴠᴇ[1]] **—groove′less,** *adj.* **—groove′like′,** *adj.* **—groov′er,** *n.*

grooved (gro͞ovd), *v.* **1.** pt. and pp. of **groove.** **—*adj.*** **2.** provided with a groove. [ɢʀᴏᴏᴠᴇ + -ᴇᴅ[2]]

groov′ing plane′, *Carpentry.* a plane for cutting grooves across grain. Also called **trenching plane.**

groov·y (gro͞o′vē), *adj.,* **groov·i·er, groov·i·est.** **1.** inclined to follow a fixed routine. **2.** *Slang.* highly stimulating or attractive: *groovy swing music; a groovy red racing car.* [ɢʀᴏᴏᴠᴇ + -ʏ[1]]

grope (grōp), *v.,* **groped, grop·ing.** **—*v.i.*** **1.** to feel about with the hands; feel one's way: *I had to grope around in the darkness for a while before I found the light switch.* **2.** to search blindly or uncertainly: *He seemed to be groping for an answer to the question.* **—*v.t.*** **3.** to seek by or as by feeling: *We watched the drunk grope his way up the stairs.* [ME *grop(ien),* OE *grāpian,* deriv. of *grāp* grasp; akin to ɢʀɪᴘᴇ, ɢʀᴀsᴘ] **—grop′er,** *n.*

grop·ing (grō′ping), *adj.* **1.** moving or going about clumsily or hesitantly; stumbling: *the groping progress of the blind.* **2.** showing or reflecting a desire to understand, esp. something that proves puzzling: *a groping scrutiny; groping expression.* [ME; see ɢʀᴏᴘᴇ, -ɪɴɢ[2]] **—grop′ing·ly,** *adv.*

Gro·pi·us (grō′pē əs; *Ger.* gʀō′pē o͝os′), *n.* **Wal·ter** (wôl′tər; *Ger.* väl′tᴇʀ), born 1883, German architect, in the U.S. since 1937.

Grop·per (grop′ər), *n.* **William,** born 1897, U.S. painter.

Gros (gʀō′), *n.* **An·toine Jean** (äɴ twaɴ′ zhäɴ), **Baron,** 1771–1835, French painter.

gros·beak (grōs′bēk′), *n.* any of various finches having a large, stout, conical bill. [< F *grosbec,* lit., large beak]

gro·schen (grō′shən), *n., pl.* **-schen.** **1.** a zinc coin of Austria, the 100th part of a schilling, equal to .0004 of a U.S. dollar. **2.** *Informal.* a German 10-pfennig piece made of nickel. **3.** any of the silver coins of various German regions first introduced in the 13th century as imitations of the French gros. [< G; MHG *grosse, grosze* < L (*denarius*) *grossus* thick (coin); akin to ɢʀᴏᴀᴛ]

gros de Lon·dres (grō′ də lôn′drə, lônd′; *Fr.* gʀō′ də lôɴ′dʀ[ə]), a cross-ribbed, silk dress fabric with ribs alternating in color or between coarse and fine yarn. [< F: lit., London gross; cf. ɢʀᴏsɢʀᴀɪɴ]

gros de Tours (grō′ də to͝or′; *Fr.* gʀō də to͞oʀ′), a ribbed silk fabric made with a two- or three-ply warp interlaced with organzine and tram filling. [< F: lit., Tours gross; cf. ɢʀᴏsɢʀᴀɪɴ]

gros·grain (grō′grān′), *n.* a heavy, corded ribbon or cloth of silk or rayon. [< F *gros grain* large grain] **—gros′grained′,** *adj.*

gros point (grō′ point′), *pl.* **gros points.** **1.** a large stitch used in embroidery. Cf. **petit point** (def. 1), **tent stitch.** **2.** Venetian point lace with raised work and large designs. [< F: large point]

gross (grōs), *adj., n., pl.* **gross** for 10, **gross·es** for 11; *v.* **—*adj.*** **1.** without deductions (opposed to *net*): *gross profits; gross sales.* **2.** unqualified; complete; rank: *a gross scoundrel.* **3.** flagrant and extreme: *gross injustice.* **4.** indelicate, indecent, obscene, or vulgar: *gross remarks.* **5.** lacking in refinement, good manners, education, etc.; unrefined. **6.** large, big, or bulky. **7.** extremely or excessively fat. **8.** thick; dense; heavy: *gross vegetation.* **9.** of or concerning only the broadest or most general considerations, aspects, etc. **—*n.*** **10.** a group of 12 dozen, or 144, things. *Abbr.:* gr, gr. **11.** *Obs.* the main body, bulk, or mass. **—*v.t.*** **12.** to make a gross profit of; earn a total of: *The company grossed over three million dollars last year.* [ME < OF *gros* large (as n., *grosse* twelve dozen) < LL *gross(us)* thick, coarse]
—Syn. 1. aggregate. **3.** shameful, outrageous, heinous, grievous. **4.** low, animal, sensual, broad. **6.** massive, great. **—Ant. 1.** partial. **4.** decent. **6.** delicate, small.

Gross (grōs), *n.* **Chaim** (ᴋʜīm), born 1904, U.S. sculptor and graphic artist, born in Austria.

Gross′ Clin′ic, The, a painting (1875) by Thomas Eakins.

Grosse Pointe (grōs′ point′, point′), a town in SE Michigan. 6631 (1960).

Grosse′ Pointe′ Park′, a city in SE Michigan, near Detroit. 15,457 (1960).

Grosse′ Pointe′ Woods′, a city in SE Michigan, near Detroit. 18,580 (1960).

gross′ na′tional prod′uct, the total monetary value of all final goods and services produced in a country during one year. *Abbr.:* GNP Cf. **national income, net national product.**

gross′ prof′it, gross receipts less the immediate cost of production.

gross′ reg′ister ton′nage, tonnage (def. 1).

gross′ ton′, **1.** a unit of measure equal to 2,240 pounds. **2.** *Naut.* Also called **gross′ reg′ister ton′.** See under **gross tonnage.**

gross′ ton′nage, *Naut.* the total volume of a vessel, expressed in units of 100 cubic feet **(gross ton),** with certain open structures, deckhouses, tanks, etc., exempted. Also called **gross register tonnage.**

gros·su·lar·ite (gros′yə lə rīt′), *n.* a mineral, calcium aluminum garnet, $Ca_3Al_2Si_3O_{12}$, occurring in gray-white to pinkish crystals. [< NL *grossulār(ia)* gooseberry (irreg. < F *groseille*) + -ɪᴛᴇ[1]]

Gross·war·dein (gʀōs′vär dīn′), *n.* German name of **Oradea.**

gross′ weight′, total weight without deduction for tare, tret, or waste.

Gros·ve·nor (grōv′nər), *n.* **Gilbert Hovey,** 1875–1966, U.S. geographer, writer, and editor.

grosz (gʀôsh), *n., pl.* **gro·szy** (gʀô′shē). an aluminum coin of Poland, the 100th part of a zloty, equivalent to about .0004 of a U.S. dollar. [< Pol < Czech *groš*; see ɢʀᴏsᴄʜᴇɴ]

Grosz (grōs), *n.* **George,** 1893–1959, U.S. painter and graphic artist, born in Germany.

grot (grot), *n.* *Chiefly Literary.* a grotto. [< F *grotte* < It *grott(a)*; see ɢʀᴏᴛᴛᴏ]

Grote (grōt), *n.* **George,** 1794–1871, English historian.

Gro·tesk (grō tesk′), *n.* (in Europe) Gothic (def. 10). [var. of ɢʀᴏᴛᴇsǫᴜᴇ]

gro·tesque (grō tesk′), *adj.* **1.** odd or unnatural in shape, appearance, or character; fantastically ugly or absurd; bizarre. **2.** of fantasy in the shaping and combination of forms, as in decorative work combining incongruous human and animal figures with scrolls, foliage, etc. **—*n.*** **3.** any grotesque object, design, or thing. [< F < It *grottesco* (as n., *grottesca* grotesque decoration such as was appar. found in excavated dwellings), deriv. of *grotta.* See ɢʀᴏᴛᴛᴏ, -ᴇsǫᴜᴇ] **—gro·tesque′ly,** *adv.* **—gro·tesque′ness,** *n.*

Grotesque work (16th century)

gro·tes·query (grō tes′kə rē), *n., pl.* **-quer·ies.** **1.** grotesque character. **2.** something grotesque. **3.** grotesque ornamental work. Also, **gro·tes′quer·ie.** [< F *grotesquerie.* See ɢʀᴏᴛᴇsǫᴜᴇ, -ᴇʀʏ]

Gro·tian (grō′shən, -shē ən), *adj.* of or pertaining to Hugo Grotius or his theories. [Gʀᴏᴛɪ(ᴜs) + -ᴀɴ] **—Gro′tian·ism,** *n.*

Gro·ti·us (grō′shē əs), *n.* **Hugo** (*Huig De Groot*), 1583–1645, Dutch jurist and statesman.

grot·to (grot′ō), *n., pl.* **-toes, -tos.** **1.** a cave or cavern. **2.** an artificial cavernlike recess or structure. [< It *grotto, grotta* < VL *crupta* subterranean passage, chamber, ᴄʀʏᴘᴛ] **—grot′toed,** *adj.* **—grot′to·like′,** *adj.*

grouch (grouch), *Informal.* **—*v.i.*** **1.** to be sulky or morose; show discontent; complain. **—*n.*** **2.** a sulky or morose person. **3.** a sulky or morose mood. [var. of obs. *grutch* < OF *grouch(er)* (to) grumble]

grouch·y (grou′chē), *adj.,* **grouch·i·er, grouch·i·est.** *Informal.* sullenly discontented; sulky; morose; ill-tempered. [ɢʀᴏᴜᴄʜ + -ʏ[1]] **—grouch′i·ly,** *adv.* **—grouch′i·ness,** *n.*

Grou·chy (gʀo͞o shē′), *n.* **Em·ma·nu·el** (e ᴍᴀ ɴʏ el′), **Marquis de,** 1766–1847, French general.

ground[1] (ground), *n.* **1.** the solid surface of the earth; firm or dry land: *to fall to the ground.* **2.** earth or soil: *stony ground.* **3.** land having an indicated character: *rising ground.* **4.** Often, **grounds. a.** a tract of land appropriated to a special use: *picnic grounds; baseball grounds.* **b.** the foundation or basis on which a theory or action rests; reason: *grounds for a statement.* **5.** subject for discussion; topic: *Careful, you're treading on delicate ground.* **6.** rational or factual support for one's position or attitude, as in a debate or argument: *on firm ground; on shaky ground.* **7.** the main surface or background in painting, decorative work, lace, etc. **8.** *Fine Arts.* **a.** a coating of some substance serving as a surface for paint, ink, or other media in art: *Lead white is a traditional ground for oil paintings.* **b.** See **ground color** (def. 2). **9.** Also called **etching ground.** an acid-resistant substance, composed of wax, gum, and resin in varying proportions, applied to the entire surface of an etching plate and through which the design is drawn with an etching needle. **10. grounds, a.** dregs or sediment: *coffee grounds.* **b.** the gardens, lawn, etc., surrounding and belonging to a building. **11.** *Elect.* a conducting connection between an electric circuit or equipment and the earth or some other conducting body. **12.** *Music.* See **ground bass.** **13.** *Naut.* the bottom of a body of water. **14.** the earth's solid or liquid surface; land or water. **15.** *Carpentry.* **a.** a strip of wood to which woodwork can be attached, set flush with the plaster finish of a room. **b.** a strip of wood or length of corner bead used at an opening as a stop for plasterwork. **16. break ground, a.** to plow. **b.** to begin excavation for a construction project. **c.** to begin upon or take preparatory measures for an undertaking. **17. cover ground, a.** to pass or travel over a certain area. **b.** to make a certain amount of progress in (a piece of work, subject, treatise, etc.); deal with: *He talked for two hours without covering any new ground.* **18. cut the ground from under someone,** to render (an argument, position, etc.) ineffective or invalid; refute: *It didn't require much effort to cut the ground from under that case.* Also, **cut the ground from under one's feet.** **19. from the ground up, a.** gradually from the most elementary level to the highest level: *He decided to learn the business from the ground up.* **b.** extensively; thoroughly: *The professor knew his subject from the ground up.* **20. gain ground, a.** to make progress; advance. **b.** to gain approval or acceptance: *The case for air-pollution control is gaining ground throughout the country.* **21. give ground,** to yield to force or forceful argument; retreat: *The disarmament talks reached an impasse when neither side would give ground on inspection proposals.* **22. hold** or **stand one's ground,** to maintain one's position; be steadfast: *The referee stood his ground, though his decision was hotly contested by the crowd.* **23. into the ground,** beyond a reasonable or necessary point (usually prec. by *run*): *You've stated your case, and you needn't run it into the ground.* **24. lose ground, a.** to lose one's advantage; suffer a reverse. **b.** to wane in popularity or acceptance; begin to fail: *Our candidate is losing ground in industrial areas.* **25. off the ground,** *Informal.* into action or well under way: *The play never got off the ground.* **26. on one's own ground,** in an area or situation that one knows well: *The only way to settle things is to meet the enemy on his own ground, since he won't come to you.* **27. on the ground,** at the place of interest or importance; actively engaged: *Minutes after the bank robbery reporters were on the ground to get the story.* **28. shift one's ground,** to change one's position in an argument or situation: *He shifted his ground whenever it seemed to his advantage to do so.* **29. suit down to the ground,** *Informal.* to be perfectly satisfactory; please greatly: *The climate suits me down to the ground.* **30. take the ground,** *Naut.* to become grounded at low water.
—*adj.* **31.** situated on or at, or adjacent to, the surface of the earth: *a ground attack.* **32.** pertaining to the ground. **33.** *Mil.* operating on land: *ground forces.*
—*v.t.* **34.** to lay or set on the ground. **35.** to place on a foundation; found; fix firmly; settle or establish. **36.** to instruct in elements or first principles. **37.** to furnish with a ground or background, as on decorative work. **38.** to cover (wallpaper) with colors or other materials before printing. **39.** *Elect.* to establish a ground for (a circuit, device, etc.). **40.** *Naut.* to cause (a vessel) to run aground. **41.** *Aeron.* to restrict (an aircraft or the like) to the ground because of bad weather, the unsatisfactory condition of the aircraft, etc.
—*v.i.* **42.** to come to or strike the ground. **43.** *Baseball.* **a.** to hit a ground ball. **b.** to ground out. **44. ground out,** *Baseball.* to be put out at first base after hitting a ground ball to the infield. [ME, OE *grund*; c. D *grond,* G *Grund*] **—ground′a·ble,** *adj.* **—ground′a·bly,** *adv.* **—ground′ed·ly,** *adv.* **—ground′ed·ness,** *n.* **—ground′ward, ground′wards,** *adv., adj.*
—Syn. 2. land, mold, loam, dirt. **5.** premise. **35.** base, set. **—Ant. 1.** sky.

ground[2] (ground), *v.* **1.** a pt. and pp. of **grind.** **—*adj.*** **2.** reduced to fine particles or dust by grinding. **3.** having the surface abraded or roughened by or as by grinding: *ground glass.*

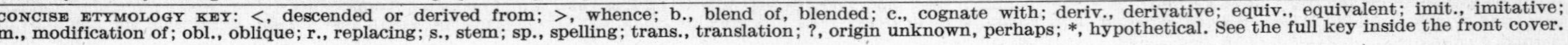
CONCISE ETYMOLOGY KEY: <, descended or derived from; >, whence; b., blend of, blended; c., cognate with; deriv., derivative; equiv., equivalent; imit., imitative; m., modification of; obl., oblique; r., replacing; s., stem; sp., spelling; trans., translation; ?, origin unknown, perhaps; *, hypothetical. See the full key inside the front cover.

ground·age (groun′dij), *n. Brit.* a tax levied on ships that anchor in a port. [ME *grondage.* See GROUND[1], -AGE]

ground′ alert′, **1.** *Mil.* the state of waiting for orders in or near combat airplanes ready to take to the air at once. **2.** the aircraft standing by during a ground alert.

ground′ bait′, bait dropped to the bottom of the water to attract fish.

ground′ ball′, *Baseball.* a batted ball that rolls or bounces along the ground. Also called **grounder.** Cf. **fly ball.**

ground′ bass′ (bās), *Music.* a short fundamental bass part continually repeated throughout a movement.

ground′ beam′, **1.** a reinforced concrete beam for supporting walls, joists, etc., at or near ground level, itself either resting directly upon the ground or supported at both ends by piers. **2.** groundsill.

ground′ bee′tle, any of numerous nocturnal, terrestrial beetles of the family *Carabidae* that feed chiefly on other insects.

ground·break·er (ground′brā′kər), *n.* a person who is an originator or pioneer in a particular activity. [GROUND[1] + BREAKER[1]]

ground′ ca′ble, *Naut.* a heavy chain for securing permanent floating moorings, as a number of mooring buoys.

ground′ ce′dar, the ground pine, *Lycopodium complanatum.*

ground′ cher′ry, **1.** Also called **husk tomato.** any of several solanaceous herbs of the genus *Physalis,* bearing an edible berry enclosed in an enlarged calyx. **2.** any of several European dwarf cherries, esp. *Prunus fruticosa.* **3.** the fruit of any of these plants.

ground′ cloth′, **1.** a covering, usually of canvas, for the floor of a stage. **2.** Also called **groundsheet.** a waterproof covering, usually of heavy canvas, spread on the ground as protection against moisture.

ground′ col′or, **1.** Also called **ground′ coat′.** a primary coat of paint; priming; base coat. **2.** the background color, as of a painting, decoration, etc.

ground′ connec′tion, *Elect.* the conductor used to establish a ground. Also called **grounding connection.**

ground′ controlled′ approach′, *Aeron.* a system in which an observer interprets radar observations of the position of an aircraft and transmits continuous instructions to the pilot for its landing. *Abbr.:* GCA Also, **ground′ control′ approach′.**

ground′ cov′er, **1.** the herbaceous plants and low shrubs in a forest, considered as a whole. **2.** any of several low, herbaceous plants used, esp. in shady places, for covering the ground in place of grass.

ground′ crew′, *Mil.* ground personnel connected with air operations, as maintenance technicians.

ground′ dove′, a very small, grayish dove, *Columbigallina passerina,* of the warmer parts of the Western Hemisphere.

ground′ effect′ machine′, *Aeron.* a vehicle that maintains a small altitude above the ground or water by forcing air downward by means of a fan and using this air as a cushion, horizontal movement usually being achieved by a separate propulsion system.

ground·er (groun′dər), *n. Baseball.* See **ground ball.** [GROUND[1] + -ER[1]]

ground′ fir′. See **ground pine** (def. 2).

ground′ floor′, **1.** the floor of a building nearest to ground level. **2.** *Informal.* an advantageous position or opportunity in a business matter, as an offer to share in the founding of a promising enterprise: *He heard of the new factory and wanted to get in on the ground floor.*

ground′ fog′, **1.** *Meteorol.* a low, often dense, fog, esp. one through which the sky and clouds above can be seen. **2.** See **radiation fog.**

ground′ glass′, **1.** *Optics.* glass that has had its polished surface removed by fine grinding and that is used to diffuse light. **2.** glass that has been ground into fine particles, esp. for use as an abrasive.

ground′ gold′-flow·er (gōld′flou′ər), a perennial herb, *Chrysopsis falcata,* of the northeastern U.S., having hairy leaves and yellow flowers and growing in sandy soil.

ground′ hem′lock, any of several prostrate evergreen shrubs of the genus *Taxus,* esp. *T. canadensis,* of eastern North America, having narrow, tapered leaves and a red, berrylike fruit.

ground′ hog′, woodchuck.

Ground′-hog Day′ (ground′hog′, -hôg′), February 2, the day on which, according to legend, the ground hog first emerges from hibernation. If it is a sunny day and he sees his shadow, he retires for the six more weeks of wintry weather that he thus predicts.

ground′ hon′eysuckle. See **bird's-foot trefoil.**

ground′ ice′. See **anchor ice.**

ground′ing connec′tion, *Elect.* See **ground connection.**

ground′ itch′, *Pathol.* a condition of the skin of the feet, caused by penetration of hookworm larvae, characterized by a blisterlike eruption and itching. Also called **water pox.**

ground′ i′vy, a trailing, labiate herb, *Glecoma hederacea,* having blue flowers. Also called **gill-over-the-ground.**

ground·keep·er (ground′kē′pər), *n.* a person who maintains or is responsible for the maintenance of a particular tract of land, as a park, cemetery, or sports field. [GROUND[1] + KEEPER]

ground′ land′lord, *Chiefly Brit.* a landlord who receives ground rent.

ground′ lay′er. See **surface boundary layer.**

ground·less (ground′lis), *adj.* without rational basis: *groundless fears.* [ME; OE *grundlēas.* See GROUND[1], -LESS] —**ground′less·ly,** *adv.* —**ground′less·ness,** *n.*

ground′ lev′el, *Physics.* See **ground state.**

ground′ lil′y. See **nodding trillium.**

ground·ling (ground′ling), *n.* **1.** a plant or animal that lives on or close to the ground. **2.** any of various fishes that live at the bottom of the water. **3.** a spectator, reader, or other person of crude or uncultivated tastes; an uncritical or uncultured person. **4.** a member of a theater audience who sits in one of the cheaper seats. [GROUND[1] + -LING[1]]

ground′ log′, *Naut.* a lead weight attached to a line, cast overboard in shoal water and allowed to pay out the line freely to show the speed of a vessel and the force of the current.

ground′ loop′, *Aeron.* a sharp horizontal loop performed, usually involuntarily, while touching the ground.

ground·mass (ground′mas′), *n.* the crystalline, granular, or glassy base or matrix of a porphyritic or other igneous rock, in which the more prominent crystals are embedded. [GROUND[1] + MASS]

ground·nut (ground′nut′), *n.* **1.** any of various plants having edible underground portions, as the peanut, *Arachis hypogaea,* and the American, climbing, leguminous vine *Apios tuberosa,* having an edible, tuberous root. **2.** the edible tuber, pod, etc., of any of these plants. Also called **potato bean, wild bean.** [GROUND[1] + NUT]

ground′ observ′er, a person stationed in a position on the ground to watch, follow, and report on flights of aircraft, esp. of enemy aircraft.

Ground′ Observ′er Corps′, *U.S.* an organization of civilian volunteers who, from observation posts on the ground, observed and reported the movement of aircraft and thereby assisted the Air Force in its efforts to detect enemy aircraft. It was active from 1949 to 1959, after which it was placed in reserve status.

ground′ owl′, *U.S. Dial.* the burrowing owl.

ground′ pine′, **1.** a European, labiate herb, *Ajuga chamaepitys,* having a resinous odor. **2.** Also called **ground fir.** any of several species of club moss, esp. *Lycopodium obscurum* and *L. complanatum.*

ground′ pink′, **1.** an annual herb, *Gilia dianthoides,* of southern California. **2.** See **moss pink.**

ground′ plan′, **1.** Also called **groundplot.** the plan of a floor of a building. **2.** first or fundamental plan.

ground′ plane′, (in perspective drawing) the theoretical horizontal plane receding from the picture plane to the horizon, beginning at the level of the base line.

ground′ plate′, **1.** *Elect.* a metal plate for making a ground connection to the earth. **2.** groundsill.

ground·plot (ground′plot′), *n.* **1.** *Aeron.* a method for obtaining the position of an aircraft by multiplying its ground speed by its time in flight and marking off the product with respect to its starting position. **2.** See **ground plan** (def. 1). [GROUND[1] + PLOT[1]]

ground′ plum′, **1.** a leguminous plant, *Astragalus caryocarpus,* of the prairie regions of North America. **2.** its plum-shaped fruit.

ground′ rattan′, a reedlike, fan palm, *Rhapis excelsa,* of China, having fan-shaped leaves, grown as an ornamental.

ground′ rent′, *Chiefly Brit.* the rent at which land is let to a tenant either for a long term or perpetually.

ground′ rob′in, *U.S. Dial.* towhee.

ground′ row′, a long, low piece of stage scenery, built to simulate part of a landscape, a building, a fence, or the like.

ground′ rule′, **1.** Usually, **ground rules.** basic or governing principles of conduct in any situation or field of endeavor: *Violation of the ground rules of social relationship usually resulted in ostracism of the offender.* **2.** *Sports.* any of certain rules specially adopted, as in baseball and softball, for dealing with situations or circumstances arising chiefly from the particular nature of the playing area or the interference of spectators.

ground·sel[1] (ground′səl), *n. Chiefly Brit.* any asteraceous plant of the genus *Senecio,* as *S. vulgaris,* a weed having small, yellow flowers. [ME *grundeswilie,* etc., OE *grundeswelge, gundeswelge;* cf. OE *gund* pus, *swelgan* to swallow, absorb (from its use in medicine); the *-r* is by folk etymology from assoc. with GROUND[1]]

ground·sel[2] (ground′səl), *n.* groundsill.

ground′ shark′, any of various requiem sharks, esp. of the genus *Carcharius.*

ground·sheet (ground′shēt′), *n.* See **ground cloth** (def. 2). [GROUND[1] + SHEET[1]]

ground·sill (ground′sil′), *n.* the lowermost sill of a framed structure, esp. one lying close to the ground. Also, **groundsel.** Also called **ground beam, ground plate.** [ME *grownsel.* See GROUND[1], SILL]

grounds′ keep′er, a groundkeeper or gardener responsible for a large tract of land, as on an estate.

ground′ sluice′, *Mining.* a trench, cut through a placer or through bedrock, through which a stream is diverted in order to dislodge and wash the gravel. —**ground′-sluic′er,** *n.*

ground·speed (ground′spēd′), *n.* the speed of an aircraft with reference to the ground. Also, **ground′ speed′.** [GROUND[1] + SPEED]

ground′ squir′rel, any of several terrestrial rodents of the squirrel family, as of the genus *Citellus* and chipmunks of the genus *Tamias.*

ground′ state′, *Physics.* the state of least energy of a particle, as an atom, or of a system of particles. Also called **ground level.**

ground′ strake′, *Naut.* See **garboard strake.**

ground′ stroke′, *Tennis.* a stroke made by hitting the ball after it has bounced from the ground. Cf. **volley** (def. 4b).

ground′ sub′stance, *Biol.* **1.** the homogeneous matrix in which the fibers and cells of connective tissue are embedded. **2.** hyaloplasm.

ground′ swell′, a broad, deep swell or rolling of the sea, due to a distant storm or gale.

ground′ ta′ble, *Archit.* See **earth table.**

ground′ tack′le, *Naut.* equipment, as anchors, chains, windlasses, etc., for mooring a vessel away from a pier or other fixed moorings.

ground-to-air (ground′tōō âr′), *adj., adv.* surface-to-air.

ground-to-ground (ground′tə ground′), *adj., adv.* surface-to-surface.

ground′ wa′ter, the water beneath the surface of the ground, consisting largely of surface water that has seeped down: the source of water in springs and wells.

ground′ wave′, *Radio.* a radio wave propagated on or near the earth's surface and affected by the ground and the troposphere.

ground·way (ground′wā′), *n. Shipbuilding.* an inclined track, usually of smooth hardwood, down which the sliding ways slide bearing the hull of a vessel being launched. Also called **standing way.** [GROUND[1] + WAY]

ground′ wire′, *Elect.* a lead from an electric apparatus to the earth or to a ground connection.

ground·wood (ground′wŏŏd′), *n. Papermaking.* wood that has been ground for making into pulp. [GROUND[2] + WOOD[1]]

ground·work (ground′wûrk′), *n.* the foundation, base, or basis of an undertaking. [GROUND[1] + WORK] —**Syn.** bottom, substructure, footing; preparation, preliminaries, prolegomena.

ground′ ze′ro, the point on the surface of the earth or water directly below, directly above, or at which an atomic or hydrogen bomb explodes.

group (grōōp), *n.* **1.** any collection or assemblage of persons or things; cluster; aggregation. **2.** a number of persons or things ranged or considered together as being related in some way. **3.** *Ethnol.* a unit of social organization less complex than a band. **4.** Also called **radical.** *Chem.* two or more atoms specifically arranged, as the hydroxyl group, –OH. Cf. **free radical.** **5.** *Ling.* **a.** (in the classification of related languages within a family) a category of a lower order than a subbranch and of a higher order than a subgroup: *the Low German group of West Germanic languages.* **b.** any grouping of languages, whether it is made on the basis of geography, genetic relationship, or something else. **6.** *Geol.* a division of stratified rocks comprising two or more formations. **7.** *Mil.* **a.** *U.S. Army.* a flexible administrative and tactical unit consisting of two or more battalions and a headquarters. **b.** *U.S. Air Force.* an administrative and operational unit subordinate to a wing, usually composed of two or more squadrons. **8.** *Music.* a section of an orchestra, comprising the instruments of the same class. **9.** *Art.* a number of figures or objects shown in an arrangement together. **10.** *Math.* an algebraic system that is closed under an associative operation, as multiplication or addition, and in which there is an identity element that, on operating on another element, leaves the second element unchanged, and in which each element has corresponding to it a unique element that, on operating on the first, results in the identity element. —*v.t.* **11.** to place or associate together in a group, as with others. **12.** to arrange in or form into a group or groups. —*v.i.* **13.** to form a group. **14.** to be part of a group. [< F *groupe* < It *gruppo* << Gmc] —**group′wise′,** *adv.*

group′ annu′ity, *Insurance.* a plan in which the members of a group, usually employees, receive annuities upon retirement.

group·er (grōō′pər), *n., pl.* (*esp. collectively*) **-er,** (*esp. referring to two or more kinds or species*), **-ers.** any of several serranoid sea basses, esp. of the genera *Epinephelus* and *Mycteroperca,* found in tropical and subtropical seas. [< Pg *garupa,* appar. repr. some South American name]

group′ flash′ing light′, *Navig.* a beacon showing intermittent groups of two or more flashes with intervals of darkness.

group′ insur′ance, life, accident, or health insurance available to a group of persons under a single contract, usually without regard to physical condition or age.

group′ mar′riage, (among primitive peoples) a form of marriage in which a group of males is united with a group of females to form a single conjugal unit. Also called **communal marriage.**

group′ occult′ing light′, *Navig.* a light occulted briefly two or more times at regular intervals.

group·oid (grōō′poid), *n. Math.* an algebraic system closed under a binary operation. Also called **monoid.** Cf. **group** (def. 10), **semigroup.** [GROUP + -OID]

group′ prac′tice, **1.** the practice of medicine by an association of physicians who work together, usually in one building. **2.** *Law.* a system in which legal services are provided by a corporation retaining and paying a number of lawyers.

group′ representa′tion, *Govt.* representation in a governing body on the basis of interests rather than by geographical location.

group′ ther′apy, *Psychiatry.* psychotherapy in which a group of patients participate, usually under the leadership of a therapist, in a discussion of their problems in an attempt to solve them.

group′ veloc′ity, *Physics.* the velocity of finite numbers of waves undergoing simple harmonic motion, equal to the phase velocity when it does not vary with the wavelengths of the waves. The group velocity of the set of waves produced in water when a stone is dropped is less than the velocity of the individual waves.

group′ with op′erators, *Math.* an algebraic system consisting of a group with an associated set of elements or operators such that the product of an operator and an element of the group is an element of the group and such that an operator times a product of elements of the group is equal to the operator times each element.

group′ work′, *Sociol.* a method, used by professional social workers, of aiding a group or members of a group toward a satisfactory personal adjustment and increased participation in community activity by exploiting the mechanisms of group life.

grouse[1] (grous), *n., pl.* **grouse, grous·es.** **1.** any of numerous gallinaceous birds of the family *Tetraonidae.* Cf. **black grouse, capercaillie, ruffed grouse, spruce grouse.** **2.** *Brit.* the red grouse. [?] —**grouse′less,** *adj.* —**grouse′-like′,** *adj.*

Ruffed grouse,
Bonasa umbellus
(Length 18 in.)

grouse[2] (grous), *v.,* **groused, grous·ing,** *n. Informal.* —*v.i.* **1.** to grumble; complain: *I've never met anyone who grouses so much about his work.* —*n.* **2.** a complaint. [?; see GROUCH] —**grous′er,** *n.*

grouse[3] (grous), *adj. Australian Slang.* excellent; great; wonderful. [?]

grout (grout), *n.* **1.** a thin, coarse mortar poured into various narrow cavities, as masonry joints, rock fissures, etc., to fill them and consolidate the adjoining objects into a solid mass. **2.** a finish coat of plaster for a ceiling or interior wall. **3.** Usually, **grouts.** lees; grounds. **4.** *Archaic.* **a.** coarse meal or porridge. **b. grouts,** groats. **—***v.t.* **5.** to fill or consolidate with grout. **6.** to use as grout. [OE *grūt;* see GRITS, GROATS, GRIT] **—grout′er,** *n.*

grout′ box′, a conical object of expanded metal, buried in poured concrete with an anchor bolt held in its inner and smaller end.

grout′lock brick′ (grout′lok′), a brick chamfered on its inner angles to allow space for vertical and horizontal reinforcing rods sealed in grout. [GROUT + LOCK[1]]

grout·y (grou′tē), *adj.*, **grout·i·er, grout·i·est.** *Dial.* sulky; surly; bad-tempered. [*grout* to grumble, sulk < ? (cf. GROUSE[2], GROUCH) + -Y[1]]

grove (grōv), *n.* **1.** a small wood or forested area, usually with no undergrowth: *Their cabin is on the other side of that grove of pines.* **2.** a small orchard or stand of fruit-bearing trees, esp. citrus trees: *We planted our first grove of lemon trees nearly twenty years ago.* [ME; OE *grāf*] **—groved,** *adj.* **—grove′less,** *adj.*

Grove (grōv), *n.* **1. Sir George,** 1820–1900, English musicologist. **2. Robert Moses** ("*Lefty*"), born 1900, U.S. baseball player. **3.** a crater in the first quadrant of the face of the moon: about 15 miles in diameter.

Grove′ Cit′y, **1.** a town in W Pennsylvania. 8368 (1960). **2.** a town in central Ohio. 8107 (1960).

grov·el (gruv′əl, grov′-), *v.i.*, **-eled, -el·ing** or (*esp. Brit.*) **-elled, -el·ling. 1.** to humble oneself or act in an abject manner, as in great fear, utter servility, etc. **2.** to lie or move with the face downward and the body prostrate, esp. in abject humility, fear, etc. **3.** to take pleasure in mean or base things. [back formation from obs. *groveling* (adv.), equiv. to obs. *grufe* face down (< Scand) + -LING[2], taken to be prp.] **—grov′el·er;** *esp. Brit.,* **grov′el·ler,** *n.* **—grov′el·ing·ly;** *esp. Brit.,* **grov′el·ling·ly,** *adv.*

Gro·ver (grō′vər), *n.* **1.** a town in SW California. 5210 (1960). **2.** a boy's given name.

Groves (grōvz), *n.* **1. Leslie Richard,** born 1896, U.S. general. **2.** a city in SE Texas. 17,304 (1960).

grow (grō), *v.*, **grew, grown, grow·ing. —***v.i.* **1.** to increase by natural development, as any living organism or part by assimilation of nutriment; increase in size or substance. **2.** to arise or issue as a natural development from an original happening, circumstance, or source: *Our friendship grew from a common interest in the theater.* **3.** to increase gradually in size, amount, etc.; become greater or larger; expand: *Over the last two decades, the influence of this group has grown to a level of national concern.* **4.** to become gradually attached or united by or as by growth: *The branches of the trees grew together, forming a natural arch.* **5.** to come to be, or become, by degrees: *to grow old.* **6.** *Naut.* to lie or extend in a certain direction, as an anchor cable. **—***v.t.* **7.** to cause to grow: *He grows corn.* **8.** to allow to grow: *to grow a beard.* **9.** to cover with a growth (used in the passive): *a field grown with corn.* **10. grow into, a.** to become large enough for: *He'll grow into his brother's suits before long.* **b.** to become mature or experienced enough for: *He grew into the job although he wasn't qualified for it when he started.* **11. grow on** or **upon, a.** to increase in influence or effect: *An uneasy feeling grew upon him as he went through the old house.* **b.** to become fixed gradually in one's mind or affections: *a village by the sea that grows on one.* **12. grow out of, a.** to become too large or mature for; outgrow: *He has grown out of all his clothes.* **b.** to originate in; develop from: *The plan grew out of a casual conversation.* **13. grow up, a.** to be or become fully grown; attain mental or physical maturity. **b.** to come into existence; arise: *New cities grew up in the desert.* [ME *grow(en),* OE *grōwan;* c. D *groeien,* OHG *grouwan,* Icel *grōa*] **—grow′a·ble,** *adj.*

—Syn. 1. develop, multiply, swell, enlarge, expand, extend. **2.** originate. **3.** wax. **7.** raise, cultivate, produce. **—Ant. 1.** decrease. **3.** wane.

Grow (grō), *n.* **Ga·lu·sha Aaron** (gə lo͞o′shə), 1822–1907, U.S. political leader: Speaker of the House 1861–63.

grow·an (grō′ən, grou′-), *n.* decomposed granite. [< Cornish **growan* (equiv. to Breton *grouan*), deriv. of *grou* gravel]

grow·er (grō′ər), *n.* **1.** a person who grows something: *He is a grower of flowers and vegetables.* **2.** a plant that grows in a certain way: *a quick grower.* [GROW + -ER[1]]

grow·ing (grō′ing), *adj.* **1.** becoming greater in quantity, size, or intensity: *growing discontent among industrial workers.* **2.** having or showing life. [OE *growende.* See GROW, -ING[2]] **—grow′ing·ly,** *adv.*

grow′ing degree′-day′, a degree-day above 41°F, used in relation to plant growth. Cf. **cooling degree-day, heating degree-day.**

grow′ing pains′, **1.** emotional difficulties experienced during adolescence and preadulthood. **2.** dull, quasi-rheumatic pains of varying degree in the limbs during childhood and adolescence, often popularly associated with the process of growing. **3.** difficulties attending any new project or any rapid development of an existing project: *a city plagued with growing pains.*

growl (groul), *v.i.* **1.** to utter a deep guttural sound of anger or hostility: *the dog growled.* **2.** to murmur or complain angrily; grumble. **3.** to rumble: *The thunder growled.* **4.** *Jazz.* to use flutter-tonguing in playing a wind instrument. **—***v.t.* **5.** to express by growling. **—***n.* **6.** the act or sound of growling. **7.** *Jazz.* the technique of flutter-tonguing. [ME *groule* to rumble (said of the bowels); c. G *grollen*] **—growl′ing·ly,** *adv.*

—Syn. 2. See **complain.**

growl·er (grou′lər), *n.* **1.** one who or that which growls. **2.** *Informal.* a pitcher, pail, or other container brought by a customer for beer. **3.** *Brit. Slang.* a four-wheeled hansom cab. **4.** *Elect.* an electromagnetic device consisting of two field poles, used for indicating short-circuited coils in armatures and for magnetizing or demagnetizing objects. **5.** an iceberg large enough to be a navigational hazard. [GROWL + -ER[1]]

grown (grōn), *adj.* **1.** advanced in growth: *a grown boy.* **2.** arrived at full growth or maturity; adult: *a grown man.* **—***v.* **3.** pp. of **grow.**

grown-up (grōn′up′), *adj.* **1.** having reached the age of maturity. **2.** characteristic of or suitable for adults: *grown-up behavior; grown-up fiction.* [adj. use of v. phrase *grow up*] **—grown′-up′ness,** *n.*

grown·up (grōn′up′), *n.* a mature, fully grown person; adult. [n. use of v. phrase *grow up*]

growth (grōth), *n.* **1.** the act or process, or a manner of growing; development; gradual increase. **2.** size or stage of development: *It hasn't yet reached its full growth.* **3.** completed development. **4.** development from a simpler to a more complex stage: *the growth of ritual forms.* **5.** development from another but related form or stage: *the growth of the nation state.* **6.** something that has grown or developed by or as by a natural process: *a growth of weeds.* **7.** *Pathol.* an abnormal increase in a mass of tissue, as a tumor. **8.** origin; source; production: *onions of English growth.* [ME (north) *growth;* c. Icel *grōthr.* See GROW, -TH[1]]

—Syn. 1. augmentation, expansion. **6.** result, outgrowth. **7.** excrescence. **—Ant. 1.** decline, decrease.

growth′ hor′mone, a hormone, produced by the anterior pituitary, that causes body growth.

Growth′ of the Soil′, a novel (1920) by Knut Hamsun.

growth′ ring′. See **annual ring.**

growth′ stock′, common stock of a company having strong prospects of substantial increase in expansion and appreciation.

groyne (groin), *n.* groin (def. 3).

groz′ing i′ron (grō′zing), **1.** (in plumbing) a hot iron for finishing soldered joints. **2.** a steel tool for cutting glass. [part trans. of D *gruisijzer,* equiv. to *gruis-* (s. of *gruizen* to crush, deriv. of *gruis* gravel; akin to OE *grūt* grit) + *ijzer* iron]

Groz·ny (grôz′nī), *n.* a city in and the capital of the Chechen-Ingush Autonomous Soviet Socialist Republic of the RSFSR, in the S Soviet Union in Europe. 240,000 (1959).

grub (grub), *n.*, *v.*, **grubbed, grub·bing. —***n.* **1.** the thick-bodied, sluggish larva of several insects, as of a scarabaeid beetle. **2.** a dull, plodding person; drudge. **3.** *Informal.* food; victuals. **—***v.t.* **4.** to dig; clear of roots, stumps, etc. **5.** to dig up by the roots; uproot (often fol. by *up* or *out*). **6.** *Slang.* to supply with food. **—***v.i.* **7.** to dig; search by or as by digging: *We grubbed through piles of old junk but couldn't find the deed.* **8.** to lead a laborious or groveling life; drudge: *She spent her days grubbing for a few pennies.* **9.** to engage in laborious research; study closely. **10.** *Slang.* to eat; take food. [ME *grubbe* (n.), *grubben* (v.); akin to OHG *grubilōn* to dig, G *grübeln* to rack (the brain), Icel *gryfja* hole, pit; see GRAVE[1], GROOVE] **—grub′ber,** *n.*

grub′ beam′, *Shipbuilding.* a curved, laminated wooden beam forming part of a rounded stern.

grub·by[1] (grub′ē), *adj.*, **-bi·er, -bi·est. 1.** dirty; slovenly: *children with grubby faces and sad eyes.* **2.** infested with or affected by grubs or larvae. **3.** contemptible. [GRUB + -Y[1]] **—grub′bi·ly,** *adv.* **—grub′bi·ness,** *n.*

grub·by[2] (grub′ē), *n., pl.* **-bies.** a small sculpin, *Myxocephalus aenus,* found off the coast of New England. [?]

grub′ hoe′, a heavy hoe for grubbing up roots, stumps, etc.

grub′ saw′, a handsaw for cutting stone.

grub·stake (grub′stāk′), *n., v.*, **-staked, -stak·ing. —***n.* **1.** provisions, outfit, etc., furnished to a prospector on condition of participating in the profits of his discoveries. **—***v.t.* **2.** to furnish with a grubstake: *I grubstaked him to two mules and supplies enough for five months.* [GRUB + STAKE[2]] **—grub′stak′er,** *n.*

Grub′ Street′, **1.** a street in London, England: formerly inhabited by many impoverished minor writers and literary hacks; now called Milton Street. **2.** petty and needy authors, or literary hacks, collectively.

grub·street (grub′strēt′), *adj.* **1.** produced by a hack; poor in quality: *a grubstreet book.* **—***n.* **2.** See **Grub Street** (def. 2).

grub·worm (grub′wûrm′), *n.* grub (def. 1). [GRUB + WORM]

grudge (gruj), *n., v.*, **grudged, grudg·ing. —***n.* **1.** a feeling of ill will or resentment: *to hold a grudge against a former opponent.* **—***v.t.* **2.** to give or permit with reluctance; submit to unwillingly: *She grudged him even the small pleasure of a night out with his friends.* **3.** to resent the good fortune of (another). **—***v.i.* **4.** to feel dissatisfaction or ill will. [ME *grudge(n), grugge(n),* var. of *gruchen* < OF *gro(u)c(h)ier* < Gmc.; cf. MHG *grogezen* to complain, cry out] **—grudge′less,** *adj.* **—grudg′er,** *n.*

—Syn. 1. bitterness, rancor, malevolence, enmity, hatred. GRUDGE, MALICE, SPITE refer to ill will held against another or others. A GRUDGE is a feeling of resentment harbored because of some real or fancied wrong: *to hold a grudge because of jealousy; She has a grudge against him.* MALICE is the state of mind which delights in doing harm, or seeing harm done, to others, whether expressing itself in an attempt seriously to injure or merely in sardonic humor: *malice in watching someone's embarrassment; to tell lies about someone out of malice.* SPITE is petty, and often sudden, resentment that manifests itself usually in trifling retaliations: *to reveal a secret out of spite.* **3.** begrudge, envy.

grudg·ing (gruj′ing), *adj.* displaying reluctance or unwillingness: *grudging acceptance of the victory of an opponent.* [GRUDGE + -ING[2]] **—grudg′ing·ly,** *adv.*

gru·el (gro͞o′əl), *n.* a light, usually thin, cooked cereal made by boiling meal, esp. oatmeal, in water or milk. [ME < MF, OF, equiv. to *gru-* (< Gmc; see GROUT) + *-el* dim. suffix]

gru·el·ing (gro͞o′ə ling, gro͞o′ling), *adj.* **1.** exhausting; very tiring; arduously severe: *a grueling race.* **—***n.* **2.** any trying or exhausting procedure or experience. Also, *esp. Brit.,* **gru′el·ling.** [slang *gruel* punishment (n.), punish (v.) + -ING[2], -ING[1]]

Gru·em·berg·er (gro͞o′əm bûr′gər), *n.* a walled plain in the third quadrant of the face of the moon: about 58 miles in diameter.

Gru·en·berg (gro͞o′ən bûrg′), *n.* **Louis,** 1884–1964, U.S. pianist and composer, born in Russia.

grue·some (gro͞o′səm), *adj.* causing one to shudder with horror; horribly repugnant; grisly. Also, **grewsome.** [obs. *grue* to shudder (c. G *grauen,* D *gruwen*) + -SOME[1]] **—grue′some·ly,** *adv.* **—grue′some·ness,** *n.*

gruff (gruf), *adj.* **1.** low and harsh; hoarse: *a gruff voice.* **2.** rough; surly: *a gruff manner.* [< MD *grof;* c. G *grob* rough, uncouth] **—gruff′ish,** *adj.* **—gruff′ly,** *adv.* **—gruff′ness,** *n.*

—Syn. 2. brusque. **—Ant. 1.** pleasant. **2.** courteous.

gruff·y (gruf′ē), *adj.*, **gruff·i·er, gruff·i·est.** gruff. [GRUFF + -Y[1]] **—gruff′i·ly,** *adv.* **—gruff′i·ness,** *n.*

gru·gru (gro͞o′gro͞o), *n.* **1.** Also, **grigri.** any of several spiny-trunked, tropical feather palms as *Acrocomia sclerocarpa,* of tropical America. **2.** Also called **gru′gru grub′, gru′gru worm′.** the larva of any of several billbugs, as *Rhynchophorus cruentatus,* which infests and feeds on the pith of palm trees, sugar cane, etc., found in South America, where it is prized as food. [< AmerSp *grugrú* < Carib]

Gruit·hui·sen (grēt′hī zən), *n.* a crater in the second quadrant of the face of the moon: about 10 miles in diameter.

grum (grum), *adj.*, **grum·mer, grum·mest.** (of a person's appearance) grim; glum; surly. [prob. b. GRIM and GLUM] **—grum′ly,** *adv.* **—grum′ness,** *n.*

grum·ble (grum′bəl), *v.*, **-bled, -bling,** *n.* **—***v.i.* **1.** to murmur or mutter in discontent. **2.** to utter low, indistinct sounds; growl. **3.** to rumble: *The thunder grumbled in the west.* **—***v.t.* **4.** to express or utter with murmuring or complaining. **—***n.* **5.** an expression of discontent; complaint; unhappy murmur; growl. **6. grumbles,** a grumbling, discontented mood. **7.** a rumble. [? freq. of OE *grymman* to wail; cf. D *grommelen,* G *grummeln,* F *grommeler* (< Gmc)] **—grum′bler,** *n.* **—grum′bling·ly,** *adv.* **—grum′bly,** *adj.*

—Syn. 1. See **complain.**

grume (gro͞om), *n.* **1.** blood when viscous. **2.** *Med.* a clot of blood. [< LL *grūm(us)* hillock]

grum·met (grum′it), *n.* grommet.

gru·mous (gro͞o′məs), *adj.* **1.** *Bot.* formed of clustered grains, granules, etc., as certain roots. **2.** having or resembling grume; clotted. [< L *grūm(us)* (see GRUME) + -OUS] **—gru′mous·ness,** *n.*

grumph·ie (grum′fē, gro͝om′pē), *n.* *Chiefly Scot.* a familiar name for a pig. Also, **grumph′y.** [*grumph* to grunt (imit.) + -IE]

grump·y (grum′pē), *adj.*, **grump·i·er, grump·i·est.** surly or ill-tempered; discontentedly irritable. Also, **grump′ish.** [GRUM, or *grump* + -Y[1]] **—grump′i·ly,** *adv.* **—grump′i·ness,** *n.*

Grun·dy (grun′dē), *n.* **Mrs.,** a narrow-minded, conventional person who is extremely critical of any breach of propriety. [after Mrs. *Grundy,* a character in the play *Speed the Plough* (1798) by Thomas Morton (1764?–1838), English playwright] **—Grun′dy·ist, Grun′dy·ite′,** *n.*

Grun·dy·ism (grun′dē iz′əm), *n.* **1.** a prudish adherence to conventionality, esp. in personal behavior. **2.** (*l.c.*) an instance of such prudishness. [GRUNDY + -ISM]

Grü·ne·wald (grY′nə vält′), *n.* **Ma·thi·as** (mä tē′äs), (*Mathias Neithardt-Gothardt*), c1470–1528, German painter and architect.

grun·ion (grun′yən), *n.* a small, slender food fish, *Leuresthes tenuis,* of the silverside family, found in southern California, that spawns at high tide in wet sand. [prob. < Sp *gruñon* grunter, deriv. of *gruñir* to grunt < L *grunnīre*]

Gru·nit·sky (grə nit′skē), *n.* **Nicolas,** born 1913, African statesman: president of the Republic of Togo since 1963.

grunt (grunt), *v.i.* **1.** to utter the deep, guttural sound characteristic of a hog. **2.** to utter a similar sound. **3.** to grumble, as in discontent. **—***v.t.* **4.** to express with a grunt. **—***n.* **5.** a sound of grunting. **6.** any food fish of the family *Pomadasyidae* (*Haemulidae*), found chiefly in tropical and subtropical seas, which emits grunting sounds. [ME *grunt(en),* OE *grunnettan,* freq. of *grun(n)ian* to grunt; c. G *grunzen,* L *grunnīre*] **—grunt′ing·ly,** *adv.*

grunt·er (grun′tər), *n.* **1.** a hog. **2.** any animal or person that grunts. **3.** grunt (def. 6). [late ME; see GRUNT, -ER[1]]

Grunth (grunt), *n.* Granth.

grunt′ing ox′, the yak.

Grus (grus, gro͞os), *n., gen.* **Gru·is** (gro͞o′is). *Astron.* the Crane, a southern constellation between Indus and Piscis Austrinus. [< L: crane; akin to Gk *géranos*]

grush·ie (grush′ē, gro͞o′shē), *adj.* *Scot.* healthy; thriving. Also, **grush.** [?]

grutch (gruch), *n., v.t., v.i.* *Brit. Dial.* grudge.

Gru·yère (gro͞o yâr′, grē-; *Fr.* grY yer′), *n.* a firm, pale-yellow cheese, made of whole milk and containing small holes, produced chiefly in France and Switzerland. Also called **Gru·yère′ cheese′.** [after *Gruyère* district in Switzerland where the cheese is made]

gr. wt., gross weight.

Gry·nae·us (grī nē′əs), *n.* *Class. Myth.* an epithet of Apollo.

gryph·on (grif′ən), *n.* *Class. Myth.* griffin[1].

GS, German silver.

Gs, gigasecond; gigaseconds.

G.S., **1.** general secretary. **2.** general staff. Also, **g.s.**

G.S.A., Girls Scouts of America.

G.S.C., General Staff Corps.

G.S.R., galvanic skin response; galvanic skin reflex.

G-string (jē′string′), *n.* **1.** a loincloth or breechcloth. **2.** a similar covering, usually decorated, worn by women entertainers, esp. in a striptease. [?]

G-stro·phan·thin (jē′strə fan′thin), *n.* *Pharm.* ouabain. [< L *g(ratus)* + STROPHANTHIN]

G-suit (jē′so͞ot′), *n.* See **anti-G suit.** [*g(ravity) suit*]

GT, gigaton; gigatons.

gt., **1.** gilt. **2.** great. **3.** (in prescriptions) a drop. [< L *gutta*]

Gt. Br., Great Britain. Also, **Gt. Brit.**

g.t.c., **1.** good till canceled. **2.** good till countermanded. Also, **G.T.C.**

gtd., guaranteed.

GTS, gas turbine ship.

gtt., (in prescriptions) drops. [< L *guttae*]

g.u., genitourinary. Also, **GU**

gua·cha·ro (gwä′chə rō′), *n., pl.* **-ros.** a nocturnal, fruit-eating, South American bird, *Steatornis caripensis,* the young of which yield an oil derived from their fat. Also called **oilbird.** [< AmerSp < Araucanian *uachar* cave]

gua·cin (gwä′sin), *n.* *Pharm.* a resin obtained from the guaco plant, used chiefly in treating rheumatism and diarrhea. [GUAC(O) + -IN[2]]

gua·co (gwä′kō), *n., pl.* **-cos. 1.** a climbing, asteraceous plant, *Mikania Guaco,* of tropical America. **2.** its medicinal leaves, or a substance obtained from them, used as an antidote for snake bites. **3.** a tropical American plant, *Aristolochia maxima,* also used for snake bites. [< AmerSp]

Gua·da·la·ja·ra (gwäd′əl ə här′ə; *Sp.* gwä′thä lä hä′rä), *n.* a city in and the capital of Jalisco, in W Mexico. 734,346 (1960).

Gua·dal·ca·nal (gwäd′əl kə nal′), *n.* one of the Solomon Islands, in the S Pacific: U.S. victory over the Japanese 1942–43. 140,000 (est. 1951); ab. 2500 sq. mi.

Gua·dal·qui·vir (gwä′thäl kē vēr′), *n.* a river in S Spain, flowing W to the Gulf of Cádiz. 374 mi. long.

Gua·da·lupe (gwäd′əl ōōp′, -əl ōō′pē), *n.* a town in SW California. 2614 (1960).

Gua·da·lupe Hi·dal·go (gwäd′əl ōōp′ hi dal′gō; *Sp.* gwä′thä lōō′pe ē thäl′gō), a city in the Federal District of Mexico: famous shrine; peace treaty 1848. 92,947 (1960). Official name, **Gustavo A. Madero.**

Gua′dalupe Moun′tains, a mountain range in S New Mexico and SW Texas, part of the Sacramento Mountains. Highest peak, Guadalupe Peak, 8751 ft.

Gua′dalupe palm′, a palm, *Erythea edulis,* of southern California, having globe-shaped, black fruit in clusters.

Gua·de·loupe (gwäd′əl ōōp′), *n.* two islands separated by a narrow channel in the Leeward Islands of the West Indies: together with five dependencies they form a department of France. 229,120 (1955); 687 sq. mi. *Cap.:* Basse-Terre.

Gua·dia·na (*Sp.* gwä thyä′nä; *Port.* gwə dyä′nə), *n.* a river in SW Europe, flowing S from central Spain through SE Portugal to the Gulf of Cádiz. 515 mi. long.

gua·guan·che (gwə gwän′chē), *n.* a barracuda, *Sphyraena guachanco,* found chiefly off the coast of Florida. [< AmerSp]

guai·a·col (gwī′ə kōl′, -kôl′, -kol′), *n. Pharm.* a slightly yellowish, oily liquid, $CH_3OC_6H_4OH$, having an aromatic odor and resembling creosote, usually obtained from guaiacum resin: used in medicine chiefly as an expectorant and local anesthetic. Also called **methylcatechol.** [GUAIAC(UM) + -OL[2]]

guai·a·cum (gwī′ə kəm), *n.* **1.** any of several tropical American, zygophyllaceous trees or shrubs of the genus *Guaiacum,* esp. *G. officinale,* of the West Indies and South America, and *G. sanctum,* of the West Indies and Florida. **2.** the hard, heavy wood of such a tree. Cf. **lignum vitae** (def. 1). **3.** a greenish-brown resin obtained from such a tree, used as a stimulant and alterative and as a remedy for rheumatism, cutaneous eruptions, etc. Also, **gui·ac** (gwī′ak) (for defs. 2, 3). [< NL < Sp *guayaco, guayacán* < Haitian]

Guai·ra (*Sp.* gwī′rä), *n.* See **La Guaira.**

gua·ji·ra (gwä hēr′ə; *Sp.* gwä hē′rä), *n., pl.* **-ji·ras** (-hēr′əz; *Sp.* -hē′räs). a Cuban peasant dance with shifting rhythms. [< AmerSp: lit., peasant woman]

Guam (gwäm), *n.* an island, belonging to the U.S., in the N Pacific, E of the Philippines: the largest of the Marianas group; U.S. naval station. 67,044 (1950); 206 sq. mi. *Cap.:* Agaña. —**Gua·ma·ni·an** (gwä mā′nē ən), *n.*

gua·ma·chil (gwə ma′chil, -mä′), *n.* a tree, *Pichecolobium dulce,* of Mexico, having thorny leafstalks, hairy, white, globe-shaped flower clusters, and black shiny seeds in spirally twisted pods from five to six inches long. Also, **cuamuchil, gua·mu·chil** (gwə mōō′chil), **huamuchil.** Also called **Madras thorn, Manila tamarind.** [< MexSp *guamúchil*]

guan (gwän), *n.* any of several large, gallinaceous birds of the family *Cracidae,* chiefly of Central and South America, related to the curassows. [< AmerSp]

gua·na·ba·na (gwə nä′bə nə), *n.* soursop. [< Sp *guanábana* < Taino]

Gua·na·ba·ra (gwä′nə bä′rə), *n.* a state in SE Brazil. 3,307,163 (1960); 452 sq. mi. *Cap.:* Rio de Janeiro.

gua·na·co (gwä nä′kō), *n., pl.* **-cos.** a wild South American ruminant, *Lama guanicoe,* of which the llama and alpaca are believed to be domesticated varieties, related to the camels. [< Sp < Quechuan *huanacu*]

Guanaco (3½ ft. high at shoulder; length to 5½ ft.)

Gua·na·jua·to (gwä′nä hwä′tō), *n.* **1.** a state in central Mexico. 1,735,490 (1960); 11,805 sq. mi. **2.** a city in and the capital of this state: center of the silver-mining region. 27,365 (1960).

gua·nase (gwä′nās), *n. Biochem.* an enzyme, found in thymus, adrenals, and pancreas, that converts guanine into xanthine. [GUAN(INE) + -ASE]

gua·nay (gwə nī′; *Sp.* gwä nī′), *n., pl.* **-nay·es** (-nī′ās; *Sp.* -nä′yes), **-nays.** a Peruvian cormorant, *Phalacrocorax bougainvillii,* a chief source of guano. Also called **guanay′ cor′morant.** [< AmerSp < Quechuan]

guan·i·dine (gwan′i dēn′, -din, gwä′ni-), *n. Chem.* a colorless, crystalline, strongly alkaline, water-soluble solid, $HN{=}C(NH_2)_2$, used chiefly in the manufacture of plastics, resins, rubber accelerators, and explosives. Also called **carbamidine, iminourea.** [GUAN(O) + -ID[3] + -INE[2]]

gua·nine (gwä′nēn), *n. Chem., Biochem.* a colorless, crystalline, water-soluble solid, $C_5H_5N_5O$, found in guano and occurring in the liver and pancreas of animals and in the scales of fishes: usually obtained as a decomposition product of yeast nucleic acids and used chiefly in biochemical research. [GUAN(O) + -INE[2]]

gua·no (gwä′nō), *n.* **1.** a natural manure composed chiefly of the excrement of sea birds, found esp. on islands near the Peruvian coast. **2.** any similar substance, as an artificial fertilizer made from fish. [< Sp: fertilizer, dung; AmerSp *huano* dung < Quechuan]

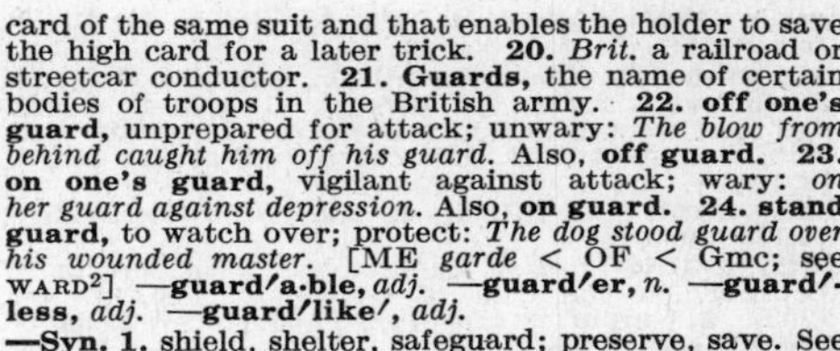

Guan·tá·na·mo (gwän tä′nə mō′; *Sp.* gwän tä′nä mô′), *n.* a city in SE Cuba: U.S. naval base. 83,684 (1953).

Guantá′namo Bay′, a bay on the SE coast of Cuba.

Gua·po·ré (*Port.* gwä pô re′; *Sp.* gwä′pô re′), *n.* **1.** a river forming part of the boundary between Brazil and Bolivia, flowing NW to the Mamoré River. 950 mi. long. **2.** former name of **Rondônia.**

guar (gwär), *n.* a leguminous plant, *Cyamopsis tetragonoloba,* grown as a forage crop, the ground seeds of which produce a sizing material for paper and textiles. [< Hindi *guār*]

guar., guaranteed.

gua·ra·cha (gwə rä′chə; *Sp.* gwä rä′chä), *n., pl.* **-chas** (-chəz; *Sp.* -chäs). **1.** a vigorous Cuban dance in triple meter. **2.** the music for this dance. [< Sp, equiv. to OSp *guar* place + *hacha* a kind of dance]

gua·ra·ni (gwär′ə nē′, gwär′ə nē′), *n., pl.* **-ni, -nis.** a paper money and monetary unit of Paraguay, equal to 100 centimos and equivalent to about .008 of a U.S. dollar. [< Sp, after GUARANÍ]

Gua·ra·ni (gwär′ə nē′), *n., pl.* **-nís, -níes,** (*esp. collectively*) **-ní. 1.** a member of a central South American people of Tupian family and affiliation. **2.** a language belonging to the Tupi-Guaraní family of languages and spoken by the Guaraní Indians. It is the chief vernacular of Paraguay. Also, **Gua′ra·ní′.**

guar·an·tee (gar′ən tē′), *n., v.,* **-teed, -tee·ing.** —*n.* **1.** guaranty (def. 1). **2.** a promise or assurance, esp. one in writing, that something is of specified quality, content, benefit, etc., or that it will perform satisfactorily for a given length of time: *a money-back guarantee.* **3.** a person who gives a guarantee or guaranty; guarantor. **4.** one to whom a guarantee is made. **5.** guaranty (def. 2). **6.** something that has the force or effect of a guaranty: *Wealth is no guarantee of happiness.* —*v.t.* **7.** to secure, as by giving or taking security. **8.** to make oneself answerable for (something) in behalf of someone else who is primarily responsible: *to guarantee the fulfillment of a contract.* **9.** to undertake to secure to another, as rights or possessions. **10.** to serve as a warrant or guaranty for. **11.** to engage (to do something). **12.** to promise (usually fol. by a clause as object): *I guarantee that I'll be there.* **13.** to engage to protect or indemnify: *to guarantee a person against loss.* [alter. of GUARANTY] —**Syn. 1.** surety, promise. **13.** insure.

guar′anteed an′nual wage′, a provision in a contract with an employer guaranteeing the employee a minimum income or work over a period of one year. Also called **annual wage.**

guar′anteed bond′, a bond issued by a corporation in which payment of the principal, interest, or both is guaranteed by another corporation.

guar′anteed stock′, stock for which dividends are guaranteed by a company other than the one issuing the stock.

guar′anteed wage′, any of various plans designed to assure certain union workers of a specified amount of income or employment during a stipulated period.

guarantee′ engineer′, a marine engineer assigned to a new vessel for a specified time by the engine builders to observe performance of machinery and to make necessary adjustments.

guar·an·tor (gar′ən tôr′, -tər), *n.* **1.** a person, group, system, etc., that guarantees: *a military organization that will be the guarantor of world peace.* **2.** a person who makes or gives a guarantee, guaranty, warrant, etc. [GUARANT(EE) + -OR[2]]

guar·an·ty (gar′ən tē′), *n., pl.* **-ties,** *v.,* **-tied, -ty·ing.** —*n.* **1.** a warrant, pledge, or formal assurance given as security that another's debt or obligation will be fulfilled. **2.** that which is taken or presented as security. **3.** the act of giving security. **4.** one who acts as a guarantor. —*v.t.* **5.** guarantee. [< AF *guarantie.* See WARRANT, -Y[3]]

guard (gärd), *v.t.* **1.** to keep safe from harm or danger; protect; watch over. **2.** to keep under close watch in order to prevent escape, misconduct, etc.: *to guard a prisoner.* **3.** to keep under control or restraint as a matter of caution or prudence: *to guard one's temper.* **4.** to provide or equip with some safeguard or protective appliance, as to prevent loss, injury, etc. **5.** *Sports.* to position oneself so as to obstruct or impede the movement or progress of (an opponent on offense): *The linebacker moved to his right to guard the end going out for a pass.* **6.** *Chess.* to protect (a piece or a square) by placing a piece in a supportive or defensive position relative to it. —*v.i.* **7.** to take precautions (usually fol. by *against*): *to guard against errors.* **8.** to give protection; keep watch; be watchful. —*n.* **9.** a person or group of persons that guards, protects, or keeps a protective or restraining watch. **10.** a person who keeps watch over prisoners or others under restraint. **11.** a body of men, esp. soldiers, charged with guarding a place from disturbance, theft, fire, etc. **12.** a close watch, as over a prisoner or other person under restraint: *to be kept under guard.* **13.** a device, appliance, or attachment that prevents injury, loss, etc. **14.** something intended or serving to guard or protect; safeguard: *insurance as a guard against emergencies.* **15.** a posture of defense or readiness, as in fencing, boxing, bayonet drill, etc. **16.** *Football.* **a.** either of the linemen stationed between a tackle and the center. **b.** the position played by this lineman. **17.** *Basketball.* either of the players stationed in the backcourt. **18.** *Chess.* a piece that supports or defends another. **19.** *Cards.* a low card that is held with a high card of the same suit and that enables the holder to save the high card for a later trick. **20.** *Brit.* a railroad or streetcar conductor. **21. Guards,** the name of certain bodies of troops in the British army. **22. off one's guard,** unprepared for attack; unwary: *The blow from behind caught him off his guard.* Also, **off guard. 23. on one's guard,** vigilant against attack; wary: *on her guard against depression.* Also, **on guard. 24. stand guard,** to watch over; protect: *The dog stood guard over his wounded master.* [ME *garde* < OF < Gmc; see WARD[2]] —**guard′a·ble,** *adj.* —**guard′er,** *n.* —**guard′less,** *adj.* —**guard′like′,** *adj.*
—**Syn. 1.** shield, shelter, safeguard; preserve, save. See **defend. 3.** hold, watch. **9.** defender, protector; watchman, guardian; guardsman, sentry, sentinel, patrol. **14.** defense, protection, aegis, security, safety; bulwark, shield. —**Ant. 1.** attack.

Guar·da·fui (gwär′də fwē′), *n.* **Cape,** a cape at the E extremity of Africa.

guard·ant (gär′dənt), *adj. Heraldry.* (of an animal) depicted full-faced but with the body seen from the side: *a lion guardant.* Also, **gardant.** [< F *gardant,* prp. of *garder.* See GUARD, -ANT]

guard′ band′, *Radio.* an unassigned range of radio frequencies either just above or just below the band of frequencies required for the signal transmitted by a broadcasting station. It helps to prevent interference in receivers between signals from different stations.

guard′ cell′, *Bot.* either of two specialized epidermal cells which flank the pore of a stoma and usually cause it to open and close.

guard′ du′ty, military duties equivalent in general to those of civilian police, but including the watching over of military prisoners at work.

guard·ed (gär′did), *adj.* **1.** cautious; careful; prudent: *to be guarded in one's speech.* **2.** protected, watched, or restrained, as by a guard. [GUARD + -ED[2]] —**guard′ed·ly,** *adv.* —**guard′ed·ness,** *n.*

guard·ee (gär′dē), *n. Brit. Informal.* guardsman (def. 2). [GUARD + -EE]

guard′ hair′, the long, usually stiff outer hair protecting the underfur in certain animals.

guard·house (gärd′hous′), *n., pl.* **-hous·es** (-hou′ziz). a building used for housing military personnel on guard duty or for the temporary detention of prisoners. [GUARD + HOUSE]

guard′house law′yer, *Mil. Slang.* an inmate of a guardhouse or brig who claims to be an authority on military law, regulations, and servicemen's rights.

Guar·di (gwär′dē), *n.* **Fran·ces·co** (frän ches′kô), 1712–93, Italian painter.

guard·i·an (gär′dē ən), *n.* **1.** a person who guards, protects, or preserves. **2.** *Law.* one who is entrusted by law with the care of the person or property, or both, of another, as a minor or some other person legally incapable of managing his own affairs. **3.** the superior of a Franciscan convent. —*adj.* **4.** guarding; protecting: *a guardian deity.* [ME *gardein* < AF. See GUARD, -IAN] —**guard′i·an·less,** *adj.*
—**Syn. 1.** protector, defender. **2.** trustee, warden, keeper.

guard·i·an ad li·tem (gär′dē ən ad lī′təm), *Law.* a person appointed by a court as guardian of an infant or other person to act on his behalf in a particular action or proceeding that may involve him. Cf. **next friend.**

guard′ian an′gel, 1. an angel believed to protect a particular person, as from danger, error, etc. **2.** a person who looks after or concerns himself with the welfare of another.

guard·i·an·ship (gär′dē ən ship′), *n.* **1.** the position and responsibilities of a guardian, esp. toward a ward. **2.** care; responsibility; charge. [GUARDIAN + -SHIP]

guard′ lock′, a lock between the entrance to a canal or basin and a tidal area.

guard′ of hon′or, a guard specially designated for welcoming or escorting distinguished guests or for accompanying a casket in a military funeral. Also called **honor guard.**

guard′ pin′, *Horol.* (in a lever escapement) a pin on the lever, meeting the safety roller in such a way as to prevent the lever from overbanking.

guard·rail (gärd′rāl′), *n.* **1.** a protective railing, as along a road, stairway, etc. **2.** *Railroads.* a rail laid parallel to a track to prevent derailment or to keep derailed rolling stock from leaving the roadbed, as on a bridge. [GUARD + RAIL[1]]

guard′ ring′, a ring that prevents another ring from slipping off a finger by being slipped on tightly after it.

guard·room (gärd′rōōm′, -rŏŏm′), *n. Mil.* a room used by guards during the period they are on duty. [GUARD + ROOM]

guard′room ta′ble, *Sp. Furniture.* a table of the Renaissance, having trestles and braced by scrolled wrought-iron rods.

guard′ ship′, 1. a warship assigned to protect a harbor. **2.** a ship under orders to maintain a higher state of readiness than the other ships in a fleet or squadron.

guards·man (gärdz′mən), *n., pl.* **-men. 1.** a man who acts as a guard. **2.** *U.S.* a member of the National Guard. [GUARD + -S[1] + MAN[1]] **3.** *Brit.* a member of any select body of troops traditionally organized to protect the person of the king. [GUARD + -S[3] + MAN[1]]

Gua·ri·ni (gwä rē′nē), *n.* **Gua·ri·no** (gwä rē′nô), 1624–83, Italian architect.

Guar·ne·ri (gwär nâr′ē; *It.* gwär ne′rē), *n.* **Giu·sep·pe An·to·nio** (jōō zep′pe än tô′nyô), (*Joseph Guarnerius*), 1683–1745, Italian violinmaker.

Guar·ne·ri·us (gwär nâr′ē əs), *n., pl.* **-us·es.** a violin made by Guarneri or by a member of his family.

Guat., Guatemala.

Gua·te·ma·la (gwä′tə mä′lə; *Sp.* gwä′te mä′lä), *n.* **1.** a republic in S Central America. 3,759,000 (est. 1960); 42,042 sq. mi. **2.** Also called **Guatema′la Cit′y.** a city in and the capital of this republic. 355,254 (est. 1957). —**Gua′te·ma′lan,** *adj., n.*

gua·va (gwä′və), *n.* **1.** any of various myrtaceous trees or shrubs of the genus *Psidium,* esp. *P. Guajava,* of tropical or subtropical America, having a berrylike fruit. **2.** the fruit, used for making jam, jelly, etc. [< Sp *guayaba* < Arawak name]

Gua·xu·pé (gwä/shōō pe/), *n.* a city in SE Brazil. 14,168 (1960).

gua·ya·be·ra (gwī/ə ber/ə; *Sp.* gwä/yä be/rä), *n., pl.* **-be·ras** (-ber/əz; *Sp.* -be/räs). **1.** a loose, smock-like shirt worn by workers in Cuba. **2.** a copy of it, worn as a sport shirt. Also called **guayabe/ra shirt/.** [< Sp]

Gua·ya·ma (gwä yä/mä), *n.* a city in S Puerto Rico. 19,183 (1960).

Guay·a·quil (gwä/yä kēl/), *n.* **1.** a seaport in W Ecuador, on the Gulf of Guayaquil. 506,037 (est. 1963). **2. Gulf of,** an arm of the Pacific in SW Ecuador.

Guay·mas (gwī/mäs, gwä/ē-), *n.* a seaport in NW Mexico 18,813 (1950).

gua·yu·le (gwä yōō/lē; *Sp.* gwä yōō/le), *n., pl.* **-les** (-lēz; *Sp.* -les). **1.** a bushlike, composite plant, *Parthenium argentatum,* of the southwestern U.S. and Mexico, the tissues of which yield a form of rubber. **2.** the rubber obtained from this plant. [< AmerSp *guayule* < Nahuatl *cuauhuli* tree gum]

gu·ber·nac·u·lum (gōō/bər nak/yə ləm), *n., pl.* **-la** (-lə). *Anat., Zool.* a part or organ that directs the movement or course of another part. [< NL, L: rudder, equiv. to *gubernā(tus)* (see GUBERNATORIAL) + *-culum* -CULE] —**gu/ber·nac/u·lar,** *adj.*

gu·ber·na·to·ri·al (gōō/bər nə tôr/ē əl, -tôr/-, gyōō/-), *adj. Chiefly U.S.* of or pertaining to a governor. [< L *gubernātōr-* (s. of *gubernātor*) steersman, GOVERNOR + -IAL]

gu·ber·ni·ya (gŏŏ ber/ni yä/), *n.* **1.** (in the Soviet Union) an administrative division of the volosts, smaller than a district. **2.** (in Russia before 1917) an administrative division equivalent to the province. [< Russ < Pol *gubernja* < L *gubern(āre)* (to) GOVERN]

guck (guk, gŏŏk), *n. Slang.* **1.** slime or oozy dirt: *fall leaves transformed to guck in a stagnant pond.* **2.** anything repulsive, esp. something loose, flowing, and slimy. [perh. b. GOO and MUCK]

gud·dle (gud/ᵊl), *v.,* **-dled, -dling,** *n. Scot.* —*v.t.* **1.** to catch (fish) by groping with the hands, as under rocks, along a river bank, etc. —*v.i.* **2.** to grope for fish under stones, along a river bank, etc. —*n.* **3.** *Informal.* a muddled affair; mix-up; confusion. [prob. imit.]

gude (gʏd), *adj., n., interj., adv. Scot. and North Eng.* good.

Gude (gʏd), *n. Scot. and North Eng.* God.

Gu·de·a (gōō dē/ə), *n.* fl. c2250 B.C., Sumerian ruler.

Gu·der·mann·i·an (gōō/dər mä/nē ən), *n. Math.* a function so defined that the tangent of the dependent variable is equal to the hyperbolic sine of the independent variable; written *gdx.* [named after C. *Gudermann* (1798–1852), German mathematician; see -IAN]

gudg·eon[1] (guj/ən), *n.* **1.** a small, European, freshwater fish, *Gobio gobio,* of the minnow family, having a threadlike barbel at each corner of the mouth, used as bait. **2.** any of certain related fishes. **3.** a person who is easily duped or cheated. **4.** a bait or allurement. —*v.t.* **5.** to dupe; cheat. [ME *gogion* < OF *go(u)jon* < L *gōbiōn-* (s. of *gōbiō*), var. of *gobius* GOBY]

gudg·eon[2] (guj/ən), *n.* **1.** *Mach.* a trunnion. **2.** a socket for the pintle of a hinge. **3.** *Naut.* a socket attached to the stern frame of a vessel, for holding the pintle of a rudder. [ME *gudyon* < OF *go(u)jon,* ? < LL *gulbia* a chisel]

gudg/eon pin/, *Brit.* See **wrist pin.**

Gud·munds·son (gʏd/mŏŏn son), *n.* **Krist·mann** (krist/män), born 1902, Icelandic novelist.

Gud·run (gŏŏd/rōōn), *n.* **1.** (in the *Volsunga Saga*) the daughter of Giuki and Grimhild and the sister of Gunnar. She marries first Sigurd and then, after Sigurd's death, Atli, whom she kills: corresponds to Kriemhild in the *Nibelungenlied.* **2.** the heroine of the Middle High German epic poem called by her name. Also, **Guthrun, Kudrun.**

Gue·dal·la (gwi dal/ə), *n.* **Philip,** 1889–1944, English writer.

guel·der-rose (gel/dər rōz/), *n.* a variety of the cranberry tree, *Viburnum Opulus roseum,* having white, sterile flowers borne in large, snowball-like clusters. [after GUELDERS]

Guel·ders (gel/dərz), *n.* Gelderland.

Guelph (gwelf), *n.* **1.** a member of the papal and popular party in medieval Italy, opposed to the Ghibellines. **2.** a member of a secret society in Italy in the early 19th century, opposed to foreign rulers and reactionary ideas. Also, **Guelf.** [< It *Guelfo* < MHG *Welf* name of founder of a princely German family] —**Guelph/ic, Guelf/ic,** *adj.* —**Guelph/ism, Guelf/ism,** *n.*

gue·mal (gwä/məl, gā/-), *n.* huemul.

Guen·e·vere (gwen/ə vēr/), *n.* a girl's given name. Also, **Guinevere.**

gue·non (gə nôn/, -non/), *n.* any of several long-tailed, African monkeys, esp. of the genus *Cercopithecus,* having a grizzled coat. [< F < ?]

guer·don (gûr/dᵊn), *Literary.* —*n.* **1.** a reward, recompense, or requital. —*v.t.* **2.** to give a guerdon to; reward. [ME < OF, var. of *werdoun* < ML *widerdo-n(um),* alter. (prob. by assoc. with L *dōnum* gift) of OHG *widarlōn,* equiv. to *widar* again, back + *lōn* reward; c. OE *witherlēan*] —**guer/don·er,** *n.* —**guer/-don·less,** *adj.*

gue·rez·a (gə rez/ə), *n.* any of several slender African monkeys of the genus *Colobus,* having a long coat of silky, usually black and white fur. Also called **colob.** [< Ethiopian native name]

guer·gal (ger gäl/), *n.* gregale.

Gue·rick·e (gâr/ə kē, -kə, gwâr/; *for 1 also Ger.* gʏ/-ri kə), *n.* **1. Ot·to von** (ôt/ō fən), 1602–86, German physicist. **2.** a walled plain in the first quadrant of the face of the moon: about 36 miles in diameter.

Gue·rick·i·an (gə rik/ē ən, gwə-), *adj.* of or pertaining to Otto von Guericke. [GUERICK(E) + -IAN]

gue·ri·don (ger/ē don/; *Fr.* gā rē dôn/), *n., pl.* **-dons** (-donz/; *Fr.* -dôn/). *Fr. Furniture.* a small table or stand, as for holding a candelabrum. [< F *guéridon,* after the proper name *Guéridon*]

gué·rite (gā rēt/; *Fr.* gā rēt/), *n., pl.* **-rites** (-rēts/; *Fr.* -rēt/). *Fr. Furniture.* a wicker chair having a tall back arched over the seat to form a hood. [< F, MF, prob. alter. of OF *garite* watchtower; see GARRET[1]]

Guer·ni·ca (gwâr/ni kə; *Sp.* ger nē/kä), *n.* **1.** Basque town in northern Spain: bombed and destroyed 1937 by German planes serving the insurgents in the Spanish civil war. **2.** (*italics.*) a painting (1937) by Pablo Picasso.

Guern·sey (gûrn/zē), *n., pl.* **-seys** for 2, 3. **1. Isle of,** one of the Channel Islands, in the English Channel. With adjacent islands: 47,198 (est. 1961); 24½ sq. mi. **2.** one of a breed of dairy cattle, raised originally on the Isle of Guernsey, producing rich, golden-colored milk. **3.** (*l.c.*) a close-fitting knitted woolen shirt much worn by seamen.

Guern/sey lil/y, a bulbous herb, *Nerine sarniensis,* of South Africa, having crimson flowers.

guerre à ou·trance (ger a ōō träns/), *French.* war to the uttermost.

Guer·re·ro (ger re/rô), *n.* a state in S Mexico. 1,189,085 (1960); 24,885 sq. mi. *Cap.:* Chilpancingo.

guer·ril·la (gə ril/ə), *n.* **1.** a member of a small independent band of soldiers that harasses the enemy by surprise raids, attacks on communication and supply lines, etc. —*adj.* **2.** pertaining to such fighters or their technique of warfare: *guerrilla warfare.* Also, **gue·ril/la.** [< Sp, dim. of *guerra* war < Gmc] —**guer·ril/la·ism, gue·ril/la·ism,** *n.*

Guesde (ged), *n.* **Jules** (zhʏl), (*Mathieu Basile*), 1845–1922, French socialist leader, editor, and writer. —**Guesd/ism,** *n.* —**Guesd/ist,** *adj., n.*

guess (ges), *v.t.* **1.** to arrive at or commit oneself to an opinion about something without having sufficient evidence to support the opinion fully: *to guess a person's weight; to guess which fist holds the white chesspiece.* **2.** to estimate or conjecture about correctly: *to guess a riddle; to guess what a thing means.* **3.** to think, believe, or suppose: *I guess I can get there in time.* —*v.i.* **4.** to form an estimate or conjecture (often fol. by *at* or *about*): *I didn't know and hated to guess. We guessed at the height of the building. It was too important to guess about.* **5.** to estimate or conjecture correctly. —*n.* **6.** an opinion which one reaches or to which one commits oneself on the basis of probability alone or in the absence of any evidence whatever. **7.** the act of forming such an opinion: *to take a guess at someone's weight.* [ME *gess(en),* prob. < Scand; cf. Sw, Dan *gisse;* c. MD *gessen.* See GET] —**guess/a·ble,** *adj.* —**guess/er,** *n.* —**guess/ing·ly,** *adv.*

—**Syn. 1.** hazard. **1, 2, 4.** GUESS, GUESS AT, CONJECTURE, SURMISE imply attempting to form an opinion as to the probable. To GUESS is to risk an opinion regarding something one does not know about; or, wholly or partly by chance, to arrive at the correct answer to a question: *to guess the outcome of a game.* GUESS AT implies more haphazard or random guessing: *to guess at the solution of a crime.* To CONJECTURE is to make inferences in the absence of sufficient evidence to establish certainty: *to conjecture the circumstances of the crime.* SURMISE implies making an intuitive conjecture which may or may not be correct: *to surmise the motives which led to it.* **3.** fancy, imagine. **6.** supposition. —**Ant. 3.** know.

guess-rope (ges/rōp/), *n.* guest-rope.

guess·ti·mate (*v.* ges/tə māt/; *n.* ges/tə mit, -māt/), *v.,* **-mat·ed, -mat·ing,** *n. Slang.* —*v.t.* **1.** to estimate without substantial facts or statistics. —*n.* **2.** an estimate arrived at by guesswork. Also, **guestimate.** [b. GUESS and ESTIMATE]

guess-warp (ges/wôrp/), *n. Naut.* **1.** Also **guest-warp.** a line from a vessel, fastened to a buoy, anchor, or stationary object for warping purposes. **2.** guest-rope. [ME *gyes warp,* equiv. to *gyes* < ? + *warp* WARP]

guess·work (ges/wûrk/), *n.* work or procedure based on or consisting of the making of guesses or conjectures. [GUESS + WORK]

guest (gest), *n.* **1.** a person who spends some time at another person's home in some social activity, as a visit, dinner, or party. **2.** one who receives the hospitality of a club, a city, or the like. **3.** a person who patronizes a hotel, restaurant, etc., for the lodging, food, or entertainment it provides. **4.** *Zool.* an inquiline. —*v.t.* **5.** to entertain as a guest. —*v.i.* **6.** *Informal.* to appear as a guest: *She is guesting on a television panel show.* [ME *gest* < Scand (cf. OIcel *gest(r)*); r. OE *g(i)est;* c. G *Gast,* Goth *gasts,* L *hostis*] —**guest/less,** *adj.*

—**Syn. 1.** company. See **visitor.**

Guest (gest), *n.* **Edgar A(lbert),** 1881–1959, U.S. journalist and writer of verse, born in England.

guest/ flag/, a rectangular white flag flown at the starboard main spreader or main yardarm of a yacht when the owner is away but guests are on board.

guest·house (gest/hous/), *n., pl.* **-hous·es** (-hou/ziz). a building, separate from a main house or establishment, for the housing of guests. [GUEST + HOUSE]

gues·ti·mate (*v.* ges/tə māt/; *n.* ges/tə mit, -māt/) *v.t.,* **-mat·ed, -mat·ing,** *n.* guesstimate.

guest/ of hon/or, **1.** a person in whose honor a dinner, party, etc., is given. **2.** a distinguished person invited to a dinner, meeting, etc., esp. on some unique occasion.

guest/ room/, a room for the lodging of guests.

guest-rope (gest/rōp/), *n. Naut.* **1.** a rope suspended from the side of a vessel or a boom as an object to which other vessels can moor, or to afford a hold for persons in such vessels. **2.** a line sent out from a vessel to a fixed object to help the vessel in warping. **3.** a line, in addition to the towrope, to steady a boat in tow. Also, **guess-rope.** Also called **guess-warp.** [*guest* < ? + ROPE]

guest-warp (gest/wôrp/), *n. Naut.* guess-warp (def. 1).

Gueux (*Fr.* gœ), *n.* See **Les Gueux.**

Gue·va·ra (ge vä/rä), *n.* **Er·nes·to** (er nes/tô), ("*Che*"), born 1928, Cuban revolutionist and political leader, born in Argentina.

guff (guff), *n. Informal.* misleading or insolent talk. [? imit.]

guf·faw (gu fô/, gə-), *n.* **1.** a loud, unrestrained burst of laughter. —*v.i.* **2.** to laugh loudly and boisterously. [? imit.]

Gug·gen·heim (gŏŏg/ən hīm/, gōō/gən-), *n.* **Daniel,** 1856–1930, U.S. industrialist and philanthropist.

Gug·gen·heim (gŏŏg/ən hīm/, gōō/gən-), *n. Games.* category (def. 4). [from the proper name]

gug·gle (gug/əl), *v.,* **-gled, -gling,** *n.* —*v.t., v.i.* **1.** to gurgle. —*n.* **2.** a guggling sound; gurgle. [imit.]

gug·let (gug/lit), *n.* goglet.

Gui., Guiana.

Gui·an·a (gē an/ə, -ä/nə; *Sp.* gyä/nä), *n.* **1.** a vast tropical region in NE South America, bounded by the Orinoco, Rio Negro, and Amazon rivers and the Atlantic. ab. 690,000 sq. mi. **2.** a coastal portion of this region, including Guyana, French Guiana, and Surinam. 1,004,000 (est. 1963); 175,275 sq. mi.

Guian/a cur/rent, an ocean current flowing northwest along the northeast coast of South America.

Gui·a·nese (gē/ə nēz/, -nēs/, gī/-), *adj., n., pl.* **-nese.** —*adj.* **1.** of or pertaining to the region of Guiana, its inhabitants, or their language. —*n.* **2.** an inhabitant or native of Guiana. Also, **Gui·an·an** (gē an/ən, -ä/nən). [GUIAN(A) + -ESE]

guib (gwib, gēb), *n.* the harnessed antelope, *Tragelaphus scriptus.* [of Afr orig.]

guid·ance (gīd/ᵊns), *n.* **1.** the act or function of guiding; leadership; direction. **2.** advice or counseling service of some sort, esp. that provided for students choosing a course of study or preparing for a specific vocation. **3.** a program of supervised care or assistance, esp. therapeutic help in the treatment of minor emotional disturbances. **4.** something that guides. **5.** the process by which the flight of a missile or rocket may be altered in speed and direction in response to controls situated either wholly in the projectile or partly at a base. [GUIDE + -ANCE]

guide (gīd), *v.,* **guid·ed, guid·ing,** *n.* —*v.t.* **1.** to assist (a person) to travel through, or reach a destination in, an area in which he does not know the way, as by accompanying him or giving him directions: *He arose and prepared to guide us through the town. Guide yourself with a road map.* **2.** to accompany (a sightseer) to show him points of interest and to explain their meaning or significance. **3.** to force (a person, object, or animal) to move in a certain path. **4.** to supply (a person) with advice or counsel, as in his practical or spiritual affairs. **5.** to supervise (someone's actions or affairs) in an advisory capacity. —*n.* **6.** one who guides, esp. one hired to guide travelers, tourists, hunters, etc. **7.** a mark, tab, or the like, to catch the eye and thus provide quick reference. **8.** a guidebook. **9.** a guidepost. **10.** a contrivance for regulating progressive motion or action: *a sewing-machine guide.* **11.** a spirit believed to direct the utterances of a medium. **12.** *Mil.* a member of a group marching in formation who sets the pattern of movement or alignment for the rest. [ME *guide(n)* < OF *guid(er)* < Gmc; cf. OE *wītan* to look after] —**guid/a·ble,** *adj.* —**guide/less,** *adj.* —**guid/er,** *n.* —**guid/ing·ly,** *adv.*

—**Syn. 1.** pilot, steer, escort. GUIDE, CONDUCT, DIRECT, LEAD imply showing the way or pointing out or determining the course to be taken. GUIDE implies continuous presence or agency in showing or indicating a course: *to guide a traveler.* To CONDUCT is to precede or escort to a place, sometimes with a degree of ceremony: *to conduct a guest to his room.* To DIRECT is to give information for guidance, or instructions or orders for a course of procedure: *to direct someone to the station.* To LEAD is to bring onward in a course, guiding by contact or by going in advance; hence, fig., to influence or induce to some course of conduct: *to lead a procession; to lead astray.* **5.** regulate, manage, govern, rule. **6.** pilot, director, conductor. **7.** sign, signal, indication, key, clue. —**Ant. 1.** follow.

guide·board (gīd/bōrd/, -bôrd/), *n.* a large board or sign, usually mounted on a post, giving directions to travelers. [GUIDE + BOARD]

guide·book (gīd/bŏŏk/), *n.* a book of directions and information for travelers, tourists, etc. [GUIDE + BOOK] —**guide/book/ish, guide/book/y,** *adj.*

guide/ cen/ter, *Mil.* a command to a marching formation to align itself behind a guide marching at the head of the formation.

guid·ed (gī/did), *adj.* **1.** accompanied by a guide: *a guided tour.* **2.** supervised or controlled: *a guided beam.* [GUIDE + -ED[2]]

guid/ed mis/sile, an aerial missile, such as a rocket, steered during its flight by radio signals, clockwork controls, etc.

guid/ed mis/sile cruis/er, a naval cruiser equipped with long-range guided missiles and missile launchers.

guide/ dog/. See **Seeing Eye dog.**

guid/ed wave/, a wave the energy of which is concentrated near a boundary or between parallel boundaries separating different materials and which has a direction of propagation parallel to these boundaries.

guide/ fos/sil. See **index fossil.**

guide/ left/, *Mil.* a command to a marching formation to align itself with a guide marching at the left side of the formation.

guide·line (gīd/līn/), *n.* **1.** a lightly marked line used as a guide, as in composing a drawing, a typed page, or a line of lettering. **2.** a rope or cord that serves to guide one's steps, esp. over rocky terrain, through underground passages, etc. **3.** a rope or wire used in guiding the movement of stage scenery or curtains being raised or lowered. **4.** any guide or indication of a future course of action: *The government laid down the guidelines on its future policy in the United Nations yesterday.* [GUIDE + LINE[1]]

guide·post (gīd/pōst/), *n.* **1.** a post, usually mounted on the roadside or at the intersection of two or more roads, bearing a sign for the guidance of travelers. **2.** a guideline. [GUIDE + POST[1]]

guide/ rail/, a track or rail designed to control the movement of an object, as a door or window.

guide/ right/, *Mil.* a command to a marching formation to align itself with a guide marching at the right side of the formation.

guide′ rope′, 1. *Aeron.* a long rope hung downward from a balloon and trailing along the ground, used to regulate the altitude of the balloon automatically, by having more or less of its weight resting on the ground, and to act as a brake. 2. rope fastened, usually at an angle, to a hoisting or towing line, to guide the object being moved.

guide′ word′, catchword (def. 2).

Gui·do (gwē′dō; *It.* gwē′dô), *n.* a boy's given name.

Gui·do d'A·rez·zo (gwē′dô dä ret′tsô), (*Guido Aretinus*) ("*Fra Guittone*"), c995–1049?, Italian monk and music theorist: reformer of musical notation. —**Gui·do·ni·an** (gwi dō′nē ən), *adj.*

gui·don (gīd′ᵊn), *n. Mil.* 1. a small flag or streamer carried as a guide, for marking or signaling, or for identification. 2. the soldier carrying it. [< MF < It *guidone*, equiv. to *guid(are)* (to) guide + *-one* n. suffix]

guid·wil·lie (gʏd′wil′ē, gwēd′-), *n., adj. Scot. Obs.* goodwilly.

Gui·enne (gwē yen′), *n.* a former province in SW France. Also, **Guyenne.**

guige (gēj, gēzh), *n. Armor.* a shoulder strap attached to the inner side of a shield. [ME *gige* < OF *guige* extra strap for shield]

guild (gild), *n.* 1. an organization of persons with related interests, goals, etc., esp. one formed for mutual aid or protection. 2. any of various medieval associations, as of merchants or tradesmen, organized to maintain standards and to protect the interests of its members and that sometimes constituted a local governing body. 3. *Bot.* a group of plants, as parasites, having a similar habit of growth and nutrition. Also, **gild.** [ME *gild(e)* < Scand (cf. OIcel *gildi* guild, payment); r. OE *gegyld* guild; akin to G *Geld* money, Goth *-gild* tax]

guil·der (gil′dər), *n.* gulden (defs. 1, 2). Also, **gilder.** [earlier *guildren*, var. of ME *guldren*, both < D *gulden* (with intrusive *-r-*)]

guild·hall (gild′hôl′), *n.* 1. *Brit.* the hall built or used by a guild or corporation for its assemblies; town hall. 2. *Hist.* the assembly hall of a guild. Also, **gildhall.** [ME; see GUILD, HALL]

guild·ship (gild′ship), *n.* 1. guild (defs. 1, 2). 2. the condition or standing of a guild member. [OE *gieldscipe*. See GUILD, -SHIP]

guilds·man (gildz′mən), *n., pl.* **-men.** a member of a guild. Also, **gildsman.** [GUILD + 's¹ + MAN¹]

guild′ so′cialism, a school of socialism developed in England in the 20th century, emphasizing decentralization and autonomy with primary control of industry in the hands of guilds of workers. —**guild′ so′cialist.** —**guild′-so′cial·is′tic,** *adj.*

guile (gīl), *n.* insidious cunning; duplicity; artful deception. [ME < OF < Gmc; akin to WILE]
—**Syn.** trickery, fraud, craft. See **deceit.**

guile·ful (gīl′fəl), *adj.* insidiously cunning; artfully deceptive; wily. [ME; see GUILE, -FUL] —**guile′ful·ly,** *adv.* —**guile′ful·ness,** *n.*

guile·less (gīl′lis), *adj.* free from guile; sincere; honest; straightforward; frank. [GUILE + -LESS] —**guile′less·ly,** *adv.* —**guile′less·ness,** *n.*
—**Syn.** artless, ingenuous, naïve, unsophisticated.

Guil·ford (gil′fərd), *n.* a boy's given name.

Guil·laume (*Fr.* gē yōm′), *n.* **Charles É·douard** (*Fr.* sharl ā dwar′), 1861–1938, Swiss physicist: Nobel prize 1920.

Guillaume′ de Ma·chaut′ (də ma shō′), 1300–77, French poet and composer.

guil·le·mot (gil′ə mot′), *n.* 1. any of several narrow-billed, alcidine birds of the genus *Cepphus*, of northern seas, as *C. grylle* (**black guillemot**), of the North Atlantic. 2. *Brit.* a murre of the genus *Uria.* [< MF, appar. dim. of *Guillaume* William]

Gui·llén (gēl yen′; *Sp.* gē lyen′), *n.* **Jor·ge** (hôr′he), born 1893, Spanish poet in the U.S.

guil·loche (gi lōsh′), *n.* 1. an ornamental band or field with paired ribbons or lines flowing in interlaced curves around a series of circular voids. 2. an ornamental and curvilinear motif of interlaced lines. [< F: graining tool; MF *goie*, dial var. of *gouge* GOUGE]

Guilloche

guil·lo·tine (*n.* gil′ə tēn′, gē′ə tēn′; *v.* gil′ə tēn′), *n., v.,* **-tined, -tin·ing.** —*n.* 1. a device for beheading persons by means of a heavy blade that is dropped between two posts that serve as guides. 2. *Surg.* an instrument for cutting the tonsils. 3. a machine consisting of a vertical blade that descends under pressure to cut or trim a rigidly clamped stack of paper. —*v.t.* 4. to behead by the guillotine. 5. to cut (a metal strip) with a guillotine shear. [named after J. J. *Guillotin* (1738–1814), French physician who urged its use]

Guillotine
A, Knife; B, Cord which releases knife; C, Hole for head of victim; D, Board to which victim is tied; E, Basket

guil′lotine amputa′tion, *Surg.* amputation of a limb by cutting directly across it, allowing no flaps.

guil′lotine shears′, a machine for shearing metal bars, slabs, etc., in which the upper blade slides between two parallel uprights. Also called **gate shear.**

guilt (gilt), *n.* 1. the fact or state of having committed an offense, crime, violation, or wrong, esp. against moral or penal law; culpability. 2. conduct involving the commission of such crimes, wrongs, etc.: *to live a life of guilt.* 3. a feeling of responsibility or remorse for some offense, crime, wrong, etc., whether real or imagined. [ME *gilt*, OE *gylt* offense]
—**Syn.** 2. criminality. —**Ant.** 1. innocence.

guilt·less (gilt′lis), *adj.* 1. free from guilt; innocent. 2. having no knowledge or experience (usually fol. by *of*): innocent: *guiltless of the ways of wicked men.* 3. destitute or devoid (usually fol. by *of*): *a house guiltless of any charm.* [ME; OE *gyltleas.* See GUILT, -LESS] —**guilt′less·ly,** *adv.* —**guilt′less·ness,** *n.*
—**Syn.** 1. See **innocent.**

guilt·y (gil′tē), *adj.,* **guilt·i·er, guilt·i·est.** 1. having committed an offense, crime, violation, or wrong, esp. against moral or penal law; justly subject to a certain accusation or penalty; culpable: *He is guilty of murder.* 2. characterized by, connected with, or involving guilt: *guilty intent.* 3. having or showing a sense of guilt, whether real or imagined: *a guilty conscience.* [ME; OE *gyltig.* See GUILT, -Y¹] —**guilt′i·ly,** *adv.* —**guilt′i·ness,** *n.*
—**Syn.** 2. criminal, felonious, culpable; illicit, nefarious.

guimpe (gimp, gamp), *n.* 1. a chemisette or yoke of lace, embroidery, or other material, worn with a dress cut low at the neck. 2. **gimp¹.** 3. a part of the habit of nuns of certain orders, consisting of a wide, stiffly starched cloth that covers the neck and shoulders. [earlier *gimp;* c. D *gimp*]

Guin., Guinea.

Guin·ea (gin′ē), *n.* 1. a coastal region in W Africa, extending from the Gambia River to the Gabon estuary. 2. Formerly, **French Guinea.** an independent republic in W Africa, on the Atlantic coast. 2,726,888 (est. 1959); ab. 96,900 sq. mi. *Cap.:* Conakry. 3. a part of the Atlantic Ocean which projects into the W coast of Africa and extends from the Ivory Coast to Gabon. 4. a former money of account of the United Kingdom, equal to 21 shillings. 5. (*l.c.*) a gold coin of Great Britain issued from 1663 to 1813, with a nominal value of 20 shillings. 6. *Informal.* See **guinea fowl.** 7. *Disparaging.* a person of Italian birth or descent. 8. *Disparaging.* any racially different foreigner. 9. (*l.c.*) *Slang.* one who does chores at a horse stable. —**Guin′e·an,** *adj.*

SENEGAL
MALI
PORT. GUINEA
Guinea
Conakry
SIERRA LEONE
ATLANTIC OCEAN
LIBERIA
IVORY COAST

Guin·ea-Bis·sau (gin′ē bi sou′), *n.* the present-day name of **Portuguese Guinea.**

Guin′ea corn′, durra.

Guin′ea Cur′rent, an ocean current flowing E along the Guinea coast of W Africa.

guin′ea fowl′, any of several African, gallinaceous birds of the family *Numididae*, esp. a common species, *Numida meleagris*, that has a bony casque on the head and dark gray plumage spotted with white and that is now domesticated and raised for its flesh and eggs.

Guinea fowl,
Numida meleagris
(Length 2 ft.)

guin′ea grains′. See **grains of paradise.**

guin′ea grass′, a perennial grass, *Panicum maximum*, of Africa, having shiny clusters of flowers in whorls, used for forage in the South.

guin′ea hen′, 1. the female of the guinea fowl. 2. any member of the guinea fowl family.

guin′ea-hen flow′er (gin′ē-hen′). See **toad lily** (def. 2).

Guin′ea pep′per, the pods of a pepper, esp. of *Capsicum Frutescens longum*, from which cayenne is ground.

guin′ea pig′, 1. a short-eared, short-tailed rodent of the genus *Cavia*, usually white, black, and tawny, used in scientific experiments, commonly regarded as the domesticated form of one of the South American wild species of cavy. 2. *Informal.* the subject of any sort of experiment. 3. Also, **guin′ea-pig′.** *Brit. Informal.* figurehead (def. 1).

Guinea pig,
Cavia porcellus
(Length 11 in.)

Guin′ea worm′, a long, slender, nematode worm, *Dracunculus medinensis*, parasitic under the skin of man and animals, common in parts of India and Africa.

Guin·e·vere (gwin′ə vēr′), *n.* 1. *Arthurian Romance.* wife of King Arthur and mistress of Lancelot. 2. Also, **Guenevere.** a girl's given name.

Guin·ness (gin′is), *n.* **Sir Alec,** born 1914, English actor.

gui·pure (gi pyŏŏr′; *Fr.* gē pʏr′), *n., pl.* **-pures** (-pyŏŏrz′; *Fr.* -pʏr′). 1. any of various laces, often heavy, made of linen, silk, etc., with the pattern connected by brides rather than by a net ground. 2. any of various laces or trimmings formerly in use, made with cords or heavy threads, metal, etc. [< MF, equiv. to *guip(er)* (to) cover or whip with silk, etc. (< Gmc; see WIPE, WHIP) + *-ure* -URE]

Güi·ral·des (gwē räl′des), *n.* **Ri·car·do** (rē kär′thō), 1886–1927, Argentine poet and short-story writer.

gui·ro (gwēr′ō; *Sp.* gē′rō), *n., pl.* **-ros.** a South American musical instrument consisting of a hollow gourd with serrated surface which is scraped with a stick. [< AmerSp *güiro*, lit., gourd, prob. < Taino]

gui·sarme (gi zärm′), *n.* a shafted weapon having as a head a curved, edged blade with a beak at the back. Also, **gisarme.** [ME < OF *g(u)isarme, gisarne*, prob. of Gmc orig.; cf. OHG *getīsarn*, lit., weeding iron, equiv to *get(an)* (to) weed (G *jäten*) + *īsarn* iron]

Guis·card (*Fr.* gēs kar′), *n.* **Ro·bert** (*Fr.* rô ber′), (*Robert de Hauteville*) c1015–85, Norman conqueror in Italy.

guise (gīz), *n., v.,* **guised, guis·ing.** —*n.* 1. general external appearance; aspect; semblance: *an old principle in a new guise.* 2. assumed appearance or mere semblance: *under the guise of friendship.* 3. style of dress: *in the guise of a shepherdess.* 4. *Archaic.* manner; mode. —*v.t.* 5. to dress; attire: *children guised as cowboys.* —*v.i.* 6. *Scot. and North Eng.* to appear or go in disguise. [ME < OF < Gmc; see WISE²]

Guise (gēz), *n.* 1. **Fran·çois de Lor·raine** (fräɴ swa′ də lô ren′), **2nd Duc de,** 1519–63, French general and statesman. 2. his son, **Hen·ri I de Lorraine** (äɴ rē′), **Duc de,** 1550–88, French general and leader of opposition to the Huguenots.

gui·tar (gi tär′), *n.* a stringed musical instrument with a long, fretted neck, a flat, somewhat violinlike body, and typically six strings, which are plucked with the fingers or with a plectrum. [< Sp *guitarr(a)* << Gk *kithára* cithara] —**gui·tar′like′,** *adj.*

Guitar

gui·tar·fish (gi tär′fish′), *n., pl.* (*esp. collectively*) **-fish,** (*esp. referring to two or more kinds or species*) **-fish·es.** any of several shark-like rays of the family *Rhinobatidae*, found in warm seas, resembling a guitar in shape.

gui·tar·ist (gi tär′ist), *n.* a performer on the guitar.

guit·guit (gwit′gwit′), *n.* any of several tropical American honeycreepers. [imit.]

Gui·try (gē′trē; *Fr.* gē trē′), *n.* **Sa·cha** (sä′shə; *Fr.* sa sha′), 1885–1957, French actor and dramatist, born in Russia.

Gui·zot (gē zō′), *n.* **Fran·çois Pierre Guil·laume** (fräɴ swa′ pyer gē yōm′), 1787–1874, French historian and statesman.

Gu·ja·rat (gŏŏj′ə rät′), *n.* 1. a region in W India, N of the Narbada River. 2. a state in W India. 20,-633,350 (1961); 72,138 sq. mi. *Cap.:* Ahmedabad. Also, **Gu′je·rat′.**

Gu·ja·ra·ti (gŏŏj′ə rä′tē), *n.* an Indic language of western India. [< Hindi < Skt *Gurjara* GUJARAT]

Gu′jarat States′, a group of former princely states, in W India; placed under a special agency (**Gu′jarat States′ A′gency**) in 1933; now divided between Gujarat and Maharashtra states.

Guj·ran·wa·la (gŏŏj′rən wä′lə), *n.* a city in NE West Pakistan. 196,154 (1961).

gu·la (gyōō′lə, gōō′-), *n., pl.* **-lae** (-lē), **-las.** 1. *Zool.* the upper part of the throat. 2. *Archit.* **a.** a molding having a large hollow, as a cavetto. **b.** ogee (def. 2). [ME < L: throat, gullet, appetite] —**gu′lar,** *adj.*

gulch (gulch), *n.* a deep, narrow ravine, esp. one marking the course of a stream or torrent. [? prob. related to *gulch* throat, a drunkard; see GULLY¹]

gul·den (gŏŏl′dən), *n., pl.* **-dens, -den.** 1. a silver coin and monetary unit of the Netherlands, equal to 100 cents and equivalent to about .28 of a U.S. dollar; florin. *Abbr.:* Gld., f., fl. 2. a former gold coin of the Netherlands; florin. 3. the monetary unit of the Netherlands Antilles, equal to 100 cents and equivalent to about .54 of a U.S. dollar. 4. the Austrian florin. 5. any of various gold coins formerly issued by German states. Also called **guilder** (for defs. 1, 2). [< D and G: lit., GOLDEN]

Gü·lek Bo·gaz (gʏ lek′ bō gäz′), Turkish name of the **Cilician Gates.**

gules (gyōōlz), *Heraldry.* —*n.* 1. the tincture, or color, red. —*adj.* 2. of the tincture, or color, red: *a lion gules.* [ME *goules* < OF *gueules* red fur neckpiece, deriv. of *gole* throat < L *gula*]

gulf (gulf), *n.* 1. a portion of an ocean or sea partly enclosed by land. 2. a deep hollow; chasm or abyss. 3. any wide separation, as in station, education, etc. 4. something that engulfs or swallows up. —*v.t.* 5. to swallow like a gulf, or as in a gulf; engulf. [ME *go(u)lf* < OF *golfe* < It *golf(o)* < LGk *kólphos* < Gk *kólpos* bosom, lap, bay] —**gulf′like′,** *adj.* —**gulf′y,** *adj.*

Gulf′ Intracoast′al Wa′terway. See under **Intracoastal Waterway.**

Gulf·port (gulf′pōrt′, -pôrt′), *n.* 1. a city in SE Mississippi, on the Gulf of Mexico. 30,204 (1960). 2. a town in W Florida. 9730 (1960).

gulf′ rupee′, rupee (def. 5).

Gulf′ States′, the States of the U.S. bordering on the Gulf of Mexico: Florida, Alabama, Mississippi, Louisiana, and Texas.

Gulf′ Stream′, 1. a warm ocean current flowing N from the Gulf of Mexico, along the E coast of the U.S., to an area off the SE coast of Newfoundland, where it becomes the western terminus of the North Atlantic Current. 2. See **Gulf Stream system.**

Gulf′ Stream′, The, a painting by Winslow Homer.

Gulf′ Stream′ sys′tem, a major ocean-current system consisting of the Gulf Stream and the Florida and North Atlantic currents. Also called **Gulf Stream.**

Gulf′ War′, a conflict (Jan.–Feb. 1991) between Iraq and the United States and its allies to expel Iraq from Kuwait.

gulf·weed (gulf′wēd′), *n.* 1. a coarse, olive-brown seaweed, *Sargassum bacciferum*, found in the Gulf Stream and tropical American seas, characterized by numerous berrylike air vessels. 2. any seaweed of the same genus. [GULF + WEED¹]

gul·gul (gul′gul), *n.* a preparation of pulverized seashells and oil, applied to the wooden hull of a ship as a protection against boring worms. [?]

Herring gull,
Larus argentatus
(Length 26 in.; wingspread 4½ ft.)

gull¹ (gul), *n.* any of numerous long-winged, web-toed, aquatic birds of the family *Laridae*, having usually white plumage with a gray back and wings. [ME *gulle*, perh. < Welsh *gwylan*, Cornish *guilan* (cf. F *goëland*)] —**gull′like′,** *adj.*

gull² (gul), *v.t.* 1. to deceive; trick; cheat. —*n.* 2. one easily deceived or cheated; a dupe. [? akin to obs. *gull* to swallow, guzzle]
—**Syn.** 1. cozen, dupe, fool, bamboozle, hoodwink.

gull·a·ble (gul′ə bəl), *adj.* gullible. —**gull′a·bil′i·ty,** *n.* —**gull′a·bly,** *adv.*

Gul·lah (gul′ə), *n.* 1. a member of a Negro people settled as slaves on the Sea Islands and the coastal regions of South Carolina, Georgia, and northeastern Florida. 2. their English dialect. [from native name of African tribe or district; perh. Angolese]

gul·let (gul′it), *n.* 1. the esophagus. 2. the throat or pharynx. 3. something like the esophagus. 4. a channel for water. 5. a gully or ravine. 6. a preparatory cut in an excavation. 7. a concavity between two saw teeth, joining them at their bases. —*v.t.* 8. to form a concavity at the base of (a saw tooth). [ME *golet* < OF *goulet* << L *gula* throat; see -ET]

gul·ley[1] (gul′ē), *n., pl.* **-leys.** gully[1] (defs. 1, 2).

gul·ley[2] (gul′ē), *n., pl.* **-leys.** *Scot. and North Eng.* gully[2].

gul·li·ble (gul′ə bəl), *adj.* easily deceived or cheated. Also, **gullable.** [GULL[2] + -IBLE] —**gul′li·bil′i·ty,** *n.* —**gul′li·bly,** *adv.*

Gul′li·ver's Trav′els (gul′ə vərz), a social and political satire (1726) by Jonathan Swift, narrating the voyages of Lemuel Gulliver to four imaginary regions: Lilliput, Brobdingnag, Laputa, and the land of the Houyhnhnms.

Gull·strand (gul′strand′; *Swed.* gōōl′stränd′), *n.* **All·var** (äl′vär), 1862–1930, Swedish oculist: Nobel prize for medicine 1911.

gul·ly[1] (gul′ē), *n., pl.* **-lies,** *v.,* **-lied, -ly·ing.** —*n.* 1. a small valley or ravine originally worn away by running water and serving as a drainageway after prolonged heavy rains. 2. a ditch or gutter. 3. *Cricket.* a. the position of a fielder between point and slips. b. the fielder occupying this position. —*v.t.* 4. to make gullies in. 5. to form (channels) by the action of water. Also, **gulley** (for defs. 1, 2). [appar. var. of GULLET, with -Y[3] r. F *-et*]

gul·ly[2] (gul′ē, gōōl′ē), *n., pl.* **-lies.** *Scot. and North Eng.* a knife, esp. a large butcher knife. Also, **gulley.** [?]

gul′ly wash′er, *Chiefly Oklahoma and Texas.* a very heavy rainstorm.

gu·los·i·ty (gyōō los′i tē), *n.* gluttony; greediness. [ME < LL *gulōsitās,* equiv. to L *gulōs(us)* (*gul(a)* throat, appetite + *-ōsus* -OSE[1]) + *-itās* -ITY]

gulp (gulp), *v.i.* 1. to gasp or choke, as when taking large drafts of a liquid. —*v.t.* 2. to swallow eagerly, or in large drafts or morsels (usually fol. by *down*): *He gulps down his food like a starving man.* 3. to suppress, subdue, or choke back as if by swallowing: *to gulp down a sob.* —*n.* 4. the act of gulping. 5. the amount swallowed at one time; mouthful. [ME *gulp(en)*; cf. D *gulpen,* Norw *glupa*] —**gulp′ing·ly,** *adv.*

gulp·y (gul′pē), *adj.* characterized by gulps or gulping. [GULP + -Y[1]]

gum[1] (gum), *n., v.,* **gummed, gum·ming.** —*n.* 1. any of various viscid, amorphous exudations from plants, hardening on exposure to air and soluble in or forming a viscid mass with water. 2. any of various similar exudations, as resin, glue, etc. 3. a preparation of such a substance, as for use in the arts, bookbinding, etc. 4. See **chewing gum.** 5. mucilage; glue. 6. rubber. 7. See **gum tree.** 8. *Philately.* the adhesive by which a postage stamp is affixed. Cf. **original gum.** 9. *Chiefly U.S. Dial.* a rubber overshoe or boot. —*v.t.* 10. to smear, stiffen, or stick together with gum. 11. to clog with or as with some gummy substance. —*v.i.* 12. to exude or form gum. 13. to become gummy; become clogged with some gummy substance. 14. **gum up the works.** See **work** (def. 16). [ME *gomme* < OF << var. of L *gummi, cummi* < Gk *kómmi*] —**gum′less,** *adj.* —**gum′like′,** *adj.*

gum[2] (gum), *n., v.,* **gummed, gum·ming.** —*n.* 1. Often, **gums.** the firm, fleshy tissue covering the alveolar parts of either jaw and enveloping the necks of the teeth. —*v.t.* 2. to shape or renew the teeth of (a saw), as by grinding. 3. **beat one's gums,** *Slang.* to talk excessively or ineffectively: *Listen, I'm tired of you beating your gums about a new fur coat!* [ME *gome,* OE *gōma* palate; akin to OIcel *gómr,* G *Gaumen* palate]

gum[3] (gum), *interj.* (used in mild oaths as a euphemism for God): *By gum!*

gum′ ammo′niac, a yellowish to brownish, sweetish but bitter and acrid, partly water-soluble gum resin, occurring in tearlike fragments and obtained from the umbelliferous plant, *Dorema ammoniacum,* of Persia: used as an expectorant in the treatment of bronchitis, externally as a counterirritant, and in the manufacture of porcelain cements. Also called **ammoniac, ammoniacum.**

gum′ ar′abic, a water-soluble, dried, gummy exudation obtained from the stems and branches of *Acacia Senegal* and other species of acacia: used as mucilage, a food thickener, an emulsifier, in inks, textile printing, and in pharmaceuticals as an excipient for tablets. Also called **acacia, gum′ aca′cia.**

gum′ ben′zoin, benzoin (def. 1). Also called **gum′ ben′jamin.**

gum·bo (gum′bō), *n., pl.* **-bos,** *adj.* —*n.* 1. the okra plant. 2. its mucilaginous pods. 3. a stew or thick soup, usually containing okra and chicken or seafood, sometimes with filé added as a thickener. 4. soil that becomes sticky and nonporous when wet. —*adj.* 5. of, pertaining to, or resembling gumbo. [< LaF *gombo, gumbo* < Bantu *kingombo,* equiv. to *ki-* prefix + *ngumbo* okra]

gum·boil (gum′boil′) *n. Pathol.* a small abscess on the gum. Also called **parulis.** [GUM[2] + BOIL[2]]

gum′bo lil′y. See **prairie lily.**

gum·bo-lim·bo (gum′bō lim′bō), *n., pl.* **-lim·bos.** a tropical American burseraceous tree, *Bursera Simaruba,* that yields a sweet, aromatic resin used in the manufacture of varnishes. Also called **gum elemi.** [of Afr orig.]

gum·bo·til (gum′bə til), *n. Geol.* a sticky clay formed by the thorough weathering of glacial drift, the thickness of the clay furnishing means for comparing relative lengths of interglacial ages. [GUMBO + *til,* var. of TILL[4]]

gum′ dam′mar, dammar (def. 1).

gum·drop (gum′drop′), *n. U.S.* a small candy made of gum arabic, gelatin, or the like, sweetened and flavored. [GUM[1] + DROP]

gum′ elas′tic, rubber[1] (def. 1).

gum′ el′emi, 1. *Chem.* elemi. 2. gumbo-limbo.

gu·mi (gōō′mē), *n.* a spreading shrub, *Elaeagnus multiflora,* of eastern Asia, having yellowish-white flowers and edible, red, scaly fruit. [< Jap]

gum·ly (gum′lē), *adj. Scot. Obs.* muddy; turbid. [alter. of GRUMLY]

gum·ma (gum′ə), *n., pl.* **gum·mas, gum·ma·ta** (gum′ə tə). *Pathol.* the rubbery, tumorlike lesion of tertiary syphilis. [< NL; see GUM[1]]

gum·ma·tous (gum′ə təs), *adj. Pathol.* 1. of the nature of or resembling a gumma. 2. pertaining to a gumma. [< NL *gummat-* (s. of *gumma*) GUMMA + -OUS]

gummed (gumd), *adj.* covered with a gummy substance. [ME; see GUM[1], -ED[2]]

gum·mite (gum′īt), *n.* a yellow to red alteration product of pitchblende and a minor ore of uranium, having a greasy luster and occurring in gumlike masses. [orig. G *Gummit.* See GUM[1], -ITE[1]]

gum·mo·sis (gu mō′sis), *n. Bot.* a pathological condition in certain plants, characterized by the excessive formation of gum. [< NL, equiv. to L *gumm(i)* GUM[1] + *-ōsis* -OSIS]

gum·mous (gum′əs), *adj.* consisting of or resembling gum; gummy. [< L *gummōs(us),* equiv. to *gumm(i)* GUM[1] + *-ōsus* -OUS]

gum·my (gum′ē), *adj.,* **-mi·er, -mi·est.** 1. of, resembling, or of the consistency of gum; viscid. 2. covered with or clogged by gum or sticky matter. 3. exuding gum. [ME; see GUM[1], -Y[1]] —**gum′mi·ness,** *n.*

gum-myr·tle (gum′mûr′təl), *n.* a smooth-barked tree, *Angophora lanceolata,* of California, having showy, white flowers and evergreen leaves. Also called **orange gum, rusty gum.**

gump (gump), *n. Dial.* a foolish, dull person. [?]

gum′ plant′, any composite plant of the genus *Grindelia,* of the western U.S., covered with a viscid secretion.

gump·tion (gump′shən), *n. Informal.* 1. initiative; aggressiveness; resourcefulness: *With his gumption he'll make a success of himself.* 2. courage; spunk; guts: *It takes gumption to quit a good paying job.* [orig. Scot] —**gump′tion·less,** *adj.* —**gump′tious,** *adj.*

gum′ rash′, *Pathol.* strophulus.

gum′ res′in, a plant exudation consisting of a mixture of gum and resin, as asafetida. —**gum′-res′i·nous,** *adj.*

gum·shoe (gum′shōō′), *n., v.,* **-shoed, -shoe·ing.** —*n.* 1. a shoe made of gum elastic or India rubber; rubber overshoe. 2. sneaker. 3. *U.S. Slang.* a. one who goes about softly, as if wearing shoes with thick rubber soles. b. a policeman or detective. —*v.i.* 4. *U.S. Slang.* to go softly as if wearing rubber shoes; move or act snoopingly or stealthily. [GUM[1] + SHOE]

gum′ thus′ (thus), frankincense.

gum′ trag′acanth, tragacanth.

gum′ tree′, 1. any tree that exudes gum, as a eucalyptus, the sour gum, the sweet gum, etc. 2. any of various other gum-yielding trees, as the sapodilla.

gum·wood (gum′wo͝od′), *n.* the wood of a gum tree, esp. the wood of the eucalyptus of Australia, or of a gum tree of the western U.S. [GUM[1] + WOOD[1]]

gun[1] (gun), *n., v.,* **gunned, gun·ning.** —*n.* 1. a metallic tube, with its stock or carriage and attachments, from which missiles are shot by the force of an explosive; a piece of ordnance. 2. any portable firearm, as a rifle, shotgun, revolver, etc. 3. a long-barreled cannon having a relatively flat trajectory. 4. any device for shooting something under pressure: *a paint gun.* 5. *Brit.* a member of a shooting party. 6. *Slang.* a person whose profession is killing; professional killer: *The gangland chiefs decided to bring in an unknown gun to do the killing.* 7. **give something the gun,** *Slang.* to put into motion or speed up: *We gave the motor the gun and drove off.* 8. **jump the gun,** *Slang.* a. to begin a race before the starting signal. b. to begin (something) prematurely; act too hastily: *I jumped the gun by putting away my winter wardrobe on the first warm day of spring.* 9. **spike someone's guns,** to frustrate or prevent someone from accomplishing his plan: *Our competitors planned a surprise reduction in their rates, but we discovered it and were able to spike their guns.* 10. **stick to one's guns,** to maintain one's position in the face of opposition; stand firm: *There was enormous pressure on them to submit, but they stuck to their guns.* —*v.i.* 11. to hunt with a gun. 12. to shoot with a gun: *No Gunning, Fishing, or Trespassing.* —*v.t.* 13. to shoot with a gun (often fol. by *down*): *The police gunned down the killer as he was making his escape.* 14. *Aeron. Slang.* to cause (an aircraft) to increase in speed very quickly. 15. to feed gasoline to, suddenly and quickly: *to gun an engine.* 16. **gun for,** a. to seek with intent to harm or kill. b. to seek; try earnestly to obtain: *He is gunning for a raise.* [ME *gunne, gonne,* appar. short for *Gunilda* (L), *gonnyld* (ME) name for engine of war; cf. Icel *Gunna,* short for *Gunnhildr* woman's name] —**gun′less,** *adj.*

gun[2] (gun), *v.* pp. of **gin**[3].

gun., gunnery.

gu·na (go͝on′ə), *n.* (in Sankhya and Vedantic philosophy) one of the three qualities of prakriti, or nature, which are activity (**rajas**), inertia (**tamas**), and harmonious balance (**sattva**). [< Skt *guṇa* thread, quality]

gun·boat (gun′bōt′), *n.* 1. a small vessel carrying mounted guns. 2. a small, armed war vessel of light draft, used in ports where the water is shallow. [GUN[1] + BOAT]

gun′ brig′, a naval brig of the 18th century having from 8 to 12 guns.

gun′ car′riage, the structure on which a gun is mounted or moved and from which it is fired.

gun·cot·ton (gun′kot′ən), *n.* a highly explosive cellulose nitrate, made by digesting clean cotton in a mixture of one part nitric acid and three parts sulfuric acid: used in making smokeless powder. [GUN[1] + COTTON]

gun′ crew′, sailors and petty officers in charge of a gun on a ship.

gun·da (go͝on′də), *n.* goonda.

gun·da·low (gun′dəlō′), *n.* a scowlike freight barge used in New England in the 19th century, esp. on certain rivers, having a rounded, bowllike bow and stern, flaring topsides, and a very short mast with a large triangular sail, similar to a lateen sail. [var. of GONDOLA]

gun′ deck′, (formerly, on a warship) any deck, other than the weather deck, that has cannons from end to end.

gun′ dog′, a dog trained to hunt game by pointing.

gun·fight (gun′fīt′), *v.,* **-fought, -fight·ing,** *n.* —*v.i.* 1. to fight with guns. —*n.* 2. a battle between people in which the principal weapon is a gun. [GUN[1] + FIGHT]

gun·fight·er (gun′fī′tər), *n.* a person highly skilled in the use of a gun and a veteran of many gunfights, esp. one living during the frontier days of the West. [GUN[1] + FIGHTER]

gun·fire (gun′fīər′), *n.* 1. the firing of a gun or guns. 2. *Mil.* the tactical use of firearms, esp. cannon, as distinguished from other weapons, as bayonets or torpedoes, and from shock or charge tactics. [GUN[1] + FIRE]

gun·flint (gun′flint′), *n.* the flint in a flintlock. [GUN[1] + FLINT]

gung ho (gung′ hō′), 1. work together: a slogan of U.S. Marines under General Carlson in World War II. 2. *Informal.* wholeheartedly, often ingenuously, loyal and enthusiastic: *a gung ho military outfit.* [< Chin]

Gu·nil·la (gə nil′ə; *Swed.* gōō nē lä′), *n.* a girl's given name.

Gun·ite (gun′īt), *n. Trademark.* a mixture of cement, sand or crushed slag, and water, sprayed over reinforcement as a lightweight concrete construction.

gunk (gungk), *n. Informal.* repulsively greasy, sticky, or slimy matter. [prob. imit.]

gunk′ hole′, *Slang.* a quiet anchorage, as in a cove, used by small yachts.

gunk·hole (gungk′hōl′), *v.i.,* **-holed, -hol·ing.** *Slang.* (of a yachtsman) to sail casually along a coast, anchoring from time to time in quiet coves and inlets. [v. use of n. phrase *gunk hole*]

gun·lock (gun′lok′), *n.* the mechanism of a firearm by which the charge is exploded. [GUN[1] + LOCK[1]]

gun·mak·er (gun′mā′kər), *n.* a person or company that makes guns. [ME; see GUN[1], MAKER] —**gun′mak′ing,** *n.*

gun·man (gun′mən), *n., pl.* **-men.** 1. *U.S.* a man armed with or expert in the use of a gun, esp. one ready to use a gun unlawfully for hire. 2. one who makes guns. [GUN[1] + MAN[1]] —**gun′man·ship′,** *n.*

gun′ met′al, 1. any of various alloys or metallic substances with a dark-gray or blackish color or finish, used for chains, belt buckles, etc. 2. Also called **gun′-metal gray′.** a dark gray with bluish or purplish tinge. 3. a bronze formerly much employed for cannon. —**gun′-met′al,** *adj.*

gun′ moll′, *Slang.* 1. a female companion of a gun-carrying criminal. 2. a female criminal, esp. one who carries a gun.

Gun·nar (go͝on′när, go͝on′ər), *n.* 1. *Scand. Legend.* a son of Giuki and Grimhild, the brother of Gudrun, and the husband of Brynhild, whom Sigurd had won for him: corresponds to Gunther in the *Nibelungenlied.* 2. a boy's given name.

gun·nel[1] (gun′əl), *n.* any of several elongated, bandlike blennies of the family *Pholididae* (*Pholidae*), esp. *Pholis gunnellus* (**rock gunnel**), of the North Atlantic. Also called **bracketed blenny.** [?]

gun·nel[2] (gun′əl), *n. Naut.* gunwale.

gun·ner (gun′ər), *n.* 1. one who works a gun or cannon. 2. *U.S. Army.* an occupational title in the artillery. 3. *U.S. Navy.* one skilled in handling ammunition and gunnery equipment. 4. *U.S. Marines.* a warrant officer who may be given any one of a number of assignments. 5. *Brit.* a. *Mil.* a private in the artillery. b. *Informal.* any officer or enlisted man assigned to the artillery. 6. one who hunts with a gun. [ME; see GUN[1], -ER[1]] —**gun′ner·ship′,** *n.*

gun·ner·y (gun′ə rē), *n.* 1. the art and science of constructing and managing guns, esp. large guns. 2. the act of firing guns. 3. guns collectively. [GUN[1] + -ERY]

gun·ning (gun′ing), *n.* 1. the act, practice, or art of shooting with guns; gunnery. 2. the hunting of game with guns. [GUN[1] + -ING[1]]

Gun·ni·son (gun′i sən), *n.* a town in central Colorado. 3477 (1960).

gun·ny (gun′ē), *n., pl.* **-nies.** a strong, coarse material made commonly from jute, esp. for bagging; burlap. [< Hindi *gonī* < Skt: sack, perh. orig. of hide; cf. *gāus* an ox]

gun·ny·sack (gun′ē sak′), *n.* a sack made of gunny or burlap. Also called **gun·ny-bag** (gun′ē bag′). [GUNNY + SACK[1]]

gun·pa·per (gun′pā′pər), *n. Mil.* a type of paper treated with nitric acid so that it has a composition similar to that of guncotton. [GUN[1] + PAPER]

gun·play (gun′plā′), *n.* the exchange of gunshots, usually with intent to wound or kill. [GUN[1] + PLAY]

gun·point (gun′point′), *n.* 1. the point or aim of a gun. 2. **at gunpoint,** under threat of being shot: *He carried out the gangster's orders at gunpoint.* [GUN[1] + POINT]

gun·pow·der (gun′pou′dər), *n.* 1. an explosive mixture of saltpeter or potassium nitrate, sulfur, and charcoal, used esp. in gunnery. 2. Also called **gun′powder tea′.** a fine variety of green China tea, each leaf of which is rolled into a little ball. [ME; see GUN[1], POWDER[1]] —**gun′pow′der·y,** *adj.*

Gun′powder Plot′, an unsuccessful plot to kill King James I and the assembled Lords and Commons by blowing up Parliament, November 5, 1605, in revenge for the laws against Roman Catholics. Cf. **Guy Fawkes Day.**

gun′ room′, 1. a room in which guns are kept. 2. *Brit.* a room for the use of junior naval officers.

gun·run·ning (gun′run′ing), *n.* the smuggling of guns or other ammunition into a country. [GUN[1] + RUNNING] —**gun′run′ner,** *n.*

gun·sel (gun′səl), *n. Slang.* 1. a catamite. 2. a criminal armed with a gun. [prob. < Yiddish *genzel* gosling < MHG *gensel* (dim. of *gans* goose); sense of def. 2, by influence of GUN[1]]

gun·shot (gun′shot′), *n.* 1. a bullet, projectile, or other shot fired from a gun. 2. the range of a gun: *out of gunshot.* 3. the shooting of a gun. —*adj.* 4. made by a gunshot. [ME; see GUN[1], SHOT[1]]

gun-shy (gun′shī′), *adj.* frightened by the shooting of a gun: *a gun-shy bird dog.*

gun·sling·er (gun′sling′ər), *n. Slang.* gunfighter. [GUN[1] + SLING[1] + -ER[1]]

gun·smith (gun′smith′), *n.* one who makes or repairs firearms. [GUN[1] + SMITH] —**gun′smith′ing,** *n.*

gun·stock (gun′stok′), *n.* the stock or support in which the barrel of a shoulder weapon is fixed. [ME; see GUN[1], STOCK]

gun·stock·ing (gun′stok′ing), *n. Naut.* a hardwood joggling plank used as a margin plank with softwood decking. [GUNSTOCK (in obs. sense of support for cannon on board ship) + -ING[1]]

gun/stock stile/, (in a door) a diminished stile having an oblique transition between the broader and narrower parts.

gun/ tack/le, *Naut.* a tackle composed of a fall rove through two single blocks and secured to one of them so as to secure a mechanical advantage of two or three, neglecting friction, depending on which is the standing and which is the running block. See diag. under **tackle.**

gun·ter (gun/tər), *n. Naut.* a jib-headed sail fastened to a vertical spar **(gun/ter yard/)** that is attached to a short mast, usually by two rings **(gun/ter i/rons),** in such a way that the spar can slide up the mast to spread the sail. Also, **gun·ther** (gun/thər). [named after Edmund GUNTER for its resemblance to an instrument using his principles]

Gun·ter (gun/tər), *n.* **Edmund,** 1581–1626, English mathematician and astronomer: inventor of various measuring instruments and scales.

gun/ter lug/, *Naut.* a standing lug having a nearly vertical yard attached to the mast in the manner of a gaff. [named after Edmund GUNTER]

Gun/ter's chain/. See under **chain** (def. 8a). [named after Edmund GUNTER]

Gun·ters·ville (gun/tərz vil), *n.* a town in NE Alabama. 6592 (1960).

Gun·ther (gun/thər *for 1;* gŏŏn/tər *for 2*), *n.* **1. John,** 1901–70, U.S. journalist and author. **2.** (in the *Nibelungenlied*) a king of Burgundy, the husband of Brunhild and the brother of Kriemhild. He was beheaded by Kriemhild in her revenge against the Burgundians for the murder of Siegfried. Cf. **Gunnar.**

gun-tot·ing (gun/tō/ting, -tōt/ən), *adj.* carrying a gun, usually a pistol, regularly.

gun·wale (gun/əl), *n. Naut.* **1.** (loosely) the upper edge of the side or bulwark of a vessel. **2.** the sheer strake of a wooden vessel; the uppermost strake beneath the plank-sheer. Also, **gunnel.** [GUN[1] + WALE[1]; a plank; so called because guns were set upon it]

gun·yah (gun/yə), *n. Australian.* **1.** an aboriginal hut or shelter. **2.** any crude bush hut or shelter. [< native Austral]

Günz (gints; *Ger.* GYNTS), *n.* the first stage of the glaciation of Eurasia during the Pleistocene. Cf. **Nebraskan** (def. 4). [after a region in the Alps; see WÜRM] —**Günz/i·an,** *adj.*

gup·py (gup/ē), *n., pl.* **-pies.** a small, fresh-water topminnow, *Lebistes reticulatus,* often kept in aquariums. [after R.J.L. *Guppy* of Trinidad, who presented specimens to the British Museum]

gur·dwa·ra (gûr/dwär ə), *n.* a sikh temple in India. [< Panjabi *gurduārā* < Skt *guru* GURU + *dvāra* door]

gurge (gûrj), *n., v.,* **gurged, gurg·ing.** —*n.* **1.** a whirlpool. **2.** Also called **gorge, gurges, whirlpool.** *Heraldry.* a charge covering the entire field of an escutcheon and having the form either of a spirallike scroll or of a number of concentric rings, the whole field having two tinctures. —*v.i.* **3.** to swirl like a whirlpool. [< L *gurge(s)* whirlpool]

gur·ges (gûr/jēz), *n., pl.* **-ges.** *Heraldry.* gurge (def. 2).

gur·gi·ta·tion (gûr/ji tā/shən), *n.* a surging rise and fall; ebullient motion, as of water. [< L *gurgitāt(us)* engulfed (ptp. of *gurgitāre,* deriv. of *gurgit-,* s. of *gurges* whirlpool; see -ATE[1]) + -ION]

gur·gle (gûr/gəl), *v.,* **-gled, -gling,** *n.* —*v.i.* **1.** to flow in a broken, irregular, noisy current: *Water gurgles from a bottle.* **2.** to make a sound as of water doing this (often used of birds or of human beings). —*v.t.* **3.** to utter or express with a gurgling sound: *He rubbed his hands together and gurgled his delight.* —*n.* **4.** act or noise of gurgling. [cf. D, MLG *gorgelen,* G *gurgeln* to GARGLE; perh. < L *gurguliō* throat] —**gur/gling·ly,** *adv.*

gur·glet (gûr/glit), *n.* goglet. [GURGLE + -ET]

gu·ri bo·ri (gōō rē/ bə rē/; *Jap.* gōō RE/ bô RE/), a form of decorative carving for Japanese metalwork, as sword mounts, in which thin alternating layers of metals of different colors, usually copper and shakudo, are cut to produce a pattern in the two colors. [< Jap, equiv. to *guri* multi-coated lacquer + *bori* carving]

Gur·kha (gŏŏr/kä; *Eng.* gûr/kə), *n., pl.* **-khas,** *(esp. collectively)* **-kha.** a member of a Rajput people, Hindu in religion, living in Nepal.

gur·nard (gûr/nərd), *n., pl. (esp. collectively)* **-nard,** *(esp. referring to two or more kinds or species)* **-nards.** **1.** any of several marine fishes of the family *Triglidae,* having a bony head armed with spines. **2.** See **flying gurnard.** [ME < OF *gornard,* prob. lit., grunter < Pr *gourgna* to grunt << L *grunnīre* to grunt]

gur·ney (gûr/nē), *n., pl.* **-neys.** a flat, padded table or stretcher with legs and wheels, for transporting patients, as to and from surgery. [?]

Gur·ney·ite (gûr/nē it/), *n.* a supporter of Joseph John Gurney (1788–1847), an English Quaker, who, on a preaching tour of America, advocated Christian evangelical principles. Cf. **Wilburite.** [*Gurney* + -ITE[1]]

gursh (gûrsh), *n.* the fractional currency unit of Saudi Arabia, the twenty-second part of a riyal, equivalent to about .001 of a U.S. dollar. Also, **girsh.** [< Ar]

gu·ru (gōō/rōō, gōō rōō/), *n. Hinduism.* a preceptor giving personal religious instruction. [< Hindi *gurū* < Skt *guru* venerable, weighty] —**gu/ru·ship/,** *n.*

Gus (gus), *n.* a boy's given name, form of **Augustus.**

gush (gush), *v.i.* **1.** to flow out or issue suddenly, copiously, or forcibly, as a fluid from confinement. **2.** to express oneself extravagantly or emotionally; talk effusively. **3.** to have a sudden, copious, or forcible flow, as of blood, tears, etc. —*v.t.* **4.** to emit suddenly, forcibly, or copiously. —*n.* **5.** a sudden, copious, or forcible outflow of a fluid. **6.** the fluid emitted. **7.** effusive language. [ME *goshe, gusche;* prob. phonesthemic in orig.; see GUST[1], RUSH[1]] —**gush/ing·ly,** *adv.*
—**Syn. 1.** pour, stream, flood. See **flow. 4.** spurt.

gush·er (gush/ər), *n.* **1.** a flowing oil well, usually of large capacity. **2.** a person who gushes. [GUSH + -ER[1]]

gush·y (gush/ē), *adj.,* **gush·i·er, gush·i·est.** given to or marked by excessively effusive talk, behavior, etc. [GUSH + -Y[1]] —**gush/i·ly,** *adv.* —**gush/i·ness,** *n.*
—**Syn.** emotional, enthusiastic, unrestrained, demonstrative, unreserved.

gus·set (gus/it), *n.* **1.** a small, triangular piece of material inserted into a shirt, shoe, etc., to improve the fit or for reinforcement. Cf. **godet** (def. 1), **gore**[3] (def. 1). **2.** a plate for uniting structural members at a joint, as in a steel frame or truss. **3.** *Armor.* **a.** Also called **voider.** an area of mail backed with cloth, for defending the armpits or other areas at joints. **b.** a small piece of plate armor at the armhole of a cuirass; pallet. [ME < OF *gousset,* deriv. of *gousse* pod, husk]

Gus·sie (gus/ē), *n.* a girl's given name, form of **Augusta.** Also, **Gusta, Gus/sy.**

gust[1] (gust), *n.* **1.** a sudden, strong blast of wind. **2.** a sudden rush or burst of water, fire, smoke, sound, etc. **3.** an outburst of passionate feeling. —*v.i.* **4.** to blow or rush in gusts. [< Scand; cf. OIcel *gustr* a gust, akin to *gjōsa, gusa* gust] —**gust/less,** *adj.*
—**Syn. 1.** See **wind**[1].

gust[2] (gust), *n.* **1.** *Archaic.* flavor or taste. **2.** *Obs.* enjoyment or gratification. —*v.t.* **3.** *Scot.* to taste; savor. [< L *gust(us)* a tasting (of food), eating a little, deriv. of *gustāre* to taste] —**gust/a·ble,** *adj., n.*

Gus·ta (gus/tə), *n.* a girl's given name, form of **Augusta.** Also, **Gussie, Gussy.**

gus·ta·tion (gu stā/shən), *n.* **1.** the act of tasting. **2.** the faculty of taste. [< L *gustātiōn-* (s. of *gustātiō*), equiv. to *gustāt(us)* (ptp. of *gustāre* to taste) + *-iōn-* -ION]

gus·ta·tive (gus/tə tiv), *adj.* gustatory. [< ML *gustātīv(us),* equiv. to L *gustāt(us)* (see GUSTATION) + *-īvus* -IVE] —**gus/ta·tive·ness,** *n.*

gus·ta·to·ry (gus/tə tōr/ē, -tôr/ē), *adj.* of or pertaining to taste or tasting. [< L *gustāt(us)* (see GUSTATION) + -ORY[1]]

Gus·tave (gus/täv; *Fr.* GYS TAV/), *n.* a boy's given name.

Gus·ta·vo A. Ma·de·ro (gōōs tä/vô ä/ mä the/rô), official name of **Guadalupe Hidalgo.**

Gus·ta·vus (gu stā/vəs, -stä/-), *n.* a boy's given name, Latin form of **Gustave.**

Gustavus I, *(Gustavus Vasa)* 1496–1560, king of Sweden 1523–60.

Gustavus II, *(Gustavus Adolphus)* ("*Lion of the North*") 1594–1632, king of Sweden 1611–32: national military hero (grandson of Gustavus I).

Gustavus III, 1746–92, king of Sweden 1771–92: economic and legal reformer.

Gustavus IV, *(Gustavus Adolphus)* 1778–1837, king of Sweden 1800, dethroned 1809 (son of Gustavus III).

Gustavus V, 1858–1950, king of Sweden 1907–50, advocator of Swedish neutrality during World Wars I and II. Also, **Gus·taf V, Gus·tav V** (gus/täv).

Gustavus VI, *(Gustaf Adolf)* 1882–1973, king of Sweden 1950–73 (son of Gustavus V). Also, **Gustav VI.**

gus·to (gus/tō), *n.* **1.** hearty or keen enjoyment, as in eating, drinking, etc., or in action or speech in general: *to tell a story with real gusto; to tackle an assignment with gusto.* **2.** individual taste or liking. [< It < L *gust(us);* see GUST[2]] —**gus/to·ish,** *adj.*

Gus·ton (gus/tən), *n.* **Philip,** born 1912, U.S. painter, born in Canada.

gust·y[1] (gus/tē), *adj.,* **gust·i·er, gust·i·est. 1.** blowing or coming in gusts, as wind, rain, storms, etc. **2.** affected or marked by gusts of wind, rain, etc.: *a gusty day.* **3.** occurring or characterized by sudden bursts or outbursts, as sound, laughter, etc. **4.** full of meaningless, pretentious talk: *an evening of gusty speechmaking.* **5.** vigorous; hearty; zestful: *a gusty, matronly woman.* [GUST[1] + -Y[1]] —**gust/i·ly,** *adv.* —**gust/i·ness,** *n.*

gust·y[2] (gus/tē, gōōs/tē), *adj.,* **gust·i·er, gust·i·est.** *Chiefly Scot.* tasty; savory; appetizing. [GUST[2] + -Y[1]]

gut (gut), *n., v.,* **gut·ted, gut·ting.** —*n.* **1.** the alimentary canal between the pylorus and the anus, or some portion of it. **2. guts, a.** the bowels or entrails. **b.** *Slang.* courage; stamina; endurance: *Climbing that cliff takes a lot of guts.* **3.** the substance forming the case of the intestine; intestinal tissue or fiber: *sheep's gut.* **4.** a preparation of the intestines of an animal, used for various purposes, as for violin strings, tennis rackets, or fishing lines. **5.** the silken substance taken from a silkworm killed when about to spin its cocoon, used in making snells for fishhooks. **6.** a narrow passage, as a channel of water or a defile between hills. **7.** *Slang.* a gut course. —*v.t.* **8.** to take out the guts or entrails of; disembowel. **9.** to plunder (a house, city, etc.) of contents: *Invaders gutted the village.* **10.** to destroy the interior of: *Fire gutted the building.* [ME *gut, guttes* (pl.), OE *guttas* (pl.), akin to *gēotan* to pour] —**gut/less,** *adj.* —**gut/like/,** *adj.*
—**Syn. 2b.** pluck.

gut·buck·et (gut/buk/it), *n.* jazz played in the raucous and high-spirited style of barrelhouse. [GUT + BUCKET]

gut/ course/, *Chiefly Northeastern U.S. Informal.* a college course for which little effort is required to receive a good or passing grade.

gu·ten A·bend (gōōt/ən ä/bənt), *German.* good evening.

gu·te Nacht (gōō/tə näKHt/), *German.* good night.

Gu·ten·berg (gōōt/ən bûrg/; *Ger.* gōōt/ən berKH/), *n.* **1. Jo·han·nes** (yō hän/əs), *(Johann Gensfleisch),* c1400–68, German printer: credited with invention of printing from movable type. **2.** a walled plain in the fourth quadrant of the face of the moon: about 45 miles in diameter.

Gu/tenberg Bi/ble, an edition of the Vulgate printed at Mainz before 1456, ascribed to Gutenberg and others: probably the first large book printed with movable type.

gu·ten Mor·gen (gōōt/ən môR/gən), *German.* good morning.

gu·ten Tag (gōōt/ən täKH/), *German.* good day.

Guth·rie (guth/rē), *n.* **1. Woodrow Wilson** *(Woody),* 1912–67, U.S. folk singer. **2.** a city in central Oklahoma: the former state capital. 9502 (1960). **3.** a boy's given name.

Guth·run (gŏŏth/rōōn), *n.* Gudrun.

Gu·tiér·rez Ná·je·ra (gōō tyeR/res nä/hā rä/), **Ma·nuel** (mä nwel/), ("*El Duque Job*"), 1859–95, Mexican poet, short-story writer, and editor.

guts·y (gut/sē), *adj.,* **guts·i·er, guts·i·est.** *Slang.* **1.** having a great deal of nerve or courage: *a gutsy lampooner of the administration.* **2.** forceful; lusty: *a gutsy style of singing.* [GUTS + -Y[1]]

gut·ta (gut/ə), *n., pl.* **gut·tae** (gut/ē). **1.** a drop, or something resembling one. **2.** Also called **drop.** *Archit.* one of a series of pendent ornaments, generally in the form of a frustum of a cone, attached to the undersides of the mutules of the Doric entablature. [< L: a drop]

gut/tae band/, regula. [*guttae* < L, pl. of *gutta* GUTTA]

gut·ta-per·cha (gut/ə pûr/chə), *n.* the concrete milky juice, nearly white when pure, of various Malaysian sapotaceous trees, esp. *Palaquium Gutta,* used in the arts, as a dental cement for temporary and root-canal fillings, and for insulating electric wires. [< Malay *gĕtah* gum, balsam + *pĕrcha* the tree producing the substance]

gut·tate (gut/āt), *adj. Biol.* resembling a drop; having droplike markings. Also, **gut/tat·ed.** [< L *guttāt(us)* speckled, spotted. See GUTTA, -ATE[1]] —**gut·ta/tion,** *n.*

gut·ta·tim (gə tā/təm, -tä/-), *adv.* (in prescriptions) drop by drop. [< L]

gut·té (gōō tā/), *adj. Heraldry.* goutté. Also, **gut·tée/.**

Gut·ten·berg (gut/ən bûrg/), *n.* a town in NE New Jersey. 5118 (1960).

gut·ter (gut/ər), *n.* **1.** a channel at the side or in the middle of a road or street, for leading off surface water. **2.** any channel, trough, or the like for carrying off fluid. **3.** a channel at the eaves or on the roof of a building, for carrying off rain water. **4.** a furrow or channel made by running water. **5.** *Bowling.* a sunken channel on each side of the alley from the line marking the limit of a fair delivery of the ball to the sunken area behind the pins. **6.** the state or abode of those who live in filth, immorality, crime, etc.: *the language of the gutter.* **7.** the pair of margins between facing pages in a bound book, magazine, or newspaper. —*v.i.* **8.** to flow in streams. **9.** (of a candle) to lose molten wax accumulated in a hollow space around the wick. **10.** (of a lamp or candle flame) to burn low or to be blown so as to be nearly extinguished. **11.** to form gutters, as water does. —*v.t.* **12.** to make gutters in; channel. **13.** to furnish with a gutter or gutters: *to gutter a new house.* [ME *gutter, goter* < AF *goutier(e),* equiv. to *goute* drop (see GOUT) + *-iere,* fem. of *-ier* -ER[2]] —**gut/ter·like/,** *adj.*

gut·ter·ing (gut/ər ing), *n.* **1.** the act of making gutters. **2.** material for making gutters. **3.** the gutters of an individual building. **4.** the melted wax or tallow of a candle. [GUTTER + -ING[1]]

gut·ter·snipe (gut/ər snīp/), *n.* one belonging to or characteristic of the lowest social group in a city. [GUTTER + SNIPE] —**gut/ter·snip/ish,** *adj.*

gut·ti·form (gut/ə fôrm/), *adj.* shaped like a drop. [GUTT(A) drop (of liquid) + -I- + -FORM]

gut·tle (gut/əl), *v.i., v.t.,* **-tled, -tling.** to eat greedily; gormandize. [GUT + -LE; cf. GUZZLE] —**gut/tler,** *n.*

gut·tur·al (gut/ər əl), *adj.* **1.** of or pertaining to the throat. **2.** harsh; throaty. **3.** *Phonet.* pertaining to or characterized by a sound articulated in the back of the mouth, as the non-English velar fricative sound (KH) or its voiced counterpart, esp. French (R). —*n.* **4.** a guttural sound. [< NL *gutturāl(is)* of the throat, equiv. to L *guttur-* gullet, throat + *-ālis* -AL[1]] —**gut/tur·al·ly,** *adv.* —**gut/tur·al·ness, gut/tur·al/i·ty, gut/tur·al·ism,** *n.*

gut·tur·al·ise (gut/ər ə līz/), *v.t., v.i.,* **-ised, -is·ing.** *Chiefly Brit.* gutturalize. —**gut/tur·al·i·sa/tion,** *n.*

gut·tur·al·ize (gut/ər ə līz/), *v.,* **-ized, -iz·ing.** —*v.t.* **1.** to speak or pronounce (something) in a guttural manner. **2.** *Phonet.* to change into, pronounce as, or supplement with a guttural or gutturalized sound. —*v.i.* **3.** to speak gutturally. [GUTTURAL + -IZE] —**gut/tur·al·i·za/tion,** *n.*

gut·tur·al·ized (gut/ər ə līzd/), *adj. Phonet.* pronounced with guttural coarticulation. Also, *esp. Brit.,* **gut/tur·al·ised/.** [GUTTURALIZE + -ED[2]]

gut·tur·o·na·sal (gut/ə rō nā/zəl), *Phonet.* —*adj.* **1.** articulated in the back of the mouth and given resonance in the nasal cavity, as the sound represented by (ng) in (ring). —*n.* **2.** a gutturonasal sound. [GUTTUR(AL) + -O- + NASAL[1]]

gut·ty (gōō/tē, gut/ē), *adj. Heraldry.* goutté.

guv (guv), *n. Chiefly Brit. Informal.* **1.** term of address used to a man, esp. by a younger man, boy, or social inferior. **2.** governor (def. 6). [by shortening]

guy[1] (gī), *n., v.,* **guyed, guy·ing.** —*n.* **1.** *Informal.* a fellow or person: *He's a nice guy.* **2.** *(often cap.) Brit.* a grotesque effigy of Guy Fawkes which is paraded through the streets and burned on Guy Fawkes Day. **3.** *Chiefly Brit. Slang.* a grotesquely dressed person. **4. give the guy to,** *Brit. Slang.* to escape from (someone); give (someone) the slip. —*v.t.* **5.** to jeer at or make fun of; ridicule. [after *Guy Fawkes*]

guy[2] (gī), *n., v.,* **guyed, guy·ing.** —*n.* **1.** a rope, cable, or appliance used to guide and steady an object being hoisted or lowered, or to secure anything likely to shift its position. —*v.t.* **2.** to guide, steady, or secure with a guy or guys. [ME *gye* < OF *guie* a guide, deriv. of *guier* to GUIDE]

Guy (gī; *Fr.* gē), *n.* a boy's given name.

Guy·a·na (gī an/ə, -ä/nə), *n.* a nation on the NE coast of South America: a former British protectorate; independence 1966; member of British Commonwealth of Nations. 628,000 (est. 1964); 82,978 sq. mi. *Cap.:* Georgetown. Formerly, **British Guiana.** See map under **Guiana.**

Guy·enne (gwē yen/), *n.* Guienne.

Guy/ Fawkes/ Day/ (gī/ fôks/), (in Britain) November 5, celebrating the anniversary of the capture of Guy Fawkes. Cf. **Gunpowder Plot.**

Guy·mon (gī/mən), *n.* a town in Oklahoma. 5768 (1960).

Guy·on (gwē yôN/), *n.* **1. Madame** *(Jeanne Marie Bouvier de la Matte),* 1648–1717, French writer. **2.** a boy's given name, form of **Gawain.**

guy·ot (gē ō/), *n.* a flat-topped seamount, found chiefly in the Pacific Ocean. [named after Arnold H. *Guyot* (1807–84), Swiss-born American geologist and geographer]

Guz·mán (gōōs män/), *n.* **Mar·tín Lu·is** (mär tēn/ lōō ēs/), born 1887, Mexican novelist, journalist, and soldier.

guz·zle (guz/əl), *v.i., v.t.,* **-zled, -zling.** to drink greedily, frequently, or plentifully: *They spent the whole night guzzling beer.* [?] —**guz/zler,** *n.*

g.v., gravimetric volume.

GW, gigawatt; gigawatts. Also, **Gw**

Gwa·li·or (gwä/lē ôr/), *n.* **1.** a former state in central India, now part of Madhya Pradesh. **2.** a city in N Madhya Pradesh. 300,600 (1961).

Gwa·ri (gwä′rē), *n., pl.* **-ris,** (*esp. collectively*) **-ri.** a member of an agricultural people of northeastern Nigeria. Also, **Gbari.**

Gwawl (gwäl), *n. Welsh Legend.* the rival of Pwyll for the hand of Rhiannon.

Gwen (gwen), *n.* a girl's given name, form of **Gwendolen, Guinevère** or **Gwyneth.** Also, **Gwen·nie** (gwen′ē), **Gweyn, Gwin, Gwynne** (gwin).

Gwen·da (gwen′də), *n.* a girl's given name, form of **Gwen.**

Gwen·do·len (gwen′dᵊlin), *n.* a girl's given name. Also, **Gwen′do·lin, Gwendolyn, Gwendolynne.**

Gwen·do·lyn (gwen′dᵊlin), *n.* a girl's given name. Also, **Gwendolen, Gwendolin, Gwen′do·lynne.**

gwine (gwīn), *v. Chiefly Southern U.S., Nonstandard.* pp. of **go.**

Gwin·nett (gwi net′), *n.* **Button,** 1735?–77, American Revolutionary leader, born in England.

Gwyd·ion (gwœd′yon), *n. Welsh Legend.* a hero, the brother and lover of Arianhrod and the father of Llew Llaw Gyffes.

Gwyn (gwin), *n.* **Eleanor** ("*Nell*"), 1650–87, English actress: mistress of Charles II. Also, **Gwynne.**

Gwyn (gwin), *n.* a pre-Christian British god, originally associated with the life after death but later regarded as a symbol of rebirth.

Gwyn·fa (gwin′fə), *n.* a girl's given name.

Gy·as (jē′əs), *n.* (in the *Aeneid*) a companion of Aeneas on the flight from Troy.

gybe (jīb), *v.i., v.t.,* **gybed, gyb·ing,** *n. Naut.* jibe[1].

Gy·gae·a (jī jē′ə), *n.* (in the *Iliad*) a lake nymph. Also, **Gy·ge** (jī′jē).

Gy·ges (jī′jēz), *n. Gk. Myth.* one of the Hecatonchires. Also, **Gy·es** (jī′ēz).

Gyl·dén (gil′dən), *n.* a walled plain in the fourth quadrant of the face of the moon: about 30 miles in diameter.

gym (jim), *n.* a gymnasium. [by shortening]

gym·el (jim′əl), *n. Music.* the technique, found in some medieval English music, of singing voice parts in parallel thirds. Also, **gimel.** [ME *gimel(es), gemel(es)* < MF *gemel, gimel* twin; see GEMEL]

gym·kha·na (jim kä′nə), *n.* **1.** a field day held for equestrians, consisting of exhibitions of horsemanship and much pageantry. **2.** a place where this is held. [m. Hindi *gendkhānā,* lit., ball-house (influenced by GYMNASTICS)]

gymn-, var. of **gymno-** before a vowel: *gymnanthous.*

gym·nan·thous (jim nan′thəs), *adj. Bot.* achlamydeous. [GYMN- + -ANTHOUS]

gym·na·si·a (jim nā′zē ə, -zhə), *n.* a pl. of **gymnasium.**

gym·na·si·arch (jim nā′zē ärk′), *n.* (in ancient Greece) a magistrate who superintended the gymnasia and public games in certain cities. [< L *gymnasiarch(us)* master of a gymnasium < Gk *gymnasíarchos,* equiv. to *gymnási(on)* (see GYMNASIUM[1]) + *archós* -ARCH] —**gym·na′si·arch′y,** *n.*

gym·na·si·ast[1] (jim nā′zē ast′), *n.* a gymnast. [GYMNASI(UM)[1] + -AST]

gym·na·si·ast[2] (jim nā′zē ast′), *n.* a student in a gymnasium. [< G < NL *gymnasiast(a).* See GYMNASIUM[2], -AST]

gym·na·si·um[1] (jim nā′zē əm), *n., pl.* **-si·ums, -si·a** (-zē ə, -zhə). **1.** a building or room designed and equipped for physical education activities. **2.** a place where Greek youths met for exercise and discussion. [< L: a public school for gymnastics < Gk *gymnásion* gymnastic school (deriv. of *gymnázein* to train, *gymnós* naked)] —**gym·na′si·al,** *adj.*

gym·na·si·um[2] (jim nā′zē əm; *Ger.* gim nä′zē o͝om′, gym-), *n.* (in continental Europe, esp. Germany) a classical school preparatory to the universities. [< G; special use of GYMNASIUM[1]]

gym·nast (jim′nast), *n.* a person trained and skilled in gymnastics, esp. a teacher of gymnastics. [< Gk *gymnast(ēs)* the trainer of the athletes, equiv. to *gymnáz(ein)* (see GYMNASIUM[1]) + *-tēs* agent suffix]

gym·nas·tic (jim nas′tik), *adj.* of or pertaining to physical exercises that develop strength and agility. Also, **gym·nas′ti·cal.** [< MF *gymnastique* < L *gymnastic(us)* < Gk *gymnastikós,* equiv. to *gymnáz(ein)* (see GYMNASIUM[1]) + *-ikos* -IC] —**gym·nas′ti·cal·ly,** *adv.*

gym·nas·tics (jim nas′tiks), *n.* **1.** (*construed as pl.*) gymnastic exercises. **2.** (*construed as sing.*) the practice or art of gymnastic exercises. [see GYMNASTIC, -ICS]

gymno-, a learned borrowing from Greek meaning "naked," "bare," "exposed," used in the formation of compound words: *gymnoplast.* Also, *esp. before a vowel,* **gymn-.** [< Gk, comb. form of *gymnós*]

gym·no·car·pous (jim′nə kär′pəs), *adj.* (of a fungus or lichen) having the apothecium open and attached to the surface of the thallus. Also, **gym·no·car·pic** (jim′nə kär′pik). Cf. **angiocarpous** (def. 2). [GYMNO- + -CARPOUS]

Gym·no·din·i·um (jim′nə din′ē əm), *n.* a genus of marine or fresh-water dinoflagellates, certain species of which cause red tide. [< NL, equiv. to *gymno-* GYMNO- + Gk *dîn(ein)* (to) whirl + NL *-ium* -IUM]

gym·nog·e·nous (jim noj′ə nəs), *adj. Zool.* naked at birth, as certain birds. [GYMNO- + -GENOUS]

gym·nog·y·nous (jim noj′ə nəs), *adj. Bot.* having a naked ovary. [GYMNO- + -GYNOUS]

gym·no·plast (jim′nə plast′), *n.* a mass of protoplasm without an enclosing wall or membrane. [GYMNO- + -PLAST]

gym·no·rhi·nal (jim′nə rīn′ᵊl), *adj.* (of a bird) having the nostrils exposed, not covered by feathers. [< NL; see GYMNO-, RHINAL]

gym·nos·o·phist (jim nos′ə fist), *n.* one of a group of ascetic Indian philosophers of the Jain sect, existing from ancient times to c1000, characterized by refusal to wear clothes and the abandonment of caste marks; a member of the Digambara sect. [< L *gymnosophist(ae)* Indian ascetic(s) < Gk *gymnosophistai* naked philosophers. See GYMNO-, SOPHIST] —**gym·nos′o·phy,** *n.*

gym·no·sperm (jim′nə spûrm′), *n. Bot.* a plant having its seeds exposed or naked, not enclosed in an ovary; conifer. Cf. **angiosperm.** [< NL *gymnosperm(ae)* name of type. See GYMNO-, -SPERM] —**gym′no·sperm′al, gym′no·sperm′ic,** *adj.* —**gym′no·sperm′ism,** *n.*

gym·no·sper·mous (jim′nə spûr′məs), *adj.* of or pertaining to a gymnosperm; having naked seeds. [< NL *gymnospermus* < Gk *gymnóspermos.* See GYMNO-, -SPERMOUS]

gym·no·spore (jim′nə spōr′, -spôr′), *n. Bot.* a naked spore, esp. one not produced in a sporangium or not having a protective envelope. [GYMNO- + -SPORE] —**gym·no·spo·rous** (jim′nə spōr′əs, -spôr′-, jim nos′pər əs), *adj.*

gym′ shoe′, a canvas shoe with a rubber sole.

gym′ suit′, any outfit prescribed for wear while participating in gymnastics or sports, usually a comfortable garment allowing freedom of movement.

gyn-, var. of **gyno-** before a vowel: *gynarchy.*

gyn·ae·ce·um[1] (jin′ə sē′əm, gī′nə-, jī′nə-), *n., pl.* **-ce·a** (-sē′ə). (among the ancient Greeks) the part of a dwelling used by women. [< L *gynaecēum* < Gk *gynaikeîon,* equiv. to *gynaik-* (s. of *gynḗ*) woman + *-eion* n. suffix of place]

gyn·ae·ce·um[2] (jin′ə sē′əm, gī′nə-, jī′nə-), *n., pl.* **-ce·a** (-sē′ə). *Bot.* gynoecium.

gy·nae·cic (ji nē′sik, -nes′ik, gī-, jī-), *adj.* gynecic.

gynaeco-, var. of **gyneco-:** *gynaecomorphous.*

gyn·ae·coc·ra·cy (jin′ə kok′rə sē, gī′nə-, jī′nə-), *n., pl.* **-cies.** gynarchy. Also, **gynecocracy.** —**gy·nae·co·crat** (ji nē′kə krat′, gī-, jī-), *n.* —**gy·nae·co·crat·ic** (ji nē′kə krat′ik, gī-, jī-; jin′ə kə-, gī′nə-, jī′nə-), *adj.*

gy·nae·col·o·gist (gī′nə kol′ə jist, jin′ə-, jī′nə-), *n.* gynecologist.

gy·nae·col·o·gy (gī′nə kol′ə jē, jin′ə-, jī′nə-), *n.* gynecology. —**gyn·ae·co·log·ic** (jin′ə kə loj′ik, gī′nə-, jī′nə-), **gyn′ae·co·log′i·cal,** *adj.*

gyn·ae·co·mas·ti·a (jin′ə kō mas′tē ə, gī′nə-, jī′nə-), *n.* gynecomastia.

gyn·ae·co·mas·ty (jin′ə kə mas′tē, gī′nə-, jī′nə-), *n.* gynecomastia. Also, **gynecomasty.**

gy·nae·co·mor·phous (ji nē′kō môr′fəs, jin′ə kō-, gī′nə-, jī′nə-), *adj.* gynecomorphous.

Gyn·ae·co·thoe·nas (jin′ə kō thē′nəs), *n. Class. Myth.* an epithet of Ares, meaning "feasted by the women."

gy·nan·dro·morph (ji nan′drə môrf′, gī-, jī-), *n. Biol.* an individual exhibiting morphological characters of both sexes. [< Gk *gýnandro(s)* of doubtful sex + -MORPH] —**gy·nan′dro·mor′phic, gy·nan′dro·mor′phous,** *adj.* —**gy·nan′dro·morph′ism, gy·nan′dro·mor′phy,** *n.*

gy·nan·drous (ji nan′drəs, gī-, jī-), *adj. Bot.* having the stamens borne on the pistil and united in a column, as in orchids. [< Gk *gýnandros* of doubtful sex. See GYN-, -ANDROUS]

gy·nan·dry (ji nan′drē, gī-, jī-), *n.* hermaphroditism. Also, **gy·nan′drism.** [< Gk *gýnandr(os)* (see GYNANDROUS) + -Y[3]]

gy·nan·ther·ous (ji nan′thər əs, gī-, jī-), *adj. Bot.* having the stamens converted into pistils by the action of frost, disease, or insects. [GYN- + ANTHER + -OUS]

gy·nar·chy (jin′är kē, gī′när-, jī′nər-), *n., pl.* **-chies.** government by a woman or women. [GYN- + -ARCHY] —**gy·narch·ic** (ji när′kik, gī-, jī-), *adj.*

gyne-, var. of **gyneco-:** *gynephobia.*

gynec-, var. of **gyneco-** before a vowel: *gynecoid.*

gy·ne·cic (ji nē′sik, -nes′ik, gī-, jī-), *adj.* of or pertaining to women. Also, **gynaecic.** [< Gk *gynaikik(ós).* See GYNEC-, -IC]

gy·ne·ci·um (ji nē′sē əm, gī-, jī-), *n., pl.* **-ci·a** (-sē ə). gynoecium.

gyneco-, a learned borrowing from Greek meaning "female," used in the formation of compound words: *gynecology.* Also, **gynaeco-, gynec-, gyne-, gyn-, -gynous, -gyny.** [< Gk, comb. form repr. *gynaik-,* s. of *gynḗ* female, woman]

gyn·e·coc·ra·cy (jin′ə kok′rə sē, gī′nə-, jī′nə-), *n., pl.* **-cies.** gynarchy. Also, **gynaecocracy.** [< Gk *gynaikokratía.* See GYNECO-, -CRACY] —**gy·ne·co·crat** (ji nē′kə krat′, gī-, jī-), *n.* —**gy·ne·co·crat·ic** (ji nē′kə krat′ik, gī-, jī-; jin′ə kə-, gī′nə-, jī′nə-), *adj.*

gyn·e·coid (jin′ə koid′, gī′nə-, jī′nə-), *adj.* of or like a woman. [GYNEC- + -OID]

gynecol., **1.** gynecological. **2.** gynecology.

gy·ne·col·o·gist (gī′nə kol′ə jist, jin′ə-, jī′nə-), *n.* a physician specializing in gynecology. Also, **gynaecologist.** [GYNECOLOG(Y) + -IST]

gy·ne·col·o·gy (gī′nə kol′ə jē, jin′ə-, jī′nə-), *n.* the branch of medical science which deals with the functions and diseases peculiar to women, esp. of the reproductive organs. Also, **gynaecology.** [GYNECO- + -LOGY] —**gyn·e·co·log·ic** (jin′ə kə loj′ik, gī′nə-, jī′nə-), **gyn′e·co·log′i·cal,** *adj.*

gyn·e·co·mas·ti·a (jin′ə kō mas′tē ə, gī′nə-, jī′nə-, ji nē′kə-, gī nē′kə-, ji nē′kə-), *n. Pathol.* abnormal enlargement of the breast in a male. [< NL; see GYNECO-, MAST-, -IA]

gyn·e·co·mas·ty (jin′ə kə mas′tē, gī′nə-, jī′nə-), *n.* gynecomastia.

gyn·e·co·mor·phous (jin′ə kō môr′fəs, gī′nə-, jī′nə-; ji nē′kə-, gī nē′kə-, jī nē′kə-), *adj. Biol.* having the form, appearance, or attributes of a female. Also, **gynaecomorphous.** [< Gk *gynaikómorphos.* See GYNECO-, -MORPHOUS]

gyn·e·cop·a·thy (jin′ə kop′ə thē, gī′nə-, jī′nə-), *n. Pathol.* any disease peculiar to women. [GYNECO- + -PATHY] —**gyn·e·co·path·ic** (jin′ə kə path′ik, gī′nə-, jī′nə-), *adj.*

gyn·e·pho·bi·a (jin′ə fō′bē ə, gī′nə-, jī′nə-), *n. Psychiatry.* an abnormal fear of women. [GYNE- + -PHOBIA]

Gyn·er·gen (jin′ər jin, -jen′, gī′nər-, jī′nər-), *n. Pharm., Trademark.* ergotamine.

gyn·i·at·rics (jin′ē a′triks, gī′nē-, jī′nē-), *n. Pathol.* the treatment of diseases peculiar to women. Also, **gyn′i·a′try.** [GYN- + -IATRIC; see -ICS]

gyno-, a learned borrowing from Greek meaning "female," "woman," used in the formation of compound words: *gynophore.* Also, *esp. before a vowel,* **gyn-.** Cf. **gyneco-.** [< Gk, comb. form of *gynḗ*]

gyn·o·base (jin′ō bās′, gī′nō-, jī′-), *n. Bot.* an elevation of the receptacle, bearing the gynoecium. [GYNO- + BASE[1]] —**gyn′o·ba′sic,** *adj.*

gyn·o·di·oe·cious (jin′ō dī ē′shəs, gī′nō-, jī′-), *adj. Bot.* having pistillate flowers on one plant and monoclinous flowers on another plant of the same species. [GYNO- + DIOECIOUS] —**gyn′o·di·oe′cious·ly,** *adv.* —**gy·no·di·oe·cism** (jī′nō dī ē′siz əm), *n.*

gy·noe·ci·um (ji nē′sē əm, gī-, jī-), *n., pl.* **-ci·a** (-sē ə). *Bot.* the pistil, or the pistils collectively, of a flower. Also, **gynaeceum, gynecium.** [< NL < Gk *gynaikeîon;* see GYNAECEUM[1]]

gyn·o·mo·noe·cious (jin′ō mə nē′shəs, gī′nō-, jī′-), *adj. Bot.* having both pistillate and monoclinous flowers on the same plant. [GYNO- + MONOECIOUS] —**gyn′o·mo·noe′cious·ly,** *adv.* —**gyn·o·mo·noe·cism** (jin′ō mə nē′siz əm, gī′nō-, jī′-), *n.*

gyn·o·phore (jin′ə fōr′, -fôr′, gī′nə-, jī′nə-), *n. Bot.* the elongated pedicel or stalk bearing the pistil in some flowers. [GYNO- + -PHORE] —**gyn′o·phor′ic,** *adj.*

gyn·o·ste·gi·um (jin′ō stē′jē əm, gī′nō-, jī′-), *n., pl.* **-gi·a** (-jē ə). *Bot.* a specialized caplike mass of tissue covering a gynoecium. [< NL; see GYNO-, STEGO-, -IUM]

gyn·o·ste·mi·um (jin′ə stē′mē əm, gī′nə-, jī′nə-), *n., pl.* **-mi·a** (-mē ə). *Bot.* the column of an orchid flower. [< NL, equiv. to *gyno-* GYNO- + Gk *stḗm(ōn)* warp, thread + NL *-ium* neut. n. suffix]

-gynous, an adjective combining form referring to the female sex: *androgynous.* [< Gk *-gynos.* See GYNO-, -OUS]

-gyny, a combining form equivalent to a combination of **gyno-,** as final element of compounds, and **-y**[3], or **-gynous** and **-y**[3], used in the formation of abstract nouns: *androgyny.*

Győr (dyœr), *n.* a city in NW Hungary. 66,000 (1956).

gyp[1] (jip), *v.,* **gypped, gyp·ping,** *n. Informal.* —*v.t.* **1.** to swindle; cheat; defraud or rob by some sharp practice. —*n.* **2.** a swindle. **3.** Also, **gyp′per.** a swindler or cheat. **4.** Also called **gypsy.** an owner of race horses who acts as his own trainer and jockey. Also, **gip.** [back formation from GYPSY, used verbally]

gyp[2] (jip), *n. Brit. Informal.* a male college servant, as at Cambridge and Durham. [perh. from GYPSY]

gyp′ joint′, **1.** a gambling house in which the games are dishonestly run. **2.** any business establishment that charges excessively for poor-quality service or goods.

gyp-room (jip′ro͞om′, -ro͝om′), *n. Brit. Slang.* a pantry, esp. one attached to a student's quarters.

gyp·se·ous (jip′sē əs), *adj.* of or pertaining to gypsum. [< LL *gypseus.* See GYPSUM, -EOUS]

gyp·sif·er·ous (jip sif′ər əs), *adj.* containing gypsum. [GYP(SUM) + -I- + -FEROUS]

gyp·soph·i·la (jip sof′ə lə), *n.* any slender, graceful herb of the genus *Gypsophila,* of Mediterranean regions, allied to the pinks and having small, panicled flowers. [< NL < Gk *gýpso(s)* chalk + *phíla* fond of (neut. pl. of *phílos*)]

gyp·sum (jip′səm), *n.* a very common mineral, hydrated calcium sulfate, $CaSO_4 \cdot 2H_2O$, occurring in crystals and in masses, soft enough to be scratched by the fingernail: used to make plaster of Paris, as an ornamental material, as a fertilizer, etc. [< L: chalk < Gk *gýpsos* chalk, gypsum]

gyp′sum pink′, babies'-breath (def. 1).

Gyp·sy (jip′sē), *n., pl.* **-sies,** *adj.* —*n.* **1.** a member of a nomadic, Caucasoid people of generally swarthy complexion, who migrated originally from India, settling in various parts of Asia, Europe, and, most recently, North America. **2.** Romany; the language of the Gypsies. **3.** (*l.c.*) a person who resembles or lives like a Gypsy. **4.** (*l.c.*) See **gypsy capstan.** **5.** (*l.c.*) See **gypsy winch.** **6.** (*l.c.*) gyp[1] (def. 4). **7.** (*l.c.*) gypsyhead. —*adj.* **8.** of or pertaining to the Gypsies. Also, **gyp′sy;** *esp. Brit.,* **Gipsy, gipsy.** [back formation of *gipcyan,* aph. var. of EGYPTIAN, from a belief that Gypsies came originally from Egypt] —**gyp′sy·dom,** *n.* —**gyp′sy·esque′, gyp′sy·ish, gyp′sy·like′, gyp·se′ian,** *adj.* —**gyp′sy·hood′,** *n.* —**gyp′sy·ism,** *n.*

gyp′sy cap′stan, *Naut.* a small capstan moved only by a motor or engine. Also, **gipsy capstan.** Also called **gypsy.**

gyp·sy·head (jip′sē hed′), *n. Naut.* a flanged drum on a winch, for winding in lines. Also called **gypsy, niggerhead.** [GYPSY + HEAD]

gyp′sy moth′, a moth, *Porthetria dispar,* introduced into the U.S. from Europe, the larvae of which feed on the foliage of shade and other trees.

gyp′sy scale′, either of two scales that often form the basis of Hungarian gypsy music.

Gypsy scales

gyp′sy set′ting, *Jewelry.* a setting, as on a ring, completely enclosing the girdle of the stone.

gyp′sy winch′, *Naut.* a small winch or crab. Also, **gipsy winch.** Also called **gypsy.**

gyr-, var. of **gyro-** before a vowel: *gyral.*

gy·ral (jī′rəl), *adj.* **1.** gyratory. **2.** *Anat.* of or pertaining to a gyrus. [GYR- + -AL[1]] —**gy′ral·ly,** *adv.*

gy·rate (*v.* jī′rāt, jī rāt′; *adj.* jī′rāt), *v.,* **-rat·ed, -rat·ing,** *adj.* —*v.i.* **1.** to move in a circle or spiral, or around a fixed point; whirl. —*adj.* **2.** *Zool.* having convolutions. [< L *gȳrāt(us)* wheeled around, turned, rounded (ptp. of *gȳrāre*). See GYR-, -ATE[1]] —**gy′ra·tor,** *n.* —**gy·ra·to·ry** (jī′rə tôr′ē, -tōr′ē), *adj.*

gy·ra·tion (jī rā′shən), *n.* act of gyrating; circular or spiral motion; revolution; rotation; whirling. [< LL *gȳrātiōn-* (s. of *gȳrātiō*). See GYRATE, -ION] —**gy·ra′tion·al,** *adj.*

gy·ra·to·ry (jī′rə tôr′ē, -tōr′ē), *adj.* moving in a circle or spiral; gyrating. [GYRAT(ION) + -ORY[1]]

gyre (jīᵊr), *n.* **1.** a ring or circle. **2.** a circular course or motion. [< L *gȳr(us)* < Gk *gŷros* ring, circle]

gy·rec·to·my (jī rek′tə mē), *n., pl.* **-mies.** *Surg.* excision of a cerebral gyrus. [GYR(US) + -ECTOMY]

gy·rene (jī′rēn, jī rēn′), *n. Slang.* a member of the U.S. Marine Corps. [GI + (MA)RINE with altered sp.]

White gyrfalcon, *Falco rusticolus candicans* (Length 2 ft.)

gyr·fal·con (jûr′fôl′kən, -fô′kən), *n.* any of several large falcons of arctic and subarctic regions, as *Falco rusticolus candicans* (**white**

gyrfalcon), having white plumage with the upper parts barred and spotted with salty- or brownish-gray. Also, **gerfalcon.** [ME *gerfaucon*, etc. < MF, OF, equiv. to *ger-* (? < OHG *giri* greedy) + *faucon* FALCON; cf. Icel *geirfalki*]

gy·ro (jī′rō), *n., pl.* **-ros. 1.** gyrocompass. **2.** gyroscope. [independent use of GYRO-]

gyro-, a learned borrowing from Greek meaning "ring," "circle," "spiral," used in the formation of compound words: *gyromagnetic; gyroscope.* Also, *esp. before a vowel,* **gyr-.** [< Gk, comb. form of *gyrós* ring, circle]

gy·ro·com·pass (jī′rō kum′pəs), *n.* a navigational compass containing a gyroscope rotor, which, when adjusted for the latitude and speed of the vessel or aircraft, indicates the direction of true north along the surface of the earth or communicates this information to one or more gyro repeaters. Also called **gyrostatic compass.** [GYRO(SCOPE) + COMPASS]

gy·ro·fre·quen·cy (jī′rō frē′kwən sē), *n., pl.* **-cies.** *Physics.* the frequency of rotation of an electron or other charged particle in a magnetic field, directly proportional to the charge of the particle and to the field strength and inversely proportional to the mass of the particle. [GYRO- + FREQUENCY]

gy′ro hori′zon, *Aeron.* See **artificial horizon** (def. 3).

gy·roi·dal (jī roid′əl), *adj.* having a spiral arrangement. [GYR- + -OID + -AL¹] **—gy·roi′dal·ly,** *adv.*

gy·ro·mag·net·ic (jī′rō mag net′ik), *adj.* of or pertaining to the magnetic properties of a rotating charged particle. [GYRO- + MAGNETIC]

gy′romagnet′ic ra′tio, *Physics.* the ratio of the magnetic moment of a rotating charged particle to its angular momentum.

gy·ron (jī′rən, -ron), *n. Heraldry.* a subordinary having the form of a triangle, usually equal to half a quarter of the escutcheon, with its apex at the fess point. [< MF, OF *giron* gusset < OHG *gēro;* c. GORE³]

gy·ron·ny (jī ron′ē, jī′rə nē), *adj. Heraldry.* divided into a number of gyrons, usually eight: *gyronny of eight.* [GYRON + -Y³; r. ME *gerundi,* etc. < MF *gironne* gyroned]

gy·ro·pi·lot (jī′rə pī′lət), *n. Aeron.* See **automatic pilot.** [GYRO(SCOPE) + PILOT]

gy·ro·plane (jī′rə plān′), *n.* autogiro. [GYRO- + PLANE¹]

gy′ro repeat′er, a navigational compass, under the control of a gyroscope, that automatically indicates true north. Also called **repeater.**

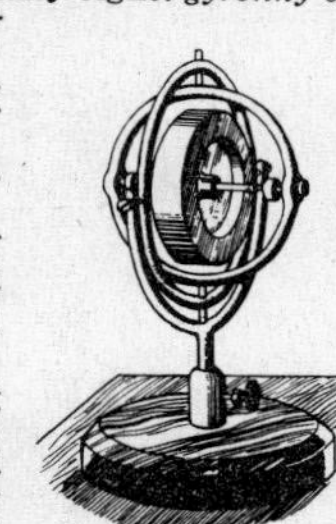
Gyroscope

gy·ro·scope (jī′rə skōp′), *n.* an apparatus consisting of a rotating wheel so mounted that its axis can turn freely in certain or all directions, and capable of maintaining the same absolute direction in space in spite of movements of the mountings and surrounding parts. Its motion is based upon the principle that a body rotating rapidly about an axis will tend to resist a disturbing change or torque by rotating slowly in a direction perpendicular to that of the disturbance: used to maintain equilibrium, determine direction, etc. Also called **gyro.** [< F; see GYRO-, -SCOPE] **—gy·ro·scop·ic** (jī′rə skop′ik), *adj.* **—gy′ro·scop′i·cal·ly,** *adv.* **—gy′ro·scop′ics,** *n.*

gy′roscop′ic sta′bilizer, gyrostabilizer.

gy·rose (jī′rōs), *adj.* marked with wavy lines. [GYR- + -OSE¹]

gy·ro·sta·bi·lized (jī′rə stā′bə līzd′), *adj.* to be stabilized by means of a gyrostabilizer. [GYRO(SCOPE) + STABILIZED]

gy·ro·sta·bi·liz·er (jī′rə stā′bə lī′zər), *n.* a device for stabilizing a seagoing vessel by counteracting its rolling motion from side to side, consisting essentially of a rotating gyroscope weighing about 1 percent of the displacement of the vessel. Also called **gyroscopic stabilizer.** [GYRO(SCOPE) + STABILIZER]

gy·ro·stat (jī′rə stat′), *n.* a modified gyroscope, consisting of a rotating wheel pivoted within a rigid case. [GYRO- + -STAT]

gy·ro·stat·ic (jī′rə stat′ik), *adj.* pertaining to the gyrostat or to gyrostatics. [GYRO- + STATIC] **—gy′ro·stat′i·cal·ly,** *adv.*

gy′rostat′ic com′pass, gyrocompass.

gy·ro·stat·ics (jī′rə stat′iks), *n.* (*construed as sing.*) *Mech.* the science that deals with the laws of rotating bodies. [GYRO- + STATICS]

gy·ro·vague (jī′rō vāg′), *n.* a vagrant monk who wandered from one monastery to another. [< F < LL *gyrovag(us),* equiv. to *gyro-* GYRO- + *vagus* strolling about; see VAGUE]

gy·rus (jī′rəs), *n., pl.* **gy·ri** (jī′rī). *Anat.* a convolution, esp. of the brain. [< L; see GYRE]

gyt·tja (yit′chä), *n. Geol.* a mud rich in organic matter, found at the bottom or near the shore of certain lakes. [< Sw, akin to *gjuta* to pour]

gyve (jīv), *n., v.,* **gyved, gyv·ing.** **—***n.* **1.** Usually, **gyves.** a shackle, esp. for the leg; fetter. **—***v.t.* **2.** to shackle. [ME *give* < ?]

H

H, h (āch), *n., pl.* **H's** or **Hs, h's** or **hs. 1.** the eighth letter of the English alphabet, a consonant. **2.** any spoken sound represented by the letter *H* or *h*, as in *hot, behave*, etc. **3.** something having the shape of an H. **4.** a written or printed representation of the letter *H* or *h*. **5.** a device, as a printer's type, for reproducing the letter *H* or *h*.

H, 1. hard. **2.** *Elect.* henry. **3.** *Slang.* heroin.

H, 1. the eighth in order or in a series. **2.** (*sometimes l.c.*) the medieval Roman numeral for 200. Cf. **Roman numerals. 3.** *Chem.* hydrogen. **4.** *Physics.* **a.** enthalpy. **b.** horizontal component of the earth's magnetic field. **c.** intensity of a magnetic field. **5.** *Music.* the letter used in German to indicate the tone B.

h, hard.

H^1, *Chem.* protium. Also, **^{1}H, H^a**

H^2, *Chem.* deuterium. Also, **^{2}H, H^b**

H^3, *Chem.* tritium. Also, **^{3}H, H^c**

h, *Physics.* See **Planck's constant.**

H., (in prescriptions) an hour. [< L *hōra*]

h., 1. harbor. **2.** hard. **3.** hardness. **4.** heavy sea. **5.** height. **6.** hence. **7.** high. **8.** *Baseball.* hit; hits. **9.** horns. **10.** hour; hours. **11.** hundred. **12.** husband. Also, **H.**

ha (hä), *interj.* (used as an exclamation of surprise, interrogation, suspicion, triumph, etc.) Also, **hah.** [ME; see HA-HA^1]

hā (hä), *n.* the 26th letter of the Arabic alphabet, representing a glottal spirant consonant sound. [< Ar]

ḥā (ḵẖä), *n.* the sixth letter of the Arabic alphabet, representing a pharyngeal spirant consonant. [< Ar]

ha, hectare; hectares.

h.a., 1. *Gunnery.* high angle. **2.** in this year. [< L *hōc annō*]

haaf (häf), *n.* deep-sea fishing grounds off the Shetland and Orkney Islands. [< Scand; cf. Icel *haf* sea; c. OE *hæf*; akin to HEAVE]

Haag (häḵẖ), *n.* **Den** (den). a Dutch name of The Hague.

Haa·kon VII (hô′ko͝on), (*Prince Carl of Denmark*) 1872–1957, king of Norway 1905–57: in exile 1940–45.

haar (här), *n. Scot. and North Eng.* a thick, wet fog along the seacoast. [north var. of HOAR]

Haar·lem (här′ləm), *n.* a city in the W Netherlands, W of Amsterdam. 171,009 (1962).

Hab., Habakkuk.

Há·ba (hä′bä), *n.* **A·lois** (ä′lois), born 1893, Czech composer.

Ha·bak·kuk (hə bak′ək, hab′ə kuk′), *n.* **1.** a Minor Prophet of the 7th century B.C. **2.** a book of the Bible bearing his name. Also, *Douay Bible,* **Ha·bac′uc.**

Ha·ba·na (ä vä′nä), *n.* Spanish name of **Havana.**

ha·ba·ne·ra (hä′bə nâr′ə *or, often,* -nyâr′ə), *n.* **1.** a dance of Cuban origin. **2.** the music for this dance, having a slow duple meter and a rhythm similar to that of a tango. **3.** (*cap.*) a popular aria ("*L'amour est un oiseau rebelle*") from Act I of Bizet's opera *Carmen*, based on a song by the Spanish composer Sebastián Yradier (1809–65). [< Sp (*danza*) *habanera* Havanan (dance). See HAVANA, -ER^2]

hab·bub (hə bo͞ob′), *n.* haboob.

Hab·da·lah (häv dä lä′; *Eng.* häv dô′lə), *n. Hebrew.* a religious ceremony observed by Jews at the conclusion of the Sabbath or a festival. Also, **Havdalah.** [lit., division]

ha·be·as cor·pus (hā′bē əs kôr′pəs), *Law.* a writ requiring a person to be brought before a judge or court, esp. for investigation of a restraint of the person's liberty, used as a protection against illegal imprisonment. [late ME < L: lit., have the body (first words of writ), equiv. to *habeās* 2nd sing. pres. subj. (with impv. force) of *habēre* to have + *corpus* body]

ha·ben·u·la (hə ben′yə lə), *n., pl.* **-lae** (-lē′). *Anat.* a narrow bandlike structure, as the stalk of the pineal body. [< L: small thong] **—ha·ben′u·lar,** *adj.*

Ha·ber (hä′bər), *n.* **Fritz** (frits), 1868–1934, German chemist: Nobel prize 1918.

hab·er·dash·er (hab′ər dash′ər), *n.* **1.** *U.S.* a dealer in men's furnishings, as shirts, ties, gloves, etc. **2.** *Chiefly Brit.* a dealer in small wares and notions, as buttons, ribbons, needles, etc. [ME *haberdasshere*]

hab·er·dash·er·y (hab′ər dash′ə rē), *n., pl.* **-er·ies. 1.** a haberdasher's shop. **2.** the goods sold there. [late ME *haberdasshrie.* See HABERDASHER, -Y^3]

hab·er·geon (hab′ər jən), *n. Armor.* **1.** a mail garment similar to the hauberk but shorter. **2.** (loosely) a hauberk. Also, **haubergeon.** [ME *haubergeoun* < MF *haubergeon*, dim. of *hauberc*; see HAUBERK]

Ha′ber proc′ess, a process for synthesizing ammonia from gaseous nitrogen and hydrogen under high pressure and temperature in the presence of a catalyst. [named after Fritz HABER]

hab·ile (hab′il), *adj.* skillful; dexterous. [late ME *habyll* < L *habil*(*is*) handy, apt; see ABLE]

ha·bil·i·ment (hə bil′ə mənt), *n.* **1. habiliments,** equipment; accouterments; furnishings: *the various habiliments of civilization.* **2.** Usually, **habiliments.** clothes as worn in a particular profession, way of life, etc. [late ME (*h*)*abylement* < MF *habillement*, equiv. to *habill*(*er*), *abill*(*ier*) (to) trim a log, hence, dress, prepare (< VL **adbiliare;* see A-^{5}, BILLET^2) + *-ment* -MENT] **—ha·bil·i·men·tal** (hə bil′ə men′tᵊl), **ha·bil′i·men′ta·ry,** *adj.* **—ha·bil′i·ment′ed,** *adj.*

ha·bil·i·tate (hə bil′i tāt′), *v.t.,* **-tat·ed, -tat·ing. 1.** *Western U.S.* to furnish money or means to work (a mine). **2.** *Archaic.* to clothe or dress. [< LL *habilitāt*(*us*) made fit, equipped (ptp. of *habilitāre*). See ABILITY, -ATE^1] **—ha·bil′i·ta′tion,** *n.* **—ha·bil′i·ta′tor,** *n.*

Ha·bi·ru (hä bē′ro͞o, hä′bē ro͞o′), *n.pl.* a nomadic people mentioned in Assyro-Babylonian literature: possibly the Hebrews. Also, **Ha·bi·ri** (hä bē′rē, hä′bē rē′). [< Babylonian *khabiru*]

hab·it^1 (hab′it), *n.* **1.** customary practice or use: *Daily bathing is an American habit.* **2.** a particular practice, custom, or usage: *the habit of shaking hands.* **3.** compulsive need, inclination, or use; addiction: *liquor habit; drug habit.* **4.** a dominant or regular disposition or tendency; prevailing character or quality: *She has a habit of looking at the bright side of things.* **5.** *Slang.* an addiction to narcotics (often prec. by *the*): *Doctors were unable to cure him of the habit.* **6.** an acquired behavior pattern regularly followed until it has become almost involuntary: *the habit of looking both ways before crossing the street.* **7.** mental character or disposition: *a habit of mind.* **8.** characteristic bodily or physical condition. **9.** the characteristic form, aspect, mode of growth, etc., of an animal or plant: *a twining habit.* **10.** the characteristic crystalline form of a mineral. **11.** garb of a particular rank, profession, religious order, etc.: *monk's habit.* **12.** the attire worn by a rider of a saddle horse. **—*v.t.* 13.** to clothe; array. [ME < L *habit*(*us*) state, style, practice, equiv. to *habi-* (var. s. of *habēre* to have) + *-tus* verbal n. suffix; r. ME *abit* < OF]
—Syn. 1. bent, wont. **2.** See **custom. 11.** dress, costume. **13.** dress, garb, attire; deck out.

hab·it^2 (hab′it), *v.t.* **1.** *Archaic.* to dwell in. **—*v.i.* 2.** *Obs.* to dwell. [ME *habit*(*en*) < L *habitā*(*re*) (to) inhabit; see HABITAT]

hab·it·a·ble (hab′i tə bəl), *adj.* capable of being inhabited. [ME *habitābil*(*is*), equiv. to *habitā*(*re*) (to) inhabit (see HABITAT) + *-bilis* -BLE; r. ME *abitable* < MF] **—hab′it·a·bil′i·ty, hab′it·a·ble·ness,** *n.* **—hab′it·a·bly,** *adv.*

hab·it·a·cle (hab′i tə kəl), *n.* **1.** a niche, as for a statue. **2.** *Obs.* a dwelling. [ME < MF < L *habitācu-l*(*um*) habitation, equiv. to *habitā*(*re*) (to) inhabit (see HABITAT) + *-culum* -CLE]

ha·bi·tan (*Fr.* A bē täɴ′), *n., pl.* **-tans** (-täɴ′). habitant^2.

hab·i·tan·cy (hab′i tᵊn sē), *n., pl.* **-cies. 1.** the act or fact of inhabiting; inhabitancy. **2.** the total number of inhabitants; population. [HABITANT + -CY]

hab·it·ant^1 (hab′i tᵊnt), *n.* an inhabitant. [< L *habitant-* (s. of *habitāns*), prp. of *habitāre* to inhabit. See HABITAT, -ANT]

ha·bi·tant^2 (hab′i tᵊnt; *Fr.* A bē täɴ′), *n., pl.* **ha·bi·tants** (hab′i tᵊnts; *Fr.* A bē täɴ′). a French settler in Canada or Louisiana, or a descendant of one, esp. a farmer. [< F, prp. of *habiter* < L *habitāre* to inhabit]

hab·i·tat (hab′i tat′), *n.* **1.** the native environment of an animal or plant; the kind of place that is natural for the life and growth of an animal or plant: *a tropical habitat.* **2.** place of abode; habitation: *Paris and New York are the major habitats of artists.* [< L: it inhabits, 3rd sing. pres. ind. of *habitāre*, freq. of *habēre* to have, hold] **—hab·i·tal·ly** (hab′i tᵊlē), *adv.*

hab·i·ta·tion (hab′i tā′shən), *n.* **1.** a place of residence; dwelling; abode. **2.** the act of inhabiting; occupancy by inhabitants. **3.** a colony or settlement; community: *Each of the scattered habitations consisted of a small number of huts.* [< L *habitātiōn-* (s. of *habitātiō*) a dwelling, equiv. to *habitāt*(*us*) inhabited (ptp. of *habitāre;* see HABITAT) + *-iōn-* -ION; r. ME (*h*)*abitacioun* < AF] **—hab′i·ta′tion·al,** *adj.*
—Syn. 1. residence, domicile, quarters.

hab·it·ed^1 (hab′i tid), *adj.* dressed or clothed, esp. in a habit: *habited nuns and monks.* [HABIT^1 + -ED^3]

hab·it·ed^2 (hab′i tid), *adj. Archaic.* inhabited. [HABIT^2 + -ED^2]

ha·bit·u·al (hə bich′o͞o əl), *adj.* **1.** of the nature of a habit; fixed by or resulting from habit: *habitual courtesy.* **2.** being such by habit: *a habitual gossip.* **3.** commonly used, as by a particular person; customary: *She took her habitual place at the table.* [< ML *habituāl*(*is*) relating to dress, condition, or habit, equiv. to L *habitu*(*s*) HABIT^1 + *-ālis* -AL^1] **—ha·bit′u·al·ly,** *adv.* **—ha·bit′u·al·ness,** *n.*
—Syn. 2. confirmed, inveterate. **3.** accustomed, regular. See **usual. —Ant. 2.** occasional. **3.** unaccustomed.

ha·bit·u·ate (hə bich′o͞o āt′), *v.t.,* **-at·ed, -at·ing. 1.** to accustom (a person, the mind, etc.) to something; make used to; acclimate: *Wealth habituated him to luxury.* **2.** *Archaic.* to frequent. [< LL *habituāt*(*us*) conditioned, constituted, (ptp. of *habituāre*), equiv. to *habitu*(*s*) HABIT^1 + *-ātus* -ATE^1] **—ha·bit′u·a′tion,** *n.*
—Syn. 1. familiarize, acclimatize, train.

hab·i·tude (hab′i to͞od′, -tyo͞od′), *n.* **1.** customary condition or character: *a healthy mental habitude.* **2.** a habit or custom: *traditional habitudes of kindliness and courtesy.* **3.** *Obs.* familiar relationship. [late ME < MF < L *habitūd*(*ō*). See HABIT^1, -TUDE] **—hab′i·tu′di·nal,** *adj.*

ha·bit·u·é (hə bich′o͞o ā′, -bich′o͞o ā′; *Fr.* A bē twā′), *n., pl.* **ha·bit·u·és** (hə bich′o͞o āz′, -bich′o͞o āz′; *Fr.* A bē twā′). a habitual frequenter of a place: *a habitué of art galleries; a habitué of bars and nightclubs.* [< F, n. use of masc. ptp. of *habituer* < LL *habituāre.* See HABITUATE]

ha·boob (hə bo͞ob′), *n.* a thick dust storm or sandstorm that blows in the deserts of North Africa and Arabia or on the plains of India. Also, **habbub, ha·boub′, ha·bub′, hubbob, hubbub.** [< Ar *habūb* a strong wind]

Habs·burg (haps′bûrg; *Ger.* häps′bo͝orḵẖ′), *n.* Hapsburg.

ha·bu·tai (hä′bə tī′), *n.* a thin, soft, durable Japanese silk, used in the manufacture of garments. Also, **ha′bu·tae′.** [< Jap *habutae*]

ha·ček (hä′chek), *n.* a mark (ˇ) placed over a consonant, as over *c* or *s* in Czech or *g* in Turkish, etc., to indicate that the sounds are palatalized, Czech *č* or *š* becoming (ch) or (sh) respectively, Turkish *ğ* becoming (y); or over a vowel, as over *e* in Czech, to indicate that the sound has a consonantal quality, *ě* becoming (ye). Also, **há′ček.** [< Czech]

ha·chure (*n.* ha sho͝or′, hash′o͝or; *v.* ha sho͝or′), *n., v.,* **-chured, -chur·ing. —*n.* 1.** one of several parallel lines drawn on a map to indicate relief features, the width of the spacing between the lines, and the breadth of the lines indicating the slope. **2.** shading composed of such lines; hatching. **—*v.t.* 3.** to indicate or shade by hachures. [< F; see HATCH^3, -URE]

ha·ci·en·da (hä′sē en′də; *Sp.* ä syen′dä), *n., pl.* **-das** (-dəz; *Sp.* -däs). (in Spanish America) **1.** a landed estate, esp. one used for farming or ranching. **2.** the main house on such an estate. **3.** a stock-raising, mining, or manufacturing establishment in the country. [< Sp < L *facienda* things to be done or made, neut. pl. of *faciendus*, fut. pass. participle of *facere* to DO^1, make]

hack^1 (hak), *v.t.* **1.** to cut, notch, slice, chop, or sever (something) with or as with heavy, irregular blows (often fol. by *up* or *down*): *to hack meat; to hack down trees.* **2.** to break up the surface of (the ground). **3.** to clear (a road, path, etc.) by cutting away vines, trees, brush, or the like: *They hacked a trail through the jungle.* **4.** to damage or injure by crude, harsh, or insensitive treatment; mutilate; mangle: *The editor hacked the story to bits.* **5.** to reduce or cut ruthlessly; trim: *The Senate* *hacked the budget almost in half before returning it to the House.* **6.** *Basketball.* to strike the arm of (an opposing ball handler): *He got a penalty for hacking the shooter.* **7.** *Brit.* to kick or kick at the shins of (an opposing player) in Rugby football. —*v.i.* **8.** to make rough cuts or notches; deal cutting blows. **9.** to cough harshly, usually in short and repeated spasms. **10.** *Brit.* to kick or kick at an opponent's shins in Rugby football. —*n.* **11.** a cut, gash, or notch. **12.** a tool, as an ax, hoe, pick, etc., for hacking. **13.** an act or an instance of hacking; a cutting blow. **14.** a short, rasping cough. **15.** a hesitation in speech. **16.** *Curling.* an indentation made in the ice at the foot score, for supporting the foot in delivering the stone. **17.** *Brit.* a gash in the skin produced by a kick, as in Rugby football. [ME *hacke(n),* OE (*tō*)*haccian* to hack to pieces; c. D *hakken,* G *hacken*] —**Syn 1.** mangle, haggle. See **cut.**

hack[2] (hak), *n.* **1.** *Brit.* **a.** a horse kept for common hire or adapted for general work, esp. ordinary riding. **b.** a saddle horse used for transportation, rather than for show, hunting, or the like. **2.** an old or worn-out horse; jade. **3.** a person, as an artist or writer, who exploits, for money, his creative ability or training in the production of dull, unimaginative, and trite work; one who produces banal and mediocre work in the hope of gaining commercial success in the arts: *As a painter, he was little more than a hack.* **4.** a professional who renounces or surrenders individual independence, integrity, belief, etc., in return for money or other reward in the performance of a task normally thought of as involving a strong personal commitment: *a political hack.* **5.** a writer who works on the staff of a publisher at a dull or routine task; someone who works as a literary drudge: *He was one among the many hacks on Grub Street.* **6.** *U.S.* a coach or carriage kept for hire; hackney. **7.** *Informal.* **a.** a taxi. **b.** Also, **hackie.** a cabdriver. —*v.t.* **8.** to make a hack of; let out for hire. **9.** to make trite or stale by frequent use; hackney. —*v.i.* **10.** *Brit.* to ride on the road at an ordinary pace, as distinguished from cross-country or military riding. **11.** *Informal.* to drive a taxi. —*adj.* **12.** hired; of a hired sort: *a hack writer; hack work.* **13.** hackneyed; trite; banal: *hack writing.* [short for HACKNEY] —**Syn. 4.** mercenary. **8.** lease, rent.

hack[3] (hak), *n.* **1.** a rack for drying food, such as fish. **2.** a rack for holding fodder for livestock. **3.** a low pile of unburnt bricks in the course of drying. **4. at hack,** *Falconry.* (of a young hawk) being trained to fly freely but to return to a hack house or hack board for food rather than to pursue quarry. —*v.t.* **5.** to place (something) on a hack, as for drying, feeding, etc. **6.** *Falconry.* to train (a young hawk) by letting it fly freely and feeding it at a hack board or a hack house. [var. of HATCH[2]]

hack·a·more (hak′ə mōr′, -môr′), *n.* **1.** a simple looped bridle, by means of which controlling pressure is exerted on the nose of a horse, used chiefly in breaking colts. **2.** *Western U.S.* any of several forms of halter used esp. for breaking horses. [alter. (by folk etym.) of Sp *jáquima* head-stall < Ar *shaqīmah*]

hack·ber·ry (hak′ber′ē, -bə rē), *n., pl.* **-ries. 1.** the small, edible, cherrylike fruit of any American, ulmaceous tree of the genus *Celtis.* **2.** a tree bearing this fruit. **3.** the wood of any of these trees. [var. of HAGBERRY]

hack′ board′, *Falconry.* a board or platform at which hawks being flown at hack are fed.

hack·but (hak′but), *n.* harquebus. [earlier *hacquebuta* < MF, var. of *haquebusch* < MD *hakebusse,* lit., hook-gun; see HARQUEBUS] —**hack·but·eer** (hak′bə tēr′), *n.*

Hack·en·sack (hak′ən sak′), *n.* a city in NE New Jersey, near New York City. 30,521 (1960).

hack·er (hak′ər), *n.* **1.** *Slang.* **a.** a skilled and enthusiastic user of computers. **b.** a person who illicitly uses or changes information in a computer system. **2.** one who or that which hacks. [HACK[1] + -ER[1]]

hack′ ham′mer, an adzlike tool for dressing stone.

hack′ house′, *Falconry.* a shed where young hawks are kept and fed while at hack.

hack·ie (hak′ē), *n. Informal.* hack[2] (def. 7b). [HACK[2] + -IE]

hack·ing (hak′ing), *n.* replacement of a single course of stonework by two or more lower courses. [HACK[1] + -ING[1]] —**hack′ing·ly,** *adv.*

hack′ing jack′et, *Chiefly Brit.* a riding jacket having a tight waist, flared skirt, slanted pockets with flaps, and slits or vents at the sides or back. Also called **hack′ing coat′.**

hack·le[1] (hak′əl), *n., v.,* **-led, -ling.** —*n.* **1.** one of the long, slender feathers on the neck or saddle of certain birds, as the domestic rooster, much used in making artificial flies for anglers. **2.** the whole neck plumage of the domestic rooster or the like. **3.** *Angling.* **a.** the legs of an artificial fly made with feathers from the neck or saddle of a rooster or other such bird. See diag. under **fly**[2]. **b.** See **hackle fly. 4.** a comb for dressing flax or hemp. —*v.t.* **5.** *Angling.* to equip with a hackle. **6.** to comb, as flax or hemp. Also, **hatchel, heckle** (for defs. 4, 6). [ME *hakell;* see HECKLE] —**hack′ler,** *n.*

hack·le[2] (hak′əl), *v.t.,* **-led, -ling.** to cut roughly; hack; mangle. [HACK[1] + -LE; c. MD *hakkelen*]

hack·le·back (hak′əl bak′), *n.* See **shovelnose sturgeon.** [HACKLE[1] + BACK[1]]

hack′le fly′, *Angling.* an artificial fly made with hackles, usually without wings. Also called **hackle.**

hack·ly (hak′lē), *adj.* rough or jagged as if hacked: *a hackly fracture.* [HACKLE[2] + -Y[1]]

hack·man (hak′mən, -man′), *n., pl.* **-men,** (-mən, -men′). *U.S.* the driver of a hack. [HACK[2] + MAN[1]]

hack·ma·tack (hak′mə tak′), *n.* **1.** the tamarack, *Larix laricina.* **2.** the wood of this tree. [earlier *hakmantak* < Algonquian]

hack·ney (hak′nē), *n., pl.* **-neys,** *adj., v.* —*n.* **1.** a horse used for ordinary riding or driving. **2.** a trotting horse used for drawing a light carriage or the like. **3.** (*cap.*) one of an English breed of horses having a high-stepping gait. **4.** a carriage or automobile for hire; cab. —*adj.* **5.** let out, employed, or done for hire. —*v.t.* **6.** to make trite, common, or stale by frequent use. **7.** to use as a hackney. [ME *hakeney,* special use of place-name *Hackney,* Middlesex, England] —**hack′ney·ism,** *n.*

hack′ney coach′, **1.** a coach available for hire. **2.** a four-wheeled carriage having six seats and drawn by two horses.

hack·neyed (hak′nēd), *adj.* made commonplace or trite; stale; banal. [HACKNEY + -ED[2]] —**Syn.** overdone, overused, worn out, threadbare. See **commonplace.**

hack·saw (hak′sô′), *n.* a saw for cutting metal, consisting typically of a narrow, fine-toothed blade fixed in a frame. Also **hack′ saw′.** See illus. under **saw.** [HACK[1] + SAW[1]]

hack′ watch′, *Naut.* See **deck watch.**

had (had), *v.* pt. and pp. of **have.**

Ha·da·mard (A DA MAR′), *n.* **Jacques Sa·lo·mon** (zhäk SA lô MÔN′), 1865–1963, French mathematician.

Had·ar (had′är, hä′där), *n.* a first magnitude star in the constellation Centaurus.

Ha·das (had′əs, hā′dəs), *n.* **Moses,** 1900–66, U.S. classical scholar, teacher, and author.

Ha·das·sah (hə dä′sə, hä-), *n.* **1.** a benevolent organization of Jewish women founded in New York City in 1912 by Henrietta Szold and concerned chiefly with bettering medical and educational facilities in Israel, forwarding Zionist activities in the U.S., and promoting world peace. **2.** Also, **Ha·das′seh.** a girl's given name. [after the Hebrew name (meaning "myrtle") of Queen Esther; see Esther 2:7]

Had·ding·ton (had′ing tən), *n.* former name of **East Lothian.**

had·dock (had′ək), *n., pl.* (*esp. collectively*) **-dock,** (*esp. referring to two or more kinds or species*) **-docks. 1.** a food fish, *Melanogrammus aeglefinus,* of the cod family, found in the North Atlantic. **2.** the rosefish, *Sebastes marinus.* [ME *haddok;* see -OCK]

Had·don (had′ən), *n.* **1. Alfred Cort** (kôrt), 1855–1940, English ethnologist, anthropologist, and writer. **2.** a town in W New Jersey. 17,099 (1960).

Had·don·field (had′ən fēld′), *n.* a town in SW New Jersey. 13,201 (1960).

Had′don Heights′, a town in SW New Jersey. 9260 (1960).

hade (hād), *n., v.,* **had·ed, had·ing.** *Geol.* —*n.* **1.** the angle between a fault plane and a vertical plane. —*v.i.* **2.** to incline from a vertical position. [?]

Ha·des (hā′dēz), *n.* **1.** *Class. Myth.* **a.** the underworld inhabited by departed souls. **b.** the god ruling the underworld; Pluto. **2.** (in the Revised Version of the New Testament) the abode or state of the dead. **3.** (*often l.c.*) hell. —**Ha·de·an** (hā dē′ən, hā′dē ən), *adj.*

Had·field (had′fēld′), *n.* **Sir Robert Abbott,** 1858–1940, English metallurgist and industrialist.

Ha·dhra·maut (hä′drä môt′), *n.* a region along the S coast of the Arabian peninsula, in the Aden protectorate. Also, **Ha′dra·maut′.** —**Ha·dhra·mau·tian** (hä′drə mô′shən), *adj., n.*

ha·dith (hä dēth′), *n., pl.* **-dith, -diths. 1.** *Islam.* a traditional account of things said or done by Muhammad or his companions. **2.** (*construed as pl.*) the entire body of such accounts. [< Ar]

hadj (haj), *n., pl.* **hadj·es.** hajj.

hadj·i (haj′ē), *n., pl.* **hadj·is.** hajji.

Had·ley (had′lē), *n.* **1. Henry Kim·ball** (kim′bəl), 1871–1937, U.S. composer and conductor. **2.** a boy's or girl's given name.

Had′ley chest′, *U.S. Furniture.* a style of chest made c1700 in Massachusetts or Connecticut, having front rails and panels carved in low relief with elaborate tulip and leaf patterns. [after *Hadley,* Massachusetts]

had·n't (had′ənt), contraction of *had not.*

Ha·dri·an (hā′drē ən), *n.* (*Publius Aelius Hadrianus*) A.D. 76–138, Roman emperor 117–138. Also, **Adrian.**

Hadrian I. See **Adrian I.**

Hadrian II. See **Adrian II.**

Hadrian III. See **Adrian III.**

Hadrian IV. See **Adrian IV.**

Hadrian V. See **Adrian V.**

Hadrian VI. See **Adrian VI.**

Ha′drian's Wall′, a wall of defense for the Roman province of Britain, constructed by Hadrian between Solway Firth and the mouth of the Tyne.

hadst (hadst), *v. Archaic.* a 2nd pers. sing. pt. of **have.**

hae (hā, ha), *v.t., auxiliary verb. Scot.* have.

haec (hīk; *Eng.* hēk), *adj., pron. Latin.* this.

haec·ce·i·ty (hek sē′i tē, hēk-), *n., pl.* **-ties.** that which makes an object what it uniquely is. Cf. **quiddity** (def. 1). [< ML *haecceitās,* lit., thisness, equiv. to L *haecce,* var. of *haec* this (fem. demonstr. adj.) + *-itās* -ITY]

Haeck·el (hek′əl), *n.* **Ernst Hein·rich** (ERNST hīn′RIKH), 1834–1919, German biologist and philosopher. —**Haeck·e·li·an** (he kē′lē ən), *adj., n.* —**Haeck′el·ism,** *n.*

haem-, var. of **hem-:** *haemangioma.*

haema-, var. of **hema-:** *haemachrome.*

haem·a·chrome (hem′ə krōm′, hē′mə-), *n.* hemachrome.

hae·mag·glu·ti·nate (hē′mə glo͞ot′ənāt′, hem′ə-), *v.t., v.i.,* **-nat·ed, -nat·ing.** hemagglutinate. —**hae′mag·glu′ti·na′tion,** *n.* —**hae·mag·glu·tin·a·tive** (hē′mə glo͞ot′ənā′tiv, -ənə tiv, hem′ə-), *adj.*

hae·mal (hē′məl), *adj.* hemal.

hae·man·gi·o·ma (hi man′jē ō′mə), *n., pl.* **-mas, -ma·ta** (-mə tə). *Pathol.* hemangioma. —**hae·man′gi·o′ma·to′sis,** *n.*

haemat-, var. of **haemato-** before a vowel: *haematoid.*

haem·a·tal (hem′ətəl, hē′mə-), *adj.* hematal.

hae·mat·ic (hi mat′ik), *adj., n.* hematic.

haem·a·tin (hem′ə tin, hē′mə-), *n. Biochem.* hematin.

haem·a·tin·ic (hem′ə tin′ik, hē′mə-), *n., adj.* hematinic.

haem·a·tite (hem′ə tīt′, hē′mə-), *n. Mineral.* hematite. —**haem·a·tit·ic** (hem′ə tit′ik, hē′mə-), *adj.*

haemato-, var. of **hemato-:** *haematocyst.* Also, *esp. before a vowel,* **haemat-.**

haem·a·to·blast (hem′ə tō blast′, hē′mə-), *n. Anat.* hematoblast.

haem·a·to·cele (hem′ə tō sēl′, hē′mə-), *n. Pathol.* hematocele.

haem·a·toc·ry·al (hem′ə tok′rē əl, hem′ə tō krī′əl, hē′mə-), *adj.* hematocryal.

haem·a·to·cyst (hem′ə tō sist, hē′mə-), *n. Pathol.* hematocyst. —**haem′a·to·cys′tis,** *n.*

haem·a·to·cyte (hem′ə tō sīt′, hē′mə-), *n.* hemocyte.

haem·a·to·gen·e·sis (hem′ə tō jen′i sis, hē′mə-), *n.* hematogenesis.

haem·a·tog·e·nous (hem′ə toj′ə nəs, hē′mə-), *adj.* hematogenous.

hae·ma·toid (hē′mə toid′, hem′ə-), *adj.* hematoid. —**hae′ma·toid′in,** *adj.*

haem·a·tol·o·gy (hem′ə tol′ə jē, hē′mə-), *n.* hematology. —**haem·a·to·log·ic** (hem′ə təloj′ik, hē′mə-), **haem′a·to·log′i·cal,** *adj.* —**haem′a·tol′o·gist,** *n.*

haem·a·to·ma (hem′ə tō′mə, hē′mə-), *n., pl.* **-mas, -ma·ta** (-mə tə). *Pathol.* hematoma.

haem·a·to·phyte (hem′ə tə fīt′, hē′mə-), *n.* hematophyte.

haem·a·to·poi·e·sis (hem′ə tō poi ē′sis, hē′mə-), *n.* hematopoiesis. —**haem·a·to·poi·et·ic** (hem′ə tō poi et′ik, hē′mə-), *adj.*

haem·a·to·sis (hem′ə tō′sis, hē′mə-), *n.* hematosis.

haem·a·to·ther·mal (hem′ə tō thûr′məl, hē′mə-), *adj.* hematothermal.

hae·ma·tox·y·lin (hē′mə tok′sə lən, hem′ə-), *n.* hematoxylin. —**hae·ma·tox·yl·ic** (hē′mə tok sil′ik, hem′ə-), *adj.*

hae·ma·tox·y·lon (hē′mə tok′sə lon′, hem′ə-), *n.* **1.** the wood of the logwood. **2.** hematoxylin.

haem·a·to·zo·on (hem′ə tə zō′on, -ən, hē′mə-), *n., pl.* **-zo·a** (-zō′ə). hematozoon. Also, **haem′a·to·zo′on.** —**haem′a·to·zo′al, haem′a·to·zo′ic,** *adj.*

hae·mic (hē′mik, hem′ik), *adj.* hemic.

hae·min (hē′min), *n. Biochem.* hemin.

haemo-, var. of **hemo-:** *haemoglobin.* Also, *esp. before a vowel,* **haem-.**

hae·mo·blast (hē′mə blast′, hem′ə-), *n. Anat.* hematoblast. [HAEMO- + -BLAST]

hae·mo·con·cen·tra·tion (hē′mə kon′sən trā′shən, hem′ə-), *n. Med.* hemoconcentration.

hae·mo·cyte (hē′mə sīt′, hem′ə-), *n.* hemocyte.

hae·mo·cy·to·blast (hē′mə sī′tə blast′, hem′ə-), *n.* hemocytoblast. —**hae′mo·cy′to·blas′tic,** *adj.*

hae·mo·dy·nam·ics (hē′mə dī nam′iks, hem′ə-), *n.* (*construed as sing.*) hemodynamics. —**hae′mo·dy·nam′ic,** *adj.*

hae·mo·glo·bin (hē′mə glō′bin, hem′ə-), *n. Biochem.* hemoglobin. —**hae′mo·glo′bic, hae′mo·glo′bin·ous,** *adj.*

hae·moid (hē′moid), *adj.* hemoid.

hae·mol·y·sin (hi mol′i sən, hē′mə lī′-, hem′ə-), *n.* hemolysin.

hae·mol·y·sis (hi mol′i sis), *n.* hemolysis. —**hae·mo·lyt·ic** (hē′mə lit′ik, hem′ə-), *adj.*

Hae·mon (hē′mən), *n. Class. Myth.* a son of Creon of Thebes who killed himself on the tomb of Antigone.

hae·mo·phil·i·a (hē′mə fil′ē ə, -fēl′yə, hem′ə-), *n. Pathol.* hemophilia. —**hae′mo·phil,** *n.*

hae·mo·phil·i·ac (hē′mə fil′ē ak′, -fē′lē-, hem′ə-), *n. Pathol.* hemophiliac.

hae·mo·phil·ic (hē′mə fil′ik, hem′ə-), *adj.* hemophilic.

haem·or·rhage (hem′ər ij, hem′rij), *n., v.,* **-rhaged, -rhag·ing.** hemorrhage. —**haem·or·rhag·ic** (hem′ə raj′ik), *adj.*

haem·or·rhoid (hem′ə roid′, hem′roid), *n. Pathol.* hemorrhoid. —**haem′or·rhoi′dal,** *adj.*

hae·mo·sta·sis (hi mos′tə sis, hē′mə stā′sis, hem′ə-), *n. Med.* hemostasis. Also, **hae·mo·sta·sia** (hē′mə stā′zhə, -zhē ə, -zē ə, hem′ə-).

hae·mo·stat (hē′mə stat′, hem′ə-), *n.* hemostat.

hae·mo·stat·ic (hē′mə stat′ik, hem′ə-), *adj., n.* hemostatic.

hae·mo·tho·rax (hē′mə thôr′aks, -thōr′-, hem′ə-), *n. Med.* hemothorax.

hae·mo·tox·in (hē′mə tok′sin, hem′ə-), *n.* hemotoxin. —**hae′mo·tox′ic,** *adj.*

Hae·mus (hē′məs), *n. Class. Myth.* a Thracian king, a son of Boreas and Orithyia: he and his wife, Rhodope, were turned into mountains for irreverently changing their names to Zeus and Hera.

Hae′mus Moun′tains, a mountain range in the first quadrant of the face of the moon forming the southeast border of Mare Serenitatis.

haen (hän), *v. Scot.* pp. of **hae.**

hae·res (hēr′ēz), *n., pl.* **hae·re·des** (hi rē′dēz). *Civil Law.* heres.

haet (hāt), *n. Scot.* hate[2].

haf·fet (haf′it), *n. Scot and North Eng.* the part of the face above the upper jaw; the cheekbone and temple. Also, **haf′fat, haf′fit.** [earlier *halfet, halfhed,* OE *healfhēafod* sinciput, equiv. to *healf* side, part, HALF + *hēafod* HEAD]

ha·fiz (hä′fiz), *n.* a title of respect for a Muslim who knows the Koran by heart. [< Ar *ḥāfiẓ* a guard, one who keeps (in memory)]

Ha·fiz (hä fiz′), *n.* (*Shams ud-din Mohammed*) c1320–89?, Persian poet.

haf·ni·um (haf′nē əm, häf′-), *n. Chem.* a metallic element having a valence of four, found in zirconium ores. *Symbol:* Hf; *at. wt.:* 178.49; *at. no.:* 72; *sp. gr.:* 12.1. [< NL *Hafn(ia)* Copenhagen + -IUM]

haft[1] (haft, häft), *n.* **1.** a handle, esp. of a knife, sword, dagger, etc. —*v.t.* **2.** to furnish with a haft or handle; set in a haft. [ME; OE *hæft* handle, lit., that which is taken, grasped; c. L *captus;* akin to G *Heft* handle] —**haft′er,** *n.*

haft[2] (haft, häft), *Scot. and North Eng.* —*n.* **1.** a permanent or accustomed residence; home. **2.** a permanent or accustomed pasture for sheep or cattle; a nonseasonal home pasture. —*v.t.* **3.** to establish in or accustom to a place of residence. **4.** to accustom (sheep or cattle) to pasturage or a specific pasture. [? akin to HAVE]

Haf·ta·rah (häf tôr′ə; *Heb.* häf tä RÄ′), *n., pl.* **-ta·roth** (-tôr′ōt; *Heb.* -tä RÔT′), **-ta·rahs.** *Judaism.* a portion of the Prophets that is chanted or read in the synagogue on the Sabbath and holy days immediately after the Parashah. Also, **Haphtarah.** [< Heb: finish, ending]

hag[1] (hag), *n.* **1.** an ugly old woman, esp. a vicious or malicious one. **2.** a witch. **3.** a hagfish. [ME *hagge*, OE **hægge*, akin to *hægtes(se)* witch, *hagorūn* spell, G *Hexe* witch] —**hag′like′,** *adj.*

hag[2] (hag, häg), *n. Brit. Dial.* **1.** a soft spot in a bog or marsh; quagmire. **2.** a firm spot or island of firm ground in a bog or marsh. **3.** an area of tree stumps and underbrush, as one left after a severe storm or where trees have been cut for timber. **4.** the projection, overhanging margin or the open face of a peat cutting; an exposed bed of peat. [ME: chasm < Scand; cf. Icel *högg* a cut, ravine]

Hag., Haggai.

Ha·gar (hā′gär, -gər), *n.* **1.** Also, *Douay Bible,* **Agar.** the mother of Ishmael. Gen. 16. **2.** a girl's given name.

hag·ber·ry (hag′ber′ē, -bə rē), *n., pl.* **-ries.** the American hackberry. [< Scand; cf. Dan *hæggebær*]

hag·born (hag′bôrn′), *adj.* born of a hag or witch. [HAG[1] + BORN]

hag·but (hag′but), *n.* harquebus. [var. of HACKBUT]

hag·don (hag′dən), *n. Brit. and Eastern Canada Dial.* any of various oceanic birds of the North Atlantic coasts of Europe and America, esp. the greater shearwater. [?]

Ha·ge·ci·us (hə gē′ sē əs), *n.* a walled plain in the fourth quadrant of the face of the moon: about 48 miles in diameter.

Ha·gen (hä′gən), *n.* (in the *Nibelungenlied*) the killer of Siegfried, himself killed by Kriemhild, Siegfried's wife.

Ha·gen (hā′gən), *n.* **Walter,** 1892–1969, U.S. golfer.

Ha·gers·town (hā′gərz toun′), *n.* a city in NW Maryland. 36,660 (1960).

hag·fish (hag′fish′), *n., pl.* (*esp. collectively*) **-fish,** (*esp. referring to two or more kinds or species*) **-fish·es.** any eel-like, marine cyclostome of the order *Hyperotreta,* having undeveloped eyes, a barbel-rimmed, circular mouth, and horny teeth for boring into the flesh of fishes to feed on their interior parts. [HAG[1] + FISH]

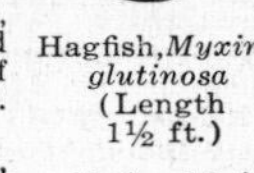

Hagfish, *Myxine glutinosa* (Length 1½ ft.)

Hag·ga·da (hə gä′də; *Heb.* hä gä dä′, -gô dô′), *n., pl.* **-doth** (-dōs, -dōt; *Heb.* -dōt′, -dōs′), **-dahs.** Haggadah (def. 1).

Hag·ga·dah (hə gä′də; *Heb.* hä gä dä′, -gô dô′), *n., pl.* **-doth** (-dōs, -dōt; *Heb.* -dōt′, -dōs′), **-dahs. 1.** a book containing the liturgy for the Seder service on the Jewish festival of Passover. **2.** Aggadah. [< Heb: narrative, akin to *higgid* to tell] —**hag·gad·ic** (hə gad′ik, -gä′dik), **hag·gad′i·cal,** *adj.*

hag·ga·dist (hə gä′dist), *n.* **1.** one of the writers of the Aggadah. **2.** one versed in the Aggadah. [HAGGAD(AH) + -IST] —**hag·ga·dis·tic** (hag′ə dis′tik), *adj.*

Hag·ga·i (hag′ē ī′, hag′ī), *n.* **1.** a Minor Prophet of the 6th century B.C. **2.** a book of the Bible bearing his name. Also, *Douay Bible,* **Aggeus.**

hag·gard (hag′ərd), *adj.* **1.** having a gaunt, wasted, or exhausted appearance, as from prolonged suffering, exertion, anxiety, etc.; worn. **2.** wild; wild-looking: *haggard eyes.* **3.** *Falconry.* (esp. of a hawk caught after it has attained adult plumage) untamed. —*n.* **4.** *Falconry.* a wild or untamed hawk caught after it has assumed adult plumage. [orig., wild female hawk. See HAG[1], -ARD] —**hag′gard·ly,** *adv.* —**hag′gard·ness,** *n.*
—**Syn. 1.** emaciated, drawn, hollow-eyed. —**Ant. 1.** robust.

Hag·gard (hag′ərd), *n.* **(Sir) H(enry) Rider,** 1856–1925, English novelist.

hagged (hagd, hag′id), *adj. Brit. Dial.* **1.** haglike. **2.** haggard (defs. 1, 2). [HAG[1] + -ED[3]]

hag·gis (hag′is), *n. Chiefly Scot.* a dish made of the heart, liver, etc., of a sheep or calf, minced with suet and oatmeal, seasoned, and boiled in the stomach of the animal. [late ME *hageys* < AF **hageis,* equiv. to *hag-* (root of *haguer* to chop, hash < MD *hacken* to HACK[1]) + *-eis* n. suffix used in cookery terms]

hag·gish (hag′ish), *adj.* of or like a hag; old and ugly. [HAG[1] + -ISH[1]] —**hag′gish·ly,** *adv.* —**hag′gish·ness,** *n.*

hag·gle (hag′əl), *v.,* **-gled, -gling,** *n.* —*v.i.* **1.** to bargain in a petty, quibbling, and naggingly quarrelsome manner: *They spent hours haggling over the price of fish.* **2.** to wrangle, dispute, or cavil: *The senators haggled interminably over the proposed bill.* —*v.t.* **3.** to mangle in cutting; hack. **4.** *Archaic.* to harass with wrangling or haggling. —*n.* **5.** the act of haggling; wrangle or dispute over terms. [late ME *hagge* to cut, chop (< Scand; cf. Icel *höggva* to HEW) + -LE] —**hag′gler,** *n.*
—**Syn. 1.** chaffer, higgle, palter. **3.** chop. **5.** argument.

ha·gi·a (ä′yē ä; *Eng.* hā′jē ə), *n.pl. Eastern Ch.* the Eucharistic elements before or after the consecration. [< LGk, n. use of neut. pl. of Gk *hágios* holy]

hag·i·arch·y (hag′ē är′kē, hā′jē-), *n., pl.* **-arch·ies.** hagiocracy. [HAGI- + -ARCHY]

hagio-, a learned borrowing from Greek meaning "saint," "holy," used in the formation of compound words: *hagiography; hagiocracy.* Also, *esp. before a vowel,* **hagi-.** [< Gk, comb. form of *hágios* holy, sacred]

hag·i·oc·ra·cy (hag′ē ok′rə sē, hā′jē-), *n., pl.* **-cies. 1.** government by a body of persons esteemed as holy. **2.** a state so governed. Also, **hagiarchy.** [HAGIO- + -CRACY]

Hag·i·og·ra·pha (hag′ē og′rə fə, hā′jē-), *n.* (*construed as sing.*) the third of the three Jewish divisions of the Old Testament, variously arranged, but usually comprising the Psalms, Proverbs, Job, Song of Solomon, Ruth, Lamentations, Ecclesiastes, Esther, Daniel, Ezra, Nehemiah, and Chronicles. Also called **the Writings.** Cf. **law**[1] (def. 21), **Prophets.** [< LL < Gk: sacred writings, equiv. to *hagio-* HAGIO- + *-grapha,* neut. pl. of *-graphos* -GRAPH]

hag·i·og·ra·pher (hag′ē og′rə fər, hā′jē-), *n.* **1.** one of the writers of the Hagiographa. **2.** a writer of lives of the saints; hagiologist. Also, **hag′i·og′ra·phist.** [< ML *hagiograph(us)* writer of sacred books (< Gk *hagiógraphos*) + -ER[1]]

hag·i·og·ra·phy (hag′ē og′rə fē, hā′jē-), *n., pl.* **-phies.** the writing and critical study of the lives of the saints; hagiology. [HAGIO- + -GRAPHY] —**hag·i·o·graph·ic** (hag′ē ə graf′ik, hā′jē-), **hag′i·o·graph′i·cal,** *adj.*

hag·i·ol·a·try (hag′ē ol′ə trē, hā′jē-), *n.* the veneration of saints. [HAGIO- + -LATRY] —**hag′i·ol′a·ter,** *n.* —**hag′i·ol′a·trous,** *adj.*

hag·i·ol·o·gy (hag′ē ol′ə jē, hā′jē-), *n., pl.* **-gies** for 2, 3. **1.** the branch of literature dealing with the lives and legends of the saints. **2.** a biography or narrative of a saint or saints. **3.** a collection of such biographies or narratives. [HAGIO- + -LOGY] —**hag·i·o·log·ic** (hag′ē ə loj′ik, hā′jē-), **hag′i·o·log′i·cal,** *adj.* —**hag′i·ol′o·gist,** *n.*

hag·i·o·scope (hag′ē ə skōp′, hā′jē-), *n.* squint (def. 12). [HAGIO- + -SCOPE] —**hag·i·o·scop·ic** (hag′ē ə skop′ik, hā′jē-), *adj.*

hag·me·nay (hog′mə nā′), *n. Scot. and North Eng.* hogmanay. Also, **hag′ma·ne′.**

Hag·no (hag′nō), *n. Class. Myth.* the Arcadian nymph of a spring who provided water whenever it was needed: one of the nymphs who tended the infant Zeus.

hag·rid·den (hag′rid′ən), *adj.* worried or tormented, as by a witch. [HAG[1] + RIDDEN]

hag·ride (hag′rīd′), *v.t.,* **-rode** or (*Archaic*) **-rid; -ridden** or (*Archaic*) **-rid; -rid·ing.** to afflict with worry, dread, want, or the like; torment. [HAG[1] + RIDE] —**hag′rid′er,** *n.*

hag·seed (hag′sēd′), *n.* offspring of a hag. [HAG[1] + SEED]

Hague (hāg), *n.* **The,** a city in the W Netherlands, near the North Sea: site of the government, royal residence and of the Permanent Court of International Justice. 604,112 (1962). Dutch, **'s Gravenhage.**

hague·ton (hak′tən), *n. Armor.* acton.

Hague′ Tribu′nal, the court of arbitration for the peaceful settlement of international disputes, established at The Hague by the international peace conference of 1899: its panel of jurists nominates a list of persons from which members of the United Nations International Court of Justice are elected. Official name, **Permanent Court of Arbitration.**

hah (hä), *interj.* ha.

ha-ha[1] (hä′hä′), *interj., n.* (used as an exclamation or representation of laughter, as in expressing amusement, derision, etc.; an onomatopoeic word indicating an amused response.) Cf. **haw-haw.** [ME, OE; imit. orig.]

ha-ha[2] (hä′hä′), *n.* a barrier consisting of a trench or ditch; a sunk fence. [< F *haha* repetitive compound based on *ha!* exclamation of surprise]

Hahn (hän), *n.* **1. Otto,** 1879–1968, German chemist: Nobel prize 1944. **2.** a crater in the first quadrant of the face of the moon: about 45 miles in diameter.

Hah·ne·mann (hä′nə mən; *Ger.* hä′nə män′), *n.* **(Chris·tian Fre·drich) Sam·u·el** (kris′chən frē′drik sam′yo͞o əl; *Ger.* kʀɪs′tē än fʀā′dʀɪkʜ zä′mo͞o el), 1755–1843, German physician: founder of homeopathy. —**Hah·ne·mann·i·an** (hä′nə man′ē ən, -mä′nē-), *adj.* —**Hah′ne·mann′ism,** *n.*

haick (hīk, hāk), *n.* haik.

Hai·da (hī′də), *n., pl.* **-das,** (*esp. collectively*) **-da** for 1. **1.** a member of an Indian people inhabiting the Queen Charlotte Islands in British Columbia and Prince of Wales Island in Alaska. **2.** the language of the Haida people. **3.** a girl's given name, form of **Haidee.**

Hai·dar A·li (hī′dər ä′lē, ä lē′), 1722–82, Islamic prince and military leader of India: ruler of Mysore 1759–82. Also, **Hyder Ali.**

Hai·dee (hā′dē), *n.* a girl's given name.

Hai·ding·er (hī′ding ər), *n.* a walled plain in the third quadrant of the face of the moon: about 15 miles in diameter.

Hai′ding·er fring′es (hī′ding ər), *Optics.* interference fringes produced by light passing through thick glass plates at near-normal incidence. [named after Wilhelm Karl von *Haidinger* (1795–1871), Australian mineralogist]

Hai·duk (hī′do͝ok), *n.* **1.** one of a class of mercenary soldiers in 16th-century Hungary. **2.** a patriotic brigand in the Slav portions of the Balkan Peninsula. **3.** a male servant or attendant dressed in Hungarian semimilitary costume. Also, **Heyduck, Heyduke, Heyduc, Heiduc, Heiduk.** [< Hung *hajdúk,* pl. of *hajdú* brigand]

Hai·fa (hī′fə), *n.* a seaport in NW Israel. 191,200 (est. 1963).

Haig (hāg), *n.* **Douglas, 1st Earl,** 1861–1928, British field marshal: commander in chief of the British forces in France 1915–18.

haik (hīk, hāk), *n.* an oblong cloth used as an outer garment by the Arabs. Also, **haick.** [< Ar *ḥā'ik, ḥayk,* akin to *ḥāk* weave]

hai·kai (hī′kī), *n., pl.* **-kai** for 2. *Pros.* **1.** an informal type of linked verse originated by Bashō, a 17th-century Japanese poet. **2.** a poem of this type. [< Jap]

hai·kal (hī′käl, hā′-), *n.* a sanctuary, esp. in the Coptic Church, separated from the choir and the nave by a screen (**hai′kal screen′**). [< Syriac *haykal,* Heb *hēkhāl* < Assyrian Babylonian *ēkallu* < Sumerian *e gal* big house, equiv. to *e* house + *gal* big]

hai·ku (hī′ko͞o), *n., pl.* **-ku** for 2. **1.** a major form of Japanese verse, written in 17 syllables and employing highly evocative allusions and comparisons. **2.** a poem written in this form. [< Jap]

hai′kwan′ tael′ (hī′kwän′), **1.** the customs unit in China, which is the basis for other local taels, equal to 1.20666 troy ounces of fine silver. **2.** liang. [< Chin (Mandarin), equiv. to *hai* sea + *kuan* gateway]

hail[1] (hāl), *v.t.* **1.** to salute or greet; welcome. **2.** to call out to in order to stop, attract attention, ask aid, etc.: *to hail a cab.* **3.** to acclaim; approve enthusiastically: *The crowds hailed the conquerors. They hailed the recent advances in medicine.* —*v.i.* **4.** to call out in order to greet, attract attention, etc.: *The people on land hailed as we passed in the night.* **5. hail from,** to have as one's place of birth or residence: *Nearly everyone here hails from a distant place.* —*n.* **6.** a shout or call to attract attention: *They answered the hail of the marooned boaters.* **7.** a salutation or greeting: *a cheerful hail.* **8.** the act of hailing. **9. within hail,** within range of hearing; audible: *The mother kept her children within hail of her voice.* —*interj.* **10.** (used as a salutation, greeting, or acclamation.) [ME *haile,* earlier *heilen,* deriv. of *hail* health < Scand; cf. Icel *heill;* c. OE *hǣl.* See WASSAIL] —**hail′er,** *n.*

hail[2] (hāl), *n.* **1.** showery precipitation in the form of irregular pellets or balls of ice more than ⅕ inch in diameter, falling from a cumulonimbus cloud. **2.** a shower or storm of such precipitation. **3.** a shower of anything: *a hail of bullets.* —*v.i.* **4.** to pour down hail (often used impersonally with *it* as subject): *It hailed the whole afternoon.* **5.** to fall or shower as hail: *Arrows hailed down on the troops as they advanced.* —*v.t.* **6.** to pour down on, as or like hail. [ME; OE *hægl,* var. of *hagol;* c. G *Hagel,* Icel *hagl*]

hail[3] (hāl), *Brit. Dial. Obs.* —*adj.* **1.** hale[1]. —*n.* **2.** fate; fortune; luck. [ME *heil* < Scand; cf. Icel *heill* HALE[1]]

Hail′ Colum′bia, *Slang.* hell (used as a euphemism): *He caught Hail Columbia for coming home late.*

Hai·le Se·las·sie (hī′lē sə las′ē, -lä′sē), (*Ras Taffari* or *Tafari*), 1891–1975, emperor of Ethiopia 1930–74: in exile 1936–41.

hail-fel·low (*n.* hāl′fel′ō; *adj.* hāl′fel′ō), *n.* **1.** Also, **hail′ fel′low, hail′-fel′low well′ met′.** a spiritedly sociable person; jolly companion. —*adj.* **2.** sociable; heartily genial: *His hail-fellow manner helped him to advance in the sales force.*

hail′ing dis′tance, 1. the distance within which the human voice can be heard: *They sailed within hailing distance of the island.* **2.** a close distance; the reach of something or someone (usually prec. by *within*): *Success is within hailing distance.*

Hail′ Mar′y. See **Ave Maria.** [ME, trans. of ML *Ave Maria*]

hail·stone (hāl′stōn′), *n.* a pellet of hail. [ME; OE *hagolstān.* See HAIL[2], STONE] —**hail′stoned′,** *adj.*

hail·storm (hāl′stôrm′), *n.* a storm with hail. [HAIL[2] + STORM]

Hai·nan (hī′nän′), *n.* **1.** an island in the South China Sea, separated from the mainland of S China by Hainan Strait; a part of Kwangtung province. 2,700,000 (est. 1956); ab. 13,200 sq. mi. **2. Strait,** a strait between this island and Luichow peninsula. 50 mi. long; 15 mi. wide.

Hai·naut (e nō′), *n.* a medieval county in territory now in SW Belgium and N France.

Haines′ Cit′y (hānz), a town in central Florida. 9135 (1960).

hain't (hānt), *Dial.* ain't; have not; has not. [orig. contr. of *have not, has not* (with loss of consonant and compensatory lengthening of *a*): influenced in use by AIN'T]

Hai·phong (hī′fong′), *n.* a seaport in North Vietnam, in NE Indochina, near the Gulf of Tonkin. 182,496 (1960).

hair (hâr), *n.* **1.** any of the numerous fine, usually cylindrical filaments growing from the skin of man and animals. **2.** an aggregate of such filaments, as that covering the human head or forming the coat of most mammals. **3.** a similar fine, filamentous outgrowth from the body of insects, spiders, etc. **4.** *Bot.* a filamentous outgrowth of the epidermis. **5.** cloth made of hair from animals, as camel and alpaca. **6.** a very small amount, degree, measure, magnitude, etc.; a fraction, as of time or space: *He lost the race by a hair.* **7. get in someone's hair,** *Slang.* to annoy or bother someone: *Their snobbishness gets in my hair.* **8. hair of the dog,** *Slang.* a drink of liquor, supposed to remedy a hangover: *Even a hair of the dog didn't help his aching head.* Also, **hair of the dog that bit one. 9. let one's hair down, a.** to relax; behave informally: *He finally let his hair down and actually cracked a joke.* **b.** to speak candidly or frankly; remove or reduce restraints: *He let his hair down and told them off.* **10. make one's hair stand on end,** to strike with horror; terrify: *The tales of the jungle made our hair stand on end.* **11. tear one's hair,** to manifest extreme anxiety, grief, or anger: *He's tearing his hair over the way he was treated by them.* Also, **tear one's hair out. 12. split hairs,** to make unnecessarily fine or petty distinctions: *To argue about whether they arrived at 2:00 o'clock or at 2:01 is just splitting hairs.* **13. to a hair,** exactly; perfect to the smallest detail: *The reproduction matched the original to a hair.* **14. without turning a hair,** showing no excitement or emotion; remaining calm: *He put out the fire without turning a hair.* Also, **not turn a hair.** [ME *heer,* OE *hǣr;* c. D, G *haar,* Icel *hār* + ME *haire* hair shirt < OF < OHG *hāria;* c. ME *here,* OE *hǣre,* Icel *hǣra*] —**hair′like′,** *adj.*

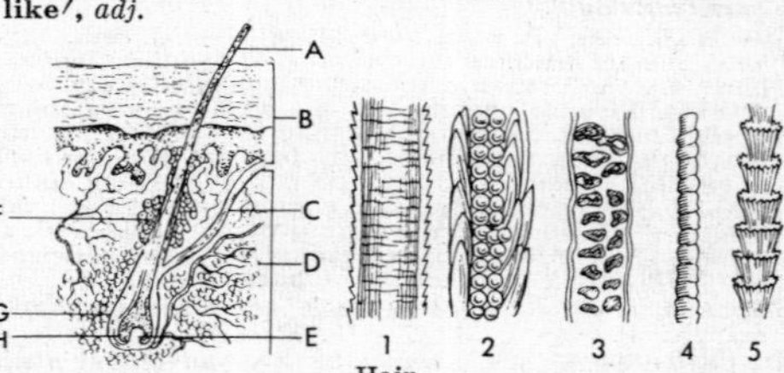

Hair
Cross section of skin containing a hair: A, Hair; B, Epidermis; C, Muscle; D, Dermis; E, Papilla; F, Sebaceous glands; G, Follicle; H, Root. Longitudinal sections of hairs: 1, Man; 2, Sable; 3, Mouse. External view: 4, Mouse; 5, Indian bat

hair·ball (hâr′bôl′), *n.* a ball of hair accumulated in the stomach or intestines of a cat or other animal as a result of the animal's licking its coat. [HAIR + BALL[1]]

hair·brained (hâr′brānd′), *adj.* harebrained.

hair·breadth (hâr′bredth′, -bretth′), *n., adj.* hair's-breadth. [HAIR + BREADTH]

hair·brush (hâr′brush′), *n.* a brush for dressing the hair. [HAIR + BRUSH[1]]

hair′brush cac′tus, a stout, spiny cactus, *Pachycereus pecten-aboriginum,* of Mexico, having purplish flowers and burlike fruits used by the Indians as combs.

hair′ cell′, *Biol.* an epithelial cell having hairlike processes, as that of the organ of Corti.

hair·cloth (hâr′klôth′, -kloth′), *n.* cloth of hair from the manes and tails of horses, woven with a cotton warp, and used for interlinings of clothes, upholstery, etc. Also called **cilice.** [HAIR + CLOTH]

hair·cut (hâr′kut′), *n.* **1.** the act or an instance of cutting the hair. **2.** the style in which the hair is cut and worn, esp. men's hair. [HAIR + CUT] —**hair′cut′ter,** *n.* —**hair′cut′ting,** *n., adj.*

hair·do (hâr′do͞o′), *n., pl.* **-dos. 1.** the style in which a woman's hair is cut, arranged, and worn; coiffure. **2.** the hair itself, esp. when newly or elaborately arranged. [HAIR + DO[1]]

hair·dress·er (hâr′dres′ər), *n.* **1.** one who arranges or cuts women's hair. **2.** *Chiefly Brit.* barber. [HAIR + DRESSER[1]]

hair·dress·ing (hâr′dres′ing), *n.* **1.** the act or process of cutting, styling, or dressing hair, esp. women's hair. **2.** the vocation or occupation of a hairdresser. **3.** a style of arranging the hair; hairdo; coiffure. **4.** a preparation, as tonic, oil, pomade, or the like, applied to the hair for increased manageability. [HAIR + DRESSING]

hair′ fol′licle, *Anat.* a small cavity from which a hair develops.

hair′ grip′, *Brit.* a bobby pin; hairpin.

hair′ hygrom′eter, a hygrometer actuated by the changes in length of a strand of human hair brought about by changes in the relative humidity.

hair·less (hâr′lis), *adj.* without hair; bald. [HAIR + -LESS] —**hair′less·ness,** *n.*

hair·line (hâr′līn′), *n.* **1.** a very slender line. **2.** the lower edge of the hair, esp. along the upper forehead: *a hairline that slowly receded.* **3.** worsted fabric woven with very fine lines or stripes. **4.** *Print.* **a.** a very thin line on the face of a type. **b.** a style of type consisting entirely of such lines. See diag. under **type. c.** a thin rule for printing fine lines. **d.** undesirable vertical lines between letters, caused by worn matrices. [HAIR + LINE[1]]

hair′ net′, a cap of loose net, as of silk or human hair, for holding the hair in place.

hair·piece (hâr′pēs′), *n.* a toupee. [HAIR + PIECE]

hair·pin (hâr′pin′), *n.* **1.** a slender U-shaped piece of wire, shell, etc., used by women to fasten up the hair or hold a headdress. —*adj.* **2.** (of a road, curve in a road, etc.) sharply curved, as in a U shape: *a hairpin turn.* [HAIR + PIN]

hair′pin meg′aron, (in pre-Hellenic Greek architecture) a free-standing megaron having a long principal chamber and a semicircular end opposite the end at which the porch is located.

hair-rais·er (hâr′rā′zər), *n.* a story, experience, etc., that is terrifying or thrilling.

hair-rais·ing (hâr′rā′zing), *adj.* terrifying: *We had a hair-raising brush with death.*

hair's-breadth (hârz′bredth′, -bretth′), *n.* **1.** a very small space or distance: *We escaped an accident by a hair's-breadth.* —*adj.* **2.** extremely narrow or close. Also, **hairs′breadth′, hairbreadth.**

hair′ seal′, any of various seals having coarse hair and no soft underfur.

hair′ shirt′, a garment of coarse haircloth, worn next to the skin by ascetics and penitents.

hair′ space′, *Print.* the thinnest metal space used to separate words, symbols, etc.

hair·split·ter (hâr′split′ər), *n.* one who makes fine or unnecessary distinctions. [HAIR + SPLITTER] —**hair′split′ting,** *n., adj.*

hair·spring (hâr′spring′), *n.* *Horol.* a fine, usually spiral, spring used for oscillating the balance of a timepiece. Also called **balance spring.** [HAIR + SPRING]

hair·streak (hâr′strēk′), *n.* any of several small, dark butterflies of the family *Lycaenidae,* having hairlike tails on the hind wings. [HAIR + STREAK]

hair′ stroke′, a fine line in writing or printing.

hair′ styl′ist, one who designs and sometimes arranges hair styles, esp. for women.

hair·tail (hâr′tāl′), *n.* cutlassfish. [HAIR + TAIL[1]; so called from the resemblance of the tail to strands of hair]

hair′ trig′ger, a trigger that allows the firing mechanism of a firearm to be operated by very slight pressure.

hair-trig·ger (hâr′trig′ər), *adj.* easily activated or set off; put into operation by the slightest impulse: *a hair-trigger temper.*

hair·worm (hâr′wûrm′), *n.* any of a number of small, slender worms of the family *Trichostrongylidae,* parasitic in the alimentary canals of various animals. [HAIR + WORM]

hair·y (hâr′ē), *adj.,* **hair·i·er, hair·i·est. 1.** covered with hair; having much hair. **2.** consisting of or resembling hair: *moss of a hairy texture.* [ME *heeri.* See HAIR, -Y[1]] —**hair′i·ness,** *n.*

Hair′y Ape′, The, a play (1922) by Eugene O'Neill.

hair·y-faced (hâr′ē fāst′), *adj.* having a face covered with hair.

hair′y-tailed mole′ (hâr′ē tāld′), a blackish North American mole, *Parascalops breweri,* having a short, hairy tail. Also, **hair′y-tail′ mole′.** Also called **Brewer's mole.**

hair′y wat′tle, a shrub, *Acacia pubescens,* having showy, yellow flowers, grown as an ornamental.

hair′y wood′pecker, a North American woodpecker, *Dendrocopos villosus,* resembling but larger than the downy woodpecker.

Hai·ti (hā′tē), *n.* **1.** a republic in the West Indies occupying the W part of the island of Hispaniola. 3,505,000 (est. 1960); 10,714 sq. mi. *Cap.:* Port-au-Prince. **2.** Also, **Hayti.** former name of **Hispaniola.**

Hai·tian (hā′shən, -tē ən), *adj.* **1.** of or pertaining to Haiti or its people. —*n.* **2.** a native or inhabitant of Haiti. **3.** See **Haitian Creole.** [HAITI + -AN]

Hai′tian Cre′ole, the creolized French that is the native language of most Haitians. Also called **Creole, Haitian.**

haj·i (haj′ē), *n., pl.* **haj·is.** hajji.

hajj (haj), *n., pl.* **hajj·es.** the pilgrimage to Mecca, which every good Muslim is supposed to make at least once in his lifetime. Also, **hadj.** [< Ar: pilgrimage]

haj·ji (haj′ē), *n., pl.* **haj·jis. 1.** a Muslim who has gone on a pilgrimage to Mecca. **2.** a Christian from Greece, Armenia, or any country of the Near East, who has visited the Holy Sepulcher at Jerusalem. Also, **hadji, haji.** [< Ar, equiv. to *hajj* pilgrimage + *-i* agent suffix]

Ha·kai (hä kī′), *n.* See **Broken Commandment, The.**

hake (hāk), *n., pl.* (*esp. collectively*) **hake,** (*esp. referring to two or more kinds or species*) **hakes. 1.** any of several marine fishes of the genus *Merluccius,* closely related to the cods, esp. *M. bilinearis,* found off the New England coast. **2.** any of several related marine fishes, esp. of the genus *Urophycis.* [ME, special use of OE *haca* hook; cf. MLG *haken* kipper salmon]

Ha·ken·kreuz (hä′kən kroits′), *n., pl.* **-kreu·ze** (-kroi′tsə). *Ger.* a swastika, esp. that used as the emblem of the Nazi party and the Third Reich. [lit., hook-cross]

Ha·ken·kreuz·ler (hä′kən kroits′lər), *n., pl.* **-ler** (-lər). *Ger.* a member of any extreme nationalist organization in Germany and Austria after World War I.

ha·kim[1] (hä kēm′), *n.* (esp. in Muslim countries) **1.** a wise or learned man. **2.** a physician. Also, **ha·keem** (hä kēm′). [< Ar *ḥakīm* wise, wise man]

ha·kim[2] (hä′kēm), *n.* (in Muslim countries) a ruler; governor; judge. [< Ar *ḥākim* governor]

Hak·luyt (hak′lit), *n.* **Richard,** 1552?–1616, English geographer and editor of explorers' narratives.

Ha·ko·da·te (hä′kô dä′te), *n.* a seaport on S Hokkaido, in N Japan. 250,457 (1964).

Hal (hal), *n.* a boy's given name, form of **Harold.**

Hal, *Chem.* halogen.

hal-, var. of **halo-** before a vowel: *halite.*

Ha·la·chah (hä lô′khə; *Heb.* hä lä khä′, -lô khô′), *n., pl.* **-la·chas,** *Heb.* **-la·chot** (-lä khôt′, -lô khôs′). Halakah. —**Ha·lach·ic** (hə lak′ik), *adj.*

Ha·laf·i·an (hə laf′ē ən), *adj.* **1.** of or belonging to the Neolithic culture chiefly of N Syria, characterized by adobe dwellings and polychrome pottery decorated with animal designs and geometric patterns. —*n.* **2.** a person who belonged to this culture. Also, **Ha·laf** (hə läf′). [after (*Tell*) *Halaf* mound in Syria; see -IAN]

Ha·la·kah (hä lô′khə; *Heb.* hä lä khä′, -lô khô′), *n., pl.* **-la·kahs,** *Heb.* **-la·koth** (-lä khôt′, -lô khôs′) for 2. **1.** the entire body of Jewish law and tradition comprising the laws of the Bible, the oral law as transcribed in the legal portion of the Talmud, and subsequent legal codes amending or modifying traditional precepts to conform to contemporary conditions. **2.** a law or tradition established by the Halakah. Also, **Halachah.** [< Heb: rule to follow, lit., way] —**Ha·lak·ic** (hə lak′ik), *adj.*

ha·la·kist (hä′lə kist, hə lä′-), *n.* **1.** one of the writers or compilers of the Halakah. **2.** one who is versed in the Halakah. Also, **ha·lach′ist,** *n.* [HALAK(AH) + -IST]

ha·la·tion (hā lā′shən, ha-), *n.* *Photog.* a blurred effect at the edges of a very light area on a photograph, caused by reflection of light through the emulsion from the surface of the film or plate. [HAL(O) + -ATION]

ha·la·vah (hä′lə vä′), *n.* halvah.

Hal·be (hal′bē), *n.* a boy's given name.

hal·berd (hal′bərd, hôl′-, hol′-; *formerly* hô′bərd), *n.* a shafted weapon with an axlike cutting blade, beak, and apical spike, used esp. in the 15th and 16th centuries. Also, **hal·bert** (hal′bərt, hôl′-, hol′-; *formerly* hô′bərt). [late ME < MF *hallebarde* < MLG *helmbarde,* equiv. to *helm* handle (c. HELM[1]) + *barde* broadax (c. MHG *barte*)]

Halberd (Head)

hal·berd·ier (hal′bər dēr′), *n.* a soldier, guard, or attendant armed with a halberd. [< MF *hallebardier.* See HALBERD, -IER]

hal·cy·on (hal′sē ən), *n.* **1.** a mythical bird, usually identified with the kingfisher, said to breed about the time of the winter solstice in a nest floating on the sea, and to have the power of charming winds and waves into calmness. **2.** any of various kingfishers, esp. of the genus *Halcyon.* **3.** (*cap.*) *Class. Myth.* Alcyone (def. 2). —*adj.* Also, **hal·cy·o·ni·an** (hal′sē ō′nē ən), **hal·cy·on·ic** (hal′sē on′ik). **4.** calm; peaceful; tranquil: *halcyon weather.* **5.** rich; wealthy; prosperous: *halcyon times of peace.* **6.** happy; joyful; carefree: *halcyon days of youth.* **7.** of or pertaining to the halcyon or kingfisher. [< L < Gk *halkyṓn,* pseudo-etymological var. of *alkyṓn* kingfisher; r. ME *alceon, alicion* < L *alcyōn* < Gk]

Hal·dane (hôl′dān), *n.* **1. John Bur·don San·der·son** (bûr′dᵊn san′dər sən), 1892–1964, English biochemist, geneticist, and writer. **2.** his father, **John Scott,** 1860–1936, Scottish physiologist and writer. **3. Richard Burdon** (*Viscount Haldane of Cloan*), 1856–1928, Scottish jurist, statesman, and writer (brother of John Scott).

hale[1] (hāl), *adj.,* **hal·er, hal·est. 1.** free from disease or infirmity; robust; vigorous: *hale and hearty men in the prime of life.* **2.** *Scot. and North Eng.* free from defect or injury. [ME (north); OE *hāl* WHOLE] —**hale′ness,** *n.* —**Syn. 1.** sound, healthy. —**Ant. 1.** sickly.

hale[2] (hāl), *v.t.,* **haled, hal·ing. 1.** to haul, pull, drag, or draw with force. **2.** to bring as by dragging: *to hale a man into court.* [ME *hale(n)* < MF *hale(r)* < Gmc; cf. D *halen* to pull, fetch; akin to OE *geholian* to get, G *holen* to fetch. See HAUL] —**hal′er,** *n.*

Hale (hāl), *n.* **1. Edward Everett,** 1822–1909, U.S. clergyman and author. **2. George El·ler·y** (el′ə rē), 1868–1938, U.S. astronomer. **3. Sir Matthew,** 1609–76, British jurist: Lord Chief Justice 1671–76. **4. Nathan,** 1755–76, American soldier hanged as a spy by the British during the American Revolution. **5. Sarah Jo·se·pha** (jō sē′fə), 1788–1879, U.S. editor and author.

Ha·le·a·ka·la (hä′le ä′kä lä′), *n.* a dormant volcano in Hawaii, on the island of Maui. Crater, 19 sq. mi.; 2000 ft. deep; 10,032 ft. above sea level.

Hale·don (hāl′dən), *n.* a town in NE New Jersey. 6161 (1960).

Ha·lei·wa (hä lā′wä), *n.* a town on NW Oahu, in central Hawaii. 2504 (1960).

ha·ler (hä′lər), *n., pl.* **-lers, -le·ru** (-lə ro͞o′). **1.** heller (def. 1). **2.** Also, **heller.** a minor coin of Czechoslovakia, the 100th part of a koruna. [< Czech < MHG *haller,* var. of *heller* HELLER]

Hales′ Cor′ners (hālz), a town in SE Wisconsin. 5549 (1960).

Hale·site (hāl′sīt), *n.* a town on NW Long Island, in SE New York. 2857 (1960).

Ha·lette (ha let′), *n.* a girl's given name.

Ha-le·vi (hä lē′vī, -lā′vē), *n.* **Judah.** See **Judah ha-Levi.**

Ha·lé·vy (A lā vē′), *n.* **1. Fro·men·tal** (frô män tAl′), (*Jacques François Fromental Élie Lévy*), 1799–1862, French composer, esp. of operas. **2.** his nephew, **Lu·do·vic** (ly dô vēk′), 1834–1908, French novelist and playwright: librettist in collaboration with Henri Meilhac.

Ha·ley·ville (hā′lē vil′), *n.* a town in NW Alabama. 3740 (1960).

half (haf, häf), *n., pl.* **halves** (havz, hävz), *adj., adv.* —*n.* **1.** one of two equal or approximately equal parts of a divisible whole, as an object, unit of measure or time, etc.; a part of a whole equal or almost equal to the remainder. **2.** *Sports.* either of two equal periods of play, usually with an intermission or rest period separating them. Cf. **quarter** (def. 9). **3.** one of two; a part of a pair. **4.** *U.S. Informal.* **a.** See **half dollar. b.** the sum of 50 cents: *Four dimes and two nickels make a half.* **5.** *Baseball.* either of the two units of play into which an inning is divided, the visiting team batting in the first unit and the home team batting in the second. **6.** *Football.* a halfback. **7.** *Brit. Informal.* **a.** a half-crown coin. **b.** the sum of a half crown; two shillings, sixpence. **c.** a half pint: *He ordered a half of ale.* **8. not the half of,** a significant yet relatively minor part of something that remains to be described in full: *He accused them of being responsible for the error, and that's not the half of the story.* Also, **not half of, not half.** —*adj.* **9.** being one of two equal or approximately equal parts of a divisible whole: *a half quart.* **10.** half or about half of anything in degree, amount, length, etc.: *at half speed; half sleeve.* **11.** partial or incomplete: *half measures.* —*adv.* **12.** in or to the extent or measure of half. **13.** in part; partly; incompletely: *half understood.* **14.** to some extent: *half recovered.* **15. by half,** by very much; by far: *She was too talented by half for her routine role.* **16. in half,** divided into halves: *The vase broke in half.* **17. not half, a.** not at all; not really: *His first attempts at painting are not half bad.* **b.** See **half** (def. 8). [ME; OE *h(e)alf;* c. G *Halb,* Icel *halfr,* Goth *halbs*]

half-and-half (haf′ən haf′, häf′ən häf′), *adj.* **1.** half one thing and half another. —*adv.* **2.** in two equal parts. —*n.* **3.** a mixture of two things, esp. in equal or nearly equal proportions. **4.** *Chiefly Brit.* a mixture of two malt liquors, esp. porter and ale. **5.** milk and light cream combined in equal parts, esp. for table use.

half′ ar′mor, plate armor that leaves the legs exposed.

half-assed (haf′ast′, häf′äst′), *adj.* *Slang* (*vulgar*). **1.** insufficient or haphazard; not fully planned or developed. **2.** incompetent; lacking sufficient ability or knowledge. **3.** unrealistic. [HALF + ASS[2] + -ED[3]]

half·back (haf′bak′, häf′-), *n.* **1.** *Football.* **a.** one of two backs who typically line up on each side of the fullback. **b.** the position played by such a back. **2.** (in soccer, Rugby, and field hockey) a player stationed near the forward line to carry out chiefly offensive duties. [HALF + BACK[1]]

half-baked (haf′bākt′, häf′-), *adj.* **1.** insufficiently cooked. **2.** not completed; insufficiently planned or prepared. **3.** lacking mature judgment or experience; unrealistic: *half-baked theorists.* **4.** *Informal.* eccentric; crazy.

half·beak (haf′bēk′, häf′-), *n.* any of several marine fishes of the family *Hemiramphidae,* having a greatly elongated lower jaw. [HALF + BEAK[1]]

half′ bind′ing, a book having a leather binding on the spine and corners, and paper or cloth sides. Also called **half leather.**

half′-blind joint′ (haf′blīnd′, häf′-), *Joinery.* a corner dovetail joint visible on one face only. Also called **lap dovetail joint.**

half′ blood′, the relation between persons having only one common parent.

half-blood (haf′blud′, häf′-), *n.* **1.** a half-breed. **2.** a person who has only one parent in common with another person, as a half sister or half brother.

half-blood·ed (haf′blud′id, häf′-), *adj.* having parents of two different breeds, races, or the like.

half′ boot′, a boot reaching about halfway to the knee.

half-bound (haf′bound′, häf′-), *adj.* bound in half binding.

half′ brau′ (brou), *Naut.* a very long, low forestaysail. [lit., half bridge; *brau,* late (pseudo-G) sp. var. of *brow* < Scand; cf. Icel *brū* bridge]

half′-breadth′ plan′ (haf′bredth′, -bretth′, häf′-), *Naval Archit.* a diagrammatic plan of one half of the hull of a vessel divided lengthwise amidships, showing water lines, stations, diagonals, and bow and buttock lines. Cf. **body plan, sheer plan.**

half-breed (haf′brēd′, häf′-), *n.* **1.** the offspring of parents of different races; one who is half-blooded. **2.** the offspring of a white person and an American Indian. —*adj.* **3.** of or pertaining to the offspring of a white person and an American Indian.

half′-a·ban′doned, *adj.*
half′-ac·cus′tomed, *adj.*
half′-ac·quaint′ed, *adj.*
half′-ac·qui·es′cent, *adj.;* **-ly,** *adv.*
half′-a′cre, *n.*
half′-ad·dressed′, *adj.*
half′-ad·mir′ing, *adj.;* **-ly,** *adv.*
half′-ad·mit′ted, *adj.;* **-ly,** *adv.*
half′-a·dream′, *adj.*
half′-af·fi′anced, *adj.*
half′-a·float′, *adj.*
half′-a·fraid′, *adj.*
half′-a·greed′, *adj.*
half′-a·like′, *adj.*
half′-a·live′, *adj.*
half′-al′tered, *adj.*
half′-A·mer′i·can, *adj.*
half′-A·mer′i·can·ized′, *adj.*
half′-An′gli·cized′, *adj.*
half′-an′gri·ly, *adv.*
half′-an′gry, *adj.*
half′-an·noyed′, *adj.*
half′-an·noy′ing, *adj.;* **-ly,** *adv.*
half′-Ar′is·to·te′lian, *adj.*
half′-armed′, *adj.*
half′-a·shamed′, *adj.*
half′-a·sham′ed·ly, *adv.*
half′-A′sian, *adj., n.*
half′-A·si·at′ic, *adj.*
half′-a·sleep′, *adj.*
half′-a·wake′, *adj.*
half′-backed′, *adj.*
half′-bald′, *adj.*
half′-banked′, *adj.*
half′-bar·bar′i·an, *adj.*
half′-bare′, *adj.*
half′-bar′rel, *n.*
half′-beg′ging, *adj.*
half′-be·gun′, *adj.*
half′-be·lieved′, *adj.*
half′-be·liev′ing, *adj.*
half′-bleached′, *adj.*
half′-blind′, *adj.;* **-ly,** *adv.*
half′-blown′, *adj.*
half′-blue′, *adj.*
half′-boiled′, *adj.*
half′-boil′ing, *adj.*

half′-bril′liant cut′ (haf′bril′yənt, häf′-), *Jewelry.* See **single cut.**

half′ broth′er, brother (def. 2).

half′ ca′dence, *Music.* a cadence ending with dominant harmony.

half-caste (haf′kast′, häf′käst′), *n.* **1.** a person of mixed race. **2.** a person of mixed European and Hindu or European and Muslim parentage. **3.** a person descended from parents of different social strata. —*adj.* **4.** of or pertaining to a half-caste.

half′ cent′, a bronze coin of the U.S., equal to one-half cent, issued at various periods between 1793 and 1857.

half′ cock′, **1.** the position of the hammer of a firearm when held halfway between the firing and retracted positions by a mechanism so that it will not operate. **2. go off at half cock,** to act or happen prematurely: *He went off at half cock and told everyone the news.* Also, **go off half-cocked.**

half-cock (haf′kok′, häf′-), *v.t.* to set the hammer of (a firearm) at half cock.

half-cocked (haf′kokt′, häf′-), *adj.* **1.** (of a firearm) at the position of half cock. **2.** *U.S.* lacking mature consideration or enough preparation; ill-considered or ill-prepared; half-baked.

half′ crown′, a cupronickel coin of Great Britain equal to 2s. 6d. and equivalent to about .35 of a U.S. dollar.

half′-dead′ escape′ment (haf′ded′, häf′-), *Horol.* a clock escapement having relatively little recoil.

half′ deck′, **1.** (in a sailing ship) the portion of the first deck below the upper or spar deck and abaft the mainmast, for quartering apprentice officers or midshipmen. **2.** (on recent sailing ships) a deckhouse for housing apprentice officers and others, as the carpenter and sailmaker. **3.** a deck on a sailing vessel, raised on and at the rear of a quarter deck. **4.** a partial forward deck on an open vessel. —**half′-deck′er,** *n.*

half-decked (haf′dekt′, häf′-), *adj.* **1.** noting a boat having its forward part decked over with all else open. **2.** noting a boat having a partial deck covering all parts immediately inboard as well as a small space forward.

half′ dime′, a silver coin of the U.S., equal to five cents, issued 1794–1805 and 1829–73.

half′ dol′lar, a silver coin of the U.S., worth 50 cents, weighing 385.8 grains to the dollar, 0.900 fine.

half′ ea′gle, a gold coin of the U.S., discontinued in 1929, equal to five dollars.

half′ frame′, **1.** *Carpentry.* See **combination frame.** **2.** *Shipbuilding.* See **half timber** (def. 1).

half′ gain′er, *Fancy Diving.* a dive in which the diver takes off facing forward and performs a half backward somersault, entering the water headfirst and facing the springboard.

half-head·ed (haf′hed′id, häf′-), *adj.* (of a bed) having posts without a canopy.

half-heart·ed (haf′här′tid, häf′-), *adj.* having or showing little enthusiasm: *a half-hearted attempt to work.* —**half′-heart′ed·ly,** *adv.* —**half′-heart′ed·ness,** *n.*
—**Syn.** indifferent, uninterested, cold, cool, perfunctory. —**Ant.** enthusiastic.

half′ hitch′, a knot or hitch made by forming a bight and passing the end of the rope around the standing part and through the bight. See illus. under **knot.**

half′ hose′, short hose; socks.

half-hour (haf′our′, -ou′ər, häf′-), *n.* **1.** a period of 30 minutes. **2.** the midpoint between the hours: *The clock struck on the half-hour.* —*adj.* **3.** of, pertaining to, or consisting of a half-hour: *half-hour programs.*

half·hour·ly (haf′our′lē, -ou′ər-, häf′-), *adj.* **1.** half-hour (def. 3). **2.** occurring every half-hour: *a half-hourly interruption.* —*adv.* **3.** at half-hour intervals: *The bell rang halfhourly.* [HALF + HOURLY]

half′ hunt′er, *Horol.* demi-hunter.

half′-lap joint′ (haf′lap′, häf′-), a joint between two timbers halved together so that a flush surface results.

half′ leath′er, *Bookbinding.* See **half binding.**

half-length (haf′lengkth′, -length′, häf′-), *n.* **1.** something that is only half a full length or height, esp. a portrait that shows only the upper half of the body, including the hands. —*adj.* **2.** of half the complete length or height.

half·life (haf′līf′, häf′-), *n., pl.* **-lives.** *Physics.* the time required for one half the atoms of a given amount of a radioactive substance to disintegrate. Also, **half′ life′.** Also called **half′-life pe′riod.** [HALF + LIFE]

half-light (haf′līt′, häf′-), *n.* light that is about half its customary brightness, or that is partially dimmed or obscured: *the half-light of early dawn; a room in half-light.*

half-mast (haf′mast′, häf′mäst′), *n.* **1.** a position approximately halfway between the top of a mast, staff, etc., and its base. —*v.t.* **2.** to place (a flag) at half-mast as a mark of respect for the dead or as a signal of distress.

half′ mod′el, *Naval Archit.* a wooden model representing half of a hull divided along the fore-and-aft midship line, formed either of a single piece or from a number of planks fastened together and usually representing molded dimensions. Cf. **block model, bread-and-butter model, lift** (def. 26), **hawk's nest model.**

half-moon (haf′mo͞on′, häf′-), *n.* **1.** the moon when, at either quadrature, half its disk is illuminated. **2.** the phase of the moon at this time. See diag. under **moon.** **3.** something having the shape of a half-moon or crescent.

half·moon (haf′mo͞on′, häf′-), *n.* an edible fish, *Medialuna californiensis,* found in southern California, having a slate-gray body. [HALF + MOON]

Half′ Moon′, the ship in which Henry Hudson made his voyage to explore America in 1609.

half′ mourn′ing, **1.** a mourning garb less somber than full mourning. **2.** the period during which it is worn.

half′ nel′son, *Wrestling.* a hold in which a wrestler, from behind his opponent, passes one arm under the corresponding arm of the opponent and locks the hand on the back of the opponent's neck. Cf. **nelson.**

half′ note′, *Music.* **1.** a note equivalent in time value to one half of a semibreve. See illus. under **note.** **2.** (formerly) the shortest note in use.

half·pace (haf′pās′, häf′-), *n.* **1.** a landing for a half-turn stair. **2.** hathpace. [pseudo-etymological var. of *hal(t)pace* < MF *hault pas* high step] —**half′paced′,** *adj.*

half′ pay′, a reduced allowance paid to a British army or navy officer when not in actual service or after retirement.

half·pen·ny (hā′pə nē, hāp′nē), *n., pl.* **half·pen·nies** for 1; **half·pence** (hā′pəns) for 2; *adj.* —*n.* **1.** a bronze coin of the United Kingdom, equal to half a penny and equivalent to about .006 of a U.S. dollar. **2.** the sum of half a penny. —*adj.* **3.** of the price or value of a halfpenny. **4.** of little value; worthless: *a halfpenny matter.* **5.** *Brit. Informal.* (of newspapers) sensational, esp. morbidly or offensively so. [ME *halfpeny.* See HALF, PENNY]

half-pike (haf′pīk′, häf′-), *n.* **1.** spontoon. **2.** a short pike formerly used by seamen boarding enemy vessels.

half′ pint′, **1.** half of a pint. **2.** *Informal.* a very short person. **3.** *Slang.* a person of little importance or influence.

half-plane (haf′plān′, häf′-), *n.* *Math.* the part of the plane on one side of a straight line of infinite length in the plane.

half′ port′, *Naut.* either of a pair of doors or flaps closing a port.

half-quar·ter·pace (haf′kwôr′tər pās′, häf′-), *n.* (on a staircase) a winder making a 45° angle at the newel.

half′ rhyme′. See **slant rhyme.**

half-round (haf′round′, häf′-), *adj.* **1.** semicircular in cross section, as a molding, piece of type, etc. —*n.* **2.** anything that is semicircular in cross section. **3.** *Print.* a curved stereotype plate.

half′-seas o′ver (haf′sēz′, häf′-), *Slang.* drunk; intoxicated; inebriated.

half′ sheave′, *Naut.* any fixed device, groove, or the like, for guiding a rope in such a way as to lessen friction upon it.

half′ shell′, either of the halves of a double-shelled creature, as of an oyster, clam, or other bivalve mollusk.

half′ sis′ter, sister (def. 2).

half′ size′, any size in women's garments designated by a fractional number from 12½ through 24½, designed for a short-waisted, full figure.

half-slip (haf′slip′, häf′-), *n.* a short petticoat worn as an underskirt.

half′ snipe′, jacksnipe (def. 1).

half′ sole′, that part of the sole of a boot or shoe which extends from the shank to the end of the toe.

half-sole (haf′sōl′, häf′-), *v.t.,* **-soled, -sol·ing.** to repair or renew (a shoe) by putting on a new half sole.

half′ sov′ereign, a gold coin of the United Kingdom, discontinued in 1917, equal to 10 shillings.

- **half′-bro′ken,** *adj.*
- **half′-bur′ied,** *adj.*
- **half′-burned′,** *adj*
- **half′-burn′ing,** *adj.*
- **half′-bush′el,** *n.*
- **half′-calf′,** *adj.*
- **half′-car′ried,** *adj.*
- **half′-cen′tu·ry,** *n., pl.,* **-ries.**
- **half′-chant′ed,** *adj.*
- **half′-Chris′tian,** *adj.*
- **half′-civ′il,** *adj.;* **-ly,** *adv.*
- **half′-civ′il·ized′,** *adj.*
- **half′-clad′,** *adj.*
- **half′-cleaned′,** *adj.*
- **half′-clear′,** *adj.;* **-ly,** *adv.*
- **half′-climb′ing,** *adj.*
- **half′-closed′,** *adj.*
- **half′-clos′ing,** *adj.*
- **half′-clothed′,** *adj.*
- **half′-coax′ing,** *adj.;* **-ly,** *adv.*
- **half′-col′ored,** *adj.*
- **half′-com·plet′ed,** *adj.*
- **half′-con·cealed′,** *adj.*
- **half′-con·ceal′ing,** *adj.*
- **half′-Con·fed′er·ate,** *adj.*
- **half′-con·fessed′,** *adj.*
- **half′-con·gealed′,** *adj.*
- **half′-con′quered,** *adj.*
- **half′-con′scious,** *adj.;* **-ly,** *adv.*
- **half′-con·serv′a·tive,** *adj.;* **-ly,** *adv.*
- **half′-con·sumed′,** *adj.*
- **half′-con′sum·mat′ed,** *adj.*
- **half′-con·temp′tu·ous,** *adj.;* **-ly,** *adv.*
- **half′-con·tent′ed,** *adj.;* **-ly,** *adv.*
- **half′-con·vict′ed,** *adj.*
- **half′-con·vinced′,** *adj.*
- **half′-con·vinc′ing,** *adj.;* **-ly,** *adv.*
- **half′-cooked′,** *adj.*
- **half′-cor′date,** *adj.*
- **half′-cor·rect′ed,** *adj.*
- **half′-cot′ton,** *adj.*
- **half′-count′ed,** *adj.*
- **half′-cov′ered,** *adj.*
- **half′-crazed′,** *adj.*
- **half′-cra′zy,** *adj.*
- **half′-Cre·ole′,** *adj.*
- **half′-crit′i·cal,** *adj.;* **-ly,** *adv.*
- **half′-crum′bled,** *adj.*
- **half′-crum′bling,** *adj.*
- **half′-cured′,** *adj.*
- **half′-cut′,** *adj.*
- **half′-Da′cron,** *adj.*
- **half′-day′,** *n.*
- **half′-dazed′,** *adj.*
- **half′-dead′,** *adj.*
- **half′-deaf′,** *adj.*
- **half′-deaf′ened,** *adj.*
- **half′-deaf′en·ing,** *adj.*
- **half′-dec′ade,** *n.*
- **half′-de·fi′ant,** *adj.;* **-ly,** *adv.*
- **half′-de′i·fied′,** *adj.*
- **half′-de·ment′ed,** *adj.*
- **half′-dem·o·crat′ic,** *adj.*
- **half′-de·mol′ished,** *adj.*
- **half′-de·nud′ed,** *adj.*
- **half′-dep′re·cat′ing,** *adj.;* **-ly,** *adv.*
- **half′-de·served′,** *adj.*
- **half′-de·serv′ed·ly,** *adv.*
- **half′-de·stroyed′,** *adj.*
- **half′-de·vel′oped,** *adj.*
- **half′-di·gest′ed,** *adj.*
- **half′-dis·crim′i·nat′ed,** *adj.*
- **half′-dis·crim′i·nat′ing,** *adj.*
- **half′-dis·posed′,** *adj.*
- **half′-di·vine′,** *adj.;* **-ly,** *adv.*
- **half′-done′,** *adj.*
- **half′-door′,** *adj.*
- **half′-doz′en,** *adj.*
- **half′-dram′,** *adj.*
- **half′-dressed′,** *adj.*
- **half′-dress′ed·ness,** *n.*
- **half′-dried′,** *adj.*
- **half′-drowned′,** *adj.*
- **half′-drown′ing,** *adj.*
- **half′-drunk′,** *adj.*
- **half′-drunk′en,** *adj.*
- **half′-dug′,** *adj.*
- **half′-dy′ing,** *adj.*
- **half′-earn′est,** *adj.;* **-ly,** *adv.*
- **half′-eat′en,** *adj.*
- **half′-ed′u·cat′ed,** *adj.*
- **half′-E·liz′a·be′than,** *adj.*
- **half′-em·braced′,** *adj.*
- **half′-em·brac′ing,** *adj.;* **-ly,** *adv.*
- **half′-en·am′ored,** *adj.*
- **half′-en·forced′,** *adj.*
- **half′-Eng′lish,** *adj.*
- **half′-e·rased′,** *adj.*
- **half′-e·vap′o·rat′ed,** *adj.*
- **half′-e·vap′o·rat′ing,** *adj.*
- **half′-ex·pect′ant,** *adj.;* **-ly,** *adv.*
- **half′-ex·ploit′ed,** *adj.*
- **half′-ex·posed′,** *adj.*
- **half′-false′,** *adj.*
- **half′-fam′ished,** *adj.*
- **half′-far′thing,** *n.*
- **half′-fas′ci·nat′ed,** *adj.*
- **half′-fas′ci·nat′ing,** *adj.;* **-ly,** *adv.*
- **half′-fed′,** *adj.*
- **half′-fem′i·nine,** *adj.*
- **half′-fer′tile,** *adj.;* **-ly,** *adv.*
- **half′-fic·ti′tious,** *adj.;* **-ly,** *adv.*
- **half′-filled′,** *adj.*
- **half′-fin′ished,** *adj.*
- **half′-flat′tered,** *adj.*
- **half′-flat′ter·ing,** *adj.;* **-ly** *adv.*
- **half′-fold′ed,** *adj.*
- **half′-for·giv′en,** *adj.*
- **half′-for·got′ten,** *adj.*
- **half′-formed′,** *adj.*
- **half′-French′,** *adj.*
- **half′-frown′ing,** *adj.;* **-ly,** *adv.*
- **half′-ful·filled′,** *adj.*
- **half′-ful·fill′ing,** *adj.*
- **half′-full′,** *adj.*
- **half′-fur′nished,** *adj.*
- **half′-gal′lon,** *n.*
- **half′-Ger′man,** *adj.*
- **half′-gill′,** *n.*
- **half′-great′,** *adj.*
- **half′-Greek′,** *adj.*
- **half′-grown′,** *adj.*
- **half′-hard′,** *adj.*
- **half′-har′vest·ed,** *adj.*
- **half′-healed′,** *adj.*
- **half′-heard′,** *adj.*
- **half′-hea′then,** *adj., n.*
- **half′-Hes′sian,** *adj.*
- **half′-hid′den,** *adj.*
- **half′-hol′i·day,** *n.*
- **half′-hol′low,** *adj.*
- **half′-hu′man,** *adj.*
- **half′-hun′gered,** *adj.*
- **half′-hyp′no·tized′,** *adj.*
- **half′-im·por′tant,** *adj.;* **-ly,** *adv.*
- **half′-inch′,** *n.*
- **half′-in·clined′,** *adj.*
- **half′-in·dig′nant,** *adj.;* **-ly,** *adv.*
- **half′-in·formed′,** *adj.*
- **half′-in·form′ing,** *adj.;* **-ly,** *adv.*
- **half′-in·gen′ious,** *adj.;* **-ly,** *adv.*
- **half′-in·gen′u·ous,** *adj.;* **-ly,** *adv.*
- **half′-in·her′it·ed,** *adj.*
- **half′-in·sin′u·at′ed,** *adj.*
- **half′-in·sin′u·at′ing,** *adj.;* **-ly,** *adv.*
- **half′-in·stinc′tive,** *adj.;* **-ly,** *adv.*
- **half′-in·tel·lec′tu·al,** *adj.;* **-ly,** *adv.*
- **half′-in·tel′li·gi·ble,** *adj.;* **-bly,** *adv.*
- **half′-in·toned′,** *adj.*
- **half′-in·tox′i·cat′ed,** *adj.*
- **half′-in·val′id,** *adj.;* **-ly,** *adv.*
- **half′-I′rish,** *adj.*
- **half′-I·tal′ian,** *adj.*
- **half′-jelled′,** *adj.*
- **half′-jok′ing,** *adj.;* **-ly,** *adv.*
- **half′-jus′ti·fied′,** *adj.*
- **half′-lan′guaged,** *adj.*
- **half′-lan′guish·ing,** *adj.*
- **half′-lapped′,** *adj.*
- **half′-Lat′in·ized′,** *adj.*
- **half′-lat′ticed,** *adj.*
- **half′-learned′,** *adj.*
- **half′-learn′ed·ly,** *adv.*
- **half′-left′,** *adj., n.*
- **half′-lib′er·al,** *adj.;* **-ly,** *adv.*
- **half′-lined′,** *adj.*
- **half′-lin′en,** *adj.*
- **half′-li′ter,** *n.*
- **half′-lived′,** *adj.*
- **half′-lu′na·tic,** *adj.*
- **half′-lunged′,** *adj.*
- **half′-mad′,** *adj.;* **-ly,** *adv.;* **-ness,** *n.*
- **half′-made′,** *adj.*
- **half′-marked′,** *adj.*
- **half′-mas′ti·cat′ed,** *adj.*
- **half′-ma·tured′,** *adj.*
- **half′-meant′,** *adj.*
- **half′-men′tal,** *adj.;* **-ly,** *adv.*
- **half′-mer′it·ed,** *adj.*
- **half′-Mex′i·can,** *adj.*
- **half′-mind′ed,** *adj.*
- **half′-min′ute,** *n.*
- **half′-mi·nute′,** *adj.*
- **half′-mis·un·der·stood′,** *adj.*
- **half′-Mo·ham′med·an,** *adj.*
- **half′-month′ly,** *adj.*
- **half′-Mos′lem,** *adj.*
- **half′-Mu·ham′mad·an,** *adj.*
- **half′-mum′bled,** *adj.*
- **half′-mum′mi·fied′,** *adj.*
- **half′-Mus′lim,** *adj.*
- **half′-na′ked,** *adj.*
- **half′-nor′mal,** *adj.;* **-ly,** *adv.*
- **half′-numb′,** *adj.*
- **half′-ny′lon,** *adj.*
- **half′-ob·lit′er·at′ed,** *adj.*
- **half′-of·fend′ed,** *adj.*
- **half′-o′pened,** *adj.*
- **half′-o·ri·en′tal,** *adj.*
- **half′-or′phan,** *n.*
- **half′-o′val,** *adj., n.*
- **half′-ox′i·dized′,** *adj.*
- **half′-peck′,** *n.*
- **half′-pet′ri·fied′,** *adj.*
- **half′-pipe′,** *n.*
- **half′-play′ful,** *adj.;* **-ly,** *adv.*
- **half′-pleased′,** *adj.*
- **half′-pleas′ing,** *adj.*
- **half′-plucked′,** *adj.*
- **half′-pound′,** *adj.*
- **half′-pound′er,** *n.*
- **half′-praised′,** *adj.*
- **half′-prais′ing,** *adj.*
- **half′-pres′ent,** *adj.*
- **half′-pro·fane′,** *adj.*
- **half′-pro·fessed′,** *adj.*
- **half′-pro′file,** *n.*
- **half′-pro·le·tar′i·an,** *adj.*
- **half′-pro·test′ed,** *adj.*
- **half′-pro·test′ing,** *adj.*
- **half′-proved′,** *adj.*
- **half′-prov′en,** *adj.*
- **half′-pro·voc′a·tive,** *adj.*
- **half′-quar′ter,** *adj.*
- **half′-ques′tion·ing,** *adj.;* **-ly,** *adv.*
- **half′-quire′,** *n.*
- **half′-quix·ot′ic,** *adj.*
- **half′-quix·ot′i·cal·ly,** *adv.*
- **half′-rad′i·cal,** *adj.;* **-ly,** *adv.*
- **half′-raw′,** *adj.*
- **half′-ray′on,** *adj.*
- **half′-re·ac′tion·ar′y,** *adj.*
- **half′-read′,** *adj.*
- **half′-rea′son·a·ble,** *adj.;* **-bly,** *adv.*
- **half′-rea′son·ing,** *adj.*
- **half′-re·bel′lious,** *adj.;* **-ly,** *adv.*
- **half′-re·claimed′,** *adj.*
- **half′-re·clined′,** *adj.*
- **half′-re·clin′ing,** *adj.*
- **half′-re·fined′,** *adj.*
- **half′-re·gained′,** *adj.*
- **half′-re·luc′tant,** *adj.;* **-ly,** *adv.*
- **half′-re·mon′strant,** *adj.*
- **half′-re·pent′ant,** *adj.*
- **half′-re·pub′li·can,** *adj.*
- **half′-ret′i·nal,** *adj.*
- **half′-re·vealed′,** *adj.*
- **half′-re·versed′,** *adj.*
- **half′-right′,** *adj., n.*
- **half′-ripe′,** *adj.*
- **half′-rip′ened,** *adj.*
- **half′-roast′ed,** *adj.*
- **half′-rod′,** *n.*
- **half′-ro·man′tic,** *adj.*
- **half′-ro·man′ti·cal·ly,** *adv.*
- **half′-rot′ted,** *adj.*
- **half′-rot′ten,** *adj.*
- **half′-rue′ful,** *adj.;* **-ly,** *adv.*
- **half′-ru′ined,** *adj.*
- **half′-Rus′sian,** *adj.*
- **half′-sag′it·tate′,** *adj.*
- **half′-sav′age,** *adj.;* **-ly,** *adv.*
- **half′-Scot′tish,** *adj.*
- **half′-sec′ond,** *adj.*
- **half′-sec′tion,** *n.*
- **half′-Se·mit′ic,** *adj.*
- **half′-sensed′,** *adj.*
- **half′-se′ri·ous,** *adj.;* **-ly,** *adv.*
- **half′-sev′ered,** *adj.*
- **half′-Shake·spear′e·an,** *adj.*
- **half′-shamed′,** *adj.*
- **half′-share′,** *n.*
- **half′-shared′,** *adj.*
- **half′-sheathed′,** *adj.*
- **half′-shod′dy,** *adj.*
- **half′-shout′ed,** *adj.*
- **half′-shut′,** *adj.*
- **half′-shy′,** *adj.;* **-ly,** *adv.*
- **half′-sight′ed,** *adj.;* **-ly,** *adv.;* **-ness,** *n.*
- **half′-silk′,** *adj.*
- **half′-sink′ing,** *adj.*
- **half′-size′,** *adj.*
- **half′-smil′ing,** *adj.;* **-ly,** *adv.*
- **half′-smoth′ered,** *adj.*
- **half′-sol′id,** *adj.*
- **half′-souled′,** *adj.*

half-staff (haf′staf′, häf′stäf′), *n.* half-mast.

half′ step′, **1.** *Music.* semitone. **2.** *Mil.* a step 15 inches long in quick time and 18 inches long in double time.

half-stuff (haf′stuf′, häf′-), *n.* (in a manufacturing process) any material half formed, esp. partly prepared pulp for making paper. Also, **half-stock** (haf′stok′, häf′-).

half-thick·ness (haf′thik′nis, häf′-), *n.* *Physics.* the thickness of an absorbing material required to reduce the intensity of a given radiation by one-half. Also called **half-value layer.**

half′ tide′, the state of the tide when halfway between high water and low water.

half′-tide dock′ (haf′tīd′), *Naut.* a basin in which a vessel awaits the opportunity to enter a wet dock accessible only around the time of high tide.

half′ tim′ber, *Shipbuilding.* **1.** Also called **half frame.** either of two timber constructions on opposite sides of a keel forming together a whole frame. **2.** any of several short timbers in a cant frame.

half-tim·bered (haf′tim′bərd, häf′-), *adj.* (of a house or building) having the frame and principal supports of timber but with the interstices filled in with masonry, plaster, or the like. Also, **half′-tim′ber.**

half′ time′, **1.** the period indicating completion of half the time allowed for an activity, such as for a football or basketball game or an examination. **2.** *Sports.* the intermission or rest period between the two halves of a football, basketball, or other game, during which spectators are often entertained by baton twirling, marching bands, or the like. —**half′-time′,** *adj.*

half′ ti′tle, **1.** Also called **bastard title.** the first printed page of certain books, appearing, after the end papers and before the title page, and containing only the title of the book. **2.** the title of any subdivision of a book that immediately precedes that subdivision, when printed on a full page by itself.

half′ tone′, *Music.* semitone.

half·tone (haf′tōn′, häf′-), *n.* **1.** Also called **middletone.** (in painting, drawing, graphics, photography, etc.) a value intermediate between light and dark. **2.** *Photoengraving.* **a.** a process in which gradation of tone is obtained by a system of minute dots produced by a screen placed in the camera a short distance in front of a sensitized plate. **b.** the metal plate made by photoengraving for reproduction by letterpress printing. **c.** a print from such a plate. Cf. **line cut.** —*adj.* **3.** pertaining to, using, used in, or produced by the halftone process: *a halftone screen; a halftone print.* [HALF + TONE]

half-track (haf′trak′, häf′-), *n.* **1.** a caterpillar tread that runs over and under the rear or driving wheels of a vehicle but is not connected with the forward wheels: used esp. on military vehicles. **2.** a motor vehicle with rear driving wheels on caterpillar treads. **3.** *Mil.* an armored vehicle equipped with half-tracks. —**half′-tracked′,** *adj.*

half-truth (haf′trōōth′, häf′-), *n., pl.* **-truths** (trōōthz). a statement which is only partly true, esp. one intended to deceive, evade blame, or the like: *Don't be satisfied with half-truths.*

half-turn·ing (haf′tûr′ning, häf′-), *n.* *Furniture.* See **split spindle.**

half′-turn stair′ (haf′tûrn′, häf′-), a staircase requiring a half turn at each landing for continued ascent and descent.

half′ twist′, **1.** *Fancy Diving.* a dive made by a half rotation of the body on its long axis. Cf. **full twist. 2.** the twisting of the body in a half turn, as in tumbling.

half′-val′ue lay′er (haf′val′yōō, häf′-), *Physics.* half-thickness.

half′ vol′ley, (in tennis, rackets, etc.) a stroke in which the ball is hit the moment it bounces from the ground.

half-vol·ley (haf′vol′ē, häf′-), *v.t., v.i.,* **-leyed, -ley·ing.** to make (a half volley). —**half′-vol′ley·er,** *n.*

half′-wave rec′tifier (haf′wāv′, häf′-), *Elect.* a rectifier that changes only one half of a cycle of alternating current into a pulsating, direct current. Cf. **full-wave rectifier.** —**half′-wave rectifica′tion.**

half·way (haf′wā′, häf′-), *adv.* **1.** to half the distance; to midpoint: *The rope reaches only halfway.* **2.** almost; nearly; just about: *He halfway surrendered to their demands.* **3. meet halfway,** to compromise with or give in partially to: *They didn't comply with all our demands, but met us halfway on the more important points.* —*adj.* **4.** midway, as between two places or points. **5.** going to or covering only half or part of the full extent; partial: *halfway measures.* [ME *half wey.* See HALF, WAY]

Half·way (haf′wā′, häf′-), *n.* a town in W Maryland. 4256 (1960).

half′way house′, **1.** an inn or stopping place situated approximately midway between two places on a road. **2.** any place considered as midway in a course.

half′ Wel′lington, a loose boot extending to just above the ankle and usually worn under the trousers.

half-wit (haf′wit′, häf′-), *n.* **1.** one who is feeble-minded. **2.** one who is foolish or senseless; dunderhead.

half-wit·ted (haf′wit′id, häf′-), *adj.* **1.** feeble-minded. **2.** foolish; stupid. —**half′-wit′ted·ly,** *adv.* —**half′-wit′ted·ness,** *n.*

hal·i·but (hal′ə bət, hol′-), *n., pl.* (*esp. collectively*) **-but,** (*esp. referring to two or more kinds or species*) **-buts. 1.** either of two large flatfishes, *Hippoglossus hippoglossus,* found in the North Atlantic, or *H. stenolepis,* found in the North Pacific, used for food. **2.** any of various other similar flatfishes. Also, **holibut.** [ME *halybutte,* equiv. to *haly* (var. of HOLY) + *butte* flat fish (< MD); so called because eaten on holy days. Cf. D *heilbot*]

hal′i·but-liv·er oil′ (hal′ə bət liv′ər, hol′-), a fixed oil extracted from the liver of the halibut, *Hippoglossus hippoglossus:* used chiefly in medicine as a source of vitamins A and D.

Hal·i·car·nas·sus (hal′ə kär nas′əs), *n.* an ancient city of Caria, in SW Asia Minor: site of the Mausoleum, one of the seven wonders of the ancient world. —**Hal′i·car·nas′si·an, Hal′i·car·nas′se·an,** *adj.*

hal·i·cot (hal′ə kō′), *n.* haricot[2].

hal·ide (hal′īd, -id, hā′līd, -lid), *Chem.* —*n.* **1.** a compound of two elements, one of which is a halogen. —*adj.* **2.** of, pertaining to, or characteristic of a halide. [HAL(OGEN) + -IDE]

hal·i·dom (hal′i dəm), *n.* **1.** a holy place, as a church or sanctuary. **2. by my halidom,** *Archaic.* upon my word; by my troth. Also, **hal·i·dome** (hal′i dōm′). [ME; OE *hāligdōm.* See HOLY, -DOM]

Hal·i·fax (hal′ə faks′), *n.* **1. Earl of,** (*Edward Frederick Lindley Wood*), 1881–1959, British statesman. **2.** a seaport in and the capital of Nova Scotia, in SE Canada. 92,511 (1961). **3.** a city in SW Yorkshire, in N England. 96,073 (1961).

Hal·i·go·ni·an (hal′ə gō′nē ən), *adj.* **1.** of or pertaining to Halifax, Nova Scotia, or to Halifax, England. —*n.* **2.** a native or inhabitant of Halifax. [< ML *Haligoni(a)* Halifax + -AN]

Hal·ir·rho·thi·us (hal′ə rō′thē əs), *n.* *Class. Myth.* a son of Poseidon slain by Ares.

hal·ite (hal′īt, hā′līt), *n.* a soft white or colorless mineral, sodium chloride, NaCl, occurring in cubical crystals with perfect cleavage; rock salt. [HAL- + -ITE[1]]

Hal·i·ther·ses (hal′ə thûr′sēz), *n.* (in the *Odyssey*) an Ithacan seer who predicted the return of Odysseus and his slaughtering of Penelope's suitors.

hal·i·to·sis (hal′i tō′sis), *n.* bad breath. [< NL; see HALITUS, -OSIS]

hal·i·tus (hal′i təs), *n., pl.* **-tus·es.** *Archaic.* breath; exhalation; vapor. [< L, equiv. to *hāl(āre)* (to) breathe, exhale + *-it-* -ITE[2] + *-us* n. suffix (4th decl.)] —**ha·lit·u·os·i·ty** (hə lich′ōō os′i tē), *n.* —**ha·lit·u·ous** (hə lich′ōō əs), *adj.*

Hal·iv·er (hal′iv ər, -ə vər), *n.* *Trademark.* See **halibut-liver oil.**

hall (hôl), *n.* **1.** a corridor or passageway in a building. **2.** the large entrance room of a house or building; vestibule; lobby. **3.** a large room or building for public gatherings; auditorium: *convention hall; concert hall.* **4.** a large building for residence, instruction, or other purposes, at a college or university. **5.** a college at a university. **6.** (in English colleges) **a.** a large room in which the members and students dine. **b.** dinner in such a room. **7.** *Chiefly Brit.* a mansion or large residence, esp. one on a large estate. **8.** *Brit. Informal.* See **music hall. 9.** the chief room in a medieval castle or similar structure, used for eating, sleeping, and entertaining. **10.** the castle, house, or similar structure of a medieval chieftain or noble. **11.** Also called **keeping room.** *Obs.* the living room or family room of a house in England or New England. [ME; OE *heall;* c. Icel *höll,* G *Halle;* akin to OE *helan* to cover, hide, L *cēlāre* to hide]

Hall (hôl), *n.* **1. Charles Francis,** 1821–71, U.S. Arctic explorer. **2. Charles Martin,** 1863–1914, U.S. chemist, metallurgist, and manufacturer. **3. Granville Stanley,** 1846–1924, U.S. psychologist and educator. **4. James Norman,** 1887–1951, U.S. novelist. **5.** a boy's given name.

hal·lah (ᴋʜä′lə; *Heb.* ᴋʜä lä′), *n., pl.* **hal·lahs,** *Heb.* **hal·loth** (ᴋʜä lōt′). challah.

Hal·lam (hal′əm), *n.* **1. Arthur Henry,** 1811–35, English poet and essayist. **2.** his father, **Henry,** 1777–1859, English historian.

hal·lan (hal′ən, hä′lən), *n.* *Scot. and North Eng.* a wall or low partition forming a small entrance foyer in a cottage and reducing drafts from the door. [late ME (north) *halland*]

hall′ bed′room, a bedroom at the end of, and having the width of, a hallway. Also called **hallroom.**

Hal·le (häl′ə), *n.* a city in SW East Germany, NW of Leipzig. 278,700 (est. 1959). Official name, **Hal·le an der Sal·le** (häl′ə än dər säl′ə).

Hal·leck (hal′ik, -ək), *n.* **1. Fitz-Green** (fits′grēn′, fits grēn′), 1790–1867, U.S. poet. **2. Henry Wa·ger** (wā′jər), 1815–72, Union general in the U.S. Civil War and writer on military subjects.

Hall′ effect′, *Physics, Elect.* the electromotive force generated in a strip of metal longitudinally conducting an electric current and subjected to a magnetic field normal to its major surface. [named after Edwin H. *Hall* (1855–1938), American physicist who discovered it]

Hal·lel (hä lāl′), *n.* *Judaism.* a liturgical prayer consisting of all or part of Psalms 113–118, recited on Passover, Shabuoth, Sukkoth, Hanukkah, and Rosh Hodesh. [< Heb: praise]

hal·le·lu·jah (hal′ə lōō′yə), *interj.* **1.** Praise ye the Lord! —*n.* **2.** an exclamation of "hallelujah!" **3.** a shout of joy, praise, or gratitude. **4.** a musical composition wholly or principally based upon the word "hallelujah". Also, **hal′le·lu′iah.** [< Heb *hallelūyāh* praise (ye) Jehovah]

Hal·letts·ville (hal′its vil′), *n.* a town in S Texas. 2808 (1960).

Hal·ley (hal′ē), *n.* **1. Edmund** or **Edmond,** 1656–1742, English astronomer. **2.** a crater in the fourth quadrant of the face of the moon: about 21 miles in diameter.

Hal′ley's Com′et, *Astron.* a comet regularly appearing over the earth every 75 or 76 years: it last appeared in 1986. [named after Edmund HALLEY who first predicted its return]

hal·liard (hal′yərd), *n.* halyard.

Hal·lie (hal′ē), *n.* a girl's given name. Also, **Hal′li, Hally.**

hal·ling (hä′ling, hal′ing), *n.* a vigorous, athletic, Norwegian folk dance. [< Norw, short for *Hallingdal* place known for this dance]

Hal·li·well (hal′i wel′, -wəl), *n.* a boy's given name.

hall·mark (hôl′märk′), *n.* **1.** an official mark or stamp indicating a standard of purity, used in marking gold and silver articles assayed by the Goldsmiths' Company of London; plate mark. **2.** any mark or special indication of genuineness, good quality, etc. **3.** any distinguishing feature or characteristic. —*v.t.* **4.** to stamp or imprint (something) with a hallmark. [after Goldsmiths' *Hall,* London, the seat of the Goldsmiths' Company + MARK[1]] —**hall′mark′er,** *n.*

hal·lo (hə lō′), *interj., n., pl.* **-los,** *v.,* **-loed, -lo·ing.** —*interj.* **1.** (used to call or answer someone, or to incite dogs in hunting.) —*n.* **2.** the cry "hallo!" **3.** a shout of exultation. —*v.i.* **4.** to call with a loud voice; shout; cry, as after hunting dogs. —*v.t.* **5.** to incite or chase (something) with shouts and cries of "hallo!" **6.** to cry "hallo" to (someone). **7.** to shout (something). Also, **halloa, halloo, hallow, hillo, hilloa, holla, hollo, holloa, holloo, hulloo.** [var. of HOLLO]

hal·loa (hə lō′, ha-), *interj., n., pl.* **-loas,** *v.i., v.t.,* **-loaed, -loa·ing.** hallo.

Hall′ of Fame′, **1.** a national shrine commemorating the names of outstanding Americans, in New York City, at New York University. **2.** a room, building, etc., set aside to honor outstanding individuals in any profession, locality, nation, or the like. **3.** a number of individuals acclaimed as outstanding in a particular profession, field of endeavor, locality, or the like: *She won a lasting place in the actors' Hall of Fame.*

hal·loo (hə lōō′), *interj., n., pl.* **-loos,** *v.i., v.t.,* **-looed, -loo·ing.** hallo.

hal·low[1] (hal′ō), *v.t.* **1.** to make holy; sanctify; consecrate. **2.** to honor as holy; consider sacred; venerate: *to hallow a battlefield.* [ME *hal(o)we(n),* OE *hālgian* (c. G *heiligen,* Icel *helga*), deriv. of *hālig* HOLY] —**hal′low·er,** *n.*

hal·low[2] (hə lō′), *interj., n., v.i., v.t.* hallo.

hal·lowed (hal′ōd; *in liturgical use often* hal′ō id), *adj.* regarded as holy; venerated; sacred: *the hallowed saints; hallowed political institutions.* [HALLOW[1] + -ED[2]] —**hal′lowed·ly,** *adv.* —**hal′lowed·ness,** *n.*
—**Syn.** blessed. See **holy.** —**Ant.** desecrated.

Hal·low·een (hal′ə wēn′, -ō ēn′, hol′-), *n.* the evening of October 31; the eve of All Saints' Day; Allhallows Eve. Also, **Hal′low·e′en′.** [(ALL)HALLOW(S) + E(V)EN[2]]

Hal·lo·well (hol′ə wel′, -wəl), *n.* a town in S Maine. 3169 (1960).

Hal·low·mas (hal′ō məs, -mas′), *n.* *Archaic.* the feast of Allhallows or All Saints' Day, on November 1. [short for ALLHALLOWMAS]

hall·room (hôl′rōōm′, -rŏŏm′), *n.* See **hall bedroom.** [HALL + (BED)ROOM]

Hall·statt·an (hôl stat′ən, häl shtät′ən), *adj.* of, pertaining to, or belonging to a variously dated early period of Iron Age culture in Europe, characterized by the use of bronze, the introduction of iron, and by artistic work in pottery, jewelry, etc. Also, **Hall·stat·ti·an** (hôl stat′ē ən, häl shtät′-), **Hall·statt** (hôl′stat, häl′shtät), **Hall·stad′tan, Hall′stadt′.** Cf. **La Tène** (def. 1). [named after *Hallstatt,* village in central Austria where remains were found; see -AN]

hall′ tree′, a stand having hooks or knobs for holding coats and hats; hatrack or clothes tree. Also called **hat tree.**

hal·lu·cal (hal′yə kəl), *adj.* of or pertaining to the hallux. [< NL *halluc-* (s. of *hallux*) HALLUX + -AL[1]]

hal·lu·ci·nate (hə lōō′sə nāt′), *v.,* **-nat·ed, -nat·ing.** —*v.t.* **1.** to affect with hallucination. —*v.i.* **2.** to have hallucinations. [< L *hallūcināt(us),* ptp. of *(h)allūcinārī* to wander in mind; see -ATE[1]] —**hal·lu′ci·na′tor,** *n.*

hal·lu·ci·na·tion (hə lōō′sə nā′shən), *n.* **1.** an apparent sensory experience of something that does not exist outside the mind; sense perception not caused by external stimuli: *to suffer from hallucinations.* **2.** the sensation caused by an hallucinatory condition or the object or scene visualized. **3.** a false notion, belief, or impression; illusion; delusion: *It is ruinous for small countries to have hallucinations of military glory.* [< L *hallūcinātiōn-* (s. of *(h)allūcinātiō*) a wandering of the mind. See HALLUCINATE, -ION] —**hal·lu′ci·na′tion·al, hal·lu·ci·na·tive** (hə lōō′sə nā′tiv, -nə tiv), *adj.*
—**Syn. 1.** phantasm, aberration. See **illusion.**

hal·lu·ci·na·to·ry (hə lōō′sə nə tôr′ē, -tōr′ē), *adj.* pertaining to or characterized by hallucination: *hallucinatory visions.* [HALLUCINATE + -ORY[1]]

hal·lu·ci·no·gen (hə lōō′sə nə jen′, hal′yə sin′ə-), *n.* a substance which produces hallucinations. [HALLUCIN(ATION) + -O- + -GEN] —**hal·lu·ci·no·gen·ic** (hə lōō′sə nō jen′ik), *adj.*

hal·lu·ci·no·sis (hə lōō′sə nō′sis), *n.* *Psychiatry.* a psychosis or state characterized and produced by hallucinations. [HALLUCIN(ATION) + -OSIS]

hal·lux (hal′əks), *n., pl.* **hal·lu·ces** (hal′yə sēz′). *Anat., Zool.* the first or innermost digit of the foot of man or of the hind foot of other air-breathing vertebrates; great toe; big toe. [< NL, alter. of LL *hallex* great toe]

Hall′wachs′ effect′ (häl′väks), *Physics.* the emission of negative electricity by a metal subjected to ultraviolet light, a type of photoelectric effect. [named after W. *Hallwachs* (1859–1922), German physicist]

hall·way (hôl′wā′), *n.* **1.** a corridor, as in a building. **2.** an entrance hall. [HALL + WAY]

Hal·ly (hal′ē), *n.* a girl's given name. Also, **Halli, Hallie.**

halm (hôm), *n.* *Brit.* haulm.

Hal·ma·he·ra (häl′mä he′rä), *n.* an island in NE Indonesia: the largest of the Moluccas. ab. 85,000; 6928 sq. mi. Also, **Hal′ma·hei′ra.** Also called **Gilolo, Jilolo.**

Halm·stad (hälm′städ′), *n.* a seaport in SW Sweden. 40,653 (1964).

---

half′-Span′ish, *adj.*
half′-spoon′ful, *adj.*
half′-spun′, *adj.*
half′-squad′ron, *n.*
half′-starved′, *adj.*
half′-starv′ing, *adj.*
half′-ster′ile, *adj.*
half′-stock′ing, *n.*
half′-sub·dued′, *adj.*
half′-sub·merged′, *adj.*
half′-suc·cess′ful, *adj.;* **-ly,** *adv.*
half′-sung′, *adj.*
half′-sunk′, *adj.*
half′-sunk′en, *adj.*
half′-syl′la·bled, *adj.*
half′-taught′, *adj.*
half′-tear′ful, *adj.;* **-ly,** *adv.*
half′-tea′spoon·ful, *adj.*
half′-tent′ed, *adj.*
half′-term′, *n.*
half′-the·at′ri·cal, *adj.*
half′-thought′, *adj.*
half′-trained′, *adj.*
half′-train′ing, *adj.*
half′-trans′lat·ed, *adj.*
half′-true′, *adj.*
half′-turned′, *adj.*
half′-un·der·stood′, *adj.*
half′-un·done′, *adj.*
half′-used′, *adj.*
half′-u′til·ized′, *adj.*
half′-veiled′, *adj.*
half′-vel′lum, *n.*
half′-ver′i·fied′, *adj.*
half′-vexed′, *adj.*
half′-wak′ing, *adj.*
half′-whis′pered, *adj.*
half′-whis′per·ing·ly, *adv.*
half′-white′, *adj.*
half′-wick′et, *n.*
half′-wild′, *adj.;* **-ly,** *adv.*
half′-will′ful, *adj.;* **-ly,** *adv.*
half′-winged′, *adj.*
half′-wom′an·ly, *adj.*
half′-won′, *adj.*
half′-wool′en, *adj.*
half′-worst′ed, *adj.*
half′-wo′ven, *adj.*
half′-writ′ten, *adj.*

ha·lo (hā′lō), *n., pl.* **-los, -loes,** *v.,* **-loed, -lo·ing.** —*n.* **1.** Also called **nimbus.** a conventional, geometric shape, usually in the form of a disk, circle, ring, or rayed structure, representing a radiant light around or above the head of a divine or sacred personage, an ancient or medieval monarch, etc. **2.** an atmosphere or quality of glory, majesty, sanctity, or the like: *the halo around Shakespeare's reputation and works. She put a halo around her son.* **3.** *Meteorol.* **a.** any of a variety of bright circles or arcs centered on the sun or moon, caused by the refraction or reflection of light by ice crystals suspended in the earth's atmosphere and exhibiting, in the case of diffraction, prismatic coloration ranging from red inside to blue outside (distinguished from *corona*). **b.** See **halo of 22°.** **4.** an undesirable bright or dark ring surrounding an image on the fluorescent screen of a television tube, due to some fault either in transmission or reception. —*v.t.* **5.** to surround with a halo. —*v.i.* **6.** *Rare.* to form a halo. [< L, acc. of *halōs* circle round sun or moon < Gk *hálōs* such a circle, disk, orig. threshing floor]

halo-, a learned borrowing from Greek meaning "salt," used in the formation of compound words (*halophyte*); sometimes specialized as a combining form of **halogen** (*halothane*). Also, *esp. before a vowel,* **hal-.** [< Gk, comb. form of *háls* salt]

Ha·lo·a (hə lō′ə), *n.* (*sometimes construed as pl.*) an annual festival held in ancient Greece in honor of Demeter, Persephone, and Dionysus.

ha′lo blight′, *Plant Pathol.* a disease of plants, characterized by small, necrotic leaf or fruit lesions surrounded by a yellowish, halolike band, caused by any of several bacteria of the genus *Pseudomonas.*

hal·o·gen (hal′ə jən, hā′lə-), *n. Chem.* any of the negative elements fluorine, chlorine, iodine, bromine, and astatine, which form binary salts by direct union with metals. [HALO- + -GEN] —**hal′o·gen·oid′,** *adj.* —**ha·log·e·nous** (hə loj′ə nəs), *adj.*

hal·o·gen·ate (hal′ə jə nāt′, hā′lə-), *v.t.,* **-at·ed, -at·ing.** *Chem.* **1.** to treat or combine with a halogen. **2.** to introduce a halogen into (an organic compound). [HALOGEN + -ATE[1]] —**hal′o·gen·a′tion** (hal′ə je nā′shən, hal oj′ə-), *n.*

hal·oid (hal′oid, hā′loid), *Chem.* —*adj.* **1.** Also, **hal·o·gen·oid** (hal′ə jə noid′, hā′lə-). resembling or derived from a halogen. —*n.* **2.** a haloid salt or derivative from a halogen. [HAL- + -OID]

ha·lo·like (hā′lō līk′), *adj.* resembling a halo. Also, **ha′lo·esque′.** [HALO + -LIKE]

Ha·lo·na (hə lō′nə), *n.* a girl's given name.

halo of 22°, *Meteorol.* a single luminous circle or arc, centered on the sun or moon, having an angular radius of nearly 22° of arc, and colors, if discernible, ranging from red inside to blue outside: the most common halo. Also called **halo.** Cf. **halo** (def. 3a).

hal·o·phile (hal′ə fīl′), *n.* a halophilous plant or animal. [HALO- + -PHILE]

ha·loph·i·lous (ha lof′ə ləs), *adj.* (of a plant or animal) thriving in a saline environment. Also, **hal·o·phil·ic** (hal′ə fil′ik). [HALO- + -PHILOUS] —**ha·loph′i·lism,** *n.*

hal·o·phyte (hal′ə fīt′), *n.* a plant which grows in salty or alkaline soil. [HALO- + -PHYTE] —**hal·o·phyt·ic** (hal′ə fit′ik), *adj.* —**hal·o·phyt·ism** (hal′ə fī tiz′əm), *n.*

hal·o·thane (hal′ə thān′), *n. Pharm.* a sweetish, volatile, slightly water-soluble, nonflammable liquid, $CF_3CHBrCl$, used as an inhalation anesthetic. [HALO- + -*thane,* as in *fluothane*]

ha·lot·ri·chite (ha lo′trə kīt′), *n.* a mineral, hydrated sulfate of iron and aluminum, $FeAl_2(SO_4)_4 \cdot 24H_2O$, occurring in yellowish fibers. [HALO- + TRICHITE]

Hals (häls), *n.* **Frans** (fräns), 1581?–1666, Dutch portrait and genre painter.

Hal·sey (hôl′zē), *n.* **William Frederick,** 1882–1959, U.S. admiral.

Häl·sing·borg (hel′sing bôr′yə), *n.* a seaport in SW Sweden, opposite Helsingør. 78,582 (1964).

halt[1] (hôlt), *v.i.* **1.** to stop; cease moving, operating, etc., either permanently or temporarily: *They halted for lunch and strolled about.* —*v.t.* **2.** to cause to halt; bring to a stop: *They halted operations during contract negotiations.* —*n.* **3.** a temporary or permanent stop. —*interj.* **4.** (used as a command to stop and stand motionless, as to troops to stop marching or by a policeman to a fleeing suspect.) [from the phrase *make halt* for G *halt machen.* See HOLD[1]]
—**Syn. 2.** hold. **3.** See **stop.**

halt[2] (hôlt), *v.i.* **1.** to falter, as in speech, reasoning, etc.; be hesitant; stumble. **2.** to be in doubt; waver between alternatives; vacillate. **3.** *Archaic.* to be lame; walk lamely; limp. —*adj.* **4.** lame; limping. —*n.* **5.** *Archaic.* lameness; a limp. [ME; OE *healt;* c. OHG *halz,* Icel *haltr,* Goth *halts,* akin to L *clādēs* damage, loss] —**halt′ing·ly,** *adv.* —**halt′ing·ness,** *n.* —**halt′less,** *adj.*

hal·ter[1] (hôl′tər), *n.* **1.** a rope or strap with a noose or headstall for leading or restraining horses or cattle. **2.** a rope with a noose for hanging criminals; the hangman's noose; gallows. **3.** death by hanging. **4.** a woman's sports waist, tied behind the neck and across the back, leaving the arms and back bare. —*v.t.* **5.** to put a halter on; restrain as by a halter. **6.** to hang (a person). [ME; OE *hælfter;* c. G *Halfter*] —**hal′ter·like′,** *adj.*

hal·ter[2] (hal′tər), *n., pl.* **hal·te·res** (hal tēr′ēz). one of a pair of slender, club-shaped appendages on the metathorax of a dipterous insect that serve to maintain its balance in flight. Also called **balancer.** [< NL, special use of L *halter* jumping weight < Gk, akin to *hállesthai* to leap]

halt·er[3] (hôl′tər), *n.* a person who halts, falters, or hesitates. [HALT[2] + -ER[1]]

halt·er[4] (hôl′tər), *n.* a person who halts or brings to a stop. [HALT[1] + -ER[1]]

Hal′tom Cit′y (hôl′təm), a city in N Texas, near Fort Worth. 23,133 (1960).

ha·lutz (khä lo͞ots′), *n., pl.* **ha·lutz·im** (khä′lo͞o tsēm′; *Eng.* khä lo͞o′tsim). *Hebrew.* a person who emigrates to Israel to establish or join a settlement for accomplishing tasks, as clearing the land, planting trees, etc., that are necessary to future development of the country. Also, **chalutz.** [lit., warrior]

hal·vah (häl vä′, häl′vä), *n.* a sweet, candylike confection of Turkish origin, consisting chiefly of ground sesame seeds and honey. Also, **halavah, hal·va′.** [< Yiddish *halva* < Rumanian < Turk *helva* < Ar *halwa* sweet confection]

halve (hav, häv), *v.t.,* **halved, halv·ing.** **1.** to divide into halves. **2.** to share equally: *to halve one's rations with a stranger.* **3.** to reduce to half. **4.** *Golf.* to play (a hole, round, or match) in the same number of strokes as one's opponent. **5. halve together,** to join (two pieces of wood) by cutting from each, at the place of joining, a portion fitting to that left solid in the other. [ME *halve(n),* deriv. of HALF]

halves (havz, hävz), *n.* **1.** pl. of **half.** **2. by halves, a.** incompletely: *to do things by halves.* **b.** half-heartedly: *better not at all than by halves.* **3. go halves,** to share equally; divide evenly: *The two brothers had always gone halves in everything.*

hal·yard (hal′yərd), *n.* any of various lines or tackles for hoisting a spar, sail, flag, etc., into position for use. Also, **halliard.** Cf. **tye.** [ME *hal(ier)* rope to haul with (see HALE[2], -IER) + YARD[1]]

Hal·y·si·tes (hal′i sī′tēz), *n.* an extinct genus comprising the chain corals. [< NL < Gk *hálys(is)* chain + -*ītēs* -ITE[1]]

ham[1] (ham), *n.* **1.** one of the rear quarters of a hog, esp. the heavy-muscled part, between hip and hock. **2.** the meat of this part. **3.** the part of the leg back of the knee. **4.** Often, **hams.** the back of the thigh, or the thigh and the buttock together. [ME *hamme,* OE *hamm* bend of the knee; c. OHG *hamma;* akin to Icel *höm* buttock, L *camur* crooked]

ham[2] (ham), *n., v.,* **hammed, ham·ming.** —*n.* **1.** *Theat. Slang.* **a.** an actor who overacts. **b.** overacting. **2.** *Informal.* an operator of an amateur radio station. —*v.i.* **3.** *Theat. Slang.* to act with exaggerated expression of emotion; overact. [short for *hamfatter,* after *The Ham-fat Man,* a Negro minstrel song celebrating an awkward man]

Ham (ham), *n.* the second son of Noah. Gen. 10:1.

Ha·ma (hä′mä, hä mä′), *n.* a city in W Syria, on the Orontes River. 107,859 (est. 1959). Ancient, **Epiphania.** Biblical name, **Hamath.**

Ham·a·dan (ham′ə dan′; *Pers.* ha mā dän′), *n.* a city in W Iran. 100,029 (1956). Ancient, **Ecbatana.**

ham·a·dry·ad (ham′ə drī′əd, -ad), *n., pl.* **-ads, -a·des** (-ə dēz′). **1.** *Class. Myth.* a dryad who is the spirit of a particular tree. **2.** See **king cobra.** [< L, s. of *Hamādryas* wood nymph < Gk, equiv. to *háma* together with (c. SAME) + *dryás* DRYAD]

ham·a·dry′as baboon′ (ham′ə drī′əs), a baboon, *Papio* (*Comopithecus*) *hamadryas,* of Ethiopia, the male of which has a mantle of long, dark hair about the head and shoulders: held sacred by the ancient Egyptians. Also called **sacred baboon.** [< NL *hamādryas* (see HAMADRYAD)]

ha·mal (hə mäl′, hə môl′), *n.* **1.** (in the Middle East and Orient) a porter. **2.** (in India) a male house servant. Also, **hammal, hamaul.** [< Ar *ḥammāl* porter, carrier, akin to *ḥamala* to carry]

Ha·ma·mat·su (hä′mä mä′tso͞o), *n.* a city on S central Honshu, in central Japan. 372,912 (1964).

ham·a·mel·i·da·ceous (ham′ə mel′i dā′shəs, -mē′li-), *adj.* belonging to the *Hamamelidaceae,* a family of shrubs and trees including the witch hazel. [< NL *hamamēlid-* (s. of Gk *hamamēlís*) kind of medlar tree + -ACEOUS. See *hama-* (in HAMADRYAD), MELON]

Ha·man (hā′mən), *n.* a powerful prince at the court of Ahasuerus, who was hanged upon exposure of his plan to destroy the Jews. Esther 3–6. Also, *Douay Bible,* **Aman.**

ha·man·tasch (hä′mən täsh′, hum′ən-, ho͝om′-), *n., pl.* **-tasch·en** (-tä′shən). *Jewish Cookery.* a triangular yeast cake filled with a mixture of poppy seeds and honey, or with prune paste, prepared esp. for the festival of Purim. [var. of Yiddish *homentasch,* equiv. to *homen* HAMAN + *tasch* pocket (G *Tasche;* c. D *tas* bag)]

ha·man·tash (hä′mən täsh′, hum′ən-, ho͝om′-), *n., pl.* **-tash·en** (-tä′shən). hamantasch.

ha·mar·ti·a (hä′mär tē′ə), *n.* (in ancient Greek tragedy) error in judgment, esp. resulting from a defect in the character of a tragic hero; the tragic flaw. [< Gk: a fault, equiv. to *hamart-* (base of *hamartánein* to err) + -*ia* -IA]

ha·mate (hā′māt), *Anat.* —*adj.* **1.** hook-shaped. **2.** having a hooklike process. —*n.* **3.** Also called **unciform.** a wedge-shaped bone of the carpus having a hooklike process projecting from the palmar surface. [< L *hāmāt(us)* hooked, equiv. to *hām(us)* hook + -*ātus* -ATE[1]]

Ha·math (hā′math), *n.* Biblical name of **Hama.**

ha·maul (hə môl′), *n.* hamal.

Ham·ble·ton (ham′bəl tən), *n.* a boy's given name, form of **Hamilton.**

Ham·ble·to·ni·an (ham′bəl tō′nē ən), *n.* **1.** one of a superior strain of American trotting horses descended from the stallion *Hambletonian.* **2.** an annual harness race for three-year-old trotters, formerly held at Goshen, New York, now at DuQuoin, Illinois.

ham·bone (ham′bōn′), *n. Theat.* (esp. in vaudeville) a performer made up in blackface and using a stereotyped Negro dialect. [HAM[1] + BONE[1]]

Ham·born (*Ger.* häm′bôrn), *n.* Duisburg.

ham·bro·line (ham′brə lēn′, -lin), *n. Naut.* right-laid, three-stranded, untarred, hemp small stuff, somewhat heavier than marline and used for lacings and seizings. Also called **ham·bro** (ham′brə, -brō). [irreg. after HAMB(U)R(G) (Germany) + -O- + LINE[1]]

ham′burg (ham′bûrg), *n.* hamburger.

Ham·burg (ham′bûrg; *for 1, 2 also Ger.* häm′bo͝ork), *n.* **1.** a state in N West Germany. 1,854,600 (1963); 288 sq. mi. **2.** a city in and the capital of this state, on the Elbe River: the largest seaport in continental Europe. 1,851,200 (1963). **3.** a town in W New York. 9145 (1960). **4.** a town in central Pennsylvania. 3747 (1960). **5.** a town in SE Arkansas. 2904 (1960).

ham·burg·er (ham′bûr′gər), *n.* **1.** Also called **Hamburg steak.** a patty of ground or chopped beef, seasoned, and fried or broiled. **2.** ground or chopped beef. **3.** a sandwich consisting of a cooked patty of ground or chopped beef between two halves of a roll or bun, or two slices of bread, often served with a slice of tomato, a slice of onion, and relishes. Also, **hamburg.** Also called **beefburger.** [short for *Hamburger steak;* see -ER[1]]

Ham′burg steak′, hamburger (def. 1).

Ham·den (ham′dən), *n.* a town in S Connecticut. 41,056 (1960).

hame (hām), *n.* either of two curved pieces lying upon the collar in the harness of an animal, to which the traces are fastened. See illus. under **harness.** [ME < MD; akin to OE *hamele* oarlock, Dan *hammel* splinter-bar, Armenian *samik* yoke pieces]

Ha·meln (hä′məln), *n.* a city in N West Germany, on the Weser River: scene of the legend of the Pied Piper of Hamelin. 50,300 (est. 1959). Also, **Ham·e·lin** (ham′ə lin).

hame′ tug′. a loop or short leather strap attaching a trace to a hame. See illus. under **harness.**

ha·metz (khä mäts′, khô mäts′; *Eng.* khô′mits), *n. Hebrew.* **1.** a food forbidden for use by Jews during the festival of Passover, esp. a baked food, as bread or cake, made with leaven or a leavening agent. **2.** a dish, kitchen utensil, or the like used in preparing or serving such food and similarly forbidden for use during Passover. Also, **chametz.**

Ham·hung (häm′ho͝ong′), *n.* a city in central North Korea. 112,184 (1944).

Ha·mil·car Bar·ca (hə mil′kär bär′kə, ham′əl kär′), c270–228 B.C., Carthaginian general and statesman (father of Hannibal).

Ham·il·ton (ham′əl tən), *n.* **1. Alexander,** 1757–1804, American statesman and writer on government: the first Secretary of the Treasury, 1789–97. **2. Edith,** 1867–1963, U.S. classical scholar and writer. **3. Lady Emma,** (*Amy,* or *Emily, Lyon*), 1765?–1815, mistress of Viscount Nelson. **4. Sir Ian Standish Monteith,** 1853–1947, British general. **5. Sir William,** 1788–1856, Scottish philosopher. **6. Sir William Rowan** (rō′ən), 1805–65, Irish mathematician and astronomer. **7.** Also called **Grand River.** a river flowing E through S Labrador into the Atlantic. 600 mi. long. **8. Mount,** a mountain of the Coast Range in California, near San Francisco: site of Lick Observatory. 4209 ft. **9.** a seaport in SE Ontario, in SE Canada, on Lake Ontario. 239,625 (1956). **10.** a city in SW Ohio. 72,354 (1960). **11.** a city in S Scotland, SE of Glasgow. 41,928 (1961). **12.** a city on central North Island, in New Zealand. 35,941 (1956). **13.** a town in central New York. 3348 (1960). **14.** a town in central Texas. 3106 (1960). **15.** a seaport in and the capital of Bermuda. 2,942 (1960). **16.** a boy's given name.

Ham·il·to·ni·an (ham′əl tō′nē ən), *adj.* **1.** pertaining to or advocating Hamiltonianism. —*n.* **2.** a supporter of Alexander Hamilton or Hamiltonianism. [HAMILTON + -IAN]

Ham·il·to·ni·an·ism (ham′əl tō′nē ə niz′əm), *n.* the political principles or doctrines held by or associated with Alexander Hamilton, esp. those stressing a strong central government and protective tariffs. Cf. **federalism.** [HAMILTONIAN + -ISM]

Ham′ilton In′let, an arm of the Atlantic in SE Labrador, estuary of Hamilton River. 150 mi. long.

Ha·mi·shah A·sar Bi·she·bat (khä mi shä′ ä sär′ bi shə bät′), *Judaism.* See **Tu Bishebat.** Also, **Hami·shah′ Asar′ Bi·she·vat′** (khä mi shô′ ô sôr′ bi shə-vät′, -shvät). [< Heb: fifteenth (day) of the month Bishebat]

Ham·ite (ham′īt), *n.* **1.** a descendant of Ham. Gen. 10:1, 6–20. **2.** a member of any of various peoples of northern and eastern Africa, as the ancient Egyptians and modern Berbers. [HAM + -ITE[1]]

Ham·it·ic (ha mit′ik, hə-), *adj.* **1.** non-Semitic but related to Semitic. —*n.* **2.** the non-Semitic portion of the language family to which Semitic belongs. [HAMITE + -IC]

Ham·it·i·cized (ha mit′i sīzd′, hə-), *adj.* exhibiting the characteristics of or influenced by speakers of Hamitic. [HAMITIC + -IZE + -ED[2]]

Ham·i·to-Se·mit·ic (ham′i tō sə mit′ik), *adj., n.* Afro-Asiatic. [comb. form of HAMITIC]

ham·let[1] (ham′lit), *n.* **1.** a small village. **2.** *Brit.* a village without a church of its own, belonging to the parish of another village or town. [ME *hamelet* < MF, equiv. to *hamel* (dim. of *ham* < Gmc; see HOME) + -*et* -ET]
—**Syn. 1.** See **community.**

ham·let[2] (ham′lit), *n., pl.* (*esp. collectively*) **-let,** (*esp. referring to two or more kinds or species*) **-lets.** any of various sea basses of the family *Serranidae,* found in the warm waters of the western Atlantic Ocean, esp. the Nassau grouper. [?]

Ham·let (ham′lit), *n.* **1.** (*italics.*) a tragedy (first printed 1603) by Shakespeare. **2.** the hero of this play. **3.** a town in S North Carolina. 4460 (1960).

Ham·lin (ham′lin), *n.* **1. Hannibal,** 1809–91, U.S. political leader: vice-president of the U.S. 1861–65. **2.** a town in central Texas. 3791 (1960). **3.** a boy's given name.

ham·mal (hə mäl′, hə môl′), *n.* hamal.

Ham·mar·skjöld (hä′mər shōld′, -shəld, ham′ər-; *Sw.* häm′är shœld′), *n.* **Dag Hjal·mar** (däg yäl′mär), 1905–61, Swedish statesman: Secretary General of the United Nations 1953–61: Nobel peace prize 1961.

ham·mer (ham′ər), *n.* **1.** a tool consisting of a solid head, usually of metal, set crosswise on a handle, used for beating metals, driving nails, etc. **2.** any of various instruments or devices resembling this in form, action, or use, as a gavel, a mallet for playing the xylophone, a lever which rings against a doorbell or buzzer, etc. **3.** *Firearms.* the part of a lock which by its fall or action causes the discharge, as by exploding the percussion cap or striking the primer or firing pin; the cock. **4.** one of the padded levers by which the strings of a piano are struck. **5.** *Track.* a metal ball, usually weighing 16 pounds, attached to a steel wire at the end of which is a grip, for throwing for distance in the hammer throw. See illus. on next page. **6.** *Anat.* the malleus. **7. under the hammer,** for sale at public auction: *The old estate and all its furnishings went under the hammer.* —*v.t.* **8.** to beat or drive (a nail, peg, etc.) with a hammer. **9.** to fasten by using hammer and nails; nail (often fol.

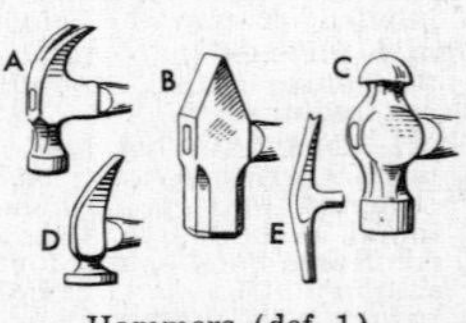

Hammers (def. 1)
A, Nail hammer; B, Engineer's hammer; C, Ball-peen hammer; D, Shoemaker's hammer; E, Carpetlayer's hammer

by *down, up,* etc.): *He spent the day hammering up announcements on fences and trees.* **10.** to assemble or build with a hammer and nails (often fol. by *together*): *He hammered together a picture frame.* **11.** to shape or ornament (metal or a metal object), by controlled and repeated blows of a hammer; beat out: *to hammer brass; to hammer a brass bowl.* **12.** to form, construct, or make with or as if with a hammer; build by repeated, vigorous, or strenuous effort (often fol. by *out* or *together*): *to hammer out an agreement; to hammer together a plot.* **13.** to pound or hit forcefully (often fol. by *out*): *to hammer out a tune on the piano; to hammer a home run; to hammer someone in the jaw.* **14.** to settle (a strong disagreement, argument, etc.); bring to an end, as by strenuous or repeated effort (usually fol. by *out*): *They hammered out their differences over a glass of beer.* **15.** to present (points in an argument, an idea, etc.) forcefully or compellingly; state strongly, aggressively, and effectively (often fol. by *home*). **16.** *Brit.* **a.** (in the London stock exchange) to dismiss (a person) from membership because of default. **b.** to depress the price of (a stock). —*v.i.* **17.** to strike blows with or as with a hammer. **18.** to make persistent or laborious attempts to finish or perfect something (sometimes fol. by *away*): *He hammered away at his speech for hours.* **19.** to reiterate; emphasize by repetition (often fol. by *away*): *The teacher hammered away at the multiplication tables.* [ME *hamer,* OE *hamor;* c. G *Hammer* hammer, Icel *hamarr* hammer, crag; orig. made of stone; akin to Russ *kamin* stone] —**ham′mer·a·ble,** *adj.* —**ham′mer·er,** *n.* —**ham′mer·like′,** *adj.*

Hammer (def. 5)

ham′mer and sick′le, **1.** the emblem of the Soviet Union, adopted in 1923 and consisting of an insignia of a hammer with its handle across the blade of a sickle and a star above. **2.** any emblem similar to this, as the flag of Communist parties in some countries outside of the Soviet Union.

ham′mer and tongs′, *Informal.* with great noise or vigor: *He went hammer and tongs at selling his idea to the prospective client.*

ham′mer beam′, *Archit.* one of a pair of short cantilevered timbers supporting a wooden arch.

ham·mer·cloth (ham′ər klôth′, -kloth′), *n., pl.* **-cloths** (-klôthz′, -klothz′, -klôths′, -kloths′). a cloth covering for the driver's seat on a horse-drawn carriage. [late ME *hamerclothe,* dissimilated var. of **hamelcloth* home-woven cloth, equiv. to *hamel* domestic (akin to Icel *heimili* homestead) + *cloth* CLOTH]

ham·mered (ham′ərd), *adj.* shaped, formed, or ornamented by a metalworker's hammer: *a hammered bowl of brass; hammered gold.* [HAMMER + -ED[2]]

Ham·mer·fest (hä′mər fest′), *n.* a seaport in N Norway: the northernmost town in Europe. 4282 (1950).

ham·mer·head (ham′ər hed′), *n.* **1.** any shark of the genus *Sphyrna,* esp. *S. zygaena,* having the head expanded laterally so as to resemble a double-headed hammer, sometimes dangerous to man. **2.** Also called **hammer-kop** (ham′ər kop′). a brown, heronlike, African bird, *Scopus umbretta,* having the head so crested as to resemble a claw hammer. **3.** See **flatheaded borer. 4.** blockhead; dunce; lout. [HAMMER + HEAD] —**ham′mer·head′ed,** *adj.*

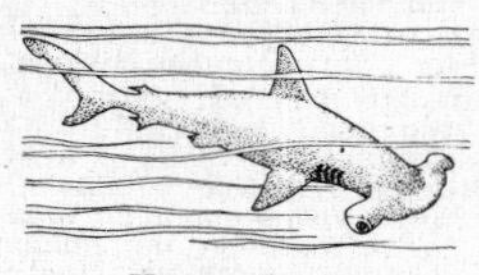
Hammerhead, *Sphyrna zygaena* (Length 15 ft.)

ham·mer·ing (ham′ər ing), *n.* **1.** the act, the process, or an instance of beating with or as with a hammer: *a metal that resists hammering; repeated hammerings from the prosecuting attorney.* **2.** a design, texture, or pattern imparted by a hammer: *the delicate hammering on a surface of gold.* [HAMMER + -ING[1]] —**ham′mer·ing·ly,** *adv.*

ham′mering glass′. See **firing glass.**

ham·mer·less (ham′ər lis), *adj.* (of a firearm) having the hammer concealed within the receiver. [HAMMER + -LESS]

ham′mer lock′, *Wrestling.* a hold in which one arm of an opponent is twisted and forced upward behind his back.

ham′mer pond′, an artificial pond for maintaining a head of water at a water mill.

Ham·mer·stein (ham′ər stīn′), *n.* **1. Oscar,** 1847?–1919, U.S. theatrical manager, born in Germany. **2.** his grandson, **Oscar II,** 1895–1960, U.S. lyricist and librettist.

ham′mer throw′, *Track.* a field event in which the hammer is thrown for distance. —**ham′mer throw′er.**

ham·mer·toe (ham′ər tō′), *n. Pathol.* **1.** a deformity of a toe in which there is a permanent angular flexion of the second and third joints. **2.** a toe having such a deformity. [HAMMER + TOE]

Ham·mett (ham′it), *n.* **(Samuel) Da·shiell** (də shēl′, dash′əl), 1894–1961, U.S. writer of detective stories.

ham·mock[1] (ham′ək), *n.* a kind of hanging bed or couch made of canvas, netted cord, or the like. [< Sp *hamac(a)* < Taino of Santo Domingo] —**ham′mock-like′,** *adj.*

ham·mock[2] (ham′ək), *n.* hummock (def. 1).

Ham·mond (ham′ənd), *n.* **1. John Hays** (hāz), 1855–1936, U.S. engineer. **2.** a city in NW Indiana, near Chicago. 111,698 (1960).

Ham′mond or′gan, *Trademark.* a musical instrument, resembling in shape an upright piano, with two keyboards, electronic tone generation, and a great variety of tone colors.

Ham·mon·ton (ham′ən tən), *n.* a town in S New Jersey. 9854 (1960).

Ham·mu·ra·bi (hä′mo͝o rä′bē, ham′o͝o-), *n.* 18th century B.C. or earlier, king of Babylonia. Also, **Ham·mu·ra·pi** (hä′mo͝o rä′pē, ham′o͝o-), **Khammurabi.** Cf. **Code of Hammurabi.**

ham·my[1] (ham′ē), *adj.,* **-mi·er, -mi·est.** resembling ham in taste, flavor, appearance, etc. [HAM[1] + -Y[1]]

ham·my[2] (ham′ē), *adj.,* **-mi·er, -mi·est.** *Informal.* **1.** characteristic of one who overacts. **2.** overacted. **3.** exaggerated. [HAM[2] + -Y[1]]

Hamp·den (hamp′dən, ham′dən), *n.* **1. John,** 1594–1643, British statesman who defended the rights of the House of Commons against Charles I. **2. Walter** (*Walter Hampden Dougherty*), 1879–1955, U.S. actor.

Hamp′den boat′, a small fishing boat used around Casco Bay, Maine, having a centerboard and formerly equipped with two spritsails and sometimes with a jib. Also called **Hampton boat.** [after *Hampden,* Maine]

ham·per[1] (ham′pər), *v.t.* **1.** to hold back; hinder; impede: *Her constant chatter hampered the progress of the work.* **2.** to interfere with; curtail: *Her ease of movement was hampered by her tight skirt.* —*n.* **3.** *Naut.* gear that, although necessary to the operations of a vessel, is sometimes in the way. [ME *hampre(n);* akin to OE *hamm* enclosure, *hemm* HEM[1]] —**ham′pered·ly,** *adv.* —**ham′pered·ness,** *n.* —**ham′per·er,** *n.*
—**Syn. 1.** obstruct, encumber, trammel, clog. See **prevent.** —**Ant. 1.** further, encourage.

ham·per[2] (ham′pər), *n.* a large basket or wickerwork receptacle, usually with a cover: *picnic hamper; clothes hamper.* [ME *hampere,* var. of *hanypere* HANAPER]

Hamp·shire (hamp′shēr, -shər), *n.* **1.** Also called **Hants.** a county in S England, including the administrative divisions of Southampton and the Isle of Wight. 1,336,084 (1961); 1650 sq. mi. *Co. seat:* Winchester. **2.** Also called **Hamp′shire Down′.** one of an English breed of sheep having a dark face, ears, and legs, noted for the rapid growth of its lambs. **3.** one of an English breed of black hogs having a broad band of white over the shoulders and front legs.

Hamp·stead (hamp′stid), *n.* a NW borough of London: residences of artists and writers. 98,902 (1961).

Hamp·ton (hamp′tən), *n.* **1. Wade** (wād), 1818–1902, Confederate general: U.S. senator 1879–91. **2.** a city in SE Virginia, on Chesapeake Bay. 89,258 (1960). **3.** a town in central Iowa. 4501 (1960). **4.** a town in SE New Hampshire. 3281 (1960).

Hamp′ton boat′. See **Hampden boat.**

Hamp′ton Roads′, a channel in SE Virginia between the mouth of the James River and Chesapeake Bay: battle between the *Monitor* and the *Merrimac* 1862.

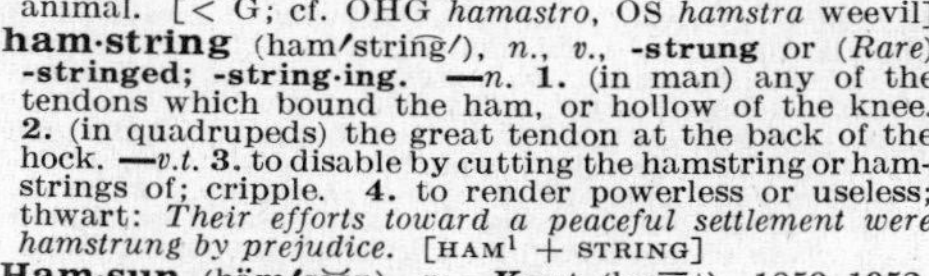
Golden hamster, *Mesocricetus auratus* (Length 7 in.)

ham·ster (ham′stər), *n.* **1.** any of several short-tailed, stout-bodied, burrowing rodents, as *Cricetus cricetus,* of Europe and Asia, having large cheek pouches. **2.** the fur of such an animal. [< G; cf. OHG *hamastro,* OS *hamstra* weevil]

ham·string (ham′string′), *n., v.,* **-strung** or (*Rare*) **-stringed; -string·ing.** —*n.* **1.** (in man) any of the tendons which bound the ham, or hollow of the knee. **2.** (in quadrupeds) the great tendon at the back of the hock. —*v.t.* **3.** to disable by cutting the hamstring or hamstrings of; cripple. **4.** to render powerless or useless; thwart: *Their efforts toward a peaceful settlement were hamstrung by prejudice.* [HAM[1] + STRING]

Ham·sun (häm′so͝on), *n.* **Knut** (kno͞ot), 1859–1952, Norwegian novelist: Nobel prize 1920.

Ham·tramck (ham tram′ik), *n.* a city in SE Michigan, completely surrounded by the city of Detroit. 34,137 (1960).

ham·u·lus (ham′yə ləs), *n., pl.* **-li** (-lī′). *Biol.* a small hook or hooklike process. [< L, equiv. to *hām(us)* hook + *-ulus* -ULE] —**ham′u·lar, ham·u·late** (ham′yə lāt′), **ham·u·lose** (ham′yə lōs′), **ham′u·lous,** *adj.*

ham·za (häm′zä), *n.* **1.** the Arabic glottal stop. **2.** the sign used in Arabic writing to mark the function of alif as a consonant and to represent the glottal stop, usually written above another letter. [< Ar *hamzah,* lit., a squeezing together]

Han (hän), *n.* **1.** a dynasty in China, 206 B.C.–A.D. 220, with an interregnum, A.D. 9–25: characterized by the revival of letters, the introduction of Buddhism, and territorial expansion. Cf. **Earlier Han, Later Han. 2.** a river flowing from central China into the Yangtze at Hankow. 900 mi. long.

han·ap (han′ap, -əp), *n.* a tall medieval or Renaissance goblet of metal or glass, having a cover and often highly decorated. [ME < MF < Gmc; cf. OE *hnæpp* bowl]

han·a·per (han′ə pər), *n.* a wicker receptacle for documents. [ME < AF (ML *hanaperium*), c. MF *hanapier* case to hold a drinking vessel, deriv. of *hanap* HANAP; see -ER[2]]

ha-Na·si (hä nä sē′), *n.* **Judah.** See **Judah ha-Nasi.** Also, **Ha·na·si′.**

hance (hans, häns), *n.* **1.** *Naut.* a local curved rise made for strength or appearance, esp. from the deck or railing level of a weather deck directly before or abaft a superstructure. **2.** *Archit.* **a.** the sharply curving portion nearest the impost at either side of an elliptical or similar arch. **b.** haunch (def. 5a). [n. use of obs. *hance* (v.), aph. var. of ENHANCE]

hanc′ing piece′ (han′sing, hän′-), *Naut.* a member used to give a hance to a ship. [HANCE + -ING[2]]

Han′ Cit′ies, Wuhan.

Han·cock (han′kok), *n.* **1. John,** 1737–93, American statesman: first signer of the Declaration of Independence. **2. Winfield Scott,** 1824–86, Union general in the Civil War. **3.** a town in NW Michigan, in the Upper Peninsula. 5022 (1960).

hand (hand), *n.* **1.** the terminal, prehensile part of the upper limb in man, consisting of the bones of the wrist or carpus, the metacarpus, fingers, and thumb. **2.** the corresponding part of the forelimb in any of the higher vertebrates. **3.** the terminal part of any limb when prehensile, as the hind foot of a monkey, the chela of a crustacean, or, in falconry, the foot of a hawk. **4.** something resembling a hand in shape or function, as various types of pointers: *the hands of a clock.* **5.** index (def. 7). **6.** a person employed in manual labor or for general duties; worker; laborer: *a factory hand; a ranch hand.* **7.** a person who performs or is capable of performing a specific work, skill or action: *a real hand at geometry; a book by several hands.* **8.** skill; workmanship; characteristic touch: *a painting that shows a master's hand.* **9.** a person, with reference to ability or skill: *He was a poor hand at running a business.* **10.** one of a ship's crew; crewman: *All hands on deck!* **11.** Often, **hands.** possession or power; control, custody, or care: *to have someone's fate in one's hands.* **12.** a position, esp. one of control, used for bargaining, negotiating, etc.: *an action to strengthen one's hand.* **13.** agency; instrumentality: *death by his own hand.* **14.** assistance; aid; active participation or cooperation in doing something: *Give me a hand with this ladder.* **15.** side; direction: *to look on either hand; on every hand; on all hands; on the right hand; on the left hand.* **16.** style of handwriting; penmanship: *He wrote in a beautiful hand.* **17.** a person's signature: *to set one's hand to a document.* **18.** a round or outburst of applause for a performer: *to get a hand.* **19.** a pledge, as of marriage: *He offered her his hand.* **20.** a linear measure equal to four inches, used esp. in determining the height of horses. **21.** *Cards.* **a.** the cards dealt to or held by each player at one time. **b.** the person holding the cards. **c.** a single part of a game, in which all the cards dealt at one time are played. **22.** *Roman Law.* manus (def. 2). **23. hands,** *Manège.* skill at manipulating the reins of a horse: *To ride well, one must have good hands.* **24.** a bunch, cluster, or bundle of various leaves, fruit, etc., as a bundle of tobacco leaves tied together or a cluster of bananas. **25.** *Mach.* the deviation of a thread or tooth from the axial direction of a screw or gear, as seen from one end looking away toward the other. **26.** *Building Trades.* **a.** the position of the hinges of a door, in terms of right and left, as seen from outside the building, room, closet, etc., to which the doorway leads. **b.** the position of the hinges of a casement sash, in terms of right and left, from inside the window. **27.** Also called **handle.** the fabric properties that can be sensed by touching the material, as resilience, smoothness, body, etc.: *the smooth hand of satin.* **28.** *Archaic.* a person considered as a source, as of information or of supply. **29. at first hand,** from the original source; directly: *I have the story at first hand.* Also, **first-hand, firsthand. 30. at hand, a.** within reach; nearby. **b.** near in time; soon. **c.** ready for use: *We keep a supply of canned goods at hand.* **31. at second hand,** from a secondary source: *Be wary of stories that you hear at second hand.* Also, **second-hand, secondhand. 32. at the hand** or **hands of,** by the action of; through the agency of: *They suffered at the hands of their stepfather.* **33. by hand,** by using the hands, as opposed to machines; manually: *lace made by hand.* **34. change hands,** to pass from one owner to another; change possession: *The property has changed hands several times in recent years.* **35. come to hand, a.** to come within one's reach or notice. **b.** to be received; arrive: *The spring stock came to hand last week.* **36. eat out of one's hand,** to be at the beck and call of another; be very attentive or servile: *She's the kind of girl who always has men eating out of her hand.* **37. force one's hand,** to prompt a person to take immediate action or to reveal his intentions: *The criticism forced the governor's hand so that he had to declare his support of the tax bill.* **38. from hand to hand,** from one person to another; having a succession of owners: *The legendary jewel went from hand to hand.* **39. from hand to mouth,** with attention only to immediate wants; improvidently: *They looked forward to a time when they would no longer have to live from hand to mouth.* **40. give someone one's hand on** or **upon something,** to give one's word; seal a bargain by or as by shaking hands: *He said the goods would be delivered within a month, and gave them his hand on it.* **41. hand and foot, a.** so as to hinder movement: *They tied him hand and foot.* **b.** slavishly; continually: *Cinderella had to wait on her stepsisters hand and foot.* **42. hand and glove,** very intimately associated: *Several high-ranking diplomats were found to be hand and glove with enemy agents.* Also, **hand in glove. 43. hand in hand, a.** with one's hand enclasped in that of another person. **b.** closely associated; concurrently; conjointly: *Doctors and nurses work hand in hand to save lives.* **44. hand over fist,** *Informal.* speedily; increasingly: *He owns a chain of restaurants and makes money hand over fist.* **45. hands down, a.** effortlessly; easily: *He won the championship hands down.* **b.** indisputably; incontestably: *It was hands down the best fight I've ever seen.* **46. hands off!** refrain from touching, striking, or interfering! keep away from!: *Hands off my hi-fi!* **47. hands up!** hold your hands above your head! give up! **48. hand to hand,** in close combat; at close quarters: *The troops fought hand to hand.* **49. have a hand in,** to have a share in; participate in: *It is impossible that she could have had a hand in this notorious crime.* **50. have one's hands full,** to have a large or excessive amount of work to handle; be constantly busy: *The Welfare Department has its hands full trying to process the growing number of applications.* **51. hold hands,** to join hands with a person of the opposite sex as a token of affection: *They have been seen holding hands in public.* **52. in hand, a.** under control: *He kept the situation well in hand.* **b.** in one's possession: *cash in hand.* **c.** in the process of consideration or settlement: *regarding the matter in hand.* **53. join hands,** to unite in a common cause; combine: *The democracies must join hands in order to survive.* **54. keep one's hand in,** to maintain interest in or some control of; remain proficient in; continue to practice: *He retired and turned the business over to his sons, but they say he keeps his hand in it. I just play enough golf to keep my hand in.* **55. lay one's hands on, a.** to obtain; acquire: *I wish I could lay my hands on a good used piano.* **b.** to seize, esp. in order to punish: *He wanted to lay his hands on the person who had backed into his car.* **c.** to impose the hands in a ceremonial fashion, as in ordination: *The bishop laid hands on the candidates.* **56. not to lift a hand,** to refuse to exert any effort; make no attempt: *She wouldn't lift a hand to help anyone.* Also, **not lift a finger. 57. off one's hands, a.** out of one's charge or care: *Now, with her invalid mother off her hands, she will be free to marry.* **b.** successfully completed; finished: *The lawyer planned a vacation as soon as the case was off his hands.* **58. on all hands, a.** by everyone; universally: *It was decided on all hands to take an excursion.* **b.** on every side; all around: *piercing glances on all hands.* Also, **on every hand. 59. on hand, a.** in one's possession; at one's disposal: *cash on hand.* **b.** about to occur; imminent: *A change of government may be on hand.* **c.** *U.S.* present: *There were not enough members on hand to constitute a quorum.* **60. on** or **upon one's hands,** under one's care or management; as one's responsibility: *He was left with a large surplus on his hands.* **61. on the other hand,** from another side or aspect; conversely: *It*

was an unfortunate experience, but, on the other hand, one can learn from one's mistakes. **62. out of hand, a.** beyond control: *to let one's temper get out of hand.* **b.** without delay; at once: *The crisis obliged him to act out of hand.* **c.** no longer in process; finished: *The case has been out of hand for some time.* **63. shake hands,** to clasp another's hand in greeting, congratulation, or agreement: *They shook hands on the proposed partnership.* **64. show one's hand,** to disclose or display one's true intentions, motives: *The impending revolution forced him to show his hand.* **65. sit on one's hands, a.** to be unenthusiastic or unappreciative; fail to applaud: *It was a lively show, but the audience sat on its hands.* **b.** to take no action; be passive or hesitant: *While hostile forces were invading the helpless country, the larger powers sat on their hands.* **66. take a hand in,** to take part in; participate in: *If the strike continues, the government will have to take a hand in the negotiations.* **67. take in hand, a.** to undertake responsibility for; assume charge: *When both parents died, an uncle took the youngster in hand.* **b.** to deal with; treat of: *We'll take the matter in hand at the next meeting.* **68. throw up one's hands,** to admit one's inadequacy, exasperation, or failure; despair: *When the general received reports of an enemy buildup, he threw up his hands.* **69. tie one's hands,** to render one powerless to act; thwart: *The provisions of the will tied his hands.* Also, **have one's hands tied. 70. tip one's hand,** to reveal one's plans or intentions before the propitious time. **71. to hand, a.** within reach; accessible. **b.** into one's possession: *A search of the attic brought some valuable antiques to hand.* **72. try one's hand (at),** to test one's skill or aptitude for: *After becoming a successful painter, he decided to try his hand at sculpture.* **73. turn** or **put one's hand to,** to set to work at; busy oneself with: *He turned his hand successfully to gardening.* **74. wash one's hands of,** to disclaim any further responsibility for; renounce interest in or support of: *He washed his hands of the entire affair.* **75. with a heavy hand, a.** with severity; oppressively: *The Law will punish offenders with a heavy hand.* **b.** in a clumsy manner; awkwardly; gracelessly: *The play was directed with a heavy hand.* **76. with a high hand,** in an arrogant or dictatorial manner; arbitrarily: *He ran the organization with a high hand.*
—v.t. 77. to deliver or pass with or as with the hand. **78.** to help, assist, guide, etc., with the hand: *He handed the elderly woman across the street.* **79.** *Naut.* **a.** to take in or furl (a sail). **b.** to haul on or otherwise handle. **80. hand down, a.** to deliver (the decision of a court): *The jury handed down a verdict of guilty.* **b.** to transmit from one to another, esp. to bequeath to posterity: *The ring had been handed down from his grandmother.* **81. hand in,** to submit; present for acceptance: *She handed in her term paper after the deadline.* **82. hand in one's checks,** *Chiefly Brit.* See **cash** (def. 7). **83. hand it to,** *Informal.* to give just credit to; pay respect to: *You have to hand it to him for getting the work out.* **84. hand off,** *Football.* to hand the ball to a member of one's team in the course of a play. **85. hand on,** to transmit; pass on (to a successor, posterity, etc.): *The silver service was handed on to the eldest daughter of the family.* **86. hand out,** to give or distribute; mete out: *People were handing out leaflets on every corner.* **87. hand over, a.** to deliver into the custody of another. **b.** to surrender control of: *He handed over his business to his sons.*
—adj. 88. of, belonging to, using, or used by the hand. **89.** made by hand. **90.** carried in or worn on the hand. **91.** operated by hand; manual. [ME, OE; c. D, G *hand*, Icel *hönd*, Goth *handus*] **—hand′like′,** *adj.*

Hand (hand), *n.* **Learned** (lûr′nid), 1872–1961, U.S. jurist.

hand′ ax′. See **broad hatchet.**

hand·bag (hand′bag′), *n.* **1.** a bag or box of leather, fabric, plastic, or the like, for carrying in the hand or under the arm or by suspending from the arm or shoulder, commonly used by women for carrying money, toilet articles, small purchases, etc. **2.** valise. [HAND + BAG]

hand·ball (hand′bôl′), *n.* **1.** a game, similar to squash, played by two or four persons who strike a small ball against a wall or walls with the hand. **2.** the small, hard rubber ball used in this game. [late ME *handballe*. See HAND, BALL[1]] **—hand′ball′er,** *n.*

hand·bar·row (hand′bar′ō), *n.* **1.** a frame with handles at each end by which it is carried. **2.** a handcart. [late ME *handberwe*. See HAND, BARROW[1]]

hand·bill (hand′bil′), *n.* a small printed bill or announcement, usually for distribution by hand. [HAND + BILL[1]]

hand·book (hand′bo͝ok′), *n.* **1.** a book of instruction or guidance, as for an occupation; manual: *a handbook of radio.* **2.** a guidebook for travelers: *a handbook of Italy.* **3.** a reference book in a particular field: *a medical handbook.* **4.** a scholarly book on a specific subject, often consisting of separate essays or articles: *a handbook of lectures on criticism.* [OE *handbōc*; revived in 19th century as counterpart to G *Handbuch*]

hand·bound (hand′bound′), *adj.* (of books) bound by hand. [HAND + BOUND[2]]

hand′ brake′, a brake operated by a hand lever.

hand·breadth (hand′bredth′, -bretth′), *n.* a unit of linear measure from 2½ to 4 inches. Also, **hand's-breadth.** [HAND + BREADTH]

hand·car (hand′kär′), *n.* *U.S.* a small railroad car or platform on four wheels propelled by a mechanism worked by hand, used on some railroads for inspecting tracks and transporting workmen. [HAND + CAR[1]]

hand·cart (hand′kärt′), *n.* a small cart drawn or pushed by hand. [HAND + CART]

hand·clap (hand′klap′), *n.* a slapping of the palm of one hand against the other, made to indicate approval or appreciation. [HAND + CLAP]

hand·clasp (hand′klasp′, -kläsp′), *n.* a clasping of hands by two or more people, as in greeting, parting, making a commitment, expressing affection, etc. [HAND + CLASP]

hand·craft (*n.* hand′kraft′, -kräft′; *v.* hand′kraft′, -kräft′), *n.* **1.** handicraft. **—v.t. 2.** to make (something) by hand. [ME; OE *handcræft*. See HANDICRAFT]

hand·craft·ed (hand′kraf′tid, -kräf′-), *adj.* made by hand; produced by a craftsman: *handcrafted leather goods.* [HANDCRAFT + -ED[3]]

hand·cuff (hand′kuf′), *n.* **1.** a ring-shaped metal device that can be locked around a prisoner's wrist, usually one of a pair connected by a short chain or linked bar; shackle. **—v.t. 2.** to put handcuffs on. **3.** to restrain or thwart (someone) by or as by handcuffing: *The amendments handcuffed the committee and prevented further action.* [HAND + CUFF[1]]

hand′ drill′, a drill held and operated by hand.

hand·ed (han′did), *adj.* **1.** having a hand or hands. **2.** having, requiring, or with the number of people, workers, or players indicated (usually used in combination): *My parents and I played a three-handed game of Canasta.* **3.** manned; staffed (usually used in combination). [HAND + -ED[3]]

hand·ed·ness (han′did nis), *n.* a tendency to use either the right hand or the left hand more frequently. [HANDED + -NESS]

Han·del (han′dəl), *n.* **George Frederick** (*Georg Friedrich Händel*), 1685–1759, German composer in England. **—Han·del·i·an** (han del′ē ən, -dē′lē-, -del′yən, -dēl′yən), *adj.*

hand·fast (hand′fast′, -fäst′), *Archaic.* **—n. 1.** a covenant, contract, or bargain completed by a handclasp, esp. a betrothal completed in this manner. **—adj. 2.** stingy; parsimonious; tight-fisted. **3.** having a firm grip or grasp. **—v.t. 4.** to betroth by joining hands. [ME (ptp.), earlier *handfest* < Scand; cf. Icel *handfestr*, ptp. of *handfesta* to betroth with a joining of hands, equiv. to *hand* HAND + *festa* to betroth, lit., make fast, FASTEN]

hand·fast·ing (hand′fas′ting, -fä′sting), *n.* **1.** a form of private marriage preliminary to a church marriage. **2.** *Obs.* betrothal. [HANDFAST + -ING[1]]

hand-feed (hand′fēd′), *v.t.*, **-fed, -feed·ing. 1.** *Agric.* to feed (animals) with apportioned amounts at regular intervals. Cf. **self-feed. 2.** to feed (an animal or person) by hand: *The students hand-fed the baby monkeys with an eye dropper.*

hand·ful (hand′fo͝ol′), *n., pl.* **-fuls. 1.** the quantity or amount that the hand can hold: *a handful of coins.* **2.** a small amount or quantity: *a handful of men.* **3.** *Informal.* a thing that or a person who is as much as one can manage or control: *The baby's tantrums made him a handful.* [ME, OE. See HAND, -FUL]

hand′ glass′, 1. a small mirror with a handle. **2.** a magnifying glass for holding in the hand.

hand′ grenade′, 1. a grenade or explosive shell that is thrown by hand and exploded either by impact or by means of a fuze. **2.** a grenade or glass missile containing a chemical, for extinguishing fire.

hand·grip (hand′grip′), *n.* **1.** the quality of the grip of a hand, as in greeting; mode of gripping, as of a handshake: *a firm handgrip; a friendly handgrip.* **2. handgrips,** hand-to-hand combat. **3.** a handle or similar part of an object affording a grip by the hand, as for lifting. [ME; OE *handgripe*. See HAND, GRIP]

hand·gun (hand′gun′), *n.* any firearm that can be held and fired with one hand; a revolver or a pistol. [HAND + GUN[1]]

hand·hold (hand′hōld′), *n.* **1.** a grip with the hand or hands. **2.** something to grip or take hold of, as a support, handle, etc. [HAND + HOLD[1]]

hand′ horn′, a forerunner of the modern French horn, developed in Germany during the mid-17th century. See illus. under **horn.**

hand·i·cap (han′dē kap′), *n., v.,* **-capped, -cap·ping. —n. 1.** a race or other contest in which certain disadvantages or advantages of weight, distance, time, etc., are placed upon competitors to equalize their chances of winning. **2.** the disadvantage or advantage itself. **3.** any disadvantage that makes success more difficult: *The main handicap of our business is lack of capital.* **4.** a physical disability. **—v.t. 5.** to place at a disadvantage; disable or burden: *He was handicapped by his age.* **6.** to subject to a disadvantageous handicap, as a competitor of recognized superiority. **7.** to assign handicaps to (competitors). **8.** *Sports.* **a.** to attempt to predict the winner of (a contest, esp. a horse race), as by comparing past performances of the contestants. **b.** to assign odds for or against (any particular contestant) winning a contest or series of contests: *He handicapped the Yankees at 2-to-1 to win the series from the Cardinals.* [orig. *hand i' cap* hand in cap, referring to a drawing before a horse race]

hand·i·capped (han′dē kapt′), *adj.* **1.** crippled or physically disabled. **2.** mentally deficient. **3.** (of a contestant) marked by, being under, or having a handicap: *a handicapped player.* [HANDICAP + -ED[3]]

hand·i·cap·per (han′dē kap′ər), *n.* *Horse Racing.* **1.** a race-track official or employee who assigns the weight a horse must carry in a race. **2.** a person employed to make predictions on the outcomes of horse races, as by a newspaper. [HANDICAP + -ER[1]]

hand·i·craft (han′dē kraft′, -kräft′), *n.* **1.** manual skill. **2.** an art, craft, or trade in which the skilled use of one's hands is required. **3.** the articles made by handicraft: *a shop offering the handicraft of various nations.* Also, **handcraft.** [ME *hendi craft* dexterous skill. See HANDY, CRAFT] **—hand′i·craft′ship,** *n.*

hand·i·crafts·man (han′dē krafts′mən, -kräfts′-), *n., pl.* **-men.** a person skilled in a handicraft; craftsman. [HANDICRAFT + 's[1] + MAN[1]] **—hand′i·crafts′man·ship′,** *n.*

Hand·ie-Talk·ie (han′dē tô′kē), *n.* *Trademark.* a portable radio receiver and transmitter.

hand·i·ly (han′di lē, -dəlē), *adv.* **1.** dexterously; expertly: *He managed the boat handily.* **2.** conveniently: *The books were handily at his side.* **3.** easily: *He came through the test handily.* [HANDY + -LY]

hand·i·ness (han′dē nis), *n.* the state or quality of being handy. [HANDY + -NESS]

hand·i·work (han′dē wûrk′), *n.* **1.** work done by hand. **2.** the characteristic quality of a particular doer or maker: *In all of Mozart's music we discover the handiwork of a genius.* **3.** the result of work done by hand: *woven mats and other handiwork; the handiwork of cabinetmakers.* [ME *handiwerk*, OE *handgeweorc*, var. of *handweorc* (c. G *Handwerk*). See HAND, Y-, WORK]

hand·ker·chief (hang′kər chif, -chēf′), *n.* **1.** a small piece of linen, silk, or other fabric, usually square, and used for personal or decorative purposes. **2.** a neckerchief or a kerchief. [HAND + KERCHIEF]

hand′kerchief ta′ble. See **corner table.**

hand-knit (hand′nit′), *v.t.*, **-knit·ted** or **-knit, -knit·ting.** to knit by hand: *She hand-knitted several sweaters for Christmas gifts.* **—hand′ knit′ter.**

han·dle (han′dəl), *n., v.,* **-dled, -dling. —n. 1.** a part of a thing made specifically to be grasped or held by the hand. **2.** that which may be held, seized, grasped, or taken advantage of in effecting a purpose: *The clue was a handle for solving the mystery.* **3.** *Slang.* a person's name, esp. given name. **4.** the total amount wagered on an event, series of events, or for an entire season or seasons, as at a gambling casino or in horse racing: *The track handle for the day was over a million dollars.* **5.** the total amount of money taken in by a business concern on one transaction, sale, or series of transactions, or during a specific period, esp. by a theater, night club, sports arena, resort hotel, or other establishment selling entertainment or dependent on special events. **6.** hand (def. 27). **7. fly off the handle,** *Informal.* to become very agitated or angry, esp. without warning: *I can't imagine why he flew off the handle like that.* [ME *handel*, OE *hand(e)le*, deriv. of HAND]
—v.t. 8. to touch, pick up, carry, or feel with the hand or hands; use the hands on; take hold of. **9.** to manage, deal with, or be responsible for: *My wife handles the household accounts. This machine handles all our billing.* **10.** to use or employ, esp. in a particular manner; manipulate: *to handle color expertly in painting.* **11.** to manage, direct, train, or control: *to handle troops.* **12.** to deal with (a subject, theme, argument, etc.): *The poem handled the problem of love and death quite interestingly.* **13.** to deal with or treat in a particular way: *to handle a person with tact.* **14.** to deal or trade in: *to handle dry goods.*
—v.i. 15. to behave or perform in a particular way when handled, directed, managed, etc.: *The troops handled well. The jet was handling poorly.* [ME *handelen*, OE *handlian* (c. G *handlen*, Icel *höndla*); deriv. of HAND] **—han′dle·a·ble,** *adj.* **—han′dle·less,** *adj.*

hand′ lead′ (led), *Navig.* a lead weighing from 5 to 15 pounds, used for sounding depths of less than 20 fathoms or 120 feet.

han·dle·bar (han′dəl bär′), *n.* **1.** Usually, **handlebars. a.** the curved steering bar of a bicycle, motorcycle, etc., placed in front of the rider and gripped by the hands. **b.** See **handlebar moustache. 2.** a bar or rod, usually of metal and having a handle at one end, used for handling, guiding, maneuvering, etc., some object. [HANDLE + BAR[1]]

han′dlebar moustache′, a man's moustache having long, curved ends that resemble handlebars.

han·dled (han′dəld), *adj.* fitted with or having a handle or handles, esp. of a specified kind (often used in combination): *a handled pot; a long-handled knife.* [HANDLE + -ED[3]]

han·dler (hand′lər), *n.* **1.** a person who or thing that handles. **2.** *Boxing.* a person who assists in the training of a fighter or is his second during a fight. **3.** a person who exhibits a dog in a bench show or field trial. [ME; see HANDLE, -ER[1]]

hand·less (hand′lis), *adj.* **1.** without hands. **2.** clumsy; awkward: *to be handless at a task.* [late ME *hand(e)les*. See HAND, -LESS]

hand′ let′ter, a brass letter, mounted in a handle, for printing on the cover of a handbound book.

hand′ lev′el, *Survey.* a leveling instrument held in the hand and used for approximate work at short distances.

han·dling (hand′ling), *n.* **1.** a touching, grasping, or using with the hands. **2.** the manner of treating or dealing with something; management; treatment. **3.** the manual or mechanical method or process by which something is moved, carried, transported, etc. **—adj. 4.** of or pertaining to the process of moving, transporting, delivering, working with, etc.: *The factory added a 10 percent handling charge for sending us the watch we saw advertised.* [ME; OE *handlung* (n.). See HANDLE, -ING[1], -ING[2]]

hand·load·er (hand′lō′dər), *n.* a marksman or hunter who loads his own cartridges by hand, as for greater accuracy or to reduce the cost. [HAND + LOADER]

hand′ log′, *Naut.* See **chip log.**

hand·loom (hand′lo͞om′), *n.* a loom operated manually, in contrast to a power loom. [HAND + LOOM[1]]

hand·loomed (hand′lo͞omd′), *adj.* handwoven. [HANDLOOM + -ED[3]]

hand·made (hand′mād′), *adj.* made by hand, rather than by machine: *the luxury of handmade shoes.* [HAND + MADE]

hand·maid (hand′mād′), *n.* **1.** a female servant or attendant. **2.** something which is necessarily subservient or subordinate to another: *Ceremony is but the handmaid of worship.* Also, **hand′maid′en.** [ME; see HAND, MAID]

hand-me-down (hand′mē doun′, han′-), *n.* **1.** an article of clothing handed down or acquired at second hand: *The younger children wore the hand-me-downs of the older ones.* **2.** a cheap, ready-made garment.

hand-off (hand′ôf′, -of′), *n.* *Football.* **1.** an offensive play in which a player, usually a back, hands the ball to a teammate. **2.** the ball itself during such a transfer: *He fumbled the hand-off.* [n. use of v. phrase *hand off*]

hand′ of writ′, *Scot.* handwriting; penmanship.

hand′ or′gan, a portable barrel organ played by means of a crank turned by hand.

hand·out (hand′out′), *n.* **1.** a portion of food or the like given to a needy person, as a beggar. **2.** *Journalism.* a press release. **3.** anything given away for nothing, as free samples of a product by an advertiser. [n. use of v. phrase *hand out*]

hand-pick (hand′pik′), *v.t.* **1.** to pick by hand. **2.** to select personally and with care: *The boss hand-picked his assistants.*

hand·rail (hand′rāl′), *n.* a rail serving as a support or guard at the side of a stairway, platform, etc. [HAND + RAIL[1]]

hand′rail bolt′, a bolt for butting two timbers together, having threads and nuts at both ends.

hand·saw (hand′sô′), *n.* any common saw with a handle at one end for manual operation with one hand. See illus. under **saw.** [HAND + SAW[1]]

hand·saw·fish (hand′sô′fish′), *n., pl.* (*esp. collectively*) **-fish,** (*esp. referring to two or more kinds or species*) **-fish·es.** a lancetfish, esp. *Alepisaurus richardsoni.* [HANDSAW + FISH, so called because of its sawlike teeth]

hand's-breadth (handz′bredth′, -bretth′), *n.* handbreadth.

hand′ screw′, **1.** a screw that can be tightened by the fingers, without the aid of a tool. **2.** Also called **wood clamp.** *Carpentry.* a clamp having two wooden jaws that are adjusted by two long screws. See illus. under **clamp.**

hand′ scroll′. See under **scroll** (def. 5).

hands-down (handz′doun′), *adj.* **1.** effortlessly achieved; easy: *a hands-down victory.* **2.** indubitable; certain: *a book destined to be a hands-down best seller.* —*adv.* **3.** easily; effortlessly: *He won the race hands-down.*

hand·sel (han′səl), *n., v.,* **-seled, -sel·ing** or (*esp. Brit.*) **-selled, -sel·ling.** —*n.* **1.** a gift or token for good luck or as an expression of good wishes, as at the beginning of the new year or when entering upon a new state, situation, or enterprise. **2.** a first installment of payment. **3.** the initial experience of anything; first encounter with or use of something taken as a token of what will follow; foretaste. —*v.t.* **4.** to give a handsel to. **5.** to inaugurate auspiciously. **6.** to use, try, or experience for the first time. Also, **hansel.** [ME *handselne* good-luck token, good-will gift, OE *handselen* manumission, lit., hand-gift (see HAND, SELL); c. Dan *handsel,* earnest money]

hand·set (hand′set′), *n., v.,* **-set, -set·ting,** *adj.* —*n.* **1.** a part of a telephone having a mouthpiece and earpiece mounted at opposite ends of a handle. —*v.t.* **2.** to set (type) by hand. —*adj.* **3.** (of type) set by hand. **4.** (of a publication) printed directly from type set by hand. [HAND + SET]

hand·sew (hand′sō′), *v.t.,* **-sewed, -sewn** or **-sewed, -sew·ing.** to sew by hand. [HAND + SEW]

hand·sewn (hand′sōn′), *adj.* sewn by hand. [HAND + SEWN]

hand·shake (hand′shāk′), *n.* a clasping and shaking of right hands by two individuals, as to symbolize greeting, congratulation, agreement, farewell, or the like. [HAND + SHAKE]

hand·shak·er (hand′shā′kər), *n.,* a person who is or is required to be overtly or ostentatiously friendly, as by his employment, aspirations, or fame: *Salesmen, politicians, and success seekers are often incurable handshakers.* [HANDSHAKE + -ER[1]] —**hand′shak′ing,** *n.*

hands-off (handz′ôf′, -of′), *adj.* **1.** characterized by nonintervention, noninterference, etc.: *the new hands-off foreign policy.* **2.** recommending or demanding nonintervention, noninterference, etc.: *a truculent, hands-off manner toward strangers.*

hand·some (han′səm), *adj.,* **-som·er, -som·est. 1.** having an attractive, well-proportioned, and imposing appearance suggestive of health and strength; good-looking: *a handsome man; a handsome woman.* **2.** having pleasing proportions, relationships, or arrangements, as of shapes, forms, colors, etc.; attractive: *a handsome house; a handsome interior.* **3.** exhibiting skill, taste, and refinement; well-made: *a handsome story; handsome furniture.* **4.** considerable, ample, or liberal in amount: *a handsome fortune.* **5.** gracious; generous: *a handsome compliment; a handsome recommendation.* **6.** dexterous; graceful: *a handsome speech.* [late ME *handsom* easy to handle (see HAND, -SOME[1]); c. D *handzaam* tractable] —**hand′some·ish,** *adj.,* —**hand′some·ness,** *n.*
—**Syn. 1.** See **beautiful. 4.** large, generous. —**Ant. 1.** ugly. **4, 5.** small.

hand′some Har′ry. See **deer grass.**

hand·some·ly (han′səm lē), *adv.* **1.** in a handsome manner. **2.** *Naut.* slowly and carefully: *Lower away handsomely.* [HANDSOME + -LY]

hand·spike (hand′spīk′), *n.* a bar used as a lever. [var. of *handspeck* < D, with assimilation to SPIKE[1]]

hand·spring (hand′spring′), *n.* an acrobatic feat in which one starts from a standing position and turns the body forward or backward in a complete circle, landing first on the hands and then on the feet. [HAND + SPRING]

hand·stand (hand′stand′), *n.* the act or an instance of supporting the body in a vertical position by balancing on the palms of the hands. Cf. **headstand.** [HAND + STAND]

hand-tai·lor (hand′tā′lər), *v.t.* **1.** to produce (a garment or the like) by individual workmanship. **2.** to make according to individual requirements.

hand′ tight′, (of a setscrew, nut, etc.) as tight as it can be made by hand, without the aid of a tool.

hand-to-hand (hand′tə hand′), *adj.* close by one's adversary; at close quarters: *hand-to-hand combat.*

hand-to-mouth (hand′tə mouth′), *adj.* offering or providing the barest livelihood, sustenance, or support; precarious; unsettled: *a hand-to-mouth existence; a hand-to-mouth salary.*

hand′ truck′, truck[1] (def. 3).

hand·weav·ing (hand′wē′ving), *n.* **1.** the art or technique of weaving on a handloom. **2.** the fabric produced by handweaving. [HAND + WEAVING]

hand·wheel (hand′hwēl′, -wēl′), *n.* a wheel, as a valve wheel, turned by hand. [HAND + WHEEL]

hand·work (hand′wûrk′), *n.* work done by hand, as distinguished from that done by machine. [ME; OE *handweorc.* See HAND, WORK] —**hand′ work′er.**

hand·worked (hand′wûrkt′), *adj.* handwrought. [HAND + WORKED]

hand·wo·ven (hand′wō′vən), *adj.* made on a handloom; handloomed. [HAND + WOVEN]

hand·write (hand′rīt′), *v.t.,* **-wrote** or (*Archaic*) **-writ; -writ·ten** or (*Archaic*) **-writ; writ·ing.** to write (something) by hand. [back formation from HANDWRITING]

hand·writ·ing (hand′rī′ting), *n.* **1.** writing done with the hand. **2.** a style or manner of writing by hand, esp. that which characterizes a particular person: *an eccentric handwriting.* **3.** *Obs.* a handwritten document; manuscript. **4. handwriting on the wall,** a premonition, portent, or clear indication, esp. of failure or disaster: *The country ignored the handwriting on the wall, and was plunged into another war.* Also, **writing on the wall.** [HAND + WRITING]

hand·wrought (hand′rôt′), *adj.* formed or shaped by hand, as metal objects. Also, **handworked.** [HAND + WROUGHT]

hand·y (han′dē), *adj.,* **hand·i·er, hand·i·est. 1.** within easy reach; conveniently available; accessible: *The aspirins are handy.* **2.** convenient or useful: *A typewriter is a handy thing to have in the house.* **3.** skillful with the hands; deft; dexterous: *a handy person.* **4.** easily manipulated or maneuvered: *a handy ship.* [HAND + -Y[1]]
—**Syn. 3.** all-round; versatile.

Han·dy (han′dē), *n.* **W**(**illiam**) **C**(**hristopher**), 1873–1958, U.S. blues composer.

hand·y-an·dy (han′dē an′dē), *n., pl.* **-dies.** a handyman. [after hero of *Handy Andy,* novel by Samuel Lover (1797–1868) Irish novelist]

hand·y·bil·ly (han′dē bil′ē), *n., pl.* **-bil·lies** (-bil′ēz). *Naut.* any of various small tackles for use on shipboard; watch tackle. [HANDY + BILLY]

hand·y·man (han′dē man′), *n., pl.* **-men.** a man hired to do various small jobs, esp. in the maintenance of an apartment building, office building, or the like. [HANDY + MAN[1]]

ha·ne·fi·yeh (hä′ne fē′ye), *n.* (in the courtyard of a mosque) a fountain for ritual washing. [< Ar: lit., thing pertaining to the faith, deriv. of *hanif* monotheist < Syriac *hanef* dissenter]

Han Fei Tzu (hän′ fā′ dzu′), died 233 B.C., Chinese philosopher and legal theorist.

Han·ford (han′fərd), *n.* **1.** a city in central California. 10,133 (1960). **2.** a locality in SE Washington, on the Columbia River: site of an atomic energy plant (**Han′ford Works′**). Cf. **Richland. 3.** a boy's given name.

hang (hang), *v.,* **hung** or (*esp. for 4, 5, 17, 22*) **hanged; hang·ing;** *n.* —*v.t.* **1.** to fasten or attach (a thing) so that it is supported only from above or at a point near its own top; suspend. **2.** to attach or suspend so as to allow free movement: *to hang a pendulum.* **3.** to place in position or fasten, so as to allow easy or ready movement. **4.** to execute by suspending from a gallows, gibbet, yardarm, or the like, as a mode of capital punishment. **5.** to suspend by the neck until dead: *He hanged himself from a beam in the attic.* **6.** to fasten to a cross; crucify. **7.** to furnish or decorate with something suspended: *to hang a room with pictures.* **8.** to fasten into position; fix at a proper angle: *to hang a scythe.* **9.** to fasten or attach (wallpaper, pictures, etc.) to a wall: *to hang pictures in a room.* **10.** to suspend (something) in front of anything: *to hang curtains on a window.* **11.** to cause (a nickname, epithet, etc.) to become associated with a person: *Friends hung that name on him.* **12.** *Slang.* to hit with (a fist, blow, punch, etc.): *He hung a left on his opponent's jaw.* **13.** *Fine Arts.* **a.** to exhibit (a painting or group of paintings): *The gallery hung his paintings in a small corner.* **b.** to put the paintings of (an art exhibition) on the wall of a gallery: *They hung the show that morning.* **14.** to attach or annex as an addition: *to hang a rider on a bill.* **15.** to make (an idea, form, etc.) dependent on a situation, structure, concept, or the like, usually derived from another source: *He hung the meaning of his puns on the current political scene.* **16.** to attach (a door or the like) to its frame by means of hinges. **17.** (used in mild curses and emphatic expressions, often as a euphemism for *damn*): *I'll be hanged if I do. Hang it all!* **18.** to keep (a jury) from rendering a verdict, as one juror by refusing to agree with the others. **19.** *Naut.* to steady (a boat) in one place against a wind or current by thrusting a pole or the like into the bottom under the boat and allowing the wind or current to push the boat side-on against the pole.
—*v.i.* **20.** to be suspended; dangle. **21.** to swing freely, as on a hinge. **22.** to be suspended by the neck, as from a gallows and suffer death in this way. **23.** to be crucified. **24.** to incline downward, jut out, or lean over or forward: *The tree hung over the edge of the lake.* **25.** to be conditioned or contingent; be dependent: *His future hangs on the outcome of their discussion.* **26.** to be doubtful or undecided; waiver or hesitate: *He hung between staying and going.* **27.** to remain unfinished or undecided; be delayed: *Let that matter hang until our next meeting.* **28.** to linger, remain, or persist: *He hung by her side, unwilling to leave.* **29.** to float or hover in the air: *Fog hung over the city.* **30.** to be oppressive, burdensome, or tedious: *guilt that hangs on one's conscience.* **31.** to remain in attention or consideration (often fol. by *on* or *upon*): *They hung on his every word.* **32.** *Fine Arts.* **a.** to be exhibited: *His works hang in most major museums.* **b.** to have one's works on display: *Rembrandt hangs in the Metropolitan Museum of Art.* **33.** to fail to agree, as a jury. **34.** to fit or drape in graceful lines: *That coat hangs well in back.* **35. hang around** or **about,** *Informal.* **a.** to spend time in a certain place or in certain company: *He hangs around with an older crowd.* **b.** to linger about; loiter: *They had stopped working and were just hanging around to talk.* **36. hang back, a.** to be reluctant to proceed or move forward: *The older pupils went straight to the podium, but the younger ones hung back out of shyness.* **b.** to refrain from taking action; hesitate: *A forward pass would have been the best call, but the quarterback hung back because his last pass had been intercepted.* **37. hang in the balance,** to be in doubt or suspense: *The wounded man's life hung in the balance.* **38. hang on, a.** to hold fast; cling to. **b.** to continue with effort; persevere: *If you can hang on for a month longer you will be free of your hardship.* **c.** to be sustained to the point of danger, tedium, etc.: *coughs that hang on for months.* **39. hang one on,** *Slang.* **a.** to strike (someone) a blow; hit: *He hung one on the bully and knocked him down.* **b.** to become extremely drunk: *Every payday he hangs one on.* **40. hang one's head.** See **head** (def. 38). **41. hang out, a.** to lean or be suspended through an opening. **b.** *Slang.* to frequent a particular place, esp. in idling away one's free time: *to hang out in a bar.* **c.** *Slang.* to reside: *The rich hang out on Park Avenue.* **d.** to suspend in open view; display: *to hang out the flag.* **42. hang over, a.** to remain to be settled; be postponed: *They will probably let the final decision hang over until next year.* **b.** to be imminent; threaten: *Destitution hangs over the town.* **43. hang together, a.** to be loyal to one another; remain united: *"We must indeed all hang together, or, most assuredly, we shall all hang separately."* **b.** to cohere: *This pancake batter doesn't hang together.* **c.** to be logical or consistent: *His version of the story does not hang together.* **44. hang up, a.** to suspend by placing on a hook, peg, or hanger. **b.** to cause or encounter delay; suspend or slow the progress of: *The accident hung up the traffic for several hours.* **c.** to break a telephone connection by replacing the receiver on the hook.
—*n.* **45.** the way in which a thing hangs. **46.** *Informal.* the precise manner of doing, using, etc., something; knack: *to get the hang of a tool.* **47.** *Informal.* meaning or thought: *to get the hang of a subject.* **48.** the least degree of care, concern, etc. (used in mild curses and emphatic expressions as a euphemism for *damn*): *He doesn't give a hang about those things.* **49.** *Naut.* **a.** loss of way due to adverse wind or current. **b.** a rake, as of a mast. [fusion of 3 verbs: (1) ME, OE *hōn* to hang, c. Goth *hāhan,* orig. **hanhan;* (2) ME *hang(i)en,* OE *hangian* to hang, c. G *hangen;* (3) ME *henge* < Scand; cf. Icel *hengja,* c. G *hängen* to hang] —**hang′a·bil′i·ty,** *n.* —**hang′a·ble,** *adj.*
—**Syn. 5.** HANG, LYNCH through a widespread misconception have been thought of as synonyms. They do have in common the meaning of "to put to death," but lynching is not always by hanging. HANG, in the sense of execute, is in accordance with a legal sentence, the method of execution being to suspend by the neck until dead. To LYNCH, however, implies the summary putting to death, by any method, of someone charged with a flagrant offense (though guilt may not have been proved). Lynching is done by private persons, usually a mob, without legal authority. **25.** depend, rely.

hang·ar (hang′ər), *n.* **1.** a shed or shelter. **2.** any enclosed structure used for housing airplanes or airships. [< F: shed, hangar; cf. ML *angārium* shed for shoeing horses < ?]

hang·bird (hang′bûrd′), *n.* *U.S. Dial.* a bird that builds a hanging nest, esp. the Baltimore oriole. [HANG + BIRD]

Hang·chow (hang′chou′; *Chin.* häng′jō′), *n.* a seaport in and the capital of Chekiang province, in E China, on Hangchow Bay. 784,000 (est. 1957).

Hang′chow Bay′, a bay of the East China Sea.

hang·dog (hang′dôg′, -dog′), *adj.* **1.** browbeaten; defeated; intimidated; abject: *He always went about with a hangdog look.* **2.** shamefaced; guilty: *He sneaked out of the room with a hangdog expression.* **3.** suitable to a degraded or contemptible person; sneaky; furtive. —*n.* **4.** *Archaic.* a degraded, contemptible person. [HANG + DOG]

hang·er (hang′ər), *n.* **1.** a shoulder-shaped frame with a hook at the top, usually of wire, wood, or plastic, for draping and hanging an article of clothing when not in use. **2.** a part of something by which it is hung, as a loop on a garment. **3.** a contrivance on which things are hung, as a hook. **4.** stirrup (def. 4). **5.** *Auto.* a double-hinged device linking the chassis with the leaf springs on vehicles having solid axles. **6.** a light saber of the 17th and 18th centuries, often worn by seamen. **7.** one who hangs something. **8.** *Sports Slang.* a scoring shot that can be made easily, as by an unguarded basketball player who has the ball close to the basket, a pool player whose object ball is on the edge of a pocket, or a handball player who receives the ball close to the front wall. [HANG + -ER[1]]

hang·er-on (hang′ər on′, -ôn′), *n., pl.* **hang·ers-on.** a person who remains in a place or with a group, another person, etc., esp. past the point when his presence is desired or in the hope of gaining some personal end; an unwanted and frequently parasitic individual: *hangers-on at the end of a party; political hangers-on.* [n. use of v. phrase *hang on;* see -ER[1]]

hang·fire (hang′fīər′), *n.* a delay in the detonation of gunpowder or other ammunition, caused by some defect in the fuze. [HANG + FIRE]

hang′ glid′er, a glider resembling a kite below which a rider is suspended in a harness. —**hang′ glid′ing.**

hang·ing (hang′ing), *n.* **1.** the act, an instance, or the form of capital punishment carried out by suspending one by the neck from a gallows, gibbet, or the like, until dead. **2.** Often, **hangings.** something that hangs or is hung on the walls of a room, as a drapery, tapestry, etc. **3.** the act of one who or that which hangs; suspension: *a careless hanging of pictures.* —*adj.* **4.** punishable by, deserving, or causing death by hanging: *a hanging crime; a hanging offense.* **5.** inclined to inflict death by hanging: *a hanging jury.* **6.** suspended; pendent; overhanging: *a hanging cliff.* **7.** situated on a steep slope or at a height: *a hanging garden.* **8.** directed downward: *a hanging look.* **9.** made, holding, or suitable for a hanging object. [ME (n., adj.); OE *hangande* (adj.). See HANG, -ING[1], -ING[2]] —**hang′ing·ly,** *adv.*

hang′ing but′tress, a structural member having the form of a buttress but supported by a corbel or cantilever rather than by its own foundation.

hang′ing com′pass, *Naut.* a compass constructed so as to be read from beneath. Also called **telltale compass.**

Hang′ing Gar′dens of Bab′ylon, ornamental gardens planted on the terraces of the ziggurats of ancient Babylon. Cf. **Seven Wonders of the World.**

hang′ing in′den′tion, *Print.* an indention of uniform amount at the beginning of each line except the first, which is of full width.

hang′ing lie′, *Golf.* a lie in which the ball is situated on a slope having a downward incline with respect to the direction that the ball is to be played.

hang′ing post′, a post from which a door, gate, etc., is hung. Also called **hinging post.**

hang′ing rail′, a rail of a door or the like to which a hinge is fastened.

hang′ing scroll′. See under **scroll** (def. 5).

hang′ing step′, a step projecting from a wall with no real or apparent support at its outer end.

hang′ing stile′, 1. the stile of a door, shutter, etc., by which it is hung. **2.** the stile of a window frame from which a casement sash is hung. **3.** See **pulley stile.** Cf. **shutting stile.**

hang′ing val′ley, 1. *Geol.* a valley, the lower end of which opens high above a shore, usually caused by the rapid erosion of a cliff. **2.** a tributary valley, the floor of which is noticeably higher than the floor of the main valley at the place of junction, usually as a result of a difference in glacial erosion.

hang′ing wall′, 1. *Mining.* the underside of the country rock overlying a vein or bed or ore. Cf. **footwall** (def. 1). **2.** *Geol.* a mass of rock overhanging a fault plane.

hang·man (hang′mən), *n., pl.* **-men.** **1.** one who hangs persons condemned to death; public executioner. **2.** a word game in which one player selects a word which the other player must guess by supplying each of its letters: for each incorrect guess a part of a stick figure of a hanged man is drawn. [ME; see HANG, MAN[1]]

hang′man's knot′, a slip noose for hanging a person, usually having eight or nine turns around the rope.

hang·nail (hang′nāl′), *n.* a small piece of partly detached skin at the side or base of the fingernail. Also called **agnail.** [ME *angenayle* corn, OE *angnægl*, equiv. to *ang-* (var. of *enge* narrow, painful; c. G *eng*) + *nægl* callus, NAIL; modern *h-* by assoc. with HANG]

hang·out (hang′out′), *n. Informal.* a place where one lives or frequently visits. [n. use of v. phrase *hang out*]

hang·o·ver (hang′ō′vər), *n.* **1.** something remaining behind from a former period or state of affairs. **2.** the disagreeable physical aftereffects of drunkenness, usually felt several hours after cessation of drinking. [n. use of v. phrase *hang over*]

hang-up (hang′up′), *n. Slang.* a preoccupation, fixation, or psychological block: *His hang-up is rockabilly.* Also, **hang′up′.**

hank (hangk), *n.* **1.** a skein, as of thread or yarn. **2.** a definite length of thread or yarn: *A hank of cotton yarn measures 840 yards.* **3.** a coil, knot, or loop: *a hank of hair.* **4.** *Naut.* a ring, link, or shackle for securing the luff of a staysail or jib to its stay or the luff or head of a gaff sail to the mast or gaff. —*v.t.* **5.** *Naut.* to fasten (a sail) by means of hanks. [ME < Scand; cf. Icel *hönk* hank, coil, skein, clasp; akin to HANG]

Hank (hangk), *n.* a boy's given name, form of **Henry.**

han·ker (hang′kər), *v.i.* to have a restless or incessant longing (often fol. by *after, for,* or an infinitive). [< Flem *hankere(n)*, nasalized freq. of D *haken* to long, hanker] —**han′ker·er,** *n.*

han·ker·ing (hang′kər ing), *n.* a longing; craving. [HANKER + -ING[1]] —**han′ker·ing·ly,** *adv.*

han·key-pan·key (hang′kē pang′kē), *n.* hanky-panky.

han·kie (hang′kē), *n.* hanky.

Han·kow (han′kou′; *Chin.* hän′kō′), *n.* a former city in E Hupeh, in E China: now part of Wuhan.

han·ky (hang′kē), *n., pl.* **-kies.** a handkerchief. Also, **hankie.** [HAN(D)K(ERCHIEF) + -Y[2]]

han·ky-pan·ky (hang′kē pang′kē), *n. Informal.* **1.** unethical behavior; mischief; deceit: *When the bank teller bought an expensive car and house, they suspected there might be some hanky-panky going on.* **2.** foolishness; playful talk or behavior. **3.** *Brit.* **a.** sleight of hand; magic. **b.** jugglery. Also, **hankey-pankey.** [rhyming compound modeled on *hocus-pocus*]

Han·ley (han′lē), *n.* a boy's given name.

Han′ley Hills′, a town in E Missouri. 3308 (1960).

Han·na (han′ə), *n.* **Marcus Alonzo** ("*Mark*"), 1837–1904, U.S. merchant and politician: senator 1897–1904.

Han·nah (han′ə), *n.* **1.** Also, *Douay Bible,* **Anna.** the mother of Samuel. I Sam. 1:20. **2.** a girl's given name.

Han·ni·bal (han′ə bəl), *n.* **1.** 247–183 B.C., Carthaginian general who crossed the Alps and invaded Italy (son of Hamilcar Barca). **2.** a port in NE Missouri, on the Mississippi: Mark Twain's boyhood home. 20,008 (1960). **3.** a boy's given name.

Han·no (han′ō), *n.* **1.** Carthaginian statesman, fl. 3rd century B.C. **2.** a crater in the fourth quadrant of the face of the moon: about 40 miles in diameter.

Han·no·ver (hä nō′vər), *n.* German name of **Hanover.**

Ha·noi (hä′noi′, ha noi′), *n.* a city in and the capital of Vietnam, in the N part, on the Songka River. 1,443,500.

Ha·no·taux (A nô tō′), *n.* **(Albert Auguste) Gabriel** (Al beʀ′ ōgʏst′ gA bʀē el′), 1853–1944, French statesman and historian.

Han·o·ver (han′ō vər), *n.* **1.** a member of the royal family which ruled Great Britain under that name from 1714 to 1901. **2.** German, **Hannover.** a former province in N West Germany; now a district in Lower Saxony. 14,944 sq. mi. **3.** German, **Hannover.** a city in and the capital of Lower Saxony, in N West Germany. 571,300 (1963). **4.** a city in S Pennsylvania. 15,538 (1960). **5.** a town in W New Hampshire. 5649 (1960).

Han·o·ve·ri·an (han′ō vēr′ē ən), *adj.* **1.** of or pertaining to the former ruling house of Hanover. —*n.* **2.** a supporter of the house of Hanover. [HANOVER + -IAN]

Hans (hanz; *Ger.* häns), *n.* a boy's given name, Germanic form of **John.**

Han·sa (han′sə, -zə), *n.* **1.** a company or guild of merchants in a medieval town. **2.** a fee paid to a merchant guild by a new member. **3.** Also called **Han′sa town′, Hansetown.** a town that is a member of the Hanseatic League. **4.** See **Hanseatic League.** [< ML; r. ME *hans, hanze* < MLG *hanse*; c. OE *hōs*, OHG, Goth *hansa* company]

Han·sard (han′sərd), *n.* the official published reports of the debates and proceedings in the British Parliament. [named after Luke *Hansard* (1752–1828) and his descendants who compiled the reports until 1889]

Han′sa yel′low, **1.** a pigment derived from coal tar, characterized chiefly by its brilliant yellow color. **2.** See **spectra yellow.** [after HANSA (? pun on *enhance*)]

Hanse (hans), *n. Rare.* Hansa.

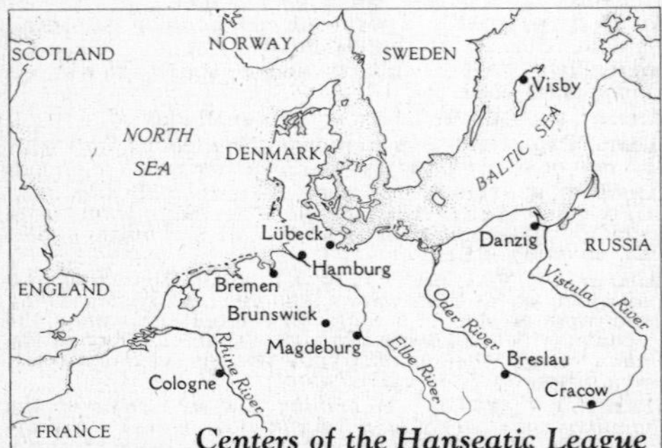

Centers of the Hanseatic League

Han·se·at·ic (han′sē at′ik), *adj.* **1.** of or pertaining to the Hanseatic League or to any of the towns belonging to it. —*n.* **2.** any of the towns belonging to the Hanseatic League. [< ML *Hanseāticus*, equiv. to *hanse* (< MLG; see HANSA) + *-āt-* -ATE[1] + *-icus* -IC]

Han′seat′ic League′, a medieval league of towns of northern Germany and adjacent countries for the promotion and protection of commerce. Also called **Hansa.**

han·sel (han′səl), *n., v.t.,* **-seled, -sel·ing** or (*esp. Brit.*) **-selled, -sel·ling.** handsel.

Han·sel and Gret·el (han′səl ən gret′əl), **1.** one of the fairy tales collected by Jakob and Wilhelm Grimm. **2.** an opera (1893) by Engelbert Humperdinck.

Han·sen (hän′sən), *n.* **1. Pe·ter An·dre·as** (pē′tər än dʀē′äs), 1795–1874, Danish astronomer. **2.** a walled plain in the first quadrant of the face of the moon: about 24 miles in diameter.

Han′sen's disease′, *Pathol.* leprosy. [named after G. H. *Hansen* (1841–1912), Norwegian physician and discoverer of leprosy-causing *Mycobacterium leprae*]

Hanse·town (hans′town′), *n.* Hansa (def. 3).

han·som (han′səm), *n.* a low-hung, two-wheeled, covered vehicle drawn by one horse, for two passengers, the driver being mounted on an elevated seat behind, and the reins running over the roof. Also called **han′som cab′.** [named after J. A. *Hansom* (1803–82), English architect who designed it]

Hansom

Han·son (han′sən), *n.* **Howard** (*Harold*), 1896–1981, U.S. composer.

Han·steen (han′stēn), *n.* a crater in the third quadrant of the face of the moon: about 32 miles in diameter.

hant (hant), *v.t., v.i., n. Dial.* haunt. Also, **ha'nt.**

han't (hānt), *Dial.* **1.** a contraction of **has not.** **2.** a contraction of **have not.**

Hants (hants), *n.* Hampshire (def. 1).

Ha·nuk·kah (hä′nŏŏ kə, -nōō kä′, -kə; *Heb.* ᴋʜä nōō kä′), *n.* a Jewish festival lasting eight days, celebrated from the 25th day of the month of Kislev to the 2nd of Tebet in commemoration of the rededication of the Temple by the Maccabees following their victory over the Syrians under Antiochus IV, characterized chiefly by the lighting of the menorah on each night of the festival. Also, **Chanukah.** Also called **Feast of Dedication, Feast of Lights.** [< Heb: lit., a dedicating]

han·u·man (hun′ŏŏ män′, hä′nŏŏ-; hun′ŏŏ män′, hä′nŏŏ-), *n., pl.* **-mans** for 1. **1.** Also called **entellus.** a langur, *Presbytis* (*Semnopithecus*) *entellus*, held sacred in India. **2.** (*cap.*) *Hindu Myth.* a monkey chief who is a conspicuous figure in the *Ramayana.* [< Hindi *Hanumān* a monkey god, hanuman < Skt *hanuman*, lit., having (big) jaws, deriv. of *hanu* jaw]

Han·yang (hän′yäng′), *n.* a former city in E China: now part of Wuhan.

hao·le (hou′lē, -lā), *n.* (among Polynesian Hawaiians) a non-Polynesian. [< Hawaiian]

hao·ma (hou′mə), *n.* **1.** a leafless, asclepiadaceous vine, *Sarcostemma acidum*, of eastern India, yielding a sour, milky juice. **2.** *Zoroastrianism.* **a.** a sacramental drink prepared with the juice of the haoma plant, milk, and water. **b.** (*cap.*) a god personifying this sacred drink. [< Avestan; c. SOMA[2]]

ha·o·ri (hou′rē; *Jap.* hä ō′ʀē), *n., pl.* **-ris,** *Jap.* **-ri.** a loose, knee-length, Japanese garment resembling a coat. [< Jap]

hap[1] (hap), *n., v.,* **happed, hap·ping.** *Archaic.* —*n.* **1.** one's luck or lot. **2.** an occurrence, happening, or accident. —*v.i.* **3.** to happen: *if it so hap.* [ME < Scand; cf. Icel *happ* luck, chance; akin to OE *gehæp* fit, convenient]

hap[2] (hap, ap), *v.t.,* **happed, hap·ping,** *n. Dial.* —*v.t.* **1.** to cover with or as with a fabric, esp. with a cloak or bedclothes. —*n.* **2.** a covering, esp. one of fabric for warmth. [ME *happe* to cover]

hap·ax le·go·me·non (hap′aks li gom′ə non′, hā′paks), *pl.* ***hap·ax le·go·me·na*** (hap′aks li gom′ə nə, hā′paks). *Greek.* a word or phrase which appears only once in a document or other official paper. [lit., something said only once]

ha'·pen·ny (hā′pə nē, hāp′nē), *n., pl.* **-nies.** *Brit.* halfpenny.

hap·haz·ard (*adj., adv.* hap haz′ərd; *n.* hap′haz′ərd), *adj.* **1.** characterized by lack of order or planning, by irregularity, or by randomness; determined by or dependent on chance; aimless. —*adv.* **2.** haphazardly. —*n.* **3.** mere chance; accident. [HAP[1] + HAZARD] —**hap·haz′ard·ness,** *n.*

hap·haz·ard·ly (hap haz′ərd lē), *adv.* at random; by chance; in a haphazard manner. [HAPHAZARD + -LY]

Haph·si·ba (haf′sə bə), *n. Douay Bible.* Hephzibah (def. 1).

Haph·ta·rah (häf tôr′ə, -tōr′ə; *Heb.* häf tä ʀä′), *n., pl.* **-ta·roth** (-tôr′ōt, -tōr′-; *Heb.* -tä ʀôt′), **-ta·rahs.** *Judaism.* Haftarah.

Ha·pi (hä′pē, ᴋʜä′pē), *n.* Apis (def. 1).

hap·less (hap′lis), *adj.* luckless; unfortunate; unlucky. [HAP[1] + -LESS] —**hap′less·ly,** *adv.* —**hap′less·ness,** *n.*

hap·lite (hap′līt), *n.* aplite. —**hap·lit·ic** (hap lit′ik), *adj.*

haplo-, a learned borrowing from Greek meaning "single," "simple," used in the formation of compound words: *haplology.* Also, *esp. before a vowel,* **hapl-.** [< Gk, comb. form of *haplóos* single, simple; akin to L *simplex*]

hap·log·ra·phy (hap log′rə fē), *n.* the accidental omission of a letter or letter group that should be repeated in writing, as in *tagme* for *tagmeme.* Cf. **dittography.** [HAPLO- + -GRAPHY]

hap·loid (hap′loid), *adj.* Also, **hap·loi′dic.** **1.** single; simple. **2.** *Biol.* pertaining to a single set of chromosomes. —*n.* **3.** *Biol.* an organism or cell having only one complete set of chromosomes, ordinarily half the normal diploid number. [HAPL- + -OID]

hap·lol·o·gy (hap lol′ə jē), *n. Gram.* the syncope of a syllable within a word, as *syllabication* for *syllabification.* [HAPLO- + -LOGY] —**hap·lo·log·ic** (hap′lə loj′ik), *adj.*

hap·lo·pi·a (hap lō′pē ə), *n. Ophthalm.* normal vision (opposed to *diplopia*). [HAPL- + -OPIA]

hap·lo·sis (hap lō′sis), *n. Biol.* the production of haploid chromosome groups during meiosis. [HAPL- + -OSIS]

hap·ly (hap′lē), *adv.* perhaps; by chance. [ME *hapliche.* See HAP[1], -LY]

hap·pen (hap′ən), *v.i.* **1.** to take place; come to pass; occur: *Something interesting is always happening in New York.* **2.** to come to pass by chance; occur without apparent reason or design; chance: *Don't ask me what caused it. It just happened, that's all.* **3.** to have the fortune or lot (to do or be as specified): *I happened to see him on the street.* **4.** to befall, as to a person or thing: *Something dreadful has happened to me.* **5.** to meet or discover by chance (usually fol. by *on* or *upon*): *to happen on a clue to a mystery.* **6.** to be, come, go, etc., casually or by chance: *My friend happened along. I happened in to see him.* [ME *hap(pe)nen.* See HAP[1], -EN[1]]

—**Syn. 1.** betide. HAPPEN, CHANCE, OCCUR refer to the taking place of an event. HAPPEN, which originally denoted the taking place by hap or chance, is now the most general word for coming to pass: *Something has happened.* CHANCE suggests the fortuitousness of an event: *It chanced to rain that day.* OCCUR is often interchangeable with HAPPEN, but is more formal, and is usually more specific as to time and event: *His death occurred the following year.*

hap·pen·ing (hap′ə ning), *n.* **1.** an occurrence or event. **2.** a dramatic or similar performance consisting chiefly of a series of discontinuous events and often involving audience participation or interaction between audience and performers. [HAPPEN + -ING[1]]

hap·pen·stance (hap′ən stans′), *n.* chance; accident. [HAPPEN + (CIRCUM)STANCE]

hap·pi·ly (hap′ə lē), *adv.* **1.** in a happy manner; with pleasure. **2.** by good fortune; luckily; providentially. **3.** with skill; aptly; appropriately: *a happily turned phrase.* [ME; see HAPPY, -LY]

hap·pi·ness (hap′ē nis), *n.* **1.** the quality or state of being happy. **2.** good fortune; pleasure; contentment; joy. **3.** aptness or felicity, as of expression. [HAPPY + -NESS]

—**Syn. 1, 2.** beatitude, blessedness, contentedness, delight, enjoyment, satisfaction. HAPPINESS, BLISS, CONTENTMENT, FELICITY imply an active or passive state of pleasure or pleasurable satisfaction. HAPPINESS results from the possession or attainment of what one considers good: *the happiness of visiting one's family.* BLISS is unalloyed happiness or supreme delight: *the bliss of perfect companionship.* CONTENTMENT is a peaceful kind of happiness in which one rests without desires, even though every wish may not have been gratified: *contentment in one's surroundings.* FELICITY is a formal word for happiness of an especially fortunate or intense kind: *to wish a young couple felicity in life.* —**Ant. 1.** misery.

hap·py (hap′ē), *adj.,* **-pi·er, -pi·est.** **1.** delighted, pleased, or glad, as over a particular thing: *to be happy to see a person.* **2.** characterized by or indicative of pleasure, contentment, or joy: *a happy mood; a happy frame of mind.* **3.** favored by fortune; fortunate or lucky: *a happy, fruitful land.* **4.** apt or felicitous, as actions, utterances, ideas, etc. **5.** obsessed by or quick to use the item indicated (usually used in combination): *a trigger-happy gangster. Everybody is gadget-happy these days.* [ME; see HAP[1], -Y[1]]

—**Syn. 1.** joyous, joyful, blithe, cheerful, merry, contented, gay, blissful, satisfied. **3.** favorable, propitious; successful, prosperous. See **fortunate. 4.** appropriate, fitting, opportune, pertinent. —**Ant. 1.** sad.

Hap·py (hap′ē), *n.* a girl's given name.

hap·py-go-luck·y (hap′ē gō luk′ē), *adj.* **1.** trusting cheerfully to luck; happily unworried or unconcerned, esp. with reference to future events or practical matters; easygoing. —*adv.* **2.** *Archaic.* by mere chance; haphazardly.

hap′py hunt′ing ground′, **1.** the Indian warrior's heaven. **2.** a place where one finds in abundance that which one needs or desires, or where one may pursue an activity without restriction: *New England attics are happy hunting grounds for antique collectors.*

hap′py war′rior, **1.** one who is undiscouraged by difficulties or opposition. **2.** (*cap.*) a nickname of Alfred E. Smith.

Haps·burg (haps′bûrg; *Ger.* häps′bŏŏʀᴋʜ′), *n.* a German princely family, prominent since the 11th century, which has furnished sovereigns to the Holy Roman Empire, Austria, Spain, etc. Also, **Habsburg.**

hap·ten (hap′ten), *n. Immunol.* a partial antigen that is incapable of stimulating antibody production when injected into an animal and that reacts with an antibody only within an artificial environment. Also, **hap·tene** (hap′tēn). [< G < Gk *hápt(ein)* to grasp + *-ēn(os)* -ENE]

hap·tics (hap′tiks), *n.* (*construed as sing.*) the branch of psychology that investigates cutaneous sense data. [*haptic* < Gk *haptik(ós)* able to grasp or perceive, equiv. to *hápt(ein)* (to) grasp, sense, perceive + *-ikos* -IC; see -ICS] —**hap′tic, hap′ti·cal,** *adj.*

hap·tom·e·ter (hap tom′i tər), *n.* a mechanical device for measuring the sense of touch. [< Gk *hápt(ein)* (to) sense, touch, grasp + -O- + -METER]

Har·a·han (har′ə han′), *n.* a town in SE Louisiana. 9275 (1960).

ha·ra-ki·ri (här′ə kēr′ē, har′ə-, har′ē-), *n.* **1.** ceremonial suicide by ripping open the abdomen with a dagger or knife: formerly practiced in Japan by members of the warrior class when disgraced or sentenced to death. **2.** suicide or any suicidal action; a self-destructive act: *political hara-kiri.* Also, **hari-kari.** [< Jap, equiv. to *hara* belly + *kiri* cut]

ha·ram (hâr′əm, har′-), *n.* harem.

ha·rangue (hə rang′), *n., v.,* **-rangued, -rangu·ing.** —*n.* **1.** a long, passionate, and vehement speech, esp. one delivered before a public gathering. **2.** any long, pompous speech or writing of a tediously hortatory or didactic nature; a sermonizing lecture or discourse. **3.** a scolding or an intense and heated verbal attack. —*v.t.* **4.** to address in a harangue. —*v.i.* **5.** to deliver a harangue. [< MF < ML *harenga* a meeting, speech made there < Gmc; cf. OHG, OS, OE *hring* RING[1]; r. late ME *arang* < MF *arenge*] —**ha·rangue′ful,** *adj.* —**ha·rangu′er,** *n.*

—**Syn. 1.** See **speech.**

Ha·rap·pa (hə rap′ə), *n.* **1.** a village in Pakistan: site or successive cities of the Indus valley civilization. **2.** a Bronze Age culture that flourished in the Indus valley of Pakistan.

Ha·rap·pan (hə rap′ən), *adj.* of or pertaining to the Bronze Age culture of Harappa. [HARAPP(A) + -AN]

Ha·rar (här′ər), *n.* a city in E Ethiopia. 38,000 (est. 1962). Also, **Harrar.**

har·ass (har′əs, hə ras′), *v.t.* **1.** to trouble by repeated attacks, incursions, etc., as in war or hostilities; harry; raid. **2.** to disturb persistently; torment, as with troubles, cares, etc.; bother continually; pester; persecute. [< F *harass(er)* (to) tire out, wear down, based on OF *harer* to sic < OHG *harēn* to cry out] —**har′ass·a·ble,** *adj.* —**har′ass·er,** *n.* —**har′ass·ing·ly,** *adv.* —**har′ass·ment,** *n.*
—**Syn. 1.** molest. **2.** badger, vex, plague, torture, hector. See **worry.**

har·assed (har′əst, hə rast′), *adj.* **1.** fatigued; careworn or burdened, as by incessant critical attacks, problems, or annoyances: *a harassed witness anticipating more questioning.* **2.** expressing vexation: *a harassed, angry cry.* [HARASS + -ED²] —**har′assed·ly,** *adv.*

Har·bin (här′bēn′, -bin), *n.* a city in central Manchuria, in NE China. 1,552,000 (est. 1957). Also called **Pinkiang.**

har·bin·ger (här′bin jər), *n.* **1.** a person who goes before and makes known the approach of another; herald. **2.** anything that foreshadows a future event; omen; sign: *Frost is a harbinger of winter.* **3.** one sent in advance of troops, a royal train, etc., to provide or secure lodgings and other accommodations. —*v.t.* **4.** to act as harbinger to; herald the coming of. [late ME *herbenger,* nasalized var. of *herbegere* < MF, dissimilated var. of *herberg(i)ere* (nom.) host, equiv. to *herberge* shelter (< Gmc; see HARBOR) + *-iere* -ER²] —**har′bin·ger·ship′,** *n.*

har·bin·ger-of-spring (här′bin jər əv spring′), *n., pl.* **har·bin·gers-of-spring.** a North American, umbelliferous herb, *Erigenia bulbosa,* having white flowers that bloom early in the spring.

Har·bo·na (här bō′nə), *n.* one of the seven eunuchs who served in the court of King Ahasuerus. Esther 1:10.

har·bor (här′bər), *n.* **1.** a portion of a body of water along the shore deep enough for anchoring a ship, and so situated with respect to coastal features, whether natural or artificial, as to provide protection from winds, waves, and currents. **2.** such a body of water having docks or port facilities. **3.** any place of shelter or refuge: *The old inn was a harbor for tired travelers.* —*v.t.* **4.** to give shelter to; offer refuge to: *They harbored the refugees who streamed across the borders.* **5.** to conceal; hide: *to harbor fugitives.* **6.** to keep or hold in the mind; maintain; entertain: *to harbor suspicion.* **7.** to house or contain. **8.** to shelter (a vessel), as in a harbor. —*v.i.* **9.** (of a vessel) to take shelter in a harbor. Also, *esp. Brit.,* **harbour.** [ME *herber(we), herberge,* OE *herebeorg* lodgings, quarters (*here* army + *(ge)beorg* refuge); c. G *Herberge*] —**har′bor·er,** *n.* —**har′bor·less,** *adj.* —**har′bor·ous,** *adj.* —**har′bor·side′,** *adv.* —**har′bor·ward,** *adv.*
—**Syn. 1.** HARBOR, HAVEN, PORT indicate a shelter for ships. A HARBOR may be naturally or artificially constructed or improved: *a fine harbor on the eastern coast.* A HAVEN is usually a natural harbor which can be utilized by ships as a place of safety; the word is common in poetic use: *a haven in time of storm; a haven of refuge.* A PORT is a HARBOR viewed esp. in its commercial relations, though it is frequently applied in the meaning of HARBOR or HAVEN also: *a thriving port; any old port in a storm.* **3.** asylum, sanctuary, retreat. **4.** protect, lodge. **6.** See **cherish.**

har·bor·age (här′bər ij), *n.* **1.** shelter for vessels, as that provided by a harbor. **2.** shelter or lodging. **3.** a place of shelter. Also, *esp. Brit.,* **harbourage.** [HARBOR + -AGE]

har′bor deck′, *Naut.* either of the two narrow fore-and-aft weather decks below and on each side of the turret deck in a turret-deck vessel.

har′bor furl′, *Naut.* a furl given to a square sail at the end of a voyage, made by gathering all loose canvas in toward the mast in a neat roll. Also called **har′bor stow′.**

har′bor mas′ter, an official who supervises operations in a harbor area and administers its rules.

har′bor seal′, a small, spotted seal, *Phoca vitulina,* of the Atlantic coasts of North America and Europe and the Pacific coast of northern North America.

har·bour (här′bər), *n., v.t., v.i. Chiefly Brit.* harbor. —**har′bour·er,** *n.* —**har′bour·less,** *adj.* —**har′bour·ous,** *adj.* —**har′bour·side′,** *adv.* —**har′bour·ward,** *adv.*

har·bour·age (här′bər ij), *n. Chiefly Brit.* harborage.

hard (härd), *adj.* **1.** not soft; solid and firm to the touch; unyielding to pressure and impenetrable or almost impenetrable. **2.** firmly formed; tight: *a hard knot.* **3.** difficult to do or accomplish; fatiguing; troublesome: *a hard task.* **4.** difficult or troublesome with respect to an action, situation, person, etc.: *hard to please; a hard time.* **5.** difficult to deal with, manage, control, overcome, or understand: *a hard problem.* **6.** involving a great deal of effort, energy, or persistence: *hard labor; hard study.* **7.** performing or carrying on work with great effort, energy, or persistence: *a hard worker.* **8.** vigorous or violent in force; severe: *a hard rain; a hard fall.* **9.** bad; unendurable; unbearable: *hard luck.* **10.** oppressive; harsh; rough: *hard treatment.* **11.** austere; severe: *a hard winter; the hard times of the Depression.* **12.** harsh or severe in dealing with others: *a hard master.* **13.** difficult to explain away; undeniable: *hard facts.* **14.** harsh or unfriendly; resentful: *hard feelings; Hard words were exchanged.* **15.** of stern judgment or close examination; searching: *a hard look.* **16.** lacking delicacy or softness; not blurred or diffused; clear and distinct; sharp; harsh: *a hard line; a hard, bright light; hard features; a hard face.* **17.** (of a photograph) contrasty. **18.** severe or rigorous in terms: *a hard bargain.* **19.** sternly realistic; dispassionate; unsentimental: *a hard, practical man; a hard view of life.* **20.** incorrigible; disreputable; tough: *a hard character.* **21.** *Chiefly Dial.* niggardly; stingy. **22.** (used to emphasize money as currency, distinguished from checks, securities, promissory notes, or other negotiable instruments): *hard cash.* **23.** (of paper money or a monetary system) supported by sufficient gold reserves and easily convertible into the currency of a foreign nation: *hard currency.* **24.** (of alcoholic beverages) **a.** containing more than 22.5 percent alcohol by volume, as whiskey and brandy as opposed to beer and wine. **b.** strong; intoxicating: *hard cider.* **25.** (of water) containing mineral salts which interfere with the action of soap. **26.** (of bread and baked goods) **a.** having a firm, crisp crust or texture: *hard rolls.* **b.** stale or tough. **27.** (of a fabric) having relatively little nap; smooth: *Silk is a harder fabric than wool or cotton.* **28.** (of the landing of a space vehicle) destroying or damaging the vehicle or its contents: *a hard landing on the moon.* **29.** (of a missile base) equipped to launch missiles from underground silos. **30.** (of a missile) capable of being launched from an underground silo. **31.** *Mil.* being underground and strongly protected from nuclear bombardment. **32.** *Rocketry.* (of a landing) made while traveling speeds of 100 to 300 miles per hour. **33.** *Agric.* noting wheats with high gluten content, milled for a bread flour as contrasted with pastry flour. **34.** *Phonet.* **a.** fortis. **b.** (of *c* and *g*) pronounced as (k) in *come* and (g) in *go,* rather than as in *cent, cello, suspicion, gem,* or *beige.* **c.** (of consonants in Slavic languages) not palatalized. Cf. **soft** (def. 24). **35.** *Ropemaking.* noting a lay having a considerable angle to the axis of the rope; short. **36. hard of hearing,** partly deaf: *Modern aids are a boon for the hard of hearing. She has been hard of hearing for years.* **37. hard up,** *Informal.* **a.** urgently in need of money. **b.** feeling a lack or need: *The country is hard up for technicians and doctors.*
—*adv.* **38.** with great exertion; with vigor or violence; strenuously: *to work hard.* **39.** earnestly, intently, or critically: *to look hard at a thing.* **40.** harshly or severely. **41.** so as to be solid, tight, or firm: *frozen hard.* **42.** with strong force or impact: *She tripped and came down hard on her back.* **43.** in a deeply affected manner; with genuine sorrow or remorse: *She took it very hard when they told her of his death.* **44.** closely; immediately; in immediate proximity: *Failure and defeat seemed hard at hand. The decision to ban students from the concerts followed hard on the heels of the riot.* **45.** to an unreasonable or extreme degree; excessively; immoderately: *He's hitting the bottle pretty hard.* **46.** *Naut.* closely, fully, or to the extreme limit: *hard aport.* **47. be hard on,** to deal harshly with; be stern: *You are being too hard on him.* **48. hard alee!** *Naut.* a command to put the tiller hard over to the lee side to head the vessel into the wind: *Ready about! Hard alee!* **49. hard by,** in close proximity to; near: *The house is hard by the river.* **50. hard over,** *Naut.* as far to one side as possible: *They put the helm hard over in an attempt to swerve.* **51. hard put to it,** in great perplexity or difficulty; at a loss: *We were hard put to it to finish the examination in the required length of time.* Also, **hard put.**
—*n.* **52.** *Naut.* a firm or paved beach or slope convenient for hauling vessels out of the water. **53.** *Brit.* **a.** a firm or solid beach or foreshore. **b.** a firm landing, jetty, or road across or adjoining the foreshore. **54.** *Brit. Slang.* See **hard labor.** [ME; OE *heard;* c. D *hard,* G *hart,* Icel *harthr,* Goth *hardus;* akin to Gk *kratýs* strong]
—**Syn. 1.** inflexible, rigid, unyielding, resisting, adamantine, flinty. See **firm¹. 3.** toilsome, burdensome, wearisome, exhausting. HARD, DIFFICULT both describe something resistant to one's efforts or one's endurance. HARD is the general word: *hard times; It was hard to endure the severe weather.* DIFFICULT means not easy, and particularly denotes that which requires special effort or skill: *a difficult task.* **5.** complex, complicated, perplexing, puzzling, intricate, knotty, tough. **6.** arduous, onerous, laborious. **8.** stormy, tempestuous. **10.** severe, rigorous, grinding, cruel, merciless, unsparing. **12.** stern, austere, strict, exacting, relentless, obdurate, adamant; unyielding, unpitying. HARD, CALLOUS, UNFEELING, UNSYMPATHETIC imply a lack of interest in, feeling for, or sympathy with others. HARD implies insensibility, either natural or acquired, so that the plight of others makes no impression on one: *a hard taskmaster.* CALLOUS may mean the same or that one is himself insensitive to hurt as the result of continued repression and indifference: *a callous answer; callous to criticism.* UNFEELING implies natural inability to feel with and for others: *an unfeeling and thoughtless remark.* UNSYMPATHETIC implies an indifference which makes no attempt to pity, etc.: *unsympathetic toward distress.* **13.** incontrovertible. **14.** unkind, unpleasant. —**Ant. 1.** soft. **3–6.** easy.

hard-and-fast (härd′ᵊn fast′, -fäst′), *adj.* strongly binding; not to be set aside or violated: *hard-and-fast rules.* —**hard′-and-fast′ness,** *n.*

hard-bake (härd′bāk′), *n. Brit.* a candy made of molasses, sugar, and butter mixed with almonds.

hard·ball (härd′bôl′), *n.* baseball as distinguished from softball. [HARD + BALL¹]

hard-bit·ten (härd′bit′ᵊn), *adj.* **1.** tough; stubborn. **2.** conditioned by battle or struggle; accustomed to conflict or difficulty and prepared for any contingency: *a hard-bitten army.* **3.** grim or severe in judgment or attitude: *a hard-bitten old teacher.* **4.** hard-boiled (defs. 2, 3). **5.** (of an animal) tending to bite vigorously or savagely.

hard·board (härd′bōrd′, -bôrd′), *n.* a material made from wood fibers compressed into sheets, having many household and industrial uses. [HARD + BOARD]

hard-boil (härd′boil′), *v.t.* to boil (an egg) until hard.

hard-boiled (härd′boild′), *adj.* **1.** boiled until hard, as an egg (distinguished from *soft-boiled*). **2.** tough; unsentimental: *a hard-boiled, vice-squad detective.* **3.** realistic; marked by a direct, clear-headed approach: *a hard-boiled appraisal of the foreign situation.* [HARD + BOILED] —**hard′-boiled′ness,** *n.*

hard′ bop′, a style of modern jazz following cool jazz in the late 1950's, marked by a harsh aggressive delivery and a strong blues feeling.

hard·bound (härd′bound′), *adj.* (of a book) bound with a stiff cover; casebound. Cf. **paperback.** [HARD + BOUND¹]

hard′ can′dy, candy, often fruit flavored, made by boiling together sugar and corn syrup.

hard′ ci′der. See under **cider.**

hard′ clam′, a quahog.

hard′ coal′, anthracite.

hard′ cop′y, **1.** *Print.* a form of readable writing or communications, as that which is typed or printed, as distinguished from perforated paper tape or cards, electromagnetic tape, or other unreadable, nonalphabetic, coded matter in a form suitable for actuating a machine. **2.** copy that is finished and ready for the printer.

hard′ core′, **1.** the permanent, dedicated, and completely faithful nucleus of a group or movement, as of a political party. **2.** an unyielding or intransigent element in a social or organizational structure; the part of a group which is difficult to deal with and resistant to change.

hard-core (härd′kōr′, -kôr′), *adj.* **1.** of, involving, or pertaining to a person or group in the hard core. **2.** obvious; blatant: *hard-core pornography.*

hard·core (härd′kōr′, -kôr′), *n.* a fill composed of small, hard lumps of rubble, brickbats, etc., used beneath foundations, roads, etc. [HARD + CORE¹]

hard′ court′, an outdoor tennis court having a concrete or asphalt surface. Cf. **clay court, grass court.**

hard·cov·er (härd′kuv′ər), *n.* **1.** a hardbound book: *Hardcovers are more durable than paperbacks.* —*adj.* **2.** hardbound: *a hardcover series.* **3.** noting or pertaining to hardcover books: *The hardcover sales were beyond expectations.* Cf. **paperback.** [HARD + COVER] —**hard′-cov′ered,** *adj.*

hard′ din′kum, *Australian Informal.* hard work; a difficult task.

hard′ disk′, *Computer Technol.* a rigid magnetic disk, often permanently mounted in a computer, on which a large quantity of data can be stored. Cf. **disk** (def. 8).

Har·de·ca·nute (här′də kə no͞ot′, -nyo͞ot′), *n.* 1019?–42, king of Denmark 1035–42, king of England 1040–42 (son of Canute). Also, **Har′di·ca·nute′, Harthacnut.**

hard·en (här′dᵊn), *v.t.* **1.** to make hard or harder: *to harden steel.* **2.** to make pitiless or unfeeling: *to harden one's heart.* **3.** to make rigid or unyielding; stiffen: *The rigors of poverty hardened his personality, preventing its natural development.* **4.** to strengthen or confirm, esp. with reference to character, intentions, feelings, etc.; reinforce. **5.** to make hardy, robust, or capable of endurance; toughen. **6.** *Mil.* to reinforce the structure of (a military or strategic installation) to protect it from nuclear bombardment. —*v.i.* **7.** to become hard or harder. **8.** to become pitiless or unfeeling. **9.** to become rigid or unyielding; stiffen: *His personality hardened over the years.* **10.** to become confirmed or strengthened: *He hardened early to a life of crime. His resistance hardened.* **11.** to become inured or toughened: *The troops hardened under constant fire.* **12.** *Com.* (of a market, prices, etc.) **a.** to cease to fluctuate; firm: *When the speculators withdrew from the market the prices hardened.* **b.** to rise higher. [ME; see HARD, -EN¹] —**hard′en·a·bil′i·ty,** *n.* —**hard′en·a·ble,** *adj.*
—**Syn. 1.** solidify, indurate; petrify, ossify. **4.** fortify, steel, brace, nerve. —**Ant. 1.** soften. **4.** weaken.

Har·den (här′dᵊn), *n.* **1. Sir Arthur,** 1865–1940, English biochemist: Nobel prize 1929. **2.** a boy's given name.

Har·den·berg (här′dᵊn berkн′), *n.* **Frie·drich von** (frē′drikн fən) ("*Novalis*"), 1772–1801, German poet.

hard·ened (här′dᵊnd), *adj.* **1.** made or become hard or harder. **2.** pitiless; unfeeling. **3.** confirmed; firmly established; inveterate; unlikely to change: *a hardened criminal.* **4.** inured; toughened: *a hardened trooper.* **5.** rigid; unyielding: *a hardened attitude.* **6.** (of a missile base) equipped to launch missiles from underground silos. **7.** (of a missile) capable of being launched from an underground silo. [HARDEN + -ED²]

hard·en·er (här′dᵊnər), *n.* **1.** one who or that which hardens. **2.** a substance mixed with paint or other protective covering to make the finish harder or more durable. **3.** *Photog.* a chemical for raising the melting point of an emulsion. [HARDEN + -ER¹]

hard·en·ing (här′dᵊning), *n.* **1.** a material which hardens another, as an alloy added to iron to make steel. **2.** the process of becoming hard or rigid. [HARDEN + -ING¹]

hard-fa·vored (härd′fā′vərd), *adj.* having a hard, unpleasant countenance. Also, *esp. Brit.,* **hard′-fa′voured.** —**hard′-fa′vored·ness;** *esp. Brit.,* **hard′-fa′voured·ness,** *n.*

hard-fea·tured (härd′fē′chərd), *adj.* having stern, harsh, or unattractive features. —**hard′-fea′tured·ness,** *n.*

hard′ fern′. See **deer fern.**

hard-fist·ed (härd′fis′tid), *adj.* **1.** stingy; miserly; close-fisted. **2.** tough-minded; ruthless: *hard-fisted gangsters.* **3.** having hard or strong hands, as a laborer. Also, **hard′fist′ed.** —**hard′-fist′ed·ness, hard′fist′ed·ness,** *n.*

hard′ goods′, durable merchandise, as automobiles, furniture, home appliances, etc. Cf. **soft goods.**

hard′ ground′, an etching ground applied to the surface of a plate held over a small flame and spread by a dabber or brayer. Cf. **soft ground** (def. 1).

hard·hack (härd′hak′), *n.* **1.** a woolly-leaved, North American, rosaceous shrub, *Spiraea tomentosa,* having terminal panicles of rose-colored or white flowers. **2.** See **shrubby cinquefoil.** [HARD + HACK¹]

hard-hand·ed (härd′han′did), *adj.* **1.** having hands hardened by toil. **2.** oppressive; tyrannical; cruel: *a hard-handed ruler.* Also, **hard′hand′ed.** —**hard′-hand′ed·ness, hard′hand′ed·ness,** *n.*

hard′ hat′, a protective helmet of metal or plastic, esp. as worn by construction workers.

hard-hat (härd′hat′), *n. Informal.* **1.** a construction worker, esp. a member of a construction workers' union. **2.** Also, **hard′ hat′, hard′hat′.** any working-class conservative, esp. one who dislikes modern liberals, long-haired students, etc.

hard′ head′, *Metal.* semirefined tin containing iron.

hard·head¹ (härd′hed′), *n.* **1.** a shrewd, practical person. **2.** a blockhead. **3.** a cyprinid fish, *Mylopharodon conocephalus,* found in the fresh waters of California. **4.** the Atlantic croaker. See under **croaker** (def. 2). **5.** See **hardhead sponge. 6.** knapweed. [HARD + HEAD]

hard·head² (härd′hed′), *n.* an alloyed silver coin of Scotland, issued in the 16th and 17th centuries, equal to one and one-half pence and later to twopence. Also called **lion.** [perh. (by folk etymology) < F *hardit,* after Philip III, named le *Hardi* the Bold (1245–85), king of France, who first issued the coin]

hard-head·ed (härd′hed′id), *adj.* **1.** not easily moved or deceived; practical; shrewd: *a hard-headed businessman.* **2.** obstinate; stubborn; willful. Also, **hard′head′ed.** —**hard′-head′ed·ly, hard′head′ed·ly,** *adv.* —**hard′-head′ed·ness, hard′head′ed·ness,** *n.*

hard′head sponge′, any of several commercial sponges, as *Spongia officinalis dura,* of the West Indies and Central America, having a harsh, elastic, resilient, fibrous skeleton.

hard-heart·ed (härd′här′tid), *adj.* unfeeling; unmerciful; pitiless. Also, **hard′heart′ed.** [ME *hard-herted.* See HARD, -HEARTED] —**hard′-heart′ed·ly, hard′heart′ed·ly,** *adv.* —**hard′-heart′ed·ness, hard′heart′ed·ness,** *n.*

har·die (här′dē), *n. Metalworking.* hardy[2].

har·di·hood (här′dē ho͝od′), *n.* **1.** hardy spirit or character; determination to survive; fortitude: *The hardihood of early settlers.* **2.** strength; power; vigor: *the hardihood of youth.* **3.** boldness or daring; courage: *hardihood of mind.* **4.** audacity; rashness. [HARDY[1] + -HOOD]

har·di·ly (här′dᵊlē), *adv.* in a hardy manner: *The plants thrived hardily.* [ME; see HARDY[1], -LY]

hard′ im′age, an image, as on a television screen, that shows excessive contrast between light and dark regions.

har·di·ment (här′dē mənt), *n. Archaic.* hardihood. [ME < OF; see HARDY[1], -MENT]

Har·din (här′dᵊn, -din), *n.* a town in S Montana. 2789 (1960).

har·di·ness (här′dē nis), *n.* **1.** the state or quality of being hardy; capacity for enduring or sustaining hardship, privation, etc.; capability of surviving under unfavorable conditions. **2.** courage; boldness; audacity. [ME; see HARDY[1], -NESS]

Har·ding (här′diŋ), *n.* **1. Warren G(amaliel),** 1865–1923, 29th president of the U.S. 1921–23. **2.** a crater in the second quadrant of the face of the moon: about 14 miles in diameter. **3.** a boy's given name.

hard′ knocks′, *U.S. Informal.* adversity or hardships.

hard′ la′bor, compulsory labor imposed upon criminals in addition to imprisonment, generally not exceeding ordinary labor in severity or amount.

hard-laid (härd′lād′), *adj. Ropemaking.* noting a rope the lay of which is at a relatively great angle to its axis; short-laid.

hard′ lines′, *Chiefly Brit. Slang.* tough luck; bad breaks.

hard·ly (härd′lē), *adv.* **1.** barely; almost not at all: *hardly any; hardly ever.* **2.** not quite: *That is hardly true.* **3.** with little likelihood: *He will hardly come now.* **4.** *Brit.* harshly or severely. **5.** *Rare.* hard. [ME; OE *heardlice.* See HARD, -LY]
—**Syn. 1.** HARDLY, BARELY, SCARCELY imply a narrow margin by which performance was, is, or will be achieved. HARDLY, though often interchangeable with SCARCELY and BARELY, usually emphasizes the idea of the difficulty involved: *We could hardly endure the winter.* BARELY emphasizes the narrowness of the margin of safety, "only just and no more": *We barely succeeded.* SCARCELY implies a very narrow margin, below satisfactory performance: *He can scarcely read.*
—**Usage.** HARDLY, BARELY, and SCARCELY all have a negative connotation, and the use of any of them with a supplementary negative is considered nonstandard, as in *I can't hardly wait* for *I can hardly wait.*

hard′ ma′ple, *U.S.* the sugar maple, *Acer saccharum.*

hard′ mass′, **1.** *Jewelry.* a hard glass used for imitating gemstones. **2.** (not in technical use) **a.** any glass for imitating gemstones, esp. emerald. **b.** any of certain synthetic gemstones. Also, **hard′ masse′.**

hard·ness (härd′nis), *n.* **1.** the state or quality of being hard: *the hardness of ice.* **2.** a relative degree or extent of this quality: *Wood of a desirable hardness.* **3.** that quality in impure water which is imparted by the presence of dissolved salts, esp. calcium sulfate or bicarbonate. **4.** *Mineral.* the comparative capacity of a substance to scratch or be scratched by another. Cf. **Mohs scale. 5.** *Metall.* the measured resistance of a metal to indention, abrasion, deformation, or machining. [ME *hardnes,* OE *heardnes.* See HARD, -NESS]

hard′ news′, *Journalism.* serious news of widespread import, concerning politics, foreign affairs, or the like, as distinguished from routine news items, feature stories, human-interest stories, etc.

hard-nosed (härd′nōzd′), *adj.* hard-headed or tough; unsentimentally practical: *a hard-nosed businessman.*

hard-of-hear·ing (härd′əv hēr′iŋ), *adj.* of, pertaining to, or having defective hearing.

Har·douin-Man·sart (ᴀʀ dwan′mäɴ sᴀʀ′), *n.* **Jules** (zhʏl). See **Mansart, Jules Hardouin-.** Also, **Hardouin′-Man·sard′.**

hard′ pal′ate. See under **palate** (def. 1).

hard·pan (härd′pan′), *n. Chiefly U.S.* **1.** any layer of firm detrital matter, as of clay, underlying soft soil. **2.** hard, unbroken ground. **3.** the fundamental or basic aspect of anything; solid foundation; underlying reality: *the hardpan of mathematical theory.* [HARD + PAN[1]]

hard′ paste′, true porcelain, made with kaolin, feldspar, quartz, or petuntse. French, **pâte dure.** Cf. **soft paste.**

hard-pressed (härd′prest′), *adj.* heavily burdened or oppressed, as by overwork; harried; put upon.

hard′-rock geol′ogy (härd′rok′), geology dealing with igneous or metamorphic rocks. Cf. **soft-rock geology.**

hard′ rub′ber, rubber vulcanized with a large amount of sulfur, usually 25–35 percent, to render it stiff and comparatively inflexible.

hards (härdz), *n.pl.* the refuse or coarser parts of flax or hemp, separated in hackling. Also, **hurds.** [ME *herdes,* OE *heordan*]

hard′ sauce′, a creamed mixture of butter and confectioners' sugar, often with flavoring and cream, used on puddings, pies, etc.

hard·scrab·ble (härd′skrab′əl), *adj.* providing meagerly in return for much effort: *the hardscrabble existence of mountainside farmers.* [HARD + SCRABBLE]

hard′ sell′, a method of advertising or selling which is direct, forceful, and insistent; high-pressure salesmanship (opposed to *soft sell*).

hard-set (härd′set′), *adj.* **1.** firmly or rigidly set; fixed: *a hard-set smile.* **2.** in a difficult position: *The army was hard-set for quite awhile before their supplies came.* **3.** determined; obstinate.

hard-shell (härd′shel′), *adj.* Also, **hard′-shelled′. 1.** having a firm, hard shell, as a crab in its normal state; not having recently molted. **2.** rigid or uncompromising. —*n.* **3.** See **hard-shell crab.**

hard′-shell clam′, quahog.

hard′-shell crab′, a crab, esp. an edible crab, that has not recently molted, therefore having a hard shell.

hard·ship (härd′ship), *n.* **1.** a condition that is difficult to endure; suffering; deprivation; oppression: *a life of hardship.* **2.** an instance or cause of this; something hard to bear, as a deprivation, lack of comfort, constant toil or danger, etc.: *They faced bravely the many hardships of frontier life.* [ME; see HARD, -SHIP]
—**Syn. 1.** trouble, affliction, burden, suffering, misfortune. HARDSHIP, PRIVATION, AUSTERITY are terms for something hard to endure. HARDSHIP applies to a circumstance in which excessive and painful effort of some kind is required, as enduring acute discomfort from cold, battling over rough terrain, and the like. PRIVATION has particular reference to lack of food, clothing, and other necessities or comforts. AUSTERITY not only includes the ideas of privation and hardship but also implies deliberate control of emotional reactions to these. —**Ant. 1.** ease.

hard′ sign′, **1.** the Cyrillic letter Ъ, ъ as used in Russian to indicate that the preceding consonant is not palatalized: not in official use since 1918. **2.** the same symbol used for the back vowel of Old Slavic from which this Russian usage and phenomenon are historically derived.

hard′ sol′der, a solder fusing at temperatures above 1200°F. Also called **brazing alloy.** Cf. **soft solder.**

hard-spun (härd′spun′), *adj.* (of yarn) compactly twisted in spinning.

hard·tack (härd′tak′), *n.* a hard, saltless biscuit, formerly much used aboard ships and for army rations. Also called **pilot biscuit, pilot bread, ship biscuit, ship bread.** [HARD + TACK[2]]

hard·tail (härd′tāl′), *n., pl.* **-tails,** (*esp. collectively*) **-tail.** See **blue runner.** [HARD + TAIL[1]]

hard′ tick′, any of numerous ticks of the family *Ixodidae,* having a hard dorsal shield and mouth parts which project from the head. Cf. **soft tick.**

hard·top (härd′top′), *n.* a style of car having a rigid metal top and no center posts between windows. Also called **hard′top convert′ible.** [HARD + TOP[1]]

hard′ tube′, *Electronics.* a very highly evacuated vacuum tube. Cf. **soft tube.**

hard·wall (härd′wôl′), *n.* a type of gypsum plaster used as a basecoat. [HARD + WALL]

hard·ware (härd′wâr′), *n.* **1.** metalware, as tools, locks, hinges, cutlery, etc. **2.** the mechanical equipment necessary for conducting an activity, usually distinguished from the theory and design which make the activity possible. **3.** weapons and combat equipment. **4.** *Computer Technol.* any electronic or mechanical equipment used in association with data processing. Cf. **software.** [HARD + WARE[1]]

hard′ wheat′, a wheat, as durum wheat, characterized by flinty, dark-colored kernels that yield a flour used in making bread, spaghetti, macaroni, etc.

Hard·wicke (härd′wik), *n.* **Sir Cedric (Webster),** 1893–1964, English actor.

hard·wood (härd′wo͝od′), *n.* **1.** the hard, compact wood or timber of various trees, as the oak, cherry, maple, mahogany, etc. **2.** a tree yielding such wood. —*adj.* **3.** made or constructed of hardwood: *a hardwood floor.* [HARD + WOOD[1]]

har·dy[1] (här′dē), *adj.,* **-di·er, -di·est. 1.** capable of enduring fatigue, hardship, exposure, etc.; sturdy; strong: *hardy animals.* **2.** (of plants) able to withstand the cold of winter in the open air. **3.** requiring great physical courage, vigor, or endurance: *the hardiest sports.* **4.** bold or daring; courageous: *hardy explorers.* **5.** unduly bold; presumptuous; foolhardy. [ME *hardi* < OF, ptp. of **hardir* to harden, make brave < Gmc; cf. Goth *-hardjan,* OE *hierdan,* etc.]
—**Syn. 1.** vigorous, robust, hale, stout, sound. **4.** intrepid, resolute, brave. —**Ant. 1.** weak. **4.** timid.

har·dy[2] (här′dē), *n., pl.* **-dies.** a chisel or fuller with a square shank for insertion into a square hole (**har′dy hole′**) in a blacksmith's anvil. [HARD + -Y[2]]

Har·dy (här′dē), *n.* **1. Godfrey Harold,** 1877–1947, English mathematician. **2. Oliver,** 1892–1957, U.S. motion-picture actor and comedian. **3. Thomas,** 1840–1928, English novelist and poet. **4.** a boy's given name.

har′dy agera′tum, the mistflower.

har′dy amaryl′lis, a showy, bulbous herb, *Lycoris squamigera,* of Japan, having fragrant, rose-lilac flowers nearly three inches wide.

hare (hâr), *n., pl.* **hares,** (*esp. collectively*) **hare,** *v.,* **hared, har·ing.** —*n.* **1.** any of several rodentlike mammals of the genus *Lepus,* of the family *Leporidae,* having long ears, a divided upper lip, and lengthened hind limbs adapted for leaping. **2.** any of the larger species of this genus, as distinguished from certain of the smaller ones known as rabbits. **3.** any of various similar animals of the same family. **4.** (*cap.*) *Astron.* the constellation Lepus. **5.** the player pursued in the game of hare and hounds. —*v.i.* **6.** *Chiefly Brit.* to run fast. [ME; OE *hara;* c. Dan *hare;* akin to G *Hase* hare, OE *hasu* gray] —**hare′like′,** *adj.*

Hare (hâr), *n.* **Augustus John Cuth·bert** (kuth′bərt), 1834–1903, English writer.

hare′ and hounds′, an outdoor game in which certain players, the hares, start off in advance on a long run, scattering small pieces of paper, called the scent, with the other players, the hounds, following the trail so marked in an effort to catch the hares before they reach a designated point. Also called **paper chase.**

hare·bell (hâr′bel′), *n.* **1.** a low, campanulaceous herb, *Campanula rotundifolia,* having blue, bell-shaped flowers. **2.** a liliaceous plant, *Scilla nonscripta,* having bell-shaped flowers. [ME; see HARE, BELL[1]]

hare·brained (hâr′brānd′), *adj.* giddy; reckless. Also, **hairbrained.** [HARE + BRAINED] —**hare′-brained′ly,** *adv.* —**hare′brained′ness,** *n.*

ha·reem (hä rēm′), *n.* harem.

hare·lip (hâr′lip′), *n.* **1.** a congenitally deformed lip, usually the upper one, in which there is a vertical fissure causing it to resemble the cleft lip of a hare. **2.** the deformity itself. Also called **cleft lip.** [HARE + LIP] —**hare′lipped′,** *adj.*

har·em (hâr′əm, har′-), *n.* **1.** that part of an Oriental palace or house reserved for the residence of women. **2.** the women in an Oriental household, including the mother, sisters, wives, concubines, daughters, entertainers, servants, etc. **3.** a group of female animals led by and mated to one male: *a stallion with a harem of five mares.* **4.** *Facetious.* a group of women associated in any way with one man or household: *The boss has a harem of three secretaries.* Also, **haram, hareem, harim.** [< Ar *ḥarīm* harem, lit., forbidden]

hare's′-foot fern′ (hârz′fo͝ot′), a fern, *Polypodium aureum,* of tropical America, having a brown, scaly rootstock and green or deep bluish-green fronds. Also called **golden polypody.**

hare·wood (hâr′wo͝od′), *n.* the greenish-gray wood of the sycamore maple, used for making furniture. [var. of obs. *airewood,* equiv. to obs. *aire* harewood (< dial. G *Ähre* << VL **acre,* L *acer* maple) + WOOD[1]]

Har·gei·sa (här gā′sə), *n.* a city in NW Somalia. 45,000 (est. 1957).

Har·greaves (här′grēvz), *n.* **James,** died 1778, English inventor of spinning machinery.

har·i·cot[1] (har′ə kō′), *n. Chiefly Brit.* **1.** any plant of the genus *Phaseolus,* esp. *P. vulgaris,* the kidney bean. **2.** the seed of any of these plants, eaten as a vegetable. [< F << Nahuatl *ayacotl* bean]

har·i·cot[2] (har′ə kō′), *n.* a stew of lamb or mutton with turnips and potatoes. Also, **halicot.** [< F; MF *hericoq* (*de mouton*)]

ha·ri·cot vert (ᴀ ʀē kō′ vᴇʀ′), *French.* See **string bean** (def. 1).

Har·i·jan (har′i jan′), *n.* a member of the group of untouchables in India. [< Skt *harijan(a)* a person dedicated to Vishnu, equiv. to *Hari* Vishnu + *jana* person]

ha·ri-ka·ri (här′ē kär′ē, har′ē kar′ē), *n.* hara-kiri.

ha·rim (hâr′əm, har′-, hä rēm′), *n.* harem.

hark (härk), *v.i.* **1.** to listen; harken (used chiefly in the imperative). —*v.t.* **2.** *Archaic.* to listen to; hear. **3. hark back, a.** (of hounds) to return along the course in order to regain a lost scent. **b.** to return to a previous subject or point; revert: *He kept harking back to his days in vaudeville.* —*n.* **4.** a hunter's shout to hounds, as to encourage them in following the scent. [ME *herk(i)e(n);* c. OFris *herkia;* akin to MD *harken,* G *horchen.* See HARKEN, HEAR]

hark·ee (här′kē), *interj.* hark ye.

hark·en (här′kən), *v.i.* **1.** to listen; give heed or attend to what is said. —*v.t.* **2.** *Archaic.* to listen to; hear. Also, **hearken.** [ME *hercnen,* OE *he(o)rcnian.* See HARK, -EN[1]] —**hark′en·er,** *n.*

Har·kins (här′kinz), *n.* **William Draper,** 1873–1951, U.S. chemist.

Hark·ness (härk′nis), *n.* **Edward Stephan,** 1874–1940, U.S. philanthropist.

harl[1] (häʀl), *Scot.* —*v.t.* **1.** to drag or pull (an object) along the ground. **2.** to troll for (fish). **3.** to plaster (the outside of a building) with roughcast. —*v.i.* **4.** to drag oneself along; move with dragging feet. **5.** to come reluctantly; sulk. —*n.* **6.** the act of dragging or pulling. **7.** a mixture of lime and gravel; roughcast. **8.** a small quantity; a scraping. Also, **harle.** [ME *harlen* to drag]

harl[2] (härl), *n.* **1.** a fiber, as of flax or hemp. **2.** *Angling.* a herl. [ME *herle* < MLG: fiber]

harl[3] (härl), *Brit. Dial.* —*n.* **1.** a knot; snarl; tangled mass. —*v.t.* **2.** to knot or twist together; entangle. **3.** to confuse. Also, **harle.** [ME *harl(en)* (to) entangle]

Har·lan (här′lən), *n.* **1. John Marshall,** 1833–1911, U.S. jurist: associate justice of the U.S. Supreme Court 1877–1911. **2.** his grandson, **John Marshall,** born 1899, U.S. jurist: associate justice of the U.S. Supreme Court since 1955. **3.** a town in W Iowa. 4350 (1960). **4.** a town in SE Kentucky. 4177 (1960). **5.** Also, **Harlen.** a boy's given name, form of **Harland.**

Har·land (här′lənd), *n.* a boy's given name.

harle[1] (häʀl), *v.t., v.i.,* **harled, harl·ing,** *n. Scot.* harl[1].

harle[2] (härl), *n., v.t.,* **harled, harl·ing.** *Brit. Dial.* harl[3].

Har′le·ian Li′brary (här′lē ən), a large library of manuscripts collected by the British statesman Robert Harley and his son and now housed in the British Museum. [< NL *Harleiān(us)* of, belonging to (Robert) HARLEY; see -AN]

Har·lem (här′ləm), *n.* **1.** a section of New York City, in the NE part of Manhattan. **2.** a tidal river in New York City, between the boroughs of Manhattan and the Bronx, which, with Spuyten Duyvil Creek, connects the Hudson and East rivers. 8 mi. long.

Har·lem·ite (här′lə mīt′), *n.* a native or inhabitant of Harlem. [HARLEM + -ITE[1]]

Har·len (här′lən), *n.* a boy's given name, form of **Harland.** Also, **Harlan.**

har·le·quin (här′lə kwin, -kin), *n.* **1.** (*often cap.*) a comic character in commedia dell'arte and the harlequinade, usually masked, dressed in multicolored, triangulated tights, and carrying a wooden sword or magic wand. **2.** a buffoon. **3.** any of various small, handsomely marked snakes. —*adj.* **4.** fancifully varied in color, decoration, etc. [< MF < ME **Herleching* (miswritten *herlething* in MS) < ML *Herla rex* King Herla (mythical figure); modern meaning from It *arlecchino* < MF *harlequin* < ME, as above] —**har′le·quin·ism,** *n.*

Harlequin

har·le·quin·ade (här′lə kwi nād′, -ki-), *n.* **1.** a pantomime, farce, or similar play in which Harlequin plays the principal part. **2.** buffoonery. [< F *arlequinade.* See HARLEQUIN, -ADE[1]]

har′lequin bug′, a black stink bug, *Murgantia histrionica,* having red and yellow markings, that feeds on cabbages and other cruciferous plants. Also called **cabbage bug, calicoback, calico bug, har′lequin cab′bage bug′.**

har′lequin duck′, a small, diving duck, *Histrionicus histrionicus,* of North America and Iceland, the male of which has bluish-gray plumage marked with black, white, and chestnut.

har·le·quin·esque (här′lə kwi nesk′, -ki-), *adj.* in the manner of a harlequin. [HARLEQUIN + -ESQUE]

har′lequin o′pal, a variety of opal having patches of various colors.

har′lequin ta′ble, a writing or dressing table having a central set of compartments that rise when drop leaves are raised.

Har·ley (här′lē), *n.* **1. Robert, 1st Earl of Oxford,** 1661–1724, British statesman. **2.** Also, **Arley.** a boy's given name.

Har′ley Street′, a street in London, England: noted for the doctors who have offices there.

Har·ling·en (här′ling ən), *n.* a city in S Texas. 41,207 (1960).

har·lot (här′lət), *n.* **1.** a lewd or promiscuous woman. **2.** a prostitute; strumpet. —*adj.* **3.** pertaining to or like a harlot; low. [ME < OF *herlot* young idler or rogue]

har·lot·ry (här′lə trē), *n., pl.* **-ries** for 2. **1.** prostitution. **2.** harlots collectively. [ME *harlotrie.* See HARLOT, -RY]

Har·low (här′lō), *n.* **1. Jean,** 1911–37, U.S. motion-picture actress. **2.** a town in W Essex, in SE England. 53,496 (1961). **3.** a boy's given name.

harm (härm), *n.* **1.** injury; damage; hurt: *to do him bodily harm.* **2.** moral injury; evil; wrong. —*v.t.* **3.** to do or cause harm to; injure; damage; hurt: *to harm one's reputation.* [ME; OE *hearm;* c. G *Harm,* Icel *harmr*] —**harm′er,** *n.*
—**Syn. 1, 2.** See **damage. 3.** maltreat, abuse. —**Ant. 1.** benefit. **3.** help.

har·mat·tan (här′mə tan′), *n.* (on the west coast of Africa) a dry, parching land breeze, charged with dust. [< WAfr *haramata* (Fanti or some other Akan speech)]

harm·ful (härm′fəl), *adj.* causing or capable of doing or causing harm; dangerous: *a harmful idea; a harmful habit.* [ME; OE *hearmful.* See HARM, -FUL] —**harm′ful·ly,** *adv.* —**harm′ful·ness,** *n.*
—**Syn.** injurious, hurtful, detrimental. —**Ant.** beneficial.

harm·less (härm′lis), *adj.* **1.** without the power or desire to do harm: *harmless play; a harmless child; a harmless Halloween prank.* **2.** without injury; unhurt; unharmed. [ME *harmles.* See HARM, -LESS] —**harm′less·ly,** *adv.* —**harm′less·ness,** *n.*

Har·mo·ni·a (här mō′nē ə), *n. Class. Myth.* the daughter of Ares and Aphrodite and wife of Cadmus.

har·mon·ic (här mon′ik), *adj.* **1.** pertaining to harmony, as distinguished from melody and rhythm. **2.** marked by harmony; in harmony; concordant; consonant. **3.** of, pertaining to, or noting a series of oscillations in which each oscillation has a frequency that is an integral multiple of the same basic frequency. **4.** *Math.* **a.** (of a set of values) related in a manner analogous to the frequencies of tones that are consonant. **b.** capable of being represented by sine and cosine functions. **c.** (of a function) satisfying the Laplace equation. —*n.* **5.** *Music.* overtone (def. 1). **6.** *Physics.* a single oscillation whose frequency is an integral multiple of the fundamental frequency. [< L *harmonic(us)* < Gk *harmonikós* musical, suitable. See HARMONY, -IC] —**har·mon′i·cal·ly,** *adv.* —**har·mon′i·cal·ness,** *n.*

har·mon·i·ca (här mon′ə kə), *n.* **1.** Also called **mouth organ.** a musical wind instrument consisting of a small rectangular case containing a set of metal reeds connected to a row of holes, over which the player places his mouth and exhales and inhales to produce the tones. **2.** any of various percussion instruments which use graduated bars of metal or other hard material as sounding elements. [n. use of fem. of L *harmonicus* HARMONIC]

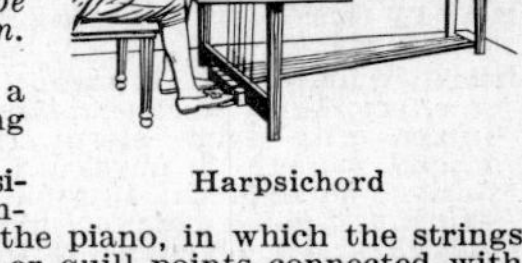
Harmonica

harmon′ic anal′ysis, *Math.* **1.** the calculation of Fourier series and integrals. **2.** the study of Fourier series and their generalization.

harmon′ic con′jugates, *Math.* two points whose cross ratio with two specified points equals −1.

harmon′ic mean′, *Statistics.* the mean obtained by taking the reciprocal of the arithmetic mean of the reciprocals of a set of nonzero numbers.

harmon′ic mi′nor scale′, *Music.* See **minor scale** (def. 1).

harmon′ic mo′tion, *Physics.* periodic motion consisting of one or more vibratory motions that are symmetric about a region of equilibrium, as the motion of a vibrating string of a musical instrument.

har·mon·i·con (här mon′ə kən), *n.* **1.** harmonica (def. 1). **2.** orchestrion. [n. use of Gk *harmonikón,* neut. of *harmonikós* HARMONIC]

harmon′ic progres′sion, *Math.* a series of numbers the reciprocals of which are in arithmetic progression.

har·mon·ics (här mon′iks), *n.* *Music.* **1.** (*construed as sing.*) the science of musical sounds. **2.** (*construed as pl.*) the partials or overtones of a fundamental tone. Cf. **overtone** (def. 1). **3.** (*construed as pl.*) the flageolet-like tones of a string (as a violin string) made to vibrate so as to bring out an overtone. [see HARMONIC, -ICS]

harmon′ic se′ries, *Math.* **1.** a series in which the reciprocals of the terms form an arithmetic progression. **2.** the divergent infinite series, $1 + \frac{1}{2} + \frac{1}{3} + \frac{1}{4} + \frac{1}{5} + \cdots$

harmon′ic tone′, *Music.* a tone produced by suppressing the fundamental tone and bringing into prominence one of its overtones.

Har·mo·ni·des (här mō′ni dēz′), *n.* (in the *Iliad*) Phereclus.

har·mo·ni·ous (här mō′nē əs), *adj.* **1.** marked by agreement in feeling or action: *a harmonious group.* **2.** forming a pleasingly consistent whole; congruous: *harmonious colors.* **3.** agreeable to the ear; tuneful; melodious. [< Gk *harmónios* melodious, lit., fitting. See HARMONY, -OUS] —**har·mo′ni·ous·ly,** *adv.* —**har·mo′ni·ous·ness,** *n.*
—**Syn. 1.** amicable, congenial; sympathetic. **2.** concordant, congruent, consonant, consistent. —**Ant. 1, 3.** discordant.

har·mo·nise (här′mə nīz′), *v.t., v.i.,* **-nised, -nis·ing.** *Chiefly Brit.* harmonize. —**har′mo·nis′a·ble,** *adj.* —**har′mo·ni·sa′tion,** *n.* —**har′mo·nis′er,** *n.*

har·mo·nist (här′mə nist), *n.* **1.** one skilled in harmony. **2.** one who makes a harmony, as of the Gospels. [HARMON(Y) + -IST]

Har·mo·nist (här′mə nist), *n.* a member of a celibate religious sect that emigrated from Germany to Pennsylvania in 1803. Also, **Harmonite.** Also called **Rappist, Rappite.** [after HARMONY, Pennsylvania; see -IST]

har·mo·nis·tic (här′mə nis′tik), *adj.* **1.** pertaining to a harmonist or harmony. **2.** pertaining to the collation and harmonizing of parallel passages, as of the Gospels. [HARMON(Y) + -ISTIC] —**har′mo·nis′ti·cal·ly,** *adv.*

Har·mo·nite (här′mə nīt′), *n.* Harmonist.

har·mo·ni·um (här mō′nē əm), *n.* an organlike keyboard instrument with small metal reeds and a pair of bellows operated by the player's feet. [Latinization of Gk *harmónion,* neut. of *harmónios* HARMONIOUS]

har·mo·nize (här′mə nīz′), *v.,* **-nized, -niz·ing.** —*v.t.* **1.** to bring into harmony, accord, or agreement: *to harmonize one's views with the existing facts.* **2.** *Music.* to accompany with appropriate harmony. —*v.i.* **3.** to be in agreement in action, sense, or feeling: *Though of different backgrounds, the members of the group harmonized with one another.* **4.** to sing in harmony. Also, *esp. Brit.,* **harmonise.** [late ME *armonise.* See HARMONY, -IZE] —**har′mo·niz′a·ble,** *adj.* —**har′mo·ni·za′tion,** *n.* —**har′mo·niz′er,** *n.*
—**Syn. 1.** reconcile, compose. **3.** agree, accord, correspond.

har·mo·ny (här′mə nē), *n., pl.* **-nies. 1.** agreement; accord; harmonious relations. **2.** a consistent, orderly, or pleasing arrangement of parts; congruity. **3.** *Music.* **a.** any simultaneous combination of tones. **b.** the simultaneous combination of tones, esp. when blended into chords pleasing to the ear; chordal structure, as distinguished from melody and rhythm. **c.** the science of the structure, relations, and practical combination of chords. **4.** an arrangement of the contents of the Gospels, either of all four or of the first three, designed to show their parallelism, mutual relations, and differences. [< L *harmoni(a)* < Gk: melody, lit., a joining (of sounds), equiv. to *harmó(s)* joint + *-ia* -Y[3]; r. ME *armonye* < MF]
—**Syn. 1.** concord, unity, peace, amity, friendship. **2.** consonance, conformity, correspondence, consistency. See **symmetry. 3.** HARMONY, MELODY in music suggest a combination of sounds from voices or musical instruments. HARMONY is the blending of simultaneous sounds of different pitch or quality, making chords: *harmony in part singing; harmony between violins and horns.* MELODY is the rhythmical combination of successive sounds of various pitch, making up the tune or air: *a tuneful melody to accompany cheerful words.*

Har·mo·ny (här′mə nē), *n.* **1.** a town in W Pennsylvania. 5106 (1960). **2.** a girl's given name.

har·most (här′most), *n.* a person serving the ancient Spartans as governor of a subject or conquered town. [< Gk *harmost(ḗs),* deriv. of *harmózein* to regulate, govern, join]

Har·mo·tho·ë (här mo′thō ē′), *n.* *Class. Myth.* the wife of Pandareus and the mother of Aëdon, Cleothera, and Merope.

har·mo·tome (här′mə tōm′), *n.* a mineral of the zeolite family, occurring in twinned crystals. [< F < Gk *harmó(s)* joint + *-tomos* -TOME] —**har·mo·tom·ic** (här′mə tom′ik), *adj.*

Harms·worth (härmz′wûrth′), *n.* **1. Alfred Charles William, Viscount Northcliffe,** 1865–1922, English journalist, publisher, and politician. **2.** his brother, **Harold Sidney, 1st Viscount Roth·er·mere** (roth′ər mēr′), 1868–1940, English publisher and politician.

Har·nack (här′näk), *n.* **A·dolf von** (ä′dôlf fən), 1851–1930, German Protestant theologian, born in Estonia.

har·ness (här′nis), *n.* **1.** the combination of straps, bands, and other parts forming the working gear of a draft animal. Cf. **yoke**[1] (def. 1). **2.** (on a loom) the frame containing heddles through which the warp is drawn and which, in combination with another such frame or other frames, forms the shed and determines the woven pattern. **3.** the equipment, as straps, bolts, gears, etc., by which a large bell is mounted and rung. **4.** *Archaic.* armor for men or horses. **5. in double harness.** See **double harness** (def. 2). **6. in harness, a.** engaged in one's usual routine of work: *After his illness he longed to get back in harness.* **b.** together as cooperating partners or equals: *Joe and I worked in harness on our last job.* —*v.t.* **7.** to put a harness on (a horse, donkey, dog, etc.); attach by a harness, as to a vehicle. **8.** to bring under conditions for effective use; gain control over for a particular end: *to harness water power; to harness the energy of the sun.* **9.** *Archaic.* to array in armor or equipments of war. [ME *harneis, herneis* < OF: baggage, equipment, ? orig. army provisions < Gmc; cf OE *here,* Icel *herr* army, OE, Icel *nest* provisions (for a journey)] —**har′ness·er,** *n.* —**har′ness·less,** *adj.* —**har′ness·like′,** *adj.*

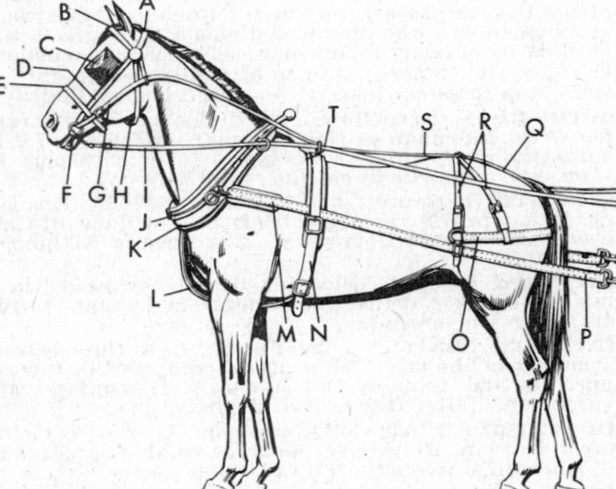

Harness of a horse
A, Crown piece; B, Front; C, Blinker; D, Cheek strap; E, Noseband; F, Bit; G, Sidecheek; H, Throatlatch; I, Reins; J, Hame; K, Collar; L, Martingale; M, Hame tug; N, Bellyband; O, Breeching; P, Trace; Q, Crupper; R, Hipstraps; S, Terret

har′ness cask′, *Naut.* a tapering wooden cask in which salt meat was formerly soaked in fresh water to rid it of the brine in which it had been preserved.

har′nessed an′telope, any of several antelopes of the genus *Tragelaphus,* found in central and southern Africa, having the body marked with white stripes and spots that resemble a harness.

har′ness eye′, *Textiles.* the eyelet on a heddle or on harness cords. Cf. **mail**[2] (def. 3).

har′ness hitch′, a hitch forming a loop around a rope, esp. one formed at the end of a bowline.

har′ness horse′, **1.** a horse used for pulling vehicles. **2.** a horse used in harness racing.

har′ness race′, a trotting or pacing race for Standardbred horses harnessed to sulkies. —**har′ness rac′ing.**

Har·nett (här′nit), *n.* **William Michael,** 1848–92, U.S. painter.

Har′ney Peak′ (här′nē), a mountain in SW South Dakota: the highest peak in the Black Hills. 7242 ft.

harns (härnz), *n.pl. Scot.* brains. [ME *hernes, harnes* earlier *hærnes* < Scand; cf. Icel *hjarni* brain; akin to G *Hirn* brain, Gk *kraníon* CRANIUM]

Har·old (har′əld), *n.* a boy's given name.

Harold I, ("*Harefoot*") died 1040, king of England 1035–40 (son of Canute).

Harold II, 1022?–66, king of England 1066: defeated by William the Conqueror at the Battle of Hastings (son of Earl Godwin).

ha·ro·seth (кнä rô′set, -rō′sis; *Eng.* hä rō′set), *n.* *Hebrew.* a mixture of chopped nuts and apples, wine, and spices that is eaten at the Seder meal on Passover. Also, **ha·ro′set, charoseth, charoset.**

Ha·roun-al-Ra·schid (hä ro͞on′äl rä shēd′; *Arab.* hä-ro͞on′är′rä shēd′), *n.* See **Harun al-Rashid.**

harp (härp), *n.* **1.** a musical instrument consisting of a triangular frame formed by a soundbox, a pillar, and a curved neck, and having strings that are stretched between the soundbox and the neck that are plucked with the fingers. **2.** anything that resembles this instrument, esp. in having a row of parallel strings or wires, as various mechanical devices, kitchen implements for slicing cheese, etc. **3.** *Disparaging.* a person of Irish birth or descent. **4.** Also called **harper.** any of several English coins issued for use in Ireland during the 16th and 17th centuries, bearing the figure of a harp on the reverse. —*v.i.* **5.** to play on a harp. —*v.t.* **6.** to play (a musical piece) on a harp. **7.** *Obs.* **a.** to recite or recount (a poem, story, etc.) to the accompaniment of a harp. **b.** to move, compel, enchant, enthrall, etc., by playing the harp. **8.** *Archaic.* to give voice or utterance to. **9. harp on** or **upon,** to dwell on persistently or tediously in speaking or writing: *She was always harping on how wonderful her daughter was.* [ME *harpe,* OE *hearpe;* c. D *harp,* G *Harfe,* Icel *harpa*] —**harp′less,** *adj.* —**harp′like′,** *adj.* —**harp′wise′,** *adv.*

Harp (def. 1)

Har·pa·lus (här′pə ləs), *n.* a crater in the second quadrant of the face of the moon: about 22 miles in diameter.

Har·pal·y·ce (här pal′i sē′), *n.* *Class. Myth.* **1.** daughter of Clymenus of Arcadia, by whom she bore a child: he slew her upon discovering that she had killed the child and had fed it to him. **2.** a huntress killed by shepherds upon whose flocks she had preyed.

harp·er (här′pər), *n.* **1.** one who plays a harp. **2.** *Numis.* harp (def. 4). [ME; OE *hearpere.* See HARP, -ER[1]]

Har·per (här′pər), *n.* a boy's given name.

Har′pers Fer′ry (här′pərz), a town in NE West Virginia at the confluence of the Shenandoah and Potomac rivers: John Brown's raid 1859. 572 (1960). Also, **Har′per's Fer′ry.**

Har′per Woods′, a city in SE Michigan, near Detroit. 19,995 (1960).

Har·pi·na (här pī′nə), *n.* *Class. Myth.* a daughter of Asopus who became the mother, by Ares, of Oenomaus.

harp·ing (här′ping), *n.* **1.** *Naut.* any of various especially thick wales for strengthening a bow. **2.** *Shipbuilding.* any of several horizontal members at the ends of a vessel for holding cant frames in position until the shell planking or plating is attached. **3.** *Obs.* the bow form of a vessel, with respect to its bluntness or sharpness: *a full harping; a lean harping.* Also, **har·pin** (här′pin) (for defs. 1, 2), **harp·ins** (här′pinz). [? HARP + -ING[1]]

harp·ist (här′pist), *n.* one who plays on the harp, esp. professionally. [HARP + -IST]

har·poon (här po͞on′), *n.* **1.** a barbed, spearlike missile attached to a rope, and thrown by hand or shot from a gun, used for killing and capturing whales and large fish. —*v.t.* **2.** to strike, catch, or kill with or as with a harpoon. [< D *harpoen* << OF *harpon* a clasp, brooch, equiv. to *harp-* (< L *harpē* < Gk: hook) + *-on* dim. suffix; aspirate *h-* by assoc. with *harpe* HARP] —**har·poon′er,** *n.* —**har·poon′like′,** *adj.*

harpoon′ gun′, a small cannon for shooting harpoons.

harp·si·chord (härp′si kôrd′), *n.* a keyboard instrument, precursor of the piano, in which the strings are plucked by leather or quill points connected with the keys, in common use from the 16th to the 18th century, and revived in the 20th. [< NL *harpichord(ium)* (with intrusive *-s-*). See HARP, -I-, CHORD[1]] —**harp′si·chord′ist,** *n.*

Harpsichord

Har·py (här′pē), *n., pl.* **-pies. 1.** *Class. Myth.* a ravenous, filthy monster having a woman's head and a bird's body. **2.** (*l.c.*) a rapacious, grasping person. **3.** (*l.c.*) a scolding, nagging, bad-tempered woman; shrew. [< L *Harpȳ(ia),* sing. of *Harpȳiae* < Gk *Hárpyiai* (pl.), lit., snatchers, akin to *harpázein* to snatch away] —**harp′y·like′,** *adj.*

har′py ea′gle, a large, powerful eagle, *Harpia harpyja,* of tropical America.

har·que·bus (här′kwə bəs), *n., pl.* **-bus·es.** any of several small-caliber long guns operated by a matchlock or wheel-lock mechanism, dating from about 1400. Also, **har′que·buse, har′que·buss, arquebus.** Also called **hackbut, hagbut.** [< MF *harquebuse* < MD *hakebusse* (with intrusive *-r-*), equiv. to *hake* hook (c. OE *haca*) + *busse* gun (lit., box) < LL *buxis* for L *buxus* BOX[1])

har·que·bus·ier (här′kwə bə sēr′), *n.* a soldier armed with a harquebus. Also, **arquebusier.** [< MF; see HARQUEBUS, -ER[2]]

Har·rar (här′ər), *n.* Harar.

har·ri·dan (har′i dən), *n.* a scolding, vicious old woman; hag. [cf. F *haridelle* a jade]

har·ri·er[1] (har′ē ər), *n.* **1.** one who or that which harries. **2.** any of several accipitrine hawks of the genus *Circus* that hunt over meadows and marshes and prey on reptiles and small birds and mammals. [HARRY + -ER[1]]

har·ri·er[2] (har′ē ər), *n.* **1.** one of a breed of medium-sized hounds, used, usually in packs, in hunting. **2.** a cross-country runner. [special use of HARRIER[1], by assoc. with HARE]

Har·ri·et (har′ē ət), *n.* a girl's given name. Also, **Har′ri·ett, Har′ri·ette, Har·ri·et·ta** (har′ē et′ə).

Har·ri·man (har′ə mən), *n.* **1. Edward Henry,** 1848–1909, U.S. financier and railroad magnate. **2.** his son, **W(illiam) A·ve·rell** (ā′vər əl), born 1891, U.S. diplomat: governor of New York 1954–58. **3.** a town in E Tennessee. 5931 (1960).

Har′ring·ton Park′ (har′ing tən), a town in NE New Jersey. 3581 (1960).

Har·ris (har′is), *n.* **1. Benjamin,** c1660–c1720, English journalist who published the first newspaper in America 1690. **2. Frank,** 1854–1931, U.S. writer, born in Ireland. **3. Joel Chan·dler** (chan′dlər, chän′-), 1848–1908, U.S. journalist, novelist, and short-story writer: creator of Uncle Remus. **4. Julie,** born 1925, U.S. actress. **5. Roy,** born 1898, U.S. composer. **6. Thaddeus William,** 1795–1856, U.S. entomologist: pioneer in applied entomology. **7.** a boy's given name.

Har·ris·burg (har′is bûrg′), *n.* **1.** a city in and the capital of Pennsylvania, in the S part, on the Susquehanna River. 79,697 (1960). **2.** a town in SE Illinois. 9171 (1960).

Har′ris Hill′, a town in W New York. 3944 (1960).

Har·ri·son (har′i sən), *n.* **1. Benjamin,** 1833–1901, 23rd president of the U.S. 1889–93. **2. Peter,** 1716–75, English architect in the U.S. **3. William Henry,** 1773–1841, U.S. general: 9th president of the U.S. 1841 (grandfather of Benjamin Harrison). **4.** a town in W Pennsylvania. 15,710 (1960). **5.** a town in N Arkansas. 6580 (1960). **6.** a town in SW Ohio. 3878 (1960). **7.** a boy's given name.

Har′rison grid′, *Horol. Rare.* See **gridiron pendulum.**

Har′rison red′, **1.** a pigment consisting of a paratoluidine toner, characterized by its brilliant red color and tendency to bleed. **2.** pimento (def. 4). [perh. after B. *Harrison* (d. 1929), American artist]

Har·ri·son·ville (har′i sən vil′), *n.* a town in W Missouri. 3510 (1960).

Har′ris Tweed′, *Trademark.* a heavy, handwoven woolen fabric made in the Outer Hebrides.

Har·rods·burg (har′ədz bûrg′), *n.* a town in central Kentucky. 6061 (1960).

Har·ro·vi·an (hə rō′vē ən), *adj.* **1.** of or pertaining to Harrow. —*n.* **2.** a pupil or former pupil of Harrow. [< NL *Harrovi(a)* Harrow + -AN]

har·row[1] (har′ō), *n.* **1.** an agricultural implement with spikelike teeth or upright disks, drawn chiefly over plowed land to level it, break up clods, root up weeds, etc. —*v.t.* **2.** to draw a harrow over (land). **3.** to disturb keenly or painfully; distress the mind, feelings, etc., of. —*v.i.* **4.** to become broken up by harrowing, as soil. [ME *harwe;* akin to Icel *herfi* harrow, D *hark* rake, Gk *krṓpion* sickle] —**har′row·er,** *n.* —**har′row·ing·ly,** *adv.*

har·row[2] (har′ō), *v.t.* *Archaic.* **1.** to ravish; violate; despoil. **2.** harry (def. 2). **3.** (of Christ) to descend into (hell) to free the righteous held captive. [ME *harwen, herwen,* OE *hergian* to HARRY] —**har′row·ment,** *n.*

Har·row (har′ō), *n.* a boarding school for boys, founded in 1571 at Harrow-on-the-Hill, England.

Har·row-on-the-Hill (har′ō on *th*ə hil′, -ôn-), *n.* an urban district in SE England, near London. 208,963 (1961).

har·rumph (hə rumf′), *v.i.* **1.** to make a low, guttural sound, as of clearing the throat (usually thought of as pompous): *Although the professor harrumphed good-naturedly, the student speaker's confidence disappeared.* **2.** to express disapproval: *Despite popular acclaim of the project, the council harrumphed.* [imit.]

har·ry (har′ē), *v.,* **-ried, -ry·ing.** —*v.t.* **1.** to harass, annoy, or prove a nuisance to by repeated attacks; worry: *to harry the enemy forces.* **2.** to ravage, as in war; devastate: *The troops harried the countryside.* —*v.i.* **3.** to make harrassing incursions. [ME *heri(en),* OE *her(g)ian* (deriv. of *here* army); c. G *(ver)heeren,* Icel *herja* to harry, lay waste]
—**Syn. 1.** molest, plague, trouble. **2.** plunder, strip, rob, pillage.

Har·ry (har′ē), *n.* a boy's given name, form of **Harold** or **Henry.**

harsh (härsh), *adj.* **1.** ungentle and unpleasant in action or effect: *harsh treatment; harsh manners.* **2.** grim or unpleasantly severe; stern; cruel; austere: *a harsh life; a harsh master.* **3.** physically uncomfortable; desolate; stark: *a harsh land.* **4.** unpleasant to the ear; grating; strident: *a harsh voice; a harsh sound.* **5.** unpleasantly rough, ragged, or coarse to the touch: *a harsh surface.* **6.** jarring to the eye or to the esthetic sense; unrefined; crude; raw: *harsh colors.* **7.** unpleasant to the taste or sense of smell; bitter; acrid: *a harsh flavor; a harsh odor.* [ME *harsk* < Scand; cf. Dan *harsk* rancid; c. G *harsch* harsh; akin to G *herb* harsh] —**harsh′ly,** *adv.* —**harsh′ness,** *n.*
—**Syn. 2.** brusque, hard, unfeeling, unkind, brutal, acrimonious, bad-tempered. See **stern**[1]. **3.** rough. **4.** discordant, dissonant, unharmonious. **6.** unesthetic.

harsh·en (här′shən), *v.t., v.i.* to make or become harsh: *Avarice had harshened his features.* [HARSH + -EN[1]]

hars·let (härs′lit), *n.* *Dial.* haslet.

harst (härst, hârst), *n., v.t., v.i.* *Scot.* harvest.

Har·stad (här′stä), *n.* a seaport in W Norway: herring fishing. 4219 (1950).

hart (härt), *n., pl.* **harts,** (*esp. collectively*) **hart.** a male of the deer, commonly the red deer, *Cervus elaphus,* esp. after its fifth year. [ME *hert,* OE *heorot;* c. D *hert,* G *Hirsch,* Icel *hjörtr;* akin to L *cervus* stag, Gk *kôrydos* crested lark]

Hart (härt), *n.* **1. Albert Bush·nell** (bo͝osh′nəl), 1854–1943, U.S. editor, historian, and educator. **2. Lo·renz** (lôr′ənts, lôr′-), 1895–1943, U.S. lyricist. **3. Moss,** 1904–61, U.S. playwright and librettist. **4. W(illiam) S(hakespeare),** 1872–1946, U.S. motion picture actor. **5.** a boy's given name.

har·tal (här täl′), *n.* (in India) a closing of shops and stopping of work, esp. as a form of passive resistance. [< Hindi, var. of *haṭtāl,* equiv. to *haṭ* shop (Skt *haṭṭa*) + *tāl* locking (Skt *tālaka* lock, bolt)]

Harte (härt), *n.* **(Francis) Bret** (bret), 1839–1902, U.S. author, esp. of short stories.

har·te·beest (här′tə bēst′, härt′bēst′), *n., pl.* **-beests,** (*esp. collectively*) **-beest. 1.** any of several large, African antelopes of the genus *Alcelaphus,* having ringed horns that curve backward. **2.** any of several related African antelopes, as certain species of the genus *Damaliscus.* [< SAfrD; see HART, BEAST]

Hartebeest,
Alcelaphus buselaphus
(4½ ft. high at shoulder; horns 1 ft.; length 6½ ft.)

Hart·ford (härt′fərd), *n.* **1. (George) Huntington, 2nd,** born 1911, U.S. businessman and patron of the arts. **2.** a port in and the capital of Connecticut, in the central part, on the Connecticut River. 162,178 (1960). **3.** a town in E Wisconsin. 5627 (1960).

Hart′ford Cit′y, a town in E Indiana. 8053 (1960).

Hart′ford fern′, a climbing or sprawling fern, *Lygodium palmatum,* of the eastern U.S., having nearly round fronds. Also called **Alice's fern.**

Har·tha·cnut (här′*th*ə kə no͞ot′, -nyo͞ot′), *n.* Hardecanute.

Hart·ley (härt′lē), *n.* **1. David,** 1705–57, English physician and philosopher. **2. Mars·den** (märz′dən), 1877–1943, U.S. painter. **3.** a boy's given name.

Hart·mann (härt′män, -mən; *Ger.* härt′män′), *n.* **1. (Karl Ro·bert) E·du·ard von** (kärl rō′bərt ā′do͞o ärt′ fən), 1842–1906, German philosopher. **2. Ni·co·la·i** (nē′kô lä′ē, nē′kô lī′), 1882–1950, German philosopher, born in Latvia.

Hart·selle (härt′sel), *n.* a town in N Alabama. 5000 (1960).

harts·horn (härts′hôrn′), *n.* **1.** the antler of a hart, formerly used as a source of ammonia. **2.** *Old Chem., Pharm.* ammonium carbonate; sal volatile. [ME *hertis horn,* OE *heortes horn.* See HART, 'S[1], HORN]

hart's-tongue (härts′tung′), *n.* a fern, *Phyllitis Scolopendrium,* having long simple fronds. Also, **harts′-tongue′.** [ME *hertis tonge.* See HART, 'S[1], TONGUE]

Harts·ville (härts′vil), *n.* a town in NE South Carolina. 6392 (1960).

Hart·well (härt′wel), *n.* a town in NE Georgia. 4599 (1960).

har·um-scar·um (hâr′əm skar′əm, har′əm skar′əm), *adj.* **1.** reckless; rash; irresponsible: *He had a harum-scarum youth.* **2.** disorganized; uncontrolled. —*adv.* **3.** recklessly; wildly: *He ran harum-scarum all over the place.* —*n.* **4.** a reckless person. **5.** *Archaic.* reckless or unpredictable behavior or action. [earlier *harum-starum* rhyming compound based on obs. *hare* to harass + STARE] —**har′um-scar′um·ness,** *n.*

Ha·run al-Ra·shid (hä ro͞on′ äl rä shēd′; *Arab.* hä-ro͞on′ är′rä shēd′), *n.* A.D. 764?–809, caliph of Baghdad 786–809: one of the greatest Abbasides, he was made almost a legendary hero in the *Arabian Nights.* Also, **Haroun-al-Raschid, Ha·run ar-Ra·shid** (hä ro͞on′ är′-rä shēd′; *Arab.* hä ro͞on′ är′rä shēd′).

Ha·ru·no·bu (här′o͞o nō′bo͞o; *Jap.* hä′ro͞o nô′bo͞o), *n.* **Su·zu·ki** (so͞o zo͞o′kē), 1720?–70, Japanese painter and printmaker.

ha·rus·pex (hə rus′peks, har′ə speks′), *n., pl.* **ha·rus·pi·ces** (hə rus′pi sēz′). (in ancient Rome) one of a class of minor priests who practiced divination, esp. from the entrails of animals killed in sacrifice. Also, **aruspex.** [< L, equiv. to *haru* (akin to *hīra* gut; see CHORD[1]) + *spec-* (s. of *specere* to look at) + *-s* nom. sing. ending]

ha·rus·pi·cy (hə rus′pi sē), *n.* divination by a haruspex. Also, **ha·rus·pi·ca·tion** (hə rus′pə kā′shən). [< L *haruspici(um),* equiv. to *haruspic-* (s. of *haruspex*) + *-ium* -Y[3]] —**ha·rus·pi·cal** (hə rus′pi kəl), *adj.*

Har·vard (här′vərd), *n.* **1. John,** 1607–38, English clergyman in U.S.: principal benefactor of Harvard College, now Harvard University. **2.** a town in N Illinois. 4248 (1960).

Har′vard beets′, sliced or diced beets cooked in a mixture of sugar, cornstarch, vinegar, and water. [after HARVARD University]

Har′vard chair′, *U.S. Furniture.* a three-legged armchair of the late 17th century, composed of turned uprights and spindles and having a triangular seat; varangian. [after HARVARD University]

Har·var·di·an (här vär′dē ən), *adj.* **1.** of or pertaining to Harvard University. —*n.* **2.** a student or alumnus of Harvard University. [HARVARD + -IAN]

Harve (härv), *n.* a boy's given name, form of **Harvey.**

har·vest (här′vist), *n.* **1.** Also, **har′vest·ing.** the gathering of crops. **2.** the season when ripened crops are gathered. **3.** a crop or yield of one growing season. **4.** a supply of anything gathered at maturity and stored: *a harvest of nuts.* **5.** the result or consequence of any act, process, or event: *The journey yielded a harvest of impressions.* **6.** (*cap., italics.*) the English title of *Regain.* —*v.t.* **7.** to gather (a crop or the like); reap. **8.** to gather the crop from: *to harvest the fields.* **9.** to gain, win, acquire, use, etc. (a prize, product, or result of any past act, process, plan, etc.). —*v.i.* **10.** to gather a crop; reap. [ME; OE *hærfest;* c. G *Herbst* autumn; akin to HARROW[1]] —**har′vest·less,** *adj.*
—**Syn. 3.** See **crop.**

har·vest·er (här′vi stər), *n.* **1.** one who harvests; reaper. **2.** any of various farm machines for harvesting field crops. **3.** an orange-brown butterfly, *Feniseca tarquinius,* the larvae of which are predacious on aphids. [HARVEST + -ER[1]]

har′vester ant′, any of several red or black ants, esp. of the genus *Pogonomyrmex,* of the southwestern U.S., that feed on and store the seeds of grasses. Also called **agricultural ant.**

har·vest·fish (här′vist fish′), *n., pl.* (*esp. collectively*) **-fish,** (*esp. referring to two or more kinds or species*) **-fishes. 1.** a butterfish of the genus *Peprilus,* esp. *P. paru* **(northern harvestfish). 2.** the butterfish *Poronotus triacanthus.* [HARVEST + FISH]

har′vest fly′. See **dog-day cicada.**

har′vest home′, **1.** the bringing home of the harvest. **2.** the time of harvesting or of gathering in the harvest. **3.** an English festival celebrated at the close of the harvest. **4.** a song sung as the harvest is brought home.

har·vest·man (här′vist mən), *n., pl.* **-men. 1.** a man engaged in harvesting. **2.** Also called **daddy-longlegs.** any of numerous arachnids of the order *Phalangida,* having a compact, rounded body and extremely long, slender legs. [HARVEST + MAN[1]]

Harvestman
Phalangium opilio

har′vest mite′, chigger (def. 1).

har′vest moon′, the moon at and about the period of fullness which is nearest to the autumnal equinox.

har′vest mouse′, **1.** an Old World field mouse, *Micromys minutus,* that builds a spherical nest among the stems of grains and other plants. **2.** any of several New World mice of the genus *Reithrodontomys* having similar habits.

har′vest tick′, chigger (def. 1).

Har·vey (här′vē), *n.* **1. William,** 1578–1657, English physician: discoverer of the circulation of the blood. **2.** a city in NE Illinois, near Chicago. 29,071 (1960). **3.** Also, **Hervey.** a boy's given name.

Har·vey·ize (här′vē īz′), *v.t.,* **-ized, -iz·ing.** *Metall.* to caseharden (a steel plate) in finely divided charcoal, as to make armor plate. [named after H. A. *Harvey* (1824–93), American steel manufacturer; see -IZE]

Har′wood Heights′ (här′wo͝od′), a town in NE Illinois. 5688 (1960).

Há·ry Já·nos (*Hung.* hä′rē yä′nôsh), an opera (1926) by Zoltán Kodály.

Harz′ Moun′tains (härts), a range of low mountains in central Germany between the Elbe and Weser rivers. Highest peak, Brocken, 3745 ft.

has (haz), *v.* a 3rd pers. sing. pres. indic. of **have.**

Ha·sa (hä′sə), *n.* a region in E Saudi Arabia, on the Persian Gulf. Also, **El Hasa.**

Ha·san (hä′sən, ha san′), *n.* (*al-Hasan*) A.D. 624?–669?, Arabian caliph: son of Ali and Fatima (brother of Husain). Also, **Hassan.**

Ha·san·lu (hä′sän lo͞o′), *n.* an archaeological site in NW Iran, S of Lake Urmia: excavated Mannaean city.

has-been (haz′bin′), *n.* one who or that which is no longer effective, successful, popular, etc.

Has·dru·bal (haz′dro͞o bəl, haz dro͞o′-), *n.* **1.** died 207 B.C., Carthaginian general (brother of Hannibal). **2.** died 221 B.C., Carthaginian general (brother-in-law of Hannibal).

Hase (häz, hä′zə), *n.* a walled plain in the fourth quadrant of the face of the moon: about 47 miles in diameter.

Ha·šek (hä′shek), *n.* **Ja·ro·slav** (yä′rô släf′), 1883–1923, Czech novelist and short-story writer.

ha·sen·pfef·fer (hä′sən fef′ər), *n.* a stew of marinated rabbit meat garnished usually with sour cream. Also, **hassenpfeffer.** [< G: lit., hare's pepper]

hash[1] (hash), *n.* **1.** a dish of diced or chopped meat and often vegetables, as of leftover corned beef, veal, etc., and potatoes, sautéed in a frying pan or of meat, potatoes, and carrots cooked together in gravy. **2.** a mess, jumble, or muddle: *a hash of unorganized facts and figures.* **3.** a reworking of old and known material: *This essay is a hash of several earlier and better works.* **4. make a hash of,** *Informal.* to spoil or botch: *The new writer made a hash of his first assignment.* **5. settle someone's hash,** *Informal.* to get rid of; subdue: *The second snub settled her hash.* —*v.t.* **6.** to chop into small pieces; mince; make into hash. **7.** to muddle or mess up: *She hashed all the information she had been given, to the confusion of everyone.* **8.** to discuss or review (something) thoroughly: *They hashed the data interminably.* **9. hash over,** *Slang.* to bring up again for consideration; discuss, esp. in review: *They hashed over their college days.* [< F *hacher* to cut up, deriv. of *hache* ax, HATCHET]

hash[2] (hash), *n.* *Slang.* hashish. [by shortening]

Hash′e·mite King′dom of Jor′dan (hash′ə mīt′), official name of **Jordan.**

hash·er (hash′ər), *n.* *Slang.* a waiter or waitress. [HASH + -ER[1]]

hash′ house′, *Slang.* a cheap, short-order restaurant.

Hash·i·mite (hash′ə mīt′), *n.* **1.** a member of any Arab dynasty in the Middle East founded by Husein ibn-Ali or his descendants. —*adj.* **2.** of or pertaining to the Hashimites. [*Hashim* great-grandfather of Muhammad + -ITE[1]]

hash·ing (hash′ing), *n.* *Radio.* interference of signals between two stations on the same or adjacent frequencies. [HASH + -ING[1]]

hash·ish (hash′ēsh, -ish), *n.* **1.** the flowering tops, leaves, etc., of Indian hemp, smoked, chewed, or drunk as a narcotic and intoxicant. **2.** any of certain preparations made from this plant. Also, **hash·eesh** (hä′shēsh). [< Ar *hashīsh,* lit., dry vegetation (e.g., hay)]

hash′ mark′, *Mil. Slang.* a service stripe.

hash-sling·er (hash′sling′ər), *n.* *Slang.* **1.** a waiter or waitress, esp. in a hash house. **2.** a short-order cook, esp. in a hash house.

Ha·sid (hä′sid; *Heb.* khä sēd′), *n., pl.* **Ha·sid·im** (hä sid′-im; *Heb.* khä′sē dēm′). *Judaism.* **1.** a member of a sect founded in Poland in the 18th century by Israel Baal Shem-Tov and characterized by its emphasis on mysticism, prayer, religious zeal, and joy. Cf. **Mitnagged. 2.** an Assidean. Also, **Chasid.** [< Heb: pious (person)] —**Ha·sid·ic** (hə sid′ik), *adj.*

Has·i·de·an (has′i dē′ən), *n.* *Judaism.* Assidean. Also, **Has′i·dae′an.**

Has·i·dism (has′i diz′əm), *n.* *Judaism.* the principles and practices of the Hasidim. Also, **Chasidism.** [HASID + -ISM]

Ha·ska·lah (hä skô′lə, hä′skə lä′; *Heb.* hä skä lä′), *n.* an 18th–19th century movement among central and eastern European Jews, begun in Germany under the leadership of Moses Mendelssohn, designed to make Jews and Judaism more cosmopolitan in character by promoting knowledge of and contributions to the secular arts and sciences and encouraging adoption of the dress, customs, and language of the general population. [< ModHeb *haskālāh* enlightenment]

Has·kell (has′kəl), *n.* a town in central Texas. 4016 (1960).

has·let (has′lit, hāz′-), *n.* the heart, liver, etc., of a hog or other animal, as used for food. [ME *hastelet* < MF: roasted meat, dim. (see -LET) of *haste* spit, piece of spit-roasted meat < Gmc; cf. OE *hearstepanne* frying pan, *hierstan* to roast, fry, D *harst* sirloin; see HEARTH]

has·lock (has′lok′), *n.* a coarse wool. [*has* neck (OE *hals*; akin to L *collum*; see COLLAR) + LOCK²]

Has·mo·ne·an (haz′mə nē′ən), *n.* a member of a priestly family of Jewish rulers and leaders in Judea in the 1st and 2nd centuries B.C. Also, **Has′mo·nae′an, Asmonean, Asmonaean.** Cf. **Maccabees.** [var. (with *h-* < Heb *kh-*) of *Asmonean* < LL *Asmōnae(us)* of *Hasmōn* (< Gk *Asmōnaios*) + -AN]

has·n't (haz′ənt), *n.* contraction of *has not.*

hasp (hasp, häsp), *n.* **1.** a clasp for a door, lid, etc., esp. one passing over a staple and fastened by a pin or a padlock. —*v.t.* **2.** to fasten with or as with a hasp. [ME; OE *hæsp, hæpse*; c. G *Haspe* hasp; akin to D *haspel* reel, Icel *hespa* skein, hasp]

Has·sam (has′əm), *n.* **(Frederick) Childe** (chīld), 1859–1935, U.S. painter and etcher.

Has·san (hä′sən, ha san′), *n.* Hasan.

Hassan II, born 1929, king of Morocco since 1961.

has·sen·pfef·fer (hä′sən fef′ər), *n.* hasenpfeffer.

has·sle (has′əl), *n. Informal.* quarrel; squabble. [var. of obs. *harsell* to irritate < MF *harcell(er)*, deriv. of *herse* harrow; see HEARSE]

has·sock (has′ək), *n.* **1.** a thick, firm cushion used as a footstool or for kneeling. **2.** ottoman (def. 6). **3.** a rank tuft of coarse grass or sedge, as in a bog. [ME; OE *hassuc* coarse grass]

hast (hast), *v. Archaic.* 2nd pers. sing. pres. indic. of **have.**

has·ta la vis·ta (äs′tä lä bēs′tä; *Eng.* hä′stə lə vē′stə), *Spanish.* until I see you until we meet; so long; good-by.

has·ta lue·go (äs′tä lwe′gō; *Eng.* hä′stə lo͞o ā′gō), *Spanish.* see you later; so long.

has·ta ma·ña·na (äs′tä mä nyä′nä; *Eng.* hä′stə mən yä′nə), *Spanish.* see you tomorrow.

has·tate (has′tāt), *adj. Bot.* (of a leaf) triangular or shaped like a halberd, with two spreading lobes at the base. [< L *hastāt(us)* armed with a spear, equiv. to *hast(a)* spear + *-ātus* -ATE¹] —**has′tate·ly,** *adv.*

Hastate leaf

haste (hāst), *n., v.,* **hast·ed, hast·ing.** —*n.* **1.** swiftness of motion; speed: *He performed his task with great haste. They felt the need for haste.* **2.** urgent need of quick action; a hurry: *to be in haste to get ahead in the world.* **3.** unnecessarily quick action; thoughtless, rash, or undue speed: *Haste makes waste.* **4. make haste,** to act or go with speed; hurry: *She made haste to tell her mother the good news.* —*v.i., v.t.* **5.** *Chiefly Literary.* to hasten. [ME < OF < OFris *hāst* haste; akin to OE *hǣst* violence, ON *heifst* hatred, Goth *haifsts* struggle] —**haste′ful,** *adj.* —**haste′ful·ly,** *adv.* —**haste′less,** *adj.* —**haste′less·ness,** *n.*
—**Syn. 1.** See **speed. 2.** flurry, bustle, ado, urgency. **3.** precipitancy, precipitation. —**Ant. 1.** sloth.

has·ten (hā′sən), *v.i.* **1.** to move or act with haste; proceed with haste; hurry: *to hasten to a place.* —*v.t.* **2.** to cause to hasten; accelerate: *to hasten someone from a room; to hasten the arrival of a happier time.* [HASTE + -EN¹] —**has′ten·er,** *n.*
—**Syn. 2.** urge, press; expedite, quicken, speed; precipitate.

Has·tings (hā′stingz), *n.* **1. Thomas,** 1860–1929, U.S. architect. **2. Warren,** 1732–1818, British statesman: first governor general of India 1773–85. **3.** a seaport in E Sussex, in SE England: William the Conqueror defeated the Saxons near here on Senlac Hill 1066. 66,346 (1961). **4.** a city in S Nebraska. 21,412 (1960). **5.** a town in SE Minnesota. 8965 (1960). **6.** a town in SW Michigan. 6375 (1960). **7.** a boy's given name.

Has·tings-on-Hud·son (hā′stingz on hud′sən, -ôn-), *n.* a town in SE New York. 8979 (1960).

hast·y (hā′stē), *adj.,* **hast·i·er, hast·i·est. 1.** moving or acting with haste; speedy; quick; hurried. **2.** made or done with haste or speed: *a hasty visit.* **3.** unduly quick; precipitate; rash: *a hasty decision.* **4.** brief; fleeting; slight; superficial: *a hasty glance.* **5.** impatient; impetuous; thoughtless; injudicious: *hasty words.* **6.** easily excited to anger; irascible: *a hasty temper.* [ME < MF *hasti*, back formation from *hastis* (pl.), equiv. to *hastif* (see HASTE, -IVE) + *-s* -S³] —**hast′i·ly,** *adv.* —**hast′i·ness,** *n.*
—**Syn. 1.** swift, rapid, fast, fleet, brisk. **3.** foolhardy, reckless, headlong, indiscreet. **6.** testy, touchy, fiery, excitable, irritable. —**Ant. 1.** slow. **3.** deliberate.

hast′y pud′ding, 1. *Chiefly Brit.* a dish made of flour or oatmeal stirred into seasoned boiling water or milk and quickly cooked. **2.** *U.S.* corn-meal mush.

hat (hat), *n., v.,* **hat·ted, hat·ting.** —*n.* **1.** a shaped covering for the head, usually with a crown and brim, esp. for wear outdoors. **2.** *Rom. Cath. Ch.* **a.** the distinctive head covering of a cardinal. **b.** the office or dignity of a cardinal. Cf. **red hat. 3. hat in hand,** humbly; respectfully: *He approached the boss, hat in hand.* **4. pass the hat,** *Informal.* to ask for contributions of money, as for charity; take up a collection: *The lodge members passed around the hat to send underprivileged children to summer camp.* **5. take off one's hat to,** to express high regard for; praise: *We took off our hats to their courage and daring.* **6. talk through one's hat,** *Informal.* to speak without knowing the facts; make unsupported or incorrect statements: *He is talking through his hat when he says he'll make the team.* **7. throw** or **toss one's hat in the ring,** to become a participant in a contest, esp. to declare one's candidacy for political office: *His friends are urging him to throw his hat in the ring.* **8. under one's hat,** *Informal.* confidential; private; secret: *I'll tell you the real story, but keep it under your hat.* —*v.t.* **9.** to provide with a hat; put a hat on. [ME; OE *hætt*; c. Icel *höttr* hood; akin to L *cassis* helmet] —**hat′less,** *adj.* —**hat′less·ness,** *n.* —**hat′like′,** *adj.*

hat·a·ble (hā′tə bəl), *adj.* hateable.

Ha·ta·su (hə tä′so͞o), *n.* Hatshepsut.

hat·band (hat′band′), *n.* **1.** a band or ribbon placed about the crown of a hat, just above the brim. **2.** a black band similarly worn as a sign of mourning. [HAT + BAND²]

Hat·bor·o (hat′bûr ō, -bur ō), *n.* a town in SE Pennsylvania. 7315 (1960).

hat·box (hat′boks′), *n.* a case or box for a hat. [HAT + BOX¹]

hatch¹ (hach), *v.t.* **1.** to bring forth (young) from the egg. **2.** to cause young to emerge from (the egg) as by brooding or incubating. **3.** to bring forth or produce; devise; create; contrive; concoct: *to hatch a scheme.* —*v.i.* **4.** to be hatched. **5.** (of a hen) to brood. —*n.* **6.** the act of hatching. **7.** that which is hatched, as a brood. [ME *hacche(n)*; akin to G *hecken* to hatch] —**hatch′a·bil′i·ty,** *n.* —**hatch′a·ble,** *adj.* —**hatch′er,** *n.*
—**Syn. 1.** incubate, brood. **3.** plan, plot.

hatch² (hach), *n.* **1.** *Naut.* **a.** an arrangement for covering and protecting a hatchway or other deck opening, generally consisting of a cover raised on a coaming. **b.** the cover itself: *Batten down the hatches!* **c.** hatchway (def. 1). **2.** an opening that serves as a doorway or window in the floor or roof of a building. **3.** the cover over such an opening. **4.** *Slang.* the throat as used for drinking: *His usual toast was a muttered "Down the hatch!"* **5.** *Aeron.* (loosely) an opening or door in an aircraft. **6.** the lower half of a divided door, both parts of which can be opened separately. **7.** a small door, grated opening, or serving counter in or attached to the wall of a building, room, etc., as for a merchant's stall. **8.** a bin or compartment built into a confined space, esp. a deep storage bin. **9.** anything resembling a hatch. [ME *hacche*, OE *hæcc* grating, hatch, half-gate; akin to D *hek* gate, railing]

hatch³ (hach), *v.t.* **1.** to mark with lines, esp. closely set parallel lines, as for shading in drawing or engraving. —*n.* **2.** a shading line in drawing or engraving. [late ME *hache* < MF *hach(er)* (to) cut up, deriv. of *hache* ax. See HATCHET]

Hatch′ Act′, either of two acts of Congress (1939, 1940), regulating expenditures, contributions, and procedures in political campaigns. [named after Carl A. Hatch (b. 1889), American lawyer and politician]

hatch′ boat′, 1. *U.S.* a small fishing vessel having covered wells for holding the catch. **2.** any vessel having its upper deck largely occupied by hatches.

hat·check (hat′chek′), *adj.* **1.** of, pertaining to, or noting the checking of hats, coats, umbrellas, etc., into temporary safekeeping. **2.** used in checking hats, coats, etc.: *a hatcheck room.* [HAT + CHECK]

hatch·el (hach′əl), *n., v.,* **-eled, -el·ing** or (*esp. Brit.*) **-elled, -el·ling.** —*n.* **1.** hackle¹ (def. 4). —*v.t.* **2.** hackle¹ (def. 6).

hatch·er·y (hach′ə rē), *n., pl.* **-er·ies.** a place for hatching eggs of hens, fish, etc., esp. a large, commercial or government site where the young are hatched, cared for, and sold or distributed. [HATCH¹ + -ERY]

hatch·et (hach′it), *n.* **1.** a small, short-handled ax having the end of the head opposite the blade in the form of a hammer, made to be used with one hand. See illus. under **ax. 2.** a tomahawk. **3.** hatchetfish. **4. bury the hatchet** or **tomahawk,** to become reconciled or reunited; make peace. **5. take up the hatchet,** to begin or resume hostilities; prepare for or go to war: *The natives are taking up the hatchet against the enemy.* [ME *hachet* < MF *hachette*, dim. (see -ET) of *hache* ax < Gmc **hapja* kind of knife; akin to Gk *kóptein* to cut] —**hatch′et-like′,** *adj.*

hatch′et door′. See **Dutch door.**

hatch′et face′, a thin face with sharp features. —**hatch′et-faced′,** *adj.*

Hatchetfish, Genus *Argyropelicus* (Length to 3½ in.)

hatch·et·fish (hach′it fish′), *n., pl.* (*esp. collectively*) **-fish,** (*esp. referring to two or more kinds or species*) **-fish·es.** any of several deep-sea fishes of the genera *Argyropelicus, Sternoptyx,* etc., found in tropical and temperate waters, having a silvery, hatchet-shaped body. [HATCHET + FISH]

hatch′et job′, *Informal.* a maliciously destructive critique or act: *After she left they did a hatchet job on the club's new member.*

hatch′et man′, *Informal.* **1.** a professional murderer. **2.** a writer or speaker who specializes in defamatory attacks, as on political candidates or public officials. **3.** one whose job it is to execute unpleasant tasks for a superior, as criticizing or dismissing employees.

hatch·ett·ite (hach′i tīt′), *n.* a soft yellowish mineral wax, darkening on exposure: found in bogs and coal beds. Also, **hatch·ett·ine** (hach′i tēn′, -tin). Also called **adipocerite.** [named after Charles Hatchett (c1765–1847), English chemist; see -ITE¹]

hatch·ing (hach′ing), *n.* a series of lines, generally parallel, used in shading or modeling, as in drawing or cartography. [HATCH³ + -ING¹]

hatch′ mast′, *U.S. Naut.* a mast near a hatch, used only for loading and unloading cargo.

hatch·ment (hach′mənt), *n. Chiefly Brit.* a square tablet, set diagonally, bearing the coat of arms of a deceased person. [var. (by syncopation and aspiration) of ACHIEVEMENT]

Hatchment

hatch·way (hach′wā′), *n.* **1.** Also called **hatch.** *Naut.* a covered opening in a deck, used as a means of passage for cargo, supplies, persons, machinery, etc. **2.** the opening of any trap door, as in a floor, ceiling, or roof. [HATCH² + WAY]

hat′ dance′, a Mexican folk dance in which the man places his sombrero on the ground as an offer of love and the woman dances on the hat's brim and then places the hat on her head to indicate her acceptance of him.

hate¹ (hāt), *v.,* **hat·ed, hat·ing,** *n.* —*v.t.* **1.** to dislike intensely or passionately; detest; feel extreme aversion for or extreme hostility toward: *to hate the enemy.* **2.** to dislike; be unwilling: *I hate to do it.* —*v.i.* **3.** to feel intense dislike, or extreme aversion or hostility. —*n.* **4.** intense dislike; extreme aversion or hostility. **5.** the object of extreme aversion or hostility. [ME *hat(i)e(n)*, OE *hatian*; c. D *haten*, Icel *hata*, Goth *hatan*, G *hassen*] —**hat′er,** *n.*
—**Syn. 1.** loathe, execrate; despise. HATE, ABHOR, DETEST, ABOMINATE imply feeling intense dislike or aversion toward something. HATE, the simple and general word, suggests passionate dislike and a feeling of enmity: *to hate autocracy.* ABHOR expresses a deep-rooted horror and a sense of repugnance or complete rejection: *to abhor cruelty; Nature abhors a vacuum.* DETEST implies intense, even vehement, dislike and antipathy, besides a sense of disdain: *to detest a combination of ignorance and arrogance.* ABOMINATE expresses a strong feeling of disgust and repulsion toward something thought of as unworthy, unlucky, and the like: *to abominate treachery.* —**Ant. 1.** love.

hate² (hāt), *n. Scot.* a bit or particle; a small quantity: *Not a hate was left.* Also, **haet.** [var. of *hae it*, Scot form of *have it.* See HAVE, IT¹]

hate·a·ble (hā′tə bəl), *adj.* meriting hatred or loathing. Also, **hatable.** [HATE¹ + -ABLE]

hate·ful (hāt′fəl), *adj.* **1.** exciting hate or deserving to be hated: *the hateful oppression of dictators.* **2.** unpleasant; dislikable; distasteful: *She found her domestic chores hateful.* **3.** full of or expressing hate; malignant; malevolent: *a hateful, denunciatory speech.* [ME; see HATE¹, -FUL] —**hate′ful·ly,** *adv.* —**hate′ful·ness,** *n.*
—**Syn. 1.** abominable, execrable, abhorrent, repugnant; invidious, loathsome. HATEFUL, OBNOXIOUS, ODIOUS, OFFENSIVE refer to that which causes strong dislike or annoyance. HATEFUL implies actually causing hatred or extremely strong dislike: *The sight of him is hateful to me.* OBNOXIOUS emphasizes causing annoyance or discomfort by objectionable qualities: *His persistence made him seem obnoxious. His piggish manners made him obnoxious to his companions.* ODIOUS emphasizes the disagreeable or displeasing: *an odious little man; odious servility.* OFFENSIVE emphasizes the distaste and resentment caused by something which may be either displeasing or insulting: *an offensive odor, remark.* —**Ant. 1.** likable, pleasant, agreeable.

hate·mon·ger (hāt′mung′gər, -mong′-), *n.* one who kindles hatred, enmity, or prejudice in others: *The senator's opponent was a hatemonger capitalizing on resentment in a poverty-stricken area.* [HATE¹ + MONGER] —**hate′mon′ger·ing,** *n.*

hate′ sheet′, a newspaper or other publication which consistently expresses biased hatred toward some race, nationality, religion, or other group.

Hat·field (hat′fēld′), *n.* **1.** Also called **Bishop's Hatfield.** a town in central Hertfordshire, in SE England. 20,504 (1961). **2.** a boy's given name.

hath (hath), *v. Archaic.* 3rd pers. sing. pres. indic. of **have.**

Hath·a·way (hath′ə wā′), *n.* **1. Anne,** 1557–1623, the wife of William Shakespeare. **2.** a boy's given name.

Hath·or (hath′ôr, -ər), *n. Egyptian Religion.* the goddess of love and joy, often represented with the head, horns, or ears of a cow.

Hath′or col′umn, a Hathor-headed column.

Hath·or-head·ed (hath′ər hed′id), *adj.* (of an ancient Egyptian column) having a capital in the form of the head of Hathor; Hathoric.

Ha·thor·ic (hə thôr′ik, -thor′-), *adj.* **1.** of or pertaining to Hathor. **2.** *Archit.* Hathor-headed. [HATHOR + -IC]

hath·pace (hath′pās′), *n.* a raised platform, as a dais. Also, **halfpace.** [var. of HALFPACE]

Ha·tik·vah (hä tēk′vä, -tik′vô, -və), *n.* the national anthem of Israel.

hat·pin (hat′pin′), *n.* a long pin for securing a woman's hat to her hair, usually having a bulbous head of colored glass, simulated pearl, or the like. [HAT + PIN]

hat·rack (hat′rak′), *n.* a frame, stand, or post having knobs or hooks for hanging hats. [HAT + RACK¹]

ha·tred (hā′trid), *n.* the feeling of one who hates; intense dislike or extreme aversion or hostility. [ME *hatereden.* See HATE¹, -RED]
—**Syn.** animosity, detestation, loathing, abomination. —**Ant.** attraction, love.

Hat·shep·sut (hat shep′so͞ot), *n.* 1495–75 B.C., queen of Egypt. Also, **Hatasu, Hat·shep·set** (hat shep′set).

Hat·ta (hat′ə), *n.* **Mohammed,** born 1902, Indonesian political leader: vice-president of the Republic of Indonesia 1945–49, 1950–56; prime minister 1948, 1949–50.

hat·ter¹ (hat′ər), *n.* a maker or seller of hats. [ME; see HAT, -ER¹]

hat·ter² (hat′ər), *n. Australian Informal.* **1.** a person who has become eccentric from living alone in a remote area. **2.** a person who lives alone in the bush, as a herder, prospector, or the like. [said to be from the phrase "as mad as a hatter"]

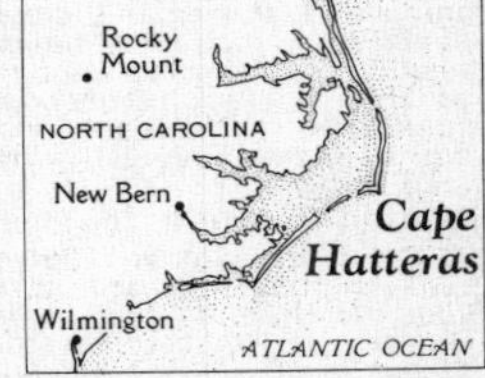

Hat·ter·as (hat′ər əs), *n.* **Cape,** a promontory on an island off the E coast of North Carolina.

Hat·ti (hat′ē), *n.* **1.** an ancient people who lived in central Anatolia before its conquest by the Hittites. **2.** (in ancient inscriptions) the Hittites or the land of the Hittites. Also, **Khatti.** —**Hat′ti·an,** *n., adj.*

Hat·tic (hat′ik), *adj.* of or pertaining to the Hatti. [HATT(I) + -IC]

Hat·ties·burg (hat′ēz bûrg′), *n.* a city in SE Mississippi. 34,989 (1960).

hat′ tree′. See **hall tree.**

hat′ trick′, 1. *Cricket.* the knocking off by one bowler of three wickets with three successive pitches: so called because formerly such a bowler was rewarded with a hat. 2. *Baseball.* a series of a base hit, a two-base hit, a three-base hit, and a home run achieved in any order by one player in one game. 3. *Ice Hockey, Soccer.* three goals or points scored by one player in one game.

Hat·tu·sas (hät′to͞o säs′), *n.* the capital of the ancient Hittite empire in Asia Minor: site of modern Boghazköy, Turkey. Also, **Khattusas.**

Hat·ty (hat′ē), *n.* a girl's given name, form of **Harriet.** Also, **Hat′tie.**

hau·ber·geon (hô′bər jən), *n.* *Armor.* habergeon.

hau·berk (hô′bûrk), *n.* *Armor.* a long defensive shirt, usually of mail, extending to the knees; byrnie. [ME < OF *hauberc*, earlier *halberc* < OHG *halsberc*, equiv. to *hals* neck (see HAWSE) + *berc* protection (see HARBOR); c. OE *healsbeorg*, Icel *halsbjörg*]

hau·er·ite (hou′ə rīt′), *n.* a rare mineral, manganese sulfide, MnS_2, occurring in brownish-black cubic crystals. [named after Franz von *Hauer* (1822–99), Austrian geologist; see -ITE[1]]

haugh (häkh, häf), *n.* *Scot. and North Eng.* a stretch of alluvial land forming part of a river valley; bottom land. [ME *halche, hawgh*, OE *healh* corner, nook]

haugh·ty (hô′tē), *adj.*, **-ti·er, -ti·est.** 1. disdainfully proud; snobbish; arrogant; supercilious: *haughty aristocrats; a haughty salesclerk.* 2. *Archaic.* exalted; lofty or noble. [obs. *haught* (sp. var. of late ME *haute* < MF << L *alt(us)* high, with *h-* < OHG *hok* high) + -Y[1]] —**haugh′ti·ly,** *adv.* —**haugh′ti·ness,** *n.*
—**Syn.** 1. lordly, disdainful, contemptuous. See **proud.**
—**Ant.** 1. humble, unpretentious, unassuming.

haul (hôl), *v.t.* 1. to pull or draw with force; move by drawing; drag: *They hauled the boat up the beach.* 2. to cart or transport; carry: *He hauled freight.* 3. to lower; cause to descend (often fol. by *down*): *to haul down the flag.* 4. to arrest or bring before a magistrate or other authority (often fol. by *before, in, to, into,* etc.): *He was hauled before the judge.* —*v.i.* 5. to pull or tug. 6. to go or come to a place, esp. with effort: *After rousting about the streets, they finally hauled into the tavern.* 7. to do carting or transport, or move freight commercially. 8. *Naut.* to sail, as in a particular direction. 9. to draw or pull a vessel up on land, as for repairs or storage. 10. *Naut.* (of the wind) to shift to a direction closer to the heading of a vessel (opposed to *veer*). 11. *Rare.* (of the wind) to change direction, shift, or veer (often fol. by *round* or *to*). 12. **haul around,** *Naut.* **a.** to brace (certain yards of a sailing vessel). **b.** (of the wind) to change in a clockwise direction. 13. **haul in with,** *Naut.* to approach. 14. **haul of all!** *Naut.* brace all yards for a new tack! 15. **haul off, a.** *Naut.* to change a ship's course so as to get further off from an object. **b.** to withdraw; leave. **c.** *Informal.* to draw back the arm in order to strike; prepare to deal a blow: *He hauled off and struck the insolent lieutenant a blow to the chin.* 16. **haul up, a.** *Informal.* to bring (before a superior) for reprimand; call to account. **b.** *U.S.* to come to a halt; stop. **c.** *Naut.* to change the course of (a sailing vessel) so as to sail closer to the wind. **d.** *Naut.* (of a sailing vessel) to come closer to the wind. **e.** *Naut.* (of a vessel) to come to a halt. —*n.* 17. the act or an instance of hauling; a strong pull or tug. 18. that which is hauled. 19. the load hauled at one time; quantity carried or transported. 20. the distance or route over which anything is hauled. 21. *Fishing.* **a.** the quantity of fish taken at one draft of the net. **b.** the draft of a fishing net. **c.** the place where a seine is hauled. 22. *Informal.* the taking or acquisition of anything, or that which is taken. 23. **long haul, a.** a relatively great period of time: *In the long haul, he'll regret having been a school dropout.* **b.** a relatively great distance: *It's a long haul from Maine to Texas.* **c.** *Naut.* the drawing up on shore of a vessel for a relatively long period of time, as for winter storage or longer. 24. **short haul, a.** a relatively small period of time: *For the short haul, he'll be able to get by on what he earns.* **b.** a relatively little distance: *The axle wouldn't break for just a short haul.* **c.** *Naut.* the drawing up on shore of a vessel for a relatively short period, as for repairs, painting, etc. [earlier *hall*, var. of HALE[2]]
—**Syn.** 1. See **draw.**

haul·age (hô′lij), *n.* 1. the act or labor of hauling. 2. the amount of force expended in hauling. 3. a charge made by a railroad for hauling cars, equipment, or commodities. [HAUL + -AGE]

haul·back (hôl′bak′), *n.* (in lumbering) a small line for pulling a cable back to its original position after it has been used to haul a log away. Also called **trip line.** [n. use of v. phrase *haul back*]

haul·er (hô′lər), *n.* 1. a person who hauls. 2. *Brit.* **a.** a commercial trucking company. **b.** a moving van or freight truck. **c.** (formerly) a worker who pulled or pushed coal carts in a coal mine. [HAUL + -ER[1]]

haul·ier (hôl′yər), *n.* *Brit. Dial.* hauler.

haulm (hôm), *n.* *Brit.* 1. stems or stalks collectively, as of grain or of peas, beans, hops, etc., as used for litter or thatching. 2. a single stem or stalk. Also, **halm.** [ME *halm*, OE *healm*; c. D, G *halm*, Icel *halmr*; akin to L *culmus* stalk, Gk *kálamos* reed]

Haunce (hôns), *n.* a boy's given name.

haunch (hônch, hänch), *n.* 1. the hip. 2. the fleshy part of the body about the hip. 3. a hind quarter of an animal. 4. the leg and loin of an animal, used for food. 5. *Archit.* **a.** Also called **hance.** either side of an arch, extending from the vertex or crown to the impost. **b.** the part of a beam projecting below a floor or roof slab. [ME *haunche* < OF *hanche* < Gmc; cf. MD *hanke* haunch, hip, G *Hanke* haunch] —**haunched,** *adj.* —**haunch′less,** *adj.*

haunch′ bone′, the ilium or hipbone.

haunt (hônt, hänt; *for 10 sometimes also* hant), *v.t.* 1. to visit habitually or appear to frequent as a spirit or ghost: *to haunt a house; to haunt a person.* 2. to recur persistently to the consciousness of; remain with: *Memories of love haunted him.* 3. to visit frequently; go to often: *He haunted the galleries and bars that the artists went to.* 4. to frequent the company of; be often with: *He haunted famous men, hoping to gain celebrity for himself.* 5. to disturb or distress; cause to have anxiety; trouble; worry: *His youthful escapades came back to haunt him.* —*v.i.* 6. to reappear continually as a spirit or ghost. 7. to visit habitually or regularly. 8. to remain persistently; loiter; stay; linger. —*n.* 9. Often, **haunts.** a place frequently visited: *to return to one's old haunts.* 10. *Chiefly Midland and Southern U.S.* a ghost. [ME *haunt(en)* < OF *hant(er)* < OE *hāmettan* to domicile, deriv. of *hām* HOME] —**haunt′er,** *n.*

haunt·ed (hôn′tid), *adj.* 1. inhabited or frequented by ghosts: *a haunted castle.* 2. obsessed; preoccupied, as with an emotion, memory, or idea: *His haunted imagination gave him no peace.* 3. disturbed; distressed; worried: *Haunted by doubt he again turned to law books on the subject.* [ME; see HAUNT, -ED[2]]

haunt·ing (hôn′ting), *adj.* 1. remaining in the consciousness; not quickly forgotten: *haunting music; haunting memories.* —*n.* 2. the act of one who or that which haunts; visitation. [ME; see HAUNT, -ING[2], -ING[1]] —**haunt′ing·ly,** *adv.*

Haupt·mann (houpt′män′), *n.* **Ger·hart** (ger′härt), 1862–1946, German dramatist, novelist, and poet: Nobel prize 1912.

hau·ri·ant (hôr′ē ənt), *adj.* *Heraldry.* (of a fish) represented as erect, with the head upward: *a dolphin hauriant.* [var. of *haurient* < L *haurient-* (s. of *hauriēns*) drawing in, prp. of *haurīre*; see -ANT, -ENT]

Hau·sa (hou′sä), *n.*, *pl.* **-sas,** (*esp. collectively*) **-sa.** 1. a member of a Negroid people of the Sudan whose culture has been strongly influenced by Islam. 2. the language of the Hausa people, an Afro-Asiatic language that is also widely used in Africa as a language of commerce. Also, **Haussa.**

Haus′dorff space′ (hous′dôrf, houz′-), *Math.* a topological space in which each pair of points can be separated by two disjoint open sets containing the points.

hau·sen (hô′zən; *Ger.* hou′zən), *n.* beluga (def. 1). [< G; OHG *hūso*]

haus·frau (hous′frou′), *n.*, *pl.* **-fraus, -frau·en** (-frou′ən). a housewife. [< G, equiv. to *Haus* HOUSE + *Frau* wife, woman]

Haus·ho·fer (hous′hō fər), *n.* **Karl,** 1860–1946, German geographer and general.

Haus·sa (hou′sä), *n.*, *pl.* **-sas,** (*esp. collectively*) **-sa.** Hausa.

Hauss·mann (hous′mən; *Fr.* ōs man′), *n.* **Georges Eu·gène** (zhôrzh œ zhen′), **Baron,** 1809–91, French administrator who improved the landscaping, street designs, and utilities systems of Paris. —**Hauss·mann·i·za·tion** (hous′mə ni zā′shən), *n.*

haust., (in prescriptions) a draught. [< L *haustus*]

haus·tel·late (hô stel′it, hô′stə lāt′), *adj.* *Zool.* 1. having a haustellum. 2. adapted for sucking, as the mouth parts of certain insects. [HAUSTELL(UM) + -ATE[1]]

haus·tel·lum (hô stel′əm), *n.*, *pl.* **haus·tel·la** (hô stel′ə). (in certain crustaceans and insects) an organ or part of the proboscis adapted for sucking blood or plant juices. [< NL, equiv. to L *haust(rum)* machine for drawing water (*haus-* (var. s. of *haurīre* to draw up) + *-trum* instrumental suffix) + *-ellum* dim. suffix]

haus·to·ri·um (hô stôr′ē əm, -stōr′-), *n.*, *pl.* **haus·to·ri·a** (hô stôr′ē ə, -stōr′-). *Bot.* an intracellular feeding organ of a parasite which does not kill the host cells but lives with them. [< NL, equiv. to L *haust(us)* drawn up, drained (ptp. of *haurīre*) + *-ōrium* -ORY[2]] —**haus·to′ri·al,** *adj.*

haut·bois (hō′boi, ō′boi), *n.*, *pl.* **-bois.** hautboy.

haut′bois straw′ber·ry, a hairy, perennial herb, *Fragaria moschata*, of Europe, having musky, dull red fruit. [so called from the shape of the curved stem]

haut·boy (hō′boi, ō′boi), *n.* *Archaic.* oboe. [< MF *hautbois*, equiv. to *haut* high (see HAUGHTY) + *bois* wood (see BUSH[1])] —**haut′boy·ist,** *n.*

haute cou·ture (ōt ko͞o tyr′), *French.* 1. high fashion; the most fashionable and influential dressmaking and designing. 2. the fashions so created. 3. the leading dressmaking establishments in the world of fashion, considered collectively.

haute cui·sine (ōt kwē zēn′), *French.* fine cooking; food preparation as an art.

haute é·cole (ō tā kôl′), *pl.* ***hautes é·coles*** (ōt zā kôl′). *French.* 1. a series of intricate steps, gaits, etc., taught to an exhibition horse. 2. dressage (def. 2). [lit., high school]

Haute-Ga·ronne (ōt ga rôn′), *n.* a department in S France. 594,633 (1962); 2458 sq. mi. *Cap.:* Toulouse.

Haute-Loire (ōt lwar′), *n.* a department in central France. 211,036 (1962); 1931 sq. mi. *Cap.:* Le Puy.

Haute-Marne (ōt marn′), *n.* a department in E France. 214,748 (1962); 2416 sq. mi. *Cap.:* Chaumont.

haute-piece (hōt′pēs′), *n.* *Armor.* a standing flange fixed to or formed on a pauldron as a protection for one side of the neck. [< F: lit., high piece]

Hautes-Alpes (ōt zalp′), *n.* a department in SE France. 87,436 (1962); 2179 sq. mi. *Cap.:* Gap.

Haute-Saône (ōt sōn′), *n.* a department in E France. 208,440 (1962); 2075 sq. mi. *Cap.:* Vesoul.

Haute-Sa·voie (ōt sa vwä′), *n.* a department in E France. 329,230 (1962); 1775 sq. mi. *Cap.:* Annecy.

Hautes-Py·ré·nées (ōt pē rā nā′), *n.* a department in SW France. 211,433 (1962); 1751 sq. mi. *Cap.:* Tarbes.

hau·teur (hō tûr′; *Fr.* ō tœr′), *n.* haughty manner or spirit; haughtiness. [< F, equiv. to *haut* high (see HAUGHTY) + *-eur*; see -OR[1]]

Haute-Vienne (ōt vyen′), *n.* a department in central France. 332,514 (1962); 2145 sq. mi. *Cap.:* Limoges.

haut monde (ō mônd′), *French.* high society.

Haut-Rhin (ō ran′), *n.* a department in NE France. 547,920 (1962); 1354 sq. mi. *Cap.:* Colmar.

ha·üy·nite (ä wē′nīt), *n.* a feldspathoid mineral, chiefly sodium aluminum silicate, having a lustrous blue color: often confused with lapis lazuli. Also, **ha·üyne** (ä wēn′). [< F *haüyne* (*Haüy* + *-(i)ne* -INE[1], named after R. *Haüy* (1743–1822), French mineralogist) + -ITE[1]]

hav, haversine.

Ha·van·a (hə van′ə), *n.* 1. Spanish, **Habana.** a seaport in and the capital of Cuba, on the NW coast. 978,400 (est. 1962). 2. a town in central Illinois. 4363 (1960). 3. a cigar made in Cuba or of Cuban tobacco.

Hav·da·la (häb dä lä′; *Eng.* häv dô′lə), *n.* *Hebrew.* Habdalah.

have (hav; *unstressed* həv, əv), *v.* and *auxiliary v.*, *pres. sing. 1st pers.* **have,** *2nd* **have** or (*Archaic*) **hast,** *3rd* **has** or (*Archaic*) **hath,** *pres. pl.* **have;** *past sing. 1st pers.* **had,** *2nd* **had** or (*Archaic*) **hadst** or **had·dest,** *3rd* **had,** *past pl.* **had;** *past part.* **had;** *pres. part.* **hav·ing,** *n.* —*v.t.* 1. to possess; own; hold for use; contain: *He has property. The work has an index.* 2. to hold, possess, or accept in some relation, as of kindred, relative position, etc.: *He wanted to marry her, but she wouldn't have him.* 3. to get, receive, or take: *to have a part in a play; to have news.* 4. to be required, compelled, or under obligation (usually fol. by an infinitive): *I have ironing to finish, and then I have to go out.* 5. to experience, undergo, or endure, as joy or pain: *Have a good time. He had a heart attack last year.* 6. to hold in mind, sight, etc.: *to have doubts.* 7. to cause to, as by command, invitation, etc.: *Have him come here at five.* 8. to be related to or be in a certain relation to: *She has three cousins. He has a kind boss.* 9. to show or exhibit in action or words: *She had the crust to refuse my invitation. Have the goodness to pass the salt.* 10. to be identified or distinguished by; possess the characteristic of: *He has a mole on his left cheek. This wood has a silky texture.* 11. to engage in or carry on: *to have a talk; to have a fight.* 12. to partake of; eat or drink: *He had cake and coffee before going to bed.* 13. to permit or allow: *I will not have it.* 14. to assert, maintain, or represent as being: *Rumor has it that she's going to be married.* 15. to know, understand, or be skilled in: *to have neither Latin nor Greek.* 16. to beget or give birth to: *to have a baby.* 17. to hold at a disadvantage: *He has you there.* 18. *Slang.* **a.** to outwit, deceive, or cheat: *The gambler had him.* **b.** to control or possess through bribery; bribe. 19. to gain possession of: *There are none to be had at that price.* 20. to hold or put in a certain position or situation: *The problem had me stumped. They had him where they wanted him.* 21. to exercise, display, or make use of: *Have pity on him.* 22. to entertain; invite or cause to be present as a companion or guest: *We had Evelyn and Everett over for dinner. He has his bodyguard with him at all times.* 23. to engage in sexual intercourse with. —*v.i.* 24. to be in possession of money and the accouterments of financial security: *There are some who have and some who have not.* —*auxiliary verb.* 25. (used with a past participle to form perfect tenses): *She has gone. It would have been an enjoyable party if he hadn't felt downcast.* 26. **had better** or **best,** ought to: *You'd better go now, it's late.* 27. **had rather** or **sooner,** to prefer: *I had much rather he go with you.* 28. **have at,** to go at vigorously; attack: *First he decided to have at his correspondence.* 29. **have done,** to cease; finish: *It seemed that they would never have done with their struggle.* 30. **have had it,** *Slang.* **a.** to become weary of or disgusted with whatever one has been doing: *I've been working like a fool, but now I've had it.* **b.** to suffer defeat; fail: *He was a great pitcher, but after this season he'll have had it.* **c.** to have had and missed a last opportunity, as to prove one's ability: *He refused to take any more excuses and told them all that they'd had it.* **d.** to become unpopular or passé: *Quiz shows have had it.* 31. **have it coming,** *Informal.* to be deserving of something that befalls one, esp. a misfortune: *When they lost their fortune, everyone said that they had it coming.* 32. **have it in for,** *Informal.* to wish harm to come to; hold a grudge against: *She has it in for intelligent students who fail to use their abilities.* 33. **have it out,** to come to an understanding or decision through discussion or combat: *We've been in disagreement about this for a long time, and I think we should have it out, once and for all.* 34. **have on, a.** to be clothed in; wear: *She had on a new dress.* **b.** to have arranged or planned: *What do you have on for Christmas?* 35. **have someone on,** *Chiefly Brit.* to tease a person; make a person the butt of a joke. Cf. **put** (def. 35). 36. **have to do with, a.** to be connected with: *I've had little to do with people of that class.* **b.** to deal with; be concerned with: *I will have nothing to do with their personal squabbles.* 37. **not having any,** *Chiefly Brit.* **a.** refusing to accept or believe the decision, information, or attitude of another: *He told me she wasn't in her apartment, but I wasn't having any and barged right in.* **b.** refusing to join a group or take part in an activity: *She wanted to dance, but I wasn't having any.* 38. **to have and to hold,** to possess legally; have permanent possession of: *The house, with the mortgage finally paid, was at last their own to have and to hold.* —*n.* 39. Usually, **haves.** an individual who or group that has wealth, social position, etc. (contrasted with *have-not*). [ME *have(n)*, *habbe(n)*, OE *habban*; c. G *haben*, Icel *hafa*, Goth *haban* to have; ? akin to HEAVE]
—**Syn.** 1. HAVE, HOLD, OCCUPY, OWN, POSSESS mean to be, in varying degrees, in possession of something. HAVE, being the most general word, admits of the widest range of application: *to have money, rights, discretion, a disease, a glimpse, an idea; to have a friend's umbrella.* To HOLD is to have in one's grasp or one's control, but not necessarily as one's own: *to hold stakes.* To OCCUPY is to hold and use, but not necessarily by any right of ownership: *to occupy a chair, a house, a position.* To OWN is to have the full rights of property in a thing, which, however, another may be holding or enjoying: *to own a house which is rented to tenants.* POSSESS is a more formal equivalent for OWN and suggests control, and often occupation, of large holdings: *to possess vast territories.* 3. obtain, gain, secure, procure. —**Ant.** 1. lack.

have·lock (hav′lok), *n.* a cap cover with a flap hanging over the back of the neck, for protection from the sun. [named after Sir Henry *Havelock* (1795–1857), English general in India]

Have·lock (hav′lok, -lək), *n.* a boy's given name.

ha·ven (hā′vən), *n.* 1. a harbor or port. 2. any place of shelter and safety; refuge; asylum. —*v.t.* 3. to shelter, as in a haven. [ME; OE *hæfen*; c. D *haven*, G *Hafen*, Icel *höfn*; akin to OE *hæf*, Icel *haf* sea] —**ha′ven·less,** *adj.* —**ha′ven·ward,** *adv.*
—**Syn.** 1. See **harbor.**

have-not (hav′not′, -not′), *n.* Usually, **have-nots.** an individual who or group that is without wealth, social position, or other material benefits (contrasted with *have*).

have·n't (hav′ənt), contraction of *have not.*

hav·er[1] (hav′ər), *n.* *Brit. Dial.* oats, taken collectively. [ME < Scand; cf. Icel *hafrar* (pl.) oats; c. D *haver*, LG *hafer*, HG *Haber*]

ha·ver[2] (hā′vər), *Scot. and North Eng.* —*n.* 1. foolish or senseless talk; nonsense. —*v.i.* 2. to talk foolishly. [?]

ha·ver·el (hā′və rəl, hăv′rəl), *n. Scot. and North Eng.* one who talks foolishly; one who havers. [HAVER² + -REL]

Hav·er·ford (hav′ər fərd), *n.* a township in SE Pennsylvania, near Philadelphia. 54,019 (1960).

Ha·ver·hill (hā′vər il, -vrəl), *n.* a city in NE Massachusetts, on the Merrimack River. 46,346 (1960).

ha·vers (hā′vərz), *interj. Scot. and North Eng.* nonsense; poppycock. [pl. of HAVER²]

hav·er·sack (hav′ər sak′), *n.* **1.** a soldier's bag for rations, extra clothing, etc. **2.** any single-strapped bag worn over one shoulder and used for carrying provisions. [earlier *havresack* < F *havresac* < G *Habersack* sack for oats. See HAVER¹, SACK¹]

Ha·ver′sian canal′ (hə vûr′zhən), (*sometimes l.c.*) a microscopic channel in bone, through which a blood vessel runs. [named after Clopton *Havers* (d. 1702), English anatomist; see -IAN]

hav·er·sine (hav′ər sīn′), *n. Trig.* one half the versed sine of a given angle or arc. *Abbr.:* hav [HA(LF) + VER(SED) + SINE¹]

Hav·er·straw (hav′ər strô′), *n.* a town in SE New York. 5771 (1960).

Hav·i·lah (hav′ə lä′, -lə), *n.* a girl's given name.

Hav·i·land (hav′ə lənd), *n.* **John,** 1792–1852, English architect, in the U.S.

hav·il·dar (hav′əl där′), *n.* (in India) a sepoy noncommissioned officer, equivalent to a sergeant. [< Hindi *ḥawāldār*]

hav·ior (hāv′yər), *n. Archaic.* **1.** behavior. **2. haviours,** manners. [sp. var. of *haviour,* alter. of late ME *havure* ownership, property (HAVE + -URE; see BEHAVIOR); r. late ME *havoir,* earlier *avoir* < MF << L *habēre* to hold, own (*h* of *havior* from HAVE)]

hav·oc (hav′ək), *n., v.,* **-ocked, -ock·ing.** —*n.* **1.** devastation; ruinous damage. **2. cry havoc,** to warn of danger or disaster. **3. play havoc with, a.** to create confusion or disorder in: *The wind played havoc with the papers on the desk.* **b.** to destroy; ruin: *The bad weather played havoc with our vacation plans.* —*v.t.* **4.** to work havoc upon; devastate. —*v.i.* **5.** to work havoc: *The fire havocked throughout the house.* [late ME *havok* < AF (in phrase *crier havok* to cry havoc, i.e., utter the command *havoc!* as signal for pillaging), MF *havot* in same sense < Gmc; akin to HEAVE] —**hav′ock·er,** *n.*
—**Syn. 1.** desolation, waste. See **ruin.**

Ha·vre (hav′ər *for 1;* hä′vrə, -vər *for 2*), *n.* **1.** a city in N Montana. 10,742 (1960). **2.** See **Le Havre.**

Hav·re de Grace (hä′vər də gräs′, hav′ər də gras′, grās′), a town in NE Maryland. 8510 (1960).

haw¹ (hô), *n.* the fruit of the Old World hawthorn, *Crataegus Oxyacantha,* or of other species of the same genus. [ME; OE *haga;* c. D *haag* hedge, Icel *hagi* pasture. Dan *have* garden]

haw² (hô), *v.i.* **1.** to hesitate or falter in or as in speech: *He hemmed and hawed around and finally said what was on his mind.* **2.** to utter a sound representing a hesitation or pause in speech: *He cleared his throat, coughed, hemmed and hawed, then managed to go on with what he was saying.* —*n.* **3.** a sound or pause of hesitation: *His confession was full of hems and haws.* [imit.]

haw³ (hô), *interj.* **1.** (used as a word of command to a horse or other draft animal, usually directing it to turn to the left.) —*v.t., v.i.* **2.** to turn or make a turn to the left: *The horse refused to haw.* Cf. **gee¹.** [appar. orig. the impv. *haw!* look! of ME *hawen,* OE *hāwian;* akin to L *cavēre* to beware]

haw⁴ (hô), *n.* the nictitating membrane of a horse, dog, etc., formerly only when inflamed. [?]

Ha·wai·i (hə wī′ē, -wä′-, -wä′yə), *n.* **1.** Formerly, **Sandwich Islands, Ter′ritory of Hawai′i.** a State of the United States comprised of the N Pacific islands of Hawaii, Kahoolawe, Kauai, Lanai, Maui, Molokai, Niihau, and Oahu: a U.S. territory 1900–59; admitted to the union 1959. 632,772 (1960); 6454 sq. mi. *Cap.:* Honolulu. **2.** the largest island of Hawaii, in the SE part. 61,332 (1960); 4021 sq. mi.

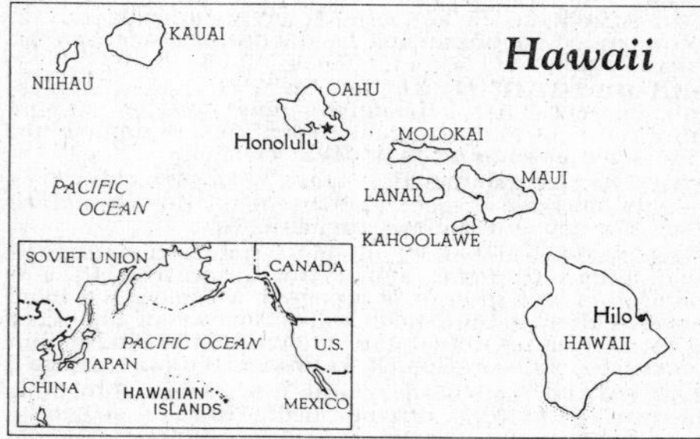

Ha·wai·ian (hə wī′ən, -wä′yən), *adj.* **1.** of or pertaining to Hawaii or the Hawaiian Islands. —*n.* **2.** a native or inhabitant of Hawaii or the Hawaiian Islands. **3.** the aboriginal language of Hawaii, a Polynesian language. [HAWAII + -AN]

Hawai′ian Is′lands, a group of islands in the N Pacific; 2090 mi. SW of San Francisco: includes the eight islands comprising the State of Hawaii and volcanic, rock, and coral islets.

Hawai′i Na′tional Park′, a large national park that includes the active volcanoes Kilauea and Mauna Loa on the island of Hawaii and the extinct crater Haleakala on Maui. 343 sq. mi.

Ha·war·den (hā′wôr′dᵊn), *n.* a town in NW Iowa. 2544 (1960).

haw·finch (hô′finch′), *n.* a European grosbeak, *Coccothraustes coccothraustes.* [HAW¹ + FINCH]

haw-haw (hô′hô′), *interj.* **1.** (used to represent the sound of a loud, boisterous laugh.) —*n.* **2.** a guffaw. [imit.; see HA-HA¹, etc.]

hawk¹ (hôk), *n.* **1.** any of numerous diurnal birds of prey either of the family *Accipitridae,* as certain accipiters, or of the family *Falconidae,* as certain falcons, caracaras, etc. **2.** any of several similar, unrelated birds, as the nighthawk. **3.** *Informal.* a person who preys on others, as a sharper. **4.** Also called **war hawk.** *Informal.* a person, esp. one in public office, who advocates war or a belligerent national attitude. —*v.i.* **5.** to fly, or hunt on the wing, like a hawk. **6.** to hunt with hawks. [ME *hauk(e),* OE *hafoc;* c. OHG *habuh,* Icel *haukr* hawk, Pol *kobuz* hobby] —**hawk′ish,** *adj.* —**hawk′like′,** *adj.*

Red-tailed hawk, *Buteo jamaicensis* (Length 2 ft.)

hawk² (hôk), *v.t.* **1.** to peddle or offer for sale by calling aloud or by going from door to door. —*v.i.* **2.** to carry wares about for sale; peddle. [back formation from HAWKER²]

hawk³ (hôk), *v.i.* **1.** to make an effort to raise phlegm from the throat; clear the throat noisily. —*v.t.* **2.** to raise by hawking: *to hawk up phlegm.* —*n.* **3.** a noisy effort to clear the throat. [imit.; see HAW²]

hawk⁴ (hôk), *n.* a small, square board with a handle underneath it, used by plasterers and masons to hold plaster or mortar being applied. [? special use of HAWK¹]

hawk·bill (hôk′bil′), *n.* See **hawksbill turtle.** [HAWK¹ + BILL²]

hawk·er¹ (hô′kər), *n.* one who hunts with hawks; a falconer. [ME; OE *hafecere.* See HAWK¹, -ER¹]

hawk·er² (hô′kər), *n.* one who offers goods for sale by shouting his wares in the street or going from door to door; peddler. [< MLG *haker* retail dealer; akin to MD *hac* in same sense]

hawk·ey (hô′kē), *n., pl.* **-eys.** *Scot. and North Eng.* hawkie.

Hawk·eye (hôk′ī′), *n., pl.* **-eyes.** a native or inhabitant of Iowa (the **Hawkeye State**) (used as a nickname). [back formation from HAWK-EYED]

hawk-eyed (hôk′īd′), *adj.* having very keen eyes: *a hawk-eyed guard.*

Hawk′eye State′, Iowa (used as a nickname).

hawk·ie (hô′kē), *n. Scot. and North Eng.* a cow, esp. a cow with a white face. Also, **hawkey.** [Scot *hawk(it)* white-marked + -IE]

hawk·ing (hô′king), *n.* the sport of hunting with hawks; falconry. [HAWK¹ + -ING¹]

Haw·kins (hô′kinz), *n.* **1. Sir Anthony Hope** ("*Anthony Hope*"), 1863–1933, English novelist and playwright. **2. Coleman,** born 1904, U.S. jazz saxophonist. **3. Sir John.** Also, **Hawkyns.** 1532–95, English slave trader and rear admiral.

Haw·kins·ville (hô′kinz vil′), *n.* a town in central Georgia. 3967 (1960).

hawk′ moth′, any of numerous moths of the family *Sphingidae,* noted for their very swift flight and ability to hover while sipping nectar from flowers. Also called **sphinx moth, hummingbird moth.**

hawk·nose (hôk′nōz′), *n.* a nose curved like the beak of a hawk. [back formation from *hawk-nosed;* see HAWK¹, NOSE, -ED³] —**hawk′nosed′,** *adj.*

hawk′ owl′, a gray and white, diurnal owl, *Surnia ulula,* of northern parts of the Northern Hemisphere, resembling a hawk in appearance and actions.

hawks·beak (hôks′bēk′), *n. Archit.* **1.** a corona having a beak as an extension of its upper part, esp. a cyma recta so used in the Greek Doric order. **2.** an echinus undercut to form a beak, as on a Greek Doric anta capital. [HAWK¹ + 's¹ + BEAK¹]

hawk's-beard (hôks′bērd′), *n.* any composite herb of the genus *Crepis,* having yellow or orange flowers. [so called because of its beardlike tufts]

hawks′bill tur′tle (hôks′bil′), a sea turtle, *Eretmochelys imbricata,* the shell of which is the source of tortoise shell. Also called **hawks′bill′, hawkbill, tortoise-shell turtle.** [HAWK¹ + 's¹ + BILL²]

hawk's-eye (hôks′ī′), *n.* a dark-green chatoyant quartz formed by the silicification of an asbestos, used for ornamental purposes.

hawk·shaw (hôk′shô′), *n.* a detective. [after *Hawkshaw,* a detective in the play *The Ticket of Leave Man* (1863) by Tom Taylor]

Hawks·moor (hôks′mŏŏr′), *n.* **Nicholas,** 1661–1736, English architect.

hawk's′ nest′ mod′el, *Naval Archit.* a half model of a vessel formed from a series of thin wooden boards sawed to the outlines of certain frames and attached perpendicularly to a plank in the proper positions. Also called **crow's nest model.**

hawk·weed (hôk′wēd′), *n.* **1.** any composite herb of the genus *Hieracium,* having yellow, orange, or red flowers. **2.** any of various related plants. [trans. of NL *hierăcium* < Gk *hierákion,* equiv. to *hierak-* (s. of *hiérax*) hawk + *-ion* neut. suffix; see WEED¹]

Haw·kyns (hô′kinz), *n.* **Sir John.** See **Hawkins, Sir John.**

Ha·worth (härth *for 1;* hô′wərth, hou′ərth *for 2*), *n.* **1. Sir Walter Norman,** 1883–1950, English chemist: Nobel prize 1937. **2.** a town in NE New Jersey. 3215 (1960).

hawse (hôz, hôs), *n., v.,* **hawsed, haws·ing.** *Naut.* —*n.* **1.** the part of a bow where the hawseholes are located. **2.** a hawsehole or hawsepipe. **3.** the distance or space between the bow of an anchored vessel and the point on the surface of the water above the anchor. **4.** the relative position or arrangement of the port and starboard anchor cables when both are used to moor a vessel. **5. to hawse,** with both bow anchors out: *a ship riding to hawse.* —*v.i.* **6.** (of a vessel) to pitch heavily at anchor. [ME *hals,* OE *heals* bow of a ship, lit., neck; c. Icel *hals* in same senses, G *Hals* neck, throat]

hawse′ bag′, *Naut.* jackass (def. 3).

hawse-fal·len (hôz′fô′lən, hôs′-), *adj. Naut.* **1.** at anchor with large waves breaking over the bow. **2.** hawse-full (def. 1).

hawse-full (hôz′fŏŏl′, hôs′-), *adj. Naut.* **1.** at anchor and pitching heavily. **2.** hawse-fallen (def. 1)

hawse·hole (hôz′hōl′, hôs′-), *n. Naut.* a hole in the stem or bow of a vessel for an anchor cable.

hawse·piece (hôz′pēs′, hôs′-), *n. Naut.* (in a wooden vessel) a massive, built-up cant frame pierced for a hawsehole. Also called **hawse′ tim′ber.**

hawse·pipe (hôz′pīp′, hôs′-), *n. Naut.* an iron or steel pipe in the stem or bow of a vessel through which an anchor cable passes. [HAWSE + PIPE¹]

haw·ser (hô′zər, -sər), *n. Naut.* a heavy rope for mooring or towing. [ME *haucer* < AF *hauceour,* equiv. to MF *hauci(er)* (to) hoist (< LL **altiāre* to raise, deriv. of L *altus* high) + *-our* -OR², -ER²]

haw′ser bend′, a knot uniting the ends of two lines.

haw·ser-laid (hô′zər lād′, -sər-), *adj. Cordage.* **1.** cable-laid (def. 1). **2.** plain-laid.

haw·thorn (hô′thôrn′), *n.* **1.** any of numerous rosaceous plants of the genus *Crataegus,* usually small trees with stiff thorns, certain species of which in the U.S. have white or pink blossoms and bright-colored fruits and are cultivated in hedges. **2.** a thorny, Old World shrub, *Crataegus Oxyacantha,* introduced into the U.S. [ME; OE *haguthorn.* See HAW¹, THORN] —**haw′thorn′y,** *adj.*

Haw·thorne (hô′thôrn′), *n.* **1. Nathaniel,** 1804–64, U.S. novelist and short-story writer. **2.** a city in California, SW of Los Angeles. 33,035 (1960). **3.** a city in NE New Jersey. 17,735 (1960). **4.** a town in W Nevada. 2838 (1960).

Haw·thorn·esque (hô′thôr nesk′), characteristic of or resembling the style, manner, or quality of the writings of Nathaniel Hawthorne. [HAWTHORNE + -ESQUE]

hay¹ (hā), *n.* **1.** grass, clover, alfalfa, etc., cut and dried for use as forage. **2.** grass mowed or intended for mowing. **3.** *Slang.* a small amount of money: *Twenty dollars an hour for doing very little certainly ain't hay.* **4. hit the hay,** *Slang.* to go to bed: *It got to be past midnight before anyone thought of hitting the hay.* **5. make hay of,** to scatter in disorder; render ineffectual: *The destruction of the manuscript made hay of two years of painstaking labor.* **6. make hay while the sun shines,** to seize an opportunity when it presents itself: *If you want to be a millionaire, you have to make hay while the sun shines.* Also, **make hay.** —*v.t.* **7.** to convert (grass) into hay. **8.** to furnish (horses, cows, etc.) with hay. —*v.i.* **9.** to cut grass, clover, or the like, and store for use as forage. [ME; OE *hēg;* c. G *Heu,* Icel *hey,* Goth *hawi.* See HEW] —**hay′ey,** *adj.*

hay² (hā), *n.* a country dance with winding movements. Also, **hey.** [< MF *haye*]

hay³ (hā), *n. Archaic.* a hedge or fence. Also, **haye.** [ME *heie,* OE *hege* hedge, fence; akin to HEDGE, HAW¹]

Hay (hā), *n.* **John Milton,** 1838–1905, U.S. statesman and author.

Ha·ya de la Tor·re (ä′yä the lä tôr′re), **Víc·tor Ra·úl** (bēk tôr′ rä ōōl′), born 1895, Peruvian political leader.

hay·cock (hā′kok′), *n.* a small conical pile of hay stacked in a hayfield while the hay is awaiting removal to a barn. [late ME; see HAY¹, COCK³]

Hay·den (hād′ᵊn), *n.* **1. Melissa** (*Mildred Herman*), born 1928, Canadian ballerina. **2.** a town in W Florida. 5471 (1960).

Hay·dn (hīd′ᵊn), *n.* **Franz Jo·seph** (fränts jō′zəf, -səf, franz; *Ger.* fränts yō′zef), 1732–1809, Austrian composer.

Hayes (hāz), *n.* **1. Carlton J(oseph) H(untley),** 1882–1964, U.S. historian, educator, and diplomat. **2. Helen** (*Helen Hayes Brown MacArthur*), born 1900, U.S. actress. **3. Roland,** born 1887, U.S. tenor. **4. Rutherford B(ir·chard)** (bur′chərd), 1822–93, 19th president of the U.S. 1877–81.

hay′ fe′ver, *Pathol.* a catarrhal affection of the mucous membranes of the eyes and respiratory tract, attacking susceptible persons usually during the summer, and due to the action of the pollen of certain plants.

hay·field (hā′fēld′), *n.* a field where grass, alfalfa, etc., are grown for making into hay. [HAY¹ + FIELD]

hay·fork (hā′fôrk′), *n.* **1.** a pitchfork. **2.** a machine for loading or unloading hay. [HAY¹ + FORK]

Hay·ley (hā′lē), *n.* a girl's given name.

hay·lift (hā′lift′), *n.* an airlift of hay for animals that have been snowed in. [HAY¹ + LIFT]

hay·loft (hā′lôft′, -loft′), *n.* a loft in a stable or barn for the storage of hay. [HAY¹ + LOFT]

hay·mak·er (hā′mā′kər), *n.* **1.** a person who or a machine that cuts hay and spreads it to dry. **2.** *Informal.* a punch delivered with great force, esp. one that results in a knockout. [late ME *heymakere.* See HAY¹, MAKER]

Hay·mar·ket (hā′mär′kit), *n.* **1.** a famous London market 1644–1830. **2.** a street in London, site of this market, known for its theaters.

Hay′market Square′, a square in Chicago: scene of a riot (**Hay′market Ri′ot**) in 1886 between police and labor unionists.

hay·mow (hā′mou′), *n.* **1.** a place in a barn where hay is stored. **2.** hay stored in a barn. [HAY¹ + MOW²]

Haynes (hānz), *n.* **El·wood** (el′wŏŏd′), 1857–1925, U.S. inventor.

Haynes·ville (hānz′vil), *n.* a town in N Louisiana. 3031 (1960).

Hay′-Paunce′fote Trea′ty (hā′pôns′fŏŏt), an agreement (1901) between the U.S. and Great Britain giving the U.S. the sole right to build a canal across Central America connecting the Atlantic and Pacific. Cf. **Clayton-Bulwer Treaty.** [named after John Milton HAY and Julian *Pauncefote* (1828–1902), English diplomat]

hay·rack (hā′rak′), *n.* **1.** a rack for holding hay for feeding horses or cattle. **2.** a rack or framework mounted on a wagon, for use in carrying hay, straw, or the like. **3.** the wagon and rack together. [HAY¹ + RACK¹]

hay·rick (hā′rik′), *n. Chiefly Brit.* a haystack. [ME *heyrek.* See HAY¹, RICK¹]

hay·ride (hā′rīd′), *n.* a pleasure ride or outing, usually at night, in an open truck or wagon partly filled with hay. [HAY¹ + RIDE]

Hays (hāz), *n.* **1. Will (Harrison),** 1879–1954, U.S. lawyer, politician, and official of the motion-picture industry. **2.** a city in central Kansas. 11,947 (1960).

hay·seed (hā′sēd′), *n.* **1.** grass seed, esp. that shaken out of hay. **2.** small bits of the chaff, straw, etc., of hay. **3.** *Informal.* an unsophisticated person from a rural area; yokel; hick. [HAY¹ + SEED]

hay·stack (hā′stak′), *n.* a stack of hay with a conical or ridged top, built up in the open air for preservation, and sometimes thatched or covered. Also, *esp. Brit.,* **hayrick.** [HAY¹ + STACK]

Hays·ville (hāz′vil), *n.* a town in central Kansas. 5836 (1960).

Hay·ti (hā′tē *for 1;* hā′tī *for 2*), *n.* **1.** a town in SE Missouri. 3737 (1960). **2.** Haiti (def. 2).

hay·ward (hā′wôrd′), *n.* an officer having charge of hedges and fences around a town common, esp. to keep cattle from breaking through and to impound stray cattle. [ME *heiward.* See HAY[3], WARD]

Hay·ward (hā′wərd), *n.* **1. Leland,** born 1902, U.S. theatrical producer. **2.** a city in central California, SE of Oakland. 72,700 (1960). **3.** a boy's given name.

hay·wire (hā′wīər′), *n.* **1.** wire used to bind bales of hay. —*adj. Informal.* **2.** in disorder: *The town is haywire after the flood.* **3.** out of control or order; crazy: *The car went haywire. He is haywire to say that.* [HAY[1] + WIRE]

Hay·wood (hā′wŏŏd′), *n.* a boy's given name. Also, **Heywood.**

ha·zan (ᴋʜä zän′; *Eng.* ᴋʜä′zən, hä′-), *n., pl.* **ha·za·nim** (ᴋʜä zä nēm′), *Eng.* **ha·zans.** *Hebrew.* a cantor of a synagogue. Also, **chazan.**

haz·ard (haz′ərd), *n.* **1.** danger; risk; peril: *The job was full of hazards.* **2.** something causing danger, peril, risk, or difficulty: *the many hazards of the big city.* **3.** the absence or lack of predictability in an event; chance; uncertainty: *There is an element of hazard in the execution of the most painstaking plans.* **4.** an unexpected or unpredictable event; accident: *We meet occasionally at hazard.* **5.** *Golf.* a bunker, sand trap, or the like, constituting an obstacle. **6.** the uncertainty of the result in throwing a die. **7.** a game played with two dice, an earlier and more complicated form of craps. **8.** something risked or staked: *All our hopes are at hazard in this new venture.* **9.** *Court Tennis.* any of the winning openings. **10.** (in English billiards) a stroke by which the player pockets the object ball (**winning hazard**) or his own ball after contact with another ball (**losing hazard**). —*v.t.* **11.** to offer (a statement, conjecture, etc.) with the possibility of facing criticism, disapproval, failure, or the like; venture: *He hazarded a guess, with trepidation, as to the outcome of the plan.* **12.** to put to the risk of being lost; expose to risk: *In making the investment, he hazarded all his savings.* **13.** to take or run the risk of (a misfortune, penalty, etc.): *Thieves hazard arrest.* **14.** to venture upon (anything of doubtful issue): *to hazard a dangerous encounter.* [ME *hasard* < OF; cf. Ar *az-zahr* the die] —**haz′ard·a·ble,** *adj.* —**haz′ard·er,** *n.* —**haz′ard·less,** *adj.*
—**Syn. 1.** See **danger. 3.** accident, fortuity, fortuitousness. **12.** stake, endanger, peril, imperil. —**Ant. 1.** safety.

Haz·ard (haz′ərd), *n.* a town in SE Kentucky. 5958 (1960).

Haz′ard of New′ For′tunes, A, a novel (1890) by William Dean Howells.

haz·ard·ous (haz′ər dəs), *adj.* **1.** full of risk; perilous; risky. **2.** dependent on chance. [HAZARD + -OUS] —**haz′ard·ous·ly,** *adv.* —**haz′ard·ous·ness,** *n.*

haze[1] (hāz), *n.* **1.** an aggregation in the atmosphere of very fine, widely dispersed, solid or liquid particles, or both, giving the air an opalescent appearance that subdues colors. **2.** vagueness or obscurity, as of the mind, perception, etc.; confused or vague thoughts, feelings, etc.: *a haze of misunderstanding.* [n. use of ME **hase,* OE *hasu,* var. of *haswa* ashen, dusky. See HAZY, HARE] —**haze′less,** *adj.*
—**Syn. 2.** See **cloud.**

haze[2] (hāz), *v.t.,* **hazed, haz·ing. 1.** to subject (freshmen, newcomers, etc.) to abusive or humiliating tricks and ridicule. **2.** *Chiefly Naut.* to harass with unnecessary or disagreeable tasks. [< MF *has(er)* (to) irritate, annoy] —**haz′er,** *n.*

ha·zel (hā′zəl), *n.* **1.** any betulaceous shrub or small tree of the genus *Corylus,* bearing edible nuts, as *C. Avellana,* of Europe, or *C. americana* and *C. cornuta,* of America. **2.** any of several other shrubs or trees, as an Australian, rhamnaceous shrub, *Pomaderris apetala.* **3.** the wood of any of these trees. **4.** the hazelnut or filbert. **5.** light reddish brown, as the color of a hazelnut. —*adj.* **6.** of or pertaining to the hazel. **7.** made of the wood of the hazel. **8.** having a light reddish-brown color. [ME *hasel,* OE *hæs(e)l;* c. G *Hasel,* Icel *hasl,* L *corylus* hazel shrub] —**ha′zel·ly,** *adj.*

Ha·zel (hā′zəl), *n.* a girl's given name

Ha·zel·belle (hā′zəl bel′), *n.* a girl's given name, form of Hazel.

Ha′zel Crest′, a town in NE Illinois. 6205 (1960).

ha′zel grouse′, a European woodland grouse, *Tetrastes bonasia,* somewhat resembling the North American ruffed grouse. Also called **ha′zel hen′.**

ha·zel·nut (hā′zəl nut′), *n.* the nut of the hazel; filbert. [ME *haselnote,* OE *hæselhnutu.* See HAZEL, NUT]

Ha′zel Park′, a city in SE Michigan, near Detroit. 25,631 (1960).

Ha·zel·wood (hā′zəl wŏŏd′), *n.* a town in E Missouri. 6045 (1960).

haze·me·ter (hāz′mē′tər), *n.* transmissometer. [HAZE[1] + -METER]

Ha·zen (hā′zən), *n.* a boy's given name.

haz·ing (hā′zing), *n.* subjection to harassment or ridicule. [HAZE[2] + -ING[1]]

Ha·zle·hurst (hā′zəl hûrst′), *n.* **1.** a town in central Georgia. 3699 (1960). **2.** a town in SW Mississippi. 3400 (1960).

Ha·zle·ton (hā′zəl tən), *n.* a city in E Pennsylvania. 32,056 (1960).

Haz·litt (haz′lit), *n.* **William,** 1778–1830, English critic and essayist.

Ha·zor (hä zōr′, -zôr′), *n.* an ancient city in Israel, N of the Sea of Galilee: extensive excavations; capital of Canaanite kingdom.

ha·zy (hā′zē), *adj.,* **-zi·er, -zi·est. 1.** characterized by the presence of haze; misty: *hazy weather.* **2.** lacking distinctness or clarity; vague; indefinite; confused: *a hazy idea.* [earlier *hawsey,* metathetic var. of ME **haswy,* OE *haswig* ashen, dusky. See HAZE[1], -Y[1]] —**ha′zi·ly,** *adv.* —**ha′zi·ness,** *n.*

HB, hard black. Also, **hb**

Hb, *Biochem.* hemoglobin.

h.b., *Football.* halfback.

H-beam (āch′bēm′), *n.* an I-beam having flanges the width of the web. Also called **H-bar** (āch′bär′).

H.B.M., His Brittanic Majesty; Her Brittanic Majesty.

HbO$_2$**,** *Biochem.* oxyhemoglobin.

H-bomb (āch′bom′), *n.* See **hydrogen bomb.**

H.C., House of Commons.

H.C.F., highest common factor. Also, **h.c.f.**

h.c.l., high cost of living.

H.C.M., His Catholic Majesty; Her Catholic Majesty.

H. Con. Res., House concurrent resolution.

hd., **1.** hand. **2.** head.

hdkf., handkerchief.

H. Doc., House document.

hdqrs., headquarters.

he[1] (hē; *unstressed* ē), *pron., nom.* **he,** *poss.* **his,** *obj.* **him;** *pl. nom.* **they,** *poss.* **their** or **theirs,** *obj.* **them;** *n., pl.* **hes;** *adj.* —*pron.* **1.** the male being in question or last mentioned; that male. **2.** anyone; that person: *He who hesitates is lost.* —*n.* **3.** a man; any male person or animal: *hes and shes.* —*adj.* **4.** *Informal.* (of plants and female animals) very large; very strong; perfect. [ME, OE (masc. nom. sing.); c. D *hij,* OS *hē,* OHG *her* he, Ir *cē* this; see HIS, HIM, SHE, HER, IT[1]]

he[2] (hā), *n.* **1.** the fifth letter of the Hebrew alphabet. **2.** any of the sounds represented by this letter. [< Heb]

HE, high explosive.

He, *Chem.* helium.

H.E., **1.** high explosive. **2.** His Eminence. **3.** His Excellency; Her Excellency.

head (hed), *n.* **1.** the upper part of the body in man, joined to the trunk by the neck, containing the brain, eyes, ears, nose, and mouth. **2.** the corresponding part of the body of an animal. **3.** the head considered as the center of the intellect, as of thought, memory, understanding, emotional control, etc.; mind; brain: *She has a head for mathematics. Keep a cool head in an emergency.* **4.** the position or place of leadership, greatest authority, or honor. **5.** one to whom others are subordinate, as the director of an institution or the manager of a department; leader or chief. **6.** a person considered with reference to his mind, disposition, attributes, status, etc.: *wise heads; crowned heads.* **7.** that part of anything that forms or is regarded as forming the top, summit, or upper end: *head of a pin; head of a page.* **8.** the foremost part or front end of anything or a forward projecting part: *head of a procession; head of a rock.* **9.** the part of a weapon, tool, etc., used for striking: *the head of a hammer.* **10.** a person or animal considered merely as one of a number, herd, or group: *ten head of cattle; a dinner at so much a head.* **11.** a culminating point, usually of a critical nature; crisis or climax: *to bring matters to a head.* **12.** the hair covering the head: *to wash one's head.* **13.** froth or foam at the top of a liquid: *the head on beer.* **14.** *Bot.* **a.** any dense flower cluster or inflorescence. **b.** any other compact part of a plant, usually at the top of the stem, as that composed of leaves in the cabbage or lettuce, of leafstalks in the celery, or of flower buds in the cauliflower. **15.** the maturated part of an abscess, boil, etc. **16.** a projecting point of a coast, esp. when high, as a cape, headland, or promontory. **17.** the obverse of a coin, as bearing a head or other principal figure (opposed to *tail*). **18.** one of the chief parts or points of a written or oral discourse; a main division of a subject, theme, or topic. **19.** something resembling a head in form or a representation of a head, as a piece of sculpture. **20.** the source of a river or stream. **21.** *Archaic.* power, strength, or force progressively gathered or gradually attained. **22. heads,** *Distilling.* alcohol produced during the initial fermentation. Cf. **tail**[1] (def. 15c). **23.** headline. **24.** *Naut.* **a.** the forepart of a vessel; bow. **b.** the upper edge of a quadrilateral sail. **c.** the upper corner of a jib-headed sail. **d.** toilet; lavatory. **e.** that part of the upper end of one spar of a mast that is overlapped by a spar above; a doubling at the upper end of a spar. **f.** that part of the upper end of a mast between the highest standing rigging and the truck. **g.** crown (def. 28). **25.** *Gram.* **a.** the member of an endocentric construction which belongs to the same form class and may play the same grammatical role as the construction itself. **b.** the member upon which another depends and to which it is subordinate. In *the first president, first president* is head and *the* is attribute, and in *first president, president* is head and *first* is attribute. **26.** the stretched membrane covering the end of a drum or similar musical instrument. **27.** *Coal Mining.* a level or road driven into the solid coal for proving or working a mine. **28.** *Mach.* any of various devices on machine tools for holding, moving, indexing, or changing tools or work, as the headstock or turret of a lathe. **29.** *Railroads.* railhead (def. 2). **30.** Also called **pressure head.** *Physics.* **a.** the vertical distance between two points in a fluid. **b.** the pressure differential resulting from this separation, expressed in terms of the vertical distance between the points. **c.** the pressure of a fluid expressed in terms of the height of a column of liquid having an equivalent pressure. **31.** the part or parts of a tape recorder which come into direct contact with the tape and serve to record, reproduce, or erase electromagnetic impulses on it. **32.** till[5]. **33.** *Photog.* a mounting for a camera, as on a tripod. **34. by** or **down by the head,** *Naut.* so loaded as to draw more water forward than aft. **35. come to a head,** to reach a crisis; culminate: *The struggle for power came to a head.* **36. give one his head,** to permit one to do as he likes; allow one freedom of choice: *She wanted to go away to college, and her parents gave her her head.* **37. go to one's head, a.** to make one confused, agitated, dizzy, or drunk: *Unlimited power went to his head. The brandy went to his head.* **b.** to make one conceited: *The adulation bestowed on him by teen-age girls went to the singer's head.* **38. hang one's head,** to become dejected or ashamed: *When he realized what he had done, he hung his head.* Also, **hide one's head. 39. head and shoulders, a.** far better, more qualified, etc.; superior: *In intelligence, he was head and shoulders above the rest of the children in the class.* **b.** *Archaic.* by force: *They pushed head and shoulders into the horsecar.* **40. head over heels, a.** headlong, as in a somersault: *He tripped and fell head over heels into the gully.* **b.** intensely; completely: *head over heels in love.* **c.** impulsively; carelessly: *They plunged head over heels into the fighting.* **41. heads up!** *Informal.* be careful! watch out for danger! **42. keep one's head,** to remain calm or poised, as in the midst of crisis or confusion: *It was fortunate that someone kept his head and called a doctor.* **43. keep one's head above water,** to remain financially solvent: *They are not rich, but they are keeping their heads above water.* **44. lay** or **put heads together,** to meet in order to discuss, consult, or scheme: *Neither of them had enough money for a tour of Europe, so they put heads together and decided to find jobs there.* **45. lose one's head,** to become uncontrolled or wildly excited: *When he thought he saw an animal in the underbrush he lost his head and began shooting recklessly.* **46. make head,** to progress or advance, esp. despite opposition; make headway: *There have been many delays, but we are at last making head.* **47. not make head or tail of,** to be unable to understand or decipher: *They couldn't make head or tail of her piteous cries.* Also, **not make heads or tails of. 48. one's head off,** extremely; excessively: *She cries her head off at every sentimental scene. He laughed his head off at the monkey's antics.* **49. on one's head,** as one's responsibility or fault: *Because of his reckless driving he now has the deaths of three persons on his head.* **50. out of one's head** or **mind,** *Chiefly U.S.* **a.** insane; crazy. **b.** delirious; irrational: *You're out of your head if you accept on those terms.* **51. over one's head, a.** to one having a prior claim or a superior position: *She went over her supervisor's head and spoke directly to a vice president.* **b.** beyond one's comprehension, ability, or resources: *The classical allusion went right over his head.* **c.** beyond one's financial resources or ability to pay: *He's lost over his head in that poker game.* **52. take into one's head,** to form a notion, purpose, or plan: *She took into her head to study medicine.* Also, **take it into one's head. 53. turn one's head, a.** to cause one to become smug or conceited: *Her recent success has completely turned her head.* **b.** to cause one to become foolish or confused: *A whirlwind romance has quite turned her head.*
—*adj.* **54.** first in rank or position; chief; leading; principal: *a head official.* **55.** of, pertaining to, or for the head (often used in combination): *headgear; headpiece.* **56.** situated at the top, front, or head of anything (often used in combination): *headline; headboard.* **57.** moving or coming from a direction in front of the head or prow of a vessel: *head sea; head tide; head current.*
—*v.t.* **58.** to go at the head of or in front of; lead; precede: *to head a list.* **59.** to outdo or excel; take the lead in or over: *to head a race; to head one's competitors in a field.* **60.** to be the head or chief of: *to head a department; to head a school.* **61.** to direct the course of; turn the head or front of in a specified direction: *I'll head the boat for the shore. Head me in the right direction and I'll walk to the store.* **62.** to go round the head of (a stream). **63.** to furnish or fit with a head. **64.** to take the head off; decapitate; behead. **65.** to poll (a tree). **66.** *Fox Hunting.* to turn aside (a fox) from its intended course. **67.** to get in front of in order to stop, turn aside, attack, etc. **68.** headline (def. 4).
—*v.i.* **69.** to move forward toward a point specified; direct one's course; go in a certain direction: *to head toward town.* **70.** to come or grow to a head; form a head: *Cabbage heads quickly.* **71.** (of a river or stream) to have the head or source where specified. **72. head off,** to go before in order to hinder the progress of; intercept: *The police headed off the fleeing driver at a railroad crossing.* [ME *he(v)ed,* OE *hēafod;* c. G *Haupt,* early Scand *haufuth,* Goth *haubith;* akin to OE *hafud-* (in *hafudland* headland), Icel *höfuth,* L *caput*] —**head′like′,** *adj.*
—**Syn. 5.** commander, director, chieftain, master, principal, superintendent, president, chairman. **54.** cardinal, foremost, first, supreme, main. **59.** surpass, beat. **60.** direct, command, rule, govern. —**Ant. 1.** foot. **54.** subordinate.

-head, a native English suffix meaning "state of being" (*godhead; maidenhead*), occurring in words now mostly archaic or obsolete, many being superseded by forms in **-hood.** [ME *-hede,* OE **-hǣdu,* akin to *-hād* -HOOD]

head·ache (hed′āk′), *n.* **1.** a pain located in the head. **2.** *Informal.* anything or any one annoying or bothersome. [ME; OE *hēafodece.* See HEAD, ACHE]

head·ach·y (hed′ā′kē), *adj.* **1.** having a headache. **2.** accompanied by or causing headaches: *a headachy cold.* [HEADACHE + -Y[1]]

head-and-tail′ light′ (hed′ən tāl′), a South American characin fish, *Hemmigrammus ocellifer,* having shiny red eyes and tail spots, often kept in aquariums. Also called **head′-and-tail′-light fish′.**

head′ arrange′ment, *Jazz, Popular Music.* a roughly outlined musical arrangement that is played from memory and is often learned by ear.

head·band (hed′band′), *n.* **1.** a band worn around the head; fillet. **2.** *Print.* a band for decorative effect at the head of a chapter or of a page in a book. **3.** a band sewed or glued to the head or tail of the back of a book, or to both, often to protect and strengthen the binding but sometimes for decoration.Cf. **tailband.** [HEAD + BAND[2]]

head·board (hed′bōrd′, -bôrd′), *n.* a board forming the head of anything, esp. of a bed. [HEAD + BOARD]

head·box (hed′boks′), *n.* (in a papermaking machine) the container in which cleaned pulp is collected for uniform distribution across the wire. [HEAD + BOX[1]]

head·cheese (hed′chēz′), *n.* a seasoned loaf made of the head meat, sometimes including the tongue or brains, of a calf or pig and molded in the natural aspic of the head. [HEAD + CHEESE[1]]

head·cloth (hed′klôth′, -kloth′), *n., pl.* **-cloths** (-klôthz′, -klothz′, -klôths′, -kloths′). any cloth for covering the head, as a turban, wimple, etc. [HEAD + CLOTH]

head′ cold′, a form of the common cold characterized esp. by nasal congestion.

head·dress (hed′dres′), *n.* **1.** a covering or decoration for the head: *a tribal headdress of feathers.* **2.** a style or manner of arranging the hair. [HEAD + DRESS]

head·ed (hed′id), *adj.* **1.** having a heading or course. **2.** shaped or grown into a head. **3.** having the mentality, personality, emotional control, or quality specified, or possessing a specified number of heads (usually used in combination): *a slow-headed student; a two-headed monster.* [ME; see HEAD, -ED[3]]

head·er (hed′ər), *n.* **1.** one who or that which removes or puts a head on something. **2.** a reaping machine that cuts off and gathers only the heads of the grain. **3.** a chamber to which the ends of a number of tubes are connected so that water or steam may pass freely from one tube to the other. **4.** *Building Trades.* **a.** a brick or stone laid in a wall or the like so that its shorter ends are exposed or parallel to the surface. Cf. **stretcher** (def. 5). **b.** a framing member crossing and supporting the ends of joists, studs, or rafters so as to transfer their weight to parallel joists, studs, or rafters. **5.** *Informal.* a plunge or dive headforemost, as into water: *He stumbled and took a header into the ditch.* [late ME *heder.* See HEAD, -ER[1]]

H S
H, Header
S, Stretcher

head′er bond′, a brickwork bond composed entirely of overlapping headers.

head·first (hed′fûrst′), *adv.* **1.** with the head in front or bent forward: *He dove headfirst into the sea.* **2.** rashly; precipitately; headforemost. [HEAD + FIRST]

head·fish (hed′fish′), *n., pl.* (*esp. collectively*) **-fish,** (*esp. referring to two or more kinds or species*) **-fish·es. 1.** See **ocean sunfish. 2.** See **sharptail mola.** [HEAD + FISH]

head·fore·most (hed′fôr′mōst′, -məst, -fôr′-), *adv.* headfirst. [HEAD + FOREMOST]

head·frame (hed′frām′), *n.* a structure supporting the hoisting sheaves at the top of a mine shaft. Also called **gallows frame.** [HEAD + FRAME]

head′ gate′, 1. a control gate at the upstream end of a canal or lock. **2.** a floodgate of a race, sluice, etc.

head·gear (hed′gēr′), *n.* **1.** any covering for the head, esp. a hat, cap, bonnet, etc. **2.** a protective covering for the head, as a steel helmet, football helmet, etc. **3.** the parts of a harness about the animal's head. **4.** *Mining.* a headframe and its machinery. [HEAD + GEAR]

head·hunt (hed′hunt′), *n.* **1.** a headhunting expedition: *The men left the village to go on a headhunt.* —*v.i.* **2.** to go headhunting. [HEAD + HUNT] —**head′hunt′er,** *n.*

head·hunt·ing (hed′hun′ting), *n.* **1.** (among certain primitive peoples) the practice of hunting down and decapitating victims and preserving their heads as trophies. **2.** the act or practice of trying to destroy the power, position, or influence of one's foes: *Headhunting is ferocious in advertising.* **3.** *Informal.* the act or practice of actively searching for new employees, esp. for highly educated, skilled, or experienced ones: *Every June the electronic manufacturers go headhunting among the newly graduated engineers.* **4.** the act or practice of firing without cause, esp. someone disliked: *Their periodic headhunting was a contributing factor to the company's failures.* —*adj.* **5.** of, pertaining to, or characteristic of headhunting: *headhunting customs; to employ headhunting tactics in business.* [HEAD + HUNTING]

head·ing (hed′ing), *n.* **1.** something that serves as a head, top, or front. **2.** a title or caption of a page, chapter, etc. **3.** a section of the subject of a discourse; a main division of a topic or theme. **4.** (loosely) the compass direction toward which a traveler or vehicle is or should be moving; course. **5.** a horizontal passage in the earth, as one made in a mine, one for ventilation or drainage, or one dug as a pilot shaft for a tunnel. **6.** *Aeron.* the angle between the axis from front to rear of an aircraft and some reference line, as magnetic north. [ME *hefding.* See HEAD, -ING[1]]

head′ing course′, (in brickwork) a course of headers. Cf. **stretching course.**

head′ing joint′, *Carpentry.* a joint formed by butting the end of one timber against the side of another.

head′ing sword′, a sword used for beheading.

head′ lamp′, headlight.

head·land (hed′lənd), *n.* **1.** a promontory extending into a large body of water. **2.** a strip of unplowed land at the ends of furrows or near a fence or border. [ME *hedeland,* OE *hēafodland.* See HEAD, LAND]

Head·land (hed′land′), *n.* a town in SE Alabama. 2650 (1960).

head·ledge (hed′lej′), *n.* *Shipbuilding.* either of two raised transverse members forming the fore and after parts of the coaming of a deck opening: used mainly of wooden construction. [HEAD + LEDGE]

head·less (hed′lis), *adj.* **1.** without a head. **2.** having the head cut off; beheaded. **3.** lacking a leader or chief. **4.** foolish; stupid; *a headless argument.* [ME *he(ve)dles,* OE *hēafodlēas.* See HEAD, -LESS] —**head′less·ness,** *n.*

head·light (hed′līt′), *n.* a light or lamp equipped with a reflector, on the front of an automobile, locomotive, etc. [HEAD + LIGHT[1]]

head·line (hed′līn′), *n., v.,* **-lined, -lin·ing.** —*n.* Also called **head. 1.** a heading in a newspaper for any written material, sometimes for an illustration, to indicate subject matter, set in larger type than that of the copy and containing one or more words and lines and often several banks. **2.** the largest such heading on the front page, usually at the top. **3.** the line at the top of a page, containing the title, pagination, etc. —*v.t.* **4.** to furnish with a headline; head. **5.** to mention or name in a headline. **6.** to publicize, feature, or star (a specific performer, product, etc.). [HEAD + LINE[1]]

head·lin·er (hed′lī′nər), *n.* *Theat. Slang.* a performer whose name appears at the head of a bill, or in larger letters than other names on the bill; star. [HEADLINE + -ER[1]]

head·lock (hed′lok′), *n.* *Wrestling.* a hold in which a wrestler locks his arm around his opponent's head. [HEAD + LOCK[1]]

head·long (hed′lông′, -long′), *adv.* **1.** with the head foremost; headfirst: *to plunge headlong into the water.* **2.** without delay; hastily: *to plunge headlong into work.* **3.** rashly; without deliberation: *to rush headlong into battle.* —*adj.* **4.** undertaken quickly and suddenly; made precipitately; hasty: *a headlong flight.* **5.** rash; impetuous: *a headlong denunciation.* **6.** done or going with the head foremost: *a headlong thrust.* **7.** *Archaic.* steep; precipitous. [late ME *hedlong,* alter. of ME *hedling.* See HEAD, -LING[2]] —**head′long′ness,** *n.* —**head′long′wise′,** *adv.*

head′ louse′. See under **louse** (def. 1).

head·man (hed′mən, -man′), *n., pl.* **-men** (-mən, -men′). **1.** a chief or leader. **2.** headsman. [ME *he(ve)dman,* OE *hēafodman.* See HEAD, MAN[1]]

head·mas·ter (hed′mas′tər, -mä′stər), *n.* **1.** (in Britain) the principal of an elementary or secondary school. **2.** (in the U.S.) a principal of a private school, esp. one for boys. [HEAD + MASTER] —**head′mas′ter·ly,** *adj.* —**head′mas′ter·ship′,** *n.*

head·mis·tress (hed′mis′tris), *n.* **1.** (in Britain) the female principal of an elementary or secondary school. **2.** (in the U.S.) a woman who is in charge of a private school, esp. one for girls. [HEAD + MISTRESS] —**head′mis′tress·ship′,** *n.*

head′ mold′, *Plant Pathol.* a disease of certain grasses, characterized by a brownish-olive, furry coating, which becomes hard and black, on the seed heads, caused by a fungus, *Helminthosporium ravelelii.*

head′ mon′ey, 1. a tax of so much per head or person. **2.** a reward paid for apprehending or killing an outlaw, fugitive, or the like.

head·most (hed′mōst′ *or, esp. Brit.,* -məst), *adj.* foremost; most advanced. [HEAD + -MOST]

head·note (hed′nōt′), *n.* a note of summary, comment, or explanation which precedes a chapter, page, etc. [HEAD + NOTE]

head-on (hed′on′, -ôn′), *adj.* **1.** (of two objects) meeting with the fronts or heads foremost: *a head-on collision.* **2.** facing the direction of forward motion or alignment; frontal. **3.** characterized by direct opposition: *a head-on confrontation.* —*adv.* **4.** with the front or head foremost, esp. in a collision: *She stepped out the kitchen door and walked head-on into the grocery boy.*

head·phone (hed′fōn′), *n.* Usually, **headphones.** a headset. [HEAD + PHONE[1]]

head·piece (hed′pēs′), *n.* **1.** a piece of armor for the head; helmet. **2.** any covering for the head. **3.** a headset. **4.** the head as the seat of the intellect; judgment. **5.** the top piece or part of any of various things. **6.** *Print.* a decorative piece at the head of a page, chapter, etc. [HEAD + PIECE]

head·pin (hed′pin′), *n.* *Bowling.* the pin standing nearest to the bowler when set up, at the head or front of the triangle; the number 1 pin. [HEAD + PIN]

head·quar·ter (hed′kwôr′tər), *v.t.* **1.** to situate in headquarters. —*v.i.* **2.** to establish one's headquarters. [back formation from HEADQUARTERS]

head·quar·ters (hed′kwôr′tərz), *n., pl.* **-ters.** (*construed as sing. or pl.*) **1.** a center of operations, as of the police, a business, etc., from which orders are issued; the chief administrative office of an organization: *The salesmen were always in touch with headquarters.* **2.** the offices or working location of a military commander, the place from which a commander customarily issues his orders. **3.** a military unit consisting of the commander, his staff, and other assistants. [HEAD + QUARTERS]

head·race (hed′rās′), *n.* the race, flume, or channel leading to a water wheel or the like. [HEAD + RACE[1]]

head·rail (hed′rāl′), *n.* a railing on a sailing vessel, extending forward from abaft the bow to the back of the figurehead. [HEAD + RAIL[1]]

head·reach (hed′rēch′), *Naut.* —*v.i.* **1.** to make headway to windward, esp. under difficulties, as in keeping off a lee shore during a storm. —*n.* **2.** the headway made by a sailing vessel under reduced sail during a storm. **3.** the distance to windward made by a sailing vessel tacking. [HEAD + REACH]

head′ reg′ister, the high register of the human voice.

head′ resist′ance, *Aeron. Obs.* the drag on the front of an aircraft.

head·rest (hed′rest′), *n.* a rest or support of any kind for the head. [HEAD + REST[1]]

head·rig (hed′rig′), *n.* (in a sawmill) the carriage and saw used in cutting a log into slabs. [HEAD + RIG[1]]

head·right (hed′rīt′), *n.* **1.** *Law.* a beneficial interest for each member of an Indian tribe in the tribal trust fund accruing from the lease of tribal oil, gas, and mineral rights, the sale of tribal lands, etc. **2.** *Amer. Hist.* a grant of land, usually 50 acres, to a settler, given by certain colonies and companies in the 17th and 18th centuries. [HEAD + RIGHT]

head·room (hed′ro͞om′, -ro͝om′), *n.* **1.** *Naut.* the clear space between two decks. **2.** Also called **headway.** clear vertical space, as between the head and sill of a doorway or between the ceiling and floor of an attic room at a certain point, esp. such height as to allow passage or comfortable occupancy. [HEAD + ROOM]

heads (hedz), *adj.* (of a coin) with the obverse facing up: *On the first toss, the coin came up heads.* [HEAD + -S[1]]

head·sail (hed′sāl′; *Naut.* hed′səl), *n.* *Naut.* **1.** any of various jibs or staysails set forward of the foremost mast of a vessel. **2.** any sail set on a foremast, esp. on a vessel having three or more masts. [HEAD + SAIL]

head·saw (hed′sô′), *n.* a saw that cuts and trims logs as they enter a mill. [HEAD + SAW[1]]

head′ sea′, *Naut.* a formation of waves running in a direction opposite to that of a vessel.

head·set (hed′set′), *n.* *Radio, Telephony.* a device consisting of one or two telephone receivers with a headband for holding them over the ears. [HEAD + SET]

head·sheet (hed′shēt′), *n.* *Naut.* **1.** foresheet (def. 1). **2. headsheets,** foresheet (def. 2). [HEAD + SHEET[2]]

head·ship (hed′ship), *n.* the position of head or chief; chief authority; leadership; supremacy. [HEAD + -SHIP]

head′ shop′, *Slang.* a shop selling drug-culture paraphernalia, such as hashish pipes, incense, psychedelic posters, etc.

head′ shrink′er, *Slang.* a psychiatrist.

heads·man (hedz′mən), *n., pl.* **-men.** a public executioner who beheads condemned persons. Also, **headman.** [HEAD + 'S[1] + MAN[1]]

head′ smut′, *Plant Pathol.* a disease of cereals and other grasses, characterized by a dark-brown, powdery mass of spores replacing the affected seed heads, caused by any of several smut fungi of the genera *Sorosporium, Sphacelotheca,* and *Ustilago.*

heads′ or tails′, 1. a gambling game in which a coin is tossed, the winner being the player who guesses which side of the coin will face up when it lands or is caught. **2.** the tossing of a coin in this manner to determine a question or choice.

head·spring (hed′spring′), *n.* **1.** the fountainhead or source of a stream. **2.** the source of anything. [late ME *hedspring.* See HEAD, SPRING]

head·stall (hed′stôl′), *n.* that part of a bridle or halter which encompasses the head of an animal. [late ME *hedstall.* See HEAD, STALL[1]]

head·stand (hed′stand′), *n.* the act or an instance of supporting the body in a vertical position by balancing on the head, usually with the aid of the hands. Cf. **handstand.** [HEAD + STAND]

head′ start′, an advantage given or acquired in any competition, as allowing one or more competitors in a race to start before the others.

head·stay (hed′stā′), *n.* (on a sailing vessel) a stay leading forward from the head of the foremost mast to the stem head or the end of the bowsprit. [HEAD + STAY[3]]

head·stock (hed′stok′), *n.* the part of a machine containing or directly supporting the moving or working parts, as the assembly supporting and driving the live spindle in a lathe. [HEAD + STOCK]

head·stone (hed′stōn′), *n.* a stone marker set at the head of a grave. [HEAD + STONE]

head·stream (hed′strēm′), *n.* a stream that is the source, or one of the sources, of a river. [HEAD + STREAM]

head·strong (hed′strông′, -strong′), *adj.* **1.** determined to have one's own way; willful; stubborn; obstinate: *a headstrong young man.* **2.** proceeding from willfulness: *a headstrong course.* [ME *heedstronge.* See HEAD, STRONG] —**head′strong′ly,** *adv.* —**head′strong′ness,** *n.*
—**Syn. 1.** See **willful.** —**Ant. 1.** tractable, docile.

heads′ up′, (used interjectionally to call attention to an impending danger or the need for immediate alertness, as a warning to hold out one's hands to catch a ball or other tossed object or to move or stand carefully to let another pass): *Heads up everybody! I'm coming through with a tray of glasses.*

heads-up (hedz′up′), *adj.* alert; quick to grasp a situation and take advantage of opportunities.

head′ swell′, *Naut.* a swell moving in a direction opposite to that of a vessel.

head′ tone′, a vocal tone in singing so produced as to bring the cavities of the nose and head into sympathetic vibration.

head·wait·er (hed′wā′tər), *n.* one in charge of waiters, busboys, etc., for an eating establishment. [HEAD + WAITER]

head·wa·ters (hed′wô′tərz, -wot′ərz), *n.pl.* the upper tributaries of a river. [HEAD + *waters,* pl. of WATER]

head·way[1] (hed′wā′), *n.* **1.** movement forward or ahead; progress in space: *The ship was unable to make much headway in the storm.* **2.** progress in general: *to make headway in a career.* **3.** rate of progress: *a slight headway against concerted opposition.* **4.** *Railroads.* the time interval between two trains, traveling in the same direction over the same track. **5. make headway,** to proceed forward; advance; progress. [(A)HEAD + WAY]

head·way[2] (hed′wā′), *n.* headroom (def. 2). [HEAD + WAY]

head·wind (hed′wind′), *n.* a wind directly opposed to the course of a vessel or aircraft. [(A)HEAD + WIND[1]]

head·work (hed′wûrk′), *n.* mental labor; thought. [HEAD + WORK] —**head′work′er,** *n.* —**head′work′ing,** *n.*

head·y (hed′ē), *adj.,* **head·i·er, head·i·est. 1.** intoxicating: *a heady wine; heady perfume.* **2.** exciting, exhilarating: *the heady news of victory.* **3.** rashly impetuous: *Her heady conduct gets her into trouble.* **4.** violent; destructive: *The coast was hit by heady winds.* **5.** clever; shrewd: *a heady scheme to win the election.* [ME *hevedy, hedy.* See HEAD, -Y[1]] —**head′i·ly,** *adv.* **head′i·ness,** *n.*

heaf (hēf), *n.* *Brit. Dial.* a sheep pasture. [alter. of HAFT[2]]

heal (hēl), *v.t.* **1.** to make whole or sound; restore to health; free from ailment. **2.** to bring to an end or conclusion, as conflicts between people, groups, etc., usually with the strong implication of restoring former amity; settle; reconcile: *They tried to heal the rift between them, but were unsuccessful.* **3.** to free from evil; cleanse; purify: *to heal the soul.* —*v.i.* **4.** to effect a cure. **5.** (of a wound, broken bone, etc.) to become whole or sound; mend; get well (often fol. by *up* or *over*). [ME *hele(n),* OE *hǣlan* (c. D *helen,* G *heilen,* Icel *heila,* Goth *hailjan*), deriv. of *hāl* HALE[1], WHOLE] —**heal′a·ble,** *adj.* —**heal′er,** *n.*
—**Syn. 1.** See **cure. 2.** compose, soothe. **3.** purge, disinfect. —**Ant. 1, 2.** irritate. **3.** soil, infect.

heal-all (hēl′ôl′), *n.* the self-heal, *Prunella vulgaris.*

heald (hēld), *n.* *Chiefly Brit.* heddle. [ME *helde,* OE *hefeld;* c. OS *hevild;* akin to Icel *hafald.* See HEAVE]

Healds·burg (hēldz′bûrg), *n.* a town in W California. 4816 (1960).

Heald·ton (hēld′tən), *n.* a town in S Oklahoma. 2898 (1960).

heal·ing (hē′ling), *adj.* **1.** curing or curative; prescribed or helping to heal. **2.** growing sound; mending; getting well. —*n.* **3.** the act or process of regaining health: *a new drug to accelerate healing.* [ME *heelyng* (adj.), *helynge* (n.), OE *hǣlinge* (n.). See HEAL, -ING[2], -ING[1]] —**heal′ing·ly,** *adv.*

heal′ing by first′ inten′tion, *Surg., Med.* See under **intention** (def. 6).

heal′ing by sec′ond inten′tion, *Surg., Med.* See under **intention** (def. 6).

health (helth), *n.* **1.** the general condition of the body or mind with reference to soundness and vigor: *good health.* **2.** soundness of body or mind; freedom from disease or ailment: *to have one's health; to lose one's health.* **3.** a polite or complimentary wish for a person's health, happiness, etc., esp. as a toast. **4.** vigor; vitality: *economic health.* [ME *helthe,* OE *hǣlth.* See HALE[1], WHOLE, -TH[1]] —**health′ward,** *adj., adv.*

health·ful (helth′fəl), *adj.* **1.** conducive to health; wholesome or salutary: *a healthful diet.* **2.** healthy: *to grow healthful after an illness.* [ME *helthful.* See HEALTH, -FUL] —**health′ful·ly,** *adv.* —**health′ful·ness,** *n.*
—**Syn. 2.** See **healthy.**

health′ insur′ance, insurance covering medical expenses and loss of income due to illness or injury of the insured.

health·y (hel′thē), *adj.,* **health·i·er, health·i·est. 1.** possessing or enjoying good health or a sound and vigorous mentality: *healthy body; a healthy mind.* **2.** pertaining to or characteristic of good health, or a sound and vigorous mind: *a healthy appearance; healthy attitudes.* **3.** conducive to health; healthful: *healthy recreations.* [HEALTH + -Y[1]] —**health′i·ly,** *adv.* —**health′i·ness,** *n.*
—**Syn. 1.** hale, hearty, robust, vigorous, strong; well. **3.** nutritious, nourishing; hygienic, salubrious; invigorating, bracing. HEALTHY, HEALTHFUL, SALUTARY,

WHOLESOME refer to that which promotes health. HEALTHY, while applied esp. to what possesses health, is also used of what is conducive to health: *a healthy climate; not a healthy place to be.* HEALTHFUL is applied chiefly to what is conducive to health: *healthful diet or exercise.* SALUTARY is applied to that which is conducive to well-being generally, as well as beneficial in preserving or in restoring health: *salutary effects; to take salutary measures.* It is used also of what is morally beneficial: *to have a salutary fear of consequences.* WHOLESOME has connotations of attractive freshness and purity; it applies to what is good for one, physically, morally, or both: *wholesome food or air; wholesome influences or advice.* —**Ant. 1.** sick.

Hea·ly (hē′lē), *n.* **Timothy Michael,** 1855–1931, Irish nationalist politician.

heap (hēp), *n.* **1.** a group of things lying one on another; pile: *a heap of stones.* **2.** *Informal.* a great quantity or number; multitude: *a heap of people.* **3.** *Slang.* an automobile, esp. a dilapidated one. **4. all of a heap,** *Informal.* **a.** overwhelmed with astonishment; amazed: *We were struck all of a heap upon hearing of the marriage.* **b.** suddenly; abruptly: *All of a heap the room was empty.* —*v.t.* **5.** to gather, put, or cast in a heap; pile (often fol. by *up, on, together,* etc.). **6.** to accumulate or amass (often fol. by *up* or *together*): *to heap up riches.* **7.** to give, assign, or bestow in great quantity; load (often fol. by *on* or *upon*): *to heap blessings upon someone; to heap work on someone.* **8.** to load, supply, or fill abundantly: *to heap a plate with food.* —*v.i.* **9.** to become heaped or piled, as sand, snow, etc.; rise in a heap or heaps (often fol. by *up*). [ME *heep,* OE *hēap;* c. D *hoop,* OHG *houf;* akin to G *Haufe*] —**heap′er,** *n.* —**heap′y,** *adj.*
—**Syn. 1.** mass, stack; cumulation; accumulation, collection. **7.** confer.

hear (hēr), *v.,* **heard** (hûrd), **hear·ing.** —*v.t.* **1.** to perceive by the ear. **2.** to learn by the ear or by being told; be informed of: *to hear news.* **3.** to listen to; give or pay attention to: *They refused to hear our side of the argument.* **4.** to be among the audience at or of (something): *to hear a recital.* **5.** to give a formal, official, or judicial hearing to (something); consider officially, as a judge, sovereign, teacher, assembly, etc.: *to hear a case.* **6.** to take or listen to the evidence or testimony of (someone): *to hear the defendant.* **7.** to listen to with favor, assent, or compliance. —*v.i.* **8.** to be capable of perceiving sound by the ear; have the faculty of perceiving sound vibrations. **9.** to receive information by the ear or otherwise: *to hear from a friend.* **10.** to listen with favor, assent, or compliance (often fol. by *of*): *I will not hear of your going.* **11.** *Chiefly Brit.* to applaud or endorse a speaker (usually used imperatively in the phrase *Hear! Hear!*). [ME *here(n),* OE *hēran, hīeran;* c. D *horen,* G *hören,* Icel *heyra,* Goth *hausjan*] —**hear′a·ble,** *adj.* —**hear′er,** *n.*
—**Syn. 1, 2.** attend. HEAR, LISTEN apply to the perception of sound. To HEAR is to have such perception by means of the auditory sense: *to hear distant bells.* To LISTEN is to give attention in order to hear and understand the meaning of a sound or sounds: *to listen to what is being said; to listen for a well-known footstep.* **7.** regard, heed. —**Ant. 7.** disregard.

hear·ing (hēr′ing), *n.* **1.** the faculty or sense by which sound is perceived. **2.** the act of perceiving sound. **3.** opportunity to be heard: *to grant a hearing.* **4.** an instance or a session in which testimony and arguments are presented, esp. before an official, as a judge in a lawsuit. **5.** a preliminary examination of the basic evidence and charges by a magistrate to determine whether criminal procedures, a trial, etc., are justified. **6.** earshot: *Their conversation was beyond my hearing.* [ME *herande, -ende.* See HEAR, -ING[1]] —**hear′ing·less,** *adj.*

hear′ing aid′, a compact, inconspicuous amplifier worn to improve one's hearing.

heark·en (här′kən), *v.i., v.t.* harken. —**heark′en·er,** *n.*

Hearn (hûrn), *n.* **Laf·cad·i·o** (laf kad′ē ō′), *(Koizumi Yakumo),* 1850–1904, U.S. journalist, novelist, and essayist, born in Greece; Japanese citizen after 1894.

Hearne (hûrn), *n.* a town in central Texas. 5072 (1960).

hear·say (hēr′sā′), *n.* **1.** unverified, unofficial information gained or acquired from another and not part of one's direct knowledge: *I pay no attention to hearsay.* **2.** an item of idle or unverified information; gossip; rumor: *a malicious hearsay.* —*adj.* **3.** of, pertaining to, or characterized by hearsay: *hearsay knowledge; a hearsay report.* [n. use of v. phrase *hear say*]

hear′say ev′idence, *Law.* testimony given by a witness based on what he has heard from another person rather than on what he himself knows or has seen or experienced.

hear′say rule′, *Law.* the rule making hearsay evidence inadmissible.

hearse (hûrs), *n.* **1.** a vehicle for conveying a dead person to the place of burial. **2.** a triangular frame for holding candles, used at the service of Tenebrae in Holy Week. **3.** a canopy erected over a tomb. [ME *herse* < MF *herce* a harrow, candle-frame < L *hirpicem,* acc. of *hirpex* harrow] —**hearse′like′,** *adj.*

Hearst (hûrst), *n.* **1.** **William Randolph,** 1863–1951, U.S. editor and publisher. **2.** his son, **William Randolph, Jr.,** born 1908, U.S. publisher and editor.

Human heart (Section)
A, Superior vena cava; B, Right atrium; C, Right ventricle; D, Left ventricle; E, Left atrium; F, Pulmonary vein; G, Pulmonary artery; H, Aorta

heart (härt), *n.* **1.** a hollow, muscular organ which by rhythmic contractions and relaxations keeps the blood in circulation throughout the body. **2.** the center of the total personality, esp. with reference to intuition, feeling, or emotion: *In your heart you know I'm an honest man.* **3.** the center of emotion, esp. as contrasted to the head as the center of the intellect: *His head told him not to fall in love, but his heart had the final say.* **4.** feeling; affection; capacity for sympathy: *to win a person's heart.* **5.** spirit, courage, or enthusiasm: *His heart sank when he walked into the room and saw their gloomy faces.* **6.** the innermost or central part of anything: *Notre Dame stands in the very heart of Paris.* **7.** the vital or essential part; core: *the heart of the matter.* **8.** the breast or bosom: *to clasp a person to one's heart.* **9.** a person (used esp. in expressions of praise or affection): *dear heart.* **10.** a conventional shape with rounded sides meeting in a point at the bottom and curving inward to a cusp at the top. **11.** a red figure or pip of this shape on a playing card. **12.** a card of the suit bearing such figures. **13. hearts, a.** *(construed as sing. or pl.)* the suit so marked: *Hearts is trump. Hearts are trump.* **b.** *(construed as sing.)* a game in which the players try to avoid taking tricks containing this suit. **14.** *Bot.* the core of a tree; the solid central part without sap or albumen. **15.** good condition for production, growth, etc., as of land or crops. **16.** Also called **core.** *Ropemaking.* a strand running through the center of a rope, the other strands being laid around it. **17. after one's own heart,** according to one's taste or preference: *There's a man after my own heart!* **18. at heart,** in reality; fundamentally; basically: *At heart she is a romantic.* **19. break one's heart,** to cause one great disappointment or sorrow, as to disappoint in love: *He left her for another woman and it broke her heart.* **20. by heart,** by memory; word for word: *They knew the song by heart.* **21. cross one's heart,** to maintain the truth of one's statement; affirm one's integrity: *That's exactly what they told me, cross my heart!* **22. do one's heart good,** to give happiness or pleasure to; delight: *It does my heart good to see you again.* **23. eat one's heart out,** to have sorrow or longing dominate one's emotions; grieve inconsolably: *She is eating her heart out over an unhappy marriage.* **24. from the bottom of one's heart,** with complete sincerity. Also, **from one's heart, from the heart.** **25. have a change of heart,** to reverse one's previous opinion or stand: *He hadn't spoken to his brother for years, but on his deathbed he had a change of heart.* **26. have a heart,** to be compassionate or merciful: *Please have a heart and give her another chance.* **27. have at heart,** to have as an object, aim, or desire: *to have another's best interests at heart.* **28. have one's heart in one's mouth,** to be very anxious or fearful: *He wanted to do the courageous thing, but his heart was in his mouth.* **29. have one's heart in the right place,** to be fundamentally kind or generous: *The old gentleman may have a stern manner, but his heart is in the right place.* **30. heart and soul,** enthusiastically; fervently; completely: *They entered heart and soul into the spirit of the holiday.* **31. in one's heart of hearts,** in one's private thoughts or feelings; deep within one: *He knew, in his heart of hearts, that the news would be bad.* **32. lose one's heart to,** to fall in love with: *He lost his heart to the prima ballerina.* Also, **lose one's heart.** **33. near one's heart,** of great interest or concern to one: *It is a cause that is very near his heart.* Also, **close to one's heart.** **34. not have the heart,** to lack the necessary courage or callousness to do something: *No one had the heart to tell him he was through as an actor.* **35. set one's heart against,** to be unalterably opposed to: *She had set her heart against selling the statue.* Also, **have one's heart set against.** **36. set one's heart at rest,** to dismiss one's anxieties: *She couldn't set her heart at rest until she knew he had returned safely.* **37. set one's heart on,** to wish for intensely; determine on: *She has set her heart on going to Europe after graduation.* Also, **have one's heart set on.** **38. take heart,** to regain one's courage; become heartened: *Her son's death was a great blow, but she eventually took heart, convinced that God had willed it.* **39. take or lay to heart, a.** to think seriously about; concern oneself with: *He took to heart his father's advice.* **b.** to be deeply affected by; grieve over: *She was prone to take criticism too much to heart.* **40. to one's heart's content,** until one is satisfied; as much or as long as one pleases: *The children played in the snow to their heart's content.* **41. wear one's heart on one's sleeve, a.** to make one's intimate feelings or personal affairs known to all: *She seemed uninvolved with him, but then she was not the kind who would wear her heart on her sleeve.* **b.** to be liable to fall in love; fall in love easily: *Wearing her heart on her sleeve, she gushed over any man who took an interest in her.* **42. with all one's heart, a.** with earnestness or zeal. **b.** with willingness; cordially: *She welcomed the visitors with all her heart.* —*v.t.* **43.** to fix in the heart: *to heart a warning.* **44.** *Archaic.* to encourage. [ME *herte,* OE *heorte;* c. D *hart,* G *Herz,* Icel *hjarta,* Goth *hairtō;* akin to L *cors,* Gk *kardiā*]

Heart (def. 10)

heart·ache (härt′āk′), *n.* emotional distress; sorrow; grief; anguish. [HEART + ACHE] —**heart′ach′ing,** *adj.*

heart′ attack′, a sudden inability of the heart to function, usually due to an embolism or increased blood pressure; heart failure.

heart′ back′. See **shield back.**

heart·beat (härt′bēt′), *n.* *Physiol.* a pulsation of the heart, including one complete systole and diastole. [HEART + BEAT]

heart′ block′, *Med.* a defect in the coordination of the heartbeat in which the atria and ventricles beat independently or the ventricles miss a beat completely.

heart·break (härt′brāk′), *n.* great sorrow, grief, or anguish. [HEART + BREAK]

heart·break·er (härt′brā′kər), *n.* a person, event, or thing causing heartbreak. [HEARTBREAK + -ER[1]]

Heart′break House′, a play (1917) by G. B. Shaw.

heart·break·ing (härt′brā′king), *adj.* causing intense anguish or sorrow. [HEARTBREAK + -ING[2]] —**heart′break′ing·ly,** *adv.*

heart·bro·ken (härt′brō′kən), *adj.* crushed with sorrow or grief. [HEART + BROKEN] —**heart′bro′ken·ly,** *adv.* —**heart′bro′ken·ness,** *n.*

heart·burn (härt′bûrn′), *n.* **1.** Also called **brash, cardialgia, pyrosis, water brash.** *Pathol.* an uneasy burning sensation in the stomach, often extending toward the esophagus, and sometimes associated with the eructation of an acid fluid. **2.** bitter jealousy; envy. [HEART + BURN[1]]

heart·burn·ing (härt′bûr′ning), *n.* rankling discontent, esp. from envy or jealousy; grudge. [HEART + BURNING]

heart′ cam′, a cam with a single lobe having the general shape of a heart.

heart′ cher′ry, **1.** a large, heart-shaped variety of sweet cherry having soft flesh. **2.** the tree bearing this fruit. Also called **gean.**

heart′ disease′, any condition of the heart which impairs its functioning.

heart·ed (här′tid), *adj.* **1.** having a specified kind of heart (now used only in combination): *hard-hearted; sad-hearted.* **2.** *Archaic.* fixed or present in the heart. [ME *iherted.* See Y-, HEART, -ED[2]] —**heart′ed·ly,** *adv.* —**heart′ed·ness,** *n.*

heart·en (här′tən), *v.t.* to give courage or confidence to; cheer. [HEART + -EN[1]] —**heart′en·er,** *n.* —**heart′en·ing·ly,** *adv.*

heart′ fail′ure, **1.** a condition in which the heart ceases to function; death. **2.** Also called **congestive heart failure.** *Med.* a condition in which the heart fails to pump blood adequately to either the systemic or the pulmonary arterial distribution.

heart·felt (härt′felt′), *adj.* deeply or sincerely felt; earnest; sincere: *heartfelt joy; heartfelt words.* [HEART + FELT[1]]

heart-free (härt′frē′), *adj.* having one's heart free; not in love.

hearth (härth), *n.* **1.** the floor of a fireplace, usually of stone, brick, etc., often extending a short distance into a room. **2.** the fireside; home: *the family hearth.* **3.** *Metall.* **a.** the lower part of a blast furnace, cupola, etc., in which the molten metal collects and from which it is tapped out. See diag. under **blast furnace.** **b.** the part of an open hearth, reverberatory furnace, etc., upon which the charge is placed and melted down or refined. **c.** a brazier or chafing dish for burning charcoal. [ME *herth(e),* OE *he(o)rth;* c. G *Herd,* D *haard;* see CARBON] —**hearth′less,** *adj.* —**hearth′stead′,** *n.*

hearth·side (härth′sīd′), *n.* fireside (def. 1). [HEARTH + SIDE[1]]

hearth·stone (härth′stōn′), *n.* **1.** a stone forming a hearth. **2.** the fireside; home. **3.** a soft stone, or a preparation of powdered stone and clay, used to whiten or scour hearths, steps, floors, etc. [ME *hertston.* See HEARTH, STONE]

heart·i·ly (här′təlē), *adv.* **1.** in a hearty manner; cordially: *He was greeted heartily.* **2.** sincerely; genuinely: *He sympathized heartily with their plight.* **3.** without restraint; exuberantly; vigorously: *They laughed heartily at his jokes.* **4.** with a hearty appetite: *They ate heartily.* **5.** zealously; enthusiastically: *The audience applauded heartily.* **6.** thoroughly; completely: *He approved heartily of her action.* [ME *hertili.* See HEARTY, -LY]

heart·ing (här′ting), *n.* the core of a masonry wall when composed of a different material from that of the facing. [ME *herting.* See HEART, -ING[1]]

Heart′ Is a Lone′ly Hunt′er, The, a novel (1940) by Carson McCullers.

heart·land (härt′land′, -lənd), *n.* that part of a region considered essential to the viability and survival of the whole, specifically, a central land area, relatively invulnerable to attack, and capable of economic and political self-sufficiency. [HEART + LAND]

heart·less (härt′lis), *adj.* **1.** unfeeling; unkind; unsympathetic; harsh; cruel: *heartless words; a heartless person.* **2.** *Archaic.* lacking courage or enthusiasm; spiritless; disheartened. [ME *herteles,* OE *heortlēas.* See HEART, -LESS] —**heart′less·ly,** *adv.* —**heart′less·ness,** *n.*

heart′-lung′ machine′ (härt′lung′), a mechanical device for replacing the functions of the heart and lungs temporarily during heart surgery by artificially inducing circulation and oxygenation.

heart′ mur′mur, *Med.* murmur (def. 3).

Heart′ of Dark′ness, a short novel (1902) by Joseph Conrad.

Heart′ of the Mat′ter, The, a novel (1948) by Graham Greene.

Heart′ of Midlo′thian, The, a historical novel (1818) by Sir Walter Scott.

heart′ point′, *Heraldry.* See **fess point.**

heart·rend·ing (härt′ren′ding), *adj.* causing or expressing intense grief, anguish, or distress. [HEART + RENDING] —**heart′rend′ing·ly,** *adv.*

hearts′ and flow′ers, *Slang.* an expression or display of maudlin sentimentality: *The graduation speech soon deteriorated into hearts and flowers.*

hearts·ease (härts′ēz′), *n.* **1.** peace of mind. **2.** the pansy, or some other plant of the genus *Viola.* **3.** the lady's-thumb. Also, **heart's′-ease′.** [ME *hertes ese.* See HEART, EASE]

heart·shake (härt′shāk′), *n.* See **star shake.** [HEART + SHAKE]

heart′ shell′, **1.** any of numerous bivalve mollusks, esp. of the families *Cardiidae* and *Carditidae,* having a heart-shaped shell. **2.** the shell itself.

heart·sick (härt′sik′), *adj.* **1.** sick at heart; extremely depressed or unhappy. **2.** characterized by or showing extreme depression. [HEART + SICK[1]] —**heart′sick′en·ing,** *adj.* —**heart′sick′ness,** *n.*

heart·some (härt′səm), *adj.* *Chiefly Scot.* **1.** giving cheer, spirit, or courage: *a heartsome wine.* **2.** cheerful; spirited. **3.** *Obs.* courageous; bold. [HEART + -SOME[1]] —**heart′some·ly,** *adv.* —**heart′some·ness,** *n.*

heart·sore (härt′sōr′, -sôr′), *adj.* **1.** sore at heart; grieved. **2.** showing grief. [HEART + SORE; cf. OE *heortsārnes* grief]

heart-strick·en (härt′strik′ən), *adj.* deeply afflicted with grief, mental anguish, etc. Also, **heart-struck** (härt′struk′). —**heart′strick′en·ly,** *adv.*

heart·strings (härt′stringz′), *n.pl.* the deepest feelings; the strongest affections: *to pull at one's heartstrings.* [HEART + STRINGS]

heart′ tamponade′, *Pathol.* tamponade (def. 2).

heart·throb (härt′throb′), *n.* **1.** a rapid beat or pulsation of the heart. **2.** a passionate or sentimental emotion. **3.** sweetheart. [HEART + THROB]

heart-to-heart (härt′tə härt′), *adj.* frank; sincere.

heart·warm·ing (härt′wôr′ming), *adj.* **1.** tenderly moving: *a heartwarming experience.* **2.** gratifying; rewarding; satisfying: *a heartwarming response to his work.* [HEART + WARMING]

heart-whole (härt′hōl′), *adj.* **1.** courageous; dauntless; stout-hearted. **2.** having the heart untouched by love. **3.** wholehearted; sincere. —**heart′-whole′ness,** *n.*

heart·wood (härt′wo͝od′), *n.* the hard central wood of the trunk of an exogenous tree; duramen. [HEART + WOOD[1]]

heart·worm (härt′wûrm′), *n. Vet. Med.* a filarial worm, *Dirofilaria immitis,* that lives in the right ventricle and pulmonary artery of dogs. [HEART + WORM]

heart·y (här′tē), *adj.,* **heart·i·er, heart·i·est,** *n., pl.* **heart·ies.** —*adj.* **1.** warm-hearted; affectionate; cordial; jovial: *a hearty welcome.* **2.** heartfelt, genuine; sincere: *hearty approval; hearty dislike.* **3.** enthusiastic or zealous; vigorous: *hearty support.* **4.** exuberant; unrestrained: *hearty laughter.* **5.** violent; forceful: *a hearty push; a hearty kick.* **6.** physically vigorous; strong and well: *hale and hearty.* **7.** substantial; abundant; nourishing: *a hearty meal.* **8.** enjoying or requiring abundant food: *a hearty appetite.* **9.** (of soil) fertile. —*n.* **10.** a brave or good fellow, esp. with reference to a fellow shipmate; chum; buddy. **11.** a sailor. [ME *herti.* See HEART, -Y[1]] —**heart′i·ly,** *adv.* —**heart′i·ness,** *n.*
—**Syn. 1.** warm, genial. **6.** healthy.

heat (hēt), *n.* **1.** the state of a body perceived as having or generating a relatively high degree of warmth. **2.** the condition or quality of being hot: *the heat of an oven.* **3.** the degree of hotness; temperature: *moderate heat.* **4.** the sensation of warmth or hotness: *unpleasant heat.* **5.** a bodily temperature higher than normal: *the heat of a fever; the feeling of heat caused by physical exertion.* **6.** added or external energy that causes a rise in temperature, expansion, evaporation, or other physical change. **7.** *Physics.* a nonmechanical energy transfer with reference to a temperature difference between a system and its surroundings or between two parts of the same system. *Symbol:* Q **8.** a hot condition of the atmosphere or physical environment; hot season or weather. **9.** a period of hot weather. **10.** a sharp, pungent flavor, as that produced by spices. **11.** warmth or intensity of feeling; vehemence; passion: *He spoke with much heat and at great length.* **12.** maximum intensity in an activity, condition, etc.; the height of any action, situation, or the like: *the heat of battle; the heat of passion.* **13.** extreme pressure, as of events, resulting in tension or strain: *In the heat of his departure he forgot his keys.* **14.** a single intense effort; a sustained, concentrated, and continuous operation: *The painting was finished at a heat.* **15.** *Sports.* **a.** a single course in or division of a race or other contest. **b.** a race or other contest in which competitors attempt to qualify for entry in the final race or contest. **16.** a single operation of heating, as of metal in a furnace, in the treating and melting of metals. **17.** an indication of high temperature, as by the condition or color of something. **18.** *Zool.* **a.** sexual excitement in animals, esp. females. **b.** the period or duration of such excitement: *to be in heat.* —*v.t.* **19.** to make hot or warm (often fol. by *up*). **20.** to excite emotionally; inflame or rouse with passion. —*v.i.* **21.** to become hot or warm (often fol. by *up*). **22.** to become excited emotionally. [ME *hete,* OE *hǣtu;* akin to G *Hitze;* see HOT] —**heat′a·ble,** *adj.* —**heat′ful,** *adj.* —**heat′less,** *adj.* —**heat′like′,** *adj.*
—**Syn. 2.** hotness, warmth, caloric. **3.** caloricity. **11.** ardor, fervor, zeal, flush, fever, excitement, impetuosity. **12.** vehemence, violence, rage. **20.** stimulate, warm, stir, animate, excite, rouse. —**Ant. 1.** coolness. **11.** indifference. **19.** cool.

heat′ bar′rier. See **thermal barrier.**

heat′ capac′ity, *Physics.* the heat required to raise the temperature of a substance one Celsius degree.

heat′ con′tent, *Thermodynamics.* enthalpy.

heat′ dev′il, a wavering, shimmering disturbance of air above or around a hot surface.

heat·ed (hē′tid), *adj.* **1.** warmed; made hot or hotter. **2.** excited; inflamed; vehement: *a heated discussion.* [HEAT + -ED[2]] —**heat′ed·ly,** *adv.* —**heat′ed·ness,** *n.*

heat′ en′gine, an engine that transforms heat into mechanical energy.

heat′ equa′tion, *Math., Physics.* the equation describing the flow of heat on a surface, $\nabla^2 \phi = \frac{1}{\alpha^2}\frac{d\phi}{dt}$, where ∇ is the Laplace operator, ϕ is a function giving the temperature at each point of the surface, α^2 is a constant, and t is the time.

heat·er (hē′tər), *n.* **1.** any of various apparatus for heating, esp. for heating water or room air. **2.** *Electronics.* the element of a vacuum tube that carries the current for heating a cathode. **3.** *Armor.* a triangular form of certain medieval shields, having one straight side, at the top, and two convex sides. **4.** *Slang.* a pistol. [HEAT + -ER[1]]

heat′ exchang′er, a device for transferring the heat of one substance to another, as from the exhaust gases to the incoming air in a regenerative furnace.

heat′ exhaus′tion, a condition characterized by faintness, rapid pulse, nausea, vomiting, profuse sweating, a cold skin, and collapse, caused by prolonged exposure to high temperatures. Also called **heat prostration.**

heath (hēth), *n.* **1.** *Brit.* a tract of open and uncultivated land; waste land overgrown with shrubs. **2.** any of various low, evergreen, ericaceous shrubs common on waste land, as the common heather, *Calluna vulgaris.* **3.** any plant of the genus *Erica,* or of the family *Ericaceae.* **4.** any of several similar but not ericaceous shrubs, as *Frankenia laevis* (**sea heath**) of the European coasts. **5. one's native heath,** the area or locality where one was born or where one's early years were spent: *He felt strangely at peace upon returning to his native heath after so many years.* [ME; OE *hǣth;* c. G *Heide,* Icel *heithr,* Goth *haithi;*| akin to OWelsh *coit* forest] —**heath′less,** *adj.* —**heath′like′,** *adj.*

Heath (hēth), *n.* **Edward (Richard George),** born 1916, British statesman: prime minister 1970–74.

heath′ as′ter, a weedy, North American aster, *Aster ericoides,* having small, white flower heads.

heath·ber·ry (hēth′ber′ē, -bə rē), *n., pl.* **-ries. 1.** crowberry. **2.** any berry found on heaths, esp. the bilberry. [OE *hæth berian.* See HEATH, BERRY]

heath·bird (hēth′bûrd′), *n. Brit. Dial.* the black grouse. [HEATH + BIRD]

heath′ cock′, *Brit. Dial.* the male of the black grouse.

hea·then (hē′thən), *n., pl.* **-thens, -then,** *adj.* —*n.* **1.** an irreligious or unenlightened person. **2.** an unconverted individual of a people that do not acknowledge the God of the Bible; one who is neither a Jew, Christian, nor Muslim; pagan. **3.** (formerly) any person neither Christian nor Jewish, esp. a member of the Islamic faith or of a polytheistic religion: *Many a knight joined the crusades to fight the heathens.* —*adj.* **4.** irreligious or unenlightened. **5.** pagan; of or pertaining to the heathen. [ME *hethen,* OE *hǣthen;* akin to G *Heide* (n.), *heidnisch* (adj.), Icel *heithingi* (n.), *heithinn* (adj.), Goth *heithnō* (n.)] —**hea′then·hood′,** *n.* —**hea′then·ness,** *n.* —**hea′then·ship′,** *n.*
—**Syn. 5.** heathenish, barbarous. HEATHEN, PAGAN are both applied to peoples who are not Christian, Jewish, or Muslim. HEATHEN is often distinctively applied to unenlightened or barbaric idolaters, esp. to primitive or ancient tribes: *heathen rites, idols.* PAGAN, though applied to any of the peoples not worshiping according to the three religions mentioned above, is most frequently used in speaking of the ancient Greeks and Romans: *a pagan poem; a pagan civilization.*

hea·then·dom (hē′thən dəm), *n.* **1.** heathenism; heathen worship or customs. **2.** heathen lands or people. [ME; OE *hǣthendōm.* See HEATHEN, -DOM]

hea·then·esse (hē′thə nes′), *n. Archaic.* **1.** heathenism. **2.** heathendom. [ME *hethenes,* OE *hǣthennes.* See HEATHEN, -NESS]

hea·then·ise (hē′thə nīz′), *v.t., v.i.,* **-ised, -is·ing.** *Chiefly Brit.* heathenize.

hea·then·ish (hē′thə nish), *adj.* **1.** of or pertaining to the heathen: *heathenish practices of idolatry.* **2.** like or befitting the heathen; barbarous. [OE *hǣthenisc.* See HEATHEN, -ISH[1]] —**hea′then·ish·ly,** *adv.* —**hea′then·ish·ness,** *n.*

hea·then·ism (hē′thə niz′əm), *n.* **1.** a belief or practice of heathens. **2.** pagan worship; idolatry. **3.** irreligion. **4.** barbaric morals or behavior; barbarism: *the heathenism of modern society.* [HEATHEN + -ISM]

hea·then·ize (hē′thə nīz′), *v.,* **-ized, -iz·ing.** —*v.t.* **1.** to make heathen or heathenish. —*v.i.* **2.** to become heathen or heathenish. **3.** to practice heathenism. Also, *esp. Brit.,* **heathenise.** [HEATHEN + -IZE]

hea·then·ry (hē′thən rē), *n.* **1.** heathenism. **2.** heathen people; the heathen. [HEATHEN + -RY]

heath·er (heth′ər), *n.* any of various heaths, esp. *Calluna vulgaris,* of England and Scotland, having small, pinkish-purple flowers. [sp. var. of *hether,* earlier *hedder, hadder, hather,* ME *hathir;* akin to HEATH] —**heath′ered,** *adj.*

heath′er bell′. See **bell heather.**

heath·er·y (heth′ə rē), *adj.* **1.** of or like heather. **2.** abounding in heather. Also, **heathy.** [HEATHER + -Y[1]] —**heath′er·i·ness,** *n.*

heath′ grass′, a European grass, *Sieglingia decumbens,* growing in spongy, wet, cold soils. Also called **heath′er grass′.**

heath′ hen′, 1. an extinct, American, gallinaceous bird, *Tympanuchus cupido cupido,* closely related to the prairie chicken. **2.** *Brit. Dial.* the female of the black grouse.

heath·y (hē′thē), *adj.,* **heath·i·er, heath·i·est.** heathery. [ME *hethy.* See HEATH, -Y[1]]

heat′ing degree′-day, a degree-day below the standard temperature of 65°F or 19°C, used in estimating fuel consumption. Cf. **cooling degree-day, growing degree-day.**

heat′ing pad′, a flexible pad, covered with fabric, containing insulated electrical heating elements for applying heat, esp. to a part of the body.

heat′ light′ning, flashes of light near the horizon on summer evenings, reflections of more distant lightning.

heat′ of condensa′tion, *Physics.* the heat liberated by a unit mass of gas at its boiling point as it condenses to a liquid: equal to the heat of vaporization.

heat′ of fu′sion, *Physics.* the heat absorbed by a unit mass of a given solid at its melting point which completely converts the solid to a liquid at the same temperature: equal to the heat of solidification. Cf. **latent heat.**

heat′ of solidifica′tion, *Physics.* the heat liberated by a unit mass of liquid at its freezing point as it solidifies: equal to the heat of fusion.

heat′ of sublima′tion, *Physics.* the heat absorbed by one gram or unit mass of a substance in the process of changing, at a constant temperature and pressure, from a solid to a gaseous state. Cf. **sublime** (def. 10).

heat′ of vaporiza′tion, *Physics.* the heat absorbed per unit mass of a given material at its boiling point which completely converts the material to a gas at the same temperature: equal to the heat of condensation. Cf. **latent heat.**

heat′ prostra′tion, *Med.* See **heat exhaustion.**

heat′ pump′, a device which, by means of a compressible refrigerant, transfers heat from one body, as the earth, air, water, etc., to another body, as a building, the process being reversible.

heat′ res′ervoir, *Thermodynamics.* a hypothetical body of infinitely large mass capable of absorbing or rejecting unlimited quantities of heat without undergoing appreciable changes in temperature, pressure, or density.

heat′ shield′, *Rocketry.* a coating or structure that surrounds part of the nose cone or other vulnerable surfaces of a spacecraft and, by heat absorption or ablation, protects them from excessive heating during reentry.

heat·stroke (hēt′strōk′), *n.* collapse or fever caused by exposure to excessive heat. [HEAT + STROKE[1]]

heat′ wave′, 1. an air mass of high temperature covering an extended area and moving relatively slowly. **2.** a more or less prolonged period of excessively warm weather.

heaume (hōm), *n.* helm[2] (def. 2). [< MF; OF *helme* < Gmc; see HELM[2]]

heave (hēv), *v.,* **heaved** or (*esp. Naut.*) **hove; heav·ing;** *n.* —*v.t.* **1.** to raise or lift with effort or force; hoist: *to heave a heavy ax.* **2.** to throw, esp. to lift and throw with effort, force, or violence: *to heave an anchor overboard; to heave a stone through a window.* **3.** *Naut.* **a.** to move into a certain position or situation: *heave a vessel aback.* **b.** to move in a certain direction: *Heave the capstan around! Heave up the anchor!* **4.** to utter laboriously or painfully: *to heave a sigh.* **5.** to cause to rise and fall with or as with a swelling motion: *to heave one's chest in breathing heavily.* **6.** to vomit; throw up: *He heaved his breakfast before noon.* **7.** *Geol.* to cause a horizontal displacement in (a stratum, vein, etc.). **8.** to haul or pull on (a rope, cable, line, etc.), as with the hands or a capstan: *Heave the anchor cable!* —*v.i.* **9.** to rise and fall in rhythmically alternate movements: *The ship heaved and rolled in the swelling sea.* **10.** to breathe with effort; pant: *He sat there heaving and puffing from the effort.* **11.** to vomit; retch. **12.** to rise as if thrust up, as a hill; swell or bulge: *The ground heaved, and small fissures appeared for miles around.* **13.** to pull or haul on a rope, cable, etc. **14.** to push, as on a capstan bar. **15.** *Naut.* **a.** to move in a certain direction or into a certain position or situation: *heave about; heave alongside; heave in stays.* **b.** (of a vessel) to rise and fall, as with a heavy beam sea. **16. heave down,** *Naut.* to careen (a vessel). **17. heave ho!** (an exclamation used by sailors, as when heaving the anchor up.) **18. heave in sight,** to rise to view, as from below the horizon: *The ship hove in sight as dawn began to break.* **19. heave out,** *Naut.* **a.** to shake loose (a reef taken in a sail). **b.** to loosen (a sail) from its gaskets in order to set it. **20. heave short,** *Naut.* to heave in slack on an anchor cable until a vessel is nearly over the anchor. **21. heave the lead.** See **lead**[2] (def. 11). **22. heave to, a.** *Naut.* to stop the headway of (a vessel), esp. by bringing the head to the wind and trimming the sails so that they act against one another. **b.** to come to a halt. —*n.* **23.** the act or effort of heaving. **24.** a throw, toss, or cast. **25.** *Geol.* the horizontal component of the apparent displacement resulting from a fault, measured in a vertical plane perpendicular to the strike. **26.** the rise and fall of the waves or swell of a sea. **27. heaves,** (*construed as sing.*) Also called **broken wind.** *Vet. Pathol.* a disease of horses, similar to asthma in man, characterized by difficult breathing. [ME *heve(n),* var. (with *-v-* from pt. and ptp.) of *hebben,* OE *hebban;* c. G *heben,* Icel *hefja,* Goth *hafjan;* akin to L *capere* to take] —**heave′less,** *adj.*
—**Syn. 1.** elevate. See **raise. 12.** surge, billow.

heave-ho (hēv′hō′), *n. Informal.* an act of rejection, dismissal, or forcible ejection, as of a lover, employee, or unruly patron: *She gave her boyfriend the old heave-ho.* [n. use of v. phrase *heave ho*]

heav·en (hev′ən), *n.* **1.** the abode of God, the angels, and the spirits of the righteous after death; the place or state of existence of the blessed after the mortal life. **2.** (*cap.*) Often, **Heavens.** the celestial powers; God. **3.** a metonym for God (used in expressions of emphasis, surprise, etc.): *For heaven's sake!* **4. heavens, a.** (used interjectionally to express emphasis, surprise, etc.): *Heavens, what a cold room!* **b.** (*construed as sing.*) a wooden roof or canopy over the outer stage of an Elizabethan theater. **5.** Usually, **heavens.** the sky, firmament, or expanse of space surrounding the earth. **6.** a place or state of supreme happiness: *a heaven on earth.* **7. move heaven and earth,** to do one's utmost to effect an end; make a supreme effort: *She promised to move heaven and earth to be there for the wedding.* [ME *heven,* OE *heofon;* c. MLG *heven;* akin to Icel *himinn,* Goth *himins,* G *Himmel*] —**heav′en·less,** *adj.*

heav·en-born (hev′ən bôrn′), *adj.* **1.** of or as of heavenly origin: *the heaven-born gods.* **2.** *Archaic.* very talented (often used ironically).

heav′en disturb′er, *Naut. Slang.* See **jolly jumper.**

heav·en·ly (hev′ən lē), *adj.* **1.** of or in the heavens: *the heavenly bodies.* **2.** of, belonging to, or coming from the heaven of God, the angels, etc. **3.** resembling or befitting heaven; blissful; beautiful: *a heavenly spot.* **4.** divine or celestial: *heavenly peace.* [ME *hevenly,* OE *heofonlīc.* See HEAVEN, -LY] —**heav′en·li·ness,** *n.*
—**Syn. 4.** supernal, sublime; seraphic, cherubic, angelic; blessed, beatific. —**Ant. 4.** infernal, hellish.

heav′enly bamboo′, nandin.

Heav′enly Cit′y. See **New Jerusalem.**

heav·en-sent (hev′ən sent′), *adj.* timely; opportune: *A heaven-sent rain revived the crops.*

heav·en·ward (hev′ən wərd), *adv.* **1.** Also, **heav′en·wards.** toward heaven. —*adj.* **2.** directed toward heaven: *heavenward prayer.* [ME *hevenward.* See HEAVEN, -WARD] —**heav′en·ward·ly,** *adv.* —**heav′en·ward·ness,** *n.*

heave′-off hinge′ (hēv′ôf′, -of′). See **loose-joint hinge.**

heav·er (hē′vər), *n.* **1.** one who or that which heaves. **2.** *Naut.* **a.** a lever inserted into a loop or between two parallel ropes and twisted in order to tauten a rope or ropes. **b.** a lever for heaving around the drum of a windlass. **c.** a T-shaped device for pushing a heavy needle through a sail. **d.** a longshoreman handling a specified type of cargo (usually used in combination): *coal heaver.* [HEAVE + -ER[1]]

heav·i·er-than-air (hev′ē ər thən âr′), *adj. Aeron.* **1.** of greater specific gravity than the air, as airplanes. **2.** of, pertaining to, or noting such aircraft.

heav·i·ly (hev′ə lē), *adv.* **1.** with a great weight or burden: *a heavily loaded wagon.* **2.** in a manner suggestive of carrying a great weight; ponderously; lumberingly: *He walked heavily across the room.* **3.** in an oppressive manner: *Cares weigh heavily upon him.* **4.** severely; intensely: *to suffer heavily.* **5.** densely; thickly: *heavily wooded.* **6.** in large amounts or in great quantities; very much: *It rained heavily on Tuesday.* **7.** without animation or vigor; in a dull manner; sluggishly: *He read his paper heavily and solemnly, and bored his listeners to tears.* [ME *hevyly,* OE *hefiglīce.* See HEAVY, -LY]

heav·i·ness (hev′ē nis), *n.* the state or quality of being heavy; weight; burden. [ME *hevinesse,* OE *hefignes.* See HEAVY, -NESS]

heav′ing-line bend′, (hē′ving līn′). See **clove hitch.**

Heav·i·side (hev′ē sīd′), *n.* **Oliver,** 1850–1925, English physicist.

Heav′iside lay′er. See **E layer.** [named after Oliver HEAVISIDE]

Heav′iside u′nit func′tion, *Math.* the function that is zero for any number less than zero and that is 1 for any number greater than or equal to zero. [named after Oliver HEAVISIDE]

heav·y (hev′ē), *adj.,* **heav·i·er, heav·i·est,** *n., pl.* **heav·ies,** *adv.* —*adj.* **1.** of great weight; hard to lift or carry: *a heavy load.* **2.** of great amount, quantity, or size; extremely large; massive: *a heavy vote; a heavy snowfall.* **3.** of great force, intensity, turbulence, etc.: *a heavy sea.* **4.** of more than the usual or average weight: *a heavy person; heavy freight.* **5.** having much weight in

proportion to bulk; being of high specific gravity: *a heavy metal.* **6.** of major import; grave; serious: *a heavy offense.* **7.** deep or intense; profound: *a heavy thinker; heavy slumber.* **8.** *Mil.* **a.** thickly armed or equipped with guns of large size. Cf. **heavy cruiser. b.** (of guns) of the more powerful sizes: *heavy weapons.* Cf. **heavy artillery. 9.** hard to bear; burdensome; harsh; oppressive: *heavy taxes.* **10.** hard to cope with; trying; difficult: *a heavy task.* **11.** being as indicated to an unusually great degree: *a heavy buyer.* **12.** broad, thick, or coarse; not delicate: *heavy lines.* **13.** weighted or laden: *air heavy with moisture.* **14.** fraught; loaded; charged: *words heavy with meaning.* **15.** depressed with trouble or sorrow; showing sorrow: *a heavy heart.* **16.** without vivacity or interest; ponderous; dull: *a heavy style.* **17.** clumsy; slow in movement or action: *a heavy gait.* **18.** loud and deep; sonorous: *a heavy sound.* **19.** (of the sky) overcast or cloudy. **20.** (of bread, baked goods, pancakes, etc.) exceptionally dense in substance; insufficiently raised or leavened; thick: *heavy doughnuts.* **21.** (of food) not easily digested. **22.** in a state of advanced pregnancy; nearing childbirth: *heavy with child; heavy with young.* **23.** having a large capacity, capable of doing rough work, or having a large output: *a heavy truck.* **24.** producing or refining basic materials, as steel or coal, used in manufacturing: *heavy industry.* **25.** *Theat.* sober, serious, or somber: *a heavy part.* **26.** *Chem.* of or pertaining to an isotope of greater than normal atomic weight, as heavy hydrogen or heavy oxygen, or to a compound containing such an element, as heavy water. —*n.* **27.** *Theat.* **a.** a villainous part or character: *Iago is the heavy in* Othello. **b.** an actor who plays villainous parts or characters. **28.** *Mil.* a gun of great weight or large caliber. —*adv.* **29.** heavily. [ME *hevi,* OE *hefig,* equiv. to *hef(e)* weight (akin to HEAVE) + *-ig* -Y[1]]
—**Syn. 1.** ponderous, massive, weighty. **9.** onerous, oppressive, grievous, cumbersome; difficult, severe; hard, harsh. **12.** blunt. **14.** HEAVY, MOMENTOUS, WEIGHTY refer to anything having a considerable amount of figurative weight. HEAVY suggests the carrying of a figurative burden: *words heavy with menace.* MOMENTOUS emphasizes the idea of great and usually serious consequences: *a momentous occasion, statement.* WEIGHTY, seldom used literally, refers to something heavy with importance, often concerned with public affairs, which may require deliberation and careful judgment: *a weighty matter, problem.* **15.** serious, grave; gloomy, sad, mournful, melancholy, morose, dejected, despondent, downcast, downhearted. **16.** tedious, tiresome, wearisome, burdensome, boring. **17.** sluggish, lumbering. **19.** lowering, gloomy. —**Ant. 1, 8–12, 15–17, 20, 21, 23, 24.** light.

heav·y-armed (hev′ē ärmd′), *adj.* (formerly) equipped with heavy arms or armor, as troops.

heav′y artil′lery, *Mil.* **1.** guns and howitzers of large caliber. **2.** *U.S.* guns and howitzers of 155-mm. caliber and larger. Cf. **light artillery** (def. 2), **medium artillery.**

heav·y-beard·ed (hev′ē bēr′did), *adj.* having a thick or dark beard.

heav′y bomb′er, *Mil.* a large plane capable of carrying heavy bomb loads for long distances, esp. at high altitudes. Cf. **light bomber, medium bomber.**

heav′y cream′, thick cream having a high percentage of butterfat.

heav′y cruis′er, a naval cruiser having eight-inch guns as its main armament. Cf. **light cruiser.**

heav·y-du·ty (hev′ē do͞o′tē, -dyo͞o′-), *adj.* made or designed to withstand a great deal of physical strain: *heavy-duty machinery.*

heav′y earth′, baryta.

heav·y-foot·ed (hev′ē fo͝ot′id), *adj.* clumsy or ponderous, as in movement, expressiveness, etc.: *music that is heavy-footed and uninspired.* —**heav′y-foot′ed·ness,** *n.*

heav·y-hand·ed (hev′ē han′did), *adj.* **1.** oppressive; harsh: *a heavy-handed master.* **2.** clumsy; graceless: *a heavy-handed treatment of the theme.* —**heav′y-hand′ed·ly,** *adv.* —**heav′y-hand′ed·ness,** *n.*

heav·y-heart·ed (hev′ē här′tid), *adj.* sorrowful; melancholy; dejected. —**heav′y-heart′ed·ly,** *adv.* —**heav′y-heart′ed·ness,** *n.*

heav′y hy′drogen, *Chem.* **1.** either of the heavy isotopes of hydrogen, esp. deuterium. **2.** deuterium.

heav·y-lad·en (hev′ē lād′ᵊn), *adj.* **1.** carrying a heavy load; heavily laden: *a heavy-laden cart.* **2.** very tired or troubled; burdened: *heavy-laden with care.* [late ME *hevy ladyn.* See HEAVY, LADEN]

heav′y min′eral oil′. See under **mineral oil.**

heav′y ni′trogen, *Chem.* the stable isotope of nitrogen having a mass number of 15.

heav′y ox′ygen, *Chem.* either of the two stable isotopes of oxygen having mass numbers of 17 and 18.

heav·y-set (hev′ē set′), *adj.* **1.** having a large body build. **2.** stout; stocky. [HEAVY + SET]

heav′y spar′, *Mineral.* barite.

heav′y wa′ter, *Chem.* water in which hydrogen atoms have been replaced by deuterium, used chiefly in nuclear reactors. *Symbol:* D_2O; *sp. gr.:* 1.1056 at 25°C.

heav·y·weight (hev′ē wāt′), *adj.* **1.** heavy in weight. **2.** of more than average weight or thickness: *a coat of heavyweight material.* **3.** noting or pertaining to a boxer, wrestler, etc., of the heaviest competitive class, esp. a professional boxer weighing over 175 pounds. **4.** of or pertaining to the weight class or division of such boxers: *a heavyweight bout.* **5.** (of a riding horse, esp. a hunter) able to carry up to 205 pounds. —*n.* **6.** a person of more than average weight. **7.** a heavyweight boxer or wrestler. **8.** *Informal.* **a.** a very influential person; one whose words carry much weight. **b.** a very intelligent person. [HEAVY + WEIGHT]

Heb, Hebrew (def. 2).

Heb., **1.** Hebrew. **2.** Hebrews.

Heb·ard·ville (heb′ərd vil′), *n.* a town in SE Georgia. 2758 (1960).

Heb·bel (heb′əl), *n.* **(Chris·ti·an) Fried·rich** (kris′tē än′ frē′drikh), 1813–63, German lyric poet and playwright.

Heb·bron·ville (heb′rən vil′), *n.* a town in S Texas. 3987 (1960).

heb·do·mad (heb′də mad′), *n.* **1.** the number seven. **2.** a period of seven successive days; week. [< L *hebdomad-* < Gk (s. of *hebdomás* week), equiv. to *hébdom(os)* seventh (see HEPTA-) + *-ad-* -AD[1]]

heb·dom·a·dal (heb dom′ə dᵊl), *adj.* **1.** taking place, coming together, or published once every seven days; weekly: *hebdomadal meetings; hebdomadal groups; hebdomadal journals.* —*n.* **2.** *Archaic.* a weekly magazine, newspaper, etc. Cf. **diurnal** (def. 7). [< LL *hebdomadāl(is).* See HEBDOMAD, -AL[1]] —**heb·dom′a·dal·ly,** *adv.*

heb·dom·a·dar·y (heb dom′ə der′ē), *n., pl.* **-dar·ies,** *adj.* —*n.* **1.** *Rom. Cath. Ch.* a member of a church or monastery appointed for one week to sing the chapter Mass and lead in the recitation of the breviary. —*adj.* **2.** hebdomadal (def. 1). [ME *ebdomadarie* < eccl. L *hebdomadāri(us).* See HEBDOMAD, -ARY]

He·be (hē′bē), *n.* **1.** *Class. Myth.* a goddess of youth and spring, the daughter of Zeus and Hera, and wife of Hercules: originally the cupbearer of the gods, but later replaced by Ganymede. **2.** a girl's given name.

he·be·phre·ni·a (hē′bə frē′nē ə), *n.* *Psychiatry.* a form of schizophrenia incident to the age of puberty, characterized by hallucinations and emotional deterioration. [< NL < Gk *hēbē* youth; see -PHRENIA] —**he·be·phren·ic** (hē′bə fren′ik), *adj.*

He·ber (hē′bər), *n.* **1. Reginald,** 1783–1826, British bishop and hymn writer. **2.** a town in central Utah. 2936 (1960).

Hé·bert (ā ber′), *n.* **Jacques Re·né** (zhäk rə nā′), ("*Père Duchesne*"), 1755–94, French journalist and revolutionary leader.

heb·e·tate (heb′i tāt′), *v.,* **-tat·ed, -tat·ing,** *adj.* —*v.t.* **1.** to make dull or blunt, as the sensitivity, a faculty, etc. —*v.i.* **2.** to become dull or blunt. —*adj.* **3.** *Bot.* having a blunt, soft point, as awns. [< L *hebetāt(us)* made dull or blunt (ptp. of *hebetāre*), equiv. to *hebet-* (s. of *hebes*) blunt, dull + *-ātus* -ATE[1]] —**heb′e·ta′tion,** *n.* —**heb′e·ta′tive,** *adj.*

he·bet·ic (hi bet′ik), *adj.* *Physiol.* pertaining to or occurring in puberty. [< Gk *hēbētik(ós)* youthful, equiv. to *hēbē* youth + *-tikos* -TIC]

heb·e·tude (heb′i to͞od′, -tyo͞od′), *n.* the state of being dull; lethargy: *moral hebetude.* [< LL *hebetūd(ō)* dullness, bluntness, equiv. to L *hebet-* (s. of *hebes*) dull + *-ūdō;* see -TUDE] —**heb′e·tu′di·nous,** *adj.*

Hebr., **1.** Hebrew. **2.** Hebrews.

He·bra·ic (hi brā′ik), *adj.* of, pertaining to, or characteristic of the Hebrews, their language, or their culture. Also, **Hebrew.** [< LL *Hebraic(us)* < Gk *Hebraïkós,* equiv. to *Hebra(îos)* HEBREW + *-ikos* -IC; r. OE *Ebrēisc*] —**He·bra′i·cal·ly,** *adv.*

He·bra·ise (hē′brā īz′, -brē-), *v.i., v.t.,* **-ised, -is·ing.** *Chiefly Brit.* Hebraize. —**He′bra·i·sa′tion,** *n.* —**He′bra·is′er,** *n.*

He·bra·ism (hē′brā iz′əm, -brē-), *n.* **1.** an expression or construction distinctive of the Hebrew language. **2.** the character, spirit, principles, or practices distinctive of the Hebrew people. [< LGk *Hebraïsm(ós),* equiv. to *Hebra-* (see HEBRAIZE) + *-ismos* -ISM]

He·bra·ist (hē′brā ist, -brē-), *n.* **1.** one versed in the Hebrew language. **2.** one imbued with the spirit of the Hebrew people or given to their principles or practices. [HEBRA(IZE) + -IST]

He·bra·is·tic (hē′brā is′tik, -brē-), *adj.* of or pertaining to Hebraists or characterized by Hebraism or Hebraisms. Also, **He′bra·is′ti·cal.** [HEBRAIST + -IC] —**He′bra·is′ti·cal·ly,** *adv.*

He·bra·ize (hē′brā īz′, -brē-), *v.,* **-ized, -iz·ing.** —*v.i.* **1.** to use expressions or constructions distinctive of the Hebrew language. —*v.t.* **2.** to make conformable to the spirit, character, principles, or practices of the Hebrew people. Also, *esp. Brit.,* **Hebraise.** [< LGk *Hebraïz(ein)* (to) speak Hebrew, behave like a Jew. See HEBREW, -IZE] —**He′bra·i·za′tion,** *n.* —**He′bra·iz′er,** *n.*

He·brew (hē′bro͞o), *n.* **1.** a member of the Semitic peoples inhabiting ancient Palestine and claiming descent from Abraham, Isaac, and Jacob; an Israelite. **2.** a Semitic language of the Afro-Asiatic family, the language of the ancient Hebrews, which, although not in a vernacular use from 100 B.C. to the present century, was retained as the scholarly and liturgical language of Jews and now is the national language of Israel. *Abbr.:* Heb —*adj.* **3.** Hebraic. **4.** noting or pertaining to the script developed from the Aramaic and early Hebraic alphabets, used since about the 3rd century B.C. for the writing of Hebrew, and later for Yiddish, Ladino, and other languages. [ME *Hebreu,* var. (with *H-* < L) of *Ebreu* < OF < ML *Ebrē(us)* for L *Hebraeus* < LGk *Hebraîos* < Aram *Hebrai;* r. OE *Ebrēas* (pl.) < ML *Ebrēī*]

He′brew cal′endar. See **Jewish calendar.**

He·brews (hē′bro͞oz), *n.* (*construed as sing.*) a book of the New Testament.

Heb·ri·des (heb′ri dēz′), *n.* (*construed as pl.*) a group of islands (**Inner Hebrides** and **Outer Hebrides**) off the W coast of and belonging to Scotland. ab. 65,000; ab. 2900 sq. mi. Also called **Western Islands.** —**Heb′ri·de′an, He·brid′i·an,** *adj.*

He·bron (hē′brən), *n.* a city in W Jordan. 42,578 (est. 1965). Arabic, **El Khalil.**

heb-sed (heb′sed′), *n.* (in ancient Egypt) a festival in which the crowning of the king was reenacted on each of two thrones, celebrated possibly to commemorate the union of Upper Egypt and Lower Egypt. Also called **sed-festival.** [< Egypt]

He·ca·be (hek′ə bē), *n.* *Class. Myth.* Hecuba (def. 1).

Hec·a·lei·us (hek′ə lī′əs), *n.* *Class. Myth.* an epithet of Zeus.

Hec·a·me·de (hek′ə mē′dē), *n.* (in the *Iliad*) a daughter of Arsinous who became the servant of Nestor during the Trojan War.

Hec·a·te (hek′ə tē; *in Shakespeare* hek′it), *n.* *Class. Myth.* a goddess of the earth and Hades, associated with sorcery, hounds, and crossroads and identified with various other goddesses, esp. Artemis. Also, **Hekate.** [< L < Gk *hekátē,* n. use of fem. of *hékatos* far-shooting, said of Apollo as sun-god] —**Hec′a·te′an, Hec′a·tae′an,** *adj.*

hec·a·tomb (hek′ə tōm′, -to͞om′), *n.* **1.** (in ancient Greece and Rome) a public sacrifice of 100 oxen to the gods. **2.** any great slaughter: *the hecatombs of modern wars.* [< L *hecatombē* < Gk *hekatómbē* the sacrifice of a hundred oxen, equiv. to *hekatón* hundred + *-bē,* comb. form of *boûs* ox]

Hec·a·ton·chi·res (hek′ə ton kī′rēz), *n.pl.* *Class. Myth.* three giants, Briareus, Cottus, and Gyges, who were the sons of Uranus and Gaea and had 50 heads and 100 arms each: they were best known for having helped the gods in their struggle against the Titans. Also, **Hec′a·ton·chei′res.**

hec·a·ton·sty·lon (hek′ə ton stī′lon), *n.* a building having 100 columns. [< Gk *hekatón* hundred + *stŷlon* (neut. of *stŷlos*) pillar]

hech·sher (hekh shär′; *Eng.* hekh′shər), *n., pl.* **hech·she·rim** (hekh shə rēm′), *Eng.* **hech·shers.** *Hebrew.* rabbinical approval of meats and other foods that comply with the ritual requirements of Jewish dietary laws, usually issued in the form of an endorsing mark or stamp on products so approved. Also, **hekhsher.** [lit., suitable]

hecht (hekht), *adj.* *Scot. Obs.* hight[1] (def. 1).

Hecht (hekt), *n.* **Ben,** 1894–1964, U.S. novelist and dramatist.

heck[1] (hek), *interj.* *Informal.* (used as a mild expression of annoyance, rejection, disgust, etc.): *What the heck do you care?* [euphemistic alter. of HELL]

heck[2] (hek), *n.* **1.** a comblike attachment on a loom, for guiding the warp threads as they are dressed for the warp beam. **2.** a device that guides yarn onto the bobbin of a spinning wheel. **3.** a gridlike arrangement of glass or metal rods below the hooks on a Jacquard loom, used for lifting all harness eyes equally or evenly. [ME *hekke,* OE *hecc,* var. of *hæcc* HATCH[2]]

heck·le (hek′əl), *v.,* **-led, -ling,** *n.* —*v.t.* **1.** to harass (a public speaker, performer, etc.) with impertinent questions, gibes, or the like; badger. **2.** hackle[1] (def. 6). —*n.* **3.** hackle[1] (def. 4). [late ME *hekele,* var. of *hechele;* akin to HACKLE[1], HATCHEL] —**heck′ler,** *n.*

hect-, var. of **hecto-** before a vowel: *hectare.*

hec·tare (hek′târ), *n.* *Metric System.* a unit of surface, or land, measure equal to 100 ares, or 10,000 square meters: equivalent to 2.471 acres. *Abbr.:* ha Also, **hektare.** [< F; see HECT-, ARE[2]]

hec·tic (hek′tik), *adj.* **1.** characterized by intense agitation, feverish excitement, confused and rapid movement, etc.: *The period preceding the trip was hectic and exhausting.* **2.** marking a particular habit or condition of body, as the fever of phthisis **(hec′tic fe′ver)** when this is attended by flushed cheeks **(hec′tic flush′),** hot skin, and emaciation. **3.** pertaining to or affected with such fever; consumptive. —*n.* **4.** a hectic fever. **5.** a hectic flush. **6.** a consumptive person. [< LL *hectic(us)* < Gk *hektikós* habitual, equiv. to *hekt-* (s. of *héxis*) state, condition + *-ikos* -IC; r. ME *etyk* < MF] —**hec′ti·cal·ly, hec′tic·ly,** *adv.* —**hec′tic·ness,** *n.*

hecto-, a learned borrowing from Greek meaning "hundred," used in the formation of compound words: *hectograph; hectogram.* Also, **hect-, hekt-, hekto-.** [< F, comb. form repr. Gk *hekatón* hundred]

hec·to·cot·y·lus (hek′tə kot′ələs), *n., pl.* **-y·li** (-ᵊlī′). *Zool.* a modified arm of the male of certain cephalopods which is used to transfer sperm into the female. [< NL, equiv. to *hecto-* HECTO- + *-cotylus* < Gk *kotýlē* cup]

hec·to·gram (hek′tə gram′), *n.* *Metric System.* a unit of 100 grams, equivalent to 3.527 ounces avoirdupois. *Abbr.:* hg Also, **hektogram;** *esp. Brit.,* **hec′to·gramme′.** [HECTO- + -GRAM[2]]

hec·to·graph (hek′tə graf′, -gräf′), *n.* **1.** a process for making copies of a letter, memorandum, etc., from a prepared gelatin surface to which the original writing has been transferred. **2.** the apparatus used. —*v.t.* **3.** to copy with the hectograph. Also, **hektograph.** [HECTO- + -GRAPH] —**hec·to·graph·ic** (hek′tə graf′ik), *adj.* —**hec·tog·ra·phy** (hek tog′rə fē), *n.*

hec·to·li·ter (hek′tə lē′tər), *n.* *Metric System.* a unit of capacity of 100 liters, equivalent to 2.8378 U.S. bushels, or 26.418 U.S. gallons. *Abbr.:* hl Also, **hektoliter;** *esp. Brit.,* **hec′to·li′tre.** [< F *hectolitre.* See HECTO-, LITER]

hec·to·me·ter (hek′tə mē′tər), *n.* *Metric System.* a unit of length equal to 100 meters, or 328.08 feet. *Abbr.:* hm Also, **hektometer;** *esp. Brit.,* **hec′to·me′tre.** [< F *hectomètre.* See HECTO-, -METER]

Hec·tor (hek′tər), *n.* **1.** *Class. Myth.* the eldest son of Priam and husband of Andromache: the greatest Trojan hero in the Trojan War, killed by Achilles. **2.** (*l.c.*) a blustering, domineering fellow; a bully. **3.** a boy's given name. —*v.t.* **4.** (*l.c.*) to treat with insolence; bully; torment: *The teacher hectored his students incessantly.* —*v.i.* **5.** (*l.c.*) to act in a blustering, domineering way; be a bully. [< L < Gk *Héktōr,* special use of adj. *héktōr* holding fast]
—**Syn. 4.** torture, persecute; badger, harass.

hec·to·stere (hek′tə stēr′), *n.* *Metric System.* a unit of capacity equal to 100 steres. Also, **hektostere.** [< F *hectostère.* See HECTO-, STERE]

Hec·u·ba (hek′yo͝o bə), *n.* **1.** Also, **Hecabe.** *Class. Myth.* the wife of Priam. **2.** (*italics.*) a tragedy (c425 B.C.) by Euripides.

he'd (hēd; *unstressed* ēd), **1.** contraction of *he had.* **2.** contraction of *he would.*

Hed·da (hed′ə), *n.* a girl's given name.

Hed·da Gab·ler (hed′ə gab′lər), a play (1890) by Henrik Ibsen.

Hed·die (hed′ē), *n.* a girl's given name. Also, **Hedy, Hedie.**

hed·dle (hed′ᵊl), *n.* one of the sets of vertical cords or wires in a loom, forming the principal part of the harness that guides the warp threads. Also, *esp. Brit.,* **heald.** [metathetic var. of HEALD]

hed·en·berg·ite (hed′ᵊn bər gīt′), *n.* a mineral of the pyroxene family, calcium ferrous silicate, $CaFe(SiO_3)_2$, occurring in crystalline limestones in the form of black crystals. [named after L. *Hedenberg,* early 19th-century Swedish chemist; see -ITE[1]]

he·der (khe′der; *Eng.* hā′dər, khā′-), *n., pl.* **ha·da·rim** (khä dä rēm′), *Eng.* **he·ders.** *Hebrew.* **1.** (esp. in Europe) a Jewish school, typically of one room, for teaching Hebrew, Bible, and prayers in the Jewish liturgy to children of elementary school age. **2.** (in the U.S.) See **Talmud Torah** (def. 1). Also, **cheder.** [lit., room]

hedge (hej), *n., v.,* **hedged, hedg·ing.** —*n.* **1.** a row of bushes or small trees planted close together, esp. when forming a fence or boundary; hedgerow: *small fields separated by hedges.* **2.** any barrier or boundary: *a hedge of stones.* **3.** an act or means of preventing complete loss of a bet, an argument, an investment, or the like, with a partially counterbalancing or qualifying one. —*v.t.* **4.** to enclose with or separate by a hedge (often fol. by *in, off, about,* etc.): *to hedge a garden.* **5.** to surround and confine, as with a hedge; hem in; restrict (often fol. by *in, about,* etc.): *He felt hedged in by the rules of language.* **6.** to surround so as to protect; guard (often fol. by *in, about,* etc.): *The tiny island, hedged in by water,* *grew to be a mighty power.* **7.** to protect with qualifications that allow for unstated contingencies or for withdrawal from commitment: *He hedged his program against attack and then presented it to the board.* **8.** to protect against a complete loss (of a bet, investment, financial position, etc.) by placing a smaller bet or bets on another contestant or other contestants, by investing in another thing or area in order to compensate for a possible loss, etc.; to mitigate a possible loss by diversifying (one's bets, investments, etc.). **9.** to prevent or hinder free movement; obstruct: *to be hedged by poverty.* **—*v.i.* 10.** to avoid a rigid commitment by qualifying or modifying a position so as to permit withdrawal; allow for escape or retreat: *He felt that he was speaking too boldly and began to hedge before they could contradict him.* **11.** to prevent complete loss of a bet by betting an additional amount or amounts against the original bet. **12.** *Finance.* to enter transactions that will protect against loss through a compensatory price movement. **13.** to hide as in a hedge; skulk. [ME, OE *hegge*; c. D *heg*, G *Hecke* hedge, Icel *heggr* bird cherry] **—hedge′less,** *adj.*

hedge′ gar′lic, an erect, cruciferous herb, *Sisymbrium officinale,* having a garliclike odor.

hedge·hog (hej′hog′, -hôg′), *n.* **1.** any of several Old World, insectivorous mammals of the genus *Erinaceus,* esp. *E. europaeus,* having spiny hairs on the back and sides. **2.** *U.S.* the porcupine. **3.** *Mil.* **a.** a defensive position, usually of considerable extent, capable of maintaining itself for a prolonged period when encircled by an advancing enemy. **b.** a portable obstacle made of crossed logs in the shape of an hour glass, usually laced with barbed wire. **c.** an obstructive device consisting of steel bars, angle irons, etc., usually embedded in concrete, designed to damage and impede the boats and tanks of a landing force on a beach. [late ME *heyghoge.* See HEDGE, HOG] **—hedge′hog′gy,** *adj.*

Hedgehog, *Erinaceus europaeus* (Length 9 in.)

hedge′hog cone′flower, a perennial herb, *Echinacea purpurea,* of the central U.S., having black, pungent roots, stout, hairy stems, and numerous rose-purple or rose-colored, cone-shaped flowers. Also called **Black Sampson.**

hedge′hog gourd′. See **teasel gourd.**

hedge·hop (hej′hop′), *v.i.,* **-hopped, -hop·ping.** to fly an airplane at a very low altitude, as for spraying crops, low-level bombing in warfare, etc. [HEDGE + HOP[1]] **—hedge′hop′per,** *n.*

hedge′ hys′sop, 1. any of several low, scrophulariaceous herbs of the genus *Gratiola,* as *G. officinalis,* of Europe. **2.** any of certain similar plants, as the skullcap *Scutellaria minor.*

hedge′ priest′, *Brit. Disparaging.* a clergyman with little education or status.

hedg·er (hej′ər), *n.* **1.** one who makes or repairs hedges. **2.** one who hedges in betting, speculating, etc. [HEDGE + -ER[1]]

hedge·row (hej′rō′), *n.* a row of bushes or trees forming a hedge. [OE *heggerewe.* See HEDGE, ROW[1]]

hedge′ spar′row, a small European oscine bird, *Prunella modularis,* which frequents hedges.

hedg·y (hej′ē), *adj.,* **hedg·i·er, hedg·i·est.** abounding in hedges. [HEDGE + -Y[1]]

Hed·ie (hed′ē), *n.* a girl's given name. Also, **Hedy, Heddie.**

He·din (he dēn′), *n.* **Sven An·ders** (sven än′dərs), 1865–1952, Swedish geographer and explorer, esp. of Asia.

He·djaz (hē jaz′; *Arab.* he zhäz′), *n.* Hejaz.

Hed·o·ne (hed′ə nē), *n.* a girl's given name.

he·don·ic (hē don′ik), *adj.* **1.** of, characterizing, or pertaining to pleasure: *a hedonic thrill.* **2.** pertaining to hedonism or hedonics. [Gk *hēdonik(ós)* pleasurable, equiv. to *hēdon(ḗ)* pleasure + *-ikos* -IC] **—he·don′i·cal·ly,** *adv.*

hedon′ic cal′culus, (in utilitarianism) appraisal of possible alternative choices in terms of the amount of pleasure to be gained and pain to be avoided in each. Also called **calculus of pleasure.**

he·don·ics (hē don′iks), *n.* (*construed as sing.*) the branch of psychology that deals with pleasurable and unpleasurable states of consciousness. [see HEDONIC, -ICS]

he·don·ism (hēd′ənniz′əm), *n.* **1.** the doctrine that pleasure or happiness is the highest good. **2.** devotion to pleasure as a way of life: *The later Roman emperors were notorious for their hedonism.* [< Gk *hēdon(ḗ)* pleasure + -ISM] **—he′don·ist,** *n., adj.* **—he′do·nis′tic,** *adj.* **—he′do·nis′ti·cal·ly,** *adv.*

-hedral, a suffix used to form adjectives corresponding to nouns with stems in **-hedron:** *polyhedral.* [-HEDR(ON) + -AL[1]]

-hedron, a learned borrowing from Greek meaning "face," used to denote geometrical solid figures having a certain form or number of faces: *polyhedron.* [< Gk *-edron,* neut. of *-edros* having bases, -sided, equiv. to *(h)édr(a)* seat, face of a geometrical form (see CATHEDRA) + *-os* adj. suffix]

Hed·wig (hed′wig), *n.* a girl's given name.

Hed·y (hed′ē), *n.* a girl's given name. Also, **Heddie, Hedie.**

hee·bie-jee·bies (hē′bē jē′bēz), *n.* (*construed as pl.*) *Slang.* a condition of extreme nervousness caused by fear, worry, strain, etc.; the jitters; the willies (usually prec. by *the*): *Just thinking about ghosts gives me the heebie-jeebies.* [rhyming compound coined by W. De Beck (1890–1942), American comic-strip cartoonist]

heed (hēd), *v.t.* **1.** to give careful attention to: *He did not heed the warning.* **—*v.i.* 2.** to give attention; have regard. **—*n.* 3.** careful attention; notice; observation (usually with *give* or *take*). [ME *hede(n),* OE *hēdan;* c. G *hüten* to guard, protect; akin to HOOD[1]] **—heed′er,** *n.*
—Syn. 1. note, observe, consider, mark. **3.** consideration, care; caution, vigilance, watchfulness. **—Ant. 1.** disregard, ignore.

heed·ful (hēd′fəl), *adj.* taking heed; attentive; mindful; thoughtful; careful: *She was always heedful of others.* [HEED + -FUL] **—heed′ful·ly,** *adv.* **—heed′ful·ness,** *n.*

heed·less (hēd′lis), *adj.* careless; thoughtless; unmindful: *Heedless of the danger, he returned to the burning building to save his dog.* [HEED + -LESS] **—heed′less·ly,** *adv.* **—heed′less·ness,** *n.*

hee·haw (hē′hô′), *n.* **1.** the braying sound made by a donkey. **2.** rude laughter. **—*v.i.* 3.** to bray. [imit. gradational compound; cf. SEESAW]

heel[1] (hēl), *n.* **1.** the back part of the foot in man, below and behind the ankle. **2.** an analogous part in other vertebrates. **3.** either hind foot or hoof of some animals, as the horse. **4.** the foot as a whole: *He was hung by the heels.* **5.** the part of a stocking, shoe, or the like covering the back part of the wearer's foot. **6.** a solid, raised base or support of leather, wood, rubber, etc., attached to the sole of a shoe or boot under the back part of the foot. **7.** something resembling the back part of the human foot in position, shape, etc.: *a heel of bread.* **8.** the rear of the palm, adjacent to the wrist. **9.** the latter or concluding part of anything: *the heel of a session.* **10.** the lower end of any of various more or less vertical objects, as rafters, spars, the sternposts of vessels, etc. **11.** *Naut.* **a.** the after end of a keel. **b.** the inner end of a bowsprit or jib boom. **12.** the crook in the head of a golf club. **13.** *Building Trades.* the exterior angle of an angle iron. **14.** *Railroads.* the end of a frog farthest from a switch. **15.** *Hort.* the base of any part, as of a cutting or tuber, that is removed from a plant for use in the propagation of that plant. **16. at one's heels,** close behind one: *The police are at his heels.* Also, **at heel. 17. cool one's heels,** to be kept waiting, esp. because of deliberate discourtesy: *The producer let the actors who were waiting to be auditioned cool their heels in the outer office.* **18. down at the heels,** having a shabby, slipshod, or slovenly appearance. Also, **down at heel, down at the heel, out at heels, out at the heels. 19. his heels,** *Cribbage.* a jack turned up as a starter, counting two points for the dealer. **20. kick up one's heels,** to have an entertaining time; frolic: *Grandfather could still kick up his heels now and then.* **21. lay by the heels, a.** to arrest and imprison. **b.** to prevail over; render ineffectual: *Superior forces laid the invaders by the heels.* **22. on** or **upon the heels of,** closely following; in quick succession of: *On the heels of the growing unemployment problem came a severe slump.* **23. show a clean pair of heels,** to leave one's pursuers or competitors behind; outrun: *The thief showed his victim a clean pair of heels.* Also, **show one's heels to. 24. take to one's heels,** to run away; take flight: *The thief took to his heels as soon as he saw someone rounding the corner.* **25. to heel, a.** close behind: *The dog followed the hunter to heel.* **b.** under control or subjugation: *The attackers were brought swiftly to heel.* **—*v.t.* 26.** to follow at the heels of; chase closely. **27.** to furnish with heels, as shoes. **28.** to perform (a dance) with the heels. **29.** *Golf.* to strike (the ball) with the heel of the club. **30.** to arm (a gamecock) with spurs. **—*v.i.* 31.** (of a dog) to follow at one's heels on command. **32.** to use the heels, as in dancing. **33. heel in,** to cover temporarily (the roots and most of the stem of a plant) with soil prior to permanent planting. [ME; OE *hēl(a);* c. D *hiel,* Icel *hæll.* See HOCK[1]] **—heel′less,** *adj.*

heel[2] (hēl), *v.i.* **1.** to incline to one side; cant; tilt: *The ship heeled in going about.* **—*v.t.* 2.** to cause to lean or cant. **—*n.* 3.** a heeling movement; a cant. [earlier *heeld,* ME *helde(n),* OE *hieldan* to lean, slope; akin to OE *heald,* Icel *hallr* sloping]

heel[3] (hēl), *n.* *Informal.* a cad; a low character: *The heel left her with three children.* [special use of HEEL[1]. See HEELER]

heel-and-toe (hēl′ən tō′), *adj.* **1.** noting a pace, as in walking contests, in which the heel of the front foot touches ground before the toes of the rear one leave it. **2.** *Naut.* noting a system of watches served alternately, on the watch-and-watch system, by the two halves of a crew.

heel′ breast′, the forward side of the heel, adjoining the shank of a shoe.

heeled (hēld), *adj.* **1.** provided with a heel or heels. **2.** provided with money; flush or wealthy (often used in combination): *one of the best-heeled families in town.* **3.** *Slang.* armed, esp. with a gun. [HEEL[1] + -ED[3]]

heel·er (hē′lər), *n.* **1.** one who heels shoes. **2.** See **ward heeler.** [HEEL[1] + -ER[1]]

heel·ing (hē′ling), *n.* *Naut.* the heel of a topmast, located at the point where the fid passes through. [HEEL[1] + -ING[1]]

heel′ing tank′, *Naut.* either of two lateral ballast tanks permitting an icebreaker to heel and crush ice to either side.

heel·piece (hēl′pēs′), *n.* **1.** *Shoemaking.* **a.** a piece of leather, wood, or other material serving as the heel of a shoe, boot, or the like. **b.** such a piece used in repairing a heel. **2.** an end piece of anything; a terminal part. [HEEL[1] + PIECE]

heel·plate (hēl′plāt′), *n.* a small metal plate attached to the heel of a shoe to protect it against excessive wear. [HEEL[1] + PLATE[1]]

heel·post (hēl′pōst′), *n.* a post made to withstand strain, forming or fitted to the end of something, as the post on which a gate or door is hinged. [HEEL[1] + POST[1]]

heel·tap (hēl′tap′), *n.* **1.** a layer of leather, metal, or the like in a shoe heel; a lift. **2.** a small portion of liquor left in a glass after drinking or in a bottle after decanting. **3.** dregs, sediment, or residue. [HEEL[1] + TAP[1]]

heel′ tap′per, a two-masted fore-and-aft schooner formerly used in fishing along the coast of New England.

Heep (hēp), *n.* **Uriah.** See **Uriah Heep.**

heer (hēr), *n.* an old unit of measure for linen and woolen yarn, equivalent to about 600 yards. [ME (Scot dial.) *heir, hair,* lit., HAIR]

Heer·len (hār′lən), *n.* a city in the SE Netherlands. 74,886 (1962).

heeze (hēz), *v.t.,* **heezed, heez·ing.** *Scot. and North Eng.* to hoist; raise; pull up. Also, **heize.** [sp. var. of *heise,* ME (north) *heis,* doublet of *hoise* HOIST]

Hef′ner can′dle (hef′nər), *Optics.* a German unit of luminous intensity, equal to 0.92 of a candela. [named after F. von *Hefner*-Alteneck (1845–1904), German electrical engineer]

heft (heft), *n.* **1.** weight; heaviness: *It was a rather flimsy chair, without much heft to it.* **2.** *Archaic.* the bulk or main part. **—*v.t.* 3.** to try the weight of by lifting and balancing, as in the hand: *He hefted the spear for a few moments, and then flung it at the foe.* **4.** to heave or lift. [HEAVE + *-t,* var. of -TH[1]] **—heft′er,** *n.*

heft·y (hef′tē), *adj.,* **heft·i·er, heft·i·est. 1.** heavy; weighty: *a hefty book.* **2.** big and strong; powerful; muscular: *a hefty fellow.* [HEFT + -Y[1]] **—heft′i·ly,** *adv.* **—hef′ti·ness,** *n.*

he·gar·i (hi gar′ē, -gâr′ē, heg′ə rē), *n.* a grain sorghum having chalky white seeds. [< Sudanese Ar; var. of Ar *hijāri* stonelike]

He·gel (hā′gəl), *n.* **Ge·org Wil·helm Frie·drich** (gā ôrkh′ vil′helm frē′drikh), 1770–1831, German philosopher.

He·gel·e·os (hi jel′ē os′), *n.* *Class. Myth.* a son of Tyrsenus.

He·ge·li·an (hā gā′lē ən, hi jē′-), *adj.* **1.** of, pertaining to, or characteristic of Hegel or his philosophical system. **—*n.* 2.** one who accepts the philosophical principles of Hegel. **3.** an authority or expert on the writings of Hegel. [HEGEL + -IAN]

Hege′lian dialec′tic, *Hegelianism.* an interpretive method, originally used to relate specific entities or events to the absolute idea, in which some assertable proposition **(thesis)** is necessarily opposed by an equally assertable and apparently contradictory proposition **(antithesis),** the mutual contradiction being reconciled on a higher level of truth by a third proposition **(synthesis).**

He·ge·li·an·ism (hā gā′lē ə niz′əm, hi jē′-), *n.* the philosophy of Hegel and his followers, characterized by the use of the Hegelian dialectic. [HEGELIAN + -ISM]

He·gem·o·ne (hi jem′ə nē), *n.* *Class. Myth.* one of the Graces worshiped at Athens.

he·gem·o·ny (hi jem′ə nē, hej′ə mō′nē), *n., pl.* **-nies. 1.** leadership or predominant influence exercised by one state over others, as in a confederation. **2.** leadership; predominance. [< Gk *hēgemonía* leadership, supremacy, equiv. to *hēgemon-* (s. of *hēgemṓn*) leader + *-ia* -Y[3]] **—heg·e·mon·ic** (hej′ə mon′ik), **heg′e·mon′i·cal,** *adj.* **—he·gem′o·nist,** *n.*

He·gi·ra (hi jī′rə, hej′ər ə), *n.* **1.** the flight of Muhammad from Mecca to Medina to escape persecution, A.D. 622: regarded as the beginning of the Muslim era. **2.** the Muslim era itself. **3.** (*l.c.*) any flight or journey to a more desirable or congenial place than where one is: *an annual hegira to Paris.* Also, **Hejira, Hijra, Hijrah.** [< ML < Ar *hijrah* a flight, departure]

he·gu·men (hi gyo͞o′men), *n.* *Eastern Ch.* the head of a monastery. Also, **he·gu·me·nos** (hi gyo͞o′mə nos′). [< ML *hēgūmen(us)* < Gk *hēgoúmenos* chief, lit., leading, prp. of *hēgeîsthai* to lead]

heh′ de′ity (he), *Egyptian Religion.* any of eight gods (the **Ogdoad**) engendered by Shu in four couples of male and female. [< Egypt]

he·huck·le·ber·ry (hē′huk′əl ber′ē), *n., pl.* **-ries.** See **swamp andromeda.**

Hei·an (hā′än′), *adj.* of or pertaining to the period in Japan, A.D. 794–1184, characterized by the modification and naturalization of ideas and institutions that were earlier introduced from China. [< Jap]

Hei·deg·ger (hī′deg ər, -di gər), *n.* **Martin,** born 1889, German philosopher and writer.

Hei·del·berg (hīd′əl burg′; *Ger.* hīd′əl berkh′), *n.* a city in NW Baden-Württemberg, in SW West Germany. 126,500 (1963).

Hei′delberg jaw′, a human lower jaw of the early Middle Pleistocene age found in 1907 near Heidelberg, Germany.

Hei′delberg man′, the primitive man reconstructed from the Heidelberg jaw.

Hei·den·stam (hā′dən stäm′), *n.* **Ver·ner von** (ver′nər fôn), 1859–1940, Swedish poet and novelist: Nobel prize 1916.

Hei·drun (hā′dro͞on, -dro͝on), *n.* *Scand. Myth.* a goat yielding mead for the fallen warriors in Valhalla.

Hei·duc (hī′do͝ok), *n.* Haiduk. Also, **Hei′duk.**

heif·er (hef′ər), *n.* a cow that has not produced a calf and is under three years of age. [ME *hayfre,* OE *hēa(h)f(o)re,* equiv. to *hēah* high + *-fore;* akin to Gk *pōris* heifer]

Hei·fetz (hī′fits), *n.* **Ja·scha** (yä′shə), 1901–87, U.S. violinist, born in Russia.

heigh[1] (hā, hī), *interj.* (an exclamation used to call attention, give encouragement, etc.)

heigh[2] (hēkh), *adj., adv., n.* *Scot.* high.

heigh-ho (hī′hō′, hā′-), *interj.* (an exclamation of surprise, exultation, melancholy, boredom, or weariness.)

height (hīt), *n.* **1.** extent or distance upward: *at a height of 500 feet.* **2.** distance upward from a given level to a fixed point: *the height from the ground to the first floor; the height of an animal at the shoulder.* **3.** the distance between the lowest and highest points of a person standing upright; stature: *She is five feet in height.* **4.** considerable or great altitude or elevation: *the height of the mountains.* **5.** Often, **heights. a.** a high place above a level; a hill or mountain: *They stood on the heights overlooking the valley.* **b.** the highest part; top; apex; summit: *In his dreams he reached the heights.* **6.** the highest point; utmost degree: *the height of power; the height of pleasure.* **7.** *Archaic.* high degree of social status. Also, **hight.** [ME; OE *hīehtho.* See HIGH, -TH[1]]
—Syn. 3. tallness. HEIGHT, ALTITUDE, ELEVATION refer to distance above a level. HEIGHT denotes extent upward (as from foot to head) as well as any measurable distance above a given level: *The tree grew to a height of ten feet. They looked down from a great height.* ALTITUDE usually refers to the distance, determined by instruments, above a given level, commonly mean sea level: *altitude of an airplane.* ELEVATION implies a distance to which something has been raised or uplifted above a level: *a hill's elevation above the surrounding country, above sea level.* **5.** prominence. **6.** peak, pinnacle; acme, zenith; culmination. **—Ant. 1, 2.** depth.
—Usage. HEIGHT, and not HEIGHTH, is considered the standard English form for this word.

height·en (hīt′ən), *v.t.* **1.** to increase the height of; make higher. **2.** to increase the degree or amount of; augment: *to heighten the value of a painting.* **3.** to strengthen, deepen, or intensify: *to heighten the plot of a story; to heighten one's awareness or appreciation; to heighten one's suffering.* **4.** to bring out the important features of, as in a drawing: *to heighten a picture with*

Chinese white. —*v.i.* **5.** to become higher. **6.** to increase: *The tension heightens as the story unfolds.* **7.** to brighten or become more intense. [HEIGHT + -EN[1]] —**height′en·er,** *n.*
—**Syn. 1.** See **elevate.**

heighth (hītth), *n. Dial.* height.

height′ of land′, divide (def. 15).

height-to-pa·per (hīt′tə pā′pər), *n. Print.* the standard height of type engravings, etc., from the foot to the face, in the U.S. 0.918 of an inch.

Hei·jo (hā′jō′), *n.* Japanese name of **Pyongyang.**

heil (hīl), *interj. German.* hail! (used as a greeting, acclamation, etc.)

Heil·bronn (hīl′brôn), *n.* a city in N Baden-Württemberg, in SW West Germany. 92,400 (1963).

Hei·li·gen·schein (hī′li gən shīn′), *n., pl.* **-schei·ne** (-shī′nə). *German.* halo; a ring of light around the shadow cast by a person's head, esp. on a dewy, sunlit lawn, caused by reflection and diffraction of light rays. [lit., saint's shining light]

Hei·lung·kiang (hā′lŏŏng′gyäng′), *n.* a province of NE China, in NE Manchuria. 14,860,000 (est. 1957); 108,880 sq. mi. *Cap.:* Harbin.

Heim·dall (hām′däl′), *n. Scand. Myth.* the god of dawn and light, and the guardian of the bridge Bifrost, famous for his eyesight and hearing: destined to kill and to be killed by Loki at Ragnarok. Also, **Heim′dal′, Heim·dallr** (hām′däl′ər).

heim·ish (hā′mish), *adj. Yiddish.* homey; unaffected.

Heim′lich maneu′ver (hīm′lik), an emergency procedure to aid a person choking on food or other objects, by an upper abdominal thrust that forces air from the lungs upward to dislodge the obstruction. [after H.J. *Heimlich* (b. 1920), U.S. physician]

Hei·ne (hī′nə), *n.* **Hein·rich** (hīn′rıкн), 1797–1856, German lyric and satiric poet, journalist, and critic.

Hei′ne-Bo·rel′ the′orem (hī′nə bō rel′), *Math.* the theorem that in a metric space every covering consisting of open sets which covers a closed and compact set has a finite collection of subsets which covers the given set. Also called **Borel-Lebesque theorem.** [named after Eduard *Heine* (1821–81), German mathematician and Émile *Borel* (1871–1956), French mathematician]

hei·nie[1] (hī′nē), *n. Disparaging.* a German, esp. a German soldier of World War I. [partly Anglicized var. of G *Heine,* familiar var. of *Heinrich* Henry; see -IE]

hei·nie[2] (hī′nē), *n. Slang.* the buttocks. [alter. of HINDER[2]; see -IE]

Hein·ie (hī′nē), *n.* a boy's given name, form of **Heinrich.**

hei·nous (hā′nəs), *adj.* hateful; odious; abominable; totally reprehensible: *a heinous offense.* [ME *heynous* < MF *haineus,* equiv. to *haine* hatred (deriv. of *hair* to HATE[1] < Gmc) + *-eus* -OUS] —**hei′nous·ly,** *adv.* —**hei′nous·ness,** *n.*
—**Syn.** wicked, infamous, flagrant, flagitious, atrocious, villainous, nefarious. —**Ant.** admirable.

Hein·rich (hīn′rik; *Ger.* hīn′rıкн), *n.* a boy's given name, Germanic form of **Henry.**

heir (âr), *n.* **1.** a person who inherits or has a right of inheritance in the property of another following the latter's death. **2.** *Law.* **a.** (in common law) a person who inherits all the property of a deceased person, as by descent, relationship, will, or legal process. **b.** *Civil Law.* a person who legally succeeds to the place of a deceased person and assumes his rights and obligations, as the liabilities for debts or the possessory rights to property. **3.** a person who inherits or is entitled to inherit the rank, title, position, etc., of another. **4.** a person, society, etc., considered as inheriting the tradition, talent, etc., of a predecessor. —*v.t.* **5.** *Chiefly Dial.* to inherit; succeed to. [ME *eir, heir* < OF < L *hērēd-* (s. of *hērēs*); akin to Gk *chērōs* bereaved] —**heir′less,** *adj.*

heir′ appar′ent, *pl.* **heirs apparent. 1.** an heir whose right is indefeasible, provided he survives the ancestor. **2.** a person whose succession to a position appears certain: *His popularity makes him the chief's heir apparent.* [ME] —**heir′ appar′ency.**

heir′ at law′, *pl.* **heirs at law.** a person who inherits, or has a right of inheritance in, the real property of one who has died without leaving a valid will.

heir·dom (âr′dəm), *n.* heirship; inheritance.

heir·ess (âr′is), *n.* a female heir, esp. a woman who has inherited or will inherit considerable wealth.

heir·loom (âr′lo͞om′), *n.* **1.** any family possession transmitted from generation to generation. **2.** *Law.* a chattel that because of its close connection with the mansion house descends to the heir, as a portrait of an ancestor, etc. [ME *heirlome.* See HEIR, LOOM[1]]

heir′ presump′tive, *pl.* **heirs presumptive.** a person who is expected to be an heir but whose expectations may be defeated by the birth of a nearer heir.

heir·ship (âr′ship), *n.* the position or rights of an heir; right of inheritance; inheritance. [ME; see HEIR, -SHIP]

Heis (hīs), *n.* a crater in the second quadrant of the face of the moon: about 8 miles in diameter.

Hei·sen·berg (hī′zən bûrg′; *Ger.* hī′zən berк′), *n.* **Wer·ner Karl** (ver′nər kärl), 1901–76, German physicist: Nobel prize 1932.

Hei′senberg uncer′tainty prin′ciple, *Physics.* See **uncertainty principle.** [named after W. K. HEISENBERG]

heist (hīst), *U.S. Slang.* —*v.t.* **1.** to rob or steal, esp. by burglary. —*n.* **2.** a robbery, esp. a burglary. [alter. of HOIST] —**heist′er,** *n.*

heize (hēz), *v.t.,* **heized, heiz·ing.** *Scot. and North Eng.* heeze.

He·jaz (hē jaz′; *Arab.* he zhäz′), *n.* a former independent kingdom in W Arabia, bordering on the Red Sea: contains the holy cities of Islam, Medina, and Mecca. ab. 2,000,000; ab. 150,000 sq. mi. *Cap.:* Mecca. Also, **Hedjaz.**

He·ji·ra (hi jī′rə, hej′ər ə), *n.* Hegira

Hek·a·te (hek′ə tē; *in Shakespeare* hek′it), *n.* Hecate. —**Hek·a·te′an, Hek′a·tae′an,** *adj.*

hekh·sher (heкн′shär; *Eng.* heкн′shər), *n., pl.* **hekh·she·rim** (heкн shə rēm′), *Eng.* **hekh·shers.** *Hebrew.* hechsher.

hek·tare (hek′târ), *n.* hectare.

hekto-, var. of **hecto-:** *hektometer.* Also, *esp. before a vowel,* **hekt-.**

hek·to·gram (hek′tə gram′), *n.* hectogram.

hek·to·graph (hek′tə graf′, -gräf′), *n., v.t.* hectograph.

hek·to·li·ter (hek′tə lē′tər), *n.* hectoliter.

hek·to·me·ter (hek′tə mē′tər), *n.* hectometer.

hek·to·stere (hek′tə stēr′), *n.* hectostere.

Hel (hel), *n. Scand. Myth.* **1.** the goddess ruling Niflheim: a daughter of Loki and Angerboda. **2.** the home of the dead; Niflheim. Also, **Hel·a** (hel′ä).

He·laine (hə lān′), *n.* a girl's given name, form of **Helen.** Also, **He·lain′.**

held (held), *v.* pt. and a pp. of **hold.**

Hel·da (hel′də), *n.* a girl's given name.

hel·den·ten·or (hel′dᵊn ten′ər; *Ger.* hel′dᵊn tā nōʀ′), *n., pl.* **-ten·ors,** *Ger.* **-te·no·re** (-tā nō′ʀə). a tenor having a brilliant, powerful voice suited to singing Wagnerian opera. Also called **heroic tenor.** [< G, equiv. to *helden* heroic (see HERO) + *Tenor* TENOR]

Hel·en (hel′ən), *n.* **1.** Also called **Hel′en of Troy′.** *Class. Myth.* the beautiful daughter of Zeus and Leda and wife of Menelaus. Her abduction by Paris was the cause of the Trojan War. **2.** a girl's given name.

Hel·e·na (hel′ə nə; *for 3 also* he lē′nə), *n.* **1. Saint,** c247–c330, mother of Constantine I. **2.** a city in and the capital of Montana, in the W part. 20,227 (1960). **3.** a girl's given name, form of **Helen.**

He·lene (hə lēn′), *n.* a girl's given name, form of **Helen.** Also, **Helyne.**

He·le·nor (hə lē′nôr), *n.* (in the *Aeneid*) a Lydian prince who accompanied Aeneas from Troy.

Hel·ga (hel′gə), *n.* a girl's given name.

Hel·go·land (hel′gō länt′), *n.* a German island in the North Sea. 148 (1953); ¼ sq. mi. Also, **Heligoland.**

He·li (hē′lī), *n. Douay Bible.* Eli (def. 1).

heli-, var. of **helio-** before a vowel: *helianthus.*

he·li·a·cal (hi lī′ə kəl), *adj. Astron.* pertaining to or occurring near the sun, esp. applied to such risings and settings of a star as are most nearly coincident with those of the sun while yet visible. Also, **he·li·ac** (hē′lē ak′). [< LL *hēliac(us)* (< Gk *hēliakós;* see HELI-, -AC) + -AL[1]] —**he·li′a·cal·ly,** *adv.*

He·li·a·dae (hə lī′ə dē′), *n.pl. Class. Myth.* the seven sons of Helius and Rhode.

He·li·a·des (hi lī′ə dēz′), *n.pl. Class. Myth.* the daughters of Helius and Clymene who were transformed into poplar trees because of their grief over the death of their brother Phaëthon.

he·li·ae·a (hē′lē ē′ə), *n.* (in ancient Athens) the dicastery. [< Gk *hēliaía* public place] —**he′li·ae′an,** *adj.*

he·li·an·thine B (hē′lē an′thin, -thēn), *Chem.* See **methyl orange.** [HELIANTH(US) + -INE[2]]

he·li·an·thus (hē′lē an′thəs), *n., pl.* **-thus·es.** any plant of the genus *Helianthus,* comprising the sunflowers. [< NL; see HELI-, -ANTHOUS] —**he·li·an·tha·ceous** (hē′lē an thā′shəs), *adj.*

he·li·ast (hē′lē ast′), *n.* (in ancient Athens) a dicast. [< Gk *hēliastḗs,* equiv. to *hēliáz(esthai)* (to) sit in the HELIAEA + *-tēs* n. suffix] —**he′li·as′tic,** *adj.*

helic-, var. of **helico-** before a vowel: *helical.*

hel·i·cal (hel′i kəl), *adj.* pertaining to or having the form of a helix; spiral. [HELIC- + -AL[1]] —**hel′i·cal·ly,** *adv.*

Helical gears

hel′ical gear′, a cylindrical gear wheel the teeth of which follow the pitch surface in a helical manner.

hel′ical rack′, *Mach.* a rack having teeth set at an oblique angle to the edges.

Hel·i·ca·on (hel′ə kā′on), *n. Class. Myth.* a son of Antenor and Theano and the husband of Laodice. Wounded in the Trojan War, he was spared by the Greeks because he had advised the Trojans to return Helen.

Hel·i·ce (hel′i sē′), *n.* an ancient city in S Greece: chief city of Achaia; center for the worship of Poseidon.

he·liced (hē′list, hel′ist), *adj.* decorated with spirals. [HELIC- (cf. F *hélice*) + -ED[3]]

hel·i·ces (hel′i sēz′), *n.* a pl. of **helix.**

hel·i·cline (hel′ə klīn′), *n.* a curved ramp. [HELI(C)- + -CLINE]

helico-, a learned borrowing from Greek meaning "spiral"; used with this meaning and as a combining form of **helix** in the formation of compound words: *helicograph.* Also, *esp. before a vowel,* **helic-.** [< Gk *heliko-,* comb. form of *hélix*]

hel·i·co·graph (hel′ə kō graf′, -gräf′), *n.* an instrument for drawing helices. [HELICO- + -GRAPH]

hel·i·coid (hel′ə koid′, hē′lə-), *adj.* **1.** coiled or curving like a spiral. —*n.* **2.** *Geom.* a warped surface generated by a straight line moving so as to cut or touch a fixed helix. [< Gk *helikoeid(ḗs)* of spiral form. See HELIC-, -OID] —**hel′i·coi′dal,** *adj.* —**hel′i·coi′dal·ly,** *adv.*

Helicon

hel·i·con (hel′ə kon′, -kən), *n.* a coiled tuba carried over the shoulder and used esp. in military bands. [prob. special use of HELICON, by assoc. with HELICO-]

Hel·i·con (hel′ə kon′, -kən), *n.* **1.** a mountain in S central Greece. 5738 ft.: regarded by ancient Greeks as the abode of Apollo and the Muses. **2.** a crater in the second quadrant of the face of the moon: about 13 miles in diameter.

Hel·i·co·ni·an (hel′ə kō′nē ən), *n.* **1.** *Class. Myth.* an epithet of Poseidon. —*adj.* **2.** of or pertaining to the Grecian Helicon or its supposed inhabitancy by Apollo and the Muses. [< L *Helicōni(us)* (< Gk *Helikṓnios;* see HELICON, -IOUS) + -AN]

hel·i·cop·ter (hel′ə kop′tər, hē′lə-), *n.* **1.** any of a class of heavier-than-air craft which are lifted and sustained in the air by rotating wings or blades turning on vertical axes by virtue of power supplied by an engine. —*v.i.* **2.** to fly in a helicopter. —*v.t.* **3.** to convey in a helicopter. [< F *hélicoptère.* See HELICO-, -PTER]

Hel·i·go·land (hel′ə gō land′), *n.* Helgoland.

he·li·o (hē′lē ō′), *n., pl.* **-os.** *Informal.* **1.** a heliogram. **2.** a heliograph. [by shortening]

helio-, a learned borrowing from Greek meaning "sun," used in the formation of compound words: *heliolatry* Also, *esp. before a vowel,* **heli-.** [< Gk, comb. form of *hḗlios* SUN]

he·li·o·cen·tric (hē′lē ō sen′trik), *adj. Astron.* **1.** measured or considered as being seen from the center of the sun. **2.** having or representing the sun as a center: *the heliocentric concept of the universe.* [HELIO- + CENTRIC] —**he′li·o·cen′tri·cal·ly,** *adv.* —**he·li·o·cen·tric·i·ty** (hē′lē ō sen tris′i tē), **he·li·o·cen·tri·cism** (hē′lē ō sen′tri siz′əm), *n.*

heliocen′tric par′allax, *Astron.* See under **parallax** (def. 2).

He·li·o·chrome (hē′lē ə krōm′), *n. Trademark.* a photograph reproducing directly the natural colors of a subject. —**he′li·o·chro′mic,** *adj.* —**he′li·o·chro′my,** *n.*

he·li·o·dor (hē′lē ə dôr′), *n.* a variety of clear yellow beryl used as a gemstone. [< G]

He·li·o·gab·a·lus (hē′lē ə gab′ə ləs), *n.* (*Varius Avitus Bassianus*) ("*Marcus Aurelius Antoninus*") A.D. 204–222, Roman emperor 218–222. Also, **Elagabalus.**

he·li·o·gram (hē′lē ə gram′), *n.* a message sent by a heliographic device. [HELIO- + -GRAM[1]]

he·li·o·graph (hē′lē ə graf′, -gräf′), *n.* **1.** a device for signaling by means of a movable mirror which reflects beams of light, esp. sunlight, to a distance. **2.** photoheliograph. **3.** *Meteorol.* an instrument for recording the duration and intensity of sunshine. —*v.t., v.i.* **4.** to communicate by heliograph. [HELIO- + -GRAPH] —**he·li·og·ra·pher** (hē′lē og′rə fər), *n.* —**he·li·o·graph·ic** (hē′lē ə graf′ik), **he′li·o·graph′i·cal,** *adj.* —**he′li·o·graph′i·cal·ly,** *adv.* —**he′li·og′ra·phy,** *n.*

he·li·o·gra·vure (hē′lē ō grə vyo͞or′, -ə grā′vyo͞or), *n. Obs.* photoengraving. [< F; see HELIO-, GRAVURE]

he·li·ol·a·try (hē′lē ol′ə trē), *n.* worship of the sun. [HELIO- + -LATRY] —**he′li·ol′a·ter,** *n.* —**he′li·ol′a·trous,** *adj.*

he·li·om·e·ter (hē′lē om′i tər), *n.* a telescope with a divided, adjustable objective, formerly used to measure small angular distances, as those between celestial bodies. [HELIO- + -METER] —**he·li·o·met·ric** (hē′lē ə me′trik), **he′li·o·met′ri·cal,** *adj.* —**he′li·o·met′ri·cal·ly,** *adv.*

He·li·op·o·lis (hē′lē op′ə lis), *n.* **1.** Biblical name, **On.** an ancient ruined city in N United Arab Republic, on the Nile delta. **2.** ancient Greek name of **Baalbek.**

He·li·os (hē′lē os′), *n.* the ancient Greek god of the sun, the son of Hyperion and Thia, and father of Phaëthon: represented as driving a chariot across the heavens; identified by the Romans with Sol; called Hyperion by Homer. Also, **He·li·us** (hē′lē əs).

he·li·o·scope (hē′lē ə skōp′), *n.* a telescope for viewing the sun, adapted to protect the eye of the viewer from the sun's glare. [HELIO- + -SCOPE] —**he·li·o·scop·ic** (hē′lē ə skop′ik), *adj.* —**he·li·os·co·py** (hē′lē os′kə pē), *n.*

he·li·o·stat (hē′lē ə stat′), *n.* an instrument consisting of a mirror moved by clockwork, for reflecting the sun's rays in a fixed direction. [< NL *heliostat(a).* See HELIO-, -STAT] —**he′li·o·stat′ic,** *adj.*

he·li·o·tax·is (hē′lē ō tak′sis), *n. Biol.* movement of an organism toward or away from sunlight. [HELIO- + -TAXIS] —**he·li·o·tac·tic** (hē′lē ō tak′tik), *adj.*

he·li·o·ther·a·py (hē′lē ō ther′ə pē), *n.* treatment of disease by means of sunlight. [HELIO- + THERAPY]

he·li·o·trope (hē′lē ə trōp′, hēl′yə- *or, esp. Brit.,* hel′yə-), *n.* **1.** *Bot.* any plant that turns toward the sun. **2.** any boraginaceous herb or shrub of the genus *Heliotropium,* esp. a garden species, *H. arborescens,* having small, fragrant, purple flowers. **3.** valerian (def. 2). **4.** a light tint of purple; reddish lavender. **5.** *Survey.* an arrangement of mirrors for reflecting sunlight from a distant point to an observation station. **6.** bloodstone. [HELIO- + -TROPE]

he·li·o·trop·ic (hē′lē ə trop′ik, -trō′pik), *adj. Bot.* turning or growing toward the light. [HELIO- + -TROPIC] —**he′li·o·trop′i·cal·ly,** *adv.*

he·li·o·tro·pin (hē′lē ə trō′pin, hē′lē o′trə pin), *n.* piperonal. [HELIOTROPE + -IN[2]]

he·li·ot·ro·pism (hē′lē o′trə piz′əm), *n.* heliotropic tendency or growth. [HELIO- + -TROPISM]

he·li·o·type (hē′lē ə tīp′), *n., v.,* **-typed, -typ·ing.** collotype. [HELIO- + -TYPE] —**he·li·o·typ·ic** (hē′lē ə tip′ik), *adj.* —**he′li·o·typ′i·cal·ly,** *adv.*

he·li·o·zo·an (hē′lē ə zō′ən), *n.* **1.** a protozoan of the order *Heliozoa,* having a spherical body and radiating pseudopods. —*adj.* **2.** Also, **he·li·o·zo·ic** (hē′lē ə zō′ik). belonging or pertaining to the *Heliozoa.* [< NL *Hēliozo(a)* name of the group (see HELIO-, -ZOA) + -AN]

hel·i·pad (hel′ə pad′, hē′lə-), *n.* a takeoff and landing area for helicopters, usually without commercial facilities. [HELI(COPTER) + PAD[1]]

hel·i·port (hel′ə pōrt′, -pôrt′, hē′lə-), *n.* a landing place for helicopters, often the roof of a building. [HELI(COPTER) + PORT[1]]

he·li·um (hē′lē əm), *n. Chem.* an inert, gaseous element present in the sun's atmosphere, certain minerals, natural gas, etc., and also occurring as a radioactive decomposition product, used as a substitute for flammable gases in dirigible balloons. *Symbol:* He; *at. wt.:* 4.0026; *at. no.:* 2; *density:* 0.1785 at 0°C and 760 mm. pressure. [< NL < Gk *hḗli(os)* the sun; see -IUM]

he·lix (hē′liks), *n., pl.* **hel·i·ces** (hel′i sēz′), **he·lix·es. 1.** a spiral. **2.** *Archit.* **a.** a spiral ornament. **b.** (in a Corinthian capital) either of two scrolls issuing from a cauliculus. Cf. **Corinthian** (def. 4). **3.** *Geom.* the curve formed by a straight line drawn on a plane when that plane is wrapped round a cylindrical surface of any kind, esp. a right circular cylinder, as the curve of a screw. Equation: $x = a \sin\theta$, $y = a \cos\theta$, $z = b\ \theta$. **4.** *Anat.* the curved fold forming most of the rim of the external ear. See diag. under **ear.** [< L: a spiral, a kind of ivy < Gk *hélix* anything twisted, cf. *helíssein* to turn, twist, roll]

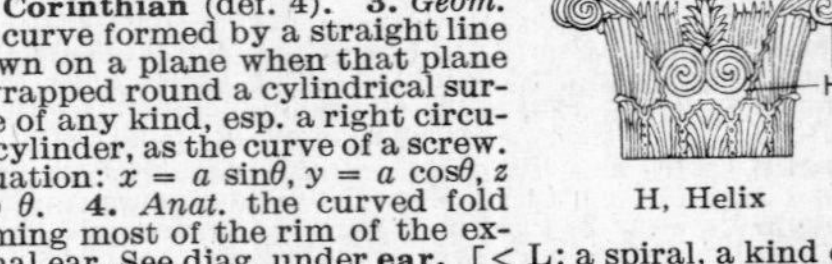

H, Helix

hell (hel), *n.* **1.** the place or state of punishment of the wicked after death; the abode of evil and condemned spirits; Gehenna or Tartarus. **2.** any place or state of torment or misery: *She made his life a hell on earth.* **3.** anything that causes torment or misery, esp. severe verbal censure; a tongue-lashing: *He expected to catch hell for coming home late.* **4.** the powers of evil. **5.** the abode of the dead; Sheol or Hades. **6.** a gambling house. **7.** a receptacle into which a tailor throws his scraps. **8.** Also called **hellbox.** *Print.* a box into which a printer throws

discarded type. **9.** the utterance of "hell" in swearing or for emphasis. **10. be hell on,** *Slang.* **a.** to be unpleasant to or painful for: *She's hell on her servants.* **b.** to be harmful to: *These country roads are hell on tires.* **11. get** or **catch hell,** *Slang.* to suffer a scolding; receive a harsh reprimand: *He'll get hell from his wife for working so late again.* **12. hell around,** *Slang.* to live or act in a wild or dissolute manner: *All they cared about was drinking and helling around.* **13. hell of a,** *Slang.* **a.** very bad, disagreeable, or difficult: *We had a hell of a trip on that bumpy road.* **b.** extraordinary; notable: *He got three minutes of applause after giving a hell of a speech.* **c.** very much of; extreme: *It was a hell of a lot of money for a movie.* **d.** very; extremely; excessively (used as an intensive): *a hell of a long trip for an old car.* **14. play hell with,** *Slang.* to deal recklessly with; bring injury or harm to: *Snowstorms played hell with the flow of city traffic.* **15. raise hell,** *Slang.* **a.** to indulge in wild celebration. **b.** to create an uproar; object violently to: *She will raise hell when she sees what your dog has done to her garden.* —*interj.* **16.** (used to express surprise, irritation, disgust, etc.) [ME, OE *hel(l)*; c. OHG *hell(i)a* (G *Hölle*), Icel *hel*, Goth *halja*; akin to OE *helan* to cover, hide, and to HULL²] —**hell′-like′,** *adj.*
—**Syn. 2.** inferno, Abaddon, pandemonium, Avernus. —**Ant. 2.** paradise.

Hell (hel), *n.* a crater in the third quadrant of the face of the moon: about 20 miles in diameter.

he'll (hēl; *unstressed* ēl, hil, il), **1.** contraction of *he will.* **2.** contraction of *he shall.*

Hel·lad·ic (he lad′ik), *adj.* of or pertaining to the Bronze Age culture on the mainland of ancient Greece c2900–1100 B.C. [< L *Helladic(us)* < Gk *Helladikós* of, from Greece, equiv. to *Hellad-* (s. of *Hellás*) Greece + *-ikos* -IC]

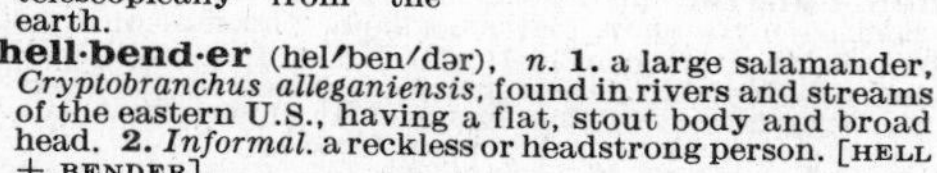

Hellbender
(Length 18 in.)

Hel·las (hel′əs), *n.* ancient Greek name of **Greece.** —**Hel·la·di·an** (he lā′dē ən), *n.* —**Hel·lad·ic** (he lad′ik), *adj.*

Hel·las (hel′əs), *n.* an area in the southern hemisphere of Mars, appearing as a light region when viewed telescopically from the earth.

hell·bend·er (hel′ben′dər), *n.* **1.** a large salamander, *Cryptobranchus alleganiensis,* found in rivers and streams of the eastern U.S., having a flat, stout body and broad head. **2.** *Informal.* a reckless or headstrong person. [HELL + BENDER]

hell·bent (hel′bent′), *adj.* *Informal.* **1.** stubbornly or recklessly determined. **2.** going at terrific speed. [HELL + BENT¹]

hell·box (hel′boks′), *n.* *Print.* hell (def. 8). [HELL + BOX¹]

hell·broth (hel′brôth′, -broth′), *n.* a magical broth prepared for an infernal purpose. [HELL + BROTH]

hell·cat (hel′kat′), *n.* **1.** a bad-tempered, unmanageable woman; shrew. **2.** a woman with magic powers derived from evil sources; witch. [HELL + CAT¹]

hell·div·er (hel′dī′vər), *n.* a grebe, esp. the pied-billed grebe. [HELL + DIVER]

Hel·le (hel′ē), *n.* *Class. Myth.* a daughter of Nephele and Athamas who, while fleeing with her brother Phrixus from a plot of their stepmother Ino, fell into the Hellespont and was drowned.

hel·le·bore (hel′ə bôr′, -bōr′), *n.* **1.** any of several ranunculaceous herbs of the genus *Helleborus,* esp. *H. niger,* the Christmas rose. **2.** Also called **false hellebore.** any of several coarse, melanthiaceous herbs of the genus *Veratrum,* as *V. album* **(European white hellebore)** and *V. viride* **(American white hellebore). 3.** the powdered root of American white hellebore, used to kill lice and caterpillars. [< Gk *helléboros*; r. earlier *ellebor(e),* ME *el(l)bre,* etc. < L *ellebor(us)*]

hel·le·bo·re·in (hel′ə bôr′ē in, -bōr′-), *n.* *Chem.* a yellow, crystalline, water-soluble, poisonous solid, $C_{37}H_{56}O_{18}$, obtained from the rhizome and root of certain hellebores, and used in medicine chiefly as a heart stimulant. [HELLEBORE + -IN²]

hel·leb·o·rin (he leb′ə rin, hel′ə bôr′in, -bōr′-), *n.* *Chem.* a colorless, crystalline, water-insoluble, poisonous solid, $C_{28}H_{36}O_6$, obtained from the rhizome and root of certain hellebores, and used in medicine chiefly as a purgative. [HELLEBOR(E) + -IN²]

Hel·len (hel′ən), *n.* *Class. Myth.* a Thessalian king, son of Deucalion and Pyrrha and eponymous ancestor of the Hellenes.

Hel·lene (hel′ēn), *n.* a Greek. [< Gk *Héllēn* a Greek; see HELLEN]

Hel·len·ic (he len′ik, -lē′nik), *adj.* **1.** of, pertaining to, or characteristic of the ancient Greeks or their language, culture, thought, etc., esp. before the time of Alexander the Great. Cf. **Hellenistic** (def. 3). —*n.* **2.** Also called **Greek.** a branch of the Indo-European family of languages, comprising a variety of ancient, medieval, and modern dialects and languages, all of them called Greek. **3.** Katharevusa. [< Gk *Hellēnik(ós)* of, pertaining to the Greeks. See HELLENE, -IC] —**Hel·len′i·cal·ly,** *adv.*

Hel·len·ise (hel′ə nīz′), *v.t., v.i.,* **-ised, -is·ing.** *Chiefly Brit.* Hellenize. —**Hel′len·i·sa′tion,** *n.* —**Hel′len·is′er,** *n.*

Hel·len·ism (hel′ə niz′əm), *n.* **1.** ancient Greek culture or ideals. **2.** the imitation or adoption of ancient Greek language, thought, customs, art, etc.: *the Hellenism of Alexandrian Jews.* **3.** the characteristics of Greek culture, esp. after the time of Alexander the Great; civilization of the Hellenistic period. [< Gk *Hellēnism(ós)* an imitation of or similarity to the Greeks. See HELLENE, -ISM]

Hel·len·ist (hel′ə nist), *n.* **1.** a person who adopts Greek speech, ideas, or customs. **2.** a person who admires or studies Greek civilization. [< Gk *Hellēnist(ḗs).* See HELLENE, -IST]

Hel·len·is·tic (hel′ə nis′tik), *adj.* **1.** pertaining to Hellenists. **2.** following or resembling Greek usage. **3.** of or pertaining to the Greeks or their language, culture, etc., after the time of Alexander the Great, when Greek characteristics were modified by foreign elements. Cf. **Hellenic** (def. 1). **4.** of or pertaining to the architecture of Greece and Greek territories from the late 3rd century through the 1st century B.C., characterized by deviations of various sorts from the proportions and arrangements of the mature Greek orders, particularly in the attenuation of the Doric order, and by innovations in plan and ornamentation. **5.** pertaining to or designating the style of the fine arts, esp. sculpture, developed in the area conquered by Alexander the Great from the end of the 4th to the 1st century B.C., chiefly characterized by delicate and highly finished modeling, dramatic, often violent movement of forms in space, representations of extreme emotion, highly individuated characterization, and a wide variety of subject matter. Cf. **archaic** (def. 5), **classical** (def. 2). [HELLENE + -ISTIC] —**Hel′len·is′ti·cal·ly,** *adv.*

Hel·len·ize (hel′ə nīz′), *v.,* **-ized, -iz·ing.** —*v.t.* **1.** to make Greek in character. —*v.i.* **2.** to adopt Greek ideas or customs. Also, *esp. Brit.,* **Hellenise.** [< Gk *Hellēníz(ein)* (to) imitate the Greeks, speak Greek. See HELLENE, -IZE] —**Hel′len·i·za′tion,** *n.* —**Hel′len·iz′er,** *n.*

hel·ler¹ (hel′ər), *n., pl.* **hel·ler. 1.** a former coin of various German states, usually equal to half a pfennig. **2.** a former bronze coin of Austria, the 100th part of a korona. **3.** haler (def. 2). [< G]

hell·er² (hel′ər), *n.* *Slang.* a noisy, wild, troublesome person. [short for HELL-RAISER]

Hel·ler·town (hel′ər toun′), *n.* a town in E Pennsylvania. 6716 (1960).

Hel·les (hel′is), *n.* **Cape,** a cape in European Turkey at the S end of Gallipoli Peninsula.

Hel·les·pont (hel′i spont′), *n.* ancient name of the **Dardanelles.** —**Hel·les·pont·ine** (hel′i spon′tin, -tīn), *adj.*

Hel·les·pon·tus (hel′is pon′tis), *n.* an area in the southern hemisphere of Mars.

hell·fire (hel′fīər′), *n.* **1.** the fire of hell. **2.** punishment in hell. [ME; see HELL, FIRE]

Hell′ Gate′, a narrow channel in the East River, in New York City.

hell·gram·mite (hel′grə mīt′), *n.* the aquatic larva of a dobsonfly, used as bait in fishing. [?]

hell·hole (hel′hōl′), *n.* **1.** a place totally lacking in comfort, cleanliness, order, etc. **2.** a place or establishment noted for its illegal or immoral practices. Also, **hell′ hole′.** [ME; see HELL, HOLE]

hell·hound (hel′hound′), *n.* **1.** a mythical watchdog of hell. **2.** a fiendish person. [ME, OE; see HELL, HOUND¹]

hel·lion (hel′yən), *n.* *Informal.* a disorderly, troublesome, or rowdy person. [HELL + *-ion,* as in *scullion, (rap)scallion*]

hell·ish (hel′ish), *adj.* **1.** of, like, or suitable to hell; infernal; vile; horrible: *It was a hellish war.* **2.** miserable; abominable; execrable: *We had a hellish time getting through traffic.* **3.** wicked; devilish: *The child's behavior was hellish most of the day.* [HELL + -ISH¹] —**hell′ish·ly,** *adv.* —**hell′ish·ness,** *n.*

hell·kite (hel′kīt′), *n.* a fiendishly cruel and wicked person. [HELL + KITE¹]

Hell·man (hel′mən), *n.* **Lillian Florence,** 1905–84, U.S. playwright.

hel·lo (he lō′, hə-, hel′ō), *interj., n., pl.* **-los,** *v.,* **-loed, -lo·ing.** —*interj.* **1.** (used to express a greeting, answer a telephone, or attract attention.) **2.** (an exclamation of surprise, wonder, elation, etc.) —*n.* **3.** the call "hello" (used as an expression of greeting): *She gave me a warm hello.* —*v.i.* **4.** to say "hello"; to cry or shout: *I helloed, but no one answered.* —*v.t.* **5.** to say "hello" to (someone): *We helloed each other as though nothing had happened.* Also, *esp. Brit.,* **hullo.** [var. of HALLO]

hell-rais·er (hel′rā′zər), *n.* *Slang.* a person or thing that raises hell, esp. habitually. [n. use of v. phrase *raise hell*; see -ER¹]

hell's′ bells′, **1.** (used interjectionally to indicate vexation or surprise.) **2.** (used interjectionally to emphasize a following remark.) [rhyming phrase]

Hell's′ Kitch′en, (in New York City) a section of midtown Manhattan, west of Times Square, formerly notorious for its slums and high rate of crime.

hell·uv·a (hel′ə və), *adj., adv.* hell (def. 12).

hell′ week′, *Informal.* the week of hazing preceding initiation into a college fraternity.

helm¹ (helm), *n.* **1.** *Naut.* **a.** a wheel or tiller by which a ship is steered. **b.** the entire steering apparatus of a ship. **c.** the angle with the fore-and-aft line made by a rudder when turned: *15-degree helm.* **d.** an imaginary tiller regarded as extending forward of the rudderpost of a ship and therefore as being moved, when the ship is turned, to the side of the fore-and-aft line opposite to that in which the rudder is turned and the ship headed: formerly referred to in most steering orders given in terms of helm position instead of rudder position. **2.** the place or post of control: *A stern taskmaster was at the helm, and things began to move more rapidly.* —*v.t.* **3.** to steer; direct. [ME *helme,* OE *helma*; c. MHG *halme, helm* handle, OIcel *hjalm* rudder] —**helm′less,** *adj.*

helm² (helm), *n.* **1.** *Meteorol.* **a.** clouds that form along the crest of the Crossfell Range in Cumberland and Westmoreland, England, before or during a helm wind. **b.** See **helm wind. 2.** Also, **heaume.** Also called **great helm.** a medieval helmet, typically formed as a single cylindrical piece with a flat or raised top, completely enclosing the head: used with field armor of the 13th and 14th centuries and with jousting armor in the 15th and early 16th centuries. —*v.t.* **3.** to furnish or cover with a helmet. [ME, OE; c. D, G *helm*; akin to OE *helan* to cover]

Hel·mand (hel′mənd), *n.* a river in S Asia, flowing SW from E Afghanistan to a lake in E Iran. 650 mi. long.

helmed (helmd), *adj.* *Heraldry.* (of a human being) depicted as wearing a helmet. [HELM² + -ED³]

hel·met (hel′mit), *n.* **1.** any of various forms of protective head covering worn by soldiers, firemen, divers, cyclists, etc. **2.** medieval armor for the head. **3.** (in fencing, singlestick, etc.) a protective device for the head and face consisting of reinforced wire mesh. **4.** anything resembling a helmet in form or position. [< MF *healmet, helmet,* dim. of *helme* HELM²] —**hel′met·ed,** *adj.* —**hel′met·like′,** *adj.*

Helmets
A, Medieval; B, Modern

hel′meted guin′ea fowl′, the common guinea fowl in its wild state. Cf. **guinea fowl.**

hel′met lin′er, *Mil.* a stiff, plastic head covering designed to be worn alone or under a steel helmet for protection.

Helm·holtz (helm′hōlts), *n.* **1. Her·mann Lud·wig Fer·di·nand von** (her′män lo͞ot′viKH fer′di nänt′ fən), 1821–94, German physiologist and physicist. **2.** a crater in the fourth quadrant of the face of the moon in the libration area: about 60 miles in diameter. —**Helm·holtz′i·an,** *adj.*

Helm′holtz free′ en′ergy, *Thermodynamics.* a quantity, expressed as the internal energy of a system minus the product of the absolute temperature and the entropy of the system, a decrease in the quantity being equal to the maximum amount of work performed on the system during a reversible change at constant temperature. Also called **Helm′holtz func′tion, work function.** Cf. **Gibbs free energy.** [named after H. L. F. von HELMHOLTZ]

hel·minth (hel′minth), *n.* a worm, esp. a parasitic worm. [< Gk *helminth-* (s. of *hélmins*) a kind of worm]

hel·min·thi·a·sis (hel′min thī′ə sis), *n.* *Pathol.* a condition characterized by worms in the body. [< NL < Gk *helminthi(ân)* (to) suffer from worms (see HELMINTH) + *-asis* -ASIS]

hel·min·thic (hel min′thik), *adj.* **1.** of, pertaining to, or caused by worms or helminths. **2.** expelling intestinal worms; anthelminthic. [HELMINTH + -IC]

hel·min·thoid (hel min′thoid, hel′min thoid′), *adj.* shaped like a helminth; vermiform; wormlike. [HELMINTH + -OID]

hel·min·thol·o·gy (hel′min thol′ə jē), *n.* the science of worms, esp. of parasitic worms. [HELMINTH + -O- + -LOGY] —**hel·min·tho·log·i·cal** (hel min′thə loj′i kəl), **hel·min′tho·log′ic,** *adj.* —**hel′min·thol′o·gist,** *n.*

helm′ port′, the opening at the stern of a ship, through which a rudder stock passes.

helms·man (helmz′mən), *n., pl.* **-men.** a person who steers a ship; steersman. [HELM¹ + 's¹ + MAN¹] —**helms′man·ship′,** *n.*

helm′ wind′ (wind), a violent northeast wind that blows in Cumberland and Westmoreland, England. Also called **helm.**

Hé·lo·ïse (el′ō ēz′; *Fr.* ā lô ēz′), *n.* **1.** 1101?–1164, French abbess: pupil and wife of Pierre Abélard. Cf. **Abélard. 2.** a girl's given name, French form of **Eloise** or **Louise.**

He·lo·ni·a (hə lō′nē ə), *n.* a girl's given name.

Hel·ot (hel′ət, hē′lət), *n.* **1.** a member of the lowest class in ancient Laconia, constituting a body of serfs who were bound to the land and were owned by the state. Cf. **Perioeci, Spartiate. 2.** (*l.c.*) a serf or slave; bondman. [< L *hēlōt(ēs)* (pl.) < Gk *heílōtes*] —**hel′ot·age,** *n.*

hel·ot·ism (hel′ə tiz′əm, hē′lə-), *n.* state or quality of being a helot; serfdom. [HELOT + -ISM]

hel·ot·ry (hel′ə trē, hē′lə-), *n.* **1.** serfdom; slavery. **2.** helots collectively. [HELOT + -RY]

help (help), *v.,* **helped** or (*esp. Dial.*) **holp; helped** or (*esp. Dial.*) **hol·pen; help·ing;** *n.; interj.* —*v.t.* **1.** to give or provide what is necessary to accomplish a task or satisfy a need; contribute strength or means to; render assistance to; cooperate effectively with; aid; assist: *He planned to help him with the work. He helped her into the cab.* **2.** to save; rescue; succor: *Help me, I'm falling!* **3.** to make easier or less difficult; contribute to; facilitate: *The exercise of restraint is certain to help the achievement of peace.* **4.** to be useful or profitable to: *Her good looks helped her career.* **5.** to refrain from; avoid (usually prec. by *can* or *cannot*): *He can't help doing it.* **6.** to relieve or break the uniformity of: *Small patches of bright color can help an otherwise dull interior.* **7.** to relieve (someone) in need, sickness, pain, or distress. **8.** to remedy, stop, or prevent: *Nothing will help now.* **9.** to serve food to at table (usually fol. by *to*): *Help her to salad.* **10.** to take or appropriate for oneself: *They helped themselves to the farmer's apples.* —*v.i.* **11.** to give aid; be of service or advantage: *Every little bit helps.* **12. help out,** to assist in an effort; be of aid to: *Her relatives helped out when she became ill.* **13. so help me,** (used as a mild oath) I am speaking the truth; on my honor: *That's exactly what happened, so help me.* —*n.* **14.** the act of helping; aid or assistance; relief or succor. **15.** one who or that which helps: *She certainly is a help around the house.* **16.** a hired helper; employee. **17.** a body of such helpers. **18.** a domestic servant or a farm laborer. **19.** means of remedying, stopping, or preventing: *The thing is done, and there is no help for it now.* **20.** *Dial.* helping (def. 2). —*interj.* **21.** (used as an exclamation to call for assistance or to attract attention.) [ME *helpe(n),* OE *helpan*; c. G *helfen*] —**help′a·ble,** *adj.*
—**Syn. 1.** encourage, befriend; support, second, uphold, back, abet. HELP, AID, ASSIST, SUCCOR agree in the idea of furnishing another with something needed, especially when the need comes at a particular time. HELP implies furnishing anything that furthers his efforts or relieves his wants or necessities. AID and ASSIST, somewhat more formal, imply especially a furthering or seconding of another's efforts. AID implies a more active helping; ASSIST implies less need and less help. To SUCCOR, still more formal and literary, is to give timely help and relief in difficulty or distress: *Succor him in his hour of need.* **3.** further, promote, foster. **6.** ameliorate. **7.** alleviate, cure, heal. **14.** support, backing. —**Ant. 3, 12, 15.** hinder. **7.** afflict.
—**Usage.** HELP BUT, in sentences like, *She's so beautiful you can't help but admire her,* has been condemned by some as being ungrammatical for *can't help admiring her.* But this objection was expressed by British grammarians and purists (like Fowler), and in American usage it can only be characterized as standard.

help·er (hel′pər), *n.* a person or thing that helps or gives assistance, support, etc.
—**Syn.** aid, assistant; supporter, backer, auxiliary, ally. [ME; see HELP, -ER¹]

help·ful (help′fəl), *adj.* giving or rendering aid or assistance; of service: *His comments were always helpful.* [ME; see HELP, -FUL] —**help′ful·ly,** *adv.* —**help′ful·ness,** *n.*
—**Syn.** useful, convenient; beneficial, advantageous. —**Ant.** useless, inconvenient.

help·ing (hel′ping), *n.* **1.** the act of one who or that which helps. **2.** a portion of food served to a person at one time: *That's his third helping of ice cream.* —*adj.* **3.** giving aid, assistance, support, or the like. [ME; see HELP, -ING[1], -ING[2]] —**help′ing·ly,** *adv.*

help′ing hand′, assistance; a degree of support: *The neighbors lent a helping hand while his wife was hospitalized.*

help·less (help′lis), *adj.* **1.** unable to help oneself; weak or dependent: *a helpless invalid.* **2.** without help, aid, or succor: *A cave-in trapped the helpless miners.* **3.** deprived of strength or power; powerless; incapacitated: *He was helpless with laughter.* **4.** bewildered; confused; perplexed: *He looked at her with a helpless expression on his face.* **5.** affording no help. [ME; see HELP, -LESS] —**help′less·ly,** *adv.* —**help′less·ness,** *n.*

help·mate (help′māt′), *n.* **1.** a companion and helper. **2.** a wife or husband. [HELP + MATE[1]]

help·meet (help′mēt′), *n.* helpmate. [from the phrase *a help meet* (i.e., suitable, like) him]

Hel·sa (hel′sə), *n.* a girl's given name, form of **Elizabeth.**

Hel·sing·ör (hel′siṉg œr′), *n.* a seaport on NE Zealand, in NE Denmark: the scene of Shakespeare's *Hamlet.* 32,636 (1960). Also called **Elsinore.**

Hel·sin·ki (hel′siṉg kē, hel siṉg′-), *n.* a seaport in and the capital of Finland, on the S coast. 445,190 (est. 1958). Swedish, **Hel·sing·fors** (hel′siṉg forz′, *Sw.* hel′siṉg-fôsh′).

hel·ter-skel·ter (hel′tər skel′tər), *adv.* **1.** in headlong and disorderly haste: *The children ran helter-skelter all over the house.* **2.** in a haphazard manner; without regard for order: *His clothes were scattered helter-skelter about the room.* —*n.* **3.** tumultuous disorder; confusion. —*adj.* **4.** carelessly hurried; confused: *They ran in a mad, helter-skelter fashion for the door.* **5.** disorderly; haphazard: *The books and papers were scattered on his desk in a helter-skelter manner.* [imit.] —**hel′ter-skel′ter·i·ness,** *n.*

helve (helv), *n., v.,* **helved, helv·ing.** —*n.* **1.** the handle of an ax, hatchet, hammer, or the like. —*v.t.* **2.** to furnish with a helve. [ME, OE *h(i)elfe*] —**helv′er,** *n.*

Hel·vel·lyn (hel vel′in), *n.* a mountain in NW England. 3118 ft.

Hel·ve·tia (hel vē′shə), *n.* **1.** an Alpine region in Roman times, corresponding to the W and N parts of Switzerland. **2.** Switzerland.

Hel·ve·tian (hel vē′shən), *adj.* **1.** of or pertaining to Helvetia or the Helvetii. **2.** Swiss. —*n.* **3.** one of the Helvetii. **4.** a Swiss. [HELVETI(A) + -AN]

Hel·vet·ic (hel vet′ik), *n.* **1.** a Swiss Protestant; Zwinglian. —*adj.* **2.** Helvetian. [HELVET(IA) + -IC]

Hel·ve·ti·i (hel vē′shē ī′), *n., pl.* the ancient Celtic inhabitants of Helvetia in the time of Julius Caesar. [< L]

Hel·vé·tius (hel vē′shəs; *Fr.* el vā syys′), *n.* **Claude A·dri·en** (klōd ā′drē ən; *Fr.* klōd A drē äN′), 1715–71, French philosopher.

He·lyne (hə lēn′, hel′in), *n.* a girl's given name, form of Helen. Also, **Helene.**

hem[1] (hem), *v.,* **hemmed, hem·ming,** *n.* —*v.t.* **1.** to enclose or confine (usually fol. by *in, around,* or *about*): *hemmed in by enemies.* **2.** to fold back and sew down the edge of (cloth, a garment, etc.); to form an edge or border on or around. —*n.* **3.** the edge made by folding back the margin of cloth and sewing it down. **4.** the edge or border of a garment, drape, etc., esp. at the bottom. **5.** the edge, border, or margin of anything. **6.** *Archit.* the raised edge forming the volute of an Ionic capital. See diag. under **volute.** [ME *hem(m),* OE *hem,* prob. akin to *hamm* enclosure]

hem[2] (hem), *interj., n., v.,* **hemmed, hem·ming.** —*interj.* **1.** (an utterance resembling a slight clearing of the throat, used to attract attention, express doubt, etc.) —*n.* **2.** the utterance or sound of "hem." —*v.i.* **3.** to utter the sound "hem." **4.** to hesitate in speaking. **5.** **hem and haw,** to speak noncommittally; avoid giving a direct answer: *He hems and haws and comes out on both sides of every question.* [imit.]

hem-, var. of **hemo-** before a vowel: *hemal.* Also, **haem-.** Cf. **haemat-.**

hema-, var. of **hemo-:** *hemacytometer.* Also, **haema-.**

he·ma·chrome (hē′mə krōm′, hem′ə-), *n.* the red coloring matter of the blood. Also, **haemachrome.** [HEMA- + -CHROME]

he·ma·cy·tom·e·ter (hē′mə sī tom′i tər, hem′ə-), *n. Med.* hemocytometer.

he·mag·glu·ti·nate (hē′mə glo͞ot′ənāt′, hem′ə-), *v.t., v.i.,* **-nat·ed, -nat·ing.** (of erythrocytes) to clump. Also, **haemagglutinate.** [HEM- + AGGLUTINATE] —**he′mag·glu′ti·na′tion,** *n.* —**he·mag·glu·tin·a·tive** (hē′mə-glo͞ot′ənā tiv, -ən ə tiv, hem′ə-), *adj.*

he·mag·glu·ti·na·tion (hē′mə glo͞ot′ənā′shən, hem′ə-), *n. Immunol.* the clumping of erythrocytes. Also, **haemagglutination.** [HEM- + AGGLUTINATION]

he·ma·gogue (hē′mə gôg′, -gog′, hem′ə-), *Med.* —*adj.* **1.** Also, **he·ma·gog·ic** (hē′mə goj′ik, hem′ə-). promoting a flow of blood. —*n.* **2.** a hemagogue agent, esp. one that promotes the flow of menstrual blood. [HEM- + -AGOGUE]

he·mal (hē′məl), *adj.* **1.** Also, **hematal.** of or pertaining to the blood or blood vessels. **2.** *Zool.* noting, pertaining to, or on the side of the body ventral to the spinal axis, containing the heart and principal blood vessels. Also, **haemal.** [HEM- + -AL[1]]

he-man (hē′man′), *n., pl.* **-men.** a strong, tough, virile man.

he·ma·nal·y·sis (hē′mə nal′i sis, hem′ə-), *n. Biochem.* an analysis, esp. of the chemical constituents, of the blood. [HEM- + ANALYSIS]

he·man·gi·o·ma (hē man′jē ō′mə), *n., pl.* **-mas, -ma·ta** (-mə tə). *Pathol.* See under **angioma.** Also, **haemangioma.** [< NL; see HEM-, ANGIOMA]

Hem·ans (hem′ənz, hē′mənz), *n.* **Mrs.** (*Felicia Dorothea Browne*), 1793–1835, English poet.

hemat-, var. of **hemato-** before a vowel: *hematic.* Also, **haemat-.**

hem·a·tal (hem′ə təl, hē′mə-), *adj.* hemal (def. 1). Also, **haematal.** [HEMAT- + -AL[1]]

hem·a·te·in (hem′ə tē′in, hē′mə-), *n. Chem.* a reddish-brown, crystalline, slightly water-soluble solid, $C_{16}H_{12}O_6$, obtained from logwood: used chiefly as a stain in microscopy. [var. of HEMATIN]

hem·a·ther·mal (hem′ə thûr′məl, hē′mə-), *adj.* warm-blooded; homoiothermal. [HEMA- + THERMAL]

he·mat·ic (hə mat′ik), *adj.* **1.** of or pertaining to blood; hemic. **2.** acting on the blood, as a medicine. —*n.* **3.** a hematic medicine. Also, **haematic.** [HEMAT- + -IC]

hem·a·tin (hem′ə tin, hē′mə-), *n.* **1.** *Biochem.* a pigment containing iron, $C_{34}H_{32}N_4O_4FeOH$, produced in the decomposition of hemoglobin, esp. under pathological conditions. **2.** (loosely) hematein. Also, **haematin, hem·a·tine** (hem′ə tēn′, -tin, hē′mə-). [HEMAT- + -IN[2]]

hem·a·tin·ic (hem′ə tin′ik, hē′mə-), *n.* **1.** a medicine, as a compound of iron, which tends to increase the amount of hematin or hemoglobin in the blood. —*adj.* **2.** of or obtained from hematin. Also, **haematinic.** [HEMATIN + -IC]

hem·a·tite (hem′ə tīt′, hē′mə-), *n.* a very common mineral, iron oxide, Fe_2O_3, occurring in steel-gray to black crystals and in red earthy masses: the principal ore of iron. Also, **haematite.** [< L *haematīte(s)* blood stone. See HEMAT-, -ITE[1]] —**hem·a·tit·ic** (hem′ə tit′ik, hē′mə-), *adj.*

hemato-, a learned borrowing from Greek equivalent to **hemo-:** *hematogenesis.* Also, **hemat-, haemat-, haemato-.** [< NL, comb. form < Gk *haimat-,* s. of *haîma* blood]

hem·a·to·blast (hem′ə tō blast′, hē′mə-), *n. Anat.* an immature blood cell, esp. a red blood cell. Also, **hemoblast, haematoblast, haemoblast.** [HEMATO- + -BLAST]

hem·a·to·cele (hem′ə tō sēl′, hē′mə-), *n. Pathol.* **1.** hemorrhage into a membranous tissue or a cavity, esp. into the cavity surrounding the testis. **2.** such a cavity. Also, **haematocele.** [HEMATO- + -CELE[2]]

hem·a·to·crit (hem′ə tō krit, hē′mə-), *n.* **1.** a centrifuge for separating the cells of the blood from the plasma. **2.** Also called **hem′atocrit val′ue.** the ratio of the volume of cells to a given volume of blood so centrifuged, expressed as a percentage. [HEMATO- + *-crit* < Gk *krit(ēs)* judge]

hem·a·toc·ry·al (hem′ə tok′rē əl, -tō krī′əl, hē′mə-), *adj.* cold-blooded, as a vertebrate. Also, **haematocryal.** [HEMATO- + CRY(O)- + -AL[1]]

hem·a·to·cyst (hem′ə tō sist′, hē′mə-), *n. Pathol.* a cyst containing blood. Also, **haematocyst.** [HEMATO- + -CYST]

hem·a·to·cyte (hem′ə tō sīt′, hē′mə-), *n.* hemocyte. Also, **haematocyte.** [HEMATO- + -CYTE]

hem·a·to·gen·e·sis (hem′ə tō jen′i sis, hē′mə-), *n.* the formation of blood. Also, **haematogenesis.** [HEMATO- + -GENESIS]

hem·a·tog·e·nous (hem′ə toj′ə nəs, hē′mə-), *adj.* **1.** originating in the blood. **2.** blood-producing. **3.** distributed or spread by way of the bloodstream, as in metastases of tumors or in infections; blood-borne. Also, **haematogenous.** [HEMATO- + -GENOUS]

he·ma·toid (hē′mə toid′, hem′ə-), *adj.* hemoid. Also, **haematoid.** [< Gk *hematoeid(ēs).* See HEMAT-, -OID]

hem·a·tol·o·gy (hem′ə tol′ə jē, hē′mə-), *n. Med.* the study of the nature, function, and diseases of the blood and of blood-forming organs. Also, **haematology.** [HEMATO- + -LOGY] —**hem·a·to·log·ic** (hem′ə təloj′ik, hē′mə-), **hem′a·to·log′i·cal,** *adj.* —**hem′a·tol′o·gist,** *n.*

hem·a·to·ma (hem′ə tō′mə, hē′mə-), *n., pl.* **-mas, -ma·ta** (-mə tə). *Pathol.* a swelling filled with extravasated blood. Also, **haematoma.** [HEMAT- + -OMA]

hem·a·to·phyte (hem′ə tō fīt′, hē′mə-), *n.* a plant microorganism, as a bacterium, that lives in the blood. Also, **haematophyte.** [HEMATO- + -PHYTE]

hem·a·to·poi·e·sis (hem′ə tō poi ē′sis, hē′mə-), *n.* the formation of blood. Also, **haematopoiesis.** [< NL *haematopoiēsis.* See HEMATO-, -POIESIS] —**hem·a·to·poi·et·ic** (hem′ə tō poi et′ik, hē′mə-), *adj.*

hem·a·to·por·phy·ri·a (hem′ə tō pôr fēr′ē ə, -fī′rē ə, hē′mə-), *n. Pathol.* porphyria. [HEMATO- + PORPHYRIA]

hem·a·to·sis (hem′ə tō′sis, hē′mə-), *n.* **1.** hematopoiesis. **2.** *Physiol.* the conversion of venous into arterial blood; oxygenation in the lungs. Also, **haematosis.** [< NL *haematōsis.* See HEMATO-, -SIS]

hem·a·to·ther·mal (hem′ə tō thûr′məl, hē′mə-), *adj.* warm-blooded; homoiothermal. Also, **haematothermal.** [HEMATO- + -THERMAL]

he·ma·tox·y·lin (hē′mə tok′sə lin, hem′ə-), *n.* a colorless or pale-yellow, crystalline compound, $C_{16}H_{14}O_6 \cdot 3H_2O$, the coloring material of logwood; used as a mordant dye and as an indicator. Also, **haematoxylin.** [HEMATO- + XYL- + -IN[2]] —**he·ma·tox·yl·ic** (hē′mə-tok sil′ik, hem′ə-), *adj.*

hem·a·to·zo·on (hem′ə tə zō′on, -ən, hē′mə-), *n., pl.* **-zo·a** (-zō′ə). an animal parasite, usually a protozoan, living in the blood. Also, **haematozoon, hem′a·to·zo′ön, haematozoön.** [HEMATO- + -ZOON] —**hem′a·to·zo′al, hem′a·to·zo′ic,** *adj.*

he·ma·tu·ri·a (hē′mə to͝or′ē ə, -tyo͝or′-, hem′ə-), *n. Pathol.* the presence of blood in the urine. [HEMAT- + -URIA] —**he′ma·tu′ric,** *adj.*

heme (hēm), *n. Biochem.* a deep-red pigment, $C_{34}H_{32}N_4O_4Fe$, consisting of ferrous iron linked to protoporphyrin and obtained from hemoglobin by treatment with acid. [shortened form of HEMATIN]

Hem′el Hemp′stead (hem′əl), a town in W Hertfordshire, in SE England. 54,816 (1961).

hem·el·y·tron (he mel′i tron′), *n., pl.* **-tra** (-trə). *Entomol.* one of the forewings of a hemipterous insect, or true bug, having a hard, thick basal portion and a thinner, membranous apex. Also, **hemielytron.** [HEM(I)- + ELYTRON] —**hem·el·y·tral** (he mel′i trəl), *adj.*

Hem·er·a (hem′ər ə), *n. Class. Myth.* a daughter of Erebus and Nyx who is sometimes identified with Eos.

hem·er·a·lo·pi·a (hem′ər ə lō′pē ə), *n. Ophthalm.* **1.** Also called **day blindness.** a condition of the eyes in which sight is normal in the night or in a dim light but is abnormally poor or wholly absent in the day or in a bright light. **2.** nyctalopia (def. 1). [< NL < Gk *hēmeralōp-* (s. of *hēmerálōps*) day blindness, equiv. to *hēmér(a)* day + *al(aós)* blind + *-opia* -OPIA] —**hem·er·a·lop·ic** (hem′ər ə lop′ik), *adj.*

He·me·ra·sia (hē′mə rā′zhə), *n. Class. Myth.* an epithet of Artemis, meaning "she who soothes."

Hem·er·o·cal·lis (hem′ər ə kal′is), *n.* the genus comprising the day lilies. [< NL < Gk *hēmerokallís,* equiv. to *hēméra* day + *kállos* beauty]

Hem′et East′ (hem′it), a town in S California. 5416 (1960).

hemi-, a learned borrowing from Greek meaning "half," used in the formation of compound words: *hemimorphic.* [< Gk *hēmi-* half; c. L *sēmi-* SEMI-]

-hemia, var. of **-emia** after *p, t, k: leucocythemia.*

hem·i·ac·e·tal (hem′ē as′i tal′), *n. Chem.* any of the class of compounds having the general formula RCH(OH)OR, where R is an organic group. [HEMI- + ACETAL]

hem·i·al·gi·a (hem′ē al′jē ə, -jə), *n. Pathol.* pain or neuralgia involving only one side of the body or head. [HEMI- + -ALGIA]

hem·i·a·nop·si·a (hem′ē ə nop′sē ə), *n. Ophthalm.* any of several conditions in which there is blindness of half of the vision of one or both eyes. Also, **hem·i·a·no·pi·a** (hem′ē ə nō′pē ə), **hemiopia.** Also called **hemiscotosis.** [HEMI- + AN-[1] + -OPSIA]

he·mic (hē′mik, hem′ik), *adj.* hematic. Also, **haemic.** [HEM- + -IC]

hem·i·cel·lu·lose (hem′i sel′yə lōs′), *n. Chem.* any of a group of gummy polysaccharides, intermediate in complexity between sugar and cellulose, which hydrolyze to monosaccharides more readily than cellulose. [HEMI- + CELLULOSE]

hem·i·chor·date (hem′i kôr′dāt), *Zool.* —*adj.* **1.** belonging or pertaining to the chordates of the subphylum *Hemichordata,* comprising small, widely distributed, marine animals, as the acorn worms. —*n.* **2.** a hemichordate animal. [HEMI- + CHORDATE]

hem·i·cra·ni·a (hem′i krā′nē ə), *n. Pathol.* pain in one side of the head; migraine. Cf. **amphicrania.** [< LL *hēmicrānia,* sp. var. of *hēmicrānium* < Gk *hēmikrānī(on)* pain on one side of the head (see HEMI-, CRANIUM) + L *-ia* -IA] —**hem·i·cran·ic** (hem′i kran′ik, -krā′nik), *adj.*

hem·i·cy·cle (hem′i sī′kəl), *n.* **1.** a semicircle. **2.** a semicircular structure. **3.** hemicyclium. [< F *hémicycle* < L *hēmicycl(ium)* < Gk *hēmikýklion.* See HEMI-, CYCLE] —**hem·i·cy·clic** (hem′i sī′klik, -sik′lik), *adj.*

hem·i·cyc·li·um (hem′i sik′lē əm), *n.* a sundial in the form of a concave quarter sphere having a rodlike gnomon lying within one radius and marked on its surface with arcs which lie in the same plane as the gnomon. Also, **hemicycle.** [< L; see HEMICYCLE]

hem·i·dem·i·sem·i·qua·ver (hem′ē dem′ē sem′ē-kwā′vər), *n. Music. Chiefly Brit.* a sixty-fourth note. [HEMI- + DEMISEMIQUAVER]

hem·i·el·y·tron (hem′ē el′i tron′), *n., pl.* **-tra** (-trə). *Entomol.* hemelytron. —**hem′i·el′y·tral,** *adj.*

hem·i·glo·bin (hē′mi glō′bin, hem′i-; hē′mi glō′bin, hem′i-), *n. Biochem.* methemoglobin. [HEMI- + GLOBIN]

hem·i·he·dral (hem′i hē′drəl), *adj.* (of a crystal) having only half the planes or faces required by the maximum symmetry of the system to which it belongs. [HEMI- + -HEDRAL] —**hem′i·he′dral·ly,** *adv.*

hem·i·hy·drate (hem′i hī′drāt), *n. Chem.* a hydrate in which there are two molecules of the compound for each molecule of water. [HEMI- + HYDRATE] —**hem′i·hy′drat·ed,** *adj.*

hem·i·kar·y·on (hem′i kar′ē on′), *n. Biol.* a haploid nucleus. Cf. **amphikaryon.** [HEMI- + Gk *káryon* nut] —**hem·i·kar·y·ot·ic** (hem′i kar′ē ot′ik), *adj.*

hem·i·me·tab·o·lous (hem′ē mi tab′ə ləs), *adj. Entomol.* undergoing incomplete metamorphosis. Also, **hem·i·met·a·bol·ic** (hem′ē met′ə bol′ik). [HEMI- + METABOLOUS] —**hem′i·me·tab′o·lism, hem′i·me·tab′o·ly,** *n.*

hem·i·mor·phic (hem′i môr′fik), *adj.* (of a crystal) having the two ends of an axis unlike in their planes or modifications; lacking a center of symmetry. [HEMI- + -MORPHIC] —**hem′i·mor′phism, hem′i·mor′phy,** *n.*

hem·i·mor·phite (hem′i môr′fīt), *n.* a mineral $Zn_4(OH)_2Si_2O_7 \cdot H_2O$, formed by the alteration of zinc minerals by silica-bearing water; calamine. [HEMIMORPH(IC) + -ITE[1]]

he·min (hē′min), *n. Biochem.* the typical, reddish-brown crystals, of microscopic size, $C_{34}H_{32}N_4O_4FeCl$, resulting when a sodium chloride crystal, a drop of glacial acetic acid, and some blood are heated on a slide: used to indicate the presence of blood. Also, **haemin.** Also called **Teichmann's crystals.** [HEM- + -IN[2]]

Hem·ing·way (hem′iṉg wā′), *n.* **Ernest (Miller),** 1898–1961, U.S. novelist, short-story writer, and journalist: Nobel prize 1954.

hem·i·o·pi·a (hem′ē ō′pē ə), *n. Ophthalm.* hemianopsia. [HEMI- + -OPIA] —**hem·i·op·ic** (hem′ē op′ik, -ō′pik), *adj.*

hem·i·pa·re·sis (hem′ē pə rē′sis, -par′i sis), *n. Pathol.* slight paralysis affecting only one side of the body. [HEMI- + PARESIS] —**hem·i·pa·ret·ic** (hem′ē pə ret′ik), *adj.*

hem·i·ple·gi·a (hem′i plē′jē ə, -jə), *n. Pathol.* paralysis of one side of the body, resulting from a disease of the brain or of the spinal cord. [< LL < Gk *hēmiplēgía.* See HEMI-, -PLEGIA] —**hem·i·ple·gic** (hem′i plē′jik, -plej′ik), *adj., n.*

hem·i·pode (hem′i pōd′), *n.* See **button quail.** [< NL *Hēmipod(ius)* name of the genus < Gk *hēmipod-* (s. of *hēmípous*) half-foot. See HEMI-, -POD] —**he·mip·o·dan** (hə mip′ə dən), *adj.*

He·mip·ter·a (hi mip′tər ə), *n.* the order comprising the hemipterous insects, esp. the true bugs. [< NL (neut. pl.); see HEMI-, -PTEROUS]

he·mip·ter·ous (hi mip′tər əs), *adj.* **1.** belonging or pertaining to the *Hemiptera,* an order of insects having forewings which are thickened and leathery at the base and membranous at the apex, comprising the true bugs. **2.** belonging or pertaining to the order *Hemiptera,* in some classifications comprising the heteropterous and homopterous insects. [HEMIPTER(A) + -OUS]

hem·i·sco·to·sis (hem′ē skə tō′sis), *n. Ophthalm.* hemianopsia. [HEMI- + SCOT- + -OSIS]

hem·i·sphere (hem′i sfēr′), *n.* **1.** half of the terrestrial globe or celestial sphere. **2.** a map or projection representing either half. **3.** the half of a sphere. **4.** *Anat.* either of the lateral halves of the cerebrum or cerebellum. [< LL *hēmisphaer(ium)* < Gk *hēmisphaírion;* r. ME *emysperie* < OF *emispere*]

hem·i·spher·ic (hem′i sfer′ik), *adj.* **1.** of or pertaining to a hemisphere. **2.** hemispherical (def. 1). [HEMISPHERE + -IC]

hem·i·spher·i·cal (hem′i sfer′i kəl), *adj.* **1.** having the form of a hemisphere. **2.** hemispheric (def. 1). [HEMI- + SPHERICAL] —**hem′i·spher′i·cal·ly,** *adv.*

hem·i·spher·oid (hem′i sfēr′oid), *n.* half of a spheroid. [HEMI- + SPHEROID] —**hem′i·spher·oi′dal,** *adj.*

hem·i·stich (hem′i stik′), *n. Pros.* **1.** the exact or approximate half of a stich, or poetic verse or line, esp. as divided by a caesura or the like. **2.** an incomplete line, or a line of less than the usual length. [< LL *hēmistichium*) < Gk *hēmistíchion* a half-verse. See HEMI-, STICH] —**he·mis·ti·chal** (hə mis′ti kəl, hem′i stik′əl), *adj.*

hem·i·ter·pene (hem′i tûr′pēn), *n.* *Chem.* See under **terpene** (def. 2). [HEMI- + TERPENE]

He·mith·e·a (hə mith′ē ə), *n.* *Class. Myth.* a daughter of Cycnus and Proclea who was amorously pursued by Achilles and swallowed up by the earth.

hem·i·trope (hem′i trōp′), *Crystall.* —*n.* **1.** twin[1] (def. 3). —*adj.* **2.** twin[1] (def. 10). [< F; see HEMI-, -TROPE] —**hem·i·trop·ic** (hem′i trop′ik), *adj.* —**hem′i·tro′pism, he·mit·ro·py** (hē mi′trə pē), *n.*

hem·i·zy·gote (hem′i zī′gōt, -zig′ōt), *n.* *Genetics.* an individual having only one of a given pair of genes. [HEMI- + ZYGOTE] —**hem·i·zy·gous** (hem′i zī′gəs), *adj.*

hem·line (hem′līn′), *n.* the bottom edge of a coat, dress, skirt, etc. [HEM[1] + LINE[1]]

hem·lock (hem′lok′), *n.* **1.** *Chiefly Brit.* a poisonous, umbelliferous herb, *Conium maculatum*, having spotted stems, finely divided leaves, and small white flowers, used medicinally as a powerful sedative. **2.** a poisonous drink made from this herb. **3.** any of various other apiaceous herbs, esp. of the genus *Cicuta*, as the water hemlock. **4.** Also called **hem′lock spruce′**, any of several coniferous trees of the genus *Tsuga*, native to the U.S., characterized by its pyramidal manner of growth. Cf. **eastern hemlock, western hemlock.** **5.** the soft, light wood of a hemlock tree, used in making paper, in the construction of buildings, etc. [ME *hemlok, humlok*, OE *hymlic, hemlic;* ? akin to OE *hymele* hop plant]

hem·mer (hem′ər), *n.* **1.** one who or that which hems. **2.** a sewing-machine attachment for hemming edges. [HEM[1] + -ER[1]]

hemo-, a learned borrowing from Greek meaning "blood," used in the formation of compound words: *hemocyte.* Also, **hem-, haem-, haemo-.** Cf. **hema-, haema-, haemat-, haemato-, hemat-, hemato-.** [< NL, comb. form repr. Gk *haîma* blood]

he·mo·blast (hē′mə blast′, hem′ə-), *n.* *Anat.* hematoblast. [HEMO- + -BLAST]

he·mo·chro·ma·to·sis (hē′mə krō′mə tō′sis, hem′ə-), *n.* *Pathol.* a rare disease chiefly of males, characterized by a bronzed skin, cirrhosis, and severe diabetes, caused by the deposit in tissue, esp. of the liver and pancreas, of hemosiderin and other pigments containing iron. Also called **bronze diabetes.** [HEMO- + CHROMAT- + -OSIS] —**he·mo·chro·ma·tot·ic** (hē′mō krō′mə tot′ik, hem′ō-), *adj.*

he·mo·con·cen·tra·tion (hē′mə kon′sən trā′shən, hem′ə-), *n.* *Med.* an increase in the concentration of cellular elements in the blood, resulting from loss of plasma. Also, **haemoconcentration.** [HEMO- + CONCENTRATION]

he·mo·cyte (hē′mə sīt′, hem′ə-), *n.* a blood cell. Also, **hematocyte, haemocyte, haematocyte.** [HEMO- + -CYTE]

he·mo·cy·to·blast (hē′mə sī′tə blast′, hem′ə-), *n.* *Anat.* a primordial cell capable of developing into any type of blood cell. Also, **haemocytoblast.** Also called **lymphoidocyte.** [HEMOCYTE + -O- + -BLAST] —**he′mo·cy′to·blas′tic,** *adj.*

he·mo·cy·tom·e·ter (hē′mō sī tom′i tər, hem′ō-), *n.* *Med.* an instrument for counting blood cells. Also, **hemacytometer.** [HEMO- + CYTO- + -METER]

he·mo·di·a (hi mō′dē ə), *n.* *Dentistry.* hypersensitivity of the teeth. [< NL *haemodia*, equiv. to Gk *haimōd(ein)* (to) be set on edge, set the teeth on edge + L *-ia* -IA]

he·mo·di·al·y·sis (hē′mə dī al′i sis, hem′ə-), *n.* *Biochem.* dialysis of the blood, esp. with an artificial kidney, for the removal of waste products. [HEMO- + DIALYSIS]

he·mo·di·a·lyz·er (hē′mō dī′ə lī′zər, hem′ō-), *n.* *Med.* See **artificial kidney.** [HEMO- + DIA- + -LYZE + -ER[1]]

he·mo·dy·nam·ics (hē′mō dī nam′iks, hem′ə-), *n.* (*construed as sing.*) the branch of physiology dealing with the forces involved in the circulation of the blood. Also, **haemodynamics.** [HEMO- + DYNAMICS] —**he′mo·dy·nam′ic,** *adj.*

he·mo·flag·el·late (hē′mə flaj′ə lāt′, hem′ə-), *n.* a flagellate that is parasitic in the blood. [HEMO- + FLAGELLATE]

he·mo·fus·cin (hē′mə fus′in, hem′ə-), *n.* *Biochem.* a yellowish-brown pigment found in the liver in certain conditions of faulty iron metabolism, as hemosiderosis. [HEMO- + FUSC(OUS) + -IN[2]]

he·mo·ge·ni·a (hē′mō jē′nē ə, -jēn′yə, hem′ō-), *n.* *Pathol.* pseudohemophilia. [HEMO- + -GEN + -IA]

he·mo·glo·bin (hē′mə glō′bin, hem′ə-; hē′mə glō′bin, hem′ə-), *n.* *Biochem.* the protein coloring matter of the red blood corpuscles, serving to convey oxygen to the tissues and occurring in reduced form (**reduced hemoglobin**) in venous blood and in combination with oxygen (**oxyhemoglobin**) in arterial blood. *Symbol:* Hb Also, **haemoglobin.** [shortening of *hematoglobulin.* See HEMO-, GLOBULIN] —**he′mo·glo′bic, he′mo·glo′bin·ous,** *adj.*

he·mo·glo·bi·nu·ri·a (hē′mə glō′bi nŏŏr′ē ə, -nyŏŏr′-, hem′ə-), *n.* *Pathol.* the presence of hemoglobin pigment in the urine. [HEMOGLOBIN + -URIA] —**he′mo·glo′bi·nu′ric,** *adj.*

he·mo·gram (hē′mə gram′, hem′ə-), *n.* *Pathol.* a graphic record of the cellular elements of the blood. [HEMO- + -GRAM[1]]

he·moid (hē′moid), *adj.* resembling blood; hematoid. Also, **haemoid.** [HEM- + -OID]

he·mol·y·sin (hi mol′i sin, hē′mə lī′-, hem′ə-), *n.* *Immunol.* a substance, as an antibody, which in cooperation with complement causes dissolution of erythrocytes. Also, **haemolysin.** [HEMO- + LYSIN]

he·mol·y·sis (hi mol′i sis), *n.* *Immunol.* the breaking down of the erythrocytes with liberation of hemoglobin. Also, **haemolysis.** [HEMO- + -LYSIS] —**he·mo·lyt·ic** (hē′mə lit′ik, hem′ə-), *adj.*

Hé·mon (ā môN′), *n.* **Louis** (lwē), 1880–1913, French novelist.

he·mo·phile (hē′mə fīl′, hem′ə-), *n.* **1.** *Pathol.* a hemophiliac. **2.** a hemophilic bacterium. —*adj.* **3.** hemophilic. [HEMO- + -PHILE]

he·mo·phil·i·a (hē′mə fil′ē ə, -fēl′yə, hem′ə-), *n.* *Pathol.* an abnormal condition of males inherited through the mother, characterized by a tendency to bleed immoderately, as from an insignificant wound, caused by improper coagulation of the blood. Also, **haemophilia.** [< NL; see HEMOPHILE, -IA]

he·mo·phil·i·ac (hē′mə fil′ē ak′, -fē′lē-, hem′ə-), *n.* *Pathol.* a person having hemophilia. Also, **haemophiliac, hemophile.** [HEMOPHILI(A) + -AC]

he·mo·phil·ic (hē′mə fil′ik, hem′ə-), *adj.* **1.** *Pathol.* affected by hemophilia. **2.** *Biol.* (of bacteria) developing best in a culture containing blood, or in blood itself. Also, **haemophilic.** [HEMOPHIL(IA) + -IC]

he·mo·phil·i·oid (hē′mə fil′ē oid′, hem′ə-), *adj.* *Pathol.* (of a disease) resembling hemophilia. [HEMOPHIL(IA) + -OID]

He·moph·i·lus (hi mof′ə ləs), *n.* *Bacteriol.* a genus of rod-shaped, parasitic, hemophilic bacteria, certain species of which, as *H. influenzae* or *H. suis*, are pathogenic for man and animals. [< NL; see HEMO-, -PHILOUS]

he·mo·pho·bi·a (hē′mə fō′bē ə, hem′ə-), *n.* *Psychiatry.* an abnormal fear of blood. [< NL; see HEMO-, -PHOBIA]

he·mop·ty·sis (hi mop′ti sis), *n.* *Med.* the expectoration of blood or bloody mucus. [< NL, equiv. to *hemo-* HEMO- + Gk *ptýsis* spitting, cf. *ptýein* to spit]

hem·or·rhage (hem′ər ij, hem′rij), *n.*, *v.*, **-rhaged, -rhag·ing.** —*n.* **1.** a discharge of blood, as from a ruptured blood vessel. —*v.i.* **2.** to bleed profusely. Also, **haemorrhage.** [< L *haemorrhag(ia)* < Gk *haimorrhagía.* See HEMO-, -RRHAGIA] —**hem·or·rhag·ic** (hem′ə raj′ik), *adj.*

hemorrhag′ic mea′sles, *Pathol.* See **black measles.**

hemorrhag′ic septice′mia, *Vet. Pathol.* an acute infectious disease of animals, caused by a bacterium of the genus *Pasteurella*, and characterized by fever, catarrhal symptoms, pneumonia, and general blood infection. Also called **pasteurellosis.** Cf. **fowl cholera, shipping fever, swine plague.**

hem·or·rhoid (hem′ə roid′, hem′roid), *n.* Usually, **hemorrhoids.** *Pathol.* a venous dilatation inside the anal sphincter of the rectum and beneath the mucous membrane (**internal hemorrhoid**), or outside the anal sphincter and beneath the surface of the skin (**external hemorrhoid**). Also, **haemorrhoid.** Also called **pile.** [< L *haemorrhoid(a)* < Gk *haimorroïda* (adj.) discharging blood] —**hem′or·rhoi′dal,** *adj.*

hem·or·rhoid·ec·to·my (hem′ə roi dek′tə mē), *n.*, *pl.* **-mies.** *Surg.* an operation for removal of hemorrhoids. [HEMORRHOID + -ECTOMY]

he·mo·sid·er·in (hē′mō sid′ər in, hem′ō-), *n.* *Biochem.* a yellowish-brown pigment containing iron, derived chiefly from hemoglobin, and found in the liver and other organs during hemosiderosis, hypochromic anemia, and other disorders of iron metabolism. [HEMO- + SIDER- + -IN[2]]

he·mo·sid·er·o·sis (hē′mō sid′ə rō′sis, hem′ō-), *n.* *Pathol.* a condition in which hemosiderin is deposited in the tissues, esp. the liver and spleen, due to the destruction of red blood cells. Cf. **hemochromatosis.** [< NL; see HEMOSIDERIN, -OSIS] —**he·mo·sid·er·ot·ic** (hē′mō sid′ə rot′ik, hem′ō-), *adj.*

he·mos·ta·sis (hi mos′tə sis, hē′mə stā′sis, hem′ə-), *n.* *Med.* **1.** the stoppage of bleeding. **2.** the stoppage of the circulation of blood in a part of the body. **3.** stagnation of blood in a part. Also, **haemostasis, he·mo·sta·sia** (hē′mə stā′zhə, -zhē ə, -zē ə, hem′ə-). [< NL; see HEMO-, STASIS]

he·mo·stat (hē′mə stat′, hem′ə-), *n.* an instrument or agent used to compress or treat bleeding vessels in order to arrest hemorrhage. Also, **haemostat.** [shortened form of HEMOSTATIC]

he·mo·stat·ic (hē′mə stat′ik, hem′ə-), *adj.* **1.** arresting hemorrhage, as a drug; styptic. **2.** pertaining to stagnation of the blood. —*n.* **3.** a hemostatic agent or substance. Also, **haemostatic.** [HEMO- + STATIC]

he·mo·ther·a·peu·tics (hē′mə ther′ə pyōō′tiks, hem′ə-), *n.* (*construed as sing.*) hemotherapy. [HEMO- + THERAPEUTICS]

he·mo·ther·a·py (hē′mə ther′ə pē, hem′ə-), *n.* *Med.* therapy by means of blood, serum, or plasma transfusion. Also, **hemotherapeutics.** [HEMO- + THERAPY]

he·mo·tho·rax (hē′mə thôr′aks, -thōr′-, hem′ə-), *n.* *Med.* the presence of blood in the pleural cavity. Also, **haemothorax.** [< NL; see HEMO-, THORAX]

he·mo·tox·in (hē′mə tok′sin, hem′ə-), *n.* *Immunol.* a hemolysin. Also, **haemotoxin.** [HEMO- + TOXIN] —**he′mo·tox′ic,** *adj.*

he·mot·ro·phe (hē mo′trə fē), *n.* *Embryol.* the material from the maternal bloodstream that nourishes a mammalian embryo following the formation of the placenta. Cf. **embryotroph.** [HEMO- + Gk *trophḗ* nourishment, food, deriv. of *tréphein* to nourish, feed] —**he·mo·troph·ic** (hē′mə trof′ik, hem′ə-), *adj.*

hemp (hemp), *n.* **1.** a tall, annual, moraceous herb, *Cannabis sativa*, native to Asia, but cultivated in many parts of the world. **2.** the tough fiber of this plant, used for making rope, coarse fabric, etc. **3.** an East Indian variety of hemp, *Cannabis sativa indica* (or *Cannabis indica*), yielding hashish, bhang, cannabin, etc. **4.** any of various plants resembling hemp. **5.** any of various fibers similar to hemp. **6.** a narcotic drug obtained from Indian hemp. [ME; OE *henep, hænep;* c. G *Hanf*, Gk *kánnabis*] —**hemp′like′,** *adj.*

hemp′ ag′rimony, a European, composite herb, *Eupatorium cannabinum*, having dull purplish flowers.

hemp·en (hem′pən), *adj.* **1.** of or pertaining to hemp. **2.** made of hemp. **3.** resembling hemp. [ME *hempyn.* See HEMP, -EN[2]]

hemp′ net′tle, **1.** a coarse, labiate weed, *Galeopsis Tetrahit*, resembling the hemp in appearance and having bristly hairs like the nettle. **2.** any other plant of the genus *Galeopsis.*

hemp·seed (hemp′sēd′), *n.* the seed of hemp, used as food for birds. [ME; see HEMP, SEED]

Hemp·stead (hemp′sted, hem′-), *n.* a village on W Long Island, in SE New York. 34,641 (1960).

hemp′ tree′. See **chaste tree.**

hemp·y (hem′pē), *adj.* *Scot.* mischievous; often in trouble for mischief. [HEMP + -Y[1]; so called because a person often in trouble was thought fit to be hanged]

hem·stitch (hem′stich′), *v.t.* **1.** to hem along a line from which threads have been drawn out, stitching the cross threads into a series of little groups. **2.** to simulate hand hemstitching by piercing the material with a large machine needle and then stitching around the perforations. —*n.* **3.** the stitch used or the needlework done in hemstitching. [HEM[1] + STITCH[1]] —**hem′stitch′er,** *n.*

hen (hen), *n.* **1.** the female of the domestic fowl. **2.** the female of any bird, esp. of a gallinaceous bird. **3.** *Informal.* a woman, esp. a busybody or gossip. [ME; OE *hen(n)* (cf. OE *hana* cock); c. G *Henne;* akin to L *canere* to sing] —**hen′like′,** *adj.* —**hen′nish,** *adj.*

hen-and-chick·ens (hen′ən chik′ənz), *n.*, *pl.* **hens-and-chickens.** **1.** any of several herbs, esp. those having offshoot or runner plants growing around the parent. **2.** a European houseleek, *Sempervivum globiferum.* **3.** See **ground ivy.**

hen·bane (hen′bān′), *n.* an Old World, solanaceous herb, *Hyoscyamus niger*, having sticky, hairy foliage of a disagreeable odor and yellowish-brown flowers, and possessing narcotic and poisonous properties esp. destructive to domestic fowls. [ME; see HEN, BANE]

hen·bit (hen′bit′), *n.* a labiate weed, *Lamium amplexicaule*, having small purplish flowers. [HEN + BIT[2]]

hence (hens), *adv.* **1.** as an inference from this fact; for this reason; therefore: *The goods were of the best quality and hence satisfactory.* **2.** from this time; from now: *They will leave a month hence.* **3.** *Rare.* **a.** henceforth; from this time on. **b.** of this moment or the present: *From hence we look back into the past.* **4.** *Archaic.* **a.** from this place; from here; away: *The inn is but a quarter mile hence.* **b.** from this world or from the living: *After a long, hard life they were taken hence.* **5.** *Obs.* from this source or origin. —*interj.* **6.** *Obs.* depart (usually used imperatively). [ME *hens, hennes*, equiv. to *henne* (OE *heonan*) + *-es* -S[1]]

hence·forth (hens′fôrth′, -fōrth′; hens′fôrth′, -fōrth′), *adv.* from now on; from this point forward. Also, **hence·for·ward** (hens′fôr′wərd, -fōr′-; hens′fôr′wərd; -fōr′-). [ME; see HENCE, FORTH]

Hench (hench), *n.* **Philip Show·al·ter** (shō′ôl tər), 1896–1965, U.S. physician: Nobel prize for medicine 1950.

hench·man (hench′mən), *n.*, *pl.* **-men.** **1.** an unscrupulous and ruthless subordinate, esp. a criminal: *The gang chief went everywhere accompanied by his henchmen.* **2.** an unscrupulous supporter or adherent of a political figure or cause, esp. one motivated by the hope of personal gain: *Hitler and his henchmen.* **3.** a trusted attendant, supporter, or follower. **4.** *Obs.* a squire or page. [ME *henchman, hensh-, henks-, hengest-*, OE *hengest* stallion (c. G *Hengst*) + *man* MAN[1]] —**hench′man·ship′,** *n.*

hendeca-, a learned borrowing from Greek meaning "eleven," used in the formation of compound words: *hendecahedron.* [comb. form repr. Gk *héndeka* eleven, equiv. to *hen-* one (neut. of *eîs*) + *déka* TEN]

hen·dec·a·gon (hen dek′ə gon′), *n.* *Rare.* a polygon having 11 angles and 11 sides. [HENDECA- + -GON] —**hen·de·cag·o·nal** (hen′də kag′ə nəl), *adj.*

hen·dec·a·he·dron (hen dek′ə hē′drən, hen′dek-), *n.*, *pl.* **-drons, -dra** (-drə). a solid figure having 11 faces. [HENDECA- + -HEDRON] —**hen·dec·a·he·dral** (hen dek′ə hē′drəl, hen′dek-), *adj.*

hen·dec·a·syl·lab·ic (hen dek′ə si lab′ik), *adj.* **1.** consisting of or pertaining to 11 syllables. —*n.* **2.** a hendecasyllable. [HENDECASYLLABLE + -IC]

hen·dec·a·syl·la·ble (hen dek′ə sil′ə bəl, hen′dek ə sil′-), *n.* a word or line of verse of 11 syllables. [< L *hendecasyllab(us)* < Gk *hendekasýllab(os).* See HENDECA-, SYLLABLE]

Hen·der·son (hen′dər sən), *n.* **1. Arthur,** 1863–1935, British statesman and labor leader: Nobel peace prize 1934. **2. David Brem·ner** (brem′nər), 1840–1906, U.S. political leader: Speaker of the House 1899–1903. **3. Fletcher** ("*Smack*"), 1898–1952, U.S. jazz pianist, arranger, and band leader. **4.** a city in NW Kentucky, on the Ohio River. 16,892 (1960). **5.** a city in N North Carolina. 12,740 (1960). **6.** a city in SE Nevada, near Las Vegas. 12,525 (1960). **7.** a town in E Texas. 9666 (1960). **8.** a town in SW Tennessee. 2691 (1960).

Hen·der·son·ville (hen′dər sən vil′), *n.* a town in W North Carolina. 5911 (1960).

hen·di·a·dys (hen dī′ə dis), *n.* *Rhet.* a figure in which a complex idea is expressed by two words connected by a copulative conjunction: "to look with eyes and envy" instead of "with envious eyes." [< ML; alter. of Gk phrase *hèn dià dyoîn* one through two, one by means of two]

Hen·don (hen′dən), *n.* a city in Middlesex, in SE England, NW of London. 151,500 (1961).

Hen·drick (hen′drik), *n.* a boy's given name, form of **Henry.**

Hen·dricks (hen′driks), *n.* **Thomas Andrews,** 1819–1885, vice-president of the U.S. 1885.

hen·e·quen (hen′ə kin), *n.* the fiber of an agave, *Agave fourcroydes*, of Yucatán, used for making ropes, coarse fabrics, etc. Also, **hen′e·quin.** [< AmerSp *geniquén* < native name]

hen′ frig′ate, *Naut. Slang.* a sailing vessel on which the captain's wife lives.

Heng·e·lo (heng′ə lō′), *n.* a city in the E Netherlands. 58,197 (1960).

Hen·gist (heng′gist, hen′jist), *n.* died A.D. 488? chief of the Jutes: with his brother Horsa led the Teutonic invasion of southern Britain c440. Also, **Hen′gest.**

hen′ hawk′. See **chicken hawk.**

hen·house (hen′hous′), *n.*, *pl.* **-hous·es** (-hou′ziz). a shelter for poultry. [HEN + HOUSE]

He·ni·o·che (hə nī′ə kē′), *n.* *Class. Myth.* an epithet of Hera, meaning "charioteer."

Hen′le's loop′ (hen′lēz). See **loop of Henle.**

Hen·ley (hen′lē), *n.* **William Ernest,** 1849–1903, English poet, critic, and editor.

Hen·ley-on-Thames (hen′lē on temz′), *n.* a city in SE Oxfordshire, in S England: annual regatta. 9131 (1961).

hen·na (hen′ə), *n.* **1.** a shrub or small tree, *Lawsonia inermis*, of Asia and the Levant. **2.** a reddish-orange dye or cosmetic made from the leaves of this plant. **3.** a color midway between red-brown and orange-brown. —*v.t.* **4.** to tint or dye with henna. [< Ar *ḥinnā′*]

Hen·ne·pin (hen′ə pin; *Fr.* en paN′), *n.* **Louis** (lwē), 1640?–1701?, Belgian Roman Catholic missionary and explorer in America.

hen·ner·y (hen′ə rē), *n.*, *pl.* **-ner·ies.** a place where fowls are kept. [HEN + -ERY]

Hen·nig (hen′ig), *n.* a boy's given name, form of **Henry.**

hen·nin (hen′in), *n.* a conical or heart-shaped hat, sometimes extremely high, with a flowing veil or piece of starched linen about the crown, worn by women in the 15th century. Also called **steeple headdress.** [< F (obs.) < ?]

He·noch (hē′nək), *n.* *Douay Bible.* Enoch (defs. 1, 2).

hen·o·the·ism (hen′ə thē iz′əm), *n.* **1.** the worship of one of a group of gods, in contrast with monotheism which teaches that only one God exists. **2.** ascription of supreme divine attributes to whichever one of several gods is addressed at the time. [< Gk *heno-*, comb. form of *hén* one (neut. of *eîs*) + THEISM] —**hen′o·the′ist,** *n.* —**hen′o·the·is′tic,** *adj.*

hen′ par′ty, *Informal.* a social gathering for women.

hen·peck (hen′pek′), *v.t.* (of a wife) to nag, scold, or regularly find fault with (her husband) in an effort to dominate. [back formation from *henpecked;* see HEN, PECK[2]]

Hen·ri (hen′rē), *n.* **Robert,** 1865–1929, U.S. painter.

hen·ri·et·ta (hen′rē et′ə), *n.* a fine wool fabric constructed in twill weave, formerly made of silk warp and worsted filling. [after *Henrietta* Maria (1609–69) queen consort of Charles I of England]

Hen·ri·et·ta (hen′rē et′ə), *n.* **1.** a town in N Texas. 3062 (1960). **2.** a girl's given name.

Hen·ri·ka (hen rē′kə), *n.* a girl's given name, form of **Henrietta.**

hen·ry (hen′rē), *n., pl.* **-ries, -rys.** *Elect.* the meter-kilogram-second unit of inductance, equal to the inductance of a circuit in which an electromotive force of one volt is produced by a current in the circuit which varies at the rate of one ampere per second. *Abbr.:* H [named after Joseph HENRY]

Hen·ry (hen′rē), *n.* **1. Joseph,** 1797–1878, U.S. physicist. **2. O.,** pen name of William Sidney Porter. **3. Patrick,** 1736–99, American patriot, orator, and statesman. **4. Cape,** a cape in SE Virginia at the mouth of the Chesapeake Bay. **5. Fort.** See **Fort Henry. 6.** a boy's given name.

Henry I, 1. ("*Beauclerc*") 1068–1135, king of England 1100–35 (son of William the Conqueror). **2.** 1008–60, king of France 1031–60.

Henry II, 1. ("*Curtmantle*") 1133–89, king of England 1154–89: first king of the Plantagenet line (grandson of Henry I of England). **2.** 1519–59, king of France 1547–59 (son of Francis I).

Henry III, 1. 1207–72, king of England 1216–72 (son of John Lackland). **2.** 1551–89, king of France 1574–89 (son of Henry II of France).

Henry IV, 1. 1050–1106, Holy Roman Emperor and King of the Germans 1056–1106. **2.** (*Bolingbroke*) ("*Henry of Lancaster*") 1367–1413, king of England 1399–1413 (son of John of Gaunt). **3.** ("*Henry of Navarre*"; "*Henry the Great*") 1553–1610, king of France 1589–1610: first of the French Bourbon kings. **4.** (*italics*) a two-part drama (Part 1, 1597?; Part 2, 1597–98?) by Shakespeare.

Henry V, 1. 1387–1422, king of England 1413–22 (son of Henry IV of Bolingbroke). **2.** (*italics*) a drama (1598–99) by Shakespeare.

Henry VI, 1. 1421–71, king of England 1422–61, 1470–71 (son of Henry V). **2.** (*italics*) a three-part drama (Part 1, 1591–92; Part 2, 1590?; Part 3, 1590?) by Shakespeare.

Henry VII, (*Henry Tudor*) 1457–1509, king of England 1485–1509: first king of the house of Tudor.

Henry VIII, 1. ("*Defender of the Faith*") 1491–1547, king of England 1509–47 (son of Henry VII). **2.** (*italics*) a drama (1612–13?) by Shakespeare.

Hen′ry Es′mond (ez′mənd), a novel (1852) by Thackeray.

Hen·ry·et·ta (hen′rē et′ə), *n.* a town in central Oklahoma. 6551 (1960).

Hen′ry of Por′tugal, ("*the Navigator*") 1394–1460, prince of Portugal: sponsor of geographic explorations.

Hen′ry's law′, *Thermodynamics.* the principle that at a constant temperature the concentration of a gas dissolved in a fluid with which it does not combine chemically is almost directly proportional to the partial pressure of the gas at the surface of the fluid. Cf. **partial pressure.** [named after William *Henry* (1774–1836), English chemist who devised it]

Hens·ley (henz′lē), *n.* a boy's given name.

Hens·lowe (henz′lō), *n.* **Philip,** died 1616, English theater manager.

hent (hent), *v.,* **hent, hent·ing,** *n.* —*v.t.* **1.** *Archaic.* to grasp; apprehend. —*n.* **2.** *Obs.* intent; purpose. [ME *hent(en),* OE *hentan*]

Hen·ty (hen′tē), *n.* **George Alfred,** 1832–1902, English journalist and novelist: writer of historical adventure stories for boys.

Hen·ze (hen′tsə), *n.* **Hans Wer·ner** (häns ver′nər), born 1926, German composer.

he·or·tol·o·gy (hē′ôr tol′ə jē), *n.* the study of the history and significance of the feasts and seasons in the ecclesiastical calendar. [< Gk *heort(ḗ)* a feast, festival + -O- + -LOGY] —**he·or·to·log·i·cal** (hē ôr′tə loj′i kəl), *adj.*

hep[1] (hep), *adj. Slang.* hip[4].

hep[2] (hut, hup, hep), *interj.* one (used in counting cadence while marching). [?]

he·par (hē′pär), *n. Chem. Obs.* any reddish-brown compound formed by the fusion of an alkali metal and sulfur or a derivative of sulfur. [< LL *hēpar* < Gk *hêpar* the liver; c. L *jecur*]

he′par cal′cis (kal′sis). See **calcium sulfide.** [*calcis* < L, gen. sing. of *calx* lime]

hep·a·rin (hep′ə rin), *n.* **1.** *Biochem.* a mucopolysaccharide acid, occurring in various tissues, esp. the liver. **2.** *Pharm.* a commercial form of this substance, obtained from the liver and lungs of domesticated animals used for food by man, that when injected into the blood prevents coagulation: used chiefly in the treatment of thrombosis. [< Gk *hêpar* the liver + -IN[2]] —**hep′a·rin·oid′,** *adj.*

hep·a·rin·ize (hep′ər ə nīz′), *v.t.,* **-ized, -iz·ing.** *Biochem.* to treat blood or plasma with heparin to prevent clotting. [HEPARIN + -IZE] —**hep′a·rin·i·za′tion,** *n.*

hepat-, var. of **hepato-** before a vowel: *hepatatrophia.*

hep·a·tat·ro·phi·a (hep′ə tə trō′fē ə), *n. Pathol.* atrophy of the liver. Also, **hep·a·tat·ro·phy** (hep′ə ta′trə fē). [HEPAT- + ATROPH(Y) + -IA]

hep·a·tec·to·mize (hep′ə tek′tə mīz′), *v.t.,* **-mized, -miz·ing.** *Surg.* to perform a hepatectomy on. [HEPATECTOM(Y) + -IZE]

hep·a·tec·to·my (hep′ə tek′tə mē), *n., pl.* **-mies.** *Surg.* excision of part or all of the liver. [HEPAT- + -ECTOMY]

he·pat·ic (hi pat′ik), *adj.* **1.** of or pertaining to the liver. **2.** acting on the liver, as a medicine. **3.** liver-colored; dark reddish-brown. **4.** *Bot.* belonging or pertaining to the liverworts. —*n.* **5.** a medicine acting on the liver. **6.** a liverwort. [< L *hēpatic(us)* < Gk *hēpatik(ós).* See HEPATO-, -IC]

he·pat·i·ca (hi pat′i kə), *n.* any ranunculaceous herb of the genus *Hepatica,* having delicate purplish, pink, or white flowers. [< ML: liverwort, n. use of fem. of L *hēpaticus* HEPATIC]

hepatico-, a combining form of **hepatic:** *hepaticoenterostomy.*

he·pat·i·co·en·ter·os·to·my (hi pat′ə kō en′tə ros′tə mē), *n., pl.* **-mies.** *Surg.* the formation of an artificial connection between a hepatic duct and the intestine. [HEPATICO- + ENTEROSTOMY]

hep·a·tise (hep′ə tīz′), *v.t.,* **-tised, -tis·ing.** *Chiefly Brit.* hepatize. —**hep′a·ti·sa′tion,** *n.*

hep·a·ti·tis (hep′ə tī′tis), *n. Pathol.* inflammation of the liver. [< Gk *hēpatîtis.* See HEPAT-, -ITIS]

hep·a·tize (hep′ə tīz′), *v.t.,* **-tized, -tiz·ing.** *Pathol.* to convert (a lung or other tissue) into liverlike tissue by engorgement. Also, *esp. Brit.,* **hepatise.** [HEPAT- + -IZE] —**hep′a·ti·za′tion,** *n.*

hepato-, a learned borrowing from Greek meaning "liver," used in the formation of compound words: *hepatotoxin.* Also, *esp. before a vowel,* **hepat-.** [comb. form repr. Gk *hēpat-,* s. of *hêpar* liver]

hep·a·tos·co·py (hep′ə tos′kə pē), *n., pl.* **-pies.** examination of the livers of sacrificed animals as a technique of divination. [HEPATO- + -SCOPY]

hep·a·to·tox·in (hep′ə tō tok′sin), *n.* a substance, as a drug, having a toxic effect on the cells of the liver. [HEPATO- + TOXIN] —**hep·a·to·tox·ic** (hep′ə tō tok′sik), *adj.*

Hep·burn (hep′bûrn′), *n.* **Katharine,** born 1909, U.S. actress.

hep·cat (hep′kat′), *n. Jazz Slang.* a performer or admirer of jazz, esp. swing. [HEP[1] + CAT[1]]

He·phaes·tus (hi fes′təs), *n.* the ancient Greek god of fire, metalworking, and handicrafts, identified by the Romans with Vulcan, sometimes believed to be the consort of Aphrodite. Also, **He·phais·tos** (hi fī′stəs).

Heph·zi·bah (hef′zi bə), *n.* **1.** Also, *Douay Bible,* **Haphsiba.** the wife of Hezekiah and the mother of Manasseh. II Kings 21:1. **2.** a name applied to Jerusalem, possibly as denoting its prophesied restoration to the Jews after the Captivity. Isa. 62:4. Cf. **Beulah.** (def. 1). **3.** Also, **Hep·si·ba** (hep′sə bə), **Hepzibah.** a girl's given name.

Hep·ple·white (hep′əl hwīt′, -wīt′), *n.* **1. George,** died 1786, English furniture designer and cabinetmaker. —*adj.* **2.** noting the style prevailing in English furniture c1780–c95, as illustrated in designs published by the firm of George Hepplewhite in 1788, reflecting Adam and Louis XVI influences.

Hepplewhite chair

hepta-, a learned borrowing from Greek meaning "seven," used in the formation of compound words: *heptahedron.* [< Gk, comb. form of *heptá* seven; c. L *septem*]

hep·ta·chlor (hep′tə klōr′, -klôr′), *n. Chem.* a white to light-tan, waxy, water-insoluble solid, $C_{10}H_5Cl_7$, used as an insecticide. [HEPTA- + CHLOR-[2]]

hep·ta·chord (hep′tə kôrd′), *n.* **1.** a musical scale of seven notes. **2.** an interval of a seventh. **3.** an ancient Greek stringed instrument. [< Gk *heptáchord(os).* See HEPTA-, CHORD[1]]

hep·tad (hep′tad), *n.* **1.** the number seven. **2.** a group of seven. **3.** *Chem.* an element, atom, or group having a valence of seven. [< Gk *heptad-* (s. of *heptás*). See HEPTA-, -AD[1]]

hep·ta·gon (hep′tə gon′), *n.* a polygon having seven angles and seven sides. [< Gk *heptágōn(os)* seven-cornered. See HEPTA-, -GON]

hep·tag·o·nal (hep tag′ə nəl), *adj.* having seven sides or angles. [HEPTAGON + -AL[1]]

Heptagon (Regular)

hep·ta·he·dron (hep′tə hē′drən), *n., pl.* **-drons, -dra** (-drə). a solid figure having seven faces. [HEPTA- + -HEDRON] —**hep′ta·he′dral, hep′ta·he′dri·cal,** *adj.*

hep·ta·hy·drate (hep′tə hī′drāt), *n. Chem.* a hydrate that contains seven molecules of water, as magnesium sulfate, $MgSO_4 \cdot 7H_2O$. [HEPTA- + HYDRATE] —**hep′ta·hy′drat·ed,** *adj.*

hep·tam·er·ous (hep tam′ər əs), *adj.* **1.** consisting of or divided into seven parts. **2.** *Bot.* (of flowers) having seven members in each whorl. [HEPTA- + -MEROUS]

hep·tam·e·ter (hep tam′i tər), *n. Pros.* a verse of seven metrical feet. [< ML *heptametr(um)* < Gk *heptámetron* a verse of seven feet. See HEPTA-, METER[2]] —**hep·ta·met·ri·cal** (hep′tə me′tri kəl), *adj.*

hep·tane (hep′tān), *n. Chem.* any of nine isomeric hydrocarbons, C_7H_{16}, of the alkane series, some of which are obtained from petroleum: used in fuels as solvents, and as chemical intermediates. [HEPT(A)- + -ANE]

hep·tan·gu·lar (hep tang′gyə lər), *adj.* having seven angles. [HEPT(A)- + ANGULAR]

hep·ta·none (hep′tə nōn′), *n. Chem.* any of three isomeric ketones having the formula $CH_3(CH_2)_4COCH_3$, $CH_3(CH_2)_3COCH_2CH_3$, or $CH_3(CH_2)_2CO(CH_2)_2CH_3$. [HEPTANE + -ONE]

hep·tar·chy (hep′tär kē), *n., pl.* **-chies. 1.** government by seven persons. **2.** an allied group of seven states or kingdoms, each under its own ruler. **3.** (*often cap.*) the seven principal concurrent early English kingdoms. [< NL; see HEPTA-, -ARCHY] —**hep′tarch, hep′tar·chist,** *n.* —**hep·tar′chic, hep·tar′chi·cal, hep·tar′chal,** *adj.*

hep·ta·stich (hep′tə stik′), *n. Pros.* a strophe, stanza, or poem consisting of seven lines or verses.

hep·ta·style (hep′tə stīl′), *adj. Archit.* **1.** having seven columns. **2.** (of a classical temple or a building in the style of one) having seven columns on one or both fronts. Also, **hep·ta·sty·lar** (hep′tə stī′lər). [HEPTA- + Gk *stŷl(os)* pillar]

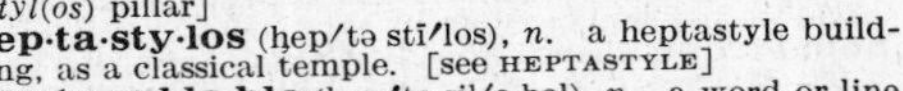

hep·ta·sty·los (hep′tə stī′los), *n.* a heptastyle building, as a classical temple. [see HEPTASTYLE]

hep·ta·syl·la·ble (hep′tə sil′ə bəl), *n.* a word or line of verse of seven syllables. [HEPTA- + SYLLABLE] —**hep·ta·syl·lab·ic** (hep′tə si lab′ik), *adj.*

Hep·ta·teuch (hep′tə to͞ok′, -tyo͞ok′), *n.* the first seven books of the Old Testament. [< LL *Heptateuch(os)* < LGk *Heptáteuchos* the first seven books of the Old Testament, equiv. to Gk *hepta-* HEPTA- + *teûchos* a book]

hep·tath·lon (hep tath′lən, -lon), *n.* an athletic contest for women comprising seven different track-and-field events and won by the contestant amassing the highest total score.

hep·ta·va·lent (hep′tə vā′lənt), *adj. Chem.* septivalent. [HEPTA- + -VALENT]

hep·tode (hep′tōd), *n. Electronics.* a vacuum tube containing seven electrodes, usually a plate, a cathode, a control electrode, and four grids. [HEPT(A)- + -ODE[2]]

her (hûr; *unstressed* hər, ər), *pron.* **1.** the objective case of **she:** *We saw her this morning. Give it to her.* **2.** the possessive case of **she** (used as an attributive adjective): *Her coat is the one on the chair. I'm sorry about her leaving. Did you mind her doing that?* Cf. **hers. 3.** the dative case of **she:** *I gave her the book.* [ME *her(e),* OE *hire,* gen. and dat. of *hēo* she (fem. of *hē* HE[1]]

her., 1. heraldic. **2.** heraldry.

He·ra (hēr′ə), *n.* **1.** Also, **Here.** the ancient Greek queen of heaven, a daughter of Cronus and Rhea and the wife and sister of Zeus, identified by the Romans with Juno.

Her·a·cle·a (her′ə klē′ə), *n.* an ancient city in S Italy, near the Gulf of Taranto: Roman defeat 280 B.C.

Her·a·cles (her′ə klēz′), *n.* **1.** Hercules (def. 1). **2.** Also called **Her′acles Fu′rens** (fyo͝or′ənz). (*italics*) a tragedy (420? B.C.) by Euripides. Also, **Herakles.** [< Gk *Hēraklês,* lit., having the glory of Hera, equiv. to *Hēr(a)* HERA + *kléos* glory, fame] —**Her′a·cle′an,** *adj.*

Her·a·clid (her′ə klid), *n., pl.* **Her·a·cli·dae** (her′ə klī′dē). a person claiming descent from Hercules, esp. one of the Dorian aristocracy of Sparta. Also, **Heraklid.** —**Her·a·cli·dan, Her·a·kli·dan** (her′ə klīd′ən), *adj.*

Her·a·cli·dae (her′ə klī′dē), *n.* a drama (429? B.C.) by Euripides. Also, **Her′a·clei′dae.** Also called **Children of Hercules.**

Her·a·cli·te·an (her′ə klī′tē ən, -klī tē′-), *adj.* **1.** of or pertaining to Heraclitus or his philosophy. —*n.* **2.** a person who believes in or advocates the philosophy of Heraclitus. Also, **Her·a·clit·ic** (her′ə klit′ik). [< L *Hēraclīte(us)* (< Gk *Hērakleíteios*) + -AN]

Her·a·cli·te·an·ism (her′ə klī′tē ə niz′əm, -klī tē′-), *n.* the philosophy of Heraclitus, maintaining the perpetual change of all things, the only abiding thing being the logos, or orderly principle, according to which the change takes place. [HERACLITEAN + -ISM]

Her·a·cli·tus (her′ə klī′təs), *n.* **1.** ("*the Obscure*") c540–c470 B.C., Greek philosopher. **2.** a walled plain in the fourth quadrant of the face of the moon: about 57 miles in diameter.

Her·a·cli·us (her′ə klī′əs, hi rak′lē əs), *n.* A.D. 575?–641, Byzantine emperor 610–641.

He·rae·a (hi rē′ə), *n.* (*sometimes construed as pl.*) a festival held in ancient Greece in honor of Hera, esp. one held in Argos every five years.

He·ra·klei·on (ē rä′klē ôn), *n.* Greek name of **Candia.**

Her·a·kles (her′ə klēz′), *n.* Heracles. —**Her′a·kle′an,** *adj.*

Her·a·klid (her′ə klid), *n.* Heraclid.

her·ald (her′əld), *n.* **1.** (formerly) a royal or official messenger, esp. one representing a monarch in an ambassadorial capacity during wartime. **2.** any messenger. **3.** one who or that which precedes or comes before; forerunner; harbinger: *the returning swallows, those heralds of spring.* **4.** one who or that which proclaims or announces: *A good newspaper should be a herald of truth.* **5.** (in the Middle Ages) an officer who arranged tournaments and other functions, announced challenges, marshaled combatants, etc., and who was later employed also to arrange processions, funerals, etc., and to regulate the use of armorial bearings. **6.** an official intermediate in rank between a king-of-arms and a pursuivant, in the Heralds' College in England or the Heralds' Office in Scotland. —*v.t.* **7.** to give tidings of; announce; proclaim: *a publicity campaign to herald a new film.* **8.** to usher in. [ME *herauld* < OF *heraut, hirauz* < Frankish *heriwald* army chief]

he·ral·dic (he ral′dik), *adj.* of, pertaining to, or characteristic of heralds or heraldry: *heraldic form; heraldic images; heraldic history; a heraldic device.* [HERALD + -IC] —**he·ral′di·cal·ly,** *adv.*

heral′dic heir′ess, a daughter of an armigerous father who has died without male issue, or whose sons have died without issue, and who therefore inherits the armorial bearings of her family. Her arms will be borne by her husband on an escutcheon of pretense and quarterly with those of her husband by their children.

her·ald·ry (her′əl drē), *n., pl.* **-ries. 1.** the science of armorial bearings. **2.** the art of blazoning armorial bearings, of settling the rights of persons to bear arms or to use certain bearings, of tracing and recording genealogies, of recording honors, and of deciding questions of precedence. **3.** the office or duty of a herald. **4.** a heraldic device, or a collection of such devices. **5.** a coat of arms; armorial bearings. **6.** heraldic symbolism. **7.** heraldic pomp or ceremony: *The coronation was marked by all the magnificence of heraldry.* [HERALD + -RY] —**her′ald·ist,** *n.*

Her′alds' Col′lege, a royal corporation in England, instituted in 1483, occupied chiefly with armorial bearings, genealogies, honors, and precedence. Also called **College of Arms.**

Her′alds' Of′fice, the official heraldic authority of Scotland. Also called **Lyon Office of Arms, Lyon Office.**

her′ald's trick′, *Heraldry.* See **engraver's trick.**

her′ald's trum′pet, a woody vine, *Beaumontia grandiflora,* of India, having large, trumpet-shaped, fragrant white flowers, and seeds that yield floss for vegetable silk.

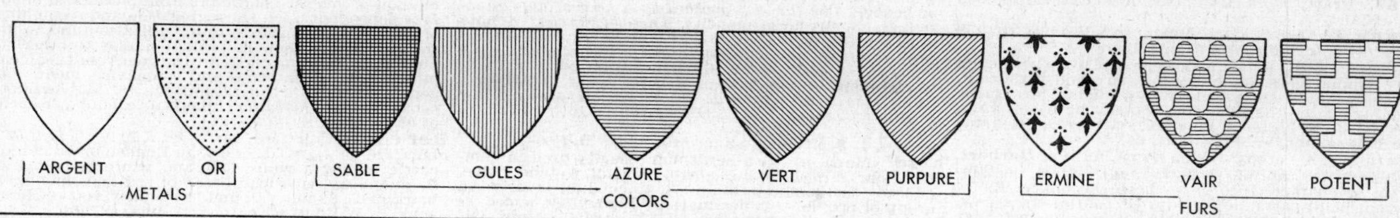

TINCTURES (as represented with engraver's tricks)

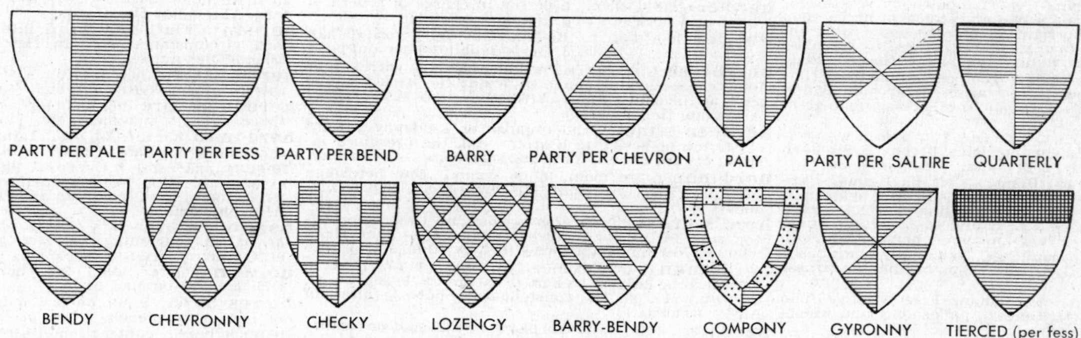

TREATMENT OF AREAS

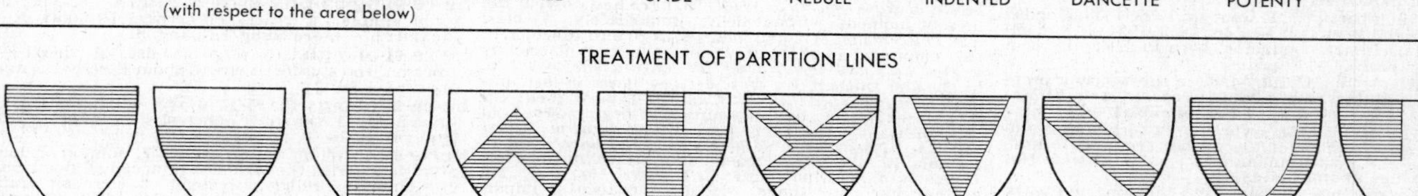

TREATMENT OF PARTITION LINES

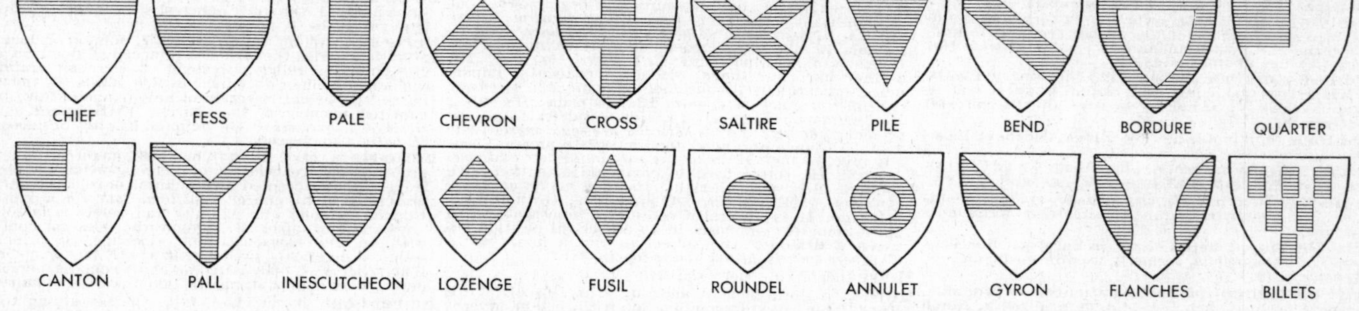

ORDINARIES AND SUBORDINARIES

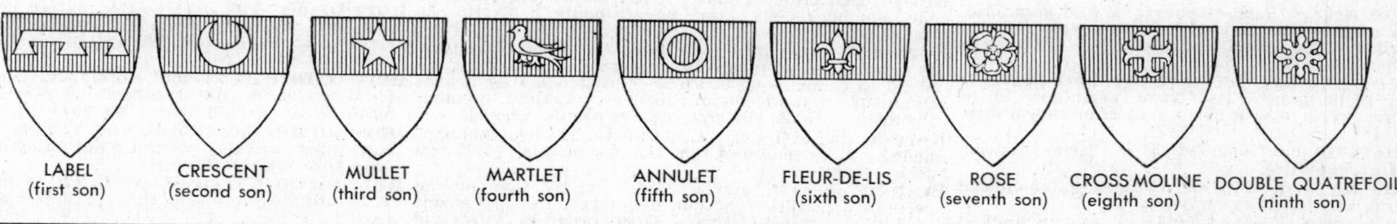

CADENCE MARKS (English system)

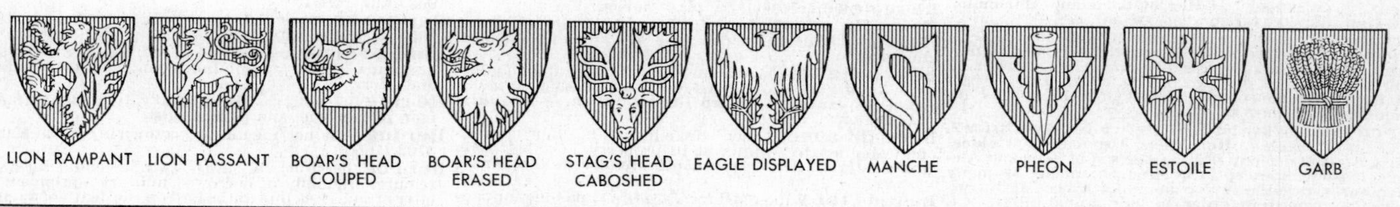

VARIOUS CHARGES

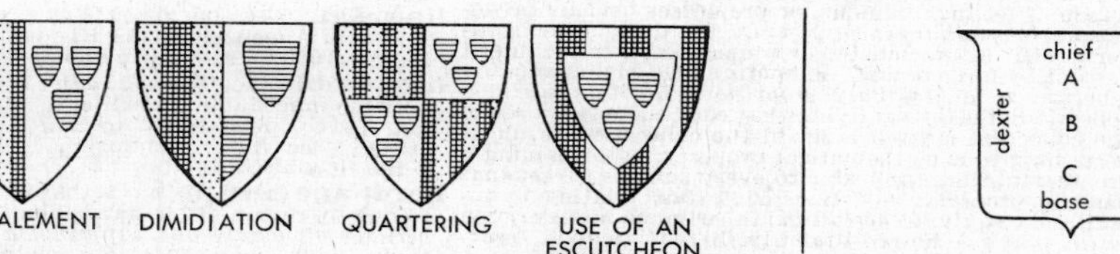

METHODS OF COMBINING DIFFERENT COATS OF ARMS

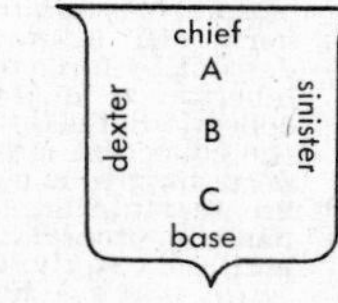

PARTS OF THE ESCUTCHEON

A—honor point

B—fess point

C—nombril

HERALDRY

He·rat (he rät′), *n.* a city in NW Afghanistan. 100,000 (est. 1964).

Hé·rault (ā rō′), *n.* a department in S France. 516,658 (1962); 2403 sq. mi. *Cap.:* Montpellier.

herb (ûrb, hûrb), *n.* **1.** a flowering plant whose stem above ground does not become woody and persistent. **2.** such a plant when valued for its medicinal properties, flavor, scent, or the like. **3.** *Archaic.* herbage. [ME *herbe* < OF *erbe, herbe* < L *herb(a)*; c. It *erba,* Sp *yerba*] —**herb′less,** *adj.* —**herb′like′,** *adj.*

Herb (hûrb), *n.* a boy's given name, form of **Herbert.**

her·ba·ceous (hûr bā′shəs, ûr-), *adj.* **1.** of, pertaining to, or characteristic of an herb; herblike. **2.** (of plants or plant parts) not woody. **3.** (of flowers, sepals, etc.) having the texture, color, etc., of an ordinary foliage leaf. [< L *herbāce(us)* grassy, like grass, equiv. to *herb(a)* grass, herbs + *-āceus* -ACEOUS] —**her·ba′ceous·ly,** *adv.*

herb·age (ûr′bij, hûr′-), *n.* **1.** nonwoody vegetation. **2.** the succulent parts, leaves and stems, of herbaceous plants. **3.** *Law.* the right to pasture one's cattle on another's land. **4.** *Brit.* vegetation grazed by animals; pasturage. [< F; see HERB, -AGE] —**her′baged,** *adj.*

herb·al (hûr′bəl, ûr′-), *adj.* **1.** of, pertaining to, or consisting of herbs. —*n.* **2.** a treatise on herbs or plants. **3.** a herbarium. [< ML *herbāl(is)* of, belonging to grass or herbs. See HERB, -AL[1]]

herb·al·ist (hûr′bə list, ûr′-), *n.* **1.** a person who collects or deals in herbs, esp. medicinal herbs. **2.** See **herb doctor. 3.** (formerly) a botanist. [HERBAL + -IST]

her·bar·i·um (hûr bâr′ē əm), *n., pl.* **-bar·i·ums, -bar·i·a** (-bâr′ē ə). **1.** a collection of dried plants systematically arranged. **2.** a room or building in which such a collection is kept. [< LL, equiv. to L *herb(a)* HERB, green vegetation + *-ārium* -ARIUM] —**her·bar′i·al,** *adj.*

her·ba·rize (hûr′bə rīz′), *v.i.,* **-rized, -riz·ing.** *Archaic.* botanize. [< L *herbār(ia)*; pl. of HERBARIUM; see -IZE]

Her·bart (her′bärt), *n.* **Jo·hann Frie·drich** (yō′hän frē′drikh), 1776–1841, German philosopher and educator.

Her·bar·ti·an (hûr bär′tē ən), *adj.* **1.** of or pertaining to Herbart's system of philosophy. —*n.* **2.** one who advocates the doctrines of Herbart. [HERBART + -IAN] —**Her·bar′ti·an·ism,** *n.*

herb′ ben′net, a perennial, European, rosaceous herb, *Geum urbanum,* having yellow flowers and an aromatic, tonic, and astringent root.

herb′ doc′tor, one who heals by the use of herbs. Also called **herbalist.**

Her·bert (hûr′bərt), *n.* **1. George,** 1593–1633, English clergyman and poet. **2. Victor,** 1859–1924, U.S. composer and orchestra conductor, born in Ireland. **3.** a boy's given name.

herb·i·cide (ûr′bi sīd′, hûr′-), *n.* a substance or preparation for killing plants, esp. weeds. [< L *herb(a)* (see HERB) + -I- + -CIDE] —**her′bi·cid′al,** *adj.*

her·bi·vore (hûr′bə vōr′, -vôr′), *n.* a herbivorous animal, esp. any member of the former group *Herbivora,* comprising the hoofed mammals. [< NL *herbivor(a)* (neut. pl.). See HERBIVOROUS]

her·biv·o·rous (hûr biv′ər əs), *adj.* feeding on plants. [< NL *herbivor(us),* equiv. to L *herb(a)* HERB + *-i-* -I- + *-vorus* -VOROUS] —**her·bi·vor·i·ty** (hûr′bə vōr′i tē, -vor′-), *n.*

Her·block (hûr′blok), *n.* See **Block, Herbert Lawrence.**

her·bo·rist (hûr′bər ist), *n.* herbalist. [< MF *herboriste,* irreg. < L *herb(a)* HERB + MF *-iste* -IST]

her·bo·rize (hûr′bə rīz′), *v.i.,* **-rized, -riz·ing.** botanize. [< F *herboris(er),* equiv. to *herbor(iste)* HERBORIST + *-iser* -IZE]

herb′ Par′is, *pl.* **herbs Paris.** a European, liliaceous herb, *Paris quadrifolia,* formerly used in medicine. [< ML *herba paris* < ?]

herb′ pa′tience, *pl.* **herbs patience.** a perennial, European herb, *Rumex Patientia,* naturalized in North America, having wavy-margined, basal leaves from eight to ten inches long, used for salads. Also called **spinach dock.**

herb′ Rob′ert, *pl.* **herbs Robert.** a wild geranium, *Geranium robertianum,* having reddish-purple flowers. Also called **fox geranium, red shanks** [< ML *herba Roberti* Robert's herb < ?]

herb·y (ûr′bē, hûr′bē), *adj.,* **herb·i·er, herb·i·est. 1.** abounding in herbs or grass. **2.** of, pertaining to, or characteristic of an herb or herbs in taste or appearance. [HERB + -Y[1]]

Her·ce·go·vi·na (her′tse gô′vi nä), *n.* Serbo-Croatian name of **Herzegovina.**

Her·cei·us (hər sē′əs, -sī′-), *n.* *Class. Myth.* an epithet of Zeus, meaning "of the courtyard."

Her·cu·la·ne·um (hûr′kyə lā′nē əm), *n.* an ancient city in SW Italy, on the Bay of Naples: buried along with Pompeii by the eruption of Mount Vesuvius in A.D. 79; partially excavated. —**Her′cu·la′ne·an, Her·cu·la·nen·sian** (hûr′kyə lə nen′shən, -sē ən), *adj.*

her·cu·le·an (hûr′kyə lē′ən, hûr kyōō′lē ən), *adj.* **1.** requiring the strength of a Hercules; very hard to perform: *Digging the tunnel was a herculean task.* **2.** having enormous strength, courage, or size. **3.** (*cap.*) of or pertaining to Hercules or his labors. [< L *Hercule(us)* of, belonging to HERCULES + -AN]

Her·cu·les (hûr′kyə lēz′), *n., gen.* **-cu·lis** (-kyə lis) for 2. **1.** Also, **Heracles, Herakles.** Also called **Alcides.** *Class. Myth.* a celebrated hero, the son of Zeus and Alcmene, possessing exceptional strength: among his many adventures were the twelve labors for his cousin Eurystheus, performed in order to gain immortality. Cf. **labors of Hercules. 2.** *Astron.* a northern constellation, between Lyra and Corona Borealis. **3.** a crater in the first quadrant of the face of the moon: about 45 miles in diameter. [< L; see HERACLES]

Her·cu·les′-club (hûr′kyə lēz klub′), *n.* **1.** Also called **prickly ash.** a prickly, rutaceous tree, *Zanthoxylum Clava-Herculis,* having a medicinal bark and berries. **2.** Also called **angelica tree, devil's-walking-stick.** a prickly, araliaceous shrub, *Aralia spinosa,* having a medicinal bark and root.

Her′cules′ Pil′lars. See **Pillars of Hercules.**

Her·cy·na (hər sī′nə), *n.* *Class. Myth.* a fountain nymph who was the playmate of Persephone.

herd[1] (hûrd), *n.* **1.** a number of animals kept, feeding, or traveling together; drove; flock: *a herd of cattle; a herd of sheep; a herd of zebras.* **2.** *Contemptuous.* a large group of people: *The star was mobbed by a herd of autograph-seekers.* **3.** any large quantity: *a herd of bicycles.* **4. ride herd on.** See **ride** (def. 25). **5. the herd,** the common people; masses: *He had no opinions of his own but simply followed the herd.* —*v.i.* **6.** to unite or go in a herd; to assemble or associate as a herd. —*v.t.* **7.** to form into or as if into a herd: *He herded everyone together to sing folk songs.* [ME; OE *heord;* c. Goth *hairda,* G *Herde*]
—**Syn. 1.** See **flock**[1]. **2.** crowd, mob. **6.** flock.

herd[2] (hûrd), *n.* **1.** a herdsman (usually used in combination): *a cowherd; a goatherd.* —*v.t.* **2.** to tend, drive, or lead (cattle, sheep, etc.). **3.** to conduct or drive (a group of people) to a destination: *The teacher herded the children into the classroom.* [ME *herd(e), hirde,* OE *hierde;* c. Goth *hairdeis,* G *Hirt(e)*; deriv. of HERD[1]]
—**Syn. 2.** guard, protect, watch.

herd·er (hûr′dər), *n.* a person in charge of a herd of cattle or a flock of sheep. [HERD[2] + -ER[1]]

Her·der (her′dər), *n.* **Jo·hann Gott·fried von** (yō′hän gôt′frēt fən), 1744–1803, German philosopher and poet.

her·dic (hûr′dik), *n.* a low-hung carriage with two or four wheels, having the entrance at the back and the seats at the side. [named after P. *Herdic,* 19th-century American, the inventor]

herd′ in′stinct, the impulse or tendency toward clustering or acting in a group, esp. the presumed instinct toward or need for gregariousness and conformity.

herd·man (hûrd′mən), *n., pl.* **-men.** *Obs.* herdsman (def. 1). [ME *hird-man,* OE *hyrdemann.* See HERD[2], MAN[1]]

herd's-grass (hûrdz′gras′, -gräs′), *n.* timothy or redtop, used for hay or pasture. [named after John *Herd,* who in 1700 found it growing in New Hampshire]

herds·man (hûrdz′mən), *n., pl.* **-men. 1.** *Chiefly Brit.* a herder; the keeper of a herd of cattle or a flock of sheep. **2.** (*cap.*) *Astron.* the constellation Boötes. [alter. of earlier HERDMAN]

here (hēr), *adv.* **1.** in this place; in this spot or locality (opposed to *there*): *Put the pen here.* **2.** to or toward this place; hither: *Come here.* **3.** at this point; at this juncture: *Here the speaker paused.* **4.** (used to call attention to some person or thing present, or to what the speaker has, offers, brings, or discovers): *Here is your paycheck. My friend here knows the circumstances.* **5.** present (used to answer roll call). **6.** in the present life or existence (often fol. by *below*): *Man wants but little here below.* **7.** under consideration, in this instance or case: *The matter here is of grave concern to us all.* **8. here and now,** at the present moment; without delay; immediately: *We must tend to the matter here and now.* **9. here and there, a.** in this place and in that; at various times or places: *He worked here and there, never for long in one town.* **b.** hither and thither: *We drove here and there in the darkness, hoping to find the right roads.* **10. here goes!** *Informal.* (expressing one's resolution in beginning a bold or unpleasant action) here I go: *You've dared me to dive from the highest board, so here goes!* **11. here's to!** (a formula in offering a toast) hail to; salutations to: *Here's to a long and happy life! Here's to you!* **12. neither here nor there,** without relevance or importance; immaterial: *The fact that her family has no money is neither here nor there.* —*n.* **13.** this place: *It's only a short distance from here.* **14.** this world; this life; the present: *The here and the hereafter are equal mysteries to man.* **15. here and now,** the immediate present (usually prec. by *the*): *Animals live only in the here and now.* —*interj.* **16.** (often used to command attention, give comfort, etc.) now; all right: *Here, let me try it. Here, don't cry.* [ME; OE *hēr;* c. G *hier,* OIcel, Goth *hēr*]
—**Usage.** It is generally considered nonstandard to place HERE, for emphasis, in an adjectival position between a demonstrative adjective and a noun, as in *This here book is the one you're looking for.*

He·re (hēr′ē), *n.* Hera (def. 1).

here-, a word element meaning "this (place)," "this (time)," etc., used in combination with certain adverbs and prepositions: *hereafter.* [ME *her-,* OE *hēr-*; special use of HERE]

here·a·bout (hēr′ə bout′), *adv.* about this place; in this neighborhood. Also, **here′a·bouts′.** [ME; see HERE-, ABOUT]

here·af·ter (hēr af′tər, -äf′-), *adv.* **1.** after this in time or order; at some future time; farther along. **2.** in the world to come. —*n.* **3.** a life or existence after death; the future beyond mortal existence. **4.** time to come; the future. [ME; OE *hērǣfter.* See HERE-, AFTER]

here·at (hēr at′), *adv.* **1.** at this time; when this happened. **2.** by reason of this; because of this. [ME *here at.* See HERE-, AT[1]]

here·by (hēr bī′, hēr′bī′), *adv.* **1.** by this, or the present, declaration, action, document, etc.; by means of this; as a result of this: *I hereby resign my office and all duties listed below.* **2.** *Obs.* nearby. [ME *here by.* See HERE-, BY]

he·re·des (hi rē′dēz), *n.* pl. of **heres.**

He·re·dia (*Fr.* ā rā dyA′; *Sp.* e re′thyä), *n.* **Jo·sé Ma·ri·a** (hô sē′ mä rē′ä), 1803–39, French poet, born in Cuba.

he·red·i·ta·ble (hə red′i tə bəl), *adj.* heritable. [< MF < L *hērēdit(āre)* (to) inherit, deriv. of *hērēd-* (s. of *hērēs*) HEIR; see -ABLE] —**he·red′i·ta·bil′i·ty,** *n.* —**he·red′i·ta·bly,** *adv.*

her·e·dit·a·ment (her′i dit′ə mənt), *n.* *Law.* any inheritable estate or interest in property. [< ML *hērēditāment(um),* deriv. of L *hērēditāre.* See HEREDITABLE, -MENT]

he·red·i·tar·y (hə red′i ter′ē), *adj.* **1.** passing, or capable of passing, naturally from parents to offspring: *Blue eyes are hereditary in our family.* **2.** of or pertaining to inheritance or heredity: *a hereditary title.* **3.** existing by reason of feeling, opinions, or prejudices held by predecessors: *a hereditary enemy.* **4.** *Law.* **a.** descending by inheritance. **b.** transmitted or transmissible in the line of descent by force of law. **c.** holding title, rights, etc., by inheritance: *a hereditary proprietor.* **5.** *Math.* **a.** (of a collection of sets) signifying that each subset of a set in the collection is itself a set in the collection. **b.** of or pertaining to a mathematical property, as containing a greatest integer, applicable to every subset of a set that has the property. [< L *hērēditāri(us)* relating to inheritance, equiv. to *hērēdit(ās)* inheritance, HEREDITY + *-ārius* -ARY] —**he·red·i·tar·i·ly** (hi red′i târ′ə lē, -red′i ter′-), *adv.* —**he·red′i·tar′i·ness,** *n.*

he·red·i·ty (hə red′i tē), *n., pl.* **-ties.** *Biol.* **1.** the transmission of genetic characters from parents to offspring. It is dependent upon the segregation and recombination of genes during meiosis and fertilization and results in the genesis of a new individual similar to others of its kind but exhibiting certain variations resulting from the interaction of the genes and the environment. **2.** the genetic characters so transmitted. [< MF *heredite* < L *hērēditāt-* (s. of *hērēditās*) inheritance, equiv. to *hērēd-* (s. of *hērēs*) HEIR + *-itāt-* -ITY]

Her·e·ford (hûr′fərd, her′ə- *for 1, 2;* her′ə fərd *for 3, 5;* hûr′fərd *for 4*), *n.* **1.** one of an English breed of red beef cattle having a white face and white body markings. **2.** one of an American breed of red hogs having white markings. **3.** a city in and the county seat of Herefordshire, in W England: cathedral. 40,431 (1961). **4.** a town in N Texas. 7652 (1960). **5.** Herefordshire.

Her·e·ford·shire (her′ə fərd shēr′, -shər), *n.* a county in W England. 130,919 (1961); 842 sq. mi. *Co. seat:* Hereford. Also called **Hereford.**

here·in (hēr in′), *adv.* **1.** in or into this place. **2.** in this fact, circumstance, etc.; in view of this. [ME; OE *hērinne.* See HERE-, IN]

here·in·af·ter (hēr′in af′tər, -äf′-), *adv.* afterward in this document, statement, etc. [HEREIN + AFTER]

here·in·be·fore (hēr′in bi fōr′, -fôr′), *adv.* before in this document, statement, etc. [HEREIN + BEFORE]

here·in·to (hēr in′tōō), *adv.* **1.** into this place. **2.** into this matter or affair. [HERE- + INTO]

he·rem (khā′rem), *n.* *Hebrew.* the most severe form of excommunication, formerly used by rabbis in sentencing wrongdoers, usually for an indefinite period of time. Also, **cherem.**

here·of (hēr uv′, -ov′), *adv.* **1.** of this: *upon the receipt hereof.* **2.** concerning this: *more hereof later.* [ME *her of,* OE *hēreof.* See HERE-, OF[1]]

here·on (hēr on′, -ôn′), *adv.* hereupon. [ME *her on,* OE *hēron.* See HERE-, ON]

he·res (hēr′ēz), *n., pl.* **he·re·des** (hi rē′dēz). *Civil Law.* an heir. Also, **haeres.** [< L, pl. of *hered-* HEIR]

here's (hērz), contraction of *here is.*

he·re·si·arch (hə rē′zē ärk′, -sē-, her′ə-), *n.* a leader in heresy; the leader of a heretical sect. [< LL *haeresiarch(a)* < Gk *hairesiárch(ēs)* the leader of a school, equiv. to *hairés(is)* HERESY + *-archēs* -ARCH]

he·re·si·mach (hə rē′zə mak′, -sə-, her′ə-), *n.* a person actively engaged in combating heresy and heretics. [< LGk *hairesimách(os),* equiv. to Gk *hairesi(s)* HERESY + *máchē* quarrel, battle]

he·re·si·og·ra·phy (hə rē′zē og′rə fē, -sē-, her′ə sē-), *n., pl.* **-phies.** a treatise on heresy. [HERESY + -O- + -GRAPHY] —**he·re′si·og′ra·pher,** *n.*

he·re·si·ol·o·gist (hə rē′zē ol′ə jist, -sē-, her′i sē-), *n.* a person who studies or writes about heresies. [HERESIOLOG(Y) + -IST]

he·re·si·ol·o·gy (hə rē′zē ol′ə jē, -sē-, her′ə sē-), *n., pl.* **-gies** for 2. **1.** the study of heresies. **2.** a heresiography. [HERESY + -O- + -LOGY]

her·e·sy (her′i sē), *n., pl.* **-sies. 1.** opinion or doctrine at variance with the orthodox or accepted doctrine, esp. of a church or religious system. **2.** the maintaining of such an opinion or doctrine. **3.** *Rom. Cath. Ch.* the willful and persistent rejection of any article of faith by a baptized member of the church. [ME *heresie* < OF *eresie* < L *haeresis* < Gk *haíresis,* lit., act of choosing, cf. *haireîn* to choose]

her·e·tic (*n.* her′i tik; *adj.* her′i tik, hə ret′ik), *n.* **1.** a professed believer who maintains religious opinions contrary to those accepted by his church or rejects doctrines prescribed by his church. **2.** *Rom. Cath. Ch.* a baptized Roman Catholic who willfully and persistently rejects any article of faith. **3.** anyone who does not conform with an established attitude, doctrine, or principle. —*adj.* **4.** heretical. [ME *heretik* < MF *heretique* < eccl. L *haeretic(us)* < LGk *hairetikós* able to choose, heretical, deriv. of *hairetós* that may be taken (verbid of *haireîn*)]

he·ret·i·cal (hə ret′i kəl), *adj.* of, pertaining to, or characteristic of heretics or heresy. [< ML *haereticāl(is).* See HERETIC, -AL[1]] —**he·ret′i·cal·ly,** *adv.* —**he·ret′i·cal·ness,** *n.*

here·to (hēr tōō′), *adv.* to this matter, document, subject, etc.; regarding this point: *attached hereto; agreeable hereto.* Also, **here·un·to** (hēr un′tōō, hēr′un tōō′). [ME *herto.* See HERE-, TO]

here·to·fore (hēr′tə fōr′, -fôr′), *adv.* before this time. [ME *heretoforn,* equiv. to *here-* HERE- + *toforn,* OE *tōforan* (*tō* TO + *foran* before; see FORE[1])]

here·un·der (hēr un′dər), *adv.* **1.** under or below this; subsequent to this. **2.** under authority of this. [ME; see HERE-, UNDER (prep.)]

here·up·on (hēr′ə pon′, -pôn′), *adv.* **1.** upon or on this. **2.** immediately following this. [ME *herupon.* See HERE-, UPON]

here·with (hēr with′, -with′), *adv.* **1.** along with this. **2.** by means of this; hereby. [ME *herwith,* OE *hērwith.* See HERE-, WITH[1]]

Her·ges·hei·mer (hûr′gəs hī′mər), *n.* **Joseph,** 1880–1954, U.S. novelist.

Her·i·go·ni·us (her′ə gō′nē əs), *n.* a crater in the third quadrant of the face of the moon: about 10 miles in diameter.

He·ring (hā′ring), *n.* **E·wald** (ā′vält), 1834–1918, German physiologist and psychologist.

Her·ing·ton (her′ing tən), *n.* a town in central Kansas. 3702 (1960).

her·i·ot (her′ē ət), *n.* *Eng. Law.* a feudal service or tribute, originally of borrowed military equipment and later of a chattel, due to the lord on the death of a tenant. [ME *heriot, heriet,* OE *heregeate, -geatu, -geatwa* war gear, equiv to *here* army + *geatwa* equipment; c. OIcel *gǫtvar* (pl.)]

He·ri·sau (*Ger.* hā′ri zou′), *n.* a town in and the capital of Appenzell Ausser Rhoden, in NE Switzerland. 14,361 (1960). French, **He·ri·sau** (ā rē zō′).

her·it·a·ble (her′i tə bəl), *adj.* **1.** capable of being inherited; inheritable; hereditary. **2.** capable of inheriting. [ME < MF, equiv. to *herit(er)* (to) inherit + *-able* -ABLE. See HEIR, HEREDITY] —**her′it·a·bil′i·ty,** *n.* —**her′it·a·bly,** *adv.*

her·it·age (her′i tij), *n.* **1.** that which comes or belongs to one by reason of birth; an inherited lot or portion: *a heritage of poverty and suffering; a national heritage of honor, pride, and courage.* **2.** something reserved for one:

the heritage of the righteous. **3.** *Law.* **a.** that which has been or may be inherited by legal descent or succession. **b.** any property, esp. land, that devolves by right of inheritance. [ME < MF, equiv. to *herit(er)* (to) inherit + *-age* -AGE; see HEIR]
—Syn. 1. estate, patrimony. See **inheritance.**

her·it·ance (her′i təns), *n. Archaic.* inheritance. [ME *herita(u)nce* < MF *heritance*, equiv. to *herit(er)* (to) inherit + *-ance* -ANCE; see HEIR]

her·i·tor (her′i tər), *n.* inheritor. Also, *referring to a woman,* **her·i·tress** (her′i tris). [alter. of ME *heriter* < MF *heritier* < L *hērēditār(ius)*; see HEREDITARY]

Her·ki·mer (hûr′kə mər), *n.* **1. Nicholas,** 1728–77, American Revolutionary general. **2.** a town in central New York. 9396 (1960).

herl (hûrl), *n.* **1.** a barb, or the barbs, of a feather, used esp. in dressing anglers' flies. **2.** an artificial fly so dressed. [ME; c. MLG *herle, harle,* LG *harl* fibre, hair of flax or hemp. See HARL[2]]

herm (hûrm), *n.* a monument consisting of a four-sided shaft, tapering inward from top to bottom and bearing a head or bust; terminal figure. Also, **herma, hermes.** Cf. **gaine, term** (def. 10). [< L *herm(a)* < Gk *hermês* statue of Hermes]

Herm (Upper part of a double herm)

Herm (hûrm), *n.* a boy's given name, form of **Herman.**

her·ma (hûr′mə), *n., pl.* **-mae** (-mē), **-mai** (-mī). herm. **—her·mae·an** (hər mē′ən), *adj.*

Her·ma (hûr′mə), *n.* a girl's given name.

Her·man (hûr′mən), *n.* **1. Woodrow** ("*Woody*"), born 1913, U.S. jazz saxophonist, clarinetist, and bandleader. **2.** a boy's given name.

Her·mann (hûr′mən *or, for 2,* her′mən), *n.* **1.** a town in central Missouri. 2536 (1960). **2.** a walled plain in the third quadrant of the face of the moon: about 10 miles in diameter.

Her′mann-Mau·guin′ sym′bol (hûr′mən mō gan′, her′män-), *Crystall.* a notation for indicating a particular point group.

her·maph·ro·dism (hûr maf′rə diz′əm), *n.* hermaphroditism. [HEMAPHROD(ITE) + -ISM]

her·maph·ro·dite (hûr maf′rə dīt′), *n.* **1.** an individual having both external and internal male and female sex organs. Cf. **pseudohermaphrodite. 2.** *Biol.* an animal, as an earthworm, or plant having normally both the male and female organs of generation. **3.** a person or thing in which two opposite qualities are combined. *—adj.* **4.** of, pertaining to, or characteristic of a hermaphrodite. **5.** combining two opposite qualities. **6.** *Bot.* monoclinous. [< L *hermaphrodīt(us)* < Gk *hermaphróditos* hemaphrodite (so called from the son of Hermes and Aphrodite, HERMAPHRODITUS)] **—her·maph·ro·dit·ic** (hər maf′rə dit′ik), **her·maph′ro·dit′i·cal, her·maph·ro·dit·ish** (hər maf′rə dī′tish), *adj.* **—her·maph′ro·dit′i·cal·ly,** *adv.*

hermaph′rodite brig′, *Naut.* a two-masted sailing vessel, square-rigged on the foremast and fore-and-aft-rigged on the mainmast. Also called **brigantine.**

Hermaphrodite brig

hermaph′rodite schoon′er, 1. a schooner used off New England c1850, rigged as a topsail schooner but with staysails in place of a gaff foresail. **2.** a two-masted sailing vessel of c1800, square-rigged on the foremast, but with an additional gaff foresail, and fore-and-aft-rigged on the mainmast.

her·maph·ro·dit·ism (hûr maf′rə dī tiz′əm), *n.* the condition of being a hermaphrodite. Also, **hermaphrodism.** [HERMAPHRODITE + -ISM]

Her·maph·ro·di·tus (hûr maf′rə dī′təs), *n. Class. Myth.* a son of Hermes and Aphrodite who, bathing in a pool haunted by a nymph (**Salmacis**) in love with him, became joined with her into a single bisexual person.

her·me·neu·tic (hûr′mə nōō′tik, -nyōō′-), *adj.* of or pertaining to hermeneutics; interpretative; explanatory. Also, **her′me·neu′ti·cal.** [< Gk *hermēneutik(ós)* of, skilled in, interpreting, equiv. to *hermēneú(ein)* (to) make clear, interpret (*hermēneús* an interpreter, deriv. of *Hermês* HERMES) + *-tikos* -TIC] **—her′me·neu′ti·cal·ly,** *adv.*

her·me·neu·tics (hûr′mə nōō′tiks, -nyōō′-), *n.* (*construed as sing.*) **1.** the science of interpretation, esp. of the Scriptures. **2.** the branch of theology which treats of the principles of Biblical exegesis. [see HERMENEUTIC, -ICS]

her·mes (hûr′mēz), *n., pl.* **-mae** (-mē), **-mai** (-mī). herm.

Her·mes (hûr′mēz), *n.* the ancient Greek herald and messenger of the gods and the god of roads, commerce, invention, cunning, and theft: identified by the Romans with Mercury.

Her′mes Tris·me·gis′tus (tris′mi jis′təs), a name given by Neoplatonists and others to the Egyptian god Thoth, who was to some extent identified with the Grecian Hermes and to whom were attributed various works embodying mystical, theosophical, astrological, and alchemical doctrines. [< ML < Gk: Hermes thrice greatest]

her·met·ic (hûr met′ik), *adj.* **1.** made airtight by fusion or sealing. **2.** of, pertaining to, or characteristic of occult science, esp. alchemy. **3.** (*cap.*) of or pertaining to Hermes Trismegistus or the writings ascribed to him. Also, **her·met′i·cal.** [< ML *hermētic(us)* of, pertaining to Hermes Trismegistus, equiv. to L *Herm(ēs)* HERMES + *-ticus* -TIC]

her·met·i·cal·ly (hûr met′ik lē), *adv.* so as to be airtight: *hermetically sealed.* [HERMETICAL + -LY]

Her·mi·a (hûr′mē ə), *n.* a girl's given name, form of **Hermione.**

Her·mi·na (hûr′mə nə), *n.* a girl's given name, form of **Hermione.** Also, **Her′mi·ne.**

Her·mi·o·ne (hûr mī′ə nē′), *n.* **1.** *Class. Myth.* the daughter of Menelaus and Helen and the wife of Orestes. **2.** a girl's given name.

Her·mis·ton (hûr′mi stən), *n.* a town in N Oregon. 4402 (1960).

her·mit (hûr′mit), *n.* **1.** a person who has withdrawn to a solitary place for a life of religious seclusion. **2.** any person living in seclusion; recluse. **3.** *Zool.* an animal of solitary habits. **4.** a spiced molasses cooky, often containing raisins or nuts. **5.** *Obs.* a beadsman. [ME *ermite, hermite, heremite* < OF < L *erēmita* < Gk *erēmítēs* one living in a desert, equiv. to *erēm(ia)* desert (deriv. of *erêmos* desolate) + *-itēs* -ITE[1]] **—her·mit′ic, her·mit′i·cal, her′mit·ish,** *adj.* **—her·mit′i·cal·ly,** *adv.* **—her′mit·like′,** *adj.* **—her′mit·ry, her′mit·ship′,** *n.*

her·mit·age (hûr′mi tij), *n.* **1.** the habitation of a hermit. **2.** any secluded place of residence or habitation; retreat. **3.** (*cap.*) a palace in Leningrad: built by Catherine II; now used as an art museum. [ME < OF. See HERMIT, -AGE]

Her·mit·age (hûr′mi tij; *Fr.* er mē tȧzh′), *n.* a full-bodied Rhone wine produced in the area of Tain-l'Ermitage, a town in SE France.

her′mit crab′, any of numerous decapod crustaceans of the genera *Pagurus, Eupagurus,* etc., which protect their soft uncovered abdomen by occupying the castoff shell of a univalve mollusk.

Hermit crab, *Pagurus pollicaris* (Length 3 in.)

Her·mite (hər mēt′; *Fr.* er mēt′), *n.* **Charles** (shȧrl), 1822–1901, French mathematician.

Hermite′ equa′tion, *Math.* a differential equation of the form, $\frac{d^2y}{dx^2} - cx\frac{dy}{dx} + cnx = 0$, where c is any constant and n is any nonnegative integer. [named after C. HERMITE]

Her·mi′tian con′jugate (hər mē′shən), *Math.* adjoint (def. 2). [named after C. HERMITE; see -IAN]

Hermi′tian ma′trix, a matrix, the entries of which are complex numbers, equal to the transpose of the matrix whose entries are the conjugates of the entries of the given matrix. [named after C. HERMITE; see -IAN]

Her′mit King′dom, a name applied to Korea during the period, c1637–c1876, when that country cut off contact with all countries except China.

Hermit of St. Augustine, *Rom. Cath. Ch.* a member of an order of mendicant friars, founded in 1256.

her′mit thrush′, a North American thrush, *Hylocichla guttata,* noted for its beautiful song.

Her·mod (her′mōōd, -mōd), *n. Scand. Myth.* a son of Odin who rode to Hel to negotiate for the return of Balder to Asgard.

Her·mon (hûr′mən), *n.* **Mount,** a mountain in SW Syria, in the Anti-Lebanon range. 9232 ft.

Her·mo′sa Beach′ (hər mō′sə), a city in SW California, near Los Angeles. 16,115 (1960).

hern[1] (hûrn), *n. Archaic.* heron.

hern[2] (hûrn, hûr′ən), *pron. Nonstandard.* hers. [ME *hiren;* by assoc. with *my, mine, thy, thine,* etc.]

her'n (hûrn, hûr′ən), *pron. Nonstandard.* hers. [var. of HERN[2]]

Her·nán·dez (er nän′des), *n.* **Jo·sé** (hô se′), 1834–1886, Argentine poet.

Hern·don (hûrn′dən), *n.* **William Henry,** 1818–91, U.S. law partner and biographer of Abraham Lincoln.

Herne (hûrn), *n.* **1. James A(hern)** (ə hûrn′), 1839–1901, U.S. actor and playwright. **2.** a city in W West Germany, in the Ruhr region. 111,200 (1963).

her·ni·a (hûr′nē ə), *n., pl.* **-ni·as, -ni·ae** (-nē ē′). *Pathol.* the protrusion of an organ or tissue through an opening in its surrounding walls, esp. in the abdominal region. [< L: a rupture] **—her′ni·al,** *adj.* **—her·ni·at·ed** (hûr′nē ā′tid), *adj.*

hernio-, a combining form of **hernia:** *herniotomy.*

her·ni·o·plas·ty (hûr′nē ə plas′tē), *n., pl.* **-ties.** *Surg.* an operation for the cure of a hernia. [HERNIO- + -PLASTY]

her·ni·or·rha·phy (hûr′nē ôr′ə fē, -or′-), *n., pl.* **-phies.** *Surg.* correction of a hernia by a suturing procedure. [HERNIO- + -RRHAPHY]

her·ni·ot·o·my (hûr′nē ot′ə mē), *n., pl.* **-mies.** *Surg.* correction of a hernia by a cutting procedure. Also called **celotomy, kelotomy.** [HERNIO- + -TOMY]

hern·shaw (hûrn′shô), *n. Brit. Dial.* a heron. [var. of HERONSEW]

he·ro (hēr′ō), *n., pl.* **-roes:** for 3 also **-ros. 1.** a man of distinguished courage or ability, admired for his brave deeds and noble qualities. **2.** a person who, in the opinion of others, has heroic qualities or has performed a heroic act and is regarded as a model or ideal: *He was a local hero when he saved the drowning child.* **3.** See **hero sandwich. 4.** the bread or roll used in making a hero sandwich. **5.** the principal male character in a story, play, film, etc. **6.** *Class. Myth.* **a.** a being of godlike prowess and beneficence who often came to be honored as a divinity. **b.** (in the Homeric period) a warrior-chieftain of special strength, courage, or ability. **c.** (in later antiquity) an immortal being; demigod. [back formation from ME *heroes* (pl.) < L *hērōs* < Gk *hḗrōs*] **—he′ro·like′,** *adj.*

He·ro (hēr′ō), *n.* **1.** *Class. Myth.* a priestess of Aphrodite who drowned herself after her lover Leander drowned while swimming the Hellespont to visit her. **2.** (*italics*) *Heros.* **3.** Also, **Heron.** (*Hero of Alexandria*) fl. c1st century A.D., Greek scientist. **4.** a girl's given name.

Her·od (her′əd), *n.* ("*the Great*") 73?–4 B.C., king of Judea 37–4.

Her′od A·grip′pa (ə grip′ə), (*Julius Agrippa*) c10 B.C.–A.D. 44, king of Judea 41–44 (grandson of Herod the Great).

Her′od An′ti·pas (an′ti pas′), died after A.D. 39, ruler of Galilee, A.D. 4–39: ordered the execution of John the Baptist and participated in the trial of Jesus.

He·ro·di·an (hi rō′dē ən), *adj.* **1.** of or pertaining to Herod the Great, his family, or its partisans. *—n.* **2.** a partisan of the house of Herod. [< L *Hērōdiān(us)* of HEROD; see -IAN]

He·ro·di·as (hə rō′dē əs), *n.* the second wife of Herod Antipas and the mother of Salome: she told Salome to ask Herod for the head of John the Baptist.

He·rod·o·tus (hi rod′ə təs), *n.* **1.** 484?–425? B.C., Greek historian. **2.** a crater in the second quadrant of the face of the moon: about 23 miles in diameter.

he·ro·ic (hi rō′ik), *adj.* Also, **he·ro′i·cal. 1.** of, pertaining to, or characteristic of a hero or heroes. **2.** suitable to the character of a hero in size or concept; daring; noble: *a heroic ambition.* **3.** having or displaying the character or attributes of a hero; extraordinarily bold, altruistic, determined, etc.: *a heroic explorer.* **4.** having or involving recourse to boldness, daring, or extreme measures: *Heroic surgery saved his life.* **5.** dealing with or describing the deeds, attributes, etc., of heroes, as in literature. **6.** of, pertaining to, or characteristic of the heroes of antiquity: *heroic mythology.* **7.** used in heroic poetry. Cf. **heroic verse. 8.** resembling heroic poetry in language or style; grandiloquent. **9.** (of style or language) lofty; extravagant; grand. **10.** being larger than life-size: *a statue of heroic proportions.* *—n.* **11.** Usually, **heroics.** See **heroic verse. 12. heroics,** extravagant language or sentiment. [< L *hērōic(us)* < Gk *hērōikós* of, pertaining to a hero. See HERO, -IC] **—he·ro′i·cal·ly,** *adv.* **—he·ro′i·cal·ness, he·ro′ic·ness, he·ro·ic·i·ty** (hēr′ō is′i tē), *n.*
—Syn. 2, 3. dauntless, valiant, valorous, gallant, brave, courageous. **8.** epic. **—Ant. 1–3.** cowardly.

hero′ic age′, 1. one of the five ages of man when, according to Hesiod, gods and demigods performed heroic and glorious deeds. **2.** any period in the history of a nation, esp. in ancient Greece and Rome, when great heroes of legend lived: *Achilles, Agamemnon, and others of Greece's heroic age.*

hero′ic cou′plet, *Pros.* a stanza consisting of two rhyming lines in iambic pentameter, esp. one forming a rhetorical unit and written in an elevated style, as, *Know then thyself, presume not God to scan / The proper study of Mankind is Man.*

hero′ic ten′or, *Music.* heldentenor.

hero′ic verse′, a form of verse adapted to the treatment of heroic or exalted themes: in classical poetry, dactylic hexameter; in English and German, iambic pentameter; and in French, the Alexandrine. An example of heroic verse is *Achilles' wrath, to Greece the direful spring/Of woes unnumbered, heavenly goddess, sing!*

her·o·in (her′ō in), *n. Pharm.* a white, crystalline, narcotic powder, $C_{17}H_{17}(OC_2H_3O)_2ON$, derived from morphine, formerly used as a sedative. The manufacture or importation of heroin is now prohibited by federal law in the U.S. because of the danger of addiction. Also called **diacetylmorphine, diamorphine.** [formerly trademark]

her·o·ine (her′ō in), *n.* **1.** a woman of heroic character; female hero. **2.** the principal female character in a story, play, film, etc. [< L *hērōīnē* < Gk *hērōínē*, fem. of *hḗrōs* HERO; see -INE[2]]

her·o·ism (her′ō iz′əm), *n.* **1.** the qualities or attributes of a hero or heroine: *He showed great heroism in battle.* **2.** heroic conduct; courageous action: *His returning into the burning building was true heroism.* [HERO + -ISM; cf. F *héroïsme*]
—Syn. 1. intrepidity, valor, prowess, gallantry, bravery, courage, daring, fortitude. **—Ant. 1.** cowardice, timidity.

Great blue heron, *Ardea herodias* (Height 4 to 5 ft.; length 4¼ ft.)

Hé·rold (ā rôld′), *n.* **Louis Joseph** (lwē zhō zef′), 1791–1833, French composer.

her·on (her′ən), *n.* any of numerous long-legged, long-necked, usually long-billed birds of the family *Ardeidae,* comprising the true herons, egrets, night herons, bitterns, etc. [ME *heiro(u)n, hero(u)n* < MF *hairon* (F *héron*) < Gmc; cf. OHG *heigir*]

He·ron (hēr′on), *n.* Hero (def. 3).

her·on·ry (her′ən rē), *n., pl.* **-ries.** a place where a colony of herons breeds. [HERON + -RY]

her·on's-bill (her′ənz bil′), *n.* any geraniaceous herb of the genus *Erodium,* having pink, purple, white, or yellow flowers and long, slender fruit. Also called **stork's-bill.**

her·on·sew (her′ən sō′, -sōō′), *n. Brit. Dial.* a heron. Also called **hernshaw.** [ME < MF *heronceau, heroncel,* dim. of *heron* HERON]

He·roph·i·le (hi rof′ə lē′), *n. Class. Myth.* a prophetess of Delphi who foretold the Trojan War.

He·roph·i·lus (hi rof′ə ləs), *n. Class. Myth.* a son of Aphrodite and Poseidon.

He·ros (hâr′ōs), *n.* a comedy (c300 B.C.) by Menander, extant only as a fragment. Also, **Hero.**

he′ro sand′wich, a large sandwich, usually consisting of a loaf of bread or long roll cut in half lengthwise and containing hot foods or a variety of ingredients, as sliced meats, cheeses, onions, tomatoes, and pickles. Also called **poor boy, submarine.**

He′ro's for′mula (hēr′ōz), *Geom.* the formula for the area of a triangle when the sides are given: for a triangle with sides a, b, and c, the area is equal to $\sqrt{s(s-a)(s-b)(s-c)}$ where s is equal to one half the perimeter of the triangle. [named after HERO of Alexandria]

he′ro wor′ship, 1. a profound reverence for great men or their memory. **2.** extravagant or excessive admiration for a personal hero.

he·ro-wor·ship (hēr′ō wûr′ship), *v.t.,* **-shiped, -shiping** or (*esp. Brit.*) **-shipped, -ship·ping.** to feel or express hero worship for: *My daughter hero-worships that actor.* **—he′ro-wor′ship·er;** *esp. Brit.,* **he′ro-wor′ship·per,** *n.*

herp., herpetology. Also, **herpet.**

her·pan·gi·na (hûr′pan jī′nə, hər pan′jə nə), *n. Pathol.* an infectious disease, esp. of children, characterized by a sudden occurrence of fever, loss of appetite, and throat ulcerations, caused by a Coxsackie virus. [HERP(ES) + ANGINA]

her·pes (hûr′pēz), *n. Pathol.* any of certain inflammatory conditions of the skin or mucous membrane, characterized by clusters of vesicles that tend to spread. [< NL: cutaneous eruption < Gk *hérpēs,* lit., a creeping, cf. *hérpein* to creep, spread] **—her·pet·ic** (hər pet′ik), *adj.*

her′pes fa·ci·a′lis (fā′shē ā′lis), *Pathol.* a vesicular eruption of the face, usually occurring on the lips, often accompanying a cold or febrile condition; herpes simplex. Also called **her′pes la·bi·a′lis** (lā′bē ā′lis). [< NL: lit., facial herpes]

her′pes sim′plex (sim′pleks), *Pathol.* an acute infection often accompanying a febrile condition, caused by a virus, characterized by the formation of groups of vesicles on the skin or mucous membrane. [< NL: lit., simple herpes]

her′pes zos′ter (zos′tər), *Pathol.* shingles. [< NL: lit., belt herpes]

her·pe·tol·o·gy (hûr′pi tol′ə jē), *n.* the branch of zoology dealing with reptiles and amphibians. [< Gk *herpetó(n)* a creeping thing (cf. *hérpein* to creep) + -LOGY] —**her·pe·to·log·ic** (hûr′pi tᵊloj′ik), **her′pe·to·log′i·cal,** *adj.* —**her′pe·to·log′i·cal·ly,** *adv.* —**her′pe·tol′o·gist,** *n.*

her·que·in (hûr′kyo͞o in,-kwēn), *n.* *Pharm.* a yellowish-brown, crystalline, slightly water-soluble, antibiotic produced by the action of *Penicillium herquei* on a suitable substrate. [< NL (*Penicillium*) *herquei* + -IN²]

Herr (heʀ), *n., pl.* **Her·ren** (heʀ′ən). the conventional German title of respect and term of address for a man, corresponding to *Mr.* or in direct address to *sir.* [< G]

Her·ren·volk (heʀ′ən fôlk′), *n., pl.* **-völ·ker** (-fœl′kəʀ). *German.* See **master race.**

Her·re·ra (eʀ ʀe′ʀä), *n.* **Fran·cis·co de** (frän thēs′kô the), ("*el Viejo*"), 1576–1656, Spanish painter and etcher.

Her·rick (her′ik), *n.* **1. Robert,** 1591–1674, English poet. **2. Robert,** 1868–1938, U.S. novelist.

Her·rin (her′in), *n.* a town in S Illinois. 9474 (1960).

her·ring (her′ing), *n., pl.* (*esp. collectively*) **-ring,** (*esp. referring to two or more kinds or species*) **-rings. 1.** an important food fish, *Clupea harengus,* found in enormous shoals in the North Atlantic. **2.** a similar fish, *Clupea pallasii,* of the North Pacific. **3.** any fish of the family *Clupeidae,* including these species and the shads, sardines, etc. **4.** any of various fishes resembling the herring but of unrelated families. [ME *hering,* OE *hǣring;* c. G *Häring*]

Herringbone

her·ring·bone (her′ing bōn′), *n.* **1.** a pattern consisting of adjoining vertical rows of slanting lines, any two contiguous lines forming either a V or an inverted V, used in masonry, textiles, embroidery, etc. **2.** *Skiing.* a method of going up a slope in which a skier sets the skis generally in the form of a V, and, with his weight on the inside edges, advances the skis by turns using the poles from behind for push and support. —*adj.* **3.** having or resembling herringbone: *herringbone tweed.* [HERRING + BONE¹]

her′ringbone bond′, a brickwork bond in which the exposed brickwork is bonded to the heart of the wall by concealed courses of bricks laid diagonally to the faces of the wall in a herringbone pattern, with the end of each brick butting against the side of the adjoining brick; a form of raking bond.

her′ringbone bridg′ing. See **cross bridging.** Also called **her′ringbone strut′ting.**

her′ringbone gear′, a helical gear having teeth that lie on the pitch cylinder in a V-shaped form so that one half of each tooth is on a right-handed helix and the other half on a left-handed helix. Also called **double-helical gear.**

Herringbone gears

her′ringbone stitch′, a catch stitch used as ornament in embroidery.

her′ring buss′ (bus), a fishing vessel of the 17th century, having two or three masts and a wide beam.

her′ring gull′, a common, large gull, *Larus argentatus,* of the Northern Hemisphere. See illus. under **gull.**

Her·ri·ot (e ʀyō′), *n.* **É·douard** (ā dwaʀ′), 1872–1957, French statesman, political leader, and author.

Herr·mann (hûr′mən), *n.* **Bernard,** born 1911, U.S. conductor and composer.

Herrn·hut·er (hârn′ho͞o′tər, hern′-), *n.* Moravian (def. 4). [< G, equiv. to *Herrnhut,* lit., Lord's safekeeping, a town near Dresden, Germany + *-er* -ER¹]

her·ry (her′ē), *v.t., v.i.,* **-ried, -ry·ing.** *Scot.* harry. —**her′ry·ment,** *n.*

hers (hûrz), *pron.* **1.** a form of the possessive case of **she** used as a predicate adjective: *The red umbrella is hers. Are you a friend of hers?* **2.** that or those belonging to her: *Hers is the biggest aspidistra on the block. Hers are the yellow ones.* [ME *hirs,* equiv. to *hire* HER + *-s* 's¹]

Her·schel (hûr′shəl, her′-; *for 4 also Yiddish* heʀ′shəl), *n.* **1. Sir John Frederick William,** 1792–1871, English astronomer. **2.** his father, **Sir William** (Friedrich Wilhelm Herschel), 1738–1822, English astronomer, born in Germany. **3.** a walled plain in the third quadrant of the face of the moon: about 28 miles in diameter. **4.** Also, **Her′shel.** a boy's given name.

Her·se (hûr′sē), *n.* *Class. Myth.* a daughter of Cecrops who was the mother, by Hermes, of Cephalus and Ceryx.

her·self (hər self′), *pron.* **1.** an emphatic appositive of *her* or *she: She herself wrote the letter.* **2.** a reflexive form of *her: She supports herself.* **3.** (used as the object of a preposition or as the direct or indirect object of a verb): *She gave herself a facial massage. He asked her for a picture of herself.* **4.** her normal or customary self: *After a few weeks of rest, she will be herself again.* [ME *hire-selfe,* OE *hire-self.* See HER, SELF]

—**Usage.** See **myself.**

Her·sey (hûr′sē, -zē), *n.* **John Richard,** born 1914, U.S. journalist, novelist, and educator.

Hersh (hûrsh), *n.* a boy's given name, form of **Herschel.**

Her·shey (hûr′shē), *n.* a town in central Pennsylvania. 6851 (1960).

Her·sil·i·a (hər sil′ē ə), *n.* *Rom. Legend.* a Sabine woman taken as a wife by Romulus.

Her·sko·witz (hûr′skə vits), *n.* **Melville (Jean),** 1895–1963, American anthropologist.

Her·ta (hûr′tə), *n.* a girl's given name, form of **Hertha.**

Her·ter (hûr′tər), *n.* **Christian Archibald,** 1895–1966 U.S. politician: Secretary of State 1959–61.

Hert·ford (här′fərd, härt′fərd), *n.* **1.** a city in and the county seat of Hertfordshire, in SE England. 15,734 (1961). **2.** Hertfordshire.

Hert·ford·shire ((här′fərd shēr′, -shər, härt′-), *n.* a county in SE England. 832,088 (1961); 632 sq. mi. *Co. seat:* Hertford. Also called **Hertford, Herts** (härts, hûrts).

Her·tha (hûr′thə), *n.* a girl's given name.

Her·to·gen·bosch, 's (*Du.* seʀ′tō кнən bôs′). See **'s Hertogenbosch.**

hertz (hûrts), *n., pl.* **hertz, hertz·es.** a unit of frequency, equal to one cycle per second. *Abbr.:* Hz [named after H. R. HERTZ]

Hertz (hûrts; *Ger.* heʀts), *n.* **1. Gu·stav** (go͝os′täf), born 1887, German physicist: Nobel prize 1925. **2. Hein·rich Ru·dolph** (hīn′ʀiкн ʀo͞o′dôlf), 1857–94, German physicist. —**Hertz·i·an** (heʀt′sē ən), *adj.*

Hertz′ effect′, *Physics.* the effect of ultraviolet radiation in lowering the sparking voltage across a spark gap: an example of photoelectric effect. [named after H. R. HERTZ]

Hertz′ian wave′, *Physics.* an electromagnetic wave produced by oscillations in an electric circuit, as a radio or radar wave: first investigated by Hertz.

Her·tzog (*Du.* heʀ′tsôкн), *n.* **James Barry Mun·nik** (mœn′ək), South African statesman and general: prime minister 1924–39.

Her·vey (hûr′vē), *n.* a boy's given name. Also, **Harvey.**

Her·ze·go·vi·na (her′tsə gō vē′nə), *n.* a former Turkish province in S Europe: a part of Austria-Hungary 1878–1914; now part of Bosnia and Herzegovina. Serbo-Croatian, **Hercegovina.** —**Her′ze·go·vi′ni·an,** *adj., n.*

Her·zl (heʀ′tsəl), *n.* **The·o·dor** (tā′ô dōʀ′), 1860–1904, Hungarian journalist: founder of the modern Zionist movement.

he's (hēz; *unstressed* ēz), contraction of *he is* or *he has.*

Hesh·van (hesh′vən, кнesh′-; *Heb.* кнesh vän′), *n.* the second month of the Jewish calendar. Also, **Cheshvan.** Also called **Marheshvan, Marcheshvan.** Cf. **Jewish calendar.** [< Heb *(mar) heshwān*]

He·si·od (hē′sē əd, hes′ē-), *n.* fl. 8th century B.C., Greek poet. —**He·si·od·ic** (hē′sē od′ik, hes′ē-), *adj.*

He·si·o·dus (hes′ē ō′dəs), *n.* a crater in the third quadrant of the face of the moon: about 28 miles in diameter.

He·si·o·ne (hi sī′ə nē′), *n.* *Class. Myth.* daughter of Laomedon, king of Troy, rescued from a sea monster by Hercules.

hes·i·tan·cy (hez′i tᵊn sē), *n., pl.* **-cies.** hesitation; indecision or disinclination. Also, **hes′i·tance.** [< LL *haesitantia* a stammering. See HESITANT, -ANCY]

hes·i·tant (hez′i tᵊnt), *adj.* **1.** hesitating; undecided or disinclined. **2.** lacking readiness of speech. [< L *haesitant-* (s. of *haesitāns,* prp. of *haesitāre*) stammering, hesitating, equiv. to *haes(us)* stuck, held fast (ptp. of *haerēre*) + *-it-* intensive and freq. suffix + *-ant-* -ANT] —**hes′i·tant·ly,** *adv.*

hes·i·tate (hez′i tāt′), *v.i.,* **-tat·ed, -tat·ing. 1.** to be reluctant or wait to act because of doubt, indecision, or disinclination: *She hesitated to take the job.* **2.** to have scruples or doubts; be unwilling: *He hesitated to break the law.* **3.** to pause: *I hesitated before reciting the next line.* **4.** to falter in speech; stammer: *Embarrassment caused the speaker to hesitate.* [< L *haesitāt(us)* stuck fast, held in place, ptp. of *haesitāre.* See HESITANT, -ATE¹] —**hes′i·tat′er, hes′i·ta′tor,** *n.* —**hes′i·tat′ing·ly,** *adv.*

—**Syn. 1.** waver, vacillate, falter. **3.** demur, delay. —**Ant. 1.** decide. **3.** hasten.

hes·i·ta·tion (hez′i tā′shən), *n.* **1.** act of hesitating; a delay due to uncertainty of mind: *His hesitation cost him the championship.* **2.** a state of doubt. **3.** a halting or faltering in speech. [< L *haesitātiōn-* (s. of *haesitātiō*) a stammering, hesitating. See HESITATE, -ION]

—**Syn. 1.** hesitancy, indecision, irresolution, vacillation. **3.** stammer.

hes′ita′tion waltz′, a waltz based on a step that consists of a pause and glide.

hes·i·ta·tive (hez′i tā′tiv), *adj.* characterized by hesitation; hesitating. [HESITATE + -IVE] —**hes′i·ta′tive·ly,** *adv.*

Hes·per (hes′pər), *n.* **1.** Hesperus. **2.** a girl's given name.

Hes·per·a (hes′pər ə), *n.* *Class. Myth.* a daughter of Erebus and Nyx.

Hes·per·e (hes′pə rē), *n.* *Class. Myth.* one of the Hesperides.

Hes·pe·ri·an (he spēr′ē ən), *adj.* **1.** western; occidental. **2.** of or pertaining to the Hesperides. —*n.* **3.** a native or inhabitant of a western land. [< L *Hesperi(us)* of, toward the West (< Gk *hespérios* western, deriv. of *hésperos* evening) + -AN]

Hes·per·i·des (he sper′i dēz′), *n.* **1.** *Class. Myth.* **a.** (*construed as pl.*) nymphs, variously given as three to seven in number, who guarded with the dragon Ladon the golden apples that were the wedding gift of Gaea to Hera. **b.** (*construed as sing.*) the garden where the golden apples were grown. **c.** (*construed as pl.*) See **Islands of the Blessed. 2.** (*italics.*) (*construed as pl.*) a collection of poems (1648) by Robert Herrick. —**Hes·per·id·i·an** (hes′pə rid′ē ən), *adj.*

hes·per·i·din (he sper′i din), *n.* *Biochem.* a crystallizable, bioflavinoid glycoside, $C_{28}H_{34}O_{15}$, occurring in most citrus fruits, esp. in the spongy envelope of oranges and lemons. [< NL; see HESPERIDIUM, -IN²]

hes·per·id·i·um (hes′pə rid′ē əm), *n., pl.* **-per·id·i·a** (-pə rid′ē ə). *Bot.* the fruit of a citrus plant, as an orange. [< NL; see HESPERIDES, -IUM] —**hes·per·i·date** (he sper′i dāt′), **hes′per·id′e·ous,** *adj.*

hes·per·i·nos (es pe′ʀē nôs′; *Eng.* hes′pər ə nos′, hes′pər ə nos′), *n.* *Gk. Orth. Ch.* vespers (def. 1). [< LGk, Gk (adj.): pertaining to evening, equiv. to *hésper(os),* *hespér(a)* evening + *-inos* -INE¹]

Hes·per·is (hes′pər is), *n.* *Class. Myth.* a daughter of Hesperus sometimes believed to be the mother, by Atlas, of the Hesperides.

Hes·per·or·nis (hes′pə rôr′nis), *n.* an extinct genus of toothed aquatic birds from the Cretaceous period of Kansas, having the rear legs modified for swimming, reaching a length of more than four feet. [< NL < Gk *Hésper(os)* HESPERUS + *órnis* bird]

Hes·per·us (hes′pər əs), *n.* an evening star, esp. Venus. Also, **Hesper.** [< L < Gk *hésperos* evening, western]

Hess (hes), *n.* **1. Dame Myra,** 1890–1965, English pianist. **2. Victor Francis,** 1883–1964, U.S. physicist, born in Austria: Nobel prize 1936. **3. Walter Rudolf,** 1881–1973, Swiss physiologist: Nobel prize for medicine 1949. **4. (Wal·ther Rich·ard) Ru·dolf** (väl′təʀ ʀiкн′-ärt ʀo͞o′dôlf), 1894–1987, German leader in the Nazi party.

Hes·se (hes′ə *for 1;* hes *for 2*), *n.* **1. Her·mann** (heʀ′-män), 1877–1962, German novelist and poet: Nobel prize 1946. **2.** German, **Hes·sen** (hes′ən). a state in E West Germany. 4,973,000 (1963); 8150 sq. mi. *Cap.:* Wiesbaden.

Hes′sel·man en′gine (hes′əl mən), a low-compression oil engine requiring a spark for ignition.

Hesse-Nas·sau (hes′nas′ô), *n.* a former state in W Germany, now part of Hesse. German, **Hes·sen-Nassau** (hes′ən näs′ou).

Hes·sian (hesh′ən), *adj.* **1.** of or pertaining to Hesse or its inhabitants. —*n.* **2.** a native or inhabitant of Hesse. **3.** a Hessian mercenary used by England during the American Revolution. **4.** a hireling or ruffian. **5.** (*l.c.*) burlap. **6.** Also called **Hes′sian and′iron.** (in the U.S.) an andiron having as an upright the figure of a Hessian soldier of the Revolutionary War. [HESSE, Germany + -IAN]

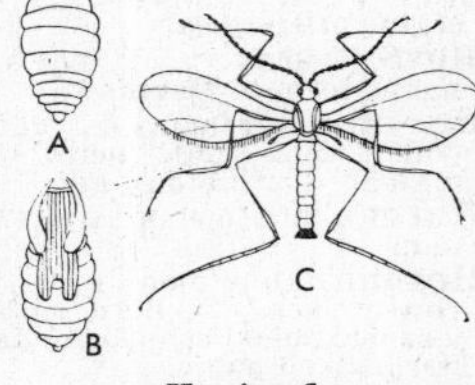

Hessian fly
A, Larva; B, Pupa;
C, Adult (male)

Hes′sian boots′, knee-high tasseled boots, fashionable in England during the early 19th century.

Hes′sian fly′, a small dipterous insect, *Phytophaga destructor,* the larvae of which feed on the stems of wheat and other grasses.

hess·ite (hes′īt), *n.* a rare mineral, silver telluride, Ag_2Te, found in silver ores: sometimes contains gold. [named after G.H. *Hess,* 19th-century Swiss chemist; see -ITE¹]

hes·so·nite (hes′ə nīt′), *n.* *Mineral.* essonite. [< Gk *hḗsson-* (s. of *hḗssōn*) less, inferior + -ITE¹]

hest (hest), *n.* *Archaic.* behest. [ME *hest(e),* OE *hǣs,* akin to *hātan* to bid]

Hes·ter (hes′tər), *n.* a girl's given name, form of **Esther.**

Hes·ti·a (hes′tē ə), *n.* the ancient Greek goddess of the hearth, identified by the Romans with Vesta.

Hes·ton and I·sle·worth (hes′tən; ī′zəl wûrth′), a city in SE England, near London. 102,897 (1961).

Hes·y·chast (hes′ə kast′), *n.* one of a sect of mystics which originated in the 14th century among the monks on Mt. Athos, Greece. [< ML *hesychast(a)* < Gk *hēsychast(ḗs)* a recluse (deriv. of *hēsychā́zein* to be quiet, be still), equiv. to *hēsych(os)* quiet, still + *-a-* thematic vowel + *-tēs* one who] —**Hes′y·chast′ic,** *adj.*

he·tae·ra (hi tēr′ə), *n., pl.* **-tae·rae** (-tēr′ē). **1.** a female paramour or concubine, esp. in ancient Greece. **2.** any woman who uses her beauty and charm to obtain wealth or social position. Also, **hetaira.** [< Gk *hetaíra*] —**he·tae′ric,** *adj.*

he·tae·rism (hi tēr′iz əm), *n.* **1.** concubinage. **2.** a social system in which the women are considered common property. Also, **he·tai·rism** (hi tīᵊr′iz əm). [HETAER(A) + -ISM] —**he·tae′rist, he·tai·rist** (hi tīᵊr′ist), *n.* —**het·ae·ris·tic** (het′ə ris′tik), **het·ai·ris·tic** (het′ī ris′tik), *adj.*

he·tai·ra (hi tīᵊr′ə), *n., pl.* **-tai·rai** (-tī′rī). hetaera. —**he·tai′ric,** *adj.*

het·er·o (het′ə rō′), *adj.* *Chem.* of or pertaining to an atom other than carbon, particularly in a cyclic compound. [independent use of HETERO-]

hetero-, a learned borrowing from Greek meaning "different," "other," used in the formation of compound words: *heterocyclic.* Also, *esp. before a vowel,* **heter-.** [comb. form of Gk *héteros* the other of two, other, different]

het·er·o·ar·o·mat·ic (het′ər ō-ar′ə mat′ik), *n.* *Chem.* a heterocyclic aromatic compound. [HETERO- + AROMATIC]

het·er·o·aux·in (het′ə rō ôk′sin), *n.* *Biochem.* See **indoleacetic acid.** [HETERO- + AUXIN]

het·er·o·cer·cal (het′ər ə sûr′kəl), *adj.* *Ichthyol.* **1.** having an unequally divided tail or caudal fin, the spinal column usually running into a much larger upper lobe. **2.** noting such a tail or caudal fin. Cf. **homocercal.** [HETERO- + Gk *kérk(os)* a tail + -AL¹] —**het·er·o·cer·cal·i·ty** (het′ər ō sər kal′i tē), *n.*

Heterocercal tail

het·er·o·chro·mat·ic (het′ər ə krō mat′ik, -ō krə-), *adj.* **1.** of, having, or pertaining to more than one color. **2.** having a pattern of mixed colors. **3.** *Genetics.* of or pertaining to heterochromatin. Also, **heterochrome.** [HETERO- + CHROMATIC] —**het·er·o·chro·ma·tism** (het′ər ə krō′mə tiz′əm), *n.*

het·er·o·chro·ma·tin (het′ər ə krō′mə tin), *n.* *Genetics.* the dense, highly stainable part of a chromosome. Cf. **euchromatin.** [HETERO- + CHROMATIN]

het·er·o·chrome (het′ər ə krōm′), *adj.* heterochromatic. [HETERO- + -CHROME]

het·er·o·chro·mo·some (het′ər ə krō′mə sōm′), *n.* *Genetics.* See **sex chromosome.** [HETERO- + CHROMOSOME]

het·er·o·chro·mous (het′ər ə krō′məs), *adj.* of different colors. [HETERO- + CHROMOUS]

het·er·och·tho·nous (het′ə rok′thə nəs), *adj.* not indigenous; foreign (opposed to *autochthonous*): *heterochthonous flora and fauna.* [HETERO- + Gk *chthṓn* the earth, land, country + -OUS]

het·er·o·clite (het′ər ə klīt′), *adj.* Also, **het·er·o·clit·ic** (het′ər ə klit′ik), **het′er·o·clit′i·cal. 1.** irregular or abnormal; anomalous. **2.** *Gram.* irregular in inflection; having inflected forms belonging to more than one class of stems. —*n.* **3.** a person or thing that deviates from the ordinary rule or form. **4.** *Gram.* a heteroclite word. [< MF < LL *heteroclit(us)* < Gk *heteróklitos*, equiv. to *hetero-* HETERO- + *-klitos*, verbid of *klínein* to bend, inflect]

het·er·o·cy·clic (het′ər ə sī′klik, -sik′lik), *adj. Chem.* **1.** of or pertaining to the branch of chemistry dealing with cyclic compounds in which at least one of the ring members is not a carbon atom. **2.** noting such compounds, as ethylene oxide, $H_2C(O)CH_2$. [HETERO- + CYCLIC] —**het·er·o·cy·cle** (het′ər ə sī′kəl), *n.*

het·er·o·dac·ty·lous (het′ə rō dak′tᵊləs), *adj. Ornith.* having the first and fourth toes directed backward, and the second and third forward, as in trogons. Also, **het′er·o·dac′tyl.** [HETERO- + Gk *-daktylos*; see DACTYL-, -OUS]

het·er·o·dox (het′ər ə doks′), *adj.* **1.** not in accordance with established or accepted doctrines or opinions, esp. in theology. **2.** holding unorthodox doctrines or opinions. [< Gk *heteródox(os)* of another opinion, equiv. to *hetero-* HETERO- + *dóx(a)* an opinion (cf. *dokein* to think, suppose) + *-os* adj. suffix] —**het′er·o·dox′ly,** *adv.*

het·er·o·dox·y (het′ər ə dok′sē), *n., pl.* **-dox·ies. 1.** heterodox state or quality. **2.** a heterodox opinion, view, etc. [< Gk *heterodoxía*. See HETERODOX, -Y[3]]

het·er·o·dyne (het′ər ə dīn′), *adj., v.,* **-dyned, -dyn·ing.** *Radio.* —*adj.* **1.** noting or pertaining to a method of changing the frequency of an incoming radio signal by adding it to a signal generated within the receiver to produce fluctuations or beats of a frequency equal to the difference between the two signals. —*v.i.* **2.** to produce a heterodyne effect. —*v.t.* **3.** to mix (a frequency) with a different frequency so as to achieve a heterodyne effect. [HETERO- + DYNE]

het·er·oe·cious (het′ə rē′shəs), *adj. Biol.* pertaining to or characterized by heteroecism. [HETER- + Gk *oikí(a)* a house, dwelling, abode + -OUS] —**het′er·oe′cious·ly,** *adv.*

het·er·oe·cism (het′ə rē′siz əm), *n. Biol.* the development of different stages of a parasitic species on different host plants, as in fungi. [HETER- + Gk *oik(ía)* a house + -ISM]

het·er·o·fer·ment·a·tive (het′ə rō fər men′tə tiv), *adj. Biochem.* producing a fermentation that results in two or more end products. Cf. **homofermentative.** [HETERO- + FERMENTATIVE]

het·er·o·gam·ete (het′ər ə gam′ēt, -ə rō gə mēt′), *n. Biol.* either of a pair of conjugating gametes differing in form, size, structure, or sex. Cf. **isogamete.** [HETERO- + GAMETE]

het·er·og·a·mous (het′ə rog′ə məs), *adj.* **1.** *Biol.* having unlike gametes, or reproducing by the union of such gametes (opposed to *isogamous*). **2.** *Bot.* having flowers or florets of two sexually different kinds (opposed to *homogamous*). [HETERO- + -GAMOUS]

het·er·og·a·my (het′ə rog′ə mē), *n.* heterogamous state. [HETERO- + -GAMY]

het·er·o·ge·ne·i·ty (het′ə rō jə nē′i tē), *n.* the quality or state of being heterogeneous; composition from dissimilar parts; disparateness. [< ML *heterogeneitās*. See HETEROGENEOUS, -ITY]

het·er·o·ge·ne·ous (het′ər ə jē′nē əs, -jēn′yəs), *adj.* **1.** different in kind; unlike; incongruous. **2.** composed of parts of different kinds; having widely dissimilar elements or constituents; not homogeneous: *The party was attended by a heterogeneous group of artists, businessmen, and social climbers.* [< ML *heterogene(us)* < Gk *heterogenēs*. See HETERO-, GENE, -OUS] —**het′er·o·ge′ne·ous·ly,** *adv.* —**het′er·o·ge′ne·ous·ness,** *n.*

het·er·o·gen·e·sis (het′ər ə jen′i sis), *n. Biol.* **1.** alternation of generations, esp. the alternation of parthenogenetic and sexual generations. **2.** abiogenesis. [HETERO- + -GENESIS]

het·er·o·ge·net·ic (het′ə rō jə net′ik), *adj.* of, pertaining to, or characterized by heterogenesis. Also, **het·er·o·gen·ic** (het′ər ə jen′ik). [HETERO- + -GENETIC] —**het′er·o·ge·net′i·cal·ly,** *adv.*

het·er·og·e·nous (het′ə roj′ə nəs), *adj. Biol., Pathol.* having its source or origin outside the organism; having a foreign origin. [HETERO- + -GENOUS]

het·er·og·e·ny (het′ə roj′ə nē), *n. Biol.* heterogenesis (def. 1). [HETERO- + -GENY]

het·er·og·o·nous (het′ə rog′ə nəs), *adj.* **1.** *Bot.* of or pertaining to monoclinous flowers of two or more kinds occurring on different individuals of the same species, the kinds differing in the relative length of stamens and pistils (opposed to *homogonous*). **2.** heterogynous. **3.** of, pertaining to, or characterized by heterogony. Also, **het·er·o·gon·ic** (het′ər ə gon′ik). [HETERO- + Gk *gón(os)* race, descent, birth + -OUS] —**het′er·og′o·nous·ly,** *adv.*

het·er·og·o·ny (het′ə rog′ə nē), *n. Biol.* **1.** the alternation of dioecious and hermaphroditic individuals in successive generations, as in certain nematodes. **2.** the alternation of parthenogenetic and sexual generations. [HETERO- + -GONY]

het·er·o·graft (het′ər ə graft′, -gräft′), *n. Surg.* a tissue or organ obtained from a member of one species and transplanted by grafting to a member of another species. Cf. **autograft, homograft.** [HETERO- + GRAFT[1]]

het·er·og·ra·phy (het′ə rog′rə fē), *n.* **1.** spelling different from that in current use. **2.** the use of the same letter or combination of letters to represent different sounds, as, in English, the use of *s* in *sit* and *easy.* [HETERO- + -GRAPHY] —**het·er·o·graph·ic** (het′ər ə graf′ik), **het′er·o·graph′i·cal,** *adj.*

het·er·og·y·nous (het′ə roj′ə nəs), *adj. Zool.* having females of two different kinds, one sexual and the other abortive or neuter, as ants. [HETERO- + -GYNOUS]

het·er·o·ki·ne·sia (het′ə rō ki nē′zhə, -zhē ə, -zē ə, -kī-), *n. Med.* the execution of movements the reverse of those one is told to make. [HETERO- + Gk *kínēs(is)* motion (see KINETIC) + -IA]

het·er·o·lec·i·thal (het′ər ə les′ə thəl), *adj. Embryol.* having an unequal distribution of yolk, as certain eggs or ova. [HETERO- + LECITHAL]

het·er·ol·o·gous (het′ə rol′ə gəs), *adj.* **1.** *Biol.* of different origin; pertaining to heterology. **2.** *Med.* consisting of dissimilar tissue, as that of another species or that of a tumor. [HETERO- + -LOGOUS]

het·er·ol·o·gy (het′ə rol′ə jē), *n.* **1.** *Biol.* the lack of correspondence of apparently similar organic structures as the result of unlike origins of constituent parts. **2.** *Pathol.* abnormality; structural difference from a type or normal standard. [HETERO- + -LOGY]

het·er·ol·y·sis (het′ə rol′i sis), *n. Biochem.* dissolution of the cells of one organism by the lysins of another. [HETERO- + -LYSIS] —**het·er·o·lyt·ic** (het′ər ə lit′ik), *adj.*

het·er·om·er·ous (het′ə rom′ər əs), *adj.* having or consisting of parts that differ in quality, number of elements, or the like: *a heteromerous flower.* [HETERO- + -MEROUS]

het·er·o·mor·phic (het′ər ə môr′fik), *adj.* **1.** *Biol.* dissimilar in shape, structure, or magnitude. **2.** *Entomol.* undergoing complete metamorphosis; possessing varying forms. [HETERO- + -MORPHIC] —**het′er·o·mor′phism, het′er·o·mor′phy,** *n.*

het·er·on·o·mous (het′ə ron′ə məs), *adj.* **1.** subject to or involving different laws. **2.** pertaining to or characterized by heteronomy. **3.** *Biol.* subject to different laws of growth or specialization. [HETERONOM(Y) + -OUS] —**het′er·on′o·mous·ly,** *adv.*

het·er·on·o·my (het′ə ron′ə mē), *n.* the condition of being under the rule or domination of another. [HETERO- + -NOMY]

het·er·o·nym (het′ər ə nim′), *n.* a word having a different sound and meaning from another, but the same spelling, as *lead* (to conduct) and *lead* (a metal). [< LGk *heterṓnym(os)*. See HETERO-, -ONYM]

het·er·on·y·mous (het′ə ron′ə məs), *adj.* **1.** of, pertaining to, or characteristic of a heteronym. **2.** having different names, as a pair of correlatives: *Father and son are heteronymous relatives.* [< LGk *heterṓnymos* having a different name. See HETERONYM, -OUS] —**het′er·on′y·mous·ly,** *adv.*

Het·er·o·ou·si·an (het′ər ō o͞o′sē ən, -ou′sē ən), *Eccles.* —*n.* **1.** a person who believes the Father and the Son to be unlike in substance or essence; an Arian (opposed to *Homoousian*). —*adj.* **2.** of or pertaining to the Heteroousians or their doctrine. Also, **Het′er·o·ü′si·an.** [< LGk *heteroousi(os)* (Gk *hetero-* HETERO- + *ousí(a)* nature, essence) + -AN]

het·er·o·phil (het′ər ə fil), *adj.* **1.** Also, **het′er·o·phil′ic.** *Immunol.* (of an antibody) having an affinity for an antigen other than its specific antigen. —*n.* **2.** *Zool., Anat.* a neutrophil. Also, **het·er·o·phile** (het′ər ə fīl′). [HETERO- + -PHIL]

het·er·oph·o·ny (het′ə rof′ə nē), *n. Music.* the simultaneous performance of the same melodic line, with slight individual variations, by two or more performers. [HETERO- + -PHONY] —**het·er·o·phon·ic** (het′ər ə fon′ik), *adj.*

het·er·o·pho·ri·a (het′ər ə fôr′ē ə, -fōr′-), *n. Ophthalm.* a latent strabismus of one or both eyes. [HETERO- + Gk *-phoria* a carrying, equiv. to *-phor(es)* -PHOROUS + *-ia* n. suffix] —**het·er·o·phor·ic** (het′ər ə fôr′ik, -for′-), *adj.*

het·er·o·phyl·lous (het′ər ə fil′əs), *adj. Bot.* having different kinds of leaves on the same plant. [HETERO- + -PHYLLOUS] —**het′er·o·phyl′ly,** *n.*

het·er·o·plas·ty (het′ər ə plas′tē), *n. Surg.* the repair of lesions with tissue from another individual or species. [HETERO- + -PLASTY] —**het′er·o·plas′tic,** *adj.*

het·er·o·po·lar (het′ər ə pō′lər), *adj. Chem.* polar (def. 3). [HETERO- + POLAR] —**het·er·o·po·lar·i·ty** (het′ər ō pō lar′i tē), *n.*

het·er·op·ter·ous (het′ə rop′tər əs), *adj.* belonging or pertaining to the *Heteroptera*, in some classifications a suborder of hemipterous insects comprising the true bugs. [< NL *Heteropter(a)* name of the class. See HETERO-, -PTEROUS]

het·er·op·tics (het′ə rop′tiks), *n.* (*construed as sing.*) incorrect or perverted perception of what is seen; hallucinatory vision. [HETER- + OPTICS]

het·er·o·sex·u·al (het′ər ə sek′sho͞o əl), *adj.* **1.** *Biol.* pertaining to the opposite sex or to both sexes. **2.** of, pertaining to, or exhibiting heterosexuality. —*n.* **3.** a heterosexual person. [HETERO- + SEXUAL]

het·er·o·sex·u·al·i·ty (het′ər ə sek′sho͞o al′i tē), *n.* sexual feeling or behavior directed toward a person or persons of the opposite sex. [HETERO- + SEXUALITY]

het·er·o·sis (het′ə rō′sis), *n. Genetics.* the increase in growth, size, fecundity, function, yield, or other characters in hybrids over those of the parents. Also called **hybrid vigor.** [< LGk *hetérōsis* an alteration. See HETERO-, -SIS]

het·er·o·sphere (het′ər ə sfēr′), *n. Meteorol. Rare.* the upper region of the atmosphere, starting approximately 50 miles above sea level, in which there are variations in the composition of chemical and atmospheric elements. Cf. **homosphere.** [HETERO- + -SPHERE]

het·er·os·por·ous (het′ə ros′pər əs, het′ər ə spôr′əs, -spōr′-), *adj. Bot.* having more than one kind of spore. [HETERO- + -SPOROUS]

het·er·os·po·ry (het′ə ros′pə rē), *n. Bot.* the production of both microspores and megaspores. [HETERO- + -SPORE + -Y[3]]

het·er·os·tra·can (het′ə ros′trə kən), *n. Paleontol.* any of several ostracoderms of the order *Heterostraci*, from the Silurian and Devonian periods, having the anterior part of the body enclosed in bony plates. [< NL *Heterostrac(i)* (pl.) name of the order, equiv. to *heter-* HETERO- + Gk *ostrak(on)* shell + -AN]

het·er·o·styled (het′ə rō stīld′), *adj.* (of a plant) having styles of different forms or lengths in the flowers. Also, **het′er·o·sty′lous.** [HETERO- + STYLED]

het·er·o·tac·tic (het′ər ə tak′tik), *adj.* of, pertaining to, or characterized by heterotaxis. Also, **het′er·o·tac′tous, het·er·o·tax·ic** (het′ər ə tak′sik). [HETERO- + Gk *takt(ós)* fixed, ordered, arranged (cf. *tássein* to arrange) + -IC]

het·er·o·tax·is (het′ər ə tak′sis), *n.* abnormal or irregular arrangement, as of parts of the body, geological strata, etc. Also, **het·er·o·tax·i·a** (het′ər ə tak′sē ə), **het′er·o·tax′y.** [HETERO- + -TAXIS]

het·er·o·tel·ic (het′ər ə tel′ik, -tē′lik), *adj.* (of an entity or event) having the purpose of its existence or occurrence outside of or apart from itself. Cf. **autotelic.** [HETERO- + TEL-[2] + -IC] —**het′er·o·tel′ism,** *n.*

het·er·o·thal·lic (het′ər ə thal′ik), *adj. Bot.* **1.** having mycelia of two unlike types both of which must participate in the sexual process. Cf. **homothallic** (def. 1). **2.** dioecious. [HETERO- + THALLIC] —**het′er·o·thal′lism,** *n.*

het·er·o·to·pi·a (het′ər ə tō′pē ə), *n. Pathol.* **1.** misplacement or displacement, as of an organ. **2.** the formation of tissue in a part where its presence is abnormal. Also, **het·er·ot·o·py** (het′ə rot′ə pē). [< NL; see HETERO-, TOP-, -IA] —**het·er·o·top·ic** (het′ər ə top′ik), **het·er·ot·o·pous** (het′ə rot′ə pəs), *adj.*

het·er·o·trich (het′ər ə trik), *n.* any ciliate of the suborder *Heterotricha*, having the body covered uniformly with short cilia. [< NL *Heterotrich(a)* name of the order. See HETERO-, TRICH-] —**het·er·ot·ri·chous** (het′ə ro′trə kəs), *adj.*

het·er·o·troph (het′ər ə trof′), *n.* a microorganism requiring a complex organic compound, as glucose, for its source of energy. Cf. **autotroph.** [HETERO- + TROPH-]

het·er·o·troph·ic (het′ər ə trof′ik), *adj. Biol.* capable of utilizing only organic materials as a source of food, as most animals and some plants (opposed to *autotrophic*). [HETERO- + -TROPHIC]

het·er·o·typ·ic (het′ər ə tip′ik), *adj. Biol.* of or pertaining to the first or reductional division in meiosis. Also, **het′er·o·typ′i·cal.** Cf. **homeotypic.** [HETERO- + *typic* (see TYPICAL)]

het·er·o·zy·go·sis (het′ər ō zī gō′sis), *n. Biol.* the state of being a heterozygote. [HETERO- + ZYGOSIS] —**het·er·o·zy·gos·i·ty** (het′ə rō zī gos′i tē), *n.*

het·er·o·zy·gote (het′ər ə zī′gōt, -zig′ōt), *n. Genetics.* a hybrid containing genes for two unlike characteristics, and therefore not breeding true to type. [HETERO- + ZYGOTE] —**het·er·o·zy·got·ic** (het′ə rō zī got′ik), *adj.*

het·er·o·zy·gous (het′ər ə zī′gəs), *adj. Biol.* **1.** having dissimilar pairs of genes for any hereditary characteristic. **2.** of or pertaining to a heterozygote. [HETERO- + Gk *zygós*, deriv. of *zygón* yolk; see -OUS]

heth (hes, ᴋʜes; *Heb.* ᴋʜet), *n.* **1.** the eighth letter of the Hebrew alphabet. **2.** the sound represented by this letter. Also, **cheth.** [< Heb]

het·man (het′mən), *n., pl.* **-mans.** a Cossack chief. [< Pol < G *Hauptmann* headman]

het·man·ate (het′mə nāt′), *n.* the authority, rule, or domain of a hetman. Also called **het′man·ship′.** [HETMAN + -ATE[1]]

HETP, *Chem.* See **hexaethyl tetraphosphate.**

Het·ty (het′ē), *n.* a girl's given name, form of **Hester** or **Esther.** Also, **Het′tie.**

het′ up′ (het), *Slang.* **1.** indignant; irate: *She was really het up about the new city tax.* **2.** enthusiastic: *John is suddenly het up about racing cars.* [*het*, dial. ptp. of *heat* + UP]

heugh (ᴋʜyo͝oᴋʜ), *n. Scot. and North Eng.* **1.** a precipice; a steep cliff, esp. one overlooking the sea. **2.** a ravine or glen with steep overhanging sides. Also, **heuch** (ᴋʜyo͝oᴋʜ). [ME *hōgh*, OE *hōh*; akin to HANG; cf. Goth *(faura) hāh* curtain]

heu·land·ite (hyo͞o′lən dīt′), *n.* a mineral of the zeolite family, hydrous calcium aluminum silicate, $CaAl_2Si_7O_{18}{\cdot}6H_2O$, occurring in igneous rocks in the form of crystals with a pearly luster. [named after Henry *Heuland*, 19th-century English mineral collector; see -ITE[1]]

Heu·ne·burg (hyo͞o′nə bûrg′), *n. Archaeol.* an excavated prehistoric site in SW Germany, near Ulm, consisting chiefly of a great fortification and indicating that the inhabitants carried on an extensive trade with cities in the eastern Mediterranean.

heu·ris·tic (hyo͝o ris′tik), *adj.* **1.** serving to indicate or point out; stimulating interest as a means of furthering investigation. **2.** (of a teaching method) encouraging the student to discover for himself. —*n.* **3.** a heuristic method or argument. [< NL *heuristic(us)*, equiv. to Gk *heur(ískein)* (to) find out, discover + L *-isticus* -ISTIC] —**heu·ris′ti·cal·ly,** *adv.*

Heus′ler al′loy (hyo͞os′lər; *Ger.* hois′lər), any of various alloys of manganese and other nonferromagnetic metals that exhibit ferromagnetism. [named after Conrad *Heusler*, 19th-century German mining engineer and chemist]

he·ve·a (hē′vē ə), *n.* See **Pará rubber.** [< NL < Sp *jebe* rubber < AmerInd]

He·ve′li·an ha′lo (hi vā′lē ən), *Astron.* a faint white halo with an angular radius of 90° that is occasionally seen around the sun or the moon, thought to be caused by the reflection and refraction of sunlight by ice crystals. [named after J. *Hevel* (1611–87), German astronomer; see -IAN]

He·ve·sy (he′ve shē), *n.* **Ge·org von** (ge ôʀg′ vôn), 1885–1966, Hungarian chemist: Nobel prize 1943.

hew (hyo͞o), *v.,* **hewed, hewed** or **hewn, hew·ing.** —*v.t.* **1.** to strike forcibly with an ax, sword, or other cutting instrument; chop; hack. **2.** to make, shape, smooth, etc., with cutting blows: *to hew a passage through the crowd; to hew a statue from marble.* **3.** to sever (a part) from a whole by means of cutting blows (usually fol. by *away, off, out, from,* etc.): *to hew branches from the tree.* **4.** to cut down; fell: *to hew wood; trees hewn down by the storm.* —*v.i.* **5.** to strike with cutting blows; cut: *He hewed more vigorously each time.* **6.** to uphold, follow closely, or conform to (usually fol. by *to*): *to hew to the tenets of one's political party.* [ME *hew(en)*, OE *hēawan*; c. G *hauen*] —**hew′a·ble,** *adj.* —**hew′er,** *n.*
—**Syn. 1.** See **cut. 2.** form.

HEW, Department of Health, Education, and Welfare.

hew′ers of wood′ and draw′ers of wa′ter, performers of menial tasks. Josh. 9:21.

Hew·ett (hyo͞o′it), *n.* a boy's given name. Also, **Hew′itt.**

Hew·ette (hyo͞o et′), *n.* a girl's given name.

Hew·lett (hyo͞o′lit), *n.* **Maurice Henry,** 1861–1923, English novelist, poet, and essayist.

hewn (hyo͞on), *adj.* **1.** felled and roughly shaped by hewing: *hewn logs.* **2.** given a rough surface: *hewn stone.* [ME *hewen*; ptp. of HEW]

hex[1] (heks), *v.t.* **1.** to bewitch; practice witchcraft on: *She must have hexed him into marrying her. He was accused of hexing his neighbors' cows because they suddenly stopped giving milk.* —*n.* **2.** a spell or charm, usually associated with witchcraft: *With all that rain, somebody must have put a hex on our picnic.* **3.** a witch. [< G *Hexe* witch; see HAG[1]] —**hex′er,** *n.*

hex[2] (heks), *adj. Informal.* hexagonal: *a bolt with a matching washer and hex nut.* [by shortening]

hexa-, a learned borrowing from Greek meaning "six," used in the formation of compound words: *hexapartite.* Also, *esp. before a vowel,* **hex-.** [comb. form repr. Gk *héx* SIX]

hex·a·ba·sic (hek′sə bā′sik), *adj. Chem.* containing six hydrogen atoms capable of being replaced or ionized: *a hexabasic acid.* [HEXA- + BASIC]

hex·a·chlo·ride (hek′sə klōr′īd, -klôr′-), *n. Chem.* a chloride containing six atoms of chlorine. [HEXA- + CHLORIDE]

hex·a·chlo·ro·phene (hek′sə klōr′ə fēn′, -klôr′-), *n. Chem.* a white, crystalline, water-insoluble powder, $(C_6HC_{13}OH)_2CH_2$, used as an antibacterial agent chiefly in toothpastes and soaps. [HEXA- + CHLORO-[2] + -PHENE]

hex·a·chord (hek′sə kôrd′), *n. Music.* a diatonic series of six tones having, in medieval music, a half step between the third and fourth tones and whole steps between the others. [< LGk *hexáchord(os)* having six strings. See HEXA-, CHORD[1]]

hex′a·co·sa·no′ic ac′id (hek′sə kō sə nō′ik, hek′-sə-), *Chem.* See **cerotic acid.** [HEXA- + Gk *eíkos(i)* twenty + -ANE + -O- + -IC]

hex·ad (hek′sad), *n.* **1.** the number six. **2.** a group or series of six. [< LL *hexad-* (s. of *hexas*) < Gk *hexad-* (s. of *hexás*) unit of six, equiv. to *héx* SIX + *-ad-* -AD[1]] —**hex·ad′ic,** *adj.*

hex′a·dec·a·no′ic ac′id (hek′sə dek′ə nō′ik, hek′-sə-), *Chem.* See **palmitic acid.** [HEXA- + DEC(A)- + -ANE + -O- + -IC]

hex·a·em·er·on (hek′sə em′ə ron′), *n.* **1.** the six days of the Creation. **2.** a written account of them, esp. the Biblical account. Gen. 1. **3.** a treatise on them. Also, **hexahemeron, hexameron.** [< LL < Gk *hexaḗmeron* period of six days, neut. of *hexaḗmeros* of six days (adj.), equiv. to *hexa-* HEXA- + *hēmér(a)* day + *-os* n. suffix] —**hex′a·em′er·ic,** *adj.*

hex·a·eth′yl tetraphos′phate (hek′sə eth′əl), *Chem.* a yellow, water-soluble, very poisonous liquid, $(C_2H_5O)_6P_4O_7$, used as an insecticide. Also called **HETP** [HEXA- + ETHYL]

hex·a·flu·o·ride (hek′sə flōō′ə rīd′, -flōr′īd, -flôr′-, -flōr′-), *n. Chem.* a fluoride containing six atoms of fluorine. [HEXA- + FLUORIDE]

hex·a·gon (hek′sə gon′, -gən), *n.* a polygon having six angles and six sides. [< Gk *hexágōn(on)*. See HEXA-, -GON]

120°

Hexagon

hex·ag·o·nal (hek sag′ə nəl), *adj.* **1.** of, pertaining to, or having the form of a hexagon. **2.** having a hexagon as a base or cross section: *a hexagonal prism.* **3.** divided into hexagons, as a surface. **4.** *Crystall.* noting or pertaining to the hexagonal system. [HEXAGON + -AL[1]] —**hex·ag′o·nal·ly,** *adv.*

hexag′onal sys′tem, *Crystall.* a system of crystallization characterized by three equal lateral axes intersecting at angles of 60° and a vertical axis of hexagonal symmetry and of different length at right angles to them.

hex·a·gram (hek′sə gram′), *n.* **1.** a six-pointed starlike figure formed of two equilateral triangles placed concentrically with each side of a triangle parallel to a side of the other and on opposite sides of the center. **2.** *Geom.* a figure of six lines. [< Gk *hexágram(mon)*. See HEXA-, -GRAM[1]] —**hex′a·gram′moid,** *adj., n.*

Hexagram

hex·a·he·dron (hek′sə hē′drən), *n., pl.* **-drons, -dra** (-drə). a solid figure having six faces. [< Gk *hexáedron*. See HEXA-, -HEDRON] —**hex′a·he′dral,** *adj.*

hex·a·hem·er·on (hek′sə hem′ə ron′), *n.* hexaemeron. —**hex′a·hem′er·ic,** *adj.*

hex·a·hy·drate (hek′sə hī′drāt), *n. Chem.* a hydrate that contains six molecules of water, as magnesium chloride, $MgCl_2 \cdot 6H_2O$. [HEXA- + HYDRATE] —**hex′a·hy′drat·ed,** *adj.*

hex·a·hy·dric (hek′sə hī′drik), *adj. Chem.* (esp. of alcohols and phenols) hexahydroxy. [HEXA- + -HYDRIC]

hex·a·hy·dro·ben·zene (hek′sə hī′drō ben′zēn, -ben zēn′), *n. Chem.* cyclohexane. [HEXA- + HYDRO-[2] + BENZENE]

hex·a·hy·dro·thy·mol (hek′sə hī′drə thī′mōl, -mōl, -mol), *n. Chem.* menthol. [HEXA- + HYDRO-[2] + THYMOL]

hex·a·hy·drox·y (hek′sə hī drok′sē), *adj. Chem.* (of a molecule) containing six hydroxyl groups. [HEXA- + HYDROXY]

hex·a·hy·drox·y·cy·clo·hex·ane (hek′sə hī drok′-sē sī′klə hek′sān), *n. Chem.* inositol. [HEXAHYDROXY + CYCLOHEXANE]

hex·am·er·al (hek sam′ər əl), *adj.* hexamerous. [HEXAMER(OUS) + -AL[1]]

hex·am·er·on (hek sam′ə ron′), *n.* hexaemeron.

hex·am·er·ous (hek sam′ər əs), *adj.* **1.** consisting of or divided into six parts. **2.** *Zool.* having a radially symmetrical arrangement of organs in six groups. **3.** *Bot.* having six members in each whorl. [< LL *hexamerus* < Gk *hexámeros* of six parts, equiv. to *hexa-* HEXA- + *mér(os)* share, part + *-os* -OUS] —**hex·am·er·ism** (hek-sam′ə riz′əm), *n.*

hex·am·e·ter (hek sam′i tər), *Pros.* —*n.* **1.** a dactylic line of six feet, as in Greek and Latin epic poetry, in which the first four feet are dactyls or spondees, the fifth is ordinarily a dactyl, and the last is a trochee or spondee, with a caesura usually following the long syllable in the third foot. **2.** any line of verse in six feet, as in English poetry. —*adj.* **3.** consisting of six metrical feet. [< L < Gk *hexámetr(os)* of six measures, equiv. to *hexa-* HEXA- + *métr(on)* measure + *-os* adj. suffix] —**hex·a·met·ric** (hek′sə me′trik), **hex′a·met′ri·cal, hex·am′e·tral,** *adj.*

hex·a·me·tho·ni·um (hek′sə mə thō′nē əm), *n. Pharm.* a ganglionic blocking agent, $[(CH_3)_3N(CH_2)_6N(CH_3)_3]^{++}$, used in the form of its chloride or bromide in the treatment of severe hypertension to lower blood pressure and increase blood flow by blocking transmission of nerve impulses which constrict blood vessels. [HEXA- + METH(YL) + (AMM)ONIUM]

hex·a·meth·yl·ene (hek′sə meth′ə lēn′), *n. Chem.* cyclohexane. [HEXA- + METHYLENE]

hex·a·meth·yl·ene·tet·ra·mine (hek′sə meth′ə-lēn te′trə mēn′), *n. Chem., Pharm.* a white, crystalline, water-soluble powder, $(CH_2)_6N_4$, used as a vulcanization accelerator, an absorbent in gas masks, in the manufacture of explosives and synthetic resins, and in medicine as a diuretic and urinary antiseptic. Also called **hexamine, methenamine.** [HEXAMETHYLENE + TETR(A)- + -AMINE]

hex·a·mine (hek′sə mēn′), *n. Chem.* hexamethylenetetramine. [HEX- + -AMINE]

hex·a·naph·thene (hek′sə naf′thēn, -nap′-), *n. Chem.* cyclohexane. [HEXA- + NAPHTHENE]

hex·ane (hek′sān), *n. Chem.* any of five isomeric hydrocarbons having the formula C_6H_{14}, of the alkane series, some of which are obtained from petroleum: used as solvents and chemical intermediates and in fuels. [HEX- + -ANE]

hex′ane·di·o′ic ac′id (hek′sān dī ō′ik), *Chem.* See **adipic acid.** [HEXA- + (BUT)ANE + DI(CARB)O(XYL)IC ACID]

hex·an·gu·lar (hek sang′gyə lər), *adj.* having six angles. [HEX- + ANGULAR] —**hex·an′gu·lar·ly,** *adv.*

hex·a·ni·trate (hek′sə nī′trāt), *n. Chem.* any compound containing six nitrate groups. [HEXA- + NITRATE]

hex′a·no′ic ac′id (hek′sə nō′ik, hek′sə-), *Chem.* See **caproic acid.** [HEXANE + -O- + -IC]

hex·a·par·tite (hek′sə pär′tīt), *adj.* sexpartite. [HEXA- + PARTITE]

hex·a·pla (hek′sə plə), *n.* (*often cap.*) an edition of a book, esp. the Old Testament, containing six versions or texts in parallel columns, esp. the one compiled by Origen. [< Gk *Hexaplâ* (title of Origen's edition), neut. pl. of *hexaploûs*, *-plóos* sixfold, equiv. to *hexa-* HEXA- + *-plo-* -fold (see PLY[2]) + *-os* adj. suffix] —**hex′a·plar, hex·a·plar·ic** (hek′sə plar′ik), **hex·a·plar·i·an** (hek′sə-plâr′ē ən), *adj.*

hex·a·pod (hek′sə pod′), *n.* **1.** an insect; a member of the class *Insecta* (formerly *Hexapoda*). —*adj.* **2.** having six feet. [< Gk *hexapod-* (s. of *hexápous*) six-footed. See HEXA-, -POD] —**hex·ap·o·dous** (hek sap′ə dəs), *adj.*

hex·ap·o·dy (hek sap′ə dē), *n., pl.* **-dies.** *Pros.* a measure consisting of six feet. [< Gk *hexapod-* (see HEXAPOD) + -Y[3]] —**hex·a·pod·ic** (hek′sə pod′ik), *adj.*

hex·ar·chy (hek′sär kē), *n., pl.* **-chies.** a group of six allied states or kingdoms, each under its own ruler. [HEX- + -ARCHY]

hex·a·stich (hek′sə stik′), *n. Pros.* a strophe, stanza, or poem consisting of six lines. Also, **hexastichon.** [< Gk *hexástich(on)*, neut. of *hexástichos* of six lines. See HEXA-, STICH[1]] —**hex·a·stich·ic** (hek′sə stik′ik), *adj.*

hex·as·ti·chon (hek sas′tə kon′), *n., pl.* **-cha** (-kə). hexastich.

hex·a·style (hek′sə stīl′), *adj. Archit.* **1.** having six columns. **2.** (of a classical temple or a building in the style of one) having six columns on one or both fronts. Also, **hex′a·sty′lar.** [see HEXASTYLOS]

hex·a·sty·los (hek′sə stī′los), *n.* a hexastyle building, as a classical temple. [< NL, L < Gk *hexa-* HEXA- + *stŷlos* pillar]

hex·a·syl·la·ble (hek′sə sil′ə bəl), *n.* a word or line of verse of six syllables. [HEXA- + SYLLABLE] —**hex·a·syl·lab·ic** (hek′sə si lab′ik), *adj.*

Hex·a·teuch (hek′sə tōōk′, -tyōōk′), *n.* the first six books of the Old Testament. [HEXA- + (PENTA)TEUCH] —**Hex′a·teuch′al,** *adj.*

hex·a·va·lent (hek′sə vā′lənt), *adj. Chem.* sexivalent. [HEXA- + -VALENT]

hex′ mark′. See **hex sign.**

hex·o·bar·bi·tal (hek′sə bär′bi tal′, -tôl′), *n. Pharm.* a compound, $C_{12}H_{16}N_2O_3$, used in the form of its sodium salt chiefly as an intravenous injection. [HEX- + -O- + BARBITAL]

hex·ode (hek′sōd), *n. Electronics.* a vacuum tube containing six electrodes, usually a plate, a cathode, a control electrode, and three grids. [HEX- + -ODE[2]]

hex·one (hek′sōn), *n. Chem.* **1.** any of various organic ketones containing six atoms of carbon in the molecule. **2.** See **methyl isobutyl ketone.** [HEX- + -ONE]

hex·os·a·mine (hek sos′ə mēn′), *n. Biochem.* any hexose derivative in which a hydroxyl group is replaced by an amino group. [HEXOSE + -AMINE]

hex·o·san (hek′sə san′), *n. Chem.* any of a group of hemicelluloses that hydrolyze to hexoses. [HEXOSE + -AN]

hex·ose (hek′sōs), *n. Chem.* any of a class of sugars containing six atoms of carbon, including glucose and fructose. [HEX- + -OSE[2]]

hex′ sign′, a magical symbol of usually stylized design for protection against evil spirits, now sometimes used for purely decorative purposes. Also called **hex mark.**

hex·yl (hek′sil), *adj. Chem.* containing a hexyl group. [HEX- + -YL] —**hex·yl′ic,** *adj.*

hex′yl group′, *Chem.* any of five univalent, isomeric groups having the formula C_6H_{13}-. Also called **hex′yl rad′ical.**

hex·yl·res·or·cin·ol (hek′sil rə zôr′sə nōl′, -nôl′, -nol′), *n. Pharm.* white or yellowish-white, needle-shaped crystals, $CH_3(CH_2)_5C_6H_3(OH)_2$, used chiefly as an antiseptic and for the expulsion of intestinal worms. [HEXYL + RESORCINOL]

hey[1] (hā), *interj.* (used as an exclamation to call attention or to express pleasure, surprise, bewilderment, etc.)

hey[2] (hā), *n.* hay[2].

hey·day[1] (hā′dā′), *n.* **1.** the stage or period of greatest vigor, strength, success, etc.; prime: *the heyday of the robber baron.* **2.** *Rare.* high spirits. Also, **hey′dey.** [var. of HIGH DAY, appar. by confusion with HEYDAY[2]]

hey·day[2] (hā′dā), *interj. Archaic.* (used as an exclamation of cheerfulness, surprise, wonder, etc.) [rhyming compound based on HEY[1]; r. *heyda* < G *hei da* hey there]

Hey·duck (hī′dōōk), *n.* Haiduk. Also, **Hey′duke, Hey′duc.**

Hey·er·dahl (hā′ər däl′), *n.* **Thor** (tōōr), born 1914, Norwegian ethnologist and author.

Hey·mans (hī′mənz; *Fr.* ə mäns′), *n.* **Cor·neille** (kôr-ne′yə), 1892–1968, Belgian physiologist: Nobel prize for medicine 1938.

Hey·rov·ský (hā′rôf skē), *n.* **Ja·ro·slav** (yä′rô släf′), 1890–1967, Czech chemist: Nobel prize 1959.

hey′ rube′, **1.** a fight between townspeople and the members of a circus or carnival. **2.** come help (used as a call to carnival or circus personnel in a fight, esp. in a fight with townspeople).

Hey·se (hī′zə), *n.* **Paul (Jo·hann von)** (poul yō′hän fən), 1830–1914, German playwright, novelist, poet, and short-story writer: Nobel prize 1910.

Hey·ward (hā′wərd), *n.* **Du·Bose** (də bōz′), 1885–1940, U.S. playwright, novelist, and poet.

Hey·wood (hā′wŏŏd), *n.* **1. John,** 1497?–1580?, English dramatist and epigrammatist. **2. Thomas,** 1573?–1641, English dramatist, poet, and actor. **3.** Also, **Haywood.** a boy's given name.

Hez·e·ki·ah (hez′ə kī′ə), *n.* a king of Judah of the 7th and 8th centuries B.C. II Kings 18. Also, *Douay Bible,* **Ezechias.** [< Heb *ḥizqīyāh* God strengthens, equiv. to *ḥizeq* strengthen + *yāh* God]

HF, See **high frequency.**

Hf, *Chem.* hafnium.

hf., half.

hf. bd., half-bound.

hf. cf., half-calf.

hf. mor., half-morocco.

HG, **1.** High German. **2.** *Brit.* Home Guard.

Hg, *Chem.* mercury. [< L *hydrargyrum*]

hg, hectogram; hectograms.

H.G., **1.** High German. **2.** His Grace; Her Grace.

hgt., height.

H.H., **1.** His Highness; Her Highness. **2.** His Holiness.

hhd, hogshead; hogsheads.

HH.D., Doctor of Humanities.

HHFA, Housing and Home Finance Agency.

H-hinge (āch′hinj′), *n.* a strap hinge having the form of an H with the joint in the crossbar.

H-hour (āch′our′, -ou′ər), *n.* the time, usually unspecified, set for the beginning of a previously planned attack.

hi (hī), *interj.* (used as an exclamation of greeting); hello! [late ME *hy*, perh. var. of *hei* HEY[1]]

H.I., Hawaiian Islands.

Hi·a·le·ah (hī′ə lē′ə), *n.* a city in SE Florida, near Miami: racetrack. 66,972 (1960).

hi·a·tus (hī ā′təs), *n., pl.* **-tus·es, -tus. 1.** a break or interruption in the continuity of a work, series, action, etc.; a missing part; gap: *Scholars attempted to fill in the hiatus in the medieval manuscript.* **2.** a gap or opening. **3.** *Gram., Pros.* the coming together, with or without break or slight pause, and without contraction, of two vowels in successive words or syllables, as in *see easily.* **4.** *Anat.* a natural fissure, cleft, or foramen in a bone or other structure. [< L: an opening, a gap, n. use of ptp. of *hiāre* to gape, to open, equiv. to *hiā-* v. s. + *-tus* ptp. suffix]

Hi·a·wath·a (hī′ə woth′ə, -wô′thə, hē′ə-), *n.* **1.** the central figure of *The Song of Hiawatha* (1855), a poem by Henry Wadsworth Longfellow. **2.** a town in NE Kansas. 3391 (1960).

hi·ba·chi (hē bä′chē), *n.* a small Japanese charcoal stove. [< Jap]

Hib·bing (hib′ing), *n.* a town in NE Minnesota: iron mining. 17,731 (1960).

hi·ber·nac·u·lum (hī′bər nak′yə ləm), *n., pl.* **-la** (-lə). **1.** a protective case or covering for winter, as of an animal or a plant bud. **2.** Also, **hi·ber·nac·le** (hī′bər-nak′əl). winter quarters, as of a hibernating animal. [< L: winter residence, equiv. to *hībernā-* (s. of *hībernāre*; see HIBERNATE) + *-culum* -CULE]

hi·ber·nal (hī bûr′nəl), *adj.* of or pertaining to winter; wintry. [< L *hībernāl(is)*, equiv. to *hībern(us)* wintry + *-ālis* -AL[1]; see HIEMAL]

hi·ber·nate (hī′bər nāt′), *v.i.,* **-nat·ed, -nat·ing. 1.** to spend the winter in close quarters in a dormant condition, as certain animals. **2.** (of people) to winter in a place with a milder climate: *Each winter finds us hibernating in Florida.* **3.** to withdraw or be in seclusion; retire. [< L *hībernāt(us)* (ptp. of *hībernāre* to spend the winter), equiv. to *hībernā-* (v. s.) + *-tus* ptp. suffix. See HIBERNAL, -ATE[1]] —**hi′ber·na′tion,** *n.* —**hi′ber·na′-tor,** *n.*

Hi·ber·ni·a (hī bûr′nē ə), *n. Literary.* Ireland.

Hi·ber·ni·an (hī bûr′nē ən), *adj.* **1.** of, pertaining to, or characteristic of Ireland or its inhabitants; Irish. —*n.* **2.** a native of Ireland. [HIBERNI(A) + -AN]

Hi·ber·ni·cise (hī bûr′ni sīz′), *v.t.,* **-cised, -cis·ing.** *Chiefly Brit.* Hibernicize.

Hi·ber·ni·cism (hī bûr′ni siz′əm), *n.* **1.** an idiom peculiar to Irish English. **2.** an Irish characteristic. Also, **Hi·ber·ni·an·ism** (hī bûr′nē ə niz′əm). [< ML *Hibernic(us)* Hibernian (*Hibern(ia)* Hibernia + *-icus* -IC) + -ISM]

Hi·ber·ni·cize (hī bûr′ni sīz′), *v.t.,* **-cized, -ciz·ing.** to make Irish in character or appearance. Also, *esp. Brit.,* **Hibernicise.** [< ML *Hibernic(us)* (see HIBERNICISM) + -IZE]

Hi·ber·no-Sax·on (hī bûr′nō sak′sən), *adj.* **1.** having the characteristics of both the Irish and English; Anglo-Irish. **2.** pertaining to or designating the style of art, esp. of manuscript illumination, developed principally during the 7th and 8th centuries A.D. in the monastic scriptoria founded by Irish missionaries, characterized chiefly by the use of zoomorphic forms elaborated in interlaced patterns and often set within a symmetrically balanced framework of geometric shapes; Anglo-Irish. Cf. **Celto-Germanic.** [*Hiberno-* comb. form of HIBERNIAN]

hi·bis·cus (hī bis′kəs, hi-), *n., pl.* **-cus·es.** any malvaceous herb, shrub, or tree of the genus *Hibiscus*, certain species of which have large, showy flowers. [< NL, L < Gk *hibískos* mallow]

hic (hik), *interj.* (an onomatopoeic word used to imitate or represent a hiccup.)

hic (hēk; *Eng.* hik), *adj., pron. Latin.* this.

hic·cup (hik′up, -əp), *n., v.,* **-cuped** or **-cupped, -cup·ing** or **-cup·ping.** —*n.* **1.** a quick, involuntary inspiration suddenly checked by closure of the glottis, producing a short, relatively sharp sound. **2.** Usually, **hiccups.** the condition of having such spasms: *She got the hiccups just as she began to speak.* —*v.i.* **3.** to make the sound of a hiccup: *The motor hiccuped as it started.* **4.** to have the hiccups. Also, **hic·cough** (hik′up, -əp). [alter. of *hocket*, *hickock*, equiv. to HIC + -OCK; akin to LG *hick* hiccup; see HOCKET]

Hic·e·ta·on (his′i tā′on), *n.* (in the *Iliad*) the brother of Priam who advised the Trojans to return Helen to Menelaus.

hic et u·bi·que (hēk′ et ōō bē′kwe; *Eng.* hik′ et yōō bī′kwē), *Latin.* here and everywhere.

Hich·ens (hich′ənz), *n.* **Robert Smythe** (smīth, smīth), 1864–1950, English novelist.

hic ja·cet (hēk′ yä′ket; *Eng.* hik jā′set), *Latin.* here lies (often used to begin epitaphs on tombstones).

hick (hik), *Informal.* —*n.* **1.** an unsophisticated, boorish, and provincial person; rube. —*adj.* **2.** pertaining to or characteristic of hicks: *hick ideas.* **3.** located in a rural area or away from a center of cultural activities: *a hick town.* [after *Hick*, familiar form of *Richard*]

hick·ey (hik′ē), *n., pl.* **-eys. 1.** any device or gadget whose name is not known or is momentarily forgotten. **2.** *Elect.* a fitting used to mount a lighting fixture in an outlet box or on a pipe or stud. **3.** *Slang.* a pimple. [orig. U.S.; perh. from surname *Hickey*]

hick′-joint point′ing (hik′joint′), *Masonry.* pointing having raked joints filled flush with the face of the masonry with a finish mortar.

Hick·ok (hik′ok), *n.* **James Butler** ("*Wild Bill*"), 1837–76, U.S. frontiersman.

hick·o·ry (hik′ə rē, hik′rē), *n., pl.* **-ries. 1.** any of several North American, juglandaceous trees of the genus *Carya*, certain species of which bear edible nuts or yield a valuable wood. Cf. **pecan, shagbark. 2.** the wood of any of these trees. **3.** a switch, stick, etc., of this wood. **4.** Also called **hick′ory cloth′, hick′ory stripe′.** a strong fabric of twill construction, used chiefly in the manufacture of work clothes. [earlier *pohickery;* akin to Algonquian *pawcohiccora* mush made of hickory nut kernels]

Hick·o·ry (hik′ə rē, hik′rē), *n.* a city in W North Carolina. 19,328 (1960).

Hick′ory East′, a town in central North Carolina. 3274 (1960).

Hick′ory Hills′, a town in NE Illinois. 2707 (1960).

hick′ory pine′. See **bristlecone pine.**

Hicks (hiks), *n.* **Edward,** 1780–1849, U.S. painter.

Hicks·ite (hik′sīt), *n.* a member of the liberal body of Quakers in the U.S., who asserted the sufficiency of the Inner Light in religious life. [after Elias *Hicks* (1748–1830), American Quaker preacher; see -ITE[1]]

Hicks·ville (hiks′vil), *n.* **1.** a town on W Long Island, in SE New York. 50,405 (1960). **2.** a town in NW Ohio. 3116 (1960).

Hicks′ yew, a hybrid yew, *Taxus media hicksi,* having a columnar manner of growth. [after *Hicks* nurseries in Westbury, New York]

hick·wall (hik′wôl′), *n. Brit. Dial.* any of certain European woodpeckers, esp. the green woodpecker. [late ME *hygh-whele,* orig. imit.]

hid (hid), *v.* pt. and a pp. of **hide.**

hid·age (hī′dij), *n. Old Eng. Law.* a tax payable to the king for every hide of land. [< ML *hīdāg(ium),* equiv. to *hīd(a)* HIDE[3] + *-agium* -AGE]

hi·dal·go (hi dal′gō; *Sp.* ē ŧħäl′gô), *n., pl.* **-gos** (-gōz; *Sp.* -gôs). a man of the lower nobility in Spain. [< Sp, contr. of *hi(jo) dalgo,* OSp *fijo dalgo* a noble, a person with property, a son with something < L *filius* son + *dē* with (lit., from) + *aliquō* something] —**hi·dal′go·ism, hi·dal′gism,** *n.*

Hi·dal·go (hi dal′gō; *Sp.* ē ŧħäl′gô), *n.* **1. Juan** (hwän), c1600–85, Spanish composer and harpist. **2.** a state in central Mexico. 994,598. (1960); 8057 sq. mi. *Cap.:* Pachuca.

Hi·dal·go y Cos·til·la (ē ŧħäl′gō ē kôs tē′yä), **Miguel** (mē gel′), 1753–1811, Mexican priest, patriot, and revolutionist.

Hi·dat·sa (hē dät′sä), *n., pl.* **-sas,** (*esp. collectively*) **-sa** for 1. **1.** a member of a Siouan people dwelling on the Missouri River. **2.** the Siouan language of the Hidatsa tribe.

hid·den (hid′ən), *adj.* **1.** concealed; obscure; covert: *hidden meaning; hidden hostility.* —*v.* **2.** pp. of **hide.** —**hid′den·ly,** *adv.* —**hid′den·ness,** *n.*
—**Syn. 1.** secret, veiled; occult.

hid·den·ite (hid′ənīt′), *n.* a rare, transparent variety of spodumene, colored yellow-green to emerald-green by chromium: used as a gem. [named after W. E. *Hidden* (1853–1918), who discovered it in 1879; see -ITE[1]]

hide[1] (hīd), *v.,* **hid, hid·den** or **hid, hid·ing,** *n.* —*v.t.* **1.** to conceal from sight; prevent from being seen or discovered. **2.** to obstruct the view of; cover up: *The sun was hidden by the clouds.* **3.** to conceal from knowledge or exposure; keep secret: *to hide one's feelings.* —*v.i.* **4.** to conceal oneself; lie concealed: *He hid in the closet.* **5. hide out,** to go into or remain in hiding: *After breaking out of jail, he hid out in a deserted farmhouse.* —*n.* **6.** *Brit.* a place of concealment for hunting or observing wildlife; hunting blind. [ME *hide(n),* OE *hȳdan;* c. OFris *hūda,* Gk *keúthein* to conceal] —**hid′a·ble,** *adj.* —**hid′er,** *n.*
—**Syn. 1.** screen, mask, cloak, veil, shroud, disguise. HIDE, CONCEAL, SECRETE mean to put out of sight or in a secret place. HIDE is the general word: *to hide or conceal one's money or purpose; A dog hides a bone.* CONCEAL, somewhat more formal, is to cover from sight: *A rock hid or concealed them from view.* SECRETE means to put away carefully, in order to keep secret: *The banker secreted the important papers.* **3.** disguise, dissemble, suppress.
—**Ant. 1.** reveal, display.

Hide
A, Head; B, Shoulder; C, Shank; D. Bend; E, Belly; F, Butt

hide[2] (hīd), *n., v.,* **hid·ed, hid·ing.** —*n.* **1.** the pelt of one of the larger animals (cow, horse, buffalo, etc.), raw or dressed. **2.** *Informal.* **a.** safety or welfare: *He's only worried about his own hide.* **b.** the skin of a human being: *Get out of here or I'll tan your hide!* **3. hide nor hair,** a trace or evidence, as of something missing: *They didn't find hide nor hair of the murder weapon.* Also, **hide or hair.** —*v.t.* **4.** *Informal.* to administer a beating to; thrash. **5.** to protect (a rope, as a boltrope of a sail) with a covering of leather. [ME; OE *hȳd;* c. D *huid,* Icel *hūth,* Dan, Sw *hud,* OHG *hūt* (G *Haut*), L *cutis* skin; see CUTICLE] —**hide′less,** *adj.*
—**Syn. 1.** See **skin.**

hide[3] (hīd), *n. Old Eng. Law.* a unit of land measurement varying from 60 to 120 acres or more depending upon local usage. [ME; OE *hīd(e), hīg(i)d* portion of land, family, equiv. to *hīg(an)* household (c. L *cīvis* citizen, Gk *keîmai* to lie, abide) + *-id* pertaining to; see CITY]

hide-and-seek (hīd′ən sēk′), *n.* a children's game in which one player at a home base gives the other players a chance to hide, then attempts to find and identify each player before he or she is able to tag the home base. Also called **hide-and-go-seek** (hīd′ən gō-sēk′).

hide·a·way (hīd′ə wā′), *n.* **1.** a place to which one can retreat; a refuge: *His hideaway is in the mountains.* —*adj.* **2.** hidden; concealed: *a hideaway bed.* [n., adj. use of v. phrase *hide away*]

hide·bound (hīd′bound′), *adj.* **1.** narrow and rigid in opinion: *a hidebound pedant.* **2.** confined to the past; extremely conservative: *a hidebound philosopher.* **3.** (of a horse, cow, etc.) having the back and ribs bound tightly by the hide. [HIDE[2] + -BOUND[1]] —**hide′bound′ness,** *n.*

hid·e·ous (hid′ē əs), *adj.* **1.** horrible or frightful to the senses; repulsive; very ugly: *a hideous monster.* **2.** shocking or revolting to the moral sense: *a hideous crime.* **3.** distressingly large: *the hideous expense of moving.* [ME *hid(ous)* (< OF *hisdos,* equiv. to *hisde* horror, fright + *-os* -OUS) + -EOUS] —**hid′e·ous·ly,** *adv.* —**hid′e·ous·ness, hid·e·os·i·ty** (hid′ē os′i tē), *n.*
—**Syn. 1, 2.** grisly, grim; repellent, detestable, odious, monstrous, dreadful, appalling, ghastly. —**Ant. 1, 2.** attractive, pleasing.

hide·out (hīd′out′), *n.* a safe place for hiding, esp. from the law. Also, **hide′-out′.** [n. use of v. phrase *hide out*]

Hi·de·yo·shi (hē′de yô′shē), *n.* **To·yo·to·mi** (tô′yô-tô′mē), 1536–98, Japanese general and statesman: prime minister and dictator of Japan 1585–98.

hid·ing[1] (hī′ding), *n.* **1.** act of concealing; concealment: *to remain in hiding.* **2.** a place or means of concealment. [ME; see HIDE[1], -ING[1]]

hid·ing[2] (hī′ding), *n. Informal.* a flogging or thrashing. [HIDE[2] + -ING[1]]

hid′ing pow′er, the ability of paint to cover completely a surface, measured in square feet of surface per gallon of paint.

hid·ro·poi·e·sis (hid′rō poi ē′sis, hī′drō-), *n.* the production of sweat. [< Gk *hidrō(s)* sweat + *poíēsis* making; see POESY] —**hid·ro·poi·et·ic** (hid′rō poi et′ik, hī′drō-), *adj.*

hi·dro·sis (hi drō′sis, hī-), *n. Pathol.* **1.** excessive perspiration due to drugs, disease, or the like. **2.** any of certain diseases characterized by sweating. [< NL, special use of Gk *hídrōsis* sweating, equiv. to *hidrō(s)* sweat + *-sis* -SIS] —**hi·drot·ic** (hi drot′ik, hī-), *adj.*

hie (hī), *v.,* **hied, hie·ing** or **hy·ing.** —*v.i.* **1.** to hasten; speed; go in haste. —*v.t.* **2.** to hasten (oneself): *Hie yourself down to this once-in-a-lifetime sale!* [ME *hie(n), hye(n),* OE *hīgian* to strive; c. D *hijgen* to pant, Gk *kī(ein)* (to) go; L *ci(ēre)* (to) cause to go]

hie·la·mon (hē′lə mən), *n. Australian.* a shield made of wood or bark, used by the aborigines. Also, **elemong, illamon.** [< native Austral]

hi·e·mal (hī′ə məl), *adj.* of or pertaining to winter; wintry. [< L *hiemāl(is)* pertaining to winter, equiv. to *hiem(s)* winter (akin to Gk *chiṓn* snow, *cheimṓn* winter, Skt *hima* cold, frost, snow) + *-ālis* -AL[1]; see HIBERNAL]

Hi·e·mis (hē ā′mis), *n.* **Mare.** See **Mare Hiemis.**

hier-, var. of **hiero-** before a vowel: *hierarchy.*

Hi·e·ra (hī′ər ə), *n. Class. Myth.* the beautiful wife of Telephus, sometimes described as a daughter of Priam, who was slain by Nireus in the Trojan War.

hi·er·a·co·sphinx (hī′ə rā′kə sfingks′), *n., pl.* **-sphinx·es, -sphin·ges** (-sfin′jēz). (in ancient Egyptian art) a hawk-headed sphinx. [< Gk *hierāko-* (comb. form of *hiérax* hawk) + SPHINX]

hi·er·arch (hī′ə rärk′, hī′rärk), *n.* **1.** a person who rules or has authority in sacred things; high priest. **2.** a person having high position or considerable authority. **3.** one of a body of officials or minor priests in certain ancient Greek temples. [< ML *hierarch(a)* < Gk *hierárchēs* steward of sacred rites, equiv. to *hier(ós)* sacred + *árch(ōn)* ruler or *arch(ós)* leader + *-ēs* n. suffix] —**hi′er·ar′chal,** *adj.*

hi·er·ar·chi·cal (hī′ə rär′ki kəl, hī rär′-), *adj.* of, belonging to, or characteristic of a hierarchy. Also, **hi′er·ar′chic.** [HIERARCH + -ICAL] —**hi′er·ar′chi·cal·ly,** *adv.*

hi·er·ar·chise (hī′ə rär kīz′, hī′rär-), *v.t.,* **-chised, -chis·ing.** *Chiefly Brit.* hierarchize.

hi·er·ar·chism (hī′ə rär′kiz əm, hī′rär kiz′-), *n.* hierarchical principles, rule, or influence. [HIERARCH(Y) + -ISM] —**hi′er·ar′chist,** *n.*

hi·er·ar·chize (hī′ə rär kīz′, hī′rär-), *v.t.,* **-chized, -chiz·ing.** to arrange in a hierarchy. Also, *esp. Brit.,* **hierarchise.** [HIERARCH(Y) + -IZE]

hi·er·ar·chy (hī′ə rär′kē, hī′rär-), *n., pl.* **-chies. 1.** any system of persons or things ranked one above another. **2.** government by ecclesiastical rulers. **3.** the power or dominion of a hierarch. **4.** an organized body of ecclesiastical officials in successive ranks or orders: *the Roman Catholic hierarchy.* **5.** one of the three divisions of the angels, each made up of three orders, conceived as constituting a graded body. **6.** Also called **celestial hierarchy.** the collective body of angels. **7.** *Ling.* the system of levels according to which a language is organized, as phonemic, morphemic, syntactic, or semantic. [< LL *hierarchi(a)* < Gk *hierarchía* rule or power of the high priest, equiv. to *hier-* HIER- + *archia* -ARCHY; r. ME *gerarchie* < MF *ierarchie* < LL *ierarchia,* var. of *hierarchia*]

hi·er·at·ic (hī′ə rat′ik, hī rat′-), *adj.* **1.** Also, **hi′er·at′i·cal.** of or pertaining to priests or the priesthood; priestly. **2.** noting or pertaining to a form of ancient Egyptian writing consisting of abridged forms of hieroglyphics, used by the priests in their records. **3.** noting or pertaining to certain styles in art whose types or methods are fixed by or as by religious tradition. —*n.* **4.** ancient Egyptian hieratic writing. [< LL *hierāticus* < Gk *hierātikós* pertaining to the priesthood, priestly, equiv. to *hier-* HIER- + *-ā-* v. suffix + *-tikos* -TIC] —**hi′er·at′i·cal·ly,** *adv.*

hiero-, a learned borrowing from Greek meaning "sacred," "priestly," used in the formation of compound words: *hierocracy.* Also, *esp. before a vowel,* **hier-.** [< Gk *hierō-,* comb. form of *hierós* holy, sacred]

hi·er·oc·ra·cy (hī′ə rok′rə sē, hī rok′-), *n., pl.* **-cies.** rule or government by priests or ecclesiastics. [HIERO- + -CRACY] —**hi·er·o·crat·ic** (hī′ər ə krat′ik, hī′rə-), **hi′er·o·crat′i·cal,** *adj.*

hi·er·o·dea·con (hī′ər ə dē′kən, hī′rə-), *n. Eastern Ch.* a monk who is also a deacon. [HIERO- + DEACON]

hi·er·o·dule (hī′ər ə do͞ol′, -dyo͞ol′, hī′rə-), *n.* a slave in an ancient Greek temple, dedicated to the service of a deity. [< Gk *hieródoul(os)* temple slave, equiv. to *hierō(n)* temple + *doûlos* slave] —**hi′er·o·du′lic,** *adj.*

hi·er·o·glyph·ic (hī′ər ə glif′ik, hī′rə-), *adj.* Also, **hi′er·o·glyph′i·cal. 1.** designating or pertaining to a pictographic script, particularly that of the ancient Egyptians, in which many of the symbols are conventionalized pictures of the thing represented by the words for which the symbols stand. **2.** inscribed with hieroglyphic symbols. **3.** hard to decipher; hard to read. —*n.* **4.** Also, **hi′er·o·glyph′.** a hieroglyphic symbol. **5.** Usually, **hieroglyphics.** hieroglyphic writing. **6.** a figure or symbol with a hidden meaning. **7. hieroglyphics,** writing, figures, characters, etc., difficult to decipher: *the confusing hieroglyphics of advanced mathematics.* [< LL *hieroglyphic(us)* < Gk *hieroglyphikós* pertaining to sacred writing. See HIERO-, GLYPHIC] —**hi′er·o·glyph′i·cal·ly,** *adv.*

Hieroglyphics

Hi′eroglyph′ic Hit′tite, an extinct language of the Anatolian branch of Indo-European, written in a pictographic script c1500–c1200 B.C. in Anatolia and c1200–c600 B.C. in Syria.

hi·er·o·glyph·ist (hī′ər ə glif′ist, hī′rə-, hī′ə rog′lə fist, hī rog′-), *n.* **1.** a person who studies hieroglyphics; hieroglyphologist. **2.** a person who writes in hieroglyphics. [HIEROGLYPH(ICS) + -IST]

hi·er·o·gly·phol·o·gy (hī′ər ə gli fol′ə jē, hī′rə-), *n.* the study of hieroglyphic writing. [HIEROGLYPH(ICS) + -O- + -LOGY] —**hi′er·o·gly·phol′o·gist,** *n.*

hi·er·o·gram (hī′ər ə gram′, hī′rə-), *n.* a sacred symbol, as an emblem, pictograph, or the like. [HIERO- + -GRAM[1]]

hi·er·o·gram·mat (hī′ər ə gram′ət, -at, hī′rə-), *n.* a writer of hierograms. Also, **hi·er·o·gram·mate** (hī′ər-ə gram′ət, -āt, hī′rə-). [< Gk *hierogrammat(eús)* sacred scribe, equiv. to *hiero-* HIERO- + *grammateús* scribe] —**hi·er·o·gram·mat·ic** (hī′ər ə grə mat′ik, hī′rə-), **hi′er·o·gram·mat′i·cal,** *adj.* —**hi′er·o·gram′ma·tist,** *n.*

hi·er·ol·a·try (hī′ə rol′ə trē, hī rol′-), *n.* worship or veneration of saints or sacred things. [HIERO- + -LATRY]

hi·er·ol·o·gy (hī′ə rol′ə jē, hī rol′-), *n.* **1.** literature or learning regarding sacred things. **2.** hagiological literature or learning. [HIERO- + -LOGY] —**hi·er·o·log·ic** (hī′ər ə loj′ik, hī′rə-), **hi′er·o·log′i·cal,** *adj.* —**hi′er·ol′o·gist,** *n.*

hi·er·o·monk (hī′ər ə mungk′, hī′rə-), *n. Eastern Ch.* a monk who is also a priest. [part. trans. of LGk or MGk *hierómonachos.* See HIERO-, MONK]

hi·er·on (hī′ə ron′), *n., pl.* **-er·a** (-ər ə). (in ancient Greece) a temple or a sacred place. [< Gk *hierón*]

Hi·er·o·nym·ic (hī′ər ə nim′ik, hī′rə-), *adj.* of or pertaining to St. Jerome. Also, **Hi′er·o·nym′i·an.** [< L *Hieronym(us)* Jerome + -IC]

Hi·er·on·y·mite (hī′ə ron′ə mīt′, hī ron′-), *n.* a member of a congregation of hermits of St. Jerome. [< L *Hieronym(us)* Jerome + -ITE[1]]

Hi·er·on·y·mus (hī′ə ron′ə məs), *n.* **Eu·se·bi·us** (yo͞o-sē′bē əs). See **Jerome, Saint.**

hi·er·o·phant (hī′ər ə fant′, hī′rə-, hī er′ə-), *n.* **1.** (in ancient Greece) an official expounder of rites of worship and sacrifice. **2.** any interpreter of sacred mysteries or esoteric principles. [< LL *hierophant(a)* < Gk *hierophántēs,* equiv. to *hiero-* HIERO- + *phántēs,* prp. of *phaínein* to show, make known] —**hi′er·o·phan′tic,** *adj.* —**hi′er·o·phan′ti·cal·ly,** *adv.*

hi·er·ur·gy (hī′ə rûr′jē, hī′rûr-), *n., pl.* **-gies.** a holy act or rite of worship. [< Gk *hierourgía,* deriv. of *hierourg(ós)* ritually sacrificing priest. See HIER-, -URGY] —**hi′er·ur′gi·cal,** *adj.*

hier wird deutsch ge·sproch·en (hēr′ virt′ doich′ gə shprōk′ən), *German.* German is spoken here. Also, **Man spricht deutsch.**

hi·fa·lu·tin (hī′fə lo͞ot′ən), *adj.* highfalutin. Also, **hi′fa·lu′tin′.**

hi-fi (hī′fī′), *n.* **1.** See **high fidelity. 2.** a radio receiver, phonograph, or other sound-reproducing apparatus possessing high fidelity. —*adj.* **3.** of, pertaining to, or characteristic of such apparatus; high-fidelity. [short form]

Hig·gin·son (hig′in sən), *n.* **Thomas Wentworth Stor·row** (stor′ō), 1823–1911, U.S. clergyman, author, and social reformer.

Hig·gins·ville (hig′inz vil′), *n.* a town in central Missouri. 4003 (1960).

hig·gle (hig′əl), *v.i.,* **-gled, -gling.** to bargain, esp. in a petty way; haggle. [appar. var. of HAGGLE]

hig·gle·dy-pig·gle·dy (hig′əl dē pig′əl dē), *adv.* **1.** in a jumbled confusion. —*adj.* **2.** confused; jumbled. [rhyming compound < ?]

hig·gler (hig′lər), *n.* a huckster or peddler. [HIGGLE + -ER[1]]

high (hī), *adj.* **1.** having a great or considerable reach or extent upward; lofty; tall: *a high wall.* **2.** having a specified extent upward: *The tree is now 20 feet high.* **3.** situated above the ground or some base; elevated: *a high platform; a high ledge.* **4.** intensified; greater than usual; exceeding the common degree or measure; strong; intense: *high speed; high color.* **5.** expensive, costly, or dear: *The price of food these days is much too high.* **6.** exalted in rank, station, estimation, etc.; of exalted character or quality: *a high official; high society.* **7.** *Music.* **a.** acute in pitch. **b.** a little sharp, or above the desired pitch. **8.** produced by relatively rapid vibrations; shrill: *the high sounds of crickets.* **9.** extending to or from an elevation: *a high dive.* **10.** great in quantity, as number, degree, force, etc.: *a high temperature.* **11.** chief; principal; main: *the high altar of a church.* **12.** of great consequence; important; grave; serious: *the high consequences of such a deed; high treason.* **13.** lofty; haughty; arrogant: *He took a high tone with his subordinates.* **14.** advanced to the utmost extent or to the culmination: *high tide.* **15.** elated; merry or hilarious: *high spirits; a high old time.* **16.** rich; extravagant; luxurious: *They have indulged in high living for years.* **17.** *Informal.* intoxicated with alcohol or narcotics: *He was so high he couldn't stand up.* **18.** remote: *high latitude; high antiquity.* **19.** extreme in opinion or doctrine, esp. religious or political: *a high Tory.* **20.** designating or pertaining to highland or inland regions. **21.** having considerable energy or potential power. **22.** *Auto.* of, pertaining to, or operating at the gear transmission ratio at

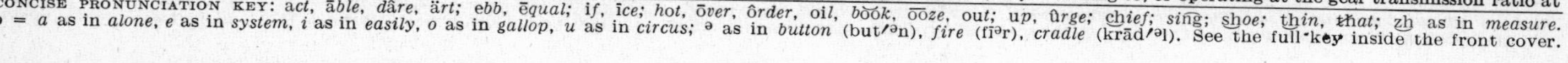
CONCISE PRONUNCIATION KEY: *act, āble, dâre, ärt; ebb, ēqual; if, īce; hot, ōver, ôrder, oil, bo͝ok, o͞oze, out; up, ûrge; chief; sing; shoe; thin, that;* zh *as in measure.* ə = *a* as in *alone,* *e* as in *system,* *i* as in *easily,* *o* as in *gallop,* *u* as in *circus;* ə as in *button* (but′ən), *fire* (fīər), *cradle* (krād′əl). See the full key inside the front cover.

which the speed of the engine crankshaft and of the drive shaft most closely correspond: *high gear.* **23.** *Phonet.* (of a vowel) articulated with the upper surface of the tongue relatively close to some portion of the palate, as the vowels of *eat* and *it,* which are high front, and those of *boot* and *put,* which are high back. Cf. **close** (def. 51), **low** (def. 31). **24.** (of meat, esp. game) tending toward a desirable or undesirable amount of decomposition; slightly tainted: *He likes his venison high.* **25.** *Metall.* containing a relatively large amount of a specified constituent (usually used in combination): *high-carbon steel.* **26.** *Baseball.* (of a pitched ball) crossing the plate at a level above the batter's shoulders: *The pitch was high and outside.* **27.** *Cards.* **a.** having greater value than other denominations or suits. **b.** able to take a trick; being a winning card. **c.** *Bridge.* having all winners: *Whose hand is high?* **28.** *Naut.* noting a wind of force 10 on the Beaufort scale, equal to a whole gale. —*adv.* **29.** at or to a high point, place, or level. **30.** in or to a high rank or estimate: *He aims high in his political ambitions.* **31.** at or to a high amount or price. **32.** in or to a high degree. **33.** luxuriously; richly; extravagantly: *They have always lived high.* **34.** *Naut.* as close to the wind as is possible while making headway with sails full. **35. fly high,** to be full of hope or elation: *His stories began to sell, and he was flying high.* **36. high and dry, a.** (of a ship) grounded so as to be entirely above water at low tide. **b.** deserted; stranded: *Her date left her high and dry.* **37. high and low,** in every possible place; everywhere: *The missing jewelry was never found, though we searched high and low for it.* —*n.* **38.** *Auto.* high gear: *He shifted from second into high.* **39.** *Informal.* See **high school. 40.** *Meteorol.* a pressure system characterized by relatively high pressure at its center. Cf. **anticyclone, low** (def. 50). **41.** *Cards.* the ace or highest trump out, esp. in games of the all fours family. **42. on high, a.** at or to a height; above. **b.** in heaven: *the powers on high.* [ME *heigh,* var. of *hegh, hey, heh,* OE *hēah, hēh;* c. D *hoog,* Icel *hār,* Sw *hög,* G *hoch* (OHG *hoh*), Goth *hauhs,* Lith *kaũkas* swelling, *kaukarā* hill]

—**Syn. 1.** HIGH, LOFTY, TALL, TOWERING refer to that which has considerable height. HIGH is a general term, and denotes either extension upward or position at a considerable height: *six feet high; a high shelf.* LOFTY denotes imposing or even inspiring height: *lofty crags.* TALL is applied either to that which is high in proportion to its breadth, or to anything higher than the average of its kind: *a tall tree, building.* TOWERING is applied to that which rises to a great or conspicuous height as compared with something else: *a towering mountain.* **6.** elevated, eminent, prominent, distinguished. **11.** head. **12.** capital. —**Ant. 1.** low.

high′ and might′y, 1. persons who are members of or identify with the higher social strata of society, esp. those who are haughty or arrogant. **2.** in an insolent, proud, or arrogant manner: *They talk high and mighty, but they owe everyone in town.* [ME *heigh and myghty* title of dignity]

high-and-might·y (hī′ən mī′tē, -ənd-), *adj.* haughty; excessively proud; arrogant.

high′-an·gle fire′ (hī′aṅg′gəl), cannon fire from a cannon set at an elevation angle exceeding that for the maximum horizontal range.

high′-angle gun′, a cannon that can be fired at a high angle of elevation.

high·ball (hī′bôl′), *n.* **1.** a drink of whiskey or other liquor diluted with water, soda, or ginger ale, and served with ice in a tall glass. **2.** *Railroads.* **a.** a signal to start a train, given with the hand or with a lamp. **b.** a signal for a train to move at full speed. —*v.i.* **3.** *Slang.* (of a train) to move at full speed. —*v.t.* **4.** to signal to (the engineer of a train) to proceed. [orig. game of chance, railway signal, later taken as a missile, shot of drink, to make the drinker high]

high′ beam′, an automobile headlight beam providing long-range illumination of a road and intended chiefly for use in driving in nonurban areas. Cf. **low beam.**

high·bind·er (hī′bīn′dər), *n.* **1.** a swindler; confidence man; cheat. **2.** a dishonest political official or leader. **3.** a member of a secret Chinese band or society employed in U.S. cities in blackmail, assassination, etc. **4.** a ruffian or rowdy.

high′ blood′ pres′sure, elevation of the arterial blood pressure or a condition resulting from it; hypertension.

high′ blow′er, a horse that produces a blowing sound when exhaling.

high·born (hī′bôrn′), *adj.* of high rank by birth. [ME; see HIGH, BORN]

high·boy (hī′boi′), *n.* *U.S. Furniture.* a tall chest of drawers on legs. [alter. of TALLBOY]

Highboy (18th century)

high·bred (hī′bred′), *adj.* **1.** of superior breed. **2.** characteristic of superior breeding: *highbred manners.* [HIGH + BRED]

high·brow (hī′brou′), *n.* **1.** a person of superior intellectual interests and tastes. **2.** *Disparaging.* a person with excessive intellectual or cultural pretensions; an intellectual snob. **3.** the crestfish. —*adj.* **4.** Also, **high′browed′.** of, pertaining to, or characteristic of a highbrow. [HIGH + BROW] —**high′brow′ism,** *n.*

high′ bunt′, *Naut.* a pronounced bunt on a furled sail, tapering sharply toward the ends of the yard (opposed to *low bunt*).

high′bush blue′ber·ry (hī′bo͝osh′), a spreading, bushy shrub, *Vaccinium corymbosum,* of eastern North America, having small, urn-shaped, white or pinkish flowers, and bluish-black edible fruit, growing from 8 to 12 feet high. [HIGH + BUSH[1]]

high′bush huck′leberry. See **black huckleberry.**

high′ camp′. See under **camp**[2] (def. 4).

high·chair (hī′châr′), *n.* a chair having a small seat, very long legs, arms, and usually a removable tray for food, for use by a young child during meals. [HIGH + CHAIR]

High′ Church′, pertaining or belonging to a party in the Anglican Church emphasizing church authority and jurisdiction and upholding the historical forms of worship (opposed to *Low Church*). [abstracted from *High Churchman*] —**High′ Church′man.**

high-class (hī′klas′, -kläs′), *adj.* of a class superior in quality or degree: *a high-class hotel.*

high-col·ored (hī′kul′ərd), *adj.* **1.** deep in color; vivid. **2.** flushed or red; florid: *a high-colored complexion.*

high′ com′edy, comedy dealing with polite society, depending largely on witty dialogue. Cf. **low comedy.**

high′ command′, 1. the leadership or highest authority of a military command or other organization. **2.** the highest headquarters of a military force.

high′ commis′sioner, 1. a representative of one sovereign member of the British Commonwealth of Nations in the country of another, having a rank and capacity generally similar to those of an ambassador. **2.** the chief of a special international commission or other organization. **3.** the head of government in a mandate, protectorate, possession, or the like.

high′ cran′berry. See **cranberry bush.**

high·dad·dy (hī′dad′ē), *n., pl.* **-dies.** *U.S. Furniture.* a highboy having no drawers in the supporting frame. [HIGH + DADDY]

high′ day′, 1. a holy or festal day. **2.** heyday[1]. [ME *heye dai* feast day]

high′er ap′sis. See under **apsis.**

high′er arith′metic, arithmetic (def. 2).

high′er crit′icism, the study of the Bible having as its object the establishment of such facts as authorship and date of composition, as well as provision of a basis for exegesis. Cf. **lower criticism.**

high′er educa′tion, education beyond high school, specifically that provided by colleges, graduate schools, and professional schools.

high′er mathemat′ics, the advanced portions of mathematics, customarily considered as embracing all beyond ordinary arithmetic, geometry, algebra, and trigonometry.

high·er-up (hī′ər up′), *n.* *Informal.* a person in a position of major authority in an organization: *You'll have to get permission from the higher-ups.* [n. use of phrase *higher up*]

High·et (hī′it), *n.* **Gilbert,** born 1906, U.S. teacher and critic, born in Scotland.

high′ explo′sive, a class of explosive, as TNT, in which the reaction is so rapid as to be practically instantaneous, used for bursting charges in shells and bombs. —**high′-ex·plo′sive,** *adj.*

high·fa·lu·tin (hī′fə lo͞ot′ən), *adj.* *Informal.* pompous; haughty; pretentious. Also, **high′fa·lu′tin′, hifalutin, hifalutin′, high·fa·lu·ting** (hī′fə lo͞o′tiṅg). [HIGH + *falutin* (perh. orig. *flutin,* var. of *fluting,* prp. of FLUTE)]

high′ fidel′ity, *Electronics.* sound reproduction over the full range of audible frequencies with very little distortion of the original signal. —**high′-fi·del′i·ty,** *adj.*

high·fli·er (hī′flī′ər), *n.* **1.** one who or that which flies high. **2.** a person who is extravagant or goes to extremes in aims, pretensions, opinions, etc. Also, **high′fly′er.** [HIGH + FLIER]

high-flown (hī′flōn′), *adj.* **1.** extravagant in aims, pretensions, etc. **2.** pretentiously lofty; bombastic: *We couldn't endure his high-flown oratory.*

high·fly·ing (hī′flī′iṅg), *adj.* **1.** moving upward to or along at a considerable height: *the dancers' highflying feet; highflying planes.* **2.** extravagant or extreme in aims, opinions, etc.: *highflying ideals about life.* [HIGH + FLYING]

high′ fre′quency, the range of frequencies in the radio spectrum between 3 and 30 megacycles per second. —**high′-fre′quen·cy,** *adj.*

high′ ful′ham. See under **fulham.**

High′ Ger′man, 1. the group of West Germanic languages that in A.D. c400–c500 underwent the second consonant shift described by Grimm's Law. The group includes German, Yiddish, Bavarian, Alemannic, and most of the dialects of central Germany. **2.** German (def. 4).

high-grade (hī′grād′), *adj.* **1.** of excellent or superior quality. **2.** (of ore) yielding a relatively large amount of the metal for which it is mined.

high-hand·ed (hī′han′did), *adj.* overbearing; arbitrary: *He has a high-handed manner.* Also, **high′hand′ed.** —**high′-hand′ed·ly, high′hand′ed·ly,** *adv.* —**high′-hand′ed·ness, high′hand′ed·ness,** *n.*

high′ hat′, 1. See **top hat. 2.** *Slang.* See **table tripod.**

high-hat (hī′hat′), *v.,* **-hat·ted, -hat·ting,** *adj.* *Informal.* —*v.t.* **1.** to snub or treat condescendingly. —*adj.* **2.** snobbish; disdainful; haughty. [v., adj. use of HIGH HAT] —**high′-hat′ter,** *n.*

high′-hat cym′bals, *Music.* a pair of cymbals mounted on a rod so that the upper cymbal can be lifted and dropped on the lower by means of a pedal.

high·hole (hī′hōl′), *n.* *U.S. Dial.* flicker[2]. Also, **high·hold·er** (hī′hōl′dər). [earlier *highwale, hewhole,* var. of HICKWALL]

High′ Ho′ly Day′, *Judaism.* Rosh Hashanah or Yom Kippur as a holy day of special significance. Also, **High′ Hol′iday.**

high′ horse′, a haughty attitude or temper; a contemptuous manner: *When he saw that his aloofness was having no effect, he came down off his high horse and joined the conversation.*

high′ hur′dles, *Track.* a race in which runners leap over hurdles three feet six inches high. Cf. **low hurdles.**

high′ i′ron, *Railroads Slang.* **1.** a main-line track. **2.** an express track.

high·jack (hī′jak′), *v.t., v.i.* hijack.

high·jack·er (hī′jak′ər), *n.* hijacker.

high′ jinks′, *Slang.* boisterous celebration or merrymaking; unrestrained fun: *The city is full of conventioneers indulging in their usual high jinks.* Also, **hijinks.**

high′ jump′, *Track.* **1.** a field event in which athletes compete in jumping for height over a crossbar supported by two upright poles, usually from a running start. **2.** a jump for height made in this event.

high′ jump′er, *Track.* a participant in the high jump.

high-key (hī′kē′), *adj.* (of a photograph) having chiefly light tones, usually with little tonal contrast.

high-keyed (hī′kēd′), *adj.* **1.** high-strung; nervous. **2.** (of a painting) having bright or chiefly pure colors.

high·land (hī′lənd), *n.* **1.** an elevated region; a plateau: *He moved to a highland far from the river.* **2. highlands,** a mountainous region or elevated part of a country. —*adj.* **3.** of, pertaining to, or characteristic of highlands. [ME; OE *heahlond.* See HIGH, LAND]

High·land (hī′lənd), *n.* **1.** a city in NW Indiana, near Chicago. 16,284 (1960). **2.** a town in SW Illinois. 4943 (1960). **3.** a town in SE New York. 2931 (1960).

High·land·er (hī′lən dər), *n.* **1.** a Gael inhabiting the Highlands of Scotland. **2.** a soldier of a Highland regiment. **3.** (*l.c.*) an inhabitant of any highland region. [HIGHLAND + -ER[1]]

High′land Falls′, a town in SE New York. 4469 (1960).

High′land fling′, fling (def. 16).

High′land Heights′, 1. a town in N Kentucky. 3491 (1960). **2.** a town in N Ohio. 2929 (1960).

High′land Park′, 1. a city in SE Michigan, within the city limits of Detroit. 38,063 (1960). **2.** a city in NE Illinois, on Lake Michigan. 25,532 (1960). **3.** a town in central New Jersey. 11,049 (1960).

High·lands (hī′ləndz), *n.* **1.** (*construed as pl.*) a mountainous region in N Scotland, N of the Grampians. **2.** (*construed as sing.*) a town in S Texas. 4336 (1960). **3.** (*construed as sing.*) a town in E New Jersey. 3536 (1960).

high-lev·el (hī′lev′əl), *adj.* **1.** undertaken by or composed of members having a high status: *They attended the high-level meeting with trepidation. It was decided that the problem could be resolved only by a high-level investigation.* **2.** having high status: *high-level personnel.* **3.** undertaken at or from a high altitude: *high-level bombing; a high-level attack.*

high·light (hī′līt′), *v.,* **-light·ed, -light·ing,** *n.* —*v.t.* **1.** to emphasize or make prominent. **2.** to create highlights in (a photograph or engraving). —*n.* **3.** Also, **high′ light′.** an important, conspicuous, memorable, or enjoyable event, scene, part, or the like: *the highlight of his talk; the highlight of the concert series.* **4.** *Art.* the point of most intense light on a represented form. [HIGH + LIGHT[1]]

high′light half′tone, dropout (def. 5).

high·line (hī′līn′), *n.* *Print., Journ.* kicker (def. 7). [HIGH + LINE[1]]

high-low (hī′lō′ *for 1, 2;* hī′lō′ *for 3*), *n.* **1.** *Chiefly Bridge.* a signal for one's partner to lead a suit, conveyed by playing a high card and then a lower card in that suit. **2.** a game of stud or draw poker in which the players having the highest and lowest ranking hands share the pot equally. **3.** Also, **high′low′.** an ankle-high, laced shoe.

high-low-jack (hī′lō′jak′), *n.* See **all fours** (def. 2).

high·ly (hī′lē), *adv.* **1.** in or to a high degree: *highly amusing; highly seasoned food.* **2.** with high appreciation or praise: *to speak highly of a person.* **3.** at or to a high price: *a highly paid consultant.* [ME *heihliche,* OE *hēalīce.* See HIGH, -LY]

High′ Mass′, *Rom. Cath. Ch.* a Mass celebrated according to the complete rite, in which the liturgy is sung, and not said, by the celebrant, who is attended by a deacon and subdeacon, and which is usually characterized by the use of music and incense; Solemn Mass. Cf. **Low Mass.** [ME; OE *hēah-mæsse*]

high′ mill′ing, a process for making fine flour, in which the grain is alternately ground and sifted a number of times. Cf. **low milling.**

high-mind·ed (hī′mīn′did), *adj.* **1.** having or showing high, exalted principles or feelings: *a high-minded ruler.* **2.** *Rare.* proud or arrogant. —**high′-mind′ed·ly,** *adv.* —**high′-mind′ed·ness,** *n.*

—**Syn. 1.** See **noble.**

high-muck-a-muck (hī′muk′ə muk′, -muk′ə muk′), *n.* *Slang.* an important or high-ranking person, esp. one who is pompous or conceited. [< Chinook jargon *hiu muckamuck,* lit., plenty food]

high-necked (hī′nekt′), *adj.* (of a garment) high at the neck.

high·ness (hī′nis), *n.* **1.** quality or state of being high; loftiness; dignity. **2.** (*cap.*) a title of honor given to members of a royal family (usually prec. by *His, Her, Your,* etc.). [ME *heyenes,* OE *hēanes.* See HIGH, -NESS]

high′ noon′, 1. the exact moment of noon. **2.** the high point of a stage or period; peak; pinnacle: *a book written at the high noon of his career.* [ME *non heye*]

high-oc·tane (hī′ok′tān), *adj.* noting a gasoline with a relatively high octane number, characterized by high efficiency and freedom from knock.

high-pitched (hī′picht′), *adj.* **1.** *Music.* played or sung at a high pitch. **2.** emotionally intense: *a high-pitched argument.* **3.** (of a roof) having an almost perpendicular slope; steep. **4.** lofty in tone or character: *high-pitched ambitions.*

high′ place′, (in ancient Semitic religions) a place of worship, usually a temple or altar on a hilltop.

High′ Point′, a city in central North Carolina. 62,063 (1960).

high-pow·er (hī′pou′ər), *adj.* **1.** (of a rifle) of a sufficiently high muzzle velocity and using a heavy enough bullet to kill large game. **2.** high-powered.

high-pow·ered (hī′pou′ərd), *adj.* **1.** extremely energetic, dynamic, and capable: *high-powered executives; high-powered workers.* **2.** of a forceful and driving character: *a high-powered political campaign; high-powered selling techniques.* **3.** capable of a high degree of magnification: *high-powered binoculars; a high-powered microscope.*

high-pres·sure (hī′presh′ər), *adj., v.,* **-sured, -sur·ing.** —*adj.* **1.** having or involving a pressure above the normal: *high-pressure steam.* **2.** vigorous; persistent;

aggressive: *high-pressure salesmanship.* —*v.t.* **3.** to employ aggressively forceful and unrelenting sales tactics on (a prospective customer): *The salesman high-pressured me into buying the car.*

high-priced (hī′prīst′), *adj.* expensive; costly. —**Syn.** See **expensive.**

high′ priest′, **1.** a chief priest. **2.** a person in a high position of power or influence; leader; arbiter: *the high priest of amateur tennis in this country; a high priest of the young painters.* **3.** *Judaism.* (from Aaronic times to about the 1st century A.D.) the priest ranking above all others in the priestly hierarchy and the only one permitted to enter the holy of holies. [ME *heiye prest*]

high′ priest′hood, **1.** the condition or office of a high priest. **2.** high priests collectively.

high-proof (hī′pro͞of′), *adj.* containing a high percentage of alcohol: *high-proof spirits.*

high′ relief′, *Sculpture.* sculptured relief in which volumes are strongly projected from the background. See illus. under **relief**[2].

High′ Ren′aissance, a style of art developed in Italy at the end of the 15th century and during the early 16th century, chiefly characterized by an emphasis on draughtsmanship, schematized, often centralized compositions, the illusion of sculptural volume in painting, and the often heroic scale of the human figure. Cf. **Early Renaissance, Venetian** (def. 2).

high′ rise′, a building, as an apartment or office building, having a comparatively large number of stories.

high-ris·er (hī′rī′zər), *n.* a bed composed of two units, one resting on the floor, the other resting on top when the piece is used as a single bed and swinging down to rest on the floor when the piece is used as a double bed.

high·road (hī′rōd′), *n.* **1.** a main road; highway. **2.** an easy or certain course: *the highroad to success.* [HIGH + ROAD]

high′ rod′, *Survey.* an extensible leveling rod, extended when in use. Also called **long rod.**

high′ school′, **1.** a school following the ordinary grammar school and consisting of grades 9 through 12. **2.** either of two schools, one (**junior high school**) corresponding to the upper grades or grade of the ordinary grammar school together with one or more years of the ordinary high school, and another (**senior high school**) corresponding to the remainder of the ordinary high school. —**high′-school′,** *adj.*

high′ school′er, a person who attends a high school; a high-school student.

high′ sea′, **1.** the sea or ocean beyond the three-mile limit or territorial waters of a country. **2.** Usually, **high seas. a.** the open, unenclosed waters of any sea or ocean; common highway. **b.** *Law.* the area within which transactions are subject to court of admiralty jurisdiction. [ME; OE *hēah-sǣ*] —**high′-sea′,** *adj.*

high′ sign′, *Slang.* a gesture, glance, or facial expression used as a signal to warn, admonish, or inform another person or other persons surreptitiously: *He gave his wife the high sign that he was bored and wanted to leave the party.*

high′ soci′ety, society (def. 9).

high-sound·ing (hī′soun′ding), *adj.* having an impressive or pretentious sound: *high-sounding titles.*

high-speed (hī′spēd′), *adj.* fit to operate or operating at a high speed: *a high-speed drill.*

high′-speed steel′ (hī′spēd′), an especially hard, heat-resistant steel for use in lathe tools and for other uses involving high friction and wear.

High·spire (hī′spīər′), *n.* a town in S Pennsylvania 2999 (1960).

high-spir·it·ed (hī′spir′i tid), *adj.* characterized by energetic enthusiasm, elation, vivacity, etc.; boldly courageous; mettlesome. —**high′-spir′it·ed·ly,** *adv.* —**high′-spir′it·ed·ness,** *n.*

high′ spir′its, a mood of joy, elation, etc.; vivacity.

high-step·ping (hī′step′ing), *adj.* **1.** seeking unrestrained pleasure, as in night clubs, parties, etc.; leading a wild and fast life: *a high-stepping girl.* **2.** (of a horse) moving with the leg raised high. —**high′-step′per,** *n.*

high-strung (hī′strung′), *adj.* at great tension; highly nervous: *high-strung nerves; a high-strung person.*

hight[1] (hīt), *adj.* **1.** *Archaic.* called or named: *Childe Harold was he hight.* —*v.t. Scot.* **2.** to promise; pledge. **3.** *Archaic.* to order; command. [ME; OE *heht,* reduplicated preterit of *hātan* to name, call, promise, command; c. G *heissen* to call, be called, mean; akin to BEHEST]

hight[2] (hīt), *n.* height.

high·tail (hī′tāl′), *v.i. Informal.* **1.** to go away or leave rapidly, esp. in escaping from something or someone: *Last we saw of him, he was hightailing down the street.* **2. hightail it,** hurry; rush; scamper: *Hightail it down to the station and see if your daddy's on the train.* [HIGH + TAIL[1]]

High′ Ta′tra. See **Tatra Mountains.**

high′ tea′, *Brit.* **1.** (traditionally) any tea at which meat is served. **2.** a late afternoon or early evening tea, roughly corresponding to a light supper in the U.S., and usually consisting of meat, salad, fruit, cake, and tea.

high-tech (hī′tek′), *n.* **1.** See **high technology. 2.** a style of design in which industrial fixtures, as metal shelving, sprinkler systems, etc., are incorporated into the decor. —*adj.* **3.** of or pertaining to high-tech or high technology.

high′ technol′ogy, any technology requiring the most sophisticated scientific equipment and advanced engineering techniques, as microelectronics, data processing, genetic engineering, or telecommunications. —**high′-tech·nol′o·gy,** *adj.*

high-ten·sion (hī′ten′shən), *adj. Elect.* subjected to or capable of operating under relatively high voltage: *high-tension wire.*

high-test (hī′test′), *adj.* (of gasoline) boiling at a relatively low temperature.

high′ tide′, **1.** the tide at high water. **2.** the time of high water. **3.** a culminating point: *the high tide of the revolution.* [ME; OE *hēah-tīd*]

high′ time′, the time just before it is too late; the appropriate time or past the appropriate time: *It's high time he found a job.*

high-toned (hī′tōnd′), *adj.* **1.** having high principles; dignified. **2.** marked by dignified, well-bred character: *He writes for a high-toned literary review.* **3.** affectedly stylish or genteel. **4.** *Archaic.* high in tone or pitch. Also, **high′-tone′.**

high′ trea′son, treason against the sovereign or state. [ME *hye tresoune*]

Hights·town (hīts′toun′), *n.* a town in central New Jersey. 4317 (1960).

high·ty-tigh·ty (hī′tē tī′tē), *interj., adj.* hoity-toity (defs. 1, 2, 5).

high-up (hī′up′), *adj., n., pl.* **-ups.** —*adj.* **1.** holding a high position or rank. —*n.* **2.** a person holding a high position or rank; higher-up. [n.; adj. use of *high up*]

high′ wa′ter, **1.** water at its greatest elevation, as in a river. **2.** See **high tide.**

high′-wa′ter mark′ (hī′wô′tər, -wot′ər), **1.** a mark showing the highest level reached by a body of water. **2.** the highest point of anything; the apex: *His speech at the conference was the high-water mark of his professional life.*

high·way (hī′wā′), *n.* **1.** a main road, esp. one between towns or cities. **2.** any public passage, either a road or waterway. **3.** any main or ordinary route, track, or course. [ME *heyewei,* OE *heiweg.* See HIGH, WAY]

high·way·man (hī′wā′mən), *n., pl.* **-men.** a holdup man, esp. one on horseback, who robs travelers along a public road. [HIGHWAY + MAN[1]]

high′ wine′, Often, **high wines.** *Distilling.* a distillate containing a high percentage of alcohol.

high′ wire′, a tightrope stretched very high above the ground.

High·wood (hī′wo͝od′), *n.* a town in NE Illinois. 4499 (1960).

high-wrought (hī′rôt′), *adj.* **1.** wrought with a great degree of skill or artistry; ornate. **2.** highly agitated; overwrought.

H.I.H., His Imperial Highness; Her Imperial Highness.

Hii·u·maa (hē′o͞o mä′), *n.* an island in the Baltic, E of and belonging to the Estonian Republic of the Soviet Union. 373 sq. mi. Danish, **Dagö.**

hi·jack (hī′jak′), *v.t.* **1.** to steal (something) in transit: *to hijack goods from a truck or train; to hijack a plane by holding a pistol to the pilot's head.* —*v.i.* **2.** to engage in such stealing. Also, **highjack.** [back formation from HIJACKER]

hi·jack·er (hī′jak′ər), *n.* a person who hijacks. Also, **highjacker.** [HIGH(WAYMAN) + *jacker,* appar. JACK[1] to hunt by night with aid of a jack light + -ER[1]]

hi·jinks (hī′jingks′), *n.* (*construed as pl.*) See **high jinks.**

Hij·ra (hij′rə), *n.* (*sometimes l.c.*) *Islam.* Hegira. Also, **Hij′rah.**

hike (hīk), *v.,* **hiked, hik·ing,** *n.* —*v.i.* **1.** to walk or march a great distance, esp. through rural areas, for pleasure, for military training, or the like. **2.** to move up or rise, as out of place or position (often fol. by *up*): *My shirt hikes up if I don't wear a belt.* **3.** to hold oneself outboard on the windward side of a heeling sailboat to reduce the amount of heel. —*v.t.* **4.** to move, draw, or raise with a jerk (often fol. by *up*): *to hike up one's socks.* **5.** to increase, often sharply and unexpectedly: *to hike the price of milk.* —*n.* **6.** a long walk or march for pleasure, for military training, or the like. **7.** an increase or rise: *a hike in wages.* [perh. dial. var. of HITCH[1]] —**hik′er,** *n.*

Hil·a·i·ra (hil′ā ī′rə), *n. Class. Myth.* the daughter of Leucippus who served as a priestess of Artemis. Also, **Hi·la·ra** (hi lâr′ə).

hi·lar·i·ous (hi lâr′ē əs, -lar′-, hī-), *adj.* **1.** boisterously gay: *a hilarious celebration.* **2.** cheerful; merry. **3.** funny; arousing merriment: *a hilarious joke; a hilarious old movie.* [< L *hilari(s)* cheerful (c. Gk *hilarós* GLAD) + -OUS] —**hi·lar′i·ous·ly,** *adv.* —**hi·lar′i·ous·ness,** *n.*

hi·lar·i·ty (hi lar′i tē, -lâr′-, hī-), *n.* **1.** boisterous gaiety. **2.** cheerfulness; mirthfulness. [earlier *hilaritie* < L *hilaritās,* equiv. to *hilari(s)* (see HILARIOUS) + *-tās* -TY[2]]
—**Syn. 1.** See **mirth.**

Hi·lar·i·us (hi lâr′ē əs), *n.* **Saint,** died A.D. 468, pope 461–468. Also, **Hil·a·rus** (hil′ar əs), **Hilary.**

Hil·a·ry (hil′ə rē), *n.* a boy's or girl's given name. Also, **Hi·laire** (hi lâr′; *Fr.* ē lεʀ′), **Hillary.**

Hil′ary of Poitiers′, **Saint,** A.D. c300–368, French bishop and theologian. French, **Hi·laire de Poi·tiers** (ē lεʀ′ də pwȧ tyā′).

Hil·bert (hil′bərt; *Ger.* hil′bεʀt), *n.* **Da·vid** (dā′vid; *Ger.* dä′vit), 1862–1943, German mathematician.

Hil′bert cube′, *Math.* the Cartesian product of a countably infinite number of copies of the closed interval from 0 to 1. [named after D. HILBERT]

Hil′bert space′, *Math.* a complete infinite-dimensional vector space on which an inner product is defined. [named after D. HILBERT]

hilch (hilsh), *Scot.* —*v.i.* **1.** to limp; hobble. —*n.* **2.** a limp. [akin to OE *hylc* bend, turn]

Hil·da (hil′də), *n.* a girl's given name, form of **Helda.**

Hil·de·brand (hil′də brand′), *n.* See **Gregory VII, Saint.** —**Hil′de·bran′di·an,** *adj., n.* —**Hil·de·brand·ine** (hil′də bran′din, -dīn), *adj.*

Hil·de·garde (hil′də gärd′), *n.* a girl's given name. Also, **Hil′de·gard′.**

Hil·des·heim (hil′des hīm′), *n.* a city in N West Germany. 98,800 (1963).

hill (hil), *n.* **1.** a natural elevation of the earth's surface, smaller than a mountain. **2.** an incline, esp. in a road: *This old jalopy won't make it up the next hill.* **3.** an artificial heap, pile, or mound: *a hill made by ants.* **4.** a small mound of earth raised about a cultivated plant or a cluster of such plants. **5.** the plant or plants so surrounded: *a hill of potatoes.* **6.** *Baseball Slang.* mound[1] (def. 6). **7. go over the hill,** *Slang.* **a.** to break out of prison. **b.** to absent oneself without leave from one's military unit. **c.** to leave suddenly or mysteriously: *Rumor has it that her husband has gone over the hill.* **8. over the hill, a.** past the crisis: *The new tax program is now over the hill.* **b.** past the peak of effectiveness or power: *He is over the hill as a professional athlete.* **9. the Hill.** See **Capitol Hill.** —*v.t.* **10.** to surround with hills: *to hill potatoes.* **11.** to form into a hill or heap. [ME; OE *hyll;* c. MD *hille,* L *coll(is)* hill, *cul(men)* top, peak, *cel(sus)* lofty, very high, Goth *hallus* rock, Lith *kal(nas)* mountain, Gk *kol(ōnós)* hill, *kol(ophṓn)* summit] —**hill′er,** *n.*
—**Syn. 1.** eminence, prominence; mound, knoll, hillock; foothill. —**Ant. 1.** hollow, valley.

Hill (hil), *n.* **1. Ambrose Pow·ell** (pou′əl), 1825–61, Confederate general in the U.S. Civil War. **2. Archi·bald Viv·i·an** (viv′ē ən), 1886–1977, English physiologist: Nobel prize for medicine 1922. **3. James Jerome,** 1838–1916, U.S. railroad builder and financier, born in Canada.

Hil·lard (hil′ərd), *n.* a boy's given name.

Hil·la·ry (hil′ə rē), *n.* **1. Sir Edmund P.,** born 1919, New Zealand mountain climber who scaled Mt. Everest 1953. **2.** Also, **Hilary, Hilaire.** a boy's or girl's given name.

hill·bil·ly (hil′bil′ē), *n., pl.* **-lies,** *adj.* —*n. Often Disparaging.* a person from a backwoods or other remote area, esp. from the mountains of the southern U.S. —*adj.* **2.** of or pertaining to a hillbilly. [HILL + *Billy,* for *William*]

hill′billy mu′sic, **1.** country-and-western music, esp. in a slick, commercialized form. **2.** folk music combined with elements of popular music in which the banjo, fiddle, and guitar are the principal instruments. It originated in the mountain region of the southern U.S.

hill′ clem′atis, a woody vine, *Clematis ligusticifolia,* of western North America, having white flowers.

Hil·lel (hil′el), *n.* ("*ha-Zaken*") c60 B.C.–A.D. 9?, Palestinian rabbi, president of the Sanhedrin and interpreter of Biblical law: first to formulate definite hermeneutic principles. Cf. **Beth Hillel.**

Hil′lel Founda′tion, *U.S.* a national organization, founded in 1924 by the B'nai B'rith, that institutes and administers programs designed to enrich the religious, cultural, and social life of Jewish college students. [named after HILLEL]

Hil·liard (hil′yərd), *n.* a town in central Ohio. 5633 (1960).

Hil·lis (hil′is), *n.* **Margaret,** born 1921, U.S. orchestra conductor.

Hill·man (hil′mən), *n.* **Sidney,** 1887–1946, U.S. labor leader, born in Lithuania.

hill′ my′na, any of several Asian birds of the genus *Gracula,* of the starling family *Sturnidae,* esp. *G. religiosa,* that has glossy black plumage and yellow neck wattles, and that is easily tamed and taught to mimic speech.

hil·lo (hil′ō, hi lō′), *interj., n., pl.* **-los,** *v.i., v.t.,* **-loed, -lo·ing.** hallo.

hil·loa (hi lō′), *interj., n., pl.* **-loas,** *v.i., v.t.,* **-loaed, -loa·ing.** hallo.

hill·ock (hil′ək), *n.* a little hill. [ME *hilloc.* See HILL, -OCK] —**hill′ocked, hill′ock·y,** *adj.*

hill′ock tree′, a tall shrub, *Melaleuca hypericifolia,* of Australia, having rich red flowers.

hill′ of beans′, *Informal.* something of trifling value; virtually nothing at all: *The whole lot of them didn't amount to a hill of beans, as far as she was concerned.*

Hills·bor·o (hilz′bûr ō, -bur ō), *n.* **1.** a town in NW Oregon. 8232 (1960). **2.** a town in central Texas. 7402 (1960). **3.** a town in SW Ohio. 5474 (1960). **4.** a town in central Illinois. 4232 (1960).

Hills·bor·ough (hilz′bûr′ō, -bur′ō), *n.* a town in W California. 7554 (1960).

Hills·dale (hilz′dāl′), *n.* **1.** a town in NE New Jersey. 8734 (1960). **2.** a town in S Michigan. 7629 (1960). **3.** a town in E Missouri. 2788 (1960).

hill·side (hil′sīd′), *n.* the side or slope of a hill. [ME, OE *hille side*]

Hill·side (hil′sīd′), *n.* **1.** a town in NE New Jersey. 22,304 (1960). **2.** a town in NE Illinois. 7794 (1960).

hill·site (hil′sīt′), *n.* a location or site on the side or top of a hill. [HILL + SITE]

hill′ sta′tion, any resort city in S Asia at a high altitude where relief may be found from the tropical heat.

hill·top (hil′top′), *n., v.,* **-topped, -top·ping.** —*n.* **1.** the top or summit of a hill. —*v.i.* **2.** *Fox Hunting.* **a.** to follow the progress of a hunt on horseback but without jumping. **b.** to follow the hunt on foot or in an automobile. [HILL + TOP[1]] —**hill′top′per,** *n.*

hill·y (hil′ē), *adj.,* **hill·i·er, hill·i·est.** **1.** full of hills; having many hills: *hilly country.* **2.** resembling a hill, elevated; steep. [ME; OE *hyllic.* See HILL, -Y[1]] —**hill′i·ness,** *n.*

Hill·yer (hil′yər), *n.* **Robert (Sil·li·man)** (sil′i mən), 1895–1961, U.S. poet and critic.

Hi·lo (hē′lō), *n.* a seaport on E Hawaii island, in SE Hawaii. 25,966 (1960).

hilt (hilt), *n.* **1.** the handle of a sword or dagger. **2.** the handle of any weapon or tool. **3. to the hilt,** to the maximum extent or degree; completely; fully: *armed to the hilt.* Also, **up to the hilt.** —*v.t.* **4.** to furnish with a hilt. [ME, OE *hilt(e);* c. MD *hilt(e),* Icel *hjalt,* OHG *helza* sword-hilt] —**hilt′less,** *adj.*

Hil·ton (hil′tən), *n.* **James,** 1900–54, English novelist.

hi·lum (hī′ləm), *n.* **1.** *Bot.* **a.** the mark or scar on a seed produced by separation from its funicle or placenta. **b.** the nucleus of a granule of starch. **2.** *Anat.* the region at which the vessels, nerves, etc., enter or emerge from a part. [< L: little thing, trifle; see NIHIL, NIL]

Hil·ver·sum (hil′vər səm), *n.* a city in the central Netherlands. 98,998 (1959).

him (him), *pron.* **1.** objective case of **he:** *I'll see him tomorrow.* **2.** the dative case of **he:** *Give him the message.* [ME, OE, dat. of *hē* HE[1]]

H.I.M., His Imperial Majesty; Her Imperial Majesty.

Hi·ma·chal Pra·desh (hi mä′chəl prə dāsh′), a union territory in N India. 1,351,144 (1961); 10,904 sq. mi.; *Cap.:* Simla.

Himala′ya ber′ry, a woody, creeping or climbing, perennial blackberry, *Rubus procerus,* of Europe, having prickly stems, white flowers, and thimble-shaped berries.

Him′ala′yan flea′bane, a perennial herb, *Erigeron multiradiatus,* of the Himalayas, having showy, purple flowers three inches wide.

Him′ala′yan musk′ rose′, a partially climbing rose, *Rosa brunoni,* of the Himalayas, having very fragrant, white flowers in thick clusters.

Him′ala′yan tahr′. See under **tahr.**

Him·a·la·yas (him′ə lā′əz, hi mäl′yəz), *n.* **the,** a mountain range extending about 1500 mi. along the border between India and Tibet. Highest peak, Mt. Everest, 29,028 ft. Also called **the Him′a·la′ya, Him′ala′ya Moun′tains.** —**Him′a·la′yan,** *adj.*

Hi·me·ji (hē′me jē′), *n.* a city on SW Honshu, in S Japan, W of Kobe. 361,179 (1964).

Hi·me·ros (hi′mə ros′), *n.* the ancient Greek god of erotic desire, closely associated with Eros.

Hi·mer·us (hī′mər əs), *n. Class. Myth.* a son of Lacedaemon who unknowingly ravished his sister Cleodice.

Himm·ler (him′lər; *Ger.* him′lər), *n.* **Hein·rich** (hīn′-riKH), 1900–45, German Nazi leader and chief of the secret police.

him·self (him self′; *medially often* im self′), *pron.* **1.** an emphatic appositive of **him** or **he**: *He himself spoke to the men.* **2.** a reflexive form of **him**: *He cut himself.* **3.** (used in absolute constructions): *Himself the soul of honor, he included many rascals among his intimates.* **4.** *Nonstandard.* (used in comparisons after *as* or *than*): *His wife is as stingy as himself.* **5.** *Nonstandard.* (used as the object of a preposition or as the direct or indirect object of a verb): *The old car only had room for himself and three others.* **6.** his normal or customary self: *He is himself again.* **7.** *Irish Eng.* a man of importance, esp. the master of the house: *Himself will be wanting an early dinner.* [ME *him selven,* OE *him selfum,* dat. sing. of *hē self*] **—Usage.** See **myself.**

Him·yar·ite (him′yə rīt′), *n.* **1.** one of an ancient people of southern Arabia speaking a Semitic language. **2.** a descendant of these people. **—*adj.*** **3.** Himyaritic. [< Ar *Himyar* (name of a tribe and an old dynasty of Yemen) + -ITE[1]]

Him·yar·it·ic (him′yə rit′ik), *adj.* **1.** of or pertaining to the Himyarites and to the remains of their civilization. **—*n.*** **2.** a Semitic language anciently spoken in southern Arabia: extinct by 1100. [HIMYARITE + -IC]

hin (hin), *n.* an ancient Hebrew unit of liquid measure equal to about one and one half gallons. [< L (Vulgate) < Gk (Septuagint) < Heb *hīn* < Egypt *hnw*]

Hi·na·ya·na (hē′nə yä′nə), *n.* the earlier of the two great schools of Buddhism, still prevalent in Ceylon, Burma, Thailand, and Cambodia, emphasizing personal salvation through one's own efforts. Also called **Theravada.** Cf. **Mahayana.** [< Skt, equiv. to *hīna* left behind (i.e., poorer) + *yāna* vehicle (lit., movement)]

Hi·na·ya·nist (hē′nə yä′nist), *n.* a Buddhist of the Hinayana school. Also called **Theravadin.** [HINAYAN(A) + -IST]

hinc il·lae la·cri·mae (hiṅk il′ī lä′kri mī′; *Eng.* hiṅk il′ē lak′ri mē), *Latin.* hence those tears.

hind[1] (hīnd), *adj.* **1.** situated in the rear or at the back; posterior: *the hind legs of an animal.* **2. on one's hind legs,** assuming a firm or independent position. [ME *hinde* (adv.), OE *hindan* from behind, at the back; c. G *hinten;* see BEHIND, HINDER[2]] **—Syn. 1.** See **back**[1].

hind[2] (hīnd), *n., pl.* **hinds,** (*esp. collectively*) **hind. 1.** *Zool.* the female of the deer, chiefly the red deer, esp. in and after the third year. **2.** any of several speckled serranid fishes of the genus *Epinephelus,* found in the warmer waters of the western Atlantic Ocean. [ME, OE; c. D *hinde,* Icel, Dan, Sw *hind,* OHG *hinta* (G, LG *Hinde*)]

hind[3] (hīnd), *n. Archaic.* **1.** a peasant or rustic. **2.** a farm laborer. [ME *hine* (sing.), *hīne* (pl.), OE *hīne,* deriv. of *hī(g)na,* gen. pl. of *hīgan* members of a household, domestics]

Hind (hīnd), *n.* a crater in the fourth quadrant of the face of the moon: about 16 miles in diameter.

Hind, Hindustani (def. 1).

Hind., **1.** Hindustan. **2.** Hindustani.

Hind′ and the Pan′ther, The, a didactic, satirical poem (1687) by John Dryden.

Hin·dar·fjall (hin′dər fyäl′), *n.* Hindfell.

hind·brain (hīnd′brān′), *n. Anat.* **1.** the rhombencephalon, being the posterior of the three primary divisions of the brain in the embryo of a vertebrate or the part of the adult brain derived from this tissue, including the cerebellum, pons, and medulla oblongata. **2.** the metencephalon. [HIND[1] + BRAIN]

Hin·de·mith (hin′də mith; *Ger.* hin′də mit), *n.* **Paul** (pôl; *Ger.* poul), 1895–1963, German composer and violist.

Hin·den·burg (hin′dən bûrg′; *Ger.* hin′dən bŏŏrk′), *n.* **1. Paul von** (poul fən; *Eng.* pôl von), (*Paul von Beneckendorff und von Hindenburg*), 1847–1934, German field marshal; 2nd president of Germany 1925–34. **2.** German name of **Zabrze.**

Hin′denburg line′, a line of elaborate fortifications established by the German army in World War I, near the French-Belgian border, from Lille SE to Metz. [named after Field Marshal HINDENBURG]

hin·der[1] (hin′dər), *v.t.* **1.** to cause delay, interruption, or difficulty in; check; retard; hamper: *The storm hindered our progress.* **2.** to prevent from doing, acting, or happening; stop: *to hinder a man from committing a crime.* **—*v.i.*** **3.** to be an obstacle or impediment. [ME *hindre(n),* OE *hindrian* to hold back, deriv. of *hinder* HINDER[2]; c. G *hindern*] **—hin′der·er,** *n.* **—hin′der·ing·ly,** *adv.*
—Syn. 1. impede, encumber, obstruct, trammel. **2.** block, thwart. See **prevent.** **—Ant. 1.** encourage.

hind·er[2] (hīn′dər), *adj.* situated at the rear or back; posterior: *the hinder part of the ship.* [ME; OE *hinder* (adv.) behind; c. G *hinter* (prep.) behind]

hind·er·most (hīn′dər mōst′ *or, esp. Brit.,* -məst), *adj. Obs.* hindmost. [HINDER[2] + -MOST]

Hind·fell (hind′fəl), *n.* (in the *Volsunga Saga*) the mountain on whose fiery top Brynhild slept until awakened by Sigurd. Also, **Hindarfjall.** Cf. **Isenstein.**

hind·gut (hīnd′gut′), *n. Embryol., Zool.* the lower part of the embryonic alimentary canal from which the colon and rectum develop. Cf. **foregut, midgut.** [HIND[1] + GUT]

Hin·di (hin′dē), *n.* **1.** the most widely spoken of the modern Indic vernaculars, esp. its best-known variety, Western Hindi. **2.** a literary language derived from Hindustani, used by Hindus. [< Hindi, Urdu, equiv. to *Hind* INDIA + -*ī* suffix of appurtenance; r. *Hinduee* < Pers *Hindūī*]

hind·most (hīnd′mōst′ *or, esp. Brit.,* -məst), *adj.* furthest behind; nearest the rear; last. [HIND[1] + -MOST]

Hin·doo (hin′do͞o), *n., pl.* **-doos,** *adj.* Hindu.

Hin·doo·ism (hin′do͞o iz′əm), *n.* Hinduism.

Hin·doo·sta·ni (hin′do͞o stä′nē, -stan′ē), *n., adj.* Hindustani. Also, **Hin·do·sta·ni** (hin′dō stä′nē, -stan′ē).

hind·quar·ter (hīnd′kwôr′tər), *n.* **1.** the posterior end of a halved carcass of beef, lamb, etc., sectioned usually between the twelfth and thirteenth ribs. **2. hindquarters.** the rear part of an animal. [HIND[1] + QUARTER]

hin·drance (hin′drəns), *n.* **1.** an impeding, stopping, preventing, or the like. **2.** the state of being hindered. **3.** a means or cause of hindering. [late ME *hinderaunce.* See HINDER[1], -ANCE]
—Syn. 3. impediment, encumbrance, obstruction, check; restraint. See **obstacle.** **—Ant. 3.** aid.

hind′ shank′. See under **shank** (def. 4).

hind·sight (hīnd′sīt′), *n.* recognition of the nature and requirements of a situation, event, etc., after its occurrence. [HIND[1] + SIGHT]

Hin·du (hin′do͞o), *n.* **1.** a person who adheres to Hinduism. **2.** any native or inhabitant of Hindustan or India. **—*adj.*** **3.** of or pertaining to the people of Hindustan or India. **4.** of or pertaining to Hindus or Hinduism. Also, **Hindoo.** [< Pers *Hindū* Indian (adj., n.), equiv. to *Hind* INDIA + -*ū* adj. suffix]

Hin′du-Ar′a·bic nu′merals (hin′do͞o ar′ə bik). See **Arabic numerals.**

Hin·du·ism (hin′do͞o iz′əm), *n.* the common religion of India, based upon the religion of the original Aryan settlers as expounded and evolved in the Vedas, the Upanishads, the Bhagavad-Gita, etc., having an extremely diversified character with many schools of philosophy and theology, many popular cults, and a large pantheon symbolizing the many attributes of a single god. Buddhism and Jainism are outside the Hindu tradition but are regarded as related religions. Also, **Hindooism.** [HINDU + -ISM]

Hin·du·ize (hin′do͞o īz′), *v.t.,* **-ized, -iz·ing.** to convert to or bring under the influence of Hinduism. [HINDU + -IZE]

Hin′du Kush′, a mountain range in S Asia, mostly in NE Afghanistan, extending W from the Himalayas. Highest peak, Tirach Mir, 25,420 ft. Also called **Hin′du Kush′ Moun′tains.**

Hin·dus (hin′dəs), *n.* **Maurice Ger·schon** (gûr′shən), born 1891, U.S. writer, born in Russia.

Hin·du·stan (hin′do͞o stän′, -stan′), *n.* **1.** Persian name of India, esp. the part N of the Deccan. **2.** the predominantly Hindu areas of India, as contrasted with the predominantly Muslim areas of Pakistan. Cf. **India.**

Hin·du·sta·ni (hin′do͞o stä′nē, -stan′ē), *n.* **1.** a standard language and lingua franca of northern India based on a dialect of Western Hindi spoken around Delhi. *Abbr.:* Hind Cf. **Hindi** (def. 2), **Urdu.** **—*adj.*** **2.** of or pertaining to Hindustan, its people, or their languages. Also, **Hindoostani, Hindostani.** [< Hindi, Urdu < Pers, equiv. to *Hindūstān* (*Hindū* HINDU + *stān* country) + -*ī* suffix of appurtenance]

hind·ward (hīnd′wərd), *adv., adj.* backward. [ME; OE *hindanweard* (adv.). See HIND[1], -WARD]

Hines (hīnz), *n.* **1. Earl** ("*Fatha*"), born 1905, U.S. jazz pianist. **2. Jerome,** born 1921, U.S. basso.

Hines·ville (hīnz′vil), *n.* a town in SE Georgia. 3174 (1960).

hinge (hinj), *n., v.,* **hinged, hing·ing.** **—*n.*** **1.** a jointed device or flexible piece on which a door, gate, shutter, lid, or other attached part turns, swings, or moves. **2.** a natural anatomical joint at which motion occurs around a transverse axis, as that of the knee or a bivalve shell. **3.** that on which something is based or depends; principle; central rule. **4.** Also called **mount.** *Philately.* a gummed sticker for affixing a stamp to a page of an album, so folded as to form a hinge, allowing the stamp to be raised to reveal the text beneath. **—*v.i.*** **5.** to depend or turn on, or as if on, a hinge (usually followed by *on* or *upon*): *Everything hinges on his decision.* **—*v.t.*** **6.** to furnish with or attach by a hinge or hinges. **7.** to attach as if by a hinge. **8.** to cause to depend; condition: *He hinged his action on future sales.* [ME *henges* (pl.), OE **hencg* (sing.); c. LG *heng(e),* MD *henge* hinge; akin to HANG] **—hinge′less,** *adj.* **—hinge′like′,** *adj.*

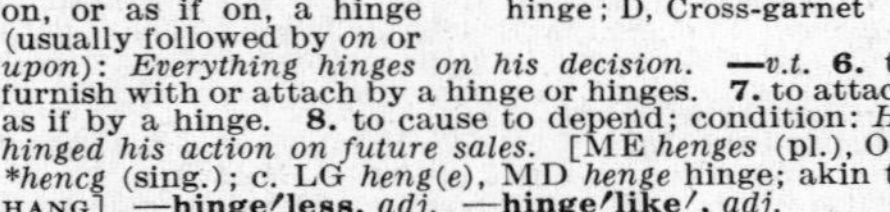

Hinges
A, Butt hinge; B, Strap-hinge; C, Backflap hinge; D, Cross-garnet

hinge′ joint′, *Anat.* ginglymus.

hinge′ strap′, a metal strap imitating the appearance of a strap hinge.

hing′ing post′. See **hanging post.**

hin·ny[1] (hin′ē), *n., pl.* **-nies.** the offspring of a female donkey and a stallion. Cf. **mule**[1] (defs. 1, 2). [obs. *hinne* (< L *hinnus* hinny) + -Y[2]]

hin·ny[2] (hin′ē), *v.i.,* **-nied, -ny·ing.** *Archaic.* to neigh; whinny. [late ME *henny* < MF *henni(r)* < L *hinnīre* (imit.)]

hi·no′ki cy′press (hi nō′kē), an evergreen tree, *Chamaecyparis obtusa,* of Japan, having scalelike leaves and orange-brown cones, grown for timber and as an ornamental. [< Jap *hinoki,* lit., fire-tree]

Hin·shel·wood (hin′shəl wo͝od′), *n.* **Sir Cyril Norman,** 1897–1967, English chemist: Nobel prize 1956.

hint (hint), *n.* **1.** an indirect or covert suggestion or implication; an intimation or clue: *Give me a hint as to his identity.* **2.** a very slight or hardly noticeable amount: *a hint of garlic in the salad dressing.* **3.** *Obs.* an occasion or opportunity. **—*v.t.*** **4.** to give a hint of: *gray skies hinting an early winter.* **—*v.i.*** **5.** to make indirect suggestion or allusion (usually fol. by *at*): *The article hinted at corruption in high places.* [var. of *hent* (n.), ME *hentne, hinten* to seize, OE *hentan,* perh. syncopated var. of **hendettan,* equiv. to *hend(an)* (to) handle (see HAND) + -*ettan* v. suffix] **—hint′er,** *n.*
—Syn. 1. allusion, insinuation, innuendo; memorandum, reminder; inkling. **4.** imply. HINT, INTIMATE, INSINUATE, SUGGEST denote the conveying of an idea to the mind indirectly or without full or explicit statement. To HINT is to convey an idea covertly or indirectly, but intelligibly: *to hint that one would like a certain present; to hint that bits of gossip might be true.* To INTIMATE is to give a barely perceptible hint, often with the purpose of influencing action: *to intimate that something may be possible.* To INSINUATE is to hint artfully, often at what one would not dare to say directly: *to insinuate something against someone's reputation.* SUGGEST denotes particularly recalling something to the mind or starting a new train of thought by means of association of ideas: *The name doesn't suggest anything to me.* **—Ant. 4.** express, declare.

hin·ter·land (hin′tər land′), *n.* **1.** an inland area supplying goods, esp. trade goods, to a port. **2.** the land lying behind a coast district. **3.** an area or sphere of influence in the unoccupied interior claimed by the state possessing the coast. **4.** Often, **hinterlands.** the remote or less developed parts of a country; back country: *The hinterlands are usually much more picturesque than the urban areas.* [< G: lit., hinder land, i.e., land behind]

Hin·ton (hin′tən, -tən), *n.* a town in SE West Virginia. 5197 (1960).

Hior·dis (hyôr′dis), *n.* (in the *Volsunga Saga*) the second wife of Sigmund and the mother of Sigurd. Also, **Hjordis.**

hip[1] (hip), *n., adj., v.,* **hipped, hip·ping.** **—*n.*** **1.** the projecting part of each side of the body formed by the side of the pelvis and the upper part of the femur and the flesh covering them; haunch. **2.** See **hip joint.** **3.** *Archit.* the inclined projecting angle formed by the junction of a sloping side and a sloping end, or of two adjacent sloping sides, of a roof. **4.** *Furniture.* knee (def. 6). **5. on** or **upon the hip,** *Archaic.* at a disadvantage: *to have someone on the hip.* **6. smite hip and thigh,** to attack unmercifully; overcome. Judg. 15:8. **—*adj.*** **7.** (esp. of a garment) extending to the hips; hiplength: *hip boots.* **—*v.t.*** **8.** (esp. of livestock) to injure or dislocate the hip of. **9.** *Archit.* to form (a roof) with a hip or hips. [ME *hipe, hupe,* OE *hype;* c. OHG *huf* (G *Hüf(te)* hip), Goth *hups* hip, loin; cf. Gk *kýbos* cube, the hollow above the hips, L *cubitus* elbow] **—hip′less,** *adj.* **—hip′like′,** *adj.*

hip[2] (hip), *n.* the ripe fruit of a rose, esp. of a wild rose. [ME *hepe,* OE *hēope* hip, briar; c. OHG *hiufo* bramble]

hip[3] (hip), *interj.* (used as a cheer or in signaling for cheers): *Hip, hip, hurrah!* [?]

hip[4] (hip), *adj.,* **hip·per, hip·pest,** *Slang.* familiar with the latest ideas, styles, developments, etc.; informed; sophisticated; knowledgeable. [?]

hip[5] (hip), *n.* hyp.

hip·bone (hip′bōn′), *n.* **1.** See **innominate bone.** **2.** the ilium. **3.** the neck of the femur. [HIP[1] + BONE[1]]

hip′ boot′, a hip-high boot, usually of rubber, worn by fishermen, firemen, etc.

hip·hug·gers (hip′hug′ərz), *n.* (*construed as pl.*) slacks that are belted or fastened at the hips rather than at the waist. [HIP[1] + HUGGER + -S[3]]

hip′ joint′, a ball-and-socket joint between the head of the femur and the innominate bone.

hip′ knob′, one of a pair of knoblike finials at the ends of the ridge of a hip roof.

hip·length (hip′leṅkth′, -leṅth′), *adj.* reaching to or covering the hips, as clothing. [HIP[1] + LENGTH]

hipp-, var. of **hippo-** before a vowel: *hipparch.*

hip·pa·lec·try·on (hip′ə lek′trē on′), *n. Class. Myth.* a four-legged beast with the foreparts of a horse and the hind parts of a rooster. [< Gk, equiv. to *hipp-* HIPP- + *alektryṓn* rooster]

Hip·pa·lus (hip′ə ləs), *n.* a walled plain in the third quadrant of the face of the moon: about 38 miles in diameter.

hip·parch (hip′ärk), *n.* (in ancient Greece) a commander of cavalry. [< Gk *hipparch(os),* equiv. to *hipp-* HIPP- + *-archos* -ARCH]

Hip·par·chus (hi pär′kəs), *n.* **1.** died 514 B.C., tyrant of Athens 527–514. **2.** c190–c125 B.C., Greek astronomer. **3.** a walled plain in the fourth quadrant of the face of the moon: about 100 miles in diameter.

hipped[1] (hipt), *adj.* **1.** having hips. **2.** having the hips as specified (usually used in combination): *broad-hipped; narrow-hipped.* **3.** (esp. of livestock) having the hip injured or dislocated. **4.** *Archit.* formed with a hip or hips, as a roof. [HIP[1] + -ED[3]]

hipped[2] (hipt), *adj. Informal.* greatly interested or preoccupied, almost to an irrational extent; obsessed (usually fol. by *on*): *He's hipped on learning to play the tuba.* [HIP[4] + -ED[3]]

hipped[3] (hipt), *adj.* **1.** Also, **hip′pish.** *Brit.* depressed; low-spirited; melancholy. **2.** vexed; annoyed. [alter. of HYP(OCHONDRIA) + -ED[3]]

Hip·pi·as (hip′ē əs), *n.* fl. 6th century B.C., tyrant of Athens (brother of Hipparchus, son of Pisistratus).

hip·pi·at·rics (hip′ē a′triks), *n.* (*construed as sing.*) the branch of veterinary medicine dealing with horses. [< Gk *hippiatrik(ós),* equiv. to *hippiatr(ós)* veterinarian (*hípp(os)* horse + *iatrós* physician) + -*ikos* -ICS] **—hip′pi·at′ric, hip′pi·at′ri·cal,** *adj.* **—hip·pi·a·trist** (hip′ē ā′trist, hi pī′ə trist), **hip·pi·a·ter** (hip′ē ā′tər), *n.*

hip·pie (hip′ē), *n.* a young person, esp. of the 1960's, who wears unconventional costumes and ornaments, rejects established institutions and values, and seeks spontaneity, direct personal relations expressing love, and expanded consciousness, usually through the use of mind-expanding drugs. Also, **hippy.** [HIP[4] + -IE]

hip·ping (hip′iṅ), *n. Shipbuilding.* a thickness of timber laid between the frames and the planking of a wooden hull to increase the breadth of the water line. [HIP[1] + -ING[1]]

hip·po (hip′ō), *n., pl.* **-pos.** *Informal.* hippopotamus. [by shortening]

Hip·po (hip′ō), *n.* See **Hippo Regius.**

hippo-, an element appearing in loan words from Greek, where it meant "horse" (*hippodrome*); on this model, used in the formation of compound words (*hippology*). Also, *esp. before a vowel,* **hipp-.** [< Gk *hippo(s)* horse; c. L *equus,* OIr *ech,* OE *eoh,* Skt *aśvas*]

hip·po·cam·pal (hip′ə kam′pəl), *adj. Anat.* of or pertaining to the hippocampus. [HIPPOCAMP(US) + -AL[1]]

hip′pocam′pal gy′rus, *Anat.* a convolution on the inner surface of the temporal lobe of the cerebrum, bordering the hippocampus. Also called **hippocam′pal convolu′tion.**

hip·po·cam·pus (hip′ə kam′pəs), *n., pl.* **-pi** (-pī). **1.** *Class. Myth.* a sea horse with two forefeet, and a body ending in the tail of a dolphin or fish. **2.** *Anat.* an enfolding of cerebral cortex into the lateral fissure of a cerebral hemisphere having the shape in cross section of a sea horse. [< L < Gk *hippókampos,* equiv. to *hippo(s)* horse + *kámpos* sea monster]

hip·po·cras (hip′ə kras′), *n.* an old medicinal cordial made of wine mixed with spices. [ME *ypocras,* appar. short for *ypocras wyn* (trans. of ML *vīnum hippocraticum;* so called because clarified by filtering through a strainer named after Hippocrates); ME *Ypocras* < ML *Hippocrās,* alter. of L *Hippocratēs* HIPPOCRATES, on model of words like *cīvitās* (nom.), *cīvitātis* (gen.)]

Hip·poc·ra·tes (hi pok′rə tēz′), *n.* ("*Father of Medicine*") c460–c360 B.C., Greek physician. **—Hip·po·crat·ic** (hip′ə krat′ik), **Hip′po·crat′i·cal,** *adj.*

Hip′pocrat′ic oath′, an oath embodying the duties and obligations of physicians, usually taken by those about to enter upon the practice of medicine.

Hip·po·crene (hip′ə krēn′, hip′ə krē′nē), *n.* a spring on Mount Helicon sacred to the Muses and regarded as a source of poetic inspiration. —**Hip′po·cre′ni·an,** *adj.*

Hip·po·cu·ri·us (hip′ə kyŏŏr′ē əs), *n.* *Class. Myth.* an epithet of Poseidon, meaning "horse-tending."

Hip·pod·a·mas (hi pod′ə məs), *n.* *Class. Myth.* the father of Perimele, who drowned her upon learning that she had been raped.

hip·po·drome (hip′ə drōm′), *n.* **1.** an arena or structure for equestrian and other spectacles. **2.** (in ancient Greece and Rome) a course or circus for horse races and chariot races. [< L *hippodrom(os)* < Gk, equiv. to *hippo-* HIPPO- + *drómos* race-course] —**hip·po·drom·ic** (hip′ə drom′ik), *adj.*

hip·po·griff (hip′ə grif′), *n.* a fabulous creature resembling a griffin but having the body and hind parts of a horse. Also, **hip′po·gryph′.** [earlier *hippogryph*, Latinized < It *ippogrifo.* See HIPPO-, GRIFFIN[1]]

Hip·pol·o·chus (hi pol′ə kəs), *n.* (in the *Iliad*) a son of Bellerophon.

hip·pol·o·gy (hi pol′ə jē), *n.* the study of horses. [HIPPO- + -LOGY] —**hip·po·log·i·cal** (hip′ə loj′i kəl), *adj.* —**hip·pol′o·gist,** *n.*

Hip·pol·y·te (hi pol′i tē′), *n.* *Class. Myth.* a queen of the Amazons, variously said to have been killed by Hercules or to have been conquered and married by Theseus. Also, **Hip·pol·y·ta** (hi pol′i tə).

Hip·pol·y·tus (hi pol′i təs), *n.* **1.** *Class. Myth.* the son of Theseus who was falsely accused by his stepmother, Phaedra, of raping her after he had rejected her advances and who was killed by Poseidon in response to the plea of Theseus. **2.** (*italics*) a tragedy (c450 B.C.) by Euripides. —**Hip·pol′y·tan,** *adj.*

Hip·pom·e·don (hi pom′i don′), *n.* *Class. Myth.* one of the Seven against Thebes.

Hip·pom·e·nes (hi pom′ə nēz′), *n.* *Class. Myth.* the successful suitor of Atalanta. Cf. **Melanion.**

Hip·pon·o·us (hi pon′ō əs), *n.* *Class. Myth.* **1.** a Trojan warrior slain by Achilles. **2.** the father of Periboea.

hip·poph·a·gist (hi pof′ə jist), *n.* a person who eats horseflesh. [HIPPOPHAG(Y) + -IST]

hip·poph·a·gy (hi pof′ə jē), *n.* the practice of eating horseflesh. Also, **hip·poph′a·gism.** [HIPPO- + -PHAGY] —**hip·poph·a·gous** (hi pof′ə gəs), *adj.*

hip·po·phile (hip′ə fil′, -fil), *n.* one who loves horses. [HIPPO- + -PHILE]

hip·po·pot·a·mus (hip′ə pot′ə məs), *n., pl.* **-mus·es, -mi** (-mī′). a large herbivorous mammal, *Hippopotamus amphibius*, having a thick hairless body, short legs, and a large head and muzzle, found in and near the rivers, lakes, etc., of Africa, and able to remain under water for a considerable time. [< L < Gk *hippopótamos* the river-horse (of Egypt), equiv. to *hippo(s)* horse + *potamós* river] —**hip·po·po·tam·ic** (hip′ə pə tam′ik), **hip·po·po·ta·mi·an** (hip′ə pə tā′mē ən), *adj.*

Hippopotamus (4½ ft. high at shoulder; length 13 ft.)

Hip·po Re·gi·us (hip′ō rē′jē əs), a seaport of ancient Numidia: St. Augustine was bishop here; the site of modern Bône, Algeria. Also called **Hippo.**

Hip·po·tho·us (hi pō′thō əs), *n.* *Class. Myth.* a son of Alope and Poseidon who was crowned king of Arcadia.

Hip·po Za·ry·tus (hip′ō zə rī′təs), ancient name of **Bizerte.**

hip·pus (hip′əs), *n.* *Med.* spasmodic contraction of the pupil of the eye. [< NL < Gk *híppos* horse, a complaint of the eye]

-hippus, var. of **hippo-** as final element of compounds: *eohippus.* [< L < Gk *-hippos*]

hip·py[1] (hip′ē), *adj.,* **-pi·er, -pi·est.** having big hips: *a hippy girl.* [HIP[1] + -Y[1]]

hip·py[2] (hip′ē), *n., pl.* **-pies.** hippie. [HIP[4] + -Y[1]]

hip′ roof′, *Archit.* a roof with sloping ends and sides; a hipped roof. See illus. under **roof.** —**hip′-roofed′,** *adj.*

hip·shot (hip′shot′), *adj.* **1.** having the hip dislocated. **2.** lame; awkward. [HIP[1] + SHOT[2]]

hip·ster (hip′stər), *n.* *Slang.* **1.** a person who is hip. **2.** a person, esp. during the 1950's, characterized by a particularly strong sense of alienation from most social intercourse and endeavor. [HIP[4] + -STER]

hi·ra·ga·na (hēr′ə gä′nə), *n.* the cursive and more widely used of the two Japanese syllabaries. Cf. **katakana.** [< Jap, equiv. to *hira* extended, flat, broad + *kana* syllabary, spelling; see KATAKANA]

Hi·ram (hī′rəm), *n.* **1.** a king of Tyre in the 10th century B.C. I Kings 5. **2.** a boy's given name.

Hi·ra·nu·ma (hē rä′nŏŏ mä′), *n.* **Baron Ki·i·chi·ro** (kē ē′chē rô′), 1867?–1952, Japanese statesman.

hir·cine (hûr′sīn, -sin), *adj.* **1.** of, pertaining to, or resembling a goat. **2.** having a goatish odor. **3.** lustful; libidinous. [< L *hircīn(us)* of a goat, equiv. to *hirc(us)* goat + *-īnus* -INE[1]]

hire (hīər), *v.,* **hired, hir·ing,** *n.* —*v.t.* **1.** to engage the services of for wages or other payment: *to hire a clerk.* **2.** to engage the temporary use of at a set price: *to hire a car.* **3.** to grant the temporary use of, or the services of, for a compensation (often fol. by *out*): *We hired ourselves out as baby-sitters. They hire out glassware for parties.* **4.** to pay for the desired action or conduct of: *They hired an investigation of her friends.* **5. hire on,** to obtain employment: *They hired on as wranglers with the rodeo.* **6. hire out,** to offer or exchange one's services for payment: *He hired himself out as a handy man.* [ME *hire(n)*, OE *hӯrian;* c. D *huren,* LG *hüren,* OFris *hēra*] —*n.* **7.** the price or compensation paid or contracted to be paid for the temporary use of something or for personal services or labor; pay: *The laborer is worthy of his hire.* **8.** the act of hiring. **9.** the state or condition of being hired. **10. for hire,** available for use or service in exchange for payment: *chauffeur-driven limousines for hire.* Also, **on hire.** [ME; OE *hӯr;* c. D *huur,* LG *hüre* (whence D *hyre,* Sw *hyra,* G *Heuer*), OFris *hēre*] —**hir′a·ble, hire′a·ble,** *adj.* —**hir′er,** *n.*

—**Syn. 1.** employ. **2, 3.** let, lease. HIRE, CHARTER, RENT refer to paying money for the use of something. HIRE is a general word, most commonly applied to paying money for labor or services, but is also used in reference to paying for the temporary use of automobiles (usually with a chauffeur), halls, etc.; in New England, it is used in speaking of borrowing money on which interest is to be paid (to distinguish from borrowing from a friend, who would not accept any interest): *to hire a gardener, a delivery truck, a hall for a convention.* CHARTER formerly meant to pay for the use of a vessel, but is now applied with increasing frequency to leasing any conveyance for the use of a group: *to charter a boat, a bus, a plane.* RENT is used in the latter sense, also, but is usually applied to paying a set sum once or at regular intervals for the use of a dwelling, room, personal effects, an automobile (which one drives oneself), etc.: *to rent a business building.* **7.** rent, rental; stipend, wages, salary.

hired′ hand′, **1.** a hired laborer, esp. on a farm or ranch; a farm hand or ranch hand. **2.** an employee.

hire·ling (hīər′ling), *n.* **1.** a person who works for payment, esp. an unimportant person who works only for the sake of payment. **2.** a venal or mercenary person. —*adj.* **3.** serving for hire. **4.** venal; mercenary. [OE *hӯrling.* See HIRE, -LING[1]]

hire′-pur′chase sys′tem (hīər′pûr′chəs), *Brit.* a system of paying for a commodity in regular installments while using it. Also called **hire′-pur′chase.**

hir′ing hall′, an employment office conducted by a union for placing members in jobs.

Hi·ro·hi·to (hēr′ō hē′tō; *Jap.* hē′rô hē′tô), *n.* ("*Showa*") born 1901, emperor of Japan since 1926.

Hi·ro·shi·ge (hēr′ō shē′gä; *Jap.* hē′rô shē′ge), *n.* **An·do** (än′dô′), ("*Tokube*"), 1797–1858, Japanese painter.

Hi·ro·shi·ma (hēr′ō shē′mə, hi rō′shi mə; *Jap.* hē′rô shē′mä), *n.* a seaport on SW Honshu, in SW Japan: first military use of atomic bomb August 6, 1945. 492,127 (1964).

hir·ple (hûr′pəl, hir′-), *v.,* **-pled, -pling,** *n.* *Brit. Dial.* —*v.i.* **1.** to walk lamely; hobble. —*n.* **2.** a crawling or limping gait. [late ME (Scot) < ?]

hir·sle (hûr′səl, hir′-), *v.i., v.t.,* **-sled, -sling.** *Scot. and North Eng.* to skid along; move or slide with friction and a grating noise. Also, **hir′sel.** [?]

hirst·ie (hir′stē), *adj.* *Scot.* histie.

hir·sute (hûr′sōōt, hûr sōōt′), *adj.* **1.** hairy; shaggy. **2.** *Bot., Zool.* covered with long, rather stiff hairs. **3.** of, pertaining to, or characteristic of hair. [< L *hirsūt(us)* rough, shaggy, bristly; akin to HORRID] —**hir′suteness,** *n.*

hir·sut·ism (hûr′sōō tiz′əm), *n.* *Med.* excessive hairiness, esp. in women. [HIRSUTE + -ISM]

hir·tel·lous (hûr tel′əs), *adj.* minutely hirsute. [< L *hirt(us)* hairy + *-ellus* dim. adj. suffix; see -OUS]

hir·u·din (hir′yə din, hir′ə-, hi rōōd′ən), *n.* *Biochem.* a gray or white, water-soluble powder obtained from the buccal gland of leeches, used in medicine chiefly as an anticoagulant. [formerly trademark]

Hir·u·din·e·a (hir′ŏŏ din′ē ə), *n.* the class comprising the leeches. [< NL; see HIRUDINEAN]

hir·u·din·e·an (hir′ŏŏ din′ē ən), *n.* **1.** any annelid worm of the class *Hirudinea*, comprising the leeches. —*adj.* **2.** belonging or pertaining to the *Hirudinea.* [< NL *Hirudine(a)* (L *hirūdin-* (s. of *hirūdō*) leech + *-e(a)* (neut.), pl. of *-eus*) + -AN]

hi·ru·di·noid (hi rōōd′ənoid′), *adj.* of, pertaining to, or resembling a leech. [HIRUDIN(EAN) + -OID]

hi·run·dine (hi run′din, -dīn), *adj.* of, pertaining to, or resembling the swallow. [< LL *hirundine(us)* of a swallow, equiv. to *hirundin-* (s. of *hirundō*) swallow + *-eus* adj. suffix; see -EOUS]

his (hiz; *unstressed* iz), *pron.* **1.** the possessive form of **he** (used as an attributive or predicative adjective): *His hat is the brown one. Do you mind his speaking first? This book is his.* **2.** that or those belonging to him: *His was the cleverest remark of all. I borrowed a tie of his.* [ME, OE, gen. of *hē* HE[1]] —**Usage.** See **me.**

his'n (hiz′ən), *pron.* *Nonstandard.* his. Also, **hisn.** [ME *hysene;* cf. HERN[2]]

His·pa·ni·a (hi spā′nē ə, -spän′yə), *n.* *Literary.* Spain.

His·pan·ic (hi span′ik), *adj.* **1.** Spanish. **2.** Latin American: *the United States and its Hispanic neighbors.* —*n.* **3.** Also, **Hispano.** an American citizen or resident of Spanish descent. [< L *hispānic(us).* See HISPANIA, -IC] —**His·pan′i·cal·ly,** *adv.*

His·pan·i·cism (hi span′i siz′əm), *n.* an idiom peculiar to Spanish. [HISPANIC + -ISM]

His·pan·i·cize (hi span′i sīz′), *v.t.,* **-cized, -ciz·ing.** (*sometimes l.c.*) **1.** to make Spanish, as in character, custom, or style. **2.** to bring under Spanish domination or influence. Also, *esp. Brit.,* **His·pan′i·cise′.** [HISPANIC + -IZE] —**His·pan′i·ci·za′tion,** *n.*

his·pa·ni·dad (ēs pä′nē thäth′), *n.* (*often cap.*) *Spanish.* hispanism, esp. as directed toward political objectives.

His·pan·io·la (his′pən yō′lə; *Sp.* ēs′pän yô′lä), *n.* an island in the West Indies, comprising the republic of Haiti and the Dominican Republic. 8,003,000 (est. 1964); 29,843 sq. mi. Formerly, **Haiti, Hayti.**

his·pa·nism (his′pə niz′əm), *n.* (*often cap.*) **1.** a movement in Latin America for the promotion of Spanish culture and influence. Cf. **hispanidad. 2.** a word, phrase, feature, etc., characteristic of or associated with Spain. [< Sp *hispanismo(o)*, equiv. to *hispan(o)* Spanish (< L *Hispānus*) + *-ismo* -ISM]

His·pa·nist (his′pə nist), *n.* a specialist in the Spanish or Portuguese language, literature, or culture. [< Sp *hispanist(a)*, equiv. to *hispān(o)* (< L *Hispānus*) + *-ista* -IST]

His·pa·no (hi spa′nō, hi spä′no), *n., pl.* **-nos.** Hispanic (def. 3).

his·pid (his′pid), *adj.* *Bot., Zool.* rough with stiff hairs, bristles, or minute spines. [< L *hispid(us)* rough, shaggy] —**his·pid′i·ty,** *n.*

his·pid·u·lous (hi spij′ə ləs), *adj.* *Bot., Zool.* covered with stiff, short hairs. [HISPID + -ULOUS]

hiss (his), *v.i.* **1.** to make or emit a sharp sound like that of the letter *s* prolonged, as a cat does, or as steam does when forced under pressure through a small opening. **2.** to express disapproval or contempt by making this sound. —*v.t.* **3.** to express disapproval of by hissing: *The audience hissed the controversial play.* **4.** to silence or drive away by hissing (usually fol. by *away, down,* etc.): *They hissed down the author when he tried to speak.* **5.** to utter with a hiss. —*n.* **6.** a hissing sound, esp. one made in disapproval. [unexplained var. of dial. *hish,* ME *hisshe(n)* (to) hiss, OE *hyscan* to jeer at, rail, deriv. of *husc* jeering; c. OS, OHG *hosc*] —**hiss′er,** *n.* —**hiss′ing·ly,** *adv.*

Hiss (his), *n.* **Alger,** born 1904, U.S. public official, accused of espionage 1948 and imprisoned for perjury 1950–54.

His·sar·lik (hi sär lik′), *n.* the modern name of the site of ancient Troy.

his·self (hi self′, hiz-), *pron.* *Nonstandard.* himself. [ME; see HIS, SELF]

hiss·ing (his′ing), *n.* **1.** the act of hissing. **2.** the sound of a hiss. **3.** *Archaic.* an occasion or object of scorn. [ME; see HISS, -ING[1]]

hist (st; *spelling pron.* hist), *interj.* **1.** (a sibilant exclamation used to attract attention, command silence, etc.) —*v.t.* **2.** to use the exclamation "hist" to. [representing in writing the sound sequence *st*]

hist-, var. of **histo-** before a vowel: *histidine.*

hist., 1. histology. **2.** historian. **3.** historical. **4.** history.

His·ta·drut (his tä drōōt′), *n.* a labor federation in Israel, founded in 1920.

his·tam·i·nase (hi stam′ə nās′), *n.* *Biochem.* an enzyme that catalyzes the decomposition of histamine, used in treating allergies. [HISTAMINE + -ASE]

his·ta·mine (his′tə mēn′, -min), *n.* *Biochem.* **1.** an amine compound, $C_5H_9N_3$, occurring in all plant and animal tissue, produced by the decomposition of histidine and released in allergic reactions, that dilates blood vessels and reduces blood pressure, stimulates gastric secretions, and causes contraction of the uterus. **2.** *Pharm.* a commercial form of this compound, obtained from histidine, and used chiefly in the diagnosis of gastric and circulatory functions. Also, **his·ta·min** (his′tə min). Cf. **antihistamine.** [HIST(IDINE) + -AMINE] —**his·ta·min·ic** (his′tə min′ik), *adj.*

his·ti·dine (his′ti dēn′, -din), *n.* *Biochem.* a crystalline, water-soluble, basic amino acid, $C_3H_3N_2CH_2CH(NH_2)COOH$, derived from fish protamines or from ptomaines when acted upon by sulfuric acid, and converted by putrefactive organisms into histamine. Also, **his·ti·din** (his′ti din). [HIST- + -ID[3] + -INE[2]]

hist·ie (his′tē), *adj.* *Scot.* (of land) barren. Also, **hirstie.** [earlier *hirstie,* equiv. to *hirst* (var. of *hurst* sandy hillock, OE *hyrst* wooded hill) + *-ie* -Y[1]]

his·ti·o·cyte (his′tē ə sīt′), *n.* *Anat.* a macrophage. [< Gk *histío(n),* dim. of *histós* web. See HISTO-, -CYTE] —**his·ti·o·cyt·ic** (his′tē ə sit′ik), *adj.*

his·ti·oid (his′tē oid′), *adj.* histoid.

histo-, a learned borrowing from Greek meaning "tissue," used in the formation of compound words: *histology.* Also, *esp. before a vowel,* **hist-.** [< Gk, comb. form of *histós* web (of a loom), tissue]

his·to·blast (his′tə blast′), *n.* *Biol.* a cell or group of cells capable of forming tissue. [HISTO- + -BLAST]

his·to·chem·is·try (his′tə kem′i strē), *n.* the branch of science dealing with the cellular and subcellular components of tissue. [HISTO- + CHEMISTRY] —**his·to·chem·i·cal** (his′tə kem′i kəl), *adj.* —**his′to·chem′i·cal·ly,** *adv.*

his·to·gen (his′tə jən, -jen′), *n.* *Bot.* a region in a plant in which tissues differentiate. [HISTO- + -GEN]

his·to·gen·e·sis (his′tə jen′i sis), *n.* *Biol.* the origin and development of tissues. [HISTO- + -GENESIS] —**his·to·ge·net·ic** (his′tə jə net′ik), *adj.* —**his′to·ge·net′i·cal·ly,** *adv.*

his·to·gram (his′tə gram′), *n.* *Statistics.* a graph of a frequency distribution in which rectangles with bases on the horizontal axis are given widths equal to the class intervals and heights equal to the corresponding frequencies. [HISTO- + -GRAM[1]]

his·tog·ra·phy (hi stog′rə fē), *n., pl.* **-phies.** a treatise on or description of organic tissues. [HISTO- + -GRAPHY] —**his·tog′ra·pher,** *n.* —**his·to·graph·ic** (his′tə graf′ik), *adj.* —**his′to·graph′i·cal·ly,** *adv.*

his·toid (his′toid), *adj.* **1.** *Pathol.* resembling normal tissue in structure, as a tumor. **2.** similar to or derived from one kind of tissue. Also, **histioid.** [HIST- + -OID]

his·tol·o·gist (hi stol′ə jist), *n.* a specialist in histology. [HISTOLOG(Y) + -IST]

his·tol·o·gy (hi stol′ə jē), *n.* **1.** the branch of biology dealing with the study of tissues. **2.** the structure, esp. the microscopic structure, of organic tissues. [HISTO- + -LOGY] —**his·to·log·i·cal** (his′tᵊloj′i kəl), **his′to·log′ic,** *adj.* —**his′to·log′i·cal·ly,** *adv.*

his·tol·y·sis (hi stol′i sis), *n.* *Biol.* disintegration or dissolution of organic tissues. [HISTO- + -LYSIS] —**his·to·lyt·ic** (his′tᵊlit′ik), *adj.*

his·to·mor·phol·o·gy (his′tō môr fol′ə jē), *n.* histology. [HISTO- + MORPHOLOGY] —**his·to·mor·pho·log·i·cal** (his′tə môr′fə loj′i kəl), *adj.* —**his′to·mor′pho·log′i·cal·ly,** *adv.*

his·tone (his′tōn), *n.* *Biochem.* any of a class of protein substances, as globin, having marked basic properties. [HIST- + -ONE]

his·to·pa·thol·o·gy (his′tō pə thol′ə jē), *n.* the science dealing with the histological structure of abnormal or diseased tissue; pathological histology. [HISTO- + PATHOLOGY] —**his·to·path·o·log·ic** (his′tə path′ə loj′ik), **his′to·path′o·log′i·cal,** *adj.* —**his′to·pa·thol′o·gist,** *n.*

his·to·phys·i·ol·o·gy (his′tə fiz′ē ol′ə jē), *n.* the branch of physiology dealing with tissues. [HISTO- + PHYSIOLOGY] —**his·to·phys·i·o·log·i·cal** (his′tə fiz′ē ə loj′i kəl), *adj.*

his·to·plas·mo·sis (his′tō plaz mō′sis), *n.* *Pathol.* a disease of the reticuloendothelial system, caused by the fungus *Histoplasma capsulatum* and characterized by fever, anemia, and emaciation. [< NL, equiv. to *Histoplasm(a)* name of the genus (see HISTO-, -PLASM) + *-ōsis* -OSIS]

his·to·ri·an (hi stôr′ē ən, -stôr′-), *n.* **1.** an expert in history; authority on history. **2.** a writer of history; chronicler. [HISTORY + -AN; r. *historien* < MF]

his·to·ri·at·ed (hi stôr′ē ā′tid, -stôr′-), *adj.* decorated with figures of people or animals, as the initials of paragraphs or the borders of the pages of a book, manuscript, etc. [< ML *historiāt(us)* (ptp. of *historiāre* to tell a story in pictures, LL: to tell a story, deriv. of L *historia* story; see HISTORY, -ATE[1]) + -ED[2]]

his·tor·ic (hi stôr′ik, -stor′-), *adj.* **1.** well-known or important in history: *a historic spot; historic occasions.* **2.** historical. [< L *historic(us)* < Gk *historikós* historical, scientific, equiv. to *histor(ía)* inquiry (see HISTORY) + *-ikos* -IC]

his·tor·i·cal (hi stôr′i kəl, -stor′-), *adj.* **1.** of, pertaining to, or characteristic of history or past events. **2.** dealing with or treating of history or past events. **3.** conforming to history; free from error in relation to history: *a historical re-enactment of the battle of Gettysburg.* **4.** of, pertaining to, or of the nature of history, as opposed to legend or fiction or as distinguished from religious belief: *It is doubtful that a historical King Arthur ever existed; a theologian's study of the historical Jesus.* **5.** narrated or mentioned in history; belonging to the past. **6.** historic (def. 1). **7.** noting or pertaining to analysis based on a comparison among several periods of development of a phenomenon, as in language, economics, etc. [< L *historic(us)* HISTORIC + -AL[1]] —**his·tor′i·cal·ly,** *adv.* —**his·tor′i·cal·ness,** *n.*

histor′ical geol′ogy, the branch of geology dealing with the history of the earth.

histor′ical linguis′tics, the study of changes in a language or group of languages over a period of time.

histor′ical mate′rialism, (in Marxist theory) the doctrine that all forms of social thought, as art or philosophy, and institutions, as the family or the state, develop as a superstructure founded on an economic base, that they reflect the character of economic relations and are altered or modified as a result of class struggles, that each ruling economic class produces the class that will destroy or replace it, and that dialectical necessity requires the eventual withering away of the state and the establishment of a classless society; the body of theory, in dialectical materialism, dealing with historical process and social causation. Cf. **economic determinism.**

histor′ical meth′od, the development of general principles by the study of the historical facts.

histor′ical nov′el, a narrative in novel form, characterized chiefly by an imaginative reconstruction of historical events and personages.

histor′ical pres′ent, *Gram.* the present tense used in narrating a past event as if it were happening at the time of narration.

histor′ical school′, **1.** a school of economists that arose in Germany in the 19th century in reaction to the principles of the classical economists, and that maintained that the factors making up an economy are variable and develop out of social institutions. **2.** *Law.* the school of jurists who maintain that law is not to be regarded so much as resulting from commands of sovereigns as from historical and social circumstances.

his·tor·i·cism (hi stôr′i siz′əm, -stor′-), *n.* **1.** a theory that history is determined by immutable laws and not by human agency. **2.** a theory that all cultural phenomena are historically determined and that historians must study each period without imposing any personal or absolute value system. **3.** a profound or excessive respect for historical institutions, as laws or traditions. **4.** a search for laws of historical evolution that would explain and predict historical phenomena. [HISTORIC + -ISM] —**his·tor′i·cist,** *n., adj.*

his·to·ric·i·ty (his′tə ris′i tē), *n.* historical authenticity. [prob. < F *historicité.* See HISTORIC, -ITY]

his·to·ried (his′tə rēd), *adj.* containing history; storied; historical: *Italy is a richly historied land.* [HISTORY + -ED[3]]

his·to·ri·og·ra·pher (hi stôr′ē og′rə fər, -stôr′-), *n.* **1.** an historian, esp. one appointed to write an official history, as of a group, period, or institution. **2.** an official historian, as of a court, institution, society, etc. [< L *historiograph(us)* < Gk *historiográph(os)* (see HISTORY, -O-, -GRAPH) + -ER[1]] —**his·to′ri·og′ra·pher·ship′,** *n.*

his·to·ri·og·ra·phy (hi stôr′ē og′rə fē, -stôr′-), *n., pl.* **-phies.** **1.** the body of literature dealing with historical matters; histories collectively. **2.** the body of techniques, theories, and principles of historical research and presentation; methods of historical scholarship. **3.** the narrative presentation of history based on a critical examination, evaluation, and selection of material from primary and secondary sources and subject to scholarly criteria. **4.** an official history: *medieval historiographies.* [< MF *historiographie* < Gk *historiographía.* See HISTORY, -O-, -GRAPHY] —**his·to·ri·o·graph·ic** (hi stôr′ē ə graf′ik, -stôr′-), **his·to′ri·o·graph′i·cal,** *adj.* —**his·to′ri·o·graph′i·cal·ly,** *adv.*

his·to·ry (his′tə rē, his′trē), *n., pl.* **-ries.** **1.** the branch of knowledge dealing with past events. **2.** a continuous, systematic narrative of past events as relating to a particular people, country, period, person, etc., usually written in chronological order: *a history of France; a medical history of the patient.* **3.** the aggregate of past events. **4.** the record of past events, esp. in connection with the human race. **5.** a past that is full of important, unusual, or interesting events: *a ship with a history.* **6.** acts, ideas, or events that will or can shape the course of the future: *First-hand observers of our space program see history in the making.* **7.** a systematic account of any set of natural phenomena, without reference to time: *a history of the American eagle.* **8.** a drama representing historical events: *Shakespeare's comedies, histories, and tragedies.* [ME *historie* < L *historia* < Gk *historía* learning or knowing by inquiry, history]
—**Syn. 2.** account, record, chronicle; annals. See **narrative.**

his·to·throm·bin (his′tə throm′bin), *n.* *Biochem.* thrombin obtained from connective tissue. [HISTO- + THROMBIN]

his·to·tome (his′tə tōm′), *n.* a microtome. [HISTO- + -TOME]

his·tot·o·my (hi stot′ə mē), *n., pl.* **-mies.** **1.** the dissection of animal or plant tissues. **2.** the cutting of tissue into thin sections for examination under a microscope; microtomy. [HISTO- + -TOMY]

his·tri·on·ic (his′trē on′ik), *adj.* Also, **his′tri·on′i·cal.** **1.** of or pertaining to actors or acting. **2.** artificial; affected. —*n.* **3.** *Archaic.* an actor. [< LL *histriōnic(us)* of actors, equiv. to *histriōn-* (s. of *histriō*) actor + *-icus* -IC] —**his′tri·on′i·cal·ly,** *adv.*

his·tri·on·ics (his′trē on′iks), *n.* (*construed as sing. or pl.*) **1.** dramatic representation; theatricals; acting. **2.** artificial behavior or speech done for effect, as insincere assumption of an emotion: *Cut out the histrionics, because we know you're not hurt.* [see HISTRIONIC, -ICS]

his·tri·o·nism (his′trē ə niz′əm), *n.* theatrical method, procedure, style, etc. [HISTRION(IC) + -ISM]

hit (hit), *v.,* **hit, hit·ting,** *n.* —*v.t.* **1.** to deal a blow or stroke: *Hit the nail with the hammer.* **2.** to come against with an impact or collision, as a missile, a flying fragment, a falling body, or the like: *The wheel hit the curb.* **3.** to reach with a missile, a weapon, a blow, or the like, as one throwing, shooting, or striking: *Did the bullet hit him?* **4.** to succeed in striking: *With his final shot he hit the mark.* **5.** *Baseball.* **a.** to make (a base hit): *He hit a single and a home run.* **b.** bat[1] (def. 14). **6.** to drive or propel by a stroke: *to hit a ball onto the green.* **7.** to have a marked effect or influence on; affect severely: *We were all hit by the depression.* **8.** to assail effectively and sharply (often fol. by *out*): *The speech hits out at warmongering.* **9.** to request or demand of: *He hit me for a loan.* **10.** to reach or attain (a specified level or amount): *Prices are expected to hit a new low. The new train can hit 100 m.p.h.* **11.** to appear in; be published in or released to: *When will this report hit the papers? What will happen when the story hits the front page?* **12.** to land on or arrive in: *The troops hit the beach at 0800. When does Harry hit town?* **13.** to give another (playing card, drink, portion, etc.) to: *With 19 showing, shall I hit you again?* **14.** to come or light upon; meet with; find: *to hit the right road.* **15.** to agree with; suit exactly: *I'm sure this purple shirt will hit Alfred's fancy.* **16.** to guess correctly: *You've hit it!* **17.** to succeed in representing or producing exactly: *to hit a likeness in a portrait.* **18.** *Informal.* to drive or propel by a stroke. **19.** *Informal.* to begin to travel on: *Let's hit the road. What time shall we hit the trail?*
—*v.i.* **20.** to strike with a missile, a weapon, or the like; deal a blow or blows: *The armies hit at dawn.* **21.** (of an internal-combustion engine) to ignite a mixture of air and fuel as intended: *This jalopy is hitting on all cylinders.* **22.** to come into collision (often fol. by *against, on,* or *upon*): *The door hit against the wall.* **23.** to come or light (usually fol. by *upon* or *on*): *to hit on a new way.* **24. hit it off,** *Informal.* to be congenial or compatible; get along; agree: *We hit it off immediately with the new neighbors. She and her brother had never really hit it off.* **25. hit off, a.** to represent or describe precisely or aptly: *In his new book he hits off the American temperament with amazing insight.* **b.** to imitate, esp. in order to satirize. **26. hit the high spots, a.** to go out on the town; go nightclubbing: *We'll hit the high spots when you come to town.* **b.** to do something in a brief, casual, superficial, or inefficient manner: *Our cleaning woman hits the high spots and that's about all. This course will hit the high spots of ancient history.*
—*n.* **27.** an impact or collision, as of one thing against another. **28.** a stroke that reaches an object; blow. **29.** a stroke of satire, censure, etc.: *a hit at complacency.* **30.** *Baseball.* See **base hit.** **31.** *Backgammon.* **a.** a game won by a player after his opponent has thrown off one or more men from the board. **b.** any winning game. **32.** a successful stroke, performance, or production; success: *The play is a hit.* **33.** an effective or telling expression or saying: *We savored the barbed hits in his reply.* **34. hit or miss,** without concern for correctness or detail; haphazardly: *The paint job had been done hit or miss.* [ME *hitte(n),* OE *hittan* < Scand; cf. Icel *hitta* to come upon (by chance), meet with] —**hit′less,** *adj.* —**hit′ta·ble,** *adj.* —**hit′ter,** *n.*
—**Syn. 1.** See **strike, beat. 29, 31, 33.** See **blow**[1].

hit-and-miss (hit′ən mis′), *adj.* sometimes operating with perfect harmony of parts and sometimes not.

hit′-and-miss′ win′dow, a window having a glazed upper sash and a lower sash with two panels with spaced slats, one of which slides completely across the other.

hit-and-run (hit′ən run′), *adj.* **1.** hitting and running away, esp. from the scene of an automobile accident: *a hit-and-run driver.* **2.** resulting from such action or conduct: *hit-and-run fatalities.* **3.** *Baseball.* pertaining to or noting a play in which a base runner begins to run to the next base as the pitcher delivers the ball to the batter, who must try to hit it in order to protect the runner. **4.** marked by taking flight immediately after a quick, concentrated attack: *a hit-and-run raid.*

hit′ bats′man, *Baseball.* a batter who, having been hit by a pitch, is awarded first base unless he has swung at the pitch or has not made a reasonable attempt to avoid being hit by it.

hitch[1] (hich), *v.t.* **1.** to fasten or tie, esp. temporarily, by means of a hook, rope, strap, etc.; tether. **2.** to harness (an animal) to a vehicle (often fol. by *up*). **3.** to raise with jerks (usually fol. by *up*); hike up: *to hitch up one's trousers.* **4.** to move or draw (something) with a jerk. **5.** to get (a ride) from someone going the same way; thumb: *to hitch a ride back to college.* **6.** *Slang.* to bind by marriage vows; unite in marriage; marry: *They got hitched in '31.* **7.** to catch, as on a projection: *He hitched his jeans on a nail and tore them.* —*v.i.* **8.** to stick, as when caught. **9.** to fasten oneself or itself to something (often fol. by *on*). **10.** to move roughly or jerkily: *The old buggy hitched along.* **11.** to hobble or limp. **12. hitch up,** to harness an animal to a vehicle: *The peasant hitched up his oxen and began to plow the fields.* —*n.* **13.** the act or fact of fastening, as to something, esp. temporarily. **14.** any of various knots or loops made to attach a rope to something in such a way as to be readily loosened. Cf. **bend**[1] (def. 16). **15.** *Mil. Slang.* a period of military service: *a three-year hitch in the Navy.* **16.** an unexpected halt, delay, or obstruction: *a hitch in our plans for the picnic.* **17.** a hitching movement; jerk or pull. **18.** a hitching gait; a hobble or limp. **19.** a fastening that joins a movable tool to the mechanism that pulls it. **20.** *Mining.* **a.** a fault having a throw less than the thickness of a coal seam being mined. **b.** a notch cut in a wall or the like to hold the end of a stull or other timber. [late ME *hytche(n)* < ?] —**hitch′er,** *n.*
—**Syn. 1.** attach, connect, hook. **2.** yoke. **16.** hindrance, catch, impediment. —**Ant. 1.** loose, loosen.

hitch[2] (hich), *n.* a minnow, *Lavinia exilicauda,* found in streams in the area of San Francisco and the Sacramento River basin. [?]

Hitch·cock (hich′kok), *n.* **1. Sir Alfred (Joseph),** 1899–1980, U.S. motion-picture and television director and producer; born in Britain. **2.** a town in S Texas. 5216 (1960).

Hitch′cock chair′, *U.S. Furniture.* a side chair of the early 19th century, which has turned legs, a turned crest rail and one or more slats in the back, and is painted or stenciled in colors or gold on black. [named after L. A. Hitchcock, 19th-century American furniture maker]

hitch·hike (hich′hīk′), *v.i.,* **-hiked, -hik·ing.** to travel by getting free automobile rides and sometimes by walking between rides. [HITCH[1] + HIKE]

hitch-hik·er (hich′hī′kər), *n.* **1.** a person who hitchhikes. **2.** a dance, deriving from the twist, in which the dancers make hand motions with the fingers clasped and the thumbs extended.

hitch′ing post′, a post to which horses, mules, etc., are tied.

hitch·y (hich′ē), *adj.,* **hitch·i·er, hitch·i·est.** moving with hitches or jerks; jerky. [HITCH[1] + -Y[1]] —**hitch′i·ly,** *adv.* —**hitch′i·ness,** *n.*

hith·er (hith′ər), *adv.* **1.** to or toward this place: *to come hither.* **2. hither and thither,** in various quarters; here and there: *They scurried hither and thither to escape the rain.* **3. hither and yon,** from here to over there, esp. to a farther place; in or to a great many places: *He looked hither and yon for the coin. She went hither and yon in search of an answer.* —*adj.* **4.** on or toward this side; nearer: *the hither side of the meadow.* [ME, OE *hider;* c. Icel *hethra,* L *citer* on this side]

hith·er·most (hith′ər mōst′ *or, esp. Brit.,* -məst), *adj.* nearest in this direction. [HITHER + -MOST]

hith·er·to (hith′ər tōō′), *adv.* **1.** up to this time; until now: *a fact hitherto unknown.* **2.** *Archaic.* to here. [ME *hiderto.* See HITHER, TO]

hith·er·ward (hith′ər wərd), *adv.* hither. Also, **hith′er·wards.** [ME, OE *hiderward.* See HITHER, -WARD]

Hit·ler (hit′lər), *n.* **Ad·olf** (ad′olf, ā′dolf; *Ger.* ä′dôlf), (*Adolf Schicklgruber*) ("*der Führer*"), 1889–1945, Nazi dictator of Germany, born in Austria: Chancellor 1933–45; dictator 1934–45.

Hit·ler·ism (hit′lə riz′əm), *n.* the doctrines, principles, and practices of the Nazi party, esp. as developed by Hitler; Nazism. [HITLER + -ISM]

Hit·ler·ite (hit′lə rīt′), *n.* **1.** an advocate or a follower of Hitlerism. —*adj.* **2.** of or pertaining to Hitler or Hitlerism. [HITLER + -ITE[1]]

hit-or-miss (hit′ər mis′), *adj.* careless; inattentive; haphazard: *The professor criticized the hit-or-miss quality of her work.*

hit-run (hit′run′), *adj.* hit-and-run (defs. 1, 2, 4).

hit-skip (hit′skip′), *adj.* hit-and-run (defs. 1, 2).

Hit·tite (hit′īt), *n.* **1.** a member of an ancient people who established a powerful empire in Asia Minor and Syria, dominant from about 1900 to 1200 B.C. **2.** an extinct language of the Anatolian branch of Indo-European, preserved in cuneiform inscriptions of the second millennium B.C. Hittite was formerly regarded by some specialists as descended from a sister language of Proto-Indo-European. Cf. **Hieroglyphic Hittite.** —*adj.* **3.** of, pertaining to, or belonging to the Hittites or their language. [< Heb *Hitt(īm)* (cf. Hittite *Khatti*) + -ITE[1]]

Hit·tit·ol·o·gy (hit′ī tol′ə jē), *n.* the study of Hittite language and culture. [HITTITE + -O- + -LOGY]

Hit′torf dark′ space′, (hit′ôrf), *Physics.* See **Crookes dark space.** [see HITTORF METHOD]

Hit′torf meth′od, *Physical Chem.* a method for determining the mobility of the ions in a given solution by measuring the amount of material transferred from one electrode compartment to the other during electrolysis. [after J. W. Hittorf (1824–1914), German physicist]

hive (hīv), *n., v.,* **hived, hiv·ing.** —*n.* **1.** an artificial shelter for honeybees; beehive. **2.** the bees inhabiting a hive. **3.** something resembling a beehive in structure or use. **4.** a place swarming with busy occupants: *a hive of industry.* **5.** a swarming or teeming multitude. —*v.t.* **6.** to gather into or cause to enter a hive. **7.** to shelter as in a hive. **8.** to store up in a hive. **9.** to store or lay away for future use or enjoyment. —*v.i.* **10.** to enter a hive. **11.** to live together in a hive. [ME; OE *hȳf;* akin to Icel *hūfr* ship's hull, L *cūpa* vat] —**hive′less,** *adj.* —**hive′like′,** *adj.* —**hiv′er,** *n.*

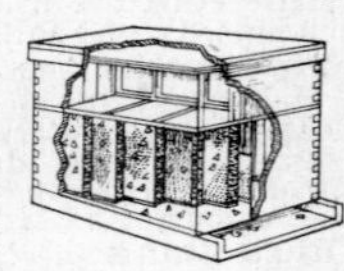

Hive (def. 1) showing removable sections holding combs

hives (hīvz), *n.* (*construed as sing. or pl.*) *Pathol.* any of various eruptive conditions of the skin, as the wheals of urticaria. [Scot < ?]

Hi·vite (hī′vīt), *n.* a member of an ancient people conquered by the Israelites.

H.J., here lies [< L *hīc jacet*]

Hjor·dis (hyôr′dis), *n.* Hiordis.

H.J. Res., House joint resolution.

H.J.S., here lies buried [< L *hīc jacet sepultus*]

hl, hectoliter; hectoliters.

H.L., House of Lords.

HLBB, Home Loan Bank Board.

Hliod (hlyōd), *n.* Liod.

h'm (hmm), *interj.* (used typically to express thoughtful absorption, hesitation, doubt, or perplexity.)

hm, hectometer; hectometers.

H.M., **1.** His Majesty. **2.** Her Majesty.

H.M.S., **1.** His Majesty's Service. **2.** Her Majesty's Service. **3.** His Majesty's Ship. **4.** Her Majesty's Ship.

H.M.S. Pinafore, an operetta (1878) with music by Sir Arthur Sullivan and libretto by Sir W. S. Gilbert.

ho[1] (hō), *interj.* **1.** (used as an exclamation of surprise, delight, exultation, etc.) **2.** (used as a call to attract attention, sometimes specially used after a word denoting a destination): *Westward ho! Land ho!* [ME]

ho[2] (hō), *interj.* (used as a command to halt or to stop an action.) [ME < OF. See WHOA]

H.O., Head Office; Home Office.

Ho, *Chem.* holmium.

ho·ac·tzin (hō ak′tsin, wäk′-), *n.* hoatzin.

Hoad (hōd), *n.* **Lew(is A.),** born 1934, Australian tennis player.

hoa·gy (hō′gē), *n., pl.* **-gies.** *Chiefly Northeastern U.S.* See **hero sandwich.** Also, **hoa′gie.** [?]

Hoang·ho (hwäng′hō′; *Chin.* hwäng′hu′), *n.* See **Hwang Ho.**

hoar (hōr, hôr), *n.* **1.** a hoary coating or appearance. **2.** hoarfrost. **3.** *Rare.* hoariness. —*adj.* **4.** *Rare.* hoary. [ME *hor,* OE *hār;* c. Icel *hārr* gray with age, OFris *hēr* gray, OHG *hēr* old (G *hehr* august, sublime)]

hoard (hōrd, hôrd), *n.* **1.** a supply or accumulation that is hidden or carefully guarded for preservation, future use, etc.: *a vast hoard of silver.* —*v.t.* **2.** to accumulate for preservation, future use, etc., in a hidden or carefully guarded place: *to hoard food during a shortage.* —*v.i.* **3.** to accumulate money, food, or the like, in a hidden or carefully guarded place for preservation, future use, etc. [ME *hord(e),* OE *hord;* c. Icel *hodd,* OHG *hort,* Goth *huzd* treasure] —**hoard′er,** *n.*

hoard·ing[1] (hōr′ding, hôr′-), *n.* **1.** the act of a person who hoards. **2. hoardings,** things that are hoarded. [HOARD + -ING[1]]

hoard·ing[2] (hōr′ding, hôr′-), *n. Brit.* **1.** a temporary fence enclosing a construction site. **2.** a billboard. [obs. *hoard* (<< OF *hourd(e)* palisade made of hurdles < Gmc; cf. G *Hürde* hurdle) + -ING[1]]

Hoare (hōr, hôr), *n.* **Sir Samuel John Gur·ney** (gûr′nē), **1st Viscount Tem·ple·wood** (tem′pəl wŏŏd′), 1880–1959, British statesman.

hoar·frost (hōr′frôst′, -frost′, hôr′-), *n.* frost (def. 2). [ME *hor-forst.* See HOAR, FROST]

hoar·hound (hōr′hound′, hôr′-), *n.* horehound.

hoarse (hōrs, hôrs), *adj.* **hoars·er, hoars·est. 1.** having a vocal tone characterized by weakness of intensity and excessive breathiness; husky: *the hoarse voice of the auctioneer.* **2.** having a raucous voice. **3.** making a harsh, low sound. [late ME *hors* < Scand; cf. Icel *hāss* (var. of **hārs*); r. ME *hoos,* OE *hās,* c. OHG *heis,* OS *hēs*] —**hoarse′ly,** *adv.* —**hoarse′ness,** *n.*
—**Syn. 1.** harsh, grating; throaty, rough.

hoars·en (hōr′sən, hôr′-), *v.t., v.i.* to make or become hoarse. [HOARSE + -EN[1]]

hoar·y (hōr′ē, hôr′ē), *adj.,* **hoar·i·er, hoar·i·est. 1.** gray or white with age. **2.** ancient or venerable. **3.** gray or white. [HOAR + -Y[1]] —**hoar′i·ly,** *adv.* —**hoar′i·ness,** *n.*

hoar·y-head·ed (hōr′ē hed′id, hôr′-), *adj.* having the gray or white hair of advanced age.

ho·at·zin (hō at′sin, wät′-), *n.* a crested, South American bird, *Opisthocomus hoazin,* the young of which have a claw on the second and third fingers of the wing. Also, **hoactzin.** [< AmerSp < Nahuatl *uatzin* pheasant]

hoax (hōks), *n.* **1.** a humorous or mischievous deception, esp. a practical joke. **2.** something intended to deceive or defraud: *The Piltdown man was a scientific hoax.* —*v.t.* **3.** to deceive by a hoax: *to hoax the public with reports of an invasion.* [HOC(U)S] —**hoax′er,** *n.*

hob[1] (hob), *n., v.,* **hobbed, hob·bing.** —*n.* **1.** a projection or shelf at the back or side of a fireplace, used for keeping food warm. **2.** a rounded peg or pin used as a target in quoits and similar games. **3.** a game in which such a peg is used. **4.** *Mach.* a milling cutter for gear and sprocket teeth, splines, threads, etc., having helically arranged teeth and fed across the work as the work is rotated. —*v.t., v.i.* **5.** *Mach.* to cut with a hob. [var. of obs. *hub* hob (in a fireplace); ? same as HUB] —**hob′ber,** *n.*

hob[2] (hob), *n.* **1.** a hobgoblin or elf. **2. play hob with,** *Informal.* to do mischief or harm to: *The little girl played hob with my radio, and now it won't work at all.* **3. raise hob with,** *Informal.* to cause a destructive commotion in; disrupt completely: *She raised such hob with her questions that the meeting broke up.* [ME, special use of *Hob,* for ROBERT or ROBIN] —**hob′like′,** *adj.*

hob-and-nob (hob′ən nob′), *adj.* close; familiar; intimate: *their hob-and-nob friendship.* [see HOBNOB]

Ho·bart (hō′bərt, *or for 1, 2,* -bärt), *n.* **1. Gar·ret Augustus** (gar′it), 1844–99, U.S. lawyer and politician: vice-president of the U.S. 1897–99. **2.** a seaport on and the capital of Tasmania, SE of Australia. 121,275 with suburbs (est. 1963). **3.** a city in NW Indiana. 18,680 (1960). **4.** Also, **Hubert.** a boy's given name.

Hob·be·ma (hob′ə mə; *Du.* hô′be mä), *n.* **Mein·dert** (min′dərt), 1638–1709, Dutch painter.

Hobbes (hobz), *n.* **Thomas,** 1588–1679, English philosopher and author.

Hobbes·i·an (hob′zē ən), *n.* **1.** a person who believes in or advocates the principles of Thomas Hobbes. —*adj.* **2.** of, pertaining to, or recalling the principles of Thomas Hobbes. [HOBBES + -IAN]

Hob·bism (hob′iz əm), *n.* the doctrines of, or those attributed to, Hobbes, esp. the doctrine of absolute submission to a royal sovereign in order to avoid the anarchic disorder resulting from the uncontrolled competition of individual interests. [HOBB(ES) + -ISM] —**Hob′bist,** *n.* —**Hob·bis′ti·cal,** *adj.*

hob·ble (hob′əl), *v.,* **-bled, -bling,** *n.* —*v.i.* **1.** to walk lamely; limp. **2.** to proceed irregularly and haltingly: *His verses hobble with their faulty meters and forced rhymes.* —*v.t.* **3.** to cause to limp: *His tight shoes hobbled him.* **4.** to fasten together the legs of (a horse, mule, etc.) by short lengths of rope to prevent free motion. **5.** to impede; hamper the progress of: *The students' inattention hobbles their learning.* —*n.* **6.** act of hobbling; an uneven, halting gait; a limp. **7.** a rope, strap, etc., used to hobble an animal. **8. hobbles,** a leg harness for controlling the gait of a pacer. **9.** *Archaic.* an awkward or difficult situation. [ME *hobele(n),* appar. akin to *hob* protuberance, uneven ground, and to D *hobbelen,* HG *hoppeln* to jolt]

hob·ble·bush (hob′əl bŏŏsh′), *n.* a North American, caprifoliaceous shrub, *Viburnum alnifolium,* having white flowers and berrylike fruit. Also called **American wayfaring tree.** [HOBBLE + BUSH[1]; so called from the fact that it obstructs the way with its branches]

hob·ble·de·hoy (hob′əl dē hoi′), *n.* **1.** an adolescent boy. **2.** an awkward, clumsy boy. [var. of *hoberdyhoy,* alliterative compound, equiv. to *hoberd* (var. of *Roberd* Robert) + -Y[2] + -*hoy* for BOY (*b > h* for alliteration)]

hob·bler (hob′lər), *n.* **1.** one who or that which hobbles. **2.** *Navig.* See **hobbling pilot.** [HOBBLE + -ER[1]]

hob′ble skirt′, a woman's skirt that is very narrow at the bottom, causing the wearer to walk in short, mincing steps.

hob′bling pi′lot, *Navig.* an unlicensed local pilot employed at a minor port. Also called **hobbler.**

Hobbs (hobz), *n.* a city in New Mexico. 26,275 (1960).

hob·by[1] (hob′ē), *n., pl.* **-bies. 1.** an activity or interest pursued for pleasure or relaxation and not as a main occupation: *His hobbies included stamp-collecting, gardening, and woodcarving.* **2.** a child's hobbyhorse. **3.** *Archaic.* a small horse. **4. ride a hobby,** to concern oneself excessively with a favorite notion or occupation. Also, **ride a hobbyhorse.** [ME *hoby(n),* prob. for *Robin,* or *Robert,* used as horse's name, as in DOBBIN] —**hob′by·ist,** *n.* —**hob′by·less,** *adj.*

hob·by[2] (hob′ē), *n., pl.* **-bies.** a small Old World falcon, *Falco subbuteo,* formerly flown at such small game as larks. [late ME *hoby* < MF *hobet,* equiv. to *hobe* falcon (? akin to OF *hober* to move) + -*et* -ET]

hob·by-horse (hob′ē hôrs′), *n.* **1.** a stick with a horse's head, or a rocking horse, ridden by children. **2.** a figure of a horse, attached at the waist of a performer in a morris dance, pantomime, etc. **3.** a pet idea or project. [HOBBY[1] + HORSE]

hob·gob·lin (hob′gob′lin), *n.* **1.** anything causing superstitious fear; a bogy. **2.** a mischievous goblin. **3.** (*cap.*) Puck (def. 1). [HOB[2] + GOBLIN]

Ho·bie (hō′bē), *n.* a boy's given name, form of **Hobart.**

hob·nail (hob′nāl′), *n.* **1.** a large-headed nail for protecting the soles of heavy boots and shoes. **2.** a small allover pattern consisting of small tufts, as on fabrics, or of small studs, as on glass. [HOB[1] + NAIL]

hob·nailed (hob′nāld′), *adj.* **1.** furnished with hobnails. **2.** rustic or loutish. [HOBNAIL + -ED[3]]

hob·nob (hob′nob′), *v.,* **-nobbed, -nob·bing,** *n.* —*v.i.* **1.** to associate on very friendly terms (often fol. by *with*): *She often hobnobs with royalty.* **2.** to drink together. —*n.* **3.** a friendly, informal chat. [from the phrase *hab or nab* have or have not, OE *hab(ban)* (to) have + *nab(ban)* not to have (*n(e)* not + *hab(ban)* (to) have)]

ho·bo (hō′bō), *n., pl.* **-bos, -boes. 1.** a tramp or vagrant. **2.** a migratory worker. [? rhyming compound based on *beau* fop, used sarcastically as greeting; see HO[1], HEY[1]] —**ho′bo·ism,** *n.*

Ho·bo·ken (hō′bō kən), *n.* a seaport in NE New Jersey, opposite New York City. 48,441 (1960).

Ho·brecht (hō′brekt; *Du.* hō′brekнt), *n.* **Ja·cob** (jā′kəb; *Du.* yä′kôp). See **Obrecht, Jacob.**

Hob·son (hob′sən), *n.* **Richmond Pear·son** (pēr′sən), 1870–1937, U.S. naval officer and politician.

Hob′son's choice′ (hob′sənz), the choice of taking either that which is offered or nothing; the absence of a real choice or alternative. [after Thomas *Hobson* (1544–1631), of Cambridge, England, who rented horses and gave his customer only one choice, that of the horse nearest the stable door]

hoc (hōk), *adj., pron. Latin.* this.

hoc an·no (hōk än′nō; *Eng.* hok an′ō), *Latin.* in this year.

Hoc·cleve (hok′lēv), *n.* **Thomas,** 1370–1450, English poet. Also, **Occleve.**

hoc est (hōk est; *Eng.* hok est), *Latin.* this is.

Hoch·hei·mer (hok′hī′mər; *Ger.* hōкн′hī′məʀ), *n.* a Rhine wine produced at Hochheim, near Mainz, Germany.

Ho Chi Minh (hō′ chē′ min′), 1890?–1969, North Vietnamese political leader: president of North Vietnam 1945–69.

Ho′ Chi′ Minh′ City′, official name of **Saigon.**

Ho′ Chi′ Minh′ Trail′, a network of jungle paths winding from North Vietnam through Laos and Cambodia into South Vietnam, used as a military supply route by North Vietnam during the Vietnam War.

hock[1] (hok), *n.* **1.** the joint in the hind leg of a horse, cow, etc., above the fetlock joint, corresponding anatomically to the ankle in man. See diag. under **horse. 2.** a corresponding joint in a fowl. —*v.t.* **3.** to hamstring. [var. of dial. *hough,* ME *ho(u)gh,* appar. back formation from ME *hokschyn,* etc., OE *hōhsinu* hock (lit., heel) sinew; see HEEL[1]]

hock[2] (hok), *n. Chiefly Brit.* any white Rhine wine. [*Hock(amore)* HOCHHEIMER]

hock[3] (hok), *v.t., n. Informal.* pawn[1] (defs. 1, 3, 6). [< D *hok* hovel, prison, debt] —**hock′er,** *n.*

hock a tchai·nik (hok′ ə chī′nik), **1.** to talk a great deal, esp. about trivial matters; gossip incessantly: *My little Elsie, all she does is sit on the phone and hock a tchainik all day.* **2.** to persist in making a fuss about something of relatively little importance. [< Yiddish: lit., to chop at a teapot]

hock·et (hok′it), *n.* a technique in medieval musical composition in which two or three voice parts are given notes or short phrases in rapid alternation, producing an erratic, hiccuping effect. [ME *hoket* hitch < MF *hocquet* hiccup, sudden interruption, equiv. to *hoc-* (imit.) + -*et* dim. suffix; see HICCUP]

hock·ey (hok′ē), *n.* **1.** See **ice hockey. 2.** See **field hockey.** [earlier *hockie,* perh., equiv. to *hock-* HOOK + -*ie* -IE]

hock′ey skate′, a tubular ice skate, having a shorter blade than a racing skate and often having a reinforced shoe for protection. Cf. **racing skate, tubular skate.**

hock′ey stick′, the stick used in field hockey or ice hockey.

Hock·ing (hok′ing), *n.* **William Ernest,** 1873–1966, U.S. philosopher.

hock·le (hok′əl), *v.,* **-led, -ling,** *n.* —*v.i.* **1.** (of a rope) to have the yarns spread and kinked through twisting in use. —*n.* **2.** the spreading and kinking of the yarns in a rope strand. [? HOCK[1] + -LE]

hock′ leg′, *Furniture.* a leg similar to a cabriole leg, but having a straight perpendicular section between the upper, convex section and the foot.

Hock leg

hock·shop (hok′shop′), *n. Informal.* a pawnshop. [HOCK[3] + SHOP]

ho·cus (hō′kəs), *v.t.,* **-cused, -cus·ing** or (*esp. Brit.*) **-cussed, -cus·sing. 1.** to play a trick on; hoax; cheat. **2.** to stupefy with drugged liquor. **3.** to drug (liquor). [short for HOCUS-POCUS]

ho·cus-po·cus (hō′kəs pō′kəs), *n., v.,* **-cused, -cus·ing** or (*esp. Brit.*) **-cussed, -cus·sing.** —*n.* **1.** a meaningless formula used in conjuring or incantation. **2.** a juggler's trick; sleight of hand. **3.** trickery; deception. **4.** unnecessarily mysterious or elaborate activity or talk to cover up a deception, magnify a simple purpose, etc. —*v.t.* **5.** to play tricks on or with. —*v.i.* **6.** to perform tricks; practice trickery or deception. [sham-Latin meaningless rhyming formula used by jugglers]

hod (hod), *n.* **1.** a portable trough for carrying mortar, bricks, etc., fixed crosswise on top of a pole and carried on the shoulder. **2.** a coal scuttle. [< MD *hodde* basket (? akin to HOOD[1]); c. MHG *hotte* (> MF, ME *hotte*)]

hod′ car′rier, a mason's assistant whose work is to carry hods of materials to the mason. Also called **hodman.**

hod·den (hod′ən), *Scot.* —*n.* **1.** coarse woolen cloth, as hand-loomed by a country weaver. —*adj.* **2.** hand-loomed. Also, **hod′din.** [?]

Ho·dei·da (hŏŏ dā′dä), *n.* the chief seaport of Yemen, in SW Arabia, on the Red Sea. 45,000. (est. 1965).

Ho·der (hô′dər), *n. Scand. Myth.* the blind god who threw a mistletoe shaft, with the help of Loki, and killed his brother Balder. Also, **Hodur.**

hodge (hoj), *n. Chiefly Brit.* an agricultural worker; farm hand. [ME *Hoge* from the proper name *Roger*]

Hodge (hoj), *n.* a boy's given name, form of **Roger.**

Hodg·en·ville (hoj′ən vil′), *n.* a town in central Kentucky: birthplace of Abraham Lincoln. 1985 (1960).

hodge·podge (hoj′poj′), *n.* a heterogeneous mixture; jumble. [var. of HOTCHPOTCH]

Hodg·es (hoj′iz), *n.* **Luther H(art·well)** (härt′wel), 1898–1974, U.S. businessman and politician: Secretary of Commerce 1961–64.

Hodg·kin (hoj′kin), *n.* **1. Alan Lloyd,** born 1914, English biophysicist: Nobel prize for medicine 1963. **2.** his cousin, **Dorothy Mary Crow·foot** (krō′fŏŏt′), born 1910, English chemist: Nobel prize 1964.

Hodg′kin's disease′, a disease characterized by progressive chronic inflammation and enlargement of the lymph nodes of the neck, armpit, groin, and mesentery, by enlargement of the spleen and occasionally of the liver and the kidneys, and by lymphoid infiltration along the blood vessels. [named after Thomas *Hodgkin* (1798–1866), London physician who described it]

hod·man (hod′mən), *n., pl.* **-men.** See **hod carrier.** [HOD + MAN[1]]

Hód·me·zö·vá·sár·hely (hôd′me zœ vä′shär hā), *n.* a city in SE Hungary. 53,000 (est. 1962).

hod·o·graph (hod′ə graf′, -gräf′), *n. Math., Mech.* the figure described by the extremity of a vector that has a fixed origin and a position vector equal to the velocity of a moving particle. [< Gk *hodō(s)* way + -o- + -GRAPH]

ho·dom·e·ter (hō dom′i tər), *n.* odometer.

Ho·dur (hô′dər), *n.* Hoder.

hoe (hō), *n., v.,* **hoed, hoe·ing.** —*n.* **1.** a long-handled implement having a thin, flat blade usually set transversely, used to break up the surface of the ground, destroy weeds, etc. **2.** any of various implements of similar form, as for mixing plaster or mortar. —*v.t.* **3.** to dig, scrape, weed, cultivate, etc., with a hoe. —*v.i.* **4.** to use a hoe. [ME *howe* < OF *houe* < Gmc; cf. MD *houwe,* OHG *houwa* mattock; akin to HEW] —**ho′er,** *n.* —**hoe′like′,** *adj.*

Hoe (hō), *n.* **1. Richard,** 1812–86, U.S. inventor and manufacturer of printing press equipment. **2.** his father **Robert,** 1784–1833, U.S. manufacturer of printing presses.

hoe·cake (hō′kāk′), *n. Southern U.S.* a cake made with corn meal, originally baked on a hoe. [HOE + CAKE]

hoe·down (hō′doun′), *n.* **1.** a community dancing party typically featuring folk and square dances accompanied by lively hillbilly tunes played on the fiddle. **2.** the hillbilly or country music typical of a hoedown. [HOE + DOWN[1]]

Hoek van Hol·land (hŏŏk vän hôl′änt), Dutch name of **Hook of Holland.**

Hoe·nir (hœ′nir), *n. Scand. Myth.* a god, one of the Vanir, who assisted in the creation of Ask and Embla by giving them reason and motion.

hoesh·in (hush′ən), *n. Scot. Archaic.* hushion.

Ho·fer (hō′fər), *n.* **An·dre·as** (än drā′əs), 1767–1810, Tyrolese patriot.

Hof·fa (hof′ə), *n.* **James Rid·dle** (rid′əl), ("Jimmy"), 1913–75?, U.S. labor leader: president of the International Brotherhood of Teamsters 1957–71.

Hoff·man (hof′mən; *Ger.* hôf′män′), *n.* **1. Au·gust Wil·helm von** (ou′gŏŏst vil′helm fən), 1818–92, German chemist. **2. E(rnst) T(he·o·dor) A(ma·de·us) (Wil·helm)** (ernst tā′ō dôr′ ä′mä dā′ŏŏs vil′helm), 1776–1822, German author, composer, and illustrator. **3. Mal·vi·na** (mal vī′nə), 1887–1966, U.S. sculptor.

Hof·mann (hof′mən; *Ger., Pol.* hôf′män′), *n.* **1. Hans,** 1880–1966, U.S. painter, born in Germany. **2. Jo·sef (Cas·i·mir)** (jō′zəf kaz′ə mir), 1876–1957, U.S. pianist and composer, born in Poland.

Hof·manns·thal (hôf′mäns täl′), *n.* **Hu·go von** (hŏŏ′gō fən), 1874–1929, Austrian poet, playwright, and librettist.

Hof·stadt·er (hof′stat′ər, -stä′tər), *n.* **1. Richard,** 1916–70, U.S. historian. **2. Robert,** born 1915, U.S. physicist: Nobel prize 1961.

Ho·fuf (hŏŏ fōōf′), *n.* a city in E Saudi Arabia. 83,000 (est. 1965). Also, **Al Hufuf, Hufuf.**

hog (hôg, hog), *n., v.,* **hogged, hog·ging.** —*n.* **1.** an omnivorous nonruminant mammal of the family *Suidae,* suborder *Artiodactyla,* and order *Ungulata;* pig, sow, or boar; swine. **2.** a domesticated swine weighing more than 120 pounds, raised for market. **3.** *Naut.* **a.** a broom for scraping the underwater parts of a vessel. **b.** See **hog piece. 4.** *Informal.* a selfish, gluttonous, or filthy person. **5.** Also, **hogg, hogget.** *Brit. Dial.* **a.** a sheep about one year old that has not been shorn. **b.** the wool shorn from such a sheep. **c.** any of several

Hog (Domestic)

other domestic animals, as a bullock, that are one year old. 6. *Railroading Slang.* a locomotive. 7. a machine for shredding wood. 8. *Curling.* a stone that stops before reaching the hog score. 9. **go the whole hog,** *Informal.* to carry to the utmost extent; do completely and unreservedly: *We went the whole hog and took a cruise around the world.* Also, **go whole hog.** 10. **live high off the hog,** *Informal.* to be in prosperous circumstances. Also, **eat high off the hog.** —*v.t.* 11. *Slang.* to appropriate selfishly; take more than one's share of. 12. to arch (the back) upward like that of a hog. 13. roach³. 14. (in machine-shop practice) to cut deeply into (a metal bar or slab) to reduce it to a shape suitable for final machining. 15. to shred (a piece of wood). —*v.i.* 16. *Naut.* (of a hull) to droop at both ends in the manner of a hog's back, or have less than the proper amount of sheer because of structural weakness; arch. Cf. **sag** (def. 6a). [ME; OE *hogg* < OBrit; cf. Welsh *hwch* swine] —**hog′like′,** *adj.*

ho·gan (hō′gôn, -gən), *n.* a Navaho Indian dwelling constructed of earth and branches and covered with mud or sod. [< Navaho]

Ho·gan (hō′gən), *n.* **Ben,** born 1912, U.S. golfer.

Ho·gans·ville (hō′gənz vil′), *n.* a town in W Georgia. 3658 (1960).

Ho·garth (hō′gärth), *n.* **William,** 1697–1764, English painter and engraver. —**Ho·garth′i·an,** *adj.*

Ho′garth chair′, *Eng. Furniture.* a Queen Anne chair having a solid splat and cabriole legs, all pieces having a cyma curve or outline. [after William HOGARTH; ? from the fact that it typified the Hogarth line]

HO gauge, a model railroad gauge of 16.5 millimeters. [*h(alf) o*]

hog·back (hôg′bak′, hog′-), *n.* *Geol.* a long, sharply crested ridge, generally formed of steeply inclined strata that are especially resistant to erosion. [HOG + BACK¹]

hog-backed (hôg′bakt′, hog′-), *adj.* cambered, as the ridge of a roof, a hill, etc.

hog·chok·er (hog′chō′kər, hôg′-), *n.* a sole, *Trinectes maculatus,* found in coastal streams from Maine to Texas and south to Panama. [so called to indicate that the fish is worthless, even as food for hogs]

hog′ chol′era, *Vet. Pathol.* a specific, acute, usually fatal, highly contagious disease of swine caused by a filterable virus, characterized by high fever, lack of appetite, diarrhea, depression, and lethargy. Also called **swine fever.**

hog·fish (hôg′fish′, hog′-), *n., pl.* (*esp. collectively*) **-fish,** (*esp. referring to two or more kinds or species*) **-fish·es.** 1. a large wrasse, *Lachnolaimus maximus,* of the western Atlantic Ocean, used for food. 2. any of various other fishes having a fancied resemblance to a hog, as the pigfish and logperch. [trans. of ML *porcopiscis* PORPOISE. See PORK, PISCES]

hog′ frame′, *Naut.* a fore-and-aft truss supporting a hull near its ends. Also called **hog truss.**

hogg (hôg, hog), *n.* *Brit. Dial.* hog (def. 5).

Hogg (hog), *n.* **James** (*"the Ettrick Shepherd"*), 1770–1835, Scottish poet.

hog·ger (hô′gər, hog′ər), *n.* 1. one who or that which hogs. 2. Also called **hog′head′.** *Railroading Slang.* a locomotive engineer. [HOG + -ER¹]

hog·ger·y (hô′gə rē, hog′ə-), *n., pl.* **-ger·ies.** 1. *Brit.* a place where hogs are kept; piggery. 2. behavior typifying a hog, as slovenliness, greed, etc. [HOG + -ERY]

hog·get (hog′it), *n.* *Brit. Dial.* hog (def. 5). [HOG + -ET]

hog·gin (hog′in, hog′in), *n.* *Brit.* a natural mixture of gravel and clay, used for making roads or paths. [?]

hog·gish (hô′gish, hog′ish), *adj.* 1. like or befitting a hog. 2. selfish; gluttonous; filthy. [HOG + -ISH¹] —**hog′gish·ly,** *adv.* —**hog′gish·ness,** *n.*

hog′ Lat′in, *Informal.* See **pig Latin.**

hog·ma·nay (hog′mə nā′), *n.* *Scot. and North Eng.* 1. the last day of the year, December 31; New Year's Eve. 2. any sweet, as an oatmeal cooky, given to children at this time. 3. the visiting of children from house to house at this time to collect their sweets. Also, **hagmenay, hagmane, hog′me·nay′, hog′ma·ne′.** [?]

hog·mol·ly (hôg′mol′ē, hog′-), *n., pl.* **-lies,** (*esp. collectively*) **-ly.** See **hog sucker.** [HOG + *molly,* alter. of MULLET]

hog′nose snake′ (hôg′nōz′, hog′-), any of several harmless, North American snakes of the genus *Heterodon,* having an upturned snout, noted for flattening its head, hissing, or playing dead when disturbed. [HOG + NOSE]

hog·nut (hôg′nut′, hog′-), *n.* 1. the nut of the brown hickory, *Carya glabra.* 2. the tree itself. 3. the pignut. 4. the earthnut, *Conopodium denudatum,* of Europe. [HOG + NUT]

hog′ pea′nut, a twining, fabaceous plant, *Amphicarpa bracteata,* bearing pods that ripen in or on the ground.

hog′ piece′, *Shipbuilding.* (in a wooden hull) a fore-and-aft timber bolted to the top of a keel to provide a good landing for the lower edges of the garboard strakes without rabbeting the upper edges of the keel. Also called **hog′ stave′, keel batten, lay board, rabbet plank.**

hog′ plum′. See **yellow mombin.**

hog′ score′, *Curling.* a line at each end of the rink, parallel to the foot score and usually seven yards in advance of the tee.

hogs·head (hôgz′hed′, hogz′-), *n.* 1. a large cask, esp. one containing from 63 to 140 gallons. 2. any of various units of liquid measure, esp. one equivalent to 63 wine gallons. *Abbr.:* hhd [ME *hoggeshed,* lit., hog's head; unexplained]

hog′ sheer′, *Naut.* a sheer in which the middle part is higher than the ends.

hog′ suck′er, any of several suckers of the genus *Hypentelium,* found in clear, cool streams of the eastern U.S., having a broad head that is concave above. Also called **hogmolly.**

hog·tie (hôg′tī′, hog′-), *v.t.,* **-tied, -ty·ing.** 1. to tie as a hog is tied, with all four feet together. 2. to hamper or thwart: *Repeated delays hogtied the investigation.* [HOG + TIE]

hog′ truss′. See **hog frame.**

Hogue (*Fr.* ôg), *n.* **La** (lA). See **La Hogue.**

hog·wash (hôg′wosh′, -wôsh′, hog′-), *n.* 1. refuse given to hogs; swill. 2. any worthless stuff. 3. meaningless or insincere talk, writing, etc. [HOG + WASH]

hog·weed (hôg′wēd′, hog′-), *n.* any of several weeds, as the ragweed or knotweed. [HOG + WEED¹]

hog-wild (hôg′wīld′, hog′-), *adj.* *Informal.* wildly or intemperately enthusiastic or excited: *They went hog-wild over that new kind of jazz.*

Ho·hen·lin·den (hō′ən lin′dən), *n.* a village in S West Germany, in Bavaria, near Munich: French victory over the Austrians 1800.

Ho·hen·lo·he (hō′ən lō′ə), *n.* a member of a German princely family, fl. 12–19th centuries.

Ho·hen·stau·fen (hō′ən shtou′fən), *n.* a member of the royal family that ruled in Germany from 1138 to 1208 and from 1215 to 1254, and in Sicily from 1194 to 1266.

Ho·hen·zol·lern (hō′ən zol′ərn; *Ger.* hō′ən tsôl′ərn), *n.* a member of the royal family that ruled in Rumania from 1866 to 1947, in Prussia from 1701 to 1918, and in the German Empire from 1871 to 1918.

Ho·ho·kam (hə hō′kəm), *adj.* 1. of, belonging to, or characteristic of an American Indian culture of the central and southern deserts of Arizona from about A.D. 450–1450, roughly contemporaneous with the Anasazi culture to the north. —*n.* 2. the Hohokam culture. [< Pima: old one]

Ho·ho·kus (hə hō′kəs), *n.* a town in NE New Jersey. 3988 (1960).

hoicks (hīks, hoiks), *interj.* *Rare.* huic. Also, **hoick** (hīk, hoik).

hoi·den (hoid′ən), *n., adj.* hoyden. —**hoi′den·ish,** *adj.*

hoi pol·loi (hoi′ pə loi′), the common people; the masses (often preceded by *the*). [< Gk: the many]

hoise (hoiz), *v.t.,* **hoised** or **hoist, hois·ing.** *Archaic.* to hoist. [late ME *hysse,* orig. sailors' cry. See HUZZA]

Hoi·sing·ton (hoi′zing tən), *n.* a town in central Kansas. 4248 (1960).

hoist (hoist), *v.t.* 1. to raise or lift, esp. by some mechanical appliance: *to hoist a flag.* 2. *Archaic.* a pt. and pp. of **hoise.** 3. **hoist with** or **by one's own petard.** See **petard** (def. 3). —*n.* 4. an apparatus for hoisting, as an elevator. 5. *Chiefly Brit.* a freight elevator. 6. act of hoisting; a lift: *Give that sofa a hoist at your end.* 7. *Naut.* **a.** the vertical dimension amidships of any square sail that is hoisted with a yard. Cf. **drop** (def. 24). **b.** the distance between the hoisted and the lowered position of such a yard. **c.** the dimension of a fore-and-aft sail along the luff. **d.** a number of flags raised together as a signal. 8. (on a flag) **a.** the vertical dimension as flown from a vertical staff. **b.** the edge running next to the staff. Cf. **fly** (def. 14). [later var. of HOISE, with *-t* as in AGAINST, etc.] —**hoist′er,** *n.*
—**Syn.** 1. elevate. See **raise.** —**Ant.** 1. lower.

hoist′ing gaff′, *Naut.* See under **gaff**¹ (def. 4). Also called **running gaff.**

hoist′ing yard′, *Naut.* a yard raised to set its sail, as an upper topsail or upper topgallant yard.

hoist·way (hoist′wā′), *n.* a vertical passage for an elevator, dumbwaiter, or the like. Also called, *esp. Brit.,* **shaftway.** [HOIST + WAY]

hoi·ty-toi·ty (hoi′tē toi′tē), *adj.* 1. assuming airs; haughty. 2. *Chiefly Brit.* giddy; flighty. —*n.* 3. a display of pretentiousness; haughtiness. 4. *Obs.* giddy behavior. —*interj.* 5. *Obs.* (used as an exclamation denoting somewhat contemptuous surprise.) Also, **highty-tighty** (for defs. 1, 2, 5). [rhyming compound based on *hoit* to romp, riot (now obs.)]

Ho·jo (hō′jō), *n.* a member of a powerful family in Japan that ruled as regents in place of the shoguns during the period 1203–1333.

ho·key (hō′kē), *adj.* *Slang.* faked; false; contrived: *That second-act curtain was just too hokey.* [irreg. HOK(UM) + -Y¹]

ho·key-po·key (hō′kē pō′kē), *n.* 1. hocus-pocus; trickery. 2. ice cream sold by street vendors. [var. of HOCUS-POCUS]

Ho·kiang (hō′kyäng′; *Chin.* hu′gyäng′), *n.* a former province in Manchuria, in NE China.

Ho·kin·son (hō′kin sən), *n.* **Helen,** c1900–49, U.S. cartoonist.

Hok·kai·do (hôk′kī dō′; *Eng.* ho kī′dō), *n.* a large island in N Japan. 5,318,797 (1964); 30,303 sq. mi. Formerly, **Yezo.**

hok·ku (hô′kōō, hok′ōō), *n., pl.* **-ku.** *Pros.* 1. the opening verse of a linked verse series. 2. haiku. [< Jap, equiv. to *hok* opening, first + *ku* hemistich]

Ho·ko Gun·to (hō′kô gōōn′tô), Japanese name of the **Pescadores.** Also called **Ho·ko·to** (hō′kô tō′).

ho·kum (hō′kəm), *n.* *Informal.* 1. nonsense; bunk. 2. elements of low comedy introduced into a play or the like for the laughs they may bring. 3. sentimental matter of an elementary or stereotyped kind introduced into a play or the like. 4. false or irrelevant material introduced into a speech, essay, etc., in order to arouse interest, excitement, or amusement. [HO(CUS-POCUS) + (BUN)CUM]

Ho·ku·sai (hō′kōō sī′, hō′kōō sī′; *Jap.* hō′kōō sī), *n.* **Ka·tsu·shi·ka** (kä′tsōō shē′kä), 1760–1849, Japanese painter and illustrator.

Hol·arc·tic (hol ärk′tik, -är′tik, hōl-), *adj.* *Zoogeog.* belonging or pertaining to a geographical division comprising the Nearctic and Palearctic regions. [HOL(O)- + ARCTIC]

Hol·bein (hōl′bīn; *Ger.* hôl′bīn), *n.* 1. **Hans** (häns), (*"the elder"*), 1465?–1524, German painter. 2. his son, **Hans** (*"the younger"*), 1497?–1543, German painter who worked chiefly in England.

Hol·brook (hōl′brŏŏk), *n.* a town in central Arizona. 3438 (1960).

HOLC, Home Owners' Loan Corporation. Also, **H.O.L.C.**

hold¹ (hōld), *v.,* **held; held** or (*Archaic*) **hold·en; hold·ing;** *n.* —*v.t.* 1. to have or keep in the hand; keep fast; grasp: *She held the purse in her right hand. He held the child's hand in his.* 2. to set aside; reserve or retain: *to hold merchandise until called for; to hold a reservation.* 3. to bear, sustain, or support, as with the hands or arms, or by any other means. 4. to keep in a specified state, relation, etc.: *He held them spellbound.* 5. to detain: *The police held him at the station house.* 6. to engage in; preside over; carry on; observe or celebrate: *to hold a meeting.* 7. to keep back from action; hinder; restrain: *Fear held him from acting.* 8. to have the ownership or use of; keep as one's own; occupy: *to hold political office.* 9. to contain or be capable of containing: *This bottle holds a quart.* 10. to have or keep in the mind; think or believe: *We hold this belief.* 11. to regard or consider: *to hold a person responsible.* 12. to decide legally. 13. to consider of a certain value; rate: *We held her best of all the applicants.* 14. to keep forcibly, as against an adversary: *Union forces held the hill.* 15. to point, aim, or direct: *He held a gun on the prisoner. The fireman held a hose on the blaze.*
—*v.i.* 16. to remain or continue in a specified state, relation, etc.: *to hold still.* 17. to remain fast; adhere; cling: *Will this button hold?* 18. to keep or maintain a grasp on something. 19. to maintain one's position against opposition; continue in resistance. 20. to agree or side (usually fol. by *with*): *to hold with new methods.* 21. to hold property by some tenure; derive title (usually fol. by *by, from, in,* or *of*). 22. to remain attached, faithful, or steadfast (usually fol. by *to*): *to hold to one's purpose.* 23. to remain valid; be in force: *The rule does not hold.* 24. to refrain or forbear (usually used imperatively). 25. **hold back, a.** to restrain or check: *Police held back the crowd.* **b.** to retain possession of; keep back: *He held back ten dollars.* **c.** to refrain from revealing; withhold: *to hold back information.* **d.** to refrain from participating or engaging in some activity: *He held back from joining in the game because he was afraid to show his ineptness.* 26. **hold down, a.** to restrain; check: *Hold down that noise!* **b.** to continue to hold and manage well: *She held down that job for years.* 27. **hold forth, a.** to extend or offer; propose. **b.** to talk at great length; harangue: *When we left, he was still holding forth on World War II.* 28. **hold in, a.** to restrain; check; curb. **b.** to contain oneself; exercise restraint: *He was raging inside, but held himself in for fear of saying something he would regret.* 29. **hold off, a.** to keep at a distance; resist; repel. **b.** to postpone action; defer: *If you hold off applying for a passport, you may not be able to get one in time.* 30. **hold on, a.** to keep a firm grip on. **b.** to keep going; continue. **c.** to maintain, as one's opinion or position. **d.** *Informal.* to stop; halt (usually used imperatively): *Hold on now! That isn't what I meant at all.* 31. **hold one's own.** See **own** (def. 4). 32. **hold one's peace.** See **peace** (def. 7). 33. **hold one's tongue.** See **tongue** (def. 24). 34. **hold out, a.** to present; offer. **b.** to stretch forth; extend. **c.** to continue to exist; last: *Will the food hold out?* **d.** to refuse to yield or submit: *The defenders held out for weeks.* **e.** *Slang.* to withhold something expected or due: *He was suspected of holding out information important to the case.* 35. **hold over, a.** to keep for future consideration or action; postpone. **b.** to remain in possession or in office beyond the regular term. **c.** to remain beyond the arranged period: *The movie was held over for a week.* **d.** *Music.* to prolong (a tone) from one measure to the next. 36. **hold up, a.** to offer; give: *She held up his father as an example to follow.* **b.** to present to notice; expose: *to hold someone up to ridicule.* **c.** to hinder; delay: *The train was held up because of the storm.* **d.** *U.S. Informal.* to stop by force in order to rob. **e.** to support; uphold: *to hold up farm prices.* **f.** to stop; halt: *They held up at the gate.* **g.** to maintain one's position or condition; endure: *They held up through all their troubles.* 37. **hold water.** See **water** (def. 16). 38. **hold with, a.** to be in agreement with; concur with: *I don't hold with his pessimistic views.* **b.** to approve of; condone: *They won't hold with such a travesty of justice.*
—*n.* 39. the act of holding fast by a grasp of the hand or by some other physical means; grasp; grip: *Take hold. Get hold of the rope.* 40. something to hold a thing by, as a handle; something to grasp, esp. for support. 41. that which holds fast or supports something else. 42. an order reserving something: *to put a hold on a library book.* 43. a controlling force or dominating influence: *to have a hold on a person.* 44. *Wrestling.* a method of seizing an opponent and keeping him in control: *a toe hold.* 45. *Music.* **a.** fermata. **b.** pause (def. 6). 46. a pause or delay, as in a continuing series. 47. a prison or prison cell. 48. a receptacle for something. 49. *Rocketry.* an unforeseen delay in the countdown prior to the launching of a missile. 50. *Archaic.* a fortified place; stronghold. [ME *hold(en),* OE *h(e)aldan;* c. OFris, Icel *halda,* OS, Goth *haldan,* G *halten* (OHG *haltan*)] —**hold′a·ble,** *adj.*
—**Syn.** 8. possess, own. See **have.** 9. See **contain.** 10. embrace, espouse, have. 11. deem, esteem, judge. 16. persist, last, endure. 17. stick.

hold² (hōld), *n.* *Naut.* 1. the entire cargo space in the hull of a vessel. 2. the cargo space in the hull of a vessel between the lowermost deck and the bottom. 3. any individual compartment of such cargo spaces, closed by bulkheads and having its own hatchway. [var. of HOLE; c. D *hol* hole, hold]

hold·all (hōld′ôl′), *n.* 1. *Brit.* a case or bag for carrying miscellaneous articles, used by travelers, soldiers, etc.; carryall. 2. a container for odds and ends. [HOLD¹ + ALL]

hold·back (hōld′bak′), *n.* 1. the iron or strap on the shaft of a vehicle to which the breeching of the harness is attached, enabling the horse to hold back or to back the vehicle. 2. a device for restraining or checking, as a doorstop, tieback, or the like. 3. a stop or delay: *a holdback in negotiations.* 4. a withholding: *the holdback of a day's pay.* [n. use of v. phrase *hold back*]

hold′ beam′, *Naut.* any of a number of beams for reinforcing the frames of a hull, bearing no decking or other load.

hold-down (hōld′doun′), *n.* a clamp for holding a metal piece, as a sheet being deep-drawn, to prevent distortion or movement. [n. use of v. phrase *hold down*]

hold·en (hōl′dən), *v.* *Archaic.* a pp. of **hold.**

Hol·den (hōl′dən, -dən), *n.* a walled plain in the fourth quadrant of the face of the moon: about 25 miles in diameter.

Hol·den·ville (hōl′dən vil′), *n.* a town in central Oklahoma. 5712 (1960).

hold·er (hōl′dər), *n.* 1. something to hold a thing with. 2. a person who has the ownership, possession, or use of something; owner; tenant. 3. *Law.* a person who has the legal right to enforce a negotiable instrument. [ME *haldere.* See HOLD¹, -ER¹] —**hold′er·ship′,** *n.*

Höl′der condi′tion (hel′dər; *Ger.* hœl′dər), *Math.* See **Lipschitz condition.**

Höl·der·lin (hœl′dər lēn′), *n.* **Jo·hann Chris·ti·an Frie·drich** (yō′hän kris′tē än′ frē′driкн), 1770–1843, German poet.

hold·fast (hōld′fast′, -fäst′), *n.* **1.** something used to hold or secure a thing in place; a catch, hook, clamp, etc. **2.** *Bot.* any of several rootlike or suckerlike organs or parts serving for attachment. [n. use of v. phrase *hold fast*]

hold·ing (hōl′ding), *n.* **1.** the act of one who or that which holds. **2.** a section of land leased or otherwise tenanted, esp. for agricultural purposes. **3.** a company owned by a holding company. **4.** Often, **holdings.** property, esp. stocks, bonds, and real estate. [ME *holdung.* See HOLD[1], -ING[1]]

hold′ing com′pany, *Finance.* a company controlling, or able to control, one or more other companies by virtue of stock ownership in these companies, usually without engaging directly in productive operations (distinguished from *parent company*).

hold′ing fur′nace, *Foundry.* a furnace for maintaining molten metal at a desired temperature.

hold′ing ground′, *Naut.* the bottom of a body of water, considered in respect to its ability to hold an anchor.

hold·out (hōld′out′), *n.* **1.** the act of holding out. **2.** an instance of this. **3.** a thing held out. **4.** a person who delays signing a contract in hopes of gaining more favorable terms: *The star was a holdout until they offered more money.* **5.** a person who declines to participate in a group activity or undertaking: *Aside from one holdout, everyone was willing to contribute.* [n. use of v. phrase *hold out*]

hold·o·ver (hōld′ō′vər), *n.* **1.** a person or thing remaining from a former period. **2.** a person who remains in a job, office, etc., after most of his associates have been replaced. **3.** *Print.* overset that can be kept for future use. **4.** a movie, play, or the like, whose engagement is continued beyond the planned closing date, usually because of good attendance. [n. use of v. phrase *hold over*]

Hol·dredge (hōl′drij), *n.* a town in S Nebraska. 5226 (1960).

hold·up (hōld′up′), *n.* **1.** *U.S. Informal.* a forcible stopping and robbing of a person. **2.** a stop or delay in the progress of something: *There was a holdup in the construction of the bridge.* **3.** *Informal.* an instance of being charged excessively. [n. use of v. phrase *hold up*]

hole (hōl), *n., v.,* **holed, hol·ing.** —*n.* **1.** an opening through something; an aperture: *a hole in the roof; a hole in my sock.* **2.** a hollow place in a solid body or mass; a cavity: *a hole in the ground.* **3.** the excavated habitation of an animal; burrow. **4.** a small, dingy, or shabby abode: *They live in a little hole in the country.* **5.** a place of solitary confinement; dungeon. **6.** an embarrassing position or predicament: *to find oneself in a hole.* **7.** *U.S.* a cove or small harbor. **8.** a fault or flaw: *They found serious holes in his reasoning.* **9.** a deep, still place in a stream: *a swimming hole.* **10.** *Sports.* **a.** a small cavity, into which a marble, ball, or the like is to be played. **b.** a score made by so playing. **11.** *Golf.* **a.** the circular opening in a green into which the ball is to be played. **b.** a part of a golf course from a tee to the hole corresponding to it, including fairway, rough, and hazards. **c.** the number of strokes taken to hit the ball from a tee into the hole corresponding to it. **12.** *Metalworking.* (in wire drawing) one reduction of a section. **13.** *Electronics.* a mobile vacancy in the electronic structure of a semiconductor which acts as a positive charge carrier and has equivalent mass. **14.** an air pocket which causes a plane or other aircraft to drop suddenly. **15. burn a hole in one's pocket,** to urge one to spend money quickly: *His inheritance was burning a hole in his pocket.* **16. hole in the wall,** a small or confining place, esp. one that is dingy, shabby, or out-of-the-way, in which a person lives or works: *Their first shop was a real hole in the wall.* **17. in a hole,** in trouble; in financial difficulty. **18. in the hole,** in debt; in straitened circumstances: *After Christmas I am always in the hole for at least a month.* **b.** *Baseball, Softball.* pitching or batting with the count of balls or balls and strikes to one's disadvantage, esp. batting with a count of two strikes and one ball or none. **c.** *Stud Poker.* being the card or one of the cards dealt face down in the first round: *a king in the hole.* **19. make a hole in,** to take a large part of: *A large bill from the dentist made a hole in her savings.* **20. pick a hole or holes in,** to find a fault or flaw in: *As soon as I presented my argument, he began to pick holes in it.* —*v.t.* **21.** to make a hole or holes in. **22.** to put or drive into a hole. **23.** *Golf.* to hit the ball into (a hole). **24.** to bore (a tunnel, passage, etc.). —*v.i.* **25.** to make a hole or holes. **26. hole out,** *Golf.* to strike the ball into a hole: *He holed out in five, one over par.* **27. hole up, a.** to go into a hole; retire for the winter, as a hibernating animal. **b.** *Slang.* to hide, as from pursuers, the police, etc.: *The police think the bank robbers are holed up in Chicago.* [ME; OE *hol* hole, cave, orig. neut. of *hol* (adj.) hollow; c. G *hohl* hollow] —**hole′less,** *adj.* —**hole′y,** *adj.*

—**Syn. 1, 2.** pit, hollow, concavity. HOLE, CAVITY, EXCAVATION refer to a hollow place in anything. HOLE is the common word for this idea: *a hole in turf.* CAVITY is a more formal or scientific term for a hollow within the body or in a substance, whether with or without a passage outward: *a cavity in a tooth; the cranial cavity.* An EXCAVATION is an extended hole made by digging out or removing material: *an excavation before the construction of a building.* **3.** den, cave; lair, retreat. **4.** hovel, shack.

hole-and-cor·ner (hōl′ən kôr′nər), *adj.* **1.** secretive; clandestine; furtive: *The political situation was full of hole-and-corner intrigue.* **2.** trivial and colorless: *She was living a hole-and-corner existence of daily drudgery.* Also, **hole-in-cor·ner** (hōl′in kôr′nər).

hole′ card′, *Stud Poker.* the card dealt face down in the first round of a deal.

hole-high (hōl′hī′), *adj. Golf.* (of a ball) lying on a point almost even with the hole.

hole′ in one′, *Golf.* ace (def. 7a).

hole·proof (hōl′prōōf′), *adj.* **1.** (of an article of clothing) designed so as to prevent holes. **2.** (of a law, legal document, etc.) constructed so as to prevent evasion or subterfuge. [HOLE + -PROOF]

hole′y dol′lar, *Australian.* the rim of a Spanish piece of eight reminted in New South Wales, 1813–29, and issued as an Australian coin worth five shillings. Also, **holy dollar.** Cf. **dump**[3] (def. 2). [so called from the hole in its center]

Hol′ger Niel′sen meth′od (hōl′gər nēl′sən). See **back pressure-arm lift method.** Also, **Hol′ger Niel′sen's meth′od.** [named after *Holger Nielsen* (d. 1955), Danish army officer who was its originator]

Hol·guín (ôl gēn′), *n.* a city in NE Cuba. 57,573 (1960).

Hol Ha·mo·ed (кнôl′ hä mô ād′), *Hebrew.* the period between the first and last two days of Passover or Sukkoth, consisting of four days during Passover and five days during Sukkoth and having less than full festival status. Also, **Chol Hamoed.** [lit., the secular part of the feast]

Ho·li (hō′lē), *n.* the Hindu spring festival. [< Hind *holī* < Skt *holi(kā)*]

hol·i·but (hol′ə bət), *n., pl.* (*esp. collectively*) **-but,** (*esp. referring to two or more kinds or species*) **-buts.** halibut.

hol·i·day (hol′i dā′), *n.* **1.** a day fixed by law or custom on which ordinary business is suspended in commemoration of some event or in honor of some person. **2.** any day of exemption from labor (distinguished from *working day*). **3.** a religious feast day; holy day. **4.** Sometimes, **holidays.** *Chiefly Brit.* a period of cessation from work or one of recreation; vacation. **5.** holy day, esp. any of several, usually commemorative, holy days observed in Judaism. **6.** (esp. in house painting) a place unintentionally left unpainted. —*adj.* **7.** of or pertaining to a festival; festive; joyous: *a holiday mood.* **8.** suitable for a holiday: *holiday attire.* —*v.i.* **9.** *Chiefly Brit.* to vacation: *to holiday at the seaside.* [ME; OE *hāligdæg.* See HOLY, DAY]

Hol·i·day (hol′i dā′), *n.* **Billie** ("*Lady Day*"), 1915–59, U.S. jazz singer.

hol·i·day·er (hol′i dā′ər), *n.* vacationist. [HOLIDAY + -ER[1]]

ho·li·er-than-thou (hō′lē ər *th*ən *th*ou′), *adj.* **1.** obnoxiously pious; sanctimonious; self-righteous. —*n.* **2.** a person who is obnoxiously pious or self-righteous.

ho·li·ly (hō′lə lē), *adv.* **1.** in a pious or devout manner. **2.** in a sacred manner. [ME; OE *hāliglīce.* See HOLY, -LY]

ho·li·ness (hō′lē nis), *n.* **1.** the quality or state of being holy; sanctity. **2.** (*cap.*) a title of the pope, formerly used also of other high ecclesiastics (usually prec. by *His* or *Your*). [ME *holynesse,* OE *hālignes.* See HOLY, -NESS]

Hol·ins·hed (hol′inz hed′, hol′in shed′), *n.* **Raphael,** died c1580, English chronicler. Also, **Hollingshead.**

Hol′inshed's Chron′icles. See **Chronicles of England, Scotland, and Ireland.**

ho·lism (hō′liz əm), *n. Philos.* the theory that whole entities, as fundamental components of reality, have an existence other than as the mere sum of their parts. [HOL(O)- + -ISM] —**ho′list,** *n.* —**ho·lis′tic,** *adj.* —**ho·lis′ti·cal·ly,** *adv.*

hol·la (hol′ə, ho lä′), *interj., n., pl.* **-las,** *v.t., v.i.,* **-laed, -la·ing.** hallo. [< MF *hola,* equiv. to *ho* ahoy + *la* there]

Hol·land (hol′ənd), *n.* **1. John Philip,** 1840–1914, Irish inventor in America. **2.** the Netherlands. **3.** a medieval county and province on the North Sea, now in North and South Holland provinces of the Netherlands. **4.** a city in W Michigan. 24,777 (1960). **5.** *Textiles.* **a.** a cotton cloth treated to produce an opaque finish, as for window shades. **b.** See **Holland finish.**

hol′lan·daise sauce′ (hol′ən dāz′, hol′ən dāz′), a rich sauce for vegetables, fish, etc., made with egg yolks, butter, lemon juice, and seasonings. [< F *sauce hollandaise* Dutch sauce]

Hol·lan·dale (hol′ən dāl′), *n.* a town in W Mississippi. 2646 (1960).

Hol·land·er (hol′ən dər), *n.* **1.** a native of the Netherlands; Dutchman. **2.** *Papermaking, Chiefly Brit.* beater (def. 4). [HOLLAND + -ER[1]]

Hol′land fin′ish, an oil and sizing or starch finish applied to cotton fabrics to increase their opacity and strength. Also called **Holland.**

Hol·lan·di·a (ho lan′dē ə), *n.* a city in and the capital of West Irian, on the NE coast, in Indonesia. 14,462 (est. 1961).

Hol·lands (hol′əndz), *n.* (*construed as sing.*) a gin, originally made in Holland, in which the juniper is mixed in the mash. Also called **Hol′land gin′.** [short for *Holland's gin*]

Hol·le (hô′le), *n. Germanic Myth.* a witchlike goddess or spirit, possibly a lunar goddess, sometimes identified with Perchta.

hol·ler[1] (hol′ər), *Informal.* —*v.i.* **1.** to cry aloud; shout: *Quit hollering into the phone.* —*v.t.* **2.** to shout (something): *He hollered insults back into the saloon.* —*n.* **3.** a loud cry used to express pain or surprise, to attract attention, to call for help, etc. [var. of HOLLO]

hol·ler[2] (hol′ər), *n. Dial.* a hollow.

Hol′ler·ith code′ (hol′ə rith), *Computer Technol.* a system for coding data into punch cards, in which each horizontal row is assigned a different value, and letters, numbers, or special characters are encoded as combinations of these values in a vertical column. [named after H. *Hollerith,* inventor of Hollerith machine (19th century)]

Hol·li·days·burg (hol′i dāz bûrg′), *n.* a town in central Pennsylvania. 6475 (1960).

Hol·lings·head (hol′ingz hed′), *n.* Holinshed.

Hol·lis (hol′is), *n.* **1.** a town in SW Oklahoma. 3006 (1960). **2.** a boy's or girl's given name.

Hol·lis·ter (hol′i stər), *n.* a town in W California. 6071 (1960).

hol·lo (hol′ō, hə lō′), *interj., n., pl.* **-los,** *v.i., v.t.,* **-loed, -lo·ing.** hallo. [var. of HOLLA]

hol·loa (hol′ō, hə lō′), *interj., n., pl.* **-loas,** *v.i., v.t.,* **-loaed, -loa·ing.** hallo.

hol·loo (hol′ōō, hə lōō′), *interj., n., pl.* **-loos,** *v.i., v.t.,* **-looed, -loo·ing.** hallo.

hol·low (hol′ō), *adj.* **1.** having a space or cavity inside; not solid; empty: *a hollow sphere.* **2.** having a depression or concavity: *a hollow surface.* **3.** sunken, as the cheeks or eyes. **4.** (of sound) not resonant; dull, muffled, or deep: *a hollow voice.* **5.** without real or significant worth; meaningless: *a hollow victory.* **6.** insincere or false: *hollow compliments.* **7.** hungry; having an empty feeling: *I feel absolutely hollow, so let's eat.* —*n.* **8.** an empty space within anything; a hole, depression, or cavity. **9.** a valley: *They took the sheep to graze in the hollow.* **10.** *Foundry.* a concavity connecting two surfaces otherwise intersecting at an obtuse angle. —*v.t.* **11.** to make hollow. **12.** to form by making hollow (often fol. by *out*): *to hollow a place in the sand; to hollow out a log.* —*v.i.* **13.** to become hollow. —*adv.* **14.** in a hollow manner: *The politician's accusations rang hollow.* **15. beat all hollow,** *Informal.* to outdo completely: *His performance beat the others all hollow.* Also, **beat hollow.** [ME *holw(e), hol(o)w,* OE *holh* a hollow place; akin to HOLE] —**hol′low·ly,** *adv.* —**hol′low·ness,** *n.*

hol′low back′, *Bookbinding.* a paper tube or roll, almost flattened, having one side glued to the back of a book and the other to the inside of the spine. —**hol′low-backed′,** *adj.*

hol·low-eyed (hol′ō īd′), *adj.* having sunken eyes.

hol·low-forge (hol′ō fōrj′, -fôrj′), *v.t.,* **-forged, -forg·ing.** to produce (a tube or vessel) by trepanning a hole in a forging and expanding it with further forging on a mandrel.

hol·low·heart·ed (hol′ō här′tid), *adj.* insincere; deceitful. [HOLLOW + HEARTED] —**hol′low·heart′ed·ness,** *n.*

Hol′low Men′, The, a poem (1925) by T. S. Eliot.

hol′low new′el, a narrow wellhole in a winding staircase.

hol′low sea′, a wave formation in which the rise from troughs to crests is very steep.

hol·low·ware (hol′ō wâr′), *n.* silver dishes, as serving dishes, having some depth (distinguished from *flatware*). [HOLLOW + WARE[1]]

hol·lus·chick (hol′əs chik′), *n., pl.* **-chick·ie** (-chik′ē). a young male fur seal. [< Russ *kholostyák* bachelor, appar. heard as *hollus* + CHICK]

hol·ly (hol′ē), *n., pl.* **-lies. 1.** any of several trees or shrubs of the genus *Ilex,* as *I. opaca* **(American holly),** the State tree of Delaware, or *I. aquifolium* **(English holly),** having glossy, spiny-toothed leaves, small, whitish flowers, and red berries. **2.** the foliage and berries, used for decoration, esp. during the Christmas season. [ME *holi(e), holyn,* OE *hole(g)n;* c. Welsh *celyn,* Ir *cuillean;* akin to D, G *hulst,* F *houx* (< G)]

American holly, *Ilex opaca*

Hol·ly (hol′ē), *n.* **1.** a town in SE Michigan. 3269 (1960). **2.** a girl's or boy's given name.

hol′ly fern′, a stiff, erect fern, *Cyrtomium falcatum,* of the warm regions of the Eastern Hemisphere, having shaggy leafstalks and fronds with hollylike segments.

Hol′ly Hill′, a town in NE Florida. 4182 (1960).

hol·ly·hock (hol′ē hok′, -hôk′), *n.* **1.** a tall, malvaceous plant, *Althea rosea,* having showy flowers of various colors. **2.** the flower itself. [ME *holihoc,* equiv. to *holi* HOLY + *hoc* mallow, OE *hocc*]

hol′ly oak′. See **holm oak.**

Hol′ly Springs′, a town in N Mississippi. 5621 (1960).

Hol·ly·wood (hol′ē wŏŏd′), *n.* **1.** the NW part of Los Angeles, California: center of the American motion-picture industry. **2.** a city in SE Florida, near Miami: seaside resort. 35,237 (1960). —**Hol′ly·wood·ite′, Hol′ly·wood′er,** *n.*

Hol·ly·wood·i·an (hol′ē wŏŏd′ē ən, hol′ē wŏŏd′-), *n.* **1.** a person who works for the motion-picture industry located in Hollywood, California. **2.** a person born or living in Hollywood, California. —*adj.* **3.** of, suitable to, or characteristic of the motion-picture industry or of the people who work in it, esp. in Hollywood, California; tawdry; emphasizing effect rather than content. **4.** of or pertaining to Hollywood or Hollywoodians. [HOLLYWOOD + -IAN]

Hol·ly·wood·ish (hol′ē wŏŏd′ish), *adj.* of, pertaining to, or resembling Hollywood, Hollywoodians, or the products of Hollywood and the motion-picture industry; highly romanticized and unrealistic: *That film was ruined by its Hollywoodish ending.* [HOLLYWOOD + -ISH[1]]

holm[1] (hōm), *n. Brit. Dial.* **1.** a low, flat tract of land beside a river or stream. **2.** a small island, esp. one in a river or lake. [ME; OE *holm;* c. Icel *holm* islet, Dan *holm,* Sw *holme* a small island, G *Holm* hill, island, Russ *kholm'* hill, L *columen, culmen* hill]

holm[2] (hōm), *n.* **1.** See **holm oak. 2.** *Brit.* a holly tree or shrub. [ME, by dissimilation from *holn,* OE *holen* HOLLY]

Holm (hōlm), *n.* **Han·ya** (hän′ye), born 1895?, U.S. dancer, choreographer, and teacher; born in Germany.

Hol·man-Hunt (hōl′mən hunt′), *n.* **William.** See **Hunt, William Holman.**

Holmes (hōmz, hōlmz), *n.* **1. John Haynes** (hānz), born 1879, U.S. clergyman. **2. Oliver Wen·dell** (wen′dəl), 1809–94, U.S. poet, novelist, essayist, and physician. **3.** his son, **Oliver Wendell,** 1841–1935, U.S. jurist: associate justice of the U.S. Supreme Court 1902–32. **4. Sherlock,** a detective in many mystery stories by Sir Arthur Conan Doyle. **5.** a boy's given name.

Holmes′ light′, a canister, attached to a life buoy or float, containing calcium carbonate and calcium phosphide, which ignite spontaneously on contact with the water, emitting conspicuous fire and smoke. [prob. from the surname *Holmes*]

hol·mic (hōl′mik), *adj. Chem.* of or containing the trivalent element holmium. [HOLM(IUM) + -IC]

hol·mi·um (hōl′mē əm), *n. Chem.* a rare-earth element found in gadolinite. *Symbol:* Ho; *at. wt.:* 164.930; *at. no.:* 67. [< NL; named after (STOCK)HOLM, Sweden; see -IUM]

holm′ oak′, an evergreen oak, *Quercus ilex,* of southern Europe, having foliage resembling that of the holly.

holo-, a learned borrowing from Greek meaning "whole," "entire," used in the formation of compound words: *holomorphic.* [< Gk, comb. form of *hólos*]

hol·o·blas·tic (hol′ə blas′tik, hō′lə-), *adj. Embryol.* (of certain eggs) undergoing total cleavage. Cf. **meroblastic.** [*holoblast* (HOLO- + -BLAST) + -IC] —**ho′lo·blas′ti·cal·ly,** *adv.*

Hol·o·caine (hol′ə kān′, hō′lə-), *n. Pharm., Trademark.* phenacaine.

hol·o·car·pic (hol′ə kär′pik, hō′lə-), *adj.* (of a fungus) having the entire thallus converted into fructifications. Also, **hol′o·car′pous.** Cf. **eucarpic.** [HOLO- + -CARPIC]

hol·o·caust (hol′ə kôst′, hō′lə-), *n.* **1.** a great or complete devastation or destruction, esp. by fire. **2.** a sacrifice completely consumed by fire; burnt offering. **3. the Holocaust,** the systematic mass extermination of European Jews in Nazi concentration camps prior to and during World War II. [ME < LL *holocaust(um)* (Vulgate) < Gk *holókauston* (Septuagint), neut. of *holókaustos* burnt whole. See HOLO-, CAUSTIC] —**hol/o·caus/tal,** *adj.* —**hol/o·caus/tic,** *adj.*

Hol·o·cene (hol/ə sēn/, hō/lə-), *Geol.* —*adj.* **1.** recent (def. 4). —*n.* **2.** recent (def. 5). [HOLO- + -CENE]

hol·o·crine (hol/ə krin, -krīn/, hō/lə-), *adj.* **1.** (of a gland) producing a secretion formed by the disintegration of the glandular cells. **2.** (of a secretion) produced by such a gland. [HOLO- + *-crine* < Gk *krīn(ein)* (to) separate]

hol·o·en·zyme (hol/ō en/zīm), *n. Biochem.* an enzyme complete in both its apoenzyme and coenzyme components. [HOLO- + ENZYME]

Hol·o·fer·nes (hol/ə fûr/nēz, hō/lə-), *n.* (in the Book of Judith) a general, serving Nebuchadnezzar, who was killed by Judith.

hol·o·go·nid·i·um (hol/ō gə nid/ē əm, hō/lō-), *n., pl.* **-nid·i·a** (-nid/ē ə). *Bot.* soredium. [< NL; see HOLO-, GONIDIUM]

ho·lo·gram (hō/lə gram, hol/ə-), *n. Optics.* a negative produced by exposing a high-resolution photographic plate, without camera or lens, near a subject illuminated by monochromatic, coherent radiation, as from a laser: when placed in a beam of coherent light a true three-dimensional image of the subject is formed. [HOLO- + -GRAM[1]]

hol·o·graph (hol/ə graf/, -gräf/, hō/lə-), *adj.* **1.** Also, **hol·o·graph·ic** (hol/ə graf/ik), **hol/o·graph/i·cal.** wholly written by the person in whose name it appears: *a holograph letter.* —*n.* **2.** a holograph writing, as a deed, will, letter, etc. [< LL *holograph(us)* < LGk *hológraphos.* See HOLO-, -GRAPH]

hol/ographic will/, *Law.* a will that is entirely in the handwriting of the testator: in some States recognized as valid without the attestation of witnesses. Cf. **nuncupative will.**

ho·log·ra·phy (hə log/rə fē), *n.* the process or technique of making holograms. [HOLO- + -GRAPHY]

hol·o·he·dral (hol/ə hē/drəl, hō/lə-), *adj.* (of a crystal) having all the planes or faces required by the maximum symmetry of the system to which it belongs. [HOLO- + -HEDRAL] —**hol/o·he/dry, hol/o·he/drism,** *n.*

hol·o·lith (hol/ə lith), *n. Jewelry.* a ring made from a single piece of stone. [HOLO- + -LITH]

hol·o·me·tab·o·lous (hol/ə mi tab/ə ləs), *adj. Entomol.* undergoing complete metamorphosis. Also, **hol·o·met·a·bol·ic** (hol/ō met/ə bol/ik). [HOLO- + Gk *meta-bólos;* see METABOLISM, -OUS] —**hol/o·me·tab/o·lism, hol/o·me·tab/o·ly,** *n.*

hol·o·mor·phic (hol/ə môr/fik), *adj. Math.* analytic (def. 5). [HOLO- + -MORPHIC] —**hol/o·mor/phism, hol/o·mor/phy,** *n.*

Hol·o·phane (hol/ə fān/, hō/lə-), *n. Trademark.* a type of glass having a surface pattern of small, lenslike areas for even diffusion of light.

hol·o·phote (hol/ə fōt/, hō/lə-), *n. Rare.* an apparatus by which practically all the light from a lighthouse lamp or the like is thrown in a desired direction. [back formation from *holophotal* (HOLO- + *-photal*); see PHOTIC, -AL[1]]

hol·o·phrase (hol/ə frāz/, hō/lə-), *n.* a word functioning as a phrase or sentence, as the imperative, *Go!* [HOLO- + PHRASE]

ho·loph·ra·sis (hə lof/rə sis), *n., pl.* **-ses** (-sēz). the expression of the ideas of a phrase or sentence in one word; polysynthesis: *a language characterized by holophrasis.* [HOLO- + Gk *phrásis;* see PHRASE]

hol·o·phras·tic (hol/ə fras/tik, hō/lə-), *adj.* **1.** using or consisting of a single word that functions as a phrase or sentence. **2.** characterized by holophrasis; polysynthetic: *a holophrastic language.* [HOLO- + *-phrastic;* see PERIPHRASTIC]

hol·o·phyt·ic (hol/ə fit/ik, hō/lə-), *adj.* (of a plant) obtaining food by synthesizing inorganic substances; autotrophic. [HOLO- + *-phytic;* see -PHYTE, -IC] —**hol·o·phyte** (hol/ə fīt/), *n.*

hol·op·neus·tic (hol/əp nōō/stik, -nyōō/-, hō/ləp-), *adj. Entomol.* having all the spiracles open, as the tracheal systems of most insects. [HOLO- + Gk *pneustik(ós)* pertaining to breathing, equiv. to *pneust(ós)* (verbid of *pnein* to breathe) + *-ikos* -IC]

hol·o·ser·i·ceous (hol/ə si rish/əs, hō/lə-), *adj. Bot., Zool.* covered with short, silky hairs. [HOLO- + SERICEOUS]

hol·o·thu·ri·an (hol/ə thōōr/ē ən, hō/lə-), *n.* **1.** any echinoderm of the class *Holothuroidea*, comprising the sea cucumbers. —*adj.* **2.** belonging or pertaining to the *Holothuroidea.* Also, **hol·o·thu·ri·oid** (hol/ə thōōr/ē-oid/). [< NL *Holothūri(a)* genus name (pl. of L *holothūrium* < Gk *holothoúrion* kind of zoophyte, equiv. to *holo-* HOLO- + *-thourion* < ?) + -AN]

Hol·o·thu·roi·de·a (hol/ə thōō roi/dē ə), *n.* the class comprising the sea cucumbers. [< NL, equiv. to *Holothūr(ia)* the genus (see HOLOTHURIAN) + *-oidea* -OIDEA]

hol·o·type (hol/ə tīp/, hō/lə-), *n. Biol.* the type specimen used in the original description of a species. [HOLO- + -TYPE] —**hol·o·typ·ic** (hol/ə tip/ik), *adj.*

hol·o·zo·ic (hol/ə zō/ik, hō/lə-), *adj. Biol.* feeding on solid food particles in the manner of most animals, as protozoans. [HOLO- + *-zoic* < Gk *zōik(ós)* of animals, equiv. to *zō(ē)* life + *-ikos* -IC]

holp (hōlp), *v.* a pt. of **help.**

hol·pen (hōl/pən), *v.* a pp. of **help.**

hols (holz), *n. pl.* Sometimes, **hol.** *Brit. Informal.* holiday (def. 4). [by shortening]

Holst (hōlst), *n.* **Gus·tav Theodore** (gōōs/täv), 1874–1934, English composer.

Holstein, *Bos taurus* (4 ft. high at shoulder)

Hol·stein (hōl/stīn; *for 1 also* hōl/stēn; *for 2 also Ger.* hōl/shtīn/), *n.* **1.** Also called **Hol·stein-Frie·sian** (hōl/stīn frē/zhən, -stēn-). one of a breed of black-and-white dairy cattle, raised originally in North Holland and Friesland, yielding large quantities of milk that has a low content of butterfat. **2.** a district in N West Germany, at the base of the peninsula of Jutland: a former duchy. Cf. **Schleswig-Holstein.**

hol·ster (hōl/stər), *n.* a leather case for a pistol, attached to a belt at the hip or over the shoulder or to a saddle. [var. of *hulster* < Sw *hölster* (> D *holster*); c. Icel *hulstr* sheath; akin to OE *heolstor* to cover, *helan* to cover, hide] —**hol/stered,** *adj.*

holt (hōlt), *n. Archaic.* **1.** a wood or grove. **2.** a wooded hill. [ME *holte,* OE *holt;* c. D *hout,* Icel *holt,* G *Holz* wood; akin to Gk *klád(os)* twig, OIr *caill* wood]

Holt (hōlt), *n.* **1. Harold Edward,** 1908–67, Australian political leader: prime minister since 1966. **2.** a town in central Michigan. 4818 (1960).

Hol·ton (hōl/tən, -tən), *n.* a town in Kansas. 3028 (1960).

Holt·ville (hōlt/vil), *n.* a town in California. 3080 (1960).

ho·lus-bo·lus (hō/ləs bō/ləs), *adv. Informal.* all at once; altogether. [mock-L rhyming compound based on phrase *whole bolus.* See WHOLE, BOLUS]

ho·ly (hō/lē), *adj.,* **-li·er, -li·est,** *n., pl.* **-lies.** —*adj.* **1.** specially recognized as or declared sacred by religious use or authority; consecrated: *holy ground.* **2.** dedicated or devoted to the service of God, the church, or religion: *a holy man.* **3.** saintly; godly; pious; devout: *a holy life.* **4.** of religious purity, exaltation, solemnity, etc.: *a holy love.* **5.** entitled to worship or profound religious reverence because of divine character or origin, or connection with God or divinity: *a holy relic; a holy image.* **6.** religious: *holy rites.* **7.** inspiring fear, awe, etc.; frightening. **8. holy terror,** a difficult or obstreperous person; a person who is a behavior problem: *Their little boy is a holy terror.* —*n.* **9.** a place of worship; a sacred place. **10.** holy things or persons collectively. [ME *holi,* OE *hālig,* var. of *hāleg,* equiv. to *hāl* WHOLE + *-eg* -Y[1]; c. D, G *heilig,* Icel *heilagr*]

—**Syn. 1.** blessed. HOLY, SACRED, CONSECRATED, HALLOWED imply possession of a sanctity which is the object of religious veneration. HOLY refers to the divine, that which has its sanctity directly from God or is connected with Him: *Remember the Sabbath day to keep it holy.* That which is SACRED, while sometimes accepted as entitled to religious veneration, may have its sanctity from human authority: *a sacred oath.* That which is CONSECRATED is specially or formally dedicated to some religious use: *a life consecrated to service.* That which is HALLOWED has been made holy by being worshiped: *a hallowed shrine.* **4.** spiritual, pure.

Ho/ly Alli/ance, a league formed by the principal sovereigns of Europe in 1815 with the professed object of promoting Christian brotherhood but the practical object of repressing democratic revolutions and institutions. The English and Turkish rulers and Pope Pius VII did not join the league.

Ho/ly Ark/, *Judaism.* a cabinet in a synagogue set into or against the wall that faces Jerusalem, for keeping the scrolls of the Torah.

Ho/ly Bi/ble, Bible (def. 1).

ho/ly bread/, 1. bread used in a Eucharistic service, both before and after consecration. **2.** *Eastern Ch.* eulogia (def. 1). **3.** *Gk. Orth. Ch.* antidoron (def. 1). [ME *holibrede*]

ho/ly cats/, *Slang.* (used as an exclamation to express surprise, wonder, confusion, etc.)

Ho/ly Cit/y, (*sometimes l.c.*) **1.** a city regarded as particularly sacred by the adherents of a religious faith, as Jerusalem by Jews and Christians, Mecca and Medina by Muslims, or Benares by Hindus. **2.** heaven.

ho/ly clo/ver, sainfoin.

Ho/ly Commun/ion, communion (def. 6).

ho/ly cow/, *Slang.* (used to express bewilderment or astonishment.)

Ho/ly Cross/, Mountain of the, a peak in central Colorado, in the Sawatch Range: snow-filled, cross-shaped crevasses. 13,996 ft.

ho/ly day/, a consecrated day or religious festival, esp. one other than Sunday. [see HOLIDAY]

ho/ly day/ of obliga/tion, 1. a day on which Roman Catholics are required to attend Mass and abstain from certain kinds of work. **2.** a day on which Episcopalians are expected to take communion.

ho/ly dol/lar, 1. *Informal.* the almighty dollar; money considered as of the utmost importance. **2,** *Australian.* See **holey dollar.**

Ho/ly Fam/ily, a representation in art of Mary, Joseph, and the infant Jesus.

Ho/ly Fa/ther, *Rom. Cath. Ch.* a title of the pope.

Ho/ly Ghost/, the third person of the Trinity. Also called **Holy Spirit.** [ME *holi gost,* OE *hālig gāst*]

Ho/ly Grail/, Grail.

ho/ly grass/, any of several fragrant, perennial grasses of the genus *Hierochloë,* esp. *H. odorata,* the vanilla grass.

Hol·y·head (hol/ē hed/), *n.* **1.** Also called **Ho/ly Is/land.** an island off the W coast of Anglesey, in NW Wales. **2.** a seaport on this island.

Ho/ly In/nocents' Day/, December 28, a day of religious observance commemorating the slaughter of the children of Bethlehem by Herod's order. Also called **Innocents' Day.**

Ho/ly Joe/, *Slang.* **1.** a chaplain, esp. in the U.S. armed forces. **2.** a minister or priest. **3.** a sanctimonious or overly pious person.

Ho/ly Lamb/, *Heraldry.* See **paschal lamb** (def. 4).

Ho/ly Land/, Palestine (def. 1).

ho/ly mack/erel, *Slang.* (used as an exclamation to express surprise or wonder.)

ho/ly Mo/ses, *Slang.* (used as an exclamation to express surprise or wonder.)

Ho/ly Mys/teries, *Eastern Ch.* **1.** the consecrated elements. **2.** (*sometimes l.c.*) the Divine Liturgy.

Ho/ly Of/fice, *Rom. Cath. Ch.* a congregation founded in 1542 to succeed the suppressed Inquisition and entrusted with matters pertaining to faith and morals, as the judgment of heresy, the application of canonical punishment, and the examination of books and prohibition of those held dangerous to faith and morals.

ho/ly of ho/lies, 1. a place of special sacredness. **2.** the innermost chamber of the Biblical tabernacle and the Temple in Jerusalem, in which the ark of the covenant was kept. **3.** *Eastern Ch.* the bema. [trans. of L *sanctum sanctōrum* (Vulgate), trans. of Gk *tò hágion tôn hagíōn,* itself trans. of Heb *qōdesh haqqodāshīm*]

ho/ly oil/, 1. consecrated oil; chrism. **2.** (esp. in the Eastern Church) oil that has been in contact with a sacred object, as a relic, and is used in various rites. [ME *holi oylle*]

Hol·yoke (hōl/yōk, hō/lē ōk/), *n.* a city in S Massachusetts, on the Connecticut River. 52,689 (1960).

Ho/ly One/, 1. God. Isa. 10:20. **2.** Jesus Christ, esp. as the Messiah. Mark 1:24; Acts 3:14.

ho/ly or/ders, 1. the rite or sacrament of ordination. **2.** the rank or status of an ordained Christian minister. **3.** the major degrees or grades of the Christian ministry.

Ho/ly Roll/er, *Disparaging and Offensive.* a member of a Pentecostal sect: so called from the ecstatic religiosity expressed during services. —**Ho/ly Roll/erism.**

Holy Roman Empire 962-1806 A.D.

Ho/ly Ro/man Em/pire, a Germanic empire located chiefly in central Europe which began with the coronation of Otto the Great, king of Germany, as Roman emperor A.D. 962, and ended with the renunciation of the Roman imperial title by Francis II in 1806, and was regarded theoretically as the continuation of the Western Empire and as the temporal form of a universal dominion whose spiritual head was the pope. It is sometimes regarded as originating with Charlemagne, who was crowned Roman emperor A.D. 800.

Ho/ly Rood/, 1. the cross on which Jesus died. **2.** (*l.c.*) a crucifix, esp. one above a rood screen. [ME *holie rode,* OE *halige rod*]

Ho/ly Sac/rament, sacrament (def. 2).

Ho/ly Sat/urday, the Saturday in Holy Week. [ME *holi Saterday*]

Ho/ly Scrip/ture, Scripture (def. 1). Also, **Ho/ly Scrip/tures.**

Ho/ly See/, 1. *Rom. Cath. Ch.* the see of Rome; the office or jurisdiction of the pope. **2.** the papal court.

Ho/ly Sep/ulcher, the sepulcher in which the body of Jesus lay between His burial and His resurrection. [ME *holie sepulcre*]

Ho/ly Spir/it, 1. the spirit of God. **2.** See **Holy Ghost.** [ME *hali spirite*]

ho·ly·stone (hō/lē stōn/), *n., v.,* **-stoned, -ston·ing.** —*n.* **1.** a block of soft sandstone used in scrubbing the decks of a vessel. —*v.t.* **2.** to scrub with a holystone. [HOLY + STONE; perh. orig. jocular or profane]

ho/ly syn/od, *Eastern Ch.* the governing council of an autocephalous church, composed of bishops and presided over by the patriarch or some other prelate.

ho/ly this/tle, lady's-thistle.

Ho/ly Thurs/day, 1. See **Ascension Day. 2.** the Thursday in Holy Week; Maundy Thursday. [ME *halewethoresday,* OE *halgan thunresdæg*]

ho·ly·tide (hō/lē tīd/), *n. Archaic.* a time of religious observances. [ME *holi tid,* OE *hālig tīd.* See HOLY, TIDE[1]]

Ho/ly Trin/ity, Trinity (def. 1). [ME *hali trinite*]

ho/ly war/, a war waged for what is supposed to be a holy purpose; religious war.

ho/ly wa/ter, water blessed by a priest. [ME *holi-water,* OE *hāligwæter*]

ho/ly wa/ter sprin/kler. See **morning star** (def. 3). Also, **ho/ly wa/ter sprin/kle.**

Ho/ly Week/, the week preceding Easter Sunday. [trans. of It *settimana santa*]

Ho/ly Wil/lie's Prayer/, a satirical poem (1786) by Robert Burns on religious hypocrisy, written in the Scottish vernacular.

Ho/ly Writ/, the Scriptures. [ME *holi writ,* OE *hālige writu* (pl.)]

Ho/ly Year/, *Rom. Cath. Ch.* a jubilee year.

hom-, var. of **homo-** before a vowel: *homonym.*

Hom·a·dus (hom/ə dəs), *n. Class. Myth.* a centaur killed by Hercules.

hom·age (hom/ij, om/-), *n.* **1.** respect or reverence paid or rendered: *In his speech he paid homage to the leaders.* **2.** the formal public acknowledgment by which a feudal tenant or vassal declared himself to be the man or vassal of his lord, owing him fealty and service. **3.** the relation thus established of a vassal to his lord. **4.** something done or given in acknowledgment or consideration of vassalage. [ME *(h)omage* < OF, equiv. to *(h)ome* man (< L *hominem,* acc. of *homo;* see *Homo*) + *-age* -AGE]

—**Syn. 1.** deference, obeisance; honor, tribute. **3.** fidelity, loyalty, devotion. —**Ant. 1.** irreverence. **3.** disloyalty.

hom·ag·er (hom/ə jər, om/-), *n.* a person who pays homage, esp. a feudal tenant or vassal. [late ME *omager* < AF. See HOMAGE, -ER[2]]

Hom·a·gy·ri·us (hom/ə jī/rē əs), *n. Class. Myth.* an epithet of Zeus, meaning "assembler."

hom·a·lo·graph·ic (hom/ə lō graf/ik), *adj.* homolographic. [< Gk *homalō(s)* even, regular + GRAPHIC]

hom·bre (hom/bər), *n. Cards.* omber.

hom·bre (ôm/bʀe; *Eng.* om/brā, -brē), *n., pl.* **-bres** (-bʀes; *Eng.* -brāz, -brēz). *Spanish.* man.

hom·burg (hom/bûrg), *n.* a felt hat with a soft crown dented lengthwise and a slightly rolled brim. [after *Homburg,* Germany, first site of its manufacture]

home (hōm), *n., adj., adv., v.,* **homed, hom·ing.** —*n.* **1.** a house, apartment, or other shelter that is the usual residence of a person, family, or household. **2.** the place in which one's domestic affections are centered. **3.** an institution for the homeless, sick, etc.: *a nursing home; an old people's home.* **4.** the dwelling place or retreat of an animal. **5.** the place or region where something is native or most common. **6.** any place of residence or refuge: *a heavenly home.* **7.** one's native place or own country. **8.** (in games) the destination or goal. **9.** *Baseball.* See **home plate. 10.** *Lacrosse.* one of three attack positions nearest the opposing goal. **11. at home, a.** in one's own house or place of residence. **b.** in one's own town or country. **c.** prepared or willing to receive social visits: *Tell him I'm not at home. We are always at home to her.* **d.** in a situation familiar to one; at ease: *She has a way of making everyone feel at home.*

e. well-informed; proficient: *to be at home in the classics.* **f.** played in one's home town or on one's own grounds: *The Yankees played two games at home and one away.* **—adj. 12.** of, pertaining to, or connected with one's home or country; domestic: *home products.* **13.** that drives or hits home; that hits the mark aimed at; to the point: *a home thrust.* **14.** *Sports.* played in a ball park, arena, or the like, that is or is assumed to be the center of operations of a team: *The pitcher didn't lose a single home game all season.* Cf. **away** (def. 14). **—adv. 15.** to, toward, or at home: *to go home.* **16.** deep; to the heart; effectively and completely. **17.** to the mark or point aimed at: *He drove the point home. Her arguments against the opposition hit home.* **18.** *Naut.* **a.** into the position desired, perfectly or to the greatest possible extent: *sails sheeted home.* **b.** in the proper, stowed position: *The anchor is home.* **c.** toward its vessel: *to bring the anchor home.* **19. bring home to,** to lay emphasis on; clarify: *The irrevocability of her decision was brought home to her.* **20. write home about,** *Informal.* to comment especially on; remark on: *The town was nothing to write home about. Her cooking is really something to write home about.* **—v.i. 21.** to go or return home. **22.** (of guided missiles, aircraft, etc.) to proceed, esp. under control of an automatic aiming mechanism, toward a specified target, as a plane, missile, location, etc. (often fol. by *in on*): *The missile homed in on the submarine.* **23.** to navigate toward a point by means of coordinates other than those given by altitudes. **24.** to have a home where specified; reside. **—v.t. 25.** to bring or send home. **26.** to provide with a home. **27.** to direct, esp. under control of an automatic aiming device, toward an airport, target, etc. [ME *hom,* OE *hām* dwelling, home; c. D *heim,* Icel *heimr,* Dan *hjem,* Sw *hem,* G *Heim* home, Goth *haims* village]
—Syn. 1. abode, dwelling, habitation; domicile, residence. See **house. 2.** hearth, fireside. **3.** asylum.

Home (hyōōm), *n.* **Lord.** See **Douglas-Hume.**

home′ base′, *Baseball.* See **home plate.**

home·bod·y (hōm′bod′ē), *n., pl.* **-bod·ies.** a person whose pleasures and activities center around the home; stay-at-home. [HOME + BODY]

home·bound (hōm′bound′), *adj.* going home: *homebound commuters.* [HOME + -BOUND[1]]

home·bred (hōm′bred′), *adj.* **1.** bred at home; native; indigenous; domestic. **2.** unpolished; unsophisticated. [HOME + BRED]

home-brew (hōm′brōō′), *n.* beer or other beverage brewed at home, as for home consumption. **—home′-brewed′,** *adj.*

Home′ Bur′ial, a poem (1914) by Robert Frost.

home·com·ing (hōm′kum′ing), *n.* **1.** a return to one's home; arrival at home. **2.** an annual event held by a college or university for visiting alumni. [ME *homcomyng;* r. ME *hamcume,* OE *hāmcyme,* equiv. to *hām* HOME + *cyme* arrival] **—home′com′er,** *n.*

Home′ Cor′ner, a town in central Indiana. 2636 (1960).

home′ econ′omics, the art and science of homemaking, including the purchase, preparation, and service of food, the selection and making of clothing, the selection of furnishings, the care of children, the care of the house, etc. **—home′ econ′omist.**

home′ fries′, slices of boiled potatoes, fried in butter or shortening. Also called **home′ fried′ pota′toes, cottage fried potatoes.**

home′ front′, the civilian sector remaining within the continental boundaries of a nation at war when its armed forces are in combat overseas, esp. when a total effort is being made to gain military victory.

home-grown (hōm′grōn′), *adj.* (esp. of fruits or vegetables) produced or grown for local consumption: *homegrown tomatoes.*

home′ guard′, a volunteer territorial force used for meeting local emergencies when the regular armed forces are needed elsewhere.

home·land (hōm′land′), *n.* one's native land. [HOME + LAND]

home·less (hōm′lis), *adj.* **1.** without a home: *a homeless child.* **2.** *Rare.* affording no home: *the homeless sea.* [OE *hāmlēas.* See HOME, -LESS] **—home′less·ly,** *adv.* **—home′less·ness,** *n.*

home·like (hōm′līk′), *adj.* like or suggestive of home; familiar; comfortable. [HOME + -LIKE] **—home′like′-ness,** *n.*
—Syn. See **simple.**

home·ly (hōm′lē), *adj.,* **-li·er, -li·est. 1.** lacking in physical attractiveness; not beautiful; unattractive: *a homely girl.* **2.** not having elegance, refinement, or cultivation. **3.** proper or suited to the home or to ordinary domestic life; plain; unpretentious: *homely fare.* **4.** commonly seen or known. **5.** very friendly. [ME *homly.* See HOME, -LY] **—home′li·ness,** *n.*
—Syn. 1, 2. SIMPLE, HOMELY (HOMEY), HOMELIKE, PLAIN imply absence of adornment or embellishment. That which is SIMPLE is not elaborate or complex: *a simple kind of dress.* In the United States, HOMELY usually suggests absence of natural beauty: *an unattractive child almost homely enough to be called ugly.* In England, the word suggests a wholesome simplicity without artificial refinement or elegance; since it characterizes that which is comfortable and attractive, it is equivalent to HOMEY: *a homely cottage.* HOMELIKE also emphasizes comfort and attractiveness, but it conveys less strongly than does HOMEY a sense of intimate security: *a homelike interior, arrangement, atmosphere.* That which is PLAIN has little or no adornment: *expensive but plain clothing.*

home·made (hōm′mād′), *adj.* **1.** made at home, locally, in the present location, etc.: *All our pastry is homemade.* **2.** made in one's own country; domestic: *I prefer a homemade car to one of those foreign models.* **3.** made, contrived, or assembled by oneself; amateurish: *the treacherous look of homemade furniture; the clumsy, homemade quality of her writing.* [HOME + MADE]

home·mak·er (hōm′mā′kər), *n.* a person who manages a home, as a housewife or housekeeper. [HOME + MAKER]

home·mak·ing (hōm′mā′king), *n.* **1.** the establishment or direction of a home; duties of a homemaker. **—adj. 2.** of or pertaining to the management of a home: *homemaking duties.* [HOME + MAKING]

home′ mis′sion, a religious mission operating within the country or territories of its supporting church. **—home′ mis′sionary.**

homeo-, a learned borrowing from Greek meaning "similar," used in the formation of compound words: *homeostatic.* Also, **homoeo-, homoio-.** [< Gk *homoio-,* comb. form of *hómoios* similar, like]

Home′ Of′fice, 1. the governmental department in Great Britain dealing with domestic matters such as elections, naturalization, and the control of police. **2.** (*l.c.*) the main office of a company.

ho·me·o·morph (hō′mē ə môrf′), *n.* any of the crystalline minerals characterized by a particular kind of homeomorphism. Also, **homoeomorph.** [HOMEO- + MORPH]

ho·me·o·mor·phism (hō′mē ə môr′fiz əm), *n.* **1.** similarity in crystalline form but not necessarily in chemical composition. **2.** *Math.* a function between two topological spaces which is continuous, one-to-one, and onto, and the inverse of which is continuous. Also, **homoeomorphism.** [HOMEOMORPH + -ISM] **—ho′me·o·mor′phic, ho′me·o·mor′phous,** *adj.*

ho·me·o·path·ic (hō′mē ə path′ik), *adj.* **1.** of, pertaining to, or according to the principles of homeopathy. **2.** practicing or advocating homeopathy. Also, **homoeopathic.** [HOMEO- + PATHIC] **—ho′me·o·path′i·cal·ly,** *adv.*

ho′meopath′ic mag′ic. See **imitative magic.**

ho·me·op·a·thist (hō′mē op′ə thist), *n.* one who practices or favors homeopathy. Also, **homoeopathist, ho·me·o·path** (hō′mē ə path′), **homoeopath.** [HOMEO- + -PATH + -IST]

ho·me·op·a·thy (hō′mē op′ə thē), *n.* the method of treating disease by drugs, given in minute doses, which would produce in a healthy person symptoms similar to those of the disease (opposed to *allopathy*). Also, **homoeopathy.** [HOMEO- + -PATHY]

ho·me·o·pla·sia (hō′mē ə plā′zhə, -zhē ə, -zē ə), *n.* *Med.* the formation of new tissue, as in healing, that is similar to the existing tissue. [HOMEO- + -PLASIA] **—ho·me·o·plas·tic** (hō′mē ə plas′tik), *adj.*

ho·me·o·sta·sis (hō′mē ə stā′sis), *n.* the tendency of a system, esp. the physiological system of higher animals, to maintain internal stability, owing to the coordinated response of its parts to any situation or stimulus tending to disturb its normal condition or function. [HOMEO- + STASIS] **—ho·me·o·stat·ic** (hō′mē ə stat′ik), *adj.* **—ho′me·o·stat′i·cal·ly,** *adv.*

ho·me·o·ther·a·py (hō′mē ə ther′ə pē), *n.* *Med.* therapy by means of an agent that is similar to but not identical with the causative agent of the disease. [HOMEO- + THERAPY]

ho·me·o·therm (hō′mē ə thûrm′, hom′ē-), *n.* homoiotherm.

ho·me·o·ther·mal (hō′mē ə thûr′məl), *adj.* homoiothermal. Also, **ho′me·o·ther′mic, ho′me·o·ther′mous.** [HOMEO- + THERMAL] **—ho′me·o·ther′my, ho′me·o·ther′mism,** *n.*

ho·me·o·typ·ic (hō′mē ə tip′ik), *adj.* *Biol.* of or pertaining to the second or equational division in meiosis. Also, **ho′me·o·typ′i·cal.** Cf. **heterotypic.** [HOMEO- + TYPE + -IC]

home·place (hōm′plās′), *n.* a person's birthplace, family home, or the like. [HOME + PLACE]

home′ plate′, *Baseball.* the base at which the batter stands and which a base runner must reach safely in order to score a run, consisting of a five-sided slab of whitened rubber set at ground level at the front corner of the diamond. Also called **home, the plate, home base.**

hom·er[1] (hō′mər), *Informal.* **—n. 1.** *Baseball.* See **home run. 2.** See **homing pigeon. —v.i. 3.** *Baseball.* to hit a home run: *Mantle homered in the ninth with one on to take the game.* [HOME + -ER[1]]

ho·mer[2] (hō′mər), *n.* a Hebrew unit of capacity equal to 10 baths in liquid measure or 10 ephahs in dry measure. Also called **kor.** [< Heb *ḥomer,* lit., heap]

Ho·mer (hō′mər), *n.* **1.** 8th century B.C., Greek epic poet: reputed author of the *Iliad* and *Odyssey.* **2. Winslow,** 1836–1910, U.S. painter and illustrator. **3.** a town in N Louisiana. 4665 (1960). **4.** a town in central New York. 3622 (1960). **5.** a boy's given name.

home′ range′, *Ecol.* the area in which an animal normally lives.

Ho·mer·ic (hō mer′ik), *adj.* **1.** of, pertaining to, or suggestive of Homer or his poetry. **2.** of heroic dimensions; grand; imposing: *Homeric feats of exploration.* [< L *Homēric(us)* < Gk *Homērikós,* equiv. to *Hómēr(os)* HOMER + *-ikos* -IC] **—Ho·mer′i·cal·ly,** *adv.*

Homer′ic laugh′ter, loud, hearty laughter; laughter of heroic dimensions.

Homer′ic sim′ile. See **epic simile.**

home·room (hōm′rōōm′, -rŏŏm′), *n.* **1.** (in a departmentalized school) the classroom in which all students in the same grade or division of a grade meet at certain times under the supervision of a teacher, who takes attendance and administers other school business. **2.** (in an elementary school) the classroom in which pupils in the same grade or division of a grade receive instruction in all subjects except those requiring special facilities. Also, **home′ room′.** [HOME + ROOM]

home′ rule′, self-government in local matters by a city, province, state, or other component part of a country.

home′ rul′er, an advocate of home rule.

home′ run′, *Baseball.* a hit that enables a batter, without the aid of a fielding error, to score a run by making a nonstop circuit of the bases.

Ho·mer·ville (hō′mər vil′), *n.* a town in S Georgia. 2634 (1960).

Home′ Sec′retary, *Brit.* the secretary of state for the Home Office.

home·sick (hōm′sik′), *adj.* ill or depressed from a longing for home. [HOME + SICK[1]] **—home′sick′-ness,** *n.*

home′ sig′nal, *Railroads.* a signal for controlling train movements into or through a route or block.

home·site (hōm′sīt′), *n.* **1.** a plot of land for a home. **2.** the home on such a plot of land. [HOME + SITE]

home·spun (hōm′spun′), *adj.* **1.** spun or made at home: *homespun cloth.* **2.** made of such cloth: *homespun clothing.* **3.** plain; unpolished; simple; rustic: *homespun humor.* **—n. 4.** a plain-weave cloth made at home, or of homespun yarn. **5.** cloth of similar appearance to that which is hand-spun and hand-woven. **6.** *Obs.* a rustic person. [HOME + SPUN]

home·stall (hōm′stôl′), *n.* *Brit.* **1.** *Dial.* a farmyard. **2.** *Obs.* a homestead. [ME *homstal,* OE *hāmsteall.* See HOME, STALL[1]]

home·stead (hōm′sted, -stid), *n.* **1.** *U.S.* a dwelling with its land and buildings, occupied by the owner as a home and exempted by a homestead law from seizure or sale for debt. **2.** any dwelling with its land and buildings. **—v.t. 3.** to settle on (land): *Pioneers homesteaded the valley.* **—v.i. 4.** to settle on a property: *They homesteaded many years ago.* [OE *hāmstede.* See HOME, STEAD]

Home·stead (hōm′sted, -stid), *n.* **1.** a town in S Florida. 9152 (1960). **2.** a town in SW Pennsylvania. 7502 (1960).

Home′stead Act′, a special act of Congress (1862) that made public lands in the West available to settlers without payment, usually in lots of 160 acres.

home·stead·er (hōm′sted′ər), *n.* **1.** the owner or holder of a homestead. **2.** *U.S.* a settler under the Homestead Act. [HOMESTEAD + -ER[1]]

home′stead law′, 1. any law exempting homesteads from seizure or sale for debt. **2.** any law making public lands available to settlers for purchase.

home·stretch (hōm′strech′), *n.* the straight part of a race track from the last turn to the finish line. Cf. **backstretch.** [HOME + STRETCH]

home′ stud′y, instruction in a subject given by mail and addressed to a student at his home.

home·town (hōm′toun′), *n.* **1.** the town or city in which a person lives or was born, or from which a person comes. **—adj. 2.** of or pertaining to a hometown: *hometown welcome; hometown attitudes; hometown lawyer.* [HOME + TOWN]

Home·town (hōm′toun′), *n.* a town in NE Illinois. 7479 (1960).

home·ward (hōm′wərd), *adv.* **1.** Also, **home′wards.** toward home. **—adj. 2.** directed toward home: *his homeward way.* [ME *homward,* OE *hāmweard.* See HOME, -WARD]

Home·wood (hōm′wŏŏd′), *n.* a city in central Alabama, near Birmingham. 20,289 (1960).

home·work (hōm′wûrk′), *n.* **1.** schoolwork assigned to be done outside the classroom. **2.** any work done at home, esp. work on contract for manufacturers or middlemen. [HOME + WORK]

home·work·er (hōm′wûr′kər, -wûr′-), *n.* a paid employee in a home, as a maid, houseman, gardener, etc. [HOME + WORKER]

home·y (hō′mē), *adj.,* **hom·i·er, hom·i·est.** comfortably informal and inviting; cozy; homelike: *a homey little inn.* Also, **homy.** [HOME + -Y[1]] **—home′y·ness, hom′i·ness,** *n.*
—Syn. See **simple.**

hom·i·ci·dal (hom′i sīd′əl), *adj.* **1.** of or pertaining to homicide. **2.** having a tendency to commit homicide. [HOMICIDE + -AL[1]] **—hom′i·ci′dal·ly,** *adv.*

hom·i·cide (hom′i sīd′), *n.* **1.** the killing of one human being by another. **2.** a person who kills another; murderer. [ME < MF < L *homicīd(ium)* a killing, *homicīd(a)* killer, equiv. to *homi-* (comb. form of *homo* man) + *-cīdium, -cīda* -CIDE]

hom·i·let·ic (hom′ə let′ik), *adj.* **1.** of or pertaining to preaching or to homilies. **2.** of the nature of a homily. **3.** of or pertaining to homiletics. Also, **hom′i·let′i·cal.** [< Gk *homilētik(ós)* affable, equiv. to *homilē-* (var. s. of *homileîn* to converse with; see HOMILY) + *-tikos* -TIC] **—hom′i·let′i·cal·ly,** *adv.*

hom·i·let·ics (hom′ə let′iks), *n.* (*construed as sing.*) the art of preaching; the branch of practical theology that treats of homilies or sermons. [see HOMILETIC, -ICS]

ho·mil·i·ar·y (ho mil′ē er′ē), *n., pl.* **-ar·ies.** a collection of homilies. [< ML *homīliāri(um)* < Gk *homīli(a)* HOMILY + L *-ārium* -ARY]

hom·i·list (hom′ə list), *n.* one who writes or delivers homilies. [HOMIL(Y) + -IST]

hom·i·ly (hom′ə lē), *n., pl.* **-lies. 1.** a religious discourse addressed to a congregation; sermon. **2.** an admonitory or moralizing discourse. [< eccl. L *homīli(a)* < Gk *homīlía* assembly, sermon, equiv. to *hómīl(os)* crowd (*hom(oû)* together + *īl(ē)* crowd) + *-ia* -Y[3]; r. ME *omelie* < MF < L, as above]

hom·ing (hō′ming), *adj.* **1.** returning home: *We saw the homing birds at dusk.* **2.** guiding or directing homeward or to a destination: *the homing instinct; a homing beacon.* [HOME + -ING[2]]

hom′ing device′, a mechanism incorporated into a guided missile, airplane, etc., that aims it toward its objective.

hom′ing pi′geon, any pigeon used to carry messages and equipped by training and breeding to fly home, often from great distances.

hom·i·nid (hom′ə nid), *n.* *Anthropol.* a member of the *Hominidae,* a family consisting of man and his ancestors. Also, **homonid, ho·min·i·an** (hō min′ē ən). [< NL *hominid(ae),* equiv. to L *homin-* (s. of *homo*) man + *-idae* -ID[2]]

hom·i·nine (hom′ə nīn′), *adj.* resembling or characteristic of man; human. [< L *homin-* (s. of *homo*) man + -INE[1]]

hom·i·noid (hom′ə noid′), *n.* a member of the *Hominoidea,* a superfamily including the great apes and man. [< L *homin-* (s. of *homo*) man + -OID]

hom·i·ny (hom′ə nē), *n.* whole or ground hulled corn from which the bran and germ have been removed by processing the whole kernels in a lye bath **(lye hominy)** or by crushing and sifting **(pearl hominy).** [< Algonquian (New England or Va.); cf. *tackhummin* to grind corn, equiv. to *ahām* he beats + *min* berry, fruit]

Hom·i·ny (hom′i nē), *n.* a town in N Oklahoma. 2866 (1960).

Homme Ar·mé, L' (lôm AR mā′), a 15th-century French secular song used by several composers in the 15th, 16th, and early 17th centuries as a cantus firmus in polyphonic masses.

Hom·mel (hom′əl), *n.* a walled plain in the fourth quadrant of the face of the moon: about 75 miles in diameter.

hom·mock (hom′ək), *n.* hummock (def. 3).

ho·mo (hō′mō), *n., pl.* **-mos.** *Slang.* a homosexual. [by shortening]

Ho·mo (hō′mō), *n.* the primate genus that includes modern man, *Homo sapiens,* and a number of closely related extinct species, as the Neanderthal man. [< L:

man; OL *hemō* the earthly one; akin to L *humus* earth, soil, *hūmānus* HUMAN, OE *guma* man, Gk *chamaí* on the ground]

homo-, an element appearing in loan words from Greek, where it meant "same" (*homology*); on this model, used in the formation of compound words (*homomorphic*). Also, *esp. before a vowel,* **hom-.** [< Gk, comb. form of *homós* one and the same; akin to Skt *sama-*; see SAME]

ho·mo·bront (hō′mə bront′, hom′ə-), *n.* isobront. [HOMO- + *-bront,* as in *isobront*]

ho·mo·cen·tric (hō′mə sen′trik, hom′ə-), *adj.* **1.** having a common center; concentric. **2.** diverging from or converging to the same point: *homocentric rays.* Also, **ho′mo·cen′tri·cal.** [HOMO- + CENTRIC] —**ho′mo·cen′tri·cal·ly,** *adv.*

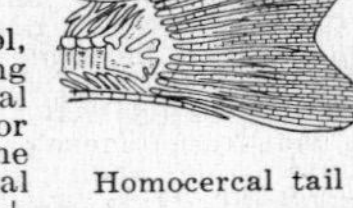
Homocercal tail

ho·mo·cer·cal (hō′mə sûr′kəl, hom′ə-), *adj. Ichthyol.* **1.** having an equally divided tail or caudal fin, the spinal column ending at or near the middle of the base of the tail. **2.** noting such a tail or caudal fin. Cf. **heterocercal.** [HOMO- + *cerc-* (< Gk *kérk(os)* tail) + -AL[1]] —**ho·mo·cer·cy** (hō′mə sûr′sē, hom′ə-), **ho·mo·cer·cal·i·ty** (hō′mə sər kal′i tē, hom′ə-), *n.*

ho·mo·chro·mat·ic (hō′mə krō mat′ik, -krə-, hom′ə-), *adj.* of or pertaining to one hue; monochromatic. Cf. **heterochromatic.** [HOMO- + CHROMATIC] —**ho·mo·chro·ma·tism** (hō′mə krō′mə tiz′əm, hom′ə-), *n.*

ho·mo·chrome (hō′mə krōm′, hom′ə-), *adj.* homochromatic. [< Gk *homóchrōm(os),* equiv. to *homo-* HOMO- + *-chromos* (*chrōm(a)* color + *-os* adj. suffix)]

ho·mo·chro·mous (hō′mə krō′məs, hom′ə-), *adj. Bot., Zool.* being all of one color, as a composite flower or flower head. [HOMOCHROME + -OUS] —**ho·mo·chro·my** (hō′mə krō′mē, hom′ə-), *n.*

ho·moch·ro·nous (hō mok′rə nəs, ho-), *adj.* (of a genetic character) occurring at the same age or period in the offspring as in the parent. [< Gk *homóchronos* of the same time. See HOMO-, CHRON-, -OUS]

ho·mo·cy·clic (hō′mə sī′klik, -sik′lik, hom′ə-), *adj. Chem.* of or noting a cyclic compound having atoms of only one element, usually carbon, in the ring. [HOMO- + CYCLIC]

ho·mo·dyne (hō′mə dīn′, hom′ə-), *adj. Radio.* of or pertaining to reception by a device that generates a varying voltage of the same or nearly the same frequency as the incoming carrier wave and combines it with the incoming signal for detection. [HOMO- + DYNE]

homoeo-, var. of **homeo-:** *homoeopathy.*

ho·moe·o·morph (hō′mē ə môrf′), *n.* homeomorph.

ho·moe·o·mor·phism (hō′mē ə môr′fiz əm), *n.* homeomorphism. —**ho′moe·o·mor′phic, ho′moe·o·mor′phous,** *adj.*

ho·moe·op·a·thist (hō′mē op′ə thist), *n.* homeopathist. Also, **ho·moe·o·path** (hō′mē ə path′).

ho·moe·op·a·thy (hō′mē op′ə thē), *n.* homeopathy. —**ho·moe·o·path·ic** (hō′mē ə path′ik), *adj.* —**ho′moe·o·path′i·cal·ly,** *adv.*

ho·mo·e·rot·i·cism (hō′mō i rot′i siz′əm), *n. Psychiatry.* a tendency to be sexually aroused by a member of the same sex. Also, **ho·mo·er·o·tism** (hō′mō er′ə tiz′əm). [HOMO- + EROTICISM] —**ho·mo·e·rot·ic** (hō′mō i rot′ik), *adj.*

ho·mo·fer·ment·a·tive (hō′mō fər men′tə tiv, hom′ō-), *adj. Biochem.* producing a fermentation that results in one end product. Cf. **heterofermentative.** [HOMO- + FERMENTATIVE]

ho·mog·a·mous (hō mog′ə məs), *adj. Bot.* **1.** having flowers or florets which do not differ sexually (opposed to *heterogamous*). **2.** having the stamens and pistils maturing simultaneously (opposed to *dichogamous*). [< Gk *homógamos* married to sisters, or to the same woman. See HOMO-, -GAMOUS]

ho·mog·a·my (hō mog′ə mē), *n.* **1.** *Bot.* state of being homogamous. **2.** interbreeding of individuals of like characteristics. [HOMO- + -GAMY]

ho·mo·ge·ne·i·ty (hō′mə jə nē′i tē, hom′ə-), *n.* composition from like parts, elements, or characteristics; state or quality of being homogeneous. Also, **ho·mo·ge·ne·ous·ness** (hō′mə jē′nē əs nis, -jēn′yəs-, hom′ə-). [< ML *homogeneitās,* equiv. to *homogene(us)* HOMOGENEOUS + *-itās* -ITY]

ho·mo·ge·ne·ous (hō′mə jē′nē əs, -jēn′yəs, hom′ə-), *adj.* **1.** composed of parts all of the same kind; not heterogeneous: *a homogeneous population.* **2.** of the same kind or nature; essentially alike: *homogeneous parts.* **3.** *Math.* **a.** having a common property throughout: *a homogeneous solid figure.* **b.** having all terms of the same degree: *a homogeneous equation.* **c.** remaining unchanged when each variable is replaced by the same specified number times the variable: *a homogeneous function.* **d.** (of an equation) formed by equating a homogeneous function to zero. **e.** relating to a function of several variables which can be written as a new function of the variables alone multiplied by a constant raised to some power. **f.** relating to a differential equation in which the derivatives can be written as a linear combination of terms containing as the variable the dependent variable of the derivative divided by the independent variable. [< ML *homogeneus,* equiv. to *homogene-* (s. of Gk *homogenḗs* of the same kind; see HOMO-, GENE) + *-us* -OUS] —**ho′mo·ge′ne·ous·ly,** *adv.*

homoge′neous coor′dinates, *Geom.* a coordinate system used in projective geometry in which a point in the plane is represented by three numbers, the ratio of the first to the third being its ordinate and the ratio of the second to the third being its abscissa in Cartesian coordinates.

ho·mo·gen·e·sis (hō′mə jen′i sis, hom′ə-), *n. Biol.* reproduction in which the offspring resemble the parents and undergo the same cycle of development. [HOMO- + GENESIS]

ho·mo·ge·net·ic (hō′mə jə net′ik, hom′ə-), *adj. Biol.* **1.** pertaining to or characterized by homogenesis. **2.** homogenous (def. 1). Also, **ho′mo·ge·net′i·cal.** [HOMO- + GENETIC] —**ho′mo·ge·net′i·cal·ly,** *adv.*

ho·mog·e·nize (hə moj′ə nīz′, hō), *v.t.,* **-nized, -niz·ing.** **1.** to form by blending unlike elements; make homogeneous; emulsify. **2.** to break up the fat globules in (milk or cream) in order to distribute them equally throughout. [HOMOGEN(EOUS) + -IZE] —**ho·mog′e·ni·za′tion,** *n.* —**ho·mog′e·niz′er,** *n.*

ho·mog·e·nous (hə moj′ə nəs, hō-), *adj.* **1.** *Biol.* corresponding in structure because of a common origin. **2.** homogeneous. **3.** homoplastic. [HOMO- + -GENOUS]

ho·mo·gen·tis′ic ac′id (hō′mə jen tis′ik, -tiz′-, hō′-), *Biochem.* a white, crystalline, water-soluble solid, $C_8H_8O_4$, an intermediate in the metabolism of tyrosine and of phenylalanine, found in the blood and urine of a person affected with alkaptonuria. [HOMO- + GENTISIC ACID]

ho·mog·e·ny (hə moj′ə nē, hō-), *n. Biol.* correspondence in form or structure, owing to a common origin. [< Gk *homogéneia* community of origin. See HOMO-, -GENY]

ho·mog·o·nous (hə mog′ə nəs, hō-), *adj. Bot.* pertaining to monoclinous flowers which do not differ in the relative length of stamens and pistils (opposed to *heterogonous*). [HOMO- + *-gonous* < Gk *-gonos* generating; see -GONY] —**ho·mog′o·nous·ly,** *adv.*

ho·mog·o·ny (hə mog′ə nē, hō-), *n. Bot.* state of being homogonous. [HOMO- + -GONY]

ho·mo·graft (hō′mə graft′, -gräft′, hom′ə-), *n. Surg.* a tissue or organ obtained from one member of a species and transplanted by grafting to another member of the same species. Also called **isograft, isoplastic graft.** Cf. **autograft, heterograft.** [HOMO- + GRAFT[1]]

hom·o·graph (hom′ə graf′, -gräf′), *n.* a word of the same written form as another but of different origin and meaning, as *homer*[1], "home run," and *homer*[2] "unit of measure." [HOMO- + -GRAPH] —**hom·o·graph·ic** (hom′ə graf′ik), *adj.*

homoio-, var. of **homeo-:** *homoiothermal.*

ho·moi·o·therm (hō moi′ə thûrm′), *n. Zool.* a homoiothermal animal. Also, **homeotherm, homotherm.** [back formation from HOMOIOTHERMAL]

ho·moi·o·ther·mal (hō moi′ə thûr′məl), *adj. Zool.* having a body temperature that is relatively constant and mostly independent of the temperature of the environment; warm-blooded (opposed to *poikilothermal*). Also, **ho·moi′o·ther′mic, ho·moi′o·ther′mous, homeothermal, homothermal.** [HOMOIO- + THERMAL] —**ho·moi′o·ther′my, ho′moi·o·ther′mism,** *n.*

Ho·moi·ou·si·an (hō′moi o͞o′sē ən, -ou′-), *n.* **1.** one of a 4th-century A.D. church party which maintained that the essence of the Son is similar to, but not the same as, that of the Father. —*adj.* **2.** relating to the Homoiousians or their belief. [< LGk *homoioúsi(os)* of like substance (*homoi-* HOMOI(O)- + *ousí(a)* substance, essence + *-os* adj. suffix) + -AN] —**Ho′moi·ou′si·an·ism,** *n.*

ho·mo·lec·i·thal (hō′mə les′ə thəl), *adj. Embryol.* having a fairly uniform distribution of yolk, as certain eggs or ova having relatively little yolk. [HOMO- + LECITHAL]

ho·mol·o·gate (hə mol′ə gāt′, hō-), *v.t.,* **-gat·ed, -gat·ing.** to approve; ratify. [< ML *homologāt(us)* (ptp. of *homologāre* < Gk *homologeîn*) (to) agree to, allow); see -ATE[1]] —**ho·mol′o·ga′tion,** *n.*

ho·mo·log·i·cal (hō′mə loj′i kəl), *adj.* homologous. Also, **ho′mo·log′ic.** [HOMOLOG(Y) + -ICAL] —**ho′mo·log′i·cal·ly,** *adv.*

ho·mol·o·gise (hə mol′ə jīz′, hō-), *v.t., v.i.,* **-gised, -gis·ing.** *Chiefly Brit.* homologize. —**ho·mol′o·gis′er,** *n.*

ho·mol·o·gize (hə mol′ə jīz′, hō-), *v.,* **-gized, -giz·ing.** —*v.t.* **1.** to make or show to be homologous. —*v.i.* **2.** to be homologous; correspond. [HOMOLOG(OUS) + -IZE] —**ho·mol′o·giz′er,** *n.*

ho·mol·o·gous (hə mol′ə gəs, hō-), *adj.* **1.** having the same or a similar relation; corresponding, as in relative position, structure, etc. **2.** *Biol.* corresponding in structure and in origin, but not necessarily in function: *The wing of a bird and the foreleg of a horse are homologous.* **3.** *Chem.* of the same chemical type, but differing by a fixed increment in certain constituents. **4.** *Immunol., Med.* pertaining to the relation between bacteria and the immune serum prepared from them. [< ML *homologus* < Gk *homólogos* agreeing, equiv. to *homo-* HOMO- + *-logos* proportional, equiv. to *log-* (s. of *lógos* proportion; see LOGOS) + *-os* -OUS]

homol′ogous chro′mosomes, *Biol.* pairs of similar chromosomes, one of maternal, the other of paternal origin, which carry the Mendelian pairs of alleles or genes.

ho·mol·o·graph·ic (hō mol′ə graf′ik), *adj.* representing parts with like proportions. Also, **homalographic.** [var. of HOMALOGRAPHIC]

homolograph′ic projec′tion, *Cartog.* an equal-area projection in which the proportion between regions of unequal area is correctly shown. Also called **Mollweide projection.**

hom·o·logue (hom′ə lôg′, -log′), *n.* **1.** something homologous. **2.** *Biol.* a homologous organ or part. **3.** *Chem.* any member of a homologous series of organic compounds: *Ethane is a homologue of the alkane series.* [< Gk *homólog(on),* neut. of *homólogos* HOMOLOGOUS]

ho·mo·lo·gu·me·na (hō′mō lə go͞o′mə nə, -gyo͞o′-), *n.* (*construed as sing.*) the books in the New Testament generally held as authoritative and canonical by the early church. Also, **ho′mo·lo·gou′me·na.** Cf. **antilegomena.** [< Gk (neut pl.), deriv. of *homologein* to agree to, allow; see HOMOLOGOUS]

ho·mol·o·gy (hə mol′ə jē, hō-), *n., pl.* **-gies.** **1.** state of being homologous; homologous relation or correspondence. **2.** *Biol.* **a.** a fundamental similarity due to community of descent. **b.** a structural similarity of two segments of one animal based on a common developmental origin. **3.** *Chem.* the similarity of organic compounds of a series in which each member differs from its adjacent compounds by a fixed increment, as by CH_2. **4.** *Math.* a classification of figures according to certain geometric properties. [< Gk *homologí(a)* agreement, equiv. to *homólog(os)* HOMOLOGOUS + *-ia* -Y[3]]

ho·mol′o·sine projec′tion (hə mol′ə sin, -sīn′, hō-), *Cartog.* an equal-area projection of the world, distorting ocean areas in order to minimize the distortion of the continents. [irreg. HOMOLO(GRAPHIC) + SINE[1]]

ho·mo·mor·phic (hō′mə môr′fik, hom′ə-), *adj. Math.* pertaining to two sets that are related by a homomorphism. [HOMO- + -MORPHIC]

ho·mo·mor·phism (hō′mə môr′fiz əm, hom′ə-), *n.* **1.** *Biol.* correspondence in form or external appearance but not in type of structure and in origin. **2.** *Bot.* possession of perfect flowers of only one kind. **3.** *Zool.* resemblance between the young and the adult. **4.** *Math.* an onto map between two sets which preserves relations between elements. Also, **ho′mo·mor′phy.** [*homomorph* (see HOMO-, -MORPH) + -ISM] —**ho′mo·mor′phous,** *adj.*

hom·o·nid (hom′ə nid), *n. Anthropol.* hominid.

hom·o·nym (hom′ə nim), *n.* **1.** a word like another in sound and spelling but different in meaning, as *chase,* to pursue, and *chase,* to ornament metal. **2.** a homophone. **3.** a homograph. **4.** a namesake. **5.** *Biol.* a name given to a species or genus which has been used at an earlier date for a different species or genus and which is therefore rejected. [< LL *homōnym(um)* < Gk *homōnymon,* neut. of *homōnymos* HOMONYMOUS] —**hom′o·nym′ic,** *adj.* —**ho·mon′y·mi·ty,** *n.*

ho·mon·y·mous (hə mon′ə məs, hō-), *adj.* of the nature of homonyms; having the same name. [< LL *homōnymus* < Gk *homṓnymos* of the same name, equiv. to *hom(o)-* HOMO- + *ónym(a)* name, -ONYM + *-os* -OUS] —**ho·mon′y·mous·ly,** *adv.*

homon′ymous construc′tion, *Gram.* a construction that consists of the same morphemes in the same order as those of another construction, as *Flying planes can be dangerous,* in which *planes* in one construction is the object of *flying,* and in another the subject of *can;* a terminal string of formatives having two or more structural descriptions.

ho·mon·y·my (hə mon′ə mē, hō-), *n.* homonymous state. [< LL *homōnymia* < Gk, equiv. to *homṓnym(os)* HOMONYMOUS + *-ia* -Y[3]]

Ho·mo·ou·si·an (hō′mō o͞o′sē ən, -ou′-, hom′ō-), *Eccles.* —*n.* **1.** one of a 4th century A.D. church party which maintained that the essence or substance of the Father and the Son is the same. (opposed to *Heteroousian*). —*adj.* **2.** of or pertaining to the Homoousians or their doctrine. Also, **Ho·mo·ü·si·an.** [< LGk *homooúsi(os)* of the same substance (Gk *hom(o)-* HOMO- + *ousí(a)* substance, essence + *-os* adj. suffix) + -AN] —**Ho′mo·ou′si·an·ism,** *n.*

hom·o·pause (hom′ə pôz′, hō′mə-), *n. Meteorol. Rare.* the boundary or transition layer between the homosphere and the heterosphere. [HOMO- + PAUSE]

hom·o·phone (hom′ə fōn′, hō′mə-), *n.* **1.** *Phonet.* a word pronounced the same as, but differing in meaning from another, whether spelled the same way or not, as *heir* and *air.* **2.** a written element that represents the same spoken unit as another, as *ks,* a homophone of *x* in English. [back formation from HOMOPHONOUS]

hom·o·phon·ic (hom′ə fon′ik, hō′mə-), *adj.* **1.** having the same sound. **2.** *Music.* having one part or melody predominating (opposed to *polyphonic*). [< Gk *homóphōn(os)* (see HOMOPHONOUS) + -IC] —**hom′o·phon′i·cal·ly,** *adv.*

ho·moph·o·nous (hə mof′ə nəs), *adj.* identical in pronunciation. [< Gk *homóphōnos* of the same sound, equiv. to *homo-* HOMO- + *phōn-* PHON- + *-os* -OUS]

ho·moph·o·ny (hə mof′ə nē), *n.* **1.** the quality or state of being homophonic. **2.** homophonic music. [< Gk *homophōnía* unison, equiv. to *homóphōn(os)* HOMOPHONOUS + *-ia* -Y[3]]

ho·mop·la·sy (hə mop′lə sē, hō′mə plas′ē, -plā′sē, hom′ə-), *n. Biol.* correspondence in form or structure, owing to a similar environment. [HOMO- + -PLASY] —**ho·mo·plas·tic** (hō′mə plas′tik, hom′ə-), *adj.*

ho·mo·po·lar (hō′mə pō′lər, hom′ə-), *adj. Chem.* of uniform polarity; not separated or changed into ions; not polar in activity. [HOMO- + POLAR] —**ho·mo·po·lar·i·ty** (hō′mə pō lar′i tē, hom′ə-), *n.*

Ho·mop·ter·a (hō mop′tər ə), *n.* the order comprising the homopterous insects. [< NL (neut. pl.); see HOMOPTEROUS]

ho·mop·ter·ous (hə mop′tər əs, hō-), *adj.* belonging or pertaining to the *Homoptera,* an order of insects closely related to the hemipterous insects (in some classifications a suborder of *Hemiptera*) but having membranous forewings and hind wings, comprising the aphids, cicadas, etc. [< Gk *homópteros.* See HOMO-, -PTEROUS]

ho·mor·gan·ic (hō′môr gan′ik, hom′ôr-), *adj. Phonet.* (of two or more speech sounds) articulated by using the same speech organ or organs, as *p, b,* and *m,* which are homorganic with respect to being labial but not with respect to being velar. Cf. **homotypical** (def. 1). [HOM(O)- + ORGANIC]

Ho·mo sa·pi·ens (hō′mō sā′pē ənz), **1.** (*italics*) modern man, the single surviving species of the genus *Homo* and of the primate family *Hominidae,* to which it belongs. **2.** mankind. [< L: man, the wise]

ho·mo·sex·u·al (hō′mə sek′sho͞o əl, -mō-), *adj.* **1.** of, pertaining to, or exhibiting homosexuality. **2.** of, pertaining to, or noting the same sex. —*n.* **3.** a homosexual person. [HOMO- + SEXUAL]

ho·mo·sex·u·al·i·ty (hō′mə sek′sho͞o al′i tē, -mō-), *n.* sexual desire or behavior directed toward a person or persons of one's own sex. [HOMO- + SEXUALITY]

ho·mo·sphere (hō′mə sfēr′, hom′ə-), *n. Meteorol. Rare.* the region of the atmosphere, extending from the earth's surface to approximately 50 miles above sea level, in which there are no gross changes in atmospheric composition. Cf. **heterosphere.** [HOMO- + -SPHERE]

ho·mos·po·rous (hə mos′pər əs, hō′mə spôr′əs, -spōr′-), *adj. Bot.* having spores of one kind only. [HOMO- + SPORE + -OUS]

ho·mos·po·ry (hə mos′pə rē, hō-), *n.* the production of a single kind of spore, neither microspore nor megaspore. [HOMO- + SPORE + -Y[3]]

ho·mo·styled (hō′mō stīld′), *adj.* (of a plant) having styles of the same form or length in all flowers. Also, **ho′mo·sty′lous, ho′mo·sty′lic.** [HOMO- + STYLED] —**ho′mo·sty′lism, ho′mo·sty′ly,** *n.*

ho·mo·tax·is (hō′mə tak′sis, hom′ə-), *n.* similarity of arrangement, as of geological strata which, though not necessarily contemporaneous, have the same relative position. [HOMO- + -TAXIS] —**ho′mo·tac′tic, ho·mo·tax·i·al** (hō′mə tak′sē əl, hom′ə-), *adj.* —**ho′mo·tax′i·al·ly,** *adv.*

ho·mo·thal·lic (hō′mə thal′ik, hom′ə-), *adj. Bot.* **1.** having all mycelia alike, the opposite sexual functions being performed by different cells of a single mycelium. Cf. **heterothallic** (def. 1). **2.** monoecious. [HOMO- + THALL(US) + -IC] —**ho′mo·thal′lism,** *n.*

ho·mo·therm (hō′mə thûrm′, hom′ə-), *n.* homoiotherm. —**ho′mo·ther′my, ho′mo·ther′mism,** *n.*

ho·mo·ther·mal (hō′mə thûr′məl, hom′ə-), *adj.* homoiothermal. Also, **ho′mo·ther′mic, ho′mo·ther′mous.**

ho·mo·thet·ic (hō′mə thet′ik, hom′ə-), *adj. Geom.* similar; similarly placed. [HOMO- + THETIC] —**ho·moth·e·ty** (hō moth′i tē, hō-), *n.*

homothet′ic transforma′tion, *Math.* See **similarity transformation.**

ho·mo·type (hō′mə tīp′, hom′ə-), *n. Biol.* an organ or part having a structure similar to that of another organ or part; homologue. [HOMO- + TYPE]

ho·mo·typ·ic (hō′mə tip′ik, hom′ə-), *adj. Biol.* **1.** of or pertaining to a homotype. **2.** homeotypic. [HOMOTYPE + -IC]

ho·mo·typ·i·cal (hō′mə tip′i kəl, hom′ə-), *adj.* **1.** *Phonet.* (of two or more speech sounds) articulated in a like manner but not with the same speech organ or organs, as the consonants of *pie* and *tie.* Cf. **homorganic. 2.** *Biol.* homotypic. [HOMOTYPE + -ICAL]

ho·mo·zy·go·sis (hō′mə zī gō′sis, -zi-, hom′ə-), *n. Biol.* the state of being a homozygote. [HOMO- + NL *zygōsis* < Gk; see ZYGO-, -OSIS]

ho·mo·zy·gote (hō′mə zī′gōt, -zig′ōt, hom′ə-), *n. Biol.* an organism with identical pairs of genes with respect to any given pair of heredity characters, and therefore breeding true to those characteristics. [HOMO- + ZYGOTE]

ho·mo·zy·gous (hō′mə zī′gəs, hom′ə-), *adj. Biol.* **1.** having identical pairs of genes for any given pair of hereditary characteristics. **2.** of or pertaining to a homozygote. [HOMO- + Gk *-zygos;* see ZYGO-, -OUS]

Homs (hôms), *n.* a city in W Syria. 152,077 (est. 1959).

ho·mun·cu·lus (hō mung′kyə ləs), *n., pl.* **-li** (-lī′). **1.** a diminutive human; midget. **2.** a fully-formed, miniature human body believed, according to some medical theories of the 16th and 17th centuries, to be contained in the spermatozoon. **3.** the human fetus. **4.** an artificially made dwarf, supposedly produced in a flask by an alchemist. —**ho·mun′cu·lar,** *adj.* [< L, equiv. to *homun-* (var. of *homin-,* s. of *homo* man) + *-culus* -CULE]

hom·y (hō′mē), *adj.,* **hom·i·er, hom·i·est.** homey.

hon (hun), *n. Informal.* **1.** (*often cap.*) honey (def. 6). **2.** honey (def. 6). [shortened form]

Hon., Honorable.

hon., **1.** honorably. **2.** *Chiefly Brit.* honorary.

Ho·nan (hō′nan′; *Chin.* hœ′nän′), *n.* **1.** a province in E China. 48,670,000 (est. 1957); 64,479 sq. mi. *Cap.:* Kaifeng. **2.** (*usually l.c.*). *Textiles.* **a.** a pongee fabric made from the filaments of the wild silkworm. **b.** a lustrous fabric simulating pongee and woven from fibers other than silk.

Hond., Honduras.

hon·da (hon′də), *n. Western U.S.* an eye at one end of a lariat through which the other end is passed to form a lasso, noose, etc. [< Sp: sling < L *funda,* perh. < Gk *sphendónē*]

Hon·do (*Jap.* hôn′dô *for 1;* hon′dō *for 2*), *n.* **1.** Honshu. **2.** a town in SW Texas. 4992 (1960).

Hon·du·ras (hon dŏŏr′əs, -dyŏŏr′-), *n.* **1.** a republic in SE Central America. 1,884,765 (1961); 43,277 sq. mi. *Cap.:* Tegucigalpa. **2.** See **British Honduras.** —**Hon·du′ran, Hon·du·ra·ne·an, Hon·du·ra·ni·an** (hon′də rā′nē ən), *adj., n.*

hone[1] (hōn), *n., v.,* **honed, hon·ing.** —*n.* **1.** a whetstone of fine, compact texture for sharpening razors. **2.** a precision tool with a mechanically rotated abrasive tip, for enlarging holes to precise dimensions. —*v.t.* **3.** to sharpen on or as on a hone: *to hone a razor.* **4.** to enlarge or finish (a hole) with a hone. [ME; OE *hān* stone, rock; c. Icel *hein* hone; akin to CONE]

hone[2] (hōn), *v.i.,* **honed, hon·ing.** *Dial.* **1.** to moan and groan. **2.** to yearn; long: *to hone for the farm life; to hone after peach pie.* [< AF *hone(r),* equiv. to OF *hogner* to grumble, growl < Gmc; cf. OS *hōnian* to abuse, revile]

Hon′ea Path′ (hun′ē), a town in NW South Carolina. 3453 (1960).

Ho·neg·ger (hon′ə gər, hō′neg′ər; *Fr.* ô ne gerʹ), *n.* **Ar·thur** (är′thər; *Fr.* AR tōōr′), 1892–1955, Swiss composer, born in France.

Hones·dale (hōnz′dāl′), *n.* a town in NE Pennsylvania. 5569 (1960).

hon·est (on′ist), *adj.* **1.** honorable in principles, intentions, and actions; upright: *an honest person.* **2.** showing uprightness and fairness: *honest dealings.* **3.** gained fairly: *honest wealth.* **4.** sincere; frank: *an honest face.* **5.** genuine or unadulterated: *honest weights; honest commodities.* **6.** respectable; having a good reputation: *an honest name.* **7.** truthful or creditable: *an honest account.* **8.** humble, plain, or unadorned. **9.** *Archaic.* chaste or virtuous. [ME *honeste* < MF < L *honest(us)* honorable, equiv. to *hones-* (var. s. of *honōs*) HONOR + *-tus* adj. suffix] —**hon′est·ness,** *n.*
—**Syn. 1.** just, incorruptible, trusty, trustworthy. **2.** fair. **4.** straightforward, candid. **5, 9.** pure. —**Ant. 1.** dishonest, corrupt.

hon′est in′jun (in′jən), *Informal.* honestly; truly: *I've never seen her before in my life, honest injun.* Also, **hon′est In′jun.** [see HONEST, INDIAN]

Hon′est John′, *U.S.* **1.** a surface-to-surface, single-stage artillery rocket. **2.** *Informal.* **a.** an honest, sincere man. **b.** a man who is so trusting and innocent that he may be easily cheated or deceived.

hon·est·ly (on′ist lē), *adv.* **1.** in an honest manner. **2.** with honesty. —*interj.* **3.** (used to express mild exasperation, disbelief, dismay, etc.): *Honestly! I want to finish this work and you keep interrupting.* [HONEST + -LY]

hon·es·ty (on′i stē), *n., pl.* **-ties.** **1.** the quality or fact of being honest; uprightness, probity, or integrity. **2.** truthfulness, sincerity, or frankness. **3.** freedom from deceit or fraud. **4.** *Bot.* a cruciferous herb, *Lunaria annua,* having purple flowers and semitransparent, satiny pods. **5.** *Obs.* chastity. [ME *honeste* < MF < L *honestās.* See HONEST, -TY[2]]
—**Syn. 1.** fairness, justice; rectitude. See **honor. 2.** candor, veracity. —**Ant. 1.** dishonesty.

hone·wort (hōn′wûrt′), *n.* any of several umbelliferous herbs of the genus *Cryptotaenia,* esp. *C. canadensis,* having white flowers. [*hone* (< ?) + WORT[2]]

hon·ey (hun′ē), *n., pl.* **hon·eys,** *adj., v.,* **hon·eyed** or **hon·ied, hon·ey·ing.** —*n.* **1.** a sweet, viscid fluid produced by bees from the nectar collected from flowers, and stored in their nests or hives as food. **2.** this substance as used in cooking or on the table as a spread or sweetener. **3.** the nectar of flowers. **4.** any of various similarly sweet, viscid products produced by insects or in other ways. **5.** something sweet, delicious, or delightful: *the honey of flattery.* **6.** (*often cap.*) darling; sweetheart (used as a term of endearment for a loved one). **7.** *Informal.* something of esp. high quality, degree of excellence, etc.: *That car is a honey. It was a honey of a first novel.* —*adj.* **8.** of or pertaining to honey; like honey; sweet. **9.** containing honey or flavored or sweetened with honey. —*v.t.* **10.** *Informal.* to talk flatteringly or endearingly to (often used with *up*). **11.** to sweeten or flavor with or as with honey. —*v.i.* **12.** *Informal.* (often fol. by *up*) to use flattery, endearing terms, etc., in an effort to obtain something of an exceptional nature: *She got where she did by honeying up to the boss.* [ME *hony,* OE *hunig;* c. D, G *honig,* Icel *hunang;* akin to Gk *knēkos* saffron] —**hon′ey·ful,** *adj.* —**hon′ey·less,** *adj.* —**hon′ey·like′,** *adj.*

hon′ey ant′, any of several ants, esp. of the genus *Myrmecocystus,* that feed on honeydew or nectar and store the excess juices in the bodies of certain worker ants.

hon·ey·bee (hun′ē bē′), *n.* a bee that collects and stores honey, esp. *Apis mellifera.* [HONEY + BEE[1]]

hon·ey·bloom (hun′ē blōōm′), *n.* See **spreading dogbane.**

hon·ey·bunch (hun′ē bunch′), *n.* sweetheart; honey (often cap. and used as a term of endearment). Also, **hon·ey·bun** (hun′ē bun′). [HONEY + BUNCH]

hon′ey buz′zard, a long-tailed, Old World hawk, *Pernis apivorus,* that feeds on small rodents, reptiles, insects, the larvae of wasps and bees, etc.

Honeycomb

hon·ey·comb (hun′ē kōm′), *n.* **1.** a structure of rows of hexagonal wax cells, formed by bees in their hive for the storage of honey, pollen, and their eggs. **2.** a piece of this containing honey and chewed as a sweet. **3.** anything whose appearance suggests such a structure, esp. in containing many small units or holes: *The building was a honeycomb of offices and showrooms.* **4.** the reticulum of a ruminant. **5.** *Textiles.* **a.** Also called **waffle cloth.** a fabric with an embossed surface woven in a pattern resembling a honeycomb. **b.** the characteristic weave of such a fabric. —*adj.* **6.** having the structure or appearance of a honeycomb. —*v.t.* **7.** to cause to be full of holes; pierce with many holes or cavities: *an old log honeycombed with ant burrows.* **8.** to penetrate in all parts: *a city honeycombed with vice.* [ME *huny-comb,* OE *hunigcamb.* See HONEY, COMB[1]]

hon′eycomb tripe′, a part of the inner lining of the stomach of the steer, calf, hog, or sheep, resembling a honeycomb in appearance and considered a table delicacy. Cf. **plain tripe.**

hon′eycomb work′, *Archit.* See **stalactite work.**

hon·ey·creep·er (hun′ē krē′pər), *n.* **1.** any of several small, usually brightly colored birds of the family *Coerebidae,* of tropical and semitropical America. **2.** any of several oscine birds of the family *Drepanididae,* indigenous to the Hawaiian Islands, the species of which exhibit extreme variations in the shape of the bill. [HONEY + CREEPER]

hon·ey·dew (hun′ē dōō′, -dyōō′), *n.* **1.** the sweet material which exudes from the leaves of certain plants in hot weather. **2.** a sugary material secreted by aphids, leafhoppers, etc. **3.** See **honeydew melon.** [HONEY + DEW] —**hon′ey·dewed′,** *adj.*

hon′eydew mel′on, a sweet-flavored, white-fleshed muskmelon having a smooth, pale-green rind.

hon′ey eat′er, any of numerous oscine birds of the family *Meliphagidae,* chiefly of Australasia, having a bill and tongue adapted for extracting the nectar from flowers.

hon·eyed (hun′ēd), *adj.* **1.** dulcet or mellifluous: *honeyed tones.* **2.** flattering or ingratiating: *honeyed words.* **3.** containing, consisting of, or resembling honey: *honeyed drinks.* Also, **honied.** [ME *honyede.* See HONEY, -ED[2]] —**hon′eyed·ly,** *adv.* —**hon′eyed·ness,** *n.*

hon′ey gild′ing, gilding of ceramics with a mixture of gold leaf and honey, later fired to fix the gold.

hon′ey guide′, any of several small, usually dull-colored birds of the family *Indicatoridae,* of Africa and southern Asia, certain species of which are noted for their habit of leading men or animals to nests of honeybees in order to feed on the honey, larvą, and wax of the nests after they have been broken open.

hon′ey lo′cust, **1.** Also called **three-thorned acacia.** a thorny, North American tree, *Gleditsia triacanthos,* having small, compound leaves and pods with a sweet pulp. **2.** See **honey mesquite.**

hon′ey mesquite′, a thorny shrub, *Prosopis juliflora,* of the West Indies.

hon·ey·moon (hun′ē mōōn′), *n.* **1.** a vacation or trip taken by a newly married couple before establishing a home. **2.** the month or so following a marriage. **3.** any period of blissful harmony: *Their entire sixty years of marriage was one long honeymoon.* **4.** any new relationship characterized by an initial period of harmony: *The honeymoon between Congress and the President was over.* —*v.i.* **5.** to spend one's honeymoon (usually fol. by *in* or *at*). [HONEY + MOON] —**hon′ey·moon′er,** *n.*

hon′eymoon bridge′, *Cards.* any of several varieties of bridge for two players.

hon′ey plant′, any plant esp. useful in furnishing nectar to bees, as the cleome or figwort.

hon′ey stom′ach, **1.** the enlarged crop of a honeybee in which nectar is transported and acted on by enzymes to form honey. **2.** the crop of an ant, bee, or other hymenopterous insect, serving as a reservoir for honeydew and nectar. Also called **hon′ey sac′.**

hon·ey·suck·er (hun′ē suk′ər), *n.* **1.** a bird that feeds on the nectar of flowers. **2.** See **honey eater.** [HONEY + SUCKER]

hon·ey·suck·le (hun′ē suk′əl), *n.* **1.** any upright or climbing, caprifoliaceous shrub of the genus *Lonicera,* certain species of which are cultivated for their fragrant white, yellow, or red tubular flowers. **2.** any of various other fragrant or ornamental plants. [ME *honiesoukel,* equiv. to *honisouke* (OE *hunisūce;* see HONEY, SUCK) + *-el* -LE] —**hon′ey·suck′led,** *adj.*

hon′eysuckle or′nament, anthemion.

hon·ey-sweet (hun′ē swēt′), *adj.* sweet as honey. [ME *hony sweete,* OE *hunig swēte*]

hon·ey·wort (hun′ē wûrt′), *n.* an herb, *Cerinthe retorta,* of Greece, having bluish-green leaves and purple-tipped, yellow flowers. [HONEY + WORT[2], so called because its flowers yield much honey]

hong (hông), *n.* **1.** (in China) a group of rooms or buildings forming a warehouse, factory, etc. **2.** one of the factories under foreign ownership formerly maintained at Canton. [< Chin (Cantonese) *hong* row, rank; equiv. to Mandarin *hang*]

Hong Kong (hông′ kông′), **1.** a British crown colony comprising the island of Hong Kong (32 sq. mi.) and the adjacent mainland bordering SE China. 3,133,131 (1961); 390 sq. mi. *Cap.:* Victoria. **2.** Victoria (def. 4). Also, **Hong′-Kong′.**

hon·ied (hun′ēd), *adj.* honeyed.

ho·ni soit qui mal y pense (ô nē swa′ kē mal ē päns′), *French.* shamed be the one who thinks evil of it: motto of the Order of the Garter.

honk (hôngk, hôngk), *n.* **1.** the cry of a goose. **2.** any similar sound. **3.** the sound of an automobile horn. —*v.i.* **4.** to emit a honk. **5.** to cause an automobile horn to emit a honk: *He drove up in front of the house and honked.* —*v.t.* **6.** to cause (an automobile horn) to emit a honk: *The driver honked his horn impatiently.* [imit.] —**honk′er,** *n.*

honk·y-tonk (hông′kē tongk′, hông′kē tôngk′), *Informal.* —*n.* **1.** a cheap, noisy, and garish nightclub or dance hall. —*adj.* **2.** of, pertaining to, or characteristic of a honky-tonk: *honky-tonk atmosphere.* **3.** characterized by or having a large number of honky-tonks: *the honky-tonk part of town.* **4.** *Music.* noting a style of ragtime piano-playing characterized by a strict two-four or four-four bass, either contrapuntal or chordal, and a melody embellished with chords and syncopated rhythms, typically performed on a piano whose strings have been muffled and given a tinny sound. [rhyming compound (with euphonic *-y-*) based on HONK]

Hon·o·lu·lu (hon′ə lōō′lōō), *n.* a seaport in and the capital of Hawaii, on S Oahu. 294,179 (1960).

hon·or (on′ər), *n.* **1.** high public esteem; fame; glory: *He has earned his position of honor.* **2.** honesty or integrity in one's beliefs and actions: *a man of honor.* **3.** a source of credit or distinction: *to be an honor to one's family.* **4.** high respect, as for worth, merit, or rank: *to be held in honor.* **5.** such respect manifested: *to be received with honor; a memorial in honor of the dead.* **6.** the privilege of being associated with or receiving a favor from a respected person, group, organization, etc.: *to have the honor of serving on a prize jury; I have the honor of introducing this evening's speaker.* **7.** Usually, **honors.** evidence, as a decoration, scroll, or title, of high rank, dignity, or distinction: *political honors.* **8.** (*usually cap.*) a deferential title, esp. for judges and mayors (prec. by *his, your,* etc.). **9. honors, a.** special rank or distinction conferred by a university, college, or school upon a student for eminence in scholarship or success in some particular subject. **b.** an advanced course of study for superior students. Cf. **honors course. 10.** chastity or purity in a woman. **11.** Also called **hon′or card′.** *Cards.* **a.** *Bridge.* any of the five highest trump cards, as an ace, king, queen, jack, or ten in the trump suit, or any of the four aces in a no-trump contract. Cf. **honor trick. b.** *Whist.* any of the four highest trump cards, as an ace, king, queen, or jack in the trump suit. **12.** *Golf.* the privilege of teeing off before the other player or side, given after the first hole to the player who or side that won the previous hole. **13. be on** or **upon one's honor,** to accept and acknowledge personal responsibility for one's actions: *We were on our honor not to cheat on the exam.* **14. do honor to, a.** to show respect to. **b.** to be a credit to: *Such good children would do honor to any mother.* **15. do the honors,** to serve or preside as host, as in introducing people, carving or serving at table, etc.: *Father did the honors at the family Thanksgiving dinner.* —*v.t.* **16.** to hold in honor or high respect; revere: *to honor one's parents.* **17.** to treat with honor. **18.** to confer honor or distinction upon. **19.** to worship (the Supreme Being). **20.** to show a courteous regard for: *to honor an invitation.* **21.** *Com.* to accept or pay (a draft, check, etc.): *All credit cards honored here.* **22.** to accept as valid and conform to the request or demands of (an official document). **23.** (in square dancing) to meet or salute with a bow. —*adj.* **24.** of, pertaining to, or noting honor. Also, *esp. Brit.,* **honour.** [ME *(h)on(o)ur* < AF (equiv. to OF *onor,* etc.) < L *honōr-* (s. of *honor,* earlier *honōs*)] —**hon′or·er,** *n.* —**hon′or·less,** *adj.*
—**Syn. 1.** distinction. **2.** probity, uprightness. HONOR, HONESTY, INTEGRITY, SINCERITY refer to the highest moral principles and the absence of deceit or fraud. HONOR denotes a fine sense of, and a strict conformity to, what is considered morally right or due: *a high sense of honor; on one's honor.* HONESTY denotes the presence of probity and particularly the absence of deceit or fraud, esp. in business dealings: *uncompromising honesty and trustworthiness.* INTEGRITY indicates a soundness of moral principle which no power or influence can impair: *a man of unquestioned integrity and dependability.* SINCERITY implies absence of dissimulation or deceit, and a strong adherence to truth: *His sincerity was evident in every word.* **4.** deference, homage; reverence, veneration. HONOR, CONSIDERATION, DISTINCTION refer to the regard in which one is held by his fellows. HONOR suggests a combination of liking and respect: *His townsmen held him in great honor.* CONSIDERATION suggests honor because of proved worth: *a man worthy of the highest consideration.* DISTINCTION suggests particular honor because of qualities or accomplishments: *He achieved distinction as a violinist at an early age.* **16.** esteem, venerate. —**Ant. 2.** dishonor, dishonesty.

Hon·or (on′ər), *n.* a boy's or girl's given name.

Ho·no·ra (hō nōr′ə, -nôr′ə), *n.* a girl's given name, form of **Honor.**

hon·or·a·ble (on′ər ə bəl), *adj.* **1.** in accordance with or characterized by principles of honor; upright: *They were all honorable men.* **2.** of high rank, dignity, or distinction; noble, illustrious, or distinguished. **3.** (*cap.*) entitling to honor or distinction: a title prefixed to the names of the younger children of British peers, from earls to barons, and to certain government officials. *Abbr.:* Hon. **4.** worthy of honor and high respect;

estimable; creditable. **5.** bringing honor or credit; consistent with honor: *an honorable peace.* Also, *esp. Brit.,* **honourable.** [ME *hono(u)rable* < AF (equiv. to MF *honorable*) < L *honōrābil(is).* See HONOR, -ABLE] —**hon′or·a·ble·ness,** *n.* —**hon′or·a·bly,** *adv.*
—**Syn. 1.** honest, noble, high-minded, just. —**Ant. 1.** ignoble.

hon′orable dis′charge, *U.S. Mil.* **1.** a discharge from military service of a person who has fulfilled his obligations efficiently, honorably, and faithfully. **2.** a certificate of such a discharge.

hon′orable or′dinary, *Heraldry.* any of the ordinaries believed to be among those that are oldest or that were the source of the other ordinaries, as the chief, pale, fess, bend, chevron, cross, and saltire. Cf. **subordinary.**

hon·or·and (on′ə rand′), *n.* the recipient of an honorary degree. [< L *honorand(us)* ger. of *honorāre* to HONOR]

hon·o·rar·i·um (on′ə râr′ē əm), *n., pl.* **-rar·i·ums, -rar·i·a** (-râr′ē ə). **1.** a reward, in recognition of acts or professional services for which custom or propriety forbids a price to be set: *The mayor was given an honorarium for delivering a speech to our club.* **2.** a fee for services rendered by a professional person. [< L: fee paid on taking office, n. use of neut. of *honōrārius* HONORARY]

hon·or·ar·y (on′ə rer′ē), *adj.* **1.** given for honor only, without the usual duties, privileges, emoluments, etc.: *The university presented the governor with an honorary degree.* **2.** holding a title or position conferred for honor only: *an honorary president.* **3.** (of an obligation) depending on one's honor for fulfillment. **4.** conferring or commemorating honor or distinction. **5.** given, made, or serving as a token of honor: *an honorary gift.* [< L *honōrāri(us)* relating to honor. See HONOR, -ARY]

hon′orary can′on, a priest attached to a cathedral but not entitled to receive a stipend or to vote in the chapter. Cf. **minor canon.**

hon′or bright′, upon my honor; really and truly: *I did sweep the floor, honor bright.*

hon′or guard′. See **guard of honor.**

Ho·no·ri·a (hō nōr′ē ə, -nôr′-), *n.* a girl's given name, form of **Honor.**

hon·or·if·ic (on′ə rif′ik), *adj.* **1.** Also, **hon′or·if′i·cal.** doing or conferring honor. **2.** conveying honor, as a title or a grammatical form used in speaking to or about a superior, elder, etc. —*n.* **3.** (in certain languages, as Chinese and Japanese) a class of forms used to show respect, esp. in direct address. **4.** a title or term of respect. [< L *honōrific(us)* honor-making. See HONOR-, -I-, -FIC] —**hon′or·if′i·cal·ly,** *adv.*

ho·no·ris cau·sa (ō nō′ʀis kou′sä; *Eng.* o nōr′is kô′zə, o nôr′-), *Latin.* as a sign of respect (usually describing an honorary college or university degree). [lit., for the sake of honor]

Ho·no·ri·us (hō nōr′ē əs, -nôr′-), *n.* **Fla·vi·us** (flā′vē əs), A.D. 384–423, Roman emperor of the West 395–423.

Honorius I, died A.D. 638, Italian ecclesiastic: pope 625–638.

Honorius II, (*Lamberto Scannabecchi*) died 1130, Italian ecclesiastic: pope 1124–30.

Honorius III, (*Cencio Savelli*) died 1227, Italian ecclesiastic: pope 1216–27.

Honorius IV, (*Giacomo Savelli*) 1210–87, Italian ecclesiastic: pope 1285–87.

hon′or point′, *Heraldry.* a point midway between the heart point and top of an escutcheon. Also called **collar point, color point.**

hon′or roll′, **1.** a list of elementary- or secondary-school pupils who have earned grades above a specific average during a semester or school year. Cf. **dean's list. 2.** a roster of names, usually in a memorial or other public place, of local citizens who have served or have died in the armed services.

hon′ors course′, a course in a university or college consisting largely of independent research terminating in a dissertation or a comprehensive examination, and earning for the student who passes it a degree with distinction.

hon′or soci′ety, (in a college, university, or secondary school) a student society which admits members on the basis of academic merit and, esp. in secondary schools, worthwhile contributions in extracurricular activities.

hon′ors of war′, *Mil.* privileges granted to a capitulating force, as of marching out of their camp or entrenchments with all their arms and with colors flying.

hon′or sys′tem, a system whereby the students at a school, the inmates in a prison, etc. are put upon their honor to observe certain rules in order to minimize administrative supervision or to promote honesty.

hon′or trick′, *Bridge.* (in certain bidding systems) a high card or set of high cards that can reasonably be expected to take a trick, the total worth of such cards in a hand being the basis for evaluating its strength and bidding.

hon·our (on′ər), *n., v.t., adj. Chiefly Brit.* honor. —**hon′our·er,** *n.* —**hon′our·less,** *adj.*

hon·our·a·ble (on′ər ə bəl), *adj. Chiefly Brit.* honorable. —**hon′our·a·ble·ness,** *n.* —**hon′our·a·bly,** *adv.*

Hon·shu (hôn′sho͞o), *n.* an island in central Japan; chief island of the country. 71,343,511 (1960); 88,851 sq. mi. Also called **Hondo.**

hooch (ho͞och), *n. Slang.* **1.** alcoholic liquor. **2.** liquor illicitly distilled and distributed. Also, **hootch.** [short for *Hoochinoo,* alter. of *Hutsnuwu,* name of Alaskan Indian tribe which made liquor]

Hooch (ho͞och; *Du.* hōᴋʜ), *n.* **Pie·ter de** (pē′tər də); *Du.* pē′tᴀʀ də), 1629?–88?, Dutch painter. Also, **Hoogh.**

hood[1] (ho͝od), *n.* **1.** a soft or flexible covering for the head and neck, either separate or attached to a cloak or the like. **2.** something resembling or suggesting such a covering, esp. in shape, as certain petals or sepals. **3.** the part of an automobile body covering the engine. **4.** *Brit.* the roof of a carriage. **5.** *Falconry.* a cover for the entire head of a hawk: used when the bird is not in pursuit of game. **6.** an ornamental ruffle or fold on the back of the shoulders of an academic gown, jurist's robe, etc. **7.** a crest or band of color on the head of certain birds and animals. —*v.t.* **8.** to furnish with a hood. **9.** to cover with, or as with, a hood. [ME *hode,* OE *hōd;* c. OFris *hōde,* D *hoed,* G *Hut* hat] —**hood′less,** *adj.* —**hood′like′,** *adj.*

hood[2] (ho͝od, ho͞od), *n. Slang.* **1.** hoodlum; gangster. **2.** a teen-age tough. [shortening of HOODLUM]

Hood (ho͝od), *n.* **1. John Bell,** 1831–79, Confederate general in the U.S. Civil War. **2. Raymond Math·ew·son** (math′yo͞o sən), 1881–1934, U.S. architect. **3. Robin.** See **Robin Hood. 4. Thomas,** 1799–1845, English poet and humorist. **5. Mount,** a volcanic peak in N Oregon, in the Cascade Range. 11,253 ft.

-hood, a native English suffix denoting state, condition, character, nature, etc., or a body of persons of a particular character or class, formerly used in the formation of nouns: *childhood; likelihood; knighthood; priesthood.* [ME *-hode, -hod,* OE *-hād* (c. G *-heit*), special use of *hād* condition, state, order, quality, rank]

hood·ed (ho͝od′id), *adj.* **1.** having, or covered with, a hood. **2.** hood-shaped. **3.** *Zool.* having on the head a hoodlike formation, crest, arrangement of colors, or the like. **4.** *Bot.* cucullate. [late ME *hodid.* See HOOD[1], -ED[3]] —**hood′ed·ness,** *n.*

hood′ed crow′, a European crow, *Corvus cornix,* having a gray body and black head, wings, and tail.

hood′ed seal′, bladdernose.

hood′ed top′, *Eng. Furniture.* a top to a secretary, chest, etc., following in outline a single- or double-curved pediment on the front of the piece. Cf. **bonnet top.**

hood′ed war′bler, a wood warbler, *Wilsonia citrina,* of the U.S., olive-green above, yellow below, and having a black head and throat with a yellow face.

hood·ie (ho͝od′ē; *Scot.* ho͞o′dē), *n. Scot.* the hooded crow. Also called **hood′ie crow′.** [HOOD[1] + -IE]

hoo·dle (ho͞od′əl), *n. Dial.* a playing marble. [?]

hood·lum (ho͞od′ləm, ho͝od′-), *n.* **1.** a gangster; racketeer. **2.** a thug. **3.** a rowdy, destructive child or adolescent: *Hoodlums broke many of the school's windows.* [? < dial. Bavarian *hodalum* a ragged beggar or rogue] —**hood′lum·ish,** *adj.* —**hood′lum·ism,** *n.*

hood·man (ho͝od′mən), *n., pl.* **-men.** *Obs.* the player who is blindfolded in hoodman-blind. [HOOD[1] + MAN]

hood·man-blind (ho͝od′mən blīnd′), *n. Archaic.* See **blindman's buff.**

hood′ mold′ing, a molding or dripstone over a door or window, as a label.

hoo·doo (ho͞o′do͞o), *n., pl.* **-doos,** *v.,* **-dooed, -doo·ing.** —*n.* **1.** bad luck. **2.** a person or thing that brings bad luck. **3.** *Geol.* **a.** a pillar of rock, usually of fantastic shape, left by erosion. **b.** See **earth pillar. 4.** voodoo. —*v.t.* **5.** to bring or cause bad luck to. [appar. var of VOODOO]

Hood′ Riv′er, a town in N Oregon. 3657 (1960).

hood·wink (ho͝od′wiŋk′), *v.t.* **1.** to deceive or trick. **2.** *Archaic.* to blindfold. **3.** *Obs.* to cover or hide. [HOOD[1] + WINK] —**hood′wink′a·ble,** *adj.* —**hood′wink′er,** *n.*

hoo·ey (ho͞o′ē), *Informal.* —*interj.* **1.** (used to express disapproval or disbelief): *Hooey! You know that's not true.* —*n.* **2.** silly or worthless talk, writing, ideas, etc.; nonsense: *That's a bunch of hooey and you know it!* [?]

hoof (ho͝of, ho͞of), *n., pl.* **hoofs** or **hooves** for 1, 2, 4; **hoof** for 3, 5; *v.* —*n.* **1.** the horny covering protecting the ends of the digits or encasing the foot in certain animals, as the ox, horse, etc. See diag. under **horse. 2.** the entire foot of a horse, donkey, etc. **3.** *Dial.* a hoofed animal, esp. one of a herd. **4.** *Informal.* the human foot. **5. on the hoof,** (of livestock) not butchered; live: *The city youngsters were seeing lambs on the hoof for the first time.* —*v.t.* **6.** *Slang.* to walk (often fol. by *it*): *Let's hoof it to the supermarket.* —*v.i.* **7.** *Slang.* to dance, esp. to tap-dance: *He's been hoofing at the Palladium.* [ME; OE *hōf;* c. OFris *hōf,* D *hoef,* G *Huf,* Icel *hōfr;* Skt *śaphás*] —**hoof′i·ness,** *n.* —**hoof′less,** *adj.* —**hoof′like′,** *adj.*

hoof′-and-mouth′ disease′ (ho͝of′ən mouth′, ho͞of′-). See **foot-and-mouth disease.**

hoof·beat (ho͝of′bēt′, ho͞of′-), *n.* the sound made by an animal's hoof in walking, running, etc. [HOOF + BEAT]

hoof·bound (ho͝of′bound′, ho͞of′-), *adj. Vet. Pathol.* (of horses) having the heels of the hoofs dry and contracted, causing lameness. [HOOF + -BOUND[1]]

hoofed (ho͝oft, ho͞oft), *adj.* having hoofs; ungulate. [HOOF + -ED[3]]

hoof·er (ho͝of′ər, ho͞o′fər), *n. Slang.* a professional dancer. [HOOF + -ER[1]]

hoof′ foot′, *Furniture.* pied-de-biche.

hoof·print (ho͝of′print′, ho͞of′-), *n.* the impression made by an animal's hoof. [HOOF + PRINT]

Hoogh (*Du.* hōᴋʜ), *n.* **Pie·ter de** (*Du.* pē′tər də). See **Hooch, Pieter de.**

Hoogh·ly (ho͞og′lē), *n.* a river in NE India, in W Bengal: the westernmost channel by which the Ganges enters the Bay of Bengal. 120 mi. long. Also, **Hugli.**

hook (ho͝ok), *n.* **1.** a curved or angular piece of metal or other hard substance for catching, pulling, holding, or suspending something. **2.** a fishhook. **3.** that which catches; snare; trap. **4.** something having a sharp curve, bend, or angle at one end, as a mark, symbol, etc. **5.** a sharp curve or angle in the length or course of anything. **6.** a curvy spit of land: *Sandy Hook.* **7.** a recurved and pointed organ or appendage of an animal or plant. **8.** *Sports.* **a.** the path described by a ball, as in baseball, bowling, or golf, that curves in a direction opposite to the throwing hand or to the side of the ball from which it was struck. **b.** a ball describing such a path. **9.** *Boxing.* a short, circular punch delivered with the elbow bent. **10.** Also called **pennant.** *Music.* a stroke or line attached to the stem of eighth notes, sixteenth notes, etc. **11.** *Metalworking.* an accidental short bend formed in a piece of bar stock during rolling. **12. hooks,** *Slang.* hands or fingers: *Get your hooks off that cake!* **13.** Also called **deck hook.** *Naut.* a triangular plate or knee that binds together the stringers and plating at each end of a vessel. **14. by hook or by crook,** by any means, whether just or unjust, legal or illegal. Also, **by hook or crook. 15. get or give the hook,** *Slang.* to receive or subject to a dismissal: *The rumor is that he got the hook.* **16. hook, line, and sinker,** *Informal.* entirely; completely: *He fell for the story — hook, line, and sinker.* **17. off the hook,** *Slang.* **a.** out of trouble; released from some difficulty: *This time there was no one around to get him off the hook.* **b.** free of obligation: *His brother paid all his bills and got him off the hook.* **18. on one's own hook,** *Informal.* on one's own initiative or responsibility; independently: *He could have gone into business with his father, but decided he would rather begin on his own hook.* **19. on the hook,** *Slang.* **a.** obliged; committed; involved: *He's already on the hook for ten thousand dollars.* **b.** subjected to a delaying tactic; waiting: *We've had him on the hook for two weeks now.* —*v.t.* **20.** to seize, fasten, suspend from, pierce, or catch hold of and draw with or as with a hook. **21.** to catch (fish) with a fishhook. **22.** *Slang.* to steal or seize by stealth. **23.** to catch or trick by artifice. **24.** (of a bull or other horned animal) to catch on the horns or attack with the horns. **25.** to catch hold of and draw (loops of yarn) through cloth with or as with a hook. **26.** to make (a rug, garment, etc.) in this fashion. **27.** *Sports.* to hit or throw (a ball) so that a hook results. **28.** *Boxing.* to deliver a hook with: *Sugar Ray hooked a right to his opponent's jaw.* **29.** *Rugby.* to push (a ball) backward with the foot in scrimmage from the front line. **30.** to make hook-shaped; crook. —*v.i.* **31.** to become attached or fastened by or as by a hook. **32.** to curve or bend like a hook. **33.** *Sports.* **a.** (of a player) to hook the ball. **b.** (of a ball) to describe a hook in course. **34.** *Slang.* to depart hastily: *We'd better hook for home.* **35. hook it,** *Slang.* to run away; depart; flee: *He hooked it when he saw the truant officer.* **36. hook up, a.** to fasten with a hook or hooks. **b.** to assemble, as a mechanical apparatus, and connect to a source of power: *to hook up a telephone.* [ME *hoke,* OE *hōc;* c. D *hoek* hook, angle, corner; akin to G *Haken,* Icel *haki*] —**hook′less,** *adj.* —**hook′like′,** *adj.*

hook·ah (ho͝ok′ə), *n.* a tobacco pipe with a long, flexible tube by which the smoke is drawn through a jar of water and thus cooled. Also, **hook′a.** [< Ar *huqqah* box, vase, pipe for smoking]

Hookah

hook′ and butt′, (in shipbuilding) a scarf joint between two wooden pieces assembled end-to-end in which each piece has a hooklike termination engaging the other piece to give the joint tensile strength. Also called **hook scarf.**

hook′ and eye′, a two-piece fastening, usually of metal, consisting of a hook attached to one part that catches onto a loop or bar attached to the part with which it is to close.

hook′ and lad′der, a fire engine with a semitrailer fitted with long, extensible ladders and other equipment. Also called **hook′-and-lad′der truck′, ladder truck.**

hook′-and-lad′der com′pany, a company of fire fighters equipped with a hook and ladder. Also called **ladder company.**

hook′ bolt′, a bolt bent in a hookline form at one end and threaded for a nut at the other.

hook′ check′, *Ice Hockey.* a maneuver for depriving an opponent of the puck by seizing it in the crook of one's stick. Cf. **check** (def. 40).

Hooke (ho͝ok), *n.* **1. Robert,** 1635–1703, English philosopher, microscopist, and physicist. **2.** a walled plain in the first quadrant of the face of the moon: about 23 miles in diameter.

hooked (ho͝okt), *adj.* **1.** bent like a hook; hook-shaped. **2.** having a hook or hooks. **3.** made with a hook or by hooking. **4.** *Slang.* **a.** addicted to narcotic drugs. **b.** addicted to or obsessed with anything: *He was hooked on television and watched it 40 hours a week.* **5.** *Slang.* married. [ME *hoked,* OE *hōkede.* See HOOK, -ED[3]] —**hook·ed·ness** (ho͝ok′id nis), *n.*

hooked′ rug′, *U.S.* a rug made by drawing loops of yarn or cloth through a foundation of burlap or the like, to form a pattern.

hook·er[1] (ho͝ok′ər), *n.* **1.** *Naut. Slang.* any old-fashioned or clumsy vessel. **2.** any fishing vessel working with hooks and lines rather than nets. [< D *hoeker,* equiv. to *hoek* HOOK + *-er* -ER[1]]

hook·er[2] (ho͝ok′ər), *n.* **1.** *Slang.* prostitute. **2.** *Slang.* a large drink of liquor. **3.** *Rugby.* a player who hooks the ball in the front line of scrummage. **4.** (*cap.*) *Offensive.* an Amish Mennonite. [HOOK + -ER[1]]

Hook·er (ho͝ok′ər), *n.* **1. Joseph,** 1814–79, Union general in the U.S. Civil War. **2. Richard,** 1554?–1600, English author and clergyman. **3. Thomas,** 1586?–1647, English Puritan clergyman: one of the founders of the colony of Connecticut.

Hook′er's green′, **1.** a medium green to strong yellowish green. **2.** a nonpermanent pigment consisting of Prussian blue mixed with gamboge, characterized chiefly by its green color. [named after W. *Hooker* (d. 1832), English illustrator]

Hooke's′ law′, *Physics.* the law that the stress on a solid substance is directly proportional to the strain produced, provided the stress is less than the elastic limit of the substance. [named after Robert HOOKE who formulated it]

hook·ey (ho͝ok′ē), *n.* hooky[2].

hook·nose (ho͝ok′nōz′), *n.* a hook-shaped nose; aquiline nose. [HOOK + NOSE]

hook-nosed (ho͝ok′nōzd′), *adj.* having a hooknose.

Hook′ of Hol′land, a cape and the harbor it forms in the SW Netherlands. Dutch, **Hoek van Holland.**

hook′ scarf′, *Shipbuilding.* See **hook and butt.**

hook′ shot′, *Basketball.* a shot with one hand in which a player extends his shooting arm to the side and brings it back over his head toward the basket as he releases the ball.

hook·swing·ing (ho͝ok′swiŋ′iŋ), *n.* a ritualistic torture, practiced among the Mandan Indians, in which a voluntary victim was suspended from hooks attached to the flesh of his back. [HOOK + SWING[1] + -ING[1]]

hook·up (ho͝ok′up′), *n.* **1.** *Electronics.* **a.** a diagram of electronic apparatus and circuits showing the connection of the different elements in one assembly or device. **b.** the elements as set up for operation. **2.** any combination of related parts; a connection. **3.** a network, as of radio or television stations. **4.** the establishment of cooperation between groups, individuals, governments, etc.; alliance. [n. use of v. phrase *hook up*]

hook·worm (hŏŏk′wûrm′), *n.* **1.** any of certain blood-sucking nematode worms, as *Ancylostoma duodenale* and *Necator americanus*, parasitic in the intestine of man and animals. **2.** Also called **hook′worm disease′.** *Pathol.* a disease caused by hookworms, characterized by severe anemia. [HOOK + WORM] —**hook′worm′y,** *adj.*

hook·y[1] (hŏŏk′ē), *adj.*, **hook·i·er, hook·i·est. 1.** full of hooks. **2.** hook-shaped. [HOOK + -Y[1]]

hook·y[2] (hŏŏk′ē), *n.* unjustifiable absence from school (usually used in the phrase *play hooky*): *On the first warm spring day the boys played hooky to go fishing.* Also, **hookey.** [? alter. of phrase *hook it* escape, make off (turned into noun by dropping the *-t*)]

hoo·li·gan (hōō′lə gən), *n.* **1.** a ruffian or hoodlum. —*adj.* **2.** of or like hooligans. [var. of *Houlihan*, Irish surname which came to be associated with rowdies] —**hoo′li·gan·ism,** *n.*

hoo·ly (hōō′lē, hy′lē), *Scot.* —*adj.* **1.** cautious; gentle. —*adv.* **2.** cautiously; gently. Also, **huly.** [ME *holy*, appar. < ON; cf. ON *hōfligr* moderate]

hoop (hōōp, hŏŏp), *n.* **1.** a circular band or ring of metal, wood, or other stiff material. **2.** such a band for holding together the staves of a cask, tub, etc. **3.** a large ring of iron, wood, plastic, etc., used as a plaything for a child to roll along the ground. **4.** a circular or ringlike object, part, figure, etc. **5.** that part of a ring which surrounds the finger. **6.** *Croquet.* a wicket. **7.** a circular band of stiff material used to expand and display a woman's skirt. **8.** See **hoop skirt. 9.** *Basketball Informal.* **a.** the metal ring from which the net is suspended; rim. **b.** the metal ring and net taken together; the basket. **10.** a decorative band, as around a mug or cup. **11.** See **hoop iron. 12.** *Naut.* See **mast hoop.** —*v.t.* **13.** to bind or fasten with or as with a hoop or hoops. **14.** to encircle; surround. [ME *hop(e)*, late OE *hōp*; c. D *hoep*] —**hoop′less,** *adj.* —**hoop′like′,** *adj.*

hoop′ back′, *Furniture.* **1.** a chair back having the uprights and crest rail in a continuous arched form. **2.** See **bow back.**

hoop′-coop plant′ (hŏŏp′kōōp′, -kŏŏp′, hōōp′-). See **Japan clover.**

hoop·er (hōō′pər, hŏŏp′ər), *n.* a person who makes or puts hoops on barrels, tubs, etc.; a cooper. [HOOP + -ER[1]]

Hoop′er rat′ing, a rating of radio and television shows based on a statistical study of the percentage of sets in a sampling that are tuned to a specific program at a given time. Also, **Hoop·e·rat·ing** (hōō′pə rā′ting). [named after Claude E. *Hooper* (d. 1954), American statistician]

Hoopes·ton (hōōps′tən), *n.* a town in E Illinois. 6606 (1960).

hoop′ i′ron, iron in the form of thin strips for bonding masonry, holding barrels together, etc.

hoop·la (hōōp′lä), *n. Slang.* **1.** bustling excitement or activity; commotion. **2.** speech or writing intended to mislead or to obscure an issue. [*hoop*, var. of WHOOP + LA[2]]

hoop·man (hōōp′mən, hŏŏp′-), *n., pl.* **-men.** *Slang.* a basketball player. [HOOP + MAN[1]]

hoo·poe (hōō′pōō), *n.* any of several Old World birds of the family *Upupidae*, esp. *Upupa epops*, of Europe, having an erectile, fanlike crest. [var. of obs. *hoopoop* (imit.); c. LG *huppup*; cf. L *upupa*]

Hoopoe,
Upupa epops
(Length 11 in.)

hoop′-pet·ti·coat narcis′sus (hōōp′pet′ē kōt′, hŏŏp′-). See **petticoat narcissus.**

hoop′ pine′. See **Moreton Bay pine.**

hoop′ skirt′, 1. a woman's skirt made to stand out and drape in a stiff bell-like shape from the waist by an undergarment framework of flexible hoops connected by tapes. **2.** the framework for such a skirt. Also called **hoop.**

hoop′ snake′, any of several harmless snakes, as *Farancia abacura*, fabled to take its tail in its mouth and roll along like a hoop.

hoop·ster (hōōp′stər, hŏŏp′-), *n. Slang.* a basketball player. [HOOP + -STER]

hoop·wood (hōōp′wŏŏd′, hŏŏp′-), *n.* See **smooth winterberry.** [HOOP + WOOD[1]]

Hoop skirt
(def. 2)

hoo·rah (hŏŏ rä′), *interj., v.i., n.* hurrah. Also, **hoo·ray** (hŏŏ rā′).

hoose·gow (hōōs′gou), *n. Slang.* a jail. Also, **hoos′gow.** [< MexSp *jusga(d)o* jail (Sp: court of justice, orig. ptp. of *juzgar* to judge) < L *jūdicāt(um)*, equiv. to *jūdic-* (s. of *jūdex*) JUDGE + *-ātum* -ATE[1]]

Hoo′sick Falls′ (hōō′sik), a town in E New York. 4023 (1960).

Hoo·sier (hōō′zhər), *n.* **1.** a native or inhabitant of Indiana (the **Hoosier State**) (used as a nickname). **2.** (*usually l.c.*) *Slang.* a hayseed; hick; bumpkin. [?] —**Hoo′sier·dom,** *n.*

Hoo′sier State′, Indiana (used as a nickname).

hoot[1] (hōōt), *v.i.* **1.** to cry out or shout, esp. in disapproval or derision. **2.** to utter the cry characteristic of an owl. **3.** to utter a similar sound. **4.** *Chiefly Brit.* to blow a horn or whistle; toot. —*v.t.* **5.** to assail with shouts of disapproval or derision: *The fans hooted the umpire.* **6.** to drive out, off, or away by hooting. **7.** to express in hoots: *to hoot one's displeasure.* —*n.* **8.** the cry of an owl. **9.** any similar sound, as an inarticulate shout. **10.** a cry or shout, esp. of disapproval or derision. **11.** *Brit.* a horn, siren, or whistle, esp. a factory whistle. **12.** Also, **hoot′er.** an owl. **13.** *Informal.* the least bit of concern, interest, or thought; trifle: *I don't give a hoot.* [ME *hoten, huten, houten* < ?] —**hoot′ing·ly,** *adv.*

hoot[2] (hōōt), *interj. Scot. and North Eng.* (used as an expression of impatience, dissatisfaction, objection, or dislike.) [?]

hootch (hōōch), *n.* hooch.

hootch·y-kootch·y (hōō′chē kōō′chē), *n., pl.* **-kootch·ies.** cooch[1]. Also, **hoot′chie-koot′chie, hoot′chy-kootch′.** [perh. alter. of HULA-HULA]

hoot·en·an·ny (hōōt′ᵊnan′ē), *n., pl.* **-nies. 1.** a social gathering or informal concert featuring folk singing and, sometimes, dancing. **2.** an informal session at which folk singers and instrumentalists perform for their own enjoyment. **3.** *Chiefly Dial.* a thingumbob. [?]

Hoo·ton (hōōt′ᵊn), *n.* **Ear·nest Albert** (ûr′nist), 1887–1954, U.S. anthropologist and writer.

hoot′ owl′, (not used scientifically) an owl that hoots, as distinguished from a screech owl.

Hoo·ver (hōō′vər), *n.* **1. Herbert (Clark),** 1874–1964, 31st president of the U.S., 1929–33. **2. J(ohn) Edgar,** 1895–1972, U.S. government official: director of the FBI 1924–72.

hoo′ver a′pron (hōō′vər), a dresslike coverall for women that ties at the waist. [named after Herbert HOOVER, so called from its popularity during his term as food administrator]

Hoo′ver Dam′, official name of **Boulder Dam.**

Hoo·ver·ville (hōō′vər vil′), *n.* a collection of huts and shacks, as at the edge of a city, housing the unemployed during the 1930's. [named after Herbert HOOVER]

hooves (hŏŏvz, hōōvz), *n.* a pl. of **hoof.**

hop[1] (hop), *v.,* **hopped, hop·ping,** *n.* —*v.i.* **1.** to make a short, bouncing leap; move by leaping with all feet off the ground. **2.** to spring or leap on one foot. **3.** to make a flight or any short, quick trip: *He hopped up to Boston for the day.* **4.** *Informal.* (of an airplane or the like) to leave the ground in beginning a flight. **5.** *Informal.* to dance. —*v.t.* **6.** to jump over; clear with a hop: *The sheep hopped the fence.* **7.** *Informal.* to board or get onto a vehicle: *to hop a train; hop a plane.* **8.** *Informal.* (of an airplane or the like) to cross by a flight. —*n.* **9.** an act of hopping; short leap. **10.** a leap on one foot. **11.** *Informal.* **a.** a flight of an airplane. **b.** a short trip. **12.** *Informal.* a dance, or dancing party. **13.** a bounce or rebound of a ball: *He caught the ball on the first hop.* [ME *hoppe(n)*, OE *hoppian*; c. G *hopfen*, Icel *hoppa*] —**hop′ping·ly,** *adv.*

hop[2] (hop), *n., v.,* **hopped, hop·ping.** —*n.* **1.** any twining, dioecious plant of the genus *Humulus*, the male flowers of which grow in panicled racemes and the female in conelike forms. **2. hops,** the dried ripe cones of the female flowers of this plant, used in brewing, medicine, etc. **3.** *Slang.* opium. —*v.t.* **4.** to treat or flavor with hops. **5. hop up,** *Slang.* **a.** to excite; make enthusiastic: *They hopped the crowd up with fiery speeches.* **b.** to add to the power of: *The kids hopped up the motor of their jalopy.* [late ME *hoppe* < MD *hoppe* (D *hop*); c. G *Hopfen* (OHG *hopfe*)]

Ho·pat·cong (hə pat′kông, -kong), *n.* a town in N New Jersey. 3391 (1960).

hop′ clo′ver, a trefoil, *Trifolium procumbens*, having withered, yellow flowers that resemble the strobiles of a hop.

hope (hōp), *n., v.,* **hoped, hop·ing.** —*n.* **1.** the feeling that what is desired is also possible, or that events may turn out for the best: *to give up hope.* **2.** a particular instance of this feeling: *the hope of winning.* **3.** grounds for this feeling in a particular instance: *There is little or no hope of his recovery.* **4.** a person in whom or thing in which expectations are centered: *The last hope of the team was that the pitcher would be in good form.* —*v.t.* **5.** to look forward to with desire and reasonable confidence. **6.** to believe, desire, or trust: *I hope that my work will be satisfactory.* —*v.i.* **7.** to feel that something desired may happen: *We hope for an early spring.* **8.** *Archaic.* to place trust; rely (usually fol. by *in*). **9. hope against hope,** to continue to hope, although the situation does not warrant it: *We are hoping against hope for a change in her condition.* [(n.) ME; OE *hopa*; c. D *hoop*, G *Hoffe*; (v.) ME *hopen*, OE *hopian*] —**hop′er,** *n.* —**hop′ing·ly,** *adv.*

—**Syn. 1.** expectancy, longing. **7.** See **expect.**

Hope (hōp), *n.* **1. Anthony,** pen name of Sir Anthony Hope Hawkins. **2. Bob** (*Leslie Townes Hope*), born 1903, U.S. comedian, born in England. **3. John,** 1868–1936, U.S. educator. **4.** a town in SW Arkansas. 8399 (1960). **5.** a girl's given name.

hope′ chest′, a chest or the like in which a young woman collects clothing, linens, and other articles toward furnishing a home of her own in anticipation of marriage.

Hope·dale (hōp′dāl′), *n.* a town in S Massachusetts. 2904 (1960).

hope·ful (hōp′fəl), *adj.* **1.** full of hope; expressing hope: *His hopeful words stimulated optimism.* **2.** exciting hope; promising advantage or success: *a hopeful prospect.* —*n.* **3.** a promising or aspiring young person: *Two pitching hopefuls joined the Mets in spring training.* [HOPE + -FUL] —**hope′ful·ness,** *n.*

—**Syn. 1.** expectant; sanguine, optimistic, confident.

hope·ful·ly (hōp′fə lē), *adv.* **1.** in a hopeful manner: *We worked hopefully and energetically, thinking we might finish first.* **2.** it is hoped; if all goes well: *Hopefully, we will get to the show on time.* [HOPEFUL + -LY]

Ho·peh (hō′pā′; *Chin.* hu′bä′), *n.* a province in NE China. 44,720,000 (est. 1957); 81,479 sq. mi. *Cap.:* Peking. Also, **Ho′pei′.** Formerly, **Chihli.**

hope·less (hōp′lis), *adj.* **1.** providing no hope; beyond hope; desperate: *a hopeless case of cancer.* **2.** without hope; despairing: *hopeless grief.* **3.** impossible of being accomplished, solved, resolved, etc.: *Balancing my budget is hopeless.* **4.** not able to learn or act, perform, or work as desired; inadequate for the purpose: *As a bridge player, you're hopeless.* [HOPE + -LESS] —**hope′less·ly,** *adv.* —**hope′less·ness,** *n.*

—**Syn. 1.** irremediable, remediless, incurable. **2.** forlorn, disconsolate, dejected. HOPELESS, DESPAIRING, DESPONDENT, DESPERATE all describe an absence of hope. HOPELESS is used of a feeling of futility and passive abandonment of oneself to fate: *Hopeless and grim, he still clung to the cliff.* DESPAIRING refers to the loss of hope in regard to a particular situation whether important or trivial; it suggests an intellectual judgment concerning probabilities: *despairing of victory; despairing of finding his gloves.* DESPONDENT always suggests melancholy and depression; it refers to an emotional state rather than to an intellectual judgment: *Despondent over ill health, he killed himself. She became despondent and suspicious.* DESPERATE conveys a suggestion of recklessness resulting from loss of hope: *As the time grew shorter, he became desperate.* DESPERATE may apply either to feelings or to situations: *a desperate remedy; The case seems hopeless but people are not yet desperate.* DESPAIRING and DESPONDENT may apply only to feelings.

Hope·still (hōp′stil), *n.* a girl's given name.

Hope·well (hōp′wel, -wəl), *n.* **1.** a city in E Virginia, on the James River. 17,895 (1960). **2.** a boy's given name.

hop·head (hop′hed′), *n. Slang.* a drug addict. [HOP[2] + HEAD]

hop′ horn′beam, any of several betulaceous trees of the genus *Ostrya*, of Europe, Asia, and North America, esp. *O. virginiana*, bearing hoplike fruiting clusters.

Ho·pi (hō′pē), *n., pl.* **-pis,** (*esp. collectively*) **-pi. 1.** a member of a Shoshonean Pueblo Indian people of northern Arizona. **2.** a Uto-Aztecan language, the language of the Hopi Indians. [< Hopi *hópitu* peaceful ones]

Hop·kins (hop′kinz), *n.* **1. Sir Frederick Gow·land** (gou′lənd), 1861–1947, English physician and biochemist: Nobel prize for medicine 1929. **2. Gerard Man·ley** (man′lē), 1844–89, English poet. **3. Harry Lloyd,** 1890–1946, U.S. government administrator and social worker. **4. Johns,** 1795–1873, U.S. financier and philanthropist. **5. Mark,** 1802–87, U.S. clergyman and educator.

Hop·kins·i·an·ism (hop kin′zē ə niz′əm), *n.* a modified Calvinism taught by Samuel Hopkins (1721–1803), which emphasized the sovereignty of God, the importance of His decrees, and the necessity of submitting to His will, accepting even damnation, if required, for His glory, and holding that ethics is merely disinterested benevolence. [*Hopkins* + -IAN + -ISM] —**Hop·kin′si·an, Hop·kin·so·ni·an** (hop′kin sō′nē ən), *adj., n.*

Hop·kin·son (hop′kin sən), *n.* **Francis,** 1737–91, American statesman and satirist.

Hop·kins·ville (hop′kinz vil′), *n.* a city in S Kentucky. 19,465 (1960).

Hop·kin·ton (hop′kin tən), *n.* a town in central Massachusetts. 2754 (1960).

Hop·les (hop′lēz), *n. Class. Myth.* a son of Ion.

hop·lite (hop′līt), *n.* a heavily-armed foot soldier of ancient Greece. [< Gk *hoplī́t(ēs)*, equiv. to *hópl(on)* piece of armor, particularly the large shield + *-ītēs* -ITE[1]] —**hop·lit·ic** (hop lit′ik), *adj.*

hop-o'-my-thumb (hop′ə mī thum′), *n.* a tiny person. [n. use of impv. phrase *hop on my thumb*]

Hop·pe (hop′ē), *n.* **Willie (William Frederick),** 1887–1959, U.S. billiards player.

hopped-up (hopt′ up′), *adj. U.S. Slang.* **1.** excited; enthusiastic; exuberant, esp. overexuberant. **2.** having an engine with added power: *a hopped-up jalopy.* **3.** drugged; doped. [adj. use of v. phrase *hop up*]

hop·per (hop′ər), *n.* **1.** one who or that which hops. **2.** any of various jumping insects, as grasshoppers, leafhoppers, etc. **3.** *Australian.* kangaroo. **4.** a funnel-shaped chamber or bin in which loose material, as grain, coal, etc., is stored temporarily, being filled through the top and later dispensed through the bottom. **5.** *Railroads.* See **hopper car. 6.** a water closet, esp. one having a funnel-shaped bowl. **7.** one of the pieces at each side of a hopper casement. **8.** *Photog.* a soft, long-haired brush for daubing lithographic ink on a treated bromide print for making a bromoil. —*v.t.* **9.** *Photog.* to daub (lithographic ink) with a hopper. [ME; see HOP[1], -ER[1]]

Hop·per (hop′ər), *n.* **1. Edward,** 1882–1967, U.S. painter and etcher. **2. (William) De Wolf** (də wŏŏlf), 1858–1935, U.S. actor.

hop′per barge′, a barge for disposing of garbage, dredged material, etc., having hoppers in the bottom through which such refuse or material can be dumped. Also called **dump scow.**

hop′per car′, *Railroads.* a freight car for bulk cargo, usually open and containing one or more bins or hoppers so that the contents can be quickly discharged through the bottom of the car.

hop′per case′ment, a casement with a sash hinged at the bottom. Also called **hop′per light′, hop′per vent′, hop′per win′dow, hospital light, hospital window.**

hop′per dredge′, a self-propelled dredge having compartments in which the dredged material can be carried and dumped through hoppers.

hop′per frame′, a window frame having one or more upper sashes hinged at the bottoms and opening inward.

hop·ping (hop′ing), *adj.* **1.** working energetically; busily engaged: *He kept the crew hopping in order to get the job out.* **2.** going from one place to another of a similar specified type (usually used in combination): *restaurant-hopping.* **3. hopping mad,** furious; enraged: *He was hopping mad when his daughter married without his permission.* [HOP[1] + -ING[2]]

hop′ping John′ (hop′in, -ing), (*sometimes l.c.*) *Southern U.S.* a dish of black-eyed peas, rice, and seasoning: traditionally served on New Year's Day because of the superstition that black-eyed peas bring good luck for the New Year.

hop·ple (hop′əl), *v.t.,* **-pled, -pling.** to hobble; tether. [? HOP[1] + -LE]

hop·sack·ing (hop′sak′ing), *n.* **1.** bagging made chiefly of hemp and jute. **2.** a coarse fabric made of cotton, wool, or other fibers and similar to burlap, used in the manufacture of wearing apparel. [HOP[2] + SACKING]

hop·scotch (hop′skoch′), *n.* a children's game in which a player tosses or kicks a small flat stone, or other object, into one of several numbered sections of a diagram marked on the pavement or ground and then hops on one foot over the lines from section to section and picks up the stone or object, usually while standing on one foot in an adjacent section. [HOP[1] + SCOTCH[1]]

hop′, step′, and jump′, *Track.* a jumping event for distance in which a participant leaps on one foot from a take-off point, lands on the same foot, steps forward on the other foot, leaps, and lands on both feet.

hop·toad (hop′tōd′), *n. U.S. Dial.* a toad. [HOP[1] + TOAD]

hop·tree (hop′trē′), *n.* any of several North American shrubs or small trees of the genus *Ptelea*, esp. *P. trifoliata*, sometimes grown as an ornamental. [HOP[2] + TREE]

hop·vine (hop′vīn′), *n.* **1.** the twining stem of the hop plant. **2.** the plant itself. [HOP[2] + VINE]

Ho·qui·am (hō′kwē əm), *n.* a city in W Washington. 10,762 (1960).

hor., 1. horizon. **2.** horizontal. **3.** horology.

ho·ra (hōr′ə, hôr′ə), *n.* a traditional Rumanian and Israeli round dance. [< ModHeb *hōrāh* < Rumanian *horă* < Turk *hora*]

Hor·ace (hôr′is, hor′-), *n.* **1.** (*Quintus Horatius Flaccus*) 65–8 B.C., Roman poet and satirist. **2.** Also, **Horatio.** a boy's given name.

Ho·rae (hōr′ē, hôr′ē), *n.pl. Class. Myth.* goddesses of the seasons, of growth and decay, and sometimes of social order, usually given as three in number, with the names Dike (Justice), Eunomia (Order), and Irene (Peace). [< L: lit., hours]

ho·ral (hōr′əl, hôr′-), *adj.* of or pertaining to an hour or hours; hourly. [< LL *hōrāl(is),* equiv. to L *hōr(a)* HOUR + *-ālis* -AL[1]]

ho·ra·ry (hōr′ə rē, hôr′-), *adj. Archaic.* **1.** pertaining to an hour; indicating the hours: *the horary circle.* **2.** occurring every hour; hourly. [< ML *hōrāri(us),* equiv. to *hōr(a)* HOUR + *-ārius* -ARY]

Ho·ra·ti·a (hə rā′shē ə, -shə, hō-, hô-), *n.* a girl's given name.

Ho·ra·tian (hə rā′shən, hō-, hô-), *adj.* **1.** of or pertaining to Horace. **2.** *Pros.* **a.** of, pertaining to, or resembling the poetic style or diction of Horace. **b.** of, pertaining to, or noting a Horatian ode. [< L *Horātiān(us),* equiv. to *Horāti(us)* HORACE + *-ānus* -AN]

Hora′tian ode′, *Pros.* an ode consisting of several stanzas all of the same form. Also called **Lesbian ode, Sapphic ode.** Cf. **Pindaric ode.**

Ho·ra·ti·i (hə rā′shē ī′, hō-, hô-), *n.pl. Rom. Legend.* three brothers who fought as champions of Rome against three other brothers (the **Curiatii**), who were the champions of Alba Longa, to determine which city should rule the other.

Ho·ra·ti·o (hə rā′shē ō′, hō-, hô-), *n.* a boy's given name. Also, **Horace.**

Ho·ra·tius (hə rā′shəs, hō-, hô-), *n.* (*Publius Horatius Cocles*) *Rom. Legend.* a hero celebrated for his defense of the bridge over the Tiber against the Etruscans.

Hor·cus (hôr′kəs), *n.* the ancient Greek god of oaths, sometimes identified with Orcus because of his role as punisher of perjurers.

horde (hōrd, hôrd), *n., v.,* **hord·ed, hord·ing.** —*n.* **1.** a large group, multitude, number, etc.; a mass or crowd: *a horde of tourists.* **2.** a tribe or troop of Asian nomads. **3.** any nomadic group. **4.** a moving pack or swarm of animals: *A horde of mosquitoes invaded the camp.* —*v.i.* **5.** to gather in a horde: *The prisoners horded together in the compound.* [earlier *hord(a)* < Pol *horda* < Mongolian *orda, ordu* camp (see URDU); *-e* perh. < F, G *horde,* but may have been added to mark length of *o,* as in BORNE, etc.]
—**Syn. 1.** mob, herd, throng.

hor·de·in (hôr′dē in), *n. Biochem.* a prolamin found in barley grain. [< F *hordéine* < L *horde(um)* barley + F *-ine* -IN[2]]

hor·de·o·lum (hôr dē′ə ləm), *n., pl.* **-la** (-lə). *Pathol.* sty[2]. [< NL, alter. of LL *hordeolus,* equiv. to L *horde(um)* barley + *-olus, -olum* dim. suffix]

Ho·reb (hōr′eb, hôr′-), *n. Bible.* a mountain sometimes identified with Mount Sinai.

hore·hound (hōr′hound′, hôr′-), *n.* **1.** a perennial, Old World herb, *Marrubium vulgare,* having downy leaves and small, whitish flowers, and containing a bitter, medicinal juice. **2.** any of various plants of the mint family. **3.** a brittle candy or lozenge flavored with horehound extract. Also, **hoarhound.** [ME *horehune,* OE *hārhūne,* equiv. to *hār* gray HOAR + *hūne* horehound]

Hor·i·con (hôr′i kon′, hor′-), *n.* a town in central Wisconsin. 2996 (1960).

hor. interm., (in prescriptions) at intermediate hours. [< L *hōrā intermediīs*]

Ho·rite (hōr′īt, hôr′-), *n.* **1.** an ancient people living in the region of the Dead Sea, possibly identical with the Hurrians. **2.** a member of this people.

ho·ri·zon (hə rī′zən), *n.* **1.** the line or circle that forms the apparent boundary between earth and sky. **2.** *Astron.* **a.** the small circle of the celestial sphere whose plane is tangent to the earth at the position of a given observer, or the plane of such a circle **(sensible horizon). b.** the great circle of the celestial sphere whose plane passes through the center of the earth and is parallel to the sensible horizon of a given position, or the plane of such a circle **(celestial horizon). 3.** the limit or range of perception, knowledge, or the like. **4.** Usually, **horizons.** the scope of a person's interest, education, understanding, etc.: *His horizons were narrow.* **5.** *Geol.* a plane in rock strata representing the deposit of a particular period and characterized by special features, as occurrence of distinctive fossil species. **6.** any of the series of distinctive layers found in a vertical cross section of any well-developed soil. [< L < Gk *horízōn* (*kýklos*) bounding (circle), equiv. to *horíz(ein)* (to) bound, limit + *-ōn* prp. suffix (nom. sing.); r. ME *orizonte* < MF < L *horizontem,* acc. of *horizōn*]

hori′zon dis′tance, 1. *Television.* the distance of the farthest point on the earth's surface visible from a transmitting antenna. **2.** *Radio.* the distance on the earth's surface reached by a direct wave: due to atmospheric refraction, sometimes greater than the visible horizon.

ho·ri·zon·less (hə rī′zən lis), *adj.* **1.** lacking or without a horizon. **2.** without hope; hopeless: [HORIZON + -LESS]

hor·i·zon·tal (hôr′i zon′tᵊl, hor′-), *adj.* **1.** at right angles to the vertical; parallel to level ground. **2.** reclining: *a horizontal position.* **3.** near, on, or parallel to the horizon. **4.** of or pertaining to the horizon. **5.** measured or contained in a plane parallel to the horizon: *a horizontal distance.* **6.** of or pertaining to a position or individual of similar status: *He received a horizontal promotion, retaining his old salary and title but with a different department of the firm.* [< L *horizont-* (s. of *horizōn*) HORIZON + -AL[1]] —**hor·i·zon·tal·i·ty** (hôr′i zon tal′i tē, hor′-), **hor′i·zon′tal·ness,** *n.* —**hor′i·zon′tal·ly,** *adv.*

hor′izon′tal bar′, *Gymnastics.* **1.** a bar fixed in a position parallel to the floor or ground, for use in chinning and other exercises. **2.** an event in gymnastic competitions, judged on strength and grace while performing specific movements on such a bar.

horizon′tal mobil′ity, *Sociol.* **1.** movement from one position to another within the same social level, as changing jobs without altering occupational status, or moving between social groups having the same social status. **2.** cultural diffusion within the same social level, as the spread of fashion within one economic class. Cf. **vertical mobility.**

hor′izon′tal sta′bilizer, *Aeron.* the horizontal surface, usually fixed, of an aircraft empennage, to which the elevator is hinged. Also called, *esp. Brit.,* **tail plane.**

hor′izon′tal un′ion, a labor union organized by skills or trades of its members rather than by industries.

hor·me (hôr′mē), *n. Psychol.* activity directed toward a goal; purposive effort. [< Gk *hormḗ* impetus, impulse] —**hor′mic,** *adj.*

hor′mic the′ory, *Psychol.* a theory that holds all behavior to be purposive, whether conscious or unconscious. [HORM(E) + -IC]

Hor·mis·das (hôr miz′dəs), *n.* **Saint,** died A.D. 523, pope 514–523.

hor·mone (hôr′mōn), *n.* **1.** *Biochem.* any of various internally secreted compounds, formed in endocrine organs, that affect the functions of specifically receptive organs or tissues when transported to them by the body fluids, as insulin, thyroxine, etc. **2.** a synthetic substance used in medicine to act like such a compound when introduced into the body. [< Gk *hormôn* (prp. of *hormáein* to set in motion, excite, stimulate), equiv. to *horm(ē)* HORME + *-ōn* prp. suffix] —**hor·mo′nal, hor·mon·ic** (hôr mon′ik, -mō′nik), *adj.*

Hor·muz (hôr′muz), *n.* **Strait of,** a strait between Iran and Trucial Oman, connecting the Persian Gulf and the Gulf of Oman. Also, **Ormuz.**

horn (hôrn), *n.* **1.** one of the bony, projecting, often curved and pointed, hollow, permanent, paired growths on the upper part of the head of certain ungulate mammals, as cattle, sheep, goats, antelopes, etc. **2.** either of the pair of solid, deciduous, usually branched, bony growths, or antlers, on the head of a deer. **3.** a similar growth, sometimes of hair, as the median horn or horns on the snout of the rhinoceros, or the tusk of the narwhal. **4.** a process projecting from the head of an animal and suggestive of such a growth, as a feeler, tentacle, crest, etc. **5.** the bony substance of which such animal growths are composed. **6.** any similar substance, as that forming tortoise shell, hoofs, nails, corns, etc. **7.** an article made of the material of an animal horn or like substance, as a thimble, a spoon, or a shoehorn. **8.** any projection or extremity resembling the horn of an animal. **9.** something resembling or suggesting an animal horn: *a drinking horn.* **10.** a part like this growth attributed to deities, demons, etc.: *the devil's horn.* **11.** Usually, **horns.** the imaginary projections on a cuckold's brow. **12.** *Music.* **a.** a wind instrument, originally formed from the hollow horn of an animal but now usually made of brass or other metal or plastic. **b.** See **French horn. 13.** something used as or resembling such a wind instrument. **14.** *Slang.* a trumpet. **15.** an instrument for sounding a warning signal: *automobile horn; fog horn.* **16.** *Aeron.* any of certain short, armlike levers on the control surfaces of an airplane. **17.** *Radio.* **a.** a tube of varying cross section used in some loudspeakers to couple the diaphragm to the sound transmitting space. **b.** *Slang.* a loudspeaker. **18.** the high protuberant part at the front and top of certain saddles; a pommel, esp. a high one. **19.** *Carpentry.* (in a door or window frame) that part of a jamb extending above the head. **20.** one of the curved extremities of a crescent, esp. of the crescent moon. **21.** a crescent-shaped tract of land. **22.** a pyramidal mountain peak, esp. one having concave faces. **23.** a symbol of power, as in the Bible: *a horn of salvation.* **24.** each of the alternatives of a dilemma. **25.** *Geol.* a mountain peak formed by the intersection of three or more glacial cinques. **26.** the narrow, more pointed part of an anvil. **27.** *Metalworking.* a projection at the side of the end of a rolled sheet or strip, caused by unevenness of the roll due to wear. **28.** *Horol.* (in a lever escapement) either of the two prongs at the end of the lever fork guarding against overbanking when the guard pin is in the crescent. **29. blow one's own horn,** to publicize or boast about one's abilities or achievements: *He's an agreeable fellow, but likes to blow his own horn.* **30. draw** or **pull in one's horns,** to restrain oneself or become less belligerent; retreat: *Since he lost so much gambling, he's drawn in his horns a bit.* **31. lock horns,** to conflict; disagree: *The administration and the staff locked horns over the proposed measures.* **32. on the horns of a dilemma,** confronted with two equally disagreeable choices: *Though badly married, she hated divorce, and so she found herself on the horns of a dilemma.* —*v.t.* **33.** to cuckold. **34.** to butt or gore with the horns. **35.** *Shipbuilding.* to set up (a frame or bulkhead of a vessel being built) at a proper angle to the keel with due regard to the inclination of the keel on the ways; plumb. **36. horn in,** *U.S. Slang.* to thrust oneself forward obtrusively; intrude or interrupt: *She could never let her husband finish a story without horning in.* —*adj.* **37.** made of horn. [ME *horn(e),* OE *horn;* c. D *horen,* Icel, Dan, Sw *horn,* G *Horn,* Goth *haurn,* L *cornu,* IrGael *côrn,* Welsh *corn;* akin to Gk *kéras* horn] —**horn′ish,** *adj.* —**horn′less,** *adj.* —**horn′less·ness,** *n.* —**horn′like′,** *adj.*

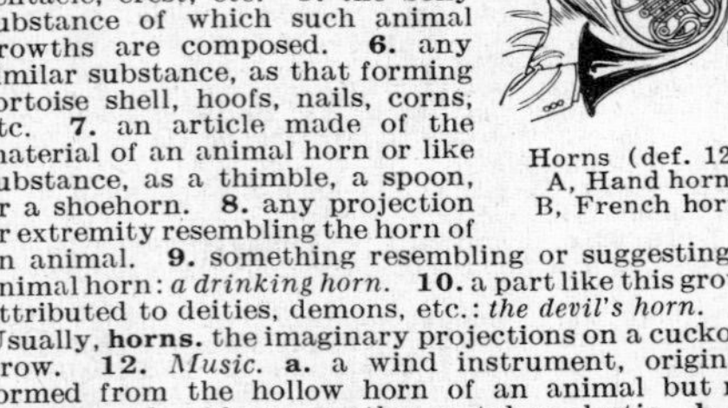

Horns (def. 12)
A, Hand horn
B, French horn

Horn (hôrn), *n.* **Cape.** See **Cape Horn.**

horn·beam (hôrn′bēm′), *n.* any betulaceous shrub or tree of the genus *Carpinus,* yielding a hard, heavy wood, as *C. caroliniana* **(American hornbeam),** of North America. [HORN + BEAM]

horn·bill (hôrn′bil′), *n.* any of several large birds of the family *Bucerotidae,* of the Old World tropics, characterized by a very large bill usually surmounted by a horny protuberance. [HORN + BILL[2]]

horn·blende (hôrn′blend′), *n.* any of the common black or greenish aluminous varieties of amphibole. [< G; see HORN, BLENDE] —**horn·blen′dic,** *adj.*

horn′blende schist′, *Petrog.* a variety of schist containing needles of hornblende which lie in parallel planes in a rock.

horn·book (hôrn′bo͝ok′), *n.* **1.** a leaf or page containing the alphabet, religious materials, etc., covered with a sheet of transparent horn and fixed in a frame with a handle, formerly used in teaching children to read. **2.** a primer, or book of rudiments. [HORN + BOOK]

horn′ bow′sprit, *Naut.* See **spike bowsprit.**

horned (hôrnd), *adj.* **1.** having horns (often used in combination): *a horned beast; blunt-horned.* **2.** having or wearing a horn-shaped protuberance, ornament, or the like: *the horned crags.* **3.** having a crescent-shaped part or form. [ME; see HORN, -ED[3]] —**horn·ed·ness** (hôr′nid nis), *n.*

horned′ di′nosaur, ceratopsian.

horned′ lark′, a lark, *Eremophila alpestris,* of the Northern Hemisphere, having a tuft of feathers on each side of the crown of the head.

horned′ liz′ard, any of several insectivorous iguanid lizards of the genus *Phrynosoma,* of western North America, having hornlike spines on the head and a flattened body covered with spiny scales. Also called **horned toad′.**

Horned lizard, Genus *Phrynosoma* (Length to 4½ in.)

horned′ pop′py. See **horn poppy.**

horned′ pout′, a bullhead, esp. the brown bullhead. Also called **hornpout.**

horned′ scream′er, a screamer, *Anhima cornuta,* of tropical South America, having a long, slender hornlike process projecting from the forehead.

horned′ vi′per, a highly venomous viper, *Cerastes cornutus,* of northern Africa and Arabia, having a scaly process resembling a horn just above each eye.

horned′ whiff′. See under **whiff**[2].

Hor′ner's meth′od (hôr′nərz), *Math.* a technique, involving successive substitutions, for approximating the real roots of an equation with real coefficients. [named after William G. *Horner* (d. 1837), English mathematician who invented it]

hor·net (hôr′nit), *n.* any of several large, stinging paper wasps of the family *Vespidae,* as *Vespa crabro* **(giant hornet),** introduced into the U.S. from Europe, or *Vespula maculata* **(bald-faced hornet** or **white-faced hornet),** of North America. [ME *harnete,* OE *hyrnet(u);* c. OHG *hornaz* (> G *Horniss*)]

hor′net's nest′, a large amount of activity, trouble, hostility, or animosity: *His investigation stirred up a hornet's nest, resulting in major shifts in personnel.*

Bald-faced hornet, *Vespula maculata* (Length 1 in.)

Hor·ney (hôr′nī), *n.* **Karen,** 1885–1952, U.S. psychiatrist and author, born in Germany.

horn′ gate′, *Foundry.* a gate having a tapering curve from bottom to top.

Horn·ie (hôʀ′nē), *n. Scot.* Satan.

hor·ni·to (hôr nē′tō; *Sp.* ôʀ nē′tō) *n., pl.* **-tos** (-tōz; *Sp.* -tôs). *Geol.* a low oven-shaped mound, such as is common in the volcanic districts of South America, usually emitting hot smoke and vapors from its sides and summit. [< Sp, equiv. to *horn(o)* oven (< L *furnus, fornus*) + *-ito* dim. suffix]

horn-mad (hôrn′mad′), *adj.* **1.** enraged enough to gore with the horns, as a bull. **2.** intensely angry; furious. —**horn′-mad′ness,** *n.*

horn′ of plen′ty, cornucopia. [trans. of L *cornūcōpia*]

horn·pipe (hôrn′pīp′), *n.* **1.** an English folk clarinet having one ox horn concealing the reed and another forming the bell. **2.** a lively jiglike dance, originally to music played on a hornpipe, performed usually by one person, and traditionally a favorite of sailors. **3.** a piece of music for or in the style of such a dance. [HORN + PIPE[1]]

horn′ pop′py, a European, papaveraceous herb, *Glaucium flavum,* having yellow flowers, naturalized along sandy shores in eastern North America. Also, **horned poppy.** Also called **sea poppy.**

horn·pout (hôrn′pout′), *n.* See **horned pout.** [by shortening]

horn-rimmed (hôrn′rimd′), *adj.* having the frames or rims made of horn, tortoise shell, or plastic that simulates either of these: *horn-rimmed glasses.*

horn-rims (hôrn′rimz′, -rimz′), *n.pl.* horn-rimmed spectacles or glasses.

Horns·by (hôrnz′bē), *n.* **Rogers,** 1896–1963, U.S. baseball player and manager.

horn′ sil′ver, cerargyrite. [trans. of G *Hornsilber*]

horn·stone (hôrn′stōn′), *n.* **1.** a variety of quartz resembling flint. **2.** an argillaceous rock baked and partly recrystallized by the heat of an igneous intrusion. [trans. of G *Hornstein*]

horn·swog·gle (hôrn′swog′əl), *v.t.,* **-gled, -gling.** *Slang.* to swindle, cheat, or hoax. [?]

horn·tail (hôrn′tāl′), *n.* any of various wasplike insects of the family *Siricidae,* the females of which have a hornlike ovipositor. [HORN + TAIL[1]]

horn′ tim′ber, *Naut.* a timber, often one of several, rising from the sternpost of a wooden vessel to support the overhang of the stern. Also called **horse timber.**

horn·worm (hôrn′wûrm′), *n.* the larva of any of several hawk moths, having a hornlike process at the rear of the abdomen. [HORN + WORM]

horn·wort (hôrn′wûrt′), *n.* any aquatic herb of the genus *Ceratophyllum,* found in ponds and slow streams. [HORN + WORT[2]]

horn·y (hôr′nē), *adj.,* **horn·i·er, horn·i·est. 1.** hornlike through hardening; callous: *horny hands.* **2.** consisting of a horn or a hornlike substance; corneous. **3.** having a horn or horns or hornlike projections. **4.** *Slang.* lustful. **5.** *Archaic.* semiopaque or somewhat translucent, like horn. [ME; see HORN, -Y[1]] —**horn′i·ly,** *adv.* —**horn′i·ness,** *n.*

horn′y cor′al, a gorgonian.

horol., horology.

hor·o·loge (hôr′ə lōj′, -loj′, hor′-), *n.* any instrument for indicating the time, esp. a sundial or an early form

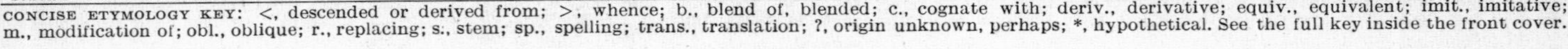
CONCISE ETYMOLOGY KEY: <, descended or derived from; >, whence; b., blend of, blended; c., cognate with; deriv., derivative; equiv., equivalent; imit., imitative; m., modification of; obl., oblique; r., replacing; s., stem; sp., spelling; trans., translation; ?, origin unknown, perhaps; *, hypothetical. See the full key inside the front cover.

of the clock. [late ME < L *hōrologium* HOROLOGIUM; r. ME *orloge* < MF < L, as above]

ho·ro·log·ic (hôr/ə loj/ik, hor/-), *adj.* **1.** of or pertaining to horology. **2.** of or pertaining to horologes. Also, **hor/o·log/i·cal.** [< L *hōrologic(us)* < Gk *hōrologikós*, equiv. to *hōrolog-* (see HOROLOGIUM) + *-ikos* -IC] —**hor/o·log/i·cal·ly,** *adv.*

ho·rol·o·gist (hō rol/ə jist, hô-), *n.* **1.** an expert in horology. **2.** a person who makes clocks or watches. Also, **ho·rol/o·ger.** [HOROLOGE + -IST]

hor·o·lo·gi·um (hôr/ə lō/jē əm, hor/-), *n., pl.* **-gi·a** (-jē ə). **1.** a building supporting or containing a timepiece, as a clock tower. **2.** (*cap.*) *Astron.* the Clock, a small southern constellation between Eridanus and Dorado. [< L < Gk *hōrológion*, equiv. to *hōrológ(os)* timeteller (*hōro-*, comb. form of *hṓra* HOUR + *-log-*, var. s. of *légein* to speak, tell, + *-os* adj. suffix) + *-ion* dim. suffix]

ho·rol·o·gy (hō rol/ə jē, hô-), *n.* the art or science of making timepieces or of measuring time. [< Gk *hōro-* (comb. form of *hṓra* HOUR) + -LOGY]

ho·rop·ter (hə rop/tər, hô-), *n.* *Ophthalm.* a curved surface in the visual field that connects those points whose images are received by corresponding points on the two retinas. [< Gk *hór(os)* boundary + *optḗr* one that looks] —**hor·op·ter·ic** (hôr/op ter/ik), *adj.*

hor·o·scope (hôr/ə skōp/, hor/-), *n.* **1.** a diagram of the heavens, showing the relative position of planets and the signs of the zodiac, for use in calculating births, foretelling events in a person's life, etc. **2.** a prediction of future events or advice for future behavior based on such a diagram. [ME, OE *horoscop(us)* < L < Gk *hōroskópos*, equiv. to *hōro-* (comb. form of *hṓra* HOUR) + *skópos* -SCOPE]

hor·o·scop·ic (hôr/ə skop/ik, -skō/pik, hor/ə-), *adj.* of or pertaining to a horoscope. [< L *hōroscopic(us)* < Gk *hōroskopikós*, equiv. to *hōroskóp(os)* HOROSCOPE + *-ikos* -IC]

ho·ros·co·py (hō ros/kə pē, hô-), *n.* the casting or taking of horoscopes. [HOROSCOPE + -Y³] —**hor·o·scop·er** (hôr/ə skō/pər, hor/-), **ho·ros·co·pist** (hō-ros/kə pist, hō-, hôr/ə skō/pist, hor/-), *n.*

hor·o·tel·ic (hôr/ə tel/ik), *adj.* *Biol.* of or pertaining to evolution at a rate standard for a given group of plants or animals. Cf. **bradytelic, tachytelic.** [< Gk *hóro(s)* boundary + *tél(os)* end, consummation + -IC] —**hor/o·tel/y,** *n.*

Hor·o·witz (hôr/ə wits, hor/-; *Russ.* hô/ʀo vits), *n.* **Vlad·i·mir** (vlad/i mēr/; *Russ.* vlä dē/miʀ), born 1904, Russian pianist, in the U.S. since 1928.

Hor·re·bow (hôr/ə bō/, hor/-), *n.* a crater in the second quadrant of the face of the moon: about 14 miles in diameter.

hor·ren·dous (hô ren/dəs, ho-), *adj.* dreadful; horrible: *a horrendous crime.* [< L *horrendus* (ger. of *horrēre* to bristle, shudder) dreadful, to be feared, equiv. to *horr-* (deriv. of *hors;* akin to HIRSUTE) + *-endus* fut. passive participial suffix] —**hor·ren/dous·ly,** *adv.*

hor·rent (hôr/ənt, hor/-), *adj.* bristling; standing erect like bristles. [< L *horrent-* (s. of *horrēns*, prp. of *horrēre* to stand on end, bristle with fear), equiv. to *horr-* (see HORRENDOUS) + *-ent-* -ENT]

hor·ri·ble (hôr/ə bəl, hor/-), *adj.* **1.** causing or tending to cause horror; dreadful: *a horrible sight.* **2.** extremely unpleasant; deplorable; disgusting: *horrible living conditions.* [ME *(h)orrible* < OF < L *horribil(is)*, equiv. to *horr-* (s. of *horrēre* to stand on end, bristle with fear) + *-ibilis* -IBLE] —**hor/ri·ble·ness,** *n.* —**hor/ri·bly,** *adv.*
—**Syn. 1.** terrible, awful, appalling, frightful; hideous, grim, ghastly, shocking, revolting, repulsive, horrid, horrendous, horrifying, dire, repellent. —**Ant. 1.** attractive.

hor·rid (hôr/id, hor/-), *adj.* **1.** such as to cause horror; dreadful; abominable. **2.** extremely unpleasant or disagreeable: *horrid weather; She thought her uncle was horrid.* [< L *horrid(us)* bristling, rough, equiv. to *horr-* (s. of *horrēre* to stand on end, bristle) + *-idus* -ID⁴] —**hor/rid·ly,** *adv.* —**hor/rid·ness,** *n.*

hor·rif·ic (hô rif/ik, ho-), *adj.* causing horror. [< L *horrific(us)*, equiv. to *horri-* (comb. form of *horrēre* to bristle with fear) + *-ficus* -FIC] —**hor·rif/i·cal·ly,** *adv.*

hor·ri·fied (hôr/ə fīd/, hor/-), *adj.* **1.** showing or indicating shock or horror: *a horrified gasp; a horrified expression.* **2.** accompanied or characterized by a feeling of horror: *horrified interest.* **3.** struck with horror; shocked: *horrified and outraged spectators.* [HORRIFY + -ED²] —**hor·ri·fied·ly** (hôr/ə fīd/lē, -fī/id-, hor/-), *adv.*

hor·ri·fy (hôr/ə fī/, hor/-), *v.t.*, **-fied, -fy·ing.** to cause to feel horror; strike with horror: *The accident horrified us all.* [< L *horrificāre* (to) cause horror, equiv. to *horri-* (comb. form of *horrēre* to bristle with fear) + *-ficāre* -FY] —**hor/ri·fi·ca/tion,** *n.* —**hor/ri·fy/ing·ly,** *adv.*
—**Syn.** frighten, terrify; revolt, repel, appall.

hor·rip·i·late (hô rip/ə lāt/, ho-), *v.t.*, **-lat·ed, -lat·ing.** to produce horripilation on. [< L *horripilāt(us)* (ptp. of *horripilāre* to bristle with hairs). See HORRIFY, PILE³, -ATE¹]

hor·rip·i·la·tion (hô rip/ə lā/shən, ho-), *n.* a bristling of the hair on the skin from cold, fear, etc.; goose flesh. [< LL *horripilātiōn-* (s. of *horripilātiō*). See HORRIPILATE, -ION]

Hor·rocks (hôr/oks, hor/-), *n.* a walled plain in the fourth quadrant of the face of the moon: about 18 miles in diameter.

hor·ror (hôr/ər, hor/-), *n.* **1.** an overwhelming and painful feeling caused by something frightfully shocking, terrifying, or revolting; a shuddering fear: *to shrink back from a corpse in horror.* **2.** anything that causes such a feeling: *killing, looting, and other horrors of war.* **3.** such a feeling as a quality or condition: *to have known the horror of slow starvation.* **4.** a strong aversion; abhorrence: *to have a horror of emotional outbursts.* **5.** *Informal.* something considered to be bad or without taste: *That hat is a horror. Her party was a horror.* **6.** **horrors,** *Slang.* **a.** extreme depression. **b.** See **delirium tremens.** **7.** *Obs.* a bristling. —*interj.* **8.** (used as a mild expression of dismay, surprise, disappointment, etc.) [< L *horr-* (s. of *horrēre* to bristle with fear) + *-or* -OR¹; r. ME *orrour* < AF < L *horrōr-*, s. of *horror*]
—**Syn. 1.** dread, dismay, consternation. See **terror. 4.** loathing, antipathy, detestation, hatred, abomination. —**Ant. 1.** serenity. **4.** attraction.

hor·ror-struck (hôr/ər struk/, hor/-), *adj.* stricken with horror; aghast. Also, **hor·ror-strick·en** (hôr/ər-strik/ən, hor/-).

Hor·sa (hôr/sə), *n.* died A.D. 455, Jutish chief (brother of Hengist).

hors con·cours (ôʀ kôɴ ko͞oʀ/), *French.* **1.** noting an artist, architect, or the like, not competing or not qualified to compete for the prizes in an exhibit or competition. **2.** noting or pertaining to a work or project submitted by such a person to an exhibit or competition. [lit., out (of the) competition]

hors de com·bat (ôʀ də kôɴ bᴀ/), *French.* out of the fight; disabled; no longer able to fight.

hors d'oeu·vre (ôr dûrv/; *Fr.* ôʀ dœ/vʀᵊ), *pl.* **hors d'oeuvre, hors d'oeuvres** (ôr dûrvz/; *Fr.* ôʀ dœ/vʀᵊ). **1.** an appetizer, as a relish or more elaborate preparation, served before or as the first course of a meal. **2.** a small bit of appetizing food, as spicy meat, fish, cheese, or an elaborate preparation of chopped or creamed foods, often served on crackers or small pieces of toast, for eating at cocktail parties or other gatherings where drinks are served with no other food. [< F: lit., out of (the) work, i.e., the main course]

horse (hôrs), *n., pl.* **hors·es,** (*esp. collectively*) **horse,** *v.*, **horsed, hors·ing,** *adj.* —*n.* **1.** a large, solid-hoofed, herbivorous quadruped, *Equus caballus*, domesticated since prehistoric times, bred in a number of varieties, and used for carrying or pulling loads, for riding, etc. **2.** a fully mature male animal of this type; stallion. **3.** any animal of the family *Equidae*, including the ass, donkey, etc. **4.** soldiers serving on horseback; cavalry: *a thousand horse.* **5.** something on which a person rides, sits, or exercises, as if astride the back of such an animal: *rocking horse.* **6.** *Gymnastics.* **a.** See **long horse. b.** See **side horse. 7.** a frame, block, etc., with legs, on which something is mounted or supported. **8.** *Carpentry.* carriage (def. 6). **9.** *Chiefly Humorous.* a man; fellow. **10.** *Slang.* horsepower. **11.** *U.S. Slang.* a crib, translation, or other illicit aid to a student's recitation. **12.** *Mining.* a mass of rock enclosed within a lode or vein. **13.** *Chess Informal.* a knight. **14.** *Naut.* **a.** traveler (def. 7b). **b.** a stout vertical cable, rigged abaft a mast, to which a spencer is hooped. **15.** *Shipbuilding.* a mold of a curved frame, esp. one used when the complexity of the curves requires laying out at full size. **16.** *U.S. Slang.* heroin. **17. back the wrong horse,** to be mistaken in judgment; support a loser. **18. beat** or **flog a dead horse,** to attempt to revive a discussion, topic, or idea that has waned, been exhausted, or proved fruitless. **19. from the horse's mouth,** *Slang.* on good authority; from a trustworthy source: *I have it straight from the horse's mouth that the boss is retiring.* **20. hold one's horses,** to check one's impulsiveness; be calm: *Hold your horses! I'm almost ready.* **21. horse of another color,** something entirely different. Also, **horse of a different color. 22. look a gift horse in the mouth,** to be critical of a gift: *Even though the car they gave you is an old jalopy, you shouldn't look a gift horse in the mouth.* **23. To horse!** mount your horse! ride! —*v.t.* **24.** to provide with a horse or horses. **25.** to set on horseback. **26.** to set or carry on a person's back or on one's own back. **27.** *Carpentry.* to cut notches for steps into (a carriage beam). **28.** *Informal.* to move around by force. **29.** *Slang.* **a.** to make (a person) the target of boisterous jokes. **b.** to perform boisterously, as a part or a scene in a play. **30.** *Naut.* **a.** to caulk (a vessel) with a hammer. **b.** to work or haze (a seaman) cruelly or unfairly. **31.** *Archaic.* to place (someone) on a person's back, in order to be flogged. —*v.i.* **32.** to mount or go on a horse. **33.** (of a mare) to be in heat. **34.** *Vulgar.* to have coitus. **35. horse around,** *Slang.* to fool around; indulge in horseplay: *They like to horse around when the work is slow.* —*adj.* **36.** of, for, or pertaining to a horse or horses: *the horse family; horse blanket.* **37.** drawn or powered by a horse or horses: *horse rake.* **38.** mounted or serving on horses: *horse troops.* **39.** unusually large. [ME, OE *hors;* c. Icel *hross*, D *ros*, G *Ross* (MHG *ros*, OHG *hros*)] —**horse/-like/,** *adj.*

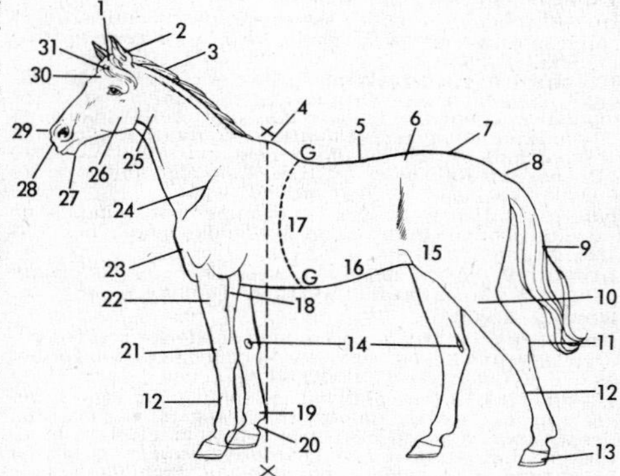

Horse
1, Poll; 2, Ear; 3, Mane; 4, Withers; 5, Back; 6, Loin; 7, Croup; 8, Dock; 9, Tail; 10, Gaskin; 11, Hock; 12, Cannon or shank; 13, Hoof; 14, Chestnut; 15, Stifle; 16, Belly; 17, Ribs; 18, Elbow; 19, Fetlock; 20, Pastern; 21, Knee; 22, Forearm; 23, Chest; 24, Shoulder; 25, Neck; 26, Cheek; 27, Chin; 28, Muzzle; 29, Nostril; 30, Forehead; 31, Forelock; GG, Girth; XX, Height

horse-and-bug·gy (hôrs/ən bug/ē), *adj.* **1.** of or pertaining to the last few generations preceding the invention of the automobile: *vivid recollections of horse-and-buggy days.* **2.** old-fashioned; outmoded: *horse-and-buggy methods.*

horse·back (hôrs/bak/), *n.* **1.** the back of a horse. **2.** *U.S.* a low, natural ridge of sand, gravel, or rock. Cf. **hogback.** —*adv.* **3.** on horseback: *to ride horseback.* [ME *horsbak.* See HORSE, BACK¹]

horse/ bean/, See **broad bean.**

horse/ block/, a step or block of stone, wood, etc., for getting on or off a horse or in or out of a vehicle.

horse/ brass/, a brass ornament, originally intended for the harness of a horse.

horse/ bri/ar, the cat briar, *Smilax rotundifolia.*

horse·car (hôrs/kär/), *n.* **1.** *U.S.* a streetcar drawn by a horse or horses. **2.** a railroad car or a truck fitted with stalls for the transportation of horses. [HORSE + CAR¹]

horse/ chest/nut, **1.** the shiny, brown, nutlike seed of a tree of the genus *Aesculus*, esp. *A. Hippocastanum.* **2.** any such tree having large, digitate leaves and upright clusters of showy white, red, or yellow flowers. [trans. of L *castanea equina*]

horse·cloth (hôrs/klôth/, -kloth/), *n., pl.* **-cloths** (-klôthz/, -klothz/; -klôths/, -kloths/). a cloth used to cover a horse, or as part of its trappings. [HORSE + CLOTH]

horse-col·lar (hôrs/kol/ər), *v.t.* *Baseball Slang.* **1.** to prevent (the opposing team) from scoring: *We horse-collared them two games out of three.* **2.** to prevent (an opposing batter) from making a base hit: *He was horse-collared his first three times up.*

horse/ conch/, a marine gastropod, *Pleuroploca gigantea*, having a yellowish, spired shell that grows to a length of two feet.

horse-cop·er (hôrs/kō/pər), *n.* *Brit.* coper.

horse-faced (hôrs/fāst/), *adj.* having a large face with lantern jaws and large teeth.

horse·feath·ers (hôrs/feth/ərz), *Slang.* —*n.* **1.** (*construed as sing. or pl.*) something not worth considering. —*interj.* **2.** rubbish; nonsense (used to express contemptuous rejection). [HORSE + FEATHERS]

horse·fish (hôrs/fish/), *n., pl.* (*esp. collectively*) **-fish,** (*esp. referring to two or more kinds or species*) **-fish·es.** moonfish (def. 1). [HORSE + FISH]

horse·flesh (hôrs/flesh/), *n.* **1.** the flesh of a horse. **2.** horses collectively, esp. for riding, racing, etc. [late ME; see HORSE, FLESH]

horse/ fly/, any of several blood-sucking, usually large flies of the family *Tabanidae*, esp. of the genus *Tabanus*, which are serious pests of horses, cattle, etc. [ME *horsfleeye*]

Horse fly, *Tabanus costalis* (Length ½ in.)

horse/ gen/tian, any weedy, caprifoliaceous plant of the genus *Triosteum*, of North America, esp. *T. perfoliatum*, having sessile leaves and purplish-brown flowers, and bearing orange fruits. Also called **horse/ gin/seng, tinker's weed, wild ipecac.**

horse/ guard/, a black and yellow sand wasp, *Bembix carolina*, of the southern U.S., that preys on flies that gather around horses and cattle.

Horse/ Guards/, **1.** a body of cavalry serving as a guard. **2.** a cavalry brigade from the household troops of the British monarch.

horse·hair (hôrs/hâr/), *n.* **1.** a hair or the hair of a horse, esp. from the mane or tail. **2.** a sturdy, glossy fabric woven of this hair. —*adj.* **3.** of or pertaining to horsehair: *a horsehair mattress.* [ME *hors here.* See HORSE, HAIR] —**horse/haired/,** *adj.*

horse·head (hôrs/hed/), *n., pl.* **-heads,** (*esp. collectively for 1*) **-head. 1.** moonfish (def. 1). **2.** an arch head, esp. on an oil-field pump. [late ME *horse heed.* See HORSE, HEAD]

Horse/head Neb/ula, a dark nebula in the constellation Orion, composed of opaque cosmic dust and resembling the head of a horse.

Horse·heads (hôrs/hedz/), *n.* a town in S New York. 7207 (1960).

horse·hide (hôrs/hīd/), *n.* **1.** the hide of a horse. **2.** leather made from the hide of a horse. **3.** *Slang.* a baseball. —*adj.* **4.** made of horsehide. [HORSE + HIDE²]

horse/ lat/itudes, *Naut.* the latitudes, approximately 30° N and S, forming the edges of the trade-wind belt, characterized by high atmospheric pressure with calms and light variable winds. [either from the climate being fatal to horses on board, or from sailors working off the dead horse (advanced pay) by that point in the voyage]

horse·laugh (hôrs/laf/, -läf/), *n.* **1.** a loud, coarse laugh, esp. of derision. —*v.i.* **2.** to utter a horselaugh. [HORSE + LAUGH] —**horse/laugh/ter,** *n.*

horse·leech (hôrs/lēch/), *n.* a large leech, as *Haemopsis marmoratis*, which infests the mouth and nasal passages of horses while they are drinking. [late ME *horsleych.* See HORSE, LEECH]

horse/less car/riage (hôrs/lis), *Archaic.* an automobile.

horse/ mack/erel, **1.** See **bluefin tuna. 2.** See **jack mackerel.**

horse·man (hôrs/mən), *n., pl.* **-men. 1.** a person who is skilled in riding a horse. **2.** a person on horseback. **3.** a person who owns, breeds, trains, or tends horses. [ME *horsman.* See HORSE, MAN¹]

horse·man·ship (hôrs/mən ship/), *n.* **1.** the art, ability, skill, or manner of a horseman. **2.** equitation. [HORSEMAN + -SHIP]

horse/ marine/, **1.** (formerly) a marine mounted on horseback or a cavalryman doing duty on shipboard. **2.** a person out of his element.

horse·mint (hôrs/mint/), *n.* **1.** Also called **apple mint.** a wild mint, *Mentha rotundifolia*, introduced into America from Europe, having spikes of purple flowers. **2.** any of various other menthaceous plants, as an erect, odorous herb, *Monarda punctata*, of America. [ME *horsminte.* See HORSE, MINT¹]

horse/ net/tle, a prickly, North American, solanaceous weed, *Solanum carolinense.*

horse/ op/era, a television play, radio drama, or motion picture about the Wild West, often presented serially and usually dealing with adventures of cowboys, gunmen, gold prospectors, settlers, etc.

horse/ par/lor, a gambling room where one can bet on horse races with a bookmaker.

horse/ pis/tol, a large pistol formerly carried by horsemen.

horse·play (hôrs/plā/), *n.* rough or boisterous play or pranks. [HORSE + PLAY] —**horse/play/ful,** *adj.*

horse·play·er (hôrs/plā/ər), *n.* a habitual better on horse races. [HORSE + PLAYER]

horse·pow·er (hôrs/pou/ər), *n.* a foot-pound-second unit of power, equivalent to 550 foot-pounds per second. [HORSE + POWER]

horse·pow·er-hour (hôrs/pou/ər our/, -ou/ər), *n.* a foot-pound-second unit of energy or work, equal to the

CONCISE PRONUNCIATION KEY: *act, āble, dâre, ärt; ebb, ēqual; if, īce; hot, ōver, ôrder, oil, bo͝ok, o͞oze, out; up, ûrge; chief; sing; shoe; thin, that;* zh *as in measure.* ə = *a* as in *alone*, *e* as in *system*, *i* as in *easily*, *o* as in *gallop*, *u* as in *circus*; ᵊ as in *button* (but/ᵊn), *fire* (fīᵊr), *cradle* (krād/ᵊl). See the full key inside the front cover.

work done by a mechanism with a power output of one horsepower over a period of one hour.

horse·pox (hôrs′poks′), *n. Vet. Pathol.* a disease in horses caused by a virus and characterized by eruptions in the mouth and on the skin. [HORSE + POX]

horse·rad·ish (hôrs′rad′ish), *n.* **1.** a cultivated, cruciferous plant, *Armoracia rusticana.* **2.** the pungent root of this plant, ground and used as a condiment and in medicine. **3.** the condiment itself, sometimes moistened with vinegar or mixed with ground beets. —*adj.* **4.** of or containing ground horseradish as a flavoring: *brisket of beef with horseradish sauce.* [HORSE + RADISH]

horse′ rake′, a large-wheeled rake drawn by a horse.

horse′'s ass′, *Slang (vulgar).* a fool.

horse′ sense′, *Informal.* plain, practical common sense.

horse·shit (hôrs′shit′, hôrsh′-), *Slang (vulgar).* —*n.* **1.** nonsense, lies, or exaggeration. —*interj.* **2.** (used to express disbelief, incredulity, etc.) [HORSE + SHIT]

horse·shoe (hôrs′sho͞o′, hôrsh′-), *n., v.,* **-shoed, -shoe·ing,** *adj.* —*n.* **1.** a U-shaped iron plate, plain or with calks, nailed to a horse's hoof to protect it from being injured by hard or rough surfaces. **2.** something U-shaped, as a valley, river bend, or other natural feature: *We picnicked in the middle of a horseshoe of trees.* **3. horseshoes,** (*construed as sing.*) a game in which horseshoes or other U-shaped pieces of metal, plastic, etc., are tossed at an iron stake 30 or 40 feet away in order to encircle it or to come closer to it than one's opponent or opponents. —*v.t.* **4.** to put horseshoes on; to shoe. —*adj.* **5.** having the shape of a horseshoe; U-shaped: *a horseshoe bend in the river.* [ME *hors shoo.* See HORSE, SHOE] —**horse′sho′er,** *n.*

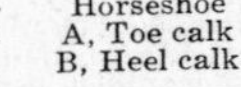

Horseshoe
A, Toe calk
B, Heel calk

horse′shoe arch′, an arch continued downward below its center or centers. Also called **Moorish arch.** See illus. under **arch.**

horse′shoe back′, *Furniture.* a bow back having a slight outward splay at its bottom.

horse′shoe crab′, any of various marine arthropods, esp. of the genus *Limulus,* with a carapace shaped somewhat like a horseshoe. Also called **king crab.**

horse′shoe mag′net, a horseshoe-shaped permanent magnet.

horse′ show′, a fashionably competitive display of the capabilities and qualities of horses and their riders or handlers, usually held as an annual event.

Horseshoe crab,
Limulus polyphemus
(Length 2 ft.)

Horse's Mouth′, The, a novel (1944) by Joyce Cary.

horse′'s neck′, a drink, either of liquor and ginger ale or ginger ale only, served with ice and having a lemon rind on the rim of the glass.

horse′ sug′ar, sweetleaf.

horse′ tail′, a ponytail.

horse·tail (hôrs′tāl′), *n.* **1.** any perennial, herbaceous, pteridophytic plant of the genus *Equisetum,* having hollow, jointed stems. **2.** a horse's tail formerly used as a Turkish military standard or as an ensign of a pasha, the number of tails increasing with the rank. [ME *horse tayle.* See HORSE, TAIL[1]]

horse′tail ag′aric, the shaggy-mane. Also called **horse′tail mush′room.**

horse′tail tree′, beefwood (def. 1).

horse′ tim′ber, *Naut.* See **horn timber.**

horse′ trade′, 1. a shrewdly conducted exchange, as of favors, objects, etc., usually resulting from or accompanied by very close bargaining. **2.** an exchanging or trading of horses.

horse-trade (hôrs′trād′), *v.i.,* **-trad·ed, -trad·ing.** to bargain or trade shrewdly.

horse′ trad′er, 1. a person who is shrewd and clever at bargaining: *Watch out for him, he's an old horse trader.* **2.** a person who trades in horses.

horse′ trad′ing, the act or fact of conducting a shrewd exchange or engaging in a horse trade; bargaining.

horse·weed (hôrs′wēd′), *n.* **1.** an asteraceous weed, *Erigeron canadense.* **2.** any of various other plants, as the wild lettuce, *Lactuca canadensis.* [HORSE + WEED[1]]

horse·whip (hôrs′hwip′, -wip′), *n., v.,* **-whipped, -whip·ping.** —*n.* **1.** a whip for controlling horses. —*v.t.* **2.** to beat with a horsewhip. [HORSE + WHIP] —**horse′whip′per,** *n.*

horse·wom·an (hôrs′wo͝om′ən), *n., pl.* **-wom·en. 1.** a woman who rides on horseback. **2.** a woman who is skilled in managing or riding horses. [HORSE + WOMAN] —**horse′wom′an·ship′,** *n.*

hors·ey (hôr′sē), *adj.,* **hors·i·er, hors·i·est.** horsy.

hors·i·ly (hôr′sə lē), *adv.* in a horsy manner. [HORSY + -LY]

hors·ing (hôr′siŋ), *n. Print.* reading proof without the assistance of a copyholder. [perh. n. use of *horse about*]

hor. som., (in prescriptions) at bedtime. [< L *hōrā somnī* at the hour of sleep]

horst (hôrst), *n.* a portion of the earth's crust, bounded on at least two sides by faults, that has been moved upward in relation to adjacent portions. Cf. **graben.** [< G: thicket; c. HURST]

Horst′ Wes′sel song′ (hôrst′ ves′əl), the official song of the Nazi party in Germany from 1933 to 1945. Also called **Horst′ Wes′sel lied′.**

hors·y (hôr′sē), *adj.,* **hors·i·er, hors·i·est. 1.** of, pertaining to, or characteristic of a horse or horses. **2.** dealing with, interested in, or devoted to horses, horseback riding, fox hunting, horse racing, etc.: *horsy talk; the horsy set in local society.* **3.** *Informal.* rather heavy and awkward in appearance: *a horsy woman.* Also, **horsey.** [HORSE + -Y[1]] —**hors′i·ness,** *n.*

hort., 1. horticultural. **2.** horticulture.

Hor·ta (hôr′tə), *n.* **Baron Victor,** 1861?–1947, Belgian architect.

hor·ta·tive (hôr′tə tiv), *adj.* hortatory. [< L *hortātīv(us),* equiv. to *hortāt(us)* (*hor-* want, desire (c. YEARN) + *-t-* v. suffix + *-ātus* -ATE[1]) + *-īvus* -IVE] —**hor′ta·tive·ly,** *adv.*

hor·ta·to·ry (hôr′tə tōr′ē, -tôr′ē), *adj.* urging to some course of conduct or action; exhorting; encouraging: *a hortatory speech.* [< LL *hortātōri(us)* encouraging, equiv. to *hortāt(us)* (see HORTATIVE) + *-ōrius* -ORY[1]] —**hor′ta·to′ri·ly,** *adv.*

Hor·tense (hôr′tens), *n.* a girl's given name.

Hor·tense′ de Beau·har·nais′ (*Fr.* ôr täns′). See **Beauharnais, Eugénie Hortense de.**

Hor·ten·si·a (hôr ten′sē ə), *n.* a shrub, *Hydrangea macrophylla,* of Japan, having pink or blue flowers in globe-shaped clusters. [< L, fem. of *Hortensius,* proper name; cf. *hortus* garden]

Hor·ten·si·us (hôr ten′sē əs), *n.* a crater in the second quadrant of the face of the moon: about 10 miles in diameter.

Hor·thy (hôr′tē), *n.* **Mi·klós von Nagy·bá·nya** (mik′lôsh fôn nod′yᵊ bä′nyo), 1863–1957, Hungarian admiral: regent of Hungary 1920–44.

hor·ti·cul·ture (hôr′tə kul′chər), *n.* **1.** the cultivation of a garden, orchard, or nursery; the cultivation of flowers, fruits, vegetables, or ornamental plants. **2.** the science and art of cultivating such plants. [< L *hort(us)* garden + (AGR)ICULTURE] —**hor′ti·cul′tur·al,** *adj.* —**hor′ti·cul′tur·ist,** *n.*

hor·tus sic·cus (hôr′təs sik′əs), a collection of dried plants; herbarium. [< L *hortus* GARDEN + *siccus* dry; see SACK[3]]

hor. un. spatio, (in prescriptions) at the end of one hour. [< L *hōrae ūnius spatiō*]

Ho·rus (hōr′əs, hôr′-), *n. Egyptian Religion.* a solar deity, regarded as either the son or the brother of Isis and Osiris, and usually represented as a falcon or as a man with the head of a falcon. [< LL < Gk *Hōros* < Egypt *Hur* hawk]

Hos., Hosea.

ho·san·na (hō zan′ə), *interj., n., pl.* **-nas,** *v.,* **-naed, -na·ing.** —*interj.* **1.** (an exclamation, originally an appeal to God for deliverance, used in praise of God or Christ.) —*n.* **2.** a cry of "hosanna." **3.** a shout of praise or adoration; an acclamation. —*v.t.* **4.** to praise, applaud, etc.: *The critics hosannaed his new play.* [< LL < Gk < Heb *hōsh(i) 'āh nnā* save, we pray; r. ME, OE *osanna* < LL]

hose (hōz), *n., pl.* **hose** for 1, 3; **hos·es** for 2, 4–6; (*Archaic*) **hos·en;** *v.,* **hosed, hos·ing.** —*n.* **1.** an article of clothing for the foot and lower part of the leg; stocking or sock. **2.** a flexible tube for conveying a liquid, as water, to a desired point: *a garden hose; a fire hose.* **3.** (clothing of men's attire in former time.) **a.** an article of clothing for the leg, extending from about the knee to the ankle and worn with knee breeches. **b.** (*construed as pl.*) knee breeches. **c.** (*construed as pl.*) tights, as were worn with, and usually attached to, a doublet. **4.** *Brit. Dial.* a sheath, or sheathing part, as that enclosing a kernel of grain. **5.** *Print.* a wooden sleeve covering the lower end of the screw of a platen press. **6.** *Golf.* hosel. —*v.t.* **7.** to water, wash, spray, or drench by means of a hose (often fol. by *down*): *to hose the garden; to hose down the ship's deck.* **8.** *Chiefly Canadian Slang.* **a.** to cheat, trick, or take advantage of. **b.** to defeat decisively. [ME, OE; c. D *hoos,* Icel *hosa,* G *Hose*] —**hose′less,** *adj.* —**hose′like′,** *adj.*

Ho·se·a (hō zē′ə, -zā′ə), *n.* **1.** a Minor Prophet of the 8th century B.C. **2.** a book of the Bible bearing his name. Also, *Douay Bible,* **Osee.** [< Heb *Hōshēa'* salvation, help]

hose·cock (hōz′kok′), *n.* a threaded exterior faucet, as for a garden hose. Also called **sillcock.** [HOSE + COCK[1]]

Ho·sein (ho͞o sīn′), *n.* Husain.

ho·sel (hō′zəl), *n. Golf.* the socket in the club head of an iron that receives the shaft. Also called **hose.** [HOSE + *-el* dim. suffix]

Ho·sha·na Rab·bah (hō shä′nə rä′bə; *Heb.* hô shä-nä′ rä bä′), the seventh day of the Jewish festival of Sukkoth, occurring on the 21st day of the month of Tishri and having a special liturgy containing a series of invocations to God for forgiveness and salvation. Also, **Hosha′nah Rab′bah.** [< Heb *hōsh(i) 'āh nnā* save, we pray + *rab(a)bah* the myriad, multitude]

ho·sier (hō′zhər), *n.* one who makes or deals in hose or stockings or goods knitted or woven like hose. [late ME *hosiare,* etc. See HOSE, -IER]

ho·sier·y (hō′zhə rē), *n.* **1.** hose or stockings of any kind. **2.** the business of a hosier. [HOSIER + -Y[3]]

hosp., hospital.

hos·pice (hos′pis), *n.* a house of shelter or rest for pilgrims, strangers, etc., esp. one kept by a religious order. [< F < L *hospit(ium)* HOSPITIUM]

hos·pi·ta·ble (hos′pi tə bəl, ho spit′ə bəl), *adj.* **1.** receiving or treating guests or strangers warmly and generously: *a hospitable family.* **2.** characterized by or betokening warmth and generosity toward guests or strangers: *a hospitable reception; a hospitable smile.* **3.** favorably receptive or open (usually fol. by *to*): *to be hospitable to new ideas; a climate hospitable to the raising of corn.* [< L *hospitā-* (s. of *hospitāre* to receive as guest) + -BLE] —**hos′pi·ta·ble·ness,** *n.* —**hos′pi·ta·bly,** *adv.*

hos·pi·tal (hos′pi tᵊl), *n.* **1.** an institution in which sick or injured persons are given medical or surgical treatment. **2.** a similar establishment for the care of animals. **3.** *Brit.* an institution supported by charity or taxes for the care of the needy, as an orphanage, old people's home, etc. **4.** a repair shop for specific portable objects: *violin hospital; doll hospital.* [ME *hospitale* < LL (neut.) n. use of L *hospitālis* hospitable, equiv. to *hospit-* (see HOSPITIUM) + *-ālis* -AL[1]]

—**Syn. 1.** retreat, clinic. HOSPITAL, ASYLUM, SANATORIUM, SANITARIUM are names of institutions for persons needing some sort of care. A HOSPITAL is an institution in which sick or injured persons are given medical or surgical treatment, therapy, etc.: *to be in a hospital recuperating from an operation; to have a baby in a hospital.* An ASYLUM is an institution (usually owned by the state) for the care of particularly afflicted or dependent persons; though it originally meant a place of refuge, the word has acquired unpleasant connotations, so that HOSPITAL is now the preferred term for that type of institution also: *an asylum for the deaf, insane, blind; an orphan asylum.* The terms SANATORIUM and SANITARIUM are sometimes used interchangeably. However, the former, stressing curative and healing measures, often means a health resort for persons needing mainly rest and recuperation in pleasant surroundings: *Nature therapy and raw foods are specialties of this sanatorium.* SANITARIUM stresses hygienic conditions, and usually has patients needing special treatment: *the sanitarium for tubercular patients.*

hos′pital bed′, a bed having a mattress base in three jointed sections so that the head, foot, or middle may be raised by a crank, allowing a patient to lie in various positions, as a therapeutic aid or for comfort.

hos′pital cor′ner, a fold on a bed sheet or blanket made by tucking the foot or head of the sheet straight under the mattress with the ends protruding and then making a diagonal fold at the side corner of the sheet and tucking this under to produce a triangular corner.

Hos·pi·tal·er (hos′pi tᵊlər), *n.* **1.** a member of the religious and military order (**Knights Hospitalers** or **Knights of St. John of Jerusalem**) originating about the time of the first Crusade (1096–99) and taking its name from a hospital at Jerusalem. **2.** (*l.c.*) a person, esp. a member of a religious order, devoted to the care of the sick or needy in hospitals. Also, **Hos′pi·tal·ler.** [HOSPITAL + -ER[2]; r. ME *hospitalier* < MF < ML *hospitālārius;* see -IER]

Hos·pi·ta·let (ôs′pē tä let′), *n.* a city in NE Spain, near Barcelona. 122,813 (1960).

hos′pital gan′grene, *Pathol.* a contagious, often fatal infection, esp. involving amputation stumps, occurring usually in crowded, ill-kept hospitals, and caused by putrefactive bacteria.

hos·pi·tal·ism (hos′pi tᵊliz′əm), *n.* **1.** hospital conditions having an adverse effect on patients. **2.** the mental and physical effects caused by such conditions. **3.** the physiological and psychological consequences of living in a foundling home. [HOSPITAL + -ISM]

hos·pi·tal·i·ty (hos′pi tal′i tē), *n., pl.* **-ties. 1.** the friendly reception and treatment of guests or strangers. **2.** the quality or disposition of receiving and treating guests and strangers in a warm, friendly, generous way. [ME *hospitalite* < MF < L *hospitālitās,* equiv. to *hospitāl(is)* (see HOSPITAL) + *-tās* -TY[2]]

hos·pi·tal·i·za·tion (hos′pi tᵊli zā′shən), *n.* **1.** an act or the state of being hospitalized. **2.** the period during which one is hospitalized: *to extend one's hospitalization.* **3.** See **hospitalization insurance.** [HOSPITALIZE + -ATION]

hospitaliza′tion insur′ance, insurance to cover, in whole or in part, the hospital bills of a subscriber or his dependents.

hos·pi·tal·ize (hos′pi tᵊlīz′), *v.t.,* **-ized, -iz·ing.** to place in a hospital for medical care or observation: *He hospitalizes patients for minor ailments.* [HOSPITAL + -IZE]

hos′pital light′. See **hopper casement.** Also called **hos′pital win′dow.**

hos·pi·tal·man (hos′pi tᵊl mən), *n., pl.* **-men.** *U.S. Navy.* an enlisted man working as a hospital assistant; corpsman. [HOSPITAL + MAN[1]]

hos′pital ship′, a ship built to serve as a hospital, esp. used to treat the wounded in wartime and accorded safe passage according to international law.

hos′pital train′, a military train equipped to transport wounded troops to a hospital.

hos·pi·ti·um (ho spish′ē əm), *n., pl.* **hos·pi·ti·a** (ho-spish′ē ə). a hospice. [< L: hospitable reception, entertainment, place of entertainment, equiv. to *hospit-* (s. of *hospes*) host, guest, stranger + *-ium* -Y[3]]

hos·po·dar (hos′pə där′), *n.* a former title of governors or princes of Walachia and Moldavia. [< Rumanian < Ukrainian *hospodár'* < *hospod'* master (akin to L *hospes;* see HOST[1]) + *-ar* suffix]

host[1] (hōst), *n.* **1.** a person who receives or entertains guests in his own home or elsewhere: *the host at a theater party.* **2.** the landlord of an inn. **3.** a living animal or plant from which a parasite obtains nutrition. **4. reckon without one's host,** to plan or calculate without taking all important factors into account. —*v.t.* **5.** to be the host at (a dinner, reception, etc.): *He hosted a reception for new members.* **6.** to act as host to: *The vice-president hosted the foreign dignitaries during their visit.* [ME *(h)oste* < MF < L *hospitem* (acc. of *hospes*) host, guest, stranger, prob. contr. of **hostipitem,* equiv. to *hosti-* (see HOST[2]) + *-pit-,* var. of *-pot-* mastery (see POTENT); akin to HOSPODAR] —**host′less,** *adj.* —**host′ly,** *adj.* —**host′ship,** *n.*

host[2] (hōst), *n.* **1.** a multitude or great number of persons or things: *a host of details.* **2.** *Archaic.* an army. [ME *(h)oste* < OF < L *host-* (s. of *hostis*) enemy, host]

Host (hōst), *n. Eccles.* the bread or wafer consecrated in the celebration of the Eucharist. [ME *hoste* < LL *hostia* Eucharistic wafer (L: victim, sacrifice); r. ME *oyst* < MF *oiste* < LL, as above; see HOUSEL]

hos·tage (hos′tij), *n., v.,* **-taged, -tag·ing.** —*n.* **1.** a person given or held as security for the performance of certain actions, promises, etc., by another. **2.** *Rare.* a security or pledge. **3.** *Obs.* the condition of a hostage. **4. hostages to fortune,** children, or a wife and children. —*v.t.* **5.** to give (someone) as a hostage: *He was hostaged to the Indians.* [ME < OF *hostage,* equiv. to *h-* (? deriv. of *host;* see HOST[2]) + *ostage* << LL **obsidātic(um)* state of being a hostage < L *obsid-* (s. of *obses*) hostage, equiv. to *ob-* OB- + *sid-* SIT + *-āticum* -AGE] —**hos′tage·ship′,** *n.*

Hostage, The, **1.** a play (1958) by Brendan Behan. **2.** French, ***L'Otage.*** a play (1911) by Paul Claudel.

hos·tel (hos′tᵊl), *n.* **1.** Also called **youth hostel.** a supervised lodging place for young people traveling by bicycle or walking. **2.** *Brit.* a residence hall at a university. **3.** an inn. —*v.i., v.t.* **4.** to travel, lodging each night at a hostel. [ME *(h)ostel* < OF < LL *hospitāle.* See HOSPITAL]

hos·tel·er (hos′tᵊlər), *n.* **1.** one who operates a hostel. **2.** one who stays at a hostel or goes hosteling. [ME; see HOSTEL, -ER[2]; akin to OF *hostelier*]

hos·tel·ry (hos′tᵊl rē), *n., pl.* **-ries.** a hostel or inn. [ME *hostelrye,* var. of *hostelerie* < MF. See HOSTEL, -RY]

hos′tel school′, (in Canada) one of a series of boarding schools operated by the federal government in the northern territories for Indian and Eskimo students.

host·ess (hō′stis), *n.* **1.** a female host; a woman who receives and entertains guests. **2.** a woman employed in a restaurant or place of amusement to receive, seat, or assist patrons. **3.** a woman employed by a railroad, bus company, airline, etc., to see that passengers are comfortable throughout a trip, usually receiving and seating them, and sometimes serving them food and drink. **4.** See **taxi dancer. 5.** a woman who manages a resort or hotel or who directs its social activities. —*v.t.* **6.** to be the hostess at (a reception, dinner, etc.): *She will hostess a shower for the new bride.* **7.** to act as hostess to: *She volunteered to hostess the garden club next season.* [ME (*h*)*ostesse* < OF. See HOST[1], -ESS] —**host′ess-ship′**, *n.*

host′ess gown′, a dressing gown or housecoat worn by women for entertaining at home.

hos·tile (hos′tᵊl or, *esp. Brit.*, -tīl), *adj.* **1.** opposed in feeling, action, or character; antagonistic: *hostile criticism.* **2.** of, pertaining to, or characteristic of an enemy: *hostile ground; a hostile nation.* **3.** characterized by antagonism. **4.** not friendly, warm, or generous; not hospitable. [< L *hostīl*(*is*), equiv. to *host*(*is*) enemy + *-īlis* -ILE] —**hos′tile·ly**, *adv.*
—**Syn. 1.** adverse, averse, contrary. HOSTILE, INIMICAL indicate that which characterizes an enemy or something injurious to one's interests. HOSTILE applies to the spirit, attitude, or action of an enemy: *They showed a hostile and menacing attitude.* INIMICAL applies to an antagonistic or injurious tendency or influence: *Their remarks were inimical to his reputation.* **2.** warlike, aggressive. —**Ant. 1, 2.** friendly. **2.** amicable. **3.** sympathetic. **4.** hospitable.

hos·til·i·ty (ho stil′i tē), *n., pl.* **-ties. 1.** a hostile state, condition, or attitude; enmity; antagonism. **2.** a hostile act. **3.** opposition or resistance to an idea, plan, project, etc. **4. hostilities, a.** acts of warfare. **b.** war. [< L *hostīlitās.* See HOSTILE, -ITY]
—**Syn. 1.** animosity, animus, ill will, unfriendliness, hatred. **4.** warfare, fighting, conflict. —**Ant. 1.** friendliness. **4.** peace.

hos·tler (hos′lər, os′lər), *n.* one who takes care of horses, esp. at an inn. [var. of HOSTELER] —**hos′tler-ship′**, *n.*

hot (hot), *adj.,* **hot·ter, hot·test,** *adv., v.,* **hot·ted, hot·ting.** —*adj.* **1.** having or communicating heat; having a high temperature: *a hot fire; hot coffee.* **2.** having or causing a sensation of great bodily heat; attended with or producing such a sensation: *He was hot with fever. Digging potatoes is a hot job.* **3.** creating a burning sensation, as on the skin or in the throat: *This ointment is hot, so apply it sparingly.* **4.** peppery or pungent: *Is this mustard hot?* **5.** having or showing intense or violent feeling; ardent or fervent; vehement; excited: *hot temper.* **6.** having a strong enthusiasm; eager: *a hot baseball fan.* **7.** lustful; lascivious. **8.** violent, furious, or intense: *the hottest battle of the war.* **9.** strong or fresh, as a scent or trail. **10.** absolutely new; fresh: *a dozen new mystery stories, hot from the press.* **11.** *Slang.* skillful in a reckless or daring way: *a hot pilot.* **12.** *Slang.* following very closely; close: *to be hot on the trail of a thief.* **13.** (of colors) extremely intense: *hot pink; hot yellow.* **14.** currently popular and commercially successful; in demand; marketable: *Frank Sinatra was the hottest singer of the 1940's. That blue dress with the short sleeves was a hot item last summer; Macy's sold hundreds of them.* **15.** *Slang.* extremely lucky, good, or favorable: *Joe's a hot crap shooter. The cards are hot for me tonight.* **16.** *Slang.* funny; absurd: *That's a hot one!* **17.** *Games.* close to the object or answer that is being sought. **18.** *Slang.* extremely exciting or interesting; sensational or scandalous: *a hot news story.* **19.** *Jazz.* **a.** (of music) emotionally intense, propulsive, and marked by aggressive attack and warm, full tone. **b.** (of a musician) skilled in playing hot jazz. **20.** *Slang.* (of a vehicle) capable of attaining extremely high speeds: *a hot new jet plane.* **21.** *Slang.* **a.** stolen recently or otherwise illegal and dangerous to possess. **b.** wanted by the police. **c.** dangerous. **22.** in the mood to perform exceedingly well, or rapidly, as during a burst of creative work: *Finish writing that story while you're still hot.* **23.** actively conducting an electric current or containing a high voltage: *a hot wire.* **24.** of, pertaining to, or noting radioactivity. **25.** *Metalworking.* noting any process involving plastic deformation of a metal at a temperature high enough to permit recrystallization due to the strain: *hot working.* **26. make it hot for,** *Informal.* to make something unpleasant for; cause trouble for: *Ever since their argument the principal has been making it hot for the new teacher.* —*adv.* **27.** in a hot manner; hotly. **28.** while hot: *Garnish with parsley and serve hot.* **29.** *Metalworking.* at a temperature high enough to permit recrystallization: *The wire was drawn hot.* —*v.t., v.i.* **30.** *Chiefly Brit. Informal.* to heat; warm (usually fol. by *up*). [ME *ho*(*o*)*t*, OE *hāt*; c. D *heet*, Icel *heitr*, Sw *het*, Dan *hed*, G *heiss*] —**hot′ly**, *adv.* —**hot′ness**, *n.*
—**Syn. 1.** heated; fiery, burning, scorching; scalding, boiling; torrid, sultry. **4.** biting, piquant, sharp, spicy. **5.** fervid; fiery, passionate, intense, excitable, animated, impetuous; angry, furious, irate, violent. —**Ant. 1.** cold.

hot′ air′, *Slang.* empty, exaggerated, or pretentious talk or writing: *The paper he read at the meeting was just so much hot air.*

hot′ bed′, *Metalworking.* an area having rails or rolls on which rolled pieces are laid to cool.

hot·bed (hot′bed′), *n.* **1.** a bottomless, boxlike, usually glass-covered structure and the bed of earth it covers, heated by fermenting manure, electrical cables, or the like, for growing plants out of season. **2.** a place or environment favoring the rapid growth or spread of something, esp. something bad: *A slum is often a hotbed of vice.* [HOT + BED]

hot′bed sash′, a window sash with sash bars parallel to its length.

hot-blood·ed (hot′blud′id), *adj.* **1.** excitable; impetuous. **2.** adventuresome, exciting, or characterized by adventure and excitement. **3.** ardent, passionate, or virile. **4.** (of livestock) of superior or pure breeding. **5.** (of horses) being a Thoroughbred or having Arab blood. —**hot′-blood′ed·ness**, *n.*

hot·box (hot′boks′), *n. Railroads.* a journal box overheated by excessive friction of an axle as a result of inadequate lubrication or the presence of foreign matter. Also, **hot′ box′**. [HOT + BOX[1]]

hot′-bulb′ en′gine (hot′bulb′), a low-compression oil engine requiring a heated bulb or cap for ignition.

hot′ but′tered rum′, a drink made with rum, hot water, and sugar, served with a lump of butter in a mug.

hot′ cake′, **1.** griddle cake; pancake. **2. sell or go like hot cakes,** to be disposed of very quickly and effortlessly, esp. in quantity: *That new recording sold like hot cakes on the first day after its release.*

hot′-cath′ode tube′ (hot′kath′ōd), *Electronics.* See **thermionic tube.**

hotch (hoch), *Scot. and North Eng.* —*v.i.* **1.** to fidget; shift one's weight from one foot to the other. —*v.t.* **2.** to cause to fidget or shiver. [late ME (north); akin to D *hotsen* to jolt, dial. G *hotzen* to move up and down, F *hocher* to jog, shake (< Gmc)]

hot·cha (hä′chä, -chə), *interj. Slang.* (used as an expression of approval or delight, now often used facetiously.) [? irreg. from HOT]

hotch·pot (hoch′pot′), *n. Law.* the bringing together of shares or properties in order to divide them equally, esp. when they are to be divided among the children of a parent dying intestate. [ME *hochepot* < AF (legal), lit., shake- pot. See HOTCH, POT[1]]

hotch·potch (hoch′poch′), *n.* **1.** a thick soup or stew of vegetables or meat, often thickened with barley. **2.** *Brit.* hodgepodge. **3.** *Law.* a hotchpot. [ME *hoche poche*, rhyming var. of HOTCHPOT]

hot′ cock′les, a children's game in which a child with his eyes covered attempts to guess who has hit him.

hot′ cold′-working, metalworking at considerable heat but below the temperature at which the metal recrystallizes: a form of cold-working.

hot′ cor′ner, *Baseball Slang.* See **third base** (def. 2).

hot′ cross′ bun′, a bun with a cross of frosting on it, eaten chiefly during Lent. Also called, *esp. Brit.*, **cross bun.**

hot′-dip coat′ing (hot′dip′), the process of coating sheets of iron or steel with molten zinc. Also called **hot galvanizing.**

hot-dipped (hot′dipt′), *adj. Metall.* coated by being dipped into molten tin or zinc.

hot′ dog′, **1.** a frankfurter. **2.** a sandwich consisting of a frankfurter in a split roll, usually eaten with mustard or relish.

hot-draw (hot′drô′), *v.t.,* **-drew, -drawn, -draw·ing.** *Metalworking.* to draw (wire, tubing, etc.) at a temperature high enough to permit recrystallization.

ho·tel (hō tel′), *n.* **1.** a commercial establishment offering lodging to transients, and often having restaurants, public rooms, shops, etc., that are available to the general public. **2.** a word used in communications to represent the letter H. [< F *hôtel* < OF *hostel* HOSTEL] —**ho·tel′less**, *adj.*
—**Syn. 1.** hostelry, hostel, guest house, motel, motor hotel. HOTEL, HOUSE, INN, TAVERN refer to establishments for the lodging or entertainment of travelers and others. HOTEL is the common word, suggesting a more or less commodious establishment with up-to-date appointments, although this is not necessarily true: *the best hotel in the city; a cheap hotel near the docks.* The word HOUSE is often used in the name of a particular hotel, the connotation being wealth and luxury: *the Parker House; the Palmer House.* INN suggests a place of homelike comfort and old-time appearance or ways; it is used for quaint or archaic effect in the names of some public houses and hotels in the U.S.: *the Pickwick Inn; the Wayside Inn.* A TAVERN, like the English PUBLIC HOUSE, is a house where liquors are sold for drinking on the premises; until recently it was archaic or dialectal in the U.S., but has been revived to substitute for *saloon*, which had unfavorable connotations: *Taverns are required to close by two o'clock in the morning.* The word has also been used in the sense of INN, esp. in New England, ever since Colonial days: *Wiggins Tavern.*

Hô·tel des In·va·lides (ō tel dā zan va lēd′), a military hospital built in Paris in the 17th and 18th centuries by Libéral Bruant and J. H. Mansart: famous for its chapel dome, the tomb of Napoleon, and as a military museum.

hô·tel de ville (ō tel′ də vēl′), *pl.* **hô·tels de ville** (ō tel′ də vēl′). *French.* a city hall. [lit., mansion of the city]

hô·tel Dieu (ō tel dyœ′), *pl.* **hô·tels Dieu** (ō tel dyœ′). *French.* a hospital. [lit., mansion of God]

ho·tel·keep·er (hō tel′kē′pər), *n.* a manager or owner of a hotel. [HOTEL + KEEPER]

ho·tel·man (hō tel′mən, -man′), *n., pl.* **-men** (-mən, -men′). hotelkeeper. [HOTEL + MAN[1]]

hotel′ rack′, the rib section of the foresaddle of lamb, mutton, or sometimes veal.

hot·foot (hot′fo͝ot′), *n., pl.* **-foots,** *v., adv.* —*n.* **1.** a practical joke in which a match, inserted surreptitiously between the sole and upper of the victim's shoe, is lit and allowed to burn down. —*v.i.* **2.** to go in great haste: *to hotfoot over to a neighbor's house.* —*adv.* **3.** with great speed in going; in haste. [ME *hot fot.* See HOT, FOOT]

hot′ gal′vanizing. See **hot-dip coating.**

hot·head (hot′hed′), *n.* a hotheaded person. [HOT + HEAD]

hot·head·ed (hot′hed′id), *adj.* **1.** hot or fiery in spirit or temper; impetuous; rash: *Hotheaded people shouldn't drive cars.* **2.** easily angered; quick to take offense. [HOT + HEADED] —**hot′head′ed·ly**, *adv.* —**hot′head′ed·ness**, *n.*

hot·house (hot′hous′), *n., pl.* **-hous·es** (-hou′ziz), *adj.* —*n.* **1.** an artificially heated greenhouse for the cultivation of tender plants. —*adj.* **2.** of, pertaining to, or noting a plant grown in a hothouse, or so fragile as to be capable of being grown only in a hothouse. **3.** overprotected, artificial, or unnaturally delicate. [HOT + HOUSE]

hot′house lamb′, a lamb born in the fall or early winter, usually reared indoors, specially fed, and marketed when from 9 to 16 weeks of age.

Ho·tien (hō′tyen′), *n.* Khotan (def. 2).

hot′ lick′, *Jazz.* lick (def. 12).

hot′ light′, *Television.* a powerful light used in television production.

hot′ line′, a direct telephone line between two officials, esp. the heads of state in Washington and Moscow, kept open for immediate communication in case of emergency, esp. to prevent an accidental atomic war.

hot′ met′al, *Print.* metallic type and printing elements produced by a casting machine; foundry type. Also called **hot type.** Cf. **cold type.**

hot′ mon′ey, *Slang.* funds transferred suddenly from one country to another chiefly to avoid depreciation in value or to take advantage of higher interest rates.

hot′ pack′, **1.** a hot towel, dressing, or the like, applied to the body to reduce swelling, relieve pain, etc. **2.** Also called **hot′ pack′ meth′od.** a method of canning food by cooking it and packing it while hot in jars or cans, then sterilizing in boiling water or steam. Cf. **cold pack.**

hot′ pep′per, **1.** any of variously shaped pungent peppers of the genus *Capsicum*, containing large amounts of capsaicin and usually having thin walls. **2.** a plant bearing such a pepper.

hot′ plate′, **1.** a portable appliance for cooking, heated formerly by a gas burner placed underneath it, now heated chiefly by an electrical unit in the appliance. **2.** a hot meal, usually consisting of meat, potato, and a vegetable, served all on one plate at a set price at a restaurant or lunch counter. **3.** a plate that has a means of retaining heat in order to prevent the food on it from becoming cold before it is eaten.

hot′ pot′, *Chiefly Brit.* mutton or beef cooked with potatoes in a covered pot.

hot′ pota′to, **1.** *Informal.* a situation or issue which is difficult, unpleasant, or risky to deal with. **2.** *Brit. Informal.* a baked potato.

hot-press (hot′pres′), *n.* **1.** a machine applying heat in conjunction with mechanical pressure, as for producing a smooth surface on paper, for expressing oil, etc. —*v.t.* **2.** to subject to treatment in a hot-press. —**hot′-press′er**, *n.*

hot′ rod′, *U.S. Slang.* a car, esp. an old one whose engine has been altered for increased speed.

hot′ rod′der, *U.S. Slang.* **1.** a driver or builder of hot rods. **2.** a fast and reckless driver.

hot-roll (hot′rōl′, -rōl′), *v.t. Metalworking.* to roll (metal) at a temperature high enough to permit recrystallization.

hot′ seat′, *Slang.* **1.** See **electric chair. 2.** a highly uncomfortable or embarrassing situation: *He's been in the hot seat because of that contract he fumbled.*

hot-short (hot′shôrt′), *adj. Metall.* (of metal) brittle at temperatures suitable for forging. [HOT + SHORT, as in *red-short*] —**hot′-short′ness**, *n.*

hot shot (hot′ shot′ *for 1;* hot′ shot′ *for 2*), **1.** incandescent shot fired to set enemy ships or buildings on fire. **2.** hotshot (defs. 4, 5).

hot·shot (hot′shot′), *Slang.* —*adj.* **1.** highly successful and aggressive: *a hotshot lawyer; a hotshot account exec.* **2.** displaying skill flamboyantly: *a hotshot ballplayer.* **3.** moving, going, or operating without a stop; fast: *a hotshot express.* —*n.* Also, **hot shot. 4.** a hotshot person or thing. **5.** a fireman; fire fighter. [HOT + SHOT[1]]

hot′ spot′, **1.** *Informal.* a nightclub. **2.** *Photog.* an area of a negative or print revealing excessive light on that part of the subject. **3.** a country or region where dangerous or difficult political situations exist or may erupt, esp. where a war, revolution, or a belligerent attitude toward other countries exists or may develop: *In the 1960's, Vietnam became a hot spot.* **4.** a section of forest or woods where fires frequently occur. **5.** an area hotter than the surrounding surface, as on the shell of a furnace.

hot-spot (hot′spot′), *v.t.,* **-spot·ted, -spot·ting.** to stop (a forest fire) at a hot spot. [v. use of HOT SPOT]

hot′ spring′, a thermal spring having waters warmer than 98°F. Cf. **warm spring.**

Hot′ Springs′, **1.** a city in central Arkansas: adjoining a national park (**Hot′ Springs′ Na′tional Park′**) noted for its thermal mineral springs. 28,337 (1960). **2.** a town in SW South Dakota. 4943 (1960). **3.** a resort village in W Virginia: site of international conference (forerunner of Food and Agriculture Organization of the United Nations) in 1943 to aid agricultural and food supply adjustments after World War II.

hot·spur (hot′spûr′), *n.* an impetuous person; a hothead. [after Sir Henry PERCY, to whom it was applied as a nickname] —**hot′spurred′**, *adj.*

hot′-stove′ league′ (hot′stōv′), devotees of a sport who meet for off-season talks.

hot′ stuff′, *Slang.* **1.** a person or thing of exceptional interest or merit. **2.** a person who is erotically stimulating or is easily aroused sexually. **3.** something unconventional, sensational, or daring: *This movie is hot stuff.*

hot′ switch′, *Radio and Television.* a rapid transfer from one point of origin to another during a broadcast.

hot·sy-tot·sy (hot′sē tot′sē), *adj. Facetious.* about as right as can be; perfect: *Everything is just hotsy-totsy.* [coined by Billie De Beck (d. 1942), American cartoonist]

hot′ tear′ (târ), *Metall.* a crack formed in hot metal during cooling, caused by an improper pouring temperature or undue restraint.

hot-tem·pered (hot′tem′pərd), *adj.* easily angered; short-tempered.

Hot·ten·tot (hot′ᵊn tot′), *n.* **1.** a member of a people of southern Africa related to the Bushmen and to various Negroid peoples. **2.** the speech of the Hottentots, consisting of two languages that belong to the Khoisan family of languages. —*adj.* **3.** of, pertaining to, or characteristic of the Hottentots or their language. [< D; the name is variously explained] —**Hot′ten·tot′ic**, *adj.*

Hot′tentot fig′, a prostrate or sprawling, perennial herb, *Mesembryanthemum edule*, of Africa, having a woody base, showy, yellow flowers about three inches wide, and fleshy, edible fruit.

Hot′tentot's bread′, **1.** elephant's-foot. **2.** the edible rhizome of this plant.

hot·ter[1] (hot′ər), *v.i. Scot. and North Eng.* **1.** to vibrate up and down; shake, totter, or rattle, as a plate on a shelf. **2.** to stammer. [< Flem *hotteren* to shake; akin to HOTCH]

hot·ter[2] (hot′ər), *adj.* comp. of **hot.**

hot′ type′, *Print.* See **hot metal.**

hot′ war′, open military conflict; armed conflict between nations: *The increasing tension of a cold war could lead to a hot war.*

hot′ wa′ter, *Informal.* trouble; a predicament: *His skipping classes will get him into real hot water when exam time comes.*

hot′-wa′ter bag′ (hot′wô′tər, -wot′ər), a bag, usually of rubber, for holding hot water to apply warmth to some part of the body, as the feet. Also called **hot′-wa′ter bot′tle.**

hot′ well′, a tank or reservoir in which hot water is collected before being recirculated, esp. condensed steam about to be returned to a boiler.

hot-work (hot′wûrk′), *v.t.* to work (metal) at a temperature high enough to permit recrystallization.

hou·ba·ra (ho͞o bär′ə), *n.* a bustard, *Chlamydotis undulata,* of northern Africa and western Asia, having long black and white plumes on each side of the neck. [< Ar *ḥubāra*]

hou·dah (hou′də), *n.* howdah.

Hou·dan (ho͞o′dan), *n.* one of a French breed of chickens having mottled black-and-white plumage. [after *Houdan,* village near Paris where these hens were bred]

Hou·di·ni (ho͞o dē′nē), *n.* **Harry** (*Erich Weiss*), 1874–1926, U.S. magician.

Hou·don (o͞o dôN′), *n.* **Jean An·toine** (zhäN äN twan′), 1741–1828, French sculptor.

hough (hok; *Scot.* hoKH), **—n. 1.** *Scot.* hock[1] (defs. 1, 2). **—v.t. 2.** *Scot.* to hamstring. **—v.i. 3.** *Brit. Dial. Obs.* to clear the throat; hack. [see HOCK[1]]

Hough (huf), *n.* **Emerson,** 1857–1923, U.S. novelist.

Hough·ton (hōt′ən), *n.* a town in NW Michigan, in the Upper Peninsula. 3393 (1960).

Houl·ton (hōl′tən, -tən), *n.* a town in E Maine. 5976 (1960).

Hou·ma (ho͞o′mə), *n.* a city in S Louisiana. 22,561 (1960).

hound[1] (hound), *n.* **1.** one of any of several breeds of dogs trained to pursue game either by sight or by scent, esp. one with a long face and large drooping ears. **2.** any dog. **3.** *Informal.* a mean, despicable fellow. **4.** *Informal.* an addict or devotee: *movie hound; autograph hound.* **5.** one of the pursuers in the game of hare and hounds. **6. follow the hounds,** *Fox Hunting.* to participate in a hunt, esp. as a member of the field. **7. ride to hounds,** *Fox Hunting.* to participate in a hunt, whether as a member of the field or of the hunt staff. **—v.t. 8.** to hunt or track with hounds, or as a hound does; pursue. **9.** to pursue or harass without respite: *She couldn't get her little brother to stop hounding her.* **10.** to incite (a hound) to pursuit or attack; urge on. **11.** *Informal.* to incite or urge (a person) to do something (usually fol. by *on*). [ME *h(o)und,* OE *hund;* c. D *hond,* Icel *hundr,* Dan, Sw *hund,* G *Hund,* Goth *hunds;* akin to L *canis,* Gk *kýōn* (gen. *kynós*), Skt *śvā́n* (gen. *śúnas*), OIr *cú* (gen. *con*); Welsh *ci* (pl. *cwn*), Tocharian A *kū*]—**hound′er,** *n.* —**hound′ish, hound′y,** *adj.* —**hound′like′,** *adj.* **—Syn. 8.** dog, follow, chase, trail. **9.** pester, annoy, persecute, bully.

hound[2] (hound), *n.* **1.** *Naut.* either of a pair of fore-and-aft members at the lower end of the head of a mast, for supporting the trestletrees, that support an upper mast at its heel. Cf. **cheek** (def. 10). **2.** a horizontal bar or brace, usually one of a pair, for strengthening the running gear of a horse-drawn wagon or the like. [ME *hūn* < Scand; cf. Icel *húnn* knob at the masthead]

hound′ dog′, *Southern U.S. Dial.* hound[1] (def. 1).

hound·fish (hound′fish′), *n., pl.* (*esp. collectively*) **-fish,** (*esp. referring to two or more kinds or species*) **-fish·es. 1.** dogfish (def. 1). **2.** a needlefish, esp. *Strongylura raphidoma.* [ME *houndfyssh.* See HOUND[1], FISH]

hound·ing (houn′ding), *n.* *Naut.* **1.** the portion of a lower mast between the cheeks or hounds and the deck. **2.** the portion of an upper mast between the cap of the mast below and the hounds above. **3.** the part of a bowsprit projecting beyond the stem. [HOUND[2] + -ING[1]]

hound's-tongue (houndz′tung′), *n.* **1.** a boraginaceous weed, *Cynoglossum officinale,* having prickly nutlets and tonguelike leaves. **2.** any other plant of the genus *Cynoglossum.* [ME; OE *hundestunge,* trans. of L *cynoglōssum* < Gk *kynóglōsson,* lit., dog-tongued object]

hound's′ tooth′, a pattern of broken or jagged checks, used on a variety of fabrics. Also called **hound's′-tooth check′.**

Hound's tooth

hound's-tooth (houndz′to͞oth′), *adj.* woven or printed with a pattern of broken or jagged checks: *a hound's-tooth coat.*

houn·skull (houn′skul′), *n.* *Armor.* a snoutlike, usually conical, visor attached to a basinet of the 14th century. [HOUND[1] + SKULL]

Hou·phouet-Boi·gny (*Fr.* o͞o fwā′bwä nyē′), *n.* **Fé·lix** (*Fr.* fā lēks′), born 1905, president of the Republic of the Ivory Coast since 1960.

houppe·lande (ho͞op′länd, -land), *n.* (in the Middle Ages) a robe or long tunic, belted or with a fitted bodice, usually having full trailing sleeves and often trimmed or lined with fur. Also, **houpe′lande.** [< F < ?]

hour (our, ou′ər), *n.* **1.** a period of time equal to 1/24th of a mean solar or civil day and equivalent to 60 minutes: *He slept for an hour.* **2.** any specific one of these 24 periods, usually reckoned in two series of 12, one series from midnight to noon and the second from noon to midnight, but sometimes reckoned in one series of 24, from midnight to midnight: *He slept for the hour between 2 and 3* A.M. *The hour for the bombardment was between 1300 and 1400.* **3.** any specific time of day; the time indicated by a timepiece: *What is the hour?* **4.** a short or limited period of time. **5.** a particular or appointed time: *What was the hour of death? What hour do you open?* **6.** a customary or usual time: *When is your dinner hour?* **7.** the present time: *the man of the hour.* **8. hours, a.** time spent in an office, factory, or the like, or for work, study, etc.: *The doctor's hours were from 10 to 4. What an employee does after hours is his own business.* **b.** customary time of going to bed and getting up: *to keep late hours.* **c.** (in the Christian church) the seven stated times of the day for prayer and devotion. **d.** the offices or services prescribed for these times. **e.** a book containing them. **9.** distance normally covered in an hour's traveling: *We live about an hour from the city.* **10.** *Astron.* **a.** a unit of measure of right ascension, etc., representing 15°, or the 24th part of a great circle. **b.** See **sidereal hour. 11.** *Educ.* **a.** a single period of class instruction, usually from 40 to 55 minutes. Cf. **clock-hour. b.** Also called **credit hour.** one unit of academic credit, usually representing attendance at one scheduled period of instruction per week throughout a semester, quarter, or term. **12. the Hours,** *Class. Myth.* the Horae. **13. one's hour, a.** Also, **one's last hour.** the instant of death: *The sick man knew that his hour had come.* **b.** any crucial moment. **—adj. 14.** of, pertaining to, or noting an hour. [ME (*h*)*oure* < AF; OF (*h*)*ore* < L *hōra* < Gk *hṓrā* time, season] —**hour′less,** *adj.*

hour′ an′gle, *Astron.* the angle, measured westward through 360°, between the celestial meridian of an observer and the hour circle of a celestial body. Cf. **sidereal hour angle.**

hour′ cir′cle, a great circle on the celestial sphere passing through the celestial poles and containing a point on the celestial sphere, as a star or the vernal equinox.

hour·glass (our′glas′, -gläs′, ou′ər-), *n.* **1.** an instrument for measuring time, consisting of two bulbs of glass joined by a narrow passage through which a quantity of sand or mercury runs in just an hour. **—adj. 2.** having a notably slim or narrow waist, midsection, or joining segment: *She has an hourglass figure.* [HOUR + GLASS]

Hourglass

hour′glass worm′, *Mach.* a worm having a concave outline following part of the circumference of its mating gear.

hour′ hand′, the hand that indicates the hours on a clock or watch.

hou·ri (ho͝or′ē, hour′ē), *n., pl.* **-ris.** one of the beautiful virgins provided in Paradise for all faithful Muslims. [< F < Pers *hūrī* < Ar *ḥūrīyah* gazelle-eyed (woman), lit., black-eyed like a gazelle]

hour·ly (our′lē, ou′ər-), *adj.* **1.** of, pertaining to, occurring, or done each successive hour. **2.** computed or totaled in terms of an hour; using an hour as a basic unit of reckoning. **3.** frequent; continual. **—adv. 4.** every hour; hour by hour. **5.** at each hour or during every hour. **6.** frequently; continually. [late ME; see HOUR, -LY]

Hou·sa·ton·ic (ho͞o′sə ton′ik), *n.* a river flowing S from NW Massachusetts through SW Connecticut to Long Island Sound near Stratford, Connecticut. 148 mi. long.

house (*n., adj.* hous; *v.* houz), *n., pl.* **hous·es** (hou′ziz), *v.,* **housed, hous·ing,** *adj.* **—n. 1.** a building in which people live; residence for human beings. **2.** a household. **3.** (*often cap.*) a family, including ancestors and descendants: *the great houses of France; the House of Hapsburg.* **4.** a building for any purpose: *a house of worship.* **5.** a theater, concert hall, or auditorium. **6.** the audience of a theater or the like. **7.** a place of shelter for an animal, bird, etc. **8.** the building in which a legislative or official deliberative body meets. **9.** (*cap.*) the body itself, esp. of a bicameral legislature: *the House of Representatives.* **10.** a quorum of such a body. **11.** (*often cap.*) a commercial establishment; business firm: *the House of Rothschild; a publishing house.* **12.** a gambling casino. **13.** the management of a commercial establishment or of a gambling casino: *rules of the house.* **14.** an advisory or deliberative group, esp. in church or college affairs. **15.** a college in an English type university. **16.** a residential hall in a college or school; dormitory. **17.** the members or residents of any such residential hall. **18.** *Informal.* a brothel; whorehouse. **19.** *Brit.* a variety of lotto or bingo played with paper and pencil, esp. by soldiers as a gambling game. **20.** Also called **parish.** *Curling.* the area enclosed by a circle 12 or 14 feet in diameter at each end of the rink, having the tee in the center. **21.** *Naut.* any enclosed shelter above the weather deck of a vessel: *bridge house; deck house.* **22.** *Astrol.* **a.** the sign of the zodiac in which a planet is felt to exert its greatest influence. **b.** one of the 12 divisions of the celestial sphere. **23. bring down the house,** *Informal.* to call forth vigorous applause from an audience; be highly successful: *The children's performances brought down the house.* **24. clean house,** to eliminate forcibly all undesirable elements: *The union finally decided it was time to clean house and regain its good reputation.* **25. dress the house,** *Theat.* **a.** to fill a theater with many people admitted on free passes. **b.** to arrange or space the seating of patrons in such a way as to make an audience appear larger or a theater or nightclub more crowded than it actually is. **26. keep house,** to maintain a home; manage a household: *She preferred staying home with her family and keeping house to continuing her career.* **27. like a house afire,** very quickly; with energy or enthusiasm: *She talks like a house afire.* **28. on the house,** as a gift from the management; free: *At the fashion show, orchid corsages for the ladies were on the house.* **29. put** or **set one's house in order, a.** to settle one's affairs. **b.** to improve one's behavior or correct one's faults: *It is easy to criticize others, but it would be better to put one's own house in order first.* **—v.t. 30.** to put or receive into a house, dwelling, or living quarters: *Over 200 students were housed in the dormitory.* **31.** to give shelter to; harbor; lodge: *to house flood victims in schools.* **32.** to provide with a place to work, study, or the like: *This office houses our executive staff.* **33.** to provide storage space for; be a receptacle for or repository of: *The library houses 600,000 books.* **34.** to remove from exposure; put in a safe place. **35.** *Naut.* **a.** to stow securely. **b.** to lower (an upper mast) and make secure, as alongside the lower mast. **c.** to heave (an anchor) home. **36.** *Carpentry.* **a.** to fit the end or edge of (a board or the like) into a gain, dado, or mortise. **b.** to form (a joint) between two pieces of wood by fitting the end or edge of one into a dado of the other. **—v.i. 37.** to take shelter; dwell. **—adj. 38.** of, pertaining to, or noting a house. **39.** for or suitable for a house: *house paint.* [ME *h(o)us,* OE *hūs;* c. D *huis,* LG *huus,* Icel *hūs,* G *Haus,* Goth *-hūs* (in *gudhūs* temple)] **—Syn. 1.** domicile. HOUSE, DWELLING, RESIDENCE, HOME are terms applied to a place to live in. DWELLING is now chiefly poetic, or used in legal or technical contexts, as in a lease or in the phrase *multiple dwelling.* RESIDENCE is characteristic of formal usage and often implies size and elegance of structure and surroundings: *the private residence of the king.* These two terms and HOUSE have always had reference to the structure to be lived in. HOME has recently taken on this meaning and become practically equivalent to HOUSE, the new meaning tending to crowd out the older connotations of family ties and domestic comfort. See **hotel. 11.** company, partnership.

House (hous), *n.* **Edward Man·dell** (man′dəl), ("*Colonel House*"), 1858–1938, U.S. diplomat.

house′ a′gent, *Brit.* **1.** a real-estate agent. **2.** a renting agent or a rent collector.

house′ arrest′, confinement of an arrested person to his residence or to a public place, as a hospital, instead of in a jail: *He was under house arrest until the day of his trial.*

house·boat (hous′bōt′), *n.* a flat-bottomed, bargelike boat fitted for use as a floating dwelling but not suited to rough water. [HOUSE + BOAT]

house·bound (hous′bound′), *adj.* restricted to the house. [HOUSE + -BOUND[1]]

house·boy (hous′boi′), *n.* houseman (def. 1). [HOUSE + BOY]

house·break (hous′brāk′), *v.t.,* **-broke, -brok·en, -break·ing.** to train (a pet) to avoid excreting indoors or to excrete in a specific place. [HOUSE + BREAK]

house·break·er (hous′brā′kər), *n.* **1.** one who breaks into and enters a house with a felonious intent. **2.** *Brit.* **a.** a wrecking company that or worker who demolishes houses and buildings, as to make room for new construction. **b.** a person who buys doors, paneled walls, etc., from standing houses, to sell as antiques; a person who dismantles a house of its valuable parts before it is torn down. [HOUSE + BREAKER] —**house′break′ing,** *n.*

house·bro·ken (hous′brō′kən), *adj.* (of a pet) trained to avoid excreting inside the house or in improper places: *a housebroken dog.* [HOUSE + BROKEN]

house′ car′, *Railroads.* any enclosed freight car.

house·carl (hous′kärl′), *n.* a member of the household troops or bodyguard of a Danish or early English king or noble. [late OE *hūscarl* < Dan *hūskarl.* See HOUSE, CARL]

house·clean (hous′klēn′), *v.t.* **1.** to subject (a house, room, etc.) to housecleaning. **—v.i. 2.** to engage in housecleaning. [back formation from HOUSECLEANING] —**house′clean′er,** *n.*

house·clean·ing (hous′klē′ning), *n.* **1.** the act of cleaning a house, room, etc., and its furnishings, esp. the act of cleaning thoroughly and completely. **2.** the act of improving or reforming by weeding out excess or corrupt personnel or of revising methods of operation. [HOUSE + CLEANING]

house·coat (hous′kōt′), *n.* a woman's long, tailored, one-piece, dresslike garment for casual wear about the house. [HOUSE + COAT]

house′ coun′sel, *Law.* a lawyer drawing a full-time salary from a corporation that he represents.

house′ crow′, a black and gray crow, *Corvus splendens,* of India.

house′ cur′tain. See **act curtain.**

house′ detec′tive, an employee of a department store, hotel, etc., engaged to prevent thefts, violations of regulations, or other forms of misconduct on the part of patrons.

house′ dick′, *Slang.* See **house detective.**

house·dress (hous′dres′), *n.* a relatively simple and inexpensive dress suitable for housework. [HOUSE + DRESS]

housed′ string′ (houzd), *Carpentry.* a string of a stair (**housed′ stair′**) receiving the ends of the risers or treads in a series of housings.

house·fa·ther (hous′fä′thər), *n.* a man responsible for a group of young people, as students, living in a dormitory, hostel, etc. [HOUSE + FATHER; cf. L *paterfamilias*]

house′ finch′, a small, common finch, *Carpodacus mexicanus,* of western North America and Mexico, the males of which have a red forehead, throat, breast, and rump.

house′ flag′, *Naut.* a flag flown by a merchant ship, bearing the emblem of its owners or operators.

house·fly (hous′flī′), *n., pl.* **-flies. 1.** a common dipterous insect, *Musca domestica,* found in nearly all parts of the world. **2.** any of several other widely distributed dipterous insects resembling the common housefly, as the stable fly. [HOUSE + FLY[2]]

Housefly, *Musca domestica* (Length ¼ in.)

house·ful (hous′fo͝ol′), *n., pl.* **-fuls.** as much or as many as a house will hold: *He had several housefuls of furniture.* [HOUSE + -FUL]

house′ fur′nishings, the furnishings of a household, as rugs, chairs, draperies, etc.

house·guest (hous′gest′), *n.* a person staying with a household as a guest for one night or longer. [HOUSE + GUEST]

house·hold (hous′hōld′, -ōld′), *n.* **1.** the people of a house collectively; a family including its servants. **—adj. 2.** of or pertaining to a household. **3.** for use in maintaining a home, esp. for use in cooking, cleaning, laundering, repairing, etc., in the home: *a household bleach.* **4.** common or usual; ordinary. [ME *houshold.* See HOUSE, HOLD[1]]

house′hold ammo′nia, diluted ammonia, often having a small quantity of detergent, used in the home for cleaning.

house′hold art′, any of the skills necessary to the efficient running of a household, as cooking or keeping a family budget.

house′hold cav′alry, (in Britain) cavalry units forming part of the ceremonial guard of the monarch.

house′hold effects′, privately owned goods, usually old or used, consisting chiefly of furniture, appliances, etc., for keeping house. Also called **house′hold goods′.** Cf. **personal effects.**

house·hold·er (hous′hōl′dər, -ōl′-), *n.* **1.** one who holds title to or occupies a house. **2.** the head of a family. [ME *housholdere.* See HOUSE, HOLDER] —**house′hold′er·ship′,** *n.*

house′hold troops′, troops guarding or attending a sovereign or his residence.

house′hold word′, a well-known phrase, name, saying, etc.; byword: *The advertising campaign is designed to make this new product a household word in every American home.*

house·hus·band (hous′huz′bənd), *n.* a man who is married to a working wife and who stays home to manage their household. [HOUSE + HUSBAND]

house·keep (hous′kēp′), *v.i.,* **-kept, -keep·ing.** to keep or maintain a house: *She has housekept for years.* [back formation from HOUSEKEEPING and HOUSEKEEPER]

house·keep·er (hous′kē′pər), *n.* **1.** a hired woman who does or directs the domestic work and planning necessary for a home, as buying food, cleaning, etc. **2.** a female employee of a hotel, hospital, etc., who supervises the cleaning staff. [late ME *howskepare.* See HOUSE, KEEPER] —**house′keep′er·like′,** *adj.*

house·keep·ing (hous′kē′piŋ), *n.* **1.** the maintenance of a house or domestic establishment. **2.** the management of household affairs. **3.** the management, care, and servicing of property and equipment of an industrial or commercial building or organization. [HOUSE + KEEPING]

hou·sel (hou′zəl), *n., v.,* **-seled, -sel·ing** or (*esp. Brit.*) **-selled, -sel·ling.** *Archaic.* —*n.* **1.** the Eucharist. **2.** the act of administering or receiving the Eucharist. —*v.t.* **3.** to administer the Eucharist to. [ME; OE *hūsl* the Eucharist, prob. orig. offering; c. Icel *hūsl,* Goth *hunsl* sacrifice, offering]

House·lan·der (hous′lən dər), *n.* **Car·yll** (kar′əl), 1901–54, English writer on Roman Catholicism.

house·leek (hous′lēk′), *n.* **1.** an Old World, crassulaceous herb, *Sempervivum tectorum,* having pink flowers and thick, succulent leaves, found growing on the roofs and walls of houses. **2.** any other plant of the genus *Sempervivum.* [late ME *howsleke.* See HOUSE, LEEK]

house·less (hous′lis), *adj.* **1.** without a house or houses. **2.** homeless. [ME *housles.* See HOUSE, -LESS] —**house′less·ness,** *n.*

house·lights (hous′līts′), *n.pl.* the lamps providing illumination of the auditorium or seating area of a theater before and after a performance. [HOUSE + LIGHT[1] + -S[3]]

house·line (hous′līn′), *n. Naut.* small stuff of three yarns of tarred hemp laid left-handed, used esp. for seizings. Also called **housing.** [HOUSE + LINE[1]]

house·maid (hous′mād′), *n.* a female servant employed in general domestic work in a home, esp. to do housework. [HOUSE + MAID] —**house′maid′y,** *adj.*

house′maid's knee′, *Pathol.* inflammation of the bursa over the anterior region of the kneepan.

house·man (hous′man′, -mən), *n., pl.* **-men** (-men′, -mən). **1.** a male servant who performs general duties in a home, hotel, etc. **2.** a man employed to maintain order; bouncer. **3.** See **house detective. 4.** one who represents the management in a gambling house. [HOUSE + MAN[1]]

house′ man′ager, a business manager responsible for managing a theater and its staff.

house′ mar′tin, a small, European swallow, *Chelidon urbica,* that builds its nest under the eaves of houses.

house·mas·ter (hous′mas′tər, -mä′stər), *n.* a man who is in charge of a house or a dormitory in a private school for boys. [HOUSE + MASTER] —**house′mas′ter·ship′,** *n.*

house·moth·er (hous′muth′ər), *n.* a woman in charge of a residence, esp. for children, students, or young women, who acts as hostess, chaperon, and occasionally as housekeeper. [HOUSE + MOTHER[1]] —**house′moth′er·ly,** *adj.*

house′ mouse′, a brownish-gray, Old World mouse, *Mus musculus,* now common in the U.S. in or near houses. See illus. under **mouse.**

house′ of assigna′tion, brothel.

House′ of Ber·nar′da Al′ba, The (ber när′də äl′bə), a drama (1941) by Federico García Lorca. Spanish, **La Casa de Bernarda Alba.**

House′ of Bur′gesses, the assembly of representatives in colonial Virginia.

house′ of cards′, a structure or plan that is insubstantial and subject to imminent collapse: *The scheme has become so overly complicated it is likely to prove to be just another house of cards.* Also called **cardcastle, cardhouse.**

House′ of Com′mons, the elective or lower house of the British Parliament.

house′ of correc′tion, a place for the confinement and reform of persons convicted of minor offenses and not regarded as confirmed criminals.

House′ of Coun′cilors, the upper house of the Japanese diet. Formerly, **House of Peers.**

House′ of Del′egates, the lower house of the General Assembly in Virginia, West Virginia, and Maryland.

house′ of deten′tion, 1. a place maintained by the civil authorities for persons charged with a crime, and sometimes for witnesses, awaiting trial. **2.** See **detention home.**

house′ of God′, a building devoted to religious worship; a church, temple, chapel, etc. Also called **house of worship, house of prayer.**

house′ of ill′ repute′, a house of prostitution; whorehouse; brothel. Also called **house′ of ill′ fame′.**

House′ of Keys′, the lower house of the legislature of the Isle of Man.

House′ of Lords′, the nonelective, upper house of the British Parliament, comprising the lords spiritual and lords temporal.

House′ of Peers′, former name of the Japanese House of Councilors.

house′ of prayer′ (prâr). See **house of God.**

house′ of prostitu′tion, brothel.

House′ of Represen′tatives, the lower legislative branch in many national and state bicameral governing bodies, as in the United States, Australia, Mexico, Japan, etc.

House′ of the Sev′en Ga′bles, The, a novel (1851) by Hawthorne.

house′ of wor′ship. See **house of God.**

house′ or′gan, a periodical issued by a business or other establishment primarily for its employees, presenting news of the activities of the firm, its executives, and employees.

house·par·ent (hous′pâr′ənt, -par′-), *n.* **1.** one of a married couple responsible for a group of young people, as students, living in a dormitory, hostel, etc., sometimes acting solely as an advisor, but often serving as host or hostess, chaperon, housekeeper, etc. **2.** a housemother or housefather. [HOUSE + PARENT]

house′ par′ty, 1. the entertainment of guests for one or more nights at one's home, a fraternity or sorority house, etc. **2.** the guests at such an affair or party: *The house party goes sailing today.*

house·phone (hous′fōn′), *n.* a telephone, as in a hotel or apartment house, that does not have a direct line to an exchange and whose calls are routed through the building's switchboard. [HOUSE + PHONE[1]]

house′ physi′cian, a resident physician in a hospital, hotel, or other public institution.

house′ place′, (in medieval architecture) a room common to all the inhabitants of a house, as a hall.

house·rais·ing (hous′rā′ziŋ), *n.* a gathering of persons in a rural community to help one of its members build a house.

house·room (hous′rōōm′, -rŏŏm′), *n.* lodging or accommodation in a house. [HOUSE + ROOM]

house·sit (hous′sit′), *v.t.,* **-sat, -sitting.** to take charge of a house while the owner is temporarily away. [HOUSE + SIT] —**house′ sit′ter.**

house′ slip′per, a slipper worn in the house or indoors, often distinguished from a bedroom slipper by having a back and heel.

house′ spar′row, a small, hardy, pugnacious weaverbird, *Passer domesticus,* of Europe, introduced into America, Australia, etc. Also called **English sparrow.**

house′ sur′geon, a surgeon who lives in a hospital in which he is on call.

house-to-house (hous′tə hous′), *adj.* **1.** conducted from one house to the next: *a house-to-house survey.* **2.** door-to-door (def. 1).

house·top (hous′top′), *n.* **1.** the top or roof of a house. **2. from the housetops,** publicly; generally: *You might as well shout it from the housetops as tell a secret to her.* [HOUSE + TOP[1]]

house′ track′, a railroad track running beside or into a building, for the receipt and delivery of freight.

house′ trail′er, a trailer fitted for use as a mobile home.

House′ Un-Amer′ican Activ′ities Commit′tee, an investigative committee of the U.S. House of Representatives. Originally created in 1938 to inquire into subversive activities in the U.S., it was commonly known at that time as the Dies Committee; it was abolished in 1975. *Abbr.:* HUAC

house·wares (hous′wârz′), *n.pl.* articles of household equipment, as kitchen utensils, glassware, etc. [HOUSE + WARE[1] + -S[3]]

house·warm·ing (hous′wôr′miŋ), *n.* a party to celebrate a person's or family's occupancy of a new house. [HOUSE + WARMING]

house·wife (hous′wīf′ or, *usually,* huz′if *for 2*), *n., pl.* **-wives** (-wīvz′), *v.* —*n.* **1.** the woman in charge of a household, esp. a wife who does all or most of the cleaning and cooking in her own household and who holds no other job. **2.** *Chiefly Brit.* a sewing box; a small case or box for needles, thread, etc. —*v.t., v.i.* **3.** *Rare.* to manage with efficiency and economy, as a household. [ME *hus(e)wif.* See HOUSE, WIFE]

house·wife·ly (hous′wīf′lē), *adj.* of, like, or befitting a housewife. [HOUSEWIFE + -LY] —**house′wife′liness,** *n.*

house·wif·er·y (hous′wī′fə rē, -wīf′rē), *n.* the function or work of a housewife; housekeeping. [late ME *huswyfery.* See HOUSEWIFE, -ERY]

house·work (hous′wûrk′), *n.* the work of cleaning, cooking, etc., to be done in housekeeping. [HOUSE + WORK]

house·wreck·er (hous′rek′ər), *n.* wrecker (def. 4). [HOUSE + WRECKER]

house′ wren′, a common, American wren, *Troglodytes aedon,* that nests around houses. See illus. under **wren.**

hous·y-hous·y (hou′sē hou′sē), *n. Brit. Informal.* house (def. 19).

hous·ing[1] (hou′ziŋ), *n.* **1.** any shelter, lodging, or dwelling place. **2.** houses collectively. **3.** the act of one who houses or puts under shelter. **4.** the providing of houses for a group or community: *the housing of an influx of laborers.* **5.** anything that covers or protects. **6.** *Mach.* a fully enclosed case and support for a mechanism. **7.** *Carpentry.* the space made in one piece of wood, or the like, for the insertion of another. **8.** *Naut.* **a.** Also called **bury.** the portion of a mast below the deck. **b.** Also called **bury.** the portion of a bowsprit abaft the forward part of the stem of a vessel. **c.** the doubling of an upper mast. **9.** a niche for a statue. [ME *husing.* See HOUSE, -ING[1]]

hous·ing[2] (hou′ziŋ), *n.* **1.** a covering of cloth for the back and flanks of a horse or other animal, for protection or ornament. **2.** Usually, **housings.** a caparison; trappings. [late ME *husynge,* equiv. to ME *hous* cloth cover (? < OF *houce* or special use of HOUSE) + *-ynge* -ING[1]]

hous·ing[3] (hou′ziŋ), *n.* houseline. [cf. D *huizing*]

Hous·man (hous′mən), *n.* **A(lfred) E(dward),** 1859–1936, English poet and classical scholar.

Hous·say (ōō sī′), *n.* **Ber·nar·do Al·ber·to** (ber när′thō äl ver′tō), 1887–1971, Argentine physiologist: Nobel prize for medicine 1947.

Hous·ton (hyōō′stən), *n.* **1. Sam(uel),** 1793–1863, U.S. soldier and political leader: president of the Republic of Texas 1836–38. **2.** a city in SE Texas: a port on a ship canal ab. 50 mi. from the Gulf of Mexico. 1,594,086. **3.** a town in central Mississippi. 2577 (1960).

hous·to·ni·a (hōō stō′nē ə), *n.* any North American, rubiaceous herb of the genus *Houstonia,* as *H. caerulea,* the common bluet or innocence. [named after Dr. W. *Houston* (d. 1733), British botanist; see -IA]

Hou·yhn·hnm (hōō in′əm, hwin′əm, win′-), *n.* (in Swift's *Gulliver's Travels*) one of a race of horses endowed with reason who rule the Yahoos, a race of degraded, brutish creatures having the form of man. [appar. alter. of WHINNY]

hove (hōv), *v.* pt. and pp. of **heave.**

hov·el (huv′əl, hov′-), *n., v.,* **-eled, -el·ing** or (*esp. Brit.*) **-elled, -el·ling.** —*n.* **1.** a small, mean dwelling house; a wretched hut. **2.** any dirty, disorganized dwelling. **3.** an open shed, as for sheltering cattle, tools, etc. —*v.t.* **4.** *Obs.* to shelter or lodge as in a hovel. [late ME *hovell* < ?]

ho·ven (hō′vən), *Vet. Pathol.* —*adj.* **1.** affected with bloat. —*n.* **2.** bloat (def. 5). [special use of ptp. of HEAVE]

hov·er (huv′ər, hov′-), *v.i.* **1.** to hang fluttering or suspended in the air: *The hawk hovered for a moment above its prey and then struck.* **2.** to keep lingering about; wait near at hand. **3.** to remain in an uncertain or irresolute state; waver: *to hover between life and death.* —*n.* **4.** the act or state of hovering. [ME *hoveren,* freq. of *hoven* to hover < ?] —**hov′er·er,** *n.* —**hov′er·ing·ly,** *adv.*
—**Syn. 1.** See **fly**[1].

Hov·er·craft (huv′ər kraft′, -kräft′), *n. Trademark.* a vehicle that can hover several feet above a relatively flat or even surface, as water, marshland, or smooth terrain, on a cushion of air provided by two or more large fans blowing downward from the chassis.

hov′ering ac′cent, *Pros.* indeterminacy as to which of two consecutive syllables in a line of verse bears the metrical stress, as in any of the first three feet of *Slow, slow, / fresh fount, / keep time / with my / salt tears.*

hov′ering act′, *Internat. Law.* **1.** an act forbidding or restricting the loitering of foreign or domestic vessels within the prescribed limits of a coastal nation. **2.** an act stipulating that foreign vessels may be boarded and their shipping manifests checked by the appropriate government officials beyond the three-mile limit of a coastal nation.

Hov·ey (huv′ē), *n.* **Richard,** 1864–1900, U.S. poet.

how[1] (hou), *adv.* **1.** in what way or manner; by what means?: *How did it happen?* **2.** to what extent, degree, etc.?: *How damaged is the car?* **3.** in what state or condition?: *How are you?* **4.** for what reason; why?: *How can you talk such nonsense?* **5.** to what effect; with what meaning?: *How is one to interpret his action?* **6.** what?: *How do you mean? If they don't have vanilla, how about chocolate?* **7.** (used as an intensifier): *How seldom I go there!* **8.** by what title or name?: *How does one address the president?* **9. and how!** *Informal.* certainly! you bet!: *Am I happy? And how!* **10. how come?** *Informal.* how is it that? why?: *How come you never visit us anymore?* **11. how so?** how does it happen to be so? why?: *You haven't any desire to go? How so?* —*conj.* **12.** the manner or way in which: *He couldn't figure out how to solve the problem.* **13.** about the manner, condition, or way in which: *I don't care how you leave your desk when you go. Be careful how you act.* **14.** in whatever manner or way; however: *You can travel how you please.* —*n.* **15.** a question concerning the way or manner in which something is done, achieved, etc.: *a child's unending whys and hows.* **16.** a way or manner of doing something: *to consider all the hows and wherefores.* **17.** a word formerly used in communications to represent the letter H. [ME *how, hu,* OE *hū;* c. OFris *hū, ho,* D *hoe;* akin to G *wie* (OHG *hweo*), Goth *hwaiwa*]

how[2] (hou), *n., adj. Scot. and North Eng.* howe.

How·ard (hou′ərd), *n.* **1. Catherine,** c1520–42, fifth wife of Henry VIII. **2. Sir Ebenezer,** 1850–1928, English town planner. **3. Henry.** See **Surrey, Henry Howard, Earl of. 4. Roy Wilson,** 1883–1964, U.S. editor and newspaper publisher. **5. Sidney (Coe)** (kō), 1891–1939, U.S. playwright and short-story writer. **6.** a boy's given name.

how·be·it (hou bē′it), *adv.* **1.** nevertheless. —*conj.* **2.** although. [ME *how be it* however it may be; parallel to ALBEIT]

how·dah (hou′də), *n.* (in the East Indies) a seat, commonly with a railing and a canopy, placed on the back of an elephant. Also, **houdah.** [< Hindi *haudah* < Ar *haudaj*]

how·die (hou′dē, ou′-; hō′dē, ō′dē), *n. Scot. and North Eng. Slang.* a midwife. Also, **howdy.** [?]

how′ do you do′, 1. (a conventional expression used in greeting a person or upon being introduced.) **2.** a greeting: *She smiled and gave him a how do you do fit for a king.*

how-do-you-do (hou′də yə dōō′), *n. Informal.* an awkward or unpleasant event or situation: *It's a fine how-do-you-do that they've refused to help us out.* Also, **how-de-do** (hou′dē dōō′).

how·dy[1] (hou′dē), *n., pl.* **-dies,** *interj. Chiefly Dial.* hello; how do you do (an expression of greeting). [from the phrase *how d(o) ye*]

how·dy[2] (hou′dē), *n., pl.* **-dies.** *Scot. and North Eng. Slang.* howdie.

howe (hou), *Scot. and North Eng.* —*n.* **1.** a hole. **2.** the hold of a ship. **3.** a hollow; dell. —*adj.* **4.** hollow. **5.** deep. Also, **how.** [ME (north and Scot), alter. of *holl;* see HOLLOW]

Howe (hou), *n.* **1. Elias,** 1819–67, U.S. inventor of the sewing machine. **2. Gordon** (*Gordie*), born 1928, U.S. ice hockey player, born in Canada. **3. Julia Ward,** 1819–1910, U.S. writer and reformer: author of the *Battle Hymn of the Republic* (wife of Samuel Gridley Howe). **4. Richard** (*Earl Howe*) ("*Black Dick*"), 1726–99, British admiral (brother of William Howe). **5. Samuel Grid·ley** (grid′lē), 1801–76, U.S. surgeon and humanitarian. **6. William, 5th Viscount,** 1729–1814, British general in the American Revolutionary War.

how·e'er (hou âr′), *adv., conj. Literary.* however.

how·el (hou′əl), *n.* a channel cut along the inside edge of a barrel stave to receive the barrelhead. [? < Dan *hövl* < MLG *hövel;* c. G *Hobel* kind of plane]

How·ell (hou′əl), *n.* **1.** a town in SE Michigan. 4861 (1960). **2.** a boy's given name.

How·ells (hou′əlz), *n.* **William Dean,** 1837–1920, U.S. author, critic, and editor.

Howe′ truss′, *Building Trades.* a truss having vertical members in tension and diagonal members in compression. See illus. under **truss.** [named after W. *How* (d. 1852), American inventor]

how·ev·er (hou ev′ər), *adv.* **1.** nevertheless; yet; on the other hand; in spite of that: *We have not yet won; however, we shall keep trying.* **2.** to whatever extent or degree; no matter how: *However much you spend, I will reimburse you.* **3.** in whatever manner: *We will allow you to travel however you please.* **4.** how; how under the circumstances: *However did you manage?* —*conj.* **5.** in whatever way, manner, or state: *Arrange your hours however you like.* [ME *hou-ever.* See HOW, EVER]
—**Syn. 1.** See **but**[1].

howff (houf, ouf; hōf, ōf), *Scot.* —*n.* **1.** an abode; a familiar shelter or resort. —*v.i.* **2.** to reside. **3.** to visit a familiar haunt. [?]

How·ie (hou′ē), *n.* a boy's given name, form of **Howard.**

how·itz·er (hou′it sər), *n. Ordn.* a cannon having a comparatively short barrel, used esp. for firing shells at a high angle of elevation, as for reaching a target behind cover, in a trench, etc. [earlier *hauwitzer* < D *houvietser* < G *Haubitze* (MHG *haufnitz* < Czech *houfnice* slingshot) + *-er* -ER[1]]

howl (houl), *v.i.* **1.** to utter a loud, prolonged, mournful cry, as that of a dog or wolf. **2.** to utter a similar cry in distress, pain, rage, etc.; wail. **3.** to make a sound like an animal howling: *The wind howls through the trees.* **4.** *Informal.* to go on a spree; enjoy oneself without restraint. —*v.t.* **5.** to utter with howls: *to howl the bad news.* **6.** to drive or force by howls (often fol. by *down*): *to howl down the opposition.* —*n.* **7.** the cry of a dog, wolf, etc. **8.** a cry or wail, as of pain, rage, protest, etc. **9.** a sound like wailing: *the howl of the wind.* **10.** a loud, scornful laugh or yell. **11.** something that causes a laugh or a scornful yell, as a joke or funny or embarrassing situation. [ME *hul(en), houle*; c. D *huilen*, G *heulen*, LG *hülen*, Dan *hyle*; with loss of *h*, Icel *ýla*]

How′land Is′land (hou′lənd), an island in the central Pacific, near the equator: U.S. aerological station and airfield. 1 sq. mi.

howl·er (hou′lər), *n.* **1.** one who or that which howls. **2.** Also called **howl′ing mon′key.** any of the large, prehensile-tailed tropical American monkeys of the genus *Alouatta*, the males of which make a howling noise. **3.** a mistake, esp. an embarrassing one in speech or writing, that evokes laughter; a humorous mistake or a funny blunder. [HOWL + -ER¹]

howl·et (hou′lit), *n.* *Brit. Dial.* an owl or owlet. [perh. < F *hulotte* wood-owl, perh. deriv. of MF *huler* to howl < Gmc; see HOWL]

howl·ing (hou′ling), *adj.* **1.** producing or uttering a howling noise: *a howling mob.* **2.** desolate, dismal, or dreary: *a howling wilderness.* **3.** *Informal.* very great; tremendous: *a howling success.* [HOWL + -ING²] —**howl′ing·ly,** *adv.*

How·rah (hou′rä), *n.* a city in E India, on the Hooghly River opposite Calcutta. 512,600 (1961).

how·so·ev·er (hou′sō ev′ər), *adv.* **1.** to whatsoever extent or degree. **2.** in whatsoever manner.

how-to (hou′to͞o′), *adj.* giving basic instructions and directions to the layman on the methods for doing or making something as a hobby or for practical use, as in carpentry, housepainting, furniture building, or a similar craft: *a how-to book.* [by shortening]

Hox·ha (hô′jä), *n.* **En·ver** (en′vər), born 1908, Albanian political leader: premier 1944–54.

hoy¹ (hoi), *n.* *Naut.* **1.** a heavy barge used in harbors. **2.** a vessel of the 17th and 18th centuries, usually sloop-rigged, used for fishing and coastal trading. [late ME *hoy(e)* < MD *hoei*]

hoy² (hoi), *interj.* **1.** (used as an exclamation to attract attention.) —*n.* **2.** a shout or hail. [ME; var. of HEY¹]

hoy·den (hoid′ən), *n.* **1.** a boisterous, ill-bred girl; a tomboy. —*adj.* **2.** boisterous; rude. Also, **hoiden.** [? < MD *heyden* boor; c. HEATHEN] —**hoy′den·ish,** *adj.* —**hoy′den·ish·ness,** *n.* —**hoy′den·ism,** *n.*

Hoyle (hoil), *n.* **1. Edmond,** 1672–1769, English authority and writer on card games. **2. according to Hoyle,** according to the rules or to the authority; correctly.

Hoyt′ Lakes′, a town in NE Minnesota. 3186 (1960).

hp, horsepower. Also, **HP**

H.P., **1.** *Elect.* high power. **2.** high pressure. **3.** high priest. **4.** horsepower. Also, **h.p.**

H.Q., headquarters. Also, **h.q., HQ.**

Hr., Herr.

hr., hour; hours. Also, **h.**

H.R., House of Representatives.

Hra·dec Krá·lo·vé (hrä′dets krä′lô ve), a town in the N Czech Republic, on the Elbe River: Austrians defeated by Prussians in Battle of Sadowa 1866. 95,588. German, **Königgrätz.**

Hr·dlič·ka (hûrd′lich kə; *Czech.* hr′dlich kä), *n.* **A·leš** (ä′lesh), 1869–1943, U.S. anthropologist, born in Czechoslovakia.

Hreid·mar (hrād′mär), *n.* (in the *Volsunga Saga*) the father of Fafnir, Otter, and Regin: he demanded wergild from the gods for killing Otter, and was killed by Fafnir when he got it.

H. Rept., House report.

H. Res., House resolution.

H.R.H., **1.** His Royal Highness. **2.** Her Royal Highness.

H.R.I.P., here rests in peace. [< L *hīc requiescit in pace*]

Hrolf (hrolf), *n.* Rollo (def. 1).

Hroz·ný (hrôz′nē), *n.* **Frie·drich** (*Germ.* frē′drikh) or **Be·dřich** (*Czech.* be′drzhikh), 1879–1952, Czech archaeologist and orientalist.

hrs., hours.

Hr·vat·ska (khr′vät skä), *n.* Serbo-Croatian name of **Croatia.**

H.S., **1.** High School. **2.** *Brit.* Home Secretary.

h.s., **1.** in this sense. [< L *hōc sensū*] **2.** (in prescriptions) at bedtime. [< L *hōrā somnī* at the hour of sleep]

H.S.H., **1.** His Serene Highness. **2.** Her Serene Highness.

Hsia (shyä), *n.* a legendary dynasty in China, the traditional dates of which are 2205–1766 B.C.

hsien (shyun), *n., pl.* **hsien.** (in popular Chinese religion) one of a group of benevolent spirits promoting good in the world. [< Chin: fairy, immortal]

Hsing·an (shing′än′), *n.* a former province in Manchuria, in NE China.

hsing shêng (shing′ shung′), the process by which many Chinese characters were formed through the combination of two symbols, one phonographic and one logographic, into a single character. [< Chin, equiv. to *hsing* form, figure + *shêng* sound, voice]

Hsin Hsüeh (shen′ shye′), *Chinese.* See **School of Mind.**

Hsi·ning (shē′ning′), *n.* Sining.

Hsin·king (shin′jing′), *n.* Changchun.

H.S.M., **1.** His Serene Majesty. **2.** Her Serene Majesty.

H-steel (āch′stēl′), *n.* a steel made to meet certain requirements for hardening rather than for specific chemical composition.

H-stretch·er (āch′strech′ər), *n.* *Furniture.* a stretcher having the form of an H.

Hsüan Chiao (shyän′ jyou′), Taoism (def. 2).

Hsüan Tsung (shyän′ dzo͝ong′), A.D. 685–762, Chinese emperor of the Tang dynasty 712–756.

Hsüan T'ung (shyän′ do͝ong′). See **Pu-yi, Henry.**

ht., height.

Hts., Heights (used in place names).

HUAC (hyo͞o′ak). See **House Un-American Activities Committee.**

Hua Kuo-feng (hwä′ kwō′fung′), born 1920?, Chinese communist leader: chairman of the Chinese Communist party and premier 1976–81.

Huam·bo (*Port.* wäm′bô), *n.* former name of **Nova Lisboa.**

hua·mu·chil (wä mo͞o′chil), *n.* guamachil.

Huang Ti (hwäng′ dē′), the legendary first emperor of China. Also called **Yellow Emperor.**

Huá·nu·co (wä′no͞o kō′), *n.* a city in central Peru. 15,180 (1951).

hua·pan·go (wə päng′gō, -pang′-; *Sp.* wä päng′gô), *n., pl.* **-gos** (-gōz; *Sp.* -gôs). a fast, rhythmic dance of Mexico, performed by couples. [< MexSp, after *Huapango*, Mexico where this type of dance originated]

hua·ra·che (wə rä′chē; *Sp.* wä rä′che), *n., pl.* **-ches** (-chēz; *Sp.* -ches). a Mexican sandal having the upper woven of leather strips. [< MexSp]

hua·ra·cho (wə rä′chō; *Sp.* wä rä′chô), *n., pl.* **-chos** (-chōz; *Sp.* -chôs). huarache.

Huás·car (wäs′kär), *n.* 1495?–1533, Inca prince of Peru (half brother of Atahualpa; son of Huayna Capac).

Huas·ca·ran (wäs′kä rän′), *n.* a mountain in W Peru, in the Andes. 22,205 ft.

Huas·tec (wäs′tek), *n., pl.* **-tecs,** (*esp. collectively*) **-tec.** **1.** a member of an Indian people of Mexico. **2.** a Mayan language, the language of the Huastecs. —**Haus·tec′an,** *adj.*

Huay·na Ca·pac (wī′nä kä′päk), c1450–1527?, Inca ruler of Peru 1493?–1527? (father of Atahualpa and Huascar). Also, **Huai′na Ca′pac.**

hub (hub), *n., v.,* **hubbed, hub·bing.** —*n.* **1.** the central part of a wheel, as that part into which the spokes are inserted. **2.** the central part or axle end from which blades or spokelike parts radiate on various devices, as on a fan or propeller. **3.** the part in central position around which all else revolves; a center of activity, authority, commerce, etc.: *the hub of one's social life; the hub of the universe.* **4. the Hub,** Boston, Massachusetts (used as a nickname). **5.** the peg or hob used as a target in quoits and similar games. **6.** any one of the holes in an electrical panel, into which connections may be plugged. **7.** *Coining.* a design of hardened steel in relief, used as a punch in making a die. **8.** *Survey.* a stake bearing a tack used to mark a theodolite position. **9.** *Metalworking.* a die forced into a metal blank. —*v.t.* **10.** *Metalworking.* to stamp (a metal blank) with a hub. [? var. of HOB¹]

hub·ba hub·ba (hub′ə hub′ə), *Slang.* (an exclamation of approval or enthusiasm, used esp. by G.I.'s of World War II in appreciation of a pretty girl.) [?]

Hub·bard (hub′ərd), *n.* **1. Elbert Green,** 1856–1915, U.S. author, editor, and printer. **2.** a town in NE Ohio. 7137 (1960).

Hub′bard squash′, **1.** a variety of winter squash having a green or yellow skin and yellow flesh. **2.** the plant bearing this fruit. [after the surname *Hubbard*]

hub·ble (hub′əl), *n.* **1.** a small hump, as on the surface of ice or a road. **2.** *Scot. and North Eng.* **a.** a heap; pile. **b.** a tumult; hubbub; uproar. [appar. short for *hubble-show*, alter. of *hubble-shubble* < MFlem *hobbelsobbel* confusedly, in an uproar]

hub·ble-bub·ble (hub′əl bub′əl), *n.* **1.** an elementary form of the hookah, in which the smoke passes through water, causing a bubbling sound. **2.** a bubbling sound. **3.** an uproar; turmoil. [rhyming compound based on BUBBLE]

hub·bly (hub′lē), *adj.* of uneven surface; rough: *hubbly ice; a hubbly road.* [? HUB (in the sense of protuberance) + -LY; c. D *hobbelig* rugged]

hub·bob (hə bob′), *n.* haboob.

hub·bub¹ (hub′ub), *n.* **1.** a loud, confused noise, as of many voices: *There was quite a hubbub in the auditorium after the announcement.* **2.** tumult; uproar. [appar. of Ir orig.; akin to ScotGael cry *ubub!* (redupl. of *ub!*) expressing aversion or contempt]
—**Syn. 1.** See **noise. 2.** disturbance, disorder, confusion. —**Ant. 1.** quiet. **2.** calm.

hub·bub² (hə bub′), *n.* haboob.

hub·by (hub′ē), *n., pl.* **-bies.** *Informal.* husband. [by shortening; see -Y²]

Hu·bert (hyo͞o′bərt), *n.* a boy's given name. Also, **Hobart.**

Hu·ber·tus·burg (ho͞o ber′təs bo͝orkh′), *n.* a castle in S East Germany, in the former province of Saxony, E of Leipzig: treaty ending the Seven Years' War signed here 1763.

hu·bris (hyo͞o′bris, ho͞o′-), *n.* excessive pride or self-confidence; arrogance. Also, **hybris.** —**hu·bris′tic,** *adj.* Cf. **sophrosyne.** [< Gk: insolence]

huck·a·back (huk′ə bak′), *n.* toweling of linen or cotton, of a distinctive absorbent weave. Also called **huck.** [?]

huck·le·ber·ry (huk′əl ber′ē), *n., pl.* **-ries,** *adj.* —*n.* **1.** the dark-blue or black, edible berry of any of various ericaceous shrubs of the genus *Gaylussacia.* **2.** the shrub itself. **3.** blueberry (def. 1). —*adj.* **4.** made with or containing huckleberries: *huckleberry pie.* [dial. var. of *hurtle-berry;* see WHORTLEBERRY]

Huck′leberry Finn′ (fin), (*The Adventures of Huckleberry Finn*) a novel (1884) by Mark Twain.

huck·ster (huk′stər), *n.* **1.** a retailer of small articles; hawker. **2.** a street peddler in fruits and vegetables. **3.** one who employs showy methods to effect a sale, win votes, etc.: *the crass methods of political hucksters.* **4.** a cheaply mercenary person. **5.** *Informal.* **a.** a persuasive and aggressive salesman. **b.** a person who works in the advertising industry, esp. one who prepares aggressive advertising for radio and television. —*v.t., v.i.* **6.** to deal, as in small articles or to make petty bargains: *to huckster fresh corn; huckster for a living.* Also, *referring to a woman,* **huck·ster·ess** (huk′stər is), **huck·stress** (huk′stris). [early ME *huccstere* (? c. MD *hokester*), equiv. to *hucc-* haggle, bargain (c. dial. G *hucken* to huckster) + *-stere* -STER] —**huck′ster·ism,** *n.*

huck·ster·er (huk′stər ər), *n.* *Archaic.* huckster.

Hud (hud), *n.* a boy's given name.

HUD (hud), *n.* Department of Housing and Urban Development.

Hud·ders·field (hud′ərz fēld′), *n.* a town in SW Yorkshire, in N England. 130,307 (1961).

hud·dle (hud′əl), *v.,* **-dled, -dling,** *n.* —*v.t.* **1.** to heap or crowd together closely. **2.** to draw (oneself) closely together, as in crouching; nestle (often fol. by *up*). **3.** *Chiefly Brit.* to do hastily and carelessly (often fol. by *up, over,* or *together*): *The novel appeared to have been huddled together.* **4.** to put on (clothes) with careless haste (often fol. by *on*). —*v.i.* **5.** to gather or crowd together in a close mass. **6.** *Football.* to get together in a huddle. **7.** to confer or consult; meet to discuss, exchange ideas, or make a decision. **8.** to crouch, curl up, or draw oneself together. —*n.* **9.** a closely gathered group, mass, or heap; bunch. **10.** confusion or disorder. **11.** a conference, or consultation, esp. a private meeting to discuss serious matters: *The delegates have been in a huddle for two hours.* **12.** *Football.* a gathering of the offensive team in a close circle behind the line of scrimmage for instructions, signals, etc., from the team captain or quarterback, usually held before each offensive play. [*hud-* (weak grade of root found in HIDE¹) + -LE; r. ME *hoder*, equiv. to *hod-* (c. *hud-*) + *-er* -ER⁶] —**hud′dler,** *n.* —**hud′dling·ly,** *adv.*

Hu·di·bras·tic (hyo͞o′də bras′tik), *adj.* **1.** of, pertaining to, or resembling the style of Samuel Butler's *Hudibras* (published 1663–78), a mock-heroic poem written in tetrameter couplets. **2.** of a playful burlesque style. —*n.* **3.** a Hudibrastic couplet or stanza. [*Hudibras* + -TIC] —**Hu′di·bras′ti·cal·ly,** *adv.*

Hud·son (hud′sən), *n.* **1. Henry,** died 1611?, English navigator and explorer. **2. William Henry,** 1841–1922, English naturalist and author. **3.** a river in E New York, flowing S to New York Bay. 306 mi. long. **4.** a town in central Massachusetts. 7897 (1960). **5.** a town in W Wisconsin. 4325 (1960). **6.** a town in S New Hampshire. 3651 (1960). **7.** a town in SE Michigan. 2546 (1960). **8.** a steam locomotive having a four-wheeled front truck, six driving wheels, and a four-wheeled rear truck. **9.** a boy's given name.

Hud′son Bay′, a large inland sea in N Canada. 850 mi. long; 600 mi. wide; 400,000 sq. mi.

Hud′son Falls′, a town in E New York. 7752 (1960).

Hud·so′ni·an cur′lew (hud sō′nē ən). See under **godwit.** [after HUDSON BAY; see -IAN]

Hud′son Riv′er School′, *Fine Arts.* a group of American painters of the mid-19th century whose works were characterized by a highly romantic treatment of landscape.

Hud′son's Bay′ blan′ket, a heavyweight, striped blanket made of wool.

Hud′son's Bay′ Com′pany, a company chartered in England in 1670 to carry on fur trading with the Indians in North America.

Hud′son seal′, muskrat fur that has been plucked and dyed to give the appearance of seal.

Hud′son Strait′, a strait connecting Hudson Bay and the Atlantic. 450 mi. long; 100 mi. wide.

Hud·son·ville (hud′sən vil′), *n.* a town in SW Michigan. 2649 (1960).

hue¹ (hyo͞o), *n.* **1.** the property of light by which the color of an object is classified as red, blue, green, or yellow in reference to the spectrum. **2.** a gradation or variety of a color; tint: *pale hues.* **3.** color: *all the hues of the rainbow.* **4.** *Obs.* form or appearance. **5.** *Obs.* complexion. [ME *hewe*, OE *hīw* form, appearance, color; c. Icel *hý* bird's down, Sw *hy* skin, complexion, Goth *hiwi* form, appearance] —**hue′less,** *adj.*

hue² (hyo͞o), *n.* outcry, as of pursuers; clamor. [ME *hu(e)* < MF: a hoot, outcry (whence *huer* to hoot, cry out)]

Hué (hwā), *n.* a seaport in central Vietnam: former capital of Annam. 103,900 (est. 1963).

hue′ and cry′, **1.** *Early Eng. Law.* the pursuit of a felon or an offender with loud outcries or clamor to give an alarm. **2.** any public clamor, protest, or alarm: *When the tax increase was announced, there was a general hue and cry.* [< AF *hu et cri.* See HUE², CRY]

hued (hyo͞od), *adj.* having the hue or color as specified (usually used in combination): *many-hued; golden-hued.* [ME *hewed*, OE *(ge)hīwod.* See HUE¹, -ED³]

Huel·va (wel′vä), *n.* a seaport in SW Spain, near the Gulf of Cádiz. 77,231 (est. 1963).

hue·mul (wā mo͞ol′), *n.* any of several yellowish-brown deer of the genus *Hippocamelus*, found in mountainous regions of South America. Also called **Andean deer, guemal.** [< AmerSp *güemul* < Araucanian *huemul*]

Huer·ta (wer′tə; *Sp.* wer′tä), *n.* **Vic·to·ria·no** (bēk′tô ryä′nô), 1854–1916, Mexican general: provisional president of Mexico 1913–14.

Hu·ey (hyo͞o′ē), *n.* a boy's given name, form of **Hugh.** Also, **Hughie.**

Hu·ey·town (hyo͞o′ē toun′), *n.* a town in central Alabama. 5997 (1960).

huff (huf), *n.* **1.** a mood of sulking anger; a fit of resentment: *He never handles disagreement logically, but always leaves in a huff.* —*v.t.* **2.** to give offense to; make angry. **3.** to treat with arrogance or contempt; bluster at; hector or bully. **4.** *Checkers.* to remove (a piece) from the board as a penalty for failing to make a compulsory capture. —*v.i.* **5.** to take offense; speak indignantly. **6.** to puff or blow; breathe heavily. **7.** *Archaic.* to swell with pride or arrogance; swagger or bluster. [imit.; see PUFF]
—**Syn. 1.** temper, passion.

huff-duff (huf′duf′), *n.* *Slang.* a device for finding and indicating the direction of the source of a high-frequency radio wave. [rhyming compound based on HUFF]

huff·ish (huf′ish), *adj.* **1.** peevish; irritable. **2.** swaggering; insolent; bullying. [HUFF + -ISH¹] —**huff′ish·ly,** *adv.* —**huff′ish·ness,** *n.*

huff·y (huf′ē), *adj.,* **huff·i·er, huff·i·est.** **1.** easily offended or touchy. **2.** offended; sulky: *a huffy mood.* [HUFF + Y¹] —**huff′i·ly,** *adv.* —**huff′i·ness,** *n.*

Hu·fuf (ho͞o fo͞of′), *n.* Hofuf.

hug (hug), *v.,* **hugged, hug·ging,** *n.* —*v.t.* **1.** to clasp tightly in the arms, esp. with affection; embrace. **2.** to cling firmly or fondly to; cherish: *to hug an opinion.* **3.** to keep close to, as in sailing, walking, moving in a direction, etc.: *to hug the shore; to hug the road.* —*v.i.* **4.** to cling together; lie close. —*n.* **5.** a tight clasp with the arms; embrace. [? < Scand; cf. Icel *hugga* to soothe, console; akin to OE *hogian* to care for] —**hug′ger,** *n.* —**hug′ging·ly,** *adv.*

huge (hyo͞oj *or often,* yo͞oj), *adj.,* **hug·er, hug·est.** **1.** extraordinarily large in bulk, quantity, or extent: *a huge ship; a huge portion of ice cream.* **2.** of unbounded extent, scope, or character; limitless. [ME *huge, hoge* < OF *ahuge, ahoge* enormous, equiv. to *a-* A-⁵ + *hoge* height

CONCISE ETYMOLOGY KEY: <, descended or derived from; >, whence; b., blend of, blended; c., cognate with; deriv., derivative; equiv., equivalent; imit., imitative; m., modification of; obl., oblique; r., replacing; s., stem; sp., spelling; translation; ?, origin unknown, perhaps; *, hypothetical. See the full key inside the front cover.

< Gmc; cf. Icel *haugr* hill, akin to HIGH] —**huge′ly,** *adv.* —**huge′ness,** *n.*

—**Syn. 1.** mammoth, gigantic, colossal; vast; stupendous; bulky. HUGE, ENORMOUS, IMMENSE, TREMENDOUS imply great magnitude. HUGE, when used of concrete objects, usually adds the idea of massiveness, bulkiness, or even shapelessness: *a huge mass of rock; a huge collection of antiques.* ENORMOUS, literally out of the norm, applies to what exceeds in extent, magnitude, or degree, a norm or standard: *an enormous iceberg; enormous curiosity.* TREMENDOUS, in informal use, applies to anything so huge as to be astonishing or to inspire awe: *a tremendous amount of equipment.* IMMENSE, literally not measurable, is particularly applicable to what is exceedingly great, without reference to a standard: *immense buildings.* All are used figuratively: *a huge success; enormous curiosity; tremendous effort; immense joy.* —**Ant. 1.** small, tiny, diminutive.

Hü·gel (hyo͞o′gəl), *n.* **Baron Friedrich von,** 1852–1925, English theologian and writer.

huge·ous (hyo͞o′jəs *or, often,* yo͞o′-), *adj.* huge. [HUGE + -OUS] —**huge′ous·ly,** *adv.* —**huge′ous·ness,** *n.*

hug·ga·ble (hug′ə bəl), *adj.* evoking a desire to hug close; inviting a close embrace; cuddly: *a huggable little girl.* [HUG + -ABLE]

hug·ger-mug·ger (hug′ər mug′ər), *n.* **1.** disorder or confusion; muddle. **2.** secrecy; reticence: *Why is there such hugger-mugger about the scheme?* —*adj.* **3.** secret or clandestine. **4.** disorderly or confused. —*v.t.* **5.** to keep secret or concealed; hush up: *to hugger-mugger an execution.* —*v.i.* **6.** to act secretly; take secret counsel. [earlier *hucker-mucker,* rhyming compound based on *mucker,* ME *mokere* to hoard]

hug·ger-mug·ger·y (hug′ər mug′ə rē), *n., pl.* **-ger·ies.** hugger-mugger (defs. 1, 2). [HUGGER-MUGGER + -Y³]

Hug·gins (hug′inz), *n.* a walled plain in the third quadrant of the face of the moon: about 42 miles in diameter.

Hugh (hyo͞o), *n.* a boy's given name.

Hugh Ca·pet (hyo͞o kā′pit, kap′it, ka pā′). See **Capet, Hugh.**

Hughes (hyo͞oz), *n.* **1. Charles Evans,** 1862–1948, U.S. jurist and statesman: Chief Justice of the U.S. 1930–41. **2. Howard (Ro·bard)** (rō′bärd), 1905–76, U.S. businessman, motion-picture producer, and aviator. **3. (John) Lang·ston** (lang′stən), 1902–67, U.S. novelist and poet. **4. Rupert,** 1872–1956, U.S. novelist and biographer. **5. Thomas,** 1822–96, English novelist, reformer, and jurist. **6. William Morris,** 1864–1952, Australian statesman, born in Wales: prime minister 1915–23.

Hugh·ie (hyo͞o′ē), *n.* a boy's given name, form of **Hugh.** Also, **Huey.**

Hu·gi (hyo͞o′gē, ho͞o′-), *n.* *Scand. Myth.* a young man, a personification of thought, who defeated Thialfi in a race.

Hu·gin (ho͞o′gin), *n.* *Scand. Myth.* one of the two ravens of Odin that brought him news from the whole world: later regarded as personifying thought. Cf. **Munin.**

Hug·li (ho͞og′lē), *n.* Hooghly.

hug-me-tight (hug′mē tīt′), *n.* a woman's short, warm, close-fitting jacket, usually knitted or crocheted and often sleeveless.

Hu·go (hyo͞o′gō; *for 1 also Fr.* Y gō′), *n.* **1. Vic·tor (Ma·rie, Viscount)** (vik′tər mə rē′; *Fr.* vēk tôʀ′ mA-ʀē′), 1802–85, French poet, novelist, and dramatist. **2.** a town in SE Oklahoma. 6287 (1960). **3.** a boy's given name.

Hu′go rose′, a showy shrub, *Rosa hugonis,* of China, having solitary, yellow flowers nearly two inches wide. Also called **Father Hugo's rose.** [named after Father *Hugo,* 19th-century missionary who introduced it to the West]

Hu·go·ton (hyo͞o′gō tᵊn, -tən), *n.* a town in SW Kansas. 2912 (1960).

Hu·gue·not (hyo͞o′gə not′), *n.* a member of the Reformed or Calvinistic communion of France in the 16th and 17th centuries; a French Protestant. [< F, perh. b. *Hugues* (name of a political leader in Geneva) and *eidgenot,* back formation from *eidgenots,* Swiss var. of G *Eidgenoss* confederate, lit., oath comrade] —**Hu′-gue·not′ic,** *adj.* —**Hu′gue·not·ism,** *n.*

huh (hu), *interj.* (used as an exclamation of surprise, bewilderment, disbelief, contempt, or the like.)

hu·ia (ho͞o′yə), *n.* an apparently extinct, crowlike bird, *Heteralocha acutirostris,* of New Zealand, noted for the completely different bill shapes of the male and female. [< Maori]

huic (hīk), *interj.* *Fox Hunting.* (used as a cry by the huntsman to encourage the hounds.)

Hui·chou (wē′jō′), *n.* Waichow.

Hui·do·bro (wē tħō′vrō), *n.* **Vi·cen·te** (bē sen′te), 1893–1948, Chilean poet.

Hui·la (wē′lä), *n.* **Mount,** a volcano in central Colombia. 18,700 ft.

huile (wēl), *n.* *French.* oil.

hui·sa·che (wē sä′chē), *n.* a tropical and subtropical shrub, *Acacia farnesiana,* having fragrant, deep-yellow flower heads. Also called **cassie, popinac, sponge tree.** [< MexSp < Nahuatl *huixachi,* equiv. to *hui(tztli)* thorn + *i(zachi)* full of]

Huis Clos (*Fr.* wē klō′). See **No Exit.**

Hui-tsung (hwē′dzo͝ong′), *n.* 1082–1135, emperor of China 1101–26: painter and patron of art.

Hui·tzi·lo·poch·tli (wē′tsē lō pōch′tlē), *n.* Uitzilopochtli.

hu′la hoop′, a tubular plastic hoop, about four feet in diameter, for rotating about the body by swinging the hips, used for physical exercise or in children's play: a craze of the 1950's.

hu·la-hu·la (ho͞o′lə ho͞o′lə), *n.* a sinuous Hawaiian native dance with intricate arm movements which tell a story in pantomime, usually danced to rhythmic drumming and accompanied by chanting. Also called **hu′la.** [< Hawaiian]

hu′la skirt′, **1.** a skirt made of long stems of grass bound to a waistband, worn typically by a hula-hula dancer. **2.** a similar skirt made of any material.

hulk (hulk), *n.* **1.** the body of an old or dismantled ship. **2.** a vessel specially built to serve as a storehouse, prison, etc., and not for sea service. **3.** *Disparaging.* a clumsy-looking or unwieldy ship or boat. **4.** a bulky or unwieldy person, object, or mass. **5.** the shell of a wrecked, burned-out, or abandoned vehicle, building, or the like. —*v.i.* **6.** to loom in bulky form; appear as a large, massive bulk: (often fol. by *up*): *The bus hulked up suddenly over the crest of the hill.* **7.** *Brit. Dial.* to lounge, slouch, or move in a heavy, loutish manner. [ME *hulke,* OE *hulc;* ? < ML *hulcus* < Gk *holkás* trading vessel, orig. towed ship, akin to *hélkein* to drag]

hulk·ing (hul′king), *adj.* bulky; heavy and clumsy. [HULK + -ING²]

hulk·y (hul′kē), *adj.,* **hulk·i·er, hulk·i·est.** hulking. [HULK + -Y¹]

hull¹ (hul), *n.* **1.** the husk, shell, or outer covering of a seed or fruit, as of a nut. **2.** the calyx of certain fruits, as the strawberry and raspberry. **3.** any covering or envelope. —*v.t.* **4.** to remove the hull of. [ME; OE *hulu* husk, pod; akin to OE *helan* to cover, hide, L *celāre* to hide, Gk *kalýptein* to cover up. See HALL, HELL, HOLE] —**hull′er,** *n.*

hull² (hul), *n.* **1.** *Naut.* the hollow, lowermost portion of a vessel, floating partially immersed in the water and supporting the remainder of the vessel. **2.** *Aeron.* **a.** the boatlike fuselage of a flying boat on which the plane lands or takes off. **b.** the cigar-shaped arrangement of girders enclosing the gasbag of a rigid dirigible. **3. hull down,** *Naut.* (of a vessel) sufficiently far away, or below the horizon, that the hull is invisible. **4. hull up,** *Naut.* (of a vessel) sufficiently near, or above the horizon, that the hull is visible. —*v.t.* **5.** to pierce (the hull of a vessel), esp. below the water line. —*v.i.* **6.** to drift without power or sails. [special use of HULL¹] —**hull′-less,** *adj.*

Hull (hul), *n.* **1. Cor·dell** (kôr′del, kôr del′), 1871–1955, U.S. statesman: Secretary of State 1933–44; Nobel peace prize 1945. **2. William,** 1753–1825, U.S. general. **3.** Official name, **Kingston-upon-Hull.** a seaport in SE Yorkshire, in E England, on the Humber River. 303,268 (1961). **4.** a city in SE Canada, on the Ottawa River opposite Ottawa. 56,929 (1961). **5.** a town in E Massachusetts. 7055 (1960).

hul·la·bal·loo (hul′ə bə lo͞o′), *n., pl.* **-loos.** hullabaloo.

hul·la·ba·loo (hul′ə bə lo͞o′), *n., pl.* **-loos.** a clamorous noise or disturbance; uproar. [appar. var. of *haloo-baloo,* rhyming compound based on Scot *baloo* lullaby]

hull′ bal′ance, (of a sailing vessel) the property of maintaining satisfactory trim and steering qualities when heeled at a normal angle.

hull′ effi′ciency, *Naval Archit.* the ratio of the quantity of work required to tow a certain hull at a given speed to that required to drive it with a certain propeller: used in propeller design.

hull′ gird′er, *Naval Archit.* the theoretical box girder formed by the continuous longitudinal members of the hull of a vessel, providing resistance to hogging and sagging.

Hull′ House′, a settlement house in Chicago, Ill., founded in 1889 by Jane Addams.

hull·ing (hul′ing), *n.* material for the framework and shell of the hull of a vessel. [HULL² + -ING¹]

hull′ing line′, *Naut.* a brail used in a sail furnished with reefing battens.

hul·lo (hə lō′), *interj., n., pl.* **-los,** *v.i., v.t.,* **-loed, -lo·ing. 1.** hallo. **2.** *Chiefly Brit.* hello.

hul·loa (hu lō′, hul′ō), *interj., n., pl.* **-loas,** *v.i., v.t.,* **-loaed, -loa·ing.** *Chiefly Brit.* hello.

hul·loo (hu lo͞o′, hul′o͞o), *interj., n., pl.* **-loos,** *v.i., v.t.,* **-looed, -loo·ing.** hallo.

hul·ly gul·ly (hul′ē gul′ē), a dance that is a modification of the frug. [?]

hu·ly (ho͞o′lē, hʏ′lē), *adj., adv.* *Scot.* hooly.

hum (hum), *v.,* **hummed, hum·ming,** *n., interj.* —*v.i.* **1.** to make a low, continuous, droning sound. **2.** to give forth an indistinct sound of mingled voices or noises. **3.** to utter an indistinct sound in hesitation, embarrassment, dissatisfaction, etc.; hem. **4.** to sing with closed lips, without articulating words. **5.** to be in a state of busy activity: *The household hummed in preparation for the reception.* **6.** *Brit. Slang.* to have a bad odor, as of stale perspiration. —*v.t.* **7.** to sound, sing, or utter by humming: *to hum a tune.* **8.** to bring, put, etc., by humming: *to hum a child to sleep.* —*n.* **9.** the act or sound of humming; an inarticulate or indistinct murmur; hem. —*interj.* **10.** (an inarticulate sound uttered in contemplation, hesitation, dissatisfaction, doubt, etc.) [ME *humme(n);* c. G *hummen* to hum; imit.; cf. HUMBLEBEE] —**hum′mer,** *n.*

hu·man (hyo͞o′mən *or, often,* yo͞o′-), *adj.* **1.** of, pertaining to, characteristic of, or having the nature of mankind: *human frailty; the human body.* **2.** consisting of people or men: *the human race.* **3.** of or pertaining to the social aspect or charcter of man: *human affairs.* **4.** sympathetic; humane: *a warmly human understanding.* —*n.* **5.** a human being. [< L *hūmān(us),* equiv. to *hūm-* (see HOMO) + *-ānus* -AN; r. ME *humain* < MF] —**hu′man·like′,** *adj.* —**hu′man·ness,** *n.*

—**Syn. 1.** HUMAN, HUMANE may refer to that which is, or should be, characteristic of human beings. In thus describing characteristics, HUMAN may refer to good and bad traits of man alike (*human kindness; human weakness*). When emphasis is placed upon the latter, HUMAN is thought of as contrasted to DIVINE: *To err is human, to forgive divine. He was only human.* HUMANE (the original spelling of HUMAN, and since 1700 restricted in meaning) takes into account only the nobler or gentler aspects of man and is often, either explicitly or implicitly, contrasted to his more ignoble or brutish aspect. A HUMANE person is, specifically, one actuated by benevolence in his treatment of his fellows, or of helpless animals; the word once had also connotations of courtesy and refinement (hence, the application of HUMANE to those branches of learning intended to refine the mind).

Hu′man Com′edy, The, a collected edition of tales and novels in 17 volumes (1842–48) by Honoré de Balzac. French, **La Comédie Humaine.**

hu·mane (hyo͞o mān′ *or, often,* yo͞o′-), *adj.* **1.** characterized by tenderness, compassion, and sympathy for men and animals, esp. for the suffering or distressed: *humane feelings.* **2.** of or pertaining to humanistic studies. [var. of HUMAN; cf. GERMANE, GERMAN] —**hu·mane′ly,** *adv.* —**hu·mane′ness,** *n.*

—**Syn. 1.** merciful, kind, kindly, kindhearted, tender, compassionate, gentle, sympathetic; benevolent, benignant, charitable. See **human.** —**Ant. 1.** brutal.

hu′man engineer′ing, 1. the manipulation of human beings chiefly through the use of psychological techniques. Cf. **psychotechnics. 2.** an applied science that coordinates the design and arrangement of physical working conditions with the capacities and requirements of the worker.

humane′ soci′ety, (*often cap.*) an organization devoted to promoting humane ideals, esp. with reference to the treatment of animals.

hu·man·ics (hyo͞o man′iks *or, often,* yo͞o-), (*construed as sing.*) the study of the nature or affairs of mankind. [HUMAN + -ICS]

hu′man-in′terest sto′ry (hyo͞o′mən in′tər ist, -trist *or, often,* yo͞o′-), a story or report, esp. in a newspaper, designed to engage attention and sympathy by enabling one to identify readily with the people, problems, and situations described.

hu·man·ise (hyo͞o′mə nīz′ *or, often,* yo͞o′-), *v.t., v.i.,* **-ised, -is·ing.** *Chiefly Brit.* humanize.

hu·man·ism (hyo͞o′mə niz′əm *or, often,* yo͞o′-), *n.* **1.** any system or mode of thought or action in which human interests, values, and dignity predominate. **2.** devotion to or study of the humanities. **3.** (*sometimes cap.*) the studies, principles, or culture of the Humanists. **4.** *Philos.* the pragmatism of F. C. S. Schiller, emphasizing the idea of creative individual thought as the basis of personal truth. [HUMAN + -ISM]

hu·man·ist (hyo͞o′mə nist *or, often,* yo͞o′-), *n.* **1.** a student of human nature or affairs. **2.** a person having a strong interest in or concern for human welfare, values, and dignity. **3.** a person devoted to or versed in the humanities. **4.** a classical scholar. **5.** (*sometimes cap.*) one of the scholars of the Renaissance who pursued and disseminated the study and understanding of the cultures of ancient Rome and Greece, and emphasized secular, individualistic, and critical thought. **6.** (*sometimes cap.*) a person who follows a form of scientific or philosophical humanism. [< It *umanist(a).* See HUMAN, -IST] —**hu′man·is′tic,** *adj.* —**hu′man·is′ti·cal·ly,** *adv.*

hu·man·i·tar·i·an (hyo͞o man′i târ′ē ən *or, often,* yo͞o-), *adj.* **1.** having concern for or helping to improve the welfare and happiness of mankind. **2.** of or pertaining to ethical or theological humanitarianism. —*n.* **3.** a person actively engaged in promoting human welfare and social reforms, as a philanthropist. **4.** a person who professes ethical or theological humanitarianism. [HUMANIT(Y) + -ARIAN]

hu·man·i·tar·i·an·ism (hyo͞o man′i târ′ē ə niz′əm *or, often,* yo͞o-), *n.* **1.** humanitarian principles or practices. **2.** *Ethics.* **a.** the doctrine that man's obligations are concerned wholly with the welfare of the human race. **b.** the doctrine that mankind may become perfect without divine aid. **3.** *Theol.* the doctrine that Jesus Christ possessed a human nature only. [HUMANITARIAN + -ISM] —**hu·man′i·tar′i·an·ist,** *n.*

hu·man·i·ty (hyo͞o man′i tē *or, often,* yo͞o-), *n., pl.* **-ties. 1.** all human beings collectively; the human race; mankind. **2.** the quality or condition of being human; human nature. **3.** the quality of being humane; kindness; benevolence. **4. the humanities, a.** the study of classical languages and classical literature. **b.** the Latin and Greek classics as a field of study. **c.** literature, philosophy, art, etc., as distinguished from the sciences. **d.** the study of literature, philosophy, art, etc. [ME *humanite* < L *hūmānitās.* See HUMAN, -ITY]

hu·man·ize (hyo͞o′mə nīz′ *or, often,* yo͞o′-), *v.,* **-ized, -iz·ing.** —*v.t.* **1.** to make humane, kind, or gentle. **2.** to make human. —*v.i.* **3.** to become human or humane. Also, *esp. Brit.,* **humanise.** [HUMAN + -IZE] —**hu′man·i·za′tion,** *n.* —**hu′man·iz′er,** *n.*

hu·man·kind (hyo͞o′mən kīnd′, -kīnd′ *or, often,* yo͞o′-), *n.* human beings collectively. [from the phrase *human kind;* modeled on *mankind*]

hu·man·ly (hyo͞o′mən lē *or, often,* yo͞o′-), *adv.* **1.** in a human manner. **2.** by human means. **3.** within the limits of human knowledge and capability: *Is it humanly possible to predict the future?* **4.** from or according to the viewpoint of mankind. [HUMAN + -LY]

hu′man na′ture, 1. the psychological and social qualities that characterize mankind, esp. in contrast with other living things. **2.** *Sociol.* the character of human conduct, generally regarded as produced by living in primary groups.

hu·man·oid (hyo͞o′mə noid′), *adj.* **1.** having human characteristics or form. —*n.* **2.** a humanoid being: *to search for humanoids in outer space.* [HUMAN + -OID]

hu·ma·num est er·ra·re (o͞o mä′no͝om est eʀ rä′ʀe; *Eng.* hyo͞o mā′nəm est e rår′ē), *Latin.* to err is human.

Hu·ma·num Ge·nus (ho͞o mä′no͝om jā′no͝os), *Latin.* The Human Race (opening words and the title of an 1884 encyclical of Pope Leo XIII on Freemasonry).

Hu·mash (ᴋʜo͞o mäsh′; *Eng.* ho͞om′əsh, ᴋʜo͞om′-), *n., pl.* **Hu·ma·shim** (ᴋʜo͞o mä shēm′; *Eng.* ho͞o mô′shim, ᴋʜo͞o-). *Hebrew.* the Pentateuch. Also, **Chumash.** [lit., law]

Hu·ma·yun (ho͞o mä′yo͞on), *n.* 1508–56, Mogul emperor of Hindustan 1530–56 (son of Baber).

Hum·ber (hum′bər), *n.* an estuary of the Ouse and Trent rivers in E England. 37 mi. long.

Hum·bert (hum′bərt), *n.* a boy's given name.

Humbert I, (*Umberto I*) 1844–1900, king of Italy 1878–1900.

hum·ble (hum′bəl, um′-), *adj.,* **-bler, -blest,** *v.,* **-bled, -bling.** —*adj.* **1.** not proud or arrogant; modest: *to be humble although successful.* **2.** having a feeling of insignificance, inferiority, subservience, etc.: *I am humble in the presence of the starry firmament. I am your humble disciple in all things of the spirit.* **3.** low in rank, importance, position, quality, etc.; lowly: *of humble origin; a humble home.* **4.** courteously respectful: *in my humble opinion.* **5.** low in height, level, etc.; small in size: *a humble member of the galaxy.* —*v.t.* **6.** to lower in condition, importance, or dignity; abase. **7.** to destroy the independence, power, or will of. **8.** to make meek: *to humble one's heart.* [ME *(h)umble* < OF < L *humil(is)* lowly, insignificant, on the ground. See HUMUS, -ILE] —**hum′ble·ness,** *n.* —**hum′bler,** *n.* —**hum′bling·ly,** *adv.* —**hum′bly,** *adv.*

—**Syn. 1.** unpretending, unpretentious. **2.** submissive; meek. **3.** unassuming, plain, common, poor. **4.** polite. **6.** mortify, shame, abash. **7.** subdue, crush, break. HUMBLE, DEGRADE, HUMILIATE suggest lowering or causing to seem lower. To HUMBLE is to bring down the pride of another or to reduce him to a state of abasement: *to humble an arrogant enemy.* To DEGRADE is to demote in rank or standing, or to reduce to a low level in condition, manners, or morals: *to degrade an officer; to degrade one's dependents.* To HUMILIATE is to make others feel or appear inadequate or unworthy, esp. in some public setting: *to humiliate a sensitive person.* —**Ant. 1, 2.** proud. **3.** noble, exalted. **4.** insolent. **6.** elevate. **8.** exalt.

hum·ble·bee (hum′bəl bē′), *n.* *Chiefly Brit.* bumblebee. [late ME *humbul-be;* akin to D *hommel* drone, G *Hummelbiene* kind of wild-bee, MLG *homelbe;* prob. akin to HUM]

hum′ble pie′, **1.** humiliation; humility forced upon someone, often under embarrassing conditions. **2.** *Obs.* a pie made of the numbles of deer or the like. **3. eat humble pie,** to be forced to apologize humbly; suffer humiliation: *After vehemently arguing, he discovered his basic illogicality and had to eat humble pie before his associates.* [earlier *an umble pie,* erroneous for *a numble pie;* see NUMBLES]

hum′ble plant′. See **sensitive plant** (def. 1).

Hum·boldt (hum′bōlt; *for 1, 2, also Ger.* ho͝om′bôlt), *n.* **1. Frie·drich Hein·rich A·lex·an·der** (frē′drIKH hīn′rIKH ä′lek sän′dər), **Baron von** (fən), 1769–1859, German naturalist, writer, and statesman. **2.** his brother, **(Karl) Wil·helm** (kärl vil′helm), **Baron von,** 1767–1835, German philologist and diplomat. **3.** a town in NW Tennessee. 8482 (1960). **4.** a town in NW Iowa. 4031 (1960).

Hum′boldt Cur′rent. See **Peru Current.**

Hum·boldt·i·a·num (hum′bōl tē ä′nəm), *n.* **Mare.** See **Mare Humboldtianum.**

Hum′boldt's Sea′. See **Mare Humboldtianum.**

hum·bug (hum′bug′), *n., v.,* **-bugged, -bug·ging,** *interj.* —*n.* **1.** a deluding trick; hoax, fraud, or deception. **2.** the quality of falseness or deception. **3.** a person who is not what he claims or pretends to be; impostor. **4.** something devoid of sense or meaning; nonsense: *a humbug of technical jargon.* **5.** *Brit.* a variety of hard mint candy. —*v.t.* **6.** to impose upon by humbug or false pretense; delude; deceive. —*v.i.* **7.** to practice humbug. —*interj.* **8.** nonsense! [?] —**hum′bug′ger,** *n.*

—**Syn. 1.** imposition. **2.** pretense, sham. **3.** pretender, deceiver, charlatan, swindler, quack, confidence man. **6.** cheat, swindle, trick, fool, dupe.

hum·bug·ger·y (hum′bug′ə rē), *n.* pretense; sham. [HUMBUG + -ERY]

hum·ding·er (hum′ding′ər), *n.* *Slang.* a person or thing of remarkable excellence or effect. [HUM + DING[1] + -ER[1]; from the fact that a missile *hums* through the air and *dings* when it strikes the mark]

hum·drum (hum′drum′), *adj.* **1.** lacking variety; dull: *a humdrum existence.* —*n.* **2.** humdrum character or routine; monotony. **3.** monotonous or tedious talk. **4.** a dull, boring fellow. [earlier *humtrum,* rhyming compound based on HUM] —**hum′drum′ness,** *n.*

Hume (hyo͞om), *n.* **1. David,** 1711–76, Scottish philosopher and historian. **2.** a boy's given name.

hu·mec·tant (hyo͞o mek′tənt), *n.* **1.** a substance that absorbs or helps another substance retain moisture, as glycerole. —*adj.* **2.** moistening; diluting. **3.** of or pertaining to a humectant or humectants. [< L *hūmectant-* (s. of *hūmectāns,* prp. of *humectāre* to moisten), equiv. to *(h)ūmect(us)* moist, damp + *-ant-* -ANT]

hu·mer·al (hyo͞o′mər əl), *adj.* **1.** *Anat., Zool.* of or pertaining to the humerus or brachium. **2.** of or pertaining to the shoulder. [< L *(h)umer(us)* HUMERUS + -AL[1]; cf. L *(h)umerāle* shoulder covering, cape]

hu′meral veil′, *Eccles.* a fringed scarf, usually white and ornamented in the middle, worn over the shoulders by a priest or subdeacon during certain parts of a High Mass.

hu·mer·us (hyo͞o′mər əs), *n., pl.* **-mer·i** (-mə rī′). *Anat., Zool.* **1.** the long bone in the arm of man extending from the shoulder to the elbow. See diagrams under **shoulder, skeleton.** **2.** brachium. **3.** a corresponding bone, structure, or region in the forelimbs of other animals or in the wings of birds or insects. [< L *(h)umerus* shoulder; c. Gk *ômos,* Goth *ams,* Skt *ámsas*]

hu·mic (hyo͞o′mik), *adj.* *Chem.* of or noting a substance, as an acid, obtained from humus. [< L *hum(us)* ground, mould + -IC]

hu·mid (hyo͞o′mid *or, often,* yo͞o′-), *adj.* moist or damp with liquid or vapor; containing a noticeable amount of moisture: *humid air.* [< L *(h)ūmid(us),* equiv. to *(h)ūm(ēre)* (to) be moist + *-idus* -ID[4]] —**hu′mid·ly,** *adv.* —**hu′mid·ness,** *n.*

—**Syn.** dank, wet. See **damp.**

hu·mid·i·fi·er (hyo͞o mid′ə fī′ər *or, often,* yo͞o-), *n.* **1.** a device for increasing the amount of water vapor in the air of a room or building, consisting of a container for water and a means for converting the water into water vapor. **2.** any device for regulating the amount of water vapor in a specific container or area. [HUMIDIFY + -ER[1]]

hu·mid·i·fy (hyo͞o mid′ə fī′ *or, often,* yo͞o-), *v.t.,* **-fied, -fy·ing.** to make humid. [HUMID + -IFY] —**hu·mid′i·fi·ca′tion,** *n.*

hu·mid·i·stat (hyo͞o mid′i stat′), *n.* an instrument for measuring and controlling humidity. Also called **hygrostat.** [HUMID + -I- + -STAT]

hu·mid·i·ty (hyo͞o mid′i tē *or, often,* yo͞o-), *n.* **1.** humid condition; dampness. **2.** See **relative humidity.** **3.** an uncomfortably high amount of relative humidity: *It's not the heat, it's the humidity that tires me out.* [late ME *humydite* < L *(h)ūmiditās.* See HUMID, -ITY]

hu·mi·dor (hyo͞o′mi dôr′), *n.* a container or storage room for cigars or other preparations of tobacco, fitted with means for keeping the tobacco suitably moist. [HUMID + -OR[2]]

hu·mil·i·ate (hyo͞o mil′ē āt′ *or, often,* yo͞o-), *v.t.,* **-at·ed, -at·ing.** to lower the pride or self-respect of; cause a painful loss of dignity to; mortify. [< LL *humiliāt(us)* (ptp. of *humiliāre* to humble), equiv. to L *humili(s)* HUMBLE + *-ātus* -ATE[1]] —**hu·mil′i·at′ing·ly,** *adv.* —**hu·mil′i·a′tor,** *n.* —**hu·mil·i·a·to·ry** (hyo͞o mil′ē ə tôr′ē, -tōr′ē *or, often,* yo͞o-), **hu·mil·i·a·tive** (hyo͞o mil′ē ā′tiv, -ē ə tiv *or, often,* yo͞o-), *adj.*

—**Syn.** dishonor, disgrace, shame; degrade, abase, debase. See **humble.** —**Ant.** exalt, honor.

hu·mil·i·at·ing (hyo͞o mil′ē ā′ting *or, often,* yo͞o-), *adj.* lowering the pride or dignity of a person; mortifying: *Such a humiliating experience was good for his overblown ego.* [HUMILIATE + -ING[2]]

hu·mil·i·a·tion (hyo͞o mil′ē ā′shən *or, often,* yo͞o-), *n.* **1.** the act or an instance of humiliating or being humiliated. **2.** the state or feeling of being humiliated; mortification. [ME < LL *humiliātiōn-* (s. of *humiliātiō*). See HUMILIATE, -ION]

—**Syn. 2.** degradation, dishonor. See **shame.**

hu·mi·lis (hyo͞o′mə lis), *adj.* *Meteorol.* (of a cloud) having a small, flattened appearance. [< NL, L: low, shallow]

hu·mil·i·ty (hyo͞o mil′i tē *or, often,* yo͞o-), *n.* the quality or condition of being humble; modest sense of one's own importance, rank, etc. [ME *humilite* < L *humilitās.* See HUMILIS, -TY[2]]

—**Syn.** lowliness, meekness, submissiveness. —**Ant.** pride.

Hum·ism (hyo͞o′miz əm), *n.* the philosophy or principles of David Hume, esp. his epistemological skepticism. [HUME + -ISM]

Hum·mels·town (hum′əlz toun′), *n.* a town in central Pennsylvania. 4474 (1960).

hum·ming (hum′ing), *adj.* **1.** making a droning sound; buzzing. **2.** very busy; briskly active: *a humming commercial center.* [HUM + -ING[2]] —**hum′ming·ly,** *adv.*

hum·ming·bird (hum′ing bûrd′), *n.* any of numerous very small, American birds of the family *Trochilidae,* characterized by the brilliant, iridescent plumage of the male, a slender bill, and narrow wings, the extremely rapid beating of which produces a humming sound: noted for their ability to hover and to fly upward, downward, and backward in a horizontal position. [HUMMING + BIRD]

Hummingbird, *Archilochus colubris* (Length 3½ in.)

hum′mingbird moth′. See **hawk moth.**

hum·mock (hum′ək), *n.* **1.** Also, **hammock.** an elevated tract of land rising above the general level of a marshy region. **2.** a knoll or hillock. **3.** Also, **hommock.** a ridge in an ice field. [*humm-* (akin to HUMP) + -OCK]

hum·mock·y (hum′ə kē), *adj.* **1.** abounding in hummocks. **2.** like a hummock. [HUMMOCK + -Y[1]]

hu·mon·gous (hyo͞o mung′gəs, -mong′- *or, often,* yo͞o-) *adj.* *Slang.* extraordinarily large. [perh. HU(GE) + MON(STROUS) + G(REAT) + (ENORM)OUS]

hu·mor (hyo͞o′mər *or, often,* yo͞o′-), *n.* **1.** a comic quality causing amusement: *the humor of a situation.* **2.** the faculty of perceiving what is amusing or comical: *His humor buoyed him up through many depressing situations.* **3.** the faculty of expressing the amusing or comical: *The author's humor came across better in the book than in the movie.* **4.** comical writing or talk in general; comical books, skits, plays, etc. **5. humors,** amusing or comical features: *humors of the occasion.* **6.** mental disposition or temperament. **7.** a temporary mood or frame of mind: *He's in a bad humor today.* **8.** a capricious or freakish inclination; whim or caprice; odd trait. **9.** *Old Physiol.* one of the four elemental fluids of the body, blood, phlegm, black bile, and yellow bile, regarded as determining, by their relative proportions, a person's physical and mental constitution. **10.** *Biol.* any animal or plant fluid, whether natural or morbid, such as the blood or lymph. **11. out of humor,** displeased; dissatisfied; cross: *The chef is feeling out of humor again and will have to be pampered.* —*v.t.* **12.** to comply with the humor or mood of in order to soothe or make content or more agreeable: *to humor a child.* **13.** to adapt or accommodate oneself to. Also, *esp. Brit.,* **humour.** [ME *(h)umour* < AF < L *(h)ūmōr-* (s. of *(h)ūmor*) moisture, fluid (medical L: body fluid), equiv. to *ūm(ēre)* (to) be wet + *-or* -OR[1]] —**hu′mor·ful,** *adj.* —**hu′mor·less,** *adj.* —**hu′mor·less·ness,** *n.*

—**Syn. 3.** HUMOR, WIT are contrasting terms that agree in referring to an ability to perceive and express a sense of the clever or amusing. HUMOR consists principally in the recognition and expression of incongruities or peculiarities present in a situation or character. It is frequently used to illustrate some fundamental absurdity in human nature or conduct, and is generally thought of as more kindly than wit: *a genial and mellow type of humor; his biting wit.* WIT is a purely intellectual manifestation of cleverness and quickness of apprehension in discovering analogies between things really unlike, and expressing them in brief, diverting, and often sharp observations or remarks. **8.** fancy, vagary. **12.** HUMOR, GRATIFY, INDULGE imply attempting to satisfy the wishes or whims of (oneself or others). To HUMOR is to comply with the mood, fancy, or caprice of another, as in order to satisfy, soothe, or manage: *to humor an invalid, a child.* To GRATIFY is to please by satisfying the likings or desires: *to gratify someone by praising him.* INDULGE suggests a yielding to wishes by way of favor or complaisance, and may imply a habitual or excessive yielding to whims: *to indulge an unreasonable demand; to indulge an irresponsible son.* —**Ant. 12.** discipline, restrain.

hu·mor·al (hyo͞o′mər əl *or, often,* yo͞o′-), *adj.* *Biol., Physiol.* of, pertaining to, or proceeding from a fluid of the body. [< ML *hūmōrāl(is).* See HUMOR, -AL[1]]

hu·mor·esque (hyo͞o′mə resk′ *or, often,* yo͞o′-), *n.* a musical composition of humorous or capricious character. [HUMOR + -ESQUE, modeled on G *Humoreske*] —**hu′mor·esque′ly,** *adv.*

hu·mor·ist (hyo͞o′mər ist *or, often,* yo͞o′-), *n.* **1.** a person who is skillful in the use of humor, as in writing, acting, etc. **2.** a person with an active sense of humor. [< ML or It *humorista.* See HUMOR, -IST] —**hu′mor·is′tic, hu′mor·is′ti·cal,** *adj.*

hu·mor·ous[1] (hyo͞o′mər əs *or, often,* yo͞o′-), *adj.* **1.** characterized by humor; funny; comic: *the humorous side of life.* **2.** having or showing the faculty of humor; droll; facetious: *a humorous person.* [HUMOR + -OUS] —**hu′mor·ous·ly,** *adv.* —**hu′mor·ous·ness,** *n.*

—**Syn. 1.** ludicrous, laughable. **2.** jocose, jocular, comic, comical. HUMOROUS, WITTY, FACETIOUS, WAGGISH imply that which arises from cleverness or a sense of fun. HUMOROUS implies a genuine sense of fun and the comic, impersonal or gently personal: *a humorous version of an incident; a humorous view of life.* WITTY implies quickness to perceive the amusing, striking, or unusual and to express it cleverly and entertainingly; it sometimes becomes rather sharp and unkind, particularly in quick repartee of a personal nature: *a witty and interesting companion; to be witty at someone else's expense.* FACETIOUS suggests a desire or attempt to be jocular or witty, often unsuccessful, inappropriate, or trifling: *a facetious treatment of a serious subject.* WAGGISH suggests the spirit of sly mischief and roguery of the constant joker (making jokes, not playing them), with no harm intended: *a waggish good humor.* —**Ant. 1, 2.** solemn, sober, serious.

hu·mor·ous[2] (hyo͞o′mər əs *or, often,* yo͞o′-), *adj.* **1.** *Archaic.* moist; wet. **2.** *Old Physiol.* pertaining or due to the bodily humors. [< LL *(h)ūmōrōsus*]

Hu·mo·rum (hyo͞o′mər əm, hyo͞o mōr′əm), *n.* **Mare.** See **Mare Humorum.**

hu·mour (hyo͞o′mər), *n., v.t.,* *Chiefly Brit.* humor. —**hu′mour·ful,** *adj.* —**hu′mour·less,** *adj.* —**hu′mour·less·ness,** *n.* —**hu′mour·some,** *adj.*

hump (hump), *n.* **1.** a rounded protuberance, esp. a fleshy protuberance on the back, as that due to abnormal curvature of the spine in man, or that normally present in certain animals such as the camel and bison. **2.** a low, rounded rise of ground; hummock. **3.** *Railroads.* (in a switchyard) a raised area down which cars pushed to its crest roll by gravity and momentum for automatic sorting through a series of preset switches. **4. the hump,** **a.** *Brit. Slang.* a fit of bad humor: *to get the hump.* **b.** *(cap.)* (in World War II) the Himalayas. **5. over the hump,** past the most difficult, time-consuming, or dangerous part or period: *The doctor says she's over the hump now and should improve steadily. If we can just get over the hump on this project, we can finish it in a month.* —*v.t.* **6.** to raise (the back) in a hump; hunch: *The cat humped its back.* **7.** *Railroads.* to sort (cars) by means of a hump. **8.** *Informal.* to exert (oneself) in a great effort. **9.** *Slang (vulgar).* to copulate with (a female). **10.** *Australian Slang.* **a.** to place or bear on the back or shoulder. **b.** to carry. —*v.i.* **11.** to rise in a hump. **12.** *Informal.* to exert oneself; to hustle or hurry. [prob. abstracted from HUMPBACKED] —**hump′less,** *adj.*

hump·back (hump′bak′), *n.* **1.** a back that is humped in a convex position because of abnormal spinal curvature; hunchback. **2.** hunchback (def. 1). **3.** a whale of the genus *Megaptera,* having a humplike back. [appar. back formation from HUMPBACKED]

hump·backed (hump′bakt′), *adj.* having a hump on the back; hunchbacked. [b. *huckbacked* (*huck* haunch + BACKED) and *crumpbacked* (OE *crump* crooked + BACKED)]

Hum·per·dinck (ho͝om′pər dingk′), *n.* **Eng·el·bert** (eng′əl bert′), 1854–1921, German composer.

humph (humf), *interj.* (an inarticulate expression resembling a snort, used to indicate disbelief, contempt, etc.).

Hum·phrey (hum′frē), *n.* **1.** *(Duke of Gloucester)* 1391–1447, English soldier and statesman (youngest son of Henry IV). **2. Doris,** 1895–1958, U.S. dancer, choreographer, and teacher. **3. Hubert H(oratio),** 1911–78, U.S. politician: vice-president 1965–69. **4.** a boy's given name.

Hum·phry Clink·er (hum′frē kling′kər), an epistolary novel (1771) by Smollett.

Hump·ty Dump·ty (hump′tē dump′tē), a character in a Mother Goose nursery rhyme: an egg that fell off a wall and could not be put together again. [rhyming compound based on *humpty;* see HUMP, -ED[3], -Y[2]]

hump·y[1] (hum′pē), *adj.,* **hump·i·er, hump·i·est.** **1.** full of humps. **2.** resembling a hump; humplike. [HUMP + -Y[1]] —**hump′i·ness,** *n.*

hum·py[2] (hum′pē), *n., pl.* **-pies.** *Australian.* any crude aborigine hut or shelter, esp. a shanty built at the edge of a town. [< native Austral]

hu·mu·lon (hyo͞o′myə lon′), *n.* *Chem.* a bitter constituent of hops, $C_{21}H_{30}O_5$, having antibiotic properties. Also, **hu·mu·lone** (hyo͞o′myə lōn′ *or, often,* yo͞o′-). [< NL *Humul(us)* genus name (special use of ML: hop plant < Gmc; cf. Icel *humall,* OE *hymele*) + -ONE]

hu·mu·hu·mu·nu·ku·nu·ku·a·pu·a·a (ho͞o′mo͞o-ho͞o′mo͞o no͞o′ko͞o no͞o′ko͞o ä′po͞o ä′ä), *n.* either of two triggerfishes, esp. *Rhinecantus aculeatus,* found among coral reefs of the tropical Indian and Pacific oceans. [< Hawaiian]

hu·mus (hyo͞o′məs *or, often,* yo͞o′-), *n.* the dark organic material in soils, produced by the decomposition of vegetable or animal matter and essential to the fertility of the earth. [< L: earth, ground] —**hu′mus·like′,** *adj.*

Hun (hun), *n.* **1.** a member of a nomadic and warlike Asian people who devastated or controlled large parts of eastern and central Europe, and who exercised their greatest power under Attila in the 5th century A.D. **2.** *(often l.c.)* a barbarous, destructive person; a vandal. **3.** *Derogatory.* **a.** a German soldier in World War I or II. **b.** a German. [sing. of *Huns,* OE *Hūnas;* c. Icel *Húnar;* akin to LL *Hunnī,* Chin *Han;* all from native name of people] —**Hun′like′,** *adj.*

Hu·nan (ho͞o′nän′), *n.* a province in S China. 36,220,000 (est. 1957); 81,274 sq. mi. *Cap.:* Changsha.

hunch (hunch), *v.t.* **1.** to thrust out or up in a hump; arch: *to hunch one's back.* **2.** to shove, push, or jostle. —*v.i.* **3.** to thrust oneself forward jerkily; lunge forward. **4.** to stand, sit, or walk in a bent posture. —*n.* **5.** a hump. **6.** *Informal.* a premonition of suspicion. **7.** a push or shove. **8.** a lump or thick piece. [appar. var. of obs. *hinch* to push, shove, kick < ?]

hunch·back (hunch′bak′), *n.* **1.** a person whose back is humped in a convex position because of abnormal spinal curvature; humpback. **2.** humpback (def. 1). [back formation from HUNCHBACKED]

hunch·backed (hunch′bakt′), *adj.* humpbacked. [b. *huckbacked* and *bunchbacked*]

Hunch′back of No′tre Dame′, The, a novel (1831) by Victor Hugo. French, **Notre Dame de Paris.**

hund., **1.** hundred. **2.** hundreds.

hun·dred (hun′drid), *n., pl.* **-dreds,** *(as after a numeral)* **-dred,** *adj.* —*n.* **1.** a cardinal number, ten times ten. **2.** a symbol for this number, as 100 or C. **3.** a set of this many persons or things: *a hundred of the men.* **4.** *U.S. Informal.* a hundred-dollar bill or the sum of one hundred dollars. **5.** *Brit. Informal.* the sum of one hundred pounds. **6.** (formerly) an administrative division of an English county. **7.** a similar division in colonial Pennsylvania, Delaware, and Virginia, and in present-day Delaware. **8.** Also called **hun′dred's place′.** *Math.* **a.** the position of the third digit to the (in a mixed number) the position of the third digit to the left of the decimal point. **b.** (in a whole number) the position of the third digit from the right. —*adj.* **9.** amounting to one hundred in number. [ME, OE (c. OFris *hunderd,* OS *hunderod,* Icel *hundrath,* D *honderd,* G *hundert*), equiv. to *hund* 100 (c. Goth *hund;* akin to L *cent(um),* Gk *(he)kat(ón),* Avestan *sat(em),* Skt *śatám,* OSlav *seto,* Russ *sto*) + *-red* tale, count, akin to Goth *rathjan* to reckon]

Hun′dred Days′, **1.** the period from March 20 to June 28, 1815, between the arrival of Napoleon in Paris, after his escape from Elba, and his abdication after the battle of Waterloo. **2.** a special session of Congress from March 9, 1933 to June 16, 1933, called by President

Roosevelt, in which important social legislation was enacted.

hun·dred·fold (hun′drid fōld′), *adj.* **1.** comprising a hundred parts or members. **2.** a hundred times as great or as much. —*adv.* **3.** in a hundredfold measure. [ME *hundredfald.* See HUNDRED, -FOLD]

hun·dred-per·cent·er (hun′drid pər sen′tər), *n.* a patriotic, sometimes jingoistic person.

hun·dredth (hun′dridth, -dritth), *adj.* **1.** next after the ninety-ninth; being the ordinal number for 100. **2.** being one of 100 equal parts. —*n.* **3.** a hundredth part, esp. of one (1/100). **4.** the hundredth member of a series. **5.** Also called **hun′dredth's place′.** (in decimal notation) the position of the second digit to the right of the decimal point. [ME *hundreth.* See HUNDRED, -TH²]

hun·dred·weight (hun′drid wāt′), *n., pl.* **-weights,** (*as after a numeral*) **-weight.** a unit of avoirdupois weight commonly equivalent to 100 pounds in the U.S. and 112 pounds in England. *Abbr.:* cwt Also called **quintal.** [HUNDRED + WEIGHT]

Hun′dred Years′′ War′, the series of wars between England and France, 1337–1453, in which England lost all her possessions in France except Calais.

Hun·e·ker (hun′ə kər), *n.* **James (Gib·bons)** (gib′ənz), 1860–1921, U.S. music critic and writer.

hung (hung), *v.* **1.** pt. and pp. of **hang.** **2. hung over,** *Slang.* suffering the effects of a hangover: *On New Year's Day they were all hung over.* **3. hung on,** *Informal.* fascinated by; extremely interested in: *He's hung on abstract art this year.* **4. hung up,** *Slang.* **a.** detained on account of a difficulty. **b.** *Baseball, Softball.* (of a base runner) trapped between bases and in danger of being tagged out.

Hung., **1.** Also, **Hung** Hungarian. **2.** Hungary.

Hun·gar·i·an (hung gâr′ē ən), *adj.* **1.** of, pertaining to, or characteristic of Hungary, its people, or their language. —*n.* **2.** a native or inhabitant of Hungary. Cf. **Magyar.** **3.** Also called **Magyar.** the language of Hungary, of the Uralic family of languages. [HUNGARY + -AN]

Hungar′ian brome′ grass′, a perennial grass, *Bromus inermis,* of Europe, grown in pastures. Also called **awnless brome grass.**

Hungar′ian gou′lash, goulash (def. 1).

Hungar′ian li′lac, a shrub, *Syringa Josikaea,* of Hungary, having slightly fragrant, deep lilac- to violet-colored flowers in slender clusters.

Hun·ga·ry (hung′gə rē), *n.* a republic in central Europe. 10,119,000 (est. 1964); 35,926 sq. mi. *Cap.:* Budapest. Hungarian, **Magyarország.**

hun·ger (hung′gər), *n.* **1.** a compelling need or desire for food. **2.** the painful sensation or state of weakness caused by need of food: *to collapse from hunger.* **3.** a strong or compelling desire or craving: *hunger for power.* —*v.i.* **4.** to feel hunger; be hungry. **5.** to have a strong desire. —*v.t.* **6.** to subject to hunger; starve. [ME, OE *hungor;* c. G *Hunger*] —**hun′ger·less,** *adj.*

hun·ger·ly (hung′gər lē), *adj.* *Archaic.* marked by a hungry look. [ME *hongerliche.* See HUNGER, -LY]

hun′ger strike′, a deliberate refusal to eat, undertaken in protest against imprisonment, improper treatment, objectionable conditions, etc. —**hun′ger strik′er.**

Hung Lou Mêng (*Chin.* hung′ lō′ mung′). See **Dream of the Red Chamber, The.**

Hung·nam (hōōng′näm′), *n.* a seaport in W North Korea. 143,600 (1944).

hun·gry (hung′grē), *adj.,* **-gri·er, -gri·est.** **1.** having a desire, craving, or need for food; feeling hunger. **2.** indicating, characteristic of, or characterized by hunger: *a lean and hungry look.* **3.** strongly or eagerly desirous. **4.** lacking needful or desirable elements; not fertile; poor: *hungry land.* **5.** marked by a scarcity of food: *Those were hungry times, during the depression years.* [ME, OE *hungrig.* See HUNGER, -Y¹] —**hun′gri·ly, hun′ger·ing·ly,** *adv.* —**hun′gri·ness,** *n.*

—**Syn. 1.** ravenous, famishing, starving. HUNGRY, FAMISHED, STARVED describe a condition resulting from a lack of food. HUNGRY is a general word, expressing various degrees of eagerness or craving for food: *hungry between meals; desperately hungry after a long fast; hungry as a bear.* FAMISHED denotes the condition of one reduced to actual suffering from want of food but sometimes is used lightly or in an exaggerated statement: *famished after being lost in a wilderness; simply famished (hungry).* STARVED denotes a condition resulting from long-continued lack or insufficiency of food, and implies enfeeblement, emaciation, or death (originally death from any cause, but now death from lack of food): *He looks thin and starved. By the end of the terrible winter, thousands had starved (to death).* It is also used exaggeratingly: *I only had two sandwiches, pie, and some milk, so I'm simply starved (hungry).* —**Ant. 1.** sated, satiated, surfeited.

Hung·tow Island (hōōng′tō′), an island off the SE coast of Taiwan. 8 mi. long.

hunk (hungk), *n.* *Informal.* a large piece or lump; chunk. [< Flem *hunke*]

hun·ker (hung′kər), *v.i.* **1.** to squat on one's heels (often fol. by *down*). —*n.* **2. on one's hunkers,** *Scot.* squatting on one's heels. [appar. *hunk* (? nasalized var. of *huck* haunch; akin to Icel *hūka* to crouch) + -ER⁶]

Hun·ker (hung′kər), *n.* a member of the conservative faction in the Democratic party in New York State, 1845–48. Cf. **Barnburner.** [?] —**Hun′ker·ism,** *n.* —**Hun′ker·ous,** *adj.* —**Hun′ker·ous·ness,** *n.*

hunks (hungks), *n.* (*construed as sing. or pl.*) **1.** a crabbed, disagreeable person. **2.** a covetous, sordid man; miser. [?]

hunk·y¹ (hung′kē), *adj.* *Slang.* **1.** satisfactory; well; right. **2.** even; leaving no balance. [?]

hunk·y² (hung′kē), *n., pl.* **hunk·ies.** (*sometimes cap.*) *U.S. Disparaging.* an unskilled or semiskilled workman of foreign birth, esp. a Hungarian. [? HUN(GARIAN) + (DO)NKEY]

hunk·y-do·ry (hung′kē dōr′ē, -dôr′ē), *adj.* *Slang.* about as well as one could wish or expect; fine; O.K. [HUNKY¹ + *dory* (< ?)]

Hun·nish (hun′ish), *adj.* **1.** of or pertaining to the Huns. **2.** (*sometimes l.c.*) barbarous; destructive. [HUN + -ISH¹] —**Hun′nish·ness,** *n.*

hunt (hunt), *v.t.* **1.** to chase or search for (game or other wild animals) for the purpose of catching or killing. **2.** to pursue with force, hostility, etc. (often fol. by *from* or *down*): *They hunted him down and strung him up.* **3.** to search for; seek; endeavor to obtain or find (often fol. by *up* or *out*): *to hunt up the most promising candidates for the position.* **4.** to search (a place) thoroughly. **5.** to scour (an area) in pursuit of game. **6.** to use or direct (a horse, hound, etc.) in chasing game. **7.** *Change Ringing.* to alter the place of (a bell) in a hunt. —*v.i.* **8.** to engage in the pursuit, capture, or killing of wild animals for food or in sport. **9.** to make a search or quest (often fol. by *for* or *after*). **10.** *Change Ringing.* to alter the place of a bell in its set according to certain rules. —*n.* **11.** an act or the practice of hunting game or other wild animals. **12.** a search; a seeking or endeavor to find. **13.** a pursuit. **14.** a body of persons associated for the purpose of hunting; an association of huntsmen. **15.** an area hunted over. **16.** *Change Ringing.* a regularly varying order of permutations in the ringing of a group of from five to twelve bells. [ME *hunte(n),* OE *huntian,* deriv. of *hunta* hunter, akin to *hentan* to pursue] —**hunt′a·ble,** *adj.* —**hunt′ed·ly,** *adv.*

—**Syn. 1.** pursue, track.

Hunt (hunt), *n.* **1. (James Henry) Leigh** (lē), 1784–1859, English essayist, poet, and editor. **2. Richard Morris,** 1828–95, U.S. architect. **3. (William) Holman** (hōl′mən), 1827–1910, English painter.

hunt′ and peck′, a slow and inefficient method of typing by looking for each key separately before striking it. Cf. **touch system.**

hunt·a·way (hun′tə wā′), *Australian.* —*n.* **1.** a sheep dog. —*adj.* **2.** (of a dog) trained to herd sheep. [n., adj. use of v. phrase *hunt away*]

hunt′ board′, **1.** *Eng. Furniture.* a semicircular drinking table, often having a groove serving as a guide for coasters and a well for unopened bottles. **2.** *U.S. Furniture.* a high sideboard table, often without drawers, used for serving breakfast before and a collation after a hunt. Also called **hunt table.**

hunt′ box′. See **hunting box.**

hunt′ but′ton, *Fox Hunting.* a button engraved with the insignia of one's hunt and worn on the coat and vest as part of the hunt uniform. See diag. under **pink coat.**

hunt·er (hun′tər), *n.* **1.** a person who hunts game or other wild animals. **2.** one who searches for or seeks something: *a fortune hunter.* **3.** a horse specially trained for quietness, stamina, and jumping ability in hunting. **4.** an animal trained to hunt game, as a dog. **5.** (*cap.*) *Astron.* the constellation Orion. **6.** Also called **hunting watch.** a watch with a hunting case. **7.** See **hunter green.** [ME *huntere.* See HUNT, -ER¹] —**hunt′er·like′,** *adj.*

Hun·ter (hun′tər), *n.* **1. John,** 1728–93, Scottish surgeon, physiologist, and biologist. **2. Robert Mer·cer Tal·ia·fer·ro** (mûr′sər tol′ə vər), 1809–87, U.S. political leader: Speaker of the House 1839–41. **3.** a boy's given name.

hunt′er green′, a dark green color of yellowish cast. Also, **hunt′er's green′.** Also called **hunter.**

hunt′er's moon′, the first full moon following the harvest moon.

hunt′er's pink′, a brilliant red often used for hunting jackets.

hunt′er's robe′, a tall, climbing plant, *Scindapsus aureus,* of the Solomon Islands, having leaves that are marked pale yellow and flowers in spikes that are enclosed in a spathe. Also called **Colombo agent, devil's-ivy.**

hunt′er tri′als, a test for hunters held under the auspices of a hunt, in which the course is laid with obstacles to simulate actual hunting conditions.

hunt·ing (hun′ting), *n.* **1.** the act of one who or that which hunts. **2.** *Elect.* the periodic oscillating of a rotating electromechanical system about a mean space position, as in a synchronous motor. —*adj.* **3.** of, for, engaged in, or used while hunting: *a hunting cap.* [ME *huntung,* OE (n.). See HUNT, -ING¹, -ING²]

hunt′ing box′, *Chiefly Brit.* a hunting lodge or house near or in a hunting area for use during the hunting season. Also called **hunt box.**

Hun·ting·burg (hun′ting bûrg′), *n.* a town in SW Indiana. 4146 (1960).

hunt′ing case′, a watchcase with a hinged cover to protect the crystal.

hunt′ing chair′, a chair having a sliding frame in front serving as a footrest.

Hunt′ing Dogs′, *Astron.* the constellation Canes Venatici.

Hun·ting·don (hun′ting dən), *n.* **1.** a town in central Pennsylvania. 7234 (1960). **2.** Huntingdonshire.

Hun·ting·don·shire (hun′ting dən shēr′, -shər), *n.* a county in E England. 79,879 (1961); 366 sq. mi. *Co. seat:* Huntingdon. Also called **Huntingdon, Hunts.**

hunt′ing ground′, a section or area for hunting game.

hunt′ing horn′, *Music.* the earliest form of the modern horn, consisting of a conical tube coiled in a circle for carrying over the shoulder, and having a flaring bell and a trumpetlike mouthpiece.

hunt′ing knife′, a large, sharp knife, usually with a handle shaped to fit a firm grip and a blade with a slight curve toward the tip that is used to skin and cut up game, or sometimes to dispatch it.

hunt′ing leop′ard, the cheetah.

hunt′ing mi′ter, *Joinery.* a curved intersection between two moldings of equal breadth, one or both curved in plan, formed by the bisection of the varying angles of intersection throughout the thickness.

hunt′ing sword′, a short, light saber of the 18th century, having a straight or slightly curved blade.

Hun·ting·ton (hun′ting tən), *n.* **1. Samuel,** 1731–96, U.S. statesman: governor of Connecticut 1786–96. **2.** a city in W West Virginia, on the Ohio River. 83,672 (1960). **3.** a city in NE Indiana. 16,185 (1960). **4.** a boy's given name.

Hun′tington Beach′, a city in SW California, SE of Los Angeles. 11,492 (1960).

Hun′tington Park′, a city in SW California, near Los Angeles. 29,920 (1960).

Hun′tington Sta′tion, a town on W Long Island, in SE New York. 23,438 (1960).

Hun′tington Woods′, a town in SE Michigan. 8746 (1960).

hunt′ing watch′, hunter (def. 6).

Hunt·ley (hunt′lē), *n.* a boy's given name.

hunt·ress (hun′tris), *n.* **1.** a woman who hunts. **2.** a mare used as a hunting horse. [ME *hunteresse.* See HUNTER, -ESS]

Hunts (hunts), *n.* Huntingdonshire.

hunts·man (hunts′mən), *n., pl.* **-men.** **1.** the member of a hunt staff who manages the hounds during the hunt. **2.** a hunter. [HUNT + 'S¹ + MAN¹] —**hunts′man·ship′,** *n.*

hunts·man's-cup (hunts′mənz kup′), *n.* any plant of the genus *Sarracenia,* esp. *S. purpurea,* the pitcher plant.

hunt's-up (hunts′up′), *n.* (formerly) a call played on a hunting horn in the morning to rouse and assemble the participants in a hunt. [from phrase *(the) hunt is up*]

Hunts·ville (hunts′vil), *n.* a city in N Alabama: rocket and missile center. 72,365 (1960).

hunt′ ta′ble. See **hunt board.**

Hun·tun (hōōn′dōōn′), *n.* a mythical Chinese being personifying chaos.

Hu·nya·di (hōō′nyo dē), *n.* **Já·nos** (yä′nôsh), 1387?–1456, Hungarian soldier and national hero. Also, **Hu′-nya·dy.**

Hu′on pine′ (hyōō′on), a taxaceous tree, *Dacrydium Franklinii,* of Tasmania. [after the *Huon* river in Tasmania]

Hu·pa (hōō′pə), *n.* an Athapaskan Indian language of NW California.

Hu·peh (hōō′pā′; *Chin.* hōō′be′), *n.* a province in central China. 30,790,000 (est. 1957); 72,394 sq. mi. *Cap.:* Wuchang.

hup·pah (KHōō pä′; *Eng.* KHŏŏp′ə), *n., pl.* **hup·pot, hup·poth** (KHōō pōt′), *Eng.* **hup·pahs.** *Hebrew.* a canopy under which the Jewish marriage ceremony is performed. Also, **chuppah.**

hur·cheon (hûr′chən), *n.* *Chiefly Scot.* **1.** a hedgehog. **2.** an urchin. [ME *hirchoun,* var. of *urchun* URCHIN]

Hurd (hûrd), *n.* a boy's given name.

hur·dies (hûr′dēz), *n.pl.* *Scot.* the buttocks. [?]

hur·dle (hûr′dəl), *n., v.,* **-dled, -dling.** —*n.* **1.** a portable barrier over which men must leap in certain running races, usually a wooden frame with a hinged inner frame that swings down under impact to prevent injury to a runner who does not clear it. **2. hurdles,** (*construed as sing.*) a race in which contestants must leap over a number of such barriers placed at specific intervals around the track. Cf. **high hurdles, low hurdles.** **3.** any of various vertical barriers, as a hedge, low wall, section of fence, etc., over which horses must jump in certain types of turf races, as a steeplechase, but esp. a man-made barrier. **4.** a difficult problem to be overcome; obstacle. **5.** *Chiefly Brit.* a movable rectangular frame of interlaced twigs, crossed bars, or the like, as for a temporary fence. **6.** a frame or sledge on which criminals were formerly drawn to the place of execution. —*v.t.* **7.** to leap over (a hurdle, barrier, fence, etc.) as in a race. **8.** to master (a difficulty, problem, etc.); overcome. **9.** to construct with hurdles; enclose with hurdles. —*v.i.* **10.** to leap over a hurdle or other barrier. [ME *hirdel, hurdel,* OE *hyrdel,* equiv. to *hyrd-* + *-l* n. suffix; c. G *Hürde* hurdle; akin to L *crātis* hurdle, wickerwork, Gk *kýrtos* basket, cage, Skt *kṛt* spin] —**hur′dler,** *n.*

Hurdy-gurdy (def. 2)

hurds (hûrdz), *n.* (*construed as pl.*) hards.

hur·dy-gur·dy (hûr′dē gûr′dē, -gûr′-), *n., pl.* **-gur·dies.** **1.** a barrel organ or similar instrument played by turning a crank. **2.** a lute- or guitar-shaped stringed musical instrument sounded by the revolution, against the strings, of a rosined wheel turned by a crank. [var. of Scot *hirdy-girdy* uproar, influenced by HURLY-BURLY] —**hur′dy-gur′dist, hur′dy-gur′dy·ist,** *n.*

hurl (hûrl), *v.t.* **1.** to throw or fling with great force or vigor. **2.** to throw or cast down. **3.** to utter with vehemence: *to hurl invective at someone.* —*v.i.* **4.** to throw a missile. **5.** *Baseball.* to pitch a ball. —*n.* **6.** a forcible or violent throw; fling. [ME *hurle,* equiv. to *hur-* (? < Gmc; see HURRY) + *-le* -LE; akin to LG *hurreln* to toss, Fris *hurreln* to roar (said of the wind), dial. G *hurlen* to roll, rumble (said of thunder)] —**hurl′er,** *n.*

—**Syn. 1.** cast, pitch.

hurl·ey (hûr′lē), *n., pl.* **hurl·eys, hurl·ies.** *Brit.* **1.** the game of hurling. **2.** the leather-covered ball used in hurling. **3.** the stick used in hurling, similar to a field hockey stick but with a wide, flat blade. **4.** *Informal.* a club or cudgel. Also, **hurly.** [HURL + *-ey,* as in *hockey*]

Hur·ley (hûr′lē), *n.* a town in N Wisconsin. 2763 (1960).

hurl·ing (hûr′ling), *n.* **1.** the act of throwing or casting, esp. with great force or strength. **2.** a traditionally Irish game played by two teams of 15 men each on a rectangular field 140 yards long, points being scored by hitting, pushing, carrying, or throwing the leather-covered ball between the goalposts at the opponent's end of the field with a wide-bladed stick resembling a hockey stick. **3.** (in parts of Britain, esp. Cornwall) a traditional, rural game in which two groups of players, using methods similar to those of football, vie for possession of a ball or other object and try to carry or hurl it into their own parish, village, farm, etc. [ME; see HURL, -ING¹]

hurl·y (hûr′lē), *n., pl.* **hurl·ies.** **1.** commotion; hurly-burly. **2.** *Brit.* hurley.

hurl·y-burl·y (hûr′lē bûr′lē, -bur′-), *n., pl.* **-burl·ies,** *adj.* —*n.* **1.** commotion; uproar; tumult. —*adj.* **2.** full of commotion; tumultuous. [alter. of *hurling (and) burling,* rhyming phrase based on HURLING in its (now obs.) sense of tumult, uproar]

Hu·rok (hyŏŏr′ok), *n.* **Sol(omon),** born 1888, U.S. impresario, born in Russia.

Hu·ron (hyŏŏr′ən, -on), *n.* **1.** a member of an Indian tribe, the northwestern member of the Iroquoian family, living west of Lake Huron. **2.** an Iroquoian language, the language of the Huron Indians. **3. Lake,** a lake between the U.S. and Canada: second largest of the Great Lakes. 23,010 sq. mi. **4.** a city in E South Dakota. 14,180 (1960). **5.** a town in N Ohio. 5197 (1960).

hur·rah (hə rä′, -rô′), *interj.* **1.** (used as an exclamation of joy, exultation, appreciation, encouragement, or the like.) —*v.i.* **2.** to shout "hurrah." —*n.* **3.** an exclamation of "hurrah." **4.** hubbub; commotion; fanfare: *He* deplored the absurd hurrah. Also, **hur·ray** (hə rā′), **hooray, hoorah.** [< G *hurra;* r. HUZZAH]

Hur·ri (ho͝or′ē), *n., pl.* **-ris,** (*esp. collectively*) **-ri,** *adj.* Hurrian.

Hur·ri·an (ho͝or′ē ən), *n.* **1.** a member of an ancient people, sometimes identified with the Horites, who lived in the Middle East during the 2nd and 3rd millenniums B.C. and who established the Mitanni kingdom about 1400 B.C. **2.** the extinct language of the Hurrians, written in a syllabic, cuneiform script but not known to be related to any other language. —*adj.* **3.** of or pertaining to the Hurrians or their language. [< Heb *Ḥorī* + -AN]

hur·ri·cane (hûr′ə kān′, hur′- *or, esp. Brit.,* -kən), *n.* **1.** a violent, tropical, cyclonic storm of the western North Atlantic, having wind speeds of or in excess of 73 miles per hour. Cf. **tropical cyclone. 2.** a storm of the most intense severity. **3.** anything suggesting a violent storm. [< Sp *huracán* < Taino *hurakán*]

hur′ricane deck′, a deck at the top of a passenger steamer, having a roof supported by light scantlings. —**hur′ri·cane-decked′,** *adj.*

hur·ri·cane-force wind (hûr′ə kān′fôrs′ wind′, -fôrs′, hur′- *or, esp. Brit.,* -kən-), a wind, not necessarily a hurricane, of Beaufort scale numbers 12–17, or having a speed of at least 73 miles per hour: the strongest of the winds.

hur′ricane lamp′, 1. a candlestick protected against draughts by a glass chimney. **2.** a kerosene or oil lantern, usually having a glass chimney.

hur′ricane lan′tern, a lantern having its flame shielded against strong winds. Also called **tornado lantern.**

hur·ried (hûr′ēd, hur′-), *adj.* **1.** moving or working rapidly, esp. forced or required to hurry, as a person. **2.** characterized by or done with hurry; hasty: *a hurried meal.* [HURRY + -ED²] —**hur′ried·ly,** *adv.* —**hur′ried·ness,** *n.*

hur·ry (hûr′ē, hur′ē), *v.,* **-ried, -ry·ing,** *n., pl.* **-ries.** —*v.i.* **1.** to move, proceed, or act with haste (often fol. by *up*): *Hurry, or we'll be late. Hurry up, it's raining out.* —*v.t.* **2.** to drive, carry, or cause to move or perform with speed. **3.** to hasten; urge forward (often fol. by *up*). **4.** to impel or perform with undue haste: *to hurry someone into a decision.* —*n.* **5.** a state of urgency or eagerness: *to be in a hurry to begin.* **6.** hurried movement or action; haste. [ME *horye(n),* perh. of imit. orig.; c. L *currere* to run; see CURRENT, SCURRY, HURL] —**hur′ry·ing·ly,** *adv.*

—**Syn. 1.** See **rush¹. 2.** hasten. **3.** accelerate, quicken; expedite, hustle. **6.** celerity; expedition, dispatch; speed, quickness; bustle, ado, precipitation, flurry, confusion, perturbation. —**Ant. 3.** delay, slow. **6.** deliberation.

hur·ry-scur·ry (hûr′ē skûr′ē, hur′ē skur′ē), *n., adv., adj., v.* **-scur·ried, -scur·ry·ing.** —*n.* **1.** headlong, disorderly haste; hurry and confusion. —*adv.* **2.** with hurrying and scurrying. **3.** confusedly; in a bustle. —*adj.* **4.** characterized by headlong, disorderly flight or haste. —*v.i.* **5.** to rush or go hurry-scurry.

hur·ry-skur·ry (hûr′ē skûr′ē, hur′ē skur′ē), *n., adv., adj., v.i.,* **-skur·ried, -skur·ry·ing.** hurry-scurry.

hur·ry-up (hûr′ē up′, hur′-), *adj.* characterized by speed or the need for speed; quick: *a hurry-up meal; a hurry-up phone call.* [adj. use of v. phrase *hurry up*]

hur·sin·ghar (hûr′sing gär′), *n.* See **night jasmine** (def. 1). [< Hindi *hārsingār*]

hurst¹ (hûrst), *n.* a casing surrounding millstones to confine the flour. [?]

hurst² (hûrst), *n.* **1.** a wooded hill. **2.** a grove. [ME; OE *hyrst;* c. LG *horst* wooded high spot; akin to Icel *hrjóstr* rough place]

Hurst (hûrst), *n.* **Fannie,** 1889–1968, U.S. novelist and short-story writer.

hurt (hûrt), *v.,* **hurt, hurt·ing,** *n., adj.* —*v.t.* **1.** to cause bodily injury to; injure: *He was badly hurt in the accident.* **2.** to cause bodily pain to or in: *The wound still hurts him.* **3.** to damage or decrease the efficiency of (a material object) by striking, rough use, improper care, etc.: *Moths can't hurt this suit, it's mothproof. Dirty oil can hurt a car's engine.* **4.** to affect adversely; harm: *to hurt one's reputation; It wouldn't hurt the lawn if you watered it more often.* **5.** to cause mental pain to; offend or grieve: *She hurt his feelings by not asking him to the party.* —*v.i.* **6.** to feel or suffer bodily or mental pain or distress: *My finger still hurts.* **7.** to cause bodily or mental pain or distress: *The blow to his pride hurt most.* **8.** to cause injury, damage, or harm. —*n.* **9.** a blow that inflicts a wound; bodily injury or the cause of such injury. **10.** injury, damage, or harm. **11.** the cause of mental pain or offense, as an insult. **12.** *Heraldry.* a roundel azure. —*adj.* **13.** physically injured: *The hurt child was taken to the hospital.* **14.** offended; suffering, as in mind: *hurt pride.* **15.** suggesting that one has been offended or is suffering in mind: *Take that hurt look off your face!* **16.** damaged: *hurt merchandise.* [ME *hurte(n)* (to) strike, hit < OF *hurte(r)* (cf. F *heurter*) ? < Gmc **hurt-* to butt; cf. MHG *hurt* an impact, Icel *hrütr* ram] —**hurt′a·ble,** *adj.*

—**Syn. 3.** mar, impair. **5.** afflict, wound. **6.** ache. **9.** See **injury. 11.** cut, slight.

hurt·er¹ (hûr′tər), *n.* a person or thing that causes hurt. [HURT + -ER¹]

hurt·er² (hûr′tər), *n.* (in a wagon or the like) a butting piece on the shoulder of an axle against which the hub strikes. [HURT + -ER²; r. ME *hurtour* < AF; MF *hurtouoir*]

hurt·ful (hûrt′fəl), *adj.* causing hurt or injury; injurious; harmful. [HURT + -FUL] —**hurt′ful·ly,** *adv.* —**hurt′ful·ness,** *n.*

—**Syn.** destructive, pernicious; noxious.

hur·tle (hûr′tᵊl), *v.,* **-tled, -tling,** *n.* —*v.i.* **1.** to rush violently; move with great speed: *The car hurtled down the highway.* **2.** to go noisily or resoundingly, as with violent or rapid motion: *The sound was deafening, as tons of snow hurtled down the mountain.* **3.** *Rare.* to strike together or against something; collide. —*v.t.* **4.** to drive violently; fling; dash. **5.** *Rare.* to dash against; collide with. —*n.* **6.** clash; collision; shock; clatter. [ME *hurtle,* equiv. to *hurt(en)* (see HURT) + *-le* -LE]

hur·tle·ber·ry (hûr′tᵊl ber′ē), *n., pl.* **-ries.** whortleberry.

hurt·less (hûrt′lis), *adj.* **1.** unhurt; uninjured. **2.** harmless; innocuous. [ME *hurtles.* See HURT, -LESS] —**hurt′less·ly,** *adv.* —**hurt′less·ness,** *n.*

hur·tling (hûrt′ling), *adj.* moving rapidly in a headlong, unrestrained manner; speeding: *a hurtling boulder.* [HURTLE + -ING²] —**hur′tling·ly,** *adv.*

Hus (hus; *Ger., Czech.* ho͞os), *n.* **Jan** (jan; *Ger., Czech.* yän). See **Huss, John.**

Hu·sain (ho͞o sīn′), *n.* (*al-Husayn*) A.D. 629?–680, Arabian caliph, the son of Ali and Fatima and the brother of Hasan. Also, **Hosein.**

hus·band (huz′bənd), *n.* **1.** a married man, esp. considered in relation to his wife. **2.** See **ship's husband. 3.** a prudent or frugal manager. **4.** *Brit.* a manager. —*v.t.* **5.** to manage, esp. with prudent economy. **6.** to use frugally; conserve: *to husband one's resources.* **7.** *Archaic.* **a.** to be or become a husband to; marry. **b.** to find a husband for. **8.** *Archaic.* to till; cultivate. [ME *husband(e),* OE *hūsbonda* master of the house < Scand; cf. Icel *hūsbōndi,* equiv. to *hūs* HOUSE + *bōndi* (*bō-,* var. of *bū-* dwell (see BOOR) + *-nd* prp. suffix + *-i* inflexional ending)] —**hus′band·er,** *n.* —**hus′band·less,** *adj.*

hus·band·age (huz′bən dij), *n.* the fees and commissions of a ship's husband. [HUSBAND + -AGE]

hus·band·man (huz′bənd mən), *n., pl.* **-men.** a farmer. [ME *husbondeman.* See HUSBAND, MAN¹]

hus·band·ry (huz′bən drē), *n.* **1.** the cultivation and production of edible crops or of animals for food; agriculture; farming. **2.** the science of raising crops or food animals. **3.** careful or thrifty management; frugality, thrift, or conservation. **4.** the management of domestic affairs, or of resources generally. [ME *housebondrie.* See HUSBAND, -RY]

Hu·sein ibn-A·li (ho͞o sīn′ ib′ən ä′lē, -ä lē′; ho͞o-sān′), 1856–1931, 1st king of Hejaz 1916–24.

hush¹ (hush), *interj.* **1.** (used as a command to be silent or quiet.) —*v.i.* **2.** to become or be silent or quiet: *They hushed as the judge walked in.* —*v.t.* **3.** to make silent; silence. **4.** to suppress mention of; keep concealed (often fol. by *up*): *They hushed up the scandal.* **5.** to calm, quiet, or allay: *to hush someone's fears.* —*n.* **6.** silence or quiet, esp. after noise. **7.** *Phonet.* either of the sibilant sounds (sh) and (zh). —*adj.* **8.** *Archaic.* silent; quiet. [appar. back formation from *husht* WHIST¹ (ME *huissht*), the *-t* being taken for ptp. suffix] —**hush·ed·ly** (hush′id lē, husht′lē), *adv.* —**hush′ful,** *adj.* —**hush′ful·ly,** *adv.*

hush² (hush), *Brit. Dial.* —*n.* **1.** the sound made by rushing waters, esp. by the sea. **2.** a rush or cascade of water, as a billow of the sea. —*v.t.* **3.** to separate (ore) from earth by washing the lighter substance away with a strong cascade of water; wash (ore) commercially. [imit. of the sound]

hush·a·by (hush′ə bī′), *v.i.* (used imperatively) to become silent; hush: *Hushaby, baby.* [HUSH¹ + (LULL)ABY]

hush-hush (hush′hush′), *adj.* highly secret or confidential: *a hush-hush report; a hush-hush political investigation.* [redupl. based on HUSH¹]

Hu Shih (ho͞o′ shœ′), 1891–1962, Chinese scholar and diplomat.

hush·ion (hush′ən), *n.* *Scot. Archaic.* a stocking without a foot; gaiter. Also, **hoeshin.** [? alter. of *huseau* (now obs.) < MF *houseau,* OF *housel,* equiv. to *house* boot + *-el* dim. suffix]

hush′ mon′ey, a bribe to keep someone silent about something esp. to keep the receiver from exposing a scandal.

hush′ pup′py, *Chiefly Southern U.S.* a small, unsweetened, corn-meal cake fried in deep fat. [so called from the fact that it was fed to dogs]

husk (husk), *n.* **1.** the dry external covering of certain fruits or seeds, esp. of an ear of corn. **2.** the enveloping or outer part of anything, esp. when dry or worthless. —*v.t.* **3.** to remove the husk from. **4.** to speak or sing in a husky voice: *He husked out his orders.* —*v.i.* **5.** to become husky: *Her voice started to husk.* [ME *huske,* equiv. to *hus-* (akin to OE *hosu* pod, husk) + *-ke,* weak var. of -OCK] —**husk′er,** *n.* —**husk′like′,** *adj.*

husk·ing (hus′king), *n.* **1.** the act of removing husks, esp. those of corn. **2.** See **husking bee.** [HUSK + -ING¹]

husk′ing bee′, a gathering of farm families to husk corn, usually as part of a celebration or party.

Hus·kis·son (hus′ki sən), *n.* **William,** 1770–1830, British statesman and financier.

husk′ toma′to. See **ground cherry** (def. 1).

husk·y¹ (hus′kē), *adj.,* **husk·i·er, husk·i·est. 1.** burly; big and strong. **2.** (of the voice) having a semiwhispered vocal tone; somewhat hoarse, as when speaking with a cold or from grief or passion. **3.** like, covered with, or full of husks. [HUSK + -Y¹] —**husk′i·ly,** *adv.* —**husk′i·ness,** *n.*

husk·y² (hus′kē), *n., pl.* **husk·ies.** *Informal.* a big, strong person. [HUSK + -Y²]

husk·y³ (hus′kē), *n., pl.* **husk·ies,** *adj.* (*sometimes cap.*) —*n.* **1.** See **Eskimo dog. 2.** See **Siberian Husky. 3.** *Chiefly Canadian.* **a.** an Eskimo. **b.** any Eskimo-Aleut language or dialect. —*adj.* **4.** *Chiefly Canadian.* Eskimo. [? var. of ESKI(MO)]

Huss (hus; *Ger., Czech.* ho͞os), *n.* **John,** 1369?–1415, Czech religious reformer and martyr. Also, **Hus.** —**Huss′ism,** *n.*

hus·sar (ho͞o zär′), *n.* **1.** (originally) one of a body of light Hungarian cavalry formed during the 15th century. **2.** one of a class of similar troops, usually with striking or flamboyant uniforms, in European armies. [< Hung *huszár,* orig. freebooter < Old Serbian *husar,* var. of *kursar* < It *corsaro* CORSAIR]

Hus·sein I (ho͞o sān′), born 1935, king of Jordan since 1953.

Hus·serl (ho͞os′erl), *n.* **Ed·mund (Gus·tav Al·brecht)** (et′mo͝ont go͞os′täf äl′brekht), 1859–1938, German philosopher born in Austria: founder of the school of philosophy called phenomenology.

Huss·ite (hus′īt), *n.* **1.** a member of the religious reformist and nationalistic movement initiated by John Huss in Bohemia in the late 14th century, maintaining a belief in the supreme authority of the Scriptures and advocating communion in both the bread and wine to laymen as well as priests. —*adj.* **2.** of or pertaining to John Huss or the Hussites. [HUSS + -ITE¹] —**Huss′it·ism,** *n.*

hus·sy (hus′ē, huz′ē), *n., pl.* **-sies. 1.** a bold or lewd woman. **2.** a mischievous or ill-behaved girl. [earlier *hussive* HOUSEWIFE]

hus·tings (hus′tingz), *n.* (*construed as sing. or pl.*) **1.** (before 1872) the temporary platform from which candidates for the British Parliament stood for nomination and addressed the electors. **2.** *Chiefly Brit.* **a.** any electioneering platform. **b.** election proceedings. **3.** Also called **hus′tings court′.** a local court in certain parts of Virginia. [ME, OE < ODan *hūs-thing* house meeting. See HOUSE, THING²]

hus·tle (hus′əl), *v.,* **-tled, -tling,** *n.* —*v.i.* **1.** to proceed or work rapidly or energetically: *to hustle about putting a house in order.* **2.** to push or force one's way; jostle or shove. **3.** *Informal.* to be aggressive, esp. in business or other financial dealings. **4.** *Slang.* **a.** to earn one's living by illicit or unethical means. **b.** (of a prostitute) to solicit clients. —*v.t.* **5.** to convey or cause to move, esp. to leave, roughly or hurriedly: *They hustled him out of the bar.* **6.** to pressure or coerce (a person) to buy or do something: *to hustle the customers into buying more drinks.* **7.** to urge, prod, or speed up: *He hustled the suspect away.* **8.** to obtain (money or the like) by aggressive or illicit means: *He could always hustle a buck or two from some sucker.* **9.** to beg or ask for money from. **10.** to sell in or work (an area), esp. by high-pressure tactics: *The souvenir venders began hustling the town at dawn.* **11.** to sell, esp. as an aggressive vender or peddler: *to hustle souvenirs.* **12.** to jostle, push, or shove roughly. **13.** *Slang.* to induce (someone) to play in a gambling game in which he will have little or no chance to win. **14.** *Slang.* to cheat; swindle: *They hustled him out of his savings.* **15.** to urge, prod, or speed up: *Hustle your work along.* —*n.* **16.** energetic activity, as in work. **17.** discourteous shoving, pushing, or jostling. **18.** *Slang.* **a.** an inducing by fraud, pressure, or aggressive deception, esp. of inexperienced or uninformed persons, to participate in an illicit scheme, dishonest gambling game, etc. **b.** such a scheme, gambling game, etc. [< D *hussel(en),* var. of *hutselen,* equiv. to *huts(en)* (to) shake, jog + *-el-* -LE]

hus·tler (hus′lər), *n.* **1.** *Informal.* an enterprising person determined to succeed; go-getter. **2.** *Slang.* a person who employs fraudulent or unscrupulous methods to obtain money; swindler. **3.** *Slang.* a prostitute; streetwalker. **4.** a person who hustles. **5.** (*cap.*) *U.S. Rocketry.* See under **discoverer** (def. 2). [HUSTLE + -ER¹]

Hus·ton (hyo͞o′stən), *n.* **1. John,** born 1906, U.S. motion-picture director and writer. **2.** his father, **Walter,** 1884–1950, U.S. actor, born in Canada.

hut (hut), *n., v.,* **hut·ted, hut·ting.** —*n.* **1.** a small or humble dwelling of simple construction, esp. one made of natural materials found close by, as of logs, grass, etc. **2.** a simple roofed shelter, often with one or two sides left open. **3.** *Mil.* a wooden or metal structure for the temporary housing of troops. —*v.t.* **4.** to furnish with a hut as temporary housing; billet. —*v.i.* **5.** to lodge or take shelter in a hut. [< F *hutte* < MHG *hütte,* OHG *hutt(e)a* < WGmc **hudjā;* akin to HIDE¹] —**hut′like′,** *adj.*

—**Syn. 1.** shed, hovel. See **cottage.**

hutch (huch), *n.* **1.** a pen or enclosed coop for small animals: *rabbit hutch.* **2.** a hut or cabin. **3.** a small shack; shanty. **4.** a chest, cupboard, bin, etc., for storage. **5.** any of various chestlike cabinets, raised on legs and having doors or drawers in front, sometimes with open shelves above. **6.** a baker's kneading trough. —*v.t.* **7.** *Rare.* to put away in or as in a hutch; hoard. [ME *hucche,* var. of *whucce,* OE *hwicce* chest; not akin to OF *huge, huche* (*ch* form appar. by contamination with English word)]

Hutch·ins (huch′inz), *n.* **Robert Maynard,** born 1899, U.S. educator.

Hutch·in·son (huch′in sən), *n.* **1. Anne Mar·bur·y** (mär′bə rē), 1591–1643, American religious liberal, born in England: banished from Massachusetts 1637. **2. Thomas,** 1711–80, American colonial administrator: royal governor of Massachusetts 1769–74; in exile after 1774. **3.** a city in central Kansas, on the Arkansas River. 37,574 (1960). **4.** a town in central Minnesota. 6207 (1960).

Hü·ther (hyo͞o′thər; *Ger.* hʏ′tər), *n.* **Ju·li·us** (jo͞ol′-yəs; *Ger.* yo͞o′lē o͞os′), 1881–1954, German painter and lithographer.

hut·ment (hut′mənt), *n.* an encampment of huts. [HUT + -MENT]

Hux·lei·an (huks′lē ən, huks lē′ən), *adj.* **1.** of, pertaining to, or characteristic or suggestive of Aldous Huxley, his writings, or his writing style: *a Huxleian nightmare of the future.* **2.** of or pertaining to Thomas Henry Huxley, his biological work, or his writings. Also, **Hux′ley·an.** [HUXLEY + -AN]

Hux·ley (huks′lē), *n.* **1. Al·dous (Leonard)** (ôl′dəs), 1894–1963, English novelist, essayist, and critic. **2. Andrew Fielding,** born 1918, English physiologist: Nobel prize for medicine 1963 (half brother of Aldous and Sir Julian Sorell). **3. Sir Julian Sor·ell** (sor′əl), born 1887, English biologist and writer (brother of Aldous). **4. Thomas Henry,** 1825–95, English biologist and writer (grandfather of Aldous and Sir Julian Sorell Huxley).

Huy·gens (hī′gənz, hoi′-; *Du.* hoi′gens), *n.* **Chris·tian** (kris′chən; *Du.* kris′tē än′), 1629–95, Dutch mathematician, physicist, and astronomer. Also, **Huy′ghens.**

Huy′gens eye′piece, *Optics.* an eyepiece consisting of two plano-convex lenses of crown glass with the plane sides facing the eye and in which the focal length of the field lens is from 1½ to 3 times the focal length of the eye lens, often completely free of lateral chromatic aberration. [named after C. HUYGENS]

Huy′gens prin′ciple, *Optics, Physics.* the principle that the shape of a wave front at a later time can be determined geometrically from its shape at a specified time by considering each point of the wave front as a source of new, secondary waves and by constructing a surface tangent to the collection of secondary waves. [named after C. HUYGENS]

Huys·mans (wēs mäns′), *n.* **Jo·ris Karl** (zhō rēs′ kärl), (*Charles Marie Georges Huysmans*), 1848–1907, French novelist.

huz·zah (hə zä′), *interj.* **1.** (used as an exclamation of joy, applause, appreciation, etc.) hurrah! —*n.* **2.** the exclamation "huzzah." —*v.i.* **3.** to shout "huzzah." —*v.t.* **4.** to salute with huzzahs: *Crowds huzzahed the triumphant hero.* [var. of earlier *hussa, hissa* sailors' cry; see HOISE]

H.V., high voltage. Also, **h.v.**

hwan (hwän, wän), *n., pl.* **hwan.** the former paper money and monetary unit of South Korea, equal to 100 chon and equivalent to about .008 of a U.S. dollar: replaced by the won in 1962. Also, **won.** [< Korean]

Hwang Hai (hwäng′ hī′), Chinese name of the **Yellow Sea.**

Hwang Ho (hwäng′ hō′; *Chin.* hwäng′ hu′), a river flowing from W China into the Gulf of Pohai. 2800 mi. long. Also, **Hoangho.** Also called **Yellow River.** See map under **Yangtze.**

hwt (hōōt), *interj. Welsh.* hoot².

Hy (hī), *n.* a boy's given name, form of **Hiram.**

hy., *Elect.* henry.

hy·a·cinth (hī′ə sinth), *n.* **1.** any bulbous, liliaceous plant of the genus *Hyacinthus,* esp. *H. orientalis,* cultivated for its spikes of fragrant, white or colored, bell-shaped flowers. **2.** a flower of such a plant. **3.** a bulb of such a plant. **4.** a plant fabled to have sprung from the blood of Hyacinthus and variously identified as iris, gladiolus, larkspur, etc. **4.** Also called **jacinth.** a reddish-orange zircon. **5.** a gem of the ancients, held to be the amethyst or sapphire. [< L *hyacinth(us)* < Gk *hyákinthos* blue larkspur, also, a gem of blue color; r. JACINTH]

Hyacinth, *Hyacinthus orientalis*

Hy·a·cinth (hī′ə sinth), *n.* a girl's given name.

hy′acinth bean′, a perennial vine, *Dolichos lablab,* of the tropical Eastern Hemisphere, having purple or white flowers and black or white seeds in a papery, beaked pod. Also called **bonavist, lablab.**

Hy·a·cin·thi·des (hī′ə sin′thi dēz′), *n.pl. Class. Myth.* the daughters of Hyacinthus who were sacrificed to save Athens from the attacking King Minos.

hy·a·cin·thin (hī′ə sin′thin), *n. Chem.* phenylacetaldehyde. [HYACINTH + -IN²]

hy·a·cin·thine (hī′ə sin′thin, -thīn), *adj.* **1.** of or like the hyacinth. **2.** adorned with hyacinths. [< L *hyacinthin(us)* < Gk *hyakínthinos.* See HYACINTH, -INE¹]

Hy·a·cin·thus (hī′ə sin′thəs), *n. Class. Myth.* a beautiful youth loved by Apollo, who accidentally killed him with a discus: from his blood sprang a flower whose petals are marked with the letters AI AI (alas!).

Hy·a·des (hī′ə dēz′), *n.pl.* **1.** *Astron.* a group of stars comprising a moving cluster in the constellation Taurus, supposed by the ancients to indicate the approach of rain when they rose with the sun. **2.** *Class. Myth.* a group of nymphs and sisters of the Pleiades who nurtured the infant Dionysus and were placed among the stars as a reward. Also, **Hy·ads** (hī′adz). [< L < Gk, equiv. to *hý(ein)* (to) rain + *-ades,* pl. of *-as* -AD]

hy·ae·na (hī ē′nə), *n.* hyena. —**hy·ae′nic,** *adj.*

hyal-, var. of **hyalo-** before a vowel: *hyalite.*

hy·a·line (*n.* hī′ə lēn′, -lin; *adj.* hī′ə lin, -līn′), *n.* **1.** Also, **hy·a·lin** (hī′ə lin). *Biochem.* a horny substance found in hydatid cysts, closely resembling chitin. **2.** something glassy or transparent. —*adj.* **3.** glassy, crystalline, or transparent. **4.** of or pertaining to glass. **5.** amorphous; not crystalline. [< LL *hyalin(us)* < Gk *hyálinos* of glass. See HYAL-, -INE¹]

hy′aline cart′ilage, *Anat.* the typical, translucent form of cartilage, containing little fibrous tissue.

hy′aline degenera′tion, *Pathol.* a condition in which normal tissue deteriorates into a homogeneous, translucent material.

hy′aline mem′brane disease′, *Pathol.* a frequently fatal disease of the lungs, occurring in the newborn, esp. premature infant, and characterized by a fibrinous membrane lining the air sacs, and associated with rapid, difficult respiration.

hy·a·lin·i·za·tion (hī′ə li ni zā′shən), *n. Pathol.* the process of becoming hyaline or undergoing hyaline degeneration. [HYALINIZE + -ATION]

hy·a·lin·ize (hī′ə lə nīz′), *v.i.,* **-ized, -iz·ing.** to become hyaline. [HYALINE + -IZE]

hy·a·lite (hī′ə līt′), *n.* a colorless variety of opal, sometimes transparent like glass, and sometimes whitish and translucent. [HYAL- + -ITE¹]

hyalo-, a learned borrowing from Greek meaning "glass," used in the formation of compound words: *hyaloplasm.* Also, *esp. before a vowel,* **hyal-.** [< Gk, comb. form of *hýalos* glass]

hy·al·o·gen (hī al′ə jin, -gen′, hī′ə lō-), *n. Biochem.* any of several water-insoluble mucoproteins that are found in certain animal tissues, as in the vitreous humor, the submaxillary glands, and the like, and that yield hyaline upon hydrolysis. [HYALO- + -GEN]

hy·a·lo·graph (hī′ə lō graf′, -gräf′), *n.* an instrument used in hyalography. [HYALO- + -GRAPH]

hy·a·log·ra·phy (hī′ə log′rə fē), *n.* the technique of writing or engraving on glass. [HYALO- + -GRAPHY] —**hy′a·log′ra·pher,** *n.*

hy·a·loid (hī′ə loid′), *n.* **1.** See **hyaloid membrane.** —*adj.* **2.** glassy; hyaline. [< Gk *hyaloeid(ḗs)* like glass. See HYAL-, -OID]

hy′aloid mem′brane, *Anat.* the delicate, pellucid, and nearly structureless membrane enclosing the vitreous humor of the eye.

hy·al·o·mere (hī al′ə mēr′, hī′ə lō-), *n. Anat.* the transparent part of a blood platelet, surrounding the chromomere. [HYALO- + -MERE]

hy·al·o·phane (hī al′ə fān′, hī′ə lō-), *n. Mineral.* a variety of orthoclase having some of the potassium replaced by barium. [HYALO- + -PHANE]

hy·al·o·plasm (hī al′ə plaz′əm, hī′ə lō-), *n. Biol.* the clear portion of the protoplasm of a cell, as distinguished from the granular and reticular portions. [HYALO- + -PLASM] —**hy·al′o·plas′mic,** *adj.*

hy′a·lu·ron′ic ac′id (hī′ə lōō ron′ik, hī′-), *Biochem.* a mucopolysaccharide found in all tissue, esp. the vitreous humor, synovial fluid, skin, and umbilical cord, yielding glucosamine, glucuronic acid, and acetic acid upon hydrolysis, and serving as a viscous agent in the ground substance of tissues and as a lubricant in joints. [HYAL- + Gk *oûron* urine + -IC]

hy·a·lu·ron·i·dase (hī′ə lōō ron′i dās′, -dāz′), *n.* **1.** *Biochem.* a mucolytic enzyme that is found in the skin of most animals, in snake venom, and in hemolytic streptococci and certain other bacteria, and that decreases the viscosity of the intercellular matrix by breaking down hyaluronic acid. **2.** *Pharm.* a commercial form of this substance, used chiefly to promote the diffusion of intradermally injected drugs. [HYAL- + Gk *oûron* urine + -ID³ + -ASE]

Hy·an·nis (hī an′is), *n.* a town in SE Massachusetts. 5139 (1960).

Hyan′nis Port′, a town in SE Massachusetts, on Nantucket Sound: summer resort.

Hy·att (hī′ət), *n.* a boy's given name.

Hy·atts·ville (hī′əts vil′), *n.* a city in central Maryland. 15,168 (1960).

hy·brid (hī′brid), *n.* **1.** the offspring of two animals or plants of different races, breeds, varieties, species, or genera. **2.** a person or group of persons produced by the interaction or crossbreeding of two unlike cultures, traditions, etc. **3.** anything derived from heterogeneous sources, or composed of elements of different or incongruous kinds: *a hybrid of the academic and business worlds.* —*adj.* **4.** bred from two distinct races, breeds, varieties, species, or genera. **5.** composite; formed or composed of heterogeneous elements. **6.** composed of elements originally drawn from different languages, as a word. [< L *hybrid(a),* var. of *hibrida* offspring of a tame sow and wild boar, mongrel]

—**Syn. 4.** HYBRID, MONGREL refer to animals or plants of mixed origin. HYBRID is the scientific term: *hybrid corn; a hybrid variety of sheep.* MONGREL, used originally of dogs to denote especially the offspring of repeated crossings of different breeds, is now extended to other animals and to plants; it is usually depreciatory, as denoting mixed, nondescript, or degenerate breed or character: *a mongrel pup.* —**Ant. 4.** purebred, thoroughbred.

hy′brid corn′, **1.** a crossbred corn, esp. the grain of corn developed by hybridization of inbred varieties. **2.** a plant grown from the grain of this corn.

hy·brid·ise (hī′bri dīz′), *v.t., v.i.,* **-ised, -is·ing.** *Chiefly Brit.* hybridize. —**hy′brid·is′a·ble,** *adj.* —**hy′brid·is′er,** *n.*

hy·brid·ism (hī′bri diz′əm), *n.* **1.** Also, **hy·brid·i·ty** (hī brid′i tē). the quality or condition of being hybrid. **2.** the production of hybrids. [HYBRID + -ISM]

hy·brid·ist (hī′bri dist), *n.* one who hybridizes; a hybridizer: *a hybridist of rare orchids.* [HYBRID + -IST]

hy·brid·ize (hī′bri dīz′), *v.,* **-ized, -iz·ing.** —*v.t.* **1.** to cause to produce hybrids; cross. **2.** to breed or cause the production of (a hybrid). **3.** to form in a hybrid manner. —*v.i.* **4.** to produce hybrids. **5.** to cause the production of hybrids by crossing different species, varieties, etc. Also, *esp. Brit.,* **hybridise.** [HYBRID + -IZE] —**hy′brid·iz′a·ble,** *adj.* —**hy′brid·iz′er,** *n.*

hy′brid perpet′ual, a cultivated variety of rose that is noted for its vigorous growth, and that blooms more or less continuously throughout the season.

hy′brid tea′, a cultivated rose originally produced chiefly by crossing the tea rose and the hybrid perpetual.

hy′brid vig′or, heterosis.

hy·bris (hī′bris), *n.* hubris. —**hy·bris′tic,** *adj.*

hyd., **1.** hydraulics. **2.** hydrostatics.

hy·dan·to·in (hī dan′tō in), *n. Pharm.* a colorless, needlelike, crystalline compound, $C_3H_4N_2O_2$, used in the synthesis of pharmaceutical substances and resins. [HYD(ROGEN + *all*)*antoin* crystal from oxidation of uric acid (see ALLANTOIS, -IN²)]

hy·da·tid (hī′də tid), *Pathol.* —*n.* **1.** a cyst with watery contents that is produced in man and animals by a tapeworm in the larval state. **2.** the encysted larva of a tapeworm; cysticercus. —*adj.* Also, **hy′da·tid′i·nous. 3.** of or pertaining to a hydatid. **4.** containing or affected by hydatids. [< Gk *hydatid-* (s. of *hydatís*) watery vesicle]

Hyde (hīd), *n.* **1. Douglas,** 1860–1949, Irish author and statesman: president of Eire 1938–45. **2. Edward.** See **Clarendon, Edward Hyde. 3.** a boy's given name.

Hyde′ Park′, **1.** a public park in London, England. **2.** a village in SE New York, on the Hudson: site of the estate and burial place of Franklin D. Roosevelt. 1979 (1960).

Hy·der·a·bad (hī′dər ə bäd′, -bad′, hī′drə-), *n.* **1.** a former state in S India: now part of Andhra Pradesh. **2.** a city in and the capital of Andhra Pradesh, in the W part. 1,251,100 (1961). **3.** a city in SE West Pakistan, in Pakistan, on the Indus River. 434,000 (est. 1961).

Hy·der A·li (hī′dər ä′lē, ä lē′). See **Haidar Ali.**

hyd·no·car·pate (hid′nō kär′pāt), *n. Chem.* a salt or ester of hydnocarpic acid. [< Gk *hýdno(n)* truffle + *karp(ós)* fruit + -ATE²]

hyd′no·car′pic ac′id (hid′nō kär′pik, hid′-), *Pharm.* a white, crystalline acid, $C_5H_7(CH_2)_{10}COOH$, obtained from chaulmoogra oil, and used in the treatment of leprosy. [< Gk *hýdno(n)* truffle + *karp(ós)* fruit + -IC]

hydr-¹, var. of **hydro-¹** before a vowel: *hydrant.*

hydr-², var. of **hydro-²** before a vowel: *hydride.*

hy·dra (hī′drə), *n., pl.* **-dras, -drae** (-drē) for 1–3, *gen.* **-drae** (-drē) for 4. **1.** (*often cap.*) *Class. Myth.* a water or marsh serpent with nine heads, each of which, if cut off, grew back as two; Hercules killed this serpent by cauterizing the necks as he cut off the heads. **2.** *Zool.* any fresh-water polyp of the genus *Hydra.* **3.** a persistent or many-sided problem that presents new obstacles as soon as one aspect is solved. **4.** (*cap.*) *Astron.* the Sea Serpent, a large southern constellation extending through 90° of the sky, being the longest of all constellations. [< L < Gk *hýdrā* water serpent, (r. ME *ydre* < MF); see OTTER]

Hydra, Genus *Hydra* (Length to ½ in.)

hy·drac·id (hī dras′id), *n. Chem.* an acid which does not contain oxygen, as hydrochloric acid, HCl. [HYDR-² + ACID]

hy·drae·mi·a (hī drē′mē ə), *n. Med.* hydremia. —**hy·drae′mic,** *adj.*

hy·dra·gogue (hī′drə gôg′, -gog′), *Med.* —*adj.* **1.** causing the discharge of watery fluid, as from the bowels. —*n.* **2.** Also, **hy′dra·gog′.** a hydragogue agent. [< L *hydragōg(us)* < Gk *hydragōgós* water-conveying, equiv. to *hydr-* HYDR-¹ + *agōgós* leading, guiding (see -AGOGUE)]

hy·dra-head·ed (hī′drə hed′id), *adj.* **1.** having many branches, divisions, authorities, facets, etc. **2.** containing many problems, difficulties, or obstacles.

hy·dral·az·ine (hī′drəl az′ēn, -in), *n. Pharm.* a compound, $C_8H_5N_2NHNH_2$, used in the form of its hydrochloride in the treatment of hypertension. [HYDR-² + (PHTH)AL(IC) + AZINE]

hy·dran·gea (hī drān′jə, -jē ə, -dran′-), *n.* **1.** any shrub of the genus *Hydrangea,* species of which are cultivated for their large showy white, pink, or blue flower clusters. **2.** a flower cluster of this shrub. [< NL < Gk *hydr-* HYDR-¹ + *angeîa,* pl. of *angeîon* vessel; so called from cup-shaped seed capsule]

hy·drant (hī′drənt), *n.* **1.** an upright pipe with a spout, nozzle, or other outlet, usually in the street, for drawing water from a main or service pipe. **2.** a water faucet. [HYDR-¹ + -ANT]

hy·dranth (hī′dranth), *n. Zool.* the terminal part of a hydroid polyp that bears the mouth and tentacles and contains the stomach region. [HYDR(A) + Gk *ánth(os)* flower]

hy·drarch (hī′drärk), *adj. Ecol.* (of a sere) originating in a wet habitat. [HYDR-¹ + -ARCH]

hy·drar·gy·rism (hī drär′jə riz′əm), *n. Pathol.* mercurialism. Also, **hy·drar·gyr·i·a** (hī′drär jir′ē ə), **hy·drar·gy·ri·a·sis** (hī drär′jə rī′ə sis). [HYDRARGYR(UM) + -ISM]

hy·drar·gy·rum (hī drär′jər əm), *n. Chem.* mercury. [< NL, equiv. to L *hydrargyr(us)* (< Gk *hydrárgyros* mercury, equiv. to *hydr-* HYDR-¹ + *árgyros* silver) + *-um,* on model of *aurum,* etc.; see -IUM] —**hy·drar·gyr·ic** (hī′drär jir′ik), *adj.*

hy·drase (hī′drās, -drāz), *n. Biochem.* any of the class of enzymes that catalyze the addition of a water molecule into a compound without causing hydrolysis. [HYDR-¹ + -ASE]

hy·dras·tine (hī dras′tēn, -tin), *n. Pharm.* an alkaloid, $C_{21}H_{21}NO_6$, that is extracted from the roots of goldenseal and forms prismatic crystals: used usually in the form of its hydrochloride, sulfate, or tartrate as a stomachic and to inhibit uterine bleeding. [HYDRAST(IS) + -INE²]

hy·dras·ti·nine (hī dras′tə nēn′, -nin), *n. Pharm.* a white, crystalline, poisonous alkaloid, $C_{11}H_{13}NO_3$, synthesized from hydrastine: used usually in the form of its hydrochloride to inhibit uterine bleeding. [HYDRASTINE + -INE²]

hy·dras·tis (hī dras′tis), *n.* goldenseal (def. 2). [< NL]

hy·drate (hī′drāt), *n., v.,* **-drat·ed, -drat·ing.** *Chem.* —*n.* **1.** any of a class of compounds containing chemically combined water. In some hydrates, as washing soda, $Na_2CO_3 \cdot 10H_2O$, the water is loosely held and is easily lost on heating; in others, as sulfuric acid, $SO_3 \cdot H_2O$, or H_2SO_4, it is strongly held as water of constitution. —*v.t., v.i.* **2.** to combine chemically with water. [HYDR-¹ + -ATE²] —**hy·dra′tion,** *n.* —**hy′dra·tor,** *n.*

hy·drat·ed (hī′drā tid), *adj.* **1.** chemically combined with water in its molecular form. **2.** (of paper pulp) beaten until gelatinous for making into water-resistant paper. [HYDRATE + -ED²]

hy′drated alu′mina, *Chem.* See **aluminum hydroxide.**

hy′drated lime′. See **slaked lime.**

hydra′tion num′ber, *Chem.* the number of molecules of water with which an ion can combine in an aqueous solution of given concentration. [HYDRATE + -ION]

hydraul., hydraulics.

hy·drau·lic (hī drô′lik, -drol′ik), *adj.* **1.** operated by, moved by, or employing water or other liquids in motion. **2.** operated by the pressure created by forcing water, oil, or another liquid through a comparatively narrow pipe or orifice. **3.** of or pertaining to water or other liquids in motion. **4.** of or pertaining to hydraulics. **5.** hardening under water, as a cement. [< L *hydraulic(us)* < Gk *hydraulikós* of a water organ. See HYDRAULUS, -IC] —**hy·drau′li·cal·ly,** *adv.*

hydrau′lic accu′mulator, **1.** an apparatus in which gas, usually air, is used as a cushion or shock absorber in a hydraulic system. **2.** (in a hydraulic system) an apparatus for storing energy.

hydrau′lic brake′, a brake operated by fluid pressures in cylinders and connecting tubular lines.

hydrau′lic cou′pling. See **fluid coupling.**

hydrau′lic flu′id, a fluid, usually of low viscosity, as oil, used in a hydraulic system.

hydrau′lic jump′, an abrupt increase in the depth of a flowing liquid with a free surface, accompanied by a corresponding decrease in the rate of flow, as a result of meeting a more level slope or an obstruction.

hydrau′lic lift′, an elevator operated by fluid pressure, esp. one used for raising automobiles in service stations and garages.

hydrau′lic machin′ery, mechanical devices such as pumps, turbines, couplings, etc., in which the flow of a liquid either causes their operation or is produced by them.

hydrau′lic min′ing, placer mining using an artificially created stream of water. Also called **hy·drau·lick·ing** (hī drô′lə king, -drol′ə king).

hydrau′lic mo′tor, a motor that converts the kinetic or potential energy of a fluid into mechanical energy.

hydrau′lic pile′, *Building Trades.* a hollow pile through which a jet of water is forced to wash away the ground beneath.

hydrau′lic press′, a machine permitting a small force applied to a small piston to produce, through fluid pressure, a large force on a large piston.

hydrau′lic ra′dius, the ratio of the cross-sectional area to the perimeter of a pipe, outlet, or the like, through which a fluid is flowing.

hydrau′lic ram′, a device by which the energy of descending water is utilized to raise a part of the water to a height greater than that of the source.

hy·drau·lics (hī drô′liks, -drol′iks), *n.* (*construed as sing.*) the science that deals with the laws governing water or other liquids in motion and their applications in engineering; practical or applied hydrodynamics. [see HYDRAULIC, -ICS]

hydrau′lic torque′ convert′er, an apparatus in which a fluid, usually oil, transmits torque from one shaft to another, producing a different torque in the other shaft. Cf. **fluid coupling.**

hy·drau·lus (hī drô′ləs), *n., pl.* **-li** (-lī), **-lus·es.** a pipe organ of ancient Greece and Rome using water pressure to maintain the air supply. Also, **hy·drau′lis.** [< L < Gk *hýdraulos* water organ, equiv. to *hydr-* HYDR-¹ + *aulós* pipe]

hy·dra·zine (hī′drə zēn′, -zin), *n.* *Chem.* **1.** a colorless, oily, fuming liquid, H_2NNH_2, that is a weak base in solution and forms a large number of salts resembling ammonium salts: used chiefly as a reducing agent and a jet-propulsion fuel. **2.** a class of substances derived by replacing one or more hydrogen atoms in hydrazine by an organic group. [HYDR-² + -INE²]

hy·dra·zo (hī draz′ō, hī′drə zō′), *adj.* *Chem.* containing the hydrazo group.

hydrazo-, a combining form representing the hydrazo group: *hydrazoic.* Also, *esp. before a vowel,* **hydraz-.** [HYDR-² + AZO-]

hy·dra·zo·ate (hī′drə zō′āt), *n.* *Chem.* a salt of hydrazoic acid; azide. [HYDRAZO- + -ATE²]

hydrazo group′, *Chem.* the bivalent group, –HNNH–. Also called **hydraz′o rad′ical.**

hy·dra·zo·ic (hī′drə zō′ik), *adj.* *Chem.* noting or pertaining to hydrazoic acid; triazoic. [HYDRAZO- + -IC]

hy′drazo′ic ac′id, *Chem.* a colorless, very explosive, poisonous liquid, HN_3, having a penetrating odor and irritating to the eyes and mucous membranes. Also called **azoimide.**

hy·dra·zone (hī′drə zōn′), *n.* *Chem.* any of a class of compounds containing the group $>C=NNH_2$. [HYDRAZ- + (KET)ONE]

hy·dre·mi·a (hī drē′mē ə), *n.* *Med.* the state of having an excess of water in the blood. Also, **hydraemia.** [HYDR-¹ + -EMIA] —**hy·dre′mic,** *adj.*

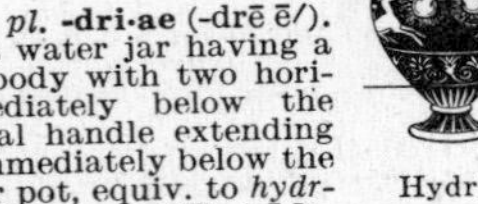
Hydria

hy·dri·a (hī′drē ə), *n., pl.* **-dri·ae** (-drē ē′). *Gk. and Rom. Antiq.* a water jar having a short neck and large body with two horizontal handles immediately below the shoulder and a vertical handle extending from the shoulder to immediately below the lip. [< L < Gk: water pot, equiv. to *hydr-* HYDR-¹ + *-ia* -IA; r. ME *ydre* < OF < L]

hy·dric¹ (hī′drik), *adj.* *Chem.* pertaining to or containing hydrogen. [HYDR-² + -IC]

hy·dric² (hī′drik), *adj.* of, pertaining to, or adapted to a wet or moist environment. [HYDR-¹ + -IC]

-hydric, a combining form of **hydric**¹: *hexahydric.*

hy·dride (hī′drīd, -drid), *n.* *Chem.* a binary compound formed by hydrogen and another, usually more electropositive, element or group, as sodium hydride, NaH, or methyl hydride, CH_4. [HYDR-² + -IDE]

hy·dri·od·ic (hī′drē od′ik), *adj.* *Chem.* of or derived from hydriodic acid. [HYDR-² + IODIC]

hy′driod′ic ac′id, *Chem.* a colorless corrosive liquid, HI, an aqueous solution of hydrogen iodide.

hy·dro (hī′drō), *n.* **1.** *Brit.* **a.** a bathhouse, hotel, or resort catering to people taking mineral-water health cures; spa. **b.** an establishment furnishing hydrotherapy. **2.** *Chiefly Canadian.* **a.** hydroelectric power. **b.** a hydroelectric power plant. [by shortening; see HYDRO-¹]

hydro-¹, a learned borrowing from Greek meaning "water," used in the formation of compound words: *hydroplane; hydrogen.* Also, *esp. before a vowel,* **hydr-¹.** [< Gk, equiv. to *hýd(ō)r* water + *-o-* -O-]

hydro-², *Chem.* a combining form of **hydrogen,** often indicating a combination of hydrogen with some negative element or radical: *hydrobromic.* Also, *esp. before a vowel,* **hydr-².**

hy·dro·a (hī drō′ə), *n.* *Pathol.* a skin condition characterized by red vesicular areas. [< NL < Gk *hidrōia* (pl.) heat spots (lit., sweat eggs), equiv. to *hidr(ōs)* sweat + *-ōia,* pl. of *ōion* egg; *-y-* of NL < *hydr-* HYDR-¹]

hy·dro·air·plane (hī′drō âr′plān′), *n.* a hydroplane. [HYDRO-¹ + AIRPLANE]

hy·dro·bomb (hī′drə bom′), *n.* an aerial torpedo equipped with a rocket engine that propels it after the torpedo has entered the water. [HYDRO-¹ + BOMB]

hy·dro·bro·mic (hī′drə brō′mik), *adj.* *Chem.* of or derived from hydrobromic acid. [HYDRO-² + BROMIC]

hy′drobro′mic ac′id, *Chem.* a colorless or faintly yellow corrosive liquid, HBr, an aqueous solution of hydrogen bromide.

hy·dro·bro·mide (hī′drə brō′mīd, -mid), *n.* *Chem.* a salt formed by the direct union of hydrobromic acid and an organic base, esp. an alkaloid, usually more soluble than the base. [HYDROBROM(IC) + -IDE]

hy·dro·car·bon (hī′drə kär′bən), *n.* *Chem.* any of a class of compounds containing only hydrogen and carbon, as an alkane, methane, CH_4, an alkene, ethylene, $CH_2=CH_2$, an alkyne, acetylene, $CH\equiv CH$, or an aromatic compound, benzene, C_6H_6. [HYDRO-² + CARBON] —**hy·dro·car·bo·na·ceous** (hī′drə kär′bə nā′shəs), *adj.*

hy·dro·cele (hī′drə sēl′), *n.* *Pathol.* an accumulation of serous fluid, usually about the testis. [< L < Gk *hydrokḗlē.* See HYDRO-¹, -CELE¹]

hy·dro·cel·lu·lose (hī′drə sel′yə lōs′), *n.* *Chem.* a gelatinous substance obtained by the partial hydrolysis of cellulose, used chiefly in the manufacture of paper, mercerized cotton, and viscose rayon. [HYDRO-¹ + CELLULOSE]

hy·dro·ce·phal·ic (hī′drō sə fal′ik), *adj.* *Pathol.* of or pertaining to hydrocephalus. Also, **hy·dro·ceph·a·lous** (hī′drə sef′ə ləs). [HYDROCEPHAL(US) + -IC]

hy·dro·ceph·a·loid (hī′drə sef′ə loid′), *adj.* *Pathol.* resembling hydrocephalus. [HYDROCEPHAL(US) + -OID]

hy·dro·ceph·a·lus (hī′drə sef′ə ləs), *n.* *Pathol.* an accumulation of serous fluid within the cranium, esp. in infancy, often causing great enlargement of the head. Also, **hy·dro·ceph·a·ly** (hī′drə sef′ə lē). [< LL *hydrocephalus (morbus)* water-headed (sickness), trans. of Gk *tò hydroképhalon (páthos).* See HYDRO-¹, -CEPHALOUS]

hy·dro·chlo·ric (hī′drə klōr′ik, -klôr′-), *adj.* *Chem.* of or derived from hydrochloric acid. [HYDRO-² + CHLORIC]

hy′drochlo′ric ac′id, *Chem.* a colorless or faintly yellow, corrosive, fuming liquid, HCl, used chiefly in chemical and industrial processes.

hy·dro·chlo·ride (hī′drə klōr′īd, -id, -klôr′-), *n.* *Chem.* a salt, esp. of an alkaloid, formed by the direct union of hydrochloric acid with an organic base that makes the organic constituent more soluble. [HYDRO-² + CHLORIDE]

hy·dro·chlo·ro·thi·a·zide (hī′drə klōr′ə thī′ə zīd′, -klôr′-), *n.* *Pharm.* a crystalline, water-insoluble powder, $C_7H_8ClN_3O_4S_2$, used as a diuretic and in the treatment of hypertension. [HYDRO-² + CHLOROTHIAZIDE]

hy′dro·cin·nam′ic al′dehyde (hī′drō si nam′ik, -drə sin′ə mik, hī′-), *Chem.* a colorless liquid, $C_6H_5CH_2CH_2CHO$, having a hyacinthlike odor, used in perfumery and flavoring. Also, **hy·dro·cin·na·mal·de·hyde** (hī′drō sin′ə mal′də hīd′). [HYDRO-² + CINNAMIC]

hy·dro·cin·nam·o·yl (hī′drō si nam′ō il), *adj.* *Chem.* containing the hydrocinnamoyl group. [HYDRO-² + CINNAMOYL]

hydrocinnam′oyl group′, *Chem.* the univalent group, $C_6H_5CH_2CH_2CO$–. Also called **hydrocinnam′oyl rad′ical.**

hy·dro·cin·nam·yl (hī′drō si nam′il, -drə sin′ə mil), *adj.* *Chem.* containing the hydrocinnamyl group. [HYDRO-² + CINNAMYL]

hydrocinnam′yl group′, *Chem.* the univalent group, $C_6H_5CH_2CH_2CH_2$–. Also called **hydrocinnam′yl rad′ical.**

hy·dro·cor·ti·sone (hī′drə kôr′ti sōn′, -zōn′), *n.* **1.** *Biochem.* a steroid hormone, $C_{21}H_{30}O_5$, of the adrenal cortex, active in carbohydrate and protein metabolism. **2.** *Pharm.* a commercial form of this compound, obtained from the adrenal glands of certain animals or synthesized, used chiefly in the form of its acetate in the treatment of arthritis and certain skin conditions. Also called **Compound F, cortisol.** [HYDRO-² + CORTISONE]

Hy·dro·cor·tone (hī′drə kôr′tōn), *n.* *Pharm., Trademark.* hydrocortisone.

hy·dro·crack·ing (hī′drə krak′ing), *n.* *Chem.* the cracking of petroleum or the like in the presence of hydrogen. [HYDRO-² + CRACKING]

hy·dro·cy·an·ic (hī′drō sī an′ik), *adj.* *Chem.* of or derived from hydrocyanic acid. [HYDRO-² + CYANIC]

hy′drocyan′ic ac′id, *Chem.* a colorless, highly poisonous liquid, HCN, an aqueous solution of hydrogen cyanide. Also called **prussic acid.**

hy·dro·de·sul·fu·ri·za·tion (hī′drō dē sul′fyər i zā′shən, -fər i-), *n.* *Chem.* desulfurization by catalytic agents of the sulfur-rich hydrocarbons obtained from petroleum or the like during cracking or hydrocracking. Also, **hy′dro·de·sul′phur·i·za′tion.** [HYDRO-² + DESULFURIZATION]

Hy·dro·Di·u·ril (hī′drō dī′ər il), *n.* *Pharm., Trademark.* hydrochlorothiazide.

hy·dro·dy·nam·ic (hī′drō dī nam′ik, -di-), *adj.* **1.** pertaining to forces in or motions of fluids. **2.** of or pertaining to hydrodynamics. [HYDRO-¹ + DYNAMIC] —**hy′dro·dy·nam′i·cal·ly,** *adv.*

hy·dro·dy·nam·ics (hī′drō dī nam′iks, -di-), *n.* (*construed as sing.*) **1.** Also called **hydromechanics.** the science of the mechanics of fluids, generally liquids, including hydrostatics and hydrokinetics. **2.** hydrokinetics. [see HYDRODYNAMIC, -ICS]

hy·dro·e·lec·tric (hī′drō i lek′trik), *adj.* pertaining to the generation and distribution of electric energy derived from the energy of falling water or any other hydraulic source. [HYDRO-¹ + ELECTRIC] —**hy·dro·e·lec·tric·i·ty** (hī′drō i lek tris′i tē, -ē′lek-), *n.*

hy·dro·flu·or·ic (hī′drə flo͞o ôr′ik, -or′-), *adj.* *Chem.* of or derived from hydrofluoric acid. [HYDRO-² + -FLUORIC]

hy′drofluor′ic ac′id, *Chem.* a colorless, fuming, corrosive liquid, HF, an aqueous solution of hydrogen fluoride, used chiefly for etching glass.

Hydrofoil (def. 3)

hy·dro·foil (hī′drə foil′), *n.* **1.** *Naval Archit.* a surface form creating a thrust against water in a direction perpendicular to the plane approximated by the surface. **2.** *Naut.* a winglike member having this form, designed to lift the hull of a moving vessel. **3.** a vessel equipped with hydrofoils. [HYDRO-¹ + FOIL²]

hy·dro·for·myl·a·tion (hī′drə fôr′mə lā′shən), *n.* *Chem.* the addition of a hydrogen atom and the formyl group to a double bond of a hydrocarbon by reaction with a mixture of carbon monoxide and hydrogen in the presence of a catalyst. [HYDRO-² + FORMYL + -ATION]

hy·dro·gen (hī′drə jən), *n.* *Chem.* a colorless, odorless, flammable gas that combines chemically with oxygen to form water: the lightest of the known elements. *Symbol:* H; *at. wt.:* 1.00797; *at. no.:* 1; *weight of one liter at 760 mm. pressure and 0°C:* .08987 g. [< F *hydrogène.* See HYDRO-¹, -GEN]

hy·dro·gen·ate (hī′drə jə nāt′, hī droj′ə-), *v.t.,* **-at·ed, -at·ing.** *Chem.* to combine or treat with hydrogen, esp. to add hydrogen to the molecule of (an unsaturated organic compound). [HYDROGEN + -ATE¹] —**hy·dro·gen·a·tion** (hī′drə jə nā′shən, hī droj′ə-), *n.*

hy′drogen bomb′, a bomb, more powerful than an atomic bomb, that derives its explosive energy from the thermonuclear fusion reaction of hydrogen isotopes. Also called **H-bomb, fusion bomb, thermonuclear bomb.**

hy′drogen bro′mide, *Chem.* a colorless gas, HBr, having a pungent odor: the anhydride of hydrobromic acid.

hy′drogen chlo′ride, *Chem.* a colorless gas, HCl, having a pungent odor: the anhydride of hydrochloric acid.

hy′drogen cy′anide, *Chem.* a colorless, poisonous gas, HCN, having a bitter almondlike odor: the anhydride of hydrocyanic acid.

hy′drogen flu′oride, *Chem.* a colorless, corrosive gas, HF, the anhydride of hydrofluoric acid, used chiefly as a catalyst and in the fluorination of hydrocarbons.

hy′drogen i′odide, *Chem.* a colorless gas, HI, having a suffocating odor: the anhydride of hydriodic acid.

hy′drogen i′on, *Chem.* ionized hydrogen of the form H^+, found in aqueous solutions of all acids.

hy·dro·gen·ise (hī′drə jə nīz′, hī droj′ə-), *v.t.,* **-ised, -is·ing.** *Chiefly Brit.* hydrogenize. —**hy′dro·gen·i·sa′tion,** *n.*

hy·dro·gen·ize (hī′drə jə nīz′, hī droj′ə-), *v.t.,* **-ized, -iz·ing.** hydrogenate. [HYDROGEN + -IZE] —**hy′dro·gen·i·za′tion,** *n.*

hy·dro·gen·ol·y·sis (hī′drō ji nol′i sis), *n., pl.* **-ses** (-sēz′). *Chem.* decomposition resulting from the interaction of a compound and hydrogen. [HYDROGEN + -O- + -LYSIS]

hy·drog·e·nous (hī droj′ə nəs), *adj.* of or containing hydrogen. [HYDROGEN + -OUS]

hy′drogen perox′ide, a colorless, unstable, oily liquid, H_2O_2, the aqueous solution of which is used chiefly as an antiseptic and a bleaching agent.

hy′drogen sul′fide, *Chem.* a colorless, flammable, water-soluble, cumulatively poisonous gas, H_2S, having the odor of rotten eggs: used chiefly in the manufacture of chemicals, in metallurgy, and as a reagent in laboratory analysis. Also called **sulfureted hydrogen.**

hy·dro·ge·ol·o·gy (hī′drō jē ol′ə jē), *n.* the science dealing with the occurrence and distribution of underground water. [HYDRO-¹ + GEOLOGY] —**hy·dro·ge·o·log·i·cal** (hī′drə jē′ə loj′i kəl), **hy′dro·ge′o·log′ic,** *adj.* —**hy′dro·ge·ol′o·gist,** *n.*

hy·dro·graph (hī′drə graf′, -gräf′), *n.* a graph of the water level or rate of flow of a body of water as a function of time, showing the seasonal change. [HYDRO-¹ + -GRAPH]

hy·drog·ra·phy (hī drog′rə fē), *n.* **1.** the science of the measurement, description, and mapping of the surface waters of the earth, with special reference to their use for navigation. **2.** those parts of a map, collectively, that represent surface waters. [HYDRO-¹ + -GRAPHY] —**hy·drog′ra·pher,** *n.* —**hy·dro·graph·ic** (hī′drə graf′ik), **hy′dro·graph′i·cal,** *adj.* —**hy′dro·graph′i·cal·ly,** *adv.*

hy·droid (hī′droid), *adj.* **1.** noting or pertaining to that form of hydrozoan which is asexual and grows into branching colonies by budding. —*n.* **2.** the phase of a hydrozoan coelenterate that consists of polyp forms usually growing as an attached colony. [HYDR(A) + -OID]

hy·dro·kin·e·ter (hī′drə kin′i tər, -drō ki nē′tər, -kī-), *n.* a device for circulating water by means of a jet of steam or water. [HYDROKINET(IC) + -ER¹]

hy·dro·ki·net·ic (hī′drō ki net′ik, -kī-), *adj.* **1.** pertaining to the motion of fluids. **2.** of or pertaining to hydrokinetics. Also, **hy′dro·ki·net′i·cal.** [HYDRO-¹ + KINETIC]

hy·dro·ki·net·ics (hī′drō ki net′iks, -kī-), *n.* (*construed as sing.*) the branch of hydrodynamics that deals with the laws governing liquids or gases in motion. Also called **hydrodynamics.** [see HYDROKINETIC, -ICS]

hy·dro·lant (hī′drə lant′), *n.* an urgent warning of navigational dangers in the Atlantic Ocean, issued by the U.S. Navy Hydrographic Office. Cf. **hydropac.** [HYDRO-¹ + (AT)LANT(IC)]

hy·dro·lase (hī′drə lās′), *n.* *Biochem.* an enzyme that catalyzes hydrolysis. Also called **hy·dro·lyst** (hī′drə-list). [HYDR-¹ + -OL¹ + -ASE]

hy′drolog′ic cy′cle, the natural sequence through which water passes into the atmosphere as water vapor, precipitates to earth in liquid or crystal form, and ultimately returns to the atmosphere through evaporation. [HYDROLOG(Y) + -IC]

hy·drol·o·gy (hī drol′ə jē), *n.* the science dealing with the occurrence, circulation, distribution, and properties of the waters of the earth and its atmosphere. [HYDRO-¹ + -LOGY] —**hy·dro·log·ic** (hī′drə loj′ik), **hy′dro·log′i·cal,** *adj.* —**hy′dro·log′i·cal·ly,** *adv.* —**hy·drol′o·gist,** *n.*

hy·drol·y·sate (hī drol′i sāt′), *n.* *Chem.* any compound formed by hydrolysis. [HYDROLYS(IS) + -ATE²]

hy·dro·lyse (hī′drə līz′), *v.t., v.i.,* **-lysed, -lys·ing.** *Chiefly Brit.* hydrolyze. —**hy′dro·lys′a·ble,** *adj.* —**hy′dro·ly·sa′tion,** *n.* —**hy′dro·lys′er,** *n.*

hy·drol·y·sis (hī drol′i sis), *n., pl.* **-ses** (-sēz′). *Chem.* decomposition in which a compound is split into other compounds by taking up the elements of water. [HYDRO-¹ + -LYSIS]

hy·dro·lyte (hī′drə līt′), *n.* *Chem.* a substance subjected to hydrolysis. [HYDRO-¹ + -LYTE¹]

hy·dro·lyt·ic (hī′drə lit′ik), *adj.* producing, noting, or resulting in hydrolysis. [HYDRO-¹ + -LYTIC]

hy·dro·lyze (hī′drə līz′), *v.t., v.i.,* **-lyzed, -lyz·ing.** to subject or be subjected to hydrolysis. Also, *esp. Brit.,* **hydrolyse.** [HYDROL(YSIS) + -IZE] —**hy′dro·lyz′a·ble,** *adj.* —**hy′dro·ly·za′tion,** *n.* —**hy′dro·lyz′er,** *n.*

hy·dro·mag·net·ics (hī′drō mag net′iks), *n.* (*construed as sing.*) magnetohydrodynamics (def. 1). [HYDRO-¹ + MAGNETICS]

hy·dro·man·cy (hī′drə man′sē), *n.* divination by means of signs observed in water. [earlier *hydromantie, -cie* < L *hydromantīa* < Gk *hydromanteía* divination by water; r. ME *ydromancye* < MF *ydromancie* < L. See HYDRO-¹, -MANCY] —**hy′dro·manc′er,** *n.* —**hy′dro·man′tic,** *adj.*

hy·dro·me·chan·ics (hī′drō mə kan′iks), *n.* (*construed as sing.*) hydrodynamics (def. 1). [HYDRO-¹ + MECHANICS] —**hy′dro·me·chan′i·cal,** *adj.*

hy·dro·me·du·sa (hī′drō mi do͞o′sə, -zə, -dyo͞o′-), *n., pl.* **-sae** (-sē). the medusa form of a hydrozoan coelenterate. [< NL; see HYDRA, -O-, MEDUSA] —**hy′dro·me·du′san,** *adj.*

hy·dro·mel (hī′drə mel′), *n.* a liquor consisting of honey and water that, when fermented, becomes mead. [< L < Gk *hydrómeli,* equiv. to *hydro-* HYDRO-¹ + *méli* honey; r. late ME *ydromel* < ML (var. of *hydromel*)]

hy·dro·met·al·lur·gy (hī′drə met′əlûr′jē), *n.* the technique or process of extracting metals at ordinary temperatures by leaching ore with liquid solvents. [HYDRO-¹ + METALLURGY] —**hy′dro·met′al·lur′gi·cal,** *adj.*

hy·dro·me·te·or (hī′drə mē′tē ər), *n.* *Meteorol.* the state or effect of liquid water or ice in the atmosphere, as rain, ice crystals, hail, fog, and clouds. Cf. **lithometeor.** [HYDRO-¹ + METEOR] —**hy′dro·me′te·or·ol′o·gy,** *n.* —**hy′dro·me′te·or·o·log′i·cal,** *adj.*

hy·drom·e·ter (hī drom′i tər), *n.* an instrument for determining the specific gravity of a liquid, consisting of a sealed cylinder and weighted bulb, that, when placed in a liquid, indicates its specific gravity by a comparison of the surface of the liquid with the graduations on the emerging stem. [HYDRO-¹ + -METER] —**hy·dro·met·ric** (hī′drə me′trik), **hy′dro·met′ri·cal,** *adj.* —**hy·drom′e·try,** *n.*

hy·dro·ni·tro·gen (hī′drə nī′trə jən), *n.* *Chem.* a compound containing only hydrogen and nitrogen. [HYDRO-² + NITROGEN]

hy·dro·pac (hī′drə pak′), *n.* an urgent warning of navigational dangers in the Pacific Ocean, issued by the U.S. Navy Hydrographic Office. Cf. **hydrolant.** [HY-DRO-¹ + PAC(IFIC)]

hy·drop·a·thy (hī drop′ə thē), *n.* the treatment of disease by the internal and external use of water; hydrotherapy. [HYDRO-¹ + -PATHY] —**hy·dro·path·ic** (hī′drə path′ik), **hy′dro·path′i·cal,** *adj.* —**hy·drop′a·thist, hy′dro·path′,** *n.*

hy·dro·per·ox·ide (hī′drō pə rok′sīd), *n. Chem.* any compound having the general formula, ROOH, where R is an element or an organic group. [HYDRO-² + PEROXIDE]

hy·dro·phane (hī′drə fān′), *n.* a partly translucent variety of opal, which becomes more translucent or transparent when immersed in water. [HYDRO-¹ + -PHANE] —**hy·droph·a·nous** (hī drof′ə nəs), *adj.*

hy·dro·phil·ic (hī′drə fil′ik), *adj. Chem.* having a strong affinity for water. [HYDRO-¹ + -PHILE + -IC]

hy·droph·i·lous (hī drof′ə ləs), *adj. Bot.* **1.** pollinated by the agency of water. **2.** hydrophytic. [< NL *hydrophilus.* See HYDRO-¹, -PHILOUS] —**hy·droph′i·ly,** *n.*

hy·dro·phobe (hī′drə fōb′), *n.* **1.** *Pathol.* a person or animal with hydrophobia. **2.** *Chem.* a hydrophobic substance. [HYDRO-¹ + -PHOBE]

hy·dro·pho·bi·a (hī′drə fō′bē ə), *n. Pathol.* **1.** rabies. **2.** an abnormal or unnatural dread of water. [< LL < Gk *hydrophobía* horror of water. See HYDRO-¹, -PHOBIA]

hy·dro·pho·bic (hī′drə fō′bik), *adj.* **1.** *Pathol.* of or pertaining to hydrophobia. **2.** *Chem.* having little or no affinity for water. [HYDROPHOBE + -IC] —**hy·dro·pho·bic·i·ty** (hī′drə fō bis′i tē), *n.*

hy·dro·phone (hī′drə fōn′), *n.* **1.** an instrument employing the principles of the microphone, used to detect the flow of water through a pipe. **2.** a device for locating sources of sound under water, as for detecting submarines by the noise of their engines. **3.** *Med.* an instrument used in auscultation, whereby sounds are intensified through a column of water. [HYDRO-¹ + -PHONE]

hy·dro·phyl·la·ceous (hī′drō fi lā′shəs), *adj.* belonging to the *Hydrophyllaceae,* a family of herbaceous plants. [*Hydrophyll(um)* genus name (see HYDRO-¹, -PHYLL) + -ACEOUS]

hy·dro·phyte (hī′drə fīt′), *n.* a plant growing in water or very moist ground. [HYDRO-¹ + -PHYTE] —**hy′dro·phyt′ism,** *n.*

hy·dro·phyt·ic (hī′drə fit′ik), *adj.* of or pertaining to a hydrophyte. [HYDROPHYTE + -IC]

hy·drop·ic (hī drop′ik), *adj.* dropsical. Also, **hy·drop′i·cal.** [< L *hydrōpic(us)* < Gk *hydrōpikós,* equiv. to *hydrōp-* (s. of *hýdrōps*) HYDROPS + *-ikos* -IC; r. ME *ydropike* < OF < L] —**hy·drop′i·cal·ly,** *adv.*

hy·dro·plane (hī′drə plān′), *n., v.,* **-planed, -plan·ing.** —*n.* **1.** an airplane provided with floats or with a boatlike underpart enabling it to land on and take off from water. **2.** an attachment to an airplane enabling it to glide on the water. **3.** a light, high-powered boat, esp. one with hydrofoils or a stepped bottom, designed to plane along the surface of the water at very high speeds. **4.** a horizontal rudder for submerging or elevating a submarine. —*v.i.* **5.** to skim over water in the manner of a hydroplane. **6.** to travel in a hydroplane. [HYDRO- + PLANE¹]

hy·dro·pneu·ma·ti·za·tion (hī′drə nōō′mə ti zā′shən, -nyōō′-), *n.* utilization of air pressure in the housing of a water turbine to keep the level of water that has been used from rising to interfere with the rotor blades. [HYDRO-¹ + PNEUMAT- + -IZATION]

hy·dro·pon·ics (hī′drə pon′iks), *n.* (*construed as sing.*) the cultivation of plants by placing the roots in liquid nutrient solutions rather than in soil; soilless growth of plants. [HYDRO-¹ + (GEO)PONICS] —**hy′dro·pon′ic,** *adj.* —**hy′dro·pon′i·cal·ly,** *adv.* —**hy·drop·o·nist** (hī drop′ə nist), *n.*

hy·drops (hī′drops), *n.* (*construed as sing.*) *Pathol.* dropsy (def. 1). Also called **hy·drop·sy** (hī′drop sē). [< L *hydrōps* < Gk *hýdrōps* dropsy, equiv. to *hydr-* HYDR-¹ + *-ōps* appearance (lit., eye, face), appar. by confusion with *ópsis* appearance] —**hy·drop′tic,** *adj.*

hy·dro·qui·none (hī′drō kwi nōn′, -drə kwin′ōn), *n. Chem.* a white, crystalline compound, $C_6H_4(OH)_2$, formed by the reduction of quinone: used chiefly in photography and to inhibit autoxidation reactions. Also called **hy·dro·quin·ol** (hī′drə kwin′ōl, -ôl, -ol), **quinol.** [HYDRO-¹ + QUINONE]

hy·dro·rhi·za (hī′drə rī′zə), *n., pl.* **-zae** (-zē). the rootlike base of a hydroid colony, by which it is attached to the substratum. [< NL; see HYDRO-¹, -RHIZA] —**hy′dro·rhi′zal,** *adj.*

hydros., hydrostatics.

hy·dro·scope (hī′drə skōp′), *n.* an optical device for viewing objects below the surface of water. [HYDRO-¹ + -SCOPE] —**hy·dro·scop·ic** (hī′drə skop′ik), **hy′dro·scop′i·cal,** *adj.* —**hy·dro·sco·pic·i·ty** (hī′drə skō pis′i tē), *n.*

hy·dro·sere (hī′drə sēr′), *n. Ecol.* a sere originating in water. [HYDRO-¹ + SERE²]

hy·dro·sol (hī′drə sol′), *n. Physical Chem.* a colloidal suspension in water. [HYDRO-¹ + SOL(UTION)]

hy·dro·so·ma (hī′drə sō′mə), *n., pl.* **-ma·ta** (-mə tə). *Zool.* hydrosome. [< NL]

hy·dro·some (hī′drə sōm′), *n. Zool.* the entire body of a compound hydrozoan. [*hydro-* (comb. form repr. HYDRA) + -SOME³]

hy·dro·sphere (hī′drə sfēr′), *n.* the water on or surrounding the surface of the globe, including the water of the oceans and the water in the atmosphere. [HYDRO-¹ + -SPHERE]

hy·dro·stat (hī′drə stat′), *n.* **1.** an electrical device for detecting the presence of water, as from overflow or leakage. **2.** any of various devices for preventing injury to a steam boiler when its water sinks below a certain level. [HYDRO-¹ + -STAT]

hy·dro·stat·ic (hī′drə stat′ik), *adj.* of or pertaining to hydrostatics. Also, **hy′dro·stat′i·cal.** [HYDRO-¹ + STATIC] —**hy′dro·stat′i·cal·ly,** *adv.*

hy·dro·stat·ics (hī′drə stat′iks), *n.* (*construed as sing.*) the branch of hydrodynamics that deals with the statics of fluids, usually confined to the equilibrium and pressure of liquids. [see HYDROSTATIC, -ICS]

hy·dro·sul·fate (hī′drə sul′fāt), *n. Chem.* a salt formed by the direct union of sulfuric acid with an organic base, esp. an alkaloid, and usually more soluble than the base. Also, **hy′dro·sul′phate.** [HYDRO-² + SULFATE]

hy·dro·sul·fide (hī′drə sul′fīd, -fid), *n. Chem.* a compound containing the univalent group, –HS. Also, **hy′dro·sul′phide.** [HYDRO-² + SULFIDE]

hy·dro·sul·fite (hī′drə sul′fīt), *n. Chem.* **1.** hyposulfite (def. 1). **2.** See **sodium hydrosulfite.** Also, **hy′dro·sul′phite.** [HYDROSULF(UROUS) + -ITE¹]

hy·dro·sul·fu·rous (hī′drō sul fyŏŏr′əs, -drō sul′fər-əs), *adj.* hyposulfurous. Also, **hy′dro·sul·phu′rous.** [HYDRO-² + SULFUROUS]

hy·dro·tax·is (hī′drə tak′sis), *n. Biol.* oriented movement toward or away from water. [HYDRO-¹ + -TAXIS] —**hy·dro·tac·tic** (hī′drə tak′tik), *adj.*

hy·dro·the·ca (hī′drə thē′kə), *n., pl.* **-cae** (-kē). *Zool.* the part of the perisarc covering a hydranth. [< NL; see HYDRO-², THECA] —**hy′dro·the′cal,** *adj.*

hy·dro·ther·a·peu·tics (hī′drō ther′ə pyōō′tiks), *n.* (*construed as sing.*) the branch of therapeutics that deals with the curative use of water. [HYDRO-¹ + THERAPEUTICS] —**hy′dro·ther′a·peu′tic,** *adj.*

hy·dro·ther·a·py (hī′drō ther′ə pē), *n.* the treatment of disease by the external use of water. [HYDRO-¹ + THERAPY] —**hy′dro·ther′a·pist,** *n.*

hy·dro·ther·mal (hī′drə thûr′məl), *adj. Geol.* noting or pertaining to the action of hot, aqueous solutions or gases within or on the surface of the earth. [HYDRO-¹ + THERMAL] —**hy′dro·ther′mal·ly,** *adv.*

hy·dro·tho·rax (hī′drə thōr′aks, -thôr′-), *n. Pathol.* the presence of serous fluid in one or both pleural cavities. [HYDRO-¹ + THORAX] —**hy·dro·tho·rac·ic** (hī′drō thə ras′ik), *adj.*

hy·dro·trop·ic (hī′drə trop′ik), *adj.* **1.** *Bot.* turning or tending toward or away from moisture. **2.** taking a particular direction with reference to moisture. [HYDRO-¹ + -TROPIC]

hy·drot·ro·pism (hī drot′rə piz′əm), *n. Biol.* **1.** oriented growth or movement in response to water. **2.** hydrotropic tendency or growth. [HYDRO-¹ + -TROPISM]

hy·drous (hī′drəs), *adj.* **1.** containing water. **2.** *Chem.* containing water or its elements in some kind of union, as in hydrates or hydroxides. [HYDR-¹ + -OUS]

hy·drox·ide (hī drok′sīd, -sid), *n. Chem.* a compound containing the hydroxyl group. [HYDR-² + OXIDE]

hy·drox·y (hī drok′sē), *adj. Chem.* hydroxyl. [HYDR-² + OXY(GEN)]

hydroxy-, a combining form of **hydroxy:** *hydroxyketone.*

hy·drox′y·a·ce′tic ac′id (hī drok′sē ə sē′tik, -ə set′ik, hī drok′-), *Chem.* See **glycolic acid.** [HYDROXY- + ACETIC]

hydrox′y ac′id, *Chem.* **1.** an organic acid containing both a carboxyl and a hydroxyl group. **2.** any of a class of organic acids containing a hydroxyl group and showing properties of both an alcohol and an acid.

hy·drox·y·ben·zene (hī drok′si ben′zēn), *n. Chem.* phenol (def. 1). [HYDROXY- + BENZENE]

hy·drox·y·ke·tone (hī drok′sē kē′tōn), *n. Chem.* a ketone containing a hydroxyl group. [HYDROXY- + KETONE]

hy·drox·yl (hī drok′sil), *adj. Chem.* containing the hydroxyl group. Also, **hydroxy.** [HYDROXY- + -YL] —**hy′drox·yl′ic,** *adj.*

hy·drox·yl·a·mine (hī drok′sil ə mēn′, -am′in), *n. Chem.* an unstable, weakly basic, crystalline compound, NH_2OH, used as a reducing agent, analytical reagent, and chemical intermediate. [HYDROXYL + -AMINE]

hydrox′yl group′, *Chem.* the univalent group, –OH, as in inorganic compounds, such as sodium hydroxide, NaOH, or as in organic compounds, such as ethyl alcohol, CH_3CH_2OH. Also called **hydrox′yl rad′ical.**

hy·drox·y·zine (hī drok′si zēn′), *n. Pharm.* an antihistaminic compound, $C_{21}H_{27}ClN_2O_2$, used in the form of its hydrochloride to induce ataraxia: a tranquilizer. [HYDROXY- + (PIPERA)ZINE]

Hy·dro·zo·a (hī′drə zō′ə), *n.* the class comprising the hydrozoans. [< NL; see HYDROZOAN]

hy·dro·zo·an (hī′drə zō′ən), *adj.* **1.** belonging or pertaining to the *Hydrozoa.* —*n.* **2.** any coelenterate of the class *Hydrozoa,* comprising solitary or colonial polyps and free-swimming medusae. [*hydrozo(a)* (see HYDRA, -ZOA) + -AN]

Hy·drus (hī′drəs), *n., gen.* **-dri** (-drī). *Astron.* the Water Snake, a southern constellation between Eridanus and Octans. [< L < Gk *hýdros* water serpent]

Spotted hyena, *Crocuta crocuta* (3 ft. high at shoulder; total length 5½ ft.; tail 1 ft.)

hy·e·na (hī ē′nə), *n.* any nocturnal carnivore of the family *Hyaenidae,* feeding chiefly on carrion. Also, **hyaena.** Cf. **brown hyena, spotted hyena, striped hyena.** [< ML *hyēna* < L *hyaena* < Gk *hýaina,* equiv. to *hu-* (s. of *hŷs*) hog + *-aina* fem. suffix; r. ME *hyane, hyene* < MF *hiene* < L] —**hy·e′nic, hy·e·nine** (hī ē′nīn, -nin), *adj.*

hy·e·noid (hī ē′noid), *adj.* resembling a hyena. Also called **hy·e·ni·form** (hī ē′nə fôrm′). [HYEN(A) + -OID]

hy·e·tal (hī′i təl), *adj.* of or pertaining to rain or rainfall. [HYET- + -AL¹]

hyeto-, a learned borrowing from Greek meaning "rain," used in the formation of compound words: *hyetology.* Also, *esp. before a vowel,* **hyet-.** [comb. form repr. Gk *hyetós* rain]

hy·et·o·graph (hī et′ə graf′, -gräf′, hī′ə tə-), *n.* a map or chart showing the average rainfall for the localities represented. [HYETO- + -GRAPH]

hy·e·tog·ra·phy (hī′i tog′rə fē), *n.* the study of the annual and geographical distribution of rainfall. [HYETO- + -GRAPHY] —**hy·e·to·graph·ic** (hī′i tə graf′ik), **hy′e·to·graph′i·cal,** *adj.* —**hy′e·to·graph′i·cal·ly,** *adv.*

hy·e·tol·o·gy (hī′i tol′ə jē), *n. Rare.* the branch of meteorology dealing with precipitation. [HYETO- + -LOGY] —**hy·e·to·log·i·cal** (hī′i təloj′i kəl), *adj.* —**hy′e·tol′o·gist,** *n.*

Hy·ge·ia (hī jē′ə), *n. Class. Myth.* the daughter of Asclepius and the ancient Greek goddess of health, identified by the Romans with Salus. [< Gk, late var. of *Hygíeia,* personification of *hygíeia* health, equiv. to *hygiḗ(s)* healthy + *-ia* -IA] —**Hy·ge′ian,** *adj.*

hy·giene (hī′jēn, -jē ēn′), *n.* **1.** Also, **hygienics.** the science that deals with the preservation of health. **2.** a condition or practice conducive to the preservation of health, as cleanliness. [< medical L *hygiēnē* (var. of *hygiēna, hygieina*) < Gk *hygieinḗ* (*téchnē*) healthful (art), fem. of *hygieinós* healthful, equiv. to *hygiḗ(s)* healthy + *-inos* -INE¹]

hy·gi·en·ic (hī′jē en′ik, hī jē′nik), *adj.* **1.** sanitary. **2.** of or pertaining to hygiene. Also, **hy′gi·en′i·cal.** [HYGIENE + -IC] —**hy′gi·en′i·cal·ly,** *adv.* —**Syn. 1.** See **sanitary.**

hy·gi·en·ics (hī′jē en′iks, hī jē′niks), *n.* (*construed as sing.*) hygiene (def. 1). [HYGIENE + -ICS]

hy·gien·ist (hī jē′nist, -jen′ist, hī′jē nist, hī′jē en′ist), *n.* an expert in hygiene. Also, **hy·ge·ist, hy·gie·ist** (hī′jē ist). [HYGIENE + -IST]

Hy·gi·nus (hi jī′nəs *for 1;* hī′gə nəs *for 2*), *n.* **1. Saint,** died A.D. 140, pope 136–140. **2.** a crater in the first quadrant of the face of the moon: about 4 miles in diameter.

hygro-, a learned borrowing from Greek meaning "wet," "moist," "moisture," used in the formation of compound words: *hygrometer.* [< Gk, comb. form of *hygrós* wet, moist]

hy·gro·gram (hī′grə gram′), *n.* the record made by a hygrograph. [HYGRO- + -GRAM¹]

hy·gro·graph (hī′grə graf′, -gräf′), *n.* a self-recording hygrometer. [HYGRO- + -GRAPH]

hy·grom·e·ter (hī grom′i tər), *n.* any instrument for measuring the water-vapor content of the atmosphere. [HYGRO- + -METER]

hy·gro·met·ric (hī′grə me′trik), *adj.* of or pertaining to the hygrometer or hygrometry. [HYGRO- + -METRIC] —**hy′gro·met′ri·cal·ly,** *adv.*

hy·grom·e·try (hī grom′i trē), *n.* the branch of physics that deals with the measurement of the humidity of air and gases. [HYGRO- + -METRY]

hy·gro·phyte (hī′grə fīt′), *n.* **1.** a plant that thrives in wet or very moist ground. **2.** a hydrophyte. [HYGRO- + -PHYTE] —**hy·gro·phyt·ic** (hī′grə fit′ik), *adj.*

hy·gro·scope (hī′grə skōp′), *n.* an instrument that indicates the approximate humidity of the air. [HYGRO- + -SCOPE]

hy·gro·scop·ic (hī′grə skop′ik), *adj.* absorbing or attracting moisture from the air. [HYGROSCOPE + -IC] —**hy′gro·scop′i·cal·ly,** *adv.* —**hy·gro·sco·pic·i·ty** (hī′grə skō pis′i tē), *n.*

hy·gro·stat (hī′grə stat′), *n.* humidistat. [HYGRO- + -STAT]

hy·gro·ther·mo·graph (hī′grō thûr′mə graf′, -gräf′), *n. Meteorol.* an instrument for recording temperature and relative humidity. [HYGRO- + THERMOGRAPH]

hy·ing (hī′ing), *v.* pp. of **hie.**

Hyk·sos (hik′sōs, -sos), *n.* a nomadic people who conquered and ruled ancient Egypt between the 13th and 18th dynasties, c1700–1580 B.C.: believed to have been a Semitic people that originally migrated into Egypt from Asia. [< Gk *Hyksṓs* < Egypt *Ḥiq shasu* leader of nomads]

hy·la (hī′lə), *n.* a tree frog of the genus *Hyla.* [< NL < Gk *hýlē* forest]

Hy·lae·us (hī lē′əs), *n. Class. Myth.* a cloud-born Arcadian centaur.

Hy·las (hī′ləs), *n. Class. Myth.* a son of Thiodamas and Menodice who was a companion of Hercules.

Hyl·lus (hil′əs), *n. Class. Myth.* **1.** a son of Hercules and Deianira who built his father's funeral pyre. **2.** a son of Hercules and Melite.

hylo-, a learned borrowing from Greek meaning "wood," "matter," used in the formation of compound words: *hylophagous; hylotheism.* [< Gk, comb. form of *hýlē* wood, matter]

hy·lo·mor·phic (hī′lə môr′fik), *adj. Philos.* (of a creature) composed of corporeal and spiritual matter. [HYLOMORPH(ISM) + -IC]

hy·lo·mor·phism (hī′lō môr′fiz əm), *n. Philos.* the theory that every physical object is composed of two principles, an unchanging prime matter and a form deprived of actuality with every substantial change of the object. [HYLO- + -MORPHISM] —**hy′lo·mor′phist,** *n.*

hy·loph·a·gous (hī lof′ə gəs), *adj.* xylophagous (def. 1). [< Gk *hylophágos.* See HYLO-, -PHAGOUS]

hy·lo·the·ism (hī′lə thē′iz əm), *n.* any philosophical doctrine identifying a god or gods with matter. [HYLO- + THEISM] —**hy′lo·the′ist,** *n., adj.* —**hy′lo·the·is′tic, hy′lo·the·is′ti·cal,** *adj.*

hy·lo·trop·ic (hī′lə trop′ik), *adj. Physical Chem.* (of a substance) capable of undergoing a change in phase, as from a liquid to a gas, with no change in the original proportions of its constituents. [HYLO- + -TROPIC]

hy·lo·zo·ism (hī′lə zō′iz əm), *n. Philos.* the doctrine that matter is inseparable from life, which is a property of matter. [HYLO- + *zo-* (s. of Gk *zōḗ*) life + -ISM] —**hy′lo·zo′ic,** *adj.* —**hy′lo·zo′ist,** *n.* —**hy′lo·zo·is′tic,** *adj.* —**hy′lo·zo·is′ti·cal·ly,** *adv.*

Hy·man (hī′mən), *n.* a boy's given name.

hy·men (hī′mən), *n. Anat.* a fold of mucous membrane partially closing the external orifice of the vagina in a virgin. [< Gk *hymḗn* skin, membrane, the virginal membrane]

Hy·men (hī′mən), *n. Class. Myth.* the god of marriage, represented as a handsome youth holding a torch, identified by the Romans with Talassio. Also called **Hy·me·nae·us** (hī′mə nē′əs).

hy·me·ne·al (hī′mə nē′əl), *adj.* **1.** of or pertaining to marriage. —*n.* **2.** marriage song. [< L *hymenae(us)* (< Gk *hyménaios* wedding song, equiv. to *Hymen* HYMEN + *-aios* pertaining to) + -AL¹] —**hy′me·ne′al·ly,** *adv.*

hy·me·ni·um (hī mē′nē əm), *n., pl.* **-ni·a** (-nē ə). *Bot.* the sporogenous layer in a fungus, composed of asci or basidia often interspersed with various sterile structures, as paraphyses. [< NL; see HYMEN(O)-, -IUM] —**hy·me′ni·al,** *adj.*

hymeno-, an element appearing in loan words from Greek, where it meant "membrane" (*hymenopteron*); on this model, used in the formation of compound words (*hymenotome*). [< Gk, comb. form of *hymḗn* membrane, hymen]

hy·me·nop·ter (hī′mə nop′tər), *n.* hymenopteron.

Hy·me·nop·ter·a (hī′mə nop′tər ə), *n.* the order comprising the hymenopterous insects. [< NL < Gk (neut. pl.). See HYMENOPTEROUS]

hy·me·nop·ter·an (hī′mə nop′tər ən), *adj.* **1.** hymenopterous. —*n.* **2.** a hymenopterous insect. [HYMENOPTER + -AN]

hy·me·nop·ter·on (hī′mə nop′tər ən), *n., pl.* **-ter·a** (-tər ə). a hymenopterous insect. [< Gk, neut. sing. of *hymenópteros* HYMENOPTEROUS]

hy·me·nop·ter·ous (hī′mə nop′tər əs), *adj.* belonging or pertaining to the *Hymenoptera*, an order of insects having, when winged, four membranous wings, and comprising the wasps, bees, ants, ichneumon flies, sawflies, etc. [< Gk *hymenópteros*. See HYMENO-, -PTEROUS]

hy·men·o·tome (hī men′ə tōm′), *n. Surg.* an instrument for cutting membrane. [HYMENO- + -TOME]

hy·men·ot·o·my (hī′mə not′ə mē), *n., pl.* **-mies.** *Surg.* **1.** incision of the hymen. **2.** incision of a membrane. [HYMENO- + -TOMY]

Hy·met·ti·us (hī met′ē əs), *n. Class. Myth.* an epithet of Zeus meaning "of Hymettus," because of an image of him there.

Hy·met·tus (hī met′əs), *n.* a mountain in SE Greece, near Athens. 3370 ft. —**Hy·met′ti·an, Hy·met′tic,** *adj.*

hymn (him), *n.* **1.** a song or ode in praise or honor of God, a deity, a nation, etc. **2.** something resembling this, as a speech, essay, or book in praise of someone or something. —*v.t.* **3.** to praise or celebrate in a hymn; express in a hymn. —*v.i.* **4.** to sing hymns. [< L *hymn(us)* < Gk *hýmnos* song in praise of gods or heroes; r. ME *ymne* (< OF) and OE *ymn*, etc. (< LL *ymnus*)] —**hymn·er** (him′ər, -nər), *n.* —**hymn′less,** *adj.* —**hymn′like′,** *adj.*

hym·nal (him′nəl), *n.* **1.** Also called **hymn′book′.** a book of hymns for use in a religious service. —*adj.* **2.** of or pertaining to hymns. [< ML *hymnāl(e)*, deriv. of neut. of *hymnālis* (adj.). See HYMN, -AL¹]

hym′nal stan′za. See **common measure** (def. 2).

hym·nar·i·um (him nâr′ē əm), *n., pl.* **-nar·i·a** (-nâr′ē ə). hymnary.

hym·na·ry (him′nə rē), *n., pl.* **-ries.** a hymnal. [< ML *hymnārium*. See HYMN, -ARY]

hym·nist (him′nist), *n.* a composer of hymns. [HYMN + -IST]

hym·no·dy (him′nə dē), *n.* **1.** the singing or the composition of hymns or sacred songs. **2.** hymns collectively, esp. the collective hymns of a specific religion, place, or period. [< ML *hymnōdi(a)* < Gk *hymnōidía* chanting of a hymn, equiv. to *hýmn(os)* HYMN + *ōidía* singing (*aoid-* sing (see ODE) + *-ia* -IA)] —**hym·nod·i·cal** (him nod′i kəl), *adj.* —**hym′no·dist,** *n.*

hym·nol·o·gy (him nol′ə jē), *n.* **1.** the study of hymns, their history, classification, etc. **2.** the composition of hymns. **3.** hymns collectively. [HYMN + -O- + -LOGY] —**hym·no·log·ic** (him′nə loj′ik), **hym′no·log′i·cal,** *adj.* —**hym′no·log′i·cal·ly,** *adv.* —**hym·nol′o·gist,** *n.*

Hymn′ to Proser′pine, a poem (1866) by Algernon Charles Swinburne.

hy·oid (hī′oid), *Anat., Zool.* —*adj.* **1.** Also, **hy·oi′dal, hy·oi′de·an.** noting or pertaining to a U-shaped bone at the root of the tongue in man, or a corresponding bone or collection of bones in animals. —*n.* **2.** the hyoid bone. See diag. under **larynx.** [< medical L *hyoīd(es)* < Gk *hyoeidḗs*, shaped like the letter hypsilon (i.e. upsilon), equiv. to *hy-* (deriv. of letter name *hŷ*, var. of *ŷ*; see UPSILON) + *-oeides* -OID]

hy·ol·i·thid (hī ol′i thid), *n.* **1.** any invertebrate of the extinct genus *Hyolithes*, most common in the Cambrian period, having a limy, univalve shell, and thought to be related to the pteropods. —*adj.* **2.** belonging or pertaining to the *Hyolithes*. [< NL *hyolithid(a)*, equiv. to *hyolith(ēs)* (see HYOID, -LITH) + *-ida* -ID²]

hy·os·cine (hī′ə sēn′, -sin), *n. Pharm.* scopolamine. [HYOSC(YAMUS) + -INE²]

hy·o·scy·a·mine (hī′ə sī′ə mēn′, -min), *n. Pharm.* a poisonous alkaloid, $C_{17}H_{23}NO_3$, obtained from henbane and other solanaceous plants: used usually in the form of its hydrobromide or sulfate salt as a sedative, analgesic, mydriatic, and antispasmodic. [HYOSCYAM(US) + -INE²]

hy·os·cy·a·mus (hī′ə sī′ə məs), *n.* the dried leaves, with or without the tops, of the henbane herb *Hyoscyamus niger*, containing the alkaloids hyoscyamine and scopolamine: used in medicine as an antispasmodic and sedative. [< NL < Gk *hyoskýamos*, equiv. to *hyós* (gen. of *hŷs* hog) + *kýamos* bean]

hyp (hip), *n. Archaic.* hypochondria. Also, **hip.** [by shortening]

hyp-, var. of **hypo-** before a vowel: *hypalgesia.*

hyp., **1.** hypotenuse. **2.** hypothesis. **3.** hypothetical.

hyp·a·byss·al (hip′ə bis′əl), *adj. Geol.* **1.** intermediate in texture between coarse-grained igneous rocks and fine-grained lava. **2.** noting any of various minor intrusions, as dikes and sills, intermediate in position between deeply situated plutonic bodies and superficial lava. [HYP- + AYBSSAL]

hyp·a·cu·sia (hip′ə kyo͞o′zhə, -zē ə, -ko͞o′-, hī′pə-), *n. Pathol.* hypoacusis. Also, **hyp·a·cu·sis** (hip′ə kyo͞o′sis, -ko͞o′-, hī′pə-). [< NL < Gk *hypákous(is)* mishearing (*hyp-* HYP- + *ákousis* hearing, equiv. to *akoú(ein)* to hear + *-sis* -SIS) + *-ia* -IA]

hyp·aes·the·sia (hip′is thē′zhə, -zhē ə, -zē ə), *n. Pathol.* hypesthesia. —**hyp·aes·the·sic** (hip′is thē′sik), *adj.*

hy·pae·thral (hi pē′thrəl, hī-), *adj.* hypethral.

hyp·al·ge·si·a (hip′al jē′zē ə, -sē ə, hī′pal-), *n. Med.* decreased sensitivity to pain (opposed to *hyperalgesia*). Also, **hy·pal·gia** (hi pal′jə, -jē ə, hī-). [HYP- + ALGESIA] —**hyp·al·ge·sic** (hip′al jē′zik, -sik, hī′pal-), *adj.*

hy·pal·la·ge (hi pal′ə jē′, hī-), *n. Rhet.* the reversal of the expected syntactic relation between two words, as in "her beauty's face" for "her face's beauty." [< L < Gk *hypallagḗ* interchange, equiv. to *hyp-* HYP- + *allagḗ* change (*all-* ALL- + *ag-* (s. of *ágein* to lead) + *-ē* n. suffix)]

Hyp·a·nis (hip′ə nis), *n.* ancient name of the **Kuban.**

hy·pan·thi·um (hi pan′thē əm, hī-), *n., pl.* **-thi·a** (-thē ə). *Bot.* a cup-shaped or tubular body, formed by the enlargement of the receptacle of a flower, bearing the sepals, petals, and stamens on its rim. [< NL < *hyp-* HYP- + *anthium* < Gk *ánthion* (*ánth(os)* flower + *-ion* dim. suffix)] —**hy·pan′thi·al,** *adj.*

hy·pas·pist (hi pas′pist, hī-), *n.* a shield bearer, esp. one of a special unit of light infantry in the Macedonian army. [< Gk *hypaspist(ḗs)* shield bearer, equiv. to *hyp-* HYP- + *aspís* shield + *-tēs* n. suffix]

Hy·pa·tia (hī pā′shə, -pat′ē ə), *n.* **1.** A.D. c370–415, Greek philosopher renowned for her beauty. **2.** a walled plain in the fourth quadrant of the face of the moon: about 30 miles in diameter.

Hyp·a·tie (hip′ə tē), *n.* a girl's given name.

hyper-, an element appearing in loan words from Greek, where it meant "over," usually implying excess or exaggeration (*hyperbole*); on this model used, especially as opposed to **hypo-**, in the formation of compound words (*hyperthyroid*). Cf. **super-.** [Gk, repr. *hypér* over, above; c. L *super;* akin to OVER]

hy·per·a·cid·i·ty (hī′pər ə sid′i tē), *n.* excessive acidity, as of the gastric juice. [HYPER- + ACIDITY] —**hy·per·ac·id** (hī′pər as′id), *adj.*

hy·per·ac·tive (hī′pər ak′tiv), *adj.* unusually or excessively active: *the child's hyperactive imagination.* [HYPER- + ACTIVE] —**hy·per·ac·tion** (hī′pər ak′shən), *n.* —**hy′per·ac·tiv′i·ty,** *n.*

hy·per·a·cu·sis (hī′pər ə kyo͞o′sis, -ko͞o′-), *n. Pathol.* excessive acuteness of the sense of hearing. Also, **hy·per·a·cou·sia** (hī′pər ə ko͞o′zhə, -zhē ə, -zē ə), **hy·per·a·cu·sia** (hī′pər ə kyo͞o′zhə, -zhē ə, -zē ə, -ko͞o-). [HYPER- + Gk *ákousis* hearing (*akoú(ein)* to hear + *-sis* -SIS)]

hy·per·ad·e·no·sis (hī′pər ad′ənō′sis), *n. Pathol.* abnormal enlargement of the glands, esp. of the lymphatic glands. [HYPER- + ADEN- + -OSIS]

hy·per·a·dre·nal·e·mi·a (hī′pər ə drēn′əlē′mē ə), *n. Pathol.* an abnormally large amount of adrenalin in the blood. Also called **hyperepinephrinemia.** [HYPER- + ADRENAL + -EMIA]

hy·per·a·dre·nal·ism (hī′pər ə drēn′əliz′əm, -ə dren′əliz′-), *n. Pathol.* a condition caused by abnormally increased secretory activity of the adrenal gland, characterized by a tendency toward increased basal metabolism and glycosuria. Also called **hy·per·a·dre·ni·a** (hī′pər ə drē′nē ə). [HYPER- + ADRENAL + -ISM]

hy·per·ae·mi·a (hī′pər ē′mē ə), *n. Pathol.* hyperemia. —**hy′per·ae′mic,** *adj.*

hy·per·aes·the·sia (hī′pər is thē′zhə, -zhē ə, -zē ə), *n. Pathol.* hyperesthesia. —**hy·per·aes·thet·ic** (hī′pər is thet′ik), *adj.*

hy·per·al·ge·si·a (hī′pər al jē′zē ə, -sē ə), *n. Med.* an exaggerated feeling or sense of pain (opposed to *hypalgesia*). Also, **hy·per·al·gi·a** (hī′pər al′jē ə, -jə). [HYPER- + ALGESIA] —**hy·per·al·ge·sic** (hī′pər al jē′zik, -sik), **hy·per·al·get·ic** (hī′pər al jet′ik), *adj.*

hy·per·an·a·ki·ne·sia (hī′pər an′ə ki nē′zhə, -zhē ə, -zē ə, -kī-), *n. Pathol.* abnormally active mechanical movement, as of the stomach or intestine. Also, **hy·per·an·a·ci·ne·sia** (hī′pər an′ə si nē′zhə, -zhē ə, -zē ə), **hy·per·an·a·ki·ne·sis** (hī′pər an′ə ki nē′sis, -kī-). [HYPER- + ANA- + Gk *-kinēsia*, deriv. of *kī́nes(is)* movement; see KINESTHESIA]

hy·per·a·phi·a (hī′pər ā′fē ə), *n. Pathol.* abnormal sensitivity to touch. [HYPER- + Gk *aph(ḗ)* touch + -IA] —**hy·per·aph·ic** (hī′pər af′ik), *adj.*

hy·per·az·o·tu·ri·a (hī′pər az′ə to͝or′ē ə, -tyo͝or′-), *n. Pathol.* an abnormally high amount of nitrogenous material in the urine. [HYPER- + AZOTE + -URIA]

hy·per·bar·ic (hī′pər bar′ik), *adj. Med.* (of an anesthetic) having a specific gravity greater than that of cerebrospinal fluid. Cf. **hypobaric.** [HYPER- + BARIC²]

hy·per·ba·ton (hī pûr′bə ton′), *n., pl.* **-ba·tons, -ba·ta** (-bə tə). *Rhet.* the use, esp. for emphasis, of a word order other than the expected or usual one, as in "Bird thou never wert." [< L < Gk: transposition, lit., overstepping, deriv. of neut. of *hyperbatós*, equiv. to *hyper-* HYPER- + *ba-* (s. of *baínein* to walk, step) + *-tos* verbal adj. suffix] —**hy·per·bat·ic** (hī′pər bat′ik), *adj.* —**hy′per·bat′i·cal·ly,** *adv.*

G H N F A A′ C B′ B F P D E

Hyperbola
DBE, GAH Opposite branches of a hyperbola; F, Focus; C, Center; AB, Transverse axis; A′B′, Conjugate axis; NCP, A diameter

hy·per·bo·la (hī pûr′bə lə), *n. Geom.* the set of points in a plane whose distances to two fixed points in the plane have a constant difference; a curve consisting of two distinct and similar branches, formed by the intersection of a plane with a right circular cone when the plane makes a greater angle with the base than does the generator of the cone. Equation: $x^2a^2 - y^2b^2 = 1$. See diag. under **conic section.** [< NL < Gk *hyperbolḗ* the geometrical term, lit., excess. See HYPERBOLE]

hy·per·bo·le (hī pûr′bə lē), *n. Rhet.* **1.** obvious and intentional exaggeration. **2.** an extravagant statement or figure of speech not intended to be taken literally, as "to wait an eternity." Cf. **litotes.** [< Gk *hyperbolḗ* excess, exaggeration, throwing beyond, equiv. to *hyper-* HYPER- + *bolḗ* throw]

hy·per·bol·ic (hī′pər bol′ik), *adj.* **1.** having the nature of hyperbole; exaggerated. **2.** using hyperbole; exaggerating. **3.** *Geom.* of or pertaining to a hyperbola. Also, **hy′per·bol′i·cal.** [HYPERBOLE + -IC] —**hy′per·bol′i·cal·ly,** *adv.*

hy′perbol′ic func′tion, *Math.* a function of an angle expressed as a relationship between the distances from a point on a hyperbola to the origin and to the coordinate axes, as hyperbolic sine, hyperbolic cosine, etc.: often expressed as combinations of exponential functions.

hyperbol′ic geom′etry, *Geom.* the branch of non-Euclidean geometry that replaces the parallel postulate of Euclidean geometry with the postulate that two distinct lines may be drawn parallel to a given line through a point not on the given line. Cf. **Riemannian geometry.**

hy·per·bo·lism (hī pûr′bə liz′əm), *n.* the use of hyperbole. [HYPERBOLE + -ISM]

hy·per·bo·lize (hī pûr′bə līz′), *v.,* **-lized, -liz·ing.** —*v.i.* **1.** to use hyperbole; exaggerate. —*v.t.* **2.** to represent or express with hyperbole or exaggeration. [HYPERBOLE + -IZE]

A B

Hyperboloids
A, Two sheet hyperboloid; B, One sheet hyperboloid

hy·per·bo·loid (hī pûr′bə loid′), *n. Math.* a quadric surface having a finite center and some of its plane sections hyperbolas. Equation: $\frac{x^2}{a^2} + \frac{y^2}{b^2} - \frac{z^2}{c^2} = 1$. [HYPERBOL(A) + -OID] —**hy·per′bo·loi′dal,** *adj.*

Hy·per·bo·re·an (hī′pər bôr′ē ən, -bôr′-, -bə rē′-), *n.* **1.** *Class. Myth.* one of a people supposed to live in a land of perpetual sunshine and abundance beyond the north wind. —*adj.* **2.** of or pertaining to the Hyperboreans. **3.** (*sometimes l.c.*) arctic; frigid. **4.** Paleosiberian. [< L *hyperbore(us)* < Gk *hyperbóre(os)* beyond the north wind, northern, polar (*hyper-* HYPER- + *boréas* the north, the north wind) + -AN; see BOREAS]

hy·per·cal·ce·mi·a (hī′pər kal sē′mē ə), *n. Pathol.* an abnormally large amount of calcium in the blood. Also, **hy′per·cal·cae′mi·a, hy·per·cal·ci·ne·mi·a, hy·per·cal·ci·nae·mi·a** (hī′pər kal′si nē′mē ə). [< NL; see HYPER-, CALC-, -EMIA]

hy·per·cal·ci·u·ri·a (hī′pər kal′si yo͝or′ē ə), *n. Pathol.* an abnormally high amount of calcium in the urine. Also, **hy·per·cal·ci·nu·ri·a** (hī′pər kal′si no͝or′ē ə, -nyo͝or′-), **hy·per·cal·cu·ri·a** (hī′pər kal kyo͝or′ē ə). [HYPER- + CALC- + -URIA]

hy·per·cap·ni·a (hī′pər kap′nē ə), *n. Med.* the presence of an excessive amount of carbon dioxide in the blood. Also called **hy·per·car·bi·a** (hī′pər kär′bē ə). [HYPER- + Gk *kapn(ós)* smoke + -IA]

hy·per·cat·a·lec·tic (hī′pər kat′əlek′tik), *adj. Pros.* (of a line of verse) containing an additional syllable after the last dipody or foot. Cf. **acatalectic** (def. 2), **catalectic.** [HYPER- + CATALECTIC]

Hy·per·chei·ri·a (hī′pər kī′rē ə), *n. Class. Myth.* an epithet of Hera, meaning "protectress."

hy·per·chlo·re·mi·a (hī′pər klō rē′mē ə, -klô-), *n. Pathol.* an abnormally large amount of chloride in the blood. Also, **hy′per·chlo·rae′mi·a.** [HYPER- + CHLOR-² + -EMIA]

hy·per·chlor·hy·dri·a (hī′pər klōr hī′drē ə, -klôr-), *n. Med.* excessive secretion of hydrochloric acid in the stomach. [HYPER- + CHLOR-¹ + HYDR-² + -IA]

hy·per·cho·les·ter·ol·e·mi·a (hī′pər kə les′tə rō lē′mē ə, -rō-), *n. Med.* the presence of an excessive amount of cholesterol in the blood. Also, **hy·per·cho·les·ter·e·mi·a** (hī′pər kə les′tə rē′mē ə). [< NL; see HYPER-, CHOLESTEROL, -EMIA]

hy·per·cho·les·ter·o·li·a (hī′pər kə les′tə rō′lē ə), *n. Pathol.* an abnormally large amount of cholesterol in the bile. [HYPER- + CHOLESTEROL + -IA]

hy·per·cho·li·a (hī′pər kō′lē ə), *n. Pathol.* an abnormally large secretion of bile. [HYPER- + CHOL- + -IA]

hy·per·con·scious (hī′pər kon′shəs), *adj.* acutely aware. [HYPER- + CONSCIOUS]

hy·per·cor·rect (hī′pər kə rekt′), *adj.* **1.** overly correct; excessively fastidious; fussy: *Her hypercorrect attitudes make her a cold and unspontaneous person.* **2.** of, pertaining to, or characterized by hypercorrection. [HYPER- + CORRECT] —**hy′per·cor·rect′ness,** *n.*

hy·per·cor·rec·tion (hī′pər kə rek′shən), *n. Ling.* an uncommon pronunciation or grammatical form or usage that results from an effort to replace incorrect or seemingly incorrect forms with correct ones, as *between you and I, Whom does she think she is?*, etc. Cf. **hyperform, hyperurbanism.** [HYPER- + CORRECTION]

hy·per·crin·ism (hī′pər krin′iz əm), *n. Pathol.* a condition caused by the abnormally large amount of secretion of any endocrine gland. Also, **hy·per·crin·e·mi·a** (hī′pər kri nē′mē ə), **hy·per·crin·i·a** (hī′pər krin′ē ə), **hy·per·cris·i·a** (hī′pər kris′ē ə). [HYPER- + (ENDO)CRINE + -ISM]

hy·per·crit·ic (hī′pər krit′ik), *n.* a person who is excessively or captiously critical. [< NL *hypercritic(us)*. See HYPER-, CRITIC]

hy·per·crit·i·cal (hī′pər krit′i kəl), *adj.* excessively or meticulously critical; overcritical. [HYPER- + CRITICAL] —**hy′per·crit′i·cal·ly,** *adv.*

hy·per·crit·i·cism (hī′pər krit′ə siz′əm), *n.* criticism that is carping or unduly harsh. [HYPER- + CRITICISM]

hy·per·cry·al·ge·si·a (hī′pər krī′al jē′zē ə, -sē ə), *n. Pathol.* abnormal sensitivity to cold. Also called **hy′per·cry′es·the′sia, hy′per·cry′aes·the′sia.** [NL; see HYPER-, CRY(O)-, ALGESIA]

hy′per·ab·sorp′tion, *n.*
hy′per·ac′cu·ra·cy, *n.*
hy′per·ac′cu·rate, *adj.*; **-ly,** *adv.*; **-ness,** *n.*
hy′per·a·cous′tics, *n.*
hy′per·ac′tion, *n.*
hy′per·ac′tive, *adj.*; **-ly,** *adv.*
hy′per·ac·tiv′i·ty, *n.*
hy′per·a·cu′i·ty, *n.*
hy′per·a·cute′, *adj.*; **-ness,** *n.*
hy′per·ad′i·pose′, *adj.*
hy′per·ad′i·pos′i·ty, *n.*
hy′per·aes′thete, *n.*
hy′per·al′i·men·ta′tion, *n.*
hy′per·al′ka·lin′i·ty, *n.*
hy′per·al′tru·ism, *n.*
hy′per·al′tru·ist, *n.*
hy′per·al′tru·is′tic, *adj.*
hy′per·an′a·bol′ic, *adj.*
hy′per·a·nab′o·lism, *n.*
hy′per·an′ar·chic, *adj.*
hy′per·an′ar·chy, *n.*
hy′per·an·gel′ic, *adj.*
hy′per·an·gel′i·cal, *adj.*; **-ly,** *adv.*
hy′per·ar′chae·o·log′i·cal, *adj.*
hy′per·bar′bar·ism, *n.*
hy′per·bar′bar·ous, *adj.*; **-ly,** *adv.*; **-ness,** *n.*
hy′per·brach′y·ce·phal′ic, *adj.*
hy′per·brach′y·ceph′a·ly, *n.*
hy′per·bran′chi·al, *adj.*
hy′per·bru′tal, *adj.*; **-ly,** *adv.*
hy′per·car′bu·ret′ed, *adj.*
hy′per·car′nal, *adj.*; **-ly,** *adv.*
hy′per·ca·tab′o·lism, *n.*
hy′per·ca·thar′sis, *n.*
hy′per·ca·thar′tic, *adj.*
hy′per·chlo′ri·na′tion, *n.*
hy′per·civ′i·li·za′tion, *n.*
hy′per·civ′i·lized′, *adj.*
hy′per·clas′si·cal, *adj.*
hy′per·clas′si·cal′i·ty, *n.*
hy′per·cli′max, *n.*
hy′per·co·ag′u·la·bil′i·ty, *n.*
hy′per·co·ag′u·la·ble, *adj.*
hy′per·com·pos′ite, *adj.*
hy′per·con′cen·tra′tion, *n.*
hy′per·con′fi·dence, *n.*
hy′per·con′fi·dent, *adj.*; **-ly,** *adv.*
hy′per·con·form′ist, *n.*
hy′per·con·form′i·ty, *n.*
hy′per·con′sci·en′tious, *adj.*; **-ly,** *adv.*; **-ness,** *n.*
hy′per·con·serv′a·tism, *n.*
hy′per·con·serv′a·tive, *adj., n.*; **-ly,** *adv.*; **-ness,** *n.*
hy′per·con′sti·tu′tion·al, *adj.*; **-ly,** *adv.*
hy′per·con′sti·tu′tion·al·ism, *n.*

hy·per·cy·the·mi·a (hī′pər sī thē′mē ə), *n.* *Pathol.* an abnormally large number of red corpuscles in the blood. [HYPER- + CYT(O)- + -HEMIA]

hy·per·cy·to·sis (hī′pər sī tō′sis), *n.* *Pathol.* an abnormally large number of cells in the blood, esp. of leukocytes. Also called **hyperleucocytosis, hyperleukocytosis.** [HYPER- + CYT- + -OSIS]

hy·per·dac·tyl·i·a (hī′pər dak til′ē ə), *n.* *Pathol.* the presence of supernumerary fingers or toes. Also, **hy·per·dac·tyl·ism** (hī′pər dak′tᵊliz′əm), **hy·per·dac·ty·ly** (hī′pər dak′tᵊ lē). [HYPER- + DACTYL- + -IA]

hy·per·du·li·a (hī′pər do͝o lē′ə, -dyo͝o-), *n.* *Rom. Cath. Theol.* the veneration offered to the Virgin Mary as the most exalted of creatures. Cf. **dulia, latria.** [< ML; see HYPER-, DULIA] —**hy·per·du·lic** (hī′pər do͞o′lik, -dyo͞o′-), **hy′per·du′li·cal,** *adj.*

hy·per·e·mi·a (hī′pər ē′mē ə), *n.* *Pathol.* an abnormally large amount of blood in any part of the body. Also, **hyperaemia.** [HYPER- + -EMIA] —**hy′per·e′mic,** *adj.*

hy·per·em·i·za·tion (hī′pər em′i zā′shən), *n.* *Med.* the artificial production of hyperemia, particularly for therapeutic purposes. [HYPEREM(IA) + -IZATION]

hy·per·en·do·crin·ism (hī′pər en′dō kri niz′əm), *n.* *Pathol.* an abnormal increase in the activity of any of the organs of internal secretion. Also, **hy·per·en·do·crin·i·a** (hī′pər en′dō krin′ē ə), **hy·per·en·do·cris·i·a** (hī′pər en′dō kris′ē ə). [HYPER- + ENDOCRINE + -ISM]

Hy·pe·re·nor (hī′pə rē′nôr), *n.* *Class. Myth.* **1.** one of the Sparti. **2.** (in the *Iliad*) the brother of Polydamas and Euphorbus: he fought in the Trojan War and was slain by Menelaus.

hy·per·ep·i·neph·ri·ne·mi·a (hī′pər ep′ə nef′rə nē′mē ə), *n.* *Pathol.* hyperadrenalemia. [HYPER- + EPINEPHRINE + -EMIA]

hy·per·ep·i·neph·ry (hī′pər ep′ə nef′rē), *n.* *Pathol.* abnormal increase in adrenal secretion, resulting in arterial tension. Also, **hy′per·ep′i·neph′ri·a.** [HYPER- + EPI- + NEPHR- + -Y³]

hy·per·es·the·sia (hī′pər is thē′zhə, -zhē ə, -zē ə), *n.* *Pathol.* an abnormally acute sense of pain, heat, cold, or touch. Also, **hyperaesthesia.** [HYPER- + -ESTHESIA] —**hy·per·es·thet·ic** (hī′pər is thet′ik), *adj.*

hy·per·eu·tec·toid (hī′pər yo͞o tek′toid), *adj.* *Metall.* **1.** (of an alloy) having more of the alloying element than the eutectoid element. **2.** (of steel) having more carbon than the 0.8 percent of eutectoid steel. [HYPER- + EUTECTOID]

hy·per·ex·ten·sion (hī′pər ik sten′shən), *n.* *Physiol.* **1.** the extension of a part of the body beyond normal limits. **2.** the state of being so extended. [HYPER- + EXTENSION]

hy′per·fine′ struc′ture (hī′pər fīn′, hī′-), *Physics.* the splitting of the lines of an atomic spectrum, produced by the angular momentum of the nucleus of the atom. Cf. **fine structure.** [HYPER- + FINE¹]

hy′per·fo′cal dis′tance (hī′pər fō′kəl, hī′-), *Photog.* the distance, at a given f number, between a camera lens and the nearest point **(hy′perfo′cal point′)** having satisfactory definition when focused at infinity. [HYPER- + FOCAL]

hy·per·form (hī′pər fôrm′), *n.* *Ling.* an uncommon pronunciation or grammatical form or usage produced by a speaker of one dialect according to an analogical rule he has formed by comparison of his own usage with that of another dialect. Cf. **hypercorrection, hyperurbanism.** [HYPER- + FORM]

hy·per·func·tion (hī′pər fungk′shən), *n.* abnormally increased function, esp. of glands or other organs (opposed to *hypofunction*). [HYPER- + FUNCTION]

hy·per·ga·lac·ti·a (hī′pər gə lak′tē ə), *n.* *Pathol.* the condition of secreting an abnormally large flow of milk. Also, **hy·per·gal·ac·to·si·a** (hī′pər gal′ak tō′sē ə), **hy·per·gal·ac·to·sis** (hī′pər gal′ak tō′sis). [HYPER- + GALACT- + -IA]

hy·per·ga·my (hī pûr′gə mē), *n.* the practice among Hindu women of marrying into a caste at least as high as their own. [HYPER- + -GAMY] —**hy·per′ga·mous,** *adj.*

hy′per·ge·o·met′ric distribu′tion (hī′pər jē′ə me′trik, hī′-), *Math.* a system of probabilities associated with finding a specified number of elements, as 5 white balls, from a given number of elements, as 10 balls, chosen from a set containing 2 kinds of elements of known quantity, as 15 white balls and 20 black balls. [HYPER- + GEOMETRIC]

hy′pergeomet′ric equa′tion, *Math.* a differential equation of the form, $(x^2-x)\frac{d^2y}{d^2x} + [(a+b+1)x-c]\frac{dy}{dx} + abx=0$ where *a, b,* and *c* are arbitrary constants.

hy′pergeomet′ric func′tion, *Math.* a function that is a solution to a hypergeometric equation.

hy·per·geus·es·the·si·a (hī′pər gyo͞o′sis thē′zē ə, -jo͞o′-), *n.* *Pathol.* an abnormal acuteness of the sense of taste. Also, **hy·per·geu·si·a** (hī′pər gyo͞o′sē ə, -jo͞o′-). [HYPER- + Gk *geûs(is)* sense of taste (verbid of *geúesthai* to taste) + ESTHESIA]

hy·per·glo·bu·li·a (hī′pər glō byo͞o′lē ə), *n.* *Pathol.* an abnormally large number of red corpuscles in the blood; hypercythemia. Also, **hy·per·glob·u·lism** (hī′pər glob′yə liz′əm). [HYPER- + GLOBULE + -IA]

hy·per·gly·ce·mi·a (hī′pər glī sē′mē ə), *n.* *Med.* an abnormally high level of glucose in the blood. Also, **hy′per·gly·cae′mi·a.** [< NL; see HYPER-, GLYCEMIA] —**hy′per·gly·ce′mic, hy′per·gly·cae′mic,** *adj.*

hy·per·gly·cis·ti·a (hī′pər glī sis′tē ə), *n.* *Pathol.* an abnormally large amount of sugar in the tissues. [HYPER- + Gk *glykýs* sweet + *-tia* -CY]

hy·per·gol (hī′pər gôl′, -gōl′, -gol′), *n.* any hypergolic agent. [HYPER- + ERG¹ + -OL¹]

hy·per·gol·ic (hī′pər gô′lik, -gol′ik, -gō′lik), *adj.* (esp. of rocket-fuel propellant constituents) igniting spontaneously upon contact with a complementary substance. [HYP(ER)- + ERG + -OL²]

hy·per·he·pat·i·a (hī′pər hi pat′ē ə, -pā′shē ə), *n.* *Pathol.* excessive liver function. [HYPER- + HEPAT- + -IA]

hy·per·hi·dro·sis (hī′pər hi drō′sis), *n.* *Physiol.* excessive sweating. Also, **hy·per·i·dro·sis** (hī′pər i drō′sis). [HYPER- + HIDROSIS]

Hy·pe·ri·on (hī pēr′ē ən), *n.* **1.** *Class. Myth.* a Titan, the father of Helios, Selene, and Eos: later identified with Apollo. **2.** *Homeric Legend.* Helios. **3.** (*italics.*) an unfinished narrative poem (1818–19) by John Keats. **4.** (*italics.*) a prose work (1839) by Longfellow. **5.** *Astron.* one of the nine satellites of Saturn. [< L < Gk *Hyperíōn,* equiv. to *hyper-* HYPER- + *iṓn* going; see ION]

hy·per·ir·ri·ta·bil·i·ty (hī′pər ir′i tə bil′i tē), *n.* extreme irritability. [HYPER- + IRRITABILITY] —**hy′per·ir′ri·ta·ble,** *adj.*

hy·per·ka·le·mi·a (hī′pər kə lē′mē ə), *n.* *Pathol.* an abnormally large amount of potassium in the blood; hyperpotassemia. Also, **hy·per·kal·i·e·mi·a** (hī′pər-kal′ē ē′mē ə). [HYPER- + NL *kal(ium)* potassium (see ALKALI, -IUM) + -EMIA] —**hy′per·ka·le′mic,** *adj.*

hy·per·ker·a·to·sis (hī′pər ker′ə tō′sis), *n.* **1.** *Pathol.* **a.** proliferation of the cells of the cornea. **b.** a thickening of the horny layer of the skin. **2.** Also called **x-disease.** *Vet. Pathol.* a condition of cattle resulting from their physical contact with or eating of objects or food contaminated by wood preservatives or machinery lubricants containing highly chlorinated naphthalenes, characterized by thickening and hardening of the skin, abnormal secretion of tears and saliva, and diarrhea. [< NL; see HYPER-, KERATOSIS] —**hy·per·ker·a·tot·ic** (hī′pər ker′ə tot′ik), *adj.*

hy·per·ki·ne·sia (hī′pər ki nē′zhə, -zhē ə, -zē ə, -kī-), *n.* *Pathol.* an abnormal amount of uncontrolled muscular action; spasm. Also, **hy·per·ki·ne·sis** (hī′pər ki nē′sis, -kī-). [HYPER- + Gk *kínēs(is)* movement + -IA] —**hy·per·ki·net·ic** (hī′pər ki net′ik, -kī-), *adj.*

hy·per·leu·co·cy·to·sis (hī′pər lo͞o′kō sī tō′sis), *n.* *Pathol.* hypercytosis. Also, **hy′per·leu′ko·cy·to′sis.** [HYPER- + LEUCOCYTOSIS]

hy·per·li·pe·mi·a (hī′pər li pē′mē ə), *n.* *Med.* excessive amounts of fat and fatty substances in the blood; lipemia. Also, **hy′per·li·pae′mi·a.** [HYPER- + LIPEMIA] —**hy′per·li·pe′mic, hy′per·li·pae′mic,** *adj.*

hy·per·meg·a·so·ma (hī′pər meg′ə sō′mə), *n.* *Pathol.* gigantism. [HYPER- + MEGA- + SOMA]

hy·per·met·a·mor·pho·sis (hī′pər met′ə môr′fə sis), *n., pl.* **-ses** (-sēz′). *Entomol.* a metamorphosis in which two or more markedly different types of larvae occur successively, as in meloid beetles. [< NL; see HYPER-, METAMORPHOSIS] —**hy′per·met′a·mor′phic,** *adj.*

hy·per·me·ter (hī pûr′mi tər), *n.* *Pros.* a verse or line containing one or more additional syllables after those proper to the meter. [HYPER- + -METER] —**hy·per·met·ric** (hī′pər me′trik), **hy′per·met′ri·cal,** *adj.*

hy·per·met·rope (hī′pər me′trōp), *n.* *Ophthalm.* a person who has hypermetropia. Also called **hyperope.** [back formation from HYPERMETROPIA]

hy·per·me·tro·pi·a (hī′pər mi trō′pē ə), *n.* *Ophthalm.* a condition of the eye in which parallel rays are focused behind the retina, distant objects being seen more distinctly than near ones; far-sightedness (opposed to *myopia*). Also called **hyperopia.** [< Gk *hypérmetr(on)* beyond measure, excessive (*hyper-* HYPER- + *métron* measure) + -OPIA] —**hy·per·met·ro·py** (hī′pər me′trə pē), *n.*

hy·per·me·trop·ic (hī′pər mə trop′ik), *adj.* *Ophthalm.* pertaining to or having hypermetropia; far-sighted. [HYPERMETROP(IA) + -IC]

hy·per·mi·cro·so·ma (hī′pər mī′krə sō′mə), *n.* *Pathol.* the state or condition of having an abnormally low stature; dwarfishness. [< NL; see HYPER-, MICROSOME]

Hy·perm·nes·tra (hī′pərm nes′trə), *n.* *Class. Myth.* the only one of the Danaides who did not kill her husband.

hy·per·mo·til·i·ty (hī′pər mō til′i tē), *n.* excessive motility of the stomach or intestine (opposed to *hypomotility*). [HYPER- + MOTILITY]

hy·per·na·tre·mi·a (hī′pər nə trē′mē ə), *n.* *Pathol.* an abnormally large quantity of sodium in the blood. Also, **hy·per·nat·ro·ne·mi·a** (hī′pər na′trə nē′mē ə). [HYPER- + NATR(IUM) + -EMIA]

hy·per·on (hī′pə ron′), *n.* *Physics.* any of several elementary particles having a mass intermediate between that of a neutron and a deutron. [HYPER- + *-on,* as in *proton, neutron*]

hy·per·ope (hī′pə rōp′), *n.* *Ophthalm.* hypermetrope. [HYPER- + Gk *ōp-* (s. of *ṓps*) eye]

hy·per·o·pi·a (hī′pə rō′pē ə), *n.* *Ophthalm.* hypermetropia. [HYPER- + -OPIA] —**hy·per·op·ic** (hī′pə rop′ik), *adj.*

hy·per·os·mi·a (hī′pə roz′mē ə), *n.* *Med.* an abnormally acute sense of smell. [HYPER- + -OSMIA] —**hy′per·os′mic,** *adj.*

hy·per·os·te·og·e·ny (hī′pə ros′tē oj′ə nē), *n.* *Pathol.* excessive bone development. [HYPER- + OSTEO- + -GENY]

hy·per·os·to·sis (hī′pər o stō′sis), *n.* *Pathol.* **1.** an increase or protuberance of bony tissue. **2.** an overgrowth of bone. [HYPER- + OSTOSIS] —**hy·per·os·tot·ic** (hī′pər o stot′ik), *adj.*

hy·per·o·var·i·a (hī′pər rō vâr′ē ə), *n.* *Med.* precocious sexuality in girls due to abnormally heavy ovarian secretion. Also, **hy·per·o·var·i·an·ism** (hī′pə rō vâr′ē ə niz′əm), **hy·per·o·va·rism** (hī′pə rō′və riz′əm). [HYPER- + NL *ovaria,* neut. pl. of OVARIUM]

hy·per·ox·e·mi·a (hī′pə rok sē′mē ə), *n.* *Pathol.* abnormal acidity of the blood. [HYPER- + OXY- + -EMIA]

hy·per·ox·ide (hī′pər ok′sīd, -sid), *n.* *Chem.* superoxide. [HYPER- + OXIDE]

hy·per·par·a·site (hī′pər par′ə sīt′), *n.* *Biol.* an organism that is parasitic on or in another parasite. [HYPER- + PARASITE] —**hy·per·par·a·sit·ic** (hī′pər-par′ə sit′ik), *adj.* —**hy′per·par′a·sit·ism,** *n.*

hy·per·par·a·thy·roid·ism (hī′pər par′ə thī′roi diz′əm), *n.* *Pathol.* a condition produced by overactivity of the parathyroid gland, characterized by softening of the bones, with consequent pain, tenderness, and a tendency to spontaneous fractures, and by muscular weakness and abdominal cramps. [HYPER- + PARATHYROID + -ISM]

hy·per·pha·gi·a (hī′pər fā′jē ə, -jə), *n.* *Med.* bulimia. [HYPER- + -PHAGIA]

hy·per·phos·phe·re·mi·a (hī′pər fos′fə rē′mē ə), *n.* *Pathol.* an abnormally large quantity of inorganic phosphorous compounds in the blood. Also, **hy·per·phos·pha·te·mi·a** (hī′pər fos′fə tē′mē ə). [HYPER- + *phospher,* obs. var. of PHOSPHOR + -EMIA]

hy·per·phys·i·cal (hī′pər fiz′i kəl), *adj.* above or beyond the physical; immaterial; supernatural. [HYPER- + PHYSICAL] —**hy′per·phys′i·cal·ly,** *adv.*

hy·per·pi·e·sia (hī′pər pī ē′zhə, -zhē ə), *n.* *Pathol.* See **essential hypertension.** Also, **hy·per·pi·e·sis** (hī′pər-pī ē′sis, -pī′ə sis). [HYPER- + Gk *píes(is)* pressure + -IA]

hy·per·pi·et·ic (hī′pər pī et′ik), *Pathol.* —*adj.* **1.** of or noting essential hypertension. —*n.* **2.** a person having essential hypertension. [HYPERPIE(SIA) + -TIC]

hy·per·pi·tu·i·ta·rism (hī′pər pi to͞o′i tə riz′əm, -tyo͞o′-), *n.* *Pathol.* **1.** overactivity of the pituitary gland. **2.** a resultant condition of this, as giantism or acromegaly. [HYPER- + PITUITAR(Y) + -ISM]

hy·per·plane (hī′pər plān′, hī′pər plān′), *n.* *Math.* a subspace of a vector space which has dimension one less than the dimension of the vector space. [HYPER- + PLANE¹]

hy·per·pla·sia (hī′pər plā′zhə, -zhē ə, -zē ə), *n.* **1.** *Pathol., Bot.* abnormal multiplication of cells. **2.** *Pathol.* enlargement of a part due to an abnormal numerical increase of its cells. [HYPER- + -PLASIA] —**hy·per·plas·tic** (hī′pər plas′tik), *adj.*

hy·per·ploid (hī′pər ploid′), *Biol.* —*adj.* **1.** having a chromosome number that is greater than but not a multiple of the diploid number. —*n.* **2.** a hyperploid cell or organism. [HYPER- + -PLOID] —**hy′per·ploi′dy,** *n.*

hy·perp·ne·a (hī′pərp nē′ə, hī′pər nē′ə), *n.* *Pathol.* abnormally energetic or labored respiration. Also, **hy·perp·noe′a.** [< NL, equiv. to *hyper-* HYPER- + *pnēa* var. of *pnoea* < Gk *pnoiē* breathing]

---

hy′per·cy′a·no′sis, *n.*
hy′per·cy′a·not′ic, *adj.*
hy′per·de′i·fi·ca′tion, *n.*
hy′per·de′i·fy′, *v.t.,* **-fied, -fy·ing.**
hy′per·del′i·ca·cy, *n.*
hy′per·del′i·cate, *adj.;* **-ly,** *adv.;* **-ness,** *n.*
hy′per·de·li′cious, *adj.;* **-ly,** *adv.;* **-ness,** *n.*
hy′per·dem′o·crat′ic, *adj.*
hy′per·di′a·bol′i·cal, *adj.;* **-ly,** *adv.;* **-ness,** *n.*
hy′per·di′as·tol′ic, *adj.*
hy′per·di·crot′ic, *adj.*
hy′per·di′cro·tism, *n.*
hy′per·dis·ten′tion, *n.*
hy′per·di·vi′sion, *n.*
hy′per·dol′i·cho·ce·phal′ic, *adj.*
hy′per·dol′i·cho·ceph′a·ly, *n.*
hy′per-Do′ri·an, *adj.*
hy′per·el′e·gance, *n.*
hy′per·el′e·gan·cy, *n.*
hy′per·el′e·gant, *adj.;* **-ly,** *adv.*
hy′per·em′e·sis, *n.*
hy′per·e·met′ic, *adj.*
hy′per·e·mo′tion·al, *adj.;* **-ly,** *adv.*
hy′per·e·mo′tive, *adj.;* **-ly,** *adv.;* **-ness,** *n.*
hy′per·e′mo·tiv′i·ty, *n.*
hy′per·em′pha·size′, *v.t.,* **-sized, -siz·ing.**
hy′per·en′er·get′ic, *adj.*
hy′per·en·thu′si·asm, *n.*
hy′per·en·thu′si·as′tic, *adj.*
hy′per·en·thu′si·as′ti·cal·ly, *adv.*
hy′per·er′e·thism, *n.*
hy′per·es′thete, *n.*
hy′per·eth′i·cal, *adj.;* **-ly,** *adv.;* **-ness,** *n.*
hy′per·ex′al·ta′tion, *n.*
hy′per·ex·cit′a·bil′i·ty, *n.*
hy′per·ex·cit′a·ble, *adj.;* **-ble·ness,** *n.;* **-bly,** *adv.*
hy′per·ex·cite′ment, *n.*
hy′per·ex·cur′sive, *adj.;* **-ly,** *adv.;* **-ness,** *n.*
hy′per·fas·tid′i·ous, *adj.;* **-ly,** *adv.;* **-ness,** *n.*
hy′per·fed′er·al·ist, *n.*
hy′per·flex′i·bil′i·ty, *n.*
hy′per·flex′i·ble, *adj.;* **-ble·ness,** *n.;* **-bly,** *adv.*
hy′per·flex′ion, *n.*
hy′per·func′tion, *n.*
hy′per·func′tion·al, *adj.;* **-ly,** *adv.*
hy′per·gen′e·sis, *n.*
hy′per·ge·net′ic, *adj.*
hy′per·ge·net′i·cal, *adj.;* **-ly,** *adv.*
hy′per·gram·mat′i·cal, *adj.;* **-ly,** *adv.;* **-ness,** *n.*
hy′per·hi·drot′ic, *adj.*
hy′per·hi·lar′i·ous, *adj.;* **-ly,** *adv.;* **-ness,** *n.*
hy′per·hy·poc′ri·sy, *n.*
hy′per·i·de′al·is′tic, *adj.*
hy′per·i·de′al·is′ti·cal·ly, *adv.*
hy′per·im·mune′, *adj.*
hy′per·im·mu′ni·ty, *n.*
hy′per·im′mu·ni·za′tion, *n.*
hy′per·im′mu·nize′, *v.t.,* **-nized, -niz·ing.**
hy′per·in′ge·nu′i·ty, *n.*
hy′per·in′tel·lec′tu·al, *adj.;* **-ly,** *adv.;* **-ness,** *n.*
hy′per·in·tel′li·gence, *n.*
hy′per·in·tel′li·gent, *adj.;* **-ly,** *adv.*
hy′per·ka·tab′o·lism, *n.*
hy′per·lac·ta′tion, *n.*
hy′per·le′thal, *adj.*
hy′per·leth′ar·gy, *n.*
hy′per·leu′co·cy·to′sis, *n.*
hy′per·leu′co·cy·tot′ic, *adj.*
hy′per·log′i·cal, *adj.;* **-ly,** *adv.;* **-ness,** *n.*
hy′per·log′i·cal′i·ty, *n.*
hy′per·lus′trous, *adj.;* **-ly,** *adv.;* **-ness,** *n.*
hy′per·mag′i·cal, *adj.;* **-ly,** *adv.*
hy′per·med′i·ca′tion, *n.*
hy′per·me·tab′o·lism, *n.*
hy′per·met′a·phor′ic, *adj.*
hy′per·met′a·phor′i·cal, *adj.*
hy′per·met′a·phys′i·cal, *adj.*
hy′per·mi·rac′u·lous, *adj.;* **-ly,** *adv.;* **-ness,** *n.*
hy′per·mod′est, *adj.;* **-ly,** *adv.;* **-ness,** *n.*
hy′per·mor′al, *adj.;* **-ly,** *adv.*
hy′per·mo′tile, *adj.*
hy′per·mo·til′i·ty, *n.*
hy′per·mys′ti·cal, *adj.;* **-ly,** *adv.;* **-ness,** *n.*
hy′per·nat′u·ral, *adj.;* **-ly,** *adv.;* **-ness,** *n.*
hy′per·neu·rot′ic, *adj.*
hy′per·ni·trog′e·nous, *adj.*
hy′per·nor′mal, *adj.;* **-ly,** *adv.;* **-ness,** *n.*
hy′per·nor·mal′i·ty, *n.*
hy′per·nu·tri′tion, *n.*
hy′per·nu′tri·tive, *adj.*
hy′per·ob·tru′sive, *adj.;* **-ly,** *adv.;* **-ness,** *n.*
hy′per·or·gan′ic, *adj.*
hy′per·or·gan′i·cal·ly, *adv.*
hy′per·or′tho·dox′, *adj.*
hy′per·or′tho·dox′y, *n.*
hy′per·or·thog′na·thous, *adj.*
hy′per·ox′y·gen·ate′, *v.t.,* **-at·ed, -at·ing.**
hy′per·ox′y·gen·a′tion, *n.*
hy′per·ox′y·gen·ize′, *v.t.,* **-ized, -iz·ing.**
hy′per·par′ox·ysm, *n.*
hy′per·pa·thet′ic, *adj.*
hy′per·pa·thet′i·cal, *adj.;* **-ly,** *adv.*
hy′per·pa′tri·ot′ic, *adj.*
hy′per·pa′tri·ot′i·cal·ly, *adv.*
hy′per·pa′tri·ot·ism, *n.*
hy′per·per·fec′tion, *n.*
hy′per·per′i·stal′sis, *n.*
hy′per·per′i·stal′tic, *adj.*
hy′per·per′son·al, *adj.;* **-ly,** *adv.*
hy′per·pig′men·ta′tion, *n.*
hy′per·pig′ment·ed, *adj.*

hy·per·pot·as·se·mi·a (hī/pər pot/ə sē/mē ə), *n. Pathol.* an abnormally large amount of potassium in the blood; hyperkalemia. [HYPER- + POTASS(IUM) + -EMIA] —**hy/per·pot/as·se/mic,** *adj.*

hy·per·pro·sex·i·a (hī/pər prō sek/sē ə), *n. Psychol.* exaggerated attention to some stimulus that one has difficulty ignoring. [HYPER- + Gk *prósex(is)* attention, equiv. to *prosech-*, s. of *prosēchein* to heed (*pros-* toward + *échein* to hold) + *-sis* -SIS + *-ia* -IA]

hy·per·py·rex·i·a (hī/pər pī rek/sē ə), *n. Pathol.* an abnormally high fever. [HYPER- + PYREXIA] —**hy·per·py·ret·ic** (hī/pər pī ret/ik), **hy/per·py·rex/i·al,** *adj.*

hy·per·se·cre·tion (hī/pər si krē/shən), *n.* an excessive secretion (opposed to *hyposecretion*). [HYPER- + SECRETION]

hy·per·sen·si·tise (hī/pər sen/si tīz/), *v.t.*, **-tised, -tis·ing.** *Chiefly Brit. Photog.* hypersensitize. —**hy/per·sen/si·ti·sa/tion,** *n.*

hy·per·sen·si·tive (hī/pər sen/si tiv), *adj.* **1.** excessively sensitive: *to be hypersensitive to criticism.* **2.** *Pathol.* allergic to a substance to which a normal individual does not react. [HYPER- + SENSITIVE] —**hy/per·sen/si·tive·ness, hy/per·sen/si·tiv/i·ty,** *n.*

hy·per·sen·si·tize (hī/pər sen/si tīz/), *v.t.*, **-tized, -tiz·ing.** *Photog.* to treat (a film or emulsion) so as to increase its speed. Also, *esp. Brit.*, **hypersensitise.** [HYPERSENSIT(IVE) + -IZE] —**hy/per·sen/si·ti·za/tion,** *n.*

hy·per·som·ni·a (hī/pər som/nē ə), *n.* sleep of abnormally long duration. [HYPER- + (IN)SOMNIA]

hy·per·son·ic (hī/pər son/ik), *adj.* noting or pertaining to speed that is at least five times that of sound in the same medium. [HYPER- + L *son(us)* sound + -IC]

hy·per·space (hī/pər spās/, hī/pər spās/), *n. Math.* a Euclidean space of dimension greater than three. [HYPER- + SPACE] —**hy·per·spa·tial** (hī/pər spā/shəl), *adj.*

hy·per·sphere (hī/pər sfēr/, hī/pər sfēr/), *n. Math.* the generalization of a sphere to more than three dimensions. [HYPER- + SPHERE] —**hy·per·spher·i·cal** (hī/pər sfer/i kəl), *adj.*

hy·per·stat·ic (hī/pər stat/ik), *adj.* redundant (def. 5b). [HYPER- + STATIC]

hy·per·sthene (hī/pər sthēn/), *n. Mineral.* an orthorhombic pyroxene consisting of a dark, platy iron magnesium silicate, found in norites and containing more than 14 percent ferrous oxide. [HYPER- + Gk *sthén(os)* strength, might; r. *hyperstene* < F *hyperstène*] —**hy·per·sthen·ic** (hī/pər sthen/ik), *adj.*

hy·per·sus·cep·ti·ble (hī/pər sə sep/tə bəl), *adj. Pathol.* hypersensitive (def. 2). [HYPER- + SUSCEPTIBLE] —**hy/per·sus·cep/ti·bil/i·ty,** *n.*

hy·per·tel·y (hī pûr/tᵊlē, hī/pər tel/ē), *n. Biol.* excessive imitation, as of color, shape, etc., without apparent usefulness. [HYPER- + TEL-² + -Y³] —**hy/per·tel/ic,** *adj.*

hy·per·ten·sin (hī/pər ten/sin), *n. Biochem.* any of several polypeptides that when activated by enzymes present in blood plasma constrict the blood vessels. Also called **angiotonin.** [HYPER- + TENSI(O)N]

hy·per·ten·sin·ase (hī/pər ten/si nās/), *n. Biochem.* an enzyme, found in animal tissues, esp. the kidney and intestine, that serves to break down hypertension. Also called **angiotonase.** [HYPERTENSIN + -ASE]

hy·per·ten·sin·o·gen (hī/pər ten sin/ə jin, -jen/), *n. Biochem.* a globulin produced by the liver, found in blood plasma and serum, and converted by renin to hypertensin. [HYPERTENSIN + -O- + -GEN]

hy·per·ten·sion (hī/pər ten/shən), *n.* **1.** excessive or extreme tension. **2.** *Pathol.* **a.** elevation of the blood pressure, esp. the diastolic pressure. **b.** an arterial disease characterized by this condition. [HYPER- + TENSION]

hy·per·ten·sive (hī/pər ten/siv), *Pathol.* —*adj.* **1.** characterized by or causing high blood pressure. —*n.* **2.** a person who has high blood pressure. [HYPER- + TENSIVE]

Hy·per·therm (hī/pər thûrm/), *n. Med., Trademark.* an apparatus for producing high fevers in patients for therapeutic purposes.

hy·per·ther·mi·a (hī/pər thûr/mē ə), *n. Med.* **1.** abnormally high fever. **2.** treatment of disease by the induction of fever, as by the injection of foreign protein or the application of heat. Also, **hy·per·ther·my** (hī/pər-thûr/mē). [< NL; see HYPER-, THERM-, -IA]

hy·per·throm·bin·e·mi·a (hī/pər throm/bi nē/mē ə), *n. Pathol.* an abnormally large amount of thrombin in the blood. [HYPER- + THROMBIN + -EMIA]

hy·per·thy·mi·a (hī/pər thī/mē ə), *n. Psychiatry.* a condition characterized by overactivity. [HYPER- + THYM(US) + -IA]

hy·per·thy·roid (hī/pər thī/roid), *adj.* **1.** of, pertaining to, or having hyperthyroidism. **2.** characterized by extreme intensity, emotionalism, or lack of restraint: *hyperthyroid journalism.* [HYPER- + THYROID]

hy·per·thy·roid·ism (hī/pər thī/roi diz/əm), *n. Pathol.* **1.** overactivity of the thyroid gland. **2.** a condition resulting from this, characterized by increased metabolism and exophthalmos. [HYPER- + THYROID + -ISM]

hy·per·ton·ic (hī/pər ton/ik), *adj.* **1.** *Physiol.* (of tissue) having a greater than normal tone. **2.** *Physical Chem.* noting a solution of higher osmotic pressure than another solution with which it is compared (opposed to *hypotonic*). Cf. **isotonic** (def. 1). [HYPER- + TONIC] —**hy·per·to·nic·i·ty** (hī/pər tō nis/i tē), *n.*

hy·per·tro·phy (hī pûr/trə fē), *n., pl.* **-phies,** *v.,* **-phied, -phy·ing.** —*n.* **1.** *Pathol., Bot.* abnormal enlargement of a part or organ; excessive growth. **2.** excessive growth or accumulation of any kind. —*v.t., v.i.* **3.** to affect with or undergo hypertrophy. [HYPER- + -TROPHY] —**hy·per·troph·ic** (hī/pər trof/ik), *adj.*

hy·per·ur·ban·ism (hī/pər ûr/bə niz/əm), *n. Ling.* an uncommon pronunciation or grammatical form or usage produced by a speaker of one dialect according to an analogical rule he has formed by comparison of his own usage with that of a more prestigious dialect he is attempting to imitate, as the pronunciation of the word two (to͞o) as (tyo͞o). Cf. **hypercorrection, hyperform.** [HYPER- + URBAN + -ISM]

hy·per·ven·ti·la·tion (hī/pər ven/tᵊlā/shən), *n. Med.* excessively rapid and deep breathing, resulting esp. in the decrease of carbon dioxide in the blood. [HYPER- + VENTILATION]

hy·per·vi·ta·min·o·sis (hī/pər vī/tə mi nō/sis), *n. Med.* an abnormal condition caused by an excessive intake of vitamins. [HYPER- + VITAMIN + -OSIS]

hyp·es·the·sia (hip/is thē/zhə, -zhē ə, -zē ə), *n. Pathol.* an abnormally weak sense of pain, heat, cold, or touch. Also, **hypaesthesia.** [HYP- + ESTHESIA] —**hyp·es·the·sic** (hip/is thē/sik), *adj.*

hy·pe·thral (hi pē/thrəl, hī-), *adj.* (of a classical building) wholly or partly open to the sky. Also, **hypaethral.** Cf. **clithral.** [< L *hypaethr(us)* (< Gk *hýpaithros* open to the sky, equiv. to *hyp-* HYP- + *aíthros* clear sky) + -AL¹]

hy·pha (hī/fə), *n., pl.* **-phae** (-fē). *Bot.* (in fungi) one of the threadlike elements of the mycelium. [< NL < Gk *hyphḗ* WEB] —**hy/phal,** *adj.*

hy·phen (hī/fən), *n.* **1.** a short line (-) used to connect the parts of a compound word or the parts of a word divided for any purpose. —*v.t.* **2.** hyphenate. [< LL < Gk *hyphén* (adv.) together, deriv. of *hyph' hén* (prep. phrase), equiv. to *hypó* under + *hén*, neut. of *heîs* one] —**hy·phen·ic** (hī fen/ik), *adj.*

hy·phen·ate (*v.* hī/fə nāt/; *adj., n.* hī/fə nit, -nāt/), *v.,* **-at·ed, -at·ing,** *adj., n.* —*v.t.* **1.** to join by a hyphen. **2.** to write with a hyphen. —*adj.* **3.** of or pertaining to something of distinct form or origin that has been joined; connected by a hyphen. —*n.* **4.** a hyphenated U.S. citizen. [HYPHEN + -ATE¹] —**hy/phen·a/tion,** *n.*

hy·phen·at·ed (hī/fə nā/tid), *adj. Chiefly Hist.* noting a naturalized citizen of the U.S. believed to be ambivalent in his loyalty: so called because of the tendency to style himself according to his former and present nationalities, using a hyphen; e.g., "German-American."

hy·phen·ise (hī/fə nīz/), *v.t.*, **-ised, -is·ing.** *Chiefly Brit.* hyphenize. —**hy/phen·i·sa/tion,** *n.*

hy·phen·ize (hī/fə nīz/), *v.t.*, **-ized, -iz·ing.** hyphenate (defs. 1, 2). [HYPHEN + -IZE] —**hy/phen·i·za/tion,** *n.*

hy·pho·po·di·um (hī/fə pō/dē əm), *n., pl.* **-di·a** (-dē ə). (in a fungus) a specialized hyphal branch, composed of one or two usually lobed cells, serving for attachment and for the absorption of food. [< NL; see HYPHA-, -PODIUM]

hypno-, a learned borrowing from Greek used, with the meaning "sleep," "hypnosis," in the formation of compound words: *hypnotherapy.* Also, *esp. before a vowel,* **hypn-.** [< Gk *hýpno(s)* sleep; see HYPNOS]

hyp·no·a·nal·y·sis (hip/nō ə nal/i sis), *n. Psychoanal.* a method of psychoanalysis in which a patient is put into hypnosis in an attempt to secure analytic data, free associations, and early emotional reactions from him. [HYPNO- + ANALYSIS] —**hyp·no·an·a·lyt·ic** (hip/nō-an/ᵊlit/ik), *adj.*

hyp·no·gen·e·sis (hip/nō jen/i sis), *n. Med.* induction of the hypnotic state. [HYPNO- + GENESIS] —**hyp·no·ge·net·ic** (hip/nō jə net/ik), *adj.*

hyp·no·graph (hip/nə graf/, -gräf/), *n.* an instrument that measures activities of the human body during sleep. [HYPNO- + -GRAPH]

hyp·noi·dal (hip noid/ᵊl), *adj. Psychol.* characterizing a state that resembles mild hypnosis but that is usually induced by other than hypnotic means. Also, **hyp/noid.** [HYPN- + -OID + -AL¹]

hyp·nol·o·gy (hip nol/ə jē), *n.* the science dealing with the phenomena of sleep. [HYPNO- + -LOGY] —**hyp·no·log·ic** (hip/nᵊloj/ik), **hyp/no·log/i·cal,** *adj.* —**hyp·nol/o·gist,** *n.*

hyp·none (hip/nōn), *n. Chem.* acetophenone. [< F; see HYPN-, -ONE]

Hyp·nos (hip/nos), *n. Class. Myth.* the god of sleep, brother of Thanatos and often regarded as a son of Erebus and Nyx: identified by the Romans with Somnus. Also, **Hypnus.** [< Gk *hýpnos* sleep << IE **swpnos*; c. OE *swefn*, L *somnus*]

hyp·no·sis (hip nō/sis), *n., pl.* **-ses** (-sēz). **1.** an artificially induced state resembling sleep, characterized by heightened susceptibility to suggestion. **2.** the production of sleep. **3.** a sleepy condition. **4.** hypnotism. [HYPN- + -OSIS]

hyp·no·sperm (hip/nə spûrm/), *n. Bot.* a hypnospore. [HYPNO- + SPERM]

hyp·no·spo·ran·gi·um (hip/nō spō ran/jē əm, -spô-), *n., pl.* **-gi·a** (-jē ə). *Bot.* a sporangium containing hypnospores. [HYPNO(SPORE) + SPORANGIUM]

hyp·no·spore (hip/nə spōr/, -spôr/), *n. Bot.* a thick-walled, asexual, resting spore. [HYPNO- + SPORE] —**hyp·no·spor·ic** (hip/nə spōr/ik, -spor/-), *adj.*

hyp·no·ther·a·py (hip/nō ther/ə pē), *n.* treatment of disease by means of hypnotism. [HYPNO- + THERAPY]

hyp·not·ic (hip not/ik), *adj.* **1.** of or pertaining to hypnosis or hypnotism. **2.** inducing or like that which induces hypnosis. **3.** susceptible to hypnotism, as a person. **4.** under the influence of hypnosis; hypnotized. **5.** inducing sleep. —*n.* **6.** an agent or drug that produces sleep; sedative. **7.** a person who is susceptible to hypnosis. **8.** a person under the influence of hypnotism. [< medical L *hypnōtic(us)* < Gk *hypnōtikós* sleep-inducing, narcotic, equiv. to *hypnō-* (var. s. of *hypnóein* to put to sleep) + *-tikos* -TIC] —**hyp·not/i·cal·ly,** *adv.*

hyp·no·tise (hip/nə tīz/), *v.t., v.i.,* **-tised, -tis·ing.** *Chiefly Brit.* hypnotize. —**hyp/no·tis/a·bil/i·ty,** *n.* —**hyp/no·tis/a·ble,** *adj.* —**hyp/no·ti·sa/tion,** *n.* —**hyp/no·tis/er,** *n.*

hyp·no·tism (hip/nə tiz/əm), *n.* **1.** the science dealing with the induction of hypnosis. **2.** the act of hypnotizing. **3.** hypnosis. [HYPNOT(IC) + ISM] —**hyp/no·tis/tic,** *adj.*

hyp·no·tist (hip/nə tist), *n.* a person who hypnotizes. [HYPNOT(IC) + -IST]

hyp·no·tize (hip/nə tīz/), *v.,* **-tized, -tiz·ing.** —*v.t.* **1.** to put in the hypnotic state. **2.** to influence, control, or direct completely, as by personal charm, words, or domination: *He really hypnotizes the women, they believe anything he tells them.* **3.** to frighten or startle so that movement is impossible: *The headlights hypnotized the deer and it just stood staring at the oncoming car.* —*v.i.* **4.** to practice hypnosis; put or be able to put others into a hypnotic state. Also, *esp. Brit.*, **hypnotise.** [HYPNOT(IC) + -IZE] —**hyp/no·tiz/a·bil/i·ty,** *n.* —**hyp/no·tiz/a·ble,** *adj.* —**hyp/no·ti·za/tion,** *n.* —**hyp/no·tiz/er,** *n.*

hyp·no·tox·in (hip/nə tok/sin), *n.* an autotoxin believed to accumulate during the state of wakefulness and to cause sleep as a result of its effect on the brain. [HYPNO- + TOXIN]

Hyp·nus (hip/nəs), *n. Class. Myth.* Hypnos.

hy·po¹ (hī/pō), *n.* See **sodium thiosulfate.** [HYPO-(SULFITE)]

hy·po² (hī/pō), *n., pl.* **-pos.** *Informal.* a hypodermic syringe or injection. [HYPO(DERMIC)]

hy·po³ (hī/pō), *n. Archaic.* hypochondria. [by shortening]

hypo-, an element appearing in loan words from Greek, where it meant "under" (*hypostasis*); on this model used, especially as opposed to **hyper-**, in the formation of compound words (*hypothyroid*). Also, *esp. before a vowel,* **hyp-.** [< Gk, comb. form of *hypó* under (prep.), below (adv.); c. L *sub*; see SUB-]

hy·po·a·cid·i·ty (hī/pō ə sid/i tē), *n.* acidity in a lesser degree than is usual or normal, as of the gastric juice. [HYPO- + ACIDITY] —**hy·po·ac·id** (hī/pō as/id), *adj.*

hy·po·a·cu·sis (hī/pō ə kyo͞o/sis, -ko͞o/-), *n. Pathol.* a deficiency in the sense of hearing. Also, **hy·po·a·cu·sia** (hī/pō ə kyo͞o/zhə, -zē ə, -ko͞o/-), **hypacusia, hypacusis.** [HYPO- + Gk *ákousis* hearing; see HYPACUSIA]

hy·po·a·de·ni·a (hī/pō ə dē/nē ə), *n. Pathol.* a deficiency of glandular activity. [HYPO- + ADEN- + -IA]

hy/po·ae·o/li·an mode/ (hī/pō ē ō/lē ən), *Music.* a plagal church mode represented on the white keys of a keyboard instrument by an ascending scale from E to E, with the final on A. [< LL *hypoaeoli(us).* See HYPO-, AEOLIAN]

hy·po·al·bu·min·e·mi·a (hī/pō al byo͞o/mi nē/mē ə), *n. Pathol.* an abnormally small quantity of albumin in the blood; hypoproteinemia. [< NL; see HYPO-, ALBUMIN, -EMIA]

hy·po·al·i·men·ta·tion (hī/pō al/ə men tā/shən), *n. Pathol.* insufficient or inadequate nourishment. Also called **subalimentation.** [HYPO- + ALIMENTATION]

hy·po·al·o·ne·mi·a (hī/pō al/ə nē/mē ə), *n. Pathol.* an abnormally small quantity of salts in the blood. [HYPO- + *alo-* (comb. form of Gk *háls* salt) + *-n-* connective + -EMIA]

hy·po·az·o·tu·ri·a (hī/pō az/ə to͝or/ē ə, -tyo͝or/-), *n. Pathol.* an abnormally low amount of nitrogenous material in the urine. [HYPO- + AZOTE + -URIA]

hy·po·bar·ic (hī/pə bar/ik), *adj. Med.* (of an anesthetic) having a specific gravity lower than that of cerebrospinal fluid. Cf. **hyperbaric.** [HYPO- + Gk *bár(os)* weight + -IC]

hy·po·ba·rop·a·thy (hī/pō bə rop/ə thē), *n. Pathol.* a condition produced in high altitudes, caused by diminished air pressure and reduced oxygen intake; mountain sickness. [HYPO- + BARO- + -PATHY]

hy·po·ba·sis (hī/pō bā/sis), *n., pl.* **-ses** (-sēz). *Archit.* **1.** the lowermost distinctively treated part of a base. **2.** a lower base beneath an upper and more important one. Also called **hypopodium.** [HYPO- + BASIS]

hy·po·blast (hī/pə blast/), *n. Embryol.* **1.** the entoderm. **2.** the cells entering into the inner layer of a young gastrula, capable of becoming entoderm and, to a certain extent, mesoderm. [HYPO- + -BLAST] —**hy/po·blas/tic,** *adj.*

hy·po·bran·chi·al (hī/pə brang/kē əl), *adj. Zool.* situated below the gills or beneath the branchial arches. [HYPO- + BRANCHIAL]

hy·po·cal·ce·mi·a (hī/pō kal sē/mē ə), *n. Pathol.* an abnormally small amount of calcium in the blood. [HYPO- + CALC- + -EMIA]

hy·po·caust (hī/pə kôst/, hip/ə-), *n.* a hollow space or system of flues in the floor or walls of an ancient Roman building or room that received and distributed the heat from a furnace. [< L *hypocaust(um)* < Gk *hypókauston* room heated from below, equiv. to *hypo-* HYPO- + *kaustón*, neut. of *kaustós* heated, burned, verbal adj.; see CAUSTIC]

hy·po·chil (hī/pə kil, hip/ə-), *n. Bot.* the lower part of the labellum of an orchid flower. [< NL *hypochil(ium)*, equiv. to *hypo-* HYPO- + *chil(ium)* < Gk *cheîl(os)* lip]

hy/per·pol/y·syl·lab/ic, *adj.*
hy/per·pol/y·syl·lab/i·cal·ly, *adv.*
hy/per·prog/na·thous, *adj.*
hy/per·pro·phet/ic, *adj.*
hy/per·pro·phet/i·cal, *adj.*; **-ly,** *adv.*
hy/per·pure/, *adj.*
hy/per·pur/ist, *n.*
hy/per·ra/tion·al, *adj.*; **-ly,** *adv.*
hy/per·re·ac/tive, *adj.*
hy/per·re/al·ize/, *v.t.*, **-ized, -iz·ing.**
hy/per·res/o·nance, *n.*
hy/per·res/o·nant, *adj.*
hy/per·rhyth/mi·cal, *adj.*
hy/per·ri·dic/u·lous, *adj.*; **-ly,** *adv.*; **-ness,** *n.*
hy/per·rit/u·al·ism, *n.*
hy/per·rit/u·a·lis/tic, *adj.*
hy/per·ro·man/tic, *adj.*
hy/per·ro·man/ti·cal·ly, *adv.*
hy/per·ro·man/ti·cism, *n.*
hy/per·saint/ly, *adj.*
hy/per·sal/i·va/tion, *n.*
hy/per·scep/ti·cal, *adj.*
hy/per·scho·las/tic, *adj.*
hy/per·scho·las/ti·cal·ly, *adv.*
hy/per·scru/pu·los/i·ty, *n.*
hy/per·scru/pu·lous, *adj.*
hy/per·sen/si·bil/i·ty, *n.*
hy/per·sen/si·ti·za/tion, *n.*
hy/per·sen/si·tize/, *v.t.*, **-tized, -tiz·ing.**
hy/per·sen/su·al, *adj.*; **-ly,** *adv.*; **-ness,** *n.*
hy/per·sen/su·al·ism, *n.*
hy/per·sen/su·ous, *adj.*; **-ly,** *adv.*; **-ness,** *n.*
hy/per·sen/ti·men/tal, *adj.*; **-ly,** *adv.*
hy/per·so·phis/ti·cat/ed, *adj.*
hy/per·so·phis/ti·ca/tion, *n.*
hy/per·spec/u·la/tive, *adj.*; **-ly,** *adv.*; **-ness,** *n.*
hy/per·sto/i·cal, *adj.*
hy/per·sub/tle, *adj.*
hy/per·sub/tle·ty, *n.*
hy/per·sug·ges/ti·bil/i·ty, *n.*
hy/per·sug·ges/ti·ble, *adj.*; **-ble·ness,** *n.*; **-bly,** *adv.*
hy/per·sys·tol/ic, *adj.*
hy/per·tech/ni·cal, *adj.*; **-ly,** *adv.*; **-ness,** *n.*
hy/per·tense/, *adj.*; **-ly,** *adv.*; **-ness,** *n.*
hy/per·ther/mal, *adj.*; **-ly,** *adv.*
hy/per·tor/rid, *adj.*
hy/per·tox/ic, *adj.*
hy/per·tox·ic/i·ty, *n.*
hy/per·trag/ic, *adj.*
hy/per·trag/i·cal, *adj.*; **-ly,** *adv.*
hy/per·trop/i·cal, *adj.*
hy/per·vas/cu·lar, *adj.*
hy/per·vas/cu·lar/i·ty, *n.*
hy/per·ve·nos/i·ty, *n.*
hy/per·vig/i·lant, *adj.*; **-ly,** *adv.*; **-ness,** *n.*
hy/per·vis·cos/i·ty, *n.*
hy/per·vis/cous, *adj.*
hy/per·vi/tal·i·za/tion, *n.*
hy/per·vi/tal·ize/, *v.t.*, **-ized, -iz·ing.**
hy/per·vo·lu/mi·nous, *adj.*

CONCISE ETYMOLOGY KEY: <, descended or derived from; >, whence; b., blend of, blended; c., cognate with; deriv., derivative; equiv., equivalent; imit., imitative; m., modification of; obl., oblique; r., replacing; s., stem; sp., spelling; trans., translation; ?, origin unknown, perhaps; *, hypothetical. See the full key inside the front cover.

hy·po·chil·i·um (hī′pə kil′ē əm, hip′ə-), *n., pl.* **-chil·i·a** (-kil′ē ə). hypochil.

hy·po·chlo·re·mi·a (hī′pō klō rē′mē ə, -klô-), *n. Pathol.* an abnormally small amount of chloride in the blood. Also, **hy·po·chlo·ri·de·mi·a** (hī′pō klōr′i dē′mē ə, -klôr′-). [HYPO- + CHLOR-[2] + -EMIA] —**hy′po·chlo·re′mic,** *adj.*

hy·po·chlor·hy·dri·a (hī′pə klōr hī′ drē ə, -klôr-), *n. Pathol.* an abnormally small amount of hydrochloric acid in the gastric secretions. Also called **hypohydrochloria.** [HYPO- + CHLOR-[2] + HYDR-[2] + -IA]

hy·po·chlor·ite (hī′pə klōr′īt, -klôr′-), *n. Chem.* a salt or ester of hypochlorous acid. [HYPO- + CHLORITE[2]]

hy·po·chlor·ous (hī′pə klōr′əs, -klôr′-), *adj. Chem.* of or derived from hypochlorous acid. [HYPO- + CHLOROUS]

hy′pochlor′ous ac′id, *Chem.* an acid, HOCl, known only in solution and in the form of its salts, whose solutions have strong bleaching properties.

hy·po·cho·les·ter·e·mi·a (hī′pō kə les′tə rē′mē ə), *n. Pathol.* a decrease in the amount of cholesterol in the blood. Also, **hy·po·cho·les·ter·i·ne·mi·a** (hī′pō kə les′tər ə nē′mē ə), **hy·po·cho·les·ter·o·le·mi·a** (hī′pō kə-les′tə rō lē′mē ə). [HYPO- + CHOLESTER(OL) + -EMIA]

hy·po·chon·dri·a (hī′pə kon′drē ə), *n.* **1.** Also, **hypochondriasis.** *Psychiatry.* an abnormal condition characterized by a depressed emotional state and imaginary ill health, referable to the physical condition of the body or one of its parts. **2.** excessive worry or talk about one's health. [< LL < Gk, neut. pl. of *hypochóndrios* pertaining to the upper abdomen (supposed seat of melancholy), equiv. to *hypo-* HYPO- + *chóndr(os)* ensiform cartilage + *-ios* adj. suffix]

hy·po·chon·dri·ac (hī′pə kon′drē ak′), *adj.* **1.** Also, **hy·po·chon·dri·a·cal** (hī′pō kon drī′ə kəl). pertaining to or suffering from hypochondria or excessive depression. **2.** produced by hypochondria. **3.** of or pertaining to the hypochondrium. —*n.* **4.** a person suffering from or subject to hypochondria. **5.** a person who worries or talks excessively about his health. [< medical L *hypochondriac(us)* < Gk *hypochondriakós* affected in the upper abdomen. See HYPOCHONDRIA, -AC] —**hy′po·chon·dri′a·cal·ly,** *adv.*

hy·po·chon·dri·a·sis (hī′pō kən drī′ə sis), *n. Psychiatry.* hypochondria (def. 1). [HYPOCHONDRI(A) + -ASIS]

hy·po·chon·dri·um (hī′pə kon′drē əm), *n., pl.* **-dri·a** (-drē ə). *Anat., Zool.* **1.** either of two regions of the abdomen of man, situated on each side of the epigastrium and above the lumbar regions. **2.** a corresponding region in certain other vertebrates. [< NL, sing. of HYPOCHONDRIA]

hy·po·chro·mi·a (hī′pə krō′mē ə), *n. Pathol.* **1.** an anemic condition due to a deficiency of hemoglobin in the red blood cells. **2.** insufficient color or pigmentation. [HYPO- + NL *-chromia* < LGk *-chrōmia*, Gk *-chrōm(os)* colored deriv. of *chrōm(a)* color; see -IA] —**hy′po·chro′mic,** *adj.*

hy′pochro′mic ane′mia, *Pathol.* an anemia characterized by an abnormally low concentration of hemoglobin in the erythrocytes, often due to iron deficiency. [HYPO- + CHROMIC]

hy·poc·o·rism (hī pok′ə riz′əm, hi-), *n.* **1.** a pet name. **2.** the practice of using a pet name. **3.** the use of forms of speech imitative of baby talk, esp. by an adult. [< Gk *hypokórisma* pet name. See HYPOCORISTIC, -ISM]

hy·po·co·ris·tic (hī′pə kō ris′tik, -kô-, hip′ə-), *adj.* endearing, as a pet name, diminutive, or euphemistic. [< Gk *hypokoristik(ós)* (dim.), equiv. to *hypokor(ízesthai)* (to) play the child, call by endearing names (*hypo-* HYPO- + *kor-* child (cf. *kórē* girl, *kóros* boy)) + *-istikos* -ISTIC] —**hy′po·co·ris′ti·cal·ly,** *adv.*

hy·po·cot·yl (hī′pə kot′əl), *n. Bot.* (in the embryo of a plant) that part of the stem below cotyledons. See diag. under **cotyledon.** [HYPO- + COTYL(EDON)] —**hy′po·cot′y·lous,** *adj.*

hy·po·cra·ter·i·form (hī′pə krə ter′ə fôrm′, -krā′tər ə-), *adj. Bot.* salverform. [HYPO- + CRATER + -I- + -FORM]

hy·po·cri·nism (hī′pə krī′niz əm), *n. Pathol.* a condition caused by an abnormally small secretion of any gland, esp. an endocrine gland. Also, **hy·po·crin·i·a** (hī′pə krin′ē ə). [HYPO- + (ENDO)CRINE + -ISM]

hy·poc·ri·sy (hi pok′rə sē), *n., pl.* **-sies.** **1.** a pretense of having a virtuous character, moral or religious beliefs or principles, etc., that one does not possess. **2.** a pretense of having some desirable or publicly approved attitude. [ME *ipocrisie* < OF < LL *hypocrisis* < Gk *hypókrisis* play acting, equiv. to *hypokrī(nesthai)* (to) play a part, explain (*hypo-* HYPO- + *krīnein* to distinguish, separate) + *-sis* -SIS; *h-* (reintroduced in 16th century) < L and Gk]
—**Syn. 1.** See **deceit.**

hyp·o·crite (hip′ə krit), *n.* **1.** a person who pretends to have moral or religious beliefs, principles, etc., he does not actually possess. **2.** a person who feigns some desirable or publicly approved attitude. [ME *ipocrite* < OF < LL *hypocrit(a)* < Gk *hypokritḗs* a stage actor, hence one who pretends to be what he is not, equiv. to *hypokrī(nesthai)* (see HYPOCRISY) + *-tēs* agent suffix] —**hyp′o·crit′i·cal,** *adj.* —**hyp′o·crit′i·cal·ly,** *adv.*
—**Syn. 1.** deceiver, dissembler, pretender, pharisee.

hy·po·cy·cloid (hī′pə sī′kloid), *n. Geom.* a curve generated by the motion of a point on the circumference of a circle which rolls internally, without slipping, on a given circle. Equation: $x = (a-b)\cos\theta + b\cos[(a-b)\theta/b]$, $y = (a-b)\sin\theta - b\sin[(a-b)\theta/b]$. [HYPO- + CYCLOID] —**hy′po·cy·cloi′dal,** *adj.*

H, Hypocycloid; P, Point tracing hypocycloid within fixed circle

hy·po·cy·to·sis (hī′pō si tō′sis), *n. Pathol.* a deficiency of the normal number of cells in the blood; cytopenia. [HYPO- + CYTO- + -SIS]

hy·po·derm (hī′pə dûrm′), *n.* **1.** *Zool.* the epidermis of an arthropod. **2.** *Bot.* hypodermis. [HYPODERM(A)] —**hy′po·der′mal,** *adj.*

hy·po·der·ma (hī′pə dûr′mə), *n. Bot., Zool.* hypodermis. [HYPO- + DERMA]

hy·po·der·mic (hī′pə dûr′mik), *adj.* **1.** characterized by the introduction of medical remedies under the skin: *hypodermic injection.* **2.** introduced under the skin: *a hypodermic medication.* **3.** pertaining to parts under the skin. **4.** stimulating; causing greater energy, awareness, etc. —*n.* **5.** a hypodermic remedy. **6.** a hypodermic injection. **7.** See **hypodermic syringe. 8.** the administration of drugs into subcutaneous body tissues. [HYPODERM(A) + -IC] —**hy′po·der′mi·cal·ly,** *adv.*

hypoder′mic nee′dle, a hollow needle used to inject solutions subcutaneously.

hypoder′mic syringe′, a small, glass, piston or barrel syringe having a detachable, hollow needle for use in injecting solutions subcutaneously.

Hypodermic syringe

hypoder′mic tab′let, *Med.* a water-soluble tablet containing medication in a base of specially recrystallized lactose, for parenteral administration.

hy·po·der·mis (hī′pə dûr′mis), *n.* **1.** *Zool.* the surface epithelium of an invertebrate when covered over by the noncellular secretion that it produces. **2.** *Bot.* a tissue or layer of cells beneath the epidermis. [HYPO- + (EPI)DERMIS]

hy′po·do′ri·an mode′ (hī′pō dōr′ē ən, -dôr′-, hip′ō-, hī′ pō-, hip′ō), *Music.* a plagal church mode represented on the white keys of a keyboard instrument by an ascending scale from A to A, with the final on D. [< LL *hypodori(us)* < Gk *hypodṓrion.* See HYPO-, DORIAN]

hy·po·dy·nam·i·a (hī′pō dī nam′ē ə, -nā′mē ə, -di-), *n. Pathol.* diminished strength; adynamia. [< NL, equiv. to *hypo-* HYPO- + Gk *dýnam(is)* power + *-ia* -IA] —**hy·po·dy·nam·ic** (hī′pō dī nam′ik), *adj.*

hy·po·en·doc·rin·ism (hī′pō en dok′rə niz′əm), *n. Pathol.* abnormally diminished activity of the internal secretion organs. Also, **hy·po·en·do·crin·i·a** (hī′pō en′dō krin′ē ə), **hy·po·en·do·cris·i·a** (hī′pō en′dō kris′ē ə). [HYPO- + ENDOCRINE + -ISM]

hy·po·eu·tec·toid (hī′pō yōō tek′toid), *adj. Metall.* (of steel) having less carbon than the 0.8 percent of eutectoid steel. [HYPO- + EUTECTOID]

hy·po·func·tion (hī′pō fungk′shən), *n.* abnormally diminished function, esp. of glands or other organs (opposed to *hyperfunction*). [HYPO- + FUNCTION]

hy·po·gas·tric (hī′pə gas′trik), *adj.* of, pertaining to, or situated in the hypogastrium. [< medical L *hypogastric(us).* See HYPOGASTR(IUM), -IC]

hy′pogas′tric ar′tery, *Anat.* See **iliac artery** (def. 3).

hy·po·gas·tri·um (hī′pə gas′trē əm), *n., pl.* **-tri·a** (-trē ə). *Anat.* the lower and median part of the abdomen. [< medical L < Gk *hypogástrion,* equiv. to *hypo-* HYPO- + *gastrion* (*gastḗr* paunch + *-ion* dim. suffix)]

hy·po·ge·al (hī′pə jē′əl), *adj.* underground; subterranean. [< L *hypogē(us)* (< Gk *hypógeios* underground, subterranean, equiv. to *hypo-* HYPO- + *gê* earth + *-ios* adj. suffix) + -AL[1]]

hy·po·gene (hī′pə jēn′, hip′ə-), *adj. Geol.* **1.** formed beneath the earth's surface, as granite (opposed to *epigene*). **2.** formed by ascending waters, as mineral or ore deposits (opposed to *supergene*). [HYPO- + *-gene,* var. of -GEN] —**hy·po·gen·ic** (hī′pə jen′ik, hip′ə-), *adj.*

hy·po·gen·e·sis (hī′pə jen′i sis), *n. Pathol.* underdevelopment of an organ or function; ateliosis. [HYPO- + GENESIS] —**hy·po·ge·net·ic** (hī′pō jə net′ik), *adj.*

hy·pog·e·nous (hī poj′ə nəs, hi-), *adj. Bot.* growing beneath, or on the under surface, as fungi on leaves. [HYPOGENE + -OUS]

hy·po·ge·ous (hī′pə jē′əs, hip′ə-), *adj.* **1.** underground; subterranean. **2.** *Bot.* growing or remaining underground. [< L *hypogēus.* See HYPOGEAL]

hy·po·ge·um (hī′pə jē′əm, hip′ə-), *n., pl.* **-ge·a** (-jē ə). **1.** *Anc. Archit.* the underground part of a building, as a vault. **2.** an underground burial chamber; a subterranean tomb. [< L *hypogēum* < Gk *hypógeion* underground chamber (neut. of *hypógeios* underground), equiv. to *hypo-* HYPO- + *gê* earth + *-ion* neut. adj. suffix]

hy·po·geu·si·a (hī′pə gyōō′sē ə, -jōō′-), *n. Pathol.* deterioration of the sense of taste. [HYPO- + Gk *geûsia* taste, equiv. to *geûs(esthai)* (to) taste + *-ia* -IA]

hy·po·glo·bu·li·a (hī′pō glo byōō′lē ə), *n. Pathol.* an abnormally low number of red cells in the blood. [< NL; see HYPO-, GLOBULE, -IA]

hy·po·glos·sal (hī′pə glos′əl, -glô′səl), *Anat.* —*adj.* **1.** situated under the tongue. —*n.* **2.** See **hypoglossal nerve.** [HYPO- + Gk *glôss(a)* tongue + -AL[1]]

hy′poglos′sal nerve′, *Anat.* either one of the twelfth pair of cranial nerves, consisting of motor fibers that innervate the muscles of the tongue.

hy·po·glot·tis (hī′pə glot′is), *n.* **1.** *Anat.* the underside of the tongue. **2.** *Pathol.* ranula. Also, **hy·po·glos·sis** (hī′pə glos′is, -glô′sis). [< Gk *hypoglōttís.* See HYPO-, GLOTTIS]

hy·po·gly·ce·mi·a (hī′pō glī sē′mē ə), *n. Pathol.* an abnormally low level of glucose in the blood. [HYPO- + Gk *glyk(ýs)* sweet + -EMIA] —**hy′po·gly·ce′mic,** *adj.*

hy·pog·na·thous (hī pog′nə thəs), *adj.* **1.** *Zool.* (of birds and insects) having the lower jaw or mandible longer than the upper. **2.** *Anthropol.* having the lower jaw longer and more projecting than the upper. [HYPO- + -GNATHOUS] —**hy·pog′na·thism,** *n.*

hy·po·gon·ad·ism (hī′pə gō′nə diz′əm, -gon′ə-), *n. Pathol.* a diminished internal secretion of the gonads. Also, **hy·po·go·nad·i·a** (hī′pō gō nad′ē ə). [HYPO- + GONAD + -ISM]

hy·pog·y·nous (hī poj′ə nəs, hi-), *adj. Bot.* **1.** situated on the receptacle beneath the pistil, as stamens, sepals, etc. **2.** having stamens, sepals, etc., so arranged. [HYPO- + -GYNOUS] —**hy·pog′y·ny,** *n.*

hy·po·he·pat·i·a (hī′pō hi pat′ē ə, -pa′shə), *n. Pathol.* deficient liver function. [HYPO- + HEPAT- + -IA]

hy·po·hi·dro·sis (hī′pō hi drō′sis), *n. Physiol.* abnormally diminished sweating. Also, **hy·po·i·dro·sis** (hī′pō i drō′sis). [HYPO- + HIDROSIS]

hy·po·hy·dro·chlo·ri·a (hī′pō hī′drə klōr′ē ə, -klôr′-), *n. Med.* hypochlorhydria. [HYPO- + HYDRO-[1] + CHLOR-[2] + -IA]

hy·po·hy·poph·y·sism (hī′pō hī pof′i siz′əm), *n. Pathol.* hypopituitarism. [HYPO- + HYPOPHYS(IS) + -ISM]

hy′poid gear′ (hī′poid), a gear resembling a bevel gear in form but designed to mesh with a similar gear in such a way that their axes would not intersect, one axis crossing over the other at approximately a right angle. [HYP(ERBOL)OID]

hy·po·in·o·se·mi·a (hī′pō in′ə sē′mē ə), *n. Pathol.* abnormally diminished formation of fibrin in the blood resulting in decreased ability to coagulate. [HYPO- + Gk *inós* (s. of *ís*) sinew, fiber + -EMIA]

hy′po i·o′ni·an mode′ (hī′pō ī ō′nē ən, hip′ō-, hī′-pō-, hip′ō-), *Music.* a plagal church mode represented on the white keys of a keyboard instrument by an ascending scale from G to G, with the final on C. [HYPO- + L *Ion(ius)* IONIAN + -IAN]

hy·po·ka·le·mi·a (hī′pō kā lē′mē ə), *n. Pathol.* an abnormally small amount of potassium in the blood; hypopotassemia. Also, **hy·po·kal·i·e·mi·a** (hī′pə kal′ē-ē′mē ə). [HYPO- + NL *kal(ium)* potassium, deriv. of *kali,* as in ALKALI + -EMIA] —**hy′po·ka·le′mic,** *adj.*

hy·po·ki·ne·mi·a (hī′pō ki nē′mē ə), *n. Pathol.* an abnormally diminished cardiac output resulting in reduced circulation rate. [HYPO- + Gk *kinē(sis)* motion (see KINESTHESIA) + -EMIA]

hy·po·ki·ne·si·a (hī′pō ki nē′zhə, -zhē ə, -zē ə, -kī-), *n. Pathol.* an abnormally diminished motor function or mobility. Also, **hy·po·ki·ne·sis** (hī′pō ki nē′sis, -kī-). [HYPO- + Gk *kīnēs(is)* motion (see KINESTHESIA) + -IA] —**hy·po·ki·net·ic** (hī′pō ki net′ik, -kī-), *adj.*

hy·po·lim·ni·on (hī′pə lim′nē on′, -nē ən, hip′ə-), *n., pl.* **-ni·a** (-nē ə). (in certain lakes) the layer of water below the thermocline. [HYPO- + Gk *límn(ē)* lake + *-ion* dim. n. suffix] —**hy·po·lim·net·ic** (hī′pō lim net′ik, hip′ō-), **hy′po·lim′ni·al,** *adj.*

Hy·pol·i·te (hi pol′i tē; *Fr.* ē pô lēt′), *n.* a boy's given name.

hy·po·lith·ic (hī′pə lith′ik, hip′ə-), *adj.* growing beneath rocks, as a plant. [HYPO- + LITHIC]

hy′po·lyd′i·an mode′ (hī′pō lid′ē ən, hip′ō-, hī′pō-, hip′ō-), *Music.* a plagal church mode represented on the white keys of a keyboard instrument by an ascending scale from C to C, with the final on F. [trans. of Gk *hypolýdios tónos*]

hy·po·ma·ni·a (hī′pə mā′nē ə, -mān′yə), *n. Psychiatry.* a mania of low intensity. [HYPO- + -MANIA] —**hy·po·man·ic** (hī′pə man′ik), *adj., n.*

hy′po·mix·o·lyd′ian mode′ (hī′pō mik′sə lid′ē ən, hip′ō-, hī′pō-, hip′ō-), *Music.* a plagal church mode represented on the white keys of a keyboard instrument by an ascending scale from A to A, with the final on D. [HYPO- + MIXOLYDIAN MODE]

hy·pom·ne·sia (hī′pom nē′zhə, -zē ə), *n. Pathol.* defective memory. Also, **hy·pom·ne·sis** (hī′pəm nē′sis). [HYPO- + (A)MNESIA]

hy·po·mo·til·i·ty (hī′pə mō til′i tē), *n.* abnormally slow motility of the stomach or intestine (opposed to *hypermotility*). [HYPO- + MOTILITY]

hy·po·my·o·to·ni·a (hī′pə mī′ə tō′nē ə), *n. Pathol.* abnormally diminished muscular tone. [HYPO- + MYOTONIA]

hy·po·nas·ty (hī′pə nas′tē), *n. Bot.* increased growth along the lower surface of an organ or part, causing it to bend upward. [HYPO- + Gk *nast(ós)* pressed close, compact + -Y[3]] —**hy′po·nas′tic,** *adj.* —**hy′po·nas′ti·cal·ly,** *adv.*

hy·po·na·tre·mi·a (hī′pō nə trē′mē ə), *n. Pathol.* an abnormally small amount of sodium in the blood. [HYPO- + NATR(IUM) + -EMIA]

hy·po·ni·trite (hī′pō nī′trīt), *n. Chem.* a salt or ester of hyponitrous acid. [HYPONITR(OUS ACID) + -ITE[1]]

hy·po·ni·trous (hī′pə nī′trəs), *adj. Chem.* of or derived from hyponitrous acid. [HYPO- + NITROUS]

hy′poni′trous ac′id, *Chem.* an unstable, crystalline acid, $H_2N_2O_2$.

hy·po·noi·a (hī′pə noi′ə), *n.* dulled mental activity; diminished function of thought. Also, **hy·po·ne·a** (hī′-pə nē′ə). Also called **hypopsychosis.** [HYPO- + -NOIA]

hy·po·pha·lan·gism (hī′pō fə lan′jiz əm), *n. Pathol.* less than the normal number of phalanges per finger or toe. [HYPO- + PHALANGE + -ISM]

hy·po·pha·ryn·go·scope (hī′pō fə ring′gə skōp′), *n. Med.* an instrument for examining the laryngopharynx. [HYPO- + PHARYNGOSCOPE]

hy·po·phar·yn·gos·co·py (hī′pə far′in gos′kə pē), *n.* examination of the laryngopharnyx. [HYPOPHARYNGOSCOPE + -Y[3]]

hy·po·phar·ynx (hī′pə far′ingks), *n., pl.* **-pha·ryn·ges** (-fə rin′jēz), **-phar·ynx·es.** (in an insect) a tonguelike lobe on the floor of the mouth. [HYPO- + PHARYNX]

hy·po·phloe·o·dal (hī′pō flē′ə dəl, hip′ə-), *adj.* living or growing beneath bark, as a lichen. Also, **hy′po·phloe′o·dic, hy′po·phloe′ous.** [HYPO- + Gk *phloiōd(ēs)* like bark (*phloi(ós)* bark + *-ōdēs* -ODE[1]) + -AL[1]]

hy·po·pho·ne·sis (hī′pō fə nē′sis, -fō-), *n. Med.* a sound of less than usual intensity in percussion or auscultation. [HYPO- + -PHONE + -SIS]

hy·po·pho·ni·a (hī′pə fō′nē ə), *n. Pathol.* an abnormally weak voice due to lack of coordination of the speech muscles. [HYPO- + -PHONIA]

hy·po·pho·ri·a (hī′pə fōr′ē ə, -fôr′-), *n. Ophthalm.* downward deviation of the visual axis of one eye. [HYPO- + NL *phoria, -phoria* state, tendency < Gk: carrying (n.), deriv. of *-phor(os)* -PHOROUS + NL *-ia* -IA]

hy·po·phos·phate (hī′pə fos′fāt), *n. Chem.* a salt or ester of hypophosphoric acid. [HYPO- + PHOSPHATE]

hy·po·phos·phite (hī′pə fos′fīt), *n. Chem.* a salt of hypophosphorous acid, as sodium hypophosphite, NaH_2PO_2. [HYPO- + PHOSPHITE]

hy·po·phos·phor·ic (hī′pə fos fôr′ik, -for′-), *adj. Chem.* of or derived from hypophosphoric acid. [HYPO- + PHOSPHORIC]

hy′pophosphor′ic ac′id, *Chem.* a tetrabasic acid, $H_4P_2O_6$, produced by the slow oxidation of phosphorous in moist air.

hy·po·phos·phor·ous (hī′pə fos′fər əs, -fos fôr′əs, -fôr′-), *adj. Chem.* of or derived from hypophosphorous acid. [HYPO- + PHOSPHOROUS]

hy′pophos′phorous ac′id, *Chem.* a colorless or yellowish, water-soluble, liquid, monobasic acid, H_3PO_2, having a sour odor, and used as a reducing agent.

hy′po·phryg′i·an mode′ (hī′pō frij′ē ən, hip′ō-, hī′pō-, hip′ō-), *Music.* a plagal church mode represented on the white keys of a keyboard instrument by an ascending scale from B to B, with the final on E. [trans. of Gk *hypophrýgia harmonía*]

hy·poph·y·ge (hī pof′i jē, hi-), *n.* apophyge (def. 2). [< Gk *hypophygḗ* flight from under, evasion < *hypo-* HYPO- + *phygḗ* flight, equiv. to *phyg(eîn)* (to) flee (c. L *fugere*) + *-ē* n. suffix]

hy·po·phyl·lous (hī′pə fil′əs, hip′ə-), *adj.* *Bot.* growing on the under surface of leaves, as a fungus. [HYPO- + -PHYLLOUS]

hy·poph·y·sec·to·mize (hī pof′i sek′tə mīz′, hi-), *v.t.*, **-mized, -miz·ing.** *Surg.* to remove the pituitary gland. [HYPOPHYSECTOMY + -IZE]

hy·poph·y·sec·to·my (hī pof′i sek′tə mē, hi-), *n.*, *pl.* **-mies.** *Surg.* excision of the pituitary gland. [HYPOPHYS(IS) + -ECTOMY]

hy·poph·y·sis (hī pof′i sis, hi-), *n.*, *pl.* **-ses** (-sēz′). *Anat.* See **pituitary gland.** [< Gk *hypóphysis* outgrowth (from below), equiv. to *hypophý(ein)* (to) grow beneath (*hypo-* HYPO- + *phy-* grow, c. BE) + *-sis* -SIS] —**hy·po·phys·e·al** (hī′pə fiz′ē əl, hip′ə-, hī pof′i sē′əl, hi-), **hy·po·phys·i·al** (hī′pə fiz′ē əl, hip′ə-), *adj.*

hy·poph·y·si·tis (hī pof′i sī′tis, hi-), *n.* *Pathol.* inflammation of the pituitary gland. [HYPOPHYS(IS) + -ITIS]

hy·po·pi·e·sis (hī′pō pī ē′sis), *n.* *Pathol.* abnormally low arterial blood pressure; hypotension. Also, **hy·po·pi·e·sia** (hī′pō pī ē′zhə, -zē ə, -shə, -sē ə). [HYPO- + Gk *piêsis* a squeezing]

hy·po·pi·tu·i·ta·rism (hī′pō pi to͞o′i tə riz′əm, -tyo͞o′-), *n.* *Pathol.* **1.** abnormally diminished activity of the pituitary gland, esp. of the anterior lobe. **2.** the condition produced by this, characterized by obesity, retention of adolescent traits, sterility, amenorrhea, and, in extreme cases, dwarfism. Also called **hypohypophysism.** [HYPO- + PITUITAR(Y) + -ISM]

hy·po·pla·si·a (hī′pə plā′zhə, -zhē ə, -zē ə), *n.* **1.** *Pathol.*, *Bot.* abnormal deficiency of cells or structural elements. **2.** *Pathol.* an underdeveloped condition in which an organ or structure remains immature or subnormal in size. Also, **hy·po·plas·ty** (hī′pō plas′tē). [HYPO- + -PLASIA] —**hy′po·plas′tic,** *adj.*

hy·po·ploid (hī′pə ploid′), *Biol.* —*adj.* **1.** having a chromosome number that is less than the diploid number. —*n.* **2.** a hypoploid cell or organism. [HYPO- + -PLOID] —**hy′po·ploid′y,** *n.*

hy·pop·ne·a (hī pop′nē ə, hi-), *n.* *Med.* abnormally shallow breathing. [< NL, equiv. to *hypo-* HYPO- + *pnēa*, *pnoea* < Gk *pnoiḗ* breathing]

hy·po·po·di·um (hī′pə pō′dē əm), *n.*, *pl.* **-di·a** (-dē ə). **1.** *Bot.* the basal portion of a petiole. **2.** *Archit.* hypobasis. [HYPO- + -PODIUM]

hy·po·po·tas·se·mi·a (hī′pō pə ta sē′mē ə), *n.* *Pathol.* an abnormally small amount of potassium in the blood. [< NL; see HYPO-, POTASS(IUM), -EMIA] —**hy′po·po·tas·se′mic,** *adj.*

hy·po·prax·i·a (hī′pə prak′sē ə), *n.* *Med.* retarded activity, inactivity, or listlessness. [HYPO- + NL *-praxia* < Gk *prâx(is)* (see PRAXIS) + NL *-ia* -IA]

hy·po·pro·sex·i·a (hī′pō prə sek′sē ə), *n.* an abnormally short attention span. [HYPO- + *-prosexia*; see HYPERPROSEXIA]

hy·po·pro·tein·e·mi·a (hī′pō prō′tē nē′mē ə, -prō′tē i nē′-), *n.* *Pathol.* an abnormally small amount of protein in the blood. [HYPO- + PROTEIN + -EMIA]

hy·po·pro·tein·o·sis (hī′pə prō′tē nō′sis, -tē i nō′sis), *n.* *Pathol.* a deficiency of protein. [HYPO- + PROTEIN + -OSIS]

hy·pop·sel·a·phe·si·a (hī′pop sel′ə fē′zē ə, hī′pə-), *n.* a deficient sense of touch. [HYPO- + Gk *psell(ós)* faltering in speech + APHES(IS) + -IA]

hy·po·psy·cho·sis (hī′pō sī kō′sis), *n.* hyponoia. [HYPO- + PSYCHOSIS]

hy·pop·ty·al·ism (hī′pə tī′ə liz′əm), *n.* *Pathol.* deficient salivary secretion. [HYPO- + PTYALISM]

hy·po·py·on (hī pō′pē on′, hi-), *n.* *Ophthalm.* an effusion of pus into the anterior chamber of the eye, containing the aqueous humor. [HYPO- + Gk *pýon* pus, discharge from a sore]

hy·por·che·ma (hī′pər kē′mə), *n.*, *pl.* **-ma·ta** (-mə tə). a lively choral ode sung in ancient Greece in honor of Apollo or Dionysus. [< Gk *hypórchēma*, equiv. to *hyp-* HYP- + *orchē-* (var. s. of *orcheîsthai* to dance with or to music) + *-ma* neut. n. suffix] —**hy·por·che·mat·ic** (hī′pər kē mat′ik), *adj.*

hy·po·sal·e·mi·a (hī′pō sa lē′mē ə), *n.* *Pathol.* an abnormally small amount of salt in the blood. [HYPO- + SAL + -EMIA]

hy·po·sar·ca (hī′pə sär′kə), *n.* extreme anasarca, or dropsy. [< L *hyposarca* < Gk *hypósarka* under the flesh. See HYPO-, SARC-]

hy·po·se·cre·tion (hī′pō si krē′shən), *n.* a diminished secretion (opposed to *hypersecretion*). [HYPO- + SECRETION]

hy·po·sen·si·tize (hī′pə sen′si tīz′), *v.t.*, **-tized, -tiz·ing.** *Med.* to cause (a person) to become less sensitive to (an agent producing an allergic reaction); desensitize. [HYPO- + SENSITIZE] —**hy′po·sen′si·ti·za′tion,** *n.*

hy·pos·mi·a (hī poz′mē ə), *n.* *Pathol.* impaired sense of smell. Also called **hy·pos·phre·si·a** (hī′pos frē′zē ə). [HYP- + -OSMIA]

hy·po·spray (hī′pō sprā′), *n.* an instrument, similar to a hypodermic syringe, but using no needle, for forcing extremely fine jets of a medicated solution through the unbroken skin. [HYPO² + SPRAY¹]

hy·pos·ta·sis (hī pos′tə sis, hi-), *n.*, *pl.* **-ses** (-sēz′). **1.** *Metaphys.* **a.** something that stands under and supports; foundation. **b.** the underlying or essential part of anything as distinguished from attributes; substance, essence, or essential principle. **2.** *Theol.* **a.** one of the three real and distinct subsistences in the one undivided substance or essence of God. **b.** a person of the Trinity. **c.** the one personality of Christ in which His two natures, human and divine, are united. **3.** *Med.* **a.** the accumulation of blood or its solid components in parts of an organ or body due to poor circulation. **b.** such sedimentation, as in a test tube. [< LL < Gk *hypóstasis* that which settles at the bottom; substance, nature, essence, equiv. to *hypo-* HYPO- + *stásis* standing, station]

hy·pos·ta·sise (hī pos′tə sīz′, hi-), *v.t.*, **-sised, -sis·ing.** *Chiefly Brit.* hypostasize.

hy·pos·ta·size (hī pos′tə sīz′, hi-), *v.t.*, **-sized, -siz·ing.** to assume the reality of (an idea, proposition, etc.); hypostatize.

hy·po·stat·ic (hī′pə stat′ik), *adj.* **1.** of or pertaining to a hypostasis; fundamental. **2.** *Theol.* pertaining to or constituting a distinct personal being or subsistence. **3.** *Med.* arising from downward pressure or from gravity. **4.** *Genetics.* (of nonallelic genes) recessive. Also, **hy′po·stat′i·cal.** [< Gk *hypostatik(ós)* pertaining to substance, equiv. to *hypostat(ós)* placed under, giving support (*hypo-* HYPO- + *sta-* STAND + *-tos* verbal adj. suffix) + *-ikos* -IC] —**hy′po·stat′i·cal·ly,** *adv.*

hy·pos·ta·tise (hī pos′tə tīz′, hi-), *v.t.*, **-tised, -tis·ing.** *Chiefly Brit.* hypostatize. —**hy·pos′ta·ti·sa′tion,** *n.*

hy·pos·ta·tize (hī pos′tə tīz′, hi-), *v.t.*, **-tized, -tiz·ing.** to treat or regard (a concept, idea, etc.) as a distinct substance or reality. [< Gk *hypóstat(os)* (see HYPOSTATIC) + -IZE] —**hy·pos′ta·ti·za′tion,** *n.*

hy·pos·the·ni·a (hī′pos thē′nē ə), *n.* *Pathol.* abnormal lack of strength; weakness. [HYPO- + STHENIA] —**hy·pos·then·ic** (hī′pos then′ik), *adj.*

hy·po·stome (hī′pə stōm′), *n.* *Zool.* any of several parts or organs of the mouth, as the labrum of a crustacean. [HYPO- + -STOME] —**hy′po·sto′mi·al,** *adj.*

hy·po·style (hī′pə stīl′, hip′ə-), *Archit.* —*adj.* **1.** having many columns carrying the roof or ceiling: *a hypostyle hall.* —*n.* **2.** a hypostyle structure. [< Gk *hypóstyl(os)* resting on pillars, equiv. to *hypo-* HYPO- + *stŷlos* pillar]

hy·po·sul·fite (hī′pə sul′fīt), *n.* *Chem.* **1.** Also called **dithionite, hydrosulfite.** a salt of hyposulfurous acid. **2.** See **sodium thiosulfate.** Also, **hy′po·sul′phite.** [HYPO- + SULFITE]

hy·po·sul·fur·ous (hī′pə sul fyo͝or′əs, -sul′fər əs), *adj.* *Chem.* of or derived from hyposulfurous acid. Also, **hy′po·sul·phur′ous.** [HYPO- + SULFUROUS]

hy′posulfur′ous ac′id, an acid, $H_2S_2O_4$, next in a series below sulfurous acid, known only in solution or in the form of its salts.

hy·po·tax·is (hī′pə tak′sis), *n.* *Gram.* dependent relation or construction, as of clauses; syntactic subordination. [< Gk *hypótaxis* subjection, equiv. to *hypo-* HYPO- + *-taxis* -TAXIS] —**hy·po·tac·tic** (hī′pə tak′tik, hip′ə-), *adj.*

hy·po·ten·sion (hī′pə ten′shən), *n.* *Pathol.* **1.** decreased or lowered blood pressure. **2.** a disease or condition characterized by this symptom. [HYPO- + TENSION]

hy·po·ten·sive (hī′pō ten′siv), *Pathol.* —*adj.* **1.** characterized by or causing low blood pressure, as shock. —*n.* **2.** a hypotensive person or agent. [HYPOTENS(ION) + -IVE]

hy·pot·e·nuse (hī pot′ənno͞os′, -nyo͞os′), *n.* *Geom.* the side of a right triangle opposite the right angle. Also, **hypothenuse.** [earlier *hypotenusa* < LL *hypotēnūsa* < Gk *hypoteínousa (grammḗ)* subtending (line) (fem. prp. of *hypoteínein* to subtend), equiv. to *hypo-* HYPO- + *tein-* stretch + *-ousa* fem. prp. suffix]

Hypotenuse 90°

Hypotenuse of a right triangle

hypoth., **1.** hypothesis. **2.** hypothetical.

hy·po·thal·a·mus (hī′pə thal′ə məs), *n.*, *pl.* **-mi** (-mī′). *Anat.* the portion of the diencephalon forming the floor of the median ventricle of the brain. [< LL; see HYPO-, THALAMUS] —**hy·po·tha·lam·ic** (hī′pō thə lam′ik, hip′ō-), *adj.*

hy·po·thal·lus (hī′pə thal′əs, hip′ə-), *n.*, *pl.* **-thal·li** (-thal′ī). *Bot.* **1.** a layer of hyphae rimming the thallus of certain lichens. **2.** a filmlike residue at the base of the sporangia of certain slime molds. [< NL; see HYPO-, THALLUS]

hy·poth·ec (hī poth′ik, hi-), *n.* *Roman and Civil Law.* **1.** a mortgage or security held by a creditor on the property of his debtor without possession of it, created either by agreement or by operation of law. **2.** (in some modern legal systems) a security interest created in immovable property. [earlier *hypotheca* < LL < Gk *hypothḗkē* deposit, pledge, mortgage (akin to *hypotithénai* to deposit as pledge). See HYPO-, THECA]

hy·poth·e·car·y (hī poth′ə ker′ē, hi-), *adj.* **1.** of or pertaining to a hypothec. **2.** created or secured by a hypothec. [HYPOTHEC + -ARY]

hy·poth·e·cate¹ (hī poth′ə kāt′, hi-), *v.t.*, **-cat·ed, -cat·ing.** **1.** to pledge to a creditor as security without delivering over; mortgage. **2.** to put in pledge by delivery, as stocks given as security for a loan. [< ML *hypothēcāt(us)*, ptp. of *hypothēcāre*. See HYPOTHEC, -ATE¹] —**hy·poth′e·ca′tion,** *n.* —**hy·poth′e·ca′tor,** *n.*

hy·poth·e·cate² (hī poth′ə kāt′, hi-), *v.i.*, *v.t.*, **-cat·ed, -cat·ing.** hypothesize. [< Gk *hypothḗk(ē)* (see HYPOTHEC) + -ATE¹] —**hy·poth′e·cat′er,** *n.*

hy·po·the·ci·um (hī′pə thē′shē əm, -sē əm), *n.*, *pl.* **-ci·a** (-shē ə, -sē ə). *Bot.* the layer of hyphal tissue directly beneath the hymenium. [HYPO- + THECIUM] —**hy′po·the′ci·al,** *adj.*

hy·poth·e·nar (hī poth′ə när′, -nər, hī′pə thē′nər), *Anat.* —*n.* **1.** the fleshly prominence on the palm at the base of the little finger. —*adj.* **2.** of, pertaining to, or situated on the hypothenar. [HYPO- + THENAR]

hy·poth·e·nuse (hī poth′ə no͞os′, -nyo͞os′), *n.* hypotenuse.

hy·po·ther·mal (hī′pə thûr′məl), *adj.* **1.** lukewarm; tepid. **2.** characterized by subnormal body temperature. [HYPO- + THERMAL]

hy·po·ther·mi·a (hī′pə thûr′mē ə), *n.* **1.** *Pathol.* subnormal body temperature. **2.** *Med.* the artificial reduction of body temperature to slow metabolic processes, usually for facilitating heart surgery. [HYPO- + THERM- + -IA]

hy·poth·e·sis (hī poth′i sis, hi-), *n.*, *pl.* **-ses** (-sēz′). **1.** a proposition, or set of propositions, set forth as an explanation for the occurrence of some specified group of phenomena, either asserted merely as a provisional conjecture to guide investigation **(working hypothesis)** or accepted as highly probable in the light of established facts. **2.** a proposition assumed as a premise in an argument. **3.** the antecedent of a conditional proposition. **4.** a mere assumption or guess. [< Gk *hypóthesis* basis, supposition. See HYPO-, THESIS] —**hy·poth′e·sist,** *n.* —**Syn. 1.** See **theory.**

hy·poth·e·sise (hī poth′i sīz′, hi-), *v.i.*, *v.t.*, **-sised, -sis·ing.** *Chiefly Brit.* hypothesize. —**hy·poth′e·sis′er,** *n.*

hy·poth·e·size (hī poth′i sīz′, hi-), *v.*, **-sized, -siz·ing.** —*v.i.* **1.** to form a hypothesis. —*v.t.* **2.** to assume by hypothesis. Also, **hypothecate².** [HYPOTHES(IS) + -IZE] —**hy·poth′e·siz′er,** *n.*

hy·po·thet·i·cal (hī′pə thet′i kəl), *adj.* **1.** assumed by hypothesis; supposed: *a hypothetical case.* **2.** of, pertaining to, involving, or characterized by hypothesis: *hypothetical reasoning.* **3.** given to making hypotheses: *a hypothetical person.* **4.** *Logic.* **a.** (of a proposition) highly conjectural; not well supported by available evidence. **b.** (of a proposition or syllogism) conditional. Also, **hy′po·thet′ic.** [< Gk *hypothetik(ós)* supposed (*hypo-* HYPO- + *the-* put (unreduplicated s. of *tithénai* to put) + *-tikos* -TIC) + -AL¹] —**hy′po·thet′i·cal·ly,** *adv.*

hypothet′ical imper′ative, *Kantianism.* a statement formulating the action necessary to attain a desired end.

hy·po·thy·roid (hī′pō thī′roid), *adj.* of, pertaining to, or having hypothyroidism. [HYPO- + THYROID]

hy·po·thy·roid·ism (hī′pə thī′roi diz′əm), *n.* *Pathol.* **1.** deficient activity of the thyroid gland. **2.** the condition produced by a deficiency of thyroid secretion, resulting in goiter, myxedema, and, in children, cretinism. [HYPOTHYROID + -ISM]

hy·po·ton·ic (hī′pə ton′ik), *adj.* **1.** *Physiol.* (of tissue) having less than the normal tone. **2.** *Physical Chem.* noting a solution of lower osmotic pressure than another solution with which it is compared (opposed to *hypertonic*). Cf. **isotonic** (def. 1). [HYPO- + TONIC] —**hy·po·to·nic·i·ty** (hī′pō tō nis′i tē), *n.*

hy·po·tra·che·li·um (hī′pō trə kē′lē əm), *n.*, *pl.* **-li·a** (-lē ə). (on a classical column) any member, as a necking, between the capital and the shaft. Cf. **trachelium.** [< L < Gk *hypotrachḗlion.* See HYPO-, TRACHELIUM]

hy·po·trich (hī′pə trik), *n.* any ciliate of the suborder *Hypotricha*, having cilia chiefly on the ventral surface. [HYPO- + TRICH-] —**hy·pot·rich·ous** (hī po′trə kəs), *adj.*

hy·po·ty·po·sis (hī′pə tī pō′sis), *n.* *Rhet.* lifelike description of a thing or scene. [< Gk *hypotýpōsis* outline, copy pattern, equiv. to *hypo-* HYPO- + *týpōsis* forming, molding (*týp(os)* beat, impression, mold + *-ōsis* -OSIS)]

hy·po·xan·thine (hī′pə zan′thēn, -thin), *n.* *Chem.* a white, crystalline, almost water-soluble, alkaloidal purine derivative, $C_5H_4N_4O$, found in animal and vegetable tissues: used chiefly in biochemical research. [HYPO- + XANTHINE] —**hy′po·xan′thic,** *adj.*

hy·pox·e·mi·a (hī′pok sē′mē ə), *n.* *Pathol.* inadequate oxygenation of the blood. [HYP- + OX(Y)- + -EMIA]

hy·pox·i·a (hī pok′sē ə), *n.* *Pathol.* a deficiency in the amount of oxygen that reaches the tissues of the body. [HYP- + OX(Y)- + -IA] —**hy·pox·ic** (hī pok′sik), *adj.*

hy·po·zeug·ma (hī′pə zo͞og′mə), *n.* *Rhet.* the use of a succession of subjects with a single predicate. [HYPO- + ZEUGMA]

hy·po·zeux·is (hī′pō zo͞ok′sis), *n.* *Rhet.* the use of a series of parallel clauses each of which has a subject and predicate, as in "I came, I saw, I conquered." [< LL < LGk < Gk *hypozeûg(nŷnai)* to put under the yoke (*hypo-* HYPO- + *zeugnŷnai* to yoke, deriv. of *zeûg(os)* yoke) + *-sis* -SIS]

Hyp·se·us (hip′sē əs, -so͞os), *n.* *Class. Myth.* a son of Peneus and Creusa who became king of the Lapiths.

hypsi-, var. of **hypso-.**

hyp·si·ceph·a·ly (hip′si sef′ə lē), *n.* *Pathol.* acrocephaly. [HYPSI- + -CEPHALY] —**hyp·si·ce·phal·ic** (hip′si sə fal′ik), **hyp′si·ceph′a·lous,** *adj.*

Hyp·sip·y·le (hip sip′ə lē′), *n.* *Class. Myth.* a queen of Lemnos who had twin sons by Jason: she was sold to Lycurgus of Nemea as a slave when the women of Lemnos discovered that she had spared her father's life at a time when the women had decided, out of jealousy, to kill all their men.

Hyp·sis·tus (hip sis′təs), *n.* *Class. Myth.* an epithet of Zeus, meaning "most high."

hypso-, a learned borrowing from Greek meaning "height," "altitude," used in the formation of compound words: *hypsometer.* Also, **hypsi-.** [< Gk, comb. form of *hýpsos* height]

hyp·sog·ra·phy (hip sog′rə fē), *n.* **1.** a branch of geography that deals with the measurement and mapping of the topography of the earth above sea level. **2.** topographical relief, esp. as represented on a map. [HYPSO- + -GRAPHY] —**hyp·so·graph·ic** (hip′sə graf′ik), **hyp′so·graph′i·cal,** *adj.*

hyp·som·e·ter (hip som′i tər), *n.* a device for determining the elevation above sea level or the reliability of a thermometer from the boiling point of liquids. [HYPSO- + -METER]

hyp·som·e·try (hip som′i trē), *n.* vertical control in mapping; the establishment of elevations or altitudes. [HYPSO- + -METRY] —**hyp·so·met·ric** (hip′sə me′trik), **hyp′so·met′ri·cal,** *adj.* —**hyp′so·met′ri·cal·ly,** *adv.* —**hyp·som′e·trist,** *n.*

hy·ra·coid (hī′rə koid′), *adj.* belonging or pertaining to the order *Hyracoidea*, comprising the hyraxes. [< NL *Hyracoid(ea)* name of the order, equiv. to *hyrac-* (s. of *hyrax*) HYRAX + *-oidea* -OID] —**hy·ra·coi·di·an** (hī′rə koi′dē ən), *adj.*, *n.*

hy·rax (hī′raks), *n.*, *pl.* **hy·rax·es, hy·ra·ces** (hī′rə sēz′). any of numerous small mammals of the order *Hyracoidea*, of Africa and the Mediterranean region, having short legs, ears, and tail, and hooflike nails on the toes. [< NL < Gk: shrewmouse]

Hyr·ca·ni·a (hər kā′nē ə), *n.* an ancient province of the Persian empire, SE of the Caspian Sea. —**Hyr·ca′ni·an,** *adj.*

Hy·ri·e (hī′rē ē′), *n.* *Class. Myth.* the mother of a child by Apollo: she was changed into a swan to relieve her grief over the death of her son.

Hyr·mi·na (hər′mi′nə), *n.* *Class. Myth.* a granddaughter of Endymion and mother, by Phorbas, of Actor.

Hyr·ne·tho (hər nē′thō), *n.* *Class. Myth.* a daughter of Temenus and a granddaughter of Aristomachus. Cf. **Deiphontes.**

Hyr·ti·us (hûr′shē əs), *n.* (in the *Iliad*) a Trojan ally.

hy·son (hī′sən), *n.* a Chinese green tea dried and prepared from twisted leaves, esp. of the early crop **(young hyson).** [< Chin (Cantonese) *hei-ch'un* blooming spring, c. Mandarin *hsi-ch'un*]

hy′son skin′, the inferior leaves that have been removed by winnowing before making hyson.

hys·sop (his′əp), *n.* **1.** an aromatic, labiate herb, *Hyssopus officinalis,* having blue flowers. **2.** *Bible.* a plant, perhaps the origan, whose twigs were used in ceremonial sprinkling. [< L *hyssōp(us)* < Gk *hýssōpos* < Sem (cf. Heb *ēzōbh*); r. ME *ysope,* OE < LL]

hyster-, var. of **hystero-** before a vowel: *hysterectomy.*

hys·ter·ec·to·mize (his′tə rek′tə mīz′), *v.t.,* **-mized, -miz·ing.** *Surg.* to perform a hysterectomy on. [HYSTERECTOM(Y) + -IZE]

hys·ter·ec·to·my (his′tə rek′tə mē), *n., pl.* **-mies.** *Surg.* excision of the uterus. [HYSTER- + -ECTOMY]

hys·ter·e·sis (his′tə rē′sis), *n.* *Physics.* **1.** the time lag exhibited by a body in reacting to changes in the forces, esp. magnetic forces, affecting it. **2.** the phenomenon exhibited by a system, often a ferromagnetic or imperfectly elastic material, in which the reaction of the system to changes is dependent upon its past reactions to change. [< Gk *hystérēsis* deficiency, state of being behind or late, whence inferior, equiv. to *hýster(os)* behind + *-ēsis* state of, result of] —**hys·ter·et·ic** (his′tə ret′ik), **hys·ter·e·si·al** (his′tə rē′sē əl), *adj.* —**hys′ter·et′i·cal·ly,** *adv.*

hys′tere′sis loop′, loop[1] (def. 6b).

hystere′sis loss′, *Physics.* the loss of energy by conversion to heat in a system exhibiting hysteresis.

hys·te·ri·a (hi stēr′ē ə, -ster′-), *n.* **1.** an uncontrollable outburst of emotion or fear, often characterized by irrationality, laughter, weeping, etc. **2.** a psychoneurotic disorder characterized by violent emotional outbreaks, disturbances of sensory and motor functions, and various abnormal effects due to autosuggestion. [HYSTER(IC) + -IA]

hys·ter·ic (hi ster′ik), *n.* **1.** Usually, **hysterics.** a fit of uncontrollable laughter or weeping; hysteria. **2.** a person subject to hysteria. —*adj.* **3.** hysterical. [< L *hysteric(us)* < Gk *hysterikós* of the womb. See HYSTER-, -IC]

hys·ter·i·cal (hi ster′i kəl), *adj.* **1.** of, pertaining to, or characterized by hysteria. **2.** uncontrollably emotional. **3.** irrational from fear, emotion, or an emotional shock. **4.** causing hysteria. **5.** suffering from or subject to hysteria. **6.** causing unrestrained laughter; very funny: *Oh, that joke is hysterical!* [< L *hysteric(us)* HYSTERIC + -AL[1]] —**hys·ter′i·cal·ly,** *adv.*

hyster′ical fe′ver, an increase in temperature without obvious cause other than hysteria.

hystero-, a learned borrowing from Greek meaning "uterus," used in the formation of compound words: *hysterotomy.* Also, *esp. before a vowel,* **hyster-.** [< Gk, comb. form of *hystéra*]

hys·ter·o·cat·a·lep·sy (his′tər ə kat′əlep′sē), *n.* *Psychiatry.* hysteria with cataleptic symptoms. [HYSTERO- + CATALEPSY]

hys·ter·o·gen·ic (his′tər ə jen′ik), *adj.* *Med.* inducing hysteria. [HYSTERO- + GENIC] —**hys·ter·og·e·ny** (his′tə roj′ə nē), *n.*

hys·ter·oid (his′tə roid′), *adj.* resembling hysteria. Also, **hys′ter·oi′dal.** [HYSTER- + -OID]

hys·ter·on prot·er·on (his′tə ron′ prot′ə ron′), **1.** *Logic.* a fallacious proof which begs the question at issue by assuming as a premise the conclusion to be proved. **2.** *Rhet.* a figure of speech in which the logical order of two elements in discourse is reversed, as in "bred and born" for "born and bred." [< LL < Gk *hýsteron* (neut. of *hýsteros*) latter + *próteron* (neut. of *próteros*) former]

hys·ter·ot·o·my (his′tə rot′ə mē), *n., pl.* **-mies.** *Surg.* the operation of cutting into the uterus, as in Caesarean section. [HYSTERO- + -TOMY]

hys·tri·co·mor·phic (his′trə kō môr′fik), *adj.* belonging or pertaining to the *Hystricomorpha,* the suborder of rodents that includes the porcupines, chinchilla, agouti, coypu, guinea pig, etc. [< L *hystric-* (s. of *hystrix* porcupine < Gk *hýstrix*) + -O- + -MORPHIC] —**hys·tric·o·morph** (hi strik′ə môrf′), *n.*

hyte (hīt), *adj.* *Scot. Archaic.* insane; mad. [?]

hy·ther·graph (hī′thər graf′, -gräf′), *n.* *Meteorol.* a climatic graph showing relationships between temperature and humidity or temperature and precipitation. [HY(DR)-[1] + THER(M) + -GRAPH]

hy·zone (hī′zōn), *n.* *Chem.* triatomic hydrogen, H_3. [HY(DROGEN + O)ZONE]

Hz., hertz.

I

I, i (ī), *n., pl.* **I's** or **Is, i's** or **is.** **1.** the ninth letter of the English alphabet, a vowel. **2.** any spoken sound represented by the letter *I* or *i*, as in *big, nice, ski,* etc. **3.** something having the shape of an I. **4.** a written or printed representation of the letter *I* or *i*. **5.** a device, as a printer's type, for reproducing the letter *I* or *i*.

I (ī), *pron., nom.* **I,** *poss.* **my** or **mine,** *obj.* **me;** *pl. nom.* **we,** *poss.* **our** or **ours,** *obj.* **us;** *n., pl.* **I's.** —*pron.* **1.** the nominative singular pronoun, used by a speaker in referring to himself. —*n.* **2.** (used to denote the narrator of a literary work written in the first person singular.) **3.** *Metaphys.* the ego. [ME *ik, ich, i;* OE *ic, ih;* c. G *ich,* Icel *ek,* L *ego,* Gk *egō,* Skt *ahām*]

I, **1.** the ninth in order or in a series. **2.** (*sometimes l.c.*) the Roman numeral for 1. Cf. **Roman numerals. 3.** *Chem.* iodine. **4.** *Elect.* current. **5.** *Logic.* See **particular affirmative.**

i, *Math.* **1.** the imaginary number $\sqrt{-1}$. **2.** a vector on the *x*-axis, having length 1.

i-, var. of **y-.**

-i-, the typical ending of the first element of compounds of Latin words, as **-o-** is of Greek words, but often used in English with a first element of any origin, if the second element is of Latin origin: *cuneiform; Frenchify.*

I., **1.** Independent. **2.** Island; Islands. **3.** Isle; Isles.

i., **1.** imperator. **2.** incisor. **3.** interest. **4.** intransitive. **5.** island. **6.** isle; isles.

I-131, *Chem.* See **iodine 131.** Also, **I 131.**

-ia, a noun suffix having restricted application in various fields, as in names of diseases (*malaria; anemia*), place names (*Italia; Rumania*), names of Roman feasts (*Lupercalia*), Latin or Latinizing plurals (*Amphibia; insignia; Reptilia*), and in other loan words from Latin (*militia*). [< NL, L, Gk, equiv. to *-i-* (formative or connective) or *-ī-* (Gk *-ei-*) + *-a,* fem. sing. or neut. pl. n. or adj. ending]

Ia., Iowa.

i.a., in absentia.

I·ac·chus (ī′ə kəs), *n.* (in the Eleusinian Mysteries) a god, usually identified with Dionysus, having Zeus, or sometimes Dionysus, as father, and Demeter, Persephone, or Semele as mother.

I·a·che (ī′ə kē′), *n.* *Class. Myth.* a nymph who was a companion of Persephone.

IAD, International Astrophysical Decade.

IADB, **1.** Inter-American Defense Board. **2.** Inter-American Development Bank.

IAEA, International Atomic Energy Agency.

I·a·go (ē ä′gō), *n.* **1.** the villain in Shakespeare's *Othello.* **2.** a boy's given name.

-ial, an adjective suffix appearing in loan words from Latin: *filial; imperial.* [< L *-iāl(is)* (m. and f.), *-iāle* (n.) adj. suffix. See -I-, -AL[1]]

I·al·me·nus (ī al′mə nəs), *n.* *Class. Myth.* a son of Ares and Astyoche who joined the Argonauts and was a leader of the Boeotians in the Trojan War.

I·al·y·sus (ī al′i səs), *n.* an ancient Mycenaean city on the island of Rhodes. Also, **I·al′y·sos.**

I.A.M., International Association of Machinists.

i·amb (ī′am, ī′amb), *n.* *Pros.* a foot of two syllables, a short followed by a long in quantitative meter, or an unstressed followed by a stressed in accentual meter, as in *Come live / with me / and be / my love.* [short for IAMBUS]

I·am·be (ī′əm bē′), *n.* *Class. Myth.* a girl who amused Demeter with bawdy stories.

i·am·bic (ī am′bik), *adj.* **1.** *Pros.* **a.** pertaining to the iamb. **b.** consisting of or employing an iamb or iambs. **2.** *Gk. Lit.* noting or pertaining to satirical poetry written in iambs. —*n.* **3.** *Pros.* **a.** an iamb. **b.** Usually, **iambics.** a verse or poem consisting of iambs. **4.** *Gk. Lit.* a satirical poem in this meter. [< L *iambic(us)* < Gk *iambikós.* See IAMBUS, -IC] —**i·am′bi·cal·ly,** *adv.*

i·am·bus (ī am′bəs), *n., pl.* **-bi** (-bī), **-bus·es.** iamb. [< L < Gk *íambos*]

I·a·mus (ī′ə məs), *n.* *Class. Myth.* a son of Evadne and Apollo who became a prophet.

I·an (ē′ən, ē′än, ī′ən), *n.* a boy's given name, Scottish form of **John.**

-ian, var. of **-an:** *amphibian; humanitarian.* [< L *-iānus.* See -I-, -AN]

-iana. See **-an, -ana.** [< L, neut. pl. of *-iānus* -IAN]

I·an·the (ī an′thē), *n.* **1.** *Class. Myth.* the wife of Iphis. **2.** a girl's given name.

I·ap·e·tus (ī ap′i təs), *n.* **1.** *Class. Myth.* a Titan, son of Uranus and Gaea and father of Atlas, Epimetheus, and Prometheus. **2.** *Astron.* one of the nine satellites of Saturn.

I·a·pig·i·a (ē′ə pij′ē ə), *n.* an area in the southern hemisphere of Mars.

I·a·pyx (ī ā′piks), *n.* *Class. Myth.* a son of Daedalus.

I·ar·bas (ī är′bəs), *n.* (in the *Aeneid*) a rejected suitor of Dido.

I·ar·da·nus (ī är′dᵊnəs), *n.* *Class. Myth.* a Lydian king who was the father of Omphale.

iar·o·vize (yär′ə vīz′), *v.t.,* **-vized, -viz·ing.** jarovize. —**iar′o·vi·za′tion,** *n.*

IAS, **1.** *Aeron.* indicated air speed. **2.** Institute for Advanced Studies. **3.** Institute of the Aeronautical Sciences.

Ia·şi (yäsh, yä′shē), *n.* Rumanian name of **Jassy.**

I·a·si·on (ī ā′zē ən), *n.* *Class. Myth.* the twin brother of Dardanus and the founder of the Trojan race.

-iasis, a noun suffix occurring in loan words from Greek: *psoriasis.* Cf. **-asis.** [< Gk, equiv. to *-iā-* (abstracted from verbs with stems so ending) + *-sis* -SIS]

I·a·so (ī ā′sō), *n.* *Class. Myth.* a daughter of Asclepius and a goddess of healing.

I·a·sus (ī′ə səs), *n.* *Class. Myth.* the father of Atalanta who abandoned her on a mountain to die because he wanted a son.

IATA, International Air Transport Association.

i·at·ric (ī a′trik, ē a′-), *adj.* of or pertaining to a physician or medicine. Also, **i·at′ri·cal.** [< Gk *iātrik(ós)* of healing, equiv. to *iātr(ós)* healer (see IATRO-) + *-ikos* -IC]

-iatrics, a combination of **-iatry** and **-ics:** *pediatrics.*

iatro-, a learned borrowing from Greek meaning "healer," "medicine," "healing," used in the formation of compound words: *iatrogenic.* [< Gk, comb. form of *iātrós* healer, equiv. to *iā(sthai)* (to) heal + *-tros* n. suffix]

i·at·ro·chem·is·try (ī a′trə kem′i strē, ē a′-), *n.* (in the 16th and 17th centuries) the study of chemistry in relation to the physiology, pathology, and treatment of disease. [IATRO- + CHEMISTRY] —**i·at·ro·chem·i·cal** (ī a′trə kem′i kəl, ē a′-), *adj.* —**i·at′ro·chem′i·cal·ly,** *adv.* —**i·at′ro·chem′ist,** *n.*

i·at·ro·gen·ic (ī a′trə jen′ik, ē a′-), *adj.* (of a neurosis or physical disorder) caused by the diagnosis, manner, or treatment of a physician or surgeon. [IATRO- + GENIC] —**i·at·ro·ge·nic·i·ty** (ī a′trō jə nis′i tē, ē a′-), *n.*

-iatry, a learned borrowing from Greek used, with the meaning "medical care," in the formation of compound words: *psychiatry.* [< Gk *iātreía* healing. See IATRO-, -Y[3]]

IATSE, International Alliance of Theatrical Stage Employees (and Moving Picture Machine Operators of the U.S. and Canada).

ib., ibidem.

I·ba·da (ē bä′dä, -də), *n.* any of the religious duties of a Muslim, including the recital of the creed, the five daily recitals of prayers, the Ramadan fast, almsgiving, and the pilgrimage to Mecca. [< Ar, equiv. to *Ibād* (see IBADHI) + *-a* n. suffix]

I·ba·dan (ē bä′dän, ē bäd′ᵊn), *n.* a city in SW Nigeria. 627,379 (1963).

I·ba·dhi (i bä′dē), *n.* *Islam.* a North African Kharijite. [< Ar, after Abdullah ibn *Ibād,* 7th-century Muslim ascetic + *-ī* suffix of appurtenance]

I·bá·ñez (ē vän′yeth), *n.* **Vi·cen·te Blas·co** (bē then′te bläs′kō). See **Blasco Ibáñez, Vicente.**

I·bar·bou·rou (ē vär vô′rô), *n.* **Jua·na de** (hwä′nä the), ("*Juana de América*"), born 1895, Uruguayan poetess.

I-beam (ī′bēm′), *n.* a rolled or extruded metal beam or shape having a cross section resembling a capital I.

I·be·ri·a (ī bēr′ē ə), *n.* **1.** Also called **Ibe′rian Penin′sula.** a peninsula in SW Europe, comprising Spain and Portugal. **2.** an ancient region S of the Caucasus in the S Soviet Union; modern Georgia.

I·be·ri·an (ī bēr′ē ən), *adj.* **1.** of or pertaining to Iberia in SW Europe, its inhabitants, or their language. **2.** *Ethnol.* noting or pertaining to a dark dolichocephalic people inhabiting parts of southern Europe and northern Africa, comprising, among others, the ancient Iberians, some of the ancient Britons, and their descendants. **3.** of or pertaining to ancient Iberia in the Caucasus or its inhabitants. —*n.* **4.** one of the ancient inhabitants of Iberia in Europe, from whom the Basques are supposed to be descended. **5.** the language of the ancient Iberians of SW Europe, not known to be related to any other language despite attempts to connect it with Basque, Berber, or the Caucasian languages. **6.** one of the ancient inhabitants of Iberia in Asia. [IBERI(A) + -AN]

I·bert (ē ber′), *n.* **Jacques Fran·çois An·toine** (zhäk fräN swa′ äN twan′), 1890–1962, French composer.

I·ber·ville, d' (dē ber vēl′), **Pierre le Moyne** (pyer lə mwan′), **Sieur,** 1661–1706, French naval officer, born in Canada: founder of the first French settlement in Louisiana 1699.

IBEW, International Brotherhood of Electrical Workers.

i·bex (ī′beks), *n., pl.* **i·bex·es, ib·i·ces** (ib′i sēz′, ī′bi-), (*esp. collectively*) **i·bex.** any of several wild goats of the genus *Capra,* found in mountainous regions of Asia, North Africa, and Europe, having long, recurved horns. [< L]

Ibex, Genus *Capra*
(About 3 ft. high at shoulder; horns to 3 ft.; length 4½ ft.)

ibid. (ib′id), ibidem.

i·bi·dem (i bē′dem; *Eng.* ib′i dəm, i bī′dəm), *adv.* *Latin.* in the same book, chapter, page, etc. [lit., there the same]

-ibility, var. of **-ability:** *reducibility.* [< L *-ibilitāt-,* equiv. to *-ibili(s)* -IBLE + *-tāt-* -TY[2]]

i·bis (ī′bis), *n., pl.* **i·bis·es** (ī′bi siz), (*esp. collectively*) **i·bis. 1.** any of several large wading birds of the family *Threskiornithidae,* of warm temperate and tropical regions, related to the herons and storks, and characterized by a long, thin, downward-curved bill. Cf. **sacred ibis. 2.** any of certain similar birds belonging to the stork family *Ciconiidae,* esp. the wood ibis, *Mycteria americana.* [ME < L < Gk < Egypt *hbj* (vowels not written)]

Sacred ibis,
Threskionis aethiopica
(Length 2½ ft.)

I·bi·za (ē vē′thä), *n.* Spanish name of **Iviza.**

-ible, var. of **-able,** occurring in words borrowed from Latin (*credible; horrible; visible*), or modeled on the Latin type (*reducible*). [< L *-ibil(is)* or *-ībil(is),* equiv. to *-i-* or *-ī-* thematic vowel + *-bilis* -BLE]

Ib·lis (ib′lēs), *n.* *Islamic Myth.* Eblis.

-ibly, var. of **-ably:** *credibly.* [-IBLE + -Y[1]]

ibn-, a prefix occurring in Arabic personal names: *ibn-Saud.* [< Ar: son (of)]

ibn-Ga·bi·rol (ib′ən gä bē′rôl), *n.* Arabic name of **Avicebron.** Also, **ibn′-Ga·bi′ral.**

ibn-Khal·dun (ib′ən khäl do͞on′), *n.* **Abd-al-Rah·man** (äb däl rä′män), 1332–1406, Arabian historian and philosopher.

ibn-Rushd (ib′ən ro͝osht′), *n.* Arabic name of **Averroës.**

ibn-Sa·ud (ib′ən sä o͞od′), *n.* **Ab·dul-A·ziz** (äb do͝ol′-ä zēz′), 1880–1953, king of Saudi Arabia 1932–53 (father of Saud ibn Abdul-Aziz).

ibn-Si·na (ib′ən sē′nä), *n.* Arabic name of **Avicenna.**

I·bo (ē′bō), *n., pl.* **I·bos,** *(esp. collectively)* **I·bo. 1.** a member of a Negro people of the lower Niger in Africa. **2.** the language of the Ibo, a Kwa language. Also, **Igbo.**

I·bot′a priv′et (ī bō′tə), a spreading shrub, *Ligustrum obtusifolium,* of Japan, having hairy leaves and nodding, white flower clusters. [< Jap *ibota* wax tree]

Ib·ra·him Pa·sha (ib′rä hēm′ pä′shä), 1789–1848, Egyptian general: governor of Syria 1833–40 (son of Mehemet Ali).

Ib·sen (ib′sən; *Norw.* ip′sən), *n.* **Hen·rik** (hen′rik), 1828–1906, Norwegian dramatist and poet.

Ib·se·ni·an (ib sē′nē ən, -sen′ē-), *adj.* of, pertaining to, or having the qualities or traits of Henrik Ibsen, his plays, or his ideas, esp. his condemnation of social convention and hypocrisy. [IBSEN + -IAN]

Ib·sen·ism (ib′sə niz′əm), *n.* **1.** a style of dramatic structure or content characteristic of Ibsen. **2.** advocacy of Ibsenian style and social ideas. [IBSEN + -ISM]

I.B.T.C.W.H., International Brotherhood of Teamsters, Chauffeurs, Warehousemen, and Helpers of America.

i·bu·pro·fen (ī′byo͞o prō′fən), *n. Pharm.* a white powdery substance, $C_{13}H_{18}O_2$, used to reduce inflammation, pain, and fever, esp. in the treatment of rheumatoid arthritis and osteoarthritis. [contraction and rearrangement of *isobutylphenyl proprionic acid,* the chemical name]

Ib·y·cus (ib′i kəs), *n.* fl. c540 B.C., Greek poet.

-ic, 1. a suffix forming adjectives from nouns or stems not used as words themselves (*poetic; metallic; Homeric*), found extensively in adjective nouns of a similar type (*public; magic*), and in nouns the adjectives of which end in *-ical* (*music; critic*). **2.** *Chem.* a suffix, specialized in opposition to *-ous,* used to show the higher of two valences: *ferric chloride.* [ME *-ic, -ik* < L *-ic(us)* -Y[1]; in many words repr. the cognate Gk *-ikos* (directly or through L); in some words r. *-ique* < F < L *-ic(us)*]

IC, *pl.* **ICs.** See **immediate constituent.**

I.C., Jesus Christ. [< L *Iesus Christus*]

i.c., (in prescriptions) between meals. [< L *inter cibōs*]

ICA, See **International Cooperation Administration.**

I·ça (ē′sä), *n.* Portuguese name of **Putumayo.**

ICAAAA *(called* ī′sē′fôr′ā′, -fôr′ā′*),* Intercollegiate Association of Amateur Athletes of America.

-ical, a combination of **-ic** and **-al**[1], used in forming adjectives from nouns (*rhetorical*), providing synonyms to words ending in *-ic* (*poetical*), and providing an adjective with additional meanings to those in the *-ic* form (*economical*). [ME < L *-icāl(is).* See -IC, -AL[1]]

ICAO, International Civil Aviation Organization.

I·car·i·a (i kâr′ē ə, ī kâr′-; *Gk.* ē′kä rē′ä), *n.* **1.** Also, **Ikaria.** a Greek island in the Aegean Sea: a part of the Southern Sporades group. 11,913 (1951); 99 sq. mi. **2.** any of the former Utopian communities founded by the followers of Étienne Cabet, esp. the one established at Nauvoo, Illinois, in 1849.

I·car·i·an (i kâr′ē ən, ī kâr′-), *adj.* **1.** of or like Icarus. **2.** of or pertaining to Icaria or its inhabitants. —*n.* **3.** an inhabitant of Icaria. [< L *Icari(us)* (< Gk *Ikários* of ICARUS) + -AN]

Icar′ian Sea′, part of the Aegean Sea, between Turkey and the Greek islands of Patmos and Leros.

I·car·i·us (i kâr′ē əs), *n. Class. Myth.* **1.** an Athenian whose hospitality to Dionysus was rewarded with instruction in wine-making. **2.** the father of Penelope.

Ic·a·rus (ik′ər əs, ī′kər-), *n. Class. Myth.* a youth who, with his father Daedalus, attempted to escape from Crete with wings of wax and feathers. Daedalus was successful but Icarus, not heeding his father's warnings, flew so high that his wings melted from the heat of the sun, and he plunged to his death in the sea.

ICBM, See **intercontinental ballistic missile.** Also, **I.C.B.M.**

I.C.C., 1. International Control Commission. **2.** Interstate Commerce Commission. Also, **ICC**

ice (īs), *n., v.,* **iced, ic·ing,** *adj.* —*n.* **1.** the solid form of water, produced by freezing; frozen water. **2.** the frozen surface of a body of water. **3.** any substance resembling this: *camphor ice.* **4.** *U.S.* a frozen dessert made of sweetened water and fruit juice. **5.** *Brit.* See **ice cream. 6.** icing, as on a cake. **7.** reserve; formality: *The ice of his manner betrayed his dislike of the new ambassador.* **8.** *Slang.* diamonds. **9.** *Slang.* **a.** protection money paid to the police by the operator of an illicit business. **b.** a fee that a ticket broker pays to a theater manager in order to receive a favorable allotment of tickets. **10. break the ice, a.** to succeed initially; make a beginning. **b.** to overcome reserve, awkwardness, or formality within a group, as in introducing persons: *The hostess broke the ice by introducing the strangers to each other.* **11. cut no ice,** *U.S. Informal.* to have no influence or importance; fail to impress: *Her father's position cuts no ice with me.* **12. on ice,** *Slang.* **a.** with a good chance of success or realization: *Now that the contract is on ice we can begin operating again.* **b.** out of activity, as in confinement or imprisonment. **c.** in a state of abeyance or readiness: *Let's put that topic on ice for the moment.* **13. on thin ice,** in a risky or delicate situation: *Without some facts to support you, you're on thin ice with that argument.* —*v.t.* **14.** to cover with ice. **15.** to change into ice; freeze. **16.** to cool with ice, as a drink. **17.** *Ice Hockey.* **a.** to hit (the puck) to the extreme end of the rink, esp. from the defensive area across the attacking area. **b.** *Canadian.* to put (a team) into formal play. **18.** to refrigerate with ice, as air. **19.** to make cold, as if with ice. **20.** to cover (cakes, buns, etc.) with icing; frost. —*v.i.* **21.** to freeze: *The sherbet is icing in the refrigerator.* **22.** to be coated with ice (often fol. by *up*): *The windshield has iced up.* —*adj.* **23.** of ice: *an ice palace.* [ME, OE *īs;* c. G *Eis,* Icel *īss*] —**ice′less,** *adj.* —**ice′like′,** *adj.*

-ice, a suffix of nouns, indicating state or quality, appearing in loan words from French: *notice.* [ME *-ice, -ise* < OF < L *-iti(us), -iti(a), -iti(um)* abstract n. suffix]

Ice., 1. Iceland. **2.** Icelandic.

ice′ age′, *Geol.* the glacial epoch.

ice′ an′chor, *Naut.* a large, hooklike device for setting in ice to anchor a vessel or to provide a hold for a hawser in warping it along. Also called **ice drag.**

ice′ a′pron, an icebreaker built upstream from a bridge pier or the like.

ice′ bag′, a bag for holding ice, applied to the head or another part of the body to be cooled. Also called **ice pack.**

ice′ beam′, *Naut.* a beam running downward from the load waterline of a vessel to reinforce the hull against ice pressure.

ice′ belt′, *Naut.* a broad belt of heavy plating on the hull of an icebreaker at the water line.

ice·berg (īs′bûrg), *n.* **1.** a large floating mass of ice, detached from a glacier and carried out to sea. **2.** *Informal.* an emotionally cold person. [half Anglicization, half adoption of D *ijsberg* ice mountain; c. G *Eisberg,* Sw *isberg*]

ice′berg let′tuce, a variety of lettuce having a cabbagelike head of crisp leaves.

ice·blink (īs′blingk′), *n.* a yellowish luminosity near the horizon or on the underside of a cloud, caused by the reflection of light from sea ice. Also called **blink.** Cf. **snowblink.** [ICE + BLINK; cf. D *ijsblink*]

ice·boat (īs′bōt′), *n.* **1.** a vehicle for rapid movement on ice, usually consisting of a T-shaped frame on three runners driven by a fore-and-aft sailing rig or, sometimes, by an engine operating a propeller. **2.** a boat for breaking through ice; icebreaker. [ICE + BOAT]

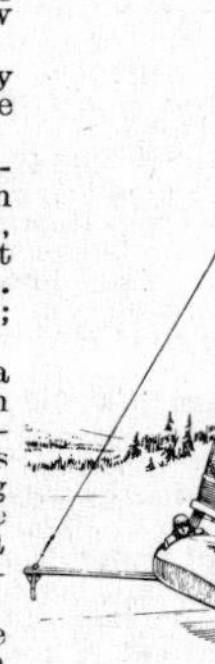

Iceboat

ice·boat·ing (īs′bō′ting), *n.* the sport of sailing or racing on ice in iceboats. [ICEBOAT + -ING[1]]

ice·bound (īs′bound′), *adj.* **1.** held fast or hemmed in by ice; frozen in: *an icebound ship.* **2.** obstructed or shut off by ice: *an icebound harbor.* [ICE + -BOUND[1]]

ice·box (īs′boks′), *n.* **1.** an insulated cabinet or chest with a partition for ice, used for preserving or cooling food, beverages, etc. **2.** any type of refrigerator. **3.** *Naut.* an enclosed area in the bottom of a vessel through which sea water can be pumped up for use in the condenser in icy waters. **4.** *Slang.* an isolation cell in a prison. [ICE + BOX[1]]

ice′box cake′, a confection made from prepared ingredients, as cookies, whipped cream, etc., that require no additional baking, chilled in a refrigerator before serving.

ice·break·er (īs′brā′kər), *n.* **1.** a vessel especially built for forcing navigable passages through ice. **2.** a tool or machine for chopping ice into small pieces. [ICE + BREAKER[1]]

ice′ bul′letin, a radio bulletin regarding ice position and movements, issued for the benefit of vessels at sea.

ice·cap (īs′kap′), *n.* a cap of ice over an area, sloping in all directions from the center. [ICE + CAP[1]]

ice′ cave′, a cave containing ice which remains unmelted during all or most of the year.

ice′ code′, a code used for reporting ice conditions affecting ship movements, having a scale of numbers from 0 to 9.

ice-cold (īs′kōld′), *adj.* **1.** cold as ice: *her ice-cold feet.* **2.** without warmth of feeling or manner; unemotional; passionless. [OE *is-calde*]

ice′ cream′, 1. a frozen food made of cream, sweetened and variously flavored. **2.** (in commercial use) a food made in imitation of this, and containing milk, egg whites, custard, cornstarch, etc.

ice′-cream cone′ (īs′krēm′), **1.** a thin, crisp, conical wafer for holding one or more scoops of ice cream. **2.** a confection consisting of an ice-cream cone, one or more scoops of ice cream, and often a topping of sprinkles, a maraschino cherry, etc.

ice′ crys′tals, *Meteorol.* precipitation consisting of small, slowly falling crystals of ice. Also called **diamond dust, frost mist, frost snow, ice needle, poudrin, snow mist.**

ice′ cube′, a small cube of ice, as one made in the freezing compartment of a refrigerator. —**ice′-cube′,** *adj.*

iced (īst), *adj.* **1.** covered with ice. **2.** cooled by means of ice: *iced tea.* **3.** *Cookery.* covered with icing. [ICE + -ED[2]]

ice′ dock′, *Naut.* an enclosed basin in icy waters in which a vessel may lie to avoid being nipped.

ice′ drag′, *Naut.* See **ice anchor.**

ice·fall (īs′fôl′), *n.* **1.** a jumbled mass of ice in a glacier. **2.** a mass of ice overhanging a precipice. **3.** a falling of ice from a glacier, iceberg, etc. [ICE + FALL]

ice′ feath′ers, a delicate structure of crystals of ice that builds on the windward side of objects. Also called **frost feathers.**

ice′ field′, a large sheet of floating ice, larger than an ice floe.

ice′ fish′ing, the act or practice of catching fish through holes cut in the ice.

ice′ floe′, 1. a large flat mass of floating ice. **2.** floe (def. 1).

ice′ flow′ers, 1. ice crystal formations on the surface of a still, slowly freezing body of water. **2.** Also called **frost flowers.** delicate tufts of frost on an ice or snow surface.

ice′ fog′, fog composed of particles of ice. Also called **frozen fog, pogonip.**

ice′ foot′, (in polar regions) a belt of ice frozen to the shore, formed chiefly as a result of the rise and fall of the tides.

ice-free (īs′frē′), *adj.* **1.** free of ice. **2.** (of a harbor or other body of water) free at all times of the year of any ice that would oppose navigation.

ice′ front′, the forward section or seaward edge of an ice shelf.

ice′ hock′ey, a game played on ice between two teams each of six players wearing skates, the object being to score goals by shooting a puck into the opponents' cage using a stick with a wooden blade set at an obtuse angle to the shaft.

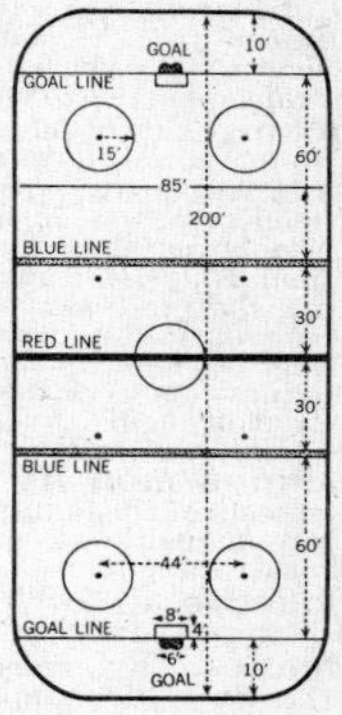

Ice hockey rink

ice·house (īs′hous′), *n., pl.* **-hous·es** (-hou′ziz). a building for storing ice. [ICE + HOUSE]

ice′ is′land, a tabular iceberg in the Arctic region.

Icel., 1. Iceland. **2.** Icelandic. Also, **Icel**

Ice·land (īs′lənd), *n.* a large island in the N Atlantic between Greenland and Scandinavia: formerly Danish; an independent republic since 1944. 189,000 (est. 1966); 39,698 sq. mi. *Cap.:* Reykjavik. —**Ice·land·er** (īs′lan′dər, -lən dər), *n.*

Ice·lan·dic (īs lan′dik), *adj.* **1.** of or pertaining to Iceland, its inhabitants, or their language. —*n.* **2.** the language of Iceland, a North Germanic language. [ICELAND + -IC]

Ice′land moss′, an edible lichen, *Cetraria islandica,* of arctic regions, containing a starchlike substance used in medicine.

Ice′land pop′py, a perennial poppy, esp. *Papaver nudicaule,* of the arctic regions, having showy orange, red, white, or yellow flowers.

Ice′land spar′, a transparent variety of calcite that is double-refracting and is used as a polarizer.

I·ce·lus (ī′sə ləs), *n.* the ancient Greek god of dreams who assumed the shapes of animals.

ice·man (īs′man′), *n., pl.* **-men.** a man engaged in gathering, storing, selling, or delivering ice. [ICE + MAN[1]]

Ice′man Com′eth, The, a play (1946) by Eugene O'Neill.

ice′ milk′, 1. a soft-textured frozen-food product made of skimmed milk. **2.** See **frozen custard.**

ice′ nee′dle, *Meteorol.* **1.** a long, thin crystal of ice. **2.** See **ice crystals.**

I·ce·ni (ī sē′nī), *n.* *(construed as sing. or pl.)* an ancient Celtic tribe of eastern England, whose queen, Boadicea, headed an insurrection against the Romans in A.D. 61. —**I·ce·nic** (ī sē′nik), *adj.*

Ice′ Observa′tion Serv′ice, the international service maintained by the U.S. Coast Guard in the North Atlantic that supplements the operation of the International Ice Patrol and is concerned chiefly with the study of ice conditions in the ocean.

ice′ pack′, 1. See **pack ice. 2.** See **ice bag. 3.** *Med.* a bathtub, or the like, filled with ice for immersing a patient for cold shock therapy.

ice′ pel′lets, *Meteorol.* precipitation consisting of particles of ice less than five millimeters in diameter, occurring either as frozen raindrops or as small hailstones. Cf. **hail**[2] (def. 1), **sleet, snow pellets.**

ice′ pick′, a pick or other tool for chipping ice.

ice′ plant′, an Old World figwort, *Mesembryanthemum crystallinum,* having leaves covered with glistening vesicles. Also called **sea fig, sea marigold.**

ice′ point′, the temperature at which a mixture of ice and air-saturated water at a pressure of one atmosphere is in equilibrium, represented by 0°C and 32°F. Cf. **steam point.**

ice′ rain′, *Rare.* freezing rain.

ice′ ram′part, a mound of earth or stones formed by the action of ice against the shore of a lake, stream, etc.

ice′ run′, the rapid breaking up or fragmentation of river ice in spring or early summer.

ice-scoured (īs′skourd′), *adj. Phys. Geog.* noting an area having surface features resulting from scouring by an advancing ice sheet during glaciation.

ice′ sheet′, 1. a broad, thick sheet of ice covering an extensive area for a long period of time. **2.** a glacier covering a large fraction of a continent.

ice′ shelf′, an ice sheet projecting into coastal waters so that the end floats.

ice′ show′, an entertainment in which performers appear on ice skates, usually in exhibitions of skill.

ice′ skate′, 1. a shoe fitted with a metal blade, for skating on ice. **2.** skate[1] (def. 3).

ice-skate (īs′skāt′), *v.i.,* **-skat·ed, -skat·ing.** to skate on ice. [v. use of ICE SKATE]

ice′ storm′, a storm of freezing rain and widespread glaze formation. Also called **silver storm.**

ice′ tongs′, 1. tongs for handling a large block of ice. **2.** a small pair of tongs for serving ice cubes.

ice′ tongue′, a section of ice at the base of and projecting from a glacier.

ice′ wa′ter, 1. melted ice. **2.** water chilled with or as with ice.

ich (ik), *n.* a disease of tropical fishes, characterized by small, white nodules on the fins, skin, and eyes, caused by a ciliate protozoan, *Ichthyophthirius multifiliis.* Also called **ichthyophthirius, ichthyophthirius disease.** [short for ICHTHYOPHTHIRIUS]

Ich·a·bod (ik′ə bod′), *n.* a boy's given name.

I·chang (ē′chäng′), *n.* a port in SW Hupeh, in central China, on the Yangtze River. 81,000 (est. 1950).

ich dien (ikh dēn′), *German.* I serve: motto of the Prince of Wales.

I Ching (ē′ jing′), an ancient Chinese book of divination, in which 64 pairs of 8 symbols are shown with various interpretations. Also called **Book of Changes.**

I Ching (Basic trigrams) A, Ch'ien; B, Tui; C, Li; D, Chen; E, Sun; F, K'an; G, Ken; H, K'un

I·chi·no·mi·ya (ē′chē nō′mē yä′), *n.* a city on central Honshu, in central Japan. 193,579 (1964).

ichn-, var. of **ichno-** before a vowel: *ichnite.*

ich·neu·mon (ik no͞o′mən, -nyo͞o′-), *n.* **1.** a slender, carnivorous mammal, *Herpestes ichneumon,* of Egypt, resembling a weasel, feeding on small mammals, reptiles, birds, etc., and believed by the ancient Egyptians to devour crocodiles' eggs. **2.** See **ichneumon fly.** [< L < Gk: lit., tracker, equiv. to *ichneú(ein)* (to) track (see ICHNO-) + *-mōn* agent suffix]

ichneu′mon fly′, any of numerous hymenopterous insects of the family *Ichneumonidae,* the larvae of which are parasitic on caterpillars and immature stages of other insects.

ich·nite (ik′nīt), *n.* *Paleontol.* a fossil footprint. [ICHN- + -ITE[1]]

ichno-, a learned borrowing from Greek meaning "track," "footstep," used in the formation of compound words: *ichnology.* Also, *esp. before a vowel,* **ichn-.** [< Gk, comb. form of *íchnos*]

ich·nog·ra·phy (ik nog′rə fē), *n., pl.* **-phies. 1.** the art of drawing ground plans. **2.** a ground plan. [< LL *ichnographia.* See ICHNO-, -GRAPHY] —**ich·no·graph·ic** (ik′nə graf′ik), **ich′no·graph′i·cal,** *adj.* —**ich′no·graph′i·cal·ly,** *adv.*

ich·nol·o·gy (ik nol′ə jē), *n.* the branch of paleontology dealing with fossil footprints. [ICHNO- + -LOGY] —**ich·no·log·i·cal** (ik′nə loj′i kəl), *adj.*

i·chor[1] (ī′kôr, ī′kər), *n.* *Class. Myth.* an ethereal fluid supposed to flow in the veins of the gods. [< Gk]

i·chor[2] (ī′kôr, ī′kər), *n.* *Pathol.* an acrid, watery discharge, as from an ulcer or wound. [< LL: sanies < Gk *ichṓr* ICHOR[1]] —**i·chor·ous** (ī′kər əs), *adj.*

ichth., ichthyology.

ich·tham·mol (ik tham′ōl, -ôl, -ol; ik′thə mōl′, -môl′, -mol′), *n.* *Pharm.* a viscous, reddish brown to brownish-black substance, obtained by the destructive distillation of bituminous schists, used in medicine chiefly as an antiseptic, analgesic, and local stimulant in skin conditions. [ICHTH(YO)- (from *ichthyosulfonate*) + AMM(ONIUM) + -OL[1]]

ich·thy·ic (ik′thē ik), *adj.* piscine. [< Gk *ichthyik(ós)* fishy. See ICHTHY-, -IC]

ichthyo-, a learned borrowing from Greek meaning "fish," used in the formation of compound words: *ichthyology.* Also, *esp. before a vowel,* **ichthy-.** [< Gk, comb. form of *ichthýs* fish]

Ich·thy·o·cen·taur (ik′thē ō sen′tôr), *n.* *Class. Myth.* a sea creature with a human head and torso, the legs of a horse, and the tail of a fish. [< Gk *ichthyokéntaur(os).* See ICHTHYO-, CENTAUR]

ich·thy·og·ra·phy (ik′thē og′rə fē), *n., pl.* **-phies.** a treatise on fishes. [ICHTHYO- + -GRAPHY] —**ich′thy·og′ra·pher,** *n.* —**ich·thy·o·graph·ic** (ik′thē ə graf′ik), *adj.*

ich·thy·oid (ik′thē oid′), *adj.* **1.** Also, **ich′thy·oi′dal.** fishlike. —*n.* **2.** any fishlike vertebrate. [< Gk *ichthyoeid(ḗs).* See ICHTHY-, -OID]

Ich·thy·ol (ik′thē ōl′, -ôl′, -ol′), *n.* *Pharm., Trademark.* ichthammol.

ichthyol., ichthyology.

ich·thy·o·lite (ik′thē ə līt′), *n.* a fossil fish. [ICHTHYO- + -LITE] —**ich·thy·o·lit·ic** (ik′thē ə lit′ik), *adj.*

ich·thy·ol·o·gy (ik′thē ol′ə jē), *n.* the branch of zoology dealing with fishes. [ICHTHYO- + -LOGY] —**ich·thy·o·log·ic** (ik′thē ə loj′ik), **ich′thy·o·log′i·cal,** *adj.* —**ich′thy·o·log′i·cal·ly,** *adv.* —**ich′thy·ol′o·gist,** *n.*

ich·thy·oph·a·gist (ik′thē of′ə jist), *n.* one who eats or subsists on fish. [ICHTHYOPHAG(Y) + -IST]

ich·thy·oph·a·gy (ik′thē of′ə jē), *n.* the practice of eating or subsisting on fish. [ICHTHYO- + -PHAGY] —**ich·thy·oph·a·gous** (ik′thē of′ə gəs), *adj.*

ich·thy·oph·thir·i·us (ik′thē of thēr′ē əs), *n.* *Ichthyol.* ich. Also called **ichthyophthir′ius disease′.** [< NL *icthyo-* IC-THYO- + *-phthirius* < Gk *phtheír* louse]

Ich·thy·or·nis (ik′thē ôr′nis), *n.* an extinct genus of toothed birds having vertebrae resembling those of fishes. [< NL; see ICHTHY-, ORNITHO-]

ich·thy·o·saur (ik′thē ə sôr′), *n.* any fishlike marine reptile of the extinct order *Ichthyosauria,* ranging from 4 to 40 feet in length and having a round, tapering body, a large head, four paddlelike flippers, and a vertical caudal fin. [see ICHTHYOSAURUS] —**ich′thy·o·sau′ri·an,** *adj.* —**ich′thy·o·sau′roid,** *adj.*

Ichthyosaur, *Stenopterygius quadriscissus* (Length 4 ft.)

ich·thy·o·saur·us (ik′thē ə sôr′əs), *n., pl.* **-us·es.** ichthyosaur. [< NL; see ICHTHYO-, -SAURUS]

ich·thy·o·sis (ik′thē ō′sis), *n.* *Pathol.* a congenital skin disease in which the epidermis continuously flakes off in large scales or plates. Also called **fishskin disease.** [< NL; see ICHTHY-, -OSIS] —**ich·thy·ot·ic** (ik′thē ot′ik), *adj.*

-ician, a combination of **-ic** and **-ian,** used to form agent nouns to stems in **-ic:** *musician; geometrician.* [-IC + -IAN; r. ME *-icien* < OF < L *-ic(a)* + *-iānus*]

i·ci·cle (ī′si kəl), *n.* a pendent, tapering mass of ice formed by the freezing of dripping water. [ME *isikel,* OE *īsgicel,* equiv. to *īs* ICE + *gicel* icicle; akin to Icel *jökul* mass of ice, glacier] —**i′ci·cled,** *adj.*

i·ci·ly (ī′sə lē), *adv.* in an icy manner: *She received him icily because of the harsh way he had treated her.* [ICY + -LY]

i·ci·ness (ī′sē nis), *n.* the state of being icy or very cold. [ICY + -NESS]

ic·ing (ī′sing), *n.* **1.** a preparation, as of confectioners' sugar, butter, vanilla extract, etc., for covering cakes, cookies, etc.; frosting. **2.** *Meteorol.* a coating of ice on a solid object. Cf. **glaze, rime**[2]. **3.** the freezing of atmospheric moisture on the surface of an aircraft. [ICE + -ING[1]]

ic′ing sug′ar, *Brit.* See **confectioners' sugar.**

i·ci on parle fran·çais (ē sē′ ôN PARL fräN se′), *French.* French is spoken here. [lit., here one speaks French]

ICJ, International Court of Justice.

ick·er (ik′ər), *n.* *Scot.* the fruit-bearing spike of any cereal plant, esp. an ear of corn. [OE *æhher, eher* (Northumbrian dial.), var. of *ēar* ear of grain; see EAR[2]]

Ick·es (ik′ēz), *n.* **Harold (Le Claire)** (lə klâr), 1874–1952, U.S. lawyer, statesman, and writer.

ick·y (ik′ē), *adj.,* **ick·i·er, ick·i·est.** *Slang.* **1.** repulsive, esp. because of excessive sweetness or sentimentality. **2.** unsophisticated or old-fashioned. **3.** sticky; viscid. [ick (< ?) + -Y[1]]

I′, Claudius, a historical novel (1934) by Robert Graves, in the form of an autobiography by the Roman emperor Claudius I.

i·con (ī′kon), *n., pl.* **i·cons. 1.** a picture, image, or other representation. **2.** *Eastern Ch.* a representation in painting, enamel, etc., of some sacred personage, as Christ or a saint or angel, itself venerated as sacred. **3.** *Logic.* a sign or representation that stands for its object by virtue of a resemblance or analogy to it. Also, **eikon, ikon** (for defs. 1, 2). [< L < Gk *eikṓn* likeness, image, figure] —**Syn. 2.** See **image.**

i·con·ic (ī kon′ik), *adj.* **1.** of, pertaining to, or characteristic of an icon, portrait, or image. **2.** *Art.* (of statues, portraits, etc.) executed according to a convention or tradition. Also, **i·con′i·cal.** [< L *īconic(us)* < Gk *eikonikós,* equiv. to *eikon-* (s. of *eikṓn*) ICON + *-ikos* -IC] —**i·con′i·cal·ly,** *adv.* —**i·co·nic·i·ty** (ī′kə nis′i tē), *n.*

I·co·ni·um (ī kō′nē əm), *n.* ancient name of **Konya.**

icono-, a learned borrowing from Greek meaning "image," "likeness," used in the formation of compound words: *iconology.* Also, *esp. before a vowel,* **icon-.** [< Gk, comb. form of *eikṓn* ICON]

i·con·o·clasm (ī kon′ə klaz′əm), *n.* the action or spirit of iconoclasts. [ICONOCL(AST) + *-asm* on model of pairs like *enthusiast: enthusiasm*]

i·con·o·clast (ī kon′ə klast′), *n.* **1.** a breaker or destroyer of images, esp. those set up for religious veneration. **2.** one who attacks cherished beliefs, traditional institutions, etc., as being based on error or superstition. [< LL *īconoclast(ēs)* < LGk *eikonoklástēs,* equiv. to Gk *eikono-* ICONO- + *-klastēs* breaker, equiv. to *klas-* (var. s. of *klân* to break) + *-tēs* agent n. suffix] —**i·con′o·clas′tic,** *adj.* —**i·con′o·clas′ti·cal·ly,** *adv.*

i·con·o·dule (ī kon′ə do͞ol′, -dyo͞ol′), *n.* a person who venerates icons and supports their use in religious worship. Also, **i·con′o·du′list.** [ICONO- + *doulia* slavery (*doûl(os)* slave, servant -Y[3])]

i·con·o·du·ly (ī kon′ə do͞o′lē, -dyo͞o′-), *n.* the veneration of images. [ICONO- + ML *dulia* service < Gk *douleia* slavery < *doûl(os)* slave + *-ia* -Y[3]] —**i·con′o·du′lic,** *adj.*

i·con·o·graph·ic (ī kon′ə graf′ik), *adj.* of or pertaining to iconography. Also, **i·con′o·graph′i·cal.** [ICONO- + -GRAPHIC]

i·co·nog·ra·phy (ī′kə nog′rə fē), *n., pl.* **-phies. 1.** symbolic representation, esp. the conventional meanings attached to an image or images. **2.** subject matter in the visual arts, esp. with reference to the conventions regarding the treatment of a subject in artistic representation. **3.** the study or analysis of subject matter and its meaning in the visual arts; iconology. **4.** *Obs.* a representation or a group of representations of a person, place, or thing, as a portrait or a collection of portraits. [< ML *īconographia* < Gk *eikonographía.* See ICONO-, -GRAPHY] —**i·con·o·graph** (ī kon′ə graf′, -gräf′), *n.* —**i′co·nog′ra·pher,** *n.*

i·co·nol·a·try (ī′kə nol′ə trē), *n.* the worship or adoration of icons. [ICONO- + -LATRY] —**i′co·nol′a·ter,** *n.* —**i′co·nol′a·trous,** *adj.*

i·co·nol·o·gy (ī′kə nol′ə jē), *n.* **1.** the historical analysis and interpretive study of symbols or images and their contextual significance; iconography. **2.** the study of icons or symbolic representations. [ICONO- + -LOGY] —**i·con·o·log·i·cal** (ī kon′əloj′i kəl, ī′kə nəloj′-), *adj.* —**i′co·nol′o·gist,** *n.*

i·con·o·scope (ī kon′ə skōp′), *n.* a television camera tube in which a beam of high-velocity electrons scans a photoemissive mosaic. Also called **ike.** Cf. **orthicon.** [formerly trademark]

i·co·nos·ta·sis (ī′kə nos′tə sis), *n., pl.* **-ses** (-sēz′). *Eastern Ch.* a partition or screen on which icons are placed, separating the sanctuary from the main part of the church. Also, **i·con·o·stas** (ī kon′ə stas′). [< eccl. L < eccl. Gk *eikonóstasis.* See ICONO-, STASIS]

i·co·sa·he·dron (ī kō′sə hē′drən, ī kos′ə-), *n., pl.* **-drons, -dra** (-drə). a solid figure having twenty faces. [< Gk *eikosáedron,* equiv. to *eikosa-* (var. of *eikosi-,* comb. form of *eíkosi* twenty) + *-edron* -HEDRON] —**i·co′sa·he′dral,** *adj.*

Icosahedron (Regular)

i·co·si·tet·ra·he·dron (ī kō′si te′trə hē′drən, ī kos′ə-), *n., pl.* **-drons, -dra** (-drə). a solid figure having 24 faces. [< Gk *eikosi-* (comb. form of *eíkosi* twenty) + TETRAHEDRON]

-ics, a suffix of nouns, originally plural as denoting things pertaining to a particular subject, but now mostly used as singular as denoting the body of matters, facts, knowledge, principles, etc., pertaining to a subject, and hence a science or art: *ethics; physics; politics; tactics.* [pl. of -IC, repr. L *-ica* (< Gk *-ika,* neut. pl. of *-ikos*), as in *rhētorica* (pl.) rhetoric book]

I.C.S., International Correspondence School.

ICSH, **1.** *Biochem.* interstitial-cell-stimulating hormone: a hormone produced by the anterior lobe of the pituitary gland that, in the female, regulates the development of the corpus luteum and, in the male, stimulates the interstitial cells of the testis to produce testosterone. **2.** *Pharm.* a commercial form of this substance, obtained from the pituitary glands of pigs and sheep. Also called **luteinizing hormone, LH**

ic·ter·ic (ik ter′ik), *adj.* *Pathol.* pertaining to or affected with icterus; jaundiced. Also, **ic·ter′i·cal.** [< L *ictericus* < Gk *ikterikós,* equiv. to *íkter(os)* jaundice + *-ikos* -IC]

ic·ter·us (ik′tər əs), *n.* *Pathol.* jaundice (def. 1). [< L < Gk *íkteros* jaundice, a yellow bird said to cure jaundice when seen]

Ic·ti·nus (ik tī′nəs), *n.* fl. mid-5th century B.C., Greek architect who together with Callicrates designed the Parthenon.

ic·tus (ik′təs), *n., pl.* **-tus·es, -tus. 1.** *Pros.* rhythmical or metrical stress. **2.** *Pathol.* **a.** a fit. **b.** a stroke, as sunstroke. [< L: a stroke, n. use of *ictus* struck (ptp. of *icere*), equiv. to *ic-* strike + *-tus* ptp. suffix] —**ic′tic,** *adj.*

i·cy (ī′sē), *adj.,* **i·ci·er, i·ci·est. 1.** made of, full of, or covered with ice. **2.** resembling ice. **3.** cold: *icy wind.* **4.** slippery: *an icy road.* **5.** without warmth of feeling; frigid: *an icy stare.* [ME *isy,* OE *īsig.* See ICE, -Y[1]]

id (id), *n.* *Psychoanal.* the part of the psyche, residing in the unconscious, that is the source of instinctive energy. Its impulses, which seek satisfaction in accordance with the pleasure principle, are modified by the ego and the superego before they are given overt expression. [special use of L *id* it, as a trans. of G *Es* primal urge]

I'd (īd), contraction of *I would, I should,* or *I had.*

-id[1], **1.** a noun suffix meaning "daughter of" (*Nereid*); used also to form names of meteors appearing to radiate in showers from particular constellations or comets (*Andromedid*). **2.** a suffix used in naming epics: *Aeneid.* [< L *-id-,* s. of *-is* fem. suffix of source or origin < Gk]

-id[2], a suffix of nouns and adjectives indicating members of a zoological family (*cichlid*), or some other group or division (*acarid; arachnid*). [back formation from NL *-idae* -IDAE and from NL *-ida* -IDA]

-id[3], var. of **-ide:** *parotid.*

-id[4], a quasi suffix common in adjectives, esp. of states which appeal to the senses: *torrid; acid.* [< L *-id(us)* adj. suffix, often with the meaning "full of"]

ID, **1.** identification. **2.** identity. **3.** inside diameter.

ID., (in Iraq) dinar; dinars.

Id., Idaho.

id., idem.

I.D., **1.** identification. **2.** identity. **3.** *Mil.* Infantry Division. **4.** Intelligence Department.

i.d., inside diameter.

I·da (ī′də), *n.* **1. Mount,** a mountain in NW Asia Minor, SE of ancient Troy. 5810 ft. **2.** Modern, **Mount Psiloriti.** the highest mountain in Crete. 8058 ft. **3.** *Class. Myth.* **a.** one of the nymphs who kept watch over the infant Zeus to protect him from being devoured by his father, Cronus. **b.** a nymph who was the mother, by Zeus, of the Dactyls. **4.** a girl's given name.

-ida, *Zool.* a suffix of the names of orders and classes: *Arachnida.* [< NL, taken as neut. pl. of L *-idēs* offspring of < Gk]

IDA, International Development Association.

Ida., Idaho.

I·da·bel (ī′də bel′), *n.* a town in SE Oklahoma. 4967 (1960).

-idae, *Zool.* a suffix of the names of families: *Canidae.* [< NL, L < Gk *-idai,* pl. of *-idēs* offspring of]

I·dae·a (ī dē′ə), *n.* *Class. Myth.* **1.** the second wife of Phineus. **2.** a nymph of Mount Ida who became the wife of Scamander and the mother of Teucer.

I·dae·an (ī dē′ən), *adj.* **1.** of, pertaining to, associated with, or inhabiting Mount Ida in Asia Minor or Crete. **2.** pertaining to or designating a style of vase painting developed in Attica during the late 8th through middle 7th century B.C., chiefly characterized by human, animal, and ornamental motifs painted in a bold, curvilinear style. Cf. **Daedalid** (def. 1). [< L *idae(us)* (< Gk *idaíos*) + -AN]

Idae′an Dac′tyl, *Class. Myth.* Dactyl.

Idae′an Moth′er, *Class. Myth.* Cybele.

I·da·ho (ī′də hō′), *n.* a State in the NW United States. 667,191 (1960); 83,557 sq. mi. *Cap.:* Boise. *Abbr.:* Id., Ida. —**I·da·ho·an** (ī′də hō′ən, ī′də hō′-), *adj., n.*

I′daho Falls′, a city in E Idaho. 33,161 (1960).

I·dal·ia (i dāl′yə), *n.* a girl's given name.

I·da·li·na (īd′əlē′nə), *n.* a girl's given name, form of **Idalia** or **Ida.** Also, **I·da·line** (īd′əlēn′).

I·das (ī′dəs), *n.* *Class. Myth.* the rival of Apollo for Marpessa.

I.D. card. See **identity card.** Also, **ID card.**

id·dhi (id′dē), *n.* *Pali.* siddhi.

-ide, a suffix used in the names of chemical compounds: *bromide.* Also, **-id.** [abstracted from OXIDE]

i·de·a (ī dē′ə, ī dē̆′), *n.* **1.** any conception existing in the mind as a result of mental understanding, awareness, or activity. **2.** a thought, conception, or notion: *That is an excellent idea.* **3.** an impression: *He gave me a general idea of how he intends to handle the new account.* **4.** an opinion, view, or belief: *His ideas on raising children are certainly strange.* **5.** a plan of action; an intention: *the idea of becoming an engineer.* **6.** a groundless supposition; fantasy. **7.** *Philos.* **a.** a concept developed by the mind. **b.** a conception of what is desirable or ought to be; ideal. **c.** (*cap.*) *Platonism.* an archetype or pattern of which the individual objects in any natural class are imperfect copies and from which they derive their being. **d.** *Kantianism.* See **idea of pure reason. 8.** *Music.* a theme, phrase, or figure. **9.** *Obs.* a likeness. **10.** *Obs.* a mental image. [< LL < Gk: pattern, equiv. to *ide-*

(s. of *idein* to see) + *-a* n. ending; r. late ME *idee* < MF < LL, as above; akin to WIT¹] —**i·de′a·ful,** *adj.* —**i·de′a·less,** *adj.*

—**Syn. 1, 2.** IDEA, THOUGHT, CONCEPTION, NOTION refer to a product of mental activity. IDEA, although it may refer to thoughts of any degree of seriousness or triviality, is commonly preferred for mental concepts considered more important or elaborate: *We pondered the idea of the fourth dimension. The idea of his arrival frightened me.* THOUGHT, which reflects its primary emphasis on the mental process, may denote any concept except the more weighty and elaborate ones: *I welcomed his thoughts on the subject. A thought came to him.* CONCEPTION suggests a thought that seems complete, individual, recent, or somewhat intricate: *The architect's conception delighted them.* NOTION suggests a fleeting, vague, or imperfect thought: *a bare notion of how to proceed.* **4.** sentiment, judgment.

i·de·a·is·tic (ī dē′ə is′tik, ī′dē ə-, ī′dē is′-), *adj.* of ideas, esp. in their abstract or symbolic character. [IDEA + -ISTIC]

i·de·al (ī dē′əl, ī dēl′), *n.* **1.** a conception of something in its perfection. **2.** a standard of perfection or excellence. **3.** a person or thing conceived as embodying such a conception or conforming to such a standard, and taken as a model for imitation. **4.** an ultimate object or aim of endeavor, esp. one of high or noble character: *He refuses to compromise any of his ideals.* **5.** something that exists only in the imagination: *To achieve the ideal is almost hopeless.* **6.** *Math.* a subring of a ring, any element of which when multipled by any element of the ring results in an element of the subring. —*adj.* **7.** conceived as constituting a standard of perfection or excellence: *ideal beauty.* **8.** regarded as perfect in its kind: *an ideal spot for a home.* **9.** existing only in the imagination; not real or practical; visionary: *an ideal marriage.* **10.** advantageous; excellent; best: *It would be ideal if she could accompany us to care for the children.* **11.** based upon an ideal or ideals: *the ideal theory of numbers.* **12.** *Philos.* **a.** existing as an archetype or Platonic Idea. **b.** pertaining to a possible state of affairs considered as highly desirable. **c.** pertaining to or of the nature of idealism. [< LL *ideāl(is).* See IDEA, -AL¹] —**i·de′al·ness,** *n.*

—**Syn. 1, 2.** epitome. IDEAL, EXAMPLE, MODEL refer to something considered as a standard to strive toward or something considered worthy of imitation. An IDEAL is a concept or standard of perfection, existing merely as an image in the mind, or based upon a person or upon conduct: *We admire the high ideals of a religious person. Sir Philip Sidney was considered the ideal in gentlemanly conduct.* An EXAMPLE is a person or his conduct or achievements regarded as worthy of being followed or imitated in a general way; or sometimes, as properly to be avoided: *an example of courage; a bad example to one's children.* A MODEL is primarily a physical shape to be closely copied, but is also a pattern for exact imitation in conduct or character: *They took their leader as a model.* **4.** intention, objective. **7.** perfect, consummate, complete. **9.** impractical, imaginary, fanciful, fantastic.

ide′al gas′, *Physics.* a gas composed of molecules on which no forces act except upon collision with one another and with the walls of the container in which the gas is enclosed; a gas obeying the ideal gas law. Also called **perfect gas.**

ide′al gas′ law′, *Physics.* the law that the product of the pressure and the volume of one gram molecule of an ideal gas is equal to the product of the absolute temperature of the gas and the universal gas constant. Also called **gas law.**

i·de·al·ise (ī dē′ə līz′), *v.t., v.i.,* **-ised, is·ing.** *Chiefly Brit.* idealize. —**i·de′al·i·sa′tion,** *n.* —**i·de′al·is′er,** *n.*

i·de·al·ism (ī dē′ə liz′əm), *n.* **1.** the cherishing or pursuit of high or noble principles, purposes, goals, etc. **2.** the practice of idealizing. **3.** something idealized; an ideal representation. **4.** *Fine Arts.* treatment of subject matter in a work of art in which a mental conception of beauty or form is stressed, characterized usually by the selection of particular features of various models and their combination into a whole according to a standard of perfection. Cf. **naturalism** (def. 2), **realism** (def. 3a). **5.** *Philos.* **a.** any system or theory that maintains that the real is of the nature of thought or that the object of external perception consists of ideas. **b.** the tendency to represent things in an ideal form, or as they might or should be rather than as they are, with emphasis on values. [IDEAL + -ISM, prob. modeled on G *Idealismus*]

i·de·al·ist (ī dē′ə list), *n.* **1.** one who cherishes or pursues high or noble principles, purposes, goals, etc. **2.** a visionary or impractical person. **3.** one who represents things as they might or should be rather than as they are. **4.** a writer or artist who treats subjects imaginatively. **5.** one who accepts the doctrines of idealism. —*adj.* **6.** idealistic. [IDEAL + -IST]

i·de·al·is·tic (ī dē′ə lis′tik, ī′dē ə-), *adj.* of or pertaining to idealism or idealists. Also, **i·de′al·is′ti·cal.** [IDEALIST + -IC] —**i·de′al·is′ti·cal·ly,** *adv.*

i·de·al·i·ty (ī′dē al′i tē), *n., pl.* **-ties.** **1.** ideal quality or character. **2.** capacity to idealize. **3.** *Philos.* existence only in idea and not in reality. [IDEAL + -ITY]

i·de·al·ize (ī dē′ə līz′), *v.,* **-ized, -iz·ing.** —*v.t.* **1.** to make ideal; represent in an ideal form or character; exalt to an ideal perfection or excellence. —*v.i.* **2.** to represent something in an ideal form; imagine or form an ideal or ideals. Also, *esp. Brit.,* **idealise.** [IDEAL + -IZE] —**i·de′al·i·za′tion,** *n.* —**i·de′al·iz′er,** *n.*

i·de·al·ly (ī dē′ə lē), *adv.* **1.** in accordance with an ideal; perfectly. **2.** in idea, thought, or imagination. **3.** in theory or principle. [IDEAL + -LY]

ide′al of pure′ rea′son, *Kantianism.* God, seen as an idea of pure reason unifying the personal soul with the cosmos.

ide′al point′, *Math.* the point at infinity in projective geometry at which parallel lines intersect.

ide′al specif′ic im′pulse, *Rocketry.* See **specific impulse** (def. 2).

ide′al type′, a construct abstracted from experience in which individual elements are combined to form a whole that is conceptually independent of empirical factors or variables, but against which particular examples of the appropriate class found in life can be measured.

ide′a man′, a creative person, esp. in a business firm; one who is capable of and responsible for providing original ideas.

i·de·a·mon·ger (ī dē′ə mung′gər, -mong′-), *n.* *Informal.* one who peddles ideas. [IDEA + MONGER]

ide′a of pure′ rea′son, *Kantianism.* any of the three undemonstrable entities (a personal soul, a cosmos, and a supreme being) implicit in the fact of a subject and an object of knowledge, and in the need for some principle uniting them. Cf. **ideal of pure reason.**

ide′a of ref′erence, *Psychiatry.* an obsessive tendency to assume that the actions or remarks of other people refer disparagingly to oneself.

i·de·ate (*v.* ī′dē āt′, ī dē′āt; *n.* ī′dē āt′, ī dē′it), *v.,* **-at·ed, -at·ing,** *n.* —*v.t.* **1.** to form in idea, thought, or imagination. —*v.i.* **2.** to form ideas; think. —*n.* **3.** ideatum. [IDE(A) + -ATE¹] —**i′de·a′tion,** *n.* —**i·de·a·tive** (ī dē′ə tiv, ī′dē ā′-), *adj.*

i·de·a·tion (ī′dē ā′shən), *n.* the process of forming ideas or images. [IDEATE + -ION]

i·de·a·tion·al (ī′dē ā′shə nəl), *adj.* of, pertaining to, or involving ideas or concepts. [IDEATION + -AL¹] —**i′de·a′tion·al·ly,** *adv.*

i·de·a·tum (ī′dē ā′təm), *n., pl.* **-ta** (-tə). *Archaic.* (in epistemology) the object of knowledge as known by the mind. Cf. **datum** (def. 5). [< NL, equiv. to L *ide(a)* IDEA + *-ātum,* neut. of *-ātus* -ATE¹]

i·dée fixe (ē dā fēks′), *pl.* **i·dées fixes** (ē dā fēks′). *French.* See **fixed idea.**

I·de·ler (id′ələr, id′lər), *n.* a walled plain in the fourth quadrant of the face of the moon: about 25 miles in diameter.

i·dem (ī′dem, id′em), *pron., adj.* *Latin.* the same as previously given or mentioned.

i·dem·fac·tor (ī′dəm fak′tər, id′əm-), *n.* *Math.* a dyadic, written *ii* + *jj* + *kk,* that leaves every vector unchanged. [IDEM + FACTOR]

i·dem·po·tent (ī′dəm pōt′ənt, id′əm-), *Math.* —*adj.* **1.** unchanged when multiplied by itself. —*n.* **2.** an element with such a property. [IDEM + POTENT¹]

i·den·tic (ī den′tik, i den′-), *adj.* **1.** identical. **2.** *Diplomacy.* (of action, notes, etc.) identical in form, as when two or more governments deal simultaneously with another government. [< ML *identic(us)* the same, equiv. to LL *ident(itās)* IDENTITY + *-icus* -IC]

i·den·ti·cal (ī den′ti kəl, i den′-), *adj.* **1.** exactly the same; being the very same: *The manager gave us the identical cottage each summer.* **2.** agreeing exactly: *identical opinions.* **3.** similar or alike in every way: *He replaced the broken dish with an identical one.* [< ML *identic(us)* IDENTIC + -AL¹] —**i·den′ti·cal·ly,** *adv.* —**i·den′ti·cal·ness,** *n.*

—**Syn. 2.** congruous, congruent, equal, matching. —**Ant. 2.** unlike, disagreeing.

iden′tical proposi′tion, *Logic.* a proposition in which the subject and predicate have the same meaning, as, "That which is mortal is not immortal."

iden′tical rhyme′, *Pros.* **1.** rhyme created by the repetition of a word. **2.** See **rime riche.**

iden′tical twin′, one of a pair of twins of the same sex, usually resembling one another closely, that develop from a single fertilized ovum. Cf. **fraternal twin.**

i·den·ti·fi·ca·tion (ī den′tə fə kā′shən, i den′-), *n.* **1.** the act of identifying; the state of being identified. **2.** something that identifies one: *He carries identification with him at all times.* **3.** *Sociol.* acceptance as one's own of the values and interests of a social group. **4.** *Psychol.* **a.** a process by which a person ascribes to himself the qualities or characteristics of another person. **b.** (in psychoanalytic theory) the transference or reaction to one person with the feelings or responses relevant to another, as the identification of a teacher with a parent. **c.** perception of another as an extension of oneself. [IDENTI(FY) + -FICATION]

identifica′tion brace′let, a bracelet, usually of linked metal, having an identification plate for the name of the wearer.

identifica′tion space′, *Math.* a topological space whose elements are the equivalence classes of a given topological space with a specified equivalence relation. Also called **quotient space.**

identifica′tion tag′, either of two oblong metal tags, issued to armed forces personnel, on which are impressed the serial number, name, etc., of the person to whom it was issued, and carried on or about the person at all times.

identifica′tion thread′. See **rogue's yarn.**

i·den·ti·fy (ī den′tə fī′, i den′-), *v.,* **-fied, -fy·ing.** —*v.t.* **1.** to recognize or establish as being a particular person or thing; verify the identity of: *to identify handwriting; to identify the bearer of a check.* **2.** to make, represent to be, or regard or treat as the same or identical: *They identified Jones with the progress of the company.* **3.** to associate in feeling, interest, action, etc. (usually fol. by *with*): *He preferred not to identify himself with that group.* **4.** *Biol.* to determine to what group (a given specimen) belongs. **5.** *Psychol.* to associate (one or oneself) with another person or a group of persons by identification. **6.** to serve as a means of identification for: *His gruff voice quickly identified him.* —*v.i.* **7.** to make oneself one with another or others: *The play was so gripping that the audience quickly identified with the actors.* [< LL *identific(āre),* equiv. to *identi(tās)* IDENTITY + *-ficāre* -FY] —**i·den′ti·fi′a·ble,** *adj.* —**i·den′ti·fi′a·ble·ness,** *n.* —**i·den′ti·fi′er,** *n.*

i·den·ti·ty (ī den′ti tē, i den′-), *n., pl.* **-ties.** **1.** state or fact of remaining the same one, as under varying aspects or conditions: *The identity of the fingerprints on the gun with his own provided evidence that he was the killer.* **2.** the condition of being oneself or itself, and not another: *He doubted his own identity.* **3.** condition or character as to who a person or what a thing is: *a case of mistaken identity.* **4.** state or fact of being the same one. **5.** exact likeness in nature or qualities: *an identity of interests.* **6.** an instance or point of sameness or likeness: *to mistake resemblances for identities.* **7.** *Math.* **a.** an equation which is valid for all values of its variables: $3 + 4 = 7$; $a^2 - b^2 = (a + b)\,(a - b)$, *for a and b real numbers.* **b.** Also called **unit element, unity.** an element in a set such that the element operating on any other element of the set leaves the second element unchanged. **c.** the property of a function or map such that each element is mapped into itself. **d.** the function or map itself. [< LL *identitās,* equiv. to L *identi(dem)* repeatedly (*idem* same + *-ti-* < ?) + *-tās* -TY²]

iden′tity card′, a card, usually of an official nature, for identifying the bearer, giving his name, address, and other personal data. Also called **ID card, I.D. card.**

iden′tity ma′trix, *Math.* a matrix that has 1 in each position on the diagonal from upper left to lower right and zero in all other positions.

ideo-, a learned borrowing from Greek meaning "idea," used in the formation of compound words: *ideology.* [comb. form < Gk *ide-* (s. of *idéa*) IDEA + -O-]

id·e·o·gram (id′ē ə gram′, ī′dē-), *n.* **1.** a written symbol that represents an idea or object directly rather than a particular word or speech sound. **2.** a written symbol that represents a morpheme or any of several morphemes, as 7, =, &. [IDEO- + -GRAM¹]

id·e·o·graph (id′ē ə graf′, -gräf′, ī′dē-), *n.* an ideogram. [IDEO- + -GRAPH] —**id·e·o·graph·ic** (id′ē ə graf′ik, ī′dē-), **id′e·o·graph′i·cal,** *adj.* —**id′e·o·graph′i·cal·ly,** *adv.*

id·e·og·ra·phy (id′ē og′rə fē, ī′dē-), *n.* the use of ideograms. [IDEO- + -GRAPHY]

i·de·o·log·ic (ī′dē ə loj′ik, id′ē-), *adj.* **1.** of or pertaining to ideology. **2.** speculative; visionary. Also, **i′de·o·log′i·cal.** [IDEOLOG(Y) + -IC] —**i′de·o·log′i·cal·ly,** *adv.*

i·de·ol·o·gise (ī′dē ol′ə jīz′, id′ē-), *v.t.,* **-gised, -gis·ing.** *Chiefly Brit.* ideologize.

i·de·ol·o·gist (ī′dē ol′ə jist, id′ē-), *n.* **1.** an expert in ideology. **2.** one who deals with systems of ideas. **3.** one advocating a particular ideology. **4.** a visionary. Also, **i·de·o·logue** (ī′dē ə lôg′, -log′, id′ē ə-, ī dē′-). [IDEOLOG(Y) + -IST]

i·de·ol·o·gize (ī′dē ol′ə jīz′, id′ē-), *v.t.,* **-gized, -giz·ing.** **1.** to explain or express ideologically: *to ideologize a political opinion.* **2.** to cause to comply with or yield to a particular ideology. Also, *esp. Brit.,* **ideologise.** [IDEOLOG(Y) + -IZE]

i·de·ol·o·gy (ī′dē ol′ə jē, id′ē-), *n., pl.* **-gies.** **1.** the body of doctrine, myth, symbol, etc., of a social movement, institution, class, or large group. **2.** such a body of doctrine, myth, etc., with reference to some political and cultural plan, as that of fascism, along with the devices for putting it into operation. **3.** *Philos.* **a.** the study of the nature and origin of ideas. **b.** a system which derives ideas exclusively from sensation. **4.** theorizing of a visionary or impractical nature. [IDEO- + -LOGY; cf. F *idéologie*]

i·de·o·mo·tor (ī′dē ə mō′tər, id′ē ə-), *adj.* *Psychol.* of or pertaining to motor activity caused by an idea. Cf. **sensorimotor** (def. 1). [IDEO- + MOTOR] —**i′de·o·mo′tion,** *n.*

ides (īdz), *n.* (*construed as sing. or pl.*) (in the ancient Roman calendar) the 15th day of March, May, July, or October, and the 13th day of the other months. [ME < MF < L *īdūs* (fem. pl.) < ?]

-ides, a Greek plural suffix appearing in scientific names: *chromolipides.* [< Gk, pl. of *-is,* suffix of source or origin. See -ID¹]

id est (id est′), *Latin.* See **i.e.**

-idia, pl. of **-idion** or **-idium.**

idio-, a learned borrowing from Greek meaning "proper to one," "peculiar," used in the formation of compound words: *idiomorphic.* [< Gk, comb. form of *ídios* own, personal, private, separate, distinct]

id·i·o·blast (id′ē ə blast′), *n.* *Bot.* a cell which differs greatly from the surrounding cells or tissue. [IDIO- + -BLAST] —**id′i·o·blas′tic,** *adj.*

id·i·o·chro·mat·ic (id′ē ə krō mat′ik, -ō krə-), *adj.* (of a mineral) deriving a characteristic color from its capacity to absorb certain light rays. [IDIO- + CHROMATIC]

id·i·oc·ra·sy (id′ē ok′rə sē), *n., pl.* **-sies.** idiosyncrasy. [< Gk *idiokrasía,* equiv. to *idio-* IDIO- + *-krasia,* equiv. to *krâs(is)* mixture + *-ia* -Y³; see IDIOSYNCRASY] —**id·i·o·crat·ic** (id′ē ə krat′ik), **id′i·o·crat′i·cal,** *adj.* —**id′i·o·crat′i·cal·ly,** *adv.*

id·i·o·cy (id′ē ə sē), *n., pl.* **-cies.** **1.** the condition of being an idiot; extreme degree of mental deficiency. **2.** utterly senseless or foolish behavior; a foolish act, statement, etc. [late ME; see IDIOT, -CY (perh. modeled on pairs like *private: privacy*)]

id·i·o·dy·nam·ic (id′ē ō dī nam′ik), *adj.* of, pertaining to, or conforming to the theories of idiodynamics. [IDIO- + DYNAMIC]

id·i·o·dy·nam·ics (id′ē ō dī nam′iks), *n.* (*construed as sing.*) a system of beliefs in psychology emphasizing the role of the personality in choosing stimuli and in organizing responses. [IDIO- + DYNAMICS]

id·i·o·glos·si·a (id′ē ə glos′ē ə, -glô′sē ə), *n.* **1.** a private form of speech invented by one child or by children who are in close contact, as twins. **2.** a pathological condition characterized by speech so distorted as to be unintelligible. [< Gk *idióglōss(os)* own-tongued (*idio-* IDIO- + *glôss(a)* tongue + *-os* adj. suffix) + *-ia* -IA] —**id′i·o·glot′tic** (id′ē ə glot′ik), *adj.*

id·i·o·graph (id′ē ə graf′, -gräf′), *n.* a mark or signature characteristic of a particular person, organization, etc.; trademark. Cf. **logotype** (def. 2). [< LGk *idiógraph(on),* n. use of neut. of Gk *idiógraphos* self-written. See IDIO-, -GRAPH]

id·i·o·graph·ic (id′ē ə graf′ik), *adj.* *Psychol.* pertaining to or involving the study of cases or events as individual units, with a view to understanding each one separately (opposed to *nomothetic*). [IDIO- + -GRAPHIC]

id·i·o·lect (id′ē ə lekt′), *n.* *Linguistics.* a person's individual speech pattern. Cf. **dialect** (def. 1). [IDIO- + *-lect* (as in *dialect*)]

id·i·om (id′ē əm), *n.* **1.** an expression whose meaning is not predictable from the usual meanings of its constituent elements, as *kick the bucket, hang one's head,* etc., or from the general grammatical rules of a language, as *the table round* for *the round table,* and which is not a constituent of a larger expression of like characteristics. **2.** a language, dialect, or style of speaking peculiar to a people. **3.** a construction or expression of one language whose parts correspond to elements in another language but whose total structure or meaning is not matched in the same way in the second language. **4.** the peculiar character or genius of a language. **5.** a distinct style or character, as in music, art, etc.: *the idiom of Bach.* [< L *idiōm(a)* < Gk, equiv. to *idiō-* (var. of *idio-* IDIO-; see IDIOT) + *-ma* n. suffix]

id·i·o·mat·ic (id′ē ə mat′ik), *adj.* **1.** peculiar to or characteristic of a particular idiom: *idiomatic French.* **2.** having a distinct style or character, esp. in the arts: *idiomatic writing; an idiomatic composer.* Also, **id′i·o·mat′i·cal.** [< LGk *idiōmatik(ós),* equiv. to *idiōmat-* (s. of *idíōma*) IDIOM + *-ikos* -IC] —**id′i·o·mat′i·cal·ly,** *adv.* —**id′i·o·mat′i·cal·ness, id·i·o·ma·tic·i·ty** (id′ē ō mə tis′i tē), *n.*

id·i·o·mor·phic (id/ē ə môr/fik), *adj.* **1.** Also called **euhedral.** (in a rock) noting or pertaining to a mineral constituent having its own characteristic outward crystalline form unaltered by the other constituents of the rock; automorphic. **2.** having its own characteristic form. [< Gk *idiómorph(os)* having an individual form (see IDIO-, -MORPHOUS) + -IC] —**id/i·o·mor/phi·cal·ly,** *adv.* —**id/i·o·mor/phism,** *n.*

-idion, a diminutive suffix occurring in loan words from Greek: *enchiridion.* Cf. **-idium.** [< Gk]

id·i·o·path·ic (id/ē ə path/ik), *adj. Pathol.* of unknown cause, as a disease. [IDIO- + -PATHIC] —**id/i·o·path/i·cal·ly,** *adv.*

id·i·op·a·thy (id/ē op/ə thē), *n., pl.* **-thies.** *Pathol.* a disease not preceded or occasioned by any other. [< NL *idiopathia* < Gk *idiopátheia* a feeling peculiar to one's self. See IDIO-, -PATHY]

id·i·o·phone (id/ē ə fōn/), *n.* a musical instrument that is made from a solid, naturally sonorous material, as a gong or a glass harmonica. [< G *Idiophon.* See IDIO-, -PHONE] —**id·i·o·phon·ic** (id/ē ə fon/ik), *adj.*

id·i·o·plasm (id/ē ə plaz/əm), *n. Biol.* See **germ plasm.** [IDIO- + -PLASM] —**id/i·o·plas/mic, id·i·o·plas·mat·ic** (id/ē ō plaz mat/ik), *adj.*

id·i·or·rhyth·mic (id/ē ə rith/mik), *adj.* **1.** (of a monk) living in a religious community of self-governing members. **2.** (of a monastery) inhabited by idiorrhythmic monks. [< Gk *idiórrhythm(os),* equiv. to *idio-* IDIO- + *rhythm(ós)* a measure, manner (see RHYTHM) + -IC] —**id/i·or·rhyth/mism, id/i·or·rhyth/my,** *n.*

id·i·o·syn·cra·sy (id/ē ə sing/krə sē, -sin/-), *n., pl.* **-sies. 1.** a characteristic, habit, mannerism, or the like, that is peculiar to an individual. **2.** the physical constitution peculiar to an individual. **3.** a peculiarity of the physical or the mental constitution, esp. susceptibility toward drugs, food, etc. Cf. **allergy** (def. 1). Also, **idiocrasy.** [< Gk *idiosynkrāsía,* equiv. to *idio-* IDIO- + *-synkrāsia,* equiv. to *syn-* SYN- + *krâs(is)* a blending + *-ia* -Y³] —**id·i·o·syn·crat·ic** (id/ē ō sin krat/ik), *adj.* —**id/i·o·syn·crat/i·cal·ly,** *adv.*
—**Syn. 1.** peculiarity, quirk.

id·i·ot (id/ē ət), *n.* **1.** an utterly foolish or senseless person. **2.** one hopelessly deficient, esp. from birth, in the ordinary mental powers; one lacking the capacity to develop beyond the mental age of three or four years. [ME < L *idiōt(a)* < Gk *idiṓtēs* private person, ignoramus, equiv. to *idiō-* (lengthened var. of *idio-* IDIO-) + *-tēs* agent n. suffix]
—**Syn. 1.** fool, halfwit; imbecile; dolt, dunce, numskull.

Idiot, The, a novel (1866) by Dostoevsky.

id/iot board/, *Television.* a mechanical apparatus, as a projector or a continuous roll of paper, for prompting during a program.

id/iot card/, *Television.* a large prompter's card, placed out of range of the camera, containing words or phrases to aid a speaker or performer during a program. Also called **id/iot sheet/.**

id·i·ot·ic (id/ē ot/ik), *adj.* of, pertaining to, or characteristic of an idiot; senselessly foolish. Also, **id/i·ot/i·cal.** [< LL *idiōtic(us)* < Gk *idiōtikós* private, ignorant. See IDIOT, -IC] —**id/i·ot/i·cal·ly,** *adv.* —**id/i·ot/i·cal·ness,** *n.*
—**Syn.** half-witted, stupid, imbecilic, fatuous, inane, asinine. —**Ant.** intelligent.

id·i·ot·ise (id/ē ə tīz/), *v.t.,* **-ised, -is·ing.** *Chiefly Brit.* idiotize.

id·i·ot·ism¹ (id/ē ə tiz/əm), *n.* **1.** idiotic conduct or action. **2.** idiocy. [IDIOT + -ISM]

id·i·ot·ism² (id/ē ə tiz/əm), *n. Obs.* an idiom. [< LL *idiōtism(us)* < Gk *idiōtismós* a vulgar phrase, peculiar way of speaking]

id·i·ot·ize (id/ē ə tīz/), *v.t.,* **-ized, -iz·ing.** to make a fool of; make idiotic. Also, *esp. Brit.,* **idiotise.** [IDIOT + -IZE]

id·i·o·trop·ic (id/ē ə trop/ik), *adj. Psychiatry.* of or characterized by introspection; introspective. [< Gk *idiótrop(os)* turned or turning to one's own (see IDIO-, -TROPE) + -IC]

id·i·ot sa·vant (id/ē ət sa vänt/, sav/ənt; *Fr.* ē dyō sa väɴ/), *pl.* **id·i·ot sa·vants,** *Fr.* **id·i·ots sa·vants** (ē dyō sa väɴ/). *Psychiatry.* a mentally defective person with a highly developed special talent, as an ability to play music, to solve complex mathematical problems mentally at great speed, etc. [< F: lit., a learned idiot]

id/iot's delight/, *Slang.* any variety of the card game solitaire.

-idium, a diminutive suffix, corresponding to **-idion,** used in zoological, biological, botanical, anatomical, and chemical terms: *peridium.* [< L < Gk *-idion* -IDION]

i·dle (īd/əl), *adj.,* **i·dler, i·dlest,** *v.,* **i·dled, i·dling,** *n.* —*adj.* **1.** not working or active; unemployed; doing nothing: *idle workmen.* **2.** not spent or filled with activity: *idle hours.* **3.** not in use or operation; not kept busy: *idle machinery.* **4.** habitually doing nothing or avoiding work; lazy. **5.** of no real worth, importance, or significance: *idle talk.* **6.** having no basis or reason; baseless; groundless: *idle fears.* **7.** frivolous; vain: *idle pleasures.* **8.** futile; ineffective: *idle threats.* **9.** useless: *idle rage.* **10.** *Mach.* noting a gear, wheel, or pulley serving only as a means of transmitting power from another idle part or a power source to a mechanism being driven. —*v.i.* **11.** to pass time in idleness. **12.** to move, loiter, or saunter idly: *to idle along the avenue.* **13.** (of a machine or mechanism) to operate without doing useful work, usually at minimum speed. —*v.t.* **14.** to pass (time) in idleness (often fol. by *away*): *to idle away the afternoon.* **15.** to cause (a person) to be idle: *The strike idled many workers.* —*n.* **16.** state or quality of being idle: *The motor was kept at an idle.* [ME, OE *īdel;* c. G *eitel*] —**i/dle·ness,** *n.* —**i/dly,** *adv.*
—**Syn. 1.** sluggish. IDLE, INDOLENT, LAZY, SLOTHFUL apply to one who is not active. To be IDLE is to be inactive or not working at a job. The word is sometimes derogatory, but not always, since one may be relaxing temporarily or may be idle through necessity: *pleasantly idle on a vacation; to be idle because one is unemployed or because supplies are lacking.* The INDOLENT person is naturally disposed to avoid exertion: *indolent and slow in movement; an indolent and contented fisherman.* The LAZY person is averse to exertion or work, and esp. to continued application; the word is usually derogatory: *too lazy to earn a living; incurably lazy.* SLOTHFUL denotes a reprehensible unwillingness to do such work as is demanded of man: *so slothful as to be a burden on others.* **5.** worthless, trivial, trifling, useless, fruitless, vain, futile, ineffectual. **7.** wasteful. **12.** See **loiter. 14.** waste. —**Ant. 1.** busy, industrious. **5.** important.

i/dle gear/, a gear placed between a driving and a driven gear to transmit motion between them. Also called **i/dler gear/.**

i/dle pul/ley, *Mach.* a loose pulley made to press or rest on a belt in order to tighten or guide it. Also called **i/dler pul/ley, jockey pulley.**

i·dler (īd/lər), *n.* **1.** one who idles. **2.** *Mach.* an idle gear, wheel, or pulley. **3.** *Railroads.* an empty freight car placed under the projecting end of an object carried by and overhanging the end of another car, so that the latter can be connected with another part of the train. **4.** *Naut.* See **day man** (def. 2). [IDLE + -ER¹]

i·dlesse (īd/les), *n. Chiefly Literary.* idleness. [IDLE + *-esse,* as in *finesse*]

i/dle wheel/, *Mach.* **1.** a wheel for transmitting power and motion between a driving and a driven part, either by friction or by means of teeth. **2.** See **idle pulley.**

I, Idle wheel

I·dle·wild (īd/əl wīld/), *n.* former name of **John F. Kennedy International Airport.**

Id·mon (id/mən), *n. Class. Myth.* an Argonaut who was the son of Apollo and Cyrene.

I·do (ē/dō), *n.* a revised and simplified form of Esperanto, put forth in 1907. [< Esperanto: lit., offspring (of Esperanto), equiv. to *id-* (< Gk; see -IDES) + *-o* n. ending] —**I/do·ism,** *n.* —**I/do·ist,** *n.* —**I/do·is/tic,** *adj.*

i·do·crase (ī/də krās/, id/ə-), *n. Mineral.* vesuvianite. [< F < Gk *eîdo(s)* form + *krâs(is)* mixture]

i·dol (īd/əl), *n.* **1.** an image or other material object representing a deity to which religious worship is addressed. **2.** *Bible.* **a.** an image of a deity other than God. **b.** the deity itself. **3.** any person or thing devotedly or excessively admired: *His political idol was Roosevelt. That unshorn, quivering, crow-voiced bumpkin is the singing idol of the teenagers.* **4.** a mere image or semblance of something, visible but without substance, as a phantom. **5.** a figment of the mind; a fantasy. **6.** a false conception or notion; fallacy. [ME < LL *īdōl(um)* < Gk *eídōlon* image, idol, deriv. of *eîdos* shape]
—**Syn. 1.** See **image. 3.** favorite, darling, pet.

I·do·la (i dō/lə), *n.* a girl's given name.

i·dol·a·ter (ī dol/ə tər), *n.* **1.** Also, **idolist.** a worshiper of idols. **2.** a person who is a devoted or excessive admirer; devotee. Also, *referring to a woman,* **i·dol·a·tress** (ī dol/ə tris). [ME *idolatrer,* equiv. to *idolatr(ie)* IDOLATRY + *-er* -ER²; *-rer* > *-er* by dissimilation]

i·dol·a·trise (ī dol/ə trīz/), *v.t., v.i.,* **-trised, -tris·ing.** *Chiefly Brit.* idolatrize. —**i·dol/a·tris/er,** *n.*

i·dol·a·trize (ī dol/ə trīz/), *v.,* **-trized, -triz·ing.** —*v.t.* **1.** to idolize. —*v.i.* **2.** to worship idols. [IDOLATR(Y) + -IZE] —**i·dol/a·triz/er,** *n.*

i·dol·a·trous (ī dol/ə trəs), *adj.* **1.** of or pertaining to idolatry. **2.** worshiping idols. **3.** blindly adoring. **4.** *Obs.* used in or designed for idolatry: *an idolatrous temple.* [IDOLATR(Y) + -OUS] —**i·dol/a·trous·ly,** *adv.* —**i·dol/a·trous·ness,** *n.*

i·dol·a·try (ī dol/ə trē), *n., pl.* **-tries. 1.** the religious worship of idols. **2.** excessive or blind adoration, reverence, devotion, etc. [ME *idolatrie* < ML *īdōlatrīa,* LL *īdōlolatrīa* (by syncope) < New Testament Gk *eidōlolatreía.* See IDOL, -LATRY]

i·dol·ise (īd/əlīz/), *v.t., v.i.,* **-ised, -is·ing.** *Chiefly Brit.* idolize. —**i/dol·i·sa/tion,** *n.* —**i/dol·is/er,** *n.*

i·dol·ism (īd/əliz/əm), *n.* **1.** idolatry. **2.** idolizing. [IDOL + -ISM]

i·dol·ist (īd/əlist), *n.* idolater (def. 1). [IDOL + -IST]

i·dol·ize (īd/əlīz/), *v.,* **-ized, -iz·ing.** —*v.t.* **1.** to regard with blind adoration, devotion, etc. —*v.i.* **2.** to practice idolatry: *to idolize as did ancient Greece and Rome.* Also, *esp. Brit.,* **idolise.** [IDOL + -IZE] —**i/dol·i·za/tion,** *n.* —**i/dol·iz/er,** *n.*

i/dols of the cave/, fallacies resulting from prejudice or personal idiosyncrasy; biased thought.

i/dols of the mar/ket place/, 1. Also called **i/dols of the fo/rum.** fallacies resulting from such cultural factors as language or custom. **2.** popular and false notions catered to for commercial or moneymaking reasons.

i/dols of the the/ater, fallacies resulting from traditional beliefs and techniques.

i/dols of the tribe/, fallacies resulting from the nature of man or from man's social organization.

I·do·me·ne·o (ē/dô me nâ/ô; *It.* ē dô me ne/ô), *n.* an opera (1781) by Wolfgang Amadeus Mozart.

I·dom·e·neus (ī dom/ə nōōs/, -nyōōs/), *n. Class. Myth.* a Cretan king and one of the leaders of the Greeks in the Trojan War.

I·do·na (i dō/nə), *n.* a girl's given name.

I·do·ne·a (i dō/nē ə), *n.* a girl's given name, form of **Idona.**

i·do·ne·ous (ī dō/nē əs), *adj.* fit; suitable. [< L *idōneus*] —**i·do·ne·i·ty** (īd/ənē/i tē), **i·do/ne·ous·ness,** *n.*

I·do·the·a (i dō/thē ə), *n.* (in the *Odyssey*) a nymph who was the daughter of Proteus.

IDP, 1. See **integrated data processing. 2.** International Driving Permit.

I·dris I (ī/dris, ī drēs/), *(Mohammed Idris Senussi)* born 1890, king of Libya since 1951.

Id·u·mae·a (id/yŏŏ mē/ə), *n.* Greek name of **Edom.** Also, **Id/u·me/a.** —**Id/u·mae/an, Id/u·me/an,** *adj., n.*

I·dun (ē/thōōn), *n. Scand. Myth.* the goddess of spring and the wife of Bragi. She kept the apples by which the Aesir were rejuvenated. Also, **I·dun·a** (ē/thōō nə), **Ithun, Ithunn.**

i·dyll (īd/əl), *n.* **1.** a poem or prose composition, usually describing pastoral scenes or events or any charmingly simple episode, appealing incident, or the like. **2.** a simple descriptive or narrative piece in verse or prose. **3.** material suitable for an idyll. **4.** an episode or scene of idyllic charm. **5.** *Music.* a composition, usually instrumental, of a pastoral or sentimental character. Also, **i/dyl.** [< L *īdyl(lium)* < Gk *eidýllion* short pastoral poem, equiv. to *eîd(os)* form + *-yllion* dim. suffix]

i·dyl·lic (ī dil/ik), *adj.* **1.** suitable for or suggestive of an idyll; charmingly simple or poetic. **2.** of, pertaining to, or characteristic of an idyll. [IDYLL + -IC] —**i·dyl/li·cal·ly,** *adv.*

i·dyl·list (īd/əlist), *n.* a writer of idylls. Also, **i/dyl·ist.** [IDYLL + -IST]

I/dylls of the King/, The, a series of poems by Tennyson, based on Arthurian legend.

-ie, var. of **-y²,** used as a hypocristic suffix of nouns: *dearie; laddie; Willie.*

IE, Indo-European.

I.E., 1. Indo-European. **2.** Industrial Engineer.

i.e., that is. [< L *id est*]

I·e·da (ī ē/də), *n.* a girl's given name, form of **Aïda.**

I·e·lene (ī/ə lēn/), *n.* a girl's given name, form of **Helen.**

-iensis, var. of **-ensis.** [< L, equiv. to *-i-* -I- + *-ēnsis* -ESE]

Ie·per (ē/pər), *n.* Flemish name of **Ypres.**

-ier, var. of **-eer:** *brigadier; halberdier.* [unstressed: ME *-ier(e),* var. of *-yer(e),* equiv. to OE *-i-* v. stem ending + *-ere* -ER¹ (in some words < OF *-ier* < L *-ārius* -ARY); stressed: var. of -EER]

I·e·ya·su (ē/ye yä/sōō), *n.* Iyeyasu.

if (if), *conj.* **1.** in case that; granting or supposing that; on condition that: *Sing if you want to. Stay home if it rains. I'll go if he goes.* **2.** even though: *an enthusiastic if small audience.* **3.** whether: *He asked if I knew Spanish.* **4.** (used to introduce an exclamatory phrase): *If only Dad could see me now!* —*n.* **5.** a supposition; uncertain possibility: *The future is full of ifs.* **6.** a condition, requirement, or stipulation: *There are too many ifs in his agreement.* [ME, var. of *yif,* OE *gif, gef;* akin to Icel *ef* if, Goth *ibai* whether, OHG *iba* condition, stipulation]
—**Syn. 1, 2.** IF, PROVIDED, PROVIDING imply a condition on which something depends. IF is general. It may be used to indicate suppositions or hypothetical conditions (often involving doubt or uncertainty): *If you like, we can go straight home. If I had known, I wouldn't have gone.* IF may mean even though: *If I am wrong, you are not right.* It may mean whenever: *If I do not understand, I ask questions.* PROVIDED always indicates some stipulation: *I will subscribe ten dollars provided that you do, too. Provided he goes, we can go along.* PROVIDING means just in case some certain thing should happen: *Providing he should come, we must have extra supplies ready.*
—**Usage.** IF meaning WHETHER, as in *I haven't decided if I'll go,* is sometimes criticized, but the usage has been established in standard English for a long time.

if, See **intermediate frequency.**

IFC, 1. International Finance Corporation. **2.** International Fisheries Commission (U.S. and Canada). **3.** International Freighting Corporation.

IFF, *Mil.* Identification, Friend or Foe: any of various electronic systems for identifying friendly aircraft or ships by eliciting automatically the appropriate response to a signal.

iff, *Math.* if and only if.

if·fy (if/ē), *adj. Informal.* full of unresolved points or questions: *an iffy problem.* [IF + -Y¹]

I.F.L.W.U., International Fur and Leather Workers' Union.

If·ni (ēf/nē), *n.* a Spanish province on the NW coast of Africa. 50,000 (est. 1964); 741 sq. mi.

I.F.S., Irish Free State.

I·fu·gao (ē/fōō gou/), *n., pl.* **-gaos,** *(esp. collectively)* **-gao.** a member of a people inhabitating Luzon, in the Philippines.

-ify, var. of **-fy** after a consonant: *intensify.* [ME *-ifie(n)* < MF *-ifi(er)* < L *-ificāre,* equiv. to *-i-* -I- + *-ficāre* -FY]

I.G., 1. Indo-Germanic. **2.** Inspector General.

Ig·bo (ig/bō), *n., pl.* **-bos,** *(esp. collectively)* **-bo.** Ibo.

I·gerne (i gûrn/), *n. Arthurian Romance.* Igraine.

Igg·dra·sil (ig/drə sil), *n.* Yggdrasil. Also, **Ig/dra·sil.**

I·glau (ē/glou), *n.* German name of **Jihlava.**

ig·loo (ig/lōō), *n., pl.* **-loos. 1.** an Eskimo house, being a dome-shaped hut usually built of blocks of hard snow. **2.** an excavation made by a seal in the snow over its breathing hole in the ice. **3.** *Mil.* a dome-shaped building for the storage of rockets or other munitions. Also, **ig/lu.** [< Eskimo *ig(d)lu* house]

ign., 1. ignition. **2.** unknown. [< L *ignotus*]

Ig·nace (ig/nāts; *Fr.* ē nyAs/), *n.* a boy's given name.

Ig·na·cia (ig nā/shə), *n.* a girl's given name.

Ig·na·tia (ig nā/shə), *n.* a girl's given name, form of **Ignacia.**

Ig·na·tius (ig nā/shəs), *n.* **1. Saint** *(Ignatius Theophorus),* A.D. c40–107?, bishop of Antioch and Apostolic Father. **2. Saint** *(Nicetas),* A.D. 799?–878, patriarch of Constantinople 846–858, 867–878. **3.** a boy's given name.

Igna/tius of Loyo/la, Saint. See **Loyola, Saint Ignatius.**

ig·ne·ous (ig/nē əs), *adj.* **1.** *Geol.* produced under conditions involving intense heat, as rocks of volcanic origin or rocks crystallized from molten magma. **2.** of, pertaining to, or characteristic of fire. [< L *igneus,* equiv. to *ign(is)* fire + *-eus* -EOUS]

ig·nes·cent (ig nes/ənt), *Rare.* —*adj.* **1.** emitting sparks of fire, as certain stones when struck with steel. **2.** bursting into flame. —*n.* **3.** an ignescent substance. [< L *ignescent-* (s. of *ignescēns* catching fire, prp. of *ignescere*), equiv. to *ign(is)* fire + *-escent-* -ESCENT]

ig·nis fat·u·us (ig/nis fach/ōō əs), *pl.* **ig·nes fat·u·i** (ig/nēz fach/ōō ī/). **1.** Also called **friar's lantern, will-o'-the-wisp.** a flitting phosphorescent light seen at night, chiefly over marshy ground, and supposed to be due to spontaneous combustion of gas from decomposed organic matter. **2.** something deluding or misleading. [< ML: lit., foolish fire]

ig·nite (ig nīt/), *v.,* **-nit·ed, -nit·ing.** —*v.t.* **1.** to set on fire; kindle. **2.** *Chem.* to heat intensely; roast. —*v.i.* **3.**

to take fire; begin to burn. [< L *ignīt(us)* ignited, set on fire (ptp. of *ignīre*), equiv. to *ign(is)* fire + *-ītus* -ITE²] —**ig·nit/a·ble, ig·nit/i·ble,** *adj.* —**ig·nit/a·bil/i·ty, ig·nit/i·bil/i·ty,** *n.*
—**Syn. 1.** See **kindle.**

ig·nit·er (ig nī/tər), *n.* **1.** one who or that which ignites. **2.** *Electronics.* the carborundum rod used to initiate the discharge in an ignitron tube. [IGNITE + -ER¹]

ig·ni·tion (ig nish/ən), *n.* **1.** act or fact of igniting; state of being ignited. **2.** (in an internal-combustion engine) the process that ignites the fuel in the cylinder. **3.** a means or device for igniting. [< ML *ignitiōn-* (s. of *ignitiō*) a setting on fire. See IGNITE, -ION]

ig·ni·tron (ig nī/tron, ig/ni tron), *n.* *Electronics.* a cathode-arc vacuum tube for conducting current when the anode is positive, having a rod of carborundum projecting into a pool of mercury. [IGNI(TER + ELEC)TRON]

ig·no·ble (ig nō/bəl), *adj.* **1.** of low character, aims, etc.; mean; base. **2.** of low grade or quality; inferior. **3.** not noble; of humble birth or station. **4.** *Falconry.* noting any hawk with short wings that chases or rakes after the quarry. [late ME < L *ignōbil(is)* unknown, inglorious, equiv. to *i-* (var. of *in-* IN-) + OL *gnōbilis* NOBLE] —**ig/no·bil/i·ty, ig·no/ble·ness,** *n.* —**ig·no/bly,** *adv.*
—**Syn. 1.** degraded, dishonorable, ignominious, contemptible, vulgar. **3.** lowly, obscure, plebeian, peasant. —**Ant. 1.** honorable. **2.** superior.

ig·no·min·i·ous (ig/nə min/ē əs), *adj.* **1.** marked by or attended with ignominy; discreditable; humiliating: *an ignominious retreat.* **2.** bearing or deserving ignominy; contemptible. [late ME < L *ignōminiōs(us).* See IGNOMINY, -OUS] —**ig/no·min/i·ous·ly,** *adv.* —**ig/no·min/i·ous·ness,** *n.*
—**Syn. 1.** degrading, disgraceful, dishonorable, shameful. **2.** despicable, ignoble.

ig·no·min·y (ig/nə min/ē), *n., pl.* **-min·ies** for 2. **1.** disgrace; dishonor; public contempt. **2.** shameful or dishonorable quality or conduct or an instance of this. [< L *ignōminia,* equiv. to *ig-* (for *in-* IN-³, abstracted, by folk etymology, from *ignōbilis* IGNOBLE) + *nōmin-* (s. of *nōmen*) NAME + *-ia* -Y³]
—**Syn. 1.** disrepute, discredit, shame, obloquy, opprobrium, odium, abasement, scandal. See **disgrace.** —**Ant. 1.** credit, honor.

ig·no·ra·mus (ig/nə rā/məs, -ram/əs), *n., pl.* **-mus·es.** an ignorant person. [< legal L: we ignore (1st pers. pl. pres. indic. of *ignōrāre* to be ignorant of, IGNORE); hence name of an ignorant lawyer in the play *Ignoramus* (1615) by G. Ruggle, whence current sense]

ig·no·rance (ig/nər əns), *n.* state or fact of being ignorant; lack of knowledge, learning, information, etc. [ME *ignora(u)nce* < L *ignōrantia.* See IGNORE, -ANCE]

ig·no·rant (ig/nər ənt), *adj.* **1.** lacking in knowledge or training; unlearned. **2.** lacking knowledge or information as to a particular subject or fact. **3.** uninformed; unaware. **4.** due to or showing lack of knowledge or training: *an ignorant statement.* [ME *ignora(u)nt* < L *ignōrant-* (s. of *ignōrāns,* prp. of *ignōrāre*), equiv. to *ignōr-* (see IGNORE) + *-ant-* -ANT] —**ig/no·rant·ly,** *adv.* —**ig/no·rant·ness,** *n.*
—**Syn. 1.** uninstructed, untutored, untaught. IGNORANT, ILLITERATE, UNLETTERED, UNEDUCATED mean lacking in knowledge or in training. IGNORANT may mean knowing little or nothing, or it may mean uninformed about a particular subject: *An ignorant person can be dangerous. I confess I'm ignorant of mathematics.* ILLITERATE originally meant lacking a knowledge of literature or similar learning, but is specifically applied to one unable to read or write: *the illiterate voter; necessary training for illiterate soldiers.* UNLETTERED is a translation of the word ILLITERATE, but emphasizes the idea of being without knowledge of or love of literature: *unlettered though highly trained in science.* UNEDUCATED refers especially to lack of schooling or to lack of access to a body of knowledge equivalent to that learned in schools: *uneducated but highly intelligent.* **2.** unenlightened, nescient. —**Ant. 1.** literate. **2.** learned.

ig·no·ra·ti·o e·len·chi (ig/nə rā/shē ō/ i leng/kī), *Logic.* the fallacy of offering proof irrelevant to the proposition in question. [< L: lit., ignorance of the refutation; see ELENCHUS]

ig·nore (ig nōr/, -nôr/), *v.t.,* **-nored, -nor·ing. 1.** to refrain from noticing or recognizing: *to ignore another's remarks.* **2.** *Law.* (of a grand jury) to reject (a bill of indictment), as on the grounds of insufficient evidence. [< L *ignōr(āre)* (to) not know, disregard, equiv. to *ignōr-* (var. of *ignār-,* s. of *ignārus* ignorant of, unknown, equiv. to *i-* IN-³ + *gnār-* KNOW) + *-ā-* thematic vowel + *-re* inf. ending] —**ig·nor/a·ble,** *adj.* —**ig·nor/er,** *n.*
—**Syn. 1.** overlook; slight, disregard, neglect. —**Ant. 1.** notice, regard.

I-go (ē/gō/), *n.* go².

Ig·o·rot (ig/ə rōt/, ē/gə-), *n., pl.* **-rots,** (*esp. collectively*) **-rot.** a member of a people of the Malay stock in northern Luzon in the Philippines, comprising various tribes, some noted as head-hunters.

I·graine (i grān/), *n.* *Arthurian Romance.* the mother of King Arthur. Also, **Igerne, Ygerne.**

Iguana,
Iguana iguana
(Length to 6 ft.)

i·gua·na (i gwä/nə), *n.* any iguanid of the genus *Iguana,* esp. the edible, arboreal *I. iguana* of tropical America, that grows to a length of more than five feet. [< Sp < Arawak *iwana*]

i·gua·nid (i gwä/nid), *n.* **1.** any of numerous lizards of the family *Iguanidae,* found in the New World, Madagascar, and several islands of the South Pacific, comprising terrestrial, semiaquatic, and arboreal species. —*adj.* **2.** belonging or pertaining to the *Iguanidae.* [< NL *Iguanid(ae),* equiv. to *Iguan(a)* name of genus (see IGUANA) + *-idae* -ID²]

i·guan·o·don (i gwä/nə don/, i gwan/ə-), *n.* a herbivorous dinosaur of the genus *Iguanodon,* from the early Cretaceous period of Europe, that grew to a length of from 15 to 30 feet and walked erect on its hind feet. [< NL < Sp *iguan(a)* IGUANA + Gk *odōn* tooth]

I·guas·sú (ē/gwä sōō/), *n.* a river in S Brazil, flowing W to the Paraná River. 380 mi. long.

I/guassú/ Falls/, a waterfall on the Iguassú River, on the boundary between Brazil and Argentina. 210 ft. high. Also called **Victoria Falls.**

I.G.Y., International Geophysical Year.

IHD, See **International Hydrological Decade.**

ihp, See **indicated horsepower.** Also, **IHP, I.H.P., i.hp., i.h.p.**

ih·ram (ē räm/), *n.* the dress worn by Muslim pilgrims to Mecca, consisting of two white cotton cloths, one worn round the waist, the other over the left shoulder. [< Ar: prohibition]

IHS, 1. Jesus. [< LL < Gk *IHΣ,* short for *IHΣOYΣ* Jesus] **2.** Jesus Savior of Men. [< L *Iēsus Hominum Salvātor*] **3.** in this sign (the cross) shalt thou conquer. [< L *In Hōc Signō Vincēs*] **4.** in this (cross) is salvation. [< L *In Hōc Salūs*]

Ij (ī), *n.* IJssel.

ij·i·thad (ij/ē thäd/), *n.* *Islam.* personal opinion concerning a question of shari'ah. [< Ar: interpretation]

ij·ma (ij mä/), *n., pl.* **ij·ma·a** (ij mä/ə). *Islam.* the consensus of all believers concerning the rightness of a belief or practice. [< Ar: consensus]

IJs·sel (ī/səl), *n.* a river in the central Netherlands, flowing N to IJssel Lake: a branch of the Rhine River. 70 mi. long. Also, **IJ, Ij.**

IJs/sel Lake/, a lake in the NW Netherlands: created by diking of the Zuider Zee. 465 sq. mi. Dutch, **IJs·sel·meer** (ī/səl mār/).

I·ka·ri·a (i kâr/ē ə, ī kâr/-; *Gk.* ē/kä rē/ä), *n.* Icaria.

ike (īk), *n.* *Slang.* Iconoscope. [modeled on *mike* for *microphone*]

Ike (īk), *n.* **1.** See **Eisenhower, Dwight David. 2.** a boy's given name.

i·ke·ba·na (ē/ke bä/nä), *n.* *Japanese.* the art of arranging flowers, esp. arrangements suitable for decorative use in the home.

I·ke·da (ē ke/dä), *n.* **Ha·ya·to** (hä yä/tô), 1899–1965, Japanese statesman: prime minister 1960–64.

I·ke·ya-Se·ki (ē ke/yä se/kē), *n.* a comet discovered in 1965 and visible briefly in late October of that year: not due to reappear before the year 2465. [after Kaoru *Ikeya* and Tsutomu *Seki,* Japanese astronomers]

Ikh·na·ton (ik nät/ən), *n.* See **Amenhotep IV.** Also, **Akhnaton.**

i·kon (ī/kon), *n.* icon (defs. 1, 2).

Il, *Chem.* illinium.

il-¹, var. of **in-²** (by assimilation) before *l: illation.*

il-², var. of **in-³** (by assimilation) before *l: illogical.*

-il, var. of **-ile:** *civil.*

I·la (ī/lə), *n.* a girl's given name.

ILA, 1. International Law Association. **2.** International Longshoreman's Association. Also, **I. L. A.**

i·lang-i·lang (ē/läng ē/läng), *n.* ylang-ylang.

Il Bar·bie·re di Si·vi·glia (*It.* ēl bär bye/re dē sē vē/lyä). See **Barber of Seville.**

Il Cor·te·gia·no (*It.* ēl kôr/te jä/nô). See **Courtier, The.**

ile-, var. of **ileo-** before a vowel: *ileac.*

-ile, a suffix of adjectives expressing capability, susceptibility, liability, aptitude, etc.: *agile; docile; ductile; fragile; prehensile; volatile.* Also, **-il.** [< L *-ilis, -īlis*]

il·e·ac¹ (il/ē ak/), *adj.* of or pertaining to the ileum. [ILE- + -AC, on model of *iliac*]

il·e·ac² (il/ē ak/), *adj.* *Pathol.* of or pertaining to ileus. [ILE(US) + -AC, on model of *iliac*]

Île de France (ēl də fräns/), **1.** a former province in N France, including Paris and the region around it. **2.** former name of **Mauritius.**

Île de Pin·gouins, L' (*Fr.* lēl də pan gwan/). See **Penguin Island.**

Île du Dia·ble (ēl dy dyä/blə), French name of **Devil's Island.**

il·e·i·tis (il/ē ī/tis), *n.* *Pathol.* inflammation of the ileum. [ILE- + -ITIS]

I·lene (ī lēn/), *n.* a girl's given name, form of **Helen.**

ileo-, a combining form of **ileum:** *ileostomy.* Also, *esp. before a vowel,* **ile-.** [< NL]

il·e·o·ce·cal (il/ē ō sē/kəl), *adj.* *Anat.* of, pertaining to, or involving the ileum and cecum. [ILEO- + *cecal,* var. of CAECAL]

il·e·o·co·li·tis (il/ē ō kə lī/tis, -kō-), *n.* *Pathol.* inflammation of the mucous membrane of the ileum and colon. [ILEO- + COLITIS]

il·e·os·to·my (il/ē os/tə mē), *n., pl.* **-mies.** *Surg.* the formation of an artificial opening into the ileum, usually of a permanent or semipermanent nature. [ILEO- + -STOMY]

Îles Co·mores (ēl kô môr/), French name of **Comoro Islands.**

Îles du Sa·lut (ēl dy sa ly/), French name of **Safety Islands.**

Il·e·tin (il/i tin), *n.* *Pharm., Trademark.* insulin (def. 2).

il·e·um (il/ē əm), *n.* **1.** *Anat.* the third and lowest division of the small intestine, extending from the jejunum to the cecum. See diag. under **intestine. 2.** *Entomol.* the anterior portion of the hindgut of an insect. [< NL, LL *īleum,* var. of L *īle* gut; by transfer, loin, flank (usually in pl.: *īlia*)]

il·e·us (il/ē əs), *n.* *Pathol.* intestinal obstruction accompanied by severe colic and characterized by abdominal pain and vomiting. [< L: colic < Gk *eileós,* equiv. to *eile-* (s. of *eilein* to roll) + *-os* n. suffix]

i·lex¹ (ī/leks), *n.* See **holm oak.** [ME < L]

i·lex² (ī/leks), *n.* **1.** any tree or shrub of the genus *Ilex.* **2.** a holly. [< NL, L]

Il·ford (il/fərd), *n.* a city in SW Essex, in SE England, near London. 178,210 (1961).

I.L.G.W.U., International Ladies' Garment Workers' Union. Also, **ILGWU**

I·lhé·us (ē lye/ōōs), *n.* a seaport in E Brazil. 56,936 (1960).

Il·i·a (il/ē ə), *n.* *Rom. Legend.* the mother of Romulus and Remus, either identified with Rhea Silvia or believed to be the daughter of Aeneas and Lavinia.

il·i·ac (il/ē ak/), *adj.* of, pertaining to, or situated near the ilium. [< LL *īliac(us)* of the flank. See ILIUM, -AC]

il/iac ar/tery, *Anat.* **1.** Also called **common iliac artery.** either of two large arteries that conduct blood to the pelvis and the legs. **2.** Also called **external iliac artery.** the outer branch of an iliac artery that becomes the femoral artery. **3.** Also called **hypogastric artery, internal iliac artery.** the inner branch of an iliac artery that conducts blood to the gluteal region.

Il·i·ad (il/ē əd), *n.* **1.** (*italics*) a Greek epic poem describing the siege of Troy, ascribed to Homer. **2.** (*sometimes l.c.*) any similar poem; a long narrative. **3.** (*often l.c.*) a long series of woes, trials, etc. [< L *Iliad-* (s. of *Ilias*) < Gk, equiv. to *Ili(on)* Troy + *-ad-* -AD] —**Il·i·ad·ic** (il/ē ad/ik), adj.

ilio-, a combining form of **ilium:** *iliocostalis.* [< NL]

il·i·o·cos·ta·lis (il/ē ō ko stal/is), *n., pl.* **-cos·ta·les** (-ko stal/ēz). *Anat.* the lateral portion of the sacrospinalis, consisting of a group of muscles, whose action assists in keeping the trunk erect and in moving the trunk and neck sideways. [< NL; see ILIO-, COSTAL]

Il·i·on (il/ī ən), *n.* Greek name of ancient Troy.

I·li·o·ne (i lī/ə nē/, il/ī ō/nē), *n.* *Class. Myth.* the oldest daughter of Priam and Hecuba, and the wife of Polymnestor.

Il·i·o·ne·us (il/ī ō/nē əs, i lī/ə nōōs/, -nyōōs/), *n.* **1.** (in the *Aeneid*) a Trojan warrior who fled from Troy with Aeneas. **2.** (in the *Iliad*) a Trojan warrior who was brutally killed by Peneleus.

I·lis·a (i lis/ə), *n.* a girl's given name, form of **Elizabeth.**

Il·i·thy·ia (il/ə thī/yə, -thī/ə), *n.* *Class. Myth.* Eileithyia.

-ility, a combination of **-(i)le** and **-ity,** used to form abstract nouns from adjectives with stems in **-(i)le:** *agility; civility; ability.* [< F *-ilité* < L *-ilitās*]

il·i·um (il/ē əm), *n., pl.* **il·i·a** (il/ē ə). *Anat.* the broad, upper portion of either innominate bone. See diag. under **pelvis.** [< NL, special use of LL *īlium,* var. of L *īle* gut, flank, groin (usually in pl.: *īlia*)]

Il·i·um (il/ē əm), *n.* Latin name of ancient Troy.

ilk¹ (ilk), *n.* **1.** family, class, or kind: *he and all his ilk.* **2. of that ilk, a.** (in Scotland) of the same family name or place: *Ross of that ilk,* i.e., *Ross of Ross.* **b.** of the same class or kind. —*adj.* **3.** same. [ME *ilke,* OE *ilca* (pron.) the same, equiv. to demonstrative *i* (cf. Goth *is* he, L *is* that) + a form of LIKE¹]

ilk² (ilk), *Chiefly Scot.* —*pron.* **1.** each. —*adj.* **2.** each; every. [ME *ilk,* north var. of *ilch,* OE *ylc* (pron.) EACH]

il·ka (il/kə), *adj., pron.* *Chiefly Scot.* ilk². [orig. phrase *ilk a* each one. See ILK², A¹]

Il·ka (il/kə), *n.* a girl's given name.

ill (il), *adj.,* **worse, worst,** *n., adv.* —*adj.* **1.** of unsound physical or mental health; unwell; sick: *She felt ill, so her teacher sent her to the nurse.* **2.** evil; wicked; bad: *of ill repute.* **3.** objectionable; unsatisfactory; poor; faulty: *ill manners.* **4.** hostile; unkindly: *ill feeling.* **5.** unfavorable; adverse: *ill fortune.* **6.** of inferior worth or ability; unskillful; inexpert: *an ill example of scholarship.* **7. ill at ease,** uncomfortable; nervous: *They were ill at ease because they didn't speak the language.* —*n.* **8.** evil: *He did ill unto his brother. Ill befell him.* **9.** harm; injury. **10.** a disease; ailment. **11.** trouble; misfortune. **12.** *Archaic.* wickedness or sin. —*adv.* **13.** in an ill manner; wickedly. **14.** unsatisfactorily; poorly: *It ill befits a man to betray old friends.* **15.** in a hostile or unfriendly manner. **16.** unfavorably; unfortunately. **17.** with displeasure or offense. **18.** faultily; improperly. **19.** with difficulty or inconvenience; scarcely: *Buying a new car is an expense we can ill afford.* [ME *ill(e)* < Scand; cf. Icel *illr* ill, bad]
—**Syn. 1.** unhealthy, ailing, diseased, afflicted. ILL, SICK mean being in bad health, not being well. ILL is the more formal word. In the U.S. the two words are used practically interchangeably except that SICK is always used when the word modifies the following noun or is used as a collective noun: *He is very sick (ill) of a fever. He looks sick (ill). a sick person; a home for the sick.* There are certain phrases, also, in which SICK is used: *sick at heart; sick for home; It makes me sick.* In England, SICK is not interchangeable with ILL, but usually has the connotation of nausea; SICK, however, is used before nouns, as a collective and in set phrases, just as in the U.S.: *He is ill. She felt ill. He looks ill; a sick man.* **2.** wrong, iniquitous. See **bad¹. 8.** mischief. **9.** hurt, pain, affliction, misery. **10.** illness, affliction. **11.** calamity. **12.** depravity. **14.** badly. —**Ant. 1.** well, healthy. **2.** good.

I'll (īl), contraction of *I will* or *I shall.*

Ill., Illinois.

ill., 1. illustrated. **2.** illustration. **3.** illustrator. **4.** most illustrious. [< L *illustrissimus*]

ill-ad·vised (il/əd vīzd/), *adj.* acting or done without due consideration; imprudent: *an ill-advised remark.* —**ill-ad·vis·ed·ly** (il/əd vī/zid lē), *adv.*

il·la·mon (ē/lə mən), *n.* *Australian.* hielamon.

Il·lam·pu (ē yäm/pōō), *n.* a peak of Mount Sorata. Cf. **Sorata.**

ill-at-ease (il/ət ēz/), *adj.* uncomfortable; uneasy.

il·la·tion (i lā/shən), *n.* **1.** act of inferring. **2.** an inference; conclusion. [< LL *illātiōn-* (s. of *illātiō*) a carrying in, equiv. to L *illāt(us)* brought in, ptp. of *infere* (*il-* IL-¹ + *lātus* brought, var. of earlier **tlātus;* see TOLERATE) + *-iōn-* -ION]

il·la·tive (il/ə tiv, i lā/tiv), *adj.* **1.** of, pertaining to, or expressing illation; inferential: *an illative word such as "therefore."* **2.** *Gram.* noting a case, as in Finnish, whose distinctive function is to indicate place into or toward which. —*n.* **3.** *Gram.* the illative case. [< LL *illātīv(us),* equiv. to *illāt-* (see ILLATION) + *-īvus* -IVE] —**il/la·tive·ly,** *adv.*

il·laud·a·ble (i lô/də bəl), *adj.* unworthy of praise; not laudable. [< LL *illaudābil(is).* See IL-², LAUDABLE] —**il·laud/a·bly,** *adv.*

ill-be·ing (il/bē/ing), *n.* state or condition of lacking health, solvency, etc. [modeled on WELL-BEING]

ill-bod·ing (il/bō/ding), *adj.* foreboding evil; inauspicious; unlucky: *ill-boding stars.*

ill-bred (il/bred/), *adj.* showing lack of proper breeding; unmannerly; rude: *He remained serene in a houseful of ill-bred children.*

ill-con·di·tioned (il/kən dish/ənd), *adj.* in a surly or bad mood, state, etc. —**ill/-con·di/tioned·ness,** *n.*

ill-con·sid·ered (il/kən sid/ərd), *adj.* lacking thorough consideration; ill-suited; unwise.

ill-dis·posed (il/di spōzd/), *adj.* **1.** unfriendly, hostile, or unsympathetic, as toward another person, an idea, etc. **2.** having an objectionable disposition. [ME] —**ill-dis·pos·ed·ness** (il/di spō/zid nis, -spōzd/-), *n.*

Ille-et-Vi·laine (ēl e vē len/), *n.* a department in W France. 614,268 (1962); 2700 sq. mi. *Cap.:* Rennes.

il·le·gal (i lē′gəl), *adj.* not legal; contrary to existing statutes, regulations, etc.; unauthorized. [< ML *illēgāl(is).* See IL-[2], LEGAL] **—il·le′gal·ly,** *adv.*
—Syn. unlawful; illegitimate; illicit; unlicensed.

il·le·gal·ise (i lē′gə līz′), *v.t.*, **-ised, -is·ing.** *Chiefly Brit.* illegalize. **—il·le′gal·i·sa′tion,** *n.*

il·le·gal·i·ty (il′ē gal′i tē), *n., pl.* **-ties.** 1. illegal condition or quality; unlawfulness. 2. an illegal act. [< ML *illēgālitās.* See ILLEGAL, -ITY]

il·le·gal·ize (i lē′gə līz′), *v.t.*, **-ized, -iz·ing.** to make illegal: *They even wanted to illegalize smoking.* Also, *esp. Brit.*, **illegalise.** [ILLEGAL + -IZE] **—il·le′gal·i·za′tion,** *n.*

il·leg·i·ble (i lej′ə bəl), *adj.* not legible; impossible or hard to read or decipher: *This letter is completely illegible.* [IL-[2] + LEGIBLE] **—il·leg′i·bil′i·ty, il·leg′i·ble·ness,** *n.* **—il·leg′i·bly,** *adv.*

il·le·git·i·ma·cy (il′i jit′ə mə sē), *n., pl.* **-cies.** state or quality of being illegitimate. [ILLEGITIMA(TE) + -CY]

il·le·git·i·mate (*adj., n.* il′i jit′ə mit; *v.* il′i jit′ə māt′), *adj., v.*, **-mat·ed, -mat·ing,** *n.* **—adj.** 1. not legitimate; unlawful; illegal: *an illegitimate action.* 2. born of parents who are not married to each other; born out of wedlock: *an illegitimate child.* 3. irregular; not in good usage. 4. *Logic.* not in accordance with the principles of valid inference. 5. *Obs.* (formerly, in London) **a.** of or pertaining to stage plays in which musical numbers were inserted because of laws which gave only a few theaters the exclusive right to produce straight dramas. **b.** acting in or producing such productions. **—v.t.** 6. to declare illegitimate. **—n.** 7. a person recognized or looked upon as illegitimate; a bastard. [IL-[2] + LEGITIMATE] **—il′le·git′i·mate·ly,** *adv.* **—il′le·git′i·mate·ness,** *n.* **il′le·git′i·ma′tion,** *n.*

il·le·git·i·ma·tise (il′i jit′ə mə tīz′), *v.t.*, **-tised, -tis·ing.** *Chiefly Brit.* illegitimatize.

il·le·git·i·ma·tize (il′i jit′ə mə tīz′), *v.t.*, **-tized, -tiz·ing.** to make illegitimate; bastardize: *The decree illegitimatized his heirs.* [ILLEGITIMATE + -IZE]

ill′ fame′, bad repute or name.

ill-fat·ed (il′fā′tid), *adj.* 1. destined, as though by fate, to an unhappy or unfortunate end: *an ill-fated voyage.* 2. bringing bad fortune.

ill-fa·vored (il′fā′vərd), *adj.* 1. unpleasant in appearance; ugly: *an ill-favored child.* 2. offensive; unpleasant; objectionable. Also, *esp. Brit.*, **ill′-fa′voured.** **—ill′-fa′vored·ly;** *esp. Brit.*, **ill′-fa′voured·ly,** *adv.* **—ill′-fa′vored·ness;** *esp. Brit.*, **ill′-fa′voured·ness,** *n.*

ill-found·ed (il′foun′did), *adj.* based on weak evidence, illogical reasoning, or the like: *an ill-founded plea for mercy.*

ill-got·ten (il′got′ən), *adj.* acquired by evil or improper means: *ill-gotten gains.*

ill′ hu′mor, a disagreeable or surly mood. **—ill′-hu′mored;** *esp. Brit.*, **ill′-hu′moured,** *adj.* **—ill′-hu′mored·ly;** *esp. Brit.*, **ill′-hu′moured·ly,** *adv.* **—ill′-hu′mored·ness;** *esp. Brit.*, **ill′-hu′moured·ness,** *n.*

Il·li·a (ē yē′ä), *n.* **Ar·tu·ro** (är to͞o′rô), born 1900, Argentine physician and statesman: president since 1963.

il·lib·er·al (i lib′ər əl, i lib′rəl), *adj.* 1. narrow-minded; bigoted. 2. *Chiefly Literary.* without culture; unscholarly; vulgar. 3. *Rare.* not generous in giving; niggardly; stingy. [< L *illīberāl(is).* See IL-[2], LIBERAL] **—il·lib′er·al′i·ty, il·lib′er·al·ness, il·lib′er·al·ism,** *n.* **—il·lib′er·al·ly,** *adv.*

il·lib·er·al·ise (i lib′ər ə līz′), *v.t.*, **-ised, -is·ing.** *Chiefly Brit.* illiberalize.

il·lib·er·al·ize (i lib′ər ə līz′), *v.t.*, **-ized, -iz·ing.** to make illiberal. [ILLIBERAL + -IZE]

Il·li·chev (i li chôf′), *n.* **Le·o·nid F.** (le o nēt′). See **Ilyichev, Leonid F.**

il·lic·it (i lis′it), *adj.* not permitted or authorized; unlicensed; unlawful. [< L *illicit(us).* See IL-[2], LICIT] **—il·lic′it·ly,** *adv.* **—il·lic′it·ness,** *n.*

Il·li·ma·ni (ē′yē mä′nē), *n.* a mountain in W Bolivia, in the Andes, near La Paz. 21,188 ft.

il·lim·it·a·ble (i lim′i tə bəl), *adj.* not limitable; limitless; boundless. [IL-[2] + LIMITABLE] **—il·lim′it·a·bil′i·ty, il·lim′it·a·ble·ness,** *n.* **—il·lim′it·a·bly,** *adv.*

il·lin·i·um (i lin′ē əm), *n.* *Chem.* (formerly) promethium. *Symbol:* Il [named after ILLINOIS; see -IUM]

Il·li·noi·an (il′ə noi′ən), *n.* 1. the third stage of the glaciation of North America during the Pleistocene. Cf. **Riss.** 2. Illinoisan. **—adj.** 3. of or pertaining to the Illinoian stage. 4. Illinoisan. [ILLINOI(S) + -AN]

Il·li·nois (il′ə noi′, -noiz′), *n.* 1. a State in the central United States: a part of the Midwest. 10,081,158 (1960); 56,400 sq. mi. *Cap.:* Springfield. *Abbr.:* Ill. 2. a river flowing SW from NE Illinois to the Mississippi River: connected by a canal with Lake Michigan. 273 mi. long.

Il·li·nois (il′ə noi′, -noiz′), *n., pl.* **-nois** (-noi′, -noiz′). 1. a member of a confederacy of North American Indians of Algonquian stock, formerly occupying Illinois and adjoining regions westward. 2. the Algonquian language of the Illinois and Miami Indians. [< F < Algonquian; akin to Shawnee *hileni,* Fox *ineniwa* man (*n* < *l* by assimilation)]

Il·li·nois·an (il′ə noi′ən, -noi′zən), *n.* 1. a native or inhabitant of Illinois. **—adj.** 2. of or pertaining to Illinois or its inhabitants. Also, **Illinoian, Il′li·nois′i·an.** [ILLINOIS + -AN]

il·liq·uid (i lik′wid), *adj.* (of an asset) not readily convertible into cash; not liquid. [IL-[2] + LIQUID] **—il·liq′uid·ly,** *adv.*

il·lit·er·a·cy (i lit′ər ə sē), *n., pl.* **-cies** for 3. 1. lack of ability to read and write. 2. state of being illiterate; lack of education. 3. a mistake in writing or speaking, felt to be characteristic of an illiterate person: *a letter that was full of illiteracies.* [ILLITERA(TE) + -CY]

il·lit·er·ate (i lit′ər it), *adj.* 1. unable to read and write: *an illiterate tribe.* 2. lacking education. 3. showing lack of culture, esp. in language and literature. 4. displaying a marked lack of knowledge in a particular field: *He is musically illiterate.* **—n.** 5. an illiterate person. [< L *illiterāt(us)* unlettered. See IL-[2], LITERATE] **—il·lit′er·ate·ly,** *adv.* **—il·lit′er·ate·ness,** *n.*
—Syn. 1. See **ignorant.**

ill-judged (il′jujd′), *adj.* injudicious; unwise.

ill-kempt (il′kempt′), *adj.* unkempt.

ill-look·ing (il′lo͝ok′ing), *adj.* *Rare.* 1. ugly. 2. sinister.

ill-man·nered (il′man′ərd), *adj.* having bad manners; impolite; discourteous; rude. [ME] **—ill′-man′nered·ly,** *adv.* **—ill′-man′nered·ness,** *n.*
—Syn. coarse, uncouth, unpolished, crude, rough; uncivil.

ill′ na′ture, unkindly or unpleasant disposition.

ill-na·tured (il′nā′chərd), *adj.* having or showing an unkindly or unpleasant disposition. **—ill′-na′tured·ly,** *adv.* **—ill′-na′tured·ness,** *n.*
—Syn. cranky, petulant, sulky, crabbed, morose, dour, gloomy, sour, crusty, bitter. See **cross.** **—Ant.** kindly, amiable.

ill·ness (il′nis), *n.* 1. state of being ill; indisposition; sickness. 2. *Obs.* wickedness. [ILL + -NESS]

il·log·ic (i loj′ik), *n.* state or quality of being illogical; illogicality: *His speech was full of illogic.* [IL-[2] + LOGIC]

il·log·i·cal (i loj′i kəl), *adj.* not logical; contrary to or disregardful of the rules of logic; unreasoning. [IL-[2] + LOGICAL] **—il·log′i·cal·ness,** *n.* **—il·log′i·cal·ly,** *adv.*

il·log·i·cal·i·ty (i loj′i kal′i tē), *n., pl.* **-ties.** 1. illogic. 2. an example of illogic: *an argument notable for its illogicalities.* [ILLOGICAL + -ITY]

ill-o·mened (il′ō′mənd), *adj.* having or attended by bad omens; ill-starred.

ill-sort·ed (il′sôr′tid), *adj.* poorly arranged; badly matched.

ill-spent (il′spent′), *adj.* misspent; wasted.

ill-starred (il′stärd′), *adj.* 1. under the influence of an evil star; ill-fated; unlucky. 2. disastrous: *an ill-starred marriage.*

ill-suit·ed (il′so͞o′tid), *adj.* not suitable; inappropriate.

ill′ tem′per, bad or irritable disposition. **—ill′-tem′pered,** *adj.* **—ill′-tem′pered·ly,** *adv.* **—ill′-tem′pered·ness,** *n.*

illth (ilth), *n.* *Rare.* useless, worthless, or injurious consumer commodities. [ILL + -TH[1], modeled on *wealth*]

ill-timed (il′tīmd′), *adj.* badly timed; inopportune.

ill-treat (il′trēt′), *v.t.* to treat badly; maltreat. **—ill′-treat′ment,** *n.*

il·lume (i lo͞om′), *v.t.*, **-lumed, -lum·ing.** *Archaic.* to illuminate. [short for ILLUMINE]

il·lu·mi·na·ble (i lo͞o′mə nə bəl), *adj.* capable of being illuminated. [< L *illūminābil(is).* See ILLUMINE, -ABLE] **—il·lu′mi·na·bil′i·ty,** *n.*

il·lu·mi·nance (i lo͞o′mə nəns), *n.* *Optics.* illumination (def. 5). [ILLUMIN(ATE) + -ANCE]

il·lu·mi·nant (i lo͞o′mə nənt), *n.* an illuminating agent or material. [< L *illūminant-* (s. of *illūmināns* lighting up, prp. of *illūmināre*), equiv. to *illūmin-* ILLUMINE + *-ant-* -ANT]

il·lu·mi·nate (*v.* i lo͞o′mə nāt′; *adj., n.* i lo͞o′mə nit, -nāt′), *v.*, **-nat·ed, -nat·ing,** *adj., n.* **—v.t.** 1. to supply with light; light up. 2. to throw light on (a subject); make lucid or clear. 3. *Chiefly Brit.* to decorate with lights, as in celebration. 4. to enlighten, as with knowledge. 5. to make resplendent or illustrious: *A smile illuminated her face. His leadership illuminated the epoch.* 6. to decorate (a letter, page, manuscript, etc.) with color, gold, or the like. **—v.i.** 7. to display lights, as in celebration. 8. to become illuminated. **—adj.** 9. *Archaic.* illuminated. 10. *Obs.* enlightened. **—n.** 11. *Archaic.* a person who is or affects to be specially enlightened. [< L *illūmināt(us)* lighted up (ptp. of *illūmināre*). See ILLUMINE, -ATE[1]] **—il·lu′mi·nat′ing·ly,** *adv.*

il·lu·mi·na·ti (i lo͞o′mə nā′tī, -nä′tē), *n.pl., sing.* **-to** (-tō). 1. persons possessing, or claiming to possess, superior enlightenment. 2. (*cap.*) a name given to different religious societies or sects because of their claim to enlightenment. [< L, pl. of *illūminātus* enlightened; see ILLUMINATE]

il·lu·mi·nat·ing (i lo͞o′mə nā′ting), *adj.* 1. that gives or casts light. 2. that informs or makes clear; enlightening. [ILLUMINATE + -ING[2]]

il·lu·mi·na·tion (i lo͞o′mə nā′shən), *n.* 1. act of illuminating. 2. fact or condition of being illuminated. 3. *Chiefly Brit.* **a.** a decoration of lights, usually colored lights. **b.** Usually, **illuminations.** a gala occasion or celebration using lights for decoration: *the illuminations at Blackpool.* 4. intellectual or spiritual enlightenment. 5. Also called **illuminance, intensity of illumination.** *Optics.* the intensity of light falling at a given place on a lighted surface; the luminous flux incident per unit area, expressed in lumens per unit of area. 6. a supply of light: *a source of illumination.* 7. decoration, as of a letter, page, or manuscript, with a painted design in color, gold, etc. [ME < eccl. L *illūminātiōn-* (s. of *illūminātiō*) spiritual enlightenment. See ILLUMINATE, -ION] **—il·lu′mi·na′tion·al,** *adj.*

Il·lu·mi·na·tions, Les (*Fr.* lā zē ly mē nä syôN′). See **Les Illuminations.**

il·lu·mi·na·tive (i lo͞o′mə nā′tiv, -nə tiv), *adj.* giving light; illuminating. [ILLUMINATE + -IVE]

il·lu·mi·na·tor (i lo͞o′mə nā′tər), *n.* 1. one who or that which illuminates. 2. a device for illuminating, as a light source with lens or a mirror for concentrating light. 3. a person who paints manuscripts, books, etc., with designs in color, gold, or the like. [late ME < LL; see ILLUMINATE, -OR[2]]

il·lu·mine (i lo͞o′min), *v.t., v.i.*, **-mined, -min·ing.** to illuminate. [ME < L *illūmin(āre)* (to) light up, equiv. to *il-* IL-[1] + *lūmin-* (s. of *lūmen*) light + *-ā-* thematic vowel + *-re* inf. suffix] **—il·lu′mi·na·ble,** *adj.*

il·lu·mi·nism (i lo͞o′mə niz′əm), *n.* 1. the doctrines or claims of Illuminati. 2. a doctrine advocating enlightenment. [ILLUMIN(ATI) + -ISM] **—il·lu′mi·nist,** *n.*

il·lu·mi·nom·e·ter (i lo͞o′mə nom′i tər), *n.* an instrument for measuring illumination. [ILLUMIN(ATION) + -O- + -METER]

illus., 1. illustrated. 2. illustration.

ill-use (*v.* il′yo͞oz′; *n.* il′yo͞os′), *v.*, **-used, -us·ing,** *n.* **—v.t.** 1. to treat badly, unjustly, cruelly, etc. **—n.** 2. Also, **ill′-us′age.** bad, unjust, or cruel treatment.

il·lu·sion (i lo͞o′zhən), *n.* 1. something that deceives by producing a false impression. 2. state or condition of being deceived; misapprehension. 3. an instance of being deceived. 4. *Psychol.* a perception that represents what is perceived in a way different from the way it is in reality. 5. a very thin, delicate tulle of silk or nylon having a cobwebbed appearance, for trimmings, veilings, and the like. 6. *Obs.* act of deceiving; deception; delusion; mockery. [ME < L *illūsiōn-* (s. of *illūsiō*) irony, mocking, equiv. to *illūs(us)* mocked, ridiculed (ptp. of *illūdere*) (*il-* IL-[1] + *lūd-* play (see LUDICROUS) + *-tus* ptp. suffix) + *-iōn-* -ION] **—il·lu′sioned,** *adj.*

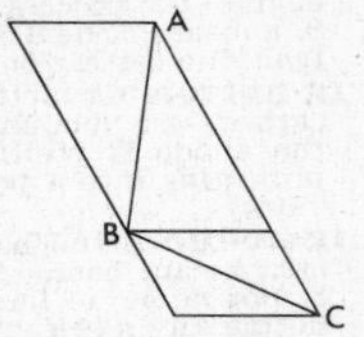

Optical illusion
Line AB equals
line BC

—Syn. 1. aberration, fantasy, chimera. ILLUSION, DELUSION, HALLUCINATION refer to mental deceptions which arise from various causes. An ILLUSION is a false mental image or conception which may be a misinterpretation of a real appearance or may be something imagined. It may be pleasing, harmless, or even useful: *A mirage is an illusion. He had an illusion that the doorman was a general.* A DELUSION is a fixed mistaken conception of something which really exists, and is not capable of correction or removal by examination or reasoning. DELUSIONS are often mischievous or harmful, as those of a fanatic or a lunatic: *the delusion that all food is poisoned.* A HALLUCINATION is a completely groundless false conception, belief, or opinion, caused by a disordered imagination; it is particularly frequent today in the pathological sense, according to which it denotes hearing or seeing something that does not exist: *hallucinations caused by nervous disorders.*

il·lu·sion·ar·y (i lo͞o′zhə ner′ē), *adj.* of, pertaining to, or characterized by illusions: *anticipated sales that were largely illusionary.* Also, **il·lu′sion·al.** [ILLUSION + -ARY]

il·lu·sion·ism (i lo͞o′zhə niz′əm), *n.* 1. *Philos.* a theory or doctrine that the material world is an illusion. 2. a technique of using pictorial methods in order to deceive the eye. Cf. **trompe l'oeil.** [ILLUSION + -ISM]

il·lu·sion·ist (i lo͞o′zhə nist), *n.* 1. a person subject to illusions. 2. a conjurer or magician who creates illusions, as by sleight of hand. 3. an adherent of illusionism. [ILLUSION + -IST]

il·lu·sion·is·tic (i lo͞o′zhə nis′tik), *adj.* of, pertaining to, or characterized by the technique or theory of illusionism. [ILLUSION + -ISTIC]

il·lu·sive (i lo͞o′siv), *adj.* illusory. [ILLUS(ORY) + -IVE] **—il·lu′sive·ly,** *adv.* **—il·lu′sive·ness,** *n.*

il·lu·so·ry (i lo͞o′sə rē, -zə-), *adj.* 1. causing illusion; deceptive. 2. of the nature of an illusion; unreal. [< LL *illūsōri(us),* equiv. to *illūsōr-* (s. of *illūsor*) mocker, deceiver (*illūs(us)* mocked (see ILLUSION) + *-or* -OR[2]) + *-ius* adj. suffix; see -ORY[1]] **—il·lu′so·ri·ly,** *adv.* **—il·lu′so·ri·ness,** *n.*
—Syn. 1. misleading, fallacious, specious, false. 2. imaginary; visionary, fancied.

illust., 1. illustrated. 2. illustration.

il·lus·trate (il′ə strāt′, i lus′trāt), *v.*, **-trat·ed, -trat·ing.** **—v.t.** 1. to make clear or intelligible, as by examples; exemplify. 2. to furnish (a book, magazine, etc.) with drawings or pictorial representations intended for elucidation or adornment. 3. *Archaic.* to enlighten. **—v.i.** 4. to clarify with examples: *To prevent misunderstandings, let me illustrate.* [< L *illustrāt(us)* made bright or clear, honored (ptp. of *illustrāre*). See IL-[1], LUSTER[1], -ATE[1]] **—il′lus·trat′a·ble,** *adj.*

il·lus·trat·ed (il′ə strā′tid), *adj.* 1. containing illustrations: *an illustrated article; an illustrated weekly.* **—n.** 2. *Brit.* a magazine or newspaper regularly containing many photographs or drawings. [ILLUSTRATE + -ED[2]]

il·lus·tra·tion (il′ə strā′shən), *n.* 1. that which illustrates, as a picture in a book, magazine, etc. 2. a comparison or an example intended for explanation or corroboration. 3. act of rendering clear; explanation; elucidation. 4. *Rare.* illustriousness; distinction. [ME < eccl. L *illustrātiōn-* (s. of *illustrātiō*) spiritual enlightenment. See ILLUSTRATE, -ION]
—Syn. 2. See **case**[1]. 2. explication.

il·lus·tra·tion·al (il′ə strā′shə nəl), *adj.* 1. of, pertaining to, or characteristic of illustrations: *illustrational art.* 2. used for purposes of illustration; serving to illustrate; illustrative: *illustrational material.* [ILLUSTRATION + -AL[1]]

il·lus·tra·tive (i lus′trə tiv, il′ə strā′tiv), *adj.* serving to illustrate: *illustrative examples.* [ILLUSTRATE + -IVE] **—il·lus′tra·tive·ly,** *adv.*

il·lus·tra·tor (il′ə strā′tər, i lus′trā tər), *n.* 1. an artist who makes illustrations. 2. one who or that which illustrates. [< LL; see ILLUSTRATE, -OR[2]]

il·lus·tri·ous (i lus′trē əs), *adj.* 1. highly distinguished; renowned; famous: *the illustrious leader of the French people.* 2. glorious, as deeds, works, etc. 3. *Obs.* luminous; bright. [< L *illustri(s)* bright, clear, famous, equiv. to *illustr(āre)* (to) brighten (see IL-[1], LUSTER[1]) + *-i(s)* adj. suffix + -OUS] **—il·lus′tri·ous·ly,** *adv.* **—il·lus′tri·ous·ness,** *n.*
—Syn. 1. celebrated, eminent, famed.

il·lu·vi·al (i lo͞o′vē əl, i lo͞ov′yəl), *adj.* of or pertaining to illuviation or illuvium. [< L *illuvi(ēs)* mud, flood, lit., what washes or is washed in (*il-* IL-[1] + *-luvi-* wash + *-ēs* n. suffix) + -AL[1]; see ALLUVIAL]

il·lu·vi·ate (i lo͞o′vē āt′), *v.i.*, **-at·ed, -at·ing.** 1. to undergo illuviation. 2. to produce illuviation. [< L *illuvi(ēs)* mud (see ILLUVIAL) + -ATE[1]]

il·lu·vi·a·tion (i lo͞o′vē ā′shən), *n.* the accumulation in one layer of soil of materials that have been leached out of another layer. [ILLUVI(AL) + -ATION]

il·lu·vi·um (i lo͞o′vē əm), *n., pl.* **-vi·ums, -vi·a** (-vē ə). the material accumulated through illuviation. [< NL; see IL-[1], ALLUVIUM]

ill′ will′, hostile feeling; antipathy; enmity: *to harbor ill will against someone.* [ME] —**ill-willed** (il′wild′), *adj.*
—**Syn.** hatred, hostility, animosity, unfriendliness. —**Ant.** benevolence.

ill-wish·er (il′wish′ər), *n.* one who wishes misfortune to another.

il·ly (il′ē, il′lē), *adv.* ill. [ILL + -LY]

Il·lyr·i·a (i lēr′ē ə), *n.* an ancient country along the E coast of the Adriatic.

Il·lyr·i·an (i lēr′ē ən), *adj.* **1.** of or pertaining to Illyria. —*n.* **2.** a native or inhabitant of Illyria. **3.** the extinct language of the Illyrians, an Indo-European language of uncertain relationship within the Indo-European language family. [ILLYRI(A) + -AN]

Il·lyr·i·cum (i lēr′ə kəm), *n.* a Roman province in ancient Illyria.

Il·lyr·i·us (i lēr′ē əs), *n.* *Class. Myth.* a son of Cadmus.

Il·ma·ri·nen (ēl′mä rē′nən), *n.* *Finnish Legend.* one of the heroes of the *Kalevala,* a smith who first forged the Sampo for Louhi and then stole it from her with the help of Vainamoinen and Lemminkainen.

il·men·ite (il′mə nīt′), *n.* a very common black mineral, iron titanate, $FeTiO_3$, occurring in crystals but more commonly massive. [named after *Ilmen,* mountain range in Urals, Russia; see -ITE[1]]

ILO, See **International Labor Organization.** Also, **I.L.O.**

I·lo·ca·no (ē′lō kä′nō), *n., pl.* **-nos,** (*esp. collectively*) **-no. 1.** a member of a people of Luzon in the Philippines. **2.** the Malayo-Polynesian, Indonesian language of the Ilocano. Also, **Ilokano.** [< Sp, equiv. to *iloc-* (< Tagalog *ilog* river) + *-ano* -AN]

I·lo·i·lo (ē′lō ē′lō), *n.* a seaport on S Panay, in the central Philippines. 137,476 (est. 1960).

I·lo·ka·no (ē′lō kä′nō), *n., pl.* **-nos,** (*esp. collectively*) **-no.** Ilocano.

I·lo·na (i lō′nə), *n.* a girl's given name, form of **Helen.** Also, **I·lo′ne.**

I·lo·ty·cin (ī′lō tī′sin), *n.* *Pharm., Trademark.* erythromycin (def. 1).

I.L.P., Independent Labour Party.

Il Pen·se·ro·so (il pen′sə rō′sō; *It.* ēl pen′se rô′sô), a poem (1632) by John Milton. Cf. **L'Allegro.**

ILS, *Aeron.* instrument landing system.

Il·se (il′sə), *n.* a girl's given name, form of **Elizabeth.**

Il·se·dore (il′si dôr′, -dōr′), *n.* a girl's given name.

Il Tro·va·to·re (il trō′və tôr′ē; *It.* ēl trô′vä tô′re), an opera (1853) by Giuseppe Verdi.

I.L.W.U., International Longshoremen's and Warehousemen's Union.

Il·ya (il′yə), *n.* a girl's given name.

Il·yi·chev (il yi chôf′), *n.* **Le·o·nid F.** (le o nēt′), born 1906, Russian journalist and government official: member of the Presidium since 1961. Also, **Illichev.**

I'm (īm), contraction of *I am.*

im-[1], var. of **in-**[2] before *b, m, p: imbrute; immingle; impassion.*

im-[2], var. of **in-**[3] before *b, m, p: imbalance; immoral; imperishable.*

im-[3], var. of **in-**[1] before *b, m, p: imbed; immure; impose.*

-im, a plural ending occurring in loan words from Hebrew: *cherubim.*

I.M., Isle of Man.

I·ma (ī′mə), *n.* a girl's given name.

im·age (im′ij), *n., v.,* **-aged, -ag·ing.** —*n.* **1.** a physical likeness or representation of a person, animal, or thing, photographed, painted, sculptured, or otherwise made visible. **2.** an optical counterpart or appearance of an object, such as is produced by reflection from a mirror, refraction by a lens, or the passage of luminous rays through a small aperture and their reception on a surface. **3.** a mental representation; idea; conception. **4.** *Psychol.* a mental representation of something previously perceived, in the absence of the original stimulus. **5.** form; appearance; semblance: *God created man in his own image.* **6.** counterpart; copy: *That child is the image of his mother.* **7.** a symbol; emblem. **8.** a type; embodiment: *Red-faced, he was the image of frustration and consternation.* **9.** a description of something in speech or writing: *Casually, almost effortlessly, he created some of the most beautiful images in the language.* **10.** an idol: *They knelt down before graven images.* **11.** *Rhet.* a figure of speech, esp. a metaphor or a simile: *With adroit turns of phrase the author created images as vivid as their presence itself.* **12.** *Math.* the point or set of points in the range corresponding to a designated point in the domain of a given function. **13.** *Archaic.* an illusion or apparition. —*v.t.* **14.** to picture or represent in the mind; imagine; conceive. **15.** to make an image of; portray in sculpture, painting, etc. **16.** to set forth in speech or writing; describe. **17.** to reflect the likeness of; mirror. **18.** to project (photographs, film, etc.) on a surface: *Familiar scenes were imaged on the screen.* **19.** to symbolize; typify. **20.** to resemble. [ME < OF, var. of *imagene* (appar. taken as base + suffix by folk etymology) < L *imāgin(em),* acc. of *imāgō* a copy, likeness; see IMITATE] —**im′age·a·ble,** *adj.* —**im′ag·er,** *n.*
—**Syn. 1, 10.** IMAGE, ICON, IDOL refer to material representations of persons or things. An IMAGE is a representation as in a statue or effigy, and is sometimes regarded as an object of worship: *to set up an image of Apollo; an image of a saint.* An ICON, in the Greek or Orthodox Eastern Church, is a representation of Christ, an angel, or a saint, in painting, relief, mosaic, or the like: *At least two icons are found in each church.* Small icons are also carried by the peasants; these are folded tablets of wood or metal, with representations of sacred subjects in enamel or in designs of black and white or silver: *An icon is honored by offerings of incense and lights.* An IDOL is an image, statue, or the like representing a deity and worshiped as such: *a wooden idol; The heathen worship idols.* And it may be used figuratively: *to make an idol of wealth.* **2.** likeness, figure, representation. **3.** notion. **6.** facsimile. —**Ant. 6.** original.

im′age dissec′tor, a form of television camera tube in which an electron image produced by a photoemitting surface is focused in the plane of an aperture and deflected past the aperture to achieve scanning. Also called **dissector tube.**

im·age·ry (im′ij rē, im′ij ə rē), *n., pl.* **-ries. 1.** the formation of mental images, figures, or likenesses of things, or of such images collectively: *a dream's dim imagery.* **2.** *Psychol.* mental images collectively, esp. those produced by the action of imagination. **3.** pictorial images. **4.** the use of rhetorical images. **5.** figurative description or illustration; rhetorical images collectively. [ME *imagerie* < MF. See IMAGE, -ERY] —**im·a·ge·ri·al** (im′ə jēr′ē əl), *adj.* —**im′a·ge′ri·al·ly,** *adv.*

im′age tube′. See **camera tube.**

im·ag·i·na·ble (i maj′ə nə bəl), *adj.* capable of being imagined or conceived. [ME < LL *imāginābil(is),* equiv. to L *imāginā(rī)* (to) IMAGINE + *-bilis* -BLE] —**i·mag′i·na·ble·ness,** *n.* —**i·mag′i·na·bly,** *adv.*

im·ag·i·nal (i maj′ə nəl), *adj.* *Entomol.* **1.** of or pertaining to an imago. **2.** having the form of an imago. [< LL *imāginal(is),* equiv. to *imāgin-* (s. of *imāgō*) IMAGE + *-ālis* -AL[1]]

im·ag·i·nar·y (i maj′ə ner′ē), *adj., n., pl.* **-ries.** —*adj.* **1.** existing only in the imagination or fancy; not real; fancied: *an imaginary illness.* —*n.* **2.** *Math.* See **imaginary number.** [ME < L *imāgināri(us),* equiv. to *imāgin-* (s. of *imāgō*) IMAGE + *-ārius* -ARY] —**i·mag′i·nar′i·ly,** *adv.* —**i·mag′i·nar′i·ness,** *n.*
—**Syn. 1.** fanciful, visionary, shadowy, chimerical, baseless, illusory. —**Ant. 1.** real.

imag′inary ax′is, *Math.* the vertical axis in an Argand diagram.

imag′inary num′ber, *Math.* **1.** the imaginary part of a complex number. **2.** Also called **pure imaginary number.** a complex number having its real part equal to zero. Also called **imaginary.**

im·ag·i·na·tion (i maj′ə nā′shən), *n.* **1.** the action of imagining, or of forming mental images or concepts of what is not actually present to the senses. **2.** the faculty of forming such images or concepts. **3.** *Psychol.* the power of reproducing images stored in the memory under the suggestion of associated images (**reproductive imagination**) or of recombining former experiences in the creation of new images directed at a specific goal or aiding in the solution of problems (**creative imagination**). **4.** the faculty of producing ideal creations consistent with reality, as in literature, as distinct from the power of creating illustrative or decorative imagery. Cf. **fancy** (def. 2). **5.** the product of imagining; a conception or mental creation, often a baseless or fanciful one. **6.** ability to meet and resolve difficulties; resourcefulness: *to solve business problems with imagination; a job that requires imagination.* **7.** (in Kantian epistemology) synthesis of data from the sensory manifold into objects by means of the categories. **8.** *Archaic.* a plan, scheme, or plot. [ME < L *imāginātiōn-* (s. of *imāginātiō*) fancy, equiv. to *imāgināt(us)* imagined, ptp. of *imāginārī* to IMAGINE (*imāgin-,* s. of *imāgō* IMAGE + *-ātus* -ATE[1]) + *-iōn-* -ION] —**i·mag′i·na′tion·al,** *adj.*
—**Syn. 4.** See **fancy.**

im·ag·i·na·tive (i maj′ə nə tiv, -nā′tiv), *adj.* **1.** characterized by or bearing evidence of imagination: *an imaginative tale.* **2.** of, pertaining to, or concerned with imagination. **3.** given to imagining, as persons. **4.** having exceptional powers of imagination. **5.** lacking truth; fanciful. [ME < LL *imāginātīv(us),* equiv. to L *imāgināt(us)* imagined (see IMAGINATION) + *-īvus* -IVE; r. ME *imaginatif* < MF] —**i·mag·i·na·tive·ly** (i maj′ə nə tiv lē, -nā′tiv-), *adv.* —**i·mag·i·na·tive·ness** (i maj′ə nə tiv nis, -nā′tiv-), *n.*

im·ag·ine (i maj′in), *v.,* **-ined, -in·ing.** —*v.t.* **1.** to form a mental image of (something not actually present to the senses). **2.** to think; believe; fancy. **3.** to assume; suppose. **4.** to conjecture; guess: *I cannot imagine whom you mean.* **5.** *Archaic.* to plan, scheme, or plot. —*v.i.* **6.** to form mental images of things not present to the senses; use the imagination. **7.** to suppose; think; conjecture. [ME *imagine(n)* < L *imāgin(ārī),* equiv. to *imāgin-* (s. of *imāgō*) IMAGE + *-ā-* thematic vowel + *-rī* inf. ending] —**i·mag′in·er,** *n.*
—**Syn. 1.** image, picture. IMAGINE, CONCEIVE, CONCEIVE OF, REALIZE refer to bringing something before the mind. To IMAGINE is, literally, to form a mental image of something: *to imagine yourself in London.* To CONCEIVE is to relate ideas or feelings to one another in a pattern: *How has the author conceived the first act of his play?* To CONCEIVE OF is to comprehend through the intellect something not perceived through the senses: *Wilson conceived of a world free from war.* To REALIZE is to make an imagined thing real or concrete to oneself, to grasp fully its implications: *to realize the extent of one's folly.*

im·ag·ism (im′ə jiz′əm), *n.* *Literature.* **1.** (*often cap.*) a theory or practice of a group of poets in England and America between 1909 and 1917 who believed that poetry should employ the language of common speech, create new rhythms, have complete freedom in subject matter, and present a clear, concentrated, and precise image. **2.** a style of poetry which employs free verse and the patterns and rhythms of common speech. [IMAGE + -ISM] —**im′ag·ist,** *n., adj.* —**im′ag·is′tic,** *adj.* —**im′ag·is′ti·cal·ly,** *adv.*

i·ma·go (i mā′gō), *n., pl.* **im·a·goes, i·ma·gi·nes** (i-maj′ə nēz′). **1.** *Entomol.* an adult insect. **2.** *Psychoanal.* an idealized concept of a loved one, formed in childhood and retained uncorrected in adult life. [< NL, L; see IMAGE]

i·mam (i mäm′), *n.* *Islam.* **1.** the officiating priest of a mosque. **2.** the title for a Muslim religious leader or chief. **3.** one of a succession of seven or twelve religious leaders, believed to be divinely inspired, of the Shiites. Also, **i·maum** (i mäm′, i mōm′). [< Ar *imām* leader, guide] —**i·mam′ship,** *n.*

i·mam·ate (i mä′māt), *n.* **1.** the office of an imam. **2.** the region or territory governed by an imam. [IMAM + -ATE[1]]

i·mam·ba·rah (i mäm′bä′rä), *n.* *Islam.* (in India) a building in which religious festivals are celebrated. [see IMARET]

I·mam·ite (i mä′mīt), *n.* *Islam.* a member of the principal sect of Shiah, believing in a succession of 12 divinely inspired imams, beginning with Ali and ending with Muhammad al-Muntazar (d. A.D. c880), who supposedly retired to a cave, later to return as the Mahdi. Also called **Twelver.** [IMAM + ITE[1]]

i·ma·ret (i mä′ret), *n.* (in Turkey) a hospice for pilgrims, travelers, etc. [< Turk < Ar *'imārah* building]

im·bal·ance (im bal′əns), *n.* **1.** state or condition of lacking balance. **2.** faulty muscular or glandular coordination. [IM-[2] + BALANCE]

im·balm (im bäm′), *v.t.* *Obs.* embalm. —**im·balm′er,** *n.* —**im·balm′ment,** *n.*

im·bark (im bärk′), *v.t., v.i.* *Obs.* embark. —**im′barka′tion, im·bark′ment,** *n.*

im·be·cile (im′bi sil, -səl *or, esp. Brit.,* -sēl′), *n.* **1.** a person of defective mentality, above the level of idiocy; one lacking the capacity to develop beyond a mental age of seven or eight years. —*adj.* **2.** mentally feeble. **3.** showing mental feebleness or incapacity. **4.** silly; absurd. **5.** *Rare.* weak or feeble. [earlier *imbecill* < L *imbēcill(us)* weak; *-ile* r. *-ill* by confusion with suffix -ILE] —**im′be·cile·ly,** *adv.*

im·be·cil·ic (im′bi sil′ik), *adj.* **1.** of, pertaining to, or characteristic of an imbecile. **2.** contemptibly silly or inappropriate: *an imbecilic suggestion.* [IMBECILE + -IC]
—**Syn. 2.** idiotic, stupid, asinine.

im·be·cil·i·ty (im′bi sil′i tē), *n., pl.* **-ties. 1.** feebleness of mind; mentality somewhat above that of idiocy. **2.** an instance or point of weakness; feebleness; incapability. **3.** silliness; absurdity. **4.** an instance of this. [earlier *imbecillity* < L *imbēcillitās.* See IMBECILE, -ITY]

im·bed (im bed′), *v.t.,* **-bed·ded, -bed·ding.** embed.

im·bibe (im bīb′), *v.,* **-bibed, -bib·ing.** —*v.t.* **1.** to consume (liquids) by drinking; drink: *He imbibed great quantities of tea.* **2.** to absorb or soak up, as water, light, heat, etc.: *The sponge imbibes water. Plants imbibe moisture from the soil.* **3.** to take or receive into the mind, as knowledge, ideas, or the like: *to imbibe a sermon; to imbibe beautiful scenery.* —*v.i.* **4.** to drink; absorb liquid or moisture: *A toast was offered before the guests imbibed.* **5.** *Obs.* to soak or saturate; imbue. [< L *imbibe(re)* (to) drink in, equiv. to *im-* IM-[1] + *bibere* to drink; r. ME *enbiben* < MF *embib(er)* < L, as above] —**im·bib′er,** *n.*
—**Syn. 1.** swallow. See **drink.**

im·bi·bi·tion (im′bi bish′ən), *n.* **1.** act of imbibing. **2.** *Physical Chem.* the absorption of solvent by a gel. **3.** *Photog.* (in color printing) absorption of dye by gelatin, as in the dye-transfer process. [late ME; see IMBIBE, -ITION] —**im′bi·bi′tion·al,** *adj.*

im·bit·ter (im bit′ər), *v.t.* embitter. —**im·bit′ter·er,** *n.* —**im·bit′ter·ment,** *n.*

im·bod·y (im bod′ē), *v.t.,* **-bod·ied, -bod·y·ing.** embody. —**im·bod′i·ment,** *n.*

im·bold·en (im bōl′dən), *v.t.* embolden.

im·bos·om (im bŏŏz′əm, -bōō′zəm), *v.t.* embosom.

im·bow·er (im bou′ər), *v.t., v.i.* embower.

im·brac·er·y (im brā′sə rē), *n., pl.* **-er·ies.** *Law.* embracery.

im·bran·gle (im brang′gəl), *v.t.,* **-gled, -gling.** embrangle.

im·brex (im′breks, -briks), *n., pl.* **-bri·ces** (-bri sēz′, -bri kās′). **1.** a convex tile, used esp. in ancient Rome to cover joints in a tile roof. **2.** *Archit.* one of the scales in ornamental imbrication. [< L, equiv. to *imbr-* (s. of *imber*) rainstorm; akin to Gk *ómbros* shower + *-ex* n. suffix]

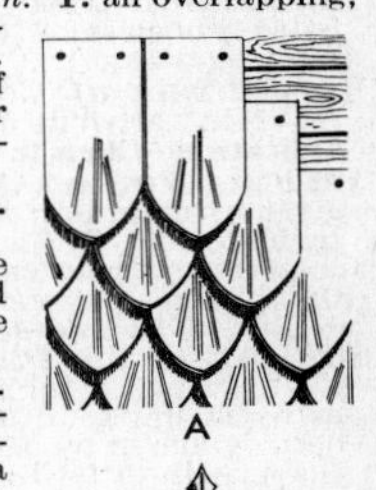

Imbricate
A, Flower bud
B, Scale of cone

im·bri·cate (*adj.* im′brə kit, -kāt′; *v.* im′brə kāt′), *adj., v.,* **-cat·ed, -cat·ing.** —*adj.* **1.** overlapping in sequence, as tiles or shingles on a roof. **2.** of, pertaining to, or resembling overlapping tiles, as decoration, drawings, etc. **3.** *Biol.* overlapping like tiles, as scales, leaves, etc. **4.** characterized by or as by overlapping shingles. —*v.t., v.i.* **5.** to overlap, as tiles or shingles. [< LL *imbricāt(us)* tiled with imbrices, shaped like such a tile or tiling (ptp. of *imbricāre,* equiv. to *imbric-* (s. of *imbrex*) IMBREX + *-ātus* -ATE[1]] —**im′bri·cate·ly,** *adv.* —**im′bri·ca′tive,** *adj.*

im·bri·ca·tion (im′brə kā′shən), *n.* **1.** an overlapping, as of tiles or shingles. **2.** a decoration or pattern resembling this. **3.** *Surg.* overlapping of layers of tissue in the closure of wounds or in the correction of defects. [IMBRICATE + -ION]

Im·bri·um (im′brē əm), *n.* **Mare.** See **Mare Imbrium.**

Im·bri·us (im′brē əs), *n.* (in the *Iliad*) a son of Mentor who joined the Trojans in the war against the Greeks and was slain by Teucer.

im·bro·glio (im brōl′yō), *n., pl.* **-glios. 1.** an intricate and perplexing state of affairs; a complicated or difficult situation. **2.** a misunderstanding, disagreement, etc., of a complicated or bitter nature, as between persons or nations. **3.** a confused heap. [< It, deriv. of *imbrogliāre* to EMBROIL]

im·brown (im broun′), *v.t., v.i.* embrown.

im·brue (im brōō′), *v.t.,* **-brued, -bru·ing. 1.** to drench in or with something that stains, esp. blood; to stain with blood: *He refused to imbrue his hands with the blood of more killing.* **2.** to impregnate or imbue (usually fol. by *with* or *in*): *They are imbrued with the follies of youth.* Also, **embrue.** [ME *enbrewe(n)* < MF *embreuv(er)* (to) cause to drink in, soak, drench < VL **imbiberāre;* see IMBIBE] —**im·brue′ment,** *n.*

im·brute (im brōōt′), *v.t., v.i.,* **-brut·ed, -brut·ing.** to degrade or sink to the level of a brute. Also, **embrute.** [IM-[1] + BRUTE] —**im·brute′ment,** *n.*

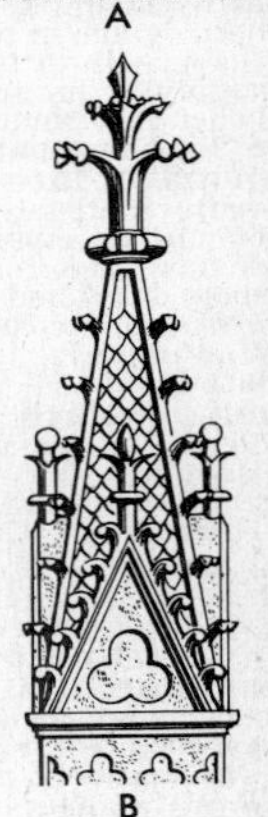

A, Imbrication of roof tiles;
B, Ornamental imbrication on pinnacle

im·bue (im byōō′), *v.t.,* **-bued, -bu·ing. 1.** to impregnate or inspire, as with feelings, opinions, etc.: *The scholar was imbued with the teachings of the ancient philosophers.* **2.** to saturate or impregnate with moisture, color, etc. **3.** to imbrue. [< L *imbue(re)* (to) wet, steep, soak] —**im·bue′ment,** *n.*
—**Syn. 1.** charge, infect, fire. **2.** permeate, infuse, tincture, soak.

IMCO, Inter-Governmental Maritime Consultive Organization.

IMF, International Monetary Fund. Also, **I.M.F.**

im·id·az·ole (im′id az′ōl, -id ə zōl′), *n. Chem.* a colorless, crystalline, water-soluble, heterocyclic compound, $C_3H_4N_2$, used chiefly in organic synthesis. Also called **glyoxaline.** [IMID(E) + AZOLE]

im·ide (im′īd, im′id), *n. Chem.* a compound derived from ammonia by replacement of two hydrogen atoms by acidic groups, characterized by the =NH group. [alter. of AMIDE] —**i·mid·ic** (i mid′ik), *adj.*

im·i·do (im′i dō′), *adj. Chem.* containing the imido group. [independent use of IMIDO-]

imido-, a combining form of **imide:** *imidogen.*

i·mid·o·gen (i mid′ə jen′, i mē′də-), *n.* the imino group, esp. in an uncombined state. [IMIDO- + -GEN]

im′ido group′, *Chem.* **1.** the bivalent group, =NH, linked to one or two acid groups. **2.** (erroneously) imino. Also called **im′ido rad′ical.**

i·mine (i mēn′, im′in), *n. Chem.* a compound containing the =NH group united with a nonacid group. [alter. of AMINE]

im·i·no (im′ə nō′), *adj. Chem.* containing the imino group. [independent use of IMINO-]

imino-, a combining form of **imine:** *iminourea.*

im′ino group′, *Chem.* the bivalent group, =NH, not linked to any acid group. Also called **im′ino rad′ical.** Cf. **imido.**

i·mi·no·u·re·a (i mē′nō yŏŏ rē′ə, i mē′nō yŏŏr′ē ə, im′ə nō yŏŏ-, im′ə nō yŏŏr′-), *n. Chem.* guanidine. [IMINO- + UREA]

imit., **1.** imitation. **2.** imitative.

im·i·ta·ble (im′i tə bəl), *adj.* capable of being imitated. [< L *imitābil(is)*, equiv. to *imitā(rī)* (to) imitate + *-bilis* -BLE] —**im′i·ta·bil′i·ty, im′i·ta·ble·ness,** *n.*

im·i·tate (im′i tāt′), *v.t.*, **-tat·ed, -tat·ing.** **1.** to follow or endeavor to follow in action or manner. **2.** to copy; mimic; counterfeit. **3.** to make a copy of; reproduce closely. **4.** to have or assume the appearance of; simulate. [< L *imitāt(us)* copied, ptp. of *imitārī*; see IMAGE] —**im′i·ta′tor,** *n.*
—**Syn. 2.** ape, mock, impersonate; simulate. **3.** IMITATE, COPY, DUPLICATE, REPRODUCE all mean to follow or try to follow an example or pattern. IMITATE is the general word for the idea: *to imitate someone's handwriting, behavior.* To COPY is to make a fairly exact imitation of an original creation: *to copy a sentence, a dress, a picture.* To DUPLICATE is to produce something which exactly resembles or corresponds to something else; both may be originals: *to duplicate the terms of two contracts.* To REPRODUCE is to make a likeness or reconstruction of an original: *to reproduce a 16th-century theater.*

im·i·ta·tion (im′i tā′shən), *n.* **1.** a result or product of imitating. **2.** act of imitating. **3.** *Sociol.* the copying of patterns of activity and thought of other groups or individuals. **4.** *Biol.* close external resemblance of an organism to some other organism or to objects in its environment. **5.** *Psychol.* the performance of an act whose stimulus is the observation of the act performed by another person. **6.** a counterfeit; copy. **7.** a literary composition that imitates the manner or subject of another author or work. **8.** *Art.* **a.** (in Aristotelian aesthetics) the representation of an object or an action as it ought to be. **b.** the representation of actuality in art or literature. **9.** *Music.* the repetition of a melodic phrase at a different pitch or key from the original or in a different voice part. —*adj.* **10.** designed to imitate a genuine or superior article or thing: *imitation leather.* **11.** *Jewelry.* noting an artificial gem no part of which is of the true gemstone. Cf. **assembled, synthetic** (def. 5). [< L *imitātiōn-* (s. of *imitātiō*). See IMITATE, -ION] —**im′i·ta′tion·al,** *adj.*

im′ita′tion dou′blet, *Jewelry.* **1.** a doublet formed entirely of glass. **2.** an imitation gem made from a single piece of glass.

Im′ita′tion of Christ′, The, a religious work (1417–21) attributed to Thomas à Kempis. Latin, **De Imitatione Christi.**

im·i·ta·tive (im′i tā′tiv), *adj.* **1.** imitating; copying; given to imitation. **2.** of, pertaining to, or characterized by imitation. **3.** *Biol.* mimetic. **4.** made in imitation of something; counterfeit. **5.** onomatopoeic. [< LL *imitātīv(us)*. See IMITATE, -IVE] —**im′i·ta′tive·ly,** *adv.* —**im′i·ta′tive·ness,** *n.*

im′itative mag′ic, magic that attempts to control the universe through the mimicking of a desired event, as by stabbing an image of an enemy in an effort to destroy him or by performing a ritual dance imitative of the growth of food in an effort to secure an abundant supply; a branch of sympathetic magic based on the belief that similar actions produce similar results. Also called **homeopathic magic.** Cf. **contagious magic.**

im·mac·u·late (i mak′yə lit), *adj.* **1.** free from spot or stain; spotlessly clean, as linen. **2.** free from moral blemish or impurity; pure; undefiled. **3.** free from fault or flaw; free from errors, as a text. **4.** *Biol.* having no spots or colored marks; unicolor. [ME *immaculat* < L *immaculāt(us)* unspotted. See IM-², MACULATE] —**im·mac′u·la·cy, im·mac′u·late·ness,** *n.* —**im·mac′u·late·ly,** *adv.*

Immac′ulate Concep′tion, *Rom. Cath. Ch.* the dogma of the unique privilege by which the Virgin Mary was conceived in her mother's womb without the stain of original sin through the anticipated merits of Jesus Christ. Cf. **virgin birth** (def. 1).

Immac′ulate Heart′, *Rom. Cath. Ch.* the physical heart of the Virgin Mary to which veneration is paid as a symbol of her charity, virtues, and role as mediatress of divine grace subordinately to Jesus Christ.

im·mane (i mān′), *adj. Archaic.* **1.** vast in size; enormous. **2.** inhumanly cruel. [< L *immān(is)*, lit., not good, equiv. to *im-* IM-² + *mānis* good; see MANES] —**im·mane′ly,** *adv.* —**im·mane′ness,** *n.*

im·ma·nent (im′ə nənt), *adj.* **1.** remaining within; indwelling; inherent. **2.** *Philos.* (of a mental act) taking place within the mind of the subject and having no effect outside of it. Cf. **transeunt. 3.** *Theol.* (of the Deity) indwelling the universe, time, etc. Cf. **transcendent** (def. 3). [< LL *immanent-* (s. of *immanēns*) staying in, (prp. of *immanēre*), equiv. to *im-* IM-¹ + *man-* stay + *-ent-* -ENT; see REMAIN] —**im′ma·nence, im′ma·nen·cy,** *n.* —**im′ma·nent·ly,** *adv.*

Im·man·u·el (i man′yŏŏ əl), *n.* **1.** the name of the Messiah as prophesied by Isaiah, often represented in Christian exegesis as being Jesus Christ. Isa. 7:14. **2.** a boy's given name. Also, **Emmanuel.** [< Heb *'immānū'el* God with us]

im·ma·te·ri·al (im′ə tēr′ē əl), *adj.* **1.** of no essential consequence; unimportant. **2.** not material; incorporeal; spiritual. [ME < ML *immāteriāl(is)*. See IM-², MATERIAL] —**im′ma·te′ri·al·ly,** *adv.* —**im′ma·te′ri·al·ness,** *n.*

im·ma·te·ri·al·ise (im′ə tēr′ē ə līz′), *v.t.*, **-ised, -is·ing.** *Chiefly Brit.* immaterialize.

im·ma·te·ri·al·ism (im′ə tēr′ē ə liz′əm), *n.* **1.** the doctrine that there is no material world, but that all things exist only in and for minds. **2.** the doctrine that only immaterial substances or spiritual beings exist. [IMMATERIAL + -ISM, modeled on *materialism*] —**im′ma·te′ri·al·ist,** *n.*

im·ma·te·ri·al·i·ty (im′ə tēr′ē al′i tē), *n., pl.* **-ties. 1.** state or character of being immaterial. **2.** something immaterial. [IMMATERIAL + -ITY]

im·ma·te·ri·al·ize (im′ə tēr′ē ə līz′), *v.t.*, **-ized, -iz·ing.** to make immaterial. Also, *esp. Brit.*, **immaterialise.** [IMMATERIAL + -IZE]

im·ma·ture (im′ə tŏŏr′, -tyŏŏr′, -chŏŏr′), *adj.* **1.** not mature, ripe, developed, perfected, etc. **2.** *Phys. Geog.* youthful. **3.** *Archaic.* premature. [< L *immātūr(us)* unripe, hence, untimely. See IM-², MATURE] —**im′ma·ture′ly,** *adv.* —**im′ma·tu′ri·ty, im′ma·ture′ness,** *n.*

im·meas·ur·a·ble (i mezh′ər ə bəl), *adj.* incapable of being measured; limitless. [late ME *inmesurable.* See IN-³, MEASURABLE] —**im·meas′ur·a·bil′i·ty, im·meas′ur·a·ble·ness,** *n.* —**im·meas′ur·a·bly,** *adv.*

im·me·di·a·cy (i mē′dē ə sē), *n.* **1.** state, condition, or quality of being immediate. **2.** *Philos.* **a.** immediate presence of an object of knowledge to the mind, without any distortions, inferences, or interpretations, and without involvement of any intermediate agencies. **b.** the direct content of the mind as distinguished from representation or cognition. [IMMEDIA(TE) + -CY]

im·me·di·ate (i mē′dē it), *adj.* **1.** occurring or accomplished without delay; instant: *an immediate reply.* **2.** of or pertaining to the present time or moment: *our immediate plans.* **3.** following without a lapse of time: *the immediate future.* **4.** having no object or space intervening; nearest or next: *in the immediate vicinity.* **5.** without intervening medium or agent; direct: *an immediate cause.* **6.** having a direct bearing: *immediate consideration.* **7.** *Philos.* directly intuited. [< ML *immediāt(us)*. See IM-², MEDIATE] —**im·me′di·ate·ness,** *n.*
—**Syn. 1.** instantaneous. **4.** close, proximate. **5.** See **direct.**

imme′diate annu′ity, *Insurance.* an annuity bought with a single premium, with payments to the annuitant to begin at the end of one payment period, as a month or a year. Cf. **deferred annuity.**

imme′diate constit′uent, *Gram.* one of the usually two largest constituents of a construction: The immediate constituents of *He ate his dinner* are *he* and *ate his dinner;* of *ate his dinner* are *ate* and *his dinner;* etc. *Abbr.:* IC Cf. **ultimate constituent.**

im·me·di·ate·ly (i mē′dē it lē), *adv.* **1.** without lapse of time; without delay; instantly; at once. **2.** without intervening medium or agent; concerning or affecting directly. **3.** with no object or space intervening. **4.** closely: *immediately in the vicinity.* —*conj.* **5.** *Chiefly Brit.* immediately that; the moment that; as soon as. [late ME; see IMMEDIATE, -LY]
—**Syn. 1.** instantaneously, forthwith. IMMEDIATELY, DIRECTLY, INSTANTLY, PRESENTLY were originally close synonyms denoting complete absence of delay or of any lapse of time. INSTANTLY is the only one retaining the meaning of action or occurrence on the instant: *He replied instantly to the accusation.* It is never used with the future tense (which must suggest a slight delay). IMMEDIATELY may have the same force: *He immediately got up;* more often, a slight delay: *The game will begin immediately.* DIRECTLY is equivalent to soon or in a little while: *You go ahead, we'll be there directly.* PRESENTLY, which once meant at once, changed to mean soon or in a little while, and, although purists insist on clinging to the sense of soon, current usage equates it with at present: *The author presently lives in San Francisco.* The expressions which have supplanted them are *right away* and *at once* (which is still usually equivalent to immediately): *He will come right away. I want to see him at once.* **2.** closely. —**Ant. 1.** later.

im·me·di·a·tism (i mē′dē ə tiz′əm), *n. U.S. Hist.* a policy for the immediate abolition of slavery. [IMMEDIATE + -ISM] —**im·me′di·a·tist,** *n.*

im·med·i·ca·ble (i med′ə kə bəl), *adj.* incurable. [< L *immedicābil(is)* incurable. See IM-², MEDICABLE] —**im·med′i·ca·ble·ness,** *n.* —**im·med′i·ca·bly,** *adv.*

Im′mel·mann turn′ (im′əl män′, -mən), a maneuver in which an airplane makes a half loop, then resumes its normal, level position by making a half roll: used to gain altitude while turning to fly in the opposite direction. [named after Max *Immelmann*, German aviator in World War I]

im·me·mo·ri·al (im′ə mōr′ē əl, -môr′-), *adj.* extending back beyond memory, record, or knowledge: *from time immemorial.* [< ML *immemoriāl(is)*. See IM-², MEMORIAL] —**im′me·mo′ri·al·ly,** *adv.*

im·mense (i mens′), *adj.* **1.** vast; huge; very great: *an immense territory.* **2.** immeasurable; boundless. **3.** *Informal.* very good; fine; splendid: *You did an immense job getting the project started.* [late ME < L *immens(us)*, equiv. to *im-* IM-² + *mensus* measured (ptp. of *mētīrī*), equiv. to *ment-* ptp. s. + *-tus* ptp. suffix] —**im·mense′ly,** *adv.* —**im·mense′ness,** *n.*
—**Syn. 1.** extensive. See **huge.**

im·men·si·ty (i men′si tē), *n., pl.* **-ties** for 3. **1.** vastness; hugeness; enormous extent: *the immensity of the Roman empire.* **2.** state or condition of being immense; boundless extent; infinity. **3.** a vast expanse; an immense quantity. [late ME < L *immensitās.* See IMMENSE, -ITY]

im·men·su·ra·ble (i men′shŏŏ rə bəl, -sər ə-), *adj.* immeasurable. [< LL *immensurābil(is)*. See IM-², MENSURABLE] —**im·men′su·ra·bil′i·ty, im·men′su·ra·ble·ness,** *n.*

im·merge (i mûrj′), *v.*, **-merged, -merg·ing.** —*v.i.* **1.** to plunge, as into a fluid. **2.** to disappear by entering into any medium, as the moon into the shadow of the sun. —*v.t.* **3.** *Rare.* to immerse. [< L *immerge(re)* (to) dip, plunge, sink. See IM-¹, MERGE] —**im·mer′gence,** *n.*

im·merse (i mûrs′), *v.t.*, **-mersed, -mers·ing. 1.** to plunge into or place under a liquid; dip; sink. **2.** to baptize by immersion. **3.** to embed; bury. **4.** to involve deeply; absorb. [< L *immers(us)* dipped, plunged into (ptp. of *immergere*), equiv. to *im-* IM-¹ + *merg-* dip + *-tus* ptp. suffix] —**im·mers′i·ble,** *adj.*
—**Syn. 1.** immerge, duck, douse. See **dip. 4.** engage.
—**Ant. 3.** disinter.

im·mersed (i mûrst′), *adj.* **1.** plunged or sunk in or as in a liquid. **2.** *Biol.* somewhat or wholly sunk in the surrounding parts, as an organ. **3.** *Rare.* baptized. [IMMERSE + -ED²]

im·mer·sion (i mûr′zhən, -shən), *n.* **1.** act of immersing. **2.** state of being immersed. **3.** baptism in which the whole body of the person is submerged in the water. **4.** state of being deeply engaged; absorption. **5.** Also called **ingress.** *Astron.* the entrance of a heavenly body into an eclipse by another body, an occultation, or a transit. Cf. **emersion** (def. 1). [late ME < LL *immersiōn-* (s. of *immersiō*) a dipping in. See IMMERSE, -ION]

im·mer·sion·ism (i mûr′zhə niz′əm, -shə-), *n.* **1.** the doctrine that immersion is essential to Christian baptism. **2.** the practice of baptism by immersion. [IMMERSION + -ISM] —**im·mer′sion·ist,** *n.*

immer′sion scale′, *Naut.* a scale showing the depth to which a vessel will be immersed under various loads. Also called **draft scale.**

im·mesh (i mesh′), *v.t.* enmesh.

im·me·thod·i·cal (im′ə thod′i kəl), *adj.* not methodical; without method. [IM-² + METHODICAL] —**im′me·thod′i·cal·ly,** *adv.* —**im′me·thod′i·cal·ness,** *n.*

im·mi·grant (im′ə grənt), *n.* **1.** one who or that which immigrates. **2.** a person who migrates to a country for permanent residence. —*adj.* **3.** of or pertaining to immigrants and immigration: *a department for immigrant affairs.* **4.** immigrating. [< L *immigrant-* (s. of *immigrāns* moving into, prp. of *immigrāre*). See IM-¹, MIGRANT]

im·mi·grate (im′ə grāt′), *v.*, **-grat·ed, -grat·ing.** —*v.i.* **1.** to pass or come into a new habitat or place of residence. **2.** to come to a country of which one is not a native, for the purpose of permanent residence. —*v.t.* **3.** to introduce as settlers: *to immigrate cheap labor.* [< L *immigrāt(us)* removed, gone into (ptp. of *immigrāre*). See IM-¹, MIGRATE] —**im′mi·gra′tor,** *n.*
—**Syn. 1.** See **migrate.**

im·mi·gra·tion (im′ə grā′shən), *n.* **1.** act of immigrating. **2.** immigrants. [IM-¹ + MIGRATION] —**im′mi·gra′tion·al, im·mi·gra·to·ry** (im′ə grə tōr′ē, -tôr′ē), *adj.*

Immigra′tion and National′ity Act′. See **McCarran-Walter Act.**

im·mi·nence (im′ə nəns), *n.* **1.** Also, **im′mi·nen·cy.** state or condition of being imminent or impending: *imminence of war.* **2.** that which is imminent; impending evil or danger. [< LL *imminentia.* See IMMINENT, -ENCE]

im·mi·nent (im′ə nənt), *adj.* **1.** likely to occur at any moment; impending: *War is imminent.* **2.** projecting or leaning forward; overhanging. [< L *imminent-* (s. of *imminēns* overhanging, prp. of *imminēre*), equiv. to *im-* IM-¹ + *min-* overhang + *-ent-* -ENT] —**im′mi·nent·ly,** *adv.* —**im′mi·nent·ness,** *n.*
—**Syn. 1.** near, at hand. IMMINENT, IMPENDING, THREATENING apply to that which menaces or portends misfortune or disaster. IMMINENT is applied usually to danger or evil that hangs, as it were, over one's head, ready to fall at any moment: *Because of recent heavy rains, a flood was imminent.* IMPENDING is similarly used, but with less suggestion of immediateness: *A reform has been impending for some time.* THREATENING is applied loosely to that which indicates coming evil, or conveys some ominous or unfavorable suggestion: *threatening weather; a threatening sky; a threatening frown.* —**Ant. 1.** distant, remote.

im·min·gle (i ming′gəl), *v.t., v.i.*, **-gled, -gling.** to mingle in; intermingle. [IM-³ + MINGLE]

im·mis·ci·ble (i mis′ə bəl), *adj.* not miscible; incapable of being mixed. [IM-² + MISCIBLE] —**im·mis′ci·bil′i·ty,** *n.* —**im·mis′ci·bly,** *adv.*

im·mit·i·ga·ble (i mit′ə gə bəl), *adj.* not mitigable; not to be mitigated. [< LL *immitigābil(is)* that cannot be softened. See IM-², MITIGABLE] —**im·mit′i·ga·bil′i·ty,** *n.* —**im·mit′i·ga·bly,** *adv.*

im·mix (i miks′), *v.t.* to mix in; mingle. [back formation from ME *immixt(e)* mixed in < L *imixt(us)* blended (ptp. of *immiscēre*), equiv. to *im-* IM-¹ + *mix-* (see MIX) + *-tus* ptp. suffix]

im·mix·ture (i miks′chər), *n.* **1.** act of immixing. **2.** state of being immixed; involvement. [< L *immixt(us)* blended (see IMMIX) + -URE; see MIXTURE]

im·mo·bile (i mō′bil, -bēl), *adj.* **1.** not mobile; immovable. **2.** incapable of moving or being moved; motionless. [ME *inmobile* < L *immōbil(is)*. See IM-², MOBILE]

im·mo·bi·lise (i mō′bə līz′), *v.t.*, **-lised, -lis·ing.** *Chiefly Brit.* immobilize. —**im·mo′bi·li·sa′tion,** *n.*

im·mo·bil·i·ty (im′ō bil′i tē), *n.* quality or condition of being immobile or irremovable. [late ME < LL *immōbilitās.* See IM-², MOBILITY]

im·mo·bi·lize (i mō′bə līz′), *v.t.*, **-lized, -liz·ing. 1.** to make immobile; fix so as to be or become immovable. **2.** *Finance.* **a.** to establish a monetary reserve by withdrawing (specie) from circulation. **b.** to create fixed capital in place of (circulating capital). **3.** to deprive of the capacity for mobilization. Also, *esp. Brit.*, **immobilise.** [IMMOBILE + -IZE; see MOBILIZE and cf. F *immobiliser*] —**im·mo′bi·li·za′tion,** *n.*

im·mod·er·a·cy (i mod′ər ə sē), *n.* immoderation. [IMMODERA(TE) + -CY]

im·mod·er·ate (i mod′ər it), *adj.* **1.** not moderate; exceeding just or reasonable limits; excessive; extreme. **2.** *Obs.* intemperate. **3.** *Obs.* without bounds. [< L *immoderāt(us)*. See IM-², MODERATE] —**im·mod′er·ate·ly,** *adv.* —**im·mod′er·ate·ness,** *n.*
—**Syn. 1.** exorbitant, unreasonable; inordinate; extravagant. —**Ant.** reasonable.

im·mod·er·a·tion (i mod′ə rā′shən), *n.* lack of moderation. [< L *immoderātiōn-* (s. of *immoderātiō*). See IM-², MODERATION]

im·mod·est (i mod′ist), *adj.* **1.** not modest in conduct, utterance, etc.; indecent; shameless. **2.** not modest in assertion or pretension; forward; impudent. [< L *immodest(us)* unrestrained, immoderate. See IM-², MODEST] **—im·mod′est·ly,** *adv.* **—im·mod′es·ty,** *n.*

Im·mo·ka·lee (i mō′kə lē′), *n.* a town in S Florida. 3224 (1960).

im·mo·late (im′ə lāt′), *v.t.*, **-lat·ed, -lat·ing. 1.** to sacrifice. **2.** to kill as a sacrificial victim, as by fire; offer in sacrifice. [< L *immolāt(us)* sprinkled with holy grits, sacrificed (ptp. of *immolāre*), equiv. to *im-* IM-¹ + *mol(a)* grits (orig. millstone; see MILL¹) + *-ātus* -ATE¹; see IMMOLATION] **—im′mo·la′tor,** *n.*

im·mo·la·tion (im′ə lā′shən), *n.* **1.** act of immolating. **2.** state of being immolated. **3.** a sacrifice. [< L *immolātiōn-* (s. of *immolātiō*) a sprinkling with holy grits in the sacrificial ceremony, hence, a sacrifice. See IMMOLATE, -ION]

im·mor·al (i môr′əl, i mor′-), *adj.* not moral; not conforming to the patterns of conduct usually accepted or established as consistent with principles of personal and social ethics. [IM-² + MORAL] **—im·mor′al·ly,** *adv.*

—Syn. bad, wicked, licentious, dissolute, dissipated, profligate, self-indulgent. IMMORAL, ABANDONED, DEPRAVED describe one who makes no attempt to curb self-indulgence. IMMORAL, referring to conduct, applies to one who acts contrary to or does not obey or conform to standards of morality; it may also mean licentious and perhaps dissipated. ABANDONED, referring to condition, applies to one hopelessly, and usually passively, sunk in wickedness and unrestrained appetites. DEPRAVED, referring to character, applies to one who voluntarily seeks evil and viciousness. IMMORAL, AMORAL, NONMORAL, and UNMORAL are sometimes confused with one another. IMMORAL means not moral and connotes evil or licentious behavior. AMORAL, NONMORAL, and UNMORAL, virtually synonymous although the first is by far the most common form, mean utterly lacking in morals (either good or bad), neither moral nor immoral. However, since, in some contexts, there is a stigma implicit in a complete lack of morals, being amoral, nonmoral, or unmoral is sometimes considered equally as reprehensible as being immoral.

im·mor·al·ise (i môr′ə līz′, i mor′-), *v.t.*, **-ised, -is·ing.** *Chiefly Brit.* immoralize.

im·mor·al·ism (i môr′ə liz′əm, i mor′-), *n.* *Philos.* indifference toward or opposition to conventional morality. [IMMORAL + -ISM]

im·mor·al·ist (i môr′ə list, i mor′-), *n.* one who advocates or practices immorality. [IMMORAL + -IST]

Immoralist, The, a novel (1902) by André Gide. French, **L'Immoraliste.**

m·mo·ral·i·ty (im′ə ral′i tē, im′ô-), *n.*, *pl.* **-ties. 1.** immoral quality, character, or conduct; wickedness; evilness. **2.** sexual misconduct; unchastity or lewdness. **3.** an immoral act. [IMMORAL + -ITY]

im·mor·al·ize (i môr′ə līz′, i mor′-), *v.t.*, **-ized, -iz·ing.** to make or cause to be immoral. Also, *esp. Brit.,* **immoralise.** [IMMORAL + -IZE]

im·mor·tal (i môr′tᵊl), *adj.* **1.** not mortal; not liable or subject to death; undying. **2.** remembered or celebrated through all time. **3.** not liable to perish or decay; imperishable; everlasting. **4.** perpetual; lasting; constant: *an immortal enemy.* **5.** of or pertaining to immortal beings or immortality. **—***n.* **6.** an immortal being. **7.** a person, esp. an author, of enduring fame. **8. the Immortals,** the 40 members of the French Academy. **9.** (*often cap.*) any of the gods of classical mythology. [ME < L *immortāl(is).* See IM-², MORTAL] **—im·mor′tal·ly,** *adv.*

immor′tal hand′, *Poker Slang.* a hand that cannot be beaten.

im·mor·tal·ise (i môr′tᵊlīz′), *v.t.*, **-ised, -is·ing.** *Chiefly Brit.* immortalize. **—im·mor′tal·is′a·ble,** *adj.* **—im·mor′tal·i·sa′tion,** *n.* **—im·mor′tal·is′er,** *n.*

im·mor·tal·i·ty (im′ôr tal′i tē), *n.* **1.** immortal condition or quality; unending life. **2.** enduring fame. [ME *immortalite* < L *immortālitās.* See IMMORTAL, -ITY]

im·mor·tal·ize (i môr′tᵊlīz′), *v.t.*, **-ized, -iz·ing. 1.** to make immortal; endow with immortality. **2.** to bestow unending fame upon; perpetuate. Also, *esp. Brit.,* **immortalise.** [IMMORTAL + -IZE] **—im·mor′ta·liz′a·ble,** *adj.* **—im·mor′tal·i·za′tion,** *n.* **—im·mor′tal·iz′er,** *n.*

im·mor·telle (im′ôr tel′), *n.* an everlasting plant or flower, esp. *Xeranthemum annuum.* [< F, n. use of fem. of *immortel* IMMORTAL]

im·mo·tile (i mōt′ᵊl), *adj.* not able to move; not motile. [IM-² + MOTILE]

im·mov·a·ble (i mo͞o′və bəl), *adj.* **1.** incapable of being moved; fixed; stationary. **2.** not moving; motionless. **3.** not subject to change; unalterable. **4.** incapable of being affected with feeling; emotionless: *an immovable heart; an immovable tyrant.* **5.** incapable of being moved from one's purpose, opinion, etc.; steadfast; unyielding. **6.** not changing from one date to another in different years: *an immovable feast.* **7.** *Law.* **a.** not liable to be removed, or permanent in place. **b.** (of property) real, as distinguished from personal. **—***n.* **8.** something immovable. **9. immovables,** *Law.* lands and the appurtenances thereof, as trees, buildings, etc. Also, **im·move′a·ble.** [ME; see IM-², MOVABLE] **—im·mov′a·bil′i·ty, im·mov′a·ble·ness, im·move′a·bil′i·ty, im·move′a·ble·ness,** *n.* **—im·mov′a·bly, im·move′a·bly,** *adv.*

im·mune (i myo͞on′), *adj.* **1.** protected from a disease or the like, as by inoculation. **2.** exempt: *He was immune from the draft.* **—***n.* **3.** one who is immune. [ME < L *immūn(is)* exempt, equiv. to *im-* IM-² + *mūn(us)* office, duty, tax + *-is* adj. suffix]

immune′ bod′y, (formerly) an antibody.

immune′ se′rum, *Med.* a serum containing naturally or artificially produced antibodies, obtained from human or animal sources.

im·mu·nise (im′yə nīz′, i myo͞o′nīz), *v.t.*, **-nised, -nis·ing.** *Chiefly Brit.* immunize. **—im′mu·ni·sa′tion,** *n.* **—im′mu·nis′er,** *n.*

im·mu·ni·ty (i myo͞o′ni tē), *n.*, *pl.* **-ties. 1.** state of being immune from or insusceptible to a particular disease or the like. **2.** exemption from any natural or usual liability. **3.** exemption from obligation, service, duty, or liability to taxation, jurisdiction, etc. **4.** special privilege. **5.** *Eccles.* **a.** the exemption of ecclesiastical persons and things from secular or civil liabilities, duties, and burdens. **b.** a particular exemption of this kind. [ME *immunite* < L *immūnitās.* See IMMUNE, -ITY]

—Syn. 2. See **exemption. 3.** franchise, license, liberty, prerogative. **—Ant. 1.** susceptibility.

im·mu·nize (im′yə nīz′, i myo͞o′nīz), *v.t.*, **-nized, -niz·ing. 1.** to make immune. **2.** to render harmless or ineffective; neutralize: *to immunize a belligerent; immunize a land mine.* Also, *esp. Brit.,* **immunise.** [IMMUNE + -IZE] **—im′mu·ni·za′tion,** *n.* **—im′mu·niz′er,** *n.*

immuno-, a combining form of **immune** or **immunity:** *immunology.*

im·mu·no·de·fi·cien·cy (im′yə nō di fish′ən sē, i myo͞o′-), *n.*, *pl.* **-cies.** a deficiency in the ability of the body's immune system to respond to antigens. [IMMUNO- + DEFICIENCY] **—im′mu·no·de·fi′cient,** *adj.*

im·mu·no·ge·net·ics (im′yə nō jə net′iks, i myo͞o′-nō-), *n.* (*construed as sing.*) **1.** the branch of immunology dealing with the study of immunity in relation to genetic makeup. **2.** the study of genetic relationships among animals by comparison of immunological reactions. [IMMUNO- + GENETICS] **—im′mu·no·ge·net′ic, im′mu·no·ge·net′i·cal,** *adj.*

im·mu·no·gen·ic (im′yə nō jen′ik, i myo͞o′nə-), *adj.* producing immunity. [IMMUNO- + -GENIC] **—im′mu·no·gen′i·cal·ly,** *adv.* **—im·mu·no·ge·nic·i·ty** (im′yə nō jə nis′i tē, i myo͞o′nō-), *n.*

immunol., immunology.

im·mu·nol·o·gy (im′yə nol′ə jē), *n.* the branch of medicine dealing with immunity from disease and the production of such immunity. [IMMUNO- + -LOGY] **—im·mu·no·log·ic** (i myo͞o′nᵊloj′ik), **im·mu′no·log′i·cal,** *adj.* **—im·mu′no·log′i·cal·ly,** *adv.* **—im′mu·nol′o·gist,** *n.*

im·mu·no·re·ac·tion (im′yə nō rē ak′shən, i myo͞o′-nō-), *n.* *Immunol.* an antigen-antibody reaction. [IMMUNO- + REACTION]

im·mure (i myo͝or′), *v.t.*, **-mured, -mur·ing. 1.** to enclose within walls. **2.** to shut in; confine. **3.** to imprison. **4.** to build into or entomb in a wall. **5.** *Obs.* to surround with walls; fortify. [< ML *immūr(āre),* equiv. to L *im-* IM-¹ + *mūr(us)* wall (see MURAL) + *-ā-* thematic vowel + *-re* inf. ending] **—im·mure′ment, im·mu·ra·tion** (im′yə rā′shən), *n.*

im·mu·si·cal (i myo͞o′zi kəl), *adj.* unmusical. [IM-² + MUSICAL] **—im·mu′si·cal·ly,** *adv.*

im·mu·ta·ble (i myo͞o′tə bəl), *adj.* not mutable; unchangeable; unalterable; changeless. [ME < L *immūtābil(is).* See IM-², MUTABLE] **—im·mu′ta·bil′i·ty, im·mu′ta·ble·ness,** *n.* **—im·mu′ta·bly,** *adv.*

Im·o·gene (im′ə jēn′), *n.* a girl's given name. Also, **Emogene, Im·o·gen** (im′ə jen′).

imp (imp), *n.* **1.** a little devil or demon; an evil spirit. **2.** a mischievous child. **3.** *Archaic.* a scion or offshoot. **4.** *Archaic.* an offspring. **—***v.t.* **5.** *Falconry.* **a.** to graft (feathers) into a wing. **b.** to furnish (a wing, tail, etc.) with feathers, as to make good losses or deficiencies and improve powers of flight. **6.** *Rare.* to add a piece to; mend or repair. [ME *impe,* OE *impa* or *impe* a shoot, graft, whence *impian* to graft; c. G *Impfen*]

Imp., 1. Emperor. [< L *Imperātor*] **2.** Empress. [< L *Imperātrix*]

imp., 1. imperative. **2.** imperfect. **3.** imperial. **4.** impersonal. **5.** implement. **6.** import. **7.** important. **8.** imported. **9.** importer. **10.** imprimatur. **11.** in the first place. [< L *imprīmīs*] **12.** imprint. **13.** imprison. **14.** improved. **15.** improvement.

im·pact (*n.* im′pakt; *v.* im pakt′), *n.* **1.** the striking of one body against another: *The impact of the colliding cars broke the windshield.* **2.** an impinging: *the impact of light on the eye.* **3.** influence; effect: *the impact of Hegel on modern philosophy.* **4.** an impacting; forcible impinging: *the tremendous impact of the shot.* **5.** the force exerted by a new idea, concept, or ideology: *the impact of atomic power; the impact of communism.* [n. use of v.] **—***v.t.* **6.** to drive or press closely or firmly into something; pack in. **7.** to fill up; congest; throng: *A vast crowd impacted St. Peter's Square.* **8.** to collide with; strike forcefully: *a rocket designed to impact the planet Mars.* **—***v.i.* **9.** to have impact or make contact forcefully (usually fol. by *on, upon, against,* etc.): *The ball impacted against the bat with a loud noise. The speaker's words suddenly impacted on the audience.* [back formation from IMPACTED]

im·pact·ed (im pak′tid), *adj.* **1.** wedged in. **2.** *Dentistry.* noting a tooth so confined in its socket as to be incapable of normal eruption. **3.** driven together; tightly packed. **4.** densely crowded; overcrowded: *an impacted school district.* [obs. *impact* adj. (< L *impact(us)* driven in, pinned to (ptp. of *impingere*), equiv. to *im-* IM-¹ + *pag-,* ptp. s. of *pangere* to drive in, + *-tus* ptp. suffix) + -ED²]

im·pac·tion (im pak′shən), *n.* **1.** act of impacting. **2.** state of being impacted; close fixation. **3.** *Dentistry.* the condition in which a tooth is impacted. [< LL *impactiōn-* (s. of *impactiō*), equiv. to L *impact(us)* driven in (see IMPACTED) + *-iōn-* -ION]

im·pact·ite (im′pak tīt′), *n.* a glassy or crystalline material composed of slag and meteoric materials, produced by the impact of a meteorite striking the earth. [IMPACT + -ITE¹]

im·pac·tive (im pak′tiv), *adj.* **1.** caused by impact: *impactive pain.* **2.** compelling or impressive: *He was deeply moved by the impactive force of the performance.* [IMPACT + -IVE]

im′pact param′eter, *Physics.* the perpendicular distance from the original center of a set of scattering particles to the original line of motion of a particle being scattered.

im·pair (im pâr′), *v.t.* **1.** to make, or cause to become, worse; diminish in value, excellence, etc.; weaken or damage: *to impair one's health; to impair negotiations.* **2.** *Obs.* to make or become worse; lessen. **—***n.* **3.** *Archaic.* impairment. [ME *empair(en), empeir(en)* (to) make worse < MF *empeir(er),* equiv. to *em-* IM-¹ + *peirer* < LL *pējōrāre,* equiv. to L *pējor* worse + *-ā-* thematic vowel + *-re* inf. suffix] **—im·pair′a·ble,** *adj.* **—im·pair′er,** *n.* **—im·pair′ment,** *n.*

—Syn. 1. See **injure. —Ant. 1.** repair.

im·pair (AN PER′), *adj.* *French.* noting any odd number.

im·pal·a (im pal′ə, -pä′lə), *n.*, *pl.* **-pal·as,** (*esp. collectively*) **-pal·a.** an African antelope, *Aepyceros melampus,* the male of which has ringed, lyre-shaped horns: noted for its leaping ability. [< Zulu]

Impala (2½ ft. high at shoulder; horns 2 ft.; total length 5½ ft.; tail 1 ft.)

im·pale (im pāl′), *v.t.*, **-paled, -pal·ing. 1.** to fix upon a sharpened stake or the like. **2.** to pierce with a sharpened stake thrust up through the body, as for torture or punishment. **3.** to fix upon, or pierce through with, anything pointed. **4.** to make helpless as if pierced through. **5.** *Rare.* to enclose with or as with pales or stakes; fence in; hem in. **6.** *Heraldry.* **a.** to marshal (two coats of arms, as the family arms of a husband and wife) on an escutcheon party per pale. **b.** (of a coat of arms) to be combined with (another coat of arms) in this way. Cf. **dimidiate** (def. 1). Also, **empale** (for defs. 1–5). [< ML *impāl(āre),* equiv. to L *im-* IM-¹ + *pāl(us)* PALE² + *-ā-* thematic vowel + *-re* inf. ending] **—im·pal′er,** *n.* **—im·pale′ment,** *n.*

im·pal·pa·ble (im pal′pə bəl), *adj.* **1.** not palpable; incapable of being perceived by the sense of touch; intangible. **2.** incapable of being readily grasped by the mind: *impalpable distinctions.* **3.** (of powder) so fine that when rubbed between the fingers no grit is felt. [IM-² + PALPABLE] **—im·pal′pa·bil′i·ty,** *n.* **—im·pal′pa·bly,** *adv.*

im·pa·na·tion (im′pə nā′shən), *n.* *Theol.* the doctrine that the body and blood of Christ are in the bread and wine after consecration. [< ML *impanātiōn-* (s. of *impanātiō*), equiv. to *impanāt(us)* embodied in bread (L *im-* IM-¹ + *pān(is)* bread + *-ātus* -ATE¹) + *-iōn-* -ION]

im·pa·na·tor (im′pə nā′tər), *n.* *Theol.* a person who maintains or holds the doctrine of impanation. [< ML; see IMPANATION, -OR²]

im·pan·el (im pan′ᵊl), *v.t.*, **-eled, -el·ing** or (*esp. Brit.*) **-elled, -el·ling. 1.** to enter on a panel or list for jury duty. **2.** to select (a jury) from the panel. **3.** to enter names on a panel or other official list. Also, **empanel.** [late ME *empanel* < AF *empanell(er).* See EM-¹, PANEL] **—im·pan′el·ment,** *n.*

im·par (im′pär), *adj.* *Anat.* unpaired; azygous. [< L: unequal. See IM-², PAR]

im·par·a·dise (im par′ə dīs′), *v.t.*, **-dised, -dis·ing. 1.** to put in or as in paradise; make supremely happy. **2.** to make into a paradise: *renovations that imparadised the spot.* [IM-¹ + PARADISE]

im·par·i·pin·nate (im par′ə pin′āt), *adj.* *Bot.* oddpinnate. [< NL *imparipinnāt(us).* See IMPAR, -I-, PINNATE]

im·par·i·syl·lab·ic (im par′ə si lab′ik), *adj.* (of a noun) not composed of the same number of syllables in all of its inflected forms, as Latin *corpus, corporis.* [IMPAR + -I- + SYLLABIC]

im·par·i·ty (im par′i tē), *n.*, *pl.* **-ties.** lack of parity or equality; disparity, difference, or inequality. [< LL *imparitās.* See IM-², PARITY¹]

im·park (im pärk′), *v.t.* **1.** to shut up, as in a park. **2.** to enclose as a park. [ME *imparke(n)* < AF *empark(er).* See EM-¹, PARK] **—im′par·ka′tion,** *n.*

im·parl (im pärl′), *v.i.* *Law.* to confer with the opposing party in a lawsuit with a view to settling the dispute amicably, out of court. [late ME *emparle* < MF *emparl(er),* equiv. to *em-* EM-¹ + *parler* to speak; see PARLIAMENT]

im·par·lance (im pär′ləns), *n.* *Law.* **1.** an extension of time granted to one party in a lawsuit to plead. **2.** a request for, or the permission granting, such a continuance. [< AF **emparlaunce,* equiv. to MF *emparl(er)* (to) IMPARL + *-aunce* -ANCE]

im·part (im pärt′), *v.t.* **1.** to make known; tell; relate: *to impart a secret.* **2.** to give; bestow; communicate. **3.** to grant a part or share of. **—***v.i.* **4.** *Archaic.* to grant a part or share; give. [late ME < L *impart(īre)* (to) share. See IM-¹, PART] **—im·part′a·ble,** *adj.* **—im′par·ta′tion, im·part′ment,** *n.* **—im·part′er,** *n.*

—Syn. 1. disclose, reveal, divulge. See **communicate. 2.** grant, cede, confer. **—Ant. 1.** conceal.

im·par·tial (im pär′shəl), *adj.* not partial or biased; fair; just: *an impartial judge.* [IM-² + PARTIAL] **—im·par·ti·al·i·ty** (im pär′shē al′i tē), **im·par′tial·ness,** *n.* **—im·par′tial·ly,** *adv.*

—Syn. unbiased, unprejudiced, equitable. See **fair¹. —Ant.** biased.

im·part·i·ble (im pär′tə bəl), *adj.* not partible; indivisible. [ME < LL *impartībil(is)* indivisible. See IM-², PARTIBLE] **—im·part′i·bil′i·ty,** *n.* **—im·part′i·bly,** *adv.*

im·pass·a·ble (im pas′ə bəl, -päs′ə-), *adj.* **1.** not passable; not allowing passage over, through, along, etc. **2.** unable to be surmounted: *an impassable obstacle to further negotiations.* **3.** unable to be circulated: *He tore the bill in half, making it impassable.* [IM-² + PASSABLE] **—im·pass′a·bil′i·ty, im·pass′a·ble·ness,** *n.* **—im·pass′a·bly,** *adv.*

im·passe (im′pas, im pas′; *Fr.* AN päs′), *n.*, *pl.* **-pass·es** (-pas iz, -pas′iz; *Fr.* -päs′). **1.** a position from which there is no escape; deadlock. **2.** a road or way that has no outlet. [< F, equiv. to *im-* IM-² + *-passe,* s. of *passer* to PASS]

im·pas·si·ble (im pas′ə bəl), *adj.* **1.** incapable of suffering pain. **2.** incapable of suffering harm. **3.** incapable of emotion; impassive. [ME < LL *impassibil(is).* See IM-², PASSIBLE] **—im·pas′si·bil′i·ty, im·pas′si·ble·ness,** *n.* **—im·pas′si·bly,** *adv.*

im·pas·sion (im pash′ən), *v.t.* to fill, or affect strongly, with passion; inflame; excite. [< It *impassion(are).* See IM-¹, PASSION]

im·pas·sion·ate (im pash′ə nit), *adj.* **1.** *Archaic.* free from passion; dispassionate. **2.** impassioned. [IM-² + PASSIONATE] **—im·pas′sion·ate·ly,** *adv.*

im·pas·sioned (im pash′ənd), *adj.* filled with passion; passionate; ardent. [IMPASSION + -ED²] **—im·pas′sioned·ly,** *adv.* **—im·pas′sioned·ness,** *n.*

—Syn. emotional, vehement, fervent, fiery. **—Ant.** apathetic.

im·pas·sive (im pas′iv), *adj.* **1.** without emotion; apathetic; unmoved. **2.** calm; serene. **3.** unconscious;

insensible. **4.** not subject to suffering. [IM-[2] + PASSIVE] —**im·pas′sive·ly,** *adv.* —**im·pas′sive·ness, im·pas·siv·i·ty** (im′pa siv′i tē), *n.*
—**Syn. 1.** emotionless, phlegmatic, stoical, indifferent, undisturbed, unperturbed. **2.** tranquil, unruffled, composed. **4.** unaffected; unflinching.

im·paste (im pāst′), *v.t.*, **-past·ed, -past·ing.** **1.** to cover with or enclose in a paste. **2.** to form into a paste. **3.** to lay on thickly, as paste. [< It *impast(are).* See IM-[1], PASTE] —**im·pas·ta·tion** (im′pa stā′shən), *n.*

im·pas·to (im pas′tō, -pä′stō), *n.* *Painting.* **1.** the laying on of paint thickly. **2.** the paint so laid on. **3.** enamel or slip applied to a ceramic object to form a decoration in low relief. [< It; see IMPASTE]

im·pa·tience (im pā′shəns), *n.* **1.** lack of patience. **2.** eager desire for relief or change; restlessness. **3.** intolerance of anything that thwarts or hinders. [ME *impacience* < L *impatientia.* See IM-[2], PATIENCE]

im·pa·ti·ens (im pā′shē enz′), *n., pl.* **-ti·ens.** any annual, balsaminaceous plant of the genus *Impatiens,* having irregular flowers in which the calyx and corolla are not clearly distinguishable. [< NL, L *impatiēns* not enduring, not bearing; see IMPATIENT]

im·pa·tient (im pā′shənt), *adj.* **1.** not patient; not bearing delay, opposition, pain, etc., with calm or patience. **2.** indicating lack of patience: *an impatient answer.* **3.** restless in desire or expectation; eagerly desirous. **4. impatient of,** intolerant of: *impatient of any interruptions.* [ME *impacient* < L *impatient-* (s. of *impatiēns*) not putting up with. See IM-[2], PATIENT] —**im·pa′tient·ly,** *adv.* —**im·pa′tient·ness,** *n.*
—**Syn. 1.** uneasy, unquiet. **1, 2.** irritable, testy, fretful, violent, hot; curt, brusque, abrupt. **3.** hasty, impetuous, precipitate, sudden. —**Ant. 1.** calm.

im·pav·id (im pav′id), *adj.* *Rare.* fearless; dauntless. [< L *impavid(us)* fearless, undaunted. See IM-[2], PAVID] —**im·pa·vid·i·ty** (im′pə vid′i tē), *n.* —**im·pav′id·ly,** *adv.*

im·pawn (im pôn′), *v.t.* *Rare.* to put in pawn; pledge. [IM-[1] + PAWN[1]]

im·peach (im pēch′), *v.t.* **1.** to accuse (a public official) before an appropriate tribunal of misconduct in office. **2.** to challenge the credibility of: *to impeach a witness.* **3.** to bring an accusation against. **4.** to call in question; cast an imputation upon: *to impeach one's motives.* **5.** to call to account. —*n.* **6.** *Obs.* impeachment. [ME *empeche(n)* < AF *empecher* < LL *impedicāre* to fetter, trap, equiv. to L *im-* IM-[1] + *pedic(a)* a fetter (see PEDI-[1], -IC) + *-ā-* thematic vowel + *-re* inf. suffix] —**im·peach′er,** *n.*

im·peach·a·ble (im pē′chə bəl), *adj.* **1.** liable to be impeached. **2.** making one subject to impeachment, as misconduct in office. [IMPEACH + -ABLE] —**im·peach′a·bil′i·ty,** *n.*

im·peach·ment (im pēch′mənt), *n.* **1.** the impeaching of a public official before an appropriate tribunal. **2.** *U.S.* (in Congress or a State legislature) the presentation of formal charges against a public official by the lower house, trial to be before the upper house. **3.** demonstration that a witness is less worthy of belief. **4.** act of impeaching. **5.** state of being impeached. [ME *empechement* < AF. See IMPEACH, -MENT]

im·pearl (im pûrl′), *v.t.* **1.** to form into drops resembling pearls. **2.** to make pearllike or pearly. **3.** *Chiefly Literary.* to adorn with pearls or pearllike drops. [IM-[1] + PEARL[1]; cf. F *emperler*]

im·pec·ca·ble (im pek′ə bəl), *adj.* **1.** faultless; irreproachable: *impeccable manners.* **2.** not liable to sin; exempt from the possibility of doing wrong. —*n.* **3.** *Rare.* an impeccable person. [< LL *impeccābil(is)* faultless, sinless. See IM-[2], PECCABLE] —**im·pec′ca·bil′i·ty,** *n.* —**im·pec′ca·bly,** *adv.*

im·pec·cant (im pek′ənt), *adj.* not sinning; sinless. [IM-[2] + PECCANT] —**im·pec′cance, im·pec′can·cy,** *n.*

im·pe·cu·ni·ous (im′pə kyōō′nē əs), *adj.* having no money; penniless; poor. [IM-[2] + *pecunious* wealthy (late ME) < L *pecūniōs(us),* equiv. to *pecūni(a)* wealth + *-ōsus* -OUS] —**im′pe·cu′ni·ous·ly,** *adv.* —**im′pe·cu′ni·ous·ness, im·pe·cu·ni·os·i·ty** (im′pə kyōō′nē os′i tē), *n.*
—**Syn.** destitute, poverty-stricken. See **poor.** —**Ant.** wealthy.

im·ped·ance (im pēd′ᵊns), *n.* **1.** *Elect.* the total opposition to alternating current by an electric circuit, equal to the square root of the sum of the squares of the resistance and reactance of the circuit and usually expressed in ohms. *Symbol:* Z **2.** Also called **mechanical impedance.** *Physics.* the ratio of the force on a system undergoing simple harmonic motion to the velocity of the particles in the system. [IMPEDE + -ANCE]

im·pede (im pēd′), *v.t.*, **-ped·ed, -ped·ing.** to retard in movement or progress by means of obstacles or hindrances; obstruct; hinder. [< L *impedī-* (s. of *impedīre* to entangle, lit., to snare the feet). See IM-[1], PEDI-[1]] —**im·ped′er,** *n.* —**im·ped·i·bil·i·ty** (im pē′də bil′i tē, -ped′ə-), *n.* —**im·ped′i·ble,** *adj.* —**im·ped′ing·ly,** *adv.*
—**Syn.** slow, delay, check, stop, block, thwart. See **prevent.** —**Ant.** advance, encourage.

im·pe·di·ent (im pē′dē ənt), *adj.* **1.** impeding; hindering. —*n.* **2.** that which impedes; hindrance. [< L *impedient-* (s. of *impediēns* entangling, prp. of *impedīre*). See IMPEDE, -ENT]

im·ped·i·ment (im ped′ə mənt), *n.* **1.** obstruction; hindrance; obstacle. **2.** some physical defect that impedes ready speech; a speech disorder: *an impediment in speech.* **3.** *Chiefly Eccles. Law.* a bar, usually of blood or affinity, to marriage: *a diriment impediment.* **4.** Usually, **impediments.** *Rare.* impedimenta. [ME < L *impedīment(um).* See IMPEDE, -MENT] —**im·ped·i·men·tal** (im ped′ə men′təl), **im·ped′i·men′ta·ry,** *adj.*
—**Syn. 1.** bar, encumbrance, check. See **obstacle.** —**Ant. 1.** help, encouragement.

im·ped·i·men·ta (im ped′ə men′tə), *n.pl.* baggage or other encumbrances that impede one's progress, esp. supplies carried with an army: *the impedimenta of the weekend skier.* [< L, pl. of *impedīmentum* IMPEDIMENT]

im·ped·i·tive (im ped′i tiv), *adj.* tending to impede; obstructive. [*impedite* to hinder (< L *impedīt(us),* ptp. of *impedīre* to IMPEDE; see -ITE[2]) + -IVE]

im·pel (im pel′), *v.t.*, **-pelled, -pel·ling.** **1.** to drive or urge forward; press on; incite or constrain to action. **2.** to drive or cause to move onward; propel; impart motion to. [late ME *impell* < L *impell(ere)* (to) strike against (something), start (it) moving, equiv. to *im-* IM-[1] + *pellere* to strike, move (something)]
—**Syn. 1.** actuate. See **compel.** —**Ant. 1.** restrain.

im·pel·lent (im pel′ənt), *adj.* **1.** impelling: *an impellent power; an impellent cause.* —*n.* **2.** that which impels; an impelling agency or force. [< L *impellent-* (s. of *impellēns* setting in motion, prp. of *impellere*). See IMPEL, -ENT]

im·pel·ler (im pel′ər), *n.* **1.** one who or that which impels. **2.** a rotor for transmitting motion, as in a centrifugal pump, blower, turbine, fluid coupling, etc. [IMPEL + -ER[1]]

im·pend (im pend′), *v.i.* **1.** to be imminent; be near at hand. **2.** to threaten or menace: *He felt that danger impended.* **3.** *Rare.* to hang or be suspended; overhang (usually fol. by *over*). [< L *impend(ere)* (to) hang over, threaten. See IM-[1], PEND]

im·pend·ent (im pen′dənt), *adj.* impending. [< L *impendent-* (s. of *impendēns* overhanging, prp. of *impendere*). See IMPEND, -ENT] —**im·pend′ence, im·pend′en·cy,** *n.*

im·pend·ing (im pen′ding), *adj.* **1.** about to happen; imminent: *their impending marriage.* **2.** imminently threatening or menacing: *an impending strike.* **3.** *Rare.* overhanging. [IMPEND + -ING[2]]
—**Syn. 1.** See **imminent.**

im·pen·e·tra·bil·i·ty (im pen′i trə bil′i tē, im′pen-), *n.* **1.** state or quality of being impenetrable. **2.** *Physics.* that property of matter by virtue of which two bodies cannot occupy the same space simultaneously. [IMPENETRA(BLE) + -BILITY]

im·pen·e·tra·ble (im pen′i trə bəl), *adj.* **1.** not penetrable; unable to be penetrated, pierced, entered, etc. **2.** inaccessible to ideas, influences, etc. **3.** incapable of being comprehended; unfathomable: *an impenetrable mystery.* **4.** *Physics.* possessing impenetrability. [late ME *impenetrabel* < L *impenetrābil(is).* See IM-[2], PENETRABLE] —**im·pen′e·tra·ble·ness,** *n.* —**im·pen′e·tra·bly,** *adv.*

im·pen·i·tent (im pen′i tᵊnt), *adj.* not penitent; obdurate. [< LL *impaenitent-* (s. of *impaenitēns*). See IM-[2], PENITENT] —**im·pen′i·tence, im·pen′i·ten·cy, im·pen′i·tent·ness,** *n.* —**im·pen′i·tent·ly,** *adv.*

imper., imperative.

im·per·a·ti·val (im per′ə tī′vəl), *adj.* of, pertaining to, or characteristic of the grammatical imperative. [IMPERATIVE + -AL[1]] —**im·per′a·ti′val·ly,** *adv.*

im·per·a·tive (im per′ə tiv), *adj.* **1.** not to be avoided or evaded: *an imperative duty.* **2.** of the nature of or expressing a command; commanding. **3.** *Gram.* noting or pertaining to the mood of the verb used in commands, requests, etc., as in *Listen! Go!* Cf. **indicative** (def. 2), **subjunctive** (def. 1). —*n.* **4.** a command. **5.** a fact that compels attention or action; obligation; need: *the imperatives of the Far Eastern situation.* **6.** *Gram.* **a.** the imperative mood. **b.** a verb in this mood. **7.** an obligatory statement, principle, or the like. [< LL *imperātiv(us),* equiv. to L *imperāt(us)* imposed, ordered, ptp. of *imperāre* (*im-* IM-[1] + *-per-* (var. of *par-,* root of *parāre* to place, set) + *-ātus* -ATE[1]) + *-īvus* -IVE] —**im·per′a·tive·ly,** *adv.* —**im·per′a·tive·ness,** *n.*
—**Syn. 1.** inescapable; indispensable, necessary, essential; exigent, compelling.

im·pe·ra·tor (im′pə rā′tər), *n.* **1.** an absolute or supreme ruler. **2.** a title of an ancient Roman emperor. **3.** a temporary title accorded a victorious general in ancient Rome. [< L; see EMPEROR] —**im·per·a·to·ri·al** (im per′ə tôr′ē əl, -tōr′-), *adj.* —**im·per′a·to′ri·al·ly,** *adv.* —**im′pe·ra′tor·ship′,** *n.*

im·per·cep·ti·ble (im′pər sep′tə bəl), *adj.* **1.** very slight, gradual, or subtle: *imperceptible gradations.* **2.** not perceptible; not perceived by or affecting the senses. —*n.* **3.** something not capable of being perceived by the senses: *metaphysical speculation about imperceptibles.* [< ML *imperceptibil(is).* See IM-[2], PERCEPTIBLE] —**im′per·cep′ti·bil′i·ty, im′per·cep′ti·ble·ness,** *n.* —**im′per·cep′ti·bly,** *adv.*

im·per·cep·tion (im′pər sep′shən), *n.* lack of perception. [IM-[2] + PERCEPTION]

im·per·cep·tive (im′pər sep′tiv), *adj.* not perceptive; lacking perception. [IM-[2] + PERCEPTIVE] —**im′per·cep·tiv′i·ty, im′per·cep′tive·ness,** *n.*

im·per·cip·i·ent (im′pər sip′ē ənt), *adj.* lacking perception; imperceptive. [IM-[2] + PERCIPIENT] —**im′per·cip′i·ence,** *n.*

imperf., imperfect.

im·per·fect (im pûr′fikt), *adj.* **1.** of, pertaining to, or characterized by defects. **2.** not perfect; lacking completeness: *imperfect vision.* **3.** *Bot.* (of a flower) diclinous. **4.** *Gram.* noting action or state still in process at some temporal point of reference, particularly in the past. **5.** *Law.* being without legal effect or support; unenforceable. **6.** *Music.* of or relating to the interval of a major or minor third or sixth. Cf. **perfect** (def. 12a). —*n.* *Gram.* **7.** the imperfect tense. **8.** another verb formation or construction with imperfect meaning. **9.** a form in the imperfect, as Latin *portābam,* "I was carrying." [< L *imperfect(us)* unfinished (see IM-[2], PERFECT); r. ME *imparfit* < MF *imparfait* < L, as above] —**im·per′fect·ly,** *adv.* —**im·per′fect·ness,** *n.*
—**Syn. 1.** defective, faulty. **2.** incomplete, underdeveloped; immature. —**Ant. 2.** complete, developed.

imper′fect contri′tion. See under **contrition** (def. 2).

imper′fect fun′gus, a fungus for which only the asexual reproductive stage is known, as any fungus of the *Fungi Imperfecti.*

im·per·fect·i·ble (im′pər fek′tə bəl), *adj.* that cannot be perfected. [IM-[2] + PERFECTIBLE] —**im′per·fect′i·bil′i·ty,** *n.*

im·per·fec·tion (im′pər fek′shən), *n.* **1.** an imperfect detail; flaw: *a law full of imperfections.* **2.** the quality or condition of being imperfect. [ME *imperfeccio(u)n* < LL *imperfectiōn-* (s. of *imperfectiō*) incompleteness. See IM-[2], PERFECTION]

im·per·fec·tive (im′pər fek′tiv), *Gram.* —*adj.* **1.** noting an aspect of the verb, as in Russian, which indicates incompleteness of the action or state at a temporal point of reference. —*n.* **2.** the imperfective aspect. **3.** a verb in this aspect. [IMPERFECT + -IVE]

imper′fect rhyme′, *Pros.* See **slant rhyme.**

im·per·fo·rate (im pûr′fər it, -fə rāt′), *adj.* **1.** Also, **im·per′fo·rat′ed.** not perforate; having no perforation. **2.** *Philately.* (of a number of stamps joined together) lacking the perforations usually separating individual stamps. —*n.* **3.** an imperforate stamp. [IM-[2] + PERFORATE] —**im·per′fo·ra′tion,** *n.*

Im·pe·ria (ēm pe′ryä), *n.* a seaport in NW Italy. 35,180 (1961).

im·pe·ri·al[1] (im pēr′ē əl), *adj.* **1.** of or pertaining to an empire. **2.** of or pertaining to an emperor or empress. **3.** characterizing the rule or authority of a sovereign state over its dependencies. **4.** of the nature or rank of an emperor or supreme ruler. **5.** of a commanding quality, manner, aspect, etc. **6.** domineering; imperious. **7.** of or befitting an emperor or empress; very fine or grand; magnificent. **8.** of special size or quality, as various products, commodities, etc. **9.** (of weights and measures) conforming to the standards legally established in Great Britain. —*n.* **10.** a size of printing or drawing paper, 22 × 30 inches in England, 23 × 33 inches in America. **11.** the top of a carriage, esp. of a diligence. **12.** a case for luggage carried there. **13.** a member of an imperial party or of imperial troops. **14.** an emperor or empress. **15.** any of various articles of special size or quality. **16. imperial octavo,** a size of book, about 8¼ × 11½ inches, untrimmed, in America, and 7½ × 11 inches, untrimmed, in England. *Abbr.:* imperial 8vo **17. imperial quarto,** *Chiefly Brit.* a size of book, about 11 × 15 inches, untrimmed. *Abbr.:* imperial 4to [ME < LL *imperiāl(is),* equiv. to L *imperi(um)* IMPERIUM + *-ālis* -AL[1]; r. ME *emperial* < MF] —**im·pe′ri·al·ly,** *adv.* —**im·pe′ri·al·ness,** *n.*

im·pe·ri·al[2] (im pēr′ē əl), *n.* a small, pointed beard beneath the lower lip. [< F *impériale,* n. use of fem. of *impérial* IMPERIAL[1]]

im·pe·ri·al[3] (im pēr′ē əl), *n.* a Russian gold coin originally worth 10 rubles and from 1897–1917 worth 15 rubles. [< Russ << ML *imperiālis* a coin, n. use of LL *imperiālis* IMPERIAL[1]]

Imperial[2]

Im·pe·ri·al (im pēr′ē əl), *n.* a town in S California. 2658 (1960).

Impe′rial Beach′, a city in SW California, near San Diego. 17,773 (1960).

Impe′rial bush′el. See under **bushel**[1] (def. 1).

impe′rial ea′gle, a brown eagle, *Aquila heliaca,* of Asia and southern Europe.

impe′rial gal′lon, a British gallon equivalent to 1⅕ U.S. gallons, or 277.42 cubic inches.

Impe′rial Hol′iday, (*sometimes l.c.*) a day of traditional significance to the entire British Empire, as the king's or queen's birthday, Victoria Day, etc., but which is not a legal or bank holiday.

im·pe·ri·al·ise (im pēr′ē ə līz′), *v.t.*, **-ised, -is·ing.** *Chiefly Brit.* imperialize. —**im·pe′ri·al·i·sa′tion,** *n.*

im·pe·ri·al·ism (im pēr′ē ə liz′əm), *n.* **1.** the policy of extending the rule or authority of an empire or nation over foreign countries, or of acquiring and holding colonies and dependencies. **2.** advocacy of imperial interests. **3.** *Brit.* the policy of so uniting the separate parts of an empire with separate governments as to secure for certain purposes a single state. **4.** imperial government. **5.** an imperial system of government. [IMPERIAL[1] + -ISM] —**im·pe′ri·al·ist,** *n., adj.* —**im·pe′ri·al·is′tic,** *adj.* —**im·pe′ri·al·is′ti·cal·ly,** *adv.*

im·pe·ri·al·ize (im pēr′ē ə līz′), *v.t.*, **-ized, -iz·ing.** **1.** to subject (a people, country, etc.) to imperial rule. **2.** to invest with imperial authority. **3.** to form into an imperial type of government. Also, *esp. Brit.,* **imperialise.** [IMPERIAL[1] + -IZE] —**im·pe′ri·al·i·za′tion,** *n.*

impe′rial jade′, transparent jadeite of gem quality; a true jade. Also called **gem jade.**

impe′rial moth′, a yellow moth, *Eacles imperialis,* having dotted wings each with a diagonal band of pinkish-brown or purple, the hairy larvae of which feed on the leaves of hickory, oak, etc.

Impe′rial Val′ley, an irrigated agricultural region in SE California, adjacent to Mexico, formerly a part of the Colorado Desert: it is largely below sea level and contains the Salton Sink.

im·per·il (im per′əl), *v.t.*, **-iled, -il·ing** or (*esp. Brit.*) **-illed, -il·ling.** to put in peril; endanger. [IM-[1] + PERIL] —**im·per′il·ment,** *n.*

im·pe·ri·ous (im pēr′ē əs), *adj.* **1.** domineering; dictatorial; overbearing: *an imperious manner; an imperious person.* **2.** urgent; imperative: *imperious need.* [< L *imperiōs(us)* commanding, tyrannical, equiv. to *imperi(um)* IMPERIUM + *-ōsus* -OUS] —**im·pe′ri·ous·ly,** *adv.* —**im·pe′ri·ous·ness,** *n.*
—**Syn. 1.** tyrannical, despotic, arrogant. **2.** necessary. —**Ant. 1.** submissive. **2.** unnecessary.

im·per·ish·a·ble (im per′i shə bəl), *adj.* not perishable; indestructible; enduring. [IM-[2] + PERISHABLE] —**im·per′ish·a·bil′i·ty, im·per′ish·a·ble·ness,** *n.* —**im·per′ish·a·bly,** *adv.*

im·pe·ri·um (im pēr′ē əm), *n., pl.* **-pe·ri·a** (-pēr′ē ə). **1.** command; supreme power. **2.** area of dominion; sphere of control or monopoly; empire. **3.** *Law.* the right to command the force of the state in order to enforce the law. [< L: command (i.e., thing commanded), empire, equiv. to *imper(āre)* (to) rule (see IMPERATIVE) + *-ium* neut. suffix]

im·pe·ri·um in im·pe·ri·o (im pe′rē ōōm′ in im pe′rē ō′; *Eng.* im pēr′ē əm in im pēr′ē ō′), *Latin.* a sovereign state within a sovereign state; enclave.

im·per·ma·nent (im pûr′mə nənt), *adj.* not permanent; transitory. [IM-[2] + PERMANENT] —**im·per′ma·nence, im·per′ma·nen·cy,** *n.* —**im·per′ma·nent·ly,** *adv.*

im·per·me·a·ble (im pûr′mē ə bəl), *adj.* **1.** not permeable; impassable. **2.** (of substances) not permitting the passage of a fluid through the pores, interstices, etc. [< LL *impermeābil(is).* See IM-[2], PERMEABLE] —**im·per′me·a·bil′i·ty, im·per′me·a·ble·ness,** *n.* —**im·per′me·a·bly,** *adv.*

im·per·mis·si·ble (im′pər mis′ə bəl), *adj.* not permissible; unallowable: *to take impermissible liberties with grammar.* [IM-[2] + PERMISSIBLE] —**im′per·mis′si·bil′i·ty,** *n.*

impers., impersonal.

im·per·son·al (im pûr′sə nᵊl), *adj.* **1.** not personal; without personal reference or connection: *an impersonal remark.* **2.** having no personality: *an impersonal deity.* **3.** *Gram.* **a.** (of a verb) having only third person singular forms and rarely if ever accompanied by an expressed subject, as Latin *pluit* "it is raining," or regularly accompanied by an empty subject word, as English *to rain* in *It is raining.* **b.** (of a pronoun or pronominal reference) indefinite, as French *on* "one." —*n.* **4.** *Gram.* an impersonal verb or pronoun. [< LL *impersōnāl(is).* See IM-[2], PERSONAL] —**im·per′son·al·ly,** *adv.*

im·per·son·al·ise (im pûr′sə nəlīz′), *v.t.*, **-ised, -is·ing.** *Chiefly Brit.* impersonalize. —**im·per′son·al·i·sa′tion,** *n.*

im·per·son·al·ism (im pûr′sə nəliz′əm), *n.* **1.** the practice of maintaining impersonal relations with individuals or groups. **2.** impersonality. [IMPERSONAL + -ISM]

im·per·son·al·i·ty (im pûr′sə nal′i tē), *n., pl.* **-ties** for 6. **1.** absence of human character or of the traits associated with the human character: *He feared the impersonality of a mechanized world.* **2.** lack of emotional involvement: *His work reflected a certain impersonality, an absence of feeling and warmth.* **3.** absence or reduction of concern for individual needs or desires: *the impersonality of an institution.* **4.** lack of a personal agent or of a known personal agent: *the impersonality of folk art.* **5.** the quality of not being concerned with particular persons: *the impersonality and universality of his interests.* **6.** something that is impersonal. [IMPERSONAL + -ITY]

im·per·son·al·ize (im pûr′sə nəlīz′), *v.t.*, **-ized, -iz·ing.** to make impersonal: *The dial system has impersonalized the telephone.* Also, *esp. Brit.*, **impersonalise.** [IMPERSONAL + -IZE] —**im·per′son·al·i·za′tion,** *n.*

im·per·son·ate (*v.* im pûr′sə nāt′; *adj.* im pûr′sə nit, -nāt′), *v.*, **-at·ed, -at·ing,** *adj.* —*v.t.* **1.** to assume the character of; pretend to be. **2.** to personate, esp. on the stage. **3.** *Rare.* to represent in personal or bodily form; personify; typify. —*adj.* **4.** embodied in a person; invested with personality. [IM-[1] + PERSON + -ATE[1]] —**im·per′son·a′tion,** *n.* —**im·per′son·a′tor,** *n.*

im·per·ti·nence (im pûr′tənəns), *n.* **1.** unmannerly intrusion or presumption; insolence. **2.** impertinent quality or action. **3.** irrelevance, inappropriateness, or absurdity. **4.** something impertinent, as an act, statement, etc. **5.** an impertinent person: *He reprimanded that impertinence, his daughter.* [IMPERTIN(ENCY) + -ENCE]

im·per·ti·nen·cy (im pûr′tənən sē), *n., pl.* **-cies.** impertinence. [< ML *impertinentia.* See IMPERTINENT, -ENCY]

im·per·ti·nent (im pûr′tənənt), *adj.* **1.** intrusive or presumptuous, as persons or their actions; rude; uncivil: *a brash, impertinent boy.* **2.** not pertinent; irrelevant: *any impertinent detail.* **3.** *Rare.* inappropriate, incongruous, or absurd. **4.** *Obs.* (of persons) trivial, silly, or absurd. [ME < LL *impertinent-* (s. of *impertinēns*) not belonging. See IM-[2], PERTINENT] —**im·per′ti·nent·ly,** *adv.* —**im·per′ti·nent·ness,** *n.*

—**Syn. 1.** fresh, bold, insulting, officious, saucy, pert, brazen. IMPERTINENT, IMPUDENT, INSOLENT refer to bold, rude, and arrogant behavior. IMPERTINENT, from its primary meaning of not pertinent and hence inappropriate or out of place, has come to imply often an unseemly intrusion into what does not concern one, or a presumptuous rudeness toward one entitled to deference or respect: *an impertinent interruption, question, manner toward a teacher.* IMPUDENT suggests a bold and shameless impertinence: *an impudent speech, young rascal.* INSOLENT suggests insulting or arrogantly contemptuous behavior: *unbearably insolent toward those in authority.* **4.** ridiculous, inane. —**Ant. 1.** polite. **4.** important, serious.

im·per·turb·a·ble (im′pər tûr′bə bəl), *adj.* incapable of being perturbed or agitated; not easily excited; calm: *imperturbable composure.* [< LL *imperturbābil(is).* See IM-[2], PERTURBABLE] —**im′per·turb′a·bil′i·ty, im′per·turb′a·ble·ness,** *n.* —**im′per·turb′a·bly,** *adv.*

—**Syn.** composed, collected, impassive, cool, unmoved.

im·per·tur·ba·tion (im′pər tər bā′shən), *n.* freedom from perturbation; tranquillity; calmness. [< LL *imperturbātiōn-* (s. of *imperturbātiō*). See IM-[2], PERTURBATION]

im·per·vi·ous (im pûr′vē əs), *adj.* **1.** not permitting penetration or passage; impenetrable: *impervious to rain; impervious to bullets.* **2.** incapable of being injured or impaired: *impervious to wear and tear.* **3.** incapable of being influenced or affected: *impervious to reason; impervious to another's suffering.* Also, **im·per′vi·a·ble.** [< L *impervius.* See IM-[2], PERVIOUS] —**im·per′vi·ous·ly,** *adv.* —**im·per′vi·ous·ness,** *n.*

im·pe·ti·go (im′pi tī′gō), *n.* *Pathol.* a contagious skin disease, esp. of children, marked by a superficial pustular eruption, particularly on the face. [< L, equiv. to *impet(ere)* (to) make for, attack (see IMPETUS) + *-īgō,* as in *vertīgo* VERTIGO] —**im·pe·tig·i·nous** (im′pi tij′ə nəs), *adj.*

im·pe·trate (im′pi trāt′), *v.t.*, **-trat·ed, -trat·ing.** **1.** to obtain by entreaty. **2.** to entreat; ask for urgently. [< L *impetrāt(us)* got by asking (ptp. of *impetrāre*), equiv. to *im-* IM-[1] + *petr-* (var. of *patr-*, root of *patrāre* to father, hence, to bring about, deriv. of *pater* father) + *-ātus* -ATE[1]] —**im′pe·tra′tion,** *n.* —**im′pe·tra′tive, im·pe·tra·to·ry** (im′pi trə tōr′ē, -tôr′ē), *adj.* —**im′pe·tra′tor,** *n.*

im·pet·u·os·i·ty (im pech′o͞o os′i tē, im′pe cho͞o-), *n., pl.* **-ties** for 2. **1.** quality or condition of being impetuous. **2.** an impetuous action. [< LL *impetuōs(us)* IMPETUOUS + -ITY]

im·pet·u·ous (im pech′o͞o əs), *adj.* **1.** of, pertaining to, or characterized by sudden or rash energy, action, emotion, etc.; impulsive: *an impetuous decision; an impetuous person.* **2.** having great impetus; moving with great force; violent: *the impetuous winds.* [ME < LL *impetuōs(us),* equiv. to L *impetu(s)* IMPETUS + *-ōsus* -OUS] —**im·pet′u·ous·ly,** *adv.* —**im·pet′u·ous·ness,** *n.*

—**Syn. 1.** eager, violent. IMPETUOUS, IMPULSIVE both refer to persons who are hasty and precipitate in action, or to actions not preceded by thought. IMPETUOUS suggests eagerness, violence, rashness: *impetuous vivacity; impetuous desire; impetuous words.* IMPULSIVE emphasizes spontaneity and lack of reflection: *an impulsive act of generosity.* —**Ant. 1.** planned, careful.

im·pe·tus (im′pi təs), *n., pl.* **-tus·es.** **1.** moving force; impulse; stimulus: *The grant for building the opera house gave impetus to the city's cultural life.* **2.** the force with which a moving body tends to maintain its velocity and overcome resistance; energy of motion. [< L: an attack, lit., a rushing into, equiv. to *impet(ere)* (to) attack (*im-* IM-[1] + *petere* to make for) + *-us* n. suffix (4th decl.)]

impf., imperfect.

imp. gal., imperial gallon.

Imp·hal (imp′hul), *n.* a city in and the capital of Manipur territory, in NE India. 102,862 (1951).

im·pi (im′pē), *n., pl.* **-pies, -pis.** a band of Kaffir warriors. [< Zulu]

im·pi·e·ty (im pī′i tē), *n., pl.* **-ties.** **1.** lack of piety; lack of reverence for God or sacred things; ungodliness. **2.** lack of dutifulness or respect. **3.** an impious act, practice, etc. [ME *impietie* < L *impietās,* equiv. to *impi(us)* IMPIOUS + *-etās,* var. of *-itās* -ITY]

im·pig·no·rate (im pig′nə rāt′), *v.t.*, **-rat·ed, -rat·ing.** to put up or give as security; pledge; mortgage. [< ML *impignorāt(us)* pledged (ptp. of *impignorāre*), equiv. to L *im-* IM-[1] + *pignor-* (s. of *pignus*) a pledge + *-ātus* -ATE[1]] —**im·pig′no·ra′tion,** *n.*

im·pinge (im pinj′), *v.*, **-pinged, -ping·ing.** —*v.i.* **1.** to strike; dash; collide (usually fol. by *on, upon,* or *against*): *rays of light impinging on the eye.* **2.** to encroach; infringe (usually fol. by *on* or *upon*): *to impinge upon another's rights.* **3.** to make an impression; affect; touch (usually fol. by *on* or *upon*): *to impinge upon the imagination; social pressures that impinge upon one's daily life.* —*v.t.* **4.** *Obs.* to come into violent contact with. [< ML *impinge(re)* (to) strike against, drive at, equiv. to L *im-* IM-[1] + *-pingere,* var. of *pangere* to fasten, drive in, fix] —**im·ping′ent,** *adj.* —**im·ping′er,** *n.* —**im·pinge′ment,** *n.*

im·pi·ous (im′pē əs), *adj.* **1.** not pious; lacking reverence for God, religious practices, etc.; irreligious; ungodly. **2.** disrespectful. [< L *impius.* See IM-[2], PIOUS] —**im′pi·ous·ly,** *adv.* —**im′pi·ous·ness,** *n.*

imp·ish (im′pish), *adj.* of, pertaining to, or characteristic of an imp; mischievous. [IMP + -ISH[1]] —**imp′ish·ly,** *adv.* —**imp′ish·ness,** *n.*

im·plac·a·ble (im plak′ə bəl, -plā′kə-), *adj.* not placable; not to be appeased or pacified; inexorable: *an implacable enemy.* [late ME < L *implācābil(is).* See IM-[2], PLACABLE] —**im·plac′a·bil′i·ty, im·plac′a·ble·ness,** *n.* —**im·plac′a·bly,** *adv.*

—**Syn.** unappeasable, unbending, merciless. See **inflexible.**

im·pla·cen·tal (im′plə sen′təl), *adj.* **1.** *Zool.* having no placenta, as a monotreme or marsupial. —*n.* **2.** an implacental mammal. Also, **im·pla·cen·tate** (im′plə-sen′tāt). [IM-[2] + PLACENTAL]

im·plant (*v.* im plant′, -plänt′; *n.* im′plant′, -plänt′), *v.t.* **1.** to instill; imbue; inculcate: *to implant sound principles in a child's mind.* **2.** to plant in something; infix: *to implant living tissue.* **3.** *Rare.* to plant: *to implant the seeds.* —*n.* **4.** *Med.* **a.** a tissue implanted into the body by grafting. **b.** a small tube containing a radioactive substance, as radium, surgically implanted in tissue for the treatment of tumors, cancer, etc. [IM-[1] + PLANT] —**im·plant′er,** *n.*

im·plan·ta·tion (im′plan tā′shən), *n.* **1.** act of implanting. **2.** state of being implanted. **3.** *Pathol.* **a.** the movement of cells to a new region. **b.** metastasis, when spontaneous. **4.** *Med.* the application of solid medicine underneath the skin. [IMPLANT + -ATION]

im·plau·si·bil·i·ty (im plô′zə bil′i tē), *n., pl.* **-ties** for 2. **1.** quality or condition of being implausible. **2.** that which is implausible. [IMPLAUSIBLE + -ITY]

im·plau·si·ble (im plô′zə bəl), *adj.* not plausible; not having the appearance of truth or credibility: *an implausible alibi.* [IM-[2] + PLAUSIBLE] —**im·plau′si·bly,** *adv.*

im·plead (im plēd′), *v.t.* **1.** to sue in a court of law. **2.** *Rare.* to accuse; impeach. **3.** *Archaic.* to plead (a suit). [ME *emplede(n)* < AF *empled(er).* See IM-[1], PLEAD] —**im·plead′a·ble,** *adj.*

im·plead·er (im plē′dər), *n.* *Law.* a procedural method by which an original party to an action may bring in a third party and make a claim against him in connection with the claim made against the original party. Also called **third party procedure.** [IMPLEAD + -ER[1]]

im·ple·ment (*n.* im′plə mənt; *v.* im′plə ment′), *n.* **1.** an instrument; tool; utensil: *agricultural implements.* **2.** an article of equipment, as household furniture, clothing, ecclesiastical vestments, or the like. **3.** a means; agent: *man as an implement of divine plan.* —*v.t.* **4.** to fulfill; perform; carry out: *Once in office, he failed to implement his campaign promises.* **5.** to put into effect according to or by means of a definite plan or procedure. **6.** to fill out or supplement. **7.** to provide with implements. [late ME < LL *implēment(um)* a filling up, equiv. to L *implē(re)* (to) fill up (*im-* IM-[1] + *plēre* to fill) + *-mentum* -MENT] —**im′ple·men′tal,** *adj.* —**im′ple·men·ta′tion,** *n.* —**im′ple·ment′er, im′ple·men′tor,** *n.*

—**Syn. 1.** See **tool.**

im·ple·tion (im plē′shən), *n.* *Rare.* **1.** act of filling. **2.** state of being filled. [< LL *implētiōn-* (s. of *implētiō*), equiv. to L *implēt(us)* filled up (ptp. of *implēre;* see IMPLEMENT) + *-iōn-* -ION]

im·pli·cate (im′plə kāt′), *v.t.*, **-cat·ed, -cat·ing.** **1.** to involve as being concerned in a matter, affair, condition, etc.: *to be implicated in a crime.* **2.** to imply as a necessary circumstance, or as something to be inferred or understood. **3.** to connect or be related intimately; affect as a consequence: *The malfunctioning of one part of the nervous system implicates another part.* **4.** *Rare.* to fold or twist together; intertwine; interlace. [< L *implicāt(us)* interwoven (ptp. of *implicāre*), equiv. to *im-* IM-[1] + *plic-* PLY[2] + *-ātus* -ATE[1]]

—**Syn. 1.** See **involve.**

im·pli·ca·tion (im′plə kā′shən), *n.* **1.** something implied or suggested as naturally to be inferred or understood: *to resent an implication of dishonesty.* **2.** act of implying: *His implication of immediate changes surprised us.* **3.** state of being implied: *to know only by implication.* **4.** *Logic.* the relation which holds between two propositions, or classes of propositions, in virtue of which one is logically deducible from the other. **5.** act of implicating: *the implication of his six accomplices.* **6.** state of being implicated: *We heard of his implication in a conspiracy.* **7.** Usually, **implications.** relationships of a close or intimate nature; involvements: *the religious implications of ancient astrology.* [ME *implicacio(u)n* < L *implicātiōn-* (s. of *implicātiō*) an interweaving, equiv. to *implicāt(us)* (see IMPLICATE) + *-iōn-* -ION] —**im′pli·ca′tion·al,** *adj.*

im·pli·ca·tive (im′plə kā′tiv, im plik′ə tiv), *adj.* tending to implicate or imply; characterized by or involving implication. [IMPLICATE + -IVE] —**im′pli·ca′tive·ly,** *adv.*

im·pli·ca·to·ry (im′plə kə tōr′ē, -tôr′ē), *adj.* implicative. [IMPLICATE + -ORY[1]]

im·plic·it (im plis′it), *adj.* **1.** unquestioning; unreserved; absolute: *implicit trust; implicit obedience; implicit confidence.* **2.** implied, rather than expressly stated: *implicit agreement.* **3.** virtually contained (usually fol. by *in*): *the drama implicit in the occasion.* **4.** *Math.* (of a function) having the dependent variable not explicitly expressed in terms of the independent variables, as $x^2 + y^2 = 1$. Cf. **explicit** (def. 4). **5.** *Obs.* entangled. [< L *implicit(us),* var. ptp. of *implicāre.* See IMPLICATE, -ITE[2]] —**im·plic′it·ly,** *adv.* —**im·plic′it·ness, im·plic′i·ty,** *n.*

implic′it differentia′tion, *Math.* a method of finding the derivative of an implicit function by taking the derivative of each term with respect to the independent variable while keeping the derivative of the dependent variable with respect to the independent variable in symbolic form and then solving that derivative.

implic′it func′tion the′orem, *Math.* a theorem that gives conditions under which a function written in implicit form can be written in explicit form.

im·plied (im plīd′), *adj.* involved, indicated, or suggested by implying; tacitly understood: *an implied rebuke; an implied compliment.* [IMPLY + -ED[2]]

im·pli·ed·ly (im plī′id lē, -plīd′-), *adv.* by implication. [IMPLIED + -LY]

im·plode (im plōd′), *v.*, **-plod·ed, -plod·ing.** —*v.i.* **1.** to burst inward (opposed to *explode*). —*v.t.* **2.** *Phonet.* to pronounce by implosion. [IM-[1] + (EX)PLODE]

im·plore (im plōr′, -plôr′), *v.*, **-plored, -plor·ing.** —*v.t.* **1.** to call upon in urgent or piteous supplication, as for aid or mercy; beseech; entreat: *They implored him to go.* **2.** to make urgent supplication for (aid, mercy, pardon, etc.): *implore forgiveness.* —*v.i.* **3.** to make urgent or piteous supplication. [< L *implōr(āre),* equiv. to *im-* IM-[1] + *plōrāre* to lament] —**im·plor′a·ble,** *adj.* —**im′plo·ra′tion,** *n.* —**im·plor·a·to·ry** (im plōr′ə tōr′ē, -plôr′ə tôr′ē), *adj.* —**im·plor′er,** *n.* —**im·plor′ing·ly,** *adv.* —**im·plor′ing·ness,** *n.*

—**Syn. 2.** crave, beg, solicit. —**Ant. 2.** spurn, reject.

im·plo·sion (im plō′zhən), *n.* **1.** the act of imploding; a bursting inward. **2.** *Phonet.* **a.** the occlusive phase of stop consonants. **b.** (of a stop consonant) the nasal release heard in the common pronunciation of *eaten, sudden,* or *mitten,* in which the vowel of the final syllable is greatly reduced. **c.** the ingressive release of a suction stop. Cf. **plosion.** [IM-[1] + (EX)PLOSION]

im·plo·sive (im plō′siv), *Phonet.* —*adj.* **1.** characterized by a partial vacuum behind the point of closure. —*n.* **2.** an implosive stop. [IM-[1] + (EX)PLOSIVE] —**im·plo′sive·ly,** *adv.*

im·plu·vi·um (im plo͞o′vē əm), *n., pl.* **-vi·a** (-vē ə). a basin or tank within a compluvium. [< L, equiv. to *im-* IM-[1] + *pluvium* (deriv. of *pluere* to rain)]

im·ply (im plī′), *v.t.*, **-plied, -ply·ing.** **1.** to involve as a necessary circumstance: *Speech implies a speaker.* **2.** (of words) to signify or mean. **3.** to indicate or suggest as something naturally to be inferred, without express statement: *His words implied a lack of faith.* **4.** *Obs.* to enfold. [ME *emplie(n)* < MF *empli(er)* < L *implicāre;* see IMPLICATE]

—**Syn. 1.** assume, include.

—**Usage.** See **infer.**

im·pol·i·cy (im pol′i sē), *n., pl.* **-cies** for 2. **1.** condition or quality of being injudicious; bad policy; inexpediency. **2.** an impolitic or injudicious act. [IM-[2] + POLICY[1]]

im·po·lite (im′pə līt′), *adj.* not polite or courteous; uncivil; rude: *an impolite reply.* [< L *impolīt(us)* rough, unpolished. See IM-[2] POLITE] —**im′po·lite′ly,** *adv.* —**im′po·lite′ness,** *n.*

—**Syn.** discourteous, disrespectful; insolent; boorish, ill-mannered, rough.

im·pol·i·tic (im pol′i tik), *adj.* inexpedient; injudicious. [IM-[2] + POLITIC] —**im·pol′i·tic·ly,** *adv.* —**im·pol′i·tic·ness,** *n.*

im·pon·der·a·bil·i·a (im pon′dər ə bil′ē ə, -bil′yə), *n.pl.* matters that cannot be precisely determined, measured, or evaluated; imponderables: *the imponderabilia surrounding human life.* [< NL, neut. pl. of ML *imponderābilis* IMPONDERABLE]

im·pon·der·a·ble (im pon′dər ə bəl), *adj.* **1.** not ponderable; that cannot be precisely determined, measured, or evaluated. —*n.* **2.** an imponderable thing, force, agency, etc. [< ML *imponderābil(is).* See IM-[2], PONDERABLE] —**im·pon′der·a·bil′i·ty, im·pon′der·a·ble·ness,** *n.* —**im·pon′der·a·bly,** *adv.*

im·pone (im pōn′), *v.t.*, **-poned, -pon·ing.** *Obs.* to wager; stake. [< L *impōne(re)* (to) put in or upon, equiv. to *im-* IM-[1] + *pōnere* to put, place; see POSITION]

im·port (*v.* im pōrt′, -pôrt′; *n.* im′pōrt, -pôrt), *v.t.* **1.** to bring in (merchandise, commodities, etc.) from a foreign country for sale, use, processing, or reexport. **2.** to bring or introduce from one use, connection, or relation into another: *foreign bodies imported into the blood; foodstuffs imported from the farm.* **3.** to convey as meaning or information, as by words, statements, actions, etc.: *Her words imported a change of attitude.* **4.** to involve as a necessary circumstance; imply: *Religion imports belief.* **5.** *Rare.* to be of consequence or importance to; concern. —*v.i.* **6.** to be of consequence or importance; matter. —*n.* **7.** that which is imported from abroad; an imported commodity or article. **8.** act of importing or bringing in; importation, as of goods from abroad: *the import of foreign cars.* **9.** meaning; implication; purport: *He felt the import of her words.* **10.** consequence or importance: *matters of great import.* [ME *importe(n)* < L *import(āre).* See IM-[1], PORT[5]] —**im·port′a·bil′i·ty,** *n.* —**im·port′a·ble,** *adj.* —**im·port′er,** *n.*

—**Syn. 3.** mean, signify. **9.** significance, sense.

im·por·tance (im pôr′təns), *n.* **1.** the quality or state of being important. **2.** important position or standing; personal or social consequence. **3.** consequential air or manner: *an air of bustling importance.* **4.** *Obs.* an im-

portant matter. **5.** *Obs.* importunity. **6.** *Obs.* import or meaning. [< ML *importantia.* See IMPORTANT, -ANCE]
—**Syn. 1.** moment, weight, concern. IMPORTANCE, CONSEQUENCE, SIGNIFICANCE refer to a quality, character, or standing such as to entitle to attention or consideration. IMPORTANCE, referring originally to the bringing or involving of noteworthy results, is the general term. CONSEQUENCE, though of the same general sense, is a weaker word, less suggestive of seriousness, dignity, or extensiveness: *The weather is a matter of consequence to the tourist, but of real importance to the farmer.* SIGNIFICANCE emphasizes the relation of the important matter to other things or people: *of great significance for economic thought.*

Impor′tance of Be′ing Ear′nest, The, a comedy (1895) by Oscar Wilde.

im·por·tant (im pôr′tᵊnt), *adj.* **1.** of much significance or consequence: *an important event.* **2.** mattering much (usually fol. by *to*): *details important to a fair decision.* **3.** of more than ordinary title to consideration or notice: *an important exception.* **4.** prominent or large: *He played an important part in national politics.* **5.** of considerable influence or authority, as a person, position, etc. **6.** of social consequence or distinction, as a person, family, etc. **7.** pompous: *When speaking, he assumes an important attitude that offends his audience.* **8.** *Obs.* importunate. [< ML *important-* (s. of *importāns* weighing, of weight, prp. of *importāre*), equiv. to *im-* IM-¹ + *port-* PORT⁵ + *-ant-* -ANT; see IMPORT] —**im·por′tant·ly,** *adv.*

im·por·ta·tion (im′pôr tā′shən, -pôr-), *n.* **1.** the bringing in of merchandise from a foreign country, for sale, use, processing, or reexport. **2.** something imported. [IMPORT + -ATION]

import′ed cur′rantworm. See under **currantworm.**

im·por·tee (im′pōr tē′, -pôr-), *n.* a person who has been imported: *a delightful new importee from the London stage.* [IMPORT + -EE]

im·por·tu·na·cy (im pôr′chə nə sē), *n.* the quality or condition of being importunate; importunateness. [IMPORTUNA(TE) + -CY]

im·por·tu·nate (im pôr′chə nit), *adj.* **1.** urgent or persistent in solicitation. **2.** pertinacious, as solicitations or demands. **3.** troublesome; annoying: *importunate demands from the children for attention.* [late ME; perh. IMPORTUNE (adj.) + -ATE¹] —**im·por′tu·nate·ly,** *adv.* —**im·por′tu·nate·ness,** *n.*

im·por·tune (im′pôr to͞on′, -tyo͞on′, im pôr′chən), *v.,* **-tuned, -tun·ing,** *adj.* —*v.t.* **1.** to beset with solicitations; demand with urgency or persistence. **2.** to make improper advances toward (a person). **3.** *Rare.* to beg for (something) urgently or persistently. **4.** *Obs.* to annoy. **5.** *Obs.* to press; impel. —*v.i.* **6.** to make urgent or persistent solicitations. **7.** to make improper advances toward another person. —*adj.* **8.** importunate. [ME (adj.) < L *importūn(us)* unsuitable, troublesome, assertive; see OPPORTUNE] —**im′por·tune′ly,** *adv.* —**im′por·tun′er,** *n.*
—**Syn. 1.** beseech, entreat, implore, supplicate, solicit. **6.** plead.

im·por·tu·ni·ty (im′pôr to͞o′ni tē, -tyo͞o′-), *n., pl.* **-ties. 1.** the state or quality of being importunate; persistence in solicitation. **2. importunities,** importunate solicitations or demands. [late ME *importunite* < L *importūnitās.* See IMPORTUNE, -ITY]

im·pose (im pōz′), *v.,* **-posed, -pos·ing.** —*v.t.* **1.** to lay on or set as something to be borne, endured, obeyed, fulfilled, paid, etc.: *to impose taxes.* **2.** to put or set by or as by authority: *to impose an arbitrary meaning upon words.* **3.** to obtrude or thrust (oneself, one's company, etc.) upon others. **4.** to pass or palm off fraudulently or deceptively: *He imposed his pretentious books on the public.* **5.** *Print.* to lay (type pages, plates, etc.) in proper order on an imposing stone or the like and secure in a chase for printing. **6.** to lay on or inflict, as a penalty. **7.** *Archaic.* to put or place on something, or in a particular place. **8.** *Obs.* to lay on (the hands) ceremonially, as in confirmation or ordination. —*v.i.* **9.** to make an impression on the mind; impose one's or its authority or influence. **10.** to obtrude oneself or one's requirements, as upon others: *Are you sure I won't impose?* **11.** to presume, as upon patience, good nature, etc. **12. impose on** or **upon, a.** to thrust oneself offensively upon others; intrude. **b.** to take unfair advantage of; misuse (influence, friendship, etc.). **c.** to defraud; cheat; deceive: *A study recently showed the shocking number of confidence men that impose on the public.* [late ME < MF *impos(er),* equiv. to *im-* IM-¹ + *poser* to POSE¹; see POSE²] —**im·pos′a·ble,** *adj.* —**im·pos′er,** *n.*

im·pos·ing (im pō′ziŋ), *adj.* very impressive; making an impression on the mind, as by great size, stately appearance, etc. [IMPOSE + -ING²] —**im·pos′ing·ly,** *adv.* —**im·pos′ing·ness,** *n.*
—**Syn.** dignified, majestic, lofty, grand, august.

impos′ing stone′, *Print.* a slab, formerly of stone but now usually of metal, resting upon a frame, on which pages of type or plates are imposed and on which type correcting in the page is done. Also called **impos′ing ta′ble.**

im·po·si·tion (im′pə zish′ən), *n.* **1.** the laying on of something as a burden, obligation, etc. **2.** something imposed, as a burden, duty, etc.; an unusual or extraordinarily burdensome requirement or task. **3.** the act of imposing by or as by authority. **4.** an instance of imposing upon a person, as by taking undue advantage of his good nature: *He did the favor but considered the request an imposition.* **5.** act of imposing fraudulently or deceptively on others; imposture. **6.** the ceremonial laying on of hands, as in confirmation or ordination. **7.** *Print.* the arrangement of page plates in proper order on a press for printing a signature. **8.** (in British schools) homework, problems, or copying exercises assigned to a student as punishment. **9.** act of putting, placing, or laying on. [ME *imposicio(u)n* < LL *impositiōn-* (s. of *impositiō*), equiv. to *imposit(us)* placed on, imposed (ptp. of *impōnere* (im- IM-¹ + *posi-,* perf. s. of *pōnere* to put, + *-tus* ptp. suffix) + *-iōn-* -ION]

im·pos·si·bil·i·ty (im pos′ə bil′i tē, im′pos-), *n., pl.* **-ties** for 2. **1.** condition or quality of being impossible. **2.** something impossible. [ME *impossibilite* < LL *impossibilitās.* See IM-², POSSIBILITY]

im·pos·si·ble (im pos′ə bəl), *adj.* **1.** not possible; unable to be, exist, happen, etc. **2.** unable to be done, performed, effected, etc. **3.** incapable of being true, as a rumor. **4.** not to be done, endured, etc., with any degree of reason or propriety: *an impossible situation.* **5.** utterly impracticable: *an impossible plan.* **6.** hopelessly unsuitable, difficult, undesirable, or objectionable: *an impossible person.* [ME < L *impossibil(is).* See IM-², POSSIBLE] —**im·pos′si·ble·ness,** *n.*

im·pos·si·bly (im pos′ə blē), *adv.* **1.** in an impossible manner. **2.** to an extent that produces hardship or prevents a solution: *The problem is impossibly difficult.* **3.** to an extreme or excessive degree: *impossibly foolish.* [IMPOSSIBLE + -LY]

im·post¹ (im′pōst), *n.* **1.** a tax; tribute; duty. **2.** a customs duty. **3.** *Horse Racing.* the weight assigned to a horse in a race. —*v.t.* **4.** to determine customs duties on, according to the kind of imports. [< LL *impost(us)* a tax, n. use of L *impostus,* var. of *impositus* imposed; see IMPOSITION] —**im′post·er,** *n.*

im·post² (im′pōst), *n. Archit.* **1.** the point of springing of an arch; spring. **2.** an architectural feature immediately beneath this point. [< F *imposte* < It *impost(a)* < fem. of L *impostus* (ptp.); see IMPOST¹]

im′post block′, dosseret.

im·pos·tor (im pos′tər), *n.* **1.** a person who imposes fraudulently upon others. **2.** a person who practices deception under an assumed character or name: *He was not the missing heir but an impostor.* [< LL, equiv. to L *impost(us)* imposed upon, deceived (ptp. of *impōnere;* see IMPOST¹) + *-or* -OR²]
—**Syn. 1.** deceiver, cheat, confidence man, charlatan, mountebank. **2.** pretender.

im·pos·tume (im pos′cho͞om, -to͞om, -tyo͞om), *n. Archaic.* an abscess. Also, **im·pos·thume** (im pos′tho͞om). [< MF *empostume,* var. of *apostume* < LL *apostūma,* var. of *apostēme* abscess < Gk: lit., separation (of pus), equiv. to *apostê(nai)* (to) separate (*apo-* APO- + *stē-* STAND + *-nai* inf. suffix) + *-ma* n. suffix; r. ME *emposteme* < MF]

im·pos·ture (im pos′chər), *n.* **1.** the action or practice of imposing fraudulently upon others. **2.** deception practiced under an assumed character or name, as by an impostor. **3.** an instance or piece of fraudulent imposition. [< LL *impostūr(a),* equiv. to L *impost(us)* deceived (see IMPOSTOR) + *-ūra* -URE] —**im·pos·trous,** (im pos′trəs), **im·pos′tur·ous,** *adj.*
—**Syn. 3.** fraud, hoax, swindle, deception, humbug, cheat.

im·po·sure (im pō′zhər), *n. Rare.* act of imposing: *the imposure of a decree.* [IMPOSE + -URE]

im·po·tence (im′pə tᵊns), *n.* **1.** the condition or quality of being impotent; weakness. **2.** complete failure of sexual power, esp. in the male. **3.** *Obs.* lack of self-restraint. Also, **im′po·ten·cy, im′po·tent·ness.** [ME, var. (see -ENCE) of *impotencie* < L *impotentia* want of self-control. See IM-², POTENCY]

im·po·tent (im′pə tᵊnt), *adj.* **1.** not potent; lacking power or ability. **2.** utterly unable (to do something). **3.** without force or effectiveness. **4.** lacking bodily strength, or physically helpless, as an aged person or a cripple. **5.** (esp. of a male) wholly lacking in sexual power. **6.** *Obs.* without restraint. [ME < L *impotent-* (s. of *impotēns*) without power over oneself or others. See IM-², POTENT¹] —**im′po·tent·ly,** *adv.*
—**Syn. 1, 2.** powerless, helpless. **3.** ineffectual, ineffective, feeble, weak.

im·pound (im pound′), *v.t.* **1.** to shut up in a pound, as a stray animal. **2.** to confine within an enclosure or within limits: *water impounded in a reservoir.* **3.** to seize, take, or appropriate summarily. **4.** to seize and retain in custody of the law, as a document for evidence. [IM-¹ + POUND³] —**im·pound′a·ble,** *adj.* —**im·pound′er,** *n.* —**im·pound′ment, im·pound·age** (im poun′dij), *n.*

im·pov·er·ish (im pov′ər ish, -pov′rish), *v.t.* **1.** to reduce to poverty: *a country impoverished by war.* **2.** to make poor in quality, productiveness, etc.; exhaust the strength or richness of: *to impoverish the soil.* [late ME *empoveris(en)* < MF *empoveriss-* (long s. of *empovrir*), equiv. to *em-* EM-¹ + *povre* POOR + *-iss* -ISH²] —**im·pov′er·ish·er,** *n.* —**im·pov′er·ish·ment,** *n.*
—**Syn. 2.** deplete, drain; weaken, enervate, fatigue, cripple. —**Ant. 1, 2.** enrich.

im·pov·er·ished (im pov′ər isht, -pov′risht), *adj.* **1.** reduced to poverty. **2.** deprived of strength, vitality, creativeness, etc.: *an impoverished attempt at humor.* **3.** (of a country, area, etc.) having few trees, flowers, birds, wild animals, etc. [IMPOVERISH + -ED²]
—**Syn. 1.** See **poor.**

im·pow·er (im pou′ər), *v.t. Obs.* empower.

im·prac·ti·ca·ble (im prak′tə kə bəl), *adj.* **1.** not practicable; incapable of being put into practice with the available means: *an impracticable plan.* **2.** unsuitable for practical use or purposes, as a device, material, etc. **3.** (of ground, places, etc.) impassable. **4.** *Rare.* (of persons) hard to deal with because of stubbornness, stupidity, etc. [IM-² + PRACTICABLE] —**im·prac′ti·ca·bil′i·ty, im·prac′ti·ca·ble·ness,** *n.* —**im·prac′ti·ca·bly,** *adv.*

im·prac·ti·cal (im prak′tə kəl), *adj.* not practical. [IM-² + PRACTICAL] —**im·prac′ti·cal′i·ty, im·prac′ti·cal·ness,** *n.*

im·pre·cate (im′prə kāt′), *v.t.,* **-cat·ed, -cat·ing.** to call down or invoke (evil or curses), as upon a person. [< L *imprecāt(us)* invoked, prayed to (ptp. of *imprecārī*), equiv. to *im-* IM-¹ + *prec-* PRAY + *-ātus* -ATE¹] —**im′pre·ca′tor,** *n.* —**im·pre·ca·to·ri·ly** (im′prə kə tōr′ə lē, -tôr′-), *adv.* —**im′pre·ca·to′ry,** *adj.*
—**Syn.** curse, execrate, anathematize, accurse, denunciate. —**Ant.** bless.

im·pre·ca·tion (im′prə kā′shən), *n.* **1.** the act of imprecating; cursing. **2.** a curse; malediction. [< L *imprecātiōn-* (s. of *imprecātiō*), equiv. to *imprecāt(us)* (see IMPRECATE) + *-iōn-* -ION]

im·pre·cise (im′pri sīs′), *adj.* not precise; not exact; vague or ill-defined. [IM-² + PRECISE] —**im′pre·cise′ly,** *adv.* —**im′pre·cise′ness,** *n.*

im·pre·ci·sion (im′pri sizh′ən), *n.* **1.** condition or quality of being imprecise or inaccurate. **2.** an instance of vagueness or inaccuracy. [IM-² + PRECISION]

im·preg·na·ble¹ (im preg′nə bəl), *adj.* **1.** strong enough to resist or withstand attack; not to be taken by force: *an impregnable fort.* **2.** not to be overcome or overthrown: *an impregnable argument.* [ME *imprenable* < MF, equiv. to *im-* IM-² + *prenable* PREGNABLE] —**im·preg′na·bil′i·ty, im·preg′na·ble·ness,** *n.* —**im·preg′na·bly,** *adv.*
—**Syn. 1.** invulnerable. **1, 2.** See **invincible. 2.** unassailable. —**Ant. 1.** vulnerable.

im·preg·na·ble² (im preg′nə bəl), *adj.* susceptible of impregnation, as an egg. [IMPREGN(ATE) + -ABLE]

im·preg·nate (*v.* im preg′nāt, im′preg-; *adj.* im preg′nit, -nāt), *v.,* **-nat·ed, -nat·ing,** *adj.* —*v.t.* **1.** to make pregnant; get with child or young. **2.** to fertilize. **3.** to charge with something infused or permeating throughout; saturate: *to impregnate a handkerchief with cheap perfume.* **4.** to fill interstices with a substance. **5.** to furnish with some actuating or modifying element infused or introduced; imbue, infect; tincture. —*adj.* **6.** impregnated. [< LL *impraegnāt(us)* impregnated, made pregnant (ptp. of *impraegnāre*), equiv. to *im-* IM-¹ + *praegn-* (see PREGNANT) + *-ātus* -ATE¹] —**im′preg·na′tion,** *n.* —**im·preg′na·tor,** *n.* —**im·preg·na·to·ry** (im preg′nə tōr′ē, -tôr′ē), *adj.*
—**Syn. 3.** permeate, infuse, penetrate.

im·pre·sa (im prā′zə; *It.* ēm pre′zä), *n., pl.* **-sas,** *It.* **-se** (-ze). *Obs.* **1.** a device or emblem. **2.** a motto. Also, **im·prese** (im prēz′). [< It: lit., undertaking, n. use of fem. of *impreso,* ptp. of *imprendere* to undertake; see EMPRISE]

im·pre·sa·ri·o (im′pri sär′ē ō′, -sâr′-; *It.* ēm′pre·sä′ryô), *n., pl.* **-sa·ri·os,** *It.* **-sa·ri** (-sä′rē). **1.** a person who organizes or manages public entertainments, esp. the manager of an opera company, ballet company, concert series, etc. **2.** any manager, director, or the like. [< It, equiv. to *impres(a)* IMPRESA + *-ario* -ARY]

im·pre·scrip·ti·ble (im′pri skrip′tə bəl), *adj. Law.* not subject to prescription. [< ML *imprescriptibil(is).* See IM-², PRESCRIPTIBLE] —**im′pre·scrip′ti·bil′i·ty,** *n.* —**im′pre·scrip′ti·bly,** *adv.*

im·press¹ (*v.* im pres′; *n.* im′pres), *v.,* **-pressed** or (*Archaic*) **-prest; -press·ing;** *n.* —*v.t.* **1.** to affect deeply or strongly in mind or feelings; influence in opinion: *He impressed us as a sincere young man.* **2.** to fix deeply or firmly on the mind or memory, as ideas, facts, etc.: *to impress a rule on a child.* **3.** to urge, as something to be remembered or done: *He impressed the need for action on them.* **4.** to press (a thing) into or on something. **5.** to impose a particular characteristic or quality upon (something): *The painter impressed his love of garish colors upon the landscape.* **6.** to produce (a mark, figure, etc.) by pressure; stamp; imprint: *He impressed his seal on the melted wax.* **7.** to apply with pressure, so as to leave a mark. **8.** to subject to or mark by pressure with something. **9.** to furnish with a mark, figure, etc., by or as by stamping. **10.** *Elect.* to produce (a voltage) or cause (a voltage) to appear or be produced on a conductor, circuit, etc. —*v.i.* **11.** to create a favorable impression; draw attention to oneself: *a child's antics calculated to impress.* —*n.* **12.** act of impressing. **13.** a mark made by or as by pressure; stamp; imprint. **14.** a distinctive character or effect imparted: *writings that bear the impress of a strong personality.* [ME *impresse(n)* < L *impress(us)* pressed into or upon, impressed (ptp. of *imprimere*), equiv. to *im-* IM-¹ + *pressus* pressed, ptp. of *primere;* see PRESS¹] —**im·press′er,** *n.*
—**Syn. 1.** move, sway, disturb; persuade.

im·press² (*v.* im pres′; *n.* im′pres), *v.,* **-pressed** or (*Archaic*) **-prest; -press·ing;** *n.* —*v.t.* **1.** to press or force into public service, as seamen. **2.** to seize or take for public use. **3.** to take or persuade into service by forceful arguments: *The neighbors were impressed into helping the family move.* —*n.* **4.** impressment. [IM-¹ + PRESS²]

im·press·i·ble (im pres′ə bəl), *adj.* capable of being impressed; impressionable. [IMPRESS¹ + -IBLE] —**im·press′i·bil′i·ty, im·press′i·ble·ness,** *n.* —**im·press′i·bly,** *adv.*

im·pres·sion (im presh′ən), *n.* **1.** a strong effect produced on the intellect, feelings, or conscience, etc. **2.** the first and immediate effect upon the mind in outward or inward perception; sensation. **3.** the effect produced by an agency or influence. **4.** a notion, remembrance, belief, etc., often of a vague or indistinct nature: *He had a general impression of lights, voices, and the clinking of silver.* **5.** a mark, indentation, figure, etc., produced by pressure. **6.** *Chiefly Print.* **a.** the process or result of printing from type, plates, etc. **b.** a printed copy from type, a plate, an engraved block, etc. **c.** one of a number of printings made at different times from the same set of type, without alteration (distinguished from *edition*). **d.** the total number of copies of a book, pamphlet, etc., printed at one time from one setting of type or from one set of plates. **7.** *Dentistry.* a mold taken, in plastic materials or plaster of Paris, of teeth and the surrounding tissues. **8.** *Metalworking.* a portion of a die having in reverse the intended form of an object to be forged. **9.** an image in the mind caused by something external to it. **10.** act of impressing; state of being impressed. **11.** an imitation of recognizable traits of famous persons, as by an entertainer: *She did her impressions of well-known singers.* [ME *impressio(u)n* < L *impressiōn-* (s. of *impressiō*), equiv. to *impress(us)* (see IMPRESS¹) + *-iōn-* -ION] —**im·pres′sion·al,** *adj.* —**im·pres′sion·al·ly,** *adv.* —**im·pres′sion·less,** *adj.*

im·pres·sion·a·ble (im presh′ə nə bəl, -presh′nə-), *adj.* **1.** easily impressed or influenced; susceptible: *an impressionable youngster.* **2.** capable of being impressed. [IMPRESSION + -ABLE; cf. F *impressionnable*] —**im·pres′sion·a·bil′i·ty, im·pres′sion·a·ble·ness,** *n.* —**im·pres′sion·a·bly,** *adv.*

im·pres·sion·ism (im presh′ə niz′əm), *n.* **1.** *Fine Arts.* **a.** (*usually cap.*) a style of painting developed in the last third of the 19th century, characterized chiefly by short brush strokes of bright colors in immediate juxtaposition to represent the effect of light on objects. **b.** a manner of painting in which the forms, colors, or tones of an object are lightly and rapidly indicated. **c.** a manner of sculpture in which volumes are partially modeled and surfaces roughened to reflect light unevenly. **2.** a theory and practice in literature which emphasizes immediate aspects of objects or actions without attention to details. **3.** a late 19th-century and early 20th-century style of musical composition in which lush harmonies, subtle rhythms, and unusual tonal colors are used to evoke moods and impressions. [IMPRESSION + -ISM; cf. G *Impressionismus,* F *impressionnisme*]

im·pres·sion·ist (im presh′ə nist), *n.* **1.** a person who adheres to the theories, methods, and practices of impressionism, esp. in the fields of painting, music, and literature. **2.** an entertainer, esp. one who imitates the mannerisms of famous personalities. —*adj.* **3.** (*usually cap.*) *Fine Arts.* of, pertaining to, or characteristic of Impressionism: *Impressionist paintings; Impressionist* artists. [< F *impressioniste.* See IMPRESSION, -IST] —**im·pres′sion·is′tic,** *adj.* —**im·pres′sion·is′ti·cal·ly,** *adv.*

im·pres·sive (im pres′iv), *adj.* having the ability to impress the mind; arousing solemn feeling; moving; admirable: *an impressive ceremony; an impressive appearance.* [IMPRESS[1] + -IVE] —**im·pres′sive·ly,** *adv.* —**im·pres′sive·ness,** *n.*
—**Syn.** imposing, awesome.

im·press·ment (im pres′mənt), *n.* the act of impressing men, property, etc., as for public service or use. [IMPRESS[2] + -MENT]

im·pres·sure (im presh′ər), *n. Archaic.* impression. [IMPRESS[1] + -URE, modeled on *pressure*]

im·prest[1] (im′prest), *n. Brit.* (formerly) a bonus or advance payment made to a soldier or sailor at enlistment. [prob. n. use of obs. v. *imprest* to advance money to < It *imprest(are)* < L *im-* IM-[1] + *praestāre* to stand surety for, equiv. to *praes* surety, bondsman (*praevids, equiv. to *praevid(ēre)* (to) foresee + *-s* nom. sing. suffix) + *stāre* to STAND]

im·prest[2] (im prest′), *v. Archaic.* pt. and pp. of **impress.**

im·pri·ma·tur (im′pri mä′tər, -mā′-, -prī-), *n.* **1.** an official license to print or publish a book, pamphlet, etc., esp. a license issued by a censor of the Roman Catholic Church. Cf. **nihil obstat. 2.** license; sanction; approval: *His book has the imprimatur of leading critics.* [< NL: let it be printed, L: let it be made by pressing upon (something); see IMPRESS[1]]

im·pri·ma·tu·ra (im prē′mə to͝or′ə), *n. Painting.* a tinted or glazed priming; underpainting. [< It *imprimitura,* equiv. to *imprimit(o)* impressed (ptp. of *imprimere;* see IMPRESS[1]) + *-ura* -URE]

im·pri·mis (im prī′mis), *adv.* in the first place. [late ME < L, contr. of phrase *in prīmīs* among the first, in the first place]

im·print (*n.* im′print; *v.* im print′), *n.* **1.** a mark made by pressure; a figure impressed or printed on something. **2.** any impression or impressed effect: *He left the imprint of his thought on all succeeding scholars.* **3.** *Bibliog.* the publisher's name, usually accompanied by the place and date of publication, printed on the title page or elsewhere in a book. **4.** the printer's name and address as indicated on any printed matter. —*v.t.* **5.** to impress (a quality, character, distinguishing mark, etc.). **6.** to produce (a mark) on something by pressure. **7.** to bestow, as a kiss. **8.** to fix firmly on the mind, memory, etc. **9.** *Psychol.* to acquire or establish by imprinting. **10.** to make an imprint upon. [IM-[1] + PRINT; r. ME *empreynte(n)* < MF *empreint(er),* deriv. of *empreinte,* fem. ptp. of *empreindre* < L *imprimere* to IMPRESS[1]] —**im·print′er,** *n.*

im·print·ing (im prin′ting), *n. Psychol.* learning occurring rapidly and very early in life, characterized chiefly by resistance to extinction or forgetfulness. [IMPRINT + -ING[1]]

im·pris·on (im priz′ən), *v.t.* **1.** to put into or confine in a prison; detain in custody. **2.** to shut up as if in a prison; hold in restraint: *imprisoned in one's memories.* [ME *enprisone(n)* < OF *enprison(er),* equiv. to *en-* EN-[1] + *prison* PRISON + *-er* inf. suffix] —**im·pris′on·er,** *n.*

im·pris·on·a·ble (im priz′ə nə bəl), *adj.* **1.** capable of being imprisoned. **2.** legally punishable by imprisonment. [IMPRISON + -ABLE]

im·pris·on·ment (im priz′ən mənt), *n.* **1.** act of imprisoning. **2.** state of being imprisoned. **3.** forcible restraint of a person against his will. [ME *enprisonement* << OF *emprison(er)* (to) IMPRISON + *-ment* -MENT]

im·prob·a·bil·i·ty (im prob′ə bil′i tē, im′prob-), *n., pl.* **-ties** for 2. **1.** the quality or condition of being improbable; unlikelihood. **2.** something improbable or unlikely. [IMPROBABLE + -ITY]

im·prob·a·ble (im prob′ə bəl), *adj.* not probable; unlikely to be true or to happen. [< L *improbābil(is).* See IM-[2], PROBABLE] —**im·prob′a·bly,** *adv.* —**im·prob′a·ble·ness,** *n.*

im·pro·bi·ty (im prō′bi tē, -prob′i tē), *n.* lack of moral principles; dishonesty; wickedness. [ME *improbite* < L *improbitās.* See IM-[2], PROBITY]

im·promp·tu (im promp′to͞o, -tyo͞o), *adj.* **1.** made or done without previous preparation: *an impromptu address to the unexpected crowds.* **2.** suddenly or hastily prepared, made, etc.: *an impromptu dinner.* **3.** improvised; having the character of an improvisation. —*adv.* **4.** without preparation: *verses written impromptu.* —*n.* **5.** something impromptu; an impromptu speech, musical composition, performance, etc. **6.** a character piece for piano common in the 19th century and having, despite its title, a clear-cut form. [< F < L *in promptū* in readiness; see PROMPT]
—**Syn. 1.** See **extemporaneous.**

im·prop·er (im prop′ər), *adj.* **1.** not proper; not strictly belonging, applicable, correct, etc.; erroneous: *He drew improper inferences from the speaker's remarks.* **2.** not in accordance with propriety of behavior, manners, etc.: *improper conduct.* **3.** unsuitable or inappropriate, as for the purpose or occasion: *improper attire.* **4.** abnormal or irregular: *improper functioning of the speech mechanism.* [< L *impropr(ius).* See IM-[2], PROPER] —**im·prop′er·ly,** *adv.* —**im·prop′er·ness,** *n.*
—**Syn. 1–3.** inapplicable, unsuited, unfit. **2.** indecorous. IMPROPER, INDECENT, UNBECOMING, UNSEEMLY are applied to that which is unfitting or not in accordance with propriety. IMPROPER has a wide range, being applied to whatever is not suitable or fitting, and often specifically to what does not conform to the standards of conventional morality: *improper diet; improper behavior in church; improper language.* INDECENT, a strong word, is applied to what is offensively contrary to standards of propriety and esp. of modesty: *indecent behavior, literature.* UNBECOMING is applied to what is especially unfitting in the person concerned: *conduct unbecoming a minister.* UNSEEMLY is applied to whatever is unfitting or improper under the circumstances: *unseemly mirth.* —**Ant. 1.** fitting. **2.** modest. **3.** suitable.

improp′er frac′tion, a fraction having the numerator greater than the denominator.

Im·pro·pe·ri·a (im′pro pēr′ē ə), *n.* (*construed as pl.*) reproach (def. 8). [< eccl. L, pl. of *improperium,* deriv. of modified s. of *improbāre* to disapprove, reject]

improp′er in′tegral, *Math.* **1.** Also called **infinite integral.** a definite integral in which one or both of the limits of integration is infinite. **2.** a definite integral in which the integrand becomes infinite at a point or points in the interval of integration.

im·pro·pri·ate (*adj.* im prō′prē it, -āt′; *v.* im prō′prē āt′), *adj., v.,* **-at·ed, -at·ing.** —*adj.* **1.** *Eng. Eccles. Law.* devolved into the hands of a layman. **2.** *Obs.* appropriated to private use. —*v.t.* **3.** *Eng. Eccles. Law.* to place (ecclesiastical property) in the hands of lay persons. **4.** *Obs.* to appropriate. [< ML *impropriāt(us)* made one's own (ptp. of *impropriāre*), equiv. to L *im-* IM-[1] + *propri(us)* one's own + *-ātus* -ATE[1]; see APPROPRIATE] —**im·pro′pri·a′tion,** *n.*

im·pro·pri·a·tor (im prō′prē ā′tər), *n.* a layman in possession of church property or revenues. [IMPROPRIATE + -OR[2]]

im·pro·pri·e·ty (im′prə prī′i tē), *n., pl.* **-ties** for 4, 5. **1.** the quality or condition of being improper; incorrectness. **2.** inappropriateness; unsuitableness. **3.** unseemliness; indecorousness. **4.** an erroneous or unsuitable expression, act, etc. **5.** an improper use of a word. [< LL *improprietās.* See IM-[2], PROPRIETY]

im·prove (im pro͞ov′), *v.,* **-proved, -prov·ing.** —*v.t.* **1.** to bring into a more desirable or excellent condition: *He took vitamins to improve his health.* **2.** to make (land) more useful, profitable, or valuable by enclosure, cultivation, etc. **3.** to increase the value of (real property) by betterments, as the construction of buildings. **4.** to make good use of; turn to account: *He improved the stopover by seeing a client with offices there.* —*v.i.* **5.** to increase in value, excellence, etc.; become better: *The military situation is improving.* **6. improve on** or **upon,** to make improvements, as by revision, addition, or emendation: *None of the younger violinists have been able to improve on his interpretation of that work.* [< AF *emprou(er)* (to) turn (something) into profit, deriv. of phrase *en prou* into profit, equiv. to *en* (see EN-[1]) + *prou* < LL *prōde* useful, back formation from L *prōdesse* to be useful; see PROUD] —**im·prov′a·ble,** *adj.* —**im·prov′a·bil′i·ty, im·prov′a·ble·ness,** *n.* —**im·prov′a·bly,** *adv.* —**im·prov′ing·ly,** *adv.*
—**Syn. 1.** amend, emend. IMPROVE, AMELIORATE, BETTER imply bringing to a more desirable state. IMPROVE usually implies remedying a lack or a felt need: *to improve a process, oneself (as by gaining more knowledge).* AMELIORATE, a formal word, implies improving oppressive, unjust, or difficult conditions: *to ameliorate working conditions.* To BETTER is to improve conditions which, though not bad, are unsatisfying: *to better an attempt, oneself (gain a higher salary).* **5.** mend, gain. —**Ant. 1, 5.** worsen.

im·prove·ment (im pro͞ov′mənt), *n.* **1.** act of improving; state of being improved. **2.** a change or addition by which a thing is improved. **3.** some thing or person that represents an advance on another in excellence or achievement: *The new landlord is a great improvement over his greedy predecessor.* **4.** a bringing into a more valuable or desirable condition, as of land or real property; a making or becoming better; betterment. **5.** something done or added to real property which increases its value. **6.** profitable use, as of a period of time. [< AF *emprouement* something profitable (especially exploitation of land). See IMPROVE, -MENT]

im·prov·er (im pro͞o′vər), *n.* **1.** one who or that which improves. **2.** a substance or agent added to improve a food, esp. as a preservative. [IMPROVE + -ER[1]]

im·prov·i·dent (im prov′i dənt), *adj.* **1.** not provident; lacking foresight; incautious; unwary. **2.** neglecting to provide for future needs. [IM-[2] + PROVIDENT] —**im·prov′i·dence,** *n.* —**im·prov′i·dent·ly,** *adv.*
—**Syn. 1.** thoughtless, careless, imprudent, heedless. **2.** shiftless, thriftless, unthrifty; wasteful, prodigal. —**Ant. 1.** prudent. **2.** economical.

im·prov·i·sa·tion (im prov′i zā′shən, im′prə vi-), *n.* **1.** act of improvising. **2.** something improvised. [IMPROVISE + -ATION] —**im·prov′i·sa′tion·al,** *adj.*

im·prov·i·sa·tor (im prov′i zā′tər, im′prə vi-), *n.* a person who improvises. [IMPROVISE + -ATOR; cf. It *improvvisatore*]

im·pro·vi·sa·to·ry (im′prə vī′zə tôr′ē, -tōr′ē, -viz′i-), *adj.* of, pertaining to, or characteristic of an improvisation or improvisator. [IMPROVISATOR + -Y[1]; see -ORY[1]] —**im·prov·i·sa·to·ri·al** (im prov′i zə tôr′ē əl, -tōr′-), *adj.* —**im·prov′i·sa·to′ri·al·ly,** *adv.*

im·pro·vise (im′prə vīz′), *v.,* **-vised, -vis·ing.** —*v.t.* **1.** to prepare or provide offhand or hastily; extemporize. **2.** to compose (verse, music, etc.) on the spur of the moment. **3.** to recite, sing, etc., extemporaneously. —*v.i.* **4.** to compose, utter, or execute anything extemporaneously: *He improvised in rhyme on subjects suggested by the audience.* [back formation from *improviso* improvised < It *improvviso* < L *imprōvīsō* suddenly. See IM-[2], PROVISO] —**im′pro·vis′er,** *n.*

im·pro·vised (im′prə vīzd′), *adj.* made or said without previous preparation. [IMPROVISE + -ED[2]] —**im·pro·vis·ed·ly** (im′prə vī′zid lē), *adv.*
—**Syn.** unpremeditated, unrehearsed, unprepared. See **extemporaneous.** —**Ant.** rehearsed.

im·prov·vi·sa·to·re (ēm′prôv vē′zä tô′re), *n., pl.* **-ri** (-rē). *Italian.* an improvisator, esp. one who extemporizes verse.

im·pru·dent (im pro͞od′ənt), *adj.* not prudent; lacking discretion. [ME < L *imprūdent-* (s. of *imprūdēns*) unforeseeing, rash. See IM-[2], PRUDENT] —**im·pru′dence, im·pru′dent·ness, im·pru′den·cy,** *n.* —**im·pru′dent·ly,** *adv.*

imp·son·ite (imp′sə nīt′), *n.* a black variety of asphaltite with a jagged fracture. [named after *Impson,* valley in Oklahoma; see -ITE[1]]

im·pu·dence (im′pyə dəns), *n.* **1.** the quality or condition of being impudent; effrontery; insolence. **2.** impudent conduct or language. **3.** *Obs.* lack of modesty; shamelessness. Also, **im′pu·den·cy.** [ME < L *impudentia* shamelessness. See IMPUDENT, -ENCE]
—**Syn. 1.** impertinence, rudeness; brass, brazenness, face, lip, boldness, presumption, sauce, pertness; nerve, gall. —**Ant. 1.** courtesy.

im·pu·dent (im′pyə dənt), *adj.* **1.** of, pertaining to, or characterized by boldness, impertinence, or effrontery: *The student was kept in for impudent behavior. The puppy gave her impudent looks as he chewed her shoe.* **2.** *Obs.* shameless or brazenly immodest. [ME < L *impudent-* (s. of *impudēns*) shameless, equiv. to *im-* IM-[2] + *pud-* (root of *pudēre* to feel shame) + *-ent-* -ENT] —**im′pu·dent·ly,** *adv.* —**im′pu·dent·ness,** *n.*
—**Syn. 1.** insulting, rude; saucy, pert, presumptuous, fresh; brazen. See **impertinent.** —**Ant. 1.** courteous.

im·pu·dic·i·ty (im′pyo͞o dis′i tē), *n.* immodesty. [< L *impudīciti(a),* equiv. to *im-* IM-[2] + *pudīcitia* modesty (*pudīc(us)* modest + *-itia* -ICE)]

im·pugn (im pyo͞on′), *v.t.* **1.** to assail by words or arguments, as statements, motives, veracity, etc.; call in question; challenge as false. **2.** *Obs.* to assail (a person) physically. [ME *impugne(n)* < MF *impugn(er)* < L *impugnāre* to attack, equiv. to *im-* IM-[1] + *pugnāre* to fight, deriv. of *pugna* a battle; see PUGNACIOUS] —**im·pugn′a·bil′i·ty,** *n.* —**im·pugn′a·ble,** *adj.* —**im·pugn′er,** *n.* —**im·pugn′ment,** *n.*
—**Syn. 1.** attack, asperse, malign, criticize, censure, abuse.

im·pu·is·sant (im pyo͞o′i sənt, im′pyo͞o is′ənt, impwis′ənt), *adj.* impotent; feeble; weak. [< MF; see IM-[2], PUISSANT] —**im·pu′is·sance,** *n.*

im·pulse (im′puls), *n.* **1.** the influence of a particular feeling, mental state, etc.: *to aid someone out of an impulse of pity; to act under a generous impulse; to strike out at someone from an angry impulse.* **2.** sudden, involuntary inclination prompting to action: *to be swayed by impulse.* **3.** an instance of this. **4.** an impelling action or force, driving onward or inducing motion. **5.** the effect of an impelling force; motion induced; impetus given. **6.** *Physiol.* a progressive wave of excitation over a nerve or muscle fiber, having either a stimulating or inhibitory effect. **7.** *Mech.* the product of the average force acting upon a body and the time during which it acts, equivalent to the change in the momentum of the body produced by such a force. **8.** *Elect.* a single, usually sudden, flow of current in one direction. [< L *impuls(us)* pressure, impulse, n. use of *impulsus* pushed on (ptp. of *impellere* to IMPEL), equiv. to *im-* IM-[1] + *pul-* (perf. s. of *pellere* to push) + *-sus* ptp. suffix]
—**Syn. 1.** stimulation, force, spur. **2.** liking, emotion, feeling.

im′pulse buy′ing, the purchasing of goods, esp. consumer goods, on impulse rather than by plan or according to need.

im′pulse roll′er, *Horol.* (in a lever escapement) the roller to which the lever imparts motion.

im′pulse tur′bine, a turbine moved by free jets of fluid striking the blades of the rotor together with the axial flow of fluid through the rotor. Cf. **reaction turbine.**

im·pul·sion (im pul′shən), *n.* **1.** the act of impelling, driving onward, or pushing. **2.** the resulting state or effect; impulse; impetus. **3.** the inciting influence of some feeling or motive; mental impulse. **4.** a constraining or inciting action exerted on the mind or conduct: *divine impulsion.* [ME < L *impulsiōn-* (s. of *impulsiō*) incitement. See IMPULSE, -ION]

im·pul·sive (im pul′siv), *adj.* **1.** actuated or swayed by emotional or involuntary impulses: *an impulsive child.* **2.** having the power or effect of impelling; characterized by impulsion: *impulsive forces.* **3.** inciting to action: *the impulsive effects of a revolutionary idea.* **4.** *Mech.* (of forces) acting momentarily; not continuous. [ME < ML *impulsīv(us).* See IMPULSE, -IVE] —**im·pul′sive·ly,** *adv.* —**im·pul′sive·ness,** *n.*
—**Syn. 1.** rash, quick, hasty. See **impetuous.**

im·pu·ni·tive (im pyo͞o′ni tiv), *adj. Psychol.* (in a frustrating situation) not condemning either oneself or others and usually justifying the situation, often accompanied by feelings of embarrassment or shame. Cf. **extrapunitive, intropunitive.** [IM-[2] + PUNITIVE]

im·pu·ni·ty (im pyo͞o′ni tē), *n.* exemption from punishment. [< L *impūnitās,* equiv. to *im-* IM-[2] + *pūnitās* punishment (*pūn-* (root of *pūnēre* to punish) + *-itās* -ITY); see PUNITIVE]
—**Syn.** See **exemption.**

im·pure (im pyo͝or′), *adj.* **1.** not pure; mixed with extraneous matter, esp. of an inferior or contaminating nature: *impure food or drugs.* **2.** modified by admixture, as color. **3.** mixed or combined with something else: *an impure style of architecture.* **4.** ceremonially unclean, as things, animals, etc. **5.** not morally pure or proper; unchaste or obscene: *impure thoughts.* **6.** marked by foreign and unsuitable or objectionable elements or characteristics, as a style of art or of literary expression. [< L *impūr(us).* See IM-[2], PURE] —**im·pure′ly,** *adv.* —**im·pure′ness,** *n.*

im·pu·ri·ty (im pyo͝or′i tē), *n., pl.* **-ties. 1.** the quality or state of being impure. **2.** Often, **impurities.** that which is or makes impure: *After the flood the authorities warned against impurities in the drinking water.* [late ME *impurite* < L *impūritās.* See IMPURE, -ITY]

im·put·a·ble (im pyo͞o′tə bəl), *adj.* able to be imputed; attributable. [< ML *imputābil(is).* See IMPUTE, -ABLE] —**im·put′a·bil′i·ty, im·put′a·ble·ness,** *n.* —**im·put′a·bly,** *adv.*

im·pu·ta·tion (im′pyo͝o tā′shən), *n.* **1.** act of imputing. **2.** an attribution, esp. of fault, crime, etc.; accusation. [< LL *imputātiōn-* (s. of *imputātiō*), equiv. to L *imputāt(us)* ascribed (ptp. of *imputāre* to IMPUTE) + *-iōn-* -ION]

im·pute (im pyo͞ot′), *v.t.,* **-put·ed, -put·ing. 1.** to attribute (something discreditable), as to a person. **2.** to attribute or ascribe: *The children imputed magical powers to the old woman.* **3.** *Law.* to charge, as with some misdemeanor. **4.** *Theol.* to attribute (righteousness, guilt, etc.) vicariously; ascribe as derived from another. **5.** *Obs.* to charge (a person) with fault. [ME *impute(n)* < L *imput(āre),* equiv. to *im-* IM-[1] + *putāre* reckon + *-re* inf. ending; see PUTATIVE] —**im·put·a·tive** (im pyo͞o′tə tiv), *adj.* —**im·put′a·tive·ly,** *adv.* —**im·put′a·tive·ness,** *n.* —**im·put′ed·ly,** *adv.* —**im·put′er,** *n.*
—**Syn. 2.** See **attribute.**

im·pu·tres·ci·ble (im′pyo͞o tres′ə bəl), *adj.* not liable to decomposition or putrefaction; incorruptible: *a tanning process to make skins imputrescible.* [< LL *imputrescibil(is).* See IM-[2], PUTRESCIBLE] —**im′pu·tres′ci·bil′i·ty,** *n.*

impv., imperative.

in (in), *prep., adv., adj., n., v.,* **inned, in·ning.** —*prep.* **1.** (used to indicate inclusion within space, a place, or limits): *walking in the park.* **2.** (used to indicate inclusion within something immaterial): *in politics; in the autumn.* **3.** (used to indicate inclusion within or occurrence during a period or limit of time): *in ancient times; a task done in ten minutes.* **4.** (used to indicate limitation or qualification, as of situation, condition, relation, manner, action, etc.): *to speak in a whisper;*

to be similar in appearance. **5.** (used to indicate means): *sketched in ink; spoken in French.* **6.** (used to indicate motion or direction from outside to a point within) into: *Let's go in the house.* **7.** (used to indicate transition from one state to another): *to break in half.* **8.** (used to indicate object or purpose): *speaking in honor of the event.* **9. in that,** because; inasmuch as: *In that you won't have time for supper, let me give you something now.* —*adv.* **10.** in or into some place, position, state, relation, etc. **11.** on the inside; within. **12.** in one's house or office. **13.** in office or power. **14.** in possession or occupancy. **15.** having the turn to play, as in a game. **16.** *Baseball.* (of an infielder or outfielder) in a position closer to home plate than usual; short: *The third baseman played in, expecting a bunt.* **17.** on good terms; in favor: *He's in with his boss, but he doubts it will last.* **18.** in vogue; in style: *Turbans are in this year.* **19.** in season: *Artichokes will soon be in.* **20. be in for,** to be bound to undergo something, esp. a disagreeable experience: *We are in for a long speech.* **21. in for it,** *Slang.* about to suffer unpleasant consequences, esp. of one's own actions or omissions: *He forgot their anniversary again, and he'll be in for it now.* Also, *Brit.,* **for it. 22. in with,** on friendly terms with; familiar with: *They are in with the junior executive set.* —*adj.* **23.** located or situated within; inner; internal: *the in part of a mechanism.* **24.** *Informal.* **a.** in favor with advanced or sophisticated people; fashionable: *the in place to dine.* **b.** comprehensible only to a special or ultrasophisticated group: *an in joke.* **25.** well-liked; included in a favored group. **26.** inward; incoming; inbound: *to put mail in the in basket; an in train.* **27.** stylish; fashionable: *Green coats will be in this fall.* **28.** plentiful; available: *Summer squash is in now.* **29.** being in power, authority, control, etc.: *a member of the in party.* **30.** playing the last nine holes of an eighteen-hole golf course (opposed to *out*): *His in score on the second round was 34.* —*n.* **31.** Usually, **ins.** persons in office or political power (distinguished from *outs*). **32.** a member of the political party in power: *The election made him an in.* **33.** pull or influence; a social advantage or connection: *He's got an in with influential people.* **34.** (in tennis, squash, handball, etc.) a return or service that lands within the in-bounds limits of a court or section of a court (opposed to *out*). —*v.t. Dial.* **35.** to take in (a crop); harvest. **36.** to enclose. [ME, OE; c. G, D, Goth *in,* Icel *ī,* L *in,* Gk *en*]

In, *Chem.* indium.

in-[1], a prefix representing English *in* (*income, indwelling, inland,* etc.) but used also as a verb-formative with transitive, intensive, or sometimes little apparent force (*intrust; inweave,* etc.). It often assumes the same phases as **in-**[2], as **en-, em-, im-**[3]. [ME, OE; see IN]

in-[2], a prefix of Latin origin meaning primarily "in," but used also as a verb-formative with the same force as **in-**[1] (*incarcerate; incantation*). Also, **il-, im-, ir-.** Cf. **em-, en-.** [< L, comb. form of *in* (prep.); c. IN]

in-[3], a prefix of Latin origin, corresponding to English *un-,* having a negative or privative force, freely used as an English formative, esp. of adjectives and their derivatives and of nouns (*inattention; indefensible; inexpensive; inorganic; invariable*). It assumes the same phonetic phases as **in-**[2] (*impartial; immeasurable; illiterate; irregular,* etc.). In French, it became *en-* and thus occurs unfelt in such words as *enemy* (French *ennemi,* Latin *inimicus,* lit., not friendly). Also, **il-, im-, ir-.** [< L; akin to AN-[1], A-[6], UN-[1]]
—**Syn.** The prefixes IN- and UN- may both have, among other uses, a negative force. IN- is the form from the classical languages (Greek and Latin) and is therefore used in learned words or in words derived from those languages: *inaccessible, inaccuracy, inadequate,* etc. UN- is the native form going back to Old English, used in words of native origin, and sometimes used in combination with words of other origins if these words are in common use: *unloving, unmanly, unfeeling, unnecessary, unsafe.* Occasionally the prefix UN- is used with a frequently used word in a common meaning, as in *unsanitary* (not clean), and IN- with the same word in a more technical sense: *insanitary* (likely to cause disease). In England the prefix IN- is more commonly used than in the United States.

-in[1], a formal element, occurring in adjectives of Greek and Latin origin, meaning "pertaining to," and (in nouns thence derived) also imitated in English (*coffin; cousin,* etc.); occurring unfelt in abstract nouns formed as nouns in Latin (*ruin*). [ME *-in, -ine* < OF < L *-inus, -ina, -inum* < Gk *-inos, -inē, -inon*]

-in[2], a noun suffix used in a special manner in chemical and mineralogical nomenclature (*glycerin; acetin,* etc.). In spelling, usage wavers between *-in* and *-ine.* In chemistry a certain distinction of use is attempted, basic substances having the termination *-ine* rather than *-in* (*aconitine; aniline,* etc.), and *-in* being restricted to certain neutral compounds, glycerides, glucosides, and proteids (*albumin; palmitin,* etc.), but this distinction is not always observed. [< NL *-ina.* See -INE[2]]

in., inch; inches.

I·na (ī′nə), *n.* a girl's given name.

-ina, a feminine suffix used in the formation of nouns of various types, esp. proper names and designations of rank, profession, etc.: *Wilhelmina; sonatina.* Cf. **-in**[2], **-ine**[2]. [<< L *-īna,* fem. of *-īnus*]

in·a·bil·i·ty (in′ə bil′i tē), *n.* lack of ability; lack of power, capacity, or means. [ME *inabilite* < ML *inhabilitās.* See IN-[3], ABILITY]
—**Syn.** incapability, incapacity, impotence, incompetence. See **disability.**

in ab·sen·tia (in ab sen′shə, -shē ə, -tē ə), *Latin.* in absence.

in ab·strac·to (in ab strak′tō), *Latin.* in the abstract.

in·ac·ces·si·ble (in′ək ses′ə bəl), *adj.* not accessible; inapproachable. [< LL *inaccessibil(is).* See IN-[3], ACCESSIBLE] —**in′ac·ces′si·bil′i·ty, in′ac·ces′si·ble·ness,** *n.* —**in′ac·ces′si·bly,** *adv.*

in·ac·cu·ra·cy (in ak′yər ə sē), *n., pl.* **-cies** for 2. **1.** the quality or state of being inaccurate. **2.** that which is inaccurate; error. [IN-[3] + ACCURACY]
—**Syn. 1.** incorrectness, erroneousness, inexactness. **2.** mistake, blunder, slip, inexactitude.

in·ac·cu·rate (in ak′yər it), *adj.* not accurate; not exact, correct, or true. [IN-[3] + ACCURATE] —**in·ac′cu·rate·ly,** *adv.* —**in·ac′cu·rate·ness,** *n.*
—**Syn.** inexact, loose; incorrect, erroneous, wrong, faulty.

In·a·chus (in′ə kəs), *n. Class. Myth.* a river god, the first king of Argos and father of Io.

in·ac·tion (in ak′shən), *n.* absence of action; idleness. [IN-[3] + ACTION]

in·ac·ti·vate (in ak′tə vāt′), *v.t.,* **-vat·ed, -vat·ing. 1.** to make inactive. **2.** *Immunol.* to stop the activity of (certain biological substances). [INACTIVE + -ATE[1]] —**in·ac′ti·va′tion,** *n.*

in·ac·tive (in ak′tiv), *adj.* **1.** not active; inert. **2.** sedentary or passive: *an inactive life.* **3.** sluggish; indolent. **4.** *Mil.* not on active duty or status. **5.** *Physical Chem.* noting a compound which does not rotate the plane of vibration of polarized light. [IN-[3] + ACTIVE] —**in·ac′tive·ly,** *adv.* —**in′ac·tiv′i·ty, in·ac′tive·ness,** *n.*
—**Syn. 1.** unmoving, immobile, inoperative. **1, 2.** INACTIVE, DORMANT, INERT, SLUGGISH, TORPID suggest lack of activity. INACTIVE indicates absence of action, indisposition to activity, or cessation of activity: *an inactive compound, life, file of papers.* DORMANT suggests the quiescence or inactivity of that which sleeps but may be roused to action: *a dormant volcano.* INERT suggests the condition of dead matter, with no inherent power of motion or action; it may also mean unable to move, or heavy and hard to move: *an inert mass; inert from hunger.* SLUGGISH expresses slowness of natural activity or of that which does not move readily or vigorously: *a sluggish stream, brain.* TORPID suggests a state of suspended physical powers, a condition particularly of animals which hibernate: *Snakes are torpid in cold weather.* **3.** lazy, idle, slothful. —**Ant. 1–3.** lively.

in·a·dapt·a·ble (in′ə dap′tə bəl), *adj.* not adaptable; incapable of being adapted. [IN-[3] + ADAPTABLE] —**in′a·dapt′a·bil′i·ty,** *n.*

in·ad·e·quate (in ad′ə kwit), *adj.* not adequate; inept; unsuitable; insufficient. [IN-[3] + ADEQUATE] —**in·ad′e·qua·cy, in·ad′e·quate·ness,** *n.* —**in·ad′e·quate·ly,** *adv.*
—**Syn.** inapt, incompetent; incommensurate; defective, imperfect, incomplete. —**Ant.** sufficient.

in·ad·mis·si·ble (in′əd mis′ə bəl), *adj.* not admissible; not allowable. [IN-[3] + ADMISSIBLE] —**in′ad·mis′si·bil′i·ty,** *n.* —**in′ad·mis′si·bly,** *adv.*

in·ad·vert·ence (in′əd vûr′tᵊns), *n.* **1.** the quality or condition of being inadvertent; heedlessness. **2.** act or effect of inattention; an oversight. [< ML *inadvertentia.* See INADVERTENCY]

in·ad·vert·en·cy (in′əd vûr′tᵊn sē), *n., pl.* **-cies.** inadvertence. [< ML *inadvertentia,* equiv. to L *in-* IN-[3] + *advert-* turn to (see ADVERT) + *-entia* -ENCY]

in·ad·vert·ent (in′əd vûr′tᵊnt), *adj.* **1.** not attentive; heedless. **2.** of, pertaining to, or characterized by lack of attention. **3.** unintentional: *an inadvertent insult.* [abstracted from INADVERTENCE, INADVERTENCY] —**in′ad·vert′ent·ly,** *adv.*
—**Syn. 1.** inattentive. **2.** thoughtless, careless, negligent.

in·ad·vis·a·ble (in′əd vī′zə bəl), *adj.* not advisable; inexpedient; unwise. [IN-[3] + ADVISABLE] —**in′ad·vis′a·bil′i·ty, in′ad·vis′a·ble·ness,** *n.* —**in′ad·vis′a·bly,** *adv.*

-inae, *Zool.* a suffix of the names of subfamilies. [< NL, L, fem. pl. of *-inus;* see -INE[1]]

in ae·ter·num (in ī ter′nŏŏm; *Eng.* in ē tûr′nəm), *Latin.* forever.

in·al·ien·a·ble (in āl′yə nə bəl, -ā′lē ə-), *adj.* not alienable; incapable of being transferred to another: *inalienable rights.* [IN-[3] + ALIENABLE] —**in·al′ien·a·bil′i·ty, in·al′ien·a·ble·ness,** *n.* —**in·al′ien·a·bly,** *adv.*

in·al·ter·a·ble (in ôl′tər ə bəl), *adj.* unalterable. [IN-[3] + ALTERABLE] —**in·al′ter·a·bil′i·ty, in·al′ter·a·ble·ness,** *n.* —**in·al′ter·a·bly,** *adv.*

in·am·o·ra·ta (in am′ə rä′tə, in′am-), *n., pl.* **-tas.** a female lover; a woman who loves or is loved. [< It *innamorata;* fem. of INNAMORATO]

in·am·o·ra·to (in am′ə rä′tō, in′am-), *n., pl.* **-tos.** a male lover. [< It *innamorato,* masc. ptp. of *innamorare* to inflame with love. See ENAMOR]

in-and-in (in′ənd in′), *adv.* repeatedly within the same family, strain, etc.: *to breed stock in-and-in.*

in-and-out (in′ənd out′), *n. Manège.* an obstacle consisting of two fences placed too far apart to be cleared in one jump and too close together to allow more than one or two strides between.

in′-and-out′ bond′, a stonework or brickwork bond having headers and stretchers alternating vertically.

in-and-out·er (in′ənd ou′tər), *n.* a person who is by turns in and out of a particular situation, condition, etc.: *an in-and-outer in government service.*

in·ane (i nān′), *adj.* **1.** lacking sense or ideas; silly: *inane questions.* **2.** empty; void. —*n.* **3.** that which is empty or void, esp. the void of infinite space: *man's venture into the boundless inane.* [< L *inān(is)*] —**in·ane′ly,** *adv.*
—**Syn. 1.** pointless. See **foolish.**

in·an·i·mate (in an′ə mit), *adj.* **1.** not animate; lifeless. **2.** spiritless; sluggish; dull. [< LL *inanimāt(us).* See IN-[3], ANIMATE] —**in·an′i·mate·ly,** *adv.* —**in·an′i·mate·ness, in·an·i·ma·tion** (in an′ə mā′shən), *n.*
—**Syn. 1.** inorganic, vegetable, mineral, inert, dead. **2.** inactive, dormant, torpid.

in·a·ni·tion (in′ə nish′ən), *n.* **1.** exhaustion from lack of nourishment; starvation. **2.** emptiness; lack of vigor; lethargy: *the inanition of his writings.* [ME < LL *inānītiōn-* (s. of *inānītiō*). See INANE, -ITION]

in·an·i·ty (i nan′i tē), *n., pl.* **-ties** for 2. **1.** lack of sense or ideas; silliness. **2.** something inane, as a remark, opinion, etc. **3.** emptiness; lack of depth or meaning. [< L *inānitās.* See INANE, -ITY]

I·nan·na (ē nä′nä), *n.* the Sumerian goddess of love and war, who reigns over heaven: identified with the Assyrian and Babylonian Ishtar.

in an·tis (in an′tis), *Archit.* **1.** (of columns in a portico) between antae. **2.** (of a portico) having columns between antae. [< L]

in·ap·peas·a·ble (in′ə pē′zə bəl), *adj.* not appeasable; not to be appeased: *inappeasable anger.* [IN-[3] + APPEASABLE]

in·ap·pe·tence (in ap′i təns), *n.* lack of appetite. Also, **in·ap′pe·ten·cy.** [IN-[3] + APPETENCE] —**in·ap′pe·tent,** *adj.*

in·ap·pli·ca·ble (in ap′lə kə bəl), *adj.* not applicable; unsuitable. [IN-[3] + APPLICABLE] —**in·ap′pli·ca·bil′i·ty, in·ap′pli·ca·ble·ness,** *n.* —**in·ap′pli·ca·bly,** *adv.*

in·ap·po·site (in ap′ə zit), *adj.* not apposite; not pertinent. [IN-[3] + APPOSITE] —**in·ap′po·site·ly,** *adv.* —**in·ap′po·site·ness,** *n.*

in·ap·pre·ci·a·ble (in′ə prē′shē ə bəl, -shə bəl), *adj.* imperceptible; insignificant: *an inappreciable difference.* [IN-[3] + LL *appreciā(re)* (to) appraise (var. of *appretiāre;* see AP-[1], PRECIOUS) + -BLE] —**in′ap·pre′ci·a·bly,** *adv.*

in·ap·pre·ci·a·tive (in′ə prē′shē ā′tiv, -shə tiv), *adj.* not appreciative; lacking in appreciation. [IN-[3] + APPRECIATIVE] —**in′ap·pre′ci·a′tive·ly,** *adv.* —**in′ap·pre′ci·a′tive·ness,** *n.*

in·ap·pre·hen·si·ble (in′ap ri hen′sə bəl), *adj.* not to be grasped by the senses or intellect. [IN-[3] + APPREHENSIBLE]

in·ap·pre·hen·sion (in′ap ri hen′shən), *n.* lack of apprehension. [IN-[3] + APPREHENSION]

in·ap·pre·hen·sive (in′ap ri hen′siv), *adj.* **1.** not apprehensive (often fol. by *of*). **2.** without apprehension. [IN-[3] + APPREHENSIVE] —**in′ap·pre·hen′sive·ly,** *adv.* —**in′ap·pre·hen′sive·ness,** *n.*

in·ap·proach·a·ble (in′ə prō′chə bəl), *adj.* **1.** not approachable. **2.** without rival. [IN-[3] + APPROACHABLE] —**in′ap·proach′a·bil′i·ty,** *n.* —**in′ap·proach′a·bly,** *adv.*

in·ap·pro·pri·ate (in′ə prō′prē it), *adj.* not appropriate; not proper or suitable. [IN-[3] + APPROPRIATE] —**in′ap·pro′pri·ate·ly,** *adv.* —**in′ap·pro′pri·ate·ness,** *n.*

in·apt (in apt′), *adj.* **1.** not apt or fitting. **2.** without aptitude or capacity. [IN-[3] + APT] —**in·apt′ly,** *adv.* —**in·apt′ness,** *n.*
—**Syn. 1.** unsuited, unsuitable, inappropriate, unfit, inapposite. **2.** incapable, clumsy, awkward. —**Ant. 1.** appropriate. **2.** capable.

Inarching

in·ap·ti·tude (in ap′ti to͞od′, -tyo͞od′), *n.* **1.** lack of aptitude; unfitness. **2.** unskillfulness; lack of dexterity. [IN-[3] + APTITUDE]

in·arch (in ärch′), *v.t. Hort.* to graft by uniting a growing branch to a stock without separating the branch from its parent stock. [IN-[2] + ARCH[1]]

in·ar·gu·a·ble (in är′gyo͞o ə bəl), *adj.* not arguable: *The premise is so obvious as to be inarguable.* [IN-[3] + ARGUABLE] —**in·ar′gu·a·bly,** *adv.*

in·arm (in ärm′), *v.t.* to hold in or as in the arms. [IN-[1] + ARM[1]]

in·ar·tic·u·late (in′är tik′yə lit), *adj.* **1.** not articulate; not uttered or emitted with expressive or intelligible modulations: *His mouth stuffed, he could utter only inarticulate sounds.* **2.** unable to use articulate speech: *inarticulate with rage.* **3.** lacking the ability to express oneself in clear and effective speech: *a brilliant writer but an inarticulate speaker.* **4.** *Anat., Zool.* not jointed; having no articulation or joint. [< LL *inarticulāt(us).* See IN-[3], ARTICULATE] —**in′ar·tic′u·late·ly,** *adv.* —**in′ar·tic′u·late·ness,** *n.*

in ar·tic·u·lo mor·tis (in är tik′o͝o lō′ môr′tis; *Eng.* in är tik′yə lō′ môr′tis), *Latin.* at the point of death.

in·ar·ti·fi·cial (in är′tə fish′əl), *adj.* **1.** not artificial; natural; artless; uncontrived. **2.** *Rare.* inartistic; crude. [< L *inartificiāl(is).* See IN-[3], ARTIFICIAL] —**in·ar′ti·fi′ci·al′i·ty, in·ar′ti·fi′cial·ness,** *n.* —**in·ar′ti·fi′cial·ly,** *adv.*

in·ar·tis·tic (in′är tis′tik), *adj.* **1.** not artistic; unaesthetic. **2.** lacking in artistic sense or appreciation. Also, **in′ar·tis′ti·cal.** [IN-[3] + ARTISTIC] —**in′ar·tis′ti·cal·ly,** *adv.*

in·as·much′ as′ (in′əz much′), **1.** in view of the fact that; seeing that; since. **2.** insofar as; to such a degree as. [ME *in as much(e) as*]
—**Syn. 1.** See **because.**

in·at·ten·tion (in′ə ten′shən), *n.* **1.** lack of attention; negligence. **2.** an act of neglect. [IN-[3] + ATTENTION]

in·at·ten·tive (in′ə ten′tiv), *adj.* not attentive. [IN-[3] + ATTENTIVE] —**in′at·ten′tive·ly,** *adv.* —**in′at·ten′tive·ness,** *n.*
—**Syn.** heedless, neglectful, oblivious, unmindful, preoccupied, vague.

in·au·di·ble (in ô′də bəl), *adj.* incapable of being heard. [IN-[3] + AUDIBLE] —**in·au′di·bil′i·ty, in·au′di·ble·ness,** *n.* —**in·au′di·bly,** *adv.*

in·au·gu·ral (in ô′gyər əl, -gər əl), *adj.* **1.** of or pertaining to an inauguration. **2.** marking the beginning of a new venture, series, etc.: *the inaugural run of the pony express.* —*n.* **3.** an address, as of a president, at the beginning of a term of office. **4.** an inaugural ceremony: *to attend the Presidential inaugural.* [obs. *inaugure* (< L *inaugur(āre)* (to) INAUGURATE) + -AL[1]]

in·au·gu·rate (in ô′gyə rāt′, -gə-), *v.t.,* **-rat·ed, -rat·ing. 1.** to make a formal beginning of; initiate; commence; begin: *World War II inaugurated the era of nuclear power.* **2.** to induct into office with formal ceremonies; install. **3.** to introduce into public use by some formal ceremony: *Plane service between the two cities was inaugurated five years ago.* [< L *inaugurāt(us)* formally installed (ptp. of *inaugurāre,* lit., to take auguries). See IN-[2], AUGUR, -ATE[1]] —**in·au′gu·ra′tion,** *n.* —**in·au′gu·ra′tor,** *n.*

Inaugura′tion Day′, the day on which the President of the United States is inaugurated, being January 20 of every year following a year whose number is divisible by four. Prior to the Twentieth Amendment to the Constitution (ratified February 6, 1933), it was March 4.

in·aus·pi·cious (in′ô spish′əs), *adj.* not auspicious; boding ill; unfavorable. [IN-[3] + AUSPICIOUS] —**in′aus·pi′cious·ly,** *adv.* —**in′aus·pi′cious·ness,** *n.*

in·be·ing (in′bē′ing), *n.* **1.** the condition of existing in something else; immanence. **2.** inward nature. [IN (adv.) + BEING]

in-be·tween (in′bi twēn′), *n.* **1.** Also, **in′be·tween′er.** one who or that which is between two extremes, two contrasting conditions, etc.: *yeses, noes, and in-betweens; for professional, amateur, and in-between.* —*adj.* **2.**

being between one thing, condition, etc., and another: *a coat for in-between weather.*

in·board (in′bōrd′, -bôrd′), *adj.* **1.** located inside a hull or aircraft. **2.** located nearer the center, as of an airplane: *the inboard end of a wing.* **3.** (of a motorboat) having the motor inboard. —*adv.* **4.** inside or toward the center of a hull or aircraft. Cf. **outboard.** [orig. phrase *in board*]

in′board pro′file, *Naval Archit.* a diagrammatic, longitudinal section of a vessel along the center line facing to port, showing the positions of the decks, transverse bulkheads, machinery, etc., in that half of the vessel.

in·board-rigged (in′bōrd′rigd′, -bôrd′-), *adj. Naut.* noting a sailing vessel, as a knockabout, having no headsails set to a bowsprit or jib boom.

in·bond (in′bond′), *adj. Masonry.* composed mainly or entirely of headers (opposed to *outbond*). [IN-[1] + BOND[1]]

in·born (in′bôrn′), *adj.* implanted by nature; innate. [OE *inboren* native]
—**Syn.** inbred, inherent, natural, native, congenital, inherited, hereditary. —**Ant.** acquired, learned.

in·bound (in′bound′), *adj.* inward bound: *inbound ships.* [IN-[1] + -BOUND[2]]

in·breathe (in′brēth′, in brēth′), *v.t.*, **-breathed, -breath·ing. 1.** to breathe in; inhale. **2.** to inspire; infuse with. [IN-[1] + BREATHE]

in·bred (in′bred′), *adj.* **1.** bred within; innate; native: *her inbred grace.* **2.** resulting from or involved in inbreeding. [ptp. of INBREED]
—**Syn. 1.** inborn.

in·breed (in′brēd′, in brēd′), *v.t.*, **-bred, -breed·ing. 1.** to breed (animals) in-and-in. **2.** *Rare.* to breed within; engender. [IN-[1] + BREED]

in·breed·ing (in′brē′ding), *n. Biol.* the mating of related individuals, as cousins, sire-daughter, brother-sister, or self-fertilized plants, which automatically fixes the genes, making them homozygous. [INBREED + -ING[1]]

in·burst (in′bûrst′), *n. Rare.* a bursting in; irruption. [IN-[1] + BURST]

in·by (in′bī′), *Brit. Dial.* —*prep.* **1.** inside; within. —*adj.* **2.** interior; inside. —*adv.* **3.** in an inward direction; closer to the center or interior. [orig. phrase *in by* near by]

Inc., incorporated.

inc., 1. engraved. [< L *incīsus*] **2.** inclosure. **3.** included. **4.** including. **5.** inclusive. **6.** income. **7.** incorporated. **8.** increase. **9.** incumbent.

In·ca (ing′kə), *n.* **1.** a member of any of the dominant groups of South American Indian peoples who established an empire in Peru prior to the Spanish conquest. **2.** a ruler or member of the royal family in the Incan empire. [< Sp < Quechua *inka* male of the blood royal] —**In·ca·ic** (ing kā′ik, in-), *adj.* —**In′can,** *n., adj.*

In·ca·bloc (ing′kə blok′), *n. Horol., Trademark.* a shockproof mounting in a watch that allows for slight longitudinal and lateral play of either end of the balance staff.

in·cage (in kāj′), *v.t.*, **-caged, -cag·ing.** encage.

in·cal·cu·la·ble (in kal′kyə lə bəl), *adj.* **1.** unable to be calculated; beyond calculation. **2.** incapable of being forecast or predicted; undeterminable. **3.** uncertain; unsure. [IN-[3] + CALCULABLE] —**in·cal′cu·la·bil′i·ty, in·cal′cu·la·ble·ness,** *n.* —**in·cal′cu·la·bly,** *adv.*

in·ca·les·cent (in′kə les′ənt), *adj.* increasing in heat or ardor. [< L *incalescent-* (s. of *incalescēns*) glowing, prp. of *incalescere.* See IN-[2], CALESCENT] —**in′ca·les′cence,** *n.*

in·can·desce (in′kən des′), *v.i., v.t.*, **-desced, -desc·ing.** to glow or cause to glow with heat. [back formation from INCANDESCENT]

in·can·des·cence (in′kən des′əns), *n.* **1.** the emission of visible light by a body, caused by its high temperature. Cf. **luminescence. 2.** the light produced by such an emission. [INCANDESC(ENT) + -ENCE]

in·can·des·cent (in′kən des′ənt), *adj.* **1.** (of light) produced by incandescence. **2.** glowing or white with heat. **3.** intensely bright; brilliant. **4.** brilliant; masterly; extraordinarily lucid: *an incandescent masterpiece; incandescent wit.* **5.** aglow with ardor, purpose, etc.: *the incandescent vitality of youth.* [< L *incandescent-* (s. of *incandescēns*), prp. of *incandescere* to glow. See IN-[2], CANDESCENT] —**in′can·des′cent·ly,** *adv.*

in′candes′cent lamp′, a lamp that emits light due to the glowing of a heated material, esp. the common electric light bulb, in which a filament is rendered luminous by the passing of an electric current through it.

in·can·ta·tion (in′kan tā′shən), *n.* **1.** the chanting or uttering of words purporting to have magical power. **2.** the formula employed; a spell or charm. **3.** magical ceremonies. **4.** magic; sorcery. **5.** repetitious wordiness used to conceal a lack of content; obfuscation: *Her prose too often resorts to incantation.* [ME < LL *incantātiōn-* (s. of *incantātiō*), equiv. to *incantāt(us)* enchanted (ptp. of *incantāre;* see ENCHANT, -ATE[1]) + *-iōn-* -ION] —**in′can·ta′tion·al,** *adj.*

in·can·ta·to·ry (in kan′tə tōr′ē, -tôr′ē), *adj.* of, pertaining to, or characteristic of incantation: *An eerie, incantatory charm pervaded the song.* [< L *incantāt(us)* (see INCANTATION) + -ORY[1]]

in·ca·pa·ble (in kā′pə bəl), *adj.* **1.** not capable. **2.** not having the necessary capacity or power to perform some specified act or function: *As an administrator, he is simply incapable.* **3.** without ordinary capability or ability; incompetent: *incapable workers.* **4. incapable of, a.** not having the capacity or power for (a specified act or function). **b.** not open to; not susceptible to or admitting: *These materials are incapable of exact measurement.* **c.** legally unqualified for. —*n.* **5.** a thoroughly incompetent person, esp. one of defective mentality. [< ML *incapābil(is).* See IN-[3], CAPABLE] —**in·ca′pa·bil′i·ty, in·ca′pa·ble·ness,** *n.* —**in·ca′pa·bly,** *adv.*
—**Syn. 1.** INCAPABLE, INCOMPETENT, INEFFICIENT, UNABLE are applied to one who or that which is lacking in ability, preparation, or power for whatever is to be done. INCAPABLE usually means inherently lacking in ability or power: *incapable of appreciating music; a bridge incapable of carrying heavy loads.* INCOMPETENT, generally used only of persons, means unfit or unqualified for a particular task: *incompetent as an administrator.* INEFFICIENT means wasteful in the use of effort or power: *an inefficient manager; inefficient methods.* UNABLE usually refers to a temporary condition of inability to do some specific thing: *unable to relax, to go to a concert.* **2.** impotent, unqualified. —**Ant. 1.** able.

in·ca·pa·cious (in′kə pā′shəs), *adj.* **1.** *Rare.* mentally incapable. **2.** *Obs.* not capacious; lacking capacity; narrow; limited. [INCAPACI(TY) + -OUS] —**in′ca·pa′cious·ness,** *n.*

in·ca·pac·i·tate (in′kə pas′i tāt′), *v.t.*, **-tat·ed, -tat·ing. 1.** to deprive of capacity; make incapable or unfit; disqualify. **2.** *Law.* to deprive of power to perform acts with legal consequences. [INCAPACIT(Y) + -ATE[1]] —**in′ca·pac′i·ta′tion,** *n.*

in·ca·pac·i·ty (in′kə pas′i tē), *n.* **1.** lack of capacity; incapability. **2.** legal disqualification. [< ML *incapācitās.* See IN-[3], CAPACITY]

in·car·cer·ate (*v.* in kär′sə rāt′; *adj.* in kär′sər it, -sə rāt′), *v.*, **-at·ed, -at·ing,** *adj.* —*v.t.* **1.** to imprison; confine. **2.** to enclose; constrict closely. —*adj.* **3.** imprisoned. [< ML *incarcerāt(us)* imprisoned (ptp. of *incarcerāre*), equiv. to *in-* IN-[2] + *carcer* prison + *-ātus* -ATE[1]] —**in·car′cer·a′tion,** *n.* —**in·car′cer·a′tive,** *adj.* —**in·car′cer·a′tor,** *n.*

in·car·di·nate (in kär′dənāt′), *v.t.*, **-nat·ed, -nat·ing. 1.** to institute as a cardinal. **2.** to institute as chief presbyter, priest, etc., in a particular church or place. [< ML *incardināt(us)* installed as chief priest (ptp. of *incardināre*), equiv. to *in* -IN-[2] + *cardin-* (see CARDINAL) + *-ātus* -ATE[1]]

in·car·di·na·tion (in kär′dənā′shən), *n.* the institution of a cleric transferred from one diocese into the clergy of another diocese. [< ML *incardinātiōn-* (s. of *incardinātiō*), equiv. to *incardināt(us)* (see INCARDINATE) + *-iōn-* -ION]

in·car·na·dine (in kär′nə dīn′, -din, -dēn′), *adj., n., v.*, **-dined, -din·ing.** —*adj.* **1.** flesh-colored; pale pink. **2.** blood-red; crimson. —*n.* **3.** an incarnadine color. —*v.t.* **4.** to make incarnadine. [< MF, fem. of *incarnadin* flesh-colored < It *incarnatino,* equiv. to *incarnat(o)* made flesh (see INCARNATE) + *-ino* -INE[1]; see CARNATION]

in·car·nal·ise (in kär′nəlīz′), *v.t.*, **-ised, -is·ing.** *Chiefly Brit.* incarnalize.

in·car·nal·ize (in kär′nəlīz′), *v.t.*, **-ized, -iz·ing.** encarnalize.

in·car·nate (*adj.* in kär′nit, -nāt; *v.* in kär′nāt), *adj., v.*, **-nat·ed, -nat·ing.** —*adj.* **1.** embodied in flesh; invested with a bodily, esp. a human, form: *a devil incarnate.* **2.** personified or typified, as a quality or idea: *chivalry incarnate.* **3.** flesh-colored or crimson. —*v.t.* **4.** to put into or represent in a concrete form, as an idea: *The thick book incarnates a complex theory.* **5.** to be the embodiment or type of: *His music incarnates the tempo of our day.* **6.** to embody in flesh; invest with a bodily, esp. a human, form: *a man who incarnated wisdom and compassion.* [late ME *incarnat* < LL *incarnāt(us)* made flesh (ptp. of *incarnāre*), equiv. to *in-* IN-[2] + *carn-* flesh (see CARNAL) + *-ātus* -ATE[1]]

in·car·na·tion (in′kär nā′shən), *n.* **1.** an incarnate being or form. **2.** a living being embodying a deity or spirit. **3.** assumption of human form or nature, as by a divine being: *the incarnation of God in Christ.* **4.** a person or thing regarded as embodying or exhibiting some quality, idea, or the like: *The leading dancer is the incarnation of grace.* **5.** act of incarnating. **6.** state of being incarnated. [ME *incarnacion* < eccl. L *incarnātiōn-* (s. of *incarnātiō*), equiv. to *incarnāt(us)* INCARNATE + *-iōn-* -ION] —**in′car·na′tion·al,** *adj.*

in·case (in kās′), *v.t.*, **-cased, -cas·ing.** encase. —**in·case′ment,** *n.*

in·cau·tion (in kô′shən), *n.* lack of caution; heedlessness; carelessness. [IN-[3] + CAUTION]

in·cau·tious (in kô′shəs), *adj.* not cautious; careless; heedless. [IN-[3] + CAUTIOUS; cf. L *incautus* unwary] —**in·cau′tious·ly,** *adv.* —**in·cau′tious·ness,** *n.*

in·cen·di·a·rism (in sen′dē ə riz′əm), *n.* **1.** act or practice of an arsonist; malicious burning. **2.** inflammatory behavior; agitation. [INCENDIAR(Y) + -ISM]

in·cen·di·ar·y (in sen′dē er′ē), *adj., n., pl.* **-ar·ies.** —*adj.* **1.** used or adapted for setting property on fire: *incendiary bombs.* **2.** of or pertaining to the criminal setting on fire of property. **3.** tending to arouse strife, sedition, etc.; inflammatory: *inceniadry speeches.* **4.** tending to inflame the senses: *an incendiary blonde.* —*n.* **5.** a person who maliciously sets fire to buildings or other property. **6.** *Mil.* a shell, bomb, or grenade containing napalm, thermite, or some other substance that burns with an intense heat. **7.** a person who stirs up strife, sedition, etc.; an agitator. [< L *incendiāri(us),* equiv. to *incendi(um)* a fire (deriv. of *incendere* to kindle) + *-ārius* -ARY]

in·cense[1] (in′sens), *n., v.*, **-censed, -cens·ing.** —*n.* **1.** an aromatic gum or other substance producing a sweet odor when burned, used esp. in religious ceremonies. **2.** the perfume or smoke arising from such a substance when burned. **3.** any pleasant perfume or fragrance. **4.** homage or adulation. —*v.t.* **5.** to perfume with incense. **6.** to burn incense for. —*v.i.* **7.** to burn or offer incense. [ME < eccl. L *incens(um),* lit., something kindled, neut. of *incensus* (ptp. of *incendere* to set on fire), equiv. to *in-* IN-[2] + *cend-* (var. of *cand-;* see CANDENT) + *-tus* ptp. suffix; r. ME *ansens, ensenz* < OF]

in·cense[2] (in sens′), *v.t.*, **-censed, -cens·ing.** to inflame with wrath; make angry; enrage. [late ME < L *incens(us)* kindled, fired (see INCENSE[1]); r. ME *encensen* < AF < L, as above] —**in·cense′ment,** *n.*
—**Syn.** anger, exasperate, provoke, irritate. See **enrage.**

in′cense ce′dar, 1. any of several pinaceous trees of the genus *Libocedrus,* esp. *L. decurrens,* of the northwestern U.S., characterized by the columnar or spirelike growth pattern of its branches. **2.** the light, soft wood of the incense cedar, *Libocedrus decurrens,* used for making pencils and railroad ties, in shipbuilding, etc.

in·cen·ter (in′sen′tər), *n. Geom.* the center of an inscribed circle; that point where the bisectors of the angles of a triangle or of a regular polygon intersect. [IN + CENTER]

in·cen·tive (in sen′tiv), *n.* **1.** that which incites to action. —*adj.* **2.** inciting, as to action; stimulating; provocative. [ME < LL *incentīv(us)* provocative, L: setting the tune, equiv. to *incent(us)* (unrecorded ptp. of *incinere* to sing) + *-īvus* -IVE] —**in·cen′tive·ly,** *adv.*
—**Syn. 1.** stimulus, spur, incitement, impulse, encouragement; goad, prod. See **motive.**

incen′tive wage′, a wage paid to promote the productivity of an employee.

in·cept (in sept′), *v.i.* **1.** *Brit.* to complete the taking of a master's or doctor's degree in a university, esp. Cambridge. —*v.t.* **2.** to take in; intussuscept. [< L *incept(us)* begun, undertaken (ptp. of *incipere*), equiv. to *in-* IN-[2] + *cep-* (var. of *cap-* take; see CAPTIVE) + *-tus* ptp. suffix] —**in·cep′tor,** *n.*

in·cep·tion (in sep′shən), *n.* **1.** beginning; start. **2.** *Brit.* **a.** the act of graduating or earning a university degree, usually a master's or doctor's degree, esp. at Cambridge University. **b.** the graduation ceremony; commencement. [late ME < L *inceptiōn-* (s. of *inceptiō*), equiv. to *incept(us)* begun (see INCEPT) + *-iōn-* -ION]
—**Syn. 1.** origin, outset, source, root, conception.

in·cep·tive (in sep′tiv), *adj.* **1.** *Gram.* (of a derived verb, or of an aspect in verb inflection) expressing the beginning of the action indicated by the underlying verb, as Latin verbs in *-sco,* which generally have inceptive force, as *calescō* "become or begin to be hot" from *caleō* "be hot." **2.** beginning; initial. —*n. Gram.* **3.** the inceptive aspect. **4.** a verb in this aspect. [< LL *inceptīv(us).* See INCEPT, -IVE] —**in·cep′tive·ly,** *adv.*
—**Syn. 1.** inchoative.

in·cer·ti·tude (in sûr′ti to͞od′, -tyo͞od′), *n.* **1.** uncertainty; doubtfulness. **2.** insecurity: *The incertitude of his position in life caused him to fear marriage.* [< LL *incertitūd(ō).* See IN-[3], CERTITUDE]

in·ces·sant (in ses′ənt), *adj.* continuing without interruption: *an incessant noise.* [late ME < LL *incessant-,* equiv. to L *in-* IN-[3] + *cessant-* (s. of *cessāns*), prp. of *cessāre* to stop work; see CEASE, -ANT] —**in·ces′san·cy, in·ces′sant·ness,** *n.* —**in·ces′sant·ly,** *adv.*
—**Syn.** ceaseless, unceasing, constant, continual, continuous, unending, never-ending, perpetual, eternal, everlasting; relentless, unrelenting, unremitting. —**Ant.** intermittent.

in·cest (in′sest), *n.* **1.** sexual intercourse between closely related persons. **2.** the crime of sexual intercourse, cohabitation, or marriage between persons within the degrees of consanguinity or affinity wherein marriage is legally forbidden. **3.** See **spiritual incest.** [ME < L *incest(us),* equiv. to *incest-* (s. of *incestus* impure: *in-* IN-[3] + *castus* CHASTE) + *-us* n. suffix (4th decl.)]

in·ces·tu·ous (in ses′cho͞o əs), *adj.* **1.** guilty of incest. **2.** involving incest. [< LL *incestuōs(us).* See INCEST, -OUS] —**in·ces′tu·ous·ly,** *adv.* —**in·ces′tu·ous·ness,** *n.*

inch[1] (inch), *n.* **1.** a unit of length, $^1/_{12}$ foot, equivalent to 2.54 centimeters. **2.** a very small amount of anything; narrow margin: *to win by an inch; to avert disaster by an inch.* **3. by inches, a.** narrowly; by a narrow margin: *escaped by inches.* **b.** Also, **inch by inch.** by small degrees or stages; gradually: *The miners worked their way through the narrow shaft by inches.* **4. every inch,** in every respect; completely: *That horse is every inch a thoroughbred.* **5. within an inch of,** nearly; close to: *He came within an inch of getting killed in the crash.* —*v.t., v.i.* **6.** to move by inches or small degrees: *We inched our way along the road.* [ME; OE *ynce* < L *uncia* twelfth part, inch, ounce. See OUNCE[1]]

inch[2] (inch), *n. Scot.* an island, esp. a small island near the seacoast. [ME < Gael *innse,* gen. of *innis* island]

In′ Chan′cery, a novel (1920) by John Galsworthy. Cf. **Forsyte Saga, The.**

inch′ mast′, *Shipbuilding.* a square stick of timber suitable for making into a mast or spar, described in terms of its breadth in inches.

inch·meal (inch′mēl′), *adv.* by inches; inch by inch; little by little (often prec. by *by*). [INCH[1] + -MEAL]

in·cho·ate (in kō′it), *adj.* **1.** just begun; incipient. **2.** rudimentary; imperfect; incomplete. **3.** not organized; lacking order: *an inchoate mass of ideas on the subject.* [< L *inchoāt(us),* var. of *incohātus* begun (ptp. of *incohāre*), equiv. to *in-* IN-[2] + *coh(um)* yoke-strap + *-ātus* -ATE[1]] —**in·cho′ate·ly,** *adv.* —**in·cho′ate·ness,** *n.*

in·cho·a·tion (in′kō ā′shən), *n.* a beginning; origin. [< LL *inchoātiōn-* (s. of *inchoātiō*). See INCHOATE, -ION]

in·cho·a·tive (in kō′ə tiv), *adj.* **1.** *Gram.* inceptive. **2.** *Archaic.* inchoate. —*n.* **3.** *Gram.* an inceptive. [< LL *inchoātīv(um) (verbum)* inceptive (verb). See INCHOATE, -IVE]

inch′ of mer′cury, a unit of atmospheric pressure, being the pressure equal to that exerted by a column of mercury one inch high under standard conditions of temperature and gravity: 33.864 millibars. *Abbr.:* in. Hg

In·chon (in′chon′), *n.* a seaport in W South Korea. 401,473 (1960). Also called **Chemulpo.** Japanese, **Jinsen.**

inch-pound (inch′pound′), *n.* one-twelfth of a foot-pound. *Abbr.:* in-lb

inch·worm (inch′wûrm′), *n.* measuringworm. [INCH[1] + WORM]

in·ci·dence (in′si dəns), *n.* **1.** the rate or range of occurrence or influence of something, esp. of something unwanted: *the high incidence of heart disease in men over 40.* **2.** a falling upon, affecting, or befalling; occurrence: *The incidence of murder that Sunday afternoon shocked the sleepy village.* **3.** *Optics, Physics.* **a.** the striking of a ray of light, beam of electrons, etc., on a surface, or the direction of striking. **b.** See **angle of incidence** (def. 1). **4.** the fact or the manner of being incident. **5.** *Geom.* partial coincidence of two figures, as of a line and a plane containing it. [ME < LL *incidentia.* See INCIDENT, -ENCE]

in·ci·dent (in′si dənt), *n.* **1.** an occurrence or event. **2.** a distinct piece of action, or an episode, as in a story, play, etc. **3.** something that occurs casually in connection with something else. **4.** something appertaining or attaching to something else. **5.** an occurrence of seemingly minor importance, esp. involving nations or factions between which relations are strained and sensitive, that can lead to serious consequences, as an outbreak of hostilities, a war, etc.: *border incident; international incident.* **6.** *Chiefly Brit.* an instance of bombing; aerial attack, esp. on a city. —*adj.* **7.** likely or apt to happen (usually fol. by *to*). **8.** naturally appertaining: *hardships incident to the life of an explorer.* **9.** conjoined or attaching, esp. as subordinate to a

principal thing. 10. falling or striking on something, as light rays. [ME < ML *incident-* (s. of *incidēns* a happening, n. use of prp. of L *incidere* to befall), equiv. to L *in-* IN-[2] + *-cid-* (var. of *cad-* fall) + *-ent-* -ENT] —**in′ci·dent·less,** *adj.*
—**Syn. 1.** happening. See **event.**

in·ci·den·tal (in′si den′t(ə)l), *adj.* **1.** happening or likely to happen in fortuitous or subordinate conjunction with something else. **2.** likely to happen or naturally appertaining (usually fol. by *to*). **3.** incurred casually and in addition to the regular or main amount: *incidental expenses.* —*n.* **4.** something incidental, as a circumstance. **5. incidentals,** minor expenses. [INCIDENT + -AL[1]] —**in′ci·den′tal·ness,** *n.*
—**Syn. 1.** casual, chance, fortuitous; contingent. —**Ant. 1.** fundamental.

in·ci·den·tal·ly (in′si den′t(ə)lē), *adv.* **1.** in an incidental manner. **2.** apart or aside from the main subject of attention, discussion, etc.; by the way. [INCIDENTAL + -LY]

in′ciden′tal mu′sic, music intended primarily to point up or accompany parts of the action of a play or to serve as transitional material between scenes.

in·ci·en·so (in′sē en′sō), *n.* a shrubby desert plant, *Encelia farinosa,* of the southwestern U.S., having silvery leaves and clusters of showy, yellow flowers. [< Sp: INCENSE]

in·cin·er·ate (in sin′ə rāt′), *v.t.,* **-at·ed, -at·ing.** to burn or reduce to ashes; cremate. [< ML *incinerāt(us)* (ptp. of *incinerāre*) < L *in-* IN-[2] + *ciner-* (s. of *cinis* ashes + *-ātus* -ATE[1]] —**in·cin′er·a′tion,** *n.*

in·cin·er·a·tor (in sin′ə rā′tər), *n.* a furnace or apparatus for incinerating. [INCINERATE + -OR[2]]

in·cip·i·ent (in sip′ē ənt), *adj.* beginning to exist or appear; in an initial stage. [< L *incipient-* (s. of *incipiēns,* prp. of *incipere* to take in hand, begin), equiv. to *in-* IN-[2] + *-cipi-* (var. of *capi-* take) + *-ent-* -ENT] —**in·cip′i·ence, in·cip′i·en·cy,** *n.* —**in·cip′i·ent·ly,** *adv.*

in·ci·pit (in′si pit; *Lat.* ing′ki pit), *n.* the introductory words or opening phrases in the text of a medieval manuscript or an early printed book. [< L: (here) begins, 3rd sing. pres. indic. of *incipere*]

in·cise (in sīz′), *v.t.,* **-cised, -cis·ing. 1.** to cut into; cut marks, figures, etc., upon. **2.** to make (marks, figures, etc.) by cutting; engrave; carve. [< L *incīs(us)* carved, cut into (ptp. of *incīdere*), equiv. to *in-* IN-[2] + *cīd-* cut + *-tus* ptp. suffix]

in·cised (in sīzd′), *adj.* **1.** cut into: *the incised gums.* **2.** made by cutting: *an incised pattern.* **3.** *Med.* made or cut cleanly, as if surgically; not ragged: *an incised wound.* **4.** (of a leaf) sharply, deeply, and somewhat irregularly notched. [INCISE + -ED[2]]

in·ci·sion (in sizh′ən), *n.* **1.** a cut, gash, or notch. **2.** act of incising. **3.** a cutting into, esp. for surgical purposes. **4.** incisiveness; keenness. [ME < L *incīsiōn-* (s. of *incīsiō*). See INCISE, -ION]

in·ci·sive (in sī′siv), *adj.* **1.** penetrating; cutting; biting; trenchant: *an incisive tone of voice.* **2.** sharp; keen; acute: *an incisive method of summarizing the issue.* **3.** adapted for cutting or piercing: *an ordinary butter knife, honed till it was incisive as a stiletto.* **4.** of or pertaining to the incisors: *the incisive teeth.* [< ML *incīsīv(us).* See INCISE, -IVE] —**in·ci′sive·ly,** *adv.* —**in·ci′sive·ness,** *n.*
—**Syn. 1.** acid, mordant; sarcastic, sardonic.

in·ci·sor (in sī′zər), *n.* *Dentistry.* one of the four anterior teeth in each jaw, used for cutting. [< NL: lit., cutter < L *incīs(us)* (see INCISE) + *-or* -OR[2]]

in·ci·so·ry (in sī′zə rē), *adj.* adapted for cutting, as the incisor teeth. [INCISOR + -Y[1]]

in·cis·ure (in sizh′ər), *n.* *Anat.* a notch, as in a bone or other structure. [< L *incīsūra.* See INCISE, -URE] —**in·cis′ur·al,** *adj.*

in·cite (in sīt′), *v.t.,* **-cit·ed, -cit·ing.** to urge on; stimulate or prompt to action: *to incite a crowd to riot.* [late ME < L *incitāre,* equiv. to *in-* IN-[2] + *citāre* to start up, excite; see CITE] —**in·cit′ant,** *adj., n.* —**in·ci·ta·tion** (in′sī tā′shən, -si-), *n.* —**in·cit′er,** *n.* —**in·cit′ing·ly,** *adv.*
—**Syn.** encourage; instigate, provoke, goad, spur, arouse, exhort; fire; induce. —**Ant.** discourage.

in·cite·ment (in sīt′mənt), *n.* **1.** act of inciting. **2.** state of being incited. **3.** that which incites; motive; incentive. [< L *incitāment(um).* See INCITE, -MENT]

in·ci·vil·i·ty (in′sə vil′i tē), *n., pl.* **-ties** for 2. **1.** the quality or condition of being uncivil; uncivil behavior or treatment. **2.** an uncivil act. [< LL *incīvīlitās.* See IN-[3], CIVILITY] —**in·civ·il** (in siv′əl), *adj.*

in·ci·vism (in′si viz′əm), *n.* lack of patriotism or interest in civic affairs. [< F *incivisme.* See IN-[3], CIVISM]

incl., 1. inclosure. 2. including. 3. inclusive.

in·clasp (in klasp′, -kläsp′), *v.t.* enclasp.

in·clear·ing (in′klēr′ing), *n.* *Brit.* **1.** a check, bill of exchange, etc., received by one member bank of a clearing house for payment to another member bank. **2.** the total amount of such items payable by one member bank. Cf. **out-clearing.** —**in′clear′er,** *n.*

in·clem·ent (in klem′ənt), *adj.* **1.** (of the weather, the elements, etc.) severe or harsh; stormy. **2.** not kind or merciful. [< L *inclēment-,* equiv. to *in-* IN-[3] + *clēment-* (s. of *clēmēns*) CLEMENT] —**in·clem′en·cy, in·clem′ent·ness,** *n.* —**in·clem′ent·ly,** *adv.*

in·clin·a·ble (in klī′nə bəl), *adj.* **1.** having a mental bent or tendency in a certain direction; inclined. **2.** favorable: *We feel that the board is inclinable to his petition.* **3.** capable of being inclined. [INCLINE + -ABLE]

in·cli·na·tion (in′klə nā′shən), *n.* **1.** a set or bent, esp. of the mind or will; a liking or preference: *Much against his inclination, he was forced to resign.* **2.** that to which one is inclined: *In sports his inclination is tennis.* **3.** act of inclining; state of being inclined. **4.** a tendency toward a certain condition, action, etc.: *the door's inclination to stick.* **5.** deviation or amount of deviation from a normal, esp. horizontal or vertical, direction or position. **6.** an inclined surface. **7.** *Math.* **a.** the angle between two lines or two planes. **b.** the angle formed by the x-axis and a given line. **8.** *Astron.* **a.** the angle between the orbital plane of a planet and another given plane, usually the ecliptic. **b.** the angle between the equatorial and orbital planes of a planet. **9.** *Magnetism.* dip (def. 30). [late ME < L *inclīnātiōn-* (s. of *inclīnātiō*), equiv. to *inclīnāt(us)* ptp. (see INCLINE, -ATE[1]) + *-iōn-* -ION] —**in′cli·na′tion·al,** *adj.*
—**Syn. 1.** leaning, tendency; propensity, proclivity, proneness, predilection, predisposition, penchant. **3.** leaning, inclining, verging, tending. **5, 6.** slope, slant, rise, fall, grade, pitch. **6.** ramp. —**Ant. 1.** dislike.

in·cli·na·to·ry (in klī′nə tôr′ē, -tōr′ē), *adj.* related to or characterized by inclination. [< L *inclīnāt(us)* (see INCLINE, -ATE[1]) + -ORY[1]] —**in·cli′na·to′ri·ly,** *adv.*

in·cline (*v.* in klīn′; *n.* in′klīn, in klīn′), *v.,* **-clined, -clin·ing,** *n.* —*v.i.* **1.** to have a mental tendency, preference, etc.; be disposed: *We incline to rest and relaxation these days.* **2.** to deviate from the vertical or horizontal; slant. **3.** to tend, in a physical sense; approximate: *The flowers incline toward blue.* **4.** to tend in character or in course of action: *a political philosophy that inclines toward the conservative.* **5.** to lean; bend. —*v.t.* **6.** to dispose (a person) in mind, habit, etc. (usually fol. by *to*): *His attitude did not incline me to help him.* **7.** to bow or bend (the head, body, etc.): *He inclined his head in greeting.* **8.** to cause to lean or bend in a particular direction. **9. incline one's ear,** to listen with favor or willingness: *to incline one's ear to another's plea.* —*n.* **10.** an inclined surface; a slope. **11.** *Railroads.* **a.** Also called **inclined plane, in′cline plane′.** a cable railway the gradient of which is approximately 45°. **b.** any railway or portion of a railway the gradient of which is too steep for ordinary locomotive adhesion alone to be effective. [late ME < L *inclīn(āre),* equiv. to *in-* IN-[2] + *-clīnāre* to bend (see LEAN[1]); r. ME *enclyne(n)* < MF] —**in·clin′er,** *n.*
—**Syn. 1.** tend, lean. **2.** lean, slope, rise, fall, pitch. **3, 4.** verge, veer.

in·clined (in klīnd′), *adj.* **1.** disposed; of a mind (usually fol. by *to*): *He was inclined to stay.* **2.** having a physical tendency; leaning. **3.** deviating in direction from the horizontal or vertical; sloping. **4.** in a direction making an angle with anything else. [INCLINE + -ED[2]]

inclined′ plane′, **1.** a plane surface inclined to the horizon, or forming with a horizontal plane any angle but a right angle. **2.** incline (def. 11a).

in·clined′-plane′ clock′ (in klīnd′plān′), a drum-shaped clock containing an unbalanced weight which, remaining constantly downward, drives the mechanism by the weight of the clock when it rolls down a special, sloped platform.

in·clin·ing (in klī′ning), *n.* **1.** inclination; disposition. **2.** *Archaic.* those who are sympathetic, as to a person or cause; party; following. [ME *enclynynge.* See INCLINE, -ING[1]]

in·cli·nom·e·ter (in′klə nom′i tər), *n.* **1.** *Aeron.* an instrument for measuring the angle an aircraft makes with the horizontal. **2.** an instrument for determining the inclination or dip of the earth's magnetic force by the dip of a magnetic needle. [INCLINE + -O- + -METER]

in·close (in klōz′), *v.t.,* **-closed, -clos·ing.** enclose. —**in·clos′er,** *n.*

in·clo·sure (in klō′zhər), *n.* enclosure.

in·clude (in klōōd′), *v.t.,* **-clud·ed, -clud·ing. 1.** to contain, embrace, or comprise, as a whole does parts or any part or element: *The package includes a book of instructions.* **2.** to place in an aggregate, class, category, or the like. **3.** to contain as a subordinate element; involve as a factor. [ME < L *inclūd(ere)* (to) shut in, equiv. to *in-* IN-[2] + *-clūdere,* var. of *claudere* to shut] —**in·clud′a·ble, in·clud′i·ble,** *adj.*
—**Syn. 1.** embody. INCLUDE, COMPREHEND, COMPRISE, EMBRACE imply containing parts of a whole. To include is to contain as a part or member, or among the parts and members, of a whole: *The list includes many new names.* To COMPREHEND is to have within the limits, scope, or range of references, as either a part or the whole number of items concerned: *The plan comprehends several projects.* To COMPRISE is to consist of, as the various parts serving to make up the whole: *This genus comprises 50 species.* EMBRACE emphasizes the extent or assortment of that which is included: *The report embraces a great variety of subjects.* —**Ant. 1.** exclude, preclude.

in·clud·ed (in klōō′did), *adj.* **1.** enclosed; embraced; comprised. **2.** *Bot.* not projecting beyond the mouth of the corolla, as stamens or a style. [INCLUDE + -ED[2]] —**in·clud′ed·ness,** *n.*

in·cluse (in′klōōs), *n.* recluse (def. 2). [ME < L *inclūs(us)* enclosed, ptp. of *inclūdere;* see INCLUDE]

in·clu·sion (in klōō′zhən), *n.* **1.** the act of including. **2.** the state of being included. **3.** that which is included. **4.** *Biol.* a body suspended in the cytoplasm, as a granule. **5.** *Mineral.* a solid body or a body of gas or liquid enclosed within the mass of a mineral. [< L *inclūsiōn-* (s. of *inclūsiō*) a shutting in, equiv. to *inclūs(us)* confined (ptp. of *inclūdere;* see INCLUDE) + *-iōn-* -ION]

inclu′sion bod′y, *Pathol.* a particle that takes a characteristic stain, found in a virus-infected cell.

inclu′sion map′, *Math.* a map of a set to itself in which each element of a given subset of the set is mapped to itself.

in·clu·sive (in klōō′siv), *adj.* **1.** including in consideration or account, as the stated limit or extremes: *from six to ten inclusive.* **2.** including a great deal, or including everything concerned; comprehensive: *an inclusive art form; an inclusive fee.* **3.** that includes; enclosing; embracing. **4. inclusive of,** including; embracing: *Europe, inclusive of the British Isles, may become united in a trade agreement if all goes well.* [< ML *inclūsīv(us)* < L *inclūs(us)* (see INCLUSION) + *-īvus* -IVE] —**in·clu′sive·ly,** *adv.* —**in·clu′sive·ness,** *n.*

inclu′sive disjunc′tion, *Logic.* See under **disjunction** (def. 2a).

in·co·er·ci·ble (in′kō ûr′sə bəl), *adj.* **1.** not coercible. **2.** *Physics.* (of a gas) incapable of being reduced to a liquid form by pressure. [IN-[3] + COERCIBLE]

in·cog (in kog′), *adj., adv., n.* *Informal.* incognita or incognito. [by shortening]

in·cog·i·ta·ble (in koj′i tə bəl), *adj.* unthinkable; unimaginable: *the incogitable daring of such an act.* [< L *incōgitābil(is)* unthinking, equiv. to *in-* IN-[3] + *cōgitābilis,* equiv. to *(cōgitā(re)* to think + *-bilis* -BLE)] —**in·cog′i·ta·bil′i·ty,** *n.*

in·cog·i·tant (in koj′i tənt), *adj.* **1.** thoughtless; inconsiderate. **2.** not having the faculty of thought. [< L *incōgitant-,* equiv. to *in-* IN-[3] + *cōgitant-* (s. of *cōgitāns*), prp. of *cōgitāre* to think; see COGITATE, -ANT] —**in·cog′i·tant·ly,** *adv.*

in·cog·ni·ta (in kog′ni tə, in′kog nē′-), *adj., adv.* **1.** (of a woman or girl) incognito. —*n.* **2.** a woman or girl who is incognita. [< It; fem. of INCOGNITO]

in·cog·ni·to (in kog′ni tō′, in′kog nē′-), *adj., adv., n., pl.* **-tos** for 3, 5. —*adj.* **1.** having one's identity concealed, as under an assumed name, esp. to avoid notice or formal attentions. —*adv.* **2.** with the real identity concealed: *to travel incognito.* —*n.* **3.** a person who is incognito. **4.** state of being incognito. **5.** the disguise or character assumed by an incognito. [< It < L *incognitus* unknown, equiv. to *in-* IN-[3] + *cognitus,* ptp. of *cognoscere* to get to know; see COGNITION]

In·cog·ni·to (in kog′ni tō′, in′kog nē′-), *n.* **Mare.** See **Mare Incognito.**

in·cog·ni·zant (in kog′ni zənt), *adj.* not cognizant; without knowledge; unaware (usually fol. by *of*). [IN-[3] + COGNIZANT] —**in·cog′ni·zance,** *n.*

in·co·her·ence (in′kō hēr′əns), *n.* **1.** the quality or state of being incoherent. **2.** something incoherent; an incoherent statement, article, speech, etc. [IN-[3] + COHERENCE]

in·co·her·en·cy (in′kō hēr′ən sē), *n., pl.* **-cies.** incoherence. [IN-[3] + COHERENCY]

in·co·her·ent (in′kō hēr′ənt), *adj.* **1.** without logical connection; disjointed; rambling: *an incoherent sentence.* **2.** characterized by such thought or language, as a person: *incoherent with rage.* **3.** not coherent or cohering: *an incoherent mixture.* **4.** without physical cohesion; loose: *incoherent dust.* **5.** without unity or harmony of elements: *an incoherent public.* **6.** without congruity of parts; uncoordinated. **7.** different or incompatible by nature, as things. [IN-[3] + COHERENT] —**in′co·her′ent·ly,** *adv.*

in·com·bus·ti·ble (in′kəm bus′tə bəl), *adj.* **1.** not combustible; incapable of being burned. —*n.* **2.** an incombustible substance. [late ME < ML *incombustibil(is).* See IN-[3], COMBUSTIBLE] —**in′com·bus′ti·bil′i·ty, in′com·bus′ti·ble·ness,** n. —**in′com·bus′ti·bly,** *adv.*

in·come (in′kum), *n.* **1.** the returns that come in periodically, esp. annually, from property, business, labor, etc.; revenue; receipts. **2.** something that comes in as an addition or increase, esp. by chance. **3.** *Archaic.* a coming in. [ME: lit., that which has come in, n. use of *incomen* (ptp. of *income* to come in), OE *incumen*] —**in′come·less,** *adj.*
—**Syn. 1.** interest, salary, wages, annuity, gain, return, earnings. —**Ant. 1.** outgo, expenditure.

in′come account′, 1. an account maintained for a particular item of revenue or income. **2.** Also called **profit and loss account.** a summary account for income and expenditures, used in closing the ledger.

in′come bond′, a bond without a guaranteed amount of interest payment, such payment being usually made only out of earnings.

in·com·er (in′kum′ər), *n.* **1.** one who comes in. **2.** *Chiefly Brit.* an immigrant. **3.** an intruder. **4.** a successor. **5.** *Hunting.* a duck, pheasant, etc., that flies toward the shooter. [IN + COMER]

in′come tax′, a tax levied on incomes; an annual government tax on personal incomes, usually graduated and providing for certain deductions and exemptions.

in·com·ing (in′kum′ing), *adj.* **1.** coming in: *the incoming tide.* **2.** succeeding, as an officeholder: *the incoming mayor.* **3.** accruing, as profit. **4.** entering, beginning, etc.: *all incoming students.* **5.** *Chiefly Brit.* immigrant. **6.** *Scot.* ensuing. —*n.* **7.** the act of coming in; arrival; advent: *the incoming of spring.* **8.** Usually, **incomings.** funds received; revenue. [IN + COMING]

in·com·men·su·ra·ble (in′kə men′shər ə bəl, -sər ə-), *adj.* **1.** not commensurable; having no common measure or standard of comparison. **2.** utterly disproportionate. **3.** *Math.* (of two or more quantities) having no common measure. —*n.* **4.** that which is incommensurable. **5.** *Math.* one of two or more incommensurable quantities. [< LL *incommensūrābil(is).* See IN-[3], COMMENSURABLE] —**in·com·men′su·ra·bil′i·ty, in′com·men′su·ra·ble·ness,** *n.* —**in′com·men′su·ra·bly,** *adv.*

in·com·men·su·rate (in′kə men′shər it, -sər it), *adj.* **1.** not commensurate; disproportionate; inadequate: *means incommensurate to our wants.* **2.** incommensurable. [IN-[3] + COMMENSURATE] —**in′com·men′su·rate·ly,** *adv.* —**in′com·men′su·rate·ness,** *n.*

in·com·mode (in′kə mōd′), *v.t.,* **-mod·ed, -mod·ing. 1.** to inconvenience or discomfort; discommode. **2.** to impede; hinder. [< L *incommod(āre),* deriv. of *incommod(us)* inconvenient, equiv. to *in-* IN-[3] + *commodus* suitable; see COMMODE]
—**Syn. 1.** disturb, trouble. **2.** delay, obstruct. —**Ant. 1.** help. **2.** expedite.

in·com·mo·di·ous (in′kə mō′dē əs), *adj.* inconvenient, as not affording sufficient space or room; uncomfortable: *incommodious hotel accommodations.* [IN-[3] + COMMODIOUS] —**in′com·mo′di·ous·ly,** *adv.* —**in′com·mo′di·ous·ness,** *n.*

in·com·mod·i·ty (in′kə mod′i tē), *n., pl.* **-ties. 1.** something inconvenient; a disadvantage or inconvenience: *The incommodities of the house are numerous.* **2.** *Obs.* the quality or state of being inconvenient. [ME < L *incommoditās.* See INCOMMODE, -ITY]

in·com·mu·ni·ca·ble (in′kə myōō′nə kə bəl), *adj.* **1.** incapable of being communicated, imparted, shared, etc. **2.** incommunicative; taciturn. [< LL *incommūnicābil(is).* See IN-[3], COMMUNICABLE] —**in′com·mu′ni·ca·bil′i·ty, in′com·mu′ni·ca·ble·ness,** *n.* —**in′com·mu′ni·ca·bly,** *adv.*

in·com·mu·ni·ca·do (in′kə myōō′nə kä′dō), *adj.* (esp. of a prisoner) deprived of communication with others. [< Sp *incomunicado.* See IN-[3], COMMUNICATE]

in·com·mu·ni·ca·tive (in′kə myōō′nə kā′tiv, -kə-tiv), *adj.* not communicative; reserved; uncommunicative. [IN-[3] + COMMUNICATIVE] —**in·com·mu·ni·ca·tive·ly** (in′kə myōō′nə kā′tiv lē, -nə kə tiv-), *adv.* —**in′com·mu′ni·ca′tive·ness,** *n.*

in·com·mut·a·ble (in′kə myōō′tə bəl), *adj.* **1.** not exchangeable. **2.** unchangeable; unalterable. [< L *incommūtābil(is).* See IN-[3], COMMUTABLE] —**in′com·mut′a·bil′i·ty, in′com·mut′a·ble·ness,** *n.* —**in′com·mut′a·bly,** *adv.*

in·com·pact (in′kəm pakt′), *adj.* not compact; loose. [IN-[3] + COMPACT[1]] —**in′com·pact′ly,** *adv.* —**in′com·pact′ness,** *n.*

in·com·pa·ra·ble (in kom′pər ə bəl, -prə bəl), *adj.* **1.** matchless or unequaled: *incomparable beauty.* **2.** not comparable; incapable of being compared to each other, as two unlike objects or qualities, or to one or more others. [ME < L *incomparābil(is)*. See IN-³, COMPARABLE] —**in·com′pa·ra·bil′i·ty, in·com′pa·ra·ble·ness,** *n.* —**in·com′pa·ra·bly,** *adv.*

in·com·pat·i·ble (in′kəm pat′ə bəl), *adj.* **1.** not compatible; incapable of existing together in harmony: *She asked for a divorce because they were utterly incompatible.* **2.** contrary or opposed in character; discordant: *incompatible colors.* **3.** that cannot coexist or be conjoined. **4.** *Logic.* **a.** (of two or more propositions) unable to be true simultaneously. **b.** (of two or more attributes of an object) unable to belong to the object simultaneously; inconsistent. **5.** (of positions, ranks, etc.) unable to be held simultaneously by one person. **6.** *Med.* of or pertaining to biological substances which interfere with one another physiologically, as different types of blood in a transfusion. **7.** *Pharm., Med.* of or pertaining to drugs which interfere with one another chemically and therefore cannot be mixed together or physiologically and cannot be prescribed together. —*n.* **8.** Usually, **incompatibles.** incompatible persons or things. **9.** an incompatible drug or the like. **10. incompatibles,** *Logic.* **a.** two or more propositions which cannot be true simultaneously. **b.** two or more attributes which cannot simultaneously belong to the same object. [< eccl. L *incompatibil(is)*. See IN-³, COMPATIBLE] —**in′com·pat′i·bil′i·ty, in′com·pat′i·ble·ness,** *n.* —**in′com·pat′i·bly,** *adv.*
—**Syn. 1.** unsuitable, unsuited. See **inconsistent. 1, 2.** unharmonious. **2.** contradictory.

in·com·pe·tence (in kom′pi təns), *n.* **1.** the quality or condition of being incompetent; lack of ability. **2.** *Law.* the condition of lacking power to act with legal effectiveness. Also, **in·com′pe·ten·cy.** [var. (with -ENCE for -ENCY) of earlier *incompetency.* See INCOMPETENT, -CY]

in·com·pe·tent (in kom′pi tənt), *adj.* **1.** not competent; lacking qualification or ability: *an incompetent candidate.* **2.** characterized by or showing incompetence: *His incompetent acting ruined the play.* **3.** *Law.* not legally qualified; inadmissible, as evidence. —*n.* **4.** an incompetent person. **5.** *Law.* a person lacking power to act with legal effectiveness. [< LL *incompetent-* (s. of *incompetēns*) unequal to. See IN-³, COMPETENT] —**in·com′pe·tent·ly,** *adv.*
—**Syn. 1.** unqualified, inadequate, unfit. See **incapable.** —**Ant. 1.** able, qualified.

in·com·plete (in′kəm plēt′), *adj.* **1.** not complete; lacking some part. **2.** *Football.* (of a forward pass) not having been completed; not caught by a receiver. **3.** *Engineering.* noting a truss the panel points of which are not entirely connected so as to form a system of triangles. Cf. **complete** (def. 7), **redundant** (def. 5c). **4.** *Logic, Philos.* (of an expression or symbol) meaningful only in a specific context. [ME < LL *incomplēt(us).* See IN-³, COMPLETE] —**in′com·plete′ly,** *adv.* —**in′com·plete′ness,** *n.*

in′complete frac′ture, a fracture in which the bone is split partially across.

in·com·ple·tion (in′kəm plē′shən), *n.* **1.** state of being incomplete; incompleteness. **2.** *Football.* an incomplete forward pass. [IN-³ + COMPLETION]

in·com·pli·ant (in′kəm plī′ənt), *adj.* **1.** not compliant; unyielding. **2.** not pliant. [IN-³ + COMPLIANT] —**in′com·pli′ance, in′com·pli′an·cy,** *n.* —**in′com·pli′ant·ly,** *adv.*

in·com·pre·hen·si·ble (in′kom pri hen′sə bəl, in-kom′-), *adj.* not comprehensible; not understandable; unintelligible. [ME < L *incomprehensibil(is).* See IN-³, COMPREHENSIBLE] —**in′com·pre·hen′si·bil′i·ty, in′com·pre·hen′si·ble·ness,** *n.* —**in′com·pre·hen′si·bly,** *adv.*

in·com·pre·hen·sive (in′kom pri hen′siv, in kom′-), *adj.* **1.** not comprehensive. **2.** not comprehending readily; having a slow or inadequate mental grasp. [IN-³ + COMPREHENSIVE] —**in′com·pre·hen′sive·ly,** *adv.* —**in′com·pre·hen′sive·ness,** *n.*

in·com·press·i·ble (in′kəm pres′ə bəl), *adj.* not compressible. [IN-³ + COMPRESSIBLE] —**in′com·press′i·bil′i·ty,** *n.* —**in′com·press′i·bly,** *adv.*

in·com·put·a·ble (in′kəm pyōō′tə bəl), *adj.* incapable of being computed; incalculable. [IN-³ + COMPUTABLE] —**in′com·put′a·bly,** *adv.*

in·con·ceiv·a·ble (in′kən sē′və bəl), *adj.* not conceivable; unimaginable; unthinkable; incredible. [IN-³ + CONCEIVABLE] —**in′con·ceiv′a·bil′i·ty, in′con·ceiv′a·ble·ness,** *n.* —**in′con·ceiv′a·bly,** *adv.*

in·con·clu·sive (in′kən klōō′siv), *adj.* **1.** not conclusive; indefinite; not resolving fully all doubts or questions: *inconclusive evidence.* **2.** without final results: *inconclusive experiments.* [IN-³ + CONCLUSIVE] —**in′con·clu′sive·ly,** *adv.* —**in′con·clu′sive·ness,** *n.*

in·con·den·sa·ble (in′kən den′sə bəl), *adj.* not condensable; incapable of being condensed. Also, **in′con·den′si·ble.** [IN-³ + CONDENSABLE] —**in′con·den′sa·bil′i·ty, in′con·den′si·bil′i·ty,** *n.*

in·con·dite (in kon′dit, -dīt), *adj.* **1.** ill-constructed; unpolished: *incondite prose.* **2.** crude; rough; unmannerly. [<L *incondit(us)* disordered, equiv. to *in-* IN-³ + *conditus* built, composed, ptp. of *condere,* (*con-* CON- + *-di-* put, set + *-tus* ptp. suffix)]

in·con·form·i·ty (in′kən fôr′mi tē), *n.* lack of conformity; failure or refusal to conform; nonconformity. [IN-³ + CONFORMITY]

in·con·gru·ent (in koŋ′grōō ənt), *adj.* not congruent; incongruous. [< L *incongruent-* (s. of *incongruēns*) inconsistent. See IN-³, CONGRUENT] —**in·con′gru·ence,** *n.* —**in·con′gru·ent·ly,** *adv.*

in·con·gru·i·ty (in′koŋ grōō′i tē), *n., pl.* **-ties** for 2. **1.** the quality or condition of being incongruous. **2.** something incongruous. [< LL *incongruitās.* See IN-³, CONGRUITY]

in·con·gru·ous (in koŋ′grōō əs), *adj.* **1.** out of keeping or place; inappropriate; unbecoming: *an incongruous effect; incongruous behavior.* **2.** not harmonious in character; inconsonant; lacking harmony of parts: *an incongruous mixture of styles.* **3.** inconsistent: *acts that were incongruous with their professed principles.* [< L *incongruus* inconsistent. See IN-³, CONGRUOUS] —**in·con′gru·ous·ly,** *adv.* —**in·con′gru·ous·ness,** *n.*
—**Syn. 1.** discrepant, unsuitable, ridiculous, ludicrous, absurd. **2.** inharmonious, discordant. **3.** contrary, contradictory; unfitting. See **inconsistent.** —**Ant. 1.** becoming, appropriate. **2.** consonant. **3.** consistent.

in·con·nu (in′kə nōō′, -nyōō′, iŋ′-; *Fr.* aN kô nʏ′), *n., pl.* **-nus** (-nōōz′, -nyōōz′; *Fr.* -nʏ′), (*esp. collectively for 2*) **-nu. 1.** a person who is unknown; a stranger. **2.** Also called **sheefish.** a game fish, *Stenodus leucichthys,* found in fresh and brackish northern waters. [< F: lit., unknown, equiv. to *in-* IN-³ + *connu,* ptp. of *connaître* to know; see CONNOISSEUR]

in·con·sec·u·tive (in′kən sek′yə tiv), *adj.* not consecutive. [IN-³ + CONSECUTIVE] —**in′con·sec′u·tive·ly,** *adv.* —**in′con·sec′u·tive·ness,** *n.*

in·con·se·quent (in kon′sə kwent′), *adj.* **1.** characterized by lack of proper sequence in thought, speech, or action. **2.** not following from the premises: *an inconsequent deduction.* **3.** characterized by lack of logical sequence; illogical; inconsecutive: *inconsequent reasoning.* **4.** irrelevant: *an inconsequent remark.* **5.** not in keeping with the general character or design; inconsistent: *inconsequent ornamentation.* **6.** without worth or consequence; trivial: *a frivolous, inconsequent young man.* [< LL *inconsequent-* (s. of *inconsequēns*) not following. See IN-³, CONSEQUENT] —**in·con′se·quence′, in·con′se·quent′ness,** *n.* —**in·con′se·quent′ly,** *adv.*

in·con·se·quen·ti·a (in′kon sə kwen′shē ə, in kon′-), *n.pl.* inconsequential details; trivia: *the inconsequentia of everyday things.* [< LL, neut. pl. of *inconsequēns.* See INCONSEQUENT, -IA]

in·con·se·quen·tial (in′kon sə kwen′shəl, in kon′-), *adj.* **1.** of no consequence; trivial. **2.** inconsequent; illogical; irrelevant. [IN-³ + CONSEQUENTIAL] —**in′con·se·quen′ti·al′i·ty,** *n.* —**in′con·se·quen′tial·ly,** *adv.*

in·con·sid·er·a·ble (in′kən sid′ər ə bəl), *adj.* **1.** small, as in value, amount, size, etc. **2.** not worthy of consideration or notice; trivial. [IN-³ + CONSIDERABLE] —**in′con·sid′er·a·ble·ness,** *n.* —**in′con·sid′er·a·bly,** *adv.*

in·con·sid·er·ate (in′kən sid′ər it), *adj.* **1.** without due regard for the rights or feelings of others: *It was inconsiderate of him to renege on his promise.* **2.** acting without consideration; thoughtless. **3.** overhasty; rash; ill-considered: *slovenly, inconsiderate reasoning.* [late ME < L *inconsīderāt(us).* See IN-³, CONSIDERATE] —**in′con·sid′er·ate·ly,** *adv.* —**in′con·sid′er·ate·ness, in′con·sid′er·a′tion,** *n.*

in·con·sist·en·cy (in′kən sis′tən sē), *n., pl.* **-cies** for 2. **1.** the quality or condition of being inconsistent. **2.** something inconsistent. Also, **in′con·sist′ence.** [IN-³ + CONSISTENCY]

in·con·sist·ent (in′kən sis′tənt), *adj.* **1.** lacking in harmony between the different parts or elements; self-contradictory: *an inconsistent story; inconsistent décor.* **2.** lacking agreement, as one thing with another or two or more things in relation to each other; at variance: *a summary that is inconsistent with the stated facts.* **3.** not consistent in principles, conduct, etc.: *All kids are inconsistent at that age.* **4.** acting at variance with professed principles. **5.** *Logic.* incompatible (def. 4b). [IN-³ + CONSISTENT] —**in′con·sist′ent·ly,** *adv.*
—**Syn. 1.** incoherent. **2.** discrepant, disagreeing, irreconcilable. INCONSISTENT, INCOMPATIBLE, INCONGRUOUS refer to things which are out of keeping with each other. That which is INCONSISTENT involves variance, discrepancy, or even contradiction, esp. from the point of view of truth, reason, or logic: *His actions are inconsistent with his statements.* INCOMPATIBLE implies incapability of close association or harmonious relationship, as from differences of nature, character, temperament, and the like: *actions incompatible with honesty of purpose; qualities which make two people incompatible.* That which is INCONGRUOUS is inappropriate or out of keeping, often to the point of being ridiculous or absurd: *Incongruous characters or situations frequently provide a basis for comedy.* —**Ant. 1.** harmonious.

in·con·sol·a·ble (in′kən sō′lə bəl), *adj.* not consolable: *inconsolable grief.* [< L *inconsōlābil(is).* See IN-³, CONSOLABLE] —**in′con·sol′a·bil′i·ty, in′con·sol′a·ble·ness,** *n.* —**in′con·sol′a·bly,** *adv.*

in·con·so·nant (in kon′sə nənt), *adj.* not consonant or in accord. [IN-³ + CONSONANT] —**in·con′so·nance,** *n.* —**in·con′so·nant·ly,** *adv.*

in·con·spic·u·ous (in′kən spik′yōō əs), *adj.* not conspicuous, noticeable, or prominent. [< LL *inconspicuus.* See IN-³, CONSPICUOUS] —**in′con·spic′u·ous·ly,** *adv.* —**in′con·spic′u·ous·ness,** *n.*

in·con·stant (in kon′stənt), *adj.* not constant; changeable; fickle; variable: *an inconstant friend; the inconstant winds.* [ME < L *inconstant-* (s. of *inconstāns*) changeable. See IN-³, CONSTANT] —**in·con′stan·cy,** *n.* —**in·con′stant·ly,** *adv.*
—**Syn.** moody, capricious, vacillating, wavering, undependable, unstable, unsettled, uncertain, mutable, mercurial, volatile. —**Ant.** steady.

in·con·sum·a·ble (in′kən sōō′mə bəl), *adj.* not consumable; incapable of being consumed. [IN-³ + CONSUMABLE] —**in′con·sum′a·bly,** *adv.*

in·con·test·a·ble (in′kən tes′tə bəl), *adj.* not contestable; not admitting of dispute; incontrovertible: *incontestable proof.* [IN-³ + CONTESTABLE] —**in′con·test′a·bil′i·ty, in′con·test′a·ble·ness,** *n.* —**in′con·test′a·bly,** *adv.*

in′contest′able clause′, a clause in a life-insurance or health-insurance policy stating that the insurer cannot contest the policy after a stated period of time.

in·con·ti·nent¹ (in kon′tᵊnənt), *adj.* **1.** *Pathol.* unable to restrain natural discharges or evacuations. **2.** unable to contain or retain (usually fol. by *of*): *incontinent of temper.* **3.** unceasing or unrestrained: *an incontinent flow of talk.* **4.** lacking in moderation or control, esp. of the sexual appetite. [ME < L *incontinent-* (s. of *incontinēns*). See IN-³, CONTINENT (adj.)] —**in·con′ti·nence, in·con′ti·nen·cy,** *n.* —**in·con′ti·nent·ly,** *adv.*

in·con·ti·nent² (in kon′tᵊnənt), *adv.* *Archaic.* immediately; at once; straightway. Also, **in·con′ti·nent·ly.** [ME < MF < LL *in continentī (tempore)* in continuous (time), i.e., without pause. See CONTINENT]

in·con·tin·u·ous (in′kən tin′yōō əs), *adj.* not continuous. [IN-³ + CONTINUOUS] —**in·con·ti·nu·i·ty** (in-kon′tᵊnōō′i tē, -nyōō′-), *n.*

in·con·trol·la·ble (in′kən trō′lə bəl), *adj.* not controllable; uncontrollable. [IN-³ + CONTROLLABLE] —**in′con·trol′la·bly,** *adv.*

in·con·tro·vert·i·ble (in′kon trə vûr′tə bəl, in-kon′-), *adj.* not controvertible; indisputable: *absolute and incontrovertible truth.* [IN-³ + CONTROVERTIBLE] —**in′con·tro·vert′i·bil′i·ty, in′con·tro·vert′i·ble·ness,** *n.* —**in′con·tro·vert′i·bly,** *adv.*
—**Syn.** incontestable, undeniable, unquestionable.

in·con·ven·ience (in′kən vēn′yəns), *n., v.,* **-ienced, -ienc·ing.** —*n.* **1.** the quality or state of being inconvenient. **2.** an inconvenient circumstance or thing; something that causes discomfort, trouble, etc. —*v.t.* **3.** to put to inconvenience; incommode: *He inconvenienced everyone by his constant telephoning.* [ME < LL *inconvenientia.* See IN-³, CONVENIENCE]

in·con·ven·ien·cy (in′kən vēn′yən sē), *n., pl.* **-cies.** inconvenience. [INCONVENIENCE + -Y³]

in·con·ven·ient (in′kən vēn′yənt), *adj.* arranged or happening in such a way as to be awkward, inopportune, disadvantageous, troublesome, etc.: *an inconvenient time for a visit.* [ME < L *inconvenient-* (s. of *inconveniēns*) not suiting. See IN-³, CONVENIENT] —**in′con·ven′ient·ly,** *adv.*
—**Syn.** untimely; annoying.

in·con·vert·i·ble (in′kən vûr′tə bəl), *adj.* **1.** (of paper money) not capable of being converted into specie. **2.** not interchangeable. [< LL *inconvertibil(is)* not alterable. See IN-³, CONVERTIBLE] —**in′con·vert′i·bil′i·ty, in′con·vert′i·ble·ness,** *n.* —**in′con·vert′i·bly,** *adv.*

in·con·vin·ci·ble (in′kən vin′sə bəl), *adj.* not convincible; incapable of being convinced. [IN-³ + CONVINCIBLE] —**in′con·vin′ci·bil′i·ty,** *n.* —**in′con·vin′ci·bly,** *adv.*

in·co·or·di·nate (in′kō ôr′dᵊnit), *adj.* not coordinate; not coordinated. Also, **in′co-or′di·nate, in′co·ör′di·nate.** [IN-³ + COORDINATE]

in·co·or·di·na·tion (in′kō ôr′dᵊnā′shən), *n.* lack of coordination. Also, **in′co-or′di·na′tion, in′co·ör′di·na′tion.** [IN-³ + COORDINATION]

incor., incorporated. Also, **incorp.**

in·cor·po·ra·ble (in kôr′pər ə bəl), *adj.* able to be incorporated. [< LL *incorpor(āre)* (to) embody + -ABLE. See INCORPORATE¹]

in·cor·po·rate¹ (*v.* in kôr′pə rāt′; *adj.* in kôr′pə rit, -prit), *v.,* **-rat·ed, -rat·ing,** *adj.* —*v.t.* **1.** to form into a corporation. **2.** to form into a society or organization. **3.** to put or introduce into a body or mass as an integral part or parts: *to incorporate revisions into a text.* **4.** to take in or include as a part or parts, as the body or a mass does: *His book incorporates his earlier essay.* **5.** to form or combine into one body or uniform substance, as ingredients. **6.** to embody: *His book incorporates all his thinking on the subject.* —*v.i.* **7.** to unite or combine so as to form one body. **8.** to form a corporation. —*adj.* **9.** incorporated, as a company. **10.** combined into one body, mass, or substance. **11.** *Archaic.* embodied. [ME < LL *incorporāt(us)* embodied. See IN-², CORPORATE] —**in·cor′po·ra′tion,** *n.* —**in·cor′po·ra′tive,** *adj.*

in·cor·po·rate² (in kôr′pər it, -prit), *adj.* *Rare.* not embodied; incorporeal. [< LL *incorporāt(us)* not embodied. See IN-³, CORPORATE]

in·cor·po·rat·ed (in kôr′pə rā′tid), *adj.* **1.** formed or constituted as a corporation. **2.** combined in one body; made part of. [INCORPORATE¹ + -ED²] —**in·cor′po·rat′ed·ness,** *n.*

incor′porated bar′, *Law.* See **integrated bar.**

in·cor·po·ra·tion (in kôr′pə rā′shən), *n.* **1.** the act of forming a corporation. **2.** *Gram.* the inclusion of the object or object reference within the inflected verb form, a type of word-formation frequent in American Indian languages. [ME *incorporacion* < LL *incorporātiōn-* (s. of *incorporātiō*), equiv. to *incorporāt(us)* (see INCORPORATE) + *-iōn-* -ION]

in·cor·po·ra·tor (in kôr′pə rā′tər), *n.* **1.** one of the signers of the articles or certificate of incorporation. **2.** one of the persons to whom the charter is granted in a corporation created by special act of the legislature. **3.** a person who incorporates. [INCORPORATE + -OR²]

in cor·po·re (in kôr′pō re′; *Eng.* in kôr′pə rē), *Latin.* in body; in substance.

in·cor·po·re·al (in′kôr pōr′ē əl, -pôr′-), *adj.* **1.** not corporeal or material; insubstantial. **2.** of, pertaining to, or characteristic of nonmaterial beings. **3.** *Law.* without material existence but existing in contemplation of law, as a franchise. [< LL *incorpore(us)* + -AL¹. See IN-³, CORPOREAL] —**in′cor·po′re·al′i·ty,** *n.* —**in′cor·po′re·al·ly,** *adv.*

in·cor·po·re·i·ty (in′kôr pə rē′i tē), *n.* **1.** quality of being incorporeal; disembodied existence or entity; incorporeality. **2.** something incorporeal, as a right, trait, characteristic, etc. [< ML *incorporeitās* < LL *incorpore(us)* bodies + *-itās* -ITY]

incorr., incorrect.

in·cor·rect (in′kə rekt′), *adj.* **1.** not correct as to fact; inaccurate: *an incorrect statement.* **2.** improper or unbecoming: *incorrect behavior; incorrect attire.* **3.** not correct in form, use, or manner: *an incorrect copy.* [ME < L *incorrect(us)* not corrected. See IN-³, CORRECT] —**in′cor·rect′ly,** *adv.* —**in′cor·rect′ness,** *n.*
—**Syn. 1.** erroneous, inexact; untrue, wrong. **2.** unsuitable, inappropriate. **3.** faulty.

in·cor·ri·gi·ble (in kôr′i jə bəl, -kor′-), *adj.* **1.** not corrigible; bad beyond correction or reform: *incorrigible behavior; an incorrigible liar.* **2.** impervious to punishment; willful; uncontrollable: *an incorrigible child.* **3.** firmly fixed; not easily changed: *an incorrigible habit.* **4.** not easily swayed or influenced: *an incorrigible optimist.* —*n.* **5.** a person who is incorrigible. [ME < LL *incorrigibil(is).* See IN-³, CORRIGIBLE] —**in·cor′ri·gi·bil′i·ty, in·cor′ri·gi·ble·ness,** *n.* —**in·cor′ri·gi·bly,** *adv.*

in·cor·rupt (in′kə rupt′), *adj.* **1.** not corrupt; not debased or perverted; morally upright. **2.** not to be corrupted; incorruptible. **3.** not vitiated by errors or alterations. **4.** *Obs.* free from decomposition or putrefaction. Also, **in′cor·rupt′ed.** [ME < L *incorrupt(us)* unspoiled. See IN-³ + CORRUPT] —**in′cor·rupt′ly,** *adv.* —**in′cor·rupt′ness,** *n.*

in·cor·rupt·i·ble (in′kə rup′tə bəl), *adj.* **1.** not corruptible; incapable of corruption: *a man of incorruptible integrity.* **2.** that cannot be perverted or bribed: *incorruptible by money.* **3.** that will not dissolve, disintegrate, decay, etc.: *an incorruptible metal.* [< LL *incorruptibil(is).* See IN-³, CORRUPTIBLE] —**in′cor·rupt′i·bil′i·ty, in′cor·rupt′i·ble·ness,** *n.* —**in′cor·rupt′i·bly,** *adv.*

in·cor·rup·tion (in′kə rup′shən), *n.* *Archaic.* incorrupt condition. [< LL *incorruptiōn-* (s. of *incorruptiō*). See IN-³, CORRUPTION]

incr., 1. increased. 2. increasing.

in·cras·sate (*v.* in kras′āt; *adj.* in kras′it, -āt), *v.*, **-sat·ed, -sat·ing,** *adj.* —*v.t.* 1. *Pharm.* to make (a liquid) thicker by addition of another substance or by evaporation. 2. *Obs.* to thicken. —*v.i.* 3. *Obs.* to become thick or thicker. —*adj.* 4. Also, **in·cras′sat·ed.** *Bot., Entomol.* thickened or swollen. [< LL *incrassāt(us)* made thick or stout (ptp. of *incrassāre*). See IN-[2], CRASS, -ATE[1]] —**in′cras·sa′tion,** *n.* —**in·cras′sa·tive,** *adj.*

in·crease (*v.* in krēs′; *n.* in′krēs), *v.*, **-creased, -creas·ing,** *n.* —*v.t.* 1. to make greater in any respect; augment; add to: *to increase taxes.* 2. to make more numerous. —*v.i.* 3. to become greater or more numerous: *Sales of automobiles increased last year.* 4. to multiply by propagation. 5. to wax, as the moon. —*n.* 6. growth or augmentation in numbers: *the increase of crime.* 7. act or process of increasing. 8. that by which something is increased. 9. the result of increasing. 10. produce of the earth. 11. product; profit; interest. 12. *Obs.* **a.** multiplication by propagation; production of offspring. **b.** offspring; progeny. [ME *increse,* var. of *encrese(n)* < AF *encres-* < MF *encreiss-,* s. of *encreistre* < L *incrēscere,* equiv. to *in-* IN-[2] + *crēscere* to grow; see CRESCENT] —**in·creas′a·ble** *adj.* —**in·creas·ed·ly** (in krē′sid lē), *adv.*

—**Syn.** 1. expand, extend, prolong. INCREASE, AUGMENT, ENLARGE may all mean to make larger. To INCREASE means to make greater, as in quantity, extent, degree: *to increase someone's salary; to increase the velocity; to increase the (degree of) concentration.* ENLARGE means to make greater in size, extent, or range: *to enlarge a building, a business, one's conceptions.* AUGMENT, a more formal word, means to make greater especially by addition from the outside: *to augment one's income (by doing extra work).* 3. dilate, expand, grow, develop, swell. 6. enlargement, expansion. —**Ant.** 1, 3. decrease.

in·creas·er (in krē′sər), *n.* 1. one who or that which increases. 2. (in plumbing) a coupling increasing in diameter at one end. Cf. **reducer** (def. 3). [INCREASE + -ER[1]]

in·creas·ing (in krē′siŋ), *adj.* 1. growing larger or greater; enlarging; augmenting. 2. *Math.* (of a function) having the property that for any two points in the domain such that one is larger than the other, the image of the larger point is greater than or equal to the image of the smaller point; nondecreasing. Cf. **decreasing.** [INCREASE + -ING[2]] —**in·creas′ing·ly,** *adv.*

in·cre·ate (in′krē āt′, in′krē āt′), *adj.* 1. not created; uncreated. 2. existing without having been created. [ME *increat* < LL *increāt(us)* not made. See IN-[3], CREATE] —**in′cre·ate′ly,** *adv.*

in·cred·i·ble (in kred′ə bəl), *adj.* 1. so extraordinary as to seem impossible: *incredible speed.* 2. not credible; unbelievable: *The plot of the book is incredible.* [ME < L *incrēdibil(is).* See IN-[3], CREDIBLE] —**in·cred′i·bil′i·ty, in·cred′i·ble·ness,** *n.* —**in·cred′i·bly,** *adv.*

in·cre·du·li·ty (in′kri do͞o′li tē, -dyo͞o′-), *n.* quality or state of being incredulous; refusal of belief. [ME *incredulite* < L *incrēdulitās.* See INCREDULOUS, -ITY]

—**Syn.** disbelief, skepticism, doubt. —**Ant.** belief.

in·cred·u·lous (in krej′ə ləs), *adj.* 1. not credulous; disinclined or indisposed to believe; skeptical. 2. indicating unbelief: *an incredulous smile.* [< L *incrēdulus.* See IN-[3], CREDULOUS] —**in·cred′u·lous·ly,** *adv.* —**in·cred′u·lous·ness,** *n.*

—**Syn.** unbelieving. See **doubtful.**

in·cre·ment (in′krə mənt, iŋ′-), *n.* 1. something added or gained; an addition or increase. 2. profit; gain. 3. act or process of increasing; growth. 4. *Math.* **a.** the difference between two values of a variable; a change, positive, negative, or zero, in an independent variable. **b.** the increase of a function due to an increase in the independent variable. [ME < L *incrēment(um)* an increase, equiv. to *incrē(scere)* (to) grow (see INCREASE) + *-mentum* -MENT] —**in·cre·men·tal** (in′krə men′tᵊl, iŋ′-), *adj.*

incremen′tal repeti′tion, *Pros.* repetition, with variation, of a refrain or other part of a poem, esp. a ballad.

in·cres·cent (in kres′ənt), *adj.* 1. increasing or waxing, as the moon. 2. *Heraldry.* (of a crescent) having the horns toward the dexter side. Cf. **decrescent** (def. 3). [< L *incrēscent-* (s. of *incrēscēns* growing, prp. of *incrēscere*), equiv. to *in-* IN-[2] + *crēsc-* grow + *-ent-* -ENT] —**in·cres′cence,** *n.*

in·cre·tion (in krē′shən), *n.* *Physiol.* 1. a substance, as an autacoid, secreted internally. 2. the process of such secretion. [IN-[2] + (SE)CRETION] —**in·cre′tion·ar′y, in·cre·to·ry** (in′kri tôr′ē, -tōr′ē), *adj.*

in·crim·i·nate (in krim′ə nāt′), *v.t.*, **-nat·ed, -nat·ing.** 1. to charge with a crime or fault: *He incriminated both men to the grand jury.* 2. to involve in an accusation; implicate: *His testimony incriminated his friend. He feared incriminating himself if he answered.* 3. to charge with responsibility for all or part of an undesirable situation, harmful effect, etc.: *to incriminate cigarettes as one cause of lung cancer.* [< ML *incrīmināt(us)* accused of a crime (ptp. of *incrīmināre*). See IN-[2], CRIMINATE] —**in·crim′i·na′tion,** *n.* —**in·crim′i·na′tor,** *n.* —**in·crim·i·na·to·ry** (in krim′ə nə tôr′ē, -tōr′ē), *adj.*

in·crust (in krust′), *v.t.* 1. to cover or line with a crust or hard coating. 2. to form into a crust. 3. to deposit as a crust. —*v.i.* 4. to form a crust: *They scraped off the barnacles incrusted on the ship's hull.* Also, **encrust.** [IN-[2] + CRUST] —**in·crust′ant,** *adj., n.*

in·crus·ta·tion (in′kru stā′shən), *n.* 1. an incrusting or being incrusted. 2. a crust or coat of anything on the surface of a body; covering, coating, or scale. 3. the inlaying or addition of enriching materials on or to a surface or an object. 4. the enriching materials inlaid on or added to a surface or an object. Also, **encrustation.** [< LL *incrustātiōn-* (s. of *incrustātiō*). See IN-[2], CRUST, -ATION]

in·cu·bate (in′kyə bāt′, iŋ′-), *v.*, **-bat·ed, -bat·ing.** —*v.t.* 1. to sit upon (eggs) for the purpose of hatching. 2. to hatch (eggs), as by sitting upon them or by artificial heat. 3. to maintain (cultures of bacteria and other microorganisms) at the most favorable temperature for development. 4. to keep at even temperature, as prematurely born infants. 5. to produce as if by hatching; give form to: *His brain was incubating schemes for raising money.* —*v.i.* 6. to sit upon eggs. 7. to undergo incubation. 8. to develop; grow; take form: *A plan was slowly incubating in her mind.* [< L *incubāt(us)* sat upon, hatched (ptp. of *incubāre*), equiv. to *in-* IN-[2] + *cub(āre)* (to) sit, lie down + *-ātus* -ATE[1]] —**in′cu·ba′tive,** *adj.*

in·cu·ba·tion (in′kyə bā′shən, iŋ′-), *n.* 1. the act or process of incubating. 2. the state of being incubated. [< L *incubātiōn-* (s. of *incubātiō*). See INCUBATE, -ION] —**in′cu·ba′tion·al, in·cu·ba·to·ry** (in′kyə bə tôr′ē, -tōr′ē, iŋ′-; in′kyo͞o bā′tə rē, iŋ′-; in kyo͞o′bə tôr′ē, -tōr′ē), *adj.*

incuba′tion patch′, a highly vascular, featherless area developed on the abdomen of certain birds that is in direct contact with eggs during incubation and provides additional warmth. Also called **brood patch.**

incuba′tion pe′riod, *Pathol.* the period between infection and the appearance of signs of a disease.

in·cu·ba·tor (in′kyə bā′tər, iŋ′-), *n.* 1. an apparatus in which eggs are hatched artificially. 2. a boxlike apparatus in which prematurely born infants are kept at a constant and suitable temperature. 3. an apparatus in which media inoculated with microorganisms are cultivated at a constant temperature favorable to the growth of these microorganisms. 4. one who or that which incubates. [< LL *incubātor.* See INCUBATE, -OR[2]]

in·cu·bous (iŋ′kyə bəs), *adj.* (of leaves) overlapping, with the upper part of each leaf covering the base of the leaf above it. Cf. **succubous.** [< L *incub(āre)* (to) lie upon (see INCUBATE) + -OUS]

in·cu·bus (in′kyə bəs, iŋ′-), *n., pl.* **-bi** (-bī′), **-bus·es.** 1. an imaginary demon or evil spirit supposed to descend upon sleeping persons, esp. one in male form fabled to have sexual intercourse with women in their sleep. Cf. **succubus** (def. 1). 2. something that weighs upon or oppresses one like a nightmare. 3. a nightmare. [< LL: a nightmare, equiv. to L *incub(āre)* (to) lie upon (see INCUBATE) + *-us* n. suffix]

in·cu·des (in kyo͞o′dēz), *n.* a pl. of **incus.**

in·cul·cate (in kul′kāt, in′kul kāt′), *v.t.*, **-cat·ed, -cat·ing.** 1. to impress by repeated statement or admonition; teach persistently and earnestly (usually fol. by *upon* or *in*): *to inculcate virtue in the young.* 2. to cause or influence (someone) to accept an idea or feeling (usually fol. by with): *Socrates inculcated his pupils with the love of truth.* [< L *inculcāt(us)* stamped or trodden in (ptp. of *inculcāre*), equiv. to *in-* IN-[2] + *culc-* (var. of *calc-,* s. of *calx* heel) + *-ātus* -ATE[1]] —**in′cul·ca′tion,** *n.* —**in·cul·ca·tive** (in kul′kə tiv), **in·cul·ca·to·ry** (in kul′kə tôr′ē, -tōr′ē), *adj.* —**in·cul′ca·tor,** *n.*

—**Syn.** 1. instill, infix, implant, ingrain.

in·cul·pa·ble (in kul′pə bəl), *adj.* not culpable; blameless; guiltless. [late ME < LL *inculpābil(is).* See IN-[3], CULPABLE] —**in·cul′pa·bil′i·ty, in·cul′pa·ble·ness,** *n.* —**in·cul′pa·bly,** *adv.*

in·cul·pate (in kul′pāt, in′kul pāt′), *v.t.*, **-pat·ed, -pat·ing.** 1. to charge with fault; blame; accuse. 2. to involve in a charge; incriminate. [< ML *inculpāt(us)* blamed (ptp. of *inculpāre*), equiv. to L *in-* IN-[2] + *culp(a)* fault + *-ātus* -ATE[1]] —**in′cul·pa′tion,** *n.*

—**Ant.** 1, 2. exonerate.

in·cul·pa·to·ry (in kul′pə tôr′ē, -tōr′ē), *adj.* tending to inculpate; imputing blame; incriminating. [INCULPATE + -ORY[1]]

in·cult (in kult′), *adj.* *Archaic.* 1. uncultivated; untilled. 2. wild; rude; unrefined. [< L *incult(us),* equiv. to *in-* IN-[3] + *cultus* tilled (ptp. of *colere*)]

in·cum·ben·cy (in kum′bən sē), *n., pl.* **-cies.** 1. the quality or state of being incumbent. 2. that which is incumbent. 3. the position or term of an incumbent. 4. a duty or obligation: *my incumbencies as head of the organization.* 5. *Rare.* an incumbent weight or mass. [INCUMBEN(T) + -CY]

in·cum·bent (in kum′bənt), *adj.* 1. holding an indicated position, role, office, etc.: *the incumbent officers of the club.* 2. obligatory (often fol. by *on* or *upon*): *a duty incumbent upon me.* 3. resting, lying, leaning, or pressing on something: *incumbent schist.* —*n.* 4. the holder of an office: *The incumbent was challenged by a fusion candidate.* 5. *Brit.* a person who holds an ecclesiastical benefice. [ME (n.) < L *incumbent-* (s. of *incumbēns* lying or leaning on, prp. of *incumbere*), equiv. to *in-* IN-[2] + *cumb-* (nasalized var. of *cub-* sit, lie; see INCUBUS) + *-ent-* -ENT] —**in·cum′bent·ly,** *adv.*

in·cum·ber (in kum′bər), *v.t.* encumber.

in·cum·brance (in kum′brəns), *n.* encumbrance.

in·cu·nab·u·la (in′kyo͞o nab′yə lə), *n.pl., sing.* **-lum** (-ləm). 1. extant copies of books produced in the earliest stages (before 1500) of printing from movable type. 2. the earliest stages or first traces of anything. [< L: swaddling-clothes, hence, beginnings, equiv. to *in-* IN-[2] + *cūnābula* (neut. pl.) cradle (*cūnā-* (s. of *cūnae,* fem. pl.) cradle + *-bula* dim. suffix)] —**in′cu·nab′u·lar,** *adj.*

in·cur (in kûr′), *v.t.*, **-curred, -cur·ring.** 1. to run or fall into (some consequence, usually undesirable or injurious): *to incur a mountain of debts.* 2. to become liable or subject to through one's own action; bring upon oneself: *to incur his displeasure.* [ME < L *incurr(ere)* (to) run into, come upon, equiv. to *in-* IN-[2] + *currere* to run; see CURRENT] —**in·cur′ra·ble,** *adj.*

in·cur·a·ble (in kyo͝or′ə bəl), *adj.* 1. not curable. —*n.* 2. a person suffering from an incurable disease. [ME < LL *incūrābili(s).* See IN-[3], CURABLE] —**in·cur′a·bil′i·ty, in·cur′a·ble·ness,** *n.* —**in·cur′a·bly,** *adv.*

in·cu·ri·ous (in kyo͝or′ē əs), *adj.* 1. not curious; not inquisitive or observant. 2. inattentive or indifferent; careless. 3. *Rare.* deficient in interest or novelty. [< L *incūriōs(us).* See IN-[3], CURIOUS] —**in·cu·ri·os·i·ty** (in′kyo͝or ē os′i tē), **in·cu′ri·ous·ness,** *n.* —**in·cu′ri·ous·ly,** *adv.*

—**Syn.** 2. uninterested, apathetic, unconcerned.

in·cur·rence (in kûr′əns, -kur′-), *n.* the act of incurring, bringing on, or subjecting oneself to something. [INCURR(ENT) + -ENCE]

in·cur·rent (in kûr′ənt, -kur′-), *adj.* carrying or relating to an inward current. [< L *incurrent-* (s. of *incurrēns*), prp. of *incurrere.* See INCUR, -ENT]

in·cur·sion (in kûr′zhən, -shən), *n.* 1. a hostile entrance into or invasion of a place or territory, esp. one of sudden character; raid: *The bandits made brief incursions on the village.* 2. a harmful inroad. 3. a running in: *the incursion of sea water.* [ME < L *incursiōn-* (s. of *incursiō*) raid, equiv. to *incurs(us)* (ptp. of *incurrere* to INCUR) + *-iōn-* -ION; see EXCURSION]

in·cur·sive (in kûr′siv), *adj.* making incursions. [INCURS(ION) + -IVE]

in·cur·vate (*adj.* in′kûr vāt′, in kûr′vit; *v.* in′kûr-vāt′, in kûr′vāt), *adj., v.*, **-vat·ed, -vat·ing.** —*adj.* 1. curved, esp. inward. —*v.t.* 2. to make curved; turn from a straight line or course; curve, esp. inward. [< L *incurvāt(us),* ptp. of *incurvāre.* See INCURVE, -ATE[1]] —**in·cur·va·ture** (in kûr′və chər), **in′cur·va′tion,** *n.*

in·curve (*v.* in kûrv′; *n.* in′kûrv′), *v.*, **-curved, -curv·ing,** *n.* —*v.t.* 1. to curve inward. —*n.* 2. Also called **inshoot.** *Baseball.* a pitch that breaks toward a batter. Cf. **outcurve.** [< L *incurv(āre)* (to) bend in, curve. See IN-[2], CURVE]

in·cus (iŋ′kəs), *n., pl.* **in·cu·des** (in kyo͞o′dēz) for 1; **in·cus** for 2. 1. *Anat.* the middle one of a chain of three small bones in the middle ear of man and other mammals. Cf. **malleus, stapes.** See diag. under **ear.** 2. Also called **anvil, anvil cloud, anvil top, thunderhead.** the spreading, anvil-shaped, upper portion of a mature cumulonimbus cloud, smooth or slightly fibrous in appearance. [< NL < L: anvil, equiv. to *incūd-* (s. of *incūdere* to hammer, beat upon) + *-s* nom. sing. ending; see INCUSE] —**in·cu·date** (iŋ′kyə dāt′, -dit, in′-), **in·cu·dal** (iŋ′kyə dᵊl, in′-), *adj.*

in·cuse (in kyo͞oz′, -kyo͞os′), *adj., n., v.*, **-cused, -cus·ing.** —*adj.* 1. hammered or stamped in, as a figure on a coin. —*n.* 2. an incuse figure or impression. —*v.t.* 3. to stamp or hammer in, as a design or figure in a coin. [< L *incūs(us)* forged with a hammer (ptp. of *incūdere*), equiv. to *in-* IN-[2] + *cūd-* beat + *-tus* ptp. suffix]

Ind (ind), *n.* 1. *Literary.* India. 2. *Obs.* the Indies.

ind-, var. of **indo-** before a vowel: *indamine.*

Ind., 1. India. 2. Also, **Ind** Indian. 3. Indiana. 4. Indies.

ind., 1. independence. 2. independent. 3. index. 4. indicated. 5. indicative. 6. indigo. 7. indirect. 8. industrial. 9. industry.

in d., (in prescriptions) daily. [< L *in diēs*]

I.N.D., in the name of God. [< L *in nōmine Deī*]

in·da·ba (in dä′bä), *n.* a conference or consultation between or with South African natives. [< Zulu]

in·da·gate (in′də gāt′), *v.t.*, **-gat·ed, -gat·ing.** *Archaic.* to investigate; research. [< L *indāgāt(us)* tracked down (ptp. of *indāgāre*), equiv. to *ind(u)* in + *-āg-* (var. s. of *agere* to drive) + *-ātus* -ATE[1]] —**in′da·ga′tion,** *n.* —**in·da·ga·tive** (in′də gā′tiv, -gə tiv), *adj.* —**in′da·ga′tor,** *n.*

in·da·mine (in′də mēn′, -min), *n.* *Chem.* any of a series of basic organic compounds derived from $H_2NC_6H_4N{=}C_6H_4{=}NH$, which form bluish and greenish salts, used in the manufacture of dyes. Cf. **quinonimine.** [IND- + AMINE]

In·dan·threne (in dan′thrēn), *n.* *Trademark.* a blue, crystalline, water-insoluble solid, $C_{28}H_{14}H_2O_4$, used as a dye for cotton and as a pigment in paints and enamels.

in·de (in′dē), *adv.* (in prescriptions) therefrom. [< L]

Ind.E., Industrial Engineer.

in·debt (in det′), *v.t.* *Rare.* to place under obligation for benefits, favors, assistance, etc., received. [orig. only ptp.; ME *endetted* < OF *endet(e),* ptp. of *endeter* + -ED[2]. See IN-[2], DEBT]

in·debt·ed (in det′id), *adj.* 1. being bound or obligated to repay a monetary loan: *He was indebted to his friend for a large sum.* 2. being under obligation to someone for favors or kindness received: *He was indebted to her for nursing him through pneumonia.* [INDEBT + -ED[2]; r. ME *endetted;* see INDEBT]

in·debt·ed·ness (in det′id nis), *n.* 1. state of being indebted. 2. an amount owed. 3. debts collectively. [INDEBTED + -NESS]

in·de·cen·cy (in dē′sən sē), *n., pl.* **-cies** for 4. 1. the quality or condition of being indecent. 2. impropriety; immodesty. 3. obscenity; indelicacy. 4. an indecent act, remark, etc. [< L *indecentia.* See INDECENT, -ENCY]

in·de·cent (in dē′sənt), *adj.* 1. offending against recognized standards of propriety or good taste; vulgar: *indecent jokes; The play was attacked for its indecent language.* 2. not decent; unbecoming or unseemly: *indecent haste.* [ME < L *indecent-* (s. of *indecēns*) unseemly. See IN-[3], DECENT] —**in·de′cent·ly,** *adv.*

—**Syn.** 1. distasteful, outrageous, indelicate, coarse, rude, gross, immodest, indecorous, obscene, filthy, lewd, licentious. See **improper.** 2. inappropriate. —**Ant.** 2. appropriate; becoming.

inde′cent assault′, a sexual offense, other than rape, committed by a male against a female.

in·de·cid·u·ate (in′di sij′o͞o āt′), *adj.* 1. *Zool.* not deciduate. 2. *Bot.* having permanent leaves. [IN-[3] + DECIDUATE]

in·de·cid·u·ous (in′di sij′o͞o əs), *adj.* *Bot.* 1. not deciduous, as leaves. 2. (of trees) evergreen. [IN-[3] + DECIDUOUS]

in·de·ci·pher·a·ble (in′di sī′fər ə bəl), *adj.* not decipherable. [IN-[3] + DECIPHERABLE] —**in′de·ci′pher·a·bil′i·ty, in′de·ci′pher·a·ble·ness,** *n.* —**in′de·ci′pher·a·bly,** *adv.*

in·de·ci·sion (in′di sizh′ən), *n.* inability to decide. [IN-[3] + DECISION]

in·de·ci·sive (in′di sī′siv), *adj.* 1. not decisive or conclusive: *a severe but indecisive battle.* 2. characterized by indecision, as persons; irresolute; undecided. 3. lacking definition; vague or indistinct: *the indecisive outline of the distant hills.* [IN-[3] + DECISIVE] —**in′de·ci′sive·ly,** *adv.* —**in′de·ci′sive·ness,** *n.*

indecl., indeclinable.

in·de·clin·a·ble (in′di klī′nə bəl), *adj.* *Gram.* not declined, especially of a word belonging to a form class most of whose members are declined, as the Latin adjective *decem,* "ten." [ME < L *indēclīnābil(is)* unchangeable. See IN-[3], DECLINABLE] —**in′de·clin′a·ble·ness,** *n.* —**in′de·clin′a·bly,** *adv.*

in·de·com·pos·a·ble (in′dē kəm pō′zə bəl), *adj.* incapable of being decomposed. [IN-[3] + DECOMPOSABLE] —**in′de·com·pos′a·ble·ness,** *n.*

in·dec·o·rous (in dek′ər əs, in′di kôr′əs, -kōr′-), *adj.* not decorous; violating propriety; unseemly. [< L *indecōrus.* See IN-[3], DECOROUS] —**in·dec′o·rous·ly,** *adv.* —**in·dec′o·rous·ness,** *n.*

—**Syn.** indecent, improper, inappropriate. —**Ant.** seemly.

in·de·co·rum (in′di kôr′əm, -kōr′-), *n.* 1. indecorous behavior or character. 2. something indecorous. [< L, neut. of *indecōrus* INDECOROUS]

CONCISE ETYMOLOGY KEY: <, descended or derived from; >, whence; b., blend of, blended; c., cognate with; deriv., derivative; equiv., equivalent; imit., imitative; m., modification of; obl., oblique; r., replacing; s., stem; sp., spelling; trans., translation; ?, origin unknown, perhaps; *, hypothetical. See the full key inside the front cover.

in·deed (in dēd′), *adv.* **1.** in fact; in reality; in truth; truly (used for emphasis, to confirm and amplify a previous statement, to indicate a concession or admission, or, interrogatively, to obtain confirmation): *Indeed, he was elected president. Did you indeed slay the dragon?* —*interj.* **2.** (used as an expression of surprise, incredulity, irony, etc.): *Indeed! I can scarcely believe it.* [orig. phrase *in deed* in fact]

indef., indefinite.

in·de·fat·i·ga·ble (in′di fat′ə gə bəl), *adj.* incapable of being tired out; not yielding to fatigue. [< L *indēfatīgābil(is)* untiring, equiv. to *in-* IN-³ + *dēfatīgā(re)* (to) tire out (see DE-, FATIGUE) + *-bilis* -BLE] —**in′de·fat′i·ga·bil′i·ty, in′de·fat′i·ga·ble·ness,** *n.* —**in′de·fat′i·ga·bly,** *adv.*

in·de·fea·si·ble (in′di fē′zə bəl), *adj.* not defeasible; not to be annulled or made void; not forfeitable. [IN-³ + DEFEASIBLE] —**in′de·fea′si·bil′i·ty, in′de·fea′si·ble·ness,** *n.* —**in′de·fea′si·bly,** *adv.*

in·de·fect·i·ble (in′di fek′tə bəl), *adj.* **1.** not defectible; not liable to defect or failure; unfailing. **2.** not liable to fault or imperfection; faultless. [IN-³ + DEFECTIBLE] —**in′de·fect′i·bil′i·ty,** *n.* —**in′de·fect′i·bly,** *adv.*

in·de·fec·tive (in′di fek′tiv), *adj. Rare.* not defective; without a flaw; indefectible. [IN-³ + DEFECTIVE]

in·de·fen·si·ble (in′di fen′sə bəl), *adj.* **1.** not justifiable; inexcusable: *indefensible behavior.* **2.** incapable of being defended against attack: *an indefensible town.* **3.** incapable of being defended against criticism or denial: *indefensible argument.* [IN-³ + DEFENSIBLE] —**in′de·fen′si·bil′i·ty, in′de·fen′si·ble·ness,** *n.* —**in′de·fen′si·bly,** *adv.*

in·de·fin·a·ble (in′di fī′nə bəl), *adj.* not definable; not readily identified, described, analyzed, or determined. [IN-³ + DEFINABLE] —**in′de·fin′a·ble·ness,** *n.* —**in′de·fin′a·bly,** *adv.*

in·def·i·nite (in def′ə nit), *adj.* **1.** not definite; without fixed or specified limit; unlimited: *an indefinite number.* **2.** not clearly defined or determined; not precise or exact: *an indefinite boundary; an indefinite date in the future.* **3.** *Gram.* **a.** (of an article) not serving to identify its modificand. **b.** (of a pronoun) not serving to identify its antecedent. **4.** *Bot.* **a.** very numerous or not easily counted, as stamens. **b.** (of an inflorescence) indeterminate. [< L *indēfīnīt(us).* See IN-³, DEFINITE] —**in·def′i·nite·ly,** *adv.* —**in·def′i·nite·ness,** *n.*
—**Syn. 1.** unspecified; indeterminate. **2.** indistinct, confused, confusing, vague, obscure, dim, equivocal, unspecific, doubtful, unsettled, uncertain. —**Ant. 1, 2.** determinate. **2.** certain, clear.

indef′inite ar′ticle, *Gram.* an article, as English *a, an,* which classes as unidentified the noun it modifies.

indef′inite in′tegral, *Math.* a representation, usually in symbolic form, of any function whose derivative is a given function. Cf. **definite integral.**

indef′inite pro′noun, *Gram.* a pronoun, as English *some, any, somebody,* which leaves unspecified the identity of its antecedent.

in·de·his·cent (in′di his′ənt), *adj. Bot.* not dehiscent; not opening at maturity. [IN-³ + DEHISCENT] —**in′de·his′cence,** *n.*

in·de·lib·er·ate (in′də lib′ər it), *adj.* done without careful planning or deliberation. [IN-³ + DELIBERATE] —**in′de·lib′er·ate·ly,** *adv.* —**in′de·lib′er·ate·ness, in′de·lib′er·a′tion,** *n.*

in·del·i·ble (in del′ə bəl), *adj.* **1.** incapable of being deleted or obliterated: *She left an indelible impression on his mind.* **2.** making indelible marks: *an indelible pencil.* [< ML *indēlēbil(is);* r. *indeleble* < L *indēlēbil(is)* indestructible. See IN-³, DELE, -BLE] —**in·del′i·bil′i·ty, in·del′i·ble·ness,** *n.* —**in·del′i·bly,** *adv.*

in·del·i·ca·cy (in del′ə kə sē), *n., pl.* **-cies** for 2. **1.** quality or condition of being indelicate. **2.** something indelicate, as language or behavior. [IN-³ + DELICACY]

in·del·i·cate (in del′ə kit), *adj.* **1.** not delicate; lacking delicacy; rough. **2.** offensive to a sense of propriety, modesty, or decency; improper, unrefined, or coarse: *indelicate language.* [IN-³ + DELICATE] —**in·del′i·cate·ly,** *adv.* —**in·del′i·cate·ness,** *n.*
—**Syn. 2.** indecorous, untactful, gauche, rude.

in·dem·ni·fi·ca·tion (in dem′nə fə kā′shən), *n.* **1.** the act of indemnifying; state of being indemnified. **2.** that which serves to indemnify; compensation. [INDEMNI(TY) + -FICATION] —**in·dem·nif·i·ca·to·ry** (in′dem nif′ə kə tôr′ē, -tōr′ē), *adj.*
—**Syn. 2.** payment, amends, reparation, indemnity, satisfaction.

in·dem·ni·fy (in dem′nə fī′), *v.t.,* **-fied, -fy·ing.** **1.** to compensate for damage or loss sustained, expense incurred, etc. **2.** to guard or secure against anticipated loss; give security against (future damage or liability). [< L *indemni(s)* without loss (see INDEMNITY) + -FY] —**in·dem′ni·fi′er,** *n.*
—**Syn. 1.** recompense, reimburse, repay.

in·dem·ni·ty (in dem′ni tē), *n., pl.* **-ties.** **1.** protection or security against damage or loss. **2.** compensation for damage or loss sustained. **3.** something paid by way of such compensation. **4.** protection, as by insurance, from liabilities or penalties incurred by one's actions. **5.** legal exemption from penalties attaching to unconstitutional or illegal actions, granted to public officers and other persons. [late ME *indem(p)nite* < legal L *indemnitās,* equiv. to L *indemni(s)* without loss (*in-* IN-³ + *demn-,* var. of *damn-* (s. of *damnum* loss) + *-is* adj. suffix) + *-tās* -TY²]

in·de·mon·stra·ble (in′di mon′strə bəl, in dem′ən-), *adj.* not demonstrable; incapable of being demonstrated or proved. [IN-³ + DEMONSTRABLE] —**in′de·mon′stra·bil′i·ty, in′de·mon′stra·ble·ness,** *n.* —**in′de·mon′stra·bly,** *adv.*

in·dene (in′dēn), *n. Chem.* a colorless, liquid hydrocarbon, C_9H_8, obtained from coal tar by fractional distillation: used chiefly in the synthesis of resins. [IND- + -ENE]

in·dent[1] (*v.* in dent′; *n.* in′dent, in dent′), *v.t.* **1.** to form deep recesses in: *The sea indents the coast.* **2.** to set in or back from the margin, as the first line of a paragraph. **3.** to sever (a document drawn up in duplicate) along an irregular line as a means of identification. **4.** to cut or tear the edge of (copies of a document) in an irregular way. **5.** to make toothlike notches in; notch. **6.** to indenture, as an apprentice. **7.** *Brit.* to draw an order upon. **8.** *Chiefly Brit.* to order, as commodities. —*v.i.* **9.** to form a recess. **10.** *Chiefly Brit.* to make out an order or requisition in duplicate. **11.** *Brit. Mil.* to make a requisition. **12.** *Obs.* **a.** to draw upon a person or thing for something. **b.** to enter into an agreement by indenture; make a compact. —*n.* **13.** a toothlike notch or deep recess; indentation. **14.** an indention. **15.** an indenture. **16.** *U.S. Hist.* a certificate issued by a State or the federal government at the close of the Revolutionary War for the principal or interest due on the public debt. **17.** *Brit.* an official requisition for stores. **18.** *Chiefly Brit.* an order for goods. [ME; back formation from INDENTED] —**in·dent′er, in·den′tor,** *n.*

in·dent[2] (*v.* in dent′; *n.* in′dent, in dent′), *v.t.* **1.** to dent; press in so as to form a dent: *to indent a pattern on metal.* **2.** to make a dent in: *Don't indent the sofa cushions.* —*n.* **3.** a dent. [ME; see IN-², DENT¹]

in·den·ta·tion (in′den tā′shən), *n.* **1.** a cut, notch, or deep recess: *various bays and indentations.* **2.** a series of incisions or notches: *the indentation of a maple leaf.* **3.** a notching or being notched. **4.** an indention. [INDENT¹ + -ATION]

in·dent·ed (in den′tid), *adj. Heraldry.* **1.** noting a partition line consisting of a series of small zigzags. **2.** (of a charge, as an ordinary) having an edge consisting of a series of small zigzags: *a fess indented.* Cf. **dancetté.** [ME < ML *indentāt(us),* equiv. to L *in-* IN-² + *dentātus* DENTATE]

in·den·tion (in den′shən), *n.* **1.** the act of indenting; state of being indented. **2.** an indentation. **3.** the indenting of a line or lines in writing or printing. **4.** the blank space left by indenting. [INDENT¹ + -ION]

in·den·ture (in den′chər), *n., v.,* **-tured, -tur·ing.** —*n.* **1.** a deed or agreement executed in two or more copies with edges correspondingly indented as a means of identification. **2.** any deed, written contract, or sealed agreement. **3.** a contract by which a person, as an apprentice, is bound to service. **4.** any official or formal list, certificate, etc., authenticated for use as a voucher or the like. **5.** the formal agreement between a group of bondholders and the debtor as to the terms of the debt. **6.** indentation. —*v.t.* **7.** to bind by indenture, as an apprentice. **8.** *Obs.* to make a depression in; indent; wrinkle; furrow. [ME < ML *indentūra.* See INDENT¹, -URE] —**in·den′ture·ship′,** *n.*

inden′tured serv′ant, *Amer. Hist.* a person who came to America and was placed under contract to work for another over a period of time, usually seven years, esp. during the 17th–19th centuries. Generally, indentured servants included redemptioners, victims of religious or political persecution, persons kidnapped for the purpose, convicts, and paupers.

in·de·pend·ence (in′di pen′dəns), *n.* **1.** Also, **independency.** state or quality of being independent. **2.** freedom from subjection, or from the influence of others. **3.** exemption from external control or support. **4.** *Archaic.* a competency. [INDEPEND(ENT) + -ENCE]
—**Syn. 1.** See **freedom.**

In·de·pend·ence (in′di pen′dəns), *n.* **1.** a city in W Missouri: starting point of the Santa Fe and Oregon trails. 62,328 (1960). **2.** a town in E Iowa. 7069 (1960). **3.** a town in N Ohio. 6868 (1960).

Independ′ence Day′, *U.S.* July 4, a holiday commemorating the adoption of the Declaration of Independence on July 4, 1776. Also called **Fourth of July.**

In′depend′ence Hall′, the building in Philadelphia where the Declaration of Independence was signed.

independ′ence of path′, *Math.* the property of a function for which the line integral has the same value along all curves between two specified points.

in·de·pend·en·cy (in′di pen′dən sē), *n., pl.* **-cies.** **1.** independence (def. 1). **2.** a territory not under the control of any other power. **3.** (*cap.*) *Eccles.* **a.** the principle that the individual congregation or church is an autonomous and equalitarian society free from any external ecclesiastical control. **b.** the polity based on this principle. [INDEPENDEN(T) + -CY]

in·de·pend·ent (in′di pen′dənt), *adj.* **1.** not influenced or controlled by others in matters of opinion, conduct, etc.; thinking or acting for oneself: *an independent thinker.* **2.** not subject to another's authority or jurisdiction; autonomous; free: *an independent businessman.* **3.** not influenced by the thought or action of others: *independent research.* **4.** not dependent; not depending or contingent upon something else for existence, operation, etc. **5.** not relying on another or others for aid or support. **6.** declining others' aid or support; refusing to be under obligation to others. **7.** possessing a competency: *to be financially independent.* **8.** sufficient to support a person without his having to work: *an independent income.* **9.** expressive of a spirit of independence; self-confident; unconstrained: *a free and independent citizen.* **10.** free from party commitments in voting: *the independent voter.* **11.** *Math.* (of a quantity or function) not depending upon another for value: *an independent variable.* **12.** *Gram.* capable of standing syntactically as a complete sentence. Cf. **dependent** (def. 4), **main**¹ (def. 4). **13.** *Logic.* **a.** (of a set of propositions) having no one proposition deducible from the others. **b.** (of a proposition) belonging to such a set. **14.** *Statistics.* **a.** (of events) having the probability of their joint occurrence equal to the product of their individual probabilities. **b.** (of an event) having its conditional probability equal to its unrestricted probability. **15.** (*cap.*) *Eccles.* of or pertaining to the Independents. **16. independent of,** irrespective of; regardless of: *Independent of monetary considerations, it was a promising position.* —*n.* **17.** an independent person or thing. **18.** *Politics.* a person who votes for candidates, measures, etc., in accordance with his own judgment and without regard to the endorsement of, or the positions taken by, any party. **19.** (*cap.*) *Eccles.* an adherent of Independency. **20.** *Brit.* a Congregationalist. [IN-³ + DEPENDENT] —**in′de·pend′ent·ly,** *adv.*

in′depend′ent var′iable, *Math.* a variable in a functional relation whose value determines the value or values of other variables, as x in the relation, $y = 3x^2$. Cf. **dependent variable.**

in·de·scrib·a·ble (in′di skrī′bə bəl), *adj.* not describable. [IN-³ + DESCRIBABLE] —**in′de·scrib′a·bil′i·ty, in′de·scrib′a·ble·ness,** *n.* —**in′de·scrib′a·bly,** *adv.*

in·de·struct·i·ble (in′di struk′tə bəl), *adj.* not destructible; that cannot be destroyed. [IN-³ + DESTRUCTIBLE] —**in′de·struct′i·bil′i·ty, in′de·struct′i·ble·ness,** *n.* —**in′de·struct′i·bly,** *adv.*

in·de·ter·mi·na·ble (in′di tûr′mə nə bəl), *adj.* **1.** not determinable; incapable of being ascertained. **2.** incapable of being decided or settled. [< LL *indētermin̄ābil(is).* See IN-³, DETERMINABLE] —**in′de·ter′mi·na·ble·ness,** *n.* —**in′de·ter′mi·na·bly,** *adv.*

in·de·ter·mi·na·cy (in′di tûr′mə nə sē), *n.* the condition or quality of being indeterminate; indetermination. [INDETERMINA(TE) + -CY]

indeter′minacy prin′ciple, *Physics.* See **uncertainty principle.**

in·de·ter·mi·nate (in′di tûr′mə nit), *adj.* **1.** not determinate; not fixed in extent; indefinite; uncertain. **2.** not clear; vague: *a cloudy and indeterminate meaning.* **3.** not established. **4.** not settled or decided. **5.** *Math.* **a.** (of a quantity) undefined, as 0/0. **b.** (of an equation) able to be satisfied by more than one value for each unknown. **6.** *Bot.* (of an inflorescence) having the axis or axes not ending in a flower or bud, thus allowing further elongation. **7.** *Engineering.* **a.** (of a structure) unable to be analyzed completely by means of the principles of statics. **b.** (of a member of a structure) subject to statically indeterminate stresses. **c.** (of a stress) unable to be determined through the principles of statics. [ME < LL *indētermināt(us).* See IN-³, DETERMINATE] —**in′de·ter′mi·nate·ly,** *adv.* —**in′de·ter′mi·nate·ness,** *n.*

in′deter′minate sen′tence, *Crim. Law.* a penalty, imposed by a court, that has relatively wide limits or no limits, as one of imprisonment for one to ten years.

in·de·ter·mi·na·tion (in′di tûr′mə nā′shən), *n.* **1.** the condition or quality of being indeterminate. **2.** an unsettled state, as of the mind. [INDETERMINATE + -ION]

in·de·ter·min·ism (in′di tûr′mə niz′əm), *n. Philos.* **1.** the doctrine that human actions, though influenced somewhat by preexisting psychological and other conditions, are not entirely governed by them but retain a certain freedom and spontaneity. **2.** the theory that the will is to some extent independent of the strength of motives, or may itself modify their strength in choice. [IN-³ + DETERMINISM] —**in′de·ter′min·ist,** *n., adj.* —**in′de·ter′min·is′tic,** *adj.*

in·dex (in′deks), *n., pl.* **-dex·es, -di·ces** (-di sēz′), *v.* —*n.* **1.** (in a nonfiction book, a dissertation, etc.) a more or less detailed alphabetical listing of names, places, and topics along with the numbers of the pages on which they are mentioned or discussed, usually included in or constituting the back matter. **2.** a sequential arrangement of material, esp. in alphabetical or numerical order. **3.** something used or serving to point out; a sign, token, or indication: *a true index of his character.* **4.** something that serves to direct attention to some fact, condition, etc.; a guiding principle. **5.** a pointer or indicator in a scientific instrument. **6.** a piece of wood, metal, or the like, serving as a pointer or indicator. **7.** Also called **fist, hand.** *Print.* a sign (☞) used to point out a particular note, paragraph, etc. **8.** a light, smooth cardboard stock. **9.** the index finger; forefinger. **10.** a number or formula expressing some property, ratio, etc., of something indicated: *index of growth; index of intelligence.* **11.** *Algebra.* **a.** an exponent. **b.** the integer n in a radical $\sqrt[n]{\ }$ defining the n-th root: $\sqrt[3]{7}$ *is a radical having index three.* **c.** a subscript or superscript indicating the position of an object in a series of similar objects, as the subscripts 1, 2, and 3 in the series x_1, x_2, x_3. **d.** See **winding number.** **12.** *Horol.* a leverlike regulator for a hairspring, bearing regulator pins under its shorter end and having beneath its longer end a calibrated arc to show the amount of acceleration or retardation. **13.** (*cap.*) *Rom. Cath. Ch.* **a.** See **Index Librorum Prohibitorum.** **b.** See **Index Expurgatorius.** **14.** (*usually cap.*) any list of forbidden or otherwise restricted material deemed morally or politically harmful by authorities: *an Index of disapproved books relating to Communism.* **15.** *Optics.* See **index of refraction.** **16.** *Obs.* **a.** a table of contents. **b.** a preface. —*v.t.* **17.** to provide with an index, as a book. **18.** to enter in an index, as a word. **19.** to serve to indicate: *warm breezes indexing the approach of spring.* **20.** to place (a book) on an official list as politically or morally harmful: *The commissar insisted on indexing the book.* **21.** to adjust (wages, taxes, etc.) according to changes in the cost of living or some other economic indicator, esp. to offset inflation. **22.** to rotate (work) on a milling machine in order to repeat the milling operation at a new position. [ME < L: informer, pointer, equiv. to *in-* IN-² + *dec-* (var. of *dic-,* perf. s. of *dīcere* to indicate) + *-s* nom. sing. ending] —**in′dex·er,** *n.* —**in·dex·i·cal** (in dek′si kəl), *adj.* —**in·dex′i·cal·ly,** *adv.* —**in′dex·less,** *adj.*

in·dex·a·tion (in′dek sā′shən), *n.* the automatic adjustment of wages, taxes, pension benefits, interest rates, or any other payments or charges to compensate for or keep pace with inflation, fluctuations in the cost of living, or some other economic indicator.

in′dex card′, a card, often relatively small, used in noting or recording information and usually filed in an index.

In·dex Ex·pur·ga·to·ri·us (in′deks ik spûr′gə tôr′ē əs, -tôr′-), *pl.* **In·di·ces Ex·pur·ga·to·ri·i** (in′di sēz′ ik-spûr′gə tôr′ē ī′, -tôr′-). *Rom. Cath. Ch.* a list of books, once listed separately but now included in the *Index Librorum Prohibitorum,* forbidden by Church authority to be read by Roman Catholics without the deletion or revision of certain passages. [< NL: lit., expurgatory index]

in′dex fin′ger, forefinger.

in′dex fos′sil, *Geol.* a widely distributed fossil, of narrow range in time, regarded as characteristic of a given geological formation, used esp. in determining the age of related formations. Also called **guide fossil.**

In·dex Li·bro·rum Pro·hib·i·to·rum (in′deks li-brôr′əm prō hib′i tôr′əm, -tôr′-, -brôr′-), *pl.* **In·di·ces Li·bro·rum Pro·hib·i·to·rum** (in′di sēz′ lī brôr′əm prō hib′i tôr′əm, -tôr′-, -brôr′-). *Rom. Cath. Ch.* a list of books which Roman Catholics are forbidden by Church authority to read without special permission, or which are not to be read unless expurgated or changed. Cf. **Index Expurgatorius.** [< NL: index of prohibited books]

in′dex num′ber, *Statistics.* a quantity whose variation over a period of time measures the change in some phenomenon.

in′dex of refrac′tion, *Optics.* a number indicating the speed of light in a given medium as either the ratio of the speed of light in a vacuum to that in the given medium **(absolute index of refraction)** or the ratio of the speed of light in a specified medium to that in the given medium **(relative index of refraction).** *Symbol:* n. Also called **index, refractive index.**

in′dex plate′, *Mach.* a plate perforated with rows of different numbers of equally spaced holes as a guide for indexing work.

in′dex set′, *Math.* a set whose elements are used to indicate the order of the elements of a sequence, series, etc.

In·di·a (in′dē ə), *n.* a republic in S Asia: comprises most of former British India and the semi-independent Indian States and Agencies; became a dominion in 1947; became fully independent on January 26, 1950, with membership in the Commonwealth of Nations. 634,700,000; 1,246,880 sq. mi. *Cap.:* New Delhi. Hindi, **Bharat.** [OE < L < Gk, equiv. to *Ind(ós)* the Indus river (< OPers *Hindu,* lit.. the river; c. Skt *sindhu*) + *-ia* -IA]

In·di·a (in′dē ə), *n.* a word used in communications to represent the letter *I.*

In′dia chintz′, a sturdy, heavyweight fabric constructed in a figured weave, used esp. in upholstery. Also called **In′dia cot′ton.**

In′dia drug′get, drugget (def. 1).

In′dia ink′, (*sometimes l.c.*) **1.** a black pigment consisting of lampblack mixed with glue or size. **2.** a liquid ink from this. Also called **Chinese ink.**

In·di·a·man (in′dē ə mən), *n., pl.* **-men.** *Naut.* See **East Indiaman.**

In·di·an (in′dē ən), *n.* **1.** Also called **American Indian, Red Indian.** a member of the aboriginal race of America or of any of the aboriginal North and South American stocks, usually excluding the Eskimos. **2.** *Informal.* any of the indigenous languages of the American Indians. **3.** a member of any of the peoples native to India or the East Indies. **4.** *Brit.* a European, esp. an Englishman, who resides or has resided in India or the East Indies. **5.** *Astron.* the constellation Indus. —*adj.* **6.** of, pertaining to, or characteristic of the American Indians or their languages. **7.** of, pertaining to, or characteristic of India or the East Indies. **8.** made of Indian corn: *Indian meal.* **9.** *Zoogeog.* oriental (def. 2). **10.** *Phytogeog.* belonging or pertaining to a geographical division comprising India south of the Himalayas, and Pakistan and Ceylon. [ME < ML *Indiān(us).* See INDIA, -AN]

In·di·an·a (in′dē an′ə), *n.* **1.** **Robert** (*Robert Clarke*), born 1928, U.S. painter of pop art. **2.** a state in the central United States: a part of the Midwest. 5,490,179; 36,291 sq. mi. *Cap.:* Indianapolis. *Abbr.:* Ind. —**In·di·an·i·an** (in′dē an′ē ən), *adj., n.*

In′dian/a bal′lot, a ballot on which the candidates are listed in separate columns by party. Also called **party-column ballot.** Cf. **Massachusetts ballot, office-block ballot.**

In′dian a′gency, headquarters of an Indian agent.

In′dian a′gent, an official representing the U.S. government in dealing with an Indian tribe or tribes.

In·di·an·ap·o·lis (in′dē ə nap′ə lis), *n.* a city in and the capital of Indiana, in the central part. 476,258 (1960).

In′dian ap′ple. See **May apple.**

In′dian bal′sam. See **Peru balsam.**

In′dian bi′son, the gaur.

In′dian bread′, **1.** See **corn bread.** **2.** tuckahoe (def. 1).

In′dian bread′root, breadroot.

In′dian cher′ry. See **yellow bush.**

In′dian club′, a metal or wooden club shaped like a large bottle, used singly or in pairs for exercising the arms.

Indian club

In′dian co′bra, a highly venomous cobra, *Naja naja,* common in India, having markings resembling a pair of spectacles on the back of the hood. Also called **spectacled cobra.**

In′dian corn′, **1.** corn[1] (def. 1). **2.** any primitive corn with variegated kernels, often used for decorative purposes. **3.** *Dial.* any coarse variety of corn grown for fodder. **4.** *Brit.* table corn; corn on the cob.

In′dian cress′, a nasturtium, *Tropaeolum majus,* of South America, having red-spotted or red-striped, yellow-orange flowers, the young flower buds and fruits being used as seasoning.

In′dian cup′. See **cup plant.**

In′dian cur′rant, a shrub, *Symphoricarpos orbiculatus,* found from South Dakota and Texas to the eastern coast of the U.S., having hairy leaves, white flowers, and reddish-purple fruit. Also called **coralberry.**

In′dian Des′ert. See **Thar Desert.**

In′dian el′ephant, any elephant of the genus *Elephas,* of India and neighboring regions. Cf. **elephant** (def. 1).

In′dian Em′pire, British India and the Indian states ruled by native princes but under indirect British control: dissolved in 1947 and absorbed into India and Pakistan.

In′dian fig′, a bushy or treelike cactus, *Opuntia Ficus-indica,* of central Mexico, having yellow flowers nearly four inches wide and juicy, red, edible fruit.

In′dian file′, in single file, as of persons walking.

In′dian giv′er, *Informal.* a person who takes back a gift that he has given. —**In′dian giv′ing.**

In′dian haw′thorn, a handsome, evergreen shrub, *Radhiolepis indica,* of southern China, having pinkish-white flowers in loose clusters.

In′dian head′er, a New England fishing schooner of c1900, having a rounded stem.

In′dian hemp′, **1.** a dogbane, *Apocynum cannabinum,* of North America, the root of which has laxative and emetic properties. **2.** hemp (def. 1). Also called **Choctaw-root.**

In′dian Hill′, a town in SW Ohio. 4526 (1960).

In′dian hip′po. See **bowman's root.**

In·di·an·ise (in′dē ə nīz′), *v.t.,* **-ised, -is·ing.** *Chiefly Brit.* Indianize. —**In′di·an·i·sa′tion,** *n.*

In·di·an·ize (in′dē ə nīz′), *v.t.,* **-ized, -iz·ing.** to make Indian or cause to become Indianlike, as in character, customs, appearance, etc. [INDIAN + -IZE] —**In′di·an·i·za′tion,** *n.*

In′dian ju′jube, an evergreen shrub or small tree, *Zizyphus mauritiana,* of India, having leaves that are rusty-hairy on the underside and small, round, red, acid fruit. Also called **cottony jujube.**

In′dian let′tuce, **1.** See **consumption weed.** **2.** See **winter purslane.**

In′dian lic′orice, a woody, East Indian, fabaceous shrub, *Abrus precatorius,* bearing seeds used for beads and having a root used as a substitute for licorice. Also called **rosary pea.**

In′dian lo′tus, a lotus, *Nelumbo nucifera,* of southern Asia, having fragrant pink or rose flowers. Also called **East Indian lotus, Egyptian lotus, sacred lotus.**

In′dian mad′der, chay[2].

In′dian mal′low, **1.** a malvaceous plant, *Abutilon Theophrasti,* having yellow flowers and velvety leaves, introduced into America from southern Asia. **2.** any of certain related species.

In′dian meal′, *Chiefly Brit.* See **corn meal.**

In′dian mil′let, **1.** durra. **2.** See **pearl millet.**

In′dian mul′berry, a small tree, *Morinda citrifolia,* found from India to Australasia, having shiny leaves, white flowers, and fleshy, yellowish fruit, yielding red and yellow dyes.

In′dian Mu′tiny. See **Sepoy Rebellion.**

In′dian O′cean, an ocean S of Asia, E of Africa, and W of Australia. 28,357,000 sq. mi.

In·di·a·no·la (in′dē ə nō′lə), *n.* **1.** a town in central Iowa. 7062 (1960). **2.** a town in W Mississippi. 6714 (1960).

In′dian paint′brush, any of several showy, scrophulariaceous herbs of the genus *Castilleja,* as *C. linariaefolia,* of the southwestern U.S.: the State flower of Wyoming.

In′dian pink′. See **fire pink.**

In′dian pipe′, a leafless, saprophytic plant, *Monotropa uniflora,* of North America and Asia, having a solitary flower and resembling a tobacco pipe.

In′dian pitch′er. See **common pitcher plant.**

In′dian pota′to. See **giant sunflower.**

In′dian pud′ding, a sweet baked pudding made of corn meal, molasses, milk, and spices.

In′dian red′, **1.** earth of a yellowish-red color, found esp. in the Persian Gulf, which serves as a pigment and as a polish for gold and silver objects. **2.** a pigment of that color prepared by oxidizing the salts of iron.

In′dian rice′, the wild rice plant.

In′dian Run′ner, one of a breed of domestic ducks.

In′dian sal′ad, waterleaf (def. 2).

In′dian san′icle. See **white snakeroot.**

In′dian silk′. See **India silk.**

In′dian States′ and A′gencies, the former semidependent states and agencies in India and Pakistan: became independent states of, or otherwise affiliated with, the republics of India and Pakistan 1947. Also called **Native States.**

In′dian sum′mer, a period of mild, dry weather, usually accompanied by a hazy atmosphere, occurring in the U.S. and Canada in late autumn or early winter.

In′dian Sum′mer of a For′syte, a novel (1918) by John Galsworthy. Cf. **Forsyte Saga, The.**

In′dian tea′. See **New Jersey tea.**

In′dian Ter′ritory, a former territory of the United States: now in E Oklahoma. ab. 31,000 sq. mi.

In′dian tobac′co, a common, American herb, *Lobelia inflata,* having small, blue flowers and inflated capsules.

In′dian tur′nip, **1.** the jack-in-the-pulpit. **2.** its root.

In′dian wolf′, a wolf, *Canis lupus pallipes,* found in Asia south of the Himalayas.

In′dian wres′tling, **1.** a form of wrestling in which two opponents, lying side by side on their backs and in opposite directions, lock corresponding legs and each attempts to force the other's leg down until one opponent is unable to remain lying flat on his back. **2.** a form of wrestling in which two opponents clasp each other's right or left hands and, placing the corresponding feet side by side, attempt to unbalance each other. **3.** a form of wrestling in which two opponents, usually facing one another across a table, rest their right or left elbows on the table and, placing their corresponding forearms upward and parallel, grip each other's hand, the object being to force the opponent's hand down so that it touches the table.

In′dian yel′low, **1.** Also called **purree, snowshoe.** an orange-yellow color. **2.** *Painting.* **a.** Also called **purree.** a yellow pigment formerly derived from the urine of cows fed on mango leaves. **b.** a pigment derived from coal tar, characterized chiefly by its yellow color and permanence.

In′dia pa′per, **1.** a fine, thin, but opaque paper made in the Orient, used chiefly in the production of thin-paper editions and for impressions of engravings. **2.** See **Bible paper.**

In′dia print′, a plain-weave cotton characterized by brilliantly colored motifs resembling those designed in India, rendered by the block-print method.

In′dia rub′ber, **1.** rubber (def. 1). **2.** a rubber eraser. **3.** *Archaic.* a rubber overshoe. Also, **in′dia rub′ber.**

In′dia silk′, a soft, lightweight fabric constructed in plain weave, woven chiefly in India. Also, **Indian silk.**

In′dia wheat′, a buckwheat, *Fagopyrum tataricum,* of India, having loose clusters of greenish or yellowish flowers, grown for soil improvement. Also called **duckwheat.**

In·dic (in′dik), *adj.* **1.** of or pertaining to India; Indian. **2.** *Ling.* of or belonging to a subbranch of Indo-Iranian that includes Sanskrit, Hindi, Urdu, Bengali, and many other Indo-European languages of India, Ceylon, and Pakistan; Indo-Aryan. [< L *Indic(us)* of India < Gk *Indikós.* See INDIA, -IC]

indic., **1.** indicating. **2.** indicative. **3.** indicator.

in·di·can (in′də kən), *n.* **1.** *Chem.* a glucoside, $C_{14}H_{17}NO_6$, which occurs in plants yielding indigo, and from which indigo is obtained. **2.** *Biochem.* indoxyl potassium sulfate, $C_8H_6O_4SK$, a component of urine. [< L *indic(um)* INDIGO + -AN]

in·di·cant (in′də kənt), *n.* **1.** that which indicates. —*adj.* **2.** *Obs.* serving to indicate; indicative. [< L *indicant-* (s. of *indicāns* pointing, prp. of *indicāre*), equiv. to *indic-* (see INDICATE) + *-ant-* -ANT]

in·di·cate (in′də kāt′), *v.t.,* **-cat·ed, -cat·ing.** **1.** to be a sign of; betoken; imply: *His hesitation indicates unwillingness.* **2.** to point out or point to; direct attention to: *to indicate a place on a map.* **3.** to show; make known: *The thermometer indicates air temperature.* **4.** to state or express, esp. briefly or in a general way: *He indicated his disapproval but did not go into detail.* **5.** *Med.* **a.** (of symptoms) to point out (a particular remedy, treatment, etc.) as suitable or necessary. **b.** to show the presence of (a condition, infection, etc.). [< L *indicāt(us)* pointed out or at (ptp. of *indicāre*), equiv. to *indic-* (s. of *index*) INDEX + *-ātus* -ATE[1]] —**in′di·cat′a·ble,** *adj.*

in′dicated horse′power, the horsepower of a reciprocating engine as shown by an indicator record. *Abbr.:* ihp, IHP, I.H.P., i.hp., i.h.p.

in·di·ca·tion (in′də kā′shən), *n.* **1.** anything serving to indicate or point out, as a sign, token, etc. **2.** *Med.* a special symptom or the like which points out a suitable remedy or treatment or shows the presence of a disease. **3.** act of indicating. **4.** the degree marked by an instrument. [< L *indicātiōn-* (s. of *indicātiō*). See INDICATE, -ION]

in·dic·a·tive (in dik′ə tiv), *adj.* **1.** indicating; pointing out; suggestive (usually fol. by *of*): *His behavior was indicative of mental disorder.* **2.** *Gram.* noting or pertaining to the mood of the verb used for ordinary objective statements, questions, etc., as the verb *plays* in *John plays football.* Cf. **imperative** (def. 3), **subjunctive** (def. 1) —*n. Gram.* **3.** the indicative mood. **4.** a verb in the indicative. [< LL *indicātīv(us).* See INDICATE, -IVE] —**in·dic′a·tive·ly,** *adv.*

in·di·ca·tor (in′də kā′tər), *n.* **1.** one who or that which indicates. **2.** a pointing or directing device, as a pointer on an instrument. **3.** an instrument which indicates the condition of a machine or the like. **4.** an instrument for measuring and recording variations of pressure in the cylinder of an engine. **5.** *Chem.* **a.** a substance which indicates the presence, and sometimes the concentration, of a certain constituent. **b.** a substance often used in a titration to indicate the point at which the reaction is complete. **6.** *Ecol.* a plant or animal that indicates, by its presence in a given area, the existence of certain environmental conditions. [< LL; see INDICATE, -OR[2]]

in·dic·a·to·ry (in dik′ə tōr′ē, -tôr′ē, in′də kə-), *adj.* serving to indicate. [< LL *indicātōri(us).* See INDICATE, -ORY[1]]

in·di·ces (in′di sēz′), *n.* a pl. of **index.**

in·di·ci·a (in dish′ē ə), *n., pl.* **-ci·a, -ci·as.** **1.** an envelope marking substituted for a stamp or a regular cancellation on each item in a large shipment of mail. **2.** Also called **indicium.** an indication; token; evidence. [< L, pl. of *indicium* INDICIUM]

in·di·cial (in dish′əl), *adj.* **1.** of, pertaining to, or resembling an indication; indicative: *behavior indicial of a personality disorder.* **2.** of, pertaining to, or resembling an index or an index finger. [INDICI(A) + -AL[1]] —**in·di′cial·ly,** *adv.*

indi′cial equa′tion, *Math.* an equation that is obtained from a given linear differential equation and that indicates whether a solution in power series form exists for the differential equation.

in·di·ci·um (in dish′ē əm), *n., pl.* **-di·ci·a** (-dish′ē ə), **-di·ci·ums.** indicia (def. 2). [< L, equiv. to *indici-* (s. of *index*) INDEX + -UM neut. sing. ending]

in·dic·o·lite (in dik′ə līt′), *n.* a dark-blue tourmaline, used as a gem. [< F; INDIGO, -LITE]

in·dict (in dīt′), *v.t.* **1.** to charge with an offense or crime; accuse of wrongdoing: *He tends to indict everyone who disagrees with him.* **2.** (of a grand jury) to bring a formal accusation against, as a means of bringing to trial: *The grand jury indicted him for murder, and he was held without bail.* [var. sp. (< ML) of INDITE] —**in·dict′er, in·dict′or,** *n.*
—**Syn. 1.** arraign. —**Ant. 1.** acquit.

in·dict·a·ble (in dī′tə bəl), *adj.* **1.** liable to being indicted, as a person. **2.** making one liable to indictment, as an offense. [INDICT + -ABLE] —**in·dict′a·bly,** *adv.*

in·dic·tion (in dik′shən), *n.* **1.** a proclamation made every 15 years in the later Roman Empire, fixing the valuation of property to be used as a basis for taxation. **2.** a tax based on such valuation. **3.** Also called **cycle of indiction.** the recurring fiscal period of 15 years in the Roman Empire, long used for dating ordinary events. **4.** a specified year in this period. **5.** the number indicating it. **6.** *Archaic.* authoritative proclamation. [ME *indiccio(u)n* < L *indictiōn-* (s. of *indictiō*) announcement, equiv. to *indict(us)* announced (ptp. of *indīcere*) + *-iōn-* -ION] —**in·dic′tion·al,** *adj.*

in·dict·ment (in dīt′mənt), *n.* **1.** act of indicting. **2.** *Law.* a formal accusation initiating a criminal case, presented by a grand jury and usually required for felonies and other serious crimes. **3.** any charge or accusation: *archaeological findings that constitute an indictment of Roman morality.* **4.** state of being indicted. [ME *enditement* < AF. See INDICT, -MENT]

In·dienne (an′dē en′; *Fr.* aN dyen′), *adj.* **1.** (of food) prepared or seasoned in East Indian style, as with curry. —*n.* **2.** (*l.c.*) fabric printed or painted in imitation of fabrics made in India. [< F, fem. of *indien* INDIAN]

in·dies (in′dēz), *n.* **the. 1.** (*construed as pl.*) See **West Indies** (def. 1). **2.** (*construed as sing.*) a region in and near S and SE Asia; India, Indochina, and the East Indies. **3.** (*construed as pl.*) See **East Indies** (def. 1).

in·dif·fer·ence (in dif′ər əns, -dif′rəns), *n.* **1.** lack of interest or concern: *She felt shocking indifference toward her children.* **2.** unimportance: *Whether or not to attend the party is a matter of indifference to him.* **3.** the quality or condition of being indifferent. **4.** mediocre quality; mediocrity. [late ME, var. of *indifferency* < L *indifferentia.* See INDIFFERENT, -ENCE, -ENCY]
—**Syn. 1.** INDIFFERENCE, UNCONCERN, LISTLESSNESS, APATHY, INSENSIBILITY all imply lack of feeling. INDIFFERENCE denotes an absence of feeling or interest; UNCONCERN, an absence of concern or solicitude, a calm or cool indifference in the face of what might be expected to cause uneasiness or apprehension; LISTLESSNESS, an absence of inclination or interest, a languid indifference to what is going on about one; APATHY, profound indifference suggestive of mental faculties either naturally sluggish or dulled by sickness or emotion. INSENSIBILITY denotes an absence of capacity for feeling or of susceptibility to emotional influences. —**Ant. 1.** eagerness, responsiveness.

in·dif·fer·en·cy (in dif′ər ən sē), *n.* *Archaic.* indifference.

in·dif·fer·ent (in dif′ər ənt, -dif′rənt), *adj.* **1.** without interest or concern; not caring; apathetic: *They criticized his indifferent attitude toward the suffering of others.* **2.** having no bias, prejudice, or preference; impartial. **3.** neutral in character or quality; neither good nor bad: *an indifferent specimen.* **4.** not particularly good, important, etc.: *an indifferent success; an indifferent performance.* **5.** of only moderate amount, extent, etc. **6.** not making a difference, or mattering, either way, as to a person. **7.** immaterial or unimportant. **8.** not essential or obligatory, as an observance. **9.** making no difference or distinction, as between persons or things: *indifferent justice.* **10.** neutral in chemical, electric, or magnetic quality. **11.** *Biol.* not differentiated or specialized, as cells or tissues. —*n.* **12.** an ethically or morally indifferent act. **13.** a person who is indifferent, esp. in matters of religion or politics. —*adv.* **14.** *Archaic.* indifferently: *I am indifferent well.* [ME < L (adj.) *indifferent-* (s. of *indifferēns*). See IN-³, DIFFERENT] —**in·dif′fer·ent·ly,** *adv.*

in·dif·fer·ent·ism (in dif′ər ən tiz′əm, -dif′rən-), *n.* **1.** systematic indifference. **2.** adiaphorism. **3.** the principle or opinion that differences of religious belief are essentially unimportant. **4.** *Philos.* the doctrine that each entity is essentially unique and at the same time essentially the same as all other entities of its kind. [< F *indifférentisme.* See INDIFFERENT, -ISM] —**in·dif′fer·ent·ist,** *n.*

in·di·gence (in′di jəns), *n.* indigent state; poverty. [ME < L *indigentia* need. See INDIGENT, -ENCE]
—**Syn.** privation, need, want, penury. —**Ant.** wealth.

in·di·gene (in′di jēn′), *n.* one who or that which is indigenous or native; a native; an autochthon. Also, **in·di·gen** (in′di jən). [< MF < L *indigen(a)* a native. See INDIGENOUS]

in·dig·e·nous (in dij′ə nəs), *adj.* **1.** originating in and characterizing a particular region or country; native (usually fol. by *to*): *the plants indigenous to Canada.* **2.** innate; inherent; natural (usually fol. by *to*): *feelings indigenous to human beings.* [< LL *indigenus* native, equiv. to L *indigen(a)* inborn (person), native (*indi-* in + *-gena* born) + *-us* -OUS] —**in·dig′e·nous·ly,** *adv.* —**in·dig′e·nous·ness, in·di·gen·i·ty** (in′di jen′i tē), *n.*
—**Syn. 1.** autochthonous, aboriginal, natural. —**Ant. 1.** foreign, alien.

in·di·gent (in′di jent), *adj.* **1.** lacking food, clothing, and other necessities of life because of poverty; needy; poor; impoverished. **2.** *Archaic.* **a.** deficient in what is requisite. **b.** destitute (usually fol. by *of*). —*n.* **3.** a person who is indigent. [ME < L *indigent-* (s. of *indigēns* needing, needy, prp. of *indigēre*), equiv. to *ind-* in + *-ig-* (var. of *eg-* want) + *-ent-* -ENT] —**in′di·gent·ly,** *adv.*
—**Syn. 1.** necessitous, penurious, distressed.

in·di·ges (in′di jēz′), *n., pl.* **in·dig·i·tes** (in dij′i tēz′). (in ancient Rome) a title applied to a Roman deified for service to his country. [< L]

in·di·gest·ed (in′di jes′tid, -dī-), *adj.* *Rare.* **1.** without arrangement or order. **2.** unformed or shapeless. **3.** not digested; undigested. **4.** not duly considered. [IN-³ + DIGESTED]

in·di·gest·i·ble (in′di jes′tə bəl, -dī-), *adj.* not digestible; not easily digested. [< L *indigestibil(is).* See IN-³, DIGESTIBLE] —**in′di·gest′i·bil′i·ty, in′di·gest′i·ble·ness,** *n.* —**in′di·gest′i·bly,** *adv.*

in·di·ges·tion (in′di jes′chən, -dī-, -jesh′-), *n.* **1.** incapability of or difficulty in digesting food; dyspepsia. **2.** an instance, or case, of this. [late ME < LL *indīgestiō-* (s. of *indīgestiō*). See IN-², DIGESTION]

in·di·ges·tive (in′di jes′tiv, -dī-), *n.* *Pathol.* attended with or suffering from indigestion; dyspeptic. [IN-³ + DIGESTIVE]

in·dig·i·ta·tion (in dij′i tā′shən), *n.* *Pathol.* intussusception, esp. of one part of an intestine into an adjacent part; invagination. [< L *indigitāt(us),* var. of *indigetāt(us)* invoked (ptp. of *indigetāre*), equiv. to *indiget-* (s. of *indigēs*) indigenous + *-ātus* -ATE¹ + -ION]

in·dign (in dīn′), *adj.* **1.** *Chiefly Literary.* undeserved. **2.** *Archaic.* unworthy. **3.** *Obs.* unbecoming or disgraceful. [late ME *indigne* < MF < L *indign(us),* equiv. to *in-* IN-³ + *dignus* worthy; see DIGNITY] —**in·dign′ly,** *adv.*

in·dig·nant (in dig′nənt), *adj.* feeling, characterized by, or expressing strong displeasure at something deemed unworthy, unjust, or base: *indignant remarks; an indignant expression on his face.* [< L *indignant-* (s. of *indignāns,* prp. of *indignārī* to deem unworthy, take offense), equiv. to *in-* IN-³ + *dign-* worthy + *-ant-* -ANT] —**in·dig′nant·ly,** *adv.*

in·dig·na·tion (in′dig nā′shən), *n.* strong displeasure at something deemed unworthy, unjust, or base; righteous anger. [ME *indignacio(u)n* < L *indignātiōn-* (s. of *indignātiō*), equiv. to *indignāt(us)* made indignant (ptp. of *indignārī*) + *-iōn-* -ION; see INDIGNANT]
—**Syn.** resentment, exasperation, wrath, ire, choler. See **anger.** —**Ant.** calm.

in·dig·ni·ty (in dig′ni tē), *n., pl.* **-ties. 1.** an injury to one's dignity; slighting or contemptuous treatment; humiliating affront, insult, or injury. **2.** *Obs.* **a.** unworthiness. **b.** disgrace or disgraceful action. [< L *indignitās* unworthiness, equiv. to *indign(us)* INDIGN + *-itās* -ITY]
—**Syn. 1.** outrage. See **insult.**

in·di·go (in′də gō′), *n., pl.* **-gos, -goes,** *adj.* —*n.* **1.** a blue dye obtained from various plants, esp. of the genus *Indigofera.* **2.** See **indigo blue** (def. 2). **3.** any leguminous plant of the genus *Indigofera.* **4.** deep violet blue. —*adj.* **5.** Also called **in′digo-blue′, in·di·got·ic** (in′də got′ik). of the color indigo. [< Sp or Pg, var. of *indico* < L *indicum* < Gk *indikón,* n. use of neut. of *Indikós* INDIC]

in′digo blue′, 1. the color indigo. —*n.* **2.** Also called **indigo, indigotin.** a dark-blue, water-insoluble, crystalline powder, $C_{16}H_{10}N_2O_2$, having a bronzelike luster, the essential coloring principle of which is contained along with other substances in the dye indigo and which can be produced synthetically.

in′digo bunt′ing, a North American bunting *Passerina cyanea,* the male of which is indigo. Also called **in′digo bird′, in′digo finch′.**

in·di·goid (in′də goid′), *adj.* **1.** of or pertaining to that group of vat dyes which have a molecular structure similar to that of indigo. —*n.* **2.** an indigoid substance. [INDIG(O) + -OID]

in′digo snake′, a large, deep blue or brown, colubrid snake, *Drymarchon corais,* ranging from the southern U.S. to South America, which invades burrows to prey on small mammals. Also called **gopher snake.**

in·dig·o·tin (in dig′ə tin, in′də gōt′ən), *n.* See **indigo blue** (def. 2). [INDIGO + hiatus-filling *-t-* + -IN²]

In·di·o (in′dē ō′), *n.* a town in S California. 9745 (1960).

in·di·rect (in′də rekt′, -dī-), *adj.* **1.** not direct in space; deviating from a straight line: *an indirect course in sailing.* **2.** coming or resulting otherwise than directly or immediately, as effects, consequences, etc.: *an indirect advantage.* **3.** not direct in action or procedure: *His methods are indirect but not dishonest.* **4.** devious; crooked; not straightforward: *He is known as a shady, indirect fellow.* **5.** not descending in a direct line of succession, as a title or inheritance. **6.** not direct in bearing, application, force, etc.: *indirect evidence.* **7.** of, pertaining to, or characteristic of indirect discourse: *an indirect quote.* [ME < ML *indīrect(us).* See IN-³, DIRECT] —**in′di·rect′ly,** *adv.* —**in′di·rect′ness,** *n.*

in′direct dis′course, discourse consisting not of an exact quotation of a speaker's words but of a version transformed from them for grammatical inclusion in a larger sentence. *He said he was hungry* is an example of indirect discourse. Cf. **direct discourse.**

in′direct′ ini′tiative, a procedure in which a statute or amendment proposed by popular petition must receive legislative consideration before being submitted to the voters.

in·di·rec·tion (in′də rek′shən, -dī-), *n.* **1.** indirect action or procedure. **2.** a roundabout course or method. **3.** a lack of direction or goal; aimlessness: *His efforts were marked by indirection and indecisiveness.* **4.** deceitful or crooked dealing. [INDIRECT + -ION, modeled on *direction*]

in′direct la′bor, labor performed, as by maintenance and clerical workers, that is not considered in computing costs per unit of production. Cf. **direct labor.**

in′direct light′ing, reflected or diffused light, used esp. in interiors to avoid glare, shadows, etc.

in′direct ob′ject, a word or group of words representing the person or thing with reference to which the action of verbs is performed, in English generally coming between the verb and the direct object or else following both and introduced by a preposition, as *to* or *for.* *The boy* is the indirect object of the verb *gave* in *He gave the boy a book* and in *He gave a book to the boy.*

in′direct pri′mary, *U.S. Politics.* a primary in which members of a party elect delegates to a party convention that in turn elects the party's candidates. Cf. **direct primary.**

in′direct tax′, a tax demanded of persons who then reimburse themselves for it at the expense of others, the tax being levied on commodities before they reach the consumer and being paid ultimately as part of their market price.

in·dis·cern·i·ble (in′di sûr′nə bəl, -zûr′-), *adj.* not discernible; imperceptible. [IN-³ + DISCERNIBLE] —**in′dis·cern′i·ble·ness, in′dis·cern′i·bil′i·ty,** *n.* —**in′dis·cern′i·bly,** *adv.*

in·dis·cerp·ti·ble (in′di sûrp′tə bəl), *adj.* not discerptible; indivisible. [IN-³ + DISCERPTIBLE] —**in′dis·cerp′ti·bil′i·ty, in′dis·cerp′ti·ble·ness,** *n.* —**in′dis·cerp′ti·bly,** *adv.*

in·dis·ci·pline (in dis′ə plin), *n.* **1.** lack of discipline: *a campus problem of student indiscipline.* **2.** an instance of this: *the indisciplines of children on holiday.* [IN-³ + DISCIPLINE]

in·dis·cov·er·a·ble (in′di skuv′ər ə bəl), *adj.* not discoverable; undiscoverable. [IN-³ + DISCOVERABLE]

in·dis·creet (in′di skrēt′), *adj.* not discreet; lacking prudence or sound judgment: *an indiscreet confidence.* [ME *indiscret* < LL *indiscrēt(us)* < L; see INDISCRETE] —**in′dis·creet′ly,** *adv.* —**in′dis·creet′ness,** *n.*

in·dis·crete (in′di skrēt′, in dis′krēt), *adj.* **1.** not discrete; not divided into parts. **2.** *Math.* trivial (def. 4). [< L *indiscrēt(us)* undivided. See IN-³, DISCRETE]

in·dis·cre·tion (in′di skresh′ən), *n.* **1.** lack of discretion; imprudence. **2.** an indiscreet act or step. [ME < LL. See IN-³, DISCRETION] —**in′dis·cre′tion·ar′y,** *adj.*

in·dis·crim·i·nate (in′di skrim′ə nit), *adj.* **1.** not discriminating; choosing at random: *indiscriminate in one's friendships.* **2.** not discriminate; haphazard: *indiscriminate slaughter.* **3.** not kept apart or divided; thrown together; jumbled: *an indiscriminate combination of colors and styles.* [IN-³ + DISCRIMINATE] —**in′dis·crim′i·nate·ly,** *adv.* —**in′dis·crim′i·nate·ness,** *n.*
—**Syn. 1.** See **miscellaneous. 3.** mixed.

in·dis·crim·i·nat·ing (in′di skrim′ə nā′ting), *adj.* not discriminating. [IN-³ + DISCRIMINATING] —**in′dis·crim′i·nat′ing·ly,** *adv.*

in·dis·crim·i·na·tion (in′di skrim′ə nā′shən), *n.* **1.** act or instance of not discriminating. **2.** quality or condition of being indiscriminate or of not discriminating; lack of discrimination. [IN-³ + DISCRIMINATION] —**in′dis·crim′i·na′tive,** *adj.*

in·dis·pen·sa·ble (in′di spen′sə bəl), *adj.* **1.** not dispensable; absolutely necessary or requisite: *an indispensable member of the staff.* **2.** incapable of being disregarded or neglected: *an indispensable obligation.* —*n.* **3.** one who or that which is indispensable. [< ML *indispensābil(is).* See IN-³, DISPENSABLE] —**in′dis·pen′sa·bil′i·ty, in′dis·pen′sa·ble·ness,** *n.* —**in′dis·pen′sa·bly,** *adv.*
—**Syn. 1.** needed. See **necessary.** —**Ant. 1–3.** unessential.

in·dis·pose (in′di spōz′), *v.t.,* **-posed, -pos·ing. 1.** to put out of the proper condition for something; make unfit; disqualify: *The croquet match indisposed me for further activity.* **2.** to make ill, esp. slightly. **3.** to disincline; render averse or unwilling: *His anger indisposed him from helping.* [back formation from INDISPOSED]

in·dis·posed (in′di spōzd′), *adj.* **1.** sick or ill, esp. slightly: *to be indisposed with a cold.* **2.** disinclined or unwilling: *indisposed to help.* [ME: out of order, not suitable. See IN-³, DISPOSED] —**in·dis·pos·ed·ness** (in′di spō′zid nis, -spōzd′-), *n.*
—**Syn. 1.** unwell. See **sick. 2.** reluctant, averse, loath.

in·dis·po·si·tion (in′dis pə zish′ən), *n.* **1.** state of being indisposed; a slight illness. **2.** disinclination; unwillingness. [late ME; see IN-³, DISPOSITION]

in·dis·put·a·ble (in′di spyo͞o′tə bəl, in dis′pyə-), *adj.* **1.** not disputable or deniable: *indisputable evidence.* **2.** unquestionably real, valid, or the like. [< LL *indisputābil(is).* See IN-³, DISPUTABLE] —**in′dis·put′a·bil′i·ty, in′dis·put′a·ble·ness,** *n.* —**in′dis·put′a·bly,** *adv.*
—**Syn. 1.** incontrovertible, incontestable, undeniable, unquestionable; evident, apparent, obvious, certain. —**Ant. 1.** questionable; uncertain.

in·dis·sol·u·ble (in′di sol′yə bəl), *adj.* **1.** not dissoluble; incapable of being dissolved, decomposed, undone, or destroyed. **2.** firm or stable. **3.** perpetually binding or obligatory. [< L *indissolūbil(is).* See IN-³, DISSOLUBLE] —**in′dis·sol′u·bil′i·ty, in′dis·sol′u·ble·ness,** *n.* —**in′dis·sol′u·bly,** *adv.*

in·dis·tinct (in′di stingkt′), *adj.* **1.** not distinct; not clearly marked or defined: *indistinct markings.* **2.** not clearly distinguishable or perceptible, as to the eye, ear, or mind: *He heard an indistinct muttering.* **3.** not distinguishing clearly: *an old man with indistinct vision and faulty hearing.* [ME < L *indistinct(us).* See IN-³, DISTINCT] —**in′dis·tinct′ly,** *adv.* —**in′dis·tinct′ness,** *n.*

in·dis·tinc·tive (in′di stingk′tiv), *adj.* **1.** without distinctive characteristics. **2.** incapable of making a distinction. [IN-³ + DISTINCTIVE] —**in′dis·tinc′tive·ly,** *adv.* —**in′dis·tinc′tive·ness,** *n.*

in·dis·tin·guish·a·ble (in′di sting′gwi shə bəl), *adj.* **1.** not distinguishable. **2.** indiscernible; imperceptible. [IN-³ + DISTINGUISHABLE] —**in′dis·tin′guish·a·ble·ness, in′dis·tin′guish·a·bil′i·ty,** *n.* —**in′dis·tin′guish·a·bly,** *adv.*

in·dite (in dīt′), *v.t.,* **-dit·ed, -dit·ing. 1.** to compose or write, as a speech, poem, etc. **2.** *Archaic.* to treat in a literary composition. **3.** *Obs.* to dictate. **4.** *Obs.* to prescribe. [ME *endite(n)* < OF *endit(er)* < VL **indictāre* < L *indict(us)* announced, hence, worded (ptp. of *indīcere*). See IN-², DICTUM] —**in·dite′ment,** *n.* —**in·dit′er,** *n.*

in·di·um (in′dē əm), *n.* *Chem.* a rare metallic element, soft, white, malleable, and easily fusible, found combined in various ores, esp. sphalerite: so-called from the two indigo-blue lines in its spectrum. *Symbol:* In; *at. wt.:* 114.82; *at. no.:* 49; *sp. gr.:* 7.3 at 20°C. [< NL < L *ind(icum)* INDIGO + -IUM]

in·di·vert·i·ble (in′də vûr′tə bəl, -dī-), *adj.* not divertible; not to be turned aside. [IN-³ + DIVERTIBLE] —**in′di·vert′i·bly,** *adv.*

individ., individual. Also, **indiv.**

in·di·vid·u·al (in′də vij′o͞o əl), *adj.* **1.** single; particular; separate: *to number individual copies of a limited edition.* **2.** existing as a distinct, indivisible entity, or considered as such: *individual parts of a tea set.* **3.** of, pertaining to, or characteristic of a particular person or thing: *individual tastes.* **4.** intended for the use of one person only: *to serve individual portions of a pizza.* **5.** distinguished by peculiar and marked characteristics; exhibiting unique or unusual qualities: *a highly individual style.* **6.** of which each is different or of a different design from the others: *a set of individual coffee cups.* —*n.* **7.** a single human being, as distinguished from a group. **8.** a person: *a strange individual.* **9.** a distinct, indivisible entity; a single thing, being, instance, or item. **10.** a group considered as a unit. **11.** *Biol.* **a.** a single or simple organism capable of independent existence. **b.** a member of a compound organism or colony. **12.** *Cards.* a duplicate-bridge tournament in which each player plays the same number of hands in partnership with every other player, individual scores for each player being kept for each hand. [ME < ML *indīviduāl(is),* equiv. to L *indīvidu(us)* indivisible (see IN-³, DIVIDE) + *-ālis* -AL¹]
—**Syn. 8.** See **person.**

in·di·vid·u·al·ise (in′də vij′o͞o ə līz′), *v.t.,* **-ised, -is·ing.** *Chiefly Brit.* individualize. —**in′di·vid′u·al·i·sa′tion,** *n.* —**in′di·vid′u·al·is′er,** *n.*

in·di·vid·u·al·ism (in′də vij′o͞o ə liz′əm), *n.* **1.** a social theory advocating the liberty, rights, or independent action of the individual. **2.** the principle or habit of independent thought or action. **3.** the pursuit of individual rather than common or collective interests; egoism. **4.** individual character; individuality. **5.** an individual peculiarity. **6.** *Philos.* **a.** the doctrine that only individual things are real. **b.** the doctrine or belief that all actions are determined by, or at least take place for, the benefit of the individual, not of the mass of men. [INDIVIDUAL + -ISM]

in·di·vid·u·al·ist (in′də vij′o͞o ə list), *n.* **1.** a person who is characterized by great independence or individuality in thought or action. **2.** an advocate of individualism. [INDIVIDUAL + -IST] —**in′di·vid′u·al·is′tic,** *adj.* —**in′di·vid′u·al·is′ti·cal·ly,** *adv.*

in·di·vid·u·al·i·ty (in′də vij′o͞o al′i tē), *n., pl.* **-ties. 1.** the particular character, or aggregate of qualities, which distinguishes one person or thing from others: *a person of marked individuality.* **2. individualities,** individual characteristics. **3.** a person or thing of individual or distinctive character. **4.** state or quality of being individual; existence as a distinct individual. **5.** the interests of the individual as distinguished from the

interests of the community. 6. *Archaic.* state or quality of being indivisible or inseparable. [INDIVIDUAL + -ITY]
—**Syn. 1.** See **character.**

in·di·vid·u·al·ize (in′də vij′o͞o ə līz′), *v.t.*, **-ized, -iz·ing.** 1. to make individual or distinctive; give an individual or distinctive character to. 2. to mention, indicate, or consider individually; specify; particularize. Also, *esp. Brit.*, **individualise.** [INDIVIDUAL + -IZE] —**in′di·vid′u·al·i·za′tion,** *n.* —**in′di·vid′u·al·iz′er,** *n.*

in′divid′ual lib′erty, the liberty of an individual to exercise freely the rights accepted as being outside of governmental control.

in·di·vid·u·al·ly (in′də vij′o͞o ə lē), *adv.* 1. in an individual or personally unique manner: *His interpretation was individually conceived.* 2. one at a time; separately: *The delegates were introduced individually.* 3. personally: *Each of us is individually responsible.* [INDIVIDUAL + -LY]

in′divid′ual med′ley, *Swimming.* a race in which the total distance is divided into three equal portions, each swimmer using the breaststroke for the first portion, the backstroke for the second, and a different stroke of his choice for the third. Cf. **medley relay** (def. 2).

in·di·vid·u·ate (in′də vij′o͞o āt′), *v.t.*, **-at·ed, -at·ing.** 1. to form into an individual or distinct entity. 2. to give an individual or distinctive character to; individualize. [< ML *individuāt(us)* made individual, ptp. of *individuāre.* See INDIVIDU(AL), -ATE[1]] —**in′di·vid′u·a′tor,** *n.*

in·di·vid·u·a·tion (in′də vij′o͞o ā′shən), *n.* 1. act of individuating. 2. state of being individuated; individual existence; individuality. 3. *Philos.* the determination or contraction of a general nature to an individual mode of existence; development of the individual from the general. [INDIVIDUATE + -ION]

in·di·vis·i·ble (in′də viz′ə bəl), *adj.* 1. not divisible; not separable into parts; incapable of being divided: *one nation indivisible.* —*n.* 2. something indivisible. [ME < LL *indīvīsibil(is).* See IN-[3], DIVISIBLE] —**in′di·vis′i·bil′i·ty, in′di·vis′i·ble·ness,** *n.* —**in′di·vis′i·bly,** *adv.*

indo-, a combining form of **indigo:** *indophenol.* Also, *esp. before a vowel,* **ind-.**

Indo-, a combining form of **India:** *Indo-European.* [< L < Gk; comb. form of L *Indus,* Gk *Indós*]

In·do-Ar·y·an (in′dō âr′ē ən, -yən, -ar′-; -är′yən), *n.* 1. a member of a people of India who are Indo-European in speech and Caucasoid in physical characteristics. —*adj.* 2. Indic (def. 2). 3. of, pertaining to, or characteristic of the Indo-Aryans.

In·do-Brit·ish (in′dō brit′ish), *adj.* of Indian and British origin, sponsorship, etc.

In·do·chi·na (in′dō chī′nə), *n.* a peninsula in SE Asia, between the Bay of Bengal and the South China Sea, comprising South Vietnam, North Vietnam, Cambodia, Laos, Thailand, Malaya, and Burma. Also called **Farther India.** Cf. **French Indochina.**

In·do-Chi·nese (in′dō chī nēz′, -nēs′), *adj., n., pl.* **-nese.** Sino-Tibetan (no longer current).

in·doc·ile (in dos′il), *adj.* not docile; not amenable to teaching or training. [< L *indocil(is).* See IN-[3], DOCILE] —**in·do·cil·i·ty** (in′dō sil′i tē), *n.*

in·doc·tri·nate (in dok′trə nāt′), *v.t.*, **-nat·ed, -nat·ing.** 1. to instruct (in a doctrine, principle, ideology, etc.). 2. to teach or inculcate. 3. to imbue (a person) with learning. [IN-[2] + ML *doctrīnāt(us)* taught, ptp. of *doctrīnāre;* see DOCTRINE, -ATE[1]] —**in·doc′tri·na′tion,** *n.* —**in·doc′tri·na′tor,** *n.*

in·doc·tri·nize (in dok′trə nīz′), *v.t.*, **-nized, -niz·ing.** indoctrinate. [INDOCTRIN(ATE) + -IZE] —**in·doc′tri·ni·za′tion,** *n.*

In·do-Eu·ro·pe·an (in′dō yo͝or′ə pē′ən), *n.* 1. a family of languages characterized by inflection, grammatical number, and, typically, gender and ablaut, and by basic vocabularies which have many correspondences, jointly in sound and in meaning, and including many politically or culturally important languages, esp. those of the Germanic, Italic, Hellenic, Slavic, and Indo-Iranian branches. Cf. **family** (def. 11), **number** (def. 19). 2. the prehistoric parent language of this family. 3. a member of any of the peoples speaking an Indo-European language. —*adj.* 4. of or belonging to Indo-European. 5. speaking an Indo-European language: *an Indo-European people.*

In·do-Eu·ro·pe·an·ist (in′dō yo͝or′ə pē′ə nist), *n.* a linguist specializing in the study, esp. the comparative study, of the Indo-European languages. [INDO-EUROPEAN + -IST]

In·do-Ger·man·ic (in′dō jər man′ik), *adj., n.* Indo-European (no longer current).

In·do-Hit·tite (in′dō hit′īt), *n.* a language family in which Proto-Anatolian and Proto-Indo-European are considered coordinate. Cf. **Hittite** (def. 2).

In·do-I·ra·ni·an (in′dō i rā′nē ən), *n.* 1. a branch of the Indo-European family of languages, including Persian, Pashto, Avestan, Kurdish, and the Indo-European languages of the Indian subcontinent. —*adj.* 2. of or belonging to Indo-Iranian.

in·dole (in′dōl), *n.* *Chem.* a colorless to yellowish solid, C_8H_7N, having a low melting point and a fecal odor, found in the oil of jasmine and clove and as a putrefaction product from animals' intestines: used in perfumery and as a reagent. [IND- + -OLE]

in′dole·a·ce′tic ac′id (in′dōl ə sē′tik, -set′ik, in′-), *Biochem.* a crystalline, water-insoluble powder, $C_8H_6NCH_2COOH$, a natural plant hormone, used esp. for stimulating growth and root formation in plant cutting. Also called **beta-indoleacetic acid, heteroauxin.** [INDOLE + ACETIC]

in′dole·bu·tyr′ic ac′id, (in′dōl byo͞o tir′ik, in′dōl-), *Biochem.* a white or yellowish, crystalline, water-insoluble powder, $C_8H_6N(CH_2)_3COOH$, which is a plant hormone similar to indoleacetic acid and used for the same purposes. [INDOLE + BUTYRIC]

in·do·lence (in′dələns), *n.* quality or state of being indolent. [< L *indolentia* painlessness. See INDOLENT, -ENCE]

in·do·lent (in′dələnt), *adj.* 1. having or showing a disposition to avoid exertion; lazy; slothful: *an indolent person.* 2. *Pathol.* causing little or no pain. [< L *indolent-* (s. of *indolēns*) < *in-* IN-[3] + *dolent-* (s. of *dolēns*) painful, prp. of *dolēre;* see DOLE[2], -ENT] —**in′do·lent·ly,** *adv.*
—**Syn. 1.** slow, inactive, sluggish, torpid. See **idle.**

in·do·log·e·nous (in′dəloj′ə nəs), *adj.* *Biochem.* producing or causing the production of indole. [INDOLE + -O- + -GENOUS]

In·do-Ma·lay·an (in′dō mə lā′ən), *adj.* of Indian and Malayan origin, sponsorship, etc.

in·dom·i·ta·bil·i·ty (in dom′i tə bil′i tē), *n.* quality or condition of being indomitable. [INDOMITABLE + -ITY]

in·dom·i·ta·ble (in dom′i tə bəl), *adj.* that cannot be subdued or overcome, as persons, pride, courage, etc.: *an indomitable warrior; indomitable valor.* [< LL *indomitābil(is)* < L *indomit(us)* untamed (< *in-* IN-[3] + *domitus,* ptp. of *domāre*) + *-ābilis* -ABLE] —**in·dom′i·ta·ble·ness,** *n.* —**in·dom′i·ta·bly,** *adv.*
—**Syn.** unconquerable, unyielding. See **invincible.**
—**Ant.** yielding.

In·do·ne·sia (in′də nē′zhə, -shə, -zē ə, -dō-), *n.* 1. See **East Indies** (def. 1). 2. **Republic of.** Formerly, **Netherlands East Indies, Dutch East Indies.** Former official name (1949), **United States of Indonesia.** a republic in the Malay Archipelago, consisting of Sumatra, Java, Celebes, the S part of Borneo, and about 3000 small islands: received independence from the Netherlands in 1949. 97,085,384 (1961); ab. 580,000 sq. mi. *Cap.:* Djakata. [INDO + Gk *nēs(os)* island + -IA]

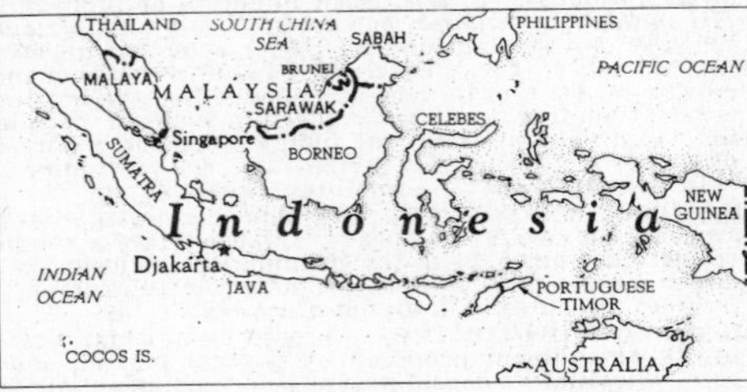

In·do·ne·sian (in′də nē′zhən, -shən, -zē ən, -dō-), *n.* 1. Also called **Malaysian.** a member of the ethnic group consisting of the natives of Indonesia, the Filipinos, and the Malays of Malaya. 2. a member of a light-colored race supposed to have been dominant in the Malay Archipelago before the Malays, and believed to constitute one element of the present mixed population of Malaysia and perhaps Polynesia. 3. Official name, **Bahasa Indonesia.** an amalgam of several Indonesian languages that is based mostly on Malay and is used as the official language of the Republic of Indonesia. 4. the westernmost subfamily of Malayo-Polynesian languages, including those of Formosa, the Philippines, the Malagasy Republic, and Indonesia, as well as Malay. —*adj.* 5. of or pertaining to the Malay Archipelago. 6. of or pertaining to Indonesia, the Indonesians, or their languages. [INDONESI(A) + -AN]

in·door (in′dōr′, -dôr′), *adj.* occurring, used, etc., in a house or building, rather than out of doors: *indoor games; an indoor grill.* [aph. var. of *within-door,* orig. phrase *within (the) door,* i.e., inside the house]

in′door base′ball, softball played indoors.

in·doors (in dōrz′, -dôrz′), *adv.* in or into a house or building: *He ran indoors.* [INDOOR + -S[1]]

In·do-Pa·cif·ic (in′dō pə sif′ik), *adj.* of or pertaining to the areas of the Indian and Pacific oceans off the coast of SE Asia.

in·do·phe·nol (in′dō fē′nōl, -nôl, -nol), *n.* *Chem.* 1. the para form of $HOC_6H_4N{=}C_6H_4{=}O$, a quinonimine derivative which is the parent substance of the blue and green indophenol dyes. 2. any derivative of this compound. 3. any of various related dyes. [INDO- + PHENOL]

In·dore (in dōr′), *n.* 1. a former state in central India: now part of Madhya Pradesh. 2. a city in W Madhya Pradesh, in central India. 394,900 (1961).

in·dorse (in dôrs′), *v.t.*, **-dorsed, -dors·ing.** endorse. —**in·dors′a·ble,** *adj.* —**in·dor·see** (in dôr sē′, in′dôr sē′), *n.* —**in·dors′er, in·dor′sor,** *n.*

in·dorse·ment (in dôrs′mənt), *n.* endorsement.

in·dox·yl (in dok′sil), *n.* *Chem.* a crystalline compound, C_8H_7NO, which is obtained by the hydrolysis of indican and is readily oxidized to furnish indigo. [IND- + (HYDR)OXYL]

In·dra (in′drə), *n.* 1. *Hinduism.* the chief of the Vedic gods, the god of rain and thunder. 2. a boy's given name.

in·draft (in′draft′, -dräft′), *n.* 1. an inward flow or current, as of air, water, etc. 2. *Archaic.* attraction; magnetism. Also, *esp. Brit.,* **in′draught′.** [IN-[1] + DRAFT]

In·dra·ni (in drä′nē), *n.* *Hindu Myth.* the consort of Indra. [see INDRA, RANEE]

Indra

in·drawn (in′drôn′), *adj.* 1. reserved; introspective: *a quiet, indrawn man.* 2. made with the breath drawn in: *an indrawn sigh.* [IN-[1] + DRAWN]

In·dre (aN′drᵊ), *n.* a department in central France. 251,432 (1962); 2667 sq. mi. *Cap.:* Châteauroux.

In·dre-et-Loire (aN drā lwar′), *n.* a department in W central France. 395,210 (1962); 2378 sq. mi. *Cap.:* Tours.

in·dri (in′drē), *n., pl.* **-dris.** a short-tailed lemur, *Indri indri,* of Madagascar, about two feet in length. [< F *indri* < Malagasy *indry* look! wrongly taken as animal's name]

In Du′bious Bat′tle, a novel (1936) by John Steinbeck.

in·du·bi·ta·bil·i·ty (in do͞o′bi tə bil′i tē, -dyo͞o′-), *n.* the quality or condition of being beyond doubt; certainty: *the indubitability of the concept.* [INDUBITABLE + -ITY]

in·du·bi·ta·ble (in do͞o′bi tə bəl, -dyo͞o′-), *adj.* that cannot be doubted; unquestionable; certain. [< L *indubitābil(is).* See IN-[3], DUBITABLE] —**in·du′bi·ta·ble·ness,** *n.* —**in·du′bi·ta·bly,** *adv.*

induc., induction.

in·duce (in do͞os′, -dyo͞os′), *v.t.*, **-duced, -duc·ing.** 1. to lead or move by persuasion or influence, as to some action, state of mind, etc.: *to induce a person to go.* 2. to bring about, produce, or cause: *Opium induces sleep.* 3. *Physics.* to produce (an electric current) by induction. 4. *Logic.* to assert or establish (a proposition about a class of phenomena) on the basis of observations on a number of particular facts. [ME < L *indūce(re)* (to) lead or bring in, introduce, equiv. to *in-* IN-[2] + *dūcere* to lead; see ADDUCE, DEDUCE, REDUCE, etc.] —**in·duc′er,** *n.* —**in·duc′i·ble,** *adj.*
—**Syn. 1.** actuate, prompt, incite, urge, spur. See **persuade.** —**Ant. 1.** dissuade.

induced′ drag′, *Aeron.* the drag force generated in the production of lift.

induced′ ra′dioactiv′ity, *Physics.* See **artificial radioactivity.**

induced′ topol′ogy, *Math.* See **relative topology.**

in·duce·ment (in do͞os′mənt, -dyo͞os′-), *n.* 1. act of inducing. 2. something that induces, motivates, or persuades; an incentive. [INDUCE + -MENT]
—**Syn. 2.** stimulus, spur, incitement; attraction, lure. See **motive.**

in·duct (in dukt′), *v.t.* 1. to install in an office, benefice, position, etc., esp. with formal ceremonies: *The committee inducted him as president.* 2. to introduce to knowledge or experience of; initiate (usually fol. by *to* or *into*): *They inducted him into the mystic rites of the order.* 3. *U.S.* to enlist (a draftee) into military service; draft. 4. to bring in as a member: *to induct one into a new profession.* [ME < L *induct(us)* led or brought in, introduced, equiv. to *induc-* (see INDUCE) + *-tus* ptp. suffix]

in·duct·ance (in duk′təns), *n.* *Elect.* 1. that property of a circuit or of a pair of circuits by which a change in current in either circuit induces, by electromagnetic induction, an electromotive force in one of the circuits. Cf. **mutual inductance, self-inductance.** 2. a piece of equipment providing inductance in a circuit or other system; inductor. [INDUCT + -ANCE]

in·duc·tee (in′duk tē′), *n.* a person inducted into military service. [INDUCT + -EE]

in·duc·tile (in duk′til), *adj.* not ductile; not pliable or yielding. [IN-[3] + DUCTILE] —**in′duc·til′i·ty,** *n.*

in·duc·tion (in duk′shən), *n.* 1. *Elect., Magnetism.* the process by which a body having electric or magnetic properties produces magnetism, an electric charge, or an electromotive force in a neighboring body without contact. Cf. **electromagnetic induction, electrostatic induction.** 2. *Logic.* **a.** any form of reasoning in which the conclusion, though supported by the premises, does not follow from them necessarily. **b.** the process of estimating the validity of observations of part of a class of facts as evidence for a proposition about the whole class. **c.** a conclusion reached by this process. 3. Also called **mathematical induction.** *Math.* a method of proving a given property true for a set of numbers by proving it true for 1 and then true for an arbitrary positive by assuming the property true for all previous positive integers and applying the principle of mathematical induction. Cf. **principle of mathematical induction.** 4. a presentation or bringing forward, as of facts, evidence, etc. 5. the act of inducing, bringing about, or causing: *induction of the hypnotic state.* 6. *Embryol.* the process by which an organizer influences the differentiation of another part. 7. the act of inducting; introduction; initiation. 8. formal installation in an office, benefice, or the like. 9. an introductory unit in a literary work, esp. in an early play; a prelude or scene, independent of the main performance but related to it. 10. *Archaic.* a preface. [ME *inducciō(u)n* < L *inductiōn-* (s. of *inductiō*). See INDUCT, -ION] —**in·duc′tion·less,** *adj.*

induc′tion coil′, *Elect.* a transformer for producing high-voltage alternating current from a low-voltage direct current, consisting essentially of two concentric coils with a common soft-iron core, a primary coil with relatively few windings of heavy wire, and a secondary coil with many turns of fine wire. Excitation of the primary coil by rapidly interrupted or variable current induces high voltage in the secondary coil.

in·duc·tive (in duk′tiv), *adj.* 1. of, pertaining to, or involving electrical or magnetic induction. 2. operating by induction: *an inductive machine.* 3. of, pertaining to, or employing logical induction: *inductive reasoning.* 4. *Embryol.* eliciting the action of an organizer. 5. serving to induce; leading or influencing (usually fol. by *to*). 6. introductory. [< LL *inductīv(us).* See INDUCT, -IVE] —**in·duc′tive·ly,** *adv.* —**in·duc′tive·ness,** *n.*
—**Syn. 3.** See **deductive.**

induc′tive capac′ity. See **dielectric constant.**

induc′tive react′ance, *Elect.* the opposition of inductance to alternating current, equal to the product of the angular frequency of the current times the self-inductance. *Symbol:* X_L Cf. **capacitive reactance.**

in·duc·tor (in duk′tər), *n.* 1. *Elect.* a device of which the primary purpose is to introduce inductance into an electric circuit. 2. a person who inducts, as into office. [< L, equiv. to *induct(us)* (see INDUCT) + *-or* -OR[2]]

in·duc·to·ther·my (in duk′tə thûr′mē), *n.* *Med.* the production of fever by means of electromagnetic induction. [formerly trademark]

in·due (in do͞o′, -dyo͞o′), *v.t.*, **-dued, -du·ing.** endue.

in·dulge (in dulj′), *v.*, **-dulged, -dulg·ing.** —*v.i.* 1. to yield to an inclination or desire; indulge oneself (often fol. by *in*): *Dessert came, but I didn't indulge. They indulged in ice cream and cake.* —*v.t.* 2. to yield to, satisfy, or gratify (desires, feelings, etc.): *to indulge one's appetite for sweets.* 3. to yield to the wishes or whims of:

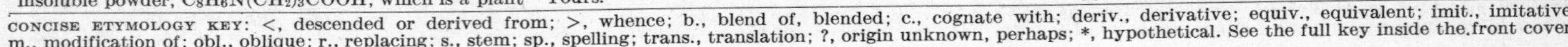
CONCISE ETYMOLOGY KEY: <, descended or derived from; >, whence; b., blend of, blended; c., cognate with; deriv., derivative; equiv., equivalent; imit., imitative; m., modification of; obl., oblique; r., replacing; s., stem; sp., spelling; trans., translation; ?, origin unknown, perhaps; *, hypothetical. See the full key inside the front cover.

to indulge a child. **4.** to allow (oneself) to follow one's will (usually fol. by *in*): *to indulge oneself in reckless spending; to indulge oneself in idle speculation.* **5.** *Com.* to grant an extension of time, for payment or performance, to (a person, company, etc.) or on (a bill, note, etc.). [< L *indulg(ēre)* (to) be long-suffering, forbearing, too kind, equiv. to *in-* IN-[2] + *-dulgēre*; akin to Gk *dolichós* long] —**in·dulg′er,** *n.* —**in·dulg′ing·ly,** *adv.* —**Syn. 3.** pamper, favor. See **humor.** —**Ant. 3.** refuse.

in·dul·gence (in dul′jəns), *n., v.,* **-genced, -genc·ing.** —*n.* **1.** the act or practice of indulging; gratification of desire. **2.** indulgent allowance or tolerance. **3.** a catering to someone's mood or whim; humoring: *The old man demanded indulgence as his due.* **4.** something granted or taken in gratification of desire: *Her favorite indulgence was candy.* **5.** *Rom. Cath. Ch.* a partial remission of the temporal punishment, esp. purgatorial atonement, which is still due for sin after absolution. Cf. **plenary indulgence. 6.** *Eng. and Scot. Hist.* (in the reigns of Charles II and James II) a grant by the king to Protestant dissenters and Roman Catholics freeing them from certain penalties imposed, by legislation, because of their religion. **7.** *Com.* an extension, through favor, of time for payment or performance. —*v.t.* **8.** *Rom. Cath. Ch.* to provide with an indulgence: *an indulgenced pilgrimage to Rome.* [ME < L *indulgentia.* See INDULGE, -ENCE]

in·dul·gen·cy (in dul′jən sē), *n., pl.* **-cies.** indulgence. [< L *indulgentia*; see -ENCY]

in·dul·gent (in dul′jənt), *adj.* characterized by or showing indulgence; benignly permissive: *an indulgent parent.* [< L *indulgent-* (s. of *indulgēns*), prp. of *indulgēre* to INDULGE; see -ENT] —**in·dul′gent·ly,** *adv.*

in·du·line (in′dyə lēn′, -lin, in′dᵊlēn′), *n.* any of a large class of dyes yielding colors similar to indigo. [IND- + -ULE + -INE[2]]

in·dult (in dult′), *n. Rom. Cath. Ch.* a faculty granted, usually for a specific period of time or for a specific case, by the pope to bishops and others, permitting them to deviate from the common law of the church. [late ME < eccl. L *indult(um)* n. use of neut. of *indultus*, ptp. of *indulgēre* to INDULGE]

in·du·men·tum (in′dŏŏ men′təm, -dyŏŏ-), *n., pl.* **-ta** (-tə), **-tums.** *Bot., Zool.* a dense, hairy covering. [< NL < LL: garment, covering, equiv. to L *indu(ere)* (to) put on, don + *-mentum* -MENT]

in·du·na (in dōō′nə), *n.* a leader among the Zulus of Africa. [< Zulu]

in·du·pli·cate (in dōō′plə kit, -kāt′, -dyōō′-), *adj. Bot.* folded or rolled inward: said of the parts of the calyx or corolla in estivation when the edges are bent abruptly toward the axis, or of leaves in vernation when the edges are rolled inward and then arranged about the axis without overlapping. Also, **in·du′pli·ca′tive.** [IN-[2] + DUPLICATE] —**in·du′pli·ca′tion,** *n.*

in·du·rate (*v.* in′dŏŏ rāt′, -dyŏŏ-; *adj.* in′dŏŏ rit, -dyŏŏ-; in dŏŏr′it, -dyŏŏr′-), *v.,* **-rat·ed, -rat·ing,** *adj.* —*v.t.* **1.** to make hard; harden, as rock, tissue, etc.: *Cold indurates the soil.* **2.** to make callous, stubborn, or unfeeling: *transgressions that indurate the heart.* **3.** to inure; accustom: *to indurate oneself to privation and suffering.* **4.** to make enduring; confirm; establish: *to indurate custom through practice.* —*v.i.* **5.** to become hard; harden. **6.** to become established or confirmed. —*adj.* **7.** hardened; callous; inured. [ME *indurat* < L *indūrāt(us)* hardened (ptp. of *indūrāre*). See IN-[2], DURE[1], -ATE[1]]

in·du·ra·tion (in′dŏŏ rā′shən, -dyŏŏ-), *n.* **1.** the act or state of indurating; state of being indurated. **2.** *Geol.* **a.** consolidation of sediments to produce sedimentary rocks. **b.** hardening of rocks by heat, pressure, cementation, etc. **3.** *Pathol.* **a.** a hardening of an area of the body as a reaction to inflammation, hyperemia, or neoplastic infiltration. **b.** an area or part of the body that has undergone such a reaction. [ME < LL *indūrātiōn-* (s. of *indūrātiō*) a hardening. See INDURATE, -ION] —**in′du·ra′tive,** *adj.*

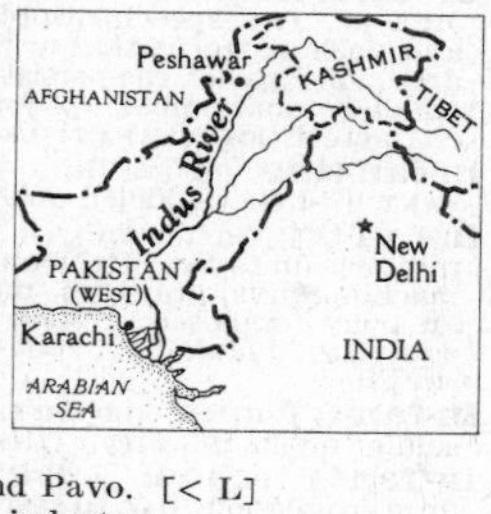

In·dus (in′dəs), *n.* a river in S Asia, flowing from W Tibet through Kashmir and Pakistan to the Arabian Sea. 1900 mi. long.

In·dus (in′dəs), *n., gen.* **-di** (-dī). *Astron.* the Indian, a southern constellation between Grus and Pavo. [< L]

indus., **1.** industrial. **2.** industry.

In′dus civiliza′tion. See **Indus valley civilization.**

in·du·si·ate (in dōō′zē it, -zhē-, -dyōō′-), *adj.* having an indusium. [< L *indusiāt(us)*, equiv. to *indūsi(um)* + *-ātus* -ATE[1]]

in·du·si·um (in dōō′zē əm, -zhē əm, -dyōō′-), *n., pl.* **-si·a** (-zē ə, -zhē ə). **1.** *Bot.* a membranous overgrowth covering the sori in ferns. **2.** *Anat., Zool.* **a.** an enveloping layer or membrane. **b.** a thin layer of gray matter on the corpus callosum. [< NL < L: kind of tunic; see INDUMENTUM] —**in·du′si·al,** *adj.*

in·dus·tri·al (in dus′trē əl), *adj.* **1.** of, pertaining to, of the nature of, or resulting from industry: *industrial production; industrial research.* **2.** having many and highly developed industries: *an industrial nation.* **3.** engaged in an industry or industries: *industrial workers.* **4.** of or pertaining to the workers in industries: *industrial training.* **5.** fashioned for use in industry: *industrial diamonds; industrial fabrics.* **6.** noting or pertaining to industrial life insurance. —*n.* **7.** an employee in some industry, esp. a manufacturing industry. **8.** a company engaged in industrial enterprises. **9.** an industrial product: *diamonds classed as industrials and nonindustrials.* **10. industrials,** stocks and bonds of industrial companies. [INDUSTRY + -AL[1]] —**in·dus′tri·al·ly,** *adv.* —**in·dus′tri·al·ness,** *n.*

indus′trial arts′, the methods of using tools and machinery, as taught in secondary and technical schools.

indus′trial design′, the art that deals with the design problems of manufactured objects, including problems of designing such objects with consideration for available materials and means of production, of designing packages, bottles, etc., for manufactured goods, of graphic design for manufactured objects, packages, etc., and other such problems. —**indus′trial design′er.**

indus′trial disease′. See **occupational disease** (def. 1).

indus′trial insur′ance. See **industrial life insurance.**

in·dus·tri·al·ise (in dus′trē ə līz′), *v.t.,* **-ised, -is·ing.** *Chiefly Brit.* industrialize. —**in·dus′tri·al·i·sa′tion,** *n.*

in·dus·tri·al·ism (in dus′trē ə liz′əm), *n.* an economic organization of society built largely on mechanized industry rather than agriculture, craftsmanship, or commerce. [INDUSTRIAL + -ISM]

in·dus·tri·al·ist (in dus′trē ə list), *n.* **1.** a person who owns, or is concerned with the management of, an industrial enterprise. —*adj.* **2.** of, pertaining to, or characterized by industrialism. [INDUSTRIAL + -IST]

in·dus·tri·al·ize (in dus′trē ə līz′), *v.,* **-ized, -iz·ing.** —*v.t.* **1.** to introduce industry into (an area) on a large scale. **2.** to convert to the ideals, methods, aims, etc., of industrialism. —*v.i.* **3.** to undergo industrialization. **4.** to follow or espouse industrialism. Also, *esp. Brit.,* **industrialise.** [INDUSTRIAL + -IZE] —**in·dus′tri·al·i·za′tion,** *n.*

indus′trial life′ insur′ance, life insurance having a relatively low face value in which premiums are paid weekly or monthly to an agent.

indus′trial park′, an area of land developed in an orderly, planned way with transportation, utilities, etc., and leased or sold to various industrial firms.

indus′trial psychol′ogy, the application of psychological principles and techniques to business and industrial problems, as in the selection of personnel, development of training programs, etc.

indus′trial revolu′tion, the totality of the changes in economic and social organization that began about 1760 in England and later in other countries, characterized chiefly by the replacement of hand tools with power-driven machines, as the power loom and the steam engine, and by the concentration of industry in large establishments.

indus′trial school′, **1.** a school for teaching one or more branches of industry. **2.** a school for educating neglected children committed to its care and training them to some form of industry.

indus′trial store′. See **company store.**

indus′trial un′ion, a labor union composed of workers in various trades and crafts within one industry.

Indus′trial Work′ers of the World′, an international industrial labor union which was organized in Chicago in 1905 and which disintegrated after 1920. *Abbr.:* I.W.W., IWW

in·dus·tri·ous (in dus′trē əs), *adj.* **1.** hard-working; working energetically and devotedly; diligent: *an industrious person.* **2.** *Obs.* skillful. [< L *industrius* < OL *indostruus*, equiv. to *indo-* in + *-stru(ere)* (to) build + *-us* -OUS] —**in·dus′tri·ous·ly,** *adv.* —**in·dus′tri·ous·ness,** *n.*
—**Syn. 1.** assiduous, sedulous, energetic. See **busy.** —**Ant. 1.** lazy, indolent.

in·dus·try (in′də strē), *n., pl.* **-tries** for 1, 2, 7. **1.** the aggregate of manufacturing or technically productive enterprises in a particular field, often named after its principal product: *the automobile industry; the steel industry.* **2.** any general business activity: *the Italian tourist industry.* **3.** trade or manufacture in general: *the rise of industry in Africa.* **4.** the ownership and management of companies, factories, etc.: *friction between labor and industry.* **5.** systematic work or labor. **6.** assiduous activity at any work or task; diligence: *His teacher praised his industry.* **7.** *Archaeol.* an assemblage of artifacts regarded as unmistakably the work of a single prehistoric group. [ME *industrie* < L *industria*, n. use of fem. of *industrius* INDUSTRIOUS]
—**Syn. 6.** application, effort, attention, devotion.

In′dus val′ley civiliza′tion, an ancient civilization that flourished in the Indus River valley, from about 2500 to 1500 B.C.: extensive archaeological excavations at the main sites of Mohenjo-Daro and Harappa in West Pakistan. Also called **Indus civilization.**

in·dwell (in dwel′), *v.,* **-dwelt, -dwell·ing.** —*v.t.* **1.** to inhabit. **2.** to possess (a person), as a principle, motivating force, etc.: *compassion that indwells the heart.* —*v.i.* **3.** to dwell (usually fol. by *in*). **4.** to abide within, as a guiding force, motivating principle, etc. (usually fol. by *in*): *a divine spirit indwelling in nature and the universe.* [ME *indwelle(n)*. See IN-[1], DWELL] —**in′dwell′er,** *n.*

In·dy, d' (daN dē′), **Vin·cent** (vaN säN′), 1851–1931, French composer.

-ine[1], a suffix of adjectives of Greek or Latin origin, meaning "of or pertaining to," "of the nature of," "made of," "like": *asinine; crystalline; equine; marine.* Cf. **-in**[1]. [< L *-īnus, -inus* < Gk *-inos*]

-ine[2], **1.** a suffix of no assignable meaning, appearing in nouns of Greek, Latin, or French origin: *doctrine; famine; routine.* **2.** a noun suffix used particularly in chemical terms (*bromine; chlorine*), and esp. in names of basic substances (*amine; aniline; caffeine; quinine; quinoline*). Cf. **-in**[2]. **3.** a suffix of feminine nouns (*heroine*), given names (*Clementine*), and titles (*landgravine*). Cf. **-ina.** [< F < L *-ina*, orig. fem. of *-inus*; also repr. Gk *-inē*, fem. n. suffix]

in·earth (in ûrth′), *v.t. Archaic.* to bury; inter. [IN-[1] + EARTH]

in·e·bri·ant (in ē′brē ənt, i nē′-), *adj.* **1.** inebriating; intoxicating. —*n.* **2.** an intoxicant. [< L *inēbriant-* (s. of *inēbriāns*, prp. of *inēbriāre* to make drunk), equiv. to *in-* IN-[2] + *ēbri(us)* drunk + *-ant-* -ANT]

in·e·bri·e·ty (in′i brī′i tē), *n.* drunkenness; intoxication. [IN-[2] + *ebriety* < L *ēbrietās*, equiv. to *ēbri(us)* drunk + *-etās* -ety, var. of -ITY]

in·e·bri·ate (*v.* in ē′brē āt′, i nē′-; *n., adj.* in ē′brē it, i nē′-), *v.,* **-at·ed, -at·ing,** *n., adj.* —*v.t.* **1.** to make drunk; intoxicate. **2.** to intoxicate mentally or emotionally; exhilarate or confuse the senses. —*n.* **3.** an intoxicated person. **4.** a habitual drunkard. —*adj.* **5.** Also, **in·e′bri·at′ed.** drunk; intoxicated. [< L *inēbriāt(us)* made drunk (ptp. of *inēbriāre*), equiv. to *in-* IN-[2] + *ēbri(us)* drunk + *-ātus* -ATE[1]] —**in·e′bri·a′tion,** *n.*
—**Syn. 4.** See **drunkard.**

in·ed·i·ble (in ed′ə bəl), *adj.* not edible; unfit to be eaten. [IN-[3] + EDIBLE] —**in·ed′i·bil′i·ty,** *n.*

in·ed·i·ta (in ed′i tə), *n.pl.* unpublished literary works: *the late author's inedita.* [< L, neut. pl. of *inēditus* not made known, equiv. to *in-* IN-[3] + *ēditus* (ptp. of *ēdere* to publish, lit., put or give out); see EDITION]

in·ed·it·ed (in ed′i tid), *adj.* **1.** unpublished: *the inedited letters of the deceased.* **2.** not edited; published without alterations, deletions, corrections, etc. [IN-[3] + EDIT + -ED[2]]

in·ed·u·ca·ble (in ej′ŏŏ kə bəl, -ed′yŏŏ-), *adj.* incapable of being educated, esp. because of some condition, as mental retardation or emotional disturbance, that prevents benefiting from instruction. [IN-[3] + EDUCABLE] —**in·ed′u·ca·bil′i·ty,** *n.*

in·ed·u·ca·tion (in ej′ŏŏ kā′shən, -ed′yŏŏ-), *n.* lack of education: *measures to remedy widespread ineducation.* [IN-[3] + EDUCATION]

in·ef·fa·ble (in ef′ə bəl), *adj.* **1.** incapable of being expressed or described; inexpressible; unspeakable: *ineffable joy.* **2.** not to be spoken; unutterable: *the ineffable name of the deity.* [late ME < L *ineffābil(is).* See IN-[3], EFFABLE] —**in·ef′fa·bil′i·ty, in·ef′fa·ble·ness,** *n.* —**in·ef′fa·bly,** *adv.*

in·ef·face·a·ble (in′i fā′sə bəl), *adj.* not effaceable; indelible: *an ineffaceable impression.* [IN-[3] + EFFACEABLE] —**in′ef·face′a·bil′i·ty,** *n.* —**in′ef·face′a·bly,** *adv.*

in·ef·fec·tive (in′i fek′tiv), *adj.* **1.** not effective; not producing results; ineffectual: *ineffective efforts; ineffective remedies.* **2.** inefficient or incompetent; incapable: *an ineffective salesman.* **3.** lacking in artistic effect, as a literary work, theatrical production, painting, etc. [IN-[3] + EFFECTIVE] —**in′ef·fec′tive·ly,** *adv.* —**in′ef·fec′tive·ness,** *n.*

in·ef·fec·tu·al (in′i fek′chŏŏ əl), *adj.* **1.** not effectual; without satisfactory or decisive effect: *an ineffectual remedy.* **2.** unavailing; futile: *His efforts to sell the house were ineffectual.* **3.** powerless; impotent. [ME; see IN-[3], EFFECTUAL] —**in′ef·fec′tu·al′i·ty, in′ef·fec′tu·al·ness,** *n.* —**in′ef·fec′tu·al·ly,** *adv.*
—**Syn. 2.** ineffective, fruitless, pointless, abortive. See **useless. 3.** feeble, weak.

in·ef·fi·ca·cious (in′ef ə kā′shəs), *adj.* not able to produce the desired effect. [IN-[3] + EFFICACIOUS] —**in′ef·fi·ca′cious·ly,** *adv.* —**in′ef·fi·ca′cious·ness, in·ef·fi·cac·i·ty** (in ef′ə kas′i tē), *n.*

in·ef·fi·ca·cy (in ef′ə kə sē), *n.* lack of power or capacity to produce the desired effect. [< LL *inefficācia.* See IN-[3], EFFICACY]

in·ef·fi·cien·cy (in′i fish′ən sē), *n., pl.* **-cies** for 2. **1.** the quality or condition of being inefficient; lack of efficiency. **2.** an instance of inefficiency: *Her work is riddled with inefficiencies.* [INEFFICIEN(T) + -CY]

in·ef·fi·cient (in′i fish′ənt), *adj.* not efficient; unable to effect or achieve the desired result with reasonable economy of means. [IN-[3] + EFFICIENT] —**in′ef·fi′cient·ly,** *adv.*
—**Syn.** See **incapable.**

in·e·las·tic (in′i las′tik), *adj.* **1.** not elastic; lacking flexibility or resilience; unyielding. **2.** *Econ.* relatively unresponsive to changes, as demand when it fails to increase in proportion to a decrease in price. Cf. **elastic** (def. 6). [IN-[3] + ELASTIC] —**in·e·las·tic·i·ty** (in′i la stis′i tē), *n.*
—**Syn. 1.** inflexible; rigid, uncompromising.

in·el·e·gance (in el′ə gəns), *n.* **1.** the quality or state of being inelegant; lack of elegance. **2.** that which is inelegant or ungraceful. [INELEG(ANT) + -ANCE]

in·el·e·gan·cy (in el′ə gən sē), *n., pl.* **-cies.** inelegance. [INELEGAN(T) + -CY]

in·el·e·gant (in el′ə gənt), *adj.* not elegant; lacking in refinement, gracefulness, or good taste. [< L *inēlegant-* (s. of *inēlegāns*). See IN-[3], ELEGANT] —**in·el′e·gant·ly,** *adv.*

in·el·i·gi·ble (in el′i jə bəl), *adj.* **1.** not eligible; not proper or suitable as a choice. **2.** legally disqualified to hold an office. **3.** legally disqualified to function as a juror, voter, witness, etc., or to become the recipient of a privilege. —*n.* **4.** a person who is ineligible, as a suitor, team member, etc. [IN-[3] + ELIGIBLE] —**in·el′i·gi·bil′i·ty, in·el′i·gi·ble·ness,** *n.* —**in·el′i·gi·bly,** *adv.*

in·el·o·quent (in el′ə kwənt), *adj.* not eloquent. [IN-[3] + ELOQUENT] —**in·el′o·quence,** *n.* —**in·el′o·quent·ly,** *adv.*

in·e·luc·ta·ble (in′i luk′tə bəl), *adj.* incapable of being evaded; inescapable: *an ineluctable destiny.* [< L *inēluctābil(is)*, equiv. to *in-* IN-[3] + *ēluctā(rī)* (to) surmount (*ē-* E- + *luctārī* to wrestle) + *-bilis* -BLE] —**in′e·luc′ta·bil′i·ty,** *n.* —**in′e·luc′ta·bly,** *adv.*

in·e·lud·i·ble (in′i lōō′də bəl), *adj.* not eludible; inescapable. [IN-[3] + ELUDE + -IBLE] —**in′e·lud′i·bly,** *adv.*

in·e·nar·ra·ble (in′i nar′ə bəl), *adj.* incapable of being described or narrated. [late ME < L *inēnarrābil(is)*, equiv. to *in-* IN-[3] + *ēnarrābilis* explicable; see E-, NARRATE, -BLE]

in·ept (in ept′, i nept′), *adj.* **1.** not apt; without skill or aptitude for a particular task or assignment: *He is inept at mechanical tasks. She is inept at dealing with people.* **2.** inappropriate; out of place. **3.** absurd or foolish: *an inept remark.* [< L *inept(us)*, equiv. to *in-* IN-[3] + *-eptus*, var. of *aptus* APT] —**in·ept′ly,** *adv.* —**in·ept′ness,** *n.*
—**Syn. 1.** unfitting, unsuited. **3.** stupid, pointless, inane. —**Ant. 1.** suited.

in·ept·i·tude (in ep′ti tōōd′, -tyōōd′, i nep′-), *n.* **1.** quality or condition of being inept. **2.** an inept act or remark. [< L *ineptitūd(ō).* See INEPT, -I-, -TUDE]

in·e·qual·i·ty (in′i kwol′i tē), *n., pl.* **-ties.** **1.** the condition of being unequal; lack of equality; disparity: *inequality of size.* **2.** social disparity: *the inequality between the rich and the poor.* **3.** disparity or inadequacy in natural endowments, as between one person and another: *a startling inequality of intellect, talents, and physical stamina.* **4.** injustice; partiality. **5.** unevenness, as of surface. **6.** an instance of unevenness. **7.** variableness, as of climate, temperament, etc. **8.** *Astron.* **a.** any component part of the departure from uniformity in astronomical phenomena, esp. in orbital motion. **b.** the amount of such a departure. **9.** *Math.* an expression or proposition that two quantities are unequal, indicated by the symbol <, signifying that the quantity preceding the symbol is less than that following, or >, signifying that the quantity preceding the symbol is greater than that following: often used in determining the possible values of a variable included in one or both quantities, as in determining the possible values of x in the expression $3x + 5 > 6x + 1$. [late ME < L *inaequālitās*. See IN-³, EQUALITY]

in·e·qui·lat·er·al (in′ē kwə lat′ər əl), *adj.* not equilateral; having unequal sides. [IN-³ + EQUILATERAL] **—in′e·qui·lat′er·al·ly,** *adv.*

in·eq·ui·ta·ble (in ek′wi tə bəl), *adj.* not equitable; unjust or unfair. [IN-³ + EQUITABLE] **—in·eq′ui·ta·ble·ness,** *n.* **—in·eq′ui·ta·bly,** *adv.*

in·eq·ui·ty (in ek′wi tē), *n., pl.* **-ties** for 2. **1.** lack of equity; unfairness. **2.** an unfair circumstance or proceeding: *His students resented his inequities in grading papers.* [IN-³ + EQUITY]

in·e·qui·valve (in ē′kwə valv′), *adj.* (of a bivalve mollusk) having the valves of the shell unequal in shape and size. [IN-³ + EQUI- + VALVE]

in·e·rad·i·ca·ble (in′i rad′ə kə bəl), *adj.* not eradicable; not capable of being eradicated, rooted out, or completely removed. [IN-³ + ERADICABLE] **—in′e·rad′i·ca·ble·ness,** *n.* **—in′e·rad′i·ca·bly,** *adv.*

in·e·ras·a·ble (in′i rā′sə bəl), *adj.* not erasable; incapable of being erased or effaced. [IN-³ + ERASABLE] **—in′e·ras′a·ble·ness,** *n.* **—in′e·ras′a·bly,** *adv.*

in·er·ra·ble (in er′ə bəl, -ûr′-), *adj.* incapable of erring; infallible. [< LL *inerrābil(is)* unerring, equiv. to L *in-* IN-³ + *errā(re)* (to) ERR + *-bilis* -BLE] **—in·er′ra·bil′i·ty, in·er′ra·ble·ness,** *n.* **—in·er′ra·bly,** *adv.*

in·er·rant (in er′ənt, -ûr′-), *adj.* free from error. [< L *inerrant-*, equiv. to *in-* IN-³ + *errant-* (s. of *errāns* wandering, prp. of *errāre*); see ERR, -ANT] **—in·er′ran·cy,** *n.* **—in·er′rant·ly,** *adv.*

in·er·rat·ic (in′i rat′ik), *adj.* not erratic or wandering; fixed: *an inerratic star.* [IN-³ + ERRATIC]

in·ert (in ûrt′, i nûrt′), *adj.* **1.** having no inherent power of action, motion, or resistance (opposed to *active*): *inert matter.* **2.** *Chem.* having little or no ability to react, as nitrogen which occurs uncombined in the atmosphere. **3.** *Pharm.* having no pharmacological action, as the excipient of a pill. **4.** inactive or sluggish by habit or nature. [< L *inert-* (s. of *iners*) unskillful, equiv. to *in-* IN-³ + *-ert-*, var. of *art-* (s. of *ars*) skill; see ART¹] **—in·ert′ly,** *adv.* **—in·ert′ness,** *n.*
—Syn. 1. immobile, unmoving, lifeless, motionless. **3.** See **inactive.**

in·ert·ance (in ûr′tᵊns, i nûr′-), *n.* *Acoustics.* the effect of inertia in an acoustic system, an impeding of the transmission of sound through the system. Also called **acoustic inertance, acoustic mass.** [INERT + -ANCE]

in·er·tia (in ûr′shə, i nûr′-), *n.* **1.** inert condition; inactivity; sluggishness. **2.** *Physics.* **a.** the property of matter by which it retains its state of rest or its velocity along a straight line so long as it is not acted upon by an external force. **b.** an analogous property of a force: *electric inertia.* **3.** *Med.* lack of activity, esp. as applied to a uterus during childbirth when its contractions have decreased or stopped. [< L: lack of skill, slothfulness. See INERT, -IA] **—in·er′tial,** *adj.*

iner′tial guid′ance, *Rocketry.* guidance of a missile solely by instruments within it that determine its course on the basis of the directions and magnitudes of acceleration which the missile undergoes in flight (distinguished from *command guidance*).

iner′tial sys′tem, *Physics.* a frame of reference in which a body remains at rest or moves with constant linear velocity unless acted upon by forces. Also called **iner′tial ref′erence frame′.** Cf. **law of motion.**

I·nes (ī′nes, ī nes′, ē′nes, ē nes′), *n.* a girl's given name, form of **Agnes.** Also, **Inez.**

in·es·cap·a·ble (in′e skā′pə bəl), *adj.* incapable of being escaped, ignored, or avoided: *inescapable responsibilities.* [IN-³ + ESCAPABLE] **—in′es·cap′a·ble·ness,** *n.* **—in′es·cap′a·bly,** *adv.*

in·es·cutch·eon (in′e skuch′ən), *n.* *Heraldry.* a charge in the form of an escutcheon, sometimes placed over the fess point so as to cover partly the other charges of the escutcheon. [IN-¹ + ESCUTCHEON]

in es·se (in es′e; *Eng.* in es′ē), *Latin.* in being; in actuality; actually existing (contrasted with *in posse*).

in·es·sen·tial (in′i sen′shəl), *adj.* **1.** not essential; not necessary; nonessential. **2.** without essence; insubstantial. **—***n.* **3.** that which is not essential. [IN-³ + ESSENTIAL] **—in′es·sen′ti·al′i·ty,** *n.*

in·es·sive (in es′iv), *Gram.* **—***adj.* **1.** noting a case, as in Finnish, whose distinctive function is to indicate place in or within which. **—***n.* **2.** the inessive case. [< L *iness(e)* to be in, at, or on, equiv. to *in-* IN-² + *esse* to be (see IS) + -IVE]

in·es·ti·ma·ble (in es′tə mə bəl), *adj.* **1.** incapable of being estimated; too great to be estimated: *the inestimable number of stars.* **2.** of incalculable value: *jewels of inestimable worth.* [ME < L *inaestimābil(is).* See IN-³, ESTIMABLE] **—in·es′ti·ma·bil′i·ty, in·es′ti·ma·ble·ness,** *n.* **—in·es′ti·ma·bly,** *adv.*

in·e·va·si·ble (in′i vā′sə bəl), *adj.* incapable of being evaded; certain: *an inevasible law of nature.* [IN-³ + *evasible* < L *ēvās(us)* (ptp. of *ēvādere* to EVADE) + -IBLE]

in·ev·i·ta·ble (in ev′i tə bəl), *adj.* **1.** unable to be avoided, evaded, or escaped; certain; necessary: *an inevitable conclusion.* **2.** sure to occur, happen, or come; unalterable: *Man's inevitable end is death.* **—***n.* **3.** that which is unavoidable. [ME < L *inēvītābil(is).* See IN-³, EVITABLE] **—in·ev′i·ta·bil′i·ty, in·ev′i·ta·ble·ness,** *n.* **—in·ev′i·ta·bly,** *adv.*

in·ex·act (in′ig zakt′), *adj.* not exact; not strictly accurate. [IN-³ + EXACT] **—in′ex·act′ly,** *adv.* **—in′ex·act′ness,** *n.*

in·ex·act·i·tude (in′ig zak′ti to͞od′, -tyo͞od′), *n.* **1.** the quality or state of being inexact or inaccurate; inexactness. **2.** an instance of this. [< F; see IN-³, EXACTITUDE]

in·ex·cus·a·ble (in′ik skyo͞o′zə bəl), *adj.* not excusable; incapable of being justified. [ME < L *inexcūsābilis*; see IN-³, EXCUSABLE] **—in′ex·cus′a·bil′i·ty, in′ex·cus′a·ble·ness,** *n.* **—in′ex·cus′a·bly,** *adv.*

in·ex·e·cu·tion (in ek′sə kyo͞o′shən, in′ek-), *n.* lack or neglect of execution. [IN-³ + EXECUTION]

in·ex·er·tion (in′ig zûr′shən), *n.* lack of exertion; inaction. [IN-³ + EXERTION]

in·ex·haust·i·ble (in′ig zôs′tə bəl), *adj.* **1.** not exhaustible; incapable of being totally depleted: *an inexhaustible supply.* **2.** unfailing; tireless: *an inexhaustible runner.* [< L *inexhaust(us)* not exhausted (see IN-³, EXHAUST) + -IBLE] **—in′ex·haust′i·bil′i·ty, in′ex·haust′i·ble·ness,** *n.* **—in′ex·haust′i·bly,** *adv.*

in·ex·ist·ent¹ (in′ig zis′tənt), *adj.* not existent; having no existence. [< LL *inexistent-* (s. of *inexistēns*) not existing. See IN-³, EXISTENT] **—in′ex·ist′ence, in′ex·ist′en·cy,** *n.*

in·ex·ist·ent² (in′ig zis′tənt), *adj.* *Archaic.* existing within; inherent. [< LL *inexistent-* (s. of *inexistēns*). See IN-², EXISTENT]

in·ex·o·ra·ble (in ek′sər ə bəl), *adj.* **1.** unyielding; unalterable: *inexorable truth; inexorable justice.* **2.** not to be persuaded, moved, or affected by prayers or entreaties: *an inexorable creditor.* [< L *inexōrābil(is).* See IN-³, EXORABLE] **—in·ex′o·ra·bil′i·ty, in·ex′o·ra·ble·ness,** *n.* **—in·ex′o·ra·bly,** *adv.*
—Syn. 2. unbending; severe, relentless, unrelenting, implacable, merciless, cruel, pitiless. See **inflexible.** **—Ant. 2.** flexible; merciful.

in·ex·pe·di·ent (in′ik spē′dē ənt), *adj.* not expedient; not suitable, judicious, or advisable. [IN-³ + EXPEDIENT] **—in′ex·pe′di·ence, in′ex·pe′di·en·cy,** *n.* **—in′ex·pe′di·ent·ly,** *adv.*

in·ex·pen·sive (in′ik spen′siv), *adj.* not expensive; not high in price; costing little. [IN-³ + EXPENSIVE] **—in′ex·pen′sive·ly,** *adv.* **—in′ex·pen′sive·ness,** *n.*
—Syn. cheap. —Ant. costly.

in·ex·pe·ri·ence (in′ik spēr′ē əns), *n.* lack of experience, or of knowledge or skill gained from experience. [< LL *inexperientia.* See IN-³, EXPERIENCE]

in·ex·pe·ri·enced (in′ik spēr′ē ənst), *adj.* not experienced; without knowledge or skill gained from experience. [INEXPERIENCE + -ED²]

in·ex·pert (in eks′pûrt, in′ik spûrt′), *adj.* not expert; unskilled. [late ME < L *inexpert(us).* See IN-³, EXPERT] **—in·ex′pert·ly,** *adv.* **—in·ex′pert·ness,** *n.*

in·ex·pi·a·ble (in eks′pē ə bəl), *adj.* **1.** not to be expiated; not allowing for expiation or atonement: *an inexpiable crime.* **2.** not to be appeased by expiation; implacable: *inexpiable hate.* [< L *inexpiābil(is).* See IN-³, EXPIABLE] **—in·ex′pi·a·ble·ness,** *n.* **—in·ex′pi·a·bly,** *adv.*

in·ex·pi·ate (in eks′pē āt′), *adj.* not expiated or atoned for: *His infamous acts remain inexpiate.* [< LL *inexpiāt(us)*, equiv. to L *in-* IN-³ + *expiātus*; see EXPIATE]

in·ex·plain·a·ble (in′ik splā′nə bəl), *adj.* not explainable; incapable of being explained; inexplicable. [IN-³ + EXPLAINABLE]

in·ex·pli·ca·ble (in eks′plə kə bəl *or, esp. Brit.,* in′ik splik′ə bəl), *adj.* not explicable; incapable of being explained. [ME < L *inexplicābil(is).* See IN-³, EXPLICABLE] **—in·ex′pli·ca·bil′i·ty, in·ex′pli·ca·ble·ness,** *n.* **—in·ex′pli·ca·bly,** *adv.*

in·ex·plic·it (in′ik splis′it), *adj.* not explicit or clear; not clearly stated. [< L *inexplicit(us)* not straightforward. See IN-³, EXPLICIT] **—in′ex·plic′it·ly,** *adv.* **—in′ex·plic′it·ness,** *n.*

in·ex·plo·sive (in′ik splō′siv), *adj.* not explosive; incapable of exploding or being exploded. [IN-³ + EXPLOSIVE]

in·ex·press·i·ble (in′ik spres′ə bəl), *adj.* **1.** not expressible; incapable of being uttered or represented in words: *a scene of inexpressible beauty.* **—***n.* **2. inexpressibles,** *Archaic.* trousers; pants. [IN-³ + EXPRESSIBLE] **—in′ex·press′i·bil′i·ty, in′ex·press′i·ble·ness,** *n.* **—in′ex·press′i·bly,** *adv.*

in·ex·pres·sive (in′ik spres′iv), *adj.* **1.** not expressive; lacking in expression. **2.** *Obs.* inexpressible. [IN-³ + EXPRESSIVE] **—in′ex·pres′sive·ly,** *adv.* **—in′ex·pres′sive·ness,** *n.*

in·ex·pug·na·ble (in′ik spug′nə bəl), *adj.* incapable of being taken by force; impregnable; unconquerable. [< L *inexpugnābil(is)*, equiv. to *in-* IN-³ + *expugnā(re)* (*expugnā(re)* (to) take by storm (*ex-* EX-¹ + *pugnāre* to fight) + *-bilis* -BLE)] **—in′ex·pug′na·bil′i·ty, in′ex·pug′na·ble·ness,** *n.* **—in′ex·pug′na·bly,** *adv.*

in·ex·pung·i·ble (in′ik spun′jə bəl), *adj.* that cannot be expunged, erased, or obliterated: *the inexpungible smell of lemon oil in the room; an inexpungible memory of our first meeting.* Also, **in·ex·punge·a·ble.** [IN-³ + EXPUNGE + -IBLE] **—in′ex·pung′i·bil′i·ty,** *n.*

in·ex·ten·si·ble (in′ik sten′sə bəl), *adj.* not extensible; incapable of being extended or stretched. [IN-³ + EXTENSIBLE] **—in′ex·ten′si·bil′i·ty,** *n.*

in ex·ten·so (in eks ten′sō; *Eng.* in ik sten′sō), *Latin.* at full length.

in·ex·tin·guish·a·ble (in′ik sting′gwi shə bəl), *adj.* not extinguishable; not to be extinguished, quenched, suppressed, or brought to an end: *inextinguishable fire; inextinguishable rage.* [IN-³ + EXTINGUISHABLE] **—in′ex·tin′guish·a·bly,** *adv.*

in·ex·tir·pa·ble (in′ik stûr′pə bəl), *adj.* incapable of being extirpated; not removable or eradicable: *an inextirpable disease.* [< L *inex(s)tirpābil(is).* See IN-³, EXTIRPABLE] **—in′ex·tir′pa·ble·ness,** *n.*

in ex·tre·mis (in eks tre′mēs; *Eng.* in ik strē′mis), *Latin.* **1.** in extremity. **2.** near death. [lit., on the outer edges, i.e. at the uttermost limit]

in·ex·tri·ca·ble (in eks′trə kə bəl), *adj.* **1.** from which one cannot extricate oneself: *an inextricable maze.* **2.** incapable of being disentangled, undone, loosed, or solved: *an inextricable knot; an inextricable grasp.* **3.** hopelessly intricate, involved, or perplexing: *inextricable confusion.* [ME < L *inextrīcābil(is).* See IN-³, EXTRICABLE] **—in·ex′tri·ca·bil′i·ty, in·ex′tri·ca·ble·ness,** *n.* **—in·ex′tri·ca·bly,** *adv.*

INF (inf), *n.* European-based U.S. nuclear weapons that were capable of striking the Soviet Union and Soviet ones that could hit Western Europe. [*I(ntermediate-range) N(uclear) F(orces)*]

inf (inf), *n.* *Math.* infimum.

Inf., **1.** infantry. **2.** infuse. [< L *infunde*]

inf., **1.** infantry. **2.** inferior. **3.** infield. **4.** infielder. **5.** infinitive. **6.** infinity. **7.** infirmary. **8.** information. **9.** below; after. [< L *infra*] **10.** (in prescriptions) **a.** infuse. [< L *infunde*] **b.** an infusion. [< L *infūsum*]

in f., in the end; finally. [< L *in fine*]

in·fal·li·ble (in fal′ə bəl), *adj.* **1.** not fallible; exempt from liability to error, as persons, their judgment, pronouncements, etc. **2.** absolutely trustworthy or sure: *an infallible rule.* **3.** unfailing in effectiveness or operation; certain: *an infallible remedy.* **4.** *Rom. Cath. Ch.* immune from fallacy or liability to error in expounding matters of faith or morals by virtue of the promise made by Christ to the Church. **—***n.* **5.** an infallible person or thing. [ME < ML *infallibil(is).* See IN-³, FALLIBLE] **—in·fal′li·bil′i·ty, in·fal′li·ble·ness,** *n.* **—in·fal′li·bly,** *adv.*
—Syn. 2, 3. See **reliable.**

in·fa·mous (in′fə məs), *adj.* **1.** having an extremely bad reputation: *an infamous city.* **2.** deserving of or causing an evil reputation; detestable; shamefully bad: *infamous conduct.* **3.** *Law.* **a.** deprived of certain rights as a citizen, as a consequence of conviction of certain offenses. **b.** of or pertaining to offenses involving such deprivation. [ME; see IN-³, FAMOUS] **—in′fa·mous·ly,** *adv.* **—in′fa·mous·ness,** *n.*
—Syn. 1. disreputable, ill-famed, notorious. **2.** disgraceful, scandalous; nefarious, odious, wicked, shocking, vile, base, heinous, villainous. **—Ant. 1.** reputable. **2.** praiseworthy.

in·fa·my (in′fə mē), *n., pl.* **-mies** for 3. **1.** evil reputation, public reproach, or strong condemnation as the result of a shameful, criminal, or outrageous act: *a day that will live in infamy.* **2.** infamous character or conduct. **3.** an infamous act or circumstance. **4.** *Law.* loss of rights, incurred by conviction of an infamous offense. [late ME *infamye* < L *infāmia*, equiv. to *infām(is)* ill-famed (*in-* IN-³ + *fām(a)* fame + *-is* adj. suffix) + *-ia* -Y³]
—Syn. 1. disrepute, obloquy, odium, opprobrium, shame. See **disgrace. —Ant. 1.** credit, honor.

in·fan·cy (in′fən sē), *n., pl.* **-cies. 1.** the state or period of being an infant; babyhood; early childhood. **2.** the corresponding period in the existence of anything: *Space science is still in its infancy.* **3.** infants collectively. **4.** *Law.* the period of life to the age of majority, usually comprising the first 21 years; minority; nonage. [< L *infantia.* See INFANT, -CY]

in·fant (in′fənt), *n.* **1.** a child during the earliest period of its life, esp. before able to walk; baby. **2.** *Law.* a person who is not of full age, esp. one who has not attained the age of 21 years; a minor. **3.** a beginner, as in experience or learning; novice: *The new candidate is a political infant.* **4.** *Rare.* anything in the first stage of existence or progress. **—***adj.* **5.** of or pertaining to infants or infancy: *infant years.* **6.** being in infancy: *an infant king.* **7.** being in the earliest stage: *an infant industry.* **8.** of or pertaining to the legal state of infancy; minor. [< L *infant-* (s. of *infāns*) not speaking, equiv. to *in-* IN-³ + *-fāns*, prp. of *fārī* to speak; r. ME *enfaunt* < AF] **—in′fant·hood′,** *n.* **—in′fant·like′,** *adj.*

in·fan·ta (in fan′tə), *n.* **1.** a daughter of the king of Spain or of Portugal. **2.** an infante's wife. [< Sp or Pg; fem. of INFANTE]

in·fan·te (in fan′tā), *n.* any son of the king of Spain or of Portugal who is not heir to the throne. [< Sp or Pg; see INFANT]

in·fan·ti·cide (in fan′ti sīd′), *n.* **1.** the act of killing an infant. **2.** a person who kills an infant. [< LL *infanticīd(ium).* See INFANT, -CIDE] **—in·fan′ti·cid′al,** *adj.*

in·fan·tile (in′fən tīl′, -til), *adj.* **1.** characteristic of or befitting an infant; babyish; childish: *infantile behavior.* **2.** of or pertaining to infants or infancy: *infantile diseases.* **3.** being in the earliest stage of development, as a land formation: *an infantile stream.* [< LL *infantil(is).* See INFANT, -ILE] **—in·fan·til·i·ty** (in′fən til′i tē), *n.*
—Syn. 1. puerile, immature, weak. See **childish.** **—Ant 1.** adult.

in′fantile paral′ysis, *Pathol.* poliomyelitis.

in·fan·ti·lism (in′fən tᵊliz′əm, -tī liz′-, in fan′tᵊliz′əm), *n.* **1.** a speech disorder characterized by speech and voice patterns that are typical of very young children. **2.** *Psychol.* the persistence in an adult of markedly childish anatomical, physiological, or psychological characteristics. [INFANTILE + -ISM]

in·fan·tine (in′fən tīn′, -tin), *adj.* infantile. [INFANT + -INE¹, modeled on MF *enfantin*]

in·fan·try (in′fən trē), *n., pl.* **-tries. 1.** soldiers or military units that fight on foot, with bayonets, rifles, machine guns, grenades, mortars, etc. **2.** a branch of an army composed of such soldiers. [< It *infanteria*, equiv. to *infante* boy, foot-soldier (see INFANT) + *-ria* -RY]

in·fan·try·man (in′fən trē mən), *n., pl.* **-men.** a soldier of the infantry. [INFANTRY + MAN¹]

in′fants' school′, *Brit.* a primary school for children from about five to seven years of age. Also, **in′fant school′.**

in·farct (in färkt′), *n.* *Pathol.* a localized area of tissue that is dying or dead, having been deprived of its blood supply because of an obstruction by embolism or thrombosis. [< NL *infarct(us)* < L: stuffed in, equiv. to *in-* IN-² + *far(c)tus* (ptp. of *farcīre*): *farc-* (see FARCE) + *-tus* ptp. suffix] **—in·farct′ed,** *adj.*

in·farc·tion (in färk′shən), *n.* *Pathol.* **1.** the formation of an infarct. **2.** an infarct. [INFARCT + -ION]

in·fare (in′fâr′), *n.* *Chiefly Dial.* a party or reception for a newly married couple. [OE *infær* a going in. See IN-¹, FARE]

in·fat·u·ate (*v.* in fach′o͞o āt′; *adj., n.* in fach′o͞o it, -āt′), *v.,* **-at·ed, -at·ing,** *adj., n.* **—***v.t.* **1.** to affect with folly; make foolish or fatuous. **2.** to inspire or possess with a foolish or unreasoning passion, as of love. **—***adj.* **3.** infatuated. **—***n.* **4.** a person who is infatuated. [< L *infatuāt(us)*, ptp. of *infatuāre.* See IN-², FATUOUS, -ATE¹] **—in·fat′u·a′tor,** *n.*

in·fat·u·at·ed (in fach′o͞o ā′tid), *adj.* characterized by foolish or irrational love or desire; blindly in love. [INFATUATE + -ED²] **—in·fat′u·at′ed·ly,** *adv.*
—Syn. fond, doting, overaffectionate.

in·fat·u·a·tion (in fach′o͞o ā′shən), *n.* **1.** act of infatuating. **2.** state of being infatuated. **3.** foolish or all-absorbing passion: *His feeling verged on infatuation.* **4.** the object of a person's infatuation: *Mildred is his latest infatuation. When I was a kid my infatuation was stamp collecting.* [< LL *infatuātiōn-* (s. of *infatuātiō*). See INFATUATE, -ION]

in·fea·si·ble (in fē′zə bəl), *adj.* not feasible; impracticable. [IN-³ + FEASIBLE] **—in·fea′si·bil′i·ty, in·fea′si·ble·ness,** *n.*

in·fect (in fekt′), *v.t.* **1.** to affect or contaminate (a person, organ, wound, etc.) with disease-producing germs. **2.** to affect with disease. **3.** to taint or contaminate with something that affects quality, character, or condition unfavorably: *to infect the air with poison gas.* **4.** to corrupt or affect morally: *The news of the gold strike infected him with greed.* **5.** to imbue with some pernicious belief, opinion, etc. **6.** to affect so as to influence feeling or action: *His courage infected the others.* **7.** *Law.* to taint with illegality, or expose to penalty, forfeiture, etc. —*v.i.* **8.** to become infected: *Neglect caused his wound to infect.* —*adj.* **9.** *Archaic.* infected. [ME *infecte(n)* < L *infect(us)* worked in, stained, tainted (ptp. of *inficere*), equiv. to *in-* IN-² + *fec-* (var. of *fac-* make) + *-tus* ptp. suffix] —**in·fect′ant,** *adj.* —**in·fect′ed·ness,** *n.* —**in·fec′tor, in·fect′er,** *n.*

in·fec·tion (in fek′shən), *n.* **1.** act or fact of infecting; state of being infected. **2.** an infecting with germs of disease, as through the medium of infected insects, air, water, clothing, etc. **3.** an infecting agency or influence. **4.** an infectious disease: *Is this infection very dangerous?* **5.** the condition of suffering an infection. **6.** corruption of another's opinions, beliefs, moral principles, etc.; moral contamination. **7.** an influence or impulse passing from one to another and affecting feeling or action. **8.** *Gram.* (in Celtic languages) assimilation in which a vowel is influenced by a following vowel or semivowel; umlaut. [ME *infeccio(u)n* < LL *infectiōn-* (s. of *infectiō*). See INFECT, -ION]

in·fec·tious (in fek′shəs), *adj.* **1.** communicable by infection, as from one person to another or from one part of the body to another: *infectious diseases.* **2.** causing or communicating infection. **3.** tending to spread from one to another: *Yawning is infectious.* **4.** *Law.* capable of contaminating with illegality; exposing to seizure or forfeiture. **5.** *Obs.* diseased. [INFECT(ION) + -IOUS] —**in·fec′tious·ly,** *adv.* —**in·fec′tious·ness,** *n.*
—**Syn. 3.** catching. See **contagious.**

infec′tious ane′mia of hors′es, *Vet. Pathol.* an infectious disease, caused by a virus, characterized by weakness and recurring fever, and transmitted by means of food and water contaminated by the urine of infected animals. Also called **equine infectious anemia, swamp fever.**

infec′tious ectrome′lia, *Vet. Pathol.* ectromelia (def. 2).

infec′tious la·ryn′go·tra·che·i′tis (lə ring′gō-trā′kē ī′tis, -ring′-), *Vet. Pathol.* a contagious disease of adult chickens, caused by a virus and characterized by inflammation and hemorrhage of the larynx and trachea and the resulting production of a blood-tinged mucus which is responsible for a rattling sound in the throat and, in many cases, for asphyxiation.

infec′tious mononucleo′sis, *Pathol.* an acute, infectious form of mononucleosis characterized by sudden fever, a benign swelling of lymph nodes, and an increase in the blood stream of leucocytes having only one nucleus. Also called **glandular fever.**

infec′tious myxomato′sis, *Vet. Pathol.* myxomatosis.

in·fec·tive (in fek′tiv), *adj.* infectious. [ME < ML *infectīv(us).* See INFECT, -IVE] —**in·fec′tive·ness, in′fec·tiv′i·ty,** *n.*

in·fe·cund (in fē′kənd, -fek′ənd), *adj.* not fecund; unfruitful; barren. [ME *infecounde* < L *infēcund(us).* See IN-³, FECUND] —**in·fe·cun·di·ty** (in′fi kun′di tē), *n.*

in·fe·lic·i·tous (in′fə lis′i təs), *adj.* **1.** not felicitous, happy, or fortunate; unhappy. **2.** inapt; inappropriate: *an infelicitous remark.* [IN-³ + FELICITOUS] —**in′fe·lic′i·tous·ly,** *adv.*

in·fe·lic·i·ty (in′fə lis′i tē), *n., pl.* **-ties** for 3, 5. **1.** the quality or state of being unhappy; unhappiness. **2.** misfortune; bad luck. **3.** an unfortunate circumstance; misfortune. **4.** inaptness or inappropriateness, as of action or expression. **5.** something inapt or infelicitous: *infelicities of style.* [ME *infelicite* < L *infēlīcitās.* See IN-³, FELICITY]

in·felt (in′felt′), *adj.* *Rare.* felt within; experienced inwardly. [IN-¹ + FELT¹]

in·feoff (in fef′, -fēf′), *v.t.* *Obs.* enfeoff. —**in·feoff′ment,** *n.*

in·fer (in fûr′), *v.,* **-ferred, -fer·ring.** —*v.t.* **1.** to derive by reasoning; conclude or judge from premises or evidence: *They inferred his displeasure from his absence.* **2.** (of facts, circumstances, statements, etc.) to indicate or involve as a conclusion; lead to. **3.** to hint; imply; suggest. **4.** to guess; speculate; surmise. —*v.i.* **5.** to draw a conclusion, as by reasoning. [< L *inferre,* equiv. to *in-* IN-² + *ferre* to bring, carry, BEAR¹] —**in·fer′a·ble, in·fer′i·ble, in·fer′ri·ble,** *adj.* —**in·fer′a·bly,** *adv.* —**in·fer′rer,** *n.*
—**Usage.** INFER in the sense of *to hint* or *imply* is often criticized, and, although it occurs in writing and is frequently heard in speech, schoolteachers and editors nevertheless regard it as a solecism for IMPLY.

in·fer·ence (in′fər əns, -frəns), *n.* **1.** the act or process of inferring. **2.** that which is inferred: *to make rash inferences.* **3.** *Logic.* **a.** the process of deriving the strict logical consequences of assumed premises. **b.** the process of arriving at some conclusion which, though it is not logically derivable from the assumed premises, possesses some degree of probability relative to the premises. **c.** a proposition reached by a process of inference. [< ML *inferentia.* See INFER, -ENCE]

in·fer·en·tial (in′fə ren′shəl), *adj.* of, pertaining to, by, or dependent upon inference. [< ML *inferenti(a).* See INFERENCE, -AL¹] —**in′fer·en′tial·ly,** *adv.*

In·fer·i (in′fə rī′), *n.pl.* *Rom. Myth.* **1.** those who live in infernal regions. **2.** the gods of the underworld.

in·fe·ri·or (in fēr′ē ər), *adj.* **1.** lower in station, rank, degree, or grade (often fol. by *to*): *a rank inferior to colonel.* **2.** lower in place or position; closer to the bottom or base: *descending into the inferior regions of the earth.* **3.** of comparatively low grade; poor in quality: *an inferior product.* **4.** less important, valuable, or excellent: *Grade B is inferior to Grade A.* **5.** working in a way that is comparatively poor or mediocre: *an inferior observer of human nature.* **6.** *Bot.* **a.** situated below some other organ. **b.** (of a calyx) inserted below the ovary. **c.** (of an ovary) having a superior calyx. **7.** *Anat., Zool.* (of an organ or part) lower in place or position; situated beneath another. **8.** *Astron.* **a.** (of a planet) having an orbit within that of the earth: applied to the planets Mercury and Venus. **b.** (of a conjunction of an inferior planet) taking place between the sun and the earth. **c.** lying below the horizon: *the inferior part of a meridian.* **9.** *Print.* written or printed low on a line of text, as the "2" in H_2O; subscript. Cf. **superior** (def. 10). —*n.* **10.** one inferior to another or others, as in rank or merit. **11.** Also called **subscript.** *Print.* a letter, number, or symbol written or printed low on a line of text. Cf. **superior** (def. 13). [ME < L, equiv. to *infer(us)* below + *-ior* comp. suffix] —**in·fe·ri·or·i·ty** (in fēr′ē ôr′i tē, -or′-), *n.* —**in·fe′ri·or·ly,** *adv.*

infe′rior goods′, *Econ.* commodities that are less in demand as consumer income rises. Cf. **superior goods.**

inferior′ity com′plex, **1.** *Psychiatry.* intense feeling of inferiority, producing a personality characterized either by extreme reticence or, as a result of overcompensation, by extreme aggressiveness. **2.** lack of self-esteem; feeling of inadequacy; lack of self-confidence.

in·fer·nal (in fûr′nəl), *adj.* **1.** *Class. Myth.* of or pertaining to the underworld. **2.** of, inhabiting, or befitting hell. **3.** hellish; fiendish; diabolical: *an infernal plot.* **4.** *Informal.* outrageous: *an infernal nuisance.* [ME < LL *infernāl(is),* equiv. to L *infern(a)* the lower regions (neut. pl. of *infernus* hellish; see INFERIOR) + *-ālis* -AL¹] —**in′fer·nal′i·ty,** *n.* —**in·fer′nal·ly,** *adv.*

infer′nal machine′, a concealed or disguised explosive device intended to destroy life or property.

in·fer·no (in fûr′nō), *n., pl.* **-nos.** **1.** hell; the infernal regions. **2.** a place or region that resembles hell: *The ironworks was an inferno of molten steel and half-naked bodies.* **3.** (*cap., italics*) the first part of Dante's *Divine Comedy,* depicting hell and the suffering of the damned. Cf. **paradise** (def. 7), **purgatory** (def. 2). Italian, **Inferno.** [< It < L *infernus* hellish]

infero-, a learned borrowing from Latin meaning "below," "lying beneath," used in the formation of compound words: *inferoanterior.* [< NL, repr. L *inferus* below]

in·fe·ro·an·te·ri·or (in′fə rō an tēr′ē ər), *adj.* below and in front. [INFERO- + ANTERIOR]

in·fer·tile (in fûr′təl *or, esp. Brit.,* -tīl), *adj.* not fertile; unproductive; sterile; barren: *infertile soil.* [< L *infertil(is).* See IN-³, FERTILE] —**in·fer′tile·ly,** *adv.* —**in′fer·til′i·ty, in·fer′tile·ness,** *n.*
—**Syn.** sterile, infecund.

in·fest (in fest′), *v.t.* **1.** to haunt or overrun in a troublesome manner, as predatory bands, destructive animals, or vermin do. **2.** to be numerous in, as anything troublesome: *the cares that infest the day.* **3.** *Archaic.* to harass. [late ME < L *infest(āre)* (to) assail, molest, deriv. of *infest(us)* hostile] —**in·fest′er,** *n.*

in·fes·ta·tion (in′fe stā′shən), *n.* **1.** the act of infesting; state of being infested. **2.** a harassing or troublesome invasion: *an infestation of ants.* [< LL *infestātiōn-* (s. of *infestātiō*). See INFEST, -ATION]

in·feu·da·tion (in′fyo͞o dā′shən), *n.* *Eng. Law.* **1.** the grant of an estate in fee. **2.** the relation of lord and vassal established by the grant and acceptance of such an estate. [< ML *infeudātiōn-* (s. of *infeudātiō*). See IN-², FEUD², -ATION]

in·fi·del (in′fi dəl), *n.* **1.** a person who has no religious faith; unbeliever. **2.** *Relig.* **a.** a person who does not accept a particular faith, esp. Christianity. **b.** (in Christian use) an unbeliever, esp. a Muslim. **c.** (in Muslim use) a person who does not accept the Islamic faith; a kaffir. **3.** (loosely) a person who disbelieves or doubts a particular theory, belief, creed, etc.; skeptic. —*adj.* **4.** without religious faith. **5.** due to or manifesting unbelief: *infidel ideas.* **6.** not accepting a particular faith, esp. Christianity or Islam; heathen. **7.** rejecting the Christian religion while accepting no other; not believing in the Bible or any Christian divine revelation. **8.** Also, **in·fi·del·ic** (in′fi del′ik). of, pertaining to, or characteristic of unbelievers or infidels. [late ME < ML *infidēl(is)* a Moslem < L: unfaithful. See IN-³, FEAL]
—**Syn. 2, 3.** See **atheist.**

in·fi·del·i·ty (in′fi del′i tē), *n., pl.* **-ties.** **1.** unfaithfulness; disloyalty. **2.** adultery. **3.** lack of religious faith, esp. Christian faith. **4.** a breach of trust; disloyalty. [ME < L *infidēlitās,* equiv. to *infidēli(s)* unfaithful (see INFIDEL) + *-tās* -TY²]

in·field (in′fēld′), *n.* **1.** *Baseball.* **a.** the diamond. **b.** the positions played by the first baseman, second baseman, third baseman, and shortstop, taken collectively. **c.** the infielders considered as a group (contrasted with *outfield*). **2.** *Track, Horse Racing.* the area enclosed by a track. **3.** *Agric.* **a.** the part of the land of a farm nearest the farmhouse. **b.** land regularly tilled. Cf. **outfield** (def. 3). [IN-¹ + FIELD]

in·field·er (in′fēl′dər), *n.* *Baseball.* any of the players stationed in the infield. [INFIELD + -ER¹]

in·fight·er (in′fī′tər), *n.* a person who engages in or is skillful at infighting. [IN + FIGHTER]

in·fight·ing (in′fī′ting), *n.* **1.** fighting at close range. **2.** fighting between rival organizations, members of a group, etc., that is kept secret from outsiders. **3.** free-for-all fighting. [IN + FIGHTING]

in·fil·trate (in fil′trāt, in′fil trāt′), *v.,* **-trat·ed, -trat·ing,** *n.* —*v.t.* **1.** to filter into or through; permeate. **2.** to cause to pass in by, or as by, filtering: *The troops infiltrated the enemy lines.* —*v.i.* **3.** to pass into or through a substance, place, etc., by or as by filtering. —*n.* **4.** that which infiltrates. **5.** *Pathol.* cells or a substance passing into the tissues and forming a morbid accumulation. [IN-² + FILTRATE] —**in·fil·tra·tive** (in fil′trā′tiv, in fil′trə-), *adj.* —**in·fil·tra·tor** (in′fil-trā′tər, in fil′trā-), *n.*

in·fil·tra·tion (in′fil trā′shən), *n.* **1.** the act or process of infiltrating; state of being infiltrated. **2.** that which infiltrates; an infiltrate. **3.** *Geol.* the deposition of dissolved minerals in the pores of a rock by the waters permeating it. **4.** *Mil.* **a.** a method of attack in which small bodies of soldiers or individual soldiers penetrate into the enemy's line at weak or unguarded points in order to assemble behind the enemy position and attack it from the rear, harass enemy rear-area installations, etc. **b.** a system of transporting troops or vehicles at extended and irregular intervals so as to avoid enemy observation or attack, esp. from the air. [INFILTRATE + -ION]

infiltra′tion gal′lery, a conduit, built in permeable earth, for collecting ground water.

in·fi·mum (in fī′məm, -fē′-), *n.* *Math.* See **greatest lower bound.** Also called **inf.** [< L, neut. of *infimus* lowest (superl. of *inferus* low)]

infin., infinitive.

in·fi·nite (in′fə nit), *adj.* **1.** immeasurably great: *a discovery of infinite importance; an infinite capacity for forgiveness.* **2.** indefinitely or exceedingly great: *infinite sums of money.* **3.** unbounded or unlimited; perfect: *God's infinite mercy.* **4.** endless or innumerable; inexhaustible: *Poets have praised woman and her infinite variety.* **5.** *Math.* **a.** not finite. **b.** (of a set) having elements that can be put into one-to-one correspondence with a subset that is not the given set. —*n.* **6.** that which is infinite. **7.** *Math.* an infinite quantity or magnitude. **8.** the boundless regions of space. **9. the Infinite** or **the Infinite Being,** God. [ME < L *infinīt(us)* boundless. See IN-³, FINITE] —**in′fi·nite·ly,** *adv.* —**in′fi·nite·ness,** *n.*

in′finite baf′fle, *Electronics.* a baffle for a loudspeaker, consisting, in theory, of an infinitely large board with a hole through which the loudspeaker is mounted, and, in practice, of a large, closed box, lined with sound-absorbent material, having a hole in one side for mounting the loudspeaker.

in′finite in′tegral, *Math.* See **improper integral** (def. 1).

in′finite prod′uct, *Math.* a sequence of numbers in which an infinite number of terms are multiplied together.

in′finite re′gress, *Philos.* causal or logical relationship of terms in a series without the possibility of a term initiating the series.

in′finite se′ries, *Math.* a sequence of numbers in which an infinite number of terms are added successively in a given pattern; the sequence of partial sums of a given sequence.

in·fin·i·tes·i·mal (in′fin i tes′ə məl), *adj.* **1.** indefinitely or exceedingly small; minute: *the infinitesimal vessels of the nervous system.* **2.** immeasurably small; less than an assignable quantity: *to an infinitesimal degree.* **3.** of, pertaining to, or involving infinitesimals. —*n.* **4.** an infinitesimal quantity. **5.** *Math.* a variable having zero as a limit. [< NL *infinitēsim(us),* equiv. to *infinīt(us)* INFINITE + *-ēsimus,* var. of *-ensimus* ordinal suffix + -AL¹] —**in′fin·i·tes′i·mal′i·ty, in′fin·i·tes′i·mal·ness,** *n.* —**in′fin·i·tes′i·mal·ly,** *adv.*

in′finites′imal cal′culus, the differential calculus and the integral calculus, considered together.

in·fin·i·ti·val (in′fin i tī′vəl), *adj.* *Gram.* of or pertaining to the infinitive. [INFINITIVE + -AL¹] —**in′fin·i·ti′val·ly,** *adv.*

in·fin·i·tive (in fin′i tiv), *Gram.* —*n.* **1.** a verb form found in many languages which functions as a noun or is used with auxiliary verbs, and which names the action or state without specifying the subject, as French *venir* "to come," Latin *esse* "to be," *fuisse* "to have been." **2.** (in English) the simple or basic form of the verb, as *come, take, eat, be,* used after auxiliary verbs, as in *I didn't come, He must be,* or this simple form preceded by a function word, as *to* in *I want to eat.* —*adj.* **3.** consisting of or containing an infinitive: *an infinitive construction.* [late ME < LL *infīnītīv(us)* indefinite, equiv. to *in-* IN-³ + *fīnītīvus* definite; see FINITE, -IVE] —**in·fin′i·tive·ly,** *adv.*

infin′itive clause′, *Gram.* a clause containing an infinitive as its main or only verb form, as *to speak clearly* in *Try to speak clearly.* Also called **infin′itive phrase′.**

in·fin·i·tize (in fin′i tīz′), *v.t.,* **-tized, -tiz·ing.** to free from limitations of space, time, circumstance, etc.; cause to become infinite. [INFINITE + -IZE]

in·fin·i·tude (in fin′i to͞od′, -tyo͞od′), *n.* **1.** infinity: *divine infinitude.* **2.** an infinite extent, amount, or number. [INFIN(ITE + MULT)ITUDE]

in·fin·i·ty (in fin′i tē), *n., pl.* **-ties.** **1.** the quality or state of being infinite: *the infinity of God.* **2.** that which is infinite. **3.** infinite space, time, or quantity: *any time short of infinity.* **4.** an infinite extent, amount, or number. **5.** an indefinitely great amount or number. **6.** *Math.* **a.** the assumed limit of a sequence, series, etc., that increases without bound. **b.** infinite distance, or an infinitely distant part of space. **7.** *Photog.* **a.** a distance between a subject and the camera so great that rays of light reflected from the subject may be regarded as parallel. **b.** a distance setting of the camera lens beyond which everything is in focus. [ME *infinite* < L *infīnitās,* equiv. to *in-* IN-³ + *fīni(s)* boundary + *-tās* -TY²]

in·firm (in fûrm′), *adj.* **1.** feeble or weak in body or health, often because of age. **2.** unsteadfast, faltering, or irresolute, as persons, the mind, etc.: *infirm of purpose.* **3.** not firm, solid, or strong: *an infirm support.* **4.** unsound or invalid, as an argument, a property title, etc. —*v.t.* **5.** *Archaic.* to invalidate. [ME *infirme* < L *infirm(us).* See IN-³, FIRM¹] —**in·firm′ly,** *adv.* —**in·firm′ness,** *n.*
—**Syn. 1, 3, 4.** weak. **2.** wavering, vacillating, indecisive. **3.** rickety, tottering, shaky, unsteady. —**Ant. 1, 2, 3.** strong.

in·fir·mar·i·an (in′fər mâr′ē ən), *n.* (in a religious house) a person who nurses the sick. [INFIRMARY + -AN]

in·fir·ma·ry (in fûr′mə rē), *n., pl.* **-ries.** **1.** a place for the care of the infirm, sick, or injured; hospital: *a school infirmary.* **2.** a dispensary. [late ME < ML *infirmāria.* See INFIRM, -ARY]

in·fir·mi·ty (in fûr′mi tē), *n., pl.* **-ties** for 1, 3. **1.** a physical weakness or ailment: *the infirmities of age.* **2.** quality or state of being infirm; lack of strength. **3.** a moral weakness or failing. [< ME *infirmite* < L *infirmitās.* See INFIRM, -ITY]

in·fix (*v.* in fiks′, in′fiks′; *n.* in′fiks′), *v.t.* **1.** to fix, fasten, or drive in: *He infixed the fatal spear.* **2.** to implant: *to infix a habit.* **3.** to infix in the mind or memory, as a fact or idea; impress. **4.** *Gram.* to add as an infix. —*v.i.* **5.** *Gram.* (of a linguistic form) to admit an infix. —*n.* **6.** *Gram.* an affix which is inserted within the body of the element to which it is added, as Latin *m* in *accumbō* "I lie down," as compared with *accubuī* "I lay down." [< L *infix(us)* fastened in, ptp. of *infīgere.* See IN-², FIX] —**in·fix·ion** (in fik′shən), *n.*
—**Syn. 3.** inculcate, instill.

in fla·gran·te de·lic·to (in flä grän′te de lik′tō; *Eng.* in flə gran′tē di lik′tō), *Latin.* in the very act of committing the offense. [lit., in blazing crime, i.e., in the heat of the evil deed]

in·flame (in flām′), *v.* **-flamed, -flam·ing.** —*v.t.* **1.** to set aflame or afire; set on fire. **2.** to redden with or as with flames: *The setting sun inflames the sky.* **3.** to kindle or excite (passions, desires, etc.). **4.** to arouse to a high degree of passion, or feeling: *His harangue inflamed the rabble.* **5.** (of an emotion, as rage) to cause to redden or grow heated: *Uncontrollable rage inflamed his face.* **6.** to incite or rouse to a state of greater violence: *His words inflamed the angry mob to riot.* **7.** to cause inflammation in: *Her eyes were inflamed with crying.* **8.** to raise (the blood, bodily tissue, etc.) to a morbid or feverish heat. —*v.i.* **9.** to burst into flame; take fire. **10.** to be kindled, as passion. **11.** to become hot with passion, as the heart. **12.** to become excessively affected with inflammation. Also, **enflame.** [IN-[2] + FLAME; r. ME *enflamme(n)* < MF *enflamm(er)* < L *inflammāre* to kindle] —**in·flam·ed·ness** (in flā′mid nis), *n.* —**in·flam′er,** *n.* —**in·flam′ing·ly,** *adv.*
—**Syn. 1.** fire. See **kindle. 3.** incite, stimulate. —**Ant. 1.** cool, soothe.

in·flam·ma·ble (in flam′ə bəl), *adj.* **1.** capable of being set on fire; combustible; flammable. **2.** easily aroused to passion or anger; excitable; irascible: *an inflammable disposition.* —*n.* **3.** something inflammable. [< ML *inflammābil(is),* equiv. to L *inflammā(re)* (to) INFLAME + *-bilis* -BLE] —**in·flam′ma·bil′i·ty, in·flam′ma·ble·ness,** *n.* —**in·flam′ma·bly,** *adv.*

in·flam·ma·tion (in′flə mā′shən), *n.* **1.** the act or fact of inflaming. **2.** the state of being inflamed. **3.** *Pathol.* redness, swelling, pain, tenderness, heat, and disturbed function of an area of the body, esp. as a reaction of tissues to injurious agents. [< L *inflammātiōn-* (s. of *inflammātiō*), equiv. to *inflammāt(us)* (ptp. of *inflammāre;* see INFLAME) + *-iōn-* -ION]

in·flam·ma·to·ry (in flam′ə tôr′ē, -tōr′ē), *adj.* **1.** tending to arouse anger, hostility, passion, etc.: *inflammatory speeches.* **2.** *Pathol.* pertaining to or attended with inflammation. [< L *inflammāt(us)* (see INFLAMMATION) + -ORY[1]] —**in·flam·ma·to·ri·ly** (in flam′ə tôr′ə lē, -tôr′-, -flam′ə tôr′-, -tōr′-), *adv.*

in·flate (in flāt′), *v.,* **-flat·ed, -flat·ing.** —*v.t.* **1.** to distend; swell or puff out; dilate: *The king cobra inflates its hood.* **2.** to distend with gas: *to inflate a balloon.* **3.** to puff up with pride, satisfaction, etc. **4.** to elate. **5.** to expand (currency, prices, etc.) unduly; raise above the previous or proper amount of value. —*v.i.* **6.** to become inflated. [< L *inflāt(us)* blown into (ptp. of *inflāre*), equiv. to *in-* IN-[2] + *flā-* blow + *-tus* ptp. suffix] —**in·flat′a·ble,** *adj.* —**in·flat′er, in·fla′tor,** *n.*
—**Syn. 1.** See **expand.** —**Ant. 1.** deflate.

in·flat·ed (in flā′tid), *adj.* **1.** distended with air or gas; swollen. **2.** puffed up, as with pride. **3.** turgid or bombastic, as language. **4.** unduly increased in level: *inflated costs.* **5.** unduly expanded in volume, as currency. **6.** *Bot.* hollow or swelled out with air: *inflated perianth.* [INFLATE + -ED[2]] —**in·flat′ed·ly,** *adv.* —**in·flat′ed·ness,** *n.*

in·fla·tion (in flā′shən), *n.* **1.** undue expansion or increase of the currency of a country, esp. by the issuing of paper money not redeemable in specie. **2.** a substantial rise of prices caused by an undue expansion in paper money or bank credit. **3.** the act of inflating. **4.** state of being inflated. [ME *inflacio(u)n* < L *inflātiōn-* (s. of *inflātiō*). See INFLATE, -ION]

in·fla·tion·ar·y (in flā′shə ner′ē), *adj.* of, pertaining to, or causing inflation: *inflationary prices.* [INFLATION + -ARY]

infla′tionary spi′ral, *Econ.* See under **spiral** (def. 7).

in·fla·tion·ism (in flā′shə niz′əm), *n.* the policy or practice of inflation through expansion of currency or bank deposits. [INFLATION + -ISM]

in·fla·tion·ist (in flā′shə nist), *n.* an advocate of inflation through expansion of currency or bank deposits. [INFLATION + -IST]

in·flect (in flekt′), *v.t.* **1.** to bend; turn from a direct line or course. **2.** to modulate (the voice). **3.** *Gram.* **a.** to apply inflection to (a word). **b.** to recite or display all or a distinct set of the inflections of (a word), in a fixed order: *to inflect Latin* amō *as* amō, amās, amat, *etc., or* nauta *as* nauta, nautae, nautae, nautam, nautā, *etc.* **4.** *Bot.* to bend in. —*v.i.* **5.** *Gram.* to be characterized by inflection. [ME *inflecte(n)* < L *inflect(ere)* (to) bend in, equiv. to *in-* IN-[2] + *flectere* to bend, curve] —**in·flect′ed·ness,** *n.* —**in·flec′tive,** *adj.* —**in·flec′tor,** *n.*

in·flec·tion (in flek′shən), *n.* **1.** modulation of the voice; change in pitch or tone of voice. **2.** Also, **flection.** *Gram.* **a.** the process or device of adding affixes to or changing the shape of a base to give it a different syntactic function without changing its form class. **b.** the paradigm of a word. **c.** a single pattern of formation of a paradigm: *noun inflection; verb inflection.* **d.** the change in the shape of a word, generally by affixation, by means of which a change of meaning or relationship to some other word or group of words is indicated. **e.** the affix added to produce this change, as the *-s* in *dogs* or the *-ed* in *played.* **f.** the systematic description of such processes in a given language, as in *serves* from *serve, sings* from *sing,* and *harder* from *hard* (contrasted with *derivation*). **3.** a bend or angle. **4.** *Math.* a change of curvature from convex to concave or vice versa. Also, *esp. Brit.,* **inflexion.** [var. sp. of *inflexion* < L *inflexiōn-* (s. of *inflexiō*) a bending. See INFLECT, -ION] —**in·flec′tion·less,** *adj.*

in·flec·tion·al (in flek′shə nəl), *adj.* **1.** of, pertaining to, or used in inflection: *an inflectional ending.* **2.** (of a language) characterized by the use of inflection: *English is an inflectional language.* [INFLECTION + -AL[1]] —**in·flec′tion·al·ly,** *adv.*

inflec′tion point′, *Math.* a point of inflection on a curve.

in·flexed (in flekst′), *adj.* *Bot., Zool.* inflected; bent or folded downward or inward: *an inflexed leaf.* [< L *inflex(us)* bent in (ptp. of *inflectere;* see INFLECT) + -ED[2]]

in·flex·i·ble (in flek′sə bəl), *adj.* **1.** not flexible; incapable of or resistant to being bent; rigid: *an inflexible rod.* **2.** of an unyielding temper, purpose, will, etc.; immovable: *He is a man with an inflexible determination.* **3.** not permitting change or variation; unalterable: *arbitrary and inflexible laws.* [< L *inflexibilis* that cannot be bent. See IN-[3], FLEXIBLE] —**in·flex′i·bil′i·ty, in·flex′i·ble·ness,** *n.* —**in·flex′i·bly,** *adv.*
—**Syn. 1.** unbendable, stiff. **2.** rigorous, stern, unrelenting, unremitting, stubborn, obstinate, intractable, obdurate, unbending, adamant. INFLEXIBLE, RELENTLESS, IMPLACABLE, INEXORABLE imply having the quality of not being turned from a purpose. INFLEXIBLE means unbending, adhering undeviatingly to a set plan, purpose, or the like: *inflexible in interpretation of rules; an inflexible will.* RELENTLESS suggests so pitiless and unremitting a pursuit of purpose as to convey a sense of inevitableness: *as relentless as the passing of time.* IMPLACABLE means incapable of being placated or appeased: *implacable in wrath.* INEXORABLE means unmoved by prayer or entreaty: *inexorable in demanding payment.* **3.** undeviating. —**Ant. 2.** amenable.

in·flex·ion (in flek′shən), *n.* *Chiefly Brit.* inflection. —**in·flex′ion·al,** *adj.* —**in·flex′ion·al·ly,** *adv.* —**in·flex′ion·less,** *adj.*

in·flict (in flikt′), *v.t.* **1.** to lay on: *to inflict a dozen lashes.* **2.** to impose as something that must be borne or suffered: *to inflict punishment.* **3.** to impose (anything unwelcome): *The regime inflicted burdensome taxes on the people.* [< L *inflict(us)* struck or dashed against (ptp. of *inflīgere*), equiv. to *in-* IN-[2] + *flīg-* (var. s. of *flīgere* to beat down) + *-tus* ptp. suffix] —**in·flict′a·ble,** *adj.* —**in·flict′er, in·flic′tor,** *n.* —**in·flic′tive,** *adj.*

in·flic·tion (in flik′shən), *n.* **1.** the act of inflicting. **2.** something inflicted, as punishment, suffering, etc. [< LL *inflictiōn-* (s. of *inflictiō*). See INFLICT, -ION]

in-flight (in′flīt′), *adj.* done, served, or shown during an air voyage: *an in-flight movie.* Also, **in′flight′.**

in·flo·res·cence (in′flō res′əns, -flô-, -flə-), *n.* **1.** a flowering or blossoming. **2.** *Bot.* **a.** the arrangement of flowers on the axis. **b.** the flowering part of a plant. **c.** a flower cluster. **d.** flowers collectively. **e.** a single flower. [< NL *inflōrescentia* < LL *inflōrescent-* (s. of *inflōrescēns* blooming, prp. of *inflōrescere*). See IN-[2], FLORA, -ESCENT] —**in′flo·res′cent,** *adj.*

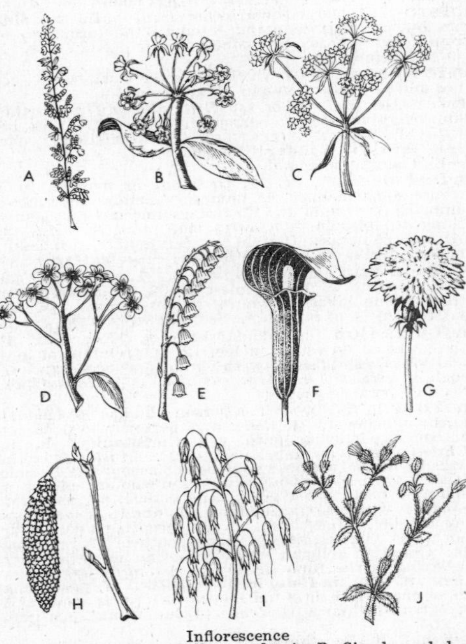

Inflorescence
A, Spike of heather, *Calluna vulgaris;* B, Simple umbel of milkweed, *Asclepias syriaca;* C, Compound umbel of water parsnip, *Sium cicutaefolium;* D, Corymb of red chokeberry, *Aronia arbutifolia;* E, Raceme of lily of the valley, *Convallaria majalis;* F, Spadix of jack-in-the-pulpit, *Arisaema triphyllum;* G, Head (anthodium) of dandelion, *Taraxacum officinale;* H, Male ament of birch, genus *Betula;* I, Panicle of oats, *Avena sativa;* J, Cyme of chickweed, genus *Cerastium*

in·flow (in′flō′), *n.* that which flows in; influx. [IN-[1] + FLOW]

in·flu·ence (in′flo͞o əns), *n., v.,* **-enced, -enc·ing.** —*n.* **1.** capacity or power of persons or things to produce effects on others by intangible or indirect means: *He used influence to get the contract.* **2.** action or process of producing effects on others by intangible or indirect means: *Her mother's influence made her stay.* **3.** a person or thing that exerts influence: *He is an influence for the good.* **4.** *Elect.* See **electrostatic induction. 5.** *Astrol.* **a.** the supposed radiation of an ethereal fluid from the stars, regarded in astrology as affecting human actions, destinies, etc. **b.** the exercise of occult power by the stars, or such power as exercised. **6.** *Archaic.* the exercise of similar power by human beings. **7.** *Obs.* influx. —*v.t.* **8.** to exercise influence on; affect; sway: *to influence a person by appealing to his weaknesses.* **9.** to move or impel (a person) to some action: *Outside factors influenced him to resign.* [ME < ML *influentia* stellar emanation, equiv. to L *influent-* (see INFLUENT) + *-ia* -Y[3]; see -ENCE] —**in′flu·ence·a·ble,** *adj.* —**in′flu·enc·er,** *n.*
—**Syn. 2.** sway, rule. See **authority. 8.** impress, bias, direct, control. **9.** incite, rouse, arouse, instigate, induce, persuade.

in·flu·ent (in′flo͞o ənt), *adj.* **1.** flowing in. —*n.* **2.** a tributary. **3.** *Ecol.* a plant or animal that has an important effect on the biotic balance in a community. [ME < L *influent-* (s. of *influēns*) inflowing. See IN-[2], FLUENT]

in·flu·en·tial (in′flo͞o en′shəl), *adj.* having or exerting influence, esp. great influence: *three influential educators.* [< ML *influenti(a)* stellar emanation (see INFLUENCE) + -AL[1]] —**in′flu·en′tial·ly,** *adv.*

in·flu·en·za (in′flo͞o en′zə), *n.* **1.** *Pathol.* an acute, extremely contagious, commonly epidemic disease, characterized by general prostration, occurring in several forms with varying symptoms, usually with nasal catarrh and bronchial inflammation, and caused by a virus. **2.** *Vet. Pathol.* an acute, contagious disease occurring in horses and swine, characterized by fever, depression, and catarrhal inflammations of the eyes, nasal passages, and bronchi, and caused by a virus. [< It < ML *influentia* INFLUENCE] —**in′flu·en′zal,** *adj.* —**in′flu·en·za·like′,** *adj.*

in·flux (in′fluks′), *n.* **1.** act of flowing in. **2.** an inflow (opposed to *outflux*): *an influx of tourists.* **3.** the place or point at which one stream flows into another or into the sea. **4.** the mouth of a stream. [< LL *influx(us)* influence of the stars, L: flowed in, ptp. of *influere.* See IN-[2], FLUX]

in·fold (in fōld′), *v.t.* enfold. —**in·fold′er,** *n.* —**in·fold′ment,** *n.*

in·form[1] (in fôrm′), *v.t.* **1.** to impart knowledge of a fact or circumstance to: *He informed them of his arrival.* **2.** to supply (oneself) with knowledge of a matter or subject: *He informed himself of all the pertinent facts.* **3.** to give character to; pervade or permeate with resulting effect on the character: *A love of nature informed his writing.* **4.** to animate or inspire. **5.** *Obs.* to train or instruct. **6.** *Obs.* to make known; disclose. **7.** *Obs.* to impart form to. —*v.i.* **8.** to give information; supply knowledge or enlightenment: *a magazine that incites more than it informs.* **9.** to furnish incriminating evidence to a prosecuting officer: *He informed on his accomplices to get a lighter sentence.* [ME *informe(n)* < L *inform(āre)* (to) form, shape, equiv. to *in-* IN-[2] + *formāre* to FORM; r. ME *enfourme(n)* < MF *enfourm(er)*] —**in·form′a·ble,** *adj.* —**in·form′ed·ly,** *adv.* —**in·form′ing·ly,** *adv.*
—**Syn. 1.** apprise; notify, advise, tell. **2.** acquaint.

in·form[2] (in fôrm′), *adj.* *Obs.* without form; formless. [< L *inform(is)* formless, deformed, equiv. to *in-* IN-[3] + *-formis* -FORM]

in·for·mal (in fôr′məl), *adj.* **1.** not according to prescribed, official, or customary forms; irregular; unofficial: *informal proceedings.* **2.** without formality or ceremony; casual: *an informal visit.* **3.** suitable to or characteristic of casual, familiar, but educated speech or writing. **4.** characterizing the second singular pronominal or verbal form, or its use, in certain languages: *the informal* tu *in French.* [IN-[3] + FORMAL[1]] —**in·for′mal·ly,** *adv.*
—**Syn. 1.** unconventional. **2.** natural, easy. **3.** See **colloquial.** —**Ant. 1.** conventional.

in·for·mal·i·ty (in′fôr mal′i tē), *n., pl.* **-ties** for 2. **1.** the state of being informal; absence of formality. **2.** an informal act. [IN-[3] + FORMALITY]

in·form·ant (in fôr′mənt), *n.* **1.** one who informs or gives information; informer. **2.** *Ling.* a native speaker of a language who supplies utterances and forms for one analyzing or learning the language. [< L *informant-* (s. of *informāns*) forming, shaping (prp. of *informāre*). See INFORM[1], -ANT]

in for·ma pau·pe·ris (in fôr′mə pô′pə ris), *Law.* without liability for costs and legal fees: *permission to sue in forma pauperis.* [< L: lit., in the style of a pauper]

in·for·ma·tion (in′fər mā′shən), *n.* **1.** knowledge communicated or received concerning a particular fact or circumstance; news: *information concerning a crime.* **2.** any knowledge gained through communication, research, instruction, etc.: *His wealth of general information is amazing.* **3.** the act or fact of informing. **4.** an office or employee for distributing information to the public: *Dial information and ask for his phone number.* **5.** *Law.* **a.** an official criminal charge presented, usually by the prosecuting officers of the state, without the interposition of a grand jury. **b.** a criminal charge, made under oath before a magistrate, of an offense punishable summarily. **6.** (in communication theory) an indication of the number of possible choices of messages, expressible as the value of some monotonic function of the number of choices, usually log to the base 2. **7.** *Computer Technol.* any data that can be coded for processing by a computer or similar device. [ME: a forming of the mind < ML, L: idea, conception. See INFORM[1], -ATION] —**in′for·ma′tion·al,** *adj.*
—**Syn. 1.** data, facts, intelligence, advice. **2.** INFORMATION, KNOWLEDGE, WISDOM are terms for human acquirements through reading, study, and practical experience. INFORMATION applies to facts told, read, or communicated which may be unorganized and even unrelated: *to pick up useful information.* KNOWLEDGE is an organized body of information, or the comprehension and understanding consequent on having acquired and organized a body of facts: *a knowledge of chemistry.* WISDOM is a knowledge of people, life, and conduct, with the facts so thoroughly assimilated as to have produced sagacity, judgment, and insight: *to use wisdom in handling people.* —**Ant. 1.** ignorance.

informa′tion retriev′al, the systematic recovery of data, as from a file, the memory bank of a computer, etc.

informa′tion the′ory, the body of theory concerned with the content and transmission of communications and the storage and retrieval of information, esp. by computers.

in·form·a·tive (in fôr′mə tiv), *adj.* giving information; instructive: *an informative book.* Also, **in·form·a·to·ry** (in fôr′mə tôr′ē, -tōr′ē). [< L *informāt(us)* (ptp. of *informāre* to INFORM[1]) + -IVE] —**in·form′a·tive·ly,** *adv.* —**in·form′a·tive·ness,** *n.*

inform′atory dou′ble, *Bridge.* a double intended to inform one's partner that one has a strong hand and that he should bid regardless of the strength of his hand. Also called **takeout double.** Cf. **business double.** [INFORMAT(ION) + -ORY[1]]

in·form·er (in fôr′mər), *n.* **1.** one who informs or communicates information or news; an informant. **2.** one who informs against another, esp. for money or other reward. [ME; see INFORM[1], -ER[1]]

inform′ing gun′, a gun fired by a warship to signal its intention to search a merchant vessel. Also called **affirming gun.**

in·for·tu·nate (in fôr′chə nit), *adj.* *Obs.* of or pertaining to infortune. [ME < L *infortūnātus,* equiv. to *in-* IN-[3] + *fortūnātus* FORTUNATE] —**in·for′tu·nate·ly,** *adv.* —**in·for′tu·nate·ness,** *n.*

in·for·tune (in fôr′chən), *n.* **1.** *Astrol.* a planet or aspect of evil influence, esp. Saturn or Mars. **2.** *Obs.* misfortune. [ME (see IN-[3], FORTUNE), trans. of L *infortūnium*]

in·fra (in′frə), *adv.* below, esp. when used in referring to parts of a text. Cf. **supra.** [< L]

infra-, a learned borrowing from Latin meaning "below," used, with second elements of any origin, in the formation of compound words: *infrasonic; infrared.* [< L, repr. *infrā*, adv. or prep.]

in·fra·cos·tal (in′frə kos′tᵊl, -kô′stᵊl), *adj.* situated below the ribs. [INFRA- + COSTAL]

in·fract (in frakt′), *v.t.* to break; violate; infringe. [< L *infract(us)* broken, bent, weakened (ptp. of *infringere*), equiv. to *in-* IN-² + *frag-* (ptp. s. of *frangere* to break) + *-tus* ptp. suffix] —**in·frac′tor,** *n.*

in·frac·tion (in frak′shən), *n.* **1.** breach; violation; infringement: *an infraction of the rules.* **2.** *Med.* an incomplete fracture of a bone. [< L *infractiōn-* (s. of *infractiō*). See INFRACT, -ION]

in·fra dig (in′frə dig′), infra dignitatem; undignified.

in·fra dig·ni·ta·tem (in′frä dig′ni tä′tem; *Eng.* in′frə dig′ni tā′təm), *Latin.* beneath (one's) dignity.

in·fra·hu·man (in′frə hyo͞o′mən), *adj.* less than human; subhuman. [INFRA- + HUMAN]

in·fra·lap·sar·i·an (in′frə lap sâr′ē ən), *n.* **1.** a person who believes in infralapsarianism. —*adj.* **2.** of or pertaining to infralapsarians or infralapsarianism. [INFRA- + L *laps(us)* a fall (see LAPSE) + -ARIAN]

in·fra·lap·sar·i·an·ism (in′frə lap sâr′ē ə niz′əm), *n.* *Theol.* the doctrine, held by Augustinians and by many Calvinists, that God planned the Creation, permitted the Fall, elected a chosen number, planned their redemption, and suffered the remainder to be eternally punished (opposed to *supralapsarianism*). [INFRALAPSARIAN + -ISM]

in·fra·mar·gin·al (in′frə mär′jə nᵊl), *adj.* below the margin; submarginal. [INFRA- + MARGINAL]

in·fran·gi·ble (in fran′jə bəl), *adj.* **1.** unbreakable: *infrangible moral strength; infrangible tableware.* **2.** inviolable: *an infrangible rule.* [< LL *infrangibil(is).* See IN-³, FRANGIBLE] —**in·fran′gi·bil′i·ty, in·fran′gi·ble·ness,** *n.* —**in·fran′gi·bly,** *adv.*

in·fra·red (in′frə red′), *n.* **1.** the part of the invisible spectrum that is contiguous to the red end of the visible spectrum and that comprises electromagnetic radiations of wavelengths from 0.8 to 1000 microns. —*adj.* **2.** noting or pertaining to the infrared or its component rays: *infrared radiation.* Also, **in′fra-red′.** Cf. **ultraviolet.** [INFRA- + RED¹]

in·fra·son·ic (in′frə son′ik), *adj.* noting or pertaining to a sound wave with a frequency below the audio-frequency range. [INFRA- + SONIC]

in·fra·son·ics (in′frə son′iks), *n.* (*construed as sing.*) the branch of science that deals with infrasonic phenomena. [see INFRASONIC, -ICS]

in·fra·struc·ture (in′frə struk′chər), *n.* **1.** the basic, underlying framework or features of a system, as the military installations, communication and transport facilities of a country. **2.** a clandestine system or framework for supporting and implementing unlawful or subversive activities.

in·fre·quen·cy (in frē′kwən sē), *n.* state of being infrequent. Also, **in·fre′quence.** [< L *infrequentia* fewness. See INFREQUENT, -ENCY]

in·fre·quent (in frē′kwənt), *adj.* **1.** happening or occurring at long intervals or rarely: *infrequent visits.* **2.** not constant, habitual, or regular: *an infrequent visitor.* **3.** not plentiful or many: *infrequent opportunities for advancement.* **4.** far apart in space. [< L *infrequent-* (s. of *infrequēns*). See IN-³, FREQUENT] —**in·fre′quent·ly,** *adv.*
—**Syn. 1, 3.** scarce, rare, uncommon.

in·fringe (in frinj′), *v.,* **-fringed, -fring·ing.** —*v.t.* **1.** to commit a breach or infraction of; violate or transgress: *to infringe a business contract; to infringe a law; to infringe the rules of etiquette.* —*v.i.* **2.** to encroach or trespass (usually fol. by *on* or *upon*): *Don't infringe on his privacy.* [< L *infringe(re)* (to) break, weaken, equiv. to *in-* IN-² + *-fringere*, var. of *frangere* to BREAK] —**in·fring′er,** *n.*
—**Syn. 1.** break, disobey. **2.** poach. See **trespass.** —**Ant. 1.** obey.

in·fringe·ment (in frinj′mənt), *n.* **1.** a breach or infraction, as of a law, right, or obligation; violation; transgression. **2.** act of infringing. [INFRINGE + -MENT]

in·fu·la (in′fyə lə), *n., pl.* **-lae** (-lē′). one of the two embroidered lappets of the miter of a bishop. [< ML, L: band, priest's fillet < ?]

in·fun·dib·u·li·form (in′fun dib′yə lə fôrm′), *adj. Bot.* funnel-shaped. [INFUNDIBUL(UM) + -I- + -FORM]

in·fun·dib·u·lum (in′fun dib′yə ləm), *n., pl.* **-la** (-lə). *Anat.* **1.** a funnel-shaped organ or part. **2.** a funnel-shaped extension of the cerebrum connecting the pituitary gland to the base of the brain. **3.** a space in the right ventricle at the base of the pulmonary artery. [< NL, L: funnel, equiv. to *infundi-* (s. of *infundere* to pour into; see IN-², FOUND³) + *-bulum* instrumental suffix] —**in′fun·dib′u·lar, in·fun·dib·u·late** (in′fun dib′yə lāt′), *adj.*

Infundibuliform corolla of morning-glory flower, *Ipomoea purpurea*

in·fu·ri·ate (*v.* in fyo͝or′ē āt′; *adj.* in fyo͝or′ē it), *v.,* **-at·ed, -at·ing,** *adj.* —*v.t.* **1.** to make furious; enrage. —*adj.* **2.** *Rare.* infuriated; enraged. [< ML *infuriāt(us)* maddened, enraged (ptp. of *infuriāre*). See IN-², FURY, -ATE¹] —**in·fu′ri·ate·ly,** *adv.* —**in·fu′ri·a′tion,** *n.*
—**Syn. 1.** anger. See **enrage.**

in·fu·ri·at·ing·ly (in fyo͝or′ē ā′ting lē), *adv.* to an irritating or exasperating degree: *to mumble infuriatingly; an infuriatingly brief visit.* [INFURIATING + -LY]

in·fus·cate (in fus′kāt), *adj. Entomol.* darkened with a fuscous or brownish tinge. Also, **in·fus′cat·ed.** [< L *infuscāt(us)* made dark or dusky, obscured (ptp. of *infuscāre*). See IN-², FUSCOUS, -ATE¹]

in·fuse (in fyo͞oz′), *v.,* **-fused, -fus·ing.** —*v.t.* **1.** to introduce, as by pouring; cause to penetrate; instill (usually fol. by *into*): *to infuse loyalty into the new employees.* **2.** to imbue or inspire (usually fol. by *with*): *The new coach infused the team with enthusiasm.* **3.** to steep or soak (leaves, bark, roots, etc.) in a liquid so as to extract the soluble properties or ingredients. **4.** *Obs.* to pour in. —*v.i.* **5.** to undergo infusion; become infused: *Leave the solution to infuse overnight.* [ME < L *infūs(us)* poured in, ptp. of *infundere.* See IN-², FUSE²] —**in·fus′er,** *n.*
—**Syn. 1.** ingrain; inculcate.

in·fu·si·ble¹ (in fyo͞o′zə bəl), *adj.* not fusible; incapable of being fused or melted. [IN-³ + FUSIBLE] —**in·fu′si·bil′i·ty, in·fu′si·ble·ness,** *n.*

in·fu·si·ble² (in fyo͞o′zə bəl), *adj.* capable of being infused. [INFUSE + -IBLE]

in·fu·sion (in fyo͞o′zhən), *n.* **1.** the act or process of infusing. **2.** that which is infused. **3.** *Pharm.* **a.** the steeping or soaking of a crude drug in water. **b.** the liquid so prepared. **4.** *Med.* **a.** the introduction of a saline or other solution into a vein. **b.** the solution used. [late ME < L *infūsiōn-* (s. of *infūsiō*). See INFUSE, -ION]

in·fu·sion·ism (in fyo͞o′zhə niz′əm), *n. Theol.* the doctrine that the soul existed in a previous state and is infused into the body at conception or birth. [INFUSION + -ISM] —**in·fu′sion·ist,** *n.*

in·fu·sive (in fyo͞o′siv), *adj.* capable of infusing; inspiring. [INFUSE + -IVE]

In·fu·so·ri·a (in′fyo͝o sôr′ē ə, -sōr′-), *n.pl.* **1.** protozoans of the class *Ciliata* (or *Ciliophora*). **2.** *Obs.* any of various microscopic organisms found in infusions of decaying organic matter. [< NL, neut. pl. of *infūsōrius.* See INFUSE, -ORY¹]

in·fu·so·ri·al (in′fyo͝o sôr′ē əl, -sōr′-), *adj.* containing or consisting of infusorians: *infusorial earth.* [INFUSORI(A) + -AL¹]

in·fu·so·ri·an (in′fyo͝o sôr′ē ən, -sōr′-), *n.* **1.** any of the Infusoria. —*adj.* **2.** infusorial. [INFUSORI(A) + -AN]

in fu·tu·ro (in fo͞o to͞o′rō; *Eng.* in fyo͞o to͝or′ō, -tyo͝or′ō), *Latin.* in the future.

-ing¹, a suffix of nouns formed from verbs, expressing the action of the verb or its result, product, material, etc. (*the art of building; a new building; cotton wadding*). It is also used to form nouns from other words than verbs (*offing; shirting*). Verbal nouns ending in *-ing* are often used attributively (*the printing trade*) and in composition (*drinking song*). In some compounds (*sewing machine*), the first element might reasonably be regarded as the participial adjective, **-ing²**, the compound thus meaning "a machine that sews," but it is commonly taken as a verbal noun, the compound being explained as "a machine for sewing." Cf. **-ing².** [ME; OE *-ing, -ung*]

-ing², a suffix forming the present participle of verbs, such participles being often used as participial adjectives: *warring factions.* Cf. **-ing¹.** [ME *-ing, inge,* r. ME *-inde, ende,* OE *-ende*]

-ing³, a native English suffix, meaning "one belonging to," "of the kind of," "one descended from," and sometimes having a diminutive force, formerly used in the formation of nouns: *farthing; shilling; bunting; gelding; whiting.* Cf. **-ling.** [ME, OE *-ing;* c. ON *-ingr, -ungr,* Goth *-ings*]

In·ga (ing′gə), *n.* a girl's given name, form of **Ingrid.**

in·gate (in′gāt′), *n. Foundry.* gate¹ (def. 12). [IN + GATE¹]

in·gath·er (in′gath̸ ər, in gath̸′ər), *v.t.* **1.** to gather or bring in, as a harvest. —*v.i.* **2.** to collect; assemble. [IN-¹ + GATHER] —**in′gath′er·er,** *n.*

in·gath·er·ing (in′gath̸′ər ing), *n.* **1.** a gathering in, esp. of farm products; a harvest. **2.** a gathering together, as of persons; assembly. [IN-¹ + GATHERING]

Inge (inj *for 1;* ing *for 2*), *n.* **1. William (Mot·ter)** (mot′ər), born 1913, U.S. playwright. **2. William Ralph,** 1860–1954, Anglican clergyman, scholar, and author: dean of St. Paul's 1911–34.

In·ge·low (in′jə lō′), *n.* **Jean,** 1820–97, English poet and novelist.

Ing·e·mar (ing′gə mär′), *n.* a boy's given name. Also, **Ingmar.**

in·gem·i·nate (in jem′ə nāt′), *v.t.,* **-nat·ed, -nat·ing.** to repeat; reiterate. [< L *ingemināt(us)* redoubled, repeated (ptp. of *ingemināre*). See IN-², GEMINATE] —**in·gem′i·na′tion,** *n.*

in·gen·er·ate¹ (in jen′ər it), *adj.* not generated; self-existent. [< LL *ingenerāt(us)* not begotten. See IN-³, GENERATE]

in·gen·er·ate² (*v.* in jen′ə rāt′; *adj.* in jen′ər it), *v.,* **-at·ed, -at·ing,** *adj. Archaic.* —*v.t.* **1.** to engender; produce. —*adj.* **2.** inborn; innate. [< L *ingenerāt(us)* implanted. See IN-², GENERATE] —**in·gen′er·ate·ly,** *adv.* —**in·gen′er·a′tion,** *n.*

in·gen·ious (in jēn′yəs), *adj.* **1.** characterized by cleverness or originality of invention or construction: *an ingenious machine.* **2.** cleverly inventive; resourceful: *an ingenious engineer; an ingenious press agent.* [ME < L *ingeniōs(us),* equiv. to *ingeni(um)* innate ability, cleverness + *-ōsus* -OUS] —**in·gen′ious·ly,** *adv.* —**in·gen′ious·ness,** *n.*
—**Syn. 2.** bright, gifted, able, resourceful; adroit. INGENIOUS, INGENUOUS are now distinct from each other and should not be confused or thought of as synonyms. INGENIOUS means clever, inventive, resourceful in contriving new explanations or methods, and the like: *an ingenious executive.* INGENUOUS means frank, candid, free from guile or deceit: *an ingenuous and sincere statement.* —**Ant. 2.** unskillful.

in·gé·nue (an′zhə no͞o′, -nyo͞o′; *Fr.* aN zhā nʏ′), *n., pl.* **-nues** (-no͞oz′, -nyo͞oz′; *Fr.* -nʏ′). **1.** the part of an ingenuous girl, esp. as represented on the stage. **2.** an actress who plays such a part or specializes in playing such parts. Also, **in′ge·nue′.** [< F, fem. of *ingénu* < L *ingenu(us)* native, inborn etc.; see INGENUOUS]

in·ge·nu·i·ty (in′jə no͞o′i tē, -nyo͞o′-), *n., pl.* **-ties** for 3. **1.** the quality of being ingenious; inventive talent: *a designer of great ingenuity.* **2.** cleverness or skillfulness of conception or design, as of things, actions, etc.: *a device of great ingenuity.* **3.** an ingenious contrivance. **4.** *Obs.* ingenuousness. [< L *ingenuitās* innate virtue, etc. (see INGENUOUS, -ITY); current senses by assoc. with INGENIOUS]

in·gen·u·ous (in jen′yo͞o əs), *adj.* **1.** free from reserve, restraint, or dissimulation. **2.** artless; innocent. [< L *ingenuus* native, inborn, honorable, tender, equiv. to *ingenu-* (s. of *ingenui,* etc., perf. of **ingignere* to implant; see IN-², GENUINE) + *-us* -OUS] —**in·gen′u·ous·ly,** *adv.* —**in·gen′u·ous·ness,** *n.*
—**Syn. 1.** frank, candid, free, open, sincere. See **ingenious. 2.** naive, guileless.

In·ger·soll (ing′gər sôl′, -sol′, -səl), *n.* **Robert Green,** 1833–99, U.S. lawyer, political leader, orator, and lecturer.

in·gest (in jest′), *v.t.* **1.** to take, as food, into the body (opposed to *egest*). **2.** *Aeron.* to draw (foreign matter) into the inlet of a jet engine, often causing damage to the engine. [< L *ingest(us)* poured, thrown into, ptp. of *ingere.* See IN-², GEST¹] —**in·gest′i·ble,** *adj.* —**in·ges′tion,** *n.* —**in·ges′tive,** *adj.*

in·ges·ta (in jes′tə), *n.pl.* substances ingested. [< NL, neut. pl. of L *ingestus.* See INGEST]

In·ghi·ra·mi (ing′gə rä′mē), *n.* a walled plain in the third quadrant of the face of the moon: about 60 miles in diameter.

in·gine (in jīn′), *n. Scot.* mental ability or genius. [< L *ingen(ium).* See ENGINE]

in·gle (ing′gəl), *n. Brit. Dial.* **1.** a fire burning in a hearth. **2.** a fireplace; hearth. [< Gael *aingeal* fire]

in·gle·nook (ing′gəl no͝ok′), *n. Chiefly Brit.* a corner by the fire; chimney corner. Also, **in′gle nook′.** [INGLE + NOOK]

in·gle·side (ing′gəl sīd′), *n. Brit. Dial.* a fireside. [INGLE + SIDE¹]

In·gle·side (ing′gəl sīd′), *n.* a town in S Texas. 3022 (1960).

In·gle·wood (ing′gəl wo͝od′), *n.* **1.** a city in SW California, near Los Angeles. 63,390 (1960). **2.** a town in Tennessee, near Nashville. 26,527 (1960).

in·glo·ri·ous (in glôr′ē əs, -glōr′-), *adj.* **1.** shameful; disgraceful: *inglorious retreat.* **2.** *Archaic.* not famous. [< L *inglōrius.* See IN-³, GLORIOUS] —**in·glo′ri·ous·ly,** *adv.* —**in·glo′ri·ous·ness,** *n.*

Ing·mar (ing′mär), *n.* a boy's given name. Also, **Ingemar.**

in·goal (in′gōl′), *n. Rugby.* the area at either end of the field between the goal line and the dead-ball line.

In God′ We′ Trust′, **1.** a motto appearing on U.S. currency. **2.** motto of Florida.

in·go·ing (in′gō′ing), *adj.* going in; entering. [IN-¹ + GOING]

in·got (ing′gət), *n.* **1.** a mass of metal cast in a convenient form for shaping, remelting, or refining. —*v.t.* **2.** to make ingots of; shape into ingots. [ME: lit., (something) poured in, equiv. to *in-* IN-¹ + *got* poured, deriv. of OE *goten,* ptp. *gēotan;* c. G *giessen,* Goth *giutan,* Icel *gjōta* to pour]

in′got i′ron, an iron of high purity made by a basic open-hearth process.

in·graft (in graft′, -gräft′), *v.t.* engraft. —**in·graft′er,** *n.* —**in·graft′ment, in′graf·ta′tion,** *n.*

in·grain (*v.* in grān′; *adj., n.* in′grān′), *v.t.* **1.** to fix deeply and firmly, as in the nature or mind. —*adj.* **2.** ingrained; firmly fixed. **3.** (of carpets) made of yarn dyed before weaving and so woven as to show a different pattern on each side; reversible. **4.** dyed in grain, or through the fiber. **5.** dyed in the yarn, or in a raw state, before manufacture. —*n.* **6.** yarn, wool, etc., dyed before manufacture. **7.** an ingrain carpet. Also, **engrain** (for defs. 1, 2). [orig. phrase (*dyed*) *in grain* (kermes)]
—**Syn. 1.** infuse, inculcate, imbue.

in·grained (in grānd′, in′grānd′), *adj.* **1.** firmly fixed; deep-rooted; inveterate: *ingrained superstition.* **2.** wrought into or through the grain or fiber. Also, **engrained.** [INGRAIN + -ED²] —**in·grain·ed·ly** (in grā′nid lē, -grānd′-), *adv.* —**in·grain′ed·ness,** *n.*

In·gram (ing′grəm), *n.* **1.** a town in SW Pennsylvania. 4730 (1960). **2.** a boy's given name.

in·grate (in′grāt), *n.* **1.** an ungrateful person. —*adj.* **2.** *Archaic.* ungrateful. [ME *ingrat* < L *ingrāt(us)* ungrateful. See IN-³, GRATEFUL] —**in′grate·ly,** *adv.*

in·gra·ti·ate (in grā′shē āt′), *v.t.,* **-at·ed, -at·ing.** to establish (oneself) in the favor or good graces of others (usually fol. by *with*): *He ingratiated himself with all the guests.* [? < early It *ingratiato,* ptp. of *ingratiare,* deriv. of phrase *in gratia* < L *in grātiam* into favor. See IN, GRACE, -ATE¹] —**in·gra′ti·a′tion,** *n.*

in·gra·ti·at·ing (in grā′shē ā′ting), *adj.* **1.** charming; agreeable; pleasing. **2.** meant to gain favor: *an ingratiating smile; an ingratiating manner.* [INGRATIATE + -ING²] —**in·gra′ti·at′ing·ly,** *adv.*

in·gra·ti·a·to·ry (in grā′shē ə tôr′ē, -tōr′ē), *adj.* serving or intended to ingratiate. [INGRATIATE + -ORY¹]

in·grat·i·tude (in grat′i to͞od′, -tyo͞od′), *n.* the state of being ungrateful; unthankfulness. [ME < ML *ingrātitūd(ō).* See IN-³, GRATITUDE]

in·gra·ves·cent (in′grə ves′ənt), *adj. Pathol.* increasing in severity, as a disease. [< L *ingravescent-* (s. of *ingravescēns*) getting heavy (prp. of *ingravescere*). See IN-², GRAVE², -ESCENT] —**in′gra·ves′cence,** *n.*

in·gre·di·ent (in grē′dē ənt), *n.* **1.** something that enters as an element into a mixture: *the ingredients of a cake.* **2.** a constituent element of anything: *the ingredients of political success.* [late ME < L *ingredient-* (s. of *ingrediēns*) going into (prp. of *ingredī*), equiv. to *in-* IN-² + *-gredient-* going; see GRADIENT]
—**Syn. 1.** See **element.** —**Ant.** whole.

In·gres (aN′grᵊ), *n.* **Jean Au·guste Do·mi·nique** (zhäN ō gʏst′ dô mē nēk′), 1780–1867, French painter.

in·gress (in′gres), *n.* **1.** the act of going in or entering. **2.** the right to enter. **3.** a means or place of entering; entryway. **4.** *Astron.* immersion (def. 5). [< L *ingress(us)* a going in, equiv. to *ingress-* (ptp. s. of *ingredī*) + *-us* n. suffix (4th decl.)] —**in·gres·sion** (in gresh′ən), *n.* —**in·gres′sive,** *adj.* —**in·gres′sive·ness,** *n.*

In·grid (ing′grid), *n.* a girl's given name.

in·group (in′gro͞op′), *n. Sociol.* a group of people sharing similar interests, attitudes, etc., and considering those outside the group as inferior or alien; a homogeneous group to which one belongs. Cf. **outgroup.** [IN-¹ + GROUP]

in·grow·ing (in′grō′ing), *adj.* **1.** growing into the flesh: *an ingrowing nail.* **2.** growing within or inward. [IN-¹ + GROWING]

in·grown (in′grōn′), *adj.* **1.** having grown into the flesh: *an ingrown toenail.* **2.** grown within or inward. [IN-¹ + GROWN]

in·growth (in′grōth′), *n.* **1.** growth inward. **2.** something formed by growth inward. [IN-¹ + GROWTH]

in·gui·nal (ing′gwə nᵊl), *adj.* of, pertaining to, or situated in the groin. [< L *inguināl(is)* of the groin, equiv. to *inguin-* (s. of *inguen*) groin + *-ālis* -AL¹]

in·gulf (in gulf′), *v.t.* engulf. **—in·gulf′ment,** *n.*

in·gur·gi·tate (in gûr′ji tāt′), *v.*, **-tat·ed, -tat·ing.** —*v.t.* **1.** to swallow greedily or in great quantity, as food. **2.** to engulf; swallow up: *The flood waters ingurgitated trees and houses.* —*v.i.* **3.** to drink or eat greedily; guzzle; swill. [< L *ingurgitāt(us)* flooded, filled (ptp. of *ingurgitāre*), equiv. to *in-* IN-[2] + *gurgit-* (s. of *gurges*) whirlpool, flood + *-ātus* -ATE[1]] **—in·gur′gi·ta′tion,** *n.*

Ing·ve·on·ic (ing′vē on′ik), *adj.* of or pertaining to Old English, Old Frisian, and Old Saxon, taken collectively. Also, **Ing′vae·on′ic, Ing·wae·on·ic, Ing·we·on·ic** (ing′wē on′ik). [< L *Inguaeon(es)* Germanic tribal group (< Gmc: lit., friends of Ing, mythical Teutonic hero) + -IC]

INH, *Pharm., Trademark.* isoniazid.

in·hab·it (in hab′it), *v.t.* **1.** to live or dwell in (a place), as persons or animals: *Small animals inhabited the woods.* **2.** to exist or be situated within; indwell: *Weird notions inhabit his mind.* —*v.i.* **3.** *Archaic.* to live or dwell, as in a place. [< L *inhabit(āre)*, equiv. to *in-* IN-[2] + *habitāre* to dwell (see HABIT[2]); r. ME *enhabite* < MF *enhabiter*] **—in·hab′it·a·ble,** *adj.* **—in·hab′it·a·bil′i·ty,** *n.* **—in·hab′i·ta′tion,** *n.*

in·hab·it·an·cy (in hab′i tən sē), *n., pl.* **-cies. 1.** place of residence; habitation. **2.** residency; occupation. Also, **in·hab′it·ance.** [INHABITAN(T) + -CY]

in·hab·it·ant (in hab′i tənt), *n.* a person or an animal that inhabits a place; permanent resident. [late ME < L *inhabitant-* (s. of *inhabitāns*) dwelling in. See INHABIT, -ANT]

in·hab·it·ed (in hab′i tid), *adj.* having inhabitants: *an inhabited island.* [INHABIT + -ED[2]] **—in·hab′it·ed·ness,** *n.*

in·hab·it·er (in hab′i tər), *n.* *Archaic.* inhabitant. [ME; see INHABIT, -ER[1]]

in·hal·ant (in hā′lənt), *adj.* **1.** used for inhaling. —*n.* **2.** an apparatus or medicine used for inhaling: *a medicated nasal inhalant.* [INHALE + -ANT]

in·ha·la·tion (in′hə lā′shən), *n.* **1.** the act of inhaling. **2.** a medicinal preparation to be inhaled. [INHALE + -ATION]

in·ha·la·tor (in′hə lā′tər), *n.* an apparatus to help one inhale air, an anesthetic, medicinal vapors, etc. [INHALE + -ATOR]

in·hale (in hāl′), *v.*, **-haled, -hal·ing.** —*v.t.* **1.** to breathe in; draw in by breathing: *to inhale air.* —*v.i.* **2.** to breathe in, esp. the smoke of cigarettes, cigars, etc.: *Do you inhale when you smoke?* [IN-[2] + (EX)HALE]

in·hal·er (in hā′lər), *n.* **1.** an apparatus used in inhaling medicinal vapors, anesthetics, etc. **2.** a respirator. **3.** one who inhales. [INHALE + -ER[1]]

In·ham·ba·ne (in′yəm bä′nə), *n.* a seaport in SE Mozambique. 68,654 (est. 1955).

in·har·mon·ic (in′här mon′ik), *adj.* not harmonic; dissonant. [IN-[3] + HARMONIC] **—in·har·mo·ny** (in här′mə nē), *n.*

in·har·mo·ni·ous (in′här mō′nē əs), *adj.* **1.** not harmonious; discordant; unmelodious. **2.** not congenial; discordant; disagreeable: *It was unpleasant to spend an evening with such an inharmonious group.* [IN-[3] + HARMONIOUS] **—in′har·mo′ni·ous·ly,** *adv.* **—in′har·mo′ni·ous·ness,** *n.*

in·haul (in′hôl′), *n.* *Naut.* any of various lines for hauling a sail, spar, etc., inward or inboard in order to stow it after use. Also, **in′haul′er.** [IN-[1] + HAUL]

in·here (in hēr′), *v.i.*, **-hered, -her·ing.** to exist permanently and inseparably in, as a quality, attribute, element, etc.; belong intrinsically; be inherent: *He analyzed the advantages that inhere in a democratic system.* [< L *inhaerēre*, equiv. to *in-* IN-[2] + *haerēre* to stick]

in·her·ence (in hēr′əns, -her′-), *n.* **1.** state or fact of inhering or being inherent. **2.** *Philos.* the relation of an attribute to its subject. [< ML *inhaerentia.* See INHERENT, -ENCE]

in·her·en·cy (in hēr′ən sē, -her′-), *n., pl.* **-cies. 1.** inherence. **2.** something inherent. [< ML *inhaerentia.* See INHERENT, -ENCY]

in·her·ent (in hēr′ənt, -her′-), *adj.* **1.** existing in something as a permanent and inseparable element, quality, or attribute: *factors inherent in the situation.* **2.** *Gram.* standing before a noun. **3.** *Obs.* inhering; infixed. [< L *inhaerent-* (s. of *inhaerēns*), prp. of *inhaerēre* to INHERE; see -ENT] **—in·her′ent·ly,** *adv.*

—Syn. 1. innate, native, inbred, ingrained.

in·her·it (in her′it), *v.t.* **1.** to take or receive (property, a right, a title, etc.) by succession or will, as an heir: *to inherit the family estate.* **2.** to succeed (a person) as heir. **3.** to receive (anything), as by succession from predecessors: *the problems of government which the new administration inherited from its predecessors.* **4.** to receive (a genetic character) by the transmission of hereditary factors. **5.** to receive as one's portion. **6.** *Obs.* to make (one) heir (usually fol. by *of*). —*v.i.* **7.** to take or receive property or the like by virtue of being heir to it. **8.** to have succession as heir. **9.** to receive qualities, powers, duties, etc., as by inheritance (fol. by *from*). [ME *en(h)erit(i)en* < MF *enheriter* < LL *inhērēditāre* to make heir. See IN-[3], HEREDITARY]

in·her·it·a·ble (in her′i tə bəl), *adj.* **1.** capable of being inherited. **2.** capable of inheriting; qualified to inherit. [late ME < AF; see IN-[2], HERITABLE] **—in·her′it·a·bil′i·ty, in·her′it·a·ble·ness,** *n.* **—in·her′it·a·bly,** *adv.*

in·her·it·ance (in her′i təns), *n.* **1.** that which is or may be inherited; any property passing at the owner's death to the heir or those entitled to succeed. **2.** the genetic characters transmitted from parent to offspring, taken collectively. **3.** something, as a quality, characteristic, or other immaterial possession, received from progenitors or predecessors as if by succession: *an inheritance of family pride.* **4.** the act or fact of inheriting by succession, as if by succession, or genetically: *to receive property by inheritance.* **5.** portion; birthright; heritage: *Absolute rule was considered the inheritance of kings.* **6.** *Obs.* right of possession; ownership. [ME *enheritance* < AF. See INHERIT, -ANCE]

—Syn. 1. patrimony; legacy, bequest. INHERITANCE, HERITAGE denote something inherited. INHERITANCE is the common term for property or any possession that comes to an heir: *He received it as an inheritance from his parents. A farm came to him by inheritance.* HERITAGE, a dignified or literary word, indicates whatever is bequeathed to a subsequent generation by an individual or by society: *our cultural heritage from Greece and Rome.*

inher′itance tax′, a tax imposed on the right of heirs to receive a decedent's property, the rate depending on the number or relationships of the heirs. Cf. **estate tax.**

in·her·it·ed (in her′i tid), *adj.* **1.** received by inheritance. **2.** *Gram.* found also in an earlier stage of the same language, esp. in the earliest reconstructed stage. [INHERIT + -ED[2]]

in·her·i·tor (in her′i tər), *n.* a person who inherits; an heir. [ME *enheritour, -er.* See INHERIT, -OR[2]]

in·her·i·trix (in her′i triks), *n., pl.* **in·her·i·tri·ces** (in her′i trī′sēz). a female inheritor; heiress. Also, **in·her·i·tress** (in her′i tris). [INHERIT + -TRIX]

in·he·sion (in hē′zhən), *n.* the state or fact of inhering; inherence. [< LL *inhaesiōn-* (s. of *inhaesiō*), equiv. to L *inhaes(us)* stuck in (ptp. of *inhaerere* to INHERE) + *-iōn-* -ION]

in. Hg, inch of mercury.

in·hib·it (in hib′it), *v.t.* **1.** to restrain, hinder, arrest, or check (an action, impulse, etc.): *to inhibit one's natural impulses.* **2.** to prohibit; forbid. **3.** *Chem.* to decrease the rate of action of or stop a chemical reaction. [late ME *inhibite* < L *inhibit(us)* held in (ptp. of *inhibēre*), equiv. to *in-* IN-[2] + *-hib-* (var. of *hab-* hold) + *-itus* -ITE[1]] **—in·hib′it·a·ble,** *adj.* **—in·hib′it·er,** *n.*

—Syn. 1. repress, discourage, obstruct. **2.** interdict. See **forbid.**

in·hi·bi·tion (in′i bish′ən, in′hi-), *n.* **1.** the act of inhibiting; state of being inhibited. **2.** *Psychol.* the blocking or holding back of one psychological process by another. **3.** *Physiol.* **a.** a restraining, arresting, or checking of the action of an organ or cell. **b.** the reduction of a reflex or other activity as the result of an antagonistic stimulation. **c.** a state created at synapses making them less excitable by other sources of stimulation. **4.** *Chem.* a stoppage or decrease in the rate of action of a chemical reaction. **5.** *Eng. Eccles. Law.* an order, esp. from a bishop, suspending a priest or an incumbent from the performance of his duties. [ME *inhibicio(u)n* < L *inhibitiōn-* (s. of *inhibitiō*). See INHIBIT, -ION]

in·hib·i·tor (in hib′i tər), *n.* **1.** *Chem.* a substance that decreases the rate of or stops completely a chemical reaction. **2.** any impurity in a mineral that prevents luminescence. Cf. **activator** (def. 2). **3.** *Rocketry.* an inert antioxidant used with solid propellants to inhibit burning on certain surfaces. **4.** an inhibiter. [INHIBIT + -OR[2]]

in·hib·i·to·ry (in hib′i tōr′ē, -tôr′ē), *adj.* serving or tending to inhibit. Also, **in·hib′i·tive.** [< ML *inhibitōri(us).* See INHIBIT, -ORY[1]]

in hoc (in hōk′; *Eng.* in hok′), *Latin.* in this; in respect to this.

in hoc sig·no vin·ces (in hōk′ sig′nō wing′kās; *Eng.* in hok′ sig′nō vin′sēz), *Latin.* in this sign shalt thou conquer: motto used by Constantine the Great, from his vision, before battle, of a cross bearing these words.

in·ho·mo·ge·ne·i·ty (in hō′mə jə nē′i tē, -hom′ə-), *n.* **1.** lack of homogeneity. **2.** that which is not homogeneous. [IN-[3] + HOMOGENEITY] **—in·ho·mo·ge·ne·ous** (in′hō mə jē′nē əs, -hom ə-), *adj.* **—in′ho·mo·ge′ne·ous·ly,** *adv.*

in·hos·pi·ta·ble (in hos′pi tə bəl, in′ho spit′ə bəl), *adj.* **1.** not inclined to, or characterized by, hospitality, as persons, actions, etc. **2.** (of a region, climate, etc.) not offering shelter, favorable conditions, etc.: *an inhospitable rocky coast.* [< ML *inhospitābil(is).* See IN-[3], HOSPITABLE] **—in·hos′pi·ta·ble·ness,** *n.* **—in·hos′pi·ta·bly,** *adv.*

in·hos·pi·tal·i·ty (in′hos pi tal′i tē, in hos′-), *n.* lack of hospitality; inhospitable attitude toward visitors, guests, etc. [< L *inhospitālitās.* See IN-[3], HOSPITALITY]

in·hu·man (in hyo͞o′mən *or, often,* -yo͞o′-), *adj.* **1.** lacking the normal human qualities of sympathy, pity, warmth, compassion, or the like; cruel; brutal: *an inhuman master.* **2.** not human. [< L *inhūmān(us)*; r. late ME *inhumain* < MF. See IN-[3], HUMAN] **—in·hu′man·ly,** *adv.* **—in·hu′man·ness,** *n.*

—Syn. 1. unfeeling, unsympathetic, cold, callous, hard, savage, brutish.

in·hu·mane (in′hyo͞o mān′ *or, often,* -yo͞o-), *adj.* not humane; lacking humanity or kindness. [var. of INHUMAN] **—in′hu·mane′ly,** *adv.*

in·hu·man·i·ty (in′hyo͞o man′i tē *or, often,* -yo͞o-), *n., pl.* **-ties** for 2. **1.** state or quality of being inhuman or inhumane; cruelty: *man's inhumanity to man.* **2.** an inhuman or inhumane act. [late ME *inhumanite* < L *inhūmānitās.* See INHUMAN, -ITY]

in·hu·ma·tion (in′hyo͞o mā′shən), *n.* the act of inhuming; burial. [INHUME + -ATION]

in·hume (in hyo͞om′), *v.t.*, **-humed, -hum·ing.** to bury; inter. [< L *inhum(āre)* < *in-* IN-[2] + *humāre* to bury < *hum(us)* earth] **—in·hum′er,** *n.*

in·im·i·cal (i nim′i kəl), *adj.* **1.** adverse in tendency or effect; harmful: *a climate inimical to health.* **2.** unfriendly; hostile: *a cold, inimical gaze.* Also, **in·im′i·ca·ble.** [< L *inimīc(us)* ENEMY + -AL[1]] **—in·im′i·cal·ly,** *adv.* **—in·im′i·cal·ness, in·im′i·cal′i·ty,** *n.*

—Syn. 1. unfavorable, noxious. **2.** antagonistic. See **hostile. —Ant. 2.** friendly.

in·im·i·ta·ble (i nim′i tə bəl), *adj.* incapable of being imitated; surpassing imitation. [< L *inimitābil(is).* See IN-[3], IMITABLE] **—in·im′i·ta·bil′i·ty, in·im′i·ta·ble·ness,** *n.* **—in·im′i·ta·bly,** *adv.*

in·i·on (in′ē ən), *n.* *Craniol.* a point at the external occipital protuberance of the skull. [< NL < Gk: nape of the neck < *in-* (s. of *is*) fiber, sinew + *-ion* dim. suffix]

in·iq·ui·tous (i nik′wi təs), *adj.* characterized by iniquity; wicked; sinful. [INIQUIT(Y) + -OUS] **—in·iq′ui·tous·ly,** *adv.* **—in·iq′ui·tous·ness,** *n.*

—Syn. flagitious, nefarious, perverse, evil, base, unjust, wrong. **—Ant.** righteous.

in·iq·ui·ty (i nik′wi tē), *n., pl.* **-ties. 1.** gross injustice; wickedness. **2.** a violation of right or duty; wicked act; sin. [ME < L *inīquitās* unevenness, unfairness, equiv. to *inīqu(us)* uneven, unfair (*in-* IN-[3] + *-īquus*, var. of *aequus* EQUI-) + *-itās* -ITY]

init., initial.

in·i·tial (i nish′əl), *adj., n., v.*, **-tialed, -tial·ing** or (*esp. Brit.*) **-tialled, -tial·ling.** —*adj.* **1.** of or pertaining to the beginning; first: *the initial step in a process.* **2.** *Phonet.* occurring at the beginning of a word or syllable, as the *f* of *fit* and the *k*-sound of *chasm* and *quay.* —*n.* **3.** an initial letter, as of a word. **4.** the first letter of a proper name. **5.** a letter of extra size or an ornamental character used at the beginning of a chapter or other division of a book or the like. —*v.t.* **6.** to mark or sign with an initial or the initials of one's name, sometimes as a token of preliminary or informal approval. [< L *initiāl(is)*, equiv. to *initi(um)* beginning (*init(us)* begun (ptp. of *inīre* to go in, enter upon), equiv. to *in-* IN-[2] + *-i-* go + *-tus* ptp. suffix + *-ium* n. suffix) + *-alis* -AL[1]] **—in·i′tial·er;** *esp. Brit.*, **in·i′tial·ler,** *n.* **—in·i′tial·ly,** *adv.*

ini′tial stabil′ity, *Naval Archit.* the resistance of a vessel to heeling. Also called **metacentric stability.**

in·i·ti·ate (*v.* i nish′ē āt′; *adj., n.* i nish′ē it, -āt′), *v.*, **-at·ed, -at·ing,** *adj., n.* —*v.t.* **1.** to begin, set going, or originate: *to initiate reforms.* **2.** to introduce into the knowledge of some art or subject. **3.** to admit with formal rites into secret knowledge, a society, etc. **4.** to propose (a measure) by initiative procedure: *to initiate a constitutional amendment.* —*adj.* **5.** initiated; begun. **6.** admitted into a society, club, etc., or into the knowledge of a subject. —*n.* **7.** a person who has been initiated. [< L *initiāt(us)* initiated (ptp. of *initiāre*), equiv. to *initi-* (see INITIAL) + *-ātus* -ATE[1]] **—in·i′ti·a′tor,** *n.*

—Syn. 1. commence; introduce, inaugurate, open. See **begin. 2.** teach, instruct, indoctrinate, train. **7.** tyro, beginner, learner, amateur, novice, pledge. **—Ant. 1.** conclude.

in·i·ti·a·tion (i nish′ē ā′shən), *n.* **1.** formal admission into a society, club, etc. **2.** the ceremonies of admission. **3.** the act of initiating. **4.** the fact of being initiated. [< L *initiātiōn-* (s. of *initiātiō*). See INITIATE, -ION]

in·i·ti·a·tive (i nish′ē ə tiv, i nish′ə-), *n.* **1.** an introductory act or step; leading action: *to take the initiative.* **2.** readiness and ability in initiating action; enterprise: *to lack initiative.* **3.** one's personal, responsible decision: *to act on one's own initiative.* **4.** *Govt.* **a.** a procedure by which a specified number of voters may propose a statute, constitutional amendment, or ordinance, and compel a popular vote on its adoption. Cf. **referendum** (def. 1). **b.** the general right or ability to present a new bill or measure, as in a legislature. —*adj.* **5.** of or pertaining to initiation; serving to initiate: *Initiative steps were taken to stop manufacture of the drug.* [INITIATE + -IVE] **—in·i′ti·a·tive·ly,** *adv.*

in·i·ti·a·to·ry (i nish′ē ə tōr′ē, -tôr′ē), *adj.* **1.** introductory; initial: *an initiatory step.* **2.** serving to initiate or admit into a society, club, etc. [INITIATE + -ORY[1]] **—in·i·ti·a·to·ri·ly** (i nish′ē ə tōr′ə lē, -tôr′-; i nish′ē ə tōr′ə lē, -tôr′-), *adv.*

in·i·ti·a·tress (i nish′ē ā′tris), *n.* a female initiator. [INITIAT(O)R + -ESS]

in·i·ti·a·trix (i nish′ē ā′triks, i nish′ē ə-), *n., pl.* **in·i·ti·a·tri·ces** (i nish′ē ā′tri sēz′, -ē ə trī′sēz), **-trix·es.** initiatress. [< LL; see INITIATE, -TRIX]

in·ject (in jekt′), *v.t.* **1.** to force (a fluid) into a passage, cavity, or tissue: *to inject a medicine into the veins.* **2.** to introduce (something new or different) into a thing: *to inject comedy into a situation.* **3.** to introduce arbitrarily or inappropriately; intrude. **4.** to interject (a remark, suggestion, etc.), as into conversation. [< L *inject(us)* thrown in (ptp. of *in(j)icere*), equiv. to *in-* IN-[2] + *-jec-* (var. of *jac-* throw) + *-tus* ptp. suffix] **—in·ject′a·ble,** *adj.*

inject., (in prescriptions) an injection. [< L *injectiō*]

in·jec·tion (in jek′shən), *n.* **1.** the act of injecting. **2.** that which is injected. **3.** a liquid injected into the body, esp. for medicinal purposes, as a hypodermic or an enema. **4.** state of being hyperemic or bloodshot. **5.** *Math.* a one-to-one function. [< L *injectiōn-* (s. of *injectiō*). See INJECT, -ION]

in·jec·tor (in jek′tər), *n.* **1.** one who or that which injects. **2.** *Mach.* **a.** a device for injecting feedwater into a boiler against high pressure by means of a jet of steam. **b.** a small multiple-plunger pump mechanism for spraying fuel into the cylinders of an internal-combustion engine. [INJECT + -OR[2]]

in·ju·di·cious (in′jo͞o dish′əs), *adj.* not judicious; showing lack of judgment; unwise; imprudent: *an injudicious decision.* [IN-[3] + JUDICIOUS] **—in′ju·di′cious·ly,** *adv.* **—in′ju·di′cious·ness,** *n.*

In·jun (in′jən), *n.* *Dial.* an American Indian. [var. of INDIAN]

in·junc·tion (in jungk′shən) *n.* **1.** *Law.* a judicial process or order requiring the person or persons to whom it is directed to do a particular act or to refrain from doing a particular act. **2.** the act or an instance of enjoining. **3.** a command; order; admonition: *the injunctions of the Lord.* [< LL *injunctiōn-* (s. of *injunctiō*), equiv. to L *injunct(us)* joined to, brought upon (ptp. of *injungere*; see ENJOIN) + *-iōn-* -ION] **—in·junc′tive,** *adj.* **—in·junc′tive·ly,** *adv.*

in·jure (in′jər), *v.t.*, **-jured, -jur·ing. 1.** to do or cause harm of any kind to; damage; hurt; impair: *to injure one's hand.* **2.** to do wrong or injustice to: *to injure a friend's feelings.* [back formation from INJURY (n.); r. *injury* (v.)] **—in′jur·a·ble,** *adj.* **—in′jur·er,** *n.*

—Syn. 1. spoil, ruin, break, mar. INJURE, IMPAIR mean to harm or damage something. INJURE is a general term referring to any kind or degree of damage: *to injure one's spine; to injure one's reputation.* To IMPAIR is to make imperfect in any way, often with a suggestion of progressive deterioration and of permanency in the result: *One's health is impaired by overwork.* **2.** maltreat, abuse. **—Ant. 1.** benefit.

in·jured (in′jərd), *adj.* **1.** wounded or harmed; damaged; hurt: *an injured arm.* **2.** offended; wronged: *an injured reputation.* **3.** displaying, or evincing, a feeling of injury; offended; reproachful: *Her face wore an injured look.* [INJURE + -ED[2]] **—in′jured·ly,** *adv.* **—in′jured·ness,** *n.*

in·ju·ri·ous (in jo͝or′ē əs), *adj.* **1.** harmful, hurtful, or detrimental, as in effect: *Injurious eating habits impaired his health.* **2.** doing or involving injury or wrong, as to another: *injurious behavior.* **3.** insulting; abusive; offensive: *an injurious statement.* [late ME < L *injūrius*, equiv. to *in-* IN-[3] + *jūri-* (s. of *jūs*) right + *-us* -OUS] **—in·ju′ri·ous·ly,** *adv.* **—in·ju′ri·ous·ness,** *n.*

—Syn. 1. damaging, deleterious, pernicious, baneful,

CONCISE ETYMOLOGY KEY: <, descended or derived from; >, whence; b., blend of, blended; c., cognate with; deriv., derivative; equiv., equivalent; imit., imitative; m., modification of; obl., oblique; r., replacing; s., stem; sp., spelling; trans., translation; ?, origin unknown, perhaps; *, hypothetical. See the full key inside the front cover.

destructive, ruinous. **2.** unjust, wrongful, prejudicial, inequitable. **3.** derogatory, defamatory, slanderous, libelous. **—Ant. 1.** beneficial. **3.** complimentary.

in·ju·ry (in′jə rē), *n., pl.* **-ju·ries. 1.** harm done or sustained: *to escape without injury.* **2.** a particular form or instance of harm: *an injury to my shoulder; an injury to my pride.* **3.** wrong or injustice done or suffered. **4.** *Law.* any wrong or violation of the rights, property, reputation, etc., of another for which legal action to recover damages may be made. **5.** *Obs.* injurious speech; calumny. [ME *injurie* < L *injūria*, n. use of fem. of *injūrius* INJURIOUS]
—Syn. 1. damage, ruin, impairment, mischief. **1–3.** INJURY, HURT, WOUND refer to material or moral impairments or wrongs. INJURY, originally denoting a wrong done or suffered, is hence used for any kind of evil, impairment, or loss, caused or sustained: *physical injury; injury to one's reputation.* HURT suggests esp. physical injury, often bodily injury attended with pain: *a bad hurt from a fall.* A WOUND is usually a physical hurt caused by cutting, shooting, etc., or an emotional hurt: *a serious wound in the shoulder; to inflict a wound by betraying someone's trust.* **—Ant. 1.** benefit.

in·jus·tice (in jus′tis), *n.* **1.** the quality or fact of being unjust; inequity. **2.** violation of the rights of others; unjust or unfair action or treatment. **3.** an unjust act; wrong; unfairness. [ME < MF < L *injustitia*. See IN-[3], JUSTICE]
—Syn. 2. injury, wrong; tort.

ink (ingk), *n.* **1.** a fluid or viscous substance used for writing or printing. **2.** a dark, protective fluid ejected by the cuttlefish and other cephalopods. **—*v.t.* 3.** to mark, stain, cover, or smear with ink: *to ink one's clothes.* [ME *inke, enke* < MF *enque* < LL *enc(austum)* < Gk *énkauston* purple ink, n. use of neut. of *énkaustos* burnt in. See EN-[2] CAUSTIC] **—ink′er,** *n.* **—ink′less,** *adj.* **—ink′like′,** *adj.*

ink′ ball′, *Print.* one of a pair of heavy pads of horsehair and cotton covered with sheepskin or buckskin and equipped with a handle, used before the invention of the ink roller for dabbing ink on type for printing.

ink·ber·ry (ingk′ber′ē, -bə rē), *n., pl.* **-ries. 1.** Also called **bearbush.** a shrub, *Ilex glabra*, having leathery, evergreen leaves and black berries. **2.** the pokeweed. **3.** the berry of either plant. [INK + BERRY]

Ink·er·man (ing′kər man′), *n.* a locality in S Crimea, in the SW Soviet Union in Europe: Russian defeat 1854.

ink·horn (ingk′hôrn′), *n.* a small container of horn or other material, formerly used to hold writing ink. [INK + HORN]

ink′horn term′, an obscure, affectedly erudite borrowing from another language, esp. Latin or Greek, as *contiguate, ingent.*

in·kie (ing′kē), *n.* inky[2].

in·kle (ing′kəl), *n.* **1.** a linen tape used for trimmings. **2.** the linen thread or yarn from which this tape is made. [?]

ink·ling (ingk′ling), *n.* **1.** a slight suggestion; hint; intimation: *He hadn't been given an inkling of what was going to happen.* **2.** a vague idea or notion; slight understanding: *They had only an inkling of how the new invention worked.* [obs. *inkle* to hint (ME *incle*) + -ING[1]; akin to OE *inca* suspicion]

ink·stand (ingk′stand′), *n.* **1.** a small stand, usually on a desk, for holding ink, pens, etc. **2.** a cuplike container for ink. [INK + STAND]

Ink·ster (ingk′stər), *n.* a city in SE Michigan, near Detroit. 39,079 (1960).

ink·well (ingk′wel′), *n.* a container for ink. Also called, *esp. Brit.,* **ink·pot** (ingk′pot′). [INK + WELL[2]]

ink·wood (ingk′wŏŏd′), *n.* a sapindaceous tree, *Exothea paniculata*, of the West Indies and Florida, yielding a hard, reddish-brown wood. [INK + WOOD[1]]

ink·y[1] (ing′kē), *adj.,* **ink·i·er, ink·i·est. 1.** black as ink: *inky shadows.* **2.** resembling ink: *The solution was an inky liquid.* **3.** stained with ink: *inky fingers.* **4.** of or pertaining to ink. **5.** consisting of or containing ink. **6.** written with ink. [INK + -Y[1]] **—ink′i·ness,** *n.*

in·ky[2] (ing′kē), *n., pl.* **-kies.** *Slang.* an incandescent lamp. Also, **inkie.** [INC(ANDESCENT) + -Y[2]]

ink′y cap′, any mushroom of the genus *Coprinus*, esp. *C. atramentarius*, whose gills disintegrate into blackish liquid after the spores mature.

in·laid (in′lād′, in lād′), *adj.* **1.** set into the surface of something: *an inlaid design on a chest.* **2.** decorated or made with a design set in the surface: *an inlaid table.* [ptp. of INLAY]

in·land (*adj.* in′lənd; *adv., n.* in′land′, -lənd), *adj.* **1.** pertaining to or situated in the interior part of a country or region: *inland cities.* **2.** *Brit.* carried on within a country; domestic; not foreign; internal: *inland mail; inland revenue.* **—*adv.* 3.** in or toward the interior of a country. **—*n.* 4.** the interior part of a country, away from the border. [ME, OE; see IN-[1], LAND]

in′land bill′, a bill of exchange drawn and payable, actually or on its face, in the same jurisdiction, as in the same country or State. Cf. **foreign bill.**

in·land·er (in′lən dər), *n.* a person living inland. [INLAND + -ER[1]]

in′land marine′ insur′ance, insurance chiefly covering risks to goods and means of transportation involved in the transporting of goods overland or by inland waterways. Cf. **ocean marine insurance.**

In′land Sea′, a sea in SW Japan, enclosed by the islands of Honshu, Shikoku, and Kyushu. 240 mi. long.

in-law (in′lô′), *n.* a relative by marriage, esp. a mother-in-law or father-in-law. [back formation from MOTHER-IN-LAW and the like]

in·law (in lô′, in′lô′), *v.t. Law.* to restore (an outlaw) to the benefits and protection of the law. [ME *inlaw-(en)*, OE *inlagian*. See IN-[1], LAW] **—in′law′ry,** *n.*

in·lay (*v.* in′lā′, in′lā′; *n.* in′lā′), *v.,* **-laid, -lay·ing,** *n.* **—*v.t.* 1.** to decorate (an object) with veneers of fine materials set in its surface: *to inlay a chest with lighter wood.* **2.** to insert or apply (layers of fine materials) in the surface of an object: *to insert marble in a tabletop.* **3.** *Hort.* to place (a fitted scion) into a prepared stock, as in a method of grafting. **—*n.* 4.** inlaid work. **5.** a veneer of fine material inserted in something else, esp. for ornament. **6.** a design or decoration made by inlaying. **7.** *Dentistry.* a filling of metal, porcelain, or the like, which is first shaped to fit a cavity and then cemented into it. **8.** *Hort.* See **inlay graft. 9.** act or process of inlaying. [IN-[1] + LAY[1]] **—in′lay′er,** *n.*

in′lay graft′, *Hort.* a graft in which the scion is matched into a place in the stock from which a piece of corresponding bark has been removed.

in-lb, inch-pound.

in·let (*n.* in′let, -lit; *v.* in′let′, in let′), *n., v.,* **-let, -let·ting.** **—*n.* 1.** an indentation of a shoreline, usually long and narrow; narrow passage between islands. **2.** a place of admission; entrance. **3.** something put in or inserted. **—*v.t.* 4.** to put in; insert. [ME; see IN, LET[1]]

in·li·er (in′lī′ər), *n. Geol.* outcrop of a formation completely surrounded by another of later date. [IN + (OUT)LIER]

in li·mi·ne (in lē′mi ne; *Eng.* in lim′i nē), *Latin.* on the threshold; at the outset.

in-line (in′līn′, in′līn′), *adj.* (of an internal-combustion engine) having the cylinders ranged side by side in one or more rows along the crankshaft.

in·line (in′līn′), *n. Printing.* an ornamented type with a white line at the center of each stroke. [IN + LINE[1]]

in loc. cit., in the place cited. [< L *in locō citātō*]

in lo·co (in lō′kō), *Latin.* in place; in the proper place.

in lo·co pa·ren·tis (in lō′kō pä ren′tēs; *Eng.* in lō′kō pə ren′tis), *Latin.* in the place of a parent; replacing a parent.

in·ly (in′lē), *adv. Chiefly Literary.* **1.** inwardly. **2.** intimately; deeply. [ME *inliche*, OE *inlīce*. See IN, -LY]

in·mate (in′māt′), *n.* **1.** a person who is confined in a hospital, prison, etc. **2.** *Archaic.* a person who dwells with another or others in the same house. [IN-[1] + MATE[1]]

in me·di·as res (in me′di äs′ res′; *Eng.* in mē′dē as′ rēz′, in mā′dē äs′ rās′), *Latin.* in the middle of things: *Homer began his story* in medias res.

in mem., in memoriam.

in me·mo·ri·am (in mə mōr′ē əm, -môr′-), in memory (of); to the memory (of); as a memorial (to). [< L]

In Memoriam A. H. H., an elegiac poem (1850) by Tennyson, on his friend Arthur Henry Hallam.

In Memory of W. B. Yeats, an elegy (1940) by W. H. Auden on the death of Yeats.

in·mesh (in mesh′), *v.t.* enmesh.

in·most (in′mōst′ *or, esp. Brit.,* -məst), *adj.* **1.** situated farthest within: *the inmost recesses of the forest.* **2.** most intimate: *one's inmost thoughts.* [ME (see IN-[1], -MOST); r. *inmest*, OE *innemest*, equiv. to *inne-* within + *-mest* -MOST]

inn (in), *n.* **1.** a commercial establishment that provides lodging, food, etc., for the public, esp. travelers; small hotel: *a country inn.* **2.** a tavern. **3.** (*cap.*) *Brit.* **a.** any of several buildings used as a place of residence for students. Cf. **Inns of Court. b.** a legal society occupying such a building. [ME, OE *in(n)* house; akin to Icel *inni*] **—inn′less,** *adj.*
—Syn. 1. hostelry. See **hotel.**

Inn (in), *n.* a river in central Europe, flowing from S Switzerland through Austria and Germany into the Danube. 320 mi. long.

inn·age (in′ij), *n.* **1.** the quantity of goods remaining in a container when received after shipment. Cf. **outage** (def. 3). **2.** *Aeron.* the amount of fuel remaining in the fuel tanks of an aircraft following a flight. Cf. **outage** (def. 4). [IN + -AGE]

in·nards (in′ərdz), *n.* (*construed as pl.*) *Informal.* **1.** the interior parts of an animal body; entrails; viscera: *He had a pain in his innards.* **2.** the internal mechanism, parts, structure, etc., of something; the interior of something: *molten lava flowing from the earth's innards.* [var. of *inwards*, n. pl. use of INWARD]

in·nate (i nāt′, in′āt), *adj.* **1.** existing in one from birth; inborn; native: *innate talent.* **2.** inherent in the essential character of something: *an innate defect in the hypothesis.* **3.** originating in or arising from the intellect or the constitution of the mind, rather than learned through experience: *man's innate knowledge of good and evil.* [< L *innāt(us)* inborn (ptp. of *innascī*), equiv. to *in-* IN-[2] + *nātus* < *nā-* (var. of *gnā-*, ptp. s. of *nascī* to be born) + *-tus* ptp. suffix] **—in·nate′ly,** *adv.* **—in·nate′ness,** *n.*
—Syn. 1. native, natural, congenital.

in·ner (in′ər), *adj.* **1.** situated farther within; interior: *an inner door.* **2.** more intimate, private, or secret: *the inner circle of his friends.* **3.** of or pertaining to the mind or spirit; mental; spiritual: *the inner life.* **4.** not obvious; hidden; obscure: *an inner meaning.* [ME; OE *innera*, comp. of *inne* within; see INMOST] **—in′ner·ly,** *adv., adj.* **—in′ner·ness,** *n.*

in′ner automor′phism, *Math.* an automorphism which maps an element *x* into an element of the form axa^{-1} where a^{-1} is the inverse of *a*. Cf. **outer automorphism.**

in′ner bar′, *Eng. Law.* a body of the King's Counsel or Queen's Counsel who sit and plead inside the dividing bar in the court, ranking above the junior counsel. Cf. **outer bar.**

in′ner bar′rister, *Eng. Law.* a barrister belonging to the inner bar. Cf. **outer barrister.**

in·ner-di·rect·ed (in′ər di rek′tid, -dī-), *adj.* guided by one's own set of values rather than external pressures. Cf. **other-directed. —in′ner-di·rec′tion,** *n.*

in′ner ear′. See **internal ear.**

In′ner Heb′rides. See under **Hebrides.**

in′ner jib′, *Naut.* a headsail immediately forward of a forestaysail or fore-topmast staysail.

In′ner Light′, (in Quakerism) the light of Christ in the soul of every man, considered as a guiding force in his life. Also called **Inner Word, Christ Within.**

in′ner man′, 1. one's spiritual or intellectual being. **2.** the stomach or appetite: *a hearty meal to satisfy the inner man.*

in′ner mis′sion, a movement, originating in the early 19th century within the evangelical churches of Germany and later spreading through Europe and America, which ministered chiefly to the material and spiritual needs of the poor and of social outcasts.

In′ner Mongo′lia, Mongolia (def. 2).

in·ner·most (in′ər mōst′ *or, esp. Brit.,* -məst), *adj.* **1.** farthest inward; inmost. **—*n.* 2.** innermost part. [INNER + -MOST] **—in′ner·most′ly,** *adv.*

in′ner prod′uct, *Math.* **1.** Also called **dot product, scalar product.** the quantity obtained by multiplying the corresponding coordinates of each of two vectors and adding the products, equal to the product of the magnitudes of the vectors and the cosine of the angle between them. **2.** the integral of the product of two real-valued functions. **3.** the integral of the product of the first of two complex-valued functions and the conjugate of the second. **4.** a complex-valued function of two vectors taken in order, whose domain is a vector space.

in·ner·spring (in′ər spring′), *adj.* having or characterized by a number of enclosed helical springs supporting padding: *an innerspring mattress; innerspring construction.* [INNER + SPRING]

In′ner Tem′ple, 1. See under **Inns of Court** (def. 1). **2.** See under **temple**[1] (def. 10).

in′ner tube′, a doughnut-shaped, flexible rubber tube inflated inside the carcass of a balloon tire to bear the weight of a vehicle.

in·ner·vate (i nûr′vāt, in′ər vāt′), *v.t.,* **-vat·ed, -vat·ing. 1.** to communicate nervous energy to; stimulate through nerves. **2.** to furnish with nerves; grow nerves into. [IN-[2] + NERVE + -ATE[1]]

in·ner·va·tion (in′ər vā′shən), *n.* **1.** the act of innervating; state of being innervated. **2.** *Anat.* the distribution of nerves to a part. [INNERVATE + -ION] **—in′ner·va′tion·al,** *adj.*

in·nerve (i nûrv′), *v.t.,* **-nerved, -nerv·ing.** to supply with nervous energy; invigorate; animate. [IN-[2] + NERVE]

In′ner Word′. See **Inner Light.**

In·ness (in′is), *n.* **George,** 1825–94, and his son **George,** 1854–1926, U.S. painters.

inn·hold·er (in′hōl′dər), *n.* innkeeper. [late ME; see INN, HOLDER]

in·ning (in′ing), *n.* **1.** *Baseball.* a division of a game during which each team has an opportunity to score until three outs have been made against it. **2.** a similar opportunity to score in certain other games, as horseshoes. **3.** an opportunity for activity; a turn: *Now the opposition will have its inning.* **4. innings, a.** (*construed as sing.*) *Cricket.* a unit of play in which the 11 members of each team have a turn at bat, the turn of a team ending after 10 players are put out or when the team declares. **b.** land reclaimed, esp. from the sea. **5.** the act of reclaiming marshy or flooded land. **6.** enclosure, as of waste land. **7.** the gathering in of crops. [ME *inninge*, OE *innung* a getting in, equiv. to *inn-(ian)* (to) go in + *-ung* -ING[1]]

inn·keep·er (in′kē′pər), *n.* a person who owns or operates an inn. [INN + KEEPER]

in·no·cence (in′ə səns), *n.* **1.** the quality or state of being innocent; freedom from sin or moral wrong. **2.** chastity: *She has not lost her innocence.* **3.** freedom from legal or specific wrong; guiltlessness: *The prisoner proved his innocence.* **4.** simplicity; guilelessness; ingenuousness. **5.** lack of knowledge or understanding; naïveté. **6.** harmlessness; innocuousness. **7.** an innocent person or thing. **8.** the North American bluet, *Houstonia caerulea.* **9.** a scrophulariaceous herb, *Collinsia verna*, having a blue-and-white flower. **10.** a related herb, *Collinsia bicolor*, of California. [ME < L *innocentia.* See INNOCENT, -ENCE]

in·no·cen·cy (in′ə sən sē), *n., pl.* **-cies.** innocence (defs. 1–6). [ME; var. of INNOCENCE]

in·no·cent (in′ə sənt), *adj.* **1.** free from moral wrong; without sin; pure: *innocent children.* **2.** free from legal or specific wrong; guiltless: *He was innocent of the crime.* **3.** not involving evil intent or motive: *an innocent misrepresentation.* **4.** free from any quality that can cause physical or moral injury; harmless: *innocent fun.* **5.** devoid (usually fol. by *of*): *a law innocent of merit.* **6.** having or showing the simplicity or naïveté of an unworldly person: *She looks so innocent you'd never guess she's a shrewd businesswoman.* **—*n.* 7.** an innocent person. **8.** a young child: *a slaughter of the innocents.* **9.** a guileless person. **10.** a simpleton or idiot. **11.** Usually, **innocents.** (*construed as sing.*) *U.S.* the bluet, *Houstonia caerulea.* [ME < L *innocent-* (s. of *innocēns*) harmless, equiv. to *in-* IN-[3] + *nocēns* harmful, prp. of *nocēre* to harm; see -ENT] **—in′no·cent·ly,** *adv.*
—Syn. 1. sinless, virtuous; faultless, impeccable, spotless, immaculate. **2.** INNOCENT, BLAMELESS, GUILTLESS imply freedom from the responsibility of having done wrong. INNOCENT may imply having done no wrong at any time, and having not even a knowledge of evil: *an innocent victim.* BLAMELESS denotes freedom from blame, esp. moral blame: *a blameless life.* GUILTLESS denotes freedom from guilt or responsibility for wrongdoing, usually in a particular instance: *guiltless of a crime.* **6.** simple, naïve, unsophisticated, artless, guileless, ingenuous. **—Ant. 1.** guilty.

In·no·cent I (in′ə sənt), **Saint,** died A.D. 417, Italian ecclesiastic: pope 401–417.

Innocent II, (*Gregorio Papareschi*) died 1143, Italian ecclesiastic: pope 1130–43.

Innocent III, (*Giovanni Lotario de' Conti*) 1161?–1216, Italian ecclesiastic: pope 1198–1216.

Innocent IV, (*Sinbaldo de Fieschi*) c1180–1254, Italian ecclesiastic: pope 1243–54.

Innocent V, (*Pierre de Tarentaise*) c1225–76, French ecclesiastic: pope 1276.

Innocent VI, (*Étienne Aubert*) died 1362, French jurist and ecclesiastic: pope 1352–62.

Innocent VII, (*Cosimo de' Migliorati*) 1336–1406, Italian ecclesiastic: pope 1404–06.

Innocent VIII, (*Gioqanni Battista Cibò*) 1432–92, Italian ecclesiastic: pope 1484–92.

Innocent IX, (*Giovanni Antonio Facchinetti*) 1519–91, Italian ecclesiastic: pope 1591.

Innocent X, (*Giambattista Pamfili*) 1574–1655, Italian ecclesiastic: pope 1644–55.

Innocent XI, (*Bendetto Odescalchi*) 1611–89, Italian ecclesiastic: pope 1676–89.

Innocent XII, (*Antonio Pignatelli*) 1615–1700, Italian ecclesiastic: pope 1691–1700.

Innocent XIII, (*Michelangelo Conti*) 1655–1724, Italian ecclesiastic: pope 1721–24.

In′nocents Abroad′, The, a satirical narrative (1869) by Mark Twain.

In′nocents′ Day′. See **Holy Innocents' Day.**

in·noc·u·ous (i nok′yo͞o əs), *adj.* **1.** not harmful or injurious; harmless: *an innocuous home remedy.* **2.** not likely to irritate or give offense; inoffensive: *a soothing, innocuous remark.* **3.** without power to interest or excite; pallid; insipid: *an innocuous novel.* [< L *innocuus.* See IN-³, NOCUOUS] —**in·noc′u·ous·ly,** *adv.* —**in·noc′u·ous·ness, in·no·cu·i·ty** (in′ə kyo͞o′i tē), *n.*

in·nom·i·nate (i nom′ə nit), *adj.* having no name; nameless; anonymous. [< LL *innōmināt(us)* unnamed. See IN-³, NOMINATE]

innom′inate ar′tery, *Anat.* an artery that arises from the arch of the aorta and divides into the right subclavian artery and right common carotid.

innom′inate bone′, *Anat.* either of the two bones forming the sides of the pelvis, each consisting of three consolidated bones, the ilium, ischium, and pubis. See diag. under **pelvis.**

innom′inate vein′, *Anat.* either of the two veins, one on each side of the base of the neck, that are formed by the union of the subclavian and internal jugular veins and unite to form the superior vena cava.

in·nom·i·ne (in nom′ə nā′, -nē′, -nō′mə nā′), *n. Music.* any of various English polyphonic instrumental compositions of the 16th and 17th centuries using an antiphon for Trinity Sunday as a cantus firmus. [< L phrase *in nōmine* in the name (of the Trinity or one of its members), a liturgical formula]

in·no·vate (in′ə vāt′), *v.,* **-vat·ed, -vat·ing.** —*v.i.* **1.** to introduce something new; make changes in anything established (often fol. by *on* or *in*): *to innovate on another's creation.* —*v.t.* **2.** to introduce (something new) for or as if for the first time: *to innovate a computer system.* **3.** *Obs.* to alter. [< L *innovāt(us)* renewed, altered (ptp. of *innovāre*), equiv. to *in-* IN-² + *novātus* (*novā(re)* (to) renew + *-tus* ptp. suffix)] —**in′no·va′tive, in·no·va·to·ry** (in′ō və tôr′ē, -tōr′ē, -vā′tə rē), *adj.* —**in′no·va′tor,** *n.*

in·no·va·tion (in′ə vā′shən), *n.* **1.** something new or different introduced: *numerous innovations in the high-school curriculum.* **2.** act of innovating; introduction of new things or methods. [< L *innovātiōn-* (s. of *innovātiō*). See INNOVATE, -ION] —**in′no·va′tion·al,** *adj.*

in·nox·ious (i nok′shəs), *adj.* harmless; innocuous. [< L *innoxius.* See IN-³, NOXIOUS] —**in·nox′ious·ly,** *adv.* —**in·nox′ious·ness,** *n.*

Inns·bruck (inz′bro͝ok; *Ger.* ins′brŏŏk), *n.* a city in W Austria, on the Inn River. 100,699 (1961).

Inns′ of Court′, 1. the four voluntary legal societies in England (**Lincoln's Inn,** the **Inner Temple,** the **Middle Temple,** and **Gray's Inn**) which have the exclusive privilege of calling candidates to the English bar after they have received such instruction and taken such examinations as the Inns provide. **2.** the buildings owned and used by the Inns.

in·nu·en·do (in′yo͞o en′dō), *n., pl.* **-dos, -does. 1.** an indirect intimation about a person or thing, esp. of a derogatory nature. **2.** *Law.* **a.** a parenthetic explanation or specification in a pleading. **b.** (in an action for slander or libel) the explanation and elucidation of the words alleged to be defamatory. **c.** the word or expression thus explained. [< L: a hint, lit., by signaling, abl. of *innuendum,* ger. of *innuere* to signal, equiv. to *in-* IN-² + *nuere* to nod]

in·nu·mer·a·ble (i no͞o′mər ə bəl, -nyo͞o′-), *adj.* **1.** very numerous. **2.** incapable of being numbered or counted. Also, **in·nu′mer·ous.** [ME < L *innumerābil(is)* countless, innumerable, equiv. to *in-* IN-³ + *numerābilis* that can be counted or numbered (*numer(us)* a number + *-ā-* connective vowel + *-bilis* -BLE)] —**in·nu′mer·a·ble·ness, in·nu′mer·a·bil′i·ty,** *n.* —**in·nu′mer·a·bly,** *adv.*
—**Syn. 1.** See **many. 2.** numberless, countless.

in·nu·tri·tion (in′no͞o trish′ən, -nyo͞o-), *n.* lack of nutrition. [IN-³ + NUTRITION] —**in′nu·tri′tious,** *adj.*

I·no (ī′nō), *n. Class. Myth.* a daughter of Cadmus and Harmonia who fled from the madness of her husband Athamas, jumped with her son into the sea, and was afterward deified as Leucothea.

in·ob·serv·ance (in′əb zûr′vəns), *n.* **1.** lack of observance; inattention: *drowsy inobservance.* **2.** nonobservance; inattentiveness: *inobservance of the rules.* [< L *inobservantia.* See IN-³, OBSERVANCE] —**in′ob·serv′ant,** *adj.* —**in′ob·serv′ant·ly,** *adv.*

in·oc·u·la·ble (i nok′yə lə bəl), *adj.* capable of being inoculated. [INOCUL(ATE) + -ABLE] —**in·oc′u·la·bil′i·ty,** *n.*

in·oc·u·lant (i nok′yə lənt), *n.* inoculum. [INOCUL(ATE) + -ANT]

in·oc·u·late (i nok′yə lāt′), *v.,* **-lat·ed, -lat·ing.** —*v.t.* **1.** to implant (a disease) in a person or animal by the introduction of germs or virus, as through a puncture, in order to produce a mild form of the disease and therefore secure immunity. **2.** to affect or treat (a person or animal) in this manner. **3.** to introduce (microorganisms) into surroundings suited to their growth, esp. into the body. **4.** to imbue (a person), as with ideas. **5.** *Metall.* to treat (molten metal) chemically to improve the microstructure. —*v.i.* **6.** to perform inoculation. [ME < L *inoculāt(us)* implanted (ptp. of *inoculāre*), equiv. to *in-* IN-² + *-oculā-* (s. of *-oculāre* to graft, deriv. of *oculus* eye, bud) + *-tus* ptp. suffix] —**in·oc·u·la·tive** (i nok′yə lā′tiv, -yə lə-), *adj.* —**in·oc′u·la′tor,** *n.*
—**Syn. 4.** indoctrinate, infuse.

in·oc·u·la·tion (i nok′yə lā′shən), *n.* **1.** act or process of inoculating. **2.** an instance of this. [ME < L *inoculātiōn-* (s. of *inoculātiō*) an engrafting. See INOCULATE, -ION]

in·oc·u·lum (i nok′yə ləm), *n., pl.* **-la** (-lə). the substance used to make an inoculation. [< NL, equiv. to *inocul(āre)* (to) INOCULATE + *-um* n. suffix]

in·o·dor·ous (in ō′dər əs), *adj.* not odorous; odorless. [< L *inodōrus.* See IN-³, ODOROUS] —**in·o′dor·ous·ly,** *adv.* —**in·o′dor·ous·ness,** *n.*

in·of·fen·sive (in′ə fen′siv), *adj.* **1.** doing no harm; harmless; unoffending: *a mild, inoffensive man.* **2.** not objectionable; not being a cause of offense. [IN-³ + OFFENSIVE] —**in′of·fen′sive·ly,** *adv.* —**in′of·fen′sive·ness,** *n.*

in·of·fi·cious (in′ə fish′əs), *adj.* **1.** *Law.* being inconsistent with moral duty and natural affection: *an inofficious will.* **2.** *Obs.* disinclined to fulfill obligations; disobliging. [< L *inofficiōs(us).* See IN-³, OFFICIOUS] —**in′of·fi′cious·ness, in·of·fi·ci·os·i·ty** (in′ə fish′ē os′i tē), *n.*

in′offi′cious will′, *Law.* a will inconsistent with the moral duty and natural affection of the testator and denying to his legitimate heirs the portions of the estate to which they are legally entitled. Also called **in′offi′cious tes′tament.** Cf. **officious will.**

in om·ni·a pa·ra·tus (in ōm′nē ä′ pä rä′to͞os; *Eng.* in om′nē ə pə rā′təs), *Latin.* prepared for all things.

I·nö·nü (i nœ ny′), *n.* **Is·met** (is met′), (*Ismet Paşa*), born 1884, president of Turkey 1938–50; prime minister 1923–24, 1925–37, 1961–65.

in·op·er·a·ble (in op′ər ə bəl), *adj.* **1.** not operable. **2.** not admitting of a surgical operation without undue risk. Cf. **operable** (def. 2). [IN-³ + OPERABLE]

in·op·er·a·tive (in op′ər ə tiv, -ə rā′tiv), *adj.* **1.** not operative; not in operation. **2.** without effect: *inoperative remedies.* [IN-³ + OPERATIVE] —**in·op′er·a·tive·ness,** *n.*

in·op·por·tune (in op′ər to͞on′, -tyo͞on′), *adj.* not opportune; inappropriate; untimely or unseasonable: *an inopportune visit; an inopportune moment.* [< LL *inopportūn(us).* See IN-³, OPPORTUNE] —**in·op′por·tune′ly,** *adv.* —**in·op′por·tune′ness, in·op′por·tu′ni·ty,** *n.*

in·or·di·nate (in ôr′dᵊnit), *adj.* **1.** not within proper limits; immoderate; excessive: *He drank an inordinate amount of wine.* **2.** disorderly; uncontrolled. **3.** unrestrained in conduct, feelings, etc.; intemperate: *an inordinate admirer of beauty; an inordinate prankster.* **4.** not regulated; irregular: *inordinate hours.* [ME *inordinat* < L *inordināt(us)* disordered, equiv. to *in-* IN-³ + *ordinātus* orderly, appointed; see ORDINATE, ORDAIN] —**in·or′di·nate·ness;** *Obs.,* **in·or·di·na·cy** (in ôr′dᵊnə sē), *n.* —**in·or′di·nate·ly,** *adv.*
—**Syn. 1.** immoderate, extreme, exorbitant, outrageous, unreasonable, disproportionate. —**Ant. 1.** reasonable.

inorg., inorganic.

in·or·gan·ic (in′ôr gan′ik), *adj.* **1.** not having the structure or organization characteristic of living bodies. **2.** not characterized by vital processes. **3.** *Chem.* noting or pertaining to compounds that are not hydrocarbons or their derivatives. Cf. **organic** (def. 1). **4.** not fundamental or related; extraneous. [IN-³ + ORGANIC] —**in′or·gan′i·cal·ly,** *adv.*

in′organ′ic chem′istry, the branch of chemistry dealing with inorganic substances.

in·or·gan·i·za·tion (in ôr′gə ni zā′shən), *n.* lack of organization. [IN-³ + ORGANIZATION]

in·os·cu·late (in os′kyə lāt′), *v.i., v.t.,* **-lat·ed, -lat·ing. 1.** to unite by openings, as arteries in anastomosis. **2.** to connect or join so as to become or make continuous, as fibers; blend. **3.** to unite intimately. [IN-² + OSCULATE] —**in·os′cu·la′tion,** *n.*

in·o·sil·i·cate (in′ə sil′ə kit, -kāt′, ī′nə-), *n. Mineral.* any silicate having a structure consisting of paired parallel chains of tetrahedral silicate groups, every other of which shares an oxygen atom with a group of the other chain, the ratio of silicon to oxygen being four to eleven. Cf. **cyclosilicate, nesosilicate, sorosilicate, tektosilicate.** [< Gk *ino-* (comb. form of *ís* fiber, sinew) + SILICATE]

in·o·si·tol (i nō′si tôl′, -tōl′, -tol′), *n.* **1.** *Biochem.* a compound, $C_6H_6(OH)_6$, widely distributed in plants and seeds as phytin, and occurring in animal tissue and in urine: an essential growth factor for animal life, present in the vitamin-B complex. **2.** *Pharm.* the commercial form of this compound, a white, sweet, crystalline solid, used chiefly in the treatment of certain liver conditions. Also called **hexahydroxycyclohexane.** [*inosite* (Gk *in-,* s. of *ís* fiber, sinew + -OSE² + -ITE¹) + -OL¹]

in·o·trop·ic (in′ə trop′ik, ī′nə-), *adj. Med.* influencing the contractility of muscular tissue. [< Gk *ino-* (comb. form of *ís* fiber, sinew) + -TROPIC]

In Our Time′ a collection of 15 short stories (1924) by Ernest Hemingway.

in·o·wer (in ō′ər), *adv. Scot.* **1.** in an inward direction; closer to the center or interior; inby. **2.** closer to the fire; nearer the hearth. [IN + OVER]

in·ox·i·dize (in ok′si dīz′), *v.t.,* **-dized, -diz·ing.** *Chem.* to keep from oxidizing. [back formation from *inoxidizable.* See IN-³, OXIDIZABLE] —**in·ox′i·diz′a·ble,** *adj.*

in pais (in pā′), *Law.* outside of court; without legal proceedings. [< MF: in the country]

in pa·ri de·lic·to (in par′ī di lik′tō), *Law.* in equal fault; equally culpable or blameworthy. [< L]

in·pa·tient (in′pā′shənt), *n.* a patient who is lodged and fed as well as treated in a hospital. [IN-¹ + PATIENT]

in pec·to·re (in pek′tō re′; *Eng.* in pek′tə rē), *Latin.* not disclosed; in secret. [lit., in the breast]

in per·pe·tu·um (in per pet′o͞o o͝om′; *Eng.* in pər pet′yo͞o əm, -pech′o͞o-), *Latin.* forever.

in per·so·nam (in pər sō′nam), *Law.* against a person, as a legal proceeding. [< L]

in pet·to (ēn pet′tô; *Eng.* in pet′ō), *Italian.* (of cardinals whom the pope appoints but does not disclose in consistory) not disclosed. [lit., in (the) breast]

in·phase (in′fāz′), *adj. Elect.* having the same phase. [orig. phrase *in phase*]

in pos·se (in pō′se; *Eng.* in pos′ē), *Latin.* in possibility; potentially (contrasted with *in esse*).

in·pour (in pōr′, -pôr′), *v.i., v.t.* to pour in. [IN-¹ + POUR]

in prae·sen·ti (in prī sen′tē; *Eng.* in prē zen′tī), *Latin.* at the present time.

In Praise′ of Fol′ly, a prose satire (1509) by Erasmus, written in Latin and directed against theologians and church dignitaries. Latin, **Moriae Encomium.**

in pro·pri·a per·so·na (in prō′prē ä′ per sō′nä; *Eng.* in prō′prē ə pər sō′nə), *Latin.* in one's own person.

in·put (in′po͝ot′), *n., adj., v.* **-put·ted, -put·ting.** —*n.* **1.** that which is put in. **2.** the power or energy supplied to a machine. **3.** the current or voltage applied to an electric or electronic circuit or device. Cf. **output** (def. 4). **4.** *Computer Technol.* **a.** information properly coded for feeding into a computer. **b.** the process of introducing data into the internal storage of a computer. **5.** the available data for solving a technical problem. **6.** *Scot.* a monetary contribution, as to charity. —*adj.* **7.** *Chiefly Computer Technol.* of or pertaining to information or equipment used for input, esp. to a computer: *an input device.* —*v.t., v.i.* **8.** *Computer Technol.* to insert or supply (information or the like) for processing by a computer or similar device: *They inputted 3000 words for sorting.* [IN-¹ + PUT, modeled on *output*]

in·quar·ta·tion (in′kwôr tā′shən), *n.* (in assaying) the addition of silver to a gold-silver alloy in order to facilitate the parting of the gold by nitric acid. [? < F *inquartation.* See IN-², QUARTER, -ATION]

in·quest (in′kwest), *n.* **1.** a legal or judicial inquiry, esp. before a jury. **2.** Also called **coroner's inquest.** an investigation into the cause of death, made by a coroner. **3.** the body of men appointed to hold such an investigation, esp. a coroner's jury. **4.** the decision or finding based on such investigation. [ME < ML *inquēst(a),* equiv. to L *in-* IN-² + *quaesīta,* pl. (taken as sing.) of *quaesītum* question (see QUEST); r. ME *enqueste* < AF]
—**Syn. 1, 2.** hearing, inquisition.

in·qui·et (in kwī′ət), *v.t. Archaic.* to destroy the peace of; disturb; disquiet. [ME *inquiet(en)* < L *inquiēt(āre).* See IN-³, QUIET²] —**in·qui′et·ly,** *adv.* —**in·qui′et·ness,** *n.*

in·qui·e·tude (in kwī′i to͞od′, -tyo͞od′), *n.* **1.** restlessness; uneasiness. **2. inquietudes,** disquieting thoughts: *beset by myriad inquietudes.* [late ME < L *inquiētūdō.* See IN-³, QUIETUDE]

in·qui·line (in′kwə līn′, -lin), *n.* **1.** *Zool.* an animal living in the nest or burrow of another animal; guest. —*adj.* **2.** of the nature of an inquiline. [< L *inquilīn(us)* tenant, equiv. to *in-* IN-² + *-quil-* (var. of *col-;* see -COLOUS) + *-īnus* -INE¹] —**in·qui·lin·i·ty** (in′kwə lin′i tē), *n.* —**in·qui·li·nous** (in′kwə lī′nəs), *adj.*

in·quire (in kwīᵊr′), *v.,* **-quired, -quir·ing.** —*v.t.* **1.** to seek to learn by asking: *to inquire a person's name.* **2.** *Obs.* to seek. **3.** *Obs.* to question (a person). —*v.i.* **4.** to seek information by questioning; ask: *to inquire about a person.* **5.** to make investigation (usually fol. by *into*): *to inquire into the incident.* **6. inquire after,** to ask about the state of health or condition of: *Friends have been calling all morning to inquire after you.* Also, **enquire.** [late ME < L *inquīre(re)* (to) seek for (see IN-², QUERY); r. ME *enquere(n)* < OF *enquerre*] —**in·quir′a·ble,** *adj.* —**in·quir′er,** *n.*
—**Syn. 1, 5.** investigate, examine, query. INQUIRE, ASK, QUESTION imply that a person (or persons) addresses another (or others) to obtain information. ASK is the general word: *to ask what time it is.* INQUIRE is more formal and always implies asking about something specific: *to inquire about a rumor.* To QUESTION implies repetition and persistence in asking; it often applies to legal examination or investigation: *to question the survivor of an accident.* —**Ant. 1.** tell.

in·quir·ing (in kwīᵊr′ing), *adj.* **1.** seeking facts, information, or knowledge: *an inquiring mind.* **2.** curious; probing; inquisitive in seeking facts: *an inquiring reporter.* **3.** scrutinizing; questioning: *He looked at his father with inquiring eyes.* [INQUIRE + -ING²] —**in·quir′ing·ly,** *adv.*

in·quir·y (in kwīᵊr′ē, in′kwə rē), *n., pl.* **-quir·ies. 1.** a seeking for truth, information, or knowledge. **2.** an investigation, as into an incident. **3.** act of inquiring, or seeking information by questioning; interrogation. **4.** a question; query. Also, **enquiry.** [INQUIRE + -Y³; r. late ME *enquery*]
—**Syn. 1.** study, scrutiny, exploration. See **investigation.** —**Ant. 4.** answer, reply.

in·qui·si·tion (in′kwi zish′ən), *n.* **1.** an official investigation, esp. one of a political or religious nature, characterized by lack of regard for individual rights, prejudice on the part of the examiners, and recklessly cruel punishments. **2.** any harsh or prolonged questioning. **3.** act of inquiring; inquiry; research. **4.** an investigation, or process of inquiry. **5.** a judicial or official inquiry. **6.** the finding of such an inquiry. **7.** the document embodying the result of such inquiry. **8.** (*cap.*) *Rom. Cath. Ch.* the special tribunal, established in the 13th century and active until early modern times, engaged chiefly in combating and punishing heresy. Cf. **Holy Office.** [ME *inquisicio(u)n* < legal L *inquīsītiōn-* (s. of *inquīsītiō*), equiv. to *inquīsīt(us)* sought for (ptp. of *inquīrere* to INQUIRE) + *-iōn-* -ION] —**in′qui·si′tion·al,** *adj.*
—**Syn. 5.** inquest, hearing.

in·qui·si·tion·ist (in′kwi zish′ə nist), *n.* an inquisitor. [INQUISITION + -IST]

in·quis·i·tive (in kwiz′i tiv), *adj.* **1.** given to inquiry or research; desirous of or eager for knowledge; curious: *an inquisitive mind.* **2.** unduly curious; prying. —*n.* **3.** an inquisitive person or persons: *thick curtains to frustrate the inquisitive.* [< LL *inquīsītīv(us),* equiv. to L *inquīsīt(us)* sought for (see INQUISITION) + *-īvus* -IVE; r. ME *inquisitif* < MF] —**in·quis′i·tive·ly,** *adv.* —**in·quis′i·tive·ness,** *n.*
—**Syn. 2.** See **curious.** —**Ant. 1, 2.** uninterested.

in·quis·i·tor (in kwiz′i tər), *n.* **1.** one who makes inquisition. **2.** a questioner, esp. an unduly curious one. **3.** one who investigates by virtue of his office. **4.** a member of the Inquisition. Also, *referring to a woman,* **in·quis·i·tress** (in kwiz′i tris). [< legal L; see INQUISITION, -OR²]

in·quis·i·to·ri·al (in kwiz′i tōr′ē əl, -tôr′-), *adj.* **1.** of or pertaining to an inquisitor or inquisitors, or inquisition. **2.** exercising the office of an inquisitor. **3.** *Law.* **a.** pertaining to a trial with one person or group inquiring into the facts and acting as both prosecutor and judge. **b.** pertaining to secret criminal prosecutions. **4.** resembling an inquisitor in harshness or intrusiveness. **5.** inquisitive; prying. [< ML *inquīsītōri(us)* (L *inquīsītōr-* INQUISITOR + *-ius* adj. suffix) + -AL¹] —**in·quis′i·to′ri·al·ly,** *adv.* —**in·quis′i·to′ri·al·ness,** *n.*

in·ra·di·us (in′rā′dē əs), *n., pl.* **-di·i** (-dē ī′), **-di·us·es.** *Geom.* the radius of the circle inscribed in a triangle. [IN + RADIUS]

in re (in rē′, rā′), in the matter of. [< L]

in rem (in rem′), *Law.* concerning a thing, as a legal proceeding for its recovery. [< L: lit., against the thing]

in re·rum na·tu·ra (in rā′ro͝om nä to͞o′rä; *Eng.* in rēr′əm nə to͝or′ə, -tyo͝or′ə), *Latin.* in the nature of things.

I.N.R.I., Jesus of Nazareth, King of the Jews. [< L *Iēsus Nazarēnus, Rēx Iūdaeōrum*]

in·rig·ger (in′rig′ər), *n.* a rowboat having oarlocks on the gunwales. [IN + RIGGER, modeled on *outrigger*]

in·road (in′rōd′), *n.* **1.** a forcible or serious encroachment: *inroads on our savings.* **2.** a hostile or predatory incursion; raid; foray. [IN-[1] + ROAD]

in·rush (in′rush′), *n.* a rushing in; influx. [IN-[1] + RUSH[1]] —**in′rush′ing,** *n., adj.*

ins., **1.** inches. **2.** *Chiefly Brit.* inscribed. **3.** inspector. **4.** insulated. **5.** insurance.

I.N.S., International News Service, a news-gathering agency: merged in 1958 with United Press to form United Press International. Also, **INS**

in sae·cu·la sae·cu·lo·rum (in sī′ko͝o lä′ sī′ko͝o-lō′ro͝om; *Eng.* in sek′yə lə sek′yə lôr′əm, -lōr′-), *Latin.* for ever and ever. [lit., for ages of ages]

in·sal·i·vate (in sal′ə vāt′), *v.t.,* **-vat·ed, -vat·ing.** to mix with saliva, as food. [IN-[2] + SALIVATE] —**in-sal′i·va′tion,** *n.*

in·sa·lu·bri·ous (in′sə lo͞o′brē əs), *adj.* unfavorable to health. [< L *insalūbri(s)* + -OUS. See IN-[3], SALUBRIOUS] —**in′sa·lu′bri·ous·ly,** *adv.* —**in·sa·lu·bri·ty** (in′sə lo͞o′bri tē), *n.*

ins′ and outs′, **1.** physical characteristics, as windings and turnings, nooks, or recesses: *the ins and outs of a subterranean passage.* **2.** intricacies; particulars; peculiarities: *the ins and outs of the tax laws.*

in·sane (in sān′), *adj.* **1.** not sane; not of sound mind; mentally deranged. **2.** characteristic of one who is mentally deranged: *insane actions.* **3.** set apart for the care and confinement of mentally deranged persons: *an insane ward; insane asylum.* **4.** utterly senseless: *an insane attempt.* [< L *insān(us).* See IN-[3], SANE] —**in-sane′ly,** *adv.* —**in·sane′ness,** *n.*
—**Syn. 1.** demented; lunatic, crazed, crazy; maniacal. See **mad. 4.** foolish, irrational.

in·san·i·tar·y (in san′i ter′ē), *adj.* not sanitary; unclean; unhealthy: *insanitary living conditions.* [IN-[3] + SANITARY] —**in·san′i·tar′i·ness,** *n.*

in·san·i·ta·tion (in san′i tā′shən), *n.* lack of sanitation or sanitary regulation; unclean or unhealthy condition. [IN-[3] + SANITATION]

in·san·i·ty (in san′i tē), *n., pl.* **-ties. 1.** condition of being insane; more or less permanent derangement of one or more psychical functions, due to disease of the mind. **2.** *Law.* such unsoundness of mind as affects legal responsibility or capacity. **3.** extreme folly; foolhardiness. [< L *insānitās.* See IN-[3], SANITY]
—**Syn. 1.** dementia, lunacy, madness, craziness, mania, aberration.

in·sa·tia·ble (in sā′shə bəl, -shē ə-), *adj.* not satiable; incapable of being satisfied: *insatiable hunger for knowledge.* [ME *insaciable* < L *insatiābil(is).* See IN-[3], SATIABLE] —**in·sa′tia·bil′i·ty, in·sa′tia·ble·ness,** *n.* —**in·sa′tia·bly,** *adv.*

in·sa·ti·ate (in sā′shē it), *adj.* insatiable: *insatiate greed.* [< L *insatiāt(us)* not filled full. See IN-[3], SATIATE] —**in·sa′ti·ate·ly,** *adv.* —**in·sa′ti·ate·ness, in-sa·ti·e·ty** (in′sə tī′i tē, in sā′shi tē, -sā′shē i-), *n.*

in·scribe (in skrīb′), *v.t.,* **-scribed, -scrib·ing. 1.** to write or engrave (words, characters, etc.). **2.** to mark (a surface) with words, characters, etc., esp. in a durable or conspicuous way. **3.** to address or dedicate (a book, photograph, etc.) informally, esp. by a handwritten note. **4.** to enroll, as on an official list. **5.** *Brit.* **a.** to issue (a loan) in the form of shares with registered stockholders. **b.** to sell (stocks). **c.** to buy (stocks). **6.** *Geom.* to draw or delineate (one figure) within another figure so that the inner lies entirely within the boundary of the outer, touching it at as many points as possible: *to inscribe a circle in a square.* [< L *inscrībe(re),* equiv. to *in-* IN-[2] + *scrībere* to write; see SCRIBE[1]] —**in·scrib′a·ble,** *adj.* —**in·scrib′a·ble·ness,** *n.* —**in·scrib′er,** *n.*

in·scrip·tion (in skrip′shən), *n.* **1.** something inscribed. **2.** a brief, usually informal dedication, as of a book, a work of art, etc. **3.** a note, as a dedication, that is inscribed and signed in a book. **4.** a historical, religious, or other record cut, impressed, painted, or written on stone, brick, metal, or other hard surface. **5.** act of inscribing. **6.** *Brit.* **a.** an issue of securities or stocks. **b.** a block of shares in a stock, as bought or sold by one person. **7.** *Pharm.* the part of a prescription indicating the drugs and the amounts to be mixed. **8.** Also called **legend.** *Numis.* the lettering in the field of a coin, medal, etc. [ME *inscripcio(u)n* < L *inscriptiōn-* (s. of *inscriptiō*), equiv. to *inscript(us)* written on (ptp. of *inscrībere* to INSCRIBE) + *-iōn-* -ION] —**in·scrip′tion·al,** *adj.* —**in·scrip′tion·less,** *adj.*

in·scrip·tive (in skrip′tiv), *adj.* of, pertaining to, or of the nature of an inscription. [< L *inscript(us)* written on (see INSCRIPTION) + -IVE] —**in·scrip′tive·ly,** *adv.*

in·scroll (in skrōl′), *v.t.* enscroll.

in·scru·ta·ble (in skro͞o′tə bəl), *adj.* **1.** incapable of being searched into or scrutinized; impenetrable to investigation. **2.** not easily understood; mysterious; unfathomable: *an inscrutable smile.* **3.** incapable of being seen through physically; physically impenetrable: *the inscrutable depths of the ocean.* [< LL *inscrūtābil(is).* See IN-[3], SCRUTABLE] —**in·scru′ta·bil′i·ty, in·scru′ta·ble·ness,** *n.* —**in·scru′ta·bly,** *adv.*
—**Syn. 1.** hidden, incomprehensible, undiscoverable, inexplicable. See **mysterious.** —**Ant. 1.** comprehensible.

in·sculp (in skulp′), *v.t. Archaic.* to carve in or on something; engrave. [ME *insculpe(n)* < L *insculp(ere),* equiv. to *in-* IN-[2] + *sculpere* to carve; see SCULPTOR]

in·sect (in′sekt), *n.* **1.** any animal of the class *Insecta,* comprising small, air-breathing arthropods having the body divided into three parts (head, thorax, and abdomen), and having three pairs of legs and usually two pairs of wings. **2.** (loosely) any small arthropod, such as a spider, tick, or centipede, having a superficial, general similarity to the *Insecta.* **3.** a contemptible person. —*adj.* **4.** of, pertaining to, like, or for an insect or insects: *insect life; insect bite; insect powder.* [< L *insect(um),* sing. of *insecta,* trans. of Gk *éntoma* insects, lit., (beings) notched, cut into; see ENTOMO-] —**in-sec′te·an, in·sec′tan, in·sec·ti·val** (in′sek tī′vəl, in-sek′tə-), *adj.* —**in′sect·like′,** *adj.*

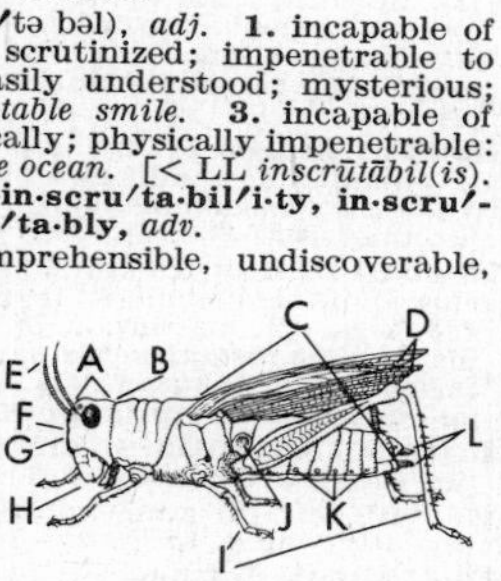

Insect (Grasshopper)
A, Head; B, Thorax; C, Abdomen; D, Wings; E, Antenna; F, Simple eye; G, Compound eye; H, Palpus; I, Legs; J, Ears; K, Spiracle; L, Ovipositor

In·sec·ta (in sek′tə), *n.* the class comprising the insects. [< NL, L, pl. of *insectum* INSECT]

in·sec·tar·i·um (in′sek târ′ē əm), *n., pl.* **-tar·i·ums, -tar·i·a** (-târ′ē ə). a place in which a collection of living insects is kept, as in a zoo. [< NL; see INSECT, -ARIUM]

in·sec·tar·y (in′sek ter′ē), *n., pl.* **-tar·ies.** a laboratory for the study of live insects, their life histories, effects on plants, reaction to insecticides, etc. [var. of INSECTARIUM]

in·sec·ti·cide (in sek′ti sīd′), *n.* **1.** a substance or preparation used for killing insects. **2.** the act of killing insects. [INSECT + -I- + -CIDE] —**in·sec′ti·cid′al,** *adj.*

in·sec·ti·fuge (in sek′tə fyo͞oj′), *n.* a substance or preparation for driving off insects. [INSECT + -I- + -FUGE]

in·sec·tile (in sek′til), *adj.* **1.** pertaining to or like an insect. **2.** consisting of insects. [INSECT + -ILE]

In·sec·tiv·o·ra (in′sek tiv′ər ə), *n.* the order comprising the insectivores. [< NL, neut. pl. of *insectivorus.* INSECTIVOROUS]

in·sec·ti·vore (in sek′tə vōr′, -vôr′), *n.* **1.** an insectivorous animal or plant. **2.** any mammal of the order *Insectivora,* comprising the moles, shrews, and Old World hedgehogs. [back formation from INSECTIVOROUS]

in·sec·tiv·o·rous (in′sek tiv′ər əs), *adj.* adapted to feeding on insects, as shrews, moles, hedgehogs, etc. [< NL *insectivorus.* See INSECT, -I-, -VOROUS]

in·sec·tol·o·gy (in′sek tol′ə jē), *n.* entomology. [INSECT + -O- + -LOGY] —**in′sec·tol′o·ger,** *n.*

in′sect wax′, *Chem.* See **Chinese wax.**

in·se·cure (in′si kyo͝or′), *adj.* **1.** exposed to danger; unsafe. **2.** not firm or safe: *insecure foundations.* **3.** subject to fear, doubt, etc.: *an insecure person.* [< ML *insēcūr(us).* See IN-[3], SECURE] —**in′se·cure′ly,** *adv.* —**in′se·cure′ness,** *n.*
—**Syn. 1.** unprotected, dangerous. **2.** unsure, risky. See **uncertain.**

in·se·cu·ri·ty (in′si kyo͝or′i tē), *n., pl.* **-ties. 1.** quality or state of being insecure; instability: *the insecurity of his financial position.* **2.** lack of assurance; self-doubt: *He is plagued by insecurity.* **3.** something insecure: *the many insecurities of life.* [< ML *insēcūritās.* See INSECURE, -ITY]

in·sem·i·nate (in sem′ə nāt′), *v.t.,* **-nat·ed, -nat·ing. 1.** to sow; inject seed into. **2.** to impregnate. **3.** to sow as seed in something; implant. [< L *insēmināt(us)* sowed in (ptp. of *insēmināre*), equiv. to *in-* IN-[2] + *sēminātus,* equiv. to *sēmina-* (s. of *sēmināre* to sow, deriv. of *sēmen* seed) + *-tus* ptp. suffix] —**in·sem′i·na′tion,** *n.*

in·sen·sate (in sen′sāt, -sit), *adj.* **1.** not endowed with sensation: *insensate stone.* **2.** without feeling or sensitivity. **3.** without sense, understanding, or judgment. [< LL *insensāt(us)* irrational. See IN-[3], SENSATE] —**in·sen′sate·ly,** *adv.* —**in·sen′sate·ness,** *n.*
—**Syn. 1.** inanimate, lifeless, inorganic. **2.** insensible. **3.** stupid, irrational, senseless, witless, dumb.

in·sen·si·bil·i·ty (in sen′sə bil′i tē), *n., pl.* **-ties. 1.** lack of physical sensibility; absence of feeling or sensation. **2.** lack of moral sensibility or susceptibility of emotion. [< LL *insensibilitās.* See INSENSIBLE, -ITY]
—**Syn. 1.** unconsciousness. **2.** See **indifference.**

in·sen·si·ble (in sen′sə bəl), *adj.* **1.** incapable of feeling or perceiving; deprived of sensation; unconscious, as a person after a violent blow. **2.** without or not subject to a particular feeling: *insensible to shame.* **3.** unconscious; unaware; inappreciative: *We are not insensible of your kindness.* **4.** not perceptible by the senses: *insensible transitions.* **5.** unresponsive in feeling. **6.** not susceptible of emotion or passion; void of any feeling. **7.** not endowed with feeling or sensation, as matter. [ME < L *insensibil(is).* See IN-[3], SENSIBLE] —**in·sen′si·bly,** *adv.*
—**Syn. 5, 6.** apathetic, unfeeling, indifferent, cool; dull, passionless, emotionless, torpid.

in·sen·si·tive (in sen′si tiv), *adj.* **1.** not sensitive: *an insensitive skin.* **2.** not susceptible to agencies or influences: *insensitive to light.* **3.** deficient in sensibility or acuteness of feeling: *an insensitive nature.* [IN-[3] + SENSITIVE] —**in·sen′si·tive·ness, in·sen′si·tiv′i·ty,** *n.*

in·sen·ti·ent (in sen′shē ənt, -shənt), *adj.* not sentient; without sensation or feeling; inanimate. [IN-[3] + SENTIENT] —**in·sen′ti·ence, in·sen′ti·en·cy,** *n.*

insep., inseparable.

in·sep·a·ra·ble (in sep′ər ə bəl, -sep′rə-), *adj.* **1.** incapable of being separated, parted, or disjoined: *inseparable companions.* —*n.* **2.** Usually, **inseparables.** inseparable objects, qualities, etc. **3.** inseparable companions or friends. [ME < L *insēparābil(is).* See IN-[3], SEPARABLE] —**in·sep′a·ra·bil′i·ty, in·sep′a·ra·ble·ness,** *n.* —**in·sep′a·ra·bly,** *adv.*

in·sert (*v.* in sûrt′; *n.* in′sûrt), *v.t.* **1.** to put or set in: *to insert a key in a lock.* **2.** to introduce or cause to be introduced into the body of something: *to insert an ad in a newspaper.* —*n.* **3.** something inserted, or to be inserted. **4.** an extra leaf, printed independently, for binding or tipping into a book or periodical, esp. a leaf consisting of an illustration or advertisement printed on different paper. **5.** any small picture, device, etc., surrounded partly or completely by body type. **6.** (in the postal service) a paper, circular, etc., placed within the folds of a newspaper or the leaves of a book, periodical, etc. **7.** *Motion Pictures, Television.* a cut-in. [< L *insert(us)* inserted (ptp. of *inserere*), equiv. to *in-* IN-[2] + *ser-* (root of *serere* to put together) + *-tus* ptp. suffix] —**in·sert′a·ble,** *adj.* —**in·sert′er,** *n.*

in·sert·ed (in sûr′tid), *adj.* **1.** *Bot.* (esp. of the parts of a flower) attached to or growing out of some part. **2.** *Anat.* having an insertion, as a muscle, tendon, or ligament; attached, as the more movable end of a muscle. [INSERT + -ED[2]]

in·ser·tion (in sûr′shən), *n.* **1.** act of inserting: *the insertion of a new part in a car.* **2.** something inserted: *an insertion into a text.* **3.** *Bot., Zool.* **a.** the manner or place of attachment, as of an organ. **b.** attachment of a part or organ, with special reference to the site or manner of such attachment. **4.** lace, embroidery, or the like, to be sewn at each edge between parts of other material. [< LL *insertiōn-* (s. of *insertiō*). See INSERT, -ION] —**in·ser′tion·al,** *adj.*

in·serv·ice (in sûr′vis, in′sûr′-), *adj.* taking place while in service: *in-service training program.*

in·ses·so·ri·al (in′ses sōr′ē əl, -sôr′-), *adj.* **1.** adapted for perching, as a bird's foot. **2.** habitually perching, as a bird. **3.** of or pertaining to birds that perch. [< NL *Insessōr(ēs)* the perching birds (L: perchers, equiv. to *insess(us)* perched on (ptp. of *insīdere,* equiv. to *in-* IN-[2] + *sīdere* to settle, alight) + *-ōrēs,* pl. of *-or* -OR[2]) + -IAL]

in·set (*n.* in′set′; *v.* in set′), *n., v.,* **-set, -set·ting.** —*n.* **1.** something inserted; an insert. **2.** a smaller picture, map, etc., inserted within the border of a larger one. **3.** influx. **4.** act of setting in. —*v.t.* **5.** to set in or insert, as an inset: *to inset a panel in a dress.* **6.** to insert an inset in: *to inset a mounting with jewels.* [IN-[1] + SET] —**in′set′ter,** *n.*

in′set ini′tial, *Print.* an initial letter, esp. of the first word of a chapter or other section of a book, magazine, etc., larger than the body type and occupying two or more lines in depth, causing body type to be set around it. Also called **drop initial.**

in·sev·er·a·ble (in sev′ər ə bəl, -sev′rə-), *adj.* unable to be severed or separated: *an inseverable alliance.* [IN-[3] + SEVERABLE] —**in·sev′er·a·bly,** *adv.*

in·sheathe (in shēth′), *v.t.,* **-sheathed, -sheath·ing.** ensheathe. Also, **in·sheath** (in shēth′).

in·shoot (in′sho͞ot′), *n.* *Baseball.* incurve (def. 2). [IN-[1] + SHOOT]

in·shore (in′shōr′, -shôr′), *adj.* **1.** close to the shore: *The ship was inshore.* **2.** lying near the shore; operating or carried on close to the shore: *inshore fishing.* —*adv.* **3.** toward the shore: *They went closer inshore.* [IN-[1] + SHORE[1]]

in·shrine (in shrīn′), *v.t.,* **-shrined, -shrin·ing.** enshrine.

in·side (*prep.* in′sīd′, in′sīd′; *adv.* in′sīd′; *n.* in′sīd′; *adj.* in′sīd′, in′-), *prep.* **1.** on the inner side or part of; within: *inside the circle; inside the envelope.* **2.** prior to the elapse of: *He promised to arrive inside an hour.* —*adv.* **3.** in or into the inner part: *to be inside; go inside.* **4.** indoors: *He plays inside on rainy days.* **5.** within one's heart, reason, etc.; by true nature; basically: *I know inside that he's not guilty. Inside, she's really very shy.* **6. inside of,** within the space or period of: *Our car broke down again inside of a mile.* —*n.* **7.** the inner part; interior: *the inside of the house.* **8.** the inner side or surface: *the inside of the hand.* **9.** Usually, **insides. a.** the inward parts of the body, esp. the stomach and intestines: *The coffee scalded my insides.* **b.** one's thoughts, feelings, etc. **10.** a select circle of power, prestige, etc.: *a man on the inside.* **11.** the shortest of several parallel, curving tracks or lanes: *The horse came up fast on the inside.* **12.** the inward nature or mind. **13.** an inside passenger or place in a coach, carriage, etc. **14. inside out, a.** with the inner side reversed to face the outside. **b.** perfectly; completely: *He knew his trade inside out.* —*adj.* **15.** situated or being on or in the inside; interior; internal: *an inside seat.* **16.** acting, employed, done, or originating within a building or place: *He used to work on the dock, but now he has an inside job.* **17.** derived from the inner circle of those concerned in and having private knowledge of a situation: *inside information.* **18.** *Baseball.* (of a pitched ball) passing between home plate and the batter: *The pitch was low and inside.* [IN + SIDE[1]]
—**Syn. 7.** INSIDE, INTERIOR both refer to the inner part or space within something. INSIDE is a common word, and is used with reference to things of any size, small or large: *the inside of a pocket.* INTERIOR, somewhat more formal, denotes the inner part or the space or the regions within; it usually suggests considerable size or extent, and sometimes a richness of decoration: *the interior of a country, of the earth; interior of a cathedral.* —**Ant. 7.** outside, exterior.

in′side job′, *Informal.* a crime committed by a person or persons closely associated with or, sometimes, in collusion with the victim: *The police, convinced that the robbery was an inside job, were proved right when the butler confessed.*

in′side loop′, *Aeron.* a loop during which the top of the airplane is on the inner side of the curve described by the course of flight. Cf. **outside loop.**

in·sid·er (in′sī′dər), *n.* **1.** one who is inside some place, society, etc. **2.** *Informal.* one who is within a limited circle of persons who understand the actual facts in a case. **3.** *Informal.* one who has some special advantage. [INSIDE + -ER[1]]

in′side straight′, *Poker.* a set of four cards, as the five, seven, eight, and nine, requiring one card of a denomination next above or below the second or third ranking cards of the set to make a straight.

in′side track′, **1.** the inner, or shorter track of a racecourse. **2.** *Informal.* an advantageous position; precedence; favor.

in·sid·i·ous (in sid′ē əs), *adj.* **1.** intended to entrap or beguile: *an insidious design.* **2.** stealthily treacherous or deceitful: *an insidious enemy.* **3.** operating or proceeding inconspicuously but with grave effect: *an insidious disease.* [< L *insidiōs(us)* deceitful, equiv. to *insidi(ae)* (pl.) an ambush (deriv. of *insidēre* to sit in) + *-ōsus* -OUS] —**in·sid′i·ous·ly,** *adv.* —**in·sid′i·ous·ness,** *n.*
—**Syn. 1.** corrupting. **2.** artful, cunning, wily, subtle, crafty.

in·sight (in′sīt′), *n.* **1.** an instance of apprehending the true nature of a thing, esp. through intuitive understanding: *an insight into the life of the village.* **2.** penetrating mental vision or discernment; faculty of seeing into inner character or underlying truth: *a man of great insight.* [ME; see IN-[1], SIGHT]
—**Syn. 2.** perception, apprehension, intuition, understanding, grasp.

in·sight·ful (in′sīt′fəl), *adj.* characterized by or displaying insight: *an insightful new treatise.* [INSIGHT + -FUL]

in·sig·ne (in sig′nē), *n.* **1.** sing. of **insignia. 2.** insignia.

in·sig·ni·a (in sig′nē ə), *n., formally a pl. of* **insigne,** *but usually used as a sing. with pl.* **-ni·a** *or* **-ni·as. 1.** a badge or distinguishing mark of office or honor: *a military insignia.* **2.** a distinguishing mark or sign of anything: *an insignia of mourning.* Also, **insigne.** [< L, pl. of *insigne* mark, badge, n. use of *insignis* distinguished (by a mark)]

in·sig·nif·i·cance (in′sig nif′ə kəns), *n.* quality or condition of being insignificant; lack of importance or consequence. [INSIGNIFIC(ANCY) + -ANCE]

in·sig·nif·i·can·cy (in′sig nif′ə kən sē), *n., pl.* **-cies** for 2. **1.** insignificance. **2.** an insignificant person or thing. [INSIGNIFICAN(T) + -CY]

in·sig·nif·i·cant (in′sig nif′ə kənt), *adj.* **1.** unimportant, trifling, or petty, as things, matters, details, etc. **2.** too small to be important: *an insignificant sum.* **3.** of no consequence, influence, or distinction, as persons. **4.** without weight of character; contemptible: *an insignificant fellow.* **5.** without meaning; meaningless, as terms. —*n.* **6.** a word, thing, or person without significance. [IN-[3] + SIGNIFICANT] —**in′sig·nif′i·cant·ly,** *adv.*

in·sin·cere (in′sin sēr′), *adj.* not sincere; not honest in the expression of actual feeling. [IN-[3] + SINCERE; cf. L *insincērus* tainted] —**in′sin·cere′ly,** *adv.*

in·sin·cer·i·ty (in′sin ser′i tē), *n., pl.* **-ties** for 2. **1.** quality of being insincere; lack of sincerity; deceitfulness. **2.** an instance of this: *He recalled her many past insincerities.* [IN-[3] + SINCERITY]

in·sin·u·ate (in sin′yo͞o āt′), *v.,* **-at·ed, -at·ing.** —*v.t.* **1.** to suggest or hint slyly: *He insinuated that she was lying.* **2.** to instill or infuse subtly or artfully, as into the mind: *The enemy propaganda insinuated doubt into the minds of the people.* **3.** to bring or introduce into a position or relation by indirect or artful methods: *to insinuate oneself into the favor of another.* —*v.i.* **4.** to make insinuations. [< L *insinuāt(us),* ptp. of *insinuāre.* See IN-[2], SINUOUS, -ATE[1]] —**in·sin·u·a·tive** (in sin′yo͞o ā′tiv, -yo͞o ə-), **in·sin·u·a·to·ry** (in sin′yo͞o ə tôr′ē, -tōr′ē), *adj.* —**in·sin′u·a′tive·ly,** *adv.* —**in·sin′u·a′tor,** *n.*
—**Syn. 1.** See **hint. 2.** introduce, inject, inculcate.

in·sin·u·at·ing (in sin′yo͞o ā′ting), *adj.* **1.** tending to instil doubts, distrust, etc.; suggestive: *an insinuating letter.* **2.** gaining favor or winning confidence by artful means: *his insinuating charm.* [INSINUATE + -ING[2]] —**in·sin′u·at′ing·ly,** *adv.*

in·sin·u·a·tion (in sin′yo͞o ā′shən), *n.* **1.** an indirect or covert suggestion or hint, esp. of a derogatory nature: *He made several nasty insinuations about his business rival.* **2.** covert or artful suggestion or hinting, as of something implied: *His methods of insinuation are most ingenious.* **3.** subtle or artful instillment into the mind. **4.** the art or power of stealing into the affections and pleasing; ingratiation: *He made his way by flattery and insinuation.* **5.** *Archaic.* a slow winding, worming, or stealing in. **6.** *Obs.* an ingratiating act or speech. [< L *insinuātiōn-* (s. of *insinuātiō*). See INSINUATE, -ION]

in·sip·id (in sip′id), *adj.* **1.** without distinctive, interesting, or attractive qualities: *an insipid tale.* **2.** without sufficient taste to be pleasing, as food or drink: *a rather insipid fruit.* [< L *insipid(us),* equiv. to *in-* IN-[3] + *-sipidus,* var. of *sapidus* SAPID] —**in′si·pid′i·ty, in·sip′id·ness,** *n.* —**in·sip′id·ly,** *adv.*
—**Syn. 1.** uninteresting, pointless, vapid. **1, 2.** flat, dull. **2.** tasteless, bland.

in·sip·i·ence (in sip′ē əns), *n. Archaic.* lack of wisdom; foolishness. [late ME < L *insipientia* foolishness, equiv. to *insipient-* (s. of *insipiēns*) foolish (*in-* IN-[3] + *-sipient-,* var. of *sapient-* SAPIENT) + *-ia;* see -ENCE] —**in·sip′i·ent,** *adj.* —**in·sip′i·ent·ly,** *adv.*

in·sist (in sist′), *v.i.* **1.** to be emphatic, firm, or resolute on some matter of desire, demand, intention, etc.: *He insists on working late every night.* **2.** to lay emphasis in assertion: *to insist on the justice of a claim.* **3.** to dwell with earnestness or emphasis (usually fol. by *on* or *upon*): *to insist on a point in a discussion.* —*v.t.* **4.** to assert or maintain firmly: *He insists that he sees the ghosts.* **5.** to demand or persist in demanding: *I insist that you see this thing through.* [< L *insist(ere)* (to) stand still on, persist in, equiv. to *in-* IN-[2] + *sistere* to stand, make stand, akin to *stare* to stand] —**in·sist′er,** *n.* —**in·sist′ing·ly,** *adv.*

in·sist·ence (in sis′təns), *n.* **1.** act or fact of insisting. **2.** quality of being insistent. [INSIST + -ENCE]

in·sist·en·cy (in sis′tən sē), *n., pl.* **-cies.** **1.** quality of being insistent; insistence. **2.** that which is insistent. [INSIST + -ENCY]

in·sist·ent (in sis′tənt), *adj.* **1.** earnest or emphatic in dwelling upon, maintaining, or demanding something; persistent; pertinacious. **2.** compelling attention or notice: *an insistent tone.* [< L *insistent-* (s. of *insistēns*), prp. of *insistere.* See INSIST, -ENT] —**in·sist′ent·ly,** *adv.*

in si·tu (in sit′o͞o; *Eng.* in sī′to͞o, -tyo͞o), *Latin.* in its original place. [lit., in place]

in·snare (in snâr′), *v.t.,* **-snared, -snar·ing.** ensnare. —**in·snare′ment,** *n.* —**in·snar′er,** *n.*

in·so·bri·e·ty (in′sə brī′i tē), *n.* lack of sobriety; intemperance or immoderation; drunkenness. [IN-[3] + SOBRIETY]

in·so·cia·ble (in sō′shə bəl), *adj.* unsociable. [< L *insociābil(is).* See IN-[3], SOCIABLE] —**in·so′cia·bil′i·ty,** *n.* —**in·so′cia·bly,** *adv.*

in·so·far (in′sə fär′, -sō-), *adv.* to such an extent (usually fol. by *as*): *I shall do what I can insofar as I am able.* [orig. phrase *in so far*]

in·so·late (in′sō lāt′), *v.t.,* **-lat·ed, -lat·ing.** to expose to the sun's rays; treat by exposure to the sun's rays. [< L *insōlāt(us)* placed in the sun, ptp. of *insōlāre.* See IN-[2], SOLI-[2], -ATE[1]]

in·so·la·tion (in′sō lā′shən), *n.* **1.** exposure to the sun's rays, esp. as a process of treatment. **2.** *Pathol.* sunstroke. **3.** *Meteorol.* solar radiation received on a given body or over a given area. [< L *insōlātiōn-* (s. of *insōlātiō*). See INSOLATE, -ION]

in·sole (in′sōl′), *n.* **1.** the inner sole of a shoe or boot. **2.** a thickness of warm or waterproof material laid as an inner sole within a shoe. [IN + SOLE[2]]

in·so·lence (in′sə ləns), *n.* **1.** contemptuously rude or impertinent behavior or speech. **2.** quality or condition of being insolent. [ME < L *insolentia.* See INSOLENT, -ENCE]

in·so·lent (in′sə lənt), *adj.* **1.** boldly rude or disrespectful; contemptuously impertinent; insulting: *an insolent reply.* —*n.* **2.** an insolent person. [ME < L *insolent-* (s. of *insolēns*) departing from custom, equiv. to *in-* IN-[3] + *sol-* (root of *solēre* to be accustomed) + *-ent-* -ENT] —**in′so·lent·ly,** *adv.*
—**Syn. 1.** brazen; contemptuous. See **impertinent.**

in·sol·u·bil·ize (in sol′yə bə līz′), *v.t.,* **-ized, -iz·ing.** to make insoluble: *to insolubilize the binder after application.* [< L *insolūbil(is)* INSOLUBLE + -IZE] —**in·sol′u·bi·li·za′tion,** *n.*

in·sol·u·ble (in sol′yə bəl), *adj.* **1.** incapable of being dissolved: *insoluble salts.* **2.** incapable of being solved: *an insoluble problem.* [< L *insolūbil(is);* r. ME *insolible* < MF *insoluble.* See IN-[3], SOLUBLE] —**in·sol′u·bil′i·ty, in·sol′u·ble·ness,** *n.* —**in·sol′u·bly,** *adv.*

in·solv·a·ble (in sol′və bəl), *adj.* incapable of being solved or explained; insoluble: *an insolvable problem.* [IN-[3] + SOLVABLE] —**in·solv′a·bil′i·ty,** *n.* —**in·solv′a·bly,** *adv.*

in·sol·ven·cy (in sol′vən sē), *n.* the condition of being insolvent; bankruptcy. [INSOLVEN(T) + -CY]

in·sol·vent (in sol′vənt), *Law.* —*adj.* **1.** not solvent; unable to satisfy creditors or discharge liabilities, either because liabilities exceed assets or because of inability to pay debts as they mature. **2.** pertaining to bankrupt persons or bankruptcy. —*n.* **3.** one who is insolvent. [IN-[3] + SOLVENT]

in·som·ni·a (in som′nē ə), *n.* inability to sleep, esp. when chronic; sleeplessness. [< L, equiv. to *insomn(is)* sleepless (*in-* IN-[3] + *somn(us)* sleep + *-is* adj. suffix) + *-ia* -IA] —**in·som′ni·ous,** *adj.*

in·som·ni·ac (in som′nē ak′), *n.* **1.** one who suffers from insomnia. —*adj.* **2.** having insomnia: *a nervous, insomniac child.* **3.** of, pertaining to, or causing insomnia: *the insomniac heat of midsummer.* [INSOMNI(A) + -AC]

in·som·no·lence (in som′nə ləns), *n.* sleeplessness; insomnia: *a troubled week of insomnolence.* Also, **in·som·no·len·cy** (in som′nə lən sē). [IN-[3] + SOMNOLENCE] —**in·som′no·lent,** *adj.* —**in·som′no·lent·ly,** *adv.*

in·so·much (in′sō much′), *adv.* **1.** to such an extent or degree; so (usually fol. by *that*). **2.** inasmuch (usually fol. by *as*). [orig. phrase *in so much*]

in·sou·ci·ance (in so͞o′sē əns; *Fr.* AN so͞o syäns′), *n.* quality of being insouciant; lack of care or concern; indifference. [< F; see INSOUCIANT, -ANCE]

in·sou·ci·ant (in so͞o′sē ənt; *Fr.* AN so͞o syän′), *adj.* free from concern; without anxiety; carefree. [< F, equiv. to *in-* IN-[3] + *souciant* worrying, prp. of *soucier* < L *sollicitāre* to disturb; see SOLICITOUS] —**in·sou′ci·ant·ly,** *adv.*

in·soul (in sōl′), *v.t.* ensoul.

insp., inspector.

in·span (in span′), *v.t.,* **-spanned, -span·ning.** *South Africa.* to yoke or harness. [< SAfrD; see IN-[1], SPAN[2]]

in·spect (in spekt′), *v.t.* **1.** to look carefully at or over; view closely and critically: *to inspect every part.* **2.** to view or examine formally or officially: *to inspect troops.* [v. use of *inspect* inspection, examination (late ME; now obs.) < L *inspect(us),* n. use of ptp. of *inspicere* to look into, inspect. See IN-[2], SPECIES] —**in·spect′a·bil′i·ty,** *n.* —**in·spect′a·ble,** *adj.* —**in·spect′ing·ly,** *adv.*
—**Syn. 1.** examine, scrutinize, investigate, study.

in·spec·tion (in spek′shən), *n.* **1.** act of inspecting or viewing, esp. carefully or critically: *an inspection of every part.* **2.** formal or official viewing or examination: *an inspection of the troops.* [ME *inspeccio(u)n* < L *inspectiōn-* (s. of *inspectiō*). See INSPECT, -ION] —**in·spec′tion·al,** *adj.*
—**Syn. 2.** See **examination.**

in·spec·tive (in spek′tiv), *adj.* **1.** given to making inspection; watchful; attentive. **2.** of or pertaining to inspection. [< LL *inspectīv(us).* See INSPECT, -IVE]

in·spec·tor (in spek′tər), *n.* **1.** one who inspects. **2.** an officer appointed to inspect. **3.** an officer of police, usually ranking next below a superintendent. [< L; see INSPECT, -OR[2]] —**in·spec′to·ral, in·spec·to·ri·al** (in′spek tôr′ē əl, -tōr′-), *adj.* —**in·spec′tor·ship′,** *n.*

in·spec·tor·ate (in spek′tər it), *n.* **1.** the office or function of an inspector. **2.** a body of inspectors. **3.** a district under an inspector. [INSPECTOR + -ATE[1]]

In·spec·tor-Gen·er·al, The (in spek′tər jen′ər əl), a comedy (1836) by Gogol.

in·sphere (in sfēr′), *v.t.,* **-sphered, -spher·ing.** ensphere.

in·spir·a·ble (in spīər′ə bəl), *adj.* capable of being inspired. [INSPIRE + -ABLE]

in·spi·ra·tion (in′spə rā′shən), *n.* **1.** an inspiring or animating action or influence: *I cannot write without inspiration.* **2.** something inspired, as a thought. **3.** a result of inspired activity. **4.** a thing or person that inspires. **5.** *Theol.* **a.** a divine influence directly and immediately exerted upon the mind or soul of a man. **b.** the divine quality of the writings or words of men so influenced. **6.** the drawing of air into the lungs; inhalation. **7.** act of inspiring; quality or state of being inspired. [ME *inspiracio(u)n* < LL *inspīrātiōn-* (s. of *inspīrātiō*). See INSPIRE, -ATION]
—**Syn. 1.** stimulus, incitement.

in·spi·ra·tion·al (in′spə rā′shə nəl), *adj.* **1.** imparting inspiration. **2.** under the influence of inspiration; inspired. **3.** of or pertaining to inspiration. [INSPIRATION + -AL[1]] —**in′spi·ra′tion·al·ly,** *adv.*

in·spir·a·to·ry (in spīər′ə tôr′ē, -tōr′ē), *adj.* of or pertaining to inspiration, or inhalation. [< L *inspīrāt(us)* breathed upon or into (ptp. of *inspīrāre;* see INSPIRE, -ATE[1]) + -ORY[1]]

in·spire (in spīər′), *v.,* **-spired, -spir·ing.** —*v.t.* **1.** to infuse an animating, quickening, or exalting influence into: *His courage inspired his followers.* **2.** to produce or arouse (a feeling, thought, etc.): *to inspire confidence in others.* **3.** to affect with a specified feeling, thought, etc.: *to inspire a person with distrust.* **4.** to influence or impel: *opposition inspired him to a greater effort.* **5.** to animate, as an influence, feeling, thought, or the like, does: *They were inspired by a belief in a better future.* **6.** to communicate or suggest by a divine or supernatural influence: *writings inspired by God.* **7.** to guide or control by divine influence. **8.** to prompt or instigate (utterances, acts, etc.) by influence, without avowal of responsibility. **9.** to give rise to, bring about, cause, etc.: *a philosophy which inspired revolution.* **10.** to take (air, gases, etc.) into the lungs in breathing; inhale. **11.** *Archaic.* to infuse (breath, life, etc.) by breathing (usually fol. by *into*). **12.** *Archaic.* to breathe into or upon. —*v.i.* **13.** to give inspiration. **14.** to inhale. [ME *inspire(n)* < L *inspīr(āre)* (to) breathe upon or into, equiv. to *in-* IN-[2] + *spīrāre* to breathe] —**in·spir·a·tive** (in spīər′ə tiv, in′spi rā′tiv), *adj.* —**in·spir′er,** *n.* —**in·spir′ing·ly,** *adv.*

in·spired (in spīərd′), *adj.* **1.** aroused, animated, or imbued with the spirit to do a certain thing, by or as if by supernatural or divine influence: *an inspired poet.* **2.** resulting from such inspiration: *an inspired poem, plan, conclusion, novel, etc.* **3.** inhaled: *Inspired air passes to the lungs.* [late ME; see INSPIRE, -ED[2]] —**in·spir·ed·ly** (in spī′rid lē, -spīərd′-), *adv.*

in·spir·it (in spir′it), *v.t.* to infuse spirit or life into; enliven. Also, **enspirit.** [IN-[2] + SPIRIT] —**in·spir′it·er,** *n.* —**in·spir′it·ing·ly,** *adv.* —**in·spir′it·ment,** *n.*

in·spis·sate (in spis′āt), *v.t., v.i.,* **-sat·ed, -sat·ing.** to thicken, as by evaporation; make or become dense. [< LL *inspissāt(us)* thickened (ptp. of *inspissāre*), equiv. to L *in-* IN-[2] + *spiss-* (base of *spissāre* to thicken, deriv. of *spissus* thick) + *-ātus* -ATE[1]] —**in′spis·sa′tion,** *n.* —**in′spis·sa′tor,** *n.*

inst., **1.** instant (def. 4). **2.** instantaneous. **3.** (*usually cap.*) institute. **4.** (*usually cap.*) institution. **5.** instructor. **6.** instrument. **7.** instrumental.

in·sta·bil·i·ty (in′stə bil′i tē), *n.* quality or state of being instable; lack of stability or firmness. [ME *instabilite* < L *instabilitās.* See IN-[3], STABILITY]

instabil′ity line′, *Meteorol.* a nonfrontal line of convective activity in the atmosphere, usually several hundred miles long but of relatively brief duration.

in·sta·ble (in stā′bəl), *adj.* not stable; unstable. [late ME < L *instabil(is).* See IN-[3], STABLE[2]]

in·stal (in stôl′), *v.t.,* **-stalled, -stal·ling.** install.

in·stall (in stôl′), *v.t.* **1.** to place in position for service or use, as a heating system, air conditioner, etc. **2.** to establish in an office, position, or place: *to install a new assistant; install oneself in new quarters.* **3.** to induct into an office or the like with ceremonies or formalities, as by seating in a stall or official seat. Also, **instal.** [late ME < ML *install(āre).* See IN-[2], STALL[1]] —**in·stall′er,** *n.*

in·stal·la·tion (in′stə lā′shən), *n.* **1.** something installed. **2.** a system of machinery or apparatus placed in position for use. **3.** act of installing. **4.** fact of being installed. **5.** *Mil.* any more or less permanent post, camp, station, base, or the like, for the support or carrying on of military activities. [< ML *installātiōn-* (s. of *installātiō*). See INSTALL, -ATION]

in·stall·ment[1] (in stôl′mənt), *n.* **1.** any of several parts into which a debt or other sum payable is divided for payment at successive fixed times: *to pay for furniture by installments.* **2.** a single portion of something furnished or issued by parts at successive times: *a magazine serial in six installments.* Also, **in·stal′ment.** [IN-[2] + obs. *(e)stallment,* equiv. to obs. *estall* arrange payment on installment plan (? < AF) + -MENT]

in·stall·ment[2] (in stôl′mənt), *n.* **1.** act of installing. **2.** fact of being installed; installation. Also, **in·stal′ment.** [INSTALL + -MENT]

install′ment plan′, *Chiefly U.S.* a system for paying a debt in fixed amounts at specified intervals.

in·stance (in′stəns), *n., v.,* **-stanced, -stanc·ing.** —*n.* **1.** a case of anything: *fresh instances of oppression.* **2.** an example put forth in proof or illustration: *to cite a few instances.* **3.** *Archaic.* urgency in speech or action. **4.** *Law.* prosecution of a case (used chiefly in the phrase *court of first instance*). **5.** *Archaic.* urgency. **6.** *Obs.* an impelling motive. **7. at the instance of,** at the urging or suggestion of: *He applied for the assistantship at the instance of his professor.* **8. for instance,** as an example; for example: *If you were to go abroad for a year, to Italy, for instance, you would get a different perspective on your own culture.* —*v.t.* **9.** to cite as an instance or example. **10.** to exemplify by an instance. —*v.i.* **11.** *Archaic.* to cite an instance. [ME < L *instantia* presence, urgency (ML: case, example). See INSTANT, -ANCE]
—**Syn. 2.** See **case**[1].

in·stan·cy (in′stən sē), *n.* **1.** quality of being instant: urgency; pressing nature. **2.** immediateness. [< L *instantia.* See INSTANCE, -ANCY]

in·stant (in′stənt), *n.* **1.** an infinitesimal or very short space of time; a moment: *not an instant too soon.* **2.** the point of time now present, or present with reference to some action or event. **3.** a particular moment: *at the instant of contact.* **4.** the present or current month: *his letter of the 12th instant. Abbr.:* inst. **5.** *Informal.* a food, beverage, etc., specially processed for quick preparation: *Some housewives resort frequently to instants.* —*adj.* **6.** succeeding without any interval of time; immediate: *instant relief.* **7.** pressing or urgent: *instant need.* **8.** noting a food or food substance requiring a minimal amount of preparation, as heating or the addition of milk or water, before being served or used: *instant coffee; instant cake mix.* **9.** *Archaic.* present, current: *the instant case before the court; the 12th of this instant May.* —*adv.* **10.** instantly. [late ME < L *instant-* (s. of *instāns*) present, urgent (prp. of *instāre*), equiv. to *in-* IN-[2] + *-stā-* stand + *-ant-* -ANT]
—**Syn. 1.** second, twinkling, flash, jiffy, trice. See **minute**[1].

in·stan·ta·ne·i·ty (in stan′tə nē′i tē, in′stən tə nē′-), *n.* quality or condition of being instantaneous: *They praised the instantaneity of his response.* [INSTANTANE(OUS) + -ITY]

in·stan·ta·ne·ous (in′stən tā′nē əs), *adj.* **1.** occurring, done, or completed in an instant: *an instantaneous explosion.* **2.** existing at or pertaining to a particular instant: *the instantaneous position of something.* [< ML *instantāneus.* See INSTANT, -AN, -EOUS] —**in′stan·ta′ne·ous·ly,** *adv.* —**in′stan·ta′ne·ous·ness,** *n.*

in′stanta′neous sound′ pres′sure, *Physics.* See **sound pressure** (def. 1).

in·stan·ter (in stan′tər), *adv.* instantly. [< legal L: urgently, equiv. to *instant-* INSTANT + *-er* adv. suffix]

in·stant·ly (in′stənt lē), *adv.* **1.** immediately; at once. **2.** *Archaic.* urgently. —*conj.* **3.** as soon as; directly: *I recognized her instantly she entered the room.* [INSTANT + -LY]
—**Syn. 1.** forthwith. See **immediately.**

in·star[1] (in′stär), *n.* an insect in any one of its periods of postembryonic growth between molts. [< NL, L: image, likeness, lit., a stand-in]

in·star[2] (in stär′), *v.t.,* **-starred, -star·ring.** **1.** to set with or as if with stars. **2.** *Archaic.* to place as a star. **3.** *Archaic.* to make a star of. [IN-[1] + STAR]

in·state (in stāt′), *v.t.,* **-stat·ed, -stat·ing.** **1.** to put or place in a certain state or position, as in an office; install. **2.** *Obs.* to endow with something. [IN-[2] + STATE (n.); see REINSTATE] —**in·state′ment,** *n.*

in sta·tu quo (in stä′to͞o kwō′; *Eng.* in stā′tyo͞o kwō′, stach′o͞o), *Latin.* in the state in which (anything was or is).

in·stau·ra·tion (in′stô rā′shən), *n.* **1.** *Archaic.* renewal; restoration; renovation; repair. **2.** *Obs.* an act of instituting, or inaugurating, something; establishment. [< L *instaurātiōn-* (s. of *instaurātiō*) a renewing, repeating. See IN-[2], STORE, -ATION] —**in·stau·ra·tor** (in′stô rā′tər), *n.*

in·stead (in sted′), *adv.* **1.** in preference; as a preferred or accepted alternative: *The city has its pleasures, but she wished instead for the quiet of country life.* **2.** as a replacement; in the place or stead of someone or something: *We asked for the father, but they sent the son instead.* **3.** **instead of,** in place of; in lieu of: *You may use milk instead of cream in this recipe.* [orig. phrase *in stead* in place]

in·step (in′step′), *n.* **1.** the arched upper surface of the foot of man between the toes and the ankle. **2.** the part of a shoe, stocking, etc., covering the instep. **3.** the front of the hind leg of a horse, cow, etc., between the hock and the pastern joint; cannon. [appar. IN-[1] + STEP]

in·sti·gate (in′stə gāt′), *v.t.*, **-gat·ed, -gat·ing.** **1.** to urge, provoke, or incite to some action or course: *to instigate the people to revolt.* **2.** to bring about by incitement; foment: *to instigate a quarrel.* [< L *instīgāt(us)* goaded on (ptp. of *instīgāre*), equiv. to *in-* IN-[2] + *-stīg-* goad, prick (see STIGMA) + *-ātus* -ATE[1]] —**in′sti·gat′ing·ly,** *adv.* —**in′sti·ga′tive,** *adj.* —**in′sti·ga′tor, in·sti·gant** (in′stə gənt), *n.*
—**Syn. 1.** induce, stimulate, encourage, push; initiate, start. **2.** arouse, provoke.

in·sti·ga·tion (in′stə gā′shən), *n.* **1.** act of instigating. **2.** state of being instigated. **3.** an incentive. [ME < L *instīgātiōn-* (s. of *instīgātiō*). See INSTIGATE, -ION]

in·stil (in stil′), *v.t.*, **-stilled, -stil·ling.** instill. —**in·stil′ment,** *n.*

in·still (in stil′), *v.t.* **1.** to infuse slowly or by degrees into the mind or feelings; insinuate; inject: *Courtesy must be instilled in childhood.* **2.** to put in drop by drop. [< L *instill(āre)*, equiv. to *in-* IN-[2] + *stillāre* to drip; see DISTILL] —**in·still′er,** *n.* —**in·still′ment,** *n.*
—**Syn. 1.** inculcate, introduce.

in·stil·la·tion (in′stə lā′shən), *n.* **1.** act of instilling. **2.** something instilled. [< L *instillātiōn-* (s. of *instillātiō*), equiv. to *instillāt(us)* instilled (ptp. of *instillāre*) + *-iōn-* -ION]

in·stil·la·tor (in′stə lā′tər), *n.* *Med.* an apparatus for putting liquid drop by drop into a cavity. [< L *instillāt(us)* (see INSTILLATION) + *-or* -OR[2]]

in·stinct[1] (in′stingkt), *n.* **1.** *Psychol.* an inborn pattern of activity or tendency to action common to a given biological species. **2.** a natural or innate impulse, inclination, or tendency. **3.** a natural aptitude or gift for something: *an instinct for art.* **4.** natural intuitive power. [< L *instinct(us)* an impulse, instigation; see INSTINCT[2]]

in·stinct[2] (in stingkt′), *adj.* **1.** infused or filled with some animating principle (usually fol. by *with*): *instinct with life.* **2.** *Obs.* urged or animated by some inner force. [< L *instinct(us)* incited, instigated (ptp. of *instinguere*), equiv. to *in-* IN-[2] + *-stinctus*, as in *distinctus* DISTINCT]

in·stinc·tive (in stingk′tiv), *adj.* **1.** of, pertaining to, or of the nature of instinct. **2.** prompted by or resulting from instinct. Also, **in·stinc·tu·al** (in stingk′cho͞o əl). [INSTINCT[1] + -IVE] —**in·stinc′tive·ly, in·stinc′tu·al·ly,** *adv.*
—**Syn. 2.** spontaneous, intuitive, unpremeditated.

in·sti·tute (in′sti to͞ot′, -tyo͞ot′), *v.*, **-tut·ed, -tut·ing,** *n.* —*v.t.* **1.** to set up; establish: *to institute a government.* **2.** to inaugurate; initiate; get under way: *to institute a new course in American literature.* **3.** to set in operation: *to institute a lawsuit.* **4.** to bring into use or practice: *to institute laws.* **5.** to establish in an office or position. **6.** *Eccles.* to assign to or invest with a spiritual charge. —*n.* **7.** a society or organization for carrying on a particular work, as of literary, scientific, or educational character. **8.** the building occupied by such a society. **9.** *Educ.* **a.** an institution, generally beyond the secondary school level, devoted to instruction in technical subjects, usually separate but sometimes organized as a part of a university. **b.** a unit within a university organized for advanced instruction and research in a relatively narrow field of subject matter. **c.** a short instructional program set up for a special group interested in some specialized type of activity. **10.** an established principle, law, custom, or organization. **11.** **institutes, a.** an elementary textbook of law designed for beginners. **b.** (*cap.*) Also called **In′stitutes of Justin′ian.** an elementary treatise on Roman law in four books, forming one of the four divisions of the Corpus Juris Civilis. **12.** something instituted. [ME < L *institūt(us)* placed, built, set up (ptp. of *instituere*), equiv. to *in-* IN-[2] + *-stitū-* (var. of *statū-*; see STATUS) + *-tus* ptp. suffix]

in·sti·tut·er (in′sti to͞o′tər, -tyo͞o′-), *n.* institutor.

in·sti·tu·tion (in′sti to͞o′shən, -tyo͞o′-), *n.* **1.** an organization, establishment, foundation, society, or the like, devoted to the promotion of a particular object, esp. one of a public, educational, or charitable character. **2.** the building devoted to such work. **3.** a concern engaged in some activity, as a retail store, insurance company, etc. **4.** *Sociol.* a well-established and structured pattern of behavior or of relationships that is accepted as a fundamental part of a culture, as marriage: *the institution of the family; the institution of slavery.* **5.** any established law, custom, etc. **6.** any familiar practice or object. **7.** act of instituting or setting up; establishment: *the institution of laws.* **8.** *Eccles.* **a.** the origination of the Eucharist, and enactment of its observance, by Christ. **b.** the investment of a clergyman with a spiritual charge. [ME < eccl. L *institūtiōn-* (s. of *institūtiō*). See INSTITUTE, -ION]

in·sti·tu·tion·al (in′sti to͞o′shə nəl, -tyo͞o′-), *adj.* **1.** of, pertaining to, or established by institution. **2.** of or pertaining to organized societies or to the buildings devoted to their work. **3.** of the nature of an institution. **4.** characterized by the blandness, drabness, uniformity, and lack of individualized attention attributed to large organizations that serve many people: *institutional food; institutional furniture.* **5.** (of advertising) having as the primary object the establishment of good will and a favorable reputation rather than the immediate sale of the product. **6.** pertaining to institutes or principles, esp. of jurisprudence. [INSTITUTION + -AL[1]] —**in′sti·tu′tion·al·ly,** *adv.*

in·sti·tu·tion·al·ise (in′sti to͞o′shə nəlīz′, -tyo͞o′-), *v.t.*, **-ised, -is·ing.** *Chiefly Brit.* institutionalize. —**in′sti·tu′tion·al·i·sa′tion,** *n.*

in·sti·tu·tion·al·ism (in′sti to͞o′shə nəliz′əm, -tyo͞o′-), *n.* **1.** the system of institutions or organized societies devoted to public, charitable, or similar purposes. **2.** strong attachment to established institutions, as of religion. **3.** the belief or theory that society must establish and maintain public institutions. **4.** the belief or policy that a church must maintain institutions of education, welfare, etc., for its members. [INSTITUTIONAL + -ISM]

in·sti·tu·tion·al·ize (in′sti to͞o′shə nəlīz′, -tyo͞o′-), *v.t.*, **-ized, -iz·ing.** **1.** to make institutional. **2.** to make into or treat as an institution. **3.** to place or confine in an institution, esp. one for the special care of mental illnesses, alcoholism, etc. Also, *esp. Brit.*, **institutionalise.** [INSTITUTIONAL + -IZE] —**in′sti·tu′tion·al·i·za′tion,** *n.*

in·sti·tu·tion·ar·y (in′sti to͞o′shə ner′ē, -tyo͞o′-), *adj.* **1.** of or pertaining to an institution or institutions; institutional. **2.** of or pertaining to institution, esp. ecclesiastical institution. [INSTITUTION + -ARY]

in·sti·tu·tive (in′sti to͞o′tiv, -tyo͞o′-), *adj.* tending or intended to institute or establish. [INSTITUTE + -IVE] —**in′sti·tu′tive·ly,** *adv.*

in·sti·tu·tor (in′sti to͞o′tər, -tyo͞o′-), *n.* **1.** one who institutes or founds. **2.** *Prot. Episc. Ch.* one who institutes a minister into a parish or church. Also, **instituter.** [< LL; see INSTITUTE, -OR[2]]

instr., **1.** instructor. **2.** instrument. **3.** instrumental.

in·stroke (in′strōk′), *n.* **1.** a stroke in an inward direction. **2.** (in an engine) the stroke during which the piston moves into the cylinder. [IN + STROKE[1]]

in·struct (in strukt′), *v.t.* **1.** to direct or command; furnish with orders or directions: *The doctor instructed me to diet.* **2.** to furnish with knowledge, esp. by a systematic method; teach; train; educate. **3.** to furnish with information; inform; apprise. **4.** *Law.* (of a judge) to guide (a jury) by outlining the legal principles involved in the case under consideration. [late ME < L *instruct(us)* equipped, trained (ptp. of *instruere*), equiv. to *in-* IN-[2] + *struc-* (perf. s. of *struere* to put together) + *-tus* ptp. suffix] —**in·struct′ed·ly,** *adv.* —**in·struct′ed·ness,** *n.* —**in·struct′i·ble,** *adj.*
—**Syn. 1.** prescribe. **2.** tutor, coach; drill, discipline; indoctrinate; school. **3.** enlighten.

in·struc·tion (in struk′shən), *n.* **1.** act or practice of instructing or teaching; education. **2.** knowledge or information imparted. **3.** an item of such knowledge or information. **4.** Usually, **instructions.** orders or directions: *The instructions are on the back of the box.* **5.** act of furnishing with authoritative directions. **6.** *Computer Technol.* a character or set of characters which together with one or more operands defines an operation and which, when taken as a unit, causes a computer to operate on the indicated quantities. [ME *instruccio(u)n* < L *instructiōn-* (s. of *instructiō*). See INSTRUCT, -ION] —**in·struc′tion·al,** *adj.*
—**Syn. 1.** tutoring, coaching; training, drill, exercise; indoctrination; schooling. **5.** command, mandate.

in·struc·tive (in struk′tiv), *adj.* **1.** serving to instruct or inform; conveying instruction, knowledge, or information. **2.** *Gram.* noting a case, as in Finnish, whose distinctive function is to indicate means by which. —*n.* **3.** *Gram.* the instructive case. [INSTRUCT + -IVE] —**in·struc′tive·ly,** *adv.* —**in·struc′tive·ness,** *n.*

in·struc·tor (in struk′tər), *n.* **1.** one who instructs; a teacher. **2.** a teacher in a college or university who ranks below an assistant professor. Also, *referring to a woman,* **in·struc·tress** (in struk′tris). [late ME < L. See INSTRUCT, -OR[2]] —**in·struc·to·ri·al** (in′struk tôr′ē əl, -tōr′-), *adj.* —**in·struc′tor·less,** *adj.* —**in·struc′tor·ship′,** *n.*
—**Syn. 1.** tutor, schoolmaster, preceptor, pedagogue.

in·stru·ment (in′strə mənt), *n.* **1.** a mechanical device or contrivance; tool; implement: *a surgeon's instruments.* **2.** a contrivance for producing musical sounds: *a stringed instrument.* **3.** that with or by which something is effected; means; agency: *an instrument of government.* **4.** a formal legal document, as a contract, promissory note, deed, grant, etc. **5.** a person used by another merely as a means to some private end. **6.** a device for measuring the present value of the quantity under observation. **7.** a mechanical or electronic measuring device, esp. one used in navigation: *landing a plane by instruments.* —*adj.* **8.** *Aeron.* relying on only instruments for navigation: *instrument flying; instrument landing.* Cf. **contact** (def. 10). —*v.t.* **9.** to equip with instruments, as a machine, manufacturing process, etc.: *to instrument a space capsule.* **10.** to arrange a composition for musical instruments; orchestrate. [ME < L *instrūmentum*) equipment, equiv. to *instru(ere)* (to) equip + *-mentum* -MENT; see INSTRUCT]
—**Syn. 1.** See **tool.**

in·stru·men·tal (in′strə men′təl), *adj.* **1.** serving as an instrument or means. **2.** of or pertaining to an instrument. **3.** performed on or written for a musical instrument or musical instruments: *instrumental music.* **4.** *Gram.* **a.** (in certain inflected languages, as Old English and Russian) noting or pertaining to a case having as its distinctive function the indication of means or agency, as Old English *beseah blīthe andweitan* "looked with a happy countenance." **b.** noting the affix or other element characteristic of this case, or a word containing such an element. **c.** similar to such a case form in function or meaning, as the Latin instrumental ablative, *gladiō*, "by means of a sword." **5.** *Obs.* helpful; useful. —*n.* *Gram.* **6.** the instrumental case. **7.** a word in the instrumental case. **8.** a construction of similar meaning. **9.** a musical composition played by an instrument or a group of instruments. Cf. **vocal** (def. 8). [ME < ML *instrūmentāl(is)*. See INSTRUMENT, -AL[1]]

in·stru·men·tal·ism (in′strə men′təliz′əm), *n.* a pragmatic philosophy maintaining that the function of thought is to be instrumental in controlling environment, and that the value of ideas is determined by their function in human experience or progress. [INSTRUMENTAL + -ISM]

in·stru·men·tal·ist (in′strə men′təlist), *n.* **1.** one who performs on a musical instrument. **2.** an advocate of instrumentalism. —*adj.* **3.** of, pertaining to, or advocating instrumentalism. [INSTRUMENTAL + -IST]

in·stru·men·tal·i·ty (in′strə men tal′i tē), *n.*, *pl.* **-ties.** **1.** quality or state of being instrumental. **2.** fact or function of serving some purpose. **3.** a means or agency. [INSTRUMENTAL + -ITY]

in·stru·men·tal·ly (in′strə men′təlē), *adv.* **1.** by or with the use of an instrument. **2.** with or on an instrument, esp. a musical instrument. [INSTRUMENTAL + -LY]

in·stru·men·ta·tion (in′strə men tā′shən), *n.* **1.** the arranging of music for instruments, esp. for an orchestra. **2.** the list of instruments for which a composition is scored. **3.** the use of, or work done by, instruments. **4.** instrumental agency; instrumentality. **5.** the science of developing, manufacturing, and utilizing instruments, esp. those used in science and industry. [INSTRUMENT (V.) + -ATION]

in′strument pan′el, *Auto.* dashboard (def. 1). Also called **in′strument board′.**

in·sub·or·di·nate (in′sə bôr′dənit), *adj.* **1.** not submitting to authority; disobedient: *an insubordinate soldier.* **2.** not lower. —*n.* **3.** one who is insubordinate. [IN-[3] + SUBORDINATE] —**in′sub·or′di·nate·ly,** *adv.* —**in′sub·or′di·na′tion,** *n.*

in·sub·stan·tial (in′səb stan′shəl), *adj.* **1.** not substantial; slight. **2.** without reality; unreal: *He lives in an insubstantial world of dreams.* [< LL *insubstantiāl(is)*. See IN-[3], SUBSTANTIAL] —**in′sub·stan′ti·al′i·ty,** *n.* —**in′sub·stan′tial·ly,** *adv.*

in·suf·fer·a·ble (in suf′ər ə bəl), *adj.* not to be endured; intolerable; unbearable: *insufferable insolence.* [IN-[3] + SUFFERABLE] —**in·suf′fer·a·ble·ness,** *n.* —**in·suf′fer·a·bly,** *adv.*

in·suf·fi·cien·cy (in′sə fish′ən sē), *n.*, *pl.* **-cies** for 2. **1.** deficiency in amount, force, or fitness; inadequateness: *insufficiency of supplies.* **2.** an instance of this. Also, **in′suf·fi′cience.** [late ME < LL *insufficientia*. See INSUFFICIENT, -CY]

in·suf·fi·cient (in′sə fish′ənt), *adj.* **1.** not sufficient; lacking in what is necessary or required: *an insufficient answer.* **2.** deficient in force, quality, or amount; inadequate: *insufficient protection.* [ME < LL *insufficient-* (s. of *insufficiēns*). See IN-[3], SUFFICIENT] —**in′suf·fi′cient·ly,** *adv.*

in·suf·flate (in suf′lāt, in′sə flāt′), *v.t.*, **-flat·ed, -flat·ing.** **1.** to blow or breathe (something) in. **2.** *Med.* to blow (air or a medicinal substance) into some opening or upon some part of the body. **3.** *Eccles.* to breathe upon, esp. upon one being baptized or upon the water of baptism. [< LL *insufflāt(us)* blown into or upon. See IN-[2], SUFFLATE] —**in′suf·fla′tion,** *n.* —**in′suf·fla′tor,** *n.*

in·su·la (in′sə lə, ins′yə-), *n.*, *pl.* **-lae** (-lē′). *Anat.* a group of convolutions situated at the base of the lateral fissure of the brain. Also called **Island of Reil.** [< NL, L: island; see ISLE]

in·su·lar (in′sə lər, ins′yə-), *adj.* **1.** of or pertaining to an island or islands: *insular possessions.* **2.** dwelling or situated on an island. **3.** forming an island: *insular rocks.* **4.** detached; standing alone; isolated. **5.** of, pertaining to, or characteristic of islanders. **6.** narrowly exclusive; illiberal: *insular attitudes toward foreigners.* **7.** *Pathol.* occurring in or characterized by one or more isolated spots, patches, or the like. **8.** *Anat.* pertaining to an island of cells or tissue, as the islets of Langerhans. —*n.* **9.** an inhabitant of an island; islander. [< LL *insulār(is)*. See INSULA, -AR[1]] —**in′su·lar·ism,** *n.* —**in·su·lar·i·ty** (in′sə lar′i tē, ins′yə-), *n.* —**in′su·lar·ly,** *adv.*

In′sular Celt′ic, a partly geographical, partly genetic grouping of Celtic languages that consists of those spoken in the British Isles in ancient times and those descended from them. Cf. **Continental Celtic.**

in·su·lar·ize (in′sə lə rīz′, ins′yə-), *v.t.*, **-ized, -iz·ing.** to make into an island or represent as insular. [INSULAR + -IZE]

in·su·late (in′sə lāt′, ins′yə-), *v.t.*, **-lat·ed, -lat·ing.** **1.** to cover or surround (an electric wire or the like) with nonconducting material. **2.** (in physics, electronics, etc.) to separate conductors by the interposition of a nonconductor in order to prevent or reduce the transfer of electricity, heat, or sound. **3.** to place in an isolated situation or condition; segregate. [< LL *insulāt(us)* made into an island. See INSULA, -ATE[1]]

in·su·la·tion (in′sə lā′shən, ins′yə-), *n.* **1.** material used for insulating. **2.** act of insulating. **3.** state of being insulated. [INSULATE + -ION]

in·su·la·tor (in′sə lā′tər, ins′yə-), *n.* **1.** *Elect.* **a.** a material of such low conductivity that the flow of current through it can usually be neglected. **b.** insulating material, often glass or porcelain, in a unit form so designed as to support a charged conductor and electrically isolate it. **2.** one who or that which insulates. [INSULATE + -OR[2]]

in·su·lin (in′sə lin, ins′yə-), *n.* **1.** *Biochem.* a hormone, produced by the islets of Langerhans of the pancreas, that regulates the metabolism of glucose and other carbohydrates. **2.** *Pharm.* any of several commercial preparations of this substance, each of which allows a particular rate of absorption into the system: obtained from the pig or ox pancreas, and used in the treatment of diabetes to restore the normal ability of the body to utilize sugars and other carbohydrates. [INSUL(A) + -IN[2]]

in·su·lin·ize (in′sə lin īz′, ins′yə-), *v.t.*, **-ized, -iz·ing.** to treat with insulin. [INSULIN + -IZE] —**in′su·li·na′tion,** *n.*

in′sulin shock′, *Pathol.* a state of collapse caused by a decrease in blood sugar resulting from the administration of excessive insulin. Also called **in′sulin reac′tion.**

In·sull (in′səl), *n.* **Samuel,** 1859–1938, U.S. public utilities magnate, born in England.

in·sult (*v.* in sult′; *n.* in′sult), *v.t.* **1.** to treat insolently or with contemptuous rudeness; affront. **2.** *Archaic.* to attack; assault. —*v.i.* **3.** *Archaic.* to behave with insolent triumph; exult contemptuously (usually fol. by *on*, *upon*, or *over*). —*n.* **4.** an insolent or contemptuously rude action or speech; affront. **5.** something having the effect of an affront: *That book is an insult to one's intelligence.* **6.** *Med.* **a.** an injury or trauma. **b.** an agent that inflicts this. **7.** *Archaic.* an attack or assault. [< L *insult(āre)* (to) jump on, insult, equiv. to *in-* IN-[2] + *-sultāre*, var. of *saltāre* to jump; see SALTANT] —**in·sult′a·ble,** *adj.* —**in·sult′er,** *n.* —**in·sult′ing·ly,** *adv.*
—**Syn. 1.** offend, scorn, injure, abuse. **4.** offense, outrage. INSULT, INDIGNITY, AFFRONT, SLIGHT imply an act which injures another's honor, self-respect, etc. IN-

SULT implies such insolence of speech or manner as deeply humiliates or wounds one's feelings and arouses to anger. INDIGNITY is especially used of inconsiderate, contemptuous treatment toward one entitled to respect. AFFRONT implies open disrespect or offense shown, as it were, to the face. SLIGHT may imply inadvertent indifference or disregard, which may also indicate ill-concealed contempt. **—Ant. 1, 4.** compliment.

in·sul·ta·tion (in′səl tā′shən), *n. Archaic.* insult. [< L *insultātiōn-* (s. of *insultātiō*), equiv. to *insultāt(us)* insulted (ptp. of *insultāre*) + *-iōn-* -ION]

in·sult·ing (in sul′ting), *adj.* tending to give or cause insult; characterized by rudeness, insolence, etc. [INSULT + -ING[2]]

in·su·per·a·ble (in so͞o′pər ə bəl), *adj.* incapable of being passed over, overcome, or surmounted: *an insuperable barrier.* [ME < L *insuperābil(is).* See IN-[3], SUPERABLE] **—in·su′per·a·bil′i·ty, in·su′per·a·ble·ness,** *n.* **—in·su′per·a·bly,** *adv.*

in·sup·port·a·ble (in′sə pōr′tə bəl, -pôr′-), *adj.* **1.** not endurable; insufferable. **2.** incapable of support, as by evidence or collected facts: *an insupportable accusation.* [< LL *insupportābil(is).* See IN-[3], SUPPORTABLE] **—in′sup·port′a·ble·ness,** *n.* **—in′sup·port′a·bly,** *adv.*

in·sup·press·i·ble (in′sə pres′ə bəl), *adj.* incapable of being suppressed: *his insuppressible humor.* [IN-[3] + SUPPRESSIBLE] **—in′sup·press′i·bly,** *adv.*

in·sur·a·ble (in sho͝or′ə bəl), *adj.* capable of being insured, as against risk of loss or harm; proper to be insured. [INSURE + -ABLE] **—in·sur′a·bil′i·ty,** *n.*

in·sur·ance (in sho͝or′əns), *n.* **1.** the act, system, or business of insuring property, life, one's person, etc., against loss or harm arising in specified contingencies, as fire, accident, death, disablement, or the like, in consideration of a payment proportionate to the risk involved. **2.** coverage by contract in which one party agrees to indemnify or reimburse another for any loss that occurs under the terms of the contract. **3.** the contract itself, set forth in a written or printed agreement or policy. **4.** the amount for which anything is insured. **5.** *Rare.* an insurance premium. [INSURE + -ANCE]

in·sur·ant (in sho͝or′ənt), *n. Rare.* a person who takes out an insurance policy. [INSURE + -ANT]

in·sure (in sho͝or′), *v.,* **-sured, -sur·ing.** **—***v.t.* **1.** to guarantee against loss or harm. **2.** to secure indemnity to or on, in case of loss, damage, or death. **3.** to issue or procure an insurance policy on or for. **4.** ensure (defs. 1–3). **—***v.i.* **5.** to issue or procure an insurance policy. [var. of ENSURE]
—Syn. 1. warrant. **4.** assure.

in·sured (in sho͝ord′), *n.* a person covered by an insurance policy. [INSURE + -ED[2]]

in·sur·er (in sho͝or′ər), *n.* **1.** *Insurance.* a person or company that contracts to indemnify another in the event of loss or damage. **2.** one who or that which insures. [INSURE + -ER[1]]

in·sur·gence (in sûr′jəns), *n.* an act of rebellion. [INSURG(ENT) + -ENCE]

in·sur·gen·cy (in sûr′jən sē), *n.* state or condition of being insurgent; insurrection against an existing government by a group not recognized as having the status of a belligerent; rebellion without a revolutionary government. [INSURGEN(T) + -CY]

in·sur·gent (in sûr′jənt), *n.* **1.** a person who rises in forcible opposition to lawful authority, esp. one who engages in armed resistance to a government or to the execution of its laws; rebel. **2.** *U.S. Politics.* a member of a section of a political party that revolts against the methods or policies of the party. **—***adj.* **3.** rising in revolt; rebellious. **4.** surging or rushing in: *The insurgent waves battered the shore.* [< L *insurgent-* (s. of *insurgēns*) rising up against, prp. of *insurgere.* See IN-[2], SURGE, -ENT]

insur′ing clause′, the clause in an insurance policy setting forth the kind and degree of coverage granted by the insurer.

in·sur·mount·a·ble (in′sər moun′tə bəl), *adj.* incapable of being surmounted, passed over, or overcome: *an insurmountable obstacle.* [IN-[3] + SURMOUNTABLE] **—in′sur·mount′a·bil′i·ty, in′sur·mount′a·ble·ness,** *n.* **—in′sur·mount′a·bly,** *adv.*

in·sur·rec·tion (in′sə rek′shən), *n.* **1.** the act or an instance of rising in arms or open rebellion against civil authority or an established government. **2.** any act or instance of revolt or open resistance to established authority. [late ME < LL *insurrectiōn-* (s. of *insurrectiō*), equiv. to *insurrect(us)* risen up against (ptp. of *insurgere*) + *-iōn-* -ION] **—in′sur·rec′tion·al,** *adj.* **—in′sur·rec′tion·al·ly,** *adv.* **—in′sur·rec′tion·ism,** *n.* **—in′sur·rec′tion·ist,** *n.*
—Syn. 1. insurgency, uprising. **2.** mutiny. See **revolt.**

in·sur·rec·tion·ar·y (in′sə rek′shə ner′ē), *adj., n., pl.* **-ar·ies.** **—***adj.* **1.** of, pertaining to, or of the nature of insurrection. **2.** given to or causing insurrection. **—***n.* **3.** a person who engages in insurrection; rebel; insurgent. [INSURRECTION + -ARY]

in·sur·rec·tion·ise (in′sə rek′shə nīz′), *v.t.,* **-ised, -is·ing.** *Chiefly Brit.* insurrectionize.

in·sur·rec·tion·ize (in′sə rek′shə nīz′), *v.t.,* **-ized, -iz·ing.** **1.** to cause insurrection in (a country or the like). **2.** to rouse (a person, group, or people) to insurgent action. [INSURRECTION + -IZE]

in·sus·cep·ti·ble (in′sə sep′tə bəl), *adj.* not susceptible; incapable of being influenced or affected (usually fol. by *of* or *to*): *insusceptible of flattery; insusceptible to infection.* [IN-[3] + SUSCEPTIBLE] **—in′sus·cep′ti·bil′i·ty,** *n.* **—in′sus·cep′ti·bly,** *adv.*

in·swathe (in swāth′), *v.t.,* **-swathed, -swath·ing.** *Rare.* enswathe. **—in·swathe′ment,** *n.*

in·swept (in′swept′), *adj.* tapering at the front or tip, as an airplane wing. [adj. use of v. phrase *swept in*]

in·swing·er (in′swing′ər), *n. Cricket.* a bowled ball that veers from off side to leg side. Cf. **outswinger.** [IN + SWINGER]

int., **1.** interest. **2.** interim. **3.** interior. **4.** interjection. **5.** internal. **6.** international. **7.** interpreter. **8.** interval. **9.** intransitive.

in·tact (in takt′), *adj.* **1.** not altered, broken or impaired; remaining uninjured, sound, or whole: *The vase remained intact despite rough handling in shipment.* **2.** not changed or diminished; not influenced or swayed: *Despite his misfortunes, his faith and optimism are still intact.* **3.** complete or whole, esp. not castrated or emasculated. **4.** having the hymen unbroken; virginal. [late ME < L *intāct(us)* untouched, equiv. to *in-* IN-[3] + *tactus,* ptp. of *tangere* to touch] **—in·tact′ly,** *adv.* **—in·tact′ness,** *n.*
—Syn. 1. See **complete.**

in·tagl·io (in tal′yō, -täl′-; *It.* ēn tä′lyô), *n., pl.* **-tagl·ios,** *It.* **-ta·gli** (-tä′lyē). **1.** a gem, seal, piece of jewelry, or the like, cut with an incised or sunken design. **2.** incised carving, as opposed to carving in relief. **3.** ornamentation with a figure or design sunk below the surface. **4.** an incised or countersunk die. **5.** a figure or design so produced. **6.** a process in which a design, text, etc., is engraved into the surface of a plate so that when ink is applied and the excess is wiped off, ink remains in the grooves and is transferred to paper in printing, as in engraving, drypoint, etching, etc. **7.** an impression or printing from such a design, engraving, etc. [< It, deriv. of *intagliare* to cut in, engrave, equiv. to *in-* IN-[2] + *tagliare* to cut < LL *tāliāre,* deriv. of L *tālea* a cutting; see TALLY]

in·take (in′tāk′), *n.* **1.** the point at which a fluid is taken into a channel, pipe, etc. **2.** the act or an instance of taking in. **3.** that which is taken in. **4.** a quantity taken in: *the intake of oxygen.* **5.** a narrowing; contraction. [n. use of v. phrase *take in*]

in·tan·gi·ble (in tan′jə bəl), *adj.* **1.** not tangible; incapable of being perceived by the sense of touch, as incorporeal or immaterial things. **2.** not definite or clear to the mind: *intangible arguments.* **3.** (of an asset) existing only in connection with something else, as the good will of a business. **—***n.* **4.** something intangible, esp. an intangible asset. [< ML *intangibil(is).* See IN-[3], TANGIBLE] **—in·tan′gi·bil′i·ty, in·tan′gi·ble·ness,** *n.* **—in·tan′gi·bly,** *adv.*

in·tar·si·a (in tär′sē ə), *n.* an art or technique of decorating a surface with inlaid patterns, esp. of wood mosaic, developed during the Renaissance. Also, **tarsia.** [IN-[2] + It *tarsia* < Ar *tarsī* an inlay] **—in·tar·si·ate** (in tär′sē āt′, -it), *adj.*

in·tar·sist (in tär′sist), *n.* a person who creates in or practices intarsia. [INTARS(IA) + -IST]

in·te·ger (in′ti jər), *n.* **1.** one of the positive or negative numbers 1, 2, 3, 4, etc., or 0; a whole number, as distinguished from a fraction or a mixed number. **2.** a complete entity. [< L: untouched, hence, undivided, whole, equiv. to *in-* IN-[3] + *-teg-* (var. of *tag-,* ptp. s. of *tangere* to touch) + *-er* adj. suffix]

in·te·ger vi·tae (in′te ger wē′tī; *Eng.* in′ti jər vī′tē), *Latin.* blameless in life; innocent. Horace, *Odes,* I.

in·te·gra·ble (in′tə grə bəl), *adj. Math.* capable of being integrated, as a mathematical function or differential equation. [INTEGR(ATE) + -ABLE] **—in′te·gra·bil′i·ty,** *n.*

in·te·gral (in′tə grəl), *adj.* **1.** of, pertaining to, or belonging as a part of the whole; constituent or component: *the integral parts of the human body.* **2.** necessary to the completeness of the whole: *This point is integral to his plan.* **3.** made up of parts which together constitute a whole. **4.** entire; complete; whole: *the integral works of a writer.* **5.** *Arith.* pertaining to or being an integer; not fractional. **6.** *Math.* pertaining to or involving integrals. **—***n.* **7.** an integral whole. **8.** *Math.* **a.** Also called **Riemann integral.** the numerical measure of the area bounded above by the graph of a given function, below by the *x-axis,* and on the sides by ordinates drawn at the endpoints of a specified interval; the limit, as the norm of partitions of the given interval approaches zero, of the sum of the products of the function evaluated at a point in each subinterval times the length of the subinterval. **b.** a primitive. **c.** any of several analogous quantities. Cf. **improper integral, line integral, multiple integral, surface integral.** [< LL *integrāl(is).* See INTEGER, -AL[1]] **—in·te·gral·i·ty** (in′tə gral′i tē), *n.* **—in′te·gral·ly,** *adv.*

in′tegral cal′culus, the branch of mathematics that deals with integrals, esp. the methods of ascertaining indefinite integrals and applying them to the solution of differential equations and the determining of areas, volumes, and lengths.

in′tegral curve′, *Math.* a curve that is a geometric representation of a functional solution to a given differential equation.

in′tegral domain′, *Math.* a commutative ring in which the cancellation law holds true. Also called **domain of integrity.**

in′tegral equa′tion, *Math.* an equation in which an integral involving a dependent variable appears.

in′tegral test′, *Math.* the theorem that a given infinite series converges if the function whose value at each integer is the corresponding term in the series is decreasing, tends to zero, and results in a finite number when integrated from one to infinity.

in·te·grand (in′tə grand′), *n. Math.* the expression to be integrated. [< L *integrand(um),* n. use of neut. of *integrandus,* ger. of *integrāre* to INTEGRATE]

in·te·grant (in′tə grənt), *adj.* **1.** making up or being a part of a whole; constituent. **—***n.* **2.** an integrant part. **3.** a solid, rigid sheet of building material composed of several layers of the same or of different materials. [< L *integrant-* (s. of *integrāns*) making whole, prp. of *integrāre.* See INTEGER, -ANT]

in·te·graph (in′tə graf′, -gräf′), *n.* integrator (def. 2). [b. INTEGRATE and -GRAPH]

in·te·grate (in′tə grāt′), *v.,* **-grat·ed, -grat·ing.** **—***v.t.* **1.** to bring together or incorporate (parts) into a whole. **2.** to make up, combine, or complete to produce a whole or a larger unit, as parts do. **3.** to unite or combine. **4.** to indicate the total amount or the mean value of. **5.** *Math.* to find the integral of. **6.** *U.S.* **a.** to combine (educational facilities, classes, and the like, previously segregated by race) into one unified system. **b.** to give or cause to give equal opportunity to members of all races, religions, and ethnic groups, esp. to Negroes, to belong to, be employed by, be customers of, or vote in (an organization, place of business, city, State, etc.): *to integrate a restaurant; to integrate a country club.* **c.** to give or cause to give equal opportunity and consideration to (a racial, religious, or ethnic group or a member of such a group): *to integrate the Negroes in Mississippi.* **—***v.i. U.S.* **6.** (of a school, neighborhood, place of business, city, etc.) to become integrated. **7.** (of a racial, religious, or ethnic group) **a.** to become integrated. **b.** to meld with and become part of the dominant culture. [< L *integrāt(us)* made whole, restored (ptp. of *integrāre*). See INTEGER, -ATE[1]] **—in′te·gra′tive,** *adj.*

in·te·grat·ed (in′tə grā′tid), *adj.* **1.** having on a basis of equal membership individuals of different racial, religious, and ethnic groups: *an integrated school.* Cf. **segregated.** **2.** combining or coordinating separate elements so as to provide a harmonious, interrelated whole: *an integrated plot; an integrated course of study.* **3.** organized or structured so that constituent units function cooperatively: *an integrated economy.* **4.** *Sociol.* of or pertaining to a group or society whose members interact on the basis of commonly held norms or values. **5.** *Psychol.* characterized by integration. [INTEGRATE + -ED[2]]

in′tegrated bar′, *Law.* (in some States) a system of bar associations to which all lawyers are required to belong. Also called **incorporated bar.**

in′tegrated da′ta proc′essing, the processing of information by systematic techniques which reduce human intervention to a minimum and which employ a language common to all the machines in the system. *Abbr.:* IDP Cf. **automatic data processing.**

in′tegrating fac′tor, *Math.* a factor that upon multiplying a differential equation with right-hand side equal to zero makes the equation integrable, usually by making the resulting expression an exact differential of some function.

in·te·gra·tion (in′tə grā′shən), *n.* **1.** the act or an instance of combining into an integral whole. **2.** behavior, as of an individual, that is in harmony with the environment. **3.** *Psychol.* the organization of the constituent elements of the personality into a coordinated, harmonious whole. **4.** *Math.* the operation of finding the integral of a function or equation, esp. solving a differential equation. **5.** *U.S.* **a.** the combination of educational and other public facilities, previously segregated by race, into one unified system. **b.** the act or an instance of integrating an organization, place of business, city, etc. **c.** the act or an instance of integrating a racial, religious, or ethnic group. [INTEGRATE + -ION; cf. L *integrātiō* renewal]

integra′tion by parts′, a method of evaluating an integral by use of the formula, $\int udv = uv - \int vdu$.

in·te·gra·tion·ist (in′tə grā′shə nist), *n. U.S.* a person who works for or favors the integration of educational and other public facilities. [INTEGRATION + -IST]

in·te·gra·tor (in′tə grā′tər), *n.* **1.** one who or that which integrates. **2.** an instrument for performing numerical integrations. [INTEGRATE + -OR[2]]

in·teg·ri·ty (in teg′ri tē), *n.* **1.** soundness of and adherence to moral principle and character; uprightness; honesty. **2.** the state of being whole, entire, or undiminished: *to preserve the integrity of the empire.* **3.** a sound, unimpaired, or perfect condition: *the integrity of the text; the integrity of a ship's hull.* [late ME *integrite* < L *integritās.* See INTEGER, -ITY]
—Syn. 1. rectitude, probity, virtue. See **honor.** **—Ant. 1.** dishonesty.

in·teg·u·ment (in teg′yə mənt), *n.* **1.** a natural covering, as a skin, shell, rind, etc. **2.** any covering, coating, enclosure, etc. [< L *integument(um)* a covering. See IN-[2], TEGUMENT]
—Syn. 1, 2. cortex. **2.** involucre, involucrum, wrapping, cloak.

in·teg·u·men·ta·ry (in teg′yə men′tə rē), *adj.* of, pertaining to, or like an integument. [INTEGUMENT + -ARY]

in·tel·lect (in′tᵊlekt′), *n.* **1.** the power or faculty of the mind by which one knows or understands, as distinguished from that by which one feels and that by which one wills; the understanding; the faculty of thinking and acquiring knowledge. **2.** capacity for thinking and acquiring knowledge, esp. of a high order; mental capacity. **3.** a particular mind or intelligence, esp. of a high order. **4.** a person possessing a great capacity for thought and knowledge. **5.** minds collectively, as of a number of persons, or the persons themselves. [ME < L *intellect(us),* equiv. to *intellect-* (ptp. s. of *intellegere* to understand; see INTELLIGENT) + *-us* n. suffix]
—Syn. 1. reason, sense, common sense, brains. See **mind.** **—Ant. 1.** inanity.

in·tel·lec·tion (in′tᵊlek′shən), *n.* **1.** the action or process of understanding; the exercise of the intellect. **2.** a particular act of the intellect. **3.** a conception or idea as the result of such an act. [late ME < ML *intellectiōn-* (s. of *intellectiō*). See INTELLECT, -ION]

in·tel·lec·tive (in′tᵊlek′tiv), *adj.* **1.** having power to understand; intelligent. **2.** of or pertaining to the intellect. [late ME < LL *intellectīv(us).* See INTELLECT, -IVE] **—in′tel·lec′tive·ly,** *adv.*

in·tel·lec·tu·al (in′tᵊlek′cho͞o əl), *adj.* **1.** appealing to or engaging the intellect: *intellectual pursuits.* **2.** of or pertaining to the intellect or its use: *intellectual powers.* **3.** directed or inclined toward things that involve the intellect: *intellectual tastes.* **4.** possessing or showing intellect or mental capacity, esp. to a high degree: *an intellectual person.* **5.** guided or developed by or relying on the intellect rather than upon emotions or feelings. **6.** characterized by or suggesting a predominance of intellect: *an intellectual way of speaking.* **—***n.* **7.** a person of superior intellect. **8.** a person who places a high value on or pursues things of interest to the intellect or the more complex forms and fields of knowledge, as aesthetic or philosophical matters, esp. on an abstract and general level. **9.** an extremely rational person; one who relies on intellect rather than on emotions or feelings. **10.** a person professionally engaged in mental labor, as a writer, teacher, etc., as distinguished from a manual laborer or businessman. **11.** **intellectuals,** *Archaic.* the mental faculties. **12.** **intellectuals,** *Obs.* things pertaining to the intellect. [ME < L *intellectuāl(is),* equiv. to *intellectu(s)* INTELLECT + *-ālis* -AL[1]] **—in′tel·lec′tu·al·ly,** *adv.* **—in′tel·lec′tu·al·ness,** *n.*
—Syn. 1, 2. mental. **4.** See **intelligent.** **—Ant. 1, 4.** animal, sensual.

in·tel·lec·tu·al·ise (in′tᵊlek′cho͞o ə līz′), *v.t., v.i.,* **-ised, -is·ing.** *Chiefly Brit.* intellectualize. **—in′tel·lec′tu·al·i·sa′tion,** *n.* **—in′tel·lec′tu·al·is′er,** *n.*

in·tel·lec·tu·al·ism (in′tᵊlek′cho͞o ə liz′əm), *n.* **1.** the exercise of the intellect. **2.** devotion to intellectual pursuits. **3.** excessive emphasis on abstract or intellectual matters, esp. with a lack of proper consideration for emotions **4.** *Philos.* **a.** the doctrine that knowledge is wholly or chiefly derived from pure reason. **b.** the belief that reason is the final principle of reality. [INTELLECTUAL + -ISM] **—in′tel·lec′tu·al·ist,** *n.* **—in′-**

tel·lec/tu·al·is/tic, *adj.* —**in/tel·lec/tu·al·is/ti·cal·ly,** *adv.*

in·tel·lec·tu·al·i·ty (in/təlek/cho͞o al/i tē), *n., pl.* **-ties. 1.** the quality or state of being intellectual. **2.** intellectual character or power. [< LL *intellectuālitās.* See INTELLECTUAL, -ITY]

in·tel·lec·tu·al·ize (in/təlek/cho͞o ə līz/), *v.,* **-ized, -iz·ing.** —*v.t.* **1.** to seek or consider the rational content or form of. **2.** to make intellectual. **3.** to analyze (something) intellectually or rationally: *to intellectualize the practice of the artist.* **4.** to ignore the emotional or psychological significance of (an action, feeling, dream, etc.) by an excessively intellectual or abstract explanation. —*v.i.* **5.** to talk or write intellectually; reason; philosophize: *to intellectualize about world problems.* Also, *esp. Brit.,* **intellectualise.** [INTELLECTUAL + -IZE] —**in/tel·lec/tu·al·i·za/tion,** *n.* —**in/tel·lec/tu·al·iz/er,** *n.*

in·tel·li·gence (in tel/i jəns), *n.* **1.** capacity for reasoning, understanding, and for similar forms of mental activity; aptitude in grasping truths, facts, meanings, etc. **2.** manifestation of such capacity: *He writes with intelligence and wit.* **3.** the faculty of understanding. **4.** knowledge of an event, circumstance, etc., received or imparted; news; information. **5.** the gathering or distribution of information, esp. secret information. **6.** *Gov.* **a.** information about an enemy or a potential enemy. **b.** the evaluated conclusions drawn from such information. **c.** an organization or agency employed in gathering such information: *military intelligence; naval intelligence.* **7.** (*often cap.*) an intelligent being, esp. an incorporeal one. **8.** interchange of information: *They have been maintaining intelligence with foreign agents for years.* [ME < L *intelligentia.* See INTELLIGENT, -ENCE]
—**Syn. 1.** See **mind. 1, 2.** discernment, reason, acumen, aptitude, penetration. —**Ant. 1, 2.** stupidity.

intel/ligence bu/reau, a government department charged with obtaining intelligence, or information, esp. for use by the armed forces. Also called **intel/ligence depart/ment, intelligence office.**

intel/ligence of/fice, 1. See **intelligence bureau. 2.** an employment agency for the placement of domestic help.

intel/ligence quo/tient, *Psychol.* mental age divided by chronological age, usually expressed as a multiple of 100. The intelligence quotient of a ten-year-old child whose mental age equals that of the average twelve-year-old is 1.2, or 120. *Abbr.:* IQ, I.Q. Cf. **achievement quotient.**

in·tel·li·genc·er (in tel/i jən sər), *n.* **1.** one who or that which conveys information. **2.** an informer; spy. [INTELLIGENCE + -ER[1]]

intel/ligence test/, *Psychol.* any of various tests, as the Binet-Simon scale, designed to measure the native mental ability or capacity of an individual. Cf. **achievement test.**

in·tel·li·gent (in tel/i jənt), *adj.* **1.** having good understanding or a high mental capacity; quick to comprehend, as persons or animals: *an intelligent student of law.* **2.** displaying or characterized by quickness of understanding, sound thought, or good judgment: *an intelligent reply.* **3.** having the faculty of reasoning and understanding; possessing intelligence: *an intelligent being.* **4.** *Archaic.* having understanding or knowledge (usually fol. by *of*). [< L *intelligent-* (s. of *intelligēns,* prp. of *intelligere,* var. of *intellegere* to understand, lit., choose between), equiv. to *intel-* (var. of *inter-* INTER-) + *-lig-* choose (var. of *leg-,* root of *legere*) + *-ent-* -ENT] —**in·tel/li·gent·ly,** *adv.*
—**Syn. 1.** bright. INTELLIGENT, INTELLECTUAL describe distinctive mental capacity. INTELLIGENT often suggests a natural quickness of understanding: *an intelligent reader.* INTELLECTUAL implies not only having a high degree of understanding, but also a capacity and taste for the higher forms of knowledge: *intellectual interests.* **2.** astute, clever, alert, bright, apt, discerning, shrewd, smart. See **sharp.** —**Ant. 1, 2.** stupid.

in·tel·li·gen·tial (in tel/i jen/shəl), *adj.* **1.** of or pertaining to the intelligence or understanding. **2.** endowed with intelligence. **3.** conveying information. [< L *intelligenti(a)* INTELLIGENCE + -AL[1]]

in·tel·li·gent·si·a (in tel/i jent/sē ə, -gent/sē ə), *n.pl.* intellectuals considered as an artistic, social, or political group, or class, esp. as an elite. [< Russ < L *intelligentia* INTELLIGENCE]

in·tel·li·gi·bil·i·ty (in tel/i jə bil/i tē), *n., pl.* **-ties** for 2. **1.** the quality or condition of being intelligible; capability of being understood. **2.** something intelligible. [INTELLIGIBLE + -ITY]

in·tel·li·gi·ble (in tel/i jə bəl), *adj.* **1.** capable of being understood; comprehensible: *an intelligible response.* **2.** *Philos.* apprehensible by the mind only; conceptual. [ME < L *intelligibil(is),* equiv. to *intellig-* (see INTELLIGENT) + *-ibilis* -IBLE] —**in·tel/li·gi·ble·ness,** *n.* —**in·tel/li·gi·bly,** *adv.*

in·tem·er·ate (in tem/ər it), *adj. Rare.* inviolate; undefiled; unsullied; pure. [< L *intemerāt(us),* equiv. to *in-* IN-[3] + *temerā-* (s. of *temerāre* to darken, hence, sully) + *-tus* ptp. suffix] —**in·tem/er·ate·ly,** *adv.* —**in·tem/er·ate·ness,** *n.*

in·tem·per·ance (in tem/pər əns, -prəns), *n.* **1.** immoderate indulgence in alcoholic beverages. **2.** excessive indulgence of a natural appetite or passion. **3.** lack of moderation or due restraint, as in action or speech. **4.** an act or instance of any of these: *a long series of intemperances.* [ME < L *intemperantia.* See IN-[3], TEMPERANCE]

in·tem·per·ate (in tem/pər it, -prit), *adj.* **1.** given to or characterized by immoderate indulgence in intoxicating drink. **2.** immoderate as regards indulgence of appetite or passion. **3.** not temperate; unrestrained; unbridled. **4.** extreme in temperature, as climate. [ME < L *intemperāt(us).* See IN-[3], TEMPERATE] —**in·tem/per·ate·ly,** *adv.* —**in·tem/per·ate·ness,** *n.*

in·tend (in tend/), *v.t.* **1.** to have in mind as something to be done or brought about: *We intend to leave in a month.* **2.** to design or mean for a particular purpose, use, recipient, etc.: *a fund intended for emergency use only.* **3.** to design to express or indicate. **4.** (of words, terms, statements, etc.) to signify. **5.** *Archaic.* to direct (the eyes, mind, etc.). —*v.i.* **6.** to have a purpose or design. **7.** *Obs.* to set out on one's course. [< L *intend(ere)* (to) stretch towards, aim at (see IN-[2], TEND[1]); r. ME *entenden* < OF *entendre*] —**in·tend/er,** *n.*
—**Syn. 1.** contemplate, plan, expect, aim, purpose. INTEND, MEAN, DESIGN, PROPOSE imply knowing what one wishes to do and setting this as a goal. To INTEND is to have in mind something willed to be done or brought about: *No offense was intended.* MEAN is a less formal word than INTEND, and often suggests less determination or purposefulness: *He means to go away.* DESIGN implies planning to effect a particular result; the things to be done have a definite relationship to one another: *to design a plan for Christmas decorations.* PROPOSE suggests setting up a program before oneself for accomplishment, or offering it for consideration: *We propose to beautify our city.*

in·tend·ance (in ten/dəns), *n.* **1.** a department of the public service, as in France, or the officials in charge of it. **2.** the official quarters of an intendant. **3.** the function of an intendant; superintendance; intendancy. [< F; see INTENDANT, -ANCE]

in·tend·an·cy (in ten/dən sē), *n., pl.* **-cies. 1.** the office or function of an intendant. **2.** a body of intendants. **3.** Also, **intendency.** a district under the charge of an intendant. [INTENDAN(T) + -CY]

in·tend·ant (in ten/dənt), *n.* **1.** a person who has the direction or management of some public business, the affairs of an establishment, etc.; a superintendent. **2.** the title of various public officials in France and elsewhere. [< F < L *intendent-* (s. of *intendēns*) attending to, prp. of *intendere.* See INTEND, -ANT]

in·tend·ed (in ten/did), *adj.* **1.** purposed; designed; intentional: *to produce the intended effect; an intended snub.* **2.** prospective: *one's intended wife.* —*n.* **3.** *Informal.* one's fiancé or fiancée. [INTEND + -ED[2]] —**in·tend/ed·ly,** *adv.* —**in·tend/ed·ness,** *n.*

in·tend·en·cy (in ten/dən sē), *n., pl.* **-cies.** intendancy (def. 3).

in·tend·ment (in tend/mənt), *n.* **1.** *Law.* the true or correct meaning of something. **2.** *Obs.* intention; design; purpose. [INTEND + -MENT; r. ME *entendement* < MF < ML *intendiment(um)*]

in·ten·er·ate (in ten/ə rāt/), *v.t.,* **-at·ed, -at·ing.** *Archaic.* to make soft or tender; soften. [IN-[2] + L *tener* TENDER[1] + -ATE[1]] —**in·ten/er·a/tion,** *n.*

intens., intensive.

in·tense (in tens/), *adj.* **1.** existing or occurring in a high or extreme degree: *intense heat.* **2.** acute, strong, or vehement, as sensations, feelings, or emotions: *The situation doesn't warrant such intense anger.* **3.** of an extreme kind; very great, strong, keen, severe, etc.: *an intense gale.* **4.** having a characteristic quality in a high degree: *The intense sunlight was blinding.* **5.** strenuous or earnest, as activity, exertion, diligence, thought, etc.: *an intense life.* **6.** exhibiting a high degree of some quality or action. **7.** having or showing great strength, strong feeling, or tension, as a person, the face, language, etc. **8.** susceptible to strong emotion; emotional: *an intense person.* [ME < L *intens(us)* stretched out, ptp. of *intendere* to INTEND. See IN-[2], TENSE[1]] —**in·tense/ly,** *adv.* —**in·tense/ness,** *n.*

in·ten·si·fi·er (in ten/sə fī/ər), *n.* **1.** one who or that which intensifies. **2.** a ram-operated device for increasing hydraulic pressure. **3.** *Gram.* an intensive. [INTENSIFY + -ER[1]]

in·ten·si·fy (in ten/sə fī/), *v.,* **-fied, -fy·ing.** —*v.t.* **1.** to make intense or more intense. **2.** to make more acute; strengthen or sharpen. **3.** *Photog.* to increase the density and contrast of (a negative). —*v.i.* **4.** to become intense or more intense. [INTENSE + -IFY] —**in·ten/si·fi·ca/tion,** *n.*
—**Syn. 1.** deepen, quicken. **2.** concentrate. See **aggravate.** —**Ant. 1.** alleviate, weaken.

in·ten·sion (in ten/shən), *n.* **1.** intensification; increase in degree. **2.** intensity; high degree. **3.** relative intensity; degree. **4.** exertion of the mind; determination. **5.** *Logic.* the set of attributes belonging to any thing to which a given term is correctly applied; connotation; comprehension. Cf. **extension** (def. 12). [< L *intensiōn-* (s. of *intensiō*). See INTENSE, -ION] —**in·ten/sion·al,** *adj.* —**in·ten/sion·al·ly,** *adv.*

in·ten·si·tom·e·ter (in ten/si tom/i tər), *n.* a device used to measure x-ray intensity in radiography in order to determine correct exposure time. [INTENSIT(Y) + -O- + -METER]

in·ten·si·ty (in ten/si tē), *n., pl.* **-ties. 1.** the quality or condition of being intense. **2.** energy, strength, concentration, vehemence, etc., as of activity, thought, or feeling: *He went at the job with great intensity.* **3.** a high or extreme degree, as of cold or heat. **4.** the degree or extent to which something is intense. **5.** a high degree of emotional excitement; depth of feeling: *The poem lacked intensity and left me cold.* **6.** *Speech.* **a.** the correlate of physical energy and the degree of loudness of a speech sound. **b.** the relative carrying power of vocal utterance. **7.** the strength or sharpness of a color due esp. to its degree of freedom from admixture with its complementary color. **8.** *Physics.* magnitude, as of energy or a force per unit of area, volume, time, etc. [INTENSE + -ITY]

inten/sity of illumina/tion, *Optics.* illumination (def. 5).

in·ten·sive (in ten/siv), *adj.* **1.** of, pertaining to, or characterized by intensity: *intensive questioning.* **2.** tending to intensify; intensifying. **3.** *Med.* **a.** increasing in intensity or degree. **b.** instituting treatment to the limit of safety. **4.** noting or pertaining to a system of agriculture involving the cultivation of limited areas, with labor and expenditures employed in raising the crop yield per unit area (opposed to *extensive*). **5.** *Gram.* indicating increased emphasis or force. *Certainly* and *tremendously* are intensive adverbs. *Myself* in *I did it myself* is an intensive pronoun. —*n.* **6.** something that intensifies. **7.** *Gram.* an intensive element or formation, as *-self* in *himself,* or Latin *-tō* in *iac-tō,* "I hurl" from *iacō,* "I throw." [late ME < ML *intensīv(us).* See INTENSE, -IVE] —**in·ten/sive·ly,** *adv.* —**in·ten/sive·ness,** *n.*

in·tent[1] (in tent/), *n.* **1.** the act or fact of intending, as to do something: *criminal intent.* **2.** that which is intended; purpose; design; intention: *The original intent of the committee was to raise funds.* **3.** *Law.* the state of a person's mind which directs his actions toward a specific object. **4.** meaning or significance. **5. to all intents and purposes,** for all practical purposes; practically speaking; virtually: *The book was, to all intents and purposes, a mere duplication of his earlier efforts.* [ME < LL *intent(us)* an aim, purpose, lit., a stretching out (n. use of L *intentus* INTENT[2]); r. ME *entent(e)* < OF]
—**Syn. 1.** See **intention. 2.** meaning; plan, plot.

in·tent[2] (in tent/), *adj.* **1.** firmly or steadfastly fixed or directed, as the eyes, mind, etc.: *an intent gaze; his intent concentration.* **2.** having the attention sharply focused or fixed on something: *intent on one's job.* **3.** determined; having the mind or will fixed on some purpose or goal: *intent on revenge.* **4.** earnest; intense: *an intent person.* [< L *intent(us),* ptp. of *intendere* to INTEND] —**in·tent/ly,** *adv.* —**in·tent/ness,** *n.*
—**Syn. 1.** resolute, concentrated. **3.** set. —**Ant. 1.** irresolute, dispersed.

in·ten·tion (in ten/shən), *n.* **1.** the act or an instance of determining mentally upon some action or result. **2.** the end or object intended; purpose. **3. intentions, a.** one's attitude toward the effect of one's actions or conduct: *a bungler with good intentions.* **b.** one's attitude with respect to marriage: *The girl began to worry that the young man's intentions might not be serious.* **4.** the act or fact of intending. **5.** *Logic.* a general concept, esp. one obtained by abstraction from the ideas or images of sensible objects **(first intention),** or one obtained by reflection on and abstraction from first intentions **(second intention). 6.** *Surg., Med.* a manner or process of healing, as in the healing of a lesion or fracture without granulation **(healing by first intention)** or the healing of a wound by granulation after suppuration **(healing by second intention). 7.** meaning or significance: *The intention of his words was clear.* **8.** *Archaic.* intentness. [ME *intencio(u)n* < L *intentiōn-* (s. of *intentiō*). See INTENT[2], -ION] —**in·ten/tion·less,** *adj.*
—**Syn. 2.** goal. INTENTION, INTENT, PURPOSE all refer to a wish which one means to carry out. INTENTION is the general word: *His intention is good.* INTENT is chiefly legal or poetical: *attack with intent to kill.* PURPOSE implies having a goal or a settled determination to achieve something: *Her strong sense of purpose is reflected in her studies.*

in·ten·tion·al (in ten/shə nəl), *adj.* **1.** done with intention or on purpose: *an intentional insult.* **2.** of or pertaining to intention or purpose. **3.** *Metaphys.* **a.** pertaining to an appearance, phenomenon, or representation in the mind; phenomenal; representational. **b.** pertaining to the capacity of the mind to refer to objects of all sorts. [INTENTION + -AL[1]] —**in·ten/tion·al/i·ty,** *n.* —**in·ten/tion·al·ly,** *adv.*
—**Syn. 1.** designed, planned, intended. See **deliberate. 2.** purposeful. —**Ant. 1.** accidental.

in·ten·tioned (in ten/shənd), *adj.* having particular or specified intentions (often used in combination): *a maliciously intentioned letter; a well-intentioned person.* [INTENTION + -ED[3]]

in·ter (in tûr/), *v.t.,* **-terred, -ter·ring. 1.** to deposit (a dead body) in a grave or tomb; bury. **2.** *Obs.* to put into the earth. [ME *entere(n)* < MF *enterr(er)* << L *in-* IN-[2] + *terra* earth]

inter-, a prefix occurring in loan words from Latin, where it meant "between," "among," "in the midst of," "mutually," "reciprocally," "together," "during" (*intercept; interest*); on this model, used in the formation of compound words (*intercom; interdepartmental*). [ME < L (in some words r. ME *entre-* < MF < L *inter-*), comb. form of *inter* (prep and adv.); see INTERIOR]

inter., 1. intermediate. **2.** interrogation. **3.** interrogative.

in·ter·ac·i·nous (in/tər as/ə nəs), *adj. Anat.* situated between the acini of a gland. [INTER- + ACINOUS]

in·ter·act (in/tər akt/), *v.i.* to act one upon another. [INTER- + ACT] —**in/ter·ac/tive,** *adj.*

in·ter·ac·tion (in/tər ak/shən), *n.* reciprocal action or influence. [INTER- + ACTION] —**in/ter·ac/tion·al,** *adj.*

in·ter·ac·tion·ism (in/tər ak/shə niz/əm), *n. Philos.* a theory that the mind and the body may each affect the other. [INTERACTION + -ISM] —**in/ter·ac/tion·ist,** *n., adj.*

in·ter a·li·a (in/ter ä/li ä/; *Eng.* in/tər ā/lē ə), *Latin.* among other things.

in·ter a·li·os (in/ter ä/li ōs/; *Eng.* in/tər ā/lē ōs/), *Latin.* among other persons.

in·ter-Al·lied (in/tər ə līd/), *adj.* between or among allied nations, esp. the Allies of World War I.

in·ter-A·mer·i·can (in/tər ə mer/i kən), *adj.* of or pertaining to some or all of the countries of North and South America.

in·ter·a·tom·ic (in/tər ə tom/ik), *adj.* between atoms. [INTER- + ATOMIC]

in·ter·bed·ded (in/tər bed/id), *adj.* (of a rock, mineral, etc.) lying between beds or strata of a different rock or mineral; interstratified. [INTER- + BEDDED]

in/ter·ab·sorp/tion, *n.*
in/ter·ac/a·dem/ic, *adj.*
in/ter·ac/a·dem/i·cal·ly, *adv.*
in/ter·ac·ces/so·ry, *adj.*
in/ter·ac·cuse/, *v.t.,* **-cused, -cus·ing.**
in/ter·a·dap/tion, *n.*
in/ter·ad/di·tive, *adj.*
in/ter·af·fil/i·a/tion, *n.*
in/ter·a/gen·cy, *n., pl.* **-cies** *adj.*
in/ter·a/gent, *n.*
in/ter·ag·glu/ti·nate/, *v.i.,* **-nat·ed, -nat·ing.**
in/ter·ag·glu/ti·na/tion, *n.*
in/ter·a·gree/, *v.t.,* **-greed, -gree·ing.**
in/ter·a·gree/ment, *n.*
in/ter·a/lar, *adj.*
in/ter·al·ve/o·lar, *adj.*
in/ter·am/bu·la/crum, *n., pl.* **-cra.**
in/ter·An/de/an, *adj.*
in/ter·an/gu·lar, *adj.*
in/ter·an/i·mate/, *v.t.,* **-mat·ed, -mat·ing.**
in/ter·an/nu·lar, *adj.*
in/ter·an·tag/o·nism, *n.*
in/ter·a·poph/y·sal, *adj.*
in/ter·ap/o·phys/e·al, *adj.*
in/ter·ap/pli·ca/tion, *n.*
in/ter·ar/bo·ra/tion, *n.*
in/ter·arch/, *v.i.*
in/ter·ar·tic/u·lar, *adj.*
in/ter·ar·tis/tic, *adj.*
in/ter·ar/y·te/noid, *adj.*
in/ter·as·so/ci·a/tion, *n.*
in/ter·as·sure/, *v.t.,* **-sured, -sur·ing.**
in/ter·as/ter·oi/dal, *adj.*
in/ter·as/tral, *adj.*
in/ter·a/tri·al, *adj.*
in/ter·at·tri/tion, *n.*
in/ter·au/lic, *adj.*
in/ter·au/ral, *adj.*
in/ter·au·ric/u·lar, *adj.*
in/ter·a·vail/a·bil/i·ty, *n.*
in/ter·a·vail/a·ble, *adj.*
in/ter·ax/i·al, *adj.*
in/ter·ax/il·lar/y, *adj.*
in/ter·ax/is, *n., pl.* **-ax·es.**
in/ter·bal/ance, *n., v.t.,* **-anced, -anc·ing.**
in/ter·band/ed, *adj.*
in/ter·bank/, *adj.*
in/ter·bel·lig/er·ent, *adj.*

in·ter·blend (in′tər blend′), *v.t., v.i.*, **-blend·ed** or **-blent, -blend·ing.** to blend one with another. [INTER- + BLEND]

in·ter·bor·ough (in′tər bûr′ō, -bur′ō), *adj.* **1.** between boroughs. **2.** located in, of, or pertaining to two or more boroughs. —*n.* **3.** a subway, streetcar, bus, etc., or a transportation system, operating between boroughs. [INTER- + BOROUGH]

in·ter·brain (in′tər brān′), *n.* the diencephalon. [INTER- + BRAIN]

in·ter·breed (in′tər brēd′), *v.*, **-bred, -breed·ing.** —*v.t.* **1.** to crossbreed. **2.** to cause to breed together. —*v.i.* **3.** to crossbreed. **4.** to breed or mate with a closely related individual, as in a small, closed population. [INTER- + BREED]

in·ter·ca·lar·y (in tûr′kə ler′ē, in′tər kal′ə rē), *adj.* **1.** interpolated; interposed; intervening. **2.** inserted or interpolated in the calendar, as an extra day, month, etc. **3.** having such an inserted day, month, etc., as a particular year. [< L *intercalāri(us)*, equiv. to *intercal(āre)* (to) INTERCALATE + *-ārius* -ARY] —**in·ter′ca·lar′i·ly,** *adv.*

inter′calary mer′istem, meristem in the internode of a stem.

in·ter·ca·late (in tûr′kə lāt′), *v.t.*, **-lat·ed, -lat·ing.** **1.** to interpolate; interpose. **2.** to insert (an extra day, month, etc.) in the calendar. [< L *intercalāt(us)* inserted (ptp. of *intercalāre*), equiv. to *inter-* INTER- + *calā-* (s. of *calāre* to summon) + *-tus* ptp. suffix] —**in·ter′ca·la′tive,** *adj.*
—**Syn. 1.** interject, introduce, insinuate.

in·ter·ca·la·tion (in tûr′kə lā′shən), *n.* **1.** the act of intercalating; insertion or interpolation, as in a series. **2.** that which is intercalated; interpolation. [< L *intercalātiōn-* (s. of *intercalātiō*). See INTERCALATE, -ION]

in′ter·car′di·nal point′ (in′tər kär′dᵊnᵊl, in′-), any of the four points of the compass midway between the cardinal points; northeast, southeast, southwest, or northwest. [INTER- + CARDINAL]

in·ter·cede (in′tər sēd′), *v.i.*, **-ced·ed, -ced·ing.** **1.** to interpose in behalf of one in difficulty or trouble, as by pleading or petition: *to intercede with the governor for a condemned man.* **2.** to mediate; attempt to reconcile differences between two people or groups. **3.** *Rom. Hist.* (of a tribune or other magistrate) to interpose a veto. [< L *intercēde(re).* See INTER-, CEDE] —**in′ter·ced′er,** *n.*
—**Syn. 1.** intervene.

in·ter·cel·lu·lar (in′tər sel′yə lər), *adj.* situated between or among cells or cellules. [INTER- + CELLULAR]

in·ter·cept (*v.* in′tər sept′; *n.* in′tər sept′), *v.t.* **1.** to take, seize, or halt (someone or something on the way from one place to another); cut off from an intended destination: *to intercept a messenger.* **2.** to stop the natural course of (light, water, etc.). **3.** to stop or check (passage, travel, etc.): *to intercept the traitor's escape.* **4.** to stop or interrupt the course, progress, or transmission of. **5.** to destroy or disperse (enemy aircraft or a missile or missiles) in the air on the way to a target. **6.** to see or overhear (a message, transmission, etc., meant for another): *We intercepted the enemy's battle plan.* **7.** *Math.* to mark off or include, as between two points or lines. **8.** *Sports.* (of a defensive player) to catch (a pass intended for a member of the offensive team): *He intercepted a pass in the end zone with a leaping catch.* **9.** to intersect. **10.** *Obs.* to prevent or cut off the operation or effect of. **11.** *Obs.* to cut off from access, sight, etc. —*n.* **12.** an interception. **13.** *Math.* **a.** an intercepted segment of a line. **b.** (in a coordinate system) the distance from the origin to the point at which a curve or line intersects an axis. [< L *intercept(us)* intercepted (ptp. of *intercipere*), equiv. to *inter-* INTER- + *-cep-* (var. of *cap-*, root of *capere* to take) + *-tus* ptp. suffix] —**in′ter·cep′tive,** *adj.*

Intercept (def. 4)
Arc of circle intercepted by line between points X and Y

in·ter·cep·tion (in′tər sep′shən), *n.* **1.** the act or an instance of intercepting. **2.** the state or fact of being intercepted. **3.** *Mil.* **a.** the engaging of an enemy force in an attempt to hinder or prevent it from carrying out its mission. **b.** the monitoring of enemy radio transmission to obtain information. [< L *interceptiōn-* (s. of *interceptiō*). See INTERCEPT, -ION]

in·ter·cep·tor (in′tər sep′tər), *n.* **1.** one who or that which intercepts. **2.** *Mil.* a fighter airplane with a high rate of climb and speed, used chiefly for the interception of enemy aircraft. Also, **in′ter·cept′er.** [< L; see INTERCEPT, -OR²]

in·ter·ces·sion (in′tər sesh′ən), *n.* **1.** the act or an instance of interceding. **2.** an interposing or pleading on behalf of a person in difficulty or trouble. **3.** a prayer to God on behalf of another or others. **4.** *Rom. Hist.* the interposing of a veto, as by a tribune. [< L *intercessiōn-* (s. of *intercessiō*), equiv. to *intercess(us)* (ptp. of *intercēdere* to INTERCEDE) + *-iōn-* -ION] —**in′ter·ces′sion·al,** *adj.*

in·ter·ces·sor (in′tər ses′ər, in′tər ses′ər), *n.* a person who intercedes. [late ME < L; see INTERCESSION, -OR²] —**in·ter·ces·so·ri·al** (in′tər si sôr′ē əl, -sōr′-), *adj.*

in·ter·ces·so·ry (in′tər ses′ə rē), *adj.* having the function of interceding: *an intercessory prayer.* [< ML *intercessōri(us).* See INTERCESSOR, -ORY¹]

in·ter·change (*v.* in′tər chānj′; *n.* in′tər chānj′), *v.*, **-changed, -chang·ing,** *n.* —*v.t.* **1.** to put each (of two things) in the place of the other. **2.** to cause (one thing) to change places with another; transpose. **3.** to give and receive (things) reciprocally; exchange: *The twins interchanged clothes frequently.* **4.** to cause to follow one another alternately: *to interchange business cares with pleasures.* —*v.i.* **5.** to occur by turns or in succession; alternate. **6.** to change places, as two persons or things, or as one with another. —*n.* **7.** the act or an instance of interchanging; reciprocal exchange: *the interchange of commodities.* **8.** a changing of places, as between two persons or things, or of one with another. **9.** alternation; alternate succession. **10.** a highway junction consisting of a system of several road levels such that vehicles may move from one road to another without crossing the stream of traffic. [INTER- + CHANGE; r. ME *entrechaunge(n)* < MF *entrechangi(er)*] —**in′ter·chang′er,** *n.*

in·ter·change·a·ble (in′tər chān′jə bəl), *adj.* **1.** (of two things) capable of being put or used in the place of each other: *interchangeable words.* **2.** (of one thing) capable of replacing or changing places with something else: *an interchangeable part.* [INTERCHANGE + -ABLE; r. late ME *entrechaungeable* < MF *entrechangeable*] —**in′ter·change′a·bil′i·ty, in′ter·change′a·ble·ness,** *n.* —**in′ter·change′a·bly,** *adv.*
—**Syn. 2.** See **exchangeable.**

in·ter·church (in′tər chûrch′), *adj.* interdenominational. [INTER- + CHURCH]

in·ter·class (in′tər klas′, -kläs′), *adj.* between classes; involving different classes. [INTER- + CLASS]

in·ter·clav·i·cle (in′tər klav′i kəl), *n.* *Zool.* a median membrane bone developed between the collarbones, or in front of the breastbone, in many vertebrates. [INTER- + CLAVICLE] —**in·ter·cla·vic·u·lar** (in′tər klə vik′yə lər), *adj.*

in·ter·col·lege (in′tər kol′ij), *adj.* intercollegiate. [INTER- + COLLEGE]

in·ter·col·le·giate (in′tər kə lē′jit, -jē it), *adj.* **1.** taking place between or participating in activities between different colleges: *intercollegiate athletics.* **2.** of, pertaining to, or representative of two or more colleges. [INTER- + COLLEGIATE]

in·ter·co·lo·ni·al (in′tər kə lō′nē əl), *adj.* **1.** between colonies, as of one country. **2.** of or pertaining to two or more colonies. [INTER- + COLONIAL] —**in′ter·co·lo′ni·al·ly,** *adv.*

in·ter·co·lum·ni·a·tion (in′tər kə lum′nē ā′shən), *n.* *Archit.* **1.** the space between two adjacent columns, usually the clear space between the lower parts of the shafts. **2.** the system of spacing between columns. [< L *intercolumni(um)* space between columns (see INTER-, COLUMN) + -ATION] —**in′ter·co·lum′nar,** *adj.*

Intercolumniation
d, diameter of shaft at base

in·ter·com (in′tər kom′), *n.* *Informal.* **1.** an intercommunication system, as of an airplane or a military tank. **2.** a microphone or receiver of an intercommunication system. [shortened form]

in·ter·com·mon (in′tər kom′ən), *v.i.* *Eng. Law.* to share in the use of a common. [INTER- + obs. *common* (v.) (var. of COMMUNE); r. ME *entrecomo(u)ne(n)* < AF *entrecomun(er)*] —**in′ter·com′mon·age,** *n.* —**in′ter·com′mon·er,** *n.*

in·ter·com·mu·ni·cate (in′tər kə myōō′nə kāt′), *v.*, **-cat·ed, -cat·ing.** —*v.i.* **1.** to communicate mutually, as people. **2.** to afford passage from one to another, as rooms. —*v.t.* **3.** to exchange (messages or communications) with one another. [< ML *intercommūnicāt(us)* (ptp.). See INTER-, COMMUNICATE] —**in′ter·com·mu′ni·ca·bil′i·ty,** *n.* —**in′ter·com·mu′ni·ca·ble,** *adj.* —**in′ter·com·mu′ni·ca′tion,** *n.* —**in·ter·com·mu·ni·ca·tive** (in′tər kə myōō′nə kā′tiv, -kə tiv), *adj.* —**in′ter·com·mu′ni·ca′tor,** *n.*

intercommunica′tion sys′tem, a communication system within a building, ship, airplane, local area, etc., with a loudspeaker or receiver for listening and a microphone for speaking at each of two or more points.

in·ter·com·mun·ion (in′tər kə myōōn′yən), *n.* **1.** mutual communion, association, or relations. **2.** *Eccles.* a communion service among members of different denominations. Cf. **close communion, open communion.** [INTER- + COMMUNION]

in·ter·com·mu·ni·ty (in′tər kə myōō′ni tē), *n.*, *pl.* **-ties,** *adj.* —*n.* **1.** common ownership, use, participation, etc. —*adj.* **2.** of, pertaining to, or between communities: *intercommunity projects.* [INTER- + COMMUNITY]

in·ter·con·fes·sion·al (in′tər kən fesh′ə nᵊl), *adj.* common to or occurring between churches having different confessions of faith. [INTER- + CONFESSIONAL]

in·ter·con·nect (in′tər kə nekt′), *v.t.* to connect, one with another. [INTER- + CONNECT] —**in′ter·con·nec′tion,** *n.*

in·ter·con·nect·ed·ness (in′tər kə nek′tid nis), *n.* the quality or condition of being interconnected; interrelatedness: *the interconnectedness of all nations working toward world peace.* [INTERCONNECT + -ED² + -NESS]

in·ter·con·so·nan·tal (in′tər kon′sə nan′tᵊl), *adj.* *Phonet.* (usually of a vowel) immediately following a consonant and preceding a consonant, as the *a* in *pat.* [INTER- + CONSONANTAL]

in·ter·con·ti·nen·tal (in′tər kon′tᵊnen′tᵊl), *adj.* **1.** of, pertaining to, or between continents: *intercontinental trade.* **2.** traveling or capable of traveling between continents: *an intercontinental jet plane.* [INTER- + CONTINENTAL]

intercontinen′tal ballis′tic mis′sile, any supersonic missile that has a range of at least 3500 nautical miles and follows a ballistic trajectory after a powered, guided launching. *Abbr.:* ICBM, I.C.B.M.

in·ter·con·ver·sion (in′tər kən vûr′zhən, -shən), *n.* conversion of each of two things into the other; reciprocal conversion. [INTER- + CONVERSION]

in·ter·con·vert (in′tər kən vûrt′), *v.t.* to subject to interconversion; interchange. [INTER- + CONVERT] —**in′ter·con·vert′i·bil′i·ty,** *n.* —**in′ter·con·vert′i·ble,** *adj.* —**in′ter·con·vert′i·bly,** *adv.*

in·ter·cool·er (in′tər kōō′lər), *n.* any device for cooling a fluid between successive heating processes, esp. for cooling a gas between successive compressions. [INTER- + COOLER]

in·ter·cos·tal (in′tər kos′tᵊl, -kô′stᵊl), *adj.* **1.** pertaining to muscles, parts, or intervals between the ribs. **2.** situated between the ribs. **3.** *Shipbuilding.* noting a structural member situated between or divided by continuous members, as frames or keelsons: *intercostal keelson; intercostal floor.* —*n.* **4.** an intercostal muscle, member, or space. [< NL *intercostāl(is).* See INTER-, COSTAL] —**in′ter·cos′tal·ly,** *adv.*

in·ter·course (in′tər kōrs′, -kôrs′), *n.* **1.** dealings or communication between individuals, groups, countries, etc. **2.** interchange of thoughts, feelings, etc. **3.** sexual relations or a sexual coupling, esp. coitus. [late ME *intercurse* < ML *intercurs(us)* communication, trading, < L: a running between. See INTER-, COURSE]

in·ter·crop (in′tər krop′), *v.*, **-cropped, -crop·ping.** *Agric.* —*v.i.* **1.** to grow one crop between the rows of another, as in an orchard, vineyard, or field. —*v.t.* **2.** to grow a crop between the rows of (another). [INTER- + CROP]

in·ter·cross (*v.* in′tər krôs′, -kros′; *n.* in′tər krôs′, -kros′), *v.t.* **1.** to cross (things), one with another. **2.** to cross (each other), as streets do; intersect. **3.** to cross in interbreeding. —*v.i.* **4.** to cross each other; intersect. **5.** to interbreed. —*n.* **6.** an instance of cross-fertilization. [INTER- + CROSS]

in·ter·crys·tal·line (in′tər kris′tᵊlin, -tᵊlīn′), *adj.* *Crystall.* situated or passing between the crystals of a substance. Cf. **transcrystalline.** [INTER- + CRYSTALLINE]

in·ter·cu·po·la (in′tər kyōō′pə lə), *n.* *Archit.* **1.** the space between an inner and an outer dome. **2.** a space between two cupolas. [INTER- + CUPOLA]

in·ter·cur·rent (in′tər kûr′ənt, -kur′-), *adj.* **1.** intervening, as of time or events. **2.** *Pathol.* (of a disease) occurring while another disease is in progress. [< L *intercurrent-* (s. of *intercurrēns*) running between, prp. of *intercurrere.* See INTER-, CURRENT] —**in′ter·cur′rence,** *n.* —**in′ter·cur′rent·ly,** *adv.*

in·ter·cut (*v.* in′tər kut′, in′tər kut′; *n.* in′tər kut′), *v.*, **-cut, -cut·ting,** *n.* *Motion Pictures, Television.* —*v.i.* **1.** to cut from one type of shot to another, as from a long shot to a close-up. —*v.t.* **2.** to interject or insert into a shot or sequence (material of another type, as animated maps used in a newscast). —*n.* **3.** a film sequence or scene produced by intercutting. [INTER- + CUT]

in·ter·de·nom·i·na·tion·al (in′tər di nom′ə nā′shə nᵊl), *adj.* common to, involving, or occurring between different religious denominations. Also called **interchurch.** [INTER- + DENOMINATIONAL] —**in′ter·de·nom′i·na′tion·al·ism,** *n.*

in·ter·den·tal (in′tər den′tᵊl), *adj.* **1.** between teeth. **2.** *Phonet.* articulated with the tip of the tongue between the upper and lower front teeth, as the fricatives (th) and (t͟h) of *thy* and *thigh.* [INTER- + DENTAL] —**in′ter·den′tal·ly,** *adv.*

in·ter·den·til (in′tər den′tᵊl, -til), *n.* *Archit.* a space between dentils. [INTER- + DENTIL]

in·ter·de·part·men·tal (in′tər dē′pärt men′tᵊl, -di pärt′-), *adj.* involving or characterized by exchange or cooperation between two or more departments, esp. of an educational institution: *an interdepartmental program.* [INTER- + DEPARTMENTAL] —**in′ter·de′part·men′tal·ly,** *adv.*

in·ter·de·pend·ent (in′tər di pen′dənt), *adj.* mutually dependent; dependent on each other. [INTER- + DEPENDENT] —**in′ter·de·pend′ence, in′ter·de·pend′en·cy,** *n.* —**in′ter·de·pend′ent·ly,** *adv.*

in·ter·dict (*n.* in′tər dikt′; *v.* in′tər dikt′), *n.* **1.** *Civil Law.* any prohibitory act or decree of a court or an administrative officer. **2.** *Rom. Cath. Ch.* a punishment

in′ter·bra′chi·al, *adj.*
in′ter·branch′, *adj.*
in′ter·bran′chi·al, *adj.*
in′ter·breath′, *adj.*
in′ter·bri·gade′, *adj.*
in′ter·bron′chi·al, *adj.*
in′ter·cap′il·lar′y, *adj.*
in′ter·car′di·nal, *adj.*
in′ter·car′pal, *adj.*
in′ter·car′pel·lar′y, *adj.*
in′ter·ca·rot′id, *adj.*
in′ter·car′ri·er, *n.*
in′ter·car′ti·lag′i·nous, *adj.*
in′ter·caste′, *adj.*
in′ter·cat′e·nat′ed, *adj.*
in′ter·caus′a·tive, *adj.*
in′ter·cav′ern·ous, *adj.*
in′ter·cen′tral, *adj.*
in′ter·cer′e·bral, *adj.*
in′ter·chaff′, *v.*
in′ter·chain′, *v.t.*
in′ter·charge′, *v.t.*, **-charged, -charg·ing.**
in′ter·chase′, *v.t.*, **-chased, -chas·ing.**
in′ter·check′, *v.t.*
in′ter·choke′, *v.t.*, **-choked, -chok·ing.**
in′ter·chon′dral, *adj.*
in′ter·cil′i·ar′y, *adj.*
in′ter·cir′cle, *v.t.*, **-cled, -cling.**
in′ter·cir′cu·late′, *v.*, **-lat·ed, -lat·ing.**
in′ter·cir′cu·la′tion, *n.*
in′ter·cit′y, *adj.*
in′ter·civ′ic, *adj.*
in′ter·civ′i·li·za′tion, *n.*
in′ter·clash′, *n.*, *v.*
in′ter·clasp′, *v.t.*
in′ter·cler′i·cal, *adj.*
in′ter·cloud′, *v.t.*
in′ter·club′, *adj.*
in′ter·coc·cyg′e·al, *adj.*
in′ter·co·he′sion, *n.*
in′ter·col′o·ni·za′tion, *n.*
in′ter·col′o·nize, *v.*, **-nized, -niz·ing.**
in′ter·co·lum′nal, *adj.*
in′ter·com′bat, *n.*
in′ter·com′bi·na′tion, *n.*
in′ter·com·bine′, *v.t.*, **-bined, -bin·ing.**
in′ter·com·mis′sion, *n.*
in′ter·com·mis′sur·al, *adj.*
in′ter·com·mu′nal, *adj.*
in′ter·com′pa·ny, *adj.*
in′ter·com′pa·ra·ble, *adj.*
in′ter·com·pare′, *v.t.*, **-pared, -par·ing.**
in′ter·com·par′i·son, *n.*
in′ter·com·plex′i·ty, *n.*
in′ter·com′pli·men′ta·ry, *adj.*
in′ter·con·cil′i·ar′y, *adj.*
in′ter·con·dens′er, *n.*
in′ter·con′dy·lar, *adj.*
in′ter·con·dyl′ic, *adj.*
in′ter·con′dy·loid′, *adj.*
in′ter·con·found′, *v.t.*
in′ter·con·tort′ed, *adj.*
in′ter·con′tra·dic′tion, *n.*
in′ter·con′tra·dic′to·ry, *adj.*
in′ter·cor′a·coid′, *adj.*
in′ter·cor′po·rate, *adj.*
in′ter·cor·pus′cu·lar, *adj.*
in′ter·cor′re·late′, *v.t.*, **-lat·ed, -lat·ing.**
in′ter·cor′re·la′tion, *n.*
in′ter·cor′ti·cal, *adj.*
in′ter·cos′mic, *adj.*
in′ter·cot′y·lar, *adj.*
in′ter·coun′ty, *adj.*
in′ter·cra′ni·al, *adj.*
in′ter·cre·ate′, *v.t.*, **-at·ed, -at·ing.**
in′ter·cri′nal, *adj.*
in′ter·cru′ral, *adj.*
in′ter·crust′, *v.t.*
in′ter·curl′, *v.*
in′ter·cus′pi·dal, *adj.*
in′ter·cys′tic, *adj.*
in′ter·de·bate′, *v.*, **-bat·ed, -bat·ing.**
in′ter·de·pen′da·bil′i·ty, *n.*
in′ter·de·pend′a·ble, *adj.*
in′ter·de·struc′tive, *adj.*; **-ly,** *adv.*; **-ness,** *n.*
in′ter·de·ter′mine, *v.t.*, **-mined, -min·ing.**
in′ter·de·ter′mi·na′tion, *n.*
in′ter·de·vour′, *v.t.*

by which the faithful, remaining in communion with the church, are forbidden certain sacraments and prohibited from participation in certain sacred acts. **3.** *Roman Law.* a general or special order of the Roman praetor forbidding or commanding an act, esp. in cases involving disputed possession. **—*v.t.* 4.** to forbid; prohibit. **5.** *Eccles.* to cut off authoritatively from certain ecclesiastical functions and privileges. **6.** to impede by steady bombardment: *Constant air attacks interdicted the enemy's advance.* [< L *interdict(us)* forbidden (ptp. of *interdīcere*), equiv. to *inter-* INTER- + *-dic-* (perf. s. of *dīcere* to speak) + *-tus* ptp. suffix; r. ME *entredit* < OF] **—in/ter·dic/tor,** *n.*

in·ter·dic·tion (in/tər dik/shən), *n.* **1.** the act or an instance of interdicting. **2.** the state of being interdicted. **3.** an interdict. **4.** steady bombardment of enemy positions, routes, or supply and communications lines for the purpose of delaying and disorganizing his progress. [< L *interdictiōn-* (s. of *interdictiō*). See INTERDICT, -ION]

in·ter·dic·to·ry (in/tər dik/tə rē), *adj.* of, pertaining to, or noting interdiction. [< LL *interdictōri(us).* See INTERDICT, -ORY[1]]

in·ter·dig·i·tate (in/tər dij/i tāt/), *v.i., v.t.,* **-tat·ed, -tat·ing.** to interlock, as or like the fingers of both hands. [INTER- + DIGITATE] **—in·ter·dig·i·ta·tion** (in/tər dij/i tā/shən), *n.*

in·ter·dis·ci·pli·nar·y (in/tər dis/ə plə ner/ē), *adj.* combining or involving two or more academic disciplines or fields of study: *The economics, history, and political science departments organized an interdisciplinary seminar on Southeast Asia.* [INTER- + DISCIPLINARY]

in·ter·dome (in/tər dōm/), *n.* the space between an inner and outer shell of a dome. [INTER- + DOME]

in·ter·est (in/tər ist, -trist), *n.* **1.** the feeling of one whose attention, concern, or curiosity is particularly engaged by something: *She has a great interest in the poetry of Donne.* **2.** that which concerns, involves, draws the attention of, or arouses the curiosity of a person: *His interests are philosophy and chess.* **3.** power of exciting such concern, involvement, etc.; quality of being interesting: *questions of great interest.* **4.** concern; importance: *a matter of primary interest.* **5.** a business, cause, or the like in which a person has a share, concern, responsibility, etc. **6.** a share, right, or title in the ownership of property, in a commercial or financial undertaking, or the like. **7.** a participation in or concern for a cause, advantage, responsibility, etc. **8.** a number or group of persons, or a party, financially interested in the same business, industry, or enterprise: *the banking interest.* **9. interests,** the group of persons or organizations having extensive financial or business power. **10.** the state of being affected by something in respect to advantage or detriment: *We need an arbiter who is without interest in the outcome.* **11.** benefit; advantage: *to have one's own interest in mind.* **12.** regard for one's own advantage or profit; self-interest: *The partnership dissolved because of their competitive interests.* **13.** influence from personal importance or capability; power of influencing the action of others. **14.** *Finance.* **a.** a sum paid or charged for the use of money or for borrowing money. **b.** the rate percent per unit of time represented by such payment or charge. **15.** something added or thrown in above an exact equivalent: *Jones paid him back with a left hook and added a right uppercut for interest.* **16. in the interest** or **interests of,** to the advantage or advancement of; in behalf of: *in the interests of good government.* **—*v.t.* 17.** to engage or excite the attention or curiosity of: *Mystery stories interested him greatly.* **18.** to concern (a person, nation, etc.) in something; involve: *The fight for peace interests all nations.* **19.** to cause to take a personal concern or share; induce to participate: *to interest a person in an enterprise.* **20.** to cause to be concerned; affect. [ME < ML, L: it concerns, lit., it is between; r. ME *interesse* < ML, L: to concern, lit., to be between. See INTER-, ESSE]

in·ter·est·ed (in/tər i stid, -tri stid, -tə res/tid), *adj.* **1.** having an interest in something; concerned: *Interested members will meet at two.* **2.** participating; having an interest or share; having money involved. **3.** having the attention or curiosity engaged: *an interested spectator.* **4.** characterized by a feeling of interest. **5.** influenced by personal or selfish motives: *an interested witness.* [INTEREST + -ED[3]] **—in/ter·est·ed·ly,** *adv.* **—in/ter·est·ed·ness,** *n.*

in·ter·es·ter·i·fi·ca·tion (in/tər i ster/ə fə kā/shən), *n. Chem.* transesterification. [INTER- + ESTERIFICATION]

in·ter·est·ing (in/tər i sting, -tri sting, -tə res/ting), *adj.* **1.** arousing a feeling of interest: *an interesting face.* **2.** engaging or exciting and holding the attention or curiosity: *an interesting book.* **3. to be in an interesting condition,** (of a woman) to be pregnant. [INTEREST + -ING[2]] **—in/ter·est·ing·ly,** *adv.* **—in/ter·est·ing·ness,** *n.*

—Syn. 2. absorbing, entertaining. INTERESTING, PLEASING, GRATIFYING mean satisfying to the mind. That which is INTERESTING occupies the mind with no connotation of pleasure or displeasure: *an interesting account of a battle.* That which is PLEASING engages the mind favorably: *a pleasing account of the wedding.* That which is GRATIFYING fulfills expectations, requirements, etc.: *a gratifying account of his whereabouts; a book gratifying in its detail.* **—Ant. 2.** dull.

in·ter·face (in/tər fās/), *n., v.,* **-faced, -fac·ing.** **—*n.* 1.** a surface regarded as the common boundary of two bodies or spaces. **2.** the facts, problems, considerations, theories, practices, etc., shared by two or more disciplines, procedures, or fields of study: *the interface of chemistry and physics.* **3.** a common boundary or interconnection between systems, equipment, concepts, or human beings. **4.** *Computer Technol.* **a.** equipment or programs designed to communicate information from one system of computing devices or programs to another. **b.** any arrangement for such communication. **—*v.t.* 5.** to bring into an interface. **—*v.i.* 6.** to be in an interface. **7.** to function as an interface. [INTER- + FACE]

in·ter·fa·cial (in/tər fā/shəl), *adj.* **1.** included between two faces. **2.** of, pertaining to, or of the nature of an interface. [INTERFACE + -IAL]

in/terfa/cial ten/sion, *Physical Chem.* the surface tension at the interface of two liquids.

in·ter·faith (in/tər fāth/), *adj.* of or operating or occurring between persons or groups belonging to different religions. [INTER- + FAITH]

in·ter·fen·es·tra·tion (in/tər fen/i strā/shən), *n.* **1.** a space between two windows. **2.** the art or process of arranging the openings in a wall. [INTER- + FENESTRATION] **—in·ter·fe·nes·tral** (in/tər fə nes/trəl), *adj.*

in·ter·fere (in/tər fēr/), *v.i.,* **-fered, -fer·ing. 1.** to come into opposition, as one thing with another, esp. with the effect of hampering action or procedure (often fol. by *with*): *Constant distractions interfere with work.* **2.** to take part in the affairs of others; meddle (often fol. by *with* or *in*): *to interfere in another's life; interfere with the disputes of others.* **3.** (of things) to strike against each other, or one against another, so as to hamper or hinder action; come into physical collision. **4.** to interpose or intervene for a particular purpose. **5.** to strike one foot or leg against the opposite foot or leg in moving, as a horse. **6.** *Sports.* **a.** to obstruct the action of an opposing player in a way barred by the rules. **b.** *Football.* to run interference for a teammate carrying the ball. **7.** *Physics.* to cause interference. **8.** to clash; come in collision; be in opposition: *The claims of two nations may interfere.* [INTER- + *fere* < L *fer(īre)* (to) strike; modeled on MF *s'entreferir*] **—in/ter·fer/er,** *n.* **—in/ter·fer/ing·ly,** *adv.*

—Syn. 2. pry, intrude, encroach, interlope. **4.** intercede.

in·ter·fer·ence (in/tər fēr/əns), *n.* **1.** the act, fact, or an instance of interfering. **2.** that which interferes. **3.** *Physics.* the process in which two or more light, sound, or electromagnetic waves of the same frequency combine to reinforce or cancel each other, the amplitude of the resulting wave being equal to the sum of the amplitudes of the combining waves. **4.** *Radio.* **a.** a jumbling of radio signals, caused by the reception of undesired ones. **b.** the signals or device producing the incoherence. **5.** *Ling.* **a.** (in bilingualism) the overlapping of two languages. **b.** deviation from the norm of either language in such a situation. **6.** the distorting or inhibiting effect of previously learned behavior on subsequent learning. **7.** *Psychol.* failure to remember one of two related events, things, etc., because of reciprocal inhibition. **8.** *Football.* **a.** the act of a teammate or of teammates running ahead of a ball-carrier and blocking prospective tacklers out of the way: *an end run with both guards running interference for the halfback.* **b.** such a teammate or such teammates: *to follow one's interference.* **c.** the prevention in a way barred by the rules of a pass receiver from catching a pass. **d.** the penalty for this. **9.** *Aerodynamics.* the occurrence, and its effects, when the aerodynamic influence of one surface of an aircraft conflicts with the influence of another surface. **10.** *Mach.* the amount by which a dimension of one part exceeds the corresponding dimension of another part into which it is to be assembled by pressing or by temperature changes. [INTERFERE + -ENCE]

interfer/ence drag/, *Aeron.* the drag on an aircraft caused by the interaction of two aerodynamic bodies.

interfer/ence mi/croscope, a microscope that utilizes light interference phenomena to create two superimposed images of an object, making possible the observation of transparent objects without using the staining technique. **—interfer/ence micros/copy.**

interfer/ence pat/tern, *Physics.* a series of alternating dark and bright bands produced as a result of light interference.

in·ter·fe·ren·tial (in/tər fə ren/shəl), *adj.* of or pertaining to interference. [INTERFERE + (DIFFER)ENTIAL]

in·ter·fer·om·e·ter (in/tər fə rom/i tər), *n.* **1.** *Optics.* a device that separates a beam of light into two ray beams, usually by means of reflection, and that brings the rays together to produce interference, used to measure wavelength, index of refraction, and astronomical distances. **2.** *Astron.* an instrument for measuring the angular separation of double stars of the diameter of giant stars by means of the interference phenomena of light emitted by these stars. [INTERFERE + -O- + -METER] **—in·ter·fer·o·met·ric** (in/tər fēr/ə me/trik), *adj.* **—in/ter·fer/o·met/ri·cal·ly,** *adv.* **—in/ter·fer·om/e·try,** *n.*

in·ter·fer·on (in/tər fēr/on), *n. Biochem.* a protein substance produced by virus-invaded cells that prevents reproduction of the virus. [INTERFERE + *-on* arbitrary suffix]

in·ter·fer·tile (in/tər fûr/tᵊl), *adj. Bot., Zool.* able to interbreed. [INTER- + FERTILE] **—in/ter·fer·til/i·ty,** *n.*

in·ter·fi·bril·lar (in/tər fī/brə lər), *adj.* situated between fibrils. Also, **in·ter·fi·bril·lar·y** (in/tər fī/brə ler/ē). [INTER- + FIBRILLAR]

in·ter·file (in/tər fīl/), *v.t.,* **-filed, -fil·ing.** to combine two or more similarly arranged sets of items, as cards, documents, etc., into a single arrangement. [INTER- + FILE[1]]

in·ter·fill·ing (in/tər fil/ing), *n. Building Trades.* a filling of materials, as brickwork between studs. [INTER- + FILLING]

in·ter·flow (*v.* in/tər flō/; *n.* in/tər flō/), *v.i.* **1.** to flow into each other; intermingle. **—*n.* 2.** an interflowing. [INTER- + FLOW]

in·ter·flu·ent (in/tər flōō/ənt), *adj.* flowing into one another; intermingling. [< L *interfluent-* (s. of *interfluēns*). See INTER-, FLUENT] **—in/ter·flu/ence,** *n.*

in·ter·fluve (in/tər flōōv/), *n.* the land area separating adjacent stream valleys. [back formation from *interfluvial* lying between streams. See INTER-, FLUVIAL] **—in/ter·flu/vi·al,** *adj.*

in·ter·fold (in/tər fōld/), *v.t.* to fold, one within another; fold together. [INTER- + FOLD[1]]

in·ter·fo·li·a·ceous (in/tər fō/lē ā/shəs), *adj. Bot.* situated between leaves, esp. opposite leaves. Also, **in·ter·fo·li·ar** (in/tər fō/lē ər). [INTER- + FOLIACEOUS]

in·ter·fuse (in/tər fyōōz/), *v.,* **-fused, -fus·ing.** **—*v.t.* 1.** to pour or pass (something) between, into, or through; infuse. **2.** to intersperse, intermingle, or permeate with something. **3.** to blend or fuse, one with another. **—*v.i.* 4.** to become blended or fused, one with another. [< L *interfūs(us)* poured between, ptp. of *interfundere.* See INTER-, FUSE[2]] **—in/ter·fu/sion,** *n.*

in·ter·ga·lac·tic (in/tər gə lak/tik), *adj.* of or existing or occurring in the space between galaxies. [INTER- + GALACTIC]

in·ter·gla·cial (in/tər glā/shəl), *adj. Geol.* occurring or formed between times of glacial action. [INTER- + GLACIAL]

in·ter·glyph (in/tər glif/), *n. Archit.* a surface between two grooves, as on a triglyph. [INTER- + GLYPH]

in·ter·gra·da·tion (in/tər grā dā/shən), *n.* **1.** the act or process of intergrading or the state of being intergraded. **2.** an evolutionary process by which different species of plants and animals tend to merge through a series of intermediate stages or grades. [INTER- + GRADATION] **—in/ter·gra·da/tion·al,** *adj.*

in·ter·grade (*n.* in/tər grād/; *v.* in/tər grād/), *n., v.,* **-grad·ed, -grad·ing.** **—*n.* 1.** an intermediate grade, form, stage, etc. **—*v.i.* 2.** to merge gradually, one into another, as different species through evolution. [INTER- + GRADE]

in·ter·group (in/tər grōōp/), *adj. Sociol.* taking place or being between groups: *intergroup relationships.* [INTER- + GROUP]

in·ter·growth (in/tər grōth/), *n.* growth or growing together, as of one thing with or into another. [INTER- + GROWTH]

in·ter·hem·i·spher·ic (in/tər hem/i sfer/ik), *adj.* of, pertaining to, or between hemispheres, as those of the earth: *interhemispheric cooperation.* [INTER- + HEMISPHERIC]

in·ter·im (in/tər im), *n.* **1.** an intervening time; meantime: *in the interim.* **2.** a temporary or provisional arrangement. **3.** (*cap.*) *Ch. Hist.* any of three provisional arrangements for the settlement of religious differences between German Protestants and Roman Catholics during the Reformation. **—*adj.* 4.** belonging to or connected with an intervening period of time; temporary: *an interim order.* **—*adv.* 5.** meantime. [< L: in the meantime]

in·ter·in·sur·ance (in/tər in shŏŏr/əns), *n.* See **reciprocal insurance.** [INTER- + INSURANCE]

in·ter·i·on·ic (in/tər ī on/ik), *adj.* between ions. [INTER- + IONIC]

in·te·ri·or (in tēr/ē ər), *adj.* **1.** being within; inside of anything; internal; further toward a center: *the interior rooms of a house.* **2.** of or pertaining to that which is within; inside: *an interior view of a house.* **3.** situated well inland from the coast or border: *the interior towns of a country.* **4.** of or pertaining to the inland. **5.** domestic: *the interior trade.* **6.** inner; private; secret: *the interior life of man.* **—*n.* 7.** the internal part; inside. **8.** *Archit.* **a.** the inside part of a building, considered as a whole from the point of view of artistic design or general effect, convenience, etc. **b.** a single room or apartment so considered. **9.** a pictorial representation of the inside of a room. **10.** the inland parts of a region, country, etc.: *the interior of Africa.* **11.** the domestic affairs of a country as distinguished from its foreign affairs: *the Department of the Interior.* **12.** the inner or inward nature or character of anything. **13.** *Math.* the largest open set contained in a given set, as the points in a circle not including the boundary. [< L, equiv. to *inter-* inward + *-ior* comp. suffix; see EXTERIOR] **—in·te·ri·or·i·ty** (in tēr/ē ôr/i tē, -or/-), *n.* **—in·te/ri·or·ly,** *adv.*

—Syn. 7. See **inside.** **—Ant. 1, 7.** exterior.

B B
A A
A A
B B

A, Interior angle; B, Exterior angle

inte/rior an/gle, *Geom.* **1.** an angle formed between parallel lines by a third line that intersects them. **2.** an angle formed within a polygon by two adjacent sides.

inte/rior ballis/tics, a branch of ballistics dealing with the motion of projectiles within the bore of a weapon.

inte/rior decora/tion, **1.** Also called **inte/rior design/.** the designing and furnishing of the interior of a house or other building, an individual apartment or

in/ter·dif/fer·en/ti·ate/, *v.t.,* **-at·ed, -at·ing.**
in/ter·dif/fer·en/ti·a/tion, *n.*
in/ter·dif·fuse/, *v.,* **-fused, -fus·ing.**
in/ter·dif·fu/sion, *n.*
in/ter·dif·fu/sive, *adj.;* **-ness,** *n.*
in/ter·dig/i·tal, *adj.;* **-ly,** *adv.*
in/ter·dis·tin/guish, *v.t.*
in/ter·dis/trict, *adj.*
in/ter·di·vi/sion, *n.*
in/ter·dor/sal, *adj.*
in/ter·e·lec/trode, *n.*
in/ter·em·brace/, *v.,* **-braced, -brac·ing.**
in/ter·em/pire, *adj.*
in/ter·en·tan/gle, *v.t.,* **-gled, -gling.**
in/ter·en·tan/gle·ment, *n.*
in/ter·ep/i·dem/ic, *adj.*
in/ter·ep/i·the/li·al, *adj.*
in/ter·e/qui·noc/tial, *adj.*
in/ter·es/tu·a·rine, *adj.*
in/ter·Eu/ro·pe/an, *adj.*
in/ter·fac/tion·al, *adj.*
in/ter·fam/i·ly, *adj.*
in/ter·fas·cic/u·lar, *adj.*
in/ter·fed/er·a/tion, *n.*
in/ter·fem/o·ral, *adj.*
in/ter·fi/brous, *adj.*
in/ter·fil/a·men/ta·ry, *adj.*
in/ter·fil/a·men/tous, *adj.*
in/ter·fi/lar, *adj.*
in/ter·fil/trate, *v.t.,* **-trat·ed, -trat·ing.**
in/ter·fil·tra/tion, *n.*
in/ter·flash/ing, *n.*
in/ter·force/, *n.*
in/ter·fra·ter/nal, *adj.;* **-ly,** *adv.*
in/ter·fric/tion, *n.*
in/ter·fron/tal, *adj.*
in/ter·ful/gent, *adj.*
in/ter·gan/gli·on/ic, *adj.*
in/ter·gen/er·at/ing, *adj.*
in/ter·gen/er·a·tive, *adj.*
in/ter·gen/er·a/tion, *n.*
in/ter·gilt/, *adj.*
in/ter·glan/du·lar, *adj.*
in/ter·glob/u·lar, *adj.*
in/ter·go/ni·al, *adj.*
in/ter·gos/sip, *v.,* **-siped, -sip·ing.**
in/ter·gov/ern·men/tal, *adj.*
in/ter·graft/, *v.i.*
in/ter·gran/u·lar, *adj.*
in/ter·grap/ple, *v.,* **-pled, -pling.**
in/ter·gu/lar, *adj.*
in/ter·gy/ral, *adj.*
in/ter·hab/i·ta/tion, *n.*
in/ter·hae/mal, *adj.*
in/ter·he/mal, *adj.*
in/ter·hos/tile, *adj.*
in/ter·hu/man, *adj.*
in/ter·hy/brid·ize/, *v.i.,* **-ized, -iz·ing.**
in/ter·im·pe/ri·al, *adj.*
in/ter·in·cor/po·ra/tion, *n.*
in/ter·in/de·pend/ence, *n.*
in/ter·in/di·cate/, *v.t.,* **-cat·ed, -cat·ing.**
in/ter·in/di·vid/u·al, *adj.*
in/ter·in/flu·ence, *v.,* **-enced, -enc·ing.**
in/ter·in/hi·bi/tion, *n.*
in/ter·in·hib/i·tive, *adj.*
in/ter·in·sert/, *v.t.*
in/ter·in/su·lar, *adj.*
in/ter·in·volve/, *v.t.,* **-volved, -volv·ing.**

office, etc. **2.** the art, business, or profession of planning this. **3.** materials used to decorate an interior.

inte′rior dec′orator, a person whose occupation is planning the decoration, including the furnishings and draperies, of homes, rooms, offices, etc. Also called **inte′rior de·sign′er.**

inte′rior drain′age, a drainage system whose waters do not continue to the ocean either on the surface or underground, but evaporate within the land area.

in·te·ri·or·ism (in tēr′ē ə riz′əm), *n. Philos.* a theory that truth is discovered by introspection rather than by examination of the outside world. [INTERIOR + -ISM] —**in·te′ri·or·ist,** *n., adj.*

inte′rior map′ping, *Math.* an open map.

inte′rior mon′ologue, *Literature.* a form of stream-of-consciousness writing which represents the inner thoughts of a character.

in·ter·is·land (in′tər ī′lənd), *adj.* being or operating between islands: *interisland traffic.* [INTER- + ISLAND]

interj., interjection.

in·ter·ja·cent (in′tər jā′sənt), *adj.* between or among others; intervening; intermediate. [< L *interjacent-* (s. of *interjacēns*) lying between, prp. of *interjacēre.* See INTER-, ADJACENT] —**in′ter·ja′cence,** *n.*

in·ter·ject (in′tər jekt′), *v.t.* **1.** to interpolate; interpose: *to interject a clarification of a previous statement.* **2.** *Obs.* to come between. [< L *interject(us)* thrown between (ptp. of *interjicere*), equiv. to *inter-* INTER- + *-jec-* (var. of *jac-*, root of *jacere* to throw) + *-tus* ptp. suffix] —**in′ter·jec′tor,** *n.*
—**Syn. 1.** insinuate, introduce, insert, intercalate.

in·ter·jec·tion (in′tər jek′shən), *n.* **1.** the act of putting between; insertion; interposition. **2.** the utterance of a word or phrase expressive of emotion; the uttering of an exclamation. **3.** something interjected, as a remark. **4.** *Gram.* **a.** any member of a class of words expressing emotion, distinguished in most languages by their use in grammatical isolation, as *Hey! Oh!* **b.** any other word or expression so used, as *Good grief! Indeed!* [ME *interjeccio(u)n* < L *interjectiōn-* (s. of *interjectiō*). See INTERJECT, -ION] —**in′ter·jec′tion·al, in·ter·jec·tur·al** (in′tər jek′chər əl), *adj.* —**in′ter·jec′tion·al·ly,** *adv.*

in·ter·jec·tion·al·ise (in′tər jek′shə nəlīz′), *v.t.,* **-ised, -is·ing.** *Chiefly Brit.* interjectionalize.

in·ter·jec·tion·al·ize (in′tər jek′shə nəlīz′), *v.t.,* **-ized, -iz·ing.** to make into an interjection. [INTERJECTIONAL + -IZE]

in·ter·jec·to·ry (in′tər jek′tə rē), *adj.* **1.** characterized by interjection; interjectional. **2.** thrust in; interjected: *an interjectory word.* [INTERJECT + -ORY[1]] —**in′ter·jec′to·ri·ly,** *adv.*

in·ter·join (in′tər join′), *v.t., v.i.* to join, one with another. [INTER- + JOIN]

in·ter·joist (in′tər joist′), *n.* a space between two joists. [INTER- + JOIST]

in·ter·ki·ne·sis (in′tər ki nē′sis, -kī-), *n. Biol.* a resting stage between any two mitotic or meiotic divisions of a cell. Also called **interphase.** [INTER- + KINESIS] —**in·ter·ki·net·ic** (in′tər ki net′ik, -kī-), *adj.*

in·ter·knit (in′tər nit′), *v.t.,* **-knit·ted** or **-knit, -knit·ting.** to knit together, one with another; intertwine. [INTER- + KNIT]

in·ter·knot (in′tər not′), *v.t., v.i.,* **-knot·ted, -knot·ting.** to tie or knot together. [INTER- + KNOT[1]]

in·ter·lace (in′tər lās′), *v.,* **-laced, -lac·ing.** —*v.i.* **1.** to cross one another, typically passing alternately over and under, as if woven together; intertwine: *Their hands interlaced. The cluster of tree tops interlaced against the sky.* —*v.t.* **2.** to unite or dispose (threads, strips, parts, branches, etc.) so as to intercross one another, passing alternately over and under; intertwine. **3.** to mingle; blend. **4.** to diversify, as with threads woven in. **5.** to intersperse; intermingle: *She interlaced the flowers with green sprigs.* [INTER- + LACE; r. ME *entrelace(n)* < MF *entrelac(er)*] —**in·ter·lac·ed·ly** (in′tər lā′sid lē), *adv.* —**in′ter·lace′ment,** *n.*

in′terlacing arcade′, an arcade, esp. a blind one, composed of arches (**in′terlacing arch′es**) so disposed and cut that each arch seems to intersect and be intersected by one or more other arches. Also called **intersecting arcade.**

Interlacing arcade

In·ter·la·ken (in′tər lä′kən, in′tər lä′kən), *n.* a town in central Switzerland between the lakes of Brienz and Thun: tourist center. 4368 (1950).

in·ter·lam·i·nate (in′tər lam′ə nāt′), *v.t.,* **-nat·ed, -nat·ing.** to interlay or lay between laminae; interstratify. [INTER- + LAMINATE] —**in′ter·lam′i·na′tion,** *n.*

in·ter·lan·guage (in′tər laŋ′gwij), *n.* a language created or used for international communication. [INTER- + LANGUAGE]

in·ter·lard (in′tər lärd′), *v.t.* **1.** to diversify by mixing in or interjecting something unique, striking, or contrasting (usually fol. by *with*): *to interlard one's speech with oaths.* **2.** (of things) to be intermixed in. **3.** *Obs.* to mix, as fat with lean. [INTER- + LARD; r. *enterlard* < MF *entrelard(er)*] —**in′ter·lar·da′tion, in′ter·lard′ment,** *n.*

in·ter·lay (in′tər lā′), *v.t.,* **-laid, -lay·ing.** **1.** to lay between; interpose. **2.** to diversify with something laid or inserted: *to interlay silver with gold.* [INTER- + LAY[1]]

in·ter·leaf (in′tər lēf′), *n., pl.* **-leaves** (-lēvz′). an additional leaf, usually blank, inserted between or bound with the regular printed leaves of a book, as to separate chapters, provide room for a reader's notes, etc. [INTER- + LEAF]

in·ter·leave (in′tər lēv′), *v.t.,* **-leaved, -leav·ing.** **1.** to provide blank leaves in (a book) for notes or written comments. **2.** to insert blank leaves between (the regular printed leaves). [INTER- + LEAVE[3]]

in′ter·li′brar·y loan′ (in′tər lī′brer ē, -brə rē, -brē, in′-), **1.** a system by which one library obtains a publication for a reader by borrowing it from another library. **2.** a loan made by this system. [INTER- + LIBRARY]

in·ter·line[1] (in′tər līn′), *v.t.,* **-lined, -lin·ing.** **1.** to write or insert (words, phrases, etc.) between the lines of writing or print. **2.** to mark or inscribe (a document, book, etc.) between the lines. [ME < ML *interlīne(āre).* See INTER-, LINE[1]]

in·ter·line[2] (in′tər līn′), *v.t.,* **-lined, -lin·ing.** to provide with an interlining. [INTER- + LINE[2]] —**in′ter·lin′er,** *n.*

in·ter·lin·e·al (in′tər lin′ē əl), *adj.* interlinear. [INTER- + LINEAL] —**in′ter·lin′e·al·ly,** *adv.*

in·ter·lin·e·ar (in′tər lin′ē ər), *adj.* **1.** situated or inserted between lines, as of the lines of print in a book: *He wanted a Latin text with an interlinear translation.* **2.** having interpolated lines; interlined. **3.** having the same text in various languages set in alternate lines: *the interlinear Bible.* —*n.* **4.** a book, esp. a textbook, having interlinear matter, as a translation. [< ML *interlīneār(is).* See INTERLINE[1], -AR[1]] —**in′ter·lin′e·ar·ly,** *adv.*

in·ter·lin·e·ate (in′tər lin′ē āt′), *v.t.,* **-at·ed, -at·ing.** interline[1]. [< ML *interlīneāt(us),* ptp. of *interlīneāre* to INTERLINE[1]; see -ATE[1]] —**in′ter·lin′e·a′tion,** *n.*

in·ter·lin·gua (in′tər liŋ′gwə), *n.* **1.** an interlanguage. **2.** (*cap.*) an artificial language developed between 1924 and 1951, based primarily upon the Romance languages, and intended mainly as a common international language for scientists. [< It; see INTER-, LINGUA]

in·ter·lin·ing[1] (in′tər lī′niŋ), *n.* **1.** an inner lining placed between the ordinary lining and the outer fabric of a garment. **2.** material, as cotton or wool, for this purpose. **3.** lining and padding quilted together. [INTERLINE[2] + -ING[1]]

in·ter·lin·ing[2] (in′tər lī′niŋ), *n.* **1.** that which is written or inserted between lines of writing or print. **2.** such insertions collectively. [INTERLINE[1] + -ING[1]]

in·ter·link (*v.* in′tər liŋk′; *n.* in′tər liŋk′), *v.t.* **1.** to link, one with another. —*n.* **2.** a connecting link. [INTER- + LINK[1]]

in·ter·lock (*v.* in′tər lok′; *n.* in′tər lok′), *v.i.* **1.** to engage or interlace, one with another: *The branches of the trees interlock to form a natural archway.* **2.** to fit into each other, as parts of machinery, so that all action is simultaneous. **3.** *Railroads.* (of switches, signals, etc.) to operate together in a prearranged order. —*v.t.* **4.** to lock one with another. **5.** to fit parts together so that all move simultaneously or in the same way. **6.** *Railroads.* to arrange (switches, signals, etc.) so that they operate together in a prearranged order. —*n.* **7.** the fact or condition of interlocking or of being interlocked. **8.** a device for preventing a mechanism from being set in motion when another mechanism is in such a position that the two operating simultaneously might produce undesirable results. **9.** *Motion Pictures.* a device for synchronizing the action of a camera and sound recorder. [INTER- + LOCK[1]] —**in′ter·lock′er,** *n.*

in′terlock′ing direc′torate, a corporate directorate one or more of whose members serve simultaneously in the directorate of another corporation or other corporations.

in·ter·lo·cu·tion (in′tər lə kyōō′shən), *n.* conversation; dialogue. [< L *interlocūtiōn-* (s. of *interlocūtiō*) a speaking between, equiv. to *interlocūt(us)* (see INTERLOCUTOR) + *-iōn-* -ION]

in·ter·loc·u·tor (in′tər lok′yə tər), *n.* **1.** the man in the middle of the line of performers of a minstrel troupe, who acts as the announcer and carries on humorous conversation and banter with the end men. **2.** a person who takes parts in a conversation or dialogue. **3.** a person who questions; interrogator. [< L *interlocūt(us)* spoken between (ptp. of *interloquī*) + -OR[2]]

in·ter·loc·u·to·ry (in′tər lok′yə tōr′ē, -tôr′ē), *adj.* **1.** of the nature of, pertaining to, or occurring in conversation: *interlocutory instruction.* **2.** interjected into the main course of speech. **3.** *Law.* **a.** pronounced during the course of an action, as a decision; not finally decisive of a case. **b.** pertaining to an intermediate decision. [< ML *interlocūtōri(us).* See INTERLOCUTOR, -ORY[1]] —**in′ter·loc′u·to′ri·ly,** *adv.*

in·ter·loc·u·tress (in′tər lok′yə tris), *n.* a female interlocutor. Also, **in′ter·loc′u·trice, interlocutrix.** [INTERLOCUT(O)R + -ESS]

in·ter·loc·u·trix (in′tər lok′yə triks), *n., pl.* **-loc·u·tri·ces** (-lok′yə trī′sēz). interlocutress. [INTERLOCU(TOR) + -TRIX]

in·ter·lope (in′tər lōp′), *v.i.,* **-loped, -lop·ing.** **1.** to intrude into some region or field of trade without a proper license. **2.** to thrust oneself into the affairs of others. [INTER- + LOPE] —**in′ter·lop′er,** *n.*
—**Syn. 2.** trespass, poach, encroach.

in·ter·lude (in′tər lōōd′), *n.* **1.** an intervening episode, period, space, etc. **2.** a short dramatic piece, esp. of a light or farcical character, formerly introduced between the parts or acts of miracle and morality plays or given as part of other entertainments. **3.** one of the early English farces or comedies, as those written by John Heywood, which grew out of such pieces. **4.** any intermediate performance or entertainment, as between the acts of a play. **5.** an instrumental passage or a piece of music rendered between the parts of a song, church service, drama, etc. [ME < ML *interlūd(ium),* equiv. to L *inter-* INTER- + *lūd(us)* play + *-ium,* neut. of *-ius* -IOUS] —**in′ter·lu′di·al,** *adj.*

in·ter·lu·nar (in′tər lōō′nər), *adj.* pertaining to the moon's monthly period of invisibility between the old moon and the new. [INTER- + LUNAR]

in·ter·lu·na·tion (in′tər lōō nā′shən), *n.* the interlunar period. [INTER- + LUNATION]

in·ter·mar·riage (in′tər mar′ij), *n.* **1.** marriage or the state of marriage between a man and woman of different races, religions, or ethnic groups, esp. between a Caucasian and a Negro or Oriental or between a Christian and a non-Christian. **2.** marriage or the state of marriage between a man and woman of different social classes. **3.** marriage or the state of marriage between a man and woman within a specific group, as required by custom or law; endogamy. **4.** marriage or the state of marriage between a man and woman belonging to the same small group, esp. if distant relatives. **5.** these types of marriage collectively. [INTER- + MARRIAGE]

in·ter·mar·ry (in′tər mar′ē), *v.i.,* **-ried, -ry·ing.** **1.** to become connected by marriage, as two families, tribes, castes, or religions. **2.** to marry within the limits of one family or of near relationship. **3.** to enter into an intermarriage. **4.** to marry. [INTER- + MARRY[1]]

in·ter·max·il·lar·y (in′tər mak′sə ler′ē), *adj.* **1.** situated between the maxillaries or upper jawbones. **2.** (in crustaceans) situated between those somites of the head which bear the maxillae. [INTER- + MAXILLARY]

in·ter·med·dle (in′tər med′əl), *v.i.,* **-dled, -dling.** to take part in a matter, esp. officiously; interfere; meddle. [INTER- + MEDDLE; r. ME *entremedle(n)* < AF *entremedl(er),* OF *entremesler*] —**in′ter·med′dler,** *n.*

in·ter·me·di·a·cy (in′tər mē′dē ə sē), *n.* the state of being intermediate or of acting intermediately. [INTERMEDIA(TE)[1] + -CY]

in·ter·me·di·ar·y (in′tər mē′dē er′ē), *adj., n., pl.* **-ar·ies.** —*adj.* **1.** being between; intermediate. **2.** acting between persons, parties, etc.; serving as an intermediate agent or agency: *an intermediary power.* —*n.* **3.** an intermediate agent or agency; a go-between or mediator. **4.** a medium or means. **5.** an intermediate form or stage. [< LL *intermedi(um)* (n.) + -ARY; see INTERMEDIATE[1]]

in·ter·me·di·ate[1] (in′tər mē′dē it), *adj.* **1.** being, situated, or acting between two points, stages, things, persons, etc.: *the intermediate stages of development.* —*n.* **2.** something intermediate, as a form or class. **3.** a person who acts between others; intermediary; mediator. **4.** *Chem.* a derivative of the initial material formed before the desired product of a chemical process. **5.** an intermediary. [< ML *intermediāt(us),* equiv. to L *intermedi(us)* intermediary (*inter-* INTER- + *medius* middle, in the middle) + *-ātus* -ATE[1]] —**in′ter·me′di·ate·ly,** *adv.* —**in′ter·me′di·ate·ness,** *n.*

in·ter·me·di·ate[2] (in′tər mē′dē āt′), *v.i.,* **-at·ed, -at·ing.** to act as an intermediary; intervene; mediate. [< ML *intermediāt(us),* ptp. of *intermediāre.* See INTER-, MEDIATE] —**in′ter·me′di·a′tion,** *n.* —**in′ter·me′di·a′tor,** *n.* —**in·ter·me·di·a·to·ry** (in′tər mē′dē ə tōr′ē, -tôr′ē), *adj.*

interme′diate card′, *Textiles.* a card used in the carding process to transfer sliver from the breaker card to the finisher card.

in′terme′diate fre′quency, *Radio.* the middle frequency in a superheterodyne receiver, at which most of the amplification takes place.

interme′diate range′ ballis′tic mis′sile, any supersonic missile that has a range of 800 to 1500 nautical miles and follows a ballistic trajectory after a powered, guided launching. *Abbr.:* IRBM, I.R.B.M.

in·ter·me′di·ate-val′ue the′orem (in′tər mē′dē it val′yōō), *Math.* the theorem that a function continuous between two points and having unequal values, *a* and *b,* at the two points takes on all values between *a* and *b.*

in′terme′diate ves′sel, a ship, somewhat slower than a passenger liner, that carries both passengers and cargo but fewer passengers than a liner and less cargo than a freighter.

in·ter·ment (in tûr′mənt), *n.* the act or a ceremony of interring; burial. [INTER- + -MENT; r. ME *enter(e)ment* < MF *enterrement*]

in′ter·met′al′lic com′pound (in′tər mə tal′ik, in′-), a compound of two or more metals. [INTER- + METALLIC]

in·ter·mez·zo (in′tər met′sō, -med′zō; *It.* ēn′termed′dzô), *n., pl.* **-zos, -zi** (-sē, -zē; *It.* -dzē). **1.** a short dramatic, musical, or other entertainment of light character introduced between the acts of a drama or opera. **2.** a short musical composition between main divisions of an extended musical work. **3.** a short, independent musical composition. [< It < LL *intermed(ium);* see INTERMEDIARY]

---

in′ter·jac′u·late′, *v.t.,* -lat·ed, -lat·ing.
in′ter·jac′u·la·to′ry, *adj.*
in′ter·judg′ment, *n.*
in′ter·ju′gal, *adj.*
in′ter·jug′u·lar, *adj.*
in′ter·junc′tion, *n.*
in′ter·la′bi·al, *adj.*
in′ter·lab′o·ra·to′ry, *adj.*
in′ter·la·cus′trine, *adj.*
in′ter·la·mel′lar, *adj.*
in′ter·lam′el·la′tion, *n.*
in′ter·lam′i·nar, *adj.*
in′ter·lap′, *v.i.,* -lapped, -lap·ping.
in′ter·lat′i·tu′di·nal, *adj.*
in′ter·lau·da′tion, *n.*
in′ter·li′bel, *v.t.,* -beled, -bel·ing or (*esp. Brit.*) -belled, -bel·ling.
in′ter·li′brar·y, *adj.*
in′ter·lie′, *v.i.,* -lay, -lain, -ly·ing.
in′ter·lig′a·men′ta·ry, *adj.*
in′ter·lig′a·men′tous, *adj.*
in′ter·light′, *n.*
in′ter·loan′, *adj.*
in′ter·loan′, *n.*
in′ter·lo′bar, *adj.*
in′ter·lo′bate, *adj.*
in′ter·lob′u·lar, *adj.*
in′ter·lo′cal, *adj.;* -ly, *adv.*
in′ter·lo′cate, *v.t.,* -cat·ed, -cat·ing.
in′ter·lo·ca′tion, *n.*
in′ter·loc′u·lar, *adj.*
in′ter·loc′u·lus, *n., pl.* -li.
in′ter·loop′, *n.*
in′ter·loop′, *v.t.*
in′ter·lot′, *v.t.,* -lot·ted, -lot·ting.
in′ter·lu′cent, *adj.*
in′ter·ma′lar, *adj.*
in′ter·mal·le′o·lar, *adj.*
in′ter·mam′ma·ry, *adj.*
in′ter·mam′mil·lar′y, *adj.*
in′ter·man·dib′u·lar, *adj.*
in′ter·ma·no′ri·al, *adj.*
in′ter·mar′gi·nal, *adj.*
in′ter·ma·rine′, *adj.*
in′ter·mas′toid, *adj.*
in′ter·mat′, *v.i.,* -mat·ted, -mat·ting.
in′ter·match′, *n., v.t.*
in′ter·maze′, *v.t.,* -mazed, -maz·ing.
in′ter·mean′, *n.*
in′ter·meas′ur·a·ble, *adj.*
in′ter·meas′ure, *v.t.,* -ured, -ur·ing.
in′ter·meet′, *v.i.,* -met, -meet·ing.
in′ter·melt′, *v.i.*
in′ter·mem′bral, *adj.*
in′ter·mem·bra′nous, *adj.*
in′ter·me·nin′ge·al, *adj.*
in′ter·men′stru·al, *adj.*
in′ter·men′tion, *v.*
in′ter·mes′en·ter′ic, *adj.*
in′ter·mesh′, *v.i.*
in′ter·mes′sage, *n.*
in′ter·met′a·car′pal, *adj.*
in′ter·me·tal′lic, *adj.*
in′ter·met′a·mer′ic, *adj.*
in′ter·met′a·tar′sal, *adj.*

in·ter·mi·gra·tion (in′tər mī grā′shən), *n.* reciprocal migration; interchange of habitat by migrating groups. [INTER- + MIGRATION]

in·ter·mi·na·ble (in tûr′mə nə bəl), *adj.* **1.** incapable of being terminated; unending: *Housecleaning is an interminable job.* **2.** monotonously or annoyingly protracted or continued: *her interminable chatter.* **3.** having no limits: *an interminable desert.* [ME < LL *interminābil(is).* See IN-³, TERMINABLE] —**in·ter′mi·na·ble·ness, in·ter′mi·na·bil′i·ty,** *n.* —**in·ter′mi·na·bly,** *adv.*

in·ter·min·gle (in′tər miŋ′gəl), *v.t., v.i.,* **-gled, -gling.** to mingle, one with another. [late ME; see INTER-, MINGLE] —**in′ter·min′gle·ment,** *n.*

in·ter·mis·sion (in′tər mish′ən), *n.* **1.** a period during which action temporarily ceases; an interval between periods of action or activity: *They studied for hours without an intermission.* **2.** a short interval between the acts of a play or parts of a public performance, usually a period of approximately 10 or 15 minutes allowing the performers and audience a rest or diversion from the performance: *We went into the lobby for a smoke during intermission.* **3.** the act or fact of intermitting; state of being intermitted: *to work without intermission.* [late ME < L *intermissiōn-* (s. of *intermissiō*) interruption, equiv. to *intermiss(us)* (ptp. of *intermittere* to INTERMIT) + *-iōn-* -ION]

in·ter·mis·sive (in′tər mis′iv), *adj.* **1.** of, pertaining to, or characterized by intermission. **2.** intermittent. [INTERMISS(ION) + -IVE]

in·ter·mit (in′tər mit′), *v.,* **-mit·ted, -mit·ting.** —*v.t.* **1.** to discontinue temporarily; suspend. —*v.i.* **2.** to stop or pause at intervals; be intermittent. **3.** to cease, stop, or break off operations for a time. [< L *intermitt(ere)* (to) leave a space between, drop (for a while), leave off, equiv. to *inter-* INTER- + *mittere* to send, let go] —**in′ter·mit′ter, in′ter·mit′tor,** *n.* —**in′ter·mit′ting·ly,** *adv.*
—**Syn. 1, 3.** interrupt. **3.** desist.

in·ter·mit·tent (in′tər mit′ᵊnt), *adj.* **1.** stopping or ceasing for a time: *an intermittent process.* **2.** alternately ceasing and beginning again: *an intermittent pain.* **3.** alternately functioning and not functioning or alternately functioning properly and improperly. **4.** (of streams, lakes, or springs) recurrent; showing water only part of the time. [< L *intermittent-* (s. of *intermittēns*) leaving off, prp. of *intermittere* to INTERMIT; see -ENT] —**in′ter·mit′tence, in′ter·mit′ten·cy,** *n.* —**in′ter·mit′tent·ly,** *adv.*
—**Syn. 1, 2.** interrupted, sporadic.

in′termit′tent cur′rent, *Elect.* a direct current that is interrupted at intervals.

in′termit′tent fe′ver, *Pathol.* a malarial fever in which feverish periods lasting a few hours alternate with periods in which the temperature is normal.

in′termit′tent move′ment, *Motion Pictures.* a mechanical motion that moves film through a camera or projector with brief pauses to allow each frame to be exposed or projected.

in·ter·mix (in′tər miks′), *v.t., v.i.* to intermingle. [back formation from *intermixt* (now *intermixed*) < L *intermixt(us)* mingled together, ptp. of *intermiscere.* See INTER-, MIX] —**in′ter·mix′a·ble,** *adj.* —**in·ter·mix·ed·ly** (in′tər mik′sid lē, -mikst′lē), *adv.*

in·ter·mix·ture (in′tər miks′chər), *n.* **1.** the act of intermixing. **2.** a mass of ingredients mixed together. **3.** something added by intermixing. [INTER- + MIXTURE]

in·ter·mo·dil·lion (in′tər mō dil′yən, -mə-), *n. Archit.* a space between two modillions. [INTER- + MODILLION]

in·ter·mod·u·la·tion (in′tər moj′ə lā′shən, -mod′yə-), *n.* the production in an electrical device of frequencies that are the sums or differences of frequencies of different inputs or of their harmonics. [INTER- + MODULATION]

in·ter·mo·lec·u·lar (in′tər mə lek′yə lər, -mō-), *adj.* existing or occurring between molecules. [INTER- + MOLECULAR]

in·ter·mon·tane (in′tər mon′tān), *adj.* situated between mountains: *an intermontane lake.* Also, **in·ter·moun·tain** (in′tər moun′tᵊn). [< L *inter-* INTER- + *montān(us),* equiv. to *mont-* (s. of *mōns*) mount + *-ānus* -ANE]

in·ter·mun·dane (in′tər mun′dān, -mun dān′), *adj.* **1.** existing in the space between worlds or heavenly bodies: *intermundane space.* **2.** *Rare.* of, pertaining to, or between heavenly bodies. [< L *inter-* INTER- + *mundān(us),* equiv. to *mund(us)* world + *-ānus* -ANE]

in·ter·mu·ral (in′tər myŏŏr′əl), *adj.* **1.** occurring or being between walls, as of buildings, cities, etc.: *A narrow, intermural forecourt.* **2.** of, pertaining to, or taking place between two or more institutions, cities, etc.: *an intermural track meet.* [< L *intermūrāl(is)* between walls. See INTER-, MURAL]

in·ter·mu·tule (in′tər myōō′chōōl), *n. Archit.* a space between two mutules. [INTER- + MUTULE]

in·tern¹ (*v.* in tûrn′; *n.* in′tûrn), *v.t.* **1.** to restrict to or confine within prescribed limits, as prisoners of war, enemy aliens, or combat troops who take refuge in a neutral country. **2.** to impound or hold within a country until the termination of a war, as a vessel of a belligerent which has put into a neutral port and remained beyond a limited period. —*n.* **3.** one who is or has been interned; internee. [< F *intern(er)* << L *intern(us)* INTERN³]

in·tern² (in′tûrn), *n.* Also, **interne. 1.** a resident member of the medical staff of a hospital, commonly a recent medical school graduate acting as assistant and serving an apprenticeship under supervision. **2.** *Educ.* See **student teacher.** —*v.i.* **3.** to be or perform the duties of an intern. [< F *interne* < L *intern(us)* INTERN³] —**in′tern·ship′,** *n.*

in·tern³ (in tûrn′), *adj. Archaic.* internal. [< L *intern(us)* inward, equiv. to *in* (see IN-²) + *-ternus* adj. suffix; see EXTERN]

in·ter·nal (in tûr′nᵊl), *adj.* **1.** situated or existing in the interior of something; interior. **2.** of, pertaining to, or noting the inside or inner part. **3.** *Pharm.* oral (def. 4). **4.** existing, occurring, or found within the limits or scope of something; intrinsic: *ideas with internal logic based upon false premises.* **5.** of or pertaining to the domestic affairs of a country: *the internal politics of a nation.* **6.** existing within the individual mind; not having objective existence: *internal malaise.* **7.** coming from, produced, or motivated by the psyche or inner recesses of the mind; subjective: *an internal response.* **8.** *Anat., Zool.* inner; not superficial; away from the surface or next to the axis of the body or of a part: *the internal carotid artery.* **9.** present or occurring within an organism or one of its parts: *an internal organ.* —*n.* **10.** Usually, **internals.** entrails; innards. **11.** an inner or intrinsic attribute. [< ML *internāl(is),* equiv. to L *intern(us)* INTERN³ + *-ālis* -AL¹] —**in′ter·nal′i·ty, in·ter′nal·ness,** *n.* —**in·ter′nal·ly,** *adv.*

inter′nal au′ditory mea′tus, *Anat.* the canal extending through the petrous portion of the temporal bone, through which pass the facial nerve and the auditory nerve and artery. See diag. under **ear.**

in·ter·nal-com·bus·tion (in tûr′nᵊl kəm bus′chən), *adj.* of or pertaining to an internal-combustion engine.

inter′nal-combus′tion en′gine, an engine of one or more working cylinders in which the process of combustion takes place within the cylinder or cylinders.

inter′nal conver′sion, *Physics.* the emission of an electron by an atom with an excited nucleus, occurring as a result of the transfer of energy from the nucleus to the electron.

inter′nal ear′, the inner portion of the ear, consisting of a bony labyrinth that is composed of a vestibule, semicircular canals, and a cochlea and that encloses a membranous labyrinth. Cf. **ear¹** (def. 1). See diag. under **ear.**

inter′nal en′ergy, *Thermodynamics.* a quantity associated with a system so that when the system undergoes an adiabatic charge, the decrease in this quantity is equal to the work done on the system. *Symbol:* U

inter′nal ev′idence, evidence found within the structure, elements, or materials of a particular work to support an opinion, thesis, or belief concerning its origin, as the spelling or vocabulary in a literary work or the brushwork or pigments used in a painting: *The internal evidence of the archaic spelling showed the manuscript to have been written before the 19th century.*

inter′nal gear′, *Mach.* a gear having teeth cut on an inner cylindrical surface.

inter′nal hem′orrhoid, *Pathol.* See under **hemorrhoid.**

inter′nal il′iac ar′tery, *Anat.* See **iliac artery** (def. 3).

in·ter·nal·ize (in tûr′nᵊlīz′), *v.t.,* **-ized, -iz·ing. 1.** to incorporate (the cultural values, mores, motives, etc., of a group), or make part of oneself, through learning and social adaptation. **2.** to make subjective or give a subjective character to. [INTERNAL + -IZE] —**in·ter′nal·i·za′tion,** *n.*

inter′nal jug′ular vein′. See under **jugular** (def. 1b).

inter′nal med′icine, the branch of medicine dealing with the diagnosis and nonsurgical treatment of diseases, esp. of adults.

inter′nal reconstruc′tion, *Historical Ling.* the hypothetical reconstruction of an earlier stage of a language or of some part of it, as its phonology, by deductions from irregularities in its present structure, as the reconstruction of a stage in English when certain instances of *r* were related to *s* in a systematic way by comparing the pair *was:were* to other pairs, as *lose:forlorn.*

inter′nal rela′tion, *Philos.* a relation between two entities such that if they had not been in this relation the nature of each would necessarily have been different. Cf. **external relation.**

inter′nal rev′enue, the revenue of a government from any domestic source, usually considered to be any source other than customs.

Inter′nal Rev′enue Serv′ice, *U.S. Govt.* the division of the Department of the Treasury that collects internal revenue, including income and excise taxes, and enforces revenue laws. Formerly, **Bureau of Internal Revenue.**

inter′nal rhyme′, *Pros.* **1.** a rhyme created by two or more words in the same line of verse. **2.** a rhyme created by words within, but not at the end of, two or more lines of a verse.

inter′nal stress′, (in metal or glass pieces, or the like) a stress existing within the material as a result of thermal changes, working, or unevenness of molecular structure. Cf. **micro-stress, residual stress.**

internat., international.

in·ter·na·tion·al (in′tər nash′ə nᵊl), *adj.* **1.** between or among nations; involving two or more nations: *international achievement of peace.* **2.** of or pertaining to two or more nations or their citizens: *a matter of international concern.* **3.** pertaining to the relations between nations: *international law.* **4.** having members or dealings in several nations: *The Mafia is an international underworld organization.* **5.** transcending national limits or a nationalistic viewpoint: *Scientific space research can be of international value.* —*n.* **6.** (*cap.*) any of several international socialist or Communist organizations formed in the 19th and 20th centuries. Cf. **First International, Second International, Third International, Fourth International, Labor and Socialist International. 7.** (*sometimes cap.*) a labor union having locals in two or more countries. **8.** any of various groups, enterprises, organizations, etc., having members or dealings in several countries (usually cap. and part of an official name). [INTER- + NATIONAL] —**in′ter·na′tion·al′i·ty,** *n.* —**in′ter·na′tion·al·ly,** *adv.*

in′terna′tional air′ mile′, mile (def. 3).

Interna′tional Associa′tion of Li′ons Clubs′, a group of service clubs, founded in 1917 and having an international membership.

Interna′tional Bank′ for Reconstruc′tion and Devel′opment, official name of the **World Bank.**

in′terna′tional can′dle, *Optics.* candle (def. 3b).

In′terna′tional Code′, a code used at sea by the navies of certain nations, using a series of flags representing digits from zero through nine.

Interna′tional Code′ of Sig′nals, a system of maritime signals adopted by many of the maritime nations of the world, using flag, semaphore, and Morse codes in which letters or letter combinations are given arbitrary designations readily understood without requiring translation.

Interna′tional Coopera′tion Administra′tion, *U.S. Govt.* the former division of the Department of State that administered all federal programs dealing with economic and technical aid to foreign countries; replaced by the Agency for International Development. *Abbr.:* ICA

Interna′tional Court′ of Jus′tice, the chief judicial agency of the United Nations, established in 1945 to decide disputes arising between nations.

in′terna′tional date′ line′. See **date line.**

In·ter·na·tio·nale (aɴ teʀ nᴀ syō nᴀl′), *n.* a revolutionary song, first sung in France in 1871 and since popular as a song of workers and Communists. [< F, short for *chanson internationale* international song]

In′terna′tional Falls′, a town in N Minnesota. 6778 (1960).

Interna′tional Geophys′ical Year′, the 18-month period from July 1, 1957 to Dec. 31, 1958, designated as a time of intensive geophysical exploration and sharing of knowledge by scientists of all countries. *Abbr.:* IGY

In′terna′tional Goth′ic, a style of Gothic art, esp. painting, developed in Europe in the late 14th and early 15th centuries, chiefly characterized by details carefully delineated in a naturalistic manner, elongated and delicately modeled forms, the use of complex perspective, and an emphasis on the decorative or ornamental aspect of drapery, foliage, or setting. Also called **International Style.**

Interna′tional Hydrolog′ical Dec′ade, a ten-year period, officially designated as 1965–74, during which participating nations undertake a program of cooperative research in hydrology. *Abbr.:* IHD

In′terna′tional Ice′ Patrol′, a yearly, U.S. Coast Guard patrol of the North Atlantic during the ice season to ascertain and warn ships of the positions of icebergs: undertaken under a 1914 international agreement between 14 maritime countries.

in·ter·na·tion·al·ise (in′tər nash′ə nᵊlīz′), *v.t.,* **-ised, -is·ing.** *Chiefly Brit.* internationalize. —**in′ter·na′tion·al·i·sa′tion,** *n.*

in·ter·na·tion·al·ism (in′tər nash′ə nᵊliz′əm), *n.* **1.** the principle of cooperation among nations, for the promotion of their common good, sometimes as contrasted with nationalism, or devotion to the interests of a particular nation. **2.** international character, relations, cooperation, or control. **3.** (*cap.*) the principles or methods of a Communist or socialist International. [INTERNATIONAL + -ISM]

in·ter·na·tion·al·ist (in′tər nash′ə nᵊlist), *n.* **1.** an advocate of internationalism. **2.** one versed in international law and relations. **3.** (*cap.*) a member or adherent of a Communist or socialist International. [INTERNATIONAL + -IST]

in·ter·na·tion·al·ize (in′tər nash′ə nᵊlīz′), *v.t.,* **-ized, -iz·ing.** to make international; bring under international control. Also, *esp. Brit.,* **internationalise.** [INTERNATIONAL + -IZE] —**in′ter·na′tion·al·i·za′tion,** *n.*

In′terna′tional La′bor Organiza′tion, a specia zed agency of the United Nations working through member nations to improve working conditions throughout the world; originally formed as an affiliate of the League of Nations. *Abbr.:* ILO, I.L.O.

in′terna′tional law′, the body of rules which civilized nations recognize as binding them in their conduct towards one another. Cf. **private international law, public international law.**

In′terna′tional Mon′etary Fund′, an international organization that promotes the stabilization of the world's currencies and maintains a monetary pool from which member nations can draw in order to correct a deficit in their balance of payments.

interna′tional Morse′ code′, a form of Morse code used in international radiotelegraphy. Also called **continental code.**

interna′tional nau′tical mile′, mile (def. 3). Also called **international air mile.**

In′terna′tional Or′ange, *Naut.* a vivid orange color, visible at a great distance and in murky weather, used to color lifesaving devices, navigational aids, etc.

Interna′tional Phonet′ic Al′phabet, the set of symbols and modifiers designed, principally on the basis of articulatory considerations, to provide a consistent and universally understood system for transcribing the speech sounds of any language: devised by the International Phonetic Association. See table under **phonetic alphabet.**

in′terna′tional pitch′, *Music.* See **diapason normal pitch.**

in′terna′tional ra′dio si′lence, a radio silence observed on vessels at sea for two three-minute periods each hour to permit distress signals to be heard.

In′terna′tional Style′, 1. See **International Gothic. 2.** the general form of architecture developed in the 1920's and 1930's by Gropius, Le Corbusier, Mies van der Rohe, and others, characterized by simple geometric forms, large untextured, often white, surfaces, large areas of glass, and general use of steel or reinforced concrete construction. **3.** (*sometimes l.c.*) any of various 20th century styles in art, as Cubism or Abstract Expressionism, that have gained wide currency in Europe, the Americas, Asia, and elsewhere.

in′terna′tional tem′perature scale′, a centigrade scale for use in measuring temperatures above −183°C in which specified values are assigned to the ice point, steam point, and melting point of gold, silver, and antimony and the boiling point of sulfur and of oxygen.

in′ter·mi′grate, *v.i.,* **-grat·ed, -grat·ing.**
in′ter·min′is·te′ri·al, *adj.*
in′ter·mo·bil′i·ty, *n.*
in′ter·mod′i·fi·ca′tion, *n.*
in′ter·mo′lar, *adj.*
in′ter·mo′men·tar′y, *adj.*
in′ter·mo′tion, *n.*
in′ter·mu·nic′i·pal, *adj.*
in′ter·mu·nic′i·pal′i·ty, *n.*
in′ter·mus′cu·lar, *adj.;* **-ly,** *adv.*
in′ter·mus′cu·lar′i·ty, *n.*
in′ter·nar′i·al, *adj.*
in′ter·na′sal, *adj.*
in′ter·na′tion, *adj.*

Interna′tional Work′ingmen's Associa′tion, official name of the **First International.**

Interna′tional Year′ of the Qui′et Sun′, *Astron.* the year 1964, in which the sun was in a state of relative quiescence, officially designated as a period for astronomical observatories of participating nations to make detailed studies of its nature. *Abbr.:* IQSY

in·terne (in′tûrn), *n.* intern[2].

in·ter·ne·cine (in′tər nē′sēn, -sīn, -nes′ēn, -nes′īn), *adj.* **1.** mutually destructive. **2.** of or pertaining to conflict or struggle within a group: *an internecine feud among proxy holders.* **3.** characterized by great slaughter. Also, **in·ter·ne·cive** (in′tər nē′siv, -nes′iv). [< L *internecīn(us)* murderous, equiv. to *internec(āre)* (to) kill out, exterminate (*inter-* INTER- + *necāre* to kill) + *-īnus* -INE[1]]

in·tern·ee (in′tûr nē′), *n.* a person who is or has been interned, as a prisoner of war. [INTERN[1] + -EE]

in·ter·neg·a·tive (in′tər neg′ə tiv), *n.* *Photog.* a color negative of a color transparency, made for purposes of duplication. [INTER- + NEGATIVE]

in·tern·ist (in′tûr nist, in tûr′nist), *n.* a physician specializing in the diagnosis and nonsurgical treatment of diseases, esp. of adults. [INTERN(AL MEDICINE) + -IST]

in·tern·ment (in tûrn′mənt), *n.* **1.** the act or an instance of interning. **2.** the state of being interned; confinement. [INTERN[1] + -MENT]

intern′ment camp′, (during wartime) a prison camp under military jurisdiction for the confinement of enemy aliens, prisoners of war, etc.

in·ter·node (in′tər nōd′), *n.* a part or space between two nodes, knots, or joints, as the portion of a plant stem between two nodes. [< L *internōd(ium).* See INTER-, NODE] —**in′ter·nod′al,** *adj.*

in·ter nos (in′ter nōs′; *Eng.* in′tər nōs′), *Latin.* between ourselves.

in·ter·nun·cial (in′tər nun′shəl), *adj.* *Anat.* (of a nerve cell or a chain of nerve cells) linking the incoming and outgoing nerve fibers of the nervous system. [INTERNUNCI(O) + -AL[1]]

in·ter·nun·ci·o (in′tər nun′shē ō′, -sē ō′), *n., pl.* **-ci·os.** a papal ambassador ranking next below a nuncio. [< It < L *internunti(us).* See INTER-, NUNCIO]

in·ter·o·ce·an·ic (in′tər ō′shē an′ik), *adj.* connecting or between oceans: *an interoceanic canal.* [INTER- + OCEANIC]

in·ter·o·cep·tive (in′tər ō sep′tiv), *adj.* *Physiol.* pertaining to interoceptors, the stimuli acting upon them, or the nerve impulses initiated by them. [INTEROCEPT(OR) + -IVE]

in·ter·o·cep·tor (in′tər ō sep′tər), *n.* *Physiol.* a receptor responding to stimuli originating from within the body. [< NL *intero-* inside (comb. form of **interus,* parallel to L *exterus* outside) + -CEPTOR]

in·ter·oc·u·lar (in′tər ok′yə lər), *adj.* being, or situated, between the eyes. [INTER- + OCULAR]

in·ter·of·fice (in′tər ô′fis, -of′is), *adj.* functioning or communicating between the offices of a company or organization; within a company: *interoffice memo.* [INTER- + OFFICE]

in·ter·os·cu·late (in′tər os′kyə lāt′), *v.i.,* **-lat·ed, -lat·ing.** **1.** to interpenetrate; inosculate. **2.** to form a connecting link. [INTER- + OSCULATE] —**in′ter·os′cu·la′tion,** *n.*

in·ter·par·ox·ys·mal (in′tər par′ok siz′məl), *adj.* *Pathol.* occurring in the period or periods between paroxysms. [INTER- + PAROXYSMAL]

in·ter·pel·lant (in′tər pel′ənt), *n.* a person who interpellates; interpellator. [< L *interpellant-* (s. of *interpellāns*) interrupting, prp. of *interpellāre,* equiv. to *inter-* INTER- + *-pellant-* speaking; see APPELLANT]

in·ter·pel·late (in′tər pel′āt, in tûr′pə lāt′), *v.t.,* **-lat·ed, -lat·ing.** to call formally upon (a minister or member of a government) in interpellation. [< L *interpellāt(us)* interrupted (ptp. of *interpellāre*), equiv. to *inter-* INTER- + *-pellā-* speak + *-tus* ptp. suffix] —**in·ter·pel·la·tor** (in′tər pel′ā tər, in tûr′pə lā′-), *n.*

in·ter·pel·la·tion (in′tər pə lā′shən, in tûr′pə-), *n.* a procedure in some legislative bodies of asking a government official to explain an act or policy, sometimes leading, in parliamentary government, to a vote of confidence or a change of government. [< L *interpellātiōn-* (s. of *interpellātiō*) interruption. See INTERPELLATE, -ION]

in·ter·pen·e·trate (in′tər pen′i trāt′), *v.,* **-trat·ed, -trat·ing.** —*v.t.* **1.** to penetrate thoroughly; permeate. **2.** to penetrate with (another substance) mutually or reciprocally. —*v.i.* **3.** to penetrate between things or parts. **4.** to penetrate each other. [INTER- + PENETRATE] —**in·ter·pen·e·tra·ble** (in′tər pen′i trə bəl), *adj.* —**in′ter·pen′e·trant,** *adj.* —**in′ter·pen′e·tra′tion,** *n.* —**in′ter·pen′e·tra′tive,** *adj.* —**in′ter·pen′e·tra′tive·ly,** *adv.*

in·ter·per·son·al (in′tər pûr′sə nəl), *adj.* **1.** existing or occurring between persons. **2.** of or pertaining to the relations between persons. [INTER- + PERSONAL]

interper′sonal the′ory, *Psychol.* the theory that personality development and behavior disorders are related to and determined by relationships between persons.

in·ter·phase (in′tər fāz′), *n.* interkinesis. [INTER- + PHASE]

in·ter·phone (in′tər fōn′), *n.* **1.** an intercommunication system using telephones to connect offices, stations, etc., as in a building or ship. **2.** a telephone used in such a system. [formerly trademark]

in·ter·plan·e·tar·y (in′tər plan′i ter′ē), *adj.* being or occurring between the planets or between a planet and the sun. [INTER- + PLANETARY]

in·ter·play (*n.* in′tər plā′; *v.* in′tər plā′), *n.* **1.** reciprocal play, action, or influence: *the interplay of plot and character.* —*v.i.* **2.** to exert influence on each other. [INTER- + PLAY]

in·ter·plead (in′tər plēd′), *v.i.,* **-plead·ed** or **-plead** or **-pled, -plead·ing.** *Law.* to litigate with each other in order to determine which of two parties is the rightful claimant against a third party. [INTER- + PLEAD; r. late ME *enterplede* < AF *enterpled(er)*]

in·ter·plead·er[1] (in′tər plē′dər), *n.* *Law.* a judicial proceeding by which, when two parties make the same claim against a third party, the rightful claimant is determined. [var. of *enterpleder* < AF (inf. used as n.)]

in·ter·plead·er[2] (in′tər plē′dər), *n.* *Law.* a party who interpleads. [INTERPLEAD + -ER[1]]

In·ter·pol (in′tər pōl′), *n.* an official international agency that coordinates the police activities of member nations. [*Inter(national) Pol(ice)*]

in·ter·po·lar (in′tər pō′lər), *adj.* connecting or being between poles: *an interpolar flight.* [INTER- + POLAR]

in·ter·po·late (in tûr′pə lāt′), *v.,* **-lat·ed, -lat·ing.** —*v.t.* **1.** to alter (a text) by the insertion of new matter, esp. deceptively or without authorization. **2.** to insert (new or spurious matter) in this manner. **3.** to introduce (something additional or extraneous) between other things or parts; interject; interpose; intercalate. **4.** *Math.* to insert, estimate, or find an intermediate term in (a sequence). —*v.i.* **5.** to make an interpolation. [< L *interpolāt(us)* furbished up, altered (ptp. of *interpolāre*), equiv. to *inter-* INTER- + *-polā-* furbish (akin to *polīre* to POLISH) + *-tus* ptp. suffix] —**in·ter·po·la·ble** (in tûr′pə lə bəl), *adj.* —**in·ter′po·lat′er, in·ter′po·la′tor,** *n.* —**in·ter′po·la′tive,** *adj.* —**in·ter′po·la′tive·ly,** *adv.*
—**Syn. 4, 5.** extrapolate.

in·ter·po·la·tion (in tûr′pə lā′shən), *n.* **1.** the act or process of interpolating or the state of being interpolated. **2.** something interpolated, as a passage introduced into a text. [< L *interpolātiōn-* (s. of *interpolātiō*). See INTERPOLATE, -ION]

in·ter·pose (in′tər pōz′), *v.,* **-posed, -pos·ing.** —*v.t.* **1.** to place between; cause to intervene: *to interpose an opaque body between a light and the eye.* **2.** to put (a barrier, obstacle, etc.) between or in the way of: *This new turn of events interposes an obstacle to our plans.* **3.** to bring (influence, action, etc.) to bear between parties, or on behalf of a party or person. **4.** to put in (a remark, question, etc.) in the midst of a conversation, discourse, or the like. —*v.i.* **5.** to come between other things; assume an intervening position or relation. **6.** to step in between parties at variance; mediate. **7.** to put in or make a remark by way of interruption. [< MF *interpose(r).* See INTER-, POSE[1]] —**in′ter·pos′a·ble,** *adj.* —**in′ter·pos′al,** *n.* —**in′ter·pos′er,** *n.* —**in′ter·pos′ing·ly,** *adv.*
—**Syn. 1.** introduce, insert, insinuate, inject. **4, 7.** interject. **6.** intervene, intercede.

in·ter·po·si·tion (in′tər pə zish′ən), *n.* **1.** the act or fact of interposing or the condition of being interposed. **2.** something interposed. **3.** *U.S.* the doctrine that an individual State may oppose any federal action it believes encroaches on its sovereignty. [ME *interposicio(u)n* < L *interpositiōn-* (s. of *interpositiō*), equiv. to *interposit(us)* placed between (ptp. of *interpōnere*) + *-iōn-* -ION]

in·ter·pret (in tûr′prit), *v.t.* **1.** to set forth the meaning of; explain; explicate; elucidate: *to interpret the hidden meaning of a parable.* **2.** to construe, or understand in a particular way: *to interpret a reply as favorable.* **3.** to bring out the meaning of (a dramatic work, music, etc.) by performance or execution. **4.** to perform or render (a song, role in a play, etc.) according to one's understanding or sensitivity: *The actor interpreted Lear as a weak, raging psychopath.* **5.** to translate. **6.** *Computer Technol.* **a.** (of data processing equipment) to translate into alphanumeric symbols and print on a punch card (the codes punched in the card). **b.** to translate (a stored program expressed in pseudocode) into machine language and to perform the indicated operations as they are translated. —*v.i.* **7.** to translate what is said in a foreign language. **8.** to explain something; give an explanation. [ME *interprete(n)* < L *interpret(ārī),* equiv. to *interpret-* (s. of *interpres* explainer; see INTER-, PRICE) + *-ā-* thematic vowel + *-rī* inf. ending] —**in·ter′pret·a·bil′i·ty, in·ter′pret·a·ble·ness,** *n.* —**in·ter′pret·a·ble,** *adj.* —**in·ter′pret·a·bly,** *adv.* —**in·ter′pret·er,** *n.* —**in·ter′pret·er·ship′,** *n.*
—**Syn. 1.** See **explain.**

in·ter·pre·ta·tion (in tûr′pri tā′shən), *n.* **1.** the act of interpreting; elucidation; explication: *This writer's work demands interpretation.* **2.** an elucidation; an explanation of the meaning of another's artistic or creative work: *His interpretation of the poem is rather ambiguous.* **3.** an understanding or conception of another's words or deeds: *Saying that his rudeness was due to his haste is a rather charitable interpretation.* **4.** a way of interpreting. **5.** the rendering of a dramatic part, music, etc., so as to bring out the meaning, or to indicate one's particular conception of it. **6.** translation. [ME *interpretacio(u)n* < L *interpretātiōn-* (s. of *interpretātiō*). See INTERPRET, -ATION] —**in·ter′pre·ta′tion·al,** *adj.*

in·ter·pre·ta·tive (in tûr′pri tā′tiv), *adj.* **1.** serving to interpret; explanatory. **2.** deduced by interpretation. **3.** made because of interpretation: *an interpretative distortion of language.* **4.** of or pertaining to those arts that require an intermediary, such as a performer, for realization, as in music or theater. [< L *interpretāt(us)* interpreted (ptp. of *interpretārī*) + -IVE] —**in·ter′pre·ta′tive·ly,** *adv.*

inter′pretative dance′, a form of modern dance in which the dancer's movements explicitly or symbolically depict an emotion, a story, or an idea.

in·ter·pre·tive (in tûr′pri tiv), *adj.* interpretative. —**in·ter′pre·tive·ly,** *adv.*

in·ter·quar′tile range′ (in′tər kwôr′tīl, -til), *Statistics.* the range of values of a frequency distribution between the first and third quartiles. [INTER- + QUARTILE]

in·ter·ra·cial (in′tər rā′shəl), *adj.* **1.** involving members of different races: *an interracial marriage.* **2.** of, for, or among persons of different races: *interracial amity.* [INTER- + RACIAL]

in·ter·ra·di·al (in′tər rā′dē əl), *adj.* situated between the radii or rays: *the interradial petals in a echinoderm.* [INTER- + RADIAL] —**in′ter·ra′di·al·ly,** *adv.*

in·ter·reg·num (in′tər reg′nəm), *n., pl.* **-nums, -na** (-nə). **1.** an interval of time between the close of a sovereign's reign and the accession of his normal or legitimate successor. **2.** any period during which a state has no ruler or only a temporary executive. **3.** any period of freedom from the usual authority. **4.** any pause or interruption in continuity. [< L, equiv. to *inter-* INTER- + *regnum* REIGN] —**in′ter·reg′nal,** *adj.*

in·ter·re·late (in′tər ri lāt′), *v.t.,* **-lat·ed, -lat·ing.** to bring into reciprocal relation. [back formation from INTERRELATED]

in·ter·re·lat·ed (in′tər ri lā′tid), *adj.* reciprocally or mutually related: *an interrelated series of experiments.* [INTER- + RELATED] —**in′ter·re·lat′ed·ly,** *adv.* —**in′ter·re·lat′ed·ness,** *n.*

in·ter·re·la·tion (in′tər ri lā′shən), *n.* reciprocal relation. [INTER- + RELATION] —**in′ter·re·la′tion·ship′,** *n.*

in·ter·rex (in′tər reks′), *n., pl.* **in·ter·re·ges** (in′tər rē′jēz). a person holding supreme authority in a state during an interregnum. [< L; see INTER-, REX]

interrog., **1.** interrogation. **2.** interrogative.

in·ter·ro·gate (in ter′ə gāt′), *v.,* **-gat·ed, -gat·ing.** —*v.t.* **1.** to ask a question or questions of (a person), esp. to seek answers or information which the person questioned considers personal or secret. **2.** to examine by questions; question formally: *The police captain interrogated the suspect.* —*v.i.* **3.** to ask questions, esp. formally or officially: *the right to interrogate.* [late ME < L *interrogāt(us)* questioned, examined (ptp. of *interrogāre*), equiv. to *inter-* INTER- + *rogā-* ask + *-tus* ptp. suffix] —**in·ter·ro·ga·ble** (in ter′ə gə bəl), *adj.* —**in·ter′ro·gat′ing·ly,** *adv.*
—**Syn. 1.** query.

in·ter·ro·ga·tion (in ter′ə gā′shən), *n.* **1.** the act of interrogating; questioning. **2.** an instance of being interrogated: *He seemed shaken after his interrogation.* **3.** a question; inquiry. **4.** an interrogation point; question mark. [ME *interrogacio(u)n* < L *interrogātiōn-* (s. of *interrogātiō*). See INTERROGATE, -ION] —**in·ter′ro·ga′tion·al,** *adj.*

interroga′tion point′. See **question mark.** Also called **interroga′tion mark′.**

in·ter·rog·a·tive (in′tə rog′ə tiv), *adj.* **1.** of, pertaining to, or conveying a question. **2.** *Gram.* forming, constituting, or used in or to form a question: *an interrogative pronoun, suffix, particle, or sentence.* —*n.* **3.** *Gram.* an interrogative word, element, or construction, as *who?* and *what?* [< LL *interrogātīv(us).* See INTERROGATE, -IVE] —**in′ter·rog′a·tive·ly,** *adv.*

in·ter·ro·ga·tor (in ter′ə gā′tər), *n.* **1.** a person who interrogates. **2.** Also called **challenger.** *Radio.* a transmitter that emits a signal to trigger a transponder. [< LL; see INTERROGATE, -OR[2]]

in·ter·ro·ga·tor-re·spon·sor (in ter′ə gā′tər ri spon′sər), *n.* *Electronics.* a radio or radar transceiver for sending a signal to a transponder and receiving and interpreting the reply.

in·ter·rog·a·to·ry (in′tə rog′ə tôr′ē, -tōr′ē), *adj., n., pl.* **-to·ries.** —*adj.* **1.** conveying a question; interrogative. —*n.* **2.** a question; inquiry. **3.** *Law.* a formal or written question. [< LL *interrogātōri(us).* See INTERROGATE, -ORY[1]] —**in·ter·rog·a·to·ri·ly** (in′tə rog′ə tôr′ə lē, -tōr′-, -rog′ə tôr′-, -tōr′-), *adv.*

in ter·ro′rem clause′ (in te rôr′em, -rōr′-), *Law.* a clause in a will stating that a beneficiary who contests the will shall lose his legacy. [< L *in terrorem* in terror]

in·ter·rupt (in′tə rupt′), *v.t.* **1.** to cause or make a break in the continuity or uniformity of (a course, process, condition, etc.). **2.** to break off or cause to cease, as in the middle of something: *He interrupted his*

in′ter·net′ted, *adj.*
in′ter·neu′ral, *adj.*
in′ter·neu·ron′ic, *adj.*
in′ter·ni′dal, *adj.*
in′ter·nu′cle·ar, *adj.*
in′ter·ol′i·var′y, *adj.*
in′ter·op′tic, *adj.*
in′ter·or′bi·tal, *adj.;* **-ly,** *adv.*
in′ter·os′cil·late′, *v.,* **-lat·ed, -lat·ing.**
in′ter·os′se·ous, *adj.*
in′ter·own′er·ship′, *n.*
in′ter·pal′a·tine′, *adj., n.*
in′ter·pal′pe·bral, *adj.*
in′ter·pap′il·lar′y, *adj.*
in′ter·pa·ren′chy·mal, *adj.*
in′ter·par′en·tal, *adj.*
in′ter·par′en·thet′ic, *adj.*
in′ter·par′en·thet′i·cal, *adj.;* **-ly,** *adv.*
in′ter·pa·ri′e·tal, *adj.*
in′ter·par′lia·ment, *adj.*
in′ter·par′lia·men′ta·ry, *adj.*
in′ter·par′ty, *adj.*
in′ter·pave′, *v.t.,* **-paved, -pav·ing.**
in′ter·peal′, *v.t.*
in′ter·pec′to·ral, *adj.*
in′ter·pe·dun′cu·lar, *adj.*
in′ter·per′me·ate′, *v.t.,* **-at·ed, -at·ing.**
in′ter·per·vade′, *v.t.,* **-vad·ed, -vad·ing.**
in′ter·per·va′sive, *adj.;* **-ly,** *adv.;* **-ness,** *n.*
in′ter·pet′a·loid′, *adj.*
in′ter·pet′a·lous, *adj.*
in′ter·pet′i·o·lar, *adj.*
in′ter·pha·lan′ge·al, *adj.*
in′ter·pla·cen′tal, *adj.*
in′ter·plait′, *v.t.*
in′ter·plant′, *v.t.*
in′ter·pledge′, *v.t.,* **-pledged, -pledg·ing.**
in′ter·pleu′ral, *adj.*
in′ter·plight′, *v.t.*
in′ter·pol′ish, *v.t.*
in′ter·pol′li·nate′, *v.,* **-nat·ed, -nat·ing.**
in′ter·por′tal, *adj.*
in′ter·pour′, *v.t.*
in′ter·pres′sure, *adj.*
in′ter·pris·mat′ic, *adj.*
in′ter·pro·duce′, *v.t.,* **-duced, -duc·ing.**
in′ter·pro·fes′sion·al, *adj.;* **-ly,** *adv.*
in′ter·pro·glot′tid·al, *adj.*
in′ter·pro·por′tion·al, *adj.*
in′ter·pro′to·plas′mic, *adj.*
in′ter·pro·vin′cial, *adj.*
in′ter·prox′i·mal, *adj.*
in′ter·pter′y·goid′, *adj.*
in′ter·pu′bic, *adj.*
in′ter·pul′mo·nar′y, *adj.*
in′ter·pu′pil·lar′y, *adj.*
in′ter·quar′rel, *v.i.,* **-reled, -rel·ing** or (*esp. Brit.*) **-relled, -rel·ling.**
in′ter·quar′ter, *n.*
in′ter·race′, *adj.*
in′ter·ra′di·ate′, *v.i.,* **-at·ed, -at·ing.**
in′ter·ra′di·a′tion, *n.*
in′ter·rail′way′, *adj.*
in′ter·ra′mal, *adj.*
in′ter·re·ceive′, *v.t.,* **-ceived, -ceiv·ing.**
in′ter·re·flect′, *v.i., v.t.*
in′ter·re·flec′tion, *n.*
in′ter·reg′i·men′tal, *adj.*
in′ter·re′gion·al, *adj.;* **-ly,** *adv.*
in′ter·reign′, *v.i.*
in′ter·re·li′gious, *adj.;* **-ly,** *adv.*
in′ter·re′nal, *adj.*
in′ter·re·pel′lent, *adj.*
in′ter·re·pul′sion, *n.*
in′ter·re·sist′, *v.*
in′ter·re·sist′ance, *n.*
in′ter·re·sist′i·bil′i·ty, *n.*
in′ter·re·spon′si·ble, *adj.*
in′ter·re·tic′u·lar, *adj.*
in′ter·re·tic′u·la′tion, *n.*
in′ter·rhyme′, *v.i.,* **-rhymed, -rhym·ing.**
in′ter·road′, *adj.*
in′ter·rule′, *v.t.,* **-ruled, -rul·ing.**
in′ter·run′, *v.t.,* **-ran, -run, -run·ning.**

work to answer the bell. **3.** to stop (a person) in the midst of doing or saying something, esp. by an interjected remark: *May I interrupt you to comment on that last remark?* **—*v.i.* 4.** to cause a break or discontinuance; interfere with action or speech, esp. by interjecting a remark: *Please don't interrupt.* [ME *interrupte(n)* < L *interrupt(us)* broken apart (ptp. of *interrumpere*), equiv. to *inter-* INTER- + *ruptus* broken; see RUPTURE] **—in′ter·rupt′ed·ly,** *adv.* **—in′ter·rupt′ed·ness,** *n.* **—in′ter·rupt′i·ble,** *adj.* **—in′ter·rup′tive,** *adj.*

—Syn. 1, 3. intermit. INTERRUPT, DISCONTINUE, SUSPEND imply breaking off something temporarily or permanently. INTERRUPT may have either meaning: *to interrupt a meeting.* To DISCONTINUE is to stop or leave off, often permanently: *to discontinue a building program.* To SUSPEND is to break off relations, operations, proceedings, privileges, etc., for a longer or shorter period, usually intending to resume at a stated time: *to suspend operations during a strike.* **—Ant. 1, 2.** continue.

in′terrupt′ed fern′, a tall fern, *Osmunda Claytoniana,* of eastern North America and eastern Asia. Also called **Clayton fern.**

in′terrupt′ed screw′, a screw having the thread interrupted in one or more places by longitudinal channels, as in the breech of a cannon or the lead screw of a lathe.

in·ter·rupt·er (in′tə rup′tər), *n.* **1.** one who or that which interrupts. **2.** *Elect.* a device for interrupting or periodically opening and closing a circuit, as in a doorbell. Also, **in′ter·rup′tor.** [INTERRUPT + -ER[1]]

in·ter·rup·tion (in′tə rup′shən), *n.* **1.** the act or an instance of interrupting or the state of being interrupted. **2.** something that interrupts. **3.** cessation; intermission. [ME *interrupcio(u)n* < L *interruptiōn-* (s. of *interruptiō*). See INTERRUPT, -ION]

in·ter·scap·u·lar (in′tər skap′yə lər), *adj.* *Anat., Zool.* between the scapulae or shoulder blades. [INTER- + SCAPULAR]

in·ter·scho·las·tic (in′tər skə las′tik), *adj.* between schools, or representative of different schools, esp. secondary schools: *interscholastic athletics.* [INTER- + SCHOLASTIC]

in·ter se (in′tər sē′; *Lat.* in′ter se′), **1.** (*italics.*) *Latin.* among themselves; between themselves. **2.** *Stockbreeding.* the mating of closely related animals to each other.

in·ter·sect (in′tər sekt′), *v.t.* **1.** to cut or divide by passing through or across: *The highway intersects the town.* **—*v.i.* 2.** to cross, as lines, wires, etc. **3.** *Geom.* to have one or more points in common: *intersecting lines.* [< L *intersect(us)* severed between (ptp. of *intersecāre*). See INTER-, -SECT]

Intersection $A \cap B$

in·ter·sec·tant (in′tər sek′tənt), *adj.* intersecting: *a stoplight at the first intersectant road.* [INTERSECT + -ANT]

intersect′ing arcade′. See **interlacing arcade.**

in·ter·sec·tion (in′tər sek′shən), *n.* **1.** a place where two or more roads meet, esp. when at least one is a major highway. **2.** any place of intersection or the act or fact of intersecting. **3.** *Math.* **a.** Also called **meet, product.** the set of elements which two or more sets have in common. *Symbol:* $\cap$ **b.** the greatest lower bound of two elements in a lattice. [< L *intersectiōn-* (s. of *intersectiō*). See INTERSECT, -ION] **—in′ter·sec′tion·al,** *adj.*

in·ter·sep·tal (in′tər sep′tᵊl), *adj.* situated between septa. [INTER- + SEPTAL]

in·ter·ses·sion (in′tər sesh′ən), *n.* a period between two academic terms or semesters. [INTER- + SESSION]

in·ter·sex (in′tər seks′), *n.* *Biol.* an individual displaying sexual characteristics intermediate between male and female. [back formation from INTERSEXUAL]

in·ter·sex·u·al (in′tər sek′sho͞o əl), *adj.* **1.** existing between the sexes. **2.** *Biol.* pertaining to or having the characteristics of an intersex. [INTER- + SEXUAL] **—in′ter·sex′u·al′i·ty, in′ter·sex′u·al·ism,** *n.* **—in′ter·sex′u·al·ly,** *adv.*

in·ter·si·de·re·al (in′tər sī dēr′ē əl), *adj.* *Rare.* interstellar. [INTER- + SIDEREAL]

in·ter·space (*n.* in′tər spās′; *v.* in′tər spās′), *n., v.,* **-spaced, -spac·ing.** **—*n.* 1.** a space between things. **2.** an intervening period of time; interval. **—*v.t.* 3.** to put a space between. **4.** to occupy or fill the space between. [INTER- + SPACE] **—in·ter·spa·tial** (in′tər spā′shəl), *adj.* **—in′ter·spa′tial·ly,** *adv.*

in·ter·sperse (in′tər spûrs′), *v.t.,* **-spersed, -spers·ing.** **1.** to scatter here and there or place at intervals among other things: *to intersperse flowers among shrubs.* **2.** to diversify with something scattered or placed at intervals: *to intersperse the shrubs with flowers.* [< L *interspers(us)* strewn among (ptp. of **interspergere*), equiv. to *inter-* INTER- + *-spersus,* var. of *sparsus,* ptp. of *spargere* to scatter; see DISPERSE] **—in·ter·spers·ed·ly** (in′tər spûr′sid lē), *adv.* **—in·ter·sper·sion** (in′tər spûr′zhən *or, esp. Brit.,* -shən), **in′ter·sper′sal,** *n.*

in·ter·stade (in′tər stād′), *n.* *Geol.* a period of time represented by an interglacial deposit. Also, **intersta·dial.** [INTER- + STADE]

in·ter·sta·di·al (in′tər stā′dē əl), *Geol.* **—*n.* 1.** a halt between successive advances or recessions of an ice sheet. **2.** interstade. **—*adj.* 3.** of or pertaining to interglacial periods or deposits. [INTER- + STADIAL]

in·ter·state (in′tər stāt′), *adj.* connecting or jointly involving states: *interstate commerce.* [INTER- + STATE]

In′terstate Com′merce Commis′sion, *U.S. Govt.* a board, consisting of eleven members, that supervises and regulates all carriers, except airplanes, engaged in interstate commerce. *Abbr.:* ICC

in·ter·stel·lar (in′tər stel′ər), *adj.* between the stars: *interstellar space.* [INTER- + STELLAR]

in·ter·stice (in tûr′stis), *n.* **1.** an intervening space. **2.** a small or narrow space or interval between things or parts, esp. when one of a series of alternating uniform spaces and parts: *The interstices between the slats of a fence.* **3.** *Rom. Cath. Ch.* the interval of time that must elapse, as required by canon law, before promotion to a higher degree of orders. **4.** an interval of time. [< LL *interstit(ium),* equiv. to *interstit-* (perf. s. of *intersistere* to stand or put between + *-ium,* neut. of *-ius* -IOUS] **—in·ter′sticed,** *adj.*

in·ter·sti·tial (in′tər stish′əl), *adj.* **1.** pertaining to, situated in, or forming interstices. **2.** *Anat.* situated between the cellular elements of a structure or part: *interstitial tissue.* **—*n.* 3.** *Crystall.* an imperfection in a crystal caused by the presence of an extra atom in an otherwise complete lattice. Cf. **vacancy** (def. 6). [< L *interstiti(um)* INTERSTICE + -AL[1]] **—in′ter·sti′tial·ly,** *adv.*

in·ter·sti′tial-cell′-stim′u·lat·ing hor′mone (in′tər stish′əl sel′stim′yə lā′ting), *Biochem.* See **ICSH.**

in·ter·strat·i·fy (in′tər strat′ə fī′), *v.,* **-fied, -fy·ing.** **—*v.i.* 1.** to lie in interposed or alternate strata. **—*v.t.* 2.** to interlay with or interpose between other strata. **3.** to arrange in alternate strata. [INTER- + STRATIFY] **—in′ter·strat′i·fi·ca′tion,** *n.*

in·ter·sub·jec·tive (in′tər səb jek′tiv), *adj.* *Philos.* comprehensible to, relating to, or used by a number of persons, as a concept or language. [INTER- + SUBJECTIVE]

in·ter·ter·ri·to·ri·al (in′tər ter′i tôr′ē əl, -tôr′-), *adj.* existing between territories: *interterritorial laws.* [INTER- + TERRITORIAL]

in·ter·tex·ture (in′tər teks′chər), *n.* **1.** the act of interweaving. **2.** the condition of being interwoven. **3.** something formed by interweaving. [INTER- + TEXTURE]

in·ter·tid·al (in′tər tīd′ᵊl), *adj.* of or pertaining to the littoral region that is above the low-water mark and below the high-water mark. [INTER- + TIDAL]

in·ter·trib·al (in′tər trī′bəl), *adj.* occurring between tribes: *intertribal warfare.* [INTER- + TRIBAL]

in·ter·tri·glyph (in′tər trī′glif′), *n.* metope. [INTER- + TRIGLYPH]

in·ter·trop·i·cal (in′tər trop′i kəl), *adj.* situated or occurring between the tropic of Cancer and the tropic of Capricorn. [INTER- + TROPICAL]

in·ter·twine (in′tər twīn′), *v.t., v.i.,* **-twined, -twin·ing.** to twine together. [INTER- + TWINE[1]] **—in′ter·twine′ment,** *n.* **—in′ter·twin′ing·ly,** *adv.*

in·ter·twist (in′tər twist′), *v.t., v.i.* **1.** to twist together. **—*n.* 2.** the act or fact of intertwisting or the condition of being intertwisted. [INTER- + TWIST] **—in′ter·twist′ing·ly,** *adv.*

In·ter·type (in′tər tīp′), *n.* *Trademark.* a typesetting machine similar to the Linotype.

in·ter·ur·ban (in′tər ûr′bən), *adj.* **1.** located in, of, or pertaining to two or more cities. **—*n.* 2.** a train, bus, etc., or a transportation system operating between cities. [INTER- + URBAN]

in·ter·val (in′tər vəl), *n.* **1.** an intervening period of time: *an interval of 50 years.* **2.** a period of cessation; pause: *intervals between the volleys of gunfire.* **3.** a space between things, points, limits, etc.; interspace: *an interval of ten feet between posts.* **4.** *Brit.* an intermission, as between the acts of a play. **5.** *Math.* **a.** the totality of points on a line between two designated points or endpoints that may or may not be included. **b.** any generalization of this to higher dimensions, as a rectangle with sides parallel to the coordinate axes. **6.** the space between soldiers or units in military formation. **7.** *Music.* the difference in pitch between two tones, as between two tones sounded simultaneously **(harmonic interval)** or between two tones sounded successively **(melodic interval). 8.** *Chiefly New Eng.* intervale. **9.** *Cards.* a period in a game for placing bets. **10. at intervals,** at particular periods of time; now and then: *At intervals, there were formal receptions at the governor's mansion to break the monotony of life on the isolated island.* [ME *intervall(e)* < L *intervall(um)* interval, lit., space between two palisades. See INTER-, WALL] **—in·ter·val·ic** (in′tər val′ik), *adj.*

in·ter·vale (in′tər vāl′), *n.* *Chiefly New Eng.* a low-lying tract of land along a river. [var. of INTERVAL; by folk etymology taken as INTER- + VALE[1]]

in′terval of conver′gence, *Math.* a region associated with a given power series such that the power series converges for all values of the variable inside the region and diverges for all values outside the region. Also called **circle of convergence.**

in·ter·val·om·e·ter (in′tər və lom′i tər), *n.* an automatic device for operating the shutter of a camera at regular intervals, as in making aerial photographs. [INTERVAL + -O- + -METER]

in·ter·vene (in′tər vēn′), *v.i.,* **-vened, -ven·ing. 1.** to come between, as in action; intercede: *to intervene in a dispute.* **2.** to occur or be between two things. **3.** to occur or happen between other events or periods: *Nothing interesting has intervened.* **4.** (of things) to occur incidentally so as to modify or hinder: *We enjoyed the picnic until a thunderstorm intervened.* **5.** to interfere with force or a threat of force: *intervene in the affairs of another country.* **6.** *Law.* to interpose and become a party to a suit pending between other parties. [< L *interven(īre)* (to) come between, equiv. to *inter-* INTER- + *venīre* to come; see CONVENE] **—in′ter·ven′er, in′ter·ve′nor,** *n.*
—Syn. 1. mediate, interpose.

in·ter·ven·ient (in′tər vēn′yənt), *adj.* **1.** intervening, as in place, time, order, or action. **2.** incidental; extraneous. **—*n.* 3.** one who intervenes. [< L *intervenient-* (s. of *interveniēns*) coming between, prp. of *intervenīre.* See INTERVENE, -ENT]

in·ter·ven·tion (in′tər ven′shən), *n.* **1.** the act or fact of intervening. **2.** interposition or interference of one state in the affairs of another: *intervention in the domestic policies of smaller nations.* [ME < LL *interventiōn-* (s. of *interventiō*) a coming between. See INTERVENE, -TION] **—in′ter·ven′tion·al,** *adj.*

in·ter·ven·tion·ist (in′tər ven′shə nist), *n.* **1.** a person who favors intervention, as in the affairs of another state. **—*adj.* 2.** of or pertaining to intervention. [INTERVENTION + -IST] **—in′ter·ven′tion·ism,** *n.*

in·ter·ver·te·bral (in′tər vûr′tə brəl), *adj.* *Anat.* situated between the vertebrae. [INTER- + VERTEBRAL] **—in′ter·ver′te·bral·ly,** *adv.*

in′terver′tebral disk′, *Anat.* the plate of fibrocartilage between the bodies of adjacent vertebrae.

in·ter·view (in′tər vyo͞o′), *n.* **1.** a conversation or meeting in which a writer or reporter asks questions of a person or persons from whom material is sought for a newspaper story, television broadcast, etc. **2.** the report of such a conversation or meeting. **3.** a formal meeting in which a person or persons question, consult, or evaluate another or others: *to arrange a job interview.* **—*v.t.* 4.** to have an interview with in order to question, consult, evaluate, or seek information from: *to interview the president.* [INTER- + VIEW; r. *enterview* < MF *entrevue,* n. use of fem. of *entrevu,* ptp. of *entrevoir* to glimpse] **—in′ter·view′a·ble,** *adj.*

in·ter·view·ee (in′tər vyo͞o ē′, in′tər vyo͞o ē′), *n.* a person who is interviewed. [INTERVIEW + -EE]

in·ter·view·er (in′tər vyo͞o′ər), *n.* **1.** a person who interviews. **2.** a peephole in an entrance door. [INTERVIEW + -ER[1]]

in·ter vi·vos (in′tər vī′vōs), *Law.* (esp. of a gift or trust) taking effect during the lifetimes of the parties involved. [< L: lit., among (the) living]

in·ter·vo·cal·ic (in′tər vō kal′ik), *adj.* *Phonet.* (usually of a consonant) immediately following a vowel and preceding a vowel, as the *v* in *cover.* [INTER- + VOCALIC] **—in′ter·vo·cal′i·cal·ly,** *adv.*

in·ter·volve (in′tər volv′), *v.t., v.i.,* **-volved, -volv·ing.** to roll, wind, or involve, one within another. [< L *inter-* INTER- + *volve(re)* (to) roll; see REVOLVE] **—in·ter·vo·lu·tion** (in′tər və lo͞o′shən), *n.*

in·ter·weave (*v.* in′tər wēv′; *n.* in′tər wēv′), *v.,* **-wove** or **-weaved; -wo·ven** or **-wove** or **-weaved; -weav·ing;** *n.* **—*v.t.* 1.** to weave together, one with another, as threads, strands, branches, roots, etc. **2.** to intermingle or combine as if by weaving: *to interweave truth with fiction.* **—*v.i.* 3.** to become woven together, interlaced, or intermingled. **—*n.* 4.** the act of interweaving or fact of being interwoven; blend: *a perfect interweave of Spanish and American cultures.* [INTER- + WEAVE] **—in′ter·weave′ment,** *n.* **—in′ter·weav′er,** *n.* **—in′ter·weav′ing·ly,** *adv.*

in·ter·wind (in′tər wīnd′), *v.t., v.i.,* **-wound** or (*Rare*) **-wind·ed; -wind·ing.** to wind together; intertwine. [INTER- + WIND[2]]

in·ter·work (in′tər wûrk′), *v.,* **-worked** or **-wrought, -work·ing.** **—*v.t.* 1.** to work or weave together; interweave. **—*v.i.* 2.** to act upon each other; interact. [INTER- + WORK]

in′ter·sale′, *n.*
in′ter·sa·lute′, *v.i.,* **-lut·ed, -lut·ing.**
in′ter·scene′, *n.*
in′ter·school′, *n.*
in′ter·sci′ence, *adj.*
in′ter·scribe′, *v.t.,* **-scribed, -scrib·ing.**
in′ter·sea′board′, *adj.*
in′ter·seg·men′tal, *adj.*
in′ter·sem′i·nal, *adj.*
in′ter·sem′i·nate′, *v.t.,* **-nat·ed, -nat·ing.**
in′ter·sen′ti·men′tal, *adj.*
in′ter·ses′a·moid′, *adj.*
in′ter·set′, *v.t.,* **-set, -set·ting.**
in′ter·shade′, *v.t.,* **-shad·ed, -shad·ing.**
in′ter·shift′ing, *adj.*
in′ter·shock′, *v.*
in′ter·shoot′, *v.,* **-shot, -shoot·ing.**
in′ter·shop′, *adj.*
in′ter·sit′u·ate′, *v.t.,* **-at·ed, -at·ing.**
in′ter·so′cial, *adj.*
in′ter·so·ci′e·tal, *adj.*
in′ter·so·ci′e·ty, *adj.*
in′ter·soil′, *v.t.*
in′ter·sole′, *v.t.,* **-soled, -sol·ing.**
in′ter·sol′u·bil′i·ty, *n.*
in′ter·sol′u·ble, *adj.*
in′ter·so′nant, *adj.*
in′ter·spe′cial, *adj.*
in′ter·spher′al, *adj.*
in′ter·spic′u·lar, *adj.*
in′ter·spi′nal, *adj.*
in′ter·spi′nous, *adj.*
in′ter·spor′al, *adj.*
in′ter·sprin′kle, *v.t.,* **-kled, -kling.**
in′ter·squeeze′, *v.t.,* **-squeezed, -squeez·ing.**
in′ter·stam′i·nal, *adj.*
in′ter·sta′tion, *adj.*
in′ter·stim′u·late′, *v.t.,* **-lat·ed, -lat·ing.**
in′ter·stim′u·la′tion, *n.*
in′ter·streak′, *v.t.*
in′ter·stream′, *adj.*
in′ter·street′, *adj.*
in′ter·stri′al, *adj.*
in′ter·stri·a′tion, *n.*
in′ter·strive′, *v.i.,* **-strove, -striv·en, -striv·ing.**
in′ter·struc′ture, *n.*
in′ter·sub·sist′ence, *n.*
in′ter·sub′sti·tu′tion, *n.*
in′ter·sys′tem, *adj.*
in′ter·sys′te·mat′ic, *adj.*
in′ter·sys′tem·at′i·cal, *adj.;* **-ly,** *adv.*
in′ter·talk′, *v.i*
in′ter·tan′gle, *v.t.,* **-gled, -gling.**
in′ter·tar′sal, *adj.*
in′ter·team′, *adj.*
in′ter·ten·tac′u·lar, *adj.*
in′ter·ter′gal, *adj.*
in′ter·ter′mi·nal, *adj.*
in′ter·thread′ed, *adj.*
in′ter·throng′ing, *adj.*
in′ter·ti′dal, *adj.*
in′ter·tinge′, *v.t.,* **-tinged, -ting·ing.**
in′ter·tis′sued, *adj.*
in′ter·touch′, *v.i.*
in′ter·town′, *adj.*
in′ter·tra·bec′u·lar, *adj.*
in′ter·trace′, *v.t.,* **-traced, -trac·ing.**
in′ter·trade′, *n., v.,* **-trad·ed, -trad·ing.**
in′ter·traf′fic, *n., v.,* **-ficked, -fick·ing.**
in′ter·trans·form′a·bil′i·ty, *n.*
in′ter·trans·form′a·ble, *adj.*
in′ter·trans·ver′sal, *adj.*
in′ter·tu′ber·al, *adj.*
in′ter·tu·ber′cu·lar, *adj.*
in′ter·tu′bu·lar, *adj.*
in′ter·un′gu·lar, *adj.*
in′ter·un′gu·late, *adj.*
in′ter·un′ion, *n., adj.*
in′ter·u′ni·ver′si·ty, *adj.*
in′ter·vag′i·nal, *adj.*
in′ter·val′ley, *n.*
in′ter·val′vu·lar, *adj.*
in′ter·va′ri·a′tion, *n.*
in′ter·va·ri′e·tal, *adj.*
in′ter·var′si·ty, *adj.*
in′ter·var′y, *v.i.,* **-var·ied, -var·y·ing.**
in′ter·vas′cu·lar, *adj.*
in′ter·vein′, *v.t.*
in′ter·vein′al, *adj.*
in′ter·vein′ous, *adj.*
in′ter·ven′tral, *adj.*
in′ter·ven·tric′u·lar, *adj.*
in′ter·ven′u·lar, *adj.*
in′ter·ver′bal, *adj.*
in′ter·ve·sic′u·lar, *adj.*
in′ter·vil′lous, *adj.*
in′ter·vis′it, *v.i.*
in′ter·vis′it·a′tion, *n.*
in′ter·vo·lute′, *adj.*
in′ter·war′, *v.i.,* **-warred, -war·ring.**
in′ter·wed′, *v.i.,* **-wed** or **-wed·ded, -wed·ding.**
in′ter·weld′, *v.t.*
in′ter·whiff′, *v.t.*
in′ter·whis′tle, *v.t.,* **-tled, -tling.**
in′ter·wish′, *v.t., n.*
in′ter·word′, *adj.*
in′ter·world′, *n.*
in′ter·wound′, *v.*
in′ter·wrap′, *v.t., v.i.,* **-wrapped, -wrap·ping.**
in′ter·wreathe′, *v.,* **-wreathed, -wreath·ing.**
in′ter·wrought′, *adj.*
in′ter·xy′la·ry, *adj.*
in′ter·zon′al, *adj.*
in′ter·zo·oe′cial, *adj.*

CONCISE PRONUNCIATION KEY: *act, āble, dâre, ärt; ebb, ēqual; if, īce; hot, ōver, ôrder, oil, bo͝ok, o͞oze, out; up, ûrge; chief; sing; shoe; thin, that;* zh as in *measure.* ə = *a* as in *alone, e* as in *system, i* as in *easily, o* as in *gallop, u* as in *circus;* ᵊ as in *button* (but′ᵊn), *fire* (fīᵊr), *cradle* (krād′ᵊl). See the full key inside the front cover.

in·tes·ta·ble (in tes′tə bəl), *adj. Law.* not legally qualified to make a will, as an infant or a lunatic. [< L *intestābil(is)* disqualified from bearing witness, hence, dishonored, equiv. to *in-* IN-[3] + *testā(rī)* (to) bear witness + *-bilis* -BLE; see TESTIFY]

in·tes·ta·cy (in tes′tə sē), *n.* the state or fact of being intestate at death. [INTESTA(TE) + -CY]

in·tes·tate (in tes′tāt, -tit), *adj.* **1.** (of a person) not having made a will: *He died intestate.* **2.** (of things) not disposed of by will: *His property remains intestate.* —*n.* **3.** one who dies intestate. [ME < L *intestāt(us)*, equiv. to *in-* IN-[3] + *testātus* TESTATE]

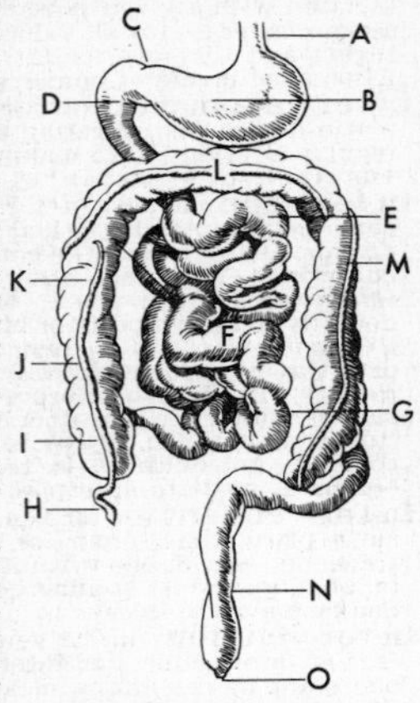

in·tes·ti·nal (in tes′tə nəl; *Brit.* in′tes tīn′əl), *adj.* **1.** of, pertaining to, or resembling the intestines. **2.** occurring, affecting, or found in the intestines. [< ML *intestīnāl(is)*. See INTESTINE, -AL[1]] —**in·tes′ti·nal·ly**, *adv.*

intes′tinal for′titude, courage; resoluteness; endurance; guts: *A job like that calls for a man with intestinal fortitude.*

in·tes·tine (in tes′tin), *n.* **1.** Usually, **intestines.** the lower part of the alimentary canal, extending from the pylorus to the anus. **2.** Also called **small intestine.** the narrow, longer part of the intestines, comprising the duodenum, jejunum, and ileum, that serves to digest and absorb nutrients. **3.** Also called **large intestine.** the broad, shorter part of the intestines, comprising the cecum, colon, and rectum, that absorbs water from and eliminates the residues of digestion. —*adj.* **4.** internal; domestic; civil: *intestine strife.* [< L *intestīn(um)*, n. use of neut. of *intestīnus* internal, equiv. to *intes-* (var. of *intus* inside) + *-tīnus* adj. suffix; see VESPERTINE]

Intestines (Human)
A, End of esophagus; B, Stomach; C, Pylorus; D, Duodenum; E, Jejunum; F, Small intestine; G, Ileum; H, Vermiform appendix; I, Cecum; J, Large intestine; K, Ascending colon; L, Transverse colon; M, Descending colon; N, Rectum; O, Anus

in·thral (in thrôl′), *v.t.*, **-thralled, -thral·ling.** enthrall. —**in·thral′ment**, *n.*

in·thrall (in thrôl′), *v.t.* enthrall. —**in·thrall′ment**, *n.*

in·throne (in thrōn′), *v.t.*, **-throned, -thron·ing.** enthrone.

in·ti·ma (in′tə mə), *n., pl.* **-mae** (-mē′). *Anat.* the innermost membrane or lining of some organ or part, esp. that of an artery, vein, or lymphatic. [< NL, n. use of fem. of L *intimus*, var. of *intumus* inmost, equiv. to *intu(s)* within + *-mus* superl. suffix] —**in′ti·mal**, *adj.*

in·ti·ma·cy (in′tə mə sē), *n., pl.* **-cies.** **1.** the state of being intimate. **2.** a close, familiar, and usually affectionate or loving, personal relationship with another person or group. **3.** a close association with or detailed knowledge or deep understanding of a place, subject, period of history, etc.: *His intimacy with Japan makes him a likely choice as ambassador to that country.* **4.** an act or expression serving as a token of familiarity, affection, or the like: *The teacher allowed his pupils the intimacy of calling him by his first name.* **5.** a quality or expression of familiarity, affection, love, or passion: *She didn't like the intimacy of his wink.* **6.** a sexually familiar act; a sexual liberty: *She let him hold her hand, but forbade him any intimacies.* **7.** the quality of affecting someone in a comfortably friendly or personally pleasing way: *The intimacy of the room was enhanced by its warm colors.* **8.** privacy, esp. an atmosphere of privacy suitable to the telling of a secret: *He refused to tell it to me except in the intimacy of his room.* [INTIMA(TE)[1] + -CY]

in·ti·mate[1] (in′tə mit), *adj.* **1.** associated in close personal relations: *an intimate friend.* **2.** characterized by or involving warm friendship or a personally close or familiar association or feeling: *an intimate handshake; an intimate gathering.* **3.** private; closely personal: *one's intimate affairs.* **4.** characterized by or suggesting privacy or intimacy; cozy: *an intimate little café.* **5.** engaged in or characterized by sexual relations. **6.** (of an association, knowledge, understanding, etc.) arising from close personal connection or familiar experience. **7.** detailed; deep: *a more intimate analysis.* **8.** showing a close union or combination of particles or elements: *an intimate mixture.* **9.** inmost; deep within. **10.** of, pertaining to, or characteristic of the inmost or essential nature; intrinsic: *the intimate structure of an organism.* **11.** of, pertaining to, or existing in the inmost depths of the mind: *intimate beliefs.* —*n.* **12.** an intimate friend or associate, esp. a confidant. [< L *intim(us)* a close friend (n. use of adj.; see INTIMA) + -ATE[1]] —**in′ti·mate·ly**, *adv.* —**in′ti·mate·ness**, *n.*
—**Syn. 1.** dear. See **familiar. 3.** privy, secret. **7.** exacting, thorough. **12.** crony.

in·ti·mate[2] (in′tə māt′), *v.t.*, **-mat·ed, -mat·ing.** **1.** to make known indirectly; hint; suggest. **2.** *Archaic.* to make known, esp. formally; announce. [< LL *intimāt(us)* made known (ptp. of *intimāre*), equiv. to *intim(us)* inmost (see INTIMA) + *-ātus* -ATE[1]] —**in′ti·mat′er**, *n.* —**in′ti·ma′tion**, *n.*
—**Syn. 1.** See **hint.**

in′timate bor′rowing, *Ling.* the borrowing of linguistic forms by one language from another when both occupy a single geographical or cultural community.

Intima′tions of Immortal′ity, (*Ode: Intimations of Immortality from Recollections of Early Childhood*) a poem (1807) by Wordsworth.

in·time (aN tēm′), *adj. French.* intimate; cozy: intime conversation; *an intime little restaurant.*

in·tim·i·date (in tim′i dāt′), *v.t.*, **-dat·ed, -dat·ing.** **1.** to make timid; inspire with fear. **2.** overawe or cow, esp. with a forceful personality or superior display of fluency, fame, wealth, etc. **3.** to force into or deter from some action by inducing fear: *to intimidate a voter into staying away from the polls.* [< ML *intimidāt(us)* made afraid (ptp. of *intimidāre*), equiv. to L *in-* IN-[2] + *timid(us)* timid, afraid + *-ātus* -ATE[1]] —**in·tim′i·da′tion**, *n.* —**in·tim′i·da′tor**, *n.* —**in·tim·i·da·to·ry** (in tim′i də tôr′ē, -tōr′ē *or, esp. Brit.*, -tim′i dā′tə rē), *adj.*
—**Syn. 1.** frighten, subdue, daunt, terrify. —**Ant. 1.** calm. **3.** encourage.

In·ti·mism (in′tə miz′əm), *n.* **1.** (*sometimes l.c.*) the style, quality, or character of the early paintings of Bonnard and Vuillard as distinguished from the works of the Nabis. **2.** (*l.c.*) a manner of painting in which domestic scenes are portrayed impressionistically. [INTIM(IST) + -ISM]

in·ti·mist (in′tə mist), *adj.* **1.** of or pertaining to the recording of intimate personal and psychological experiences as a basis for art, literature, etc.: *an example of the intimist novel.* —*n.* **2.** an intimist painter, writer, etc. [< F *intimiste*, equiv. to *intime* INTIMATE[1] + *-iste* -IST]

in·ti·miste (aN tē mēst′), *adj. French.* intimist.

in·tinc·tion (in tingk′shən), *n.* (in a communion service) the act of steeping the bread or wafer in the wine in order to enable the communicant to receive the two elements conjointly. [< LL *intinctiōn-* (s. of *intinctiō*) a dipping in, equiv. to *intinct(us)* (see IN-[2], TINT[1]) + *-iōn-* -ION]

in·tine (in′tēn, -tīn), *n. Bot.* the inner coat of a spore, esp. a pollen grain. [<< L *int(us)* within + -INE[2]]

in·ti·tle (in tīt′əl), *v.t.*, **-tled, -tling.** entitle.

in·tit·ule (in tit′yo͞ol), *v.t.*, **-uled, -ul·ing.** *Archaic.* to give a title to; entitle. [< LL *intitul(āre)*, equiv. to L *in-* IN-[2] *titul(us)* TITLE; r. late ME *entitule* < MF *entitul(er)*] —**in·tit′u·la′tion**, *n.*

in·to (in′to͞o; *unstressed* in′to͝o, -tə), *prep.* **1.** to the inside of; in toward: *He walked into the room. The train chugged into the station.* **2.** toward or in the direction of: *going into town; veered into the wind.* **3.** to a point of contact with; against: *backed into a parked car.* **4.** (used to indicate insertion or immersion in): *plugged into the socket.* **5.** (used to indicate entry, inclusion, or introduction in a place or condition): *received into the church; voted into membership.* **6.** to the state, condition, or form assumed or brought about: *went into shock; lapsed into disrepair; translated into another language.* **7.** to the occupation, action, possession, circumstance, or acceptance of: *went into banking; coerced into complying.* **8.** (used to indicate a continuing extent in time or space): *lasted into the night; a line of men far into the distance.* **9.** (used to indicate the number to be divided by another number): *2 into 20 equals 10.* —*adj.* **10.** *Math.* pertaining to a function or map from one set to another set, the range of which is a proper subset of the second set, as the function *f*, from the set of all integers into the set of all perfect squares where $f(x) = x^2$ for every integer. [ME, OE; see IN, TO]

in·toed (in′tōd′), *adj.* having inwardly turned toes. [IN-[1] + TOED]

in·tol·er·a·ble (in tol′ər ə bəl), *adj.* **1.** not tolerable; unendurable; insufferable: *intolerable agony.* **2.** excessive. [ME < L *intolerābil(is)*. See IN-[3], TOLERABLE] —**in·tol′er·a·bil′i·ty, in·tol′er·a·ble·ness**, *n.* —**in·tol′er·a·bly**, *adv.*
—**Syn. 1.** unbearable, insupportable. —**Ant. 1.** endurable.

in·tol·er·ance (in tol′ər əns), *n.* **1.** lack of toleration; indisposition to tolerate contrary opinions or beliefs, persons of different races or backgrounds, etc. **2.** incapacity or indisposition to bear or endure: *intolerance of heat.* **3.** sensitivity or an allergy to a food, drug, etc. **4.** an intolerant act. [< L *intolerantia*. See INTOLERANT, -ANCE]

in·tol·er·ant (in tol′ər ənt), *adj.* **1.** not tolerating beliefs, opinions, usages, manners, etc., different from one's own, as in political or religious matters; bigoted. **2.** unable or indisposed to tolerate or endure (usually fol. by *of*): *intolerant of excesses.* —*n.* **3.** an intolerant person; bigot. [< L *intolerant-* (s. of *intolerāns*) impatient. See IN-[3], TOLERANT] —**in·tol′er·ant·ly**, *adv.*
—**Syn. 1.** illiberal, narrow, proscriptive, prejudiced, biased, dictatorial, totalitarian. INTOLERANT, FANATICAL, BIGOTED refer to strongly illiberal attitudes. INTOLERANT refers to an active refusal to allow others to have or put into practice beliefs different from one's own: *intolerant in politics; intolerant of other customs.* BIGOTED is to be so emotionally or subjectively attached to one's own belief as to be unthinkingly hostile to all others: *a bigoted person.* FANATICAL applies to unreasonable or extreme action in maintaining one's beliefs and practices without necessary reference to others: *a fanatical religious sect.*
—**Ant. 1.** liberal.

in·tomb (in to͞om′), *v.t.* entomb. —**in·tomb′ment**, *n.*

in·to·na·co (in ton′ə kō′, -tō′nə-; *It.* in tô′nä kô), *n., pl.* **-cos,** *It.* **-ci** (-chē). (formerly in fresco painting) the last and finest coat of plaster, usually applied in sections and painted while still damp with colors ground in water or a lime-water mixture. Cf. **arriccio, trullisatio.** [< It, equiv. to *intonac(are)* (to) coat (*in-* IN-[2] + VL **tunicāre*, back formation from L *tunicātus* wearing a tunic) + *-o* n. suffix]

in·to·nate (in′tō nāt′, -tə-), *v.t.*, **-nat·ed, -nat·ing.** **1.** to utter with a particular tone or modulation of voice. **2.** to intone; chant. [< ML *intonāt(us)* intoned, ptp. of *intonāre*. See IN-[2] TONE, -ATE[1]]

in·to·na·tion (in′tō nā′shən, -tə-), *n.* **1.** the pattern or melody of pitch changes in connected speech, esp. the pitch pattern of a sentence, which distinguishes kinds of sentences or speakers of different language cultures. **2.** the act or manner of intonating. **3.** the manner of producing musical tones, specifically the relation in pitch of tones to their key or harmony. **4.** that which is intoned or chanted. **5.** the opening phrase in a Gregorian chant, usually sung by one or two voices. [< ML *intonātiōn-* (s. of *intonātiō*). See INTONATE, -ION] —**in′to·na′tion·al**, *adj.*

in·tone (in tōn′), *v.*, **-toned, -ton·ing.** —*v.t.* **1.** to utter with a particular tone or voice modulation. **2.** to give tone or variety of tone to; vocalize. **3.** to utter in a singing voice (the first tones of a section in a liturgical service). **4.** to recite or chant in monotone. —*v.i.* **5.** to speak or recite in a singing voice, esp. in monotone; chant. **6.** *Music.* to produce a tone, or a particular series of tones, like a scale, esp. with the voice. [< ML *inton(āre)*; r. late ME *entone* < MF *enton(er)*] —**in·ton′er**, *n.*

in·tor·sion (in tôr′shən), *n.* a twisting or winding about an axis or fixed point, as of the stem of a plant. [< LL *intorsiōn-* (s. of *intorsiō*). See IN-[2], TORSION]

in·tort (in tôrt′), *v.t.* to twist inward about an axis or fixed point; curl; wind: *intorted horns.* [< L *intort(us)* turned or twisted in, var. ptp. of *intorquēre*. See IN-[2], TORT]

in·tor·tus (in tôr′təs), *adj. Meteorol.* (of a cloud) having very irregular filaments that often look entangled. [< L: INTORT]

in to·to (in tō′tō), *Latin.* in all; in the whole; wholly.

in·town (in′toun′, in toun′), *adj.* being in the central or metropolitan area of a city: *an intown motel.* [IN + TOWN]

in·tox·i·cant (in tok′sə kənt), *adj.* **1.** intoxicating or exhilarating: *a highly intoxicant drink; the clear, intoxicant air of the mountains.* —*n.* **2.** an intoxicating agent, as liquor or certain drugs. [< ML *intoxicant-* (s. of *intoxicāns*) poisoning, prp. of *intoxicāre*. See IN-[2], TOXICANT]

in·tox·i·cate (*v.* in tok′sə kāt′; *adj.* in tok′sə kit, -kāt′), *v.*, **-cat·ed, -cat·ing,** *adj.* —*v.t.* **1.** to affect temporarily with diminished control over the physical and mental powers, by means of alcoholic liquor, a drug, or other substance, esp. to stupefy or excite with liquor. **2.** to make enthusiastic; elate strongly, as by intoxicants; exhilarate: *The prospect of success intoxicates me.* **3.** *Pathol.* to poison. —*v.i.* **4.** to cause or produce intoxication: *having the power to intoxicate.* —*adj.* **5.** *Archaic.* intoxicated. [< ML *intoxicāt(us)* poisoned, ptp. of *intoxicāre*. See IN-[2], TOXIC, -ATE[1]] —**in·tox·i·ca·ble** (in tok′sə kə bəl), *adj.* —**in·tox′i·ca′tor**, *n.*

in·tox·i·cat·ed (in tok′sə kā′tid), *adj.* **1.** drunk; inebriated. **2.** mentally or emotionally exhilarated. [INTOXICATE + -ED[2]] —**in·tox′i·cat′ed·ly**, *adv.*

in·tox·i·cat·ing (in tok′sə kā′ting), *adj.* **1.** causing or capable of causing intoxication: *intoxicating beverages.* **2.** (of alcoholic beverages) being distilled rather than fermented. **3.** exhilarating: *an intoxicating idea.* [INTOXICATE + -ING[2]] —**in·tox′i·cat′ing·ly**, *adv.*

in·tox·i·ca·tion (in tok′sə kā′shən), *n.* **1.** inebriation; drunkenness. **2.** the act or an instance of intoxicating. **3.** overpowering excitement of the mind or emotions. **4.** *Pathol.* poisoning. [< ML *intoxicātiōn-* (s. of *intoxicātiō*) a poisoning. See INTOXICATE, -ION]

in·tox·i·ca·tive (in tok′sə kā′tiv), *adj. Archaic.* **1.** of or pertaining to intoxicants or intoxication. **2.** intoxicating. [INTOXICATE + -IVE] —**in·tox′i·ca′tive·ly**, *adv.*

intr., **1.** intransitive. **2.** introduce. **3.** introduced. **4.** introducing. **5.** introduction. **6.** introductory.

intra-, a learned borrowing from Latin meaning "within," used in the formation of compound words: *intramural.* Cf. **intro-.** [< LL, repr. L *intrā* (adv. and prep.); akin to INTERIOR, INTER-]

in·tra·ab·dom·i·nal (in′trə ab dom′ə nəl), *adj. Anat.* **1.** being within the abdomen. **2.** going into the abdomen, as an injection. —**in′tra·ab·dom′i·nal·ly**, *adv.*

in·tra·a·tom·ic (in′trə ə tom′ik), *adj.* within an atom or atoms.

in·tra·car·di·ac (in′trə kär′dē ak′), *adj.* endocardial. [INTRA- + CARDIAC]

in·tra·cel·lu·lar (in′trə sel′yə lər), *adj.* within a cell or cells. [INTRA- + CELLULAR] —**in′tra·cel′lu·lar·ly**, *adv.*

In′tra·coast′al Wa′terway (in′trə kō′stəl, in′-), a mostly inland water route, partly natural and partly artificial, extending 1550 mi. along the Atlantic coast from Boston to Florida Bay **(Atlantic Intracoastal Waterway)** and 1116 mi. along the Gulf coast from Carrabelle, Florida to Brownsville, Texas **(Gulf Intracoastal Waterway)**: constructed to protect small commercial and pleasure craft from the hazards of the open sea.

in·tra·cra·ni·al (in′trə krā′nē əl), *adj.* being within the cranium or skull. [INTRA- + CRANIAL]

in·trac·ta·ble (in trak′tə bəl), *adj.* **1.** not docile; stubborn; obstinate: *an intractable disposition.* **2.** (of things) hard to shape or work with; unmanageable. **3.** resisting treatment or cure: *an intractable malady.* —*n.* **4.** an intractable person. [< L *intractābil(is)*. See IN-[3], TRACTABLE] —**in·trac′ta·bil′i·ty, in·trac′ta·ble·ness**, *n.* —**in·trac′ta·bly**, *adv.*
—**Syn. 1.** perverse, headstrong, dogged, obdurate, stony, willful, froward. **1, 2.** fractious, refractory, unbending, inflexible, adamant, unyielding. —**Ant. 1.** amiable. **1, 2.** amenable, flexible.

in·tra·cu·ta·ne·ous (in′trə kyo͞o tā′nē əs), *adj. Anat.* intradermal. [INTRA- + CUTANEOUS] —**in′tra·cu·ta′ne·ous·ly**, *adv.*

in·tra·der·mal (in′trə dûr′məl), *adj. Anat.* **1.** being within the skin. **2.** going between the layers of the skin, as an injection. Also, **in′tra·der′mic.** [INTRA- + DERM(A)[1] + -AL[1]] —**in′tra·der′mal·ly, in′tra·der′mi·cal·ly**, *adv.*

in·tra·dos (in′trə dos′, -dōs′, in trā′dos, -dōs), *n., pl.* **-dos** (-dōz′, -dōz), **-dos·es.** *Archit.* the interior curve or surface of an arch or vault. Cf. **extrados.** [< F, equiv. to *infra-* INFRA- + *dos* back; see DOSSER]

in·tra·mar·gin·al (in′trə mär′jə nəl), *adj.* existing or occurring within a margin or limit. [INTRA- + MARGINAL]

in·tra·mo·lec·u·lar (in′trə mə lek′yə lər, -mō-), *adj.* existing or occurring within the molecule or molecules. [INTRA- + MOLECULAR]

in·tra·mun·dane (in′trə mun′dān, -mun dān′), *adj.* existing or occurring within the material world. [INTRA- + MUNDANE]

in·tra·mu·ral (in′trə myo͝or′əl), *adj.* **1.** involving representatives of a single school: *intramural athletics.* **2.** within the walls, boundaries, or enclosing units, as of a city, institution, building, etc. Cf. **extramural. 3.** *Anat.* being within the substance of a wall, as of an organ. [INTRA- + MURAL]

in·tra mu·ros (in′trä mo͞o′rōs; *Eng.* in′trə myo͝or′ōs), *Latin.* within the walls, as of a city.

in·tra·mus·cu·lar (in′trə mus′kyə lər), *adj.* located or occurring within a muscle. [INTRA- + MUSCULAR] —**in′tra·mus′cu·lar·ly**, *adv.*

in trans., in transit; en route. [< L *in transitū*]

intrans., intransitive.

in·tran·si·gent (in tran′si jənt), *adj.* **1.** uncompromising; inflexible; adamant; unyielding; irreconcilable. —*n.* **2.** one who is adamant or inflexible, as in politics. Also, **in·tran′si·geant.** [< Sp *intransigent(e)*, equiv. to in- IN-^{3} + *transigente* compromising (prp. of *transigir*) < L *transigent-* (s. of *transigēns*, prp. of *transigere* to come to an agreement); see TRANSACT] —**in·tran′si·gence, in·tran′si·gen·cy, in·tran′si·geance, in·tran′si·gean·cy,** *n.* —**in·tran′si·gent·ly, in·tran′si·geant·ly,** *adv.*

in·tran·si·tive (in tran′si tiv), *adj.* **1.** noting or having the quality of an intransitive verb. —*n.* **2.** See **intransitive verb.** [< L *intransitīv(us).* See IN-^{3}, TRANSITIVE] —**in·tran′si·tive·ly,** *adv.* —**in·tran′si·tive·ness,** *n.*

intran′sitive verb′, a verb that indicates a complete action without being accompanied by a direct object, as *sit, lie,* etc., and, in English, that does not form a passive.

in tran·si·tu (in trän′si to͞o′; *Eng.* in tran′si to͞o′, -tyo͞o′), *Latin.* in transit; on the way.

in·trant (in′trənt), *n.* *Archaic.* one who enters (a college, association, etc.); entrant. [< L *intrant-* (s. of *intrāns*) entering, prp. of *intrāre* to ENTER]

in·tra·nu·cle·ar (in′trə no͞o′klē ər, -nyo͞o′-), *adj.* existing or taking place within a nucleus. [INTRA- + NUCLEAR]

in·tra·psy·chic (in′trə sī′kik), *adj.* *Psychol.* from or within the mind or self: *intrapsychic conflict.* [INTRA- + PSYCHIC] —**in′tra·psy′chi·cal·ly,** *adv.*

in·tra·spi·nal (in′trə spīn′əl), *adj.* *Anat.* **1.** being within the spine. **2.** going into the spinal canal, as an injection. [INTRA- + SPINAL] —**in′tra·spi′nal·ly,** *adv.*

in·tra·state (in′trə stāt′), *adj.* existing or occurring within a state, esp. one of the United States: *intrastate commerce.* Cf. **interstate.** [INTRA- + STATE]

in·tra·tel·lu·ric (in′trə tə lo͝or′ik), *adj.* **1.** *Geol.* located in, taking place in, or resulting from action beneath the lithosphere. **2.** *Petrog.* noting or pertaining to crystallization of an eruptive rock previous to its extrusion on the surface. [INTRA- + TELLURIC^1]

in·tra·u·ter·ine (in′trə yo͞o′tər in, -tə rīn′), *adj.* located or occurring within the uterus. [INTRA- + UTERINE]

intrau′terine device′. See **IUD.**

in·trav·a·sa·tion (in trav′ə sā′shən), *n.* *Pathol.* the entrance of foreign matter into a blood vessel of the body. [INTRA- + (EXTRA)VASATION]

in·tra·vas·cu·lar (in′trə vas′kyə lər), *adj.* within the blood vessels. [INTRA- + VASCULAR]

in·tra·ve·nous (in′trə vē′nəs), *adj.* **1.** within a vein or the veins. **2.** of, pertaining to, employed in, or administered by an injection into the vein: *intravenous needle; intravenous solution; intravenous feeding.* [INTRA- + VENOUS] —**in·tra·ve′nous·ly,** *adv.*

in′trave′nous drip′, *Med.* drip (def. 12).

in·tra vi·res (in′trə vī′rēz), *Law.* within the legal power or authority of an individual or corporation (opposed to *ultra vires*). [< L: within the powers]

in·tra·vi·tal (in′trə vīt′əl), *adj.* *Biol.* occurring during life. [INTRA- + VITAL]

in·tra vi·tam (in′trə vī′tam), *Biol.* during life: *the staining of tissues intra vitam.* [< L]

in·treat (in trēt′), *v.t., v.i.* *Archaic.* entreat.

in·trench (in trench′), *v.t., v.i.* entrench. —**in·trench′er,** *n.* —**in·trench′ment,** *n.*

intrench′ing tool′, a small, collapsible spade used by a soldier in the field for digging foxholes and the like. Also, **entrenching tool.**

in·trep·id (in trep′id), *adj.* fearless; dauntless: *an intrepid explorer.* [< L *intrepid(us),* equiv. to *in-* IN-^{3} + *trepidus* anxious; see TREPIDATION] —**in′tre·pid′i·ty, in·trep′id·ness,** *n.* —**in·trep′id·ly,** *adv.*
—**Syn.** brave, courageous, bold. —**Ant.** timid.

Int. Rev., Internal Revenue.

in·tri·ca·cy (in′trə kə sē), *n., pl.* **-cies.** **1.** intricate character or state. **2.** an intricate part, action, etc. [INTRICA(TE) + -CY]

in·tri·cate (in′trə kit), *adj.* **1.** entangled or involved; having many interrelated parts or facets: *an intricate maze of paths amid the shrubbery.* **2.** complex; complicated; hard to understand: *an intricate machine.* [< L *intrīcāt(us)* entangled (ptp. of *intrīcāre*), equiv. to *in-* IN-^{2} + *trīc(ae)* perplexities + *-ātus* -ATE^1] —**in′tri·cate·ly,** *adv.* —**in′tri·cate·ness,** *n.*
—**Syn. 1.** knotty, tangled, labyrinthine.

in·tri·gant (in′trə gənt; *Fr.* AN trē gäN′), *n., pl.* **-gants** (-gənts; *Fr.* -gäN′). a person who engages in intrigue or intrigues. Also, **in′tri·guant.** [< F < It *intrigante,* prp. of *intrigare* to INTRIGUE]

in·tri·gante (in′trə gant′, -gänt′; *Fr.* AN trē gäNt′), *n., pl.* **-gantes** (-gants′, -gänts′; *Fr.* -gäNt′). a female intrigant. Also, **in′tri·guante′.** [< F; fem. of INTRIGANT]

in·trigue (*v.* in trēg′; *n.* in trēg′, in′trēg), *v.,* **-trigued, -tri·guing,** *n.* —*v.t.* **1.** to arouse the curiosity or interest of by unusual, unique, new, or otherwise fascinating qualities. **2.** to interest or appeal to: *The simplicity of your plan intrigues me, but I wonder if it would work.* **3.** to beguile by appeal to the curiosity, fancy, or interest (usually fol. by *into*): *to intrigue one's way into another's notice.* **4.** to puzzle; cause to ponder: *I am intrigued by this event.* **5.** to accomplish or force by crafty plotting or underhand machinations. **6.** *Obs.* to entangle. **7.** *Obs.* to trick or cheat. **8.** *Obs.* to plot for. —*v.i.* **9.** to plot craftily or use underhand machinations. **10.** to carry on a clandestine or illicit love affair. —*n.* **11.** the use of underhand machinations or deceitful stratagems. **12.** such a machination or stratagem or a series of them; a plot or crafty dealing: *political intrigues.* **13.** a clandestine or illicit love affair. **14.** the series of complications forming the plot of a play. [< F *intrigue(r)* < It *intrigare* < L *intrīcāre* to entangle; see INTRICATE] —**in·tri′guer,** *n.* —**in·tri′guing·ly,** *adv.*
—**Syn. 1.** interest, attract, fascinate. **9.** manipulate. **11, 12.** manipulation.

in·trin·sic (in trin′sik, -zik), *adj.* **1.** belonging to a thing by its very nature: *intrinsic merit.* **2.** *Anat.* (of certain muscles, nerves, etc.) belonging to or lying within a given part. Also, **in·trin′si·cal.** [< ML *intrinsec(us)* inward (adj.), L (adv.), equiv. to *intrin-* (*int(e)r-,* as in *interior* + *-in* locative suffix) + *secus* beside, deriv. of *sequī* to follow] —**in·trin′si·cal·ly,** *adv.*
—**Syn. 1.** native, innate, natural, true, real. —**Ant. 1.** extrinsic.

in·tro (in′trō), *n., pl.* **-tros.** *Informal.* **1.** an introduction. **2.** the introductory passage of a piece for a jazz or dance band. [shortened form of INTRODUCTION]

intro-, a prefix, meaning "inwardly," "within," occurring in loan words from Latin (*introspection*); occasionally used in the formation of new words (*introjection*). Cf. **intra-.** [< L, repr. *intrō* (adv.) inwardly, within]

intro., **1.** introduce. **2.** introduced. **3.** introducing. **4.** introduction. **5.** introductory. Also, **introd.**

in·tro·duce (in′trə do͞os′, -dyo͞os′), *v.t.,* **-duced, -duc·ing.** **1.** to present (a person or persons) to another or others so as to make acquainted. **2.** to make (two or more persons) acquainted with one another: *Will you introduce us?* **3.** to present (a person, product, etc.) to a particular group of individuals or to the general public for or as if for the first time by a formal act, announcement, series of recommendations or events, etc.: *an advertising campaign to introduce a new soap product to the public; to introduce a debutante to society.* **4.** to bring (a person) to first knowledge or experience of something: *to introduce someone to skiing.* **5.** to create, bring into notice, use, etc., for or as if for the first time; institute: *to introduce a new concept in architectural design.* **6.** to suggest, propose, or advance for or as if for the first time: *to introduce a theory of geological evolution.* **7.** to present for official consideration or action, as a legislative bill. **8.** to begin; lead into; preface: *to introduce a speech with an amusing anecdote.* **9.** to put or place into something for the first time; insert: *to introduce a figure into a design.* **10.** to bring in or establish, as something foreign or alien: *The Japanese beetle was introduced into America.* **11.** to present (a speaker, performer, etc.) to an audience. **12.** to present (a person) at a royal court. [late ME < L *intrōdūce(re)* (to) lead inside, equiv. to *intrō-* INTRO- + *dūcere* to lead; see DUKE] —**in′tro·duc′er,** *n.* —**in′tro·duc′i·ble,** *adj.*
—**Syn. 1, 2.** INTRODUCE, PRESENT mean to bring persons into personal acquaintance with each other, as by announcement of names and the like. INTRODUCE is the ordinary term, referring to making persons acquainted who are ostensibly equals: *to introduce a friend to one's sister.* PRESENT, a more formal term, suggests a degree of ceremony in the process, and implies (if only as a matter of compliment) superior dignity, rank, or importance in the person to whom another is presented: *to present a visitor to the president.*

in·tro·duc·tion (in′trə duk′shən), *n.* **1.** the act of introducing or the state of being introduced. **2.** a formal presentation of one person to another or others. **3.** something introduced. **4.** a preliminary part, as of a book, musical composition, or the like, leading up to the main part. **5.** an elementary treatise: *an introduction to botany.* **6.** the act or an instance of inserting. [ME *introduccion* < L *intrōductiōn-* (s. of *intrōductiō*). See INTRODUCE, -TION]
—**Syn. 4.** INTRODUCTION, FOREWORD, PREFACE refer to material given at the front of a book to explain or introduce it to the reader. An INTRODUCTION is a formal preliminary statement or guide to the book: *His purpose is stated in the introduction.* A FOREWORD is often an informal statement made to the reader. It is the same as PREFACE, but FOREWORD was substituted for it when the restoration of native terms was in vogue: *an unusual foreword; a short preface.*

in·tro·duc·to·ry (in′trə duk′tə rē), *adj.* serving to introduce; preliminary; prefatory. Also, **in′tro·duc′tive.** [ME < LL *intrōductōri(us),* equiv. to L *intrōduct(us)* led inside (ptp. of *introducere*) + *-ōrius* -ORY^1] —**in′tro·duc′to·ri·ly,** *adv.* —**in′tro·duc′to·ri·ness,** *n.*
—**Syn.** See **preliminary.**

in·tro·it (in′trō it, -troit), *n.* **1.** *Rom. Cath. Ch.* a part of a psalm with antiphon recited by the celebrant of the Mass at the foot of the altar and, at High Mass, sung by the choir when the priest begins the Mass. **2.** *Anglican Ch., Lutheran Ch.* a psalm or anthem sung as the celebrant of the Holy Communion enters the sanctuary. **3.** a choral response sung at the beginning of a religious service. [< eccl. L *introit(us)*; L: entrance, beginning, equiv. to *introit-* (ptp. s. of *introīre* to go in) + *-us* n. suffix (4th decl.)]

in·tro·ject (in′trə jekt′), *v.t., v.i.* *Psychoanal.* to incorporate by introjection. [back formation from INTROJECTION]

in·tro·jec·tion (in′trə jek′shən), *n.* *Psychoanal.* an unconscious psychic process by which a person incorporates into his own psychic apparatus an image representing an external object or individual. [INTRO- + (IN)JECTION]

in·tro·mit (in′trə mit′), *v.t.,* **-mit·ted, -mit·ting.** to send, put, or let in; introduce; admit. [ME *intromitte(n)* < L *intrōmitt(ere)* (to) send in, equiv. to *intrō-* INTRO- + *mittere* to send] —**in·tro·mis·si·bil·i·ty** (in′trə mis′ə bil′i tē), *n.* —**in′tro·mis′si·ble,** *adj.* —**in·tro·mis·sion** (in′trə mish′ən), *n.* —**in′tro·mis′sive,** *adj.* —**in′tro·mit′tent,** *adj.* —**in′tro·mit′ter,** *n.*

in·tro·pu·ni·tive (in′trə pyo͞o′ni tiv), *adj.* *Psychol.* (in a frustrating situation) directing one's hostility inward, toward oneself, and experiencing guilt, remorse, etc. Cf. **extrapunitive, impunitive.** [INTRO- + PUNITIVE]

in·trorse (in trôrs′), *adj.* *Bot.* turned or facing inward, as anthers that open toward the gynoecium. [< L *intrors(us),* contr. of *intrōversus* toward the inside. See INTRO-, VERSUS] —**in·trorse′ly,** *adv.*

in·tro·scope (in′trə skōp′), *n.* *Optics.* an instrument for the examination of the interior of a tube, as a gun barrel, consisting of a low-power microscope that has a source of light and an adjustable objective lens which can be lowered into the tube. [INTRO- + -SCOPE]

in·tro·spect (in′trə spekt′), *v.i.* **1.** to practice introspection; consider one's own internal state or feelings. —*v.t.* **2.** to look into or examine (one's own mind, feelings, etc.): *an effort to introspect his true feelings.* [back formation from INTROSPECTION] —**in′tro·spect′a·ble, in′tro·spect′i·ble,** *adj.* —**in′tro·spec′tive,** *adj.* —**in′tro·spec′tive·ly,** *adv.* —**in′tro·spec′tive·ness,** *n.* —**in′tro·spec′tor,** *n.*

in·tro·spec·tion (in′trə spek′shən), *n.* **1.** observation or examination of one's own mental and emotional state, mental processes, etc.; act of looking within oneself. **2.** the quality, tendency, or disposition to do this. **3.** See **sympathetic introspection.** [< L *intrōspect(us)* looked within (ptp. of *intrōspicere,* equiv. to *intrō-* INTRO- + *-spicere,* var. of *specere* to look) + -ION] —**in′tro·spec′tion·al,** *adj.* —**in′tro·spec′tion·ist,** *n., adj.*

in·tro·sus·cep·tion (in′trə sə sep′shən), *n.* *Rare.* intussusception. [INTRO- + (INTUS)SUSCEPTION]

in·tro·ver·sion (in′trə vûr′zhən, -shən, in′trə vûr′-), *n.* **1.** the act of introverting. **2.** the state of being introverted. **3.** the quality, tendency, or disposition of being introverted. **4.** *Psychol.* **a.** the act of directing one's interest inward or to things within the self. **b.** the state of being concerned primarily with things within the self, with one's own thoughts and feelings rather than with the external environment. Cf. **extroversion.** [< NL *intrōversiōn-* (s. of *intrōversiō*). See INTRO-, VERSION] —**in·tro·ver·sive** (in′trə vûr′siv), **in·tro·ver·tive** (in′trə vûr′tiv), *adj.*

in·tro·vert (*n., adj.* in′trə vûrt′; *v.* in′trə vûrt′), *n.* **1.** *Psychol.* a person characterized by concern primarily with his own thoughts and feelings (opposed to *extravert*). **2.** *Informal.* a shy person. **3.** *Zool.* a part that is or can be introverted. —*adj.* **4.** *Psychol.* marked by introversion. —*v.t.* **5.** to turn inward: *to introvert one's anger.* **6.** *Psychol.* to direct (the mind, one's interest, etc.) inward or to things within the self. **7.** *Zool.* to insheathe a part of, within another part; invaginate. [INTRO- + (IN)VERT]

in·trude (in tro͞od′), *v.,* **-trud·ed, -trud·ing.** —*v.t.* **1.** to thrust or bring in without reason, permission, or welcome. **2.** *Geol.* to thrust or force in. **3.** to install (a cleric) in a church contrary to the wishes of its members. —*v.i.* **4.** to thrust oneself without invitation or welcome: *to intrude upon his privacy.* [< L *intrūde(re)* (to) push in, equiv. to *in-* IN-^{2} + *trūdere* to push; see PROTRUDE] —**in·trud′er,** *n.* —**in·trud′ing·ly,** *adv.*
—**Syn. 4.** interfere, interlope. See **trespass.**

Intrud′er in the Dust′, a novel (1948) by William Faulkner.

in·tru·sion (in tro͞o′zhən), *n.* **1.** the act or an instance of intruding. **2.** the state of being intruded. **3.** *Law.* **a.** an illegal act of entering, seizing, or taking possession of another's property. **b.** a wrongful entry after the determination of a particular estate, made before the remainderman or reversioner has entered. **4.** *Geol.* **a.** the forcing of extraneous matter, as molten rock, into some other formation. **b.** the matter forced in. [ME < ML (legal) *intrūsiōn-* (s. of *intrūsiō*), equiv. to L *intrūs(us)* pushed in (ptp. of *intrūdere* to INTRUDE) + *-iōn-* -ION] —**in·tru′sion·al,** *adj.*

in·tru·sive (in tro͞o′siv), *adj.* **1.** intruding; thrusting in. **2.** characterized by or involving intrusion. **3.** tending or apt to intrude; coming unbidden or without welcome: *an intrusive person; intrusive memories of a lost love.* **4.** *Petrol.* **a.** (of a rock) having been forced, while molten or plastic, into fissures or other openings or between layers of other rocks. **b.** noting or pertaining to plutonic rocks. **5.** *Phonet.* excrescent (def. 2). [late ME; see INTRUSION, -IVE] —**in·tru′sive·ly,** *adv.* —**in·tru′sive·ness,** *n.*
—**Syn. 3.** annoying, bothersome, interfering, distracting, irksome, worrisome, troublesome, irritating, disturbing.

in·trust (in trust′), *v.t.* entrust.

in·tu·bate (in′to͝o bāt′, -tyo͝o-), *v.t.,* **-bat·ed, -bat·ing.** *Med.* **1.** to insert a tube into (the larynx or the like). **2.** to treat by inserting a tube, as into the larynx. [IN-^{2} + TUBATE] —**in′tu·ba′tion,** *n.*

in·tu·it (in to͞o′it, -tyo͞o′-; in′to͞o it, -tyo͞o-), *v.t., v.i.* to know or receive by intuition. [back formation from INTUITION] —**in·tu′it·a·ble,** *adj.*

in·tu·i·tion (in′to͞o ish′ən, -tyo͞o-), *n.* **1.** direct perception of truth, fact, etc., independent of any reasoning process; immediate apprehension. **2.** a fact, a truth, etc., perceived in this way. **3.** a keen and quick insight. **4.** the quality or ability of having such direct perception or quick insight. **5.** *Philos.* **a.** an immediate cognition of an object not inferred or determined by a previous cognition of the same object. **b.** any object or truth so discerned. **c.** pure, untaught, noninferential knowledge. [< LL *intuitiōn-* (s. of *intuitiō*) contemplation, equiv. to L *intuit(us)* gazed at, contemplated (ptp. of *intuērī*) + *-iōn-* -ION. See IN-^{2}, TUITION] —**in′tu·i′tion·less,** *adj.*

in·tu·i·tion·al (in′to͞o ish′ə nəl, -tyo͞o-), *adj.* **1.** pertaining to or of the nature of intuition. **2.** characterized by intuition; having intuition. **3.** based on intuition as a principle. [INTUITION + -AL^1] —**in′tu·i′tion·al·ly,** *adv.*

in·tu·i·tion·al·ism (in′to͞o ish′ə nəliz′əm, -tyo͞o-), *n.* intuitionism. [INTUITIONAL + -ISM] —**in′tu·i′tion·al·ist,** *n.*

in·tu·i·tion·ism (in′to͞o ish′ə niz′əm, -tyo͞o-), *n.* **1.** *Ethics.* the doctrine that moral values and duties can be discerned directly. **2.** *Metaphys.* **a.** the doctrine that in perception external objects are given immediately, without the intervention of a representative idea. **b.** the doctrine that knowledge rests upon axiomatic truths discerned directly. [INTUITION + -ISM] —**in′tu·i′tion·ist,** *n., adj.*

in·tu·i·tive (in to͞o′i tiv, -tyo͞o′-), *adj.* **1.** perceiving by intuition, as a person, the mind, etc. **2.** perceived by, resulting from, or involving intuition: *intuitive knowledge.* **3.** having or possessing intuition: *an intuitive person.* **4.** capable of being perceived or known by intuition. [< ML *intuitīv(us).* See INTUITION, -IVE] —**in·tu′i·tive·ly,** *adv.* —**in·tu′i·tive·ness,** *n.*

in·tu·i·tiv·ism (in to͞o′i ti viz′əm, -tyo͞o′-), *n.* **1.** ethical intuitionism. **2.** intuitive perception; insight. [INTUITIVE + -ISM] —**in·tu′i·tiv·ist,** *n.*

in·tu·mesce (in′to͝o mes′, -tyo͝o-), *v.i.,* **-mesced, -mes·cing.** **1.** to swell up, as with heat; become tumid. **2.** to bubble up. [< L *intumēsce(re)* (to) swell up, equiv. to *in-* IN-^{2} + *tumēscere,* equiv. to *tum(ēre)* (to) swell + *-escere* -ESCE]

in·tu·mes·cence (in′to͝o mes′əns, -tyo͝o-), *n.* **1.** a swelling up, as with congestion. **2.** the state of being swollen. **3.** a swollen mass. [< F; see INTUMESCE, -ENCE] —**in′tu·mes′cent,** *adj.*

in·turn (in′tûrn′), *n.* an inward turn or curve around an axis or fixed point. [IN-^{1} + TURN] —**in′turned′,** *adj.*

in·tus·sus·cept (in′təs sə sept′), *v.t.* to take within, as one part of the intestine into an adjacent part; invaginate. [back formation from INTUSSUSCEPTION] —**in′tus·sus·cep′tive,** *adj.*

in·tus·sus·cep·tion (in′təs sə sep′shən), *n.* **1.** a taking within. **2.** *Biol.* growth of a cell wall by the deposition of new particles among the existing particles of the wall. Cf. **apposition** (def. 4). **3.** Also called **invagination.** *Pathol.* the slipping of one part within another, as of the intestine. [< L *intus* within + *susceptiō-* (s. of *susceptiō*) an undertaking, equiv. to *suscept(us)* taken up (ptp. of *suscipere;* see SUSCEPTIBLE) + *-iōn-* -ION]

in·twine (in twīn′), *v.t., v.i.,* **-twined, -twin·ing.** entwine. —**in·twine′ment,** *n.*

In·u·it (in′o͞o it, -yo͞o-), *n., pl.* **-its,** (*esp. collectively*) **-it. 1.** a member of the Eskimo peoples inhabiting the northernmost regions of North America from Alaska to Greenland: this term is preferred to Eskimo among the Inuit people, and is used officially by the Canadian government. **2.** the language of the Inuit, a member of the Eskimo-Aleut family. [< Inuit: people, pl. of *inuk* person]

in·u·lase (in′yə lās′), *n. Biochem.* an enzyme that converts inulin into levulose. [INUL(IN) + -ASE]

in·u·lin (in′yə lin), *n. Chem.* a polysaccharide, $(C_6H_{10}O_5)_n$, obtained from the roots of certain plants, esp. elecampane, dahlia, and Jerusalem artichoke, which undergoes hydrolysis to the dextrorotatory form of fructose: used chiefly as an ingredient in diabetic bread and as a reagent in diagnosing kidney function. Also called **alant starch.** [< NL *Inul(a)* a genus of plants (L: elecampane) + -IN[2]]

in·unc·tion (in ungk′shən), *n.* **1.** the act of anointing. **2.** *Med.* the rubbing in of an oil or ointment. **3.** *Pharm.* an unguent. [late ME < L *inunctiōn-* (s. of *inunctiō*), equiv. to *inunct(us)* anointed (ptp. of *inungere*) + *-iōn-* -ION. See IN-[2], UNCTION]

in·un·dant (in un′dənt), *adj.* **1.** flooding or overflowing. **2.** overwhelming with force, numbers, etc. [< L *inundant-* (s. of *inundāns*) overflowing, prp. of *inundāre;* see INUNDATE]

in·un·date (in′ən dāt′, -un-, in un′dāt), *v.t.,* **-dat·ed, -dat·ing. 1.** to flood; overspread with water; overflow. **2.** to overspread or overwhelm: *inundated with requests.* [< L *inundāt(us)* flooded, inundated (ptp. of *inundāre*), equiv. to *in-* -IN-[2] + *und(a)* wave + *-ātus* -ATE[1]] —**in′un·da′tion,** *n.* —**in′un·da′tor,** *n.*
—**Syn. 1.** See **flood. 2.** glut.

in·ur·bane (in′ûr bān′), *adj.* not urbane; lacking in courtesy, refinement, etc. [IN-[3] + URBANE] —**in·ur·ban·i·ty** (in′ûr ban′i tē), **in′ur·bane′ness,** *n.* —**in′ur·bane′ly,** *adv.*

in·ure (in yŏŏr′, i nŏŏr′), *v.,* **-ured, -ur·ing.** —*v.t.* **1.** to toughen or harden by exercise; accustom; habituate (usually fol. by *to*): *to inure a person to hardship.* —*v.i.* **2.** to come into use; take or have effect. **3.** to become beneficial or advantageous. Also, **enure.** [v. use of phrase *in ure* < AF *en ure* in use, at work, equiv. to *en* in + *ure* < L *opera,* pl. of *opus* work; r. late ME *enure* < AF *en ure*] —**in·ur·ed·ness** (in yŏŏr′id nis, i nŏŏr′-, in yŏŏrd′-, i nŏŏrd′-), *n.* —**in·ure′ment,** *n.*

in·urn (in ûrn′), *v.t.* **1.** to put into an urn, esp. a funeral urn. **2.** to bury; inter. [IN-[2] + URN] —**in·urn′ment,** *n.*

in u·ter·o (in yo͞o′tə rō′), in the uterus; unborn. [< L]

in·u·tile (in yo͞o′til), *adj.* useless; of no use or service. [late ME < L *inūtil(is).* See IN-[3], UTILE] —**in·u′tile·ly,** *adv.*

in·u·til·i·ty (in′yo͞o til′i tē), *n., pl.* **-ties. 1.** uselessness. **2.** a useless thing or person. [< L *inūtilitās.* See INUTILE, -ITY]

inv., 1. he invented it; she invented it. [< L *invēnit*] **2.** invented. **3.** invention. **4.** inventor. **5.** inventory. **6.** invoice.

in va·cu·o (in wä′ko͞o ō′; *Eng.* in vak′yo͞o ō′), *Latin.* **1.** in a vacuum. **2.** in isolation.

in·vade (in vād′), *v.,* **-vad·ed, -vad·ing.** —*v.t.* **1.** to enter forcefully as an enemy; go into with hostile intent: *Germany invaded Czechoslovakia.* **2.** to enter like an enemy: *Locusts invaded the fields.* **3.** to enter as if to take possession: *to invade a neighbor's home.* **4.** to enter and affect injuriously or destructively, as disease: *viruses that invade the blood stream.* **5.** to intrude upon: *to invade the privacy of a family.* **6.** to encroach or infringe upon: *to invade the rights of citizens.* **7.** to permeate: *The smell of baking invades the house.* **8.** to penetrate; spread into or over: *The population boom has caused city dwellers to invade the suburbs.* —*v.i.* **9.** to make an invasion. [< L *invāde(re),* equiv. to *in-* IN-[2] + *vādere* to go; see WADE] —**in·vad′a·ble,** *adj.* —**in·vad′er,** *n.*

in·vag·i·na·ble (in vaj′ə nə bəl), *adj.* capable of being invaginated; susceptible of invagination. [INVAGIN(ATE) + -ABLE]

in·vag·i·nate (*v.* in vaj′ə nāt′; *adj.* in vaj′ə nit, -nāt′), *v.,* **-nat·ed, -nat·ing,** *adj.* —*v.t.* **1.** to insert or receive, as into a sheath; sheathe. **2.** to fold or draw (a tubular organ) back within itself; introvert; intussuscept. —*v.i.* **3.** to become invaginated; undergo invagination. **4.** to form a pocket by turning in. —*adj.* **5.** folded or turned back upon itself. **6.** sheathed. [< ML *invāgināt(us)* sheathed in, ptp. of *invāgināre.* See IN-[2], VAGINATE]

in·vag·i·na·tion (in vaj′ə nā′shən), *n.* **1.** the act or process of invaginating. **2.** *Embryol.* the inward movement of a portion of the wall of a blastula in the formation of a gastrula. **3.** *Pathol.* intussusception (def. 3). [INVAGINATE + -ION]

in·va·lid[1] (in′və lid; *Brit.* in′və lēd′), *n.* **1.** an infirm or sickly person. **2.** a person who is too sick, weak, or old to care for himself; a person disabled by sickness or age: *a hopeless invalid.* **3.** *Archaic.* a member of the armed forces disabled for active service. —*adj.* **4.** unable to care for oneself due to sickness, age, or a disability: *his invalid sister.* **5.** of or for invalids: *invalid diets.* **6.** (of things) in poor or weakened condition: *the invalid state of his rocking chair.* —*v.t.* **7.** to affect with disease; make an invalid: *He was invalided for life.* **8.** to remove from or classify as not able to perform active service, as an invalid. **9.** *Brit.* to remove or evacuate (military personnel) from an active theater of operations because of injury or illness. —*v.i. Archaic.* **10.** to become an invalid. [< L *invalid(us)* weak. See IN-[3], VALID]

in·val·id[2] (in val′id), *adj.* **1.** not valid; without force or foundation; indefensible. **2.** deficient in substance or cogency; weak. **3.** void or without legal force, as a contract. [< ML *invalid(us)* not legally valid. See IN-[3], VALID] —**in·val′id·ly,** *adv.* —**in·val′id·ness,** *n.*

in·val·i·date (in val′i dāt′), *v.t.,* **-dat·ed, -dat·ing. 1.** to render invalid; discredit. **2.** to deprive of legal force or efficacy. [INVALID[2] + -ATE[1]] —**in·val′i·da′tion,** *n.* —**in·val′i·da′tor,** *n.*

in·va·lid·ism (in′və li diz′əm), *n.* prolonged ill health. [INVALID[1] + -ISM]

in·va·lid·i·ty[1] (in′və lid′i tē), *n.* lack of validity. [< ML *invaliditās.* See INVALID[2], -ITY]

in·va·lid·i·ty[2] (in′və lid′i tē), *n.* invalidism. [INVALID[1] + -ITY]

in·val·u·a·ble (in val′yo͞o ə bəl), *adj.* beyond calculable or appraisable value; of inestimable worth; priceless. [IN-[3] + VALUABLE capable of valuation (obs. sense)] —**in·val′u·a·ble·ness,** *n.* —**in·val′u·a·bly,** *adv.*
—**Syn.** precious. —**Ant.** worthless.

In·var (in vär′), *n. Trademark.* an iron alloy containing 35.5 percent nickel and having a very low coefficient of expansion at atmospheric temperatures.

in·var·i·a·ble (in vâr′ē ə bəl), *adj.* **1.** not variable or capable of being varied; unchangeable; static or constant. —*n.* **2.** that which is invariable; a constant. [late ME; see IN-[3], VARIABLE] —**in·var′i·a·bil′i·ty, in·var′i·a·ble·ness,** *n.* —**in·var′i·a·bly,** *adv.*
—**Syn. 1.** unalterable, unchanging, changeless, invariant, unvarying, immutable, uniform. —**Ant. 1.** changing.

in·var·i·ant (in vâr′ē ənt), *adj.* **1.** unvarying; invariable; constant. **2.** *Math.* normal (def. 4e). —*n.* **3.** *Math.* a quantity or expression that is constant throughout a certain range of conditions. [IN-[3] + VARIANT] —**in·var′i·ant·ly,** *adv.*

in·va·sion (in vā′zhən), *n.* **1.** the act or an instance of invading or entering as an enemy, esp. by an army. **2.** the entrance or advent of anything troublesome or harmful, as disease. **3.** entrance as if to take possession or overrun. **4.** infringement by intrusion: *invasion of privacy.* [< LL *invāsiōn-* (s. of *invāsiō*), equiv. to *invās(us)* invaded (ptp.) of *invādere*) + *-iōn-* -ION; see INVADE]

in·va·sive (in vā′siv), *adj.* **1.** characterized by or involving invasion; offensive: *invasive war.* **2.** invading, or tending to invade; intrusive. [late ME < ML *invāsīv(us).* See INVASION, -IVE]

in·vect·ed (in vek′tid), *adj. Heraldry.* **1.** noting an edge of a charge, as an ordinary, consisting of a series of small convex curves. **2.** (of a charge, as an ordinary) having such an edge: *a chevron invected.* Cf. **engrailed.** [< L *invect(us)* driven into (see INVECTIVE) + -ED[2]]

in·vec·tive (in vek′tiv), *n.* **1.** vehement denunciation; an utterance of violent censure or reproach. **2.** a railing accusation; vituperation. **3.** an insulting or abusive word or expression. —*adj.* **4.** vituperative; denunciatory; censoriously abusive. [< LL *invectīv(us)* abusive, equiv. to L *invect(us)* driven into, attacked (ptp. of *invehī* to INVEIGH) + *-īvus* -IVE] —**in·vec′tive·ly,** *adv.* —**in·vec′tive·ness,** *n.*
—**Syn. 1.** contumely, scorn. See **abuse.**

in·veigh (in vā′), *v.i.* to protest strongly or attack vehemently with words; rail (usually fol. by *against*): *to inveigh against isolationism.* [ME *inveh* < L *inveh(ī)* (to) burst into, attack, equiv. to *in-* IN-[2] + *vehī* to sail, ride, drive] —**in·veigh′er,** *n.*

in·vei·gle (in vē′gəl, -vā′gəl), *v.t.,* **-gled, -gling. 1.** to entice, lure, or ensnare by flattery or artful talk or inducements (usually fol. by *into*): *to inveigle a person into playing bridge.* **2.** to acquire, win, or obtain by beguiling talk or methods (usually fol. by *from* or *away*): *to inveigle a theater pass from a person.* [var. of *envegle* < AF *enveogl(er),* equiv. to *en-* EN-[1] + OF *(a)vogler* to blind, deriv. of *avogle* blind < ML *abocul(us)* eyeless, adj. use of phrase *ab oculis,* lit., from eyes. See AB-, OCULAR] —**in·vei′gle·ment,** *n.* —**in·vei′gler,** *n.*
—**Syn. 1.** induce, beguile, persuade. **2.** enmesh.

in·ve·nit (in wā′nit; *Eng.* in vā′nit), *Latin.* he invented it; she invented it.

in·vent (in vent′), *v.t.* **1.** to originate as a product of one's own contrivance: *to invent a machine.* **2.** to produce or create with the imagination: *to invent a story.* **3.** to make up or fabricate (something fictitious or false): *to invent excuses.* **4.** *Obs.* to come upon; find. [late ME *invente* < L *invent(us)* found (ptp. of *invenīre*), equiv. to *in-* IN-[2] + *ven-* come + *-tus* ptp. suffix] —**in·vent′i·ble, in·vent′a·ble,** *adj.*
—**Syn. 1.** devise, contrive. See **discover. 2.** imagine, conceive. **3.** concoct.

in·vent·er (in ven′tər), *n. Rare.* inventor.

in·ven·tion (in ven′shən), *n.* **1.** the act of inventing. **2.** *Patent Law.* the conception of an idea and the means or apparatus by which the result is obtained. **3.** anything invented or devised. **4.** the exercise of imaginative or creative power in literature, art, or music. **5.** the act or an instance of producing or creating by exercise of the imagination. **6.** the power or faculty of inventing, devising, or originating. **7.** something fabricated, as a false statement. **8.** *Sociol.* the creation of a new culture trait, pattern, etc. **9.** *Music.* a short piece, contrapuntal in nature, generally based on one subject. **10.** *Rhet.* (traditionally) one of the five steps in speech preparation, the process of choosing ideas appropriate to the subject, audience, and occasion. **11.** *Archaic.* the act of finding. [ME *invencio(u)n* < L *inventiōn-* (s. of *inventiō*) a finding out, equiv. to *invent(us)* (see INVENT) + *-iōn-* -ION] —**in·ven′tion·al,** *adj.* —**in·ven′tion·less,** *adj.*

in·ven·tive (in ven′tiv), *adj.* **1.** apt at inventing, devising, or contriving. **2.** apt at creating with the imagination. **3.** having the function of inventing. **4.** pertaining to, involving, or showing invention. [INVENT + -IVE; r. late ME *inventif* < MF] —**in·ven′tive·ly,** *adv.* —**in·ven′tive·ness,** *n.*

in·ven·tor (in ven′tər), *n.* a person who invents, esp. one who devises some new process, appliance, machine, or article; one who makes inventions. [< L; see INVENT, -OR[2]]

in·ven·to·ry (in′vən tôr′ē, -tōr′ē), *n., pl.* **-to·ries,** *v.,* **-to·ried, -to·ry·ing.** —*n.* **1.** a detailed, often descriptive, list of articles, giving the code number, quantity, and value of each; catalog. **2.** a formal list of movables, as of a merchant's stock of goods. **3.** a formal list of the property of a person or estate. **4.** a complete listing of merchandise or stock on hand, work in progress, raw materials, finished goods on hand, etc., made each year by a business concern. **5.** the objects or items represented on such a list, as a merchant's stock of goods. **6.** the aggregate value of a stock of goods. **7.** a catalog of natural resources, esp. a count or estimate of wildlife and game in a particular area. **8.** a tally of one's personality traits, aptitudes, skills, etc., for use in counseling and guidance. **9.** the act of making a catalog or detailed listing. —*v.t.* **10.** to make an inventory of; enter in an inventory; catalog. **11.** to summarize: *a book that inventories the progress in chemistry.* —*v.i.* **12.** to have value as shown by an inventory: *stock that inventories at two million dollars.* [< ML *inventōri(um)* (see INVENT, -ORY[2]); r. LL *inventārium,* equiv. to L *invent(us)* found + *-ārium* -ARY] —**in′ven·to′ri·a·ble,** *adj.* —**in′ven·to′ri·al,** *adj.* —**in′ven·to′ri·al·ly,** *adv.*
—**Syn. 1.** roster, record, register, account. See **list**[1].

in·ve·rac·i·ty (in′və ras′i tē), *n., pl.* **-ties** for 2. **1.** untruthfulness; mendacity. **2.** an untruth; falsehood. [IN-[3] + VERACITY]

In·ver·car·gill (in′vər kär′gil), *n.* a city on S South Island, in New Zealand. 41,088 (1961).

In·ver·ness (in′vər nes′), *n.* **1.** Also called **In·ver·ness·shire** (in′vər nes′shēr, -shər). a county in NW Scotland. 84,425 (1961); 4211 sq. mi. **2.** its county seat: a seaport. 28,115 (1951). **3.** (*often l.c.*) an overcoat with a long, removable cape (**Inverness′ cape′**). **4.** (*often l.c.*) a sleeveless, usually long cape of wool or worsted, in a plaid pattern, close-fitting at the neck and hanging loose from the shoulders.

in·verse (*adj., n.* in vûrs′, in′vûrs; *v.* in vûrs′), *adj., n., v.,* **-versed, -vers·ing.** —*adj.* **1.** reversed in position, direction, or tendency: *inverse order.* **2.** *Math.* **a.** (of a proportion) containing terms of which an increase in one results in a decrease in another. A term is said to be in inverse proportion to another term if it increases (or decreases) as the other decreases (or increases). **b.** of or pertaining to an inverse function. Cf. **direct** (def. 16). **3.** inverted; turned upside down. —*n.* **4.** an inverted state or condition. **5.** that which is inverse; the direct opposite. **6.** *Math.* **a.** an element of an algebraic system, as a group, corresponding to a given element such that its product or sum with the given element is the identity element. **b.** See **inverse function. c.** a point related to a given point so that it is situated on the same radius, extended if necessary, of a given circle or sphere and so that the product of the distances of the two points from the center equals the square of the radius of the circle or sphere. **d.** the set of such inverses of the points of a given set, as the points on a curve. —*v.t.* **7.** to invert. [< L *invers(us),* lit., turned in, i.e., inside out or upside down, ptp. of *invertere.* See IN-[2], VERSUS]

inverse′ cose′cant, *Trig.* See **arc cosecant.**

in′verse co′sine, *Trig.* See **arc cosine.**

inverse′ cotan′gent, *Trig.* See **arc cotangent.**

in′verse feed′back, *Electronics.* See under **feedback** (def. 1).

in′verse func′tion, *Math.* the function that replaces another function when the dependent and independent variables of the first function are interchanged for an appropriate set of values of the dependent variable. In $y = \sin x$ and $x = \text{arc} \sin y$, the inverse function of *sin* is *arc sine.*

in′verse im′age, *Math.* the point or set of points in the domain of a function corresponding to a given point or set of points in the range of the function. Also called **counter image.**

in·verse·ly (in vûrs′lē), *adv.* **1.** in an inverse manner. **2.** *Math.* in inverse proportion. [INVERSE + -LY]

in′verse se′cant, *Trig.* See **arc secant.**

in′verse sine′, *Trig.* See **arc sine.**

in′verse square′ law′, *Physics, Optics.* one of several laws relating two quantities such that one quantity varies inversely as the square of the other, as the law that the illumination produced on a screen by a point source varies inversely as the square of the distance of the screen from the source.

in′verse tan′gent, *Trig.* See **arc tangent.**

in·ver·sion (in vûr′zhən, -shən), *n.* **1.** the act or an instance of inverting. **2.** the state of being inverted. **3.** anything that is inverted. **4.** *Rhet.* reversal of the usual or natural order of words; anastrophe. **5.** *Gram.* any change from a basic word order or syntactic sequence, as in the placement of a subject after an auxiliary verb in a question or after the verb in an exclamation, as "When will you go?" and "How beautiful is the rose!" **6.** *Anat.* the turning inward of a part, as the foot. **7.** *Chem.* **a.** a hydrolysis of certain carbohydrates, as cane sugar, which results in a reversal of direction of the rotatory power of the carbohydrate solution, the plane of polarized light being bent from right to left or vice versa. **b.** a reaction in which a starting material of one optical configuration forms a product of the opposite configuration. **8.** *Music.* **a.** the process, or result, of transposing the tones of an interval or chord so that the original bass becomes an upper voice. **b.** (in counterpoint) the transposition of the upper voice part below the lower, and vice versa. **c.** presentation of a melody in contrary motion to its original form. **9.** *Psychiatry.* assumption of the sexual role of the opposite sex; homosexuality. **10.** *Genetics.* change in position of a chromosome segment such that the linear order of the genes is reversed. **11.** *Phonet.* retroflexion (def. 3). **12.** *Meteorol.* a reversal in the normal temperature lapse rate, the temperature rising with increased elevation instead of falling. **13.** *Electricity.* a converting of direct current into alternating current. **14.** *Math.* the operation of forming the inverse of a point, curve, function, etc. [< L *inversiōn-* (s. of *inversiō*) a turning in. See INVERSE, -ION]

inver′sion cast′ing, 1. *Metall.* casting from an electric furnace inverted over the mold. **2.** *Foundry.* a process of casting, used esp. for small statuary or the like, in which the mold is inverted after the outer surfaces have hardened so as to drain off the molten metal at the center.

inver′sion cen′ter, *Crystall.* See **center of symmetry.**

in·ver·sive (in vûr′siv), *adj.* noting, pertaining to, or characterized by inversion. [INVERS(ION) + -IVE]

in·ver·sor (in vûr′sər), *n.* an instrument for drawing a curve and its inverse simultaneously. [INVERSE + -OR[2]]

in·vert (*v.* in vûrt′; *adj., n.* in′vûrt), *v.t.* **1.** to turn upside down. **2.** to reverse in position, direction, or relationship. **3.** to turn or change to the opposite or contrary, as in nature, bearing, or effect: *to invert a process.* **4.** to turn inward or back upon itself. **5.** to turn inside out. **6.** *Chem.* to subject to inversion. **7.** *Music.* to subject to musical inversion. **8.** *Phonet.* to articulate as a retroflex vowel. —*v.i.* **9.** *Chem.* to

become inverted. —*adj.* **10.** *Chem.* subjected to inversion. —*n.* **11.** one who or that which is inverted. **12.** a homosexual. **13.** (in plumbing) that portion of the interior of a drain or sewer pipe where the liquid is deepest. **14.** an inverted arch or vault. **15.** *Philately.* a two-colored postage stamp with all or part of the central design printed upside down in relation to the inscription. [< L *invert(ere)* (to) turn the wrong way round, equiv. to *in-* IN-² + *vertere* to turn] —**in·vert′er,** *n.* —**in·vert′i·bil′i·ty,** *n.* —**in·vert′i·ble,** *adj.*
—**Syn. 2.** See **reverse.**

in·vert·ase (in vûr′tās), *n.* *Biochem.* an enzyme, occurring in yeast and in the digestive juices of animals, that causes the inversion of cane sugar into invert sugar. Also, **invertin.** Also called **sucrase.** [INVERT + -ASE]

in·ver·te·brate (in vûr′tə brit, -brāt′), *adj.* **1.** *Zool.* **a.** not vertebrate; without a backbone. **b.** of or pertaining to creatures without a backbone. **2.** without strength of character. —*n.* **3.** an invertebrate animal. **4.** a person who lacks strength of character. [< NL *invertebrāt(us).* See IN-³, VERTEBRATE] —**in·ver·te·bra·cy** (in vûr′tə brə sē), **in·ver′te·brate·ness,** *n.*

invert′ed com′ma, *Brit.* See **quotation mark.** Also called **turned comma.**

invert′ed king′ post′ truss′, a truss, used esp. in bridges and sloping roofs, having a V-shaped tension member, suspended from the ends of an upper chord, which supports the foot of a central strut. Also called **simple Fink truss.**

invert′ed mor′dent, *Music.* a melodic embellishment consisting of a rapid alternation of a principal tone with an auxiliary tone one degree above it. Also called **pralltriller.**

invert′ed pleat′, a reverse box pleat, having the flat fold turned in.

invert′ible coun′terpoint, *Music.* counterpoint in which the voices, while retaining their original form, may be interchanged above or below one another in any order.

in·ver·tin (in vûr′tᵊn), *n.* *Biochem.* invertase. [INVERT + -IN²]

in·ver·tor (in vûr′tər), *n.* *Elect.* a converter. [< NL; see INVERT, -OR²]

in′vert soap′, *Chem.* See **cationic detergent.**

in′vert sug′ar, a mixture of the dextrorotatory forms of glucose and fructose, formed naturally in fruits and produced artificially in syrups or fondants by treating cane sugar with acids.

in·vest (in vest′), *v.t.* **1.** to put (money) to use, by purchase or expenditure, in something offering profitable returns, esp. interest or income. **2.** to spend: *to invest large sums in books.* **3.** to use, give, or devote (time, talent, etc.) as for a purpose or to achieve something: *He invested a lot of time in trying to help retarded children.* **4.** to furnish with power, authority, rank, etc.: *The Constitution invests the President with the power of veto.* **5.** to settle or secure a power, right, etc., in the possession of; vest: *Feudalism invested the lords with absolute authority over the lives of their vassals.* **6.** to endow with a quality or characteristic: *to invest a friend with every virtue.* **7.** to infuse or belong to, as a quality or characteristic does: *Goodness invests his every action.* **8.** *Foundry.* to surround (a pattern) with an investment. **9.** to provide with the insignia of office. **10.** to install in an office or position. **11.** to clothe; attire; dress. **12.** to cover or adorn, as an article of attire does. **13.** to cover, surround, or envelop, as if with a garment, or like a garment: *Spring invests the trees with leaves.* **14.** to surround (a place) with military forces or works so as to prevent approach or escape; besiege. —*v.i.* **15.** to invest money. **16.** to make an investment: *to invest in oil stock; to invest in a new hat.* [late ME < ML *invest(īre)* (to) install, invest (money), surround, clothe in, L: to clothe in, equiv. to *in-* IN-² + *vestīre* to clothe, deriv. of *vest(is)* garment; see VEST] —**in·vest′a·ble, in·vest′i·ble,** *adj.* —**in·ves′tor,** *n.*

in·ves·ti·ga·ble (in ves′tə gə bəl), *adj.* capable of being investigated. [< LL *investīgābil(is),* equiv. to L *investīgā(re)* (to) track down (see INVESTIGATE) + *-bilis* -BLE]

in·ves·ti·gate (in ves′tə gāt′), *v.,* **-gat·ed, -gat·ing.** —*v.t.* **1.** to search or inquire into systematically; search or examine into the particulars of; examine in detail. **2.** to examine the particulars of in an attempt to learn the facts about something hidden, unique, or complex, esp. in search of a motive, cause, or culprit: *to investigate a murder.* —*v.i.* **3.** to make inquiry, examination, or investigation. [< L *investīgāt(us)* tracked down, esp. with dogs, ptp. of *investīgāre.* See IN-², VESTIGE, -ATE¹] —**in·ves′ti·ga′tive, in·ves·ti·ga·to·ry** (in ves′tə gə tôr′ē, -tōr′ē), *adj.* —**in·ves′ti·ga′tor,** *n.*

in·ves·ti·ga·tion (in ves′tə gā′shən), *n.* **1.** the act or process of investigating or the condition of being investigated. **2.** a searching inquiry for ascertaining facts; a detailed or careful examination. [ME *investigacio(u)n* < L *investīgātiōn-* (s. of *investīgātiō*). See INVESTIGATE, -ION] —**in·ves′ti·ga′tion·al,** *adj.*
—**Syn. 1, 2.** scrutiny, exploration. INVESTIGATION, EXAMINATION, INQUIRY, RESEARCH express the idea of an active effort to find out something. An INVESTIGATION is a systematic, minute, and thorough attempt to learn the facts about something complex or hidden: it is often formal and official: *an investigation of a bank failure.* An EXAMINATION is an orderly attempt to obtain information about or to make a test of something, often something presented for observation: *a physical examination.* An INQUIRY is an investigation made by asking questions rather than by inspection, or by study of available evidence: *an inquiry into a proposed bond issue.* RESEARCH is careful and sustained investigation usually into a subject covering a wide range, or into remote recesses of knowledge: *chemical research.*

in·ves·ti·tive (in ves′ti tiv), *adj.* **1.** of, pertaining to, or empowered to invest: *an investitive act.* **2.** of or pertaining to investiture. [< ML *investīt(us)* (see INVESTITURE) + -IVE]

in·ves·ti·ture (in ves′ti chər), *n.* **1.** the act or process of investing. **2.** *Brit.* the formal bestowal, confirmation, presentation of rank, office, or of a possessory or prescriptive right, usually involving the giving of insignia or an official title. **3.** the state of being invested, as with a garment, quality, office, etc. **4.** that which covers or adorns. **5.** *Archaic.* that which invests. [ME < ML *investītūra,* equiv. to *investīt(us)* installed (ptp. of *investīre;* see INVEST) + *-ūra* -URE]

in·vest·ment (in vest′mənt), *n.* **1.** the investing of money or capital in order to secure profitable returns, esp. interest or income. **2.** a particular instance or mode of investing. **3.** a thing invested in, as a business, a quantity of shares of stock, etc. **4.** that which is invested, or a sum invested. **5.** the act or fact of investing or state of being invested, as with a garment. **6.** a devoting, using, or giving of time, talent, emotional energy, etc., as for a purpose or to achieve something: *His investment in the project included more time and worry than he cared to remember.* **7.** *Biol.* any covering, coating, outer layer, or integument, as of an animal or vegetable body. **8.** the act of investing with a quality, attribute, etc. **9.** investiture with an office, dignity, or right. **10.** a siege; the surrounding of a place with military forces or works, as in besieging. **11.** *Foundry.* a refractory material applied in a plastic state to a pattern to make a mold. **12.** *Archaic.* a garment or vestment. [INVEST + -MENT]

invest′ment bank′, a financial institution that deals chiefly in the underwriting of new securities. —**invest′ment bank′er.** —**invest′ment bank′ing.**

invest′ment cast′ing, *Foundry.* a casting process in which an expendable pattern is surrounded by an investment compound and then baked so that the investment is hardened to form a mold and the pattern material may be melted and run off. Also called **precision casting.** Cf. **lost-wax process.**

invest′ment com′pany, a company that invests its funds in other companies and issues its own securities against these investments. Also called **invest′ment trust′.**

invest′ment mold′, *Foundry.* a mold made of an investment compound.

in·vet·er·a·cy (in vet′ər ə sē), *n.* the quality or state of being inveterate or deeply ingrained: *the inveteracy of people's prejudices.* [INVETERA(TE) + -CY]

in·vet·er·ate (in vet′ər it), *adj.* **1.** confirmed in a habit, practice, feeling, or the like: *an inveterate gambler.* **2.** firmly established by long continuance, as a disease, habit, practice, feeling, etc.; chronic; continuous. [ME < L *inveterāt(us)* grown old, deep-rooted (ptp. of *inveterāre*), equiv. to *in-* IN-² + *veter-* (s. of *vetus*) old + *-ātus* -ATE¹] —**in·vet′er·ate·ly,** *adv.* —**in·vet′er·ate·ness,** *n.*
—**Syn. 1.** hardened. **2.** set, fixed, rooted.

in·vid·i·ous (in vid′ē əs), *adj.* **1.** causing or tending to cause animosity, resentment, or envious dislike: *an invidious honor.* **2.** calculated to excite ill will or resentment or give offense; hateful: *invidious remarks.* **3.** offensively or unfairly discriminating; harmful; injurious: *invidious comparisons.* **4.** *Obs.* envious. [< L *invidiōs(us)* envious, envied, hateful, equiv. to *invidi(a)* ENVY + *-ōsus* -OUS] —**in·vid′i·ous·ly,** *adv.* —**in·vid′i·ous·ness,** *n.*

in·vig·i·late (in vij′ə lāt′), *v.i.,* **-lat·ed, -lat·ing. 1.** *Brit.* to keep watch over students at an examination. **2.** *Obs.* to keep watch. [< L *invigilāt(us)* watched over (ptp. of *invigilāre*), equiv. to *in-* IN-² + *vigilā-* (s. of *vigilāre* to watch; see VIGIL) + *-tus* ptp. suffix] —**in·vig′i·la′tion,** *n.* —**in·vig′i·la′tor,** *n.*

in·vig·or·ant (in vig′ər ənt), *n.* a tonic. [INVIGOR(ATE) + -ANT]

in·vig·or·ate (in vig′ə rāt′), *v.t.,* **-at·ed, -at·ing.** to give vigor to; fill with life and energy: *to invigorate the body.* [IN-² + *vigorate;* see VIGOR, -ATE¹] —**in·vig′or·at′ing·ly,** *adv.* —**in·vig′or·a′tion,** *n.* —**in·vig′or·a′tive,** *adj.* —**in·vig′or·a′tive·ly,** *adv.* —**in·vig′or·a′tor,** *n.*
—**Syn.** strengthen, vitalize, energize. See **animate.**

in·vin·ci·ble (in vin′sə bəl), *adj.* **1.** incapable of being conquered, defeated, or subdued: *an invincible opponent.* **2.** insuperable; insurmountable: *invincible difficulties.* [ME < LL *invincibil(is).* See IN-³, VINCIBLE] —**in·vin′ci·bil′i·ty, in·vin′ci·ble·ness,** *n.* —**in·vin′ci·bly,** *adv.*
—**Syn. 1.** unyielding. INVINCIBLE, IMPREGNABLE, INDOMITABLE suggest that which cannot be overcome or mastered. INVINCIBLE is applied to that which cannot be conquered in combat or war, or overcome or subdued in any manner: *an invincible army; invincible courage.* IMPREGNABLE is applied to a place or position that cannot be taken by assault or siege, and hence to whatever is proof against attack: *an impregnable fortress; impregnable virtue.* INDOMITABLE implies having an unyielding spirit, or stubborn persistence in the face of opposition or difficulty: *indomitable will.* —**Ant. 1.** conquerable.

Invin′cible Arma′da, Armada.

in vi·no ve·ri·tas (in wē′nō we′ri täs′; *Eng.* in vī′nō ver′i tas′, vē′nō), *Latin.* in wine there is truth.

in·vi·o·la·ble (in vī′ə lə bəl), *adj.* **1.** prohibiting violation; secure from destruction, violence, infringement or desecration: *an inviolable sanctuary.* **2.** incapable of being violated; incorruptible; unassailable: *inviolable secrecy; an inviolable conscience.* [< L *inviolābil(is).* See IN-³, VIOLABLE] —**in·vi′o·la·bil′i·ty, in·vi′o·la·ble·ness,** *n.* —**in·vi′o·la·bly,** *adv.*

in·vi·o·late (in vī′ə lit, -lāt′), *adj.* **1.** free from violation, injury, desecration, or outrage. **2.** undisturbed; untouched. **3.** unbroken: *that promise which remains inviolate.* **4.** not infringed. [< L *inviolāt(us)* unhurt, inviolable. See IN-³, VIOLATE] —**in·vi·o·la·cy** (in vī′ə lə sē), **in·vi′o·late·ness,** *n.* —**in·vi′o·late·ly,** *adv.*

in·vis·i·ble (in viz′ə bəl), *adj.* **1.** not visible; not perceptible by the eye: *invisible fluid.* **2.** withdrawn from or out of sight; hidden: *an invisible seam.* **3.** not perceptible or discernible by the mind: *invisible differences.* **4.** not ordinarily found in financial statements or reflected in statistics or a listing: *Good will is an invisible asset to a business.* **5.** concealed from public knowledge. —*n.* **6.** an invisible thing or being. **7. the invisible,** the unseen or spiritual world. [ME < L *invīsibil(is).* See IN-³, VISIBLE] —**in·vis′i·bil′i·ty, in·vis′i·ble·ness,** *n.* —**in·vis′i·bly,** *adv.*

invis′ible glass′, 1. glass which has been curved to eliminate reflections. **2.** a glass plate with transparent molecular coatings on both sides that eliminate surface reflections, used for optical purposes.

invis′ible hand′, (in the economics of Adam Smith) the underlying principle that assures the optimum level of economic welfare of a society when each person acts in self-interest.

invis′ible ink′. See **sympathetic ink.**

invis′ible shad′ow, (in architectural shades and shadows) a three-dimensional space occupied by the shadow projected by a solid and within which a surface is in shadow.

in·vi·ta·tion (in′vi tā′shən), *n.* **1.** the act of inviting. **2.** the written or spoken form with which a person is invited. **3.** something offered as a suggestion: *an invitation to consider a merger.* **4.** attraction or incentive; allurement. **5.** a provocation: *The article was an invitation for public protest against the newspaper.* —*adj.* **6.** Also, **in′vi·ta′tion·al.** *Sports.* restricted to individuals or teams invited by the sponsor, as a track meet or basketball tournament. [< L *invītātiōn-* (s. of *invītātiō*), equiv. to *invītāt(us)* invited (ptp. of *invītāre*) + *-iōn-* -ION]

In·vi·ta·tion au Châ·teau, L′ (*Fr.* lan vē tä syôn′ ō shä tō′). See **Ring Round the Moon.**

in·vi·ta·to·ry (in vī′tə tôr′ē, -tōr′ē), *adj.* serving to invite; conveying an invitation. [ME < LL *invītātōri(us).* See INVITE, -ATE¹, -ORY¹]

in·vite (*v.* in vīt′; *n.* in′vīt), *v.,* **-vit·ed, -vit·ing,** *n.* —*v.t.* **1.** to ask or request the presence or participation of in a kindly, courteous, or complimentary way, esp. to ask or request to come or go to some place, gathering, entertainment, etc., or to do something: *to invite friends to dinner.* **2.** to request politely or formally: *to invite donations.* **3.** to act so as to bring on or render probable: *to invite danger by fast driving.* **4.** to call forth or give occasion for: *That big hat invites laughter.* **5.** to attract, allure, entice, or tempt. —*v.i.* **6.** to give invitation; offer attractions or allurements. —*n.* **7.** *Chiefly Dial.* an invitation. [< L *invīt(āre)*] —**in·vit′er,** *n.*
—**Syn. 1.** bid. See **call. 2.** solicit. **5.** lure, draw.

in·vit·ing (in vī′ting), *adj.* offering an invitation, esp. one of an attractive, alluring, or tempting nature: *an inviting offer.* [INVITE + -ING²] —**in·vit′ing·ly,** *adv.* —**in·vit′ing·ness,** *n.*

in vi·tro (in vē′trō), *Biol.* within an artificial environment, as a test tube: *the cultivation of tissues in vitro.* Cf. **in vivo.** [< L: lit., in glass]

in vi·vo (in vē′vō), *Biol.* within a living organism: *the cultivation of tissues in vivo.* Cf. **in vitro.** [< L: in something alive]

in·vo·cate (in′və kāt′), *v.t.,* **-cat·ed, -cat·ing.** *Archaic.* invoke. [< L *invocāt(us)* called upon (ptp. of *invocāre*), equiv. to *in-* IN-² + *vocā-* (s. of *vocāre* to call) + *-tus* ptp. suffix] —**in·voc·a·tive** (in vok′ə tiv, in′və kā′tiv), *adj.* —**in′vo·ca′tor,** *n.*

in·vo·ca·tion (in′və kā′shən), *n.* **1.** the act of invoking or calling upon a deity, spirit, etc., for aid, protection, inspiration, or the like; supplication. **2.** any petitioning or supplication for help or aid. **3.** a form of prayer invoking God's presence, said esp. at the beginning of a public ceremony. **4.** an entreaty for aid and guidance from a Muse, deity, etc., at the beginning of an epic or epiclike poem. **5.** the act of calling upon a spirit by incantation. **6.** the magic formula used to conjure up a spirit; incantation. **7.** the act of calling upon or referring to something, as a concept, document, etc., for support and justification in a particular circumstance. **8.** the enforcing or use of a legal or moral precept or right. [ME *invocacio(u)n* < L *invocātiōn-* (s. of *invocātiō*). See INVOCATE, -ION]

in·voc·a·to·ry (in vok′ə tôr′ē, -tōr′ē), *adj.* of, pertaining to, or characteristic of invocation. [INVOCATE + -ORY¹]

in·voice (in′vois), *n., v.,* **-voiced, -voic·ing.** —*n.* **1.** an itemization of goods purchased or services provided, together with the charges and terms. **2.** an itemized bill containing the prices which comprise the total charge. **3.** *Rare.* the merchandise or shipment itself. —*v.t.* **4.** to present an invoice to: *The manufacturer invoiced our company for two typewriters.* **5.** to present an invoice for: *five chairs invoiced and shipped last month.* [var. of *invoyes,* pl. of obs. *invoy,* r. *envoy* < MF: message; see ENVOY²]

in·voke (in vōk′), *v.t.,* **-voked, -vok·ing. 1.** to call for with earnest desire; make supplication or pray for: *to invoke God's mercy.* **2.** to call on (a deity, Muse, etc.), as in prayer or supplication. **3.** to declare to be binding or in effect: *to invoke the Taft-Hartley Act; to invoke a veto.* **4.** to appeal to, as for confirmation. **5.** to petition or call on for help or aid. **6.** to call forth or upon (a spirit) by incantation. **7.** to cause, call forth, or bring about. [late ME < L *invoc(āre),* equiv. to *in-* IN-² + *vocāre* to call, akin to *vox* VOICE] —**in·vo′ca·ble,** *adj.* —**in·vok′er,** *n.*

in·vo·lu·cel (in vol′yə sel′), *n.* *Bot.* a secondary involucre, as in a compound cluster of flowers. [< NL *involūcell(um),* equiv. to *involū-c(rum),* INVOLUCRUM + *-ellum* dim. suffix] —**in·vol·u·cel·ate** (in vol′yə sel′it), **in·vol·u·cel·at·ed** (in vol′yə sel′ā tid), *adj.*

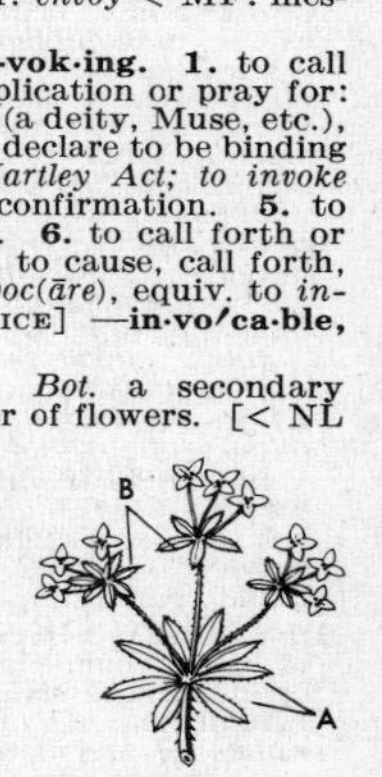

in·vo·lu·crate (in′və lo͞o′krit, -krāt), *adj.* having an involucre. [INVOLUCR(E) + -ATE¹]

in·vo·lu·cre (in′və lo͞o′kər), *n.* **1.** *Bot.* a collection or rosette of bracts subtending a flower cluster, umbel, or the like. **2.** a covering, esp. a membranous one. [< MF < L; see INVOLUCRUM] —**in′vo·lu′cral,** *adj.*

B
A

A, Involucre
B, Involucel

in·vo·lu·crum (in′və lo͞o′krəm), *n., pl.* **-cra** (-krə). involucre. [< NL, L: a wrap, cover, equiv. to *involū-* (ptp. s. of *involvere* to wrap, cover; see INVOLUTE) + *-crum* n. suffix]

in·vol·un·tar·y (in vol′ən ter′ē), *adj.* **1.** not voluntary; independent of one's will or done or made otherwise than by one's own choice: *an involuntary listener; involuntary servitude.* **2.** unintentional; unconscious: *an involuntary gesture.* **3.** *Physiol.* acting independently of or done or occurring without volition: *involuntary muscles.* [< LL *involuntāri(us).* See IN-³, VOLUNTARY] —**in·vol·un·tar·i·ly** (in vol′ən ter′ə lē, -vol′ən târ′-), *adv.* —**in·vol·un·tar·i·ness** (in vol′ən ter′ē nis, -vol′ən târ′-), *n.*
—**Syn. 1, 3.** See **automatic. 2.** instinctive. **3.** reflex, uncontrolled. —**Ant. 2.** intentional.

in·vo·lute (*adj., n.* in′və lo͞ot′; *v.* in′və lo͞ot′, in′və-lo͞ot′), *adj., n., v.,* **-lut·ed, -lut·ing.** —*adj.* **1.** involved; intricate; complex. **2.** curled or curved inward or spirally. 3. *Bot.* rolled inward from the edge, as a leaf. 4. *Zool.* (of shells) having the whorls closely wound. —*n.* 5. *Geom.* any curve of which a given curve is the evolute. —*v.i.* 6. to roll or curl up; become involute. 7. to return to a normal shape, size, or state. [< L *involūt(us)* rolled in or up (ptp. of *involvere*), equiv. to *in-* IN-[2] + *volū-* (ptp. s. of *volere* to roll) + *-tus* ptp. suffix]

in·vo·lut·ed (in′və lo͞o′tid, in′və lo͞o′tid), *adj.* 1. curving or curling inward. 2. having an involved or complex nature. 3. having resumed its normal size, shape, or condition. [INVOLUTE + -ED[2]]

in′volute teeth′, (in gears) teeth having a profile which is the involute of a circle.

A, Involute leaves of white lotus, *Nymphaea lotus;* B, Transverse section

in·vo·lu·tion (in′və lo͞o′shən), *n.* 1. the act or an instance of involving or entangling; involvement. 2. the state of being involved. 3. something complicated. 4. *Bot., Zool.* a. a rolling up or folding in upon itself. b. a part so formed. 5. *Biol.* retrograde development; degeneration. 6. *Physiol.* the regressive changes in the body occurring with old age. 7. *Embryol.* the inward movement of cells around the blastopore in the formation of a gastrula. 8. *Gram.* a complex construction in which the subject is separated from its predicate by intervening clauses or phrases. 9. *Math.* a. a function that is its own inverse. b. *Obsolesc.* the raising of a quantity or expression to any given power. [< ML *involūtiōn-* (s. of *involūtiō*). See INVOLUTE, -ION]

Involute produced by string r, unwinding about curve A. Locus of points p equals the involute

in·vo·lu·tion·al (in′və lo͞o′shə nəl), *adj.* 1. of, pertaining to, or characteristic of involutional melancholia: *involutional symptoms.* —*n.* 2. a person who suffers from involutional melancholia. [INVOLUTION + -AL[1]]

involu′tional melancho′lia, *Psychiatry.* extreme depression occurring during the climacteric and characterized by feelings of guilt, hypochondria, insomnia, etc.

in·volve (in volv′), *v.t.*, **-volved, -volv·ing.** 1. to include as a necessary circumstance, condition, or consequence; imply; entail: *This job involves lots of hard work.* 2. to affect, as something within the scope of operation. 3. to include, contain, or comprehend within itself or its scope. 4. to bring into an intricate or complicated form or condition. 5. to bring into difficulties (usually fol. by *with*): *a plot to involve one government in a war with another.* 6. to cause to be troublesomely associated or concerned, as in something embarrassing or unfavorable: *Don't involve me in your quarrel!* 7. to combine inextricably (usually fol. by *with*). 8. to implicate, as in guilt or crime, or in any matter or affair. 9. to engage the interests or emotions or commitment of. 10. to preoccupy or absorb fully (usually used passively or reflexively): *You are much too involved with the problem to see it clearly.* 11. to envelop or enfold, as if with a wrapping. 12. to swallow up, engulf, or overwhelm. 13. *Archaic.* to roll, surround, or shroud, as in a wrapping. 14. *Archaic.* to roll up on itself; wind spirally; coil; wreathe. 15. *Math. Obs.* to raise to a given power. [ME *involve(n)* < L *involv(ere)* (to) roll in or up, equiv. to *in-* IN-[2] + *volvere* to roll; see REVOLVE] —**in·volve′ment,** *n.* —**in·volv′er,** *n.*

—**Syn.** 1. embrace, contain, comprehend, comprise. 5, 6, 8. INVOLVE, ENTANGLE, IMPLICATE imply getting a person connected or bound up with something from which it is difficult for him to extricate himself. To INVOLVE is to bring more or less deeply into something, esp. of a complicated, embarrassing, or troublesome nature: *to involve someone in debt.* To ENTANGLE (usually pass. or reflex.) is to involve so deeply in a tangle as to confuse and make helpless: *to entangle oneself in a mass of contradictory statements.* To IMPLICATE is to connect a person with something discreditable or wrong: *implicated in a plot.* —**Ant.** 6. extricate.

in·volved (in volvd′), *adj.* 1. intricate; complex. 2. implicated: *More than one person is involved in this crime.* 3. concerned in an affair, esp. in a way likely to cause danger or unpleasantness: *I didn't call the police because I didn't want to get involved.* 4. committed or engaged, as in a political cause, artistic movement, etc.: *The Civil Rights demonstration attracted the involved young people of the area.* 5. *Obs.* involute (def. 3). [INVOLVE + -ED[2]] —**in·volv·ed·ly** (in vol′vid lē, -volvd′-), *adv.* —**in·volv′ed·ness,** *n.*

—**Syn.** 1. complicated, knotty, tangled, perplexing. —**Ant.** 1. simple.

invt., inventory.

in·vul·ner·a·ble (in vul′nər ə bəl), *adj.* 1. incapable of being wounded, hurt, or damaged. 2. proof against or immune to attack: *A strong navy made Great Britain invulnerable.* [< L *invulnerābil(is).* See IN-[3], VULNERABLE] —**in·vul′ner·a·bil′i·ty, in·vul′ner·a·ble·ness,** *n.* —**in·vul′ner·a·bly,** *adv.*

in·wale (in′wāl′), *n. Naut.* 1. (in an open boat) a horizontal timber binding together the frames along the top strake. 2. a strip of reinforcing material within a gunwale. 3. *Obs.* gunwale. [IN + WALE[1]]

in·wall (in wôl′), *v.t.* 1. to enclose with a wall. —*n.* 2. an inner wall. 3. *Metall.* an inwardly sloping wall above the bosh of a blast furnace. [IN-[1] + WALL]

in·ward (in′wərd), *adv.* Also, **in′wards.** 1. toward the inside, interior, or center, as of a place, space, body, etc. 2. into or toward the mind or soul: *He turned his thoughts inward.* 3. *Obs.* on the inside or interior: *terrible on the outside, but inward, beautiful.* 4. *Obs.* in the mind or soul; mentally or spiritually: *inward pained.* —*adj.* 5. proceeding or directed toward the inside or interior. 6. situated within or in or on the inside; interior; internal: *an inward room.* 7. pertaining to the inside or inner part. 8. located within the body: *the inward parts.* 9. pertaining to the inside of the body: *inward convulsions.* 10. inland: *inward passage.* 11. mental or spiritual; inner: *inward peace.* 12. muffled or indistinct, as the voice. 13. private or secret. 14. *Archaic.* pertaining to the homeland; domestic. 15. *Obs.* closely personal; intimate; familiar. —*n.* 16. the inward or internal part; the inside. 17. **inwards,** the inward parts of the body; entrails; innards. [ME; OE *inweard.* See IN, -WARD]

in·ward·ly (in′wərd lē), *adv.* 1. in or on, or with reference to, the inside or inner part; internally. 2. privately; secretly: *Inwardly, he disliked his guest.* 3. within the self; toward one's innermost being; mentally or spiritually: *look inwardly and try to discover the truth.* 4. in low tones; not aloud. 5. *Obs.* toward the inside, interior, or center. [ME *inwardli,* OE *inweardlīce.* See INWARD, -LY]

in·ward·ness (in′wərd nis), *n.* 1. the state of being inward or internal: *the inwardness of the body's organs.* 2. depth of thought or feeling; concern with one's own affairs and oneself; introspection. 3. preoccupation with what concerns man's inner nature; spirituality. 4. the fundamental or intrinsic character of something; essence. 5. inner meaning or significance. 6. *Obs.* intimacy. [ME; see INWARD, -NESS]

in·weave (in wēv′), *v.t.*, **-wove** or **-weaved; -wo·ven** or **-wove** or **-weaved; -weav·ing.** 1. to weave in or together. 2. to introduce into or as into a fabric in weaving. 3. to combine or diversify with something woven in. Also, **enweave.** [IN-[1] + WEAVE]

in·wind (in wīnd′), *v.t.*, **-wound, -wind·ing.** enwind.

in·wrap (in rap′), *v.t.*, **-wrapped, -wrap·ping.** enwrap.

in·wreathe (in rēth′), *v.t.*, **-wreathed, -wreath·ing.** enwreathe.

in·wrought (in rôt′), *adj.* 1. worked in or closely combined with something. 2. *Archaic.* wrought or worked with something by way of decoration. 3. *Archaic.* wrought or worked in, as a decorative pattern. Also, **enwrought.** [IN-[1] + WROUGHT]

I·o (ī′ō), *n.* 1. *Class. Myth.* the daughter of Inachus who, being loved by Zeus, was transformed into a white heifer and was, at the wish of Hera, first guarded by Argus and later pursued through the world by a gadfly until she reached Egypt, where she resumed her true shape: identified by the Egyptians with Isis. 2. *Astron.* one of the 12 satellities of Jupiter.

I·o (ī′ō), *n., pl.* **I·os.** See **Io moth.**

Io, *Chem.* ionium.

Io., Iowa.

Io·an·ni·na (yô ä′nē nä′, yä′nē nä′), *n.* a city in NW Greece. 32,315 (1951). Serbian, **Janina, Yanina.**

I·ob·a·tes (ī ob′ə tēz′), *n. Class. Myth.* a Lycian king commissioned by his son-in-law, Proetus, to kill Bellerophon: after surviving ordeals designed to destroy him, Bellerophon was believed to be divinely protected, and Iobates gave him half his kingdom.

iod-, var. of **iodo-** before a vowel: *iodic.*

I·od·a·ma (ī od′ə mə), *n. Class. Myth.* a priestess of Athena who saw the Gorgon's head on the shield of Athena and was turned to stone.

i·o·date (ī′ə dāt′), *n., v.*, **-dat·ed, -dat·ing.** —*n.* 1. *Chem.* a salt of iodic acid, as sodium iodate, $NaIO_3$. —*v.t.* 2. to iodize. [IOD- + -ATE[2]] —**i′o·da′tion,** *n.*

i·od·ic (ī od′ik), *adj. Chem.* containing iodine, esp. in the pentavalent state. [IOD- + -IC]

iod′ic ac′id, *Chem.* a colorless or white, crystalline, water-soluble solid, HIO_3, used chiefly as a reagent.

i·o·dide (ī′ə dīd′, -did), *n. Chem.* 1. a salt of hydriotic acid consisting of two elements, one of which is iodine, as sodium iodide, NaI. 2. a compound containing iodine, as methyl iodide. [IOD- + -IDE]

i·o·dim·e·try (ī′ə dim′i trē), *n. Chem.* iodometry. —**i·o·di·met·ric** (ī′ō də me′trik), *adj.*

i·o·dine (ī′ə dīn′, -din; *in Chem.* ī′ə dēn′), *n. Chem.* a nonmetallic halogen element occurring at ordinary temperatures as a grayish-black, crystalline solid that sublimes to a dense violet vapor when heated: used in medicine as an antiseptic. *Symbol:* I; *at. wt.:* 126.904; *at. no.:* 53; *sp. gr.:* (solid) 4.93 at 20°C. Also, **i·o·din** (ī′ə din). [< NL *iōd(um)* (< Gk *iōdēs,* orig. rust-colored, but by folk-etymology taken as *ī(on)* violet + *-ōdēs* -ODE[1]) + -INE[2]]

iodine 131, *Chem.* a radioactive isotope of iodine having a mass number 131 and a half life of 8.6 days, used in the diagnosis and treatment of disorders of the thyroid gland. Also called **I-131, I 131, radioiodine.**

i·o·dism (ī′ə diz′əm), *n. Pathol.* poisoning caused by sensitivity to or overuse of iodine or its compounds. [IOD- + -ISM]

i·o·dize (ī′ə dīz′), *v.t.*, **-dized, -diz·ing.** to treat, impregnate, or affect with iodine or an iodide. [IOD- + -IZE] —**i′o·di·za′tion,** *n.* —**i′o·diz′er,** *n.*

iodo-, a combining form of **iodine:** *iodometry.* Also, *esp. before a vowel,* **iod-.** [comb. form repr. NL *iōdum* iodine]

i·o·do·form (ī ō′də fôrm′, ī od′ə-), *n. Chem.* a yellowish, crystalline, water-insoluble solid, CHI_3, analogous to chloroform, and having a penetrating odor: used chiefly as an antiseptic. Also called **triiodomethane.** [IODO- + -FORM]

I·o·dol (ī′ə dōl′, -dôl′, -dol′), *n. Pharm., Trademark.* tetraiodopyrrole.

i·o·dom·e·try (ī′ə dom′i trē), *n. Chem.* a volumetric analytical procedure for determining iodine or materials that will liberate iodine or react with iodine. Also, **iodimetry.** [IODO- + -METRY] —**i·o·do·met·ric** (ī′ō də me′trik), *adj.* —**i′o·do·met′ri·cal·ly,** *adv.*

i·o·dous (ī ō′dəs, ī od′əs), *adj.* 1. *Chem.* containing iodine, esp. in the trivalent state. 2. pertaining to or resembling iodine. [IOD- + -OUS]

I.O.F., Independent Order of Foresters.

I·o·la (ī ō′lə), *n.* 1. a town in SE Kansas. 6885 (1960). 2. a girl's given name, form of **Viola.**

I·o·lan·the (ī′ə lan′thē), *n.* a girl's given name.

I·o·lan·the (ī′ə lan′thē), *n.* an operetta (1882) by Sir William S. Gilbert and Sir Arthur Sullivan.

I·o·la·us (ī′ə lā′əs), *n. Class. Myth.* a son of Iphicles who was the nephew and trusted companion of Hercules.

I·o·le (ī′ə lē′), *n. Class. Myth.* a daughter of Eurytus who became the wife of Hyllus.

i·o·lite (ī′ə līt′), *n.* cordierite. [< Gk *ío(n)* the violet + -LITE]

I′o moth′, a showy, yellow moth, *Automeris io,* of North America, having a prominent, pink and bluish eyespot on each hind wing. [named after Io]

i·on (ī′ən, ī′on), *n.* 1. *Physics, Chem.* an electrically charged atom or group of atoms formed by the loss or gain of one or more electrons, as a cation **(positive ion),** which is created by electron loss and is attracted to the cathode in electrolysis, or as an anion **(negative ion),** which is created by an electron gain and is attracted to the anode. The valence of an ion is equal to the number of electrons lost or gained and is indicated by a plus sign for cations and a minus sign for anions, thus: Na^+, Cl^-, Ca^{++}, S= 2. one of the electrically charged particles formed in a gas by electric discharge or the like. [< Gk *íon* going, neut. prp. of *iénai* to go]

I·on (ī′on), *n.* a drama (415? B.C.) by Euripides:

-ion, a suffix, appearing in words of Latin origin, denoting action or condition, used in Latin and in English to form nouns from stems of Latin adjectives (*communion; union*), verbs (*legion; opinion*), and esp. past participles (*allusion; creation; fusion; notion; torsion*). Also, **-ation, -ition, -tion.** Cf. **-cion, -xion.** [< L *-iōn-* (s. of *-iō*) suffix forming nouns, esp. on ptp. stems; r. ME *-ioun* < AF < L *-iōn-*]

Ion., Ionic.

I·o·na (ī ō′nə), *n.* 1. an island in the Hebrides, off the W coast of Scotland: center of early Celtic Christianity. 2. a girl's given name.

i′on cham′ber, *Physics.* See **ionization chamber.**

Io·nes·co (yə nes′kō, ē ə-), *n.* **Eu·gène** (*Fr.* œ zhen′; *Eng.* yo͞o jēn′, yo͞o′jēn), born 1912, French playwright born in Rumania.

i′on exchange′, the process of reciprocal transfer of ions between a solution and a resin or other suitable solid.

I·o·ni·a (ī ō′nē ə), *n.* 1. an ancient region on the W coast of Asia Minor and on adjacent islands in the Aegean: colonized by the ancient Greeks. 2. a town in central Michigan. 6754 (1960).

I·o·ni·an (ī ō′nē ən), *adj.* 1. of or pertaining to Ionia. 2. of or pertaining to the branch of the Greek people named from Ion, their legendary founder. —*n.* 3. a member of one of the four main divisions of the prehistoric Greeks who invaded the Greek mainland and, after the Dorian invasions, emigrated to the Aegean islands and the coast of Asia Minor. Cf. **Achaean** (def. 5), **Aeolian** (def. 2), **Dorian** (def. 2). 4. an Ionian Greek. [IONI(A) + -AN]

Io′nian Is′lands, a group of Greek islands including Corfu, Levkas, Ithaca, Cephalonia, Paxos, and Zante off the W coast of Greece, and Cerigo off the S coast.

Io′nian mode′, *Music.* an authentic church mode represented on the white keys of a keyboard instrument by an ascending scale from C to C.

Io′nian Sea′, an arm of the Mediterranean between S Italy, E Sicily, and Greece.

i·on·ic (ī on′ik), *adj.* 1. of or pertaining to ions. 2. pertaining to or occurring in the form of ions. [ION + -IC]

I·on·ic (ī on′ik), *adj.* 1. *Archit.* noting or pertaining to one of the five classical orders that in ancient Greece consisted of a fluted column with a molded base and a capital composed of four volutes, usually parallel to the architrave with a pulvinus connecting a pair on each side of the column, and an entablature typically consisting of an architrave of three fascias, a richly ornamented frieze, and a cornice corbeled out on egg-and-dart and dentil moldings, with the frieze sometimes omitted. Roman and Renaissance examples are often more elaborate, and usually set the volutes of the capitals at 45° to the architrave. Cf. **composite** (def. 3), **Corinthian** (def. 4), **Doric** (def. 3), **Tuscan** (def. 2). See illus. under **order.** 2. *Pros.* noting or employing a foot consisting either of two long followed by two short syllables **(greater Ionic),** or of two short followed by two long syllables **(lesser Ionic).** 3. noting or pertaining to that variety of the eastern branch of the early Greek alphabet that was used for the writing of the Ionic dialect and that became the variety used for all dialects of Greek from the 4th century B.C. to the present. 4. of or pertaining to Ionia or the Ionians. —*n.* 5. *Pros.* an Ionic foot, verse, or meter. 6. the dialect of ancient Greek spoken in Euboea, the Cyclades, and on the mainland of Asia Minor at Miletus and elsewhere. 7. Also, **ionic.** *Print.* a style of type. [< L *Iōnic(us)* < Gk *Iōnikós* of Ionia; see -IC]

ion′ic bond′, *Chem.* electrovalence (def. 2).

i·on·ise (ī′ə nīz′), *v.t., v.i.*, **-ised, -is·ing.** *Chiefly Brit.* ionize. —**i′on·is′a·ble,** *adj.* —**i′on·i·sa′tion,** *n.* —**i′on·is′er,** *n.*

i·o·ni·um (ī ō′nē əm), *n. Chem.* a naturally occurring radioactive isotope of thorium. *Symbol:* Io; *at. no.:* 90; *at. wt.:* 230. [ION + -IUM]

ioniza′tion cham′ber, *Physics.* an apparatus for detecting and analyzing ionizing radiation, consisting of a vessel filled with a gas at normal or lower than normal pressure and fitted with two electrodes such that the current between the electrodes is a function of the amount of ionization. Also called **ion chamber.**

i·on·ize (ī′ə nīz′), *v.*, **-ized, -iz·ing.** —*v.t.* 1. to separate or change into ions. 2. to produce ions in. —*v.i.* 3. to become changed into the form of ions, as by dissolving. Also, *esp. Brit.,* **ionise.** [ION + -IZE] —**i′on·iz′a·ble,** *adj.* —**i′on·i·za′tion,** *n.* —**i′on·iz′er,** *n.*

i·on·o·gen (ī on′ə jin, -jen′), *n. Physics, Chem.* any substance capable of producing ions, as an electrolyte. [ION + -O- + -GEN] —**i·on·o·gen·ic** (ī on′ə jen′ik), *adj.*

i·on·o·mer (ī on′ə mər), *n. Chem.* any of a class of plastics that because of its ionic bonding action is capable of conducting electric current. [ION + -O- + (POLY)MER]

i·o·none (ī′ə nōn′), *n. Chem.* a light-yellow to colorless, slightly water-soluble liquid that is either one or a mixture of two unsaturated ketones having the formula $C_{13}H_{20}O$, used chiefly in perfumery. [formerly trademark]

i·on·o·pause (ī on′ə pôz′), *n.* the transitional zone between the ionosphere and the mesosphere. [ION + -O- + PAUSE]

i·on·o·sphere (ī on′ə sfēr′), *n.* 1. the region of the earth's atmosphere between the stratosphere and the exosphere, consisting of several ionized layers and extending from about 50 to 250 miles above the surface of the earth. 2. *Obs.* See **E layer.** [ION + -O- + -SPHERE] —**i·on·o·spher·ic** (ī on′ə sfer′ik), *adj.*

i′on propul′sion, *Rocketry.* a projected type of propulsion for vehicles in outer space, the exhaust consisting of positive ions and negative electrons repelled from the vehicle by electrostatic forces, resulting in a very high exhaust velocity.

I.O.O.F., Independent Order of Odd Fellows.

-ior, a suffix of comparatives appearing in words of Latin origin: *superior; ulterior; junior.* [< L *-ior,* masc. and fem. of comp. adjs.]

Ior·mun·gandr (yôr′mo͝on gän′dər), *n.* Jormungandr.

Iosh·kar-O·la (yosh kär′o lä′), *n.* a city in and the capital of the Mari Autonomous Soviet Socialist Republic, in the RSFSR, in the central Soviet Union in Europe. 88,000 (1959). Also, **Yoshkar-Ola.**

i·o·ta (ī ō′tə), *n.* **1.** a very small quantity; jot; whit. **2.** the ninth letter of the Greek alphabet (Ι, ι). **3.** the vowel sound represented by this letter. [< L < Gk *iôta* < Sem; cf. Heb *yōdh*]
—**Syn. 1.** bit, particle, atom, grain, mite.

i·o·ta·cism (ī ō′tə siz′əm), *n.* conversion of other vowel sounds into that of iota, English (ē). [< LL *iōtacism(us)* < Gk *iōtakismós.* See IOTA, -AC, -ISM]

IOU, a written acknowledgment of a debt, esp. an informal one consisting only of the sum owed and the debtor's signature. Also, **I.O.U.** [repr. *I owe you*]

-ious, a combination of **-i-** and **-ous,** used to form adjectives; added to stems chiefly of Latin origin: *odious, religious, various.* Cf. **-eous.** [ME << L *-iōsus* (see -I-, -OSE[1]) and L *-ius* (masc. sing. ending of adjs., as in *varius*)]

I·o·wa (ī′ə wə; *sometimes* ī′ə wā′), *n., pl.* **-was,** (*esp. collectively*) **-wa** for 3. **1.** a State in the central United States: a part of the Midwest. 2,757,537 (1960); 56,280 sq. mi. *Cap.:* Des Moines. *Abbr.:* Ia., Io. **2.** a river flowing SE from N Iowa to the Mississippi River. 291 mi. long. **3.** a member of an American Indian people originally of Iowa, Missouri, and Minnesota but now of Oklahoma, Nebraska, and Kansas. **4.** a Siouan dialect that is the language of the Iowa Indians.

I′owa Cit′y, a city in SE Iowa. 33,443 (1960).

I′owa Falls′, a town in central Iowa. 5565 (1960).

I′owa Park′, a town in N Texas. 3295 (1960).

I·ox·us (ī ok′səs), *n.* a grandson of Theseus and Perigune.

IPA, 1. International Phonetic Alphabet. **2.** International Phonetic Association. **3.** International Press Association. Also, **I.P.A.**

IPBM, interplanetary ballistic missile. Also, **I.P.B.M.**

ip·e·cac (ip′ə kak′), *n.* **1.** the dried root of either of two shrubby, South American, rubiaceous plants, *Cephaelis Ipecacuanha* or *C. acuminata.* **2.** the plants themselves. **3.** a drug consisting of the dried roots of these plants, used as an emetic, purgative, etc., and as the source of emetine. Also, **ip·e·cac·u·an·ha** (ip′ə kak′yo͞o an′ə). [short for *ipecacuanha* < Pg < Tupi *ipekaaguéne,* equiv. to *ipeh* low + *kaá* leaves + *guéne* vomit]

ip′ecac spurge′, a spurge, *Euphorbia Ipecacuanhae,* of the eastern U.S.

iph, inches per hour.

i.p.h., 1. *Print.* impressions per hour. **2.** inches per hour.

Iph·i·a·nas·sa (if′ē ə nas′ə), *n.* **1.** (in the *Iliad*) a daughter of Agamemnon, offered to Achilles as a wife if he would return to battle against the Trojans. **2.** a daughter of Proetus and Antia who, with her sisters Iphinoë and Lysippe, was inflicted with madness for her irreverence toward the gods.

Iph·i·cles (if′ə klēz′, ī′fə-), *n. Class. Myth.* a son of Alcmene and Amphitryon, the brother of Hercules.

I·phid·a·mas (i fid′ə məs), *n.* (in the *Iliad*) the son of Antenor and Theano, who was killed by Agamemnon.

Iph·i·ge·ni·a (if′i jə nī′ə, -nē′ə), *n.* **1.** *Class. Myth.* the daughter of Agamemnon and Clytemnestra and sister of Orestes and Electra: when she was about to be sacrificed to ensure a wind to take the Greek ships to Troy, she was saved by Artemis, whose priestess she became. **2.** a girl's given name.

Iphigeni′a in Au′lis (ô′lis), **1.** a tragedy (408? B.C.) by Euripides. **2.** an opera (1774) by Christoph Willibald von Gluck.

Iphigeni′a in Tau′ris (tôr′is), **1.** a drama (413? B.C.) by Euripides. **2.** an opera (1779) by Christoph Willibald von Gluck.

Iph·i·me·di·a (if′ə mə dī′ə), *n. Class. Myth.* the wife of Aloeus and the mother, by Poseidon, of Otus and Ephialtes.

I·phin·o·ë (i fin′ō ē′), *n. Class. Myth.* **1.** a daughter of Antia and Proetus who was inflicted with madness for her irreverence toward the gods. Cf. **Iphianassa** (def. 2). **2.** the woman who brought Queen Hypsipyle's message of welcome to Jason and the Argonauts.

I·phis (ī′fis), *n. Class. Myth.* **1.** a Cretan maiden, reared as a boy by her mother because her father ordered that all of his daughters be killed: Io changed her into a man when she fell in love with the beautiful Ianthe. **2.** a son of Alector.

I·phi·ti·on (i fish′ē on′), *n.* (in the *Iliad*) a Trojan warrior slain by Achilles.

Iph·i·tus (if′i təs, ī′fi-), *n. Class. Myth.* a son of Eurytus and the brother of Iole who joined the Argonauts.

Iph·thi·me (if′thə mē′, if thī′mē), *n.* (in the *Odyssey*) a sister of Penelope.

I·pia·les (ē pyä′les), *n.* a city in SW Colombia. 11,569 (1951).

Ip·i·u·tak (ip′ē yo͞o′tak), *adj.* of, pertaining to, or characteristic of an Eskimo culture of Alaska lasting from A.D. 100–600. [named after site where cultural relics were found]

ipm, inches per minute. Also, **i.p.m.**

I·poc·to·nus (i pok′tə nəs), *n. Class. Myth.* an epithet of Hercules, meaning "worm-killer," in reference to his protection of vines.

I·poh (ē′pō), *n.* a city in central Perak, on the SW Malay peninsula, in Malaysia. 125,770 (1957).

ip·o·moe·a (ip′ə mē′ə, ī′pə-), *n.* **1.** any convolvulaceous plant of the genus *Ipomoea,* certain species of which are cultivated for their large, showy flowers. **2.** the dried root of the plant *Ipomoea orizabensis,* yielding a resin used as a cathartic. [< NL < Gk *ip-* (s. of *íps*) worm + *homoîa,* neut. pl. of *homoîos* like; see HOMEO-]

Ip·po·li·tov-I·va·nov (i po lē′tof i vä′nof), *n.* **Mi·kha·il Mi·khai·lo·vich** (mi kHä ēl′ mi kHī′lo vich), 1857–1935, Russian composer.

ipr, inches per revolution. Also, **i.p.r.**

i·pro·ni·a·zid (ī′prə nī′ə zid), *n. Pharm.* a compound, $C_9H_{13}N_3O$, used in the form of its crystalline, water-soluble dihydrochloride for the treatment of mental depression. [I(SO)PRO(PYL) + NI(COTINE) + AZ- + -ID[4]]

ips, inches per second. Also, **i.p.s.**

Ip·sam·bul (ip′sam bo͞ol′), *n.* See **Abu Simbel.**

ip·se dix·it (ip′se dik′sit; *Eng.* ip′sē dik′sit), *Latin.* **1.** he himself said it. **2.** an assertion without proof.

ip·sis·si·ma ver·ba (ip sis′si mä′ weʀ′bä; *Eng.* ip-sis′ə mə vûr′bə), *Latin.* the very words; verbatim.

ip·so fac·to (ip′sō fak′tō), by the fact itself; by the very nature of the deed: *to be condemned ipso facto.* [< L]

ip·so ju·re (ip′sō yo͞o′ʀe; *Eng.* ip′sō jo͝or′ē), *Latin.* by the law itself; by operation of law.

Ip·sus (ip′səs), *n.* an ancient village in central Asia Minor, in Phrygia: the scene of a battle (301 B.C.) between the successors of Alexander the Great.

Ips·wich (ip′swich), *n.* **1.** a city in SE Suffolk, in E England. 117,325 (1961). **2.** a town in NE Massachusetts. 4617 (1960).

IPY, International Polar Year.

IQ, *Psychol.* See **intelligence quotient.** Also, **I.Q.**

i.q., the same as. [< L *idem quod*]

Iq·bal (ik bäl′), *n.* **Muhammad,** 1873–1938, Pakistani poet.

IQSY, *Astron.* See **International Year of the Quiet Sun.**

I·qui·que (ē kē′ke), *n.* a seaport in N Chile. 64,900.

I·qui·tos (ē kē′tôs), *n.* a city in NE Peru, on the upper Amazon. 51,730 (est. 1957).

IR, 1. infrared. **2.** intelligence ratio.

Ir, Irish.

Ir, *Chem.* iridium.

ir-[1], var. of **in-**[2] (by assimilation) before *r: irradiate.*

ir-[2], var. of **in-**[3] (by assimilation) before *r: irreducible.*

Ir., 1. Ireland. **2.** Irish.

I.R., 1. immediate reserve. **2.** infantry reserve. **3.** intelligence ratio. **4.** internal revenue.

I·ra (ī′rə), *n.* a boy's or girl's name.

I.R.A., 1. individual retirement account: a savings plan that allows individuals to put aside money that is tax free until retirement. **2.** Irish Republican Army. Also, **IRA**

i·ra·cund (ī′rə kund′), *adj.* prone to anger; irascible. [< L *īrācund(us)* irascible, equiv. to *īrā-* (see IRATE) + *-cundus* inclined to, adj. suffix] —**i′ra·cun′di·ty,** *n.*

i·ra·de (*Turk.* i rä′de), *n.* a decree of a Muslim ruler. [< Turk < Ar *irādah* will, wish]

I·rak (i rak′; *Pers.* ē räk′), *n.* Iraq.

I·ra·ki (i rak′ē; *Pers.* ē rä′kē), *n., pl.* **-kis,** *adj.* Iraqi.

I·ran (i ran′, ī ran′; *Pers.* ē rän′), *n.* a republic in SW Asia. 22,860,000 (est. 1964); ab. 635,000 sq. mi. *Cap.:* Teheran. Formerly (until 1935), **Persia.**

Iran., Iranian.

I·ra·ni·an (i rā′nē ən, ī rā′-), *adj.* **1.** of or pertaining to Iran, its inhabitants, or their language. **2.** of or pertaining to Iranian. —*n.* **3.** a subbranch of the Indo-European family of languages, including esp. Persian, Pashto, Avestan, and Kurdish. **4.** an inhabitant of Iran; Persian. Also, **I·ra·ni** (i rä′nē) (for defs. 1, 4). [IRAN + -IAN]

Ira′nian Plateau′, a plateau in SW Asia, mostly in Iran, extending from the Tigris to the Indus rivers. 1,000,000 sq. mi.

I·raq (i rak′; *Pers.* ē-räk′), *n.* a republic in SW Asia, N of Saudi Arabia and W of Iran, centering in the Tigris-Euphrates basin of Mesopotamia. 8,261,527 (1965); 172,000 sq. mi. *Cap.:* Baghdad. Also, **Irak.**

I·ra·qi (i rak′ē; *Pers.* ē rä′kē), *n., pl.* **-qis,** *adj.* —*n.* **1.** a native of Iraq. **2.** Also, **Ira′qi Ar′abic.** the dialect of Arabic spoken in Iraq. —*adj.* **3.** of or pertaining to Iraq, its inhabitants, or their language. Also, **Iraki.** [< Ar *'Irāqī,* equiv. to *'Irāq* IRAQ + *-ī* suffix of appurtenance]

i·ras·ci·ble (i ras′ə bəl), *adj.* **1.** easily provoked to anger: *an irascible old man.* **2.** characterized or produced by anger: *an irascible response.* [ME *irascibel* < LL *īrascibil(is),* equiv. to L *īrasc-* (s. of *īrascī* to grow angry; see IRE, -ESCE) + *-ibilis* -IBLE] —**i·ras′ci·bil′i·ty, i·ras′ci·ble·ness,** *n.* —**i·ras′ci·bly,** *adv.*

i·rate (ī′rāt, ī rāt′), *adj.* **1.** angry; enraged. **2.** arising from or characterized by anger: *an irate reply.* [< L *īrāt(us)* angered (ptp. of *īrascī*). See IRE, -ATE[1]] —**i·rate′ly,** *adv.*
—**Syn. 1.** furious, irritated, provoked. —**Ant. 1.** calm.

I·ra·zu (ē′rä so͞o′), *n.* **Mount,** a volcano in central Costa Rica. 11,200 ft.

IRBM, See **intermediate range ballistic missile.** Also, **I.R.B.M.**

ire (īᵊr), *n.* anger; wrath. [ME < OF < L *īra* anger] —**ire′less,** *adj.*
—**Syn.** fury, rage, choler, spleen.

Ire., Ireland.

Ire·dell (īᵊr′del), *n.* **James,** 1751–99, associate justice of U.S. Supreme Court, 1790–99.

ire·ful (īᵊr′fəl), *adj.* **1.** full of ire; wrathful: *an ireful look.* **2.** easily roused to anger; irascible. [ME; see IRE, -FUL] —**ire′ful·ly,** *adv.* —**ire′ful·ness,** *n.*

Ire·land (īᵊr′lənd), *n.* **1.** Also called **Emerald Isle.** *Literary,* **Hibernia.** a large western island of the British Isles, comprising Northern Ireland and the Republic of Ireland. 4,243,383 (1961); 32,375 sq. mi. **2. Republic of.** Formerly, **Irish Free State** (1922–37), **Eire** (1937–49). a republic occupying most of the island of Ireland: formerly associated with the British Commonwealth of Nations. 2,818,341 (1961); 27,137 sq. mi. *Cap.:* Dublin. **3.** *Heraldry.* a coat of arms blazoned as follows: Azure, a harp or stringed argent. —**Ire′land·er,** *n.*

I·re·ne (ī rē′nē *for 1;* ī rēn′, ī rē′nē *for 2*), *n.* **1.** *Class. Myth.* one of the Horae, the personification of peace. **2.** Also, **I·re·na** (ī rē′nə, i rā′nə), **Irina.** a girl's given name.

i·ren·ic (ī ren′ik, ī rē′nik), *adj.* tending to promote peace; peaceful. Also, **i·ren′i·cal.** [< Gk *eirēnik(ós),* equiv. to *eirḗn(ē)* peace + *-ikos* -IC] —**i·ren′i·cal·ly,** *adv.*

i·ren·ics (ī ren′iks, ī rē′niks), *n.* (*construed as sing.*) the branch of theology dealing with the promotion of peace and conciliation among Christian churches. Cf. **polemics** (def. 2). [see IRENIC, -ICS]

IrGael, Irish Gaelic.

Ir·gun (ir go͞on′), *n.* a militant Zionist underground group, active chiefly during the period of British control of Palestine.

Ir·gun·ist (ir go͞o′nist), *n.* a member of the Irgun. [IRGUN + -IST]

I·ri·cise (ī′ri sīz′), *v.t.,* **-cised, -cis·ing.** (*sometimes l.c.*) *Chiefly Brit.* Irishize.

I·ri·cism (ī′ri siz′əm), *n.* Irishism.

I·ri·cize (ī′ri sīz′), *v.t.,* **-cized, -ciz·ing.** (*sometimes l.c.*) Irishize.

irid-, var. of **irido-** before a vowel: *iridectomy.*

ir·i·da·ceous (ir′i dā′shəs, ī′ri-), *adj.* **1.** belonging to the *Iridacea,* or iris family of plants, including certain flags, the crocus, gladiolus, and freesia. **2.** resembling or pertaining to plants of the genus *Iris.* [IRID- + -ACEOUS]

ir·i·dec·tome (ir′i dek′tōm, ī′ri-), *n. Surg.* a slender cutting instrument used in performing an iridectomy. [IRID- + EC- + -TOME]

ir·i·dec·to·mise (ir′i dek′tə mīz′, ī′rə-), *v.t.,* **-mised, -mis·ing.** *Chiefly Brit.* iridectomize.

ir·i·dec·to·mize (ir′i dek′tə mīz′, ī′ri-), *v.t.,* **-mized, -miz·ing.** *Surg.* to perform an iridectomy on. [IRIDECTOM(Y) + -IZE]

ir·i·dec·to·my (ir′i dek′tə mē, ī′ri-), *n., pl.* **-mies.** *Surg.* excision of part of the iris. [IRID- + -ECTOMY]

ir·i·des (ir′i dēz′, ī′ri-), *n.* a pl. of **iris.**

ir·i·des·cence (ir′i des′əns), *n.* iridescent quality; a play of lustrous, changing colors. [IRID- + -ESCENCE]

ir·i·des·cent (ir′i des′ənt), *adj.* **1.** displaying a play of lustrous colors like those of the rainbow. —*n.* **2.** an iridescent cloth, material, or other substance: *new fall dresses of imported iridescents.* [IRID- + -ESCENT] —**ir′i·des′cent·ly,** *adv.*

ir′ides′cent sea′weed, a red alga, *Iridophycus coriaceum,* found on the Pacific coast of North America, having broad, leathery, iridescent blades.

i·rid·ic (i rid′ik, ī rid′-), *adj. Chem.* of or containing iridium, esp. in the tetravalent state. [IRID- + -IC]

i·rid·i·um (i rid′ē əm, ī rid′-), *n. Chem.* a precious metallic element resembling platinum: used in platinum alloys and for the points of gold pens. *Symbol:* Ir; *at. wt.:* 192.2; *at. no.:* 77; *sp. gr.:* 22.4 at 20°C. [< NL; see IRID-, -IUM]

ir·i·dize (ir′i dīz′, ī′ri-), *v.t.,* **-dized, -diz·ing.** to cover with iridium. [IRID- + -IZE] —**ir′i·di·za′tion,** *n.*

irido-, a combining form of Latin origin used, with the meanings "rainbow," "iridescent," "iris (of the eye)," "*Iris* (the genus)," and "iridium," in the formation of compound words: *iridopupillary; iridosmine; iridotomy.* Also, *esp. before a vowel,* **irid-.** [comb. form repr. NL, L, Gk *īrid-* (s. of *îris*) rainbow, iris, etc.; see IRIS]

ir·i·do·cap·su·li·tis (ir′i dō kap′sə lī′tis, ī′ri-), *n. Pathol.* inflammation of the iris and the capsule of the lens. [IRIDO- + CAPSULE + -ITIS]

ir·i·do·cho·roid·i·tis (ir′i dō kôr′oi dī′tis, -kōr′-, ī′-ri-), *n. Pathol.* inflammation of the iris and the choroid. [< NL; see IRIDO-, CHOROID, -ITIS]

ir·i·do·cy·cli·tis (ir′i dō si klī′tis, ī′ri-), *n. Pathol.* inflammation of the iris and the ciliary body. [IRIDO- + *cyclitis;* see CYCL-, -ITIS]

ir·i·do·pu·pil·lar·y (ir′i dō pyo͞o′pə ler′ē, ī′ri-), *adj. Ophthalm.* pertaining to the iris and the pupil. [IRIDO- + PUPILLARY[2]]

ir·i·dos·mine (ir′i doz′min, -dos′-, ī′ri-), *n.* a native alloy of iridium and osmium, usually containing some rhodium, ruthenium, platinum, etc., used esp. for the points of gold pens. Also, **ir·i·dos·mi·um** (ir′i doz′mē-əm, -dos′-, ī′ri-). Also called **osmiridium.** [IRID- + OSM(IUM) + -INE[2]]

ir·i·dot·o·my (ir′i dot′ə mē, ī′ri-), *n., pl.* **-mies.** *Surg.* the formation of an artificial pupil by transverse division of fibers of the iris. [IRIDO- + -TOMY]

ir·i·dous (ir′i dəs, ī′ri-), *adj. Chem.* containing trivalent iridium. [IRID- + -OUS]

Ir·i·dum (ir′i dəm), *n.* **Sinus.** See **Sinus Iridum.**

I·ri·na (ī rē′nə), *n.* a girl's given name. Also, **Irene, Irena.**

i·ris (ī′ris), *n., pl.* **i·ris·es, ir·i·des** (ir′i dēz′, ī′ri-), *v.* —*n.* **1.** *Anat.* the contractile, circular diaphragm forming the colored portion of the eye and containing a circular opening, the pupil, in its center. See diag. under **eye. 2.** *Bot.* any plant of the genus *Iris,* having showy flowers and sword-shaped leaves. **3.** a flower of this plant. **4.** (*cap.*) *Class. Myth.* a messenger of the gods, regarded as the goddess of the rainbow. **5.** a rainbow. **6.** any appearance resembling a rainbow. **7.** *Motion Pictures, Television.* an iris-in or iris-out. **8.** *Mineral.* a variety of quartz having a fracture showing iridescence. —*v.i.* **9.** *Motion Pictures.* to begin or end a take or scene with an iris-in or iris-out, achieved by manipulation of an iris diaphragm on the camera or by editing the film. [ME < L: crystal < Gk: rainbow, goddess; in some senses < NL, L: flag or NL < Gk: diaphragm of eye]

Iris (bearded), *Iris pallida*

I·ris (ī′ris), *n.* a girl's given name.

i·ris·a·tion (ī′ri sā′shən), *n.* the effect or quality of being iridescent; iridescence. [IRIS + -ATION]

i′ris di′aphragm, *Optics, Photog.* a composite diaphragm with a central aperture readily adjustable for size, used to regulate the amount of light admitted to a lens or optical system.

I·rish (ī′rish), *adj.* **1.** of, pertaining to, or characteristic of Ireland or its inhabitants. —*n.* **2.** the inhabitants of Ireland and their descendants elsewhere. **3.** the aboriginal Celtic-speaking people of Ireland. **4.** the Celtic language of Ireland in its historical or modern form. Cf. **Middle Irish, Old Irish. 5.** See **Irish English.** [ME; OE *Ir(as)* people of Ireland (c. Icel *Īrar*); see -ISH[1]] —**I′rish·ly,** *adv.*

I′rish boat′, a small fishing boat used around Boston in the late 19th century, derived from an Irish model and having a cutter rig. Also called **Boston hooker, dundavoe.**

I′rish bridge′, *Brit.* a paved ford.

I′rish bull′, a paradoxical statement that appears to make sense.

I′rish Chris′tian Broth′er. See **Brother of the Christian Schools** (def. 2).

I′rish cof′fee, a mixture of hot coffee and Irish whiskey, sweetened and topped with whipped cream.

I′rish dai′sy, the dandelion, *Taraxacum officinale.*

I′rish Eng′lish, **1.** the English dialects spoken in Ireland. **2.** the standard English of Ireland. Also called **Irish.**

I′rish Free′ State′, former name of the Republic of Ireland. Gaelic, **Saorstat Eireann, Saorstat.**

I′rish Gael′ic, Gaelic as used in Ireland.

I·rish·ise (ī′ri shīz′), *v.t.,* **-ised, -is·ing.** (*sometimes l.c.*) *Chiefly Brit.* Irishize.

I·rish·ism (ī′ri shiz′əm), *n.* a custom, manner, practice, idiom, etc., characteristic of the Irish. Also, **Iricism.** [IRISH + -ISM]

I·rish·ize (ī′ri shīz′), *v.t.,* **-ized, -iz·ing.** (*sometimes l.c.*) to make Irish, as in character, custom, etc.; give an Irish character to. Also, **Iricize,** or, *esp. Brit.,* **Iricise, Irishise.** [IRISH + -IZE]

I′rish lord′, any of several marine sculpins of the genus *Hemilepidotus,* found from Alaska to northern California.

I·rish·man (ī′rish mən), *n., pl.* **-men. 1.** a man born in Ireland or of Irish ancestry. **2.** a native or inhabitant of Ireland. [IRISH + MAN[1]]

I′rish moss′, a purplish-brown, cartilaginous seaweed, *Chondrus crispus,* of the Atlantic coasts of Europe and North America. Also called **carrageen.**

I′rish Pale′, pale[2] (def. 6).

I′rish pen′nant, *Naut. Slang.* **1.** Also called **cow's tail, dead men.** an unwhipped rope end. **2.** any strand or rope end left hanging untidily.

I′rish pota′to, potato (def. 1).

I′rish Repub′lican Ar′my, a secret Irish nationalist organization founded to work for Irish independence from Great Britain and suppressed by the Irish government in 1936.

I′rish Sea′, a part of the Atlantic between Ireland and England.

Irish setter (27 in. high at shoulder)

I′rish set′ter, one of an Irish breed of setters having a golden-chestnut or mahogany-red coat.

I′rish stew′, a stew usually made of mutton, lamb, or beef, with potatoes, onions, etc.

I′rish ter′rier, one of an Irish breed of terriers having a dense, wiry, reddish coat.

I′rish tweed′, a sturdy fabric of light warp and dark filling, used in men's suits and coats.

I′rish wa′ter span′iel, one of an Irish breed of large water spaniels having a thick, curly, liver-colored coat, a topknot of long, loose curls, and a thin, tapering tail covered with short hair. See illus. under **water spaniel.**

Irish terrier (18 in. high at shoulder)

I′rish whis′key, any whiskey made in Ireland, characteristically a product of barley.

I′rish wolf′hound, one of an Irish breed of large, tall dogs having a rough, wiry coat ranging in color from white to brindle to black.

I·rish·wom·an (ī′rish wŏŏm′ən), *n., pl.* **-wom·en.** a woman born in Ireland or of Irish ancestry. [IRISH + WOMAN]

I′rish yew′, an evergreen plant, *Taxus baccata stricta,* of Eurasia and northern Africa, having upright branches and dark green foliage.

Irish wolfhound (32 in. high at shoulder)

i·ris-in (ī′ris in′), *n. Motion Pictures, Television.* the gradual appearance of an image or scene through an expanding circle.

i·ris-out (ī′ris out′), *n. Motion Pictures, Television.* the gradual disappearance of an image or scene through a contracting circle.

i′ris shut′ter, a camera shutter having a group of overlapping blades that open and close at the center when exposing film.

i·ri·tis (ī rī′tis), *n. Ophthalm.* inflammation of the iris of the eye. [IR(IS) + -ITIS] —**i·rit·ic** (ī rit′ik), *adj.*

Ir·ja (ûr′yə), *n.* a girl's given name.

irk (ûrk), *v.t.* to irritate, annoy, or exasperate: *It irked him to wait.* [ME *irk(en)* (to) grow tired, tire < Scand; cf. Icel *yrkja* to work, c. OE *wyrcan;* see WORK] —**Syn.** chafe, fret, bother; tire.

irk·some (ûrk′səm), *adj.* **1.** annoying; irritating; distressing; tiresome: *irksome restrictions.* **2.** *Obs.* causing weariness or disgust. [IRK + -SOME[1]] —**irk′some·ly,** *adv.* —**irk′some·ness,** *n.*

Ir·kutsk (ir ko͞otsk′), *n.* a city in the S RSFSR, in the S Soviet Union in Asia, W of Lake Baikal. 365,000 (1957).

Irl (ûrl), *n.* a boy's given name, form of **Earl.**

Ir·ma (ûr′mə), *n.* a girl's given name, form of **Erma** or **Irmina.**

Ir·mi·na (ûr mē′nə), *n.* a girl's given name.

Ir′min·ger Cur′rent (ûr′ming gər), a branch of the North Atlantic Current, flowing N past the W coast of Iceland and then W.

IRO, International Refugee Organization.

i·ron (ī′ərn), *n.* **1.** *Chem.* a ductile, malleable, silver-white metallic element, scarcely known in a pure condition, but much used in its crude or impure carbon-containing forms for making tools, implements, machinery, etc. *Symbol:* Fe; *at. wt.:* 55.847; *at. no.:* 26; *sp. gr.:* 7.86 at 20°C. Cf. **pig iron, cast iron, steel, wrought iron. 2.** something hard, strong, rigid, unyielding, or the like: *hearts of iron.* **3.** an instrument, utensil, weapon, etc., made of iron. **4.** an iron implement used, when heated, to press or smooth clothes, linens, etc. **5.** *Golf.* one of a series of nine iron-headed clubs having progressively sloped-back faces, used for driving or lofting the ball. Cf. **wood[1]** (def. 8). **6.** a branding iron. **7.** any of several tools, structural members, etc., of metals other than iron. **8.** the blade of a carpenter's plane. **9.** *Slang.* a pistol. **10.** a harpoon. **11.** *Med.* a preparation of iron or containing iron, used chiefly in the treatment of anemia, or as a styptic and astringent. **12. irons,** shackles or fetters: *Put him in irons!* **13.** *Archaic.* a sword. **14. in irons,** *Naut.* **a.** (of a sailing vessel) unable to maneuver because of the position of the sails with relation to the direction of the wind. Cf. **stay[3]** (def. 2b). **b.** (of a towing vessel) unable to maneuver because of tension on the towing line. **15. in** or **into irons,** in shackles or fetters. **16. irons in the fire,** matters with which one is immediately concerned; undertakings; projects: *He had other irons in the fire, so that one failure would not destroy him.* **17. strike while the iron is hot,** to act quickly when an opportunity presents itself. —*adj.* **18.** of, containing, or made of iron. **19.** resembling iron in firmness, strength, color, etc.: *an iron will.* **20.** stern; harsh; cruel. **21.** inflexible; unrelenting. **22.** strong; robust; healthy. **23.** holding or binding strongly: *an iron grip.* **24.** irritating or harsh in tone: *the foghorn's iron voice.* **25.** *Archaic.* of or pertaining to the iron age. **26.** *Archaic.* degenerate; debased; wicked. —*v.t.* **27.** to smooth or press with a heated iron, as clothes, linens, etc. **28.** to furnish, mount, or arm with iron. **29.** to shackle or fetter with irons. **30.** *Metalworking.* to smooth and thin the walls of (an object being deep-drawn). —*v.i.* **31.** to press clothes, linens, etc., with an iron. **32. iron out,** *Informal.* **a.** to iron or press (an item of clothing or the like). **b.** to remove (wrinkles) from by ironing. **c.** to smooth out; clear up (difficulties, disagreements, etc.): *The problem should have been ironed out months ago.* [ME, OE *īren,* var. of *īsen* (c. G *Eisen*), *īsern* (c. Goth *eisarn*); akin to OIr *īarn*] —**i′ron·less,** *adj.*

I′ron Age′, **1.** the period in the history of mankind, following the Stone Age and the Bronze Age, marked by the use of implements and weapons made of iron. **2.** (*l.c.*) *Class. Myth.* the present age, following the bronze age; the last and worst of the four ages of man, characterized by danger, corruption, and toil. **3.** (*l.c.*) *Archaic.* any age or period of degeneracy or wickedness.

i′ron ammo′nium ox′alate, *Chem.* See **ferric ammonium oxalate.**

i·ron·bark (ī′ərn bärk′), *n.* any of the various Australian eucalyptuses having a hard, solid bark, as *Eucalyptus resinifera,* a tall tree yielding a valuable timber and a gum. [IRON + BARK[2]]

i′ron blue′, any of the class of blue pigments having a high tinting strength and ranging in shade and in coloring properties from reddish-blue to jet blue: used chiefly in the manufacture of paints and printing inks.

i·ron·bound (ī′ərn bound′), *adj.* **1.** bound with iron. **2.** rock-bound; rugged. **3.** hard; rigid; unyielding. [ME; see IRON, -BOUND[1]]

i′ron brick′, *Masonry.* brick having a sprinkling of dark spots caused by the presence of iron salts.

i·ron·clad (*adj.* ī′ərn klad′; *n.* ī′ərn klad′), *adj.* **1.** covered or cased with iron plates, as a vessel for naval warfare; armor-plated. **2.** very rigid or exacting; inflexible; unbreakable: *an ironclad contract.* —*n.* **3.** a warship of the middle or late 19th century having iron or steel armor plating with a heavy wooden backing. [IRON + CLAD]

I′ron Cross′, a German medal awarded for outstanding bravery or service during wartime.

i′ron cur′tain, **1.** a barrier to understanding and the exchange of information and ideas created by ideological, political, and military hostility of one country toward another or others, esp. such a barrier between Soviet Russia, or areas controlled by it, and other countries. **2.** an impenetrable barrier to communication or information, esp. as imposed by rigid censorship and secrecy. [used by Winston Churchill in 1946 to describe the line of demarcation between Western Europe and the Russian zone of influence]

I·ron·dale (ī′ərn dāl′), *n.* a town in central Alabama. 3501 (1960).

I′ron Duke′, epithet of the first Duke of Wellington.

i·rone (ī rōn′, ī′rōn), *n. Chem.* a colorless liquid of isomeric, unsaturated ketones having the formula $C_{14}H_{22}O$, obtained from orris root: used in perfumery for its violet color. [IR(IS) + -ONE]

i·ron·er (ī′ər nər), *n.* one who or that which irons. [IRON + -ER]

i·ron·fist·ed (ī′ərn fis′tid), *adj.* **1.** ruthless and tyrannical. **2.** stingy; tight-fisted. [IRON + FISTED]

i′ron gang′, *Australian.* See **chain gang.**

I′ron Gate′, a gorge cut by the Danube through the Carpathian Mountains, between Yugoslavia and SW Rumania. 2 mi. long. Also, **I′ron Gates′.**

i′ron gray′, a gray like that of freshly broken iron. [OE *īsengrǣg*] —**i′ron-gray′,** *adj.*

I′ron Guard′, a Rumanian fascist party that was extremely nationalistic and anti-Semitic, eliminated after World War II. —**I′ron-Guard′,** *adj.*

i′ron hand′, strict or harsh control: *He governed the country with an iron hand.*

i·ron·hand·ed (ī′ərn han′did), *adj.* having or governing with an iron hand. [IRON + HANDED] —**i′ron·hand′ed·ly,** *adv.* —**i′ron·hand′ed·ness,** *n.*

i′ron hat′, *Geol.* gossan.

i·ron-heart·ed (ī′ərn här′tid), *adj. Informal.* cruel; heartless; unfeeling. —**i′ron-heart′ed·ly,** *adv.* —**i′ron-heart′ed·ness,** *n.*

i′ron horse′, *Archaic.* a locomotive.

i·ron·ic (ī ron′ik), *adj.* **1.** containing or exemplifying irony: *an ironic novel; an ironic remark.* **2.** ironical. [< LL *īrōnic(us)* < Gk *eirōnikós.* See IRONY, -IC]

i·ron·i·cal (ī ron′i kəl), *adj.* **1.** pertaining to, of the nature of, exhibiting, or characterized by irony or mockery: *an ironical compliment; an ironical smile.* **2.** using or prone to irony: *an ironical speaker.* [IRONIC + -AL[1]] —**i·ron′i·cal·ly,** *adv.* —**i·ron′i·cal·ness,** *n.* —**Syn. 1, 2.** sarcastic, sardonic.

i·ron·ing (ī′ər ning), *n.* **1.** the act or process of smoothing or pressing with a heated iron, as clothes, linens, etc. **2.** articles of clothing or the like that have been or are to be ironed. [IRON + -ING[1]]

i′roning board′, a flat, cloth-covered board or other surface, often foldable and having legs, on which clothing, linens, or similar articles are ironed.

i·ro·nist (ī′rə nist), *n.* a person who uses irony habitually, esp. a writer. [IRON(Y)[1] + -IST]

i·ron-jawed (ī′ərn jôd′), *adj.* **1.** having a jaw of or like iron: *iron-jawed press; iron-jawed fighter.* **2.** fiercely determined: *iron-jawed will.*

i′ron law′ of wag′es, *Econ.* the doctrine or theory that wages tend toward a level sufficient only to maintain a subsistence standard of living. Also called **brazen law of wages.**

i·ron·like (ī′ərn līk′), *adj.* resembling iron in strength or hardness. [IRON + -LIKE]

i′ron lung′, a chamber, used esp. in the treatment of certain forms of infantile paralysis, that encloses the chest area and in which alternate pulsations of high and low pressure are used to force normal lung movements, or air into and out of the lungs.

i′ron man′, *Slang.* **1.** a person who can be depended upon to perform a given task or job tirelessly and with uniform efficiency. **2.** a machine that performs a job formerly done by hand. **3.** a dollar bill or a silver dollar.

i·ron·mas·ter (ī′ərn mas′tər, -mä′stər), *n. Chiefly Brit.* the master of a foundry or ironworks; a manufacturer of iron. [IRON + MASTER]

i′ron mold′, a stain on cloth or the like made by rusty iron or by ink pigmented with an iron derivative.

i·ron·mon·ger (ī′ərn mung′gər, -mong′gər), *n. Chiefly Brit.* a dealer in hardware. [ME; see IRON, MONGER]

i·ron·mon·ger·y (ī′ərn mung′gə rē, -mong′-), *n., pl.* **-ger·ies.** *Brit.* **1.** a hardware store or business. **2.** the stock of a hardware store; hardware. [IRONMONGER + -Y[3]]

I′ron Moun′tain, a town in NW Michigan, in the Upper Peninsula. 9299 (1960).

i′ron perchlo′ride, *Chem.* See **ferric chloride.**

i′ron put′ty, a compound of iron oxide and boiled linseed oil for calking pipe joints.

i′ron py′rites, **1.** pyrite; fool's gold. **2.** marcasite. **3.** pyrrhotite.

I′ron Riv′er, a town in NW Michigan, in the Upper Peninsula. 3754 (1960).

i′ron rust′, rust (def. 1).

i·ron-sick (ī′ərn sik′), *adj. Naut.* noting a wooden hull, fastened with iron, in which chemical interaction between the iron and the wood has resulted in the decay of both; nail-sick. —**i′ron sick′ness.**

i·ron·side (ī′ərn sīd′), *n.* **1.** a person with great power of endurance or resistance. **2.** (*cap.*) an epithet or nickname of Edmund II of England. **3.** (*cap.*) Usually, **Ironsides. a.** (*construed as sing.*) a nickname of Oliver Cromwell. **b.** the soldiers serving under Cromwell. **4. ironsides,** (*usually construed as sing.*) **a.** an ironclad. **b.** *Eastern U.S.* scup. [ME; see IRON, SIDE[1]]

i·ron·smith (ī′ərn smith′), *n.* a worker in iron; blacksmith. [ME *irensmith,* OE *īsensmith.* See IRON, SMITH]

i′ron so′dium ox′alate, *Chem.* See **ferric sodium oxalate.**

i′ron sponge′, *Metall.* See **sponge iron.**

i·ron·stone (ī′ərn stōn′), *n.* **1.** any iron-bearing mineral or rock with siliceous impurities. **2.** Also called **i′ronstone chi′na.** a hard white stoneware. [IRON + STONE]

i′ron sul′fate. See **ferrous sulfate.**

I·ron·ton (ī′ərn tən), *n.* a city in S Ohio, on the Ohio River. 15,747 (1960).

i′ron trichlo′ride, *Chem.* See **ferric chloride.**

i′ron vit′riol, *Chem.* See **ferrous sulfate.**

i·ron·ware (ī′ərn wâr′), *n.* articles of iron, as pots, kettles, tools, etc.; hardware. [late ME; see IRON, WARE[1]]

i·ron·weed (ī′ərn wēd′), *n.* any of certain North American, composite plants of the genus *Vernonia,* having tubular, chiefly purple or red flowers. [IRON + WEED[1]]

i·ron·wood (ī′ərn wŏŏd′), *n.* **1.** any of various trees yielding a hard, heavy wood, as the American hornbeam, *Caprinus caroliniana,* or *Lyonothamnus floribundus,* found on the islands off the coast of southern California. **2.** the wood of any of these trees. [IRON + WOOD[1]]

i·ron·work (ī′ərn wûrk′), *n.* **1.** work in iron. **2.** objects or parts of objects made of iron: *ornamental ironwork.* [late ME; see IRON, WORK]

i·ron·work·er (ī′ərn wûr′kər), *n.* **1.** a worker in iron. **2.** a person employed in an ironworks. **3.** a person who works with structural steel. [IRON + WORKER]

i·ron·work·ing (ī′ərn wûr′king), *n.* the method of fashioning articles from iron. [IRONWORK + -ING[1]]

i·ron·works (ī′ərn wûrks′), *n.* (*construed as sing.* or *pl.*) an establishment where iron is smelted or where it is cast or wrought. [IRON + WORKS]

i·ro·ny[1] (ī′rə nē, ī′ər-), *n., pl.* **-nies. 1.** a figure of speech in which the literal meaning of a location is the opposite of that intended, esp., as in the Greek sense, when the locution understates the effect intended. **2.** an utterance or the use of words to express a meaning which is different from, and often the direct opposite of, the literal meaning. **3.** *Lit.* **a.** a technique of indicating, as through character or plot development, an intention or attitude opposite to that which is actually or ostensibly stated. **b.** (esp. in contemporary writing) a manner of organizing a work so as to give full expression to contradictory or complementary impulses, attitudes, etc., esp. as a means of indicating detachment from a subject, theme, or emotion. **4.** See **Socratic irony. 5.** See **dramatic irony. 6.** an outcome of events contrary to what was, or might have been, expected. **7.** the incongruity of this. **8.** an objectively sardonic style of speech or writing. **9.** an objectively or humorously sardonic utterance, disposition, quality, etc. [< L *īrōnīa* < Gk *eirōneía*, equiv. to *eírōn* a dissembler + *-eia* -Y³]

—Syn. 1, 3. IRONY, SARCASM, SATIRE indicate mockery of something or someone. The essential feature of IRONY is the indirect presentation of a contradiction between an action or expression and the context in which it occurs. In the figure of speech, emphasis is placed on the opposition between the literal and intended meaning of a statement; one thing is said and its opposite implied, as in the comment, "Beautiful weather, isn't it?" made when it is raining or nasty. Ironic literature exploits, in addition to the rhetorical figure, such devices as character development, situation, and plot to stress the paradoxical nature of reality or the contrast between an ideal and actual condition, set of circumstances, etc., frequently in such a way as to stress the absurdity present in the contradiction between substance and form. Pope's *Rape of the Lock*, for example, deals with a trivial situation in terms and forms appropriate to the most solemn and heroic of circumstances. The heavy apparatus of mythology and allegory is used in the poem to show a multitude of nymphs, sylphs, gnomes, and mortals warring bitterly and heroically over a curl of hair stolen from a lovely and flighty young girl by one of her admirers at a card party. Neither faction wins the prize, for the lock is finally placed in the heavens. IRONY differs from SARCASM in greater subtlety and wit. In SARCASM ridicule or mockery is used harshly, often crudely and contemptuously, for destructive purposes. It may be used in an indirect manner, and have the form of irony, as in "What a fine musician you turned out to be!" or it may be used in the form of a direct statement, "You couldn't play one piece correctly if you had two assistants." The distinctive quality of SARCASM is present in the spoken word and manifested chiefly by vocal inflection, whereas SATIRE and IRONY, arising originally as literary and rhetorical forms, are exhibited in the organization or structuring of either language or literary material. SATIRE usually implies the use of irony or sarcasm for censorious or critical purposes and is often directed at public figures or institutions, conventional behavior, political situations, etc.

i·ron·y² (ī′ər nē), *adj.* consisting of, containing, or resembling iron. [ME; see IRON, -Y¹]

Ir·o·quoi·an (ir′ə kwoi′ən), *adj.* **1.** belonging to or constituting a linguistic family of the Iroquoian-Caddoan stock of North American Indians of Canada and the eastern U.S., including the Iroquois confederacy, the Cherokees, Wyandots or Hurons, Eries, and others. **2.** of, pertaining to, or characteristic of the Iroquois Indians. [IROQUOI(S) + -AN]

Ir·o·quois (ir′ə kwoi′, -kwoiz′), *n., pl.* **-quois,** *adj.* **—n. 1.** a member of the Indian confederacy, the Five Nations, comprising the Mohawks, Oneidas, Onondagas, Cayugas, and Senecas, and, later, the Tuscaroras. **—adj. 2.** belonging or relating to the Iroquois or their tribes. [< F < Algonquian *irinakhoiw*, lit., real adders]

Ir·ra (ēr′ä), *n.* the Akkadian god of pestilence.

ir·ra·di·ance (i rā′dē əns), *n.* *Physics.* incident flux of radiant energy per unit area. Also, **irradiation.** [IR-¹ + RADIANCE]

ir·ra·di·ant (i rā′dē ənt), *adj.* irradiating; radiant; shining. [< L *irradiant-*, (s. of *irradiāns*) shining upon, prp. of *irradiāre*. See IR-¹, RADIANT]

ir·ra·di·ate (*v.* i rā′dē āt′; *adj.* i rā′dē it, -āt′), *v.*, **-at·ed, -at·ing,** *adj.* **—v.t. 1.** to shed rays of light upon; illuminate. **2.** to illumine intellectually or spiritually. **3.** to brighten as if with light. **4.** to radiate (light, illumination, etc.). **5.** to heat with radiant energy. **6.** to cure by being exposed to radiation, as of ultraviolet light. **7.** to expose to radiation. **—v.i. 8.** *Archaic.* to emit rays; shine. **9.** *Archaic.* to become radiant. **—adj. 10.** irradiated; bright. [< L *irradiāt(us)* illumined, ptp. of *irradiāre.* See IR-¹, RADIATE] **—ir·ra′di·at′ing·ly,** *adv.* **—ir·ra′di·a′tive,** *adj.* **—ir·ra′di·a′tor,** *n.*

ir·ra·di·a·tion (i rā′dē ā′shən), *n.* **1.** the act of irradiating. **2.** the state of being irradiated. **3.** intellectual or spiritual enlightenment. **4.** a ray of light; beam. **5.** *Optics.* the apparent enlargement of an object when seen against a dark background. **6.** the use of x-rays or other radiations for the treatment of disease, the making of x-ray photographs, the manufacture of vitamin D, etc. **7.** exposure or the process of exposure to x-rays or other radiation. **8.** irradiance. [< LL *irradiātiōn-* (s. of *irradiātiō*). See IR-¹, RADIATION]

ir·ra·tion·al (i rash′ə nᵊl), *adj.* **1.** without the faculty of, or not endowed with, reason: *irrational animals.* **2.** temporarily without the faculty of reason; deprived of reason. **3.** without or deprived of sound judgment. **4.** not in accordance with reason; utterly illogical: *irrational fear.* **5.** *Math.* **a.** (of a number) not capable of being expressed exactly as a ratio of two integers. **b.** (of a function) not capable of being expressed exactly as a ratio of two polynomials. **6.** *Algebra.* (of an equation) having an unknown under a radical sign or, alternately, with a fractional exponent. **7.** *Gk. and Lat. Pros.* **a.** of or pertaining to a substitution in the normal metrical pattern, esp. a long syllable for a short syllable. **b.** noting a foot containing such a substitution. **—n. 8.** *Math.* See **irrational number.** [late ME < L *irratiōnāl(is).* See IR-², RATIONAL] **—ir·ra′tion·al·ly,** *adv.* **—ir·ra′tion·al·ness,** *n.*

—Syn. 4. unreasonable, ridiculous; insensate.

ir·ra·tion·al·ise (i rash′ə nᵊlīz′), *v.t.*, **-ised, -is·ing.** *Chiefly Brit.* irrationalize.

ir·ra·tion·al·ism (i rash′ə nᵊliz′əm), *n.* **1.** irrationality in thought or action. **2.** an attitude or set of beliefs having a nonrational basis. **3.** a theory that nonrational forces govern the universe. [IRRATIONAL + -ISM] **—ir·ra′tion·al·ist,** *adj., n.* **—ir·ra′tion·al·is′tic,** *adj.*

ir·ra·tion·al·i·ty (i rash′ə nal′i tē), *n., pl.* **-ties. 1.** the quality or condition of being irrational. **2.** an irrational, illogical, or absurd action, thought, etc. [IRRATIONAL + -ITY]

ir·ra·tion·al·ize (i rash′ə nᵊlīz′), *v.t.*, **-ized, -iz·ing.** to make or cause to be irrational. Also, *esp. Brit.*, **irrationalise.** [IRRATIONAL + -IZE]

irra′tional num′ber, *Math.* a number that cannot be exactly expressed as a ratio of two integers.

Ir·ra·wad·dy (ir′ə wod′ē, -wô′dē), *n.* a river flowing S through Burma to the Bay of Bengal. 1250 mi. long.

ir·re·but·ta·ble (ir′i but′ə bəl), *adj.* not rebuttable; incapable of being rebutted or refuted. [IR-² + REBUTTABLE]

ir·re·claim·a·ble (ir′i klā′mə bəl), *adj.* not reclaimable; incapable of being reclaimed or reformed: *an irreclaimable swamp; irreclaimable offenders.* [IR-² + RECLAIMABLE] **—ir′re·claim′a·bil′i·ty, ir′re·claim′a·ble·ness,** *n.* **—ir′re·claim′a·bly,** *adv.*

ir·rec·on·cil·a·ble (i rek′ən sī′lə bəl, i rek′ən sī′-), *adj.* **1.** incapable of being brought into harmony or adjustment; incompatible: *two irreconcilable statements.* **2.** incapable of being made to acquiesce or compromise; implacably opposed: *irreconcilable enemies.* **—n. 3.** one who or that which is irreconcilable. **4.** a person who remains opposed to agreement or compromise. [IR-² + RECONCILABLE] **—ir·rec′on·cil′a·bil′i·ty, ir·rec′on·cil′a·ble·ness,** *n.* **—ir·rec′on·cil′a·bly,** *adv.*

ir·re·cov·er·a·ble (ir′i kuv′ər ə bəl), *adj.* **1.** incapable of being recovered or regained: *an irrecoverable debt.* **2.** unable to be remedied or rectified; irretrievable: *an irrecoverable fall from grace.* [IR-² + RECOVERABLE] **—ir′re·cov′er·a·ble·ness,** *n.* **—ir′re·cov′er·a·bly,** *adv.*

ir·re·cu·sa·ble (ir′i kyōō′zə bəl), *adj.* not to be objected to or rejected. [< LL *irrecūsābil(is).* See IR-², RECUSE, -ABLE] **—ir′re·cu′sa·bly,** *adv.*

ir·re·deem·a·ble (ir′i dē′mə bəl), *adj.* **1.** not redeemable; incapable of being bought back or paid off. **2.** not convertible into specie, as paper money. **3.** beyond redemption; irreclaimable. **4.** irremediable; irreparable; hopeless. [IR-² + REDEEMABLE] **—ir′re·deem′a·bil′i·ty, ir′re·deem′a·ble·ness,** *n.* **—ir′re·deem′a·bly,** *adv.*

ir·re·den·ta (ir′i den′tə), *n.* a region that is under the political jurisdiction of one nation but is related to another by reason of cultural, historical, and ethnic ties. [< It *(Italia) irredenta* (Italy) unredeemed; see IRREDENTIST]

ir·re·den·tist (ir′i den′tist), *n.* **1.** *(usually cap.)* a member of an Italian association that became prominent in 1878, advocating the redemption, or the incorporation into Italy, of certain neighboring regions **(Italia irredenta)** having a primarily Italian population. **2.** a member of a party in any country advocating the acquisition of some region included in another country by reason of cultural, historical, ethnic, racial, or other ties. **—adj. 3.** pertaining to or supporting such a party or its doctrine. [< It *irredentist(a),* equiv. to *(Italia) irredent(a)* (Italy) unredeemed (fem. of *irredento,* equiv. to *ir-* IR-² + *redento* < L *redemptus;* see REDEMPTION) + *-ista* -IST] **—ir′re·den′tism,** *n.*

ir·re·duc·i·ble (ir′i dōō′sə bəl, -dyōō′-), *adj.* **1.** not reducible; incapable of being reduced or of being diminished or simplified further: *the irreducible minimum.* **2.** incapable of being brought into a different condition or form. **3.** *Math.* **a.** of or pertaining to a polynomial that cannot be factored. **b.** of or pertaining to a group that cannot be written as the direct product of two of its subgroups. [IR-² + REDUCIBLE] **—ir′re·duc′i·bil′i·ty, ir′re·duc′i·ble·ness,** *n.* **—ir′re·duc′i·bly,** *adv.*

ir·re·form·a·ble (ir′i fôr′mə bəl), *adj.* **1.** insusceptible to reforming influences; incorrigible. **2.** of a finality or excellence rendering major improvement impossible, as a doctrine or judgment. [IR-² + REFORM¹ + -ABLE]

ir·ref·ra·ga·ble (i ref′rə gə bəl), *adj.* not to be refuted; undeniable. [< LL *irrefragābil(is),* equiv. to L *ir-* IR-² + *refragā(rī)* (to) resist, oppose + *-bilis* -BLE] **—ir·ref′ra·ga·bil′i·ty, ir·ref′ra·ga·ble·ness,** *n.* **—ir·ref′ra·ga·bly,** *adv.*

ir·re·fran·gi·ble (ir′i fran′jə bəl), *adj.* **1.** not to be broken or violated; inviolable: *an irrefrangible rule of etiquette.* **2.** incapable of being refracted: *X-rays are irrefrangible.* [IR-² + REFRANGIBLE] **—ir′re·fran′gi·bil′i·ty, ir′re·fran′gi·ble·ness,** *n.* **—ir′re·fran′gi·bly,** *adv.*

ir·ref·u·ta·ble (i ref′yə tə bəl, ir′i fyōō′tə bəl), *adj.* not refutable; incontrovertible: *irrefutable logic.* [< LL *irrefūtābil(is).* See IR-², REFUTABLE] **—ir·ref′u·ta·bil′i·ty, ir·ref′u·ta·ble·ness,** *n.* **—ir·ref′u·ta·bly,** *adv.*

irreg., 1. irregular. **2.** irregularly.

ir·re·gard·less (ir′i gärd′lis), *adj.* *Nonstandard.* regardless. [IR(RESPECTIVE) + REGARDLESS]

—Usage. IRREGARDLESS is considered nonstandard because it is redundant: once the negative idea is expressed by the *-less* ending, it is poor style to add the negative *ir-* prefix to express the same idea. Nonetheless, it does creep into the speech of good English speakers, perhaps as a result of attempting greater emphasis.

ir·reg·u·lar (i reg′yə lər), *adj.* **1.** without symmetry, even shape, formal arrangement, etc.: *an irregular pattern.* **2.** not characterized by any fixed principle, method, continuity, or rate: *irregular intervals.* **3.** not according to rule, or to the accepted principle, method, course, order, etc. **4.** not conforming to established rules, customs, etiquette, morality, etc. **5.** *Bot.* **a.** not uniform. **b.** (of a flower) having the members of some or all of its floral circles or whorls differing from one another in size or shape, or extent of union. **6.** *Gram.* not conforming to the prevalent pattern or patterns of formation, inflection, construction, etc., of a language; having a rule descriptive of a very small number of items: *The English verbs "keep" and "see" are irregular in their inflections.* **7.** *Mil.* (formerly, of troops) not belonging to an organized group of the established forces. **8.** flawed, damaged, or failing to meet a specific standard of manufactured goods: *a sale of slightly irregular shirts.* **—n. 9.** one who or that which is irregular. **10.** a product or item containing a flaw or not meeting a specific standard of quality and that therefore cannot be sold as first-quality merchandise. **11.** *Mil.* a soldier not of a regular military force, as a guerrilla or partisan. [< LL *irregulār(is)* (see IR-², REGULAR); r. ME *irreguler* < MF] **—ir·reg′u·lar·ly,** *adv.*

—Syn. 1. unsymmetrical, uneven. **2.** unmethodical, unsystematic; disorderly, capricious, erratic, eccentric, lawless. **3.** anomalous, unusual. IRREGULAR, ABNORMAL, EXCEPTIONAL imply a deviation from the regular, the normal, the ordinary, or the usual. IRREGULAR, not according to rule, refers to any deviation, as in form, arrangement, action, and the like; it may imply such deviation as a mere fact, or as regrettable, or even censurable. ABNORMAL means a deviation from the common rule, often implying that this results in an abberrant or regrettably strange form or nature of a thing: *abnormal lack of emotion; A two-headed calf is abnormal.* EXCEPTIONAL means out of the ordinary or unusual; it may refer merely to the rarity of occurrence, or to the superiority of quality: *an exceptional case; an exceptional mind.* Because of the stigma of ABNORMAL, EXCEPTIONAL is today frequently substituted for it in contexts where such a euphemism may be thought to be appropriate: *a school for exceptional children* (children who are abnormal in behavior, mental capacity, or the like).

ir·reg·u·lar·i·ty (i reg′yə lar′i tē), *n., pl.* **-ties** for 2, 3. **1.** quality or state of being irregular. **2.** something irregular. **3.** a breach of rules, customs, etiquette, morality, etc. [ME *irregularite* < OF < ML *irregulāritās.* See IR-², REGULARITY]

ir·rel·a·tive (i rel′ə tiv), *adj.* **1.** not relative; without relation (usually fol. by *to*). **2.** not pertinent; irrelevant. [IR-² + RELATIVE] **—ir·rel′a·tive·ly,** *adv.* **—ir·rel′a·tive·ness,** *n.*

ir·rel·e·vance (i rel′ə vəns), *n.* **1.** the quality or condition of being irrelevant. **2.** an irrelevant thing, act, etc. [IR-² + RELEVANCE]

ir·rel·e·van·cy (i rel′ə vən sē), *n., pl.* **-cies.** irrelevance. [IR-² + RELEVANCY]

ir·rel·e·vant (i rel′ə vənt), *adj.* **1.** not relevant; not applicable or pertinent: *His lectures often stray to interesting but irrelevant subjects.* **2.** *Law.* (of evidence) having no probative value upon any issue in the case. [IR-² + RELEVANT] **—ir·rel′e·vant·ly,** *adv.*

ir·re·liev·a·ble (ir′i lē′və bəl), *adj.* not relievable; incapable of being relieved. [IR-² + RELIEVABLE]

ir·re·li·gion (ir′i lij′ən), *n.* **1.** lack of religion. **2.** hostility to or disregard of religion; impiety. [< L *irreligiōn-* (s. of *irreligiō*). See IR-², RELIGION] **—ir′re·li′gion·ist,** *n.*

ir·re·li·gious (ir′i lij′əs), *adj.* **1.** not religious; not practicing a religion and feeling no religious impulses or emotions. **2.** showing or characterized by a lack of religion. **3.** showing disregard for or hostility to religion: *His irreligious statements are offensive.* [< L *irreligiōs(us).* See IR-², RELIGIOUS] **—ir′re·li′gious·ly,** *adv.* **—ir′re·li′gious·ness, ir·re·lig·i·os·i·ty** (ir′i lij′ē os′i tē), *n.*

ir·rem·e·a·ble (i rem′ē ə bəl, i rē′mē-), *adj.* permitting no return to the original place or condition; irreversible. [< L *irremeābil(is),* equiv. to *ir-* IR-² + *remeā(re)* (to) come back (*re-* RE- + *meāre* to go) + *-bilis* -BLE] **—ir·rem′e·a·bly,** *adv.*

ir·re·me·di·a·ble (ir′i mē′dē ə bəl), *adj.* not admitting of remedy, cure, or repair: *irremediable disease; irremediable conduct.* [< L *irremediābil(is).* See IR-², REMEDIABLE] **—ir′re·me′di·a·ble·ness,** *n.* **—ir′re·me′di·a·bly,** *adv.*

ir·re·mis·si·ble (ir′i mis′ə bəl), *adj.* **1.** not remissible; unpardonable, as a sin. **2.** unable to be remitted or postponed, as a duty. [ME < LL *irremissibil(is).* See IR-², REMISSIBLE] **—ir′re·mis′si·bil′i·ty, ir′re·mis′si·ble·ness,** *n.* **—ir′re·mis′si·bly,** *adv.*

ir·re·mov·a·ble (ir′i mōō′və bəl), *adj.* not removable. [IR-² + REMOVABLE] **—ir′re·mov′a·bil′i·ty, ir′re·mov′a·ble·ness,** *n.* **—ir′re·mov′a·bly,** *adv.*

ir·rep·a·ra·ble (i rep′ər ə bəl), *adj.* not reparable; incapable of being rectified, remedied, or made good: *an irreparable mistake.* [ME < L *irreparābil(is).* See IR-², REPARABLE] **—ir·rep′a·ra·bil′i·ty, ir·rep′a·ra·ble·ness,** *n.* **—ir·rep′a·ra·bly,** *adv.*

ir·re·peal·a·ble (ir′i pē′lə bəl), *adj.* incapable of being repealed or revoked. [IR-² + REPEALABLE] **—ir′re·peal′a·bil′i·ty, ir′re·peal′a·ble·ness,** *n.* **—ir′re·peal′a·bly,** *adv.*

ir·re·place·a·ble (ir′i plā′sə bəl), *adj.* incapable of being replaced; unique: *an irreplaceable antique.* [IR-² + REPLACEABLE] **—ir′re·place′a·bly,** *adv.*

ir·re·plev·i·sa·ble (ir′i plev′i sə bəl), *adj.* *Law.* not replevisable; not capable of being replevied. Also, **ir·re·plev·i·a·ble** (ir′i plev′ē ə bəl). [IR-² + REPLEVISABLE]

ir·re·press·i·ble (ir′i pres′ə bəl), *adj.* incapable of being repressed or restrained; uncontrollable: *an irrepressible urge to have a chocolate malt.* [IR-² + REPRESSIBLE] **—ir′re·press′i·bil′i·ty, ir′re·press′i·ble·ness,** *n.* **—ir′re·press′i·bly,** *adv.*

ir·re·proach·a·ble (ir′i prō′chə bəl), *adj.* not reproachable; free from blame. [IR-² + REPROACHABLE] **—ir′re·proach′a·ble·ness, ir′re·proach′a·bil′i·ty,** *n.* **—ir′re·proach′a·bly,** *adv.*

ir·re·sist·i·ble (ir′i zis′tə bəl), *adj.* **1.** not resistible; incapable of being resisted or withstood: *an irresistible impulse.* **2.** extremely tempting or enticing, esp. tempting to own or possess: *She saw an irresistible hat in the store window.* **3.** loveable, esp. calling forth warm feeling of protective love: *an irresistible little puppy.* **—n. 4.** an irresistible person or thing. [< LL *irresistibil(is).* See IR-², RESISTIBLE] **—ir′re·sist′i·bil′i·ty, ir′re·sist′i·ble·ness,** *n.* **—ir′re·sist′i·bly,** *adv.*

ir·res·o·lu·ble (ir′i zol′yə bəl, i rez′əl yə bəl), *adj.* **1.** incapable of being solved, explained, or clarified. **2.**

Archaic. incapable of being resolved into component parts; insoluble. **3.** *Archaic.* incapable of being relieved. [< L *irresolūbil(is).* See IR-[2], RESOLUBLE] **—ir′re·sol′u·bil′i·ty,** *n.*

ir·res·o·lute (i rez′ə lo͞ot′), *adj.* not resolute; doubtful or undecided; infirm of purpose; vacillating. [IR-[2] + RESOLUTE] **—ir·res′o·lute′ly,** *adv.* **—ir·res′o·lute′ness,** *n.*

ir·res·o·lu·tion (i rez′ə lo͞o′shən), *n.* lack of resolution; lack of decision or purpose; vacillation. [IRRESOLUTE + -ION]

ir·re·solv·a·ble (ir′i zol′və bəl), *adj.* not resolvable; incapable of being resolved, analyzable, or solvable. [IR-[2] + RESOLVABLE] **—ir′re·solv′a·bil′i·ty, ir′re·solv′a·ble·ness,** *n.*

ir·re·spec·tive (ir′i spek′tiv), *adj.* without regard to something else, esp. something specified; ignoring or discounting (usually fol. by *of*): *Irrespective of my wishes, I should go.* [IR-[2] + RESPECTIVE] **—ir′re·spec′tive·ly,** *adv.*

ir·re·spir·a·ble (ir′i spīər′ə bəl, i res′pi rə bəl), *adj.* not respirable; unfit for breathing. [< LL *irrespīrābil(is).* See IR-[2], RESPIRABLE]

ir·re·spon·si·ble (ir′i spon′sə bəl), *adj.* **1.** said, done, or characterized by a lack of a sense of responsibility: *irresponsible attitudes; His reckless driving and his refusal to work show him to be completely irresponsible.* **2.** not capable of or qualified for responsibility, as due to age, circumstances, a mental deficiency, etc.: *The bank refused to grant the youth a loan because it considers minors irresponsible.* **3.** not responsible, answerable, or accountable to higher authority: *I would love to be as irresponsible as a king.* **—***n.* **4.** an irresponsible person. [IR-[2] + RESPONSIBLE] **—ir′re·spon′si·bil′i·ty, ir′re·spon′si·ble·ness,** *n.* **—ir′re·spon′si·bly,** *adv.*

ir·re·spon·sive (ir′i spon′siv), *adj.* not responsive; not responding, or not responding readily, as in speech, action, or feeling. [IR-[2] + RESPONSIVE] **—ir′re·spon′sive·ness,** *n.*

ir·re·ten·tive (ir′i ten′tiv), *adj.* not retentive; lacking power to retain, esp. mentally. [IR-[2] + RETENTIVE] **—ir′re·ten′tive·ness, ir′re·ten′tion,** *n.*

ir·re·trace·a·ble (ir′i trā′sə bəl), *adj.* not retraceable; unable to be retraced: *an irretraceable crime.* [IR-[2] + RETRACEABLE] **—ir′re·trace′a·bly,** *adv.*

ir·re·triev·a·ble (ir′i trē′və bəl), *adj.* not retrievable; irrecoverable; irreparable. [IR-[2] + RETRIEVABLE] **—ir′re·triev′a·bil′i·ty, ir′re·triev′a·ble·ness,** *n.* **—ir′re·triev′a·bly,** *adv.*

ir·rev·er·ence (i rev′ər əns), *n.* **1.** the quality of being irreverent; lack of reverence or respect. **2.** an irreverent act or statement. **3.** the condition of not being reverenced, venerated, respected, etc. [ME < L *irreverentia.* See IR-[2], REVERENCE]

ir·rev·er·ent (i rev′ər ənt), *adj.* not reverent; manifesting or characterized by irreverence; deficient in veneration or respect: *an irreverent reply.* [< L *irreverent-* (s. of *irreverēns*) disrespectful. See IR-[2], REVERENT] **—ir·rev′er·ent·ly,** *adv.*

ir·re·vers·i·ble (ir′i vûr′sə bəl), *adj.* not reversible; incapable of being changed or reversed: *His refusal is irreversible.* [IR-[2] + REVERSIBLE] **—ir′re·vers′i·bil′i·ty, ir′re·vers′i·ble·ness,** *n.* **—ir′re·vers′i·bly,** *adv.*

ir·rev·o·ca·ble (i rev′ə kə bəl), *adj.* not to be revoked or recalled; unable to be repealed or annulled: *an irrevocable decree.* [ME < L *irrevocābil(is).* See IR-[2], REVOCABLE] **—ir·rev′o·ca·bil′i·ty, ir·rev′o·ca·ble·ness,** *n.* **—ir·rev′o·ca·bly,** *adv.*

ir·ri·ga·ble (ir′i gə bəl), *adj.* capable of being irrigated. [IRRIG(ATE) + -ABLE] **—ir′ri·ga·bly,** *adv.*

ir·ri·gate (ir′ə gāt′), *v.t.*, **-gat·ed, -gat·ing. 1.** to supply (land) with water by artificial means, as by diverting streams, flooding, or spraying. **2.** *Med.* to supply or wash (an orifice, wound, etc.) with a spray or a flow of some liquid. **3.** to moisten; wet. [< L *irrigāt(us)* watered (ptp. of *irrigāre*), equiv. to *ir-* IR-[1] + *rigā-* (s. of *rigāre* to lead water) + *-tus* ptp. suffix] **—ir′ri·ga′tor,** *n.*

ir·ri·ga·tion (ir′ə gā′shən), *n.* **1.** the artificial application of water to land to assist in the production of crops. **2.** *Med.* the covering or washing out of anything with water or other liquid for the purpose of making or keeping it moist, as in local medical treatment. **3.** the state of being irrigated. [< L *irrigātiōn-* (s. of *irrigātiō*). See IRRIGATE, -ION] **—ir′ri·ga′tion·al,** *adj.*

ir·ri·ga·tive (ir′ə gā′tiv), *adj.* serving for or pertaining to irrigation. [IRRIGATE + -IVE]

ir·rig·u·ous (i rig′yo͞o əs), *adj.* *Archaic.* well-watered, as land. [< L *irriguus,* equiv. to *ir-* IR-[1] + *riguus* watered, watering (*rig(āre)* (to) water + *-uus* -UOUS)]

ir·ri·ta·bil·i·ty (ir′i tə bil′i tē), *n., pl.* **-ties. 1.** the quality or state of being irritable. **2.** *Physiol., Biol.* the ability to be excited to a characteristic action or function by the application of some stimulus: *Protoplasm displays irritability by responding to heat.* [< L *irrītābilitās.* See IRRITABLE, -ITY]

ir·ri·ta·ble (ir′i tə bəl), *adj.* **1.** easily irritated; readily excited to impatience or anger. **2.** *Physiol., Biol.* displaying irritability. **3.** *Pathol.* susceptible to physical irritation; likely to shrink, become inflamed, etc., when stimulated: *an irritable wound.* [< L *irrītābil(is),* equiv. to *irrītā(re)* (to) IRRITATE + *-bilis* -BLE] **—ir′ri·ta·ble·ness,** *n.* **—ir′ri·ta·bly,** *adv.*

—Syn. 1. testy, touchy, snappish, petulant, resentful.

ir′ritable heart′, *Pathol.* See **cardiac neurosis.**

ir·ri·tant (ir′i tᵊnt), *adj.* **1.** irritating; tending to cause irritation. **—***n.* **2.** anything that irritates. **3.** *Pathol., Med.* a biological, chemical, or physical agent that stimulates a characteristic function or elicits a response, esp. an inflammatory response. [< L *irrītant-* (s. of *irrītāns*) irritating, prp. of *irrītāre.* See IRRITATE, -ANT] **—ir′ri·tan·cy,** *n.*

ir·ri·tate (ir′i tāt′), *v.*, **-tat·ed, -tat·ing. —***v.t.* **1.** to excite to impatience or anger. **2.** *Physiol., Biol.* to excite (a living system) to some characteristic action or function. **3.** *Pathol.* to bring (a body part) to an abnormally excited or sensitive condition. **—***v.i.* **4.** to cause impatience or anger: *a provocation that irritates more than it rouses to ambition.* [< L *irrītāt(us)* aroused to anger (ptp. of *irrītāre*), equiv. to *ir-* IR-[1] + *-rītā-* arouse, excite (< ?) + *-tus* ptp. suffix] **—ir′ri·ta′tor,** *n.*

—Syn. 1. vex, chafe, fret, gall; nettle, ruffle, pique; incense, enrage, infuriate, inflame. IRRITATE, EXASPERATE, PROVOKE mean to annoy or stir to anger. To IRRITATE is to excite to impatience or angry feeling, often of no great depth or duration: *to irritate by refusing to explain an action.* To EXASPERATE is to irritate to a point where self-control is threatened or lost: *to exasperate by continual delays and excuses.* To PROVOKE is to stir to a sudden, strong feeling of resentful anger as by unwarrantable acts or wanton annoyance: *to tease and provoke an animal until it attacks.*

ir·ri·tat·ed (ir′i tā′tid), *adj.* **1.** annoyed. **2.** inflamed or made raw, as a part of the body. [IRRITATE + -ED[2]] **—ir′ri·tat′ed·ly,** *adv.*

ir·ri·tat·ing (ir′i tā′ting), *adj.* causing irritation; provoking: *irritating querulousness.* [IRRITATE + -ING[2]] **—ir′ri·tat′ing·ly,** *adv.*

ir·ri·ta·tion (ir′i tā′shən), *n.* **1.** the act or fact of irritating or the state of being irritated. **2.** *Physiol., Pathol.* **a.** the bringing of a bodily part or organ to an abnormally excited or sensitive condition. **b.** the condition itself. [< L *irrītātiōn-* (s. of *irrītātiō*). See IRRITATE, -ION]

ir·ri·ta·tive (ir′i tā′tiv), *adj.* **1.** serving or tending to irritate. **2.** *Pathol.* characterized or produced by irritation of some body part: *an irritative fever.* [IRRITATE + -IVE] **—ir′ri·ta′tive·ness,** *n.*

ir·ro·rate (ir′ə rāt′, i rōr′it, i rôr′-), *adj.* *Zool.* marked with small spots of color; speckled. Also, **ir′ro·rat′ed.** [< L *irrōrāt(us)* bedewed (ptp. of *irrōrāre*), equiv. to *ir-* IR-[1] + *rōrā-* (*rōr-,* s. of *rōs* dew + *-ā-* thematic vowel) + *-tus* ptp. suffix] **—ir′ro·ra′tion,** *n.*

ir·ro·ta·tion·al (ir′ō tā′shə nᵊl), *adj.* **1.** not having rotation. **2.** *Math.* conservative (def. 7). [IR-[2] + ROTATIONAL] **—ir′ro·ta′tion·al·ly,** *adv.*

ir·rupt (i rupt′), *v.i.* **1.** to intrude suddenly or with force. **2.** to manifest violent activity or emotion, as a group of persons. **3.** (of animals) to increase suddenly in numbers through a lessening of the number of deaths. [< L *irrupt(us);* see IRRUPTION]

ir·rup·tion (i rup′shən), *n.* a breaking or bursting in; a violent incursion or invasion. [< L *irruptiōn-* (s. of *irruptiō*), equiv. to *irrupt(us)* broken into (ptp. of *irrumpere;* see IR-[1], RUPTURE) + *-iōn-* -ION]

ir·rup·tive (i rup′tiv), *adj.* **1.** of, pertaining to, or characterized by irruption. **2.** irrupting or tending to irrupt. **3.** *Petrol.* intrusive. [IRRUPT + -IVE] **—ir·rup′tive·ly,** *adv.*

IRS, Internal Revenue Service.

Ir·tish (ir tish′), *n.* a river in central Asia, flowing NW from the Altai Mountains in China through the W Soviet Union in Asia to the Ob River. ab. 1840 mi. long. Also, **Ir·tysh′.**

I·rus (ī′rəs), *n.* (in the *Odyssey*) Arnaeus.

Ir·vine (ûr′vin), *n.* **1.** a town in central Kentucky. 2955 (1960). **2.** a boy's given name.

Ir·ving (ûr′ving), *n.* **1. Sir Henry** (*John Henry Brodribb*), 1838–1905, English actor. **2. Washington,** 1783–1859, U.S. essayist, story writer, and historian. **3.** a city in NE Texas, near Dallas. 45,985 (1960). **4.** Also, **Ervin, Erwin, Ir·vin** (ûr′vin), **Irvine, Irwin.** a boy's given name.

Ir·ving·ton (ûr′ving tən), *n.* **1.** a town in NE New Jersey, near Newark. 59,379 (1960). **2.** a town in SE New York. 5494 (1960).

Ir·win (ûr′win), *n.* **1. Wallace,** 1875–1959, U.S. journalist and humorist. **2.** his brother **William Henry** ("*Will*"), 1873–1948, U.S. novelist, short-story writer, and journalist. **3.** a town in SW Pennsylvania. 4270 (1960). **4.** Also, **Ervin, Erwin, Irvin, Irvine, Irving.** a boy's given name.

is (iz), *v.* **1.** 3rd pers. sing. pres. indic. of **be. 2. as is.** See **as** (def. 18). [ME, OE; c. D *is,* Icel *es, er;* akin to G, Goth *ist,* L *est,* Gk *esti,* Skt *asti*]

is-, var. of **iso-** before a vowel: *isallobar.*

Is., **1.** Isaiah. **2.** island. **3.** isle.

is., **1.** island. **2.** isle.

Isa., Isaiah.

I·saac (ī′zək), *n.* **1.** a son of Abraham and Sarah, and father of Jacob. Gen. 21:1–4. **2.** a boy's given name.

I·saacs (ī′zəks), *n.* **1. Sir Isaac Alfred,** 1855–1948, Australian jurist: governor general of Australia 1931–36. **2. Jorge,** 1837–95, Colombian novelist.

Is·a·bel (iz′ə bel′), *n.* a girl's given name. Also, **Is′a·belle′, Is·a·bel·la** (iz′ə bel′ə).

Is·a·bel·la (iz′ə bel′ə), *n.* (*or the Pot of Basil*) a narrative poem (1820) by John Keats.

Isabella I, ("*the Catholic*") 1451–1504, wife of Ferdinand V: queen of Castile 1474–1504; joint ruler of Aragon 1479–1504.

is·ab·nor·mal (īs′ab nôr′məl), *n.* *Meteorol.* a line on a map or chart connecting points having an equal deviation from the normal of some meteorological quantity. Also, **isoabnormal.** Cf. **isanomal.** [IS- + ABNORMAL]

is·a·cous·tic (ī′sə ko͞o′stik *or, esp. Brit.,* ī′sə kou′-), *adj.* of or pertaining to two sounds of equal intensity. [IS- + ACOUSTIC]

Is·a·do·ra (iz′ə dōr′ə, -dôr′ə), *n.* a girl's given name. Also, **Isidora.**

Is·a·dore (iz′ə dōr′, -dôr′), *n.* a boy's given name. Also, **Isidor, Isidore.**

i·sa·go·ge (ī′sə gō′jē, ī′sə gō′jē), *n.* **1.** an introduction, esp. a scholarly introduction to a field of study or research. **2.** isagogics. [< L < Gk *eisagōgḗ,* equiv. to *eiság(ein)* (to) introduce (*eis-* into + *ágein* to lead) + *-ōgē* verbid n. suffix]

i·sa·gog·ic (ī′sə goj′ik), *adj.* **1.** introductory, esp. to the interpretation of the Bible. **—***n.* **2.** isagogics. [< L *īsagōgic(us)* < Gk *eisagōgikós.* See ISAGOGE, -IC] **—i′sa·gog′i·cal·ly,** *adv.*

i·sa·gog·ics (ī′sə goj′iks), *n.* (*construed as sing.*) **1.** introductory studies. **2.** the branch of theology which is introductory to exegesis and the literary history of the Bible. Also, **isagogic, isagoge.** [see ISAGOGIC, -ICS]

I·sai (ī′zī), *n.* Jesse.

I·sa·iah (ī zā′ə *or, esp. Brit.,* ī zī′ə), *n.* Also, *Douay Bible,* **I·sa·ias** (ī zā′əs, ī zī′əs). **1.** a Major Prophet of the 8th century B.C. **2.** a book of the Bible bearing his name. **3.** a boy's given name. [< Heb *Yesha 'yahu,* lit., Jehovah's salvation]

I·sa·ian (ī zā′ən *or, esp. Brit.,* ī zī′-), *adj.* of, pertaining to, or characteristic of Isaiah or of the book of the Bible bearing his name. Also, **I·sa·ian·ic** (ī′zā an′ik *or, esp. Brit.,* ī′zī-). [ISAI(AH) + -AN]

is·al·lo·bar (ī sal′ə bär′), *n.* *Meteorol.* a line on a weather map or chart connecting points having equal pressure changes. [IS- + ALLO- + -BAR]

is·al·lo·therm (ī sal′ə thûrm′), *n.* *Meteorol.* a line on a weather map or chart connecting points having equal temperature variations within a given period of time. [IS- + ALLO- + -THERM]

I·san·der (ī san′dər), *n.* (in the *Iliad*) a son of Bellerophon who was killed by Ares.

is·an·drous (ī san′drəs), *adj.* *Bot.* having the stamens similar to each other and equal in number to the petals. [IS- + ANDROUS]

is·a·nom·al (ī′sə nom′əl), *n.* *Meteorol.* a line on a map or chart connecting points having an equal anomaly of a meteorological quantity. Cf. **isadnormal.** [IS- + *-anomal,* back formation from ANOMALOUS] **—is′a·nom′a·lous,** *adj.*

is·an·thous (ī san′thəs), *adj.* *Bot.* having regular flowers. [< NL *isanthus.* See IS-, -ANTHOUS]

I·sar (ē′zär), *n.* a river in central Europe, flowing NE from W Austria through S West Germany to the Danube River. 215 mi. long.

i·sa·rithm (ī′sə rith′əm), *n.* isopleth. [IS- + *-arithm,* as in *logarithm*]

i·sa·tin (ī′sə tin), *n.* *Chem.* a yellowish-red or orange, crystalline, water-soluble solid, $C_8H_5NO_2$, used chiefly in the synthesis of vat dyes. [< Gk *isát(is)* woad + -IN[2]]

-isation, var. of **-ization.**

is·aux·e·sis (ī′sôg zē′sis, ī′sôk sē′-), *n.* *Biol.* growth of a part at the same rate as that of the whole organism. Cf. **bradyauxesis, tachyauxesis.** [IS- + AUXESIS] **—is·aux·et·ic** (ī′sôg zet′ik, ī′sôk set′-), *adj.*

is·ba (iz bä′), *n.* (in Russia) a log hut. Also, **izba.** [< Russ *izba,* ORuss *istuba* < Gmc; cf. G *Stube,* c. OE *stofa* bathroom; see STOVE[1]]

Is·car·i·ot (i skar′ē ət), *n.* **1.** the surname of Judas, the betrayer of Jesus. Mark 3:19; 14:10,11. **2.** one who betrays another; traitor. [< L *Iscariōta* < Gk *Iskariṓtēs* < Heb *īsh-qeriyōth* man of *Kerioth* a village in Palestine] **—Is·car·i·ot·ic** (i skar′ē ot′ik), **Is·car′i·ot′i·cal,** *adj.* **—Is·car′i·ot·ism,** *n.*

isch-, a learned borrowing from Greek meaning "to check," used in the formation of compound words: *ischemia.* [comb. form repr. Gk *ischein* to suppress, check]

is·che·mi·a (i skē′mē ə), *n.* *Pathol.* local anemia produced by local obstacles to the arterial flow. Also, **is·chae′mi·a.** [ISCH- + -EMIA] **—is·che·mic, is·chae·mic** (i skē′mik, -skem′ik), *adj.*

Is·chep·o·lis (i skep′ə lis), *n.* *Class. Myth.* a son of Alcathous who was killed on the Calydonian Boar Hunt.

Is·chia (ē′skyä), *n.* **1.** an Italian island in the Tyrrhenian Sea, W of Naples: earthquake 1883. 10,385 (1951); 18 sq. mi. **2.** a seaport on this island. 3188 (1951).

is·chi·ad·ic (is′kē ad′ik), *adj.* pertaining to the ischium; sciatic. Also, **is·chi·at·ic** (is′kē at′ik), **is·chi·al** (is′kē əl). [< L *ischiadic(us)* < Gk *ischiadikós,* equiv. to *ischiad-* (s. of *ischiás*) hip-pain + *-ikos* -IC]

is·chi·um (is′kē əm), *n., pl.* **-chi·a** (-kē ə). *Anat.* **1.** the lower portion of either innominate bone. See diag. under **pelvis. 2.** either of the bones on which the body rests when sitting. [< L < Gk *ischíon* hip-joint]

Is·chys (is′kis), *n.* *Class. Myth.* a youth who was slain after committing an act of infidelity with Coronis, the beloved of Apollo.

-ise[1], var. of **-ize:** *organise.*

-ise[2], a noun suffix, occurring in loan words from French, indicating quality, condition, or function: *franchise; merchandise.* Cf. **-ice.** [ME < OF *-ise,* var. of -ICE]

I′sen·heim Al′tarpiece (ē′zən hīm′), an altarpiece (1510?–15?) painted by Matthias Grünewald.

I·sen·land (ē′sən land′, -lənd, ē′zən-; *Ger.* ē′zən länt′), *n.* (in the *Nibelungenlied*) the country of Brynhild, usually identified with Iceland.

I·sen·stein (ē′sən stīn′, ē′zən-; *Ger.* ē′zən shtīn′), *n.* (in the *Nibelungenlied*) the home of Brunhild in Isenland. Cf. **Hindfell.**

is·en·thal·pic (ī′sən thal′pik, ī′zən-), *adj.* *Thermodynamics.* pertaining to or characterized by constant enthalpy. [IS- + ENTHALPIC]

is·en·trope (ī′sən trōp′, ī′zən-), *n.* a line on a map or chart joining points having equal entropy. [back formation from ISENTROPIC]

is·en·trop·ic (ī′sən trop′ik, ī′zən-), *adj.* **1.** *Thermodynamics.* having a constant entropy. **2.** of or pertaining to an isentrope. [IS- + *entropic* (see ENTROPY, -IC)]

I·sère (ē zâr′), *n.* **1.** a river in SE France, flowing from the Alps to the Rhone River. 150 mi. long. **2.** a department in SE France. 729,789 (1962); 3180 sq. mi. *Cap.:* Grenoble.

I·seult (i so͞olt′), *n.* **1.** Also, **Yseult.** German, **Isolde.** *Arthurian Romance.* **a.** the daughter of King Angush of Ireland who became the wife of King Mark of Cornwall: she was the beloved of Tristram. **b.** daughter of the king of Brittany, and wife of Tristram. **2.** a girl's given name.

Is·fa·han (is′fə hän′), *n.* a city in central Iran: the capital of Persia from the 16th into the 18th century. 339,909 (est. 1963). Also, **Ispahan.**

-ish[1], **1.** a suffix used to form adjectives from nouns, with the sense of "belonging to" (*British; Danish; English; Spanish*); "after the manner of," "having the characteristics of," "like" (*babyish; girlish; mulish*); "addicted to," "inclined or tending to" (*bookish; freakish*). **2.** a suffix used to form adjectives from other adjectives, with the sense of "somewhat," "rather" (*oldish; reddish; sweetish*). [ME; OE *-isc;* c. G *-isch,* Goth *-iska,* Gk *-iskos;* akin to -ESQUE]

—Syn. The suffixes -ISH, -LIKE, -LY, agree in indicating that something resembles something else. One of the common meanings of -ISH is derogatory; that is, it indicates that something has the bad qualities of something else, or that it has qualities similar which are not suitable to it: *childish; mannish* (of a woman). The suffix -LIKE, in the formation of adjectives, is usually complimentary: *childlike innocence; godlike serenity.* In an adverbial function, it may be slightly disparaging: *Manlike, he wanted to run the show.* The suffix -LY, when it means having the nature or character of, is distinctly complimentary: *kingly; manly; motherly.*

-ish², a suffix occurring in *i*-stem verbs borrowed from French: *ravish.* [< F *-iss-*, extended s. of verbs in *-ir* << L *-isc-*, in inceptive verbs]

Ish·bo·sheth (ish bō′shith), *n.* a son and successor of Saul. II Sam. 2–4. Also, *Douay Bible,* **Esh-baal.**

Ish·er·wood (ish′ər wo͝od′), *n.* **Christopher (William Brad·shaw)** (brad′shô), born 1904, English poet, novelist, and playwright; in the U.S. since 1938.

Ish′erwood fram′ing, *Naval Archit.* a system for framing steel vessels in which light, closely spaced, longitudinal frames are connected by heavy, widely spaced transverse frames with deep webs. Also called **Ish′erwood sys′tem, longitudinal framing.** [named after B. F. *Isherwood* (1822–1915), American engineer]

Ish·i·ha′ra test′ (ish′ē här′ə), *Ophthalm.* a test for determining color blindness by means of a series of cards each having colored dots that form one pattern to the normal eye and a different pattern to the eye that is color-blind. Also, **Ish′i·ha′ra's test′.** [named after S. *Ishihara* (b. 1879), Japanese eye specialist, who first made it]

i·shi·me (ē′shē mā′; *Jap.* ē′shē me′), *n.* an irregular, slightly roughened texture given to a piece of Japanese metalwork, as a sword mount. [< Jap]

Ish·ma·el (ish′mē əl, -mā-), *n.* **1.** Also, *Douay Bible,* **Ismael.** the son of Abraham and Hagar: both he and Hagar were cast out of Abraham's family by Sarah. Gen. 16:11, 12. **2.** any outcast. [< Heb *Yishmā'ēl*, lit., God will hear]

Ish·ma·el·ite (ish′mē ə līt′, -mā ə-, -mə-), *n.* **1.** a descendant of Ishmael, the traditional ancestor of the Arab peoples. **2.** a wanderer or outcast. [ISHMAEL + -ITE¹] —**Ish′ma·el·it′ish,** *adj.*

Ish·pe·ming (ish′pə ming), *n.* a town in NW Michigan, in the Upper Peninsula. 8857 (1960).

Ish·tar (ish′tär), *n.* the Assyrian and Babylonian goddess of love and war, identified with the Phoenician Astarte, the Semitic Ashtoreth, and the Sumerian Inanna. Also called **Mylitta.**

I·shum (ē′shəm), *n.* the Akkadian god of fire and the companion of Irra.

Ish·va·ra (ēsh′wər ə), *n.* *Hinduism.* a personal and supreme god, supposed in dvaita Vedantism to be included with the world and Atman within Brahman.

Is·i·ac (is′ē ak′, iz′-, ī′sē-), *adj.* of or pertaining to Isis or the worship of Isis. Also, **I·si·a·cal** (i sī′ə kəl, ī sī′-). [< L *Isiac(us)* < Gk *Isiakós.* See ISIS, -AC]

i·sid·i·oid (ī sid′ē oid′), *adj.* of, pertaining to, or resembling an isidium. [ISIDI(UM) + -OID]

i·sid·i·um (ī sid′ē əm), *n., pl.* **i·sid·i·a** (ī sid′ē ə). *Bot.* a coralloid outgrowth from the thallus in certain lichens. [<NL, deriv. of *Isid-* (s. of *Isis*) ISIS (from the hornlike appearance of the growth); see -IUM]

Is·i·dor (iz′i dôr′, -dôr′), *n.* a boy's given name. Also, **Isadore, Is′i·dore′.**

Is·i·do·ra (iz′i dôr′ə, -dôr′ə), *n.* a girl's given name. Also, **Isadora.**

Is′idore of Seville′, Saint (*Isidorus Hispalensis*), A.D. c570–636, Spanish archbishop, historian, and encyclopedist. —**Is′i·do′ri·an, Is′i·do′re·an,** *adj.*

Is·i·do·rus (iz′i dôr′əs, -dôr′-), *n.* a crater in the fourth quadrant of the face of the moon: about 30 miles in diameter.

Is·in (is′in), *n.* an ancient Sumerian city in S Iraq: archaeological site.

i·sin·glass (ī′zen glas′, -gläs′, ī′zing-), *n.* **1.** a pure, transparent or translucent form of gelatin, obtained from the air bladders of certain fish, esp. the sturgeon: used in glue and jellies and as a clarifying agent. **2.** mica. [< MD *huysenblase* (with *glass* for *blase* by folk etymology), lit., sturgeon bladder; c. G *Hausenblase*]

I·sis (ī′sis), *n.* **1.** *Egyptian Religion.* a goddess of fertility, the sister and wife of Osiris and mother of Horus, and usually represented as a woman with a cow's horns with the solar disk between them: later worshiped in the Greek and Roman empires. **2.** a girl's given name. [< L < Gk < Egypt *Ese*]

Isis

Is·kan·da·ri·yah (*Arab.* is kan′da rē′yä), *n.* Al-Iskandariyah.

Is·kan·der Bey (is kan′dər bā′), Scanderbeg.

Is·ken·de·run (is ken′də ro͞on′), *n.* **1.** Formerly, **Alexandretta.** a seaport in S Turkey, on the Gulf of Iskenderun. 69,259 (1965). **2. Gulf of,** an inlet of the Mediterranean, off the S coast of Turkey. 45 mi. long; 28 mi. wide.

isl., 1. island. **2.** isle. Also, **Isl.**

Is·la de Pas·cua (ēs′lä ᵺe päs′kwä), Spanish name of **Easter Island.**

Is·lam (is′ləm, iz′-, is läm′), *n.* **1.** the religious faith of Muslims, based on the words and religious system founded by the prophet Muhammad and taught by the Koran, the basic principle of which is absolute submission to a unique and personal god, Allah. **2.** the whole body of Muslim believers, their civilization, and the countries in which theirs is the dominant religion. [< Ar: submission (to God), verbid of *aslama* to surrender] —**Is·lam·ic** (is lam′ik, -läm′ik, iz-), **Is·lam·it·ic** (is′lə mit′ik, iz′-), *adj.*

Islam′ic cal′endar, a calendar of 12 lunar months, each beginning with the new moon.

Islam′ic Repub′lic of Maurita′nia, official name of **Mauritania.**

Is·lam·ise (is′lə mīz′, iz′-), *v.i., v.t.,* **-ised, -is·ing.** *Chiefly Brit.* Islamize. —**Is′lam·i·sa′tion,** *n.*

Is·lam·ism (is′lə miz′əm, iz′-), *n.* the religion of Islam. [ISLAM + -ISM]

Is·lam·ite (is′lə mīt′, iz′-), *n.* a Muslim. [ISLAM + -ITE¹]

Is·lam·ize (is′lə mīz′, iz′-), *v.i., v.t.,* **-ized, -iz·ing.** to convert to or bring under the influence of Islam. Also, *esp. Brit.,* **Islamise.** [ISLAM + -IZE] —**Is′lam·i·za′tion,** *n.*

is·land (ī′lənd), *n.* **1.** a tract of land completely surrounded by water, and not large enough to be called a continent. **2.** a clump of woodland in a prairie. **3.** an isolated hill. **4.** something resembling an island, esp. in being isolated or having little or no direct communication with others. **5.** a platform in the middle of a street, at a crossing, for the safety of pedestrians. **6.** *Railroads.* a platform or building between sets of tracks. **7.** *Anat.* an isolated portion of tissue differing in structure from the surrounding tissue. —*v.t.* **8.** to make into an island. **9.** to dot with islands. **10.** to place on an island; isolate. [ME *iland*, OE *ī(g)land*, var. of *īegland*, equiv. to *īeg* island (c. Icel *ey*) + *land* LAND; sp. with *-s-* by assoc. with ISLE] —**is′land·ish,** *adj.* —**is′land·less,** *adj.* —**is′land·like′,** *adj.*

is′land arc′, a curved chain of islands, as the Aleutians or Antilles, usually convex toward the ocean and enclosing a deep-sea basin.

is·land·er (ī′lən dər), *n.* a native or inhabitant of an island. [ISLAND + -ER¹]

is′land myr′tle. See **tree myrtle.**

is′land of Lang′erhans. See **islet of Langerhans.**

is′land of Reil′ (rīl), *Anat.* insula. [named after J. C. *Reil* (d. 1813), German physician]

Is′land of the Sun′, *Class. Myth.* Sicily: the island where Helius kept his oxen.

Is′land Park′, a town on S Long Island, in SE New York. 3846 (1960).

Is′lands of the Blessed′, *Class. Myth.* islands in the ocean at the remotest western end of the world, to which the souls of heroes and good men were said to be transported after death. Also called **Hesperides.**

is′land u′niverse, an external galaxy.

Is·las Mal·vi·nas (ēs′läs mäl vē′näs), Spanish name of the **Falkland Islands.**

isle (īl), *n., v.,* **isled, isl·ing.** —*n.* **1.** a small island. **2.** any island. —*v.t.* **3.** to make into or as into an isle. **4.** to place on or as on an isle. [ME *i(s)le* < OF < L *insula*] —**isle′less,** *adj.*

Isle′ of Capri′, *Literary.* Capri (def. 1).

Isle′ of Man′. See **Man, Isle of.**

Isle′ of Pines′. See **Pines, Isle of.**

Isle′ of Shoals′ boat′, a sailing boat formerly used in Ipswich Bay, Massachusetts, rigged with two spritsails or gaff sails.

Isle′ of Wight′. See **Wight, Isle of.**

Isle′ Roy′ale (roi′əl), an island in Lake Superior: a part of Michigan; a national park. 208 sq. mi.

is·let (ī′lit), *n.* a very small island. [< MF *islette.* See ISLE, -ET] —**is′let·ed,** *adj.*

is′let of Lang′erhans, *Anat.* any of several masses of endocrine cells in the pancreas that secrete insulin. Also, **island of Langerhans.** [named after P. *Langerhans* (1847–88), German anatomist, who first described them]

Is·ling·ton (iz′ling tən), *n.* a borough of N London, England. 228,833 (1961).

isls., islands.

ism (iz′əm), *n.* a distinctive doctrine, theory, system, or practice: *This is the age of isms.* [abstracted from words so ending]

-ism, a suffix appearing in loan words from Greek, where it was used to form action nouns from verbs (*baptism*); on this model, used as a productive suffix in the formation of nouns denoting action or practice, state or condition, principles, doctrines, a usage or characteristic, etc. (*criticism; barbarism; Darwinism; despotism; plagiarism; realism; witticism*). Cf. **-ist, -ize.** [< Gk *-ism(os), -ism(a)* n. suffixes, often directly, often through L *-ismus, -isma,* sometimes through F *-isme,* G *-ismus*]

Is·ma·el (is′mē əl, -mā-), *n.* *Douay Bible.* Ishmael (def. 1).

Is·ma·il·i·an (is′mā il′ē ən), *n.* *Islam.* a member of the Ismailiya sect. Also, **Is·ma·il·i** (is′mā il′ē). Also called **Sevener.** [after *Ismaili* follower of *Ismail* (d. A.D. 760), elder son of the imam Djafar, but disinherited by his father: see -AN]

Is·ma·i·li·ya (is′mä ē lē′yä), *n.* *Islam.* a sect of the Shiah, including in their number the Assassins and the Druses, having an esoteric philosophy and asserting Ismail to be the seventh divinely inspired imam in the succession from Ali. [< Ar; see ISMAILIAN]

Is·ma·il Pa·sha (is mä′ēl pä′shä), 1830–95, viceroy and khedive of Egypt 1863–79.

Is·ma·rus (is′mər əs), *n.* *Class. Myth.* a city of the Cicones, plundered by Odysseus on his return from Troy.

Is·me·ne (is mē′nē, iz-), *n.* *Class. Myth.* a daughter of Oedipus and Jocasta who was afraid to join Antigone in her forbidden burial of their brother Polynices.

Is·me·ne (is mē′nē, iz-), *n.* a genus of bulbous, perennial, South American herbs, usually included in the genus *Hemerocallis.* [< NL; named after ISMENE]

Is·me·nus (is mē′nəs), *n.* *Class. Myth.* a son of Asopus and Metope.

is·nad (is näd′), *n.* *Islam.* the chain of testimony by which a hadith is transmitted. [< Ar]

isn't (iz′ənt), contraction of *is not.*

iso-, 1. a learned borrowing from Greek meaning "equal," used in the formation of compound words: *isochromatic.* **2.** *Chem.* a prefix added to the name of one compound to denote another isomeric with it. Also, *esp. before a vowel,* **is-.** [< Gk, comb. form of *ísos* equal]

i·so·ab·nor·mal (ī′sō ab nôr′məl), *n.* isabnormal.

i·so·ag·glu·ti·na·tion (ī′sō ə glo͞ot′ᵊnā′shən), *n.* *Med.* the clumping of the red blood cells of an animal by a transfusion from another animal of the same species. [ISO- + AGGLUTINATION] —**i·so·ag·glu·ti·na·tive** (ī′sō ə glo͞ot′ᵊnā′tiv, -ᵊnə-), *adj.*

i·so·ag·glu·ti·nin (ī′sō ə glo͞ot′ᵊnin), *n.* an agglutinin which can effect isoagglutination. [ISO- + AGGLUTININ]

i·so·am·yl (ī′sō am′il), *adj.* *Chem.* containing the isoamyl group; isopentyl. [ISO- + AMYL]

i′soam′yl ac′etate, *Chem.* a colorless liquid, $CH_3COOCH_2CH_2CH(CH_3)_2$, used in flavorings, perfumery, and as a solvent. Cf. **banana oil** (def. 1).

i′soam′yl ben′zoate, *Chem.* a colorless liquid, $C_6H_5COOCH_2CH_2CH(CH_3)_2$, having a sharp, fruitlike odor: used in cosmetics.

i′soam′yl ben′zyl e′ther, *Chem.* a colorless liquid, $(CH_3)_2CHCH_2CH_2OCH_2C_6H_5$, used in soap perfumes. Also called **benzyl isoamyl ether.**

isoam′yl group′, *Chem.* the univalent group, $(CH_3)_2CHCH_2CH_2$–. Also called **isoam′yl rad′ical.** Cf. **amyl group, pentyl group.**

i′soam′yl ni′trite, *Pharm.* See **amyl nitrite.**

isoam′yl salic′ylate, *Chem.* a colorless, sometimes slightly yellow, synthetic oil, $HOC_6H_4CO_2CH_2CH_2CH(CH_3)_2$, having an orchidlike odor: used in perfumery.

i·so·bar (ī′sə bär′), *n.* **1.** *Meteorol.* a line drawn on a weather map or chart that connects all points having the same barometric pressure, reduced to sea level, at a specified time or over a certain period. **2.** Also, **i·so·bare** (ī′sə bâr′). *Physics, Chem.* one of two or more atoms having equal atomic weights but different atomic numbers. Cf. **isotope.** [< Gk *isobar(ḗs)* of equal weight. See ISO-, BARO-] —**i′so·bar′ism,** *n.*

i·so·bar·ic (ī′sə bar′ik), *adj.* *Meteorol.* **1.** having or showing equal barometric pressure. **2.** of or pertaining to isobars. [ISOBAR + -IC]

i·so·bath (ī′sə bath′), *n.* **1.** an imaginary line or one drawn on a map connecting all points of equal depth below the surface of a body of water. **2.** a similar line for indicating the depth below the surface of the earth of a particular geological stratum. [< Gk *isobath(ḗs)* of equal depth. See ISO-, BATHO-]

i·so·bath·ic (ī′sə bath′ik), *adj.* **1.** having the same depth. **2.** of or pertaining to an isobath. [ISOBATH + -IC]

i·so·bath·y·therm (ī′sə bath′ə thûrm′), *n.* a line on a chart or diagram of a body of water, connecting depths having the same temperature. [ISO- + BATHY- + THERM] —**i′so·bath′y·ther′mal, i′so·bath′y·ther′mic,** *adj.*

i·so·bront (ī′sə bront′), *n.* *Meteorol.* a line on a weather map or chart connecting various points where the same phase of thunderstorm activity occurs simultaneously. Also called **homobront.** [ISO- + *-bront* < Gk *brontḗ* thunder]

i·so·bu·tane (ī′sə byo͞o′tān, -byo͞o tān′), *n.* *Chem.* a colorless, flammable gas, $(CH_3)_3CH$, used as a fuel, as a refrigerant, and in the manufacture of gasoline by alkylation. [ISO- + BUTANE]

i·so·bu·tyl·ene (ī′sə byo͞ot′ᵊlēn′), *n.* *Chem.* a colorless, very volatile liquid or flammable gas, $(CH_3)_2C{=}CH_2$, used chiefly in the manufacture of butyl rubber. Also, **i·so·bu·tene** (ī′sə byo͞o′tēn). [ISO- + BUTYLENE]

i′so·bu′tyl pro′pionate (ī′sə byo͞o′til, -byo͞ot′ᵊl, ī′sə-), *Chem.* a colorless liquid, $CH_3CH_2COOCH_2CH(CH_3)_2$, used chiefly as a paint, varnish, and lacquer solvent. [ISO- + BUTYL]

i·so·car·pic (ī′sə kär′pik), *adj.* *Bot.* having carpels equal in number to the other floral parts. [ISO- + -CARPIC]

i·so·ce·phal·ic (ī′sō sə fal′ik), *adj.* *Fine Arts.* (of a composition) having the heads of all figures on approximately the same level. Also, **i·so·ceph·a·lous** (ī′sō sef′ə ləs). [ISO- + CEPHALIC] —**i·so·ceph·a·ly** (ī′sō sef′ə lē), *n.*

i·so·ce·rau·nic (ī′sō si rô′nik), *adj.* *Meteorol.* representing, having, or indicating equality in the frequency, intensity, or simultaneity of thunderstorms: *isoceraunic line; isoceraunic map.* Also, **isokeraunic.** [ISO- + *ceraun-* < Gk *keraun(ós)* thunderbolt + -IC]

i·so·chasm (ī′sə kaz′əm), *n.* *Meteorol.* a line on a map or chart connecting points where auroras are observed with equal frequency. [ISO- + CHASM] —**i′so·chas′mic,** *adj.*

i·so·cheim (ī′sə kīm′), *n.* *Climatology.* a line on a map connecting points that have the same mean winter temperature. Also, **i′so·chime′.** [ISO- + *-cheim* < Gk *cheima* winter cold] —**i′so·chei′mal, i·so·chei·me·nal** (ī′sə kī′mə nᵊl), **i′so·cheim′ic,** *adj.*

i·so·chor (ī′sə kôr′), *n.* *Physics.* a curve graphing temperature against pressure with volume held constant. Also, **i′so·chore′.** [ISO- + *-chor* < Gk *chṓra* place, land] —**i·so·chor·ic** (ī′sə kôr′ik, -kor′-), *adj.*

i·so·chro·mat·ic (ī′sə krō mat′ik, ī′sō krə-), *adj.* **1.** *Optics.* having the same color or tint. **2.** orthochromatic. [ISO- + CHROMATIC]

i·soch·ro·nal (ī sok′rə nᵊl), *adj.* **1.** equal or uniform in time. **2.** performed in equal intervals of time. **3.** characterized by motions or vibrations of equal duration. [< NL *isochron(us)* (< Gk *isóchronos* equal in age or time; see ISO-, CHRON-) + -AL¹] —**i·soch′ro·nal·ly,** *adv.*

i·so·chrone (ī′sə krōn′), *n.* a line, as on a map, composed of all points having some property simultaneously, as in having the same delay in receiving a radio signal from a given source or requiring the same time to be reached by available transportation from a given center. [back formation from ISOCHRONOUS or ISOCHRONAL]

i·soch·ro·nism (ī sok′rə niz′əm), *n.* an isochronal character or action. [ISOCHRONE + -ISM]

i·soch·ro·nize (ī sok′rə nīz′), *v.t.,* **-nized, -niz·ing.** to make isochronal. [ISOCHRONE + -IZE]

i·soch·ro·nous (ī sok′rə nəs), *adj.* isochronal. [< NL *isochronus.* See ISOCHRONAL, -OUS] —**i·soch′ro·nous·ly,** *adv.*

i·soch·ro·ny (ī sok′rə nē), *n.* the state or an instance of occurring at the same time; contemporaneity. [ISOCHRONE + -Y³]

i·soch·ro·ous (ī sok′rō əs), *adj.* having the same color throughout. Also, **i·soch′ro·öus.** [ISO- + -CHROOUS]

i·so·cli·nal (ī′sə klīn′ᵊl, ī′sō-), *adj.* **1.** of or pertaining to equal direction of inclination; inclining or dipping in the same direction. **2.** noting or pertaining to an isoclinic line. **3.** *Geol.* noting or pertaining to a fold of strata which is of the nature of an isocline. —*n.* **4.** See **isoclinic line.** Also, **i·so·clin·ic** (ī′sə klin′ik, ī′sō-). [ISO- + *-clinal* < Gk *klín(ein)* (to) slope + -AL¹]

i·so·cline (ī′sə klīn′), *n.* *Geol.* a fold of strata so tightly compressed that the parts on each side dip in the same direction. [back formation from ISOCLINAL]

i′soclin′ic line′, an imaginary line connecting points on the earth's surface having equal magnetic dip. Also called **isoclinic, isoclinal.**

i·soc·ra·cy (ī sok′rə sē), *n., pl.* **-cies.** a government in which all have equal political power. [< Gk *isokratía.* See ISO-, -CRACY] —**i·so·crat** (ī′sə krat′), *n.* —**i′so·crat′ic,** *adj.*

I·soc·ra·tes (ī sok′rə tēz′), *n.* 436–338 B.C., Athenian orator.

i·so·cy·a·nate (ī′sə sī′ə nāt′), *n.* *Chem.* **1.** a salt or ester of isocyanic acid. **2.** any compound containing the univalent group, –NCO. [ISOCYAN(IC ACID) + -ATE²]

i′so·cy·an′ic ac′id (ī′sō sī an′ik, ī′sō-), *Chem.* an unstable acid, HN=C=O, tautomeric with cyanic acid, known only in the form of its salts. [ISO- + CYANIC ACID]

i·so·cy·a·nide (ī′sə sī′ə nīd′, -nid), *n. Chem.* a compound containing an isocyano group. Also called **carbylamine.** [ISO- + CYANIDE]

i·so·cy·a·nine (ī′sə sī′ə nēn′, -nin), *n. Chem.* a member of the group of cyanine dyes. Cf. **cyanine.** [ISO- + CYANINE]

i·so·cy·a·no (ī′sə sī′ə nō′), *adj. Chem.* containing an isocyano group. [ISO- + CYANO]

isocy′ano group′, *Chem.* the univalent group, –N≡C or –N≡C. Also called **isocy′ano rad′ical.**

i·so·def (ī′sə def′), *n.* uniform deficiency, esp. a line connecting points of equal deviation from a mean, as on a chart, graph, etc. [ISO- + DEF(ICIENCY)]

i·so·di·a·met·ric (ī′sə dī′ə me′trik), *adj.* **1.** having equal diameters or axes. **2.** *Bot.* having the diameter similar throughout, as a cell. **3.** (of crystals) having two, or three, equal horizontal axes and a third, or fourth, unequal axis at right angles thereto. [ISO- + DIAMETRIC]

i·so·di·mor·phism (ī′sō dī môr′fiz əm), *n. Crystall.* isomorphism between the forms of two dimorphous substances. [ISO- + DIMORPHISM] —**i′so·di·mor′phous, i′so·di·mor′phic,** *adj.*

i·so·dom·ic (ī′sə dom′ik), *adj. Archit.* (of ashlar) composed of stones of uniform size. [ISODOM(UM) + -IC]

i·sod·o·mum (ī sod′ə məm), *n.* See **opus isodomum.** [< NL < Gk *isódomon*, n. use of neut. of *isódomos* with equal layers or rows. See ISO-, DOME]

i·so·dose (ī′sə dōs′), *adj.* of or pertaining to points of equal intensity of radiation in a contaminated region: *isodose map; isodose lines.* [ISO- + DOSE]

i·so·dros·o·therm (ī′sə dros′ə thûrm′), *n. Meteorol.* a line on a weather map or chart connecting points having an equal dew point. [ISO- + Gk *dróso(s)* dew + THERM]

i·so·dy·nam·ic (ī′sō dī nam′ik, -di-), *adj.* **1.** pertaining to or characterized by equality of force, intensity, or the like. **2.** noting or pertaining to an imaginary line on the earth's surface connecting points of equal horizontal intensity of the earth's magnetic field. Also, **i′so·dy·nam′i·cal.** [ISO- + DYNAMIC]

i·so·e·las·tic (ī′sō i las′tik), *adj. Physics.* noting or pertaining to a substance or system exhibiting uniform elasticity throughout. [ISO- + ELASTIC]

i·so·e·lec′tric point′ (ī′sō i lek′trik), *Chem.* the *p*H at which a substance is electrically neutral or at which it is at its minimum ionization. [ISO- + ELECTRIC]

i·so·e·lec·tron·ic (ī′sō i lek tron′ik, -ē′lek-), *adj. Physics, Chem.* **1.** noting or pertaining to atoms and ions having an equal number of electrons. **2.** noting or pertaining to atoms, radicals, or ions having either an equal number of electrons or an equal number of valence electrons. [ISO- + ELECTRONIC]

i·so·gam·ete (ī′sə gam′ēt, ī′sō gə mēt′), *n. Biol.* one of a pair of conjugating gametes, exhibiting no differences in form, size, structure, or sex. Cf. **heterogamete.** [ISO- + GAMETE] —**i·so·ga·met·ic** (ī′sō gə met′ik), *adj.*

i·sog·a·mous (ī sog′ə məs), *adj. Biol.* having two similar gametes in which no differentiation can be distinguished, or reproducing by the union of such gametes (opposed to *heterogamous*). [ISO- + -GAMOUS]

i·sog·a·my (ī sog′ə mē), *n. Biol.* the fusion of two gametes of similar form, as in certain algae. [ISO- + -GAMY]

i·sog·e·nous (ī soj′ə nəs), *adj. Biol.* of the same or similar origin, as parts derived from the same or corresponding tissues of the embryo. [ISO- + -GENOUS] —**i·sog′e·ny,** *n.*

i·so·ge·o·therm (ī′sə jē′ə thûrm′), *n.* an imaginary line on the earth's surface connecting all points having the same mean temperature. Also, **geoisotherm.** [ISO- + GEO- + THERM] —**i′so·ge′o·ther′mal, i′so·ge′o·ther′mic,** *adj.*

i·so·gloss (ī′sə glôs′, -glos′), *n.* (in the study of the geographical distribution of a dialect) a line on a map separating two localities which differ in a feature of their speech, as in the use of a certain word, phoneme, etc. [ISO- + GLOSS[2]] —**i′so·glos′sal,** *adj.*

i·so·gon (ī′sə gon′), *n.* a polygon having all angles equal. [ISO- + -GON]

i·sog·o·nal (ī sog′ə nᵊl), *adj.* **1.** equiangular; isogonic. —*n.* **2.** See **isogonal line.** [< Gk *isogṓn(ios)* equiangular (see ISO-, -GON) + -AL[1]] —**i·so·go·nal·i·ty** (ī′sə gə nal′i tē), *n.* —**i·sog′o·nal·ly,** *adv.*

isog′onal line′, an imaginary line, or one drawn on a map, connecting all points of equal declination of the earth's magnetic field. Also called **isogone.**

i·so·gone (ī′sə gōn′), *n.* See **isogonal line.** [shortened form]

i·so·gon·ic (ī′sə gon′ik), *adj.* **1.** having or pertaining to equal angles. **2.** noting or pertaining to an isogonal line. —*n.* **3.** See **isogonal line.** [< Gk *isogṓn(ios)* having equal angles (see ISO-, -GON) + -IC]

i·so·gra·di·ent (ī′sə grā′dē ənt), *n. Meteorol.* a line on a weather map or chart connecting points having the same horizontal gradient of a meteorological quantity, as temperature, pressure, or the like. [ISO- + GRADIENT]

i·so·graft (ī′sə graft′, -gräft′), *n. Surg.* homograft. [ISO- + GRAFT[1]]

i·so·gram (ī′sə gram′), *n. Meteorol., Geog.* a line representing equality with respect to a given variable, used to relate points on maps, charts, etc. Also called **isoline.** [ISO- + -GRAM[1]]

i·so·graph (ī′sə graf′, -gräf′), *n.* (in the study of the geographical distribution of a dialect) a line drawn on a map to indicate areas having common linguistic characteristics. [ISO- + -GRAPH] —**i·so·graph·ic** (ī′sə graf′ik), **i′so·graph′i·cal,** *adj.* —**i′so·graph′i·cal·ly,** *adv.*

i·so·griv (ī′sə griv′), *n.* a line on a map or chart connecting points of uniform grid variation. [ISO- + GRIV(ATION)]

i·so·ha·line (ī′sə hā′lēn, -līn, -hal′ēn, -īn), *n.* a line drawn on a map or chart of the ocean connecting all points of equal salinity. Also, **i·so·hal·sine** (ī′sə hal′sēn, -sīn). [ISO- + Gk *hálin(os)* salty; see HAL-, -INE[1]]

i·so·hel (ī′sə hel′), *n. Meteorol.* a line on a weather map or chart connecting points that receive equal amounts of sunshine. [ISO- + Gk *hḗl(ios)* sun]

i·so·hume (ī′sə hyōōm′), *n. Meteorol.* a line on a weather map or chart connecting points of equal relative humidity. [ISO- + HUM(IDITY)]

i·so·hy·et (ī′sə hī′ət), *n.* a line drawn on a map connecting points having equal rainfall at a certain time or for a stated period. [ISO- + Gk *hyet(ós)* rain] —**i′so·hy′et·al,** *adj.*

i′so·i·on′ic point′ (ī′sō ī on′ik, ī′sō-), *Chem.* the hydrogen ion concentration at which the concentration of the dipolar ion is at a maximum. [ISO- + IONIC]

i·so·ke·rau·nic (ī′sō ki rô′nik), *adj.* isoceraunic.

i·so·la·ble (ī′sə lə bəl, is′ə-), *adj.* capable of being isolated. [ISOL(ATE) + -ABLE] —**i′so·la·bil′i·ty,** *n.*

i·so·lat·a·ble (ī′sə lā′tə bəl, is′ə-), *adj.* isolable. [ISOLATE + -ABLE]

i·so·late (*v.* ī′sə lāt′, is′ə-; *adj.* ī′sə lit, is′ə-), *v.,* **-lat·ed, -lat·ing,** *adj.* —*v.t.* **1.** to set or place apart; detach or separate so as to be alone. **2.** *Med.* to keep (an infected person) from contact with noninfected ones; quarantine. **3.** *Chem., Bacteriol.* to obtain (a substance or microorganism) in an uncombined or pure state. **4.** *Elect.* to insulate. —*adj.* **5.** isolated. [back formation from ISOLATED] —**i′so·la′tor,** *n.*

i·so·lat·ed (ī′sə lā′tid, is′ə-), *adj.* **1.** separated from other persons or things; alone; solitary. **2.** *Math.* **a.** (of a singularity of a function of a complex variable) having a neighborhood containing no other singular point. **b.** (of a point in a subset of a topological space) having a neighborhood containing no other point of the set. [< It *isolat(o)* (< L *insulātus*; see INSULATE) + -ED[2]] —**i′so·lat′ed·ly,** *adv.*

i′solating lan′guage, a language which uses few or no bound forms.

i·so·la·tion (ī′sə lā′shən, is′ə-), *n.* **1.** the act or an instance of isolating. **2.** the state of being isolated. **3.** the complete separation from others of a person suffering from contagious or infectious disease; quarantine. **4.** the separation of a nation from other nations by isolationism. **5.** *Psychoanal.* a process whereby an idea or memory is divested of its emotional component. **6.** *Sociol.* See **social isolation.** [ISOLATE + -ION] —**Syn. 2.** See **solitude. 3.** segregation.

isola′tion booth′, a soundproof booth located within a television studio, used to control the parts of the show that will be heard by the occupant.

i·so·la·tion·ism (ī′sə lā′shə niz′əm, is′ə-), *n.* the policy or doctrine of isolating one's country from the affairs of other nations by declining to enter into alliances, foreign economic commitments, international agreements, etc., seeking to devote the entire efforts of one's country to its own advancement and remain at peace by avoiding foreign entanglements and responsibilities. [ISOLATION + -ISM]

i·so·la·tion·ist (ī′sə lā′shə nist, is′ə-), *n.* a person who favors or works for isolationism. [ISOLATION + -IST]

i·so·la·tive (ī′sə lā′tiv, is′ə-), *adj.* noting a change in part of the sound of a word made independently of the phonetic environment of that part. [ISOLATE + -IVE]

I·sol·da (i zōl′də), *n.* a girl's given name, form of **Iseult.**

I·solde (i sōld′, i sōl′də; *Ger.* ē zôl′də), *n.* German name of **Iseult.**

i·so·lec·i·thal (ī′sə les′ə thəl), *adj. Embryol.* homolecithal. [ISO- + LECITHAL]

i·so·leu·cine (ī′sə lōō′sēn, -sin), *n. Biochem.* a crystalline amino acid, $C_2H_5CH(CH_3)CH(NH_2)COOH$, occurring in casein, essential to the nutrition of man and animals. [ISO- + LEUCINE]

i·so·line (ī′sə līn′), *n.* isogram. [ISO- + LINE[1]]

i·sol·o·gous (ī sol′ə gəs), *adj. Chem.* (of two or more organic carbon compounds) similar chemically but differing from one another by other than nCH_2, as ethane, $H_3C–CH_3$, ethylene, $H_2C=CH_2$, and acetylene, HC≡CH. [ISO- + (HOMO)LOGOUS]

i·so·logue (ī′sə lôg′, -log′), *n. Chem.* one of two or more isologous compounds. Also, **i′so·log′.** [back formation from ISOLOGOUS, modeled after *homologue: homologous*]

i·so·mag·net·ic (ī′sō mag net′ik), *adj.* **1.** noting or pertaining to an imaginary line on the earth's surface, or a corresponding line on a map or the like, connecting places which have the same magnetic elements. —*n.* **2.** an isomagnetic line. [ISO- + MAGNETIC]

i·so·mer (ī′sə mər), *n.* **1.** *Chem.* a compound displaying isomerism with one or more other compounds. **2.** Also called **nuclear isomer.** *Physics.* a nuclide that exhibits isomerism with one or more other nuclides. [back formation from ISOMERIC]

i·so·mer·ic (ī′sə mer′ik), *adj.* of, pertaining to, or displaying isomerism. [< Gk *isomer(ḗs)* having equal parts (see ISO-, -MERE) + -IC] —**i′so·mer′i·cal·ly,** *adv.*

i·som·er·ism (ī som′ə riz′əm), *n.* **1.** *Chem.* the relation of two or more compounds, radicals, or ions that are composed of the same kinds and numbers of atoms but differ from each other in structural arrangement **(structural isomerism),** as CH_3OCH_3 and CH_3CH_2OH, or in the arrangement of their atoms in space and therefore in one or more properties. Cf. **optical isomerism, stereoisomerism. 2.** Also called **nuclear isomerism.** *Physics.* the relation of two or more nuclides that have the same atomic number and mass number but different energy levels and half-lives. **3.** *Chem., Physics.* the phenomenon characterized by such a relation. **4.** the state or condition of being isomerous. [ISOMERIC + -ISM]

i·som·er·ize (ī som′ə rīz′), *v.i., v.t.,* **-ized, -iz·ing.** *Chem.* to convert into an isomer. [ISOMER + -IZE] —**i·som′er·i·za′tion,** *n.*

i·som·er·ous (ī som′ər əs), *adj.* **1.** having an equal number of parts, markings, etc. **2.** *Bot.* (of a flower) having the same number of members in each whorl. [ISO- + -MERE + -OUS]

i·so·met·ric (ī′sə me′trik), *adj.* Also, **i′so·met′ri·cal. 1.** of, pertaining to, or having equality of measure. **2.** *Crystall.* noting or pertaining to that system of crystallization which is characterized by three equal axes at right angles to one another. **3.** *Pros.* of equal measure; made up of regular feet. **4.** *Drafting.* designating a method of projection **(i′somet′ric projec′tion)** in which a three-dimensional object is represented by a drawing **(i′somet′ric draw′ing)** having the horizontal edges of the object drawn usually at a 30° angle and all verticals projected perpendicularly from a horizontal base, all lines being drawn to scale. Cf. **axonometric, cabinet** (def. 17), **oblique** (def. 13). —*n.* **5.** an isometric drawing. **6.** Also, **i′somet′ric line′.** *Physics.* a line graphing temperature against pressure with volume held constant. **7. isometrics,** isometric exercises collectively. [< Gk *isometr(ía)* ISOMETRY + -IC] —**i′so·met′ri·cal·ly,** *adv.*

A B C

Isometric (def. 4)
A, Axonometric
B, Oblique
C, Cabinet

i′somet′ric ex′ercise, any of various exercises to strengthen specific muscles or shape the figure that, instead of depending on strenuous physical activity, pit one muscle or part of the body against another or against an immovable object in a strong but motionless pressing, pushing, pulling, flexing, or contracting, as by pressing the fist of one hand against the palm of the other, pushing downward against a desk, pulling upward on a chair in which one is sitting, etc.

i·so·me·tro·pi·a (ī′sō mə trō′pē ə), *n. Ophthalm.* a condition in which the refraction is the same in the two eyes. [< Gk *isómetr(os)* of equal measure (see ISO-, -METER) + -OPIA]

i·som·e·try (ī som′i trē), *n.* **1.** equality of measure. **2.** *Geog.* equality with respect to height above sea level. **3.** *Math.* a function from one metric space onto a second metric space having the property that the distance between two points in the first space is equal to the distance between the image points in the second space. [< Gk *isometría.* See ISO-, -METRY]

i·so·morph (ī′sə môrf′), *n.* **1.** an organism which is isomorphic with another or others. **2.** an isomorphous substance. [back formation from ISOMORPHOUS]

i·so·mor·phic (ī′sə môr′fik), *adj.* **1.** *Biol.* different in ancestry, but having the same form or appearance. **2.** *Chem., Crystall.* isomorphous. **3.** *Math.* pertaining to two sets related by an isomorphism. [ISO- + -MORPHIC]

i·so·mor·phism (ī′sə môr′fiz əm), *n.* **1.** the state or property of being isomorphous or isomorphic. **2.** *Math.* a one-to-one relation onto the map between two sets, which preserves the relations existing between elements in its domain. [ISOMORPH(OUS) + -ISM]

i·so·mor·phous (ī′sə môr′fəs), *adj. Chem., Crystall.* **1.** (of a compound) capable of crystallizing in a form similar to that of another compound. **2.** (of an element) capable of crystallizing in a form similar to that of another element when combined with the same atom or group. [ISO- + -MORPHOUS]

i·so·neph (ī′sə nef′), *n. Meteorol.* a line on a weather map or chart connecting points having the same amount of cloudiness. [ISO- + Gk *néph(os)* cloud] —**i·so·ne·phel·ic** (ī′sō nə fel′ik), *adj.*

i·so·ni·a·zid (ī′sə nī′ə zid), *n. Pharm.* a white, crystalline, water-soluble solid, $C_5H_4NCONHNH_2$, used in medicine in the treatment of tuberculosis. [short for ISONICOTINIC ACID HYDRAZIDE]

i′so·nic·o·tin′ic ac′id hy′dra·zide (ī′sə nik′ə-tin′ik; hī′drə zīd′, -zid), *Chem.* isoniazid. [ISO- + NICOTINIC ACID + HYDRAZ(INE) + -IDE]

i·son·o·my (ī son′ə mē), *n.* equality of political rights. [< Gk *isonomía.* See ISO-, -NOMY] —**i·so·nom·ic** (ī′sə-nom′ik), **i·son′o·mous,** *adj.*

I·son·zo (ē zôn′tsô), *n.* a river in S Europe, flowing S from the Julian Alps in Yugoslavia to the Gulf of Trieste in Italy. 75 mi. long.

i·so·oc·tane (ī′sō ok′tān), *n. Chem.* the octane, $(CH_3)_3CCH_2CH(CH_3)_2$, used as one of the standards in establishing the octane number of a fuel. Cf. **octane number.** [ISO- + OCTANE]

i·so·os·mot·ic (ī′sō oz mot′ik, -os-), *adj. Physical Chem.* of or noting solutions that exert equal pressure against the semipermeable membrane separating them.

i·so·pach (ī′sə pak′), *n.* an imaginary line or one drawn on a map connecting all points of equal thickness in a particular geological formation. [ISO- + Gk *pách(os)* thickness]

i·so·pach·ous (ī′sə pak′əs), *adj.* **1.** having the same thickness. **2.** of or pertaining to an isopach. [ISOPACH + -OUS]

i·so·pag (ī′sə pag′), *n.* an imaginary line or one drawn on a map connecting all points where ice exists at approximately the same period during winter. [ISO- + Gk *pág(os)* frost]

i·so·pec·tic (ī′sə pek′tik), *n.* an imaginary line or one drawn on a map connecting all points where ice starts to form at approximately the same period during winter. [ISO- + Gk *pēktik(ós)* freezing; see PECTIC]

i·sop·e·din (ī sop′i din, ī′sə pēd′ᵊn), *n. Ichthyol.* the underlying layer of a ganoid scale, composed of connective tissue embedded with bone. Also, **i·sop·e·dine** (ī sop′i din, -dēn′, -dīn′). [ISO- + Gk *pedīn(ós)* level]

i·so·pen·tyl (ī′sə pen′til), *adj. Chem.* isoamyl. [ISO- + PENT(A)- + -YL]

i·so·pe·rim·e·ter (ī′sō pə rim′i tər), *n.* any of a number of figures having equal perimeters. [ISO- + PERIMETER]

i·so·pe·rim·e·try (ī′sō pə rim′i trē), *n.* the study of isoperimeters. [ISOPERIMET(E)R + -Y[3]] —**i·so·per·i·met·ric** (ī′sə per′ə me′trik), **i′so·per′i·met′ri·cal,** *adj.*

i·so·pet·a·lous (ī′sə pet′ᵊləs), *adj. Bot.* having petals similar in form and size. [ISO- + PETALOUS]

i′so·phthal′ic ac′id (ī′sə thal′ik, ī′sə-), *Chem.* a colorless, crystalline, slightly water-soluble solid, $C_6H_4(COOH)_2$, the meta isomer of phthalic acid: used chiefly in the manufacture of resins and plasticizers. [ISO- + PHTHALIC]

i·so·pi·es·tic (ī′sō pī es′tik), *adj.* **1.** of or noting equal pressure; isobaric. —*n.* **2.** isobar (def.1). [ISO- + Gk *piest(ós)* compressible (verbid of *piézein* to press) + -IC] —**i′so·pi·es′ti·cal·ly,** *adv.*

i′so·plas′tic graft′ (ī′sə plas′tik, ī′sə-), *Surg.* homograft. [ISO- + PLASTIC]

i·so·pleth (ī′sə pleth′), *n.* a line drawn on a map through all points having the same numerical value, as of a population figure, geographic measurement, etc. Also called **isarithm.** [< Gk *isoplēth(ḗs)* equal in number, equiv. to *iso-* ISO- + *plêth(os)* a great number + *-ēs* adj. suffix]

i·so·pod (ī′sə pod′), *n.* **1.** any fresh-water, marine, or terrestrial crustacean of the order or suborder *Isopoda*, having seven pairs of legs, and having a body flattened dorsoventrally. —*adj.* **2.** of, pertaining to, or characteristic of the *Isopoda.* **3.** having the feet all alike, or similar in character. [< NL *Isopod(a)* name of genus type. See ISO-, -POD] —**i·sop·o·dan** (ī sop′ə dᵊn), *adj., n.* —**i·sop′o·dous,** *adj.*

i·so·pol·i·ty (ī′sə pol′i tē), *n.* equal rights of citizenship, as in different communities; mutual political rights. [ISO- + POLITY] —**i·so·po·lit·i·cal** (ī′sə pə lit′i kəl), *adj.*

i·so·por (ī′sə pôr′), *n.* an imaginary line on the earth's surface connecting points of equal annual change in the declination, inclination, or other components of the earth's magnetic field. Also called **i′sopor′ic line′.** [ISO- + Gk *pór(os)* path, PORE²] —**i′so·por′ic,** *adj.*

i·so·prene (ī′sə prēn′), *n.* *Chem.* a colorless, volatile, water-insoluble liquid, $CH_2{=}C(CH_3)CH{=}CH_2$, of the terpene class, usually obtained from rubber or from oil of turpentine by pyrolysis: used chiefly in the manufacture of synthetic rubber by polymerization. [ISO- + *-pr-* (< ?) + -ENE; see TERPENE]

i·so·pro·pa·nol (ī′sə prō′pə nōl′, -nôl′, -nol′), *n.* See **isopropyl alcohol.** [ISO- + PROPANE + -OL¹]

i·so·pro·pyl (ī′sə prō′pil), *adj.* *Chem.* containing the isopropyl group. [ISO- + PROPYL]

i′sopro′pyl al′cohol, *Chem.* a colorless, flammable, water-soluble liquid, $CH_3CHOHCH_3$, produced from propylene by the action of sulfuric acid and hydrolysis: used chiefly in the manufacture of antifreeze and rubbing alcohol and as a solvent. Also called **dimethylcarbinol, secondary propyl alcohol.**

i′sopro′pyl e′ther, *Chem.* a colorless, volatile, flammable, slightly water-soluble liquid, $(CH_3)_2CHOCH(CH_3)_2$, used chiefly as a solvent for waxes, fats, and resins.

isopro′pyl group′, *Chem.* the univalent group, $(CH_3)_2CH–$, an isomer of the propyl group. Also called **isopro′pyl rad′ical.**

i·so·pro·pyl·i·dene·ac·e·tone (ī′sə prō pil′i dēn-as′i tōn′), *n.* *Chem.* See **mesityl oxide.** [ISO- + PROPYL + -ID³ + -ENE + ACETONE]

isopro′pyl mepro′bamate, *Pharm.* carisoprodol.

i·so·pyc·nic (ī′sə pik′nik), *adj.* **1.** Also, **i·so·pyc·nal** (ī′sə pik′nᵊl). having the same density. —*n.* **2.** an imaginary line or one drawn on a map connecting all points having the same density, as of water or air. [ISO- + *pycnic*, var. of PYKNIC]

i·so·pyre (ī′sə pīᵊr′), *n.* *Mineral.* an impure variety of opal, containing alumina, lime, and iron sesquioxide. [ISO- + Gk *pŷr* fire]

i·so·rhythm (ī′sə rith′əm), *n.* *Music.* a structural feature characteristic of the Ars Nova motet, consisting of a single rhythmic phrase pattern repeated, usually in the tenor, throughout the composition. [ISO- + RHYTHM] —**i·so·rhyth·mic** (ī′sə rith′mik), *adj.* —**i′so·rhyth′mi·cal·ly,** *adv.*

i·sos·ce·les (ī sos′ə lēz′), *adj.* (of a straight-sided plane figure) having two sides equal: *an isosceles triangle; an isosceles trapezoid.* See diag. under **triangle.** [< LL < Gk *isoskelḗs* with equal legs, equiv. to *iso-* ISO- + *skél(os)* leg + *-ēs* adj. suffix]

i·so·seis·mic (ī′sə sīz′mik, -sīs′-), *adj.* **1.** noting or pertaining to equal intensity of earthquake shock. **2.** noting or pertaining to an imaginary line on the earth's surface connecting points characterized by such intensity. —*n.* **3.** an isoseismic line. Also, **i′so·seis′mal.** [ISO- + SEISMIC]

i·sos·ta·sy (ī sos′tə sē), *n.* **1.** *Geol.* the equilibrium of the earth's crust, a condition in which the forces tending to elevate balance those tending to depress. **2.** the state in which pressures from every side are equal. Also, **i·sos′ta·cy.** [ISO- + *-stasy* < Gk *-stasia*; see STASIS, -Y³]

i·so·stat·ic (ī′sə stat′ik), *adj.* of, pertaining to, or characterized by isostasy. [ISO- + STATIC] —**i′so·stat′i·cal·ly,** *adv.*

i·so·ste·mo·nous (ī′sə stē′mə nəs, -stem′ə-), *adj.* *Bot.* having stamens equal in number to the sepals or petals. [ISO- + Gk *stḗmōn* thread + -OUS] —**i′so·ste′mo·ny,** *n.*

i·so·stere (ī′sə stēr′), *n.* **1.** *Chem.* a compound isosteric with one or more other compounds. **2.** *Meteorol.* a line on a map or chart connecting points of equal atmospheric density. [ISO- + Gk *stere(ós)* solid, hard]

i·so·ster·ic (ī′sə ster′ik), *adj.* *Chem.* having the same number of valence electrons in the same configuration but differing in the kinds and numbers of atoms. [ISOSTERE + -IC]

i·sos·ter·ism (ī sos′tə riz′əm), *n.* **1.** *Chem.* the quality or state of being isosteric. **2.** *Pharm.* the theory that isosteric compounds have identical or similar pharmacological action. [ISOSTERE + -ISM]

i·so·struc·tur·al (ī′sə struk′chər əl), *adj.* *Crystall.* (of two objects) having the same crystal structure but not necessarily a similar chemical composition. [ISO- + STRUCTURAL]

i·so·tac (ī′sə tak′), *n.* an imaginary line or one drawn on a map connecting all points where ice starts to melt at approximately the same period during spring. [ISO- + Gk *tak(ênai)* (to) melt or *tak(éros)* melting]

i·so·tach (ī′sə tak′), *n.* *Meteorol.* a line on a weather map or chart connecting points where winds of equal speeds have been recorded. [ISO- + *-tach* < Gk *tach(ýs)* swift; see TACHY-]

i·so·ten·i·scope (ī′sə ten′i skōp′), *n.* an instrument for measuring vapor pressure. [ISO- + *-ten-* (? root of L *tenēre* to hold) + -I- + -SCOPE]

i·so·there (ī′sə thēr′), *n.* *Climatol.* a line on a weather map or chart connecting points that have the same mean summer temperature. [ISO- + Gk *-there-*, var. s. of *théros* summer] —**i·soth·er·al** (ī soth′ər əl), *adj.*

i·so·therm (ī′sə thûrm′), *n.* **1.** *Meteorol.* a line on a weather map or chart connecting points having equal temperature. **2.** *Physics.* a curve on which every point represents the same temperature. [back formation from ISOTHERMAL]

i·so·ther·mal (ī′sə thûr′məl), *adj.* **1.** occurring at constant temperature. **2.** pertaining to an isotherm. —*n.* **3.** *Climatol.* an isotherm. [< F *isotherme* isothermal (< Gk *iso-* ISO- + *thermē* heat) + -AL¹] —**i′so·ther′mal·ly,** *adv.*

i′sother′mal line′, *Physics.* a line on which every point represents the same temperature.

i′sother′mal proc′ess, a process that takes place without change in temperature.

i·so·ther·mo·bath (ī′sə thûr′mə bath′, -bäth′), *n., pl.* **-baths** (-bathz′, -bäthz′). a line drawn on a diagram of a vertical section of the ocean connecting all points having equal temperature. [ISOTHERM + -O- + Gk *báth(os)* depth] —**i′so·ther′mo·bath′ic,** *adj.*

i·so·thi·o·cy·a·no (ī′sə thī′ō sī′ə nō′), *adj.* *Chem.* containing the isothiocyano group. [ISO- + THIO- + CYANO-³]

isothiocy′ano group′, *Chem.* the univalent group, $-N{=}C{=}S$. Also called **isothiocy′ano rad′ical.**

i·so·tim·ic (ī′sə tim′ik), *adj.* (of a line or surface in space) having an equal value of some quantity at a given time. [ISO- + TIME + -IC]

i·so·tone (ī′sə tōn′), *n.* *Physics.* one of two or more atoms having an equal number of neutrons but different atomic numbers. [ISO- + TONE]

i·so·ton·ic (ī′sə ton′ik), *adj.* **1.** *Physical Chem.* noting or pertaining to solutions characterized by equal osmotic pressure. Cf. **hypertonic** (def. 2), **hypotonic** (def. 2). **2.** *Physiol.* **a.** noting or pertaining to a solution containing just enough salt to prevent the destruction of the erythrocytes when added to the blood. **b.** noting or pertaining to a contraction of a muscle when under constant tension. **3.** *Music.* of or characterized by equal tones. [< Gk *isótonos* having equal accent or tone (see ISO-, TONE) + -IC] —**i·so·to·nic·i·ty** (ī′sə tō nis′i tē), *n.*

soton′ic so′dium chlo′ride solu′tion, *Pharm.* an aqueous solution of 0.9 percent sodium chloride, isotonic with the blood and tissue fluid, used in medicine chiefly for bathing tissue and, in sterile form, as a solvent for drugs which are to be administered parenterally to replace body fluids. Also called **normal saline solution, physiological salt solution, physiological sodium chloride solution.** Cf. **Ringer's solution.**

i·so·tope (ī′sə tōp′), *n.* *Chem.* any of two or more forms of a chemical element, having the same number of protons in the nucleus, or the same atomic number, but having different numbers of neutrons in the nucleus, or different atomic weights. There are 275 isotopes of the 81 stable elements, in addition to over 800 radioactive isotopes, and every element has known isotopic forms. Isotopes of a single element possess almost identical properties. [ISO- + Gk *tóp(os)* place] —**i·so·top·ic** (ī′sə top′ik), *adj.*

i·sot·o·py (ī sot′ə pē, ī′sə tō′pē), *n.* the quality or condition of being isotopic; isotopic character. [ISOTOPE + -Y³]

i·so·trop·ic (ī′sə trop′ik), *adj.* **1.** *Physics.* of equal physical properties along all axes. Cf. **anisotropic** (def. 1). **2.** *Zool.* lacking axes which are predetermined, as in some eggs. Also, **i·sot·ro·pous** (ī so′trə pəs). [ISO- + -TROPIC]

i·sot·ro·py (ī so′trə pē), *n.* the quality or condition of being isotropic; isotropic property. [ISO- + -TROPY]

i·so·type (ī′sə tīp′), *n.* **1.** a drawing, diagram, or other symbol that represents a specific quantity of or other fact about the thing depicted: *Every isotype of a house on that chart represents a million new houses.* **2.** a statistical graph, chart, diagram, etc., which employs such symbols. [ISO- + TYPE]

i·so·typ·ic (ī′sə tip′ik), *adj.* **1.** of or pertaining to an isotype. **2.** *Crystall.* (of two objects) isostructural and of similar chemical composition. Also, **i′so·typ′i·cal.** [ISOTYPE + -IC]

Is·pa·han (is′pə hän′, is′pə han′), *n.* **1.** Isfahan. **2.** a Persian rug characterized by hand-tied knots and ornamented with floral and animal patterns, usually on a deep red, blue, or green background.

Is·ra·el (iz′rē əl, -rā-), *n.* **1.** a republic in SW Asia, on the Mediterranean: formed as a Jewish state May 1948. 3,921,700 (1983); 7984 sq. mi. *Cap.:* Jerusalem. **2.** the people traditionally descended from Jacob; the Hebrew or Jewish people. **3.** a name given to Jacob after he had wrestled with the angel. Gen. 32: 28. **4.** the northern kingdom of the Hebrews, including the ten tribes, sometimes called by the name of the chief tribe, Ephraim. *Cap.:* Samaria. **5.** a group considered by its members or by others as God's chosen people. **6.** a boy's given name. [ME, OE < L < Gk < Heb *Yisrā'ēl*, lit., wrestler with God]

Is′rael ben El·i·e′zer (ben el′ē ē′zər, -ā′zər). See **Baal Shem-Tov.**

Is·rae·li (iz rā′lē), *n., pl.* **-lis,** (*esp. collectively*) **-li,** *adj.* —*n.* **1.** a native or inhabitant of modern Israel. —*adj.* **2.** of or pertaining to modern Israel or its inhabitants. [< NHeb *Yisre'ēlī*, equiv. to *Yisrā'ēl* ISRAEL + *-ī* suffix of appurtenance]

Is·ra·el·ite (iz′rē ə līt′, -rā-), *n.* **1.** a descendant of Jacob, esp. a member of the Hebrew people who inhabited the ancient kingdom of Israel. **2.** one of a group considered by its members or by others as God's chosen people. —*adj.* **3.** of or pertaining to ancient Israel or its people; Hebrew. [ISRAEL + -ITE¹]

Is·ra·el·it·ish (iz′rē ə lī′tish, -rā-), *adj.* of or pertaining to the Israelites; Hebrew. Also, **Is·ra·el·it·ic** (iz′rē ə lit′ik, -rā-). [ISRAELITE + -ISH¹]

Is·ra·fil (iz′rə fēl′), *n.* *Islamic Myth.* the angel who will sound the trumpet announcing the end of the world.

Is·sa·char (is′ə kär′), *n.* **1.** a son of Jacob and Leah. Gen. 30:18. **2.** one of the 12 tribes of Israel.

Is·sa·char·ite (is′ə kə rīt′), *n.* a member of the tribe of Issachar. [ISSACHAR + -ITE¹]

Is·sei (ēs′sā′), *n., pl.* **-sei.** a Japanese immigrant to the U.S. Also, **is′sei′.** Cf. **Kibei, Nisei, Sansei.** [< Jap, equiv. to *is* first + *sei* generation]

is·su·a·ble (ish′o͞o ə bəl), *adj.* **1.** able to be issued or to issue. **2.** forthcoming; receivable. **3.** *Law.* admitting of issue being taken. [ISSUE + -ABLE] —**is′su·a·bly,** *adv.*

is·su·ance (ish′o͞o əns), *n.* **1.** the act of issuing. **2.** issue. [ISSU(ANT) + -ANCE]

is·su·ant (ish′o͞o ənt), *adj.* **1.** *Heraldry.* (of a beast) represented with the body erect and only the forepart visible: *a lion issuant.* **2.** *Rare.* emerging from a place. [ISSUE + -ANT]

is·sue (ish′o͞o *or, esp. Brit.,* is′yo͞o), *n., v.,* **-sued, -suing.** —*n.* **1.** the act of sending out or putting forth; promulgation; distribution. **2.** that which is printed or published and distributed, esp. a given number of a periodical: *Have you seen the latest issue of the magazine?* **3.** that which is sent out or put forth in any form. **4.** a quantity sent out or put forth at one time: *a new issue of commemorative stamps.* **5.** a point in question or a matter that is in dispute, as between contending parties in an action at law. **6.** a point, matter, or dispute, the decision of which is of special or public importance: *the political issues.* **7.** a point the decision of which determines a matter: *The real issue in the strike was not money but the right to bargain collectively.* **8.** a point at which a matter is ready for decision: *to bring a case to an issue.* **9.** something proceeding from any source, as a product, effect, result, or consequence: *His words were the issue of an intelligent man.* **10.** the ultimate result, event, or outcome of a proceeding, affair, etc.: *the issue of a contest.* **11.** a distribution of food rations, clothing, equipment, or ammunition to a number of officers or enlisted men, or to a military unit. **12.** offspring; progeny: *to die without issue.* **13.** a going, coming, passing, or flowing out: *free issue and entry.* **14.** a place or means of egress; outlet or exit. **15.** that which comes out, as an outflowing stream. **16.** *Pathol.* **a.** a discharge of blood, pus, or the like. **b.** an incision, ulcer, or the like, emitting such a discharge. **17.** *Law.* the yield or profit from land or other property. **18.** the printing of copies of a work from the original setting of type with some slight changes: *The third issue of the poem contains the final change in the 24th line.* **19.** *Obs.* a proceeding or action. **20. at issue, a.** being disputed or under discussion. **b.** being at opposite viewpoints; in disagreement: *Medical men are still at issue over the proper use of tranquilizers.* **21. join issue, a.** to enter into controversy or take exception to. **b.** to submit an issue jointly for legal decision. **22. take issue,** to disagree with; dispute: *He took issue with me on my proposal for a new advertising campaign.* —*v.t.* **23.** to put out; deliver for use, sale, etc.; put into circulation. **24.** to mint, print, or publish for sale or distribution: *to issue a new coin; to issue a new book.* **25.** to distribute (food, clothing, etc.) to one or more officers or enlisted men or to a military unit. **26.** to send out; discharge; emit. —*v.i.* **27.** to go, pass, or flow out; come forth; emerge: *to issue forth to battle.* **28.** to be sent, put forth, or distributed authoritatively or publicly, as a writ, money, etc. **29.** to be published, as a book. **30.** to originate or proceed from any source. **31.** to arise as a result or consequence; result. **32.** *Chiefly Law.* to proceed as offspring, or be born or descended. **33.** *Chiefly Law.* to come as a yield or profit, as from land. **34.** to result: *a reaction which issues from the stimulus.* **35.** *Archaic.* to have the specified outcome, result, etc. (often fol. by *in*). **36.** *Obs.* to end; terminate. [ME < MF: place or passage out; OF *(e)issue* < VL **exuta*, n. use of fem. of **exutus*, r. L *exitus* (ptp. of *exīre* to go out); see EXIT] —**is′sue·less,** *adj.* —**is′su·er,** *n.*
—**Syn. 2.** copy, number, edition, printing. **5–7.** crux. **6, 7.** problem, question. **10.** upshot, conclusion, end. **27.** See **emerge. 30.** flow, emanate, arise, spring. **31.** ensue. —**Ant. 27.** return.

is′sue par′, *Finance.* See under **par** (def. 3b).

Is·sus (is′əs), *n.* an ancient town in Asia Minor, in Cilicia: victory of Alexander the Great over Darius III 333 B.C.

Is·syk-Kul (is′ik ko͝ol′), *n.* a mountain lake in the SW Soviet Union in Asia. 2250 sq. mi.

-ist, a suffix of nouns, often accompanying verbs ending in *-ize* or nouns ending in *-ism*, denoting one who practices or is concerned with something, or holds certain principles, doctrines, etc.: *apologist; dramatist; machinist; novelist; realist; socialist; Thomist.* Cf. **-ism, -istic, -ize.** [ME *-iste*, < L *-ista* < Gk *-istēs*; in some words, repr. F *-iste*, G *-ist*, It *-ista*, etc., << L < Gk, as above]

Is·tan·bul (is′tan bo͞ol′, -tän-; *Turk.* is täm′bo͝ol), *n.* a port in NW Turkey, on the European side of the Bosporus: built by Constantine I on the site of ancient Byzantium; capital of the Eastern Roman Empire and of the Ottoman Empire; capital removed to Ankara 1923. 1,750,642 (1965). Also, **Stambul, Stamboul.** Formerly (A.D. 330–1930), **Constantinople.**

i·stes·so tem·po, l' (li stes′ō tem′pō; *It.* lē stes′sō tem′pō), *Music.* See **l'istesso tempo.**

Isth., isthmus. Also, **isth.**

isth·mec·to·my (is mek′tə mē), *n., pl.* **-mies.** *Surg.* excision of an isthmus, particularly the isthmus of the thyroid gland. [ISTHM(US) + -ECTOMY]

isth·mi·an (is′mē ən), *adj.* **1.** of or pertaining to an isthmus. **2.** (*cap.*) of or pertaining to the Isthmus of Corinth or the Isthmus of Panama. —*n.* **3.** a native or inhabitant of an isthmus. [< L *isthmi(us)* (< Gk *isthmios* of a neck of land, equiv. to *isthm(ós)* neck + *-ios* adj. suffix) + -AN]

Isth′mian Games′, one of the great national festivals of ancient Greece, held every two years on the Isthmus of Corinth.

isth·mus (is′məs), *n., pl.* **-mus·es, -mi** (-mī). **1.** a narrow strip of land, bordered on both sides by water, connecting two larger bodies of land. **2.** *Anat., Zool.* a connecting, usually narrow, part, organ, or passage, esp. when joining structures or cavities larger than itself. **3.** *Ichthyol.* the narrow fleshy area between the sides of the lower jaw of a fish. [< L < Gk *isthmós* neck (of land)] —**isth′moid,** *adj.*

-istic, a suffix of adjectives (and in the plural, of nouns from adjectives) formed from nouns in *-ist* and having reference to such nouns, or to associated nouns in *-ism* (*deistic; euphuistic; puristic*). In nouns, it usually has a plural form (*linguistics*). Cf. **-ist, -ic, -ics.** [< L *-istic(us)* < Gk *-istikos*; in some words, for *-istique* < F]

-istical, a combination of **-istic** and **-al**[1].

-istics, a combination of **-ist** and **-ics.**

is·tle (ist/lē), *n.* a fiber from any of several tropical American plants of the genera *Agave, Yucca,* or *Fourcroza,* used in making bagging, carpets, etc. Also, **ixtle.** [< MexSp *ixtle* < Nahuatl *ixtli*]

Is·tri·a (is/trē ə; *It.* ēs/tryä), *n.* a peninsula in W Croatia, projecting into the N Adriatic. —**Is/tri·an,** *adj., n.*

I·sus (ī/səs), *n.* (in the *Iliad*) an illegitimate son of King Priam killed in battle by Agamemnon.

it[1] (it), *pron., nom.* **it,** *poss.* **its** or (*Obs. or Dial.*) **it,** *obj.* **it;** *pl. nom.* **they,** *poss.* **their** or **theirs,** *obj.* **them;** *n.* —*pron.* **1.** (used to represent an inanimate thing understood, previously mentioned or about to be mentioned): *It has whitewall tires and red upholstery. Although he didn't like it, I decided to see the movie anyway. You can't tell a book by its cover.* **2.** (used to represent a person or animal understood, previously mentioned or about to be mentioned whose gender is unknown or disregarded): *It was the largest ever caught off the Florida coast. Who was it? It was John. The horse had its saddle on.* **3.** (used to represent a group understood or previously stated): *It passed the bill over the governor's veto. The jury returned to its box.* **4.** (used to represent a concept or abstract idea understood or previously stated): *It all started with Adam and Eve. He has been taught to believe it all his life. Its chief proponents were the conservatives.* **5.** (used to represent an action or activity understood, previously mentioned or about to be mentioned): *Since you don't like it, you don't have to go skiing.* **6.** (used as the impersonal subject of the verb *to be*): *It is six o'clock. It is foggy. It is five miles to town.* **7.** (used in statements expressing an action, condition, fact, circumstance, or situation without reference to an agent): *It rained last night. If it weren't for Edna, I wouldn't go. Its having rained for only one hour didn't help the crops.* **8.** (used in referring to something as the origin or cause of pain, pleasure, etc.): *It pleases me to hear that. Where does it hurt? It grieves me that you can't go.* **9.** (used in referring to a source not specifically named or described): *It is said that love is blind. It is written that dead men tell no tales.* **10.** (used as an anticipatory subject or object to make a sentence longer or more eloquent or to make or shift emphasis): *It is necessary that every man do his duty. It was then that he saw the gun.* —*n.* **11.** (in children's games) the player called upon to perform some task, as in tag, the one who must catch the other players. **12.** the general state of affairs; circumstances, fate, or life in general: *How's it going with you?* **13. be with it,** *Slang.* **a.** to be attentive or alert: *She tried, but just wasn't with it.* **b.** to be understanding or appreciative of something, as jazz. **c.** *Carnival Slang.* to be a member of the carnival. **14. get with it,** *Slang.* to become active or interested: *He was warned to get with it or resign.* **15. have it,** *Slang.* **a.** to be physically attractive; to exude sex appeal: *That new blonde really has it.* **b.** to love someone: *She really has it bad for him.* **c.** to possess the requisite abilities for something; to be talented, skilled, adept, or proficient: *That new quarterback really has it. In this business you either have it or you don't.* [ME, var. of ME, OE *hit,* neut. of HE[1]]

it[2] (it), *n. Brit. Informal.* sweet vermouth: *gin and it.* [*It(alian vermouth)*]

it·a (it/ə), *adv.* (in prescriptions) in such a manner. [< L]

I·ta·bu·na (ē/tə bōō/nə), *n.* a city in E Brazil. 67,687 (1960).

it·a·col·u·mite (it/ə kol/yə mīt/), *n.* a sandstone consisting of interlocking quartz grains and mica scales, found principally in Brazil and North Carolina, and noted for its flexibility when in thin slabs. [named after *Itacolumi,* mountain in Brazil; see ITE[1]]

I·ta·ja·í (ē/tə zhə ē/), *n.* a seaport in S Brazil. 38,889 (1960).

Ital., **1.** Italian. **2.** Italic. **3.** Italy. Also, **It.**

ital., italic; italics.

I·ta·lia (ē tä/lyä), *n.* Italian name of **Italy.**

Ita/lia ir·re·den/ta (*It.* ēr/Rē den/tä). See under **irredentist** (def. 1).

I·tal·ian (i tal/yən), *adj.* **1.** of or pertaining to Italy, its people, or their language. —*n.* **2.** a native or inhabitant of Italy, or a person of Italian descent. **3.** a Romance language, the language of Italy, official also in Switzerland. [ME < L *Italiān(us).* See ITALY, -AN] —**I·tal/ian·esque/,** *adj.*

Ital/ian as/ter, a perennial herb, *Aster Amellus,* of Eurasia, having clustered, purple flower heads.

I·tal·ian·ate (*adj.* i tal/yə nāt/, -nit; *v.* i tal/yə nāt/), *adj., v.,* **-at·ed, -at·ing.** —*adj.* **1.** Italianized; conforming to the Italian type or style or to Italian customs, manners, etc. —*v.t.* **2.** to Italianize. [< It *italianato.* See ITALIAN, -ATE[1]] —**I·tal/ian·ate/ly,** *adv.* —**I·tal/ian·a/tion,** *n.*

Ital/ian clo/ver. See **crimson clover.**

Ital/ian corn/ sal/ad, an annual herb, *Valerianella eriocarpa,* of southern Europe, having spoon-shaped, hairy leaves and pale-blue flowers.

Ital/ian cy/press, a tree, *Cupressus sempervirens,* of southern Europe and southwestern Asia, having flattened twigs and four-sided leaves.

Ital/ian East/ Af/rica, a former Italian territory in E Africa, formed in 1936 by the merging of Eritrea and Italian Somaliland with newly conquered Ethiopia: taken by the British Imperial forces 1941.

Ital/ian grey/hound, one of an Italian breed of toy dogs resembling a greyhound.

Ital/ian hand/, **1.** a medieval script, used in early printing and later considered a standard of fine handwriting. **2.** meddling, interference, or craftiness of a subtle nature: *I sense his fine Italian hand in this matter.*

Ital/ian hon/eysuckle, a honeysuckle, *Lonicera Caprifolium,* of Europe and western Asia.

I·tal·ian·ise (i tal/yə nīz/), *v.i., v.t.,* **-ised, -is·ing.** *Chiefly Brit.* Italianize. —**I·tal/ian·i·sa/tion,** *n.*

I·tal·ian·ism (i tal/yə niz/əm), *n.* **1.** an Italian practice, trait, or idiom. **2.** Italian quality or spirit. [ITALIAN + -ISM]

I·tal·ian·ist (i tal/yə nist), *n.* one who specializes in the study of Italy, the Italian people, or the Italian language. [ITALIAN + -IST]

I·tal·ian·ize (i tal/yə nīz/), *v.,* **-ized, -iz·ing.** —*v.i.* **1.** to become Italian in manner, character, etc. **2.** to speak Italian. —*v.t.* **3.** to make Italian, esp. in manner, character, etc. Also, *esp. Brit.,* **Italianise.** [ITALIAN + -IZE] —**I·tal/ian·i·za/tion,** *n.*

I·tal·ian·iz·er (i tal/yə nī/zər), *n.* one who or that which Italianizes: *In matters of food and dress, he is an Italianizer.* [ITALIANIZE + -ER[1]]

Ital/ian jas/mine, an evergreen shrub, *Jasminum humile,* having fragrant, golden-yellow flowers.

Ital/ian reed/. See **giant reed.**

Ital/ian rye/ grass/, a European annual grass, *Lolium multiflorum,* naturalized in North America, having flowering spikes and used as a winter turf. Also called **Australian rye grass.**

Ital/ian Soma/liland, a former Italian colony and trust territory in E Africa: now part of the republic of Somalia.

Ital/ian son/net. See **Petrarchan sonnet.**

i·tal·ic (i tal/ik, ī tal/-), *adj.* **1.** designating or pertaining to a style of printing types in which the letters usually slope to the right, patterned upon a compact manuscript hand, and used for emphasis, to separate different kinds of information, etc. **2.** (*cap.*) of or pertaining to Italy, esp. ancient Italy or its tribes. —*n.* **3.** Often, **italics.** italic type. **4.** (*cap.*) *Ling.* a branch of the Indo-European family of languages, including ancient Latin, Oscan, Umbrian and modern Romance, and closely related to Celtic. [< L *Italic(us)* < Gk *Italikós,* equiv. to *Ital(ía)* ITALY + *-ikos* -IC]

I·tal·i·cism (i tal/i siz/əm), *n.* Italianism, esp. an idiom or a characteristic of the Italian language. [ITALIC + -ISM]

i·tal·i·cize (i tal/i sīz/, ī tal/-), *v.,* **-cized, -ciz·ing.** —*v.t.* **1.** to print in italic type. **2.** to underscore with a single line, as in indicating italics. —*v.i.* **3.** to use italics. [ITALIC + -IZE] —**i·tal/i·ci·za/tion,** *n.*

I·tal·o·phile (i tal/ə fīl/, it/əlō-), *n.* **1.** one who admires Italian customs, traditions, etc. —*adj.* **2.** Also, **I·tal·o·phil** (i tal/ə fil, it/əlō-). favoring Italian customs, manners, traditions, etc. [ITAL(IAN) + -O- + -PHILE]

It·a·ly (it/əlē), *n.* a republic in S Europe, comprising a peninsula S of the Alps and Sicily, Sardinia, Elbe, and other smaller islands: a kingdom 1870–1946. 50,463,762 (1961); 116,294 sq. mi. *Cap.:* Rome. Italian, **Italia.**

I·ta·pe·ti·nin·ga (ē/tə pe/tē nēnḡ/gə), *n.* a city in E Brazil. 30,403 (1960).

I·tas·ca (ī tas/kə), *n.* **1. Lake,** a lake in N Minnesota: one of the sources of the Mississippi River. **2.** a town in NE Illinois. 3564 (1960).

itch (ich), *v.i.* **1.** to have or feel a peculiar tingling or uneasy irritation of the skin which causes a desire to scratch the part affected. **2.** to cause such a feeling: *This shirt itches.* **3.** to have a desire to do or to get something: *to itch after fame.* —*v.t.* **4.** to cause to have an itch: *His wool shirt always itches him.* **5.** to annoy; irritate: *His remarks itched me.* —*n.* **6.** the sensation of itching. **7.** an uneasy or restless desire or longing: *an itch for excitement.* **8.** a contagious disease caused by the itch mite, which burrows into the skin (usually prec. by *the*). Cf. **mange, scabies.** [ME *(y)icchen,* OE *gicc(e)an;* akin to G *jucken,* D *jeuken*]

itch·ing (ich/ing), *adj.* **1.** of, pertaining to, or characterized by an irritating sensation of the skin. **2.** of, pertaining to, or having a longing or desire to do or to have something: *An itching public anxiously awaits his announcement.* **3.** characterized by a restless desire for action, adventure, activity, etc.; marked by restlessness: *An itching impulse for adventure has led him into some dangerous situations.* **4.** characterized by a desire for money and material possessions; acquisitive; avaricious: *This moneylender had an itching palm always ready to wring another dollar from a customer.* —*n.* **5.** itch. [ME (n., adj.), OE (adj.). See ITCH, -ING[2], -ING[1]] —**itch/ing·ly,** *adv.*

itch/ mite/, a parasitic mite, *Sarcoptes scabiei,* causing itch or scabies in man and a form of mange in animals.

itch·y (ich/ē), *adj.,* **itch·i·er, itch·i·est.** **1.** having or causing an itching sensation. **2.** characterized by itching. [OE *giccig.* See ITCH, -Y[1]] —**itch/i·ness,** *n.*

-ite[1], a suffix of nouns denoting esp. persons associated with a place, tribe, leader, doctrine, system, etc. (*Campbellite; Israelite; laborite*); minerals and fossils (*ammonite; anthracite*); explosives (*cordite; dynamite*); chemical compounds, esp. salts of acids whose names end in *-ous* (*phosphite; sulfite*); pharmaceutical and commercial products (*vulcanite*); a member or component of a part of the body (*somite*). Cf. **-itis.** [ME < L *-ita* < Gk *-ītēs;* often directly < Gk; in some words repr. F *-ite,* G *-it,* etc., < L < Gk, as above]

-ite[2], a suffix forming adjectives and nouns from adjectives, and from some verbs: *composite; opposite; erudite; requisite.* [< L *-itus* or *-ītus* ptp. suffix]

i·tem (*n., v.* ī/təm; *adv.* ī/tem), *n.* **1.** a separate article or particular: *50 items on the list.* **2.** a separate piece of information or news, as a short paragraph in a newspaper. **3.** *Slang.* something suitable for a news paragraph or as a topic of gossip, esp. something that is sensational or scandalous: *I understand the band leader and the new girl singer are an item.* **4.** a word formerly used in communications to represent the letter I. **5.** *Obs.* **a.** an admonition or warning. **b.** an intimation or hint. —*v.t. Archaic.* **6.** to set down or enter as an item, or by or in items. **7.** to make a note or memorandum of. —*adv.* **8.** *Obs. or Archaic.* likewise. [< L: likewise]
—**Syn. 1.** thing; heading, entry.

i·tem·ize (ī/tə mīz/), *v.t.,* **-ized, -iz·ing.** to state by items; give the particulars of; list the individual units or parts of: *to itemize an account.* [ITEM + -IZE] —**i/tem·i·za/tion,** *n.* —**i/tem·iz/er,** *n.*

i·tem·ized (ī/tə mīzd/), *adj.* with each item separately listed with its own pertinent information: *an itemized bill.* [ITEMIZE + -ED[2]]

i/tem ve/to, *U.S.* (in certain States) the power of the governor to veto particular items of a bill without having to veto the whole bill.

it·er (it/ər, ī/tər), *n. Anat.* a canal or passage, as the aqueduct of Sylvius. [< L: a walking, hence passage, road, right of way, journey, akin to *īre* to go]

it·er·ance (it/ər əns), *n.* iteration. [ITER(ANT) + -ANCE]

it·er·ant (it/ər ənt), *adj.* characterized by repetition; repeating. [< L *iterant-* (s. of *iterāns*) repeating, prp. of *iterāre.* See ITERATE, -ANT]

it·er·ate (it/ə rāt/), *v.t.,* **-at·ed, -at·ing.** **1.** to utter again or repeatedly. **2.** to do (something) over again or repeatedly. [< L *iterāt(us)* repeated (ptp. of *iterāre*), equiv. to *iter-* (s. of *iterum*) again + *-ātus* -ATE[1]] —**it/er·a/tion,** *n.*
—**Syn. 1.** reiterate, repeat, rehearse.

it/erated in/tegral, *Math.* a double integral that can be evaluated by integrating the integrand with respect to one variable and integrating the resulting function with respect to the second variable.

it·er·a·tive (it/ə rā/tiv, -ər ə tiv), *adj.* **1.** repeating; making repetition; repetitious. **2.** *Gram.* frequentative. [< LL *iterātīv(us).* See ITERATE, -IVE] —**it/er·a/tive·ly,** *adv.* —**it/er·a/tive·ness,** *n.*

Ith·a·ca (ith/ə kə), *n.* **1.** one of the Ionian Islands, off the W coast of Greece: legendary home of Ulysses. 5803 (1951); 37 sq. mi. **2.** a city in S New York at the S end of Cayuga Lake. 28,799 (1960). **3.** a town in central Michigan. 2611 (1960). —**Ith/a·can,** *adj.*

ith·er (ith/ər), *adj., pron., adv. Brit. Dial.* other. —**ith/er·ness,** *n.*

I·tho·ma·tas (i thō/mə təs), *n. Class. Myth.* Zeus: so called because Mount Ithome was dedicated to him.

I·tho·me (i thō/mē), *n.* **1. Mount,** a mountain in SW Greece, in SW Peloponnesus. 2630 ft. **2.** in ancient geography, a fortress of Messenia on Mount Ithome. **3.** *Class. Myth.* one of the nymphs who reared Zeus.

I·thunn (ē/thōōn), *n.* Idun. Also, **I/thun.**

I·thu/ri·el's-spear/ (i thŏŏr/ē əlz spēr/), *n.* See **triplet lily.** [from phrase *Ithuriel with his spear* in *Paradise Lost*]

ith·y·phal·lic (ith/ə fal/ik), *adj.* **1.** of or pertaining to the phallus carried in ancient festivals of Bacchus. **2.** grossly indecent; obscene. **3.** *Class. Pros.* noting or pertaining to any of several meters employed in hymns sung in Bacchic processions. —*n.* **4.** a poem in ithyphallic meter. **5.** an indecent poem. [< LL *īthyphallic(us)* < Gk *īthyphallikós,* equiv. to *īthýphall(os)* erect phallus + *-ikos* -IC]

-itic, a combination of **-ite**[1] and **-ic,** used to form adjectives from nouns ending in **-ite:** *Semitic.* [< L -ITICUS < Gk *-itikos,* equiv. to *it(is)* -ITIS + *-ikos* -IC; in some words repr. F *-itique* < L < Gk, as above]

i·tin·er·an·cy (ī tin/ər ən sē, i tin/-), *n.* **1.** the act of traveling from place to place. **2.** a going around from place to place in the discharge of duty or the conducting of business. **3.** a body of itinerants, as ministers, judges, salesmen, etc. **4.** the state of being itinerant. **5.** the system of rotation governing the ministry of the Methodist Church. Also, **i·tin·er·a·cy** (ī tin/ər ə sē, i tin/-). [ITINERAN(T) + -CY]

i·tin·er·ant (ī tin/ər ənt, i tin/-), *adj.* **1.** traveling from place to place, esp. on a circuit, as a minister, judge, or salesman; itinerating; journeying. **2.** characterized by such traveling: *Itinerant preaching has its advantages and disadvantages.* **3.** working in one place for a comparatively short time and then moving on to work in another place, usually as a physical or outdoor laborer; characterized by alternating periods of working and wandering: *an itinerant farm hand.* —*n.* **4.** a person who travels from place to place, esp. for duty or business. **5.** a person who alternates between working and wandering. [< LL *itinerant-* (s. of *itinerāns*) journeying (prp. of *itinerārī* to journey), equiv. to *itiner-* (s. of *iter*) journey + *-ant-* -ANT] —**i·tin/er·ant·ly,** *adv.*
—**Syn. 1, 3.** wandering, nomadic, migratory, unsettled, roving, roaming; peripatetic. —**Ant. 1.** settled.

i·tin·er·ar·i·um (ī tin/ə râr/ē əm), *n., pl.* **-er·ar·i·a** (-ə râr/ē ə), **-er·ar·i·ums.** *Rom. Cath. Ch.* a prayer in the breviary, used by a priest about to begin a journey. [< ML; see ITINERARY]

i·tin·er·ar·y (ī tin/ə rer/ē, i tin/-), *n., pl.* **-ar·ies,** *adj.* —*n.* **1.** a line of travel; route. **2.** a detailed plan for a journey, esp. a list of places to visit; plan of travel. **3.** an account of a journey; a record of travel. **4.** a book describing a route or routes of travel with information helpful to travelers; guidebook for travelers. —*adj.* **5.** of or pertaining to travel or travel routes. **6.** *Obs.* itinerant. [late ME < LL *itinerāri(um),* n. use of neut. of *itinerārius* of a journey, equiv. to *itiner-* (s. of *iter*) journey + *-ārius* -ARY]

i·tin·er·ate (ī tin/ə rāt/, i tin/-), *v.i.,* **-at·ed, -at·ing.** to go from place to place, esp. in a regular circuit, as a preacher or judge. [< LL *itinerāt(us)* traveled (ptp. of *itinerārī*), equiv. to L *itiner-* (s. of *iter*) journey + *-ātus* -ATE[1]] —**i·tin/er·a/tion,** *n.*

-ition, a compound suffix of nouns, being *-tion* with a preceding original or formative vowel, or, in other words, a combination of **-ite**[2] and **-ion:** *expedition; extradition.* [< L *-itiōn-* or *-ītiōn-,* s. of *-itiō* or *-ītiō.* See -ITE[2], -ION]

-itious, a compound suffix occurring in adjectives of Latin origin (*adventitious*) and with adjectives, formed in Latin or English, associated with nouns ending in *-ition* (*ambitious; expeditious*). Cf. **-ite**[2], **-ous.** [< L *-icius* or *-īcius* (as in *adventitious*); and < L *-itiōsus* or *-ītiōsus* (as in *ambitious*)]

-itis, a learned borrowing from Greek, used esp. in pathological terms to denote inflammation of an organ (*bronchitis; gastritis; neuritis*) and hence extended in meaning to include abnormal states or conditions, excesses, tendencies, obsessions, etc. (*telephonitis; baseballitis*). [< NL (or L) < Gk]

-itive, a suffix occurring in substantives of Latin origin: *definitive; fugitive.* [< L *-itīv(us)* or *-ītīv(us)*]

it'll (it/əl), **1.** a contraction of *it will.* **2.** contraction of *it shall.*

I·to (ē/tô/), *n.* **Marquis Hi·ro·bu·mi** (hē/Rô bōō/mē), 1841–1909, Japanese statesman.

ITO, International Trade Organization.

-itol, *Chem.* a suffix used in names of alcohols containing more than one hydroxyl group: *inositol.* [-ITE[1] + -OL[1]]

I·to·ni·a (i tō/nē ə), *n. Class. Myth.* an epithet of Athena.

I·to·ni·us (i tō/nē əs), *n. Class. Myth.* a Boeotian, sometimes believed to be the father of Athena.

I·to su·ka·shi (ē tô/ sə kä/shē; *Jap.* ē tô/ sōō-kä/shē, sə-), a form of decoration for a tsuba consisting of intricately sawed fretwork. [< Jap]

it's (its), **1.** a contraction of *it is: It's starting to rain.* **2.** contraction of *it has: It's been a long time.*

its (its), *pron.* the possessive form of **it** (used as an attributive adjective): *The book has lost its jacket. I'm sorry about its being so late.* [IT[1] + (HI)S]
—**Usage.** See **me.**

it·self (it self′), *pron.* **1.** a reflexive form of **it:** *The battery recharges itself.* **2.** an emphatic appositive of **it, which, that, this,** or a noun: *which itself is also true; Even without flowers, the bowl itself is beautiful.* **3.** (used as the object of a preposition or as the direct or indirect object of a verb): *The chameleon's ability to change color is a protection for itself.* **4.** its normal or customary self: *After much tender care, the puppy was soon itself again.* [ME; OE *hit self.* See IT[1], SELF] **—Usage.** See **myself.**

it·ty-bit·ty (it′ē bit′ē), *adj. Babytalk.* small; tiny. Also, **it·sy-bit·sy** (it′sē bit′sē). [alter. of *little bit*]

ITU, International Telecommunication Union.

I.T.U., International Typographical Union.

I·tur·bi (i tûr′bē, ē tōōr′bē), *n.* **José,** 1895–1980, U.S. pianist, conductor, and composer; born in Spain.

I·tur·bi·de (ē′tōōr bē′the), *n.* **A·gus·tín de** (ä′gōōs tēn′ de), 1783–1824, Mexican soldier and revolutionary: as Augustín I, emperor of Mexico 1822–23.

-ity, a suffix used to form abstract nouns expressing state or condition: *jollity; civility; Latinity.* [var. of *-itie,* ME *-ite* < OF < L *-itāt-* (s. of *-itās*); in many words repr. L *-itās* directly]

It·y·lus (it′ᵊləs, īt′-), *n. Class. Myth.* the only child of Aëdon and Zethus, mistakenly killed by his mother.

I·tys (ī′tis, it′is), *n. Class. Myth.* the son of Tereus and Procne who was murdered and served as a meal to Tereus by Procne and her sister Philomela.

IU, 1. immunizing unit. **2.** international unit.

IUD, any small, mechanical device for semipermanent insertion in the uterus as a contraceptive. Also called **intrauterine device, loop, coil.** [*i(ntra)u(terine) d(evice)*]

I·u·lus (ī yōō′ləs), *n. Class. Myth.* Ascanius.

-ium, a suffix occurring in loan words from Latin (*tedium*); specialized in chemical terminology to form names of elements (*barium*). [< NL, L, neut. suffix]

I.V., initial velocity.

i.v., 1. increased value. **2.** initial velocity. **3.** intravenous. **4.** invoice value.

I·van (ī′vən), *n.* a boy's given name, Russian form of **John.**

I·van III (ī′vən; *Russ.* i vän′), ("*Ivan the Great*") 1440–1505, grand duke of Muscovy 1462–1505.

Ivan IV, ("*Ivan the Terrible*") 1530–84, first czar of Russia 1547–84.

I·van·hoe (ī′vən hō′), *n.* a novel (1819) by Sir Walter Scott about England in the 12th century.

I·va·nov (i vä′nof), *n.* **Vse·vo·lod Vya·che·sla·vo·vich** (fse′vo lot vyä che slä′vo vich), 1895–1963, Russian playwright.

I·va·no·vo (i vä′no vo), *n.* a city in the W RSFSR, in the central Soviet Union in Europe, NE of Moscow. 332,000 (1959). Formerly, **Iva′novo Voz·ne·sensk** (voz ne sensk′).

I·var (ī′vər, ē′vər), *n.* a boy's or girl's given name.

I've (īv), contraction of *I have.*

-ive, a suffix of adjectives (and nouns of adjectival origin) expressing tendency, disposition, function, connection, etc.: *active; corrective; destructive; detective; passive; sportive.* Cf. **-ative, -itive.** [< L *-īv(us)*; in some words. repr. F *-ive,* fem. of *-if*]

Ives (īvz), *n.* **1. Burl (I·cle Ivanhoe)** (bûrl ik′əl), born 1909, U.S. actor and folk singer. **2. Charles Edward,** 1874–1954, U.S. composer. **3. Frederick Eugene,** 1856–1937, U.S. inventor. **4. James Mer·ritt** (mer′it), 1824–95, U.S. lithographer. Cf. **Currier. 5.** a boy's given name.

i·vied (ī′vēd), *adj.* covered or overgrown with ivy: *ivied walls.* [IVY + -ED[3]]

I·vis (ī′vis), *n.* a girl's given name.

I·vi·za (ē vē′sä), *n.* a Spanish island in the SW Balearic Islands, in the W Mediterranean Sea. Spanish, **Ibiza.**

I·vor (ī′vər, ē′vər), *n.* a boy's given name.

i·vo·ry (ī′və rē, īv′rē), *n., pl.* **-ries,** *adj.* **—***n.* **1.** the hard white substance, a variety of dentine, composing the main part of the tusks of the elephant, walrus, etc. **2.** this substance when taken from a dead animal and used to make carvings, billiard balls, etc. **3.** some substance resembling this. **4.** an article made of this substance, as a carving or a billiard ball. **5.** a tusk, as of an elephant. **6.** dentine of any kind. **7.** *Slang.* a tooth, or the teeth. **8. ivories,** *Slang.* **a.** the keys of a piano or of a similar keyboard instrument. **b.** dice. **9.** Also called **vegetable ivory.** the hard endosperm of the ivory nut, used for ornamental purposes, for buttons, etc. **10.** a creamy or yellowish white. **11.** a smooth paper finish produced by coating with beeswax before calendering. **—***adj.* **12.** consisting or made of ivory. **13.** of the color ivory. [ME < OF *ivurie* < L *ebore(us)* (adj.), equiv. to *ebor-* (s. of *ebur*) ivory + *-eus* adj. suffix] **—i′vo·ry·like′,** *adj.*

i′vo·ry-billed wood′pecker (ī′və rē bild′, īv′rē-), a large, nearly extinct, black and white woodpecker, *Campephilus principalis,* of the southern U.S., having an ivory-colored bill.

MALI
UPPER VOLTA
GUINEA
Ivory Coast
LIBERIA
GHANA
Abidjan
ATLANTIC OCEAN

i′vory black′, a fine black pigment made by calcining ivory.

I′vory Coast′, a republic in W Africa: formerly part of French West Africa. 3,800,000 (est. 1965); 127,520 sq. mi. *Cap.:* Abidjan.

i′vory gull′, a white, arctic gull, *Pagophila eburnea.*

i′vory nut′, 1. the seed of a low, South American palm, *Phytelephas macrocarpa,* yielding vegetable ivory. **2.** a similar seed from other palms.

i′vory palm′, the palm bearing the common ivory nut.

i′vory tow′er, 1. a place or situation remote from worldly or practical affairs: *The laboratory was for him an ivory tower where he could pursue his love of theoretical science in perfect contentment.* **2.** an attitude of aloofness from or disdain or disregard for worldly or practical affairs: *Living in an ivory tower, he had no understanding of politics.* **—i′vo·ry-tow′er·ish,** *adj.* **—i′vo·ry-tow′er·ish·ness,** *n.*

i·vo·ry-tow·ered (ī′və rē tou′ərd, īv′rē-), *adj.* remote from practical considerations or from everyday existence. [IVORY TOWER + -ED[2]]

i·vo·ry-tow·er·ism (ī′və rē tou′ə riz′əm, īv′rē-), *n.* cultivation of or adherence to an attitude of indifference toward worldliness, popular trends, or matters that are outside one's circle of interest. [IVORY TOWER + -ISM] **i′vo·ry-tow′er·ist, i′vo·ry-tow′er·ite′,** *n.*

i·vo·ry·type (ī′və rē tīp′, īv′rē-), *n. Obs.* a photograph consisting of two prints of the same image, a weaker one, made transparent with varnish and colored on the back, laid over a stronger one. [IVORY + -TYPE]

i·vo·ry-white (ī′və rē hwīt′, -wīt′, īv′rē-), *adj.* of a creamy or yellowish white in color.

-ivus, a suffix appearing in Latin scientific names: *exfoliativus.* Cf. **-ive.** [< NL, L]

i·vy (ī′vē), *n., pl.* **i·vies. 1.** Also called **English ivy.** a climbing vine, *Hedera helix,* having smooth, shiny, evergreen leaves, small, yellowish flowers, and black berries, grown as an ornamental. **2.** any of various other climbing or trailing plants. **3.** (*usually cap.*) See **Ivy League.** [ME; OE *īfig*; akin to G *Efeu*] **—i′vy·like′,** *adj.*

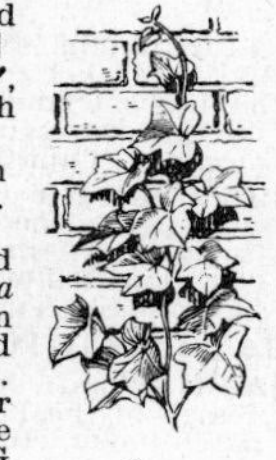
Ivy, *Hedera helix*

I·vy (ī′vē), *n.* a girl's given name.

i·vy·ber·ry (ī′vē ber′ē), *n., pl.* **-ries.** the wintergreen, *Gaultheria procumbens.* [IVY + BERRY]

i′vy gera′nium, a trailing, perennial herb, *Pelargonium peltatum,* of South Africa, having a fleshy stem which becomes woody with age, glossy, ivy-shaped leaves, and clusters of flowers ranging from white to deep rose in color.

I′vy League′, 1. a group of colleges and universities in the northeastern U.S., esp. Yale, Harvard, Princeton, Columbia, Dartmouth, Cornell, Pennsylvania, and Brown, having a reputation for high scholastic achievement and social prestige. **2.** of, pertaining to, or characteristic of Ivy League colleges or their students and graduates: *an Ivy League education; an Ivy League suit.*

I′vy Lea′guer, a student or alumnus of an Ivy League college. [IVY LEAGUE + -ER[1]]

i′vy vine′, 1. a vinelike plant, *Ampelopsis cordata,* of the U.S., differing from the grape vine, esp. in having a corolla of wholly separate petals. **2.** See **Virginia creeper.**

I.W., Isle of Wight.

i.w., 1. inside width. **2.** isotopic weight.

i·wis (i wis′), *adv. Obs.* certainly. Also, **ywis.** [ME, adv. use of neut. of OE *gewiss* (adj.) certain; c. D *gewis,* G *gewiss* certain, certainly; akin to WIT[2]]

I·wo (ē′wō), *n.* a city in SW Nigeria. 100,006 (1953).

I·wo Ji·ma (ē′wə jē′mə, ē′wō; *Jap.* ē′wô jē′mä), one of the Volcano Islands, in the N Pacific, S of Japan: captured by U.S. forces 1945.

I.W.W. See **Industrial Workers of the World.** Also, **IWW**

I.X., Jesus Christ. Also, **IX** [< Gk *Iēsoûs Christós*]

Ix·elles (ēk sel′), *n.* a city in central Belgium, near Brussels. 94,007 (est. 1964). Flemish, **Elsene.**

ix·i·a (ik′sē ə), *n.* any iridaceous plant of the genus *Ixia,* of southern Africa, having sword-shaped leaves and showy, ornamental flowers. [< NL < Gk: birdlime, equiv. to *ix(ós)* mistletoe, birdlime (made with mistletoe berries) + *-ia* -IA]

Ix·i·on (ik sī′ən), *n. Class. Myth.* a king of the Lapithae who was punished by Zeus for his love for Hera by being bound on an eternally revolving wheel in Tartarus. **—Ix·i·o·ni·an** (ik′sē ō′nē ən), *adj.*

ix·od·id (ik sod′id, -sō′did, ik′sə did), *n.* **1.** any of numerous ticks of the family *Ixodidae,* comprising the hard ticks. **—***adj.* **2.** belonging or pertaining to the family *Ixodidae.* [< NL *Ixodid(ae)* name of the family, equiv. to *Ixod(es)* name of the genus (< Gk: like birdlime, equiv. to *ix(ós)* birdlime + *-ōdēs* -ODE[1]) + *-idae* -ID[2]]

Ix·ta·ci·huatl (ēs′tä sē′wätᵊl), *n.* an extinct volcano in S central Mexico, SE of Mexico City. 17,342 ft. Also, **Ix·tac·ci·huatl** (ēs′täk sē wätᵊl), **Iztaccihuatl.**

ix·tle (iks′tlē, ist′lē), *n.* istle.

I·yar (ē′yär; *Heb.* ē YÄR′), *n.* a month of the Jewish calendar. Also, **Iy′yar.** Cf. **Jewish calendar.** [< Heb]

I·ye·ya·su (ē′ye yä′sōō), *n.* **To·ku·ga·wa** (tô′kōō gä′wä), 1542–1616, Japanese general and statesman. Also, **Ieyasu.**

I·ynx (ī′iŋks), *n. Class. Myth.* a daughter of Pan and Echo.

I·za·na·gi (ē′zä nä′gē), *n.* the Japanese god who fathered the islands and gods of Japan by a union with his sister Izanami.

I·za·na·mi (ē′zä nä′mē), *n.* a Japanese goddess, the sister of Izanagi.

iz·ard (iz′ərd), *n.* a chamois that inhabits the Pyrenees. [< F, var. of *isard* < dial. (Gascon) *isart*]

Iz·ard (iz′ərd), *n.* **Ralph,** 1742–1804, U.S. diplomat and politician.

-ization, a combination of **-ize** and **-ation:** *civilization.*

iz·ba (iz bä′), *n.* isba.

-ize, a suffix of verbs having the sense, intransitively, of following some line of action, practice, policy, etc. (*Atticize; apologize; economize; theorize; tyrannize*), or of becoming as indicated (*crystallize; oxidize*); and transitively, of acting toward or upon, treating, or affecting in a particular way (*baptize; colonize; patronize; stigmatize*), or of making or rendering as indicated (*civilize; legalize; mobilize; realize*). Also, **-ise**[1]. Cf. **-ism** and **-ist.** [< LL *-iz(āre)* < Gk *-izein*; r. ME *-ise(n)* < OF *-ise(r)*]

I·zhevsk (i zhefsk′), *n.* a city in and the capital of the Udmurt Autonomous Soviet Socialist Republic, in the RSFSR, in the E Soviet Union in Europe. 283,000 (1959).

Iz·mir (iz′mēr), *n.* **1.** Formerly, **Smyrna.** a seaport in W Turkey on the Gulf of Izmir: important city of Asia Minor from ancient times. 417,413 (1965). **2. Gulf of.** Formerly, **Gulf of Smyrna.** arm of the Aegean Sea in W Turkey. 35 mi. long; 14 mi. wide.

Iz·tac·ci·huatl (ēs′täk sē′wätᵊl), *n.* Ixtaccihuatl.

Iz·ves·ti·a (iz ves′tē ə), *n.* the official newspaper of the Soviet government.

Iz·zak (ī′zək), *n.* a boy's given name, form of **Isaac.**

iz·zard (iz′ərd), *n. Chiefly Dial.* the letter Z. [var. of ZED]

iz·zat (iz′ət), *n.* **1.** personal dignity or honor. **2.** personal prestige. [< Hindi *'izzat*]

J, j (jā), *n., pl.* **J's** or **Js, j's** or **js.** **1.** the 10th letter of the English alphabet, a consonant. **2.** any spoken sound represented by the letter *J* or *j*, as in *judge, rajah, major,* etc. **3.** something having the shape of a J. **4.** a written or printed representation of the letter *J* or *j*. **5.** a device, as a printer's type, for reproducing the letter *J* or *j*.

J, *Physics.* joule. Also, **j**

J, **1.** the 10th in order or in a series, or, when *I* is omitted, the 9th. **2.** (*sometimes l.c.*) the medieval Roman numeral for 1. Cf. **Roman numerals.**

j, **1.** *Math.* a vector on the y-axis, having length 1 unit. **2.** *Engineering.* the imaginary number $\sqrt{-1}$.

J., **1.** Journal. **2.** Judge. **3.** Justice.

ja (yä), *adv. German.* yes.

Ja., January.

J.A., **1.** Joint Agent. **2.** Judge Advocate.

jab (jab), *v.,* **jabbed, jab·bing,** *n.* **—***v.t., v.i.* **1.** to poke, or thrust smartly or sharply, as with the end or point of something. **2.** to punch, esp. with a short, quick blow. **—***n.* **3.** a poke with the end or point of something; a smart or sharp thrust. **4.** a short, quick blow. Also, **job.** [var., orig. Scot, of JOB²] **—jab′bing·ly,** *adv.*

Ja·bal (jā′bəl), *n.* a son of Lamech, and the progenitor of nomadic shepherds. Gen. 4:20.

Jab·al al-Duruz (jeb′əl ed dro͞oz′). See **Jebel ed Druz.**

Jab·al·pur (jub′əl pôr′), *n.* a city in central Madhya Pradesh, in central India. 295,400 (1961). Also, **Jubbulpore.**

jab·ber (jab′ər), *v.t., v.i.* **1.** to talk or utter rapidly, indistinctly, imperfectly, or nonsensically; chatter. **—***n.* **2.** rapid, indistinct, or nonsensical talk; gibberish. [appar. imit.; cf. GIBBER¹, GAB¹] **—jab′ber·er,** *n.* **—jab′ber·ing·ly,** *adv.*

Jab·ber·wock·y (jab′ər wok′ē), *n., pl.* **-wock·ies,** *adj.* **—***n.* **1.** a parody of language consisting of meaningless syllables; nonsense; gibberish. **2.** an example of writing or speech consisting of or containing such meaningless syllables. **—***adj.* **3.** consisting of or comparable to Jabberwocky; characterized by an absence of intelligible meaning. Also, **Jab·ber·wock** (jab′ər wok′). [coined by Lewis Carroll in *Jabberwocky,* poem in *Through the Looking Glass*]

Ja·bez (jā′biz), *n.* a boy's given name.

Ja·bir (jä′bir), *n.* Geber.

jab·i·ru (jab′ə ro͞o′), *n.* a large stork, *Jabiru mycteria,* of the warmer regions of America. [< Pg < Tupi-Guarani *jabirú*]

jab·o·ran·di (jab′ə ran′dē), *n., pl.* **-dis.** **1.** any of several South American, rutaceous shrubs of the genus *Pilocarpus.* **2.** the dried leaflets of certain of these plants, esp. *Pilocarpus jaborandi,* containing the alkaloid pilocarpine used in medicine chiefly to produce sweating, to promote the flow of saliva, to contract the pupil of the eye, and for glaucoma. [< Pg < Tupi-Guarani *yaborandí*]

ja·bot (zha bō′ *or, esp. Brit.,* zhab′ō), *n.* a falling ruffle, cascade, or other arrangement of lace, embroidery, or the like, worn at the neck or the front of the waist by women and formerly by men. [< F: lit., bird's crop; akin to OF *gave* throat, bird's crop < ?]

Ja·brud (jab′ro͝od), *n. Archaeol.* a Paleolithic site in SW Syria, in the Anti-Lebanon mountain range.

ja·bu·ran (jä′bo͞o rän′), *n., pl.* **-ran.** an evergreen plant, *Ophiopogon Jaburan,* of Japan, having cordlike roots, white flowers, and violet-blue, berrylike fruit. [< Jap]

Jac (jak), *n.* a boy's given name, form of **Jack.**

J.A.C., Junior Association of Commerce.

ja·cal (hə käl′), *n.* a form of construction used in the SW U.S. and Mexico, consisting of a number of thin stakes driven into the ground close together and plastered with mud. [< MexSp < Nahuatl *xacalli,* short for *xamitl calli* adobe house]

Jac·a·lyn (jak′ə lin), *n.* a girl's given name. Also, **Jac′a·lin, Jac′a·linne, Jackelyn, Jacqueline, Jacquelyn, Jacquelynne.**

jac·a·mar (jak′ə mär′), *n.* any tropical American bird of the family *Galbulidae,* having a long bill and usually metallic green plumage above. [< F < Tupi *jacamáciri*]

ja·ça·na (zhä′sə nä′), *n.* any of several tropical, ploverlike, aquatic birds of the family *Jacanidae,* most of them having extremely long toes and claws for walking on floating water plants. Also called **lily-trotter.** [< Pg *jaçanã* < Tupi-Guarani *jasanã*]

jac·a·ran·da (jak′ə ran′də), *n.* **1.** any tropical American, bignoniaceous tree of the genus *Jacaranda.* **2.** the fragrant, ornamental wood of any of these trees. **3.** any of various related or similar trees. **4.** their wood. [< Pg *jacarandá* < Tupi-Guarani *yacarandá*]

Ja·car·ta (jə kär′tə), *n.* Djakarta.

jacht (yäKHt), *n.* any of various small, ornate sailing vessels of the 17th century, used as pleasure boats, dispatch boats, etc. [earlier form of YACHT]

ja·cinth (jā′sinth, jas′inth), *n.* hyacinth (def. 4). [< LL *jacinth(us),* L *hyacinthus* HYACINTH; r. ME *jacin(c)t* < OF *jacin(c)te* < LL *jacin(c)t(us)*]

Ja·cinth (jā′sinth, jas′inth), *n.* a girl's given name, form of **Hyacinth.**

Ja·cin′to Cit′y (jə sin′tō), a town in S Texas. 9547 (1960).

jack¹ (jak), *n.* **1.** any of various portable devices for lifting heavy objects short heights, using various mechanical, pneumatic, or hydraulic methods. **2.** Also called **knave.** *Cards.* a playing card bearing the picture of a servant or soldier. **3.** a device for turning a spit. **4.** Also called **clock jack, jacquemart.** *Horol.* a mechanical figure which strikes a clock bell. **5.** Also called **jackstone.** *Games.* **a.** one of a set of small metal objects having six points, used in the game of jacks. **b.** one of any other set of objects, as pebbles, stones, etc., used in the game of jacks. **c. jacks,** (*construed as sing.*) a children's game in which small metal objects, or stones, pebbles, or the like, are tossed, caught, and moved on the ground in a number of prescribed ways, usually while bouncing a rubber ball. **6.** (*cap.*) *Informal.* fellow; buddy; man (usually used in addressing a stranger): *Hey, Jack, which way to Jersey?* **7.** *Lawn Bowling.* a small, usually white bowl or ball used as a mark for the bowlers to aim at. **8.** a small flag flown at the jack staff of a vessel, consisting of a small national ensign or merchant flag, of the union of a national ensign, or of some distinctive design usually symbolizing the nationality of the vessel. Cf. **union jack** (defs. 1, 2). **9.** a jackass. **10.** See **jack rabbit.** **11.** *Elect.* a connecting device in an electrical circuit designed for the insertion of a plug. **12.** (*cap.*) sailor. **13.** *Naut.* **a.** Also called **jack crosstree.** either of a pair of iron or steel crosstrees at the head of a topgallant mast, used to hold royal shrouds away from the mast. **b.** a two-masted, fore-and-aft-rigged fishing schooner used off Newfoundland. **c.** See **mast funnel.** **14.** *Slang.* money: *He won a lot of jack at the races.* **15.** a small wooden rod in the mechanism of a harpsichord, spinet, or virginal that rises when the key is depressed and causes the attached plectrum to strike the string. **16.** any of several carangid fishes, esp. of the genus *Caranx,* as *C. hippos* (**crevalle jack**), of the western Atlantic Ocean. **17.** a lumberjack. **18.** *U.S.* applejack. **19.** *Falconry.* the male of a kestrel, hobby, or esp. of a merlin. **20.** *Theat.* See **brace jack.** **21.** *U.S.* jacklight. **22. every man jack,** everyone without exception: *They presented a formidable opposition, every man jack of them.* **—***v.t.* **23.** to lift or move (something) with or as with a jack (usually fol. by *up*): *to jack a car up.* **24.** *Informal.* to increase, accelerate, or raise (prices, wages, speed, etc.) (usually fol. by *up*). **25.** *U.S.* to seek (game or fish) with a jacklight. **—***v.i.* **26.** *U.S.* to fish or hunt with the aid of a jacklight. **—***adj.* **27.** *Carpentry.* having a height or length less than that of most of the others in a structure; cripple: *jack rafter; jack truss.* [ME *jakke, Jakke,* var. of *Jakken,* dissimilated var. of *Jankin,* equiv. to *Jan* JOHN + *-kin* -KIN]

jack² (jak), *n.* **1.** a Polynesian, moraceous tree, *Artocarpus heterophyllus,* bearing a fruit resembling bread fruit. **2.** the fruit itself, which may weigh up to 70 pounds. [< Pg *jac(a)* < Malayalam *chakka*]

jack³ (jak), *n.* **1.** a defensive coat, usually of leather, worn by foot soldiers and others. **2.** *Archaic.* a container for liquor, originally of waxed leather coated with tar. [ME *jakke* < MF *jaque(s),* perh. < Sp *jacō* JACKET (< ?), but perh. special use of MF *jacque(s)* peasant << LL *Jacōbus* JACOB]

Jack (jak), *n.* a boy's given name, form of **Jacob** or **John.**

jack-, a combining form of **jack**¹: *jackstay.*

jack-a-dan·dy (jak′ə dan′dē), *n., pl.* **-dies.** dandy (def. 1). [JACK- + *-a-* (< ?) + DANDY] **—jack′-a-dan′dy·ism,** *n.*

jack·al (jak′əl, -ôl), *n.* **1.** any of several wild dogs of the genus *Canis,* esp. *Canis aureus,* of Asia and Africa, which hunt in packs at night and which formerly were believed to hunt prey for the lion. **2.** one who performs menial or degrading tasks for another. **3.** one who performs dishonest or base deeds for his own or another's gain. [< Turk *çakāl* < Pers *shag(h)āl*; c. Skt *śrgāla*]

Jackal, *Canis aureus* (Total length 3 ft.; tail 1 ft.)

jack·a·napes (jak′ə nāps′), *n.* **1.** an impertinent, presumptuous young man; whippersnapper. **2.** an impudent, mischievous child. **3.** *Archaic.* an ape or monkey. [late ME *Jakken-apes,* lit., jack (i.e., man) of the ape, nickname of William de la Pole (1396–1450), Duke of Suffolk, whose badge was an ape's clog and chain]

jack′ arch′, **1.** See **flat arch.** **2.** a crudely built arch, as a French arch.

jack·a·roo (jak′ə ro͞o′), *n., pl.* **-roos,** *v.i.,* **-rooed, -roo·ing.** *Australian.* jackeroo.

jack·ass (jak′as′), *n.* **1.** a male donkey. **2.** a fool, dolt, or blockhead; ass. **3.** Also called **hawse bag.** *Naut.* a stuffed bag for stopping a hawsehole. [JACK- + ASS¹] **—jack′ass′er·y, jack′ass′ism, jack′ass′ness,** *n.*

jack′ass bark′, *Naut.* **1.** a barkentine square-rigged on the mainmast above a gaff mainsail. **2.** a sailing vessel having four or more masts, the foremast and mainmast being wholly square-rigged, the others being fore-and-aft-rigged. **3.** any sailing vessel of three or more masts carrying an otherwise nameless rig.

jack′ass brig′, *Naut.* a two-masted sailing vessel square-rigged on the foremast with a fore-and-aft mainsail: brigantine.

jack′ass gun′ter, *Naut.* a gunter having a wire rope with a traveler in place of the usual upper iron. Also called **bastard gunter.**

jack′ass rig′, *Naut.* a rig of sails not conforming to a recognized type.

jack′ bean′, **1.** a bushy, leguminous plant, *Canavalia ensiformis,* of tropical regions, grown esp. for forage. **2.** the white seeds of this plant.

jack′ block′, *Naut.* a block used in raising or lowering a topgallant yard.

jack·boot (jak′bo͞ot′), *n.* a large leather boot reaching up over the knee. [JACK- + BOOT¹] **—jack′boot′ed,** *adj.*

jack′ chain′, a chain having open links in the form of a figure 8, with one loop at right angles to the other.

jack′ cheese′, Monterey (def. 2).

jack′ cross′tree, *Naut.* jack¹ (def. 13a).

jack·daw (jak′dô′), *n.* **1.** a glossy, black, European bird, *Corvus monedula,* of the crow family, that nests in towers, ruins, etc. **2.** See **boat-tailed grackle.** [JACK- + DAW]

Jack·e·lyn (jak′ə lin), *n.* a girl's given name. Also, **Jacalin, Jacalinne, Jacalyn, Jacqueline, Jacquelyn, Jacquelynne.**

jack·e·roo (jak′ə ro͞o′), *n., pl.* **-roos,** *v.,* **-rooed, -roo·ing.** *Australian.* —*n.* **1.** an inexperienced young man working as a novice on a sheep station. —*v.i.* **2.** to work as a novice on a sheep station. **3.** to lead the wandering, carefree life of a young man without responsibilities. Also, **jackaroo.** [JACK- + (KANG)AROO]

jack·et (jak′it), *n.* **1.** a short coat, in any of various forms, usually opening down the front. **2.** something designed to be placed around the upper part of the body for a specific purpose other than clothing: *a life jacket.* **3.** a protective outer covering. **4.** the skin of a potato, esp. when it has been cooked. **5.** See **book jacket. 6.** the cover of a paper-bound book, usually bearing a colorful illustration. **7.** a paper or cardboard envelope for protecting a phonograph record. **8.** a metal casing, as the steel covering of a cannon, the steel cover around the core of a bullet, or the water jacket on certain types of machine guns. **9.** a folded paper or open envelope containing an official document. —*v.t.* **10.** to put a jacket on (someone or something). [late ME *jaket* < MF *ja(c)quet,* equiv. to *jaque* JACK[3] + *-et* -ET] —**jack′et·ed,** *adj.* —**jack′et·less,** *adj.* —**jack′et·like′,** *adj.*

jack·ey (jak′ē), *n. Brit. Slang.* Jacky (def. 2).

jack·fish (jak′fish′), *n., pl., (esp. collectively)* **-fish,** *(esp. referring to two or more kinds or species)* **-fish·es.** *U.S. Dial.* **1.** any of several pikes, esp. the northern pike. **2.** the sauger. [JACK- + FISH]

Jack′ Frost′, frost or freezing cold personified.

jack·fruit (jak′fro͞ot′), *n.* a large, tropical, milky-juiced tree, *Artocarpus integrifolia,* having stiff, glossy, green leaves, cultivated for its very large, edible fruit and seeds. Also called **jak.** [JACK[2] + FRUIT]

jack·ham·mer (jak′ham′ər), *n.* a portable rock drill operated by compressed air. [JACK- + HAMMER]

Jack·ie (jak′ē), *n.* **1.** a girl's given name, form of **Jacqueline. 2.** a boy's given name, form of **Jack.** Also, **Jacky.**

jack-in-a-box (jak′in ə boks′), *n., pl.* **-box·es. 1.** a tropical tree, *Hernandia sonora,* bearing a nut enclosed in an inflated involucre. **2.** jack-in-the-box.

jack′ing en′gine, an engine for moving an idle reciprocating engine or turbine to permit inspection and repairs. Also called **turning engine.**

jack-in-the-box (jak′in *th*ə boks′), *n., pl.* **-box·es.** a toy consisting of a box from which, upon release of its lid, an enclosed figure springs up. Also, **jack-in-a-box.**

jack-in-the-pul·pit (jak′in *th*ə po͝ol′pit, -pul′-), *n., pl.* **-pul·pits.** an araceous herb, *Arisaema atrorubens (A. triphyllum),* of North America, having an upright spadix arched over by a spathe.

Jack-in-the-pulpit

Jack′ Ketch′ (kech), *Brit. Slang.* a public executioner or hangman. [after *John Ketch* (1663?–86), English executioner noted for brutality]

jack·knife (jak′nīf′), *n., pl.* **-knives. 1.** a large pocketknife. **2.** *Fancy Diving.* a dive in which the diver bends in midair to touch his toes and straightens out immediately before entering the water. [JACK- + KNIFE]

jack′knife clam′. See **razor clam.**

jack·knife-fish (jak′nīf′fish′), *n., pl.* **-fish·es,** *(esp. collectively)* **-fish.** *Ichthyol.* a black and white, American drum, *Equetus lanceolatus,* found in tropical areas of the Atlantic Ocean, having an elongated dorsal fin that is held erect.

jack′ lad′der, 1. *Naut.* See **Jacob's ladder** (def. 2a). **2.** *Lumbering.* See **bull chain.**

jack·leg (jak′leg′), *adj.* **1.** unskilled; untrained for one's work. **2.** unscrupulous or without the accepted standards of one's profession. **3.** makeshift. [alter. of BLACKLEG; *jack* r. *black,* with which it rhymes]

jack·light (jak′līt′), *n.* a portable cresset, oil-burning lantern, or electric light used in hunting or fishing at night. [JACK- + LIGHT[1]]

jack·light·er (jak′lī′tər), *n. U.S.* **1.** a person who fishes or hunts at night with the aid of a jacklight. **2.** a person who illegally hunts deer at night using a jacklight. [JACKLIGHT + -ER[1]]

jack′ mack′erel, a mackerellike food fish, *Trachurus symmetricus,* found along the Pacific coast of the U.S.

Jack′ Mor′mon, 1. a non-Mormon living amicably with Mormons. **2.** a Mormon not active in the church or strict in his adherence to Mormon principles. Also, **Jack′ Mor′mon.**

jack′ oak′, the blackjack, *Quercus marilandica.*

jack-of-all-trades (jak′əv ôl′trādz′), *n., pl.* **jacks-of-all-trades.** a man who is adept at many different trades or different kinds of work requiring manual skills.

jack-o'-lan·tern (jak′ə lan′tərn), *n.* **1.** a hollowed pumpkin with openings cut to represent human eyes, nose, and mouth and in which a candle or other light may be placed, traditionally made for display at Halloween. **2.** a commercially made lantern resembling this. **3.** any phenomenon of light, as a corposant or an ignis fatuus.

jack·pile (jak′pīl′), *n. Building Trades.* a pile driven by a jack. [JACK- + PILE[2]]

jack·pil·ing (jak′pī′ling), *n.* a number of jackpiles. [JACKPILE + -ING[1]]

jack′ pine′, a pine, *Pinus Banksiana,* found on tracts of poor, rocky almost barren land in Canada and the northern U.S. Also called **gray pine.**

jack′ plane′, *Carpentry.* a plane for rough surfacing. See illus. under **plane**[2].

jack′ post′, a post for supporting a floor beam, having two telescoping sections, adjustable to any height.

jack·pot (jak′pot′), *n.* **1.** *Poker.* a pot that accumulates until a player opens the betting with a pair of predetermined denomination, usually jacks or better. **2.** the chief prize or the cumulative stakes in any game or contest, as in bingo, in a quiz contest, on a slot machine, etc. **3.** *Informal.* an outstanding reward or success. **4. hit the jackpot,** *Slang.* to achieve a sensational success; have sudden luck: *The firm has hit the jackpot with its new line of products.* Also, **jack′ pot′.** [?]

jack′ rab′bit, any of various large hares of western North America, having very long hind legs and long ears. [JACK(ASS) + RABBIT; so named from the size of its ears]

Whitetail jack rabbit, *Lepus townsendii* (Length 22 in.; ears 5 in.)

jack′ raft′er, a rafter having less than the full length of the roof slope, as one meeting a hip or a valley.

jack′ rod′, *Naut.* a horizontal metal rod or tube to which an awning or other cloth may be seized to support it. Also called **jackstay.**

jack′ rope′, *Naut.* **1.** a rope for bending the foot of a sail to a boom. **2.** a line that is rove through grommets on the reef band of a square sail, and to which lanyards from the jackstay on the yard are toggled to reef the sail.

Jack′ Rose′, a cocktail made with apple brandy, lime or lemon juice, and grenadine. [short for *jacqueminot (rose);* named after J. M. *Jacqueminot* (1787–1865), French nobleman and general]

Jacks·bor·o (jaks′bûr ō, -bur ō), *n.* a town in N Texas. 3816 (1960).

jack·screw (jak′skro͞o′), *n.* a jack consisting of a screw steadied by a threaded support and carrying a plate or other part bearing the load. [JACK- + SCREW]

jack·shaft (jak′shaft′, -shäft′), *n. Mach.* **1.** Also called **countershaft.** a short shaft, connected by belting, gears, etc., that transmits motion from a motor or engine to a machine or machines being driven. **2.** a shaft on which an idle wheel or fairlead turns. [JACK- + SHAFT]

jack·smelt (jak′smelt′), *n., pl.* **-smelts,** *(esp. collectively)* **-smelt.** a large silversides, *Atherinopsis californiensis,* found along the coast of California, that grows to a length of 22 inches. [JACK- + SMELT[2]]

jack·snipe (jak′snīp′), *n., pl. (esp. collectively)* **-snipe,** *(esp. referring to two or more kinds or species)* **-snipes. 1.** Also called **half snipe.** a small, short-billed snipe, *Limnocryptes minimus,* of Europe and Asia. **2.** any of several related snipes. **3.** See **pectoral sandpiper.** [JACK- + SNIPE]

Jack·son (jak′sən), *n.* **1. Andrew** (*"Old Hickory"*), 1767–1845, U.S. general: 7th president of the U.S. 1829–37. **2. Lady Barbara** (*Barbara Ward*), born 1914, English economist and author. **3. Helen Hunt** (*Helen Maria Fiske*), 1830–85, U.S. novelist and poet. **4. Robert Hough·wout** (hou′ət), 1892–1954, U.S. jurist: associate justice of the U.S. Supreme Court 1941–54. **5. Thomas Jonathan** (*"Stonewall Jackson"*), 1824–63, Confederate general in the U.S. Civil War. **6.** a city in and the capital of Mississippi, in the central part. 144,422 (1960). **7.** a city in S Michigan. 50,720 (1960). **8.** a city in W Tennessee. 33,849 (1960). **9.** a town in S Ohio. 6980 (1960). **10.** a town in SW Alabama. 4959 (1960). **11.** a town in SE Missouri. 4875 (1960). **12.** a town in SW Minnesota. 3370 (1960). **13.** a town in central Georgia. 2545 (1960). **14.** a boy's given name.

Jack′son Day′, January 8, a holiday commemorating Andrew Jackson's victory at the Battle of New Orleans in 1815: a legal holiday in Louisiana.

Jack·so·ni·an (jak sō′nē ən), *adj.* **1.** of or pertaining to Andrew Jackson, his ideas, the period of his presidency, and the political principles and social values associated with him: *Jacksonian democracy.* —*n.* **2.** a follower of Jackson. [JACKSON + -IAN]

Jack·son·ism (jak′sə niz′əm), *n.* the group of political principles or attitudes associated with Andrew Jackson. [JACKSON + -ISM]

Jack·son·ville (jak′sən vil′), *n.* **1.** a seaport in NE Florida, on the St. John's River. 201,030 (1960). **2.** a city in W Illinois. 21,690 (1960). **3.** a city in SE North Carolina. 13,491 (1960). **4.** a town in E Texas. 9590 (1960). **5.** a town in E Alabama. 5678 (1960).

jack-span·iard (jak′span′yərd), *n.* (in the West Indies) any of several reddish or brownish paper wasps of the genus *Polistes* that build flat, open nests.

jack′ staff′, a flagstaff at the bow of a vessel, on which a jack is flown.

jack·stay (jak′stā′), *n. Naut.* **1.** a rod or batten, following a yard, gaff, or boom, to which one edge of a sail is bent. **2.** a rail for guiding the movement of the hanks of a sail. **3.** a transverse stay for stiffening a mast having a gaff sail, coming downward and outward from the head of the mast, passing over a spreader at the level of the gaff, then inclining inward to the mast again near the foot. **4.** See **jack rod.** [JACK- + STAY[3]]

jack·stone (jak′stōn′), *n.* **1.** jack[1] (def. 5a, b). **2. jackstones,** *(construed as sing.)* jack[1] (def. 5c). [earlier *chackstone,* alter. of *checkstone* pebble < ?]

jack·straw (jak′strô′), *n.* **1.** a straw-stuffed figure of a man; scarecrow. **2.** an insignificant person. **3.** one of a group of strips of wood or similar objects, as straws or toothpicks, used in the game of jackstraws. **4. jackstraws,** *(construed as sing.)* a game in which players compete in picking up, one by one, as many jackstraws as possible without disturbing the heap. [after *Jack Straw,* name or nickname of one of the leaders of the rebellion headed by Wat Tyler in 1381 in England]

jack-tar (jak′tär′), *n.* a sailor. Also, **Jack′ Tar′.**

jack′ tow′el, a long towel with the ends sewed together, for hanging on a roller.

jack′ truss′, any of a number of trapezoidal trusses for supporting those areas of a hip roof not beneath the peak or ridge, parallel to the truss or trusses that meet at the peak or ridge.

Jack·y (jak′ē), *n., pl.* **Jack·ies. 1.** *(often l.c.)* a sailor. **2.** *(usually l.c.)* Also, **jackey.** *Brit. Slang.* gin[1]. **3.** Also, **Jackie.** a boy's given name, form of **Jack. 4.** a girl's given name, form of **Jacqueline.**

jack·yard (jak′yärd′), *n. Naut.* a small, inclined spar upholding the head of a quadrangular gaff topsail (**jack′yard top′sail, jack′yard′er,** or **lug topsail**), similar in form to a lugsail. Also called **jenny yard.** [JACK- + YARD[2]]

Jac·mel (*Fr.* zhak mel′), *n.* a seaport in S Haiti. 9397 (est. 1957).

Ja·cob (jā′kəb *for 1, 3; Fr.* zhä kôb′), *n.* **1.** the second son of Isaac, the twin brother of Esau, and father of the 12 patriarchs. Gen. 25:24–34. **2. Fran·çois** (fräN swA′), born 1920, French geneticist: Nobel Prize for medicine 1965. **3.** a boy's given name.

Jacobean chair, c1620

Ja·co·ba (jə kō′bə), *n.* a girl's given name. Also **Jakoba.**

Ja·cob ben Ash·er (jā′kəb ben ash′ər), c1269–c1340, Hebrew commentator on the Bible and codifier of Jewish law.

Jac·o·be·an (jak′ə bē′ən), *adj.* **1.** of or pertaining to James I of England or to his period. **2.** noting or pertaining to the style of architecture and furnishings prevailing in England in the first half of the 17th century, continuing the Elizabethan style with a gradual introduction of Italian models in architecture and increased elaboration of forms and motifs in furnishings. **3.** of or pertaining to the style of literature and drama produced during the early 17th century. —*n.* **4.** a writer, statesman, or other personage of the Jacobean period. [< NL *jacobae(us)* of JACOB (Latinized form of *James*) + -AN]

Jac·o·be·than (jak′ə bē′*th*ən), *adj.* noting or pertaining to the architecture of England at the beginning of the 17th century. [JACO(BEAN) + (ELIZA)BETHAN]

Ja·co·bi (yä kō′bē *for 1;* jə kō′bē *for 2*), *n.* **1. Karl Gus·tav Ja·kob** (kärl go͝os′täf yä′kōp), 1804–1851, German mathematician. **2.** a walled plain in the fourth quadrant of the face of the moon: about 41 miles in diameter.

Ja·co·bi·an (jə kō′bē ən, yə-), *Math.* —*n.* **1.** a function of a set of *n* functions, where *n* is a positive integer, whose value at a point *x* is a determinant, the rows of which are the *n* partial derivatives of each function evaluated at *x.* —*adj.* **2.** of or pertaining to a Jacobian. [named after K. G. J. JAKOBI; see -AN]

Jac·o·bin (jak′ə bin), *n.* **1.** (in the French Revolution) a member of a radical society or club of revolutionaries that promoted the Reign of Terror and other extreme measures, active chiefly from 1789 to 1794: so called from the Dominican convent in Paris, where they originally met. **2.** an extreme radical, esp. in politics. **3.** Dominican. **4.** *(l.c.)* one of a fancy breed of domestic pigeons having neck feathers that hang over the head like a hood. [ME *Jacobin* < OF *(frere) jacobin* < ML *(frater) Jacobīn(us).* See JACOB, -IN[1]] —**Jac′o·bin′ic, Jac′o·bin′i·cal,** *adj.* —**Jac′o·bin′i·cal·ly,** *adv.*

Ja·co·bi·na (jak′ə bē′nə), *n.* a girl's given name. Also, **Ja·co·bine** (jā′kə bēn′).

Jac·o·bin·ise (jak′ə bi nīz′), *v.t.,* **-ised, -is·ing.** *Chiefly Brit.* Jacobinize. —**Jac′o·bin′i·sa′tion,** *n.*

Jac·o·bin·ism (jak′ə bi niz′əm), *n.* **1.** the political principles of the Jacobins. **2.** extreme radicalism, esp. in politics. [JACOBIN + -ISM]

Jac·o·bin·ize (jak′ə bi nīz′), *v.t.,* **-ized, -iz·ing.** to imbue with Jacobinism. [JACOBIN + -IZE] —**Jac′o·bin′i·za′tion,** *n.*

Jac·o·bite (jak′ə bīt′), *n.* **1.** a partisan or adherent of James II of England after his overthrow (1688), or of the Stuarts. **2.** a member of the Syrian Monophysitic church, which was founded in the 6th century A.D. and was governed by the patriarch of Antioch. [*Jacob-* (Latinized form of *James*) + -ITE[1]] —**Jac·o·bit·ic** (jak′ə bit′ik), **Jac′o·bit′i·cal,** *adj.* —**Jac′o·bit′i·cal·ly,** *adv.* —**Jac·o·bite·ly** (jak′ə bīt′lē), *adv.* —**Jac·o·bit·ish** (jak′ə bī′tish), *adj.* —**Jac′o·bit′ish·ly,** *adv.*

Jac′obite glass′, an English drinking glass of the late 17th or early 18th century, engraved with Jacobite mottoes and symbols.

Jac·o·bit·ism (jak′ə bī tiz′əm), *n.* the principles or aims of the Jacobites. [JACOBITE + -ISM]

Ja·cob·sen (yä′kôb sən), *n.* **Jens Pe·ter** (yens pā′tər), 1847–85, Danish novelist.

ja·cobs·ite (jā′kəb zīt′), *n.* a rare magnetic mineral, manganese iron oxide, $MnFe_2O_4$, similar to magnetite. [named after *Jacobs(berg)* Swedish locality; see -ITE[1]]

Ja′cob's lad′der, 1. a ladder, seen by Jacob in a dream, reaching from the earth to heaven. Gen. 28:12. **2.** *Naut.* **a.** Also called **jack ladder, pilot ladder.** a hanging ladder having ropes or chains supporting wooden or metal rungs or steps. **b.** any ladderlike arrangement aloft other than one of rattled shrouds.

Ja·cob's-lad·der (jā′kəbz lad′ər), *n.* **1.** Also called **charity, Greek valerian.** a garden plant, *Polemonium caeruleum,* whose leaves have a ladderlike arrangement. **2.** any of certain related plants.

Ja′cob·son's or′gan (jā′kəb sənz), *Anat., Zool.* either of a pair of blind, tubular sacs in the roof of the mouth, vestigial in man but well-developed in many animals, opening into the mouth and believed to function in olfaction. [named after L. L. *Jacobson* (d. 1843), Danish anatomist]

Ja′cob's staff′, *pl.* **Jacob's staves. 1.** cross-staff. **2.** *Survey.* a pole providing a firm support for a compass or other instrument.

ja·co·bus (jə kō′bəs), *n., pl.* **-bus·es.** a former gold coin of England issued by James I. [Latinized form of *James*]

jac·o·net (jak′ə net′), *n.* **1.** a cotton fabric of light weight, usually finished as cambric, lawn, organdy, voile, etc., and much used in the manufacture of clothing and bandages. **2.** a cotton fabric with one glazed surface, often used as a lining for the spines of books. [< Urdu *jagannāthī,* after *Jagannāthpūrī* in Orissa, India, where cloth was first made]

jac·quard (jak′ärd, jə kärd′; *Fr.* zhA kAR′), *n.* *(often cap.)* fabric produced on a Jacquard loom. [named after J. M. *Jacquard.* See JACQUARD LOOM]

Jac′quard card′, (in a Jacquard loom) one of a series of perforated cards that control the manipulation of the warp threads and determine the intricate pattern woven on the material.

Jac′quard har′ness, (in Jacquard weaving) the unit between the loom proper and the Jacquard head motion, comprising a group of cords that are manipulated in such a way as to raise and lower the warp threads in a pattern determined by the Jacquard cards. Also called **tie-up.**

Jac′quard head′ mo′tion, an apparatus or mechanism, located above a Jacquard loom, containing the cards that control the harness action.

Jac′quard loom′, a pattern loom for weaving elaborate designs. [named after J. M. *Jacquard* (1757–1834), French inventor]

Jac′quard weave′, an intricate weave structure constructed from a variety of basic weaves and producing elaborate patterns in fabric woven on a Jacquard loom.

Jac·que·line (jak′ə lin, -lēn′, jak′wə-; *Fr.* zhäkᵊ lēn′), *n.* a girl's given name. Also, **Jacalin, Jacalinne, Jacalyn, Jackelyn, Jac′que·lyn, Jac′que·lynne.**

jacque·mart (zhäk mär′), *n. Horol.* jack[1] (def. 4). [appar., equiv. to F *Jacque(s)* James + *mart(eau)* hammer]

Jac·que·rie (zhäkᵊ rē′), *n.* **1.** the revolt of the peasants of northern France against the nobles in 1358. **2.** (*l.c.*) any peasant revolt. [< F, MF: peasantry, equiv. to *jaque(s)* peasant (see JACK[3]) + *-rie* -RY]

Jacques (zhäk), *n.* a boy's given name, French form of **Jacob** or **James.**

Jacques Bon·homme (zhäk bô nôm′), the contemptuous title given by the nobles to the peasants in the revolt of the Jacquerie and adopted by the peasants in subsequent revolts. [< F: lit., James goodfellow; see JACK[3]]

Jac·quette (jə ket′; *Fr.* zhä ket′), *n.* a girl's given name, form of **Jacqueline.** Also, **Jac·quet·ta** (jə ket′ə).

jac·ta·tion (jak tā′shən), *n.* **1.** boasting; bragging. **2.** *Pathol.* a restless tossing of the body. [< L *jactātiōn-* (s. of *jactātiō*) bragging, equiv. to *jactāt(us)* (ptp. of *jactāre,* freq. of *jacere* to throw) + *-iōn-* -ION]

jac·te·leg (jak′tə leg′), *n. Brit. Dial.* jockteleg.

jac·ti·ta·tion (jak′ti tā′shən), *n.* **1.** *Law.* a false boast or claim that causes injury to another. **2.** *Pathol.* jactation (def. 2). [< LL *jactitātiōn-* (s. of *jactitātiō*) tossing, equiv. to *jactitāt(us)* (ptp. of *jactitāre,* freq. of *jactāre* to throw about; see JACTATION) + *-iōn-* -ION]

jac·u·late (jak′yə lāt′), *v.t.,* **-lat·ed, -lat·ing.** to throw or hurl (a dart, javelin, etc.). [< L *jaculāt(us)* (ptp. of *jaculārī* to throw the javelin), equiv. to *jacul(um)* javelin (n. use of neut. of *jaculus* (adj.) hurling, equiv. to *jac-* hurl + *-ulus* adj. suffix) + *-ātus* -ATE[1]] —**jac′u·la′tion,** *n.* —**jac′u·la′tor,** *n.* —**jac·u·la·to·ry** (jak′yə lə tôr′ē, -tōr′ē), *adj.*

jac·u·lif·er·ous (jak′yə lif′ər əs), *adj. Bot., Zool.* having dartlike spines. [< NL *jaculifer* dart-bearing (*jaculi-,* comb. form of L *jaculum* dart, + *-fer* bearing) + -OUS; see JACULATE]

jad (jäd), *n. Brit. Dial.* (in stone quarries) a long, deep cutting from which blocks of stone will be detached. [?]

jad·der (jad′ər), *n. Brit. Dial.* one who works in a stone quarry; stone cutter. [JAD + -ER[1]]

jade[1] (jād), *n.* **1.** either of two minerals, jadeite or nephrite, sometimes green, highly esteemed as an ornamental stone for carvings, jewelry, etc. **2.** an object, as a carving, made from this material. **3.** Also called **jade′ green′.** green, varying from bluish green to yellowish green. [< F < It *giada* < obs. Sp (*piedra de*) *ijada* (stone of) flank < L *īli-* flank (see ILIUM) + *-ata* -ATE[1]; so called because supposed to cure nephritic colic] —**jade′like′,** *adj.*

jade[2] (jād), *n., v.,* **jad·ed, jad·ing.** —*n.* **1.** a worn-out, broken-down, worthless, or vicious horse. **2.** a worthless, vicious, or disreputable woman. —*v.t., v.i.* **3.** to make or become dull, worn-out, or weary, as from overwork or overuse. [?] —**jad′ish,** *adj.* —**jad′ish·ly,** *adv.* —**jad′ish·ness,** *n.*
—**Syn. 3.** exhaust, enervate; sate, satiate.

jad·ed (jā′did), *adj.* **1.** worn out or wearied, as by overwork or overuse. **2.** dulled or satiated by overindulgence: *a jaded appetite.* **3.** dissipated: *a jaded woman.* [JADE[2] + -ED[2]] —**jad′ed·ly,** *adv.* —**jad′ed·ness,** *n.*

jade-green (jād′grēn′), *adj.* of the color of jade.

jade·ite (jā′dīt), *n.* a mineral, essentially sodium aluminum silicate, $NaAlSi_2O_6$, occurring in tough masses, whitish to dark green: a form of jade. [JADE[1] + -ITE[1]]

Ja·dot·ville (*Fr.* zhä dō vēl′), *n.* a city in the S Republic of the Congo. 74,478 (est. 1958).

jae·ger (yā′gər; *for 1 also* jā′gər), *n.* **1.** any of several rapacious sea birds of the family *Stercorariidae* that pursue weaker birds in order to make them drop their prey. **2.** a hunter. **3.** a member of any of certain groups of sharpshooters in the German or Austrian army. Also, **jager, jäger, yager** (for defs. 2, 3). [< G *Jäger* hunter, equiv. to *jag(en)* (to) hunt + *-er* -ER[1]]

Ja·el (jā′əl), *n.* the woman who killed Sisera by hammering a tent pin through his head as he slept. Judges 4:17–22. Also, *Douay Bible,* **Jahel.**

Ja·én (hä en′), *n.* a city in S Spain, NNW of Granada. 65,678 (est. 1963).

Jaf·fa (jaf′ə; *locally* yä′fä), *n.* a seaport in W Israel, part of Tel-Aviv. Ancient, **Joppa.**

Jaff·na (jaf′nə), *n.* a seaport in N Ceylon. 94,248 (1963).

jag[1] (jag), *n., v.,* **jag·ged, jag·ging.** —*n.* **1.** a sharp projection on an edge or surface. —*v.t.* **2.** to cut or slash, esp. in points or pendants along the edge; form notches, teeth, or ragged points in. [late ME *jagge* (n.), *jaggen* (v.) < ?] —**jag′less,** *adj.*

jag[2] (jag), *n.* **1.** *Dial.* a load, as of hay or wood. **2.** a state of intoxication from liquor. **3.** *Informal.* a spree; binge: *He went on an eating jag and gained twenty pounds in two weeks. Her last crying jag was the worst so far.* [perh. orig. load of broom or furze (OE *ceacga* broom, furze)]

J.A.G., Judge Advocate General.

ja·ga·mo·han (jug′ə mō hun′), *n.* a porch of a Brahman temple. [< Hindi]

Jag·an·nath (jug′ə nät′, -nôt′), *n.* **1.** *Hinduism.* a name of Krishna or Vishnu. **2.** Juggernaut (def. 3). Also, **Jag·an·na·tha** (jug′ə nät′hə), **Jagganath.** [var. of JUGGERNAUT]

Jag·a·tai (jag′ə tī′), *n.* Chagatai. Also, **Jag′ha·tai′.** —**Jag·a·ta·ic** (jag′ə tā′ik), *adj.*

Ja·gel·lo (yä gel′ō), *n., pl.* **-los.** a member of a dynasty ruling in Bohemia, Hungary, Lithuania, and Poland in the 14th–16th centuries. Also, **Jagiello.** —**Ja·gel·lon** (yä gel′lon, yä′gə lōn′), **Ja′gel·lo′ni·an,** *adj.*

ja·ger (yä′gər), *n.* jaeger (defs. 2, 3). Also, **jä′ger.**

Jag·ga·nath (jug′ə nät′, -nôt′), *n.* Jagannath.

jag·ged (jag′id), *adj.* having ragged notches, points, or teeth; zigzag: *the jagged edge of a saw; a jagged wound.* [JAG[1] + -ED[2]] —**jag′ged·ly,** *adv.* —**jag′ged·ness,** *n.*

jag·ger·y (jag′ə rē), *n.* a coarse, dark sugar, esp. that made from the sap of East Indian palm trees. Also, **jag′gar·y, jag′gher·y.** [< Hindi *jāgrī*]

jag·gy (jag′ē), *adj.,* **-gi·er, -gi·est.** jagged; notched. [JAG[1] + -Y[1]]

Ja·giel·lo (yä gyel′ō), *n., pl.* **-los.** Jagello. —**Ja·giel·lon** (yä′gyə lōn′, yä′gyə lōn′), **Ja′giel·lo′ni·an,** *adj.*

jag·uar (jag′wär), *n.* a large, ferocious, spotted feline, *Panthera onca,* of tropical America. [< Pg < Tupi *jaguara*]

Jaguar
(Total length 7 ft.; tail 2 ft.)

ja·gua·run·di (jä′gwə run′dē), *n., pl.* **-dis.** a short-legged, long-bodied, South American cat, *Felis eyra.* [< Pg < Tupi]

Ja·han·gir (yə hän′gēr), *n.* 1569–1627, 4th Mogul emperor in India 1605–27 (son of Akbar). Also, **Jehangir.**

Ja·hel (jā′əl), *n. Douay Bible.* Jael.

Jahr·zeit (yär′tsīt, yôr′-), *n. Judaism.* Yahrzeit.

Jah·veh (yä′ve), *n.* Yahweh. Also, **Jah′ve, Jah·weh, Jah·we** (yä′we).

Jah·vism (yä′viz əm), *n.* Yahwism. Also, **Jah·wism** (yä′wiz əm).

Jah·vist (yä′vist), *n.* Yahwist. Also, **Jah·wist** (yä′wist). —**Jah·vis′tic, Jah·wis′tic,** *adj.*

jai a·lai (hī′ lī′, hī′ ə lī′, hī′ ə lī′), a game resembling handball, played on a three-walled court between two, four, or six players who are equipped with a long, curved wicker basket or cesta strapped to the wrist for catching and throwing the small, hard ball against the front wall. Cf. **cancha, fronton.** [< Sp < Basque, equiv. to *jai* game + *alai* merry]

jail (jāl), *n.* **1.** a prison, esp. one for the detention of persons awaiting trial or convicted of minor offenses. —*v.t.* **2.** to take into or hold in lawful custody; imprison. Also, *Brit.,* **gaol.** [ME *jaile* < OF *jaiole* cage < LL *caveola,* equiv. to L *cave(a)* enclosure (see CAVE[1]) + *-ola* dim. suffix] —**jail′less,** *adj.* —**jail′like′,** *adj.*

jail·bait (jāl′bāt′), *n. Slang.* **1.** a girl with whom sexual intercourse is punishable as statutory rape because of her youth. **2.** a sexually attractive young girl. **3.** any temptation to commit a crime punishable by imprisonment. [JAIL + BAIT]

jail·bird (jāl′bûrd′), *n.* one who is or has been confined in jail. [JAIL + BIRD]

jail·break (jāl′brāk′), *n.* an escape from prison by forcible means. [JAIL + BREAK]

jail′ deliv′ery, **1.** a liberation of persons from prison, esp. by force. **2.** the act of clearing a jail of prisoners by bringing them to trial, as at the assizes in England.

jail·er (jā′lər), *n.* a person who is in charge of a jail, esp. a small jail. Also, **jail′or.** [ME *jayler, jaioler* < OF *jaiolier.* See JAIL, -ER[2]]

jail·house (jāl′hous′), *n., pl.* **-hous·es** (-hou′ziz). a building used as a jail. [JAIL + HOUSE]

Jain (jīn), *n.* **1.** an adherent of Jainism. —*adj.* **2.** of or pertaining to the Jains or Jainism. Also, **Jai·na** (jī′nə), **Jain′ist.** [< Hindi: saint, lit., one who overcomes < Skt *jaina*]

Jain·ism (jī′niz əm), *n.* a dualistic, ascetic religion founded in the 6th century B.C. by a Hindu reformer as a revolt against the caste system and the vague world spirit of Hinduism. [JAIN + -ISM]

Jai·pur (jī′pŏŏr), *n.* **1.** a former state in N India, now part of Rajasthan. **2.** a city in and the capital of Rajasthan, in N India: known as the "pink city" because of its buildings of that color. 403,400 (1961).

jak (jak), *n.* jackfruit.

Ja·kar·ta (jə kär′tə), *n.* Djakarta.

jake[1] (jāk), *adj. Slang.* satisfactory; O.K.: *Everything's jake with me.* [?]

jake[2] (jāk), *n.* a two-masted, fore-and-aft-rigged schooner of the Canadian Maritime Provinces. [perh. special use of JAKE]

Jake (jāk), *n.* a boy's given name, form of **Jacob.**

jakes (jāks), *n.* (*usually construed as pl.*) *Chiefly Dial.* an outdoor privy; outhouse. [< F *Jacques,* proper name]

Ja·ko·ba (jə kō′bə), *n.* a girl's given name. Also, **Jacoba.**

Ja·kob·son (yä′kəb sən), *n.* **Ro·man** (rō′män, -mən), born 1896, U.S. linguist and scholar, born in Russia.

Jal (jal), *n.* a town in SE New Mexico. 3051 (1960).

Ja·lal ud-din Ru·mi (jä läl′ ŏŏd dēn′ rōō′mē, ŏŏd-, ja-), 1207–73, Persian poet and mystic.

jal·ap (jal′əp), *n.* **1.** the dried tuberous root of any of several convolvulaceous plants, esp. *Ipomoea Purga* (*Exogonium Jalapa*), or the light yellowish powder derived from it, used in medicine chiefly as a purgative. **2.** any of these plants. [< MF < Sp (*purga de*) *Jalapa* purgative from JALAPA] —**ja·lap·ic** (jə lap′ik), *adj.*

Ja·la·pa (hä lä′pä), *n.* a city in and the capital of Vera Cruz, in E Mexico. 66,509 (1960).

jal·a·pin (jal′ə pin), *n.* a resin which is one of the purgative principles of jalap. [< NL *jalāp(a)* JALAP + -IN[2]]

ja·lee (jä′lē), *n.* (in Indian architecture) decorated and pierced slabs of marble used as a screen. [< Hindi *jālī* network]

Ja·lis·co (hä lēs′kō), *n.* a state in W Mexico, 2,443,261 (1960); 31,152 sq. mi. *Cap.:* Guadalajara.

ja·lop·y (jə lop′ē), *n., pl.* **-lop·ies.** *Informal.* an old, decrepit, or unpretentious automobile. [?]

ja·lor (jä′lər), *n.* any of a wide variety of East Indian rowing and sailing vessels. Also, **ja′lur.** [?]

jal·ou·sie (jal′ə sē′ *or, esp. Brit.,* zhal′ŏŏ zē′), *n.* **1.** a type of blind or shutter made with horizontal slats fixed at an angle to admit light and air but exclude rain and the rays of the sun. **2.** a window made of glass slats of a similar nature. [< F; OF *gelosie* latticework, JEALOUSY] —**jal′ou·sied′,** *adj.*

jam[1] (jam), *v.,* **jammed, jam·ming,** *n.* —*v.t.* **1.** to press, squeeze, or wedge tightly between bodies or surfaces, so that motion or extrication is made difficult or impossible: *The ship was jammed between two rocks.* **2.** to bruise or crush by squeezing: *He jammed his hand in the door.* **3.** to press, push, or thrust violently, as into a confined space or against some object: *She jammed her foot on the brake.* **4.** to fill or block up by crowding; pack or obstruct: *Crowds jam the doors.* **5.** to put or place in position with a violent gesture (often fol. by *on*): *He jammed his hat on and stalked out of the room.* **6.** to make (something) unworkable by causing parts to become stuck, blocked, caught, displaced, etc.: *He jammed the rifle by forcing the cartridge in backward.* **7.** *Radio.* **a.** to interfere with (radio signals or the like) by sending out others of approximately the same frequency. **b.** (of radio signals or the like) to interfere with (other signals). **8.** *Naut.* to head (a sailing vessel) as nearly as possible into the wind without putting it in stays or putting it wholly aback. —*v.i.* **9.** to become stuck, wedged, fixed, blocked, etc.: *This door jams.* **10.** to press or push violently, as into a confined space or against one another: *They jammed into the elevator.* **11.** (of a machine, part, etc.) to become unworkable, as through the wedging or displacement of a part. **12.** *Jazz.* to participate in a jam session. —*n.* **13.** the act of jamming or the state of being jammed. **14.** a mass of objects, vehicles, etc., jammed together or otherwise unable to move except slowly: *a log jam; a traffic jam.* **15.** *Informal.* a difficult or embarrassing situation; fix: *He got himself into a jam with the tax people.* Also, **jamb** (for defs. 1–10, 13, 14). [appar. imit.; cf. CHAMP[1], DAM[1]]
—**Syn. 1.** crowd; ram, force.

jam[2] (jam), *n.* a preserve of whole fruit, slightly crushed, boiled with sugar. [? special use of JAM[1]] —**jam′like′,** **jam′my,** *adj.*

Jam., Jamaica.

Ja·mai·ca (jə mā′kə), *n.* an island in the West Indies, S of Cuba: formerly a British colony; became independent in 1962 with dominion status in the British Commonwealth of Nations. 1,606,546 (1960); 4413 sq. mi. *Cap.:* Kingston.

Jamai′ca gin′ger, **1.** ginger from Jamaica. **2.** a ginger extract used as a flavoring. **3.** powdered ginger root used for medicinal purposes.

Jamai′ca gold′ fern′, an evergreen fern, *Pityrogramma sulphurea,* of the West Indies, the undersides of the leaves being covered with a pale-yellow, powderlike substance.

Jamai′ca hon′eysuckle. See **yellow granadilla.**

Ja·mai·can (jə mā′kən), *adj.* **1.** of or pertaining to the island of Jamaica or its inhabitants. —*n.* **2.** a native or an inhabitant of Jamaica. [JAMAIC(A) + -AN]

Jamai′ca rum′, a heavy, pungent, slowly fermented rum made in Jamaica.

Jamai′ca shorts′, shorts extending to the middle of the thigh, worn by women for informal dress.

Ja·mal·pur (jə mäl′pŏŏr), *n.* a city in N East Pakistan province, in Pakistan.

Ja·mal ud-Din (jä mäl′ ŏŏd dēn′), (*Jamal ud-Din al-Afghani*) 1838–97, Muslim educator and political leader, born in Persia: founder of modern Pan-Islamism.

jamb[1] (jam), *n.* **1.** *Archit., Building Trades.* **a.** either of the sides of an opening. **b.** either of two stones, timbers, etc., forming the sidepieces for the frame of an opening. **2.** *Armor.* greave. Also, **jambe.** [ME *jambe* < MF: leg, jamb < LL *gamba* leg, var. of *camba* hock, fetlock < Gk *kámpē* joint, something jointed]

jamb[2] (jam), *v.t., v.i., n.* jam[1] (defs. 1–10, 13, 14).

jam·ba·lay·a (jum′bə lī′ə), *n.* a cooked dish of Creole origin, consisting of rice, herbs, vegetables, esp. tomatoes, onions, and peppers, and meat or fish, generally ham or shrimp. [< LaF < Pr *jambalaia*]

jam·bart (*Fr.* zhän bar′), *n., pl.* **-barts** (*Fr.* -bar′). *Armor.* greave. [var. of *jamber,* ME *jaumber* < AF *jaumbere,* OF *jambiere,* equiv. to *jambe* leg (see JAMB[1]) + *-iere* -IER; see -ART]

jam·beau (jam′bō), *n., pl.* **-beaux** (-bōz). **1.** *Armor.* greave. **2.** a spikefish, *Parahollardia lineata,* found in the deep waters of the Atlantic Ocean. [ME < AF, equiv. to *jambe* leg (see JAMB[1]) + *-eau* < L *-ellus* n. suffix]

Jam·bi (jäm′bē), *n.* Djambi.

jam·bi·ya (jam bē′yə), *n.* an Arabian knife having a curved, double-edged blade, usually with a central rib. [< Ar]

jam·bo·ree (jam′bə rē′), *n.* **1.** *Informal.* a carousal; any noisy merrymaking. **2.** a large gathering of members of the Boy Scouts, usually nation-wide or international in scope (distinguished from *camporee*). **3.** a large gathering, as of a political party, the teams of a sporting league, etc., often including a program of speeches, entertainment, or the like. [appar. b. JABBER and SHIVAREE, with *m* from JAM[1] crowd]

jam·bos (jam′bos, -bōs), *n.* See **rose apple.** [< NL, var. of *jambosa* < E *jamb(o)* rose apple (< Hindi *jambu* < Skt) + L (*r*)*osa* ROSE[1]]

jam·boy (jam′boi), *n. Armor.* tonlet. [? var. of JAMBEAU]

jamb·stone (jam′stōn′), *n. Masonry.* a stone, or one of the stones, forming one jamb of an opening. [JAMB[1] + STONE]

James (jāmz), *n.* **1.** Also called **James′ the Great′.** one of the 12 apostles, the son of Zebedee and brother of the apostle John. Matt. 4:21. **2.** the person identified in Gal. 1:19 as the Lord's brother: probably the author of the Epistle of St. James. **3.** Also called **James′ the Less′.** ("*James the son of Alphaeus*") one of the 12 apostles. Matt. 10:3; Mark 3:18; Luke 6:15. **4. Henry,** 1811–82, U.S. philosopher and author (father of Henry and William James). **5. Henry,** 1843–1916, U.S. novelist and critic in England (brother of William James). **6. Jesse (Wood·son)** (wŏŏd′sən), 1847–82, U.S. outlaw and legendary figure. **7. Will,** 1892–1942, U.S. author and illustrator. **8. William,** 1842–1910, U.S. psychologist and philosopher (brother of Henry James). **9.** one of the books of the New Testament. **10.** a boy's given name.

James I, 1566–1625, king of England and Ireland 1603–25; as James VI, king of Scotland 1567–1625 (son of Mary Stuart).

James II, 1633–1701, king of England, Ireland, and Scotland 1685–88 (son of Charles I of England).

James III. See **Stuart, James Francis Edward.**

James VI. See **James I.**

James′ Bay′, the S arm of Hudson Bay, in E Canada between Ontario and Quebec provinces. 300 mi. long; 160 mi. wide.

James·burg (jāmz′bûrg), *n.* a town in E New Jersey. 2853 (1960).

James′ Ed′ward. See **Stuart, James Francis Edward.**

James·i·an (jām′zē ən), *adj.* **1.** of, pertaining to, or characteristic of the novelist Henry James or his writings. **2.** of, pertaining to, or suggestive of William James or his philosophy. —*n.* **3.** a student of the works of Henry James. **4.** a follower or adherent of the philosophy of William James. Also, **James′e·an.** [JAMES + -IAN]

Jame·son (jām′sən), *n.* **Sir Leander Starr** (stär), ("*Doctor Jameson*"), 1853–1917, Scottish physician and statesman: colonial administrator in South Africa.

jame·son·ite (jām′sə nīt′), *n.* a mineral, lead and iron antimony sulfide. [named after Robert *Jameson* (1774–1854), Scottish scientist; see -ITE[1]]

James′ Range′, a mountain range in central Australia.

James′ Riv′er, 1. a river flowing E from the W part of Virginia to Chesapeake Bay. 340 mi. long. **2.** a river flowing S from central North Dakota through South Dakota to the Missouri River. 710 mi. long.

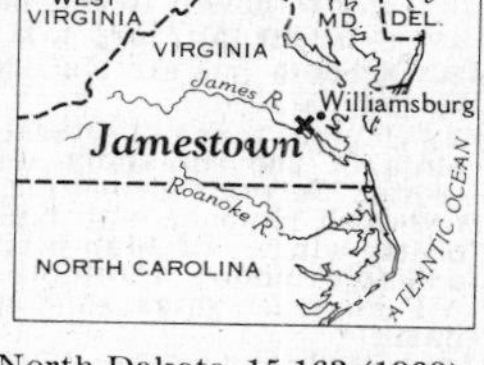

James·town (jāmz′toun′), *n.* **1.** a village in E Virginia: first permanent English settlement in North America 1607; restored 1957. **2.** a city in SW New York. 41,818 (1960). **3.** a city in central North Dakota. 15,163 (1960).

Ja·mie (jā′mē), *n.* a boy's given name, form of **James.**

Ja′mie Green′, *Naut.* **1.** a quadrangular fore-and-aft sail set under a bowsprit and jib boom when the wind is abeam. **2.** a water sail set beneath the after boom of a schooner or the like when the wind is astern or on the quarter. Also, **Jimmy Green.** [special use of arbitrary proper name]

Jam·mu and Kash·mir (jum′o͞o; kash′mēr, kash-mēr′), official name of **Kashmir.**

jam′ nut′. See **lock nut** (def. 2).

jam-pack (jam′pak′), *v.t.* to fill or pack to the greatest possible extent: *We jam-packed the basket with all kinds of fruit.*

jam′ ses′sion, *Jazz.* **1.** a meeting of a group of musicians to play for their own enjoyment. **2.** an impromptu jazz performance or special performance by jazz musicians who do not regularly play together. [? JAM[1], or ? shortening of JAMBOREE]

Jam·shed·pur (jam′shed po͝or′), *n.* a city in SE Bihar, in NE India. 303,500 (1961).

Jam·shid (jam shēd′), *n.* *Persian Myth.* the king of the peris who, given a human form as punishment for his boast of immortality, became a powerful and wonder-working Persian king. Also, **Jam·shyd′.**

Jan (jan), *n.* **1.** a boy's given name, form of **John.** **2.** a girl's given name, form of **Janet.**

Jan., January.

Ja·ná·ček (yä′nä chek′), *n.* **Le·oš** (le′ôsh), 1854–1928, Czech composer.

jane (jān), *n.* *Slang.* a girl or woman. [special use of the proper name]

Jane (jān), *n.* a girl's given name. Also, **Jayn, Jayne, Jaynne.**

Jane′ Doe′ (dō), a fictitious female person named in legal proceedings where the true name of the party in question is not known. [fem. of JOHN DOE]

Jane Eyre (jān′ âr′), a novel (1847) by Charlotte Brontë.

Janes·ville (jānz′vil), *n.* a city in S Wisconsin. 35,164 (1960).

Ja·net (zhA ne′ *for 1;* jan′it *for 2*), *n.* **1. Pierre Ma·rie Fé·lix** (pyer mA rē′ fā lēks′), 1859–1947, French psychologist and neurologist. **2.** Also, **Ja·net·ta** (jə net′ə). a girl's given name, form of **Jane.**

jan·gle (jang′gəl), *v.,* **-gled, -gling,** *n.* —*v.i.* **1.** to produce a harsh, discordant sound, as two small, thin pieces of metal hitting together: *The charms on her bracelet jangle as she moves.* **2.** to speak angrily; wrangle. —*v.t.* **3.** to cause to make a harsh, discordant, usually metallic sound: *He jangled the pots and pans.* **4.** to cause to become irritated or upset: *The whine of the motors jangled his nerves.* —*n.* **5.** a harsh or discordant sound. **6.** an argument, dispute, or quarrel. [ME *jangle(n)* < OF *jangle(r)* < Gmc; cf. MD *jangelen* to haggle, whine] —**jan′gler,** *n.* —**jan′gly,** *adj.*

Jan·ice (jan′is), *n.* a girl's given name, form of **Jane.** Also, **Jan′is, Janys.**

Ja·nic·u·lum (jə nik′yə ləm), *n.* a ridge near the Tiber in Rome, Italy. —**Ja·nic′u·lan,** *adj.*

Ja·nie (jā′nē), *n.* a girl's given name, form of **Jane.** Also, **Ja′ney, Jany, Janye.**

jan·i·form (jan′ə fôrm′), *adj.* Janus-faced. [JAN(US) + -I- + -FORM]

Ja·ni·na (yä′nē nä′), *n.* Serbian name of **Ioannina.**

Jan·is·sar·y (jan′i ser′ē), *n., pl.* **-sar·ies.** (*sometimes l.c.*) **1.** any soldier in the Turkish army. **2.** a member of an elite military unit of the Turkish army organized in the 14th century and abolished in 1826 after it revolted against the Sultan. Also, **Janizary.** [< ML *janizari* < Turk *yeniçeri*, equiv. to *veni* new + *çeri* soldiery, militia] —**Jan·is·sar·ian** (jan′i sâr′ē ən), *adj.*

Jan′issary mu′sic, music characteristic of or imitative of that played by a Turkish military band, typically employing cymbals, triangles, bass drum, and Turkish crescents.

jan·i·tor (jan′i tər), *n.* **1.** a person employed in an apartment house, office building, etc., to clean the public areas, remove garbage, and serve as a general handyman. **2.** a doorkeeper or porter. [< L *jānitor* doorkeeper, equiv. to *jāni-* (comb. form of *jānus* doorway, covered passage) + *-tor* -TOR] —**jan·i·to·ri·al** (jan′i-tôr′ē əl, -tōr′-), *adj.* —**jan′i·tor·ship′,** *n.*

jan·i·tress (jan′i tris), *n.* a woman employed in an apartment house, office building, etc., to clean the public areas, remove garbage, and the like. [JANI(TOR) + -TRESS]

Jan·i·zar·y (jan′i zer′ē), *n., pl.* **-zar·ies.** (*sometimes l.c.*) Janissary. —**Jan·i·zar·i·an** (jan′i zâr′ē ən), *adj.*

Jan May·en (yän′ mī′en), a volcanic island in the Arctic Ocean between Greenland and Norway: a possession of Norway. 144 sq. mi.

jan·nock (jan′ək), *adj.* *Brit., Australian Informal.* honest; fair; straightforward. Also, **jonnick.** [?]

Jan·sen (jan′sən; *Du.* yän′sən), *n.* **Cor·ne·lis Ot·to** (kôR nā′lis ot′ō), (*Cornelius Jansenius*), 1585–1638, Dutch Roman Catholic theologian.

Jan·sen·ism (jan′sə niz′əm), *n.* the doctrinal system of Cornelis Jansen and his followers, denying free will and maintaining that human nature is corrupt and that Christ died for the elect and not for all men. [< F *jansénisme.* See JANSEN, -ISM] —**Jan′sen·ist,** *n.* —**Jan′sen·is′tic, Jan′sen·is′ti·cal,** *adj.*

Jans·sen (jan′sən), *n.* a walled plain in the fourth quadrant of the face of the moon: about 100 miles in diameter.

Jan·u·ar·i·us (jan′yo͞o âr′ē əs), *n.* **Saint,** A.D. 272?–305?, Italian ecclesiastic and martyr: patron saint of Naples. Italian, **San Gennaro.**

Jan·u·ar·y (jan′yo͞o er′ē), *n., pl.* **-ar·ies.** the first month of the year, containing 31 days. [< L *Jānuāri(us)*, equiv. to *Jānu(s)* JANUS + *-ārius* -ARY]

Ja·nus (jā′nəs), *n.* an ancient Roman god of doorways, of beginnings, and of the rising and setting of the sun, usually represented as having one head with two bearded faces back to back, looking in opposite directions. [< L, special use of *jānus* doorway, archway; arcade]

Ja′nus cloth′, a worsted fabric, each side of which has a different color.

Ja·nus-faced (jā′nəs fāst′), *adj.* **1.** having two faces, one looking forward, one looking backward, as the Roman deity Janus. **2.** having two contrasting aspects, as the alternation of mood in a capricious person: *a Janus-faced mingling of entreaties with curses.* **3.** two-faced; deceitful. **4.** aware of or concerned with polarities; seeing different and contrasting aspects: *a Janus-faced view of history.* **5.** having or containing contrasting characteristics: *a Janus-faced policy.*

Ja·ny (jā′nē), *n.* a girl's given name, form of **Jane.** Also, **Janey, Janie, Ja′nye.**

Janys (jan′is), *n.* a girl's given name. Also, **Janice, Janis.**

Jap (jap), *n.* *Often Disparaging.* a Japanese. [clipped form]

Jap., Japanese. Also, **Jap**

ja·pan (jə pan′), *n., adj., v.,* **-panned, -pan·ning.** —*n.* **1.** any of various hard, durable, black varnishes, originally from Japan, for coating wood, metal, or other surfaces. **2.** work varnished and figured in the Japanese manner. **3. Japans,** (in the 19th century) the pseudo-Oriental decorative motifs or patterns used on English porcelain of the 18th and 19th centuries. —*adj.* **4.** of or pertaining to japan. —*v.t.* **5.** to varnish with japan; lacquer. **6.** to coat with any material which gives a hard, black gloss. [special use of JAPAN] —**ja·pan′ner,** *n.*

Ja·pan (jə pan′), *n.* a constitutional monarchy on a chain of islands off the E coast of Asia: main islands, Hokkaido, Honshu, Kyushu, and Shikoku. 120,020,000; 141,529 sq. mi. *Cap.:* Tokyo. Japanese, **Nihon, Nippon.**

Japan., Japanese.

Japan′ ce′dar, a pinaceous tree, *Cryptomeria japonica,* of Japan, characterized by the pyramidal manner of growth of its branches. Also called **Japanese cedar, sugi.**

Japan′ clo′ver, a drought-resistant, perennial bush clover, *Lespedeza striata,* introduced to the southern Atlantic states from Asia, having numerous tiny trifoliate leaves valued for pasturage and hay. Also called **hoop-coop plant.**

Japan′ Cur′rent, a warm ocean current in the Pacific, flowing N along the E coast of Formosa, NE along the E coast of Japan, and continuing in an easterly direction into the open Pacific. Also called **Japan Stream, Kuroshio, Black Stream.**

Jap·a·nese (jap′ə nēz′, -nēs′), *adj., n., pl.* **-nese.** —*adj.* **1.** of, pertaining to, or characteristic of Japan, its people, or their language. —*n.* **2.** a native of Japan. **3.** the language of Japan, not known to be related to any other language. [JAPAN + -ESE]

Jap′anese androm′eda, an Asian evergreen shrub, *Pieris japonica,* having broad, glossy leaves and clusters of whitish blossoms. Also called **andromeda.**

Jap′anese anem′one, a perennial garden herb, *Anemone japonica,* of eastern Asia, having purplish or reddish flowers.

Japanese′ arborvi′tae, a Japanese tree, *Thuja standishii,* having spreading branches with bright-green leaves.

Jap′anese ar′tichoke. See **Chinese artichoke.**

Jap′anese bar′berry, a barberry, *Berberis Thunbergii,* of Japan, having yellow flowers and bearing bright-red fruit.

Jap′anese bee′tle, a scarabaeid beetle, *Popillia japonica,* introduced into the eastern U.S. from Japan, the adult of which feeds on the foliage of fruit and other trees, and the larva of which feeds on plant roots.

Jap′anese black′ pine′, a pine. *Pinus Thunbergii.* of Japan, grown as a seaside ornamental in the U.S.

Jap′anese bur′net, a perennial herb, *Sanguisorba obtusa,* of Japan, having small, red flowers in showy, short spikes.

Jap′anese ce′dar. See **Japan cedar.**

Jap′anese chest′nut. See under **chestnut** (def. 2).

Jap′anese clem′atis, a woody vine, *Clematis paniculata,* of Japan, having dense clusters of fragrant, white flowers and plumed fruit.

Jap′anese flow′ering cher′ry, any of various ornamental hybrid cherry trees developed in Japan, having white or pink blossoms and inedible fruit. Also called **Jap′anese cher′ry.**

Jap′anese gel′atin, agar (def. 1). Also called **Jap′anese i′singlass.**

Jap′anese hol′ly, an evergreen shrub, *Ilex crenata,* of Japan, having black fruit and box-shaped foliage.

Jap′anese hon′eysuckle, a climbing honeysuckle, *Lonicera japonica,* introduced into the eastern U.S. from Asia, having fragrant, white flowers that fade to yellow.

Jap′anese i′vy. See **Boston ivy.**

Jap′anese lan′tern. See **Chinese lantern.**

Jap′anese larch′, a tree, *Larix leptolepsis,* of Japan, having bluish-green leaves and egg-shaped cones.

Jap′anese lau′rel, an evergreen shrub, *Aucuba japonica,* of eastern Asia, having dark-green, glossy leaves and scarlet berries.

Jap′anese lawn′ grass′. See **Korean lawn grass.**

Jap′anese leaf′. See **Chinese evergreen.**

Jap′anese lil′y, a bulbous herb, *Lilium speciosum,* of Japan, having drooping, fragrant, white flowers with rose-red spots.

Jap′anese ma′ple, a small, graceful tree, *Acer palmatum,* of Korea and Japan, having small, purple flowers and winged fruit, the foliage turning bright red in autumn. Also called **full-moon maple.**

Jap′anese morn′ing-glory, any of several cultivated morning-glories of Japan that are derived from *Ipomoea Nils* and have large, showy flowers with scalloped, ruffled, or fringed margins.

Jap′anese pago′da tree′. See **pagoda tree.**

Jap′anese pa′per, paper of a high rag content, used for woodcuts, engravings, etc.

Jap′anese pear′, a tree, *Pyrus pyrifolia,* of China, having bristly toothed leaves and apple-shaped, brownish, hard-fleshed fruit. Also called **sand pear.**

Jap′anese persim′mon, 1. the soft, orange or reddish, edible fruit of an Asian tree, *Diospyros Kaki.* **2.** the tree itself.

Jap′anese quince′, a flowering quince, *Chaenomeles lagenaria,* of Japan, having scarlet flowers and yellowish-green fruit.

Jap′anese riv′er fe′ver, an infectious disease occurring chiefly in Japan and the East Indies, caused by the organism *Rickettsia tsutsugamushi,* transmitted by mites through biting. Also called **scrub typhus, tsutsugamushi disease.**

Jap′anese silk′, raw silk of usually high quality produced in Japan, used in the manufacture of such fabrics as shantung, habutai, etc.

Jap′anese span′iel, one of a Japanese breed of toy dogs having a long, silky, black and white or red and white coat and a tail carried over the back.

Jap′anese spurge′, a low, perennial, Japanese herb, *Pachysandra terminalis,* having spikes of white flowers, grown as a ground cover.

Jap′anese tree′ pe′ony, a shrubby plant, *Paeonia suffruticosa,* of China, having rose-red or white flowers nearly 12 inches wide.

Jap′anese wiste′ria, a wisteria, *Wisteria floribunda,* of Japan, having violet or violet-blue flowers, grown in the U.S. as an ornamental.

Jap′anese wolf′, a wolf, *Canis lupus hodophylax,* of Japan.

Jap′anese yew′, a yew, *Taxus cuspidata,* of Japan, grown as an ornamental.

Jap·a·nesque (jap′ə nesk′), *adj.* having a Japanese style. [JAPAN + -ESQUE]

Ja·pan·ism (jə pan′iz əm), *n.* **1.** devotion to or preference for Japan and its institutions. **2.** a custom, trait, or thing, peculiar to Japan or its citizens. Also, **Japonism.** [< F *japonisme,* equiv. to *Japon* JAPAN + *-isme* -ISM]

Japan′ Stream′. See **Japan Current.**

Japan′ tea′, light, unfermented tea common to Japan.

Japan′ wax′, a pale-yellow, waxy, water-insoluble solid obtained from the fruit of certain sumacs, esp. *Rhus succedanea,* native to Japan and China: used chiefly in the manufacture of candles, furniture polishes, and floor waxes. Also called **Japan′ tal′low, sumac wax.**

jape (jāp), *v.,* **japed, jap·ing,** *n.* —*v.i.* **1.** to jest; joke; gibe. —*v.t.* **2.** to mock or make fun of. —*n.* **3.** a joke; jest; quip. **4.** a trick or practical joke. [ME *jape(n),* perh. < OF *jabe(r)* (to) mock, deride] —**jap′er,** *n.* —**jap′er·y,** *n.* —**jap′ing·ly,** *adv.*

Ja·pheth (jā′fith), *n.* a son of Noah. Gen. 5:32. [< LL < Gk *Iapheth* < Heb *Yepheth* increase]

Ja·phet·ic (jə fet′ik), *adj.* **1.** of or pertaining to Japheth. **2.** of, pertaining to, or noting a group of languages of the Caucasus, Mesopotamia, Asia Minor, and southern Europe considered by the linguist N. Ja. Marr (1864–1934) as representing a stage in language development prior to the stage including Indo-European and Semitic. Japhetic theory dominated Soviet linguistic scholarship until its official repudiation in 1950. [*Japhet-* (comb. form of JAPHETH) + -IC]

ja·pon·i·ca (jə pon′ə kə), *n.* **1.** the camellia, *Camellia japonica.* **2.** See **Japanese quince.** [< NL, equiv. to *Japon(ia)* JAPAN + *-ica,* fem. of *-icus* -IC]

Jap·o·nism (jap′ə niz′əm), *n.* Japanism.

Ja·pu·rá (*Port.* zhä′po͞o rä′), *n.* a river flowing E from the Andes in SW Colombia through NW Brazil to the Amazon. 1750 mi. long. Also, **Yapurá.**

ja·pyg·id (jə pij′id), *n.* any eyeless, wingless, primitive insect of the family *Japygidae,* having a pair of pincers at the rear of its abdomen. [< NL *japygid(a),* equiv. to *Japygi(a)* old Italian kingdom + *-ida* -ID[2]]

Jaque·lee (jak lē′), *n.* a girl's given name.

Ja·ques (jā′kwēz, -kwiz, jāks), *n.* a disillusioned and satirical observer of life, in Shakespeare's *As You Like It.* —**Ja·que·si·an** (jā kwē′zē ən), *adj.*

Jaques-Dal·croze (*Fr.* zhäk′dAl krōz′), *n.* **É·mile** (*Fr.* ā mēl′), 1865–1950, Swiss composer and teacher.

jar[1] (jär), *n.* **1.** a broad-mouthed container, usually cylindrical and of glass or earthenware. **2.** the quantity such a container can or does hold. [< MF *jarre* < OPr *jarra* < Ar *jarrah* earthen water-vessel] —**jar′less,** *adj.*

jar² (jär), *v.*, **jarred, jar·ring,** *n.* —*v.i.* **1.** to produce a harsh, grating sound; sound discordantly: *The chalk jarred against the blackboard.* **2.** to have a harshly unpleasant or perturbing effect on one's nerves, feelings, thoughts, etc.: *Nonsensical chatter jars on his ears.* **3.** to vibrate audibly; rattle: *The window jarred in the frame.* **4.** to vibrate or shake. **5.** to conflict, clash, or disagree. —*v.t.* **6.** to cause to sound harshly or discordantly. **7.** to cause to rattle or shake. **8.** to have a sudden and unpleasant effect upon (the feelings, nerves, etc.): *The burglary violently jarred her sense of security.* —*n.* **9.** a harsh, grating sound. **10.** a discordant sound or combination of sounds. **11.** a jolt or shake; a vibrating movement, as from concussion. **12.** a sudden unpleasant effect upon the mind or feelings; shock. **13.** a quarrel or disagreement, esp. a minor one. [? OE *cearr(an)* (to) creak] —**jar′ring·ly,** *adv.*

jar³ (jär), *n.* **1.** *Archaic.* a turn or turning. **2. on the jar,** partly opened; ajar: *The window was on the jar to admit the soft spring breeze.* [var. of CHAR³, CHARE; cf. AJAR²]

Ja·rash (jar′äsh), *n.* Jerash.

jar·din an·glais (zhar dan äN gle′), *pl.* **jar·dins an·glais** (zhar dan äN gle′, -dan zäN-). *French.* (in Europe) a landscape garden having winding paths and irregular planting in supposed imitation of English practice. [lit., English garden]

jar·din chi·nois (zhar dan shē nwa′), *pl.* **jar·dins chi·nois** (zhar dan shē nwa′). *French.* an imitation of a Chinese garden, popular in the 18th century. [lit., Chinese garden]

jar·di·niere (jär′dᵊnēr′), *n.* **1.** an ornamental receptacle or stand for holding plants, flowers, etc. **2.** various vegetables diced and boiled or glazed, each type usually separately, used for garnishing meat or poultry. [< F, fem. of *jardinier* gardener, equiv. to OF *jardin* GARDEN + *-ier* -ER²]

jar·gon¹ (jär′gən, -gon), *n.* **1.** the language, esp. the vocabulary, peculiar to a particular trade, profession, or group: *medical jargon; plumbers' jargon.* **2.** unintelligible or meaningless talk or writing; gibberish. **3.** any talk or writing which one does not understand. **4.** pidgin. **5.** a kind of speech abounding in uncommon or unfamiliar words, and often vague in meaning. —*v.i.* **6.** to utter or talk jargon or a jargon. [ME *jargoun* < MF *jargon;* akin to GARGLE] —**jar′gon·al, jar′gon·is′tic,** *adj.* —**jar′gon·ish, jar′gon·esque′,** *adj.* —**jar′gon·ist, jar′gon·eer′,** *n.*
—**Syn. 1.** See **language. 2.** babble, gabble, twaddle, nonsense.

jar·gon² (jär′gon), *n.* a colorless to smoky gem variety of zircon. Also, **jar·goon** (jär go͞on′). [< F < It *giargone* << Pers *zargūn* gold-colored]

jar·gon·ise (jär′gə nīz′), *v.i., v.t.,* **-ised, -is·ing.** *Chiefly Brit.* jargonize. —**jar′gon·i·sa′tion,** *n.*

jar·gon·ize (jär′gə nīz′), *v.,* **-ized, -iz·ing.** —*v.i.* **1.** to talk jargon or a jargon. —*v.t.* **2.** to translate into jargon. [JARGON¹ + -IZE] —**jar′gon·i·za′tion,** *n.*

jarl (yärl), *n.* *Scand. Hist.* a chieftain; earl. [< ON; cf. Icel *jarl;* see EARL] —**jarl′dom,** *n.*

jar·less (jär′lis), *adj.* free from jarring or shaking. [JAR² + -LESS]

jar·o·site (jar′ə sīt′, jə rō′sit), *n.* a yellowish or brownish mineral, $K_2Fe_6(SO_4)_4(OH)_{12}$, occurring in small crystals or large masses. [named after Barranco *Jaroso* (in Almeria, Spain); see -ITE¹]

jar·o·vize (yär′ə vīz′), *v.t.,* **-vized, -viz·ing.** to vernalize. Also, **iarovize, yarovize.** [< Russ *yarov(oe)* spring grain (deriv. of *yara* spring; c. YEAR) + -IZE] —**jar′o·vi·za′tion,** *n.*

Jar·rell (jar′əl, jə rel′), *n.* **Randall,** 1914–65, U.S. poet and critic.

Jar·row (jar′ō), *n.* a seaport in NE Durham, in NE England, at the mouth of the Tyne River. 28,752 (1961).

Jar·ry (zha rē′), *n.* **Al·fred** (al fred′), 1873–1907, French poet and playwright.

jar·vey (jär′vē), *n., pl.* **-veys.** *Irish Eng.* **1.** a hackney coachman. **2.** a hackney coach. Also, **jar′vie, jarvy.** [special use of *Jarvey,* var. of *Jarvis* proper name]

jar·vy (jär′vē), *n., pl.* **-vies.** *Irish Eng.* jarvey.

Jas., *Bible.* James.

Ja·scha (yä′shə), *n.* a boy's given name, Russian form of **Jacob** or **James.**

ja·sey (jā′zē), *n., pl.* **-seys.** *Brit. Informal.* a wig, esp. a worsted one. Also, **jasy, jazey, jazy.** [var. of JERSEY] —**ja′seyed,** *adj.*

jas·mine (jaz′min, jas′-), *n.* **1.** any of several oleaceous shrubs or vines of the genus *Jasminum,* having fragrant flowers. **2.** any of several other plants having similar fragrant flowers, as the Caroline jessamine. **3.** the fragrance itself. **4.** a pale-yellow color. Also, **jessamine.** [< MF *jasmin,* var. of *jassemin* < Ar *yās(a)mīn* < Pers *yāsmīn*] —**jas′mined,** *adj.* —**jas′mine·like′,** *adj.*

Jas·mine (jaz′min, jas′-), *n.* a girl's given name. Also **Jas′min, Jas·mi·na** (jaz′mə nə, jas′-).

jas′mine tea′, tea scented with jasmine blossoms.

Ja·son (jā′sən), *n.* **1.** *Class. Myth.* a hero, the leader of the Argonauts, who at the request of his uncle Pelias retrieved the Golden Fleece from King Aeëtes of Colchis with the help of Medea. **2.** a boy's given name.

jas·pé (ja spā′; *Fr.* zha spā′), *adj.* given a veined and spotted appearance imitating jasper. [< F: mottled, ptp. of *jasper* to mottle, deriv. of *jaspe* JASPER¹]

jas·per¹ (jas′pər), *n.* **1.** a compact, opaque, often highly colored, cryptocrystalline variety of quartz, often used in decorative carvings. **2.** Also called **cameo ware, jas′per·ware′,** a fine, hard stoneware invented c1775 by Wedgwood, basically white but usually stained various colors by metallic oxides. [ME *jaspe, jaspre* < MF; OF *jaspe* < L *iaspis* < Gk < ?] —**jas′per·at′ed, jas′pered,** *adj.* —**jas′per·oid′,** *adj.*

jas·per² (jas′pər), *n.* *Slang.* a fellow; guy. [special use of proper name *Jasper*]

Jas·per (jas′pər), *n.* **1.** a city in NW Alabama. 10,799 (1960). **2.** a town in SW Indiana. 6737 (1960). **3.** a town in E Texas. 4889 (1960). **4.** a boy's given name, form of **Caspar.**

Jas′per dip′, white jasperware colored by painting or by dipping.

Jas′per Park′, a national park in the Canadian Rockies in W Alberta, in SW Canada.

Jas·pers (yäs′pərs), *n.* **Karl** (kärl), 1883–1969, German philosopher.

jas·per·y (jas′pə rē), *adj.* **1.** containing or composed of jasper. **2.** resembling jasper. [JASPER¹ + -Y¹]

jass (yäs), *n.* **1.** a card game for two persons that is played with a 36-card pack made by removing all cards below the sixes from a regular 52-card pack, in which point values are assigned to certain melds and to certain cards taken in tricks. **2.** Also, **jasz.** the jack of trumps in klaberjass. [< G (Swiss)]

Jas·sy (yä′sē), *n.* a city in NE Rumania. 123,558 (est. 1964). Also, **Yassy.** Rumanian, **Iaşi.**

ja·sy (jā′zē), *n., pl.* **-sies.** *Brit. Informal.* jasey.

Jat (jät, jôt), *n.* a member of an Indo-Aryan people living mainly in northwestern India. In early times they offered vigorous resistance to the Muslim invaders of India.

Ja·ta·ka (jä′tə kə), *n.* *Buddhism.* a collection of fables, many concerning former lives of the Buddha.

ja·to (jā′tō), *n., pl.* **-tos.** a jet-assisted takeoff, esp. one using auxiliary rocket motors that are jettisoned at the completion of the takeoff. [*j(et) a(ssisted) t(ake)-o(ff)*]

jauk (jäk, jôk), *v.i.* *Scot.* to dally; dawdle. [?]

jaun·dice (jôn′dis, jän′-), *n., v.,* **-diced, -dic·ing.** —*n.* **1.** Also called **icterus.** *Pathol.* an abnormal body condition due to an increase of bile pigments in the blood, characterized by yellowness of the skin, of the whites of the eyes, etc., by lassitude, and by loss of appetite. **2.** grasserie. **3.** a state of feeling in which views are prejudiced or judgment is distorted. —*v.t.* **4.** to distort or prejudice, as with envy, resentment, etc.: *His social position jaundiced his view of things.* [ME *jaundis* < OF *jaunisse,* equiv. to *jaun(e)* yellow (< L *galbinus* pale green) + *-isse* -ICE]

jaun·diced (jôn′dist, jän′-), *adj.* **1.** affected with or colored by or as by jaundice: *jaundiced skin.* **2.** affected with or exhibiting prejudice, often resulting from a particular experience, social position, etc.: *a jaundiced viewpoint.* [JAUNDICE + -ED³]

jaunt (jônt, jänt), *v.i.* **1.** to make a short journey, esp. for pleasure. —*n.* **2.** such a journey. [?] —**jaunt′ing·ly,** *adv.*
—**Syn. 2.** See **excursion.**

jaunt′ing car′, a light, two-wheeled, one-horse cart, common in Ireland, having two seats set back to back and having a perch in front for the driver.

jaun·ty (jôn′tē, jän′-), *adj.,* **-ti·er, -ti·est. 1.** easy and sprightly in manner or bearing: *a jaunty step.* **2.** smartly trim or effective, as clothing: *a jaunty hat.* [< F *gentil* noble, gentle, GENTEEL] —**jaun′ti·ly,** *adv.* —**jaun′ti·ness,** *n.*

jaup (jôp, jäp), *n.* *Scot. and North Eng.* **1.** a splash, spurt, or drop of water. **2.** a spot or stain, as from a splash of water or mud. Also, **jawp.** [? akin to JAW²]

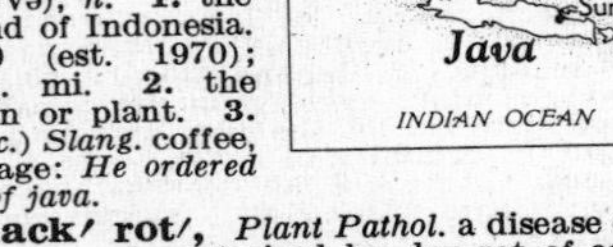

Jau·rès (zhō res′), *n.* **Jean Lé·on** (zhäN lā ôN′), 1859–1914, French socialist and author.

Jav., Javanese.

Ja·va (jä′və), *n.* **1.** the main island of Indonesia. 75,000,000 (est. 1970); 48,920 sq. mi. **2.** the coffee bean or plant. **3.** (*usually l.c.*) *Slang.* coffee, the beverage: *He ordered two cups of java.*

Ja′va black′ rot′, *Plant Pathol.* a disease of stored sweet potatoes, characterized by dry rot of and black protuberances on the tubers, caused by a fungus, *Diplodia tubericola.*

Ja′va cot′ton, kapok.

Ja′va fig′, a large, smooth tree, *Ficus benjamina,* of southeastern Asia, having leathery leaves and round fruit. Also called **Java willow.**

Ja′va man′, the hominid genus *Pithecanthropus.*

Jav·a·nese (jav′ə nēz′, -nēs′), *adj., n., pl.* **-nese.** —*adj.* **1.** of or pertaining to the island of Java, its people, or their language. —*n.* **2.** a member of the native Malayan race of Java, esp. of that branch of it in the central part of the island. **3.** the language of central Java, of the Malayo-Polynesian family. [*Javan* (JAV(A) + -AN) + -ESE]

jav·a·nine (jav′ə nēn′, -nin), *n.* *Pharm.* a crystalline, water-soluble alkaloid obtained from cinchona bark, used in medicine as an agent for stimulating the stomach and as a substitute for quinine. [< NL *javan(ica)* (name of a genus) + -INE²]

Ja·va·ry (zhä′vä rē′), *n.* a river in E South America, flowing NE from Peru to the upper Amazon, forming part of the boundary between Peru and Brazil. 650 mi. long. Also, **Ja′va·ri′.**

Ja′va Sea′, a sea between Java and Borneo.

Ja′va spar′row, a finchlike bird, *Padda oryzivora,* of the East Indies and Malaya, having gray plumage tinged with pink on the belly, often kept as a pet.

Ja′va wil′low. See **Java fig.**

jave·lin (jav′lin, jav′ə lin), *n.* **1.** a light spear, usually thrown by hand. **2.** *Track.* **a.** a spearlike shaft about 8½ feet long and usually made of wood, used in throwing for distance. **b.** Also called **jave′lin throw′,** a competitive field event consisting in throwing the javelin for distance. —*v.t.* **3.** to strike or pierce with or as with a javelin. [< MF *javeline,* equiv. to *javel-* (? < Celt) + *-ine* -INE²]

Ja·vel′ wa′ter (zhə vel′), sodium hypochlorite, NaOCl, dissolved in water, used as a bleach, antiseptic etc. Also, **Javelle′ wa′ter.** [trans. of F *eau de Javel* after *Javel* former town, now in the city of Paris]

jaw¹ (jô), *n.* **1.** either of two bones, the mandible or maxilla, forming the framework of the mouth. **2.** the part of the face covering these bones, the mouth, or the mouth parts collectively: *His jaw is swollen.* **3. jaws,** anything resembling a pair of jaws or evoking the concept of grasping and holding: *the jaws of a gorge; the jaws of death.* **4.** *Mach.* **a.** one of two or more parts, as of a machine, that grasp or hold something: *the jaws of a vise.* **b.** any of two or more protruding parts for attaching to or meshing with similar parts. **5.** Often, **jaws.** Also called **throat.** *Naut.* a forked piece at the end of a gaff, fitting halfway around the mast. **6.** *Slang.* offensive talk. —*v.i.* *Slang.* **7.** to talk; gossip. **8.** to scold or use abusive language. —*v.t.* **9.** *Slang.* to scold. [ME *jowe* < OF *joue;* akin to It *gota* cheek] —**jaw′less,** *adj.*

jaw² (jô), *Scot. and North Eng.* —*n.* **1.** a swelling wave of water; billow. —*v.i.* **2.** (of liquid) to surge, splash, or dash forward, as in waves. —*v.t.* **3.** to pour or splash (liquid). [? akin to JAUP]

ja·wan (jə wän′), *n.* a common soldier of the Indian army. [< Urdu *jawān*]

jaw·bone (jô′bōn′), *n., v.,* **-boned, -bon·ing,** *adj.* —*n.* **1.** a bone of either jaw; a maxilla or mandible. **2.** the bone of the lower jaw; mandible. —*v.t.* **3.** *Informal.* to attempt to convince or influence (a person, company, etc.) by moral persuasion instead of by using force or authority. —*adj.* **4.** *Informal.* obtained by or resorting to such a practice: *jawbone controls.* [JAW¹ + BONE¹]

jaw·break·er (jô′brā′kər), *n.* **1.** *Informal.* any word that is hard to pronounce. **2.** a very hard, opaque ball of candy. **3.** Also called **jaw′ crush′er.** a machine to break up ore, consisting of a fixed plate and a hinged jaw moved by a toggle joint. [JAW¹ + BREAKER¹] —**jaw′break′ing,** *adj.* —**jaw′break′ing·ly,** *adv.*

jaw·fish (jô′fish′), *n., pl.* (*esp. collectively*) **-fish,** (*esp. referring to two or more kinds or species*) **-fish·es.** any of several large-mouthed fishes of the family *Opisthognathidae,* living in holes in the sandy bottom of warm seas. [JAW¹ + FISH]

Jaw·len·sky (you len′skē), *n.* **A·le·xej von** (ä′le ksā′ fən), 1864?–1941, German painter, born in Russia.

jaw·like (jô′līk′), *adj.* resembling a jaw or pair of jaws. [JAW¹ + -LIKE]

jawp (jôp, jäp), *n.* *Scot. and North Eng.* jaup.

jaw·rope (jô′rōp′), *n.* *Naut.* a rope tied across the jaw of a gaff to hold it to the mast. [JAW¹ + ROPE]

jaw's-harp (jôz′härp′), *n.* jew's-harp.

Jax·ar·tes (jak sär′tēz), *n.* ancient name of **Syr Darya.**

jay (jā), *n.* **1.** any of several noisy, mischievous, corvine birds of the subfamily *Garrulinae,* as the common, crested *Garrulus glandarius,* of the Old World, having brownish plumage with blue, black, and white barring on the wings. Cf. **blue jay, Canada jay. 2.** *Informal.* a simple-minded or gullible person; simpleton. [ME < MF *jai* < LL *gāius, gāia,* special use of L *Gāius* man's name]

Jay (jā), *n.* **1. John,** 1745–1829, U.S. statesman and jurist: 1st Chief Justice of the U.S. 1789–95. **2.** a boy's given name.

jay·bird (jā′bûrd′), *n.* jay. [JAY + BIRD]

Jay·cee (jā′sē′), *n.* a member of a civic group for young men (**Unit′ed States′ Jay′cees′**). [from *J(unior) C(hamber)* in its original name *United States Junior Chamber of Commerce*]

Jay·hawk·er (jā′hô′kər), *n.* **1.** a native or inhabitant of Kansas (the **Jayhawker State**) (used as a nickname). **2.** (*sometimes l.c.*) a plundering marauder, esp. one of the antislavery guerrillas in Kansas, Missouri, and other border States before and during the Civil War. [? *jay hawk* (a bird, but unattested) + -ER¹]

Jay′hawker State′, Kansas (used as a nickname).

Jayne (jān), *n.* a girl's given name. Also, **Jane, Jayn, Jaynne.**

Jay's′ Trea′ty, *U.S. Hist.* the agreement in 1794 between England and the U.S. by which limited trade relations were established, England agreed to give up its forts in the northwestern frontier, and a joint commission was set up to settle border disputes. Also, **Jay′ Trea′ty.** [named after John JAY]

jay·vee (jā′vē′), *n.* *Sports Informal.* **1.** a player on the junior varsity. **2.** See **junior varsity.** [pronunciation of *JV,* abbr. for *junior varsity*]

jay·walk (jā′wôk′), *v.i.* to cross a street at other than a regular crossing or to cross in a heedless manner, as against traffic lights. [JAY + WALK] —**jay′walk′er,** *n.*

ja·zey (jā′zē), *n., pl.* **-zeys.** *Brit. Informal.* jasey.

ja·zy (jā′zē), *n., pl.* **-zies.** *Brit. Informal.* jasey.

jazz (jaz), *n.* **1.** music originating in New Orleans around the beginning of the 20th century and subsequently developing through various increasingly complex styles, generally marked by intricate, propulsive rhythms, polyphonic ensemble playing, improvisatory, virtuosic solos, melodic freedom, and a harmonic idiom ranging from simple diatonicism through chromaticism to, in recent developments, atonality. **2.** a style of dance music, popular esp. in the 1920's, arranged for a large band and marked by some of the features of true jazz. **3.** dancing or a dance performed to such music, as with violent bodily motions and gestures. **4.** *Slang.* liveliness; spirit. **5.** *Slang.* insincere, exaggerated, or pretentious talk: *Don't give me any of that jazz about your great job!* —*adj.* **6.** of, pertaining to, characteristic of, or noting jazz. —*v.t.* **7.** to play (music) in the manner of jazz. **8.** *Slang.* **a.** to put vigor or liveliness into (often fol. by *up*). **b.** to accelerate (often fol. by *up*). —*v.i.* **9.** to dance to jazz music. **10.** to play or perform jazz music. **11.** *Slang.* to act or proceed with great energy or liveliness. [?] —**jazz′er,** *n.*

jazz′ band′, a band specializing in jazz, and consisting typically of trumpet, trombone, clarinet, saxophone, piano, double bass, and percussion.

jazz·man (jaz′man′, -mən), *n., pl.* **-men** (-men′, -mən). an instrumentalist who plays jazz. [JAZZ + MAN¹]

jazz′ sing′er, a singer whose vocal technique is similar to that of a musical instrument, and whose singing has a strong jazz feeling, chiefly imparted through phrasing, melodic improvisation, and rhythmic subtlety.

jazz·y (jaz′ē), *adj.,* **jazz·i·er, jazz·i·est.** *Slang.* **1.** pertaining to or suggestive of jazz music. **2.** wildly active or lively. [JAZZ + -Y¹] —**jazz′i·ly,** *adv.* —**jazz′i·ness,** *n.*

J.C., 1. Jesus Christ. **2.** Julius Caesar. **3.** jurisconsult. [< L *juris consultus*]

J.C.B., 1. Bachelor of Canon Law. [< L *Juris Canonici Baccalaureus*] **2.** Bachelor of Civil Law. [< L *Juris Civilis Baccalaureus*]

J.C.D., 1. Doctor of Canon Law. [< L *Juris Canonici Doctor*] **2.** Doctor of Civil Law. [< L *Juris Civilis Doctor*]

J.C.L., Licentiate in Canon Law. [< L *Juris Canonici Licentiātus*]

J.C.S., Joint Chiefs of Staff. Also, **JCS**

jct., junction. Also, **jctn.**

JD, *Informal.* **1.** juvenile delinquency. **2.** juvenile delinquent.

JD., dinar (def. 5).

J.D., 1. See **Julian Day. 2.** Doctor of Law. [< L *Juris Doctor*] **3.** Doctor of Jurisprudence. [< L *Juris Doctor*] **4.** Doctor of Laws. [< *Jurum Doctor*] **5.** *Informal.* **a.** juvenile delinquency. **b.** juvenile delinquent.

Je., June.

jeal·ous (jel′əs), *adj.* **1.** feeling resentment against a person because of his rivalry, success, or advantages (often fol. by *of*): *He was jealous of his rich brother.* **2.** feeling resentment because of another's success, advantage, etc. (often fol. by *of*): *He was jealous of his brother's wealth.* **3.** characterized by or proceeding from suspicious fears or envious resentment: *jealous intrigues.* **4.** inclined to or troubled by suspicions or fears of rivalry, unfaithfulness, etc., as in love or aims: *a jealous husband.* **5.** solicitous or vigilant in maintaining or guarding something: *The American people are jealous of their freedom.* **6.** *Bible.* intolerant of unfaithfulness or rivalry: *The Lord is a jealous God.* [ME *jelous, gelos* < OF *gelos* (F *jaloux*) < VL **zēlōs(us)*, equiv. to LL *zēl(us)* ZEAL + *-ōsus* -OSE[1]] **—jeal′ous·ly,** *adv.* **—jeal′ous·ness,** *n.*

jeal·ous·y (jel′ə sē), *n., pl.* **-ous·ies** for 4. **1.** jealous resentment against a rival, a person enjoying success or advantage, etc., or against another's success or advantage itself. **2.** mental uneasiness from suspicion or fear of rivalry, unfaithfulness, etc., as in love or aims. **3.** vigilance in maintaining or guarding something. **4.** a jealous feeling, disposition, state, or mood. [ME *gelusie, jelosie* < OF *gelosie*, equiv. to *gelos* JEALOUS + *-ie* -Y[3]]

jean (jēn *or, esp. Brit.,* jān), *n.* **1.** Sometimes, **jeans.** a stout twilled cotton fabric. **2. jeans,** (*construed as pl.*) **a.** a garment, as overalls or trousers, made of this fabric. **b.** sturdy, low-waisted slacks with high patch pockets, cut and sewn in the style of work pants, esp. as worn by teenagers of both sexes. Cf. **blue jeans, Levis. c.** *Slang.* trousers. [short for *jean fustian* Genoa fustian, late ME *Gene* GENOA + FUSTIAN]

Jean (jēn *for 2; Fr.* zhäN *for 1, 2*), *n.* **1. Grand Duke,** born 1921, sovereign of Luxembourg since 1964 (son of Grand Duchess Charlotte). **2.** a girl's or boy's given name.

Jean-Chris·tophe (zhäN krēs tôf′), *n.* a novel (1906–12) by Romain Rolland.

Jean·er·ette (jen′ə ret′), *n.* a town in S Louisiana. 5568 (1960).

Jeanne d'Arc (zhän dark′), French name of **Joan of Arc.**

Jean·nette (jə net′), *n.* **1.** a city in W Pennsylvania, near Pittsburgh. 16,565 (1960). **2.** Also, **Jean·net·ta** (jə net′ə), **Jean·ette** (jə net′; *Fr.* zhä net′). a girl's given name, form of **Jean.**

Jean·nie (jē′nē), *n.* a girl's given name, form of **Jean.** Also, **Jean′ie, Jeanne** (jēn; *Fr.* zhän), **Jean′nye.**

Jeans (jēns), *n.* **Sir James (Hop·wood)** (hop′wo͝od), 1877–1946, English astrophysicist and author.

Jebb (jeb), *n.* **Sir Richard Clav·er·house** (klav′ər hous′), 1841–1905, Scottish scholar of classical Greek.

jeb·el (jeb′əl), *n.* djebel.

Jeb·el ed Druz (jeb′əl ed dro͞oz′), a mountainous region in S Syria: inhabited by Druses. ab. 2700 sq. mi. Also, **Jeb′el el Druz′, Jabal al-Duruz, Jeb·el Druze** (jeb′əl dro͞oz′), **Djebel Druze.**

Jeb·el Mu·sa (jeb′əl mo͞o′sä), a mountain in NW Morocco, opposite Gibraltar: one of the Pillars of Hercules. 2775 ft. Ancient, **Abyla.**

Je·bus (jē′bəs), *n.* an ancient Canaanite city taken by David: it later became Jerusalem.

Jeb·us·ite (jeb′yə sīt′), *n.* a member of an ancient Canaanite people that lived in Jebus. [JEBUS + -ITE[1]] **—Jeb·u·sit·ic** (jeb′yə sit′ik), **Jeb′u·sit′i·cal, Jeb·u·sit·ish** (jeb′yə sī′tish), *adj.*

Jed·burgh (jed′bûr ō, -bur ō, -bər ə), *n.* a border town in SE Scotland: ruins of a great abbey. 3679 (est. 1964).

Jed·da (jed′də), *n.* Jidda.

jed′ding ax′ (jed′ing), a stonemason's ax, similar to a kevel, having a head with one flat and one pointed face. [*jedding*, var. of *jadding* (JAD + -ING[2])]

jee (jē), *interj., v.i., v.t.,* **jeed, jee·ing.** gee[1].

jeep (jēp), *n.* a small military motor vehicle having four-wheel drive. [? special use of *jeep*, name of fabulous animal in comic strip "Popeye," or alter. of G.P. (for General Purpose Vehicle), or both]

jeep′ car′rier, *U.S. Navy.* an antisubmarine escort carrier.

jee·pers (jē′pərz), *interj.* (used as a mild exclamation of surprise or emotion.) Also, **jee′pers cree′pers** (krē′pərz). [euphemism for *Jesus*]

jeer[1] (jēr), *v.i.* **1.** to speak or shout derisively; scoff or gibe rudely: *Don't jeer unless you can do better.* **—*v.t.*** **2.** to shout derisively at. **3.** to treat with scoffs or derision; mock. **4.** to drive away by derisive shouts (fol. by *out of, off,* etc.): *They jeered the speaker off the stage.* **—*n.*** **5.** a jeering utterance; derisive or rude gibe. [< ?; cf. OE *cēir* clamor, akin to *cēgan* to call out] **—jeer′er,** *n.* **—jeer′ing·ly,** *adv.*
—Syn. 1. sneer; jest. See **scoff. 2.** deride, mock, taunt, ridicule, flout, fleer.

jeer[2] (jēr), *n.* Often, **jeers.** *Naut.* any of various combinations of tackles for raising or lowering heavy yards. [JEE + -ER[1]]

jeez (jēz), *interj.* (used as a mild expression of surprise, disappointment, astonishment, etc.) [euphemistic shortening of *Jesus*]

je·fe (he′fe; *Eng.* hā′fā), *n., pl.* **-fes** (-fes; *Eng.* -fāz). *Spanish.* leader; chief; boss.

Jeff (jef), *n.* a boy's given name, form of **Jeffrey.**

Jef·fers (jef′ərz), *n.* **(John) Robinson,** 1887–1962, U.S. poet.

Jef·fer·son (jef′ər sən), *n.* **1. Joseph,** 1829–1905, U.S. actor. **2. Thomas,** 1743–1826, U.S. statesman, diplomat, architect, and author: 3rd president of the U.S. 1801–09. **3.** a town in SW Pennsylvania. 8280 (1960). **4.** a town in central Iowa. 4570 (1960). **5.** a town in S Wisconsin. 4548 (1960). **6.** a town in E Texas. 3082 (1960). **7.** a town in NE Ohio. 2774 (1960). **8.** a boy's given name.

Jef′ferson Cit′y, 1. a city in and the capital of Missouri, in the central part, on the Missouri River. 28,228 (1960). **2.** a town in E Tennessee. 4550 (1960).

Jef′ferson Day′, April 13, Thomas Jefferson's birthday, a legal holiday in certain States, sometimes celebrated by the Democratic party by the holding of fund-raising dinners.

Jef·fer·so·ni·an (jef′ər sō′nē ən), *adj.* **1.** pertaining to or advocating the political principles and doctrines of Thomas Jefferson, esp. those stressing minimum control by the central government, the inalienable rights of the individual, and the superiority of an agrarian economy and rural society. **—*n.*** **2.** a supporter of Thomas Jefferson or Jeffersonianism. [JEFFERSON + -IAN] **—Jef′fer·so′ni·an·ism,** *n.*

Jef·fer·son·town (jef′ər sən toun′), *n.* a town in N Kentucky. 3431 (1960).

Jef·fer·son·ville (jef′ər sən vil), *n.* a city in S Indiana, on the Ohio River. 19,522 (1960).

Jef·frey (jef′rē), *n.* **1. Francis** ("*Lord Jeffrey*"), 1773–1850, Scottish jurist, editor, and critic. **2.** a boy's given name.

Jef·freys (jef′rēz), *n.* **George** (*1st Baron Jeffreys of Wem*), 1648–89, English jurist.

Jef·fries (jef′rēz), *n.* **James J.,** 1875–1953, U.S. boxer: world heavyweight champion 1899–1905.

Jeh (jā), *n.* *Zoroastrianism.* a female demon who was the companion of Angra Mainyu and was believed to have corrupted the female sex: sometimes considered to be the first woman.

je·had (jē häd′), *n.* jihad.

Je·han·gir (yə hän′gēr), *n.* Jahangir.

Je·hoi·a·da (ji hoi′ə də), *n.* a priest of Judah who led the revolt against Athalia. II Kings 11:1–16. Also, *Douay Bible,* **Joiada.**

Je·hol (jə hōl′, rā′hō′; *Chin.* zhu′hu′, ru′-), *n.* **1.** a region and former province in NE China: incorporated into Manchukuo by the Japanese 1932–1945. 74,297 sq. mi. **2.** Chengteh.

Je·hosh·a·phat (ji hosh′ə fat′, -hos′-), *n.* a king of Judah, son of Asa, who reigned in the 9th century B.C. I Kings 22:41–50.

Je·ho·vah (ji hō′və), *n.* **1.** a name of God in the Old Testament, an erroneous rendering of the ineffable name, JHVH, in the Hebrew Scriptures. **2.** (in modern Christian use) God. **—Je·ho·vic** (ji hō′vik), *adj.*

Jeho′vah God′, (among the Jehovah's Witnesses) God.

Jeho′vah's Wit′nesses, a Christian sect, founded in the U. S. in the late 19th century, that believes in the imminent end of the world and the establishment of a theocracy under God's rule.

Je·ho·vist (ji hō′vist), *n.* Yahwist. [JEHOV(AH) + -IST] **—Je·ho′vism,** *n.* **—Je·ho·vis·tic** (jē′hō vis′tik), *adj.*

Je·hu (jē′hyo͞o), *n.* **1.** a king of Israel noted for his furious chariot attacks. II Kings 9. **2.** (*l.c.*) a fast driver. **3.** (*l.c.*) *Slang.* any driver. **4.** a boy's given name.

jejun-, var. of **jejuno-** before a vowel: *jejunectomy.*

je·june (ji jo͞on′), *adj.* **1.** deficient or lacking in nutritive value: *a jejune diet.* **2.** without interest; dull; insipid: *a jejune novel.* **3.** lacking knowledge or experience; uninformed: *jejune attempts to design a house.* **4.** juvenile; immature; childish: *jejune behavior toward others.* [< L *jējūn(us)* empty, poor, mean] **—je·june′ly,** *adv.* **—je·june′ness, je·ju·ni·ty** (ji jo͞o′ni tē), *n.*

je·ju·nec·to·my (ji jo͞o nek′tə mē, jē′jo͞o-), *n., pl.* **-mies.** *Surg.* excision of part or all of the jejunum. [JEJUN- + -ECTOMY]

jejuno-, a combining form of **jejunum:** *jejunostomy.*

je·ju·nos·to·my (ji jo͞o nos′tə mē, jē′jo͞o-), *n., pl.* **-mies.** *Surg.* the formation of a permanent, artificial opening through the abdominal wall into the jejunum. [JEJUNO- + -STOMY]

je·ju·num (ji jo͞o′nəm), *n.* *Anat.* the middle portion of the small intestine, between the duodenum and the ileum. See diag. under **intestine.** [< L *jējūnum*, n. use of neut. of *jējūnus* empty; so called because thought to be empty after death] **—je·ju′nal,** *adj.*

Je′kyll and Hyde′ (je′kəl, jek′əl), a person marked by dual personality, one aspect of which is good and the other bad. [after the protagonist of *Dr. Jekyll and Mr. Hyde*]

jell (jel), *v.i.* **1.** to congeal; become jellylike in consistency. **2.** to become clear, substantial, or definite; crystallize: *The plan didn't begin to jell until a consultant was called in.* **—*n.*** **3.** jelly. [back formation from JELLY]

jel·la·ba (jə lä′bə), *n.* djellabah. Also, **jel·lab, je·lab** (jə läb′).

jel·lib (jə lēb′), *n.* djellabah. Also, **je·lib′.**

Jel·li·coe (jel′ə kō′), *n.* **John Rush·worth** (rush′wûrth′), **1st Earl,** 1859–1935, British admiral.

jel·lied (jel′ēd), *adj.* **1.** congealed or brought to the consistency of jelly: *jellied consommé.* **2.** containing or spread over with jelly or syrup: *a jellied apple.* [JELLY + -ED[2]] **—jel′lied·ness,** *n.*

jel·li·fy (jel′ə fī′), *v.,* **-fied, -fy·ing.** **—*v.t.*** **1.** to make into a jelly; reduce to a gelatinous state. **—*v.i.*** **2.** to turn into jelly; become gelatinous. [JELLY + -FY] **—jel′li·fi·ca′tion,** *n.*

Jell-O (jel′ō), *n.* *Trademark.* a dessert made from a mixture of gelatin, sugar, and fruit flavoring, dissolved in hot water and chilled until firm.

jel·ly (jel′ē), *n., pl.* **-lies,** *v.,* **-lied, -ly·ing,** *adj.* **—*n.*** **1.** a food preparation of a soft, elastic consistency due to the presence of gelatin, pectin, etc., as fruit juice boiled down with sugar and used as a sweet spread for bread and toast, as a filling for cakes, doughnuts, etc. **2.** anything of the consistency of jelly. **—*v.t., v.i.*** **3.** to bring or come to the consistency of jelly. **—*adj.*** **4.** containing or made, spread, or topped with jelly: *jelly donuts.* [ME *gely* < OF *gelee* (frozen) jelly < LL **gelāta* frozen, equiv. to L *gel-* freeze + *-āta* -ATE[1]] **—jel′ly·like′,** *adj.*

jel·ly·bean (jel′ē bēn′), *n.* a bean-shaped, usually brightly colored candy with a hard sugar coating and a firm gelatinous filling. [JELLY + BEAN]

jel′ly dough′nut, a raised doughnut filled with jelly or jam.

Jellyfish, Class *Scyphozoa*

jel·ly·fish (jel′ē fish′), *n., pl.* (*esp. collectively*) **-fish,** (*esp. referring to two or more kinds or species*) **-fish·es.**

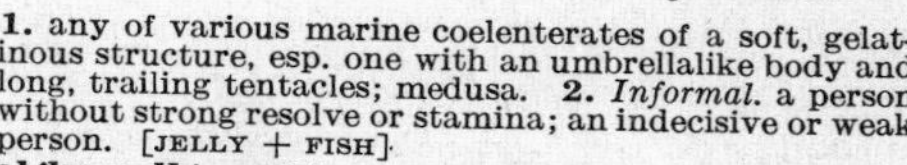

1. any of various marine coelenterates of a soft, gelatinous structure, esp. one with an umbrellalike body and long, trailing tentacles; medusa. **2.** *Informal.* a person without strong resolve or stamina; an indecisive or weak person. [JELLY + FISH]

jel′ly roll′, a thin, rectangular layer of sponge cake, spread with fruit jelly and rolled up.

jem·a·dar (jem′ə där′), *n.* (in India) **1.** any of various government officials. **2.** the supervisor of a staff of servants. **3.** a native officer in a sepoy regiment, corresponding in rank to a lieutenant. [< Urdu *jamadar*, var. of *jamdar* < Pers < Ar *jam'* aggregation (of men) + Pers *dār* holding, leader of]

Je·mappes (zhə map′), *n.* a town in SW Belgium, near Mons: French victory over Austrians 1792. 12,766 (est. 1964).

Je·mi·ma (jə mī′mə), *n.* a girl's given name.

jem·my (jem′ē), *v.,* **-mied, -my·ing,** *n., pl.* **-mies.** *Brit.* **—*v.t.*** **1.** jimmy[1]. **—*n.*** **2.** jimmy[1]. **3.** *Slang.* an overcoat. **4.** the baked head of a sheep.

jen (zhun, run), *n.* (in Chinese philosophy) a compassionate love for humanity or for the world as a whole. [< Chin (Peking)]

Je·na (yā′nä), *n.* a city in S East Germany: Napoleon decisively defeated the Prussians here in 1806. 83,073 (est. 1955).

je ne sais quoi (zhənə se kwa′), *French.* an indefinable, elusive quality, esp. a pleasing one: *She has a certain* je ne sais quoi *that charms everybody.* [lit., I don't know what]

Jen·ghis Khan (jen′giz kän′, jeng′-). See **Genghis Khan.** Also, **Jen′ghiz Khan′.**

Jen·ice (jen′is), *n.* a girl's given name, form of **Janice.**

Jen·kins (jeng′kins), *n.* a town in SE Kentucky. 3202 (1960).

Jen·kin·son (jeng′kin sən), *n.* **Robert Banks, 2nd Earl of Liverpool,** 1770–1828, British statesman: prime minister 1812–27.

Jen·kin·town (jeng′kin toun′), *n.* a town in SE Pennsylvania. 5017 (1960).

jên-min-piao (zhun′men′pyou′, run′-), *n., pl.* **jên-min-piao.** the monetary unit of China, equal to 10 chiao or 100 fen, and equivalent to about .41 of a U.S. dollar. *Abbr.:* JMP Also, **jên-min-pi** (zhun′men′pē′, run′-). [< Chin]

Jen·ne (jen′ē), *n.* a girl's given name, form of **Jennifer.** Also, **Jen′nie, Jenny.**

Jen·ner (jen′ər), *n.* **1. Edward,** 1749–1823, English physician: discoverer of smallpox vaccine. **2. Sir William,** 1815–98, English physician and pathologist.

jen·net (jen′it), *n.* **1.** a small Spanish horse. **2.** a female ass or donkey. Also, **genet.** [late ME < MF *genet* < Catalan, var. of *ginet* horse of the Zenete kind < Ar *zinētī*, dial. var. of *zanātī* pertaining to the Zenete tribe (of Moors) after *Zanātah* the Zenetes]

Jen·ni·fer (jen′ə fər), *n.* a girl's given name, form of **Guinevere.**

Jen·nings (jen′ingz), *n.* a city in E Missouri, near St. Louis. 19,965 (1960).

jen·ny[1] (jen′ē), *n., pl.* **-nies. 1.** See **spinning jenny. 2.** the female of certain animals, esp. a female donkey or a female bird: *a jenny wren.* [special use of JENNY]

jen·ny[2] (jen′ē), *n., pl.* **-nies.** *Naut. Slang.* genoa. Also, **jen′nie.** [by alter.]

Jen·ny (jen′ē) *n.* a girl's given name, form of **Jennifer.** Also, **Jenne, Jennie.**

jen′ny yard′, *Naut.* jackyard.

Jen·seits von Gut und Bö·se (*Ger.* yen′zīts gʏ′tə o͝ont bœ′zə). See **Beyond Good and Evil.**

Jen·sen (yen′zən *for 1;* yen′sən *for 2*), *n.* **1. J. Hans D.** (häns), born 1907, German physicist: Nobel prize 1963. **2. Jo·han·nes Vil·helm** (yō hä′nəs vil′helm), 1873–1950, Danish poet and novelist: Nobel prize 1944.

Je·nů·fa (yā′no͞o fə), *n.* an opera (1904) by Leoš Janáček.

jeop·ard·ise (jep′ər dīz′), *v.t.,* **-ised, -is·ing.** *Chiefly Brit.* jeopardize.

jeop·ard·ize (jep′ər dīz′), *v.t.,* **-ized, -iz·ing.** to put in jeopardy; hazard; risk; imperil: *He jeopardized his life every time he dived from the tower.* Also, **jeop′ard.** [JEOPARD(Y) + -IZE]

jeop·ard·ous (jep′ər dəs), *adj.* perilous; hazardous; risky. [late ME *jeopartous*, equiv. to *j(e)upart(i)* (see JEOPARDY) + *-ous* -OUS] **—jeop′ard·ous·ly,** *adv.* **—jeop′ard·ous·ness,** *n.*
—Syn. dangerous.

jeop·ard·y (jep′ər dē), *n., pl.* **-dies. 1.** hazard or risk of or exposure to loss, harm, death, or injury: *For a moment his life was in jeopardy.* **2.** peril or danger: *The spy was in jeopardy of being discovered.* **3.** *Law.* the danger or hazard of being found guilty, and of consequent punishment, undergone by criminal defendants on trial. [ME *j(e)uparti*, etc. < AF, OF: lit., divided game or play, hence, uncertain chance, problem (in chess or love), equiv. to *j(e)u* play, game (< L *jocus* JOKE) + *parti*, ptp. of *partir* to divide; see PARTY]
—Syn. 1, 2. See **danger. —Ant. 1, 2.** security.

Jeph·thah (jef′thə), *n.* **1.** Also, *Douay Bible,* **Jeph·te** (jef′tə). a judge of Israel. Judges 11, 12. **2.** a boy's given name.

Je·quié (zhə kye′), *n.* a city in E Brazil. 50,484 (1960).

je·quir·i·ty (jə kwir′i tē), *n., pl.* **-ties. 1.** the Indian licorice, *Abrus precatorius.* **2.** Also called **jequir′ity beans′.** the seeds of this plant. [< Pg *jequiriti* < Tupi-Guarani *jekiritī*; cf. F *jéquirity* (< E)]

jer (yer), *n.* **1.** *Slavic Ling.* either of two letters (Ъ, Ь) of the Cyrillic alphabet used, as in Old Church Slavonic, to indicate two short vowels, or, as in Russian, to indicate that the preceding consonant is hard or soft. Cf. **hard sign, soft sign. 2.** either of the very short vowels represented by these signs, being front jer (Ь, usually transcribed as ĭ) and back jer (Ъ, usually transcribed as ŭ).

Jer., 1. *Bible.* Jeremiah. **2.** Jersey.

Je·rash (jer′äsh), *n.* a town in N Jordan, N of Amman: Roman ruins. 4018 (1962). Also, **Jarash.**

Jer·ba (jer′bə), *n.* Djerba.

jer·bo·a (jər bō′ə), *n.* any of various mouselike rodents of North Africa and Asia, as of the genera *Jaculus, Dipus,* etc., with long hind legs used for jumping. [< NL < Ar *yarbū'*]

je·reed (jə rēd′), *n.* a blunt wooden javelin used in games by horsemen in certain Muslim countries in the Middle East. Also, **jerid, jerreed, jerrid.** [< Ar *jarīd* rod, shaft]

Jerboa, *Jaculus jaculus* (Total length 13 in.; tail 8 in.)

jer·e·mi·ad (jer′ə mī′ad), *n.* a lamentation; mournful complaint. [JEREMI(AH) + -AD]

Jer·e·mi·ah (jer′ə mī′ə), *n.* **1.** a Major Prophet of the 6th and 7th centuries B.C. **2.** a book of the Bible bearing his name. **3.** a boy's given name. Also, *Douay Bible,* **Jer·e·mi·as** (jer′ə mī′əs) (for defs. 1, 2). —**Jer′e·mi′an, Jer·e·mi·an·ic** (jer′ə mī an′ik), *adj.*

Jé·ré·mie (zhā rā mē′), *n.* a seaport in SW Haiti. 12,012 (est. 1957).

Jer·e·my (jer′ə mē), *n.* a boy's given name, form of **Jeremiah.**

Je·rez (he reth′, -res′), *n.* **1.** Also called **Jerez′ de la Fron·te′ra** (de lä frôn te′rä). Formerly, **Xeres.** a city in SW Spain: noted for its sherry. 119,342 (est. 1957). —*adj.* **2.** pertaining to, characteristic of, resembling, or noting sherry from Jerez.

Jer·i (jer′ē), *n.* a girl's given name, form of **Geraldine.** Also, **Jer′re, Jerri, Jerrie, Jerry.**

Jer·i·cho (jer′ə kō′), *n.* an ancient city of Palestine, N of the Dead Sea.

je·rid (jə rēd′), *n.* jereed.

Jer·is (jer′is), *n.* a boy's given name.

Je·ri·tza (ye′rē tsä′), *n.* **Ma·ri·a** (mä rē′ä), 1887–1982, Austrian operatic soprano.

jerk[1] (jûrk), *n.* **1.** a quick, sharp pull, thrust, twist, throw, or the like; a sudden start: *The train started with a jerk.* **2.** a spasmodic, usually involuntary, muscular movement, as the reflex action of pulling the hand away from a flame. **3.** any sudden, quick movement of the body, as in dodging something. **4.** *Slang.* a naïve, fatuous, or foolishly inconsequential person. **5.** (in weight lifting) the raising of a weight from shoulder height to above the head by straightening the arms. **6. jerks,** *Brit. Informal.* See **physical jerks. 7.** a dance, deriving from the twist, in which the dancers alternately thrust out their pelvises and their shoulders. **8. the jerks,** *U.S.* paroxysms or violent spasmodic muscular movements, as resulting from excitement evoked by some religious services. —*v.t.* **9.** to pull, twist, move, thrust, or throw with a quick, suddenly arrested motion: *She jerked the child by the hand.* **10.** to utter in a broken, spasmodic way. **11.** to draw (water or the like) from a source. **12.** *Informal.* to prepare, dispense, and serve (sodas, ice cream, etc.) at a soda fountain. —*v.i.* **13.** to give a jerk or jerks. **14.** to move with a quick, sharp motion; move spasmodically. **15.** to talk in a broken, spasmodic way: *She jerked along through her story.* **16.** *Informal.* to work as a soda jerk. **17.** to dance the jerk. [? dial. var. of *yerk* to draw stitches tight (shoemaker's term), thus making the shoe ready to wear, OE *gearc(ian)* (to) prepare, make ready] —**jerk′er,** *n.* —**jerk′ing·ly,** *adv.*

jerk[2] (jûrk), *v.t.* **1.** to preserve meat, esp. beef (**jerked′ beef′**), by cutting in strips and curing by drying in the sun. —*n.* **2.** jerky[2]. [back formation from JERKY[2]]

jer·kin (jûr′kin), *n.* a close-fitting jacket or short coat, as one of leather worn in the 16th and 17th centuries. [?]

jer·kin·head (jûr′kin hed′), *n.* a roof having a hipped end truncating a gable. Also called **shreadhead.** [?]

Jerkin

jerk·wa·ter (jûrk′wô′tər, -wot′ər), *Informal.* —*n.* **1.** a train not running on the main line. —*adj.* **2.** off the main line: *a jerkwater train.* **3.** ridiculously insignificant and out-of-the-way: *a jerkwater town.* [JERK[1] + WATER; so called from the jerking (i.e., drawing) of water to fill buckets for supplying a steam locomotive that has run short]

jerk·y[1] (jûr′kē), *adj.,* **jerk·i·er, jerk·i·est. 1.** characterized by jerks or sudden starts; spasmodic. **2.** *Slang.* silly; foolish; ridiculous. [JERK[1] + -Y[1]] —**jerk′i·ly,** *adv.* —**jerk′i·ness,** *n.*

jerk·y[2] (jûr′kē), *n.* meat, esp. beef, that has been jerked. Also, **jerk.** [popular alter. of CHARQUI]

Jer·myn (jûr′min), *n.* a town in NE Pennsylvania. 2568 (1960).

Jer·o·bo·am (jer′ə bō′əm), *n.* **1.** the first king of the Biblical kingdom of the Hebrews in N Palestine. **2.** (*l.c.*) a wine bottle having a capacity of about 4/5 gal.

Jer·old (jer′əld), *n.* a boy's given name, form of **Gerald.** Also, **Jer′rold.**

Je·rome (jə rōm′; *for 1 also* jer′əm), *n.* **1. Saint** (*Eusebius Hieronymus*), A.D. c340–420, Christian ascetic and biblical scholar: chief preparer of the Vulgate version of the Bible. **2. Jerome K(lap·ka)** (klap′kə), 1859–1927, English humorist and playwright. **3.** a town in S Idaho. 4761 (1960). **4.** a boy's given name.

Jer·o·ni·ma (jer′ə nē′mə), *n.* a girl's given name.

jer·reed (jə rēd′), *n.* jereed. Also, **jer·rid′.**

Jer·rie (jer′ē), *n.* a girl's given name, form of **Geraldine.** Also, **Jeri, Jer′re, Jer′ri, Jerry.**

jer·ry (jer′ē), *adj. Building Trades Slang.* of inferior materials or workmanship. [short for JERRY-BUILT]

Jer·ry (jer′ē), *n., pl.* **-ries.** *Chiefly Brit. Informal.* **1.** a German. **2.** Germans collectively. [GER(MAN) + -Y[1]]

Jer·ry (jer′ē), *n., pl.* **-ries.** (*often l.c.*) *Slang.* See **chamber pot.** [short for JEROBOAM]

Jer·ry (jer′ē), *n.* **1.** a boy's given name, form of **Gerald, Gerard, Jeremiah,** and **Jerome. 2.** Also, **Jeri, Jerre, Jerri, Jerrie.** a girl's given name, form of **Geraldine.**

jer·ry-build (jer′ē bild′), *v.t.,* **-built, -build·ing.** to build cheaply and flimsily. [back formation from *jerry-builder.* See JERRY (chamber pot), BUILD] —**jer′ry-build′er,** *n.*

jer·ry-built (jer′ē bilt′), *adj.* **1.** built cheaply and flimsily. **2.** contrived or developed in a haphazard, unsubstantial fashion, as a project, organization, etc. [*jerry* (as in JERRY-BUILD) + BUILT]

jer′ry can′, 1. Also called **blitz can.** *Mil.* a narrow, flat-sided, five-gallon container for fluids, as fuel. **2.** *Brit.* a can with a capacity of 4½ imperial gallons. Also, **jer′ry·can′.** [*jerry,* short for JEROBOAM]

jer·sey (jûr′zē), *n., pl.* **-seys. 1.** a close-fitting, knitted sweater or shirt, worn by seamen, athletes, etc. **2.** a similar knitted garment of wool, silk, or the like, worn by women. **3.** (*cap.*) one of a breed of dairy cattle, raised originally on the island of Jersey, producing milk having a high content of butterfat. **4.** See **jersey cloth.** [after JERSEY] —**jer′seyed,** *adj.*

Jer·sey (jûr′zē), *n.* **1.** a British island in the English Channel: the largest of the Channel Islands. 57,200 (1961); 45 sq. mi. *Cap.:* St. Helier. **2.** See **New Jersey.** —**Jer′sey·an,** *n., adj.* —**Jer′sey·ite′,** *n.*

Jer′sey Cit′y, a seaport in NE New Jersey, opposite New York City. 276,101 (1960).

jer′sey cloth′, a machine-knitted or machine-woven fabric of wool, nylon, rayon, silk, etc., used for garments. Also called **jersey.**

Jer′sey Shore′, a town in central Pennsylvania. 5613 (1960).

Jer·sey·ville (jûr′zē vil), *n.* a town in W Illinois. 7420 (1960).

Jer·ub·baal (jer′ə bāl′), *n.* Gideon (def. 1).

Je·ru·sa·lem (ji rōō′sə ləm), *n.* a city in Israel: an ancient holy city; the principal city of Palestine; a center of pilgrimage for Jews, Christians, and Muslims; divided between Israel and Jordan 1948 and unified by Israeli occupation in 1967; the capital of Israel since 1950. 355,500. —**Je·ru′sa·lem·ite′,** *adj., n.*

Jeru′salem ar′tichoke, 1. a sunflower, *Helianthus tuberosus,* having edible, tuberous, underground stems or rootstocks. **2.** the tuber itself. Also called **Canada potato.** [popular alter. of It *girasole articiocco* edible sunflower. See GIRASOL, ARTICHOKE]

Jeru′salem cher′ry, an Old World, solanaceous plant, *Solanum Pseudo-Capsicum,* having white flowers and bearing round, scarlet or yellow fruits, cultivated as an ornamental.

Jeru′salem cross′, 1. a cross whose four arms are each capped with a crossbar. See illus. under **cross. 2.** See **scarlet lychnis.**

Jeru′salem date′, butterfly-flower.

Jeru′salem Deliv′ered, an epic poem (1581) by Tasso. Italian, **Gerusalemme Liberata.**

Jeru′salem oak′. See **feather geranium.**

Jeru′salem sage′, a perennial herb, *Phlomis fruticosa,* of southern Europe, having yellowish, hairy branches and numerous yellow flowers.

Jer·vis (jûr′vis), *n.* a boy's given name.

Jes·per·sen (yes′pər sən, jes′-), *n.* **(Jens) Ot·to (Har·ry)** (yens ot′ō här′ē), 1860–1943, Danish philologist.

jess (jes), *Falconry.* —*n.* **1.** a short strap fastened round the leg of a hawk and attached to the leash. —*v.t.* **2.** to put jesses on (a hawk). Also, *esp. Brit.,* **jesse.** [ME *ges* < OF *ges, gez, getz* (nom.) (*get* acc. < F *jet* JET[1]) << L *jact(us)* a throwing, n. use of *jactus* (ptp. of *jacere* to throw), equiv. to *jac-* + *-tus* ptp. suffix]

Jess (jes), *n.* a boy's given name, form of **Jesse** or **Jessie.**

jes·sa·mine (jes′ə min), *n.* jasmine.

Jes·sa·myn (jes′ə min), *n.* a girl's given name, form of **Jasmine.** Also, **Jes·mine** (jez′min), **Jes′sa·mine.**

jes·sant (jes′ənt), *adj. Heraldry.* **1.** shooting up, as a plant. **2.** coming forth; issuant. [< MF *gesant* (prp. of *gesir* << L *jacēre* to lie), equiv. to *ges-* lie + *-ant* -ANT]

jesse (jes), *n., v.t.,* **jessed, jess·ing.** *Chiefly Brit.* jess.

Jes·se (jes′ē), *n.* **1.** Also, *Douay Bible,* **Isai.** the father of David. I Sam. 16. **2.** Also, **Jessie.** a boy's given name.

Jes·sel·ton (jes′əl tən), *n.* a seaport in NW Sabah, in Malaysia: the capital of the former British North Borneo. 15,500 (est. 1957).

Jes′se tree′. See **tree of Jesse.**

Jes′se win′dow, a church window having a representation of the tree of Jesse.

Jes·si·ca (jes′ə kə), *n.* a girl's given name, form of **Johanna.**

Jes·sie (jes′ē), *n.* **1.** a girl's given name, form of **Jessica. 2.** Also, **Jesse.** a boy's given name. Also, **Jes′sy.**

jest (jest), *n.* **1.** a joke or witty remark; witticism. **2.** a bantering remark; a piece of good-natured ridicule. **3.** sport or fun: *to speak half in jest, half in earnest.* **4.** the object of laughter, sport, or mockery; laughingstock. **5.** *Obs.* an exploit. Cf. **gest**[1]. —*v.i.* **6.** to speak in a playful, humorous, or facetious way; joke. **7.** to speak or act in mere sport, rather than in earnest; trifle (often fol. by *with*): *Please don't jest with me.* **8.** to utter derisive speeches; gibe or scoff. —*v.t.* **9.** to deride or joke at; banter. [var. sp. of GEST[1]] —**jest′ful,** *adj.* —**Syn. 1.** quip. See **joke. 2.** jape, gibe. **4.** butt.

jest·book (jest′bŏŏk′), *n.* a book of jests or jokes.

jest·er (jes′tər), *n.* **1.** a person who is given to witticisms, jokes, and pranks. **2.** a professional fool or clown, kept by a prince or noble, esp. during the Middle Ages. [ME *gester.* See GEST[1], -ER[1]]

jest·ing (jes′ting), *adj.* **1.** given to making jests; playful. **2.** fit for joking; unimportant; trivial: *This is no jesting matter.* —*n.* **3.** pleasantry; triviality. [JEST + -ING[2], -ING[1]] —**jest′ing·ly,** *adv.*

Je·su (jē′zōō, -sōō, jā′-, yā′-), *n. Literary.* Jesus. [< L, obl. (usually voc.) form of JESUS]

Jes·u·it (jezh′ōō it, jez′yōō-, jez′ōō-), *n.* **1.** a member of a Roman Catholic religious order (**Society of Jesus**) founded by Ignatius Loyola in 1534. **2.** (*usually l.c.*) *Offensive.* a crafty, intriguing, or equivocating person: so called in allusion to the methods ascribed to the order by its opponents. —*adj.* **3.** Also, **Jes′u·it′ic, Jes′u·it′i·cal, Jes′u·it·ist.** of or pertaining to Jesuits or Jesuitism. [< NL *Jēsuit(a),* equiv. to L *Jēsu(s)* + *-ita* -ITE[1]] —**Jes′u·it′i·cal·ly,** *adv.*

Jes·u·it·ise (jezh′ōō i tīz′, jez′yōō-, jez′ōō-), *v.t., v.i.,* **-ised, -is·ing.** *Chiefly Brit.* Jesuitize. —**Jes′u·it·i·sa′tion,** *n.*

Jes·u·it·ism (jezh′ōō i tiz′əm, jez′yōō-, jez′ōō-), *n.* **1.** the system, principles, or practices of the Jesuits. **2.** (*usually l.c.*) *Disparaging.* an unethical principle or practice, such as casuistry or equivocation, ascribed to the Jesuits by their opponents. Also, **Jes′u·it·ry.** [JESUIT + -ISM]

Jes·u·it·ize (jezh′ōō i tīz′, jez′yōō-, jez′ōō-), *v.t., v.i.,* **-ized, -iz·ing.** to make Jesuit or to become a Jesuit. Also, *esp. Brit.,* **Jesuitise.** [JESUIT + -IZE] —**Jes′u·it·i·za′tion,** *n.*

Jes′uits′ res′in, copaiba.

Jes′uit ware′, Chinese porcelain of the early 18th century, decorated with Christian motifs, usually in black and gold on a white background.

Jes·up (jes′əp), *n.* a town in SE Georgia. 7304 (1960).

Je·sus (jē′zəs), *n.* **1.** Also called **Jesus Christ, Christ Jesus, Je′sus of Naz′areth.** born 4? B.C., crucified A.D. 29?, the founder of the Christian religion. **2.** ("*the Son of Sirach*") the author of the Apocryphal book of Ecclesiasticus, who lived in the 3rd century B.C. **3.** *Christian Science.* the highest human example of God's nature expressed through man. **4.** Also, **Je·sús** (*Sp.* he sōōs′). a boy's given name. —*interj.* **5.** (used as an oath or strong expression of disbelief, dismay, awe, disappointment, pain, or the like.) [ME, OE < LL < Gk *Iēsoûs* < Heb *Yēshūa'*, syncopated var. of *Yehōshūa'* God is help]

Je′sus Christ′, 1. Jesus (def. 1). **2.** Jesus (def. 5).

jet[1] (jet), *n., v.,* **jet·ted, jet·ting,** *adj.* —*n.* **1.** a free or submerged stream of a liquid, gas, or small solid particles forcefully shooting forth from a nozzle, orifice, etc. **2.** something that issues in such a stream, as water or gas. **3.** a spout or nozzle for emitting liquid or gas: *a gas jet.* **4.** See **jet plane. 5.** See **jet engine.** —*v.t.* **6.** to shoot (something) forth in a stream; spout. **7.** to place (a pile or the like) by eroding the ground beneath it with a jet of water or of water and compressed air. —*v.i.* **8.** to be shot forth in a stream. **9.** to move or travel by means of jet propulsion: *The octopus jetted away from danger.* **10.** to travel by or as by jet plane: *to jet to Las Vegas for the weekend.* **11.** to move or travel rapidly: *The star halfback jetted toward the goal line.* —*adj.* **12.** of, pertaining to, associated with, or noting a jet, jet engine, or jet plane: *jet pilot; jet exhaust.* **13.** in the form of or producing a jet or jet propulsion: *jet nozzle; jet engine.* **14.** by means of a jet airplane: *a jet trip; jet transportation.* [< MF *jet(er)* (to) throw < LL **jectāre,* alter. of L *jactāre,* equiv. to *jac-* throw + *t-* freq. suffix + *-āre* inf. suffix] —**jet′ting·ly,** *adv.*

jet[2] (jet), *n.* **1.** a compact black coal, susceptible of a high polish, used for making beads, jewelry, buttons, etc. **2.** a deep glossy black. **3.** *Obs.* black marble. —*adj.* **4.** consisting or made of jet. **5.** of the color jet; black as jet. [ME *jet, get* < OF *jaiet* << L *gagāt(ēs)* < Gk (*líthos*) *gagátēs* Gagatic (stone), named after *Gágai,* town in Lycia; r. OE *gagāt-stān* jet stone]

jet·a·va·tor (jet′ə vā′tər), *n. Rocketry.* an extension of the exhaust nozzle of a rocket, for controlling the direction of the exhaust gases. [JET[1] + (EL)EVATOR]

jet-black (jet′blak′), *adj.* deep-black: *jet-black hair.*

jet′ condens′er, a steam condenser in which a jet of water is sprayed into the condenser chamber.

je·té (zhə tā′), *n., pl.* **-tés** (-tāz′; *Fr.* -tā′). *Ballet.* a jump forward, backward, or to the side, from one foot to the other. [< F: lit., thrown, ptp. of *jeter* to throw; see JET[1]]

jet′-e·nam·elled ware′ (jet′i nam′əld), English Worcester porcelain ware of the 18th century, transfer-printed in black.

jet′ en′gine, an engine, esp. an aircraft engine, that produces forward motion by the rearward exhaust of a jet of fluid or heated air and gases. Also called **jet′ mo′tor.**

Jeth·ra (jeth′rə), *n.* a girl's given name.

Jeth·ro (jeth′rō), *n.* **1.** the father-in-law of Moses. Ex. 3:1. **2.** a boy's given name.

jet·lin·er (jet′lī′nər), *n.* a commercial jet plane. [JET[1] + (AIR)LINER]

jet′ plane′, an airplane moved by jet propulsion.

jet·port (jet′pôrt′, -pōrt′), *n.* an airport for jet airplanes. [JET[1] + PORT[1]]

jet-pro·pelled (jet′prə peld′), *adj.* **1.** propelled by a jet engine or engines. **2.** having a force or speed suggesting something propelled by a jet engine; fast or powerful.

jet′ propul′sion, the propulsion of a body by its reaction to a force ejecting a gas or a liquid from it. —**jet′-pro·pul′sion,** *adj.*

jet·sam (jet′səm), *n.* goods cast overboard deliberately, as to lighten a vessel or improve its stability in an emergency, which sink where jettisoned or are washed ashore. Also, **jet′som.** Cf. **flotsam, lagan.** [alter. of *jetson,* syncopated var. of JETTISON]

jet′ set′, an ultrafashionable social set composed of people who are reputed to spend much of their leisure time in intercontinental travel from resort to resort by jetliner.

jet′ stream′, 1. strong, generally westerly winds concentrated in a relatively narrow and shallow stream in the upper troposphere. **2.** the exhaust of a rocket engine.

Jet·tie (jet′ē), *n.* a girl's given name.

jet·ti·son (jet′i sən, -zən), *n.* **1.** the act of casting goods overboard to lighten a vessel or aircraft or to improve its stability in an emergency. **2.** jetsam. —*v.t.* **3.** to cast (goods) overboard in order to lighten a vessel or aircraft or to improve its stability in an emergency. **4.** to throw off (an obstacle or burden). **5.** *Cards Slang.* to discard (an unwanted card or cards). [ME *jetteson* < AF; OF *getaison* << L *jactātiōn-* (s. of *jactātiō*) JACTATION] —**jet′ti·son·a·ble,** *adj.*

jet·ton (jet′ən), *n.* an inscribed counter or token. [< F *jeton,* equiv. to *jet(er)* (to) throw, cast up (accounts) reckon (see JET[1]) + *-on* n. suffix]

jet·ty[1] (jet′ē), *n., pl.* **-ties,** *v.,* **-tied, -ty·ing.** —*n.* **1.** a pier or structure of stones, piles, or the like, projecting into the sea or other body of water to protect a harbor, deflect the current, etc. **2.** a wharf or landing pier. **3.** the piles or wooden structure protecting a pier. **4.** Also, **jutty.** *Archit.* an overhang, as of an upper story beyond a lower. —*v.t.* **5.** to construct (part of a building) so that it projects beyond lower construction: **jutty.**

CONCISE ETYMOLOGY KEY: <, descended or derived from; >, whence; b., blend of, blended; c., cognate with; deriv., derivative; equiv., equivalent; imit., imitative; m., modification of; obl., oblique; r., replacing; s., stem; sp., spelling; translation; ?, origin unknown, perhaps; *, hypothetical. See the full key inside the front cover.

[ME *get(t)ey* < OF *jetee*, lit., something thrown out, a projection, n. use of *jetee*, fem. ptp. of *jeter* to throw; see JET[1]]

jet·ty[2] (jet′ē), *adj.* **1.** made of jet. **2.** resembling jet, esp. in color; of a deep, glossy black. [JET[2] + -Y[1]] **—jet′ti·ness,** *n.*

jet′ wash′, *Aeron.* the backwash caused by a jet engine.

jeu (zhœ), *n., pl.* **jeux** (zhœ). *French.* a game.

jeu de mots (zhœdᵊ mō′), *pl.* **jeux de mots** (zhœdᵊ mō′). *French.* a pun. [lit., play of words]

jeu d'es·prit (zhœ des prē′), *pl.* **jeux d'es·prit** (zhœ des prē′). *French.* **1.** a witticism. **2.** a literary work showing keen wit or intelligence rather than profundity. [lit., play of spirit]

jeune fille (zhœn fē′yᵊ), *pl.* **jeunes filles** (zhœn fē′yᵊ). *French.* a young, unmarried girl.

jeune pre·mier (*Fr.* zhœn prə myā′), *pl.* **jeunes pre·miers** (*Fr.* zhœn prə myā′). *Theat.* **1.** the juvenile lead in a play. **2.** an actor who plays such a role. [< F: lit., young first (actor)]

jeune pre·mière (*Fr.* zhœn prə myer′), *pl.* **jeunes pre·mières** (*Fr.* zhœn prə myer′). *Theat.* a young actress who is the juvenile lead in a play. [< F: lit., young first (actress)]

jeu·nesse do·rée (zhœ nes′ dô rā′), *French.* wealthy, stylish, sophisticated young people. [lit., gilded youth]

Jev·ons (jev′ənz), *n.* **William Stanley,** 1835–82, English economist and logician.

Jew (jōō), *n.* **1.** a person whose religion is Judaism. **2.** one of a scattered group of people that traces its descent from the Biblical Hebrews or from postexilic adherents of Judaism; Israelite. **3.** a subject of the ancient kingdom of Israel. **—*adj.*** **4.** *Offensive.* of Jews; Jewish. **—*v.t.*** **5.** (*l.c.*) *Offensive.* to bargain sharply with; beat down in price (often fol. by *down*). [ME *jewe, giu, gyu, ju* OF *juiu, juieu, gyu* < LL *jūdē(us),* L *jūdaeus* < Gk *ioudaîos* < Aram *yehūdāi*, c. Heb *yehūdī* Jew, deriv. of *yehūdāh* JUDAH; r. OE *iūdēas* Jews < LL *jūdē(us)* + OE *-as* pl. ending]

Jew., Jewish.

Jew-bait·ing (jōō′bā′ting), *n.* active anti-Semitism. **—Jew′-bait′er,** *n.*

jew·el (jōō′əl), *n., v.,* **-eled, -el·ing** or (*esp. Brit.*) **-elled, -el·ling.** **—*n.*** **1.** a cut and polished precious stone; gem. **2.** a fashioned ornament for personal adornment, esp. of a precious metal set with gems. **3.** a precious possession. **4.** *Informal.* a person of great worth or rare excellence: *She's a little jewel, so good, so kind.* **5.** a durable bearing used in fine timepieces and other delicate instruments, made of natural or synthetic precious stone or other very hard material. **6.** an ornamental boss of glass, sometimes cut with facets, in stained-glass work. **7.** something resembling a jewel in appearance, ornamental effect, or the like, as a star, dewdrop, etc. **—*v.t.*** **8.** to set or adorn with jewels. [ME *jouel juel* < AF *jeul*, OF *jouel, joel* < VL **jocāle* plaything, n. use of neut. of **jocālis* (adj.) of play, equiv. to L *joc(us)* JOKE + *-ālis* AL[1]] **—jew′el·like′,** *adj.*

Jew·el (jōō′əl), *n.* a girl's given name.

jew′el block′, *Naut.* a block at the end of a yard or gaff for supporting a signal or ensign halyard. Also called **dasher block.**

jew′el case′, a box or small chest, often lined in a soft fabric and fitted with compartments, designed for holding jewelry. Also called **jew′el box′.**

jew·el·er (jōō′ə lər), *n.* one who designs, makes, sells, or repairs jewelry, watches, etc.; one who deals in jewels. Also, *esp. Brit.,* **jew′el·ler.** [ME *jueler* < AF *jueler*, MF *juelier.* See JEWEL, -ER[2]]

jew′elers' put′ty. See **putty powder.**

jew′elers' rouge′, colcothar.

jew·el·fish (jōō′əl fish′), *n., pl.* **-fish·es,** (*esp. collectively*) **-fish.** a brightly-colored cichlid fish, *Hemichromis bimaculatus*, found in Africa, often kept in aquariums. [JEWEL + FISH]

jew·el·ry (jōō′əl rē), *n.* **1.** a number of articles of gold, silver, precious stones, etc., for personal adornment. **2.** any ornament for personal adornment, as a necklace, cufflinks, etc., including those of base metals, glass, plastic, or the like. Also, *esp. Brit.,* **jew′el·ler·y.** [ME *jueirie* < OF *juelerie*, equiv. to *juel* JEWEL + *-erie* -ERY]

jew·el·weed (jōō′əl wēd′), *n.* any of several plants of the genus *Impatiens*, esp. *I. biflora*, having orange-yellow flowers spotted with reddish brown, or *I. pallida*, having yellow flowers sometimes spotted with brownish red. Cf. **touch-me-not.** [JEWEL + WEED[1]]

Jew·ess (jōō′is), *n.* *Often Offensive.* a Jewish girl or woman. [ME *jewesse.* See JEW, -ESS]

Jew·ett (jōō′it), *n.* **Sarah Orne** (ôrn), 1849–1909, U.S. short-story writer and novelist.

Jew′ett Cit′y, a town in SE Connecticut. 3608 (1960).

jew·fish (jōō′fish′), *n., pl.,* (*esp. collectively*) **-fish,** (*esp. referring to two or more kinds or species*) **-fish·es.** any of several very large fishes, esp. of the family *Serranidae*, as the giant sea bass and the groupers *Epinephelus itajara* and *E. nigritus*, found in the tropical Atlantic Ocean. [? JEW + FISH]

Jew·ish (jōō′ish), *adj.* **1.** of, pertaining to, characteristic of, or noting the Jews: *Jewish customs.* **2.** Yiddish: *the Jewish language.* **—*n.*** **3.** *Informal.* Yiddish. [JEW + -ISH[1]; r. OE *iūdēisc* < LL *iūdē(us)* Jew + OE *-isc* -ish] **—Jew′ish·ly,** *adv.* **—Jew′ish·ness,** *n.*

Jew′ish Auton′omous Re′gion, an autonomous region in the Khabarovsk territory of the Russian Federation in E Siberia. 216,000; 13,900 sq. mi. *Cap.:* Birobidzhan.

Jew′ish cal′endar, the lunisolar calendar used by Jews, as for determining religious holidays, that is reckoned from 3761 B.C. and was established by Hillel II in the 4th century A.D., the calendar year consisting of 353 days **(defective year),** 354 days **(regular year),** or 355 days **(perfect** or **abundant year)** and containing 12 months: Tishri, Heshvan, Kislev, Tebet, Shebat, Adar, Nisan, Iyar, Sivan, Tammuz, Ab, and Elul, with the 29-day intercalary month of Veadar added 7 times in every 19-year cycle in order to adjust the calendar to the solar cycle. The Jewish ecclesiastical year begins with Nisan and the civil year with Tishri. Also called **Hebrew calendar.**

Jew·ish·ness (jōō′ish nis), *n.* the state or quality of being Jewish. [JEWISH + -NESS]

Jew′ of Mal′ta, The, a blank-verse drama (1592?) by Christopher Marlowe.

Jew·ry (jōō′rē), *n., pl.* **-ries.** **1.** the Jewish people collectively. **2.** a district inhabited mainly by Jews; ghetto. **3.** *Archaic.* Judea. [ME *jewerie* < AF *juerie* (OF *juierie*), equiv. to *ju* JEW + *-erie* -ERY]

Jew's-harp (Length about 3 in.)

jew's-harp (jōōz′härp′), *n.* **1.** a small, simple musical instrument consisting of a lyre-shaped metal frame containing a metal tongue, which is plucked while the frame is held in the teeth. **2.** See **nodding trillium.** Also, **jews'-harp′.** [? jocular; earlier called *Jew's trump*]

Jez·e·bel (jez′ə bel′, -bəl), *n.* **1.** Also, *Douay Bible,* **Jez′a·bel′.** the wife of Ahab, king of Israel. I Kings 16:31. **2.** a wicked, shameless, abandoned woman. **—Jez·e·bel·i·an** (jez′ə bē′lē ən), **Jez·e·bel·ish** (jez′ə bel′ish), *adj.*

Jez·re·el (jez′rē əl, jez rēl′), *n.* **Plain of,** Esdraelon. **—Jez′re·el·ite′,** *n.*

JFK, John Fitzgerald Kennedy.

jg, junior grade. Also, **j.g.**

Jhan·si (jän′sē), *n.* a city in SW Uttar Pradesh, in central India. 140,200 (1961).

Jhe·lum (jā′ləm), *n.* a river in S Asia, flowing from S Kashmir into the Chenab River in Pakistan. 450 mi. long.

JHS, IHS (defs. 1, 2).

JHVH, YHVH. Also, **JHWH** [repr. Heb *J(a)hv(e)h* God]

jib[1] (jib), *n.* *Naut.* **1.** any of various triangular sails set forward of a forestaysail or fore-topmast staysail. Cf. **flying jib, inner jib, outer jib.** **2.** the inner one of two such sails, set inward from a flying jib. **3. cut of one's jib,** *Informal.* one's general appearance or manner of dressing: *I could tell by the cut of his jib that he wasn't the kind of person I'd want to deal with.* **—*adj.*** **4.** of or pertaining to a jib: *jib boom; jib clew.* [?]

jib[2] (jib), *v.i., v.t.,* **jibbed, jib·bing,** *n.* jibe[1]. Also, **jibb.**

jib[3] (jib), *v.,* **jibbed, jib·bing,** *n.* *Chiefly Brit.* **—*v.i.*** **1.** to move restively sidewise or backward instead of forward, as an animal in harness; balk. **2.** to balk at doing something; defer action; procrastinate. **—*n.*** **3.** a horse or other animal that jibs. [? special use of JIB[2]]

jib[4] (jib), *n.* the projecting arm of a crane; the boom of a derrick. [appar. short for GIBBET]

jib·ba (jib′ə), *n.* a long, collarless coat or smock worn by Muslims. Also, **djibbah, jib′bah.** [< EgyptAr *jibbah*, var. of Ar *jubbah*]

jib·ber (jib′ər), *n.* *Chiefly. Brit.* one who or that which jibs. [JIB[3] + -ER[1]]

jib′ber the kib′ber (jib′ər, kib′ər), *Naut. Slang.* to lure a vessel aground in order to plunder it by displaying a bobbing light from the shore, simulating a light on a vessel, to make it appear to the vessel to be wrecked that it has more sea room than it actually does.

jib′ boom′, *Naut.* a spar forming a continuation of a bowsprit. Also, **jib′boom′.**

jib′ cat′, *U.S. Naut.* a catboat with a bowsprit and a jib.

jib′ crane′, a crane having an arm guyed at a fixed angle to the head of a rotating mast.

jib′ door′, a door built flush with a partition, esp. in order to be invisible or inconspicuous.

jibe[1] (jīb), *v.,* **jibed, jib·ing,** *n.* *Naut.* **—*v.i.*** **1.** to shift from one side to the other when running before the wind, as a fore-and-aft sail or its boom. **2.** to alter course so that a fore-and-aft sail shifts in this manner. **—*v.t.*** **3.** to cause to jibe. **—*n.*** **4.** act of jibing. Also, **gibe, gybe, jib.** [var. of *gybe* < D *gijbe(n)*]

jibe[2] (jīb), *v.t., v.i.,* **jibed, jib·ing,** *n.* gibe[1]. **—jib′er,** *n.* **—jib′ing·ly,** *adv.*

jibe[3] (jīb), *v.i.,* **jibed, jib·ing.** to be in harmony or accord with; agree: *The report does not quite jibe with the commissioner's observations.* [?]

jib′ guy′, *Naut.* one of two or more horizontal stays for a jib boom.

jib-head·ed (jib′hed′id), *adj.* *Naut.* **1.** (of a sail) having a pointed head. **2.** (of a rig) having all sails triangular, as a Marconi rig.

jib′ sheet′, *Naut.* either of the sheets of a jib clew.

jib′ stay′, *Naut.* a stay on which a jib is set. Also, **jib′stay′.**

jib′ top′sail, *Naut.* a triangular headsail shaped like a jib but set well above the jib boom. Also called **jib-o-jib** (jib′ə jib′), **jib′ber jib′.**

Ji·bu·ti (jē bōō′tē), *n.* Djibouti.

Jid·da (jid′də), *n.* the seaport of Mecca, in W Saudi Arabia, on the Red Sea. 160,000 (est. 1956). Also, **Jedda.**

jif·fy (jif′ē), *n., pl.* **-fies.** *Informal.* a very short time: *to do something in a jiffy.* [?]

jig[1] (jig), *n., v.,* **jigged, jig·ging.** **—*n.*** **1.** *Mach.* a plate, box, or open frame for holding work and for guiding a machine tool to the work, used esp. for locating and spacing drilled holes; fixture. **2.** *Angling.* any of several devices or lures, esp. a hook or gang of hooks weighted with metal and dressed with hair, feathers, etc., for jerking up and down or for drawing through the water to attract fish. **3.** an apparatus for separating ore from gangue and other materials by shaking in or treating with water. **4.** a cloth-dyeing machine in which the material, guided by rollers, is passed at full width through a dye solution in an open vat. **5.** *Naut.* jigger[1] (def. 2c). **—*v.t.*** **6.** to treat, cut, produce, etc., with a jig. **—*v.i.*** **7.** to use a jig. **8.** to fish with a jig. [var. of GAUGE; cf. *jeg* templet]

jig[2] (jig), *n., v.,* **jigged, jig·ging.** **—*n.*** **1.** a rapid, lively, springy, irregular dance for one or more persons, usually in triple meter. **2.** a piece of music for or in the rhythm of such a dance. **3.** *Obs.* prank; trick. **4. the jig is up,** *Slang.* it is hopeless; no chance remains: *When the burglar heard the police siren, he knew the jig was up.* **—*v.t.*** **5.** to dance (a jig or any lively dance). **6.** to sing or play in the time or rhythm of a jig: *to jig a tune.* **7.** to move with a jerky or bobbing motion; jerk up and down or to and fro. **—*v.i.*** **8.** to dance or play a jig. **9.** to move with a quick, jerky motion; hop; bob. [appar. var. of JOG[1]] **—jig′like′, jig′gish,** *adj.*

jig[3] (jig), *n.* (formerly used in communications to represent the letter J.)

jig[4] (jig), *n.* *Disparaging and Offensive.* a Negro. [shortened form of JIGGER[2]]

jig·a·boo (jig′ə bōō′), *n., pl.* **-boos.** *Disparaging and Offensive.* a Negro. [? JIGGER[2] + BOO]

jig·ger[1] (jig′ər), *n.* **1.** one who or that which jigs. **2.** *Naut.* **a.** the lowermost sail set on a jiggermast. **b.** jiggermast. **c.** a light tackle, as a gun tackle. **3.** any of various mechanical devices, many of which have a jerky or jolting motion. **4.** *Informal.* some contrivance, article, or part that one cannot or will not name more precisely: *What is that little jigger on the pistol?* **5.** *Ceram.* a machine for forming plates or the like in a plaster mold rotating beneath a templet. **6.** a jig for separating ore. **7.** a jig for fishing. **8.** *Golf.* a club with an iron head intermediate between a mashie and a midiron, now rarely used. **9.** *Billiards, Pool.* a bridge. **10.** *U.S.* **a.** a 1½ ounce measure used in cocktail recipes. **b.** a small whiskey glass holding 1½ ounces. **—*adj.*** **11.** *Naut.* **a.** of or pertaining to a jiggermast. **b.** noting or pertaining to a sail, yard, boom, etc., or to any rigging belonging to a jigger lower mast or to some upper mast of a jiggermast. **c.** noting any stay running aft and upward to the head of a jigger lower mast or of some specified upper mast of a jiggermast: *jigger topmast stay.* [JIG[1] + -ER[1]]

jig·ger[2] (jig′ər), *n.* **1.** Also called **jig′ger flea′.** chigoe. **2.** chigger. [var. of CHIGGER]

jig·gered (jig′ərd), *adj.* *Informal.* confounded; blamed; damned: *I'm jiggered if I know what that means.* [? euphemistic alter. of *buggered;* see BUGGER]

jig·ger·mast (jig′ər məst), *n.* *Naut.* **1.** a small mast set well aft in a yawl, ketch, or dandy; mizzenmast. **2.** the fourth mast from forward in a vessel having five or more masts. Also, **jig′ger mast′.** Also called **jigger.** [JIGGER[1] + MAST[1]]

jig·gers (jig′ərz), *interj.* *Slang.* watch out: *Jiggers, the cops are coming!* [? *jigger,* as in JIGGERED + -S[1]]

jig·ger·y-pok·er·y (jig′ə rē pō′kə rē), *n.* *Chiefly Brit.* **1.** false pretense; fraud; humbug. **2.** sly, underhanded action. **3.** manipulation: *After a little jiggery-pokery, the engine started.* [alter. of *joukery-pawkery.* See JOUK, PAWKY, -ERY]

jig·ging (jig′ing), *n.* *Naut. Obs.* the sails set above the moonrakers, taken as a whole; flying kites; jolly jumpers. [JIG[1] + -ING[1]]

jig·gle (jig′əl), *v.,* **-gled, -gling,** *n.* **—*v.t., v.i.*** **1.** to move up and down or to and fro with short, quick jerks. **—*n.*** **2.** a jiggling movement. [JIG[2] + -LE] **—jig′gly,** *adj.*

jig′ saw′, a narrow saw, mounted vertically in a frame, for cutting curves or other difficult lines. [*jig,* var. of GIG[1]]

jig·saw (jig′sô′), *v.,* **-sawed, -sawed** or **-sawn, -saw·ing,** *adj., n.* **—*v.t.*** **1.** to cut or form with a jig saw. **—*adj.*** **2.** formed by or as if by a jig saw: *jigsaw ornamentation.* **—*n.*** **3.** See **jig saw.** [v., adj., n. use of JIG SAW]

jig′saw puz′zle, a set of irregularly colored pieces of pasteboard, wood, or the like, which when fitted together form a picture.

ji·had (ji häd′), *n.* **1.** a holy war undertaken as a sacred duty by Muslims. **2.** any vigorous, often bitter crusade for an idea or principle. Also, **jehad.** [< Ar *jihād* struggle; strife]

jill (jil), *n.* (*sometimes cap.*) **1.** a girl or young woman. **2.** a sweetheart. [special use of proper name *Jill*]

Jill (jil), *n.* a girl's given name.

jill·et (jil′it), *n.* *Scot.* a giddy or flirtatious girl or young woman. [earlier *gillot*, equiv. to *Gill* JILL + *-ot* (< F *-otte* as in *Charlotte*)]

jil·lion (jil′yən), *Informal.* **—*n.*** **1.** a fanciful number suggesting a very large quantity. **—*adj.*** **2.** of or noting such a quantity: *a jillion problems.* [*j-* (arbitrary letter) + *-illion*, as in *million*]

Ji·lo·lo (jī lō′lō), *n.* Halmahera.

jilt (jilt), *v.t.* **1.** to reject or cast aside (a lover or sweetheart) after encouragement or engagement. **—*n.*** **2.** a woman who jilts a lover. [*jilt* harlot, syncopated var. of JILLET] **—jilt′er,** *n.*

jīm (jēm), *n.* the fifth letter of the Arabic alphabet. [< Ar]

Jim (jim), *n.* a boy's given name, form of **James.**

Jim Crow (jim′ krō′), **1.** a practice or policy of segregating or discriminating against Negroes, as in public places, public vehicles, employment, etc. **2.** *Disparaging.* Negro. [so called from the name of a song sung by Thomas Rice (1808–60) in a Negro minstrel show] **—Jim′-Crow′, jim′-crow′,** *adj.*

Jim′ Crow′ism (krō′iz əm), **1.** See **Jim Crow** (def. 1). **2.** anti-Negro sentiment. [JIM CROW + -ISM]

jim-dan·dy (jim′dan′dē), *adj.* *Informal.* of superior quality; excellent: *a jim-dandy sports car.* [special use of *Jim* proper name + DANDY[1]]

jim′ dash′ (jim), *Print., Journalism.* a dash, often three ems long, used within a headline, between the headline and the main body of printed matter, between items in a single column, or between related but different material within a story. [*jim,* prob. special use of *Jim* proper name]

Ji·mé·nez (hē me′neth), *n.* **Juan Ra·món** (hwän rä-môn′), 1881–1958, Spanish poet: Nobel prize 1956.

Ji·mé·nez de Cis·ne·ros (hē me′neth de thēs ne′rôs), **Fran·cis·co** (frän thēs′kō), 1436–1517, Spanish cardinal and statesman. Also called **Ximenes.**

Ji·mé·nez de Que·sa·da (hē me′neth de ke sä′thä, -me′nes), **Gon·za·lo** (gôn thä′lō, -sä-), 1497?–1579, Spanish explorer and conqueror in South America.

ji·mi·ga·ki (jē mē′gä kē′), *n.* a polished surface on Japanese metalwork, as a sword mount. [< Jap, equiv. to *jimi* plainly + *gaki* drawn, painted]

jim·i·ny (jim′ə nē), *interj.* (a mild exclamation of surprise, emotion, or awe.) Also, **jim′mi·ny.** [obs. form of GEMINI, ? alter. of L *Jesu Domine* Lord Jesus!]

jim·jams (jim′jamz′), *n.* (*construed as pl.*) *Slang.* **1.** excessive nervousness; the jitters. **2.** See **delirium tremens.** [repetitive compound with gradation, based on JAM[1]. Cf. *flim-flam, jingle-jangle,* etc.]

Jim·mie (jim′ē), *n.* **1.** a boy's given name, form of **James.** **2.** Also, **Jymmye.** a girl's given name. Also, **Jim′my.**

jim·my[1] (jim′ē), *n., pl.* **-mies,** *v.,* **-mied, -my·ing.** **—*n.*** **1.** a short crowbar. **—*v.t.*** **2.** to force open (a door, window, etc.) with a jimmy: *The burglar got in by jimmy-*

ing the back door. Also, *esp. Brit.,* **jemmy.** [special use of JIMMY; cf. JACK[1]]

jim·my[2] (jim′ē), *n., pl.* **-mies.** *Australian Slang.* an immigrant. [rhyming slang; *Jimmy* (Grant, with *immigrant*)]

Jim′my Green′ (jim′ē), *Naut.* See **Jamie Green.**

jimp (jimp), *adj. Scot. and North Eng.* **1.** slender; trim; delicate. **2.** scant; barely sufficient; small. Also, **gimp.** [? var. of *gim* smart, spruce, adj. use of GEM (*i* < OE *gim* jewel < L *gemma*)] —**jimp′ly,** *adv.* —**jimp′ness,** *n.*

jim′son weed′ (jim′sən), a coarse, rank-smelling weed, *Datura Stramonium,* having white flowers and poisonous leaves. Also, **Jim′son weed′.** [var. of *Jamestown weed,* after JAMESTOWN, Virginia]

Jim Thorpe (jim′ thôrp′), **1.** See **Thorpe, James Francis. 2.** a town in E Pennsylvania. 5945 (1960).

jin[1] (jin), *n., pl.* **jins,** (*esp. collectively*) **jin.** *Islamic Myth.* jinn.

jin[2] (jin), *n. Australian Informal.* gin[6].

jin·gal (jin′gəl), *n.* a large musket fired from a rest, often mounted on a carriage: formerly used by natives in India, China, etc. Also, **gingal, gingall.** [< Hindi *janjāl*]

jin·gle (jing′gəl), *v.,* **-gled, -gling,** *n.* —*v.i.* **1.** to make clinking or tinkling sounds, as coins, keys, or other light, resonant metal objects, when struck together repeatedly: *His spurs jingled as he walked.* **2.** to move or proceed with such sounds: *The sleigh, decorated with bells, jingled along the snowy road.* **3.** to sound in a light, repetitious manner suggestive of this, as verse, sequence of words, piece of music, etc.: *That tune jingles nicely.* **4.** to make rhymes. —*v.t.* **5.** to cause to jingle: *He jingled the coins in his pocket.* —*n.* **6.** a tinkling or clinking sound, as of small bells or of small pieces of resonant metal repeatedly struck one against another. **7.** something that makes such a sound, as a small bell or a metal pendant. **8.** a succession of like or repetitious sounds, as in music or verse. **9.** a piece of verse having such a succession of sounds, usually of a humorous, superficial, or nonsensical character. **10.** such a verse set to music. **11.** *Irish Eng. and Australian.* a loosely sprung, two-wheeled, roofed carriage, usually used as a hackney coach. [ME *gyngle(n),* appar. imit.; cf. D *jengelen*] —**jin′gler,** *n.* —**jin′gling·ly,** *adv.*

jin′gle bell′, 1. *U.S. Naut.* a bell located in the engine room of a vessel to signal directions from the pilot house. **2.** a sleigh bell.

jin′gle shell′, 1. any of several marine, bivalve mollusks of the genus *Anomia,* having a thin, pearly shell with a conspicuous hole or notch near the hinge of the lower valve. **2.** the shell itself.

jing′ling John′ny, *Music.* crescent (def. 7).

jin·gly (jing′glē), *adj.* characterized by or resembling a jingle. [JINGLE + -Y[1]]

jin·go (jing′gō), *n., pl.* **-goes,** *adj.* —*n.* **1.** a person who professes his patriotism loudly and excessively, favoring preparedness for war and an aggressive foreign policy; chauvinist. **2.** *Eng. Hist.* a Conservative supporter of Disraeli's policy in the Near East during the period 1877–78. **3. by jingo!** *Informal.* (an exclamation used to emphasize the truth or importance of a foregoing statement, or to express astonishment, approval, etc.): *I know you can do it, by jingo!* —*adj.* **4.** of jingoes. **5.** characterized by jingoism. [orig. conjurer's call *hey jingo* appear! come forth! (opposed to *hey presto* hasten away!), taken into general use in the phrase *by Jingo,* euphemism for *by God;* chauvinistic sense from *by Jingo* in political song supporting use of British forces against Russia in 1878]

jin·go·ism (jing′gō iz′əm), *n.* the spirit, policy, or practice of jingoes; bellicose chauvinism. [JINGO + -ISM] —**jin′go·ist,** *n., adj.* —**jin′go·is′tic, jin′go·ish,** *adj.* —**jin′go·is′ti·cal·ly,** *adv.*

jin·gu (jing′gōō′), *n.* an important Shinto shrine. [< Jap]

jin·ja (jin′jä′), *n.* **1.** *Shinto.* a shrine. —*adj.* **2.** (*cap.*) Kokka. [< Jap]

Jin·ja (jin′jä), *n.* a city in central Uganda, on Lake Victoria. 29,741 (1959).

jink (jingk), *n.* **1. jinks,** prankish or frolicsome activities. **2.** *Brit. Dial.* chink. [? var. of dial. *chink* to gasp violently; akin to OE *cincung* boisterous laughter]

jin·ker (jing′kər), *n. Australian* **1.** a racing sulky. **2.** any of various carts or trailers used to transport logs and timber. [var. of *janker* (Scot) < ?]

jinn (jin), *n., pl.* **jinns,** (*esp. collectively*) **jinn.** *Islamic Myth.* any of a class of spirits, lower than the angels, capable of appearing in human and animal forms, and influencing mankind for good and evil. Also, **jin·ni** (ji nē′, jin′ē), **djin, djinn, djinni, jin.** [pl. of Ar *jinnī* demon]

Jin·nah (jin′ə), *n.* **Mohammed Ali** ("*Quaid-i-Azam*"), 1876–1948, Muslim leader in India: 1st governor general of Pakistan 1947–48.

jin·rik·i·sha (jin rik′shô, -shä), *n.* (in Japan, the Philippines, etc.) a small, two-wheeled passenger vehicle with a folding top, pulled by one man. Also, **jin·rick′sha, jin·rick′shaw, jin·rik′sha.** Also called **rickshaw, ricksha.** [< Jap, equiv. to *jin* man + *riki* power + *sha* vehicle]

Jin·sen (jin′sen′), *n.* Japanese name of **Inchon.**

jinx (jingks), *n.* **1.** a person, thing, or influence supposed to bring bad luck. —*v.t. Informal.* **2.** to bring bad luck to; place a jinx on: *The pilot felt that the flight had been jinxed.* **3.** to destroy the point of: *His sudden laugh jinxed the host's joke.* [< L *jynx* < Gk *íynx* wryneck (bird used in divination and magic)]

Jinx (jingks), *n.* a girl's given name.

ji·pi·ja·pa (hē′pē hä′pä), *n.* **1.** a tropical American, palmlike plant, *Carludovica palmata.* **2.** a Panama hat made from the young leaves of this plant. [< AmerSp *jipijapa,* after *Jipijapa,* town in Ecuador]

jit·ney (jit′nē), *n., pl.* **-neys,** *v.,* **-neyed, -ney·ing.** —*n.* **1.** a small passenger bus following a regular route at varying hours, originally charging each passenger five cents. **2.** *Slang.* a nickel; five-cent piece. —*v.t., v.i.* **3.** to carry or ride in a jitney. [?]

jit·ter (jit′ər), *n.* **1. jitters,** nervousness; a feeling of fright or uneasiness (usually prec. by *the*): *The whole city had the jitters from the bombing.* —*v.i.* **2.** to behave nervously. [var. of *chitter* to shiver (ME *chiteren*), itself gradational var. of CHATTER]

jit·ter·bug (jit′ər bug′), *n., v.,* **-bugged, -bug·ging.** —*n.* **1.** a strenuously athletic dance consisting of a few standardized steps augmented by twirls, splits, somersaults, etc., popular esp. in the early 1940's and performed chiefly to boogie-woogie and swing. **2.** one who dances the jitterbug. **3.** a broad, reinforced wire mesh for tamping crushed stone. —*v.i.* **4.** to dance the jitterbug. [JITTER + BUG[1]]

jit·ter·y (jit′ə rē), *adj.* tense; strained; nervous; shaky: *The stern face of the customs officer made him feel jittery.* [JITTER + -Y[1]]

jiu·jit·su (jōō jit′sōō), *n.* jujitsu. Also, **jiu·jut′su.**

ji·va (jē′və), *n.* **1.** *Hinduism.* the individual soul, regarded as a particular manifestation of Atman. **2.** *Jainism.* **a.** the individual soul or life monad, compared to a transparent crystal stained by karmic matter with colors or lesyas of varying hues. **b.** all such monads collectively, regarded as the animating principle of the universe. Also called **ji·vat·ma** (jē vät′mə). [< Skt: lit., living]

Ji·va·ro (hē′vä rô), *n., pl.* **-ros** (-rôs), (*esp. collectively*) **-ro.** a member of an Indian people of Ecuador and Peru noted for their practice of shrinking human heads. [< Sp *jíbaro* < native name]

jive (jīv), *n., v.,* **jived, jiv·ing.** —*n.* **1.** swing music. **2.** *Slang.* the jargon of the jazz and entertainment worlds, or of narcotic addicts. **3.** *Slang.* unintelligible, meaningless, or deceptive talk. —*v.i.* **4.** to play jive, **5.** to dance to jive; jitterbug. —*v.t.* **6.** *Slang.* to fool or kid (someone); talk jive to. [?]

jiz·ya (jiz′yə), *n.* (formerly) a poll tax imposed on non-Muslims by the Moguls in India. Also, **jiz′yah.** [< Ar]

JJ., **1.** Judges. **2.** Justices.

Jl., July.

JMP, jēn-min-piao.

jna·na (jənyä′nə, gənyä′-), *n. Hinduism.* knowledge acquired through meditation and study as a means of reaching Brahman. Also called **Brahmajnana.** Cf. **bhakti** (def. 1), **karma** (def. 1). [< Skt *jñāna*]

jna·na-mar·ga (jənyä′nə mär′gə, gənyä′-), *n. Hinduism.* See under **marga.**

Jno., John.

jo (jō), *n., pl.* **joes.** *Scot.* beloved one; darling; sweetheart. Also, **joe.** [var. of JOY]

Jo (jō), *n.* **1.** a girl's given name, form of **Josephine. 2.** Also, **Joe.** a boy's given name, form of **Joseph.**

Jo·ab (jō′ab), *n.* a commander of David's army and the slayer of Abner and Absalom. II Sam. 3:27; 18:14.

Jo·a·chim (yō′ä кнim, yō ä′-), *n.* **1. Jo·seph** (yō′zef), 1831–1907, Hungarian violinist and composer. **2.** a boy's given name.

Joan (jōn), *n.* **1.** ("*Fair Maid of Kent*") 1328–85, wife of Edward, the Black Prince, and mother of Richard II. **2.** a fictitious female pope about A.D. 855–858. **3.** a girl's given name.

Jo·anne (jō an′), *n.* a girl's given name. Also, **Jo·ann′, Jo Ann′, Jo·an·na** (jō an′ə).

jo·an·nes (jō an′ēz), *n., pl.* **-nes.** johannes.

Joan′ of Arc′ (ärk), **Saint** ("*the Maid of Orleans*"), 1412?–31, French national heroine and martyr who raised the siege of Orleans. French, **Jeanne d'Arc.**

Jo·ão Pes·so·a (zhōō oun′ pe sô′ə), a seaport in NE Brazil. 137,788 (1960).

Jo·ash (jō′ash), *n.* a king of Judah, reigned 837?–800? B.C., successor of Athaliah. II Kings 13:10–13. Also, *Douay Bible,* **Jo·as** (jō′as).

job[1] (job), *n., v.,* **jobbed, job·bing,** *adj.* —*n.* **1.** a piece of work, esp. a specific task done as part of the routine of one's occupation, or for an agreed price: *It was the secretary's job to open the mail. She gave him the job of mowing the lawn.* **2.** anything one has to do; duty; responsibility: *It is your job to be on time.* **3.** a post of employment: *She was seeking a job as a secretary.* **4.** an affair, matter, occurrence, or state of affairs: *to make the best of a bad job.* **5.** the unit or material being worked upon: *The housing project was a long and costly job.* **6.** the process of working: *It was a tedious job.* **7.** a public or official act or decision carried through for the sake of improper private gain. **8.** *Slang.* a theft or similar criminal action: *The police caught the gang that pulled that bank job.* **9.** *Slang.* an object or person, esp. a remarkable one: *I like that blonde job in the red dress.* **10. on the job,** *Slang.* alert; observant: *The cops were on the job and caught them red-handed.* —*v.i.* **11.** to work at jobs or odd pieces of work; work by the piece. **12.** to do business as a jobber. **13.** to turn public business, planning, etc., improperly to private gain. —*v.t.* **14.** to buy in large quantities, as from wholesalers or manufacturers, and sell to dealers in smaller quantities: *He jobs shoes in Ohio and Indiana.* **15.** to assign or give (work, a contract for work, etc.) in separate portions, as among different contractors or workmen (often fol. by *out*): *He jobbed out the contract to a number of small outfits.* **16.** to carry on (public or official business) for improper private gain. **17.** to dispose of: *His party jobbed him when he sought a second term in office.* **18.** to swindle or trick (someone): *They jobbed him out of his property.* —*adj.* **19.** of or for a particular job or transaction. **20.** bought, sold, or handled together: *He's too big a customer to buy in less than job quantities.* [?]
—**Syn. 3.** See **position.**

job[2] (job), *v.t., v.i.,* **jobbed, job·bing,** *n.* jab. [ME *jobbe(n)* < ?]

Job (jōb), *n.* **1.** the central figure in an Old Testament parable of the righteous sufferer. **2.** a book of the Bible bearing his name. **3.** (*italics*) a ballet (1930) by Ralph Vaughan Williams. **4.** a boy's given name.

job′ anal′ysis, a detailed study of the requirements necessary to complete a job, taking into consideration chiefly the order of operation, material and machinery needed, and the necessary qualifications of workers.

Jo. Bapt., John the Baptist.

job·ber (job′ər), *n.* **1.** a wholesale merchant, esp. one selling to retailers. **2.** a pieceworker. **3.** (formerly) a merchant who deals in special, odd, or job lots. **4.** one who practices jobbery. [JOB[1] + -ER[1]]

job·ber·y (job′ə rē), *n.* the conduct of public or official business for the sake of improper private gain. [JOBBER + -Y[3]]

job′ case′, *Print.* any of various cases for holding types, esp. one of several that accommodate both upper-case and lower-case letters. Cf. **California job case, case**[2] (def. 7).

job′ classifica′tion, an arrangement of different types of employment within a company or industry, according to the skill, experience, or training required.

Job′ Corps′, *U.S.* an organization, under the auspices of the OEO, that operates rural conservation camps and urban training centers for poor youths.

job′ cost′ing. See **job-order costing.**

job′ descrip′tion, an abstract of a job analysis containing the classification of and requirements for a job, used in hiring and placing prospective employees.

job·hold·er (job′hōl′dər), *n.* **1.** a person who has a regular job. **2.** a government employee. [JOB[1] + HOLDER]

Jo·bi·na (jō bē′nə), *n.* a girl's given name. Also, **Jo·by′na.**

job·less (job′lis), *adj.* **1.** without a job. **2.** noting or pertaining to persons without jobs, esp. to those of working age who are seeking employment. —*n.* **3.** (*construed as pl.*) unemployed people collectively, esp. those of working age who are seeking a job (usually prec. by *the*). [JOB[1] + -LESS] —**job′less·ness,** *n.*

job′ lot′, 1. a large, often assorted quantity of goods sold or handled as a single transaction. **2.** a miscellaneous quantity; a quantity of odds and ends.

job′ or′der, a written order to a workman or group of workmen to perform a certain job.

job′-order cost′ing (job′ôr′dər), a method of cost accounting by which the total cost of a given unit or quantity is determined by computing the costs that go into making a product as it moves through the manufacturing process. Also called **job costing.** Cf. **process costing.**

job′ print′er, a printer who does miscellaneous work, as distinguished from one who works solely on books, periodicals, etc. —**job′ print′ing.**

Job's′ com′forter, a person who unwittingly or maliciously depresses or discourages someone while attempting to console him.

Job's-tears (jōbz′tērz′), *n.* **1.** (*construed as pl.*) the hard, nearly globular involucres that surround the female flowers of an Asian grass, *Coix Lacryma-Jobi,* and which when ripe are used as beads. **2.** (*construed as sing.*) the grass itself.

job′ tick′et, 1. a slip accompanying a job order and used for giving instructions or for recording time spent on the work. **2.** See **job order.**

job′ work′, 1. miscellaneous printing work, as distinguished from books, periodicals, etc. **2.** work done by the job.

Jo·cas·ta (jō kas′tə), *n.* **1.** *Class. Myth.* a queen of Thebes, the wife of Laius and the mother, later the wife, of Oedipus, by whom she became the mother of Eteocles, Polynices, and Antigone: called Epicaste by Homer. **2.** a girl's given name. Also, **Jo·cas′te.**

Joc·e·lyn (jos′ə lin), *n.* a girl's given name. Also, **Joc′e·lin, Joc′e·line, Joc′e·lynne, Joselyn.**

Joch·e·bed (jok′ə bed′), *n.* the mother of Aaron and Moses. Ex. 6:20. Also, *Douay Bible,* **Joch′a·bed.**

jock[1] (jok), *n. Informal.* jockey (def. 1). [shortened form]

jock[2] (jok), *n.* **1.** a jockstrap. **2.** *Slang.* an athlete. [by shortening from JOCKSTRAP]

Jock (jok), *n.* **1.** *Scot. and Irish Eng.* **a.** a nickname for **John. b.** an innocent lad; a country boy. **2.** *Brit. Informal.* a Scottish soldier. **3.** a boy's given name.

jock·ey (jok′ē), *n., pl.* **-eys,** *v.,* **-eyed, -ey·ing.** —*n.* **1.** a person who professionally rides horses in races. **2.** *Informal.* a person who pilots, operates, or guides the movement of something, as an airplane or automobile. —*v.t.* **3.** to ride (a horse) as a jockey. **4.** *Informal.* to operate or guide the movement of; pilot; drive. **5.** to move, bring, put, etc., by skillful maneuvering: *He jockeyed the sofa through the door.* **6.** to trick or cheat: *The huckster jockeyed them into buying worthless securities.* **7.** to manipulate cleverly or trickily: *He jockeyed himself into office.* —*v.i.* **8.** to aim at an advantage by skillful maneuvering. **9.** to act trickily; seek an advantage by trickery. [JOCK + -EY[2]] —**jock′ey·like′, jock′ey·ish,** *adj.* —**jock′ey·ship′,** *n.*

jock′ey cap′, a cap with a long visor, worn by jockeys.

jock′ey club′, 1. an association for the regulating and promoting of thoroughbred horse racing, usually composed of racing officials and thoroughbred owners at a specific race track or in a particular region. **2.** a section at a racetrack reserved for members of such an association, containing box seats, a restaurant, and sometimes rooms for social gatherings.

jock′ey pul′ley, *Mach.* See **idle pulley.**

jock·o (jok′ō), *n., pl.* **jock·os. 1.** a chimpanzee. **2.** any monkey. [< F, alter. of a word of a Bantu language (of Gabon) *ngeko*]

Jock·o (jok′ō), *n.* a boy's given name, form of **Jock.**

Jock′ Scot′, *Angling.* an artificial fly having a yellow floss body, black silk tag, scarlet and yellow tail, wings of scarlet and of jungle cock feathers spotted with yellow and gray, and hackle of guinea fowl and grouse feathers. Also, **Jock′ Scott′.** [special use of JOCK + *Scot,* a regional allusion]

jock·strap (jok′strap′), *n.* an elastic supporter for the genitals, worn by men esp. while participating in athletics. Also called **athletic supporter.** [*jock* male organ (var. of JACK[1] male; see JOCK) + STRAP]

jock·te·leg (jok′tə leg′), *n. Brit. Dial.* a large clasp knife or pocketknife; jackknife. Also, **jacteleg, joktaleg.** [?]

jo·cose (jō kōs′), *adj.* given to or characterized by joking; jesting; humorous; playful: *a jocose and amusing manner.* [< L *jocōs(us),* equiv. to *joc(us)* JOKE + *-ōsus* -OSE[1]] —**jo·cose′ly,** *adv.* —**jo·cose′ness,** *n.*
—**Syn.** facetious, waggish, witty, funny, droll, comical, sportive, merry. See **jovial.**

jo·cos·i·ty (jō kos′i tē), *n., pl.* **-ties. 1.** state or quality of being jocose. **2.** joking or jesting. **3.** a joke or jest. [JOCOSE + -ITY]

joc·u·lar (jok′yə lər), *adj.* given to, characterized by, intended for, or suited to joking or jesting; waggish; facetious: *jocular remarks about opera stars.* [< L *joculār(is),* equiv. to *jocul(us)* little joke (*joc(us)* joke + *-ulus* -ULE) + *-āris* -AR[1]] —**joc′u·lar·ly,** *adv.*
—**Syn.** See **jovial.**

joc·u·lar·i·ty (jok′yə lar′i tē), *n., pl.* **-ties. 1.** state or quality of being jocular. **2.** jocular speech or behavior. **3.** a jocular remark or act. [JOCULAR + -ITY]

joc·und (jok′ənd, jō′kənd), *adj.* cheerful; merry; gay; blithe; glad: *a witty and jocund group.* [ME *joc(o)und* <

LL *jocund(us)*, alter. of L *jūcundus* pleasant, equiv. to *ju(vāre)* (to) please + *-cundus* adj. suffix] —**joc′und·ly**, *adv.*
—Syn. joyous, joyful, blithesome, jolly. See **jovial.**

jo·cun·di·ty (jō kun′di tē), *n., pl.* **-ties** for 2. **1.** the state or an instance of being jocund; gaiety. **2.** a jocund remark or act. [JOCUND + -ITY]

Jo·dean (jō dēn′), *n.* a girl's given name. Also, **Jo·deen′, Jo·dene′, Jo·dine′, Jo·dyn′, Jo·dynne′.**

jodh·pur (jod′pər, jōd′-), *n.* **1. jodhpurs,** (*construed as pl.*) riding breeches cut very full over the hips and tapering at the knees to become tight fitting from knees to ankles. **2.** Also called **jodh′pur shoe′, jodh′pur boot′.** an ankle-high shoe for wearing with such breeches, having a strap that encircles the ankle and buckles on the side. Cf. **chukka boot.** [after JODHPUR]

Jodh·pur (jōd′pŏŏr), *n.* **1.** Also called **Marwar.** a former state in NW India, now in Rajasthan. **2.** a city in W Rajasthan, in NW India. 224,800 (1961).

Jo·di (jō′dē), *n.* a girl's given name.

Jo. Div., John the Divine.

Jodl (yōd′əl), *n.* **Al·fred** (äl′frāt), 1892?–1946, German general: signed the surrender of Germany on behalf of the German high command in World War II.

Jo·do (jō′dō), *n.* *Japanese.* See **Pure Land.**

Jod′rell Bank′ (jō′drəl), a site in NE Cheshire, England: world's largest radio telescope.

Jo·dy (jō′dē), *n.* a boy's given name.

joe[1] (jō), *n.* *Scot.* jo.

joe[2] (jō), *n.* (*often cap.*) *Slang.* fellow; guy: *See that joe sitting at the bar? He's a good joe.* [special use of JOE]

Joe (jō), *n.* a boy's given name, form of **Joseph.** Also, **Jo.**

Joe′ Blow′, *Slang.* an average citizen; man in the street. Also called **Joe Doakes.** [rhyming phrase. See JOE[2], BLOW[2]]

Joe′ Col′lege, a personification of a typical U.S. college boy. [modeled on JOE BLOW]

Joe′ Doakes′ (dōks), *pl.* **Joe Doakes.** *Slang.* See **Joe Blow.**

Jo·el (jō′əl), *n.* **1.** a Minor Prophet of the postexilic period. **2.** a book of the Bible bearing his name. **3.** a boy's given name.

Joe′ Mil′ler (mil′ər), **1.** a book of jokes. **2.** an old, familiar joke; chestnut. [after *Joe Miller's Jestbook* (1739) by John Mottley]

Jo·en·suu (yô′en sōō′), *n.* a city in SE Finland. 31,826 (est. 1965).

joe-pye′ weed′ (jō′pī′), **1.** Also called **purple boneset.** a tall, composite weed, *Eupatorium purpureum*, of North America, having clusters of pinkish or purple flowers. **2.** Also called **spotted joe-pye weed.** a related plant, *E. maculatum*, having similar flowers and stems that are often spotted with purple. [?]

Jo. Evang., John the Evangelist.

jo·ey[1] (jō′ē), *n., pl.* **-eys.** *Australian.* **1.** any young animal, esp. a kangaroo. **2.** a young child. [< native Austral]

jo·ey[2] (jō′ē), *n., pl.* **-eys.** *Brit. Slang.* **1.** a threepenny piece. **2.** (formerly) a fourpenny piece. [after *Joseph Hume* (1777–1855), English politician who favored the coinage of the fourpenny piece]

Jo·ey (jō′ē), *n., pl.* **Jo·eys.** a clown, esp. in the circus or pantomime and puppet theater. [dim. of *Joseph*, after Joseph GRIMALDI]

Jo·ey (jō′ē), *n.* a boy's given name, form of **Joe** or **Joseph.**

jo′ey glass′, a small tumbler of the 17th century; dram glass.

Jof·fre (zhô′frᵊ), *n.* **Jo·seph Jacques Cé·saire** (zhō zef′ zhäk sā zer′), 1852–1931, French general in World War I.

jog[1] (jog), *v.,* **jogged, jog·ging,** *n.* **—***v.t.* **1.** to move or shake with a push or jerk: *The horseman jogged the reins lightly.* **2.** to cause to function with a jolt for a moment or in a series of disconnected motions: *He jogged the motor and started the machine.* **3.** to push slightly, as to arouse the attention; nudge: *She jogged his elbow when she wanted to be introduced to his friend.* **4.** to stir or jolt into activity, as by a hint or reminder: *to jog a person's memory.* **5.** to cause (a horse) to go at a steady trot. **6.** *Print.* to align the edges of (a stack of sheets of paper of the same size) by jolting them gently on their edges. **—***v.i.* **7.** to move with a jolt or jerk: *His briefcase jogged against his leg as he walked.* **8.** to go or travel with a jolting pace or motion: *The clumsy cart jogged down the bumpy road.* **9.** to run or ride at a steady trot: *They jogged to the stable.* **10.** to run at a leisurely, slow pace, raising the knees high, esp. as an outdoor exercise. **11.** to go in a desultory or humdrum fashion (usually fol. by *on* or *along*): *He just jogged along, getting by however he could.* **—***n.* **12.** a shake; slight push; nudge. **13.** a steady trot, as of a horse. **14.** the act of jogging. [b. *jot* to jog (now dial.) and *shog* to shake, jog (late ME *shoggen*)] —**jog′ger,** *n.*

jog[2] (jog), *n.* **1.** an irregularity of line or surface; projection; notch. **2.** *Theat.* a narrow flat placed at right angles to another flat to make a corner, used esp. in sets representing an interior. [var. of JAG[1]]

jog·gle (jog′əl), *v.,* **-gled, -gling,** *n.* **—***v.t.* **1.** to shake slightly; move to and fro, as by repeated jerks; jiggle: *She joggled the key in the lock a couple of times before getting the door open.* **2.** to cause (something) to shake or totter as by a sudden, slight push. **3.** to join or fasten by fitting a projection into a recess. **4.** to fit or fasten with dowels. **—***v.i.* **5.** to move irregularly; have a jogging or jolting motion; shake. **—***n.* **6.** the act of joggling. **7.** a slight shake or jolt. **8.** a moving with jolts or jerks. **9.** a projection on one of two joining objects fitting into a corresponding recess in the other to prevent slipping. **10.** *Carpentry.* an enlarged area, as of a post or king post, for supporting the foot of a strut, brace, etc. [JOG[1] + -LE] —**jog′gler,** *n.*

jog′gle post′, **1** a wooden king post having notches or raised areas for receiving and supporting the feet of struts. **2.** a post formed of timbers joggled together. Also, **jog′gle piece′.**

jog′gling plank′, *Naut.* a curved margin plank having a joggled inner edge so that the ends of deck planks can butt against the joggles. Cf. **gunstocking.**

Jog·ja·kar·ta (jōg′yä kär′tä), *n.* a city in central Java, in S Indonesia. 312,698 (1961). Also, **Jokjakarta.** Dutch. **Djokjakarta.**

jog′ trot′, **1.** a slow, regular, jolting pace, as of a horse. **2.** an uneventful, humdrum way of living, doing something, etc.: *a sleepy little town where life proceeded at a jog trot.*

Jo·han·an ben Zak·ka·i (jō han′ən ben zak′ā ī′), died A.D. c80, Palestinian rabbi: leading Pharisaic teacher and disciple of Hillel.

Jo·hann (yō′hän), *n.* a boy's given name, Germanic form of **John.**

Jo·han·na (jō han′ə, -an′ə), *n.* a girl's given name.

jo·han·nes (jō han′ēz), *n., pl.* **-nes.** a gold coin formerly used as currency in Portugal, first issued in the early 18th century. Also, **joannes.** [after the name *Joannes* (John V, of Portugal) on coin. See JOHN]

Jo·han·nes (yō hä′nis, -han′is), *n.* a boy's given name, form of **John.**

Jo·han·nes·burg (jō han′is bûrg′; *Du.* yō hän′əs-bœrkh′), *n.* a city in S Transvaal, in the N Republic of South Africa. 595,083 (1960).

Jo·han·nine (jō han′in, -īn), *adj.* of or pertaining to the apostle John or to the books in the New Testament attributed to him. [*Johann(es)* John (equiv. of Gk *Iōánnēs*) + -INE[1]]

Jo·han·nis·berg·er (yō hän′is ber′gər), *n.* any of the white wines from the Johannisberg vineyards of the Rheingau wine region of West Germany.

john (jon), *n.* *Slang.* toilet; bathroom. [special use of JOHN]

John (jon), *n.* **1.** the apostle John, believed to be the author of the fourth Gospel, three Epistles, and the book of Revelation. **2.** See **John the Baptist. 3.** (*John Lackland*) 1167?–1216, king of England 1199–1216; signer of the Magna Charta 1215 (son of Henry II of England). **4. Augustus Edwin,** 1878–1961, Welsh painter and etcher. **5.** the fourth Gospel: the Gospel of St. John. **6.** any of the three Epistles of John: I, II, or III John. **7.** *Slang.* a woman's lover. **8.** *Slang.* a prostitute's customer. **9.** a boy's given name. [ME *Joh(a)n*, OE *Iōhannis* < ML *Iō(h)annēs* < Gk *Iōánnēs* < Heb *Yōḥānān*, deriv. of *Yehōḥānān* God has been gracious]

John I, **1. Saint,** died A.D. 526, Italian ecclesiastic: pope 523–526. **2.** ("*the Great*") 1357–1433, king of Portugal 1385–1433.

John II, (*Mercurius*) died A.D. 535, Italian ecclesiastic: pope 533–535.

John III, **1.** (*Catelinus*) died A.D. 574, Italian ecclesiastic: pope 561–574. **2.** (*John Sobieski*) 1624–96, king of Poland 1674–96.

John IV, died A.D. 642, pope 640–642.

John V, died A.D. 686, pope 685–686.

John VI, died A.D. 705, Greek ecclesiastic: pope 701–705.

John VII, died A.D. 707, Greek ecclesiastic: pope 705–707.

John VIII, died A.D. 882, Italian ecclesiastic: pope 872–882.

John IX, died A.D. 900, Italian ecclesiastic: pope 898–900.

John X, died A.D. 929?, Italian ecclesiastic: pope 914–928.

John XI, died A.D. 936, Italian ecclesiastic: pope 931–936.

John XII, (*Octavian*) died A.D. 964, Italian ecclesiastic: pope 955–964.

John XIII, died A.D. 972, Italian ecclesiastic: pope 965–972.

John XIV, died A.D. 984, pope 983–984.

John XV, died A.D. 996, Italian ecclesiastic: pope 985–996.

John XVII, (*Sicco*) died 1003, pope 1003.

John XVIII, (*Fasanus*) died 1009, Italian ecclesiastic: pope 1003–09.

John XIX, died 1032, pope 1024–32.

John XXI, (*Petrus Hispanus*) died 1277, Portuguese ecclesiastic: pope 1276–77.

John XXII, (*Jacques Duèse*) c1244–1334, French ecclesiastic: pope 1316–34.

John XXIII, (*Angelo Giuseppe Roncalli*) 1881–1963, Italian ecclesiastic: pope 1958–63.

John′ Bar′leycorn, a humorous personification of barley as used in malt liquor, of malt liquor itself, or of any intoxicating liquor.

John′ Birch′ Soci′ety, an ultraconservative organization, founded in December, 1958, by Robert Welch, Jr., chiefly to combat alleged communist activities in the U.S. [named after *John Birch* (d. 1945), American USAF captain]

John′ Brown′s′ Bod′y, a long narrative poem (1928) by Stephen Vincent Benét, about the American Civil War.

John′ Bull′, **1.** the English people. **2.** the typical Englishman. [after *John Bull*, chief character in Arbuthnot's allegory *The History of John Bull* (1712)] —**John′ Bull′ish.** —**John′ Bull′ishness.** —**John′ Bull′ism.**

John′ Doe′, **1.** a fictitious personage in legal proceedings, used esp. as the first such name when two or more persons whose real names cannot be ascertained are involved. Cf. **Richard Roe. 2.** an anonymous, average man.

John′ Do′ry (dôr′ē, dôr′ē), any compressed, marine fish of the family *Zeidae*, esp. *Zeus faber*, found in Europe, having long spines in the dorsal fin. [JOHN + DORY[2]; jocular, modeled on JOHN DOE]

Joh′ne's disease′ (yō′nəz), *Vet. Pathol.* a chronic diarrheal disease of cattle and sheep caused by infection with an organism related to the tubercle bacillus *Mycobacterium paratuberculosis*. Also called **mycobacterium paratuberculosis.** [named after H. A. *Johne* (1839–1910), German scientist]

John′ F. Ken′nedy Interna′tional Air′port, international airport for New York, on SW Long Island. Formerly, **Idlewild.**

John′ Ga′briel Bork′man (bôrk′mən), a play (1896) by Henrik Ibsen.

John′ Han′cock, **1.** See **Hancock, John. 2.** *Informal.* one's signature. [after John HANCOCK, from the boldness and legibility of his signature]

John′ Hen′ry, *pl.* **John Henries.** *Informal.* a person's signature: *Just put your John Henry on that check.* [from the proper name]

joh·nin (yō′nin), *n.* *Vet. Med.* a sterile solution prepared from the growth products of the bacillus *Mycobacterium paratuberculosis*, used chiefly in the diagnosis of Johne's disease. Also called **paratuberculin.** [*john-* (see JOHNE'S DISEASE) + -IN[2]]

John·na (jon′ə), *n.* a girl's given name.

John·ny (jon′ē), *n., pl.* **-nies** for 1, 2. **1.** (*sometimes l.c.*) *Slang.* a familiar term of address for a man or boy. **2.** (*sometimes l.c.*) *Slang.* a short collarless gown that is fastened in back and is worn by hospital bed patients. **3.** a boy's given name, form of **John. 4.** a girl's given name. Also, **John′nie.** [JOHN + -Y[2]]

john·ny·cake (jon′ē kāk′), *n.* *U.S.* a cake or bread made of corn meal and water or milk. Also, **john′ny cake′.** [? obs. *jonakin, jonikin* (appar. of AmerInd orig.) kind of griddlecake + CAKE]

John′ny col′lar, (*often l.c.*) a small standing collar, as on a shirtwaist or dress bodice, with close-fitting neckline.

John·ny-come-late·ly (jon′ē kum′lāt′lē), *n., pl.* **John·ny-come-late·lies, John·nies-come-late·ly.** a late arrival or participant: *the Johnny-come-latelies producing mystery films after the trend had ended.* Also, **John′nie-come-late′ly.** [from the proper name JOHNNY]

John·ny-jump-up (jon′ē jump′up′), *n.* *U.S.* **1.** any of certain violets, esp. *Viola Kitaibeliana Rafinesquii*. **2.** a small form of the pansy, *Viola tricolor*. [so called from its rapid rate of growth]

John′ny-on-the-spot′, *Informal.* one who is on hand to perform a duty, seize an opportunity, etc.: *a Johnny-on-the-spot with an answer to any question.*

John′ny Reb′ (reb), *Informal.* **1.** *U.S. Hist.* a Confederate soldier. **2.** a native or inhabitant of the southern U.S., esp. of one of the former Confederate States; Southerner.

John′ny smok′ers. See **prairie smoke.**

John′ of Aus′tria, ("*Don John*") 1547?–78, Spanish general: victor at the battle of Lepanto.

John′ of Gaunt′ (gônt, gänt), (*Duke of Lancaster*) 1340–99, English soldier and statesman: 4th son of Edward III; founder of the royal house of Lancaster (father of Henry IV of England).

John′ of Ley′den (līd′ᵊn), (*Jan Beuckelszoon* or *Bockhold*) 1509–36, Dutch Anabaptist.

John′ of Salis′bury, c1115–80, English prelate and scholar.

John′ of the Cross′, **Saint** (*Juan de Yepis y Álvarez*), 1542–91, Spanish mystic, writer, and theologian: co-founder with Saint Theresa of the order of Discalced Carmelites. Spanish, **San Juan de la Cruz.**

John′ o'Groat's′ House′ (ə grōts′, ə grōts′), the northern tip of Scotland, near Duncansby Head, NE Caithness, traditionally thought of as the northernmost point of Britain: *from Land's End to John o'Groat's House.* Also called **John′ o'Groat's′.**

John Paul I, (*Albino Luciani*) 1912–78, Italian ecclesiastic: pope 1978.

John Paul II, (*Karol Wojtyla*) born 1920, Polish ecclesiastic: pope since 1978.

Johns (jonz), *n.* **Jasper,** born 1930, U.S. painter.

John·son (jon′sən), *n.* **1. Andrew,** 1808–75, 17th president of the U.S. 1865–69. **2. Charles Spur·geon** (spûr′jən), 1893–1956, U.S. educator and sociologist. **3. Gerald White,** born 1890, U.S. writer. **4. Jack** (*John Arthur*), 1878–1946, U.S. heavyweight prize fighter: world champion 1908–15. **5. James Wel·don** (wel′dən), 1871–1938, U.S. poet and essayist. **6. Lyn·don Baines** (lin′dən bānz), 1908–73, 36th president of the U.S. 1963–69. **7. Philip C(ortelyou),** born 1906, U.S. architect and author. **8. Richard Men·tor** (men′tər, -tôr), 1780–1850, vice-president of the U.S. 1837–41. **9. Samuel** ("*Dr. Johnson*"), 1709–84, English lexicographer, critic, poet, and conversationalist. **10. Walter Perry** ("*Big Train*"), 1887–1946, U.S. baseball player. **11. Sir William,** 1715–74, British colonial administrator in America, born in Ireland.

John·son·burg (jon′sən bûrg′), *n.* a town in central Pennsylvania. 4966 (1960).

John′son Cit′y, **1.** a city in NE Tennessee. 29,892 (1960). **2.** a city in S New York. 19,118 (1960).

John·son·ese (jon′sə nēz′, -nēs′), *n.* a literary style characterized by pompous phraseology and an excessively Latinate vocabulary: from the style of writing practiced by Samuel Johnson. [JOHNSON + -ESE]

John′son grass′, a perennial sorghum, *Sorghum halepense*, that spreads by creeping rhizomes, grown for fodder. Also called **Aleppo grass, Means grass.** [named after William *Johnson*, American agriculturist who first planted it in 1840]

John·so·ni·an (jon sō′nē ən), *adj.* **1.** of, pertaining to, or characteristic of Samuel Johnson or his works. **2.** having the quality of Johnsonese. **—***n.* **3.** a person who writes in the Johnsonian style. **4.** a teacher or critic who specializes in the works of Samuel Johnson. [JOHNSON + -IAN] —**John·so′ni·an·ism,** *n.* —**John·so′ni·an·ly,** *adv.*

John·ston (jon′stən, -sən), *n.* **1. Albert Sidney,** 1803–62, Confederate general in the U.S. Civil War. **2. Joseph Eggleston,** 1807–91, Confederate general in the U.S. Civil War. **3. Mary,** 1870–1936, U.S. writer.

John′ston Cit′y, a town in S Illinois. 3891 (1960).

John′ston's or′gan (jon′stənz), *Entomol.* a sense organ in the second segment of the antenna of an insect, sensitive to movements of the antenna's flagellum, as when the insect is in flight. [named after Christopher *Johnston* (d. 1891), American physician]

Johns·town (jonz′toun′), *n.* **1.** a city in SW Pennsylvania: disastrous flood 1889. 53,949 (1960). **2.** a town in central Ohio. 2881 (1960).

John′ the Bap′tist, the forerunner and baptizer of Jesus. Matt. 3.

Jo·hore (jə hōr′, -hôr′), *n.* **1.** a state in Malaysia, on S Malay Peninsula. 1,064,814 (est. 1961); 7330 sq. mi. **2.** a city in and the capital of this state, in the S part. 672,590 (1957).

Joi·a·da (joi′ə də), *n.* *Douay Bible.* Jehoiada.

joie de vi·vre (zhwadᵊ vē′vrᵊ), *French.* a delight in being alive, esp. as expressed in a keen, carefree enjoyment of living. [lit., joy of living]

join (join), *v.t.* **1.** to bring in contact, connect, or bring or put together: *to join hands; to join pages with a staple.* **2.** to come into contact or union with: *The brook joins the river.* **3.** to bring together in a particular relation or for a specific purpose, action, etc.; unite: *to join forces.* **4.** to become a member of (a society, party, etc.): *to join a club.* **5.** to enlist in (one of the armed forces): *to join the Navy.* **6.** to come into the company of; meet or accompany: *I'll join you later.* **7.** to participate with (someone) in some act or activity: *My wife joins me in thanking you for the gift.* **8.** to unite in marriage. **9.** to meet or engage in (battle, conflict, etc.): *The opposing armies joined battle in the valley.* **10.** to adjoin: *His land joins mine.* **11.** to draw a curve or straight line between: *to join two points on a graph.* —*v.i.* **12.** to come into or be in contact or connection: *a place where cliffs and sea join.* **13.** to become united, associated, or combined; associate or ally oneself (usually fol. by *with*): *Please join with us in our campaign.* **14.** to take part with others (often fol. by *in*): *Let's all join in.* **15.** to be contiguous or close; lie or come together; form a junction: *Our farms join along the river.* **16.** to enlist in one of the armed forces (often fol. by *up*): *He joined up to fight for his country.* **17.** *Obs.* to meet in battle or conflict. —*n.* **18.** a joining. **19.** a place or line of joining; seam. **20.** *Math.* union (def. 10a). [ME *joine(n)* < OF *joign-* (root of *joindre* to join) < L *jung(ere)* (to) YOKE, join] —**join′a·ble,** *adj.*

—**Syn. 1.** link, couple, fasten, attach; conjoin, combine; associate, consolidate, amalgamate. JOIN, CONNECT, UNITE all imply bringing two or more things together more or less closely. JOIN may refer to a connection or association of any degree of closeness, but often implies direct contact: *One joins the corners of a mortise together.* CONNECT implies a joining as by a tie, link, wire, etc.: *One connects two batteries.* UNITE implies a close joining of two or more things, so as to form one: *One unites layers of veneer sheets to form plywood.* **10.** abut, border. —**Ant.** separate, divide.

join·der (join′dər), *n.* **1.** the act of joining. **2.** *Law.* **a.** the joining of causes of action in a suit. **b.** the joining of parties in a suit. **c.** the acceptance by a party to an action of an issue tendered. [< F *joindre.* See JOIN, -ER³]

join·er (joi′nər), *n.* **1.** one who or that which joins. **2.** a carpenter, esp. one who constructs doors, window sashes, paneling, and other permanent woodwork, esp. for interiors. **3.** a person who belongs to many clubs, associations, societies, etc., as from indiscriminate enthusiasm, for increased status, to make business or social contacts, or the like. [JOIN + -ER¹; r. ME *joinour* < AF *joignour,* equiv. to *joign-* (see JOIN) + *-our* -OR²]

join′er bulk′head, *Shipbuilding.* See **partition bulkhead.**

join′er door′, *Shipbuilding.* a door of wood or light metal set in a nonwatertight bulkhead.

join·er·y (joi′nə rē), *n.* **1.** the craft or trade of a joiner. **2.** woodwork made by a joiner. [JOINER + -Y³]

joint (joint), *n.* **1.** the place at which two things, or separate parts of one thing, are joined or united, either rigidly or in such a way as to admit of motion; juncture. **2.** *Anat., Zool.* **a.** the movable or fixed place or part where two bones or elements of a skeleton join. **b.** the form or structure of such a part, as a ball-and-socket, hinge, or other arrangement. **3.** *Biol.* **a.** a part, esp. of a plant, insect, etc., connected with another part by an articulation, node, or the like. **b.** a portion between two articulations, nodes, or the like. **4.** *Bot.* the part of a stem from which a branch or leaf grows; node. **5.** one of the large portions into which a section of meat is divided by a butcher, as the shoulder or leg, esp. as served at table. **6.** *Geol.* a fracture plane in rocks, generally at right angles to the bedding of sedimentary rocks and variously oriented in igneous and metamorphic rocks, commonly arranged in two or more sets of parallel intersecting systems. **7.** *Slang.* a dirty or disreputable place of public accommodation, esp. a cheap restaurant or nightclub. **8.** *Slang.* place; establishment: *We stayed in a very classy joint near the ocean.* **9.** *Slang.* a marijuana cigarette. **10. out of joint, a.** dislocated, as a bone. **b.** in an unfavorable state; inauspicious: *The time is out of joint.* **c.** out of keeping; inappropriate: *Such behavior seems wholly out of joint with their fine upbringing.* —*adj.* **11.** shared by or common to two or more: *a joint obligation.* **12.** sharing or acting in common: *joint members of a committee.* **13.** joined or associated, as in relation, interest, or action: *joint owners.* **14.** undertaken or produced by two or more in conjunction or in common: *a joint reply; a joint effort.* **15.** *Law.* joined together in obligation or ownership: *joint heirs.* **16.** *Parl. Proc.* of or pertaining to both branches of a bicameral legislature. **17.** pertaining to or noting diplomatic action in which two or more governments are formally united. —*v.t.* **18.** to unite by a joint or joints. **19.** to form or provide with a joint or joints. **20.** to cut (a fowl, piece of meat, etc.) at the joint; divide at a joint; separate into pieces at the joints: *to joint a chicken.* **21.** *Carpentry.* **a.** to prepare (a board or the like) for fitting in a joint. **b.** to true the bottom of (a wooden plane body) so that it will move evenly along the surface of the work. **22.** to file the teeth of (a saw) to uniform height. **23.** *Masonry.* to finish (a mortar joint), as by striking. —*v.i.* **24.** to fit together by or as by joints: *The cinder blocks jointed neatly.* [ME < OF *joint, jointe* < L *junct(um), juncta,* n. use of neut. and fem. of *junctus* (ptp. of *jungere* to join), equiv. to *junc-* (var. of *jung-* join) + *-tus* ptp. suffix]

joint′ account′, a bank account in the names of two or more persons or parties and subject to withdrawals by each.

joint′ and last′ survi′vor annu′ity, *Insurance.* an annuity payable until the death of the last of two or more designated persons, though sometimes with reduced amounts after the first such person dies.

joint′ bar′, a steel member for maintaining a rigid joint between two rail ends.

Joint′ Chiefs′ of Staff′, *U.S.* the Chiefs of Staff of the Army and the Air Force and the Chief of Naval Operations, together with a chairman selected from one of the branches of the armed forces, serving as the principal military advisory body to the President, the National Security Council, and the Secretary of Defense.

joint′ commit′tee, *Govt.* a committee appointed from both houses of a bicameral legislature in order to reach a compromise on their differences concerning a particular issue.

joint·ed (join′tid), *adj.* **1.** having or provided with joints. **2.** formed with knots or nodes. [JOINT + -ED³] —**joint′ed·ly,** *adv.* —**joint′ed·ness,** *n.*

joint·er (join′tər), *n.* **1.** one who or that which joints. **2.** a tool or machine used in making joints. **3.** *Agric.* a device with a triangular head, used with a plow to bury trash. **4.** *Law Obs.* a man who holds a jointure. [JOINT + -ER¹]

joint′er plane′, *Carpentry.* a plane for truing the edges of boards, planing large surfaces, etc.

joint′ ill′, *Vet. Pathol.* a disease of young foals characterized by swollen inflamed joints, high fever, and usually by death a few days after birth. Also called **navel ill, pyosepticemia.**

joint·less (joint′lis), *adj.* **1.** without a joint; lacking a joint. **2.** (of an object) formed as a single piece, without jointing. [JOINT + -LESS]

joint′ life′ annu′ity, *Insurance.* an annuity, the payments of which cease at the death of the first of two or more specified persons.

joint′ life′ insur′ance, life insurance covering two or more persons, the benefits of which are paid after the first person dies.

joint·ly (joint′lē), *adv.* together; in combination; in common: *My brother and I own the farm jointly.* [JOINT + -LY]

joint′ resolu′tion, a resolution adopted by both branches of a bicameral legislative assembly and requiring the signature of the chief executive to become law.

joint·ress (join′tris), *n.* *Law.* a woman on whom a jointure has been settled. [JOINT(E)R + -ESS]

joint′ run′ner, (in plumbing) incombustible materials, as asbestos, for packing a joint to be calked with lead.

joint′ ses′sion, a joint meeting, as of both houses of a bicameral legislature.

joint′ stock′, **1.** stock or capital divided into a number of shares. **2.** a pool of stock held in common.

joint′-stock′ com′pany (joint′stok′), **1.** *U.S.* an association of individuals in a business enterprise with transferable shares of stock, much like a corporation except that stockholders are liable for the debts of the business. **2.** *Brit.* an incorporated business with transferable shares and with shareholders having either limited or unlimited liability for debts of the business.

joint′ stool′, a low wood stool having turned legs with all parts joined by a mortise joint.

join·ture (join′chər), *n.* *Law.* **1.** an estate or property settled on a woman in consideration of marriage, to be owned by her after her husband's death. **2.** *Obs.* a joint tenancy limited in favor of a man and his wife. [ME < OF < L *junctūr(a),* equiv. to *junct-* (see JOINT) + *-ūra* -URE] —**join′tured,** *adj.* —**join′ture·less,** *adj.*

joint·weed (joint′wēd′), *n.* an American, polygonaceous herb, *Polygonella articulata,* having many-jointed, spikelike racemes of small, white or rose-colored flowers. [JOINT + WEED¹]

joint·worm (joint′wûrm′), *n.* the larva of any of several chalcid flies of the family *Eurytomidae,* esp. of the genus *Harmolita,* that feeds in the stems of grasses. Also called **strawworm.** [JOINT + WORM]

Join·vi·le (zhoinn vē′le), *n.* a seaport in S Brazil. 55,553 (1960). Also, **Joinville.**

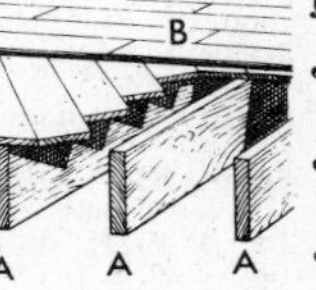

A, Joist
B, Floor boards

Join·ville (*Fr.* zhwan vēl′ *for 1; Port.* zhoinn vē′le *for 2*), *n.* **1. Jean de** (zhän də), 1224?–1317, French chronicler. **2.** Joinvile.

joist (joist), *n.* **1.** any of a number of small, parallel beams of timber, steel, reinforced concrete, etc., for supporting floors, ceilings, etc. —*v.t.* **2.** to furnish with or fix on joists. [ME *giste* < OF < LL **jacit(um)* support, n. use of neut. of *jacitus* (ptp. of *jacēre* to lie), equiv. to *jaci-* lie + *-tus* ptp. suffix] —**joist′less,** *adj.*

jo·jo·ba (hō hō′bə), *n.* an evergreen shrub, *Simmondsia californica,* of southwestern North America, bearing oily seeds and an edible fruit. [< MexSp]

Jó·kai (yō′koi), *n.* **Mau·rus** (mou′ro͝os) or **Mór** (môr), 1825–1904, Hungarian novelist.

joke (jōk), *n., v.,* **joked, jok·ing.** —*n.* **1.** something said or done to provoke laughter or amusement, as a witticism, a short and amusing narrative, a prankish act, etc.: *He tells very funny jokes. She played a joke on him.* **2.** something that is amusing or ridiculous; an object of jesting; a thing, situation, or person laughed at rather than taken seriously: *Her cooking is the neighborhood joke. His debut as a virtuoso violinist was a joke.* **3.** a matter for joking about; trifling matter: *The loss was no joke.* **4.** something that does not present the expected challenge; something very easy: *The test was a joke for the whole class.* **5.** See **practical joke.** —*v.i.* **6.** to speak or act in a playful or merry way: *He was always joking with us.* **7.** to say something in fun or sport, rather than in earnest: *He didn't really mean it; he was only joking.* —*v.t.* **8.** to subject to jokes; make fun of; tease. **9.** to obtain by joking: *The comedian joked coins from the audience.* [< L *joc(us)* jest] —**joke′less,** *adj.* —**jok′ing·ly,** *adv.*

—**Syn. 1.** witticism, jape, prank, quip, quirk, sally, raillery. JOKE, JEST refer to something said (or done) in sport, or to cause amusement. A JOKE is something said or done for the sake of exciting laughter; it may be raillery, a witty remark, or a prank or trick: *to tell a joke.* JEST, today a more formal word, nearly always refers to joking language and is more suggestive of scoffing or ridicule than is JOKE: *to speak in jest.*

joke·book (jōk′bo͝ok′), *n.* a book of jokes. [JOKE + BOOK]

jok·er (jō′kər), *n.* **1.** a person who jokes. **2.** one of two extra playing cards in a pack, usually imprinted with the figure of a jester, used in some games as the highest card or as a wild card. **3.** *U.S.* a clause or expression inserted in a legislative bill with the unavowed object of defeating the ostensible purpose of the bill if passed. **4.** a seemingly minor, unsuspected clause or wording that is put into an agreement, legal document, etc., to change its effect. **5.** an unexpected or final fact, factor, or condition that changes or reverses a situation or result completely: *He gave her a beautiful diamond engagement ring, but the joker was that it was stolen!* **6.** any method, trick, or expedient for getting the better of another: *They pulled a joker on us to get better seats.* **7.** *Informal.* a man; fellow; chap: *That joker's earning twice as much as I am.* **8.** one who thinks himself funny; prankster: *Who's the joker who put toothpaste in the éclairs?* **9.** *Informal.* a wise guy; wiseacre; smart aleck: *Tell that joker to stop using my parking space.* [JOKE + -ER¹]

joke·ster (jōk′stər), *n.* a joker, esp. a practical joker. [JOKE + -STER]

Jok·ja·kar·ta (jok′yä kär′tä), *n.* Jogjakarta.

jok·ta·leg (jok′tə leg′), *n.* *Brit. Dial.* jockteleg.

jole (jōl), *n.* jowl².

Jo·li·et (jō′lē et′, jō′lē et′; *for 1 also Fr.* zhô lye′), *n.* **1. Louis** (lwē), 1645–1700, French explorer of the Mississippi, born in Canada. **2.** a city in NE Illinois. 66,780 (1960).

Jo·liot-Cu·rie (zhô lyō′kү rē′), *n.* **1. I·rène** (ē ren′), (*Irène Curie*), 1897–1956, French nuclear physicist: Nobel prize for chemistry 1935 (daughter of Pierre and Marie Curie). **2.** her husband, **(Jean) Fré·dé·ric** (zhän frā dā rēk′), (*Jean Frédéric Joliot*), 1900–58, French nuclear physicist: Nobel prize for chemistry 1935. **3.** a ring formation in the averted hemisphere or far side of the moon.

Jo·li·vet (zhô lē ve′), *n.* **An·dré** (än drā′), born 1905, French composer.

jol·li·er (jol′ē ər), *n.* *Informal.* a person who jollies, esp. a person who uses teasing flattery in order to gain a desired aim. [JOLLY + -ER¹]

jol·li·fi·ca·tion (jol′ə fə kā′shən), *n.* jolly merrymaking; jolly festivity. [JOLLY + -FICATION]

jol·li·fy (jol′ə fī′), *v.t., v.i.,* **-fied, -fy·ing.** *Informal.* to make or become jolly or merry. [JOLLY + -FY]

jol·li·ty (jol′i tē), *n., pl.* **-ties. 1.** jolly mood, condition, or activity; gaiety. **2. jollities,** jolly festivities. [ME *jolite* < OF, equiv. to *joli(f)* gay (see JOLLY) + *-te* -TY²]

—**Syn. 1.** See **mirth.**

jol·ly (jol′ē), *adj.,* **-li·er, -li·est,** *v.,* **-lied, -ly·ing,** *n., pl.* **-lies,** *adv.* —*adj.* **1.** in good spirits; gay; merry: *In a moment he was as jolly as ever.* **2.** cheerfully festive or convivial: *a jolly party.* **3.** joyous; happy: *Christmas is a jolly season.* **4.** *Chiefly Brit. Informal.* delightful; charming. **5.** *Brit.* **a.** *Informal.* great; thorough: *a jolly blunderer.* **b.** *Slang.* slightly drunk; tipsy. —*v.t.* **6.** *Informal.* to talk or act agreeably to (a person) in order to keep him in good humor, esp. in the hope of gaining something: *They jollied him along until the job was done.* —*v.i.* **7.** *Informal.* to jolly a person. —*n.* **8.** *Informal.* the practice or an instance of jollying a person. —*adv.* **9.** *Brit. Informal.* extremely; very: *jolly well.* [ME *joli, jolif* < OF *jolif, joli* gay, equiv. to *jol-* (prob. < ON; cf. Icel *jōl* YULE) + *-if* -IVE] —**jol′li·ly,** *adv.* —**jol′li·ness,** *n.*

—**Syn. 1–3.** glad, spirited, jovial, sportive, playful. See **gay.** —**Ant. 1–3.** gloomy, melancholy.

Jol′ly bal′ance (jol′ē; *Ger.* yôl′ē), a spring balance used for determining the density of a sample by comparison of its weight in air and water. [named after Philipp von *Jolly* (d. 1884), German physicist]

jol′ly boat′, *Naut.* **1.** a light boat carried at the stern of a sailing vessel. **2.** a small pleasure sailboat for use in sheltered waters. [*jolly* < Dan *jolle* YAWL]

jol′ly jump′er, *Naut.* any light sail set above a skysail; flying kite.

Jol′ly Rog′er (roj′ər), a flag flown by pirates, having the device of a white skull and crossbones on a black field.

Jo·lo (hô lô′), *n.* **1.** an island in the SW Philippines: the main island of the Sulu Archipelago. 116,000 (est. 1948); 345 sq. mi. **2.** a seaport on this island. 18,282 (1948).

Jol·son (jōl′sən), *n.* **Al** (*Asa Yoelson*), 1886–1950, U.S. actor and singer, born in Russia.

jolt (jōlt), *v.t.* **1.** to jar, shake, or cause to move by or as by a sudden rough thrust; shake up roughly: *The truck jolted its passengers over the uneven road.* **2.** to knock sharply so as to dislodge: *He jolted the nail free with a stone.* **3.** to stun with a blow, esp. in boxing. **4.** to shock psychologically: *The war jolted us all.* **5.** to bring to a desired state sharply or abruptly: *to jolt a person into awareness.* **6.** to make active, as by using an abrupt, sharp, or rough manner: *to jolt someone's memory.* **7.** to interfere with or intrude upon, esp. in a rough or crude manner; interrupt disturbingly. —*v.i.* **8.** to move with a sharp jerk or a series of sharp jerks: *The car with the flat tire jolted to a halt.* —*n.* **9.** a jolting shock, movement, or blow: *The automobile gave a sudden jolt.* **10.** an emotional or psychological shock: *The news gave me quite a jolt.* **11.** that which causes such a shock: *The news was a jolt to me.* **12.** a sudden, unexpected rejection or defeat: *Their policy got a rude jolt from the wide-spread opposition.* **13.** *Slang.* a prison sentence. **14.** *Slang.* an injection of a narcotic. **15.** a bracing dose of something: *a jolt of whiskey; a jolt of fresh air.* [b. *jot* to jolt and *joll* to bump, both now dial.] —**jolt′er,** *n.* —**jolt′ing·ly,** *adv.* —**jolt′less,** *adj.*

jolt·y (jōl′tē), *adj.,* **jolt·i·er, jolt·i·est.** full of jolts; bumpy. [JOLT + -Y¹] —**jolt′i·ness,** *n.*

Jon (jon), *n.* a boy's given name, form of **John.**

Jo·nah (jō′nə), *n.* **1.** a Minor Prophet who, for his impiety, was thrown overboard from his ship and swallowed by a large fish, remaining in its belly for three days before being cast up onto the shore unhurt. **2.** a book of the Bible bearing his name. **3.** any person or thing regarded as bringing bad luck. **4.** a boy's given name. Also, **Jo·nas** (jō′nəs). —**Jo′nah·esque′,** *adj.*

Jon·a·than (jon′ə thən), *n.* **1.** a son of Saul and friend of David. I Sam. 18–20. **2.** *Archaic.* an American, esp. a New Englander. Cf. **Brother Jonathan. 3.** a boy's given name.

Jon·a·than (jon′ə thən), *n.* *Hort.* **1.** a variety of red apple that matures in early autumn. **2.** the tree bearing this fruit. [named after *Jonathan* Hasbrouck (d. 1846), American jurist]

Jon′athan spot′, *Plant Pathol.* a disease of stored apples, esp. the Jonathan, characterized by circular lesions on the fruit.

Jones (jōnz), *n.* **1. An·son** (an′sən), 1798–1858, president of the Republic of Texas. **2. Ca·sey** (kā′sē), (*John Luther Jones*), 1864–1900, U.S. locomotive engineer: folk hero of ballads, stories, and plays. **3. Daniel,** 1881–1967, English phonetician. **4. Ernest,** 1879–1958, Welsh psychoanalyst. **5. Henry Arthur,** 1851–1929, English dramatist. **6. Howard Mum·ford** (mum′fərd), 1892–1980, U.S. educator and critic. **7. In·i·go** (in′ə gō′), 1573–1652, English architect. **8. John Paul** (*John Paul*), 1747–92, American naval commander in the Revolutionary War, born in Scotland. **9. John Win·ston** (win′stən), 1791–1848, U.S. politician: Speaker of the House 1843–45. **10. Robert Tyre** (tīər), ("*Bobby*"), born 1902, U.S. golfer. **11. Rufus Matthew,** 1863–1948, U.S. Quaker, teacher, author, and humanitarian.

Jones·bor·o (jōnz′bûr ō, -bur ō), *n.* **1.** a city in NE Arkansas. 21,418 (1960). **2.** a town in central Louisiana. 3848 (1960). **3.** a town in central Georgia. 3014 (1960).

Jones·es (jōn′ziz), *n.pl.* one's social equals, esp. one's neighbors: *Keeping up with the Joneses is the only thing she's concerned about.* [pl. of *Jones,* common proper name]

jon·gleur (jong′glər; *Fr.* zhôn glœr′), *n., pl.* **-gleurs** (-glərz; *Fr.* -glœr′). (in medieval France and Norman England) an itinerant minstrel or entertainer who sang songs, often of his own composition, and told stories. [< F; MF *jougleur* (? by misreading, *ou* being read *on*), OF *jogleor* < L *joculātor* joker, equiv. to *joculāt(us),* ptp. of *joculārī* to joke (*jocul-* (see JOCULAR) + *-ātus* -ATE[1]) + *-or* -OR[2]]

Jon′ker di′amond (jong′kər), a diamond weighing 726 carats, discovered in the Transvaal in 1934 and cut into 12 pieces.

Jön·kö·ping (yœn′chœ ping), *n.* a city in S Sweden. 52,576 (1965).

jon·nick (jon′ik), *adj.* *Brit., Australian Informal.* jannock.

jon·quil (jong′kwil, jon′-), *n.* a narcissus, *Narcissus Jonquilla,* having long, narrow, rushlike leaves and fragrant, yellow or white flowers. [< F *jonquille* < Sp *junquilla,* equiv. to *junc(o)* rush, reed (< L *juncus*) + *-illa* dim. suffix]

Jon·quil (jong′kwil, jon′-), *n.* a girl's given name.

Jon·son (jon′sən), *n.* **Ben,** 1573?–1637, English dramatist and poet. —**Jon·so·ni·an** (jon sō′nē ən), *adj.*

jook[1] (jo͝ok, jo͝ok), *n.* *Slang.* See **juke joint.** Also called **jook′ joint′.**

jook[2] (jo͝ok), *n., v.t., v.i.* *Scot.* jouk.

Jooss (yōs), *n.* **Kurt** (ko͝ort), born 1901, German ballet dancer and choreographer.

Jop·lin (jop′lin), *n.* a city in SW Missouri. 38,958 (1960).

Jop·pa (jop′ə), *n.* ancient name of **Jaffa.**

Jor·daens (yôr′däns), *n.* **Ja·cob** (yä′kôp), 1593–1678, Flemish painter.

jor·dan (jôr′dən), *n.* *Obs.* See **chamber pot.** [ME *jurdan* urinal, perh. after JORDAN, the river, by coarse jesting]

Jor·dan (jôr′dən; *for 2 also Fr.* zhôr dän′), *n.* **1. David Starr** (stär), 1851–1931, U.S. biologist and educator. **2. Ma·rie En·ne·mond Ca·mille** (ma rē′ en° môn′ ka mē′y°), 1838–1922, French mathematician. **3.** Official name, **Hashemite Kingdom of Jordan.** a country in SW Asia, consisting of the former Trans-Jordan and a part of Palestine. 1,860,443 (est. 1965); 37,264 sq. mi. *Cap.:* Amman. **4.** a river in SW Asia, flowing from S Lebanon through the Sea of Galilee, then S between Israel and Jordan through W Jordan into the Dead Sea. 200 mi. long.

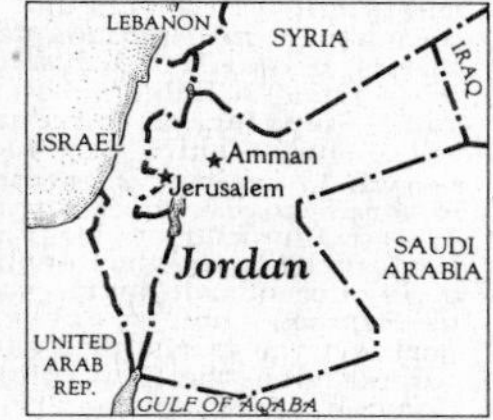

Jor′dan al′mond, a large, hard-shelled, Spanish almond used esp. in confectionery. [alter. of ME *jardyne almaund* garden almond, equiv. to *jardyne* (see JARDINIERE) + *almaund* ALMOND]

Jordan′ arc′, *Math.* See **simple arc.** [named after M. E. C. JORDAN]

Jordan′ curve′, *Math.* See **simple closed curve.** [named after M. E. C. JORDAN]

Jordan′ curve′ the′orem, *Math.* the theorem that the complement of a simple closed curve can be expressed as the union of two disjoint sets, each having as boundary the given curve. Cf. **simple closed curve.** [named after M. E. C. JORDAN]

Jor′dan en′gine, a machine for beating and refining pulp, used in manufacturing certain grades of paper. [named after Joseph *Jordan* (1859–60), American inventor, who developed it]

Jor·dan′-Höl′der the′orem (zhôr dän′hœl′dər), *Math.* the theorem that for any two composition series of a group, an isomorphism exists between the corresponding quotient groups of each series, taken in some specified order.

Jor·mun·gandr (yôr′mo͝on gän′dər), *n.* See **Midgard serpent.** Also, **Iormungandr.**

jor·na·da (hôr nä′də; *Sp.* hôr nä′thä), *n., pl.* **-das** (-dəz; *Sp.* -thäs). *Southwestern U.S.* a full day's travel across a desert without a stop for taking on water. [< Sp < OPr *jornada,* equiv. to *jorn-* (< LL *diurn(um)* day) + *-ada* (< L *-āta* fem. perfective suffix)]

jo·ro·po (hə rō′pō; *Sp.* hô rô′pô), *n., pl.* **-pos** (-pōz; *Sp.* -pôs). a Venezuelan ballroom dance in quick triple meter. [< AmerSp]

jo·rum (jôr′əm, jōr′-), *n.* **1.** a large bowl or vessel for holding drink. **2.** the contents of such a vessel: *a jorum of punch.* **3.** a great quantity. [said to be named after *Joram,* who brought vessels of silver, gold, and brass to David (2 Samuel 8:10)]

Jos (jôs), *n.* a city in central Nigeria. 31,582 (1953).

Jos·e·lyn (jos′ə lin), *n.* a girl's given name. Also, **Jocelin, Joceline, Jocelyn, Jocelynne.**

Jo·sep (jō′səp), *n.* a boy's given name, form of **Joseph.**

Jo·seph (jō′zəf, -səf), *n.* **1.** the first son of Jacob and Rachel: sold into slavery by his brothers. Gen. 30:22–24; 37. **2.** the husband of Mary who was the mother of Jesus. Matt. 1:16–25. **3.** (*l.c.*) a long coat buttoning in the front, worn esp. by women as part of their riding habit in colonial America. **4.** a boy's given name.

Joseph II, 1741–90, emperor of the Holy Roman Empire 1765–90 (son of Francis I; brother of Leopold II and Marie Antoinette).

Jo·se·phine (jō′zə fēn′, -sə-), *n.* **1. Empress** (*Marie Joséphine Rose Tascher de la Pagerie*). See **Beauharnais, Joséphine de. 2.** a girl's given name.

Jo·se·phine's-lil·y (jō′zə fēnz′lil′ē, -sə-), *n.* a perennial herb, *Brunsuigia josephinae,* of South Africa, having showy, lilylike, red flowers. [named after the Empress JOSEPHINE]

Jo′seph of Ar·i·ma·thae′a (ar′ə mə thē′ə), a member of the Sanhedrin who placed the body of Jesus in the tomb. Matt. 27:57–60; Mark 15:43.

Jo·seph's-coat (jō′zəfs kōt′, -səfs-), *n.* an annual herb, *Amaranthus tricolor,* having stalkless, headlike clusters of flowers and sometimes blotched and colored leaves. Also called **fountain plant.** [after JOSEPH (def. 1) and his coat of many colors]

Jo·se·phus (jō sē′fəs), *n.* **Fla·vi·us** (flā′vē əs), (*Joseph ben Matthias*), A.D. 37?–c100, Jewish historian and general.

Jo·ser (jō′sər), *n.* a boy's given name, form of **Joseph.**

josh (josh), *Informal.* —*v.t., v.i.* **1.** to chaff; banter in a teasing way. —*n.* **2.** good-natured banter. [? b. JOKE and BOSH] —**josh′er,** *n.*

Josh (josh), *n.* a boy's given name, form of **Joshua.**

Josh., Joshua.

Josh·u·a (josh′o͞o ə), *n.* **1.** the successor of Moses as leader of the Israelites. Deut. 31:14,23; 34:9. **2.** a book of the Bible bearing his name. **3.** a boy's given name. Also, *Douay Bible,* **Josue** (for defs. 1, 2).

Josh′ua tree′, a tree, *Yucca brevifolia,* growing in arid or desert regions of the southwestern U.S. Also called **tree yucca.**

Jo·si·ah (jō sī′ə), *n.* **1.** Also, *Douay Bible,* **Jo·si·as** (jō sī′əs). a king of Judah, reigned 640?–609? B.C. II Kings 22. **2.** a boy's given name. [<< Heb *Yōshīyāh* God upholds]

Jo·sie (jō′sē, -zē), *n.* a girl's given name, form of **Josephine.**

jos·kin (jos′kin), *n.* *Chiefly Brit. Slang.* a bumpkin. [? alter. of BUMPKIN, with dial. *joss* to jostle, bump r. *bump-*]

Jos·quin des Prés (zhôs kan dā prā′). See **Des Prés, Josquin.**

joss[1] (jos), *n.* a Chinese house idol or cult image. [< pidgin E < Pg *deos* < L *deus* god]

joss[2] (jos), *n.* *Brit., Australian Informal.* a foreman or boss. [?]

jos·ser (jos′ər), *n.* *Brit. Slang.* fellow, esp. one who is or is made to appear foolish or simple-minded. [?]

joss′ house′, a Chinese temple for idol worship.

joss′ stick′, a slender stick of a dried, fragrant paste, burned by the Chinese as incense before a joss.

jos·tle (jos′əl), *v.,* **-tled, -tling,** *n.* —*v.t.* **1.** to bump, push, shove, or brush roughly or rudely against; elbow roughly; hustle. **2.** to drive or force by, or as by, pushing or shoving: *The crowd jostled him into the subway.* **3.** to exist in close contact or proximity with: *The three families jostle each other in the small house.* **4.** to contend with: *The candidates jostled each other to win the election.* **5.** to unsettle; disturb: *The thought jostled her complacency.* —*v.i.* **6.** to bump, shove, push, or brush against as in passing or in a crowd (often fol. by *with* or *against*): *He jostled against the crowd.* **7.** to exist in close contact or proximity with someone or something. **8.** to compete; contend. —*n.* **9.** a shock, push, bump, or brush against someone or something. Also, **justle.** [var. (in ME, var. sp.) of *justle,* equiv. to *juste(n)* (to) JOUST + -LE] —**jos′tle·ment,** *n.* —**jos′tler,** *n.*

Jos·u·e (jos′yo͞o ē), *n.* *Douay Bible.* Joshua (defs. 1, 2).

jot (jot), *v.,* **jot·ted, jot·ting,** *n.* —*v.t.* **1.** to write or mark down quickly or briefly (usually fol. by *down*): *Jot down his license number.* —*n.* **2.** the least part of something; a little bit: *I don't care a jot.* **2. not a jot or tittle,** not a bit; not at all: *The world situation matters not a jot or tittle to him.* [< L *jota* < Gk *iôta* IOTA]

jo·ta (hō′tə; *Sp.* hô′tä), *n., pl.* **-tas** (-təz; *Sp.* -täs). **1.** a Spanish dance in triple meter, performed by a couple and marked by complex rhythms executed with the heels and castanets. **2.** the music for this dance. [< Sp, prob. OSp *sota* dance, deriv. of *sotar* to dance < L *saltāre*]

jot·ter (jot′ər), *n.* **1.** a person who jots things down. **2.** a small notebook. [JOT + -ER[1]]

jot·ting (jot′ing), *n.* **1.** the act of one who jots. **2.** a quickly written or brief note; memorandum. [JOT + -ING[1]] —**jot′ty,** *adj.*

Jo·tun (yô′to͞on), *n.* *Scand. Myth.* any of a race of giants frequently in conflict with the gods. Also, **Jo′tunn, Jö·tunn** (yœ′to͞on). [< Icel *jötunn* giant; c. OE *eoten;* akin to EAT]

Jo·tun·heim (yô′to͞on hām′), *n.* *Scand. Myth.* the outer world, or realm of giants; Utgard. Also, **Jo′tunn·heim′, Jö·tun·heim, Jö·tunn·heim** (yœ′to͞on hām′). [< Icel, equiv. to *jötunn* giant + *heimr* world, HOME]

Jou·bert (zho͞o ber′), *n.* **Jo·seph** (zhō zef′), 1754–1824, French moralist and essayist.

Jou·haux (zho͞o ō′), *n.* **Lé·on** (lā ôn′), 1879–1954, French labor leader and politician: Nobel peace prize 1951.

jouk (jo͞ok), *Scot.* —*n.* **1.** a sudden, elusive movement. —*v.t., v.i.* **2.** to dodge or duck. Also, **jook.** [appar. var. of DUCK[2]]

Jou·ka·hai·nen (you′kə hī′nen), *n.* *Finnish Legend.* a Lapp magician who tried to kill Väinämöinen.

joule (jo͞ol, joul), *n.* *Physics.* the meter-kilogram-second unit of work or energy, equal to the work done by a force of one newton when its point of application moves through a distance of one meter in the direction of the force: equivalent to 10^7 ergs and one watt-second. *Abbr.:* J, j Also called **newton-meter.** [named after J. P. JOULE]

Joule (jo͞ol, joul), *n.* **James Prescott,** 1818–89, English physicist.

Joule's′ law′, *Physics.* **1.** the principle that the rate of production of heat by a constant direct current is directly proportional to the resistance of the circuit and to the square of the current. **2.** the principle that the internal energy of a given mass of an ideal gas is a function of its temperature alone. [named after J. P. JOULE]

Joule′-Thom′son effect′ (jo͞ol′tom′sən, joul′-), *Thermodynamics.* the change of temperature that a gas exhibits during a throttling process, shown by passing the gas through a small aperture or porous plug into a region of low pressure. Cf. **free expansion.** [named after J. P. JOULE and Sir William THOMSON]

jounce (jouns), *v.,* **jounced, jounc·ing,** *n.* —*v.t., v.i.* **1.** to move joltingly or roughly up and down; bounce. —*n.* **2.** a jolting fall or bounce. [late ME, appar. b. *joll* to bump (now obs.) and BOUNCE]

jour., **1.** journal. **2.** journeyman.

Jour·dan (zho͞or dän′), *n.* **Jean Bap·tiste** (zhän ba-tēst′), **Count,** 1762–1833, French marshal.

journ., journalism.

jour·nal (jûr′nəl), *n.* **1.** a daily record, as of occurrences, experiences, or observations: *She kept a journal during her European trip.* **2.** a record, usually daily, of the proceedings and transactions of a legislative body, an organization, etc. **3.** a newspaper, esp. a daily one. **4.** any periodical or magazine, as one published for a learned society or profession: *the October issue of* The Journal of Higher Education. **5.** *Bookkeeping.* **a.** a daybook. **b.** (in the double-entry method) a book into which all transactions are entered from the daybook or blotter to facilitate posting into the ledger. **6.** *Naut.* a log or logbook. **7.** *Mach.* the portion of a shaft or axle contained by a plain bearing. [ME < OF *journal* daily < L *diurnāl(is)* DIURNAL] —**jour′nal·ar′y,** *adj.* —**jour′nal·ish,** *adj.*

jour′nal box′, *Mach.* a box or housing for a journal and its bearing.

jour′nal bronze′, an alloy of about 83 percent copper, 13 percent tin, 3 percent zinc, and 1 percent lead.

jour·nal·ese (jûr′nəlēz′, -nəlēs′), *n.* **1.** a manner of writing or speaking characterized by neologism, archness, faulty or unusual syntax, etc., used by some journalists, esp. certain columnists, and conceived of as typifying the journalistic style. **2.** writing or expression in this manner: *Get that journalese out of your copy!* —*adj.* **3.** of, pertaining to, or characterized by this manner (often used predicatively): *That word's not English, it's journalese.* [JOURNAL + -ESE]

jour·nal in·time (zho͞or nal an tēm′), *pl.* **jour·naux in·times** (zho͞or nō zan tēm′). *French.* a diary.

jour·nal·ise (jûr′nəlīz′), *v.i., v.t.,* **-ised, -is·ing.** *Chiefly Brit.* journalize.

jour·nal·ism (jûr′nəliz′əm), *n.* **1.** the occupation of reporting, writing, editing, photographing, or broadcasting news or of conducting any news organization as a business. **2.** press[1] (def. 27). **3.** a course of study preparing students for careers in reporting, writing, and editing for newspapers and magazines. **4.** writing that reflects superficial thought and research, a popular slant, and hurried composition, conceived of as exemplifying newspaper or popular magazine writing as distinguished from scholarly writing: *He calls himself a historian, but his books are mere journalism.* [< F *journalisme.* See JOURNAL, -ISM]

jour·nal·ist (jûr′nəlist), *n.* **1.** a person who practices the occupation of journalism. **2.** a person who keeps a journal, diary, or other record of daily events. [JOURNAL + -IST]

jour·nal·is·tic (jûr′nəlis′tik), *adj.* of, pertaining to, or characteristic of journalists or journalism. [JOURNALIST + -IC] —**jour′nal·is′ti·cal·ly,** *adv.*

jour·nal·ize (jûr′nəlīz′), *v.,* **-ized, -iz·ing.** —*v.t.* **1.** to enter or record in a journal. **2.** to tell or relate, as done in a journal. **3.** (in double-entry bookkeeping) to enter in a journal, preparatory to posting to the ledger. —*v.i.* **4.** to keep or make entries in a journal. Also, *esp. Brit.,* **journalise.** [JOURNAL + -IZE] —**jour′nal·i·za′tion,** *n.* —**jour′nal·iz′er,** *n.*

Jour′nal of the Plague′ Year′, A, a fictitious history (1722) by Daniel Defoe, purporting to be the authentic account of a resident of London during the year of the Great Plague.

jour·ney (jûr′nē), *n., pl.* **-neys,** *v.,* **-neyed, -ney·ing.** —*n.* **1.** travel from one place to another, usually taking a rather long time: *a six-day journey over the desert.* **2.** a distance, course, or area traveled or suitable for traveling: *a desert journey.* **3.** a period of travel: *a week's journey.* **4.** passage or progress from one stage to another: *the journey to success.* —*v.i.* **5.** to make a journey; travel. [ME *journee* day < OF < VL **diurnāta* a day's time, day's work, etc., equiv. to L *diurn(us)* daily + *-āta* perfective suffix (fem.)] —**jour′ney·er,** *n.*
—**Syn. 1.** excursion, jaunt, tour. See **trip. 5.** roam, rove; peregrinate.

jour·ney·man (jûr′nē mən), *n., pl.* **-men. 1.** a person who has served his apprenticeship at a trade or handicraft and is certified to work at it for another. **2.** *Obs.* a person hired to do work for another, usually for a day. [JOURNEY a day's work (obs.) + MAN[1]]

jour·ney·work (jûr′nē wûrk′), *n.* **1.** the work of a journeyman. **2.** necessary, routine, or servile work. [JOURNEY a day's work (obs.) + WORK]

joust (joust, just, jo͞ost), *n.* **1.** single combat in which two armored knights on horseback opposed each other with weapons of war, as the lance, sword, mace, etc. **2.** (in late medieval history) this type of combat fought in a highly formalized manner as part of a tournament. **3. jousts,** tournament. —*v.i.* **4.** to contend in a joust or tournament. Also, **just.** [ME *jouste* < OF *jouste, joste,* deriv. of *joster, jouster* to tilt in the lists < VL **juxtāre* to approach, clash, deriv. of L *juxtā* approaching, bordering] —**joust′er,** *n.*

Jouve (zho͞ov), *n.* **Pierre Jean** (pyer zhän), born 1887, French writer.

Jove (jōv), *n.* **1.** Jupiter (def. 1). **2.** *Archaic.* the planet Jupiter. **3. by Jove!** (an exclamation used to emphasize a previous remark or to express surprise, approval, etc.): *It was a good fight, by Jove!* [ME < L *Jov-* root of sky-god's name (nom. *Juppiter*). See TUESDAY]

jo·vi·al (jō′vē əl), *adj.* **1.** endowed with or characterized by a hearty, joyous humor or a spirit of good fellowship: *a jovial little man.* **2.** (*cap.*) of or pertaining to the god Jove, or Jupiter. [< L *joviāl(is)* of Jupiter (the planet, supposed to exert a happy influence), equiv. to *jovi-* (see JOVIAN) + *-ālis* -AL[1]] —**jo′vi·al·ly,** *adv.* —**jo′vi·al·ness,** *n.*
—**Syn. 1.** merry, jolly, convivial, gay, joyful, mirthful. JOVIAL, JOCOSE, JOCULAR, JOCUND agree in referring to someone who is in a good humor. JOVIAL suggests a hearty, joyous humor: *a jovial person.* JOCOSE refers to that which causes laughter; it suggests someone who is playful and given to jesting: *with jocose and comical airs.* JOCULAR means humorous, facetious, mirthful, and waggish: *jocular enough to keep up the spirits of all around him.* JOCUND, now a literary word, suggests a cheerful, light-hearted, and sprightly gaiety: *glad and jocund company.* —**Ant. 1.** gloomy.

jo·vi·al·i·ty (jō′vē al′i tē), *n.* the state or quality of being jovial; merriment; jollity. [JOVIAL + -ITY; cf. F *jovialité*]
—**Syn.** See **mirth.**

Jo·vi·an (jō′vē ən), *adj.* **1.** of or pertaining to the Roman god Jupiter. **2.** of or pertaining to the planet Jupiter. [< L *Jovi-* (comb. form of *Juppiter*) + -AN] —**Jo′vi·an·ly,** *adv.*

Jo·vi·an (jō′vē ən), *n.* (*Flavius Claudius Jovianus*) A.D. 331?–364, Roman emperor 363–364.

jow (jou, jō), *Scot.* —*n.* **1.** the ringing, tolling, or sound of a bell. —*v.t.* **2.** to ring or toll (a bell). **3.** to hit or strike (esp. the head). —*v.i.* **4.** to rock from side to side. [var. of *joll* (now dial.), ME *jolle(n)* (to) strike < ?]

Jow·ett (jou′it), *n.* **Benjamin,** 1817–93, English educator and Greek scholar.

jowl[1] (joul, jōl), *n.* **1.** a jaw, esp. the lower jaw. **2.** the cheek. [ME *chawl, chavell,* OE *ceafl* jaw; c. D *kevel,* G *Kiefer,* Icel *kjaptr*] —**jowled,** *adj.*

jowl[2] (joul, jōl), *n.* **1.** a fold of flesh hanging from the jaw, as of a fat person. **2.** the meat of the cheek of a hog. **3.** the dewlap of cattle. **4.** the wattle of fowls. Also, **jole.** [ME *cholle,* OE *ceole* throat; c. G *Kehle* throat]

jowl·y (jou′lē, jō′-), *adj.,* **jowl·i·er, jowl·i·est.** having prominent jowls. [JOWL[1] + -Y[1]]

joy (joi), *n.* **1.** the emotion of great delight or happiness caused by something good or satisfying; keen pleasure: *She felt the joy of seeing her son's success.* **2.** a source or cause of keen pleasure or delight: *His handling of prose is a pure joy.* **3.** the expression or display of glad feeling; festive gaiety. **4.** state of happiness or felicity. —*v.i.* **5.** to feel joy; be glad; rejoice. —*v.t.* **6.** *Obs.* to gladden. [ME *joy(e)* < OF *jore, joye* < LL *gaudia,* neut. pl. (taken as fem. sing.) of L *gaudium* joy, equiv. to *gaud-* (base of *gaudēre* to be glad) + *-ium* n. suffix]
—**Syn. 1.** rapture. **4.** bliss. See **pleasure.** —**Ant. 1, 3.** misery.

Joy (joi), *n.* a girl's given name. Also, **Joye.**

joy·ance (joi′əns), *n.* *Archaic.* joyous feeling; gladness. [JOY + -ANCE (coined by Spenser)]

Joyce (jois), *n.* **1. James (Augustine Aloysius),** 1882–1941, Irish novelist. **2. William** ("*Lord Haw-Haw*"), 1906–46, U.S. and English Nazi propagandist in Germany. **3.** a girl's or boy's given name.

Joyc·e·an (joi′sē ən), *adj.* **1.** of, pertaining to, or characteristic of James Joyce or his work. —*n.* **2.** a student of the life and work of James Joyce. **3.** a person who favors or advocates the work, style, or methods of James Joyce. **4.** an imitator of James Joyce. [JOYCE + -AN]

joy·ful (joi′fəl), *adj.* **1.** full of joy, as a person, the heart, etc.; glad; delighted. **2.** showing or expressing joy, as looks, actions, speech, etc. **3.** causing or bringing joy, as an event, a sight, news, etc.; delightful. [ME; see JOY, -FUL] —**joy′ful·ly,** *adj.* —**joy′ful·ness,** *n.*
—**Syn. 1.** joyous, happy, blithe; buoyant, elated, jubilant. See **gay.** —**Ant. 1.** melancholy.

joy·less (joi′lis), *adj.* **1.** without joy or gladness; unhappy: *the joyless days of the war.* **2.** causing no joy or pleasure. [ME *joyles.* See JOY, -LESS] —**joy′less·ly,** *adv.* —**joy′less·ness,** *n.*
—**Syn. 1.** sad, cheerless, gloomy, dismal, miserable. —**Ant. 1.** joyous.

Joy′ of Life′, The, a painting (1905–06) by Henri Matisse.

joy·ous (joi′əs), *adj.* joyful; happy; jubilant. [ME < AF; OF *joios,* etc. See JOY, -OUS] —**joy′ous·ly,** *adv.* —**joy′ous·ness,** *n.*

joy′ ride′, *Informal.* **1.** a pleasure ride in an automobile. **2.** a short ride in an automobile driven recklessly or used without the owner's permission. **3.** a brief, emotionally exciting interlude. —**joy′ rid′er.** —**joy′ rid′ing.**

joy-ride (joi′rīd′), *v.i.,* **-rode, -rid·den, -rid·ing.** *Informal.* to go on a joy ride.

joy′ stick′, *Aeron. Informal.* the control stick of an airplane. [appar. so called from the joy that controlling the plane gives]

JP, jet propulsion.

J.P., Justice of the Peace.

Jr., **1.** Journal. **2.** Junior.

jr., junior.

J.S.D., Doctor of the Science of Law; Doctor of Juristic Science.

Ju (RO͞O), *n.* **1.** Confucian (def. 2). **2.** one of the tutors of aristocratic origin working during the Chou dynasty.

Ju., June.

Juan (wän; *Sp.* hwän), *n.* a boy's given name, Spanish form of **John.**

Jua·na (wä′nə; *Sp.* hwä′nä), *n.* a girl's given name.

Juan Car·los (wän kär′lōs), **Prince** (*Juan Carlos Alfonso Victor María de Borbón y Borbón*), born 1938, Spanish nobleman, born in Italy.

Ju·an de Fu·ca (jo͞o′ən di fyo͞o′kə; *Sp.* hwän′ de fo͞o′kä), a strait between Vancouver Island and NW Washington. 100 mi. long; 15–20 mi. wide. Also called **Ju′an de Fu′ca Strait′.**

Juan de la Cruz (*Sp.* hwän de lä kro͞oth, kro͞os), **San.** See **John of the Cross, Saint.**

Ju·an Fer·nán·dez (jo͞o′ən fər nan′dez; *Sp.* hwän′ fer nän′deth), a group of three islands in the S Pacific, 400 miles W of and belonging to Chile: Alexander Selkirk, the alleged prototype of *Robinson Crusoe,* was marooned here 1704.

Jua·ni·ta (wä nē′tə; *Sp.* hwä nē′tä), *n.* a girl's given name.

Juá·rez (wär′ez; *Sp.* hwä′res), *n.* **1. Be·ni·to (Pa·blo)** (be nē′tô pä′blô), 1806–72, president of Mexico 1858–72. **2. Ciudad.** See **Ciudad Juárez.**

ju·ba (jo͞o′bə), *n.* a lively dance accompanied by rhythmic hand clapping, developed by plantation Negroes of the U.S. [?]

Ju·ba (jo͞o′bä), *n.* **1.** a river in E Africa, flowing S from S Ethiopia through Somalia to the Indian Ocean. 1000 mi. long. Italian, **Giuba.** **2.** a city in S Sudan, on the White Nile. 10,660 (1960).

Ju·bal (jo͞o′bəl), *n.* son of Lamech and Adah: the progenitor of musicians and those who produce musical instruments. Gen 4:21.

ju·bate (jo͞o′bāt), *adj.* *Zool.* covered with long hairs resembling a mane. [< NL *jubāt(us)* maned, equiv. to L *jub(a)* mane + *-ātus* -ATE[1]]

jub·bah (jo͝ob′bə), *n.* a long outer garment with long sleeves, worn in Muslim countries. [< Ar]

Jub·bul·pore (jub′əl pôr′), *n.* Jabalpur.

ju·be (jo͞o′bē), *n.* *Archit.* **1.** a screen with an upper platform, separating the choir of a church from the nave and often supporting a rood. **2.** a rood loft. [< L *jubē,* first word of prayer beginning *Jubē, Domine, benedicere* consent, O Lord, to bless, said at or near the rood screen]

ju·bi·lant (jo͞o′bə lənt), *adj.* **1.** showing great joy or triumph; rejoicing; exultant: *the cheers of jubilant victors.* **2.** expressing joy or exultation: *The mood of his poetry is sometimes mournful, sometimes jubilant.* [< L *jūbilant-* (s. of *jūbilāns,* prp. of *jūbilāre* to shout for joy), equiv. to *jūbil-* shout + *-ant-* -ANT] —**ju′bi·lance, ju′bi·lan·cy,** *n.* —**ju′bi·lant·ly,** *adv.*

ju·bi·late (jo͞o′bə lāt′), *v.i.,* **-lat·ed, -lat·ing.** **1.** to show or feel great joy; rejoice; exult. **2.** to celebrate a jubilee or joyful occasion. [< L *jūbilāt(us)* (ptp. of *jūbilāre* to shout for joy), equiv. to *jūbil-* shout + *-ātus* -ATE[1]] —**ju·bi·la·to·ry** (jo͞o′bə lə tôr′ē, -tōr′ē), *adj.*

Ju·bi·la·te (jo͞o′bə lä′tē, -lā′tē), *n.* **1.** Also called **Ju′bi·la′te Sun′day.** the third Sunday after Easter: so called from the first word of the 65th Psalm in the Vulgate, which is used as the introit. **2.** a musical setting of this psalm. [< L *jūbilāte* shout ye for joy]

ju·bi·la·ti·o (jo͞o′bə lä′shē ō′), *n.* jubilus. [< L: JUBILATION]

ju·bi·la·tion (jo͞o′bə lā′shən), *n.* **1.** a feeling of joy or exultation: *Their jubilation didn't last long; the following week they lost the game.* **2.** act of rejoicing or jubilating; exultation. **3.** a joyful or festive celebration. [< L *jūbilātiōn-* (s. of *jūbilātiō*) a shouting for joy, equiv. to *jūbilāt-* (see JUBILATE) + *-iōn-* -ION; r. ME *jubilacioun* < AF]

ju·bi·lee (jo͞o′bə lē′, jo͞o′bə lē′), *n.* **1.** the celebration of any of certain anniversaries, as the 25th (**silver jubilee**), 50th (**golden jubilee**), or 60th or 75th (**diamond jubilee**). **2.** the completion of 50 years of existence, activity, or the like, or its celebration: *Our college will celebrate its jubilee next year.* **3.** any season or occasion of rejoicing or festivity. **4.** rejoicing or jubilation. **5.** *Rom. Cath. Ch.* **a.** an appointed year or other period, ordinarily every 25 years (**ordinary jubilee**), in which a plenary indulgence is granted upon repentance and the performance of certain religious acts. **b.** a period of time (**extraordinary jubilee**) declared by the pope as a time of rejoicing, as for an anniversary, when a plenary indulgence is granted upon repentance and the performance of certain religious acts. **c.** Also called **ju′bilee indul′gence.** the plenary indulgence granted during such a period. **6.** Also, **Ju′bi·le′.** *Chiefly Biblical.* a yearlong period to be observed by Jews once every 50 years, during which Jewish slaves were to be freed, alienated lands were to be restored to the original owner or his heir, the fields were to be left untilled, and all agricultural labors were to be suspended. Lev. 25. Cf. **sabbatical year** (def. 2). **7.** a Negro folk song concerned with future happiness or deliverance from tribulation. —*adj.* **8.** flambé (def. 1). [ME < MF *jubile* < eccl. L < *jūbilaeus* < eccl. Gk *iōbēlaios* (with *ō* and *ē* > *u* and *i* by assimilation to L *jūbilāre* to shout for joy) < Heb *yōbhēl* ram's horn, jubilee]

Ju′bilee′ rig′, *Brit. Naut.* a square rig introduced in 1897, having very wide yards and stump topgallant masts. [named after Queen Victoria's second jubilee]

ju·bi·lus (jo͞o′bə ləs), *n., pl.* **-li** (-lī′). *Liturgy.* (in Roman Catholic music) a rejoicing, melodic group of tones to which is chanted the last "a" of the second and third alleluias, often following the gradual of the Mass. Also, **jubilatio.** [< ML: shout of joy, L *jūbilum* a wild cry, shepherd's song; see JUBILATE]

Jud., **1.** Judges. **2.** Judith (Apocrypha).

jud., **1.** judge. **2.** judgment. **3.** judicial. **4.** judiciary.

Ju·da (jo͞o′də), *n.* *Douay Bible.* Judah (defs. 1–3).

Ju·dae·a (jo͞o dē′ə), *n.* Judea. —**Ju·dae′an,** *adj., n.*

Ju·dah (jo͞o′də), *n.* **1.** the fourth son of Jacob and Leah. Gen. 29:35. **2.** one of the 12 tribes of Israel. **3.** the Biblical kingdom of the Hebrews in S Palestine, including the tribes of Judah and Benjamin. Cf. **Ephraim** (def. 3). **4.** a boy's given name. Also, *Douay Bible,* **Juda** (for defs. 1–3).

Ju′dah ha-Le′vi (hä lē′vī), (*Judah ben Samuel Halevi*) 1085–1140, Spanish rabbi, physician, poet, and philosopher. Also, **Ju′dah Ha·le′vi.**

Ju′dah ha-Na·si′ (hä nä sē′), A.D. c135–c210, Jewish rabbi and scholar. Also, **Ju′dah Ha·na·si′.** Also called **Judah I.**

Ju·dah·ite (jo͞o′də īt′), *n.* **1.** a member of the tribe of Judah or of the kingdom of Judah. —*adj.* **2.** of or pertaining to the tribe or kingdom of Judah. [JUDAH + -ITE[1]]

Ju·da·ic (jo͞o dā′ik), *adj.* **1.** of or pertaining to Judaism: *the Judaic idea of justice.* **2.** of or pertaining to the Jews; Jewish. [< L *jūdaic(us)* < Gk *ioudaikós,* equiv. to *Ioudaî(os)* Jew + *-ikos* -IC] —**Ju·da′i·cal·ly,** *adv.*

Ju·da·i·ca (jo͞o dā′i kə), *n.pl.* things Jewish, esp. when of a historical or literary nature, as books about Jewish life and customs. [< L, neut. pl. of *jūdaicus* JUDAIC]

Ju·da·ise (jo͞o′dē īz′, -dā-), *v.i., v.t.,* **-ised, -is·ing.** *Chiefly Brit.* Judaize. —**Ju′da·i·sa′tion,** *n.* —**Ju′da·is′er,** *n.*

Ju·da·ism (jo͞o′dē iz′əm, -dā-), *n.* **1.** the monotheistic religion of the Jews, having its ethical, ceremonial, and legal foundation in the precepts of the Old Testament and in the teachings and commentaries of the rabbis as found chiefly in the Talmud. Cf. **Conservative Jew, Orthodox Jew, Reform Jew.** **2.** belief in and conformity to this religion, its practices, and ceremonies. **3.** this religion considered as forming the basis of the cultural and social identity of the Jews: *He called assimilation a threat to American Judaism.* **4.** Jews collectively. [< L *jūdaism(us)* < Gk *ioudaismós,* equiv. to *Ioudaî(os)* Jew + *-ismos* -ISM]

Ju·da·ist (jo͞o′dē ist, -dā-), *n.* **1.** an adherent or supporter of Judaism. **2.** (in the early Christian church) a convert from Judaism who followed or advocated Jewish rites or practices. [JUDA(ISM) + -IST] —**Ju′da·is′tic,** *adj.* —**Ju′da·is′ti·cal·ly,** *adv.*

Ju·da·ize (jo͞o′dē īz′, -dā-), *v.,* **-ized, -iz·ing.** —*v.i.* **1.** to conform to the spirit, character, principles, or practices of Judaism. —*v.t.* **2.** to bring into conformity with Judaism. Also, *esp. Brit.,* **Judaise.** [< LL *jūdaiz(āre)* < Gk *ioudaízein,* equiv. to *Ioudaî(os)* Jew + *-izein* -IZE] —**Ju′da·i·za′tion,** *n.* —**Ju′da·iz′er,** *n.*

Ju·das (jo͞o′dəs), *n.* **1.** Judas Iscariot, the disciple who betrayed Jesus. Mark 3:19. **2.** one treacherous enough to betray a friend; traitor. **3.** one of the 12 apostles (not Judas Iscariot). Luke 6:16; Acts 1:13; John 14:22. **4.** a brother of James (and possibly of Jesus). Matt. 3:55; Mark 6:3. **5.** (*usually l.c.*) Also called **ju′das hole′.** a peephole, as in an entrance door or the door of a prison cell. —*adj.* **6.** used as a decoy to lead other animals to slaughter: *A Judas goat led sheep into the abattoir.* —**Ju′das-like′,** *adj.*

Ju′das Maccabae′us. See **Maccabaeus, Judas.**

Ju′das Priest′, (an exclamation of exasperation or disgust.) [euphemism for *Jesus Christ*]

Ju′das tree′, **1.** a Eurasian, purple-flowered, leguminous tree, *Cercis Siliquastrum,* supposed to be the kind upon which Judas hanged himself. **2.** any of various other trees of the same genus, as the redbud.

Judd (jud), *n.* a boy's given name.

Jude (jo͞od), *n.* **1.** a book of the New Testament. **2.** the author of this book, sometimes identified with Judas, the brother of James. **3.** a boy's given name, form of **Judd** or **Judah.**

Ju·de·a (jo͞o dē′ə), *n.* the S region of ancient Palestine: existed under Persian, Greek, and Roman rule; now absorbed by SW Israel and W Jordan. Also, **Judaea.**

Ju·de·an (jo͞o dē′ən), *adj.* **1.** of or pertaining to Judea. —*n.* **2.** a native or inhabitant of Judea. Also, **Judaean.** [JUDE(A) + -AN]

Jude′ the Obscure′, a novel (1895) by Thomas Hardy.

Ju·dette (jo͞o det′), *n.* a girl's given name, form of **Judith.**

Judg., Judges.

judge (juj), *n., v.,* **judged, judg·ing.** —*n.* **1.** a public officer authorized to hear and determine causes in a court of law; a magistrate charged with the administering of justice. **2.** a person appointed to decide in any competition or contest; authorized arbiter: *the judges of a beauty contest.* **3.** one qualified to pass a critical judgment: *He is a good judge of horses.* **4.** an administrative head of Israel in the period between the death of Joshua and the accession to the throne by Saul. —*v.t.* **5.** to pass legal judgment on; pass sentence on (a person): *The court judged him guilty.* **6.** to hear evidence or legal arguments in (a case) in order to pass judgment; try: *The Supreme Court is judging that case.* **7.** to form a judgment or opinion of or upon; decide upon critically: *You can't judge a book by its cover.* **8.** to decide or decree judicially or authoritatively: *The censor judged the book obscene and forbade its sale.* **9.** to infer, think, or hold as an opinion: *He judged her to be correct.* **10.** to make a careful guess about; estimate: *We judged the distance to be about four miles.* **11.** (of the Hebrew judges) to govern. —*v.i.* **12.** to act as a judge; pass judgment: *No one would judge between us.* **13.** to form an opinion or estimate: *I have heard the evidence and will judge accordingly.* **14.** to make a mental judgment. [ME *jugge(n)* < AF *juge(r),* OF *jugier* < L *jūdicāre* to judge, equiv. to *jūdic-* (s. of *jūdex*) a judge + *-āre* inf. suffix] —**judge′a·ble,** *adj.* —**judg′er,** *n.* —**judge′less,** *adj.* —**judge′like′,** *adj.* —**judge′ship,** *n.* —**judg′ing·ly,** *adv.*
—**Syn. 1.** justice. **2.** arbitrator. JUDGE, REFEREE, UMPIRE refer to one who is entrusted with decisions affecting others. JUDGE, in its legal and other uses, implies particularly that one has qualifications and authority for giving decisions in matters at issue: *a judge appointed to the Supreme Court.* A REFEREE usually examines and reports on the merits of a case as an aid to a court. An UMPIRE gives the final ruling when arbitrators of a case disagree. **3.** connoisseur, critic. **9.** conclude, determine; consider, regard. **12.** adjudge, adjudicate.

judge′ ad′vocate, *pl.* **judge advocates.** *Mil., Navy.* a staff officer designated as legal adviser to a commander and charged with the administration of military justice.

judge′ ad′vocate gen′eral, *pl.* **judge advocates general, judge advocate generals.** *Mil.* the chief legal officer of an army, navy, or air force.

Judge′ and His Hang′man, The, a novel (1952) by Friedrich Dürrenmatt. German, **Der Richter und sein Henker.**

Judge′ Lynch′, the personification of lynch law.

judge-made (juj′mād′), *adj.* established by a court, as by an application or interpretation of a law that is allegedly contrary to the intentions of the enacting body or by a decision that is allegedly an attempt to legislate.

Judg·es (juj′iz), *n.* (*construed as sing.*) a book of the Bible containing the history of the judges.

judg·mat·ic (juj mat′ik), *adj.* judicious. Also, **judg·mat′i·cal.** [JUDG(MENT) + (DOG)MATIC] —**judg·mat′i·cal·ly,** *adv.*

judg·ment (juj′mənt), *n.* **1.** the act or an instance of judging. **2.** *Law.* **a.** the judicial decision of a cause in court. **b.** the obligation, esp. a debt, arising from a judicial decision. **c.** the certificate embodying such a decision and issued against the obligor, esp. a debtor. **3.** the ability to judge, make a decision, or form an opinion objectively, authoritatively, and wisely, esp. in matters affecting action; good sense; discretion: *a man of sound judgment.* **4.** demonstration or exercise of such ability or capacity: *The major was decorated for the judgment he showed under fire.* **5.** the forming of an opinion, estimate, notion, or conclusion, as from circumstances presented to the mind: *Our judgment of the cause of his failure must rest on the evidence.* **6.** the opinion formed: *He regretted his hasty judgment.* **7.** a misfortune regarded as inflicted by divine sentence, as for sin. **8.** (*usually cap.*) Also called **Last Judgment.** the final trial of all mankind, both the living and dead, at the end of the world. Also, *esp. Brit.,* **judge′ment.** [ME *jug(g)ement* < OF *jugement,* equiv. to *juge-* (s. of *jugier* to JUDGE) + *-ment* -MENT] —**judg·men·tal;** *esp. Brit.,* **judge·men·tal** (juj men′tᵊl), *adj.*
—**Syn. 1.** determination. **2a.** verdict, decree. **3.** understanding; discrimination, discernment, perspicacity, penetration; sagacity, wisdom, intelligence, prudence, brains, common sense, taste.

Judg′ment Book′, *Theol.* the book from which all men will be judged at the Last Judgment, containing a full record of their acts.

Judg′ment Day′, **1.** the day of the Last Judgment; doomsday. **2.** (*italics*) a novel (1935) by James T. Farrell. Cf. **Studs Lonigan.**

judg′ment debt′, a debt established or confirmed by decree of a court of law.

judg′ment note′, a note that expressly authorizes a creditor, in case of default, to seek a judgment in court without notifying the debtor.

Judg′ment of Par′is, *Class. Myth.* the decision by

Paris to award Aphrodite the apple of discord competed for by Aphrodite, Athena, and Hera.

ju·di·ca·ble (jo͞o′də kə bəl), *adj.* capable of being or liable to be judged or tried. [< LL *jūdicābil(is)*, equiv. to *jūdic(āre)* (to) JUDGE + *-ābilis* -ABLE]

ju·di·ca·tive (jo͞o′də kā′tiv), *adj.* having ability to judge; judging: *the judicative faculty.* [< ML *jūdicātīv(us)*, equiv. to L *jūdic-* (see JUDGE) + *-ātīvus* -ATIVE]

ju·di·ca·tor (jo͞o′də kā′tər), *n.* a person who acts as judge or sits in judgment. [< LL, equiv. to L *jūdicāt(us)* (ptp. of *jūdicāre* to JUDGE; see ATE[1]) + *-or* -OR[2]] —**ju·di·ca·to·ri·al** (jo͞o′də kə tôr′ē əl, -tōr′-), *adj.*

ju·di·ca·to·ry (jo͞o′də kə tôr′ē, -tōr′ē), *adj., n., pl.* **-to·ries.** —*adj.* **1.** of or pertaining to judgment or the administration of justice; judiciary: *judicatory power.* —*n.* **2.** a court of law and justice; tribunal; judiciary. **3.** the administration of justice. [< ML *jūdicātōr(ium)* law court, equiv. to L *jūdic-* (see JUDGE) + *-āt(us)* -ATE[1] + *-ōrium* -ORY[2]]

ju·di·ca·ture (jo͞o′də kā′chər), *n.* **1.** the administration of justice, as by judges or courts. **2.** the office, function, or authority of a judge. **3.** the jurisdiction of a judge or court. **4.** a body of judges. **5.** the power of administering justice by legal trial and determination. [< ML *jūdicātūr(a)*, equiv. to L *jūdic-* (see JUDGE) + *-āt(us)* -ATE[1] + *-ūra* -URE]

ju·di·ci·a·ble (jo͞o dish′ē ə bəl), *adj.* capable of being judged or tried. [< L *jūdici(um)* judgment (see JUDGE) + -ABLE]

ju·di·cial (jo͞o dish′əl), *adj.* **1.** pertaining to judgment in courts of justice or to the administration of justice: *judicial proceedings.* **2.** pertaining to courts of law or to judges: *judicial functions.* **3.** of or pertaining to a judge; proper to the character of a judge; judgelike: *judicial gravity.* **4.** inclined to make or give judgments; critical; discriminating: *a judicial mind.* **5.** decreed, sanctioned, or enforced by a court. **6.** giving or seeking judgment, as in a dispute or contest; determinative: *a judicial duel over lands.* **7.** inflicted by God as a judgment or punishment. [< L *jūdiciāl(is)* of the law courts, equiv. to *jūdici(um)* judgment (see JUDGE) + *-ālis* -AL[1]] —**ju·di′cial·ly,** *adv.* —**ju·di′cial·ness,** *n.*
—**Syn. 1, 2.** juridical. **2.** forensic. **4.** See **judicious.**

judi′cial con′ference, *Law.* a conference of judges held to discuss improvements in methods or judicial procedure through court rules or otherwise.

judi′cial review′, *U.S.* the power of a court to adjudicate the constitutionality of the laws of a government or the acts of a government official.

judi′cial separa′tion, *Law.* a decree of legal separation of husband and wife that does not dissolve the marriage bond. Also called **limited divorce.**

ju·di·ci·ar·y (jo͞o dish′ē er′ē, -dish′ə rē), *adj., n., pl.* **-ar·ies.** —*adj.* **1.** pertaining to judgment in courts of justice or to courts or judges; judicial. —*n.* **2.** the judicial branch of government. **3.** the system of courts of justice in a country. **4.** judges collectively. [orig. adj. < L *jūdiciāri(us)* of the law courts, equiv. to *jūdici(um)* judgment (see JUDGE) + *-ārius* -ARY] —**ju·di′ci·ar′i·ly,** *adv.*

ju·di·cious (jo͞o dish′əs), *adj.* **1.** using or showing judgment as to action or practical expediency; discreet, prudent, or politic: *judicious use of money.* **2.** having, exercising, or characterized by good judgment; wise, sensible, or well-advised: *a judicious selection.* [< L *jūdici(um)* judgment (see JUDGE) + -OUS; cf. It *giudizioso*, F *judicieux*] —**ju·di′cious·ly,** *adv.* —**ju·di′cious·ness,** *n.*
—**Syn. 1.** See **practical. 2.** rational, reasonable, sober, sound, sagacious, enlightened, considered. JUDICIOUS, JUDICIAL both refer to a balanced and wise judgment. JUDICIOUS implies the possession and use of discerning and discriminating judgment: *a judicious use of one's time.* JUDICIAL has connotations of judgments made in a courtroom, and refers to a fair and impartial kind of judgment: *cool and judicial in examining the facts.* —**Ant. 1.** imprudent. **2.** silly, unreasonable.

Ju·dith (jo͞o′dith), *n.* **1.** a devoutly religious woman of the ancient Jews who saved her town from conquest by entering the camp of the besieging Assyrian army and cutting off the head of its commander, Holofernes, while he slept. **2.** a book of the Apocrypha and Douay Bible bearing her name. **3.** a girl's given name. [<< Heb *Yehūdīth* Jewess]

ju·do (jo͞o′dō), *n.* **1.** a method of defending oneself or fighting without the use of weapons, based on jujitsu but differing from it in banning dangerous throws and blows and stressing the athletic or sport element. **2.** the sport of fighting by this method. Cf. **jujitsu, karate.** —*adj.* **3.** of or pertaining to this fighting method or sport. [< Jap, equiv. to *jū* soft + *dō* art] —**ju′do·ist,** *n.*

ju·do·ka (jo͞o′dō kä′, jo͞o′dō kä′), *n., pl.* **-kas, -ka.** **1.** a contestant in a judo match. **2.** a judo expert. [< Jap, equiv. to *jūdō* JUDO + *ka* n. suffix]

Ju·dy (jo͞o′dē), *n.* **1.** the wife of Punch in the puppet show called *Punch and Judy.* **2.** Also, **Ju′die.** a girl's given name, form of **Judith.**

jug[1] (jug), *n., v.,* **jugged, jug·ging.** —*n.* **1.** a container for liquid, usually made of pottery, metal, or glass, commonly having a handle, often a spout or lip, and sometimes a lid or cork. **2.** the contents of such a container; jugful. **3.** a deep vessel, usually of earthenware, with a handle and a narrow neck stopped by a cork. **4.** *Slang.* jail; prison. —*v.t.* **5.** to put into a jug. **6.** to stew (meat) in an earthenware jug. **7.** *Slang.* to commit to jail; imprison. [? special use of *Jug* hypocoristic var. of *Joan*, woman's name]

jug[2] (jug), *n., v.,* **jugged, jug·ging.** —*n.* **1.** a sound made by a bird, esp. a nightingale. —*v.i.* **2.** to make such a sound. [imit.]

ju·gal (jo͞o′gəl), *adj.* **1.** of or pertaining to the cheek or the cheekbone. **2.** *Entomol.* pertaining to, involving, or situated near the jugum. [< L *jugāl(is)*, equiv. to *jug(um)* YOKE + *-ālis* -AL[1]]

ju′gal bone′, **1.** (in man) the cheekbone. **2.** a corresponding bone in animals.

ju′gal fur′row, (in certain insects) the crease, between the anal and jugal veins, along which the wing folds.

ju·gate (jo͞o′gāt, -git), *adj.* **1.** *Bot.* having the leaflets in pairs, as a pinnate leaf. **2.** *Entomol.* having a jugum. **3.** (of two or more portraits on a coin, medal, or escutcheon) overlapping. [< L *jug(um)* YOKE + -ATE[1]]

Ju·gend·stil (yo͞o′gənt shtēl′), *n.* (*sometimes l.c.*) *Fine Arts.* Art Nouveau as practiced in German-speaking countries. [< G, equiv. to *Jugend* youth + *Stil* style]

jug·ful (jug′fo͝ol), *n., pl.* **-fuls.** enough to fill a jug. [JUG[1] + -FUL]

jugged′ hare′, a stew made of wild rabbit, usually cooked in an earthenware or stone pot.

Jug·ger·naut (jug′ər nôt′), *n.* **1.** (*often l.c.*) any large, overpowering, destructive force or object, as war, a giant battleship, a powerful football team, etc. **2.** (*often l.c.*) anything requiring blind devotion or cruel sacrifice. **3.** Also called **Jagannath.** an idol of Krishna, at Puri in Orissa, India, annually drawn on an enormous cart under whose wheels devotees are said to have thrown themselves to be crushed. [< Hindi *Jagannāth* < Skt *Jagannātha* lord of the world (i.e., the god Vishnu), equiv. to *jagat* world + *nātha* lord] —**Jug′ger·naut′ish,** *adj.*

jug·gins (jug′inz), *n., pl.* **-gins·es.** *Chiefly Brit.* a simpleton. [?]

jug·gle (jug′əl), *v.,* **-gled, -gling,** *n.* —*v.t.* **1.** to keep (several objects, as balls, plates, ten pins, or knives) in continuous motion in the air simultaneously by tossing and catching. **2.** to hold, catch, carry, or balance precariously; almost drop and then catch hold again: *The center fielder juggled the ball, but finally made the catch.* **3.** to alter or manipulate in order to deceive, as by subterfuge or trickery: *to juggle accounts; to juggle the facts.* —*v.i.* **4.** to perform feats of manual or bodily dexterity, as tossing up and keeping in continuous motion a number of balls, plates, knives, etc. **5.** to use artifice or trickery. —*n.* **6.** the act or fact of juggling. [ME *jog(e)len* < OF *jogle(r)* (to) serve as buffoon or jester < LL *joculāre* to joke (r. L *joculārī*), equiv. to L *jocul(us)* (*joc(us)* JOKE + *-ulus* -ULE) + *-āre* inf. suffix] —**jug′gling·ly,** *adv.*

jug·gler (jug′lər), *n.* **1.** one who performs juggling feats, as with balls, knives, etc. **2.** one who deceives by trickery; trickster. [ME *joglere* < OF *jogler* (nom.) < L *joculātor* joker, equiv. to *joculāt(us)*, ptp. of *joculārī* to joke (*jocul-* (see JUGGLE) + *-ātus* -ATE[1]) + *-or* -OR[2]; r. OE *gēogelere* magician, c. G *gaukler*]

jug·gler·y (jug′lə rē), *n., pl.* **-gler·ies.** **1.** the art or practice of a juggler, esp. sleight of hand. **2.** the performance of juggling feats. **3.** any trickery or deception. [ME *jogel(e)rie* < OF *joglerie*, equiv. to *jogler* JUGGLER + *-ie* -Y[3]]

jug·head (jug′hed′), *n.* *Chiefly Western and Midland U.S.* a stupid person. [JUG[1] + HEAD]

ju·glan·da·ceous (jo͞o′glan dā′shəs), *adj.* belonging to the *Juglandaceae*, or walnut, family of trees. [< NL *Juglandace(ae)* walnut family (L *jugland-*, s. of *juglans* walnut + *-aceae* -ACEAE) + -OUS]

Ju·go·slav (yo͞o′gō släv′, -slav′), *n., adj.* Yugoslav. Also, **Ju′go-Slav′.** —**Ju′go·slav′ic,** *adj.*

Ju·go·sla·vi·a (yo͞o′gō slä′vē ə), *n.* Yugoslavia. —**Ju′go·sla′vi·an,** *adj., n.*

jug·u·lar (jug′yə lər, jo͞o′gyə-), *adj.* **1.** *Anat.* **a.** of or pertaining to the throat or neck. **b.** noting or pertaining to any of certain large veins of the neck, esp. one (**external jugular vein**) collecting blood from the superficial parts of the head, or one (**internal jugular vein**) collecting blood from within the skull. **2.** (of a fish) having the pelvic fins at the throat, before the pectoral fins. —*n.* **3.** *Anat.* a jugular vein. [< LL *jugulār(is)*, equiv. to L *jugul(um)* throat (see JUGULATE) + *-āris* -AR[1]]

ju·gu·late (jo͞o′gyə lāt′), *v.t.,* **-lat·ed, -lat·ing.** **1.** to check or suppress (disease) by extreme measures. **2.** to cut the throat of; kill. [< L *jugulāt(us)* (ptp. of *jugulāre* to cut the throat of), equiv. to *jugul(um)* throat (dim. of *jugum* YOKE) + *-ātus* -ATE[1]] —**ju′gu·la′tion,** *n.*

ju·gum (jo͞o′gəm), *n.* *Entomol.* the posterior basal area or lobe in the forewing of certain insects, sometimes serving to couple the forewings and hind wings in flight. [< NL, L: YOKE]

Ju·gur·tha (jo͞o gûr′thə), *n.* died 104 B.C., king of Numidia 113–104. —**Ju·gur′thine** (jo͞o gûr′thin, -thīn), *adj.*

juice (jo͞os), *n., v.,* **juiced, juic·ing.** —*n.* **1.** the liquid part or contents of plant or animal substance. **2.** the natural fluids of an animal body: *gastric juices.* **3.** the natural fluid, fluid content, or liquid part that can be extracted from a plant or one of its parts, esp. of a fruit: *orange juice.* **4.** essence, strength, or vitality: *He might be an old man, but he's still got the juice of life.* **5.** any extracted liquid. **6.** *U.S. Slang.* **a.** electricity or electric power. **b.** gasoline, fuel oil, etc., used to run an engine. **7. stew in one's own juice.** See **stew** (def. 5). —*v.t.* **8.** *Informal.* to extract juice from. **9. juice up, a.** to add more power, energy, or speed to; accelerate. **b.** to make exciting or spectacular: *They juiced up the movie by adding some battle scenes.* [ME *ju(i)s* < OF *jus* < L *jūs* broth, soup, sauce, juice] —**juice′less,** *adj.*

juic·er (jo͞o′sər), *n.* **1.** a kitchen appliance for extracting juice from fruits and vegetables. **2.** a stage electrician who works on the lighting of motion-picture, television, and theatrical sets. [JUICE + -ER[1]]

juic·y (jo͞o′sē), *adj.,* **juic·i·er, juic·i·est.** **1.** full of juice; succulent: *a juicy pear.* **2.** very interesting or colorful, esp. when slightly improper: *a juicy bit of gossip about the neighbors.* [ME *j(o)usy.* See JUICE, -Y[1]] —**juic′i·ly,** *adv.* —**juic′i·ness,** *n.*

Juif Er·rant, Le (*Fr.* lə zhwē fe RäN′). See **Wandering Jew, The.**

ju·jit·su (jo͞o jit′so͞o), *n.* a method of developed in Japan of defending oneself without the use of weapons by using the strength and weight of an adversary to disable him. Also, **jiujitsu, jiujutsu, jujutsu.** Cf. **judo, karate.** [< Jap, equiv. to *jū* soft, pliant + *jitsu* art]

ju·ju (jo͞o′jo͞o), *n.* **1.** an object venerated superstitiously and used as a fetish or amulet by native tribes of West Africa. **2.** the magical power attributed to such an object. **3.** a ban or interdiction effected by it. [< Hausa *djudju* fetish] —**ju′ju·ism,** *n.* —**ju′ju·ist,** *n.*

ju·jube (jo͞o′jo͞ob), *n.* **1.** the edible, plumlike fruit of any of certain Old World trees of the genus *Zizyphus.* **2.** any tree producing this fruit. **3.** a small candy or lozenge of gum arabic, gelatin, or the like, and fruit flavoring. [late ME < ML *jujub(a)* < L *zizyph(um)* < Gk *zízyphon* jujube tree]

ju·jut·su (jo͞o jut′so͞o, -jo͝ot′-), *n.* jujitsu.

Ju·juy (ho͞o hwē′), *n.* a city in NW Argentina. 72,150 (1965).

juke·box (jo͞ok′boks′), *n.* a coin-operated phonograph, typically in a gaudy, illuminated cabinet, having a variety of records that can be selected by pushbutton. Also called **juke.** [JUKE (JOINT) + BOX[1]]

juke′ house′, *Southern U.S.* **1.** a cheap roadhouse. **2.** a brothel.

juke′ joint′, an establishment where one can eat, drink, and, usually, dance to music provided by a jukebox. Also, **jook joint, jook.** [< Gullah *juke house* bawdy-house (cf. Bambara *dzugu* wicked); *joint* r. *house* for alliteration's sake]

Jukes (jo͞oks), *n.* the fictitious name of an actual New York family whose history over several generations showed a high incidence of disease, delinquency, and poverty. Cf. **Kallikak.**

Jul., July.

ju·lep (jo͞o′lip), *n.* **1.** a sweet drink, variously prepared and sometimes medicated. **2.** See **mint julep.** [ME < MF < Ar *julāb* < Pers *gulāb*, equiv. to *gul* rose + *āb* water]

Jules (jo͞olz; *Fr.* zhyl), *n.* a boy's given name, French form of **Julius.**

Jul·ia (jo͞ol′yə), *n.* a girl's given name.

Jul·ian (jo͞ol′yən), *n.* **1.** (*Flavius Claudius Julianus*) ("*the Apostate*") A.D. 331–363, Roman emperor 361–363. **2.** a boy's given name, form of **Julius.**

Jul·ian (jo͞ol′yən), *adj.* of, pertaining to, or characteristic of Julius Caesar. [< L *juliān(us)*, equiv. to *Juli(us)* + *-ānus* -AN]

Ju·li·an·a (jo͞o′lē an′ə; *for 1 also Du.* yY′lē ä′nä), *n.* **1.** (*Juliana Louise Emma Marie Wilhelmina*) born 1909, queen of the Netherlands since 1948 (daughter of Wilhelmina I). **2.** Also, **Ju′li·an′na, Ju·li·anne** (jo͞o′lē-an′). a girl's given name, form of **Julia.**

Jul′ian Alps′, a mountain range in N Slovenia. Highest peak, Mt. Triglav, 9394 ft.

Jul′ian cal′endar, the calendar established by Julius Caesar in 46 B.C., fixing the length of the year at 365 days and at 366 days every fourth year. There are 12 months of 30 or 31 days, except for February (which has 28 days with the exception of every fourth year, or leap year, when it has 29 days). Cf. **Gregorian calendar.**

Jul′ian Day′, *Astron.* a serial number equal to the number of days elapsed since January 1, 4713 B.C., proposed by Joseph Scalizer in 1582 and used in astronomical calculations: *January 1, 1965, at noon, Greenwich Civil Time, was Julian Day 2,438,762.0.* *Abbr.:* J.D.

Ju·lie (jo͞o′lē), *n.* a girl's given name, form of **Julia.**

ju·li·enne (jo͞o′lē en′; *Fr.* zhY lyen′), *adj.* **1.** (of food, esp. vegetables) cut into thin strips or small, matchlike pieces. —*n.* **2.** a clear soup garnished, before serving, with julienne vegetables. [< F, special use of *Julienne* woman's name]

Ju·li·et (jo͞o′lē ət, jo͞o′lē et′; *esp for 1* jo͞ol′yət), *n.* **1.** the heroine of Shakespeare's *Romeo and Juliet.* **2.** (used in communications to represent the letter *J*). **3.** Also, **Ju′li·ette′.** a girl's given name, form of **Julia.**

Ju′liet cap′, a skullcap, often set with pearls or other gems, worn by women for semiformal or bridal wear. [named after JULIET (def. 1)]

Jul·ius (jo͞ol′yəs), *n.* a boy's given name.

Julius I, Saint, died A.D. 352, Italian ecclesiastic: pope 337–352.

Julius II, (*Giuliano della Rovere*) 1443—1513, Italian ecclesiastic: pope 1503–13.

Julius III, (*Giammaria Ciocchi del Monte* or *Giovanni Maria del Monte*) 1487–1555, Italian ecclesiastic: pope 1550–55.

Jul′ius Cae′sar, **1.** See **Caesar, Gaius Julius.** **2.** (*italics*) a tragedy (1600?) by Shakespeare.

Jul·lun·dur (jul′ən dər), *n.* a city in central Punjab, in NW India. 222,600 (1961).

Ju·ly (jo͞o lī′, jə lī′), *n., pl.* **-lies.** the seventh month of the year, containing 31 days. [ME *julie* < AF < L *Julius* (CAESAR), after whom it was named; r. OE *Julius* < L; ME *ju(i)l* < OF]

Ju·ma·da (jo͝o mä′dä), *n.* either of two successive months of the Muslim year, the fifth (**Jumada I**) or the sixth (**Jumada II**). [< Ar]

jum·ble (jum′bəl), *v.,* **-bled, -bling,** *n.* —*v.t.* **1.** to mix in a confused mass; put or throw together without order. **2.** to confuse mentally; muddle. —*v.i.* **3.** to be mixed together in a disorderly heap or mass. **4.** to meet or come together confusedly. —*n.* **5.** a mixed or disordered heap or mass. **6.** a confused mixture; medley. **7.** a state of confusion or disorder. **8.** Also, **jum′bal.** a small, round, flat cake with a hole in the middle. [? b. *joll* to bump (now dial.) and TUMBLE] —**jum′ble·ment,** *n.* —**jum′bler,** *n.* —**jum′bling·ly,** *adv.*
—**Syn. 7.** muddle, hodgepodge; farrago, gallimaufry; mess; chaos. —**Ant. 1.** separate. **7.** order.

jum·bled (jum′bəld), *adj.* without order or coherence; chaotic. [JUMBLE + -ED[2]]

jum′ble sale′, *Chiefly Brit.* See **rummage sale.**

jum·bo (jum′bō), *n., pl.* **-bos,** *adj.* —*n.* **1.** *Informal.* a very large person, animal, or thing. **2.** *U.S. Naut.* **a.** a forestaysail having a boom (**jum′bo boom′**) along its foot, used esp. on schooners. **b.** a sail used in place of a course on a square-rigged vessel, having the form of an isosceles triangle set apex downward. **c.** a narrow triangular sail set point downward in place of a foresail on a topsail schooner. —*adj.* **3.** very large. [after *Jumbo*, name of large elephant in Barnum's show < Swahili *jumbe* chief]

jum·buck (jum′buk), *n.* *Australian.* a sheep. [from native Austral]

Jum·na (jum′nə), *n.* a river in N India, flowing SE from the Himalayas to the Ganges at Allahabad. 860 mi. long.

jump (jump), *v.i.* **1.** to spring clear of the ground or other support by a sudden muscular effort; leap: *to jump into the air; to jump out a window; to jump onto a moving train.* **2.** to rise suddenly or quickly: *He jumped from his seat when she entered.* **3.** to move or jerk suddenly, as from surprise or shock: *He jumped when the firecracker exploded.* **4.** *Informal.* to obey quickly; hustle: *The waiter was told to jump when the captain signaled.* **5.** *Slang.* to be full of activity; bustle: *The whole town is jumping with excitement.* **6.** to start a campaign, program, military attack, etc.; launch an activity, esp. of major proportions (usually fol. by *off*): *The march jumped off early in the morning.* **7.** *Checkers.* to move a man from one side of an opponent's man to a vacant square on the other, thus capturing it. **8.** to rise suddenly in amount, price, etc.: *Costs jumped again this*

quarter. **9.** to pass abruptly, ignoring intervening steps or deliberation: *to jump to a conclusion.* **10.** to change abruptly: *The traffic light jumped from green to red.* **11.** to move or change suddenly, haphazardly, aimlessly, or after a short period: *He jumped from job to job.* **12.** to pass or go aimlessly: *He jumped from one thing to another without being able to concentrate on anything.* **13.** to omit letters, numbers, etc.; skip: *This typewriter jumps and needs repairing.* **14.** to parachute from an airplane. **15.** to take eagerly; seize (often fol. by *at*): *He jumped at the offer.* **16.** to enter into something with vigor (usually fol. by *in* or *into*): *He jumped into the discussion right away.* **17.** to advance rapidly from one level to another, esp. in rank; pass through or skip intermediate stages in a forward or upward progression: *He jumped from clerk to general manager in a year.* **18.** *Motion Pictures.* (of a shot or frame) to fail to line up properly with the preceding or following shots because of a mechanical fault in the camera or projector. **19.** *Bridge.* to bid more than is necessary to reach the next bidding level, esp. as a signal to one's partner: *She jumped from three clubs to four spades.* **20.** *Journalism.* (of newspaper copy) to continue on a subsequent page, following intervening copy (opposed to *turn*). —*v.t.* **21.** to leap or spring over: *to jump a stream.* **22.** to cause to leap: *She jumped the horse over the fence.* **23.** to skip or pass over; bypass: *to jump the third grade in school.* **24.** to elevate or advance, esp. in rank, by causing to skip or pass rapidly through intermediate stages: *The college jumped him from instructor to full professor.* **25.** to anticipate or start before (the proper time, circumstances, etc.): *One car jumped the red light and collided with a truck.* **26.** to increase sharply: *The store jumped its prices to offset heavy expenditures.* **27.** *Checkers.* to capture (an opponent's man) by leaping over it to an unoccupied square. **28.** *Informal.* to attack without warning, as from ambush: *The thugs jumped him in a dark alley.* **29.** *Bridge.* to raise (the bid) by more than necessary to reach the next bidding level, esp. as a signal to one's partner. **30.** *Informal.* **a.** to abscond from; leave: *The robbers jumped town.* **b.** to flee or escape from. **31.** to seize or occupy illegally or forceably (a mining claim or the like), as on the ground of some flaw in the holder's title. **32.** (of trains, trolleys, etc.) to spring off or leave (the track). **33.** to get on board (a train, bus, etc.) quickly or with little planning or preparation for the trip: *He jumped a plane for Chicago.* **34.** *Journalism.* to continue (a story) from one page to another over intervening copy. **35.** *Metalworking.* to thicken (a bar or the like) by striking its end; upset (often fol. by *up*). **36.** **jump aboard** or **on board,** to join a group, activity, etc., esp. one that has been operating or functioning for some time: *After some hesitation, he jumped aboard and contributed heavily to the campaign.* **37. jump all over someone,** *Slang.* to reprimand; criticize. **38. jump bail.** See **bail**[1] (def. 7). **39. jump down someone's throat.** See **throat** (def. 11). **40. jump in** or **into with both feet,** to join or enter into exuberantly, eagerly, hastily, etc.: *Although Hal didn't know what the trouble was, he jumped in with both feet and started trying to clean up the mess.* **41. jump on,** *Informal.* to rebuke; reprimand: *He'll jump on anyone who contradicts him.* **42. jump on the bandwagon,** to join or support a successful or winning group, activity, candidate, etc.: *The business people finally jumped on the bandwagon, too, and the candidate won by a landslide.* **43. jump ship,** *Naut.* (of a crew member) to desert from a vessel; leave a vessel before the time agreed upon. **44. jump the gun.** See **gun**[1] (def. 8). —*n.* **45.** the act or an instance of jumping; leap. **46.** a space, obstacle, apparatus, or the like, cleared or to be cleared in a leap. **47.** *Informal.* a short or hurried journey. **48.** a descent by parachute from an airplane. **49.** a sudden rise in amount, price, etc.: *a jump in the stock market.* **50.** a sudden upward or other movement of an inanimate object. **51.** an abrupt transition from one point or thing to another, with omission of what intervenes: *In his book the writer made an unexplained jump from one topic to another.* **52.** a move or one of a series of moves: *The gangster stayed one jump ahead of the police.* **53.** *Sports.* any of several contests which feature a leap or jump. Cf **broad jump, high jump.** **54.** *Motion Pictures.* a break in the continuity of action due to a failure to match the action of one shot with the following one of the same scene. **55.** a sudden start as from nervous excitement: *She gave a jump when the firecracker went off.* **56.** *Checkers.* the act of taking an opponent's man by leaping over it to an unoccupied square. **57. the jumps,** restlessness; nervousness; anxiety: *I've got the jumps today.* **58.** Also called **breakover.** *Journalism.* the part of a story continued on another page. **59.** *Math.* the difference in limit values at a jump discontinuity of a given function. **60. get** or **have the jump on,** *Informal.* to get or have a head start or an initial advantage: *They got the jump on us in selling the item, but we finally caught up.* **61. on the jump,** in a hurry; running about: *Her lively youngsters keep her on the jump.* —*adj.* **62.** *Jazz.* **a.** of, pertaining to, or characteristic of swing. **b.** of, pertaining to, or characteristic of jazz; played at a bright tempo. —*adv.* **63.** *Obs.* exactly; precisely. [cf. Dan *gumpe* to jolt, *gimpe* to move up and down, Sw *gumpa,* LG *gumpen* to jump] —**jump′a·ble,** *adj.* —**jump′ing·ly,** *adv.*
—**Syn. 1.** JUMP, LEAP, VAULT imply propelling oneself by a muscular effort, either into the air or from one position or place to another. JUMP and LEAP are often used interchangeably, but JUMP indicates more particularly the springing movement of the feet in leaving the ground or support: *to jump up and down.* LEAP (which formerly also meant to run) indicates the passage, by a springing movement of the legs, from one point or position to another: *to leap across a brook.* VAULT implies leaping, esp. with the aid of the hands or some instrument, over or upon something: *to vault (over) a fence.* **45.** spring, bound, vault; skip, hop, caper.

jump′ ball′, *Basketball.* a ball tossed into the air above and between two opposing players by the referee in putting the ball into play.

jump′ bid′, *Bridge.* a bid higher than necessary to reach the next bidding level, usually to indicate exceptional strength.

jump′ di′al, a timepiece dial in which the numbers are seen through apertures.

jump′ discontinu′ity, *Math.* a discontinuity of a function at a point where the function has finite, but unequal, limits as the independent variable approaches the point from the left and from the right. Cf. **jump** (def. 59).

jump·er[1] (jum′pər), *n.* **1.** one who or that which jumps. **2.** *Sports.* a participant in a jumping event, as in track or skiing. **3.** *Manège.* a horse specially trained to jump obstacles. **4.** a boring tool or device worked with a jumping motion. **5.** Also called **jump wire.** *Elect.* a short length of conductor used to make a connection, usually temporary, between terminals of a circuit or to bypass a circuit. **6.** a kind of sled. **7.** Also called **jumper stay.** *Naut.* a line preventing the end of a spar from being lifted out of place. **8.** any of various fishes that leap from the water, as the striped mullet or jump-rock. [JUMP + -ER[1]]

jump·er[2] (jum′pər), *n.* **1.** a one-piece, sleeveless dress, or a skirt with straps and a complete or partial bodice, usually worn over a blouse by women and children. **2.** a loose outer jacket worn esp. by workmen and sailors. **3.** *Brit.* a pullover sweater. **4. jumpers,** rompers. [obs. *jump* short coat (nasalized var. of JUPE) + -ER[1]]

jump′er stay′, *Naut.* **1.** Also called **preventer backstay, preventer stay.** a supplementary backstay set up temporarily abaft the permanent backstays to reinforce a mast under a press of sail. **2.** a wire running from the foremost funnel of a powered vessel to the foremast as a support for signal halyards. **3.** (on a fore-and-aft-rigged yacht) a short stay used as a reinforcement for the upper part of a mast, passing from the masthead over a projecting strut to a point on the mast below the head of the forestay or jib stay. **4.** a stay leading from the bottom of a martingale boom to the end of a jib boom on a small sailing vessel. **5.** jumper[1] (def. 7).

jump′ head′, *Journalism.* the headline printed over the continued portion of a story in a newspaper, magazine, etc., usually condensed from the main headline.

jump′ing bean′, the seed of any of certain Mexican, euphorbiaceous plants of the genera *Sebastiania* and *Sapium,* which is inhabited by the larva of a small moth whose movements cause the seed to move about or jump. Also called **Mexican jumping bean.**

jump′ing jack′, a toy consisting of a jointed figure which is made to jump, move, or dance by pulling a string or stick attached to it.

jump′ing-off′ place′ (jum′piŋ ôf′, -of′), **1.** an out-of-the-way place; the farthest limit of anything settled or civilized. **2.** a place for use as a starting point: *They used France as the jumping-off place in their study of Europe.*

jump′ing spi′der, any of several hairy, often brightly colored spiders, of the family *Salticidae,* that stalk and jump upon their prey instead of snaring it in a web.

jump′ line′, *Journalism.* a line of type identifying the page on or from which a newspaper story is continued.

jump·mas·ter (jump′mas′tər, -mä′stər), *n.* a person who supervises the jumping of paratroopers or other parachutists. [JUMP + MASTER]

jump-off (jump′ôf′, -of′), *n.* **1.** the act of jumping off. **2.** a place for jumping off. **3.** a point of departure, as of a race or a military attack. **4.** the start of such a departure. **5.** a supplementary contest among horses tied for first place in a jumping contest. [n. use of v. phrase]

jump′ pass′, *Football, Basketball.* a pass in which a player leaps into the air and throws the ball to a teammate before returning to the ground.

jump·rock (jump′rok′), *n.* any of several fresh-water suckers of the genus *Moxostoma,* found in the southeastern U.S. [? JUMP + ROCK[1]]

jump′ rope′, **1.** a girl's game in which a rope is swung over and under the standing jumper, who must leap over it each time it reaches her feet. **2.** the rope used. Also called **skip rope.**

jump′ seat′, a movable or folding seat, as in a carriage or automobile.

jump-shift (jump′shift′), *n.* *Bridge.* a jump bid in a suit different from the suit just bid by one's partner.

jump′ shot′, *Basketball.* a shot with one or both hands in which a player leaps into the air and shoots the ball at the basket the moment that he reaches the highest point of the leap.

jump′ spark′, *Elect.* spark[1] (def. 2).

jump′ suit′, **1.** a one-piece paratrooper's uniform worn for jumping. **2.** an article of women's clothing styled after this.

jump′ turn′, *Skiing.* a turn in which a skier plants one or both poles in the snow in advance of the forward ski, bends close to the ground, and pivots in the air around the pole or poles.

jump′ wire′, *Elect.* jumper[1] (def. 5).

jump·y (jum′pē), *adj.,* **jump·i·er, jump·i·est.** **1.** subject to sudden, involuntary starts, esp. from nervousness, fear, excitement, etc. **2.** very nervous; apprehensive. **3.** characterized by sudden starts, jerks, or jumps: *a jumpy railroad car; a jumpy narrative.* [JUMP + -Y[1]] —**jump′i·ly,** *adv.* —**jump′i·ness,** *n.*

Jun., **1.** June. **2.** Junior.

Junc., Junction.

jun·ca·ceous (juŋ kā′shəs), *adj.* belonging or pertaining to the *Juncaceae,* or rush, family of plants. [< NL *juncace(ae)* rush family (L *junc(us)* rush + *-aceae* -ACEAE) + -OUS]

jun·co (juŋ′kō), *n., pl.* **-cos.** any of several small North American finches of the genus *Junco,* as *J. hyemalis* **(slate-colored junco),** having slate-gray and white plumage. Also called **snowbird.** [< Sp: rush, bird found in rush-beds < L *juncus* rush]

junc·tion (juŋk′shən), *n.* **1.** the act of joining; combining. **2.** the state of being joined; union. **3.** a place or point where two or more things are joined together, as a seam, joint, etc. **4.** a place or point where two or more things meet or converge. **5.** a place or station where railroad lines meet, cross, or diverge. **6.** an intersection of highways or roads. **7.** something that joins other things together: *He used the device as a junction between the branch circuit and the main power lines.* [< L *junctiōn-* (s. of *junctiō*), equiv. to *junct(us),* ptp. of *jungere* to join (*junc-,* var. of *jung-* join + *-tus* ptp. suffix) + *-iōn-* -ION] —**junc′tion·al,** *adj.*
—**Syn. 3.** union, linkage, coupling; welt. **7.** connection. JUNCTION, JUNCTURE refer to a place, line, or point at which two or more things join. A JUNCTION is also a place where things come together: *the junction of two rivers.* A JUNCTURE is a line or point at which two bodies are joined, or a point of exigency or crisis in time: *the juncture of the head and neck; a critical juncture in a struggle.*

Junc′tion Cit′y, a city in NE Kansas. 18,700 (1960).

junc·ture (juŋk′chər), *n.* **1.** a point of time, esp. one made critical or important by a concurrence of circumstances: *At this juncture, we must decide whether to stay or to go.* **2.** a very serious state of affairs; crisis: *The matter has reached a juncture, and a decision must be made.* **3.** the line or point at which two bodies are joined; joint or articulation; seam. **4.** the act of joining. **5.** the state of being joined. **6.** something by which two things are joined. **7.** *Gram.* a distinctive sound feature or modification of a sound feature marking the phonological boundary of a word, clause, or sentence. [< L *junctūr(a),* equiv. to *junct(us)* (see JUNCTION) + *-ūra* -URE]
—**Syn. 1, 3.** See **junction.**

jun·dy (jun′dē), *n., pl.* **-dies,** *v.,* **-died, -dy·ing.** *Scot.* —*n.* **1.** a shove; push. —*v.t., v.i.* **2.** to jostle; shove; push. [? akin to JAUNT]

June (jo͞on), *n.* **1.** the sixth month of the year, containing 30 days. **2.** a girl's given name. [ME *jun(e),* OE *iuni(us)* < L *(mensis) Jūnius* after the clan name; r. ME *juyng* < OF *juin(g)* < L, as above]

Ju·neau (jo͞o′nō), *n.* a seaport in and the capital of Alaska, in the SE part. 6797 (1960).

June bug, *Phyllophaga fusca* (Length 1 in.)

June·ber·ry (jo͞on′ber′ē, -bə rē), *n., pl.* **-ries.** the American serviceberry, *Amelanchier canadensis.* [JUNE + BERRY]

June′ bug′, **1.** Also called **May beetle.** any of several large, brown scarabaeid beetles of the genus *Phyllophaga,* appearing in late spring and early summer. **2.** See **green June beetle.**

June′ grass′. See **Kentucky bluegrass.**

June·teenth (jo͞on tēnth′), *n.* an annual celebration held on June 19th by the Negroes of Texas to commemorate their emancipation. [JUNE + (NINE)TEENTH]

Jung (yo͝oŋ), *n.* **Carl Gus·tav** (kärl go͝os′täf), 1875–1961, Swiss psychiatrist and psychologist.

Jün·ger (yo͝oŋ′ər; *Ger.* YYŊ′ər), *n.* **Ernst** (ûrnst; *Ger.* ERNST), born 1895, German author.

Jung·frau (yo͝oŋ′frou′), *n.* a mountain in S Switzerland, in the Bernese Alps. 13,668 ft.

Jung·gram·ma·ti·ker (yo͝oŋ′grä mä tē kər), *n.* *Linguistics, German.* a group of linguists of the late 19th century who held that phonetic laws are universally valid and allow of no exceptions. [lit., young grammarians]

Jung·i·an (yo͝oŋ′ē ən), *adj.* **1.** of or pertaining to Carl G. Jung or his theories, esp. of archetypes and the collective unconscious. —*n.* **2.** an advocate or follower of Jung's theories. [JUNG + -IAN]

jun·gle (juŋ′gəl), *n.* **1.** a wild land overgrown with dense vegetation, often nearly impenetrable, esp. tropical vegetation or a tropical rain forest. **2.** a tract of such land. **3.** a wilderness of dense overgrowth; a piece of swampy, thick-set forest land. **4.** any confused mass or agglomeration of objects; jumble: *a jungle of wrecked automobiles.* **5.** something that baffles or perplexes; maze: *a jungle of legal double-talk.* **6.** a scene of violence and struggle for survival: *The neglected prison was a jungle for its inmates.* **7.** a place or situation of ruthless competition: *the advertising jungle.* **8.** *U.S. Slang.* a hobo camp. [< Hindi *jangal* < Skt *jangala* wilderness] —**jun′gled,** *adj.*

Jungle, The, a novel (1906) by Upton Sinclair.

Jun′gle Books′, The, a series of jungle stories in two volumes (1894, 1895) by Rudyard Kipling.

jun′gle cock′, the male of the jungle fowl.

jun′gle fe′ver, *Pathol.* a severe variety of malarial fever occurring in the East Indies and the tropics.

jun′gle fowl′, any of several East Indian, gallinaceous birds of the genus *Gallus,* as *G. gallus* **(red jungle fowl)** believed to be the ancestor of the domestic fowl.

jun′gle gera′nium, flame-of-the-woods.

Jun·gle·gym (juŋ′gəl jim′), *n.* *Trademark.* a three-dimensional framework of metal bars used as a climbing apparatus in a children's playground.

jun′gle hen′, the female of the jungle fowl.

jun′gle rot′, *Pathol.* any cutaneous disease or condition caused or induced by a tropical climate.

jun·gly (juŋ′glē), *adj.* resembling or suggesting a jungle. [JUNGLE + -Y[1]]

jun·ior (jo͞on′yər), *adj.* **1.** younger (usually designating the younger of two men bearing the same full name, as a son named after his father; often written as *Jr.* or *jr.* following the name): *May I speak with the junior Mr. Hansen? Mr. Edward Andrew Hansen, Jr.* Cf. **senior** (def. 1). **2.** of more recent appointment or admission, as to an office or status; of lower rank or standing: *a junior partner.* **3.** (in American universities, colleges, and schools) noting or pertaining to the class or year next below that of the senior. **4.** *Law.* subordinate to preferred creditors, mortgagees, and the like. **5.** of later date; subsequent to: *His appointment is junior to mine by six months.* **6.** composed of younger members: *The junior division of the camp went on the hike.* **7.** (of an iron or steel shape) relatively small, but rolled to a standard form. —*n.* **8.** a person who is younger than another. **9.** a person who is newer or of lower rank in an office, class, profession, etc.; subordinate. **10.** a student who is in the next to the final year of a course of study. **11.** a range of odd-numbered garment sizes, chiefly from 5–15, designed for short-waisted women and for girls. **12.** *Informal.* (esp. in direct address) an annoying, flippant, or disrespectful youth: *Look, junior, I didn't ask your opinion.* [< L *jūnior* younger]

jun·ior·ate (jo͞on′yə rāt′), *n.* **1.** the two-year course of study for a Jesuit novice in preparation for the course in philosophy. **2.** a seminary for this course. [JUNIOR + -ATE[1]]

jun′ior col′lege, 1. a collegiate institution offering courses only through the first one or two years of college instruction and granting a certificate of title instead of a degree. 2. a division of a college or university offering general courses during the first two years of instruction or fulfilling administrative duties applicable to freshmen and sophomores.

jun′ior coun′sel, *Eng. Law.* 1. a body of barristers who are lower in rank than the King's Counsel or Queen's Counsel, and who plead outside the bar in the court. 2. a member of this body of barristers.

jun′ior high′ school′. See under **high school** (def. 2).

jun·ior·i·ty (jo͞on yôr′i tē, -yor′-), *n.* the state or fact of being junior in age, rank, standing, etc. [JUNIOR + -ITY]

Jun′ior League′, any local branch of a women's organization (**Associa′tion of the Jun′ior Leagues′ of Amer′ica, Inc.**), the members of which are engaged in volunteer welfare work, in civic affairs, etc. —**Jun′ior Lea′guer.**

jun′ior miss′, *Informal.* a girl in her early or middle teens.

jun′ior school′, *Brit.* a school for children aged seven to eleven, similar to a U.S. elementary school.

jun′ior var′sity, *Sports.* a team that consists of players who failed to make the varsity because of lack of experience or skill and that often competes against other teams of similar composition or ability.

ju·ni·per (jo͞o′nə pər), *n.* 1. any evergreen, coniferous shrub or tree of the genus *Juniperus,* esp. *J. communis,* having cones that form purple berries used in flavoring gin and in medicine as a diuretic. 2. a tree mentioned in the Old Testament, said to be the retem. [ME *junipere* < L *jūniper(us)*]

ju′niper ber′ry. See **box huckleberry.**

Jun·ius (jo͞on′yəs), *n.* 1. the pen name of the unknown author of a series of letters published in a London newspaper (1769–72), attacking the British king and his ministers' abuse of royal prerogative in denying John Wilkes his seat in Parliament. 2. **Franciscus,** 1589–1677, English philologist, born in Germany.

junk[1] (jungk), *n.* 1. any old or discarded material, as metal, paper, rags, etc. 2. anything that is regarded as worthless, meaningless, contemptible, or mere trash. 3. old cable or cordage used when untwisted for making gaskets, swabs, oakum, etc. 4. *Naut. Slang.* See **salt junk.** —*v.t.* 5. *Informal.* to cast aside as junk; discard as no longer of use. —*adj.* 6. cheap, unwanted, or trashy. [ME *jonke* < ?]

Junk[2]

junk[2] (jungk), *n.* a seagoing ship used in Chinese and other waters, having square sails spread by battens, a high stern, and usually a flat bottom. [< Pg *junc(o)* a kind of sailboat < Javanese *jon*]

junk[3] (jungk), *n.* *Informal.* narcotics, esp. heroin. [? special use of JUNK[1]]

junk′ bond′, any corporate bond with a low rating and a high yield, esp. one involving high risk.

Jun·ker (yo͝ong′kər), *n.* 1. a member of a class of aristocratic landholders, esp. in East Prussia, strongly devoted to militarism and authoritarianism, from among whom the German military forces recruited a large number of its officers. 2. a young German, esp. Prussian, nobleman. 3. a German official or military officer who is narrow-minded, haughty, and overbearing. [< G; OHG *junchērr(o),* equiv. to *junc* YOUNG + *hērro* HERR]

Jun·ker·dom (yo͝ong′kər dəm), *n.* 1. the Junkers as a group. 2. (*sometimes l.c.*) the condition or character of a Junker. 3. (*sometimes l.c.*) the spirit or policy of the Junkers; Junkerism. [JUNKER + -DOM]

Jun·ker·ism (yo͝ong′kə riz′əm), *n.* (*sometimes l.c.*) the spirit or policy of the Junkers. [JUNKER + -ISM]

Jun·kers (yo͝ong′kərs), *n.* **Hu·go** (ho͞o′gō), 1859–1935, German aircraft designer and builder.

jun·ket (jung′kit), *n.* 1. a sweet, custardlike food of flavored milk curded with rennet. 2. a pleasure excursion, as a picnic or outing. 3. a trip, as by an official or legislative committee, paid out of public funds and ostensibly to obtain information. —*v.i.* 4. to feast, picnic, or go on a pleasure excursion. —*v.t.* 5. to entertain; feast; regale. [ME *jonket* < OF (dial.) *jonquette* rush basket, equiv. to *jonc* (< L *juncus* reed) + *-ette* -ETTE] —**jun′ket·ter, jun·ke·teer** (jung′ki tēr′), *n.* —**Syn. 2.** See **excursion.**

junk′ food′, food that is low in nutritional value and usually high in calories, as potato chips.

junk·ie (jung′kē), *n.* *Informal.* a drug addict, esp. one addicted to heroin. [JUNK[3] + -IE]

junk′ jew′elry, cheap costume jewelry.

junk′ mail′, *Informal.* unsolicited commercial mail.

junk·man[1] (jungk′man′), *n., pl.* **-men.** a dealer in resaleable, used metal, paper, rags, and other junk. [JUNK[1] + MAN[1]]

junk·man[2] (jungk′mən, -man′), *n., pl.* **-men** (-mən, -men′). a crew member of a junk. [JUNK[2] + MAN[1]]

junk′ ring′, (in certain internal-combustion engines) a ring on a detachable cylinder head for compressing other rings intended to prevent the loss of pressure from the cylinder. [JUNK[1] + RING[1]; orig. a ring that held oakum in place]

junk·yard (junk′yärd′), *n.* a yard for the collection, storage, and resale of junk. [JUNK[1] + YARD[2]]

Ju·no (jo͞o′nō), *n.* 1. the ancient Roman queen of heaven, a daughter of Saturn and the wife and sister of Jupiter: the protectress of women and marriage, identified with the Greek goddess Hera. 2. *Astron.* the fourth largest and one of the four brightest asteroids.

Ju′no and the Pay′cock (pā′kok), a play (1924) by Sean O'Casey.

Ju·no·esque (jo͞o′nō esk′), *adj.* (of a woman) stately; regal. [JUNO + -ESQUE]

Ju·not (zhʏ nō′), *n.* **An·doche** (äN dôsh′), (*Duc d'Abrantès*), 1771–1813, French marshal.

jun·ta (ho͞on′tə, ho͞on′-, jun′-, hun′-), *n.* 1. a small group ruling a country, esp. immediately after a coup d'état and before a legally constituted government has been instituted. 2. a council. 3. a deliberative or administrative council, esp. in Spain and Latin America. 4. junto. [< Sp: a meeting, n. use of fem. of L *junctus* (ptp. of *jungere* to JOIN); see JUNCTION]

jun·to (jun′tō), *n., pl.* **-tos.** a self-appointed committee, esp. with political aims; cabal. [alter. of JUNTA]

jupe (jo͞op), *n.* *Scot. and North Eng.* 1. a woman's jacket, kirtle, or bodice. 2. **jupes,** stays; stiffeners. 3. *Obs.* a man's loose jacket, tunic, or kirtle. [ME *ju(i)pe* < OF *jupe* < Ar *jubbah* JUBBAH]

Ju·pi·ter (jo͞o′pi tər), *n.* 1. Also called **Jove.** the supreme deity of the ancient Romans: the god of the heavens and of weather, identified with the Greek god Zeus. 2. *Astron.* the planet fifth in order from the sun, having a diameter of 88,640 miles, a mean distance from the sun of 483,000,000 miles, a period of revolution of 11.86 years, and 12 satellites. It is the largest planet in the solar system. 3. *U.S.* an intermediate-range ballistic missile powered by a single liquid-fueled rocket engine.

Ju·pi·ter's-beard (jo͞o′pi tərz bērd′), *n.* See **red valerian.**

Ju′piter Sym′phony, the symphony no. 41 in C major (1788), K.551, by Wolfgang Amadeus Mozart.

ju·pon (jo͞o′pon, jo͞o pon′; *Fr.* zhʏ pôN′), *n., pl.* **-pons** (-ponz, -ponz′; *Fr.* -pôN′). a close-fitting tunic, usually padded and bearing heraldic arms, worn over armor. Also, **gipon.** [ME *jopo(u)n* < MF *jupon,* equiv. to OF *jupe* JUPE + *-on* aug. suffix]

ju·ra (jo͝or′ə), *n.* pl. of **jus.**

Ju·ra (jo͝or′ə), *n.* 1. Jurassic (def. 2). 2. a department in E France. 225,682 (1962); 1952 sq. mi. *Cap.:* Lons-le-Saunier. 3. See **Jura Mountains** (def. 1).

ju·ral (jo͝or′əl), *adj.* 1. pertaining to law; legal. 2. pertaining to rights and obligations. [< L *jur-* (s. of *jūs*) law + -AL[1]] —**ju′ral·ly,** *adv.*

ju·ra·men·ta·do (*Sp.* ho͞o′rä men tä′ᵺō), *n., pl.* **-dos** (-ᵺōs). (formerly) a Muslim, esp. a Moro, bound by an oath to be killed fighting against Christians and other infidels. [< Sp: lit., (one) sworn (ptp. of *juramentar* to swear), equiv. to *jurament-* (< LL *jūrāmentum* oath, equiv. to *jūrā-* swear + *-mentum* -MENT) + *-ado* -ATE[1]; see JURANT]

Ju′ra Moun′tains (jo͝or′ə; *Fr.* zhʏ RA′), 1. Also called **Jura.** a mountain range in W central Europe, between France and Switzerland, extending from the Rhine to the Rhone. Highest peak, Crêt de la Neige, 5654 ft. 2. a mountain range in the second quadrant of the face of the moon forming the northern border of Sinus Iridum.

ju·rant (jo͝or′ənt), *Rare.* —*adj.* 1. taking an oath; swearing. —*n.* 2. a person who takes an oath. [< L *jūrant-* (s. of *jūrāns,* prp. of *jūrāre* to swear), equiv. to *jūr-* swear + *-ant-* -ANT]

Ju·ras·sic (jo͝o ras′ik), *Geol.* —*adj.* 1. noting or pertaining to a period of the Mesozoic epoch, occurring from 135,000,000 to 180,000,000 years ago and characterized by the presence of dinosaurs and conifers. See table under **era.** —*n.* 2. Also, **Jura.** the Jurassic period or system. [JUR(A) + *-assic,* suffix abstracted from TRIASSIC; cf. F *jurassique*]

ju·rat (jo͝or′at), *n.* 1. *Law.* a certificate on an affidavit, by the officer, showing by whom, when, and before whom it was sworn to. 2. a sworn officer; a magistrate; a member of a permanent jury. [< ML *jūrāt(us)* sworn man, n. use of L ptp. of *jūrāre* to swear, equiv. to *jūr-* swear + *-ātus* -ATE[1]]

ju·ra·tion (jo͝o rā′shən), *n.* an act of taking or administering an oath. [< LL *jūrātiōn-* (s. of *jūrātiō*), equiv. to *jūrāt(us)* (see JURAT) + *-iōn-* -ION]

ju·ra·to·ry (jo͝or′ə tōr′ē, -tôr′ē), *adj.* pertaining to, constituting, or expressed in an oath. [< LL *jūrātōri(us)* sworn to, equiv. to L *jūrāt(us)* sworn (see JURAT) + *-ōrius* -ORY[1]]

Jur. D., Doctor of Law. [< L *Juris Doctor*]

ju·re di·vi·no (yo͞o′re di wē′nō; *Eng.* jo͝or′ē di vī′nō), *Latin.* by divine law.

ju·re hu·ma·no (yo͞o′re o͞o mä′nō; *Eng.* jo͝or′ē hyo͞o-mā′nō), *Latin.* by human law.

ju·rel (ho͞o rel′), *n.* any of several carangid food fishes, esp. of the genus *Caranx,* found in warm seas. [< Sp < Catalan *sorell,* prob. < L *saur(us)* < Gk *saûros* lizard]

ju·rid·i·cal (jo͝o rid′i kəl), *adj.* 1. of or pertaining to the administration of justice. 2. of or pertaining to law or jurisprudence; legal. Also **ju·rid′ic.** [< L *jūridic(us)* (*jūri-,* comb. form of *jūs* law + *dic-,* base of *dicere* to say) + -AL[1]] —**ju·rid′i·cal·ly,** *adv.*

jurid′ical days′, days in court on which law is administered; days on which the court can lawfully sit.

ju·ris·con·sult (jo͝or′is kən sult′, -kon′sult), *n.* 1. *Roman and Civil Law.* a person authorized to give legal advice. 2. *Civil Law.* a master of the civil law. *Abbr.:* J.C. [< L *jūris consultus* one skilled in the law. See JUS, CONSULT]

ju·ris·dic·tion (jo͝or′is dik′shən), *n.* 1. the right, power, or authority to administer justice by hearing and determining controversies. 2. power; authority; control: *He has jurisdiction over all American soldiers in the area.* 3. the extent or range of judicial or other authority: *This case comes under the jurisdiction of the Crown.* 4. the territory over which authority is exercised: *All islands to the northwest are his jurisdiction.* [ME < L *jūrisdictiōn-* (see JUS, DICTION); r. ME *jurediccioun* < OF *juredicion* < L, as above] —**ju′ris·dic′tive,** *adj.* —**ju′ris·dic′tion·al·ly,** *adv.*

jurisp., jurisprudence.

ju·ris·pru·dence (jo͝or′is pro͞od′əns), *n.* 1. the science or philosophy of law. 2. a body or system of laws. 3. a department of law: *medical jurisprudence.* 4. *Civil Law.* decisions of courts, esp. of reviewing tribunals. [< L *jūris prūdentia* knowledge of the law. See JUS, PRUDENCE] —**ju·ris·pru·den·tial** (jo͝or′is pro͞o den′shəl), *adj.* —**ju′ris·pru·den′tial·ly,** *adv.*

ju·ris·pru·dent (jo͝or′is pro͞od′ənt), *adj.* 1. versed in jurisprudence. —*n.* 2. a person versed in jurisprudence. [JURISPRUD(ENCE) + -ENT]

ju·rist (jo͝or′ist), *n.* 1. a lawyer. 2. a judge. 3. a person versed in the law. 4. a person who writes on the subject of law. [< F *juriste* < ML *jurist(a).* See JUS, -IST]

ju·ris·tic (jo͝o ris′tik), *adj.* of or pertaining to a jurist or to jurisprudence; juridical. Also, **ju·ris′ti·cal.** [JURIST + -IC] —**ju·ris′ti·cal·ly,** *adv.*

juris′tic act′, an act by an individual that changes, ends, or affects a legal right but is not in itself an exercise of legal authority.

juris′tic per′son, *Law.* See under **person** (def. 11).

Jur. M., Master of Jurisprudence.

ju·ror (jo͝or′ər), *n.* 1. one of a body of persons sworn to deliver a verdict in a case submitted to them; member of a jury. 2. one of the panel from which a jury is selected. 3. any of a group of people who judge a competition. 4. one who has taken an oath or sworn allegiance. [ME *jurour* < AF (cf. OF *jureur*), equiv. to OF *jur(er)* (to) swear (< L *jūrāre*) + *-our* -OR[2]]

Ju·ru·á (zho͞o′ro͞o ä′), *n.* a river in E and W South America, flowing NE from E Peru through W Brazil to the Amazon. 1200 mi. long.

ju·ry[1] (jo͝or′ē), *n., pl.* **-ries.** 1. a body of persons sworn to render a verdict or true answer on a question or questions officially submitted to them. 2. such a body selected according to law and sworn to inquire into or determine the facts concerning a cause or an accusation submitted to them and to render a verdict to a court. Cf. **grand jury, petty jury.** 3. a body of persons chosen to adjudge prizes, awards, etc., as in a competition. [ME *jurie, juree,* < OF *juree* oath, juridical inquiry, n. use of *juree,* fem. ptp. of *jurer* to swear] —**ju′ry·less,** *adj.*

ju·ry[2] (jo͝or′ē), *adj.* *Naut.* makeshift or temporary, as for an emergency. [?]

ju′ry list′, *Law.* a list of persons eligible to serve as jurors.

ju·ry·man (jo͝or′ē mən), *n., pl.* **-men.** a juror. [JURY[1] + MAN[1]]

ju′ry mast′, *Naut.* a temporary mast replacing one that has been broken or carried away. [JURY[2] + MAST[1]]

ju·ry-pack·ing (jo͝or′ē pak′ing), *n.* the lawyer's practice of contriving that the majority of those chosen for a jury will be persons known or likely to have preconceptions or partialities affecting the issue at hand, as by disqualifying people in specific age or economic groups.

ju·ry-rig (jo͝or′ē rig′), *n., v.,* **-rigged, -rig·ging.** *Naut.* —*n.* 1. a temporary rig to replace a permanent rig that has been disabled, lost overboard, etc. —*v.t.* 2. to replace (a rudder, mast, etc.) with a jury-rig: *We jury-rigged a fore-topmast after the storm had snapped ours off.*

ju·ry-rigged (jo͝or′ē rigd′), *adj.* *Naut.* temporarily rigged in a makeshift fashion. [JURY-RIG + -ED[3]]

ju′ry room′, a private room, adjacent to a courtroom, where trial juries deliberate verdicts.

ju′ry wheel′, *Law.* a revolving device containing the names of the persons on a jury list, from which are drawn, at random, the names of the jurors who are to constitute a given panel.

ju·ry·wom·an (jo͝or′ē wo͝om′ən), *n., pl.* **-wom·en.** a female juror. [JURY[1] + WOMAN]

jus (jus; *Lat.* yo͞os), *n., pl.* **ju·ra** (jo͝or′ə; *Lat.* yo͞o′re). *Law.* 1. a right. 2. law as a system or in the abstract. [< L *jūs* law, right, gen. sing. *jūris,* nom pl. *jūra,* comb. form *jūri-*]

jus (zhʏ; *Eng.* zho͞os, jo͞os), *n.* *French.* juice; gravy. Cf. **au jus.**

jus ca·no·ni·cum (yo͞os′ kä nō′ni ko͞om′; *Eng.* jus′ kə non′ə kəm), *Latin.* See **canon law.**

jus ci·vi·le (jus′ si vī′lē), *Roman Law.* the rules and principles of law derived from the customs and legislation of Rome, as opposed to those derived from the customs of all nations (**jus gentium**) or from fundamental ideas of right and wrong implicit in the human mind (**jus naturale**). [< L: civil law]

jus di·vi·num (yo͞os′ di wē′no͞om; *Eng.* jus′ di vī′nəm), *Latin.* divine law.

jus gen·ti·um (jus′ jen′shē əm), *Roman Law.* See under **jus civile.** [< L: law of the nations]

jus na·tu·ra·le (jus′ nach′ə rā′lē, nat′yo͞o-), *Roman Law.* See under **jus civile.** Also, **jus na·tu·rae** (jus nach′ə rē′, nat′yo͞o-). [< L: natural law]

jus post·li·mi·ni·i (jus′ pōst′lə min′ē ī′), *Internat. Law.* postliminy. [< L: right of postliminy]

jus pri·mae noc·tis (jus′ prī′mē nok′tis). See **droit du seigneur.**

jus san·gui·nis (jus′ sang′gwə nis), *Law.* the principle that the country of citizenship of a child is determined by the country of citizenship of his parents. Cf. **jus soli.** [< L: right of blood]

Jus·se·rand (zhʏsᵊ räN′), *n.* **Jean** (**A·dri·en An·toine**) **Jules** (zhäN A drē äN′ äN twAN′ zhʏl), 1855–1932, French diplomat, historian, and essayist.

jus·sive (jus′iv), *Gram.* —*adj.* 1. expressing a mild command. The jussive mood occurs in the Semitic languages. —*n.* 2. a jussive form, mood, case, construction, or word. [< L *jūss(us)* (ptp. of *jubēre* to command), equiv. to *jūs-* (var. of *jūb-*) + *-sus* (var. of *-tus*) ptp. suffix]

jus so·li (jus sō′lī), *Law.* the principle that the country of citizenship of a child is determined by his country of birth. Cf. **jus sanguinis.** [< L: right of soil (land)]

just[1] (just), *adj.* 1. guided by truth, reason, justice, and fairness: *We hope to be just in our understanding of such difficult situations.* 2. done or made according to principle; equitable; proper: *a just reply.* 3. based on right; rightful; lawful: *a just claim.* 4. agreeable to truth or fact; true; correct: *a just analysis.* 5. given or awarded rightly; deserved, as a sentence, punishment, reward, etc.: *just deserts.* 6. in accordance with standards or requirements; proper or right: *just proportions.* 7. (esp. in Biblical use) righteous. 8. actual, real, or genuine. —*adv.* 9. within a brief preceding time; but a moment before: *The sun just came out.* 10. exactly or precisely: *This is just what I mean.* 11. by a narrow margin; barely: *It just missed the mark.* 12. only or merely: *He was just a clerk until he became ambitious. It was just one of those things.* 13. actually; really; positively: *The weather is just glorious.* [ME < L *jūst(us)* righteous, equiv. to *jūs* law, right + *-tus* adj. suffix]
—**Syn. 1.** upright; equitable, fair, impartial. **3.** legitimate, legal. **4.** accurate, exact; honest. **5.** merited, appropriate, condign, suited, apt, due. **7.** good, honest, pure, conscientious, honorable. —**Ant. 1.** biased. **4.** untrue. **5.** unjustified.

just[2] (just), *n., v.i.* joust. —**just′er,** *n.*

Jus·ta (jus′tə), *n.* a girl's given name, form of **Justina.**

just·au·corps (zho͞o′stə kōr′, -kôr′; *Fr.* zhʏst ō kôR′), *n., pl.* **-corps** (-kōr′, -kôr′; *Fr.* -kôR′). a close-fitting knee-length coat, characterized by wide turned-back cuffs and stiff flared skirts, much used, esp. by men, in the 17th and 18th centuries. Also called **justicoat.** [< F *juste au corps* fitting to the body]

juste-mi·lieu (zhʏst mē lyœ′), *n., pl.* **juste-mi·lieux** (zhʏst mē lyœ′). *French.* a point between two extremes; the golden mean. [lit., exact middle]

Jus·ten (jus′tin), *n.* a boy's given name.

jus·tice (jus′tis), *n.* **1.** the quality of being just; righteousness, equitableness, or moral rightness: *to uphold the justice of a cause.* **2.** rightfulness or lawfulness, as of a claim or title; justness of ground or reason: *to complain with justice.* **3.** the moral principle determining just conduct. **4.** conformity to this principle, as manifested in conduct; just conduct, dealing, or treatment. **5.** the administering of deserved punishment or reward. **6.** the maintenance or administration of what is just by law, as by judicial or other proceedings: *a court of justice.* **7.** judgment of persons or causes by judicial process: *to administer justice in a community.* **8.** a judicial officer; a judge or magistrate. **9. bring to justice,** to cause to come before a court for trial or to receive punishment for one's misdeeds: *The murderer was brought to justice, and the case was closed.* **10. do justice, a.** to treat justly or fairly. **b.** to appreciate properly: *We must see this play again to do it justice.* **c.** to act in accordance with one's abilities or potentialities; acquit oneself well: *He finally got a role in which he could do himself justice as an actor.* [ME < OF < L *jūstitia,* equiv. to *jūst(us)* JUST[1] + *-itia* -ICE] —**jus′tice·less,** *adj.* —**jus′tice·like′,** *adj.*

Jus·tice (jus′tis), *n.* a town in NE Illinois. 2803 (1960).

jus′tice of the peace′, a local public officer, usually having jurisdiction to try and determine minor civil and criminal cases and to hold preliminary examinations of persons accused of more serious crimes, and having authority to administer oaths, solemnize marriages, etc.

jus·tic·er (jus′ti sər), *n. Archaic.* a judge or magistrate. [ME < AF (cf. OF *justicier*); see JUSTICIARY]

jus·tice·ship (jus′tis ship′), *n.* the office of a justice. [JUSTICE + -SHIP]

jus′tices in eyre′, *Old Eng. Law.* See under **eyre** (def. 2a).

jus·ti·ci·a·ble (ju stish′ē ə bəl), *adj. Law.* capable of being settled by law or by the action of a court: *a justiciable dispute.* [< AF < ML *justitiābil(is).* See JUSTICE, -ABLE] —**jus·ti′ci·a·bil′i·ty,** *n.*

jus·ti·ci·ar (ju stish′ē ər), *n.* **1.** a high judicial officer in medieval England. **2.** the chief political and judicial officer in England from the reign of William I to that of Henry III. **3.** justiciary (def. 2). [ME < ML *justi-ciār(ius)* JUSTICIARY; see -AR[2]] —**jus·ti′ci·ar·ship′,** *n.*

jus·ti·ci·ar·y (ju stish′ē er′ē), *adj., n., pl.* **-ar·ies.** —*adj.* **1.** of or pertaining to the administration of justice. —*n.* **2.** the office or jurisdiction of a justiciar. **3.** justiciar. [< ML *justiciārius.* See JUSTICE, -ARY]

jus·ti·coat (jus′tə kōt′), *n.* justaucorps. [Anglicized form]

jus·ti·fi·a·ble (jus′tə fī′ə bəl, jus′tə fī′-), *adj.* capable of being justified; that can be shown to be or can be defended as being just or right; defensible: *justifiable homicide.* [< MF; see JUSTIFY, -ABLE] —**jus′ti·fi′a·bil′i·ty, jus′ti·fi′a·ble·ness,** *n.* —**jus′ti·fi′a·bly,** *adv.*

justifi′able abor′tion. See **therapeutic abortion.**

jus·ti·fi·ca·tion (jus′tə fə kā′shən), *n.* **1.** a reason, fact, circumstance, or explanation that justifies or defends: *His insulting her was ample justification for her to leave the party.* **2.** act of justifying: *Her justification of her son's crime sounded ludicrous to the jury.* **3.** the state of being justified. **4.** Also called **justifica′tion by faith′.** *Theol.* the act of God whereby man is made or accounted just, or free from guilt or penalty of sin. **5.** *Print.* the spacing of words and letters within a line of type so that all full lines in a column have even margins on the left and on the right. [ME < LL *justi-ficātiōn-* (s. of *justificātiō*), equiv. to *justificā(re)* (to) JUSTIFY + *-tiōn-* -TION]

jus·tif·i·ca·to·ry (ju stif′ə kə tôr′ē, -tōr′ē, jus′tə fə-kā′tə rē), *adj.* serving to justify; providing justification. Also, **jus·ti·fi·ca·tive** (jus′tə fə kā′tiv). [< LL *justi-ficāt(us)* (ptp. of *justificāre* to JUSTIFY), equiv. to *justi-fic-* make just + *-ātus* -ATE[1] + -ORY[1]]

jus·ti·fi·er (jus′tə fī′ər), *n.* one who or that which justifies. [JUSTIFY + -ER[1]]

jus·ti·fy (jus′tə fī′), *v.,* **-fied, -fy·ing.** —*v.t.* **1.** to show (an act, claim, statement, etc.) to be just, right, or warranted: *The end does not always justify the means.* **2.** to defend or uphold as blameless, just, or right: *Don't try to justify his rudeness.* **3.** declare guiltless; absolve; acquit. **4.** *Print.* to make (a line of type) a desired length by spacing the words and letters in it, esp. so that full lines in a column have even margins on the left and on the right. **5.** *Type Founding.* to level and square (a strike). —*v.i.* **6.** *Law.* **a.** to show a satisfactory reason or excuse for something done. **b.** to qualify as bail or surety. **7.** *Print.* (of a line of type) to fit exactly into a desired length. [ME *justifi(en)* < OF *justifie(r)* < L *justificāre,* equiv. to *justi-* (comb. form of *justus* JUST[1]) + *-ficāre* -FY] —**jus′ti·fy′ing·ly,** *adv.*
—**Syn. 2.** vindicate; exonerate, exculpate; warrant, excuse. —**Ant. 2.** accuse, condemn.

Jus·tin (jus′tin; *Fr.* zhʏs taN′; *Ger.* yŏŏs tēn′), *n.* a boy's given name.

Jus·ti·na (ju stē′nə, -stī′-), *n.* a girl's given name. Also, **Justine.**

Jus·tine (ju stēn′; *Fr.* zhʏs tēn′), *n.* a girl's given name. Also, **Justina.**

Jus·tin·i·an I (ju stin′ē ən), (*Flavius Anicius Justinianus*) ("*Justinian the Great*") A.D. 483–565, Byzantine emperor 527–565.

Justin′ian Code′, the body of Roman law that was codified and promulgated under Justinian I.

Jus·tin·i·a·ni·an (ju stin′ē ā′nē ən), *adj.* of or pertaining to Justinian I or the Byzantine dynasty (A.D. 518–610) named after him. Also, **Jus·tin′i·a′ne·an.** [JUSTINIAN + -IAN]

Jus·tin Mar·tyr (jus′tin mär′tər), **Saint,** A.D. c100–163?, early church historian and philosopher.

just′ intona′tion, *Music.* a system of tuning based on the pure perfect fifth and major third.

Jus·ti·ti·a (ju stish′ē ə), *n.* the ancient Roman personification of justice.

jus·ti·ti·a om·ni·bus (yōō stit′ē ä′ ōm′ni bŏŏs′; *Eng.* ju stish′ē ə om′nə bəs), *Latin.* justice to all: motto of the District of Columbia.

jus·tle (jus′əl), *v.t., v.i.,* **-tled, -tling,** *n.* jostle.

just·ly (just′lē), *adv.* **1.** in a just manner; honestly; fairly. **2.** in conformity to fact or rule; accurately. **3.** deservedly; as deserved. [ME; see JUST[1], -LY]

just·ness (just′nis), *n.* **1.** the quality or state of being just, equitable, or right; lawfulness: *His justness is seldom to be doubted.* **2.** conformity to fact or rule; correctness; exactness; accuracy. [ME *justnesse.* See JUST[1], -NESS]

just′ no′ticeable dif′ference, *Psychol.* the smallest perceptible difference between two stimuli.

jut (jut), *v.,* **jut·ted, jut·ting,** *n.* —*v.i.* **1.** to extend beyond the main body or line; project; protrude (often fol. by *out*): *The narrow strip of land juts out into the bay.* —*n.* **2.** something that juts out; a projecting or protruding point. [var. of JET[1]] —**jut′ting·ly,** *adv.*

jute (jōōt), *n.* **1.** a strong, coarse fiber used for making burlap, gunny, cordage, etc., obtained from two East Indian tiliaceous plants, *Corchorus capsularis* and *C. olitorius.* **2.** either of these plants. **3.** any plant of the same genus. [< Bengali *jhuto* < Skt *jūta* braid (of hair)] —**jute′like′,** *adj.*

Jute (jōōt), *n.* a member of a continental Germanic tribe, probably from Jutland, that invaded Britain in the 5th century A.D. and settled in Kent. [OE (north) *Iuti,* later misread as *Juti,* whence modern form] —**Jut′ish,** *adj.*

jute′ board′, a strong, bendable cardboard made from rags and sulfite, used chiefly in the manufacture of shipping cartons.

Jut·land (jut′lənd), *n.* a peninsula comprising the continental portion of Denmark: a major naval engagement between the British and German fleets was fought west of this peninsula 1916. 1,659,609 (1960); 11,441 sq. mi. Danish, **Jylland.** —**Jut′land·er,** *n.* —**Jut′land·ish,** *adj.*

jut·ty (jut′ē), *n., pl.* **-ties,** *v.,* **-tied, -ty·ing.** —*n.* **1.** jetty[1] (def. 4). —*v.i., v.t.* **2.** *Obs.* to project beyond.

Ju·tur·na (jōō tûr′nə), *n. Class. Myth.* a nymph who was loved by Jupiter and was immortalized by him as the goddess of lakes and streams: she vainly attempted to save her brother, Turnus, from death at the hands of Aeneas.

Ju·var·ra (yōō vär′rä), *n.* **Fi·lip·po** (fē lēp′pô), 1678–1736, Italian architect. Also, **Ju·va′ra.**

Ju·ve·nal (jōō′və nəl), *n.* (*Decimus Junius Juvenalis*) A.D. c60–140, Roman poet. —**Ju·ve·na·li·an** (jōō′və-nā′lē ən), *adj.*

ju′ve·nal plum′age (jōō′və nəl), *Ornith.* the first plumage of birds, composed of contour feathers, which in certain species follows the molt of natal down and in other species follows the naked nestling stage. [< L *juvenāl(is)* youthful, equiv. to *juven(is)* young man or woman + *-ālis* -AL[1]]

ju·ve·nes·cent (jōō′və nes′ənt), *adj.* **1.** being or becoming youthful; young. **2.** young in appearance. **3.** having the power to make young or youthful: *a juvenescent elixir.* [< L *juvenēscent-* (s. of *juvenēscēns,* prp. of *juvenēscere* to become youthful), equiv. to *juven-* young (see JUVENILE) + *-ēscent-* -ESCENT] —**ju′ve·nes′cence,** *n.*

ju·ve·nile (jōō′və nəl, -nil, -nīl′), *adj.* **1.** pertaining to, characteristic of, or suitable or intended for young persons: *juvenile behavior; juvenile books.* **2.** young; youthful: *juvenile years.* **3.** immature; childish; infantile: *His juvenile tantrums are not in keeping with his age.* —*n.* **4.** a young person; youth. **5.** *Theat.* **a.** a youthful male role. **b.** an actor who plays such parts. **6.** *Ornith.* a young bird in the stage when it has fledged, if altricial, or has replaced down of hatching, if precocial. **7.** a two-year-old race horse. **8.** a book for children. [< L: neut. of *juvenīlis* youthful, equiv. to *juven(is)* youthful + *-īlis* -ILE] —**ju′ve·nile·ly,** *adv.* —**ju′ve·nile·ness,** *n.*
—**Syn. 1.** See **young.**

ju′venile court′, a law court having jurisdiction over youths, generally of less than 18 years.

ju′venile delin′quency, behavior of a child or youth that is so marked by violation of law, persistent mischievousness, anti-social behavior, disobedience, or intractability, as to thwart correction by parents and to constitute a matter for action by the juvenile courts.

ju′venile delin′quent, 1. a minor who cannot be controlled by parental authority and commits antisocial or criminal acts, as vandalism, violence, etc. **2.** a child or youth characterized by juvenile delinquency.

ju′venile of′ficer, a police officer concerned with juvenile delinquents.

ju·ve·nil·i·a (jōō′və nil′ē ə, -nil′yə), *n.pl.* **1.** works, esp. writings, produced in youth: *His juvenilia were more successful than his mature writings.* **2.** literary or artistic productions suitable or designed for the young: *publishers of juvenilia.* [< L, pl. of *juvenīlis* JUVENILE]

ju·ve·nil·i·ty (jōō′və nil′i tē), *n., pl.* **-ties. 1.** juvenile state, character, or manner. **2. juvenilities,** youthful qualities or acts. **3.** young persons collectively. [JUVENILE + -ITY]

Ju·ven·ta Fons (yōō ven′tä fons′), an area in the southern hemisphere of Mars, appearing as a dark region when viewed telescopically from the earth.

Ju·ven·tas (jōō ven′təs), *n.* the ancient Roman goddess who protected the men of military age. [< L: youth]

juxta-, a learned borrowing from Latin meaning "beside," "near," used in the formation of compound words: *juxtaposition.* [< L *juxtā*]

jux·ta·pose (juk′stə pōz′), *v.t.,* **-posed, -pos·ing.** to place close together or side by side, esp. for comparison or contrast. [back formation from JUXTAPOSITION]

jux·ta·po·si·tion (juk′stə pə zish′ən), *n.* **1.** a placing close together or side by side, esp. for comparison or contrast. **2.** the situation of being close together or side by side. [JUXTA- + POSITION] —**jux′ta·po·si′tion·al,** *adj.*

JV, junior varsity. Also, **J.V.**

J.W.V., Jewish War Veterans.

Jy., July.

Jyl·land (yʏl′län), *n.* Danish name of **Jutland.**

Jym·mye (jim′ē), *n.* a girl's given name. Also, **Jimmie, Jimmy.**

j'y suis, j'y reste (zhē swē′, zhē rest′), *French.* Here I am, here I stay (attributed to Count de MacMahon, at the taking of the Malakoff fortifications in the Crimean War).

Jy·väs·ky·lä (yʏ′väs kʏ′lä), *n.* a city in S central Finland. 51,810 (est. 1965).

K

K, k (kā), *n., pl.* **K's** or **Ks, k's** or **ks. 1.** the 11th letter of the English alphabet, a consonant. **2.** any sound represented by the letter *K* or *k*, as in *bilk, kit, sick,* etc. **3.** something having the shape of a K. **4.** a written or printed representation of the letter *K* or *k*. **5.** a device, as a printer's type, for reproducing the letter *K* or *k*.

K, 1. *Chess.* king. **2.** Kelvin. **3.** *Music.* K.V. **4.** *Computer Technol. Informal.* the number 1000: *The price of the equipment is about $65K.* [abbr. of KILO]

K, 1. the 11th in order or in a series, or, when *I* is omitted, the 10th. **2.** (*sometimes l.c.*) the medieval Roman numeral for 250. Cf. **Roman numerals. 3.** *Computer Technol.* the number 1024 or 2^{10}: *A binary 32K memory has 32,768 positions.* **4.** *Baseball.* strike-out; strike-outs.

k, *Math.* a vector on the z-axis, having length 1 unit.

K., 1. kip; kips. **2.** *Music.* Kirkpatrick (referring to a chronological catalog of the sonatas of Domenico Scarlatti compiled by Ralph Kirkpatrick, born 1911, U.S. harpsichordist; used with a number to identify a specific work). **3.** Knight. **4.** *Music.* Köchel (referring to a chronological catalog of the works of Mozart originally compiled by Ludwig von Köchel, 1800–1877, Austrian musicologist; used with a number to identify a specific work). Also, **K.V.**

k., 1. *Elect.* capacity. **2.** karat. **3.** kilogram; kilograms. **4.** *Chess.* king. **5.** knight. **6.** knot. **7.** kopeck.

K2, *n.* a mountain in N Kashmir, in the Karakoram range: second highest peak in the world. 28,250 ft. Also called **Godwin Austen, Dapsang.**

K-9 corps, *U.S.* a group of dogs trained as messengers, watchdogs, or fighters.

kA, kiloampere; kiloamperes.

ka (kä), *n.* *Egyptian Religion.* a spiritual entity, an aspect of the individual, believed to live within the body during life and to survive it after death. [< Egypt]

Kaa·ba (kä′bə, kä′ə bə), *n.* **1.** a small, cubical building in the courtyard of the Great Mosque at Mecca containing a sacred black stone: the chief objective of Muslim pilgrimages. **2.** one of several replicas of this building, sacred to pre-Islamic Arabs. Also, **Caaba.** [< Ar *ka'abah* a square building, deriv. of *ka'b* cube]

Kaap·stad (käp′stät), *n.* Afrikaans name of **Cape Town.**

kab (kab), *n.* cab².

kab·a·la (kab′ə lə, kə bä′lə), *n.* cabala. Also, **kab′ba·la.**

Ka·ba·lev·sky (kä′bə lef′skē), *n.* **Dmi·tri** (dmē′trē), born 1904, Russian composer.

Ka·bar·di·an (kə bär′dē ən), *n.* an eastern Circassian language of the Kabardino-Balkar A.S.S.R. [KABARD(INO-BALKAR A.S.S.R.) + -IAN]

Kab·ar·di′no-Bal·kar′ Auton′omous Re·pub′lic (kab′ər dē′nō bôl kär′, -bal-, -bôl′kär, -bal′-; *Russ.* kə bur dyē′nə bul kär′), an autonomous republic in the Russian Federation in N Caucasia, N of the Georgian Republic. 675,000; 4747 sq. mi. *Cap.:* Nalchik.

Ka·bei·ri (kə bī′rī), *n.pl.* Cabiri.

Ka·bi·nett·wein (kä′bi net′vīn′), *n.* *German.* See **cabinet wine.**

Ka·bir (kə bēr′), *n.* fl. late 15th century, Hindu religious reformer.

ka·bob (kə bob′), *n.* **1.** Usually, **kabobs.** small pieces of meat, seasoned and broiled, often with tomatoes, green peppers, onions, or other vegetables, usually on a skewer. **2.** (in Anglo-Indian use) roast meat. Also, **cabob, kebab, kebob, ka·bab′.** [< Ar, Hindi *kabāb* < Turk *kebab* roast meat. See SHISH KEBAB]

ka·bu·ki (kä bo͞o′kē, kə-, kä′bo͞o kē), *n.* popular drama of Japan, developed chiefly in the 17th century, characterized by elaborate costuming, rhythmic dialogue, stylized acting, music, and dancing, and by the performance of both male and female roles by male actors. Cf. **Nō.** [< Jap, equiv. to *kabu* music and dancing + *ki* spirit, style]

Ka·bul (kä′bo͝ol), *n.* **1.** a city in and the capital of Afghanistan, in the NE part. 300,000 (est. 1964). **2.** a river flowing E from NE Afghanistan to the Indus River in Pakistan. 360 mi. long.

ka·bu·to ga·ne (kä′bo͞o tō′ gä nā′; *Jap.* kä′bo͞o tô′ gä ne′), *pl.* **ka·bu·to ga·ne.** the pommel of a tachi. [< Jap: lit., headpiece metal]

ka·bu·zu·chi (kä bo͞o′zo͞o chē′), *n., pl.* **-chi.** the pommel of a Japanese sword; kashira. [< Jap, equiv. to *kabu* stub + *zuchi* hammer]

Ka·byle (kə bīl′), *n.* **1.** a member of a branch of the Berber race dwelling in Algeria and Tunisia. **2.** a Berber language spoken by the Kabyles. [< Ar *qabā'il*, pl. of *qabīlah* tribe]

ka·cha (kuch′ə), *adj.* kutcha. Also, **kach·cha** (kuch′chə).

ka·chi·na (kə chē′nə), *n.* any of various ancestral spirits deified by the Hopi Indians and impersonated in religious rituals by masked dancers. Also, **katcina, katchina.** [< Hopi: supernatural]

kachi′na doll′, a Hopi Indian doll carved from cottonwood root in representation of a kachina and given as a gift to a child or used as a household decoration.

Ka·dai (kä′dī), *n.* **1.** a group of languages related to the Thai group and spoken by a small population in southern China and northern Vietnam. **2.** a language family consisting of this group and the Thai group. —*adj.* **3.** of or pertaining to Kadai.

Ká·dár (kä′där), *n.* **Já·nos** (yä′nôsh), born 1912, Hungarian political leader: premier 1956–58 and 1961–65; First Secretary of Hungarian Communist party since 1956. Hungarian, **János Ká·dár** (yä′nôsh kä′där).

Kad·dish (kä′dish; *Heb.* kä dēsh′), *n., pl.* **Kad·di·shim** (kä dish′im; *Heb.* kä dē shēm′). *Judaism.* **1.** (*italics*) a liturgical prayer, consisting of three or six verses, recited at given points during each of the three daily services and on certain other occasions. **2.** (*italics*) Also called **Mourner's Kaddish.** the five-verse form of this prayer that is recited at given points during each of the three daily services by one observing the mourning period of 11 months, beginning on the day of burial, for a deceased parent, brother, or other close relative, and by one observing the anniversary of such a death. **3. Kaddishim,** persons who recite this prayer. [< Aram *qaddīsh* holy (one)]

ka·di (kä′dē, kā′dē), *n., pl.* **-dis.** cadi.

Ka·diak′ bear′ (kəd yak′, -yäk′). See **Kodiak bear.**

Ka·di·yev·ka (kä dē′yəf kä), *n.* a city in the E Ukraine, in the S Soviet Union in Europe. 192,000 (est. 1962).

Ka·du·na (kə do͞o′nə), *n.* a city in central Nigeria. 149,910 (1963).

kāf (käf), *n.* the 22nd letter of the Arabic alphabet, representing a velar stop consonant sound. [< Ar; c. Heb *kaph*, lit., palm (of the hand)]

kaf·fee klatsch (kä′fā kläch′, klach′, -fē). See **coffee klatsch.**

Kaf·fir (kaf′ər, kä′fər), *n., pl.* **-firs,** (*esp. collectively*) **-fir. 1.** *Usually Disparaging.* a member of a South African Negroid race inhabiting parts of the Cape of Good Hope, Natal, etc. **2.** *Often Disparaging.* Xhosa. **3.** (*l.c.*) kafir (def. 4). **4.** (*l.c.*) *Islam.* an infidel. [< Ar *kāfir* unbeliever, infidel, skeptic]

Kaf′fir bean′ tree′, a tree, *Schotia latifolia*, of South Africa, having pinkish flowers.

kaf·fi·yeh (kə fē′yə), *n.* an Arab headdress made from a diagonally folded square of cloth, held in place by an agal wound around the head. Also, **keffiyeh, kufiyeh, kuffieh.** [< Ar *kaffiyah*, var. of *kuffiyeh*; see COIF¹]

Kaf·frar·i·a (kə frâr′ē ə), *n.* a region in the S Republic of South Africa: inhabited mostly by Kaffirs. —**Kaf·frar′i·an,** *adj., n.*

Kaf·ir (kaf′ər, kä′fər), *n., pl.* **-irs,** (*esp. collectively*) **-ir. 1.** a member of an Indo-European people of Nuristan. **2.** (*l.c.*) *Islam.* kaffir (def. 4). **3.** Kaffir (defs. 1, 2). **4.** (*l.c.*) Also, **kaffir, kaf′ir corn′,** a grain sorghum, *Sorghum vulgare caffrorum*, having stout, short-jointed, leafy stalks, introduced into the U.S. from southern Africa. [< Ar; see KAFFIR]

Ka·fi·ri·stan (kä′fi ri stän′), *n.* former name of **Nuristan.**

Kaf′ir lil′y. See **crimson flag.**

Kaf·ka (käf′kä, -kə), *n.* **Franz** (fränts), 1883–1924, Austrian novelist and short-story writer.

Kaf·re (kaf′rā, käf′-), *n.* Khafre.

kaf·tan (kaf′tən, käf tän′), *n.* caftan.

Ka·ga·no·vich (kä′gä nô′vich), *n.* **La·zar Moi·se·e·vich** (lä′zär moi se′yə vich), born 1893, Russian politician and government administrator.

Ka·ga·wa (kä′gä wä′), *n.* **To·yo·hi·ko** (tô′yô hē′kô), 1888–1960, Japanese social reformer and religious leader.

Ka·ge·ra (kä gâr′ə), *n.* a river in equatorial Africa flowing into Lake Victoria from the west: the most remote headstream of the Nile. 430 mi. long.

Ka·gi (kä′gē′), *n.* Japanese name of Chiayi.

ka·go (kä′gō), *n., pl.* **-gos.** (in Japan) a small basketwork palanquin strung from a pole each end of which rests on the shoulder of a bearer. [< Jap: basket, cage]

Ka·go·shi·ma (kä′gô shē′mä), *n.* a seaport on S Kyushu, in SW Japan. 314,084 (1964).

ka·gu (kä′go͞o), *n.* a raillike bird, *Rhinochetus Jubatus*, of the island of New Caledonia, having a gray body, black and white wings, and a long, shaggy crest. [from native word in New Caledonia]

Kah·lú·a (kä lo͞o′ä, kə lo͞o′ə), *n.* *Trademark.* a liqueur flavored with coffee, made in Mexico.

Kahn (kän), *n.* **Louis I.,** born 1901, U.S. architect, born in Estonia.

Kahn′ test′ (kän), *Med.* a test for syphilis in which the formation of a macroscopic precipitate in a mixture of the patient's serum and an antigen indicates a syphilitic condition. Cf. **Kline test.** [named after R. L. *Kahn* (b. 1887), American bacteriologist, its originator]

Ka·hoo·la·we (kä′ho͞o lä′wē), *n.* an island in central Hawaii, S of Maui: uninhabited. 45 sq. mi.

Ka·hu·lu·i (kä′ho͞o lo͞o′ē), *n.* a town on N Maui, in central Hawaii. 4223 (1960).

ka·hu·na (kə ho͞o′nə), *n.* (in Hawaii) a native medicine man or priest. [< Hawaiian]

kai·ak (kī′ak), *n.* kayak.

Kai′do crab′ ap′ple (kī′dō), a small tree, *Malus micromalus*, having shiny leaves, deep-pink flowers, and red fruit.

Kai·e·teur (kī′e to͝or′), *n.* a waterfall in central Guyana, on a tributary of the Essequibo River. 741 ft. high. Also called **Kaieteur′ Falls′.**

kaif (kīf), *n.* kef.

Kai·feng (kī′fung′), *n.* a city in and the capital of Honan, in E China. 299,100 (est. 1959).

kail (kāl), *n.* kale.

Kai·las·a (kī lä′sə), *n.* a Brahmanical temple dedicated to Siva, at Ellora, India: architecturally one of the finest of ancient cave temples.

Kai·lu·a (kī lo͞o′ä), *n.* a city on SE Oahu, in Hawaii. With Lanikai, 25,622 (1960).

kail·yard (kāl′yärd′), *n.* *Scot.* kaleyard.

kail′yard school′. See **kaleyard school.** —**kail′yard′er,** *n.* —**kail′yard′ism,** *n.*

kain (kān), *n.* *Scot.* cain.

kain (kīn), *n.* *Malay.* sarong.

Kain (kān), *n.* a boy's given name. Also, **Kane, Kayne.**

Kain·gang (kīn′gang′), *n., pl.* **-gangs,** (*esp. collectively*) **-gang.** Caingang.

kai·nite (kī′nīt, kā′nīt), *n.* a mineral, hydrous sulfate of magnesium and potassium chloride, occurring in granular crystalline masses, a source of potassium salts. [< G *Kainit*. See CAINO-, -ITE¹]

Kair·ouan (*Fr.* ker wän′), *n.* a city in NE Tunisia: a holy city of Islam. 33,968 (1956). Also, **Kair·wan** (kīər wän′).

kai·ser (kī′zər), *n.* **1.** a German emperor. **2.** an Austrian emperor. **3.** *Hist.* a ruler of the Holy Roman Empire. **4.** a person who exercises or seeks to exercise absolute authority; an autocrat. [< G << L *Caesar* emperor, special use of proper name (see CAESAR); r. ME (north) *caisere* (OE *cāsere*) and ME *keisere* (< Scand; cf. Icel *keisari*) << L *Caesar*, as above]

Kai·ser (kī′zər), *n.* **1. Henry J(ohn),** 1882–1967, U.S. industrialist. **2.** a walled plain in the fourth quadrant of the face of the moon: about 34 miles in diameter.

kai·ser·dom (kī′zər dəm), *n.* **1.** the rank or position of a kaiser. **2.** the area under the rule of a kaiser. [prob. trans. of G *Kaisertum*. See KAISER, -DOM]

kai·ser·ism (kī′zə riz′əm), *n.* autocratic rule, like that of a German kaiser. [KAISER + -ISM]

kai·ser·ship (kī′zər ship′), *n.* the office of kaiser. [KAISER + -SHIP]

Kai·sers·lau·tern (kī′zərs lou′tərn), *n.* a city in S Rhineland-Palatinate, in SW West Germany. 86,900 (1963).

k'ai shu (kī′ sho͞o′), a variety of Chinese script developed in the 4th century A.D. and considered to be standard since that time. [< Chin: lit., model script]

Ka·jaa·ni (kä′yä nē), *n.* a city in central Finland. 17,112 (est. 1965).

Ka·jar (kä jär′), *n.* a dynasty that ruled Persia 1794–1925.

kaj·e·put (kaj′ə pət, -po͝ot′), *n.* cajuput.

ka·ka (kä′kə), *n.* any of several New Zealand parrots of the genus *Nestor*, esp. *N. meridionalis*, having chiefly greenish and olive-brown plumage. [< Maori; ? imit. of the bird's cry]

ka·ka·po (kä′kä pō′), *n., pl.* **-pos** (-pōz′). a large, almost flightless, nocturnal parrot, *Strigops habroptilus*, of New Zealand. [< Maori: lit., night kaka]

ka·ke·mo·no (kä′ke mô′nô; *Eng.* kä′kə mō′nō), *n., pl.* **-no,** *Eng.* **-nos.** *Japanese.* a vertical hanging scroll containing either text or a painting, intended to be viewed on a wall and rolled when not in use. Cf. **makimono.** [lit., hanging object]

ka·ki (kä′kē), *n., pl.* **-kis. 1.** the Japanese persimmon tree. **2.** the fruit of this tree. [< Jap]

kak·is·toc·ra·cy (kak′i stok′rə sē), *n., pl.* **-cies.** government by the worst men in the state. [< Gk *kákisto(s)*, superl. of *kakós* bad + -CRACY] —**ka·kis·to·crat·i·cal** (kə kis′tə krat′i kəl), *adj.*

kal., kalends.

ka·la-a·zar (kä′lä ä zär′, kä′lä az′ər), *n. Pathol.* a chronic, usually fatal disease occurring in India, Assam, and other tropical areas of Asia, characterized by irregular fever, enlargement of the spleen, hemorrhages, and emaciation, and caused by the protozoan *Leishmania donovani*. Also called **Dumdum fever, visceral leishmaniasis.** [< Hindi, equiv. to *kālā* black + Pers *āzār* disease]

Ka·la·ha·ri (kä′lä hä′rē), *n.* a desert region in SW Africa, largely in Botswana. 3,500,000 sq. mi.

Ka·lakh (kä′läкн), *n.* an ancient Assyrian city on the Tigris River: its ruins are at Nimrud near Mosul in N Iraq. Biblical name, **Calah.**

ka·lam (kə läm′), *n. Islam.* **1.** a rationalistic school of theology originating in the 9th century A.D., asserting the existence of God as a prime mover and the freedom of the will. **2.** the word of Allah. [< Ar: word] —**Ka·lam′ist,** *n.*

Kal·a·ma·zoo (kal′ə mə zo͞o′), *n.* a city in SW Michigan. 82,089 (1960).

kal′a·mein work′ (kal′ə mīn′), *Building Trades.* cladding of wooden doors and windows with galvanized sheet steel. [*kalamein* orig. trademark]

kal·an·cho·e (kal′ən kō′ē, kə lang′kō ē), *n.* any of several chiefly African and Asian tropical herbs or shrubs of the genus *Kalanchoe*, certain species of which are cultivated as ornamentals. [< NL]

Ka·lat (kə lät′), *n.* a region in S Baluchistan, in SW West Pakistan. Also, **Khelat.**

kal·a·thos (kal′ə thos′), *n., pl.* **-thoi** (-thoi′). *Gk. and Rom. Antiq.* a fruit basket having a conventionalized shape of a lily, often used in ancient art as a symbol of fertility. Also, **calathus.** [< Gk, whence also L *calathus*]

Kalb (kalb; *Ger.* kälp), *n.* **Jo·hann** (yō′hän), ("*Baron de Kalb*"), 1721–80, German general in the American Revolutionary Army.

kale (kāl), *n.* **1.** Also called **borecole.** a cabbagelike plant, *Brassica oleracea acephala*, having curled or wrinkled leaves: used as a vegetable. **2.** *Scot.* cabbage. **3.** *U.S. Slang.* money. Also, **kail.** [ME *cale*, north var. of COLE]

ka·lei·do·scope (kə lī′də skōp′), *n.* an optical instrument in which bits of glass, beads, etc., held loosely at the end of a rotating tube are shown in continually changing symmetrical forms by reflection in three mirrors placed at 60° angles to each other. [< Gk *kal(ós)* beautiful + *eîdo(s)* shape + -SCOPE]

ka·lei·do·scop·ic (kə lī′də skop′ik), *adj.* **1.** of, pertaining to, or created by a kaleidoscope. **2.** changing form, pattern, color, etc, in a manner suggesting a kaleidoscope. **3.** continually shifting from one set of relations to another; rapidly changing: *the kaleidoscopic events of the past year.* **4.** extremely complex and varied: *a kaleidoscopic view of history.* Also, **ka·lei′do·scop′i·cal.** [KALEIDOSCOPE + -IC] —**ka·lei′do·scop′i·cal·ly,** *adv.*

ka·le·ma (kə lā′mə), *n.* a very heavy surf that occurs on the coast of Guinea, in W Africa. [< Pg < a WAfr language]

kal·en·dar (kal′ən dər), *n.* calendar. —**kal·en·dar·i·al** (kal′ən dâr′ē əl), *adj.*

kal·ends (kal′əndz), *n.* (*usually construed as pl.*) calends.

Ka·le·va (kä′le və), *n.* a hero and progenitor of heroes in Finnish and Estonian folk epics.

Ka·le·va·la (kä′lə vä′lə; *Fin.* kä′le vä′lə), *n.* **1.** (*italics*) the national epic of Finland (1835, enlarged 1849), compiled and arranged by Elias Lönnrot from popular lays of the Middle Ages. **2.** the home or land of Kaleva; Finland. [< Finn, equiv. to *kaleva* hero's + *-la* dwelling place]

kale·yard (kāl′yärd′), *n. Scot.* See **kitchen garden.** Also, **kail·yard.** [KALE + YARD²]

kale′yard school′, a school of writers describing homely life in Scotland, with much use of Scottish dialect: in vogue toward the close of the 19th century, when books by Sir James M. Barrie and others were appearing. Also, **kail·yard school.**

Kal·gan (käl′gän′), *n.* former name of **Wanchüan.**

Kal·goor·lie (kal go͝or′lē), *n.* a city in SW Australia: chief center of gold-mining industry in Australia. 9696, with suburbs 21,773 (1961).

kal·i (kal′ē, kā′lē), *n., pl.* **kal·is.** a glasswort. [< Ar *qalīy*; see ALKALI]

Kali

Ka·li (kä′lē), *n. Hinduism.* a goddess personifying creation and destruction, sometimes considered as the active, differentiated counterpart of Brahman.

ka·li·an (käl yän′), *n.* a Persian tobacco pipe in which the smoke is drawn through water; hookah. [< Pers *qalyān*]

Ka·li·da·sa (kä′li dä′sə), *n.* fl. 5th century A.D., Hindu dramatist and poet. Also, **Kā′li·dā′sa.**

ka·lif (kā′lif, kal′if), *n.* caliph.

kal·i·fate (kal′ə fāt′, -fit), *n.* caliphate.

Ka·li·man·tan (kä′lē män′tän), *n.* Indonesian name of Borneo, esp. referring to the southern, or Indonesian, part.

Ka·li·nin (kä lē′nin), *n.* **1. Mi·kha·il Iva·no·vich** (mi кнä ēl′ i vä′no vich), 1875–1946, Russian revolutionary: president of the U.S.S.R. 1923–46. **2.** Former name of **Tver.**

Ka·li·nin·grad (kä lē′nin gräd′), *n.* a seaport in the W RSFSR, in the W Soviet Union in Europe, on the Bay of Danzig. 247,000 (est. 1964). German, **Königsberg.**

kal·i·nite (kal′ə nīt′, kā′lə-), *n.* a mineral, hydrous sulfate of potassium and aluminum, occurring in lava. [< NL *kali(um)* KALI, alkali + hiatus-filling *-n-* + -ITE¹]

ka·liph (kā′lif, kal′if), *n.* caliph.

Kal·i·spel (kal′i spel′), *n.* a Salishan language used by the Flathead Indians of Montana and by some neighboring tribes in Idaho and the western part of Washington State.

Kal·i·spell (kal′i spel′), *n.* a city in NW Montana. 10,151 (1960).

Ka·lisz (kä′lish), *n.* a city in central Poland. 73,000 (est. 1963). German, **Ka·lisch** (kä′lish).

Ka·li Yu·ga (kul′ē yo͝og′ə), *Hinduism.* the fourth and present age of the world, full of conflict and sin. [< Skt *kaliyuga*, equiv. to *kali* unlucky cast in dice + *yuga* YOKE¹]

Kal·li·kak (kal′ə kak′), *n.* the fictitious name of an actual New Jersey family whose history over several generations showed a high incidence of disease, delinquency, and poverty. Cf. **Jukes.**

Kal·man (kôl′mən, kal′-), *n.* a boy's given name, form of **Clement.**

Kal·mar (käl′mär), *n.* a seaport in SE Sweden, on Kalmar Sound. 31,905 (1963). —**Kal·mar·i·an** (kal mâr′ē ən), *adj.*

Kal′mar Sound′, a strait between SE Sweden and Öland Island. 85 mi. long; 14 mi. wide.

kal·mi·a (kal′mē ə), *n.* any North American, evergreen, ericaceous shrub of the genus *Kalmia*, having showy flowers, as the mountain laurel. [named after Peter *Kalm* (1715–79), Swedish botanist; see -IA]

Kal·muck (kal′muk), *n.* **1.** a member of any of a group of Buddhistic Mongol tribes of a region extending from western China to the valley of the lower Volga River. **2.** a Mongolian language used by that part of the Kalmuck people that was formerly powerful in NW China, specifically in Ozungaria, and is now relocated NW of the Caspian Sea. Also, **Kal′muk.**

Kal·myk·i·a (kal mik′ē ə; *Russ.* kul mi′kyə), *n.* an autonomous republic in the Russian Federation in Europe, on the NW shore of the Caspian Sea. 293,000; 75,900 sq. mi. *Cap.:* Elista. Also, **Kal·myk′i·ya.** Official name, **Kal·myk′ Auton′omous Repub′lic** (kal mik′).

ka·long (kä′long), *n.* a flying fox of the genus *Pteropus*. [< Javanese]

kal·pa (kul′pə), *n. Hinduism, Buddhism.* one of the ages of the world, the present one being the fourth. [< Skt]

kal·pak (kal′pak), *n.* calpac.

kal·pis (kal′pis), *n.* a form of the hydria. [< Gk]

kal·so·mine (kal′sə mīn′, -min), *n., v.t.,* **-mined, -min·ing.** calcimine. —**kal′so·min′er,** *n.*

Kalpis

kalt·e·mail (kält′tə mīl′), *n.* a technique of ceramic decoration of the 16th and 17th centuries, consisting of the application of a hard lacquer without subsequent firing. [< G, equiv. to *kalt* cold + *Email* enamel]

Ka·lu·ga (kä lo͞o′gä), *n.* a city in the W RSFSR, in the central Soviet Union in Europe, SW of Moscow. 164,000 (est. 1964).

Ka·ma (kä′mä), *n.* a river in the E Soviet Union in Europe, flowing from the central Ural mountain region into the Volga River S of Kazan. 1200 mi. long.

Ka·ma (kä′mə), *n.* **1.** *Hindu Myth.* the god of erotic desire, sometimes seen as an aspect of the god whose other aspect is Mara, or death. **2.** (*l.c.*) the attachment to temporal things personified by this god. **3.** a girl's given name. [< Skt, special use of *kāma* love, lust]

kam·a·cite (kam′ə sīt′), *n.* a nickel-iron alloy found in meteorites. [< G (obs.) *Kamacit* < Gk *kamak-* (s. of *kámax*) pole + G *-it* -ITE¹]

Ka·ma·dhe·nu (kä′mə dā′no͞o), *n. Hindu Myth.* a celestial cow whose milk is life, and one of whose milkings is the visible world. [< Skt, equiv. to *kāma* love + *dhenū* yielding milk, milch cow]

Ka·ma·ku·ra (kä′mä ko͞o′rä), *n.* a city on S Honshu, in central Japan: great bronze statue of Buddha. 113,227 (1964).

ka·ma·la (kə mā′lə, kam′ə lə), *n.* a powder from the capsules of an East Indian, euphorbiaceous tree, *Malotus philippinensis*, used as a yellow dye and in medicine as an anthelmintic. [< Skt < Dravidian; cf. Kanarese *kōmale*]

Ka·ma·lo·ka (kä′mə lō′kə), *n. Hinduism.* a world after death in which souls undergo pleasures and pains within the grasp of kama. [< Skt: lit., love-brightness]

Ka·ma-Ma·ra (kä′mə mär′ə), *n. Hindu Myth.* a god of erotic desire and death, whose two aspects are personified as Kama and Mara.

ka·ma·shi·mo za·shi (kä mä′shē mō′ zä shē′; *Jap.* kä mä′shē mô′ zä shē′), *pl.* **ka·ma·shi·mo za·shi.** a short Japanese sword worn with court or ceremonial dress. [< Jap, equiv. to *kamashimo* court costume + *zashi* for wear with]

Ka·ma·su·tra (kä′mə so͞o′trə), *n.* an ancient Hindu text on mystical erotics.

kam·bal (kum′bəl), *n.* (in India) a blanket or shawl made of coarse wool. [< Hindi < Skt *kambala*]

Kam·chat·ka (kam chät′kə; *Russ.* käm chät′kä), *n.* a peninsula in the E Soviet Union in Asia, extending S between the Bering Sea and the Sea of Okhotsk. 750 mi. long; 104,200 sq. mi. —**Kam·chat′kan,** *adj., n.*

kame¹ (kām), *n. Phys. Geog.* a ridge or mound of detrital material, esp. of stratified sand and gravel, left by a retreating ice sheet. [ME (north) *camb* comb, OE *camb*; see COMB¹]

kame² (kām), *n. Scot.* combe. [dial. var. of COMB²]

Ka·me·ha·me·ha I (kä mā′hä mā′hä, kə mā′ə mā′ə), ("*the Great*") 1737?–1819, king of the Hawaiian Islands 1810–19.

Kame′hame′ha Day′, the date, June 11, observed in Hawaii as a holiday in celebration of the birth of Kamehameha I.

ka·me·lau·ki·on (kä mē läf′kē ôn; *Eng.* kam′ə lô′kē-on′, käm′ə lou′-), *n., pl.* **-ki·a** (-kē ä; *Eng.* -kē ə), **-ki·ons.** *Gk. Orth. Ch.* a tall, black, brimless, flat-topped hat, worn by the clergy of the Eastern Church. [< MGk *kamēlaúkion* from the fact that it is made of camel's hair]

Ka·mensk-U·ral·ski (kä′mənsk o͞o räl′ski), *n.* a city in the W RSFSR, in the W Soviet Union in Asia, near the Ural mountains. 152,000 (est. 1962). Also, **Ka′mensk U·ral′skiy.**

Ka·me·rad (kä′mə rät′), *n. German.* comrade (used as a shout of surrender).

Ka·mer·lingh On·nes (kä′mər ling ô′nəs), **Hei·ke** (hī′kə), 1853–1926, Dutch physicist: Nobel prize 1913.

Ka·me·run (kä′mə ro͞on′), *n.* German name of **Cameroons.**

ka·mi (kä′mē), *n., pl.* **-mi.** *Japanese.* a divine being or force.

Ka·mi·ka·ze (kä′mə kä′zē), *n.* **1.** a member of a corps in the Japanese air force, charged with the suicidal mission of crashing his aircraft, laden with explosives, into an enemy target, esp. a ship, during World War II. **2.** an airplane used for this purpose. —*adj.* **3.** of, pertaining to, undertaken by, or characteristic of a Kamikaze: *a Kamikaze pilot; a Kamikaze attack.* [< Jap, equiv. to *kami* divine + *kaze* wind]

Ka·mi·na (kä mē′nä), *n.* a city in the S Republic of the Congo. 32,100 (est. 1954).

Kam·loops (kam′lo͞ops), *n.* a city in S British Columbia, in SW Canada. 10,076 (1961).

Kam·pa·la (käm pä′lä), *n.* a city in and the capital of Uganda, in the central part. 46,714 (1959).

kam·pong (käm′pông, -pong, käm pông′ -pong′), *n.* a small village or community of houses in Malay-speaking lands. Also, **campong.** [< Malay]

Kam·pu·che·a (kam′po͞o chē′ə), *n.* **Democratic,** official name of **Cambodia.** —**Kam′pu·che′an,** *adj., n.*

kam·py·lite (kam′pə līt′), *n.* campylite.

kam·seen (kam sēn′), *n.* khamsin. Also, **kam′sin.**

Kan., Kansas.

ka·na (kä′nä, -nə), *n.* the Japanese syllabic script, consisting of 73 symbols and having two written varieties. Cf. **hiragana, katakana.** [< Jap: lit., pretended letters (so called because KANJI are considered the real letters)]

Ka·nak·a (kə nak′ə, kan′ə kə), *n.* **1.** a native Hawaiian. **2.** a South Sea islander. [< Hawaiian: man]

ka·na·ma·ji·ri (kä′nə mä′jə rē; *Jap.* kä′nä mä′jē rē′), *n.* the standard script of modern Japanese, in which Chinese-derived characters, or kanji, are used for root elements, supplemented by kana for inflections and particles and sometimes for indication of the Japanese pronunciation of kanji. [< Jap: lit., kana mixture]

ka·na·mo·no (kə nä′mō nō′; *Jap.* kä nä′mô nô′), *n.pl.* Japanese sword mounts. [< Jap, equiv. to *kana* metal + *mono* fittings]

Ka·na·nur (kun′ə no͝or′), *n.* Cannanore.

Ka·na·ra (kə när′ə, kun′ər ə), *n.* a region in SW India, on the Deccan Plateau. ab. 60,000 sq. mi. Also, **Canara.**

Ka·na·rak (kə när′uk), *n.* Konarak.

Ka·na·rese (kä′nə rēz′, -rēs′), *adj., n., pl.* **-rese.** —*adj.* **1.** of or pertaining to Kanara, a part of the Maharashtra province in W India. —*n.* **2.** one of a Dravidian people of Kanara, in SW India. **3.** Kannada. Also, **Canarese.** [KANAR(A) + -ESE]

Ka·na·za·wa (kä′nä zä′wä), *n.* a seaport on W Honshu, in central Japan. 327,703 (1964).

Kan·chen·jun·ga (kän′chən jo͝ong′gə), *n.* a mountain in S Asia, between NE India and Nepal, in the E Himalayas: third highest in the world. 28,146 ft. Also, **Kan·chan·jan·ga** (kän′chən jäng′gə), **Kinchinjunga.**

Kan·da·har (kun′də här′), *n.* a city in S Afghanistan. 100,000 (est. 1964).

Kan·din·sky (kan din′skē; *Russ.* kän dēn′ski), *n.* **Was·si·ly** (vas′ə lē) or **Va·si·li** (vas′ə lē; *Russ.* vä sē′-li), 1866–1944, Russian painter. Also, **Kan·din′ski.**

Kan·dy (kan′dē, kän′dē), *n.* a city in central Ceylon: famous Buddhist temples. 67,768 (1963).

kane (kān), *n. Scot.* cain.

Kane (kān), *n.* **1.** a town in N Pennsylvania. 5380 (1960). **2.** a walled plain in the first quadrant of the face of the moon: about 33 miles in diameter. **3.** Also, **Kain, Kayne.** a boy's given name.

ka·neel·hart (kə nēl′härt), *n.* **1.** a lauraceous tree, *Licaria cayennensis*, of Central and South America. **2.** the very hard, durable wood of this tree. [prob. < D, equiv. to *kaneel* cinnamon (MD *caneel* < MF *canelle* < ML *canella*; see CANELLA) + *hart* HEART]

Ka·ne·o·he (kä′nā ō′-hā), *n.* a town on E Oahu, in Hawaii. 14,414 (1960).

kang (käng), *n.* (in Chinese buildings) a masonry stove for sitting or sleeping upon. [< Chin (Peking)]

Great gray kangaroo, *Macropus giganteus* (Total length 7½ ft.; tail 3½ ft.)

kan·ga·roo (kang′gə-ro͞o′), *n., pl.* **-roos,** (*esp. collectively*) **-roo.** any herbivorous marsupial of the family *Macropodidae*, of

CONCISE ETYMOLOGY KEY: <, descended or derived from; >, whence; b., blend of, blended; c., cognate with; deriv., derivative; equiv., equivalent; imit., imitative; m., modification of; obl., oblique; r., replacing; s., stem; sp., spelling; trans., translation; ?, origin unknown, perhaps; *, hypothetical. See the full key inside the front cover.

Australia and adjacent islands, having a small head, short forelimbs, powerful hind legs used for leaping, and a long, thick tail serving as a support and balance. [? < native Austral] —**kan′ga·roo′like′,** *adj.*

kan′garoo court′, **1.** a self-appointed or mob-operated tribunal, usually disregarding or parodying existing principles of law, human rights, etc., esp. one constituted by criminals, as in prison, to settle disputes among themselves. **2.** any crudely or irregularly operated court, esp. one so controlled as to render a fair trial impossible. **3.** a humorous burlesque of judicial procedure, conducted for the amusement of the participants, as a satire on social conditions or the like.

kan·ga·roo·ing (kang′gə ro͞o′ing), *n.* *Australian.* the art or practice of hunting kangaroos. [KANGAROO + -ING[1]]

kangaroo′ rat′, **1.** any of various small jumping rodents of the family *Heteromyidae,* of Mexico and the western U.S., such as those of the genus *Dipodomys.* **2.** an Australian rodent of the genus *Notomys,* found in arid areas.

Kangaroo rat, *Dipodomys phillipsii* (Total length 13 in.; tail 7 in.)

kangaroo′ thorn′, a spiny shrub, *Acacia armata,* having bright-yellow flower heads, grown as an ornamental.

kangaroo′ vine′, a vine, *Cissus antarctica,* of Australia, having shiny, leathery leaves.

K'ang Hsi (käng′ shē′), (*Shêng-tsu*) 1654?–1722, Chinese emperor of the Ch'ing dynasty 1662–1722.

K'ang Tê (käng′ du′). See **Pu-yi, Henry.** Also, **Kang′ Teh′.**

kan·ji (kän′jē), *n., pl.* **-ji, -jis. 1.** a system of Japanese writing using Chinese-derived characters. **2.** any one of these characters. [< Jap, equiv. to *kan* Chinese + *ji* ideograph]

Kan·ka·kee (kang′kə kē′), *n.* a city in NE Illinois. 27,666 (1960).

Kan·kan (*Fr.* käɴ käɴ′), *n.* a city in the E Guinea republic. 24,600 (1955).

Kan·na·da (kä′nə də, kan′ə-), *n.* a Dravidian language used in most of Madras state in southern India. Also called **Kanarese.**

Kan·nap·o·lis (kə nap′ə lis), *n.* a city in W North Carolina. 34,647 (1960).

Ka·no (kä′nō), *n.* a city in N Nigeria. 295,432 (1963).

ka·no·ne (kə nō′nə), *n., pl.* **-nen** (-nən). *Rare.* a person who excels in skiing. [< G: lit., cannon < It *cannone;* see CANNON]

Kan·pur (kän′po͝or), *n.* Indian name of **Cawnpore.**

kans (käns), *n.* an Indian grass, *Saccharum spontaneum,* used, in some areas, for fodder, thatching, etc., and constituting, in other areas, a troublesome weed. Also called **kans grass.** [< Hindi *kās* < Skt *kāsa*]

Kans., Kansas.

Kan·sa (kän′sə), *n.* *Hindu Legend.* a tyrannical king killed by Krishna.

Kan·san (kan′zən), *adj.* **1.** of or pertaining to the State of Kansas. **2.** *Geol.* of or pertaining to the Kansan. —*n.* **3.** a native or inhabitant of Kansas. **4.** *Geol.* the second stage of the glaciation of North America during the Pleistocene. Cf. **Mindel.** [KANS(AS) + -AN]

Kan·sas (kan′zəs), *n.* **1.** a State in the central United States: a part of the Midwest. 2,178,611 (1960); 82,276 sq. mi. *Cap.:* Topeka. *Abbr.:* Kans., Kan. **2.** a river in NE Kansas, flowing E to the Missouri River. 169 mi. long.

Kan′sas Cit′y, **1.** a city in W Missouri, at the confluence of the Kansas and Missouri rivers. 475,539 (1960). **2.** a city in NE Kansas, adjacent to Kansas City, Missouri. 121,901 (1960).

Kan′sas Cit′y style′, a style of jazz developed in Kansas City, Missouri, in the early 1930's, marked by a strong blues flavoring, the use of riffs as a characteristic formal device, and by a less pronounced beat than the New Orleans or Chicago style of jazz.

Kan′sas gay′-feath·er (gā′feth′ər). See **prairie button snakeroot.**

Kan′sas-Ne·bras′ka Act′ (kan′zəs nə bras′kə), *U.S. Hist.* the act of Congress in 1854 annulling the Missouri Compromise, providing for the organization of the Territories of Kansas and Nebraska, and permitting these Territories self-determination on the question of slavery.

kans′ grass′, kans.

Kan·su (kan′so͞o′; *Chin.* gän′so͞o′), *n.* a province in NW China. 12,800,000 (est. 1957); 137,104 sq. mi. *Cap.:* Lanchow.

Kant (kant; *Ger.* känt), *n.* **1. Im·man·u·el** (i man′yo͞o əl; *Ger.* i mä′no͞o el′), 1724–1804, German philosopher. **2.** a crater in the fourth quadrant of the face of the moon: about 22 miles in diameter.

kan·tar (kän tär′), *n.* (in eastern Mediterranean countries) a unit of weight corresponding to the hundredweight, but varying in different localities. [< Ar *qinṭār* << L *centenārium;* see QUINTAL]

kan·te·le (kän′tᵊlə, kan′-), *n.* an ancient Finnish instrument resembling a psaltery. [< Finn]

kan·tha·ros (kan′thər əs), *n., pl.* **-tha·roi** (-thə roi′). *Gk. and Rom. Antiq.* a cup in the shape of a deep bowl set upon a stem terminating in a foot, having two handles rising from the brim and curving downward to join the body immediately above its juncture with the stem: used for libations offered in honor of Dionysus. Also, **cantharus.** [< Gk]

Kantharos

Kant·i·an (kan′tē ən), *adj.* **1.** of, pertaining to, or resembling the philosophy of Kant. —*n.* **2.** an adherent of Kantianism. [KANT + -IAN]

Kant·i·an·ism (kan′tē ə niz′əm), *n.* the philosophy of Kant, maintaining that the mind, because of its nature, cannot know things as they are but rather interprets the data presented to it as spatiotemporal phenomena, and that the reason, either in order to give a meaningful ground for experience or in order to make ethical conduct possible, may postulate things unknowable to it, as the existence of a god and of a personal, immortal, and self-determining soul. —**Kant′ ist,** *n.*

Kan·tor (kan′tər), *n.* **Mac·Kin·lay** (mə kin′lē), born 1904, U.S. novelist.

kan·zu (kan′zo͞o), *n.* a long white robe worn esp. by men in central Africa. [< Swahili]

Kao·hsiung (gou′shyo͞ong′), *n.* a seaport on SW Taiwan. 539,771 (est. 1963). Also called **Takao.**

Ka·o·lack (kä′ō lak, kou′lak), *n.* a city in W Senegal. 46,800 (1957). Also, **Ka′o·lak.**

ka·o·li·ang (kä′ō lē ang′), *n.* a variety of grain sorghum. [< Chin (Mandarin) *kao* tall + *liang* millet, grain]

ka·o·lin (kā′ə lin), *n.* a fine white clay used in the manufacture of porcelain. Also, **ka′o·line.** [< F < Chin *Kaoling* name of a mountain in China which yielded the first kaolin sent to Europe (*kao* high + *ling* hill)] —**ka′o·lin′ic,** *adj.*

ka·o·lin·ise (kā′ə lə nīz′), *v.t.,* **-ised, -is·ing.** *Chiefly Brit.* kaolinize. —**ka′o·lin·i·sa′tion,** *n.*

ka·o·lin·ite (kā′ə lə nīt′), *n.* a very common mineral, hydrated aluminum disilicate, $Al_2Si_2O_5(OH)_4$, formed by the alteration of other minerals: the commonest constituent of kaolin. [KAOLIN + -ITE[1]]

ka·o·lin·ize (kā′ə lə nīz′), *v.t.,* **-ized, -iz·ing.** to convert (minerals containing kaolinite) into kaolin by weathering. Also, *esp. Brit.,* **kaolinise.** [KAOLIN + -IZE] —**ka′o·lin·i·za′tion,** *n.*

ka·on (kā′on), *n.* *Physics.* K-meson. [*ka* (name of letter *k*) + (MES)ON[1]]

Kao Tsu (*Chin.* gou′ dzo͞o′), **1.** See **Li Yüan. 2.** See **Chao K'uang-yin.**

Ka·pa·a (kä pä′ä), *n.* a town on E Kauai, in NW Hawaii. 3439 (1960).

Ka·pell (kə pel′), *n.* **William,** 1922–53, U.S. pianist.

Ka·pell·meis·ter (kä pel′mī′stər), *n., pl.* **-ter. 1.** a choirmaster. **2.** a conductor of an orchestra. **3.** bandmaster. [< G; see CHAPEL, MASTER]

kaph (käf, kôf), *n.* **1.** the 11th letter of the Hebrew alphabet. **2.** the consonant sound represented by this letter. Also, **caph.** [< Heb: lit., palm of the hand]

Ka·pi·la (kä′pi lə), *n.* fl. early 6th century B.C., Hindu philosopher: reputed founder of the Sandkhya system of Hindu philosophy.

Ka·pi·tal, Das (*Ger.* däs kä′pi täl′). See **Das Kapital.**

Kap·lan (kap′lən), *n.* **1. Mor·de·cai Me·na·hem** (môr′də kī′ mä′nä hem′, mä nä′hem), born 1881, U.S. religious leader and educator, born in Lithuania: founder of the Reconstruction movement in Judaism. **2.** a town in S Louisiana. 5267 (1960).

ka·pok (kā′pok, kap′ək), *n.* the silky down which invests the seeds of a silk-cotton tree (**ka′pok tree′**), *Ceiba pentandra,* of the East Indies, Africa, and tropical America: used for stuffing pillows, life jackets, etc., and for sound insulation. Also called **Java cotton.** [< Malay *kāpoq*]

ka′pok oil′, a yellowish-green oil expressed from the seeds of the kapok tree, used esp. in foods and in the manufacture of soap.

ka·po·te (kə pō′tə), *n.* a long coat worn esp. by male Jews of eastern Europe. [< Yiddish < F *capote* CAPOTE]

kap·pa (kap′ə), *n.* **1.** the 10th letter of the Greek alphabet (K, κ). **2.** the consonant sound represented by this letter. [< Gk < Sem; see KAPH]

kap′pa me′son, *Physics.* K-meson.

ka·pu·ka (kä′pə kə), *n.* a tree, *Griselinia littoralis,* of New Zealand, having brown, hairy twigs and small, greenish flowers. [< Maori]

ka·put (kä po͝ot′, -po͞ot′, kə-), *adj.* *Slang.* ruined; done for; demolished. [< G: orig. trickless (in game of piquet) < F (*être*) *capot* (to be) without tricks, i.e., make zero score]

ka·ra·bu·ran (kar′ə byo͞o rän′), *n.* a severe, dust-laden, northeast wind blowing during the spring and summer in central Asia. Also called **black buran, black storm.** [< Turk, equiv. to *kara* black + *buran* whirlwind, storm]

Ka·ra·chai′-Cher·kess′ Auton′omous Re′gion (kär′ə chi′chər kes′; *Russ.* kə ʀu chyī′chyiʀ kyes′), an autonomous region in the Russian Federation in Europe, in the Caucasus. 369,000; 5442 sq. mi. *Cap.:* Cherkess.

Ka·ra·chi (kə rä′chē), *n.* a seaport in S West Pakistan, near the Indus delta: former capital of Pakistan. 1,916,000 (est. 1961).

Ka·ra·fu·to (kä′ʀä fo͞o′tô), *n.* Japanese name of the southern, Japanese part of Sakhalin.

Ka·ra·gan·da (kä′ʀä gän′dä), *n.* a city in W Kazakstan, in the SW Soviet Union in Asia. 398,000 (1959).

Kar·a·ite (kâr′ə īt′), *n.* *Judaism.* a member of a sect, founded in Persia in the 8th century A.D. by the religious leader Anan ben David, which rejected the Talmud and the teachings and traditions of the rabbis in favor of strict adherence to the Bible as the single authoritative source of Jewish law and practice. Cf. **Rabbinite.** [< Heb *q'rā(īm)* scripturalists (*qārā* to read + *-īm,* pl. of *-ī* suffix of appurtenance) + -ITE[1]] —**Kar·a·ism** (kâr′ə iz′əm), **Kar·a·it·ism** (kâr′ə ī tiz′əm), *n.* —**Kar·a·it·ic** (kâr′ə it′ik), *adj.*

Ka·ra·jan (kar′ə yən; *Ger.* kä′ʀä yän), *n.* **Her·bert von** (hûr′bərt von; *Ger.* heʀ′bəʀt fən), born 1908, Austrian conductor.

Ka·ra-Kal·pak (kə rä′kəl päk′, kär ə-), *n.* **1.** one of a Mongolian people living in the Kara-Kalpak Republic and adjacent areas. **2.** the Turkic language of the Kara-Kalpaks.

Kara-Kalpak′ Auton′omous Repub′lic, an autonomous republic in NW Uzbekistan. 904,000; 63,938 sq. mi. *Cap.:* Nukas.

Ka·ra·ko·ram (kär′ə kōr′əm, -kôr′-), *n.* **1.** Also called **Mustagh.** a mountain range in NW India, in N Kashmir. Highest peak, K2, 28,250 ft. **2.** a pass traversing this range, on the route from NE Kashmir to Sinkiang province in China. 18,300 ft.

Ka·ra·ko·rum (kär′ə kōr′əm, -kôr′-), *n.* a ruined city in central Mongolian People's Republic: capital of the Mongol Empire in the 13th century.

kar·a·kul (kar′ə kəl), *n.* **1.** one of an Asian breed of sheep the young of which have a black fleece, the adults a brown or gray one. **2.** caracul (def. 1). [orig. place name, widely used in Turkestan, esp. in naming lakes; cf. Turk *kara* black, *kul* lake]

Ka·ra Kum (kä ʀä′ ko͞om′), a desert in the SW Soviet Union in Asia, largely in Turkmenistan, S of the Aral Sea. ab. 110,000 sq. mi. Also, **Qara Qum.**

Ka·ra·mi (kä ʀä′mē), *n.* **Ra·shid** (ʀa shēd′), born 1921, Lebanese lawyer and statesman: prime minister 1955–56, 1958–60, 1961–64, and 1965–66. Also, **Ka·ra·meh** (kä ʀä′mē, -me).

ka·ran·da (kə run′də), *n.* a shrub or small tree, *Carissa Carandas,* of India, having white or pink flowers and reddish-black berries. [< Hindi < Skt *karamardaka*]

ka·ra·o·ke (kar′ē ō′kē), *n.* an act of singing along to a music video, esp. one from which the original vocals have been electronically eliminated. [< Japn, = *kara* empty + *oke* orchestra]

Ka′ra Sea′ (kär′ə), an arm of the Arctic Ocean between Novaya Zemlya and the N Soviet Union.

kar·at (kar′ət), *n.* a unit for measuring the fineness of gold, pure gold being 24 karats fine. *Abbr.:* k., kt. [sp. var. of CARAT]

ka·ra·te (kə rä′tē), *n.* a method developed in Japan of defending oneself without the use of weapons by striking sensitive areas on an attacker's body with the hands, elbows, knees, or feet. Cf. **judo, jujitsu.** [< Jap: lit., empty hands]

Kar·ba·la (kär′bə lə), *n.* Kerbela.

Ka·re·lia (kə rēl′yə; *Russ.* kä re′li ä′), *n.* **1.** a region in the NW Soviet Union in Europe, comprising Lake Ladoga and Onega Lake and the adjoining area along the E border of Finland. **2.** See **Karelian Autonomous Republic.**

Ka·re·li·an (kə rē′lē ən, -rēl′yən), *adj.* **1.** of or pertaining to Karelia, its people, or their language. —*n.* **2.** a native or inhabitant of Karelia. **3.** the Uralic language of the Karelians, sometimes regarded as a dialect of Finnish. [KARELI(A) + -AN]

Kare′lian Auton′omous Repub′lic, an autonomous republic in the NW Russian Federation in Europe. Also called **Karalia.** 792,000; 66,500 sq. mi. *Cap.:* Petrozavodsk.

Kare′lian Isth′mus, a narrow strip of land between Lake Ladoga and the Gulf of Finland: part of the Soviet Union since 1945.

Ka·ren (kə ren′ *for 1–3, 5;* kar′ən, kär′- *for 4*), *n., pl.* **-rens,** (*esp. collectively*) **-ren,** *adj.* —*n.* **1.** a group of people of eastern and southern Burma. **2.** one of these people. **3.** the language of the Karen, a Sino-Tibetan language of the Tibeto-Burman branch. **4.** Also, **Kar′in, Karyn, Karynne.** a girl's given name, form of **Carin.** —*adj.* **5.** of or pertaining to these people or their language.

Karl (kärl), *n.* a boy's given name, form of **Charles.** Also, **Carl.**

Kar·la (kär′lə), *n.* a girl's given name, form of **Caroline.** Also, **Carla.**

Karl·feldt (käʀl′felt), *n.* **E·rik Ax·el** (ā′ʀik äk′səl), 1864–1931, Swedish poet: Nobel prize posthumously 1931.

Karl-Marx-Stadt (kärl′märks′shtät′), *n.* a city in S East Germany. 286,266 (est. 1959). Formerly, until 1953, **Chemnitz.**

Kar·lo·vy Va·ry (kär′lə vē vär′ē; *Czech.* käʀ′lô vi vä′ʀi), a city in W Czech Republic: mineral springs; Carlsbad Decrees (1819). 60,950. German, **Karlsbad.** Formerly, **Carlsbad.**

Karls·bad (käʀls′bät′; *Eng.* kärlz′bad), *n.* German name of **Carlsbad.**

Karls·ruh·e (kärlz′ro͞o′ə), *n.* a city in SW West Germany: capital of the former state of Baden. 249,500 (1963).

Karl·stad (kärl′städ), *n.* a city in S Sweden. 47,416 (1965).

kar·ma (kär′mə), *n.* **1.** *Hinduism, Buddhism.* action, seen as bringing upon oneself inevitable results, good or bad, either in this life or in a reincarnation: in Hinduism one of the means of reaching Brahman. Cf. **bhakti** (def. 1), **jnana. 2.** *Theosophy.* the cosmic principle according to which each person is rewarded or punished in one incarnation according to his deeds in the previous incarnation. **3.** fate; destiny. [< Skt: work, deed, fate (*kar-* do, make + *-ma* action of, result of)] —**kar′mic,** *adj.*

Kar·ma (kär′mə), *n.* a girl's given name. Also, **Carma.**

kar·ma·dha·ra·ya (kär′mä dä rä′yä), *n.* *Linguistics.* a compound of two words in which the first is an adjective and the second a substantive, as *blackbird, gentleman, grandson,* etc. [< Skt, equiv. to *karma* KARMA + *dhāraya* that keeps up or to]

kar·ma·mar·ga (kär′mə mär′gə), *n.* *Hinduism.* See under **marga.**

Kar′man trail′ (kär′män), *Mech.* a series of vortices arranged in two rows and alternately spaced, created in the wake of a long cylinder moving through a fluid. Also called **Kar′man street′ of vor′tices.** [named after Theodor von *Kármán* (1881–1963), Hungarian-born physicist and aeronautical engineer]

Kar·nak (kär′nak), *n.* a village in the E United Arab Republic, on the Nile: the northern part of the ruins of ancient Thebes.

Karnes′ Cit′y (kärnz), a town in S Texas. 2593 (1960).

ka·ro (kär′ō), *n., pl.* **-ros.** a shrub or small tree, *Pittosporum crassifolium,* of New Zealand, having shiny leaves with a white, felty underside, red flowers, and densely hairy fruit. [< Maori]

Kar·o·line (kar′ə lin′, -lin), *n.* a girl's given name. Also, **Caroline.**

ka·ross (kə ros′), *n.* a mantle of animal skins worn by tribesmen in southern Africa. [< SAfrD *karos*, perh. < Hottentot]

kar·pas (kär päs′), *n. Hebrew.* a piece of parsley, celery, or similar green vegetable that is dipped in salt water and eaten at the Seder meal on Passover.

Kar·rer (kär′ər), *n.* **Paul,** born 1889, Swiss chemist, born in Russia: Nobel prize 1937.

kar·ri-tree (kar′ē trē′), *n.* See **princess tree.** [?]

Kar·roo (kə ro͞o′), *n., pl.* **-roos** for 2. **1.** a vast plateau in the S Republic of South Africa, in Cape of Good Hope province. 100,000 sq. mi.; 3000–4000 ft. above sea level. **2.** (*l.c.*) one of the arid tablelands with red clay soil, in South Africa. [< SAfrD *karo* < Hottentot *garo* desert]

kar·ru·sel (kar′ə sel′, kar′ə sel′), *n. Horol.* a device for minimizing positional error, similar to the tourbillion but rotating once every 52½ minutes. [prob. alter. of CARROUSEL]

Kars (kärs), *n.* a city in NE Turkey. 14,236 (1965).

karst (kärst), *n. Geol.* an area of limestone formations characterized by sinks, ravines, and underground streams. [< G, special use of *Karst*, name of limestone plateau north of Trieste] —**karst′ic,** *adj.*

Kart·ti·ke·ya (kär′ti kā′yə), *n.* the Hindu god of bravery.

ka·ru·na (ku′ro͝o nä′), *n. Buddhism.* the universal compassion of a Boddhisattva. [< Skt *karuṇā*]

Kar·yn (kar′ən, kär′-), *n.* a girl's given name, form of **Carin.** Also, **Karen, Karin, Kar′ynne.**

karyo-, a learned borrowing from Greek used, with the meaning "nucleus of a cell," in the formation of compound words: *karyotin.* Also, **caryo-.** [< Gk, comb. form of *káryon* nut, kernel]

kar·y·og·a·my (kar′ē og′ə mē), *n. Biol.* the fusion of the nuclei of cells, as in fertilization. [KARYO- + -GAMY] —**kar·y·o·gam·ic** (kar′ē ə gam′ik), *adj.*

kar·y·o·ki·ne·sis (kar′ē ō ki nē′sis, -kī-), *n. Biol.* **1.** mitosis. **2.** the series of active changes which take place in the nucleus of a living cell in the process of division. [KARYO- + Gk *kínesis* motion (*kinē-*, verbid s. of *kinein* to move, + *-sis* -SIS)] —**kar·y·o·ki·net·ic** (kar′ē ō ki net′ik, -kī-), *adj.*

kar·y·o·lymph (kar′ē ə limf′), *n. Bot.* the transparent or translucent fluid in a nucleus. [KARYO- + LYMPH]

kar·y·ol·y·sis (kar′ē ol′i sis), *n. Biol.* the dissolution of a cell nucleus. [KARYO- + -LYSIS] —**kar·y·o·lit·ic** (kar′ē ə lit′ik), *adj.*

kar·y·om·i·tome (kar′ē om′i tōm′), *n. Biol.* the network or reticulum in the nucleus of a cell. [KARYO- + *mitome* < G *Mitom* network < Gk *mít(os)* thread + *-ōma* -OMA]

kar·y·o·plasm (kar′ē ə plaz′əm), *n. Biol.* the substance of the nucleus of a cell. [KARYO- + -PLASM] —**kar′y·o·plas′mic, kar·y·o·plas·mat·ic** (kar′ē ō plaz mat′ik), *adj.*

kar·y·o·some (kar′ē ə sōm′), *n. Biol.* **1.** any of several masses of chromatin in the reticulum of a cell nucleus. **2.** the nucleus of a cell. **3.** a chromosome. [KARYO- + -SOME³]

kar·y·o·tin (kar′ē ō′tin), *n. Biol.* nuclear material; chromatin. [KARYO- + (CHROMA)TIN]

kar·y·o·type (kar′ē ə tīp′), *n. Genetics.* the sum total of the morphological characteristics of the chromosomes in a cell. [KARYO- + TYPE] —**kar·y·o·typ·ic** (kar′ē ə-tip′ik), **kar′y·o·typ′i·cal,** *adj.*

kas (käs), *n.* (in Holland and in Dutch colonies) a large cabinet of the 17th and 18th centuries, having two doors and often a number of drawers at the bottom, and usually having an elaborately painted or carved decoration with a heavy cornice. [< D; see CASE²]

Kas., Kansas.

Kas·a·vu·bu (kas′ə vo͞o′bo͞o, kä′sä-), *n.* **Joseph,** born 1917?, African political leader: president of the Republic of the Congo since 1960.

Kas·bah (kaz′bə, -bä, käz′-), *n.* the older, native quarter of Algiers, in N Algeria. Also, **Casbah.**

Kas·bek (käz bek′), *n.* Kazbek.

Kä·se (kā′zə), *German.* cheese.

ka·sha (kä′shə), *n.* **1.** *Eastern European Cookery.* a cooked food prepared from hulled and crushed grain, esp. buckwheat; mush. **2.** hulled and crushed grain; groats, esp. of buckwheat. [< Russ]

Kash·a (kash′ə), *n. Trademark.* a soft fabric of wool and goat's hair, having a napped surface and a slight crosswise streak.

ka·sher (kä′shər), *adj., n., v.t.* kosher.

Kash·gar (käsh′gär′), *n.* a city in W Sinkiang, in extreme W China. 91,000 (est. 1957). Also called **Shufu.**

kash′gar tam′arisk (käsh′gär), a hairy shrub, *Tamarix hispida*, found in the region east of the Caspian Sea, having pink flowers in dense terminal clusters.

ka·shi·ra (kə shēr′ə; *Jap.* kä shē′rä), *n., pl.* **-ra.** the pommel of a Japanese sword, usually decorated to match the fuchi; kabuzuchi. [< Jap: lit., head, cap]

kash·mir (kazh′mēr, kash′-), *n.* cashmere.

Kash·mir (kash′mēr, kash mēr′), *n.* a state in SW Asia, adjacent to India, Pakistan, Sinkiang, and Tibet: sovereignty in dispute between India and Pakistan since 1947. 4,750,000 (est. 1959), of which 3,560,976 (1961) live in the part occupied by India; 82,258 sq. mi. *Cap.:* Srinagar. Also, **Cashmere.** Official name, **Jammu and Kashmir.**

Kash·mir·i (kash mēr′ē), *n., pl.* **-mir·is,** (*esp. collectively*) **-mir·i.** **1.** a native or inhabitant of Kashmir. **2.** the Indo-Iranian language of the Kashmiri.

Kash·mir·i·an (kash mēr′ē ən), *adj.* **1.** of, pertaining to, or characteristic of Kashmir or the Kashmiri. —*n.* **2.** a Kashmiri. [KASHMIR + -IAN]

Kash′mir rug′, an Oriental handmade rug, woven flat without pile, and having the patterns which entirely cover its surface embroidered with colored yarns.

kash·ruth (käsh ro͞ot′), *n. Hebrew.* **1.** the body of dietary laws prescribed for Jews: *an observer of* kashruth. **2.** fitness for use with respect to Jewish law: *the* kashruth *of a religious object.* Also, **kash·rut′.** [lit., fitness]

Kas·per (kas′pər), *n.* a boy's given name, form of **Caspar.**

Kas·sa (kosh′sho), *n.* Hungarian name of **Košice.**

Kas·sa·la (kä′sä lä′), *n.* a city in the E Sudan, near Eritrea. 35,621 (1956).

Kas·sa·pa (kä shup′ə), *n.* Kasyapa.

Kas·sel (käs′əl), *n.* a city in E West Germany. 211,800 (1963). Also, **Cassel.**

Kas·sem (käs sem′, kä′sem), *n.* **Ab·dul Ka·rim** (äb′do͝ol kä rēm′), 1914–63, Iraqi general and statesman: premier 1958–63.

Kas·site (kas′īt), *n.* a member of an ancient people related to the Elamites, who ruled Babylonia from c1650 to c1100 B.C. Also, **Cassite.**

Käst·ner (kast′nər; *for 1 also Ger.* kest′nər), *n.* **1.** **E·rich** (ā′rikh), born 1899, German writer. **2.** a walled plain in the fourth quadrant of the face of the moon: about 75 miles in diameter.

Kas·tro (*Gk.* käs′trô), *n.* Mytilene (def. 2).

Ka·strop-Rau·xel (*Ger.* käs′trôp rouk′səl), *n.* Castrop-Rauxel.

Kas·ya·pa (käsh yup′ə), *n.* an important disciple of the Buddha who called together a council of arhats after the death of the Buddha to compose the Pali Canon. Also, **Kassapa.**

kat (kät), *n.* an evergreen shrub, *Catha edulis*, of Arabia and Africa, the leaves of which are used as a narcotic when chewed or made into a beverage. Also, **khat.** [< Ar *qāt*]

kata-, var. of **cata-.** Also, **kat-, kath-.**

ka·tab·a·sis (kə tab′ə sis), *n., pl.* **-ses** (-sēz′). **1.** a march from the interior of a country to the coast, as that of the ten thousand Greeks after their defeat and the death of Cyrus the Younger at Cunaxa. **2.** a retreat, esp. a military retreat. Cf. **anabasis.** [< Gk *katábasis* a going down, descent, equiv. to *kataba-* (s. of *katabaínein* to go down) + *-sis* -SIS. See KATA-, BASIS]

kat·a·bat·ic (kat′ə bat′ik), *adj. Meteorol.* (of a wind or air current) moving downward or down a slope. Cf. **anabatic** (def. 1). [< Gk *katabatik(ós)* pertaining to going down, equiv. to *kata-* KATA- + *ba-* (s. of *baínein* to go) + *-tikos* -TIC]

ka·tab·o·lism (kə tab′ə liz′əm), *n.* catabolism. —**kat·a·bol·ic** (kat′ə bol′ik), *adj.* —**kat′a·bol′i·cal·ly,** *adv.*

Ka·tah·din (kə tä′din), *n.* **Mount,** the highest peak in Maine, in the central part. 5273 ft.

ka·ta·ka·na (kä′tə kä′nə; *Jap.* kä′tä kä′nä), *n.* the more angular, less commonly used of the two Japanese syllabaries. Cf. **hiragana.** [< Jap, equiv. to *kata* side, form, formal + *kana* syllabary; see HIRAGANA]

kat·a·lase (kat′əlās′), *n. Biochem.* **1.** catalase. **2.** peroxidase.

ka·tal·y·sis (kə tal′i sis), *n., pl.* **-ses** (-sēz′). *Chem.* catalysis.

kat·a·lyst (kat′əlist), *n. Chem.* catalyst.

kat·a·lyze (kat′əlīz′), *v.t.,* **-lyzed, -lyz·ing.** *Chem.* catalyze. —**kat′a·lyz′er,** *n.*

kat·a·mor·phism (kat′ə môr′fiz əm), *n. Geol.* metamorphism, occurring at or near the earth's surface, which changes complex minerals to simple minerals. Cf. **anamorphism.** [KATA- + -MORPHISM] —**kat′a·mor′phic,** *adj.*

ka·ta·na (kə tä′nə; *Jap.* kä tä′nä), *n., pl.* **-na.** the long fighting sword of a Japanese samurai, having a gently curved blade with a single edge and a long handle continuing the curve: occasionally equipped with a kogai and kozuka. Cf. **wakizashi.** [< Jap: sword]

Ka·tan·ga (kə täng′gə, -tang′-), *n.* a province in the SE Republic of the Congo: important mining area. 1,687,683 (est. 1959); 191,878 sq. mi. *Cap.:* Elisabethville.

Kat·ang·ese (kat′äng gēz′, -gēs′, -ang-), *n., pl.* **-ese,** *adj.* —*n.* **1.** a native or inhabitant of Katanga. —*adj.* **2.** of or pertaining to Katanga or its people. Also, **Ka·tan·gan** (kə täng′gən, -tang′-). [KATANG(A) + -ESE]

kat·a·pla·sia (kat′ə plā′zhə, -zhē ə, -zē ə), *n.* cataplasia.

ka·tár (kə tär′), *n.* an Indian dagger having a broad blade with a hilt formed by two parallel longitudinal bars, between which are one or two crosspieces as a grip. [< Hindi]

Ka·tar (kot′or), *n.* Qatar.

kat·a·to·ni·a (kat′ə tō′nē ə, -tōn′yə), *n. Psychiatry.* catatonia. —**kat·a·ton·ic** (kat′ə ton′ik), *adj.*

Ka·ta·yev (kä tä′yef), *n.* **Va·len·tin Pe·tro·vich** (vä′len tēn pe trô′vich), born 1897, Russian writer.

ka·tci·na (kə chē′nə), *n.* kachina. Also, **ka·tchi′na.**

Kate (kāt), *n.* a girl's given name, form of **Katherine** or **Catherine.**

Kat·e·ri (kat′ə rē), *n.* a girl's given name, form of **Katherine.**

Ka·tha·re·vu·sa (kä′thə rev′ə sä′, -sə, kath′ə-; *Gk.* kä′thä re′vo͞o sä), *n.* the puristic Modern Greek literary language (opposed to *demotic*). Also called **Hellenic.**

ka·thar·sis (kə thär′sis), *n.* catharsis. —**ka·thar·tic** (kə thär′tik), *adj.*

Kath·er·ine (kath′ər in, kath′rin), *n.* a girl's given name. Also, **Catherine, Catheryn, Kath′a·rine, Kathryn, Kath·rynne** (kath′rin).

Ka·thi·a·war (kä′tē ä wär′), *n.* a peninsula on the W coast of India.

Kath·ie (kath′ē), *n.* a girl's given name, form of **Katherine** and **Kathleen.** Also, **Cathy, Cathie, Kathy.**

ka·this·ma (kä′thēz mä, kə thiz′mə), *n., pl.* **ka·this·ma·ta** (kä thēz′mä tä, kə thiz′mə tə). one of the 20 divisions of the Psalter in the Greek rite. Also, **cathisma.** [< MGk, Gk: seat, equiv. to *kathíz(ein)* (to) sit down (*kata-* KATA- + *hizein* to sit down) + *-ma* n. suffix]

Kath·lee (kath′lē, kath lē′), *n.* a girl's given name.

Kath·leen (kath′lēn, kath lēn′), *n.* a girl's given name, form of **Katherine.** Also, **Kath′lene, Kath·lyn, Kathlynne** (kath′lin).

kath·ode (kath′ōd), *n.* cathode. —**ka·thod·ic** (kə-thod′ik), **kath·o·dal** (kath′ə dəl), *adj.*

ka·thol·i·kos (kə thol′ə kəs, -kos′), *n., pl.* **-kos·es, -koi** (-koi′). catholicos.

Kath·y (kath′ē), *n.* a girl's given name, form of **Katherine** and **Kathleen.** Also, **Cathy, Cathie, Kathie.**

kat·i·on (kat′ī′ən), *n. Physical Chem.* cation.

Kat·mai (kat′mī), *n.* **1.** **Mount,** an active volcano in SW Alaska. 7500 ft. **2.** a national monument including Mt. Katmai and the Valley of Ten Thousand Smokes. 4215 sq. mi.

Kat·man·du (kät′män do͞o′), *n.* a city in and the capital of Nepal, in the E part. 122,507 (est. 1961). Also, **Kath′man·du′.**

Ka·to·wi·ce (kä′tô vē′tse), *n.* a city in S Poland. 281,000 (est. 1963). German, **Kat·to·witz** (kä′tō vits).

Ka·tri·na (kə trē′nə), *n.* a girl's given name, form of **Katherine.** Also, **Caterina, Ka·try′na.**

Kat·rine (ka′trin), *n.* **Loch,** a lake in central Scotland. 8 mi. long.

kat′su·ra tree′ (kät′sər ə), a Japanese tree, *Cercidiphyllum japonicum*, often cultivated as an ornamental in the U.S. [*katsura* < Jap]

Kat·te·gat (kat′ə gat′), *n.* a strait between Jutland and Sweden. 40–70 mi. wide. Also, **Cattegat.**

ka·ty·did (kā′tē did), *n.* any of several large, usually green, American long-horned grasshoppers, the males of which produce a characteristic song. [imit.]

katz·en·jam·mer (kat′sən jam′ər), *n.* **1.** the discomfort and illness experienced as the aftereffects of excessive drinking; hangover: *He tried to cure his katzenjammer with aspirin.* **2.** uneasiness; anguish; distress: *He showed the symptoms of that psychological katzenjammer newcomers know so well.* **3.** uproar; clamor: *His speech produced a public katzenjammer which forced him to retract certain statements.* [< G, equiv. to *Katzen* (pl. of *Katze* CAT¹) + *Jammer* discomfort, OHG *jāmar* (n. and adj.)]

Katydid, *Microcentrum rhombifolium* (Length 2 in.)

Ka·u·a·i (kä′o͞o ä′ē), *n.* an island in NW Hawaii. 28,176 (1960); 511 sq. mi.

kauch (käkh), *n. Scot.* kiaugh.

Kauf·man (kôf′mən), *n.* **1.** **George S(imon),** 1889–1961, U.S. dramatist and journalist. **2.** a town in NE Texas. 3087 (1960).

Kau·nas (kou′näs), *n.* a city in S central Lithuania, in the W Soviet Union in Europe. 214,000 (1959). Russian, **Kovno.**

Kau·ra·vas (kou′rə väz′), *n.* (*construed as pl.*) (in the Mahabharata) the cousins and enemies of the Pandavas. Also, **Kurus.**

kau·ri (kou′rē), *n., pl.* **-ris.** **1.** Also, **kau′ri pine′.** a tall, coniferous tree, *Agathis australis*, of New Zealand, yielding a valuable timber and a resin. **2.** the wood of this tree. **3.** any of various other trees of the genus *Agathis.* **4.** See **kauri resin.** [< Maori]

kau′ri res′in, a hard resin obtained from the bark of the kauri or found, sometimes in masses of as much as 100 pounds, in the soil where the tree has grown: used chiefly in making varnish. Also, **kauri, kau′ri gum′, kau′ri co′pal.**

kau·ry (kou′rē), *n., pl.* **-ries.** kauri.

Kaut·sky (kout′skē), *n.* **Karl Johann** (kärl′ yō′-hän), 1854–1938, German socialist writer and editor.

ka·va (kä′və), *n.* **1.** a Polynesian, piperaceous shrub, *Piper methysticum*, the roots of which are used in making a beverage. **2.** a beverage, producing euphoria, made from the roots of the kava. [< Polynesian (first recorded from Tonga Islands): lit., bitter] —**Ka·va·ic** (kə vā′ik), *adj.*

Ka·val·la (kə val′ə; *Gk.* kä vä′lä), *n.* a seaport in E Greece. 44,517 (1961).

Ka·va·phis (kä vä′fēs), *n.* **Constantine.** See **Cavafy, Constantine.**

kav·er (kav′ər), *n.* caver.

Ka·ver·i (kô′və rē), *n.* Cauvery.

Ka·ve·rin (kä vā′rin), *n.* **Ve·nia·min** (ve nyä mēn′), (*Veniamin Aleksandrovich Zilberg*), born 1902, Russian novelist.

Ka·vir′ Des′ert (kä vēr′), Dasht-i-Kavir.

Ka·wa·gu·chi (kä′wä go͞o′chē), *n.* a city on SE Honshu, in central Japan, N of Tokyo. 222,191 (1964).

Ka·wa·sa·ki (kä′wä sä′kē), *n.* a seaport on SE Honshu, in central Japan, SW of Tokyo. 789,303 (1964).

Kay (kā), *n.* **1.** **Sir,** *Arthurian Romance.* the rude, boastful foster brother and seneschal of Arthur. **2.** a boy's or girl's given name.

kay·ak (kī′ak), *n.* **1.** an Eskimo hunting craft with a skin cover on a light framework, made watertight by flexible closure around the waist of the occupant. **2.** a small boat resembling this, made commercially, for use in sports, of a variety of materials. Also, **kaiak, kyak, kyack.** [< Eskimo]

Kayes (kāz), *n.* a city in W Mali. 29,500 (1957).

Ka·yi·ban·da (kä′yi bän′də), *n.* **Gré·goire** (grā gwär′; *Fr.* grā gwar′), born 1924, president of the Republic of Rwanda since 1962.

Kayne (kān), *n.* a boy's given name. Also, **Kain, Kane.**

kay·o (kā′ō′), *n., pl.* **kay·os,** *v.,* **kay·oed, kay·o·ing.** *Slang.* —*n.* **1.** a knockout in boxing. —*v.t.* **2.** to knock unconscious in a boxing match. [*kay* (letter *k*) + *o* (letter *o*), var. of *k.o.*, abbr. of *knockout*]

Kay·se·ri (kī′se rē′), *n.* a city in central Turkey. 126,913 (1965). Ancient, **Caesarea.**

Kays·ville (kāz′vil), *n.* a town in N Utah. 3608 (1960).

ka·za·chok (kə zä chôk′), *n., pl.* **-zach·ki** (-zäch kē′). a lively, Slavic folk dance for solo male dancer, marked esp. by the prisiadka. Also called **kazatsky, kazatske.** [< Russ]

Ka·zakh (kə zäk′), *n.* **1.** a member of a nomadic Muslim people living mainly in Kazakhstan. **2.** the Turkic language of the Kazakh people. Also, **Ka·zak′.**

Ka·zakh·stan (kä′zäk stän′; *Russ.* kə zukh stän′), *n.* a republic in central Asia, NE of the Caspian Sea and W of China. 14,685,000; 1,064,092 sq. mi. *Cap.:* Alma-Ata. Formerly, **Kazakh′ So′viet So′cialist Repub′lic.**

Ka·zan (kə zan′, -zän′; *for 2 also Russ.* ku zän′), *n.* **1. E·li·a** (i lī′ə, ēl′yə), born 1909, U.S. film and stage director and novelist, born in Turkey. **2.** a city in and capital of the Tatar Autonomous Republic in the SE Russian Federation in Europe, near the Volga River. 993,000.

Ka·zant·za·kis (kaz′ən zak′is, kä′zən zä′kis; *Gk.* kä′zändzä′kēs), *n.* **Ni·kos** (nē′kôs), 1883–1957, Greek poet and novelist.

ka·zat·sky (kə zät′skē), *n., pl.* **-skies.** kazachok. Also, **ka·zat′ske.**

Kaz·bek (käz bek′), *n.* **Mount,** an extinct volcano in the S Soviet Union in Europe, in the central Caucasus Mountains. 16,541 ft. Also, **Kasbek.**

ka·zoo (kə zo͞o′), *n., pl.* **-zoos.** a musical toy consisting of a tube that is open at both ends and has a hole in the side covered with parchment or membrane, against which the performer sings or hums. Also called **mirliton.**

KB, *Chess.* king's bishop.

kb, kilobar; kilobars.

K.B., **1.** King's Bench. **2.** Knight Bachelor.

K.B.E., Knight Commander of the British Empire.

KBP, *Chess.* king's bishop's pawn.

kc, **1.** kilocycle; kilocycles. **2.** kilocycles per second. **3.** kilocurie; kilocuries.

K.C., **1.** King's Counsel. **2.** Knight Commander. **3.** Knights of Columbus.

kcal, kilocalorie; kilocalories.

K.C.B., Knight Commander of the Bath.

kCi, kilocurie; kilocuries.

K.C.M.G., Knight Commander of the Order of St. Michael and St. George.

Kčs., koruna.

kc/s, kilocycles per second. Also, **kc/sec**

K.C.S.I., Knight Commander of the Order of the Star of India.

K.C.V.O., Knight Commander of the (Royal) Victorian Order.

KD, *Com.* knocked-down.

KD., dinar (def. 6).

ke·a (kā′ə, kē′ə), *n.* a large, greenish New Zealand parrot, *Nestor notabilis.* [< Maori]

Ke·a (ke′ä), *n.* Keos.

Kean (kēn), *n.* **Edmund,** 1787–1833, English actor, esp. known for performance of Shakespearean roles.

Keans·burg (kēnz′bûrg), *n.* a town in E New Jersey. 6854 (1960).

keap (kāp), *v.t., n. Scot. and North Eng.* kep.

Kear·ney (kär′nē), *n.* a city in S Nebraska, on the Platte. 14,210 (1960).

Kearns (kûrnz), *n.* a town in N Utah, near Salt Lake City. 17,172 (1960).

Kear·ny (kär′nē), *n.* **1. Philip,** 1814–62, U.S. general. **2.** a city in NE New Jersey, near Newark. 37,472 (1960).

keat (kēt), *n.* keet.

Keats (kēts), *n.* **John,** 1795–1821, English poet. —**Keats′i·an,** *adj.*

Keb (keb), *n. Egyptian Religion.* Geb.

ke·bab (kā′bob, kə bob′), *n.* kabob.

ke·bar (kā′bər), *n. Scot.* caber.

keb·buck (keb′ək), *n. Brit. Dial.* an entire cheese. [late ME *cabok* (Scot dial.) < ?; cf. ScotGael *ceapag* (not in Ir), perh. < Scot]

keb·lah (keb′lə), *n.* kiblah.

Ke·ble (kē′bəl), *n.* **John,** 1792–1866, English clergyman and poet.

Kech·ua (kech′wä, -wə), *n., pl.* **-uas,** (*esp. collectively*) **-ua.** Quechua.

Kech·uan (kech′wən), *adj., n., pl.* **-uans,** (*esp. collectively*) **-uan.** —*adj.* **1.** Quechuan. —*n.* **2.** Quechua.

keck (kek), *v.i.* **1.** to retch; be nauseated. **2.** to feel or show disgust or strong dislike. [? akin to CHOKE]

keck·ling (kek′ling), *n. Naut.* old rope wound around a cable as a protection against chafing. [*keckle* < ? + -ING[1]]

keck·sy (kek′sē), *n., pl.* **-sies.** *Brit. Dial.* kex. [back formation from *keckses, kexes,* pl. of KEX]

Kecs·ke·mét (kech′ke māt′), *n.* a city in central Hungary. 66,819 (1960).

ked (ked), *n.* See **sheep tick.** [earlier *cade* < ?]

Ke·dah (kā′dä), *n.* a state in Malaysia, on the SW Malay Peninsula. 783,993 (est. 1961); 3660 sq. mi. *Cap.:* Alor Star.

Ke·dar (kē′dər), *n.* **1.** the second son of Ishmael. Gen. 25:13. **2.** an ancient Arabian tribe descended from Kedar.

Ke·dar·ite (kē′də rīt′), *n.* **1.** a member of the tribe of Kedar. —*adj.* **2.** of or pertaining to the tribe of Kedar or the Kedarites. [KEDAR + -ITE[1]]

ked·dah (ked′ə), *n.* kheda.

kedge (kej), *v.,* **kedged, kedg·ing,** *n. Naut.* —*v.t.* **1.** to warp or pull (a vessel) along by hauling on the cable of an anchor carried out from the vessel and dropped. —*v.i.* **2.** (of a vessel) to move by being kedged. —*n.* **3.** Also called **kedge′ an′chor.** a small anchor used in kedging. [akin to ME *caggen* to fasten]

ked·ger·ee (kej′ə rē′), *n.* **1.** *East Indian Cookery.* a cooked dish consisting of rice, lentils, and spices. **2.** a cooked dish of rice, fish, hard-boiled eggs, butter, cream, and seasonings. [< Hindi *khicṛī, khicarī*]

Ke·dron (kē′drən), *n.* a ravine in Jordan, E of Jerusalem. Also, **Kidron.**

Ke·du·shah (kə do͞o shä′, -do͞o′shō), *n., pl.* **-du·shoth** (-do͞o shōt′, -do͞o′shōs). *Judaism.* a liturgical prayer of varying form that is recited after the third blessing of the *Amidah* during the repetition of this prayer by the cantor. [< Heb *qedhushshāh* holiness]

ke·ef (kē ef′), *n.* kef (def. 2).

Kee′go Har′bor (kē′gō), a town in SE Michigan. 2761 (1960).

keek (kēk), *v.i. Scot. and North Eng.* to peep; look furtively. [ME *kike(n),* c. or < MD, MLG *kiken*]

keel[1] (kēl), *n.* **1.** *Naut.* **a.** a central fore-and-aft structural member in the bottom of a hull, extending from the stem to the sternpost and having the floors or frames attached to it, usually at right angles: sometimes projecting from the bottom of the hull to provide stability. **b.** any of various barges or bargelike sailing vessels, esp. those on the Humber in England. **2.** *Poetic.* a ship or other vessel. **3.** a part corresponding to a ship's keel in some other structure, as in a dirigible balloon. **4.** (*cap.*) *Astron.* the constellation Carina. **5.** *Bot., Zool.* a longitudinal ridge, as on a leaf or bone; a carina. **6.** Also called **brace molding.** *Archit.* a projecting molding the profile of which consists of two ogees symmetrically disposed about an arris or fillet. **7. on an even keel,** in a state of balance; steady; steadily: *The affairs of state are seldom on an even keel for long.* —*v.t., v.i.* **8.** to turn or upset so as to bring the wrong side or part uppermost. **9. keel over,** to fall or faint without warning: *Several cadets keeled over from the heat during the parade.* [ME *kele* < Scand; cf. Icel *kjölr*] —**keel′less,** *adj.*

keel[2] (kēl), *n. Vet. Pathol.* a fatal disease of domestic ducks. [n. use of KEEL[1] (v.)]

keel[3] (kēl), *n. Brit. Dial.* **1.** keelboat. **2.** a keelboat load of coal; the amount of coal carried by one keelboat. **3.** a measure of coal equivalent to 21 tons and 4 hundredweight. [late ME *kele* < MD *kiel;* c. OE *cēol,* G *Kiel* ship]

keel[4] (kēl), *v.t. Archaic.* to cool, esp. by stirring. [ME *kele(n),* OE *celan;* akin to COOL]

keel[5] (kēl), *n.* a red ocher stain used for marking sheep, lumber, etc.; ruddle. [late ME *keyle* (north dial.); cf. Gael *cil* (? < E)]

keel·age (kē′lij), *n.* a toll on a merchant ship entering a port. [KEEL[1] + -AGE]

keel′ bat′ten, *Shipbuilding.* See **hog piece.**

keel·boat (kēl′bōt′), *n. U.S.* a roughly built, shallow freight boat, formerly used on the Mississippi and its tributaries, having a keel to permit sailing into the wind. [KEEL[3] + BOAT]

keel·boat·man (kēl′bōt′mən), *n., pl.* **-men.** a member of the crew of a keelboat. [KEELBOAT + MAN]

Kee·ler (kē′lər), *n.* **William H.** ("*Wee Willy*"), 1872–1923, U.S. baseball player.

Kee·ley (kē′lē), *n.* **Leslie En·raught** (en′rôt), 1834–1900, U.S. physician.

keel·haul (kēl′hôl′), *v.t.* **1.** *Naut.* to haul (an offender) under the bottom of a vessel and up on the other side as a punishment. **2.** to rebuke severely. Also, **keel·hale** (kēl′hāl). Also called **keel·drag** (kēl′drag′), **keel·rake** (kēl′rāk′). [< D *kielhal(en).* See KEEL[1], HAUL]

Kee·lie (kē′lē), *n.* a girl's given name. Also, **Kee′ley, Kee′ly.**

Kee′ling Is′lands (kē′ling). See **Cocos Islands.**

keel·less (kēl′lis), *adj.* having no keel, as a vessel.

keel′ rail′, *Naut.* See **bilge rail.**

keel·son (kel′sən, kēl′-), *n. Naut.* any of various fore-and-aft structural members lying above or parallel to the keel in the bottom of a hull. Also, **kelson.** [< LG *kielswin,* lit., keel swine < Scand; cf. Sw *kjölsvin,* appar. dissimilated var. of *kjölsvill.* See KEEL[1], SILL]

Kee·lung (kē′lo͞ong′), *n.* a seaport on the N coast of Taiwan. 194,006 (1957). Also, **Chilung.** Japanese, **Kiirun.**

keel′ ves′sel, any of various types of sailing vessels in which a fixed, projecting keel gives lateral resistance.

keen[1] (kēn), *adj.* **1.** finely sharpened; so shaped as to cut or pierce substances readily: *a keen edge.* **2.** sharp, piercing, or biting: *a keen wind; keen satire.* **3.** characterized by strength and distinctness of perception; extremely sensitive or responsive: *keen eyes; keen ears.* **4.** having or showing great mental penetration or acumen: *keen reasoning.* **5.** animated by or showing strong feeling or desire: *keen competition.* **6.** intense, as feeling, desire, etc.: *keen ambition; keen jealousy.* **7.** ardent, eager; interested (often fol. by *about, for,* etc., or an infinitive): *She is really keen about the trip.* **8.** *Slang.* great; wonderful; marvelous. [ME *kene,* OE *cēne;* c. G *kühn* bold, OIcel *koenn* wise, skilful; akin to CAN[1], KNOW[1]] —**keen′ly,** *adv.* —**keen′ness,** *n.*

—**Syn. 1, 4.** See **sharp. 2.** cutting, bitter, poignant, caustic, acrimonious. **3.** piercing, penetrating, acute, sensitive. **4.** discerning, acute, astute, sagacious, quick, shrewd, clever. **7.** earnest, fervid. —**Ant. 1, 3, 4.** dull.

keen[2] (kēn), *n.* **1.** a wailing lament for the dead. —*v.i.* **2.** to wail in lamentation for the dead. [< Ir *caoine* (n.), *caoin-* (v.; s. of *caoinim*) lament] —**keen′er,** *n.*

Keen (kēn), *n.* a boy's given name.

Kee·nan (kē′nən), *n.* a boy's given name.

Keene (kēn), *n.* a city in SW New Hampshire. 17,562 (1960).

Keene's′ cement′ (kēnz), *Trademark.* a hard, white finish plaster.

keen·ing (kē′ning), *n.* **1.** act of a person who keens. **2.** a wail or lamentation; keen. [KEEN[2] + -ING[1]]

keep (kēp), *v.,* **kept, keep·ing,** *n.* —*v.t.* **1.** to maintain (some action), esp. in accordance with specific requirements, a promise, etc.: *to keep watch; to keep step; to keep silence.* **2.** to cause to continue in a given place, position, state, course, or action: *to keep a light burning; to keep a child happy.* **3.** to maintain in condition or order, as by care and labor: *He keeps his car in good condition.* **4.** to maintain in usable condition; preserve: *If you want to keep meat for a long time, freeze it.* **5.** to hold in custody or under guard, as a prisoner; prevent from coming or going: *They kept him in jail.* **6.** to have regularly in stock and for sale: *to keep a large supply of machine parts.* **7.** to maintain in one's service or for one's use or enjoyment: *to keep a car and chauffeur.* **8.** to associate with: *She keeps very rough company.* **9.** to have the care, charge, or custody of: *She keeps my dog when I travel.* **10.** to withhold from the knowledge of others: *to keep a secret.* **11.** to withhold from use; reserve: *I'll keep this toy until you learn to behave. Keep the good wine for company.* **12.** to hold back or restrain: *They kept the child from talking.* **13.** to maintain by writing: *to keep a diary.* **14.** to record (business transactions, daily occurrences, etc.) regularly: *to keep records.* **15.** to observe; pay obedient regard to (a law, rule, promise, etc.). **16.** to conform to; follow; fulfill: *to keep one's word.* **17.** to observe (a season, festival, etc.) with formalities or rites: *to keep Christmas.* **18.** to maintain or carry on, as an establishment, business, etc.; to manage. **19.** to guard; protect: *He kept her from harm.* **20.** to maintain or support: *He cannot keep a wife on his income.* **21.** to support in return for sexual favors: *to keep a mistress.* **22.** to take care of; tend: *to keep sheep.* **23.** to raise (livestock): *These farmers keep goats and cattle.* **24.** to remain in (a place, spot, etc.): *Please keep your seats.* **25.** to maintain one's position in or on: *He kept the job.* **26.** to continue to follow (a path, track, course, etc.). **27.** to continue to hold or have. **28.** to save, hold, or retain in possession. **29.** to maintain in active existence as an assembly, court, fair, etc.

—*v.i.* **30.** to continue in an action, course, position, state, etc.: *to keep in sight; to keep going.* **31.** to remain, or continue to be, as specified: *to keep cool.* **32.** to remain or stay in a place: *to keep indoors.* **33.** to continue unimpaired or without spoiling: *The milk will keep on ice.* **34.** to admit of being reserved for a future occasion. **35.** to keep oneself or itself (fol. by *away, back, off, out,* etc.): *Keep off the grass.* **36.** to restrain oneself: *try to keep from smiling.* **37. keep at,** to persist in; be steadfast: *You'll never master your French unless you keep at it.* **38. keep back, a.** to hold in check; restrain: *The dikes kept back the floodwaters.* **b.** to stay away from: *The crowds would not keep back from the barrier.* **c.** to refuse to reveal: *The prisoner was keeping back vital information.* **39. keep in with,** *Informal.* to stay in someone's favor; be on good terms with: *She is a social climber who makes certain to keep in with all the right people.* **40. keep on,** to continue; persist: *If you keep on singing they'll ask you to leave.* **41. keep tab** or **tabs on.** See **tab**[1] (def. 9). **42. keep time.** See **time** (def. 41). **43. keep to, a.** to adhere to; conform to: *She keeps to the rules. Don't vacillate! Keep to your argument.* **b.** to confine oneself to: *to keep to one's bed.* **44. keep to oneself, a.** to remain aloof from the society of others. **b.** to hold (something) as secret or confidential: *I'll tell you only if you promise to keep it to yourself.* **45. keep track of.** See **track** (def. 16). **46. keep up, a.** to maintain an equal rate of speed, activity, or progress with another or others. **b.** to persevere; continue. **c.** to maintain the good condition of; keep in repair. **d.** Also, **keep up on** or **with.** to stay informed: *to keep up on current events.*

—*n.* **47.** subsistence; board and lodging: *to work for one's keep.* **48.** the innermost and strongest structure or central tower of a medieval castle. **49. keeps,** (*construed as sing.*) a game of marbles in which the players keep the marbles they have won. **50. for keeps,** *Informal.* **a.** under the stipulation that one keeps one's winnings. **b.** with serious intent or purpose. **c.** finally; permanently: *They decided to settle the controversy for keeps.* [ME *kepe(n),* OE *cēpan* to observe, heed, watch, await, take; perh. akin to OE *gecōp* proper, fitting, *capian* to look, OIcel *kōpa* to stare] —**keep′a·ble,** *adj.*

—**Syn. 2.** KEEP, RESERVE, RETAIN, WITHHOLD refer to having and holding in possession. KEEP (a common word) and RETAIN (a more formal one) agree in meaning to continue to have or hold, as opposed to losing, parting with, or giving up: *to keep a book for a week.* To RESERVE is to keep for some future use, occasion, or recipient, or to hold back for a time: *to reserve judgment.* To WITHHOLD is generally to hold back altogether: *to withhold help.* **3.** preserve. **5.** detain, hold, confine. **48.** donjon, dungeon, stronghold. —**Ant. 3.** lose. **5.** release.

keep·er (kē′pər), *n.* **1.** a person who guards or watches, as at a prison, gate, etc. **2.** a person who assumes responsibility for another's behavior: *He refused to be his brother's keeper.* **3.** a person who owns or operates a business, esp. a small retail establishment: *a shop keeper.* **4.** a person who is responsible for the maintenance of something: *the keeper at a zoo.* **5.** a person charged with responsibility for the preservation and conservation of something valuable, as a curator, game warden, etc. **6.** a person who conforms to or abides by a requirement: *a keeper of his word.* **7.** something that serves to hold in place, retain, etc., as on a door lock. **8.** something that lasts well, as a fruit. **9.** See **guard ring. 10.** *Football.* a play in which the quarterback retains the ball and runs with it, usually after faking a hand-off or pass. **11.** strike (def. 74). **12.** an iron or steel bar placed across the poles of a permanent horseshoe magnet for preserving the strength of the magnet during storage. **13.** a fish that is of sufficient size to be caught and retained without violating the law. [ME *keper.* See KEEP, -ER[1]] —**keep′er·less,** *adj.* —**keep′er·ship′,** *n.*

—**Syn. 1.** guard, warden, jailer. **2.** custodian, guardian.

keep′er hook′, *Theat.* an S-shaped hook for securing doors, windows, etc., or for fastening a batten to a flat.

keep·ing (kē′ping), *n.* **1.** logical conformity in things or elements associated together: *His deeds are in keeping with his character but out of keeping with his words.* **2.** act of one who or that which keeps; observance, custody, or care. **3.** maintenance or keep. **4.** holding, reserving, or retaining. [ME *keping.* See KEEP, -ING[1]]

—**Syn. 1.** agreement, congruity, harmony. **2.** protection, care, charge, guardianship. See **custody.**

keep′ing room′, *Obs.* hall (def. 11).

keep·sake (kēp′sāk′), *n.* anything kept, or given to be kept, as a token of friendship or affection; remembrance. [KEEP (v.) + SAKE[1]]

kees·hond (kās′hond′), *n., pl.* **-hon·den** (-hon′dən). one of a Dutch breed of small dogs having thick, silver-gray hair tipped with black and a tail carried over the back. [< D, prob. special use of *Kees* (shortening of *Cornelius,* proper name) + *hond* dog; see HOUND[1]]

Keeshond (18 in. high at shoulder)

keet (kēt), *n.* the young of the guinea fowl. Also, **keat.** [imit.]

Kee·wa·tin (kē wä′tin), *n.* a district in the Northwest Territories, in N. Canada. 228,160 sq. mi.

kef (kāf), *n.* (in the Middle East) **1.** a state of drowsy contentment, esp. from the use of a narcotic. **2.** Also, **keef.** a substance, esp. a smoking preparation of hemp leaves, used to produce this state. Also, **kaif, kief, kif.** [< Ar, var. of *kaif* well-being, pleasure]

Ke·fau·ver (kē′fô vər), *n.* **Es·tes** (es′tis), 1903–63, U.S. political leader: U.S. senator 1949–63.

kef·fi·yeh (kə fē′ə), *n.* kaffiyeh.

keg (keg), *n.* **1.** a small cask or barrel, usually holding from 5 to 10 gallons. **2.** a unit of weight, equal to 100 pounds, used for nails. [late ME *cag* < Scand; cf. Icel *kaggi*]

keg·ler (keg′lər), *n. Slang.* a participant in a bowling game, as candlepins or tenpins. Also, **keg·el·er** (keg′ə lər, keg′lər). [< G, equiv. to *Kegel* (nine)pin + *-er* -ER¹]

ke·hil·lah (kə hil′ə; *Heb.* kə hē lä′), *n., pl.* **-hil·loth** (-hil′ōt; *Heb.* -hē lôt′). the organization of the Jewish population of a community that deals with charities and other communal affairs. [< Heb *qəhillāh* community]

kei·ap·ple (kī′ap′əl), *n.* a thorny shrub or small tree, *Dovyalis caffra,* of South Africa, having round, yellow, juicy-pulped, cranberry-flavored fruit that is edible only when cooked. [after Great *Kei,* river in Cape Province, South Africa]

Kei·fer (kī′fər), *n.* **Joseph Warren,** 1836–1932, U.S. lawyer and politician: Speaker of the House 1881–83.

Kei·jo (kā′jō′; *Eng.* kā jō′), *n.* Japanese name of **Seoul.**

keir (kēr), *n.* kier.

Kei·ta (kā′tä), *n.* **Mo·di·bo** (mô dē′bô), 1915–77, African statesman: president of the Republic of Mali 1960–68.

Kei·tel (kīt′əl), *n.* **Wil·helm** (vil′helm), 1882–1946, German marshal: chief of the Nazi supreme command 1938–45.

Keith (kēth), *n.* **1. Sir Arthur,** 1866–1955, Scottish anthropologist. **2.** a boy's given name.

keit·lo·a (kīt′lō ə, kāt′-), *n.* a variety of the black rhinoceros having the posterior horn equal to or longer than the anterior horn. [< Bantu *khetlwa*]

Kei·zer (kī′zər), *n.* a town in NW Oregon. 5288 (1960).

Kek·ko·nen (kek′ō nen′), *n.* **Ur·ho Ka·le·va** (o͝or′hô kä′le vä′). born 1900, Finnish statesman: president since 1956.

Ke′ku·lé's for′mula (kā′kə lāz′), *Chem.* the structural formula of benzene represented as a hexagonal ring with alternate single and double bonds between the carbon atoms. Cf. **benzene ring.** See diag. under **benzene ring.** [named after Friedrich August KEKULÉ VON STRADONITZ]

Ke·ku·lé von Stra·do·nitz (kā′kə lā′ fən shträ′dō-nits), **Frie·drich Au·gust** (frē′drikh ou′go͝ost), 1829–96, German chemist.

Ke·lan·tan (kə län tän′), *n.* a state in Malaysia, on SE Malay Peninsula. 570,998 (est. 1961); 5750 sq. mi. *Cap.:* Kota Bahru.

Kel·cey (kel′sē), *n.* a boy's given name. Also, **Kel′sey.**

kel·e·be (kel′ə bē), *n. Gk. and Rom. Antiq.* a mixing bowl, characterized by a wide neck and flanged lip from which extend two vertical handles to the shoulder of an oval body, used to mix wine and water. Also called **column krater.** Cf. **krater.** [< Gk]

kel·ek (kel′ek), *n.* a raft or float of Iraq and Armenia, supported on inflated animal skins. [< Turk]

kel·ep (kel′ep, kə lep′), *n.* a stinging ant, *Ectatomma tuberculatum,* introduced into the U.S. from Guatemala, which preys on the boll weevil. [< Kekchi, a native Guatemalan language]

kel·leg (kel′ig), *n.* killick. Also, **kel·lick, kel·lock** (kel′ək).

Kel·ler (kel′ər), *n.* **1. Gottfried,** 1819–90, Swiss novelist. **2. Helen (Adams),** 1880–1968, U.S. blind and deaf lecturer, author, and educator of the blind: educated by Annie Sullivan.

kel·let (kel′it), *n. Naut.* a weight that is slid part of the way down the cable of a cast anchor to resist some of the drag imparted by the motion of the boat by making the lower part of the chain more nearly parallel to the bottom. Also called **sentinel.** [var. of KILLICK]

kel·li·on (ke lē′on), *n., pl.* **-li·a** (-lē′ə). *Eastern Ch.* **1.** a small community of monks. **2.** a cell in a monastery. [< LGk: little cell, equiv. to L *cell(a)* CELL + Gk *-ion* dim. suffix]

Kell′ner eye′piece (kel′nər), *Optics.* a Ramsden eyepiece having an achromatic lens, used in binoculars.

Kel·logg (kel′ôg, -og, -əg), *n.* **1. Frank Billings,** 1856–1937, U.S. statesman: Secretary of State 1925–29; Nobel peace prize 1929. **2.** a town in N Idaho. 5061 (1960).

Kel′logg-Bri·and′ Pact′ (kel′ôg brē änd′, -brē äN′, -og-, -əg-), the multilateral pact outlawing war and agreeing to peaceful means to settle international disputes, originally signed in 1928 by 15 nations, later joined by 49 others. Also called **Kel′logg Peace′ Pact′.** [named after F. B. KELLOGG and A. BRIAND]

Kells′, Book′ of. See **Book of Kells.**

kel·ly (kel′ē), *n., pl.* **-lies, -lys.** *Informal.* a man's stiff hat, as a derby or straw skimmer. [special use of surname *Kelly,* taken as standing for stage Irishman, with derby hat on]

Kel·ly (kel′ē), *n.* **1. Emmett (Leo),** 1898–1979, U.S. clown and pantomimist. **2. George (Edward),** 1887–1974, U.S. playwright and actor. **3.** Also, **Kel′lie.** a boy's or girl's given name.

kel′ly green′, a strong yellow-green.

ke·loid (kē′loid), *n. Pathol.* a kind of fibrous tumor forming hard, irregular, clawlike excrescences upon the skin. Also, **cheloid.** [*kel(is)* keloid (< Gk: stain, spot) + -OID] —**ke·loi′dal,** *adj.*

ke·lot·o·my (kə lot′ə mē), *n., pl.* **-mies.** *Surg.* herniotomy. [< Gk *kēl(ē)* rupture + -o- + -TOMY]

kelp (kelp), *n.* **1.** any large, brown seaweed of the family *Laminariaceae.* See illus. under **stipe. 2.** the ash of such seaweeds. —*v.i.* **3.** to burn such seaweed for its ash. [? ME *culp* < ?]

kelp′ crab′, any of several spider crabs commonly found in kelp beds along the Pacific coast of North America.

kelp·fish (kelp′fish′), *n., pl.* (*esp. collectively*) **-fish,** (*esp. referring to two or more kinds or species*) **-fish·es. 1.** any of several clinid fishes that live among kelp. Cf. **kelp greenling. 2.** any of various other fishes that live among kelp. [KELP + FISH]

kelp′ green′ling, a food and game fish, *Hexagrammos decagrammus,* living in the kelp along the Pacific coast of North America.

kel·pie¹ (kel′pē), *n.* (in Scottish legends) a water spirit, usually having the form of a horse, reputed to cause drownings or to warn those in danger of drowning. [?]

kel·pie² (kel′pē), *n. Australian.* one of a breed of medium-sized dogs, used for herding sheep. [after the name of one of these dogs]

kel·py (kel′pē), *n., pl.* **-pies.** kelpie¹.

Kel·so (kel′sō), *n.* a town in SW Washington. 8379 (1960).

kel·son (kel′sən), *n.* keelson.

kelt (kelt), *n.* a salmon that was spawned. [ME (north) < ?]

Kelt (kelt), *n.* Celt. —**Kel′tic,** *n., adj.* —**Kel′ti·cal·ly,** *adv.*

kel·ter (kel′tər), *n. Chiefly Brit. Dial.* kilter.

Kel·vin (kel′vin), *n.* **1. William Thomson, 1st Baron,** 1824–1907, English physicist and mathematician. —*adj.* **2.** *Physics.* **a.** noting or pertaining to an absolute scale of temperature (**Kel′vin scale′**) in which the degree intervals are equal to those of the Celsius scale and in which 0° Kelvin equals −273.16° Celsius. **b.** (*l.c.*) a unit of temperature change equal to one degree on the Kelvin scale. *Abbr.:* K Cf. **absolute scale, Rankine** (def. 2). **3.** Also, **Kel·win** (kel′win). a boy's given name.

Kel′vin effect′, *Physics.* See **Thomson effect.** [named after Lord KELVIN]

Ke·mal A·ta·türk (ke mäl′ ä′tä tyrk′), (*Mustafa* or *Mustapha Kemal*) ("*Kemal Pasha*") 1881–1938, Turkish general: president of Turkey 1923–38.

Ke·mal·ism (kə mä′liz əm), *n.* the group of principles advocated by Kemal Atatürk. [KEMAL + -ISM] —**Ke·mal′ist,** *n., adj.*

Kem·ble (kem′bəl), *n.* **1. Frances Anne** or **Fanny** (*Mrs. Butler*), 1809–93, English actress and author. **2.** her uncle, **John Philip,** 1757–1823, English actor.

Ke·me·ro·vo (ke′me ro vo), *n.* a city in the S RSFSR, in the S Soviet Union in Asia. 343,000 (est. 1964).

Ke·mi (kem′ē), *n.* a seaport in W Finland, on the Gulf of Bothnia. 20,148 (1960).

kemp¹ (kemp) *n.* **1.** *Brit. Dial.* **a.** (formerly) a strong, brave warrior. **b.** an athlete, esp. a champion. **c.** a professional fighter. **d.** an impetuous or roguish young man. **2.** *Scot. and North Eng.* a contest, as between two athletes or two groups of workers, esp. a reaping contest between farm workers. —*v.i.* **3.** *Scot. and North Eng.* to contest, fight, or strive, esp. to strive in a reaping contest. [ME *kempe,* OE *cempa* (c. OS *kempio,* Icel *kappi*) < L *campiō* CHAMPION]

kemp² (kemp), *n.* a short, coarse, brittle fiber, used chiefly in the manufacture of carpets. [ME *kempe* coarse (said of hair); akin to OE *cenep* mustache, bristly object, OIcel *kanpr* mustache, cat's whiskers] —**kemp′y,** *adj.*

Kemp (kemp), *n.* a boy's given name.

Kem·pis (kem′pis), *n.* **Thomas à,** 1379?–1471, German ecclesiastic and author.

ken¹ (ken), *n., v.,* **kenned** or **kent, ken·ning.** —*n.* **1.** knowledge or cognizance; mental perception: *an idea beyond one's ken.* **2.** range of sight or vision. —*v.t.* **3.** *Chiefly Scot.* **a.** to know, have knowledge of or about, or be acquainted with (a person or thing). **b.** to understand or perceive (an idea or situation). **4.** *Scots Law.* to acknowledge as heir; recognize by a judicial act. **5.** *Archaic.* to see; descry; recognize. **6.** *Brit. Dial. Archaic.* **a.** to declare, acknowledge, or confess (something). **b.** to teach, direct, or guide (someone). —*v.i.* **7.** *Brit. Dial.* **a.** to have knowledge of something. **b.** to understand. [ME *kenne(n)* (to) make known, see, know, OE *cennan* to make known, declare; c. Icel *kenna,* G *kennen;* akin to CAN¹]

ken² (ken), *n., pl.* **ken.** a Japanese sword having a straight, double-edged blade. Also called **tsurugi.** [< Jap: sword, blade]

Ken (ken), *n.* a boy's given name, form of **Kendall, Kenley,** or **Kenneth.**

Ken., Kentucky.

ke·naf (kə naf′), *n.* ambary. [< Pers]

kench (kench), *n. U.S.* a deep bin in which animal skins and fish are salted. [?]

Ken′dal green′ (ken′dəl), **1.** coarse woolen cloth, green in color. **2.** green produced by a dye extracted from the woadwaxen plant. [after *Kendal,* town in Westmoreland, England]

Ken·dall (ken′dəl), *n.* **1. Edward Calvin,** 1886–1972, U.S. biochemist: Nobel prize for medicine 1950. **2.** a boy's given name.

Ken·dall·ville (ken′dəl vil), *n.* a town in NE Indiana. 6765 (1960).

Ken′dal sneck′ bent′, *Angling.* a fishhook having a wide, squarish bend. [prob. after *Kendal,* England]

ken·do (ken dô′; *Eng.* ken′dō), *n. Japanese.* a form of fencing with bamboo staves, head guards, and protective garments. —**ken′do·ist,** *n.*

Ken·dra (ken′drə), *n.* a boy's or girl's given name.

Ken·drew (ken′dro͞o), *n.* **John C(ow·dery)** (kō′drē), born 1917, English scientist: Nobel prize for chemistry 1962.

Ken·e·dy (ken′i dē), *n.* a town in S Texas. 4301 (1960).

Ken·horst (ken′hôrst), *n.* a town in central Pennsylvania. 2815 (1960).

Ken·il·worth (ken′əl wûrth′), *n.* **1.** a town in central Warwickshire, in central England, SE of Birmingham. 14,427 (1961). **2.** a town in NE New Jersey. 8379 (1960). **3.** a town in NE Illinois. 2959 (1960).

Ken′ilworth i′vy, a European, climbing vine, *Cymbalaria muralis,* having small, lilac-blue flowers. Also called **coliseum ivy.** [after KENILWORTH (def. 1) and its castle]

Ken·ley (ken′lē), *n.* a boy's given name.

Ken·more (ken′mōr′, -môr′), *n.* a city in NW New York, near Buffalo. 21,261 (1960).

Kenn (ken), *n.* a boy's given name.

Ken·nan (ken′ən), *n.* **1. George Frost,** born 1904, U.S. author and diplomat. **2.** a boy's given name.

Ken·ne·bec (ken′ə bek′), *n.* a river flowing S through W Maine to the Atlantic. 164 mi. long.

Ken·ne·bunk (ken′ə bungk′), *n.* a town in SW Maine. 2804 (1960).

Ken·ne·dy (ken′i dē), *n.* **1. Anthony M.,** born 1936, associate justice of the U.S. Supreme Court since 1988. **2. Edward Moore** ("Ted"), born 1932, U.S. political leader: senator from Massachusetts since 1963. **3. John Fitzgerald,** 1917–63, 35th president of the U.S. 1961–63. **4. Joseph Patrick,** 1888–1969, U.S. financier and diplomat (father of John Fitzgerald, Robert Francis, and Edward Moore). **5. Robert Francis,** 1925–68, U.S. political leader and government official: attorney general 1961–64; senator from New York 1965–68. **6. Cape,** former name (1963–73) of Cape Canaveral. **7. John F., International Airport.** See **John F. Kennedy International Airport.**

ken·nel¹ (ken′əl), *n., v.,* **-neled, -nel·ing** or (*esp. Brit.*) **-nelled, -nel·ling.** —*n.* **1.** a house for a dog or dogs. **2.** Often, **kennels.** an establishment where dogs are bred, raised, trained, or boarded. **3.** the hole or lair of an animal, esp. a fox. **4.** a wretched abode likened to a doghouse. —*v.t.* **5.** to put into or keep in a kennel: *to kennel a dog for a week.* —*v.i.* **6.** to take shelter or lodge in a kennel. [ME *kenel* < AF *kenil (F *chenil*) < VL **canīle* (L *can(is)* dog + *-īle* suffix of place)]

ken·nel² (ken′əl), *n.* a gutter or open sewer. [var. of *cannel,* ME *canel* CHANNEL¹]

ken′nel club′, an association of dog breeders, usually concerned only with certain breeds of dogs.

Ken′nel·ly-Heav′i·side lay′er (ken′əl ē hev′ē sīd′). See **E layer.** [named after A.W. *Kennelly* (d. 1939), American electrical engineer and O. *Heaviside* (d. 1925), English physicist]

Ken·ner (ken′ər), *n.* a city in SE Louisiana, near New Orleans. 17,037 (1960).

Ken′ne·saw Moun′tain (ken′i sô′), a mountain in N Georgia, near Atlanta: battle 1864. 1809 ft.

Ken·neth (ken′ith), *n.* a boy's given name.

Ken′nett Square′, a town in SE Pennsylvania.

Ken·ne·wick (ken′ə wik), *n.* a city in S Washington, on the Columbia. 14,244 (1960).

ken·ning (ken′ing), *n.* a conventional and poetic phrase used for or in addition to the usual name of a person or thing, esp. in Icelandic and Anglo-Saxon verse, as "a wave traveler" for "a boat." [< Icel; see KEN¹, -ING¹]

Ken·ny (ken′ē), *n.* **1. Elizabeth** ("*Sister Kenny*"), 1886–1952, Australian nurse: researcher in poliomyelitis therapy. **2.** Also, **Ken′ney, Ken′nie.** a boy's given name, form of **Kenneth.**

Ken′ny meth′od, *Med.* a method of treating poliomyelitis, in which hot, moist packs are applied to affected muscles to relieve spasms and pain, and a regimen of exercises is prescribed to prevent deformities and to strengthen the muscles. Also called **Ken′ny treat′ment.** [named after Elizabeth KENNY]

ke·no (kē′nō), *n.* a game of chance, adapted from lotto for gambling purposes. [< F *quine* five winning numbers (<< L *quīnī* five each) + (LOTT)O]

ke·no·gen·e·sis (kē′nō jen′i sis, ken′ō-), *n.* cenogenesis. —**ke·no·ge·net·ic** (kē′nō jə net′ik, ken′ō-), *adj.* —**ke′no·ge·net′i·cal·ly,** *adv.*

Ke·no·sha (ki nō′shə), *n.* a port in SE Wisconsin, on Lake Michigan. 67,899 (1960).

ke·no·sis (ki nō′sis), *n. Theol.* **1.** the humbling of Christ and His renunciation of divine attributes through taking on the form of a servant and suffering for mankind. **2.** any doctrine or concept concerning this. [< Gk: an emptying (*ken(oûn)* (to) empty out, drain + *-ōsis* -OSIS)] —**ke·not·ic** (ki not′ik), *adj.*

Ke·no·va (kə nō′və), *n.* a town in W West Virginia. 4577 (1960).

Ken·sing·ton (ken′zing tən), *n.* a borough of W London, England. 170,891 (1961).

ken·speck·le (ken′spek′əl), *adj. Scot. and North Eng.* conspicuous; easily seen or recognized. Also, **ken′speck′led.** [*kenspeck* (< Scand; cf. Sw *känspak* quick at recognizing, lit., know-clever) + -LE; see KEN¹]

Kent (kent), *n.* **1. James,** 1763–1847, U.S. jurist. **2. Rock·well** (rok′wel′, -wəl), 1882–1971, U.S. illustrator, painter, and writer. **3. William,** 1685–1748, English painter, architect, and landscape gardener. **4.** a county in SE England. 1,701,083 (1961); 1525 sq. mi. *Cap.:* Maidstone. **5.** an ancient English kingdom in SE Great Britain. See map under **Mercia. 6.** a city in NE Ohio. 17,836 (1960). **7.** a town in central Washington. 9017 (1960). **8.** a boy's given name.

Kent·ish (ken′tish), *adj.* of or pertaining to Kent or its people. [ME *Kentissh,* OE *Centisc.* See KENT, -ISH¹]

Kent′ish fire′, *Brit.* prolonged clapping by an audience, esp. in unison, indicating impatience or disapproval. [said to have originated in *Kent,* England, in the 19th century as an indication of opposition to speakers favoring the Catholic Relief Bill]

Kent·ish·man (ken′tish mən), *n., pl.* **-men.** a man native to or inhabiting Kent, England. [KENTISH + MAN¹]

Kent′ish trac′ery, *Archit.* tracery, originating in Kent in the 14th century, having cusps with split ends.

kent·ledge (kent′lij), *n. Naut.* pig iron used as permanent ballast. [?]

Ken·ton (ken′tən), *n.* **1.** a town in central Ohio. 8747 (1960). **2.** a boy's given name.

Ken·tuck·y (kən tuk′ē), *n.* **1.** a State in the E central United States. 3,038,156 (1960); 40,395 sq. mi. *Cap.:* Frankfort. *Abbr.:* Ky., Ken. **2.** a river flowing NW from E Kentucky to the Ohio River. 259 mi. long. —**Ken·tuck′i·an,** *adj., n.*

Ken·tuck′y blue′grass, a grass, *Poa pratensis,* of the Mississippi valley, used for pasturage and hay.

Kentuck′y cof′fee tree′, a tall, North American tree, *Gymnocladus dioica,* whose seeds (**Kentuck′y cof′fee beans′**) were formerly used as a substitute for coffee beans.

Kentuck′y colo′nel, an unofficial, honorary title conferred in Kentucky.

Kentuck′y Der′by, a horse race for 3-year-olds, run annually since 1875, on the first Saturday in May, at Churchill Downs in Louisville, Kentucky.

Kentuck′y ri′fle, a muzzleloading flintlock rifle developed near Lancaster, Pennsylvania, in the early 18th century. Also called **Pennsylvania rifle.**

Kentuck′y war′bler, a wood warbler, *Oporornis formosus,* of the U.S., olive-green above, yellow below, and marked with black on the face.

Kentuck′y wind′age, *U.S. Slang.* a method of correcting for windage, gravity, etc., by aiming a weapon to one side of the target instead of by adjusting the sights.

Kent·wood (kent′wo͝od′), *n.* a town in SE Louisiana. 2607 (1960).

Ken·ya (kēn′yə, ken′-), *n.* **1.** a republic in E Africa: member of the British Commonwealth; formerly a British crown colony and protectorate. 6,551,000 (est. 1960); 223,478 sq. mi. *Cap.:* Nairobi. **2. Mount,** an extinct volcano in central Kenya. 17,040 ft. —**Ken′yan,** *adj., n.*

Ken·yat·ta (ken yä′tə), *n.* **Jo·mo** (jō′mō), 1893?–1978, African anthropologist, educator, and political leader in Kenya.

Ken·yon (ken′yən), *n.* **1. John Samuel,** 1874–1959, U.S. phonetician and educator. **2.** a boy's given name.

Ke·o·kuk (kē′ə kuk′), *n.* a city in SE Iowa, on the Mississippi River: large power dam. 16,316 (1960).

Ke·os (ke′ōs), *n.* a Greek island in the Aegean, off the SE coast of the Greek mainland. 3108 (1951); 56 sq. mi. Also called **Kea, Zea.**

kep (kep), *v.,* **kepped; keppen** or **kip·pen** (kip′ən); **kep·ping,** *n. Scot. and North Eng.* —*v.t.* **1.** to detain, intercept, or stop (a person or object); keep. **2.** to catch or grab at (a person or object), esp. to prevent from falling. —*n.* **3.** *Obs.* a basket. Also, **keap.** [back formation from KEPT]

Ke·phal·le·ni·a (ke fä′lē nē′ä), *n.* Greek name of **Cephalonia.**

kep·i (kā′pē, kep′ē), *n., pl.* **kep·is.** a French military cap with a flat circular top and a nearly horizontal visor. [< F *képi* < SwissG *Käppi* (*Kapp*(*e*) CAP + *-i* dim. suffix)]

Kepi

Kep·ler (kep′lər), *n.* **1. Jo·hann** (yō′hän), 1571–1630, German astronomer. **2.** a crater in the second quadrant of the face of the moon having an extensive ray system: about 22 miles in diameter. —**Kep·ler·i·an** (kep lēr′ē ən), *adj.*

Kep′ler tel′escope. See **astronomical telescope.** [named after Johann KEPLER]

kep·pen (kep′ən), *v. Brit.* a pp. of **kep.**

kept (kept), *v.* **1.** pt. and pp. of **keep.** —*adj.* **2.** having the expression of principles, ideas, etc., controlled, dominated, or determined by one whose money provides support: *a kept press; a kept writer.*

Ker (kûr), *n., pl.* **Ke·res** (kēr′ēz). *Class. Myth.* a spirit associated with death and sometimes identified with the Furies.

Ker·ak (ker′äk, ke räk′), *n.* a town in W Jordan, near the S Dead Sea: ancient citadel of the Moabites. 8184 (est. 1965). Also, **Krak, El Kerak.** Formerly, **Le Crac.** Ancient, **Kir Moab.**

Ker·a·la (kā′rə lə), *n.* a state in SW India: formerly the regions of Travancore and Cochin. 16,903,715 (1961); 15,035 sq. mi. *Cap.:* Trivandrum.

ke·ram·ic (kə ram′ik), *adj.* ceramic.

ke·ram·ics (kə ram′iks), *n.* (*construed as sing. or pl.*) ceramics.

kerat-, var. of **kerato-** before a vowel: *keratitis.*

ker·a·tal·gia (ker′ə tal′jə, -jē ə), *n. Pathol.* pain in the cornea. [KERAT- + -ALGIA]

ker·a·tec·ta·sia (ker′ə tek tā′zhə, -zhē ə, -zē ə), *n. Pathol.* protrusion of the cornea; keratoconus. [KERAT- + Gk *éktas*(*is*) extension (*ek-* EC- + *ta-,* var. s. of *teinein* to stretch + *-sis* -SIS) + -IA]

ker·a·tec·to·my (ker′ə tek′tə mē), *n., pl.* **-mies.** *Surg.* excision of part of the cornea. [KERAT- + -ECTOMY]

ker·a·tin (ker′ə tin), *n. Zool.* a scleroprotein or albuminoid substance, found in the dead outer corneal skin layer, and in horn, hair, feathers, hoofs, nails, claws, bills, etc. Also, **ceratin.** [KERAT- + -IN²]

ker·a·tin·ize (ker′ət ə nīz′), *v.t., v.i.,* **-ized, -iz·ing.** to make or become keratinous. [KERATIN + -IZE] —**ker′a·tin·i·za′tion,** *n.*

ke·rat·i·nous (kə rat′ən əs), *adj.* composed of or resembling keratin; horny. [KERATIN + -OUS]

ker·a·ti·tis (ker′ə tī′tis), *n. Pathol.* inflammation of the cornea. [KERAT- + -ITIS]

kerato-, var. of **cerat-:** *keratogenous.* Also, *esp. before a vowel,* **kerat-.**

ker·a·to·co·nus (ker′ə tō kō′nəs), *n., pl.* **-ni.** *Pathol.* a conical protrusion of the cornea. [KERATO- + L *cōnus* CONE]

ker·a·tode (ker′ə tōd′), *n.* the horny, fibrous substance forming the skeleton of certain sponges. Also, **keratose.** [< Gk *keratṓd*(*ēs*) hornlike. See KERAT-, -ODE¹]

ker·a·to·der·ma (ker′ə tō dûr′mə), *n. Pathol.* keratosis. Also, **ker·a·to·der·mi·a** (ker′ə tō dûr′mē ə). [KERATO- + DERMA]

ker·a·tog·e·nous (ker′ə toj′ə nəs), *adj.* producing horn or a horny substance. [KERATO- + -GENOUS]

ker·a·toid (ker′ə toid′), *adj.* resembling horn; horny. [< Gk *keratoeid*(*ēs*) hornlike. See KERAT-, -OID]

ker·a·to·ma (ker′ə tō′mə), *n., pl.* **-mas, -ma·ta** (-mə tə). *Pathol.* keratosis. [KERAT- + -OMA]

ker·a·tom·e·ter (ker′ə tom′i tər), *n. Ophthalm.* an instrument for measuring the curvature of the cornea. [KERATO- + -METER] —**ker·a·to·met·ric** (ker′ə tō me′trik), *adj.* —**ker·a·tom·e·try** (ker′ə tom′i trē), *n.*

ker·a·to·plas·ty (ker′ə tō plas′tē), *n., pl.* **-ties.** a plastic surgical operation upon the cornea, esp. a corneal transplantation. [KERATO- + -PLASTY] —**ker′a·to·plas′tic,** *adj.*

ker·a·to·scope (ker′ə tə skōp′), *n. Ophthalm.* an instrument, as Placido's disk, for determining the symmetry of the curvature of the cornea. [KERATO- + -SCOPE] —**ker·a·tos·co·py** (ker′ə tos′kə pē), *n.*

ker·a·tose (ker′ə tōs′), *adj.* **1.** having a skeleton formed of horny fibers, as certain sponges. —*n.* **2.** keratode. [KERAT- + -OSE¹]

ker·a·to·sis (ker′ə tō′sis), *n., pl.* **-ses** (-sēz). *Pathol.* **1.** any skin disease characterized by a horny growth. **2.** any horny growth. Also, **keratoderma, keratoma.** [KERAT- + -OSIS] —**ker′a·to′sic, ker·a·tot·ic** (ker′ə tot′ik), *adj.*

ker·a·tot·o·my (ker′ə tot′ə mē), *n., pl.* **-mies.** *Surg.* incision of the cornea. [KERATO- + -TOMY]

kerb (kûrb), *n., v.t. Brit.* curb (defs. 1, 15).

Ker·be·la (kûr′bə lə), *n.* a town in central Iraq: holy city of the Shiah sect. 60,804 (1957). Also, **Karbala.**

kerb·ing (kûr′biŋ), *n. Brit.* curbing.

kerb′ mar′ket, *Brit.* curb (def. 3). Also, **kerb′stone mar′ket.**

kerb·stone (kûrb′stōn′), *n. Brit.* curbstone.

Ker·by (kûr′bē), *n.* a boy's given name. Also, **Kirby.**

Kerch (kerch), *n.* **1.** a seaport in E Crimea, in the SW RSFSR, in the SW Soviet Union in Europe, on Kerch Strait. 99,000 (1959). **2.** a strait in the SW Soviet Union in Europe, connecting the Sea of Azov and the Black Sea. 25 mi. long.

ker·chief (kûr′chif), *n.* **1.** a cloth worn as a head covering, esp. by women. **2.** such a cloth worn about the neck or shoulders. [ME *kerchef,* syncopated var. of *keverchef* < OF *cuevrechef,* lit., cover (the) head. See COVER, CHIEF] —**ker′chiefed, ker′chieft,** *adj.*

Ke·ren·ski (ke ren′skī), *n.* **A·le·ksan·dr Fe·o·do·ro·vich** (ä′le ksän′dər fe ō′do ʀō′vich), 1881–1970, Russian revolutionary leader: premier 1917; in the U.S. after 1946. Also, **Ke·ren′sky.**

Ker·e·san (ker′i sən), *n.* a family of languages spoken by Pueblo tribes of the Rio Grande valley and neighboring areas.

kerf (kûrf), *n.* **1.** a cut or incision made by a saw or the like in a piece of wood. —*v.t.* **2.** to make a kerf or kerfs in (a piece of wood). Also, **curf.** [ME *kerf, kirf,* OE *cyrf* a cutting (c. OFris *kerf*); akin to CARVE]

ker·flop (kər flop′), *adv.* with or as if with a flop: *He fell kerflop into the chair.* [imit.]

Ker·gue·len (kûr′gə len′), *n.* a desolate island in the S Indian Ocean: a possession of France. 1400 sq. mi. French, **Ker·gué·len** (ker gā len′).

Ker·ki (ker kē′), *n.* a city in E Turkmenistan, in the S Soviet Union in Asia: trade center. 20,000 (est. 1961).

Ker·ky·ra (keʀ′kē rä), *n.* Greek name of **Corfu.**

Ker·man (kər män′), *n.* a city in SE Iran. 62,175 (1956).

Ker·man·shah (kər män′shä′), *n.* **1.** a city in W Iran. 125,181 (1956). **2.** Kirman.

ker·mes (kûr′mēz), *n.* **1.** a red dye formerly prepared from the dried bodies of the females of a scale insect, *Kermes ilices,* which lives on certain oaks of the Mediterranean region. **2.** the small evergreen oak, *Quercus coccifera,* on which this insect is found. [earlier *chermez* < OIt *chermes* < Ar *qirmiz* < Pers; see CRIMSON]

ker·mes·ite (kûr′mē zīt′, -mi sīt′, kûr mes′īt), *n.* a mineral, antimony oxysulfide, Sb_2S_2O, occurring usually in tufts of red capillary crystals. [KERMES + -ITE¹]

ker·mis (kûr′mis), *n.* **1.** (in the Low Countries) an annual fair or festival at which there are games, merrymaking, etc. **2.** a similar entertainment, usually for charitable purposes. Also, **ker′mess, kirmess.** [< D, earlier *ker*(*c*)*misse* (*kerc* CHURCH + *misse* MASS); orig. a fair at the dedication of a church]

Ker·mit (kûr′mit), *n.* a boy's given name.

kern¹ (kûrn), *n. Archaic.* **1.** a band of lightly armed foot soldiers of ancient Ireland. **2.** (in Ireland and the Scottish Highlands) a soldier. **3.** an Irish peasant, esp. a crude or boorish one. Also, **kerne.** [ME *kerne* < Ir *ceithern* band of foot soldiers; see CATERAN]

kern² (kûrn), *Print.* —*n.* **1.** a part of the face of a type projecting beyond the body or shank, as in certain italic letters. —*v.t.* **2.** to form or furnish with a kern, as a type or letter. [< F *carne* corner of type << L *cardin-* (s. of *cardō*) hinge]

kern³ (kûrn), *Brit. Dial.* —*v.i.* **1.** (of a tree or plant) to produce or form kernels, hard grain, or seed. —*v.t.* **2.** to cause to granulate, esp. to granulate salt. **3.** to cover with crystalline grains of salt; salt (meat). —*n.* **4.** *Obs.* a kernel, as of a nut; a grain, as of sand or wheat. [ME *kern*(*e*), *curne;* see CORN¹]

kern⁴ (kûrn), *n. Engineering.* **1.** the central area of any horizontal section of a wall, column, etc., within which the resultant forces of all compressive loads must pass if there is to be only compression at that point. **2.** a particle of dust, pollen, or the like. [< G: core, kernel]

kern⁵ (kûʀn), *v.t., v.i., n. Scot. and North Eng.* churn.

kern⁶ (kûʀn), *n. Scot. and North Eng.* kirn².

Kern (kûrn), *n.* **Jerome (David),** 1885–1945, U.S. composer.

kern′ count′er. See **dust counter.**

ker·nel (kûr′nəl), *n., v.,* **-neled, -nel·ing** or (*esp. Brit.*) **-nelled, -nel·ling.** —*n.* **1.** the softer, usually edible part contained in the shell of a nut or the stone of a fruit. **2.** the body of a seed within its husk or integuments. **3.** a whole seed grain, as of wheat or corn. **4.** *Math.* the set of elements that a given function from one set to a second set maps into the identity of the second set. **5.** the central part of anything; the nucleus; the core: *His leadership and imagination are the kernel of the organization.* **6.** Also called **rumpf.** *Physical Chem.* the remainder of an atom after the valence electrons have been removed. —*v.t.* **7.** to enclose as a kernel. [ME *kirnel,* OE *cyrnel,* dim. of *corn* CORN¹] —**ker′nel·less,** *adj.* —**ker′nel·ly,** *adj.*

ker′nel smut′, *Plant Pathol.* a disease of sorghum and other grasses in which the grains are replaced by the black spores of a smut fungus, esp. of the genera *Tilletia* and *Sphacelotheca.*

Ker·ners·ville (kûr′nərz vil), *n.* a town in central North Carolina. 2942 (1960).

kern·ite (kûr′nīt), *n.* a mineral, hydrated sodium borate, $Na_2B_4O_7{\cdot}4H_2O$, occurring in transparent colorless crystals: the principal source of boron compounds in the U.S. [named after *Kern* County, California; see -ITE¹]

ker·nos (kûr′nos), *n., pl.* **-noi** (-noi). *Gk. Antiq.* a Mycenaean ceramic piece usually in the form of a ring to which were attached a number of cups or vases. [< Gk]

ker·o (kâr′ō), *n., pl.* **ker·os.** a wooden vessel, as a beaker, made by the Incas. [< native name]

ker·o·gen (ker′ə jən, -jen′), *n.* the bituminous matter in oil shale, from which shale oil is obtained. [< Gk *kērō*(*s*) wax + -GEN]

ker·o·sene (ker′ə sēn′, kar′-, ker′ə sēn′, kar′-), *n.* a mixture of liquid hydrocarbons obtained by distilling petroleum, bituminous shale, or the like: used chiefly in lamps as a fuel, and as a solvent for cleaning. Also, **ker′o·sine′.** [irreg. < Gk *kērós* wax + -ENE]

Ker·ou·ac (ker′o͞o ak′), *n.* **Jack** (*Jean-Louis Lefris de Kérouac*) 1922–69, U.S. novelist, born in Canada.

ker·plunk (kər pluŋk′), *adv.* with or as with a muffled thud: *The huge stone hit the water kerplunk.* [imit.]

Kerr (kûr *or, for 2,* kär), *n.* **1. Clark,** born 1911, U.S. educator: president of the University of California at Berkeley since 1958. **2. Michael Crawford,** 1827–76, U.S. politician: Speaker of the House 1875–76. **3. Walter F.,** born 1913, U.S. drama critic and author. **4.** Also, **Carr.** a boy's given name.

Kerr′ cell′ (kär, kûr), *Physics.* a transparent cell filled with a fluid, usually nitrobenzene, and containing two electrodes placed between two polarizing light filters, suitable for demonstrating the Kerr effect and often used as a high-speed camera shutter.

Kerr′ effect′, *Physics.* the double refraction of light in certain substances, produced by an electric field. [named after John *Kerr* (1824–1907), Scottish physicist]

Kerr·ville (kûr′vil), *n.* a town in SW Texas. 8901 (1960).

ker·ry (ker′ē), *n., pl.* **-ries.** one of an Irish breed of small, black dairy cattle. [after KERRY, home of the breed]

Ker·ry (ker′ē), *n.* **1.** a county in W Munster province, in the SW Republic of Ireland. 116,458 (1961): 1815 sq. mi. *Co. seat:* Tralee. **2.** a boy's given name, form of **Kerr.**

Ker′ry blue′ ter′rier, one of an Irish breed of terriers having a soft, wavy, bluish-gray coat.

Kerry blue terrier (18½ in. high at shoulder)

ker·sey (kûr′zē), *n., pl.* **-seys,** *adj.* —*n.* **1.** a heavy overcoating of wool or wool and cotton, similar to beaver and melton. **2.** a coarse twilled woolen cloth with a cotton warp. —*adj.* **3.** of or pertaining to fabrics made of kersey. [ME; ? after *Kersey,* in Suffolk, England]

ker·sey·mere (kûr′zi mēr′), *n.* a heavily fulled woolen cloth constructed in fancy twill weave. [KERSEY + (CASSI)MERE]

Kerst (kûrst), *n.* **Donald William,** born 1911, U.S. physicist.

ke·rug·ma (ki rug′mə), *n., pl.* **-ma·ta** (-mə tə). kerygma.

Ker·win (kûr′win), *n.* a boy's given name.

ke·ryg·ma (ki rig′mə), *n., pl.* **-ma·ta** (-mə tə). the preaching of the gospel of Christ, esp. in the manner of the early church. Also, **kerugma.** [< Gk: proclamation, preaching, equiv. to *kērý*(*ssein*) (to) proclaim, preach + *-ma* n. suffix] —**ker·yg·mat·ic** (ker′ig mat′ik), *adj.*

Kes·sel·ring (kes′əl riŋ; *Ger.* kes′əl ʀiŋ), *n.* **Al·bert** (al′bərt; *Ger.* äl′bert), 1885–1960, German field marshal.

kes·trel (kes′trəl), *n.* **1.** a common small falcon, *Falco tinnunculus,* of northern parts of the Eastern Hemisphere, notable for hovering in the air with its head to the wind. **2.** any of several related small falcons, as the sparrow hawk, *Falco sparverius.* [late ME *castrell* < MF *quercelle* (by metathesis), var. of *crecerelle,* of disputed orig.]

ket-, var. of **keto-** before a vowel: *ketene.*

ketch (kech), *n. Naut.* a sailing vessel rigged fore and aft on two masts, the larger, forward, being the mainmast and the after stepped forward of the rudderpost, being the mizzen or jigger. Cf. **yawl¹** (def. 2). [ME *cache,* appar. n. use of *cache* to CATCH]

Ketch

Ketch·i·kan (kech′ə kan′), *n.* a seaport in SE Alaska. 6483 (1960).

ketch-rigged (kech′rigd′), *adj.* rigged in the manner of a ketch.

ketch·up (kech′əp, kach′-), *n.* any of various sauces for meat, fish, etc.: *tomato ketchup; mushroom ketchup.* Also, **catchup, catsup.** [< Chin (Amoy dial.) *ke-tsiap* pickled-fish brine]

ke·tene (kē′tēn), *n. Chem.* **1.** a colorless, poisonous gas, $H_2C{=}C{=}O$, irritating to the lungs, prepared from acetone or acetic acid by pyrolysis: used chiefly in the manufacture of certain commercial chemicals, as acetic anhydride and aspirin. **2.** a class of compounds having the type formulas $RHC{=}C{=}O$ and $R_2C{=}C{=}O$ where R is a radical. [KET- + -ENE]

ke·to (kē′tō), *adj. Chem.* of or derived from a ketone. [KETO(NE)]

keto-, a combining form of **ketone:** *ketolysis.* Also, *esp. before a vowel,* **ket-.**

ke/to-e/nol tautom/erism (kē/tō ē/nōl, -nôl, -nol), *Chem.* a type of tautomerism in which the individual tautomers are alternately a keto form and an enol.

ke/to form/, *Chem.* (in a keto-enol tautomeric substance) the form with the characteristics of a ketone.

ke·to·gen·e·sis (kē/tō jen/i sis), *n. Med.* the production of ketone bodies in the body, as in diabetes mellitus. [KETO- + GENESIS] —**ke·to·ge·net·ic** (kē/tō jə net/ik), *adj.*

ke·to·hex·ose (kē/tō hek/sōs), *n. Chem.* any of a class of sugars composed of six carbon atoms and a ketone group, as fructose. [KETO- + HEXOSE]

ke·tol·y·sis (ki tol/i sis), *n., pl.* **-ses** (-sēz/). *Chem.* the breaking down of ketones. [KETO- + -LYSIS] —**ke·to·lyt·ic** (kēt/əlit/ik), *adj.*

ke·tone (kē/tōn), *n. Chem.* any of a class of organic compounds containing a carbonyl group, > C=O, attached to two organic groups, as CH_3COCH_3 or $CH_3COC_2H_5$. —*adj.* **2.** containing the ketone group. [< G *Keton,* aph. alter. of *Aceton* ACETONE] —**ke·ton·ic** (ki ton/ik), *adj.*

ke/tone bod/y, *Biochem.* any of three compounds, acetoacetic acid, beta-hydroxybutyric acid, or acetone, that are intermediate in the metabolism of fatty acids and that are found in abnormal quantities in the blood and urine during certain pathological conditions, as diabetes mellitus. Also called **acetone body.**

ke/tone group/, *Chem.* the characteristic group occurring in ketones that consists of the carbonyl group attached to two other organic groups. Also called **ke/tone rad/ical.**

ke·to·ne·mi·a (kē/tō nē/mē ə), *n. Med.* the presence of ketone bodies in the blood. [KETONE + -EMIA]

ke·to·nu·ri·a (kē/tō nŏŏr/ē ə, -nyŏŏr/-), *n. Med.* the presence of ketone bodies in the urine. [KETONE + -URIA]

ke·tose (kē/tōs), *n. Chem.* a monosaccharide that contains a ketone group. [KET- + -OSE[2]]

ke·to·sis (ki tō/sis), *n. Pathol.* the accumulation of excessive ketones in the body, as in diabetic acidosis. [KET- + -OSIS]

Ket·ter·ing (ket/ər ing), *n.* **1.** **Charles Franklin,** 1876–1958, U.S. engineer and inventor. **2.** a city in SW Ohio. 54,462 (1960).

ket·tle (ket/əl), *n.* **1.** a container in which to boil liquids, cook foods, etc.; pot. **2.** a teakettle. **3.** a kettledrum. **4.** See **kettle hole.** [ME *ketel* < Scand; cf. Icel *ketill;* c. OE *citel,* G *Kessel;* all < L *cat(illus),* dim. of *catinus* pot]

ket/tle base/, a bombé base to a piece of furniture.

ket·tle-bot·tom (ket/əl bot/əm), *adj. Naut.* noting a type of hull formerly used for merchant sailing vessels, characterized by a very wide bottom with very slight deadrise and a large amount of tumble home with concave topsides and a narrow upper deck: used to minimize taxation under former rules of tonnage measurement.

ket·tle·drum (ket/əl drum/), *n.* a drum consisting of a hollow hemisphere of brass or copper over which is stretched a skin, the tension of which can be modified by hand screws or foot pedals for tuning. [KETTLE + DRUM[1]]

Kettledrum

ket·tle·drum·mer (ket/əl drum/ər), *n.* a person who plays kettledrums. [KETTLEDRUM + -ER[1]]

ket/tle hat/, *Armor.* See **chapel de fer.**

ket/tle hole/, *Geol.* a kettle-shaped depression in rock or detrital material, esp. in glacial drift. Also called **kettle.**

ket/tle of fish/, **1.** an awkward situation; muddle; mess: *He's managed to get himself into a fine kettle of fish!* **2.** a state of affairs; a matter under consideration: *The new proposal is quite a different kettle of fish from the last one.*

ket/tle stitch/, *Bookbinding.* (in handsewing) a knot tied in the thread that links one section to the next. [part trans. of G *Kettlestich,* equiv. to *Kettel* little chain (dim. of *Kette* chain, OHG *ketīna* < L *catēna*) + *Stich* STITCH]

ke·tu·bah (kə tōō bä/, kə tōō/bə), *n., pl.* **-both** (-bōt/), *Eng.* **-bahs.** *Hebrew.* the formal contract joining a man and woman in a Jewish marriage and including specific arrangements for securing her financial condition in the event that he dies or divorces her. [lit., something written]

Ke·tu·bim (kə tōō bēm/), *n. Hebrew.* the Hagiographa. Also, **Ke·tu·vim** (kə tōō vēm/). Cf. **Tanach.** [lit., writings]

Ke·tur·ah (ki tŏŏr/ə), *n.* the second wife of Abraham. Gen. 25:1. Also, *Douay Bible,* **Cetura.**

keV, See **kiloelectron volt.**

ke·va·lin (kā/və lin), *n. Jainism.* one who is free of karmic matter, detached, and omniscient; Tirthankara. [< Skt *kevala* alone, sole]

kev·el[1] (kev/əl), *n. Naut.* a sturdy bit, bollard, etc., on which the heavier hawsers of a ship may be secured. Also, **cavel, cavil, kev/il.** [ME *kevile* < AF < L *clāvicul(a)* little key (*clāvi(s)* key + *-cula* -CULE, -CLE)]

kev·el[2] (kev/əl), *n.* a hammer for the rough dressing of stone, having one square face and one pyramidal face. Also, **cavel, cavil, gavel.** [ME *kevell* < ?]

Kev·in (kev/in), *n.* a boy's given name.

Kew (kyōō), *n.* a part of Richmond, in NE Surrey, in SE England: famous botanical gardens (**Kew/ Gar/dens**). 4362 (1951).

Ke·wa·nee (kē wô/nē), *n.* a city in NW Illinois. 16,324 (1960).

Ke·wau·nee (kē wô/nē), *n.* a town in E Wisconsin. 2772 (1960).

kew·pie (kyōō/pē), *n.* a minor benevolent sprite or pixie, usually described in folklore as having the form of a plump, winged child, similar to a cherub or cupid. [alter. of CUPID]

Kew·pie (kyōō/pē), *n. Trademark.* a small, very plump doll, usually made of plaster or celluloid.

kex (keks), *n. Brit. Dial.* the dry, usually hollow stem or stalk of various herbaceous plants, esp. of large umbelliferous plants, as cow parsnip, wild chervil, etc. [ME < ?]

key[1] (kē), *n., pl.* **keys,** *adj., v.,* **keyed, key·ing.** —*n.* **1.** a metal instrument for operating a lock by moving its bolt. **2.** a means of attaining, understanding, solving, etc.: *the key to success; the key to a problem.* **3.** a book, pamphlet, or the like, containing the solutions or translations of material given elsewhere, as testing exercises. **4.** a systematic explanation of abbreviations, symbols, etc., used in a dictionary, map, etc. Cf. **legend** (def. 4). **5.** the system, method, pattern, etc., used to decode or decipher a cryptogram, as a code book, machine setting, key word, or the like. **6.** something that secures or controls entrance to a place: *Gibraltar is the key to the Mediterranean.* **7.** a pin, bolt, wedge, or other piece inserted in a hole or space to lock or hold parts of a mechanism or structure together; a cotter. **8.** a small piece of steel fitting into matching slots of a hub of a wheel or the like and the shaft on which it is mounted so that torque is transmitted from one to the other. **9.** a contrivance for grasping and turning a bolt, nut, etc. **10.** one of a set of levers or parts pressed in operating a typewriter, calculating machine, etc. **11.** a manually operated lever for opening and closing an electric current, used to produce signals in telegraphy. **12.** *Music.* **a.** (in a keyboard instrument) one of the levers that when depressed by the performer sets in motion the playing mechanism. **b.** (on a woodwind instrument) a metal lever that opens and closes a vent. **c.** the keynote or tonic of a scale. **d.** the relationship perceived between all tones in a given unit of music to a single tone or a keynote; tonality. **e.** the principal tonality of a composition: *a symphony in the key of C minor.* **13.** tone or pitch, as of voice: *to speak in a high key.* **14.** mood or characteristic style, as of expression or thought: *He writes in a melancholy key.* **15.** degree of intensity, as of feeling or action. **16.** (in a series of advertisements soliciting replies) a unique code inserted for each medium used, to determine the relative effectiveness of the media. **17.** *Elect.* **a.** a device for opening and closing electrical contacts. **b.** a hand-operated switching device ordinarily formed of concealed spring contacts with an exposed handle or push button, capable of switching one or more parts of a circuit. **18.** *Bot., Zool.* a systematic tabular classification of the significant characteristics of the members of a group of organisms to facilitate identification and comparison. **19.** *Masonry.* a keystone. **20.** *Building Trades.* any grooving or roughness applied to a surface to improve its bond with another surface. **21.** *Masonry, Carpentry.* a wedge, as for tightening a joint or splitting a stone or timber. **22.** *Carpentry.* a small piece of wood set into a timber across the grain to prevent warping. **23.** *Archit.* (in a ribbed vault) a stone, as a boss, at the intersection of two or more ribs. **24.** *Photog.* the dominant tonal value of a picture. **25.** *Painting.* the tonal value and intensity of a color or range of colors: *The palette of the Impressionists was generally in a high key. Rembrandt's colors are characterized by their low key.* **26.** *Bot.* a samara. **27.** (*cap.*) a member of the House of Keys. **28.** **keys,** spiritual authority. **29.** **power of the keys,** the authority of a pope in ecclesiastical matters, vested in him as successor of St. Peter. —*adj.* **30.** chief; major; important; essential: *a key man in the company; the key industries of Canada.* —*v.t.* **31.** to regulate or adjust (actions, thoughts, speech, etc.) to a particular state or activity: *to key one's speech to the level of the audience.* **32.** *Music.* to regulate the key or pitch of. **33.** *Painting.* **a.** to paint (a picture) in a given key. **b.** to adjust the colors in (a painting) to a particular hue: *He keyed the painting to brown.* **34.** to fasten, secure, or adjust with a key, wedge, or the like, as parts of a mechanism. **35.** to provide with a key or keys. **36.** (in the layout of newspapers, magazines, etc.) to identify, through signs or symbols, the positions of illustrations or pieces of copy in a dummy. **37.** to lock with or as with a key. **38.** *Masonry.* to provide (an arch or vault) with a keystone. **39.** **key up, a.** to bring to a particular degree of intensity of feeling, excitement, energy, etc.: *The party keyed him up to such a degree that he got hysterical.* **b.** to raise (a piece of masonry) by the insertion of a wedge or wedges. **c.** to raise (the haunches of an arch) by the insertion of a voussoir. [ME *key(e), kay(e),* OE *cæg, cǣge;* c. OFris *kei, kai*]

key[2] (kē), *n., pl.* **keys.** a reef or low island; cay. [< Sp *cay(o),* prob. < Arawak]

Key (kē), *n.* **Francis Scott,** 1780–1843, U.S. lawyer: author of *The Star-Spangled Banner.*

key·board (kē/bōrd/, -bôrd/), *n.* **1.** the row or set of keys in a piano, typewriter, etc. **2.** any of two or more sets of keys, as in large organs or harpsichords. [KEY[1] + BOARD]

key/ case/, a small case of leather, plastic, etc., in which keys are carried.

key/ club/, a private night club to which each member has a door key.

keyed (kēd), *adj.* **1.** fitted with keys. **2.** fastened or secured by a key. **3.** *Music.* pitched in a specific key. **4.** reinforced by a keystone. [KEY[1] + -ED[3]]

key/ fruit/, *Bot.* a samara.

key·hole (kē/hōl/), *n.* **1.** a hole for inserting a key in a lock, esp. one in the shape of a circle with a rectangle having a width smaller than the diameter of the circle projecting from the bottom. **2.** *Basketball.* the area at each end of the court that is bounded by two lines extending from the end line parallel to and equidistant from the sidelines and terminating in a circle around the foul line. —*adj.* **3.** extremely private or intimate, esp. with reference to information gained as if by peeping through a keyhole. **4.** snooping and intrusive: *a keyhole investigator.* [KEY[1] + HOLE]

key/hole saw/, a compass saw for cutting keyholes, etc.

Key/ Lar/go (lär/gō), one of the islands in the Florida Keys. 30 mi. long; 2 mi. wide.

key·less (kē/lis), *adj.* **1.** lacking a key or keys. **2.** requiring no key or keys. [KEY[1] + -LESS]

key·man (kē/man/), *n., pl.* **-men.** a person highly important or essential to the functioning of an organization, as a team, business, etc. [KEY[1] + MAN[1]]

key/man insur/ance, life insurance taken out by a business firm on a vital member or employee of that firm, with the firm as beneficiary.

key/ mon/ey, **1.** an amount of money paid, often secretly, to a landlord, superintendent, or current tenant by a person wanting to get future tenancy. **2.** (chiefly in Europe) advance rent or security required of a new tenant on signing a lease for an apartment or house and given in exchange for the key.

Keynes (kānz), *n.* **John May·nard** (mā/nərd, -närd), **1st Baron,** 1883–1946, English economist and writer.

Keynes·i·an (kān/zē ən), *adj.* **1.** of or pertaining to the economic theories, doctrines, or policies of Keynes or his followers, esp. the policy of maintaining high employment and controlling inflation by varying the interest rates, tax rates, and public expenditure. —*n.* **2.** one who maintains or supports the economic theories, doctrines, or policies of Keynes. [KEYNES + -IAN]

Keynes·i·an·ism (kān/zē ə niz/əm), *n.* the group of theories and programs of John Maynard Keynes and his followers, esp. the advocacy of governmental programs for the issuance of currency and for budgeting so as to maintain a high level of employment. [KEYNESIAN + -ISM]

key·note (kē/nōt/), *n., v.,* **-not·ed, -not·ing.** —*n.* **1.** *Music.* the note or tone on which a key or system of tones is founded; the tonic. **2.** the main idea or central principle of a speech, program, thought, action, etc. **3.** the policy line to be followed, as by a party in a political campaign, and which is set forth authoritatively in advance by a keynote address or other formal announcement. —*v.t.* **4.** to announce the policy of (a political party, campaign, assembly, etc.): *The governor will keynote the convention.* **5.** *Music.* to give the keynote of. [KEY[1] + NOTE]

key/note address/, a speech, as at a political convention, which presents important issues, principles, policies, etc. Also called **key/note speech/.**

key·not·er (kē/nō/tər), *n.* a person who delivers a keynote address. [KEYNOTE + -ER[1]]

key/ plate/, *Print.* (in color printing) the plate providing the greatest definition of detail, usually the black plate, on which the other plates are registered.

Key·port (kē/pōrt/, -pôrt/), *n.* a town in E New Jersey. 6440 (1960).

key/ punch/, **1.** a machine, operated by a keyboard, for coding information by punching holes in cards in certain patterns. **2.** Also called **card punch.** a device having a typewriterlike keyboard, for punching holes in a punch card or paper tape.

key·punch (kē/punch/), *v.t.* to punch holes in (a punch card or paper tape), using a key punch. [v. use of KEY PUNCH] —**key/punch/er,** *n.*

key/ ring/, a ring, usually of metal, for holding keys.

key/ scarf/, *Shipbuilding.* any of various scarf joints in which the overlapping parts are keyed together.

Key·ser (kī/zər), *n.* a town in NE West Virginia. 6192 (1960).

Key·ser·ling (kī/zər ling), *n.* **Her·mann A·le·xan·der** (her/män ä/le ksän/dər), **Count,** 1880–1946, German philosopher and writer.

key/ sig/nature, *Music.* (in notation) the group of sharps or flats placed after the clef to indicate the tonality of the music following.

key·slot (kē/slot/), *n.* a short, curved slot cut into a shaft for a Woodruff key. Cf. **keyway** (def. 1). [KEY[1] + SLOT[1]]

key/ sta/tion, a radio or television station that is the origin of most network broadcasting.

key·stone (kē/stōn/), *n.* **1.** the wedge-shaped piece at the summit of an arch, regarded as holding the other pieces in place. See diag. under **arch.** **2.** something on which associated things depend: *the keystone of one's philosophy.* **3.** Also called **key/stone sack/.** *Baseball Slang.* See **second base** (def. 1). [KEY[1] + STONE]

key/stone joist/, a reinforced-concrete joist with sloping sides and the top wider than the bottom.

Key·ston·er (kē/stō/nər), *n. Informal.* a native or inhabitant of Pennsylvania (the **Keystone State**) (used as a nickname). [KEYSTONE (STATE) + -ER[1]]

Key/stone State/, Pennsylvania (used as a nickname).

key·stroke (kē/strōk/), *n.* one stroke of any key on a machine operated by a keyboard, as a typewriter, key punch, linotype, etc.: *She can do 3,000 keystrokes an hour.* [KEY[1] + STROKE[1]]

key·way (kē/wā/), *n.* **1.** Also called **key/ seat/.** *Mach.* a groove in a shaft, the hub of a wheel, etc., for receiving part of a key holding it to another part. **2.** a slot in a lock for receiving and guiding the key. **3.** (in poured-concrete construction) a longitudinal groove in a footing, or in a pour that has set, providing a key for newly poured concrete. **4.** a depression or slot carved into rock to provide a bond or anchorage for a structure, as a dam. [KEY[1] + WAY]

Key/ West/, **1.** an island in S Florida, in the Gulf of Mexico. **2.** a seaport on this island: the southernmost city in the U.S.; naval base. 33,956 (1960).

key/ word/, **1.** a word which serves as a key, as to the meaning of another word, a sentence, passage, or the like. **2.** a word used to encipher or decipher a cryptogram, as a pattern for a transposition procedure, the basis for a complex substitution, or the like.

kG, kilogauss; kilogausses.

kg, kilogram; kilograms.

K.G., Knight of the Garter.

kgf, kilogram-force.

kg-m, kilogram-meter; kilogram-meters.

kgr, kilograin; kilograins.

khā (KHä), *n.* the seventh letter of the Arabic alphabet, representing a velar spirant consonant sound. [< Ar]

Kha·ba·rovsk (KHä bä/rofsk), *n.* **1.** Formerly, **Far Eastern Region.** an administrative division of the RSFSR in the E Soviet Union in Asia. 1,250,000 (1959); 965,400 sq. mi. **2.** a port in and the capital of this territory, in the SE part, on the Amur River. 322,000 (1959).

Kha·bur (*Arab.* khä bo͝or′), *n.* a river in W Asia, flowing S from SE Turkey through NE Syria to the Euphrates. 200 mi. long.

Kha·cha·tu·ri·an (kä′chə to͝or′ē ən, kach′ə-; *Russ.* khä′chä to͞o ryän′), *n.* **A·ram** (ä räm′), 1903–78, Russian composer, born in Armenia.

khad·dar (kä′dər), *n.* a plain-weave cotton fabric produced in India. Also, **kha·di** (kä′dē). [< Hindi *khādar*]

Kha·fa·je (khä′fä yā′, kä′-), *n.* the site of an ancient city in E Iraq: occupied at different times by the Akkadians and Sumerians. Also, **Kha′fa·jeh.**

Khaf·re (kaf′rā, käf′-), *n.* (*Chephren*) c2800 B.C., Egyptian king of the 4th dynasty; builder of 2nd pyramid at El Giza (brother of Cheops). Also, **Kafre.**

Khai′bar Pass′ (kī′bər). See **Khyber Pass.**

Khakass′ Auton′omous Re′gion, an autonomous region in the Russian Federation, in S Siberia. 500,000; 19,161 sq. mi. *Cap.:* Abakan.

khak·i (kak′ē, kä′kē), *n., pl.* **khak·is,** *adj.* —*n.* **1.** dull yellowish brown. **2.** a stout twilled cotton uniform cloth of this color. **3.** a similar fabric of wool. —*adj.* **4.** of the color of khaki. **5.** made of khaki. [< Urdu < Pers: dusty (*khāk* dust + -ī suffix of appurtenance)] —**khak′i·like′,** *adj.*

khak·is (kak′ēz, kä′kēz), *n.* (*construed as pl.*) **1.** khaki slacks or trousers. **2.** a khaki military uniform. [pl. of KHAKI]

kha·lif (kə lēf′, kā′lif, kal′if), *n.* caliph. Also, **kha·li·fa** (kə lē′fə).

khal·i·fate (kal′ə fāt′, -fit), *n.* caliphate.

Khal·kha (kal′kə), *n.* an Altaic language that is the official language of the Mongolian People's Republic and the chief vernacular of the eastern half of the country.

Khal·ki·di·ke (khäl′kə thē′kē), *n.* Greek name of **Chalcidice.**

Khal·kis (*Gk.* khäl kēs′), *n.* Chalcis.

khal·sa (käl′sə), *n.* a martial fraternity originated in 1675 and remaining as one of the closely-knit communities of the Sikhs. [< Hindi *khālṣa* lit., pure << Ar *khālisah*]

kham·sin (kam′sin, kam sēn′), *n.* a hot southerly wind, varying from SE to SW, that blows regularly in Egypt for about 50 days, commencing about the middle of March. Also, **kamseen, kamsin.** [< Ar: lit., fifty]

khan[1] (kän, kan), *n.* **1.** (in the Altaic group of languages) a title held by hereditary rulers or tribal chiefs. **2.** the supreme ruler of the Tatar tribes, as well as emperor of China, during the Middle Ages: a descendant of Genghis Khan. **3.** a title of respect used in Iran, Afghanistan, Pakistan, India, and other countries of Asia. [late ME *Ca(a)n, Chan* << Turkic *Khān,* appar. contr. of *Khāgān,* equiv. to Turk *kağan* ruler]

khan[2] (kän, kan), *n.* an inn or caravansary. [< Ar < Pers; r. late ME *alchan* < Ar (*al* the + *khān*)]

khan·ate (kä′nāt, kan′āt), *n.* the area governed by a khan. [KHAN[1] + -ATE[1]]

khan·da (kän′də), *n.* an Indian sword, having a broad, usually single-edged blade and a disklike pommel with a point. [var. of *khanjar* < Pers: dagger]

Khanh (kän), *n.* **Ngu·yen** (ᵊŋgo͞o′yen), born 1927, Vietnamese army officer and statesman.

Kha·nia (khä nyä′), *n.* Greek name of **Canea.**

khan·sa·mah (kän′sə mä′), *n. Anglo-Indian.* **1.** a native house steward or butler. **2.** a native male servant. [< Hindi *khānsāmā* < Pers *khānsāmān,* equiv. to *khān* master + *sāmān* stores]

kha·rif (kə rēf′), *n.* (in India) a crop sown in early summer for harvesting in the autumn. [< Hindi < Ar *kharīf,* lit., gathered]

Kha·ri·jite (kär′ə jīt′), *n. Islam.* a member of an orthodox sect emphasizing the importance of strict adherence to Muslim principles of conduct, and advocating the killing of anyone seriously violating those principles. [< Ar *khārij(ī)* dissenter + -ITE[1]]

Khar·kov (kär′kof, -kov; *Russ.* khär′kof), *n.* a city in the E Ukraine, in the S Soviet Union in Europe: former capital of the Ukraine. 1,070,000 (1965).

Khar·toum (kär to͞om′), *n.* a city in and the capital of the Sudan, at the junction of the White and Blue Nile rivers: besieged 1885; retaken by the British 1898. 160,000 (est. 1970). Also, **Khar·tum′.**

Khartoum′ North′, a city in E Sudan, on the Blue Nile River, opposite Khartoum. 58,000 (est. 1964).

Kha·si (kä′sē), *n.* an Austroasiatic language of Assam, in NE India.

Khas·ko·vo (khäs′ko vo), *n.* a city in S Bulgaria. 27,394 (1956).

khat (kät), *n.* kat.

kha·tri (ku′trē), *n.* a person who belongs to a Hindu mercantile caste alleged to originate with the kshatriyas. [< Hindi < Skt *kṣatriya*]

Khat·ti (khat′ē), *n.* Hatti. —**Khat′tish,** *adj.*

Khat·tu·sas (khät′to͞o säs′), *n.* Hattusas.

Khay·yám (kī yäm′, -yam′), *n.* **Omar.** See **Omar Khayyám.**

khed·a (ked′ə), *n.* (in India) an enclosure constructed to ensnare wild elephants. Also, **keddah, khed′ah.** [< Hindi]

khe·dive (kə dēv′), *n.* the title of the Turkish viceroys in Egypt from 1867 to 1914. [< F *khédive* < Turk *hidiv* < Pers *khidīw* prince] —**khe·di′val, khe·di·vi·al** (kə dē′vē əl), *adj.* —**khe·di·vi·ate** (kə dē′vē it, -āt′), **khe·di·vate** (kə dē′vit, -vāt′), *n.*

Khe·lat (kə lät′), *n.* Kalat.

Kher·son (kher sôn′), *n.* a port in the S Ukraine, in the SW Soviet Union in Europe, on the Dnieper River, near the Black Sea. 200,000 (est. 1964).

khid·mat·gar (kid′mət gär′), *n.* (in India) a waiter. Also, **khid′mut·gar′, khit·mat·gar, khit·mut·gar** (kit′mət gär′). [< Urdu < Pers, equiv. to *khidmat* service (< Ar *khidmah*) + *-gār* agent suffix]

Khi·os (khē′ôs; *Eng.* kī′os), *n.* Greek name of **Chios.**

Khir·bet Qum·ran (kēr′bet ko͝om′rän), an archaeological site in Jordan, near the NW coast of the Dead Sea: Dead Sea Scrolls found here. Also, **Khir′bet Qûm′ran.**

Khi·va (khē′vä), *n.* a former Asian khanate along the Amu Darya River, S of the Aral Sea: now divided between the Uzbek and Turkman republics of the Soviet Union.

Khlyst (klist), *n., pl.* **Khlys·ty** (kli stē′), **Khlysts.** a member of a rigorously ascetic Russian sect originating in the 17th century, and believing that each successive leader of the sect was an incarnation of Christ. [< Russ: lit., riding whip]

Khmer (kmer), *n.* **1.** a member of a people in Cambodia whose ancestors established an empire about the 5th century A.D. and who reached their zenith during the 9th to the 12th centuries when they dominated most of Indo-China. **2.** an Austroasiatic language that is the official language of Cambodia.

Khmer′ Repub′lic, former name of **Cambodia.**

Khnum (khno͞om), *n. Egyptian Religion.* a god in the form of a ram who created human beings from clay on a potter's wheel.

Khoi·san (koi′sän), *n.* **1.** a family of languages indigenous to southern Africa and including the languages of the Bushmen and the Hottentots. —*adj.* **2.** of or belonging to Khoisan.

kho·ja (kō′jə) *n.* **1.** a teacher in a Muslim school. **2.** (*cap.*) a member of a subsect of the Muslims in India. [< Pers *khwāja*]

Kho·mei·ni ((khō mā′nē, khō-), *n.* **Ru·hol·lah** (ro͞o hō′lə), born 1900?, Iranian Islamic leader: de facto head of state since 1979.

Khond (kond), *n.* a member of an outcaste Dravidian people of the state of Orissa in eastern India.

Kho·tan (khō′tän′), *n.* **1.** an oasis in W China, in SW Sinkiang. **2.** Also, **Hotien.** the chief city in this oasis. 50,000 (est. 1950).

Khru·shchev (kro͞osh′chef, -chôf, kro͞osh′-; *Russ.* khro͞o shchôf′), *n.* **Ni·ki·ta S(er·gey·e·vich)** (ni kē′tə sər gā′ə vich; *Russ.* ni kē′tä ser ge′ye vich), 1894–1971, Russian political leader: premier of the U.S.S.R. 1958–64.

Khu·fu (ko͞o′fo͞o), *n.* Cheops.

khus-khus (kus′kəs), *n.* vetiver (def. 2). [< Pers, Hindi *khaskhas*]

Khut·bah (kho͝ot′bə), *n. Islam.* a sermon preached by an imam in a mosque at the time of the Friday noon prayer. [< Ar, akin to *khaṭaba* to preach]

Khu·zis·tan (kho͞o′zis tän′), *n.* a province in SW Iran, on the Persian Gulf. 2,065,108 (1956); ab. 35,000 sq. mi. *Cap.:* Khorramshahr.

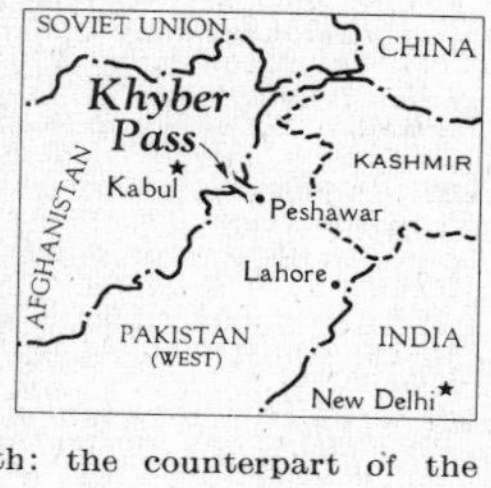

Khy′ber knife′ (kī′bər), a long Indian knife having a triangular, single-edged blade with the handle set off center toward the back.

Khy′ber Pass′, the chief mountain pass between Pakistan and Afghanistan, W of Peshawar. 33 mi. long; 6825 ft. high. Also called **Khaibar Pass.**

kHz, kilohertz.

Ki (kē), *n.* the Sumerian goddess personifying earth: the counterpart of the Akkadian Aruru.

Ki., Kings.

ki·a·boo′ca wood′ (kī′ə bo͞o′kə). See **Padouk wood.** [?]

ki·ang (kē äng′), *n.* a wild ass, *Equus hemionus kiang,* of Tibet and Mongolia. [< Tibetan *(r)kyan*]

Kiang·ling (kyäng′ling′; *Chin.* jyäng′ling′), *n.* a city in S Hupeh, in central China, on the Yangtze. ab. 15,000. Also, **Chiangling.** Formerly, **Kingchow.**

Kiang·si (kyäng′sē′; *Chin.* jyäng′sē′), *n.* a province in SE China. 18,610,000 (est. 1957); 63,629 sq. mi. *Cap.:* Nanchang.

Kiang·su (kyäng′so͞o′; *Chin.* jyäng′so͞o′), *n.* a maritime province in E China. 45,230,000 (est. 1957); 40,927 sq. mi. *Cap.:* Nanking.

Kiao·chow (kyou′chou′; *Chin.* jyou′jō′), *n.* **1.** a territory on the Shantung peninsula, in E China, around Kiaochow Bay: leased to Germany 1898–1914. ab. 200 sq. mi. Chief city, Tsingtao. **2. Bay,** an inlet of the Yellow Sea in E China, in Shantung province. 20 mi. long; 15 mi. wide.

KIAS, knot indicated airspeed.

kiaugh (kyäkh), *n. Scot.* trouble; worry. Also, **kauch.** [? < Gael; cf. Ir *ciach* oppression, *ciachdha* distressed, troubled]

kib·ble[1] (kib′əl), *v.,* **-bled, -bling,** *n.* —*v.t.* **1.** to grind or divide into relatively large particles or pellets, as coarse-ground meal or prepared dry dog food. —*n.* **2.** grains or pellets resulting from a kibbling process: *Give the cat some kibble.* [?]

kib·ble[2] (kib′əl), *n. Brit.* an iron bucket used in mines for hoisting ore. [< G *Kübel* pail, vat]

kib·butz (ki bo͝ots′, -bo͞ots′), *n., pl.* **-but·zim** (-bo͝ot sēm′). (in Israel) a community, chiefly agricultural, organized under collectivist principles. [< ModHeb *qibbūṣ,* lit., gathering]

kib·butz·nik (ki bo͝ots′nik, -bo͞ots′-), *n.* a member of a kibbutz. [< Yiddish *kibutsnik,* equiv. to *kibuts* KIBBUTZ + *-nik* suffix of appurtenance]

kibe (kīb), *n. Med. Obs.* a chapped or ulcerated chilblain, esp. on the heel. [ME *kybe,* perh. < Welsh *cibi*]

Ki·bei (kē′bā′), *n., pl.* **-bei.** a person of Japanese descent, born in the U.S. and educated in Japan (distinguished from *Nisei*). Also, **kibei.** Cf. **Issei, Sansei, Nisei.** [< Jap]

kib·itz (kib′its), *v.i. Informal.* to act as a kibitzer. [< Yiddish *kibitzen,* equiv. to G *kiebitzen,* deriv. of *Kiebitz* busybody, lit., lapwing, plover]

kib·itz·er (kib′it sər), *n. Informal.* **1.** a spectator at a card game who looks at the players' cards over their shoulders. **2.** a giver of uninvited or unwanted advice. **3.** a person who jokes, chitchats, or makes wisecracks, esp. while others are trying to work or to discuss something seriously. [< Yiddish; see KIBITZ, -ER[1]]

kib·lah (kib′lä), *n. Islam.* **1.** the point toward which Muslims turn to pray, esp. the sacred stone in the Kaaba at Mecca. **2.** the direction of this from a given place. Also, **kib′la, qibla.** [< Ar *qiblah* something placed opposite, akin to *qabala* to be opposite]

ki·bosh (kī′bosh, ki bosh′), *n. Informal.* **1.** nonsense. **2. put the kibosh on,** to render inactive or ineffective; squelch; check: *Another such injury may put the kibosh on his athletic career.* [?]

kick (kik), *v.t.* **1.** to strike with the foot: *He kicked the ball.* **2.** to make (a car) increase in speed, esp. in auto racing: *He kicked his car into high gear.* **3.** *Football.* to score (a field goal or a conversion) by place-kicking or drop-kicking the ball. **4.** to strike in recoiling: *The gun kicked his shoulder.* **5.** *Poker Slang.* raise (def. 24). **6.** to drive, force, make, etc., by or as by kicks. —*v.i.* **7.** to make a rapid, forceful thrust with the foot: *He kicked at the ball. You have to kick rapidly when using a crawl stroke.* **8.** to have a tendency to strike with the foot or feet: *That horse kicks when you walk into his stall.* **9.** *Informal.* to resist, object, or complain. **10.** to recoil, as a firearm when fired. **11.** to be actively or vigorously involved: *He's still around and kicking.* **12. kick about,** to move from place to place frequently: *He kicked about a good deal before settling down.* **13. kick around,** *Slang.* **a.** to treat (someone) harshly or inconsiderately. **b.** to consider, discuss, or speculate about (a proposal, project, etc.). **c.** to experiment with. **d.** to change one's residence or job frequently: *He has been kicking around Europe since his discharge from the army.* **14. kick back,** **a.** *Informal.* to recoil, esp. vigorously or unexpectedly. **b.** *Slang.* to give someone a kickback. **c.** *Slang.* to return (stolen property, money, etc.) to the owner. **15. kick in,** *Slang.* **a.** to contribute one's share, esp. in money. **b.** to die: *He kicked in after a long and painful illness.* **16. kick off, a.** *Football.* to begin play or begin play again by a kickoff: *The Giants won the toss and elected to kick off.* **b.** *Slang.* to die. **c.** *Informal.* to initiate (an undertaking, meeting, etc.); begin: *A rally tomorrow night will kick off the campaign.* **17. kick out,** *Informal.* to dismiss or oust someone: *They have been kicked out of the country club.* **18. kick over,** *Informal.* (of an internal combustion engine) to begin ignition; turn over: *The engine kicked over a few times but we couldn't get it started.* **19. kick the bucket.** See **bucket** (def. 11). **20. kick the habit,** to get over an addiction, habit, etc.: *He tried in vain to kick the cigarette habit.* **21. kick upstairs.** See **upstairs** (def. 4). **22. kick up, a.** to drive or force upward by kicking. **b.** to stir up (trouble); make or cause (a disturbance, scene, etc.): *The two dogs, left locked up in the apartment, kicked up a tremendous row.* —*n.* **23.** the act of kicking; a blow or thrust with the foot. **24.** power or disposition to kick: *That horse has a mean kick.* **25.** a recoil, as of a gun. **26.** *Informal.* an objection or complaint. **27.** *Informal.* **a.** a stimulating or intoxicating quality in alcoholic drink. **b.** vigor, energy, or vim. **28.** *Slang.* **a.** thrill; pleasurable excitement: *His biggest kick comes from telling about the victory.* **b.** a strong but temporary interest, often an activity: *Making mobiles is his latest kick.* **29.** a pocket. **30.** *Football.* **a.** an instance of kicking the ball. **b.** any method of kicking the ball: *place kick.* **c.** a kicked ball. **d.** the distance such a ball travels. **e.** a turn at kicking the ball. **31.** *Glassmaking.* a solid glass base or an indentation at the base of drinking glasses, bottles, etc., which reduces the liquid capacity of the glassware. **32.** *Brit. Slang.* sixpence. [ME *kike(n),* ?< Scand; cf. Icel *keikja* to bend backward, bend the knees (in wrestling)] —**kick′a·ble,** *adj.* —**kick′less,** *adj.*

—**Syn. 1.** boot. **9.** remonstrate; oppose. **9, 26a.** grumble, growl, grouch, moan; protest, protestation, grievance.

Kick·a·poo (kik′ə po͞o′), *n.* a dialect of the Fox language.

kick·back (kik′bak′), *n. Informal.* **1.** a response, usually vigorous. **2.** a percentage of income given to a person in a position of power or influence as payment for having made the income possible: usually considered improper or immoral. **3.** a rebate, usually given secretively by a seller to a buyer or to one who influenced the buyer. **4.** the practice of an employer, foreman, or person in a supervisory position of taking back a portion of the wages due workers. [n. use of v. phrase *kick back*]

kick·ball (kik′bôl′), *n.* a children's playground game, similar to baseball, in which a large inflated ball, as a soccer ball, is kicked instead of being batted. [KICK + BALL[1]]

kick·board (kik′bōrd′, -bôrd′), *n. Swimming.* a buoyant, usually small board that is used to support the arms of a swimmer, used chiefly in practicing kicking movements. [KICK + BOARD]

kick·er (kik′ər), *n.* **1.** one who or that which kicks. **2.** *Informal.* an essential part of an agreement, contract, or the like, regarded as unfair or disadvantageous. **3.** *Draw Poker.* a card, usually an ace or face card, held with a pair or three of a kind in the hope of drawing a matching card. **4.** (in concrete construction) a low plinth at the base of a column. **5.** *Naut.* **a.** a small, low-powered outboard motor. **b.** an auxiliary engine on a sailing vessel. **6.** *Slang.* the alcoholic liquor in a mixed drink. **7.** Also called **eyebrow, highline, overline, teaser.** *Print., Journ.* a short line of copy set in a distinctive type above a headline and intended to call attention to it. **8.** *Metall.* a charge of high-carbon iron which produces a vigorous boil when charged into an open-hearth furnace containing slag and molten metal of lower carbon content. [KICK + -ER[1]]

kick′ing tack′le, *Naut.* See **relieving tackle.**

kick·off (kik′ôf′, -of′), *n.* **1.** *Football.* a place kick or a drop kick from the 40-yard line of the team kicking at the beginning of the first and third periods or after the team kicking has scored a touchdown or field goal. **2.** *Informal.* the initial stage of something: *the campaign kickoff; the kickoff of his new TV series.* Also, **kick′-off′.** [n. use of v. phrase *kick off*]

kick′ plate′, a metal plate fastened to the bottom of a door to resist blows and scratches. Also, **kick′plate′.**

kick′ pleat′, an inverted pleat extending upward six to ten inches from the hemline at the back of a narrow skirt, to allow freedom in walking.

kick·shaw (kik′shô′), *n.* **1.** a tidbit or delicacy, esp. one served as an appetizer or hors d'oeuvre. **2.** something showy but without value; trinket; trifle. [back formation from *kickshaws* < F *quelque chose* something (by folk etymology)]

kick·stand (kik′stand′), *n.* a device for supporting a bicycle or motorcycle when not in use, pivoted to the rear axle in such a way that it can be kicked down below the rear wheel. [KICK + STAND]

kick′ start′er, a starter, as of a motorcycle, that operates by a downward kick on a pedal. Also called **kick′ start′.**

kick′ turn′, *Skiing.* a turn from a stationary position in which a skier lifts one ski to a point where the heel is nearly at right angles to the snow, then faces the ski outward, sets it down in the direction to be turned, and swings the other ski around so that both skis are parallel.

kick·up (kik′up′), *n. Informal.* a fuss; commotion; row: *They instigated a real kickup about the new rules.* [n. use of v. phrase *kick up*]

kick·wheel (kik′hwēl′, -wēl′), *n.* a potter's wheel rotated by kicking. [KICK + WHEEL]

Kic·va (kik′və), *n. Welsh Legend.* the wife of Pryderi.

kid[1] (kid), *n., v.,* **kid·ded, kid·ding.** —*n.* **1.** a young goat. **2.** leather made from the skin of a kid or goat, used in making shoes and gloves. **3.** a glove made from this leather. **4.** *Informal.* a child or young person. —*v.i., v.t.* **5.** (of a goat) to give birth to (young). [ME *kide* < Scand; cf. Shetlandic *kidi* lamb, akin to Icel *kith* kid] —**kid′dish·ness,** *n.* —**kid′like′,** *adj.*

kid[2] (kid), *v.,* **kid·ded, kid·ding.** *Informal.* —*v.t.* **1.** to tease; banter; jest with: *She is always kidded about her accent.* **2.** to humbug or fool. —*v.i.* **3.** to speak or act deceptively in jest; jest. [? special use of KID[1]] —**kid′der,** *n.* —**kid′ding·ly,** *adv.*

kid[3] (kid), *n.* a tublike wooden container in which food is served to sailors. [ME; ? var. of KIT[1]]

Kid (kid), *n.* **Thomas.** See **Kyd, Thomas.**

Kidd (kid), *n.* **1. Michael,** born 1919, U.S. dancer and choreographer. **2. William** ("*Captain Kidd*"), 1645?–1701, Scottish navigator and privateer: hanged for piracy.

Kid·der·min·ster (kid′ər min′stər), *n.* an ingrain carpet 36 inches wide. [after the town in Worcestershire, England, where first made]

kid′die car′ (kid′ē), **1.** a car for a small child, having three wheels and pushed with the feet. **2.** a small tricycle. Also, **kid′dy car′.**

kid·ding (kid′ing), *n.* fagoting (def. 2). [ME *kid* fagot, later *kid* (v.) + -ING[1]]

kid·do (kid′ō), *n., pl.* **-dos, -does.** a familiar form of address. [KID[1] + *-o* suffix of association]

Kid·dush (kē do͞osh′; *Eng.* kid′əsh), *n. Judaism.* the blessing or prayer, differing in form according to the occasion, that is recited over a cup of wine or over bread on the eve of the Sabbath or a festival. [< Heb *qiddūsh* sanctification]

kid·dy (kid′ē), *n., pl.* **-dies.** *Informal.* a child. Also, **kid′die.** [KID[1] + -Y[2]]

kid′ gloves′, 1. gloves made of kid leather. **2. handle with kid gloves,** to treat with extreme tact or gentleness: *Such overly sensitive people must be handled with kid gloves.*

kid·nap (kid′nap), *v.t.,* **-napped** or **-naped, -nap·ping** or **-nap·ing.** to steal, carry off, or abduct (a person) by force or fraud, esp. for use as a hostage or to extract ransom. [KID[1] + *nap,* var. of NAB] —**kid′nap·er;** *esp. Brit.,* **kid′nap·per,** *n.*

Kid·napped (kid′napt), *n.* a novel (1886) by Robert Louis Stevenson.

kid·ney (kid′nē), *n., pl.* **-neys. 1.** *Anat.* either of a pair of bean-shaped, glandular organs in the back part of the abdominal cavity which excrete urine. **2.** a corresponding organ in other vertebrate animals, or an organ of like function in invertebrates. **3.** the meat of an animal's kidney used as food. **4.** constitution or temperament: *He was a quiet child, of a different kidney from his boisterous brothers.* **5.** kind, sort, or class: *He is only at ease with men of his own kidney.* [ME *kidenei,* equiv. to *kiden-* (of unknown meaning and orig.) + *-ei,* OE *ǣg* EGG[1]] —**kid′neylike′,** *adj.*

Human kidney (Section) A, Adrenal gland; B, Cortex; C, Papilla; D, Pelvis; E, Ureter

kid′ney bean′, 1. the common bean, *Phaseolus vulgaris.* **2.** its kidney-shaped seed.

kid′ney cor′puscle, (not used scientifically) See **Malpighian corpuscle.**

kid·ney-shaped (kid′nē shāpt′), *adj.* having the general shape of a long oval indented at one side; reniform: *a kidney-shaped table.*

kid′ney stone′, *Pathol.* an abnormal stone, or concretion, composed primarily of oxalates and phosphates, found in the kidney. Also called **renal calculus.**

kid′ney vetch′, an Old World, leguminous herb, *Anthyllis Vulneraria,* formerly used as a remedy for kidney diseases. Also called **woundwort.**

kid′ney worm′, any of various large nematodes parasitic in the kidneys, esp. *Stephanurus dentatus,* found in pigs.

kid·ney·wort (kid′nē wûrt′), *n.* **1.** the navelwort, *Cotyledon umbilica.* **2.** coyote-brush. [KIDNEY + WORT[2], from its use in treating kidney ailments]

Ki·dron (kē′drən), *n.* Kedron.

kid·skin (kid′skin′), *n.* **1.** leather made from the skin of a young goat; kid. —*adj.* **2.** made of kidskin: *kidskin gloves.* [KID[1] + SKIN]

kid′ stuff′, 1. something appropriate only for children. **2.** something very easy or simple.

kief (kēf), *n.* kef.

Kief·fer (kē′fər), *n.* **1.** a large, brownish-red, hybrid variety of pear. **2.** the tree bearing this fruit. [named after Peter *Kieffer* (1812–90), American botanist]

Kiel (kēl), *n.* the capital of Schleswig-Holstein in N Germany, at the Baltic end of the Kiel Canal. 260,900.

kiel·ba·sa (kil bä′sə, kēl-), *n., pl.* **-sas, -sy** (-sē). a smoked sausage of coarsely chopped beef and pork, flavored with garlic and spices and often bottled in brine. Also called **Polish sausage.** [< Pol *kiełbasa* sausage]

Kiel′ Canal′, a canal connecting the North and Baltic seas. 61 mi. long.

Kiel·ce (kyel′tse), *n.* a city in S Poland. 96,000 (est. 1963).

Kien Lung (kyen′ lo͝ong′). See **Ch'ien Lung.**

kier (kēr), *n.* a large vat in which fibers, yarns, or fabrics are boiled, bleached, or dyed. Also, **keir.** [< Scand; cf. Icel *ker* tub]

Kier·ke·gaard (kēr′kə gärd′; *Dan.* kēr′kə gôr′), *n.* **Sö·ren Aa·bye** (sœ′rən ô′by), 1813–55, Danish philosopher and theologian.

Kier·ke·gaard·i·an (kēr′kə gär′dē ən, kēr′kə gär′-), *adj.* **1.** of, pertaining to, or resembling the philosophy or religious views of Kierkegaard. —*n.* **2.** an adherent of the views of Kierkegaard. [KIERKEGAARD + -IAN] —**Kier′ke·gaard′i·an·ism,** *n.*

kie·sel·guhr (kē′zəl go͝or′), *n.* See **diatomaceous earth.** [< G, equiv. to *Kiesel* flint + *Gu(h)r* earthy deposit]

kie·ser·ite (kē′zə rīt′), *n.* a mineral, hydrous magnesium sulfate, having a white or yellowish color and found with salt deposits. [< G *Kieserit,* named after D. G. *Kieser,* German physician; see -ITE[1]]

Ki·ev (kē′ef), *n.* a city in and the capital of the Ukraine in the SW Soviet Union in Europe, on the Dnieper River. 1,332,000 (1965).

Ki·ev·an (kē′ef ən, -ev ən), *adj.* **1.** of or pertaining to Kiev. **2.** of or pertaining to the period in Russian history (11th and 12th centuries) when Kiev was the political center of a loose federation of states: *Kievan Russia.* —*n.* **3.** a native or inhabitant of Kiev. [KIEV + -AN]

kif (kif), *n.* kef.

Ki·ga·li (kē gä′lē), *n.* a town in and the capital of Rwanda in the central part. 5000 (est. 1962).

Ki·i·run (kē′ē ro͞on′), *n.* Japanese name of Keelung.

kike (kīk), *n. Disparaging and Offensive.* a person of Jewish religion or descent. [appar. modeled on *hike* Italian, itself modeled on *mike* Irishman, short for *Michael*]

Ki·ku·yu (ki ko͞o′yo͞o), *n., pl.* **-yus,** (*esp. collectively*) **-yu. 1.** a member of a Negroid people of Kenya having an agricultural economy and notable as being the originators of the Mau Mau. **2.** the language of the Kikuyu, a Bantu language.

Ki·kwit (kē′kwēt), *n.* a city in W Zaire. 11,000 (est. 1962).

kil., kilometer; kilometers.

Ki·lau·e·a (kē′lou ā′ä), *n.* a crater on Mauna Loa volcano, on SE Hawaii island, in Hawaii. 2 mi. wide; 4040 ft. high.

Kil·dare (kil dâr′), *n.* a county in Leinster, in the E Republic of Ireland. 64,420 (1961); 654 sq. mi. *Co. seat:* Kildare.

kil·der·kin (kil′dər kin), *n.* **1.** a unit of capacity, usually equal to half a barrel or two firkins. **2.** an English unit of capacity, equal to 18 imperial gallons. [ME *kilderkyn,* dissimilated var. of *kinderkin* < MD, equiv. to *kinder* (<< Ar *qinṭār* QUINTAL) + *-kin* -KIN]

kil·erg (kil′ûrg′), *n. Physics.* (no longer current) a unit of work or energy, equal to 1000 ergs. [KIL(O)- + ERG[1]]

ki·ley (kī′lē), *n., pl.* **-leys.** *Australian.* kylie.

kil·ij (kil′izh), *n.* a Turkish saber with a crescent-shaped blade, sharp on the entire convex edge and sharp on the opposite edge for about eight inches back from the point. [< Turk]

Kil·i·man·ja·ro (kil′ə mən jär′ō), *n.* a volcanic mountain in N Tanzania: highest peak in Africa. 19,321 ft.

Kil·ken·ny (kil ken′ē), *n.* **1.** a county in Leinster, in the SE Republic of Ireland. 61,668 (1961); 796 sq. mi. **2.** its county seat. 10,159 (1961).

Kilken′ny cats′, a pair of proverbial cats in Ireland who fought until only their tails were left.

kill[1] (kil), *v.t.* **1.** to deprive (any living creature or thing) of life in any manner; cause the death of; slay. **2.** to destroy; do away with; extinguish: *His response killed our hopes. Heavy injuries killed our chances of winning the game.* **3.** to destroy or neutralize the active qualities of: *to kill the effect of poison by diluting it.* **4.** to spoil the effect of: *His extra brushwork killed the painting.* **5.** to cause (time) to be consumed with seeming rapidity or with a minimum of boredom, esp. by engaging in some easy activity or amusement of passing interest: *I had to kill three hours before train time, so I went to the movies.* **6.** to spend (time) unprofitably: *He killed ten good years on that job.* **7.** to overcome completely or with irresistible effect: *That giggle of hers kills me.* **8.** to muffle or deaden: *This carpet kills the sound of footsteps.* **9.** to tire completely; exhaust: *The long hike killed us.* **10.** to cancel publication of (a word, paragraph, item, etc.), esp. after it has been set in type. **11.** to defeat or veto (a legislative bill, etc.). **12.** *Elect.* to render (a circuit) dead. **13.** to stop the operation of (machinery, engines, etc.): *He killed the motor and the car slowed down.* **14.** *Tennis.* to hit (a ball) with such force that its return is impossible. **15.** *Metall.* **a.** to deoxidize (steel) before teeming it into an ingot mold. **b.** to eliminate springiness from (wire or the like). **c.** to cold-roll (sheet metal) after its final heat treatment in order to eliminate distortion. **16.** *Ice Hockey.* to prevent the opposing team from scoring in the course of (a penalty being served by a teammate or teammates). **17.** *Informal.* to consume completely: *They killed a bottle of bourbon between them.* —*v.i.* **18.** to inflict or cause death. **19.** to commit murder. **20.** to be killed. **21.** to overcome completely; produce an irresistible effect: *She was dressed to kill.* **22. kill off, a.** to destroy completely; kill, esp. successively or indiscriminately: *The invaders killed off all the inhabitants of the town.* **b.** *Slang.* to extinguish; eliminate: *That bus ride every day kills off all of my energy.* **23. kill with kindness,** to overdo in one's efforts to be kind: *The maiden aunts would kill their nephews and nieces with kindness.* —*n.* **24.** the act of killing, esp. game: *The hounds moved in for the kill.* **25.** an animal or animals killed. [ME *cull(en), kill(en),* OE **cyllan;* c. dial. G *küllen* (Westphalian); akin to OE *-colla,* in *morgencolla* morning-killer. See QUELL] —**kill′a·ble,** *adj.*

—**Syn. 1.** slaughter, massacre, butcher; hang, electrocute, behead, guillotine, strangle, garrote; assassinate. KILL, EXECUTE, MURDER all mean to deprive of life. KILL is the general word, with no implication of the manner of killing, the agent or cause or the nature of what is killed (whether human being, animal, or plant): *to kill a person.* EXECUTE is used with reference to the putting to death of one in accordance with a legal sentence, no matter what the means are: *to execute a criminal.* MURDER is used of killing a human being unlawfully: *He murdered him for his money.*

kill[2] (kil), *n. U.S. Dial.* a channel; a creek; a stream; a river. [< D *kil,* MD *kille* channel; akin to Icel *kīll* creek, inlet]

Kil·lar·ney (ki lär′nē), *n.* **1.** a town in the SW Republic of Ireland. 6298 (1951). **2. Lakes of,** three lakes in SW Ireland.

kill·dee (kil′dē), *n. U.S. Dial.* killdeer.

kill·deer (kil′dēr′), *n.* an American plover, *Charadrius vociferus,* having two black bands around the upper breast. Also called **kill′deer plov′er.** [imit.]

Kil·leen (ki lēn′), *n.* a city in central Texas. 23,377 (1960).

kill·er (kil′ər), *n.* **1.** one who or that which kills. **2.** See **killer whale. 3.** a device used by a post office for printing cancellations on postage stamps. **4.** a mark of cancellation made on a postage stamp. **5.** *Slang.* something or someone having a formidable impact: *That flowered hat is a real killer.* [KILL[1] + -ER[1]]

kill′er bee′, a honeybee of African origin, released in South America in the 1950's, noted for aggressively attacking in swarms when disturbed.

kill·er-dill·er (kil′ər dil′ər), *n. Slang.* killer (def. 5). [rhyming compound]

kill′er whale′, any of several predatory dolphins, esp. the black and white *Grampus orca,* found in all seas.

kil·lick (kil′ik), *n.* **1.** a small anchor or weight for mooring a boat, sometimes consisting of a stone secured by pieces of wood. **2.** any anchor. Also, **kelleg, kellick, kellock, killock, killoch.** [?]

kil·lic·kin·nic (kil′ə kə nik′), *n.* kinnikinnick. Also, **kil′li·ki·nic′, kil′lic·kin·nick′.**

Kil·lie·cran·kie (kil′ē krang′kē), *n.* a mountain pass in central Scotland, in the Grampians.

kil·li·fish (kil′ē fish′), *n., pl.,* (*esp. collectively*) **-fish,** (*esp. referring to two or more kinds or species*) **-fish·es. 1.** any of several small, oviparous cyprinodont fishes, esp. of the genus *Fundulus,* found in salt, brackish, and fresh waters. **2.** any of several livebearers. Cf. **least killifish.** [? KILL[2] + -I- + FISH]

kill·ing (kil′ing), *n.* **1.** the act of one who or that which kills. **2.** the total game killed on a hunt. **3.** *Informal.* a stroke of extraordinary success, as in stock market speculation. —*adj.* **4.** that kills. **5.** exhausting: *a killing pace.* **6.** *Informal.* irresistibly funny. [late ME; see KILL[1], -ING[1], -ING[2]] —**kill′ing·ly,** *adv.*

kill′ing frost′, the occurrence of temperatures cold enough to kill all but the hardiest vegetation, esp. the last such occurrence in spring and the first in fall, events which limit the agricultural growing season.

kill·joy (kil′joi′), *n.* one who or that which spoils the joy or pleasure of others.

kil·lock (kil′ək), *n.* killick. Also, **kil′loch.**

Kil·mar·nock (kil mär′nək), *n.* a city in SW Scotland, SW of Glasgow. 47,509 (1961).

Kil·mer (kil′mər), *n.* **1. (Alfred) Joyce,** 1886–1918, U.S. poet and journalist. **2.** a boy's given name.

kiln (kil, kiln), *n.* **1.** a furnace or oven for burning, baking, or drying something, esp. one for calcining limestone or one for baking bricks. —*v.t.* **2.** to burn, bake, or treat in a kiln. [ME *kiln(e),* OE *cyl(e)n* < L *culīna* kitchen]

kiln-dry (kil′drī′, kiln′-), *v.t.,* **-dried, -dry·ing.** to dry in a kiln.

kil·o (kil′ō, kē′lō), *n., pl.* **kil·os. 1.** kilogram. **2.** kilometer. **3.** (a word used in communications to represent the letter K.) *Abbr.:* K [shortened form]

kilo-, a Greek prefix meaning "thousand," introduced from French in the nomenclature of the metric system (*kiloliter*); on this model, used in the formation of compound words in other scientific systems of measurement (*kilowatt*). [< F, repr. Gk *chílioi* a thousand]

kil·o·am·pere (kil′ō am′pēr), *n. Elect.* a unit of electric current, equal to 1000 amperes. *Abbr.:* kA [KILO- + AMPERE]

kil·o·bar (kil′ə bär′), *n.* a unit of pressure, equal to 14,500 pounds per square inch. *Abbr.:* kb [KILO- + BAR[1]]

kil·o·bit (kil′ə bit′), *n. Computer Technol.* **1.** 1024(2^{10}) bits. **2.** (loosely) one thousand bits.

kil·o·byte (kil′ə bīt′), *n. Computer Technol.* **1.** 1024 (2^{10}) bytes: abbreviated to "K" to describe memory capacity: *a computer with 128K.* **2.** (loosely) one thousand bytes.

kil·o·cal·o·rie (kil′ə kal′ə rē), *n. Physics.* calorie (def. 1a). *Abbr.:* kcal Also called **kil′ogram cal′orie.** [KILO- + CALORIE]

kil·o·cu·rie (kil′ə kyo͝or′ē, -kyo͝o rē′), *n.* a unit of radioactivity, equal to 1000 curies. *Abbr.:* kCi, kc [KILO- + CURIE]

kil·o·cy·cle (kil′ə sī′kəl), *n.* a unit equal to 1000 cycles: used esp. in radio as 1000 cycles per second for expressing the frequency of electromagnetic waves; kilohertz. The term kilohertz is now preferred in technical use. *Abbr.:* kc [KILO- + CYCLE]

kil·o·dyne (kil′ə dīn′), *n. Physics.* a unit of force, equal to 1000 dynes. [KILO- + DYNE]

kil′o·e·lec′tron volt′ (kil′ō i lek′tron), one thousand electron-volts. *Abbr.:* keV, kev [KILO- + ELECTRON]

kil·o·gauss (kil′ə gous′), *n. Elect.* a unit of magnetic induction, equal to 1000 gauss. *Abbr.:* kG [KILO- + GAUSS]

kil·o·grain (kil′ə grān′), *n.* one thousand grains. *Abbr.:* kgr [KILO- + GRAIN]

kil·o·gram (kil′ə gram′), *n. Metric System.* a unit of mass and weight, equal to 1000 grams, and equivalent to 2.2046 pounds avoirdupois. *Abbr.:* kg, kg. Also, *esp. Brit.,* **kil′o·gramme′.** [< F *kilogramme.* See KILO-, -GRAM[2]]

kil·o·gram-force (kil′ə gram′fōrs′, -fôrs′), *n. Physics.* a meter-kilogram-second unit of force, equal to the force that produces an acceleration equal to the acceleration of gravity, when acting on a mass of one kilogram. *Abbr.:* kgf

kil·o·gram-me·ter (kil′ə gram′mē′tər), *n. Physics.* a meter-kilogram-second unit of work or energy, equal to the work done by a force of one kilogram when its point of application moves through a distance of one meter in the direction of the force; approximately 7.2 foot-pounds. *Abbr.:* kg-m Also, *esp. Brit.,* **kil′o·gramme′-me′tre.**

kil·o·hertz (kil′ə hûrtz′), *n. Physics.* a unit of frequency, equal to 1000 cycles per second. *Abbr.:* kHz [KILO- + HERTZ]

kil·ohm (kil′ōm′), *n. Elect.* a unit of resistance, equal to 1000 ohms. *Abbr.:* kΩ [KIL(O)- + OHM]

kil·o·joule (kil′ə jo͞ol′, -joul′), *n. Physics.* a unit of work or of energy, equal to 1000 joules. *Abbr.:* kJ, kj [KILO- + JOULE]

kil·o·line (kil′ə līn′), *n. Elect.* a unit of magnetic flux, equal to 1000 maxwells. [KILO- + LINE[1]]

kil·o·li·ter (kil′ə lē′tər), *n. Metric System.* one thousand liters; a cubic meter. Also, *esp. Brit.,* **kil′o·li′tre.** [< F *kilolitre.* See KILO-, LITER]

kil·o·lu·men (kil′ə lo͞o′mən), *n.* a unit of luminous flux, equal to 1000 lumens. [KILO- + LUMEN]

kilom., kilometer; kilometers.

kil·o·meg·a·cy·cle (kil′ə meg′ə sī′kəl), *n.* a unit of frequency, equal to 10^9 cycles per second. *Abbr.:* kMc [KILO- + MEGACYCLE]

kil·o·me·ter (kil′ə mē′tər *or, often,* ki lom′i tər), *n. Metric System.* a unit of length, the common measure of distances equal to 1000 meters, and equivalent to 3280.8 feet or 0.621 mile. *Abbr.:* km, km. Also, *esp. Brit.,* **kil′o·me′tre.** [< F *kilomètre.* See KILO-, METER[1]] —**kil·o·met·ric** (kil′ə me′trik), **kil′o·met′ri·cal,** *adj.*

kil·o·mole (kil′ə mōl′), *n.* one thousand moles. *Abbr.:* kmole [KILO- + MOLE[1]]

kil·o·oer·sted (kil′ō ûr′sted), *n.* a unit of magnetic intensity, equal to 1000 oersteds. *Abbr.:* kOe

kil·o·par·sec (kil′ə pär′sec′), *n.* a unit of distance, equal to 1000 parsecs. *Abbr.:* kpc [KILO- + PARSEC]

kil·o·poise (kil′ə poiz′), *n.* a unit of viscosity, equal to 1000 poises. [KILO- + POISE[2]]

kil·o·pound (kil′ə pound′), *n.* one thousand pounds. [KILO- + POUND[2]]

kil·o·stere (kil′ə stēr′), *n.* one thousand steres. [KILO- + STERE]

kil·o·ton (kil′ə tun′), *n.* **1.** one thousand tons. **2.** an explosive force equal to that of 1000 tons of TNT. [KILO- + TON[1]]

kil·o·var (kil′ə vär′), *n. Elect.* a unit of reactive power, equal to 1000 vars. *Abbr.:* kVAr, kvar [KILO- + VAR]

kil·o·var-hour (kil′ə vär′ our′, -ou′ər), *n. Elect.* a unit of reactive power multiplied by time, equivalent to that transferred or expended in one hour by one kilovar of reactive power.

kil·o·volt (kil′ə vōlt′), *n. Elect.* a unit of electromotive force, equal to 1000 volts. *Abbr.:* kV, kv [KILO- + VOLT[1]]

kil·o·volt-am·pere (kil′ə vōlt′am′pēr), *n.* an electrical unit, equal to 1000 volt-amperes. *Abbr.:* kVA, kva

kil·o·volt-am·pere-hour (kil′ə vōlt′am′pēr our′, -ou′ər), *n.* kilovolt-amperes per hour. *Abbr.:* kVAH, kvah

kil·o·watt (kil′ə wot′), *n. Elect.* a unit of power, equal to 1000 watts. *Abbr.:* kw. [KILO- + WATT]

kil·o·watt-hour (kil′ə wot′our′, -ou′ər), *n. Elect.* a unit of energy, equivalent to the energy transferred or expended in one hour by one kilowatt of power; approximately 1.34 horsepower-hour. *Abbr.:* kWh, kwhr

Kil·pat·rick (kil pa′trik), *n.* **Hugh Jud·son** (jud′sən), 1836–81, Union general in the U.S. Civil War.

Kil·roy (kil′roi′), *n.* **1.** a fictitious American soldier, created by American troops who regularly left the inscription "Kilroy was here" on walls, property, etc., all over the world in the years during and after World War II. **2.** someone who travels a great deal.

kilt (kilt), *n.* **1.** any short, pleated skirt, esp. a tartan wrap-around, as that worn by men in the Scottish Highlands. —*v.t.* **2.** to draw or tuck up, as the skirt, about oneself. **3.** to provide (a skirt) with kilt pleats. [ME *kylte,* ? < Scand; cf. Dan *kilte* to tuck up] —**kilt′like′,** *adj.*

kilt·ed (kil′tid), *adj.* **1.** wearing a kilt. **2.** gathered in pleats; pleated. [KILT + -ED[3]]

kil·ter (kil′tər), *n.* **1.** *Informal.* good condition; order: *The engine was out of kilter.* **2.** *Poker.* skeet[2]. [?]

kilt·ie (kil′tē), *n.* **1.** a person who wears a kilt, esp. a member of a regiment in which the kilt is worn as part of the dress uniform. **2.** a sports shoe having a leather fringed flap that covers the lacing. [KILT + -IE]

kilt·ing (kil′ting), *n.* an arrangement of kilt pleats. [KILT + -ING[1]]

kilt′ pleat′, a large vertical pleat overlapping one adjoining pleat and being overlapped by the other, as on a kilt.

Kil·wich (kil′wiKH), *n. Welsh Legend.* a prince who performed five labors in order to marry Olwen.

Kim (kim), *n.* a boy's or girl's given name.

Kim (kim), *n.* a novel (1901) by Rudyard Kipling.

Kim·ball (kim′bəl), *n.* **1.** a town in W Nebraska. 4384 (1960). **2.** a boy's given name.

Kim·ber·ley (kim′bər lē), *n.* **1.** a city in E Cape of Good Hope province, in the central Republic of South Africa: diamond mines. 77,180 with suburbs (1960). **2.** a boy's or girl's given name.

kim·ber·lite (kim′bər līt′), *n.* a variety of mica peridotite, low in silica content and high in magnesium content, in which diamonds are formed. [named after KIMBERLEY; see -ITE[1]]

Kim·ber·ly (kim′bər lē), *n.* a town in E Wisconsin. 5322 (1960).

kim·chi (kim′chē), *n.* (in Korea) a pickled or fermented mixture, usually of cabbage, onions, and fish variously seasoned, as with garlic, horseradish, red peppers, and ginger. Also, **kim′chee.** [< Korean]

kim·mer (kim′ər), *n. Scot.* cummer.

ki·mo·no (kə mō′nə, -nō), *n., pl.* **-nos.** **1.** a loose, wide-sleeved robe, fastened at the waist with a wide sash, characteristic of Japanese costume. **2.** a woman's loose dressing gown. [< Jap: clothing, garb] —**ki·mo′noed,** *adj.*

kin (kin), *n.* **1.** one's relatives collectively; kinsfolk. **2.** family relationship or kinship. **3.** a group of persons descended from a common ancestor, or constituting a family, clan, tribe, or race. **4.** a relative or kinsman. **5.** someone or something of the same or similar kind: *He was interested in the techniques used by the propagandist and his kin, the ad man. Traditional philosophy and its kin, theology, have come upon hard days.* **6. of kin,** of the same family; related; akin: *Although their surnames are identical they are not of kin.* —*adj.* **7.** of the same family; related; akin. **8.** of the same kind or nature; having affinity. [ME; OE *cynn;* c. OS, OHG *kunni,* Icel *kyn,* Goth *kuni;* akin to L *genus,* Gk *génos,* Skt *jánas.* See GENDER] —**kin′less,** *adj.*

-kin, a diminutive suffix of nouns: *lambkin.* [ME < MD, MLG *-ken;* c. G *-chen*]

Kin·a·ba·lu (kin′ə bə lo͞o′), *n.* a mountain in central Sabah: highest peak on the island of Borneo. 13,455 ft. Also, **Kin′a·bu·lu′.**

kin·aes·the·sia (kin′is thē′zhə), *n.* kinesthesia. Also, **kin′aes·the′sis.** —**kin·aes·thet·ic** (kin′is thet′ik), *adj.*

ki·nase (kī′nās, kin′ās), *n. Biochem.* a substance that causes a zymogen to change into an enzyme. [KIN(ETIC) + -ASE]

Ki·nau (ki nou′), *n.* a walled plain in the fourth quadrant of the face of the moon: about 26 miles in diameter.

Kin·car·dine (kin kär′din), *n.* a county in E Scotland. 48,810 (1961); 379 sq. mi. *Co. seat:* Stonehaven. Also called **Kin·car·dine·shire** (kin kär′din shēr′, -shər).

kin·chin (kin′chin), *n. Slang, Chiefly Brit.* a child. [< G *Kindchen,* dim. of *Kind* child. See KIND[2], -KIN]

Kin·chin·jun·ga (kin′chin jo͝on′gä), *n.* Kanchenjunga.

kind[1] (kīnd), *adj.* **1.** of a good or benevolent nature or disposition, as a person: *a kind old lady.* **2.** having, showing, or proceeding from benevolence: *kind words.* **3.** indulgent, considerate, or helpful (often fol. by *to*): *to be kind to animals.* **4.** mild; gentle; clement: *kind weather.* **5.** *Archaic.* loving. [ME *kind(e)* natural, well-disposed, OE *gecynde* natural. See KIND[2]]

—**Syn. 1.** mild, benign, benignant, humane, gentle, tender, compassionate. KIND, GRACIOUS, KINDHEARTED, KINDLY imply a sympathetic attitude toward others, and a willingness to do good or give pleasure. KIND implies a deep-seated characteristic shown either habitually or on occasion by considerate behavior: *a kind father.* GRACIOUS often refers to kindness from a superior or older person to a subordinate, an inferior, a child, etc.: *a gracious monarch.* KINDHEARTED implies an emotionally sympathetic nature, sometimes easily imposed upon: *a kindhearted old woman.* KINDLY, a mild word, refers usually to general disposition, appearance, manner, etc.: *a kindly face.* —**Ant. 1.** cruel.

kind[2] (kīnd), *n.* **1.** a class or group of individual objects, people, animals, etc., of the same nature or character or classified together because they have traits in common; category: *Our dog is the same kind as theirs. What kind of house do you live in?* **2.** nature or character as determining likeness or difference between things: *These differ in degree rather than in kind.* **3.** a person or thing as being of a particular character or class: *He is a strange kind of hero.* **4.** a more or less adequate or inadequate example of something; sort: *The vines formed a kind of roof.* **5.** *Archaic.* **a.** the nature, or natural disposition or character. **b.** manner; form. **6.** *Obs.* gender; sex. **7. in kind, a.** in something of the same kind or in the same way as that received or borne: *She will be repaid in kind for her rudeness.* **b.** in produce or commodities instead of money: *In colonial times, payment was often made in kind.* **8. kind of,** *Informal.* to some extent; somewhat; rather: *The room was kind of dark.* **9. of a kind,** of the same class, nature, character, etc.: *They are two of a kind.* [ME *kinde,* OE *gecynd* nature, race, origin; c. Icel *kyndi,* OHG *kikunt,* L *gēns, gentis.* See KIN]

—**Syn. 1.** order, genus, species; race, breed; set.

—**Usage 8.** KIND OF and SORT OF are frowned upon by teachers and others who are concerned with careful writing because both phrases characterize a vagueness in thinking and betoken a writer's or speaker's inadequacy in expression. If one wishes to convey uncertainty or vagueness, he is better advised to use RATHER, QUITE, or even the relatively meaningless SOMEWHAT, any of which, before an adjective or adverb, yield the same sense but are less objectionable: *The movie was rather (or quite) good.* (Not, *kind of good.*) *He is feeling somewhat better today.* Before a noun or noun phrase, even SOMETHING LIKE is preferred to KIND OF, SORT OF: *The house is something like a castle,* or *The house resembles a castle.* (Not, *kind of* or *sort of like a castle.*)

kin·der·gar·ten (kin′dər gär′tən, -dən), *n.* a school for furthering the intellectual, physical, and social development of young children, usually five-year-olds, by means of games, creative activities, nature study, etc. [< G: lit., children's garden, equiv. to *Kinder* children (see KIND[2]) + *Garten* GARDEN]

kin·der·gart·ner (kin′dər gärt′nər, -gärd′-), *n.* **1.** a child who attends a kindergarten. **2.** a kindergarten teacher. Also, **kin′der·gar′ten·er.** [< G *Kindergärtner.* See KINDERGARTEN, -ER[1]]

Kind·er·tot·en·lied·er (*Ger.* kin′dər tōt′ən lē′dər), *n.* a song cycle (1902), by Gustav Mahler, consisting of five songs set to poems by Friedrich Rückert.

kind·heart·ed (kīnd′här′tid), *adj.* having or showing kindness: *a kindhearted, motherly woman.* [KIND[1] + HEARTED] —**kind′heart′ed·ly,** *adv.* —**kind′heart′ed·ness,** *n.*

—**Syn.** See **kind**[1].

kind·jal (kind′jäl), *n.* a double-edged knife of the Caucasus, having a broad blade with edges parallel for most of their length, terminating in a long, sharp point. [< South Caucasian]

kin·dle[1] (kin′dəl), *v.,* **-dled, -dling.** —*v.t.* **1.** to start (a fire); cause (a flame, blaze, etc.) to spring up. **2.** to set fire to or ignite (fuel or any combustible matter). **3.** to excite; stir up or set going; animate, rouse, or inflame: *He kindled their hopes of victory.* **4.** to light up, illuminate, or make bright: *The moon kindled the countryside. Happiness kindled her eyes.* —*v.i.* **5.** to begin to burn, as combustible matter, a light, fire, or flame. **6.** to become roused, ardent, or inflamed. **7.** to become lighted up, bright, or glowing, as the sky at dawn or the eyes with ardor. [ME *kindle(n)* < Scand; cf. OSw *quindla* to set fire to, Icel *kynda* to kindle] —**kin′dler,** *n.*

—**Syn. 1–3.** fire, light. KINDLE, IGNITE, INFLAME imply setting something on fire. To KINDLE is especially to cause something gradually to begin burning; it is often used figuratively: *to kindle someone's interest.* To IGNITE is to set something on fire with a sudden burst of flame: *to ignite dangerous hatreds.* INFLAME, a literary word meaning to set aflame, is now found chiefly in figurative uses, as referring to unnaturally hot, sore, or swollen conditions in the body, or to exciting the mind by strong emotion: *The wound was greatly inflamed.* **3.** arouse, awaken, bestir, incite, stimulate.

kin·dle[2] (kin′dəl), *v.,* **-dled, -dling,** *n.* —*v.t.* **1.** (of animals, esp. rabbits) to bear (young); produce (offspring). —*v.i.* **2.** (of animals, esp. rabbits) to give birth, as to a litter. —*n.* **3.** a litter of kittens, rabbits, etc. [ME, v. use of *kindle* young, offspring, equiv. to *kind-* (OE *gecynd* offspring; see KIND[2]) + *-le* -LE]

kind·less (kīnd′lis), *adj.* **1.** lacking kindness; unkind. **2.** *Obs.* unnatural; inhuman. [ME; see KIND[1], -LESS] —**kind′less·ly,** *adv.*

kind·li·ness (kīnd′lē nis), *n.* **1.** the state or quality of being kindly; benevolence. **2.** a kindly deed. [late ME; see KINDLY, -NESS]

kin·dling (kind′ling), *n.* **1.** material that can be readily ignited, used in starting a fire. **2.** the act of one who kindles. [ME; see KINDLE[1], -ING[1]]

kind·ly (kīnd′lē), *adj.,* **-li·er, -li·est,** *adv.* —*adj.* **1.** having, showing, or proceeding from a benevolent disposition or spirit; kindhearted; good-natured; sympathetic: *kindly people.* **2.** gentle or mild, as rule or laws. **3.** pleasant, agreeable, or benign: *a kindly climate.* **4.** favorable, as soil for crops. —*adv.* **5.** in a kind manner; with sympathetic or helpful kindness. **6.** cordially or heartily: *We thank you kindly.* **7.** with liking; favorably: *to take kindly to an idea.* **8.** obligingly; please: *Would you kindly close the door?* [ME *kyndly,* OE *(ge)cyndelic* natural. See KIND[1], -LY]

—**Syn. 1.** See **kind**[1].

kind·ness (kīnd′nis), *n.* **1.** the state or quality of being kind: *kindness to animals.* **2.** a kind act: *his many kindnesses to me.* **3.** kind behavior: *I will never forget your kindness.* **4.** friendly feeling; liking. [ME *kindenes.* See KIND[1], -NESS]

—**Syn. 1, 3.** benignity, benevolence, beneficence, humanity, generosity, charity, sympathy, compassion, tenderness. **2.** good turn. —**Ant. 1.** malevolence. **3.** cruelty.

kin·dred (kin′drid), *n.* **1.** a body of persons related to another; family, tribe, or race. **2.** one's relatives collectively; kinfolk; kin. **3.** relationship by birth or descent, or sometimes by marriage; kinship. **4.** natural relationship; affinity. —*adj.* **5.** associated by origin, nature, qualities, etc.: *kindred languages.* **6.** having the same belief, attitude, or feeling: *We are kindred spirits on that subject.* **7.** related by birth or descent; having kinship: *kindred tribes.* **8.** belonging to kin or relatives: *kindred blood.* [ME, var. (with epenthetic *d*) of *kinred-(en).* See KIN, -RED] —**kin′dred·less,** *adj.* —**kin′dred·ly,** *adv.* —**kin′dred·ness,** *n.* —**kin′dred·ship′,** *n.*

Kin·du (kin′do͞o), *n.* a city in the E Republic of the Congo. 14,200 (est. 1954).

kine[1] (kīn), *n. Archaic.* pl. of **cow**[1]. [ME *kyn,* OE *cȳ* (nom., acc.), *cȳna* (gen.), pl. forms of *cū* cow[1]]

kin·e[2] (kin′ē), *n.* kinescope (def. 1). [shortened form]

kin·e·ma (kin′ə mə), *n. Brit.* cinema.

kin′emat′ic pair′, *Mech.* pair (def. 10).

kin·e·mat·ics (kin′ə mat′iks, kī′nə-), *n.* (*construed as sing.*) **1.** the branch of mechanics that deals with pure motion, without reference to the masses or forces involved in it. **2.** Also called **applied kinematics.** the theory of mechanical contrivance for converting one kind of motion into another. [< Gk *kīnēmat-* (s. of *kīnēma* movement; see CINEMA) + -ICS] —**kin′e·mat′ic, kin′e·mat′i·cal,** *adj.* —**kin′e·mat′i·cal·ly,** *adv.*

kinemat′ic viscos′ity, *Physics.* the coefficient of viscosity of a fluid divided by the density, usually measured in stokes.

kin·e·mat·o·graph (kin′ə mat′ə graf′, -gräf′), *n.* cinematograph. —**kin·e·ma·tog·ra·pher** (kin′ə mə tog′rə fər), *n.* —**kin·e·mat·o·graph·ic** (kin′ə mat′ə graf′ik), **kin′e·mat′o·graph′i·cal,** *adj.* —**kin′e·mat′o·graph′i·cal·ly,** *adv.* —**kin′e·ma·tog′ra·phy,** *n.*

kin·e·scope (kin′i skōp′), *n., v.,* **-scoped, -scop·ing.** *Television.* —*n.* **1.** Also, **kine.** (*cap.*) *Trademark.* a cathode ray tube with a fluorescent screen on which an image is reproduced by a directed beam of electrons. **2.** the recording of a television program on motion picture film for later broadcasting. —*v.t.* **3.** to record (a program) on motion picture film for later broadcasting.

ki·ne·sics (ki nē′siks, kī-), *n.* (*construed as sing.*) the study of body motion as related to speech. [< Gk *kīnēs(is)* (see KINESIOLOGY) + -ICS] —**ki·ne′sic,** *adj.* —**ki·ne′si·cal·ly,** *adv.*

ki·ne·si·ol·o·gy (ki nē′sē ol′ə jē, -zē-, kī-), *n.* the science dealing with the interrelationship of the physiological processes and anatomy of the human body with respect to movement. [< Gk *kīnēsi(s)* movement (*kīnē-,* verbid s. of *kīnein* to move + *-sis* -SIS) + -O- + -LOGY]

kin·es·the·sia (kin′is thē′zhə), *n.* the sensation of movement or strain in muscles, tendons, and joints; muscle sense. Also, **kinaesthesia, kin′es·the′sis.** [< Gk *kin(eîn)* (to) move, set in motion + ESTHESIA] —**kin·es·thet·ic** (kin′is thet′ik), *adj.*

ki·net·ic (ki net′ik, kī-), *adj.* **1.** pertaining to motion. **2.** caused by motion: *kinetic energy.* **3.** characterized by movement: *Dance is a kinetic art. The mobile is a form of kinetic sculpture.* [< Gk *kīnētik(ós)* moving, equiv. to *kīnē-* (verbid s. of *kīnein* to move) + *-tikos* -TIC] —**ki·net′i·cal·ly,** *adv.*

kinet′ic en′ergy, *Physics.* the energy of a body or a system with respect to the motion of the body or of the particles in the system. Cf. **potential energy.**

kinet′ic poten′tial, *Physics.* the kinetic energy minus the potential energy in a system obeying the principle of conservation of energy. *Symbol:* L Also called **Lagrangian function.**

ki·net·ics (ki net′iks, kī-), *n.* (*construed as sing.*) the branch of mechanics that deals with the actions of forces in producing or changing the motion of masses. [see KINETIC, -ICS]

kinet′ic the′ory of gas′es, *Physics.* a theory that the particles in a gas move freely and rapidly along straight lines but often collide, resulting in variations in their velocity and direction. Pressure is interpreted as arising from the impacts of these particles with the walls of a container. Other macroscopic variables are similarly treated.

kinet′ic the′ory of heat′, *Physics.* a theory that the temperature of a body is determined by the average kinetic energy of its particles and that an inflow of heat increases this energy.

kinet′ic the′ory of mat′ter, *Physics.* a theory that matter is composed of small particles, all in random motion.

ki·ne·to·graph (ki nē′tə graf′, -gräf′), *n.* a camera for taking pictures for a kinetoscope. [< Gk *kīnētó(s)* movable (*kīnē-*, verbid s. of *kīneîn* to move + *-tos* adj. suffix) + -GRAPH] —**ki·ne·tog·ra·pher** (kin′i tog′rə fər), *n.* —**ki·ne·to·graph·ic** (ki nē′tə graf′ik), *adj.* —**kin′e·tog′ra·phy,** *n.*

ki·ne·to·scope (ki nē′tə skōp′), *n.* an early motion-picture device, invented by Edison, in which the film passed beneath a peephole and was seen by a single viewer. [*kineto-* (see KINETOGRAPH) + -SCOPE] —**ki·ne·to·scop·ic** (ki nē′tə skop′ik), *adj.*

kin·e·to·sis (kin′i tō′sis, kī′nə-), *n.* *Pathol.* any condition caused by motion of the body, as seasickness. [< Gk *kīnēt(ós)* movable (see KINETOGRAPH) + -OSIS]

kin·folk (kin′fōk′), *n.pl.* relatives or kindred. Also, **kin′folks′, kinsfolk.** [KIN + FOLK]

king (king), *n.* **1.** a male sovereign or monarch; a man who holds by life tenure, and usually by hereditary right, the chief authority over a country and people. **2.** (*cap.*) God or Christ: *King of kings; King of Heaven.* **3.** a person or thing preeminent in its class: *He was an oil king. The lion is the king of the beasts.* **4.** a playing card bearing a picture of a king. **5.** *Chess.* the chief piece of each color in the game of chess, moved one square at a time in any direction. **6.** *Checkers.* a man that has been moved entirely across the board and has been crowned, thus allowing it to be moved in any direction. **7.** *Entomol.* a fertile male termite. **8.** a word formerly used in communications to represent the letter K. —*v.t.* **9.** to make a king of; cause to be or become a king. —*v.i.* **10.** to reign as king. **11.** to play the king; behave in an imperious or pretentious manner (usually fol. by *it*): *He kinged it over all the other kids on the block.* [ME, OE *cyng, cyni(n)g*; c. G *König*, D *koning*, Icel *konungr*, Sw *konung*, Dan *konge*. See KIN, -ING[1]] —**king′less,** *adj.* —**king′less·ness,** *n.* —**king′like′,** *adj.*

King (king), *n.* **1. Ernest Joseph,** 1878–1956, U.S. naval officer. **2. Martin Luther,** 1929–68, U.S. Baptist minister: civil-rights leader; Nobel peace prize 1964. **3. Rufus,** 1755–1827, U.S. political leader and statesman. **4. William Lyon Mackenzie,** 1874–1950, Canadian statesman: prime minister 1921–26, 1926–30, 1935–48. **5. William Rufus De·Vane** (də vān′), 1786–1853, vice-president of the U.S. 1853.

king·bird (king′bûrd′), *n.* any of several American tyrant flycatchers of the genus *Tyrannus*, esp. *T. tyrannus* **(eastern kingbird),** of North America, having grayish-black plumage with a white-tipped tail. [KING + BIRD]

king·bolt (king′bōlt′), *n.* **1.** a vertical bolt connecting the body of a horse-drawn vehicle with the fore axle, the body of a railroad car with a truck, etc. **2.** (in a roof truss) an iron or steel rod serving as a king post. Also called **king rod.** [KING + BOLT[1]]

king′ bridge′, *Naut.* a truss connecting two king posts or the uprights of a goal post mast.

King′ Charles′ span′iel, a variety of the English toy spaniel having a black-and-tan coat. [after *Charles* II of England from his liking for this variety]

King·chow (ging′jō′), *n.* former name of **Kiangling.**

King′ Cit′y, a town in W California. 2937 (1960).

king′ clos′er, *Masonry.* **1.** a brick of regular length and thickness, used in building corners, having a long bevel from a point on one side to one about halfway across the adjacent end. **2.** a brick of three-quarter length for finishing a course at the end. Also, **king′ clo′sure.**

king′ co′bra, a cobra, *Naja* (*Ophiophagus*) *hannah*, of southeastern Asia and the East Indies, that grows to a length of more than 15 feet: the largest of the venomous snakes. Also called **hamadryad.**

king′ crab′, 1. See **horseshoe crab. 2.** Also called **Alaskan crab.** a large, edible crab, *Paralithodes camtschatica*, found in the North Pacific, esp. along the coasts of Alaska and Japan.

king·craft (king′kraft′, -kräft′), *n.* the art of ruling as king; royal statesmanship. [KING + CRAFT]

king·cup (king′kup′), *n.* **1.** any of various common buttercups, as *Ranunculus bulbosus.* **2.** *Chiefly Brit.* the marsh marigold. [KING + CUP]

king′ dev′il, any of several European hawkweeds introduced into northeastern North America, where they are troublesome weeds.

king·dom (king′dəm), *n.* **1.** a state or government having a king or queen as its head. **2.** anything conceived as constituting a realm or sphere of independent action or control: *the kingdom of thought.* **3.** a realm or province of nature, esp. one of the three great divisions of natural objects: *the animal, vegetable, and mineral kingdoms.* **4.** the spiritual sovereignty of God or Christ. **5.** the domain over which this extends, whether in heaven or on earth. [ME; OE *cyningdōm.* See KING, -DOM] —**king′dom·less,** *adj.*

—**Syn. 1.** KINGDOM, MONARCHY, REALM refer to the state or domain ruled by a king or queen. A KINGDOM is a governmental unit ruled by a king or queen: *the kingdom of Norway.* A MONARCHY is primarily a form of government in which a single person is sovereign; it is also the type of power exercised by the monarch: *This kingdom is not an absolute monarchy.* A REALM is the domain, including the subjects, over which the king has jurisdiction; figuratively, a sphere of power or influence: *the laws of the realm.* **2.** dominion, empire, domain.

king′dom come′, the next world; the condition or state of having died. [abstracted from the phrase *Thy kingdom come* in the Lord's Prayer]

King′dom Hall′, any meeting place of Jehovah's Witnesses for religious services.

king′dom of ends′, (in Kantian ethics) a metaphorical realm to which belong those persons acting and being acted upon in accordance with moral law.

king·fish (king′fish′), *n., pl.* (*esp. collectively*) **-fish,** (*esp. referring to two or more kinds or species*) **-fish·es. 1.** any of several marine food fishes of the drum family, esp. of the genus *Menticirrhus*, found in the eastern U.S. **2.** a marine food fish, *Genyonemus lineatus*, found off the Californian coast. **3.** See **king mackerel. 4.** a large game fish, *Seriola grandis*, found in Australia and New Zealand, closely related to the yellowtail. **5.** any of various other fishes noted esp. for their size. [KING + FISH]

Belted kingfisher, *Megaceryle alcyon* (Length 13 in.)

king·fish·er (king′fish′ər), *n.* any of numerous fish- or insect-eating birds of the family *Alcedinidae* that have a large head and a long, stout bill and are usually crested and brilliantly colored. [KING + FISHER; r. *king's fisher*, late ME *kynggs fischare*]

King·fish·er (king′fish′ər), *n.* a town in central Oklahoma. 3249 (1960).

king′fisher dai′sy, a tender, annual shrub, *Felicia bergeriana*, of South Africa, having grasslike leaves and solitary, bright-blue flowers.

King′ George′s War′, a war (1744–48) waged by England and its colonies against France, constituting the North American phase of the War of the Austrian Succession.

king·hood (king′ho͝od), *n.* the state of being king; kingship. [ME *kinghod.* See KING, -HOOD]

King′ Horn′, the earliest extant verse romance (late 13th century) in the English language.

King′ James′ Ver′sion. See **Authorized Version.** Also called **King′ James′′ Bi′ble.**

King′ John′, a drama (1596–97?) by Shakespeare.

King·lake (king′lāk′), *n.* **Alexander William,** 1809–91, English historian.

King′ Lear′ (lēr), a tragedy (1606) by Shakespeare.

king·less (king′lis), *adj.* without a king. [ME; see KING, -LESS]

king·let (king′lit), *n.* **1.** a king ruling over a small country or territory. **2.** any of several small, greenish, crested birds of the genus *Regulus.* Cf. **goldcrest, golden-crowned kinglet, ruby-crowned kinglet.** [KING + -LET]

king·ly (king′lē), *adj.,* **-li·er, -li·est,** *adv.* —*adj.* **1.** having the rank of king. **2.** consisting of kings or of royal rank: *a guest list of kingly personages.* **3.** stately or splendid, as resembling, suggesting, or befitting a king; regal: *He strode into the room with a kingly air.* **4.** pertaining or proper to a king or kings: *kingly power.* —*adv.* **5.** in the manner of a king; regally. [ME; see KING, -LY] —**king′li·ness,** *n.*

—**Syn. 3, 4.** princely, sovereign, majestic, august, magnificent, exalted, grand. KINGLY, REGAL, ROYAL refer to that which is closely associated with a king, or is suitable for one. What is KINGLY may either belong to a king, or be befitting, worthy of, or like a king: *a kingly presence, appearance, graciousness.* REGAL is especially applied to the office of kingship or the outward manifestations of grandeur and majesty: *regal authority, bearing, splendor, munificence.* ROYAL is applied especially to what pertains to or is associated with the person of a monarch: *the royal family, word, robes, salute; a royal residence.* —**Ant. 3, 4.** lowly.

king′ mack′erel, a game fish, *Scomberomorus cavalla*, found in the western Atlantic Ocean.

king·mak·er (king′mā′kər), *n.* a person who has sufficient power and influence to choose a ruler or a candidate for public office. [KING + MAKER] —**king′mak′ing,** *n., adj.*

King·man (king′mən), *n.* **1.** a town in W Arizona. 4525 (1960). **2.** a town in S Kansas. 3582 (1960).

king-of-arms (king′əv ärmz′), *n., pl.* **kings-of-arms.** a title of certain of the principal heralds of England and certain other kingdoms empowered by their sovereigns to grant armorial bearings. [late ME *king of armes.* See KING, ARM[2]]

king′ of beasts′, the lion.

king′ of kings′, a king having other kings subject to him.

King′ of kings′, 1. Christ; Jesus. **2.** God; Jehovah. Also, **King′ of Kings′.**

king′ of the for′est, the oak tree.

king-of-the-her·rings (king′əv thə her′ingz), *n., pl.* **king-of-the-herrings.** oarfish.

king′ of the hill′, a game in which each person attempts to climb to the top of some point, as a mound of earth, and to prevent all others from pushing or pulling him off the top. Also called **king′ of the moun′tain.**

king-of-the-salm·on (king′əv thə sam′ən), *n., pl.* **king-of-the-salm·on.** a ribbonfish, *Trachypterus trachypterus*, found in northern parts of the Pacific Ocean.

king′ pen′guin, a large penguin, *Aptenodytes patagonicus*, found on islands bordering the Antarctic Circle.

King′ Phil′ip's War′, the war (1675–76) between New England colonists and a confederation of Indians under their leader, King Philip.

king·pin (king′pin′), *n.* **1.** *Bowling.* **a.** See **headpin. b.** the pin at the center; the number five pin. **2.** *Informal.* the person of chief importance in a corporation, undertaking, etc. **3.** *Informal.* the chief element of any system or the like. **4.** a kingbolt. [KING + PIN]

king′ plank′, *Shipbuilding.* a plank running along the center line of a deck, into which all other planks are fitted.

King post
A, King post; B, Tie beam; C, Strut; D, Principal rafter; E, Purlin; F, Common rafter

king′ post′, 1. a vertical suspension member depending from the apex of a triangular roof truss to support the feet of struts or the middle of a tie beam or rod. **2.** *Mach.* a rotating or stationary column for supporting the tackle or booms used in lifting. Also, **king′post′, king′-post′.**

king′ rail′, a large, long-billed rail, *Rallus elegans*, of North America, having reddish-brown plumage.

king′ rod′, kingbolt.

Kings (kingz), *n.* (*construed as sing.*) **1.** either of two books of the Bible, I Kings or II Kings, which contain the history of the kings of Israel and Judah. **2.** *Douay Bible.* one of the four books of the Old Testament, I, II, III, or IV Kings, corresponding to I and II Samuel and I and II Kings in the Authorized Version.

king′ salm′on. See **chinook salmon.**

King's′ Bench′, *Brit. Law.* a court, originally the principal court for criminal cases, gradually acquiring a civil jurisdiction concurrent with that of the Court of Common Pleas, and also possessing appellate jurisdiction over the Court of Common Pleas. Also called, *when a queen is sovereign,* **Queen's Bench.**

King's′ Birth′day, an imperial holiday in Britain and most of the Commonwealth countries, celebrating the birthday of a reigning monarch, on either the birth date or an arbitrary date chosen by the monarch. Also called, *when a queen is sovereign,* **Queen's Birthday.**

king's′ boun′ty, *Brit.* a grant, given in the royal name, to a mother of triplets. Also, **King's′ boun′ty, King's′ Boun′ty.** Also called, *when a queen is sovereign,* **queen's bounty.**

Kings·burg (kingz′bûrg), *n.* a town in central California. 3093 (1960).

Kings′ Can′yon Na′tional Park′, a national park in E California: deep granite gorges; giant sequoias; mountains. 708 sq. mi.

King's′ Cham′pion. See under **Champion of England.**

King's′ clo′ver. See **yellow melilot.**

king's′ col′our, *Brit.* **1.** a white ceremonial ensign with a royal cipher, flown on special occasions by the Royal Navy. **2.** the union jack as an emblem on the regimental colors of a British military unit. **3. king's colours,** a pair of silk flags with the royal cipher, announcing the monarch's presence. Also, **King's′ col′our, King's′ Col′our.** Also called, *when a queen is sovereign,* **queen's colour.**

king's′ Coun′sel, *Brit. Law.* **1.** a body of barristers of a higher status who are specially appointed to be the Crown's counsel, and who are permitted to plead inside the bar in the court. **2.** a member of this body of barristers. **3.** an honorary title conferred on a successful barrister when the sovereign is a king, originally for services in representing the crown but now as a mark of professional distinction. Also called, *when a queen is sovereign,* **queen's Counsel.**

king's′ Eng′lish, educated or correct English speech or usage, esp. of England. Also called, *when a queen is sovereign,* **queen's English.**

king's′ ev′idence, *Brit. Law.* evidence for the crown given by an accused person against his alleged accomplices. Also called, *when a queen is sovereign,* **queen's evidence.** Cf. **state's evidence.**

king's′ e′vil, scrofula: so called because it was supposed to be curable by the touch of the reigning sovereign. [ME *kynges evel*]

Kings·ford (kingz′fərd), *n.* a town in NW Michigan, in the Upper Peninsula. 5084 (1960).

king's′ high′way, *Brit.* a highway built by the national government. Also, **King's′ high′way, King's′ High′way.**

king·ship (king′ship), *n.* **1.** the state, office, or dignity of a king. **2.** rule by a king; monarchy. **3.** aptitude for kingly duties. **4.** (*cap.*) a title used in referring to a king; Majesty (prec. by *his* or *your*). [ME *kingscip.* See KING, -SHIP]

king-size (king′sīz′), *adj.* larger than the usual size. Also, **king′-sized′.**

Kings·ley (kingz′lē), *n.* **1. Charles,** 1819–75, English clergyman, novelist, and poet. **2. Sidney,** born 1906, U.S. playwright. **3.** a boy's given name.

King's′ mark′, one of the marks composing a hallmark, consisting of the head of a leopard, formerly a crowned head.

Kings′ Moun′tain, 1. a ridge in N South Carolina: American victory over the British 1780. **2.** a town in SW North Carolina. 8008 (1960).

king·snake (king′snāk′), *n.* any of several New World constrictors of the genus *Lampropeltis*, that often feed on other snakes. Also, **king′ snake′.** [KING + SNAKE]

Kings′ Park′, a town in NW Long Island, in SE New York. 4949 (1960).

king's′ pat′tern, a spoon pattern of the 19th century having a stem decorated with threads, scrolls, and shell motifs.

king's′-pawn o′penings (kingz′pôn′), (*construed as sing.*) a class of chess openings in which the pawn in front of the king is advanced two squares on the first move.

Kings′ Point′, a town on NW Long Island, in SE New York. 5410 (1960).

Kings·port (kingz′pōrt′, -pôrt′), *n.* a city in NE Tennessee. 26,314 (1960).

King's′ Proc′tor, a British judiciary officer who may intervene in probate, nullity, or divorce actions when collusion, suppression of evidence, or other irregularities are alleged. Also called, *when a queen is sovereign,* **Queen's Proctor.**

king's′ ran′som, an extremely large amount of money: *The painting was sold for a king's ransom.*

King's′ Remem′brancer, (in Great Britain) a judiciary official who collects debts owed to the king. Also called, *when a queen is sovereign,* **Queen's Remembrancer.**

king's′ scout′, (in Great Britain) a boy scout who has achieved the highest level of scouting: similar to the U.S. eagle scout. Also called, *when a queen is sovereign,* **queen's scout.**

king's′ shil′ling, (until 1879) a shilling given a recruit in the British army to bind his enlistment contract. Also called, *when a queen is sovereign,* **queen's shilling.**

King's′ speech′, (in the British parliament) a speech reviewing domestic conditions and foreign relations, prepared by the ministry in the name of the sovereign, and read at the opening of the Parliament either by the sovereign in person or by commission. Also called, *when a queen is sovereign,* **Queen's speech.**

Kings·ton (kingz′tən, king′stən), *n.* **1.** a seaport in and the capital of Jamaica. 376,520 (1960). **2.** a port in SE Ontario, in SE Canada, on Lake Ontario: Royal Military College of Canada. 53,526 (1961). **3.** a city in

SE New York, on the Hudson River. 29,260 (1960). **4.** a borough in E Pennsylvania, on the Susquehanna River opposite Wilkes-Barre. 61,055 (1960). **5.** a town in S Rhode Island. 2616 (1960).

Kings·ton-up·on-Hull (kiŋz′tən ə pon′hul′, kiŋ′stən-), *n.* official name of **Hull.**

Kings·tree (kiŋz′trē′), *n.* a town in central South Carolina. 3847 (1960).

Kings·ville (kiŋz′vil), *n.* a city in S Texas. 25,297 (1960).

king's′ weath′er, *Brit. Informal.* fine weather; weather fit for a king.

King·teh·chen (giŋ′du′jen′), *n.* former name of **Fowliang.**

king′ truss′, *Building Trades.* a truss having a king post.

Kin·gu (kin′go͞o), *n.* (in Akkadian myth) a son of Apsu and Tiamat whose blood Ea and Marduk used in creating mankind.

king′ vul′ture, a large, black and white vulture, *Sarcorhamphus papa,* of Central and South America, having colorful wattles and wartlike protuberances on its head and neck.

king·whit·ing (kiŋ′hwī′tiŋ, -wī′-), *n., pl.* **-ings,** (*esp. collectively*) **-ing.** See **northern kingfish.**

King′ Wil′liam's War′, the war (1689–97) in which England and its American colonies and Indian allies opposed France and its Indian allies and which constituted the American phase of the War of the Grand Alliance.

king·wood (kiŋ′wo͝od′), *n.* **1.** a Brazilian wood streaked with violet tints, used esp. in cabinetwork. **2.** the tree, *Dalbergia cearensis,* which yields it. [KING + WOOD¹]

King·wood (kiŋ′wo͝od′), *n.* a town in N West Virginia. 2530 (1960).

kink (kiŋk), *n.* **1.** a twist or curl, as in a thread, rope, or hair, caused by its doubling or bending upon itself. **2.** a muscular stiffness or soreness, as in the neck or back. **3.** a flaw or imperfection likely to hinder the successful operation of something, as a machine, plan, etc.: *There are still a few kinks to be worked out of the plan before we start production.* **4.** a mental twist; notion; whim or crotchet. —*v.t., v.i.* **5.** to form, or cause to form, a kink or kinks, as a rope. [< D: a twist in a rope; cf. Icel *kinka* to nod, *kikna* to bend the knee]

Kin·kaid (kin kād′), *n.* **Thomas Cas·sin** (kas′in), born 1888, U.S. admiral.

Kinkaid′ Act′, *U.S. Hist.* an act of Congress (1904) providing for the granting of 640-acre homesteads to settlers in western Nebraska. [named after Moses *Kinkaid* (1854–1922), American Congressman]

Kin·kaid·er (kin kā′dər), *n.* *U.S. Hist.* a person who received free land under the provisions of the Kinkaid Act. [KINKAID (ACT) + -ER¹]

kin·ka·jou (kiŋ′kə jo͞o′), *n.* a brownish, arboreal mammal, *Potos flavus,* of Central and South America, having a prehensile tail, related to the raccoon and coati. [< F *quincajou* < Sp *quincajú* < Pg *kinkaju* < Tupi]

Kinkajou (Length 3 ft.)

kin·kle (kiŋ′kəl), *n.* a little kink. [KINK + -LE] —**kin′kled, kink′ly,** *adj.*

kink·y (kiŋ′kē), *adj.,* **kink·i·er, kink·i·est. 1.** full of kinks; closely twisted: *a kinky rope.* **2.** (of hair) closely or tightly curled. [KINK + -Y¹] —**kink′i·ly,** *adv.* —**kink′i·ness,** *n.*

kin·less (kin′lis), *adj.* without kin; having no relatives.

Kin·loch (kin′lok), *n.* a town in E Missouri. 6501 (1960).

Kin·ne·lon (ken′ᵊlən, kin′-), *n.* a town in N New Jersey. 4431 (1960).

kin·ni·kin·nick (kin′ə kə nik′), *n.* **1.** a mixture of bark, dried leaves, and sometimes tobacco, formerly smoked by the Indians and pioneers in the Ohio valley. **2.** any of various plants used in this mixture, as the bearberry, *Arctostaphylos Uva-ursi,* or the silky cornel, *Cornus Amomum.* Also, **kin′ni·kin·nic′, kin′ni·ki·nick′, kin′ni·ki·nic′, kin′ni·kin·nik′, killickinnic.** [< Algonquian (Ojibwa): lit., that which is mixed]

ki·no (kē′nō), *n., pl.* **-nos.** (in Europe) a motion picture theater; cinema. [< G (by shortening) *Kinematograph* < F *cinématographe* CINEMATOGRAPH]

ki′no gum′ (kē′nō), the reddish or black, catechulike inspissated juice or gum of certain tropical trees, esp. that from *Pterocarpus Marsupium,* a tall, fabaceous tree of India and Ceylon, used in medicine, tanning, etc. [appar. var. of Mandingo *keno* kind of gum]

ki·noo (ki no͞o′), *n., pl.* **-noos.** *Naut.* cunner².

Kin·ross (kin rôs′, -ros′), *n.* a county in E Scotland. 6704 (1961); 82 sq. mi. *Co. seat:* Kinross. Also called **Kinross-shire** (kin rôs′shēr, -shər, -ros′-).

Kin·sey (kin′zē), *n.* **Alfred Charles,** 1894–1956, U.S. zoologist and biologist.

kins·folk (kinz′fōk′), *n.pl.* kinfolk. [late ME *kynsefolk* (see KIN, FOLK), modeled on *kinsman*]

Kin·sha·sa (kin′shä sä), *n.* a port in and capital of the Democratic Republic of the Congo, in the NW part, on the Congo River. 402,492 (est. 1959). Formerly, **Léopoldville.**

kin·ship (kin′ship), *n.* **1.** the state or fact of being of kin; family relationship. **2.** relationship by nature, qualities, etc.; affinity. [KIN + -SHIP] —**Syn. 1.** See **relationship. 1, 2.** connection. **2.** bearing.

kins·man (kinz′mən), *n., pl.* **-men. 1.** a blood relative, esp. a male. **2.** a relative by marriage. **3.** a person of the same race. [early ME *cunnes man, kynnes man.* See KIN, 's¹, MAN¹]

Kin·ston (kin′stən), *n.* a city in E North Carolina. 24,819 (1960).

kins·wom·an (kinz′wo͝om′ən), *n., pl.* **-wom·en.** a female relative. [ME; see KIN, 's¹, WOMAN, modeled on *kinsman*]

Kio·ga (kyō′gə), *n.* **Lake.** See **Kyoga, Lake.**

ki·o·nec·to·my (kī′ə nek′tə mē), *n., pl.* **-mies.** *Surg.* uvulectomy. [< Gk *kīōn* uvula + -ECTOMY]

ki·o·not·o·my (kī′ə not′ə mē), *n., pl.* **-mies.** *Surg.* uvulotomy. [< Gk *kīōn* uvula + -o- + -TOMY]

ki·osk (kē osk′, kī′osk), *n.* **1.** a kind of open pavilion or summerhouse common in Turkey and Iran. **2.** a similar structure used as a bandstand, as a newsstand, etc. [< F *kiosque* stand in a public park < Turk *kösk* (palatal *k*) villa < Pers *kūshk* garden pavilion]

Kio·to (kē ō′tō; *Jap.* kyô′tô), *n.* Kyoto.

ki·ot·o·my (kī ot′ə mē), *n., pl.* **-mies.** *Surg.* uvulotomy. [syncopated var. of KIONOTOMY]

Ki·o·wa (kī′ə wə), *n., pl.* **-was,** (*esp. collectively*) **-wa. 1.** a member of a Plains Indian people of the southwestern U.S. **2.** a Uto-Aztecan language that is most closely related to Tanoan and is the language of the Kiowa people.

kip¹ (kip), *n.* **1.** the hide of a young or small beast. **2.** a bundle or set of such hides. [ME *kipp* < MD, MLG *kip* pack (of hides); akin to Icel *kippa* bundle]

kip² (kip), *n.* a unit of weight equal to 1000 pounds. [KI(LO) + P(OUND)²]

kip³ (kip), *n.* a paper money and monetary unit of Laos, equal to 100 at, and equivalent to about .0126 of a U.S. dollar. *Abbr.:* K. [< Thai]

kip-ft, one thousand foot-pounds.

Kip·ling (kip′liŋ), *n.* **(Joseph) Rud·yard** (rud′yərd), 1865–1936, English author: Nobel prize 1907.

Kip·nis (kip′nis; *Russ.* kip nēs′), *n.* **Al·ex·an·der** (al′ig zan′dər; *Russ.* ä′le ksän′dər), born 1891, Russian singer in the U.S.

kip·pen (kip′in), *v.* *Brit.* a pp. of **kep.**

kip·per (kip′ər), *n.* **1.** a kippered fish, esp. a herring. **2.** a method of curing fish by splitting, salting, drying, and smoking. **3.** *Australian Informal.* a young, male aborigine, usually 14 to 16 years old, who has recently undergone his tribal initiation rite. —*v.t.* **4.** to cure (herring, salmon, etc.) by cleaning, salting, etc., and drying in the air or in smoke. [ME *kypre,* OE *cypera* spawning salmon, appar. deriv. of *cyperen* of copper, i.e., copper-colored]

ki·pu·ka (kē po͞o′kä), *n.* (in Hawaii) a tract of land surrounded by recent lava flows. [< Hawaiian]

kir·by (kûr′bē), *n., pl.* **-bies.** *Angling.* a fishhook having an even bend. Also called **kir′by hook′.** [after the proper name]

Kir·by-Smith (kûr′bē smith′), *n.* **Edmund,** 1824–93, U.S. Confederate general.

Kirch (kûrch), *n.* a crater in the second quadrant of the face of the moon: about 7 miles in diameter.

Kirch·er (kûrch′ər), *n.* a crater in the third quadrant of the face of the moon: about 51 miles in diameter.

Kirch·hoff (kērkh′hôf), *n.* **Gus·tav Ro·bert** (go͝os′täf rō′bert), 1824–87, German physicist.

Kirch′hoff's law′, *Physics, Elect.* **1.** the law that the algebraic sum of the currents flowing toward any point in an electric network is zero. **2.** the law that the algebraic sum of the products of the current and resistance in the conductors forming a closed loop in a network is equal to the algebraic sum of the electromotive forces in the loop. [named after G. R. KIRCHHOFF]

Kir·choff (kûr′chôf), *n.* a crater in the first quadrant of the face of the moon: about 17 miles in diameter.

Kir·ghiz (kir gēz′), *n., pl.* **-ghiz, -ghiz·es. 1.** one of a people of Mongolian physical type and Turkic speech, dwelling chiefly in west central Asia. **2.** their language.

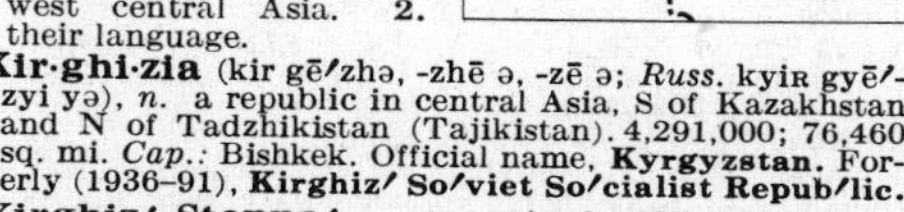

Kir·ghi·zia (kir gē′zhə, -zhē ə, -zē ə; *Russ.* kyir gyē′zyi yə), *n.* a republic in central Asia, S of Kazakhstan and N of Tadzhikistan (Tajikistan). 4,291,000; 76,460 sq. mi. *Cap.:* Bishkek. Official name, **Kyrgyzstan.** Formerly (1936–91), **Kirghiz′ So′viet So′cialist Repub′lic.**

Kirghiz′ Steppe′, a steppe in the SW Soviet Union in Asia, in Kazakstan. Also called **The Steppes.**

Ki·ri·len·ko (ki ri leng′ko), *n.* **An·drei** (än drā′), born 1906, Russian government official: alternate member of the Presidium since 1962.

Ki·rin (kē′rin′), *n.* **1.** a province in central Manchuria, in NE China. 12,550,000 (est. 1957); 72,201 sq. mi. **2.** the capital of this province: a port on the Sungari River. 568,000 (est. 1957).

kirk (kûrk; *Scot.* kirk), *n.* **1.** *Scot. and North Eng.* a church. **2. the Kirk,** (among the English) the Church of Scotland (Presbyterian), as distinguished from the Church of England or the Scottish Episcopal Church. [ME < Scand; cf. Icel *kirkja* CHURCH] —**kirk′like′,** *adj.*

Kirk (kûrk), *n.* **1. Grayson (Louis),** born 1903, U.S. educator: president of Columbia University since 1953.

Kirk·cal·dy (kûr kôl′dē, -kô′dē, -kä′-), *n.* a city in SE Fife, in E Scotland, on the Firth of Forth. 52,371 (1961).

Kirk·cud·bright (kər ko͞o′brē), *n.* a county in SW Scotland. 28,877 (1961); 896 sq. mi. *Co. seat:* Kirkcudbright. Also called **Kirk·cud·bright·shire** (kər ko͞o′brē shēr′, -shər).

Kir·ke·nes (chēr′kə nes′), *n.* a seaport in NE Norway. 3596 (1950).

Kirk·land (kûrk′lənd), *n.* **1. Jack,** born 1901, U.S. writer and playwright. **2.** a town in central Washington. 6025 (1960).

kirk·man (kûrk′mən; *Scot.* kirk′mən), *n., pl.* **-men.** *Scot. and North Eng.* **1.** a member or follower of the Kirk. **2.** an ecclesiastic; churchman. [KIRK + MAN¹]

Kir·kuk (kir ko͝ok′), *n.* a city in N Iraq. 176,794 (est. 1963).

Kirk·wall (kûrk′wôl′, -wəl), *n.* a town on Pomona island, NE of Scotland: county seat of Orkney. 4293 (est. 1964).

Kirk·wood (kûrk′wo͝od′), *n.* a city in E Missouri, near St. Louis. 29,421 (1960).

Kir·man (kir män′), *n.* a Persian rug marked by ornate flowing designs and light, muted colors. Also, **Kir·man·shah** (kir′män shä′), **Kermanshah.** [after KERMAN]

kir·mess (kûr′mis), *n.* kermis.

Kir Mo·ab (kûr mō′ab), ancient name of **Kerak.**

kirn¹ (kûrn; *Scot.* kirn), *Scot. and North Eng.* —*v.t., v.i.* **1.** to churn. —*n.* **2.** a churn. Also, **kern.** [ME *kirne* < Scand; cf. Icel *kirna;* c. CHURN]

kirn² (kûrn; *Scot.* kirn), *n.* *Scot. and North Eng.* **1.** a harvest celebration; a feast or party celebrating a successful harvest. **2.** the harvesting of the last handful of corn, noting either the end of the harvest season or the winning of a race against other reapers. Cf. **kemp¹** (def. 2). Also, **kern, kurn.** [akin to CORN¹]

Ki·rov (kē′rof), *n.* a city in the RSFSR, in the E Soviet Union in Europe. 292,000 (est. 1964). Formerly, **Vyatka.**

Ki·ro·va·bad (kē′ro vä bät′), *n.* a city in NW Azerbaijan, in the S Soviet Union in Europe. 126,000 (est. 1962). Formerly, **Elisavetpol, Gandzha.**

Ki·ro·vo·grad (kē′ro vo grät′), *n.* a city in the S central Ukraine, in the SW Soviet Union in Europe. 150,000 (est. 1964). Formerly, **Elisavetgrad, Zinovievsk.**

kir·pan (kir pän′), *n.* a small dagger worn by orthodox Sikhs. [< Panjabi and Hindi < Skt *kṛpāṇa* sword]

kirsch·was·ser (kērsh′vä′sər), *n.* a fragrant, colorless, unaged brandy distilled from a fermented mash of cherries, produced esp. in West Germany, Switzerland, and Alsace, France. Also called **kirsch.** [< G, equiv. to *Kirsch(e)* CHERRY + *Wasser* WATER]

Kir·sten (kûr′stən, kēr′-; *Nor.* khish′tən, khir′stən), *n.* a girl's given name.

Kirt′land's war′bler (kûrt′ləndz), a wood warbler, *Dendroica kirtlandii,* of the north central U.S., bluish gray above, striped with black and pale yellow below. [named after Jared *Kirtland* (1793–1877), American naturalist]

kir·tle (kûr′tᵊl), *n.* **1.** a woman's loose gown, worn in the Middle Ages. **2.** *Obs.* a man's tunic or coat. [ME *kirtel,* OE *cyrtel,* appar., equiv. to *cyrt(an)* (to) shorten (<< L *curtus* shortened) + *-el* -LE] —**kir′tled,** *adj.*

Ki·ru·na (kē′ry nä), *n.* a city in N Sweden: important iron-mining center. 28,226 (1965).

ki·san (kē′sän), *n.* (in India) a peasant. [< Hindi *kisān* < Skt *kṛṣāṇa* one who plows]

Ki·san·ga·ni (ki zäng′gä nē), *n.* a city in the N Democratic Republic of the Congo, on the Congo River. 126,533 (est. 1959). Formerly, **Stanleyville.**

Ki·se·levsk (ki se lyôfsk′), *n.* a city in the S RSFSR, in the Soviet Union in Asia. 142,000 (est. 1962).

kish (kish), *n.* *Metall.* **1.** a mixture of graphite and slag separated from and floating on the surface of molten pig iron or cast iron as it cools. **2.** dross on the surface of molten lead. [< G *Kies* gravel, pyrites; akin to OE *cisel* gravel]

Kish (kish), *n.* an ancient Sumerian and Akkadian city: its site is 8 miles east of the site of Babylon in S Iraq.

Ki·shi (kē′shē), *n.* **No·bu·su·ke** (nô′bo͝o so͞o′ke), born 1896, Japanese statesman: premier 1958–60.

Ki·shi·nev (kish′ə nef′, -nôf′; *Russ.* kyi shi nyôf′), *n.* a city in and the capital of Moldavia (Moldova), in the central part. 503,000. Rumanian, **Chişinău.**

kish·ke (kish′kə), *n.* *Jewish Cookery.* a beef or fowl intestine stuffed with a mixture, as of flour, fat, onion, and seasonings, and roasted. Also called **stuffed derma.** [< Yiddish < Slav; cf. Pol *kiszka* sausage]

Kis·lev (kis′ləv; *Heb.* kēs lev′), *n.* a month of the Jewish calendar. Cf. **Jewish calendar.** [< Heb]

kis·met (kiz′mit, kis′-), *n.* fate; destiny. Also, **kis·mat** (kiz′mət, kis′-). [< Turk < Pers *qismat* < Ar *qisma(t)* division, portion, lot, fate, akin to *qasama* to divide]

kiss (kis), *v.t.* **1.** to touch or press with the lips slightly pursed in token of greeting, affection, love, reverence, etc.: *He kissed his wife. He kissed the Pope's ring.* **2.** to join lips with: *She kissed him and left.* **3.** to touch gently or lightly: *The breeze kissed her face.* **4.** *Billiards, Pool.* (of a ball) to make slight contact with or brush (another ball). **5.** to put, bring, take, etc., by, or as if by, kissing: *She kissed the baby's tears away.* —*v.i.* **6.** to join lips in respect, affection, love, or passion: *They kissed passionately.* **7.** to express a thought, feeling, etc., by a contact of the lips: *They kissed good-by at the station.* **8.** *Billiards, Pool.* (of a ball) to carom gently off or touch another ball. **9. kiss off,** *Slang.* to reject; dismiss; ignore: *He kissed off their objections with a wave of his hand.* —*n.* **10.** the act of kissing. **11.** a slight touch or contact. **12.** *Billiards, Pool.* the slight touch of one ball by another. **13.** a baked confection of egg whites and confectioners' sugar, served as a cooky. **14.** a piece of toffeelike confectionery, sometimes containing nuts, coconut, or the like. [ME *kiss(en),* OE *cyssan* (c. G *küssen,* Icel *kyssa*), deriv. of OE *coss* a kiss; c. Icel *koss,* G *Küss*] —**kiss′a·bil′i·ty,** *n.*

kiss·a·ble (kis′ə bəl), *adj.* (of a person, esp. a woman) inviting kissing through being physically attractive. —**kiss′a·ble·ness,** *n.* —**kiss′a·bly,** *adv.*

kiss·er (kis′ər), *n.* **1.** one who or that which kisses. **2.** *Slang.* **a.** the face. **b.** the mouth. [KISS + -ER¹]

Kis·sim·mee (ki sim′ē), *n.* a town in central Florida. 6845 (1960).

kiss′ing bug′, 1. *Informal.* **a.** a person much given to kissing. **b.** an irresistible desire to kiss or be kissed: *She's got the kissing bug.* **2.** any of several assassin bugs that attack man, sometimes inflicting painful bites.

kiss′ing cous′in. See under **kissing kin.**

kiss′ing gate′, *Brit. Dial.* a gate hung in a narrow enclosure having the shape of a U or V, allowing only one person to pass at a time.

kiss′ing gour′ami, a whitish labyrinth fish, *Helostoma temmincki,* found in southeastern Asia, noted for the habit of pressing its fleshy, protrusible lips against those of another, often kept in aquariums.

kiss′ing kin′, any more or less distant kin familiar enough to be greeted with a kiss, as a cousin (**kissing cousin**).

kiss·ing·ly (kis′iŋ lē), *adv.* lightly; gently.

kiss′ of death′, a fatal or destructive relationship or action: *The support of the Communist group was the kiss of death to the candidate.*

kiss-off (kis′ôf′, -of′), *n.* **1.** *Slang.* act or instance of dismissing a person or thing: *It wasn't easy giving the old man the kiss-off after he served the company so faithfully for so long.* **2.** *Billiards, Pool.* kiss (def. 12). [n. use of v. phrase *kiss off*]

kiss′ of peace′, 1. (in certain Christian churches) a ceremonial embrace given as a token of Christian love and unity. 2. a ceremonial kiss formerly given, esp. at a baptism or Eucharistic service, as a token of Christian love and unity. Also called **pax.**

kist[1] (kist), *n. Scot. and North Eng.* **1.** a coffer; a money chest. **2.** any chest-like container; a box, trunk, or basket. **3.** a coffin, esp. a stone one; a sarcophagus. [ME *kiste* < Scand; cf. Icel *kista* CHEST]

kist[2] (kist), *n.* cist[2].

Kist·na (kist′nə), *n.* a river in S India, flowing E from the Western Ghats to the Bay of Bengal. 800 mi. long.

kist·vaen (kist′vīn′), *n.* cist[2]. [< Welsh *cist faen* stone coffin, equiv. to *cist* coffin (see CIST[2] + *faen*) lenited var. of *maen* stone; see MENHIR]

Ki·su·mu (kē so͞o′mo͞o), *n.* a city in W Kenya. 23,526 (1962).

kis·wah (kis′wä), *n. Islam.* a decorative veil draped over the walls of the Kaaba, now made of black brocade embroidered in gold with inscriptions from the Koran. [< Ar]

kit[1] (kit), *n., v.,* **kit·ted, kit·ting.** —*n.* **1.** a set or collection of tools, supplies, instructional matter, etc., for a specific purpose: *a first-aid kit; a selling kit.* **2.** the case for containing these. **3.** such a case and its contents. **4.** *Chiefly Brit.* a costume or outfit of clothing, esp. for a specific purpose: *ski kit; dancing kit; battle kit.* **5.** *Informal.* a set, lot, or collection of things or persons. **6.** a wooden tub, pail, etc., usually circular. **7. kit and caboodle,** or **boodle,** *Informal.* the whole lot of persons or things; all of something (often prec. by *whole*): *We took along the whole kit and caboodle in the station wagon.* —*v.t.* **8.** *Chiefly Brit.* to outfit or equip. [ME *kyt, kitt* < MD *kitte* jug, tankard]

kit[2] (kit), *n.* a violin or rebec small enough to be carried in the pocket, used by dancing masters in the 17th and 18th centuries. Also called **pochette, sourdine.** [?]

kit[3] (kit), *n.* kitten. [shortened form]

Kit (kit), *n.* **1.** a boy's given name, form of **Christopher. 2.** a girl's given name, form of **Catherine** or **Katherine.**

kit·am·bil·la (kit′əm bil′ə), *n.* a shrub or small tree, *Dovyalis hebecarpa,* of India and Ceylon, having velvety, maroon-purple fruit. Also called **Ceylon gooseberry.** [< Singhalese *kätämbilla*]

Ki·ta·sa·to (kē′tä sä′tō), *n.* **Shi·ba·sa·bu·ro** (shē bä′sä bo͞o′rō), 1852–1931, Japanese bacteriologist.

kit′ bag′, a knapsack, as for a soldier.

kitch·en (kich′ən), *n.* **1.** a room or place equipped for cooking. **2.** the culinary department; cuisine: *This restaurant has a fine Italian kitchen.* —*adj.* **3.** of, pertaining to, or designed for use in a kitchen: *kitchen window; kitchen curtains.* **4.** employed in or assigned to a kitchen: *kitchen help.* **5.** characteristic of the primarily oral forms of a language, as that used in a region geographically distant from where the standard tongue is spoken. **b.** (of a language) inferior, mongrel: *kitchen Latin.* [ME *kichene,* OE *cycene* << L *coquīna,* equiv. to *coqu(ere)* (to) cook + *-īna* -INE[1]] —**kitch′en·less,** *adj.* —**kitch′en·y,** *adj.*

kitch′en cab′inet, 1. a group of unofficial advisers on whom a head of government appears to rely heavily. **2.** a cupboard built into a kitchen or a chest of drawers, often of metal, for kitchen use, as for dishes and silverware.

kitch·en·er (kich′ə nər), *n.* **1.** a person employed in, or in charge of, a kitchen. **2.** an elaborate kitchen stove. [late ME; see KITCHEN, -ER[2]]

Kitch·e·ner (kich′ə nər), *n.* **1. Horatio Herbert** (*1st Earl Kitchener of Khartoum and of Broome*), 1850–1916, English field marshal and statesman. **2.** a city in S Ontario, in SE Canada. 74,485 with suburbs (1961).

kitch·en·ette (kich′ə net′), *n.* a very small, compact kitchen. Also, **kitch′en·et′.** [KITCHEN + -ETTE]

kitch′en gar′den, a garden where vegetables, herbs, and fruit are grown for one's own use. —**kitch′en gar′dener.**

kitch·en·maid (kich′ən mād′), *n.* a female servant who assists the cook. [KITCHEN + MAID]

kitch′en match′, a wooden friction match with a large head, used esp. for igniting gas ovens or burners.

kitch′en mid′den, a mound consisting of shells of edible mollusks and other refuse, marking the site of a prehistoric human habitation. [trans. of Dan *kökkenmödding*]

kitch′en police′, *Mil.* **1.** duty as assistant to the cooks. *Abbr.:* K.P. **2.** soldiers detailed by roster or as punishment to assist in kitchen duties.

kitch·en·ware (kich′ən wâr′), *n.* cooking equipment or utensils. [KITCHEN + WARE[1]]

Kitch′in rud′der (kich′in), a device for maneuvering, reversing, or improving the forward speed of a small, propeller-driven craft, consisting of a pair of curved blades, pivoted at top and bottom and rotated independently of one another around the propeller so as to concentrate its wake, divert it to one side or the other, or reverse its thrust in a forward direction.

kite[1] (kīt), *n., v.,* **kit·ed, kit·ing.** —*n.* **1.** a light frame covered with some thin material, to be flown in the wind at the end of a long string. **2.** any of several small birds of the hawk family *Accipitridae* that have long, pointed wings, that feed on insects, carrion, small reptiles, rodents, and birds, and that are noted for their graceful, gliding flight. Cf. **black kite, swallow-tailed kite, white-tailed kite. 3.** *Naut.* See **flying kite. 4.** *Com.* a fictitious negotiable instrument, not representing any actual transaction, used for raising money or sustaining credit. **5.** *Obs.* a person who preys on others; a sharper. —*v.i.* **6.** *Informal.* to fly or move with a rapid or easy motion like that of a kite. **7.** *Com.* to obtain money or credit through kites. —*v.t.* **8.** *Com.* to employ as a kite. [ME *kyte,* OE *cӯta* kite, bittern; akin to G *Kauz* owl] —**kit′er,** *n.* —**kite′like′,** *adj.*

kite[2] (kīt), *n. Scot. and North Eng.* kyte.

kite′ wind′er (wīn′dər), a triangular winder on a staircase.

kith (kith), *n.* **1.** acquaintances, friends, neighbors, or the like; persons living in the same general locality and forming a more or less cohesive group. **2.** kindred. **3.** a group of people living in the same area and forming a culture with a common language, customs, economy, etc., usually endogamous. [ME; OE *cӯth,* earlier *cӯththu* kinship, knowledge, equiv. to *cūth* known (see UNCOUTH) + *-thu* -TH[1]; akin to Goth *kunthi,* G *Kunde* knowledge]

kith′ and kin′, acquaintances and relatives.

kith·a·ra (kith′ər ə), *n.* a musical instrument of ancient Greece consisting of an elaborate wooden soundbox having two arms connected by a yoke to which the upper ends of the strings are attached. Also, **cithara.** [< L < Gk *kithárā* lyre]

Kithara

kithe (kīth), *v.t., v.i.,* **kithed, kith·ing.** *Scot. and North Eng.* **1.** to make known by action; show; demonstrate; prove. **2.** *Obs.* to make known by words; announce; declare; proclaim. Also, **kythe.** [ME *kithe(n),* OE *cӯthan* to make known, deriv. of *cūth* known; see UNCOUTH]

kit·ling (kit′ling), *n. Brit. Dial.* the young of any animal, esp. a young cat; kitten; kit. [ME *kiteling* < Scand; cf. Icel *ketlingr.* See CAT[1], -LING[1]]

kitsch (kich), *n.* art or literature judged to have little or no aesthetic value, esp. when produced to satisfy popular taste. [< G, deriv. of *kitschen* to throw together a work of art < dial.]

Ki Tse (gē′ dzu′), 12th century B.C., legendary Chinese founder of Korea. Also, **Chi-tsë, Chi-tzŭ.**

Kit·tan·ning (ki tan′ing), *n.* a town in central Pennsylvania. 6793 (1960).

kit·tel (kit′əl), *n. Yiddish.* a white robe used by Jews, esp. Orthodox Jews, as a ceremonial garment for men and as a burial shroud for both sexes: worn during worship on Rosh Hashanah and Yom Kippur, by a bridegroom during the wedding ceremony, and by the leader of the Seder on Passover.

kit·ten (kit′ən), *n.* **1.** a young cat. —*v.t., v.i.* **2.** (of cats) to give birth; bear. [ME *kitoun,* appar. b. *kiteling* KITLING and MF *chitoun,* var. of *chaton* kitten] —**kit′ten·like′,** *adj.*

kit·ten·ish (kit′ənish), *adj.* artlessly playful like a kitten. [KITTEN + -ISH[1]] —**kit′ten·ish·ly,** *adv.* —**kit′ten·ish·ness,** *n.*

Kit·ter·y (kit′ə rē), *n.* a town in SW Maine. 8051 (1960).

Kit·tie (kit′ē), *n.* a girl's given name, form of **Katherine** or **Catherine.** Also, **Kitty.**

Kit·ti·ka·chorn (kē′tē kä chôrn′), *n.* **Tha·nom** (thä-nôm′), born 1911, Thai statesman: premier 1963–73.

kit·ti·wake (kit′ē wāk′), *n.* either of two gulls of the genus *Rissa,* having the hind toe very short or rudimentary. [imit.]

kit·tle (kit′əl), *v.,* **-tled, -tling,** *adj.,* **-tler, -tlest.** *Brit. Dial.* —*v.t.* **1.** to tickle with the fingers; agitate or stir, as with a spoon. **2.** to excite or rouse (a person), esp. by flattery or strong words. —*adj.* **3.** ticklish; fidgety. **4.** requiring skill or caution; precarious. [late ME *kytylle, ketil,* OE **cytelian* (whence *citelung* tickling); c. MHG *kützeln;* akin to Icel *kitla,* G *kitzeln* to tickle]

Kit·tredge (ki′trij), *n.* **George Ly·man** (lī′mən), 1860–1941, U.S. Shakespearean scholar and philologist.

kit·ty[1] (kit′ē), *n., pl.* **-ties. 1.** a kitten. **2.** a pet name for a cat. [KIT[3] + -Y[2]]

kit·ty[2] (kit′ē), *n., pl.* **-ties. 1.** a fund, collection, or accumulation, usually of small amounts of money or goods; savings or reserve. **2.** a pool into which each player in a card game puts a certain amount of his winnings for some special purpose, as to pay for refreshments. **3.** the cards left over after a deal which may be used by the highest bidder. [KIT[1] + -Y[2]]

Kit·ty (kit′ē), *n.* a girl's given name, form of **Katherine** or **Catherine.** Also, **Kittie.**

kit·ty-cor·nered (kit′ē kôr′nərd), *adj., adv. U.S. Informal.* cater-cornered. Also, **kit′ty-cor′ner.**

Kit·ty·hawk (kit′ē hôk′), *n.* a village in NE North Carolina: Wright brothers' airplane flight 1903.

Ki·twe (kē′twä), *n.* a city in N Zambia. 350,000.

Kiung·chow (kyo͝ong′chō′, -chou′; *Chin.* gyo͝ong′jō′), *n.* a seaport on S Hainan island, in S China. ab. 59,000. Also, **Kiung·shan** (kyo͝ong′shän′; *Chin.* gyo͝ong′shän′).

Kiu·shu (kyo͞o′sho͞o′), *n.* Kyushu.

ki·va (kē′və), *n.* a large chamber, often wholly or partly underground, in a Pueblo Indian village, used for religious ceremonies and other purposes. [< Hopi]

Ki·wa·nis (ki wä′nis), *n.* an organization founded in 1915 for the promulgation of higher ideals in business, industrial, and professional life. [said to be < AmerInd: to make oneself known] —**ki·wa′ni·an,** *n.*

ki·wi (kē′wē), *n., pl.* **-wis. 1.** any of several flightless, ratite birds of the genus *Apteryx,* of New Zealand, allied to the extinct moas. **2.** *Slang.* a member of an air service, as in World War I, who is confined to ground duty. **3.** *Australian Informal.* a New Zealander. **4.** the egg-shaped berry of the shrub *Actinidia chinensis,* native to China but cultivated in New Zealand, having a thin brown skin and tart green flesh. [< Maori]

Kiwi, *Apteryx australis* (Total length to 28 in.; bill 6 in.)

ki·yas (kē yäs′), *n. Islam.* giyas.

ki·yi (kē′yē), *n.* a small whitefish, *Coregonus kiyi,* found in the deeper waters of the Great Lakes, related to the whitefishes. [?]

Ki·zil Ir·mak (ki zil′ ēr mäk′), a river flowing N through central Turkey to the Black Sea. 600 mi. long.

Ki·zil Kho·to (ki zil′ khō′tō), Kyzyl.

Ki·zil Kum (ki zil′ ko͞om′). See **Kyzyl Kum.**

kJ, kilojoule; kilojoules. Also, **kj**

Kjö·len (chœ′lən), *n.* a mountain range between Norway and Sweden. Highest peak, Mt. Kebnekaise, 7005 ft.

K.K.K., Ku Klux Klan. Also, **KKK**

KKt, *Chess.* king's knight.

KKtP, *Chess.* king's knight's pawn.

kl., kiloliter. Also, **kl**

kla·ber·jass (klä′bər yäs′), *n.* a card game played with a 32-card pack made by removing all cards below the sevens from a regular 52-card pack, in which scoring values are assigned to certain cards taken in tricks, to sequences in the same suit, to the king and queen of trumps, and to the last trick. [< G]

Kla·bund (klä bo͝ont′), *n.* (*Alfred Henschke*) 1890?–1928, German poet, novelist, and playwright.

Kla·gen·furt (klä′gən fo͝ort′), *n.* a city in S Austria. 67,782 (1961).

Klai·pe·da (klī′pe də; *Eng.* klī′pi də), *n.* **1.** a seaport in NW Lithuania, on the Baltic. 204,000. **2.** a former German Territory including this seaport: now a part of Lithuania. 1092 sq. mi. German, **Memel.**

Klam·ath (klam′əth), *n.* a river flowing from SW Oregon through NW California into the Pacific. 250 mi. long.

Klam·ath (klam′əth), *n., pl.* **-aths,** (*esp. collectively*) **-ath.** a member of an American Indian people belonging to the Lutuamian group and located in southern Oregon.

Klam′ath Falls′, a city in SW Oregon. 16,949 (1960).

Klam′ath Lakes′, two lakes which drain into the Klamath River: one lake (**Upper Klamath Lake**) is in SW Oregon, and the other (**Lower Klamath Lake**) is in N California.

Klam′ath weed′, the St.-John's-wort, *Hypericum perforatum.* [after the KLAMATH river]

Klan (klan), *n.* **1.** See **Ku Klux Klan. 2.** a chapter of the Ku Klux Klan. —**Klan′ism,** *n.*

Klans·man (klanz′mən), *n., pl.* **-men.** a member of the Ku Klux Klan. [KLAN + 'S[1] + MAN[1]]

Klapp·vi·sier (kläp′vi zēr′), *n. Armor.* a visor attached by a hinge at the top: used on basinets of the 14th century. [< G: flap visor]

Klap·roth (klap′rōth, -rôth), *n.* a walled plain in the third quadrant of the face of the moon: about 60 miles in diameter.

Klau·sen·burg (klou′zən bo͝orkh′), *n.* German name of **Cluj.**

klav·ern (klav′ərn), *n.* **1.** a local branch of the Ku Klux Klan. **2.** a meeting place of the Ku Klux Klan.

kla·vier (klə vēr′, klav′ē ər, klä′vē-), *n.* clavier[2].

klax·on (klak′sən), *n.* a loud electric horn for automobiles, trucks, etc. [formerly trademark]

klea·gle (klē′gəl), *n.* an official of the Ku Klux Klan.

Klé·ber (klā ber′), *n.* **Jean Bap·tiste** (zhän ba tēst′), 1753–1800, French general.

Klebs (klebz; *Ger.* kläps), *n.* **Ed·win** (ed′win; *Ger.* et′vēn), 1834–1913, German pathologist and bacteriologist.

kleb·si·el·la (kleb′zē el′ə, klep′sē-), *n. Bacteriol.* any of several rod-shaped, aerobic bacteria of the genus *Klebsiella,* certain species of which, as *K. pneumoniae,* are found in the respiratory, intestinal, and genitourinary tracts of man and animals and are sometimes pathogenic. [< NL, named after E. KLEBS]

Klebs′-Löf′fler bacil′lus (klebz′lef′lər; *Ger.* kläps′lœf′lər), a bacterium, *Corynebacterium diphtheriae,* which causes diphtheria. [named after E. KLEBS and F. A. J. LÖFFLER]

Klee (klā), *n.* **Paul** (poul), 1879–1940, Swiss painter and etcher.

Kleen·ex (klē′neks), *n. Trademark.* a soft, disposable paper tissue, used esp. as a handkerchief.

Klei·ber (klī′bər), *n.* **E·rich** (ā′rikh), 1890–1956, Austrian orchestra conductor.

kleig′ light′ (klēg). See **klieg light.**

Klein (klīn), *n.* **1. Fe·lix** (fē′liks; *Ger.* fā′liks), 1849–1925, German mathematician. **2.** a crater in the fourth quadrant of the face of the moon.

Klein′ bot′tle, *Geom.* a one-sided figure consisting of a tapered tube the narrow end of which is bent back, run through the side of the tube, and flared to join the wide end, thereby allowing any two points on the figure to be joined by an unbroken line. [named after Felix KLEIN]

Kleist (klīst), *n.* **(Bernd) Hein·rich (Wil·helm) von** (bernt hīn′rikh vil′helm fən), 1777–1811, German poet, dramatist, and story writer. —**Kleist′i·an,** *adj.*

Klem·pe·rer (klem′pər ər), *n.* **Otto,** 1885–1973, German orchestra conductor.

klepht (kleft), *n.* a Greek or Albanian brigand, exalted in the war of Greek independence as a patriotic robber; guerrilla. [< ModGk *klépht(ēs),* var. of Gk *kléptēs* thief, rogue; see KLEPTOMANIA] —**kleph′tic,** *adj.*

klep·to·ma·ni·a (klep′tə mā′nē ə, -mān′yə), *n. Psychol.* an irresistible impulse to steal, esp. in the absence of economic motive. Also, **cleptomania.** [*klepto-* (repr. Gk *kléptēs* thief) + -MANIA]

klep·to·ma·ni·ac (klep′tə mā′nē ak′), *n. Psychol.* one who has kleptomania. Also, **cleptomaniac.** [KLEPTOMANI(A) + -AC]

klesh·a (klesh′ə), *n. Yoga.* any of the five hindrances to enlightenment, which are ignorance or avidya, egocentricity, attachments, aversions, and the instinctive will to live. [< Skt: feeling, lit., pain]

Kle·ve (klā′və), *n.* German name of **Cleves.**

klieg′ eyes′ (klēg), inflammation and edema of the eyes as a result of prolonged exposure to arc lights, as the klieg lights of the motion-picture industry.

klieg′ light′, a flood light with an arc-light source used in motion-picture studios to project a beam of high actinic power. [named after J. H. *Kliegl* (1869–1959) and his brother Anton, German-born American inventors]

Klimt (klimt), *n.* **Gus·tav** (go͝os′täf), 1862–1918, Austrian painter.

K-line (kā′līn′), *n. Physics.* one of a series of lines (**K-series**) in the x-ray spectrum of an atom corresponding to radiation (**K-radiation**) caused by the transition of an electron to the K-shell.

Kline (klīn), *n.* **Franz (Jo·sef)** (franz jō′zəf, frants, fränts), 1910–62, U.S. painter.

Kline′ test′, *Med.* a test for syphilis in which the formation of a microscopic precipitate in a mixture of the patient's serum and an antigen indicates a syphilitic condition. Cf. **Kahn test.** [named after Benjamin S. *Kline* (b. 1886), American developer of test]

klip·pe (klip′ə), *n. Numis.* a square or lozenge-shaped coin. [< G < Sw *klippa* to cut; see CLIP[1]]

klip·spring·er (klip′spring′ər), *n.* a small, active African antelope, *Oreotragus oreotragus,* of mountainous regions from the Cape of Good Hope to Ethiopia. [< SAfrD: lit., rock-springer]

klis·mos (kliz′mos), *n., pl.* **-moi** (-moi). an ancient Greek chair, having a deep top rail curving forward from the back, and having legs curving upwards and inwards: imitated during various classical revivals, esp. in the early 19th century. [< Gk, akin to *klinein* to LEAN¹]

klis·ter (klis′tər), *n.* a sticky wax for use on skis, as for slopes where the snow is excessively wet. [< Norw < MLG; c. G *Kleister* paste]

Klon·dike (klon′dīk), *n.* **1.** a region of the Yukon territory in NW Canada: gold rush 1897–98. **2.** a river in this region, flowing into the Yukon. 90 mi. long. **3.** (*l.c.*) *Cards.* a variety of solitaire.

klong (klông, klong), *n.* (in Thailand) a canal: *the klongs of Bangkok.* [< Thai]

kloof (klo͞of), *n.* (in Africa) a deep glen; ravine. [< SAfrD; akin to CLEAVE²]

Klop·stock (klôp′shtôk′), *n.* **Frie·drich Gott·lieb** (frē′drīkн gôt′lēp), 1724–1803, German poet.

klös·se (klā′sə, klās; *Ger.* klœ′sə), *n.* (*construed as pl.*) *German Cookery.* dumplings. Also, **kloes′se.** [< G, pl. of *Kloss* ball of dough, dumpling]

kluck (kluk), *v.i., v.t., n.* cluck¹.

Kluck (klo͝ok), *n.* **A·le·xan·der von** (ä′le ksän′dər fon), 1846–1934, German general.

Kluck·hohn (kluk′hōn), *n.* **Clyde** (**Kay Ma·ben**) (mā′bən), 1905–60, American anthropologist.

klutz (kluts), *n. Slang.* **1.** a clumsy, awkward person. **2.** a stupid or foolish person; blockhead. [< G *Klotz*, lit., block of wood; akin to CLOT] —**klutz′y,** *adj.*

Kly·don·o·graph (klī don′ə graf′, -gräf′), *n. Trademark.* an instrument for recording photographically a surge of voltage, as in a power line.

Klys·tron (klis′tron, klī′strən), *n. Trademark.* a vacuum tube containing an electron gun, a resonator which changes the velocity of the electron beam in accordance with a signal (**buncher resonator**), a drift tube in which the electron velocity does not change, another resonator which abstracts energy from the electron beam (**catcher resonator**), and an electrode which collects the electrons (**collector electrode**). It has several ultra-high-frequency applications. Cf. **resonator** (def. 4).

km, kilometer; kilometers.

km., **1.** kilometer; kilometers. **2.** kingdom.

kMc, kilomegacycle; kilomegacycles.

K-me·son (kā′mē′son, -mes′on), *n. Physics.* a meson having a mass approximately half that of a proton, existing with either zero charge or positive or negative charge equal in magnitude to that of an electron. Also called **kaon, kappa meson.**

kmole. See **kilomole.**

km/sec, kilometers per second.

kn, knot; knots.

kn., kronen.

knack (nak), *n.* **1.** a talent or aptitude: *He had a knack for saying the right thing when necessary.* **2.** a sharp, cracking sound. [ME *knack* trick, perh. same word as *knak* sharp sounding blow, rap, cracking noise; imit.] —**Syn. 1.** aptness, facility, dexterity.

knäck·e·bröd (nek′ə bro͞od′, -bred′; *Sw.* knek′ə-brœd′), *n.* flat, thin, brittle unleavened rye bread. [< Sw, equiv. to *knäcke* to break + *bröd* bread]

knack·er (nak′ər), *n. Brit.* **1.** a person who buys animal carcasses or slaughters useless livestock for a knackery or rendering works. **2.** a person who buys and dismembers old houses, ships, etc., to salvage usable parts, selling the rest as scrap. **3.** *Dial.* an old, sick, or useless farm animal, esp. a horse. **4.** *Obs.* a harness maker; a saddler. [*knack* (< Scand; cf. Icel *hnakkr* nape of the neck, saddle) + -ER¹]

knack·er·y (nak′ə rē), *n. Brit.* See **rendering works.** [KNACK(ER) + -ERY]

knack·wurst (nok′wûrst, -wo͝orst), *n.* a short, thick, highly seasoned sausage. Also, **knockwurst.** [< G, equiv. to *knacke(n)* (to) crack, break + *Wurst* sausage. Cf. KNACK]

knag·gy (nag′ē), *adj.*, **-gi·er, -gi·est.** knotty; rough with knots. [ME *knag* spur, projection, peg (c. G *Knagge* knot, peg) + -Y¹]

knai·del (knād′əl), *n., pl.* **knai·dlach** (knād′ləкн, -läкн). *Jewish Cookery.* a dumpling or small ball of matzo meal, eggs, and salt, often mixed with another foodstuff, as ground almonds or grated potato, usually served in soup. [< Yiddish *kneydel* dumpling, ball; c. G *Knödel*]

knap¹ (nap), *n. Dial.* a crest or summit of a small hill. [ME; OE *cnæpp* top, summit; c. Icel *knappr* knob]

knap² (nap), *v.i., v.t.*, **knapped, knap·ping.** *Chiefly Brit. Dial.* **1.** to strike smartly; rap. **2.** to break off abruptly. **3.** to chip or become chipped, as a flint or stone. **4.** to bite suddenly or quickly. [late ME; c. D *knap* (n.), *knappen* (v.) crack; orig. imit.] —**knap′per,** *n.*

knap·sack (nap′sak′), *n.* a leather or canvas case for clothes and other supplies, carried on the back by soldiers, hikers, and the like. [< LG *knappsack*, lit., bite-sack, equiv. to *knapp* a bite (of food) + *sack* SACK¹; cf. dial. E *knap* to snap up, eat greedily] —**knap′sacked′,** *adj.*

knap·weed (nap′wēd′), *n.* any composite plant of the genus *Centaurea*, esp. the perennial, weedy *C. nigra*, having rose-purple flowers set on a dark-colored knob-like involucre. Also called **hardhead, Spanish button.** [late ME *knopwed*. See KNOP, WEED¹]

knar (när), *n.* a knot on a tree or in wood. [ME *knarre*; c. D *knar*, LG *knarre*] —**knarred, knar′ry,** *adj.*

knave (nāv), *n.* **1.** an unprincipled or dishonest person. **2.** *Cards.* jack¹ (def. 2). **3.** *Archaic.* a male servant or man of humble position. [ME; OE *cnafa*; c. G *Knabe* boy; akin to Icel *knapi* page, boy]
—**Syn. 1.** blackguard, villain, scamp, scapegrace. KNAVE, RASCAL, ROGUE, SCOUNDREL are disparaging terms applied to persons considered base, dishonest, or worthless. KNAVE, formerly merely a boy or servant, in modern use emphasizes baseness of nature and intention: *a dishonest and swindling knave.* RASCAL suggests shrewdness and trickery in dishonesty: *a plausible rascal.* A ROGUE is a worthless fellow who sometimes preys extensively upon the community by fraud: *photographs of criminals in a rogues' gallery.* A SCOUNDREL is a blackguard and rogue of the worst sort: *a thorough scoundrel.* RASCAL and ROGUE are often used affectionately or humorously (*an entertaining rascal; a saucy rogue*), but KNAVE and SCOUNDREL are not. —**Ant.** hero.

knav·er·y (nā′və rē), *n., pl.* **-er·ies.** **1.** action or practice characteristic of a knave. **2.** unprincipled or dishonest dealing; trickery. **3.** a knavish act or practice. [KNAVE + -ERY]

knav·ish (nā′vish), *adj.* **1.** like or befitting a knave; dishonest. **2.** waggish; mischievous. [ME *knavyssh*. See KNAVE, -ISH¹] —**knav′ish·ly,** *adv.* —**knav′ish·ness,** *n.*

knead (nēd), *v.t.* **1.** to work (dough, clay, etc.) into a uniform mixture by pressing, folding, and stretching. **2.** to manipulate by similar movements, as the body in a massage. **3.** to make by kneading. **4.** to make kneading movements with: *She kneaded her fist into her palm.* [ME *knede(n)*, OE *cnedan*; c. G *kneten*, D *kneden*] —**knead′a·bil′i·ty,** *n.* —**knead′a·ble,** *adj.* —**knead′er,** *n.* —**knead′ing·ly,** *adv.*

knead′ed but′ter. See **beurre manié.**

knee (nē), *n., v.,* **kneed, knee·ing.** —*n.* **1.** *Anat.* the joint on the human leg that allows for movement between the femur and tibia and is protected by the patella; the central area of the leg in man between the thigh and the lower leg. See diag. under **skeleton.** **2.** the corresponding joint or region in the hind leg of a quadruped; stifle. **3.** a joint or region likened to this but not anatomically homologous with it, as the tarsal joint of a bird, the carpal joint in the forelimb of the horse or cow, etc. **4.** the part of a garment covering the knee. **5.** something resembling a bent knee, esp. a rigid or braced angle between two framing members. **6.** Also called **hip, shoulder.** *Furniture.* the inward curve toward the top of a cabriole leg. **7.** *Building Trades.* **a.** the junction of the top and either of the uprights of a bent. **b.** a curved member for reinforcing the junction of two pieces meeting at an angle. **8.** Also called **kneeler.** a stone cut to follow a sharp return angle. **9. bring someone to his knees,** to force someone into submission or compliance: *After months of haggling he brought the owner to his knees and bought the property at a reasonable price.* —*v.t.* **10.** to strike or touch with the knee. **11.** to secure (a structure, as a bent) with a knee. —*v.i.* **12.** *Obs.* to go down on the knees; kneel. [ME *cneo, kne*, OE *cnēo(w)*; c. G, D *knie*, Icel *knē*, Goth *kniu*, L *genu*, Gk *góny*, Skt *jānu* knee]

knee′ ac′tion, **1.** *Auto.* a form of suspension for the front wheels of a vehicle permitting each wheel to rise and fall independent of the other. **2.** limited and temporary bending at a joint provided to relieve a structure or machine part under stress.

knee′ bend′, a physical exercise in which a person starts from an erect position, moves to a squatting position, and returns to the original position without using the hands to support the body.

knee′ brace′, *Building Trades.* a diagonal member for bracing the angle between two joined members, as a stud or column and a joist or rafter, being joined to each partway along its length.

knee′ breech′es, breeches (def. 1).

knee·cap (nē′kap′), *n.* **1.** the patella. **2.** a protective covering, usually knitted, for the knee. [KNEE + CAP]

knee′ cop′, *Armor.* poleyn.

knee-deep (nē′dēp′), *adj.* **1.** so deep as to reach the knees: *I had to get out and walk to the house in knee-deep mud.* **2.** submerged or covered by something having such depth: *They were knee-deep in water.* **3.** embroiled; enmeshed; involved: *He was knee-deep in trouble.*

knee-high (nē′hī′), *adj.* as high as the knees.

knee·hole (nē′hōl′), *n.* an open space for the knees, as under a desk. [KNEE + HOLE]

knee′ jerk′, a reflex extension of the leg, caused by contraction of the quadriceps, resulting from a sharp tap on the patellar tendon; patellar reflex.

kneel (nēl), *v.*, **knelt** or **kneeled, kneel·ing,** *n.* —*v.i.* **1.** to fall or rest on the knees or a knee. —*n.* **2.** the action or position of kneeling. [ME *knele(n)*, OE *cnēowlian* (c. LG *knelen*, D *knielen*). See KNEE, -LE] —**kneel′ing·ly,** *adv.*

kneel·er (nē′lər), *n.* **1.** one who or that which kneels. **2.** a bench, pad, or the like, to kneel on. **3.** a stone for supporting inclined masonry, as coping stones. **4.** knee (def. 8). [ME; see KNEEL, -ER¹]

knee·pad (nē′pad′), *n.* a pad to protect the knee. [KNEE + PAD¹]

knee·pan (nē′pan′), *n.* the kneecap or patella. [KNEE + PAN¹]

knee·piece (nē′pēs′), *n.* a piece of armor for protecting the knee, as a poleyn. [KNEE + PIECE]

knee′ raft′er, **1.** a rafter for maintaining the angle between a principal rafter and a tie or collar beam. **2.** a rafter bent downward at the lower end. Also called **crook rafter.**

knee-sprung (nē′sprung′), *adj. Vet. Pathol.* (of a horse, mule, etc.) having a forward bowing of the knee caused by inflammatory shortening of the flexor tendons.

knell (nel), *n.* **1.** the sound made by a bell rung slowly for a death or a funeral. **2.** any sound announcing the death of a person or the end, extinction, failure, etc., of something: *the knell of parting day.* **3.** any mournful sound. —*v.i.* **4.** to sound, as a bell, esp. a funeral bell. **5.** to give forth a mournful, ominous, or warning sound. —*v.t.* **6.** to proclaim or summon by, or as by, a bell. [ME *knel*, OE *cynll* (n.); ME *knellen, knyllen*, OE *cyllan* (v.); c. Icel *knylla* to beat, strike; akin to D *knal* bang, *knallen* to bang, G *Knall* explosion, *knallen* to explode]

knelt (nelt), *v.* a pt. and pp. of **kneel.**

Knes·set (knes′et), *n.* the parliament of Israel. Also, **Knes·seth** (knes′et). [< Heb: lit., gathering]

knew (no͞o, nyo͞o), *v.* pt. of **know.**

Knick·er·bock·er (nik′ər bok′ər), *n.* **1.** a descendant of the Dutch settlers of New York. **2.** any New Yorker. [generalized from Diedrich *Knickerbocker*, fictitious author of Washington Irving's *History of New York*]

knick·ered (nik′ərd), *adj.* wearing knickers. [KNICKER(S) + -ED³]

knick·ers (nik′ərz), *n.* (*construed as pl.*) **1.** loosely fitting short breeches gathered in at the knee. **2.** a bloomerlike undergarment worn by women. Also, **knick·er·bock·ers** (nik′ər bok′ərz). [shortened form of *knickerbockers*, pl. of *knickerbocker*, special use of KNICKERBOCKER] —**knick′ered, knick′er·bock′ered,** *adj.*

knick·knack (nik′nak′), *n.* **1.** a pleasing trifle; a trinket or gimcrack. **2.** a bit of bric-à-brac. Also, **nick-nack.** [gradational compound based on KNACK in obs. sense of toy] —**knick′knacked′,** *adj.* —**knick′knack′y,** *adj.*

Knies (knēs), *n.* **Karl Gus·tav A·dolf** (kärl go͝os′täf ä′dôlf), 1821–98, German statistician and historical economist.

knife (nīf), *n., pl.* **knives,** *v.,* **knifed, knif·ing.** —*n.* **1.** an instrument for cutting, consisting essentially of a thin, sharp-edged, metal blade fitted with a handle. **2.** a knifelike weapon; dagger; short sword. **3.** any blade for cutting, as in a tool or machine. **4. under the knife,** in surgery; undergoing an operation: *The patient is still under the knife.* —*v.t.* **5.** to apply a knife to; cut, stab, etc., with a knife. **6.** to attempt to defeat or undermine in a secret or underhanded way. —*v.i.* **7.** to move or cleave through something with or as if with a knife: *The ship knifed through the heavy seas.* [ME *knif*, OE *cnīf*; c. Icel *knīfr*, D *knijf*, G *Kneif*] —**knife′less,** *adj.* —**knife′like′,** *adj.* —**knif′er,** *n.*

knife′ aca′cia, a stout shrub, *Acacia cultriformis*, having knife-shaped phyllodia and yellow flower heads.

knife′ box′, *Furniture.* an ornamental box, closed with a lid, for containing table knives.

knife′ edge′, **1.** the cutting edge of a knife. **2.** anything very sharp. **3.** a wedge on the fine edge of which a scale beam, pendulum, or the like, oscillates.

knife-edged (nīf′ejd′), *adj.* having a thin, sharp edge.

knife′ pleat′, a sharply creased narrow pleat, usually one of a series folded in the same direction.

knife′ switch′, *Elect.* a form of air switch in which a moving element, usually a hinged blade, is placed between two contact clips.

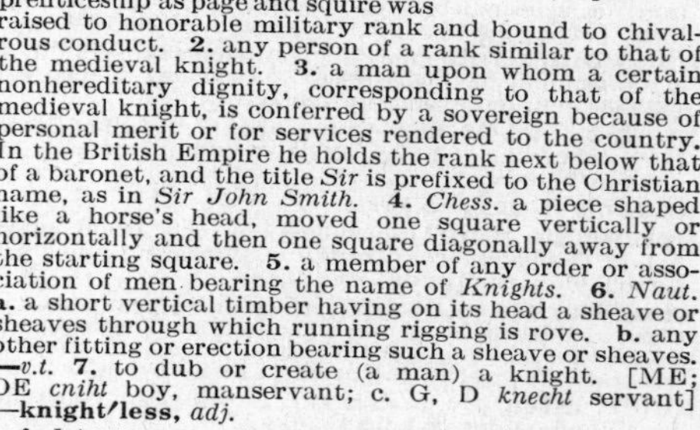

Knife box (18th century) A, Closed B, Open

knight (nīt), *n.* **1.** *Medieval Hist.* **a.** a mounted soldier serving under a feudal superior. **b.** a man, usually of noble birth, who after an apprenticeship as page and squire was raised to honorable military rank and bound to chivalrous conduct. **2.** any person of a rank similar to that of the medieval knight. **3.** a man upon whom a certain nonhereditary dignity, corresponding to that of the medieval knight, is conferred by a sovereign because of personal merit or for services rendered to the country. In the British Empire he holds the rank next below that of a baronet, and the title *Sir* is prefixed to the Christian name, as in *Sir John Smith.* **4.** *Chess.* a piece shaped like a horse's head, moved one square vertically or horizontally and then one square diagonally away from the starting square. **5.** a member of any order or association of men bearing the name of *Knights.* **6.** *Naut.* **a.** a short vertical timber having on its head a sheave or sheaves through which running rigging is rove. **b.** any other fitting or erection bearing such a sheave or sheaves. —*v.t.* **7.** to dub or create (a man) a knight. [ME; OE *cniht* boy, manservant; c. G, D *knecht* servant] —**knight′less,** *adj.*

Knight (nīt), *n.* **1. Eric,** 1897–1943, U.S. novelist, born in England. **2. Frank Hy·ne·man** (hī′nə mən), born 1885, U.S. economist.

knight′ bach′elor, *pl.* **knights bachelors, knight bachelors.** bachelor (def. 3).

knight′ banneret′, *pl.* **knights bannerets.** banneret¹ (def. 2).

Knight′, Death′ and the Dev′il, an engraving (1513) by Albrecht Dürer.

knight-er·rant (nīt′er′ənt), *n., pl.* **knights-er·rant.** *Hist.* a wandering knight; a knight who traveled in search of adventures, to exhibit military skill, etc. [ME; see KNIGHT, ERRANT]

knight-er·rant·ry (nīt′er′ən trē), *n., pl.* **-er·rant·ries.** **1.** the behavior, vocation, or character of a knight-errant or of knights-errant. **2.** quixotic conduct or action. [KNIGHT-ERRANT + -RY]

knight·head (nīt′hed′), *n.* **1.** *Naut.* either of a pair of upright members flanking and securing the bowsprit of a vessel at the bow, often used as mooring bitts; apostle. **2.** a plate at the fore end of a topgallant forecastle, on an iron or steel sailing ship, through which a spike bowsprit passes. [KNIGHT + -HEAD]

knight·hood (nīt′ho͝od), *n.* **1.** the rank or dignity of a knight. **2.** the profession or vocation of a knight. **3.** knightly character or qualities. **4.** the body of knights. [ME *knighthod*, OE *cnihthād*. See KNIGHT, -HOOD]

knight·ly (nīt′lē), *adj.* **1.** of or belonging to a knight: *knightly armor.* **2.** characteristic of a knight; noble and courageous: *knightly deeds.* **3.** being or resembling a knight. **4.** composed of knights. —*adv.* **5.** in a manner befitting a knight. [ME; OE *cnihtlīc*. See KNIGHT, -LY] —**knight′li·ness,** *n.*

Knights, The, a comedy (424 B.C.) by Aristophanes.

Knights′ Hos′pitalers. See under **Hospitaler** (def. 1).

Knights′ of Colum′bus, an international fraternal and benevolent organization of Roman Catholic men, founded in New Haven, Connecticut, in 1882.

Knights′ of La′bor, a secret workingmen's organization formed in 1869 to defend the interests of labor.

Knights′ of Mal′ta, the order of Hospitalers.

Knights′ of Pyth′ias, a fraternal order founded in Washington, D.C., in 1864.

Knights′ of St. John′ of Jeru′salem. See under **Hospitaler** (def. 1).

Knights′ of the Ku′ Klux′ Klan′. See **Ku Klux Klan** (def. 2).

Knights′ of the Round′ Ta′ble, a legendary order of knights created by King Arthur.

knight's-spur (nīts′spûr′), *n.* See **field larkspur.**

Knights′ Tem′plars, **1.** a Masonic order in the U.S. claiming descent from the Medieval order of Templars. **2.** a pl. of **Knight Templar.**

Knight′ Tem′plar, *pl.* **Knights Templars, Knights Templar.** Templar.

knish (knish), *n. Jewish Cookery.* a fried or baked turnover or roll of dough with a filling, as of meat, cheese, or potato. [< Yiddish < Pol *knysz;* c. Russ *knish* kind of cake]

knit (nit), *v.,* **knit·ted** or **knit, knit·ting,** *n.* —*v.t.* **1.** to make (a garment, fabric, etc.) by joining loops of yarn, either by hand with knitting needles or by machine. **2.** to join closely and firmly together, as members or parts. **3.** to contract into folds or wrinkles: *to knit the brow.* **4.** to form or bring (something nonmaterial) into being: *He knitted his theory from the ideas of others.* —*v.i.* **5.** to become closely and firmly joined together; grow together, as broken bones do. **6.** to contract into folds or wrinkles, as the brow. **7.** to become closely and intimately united. —*n.* **8.** fabric produced by interlooping of a yarn or yarns. **9.** a knitted garment. [ME *knitte,* OE *cnytt(an)* (to) tie; c. G *knütten;* see KNOT[1]] —**knit′ta·ble,** *adj.* —**knit′ter,** *n.*

knit·ted (nit′id), *adj.* made by knitting, as a cloth article: *a knitted bedspread.* [KNIT + -ED[2]]

knit·ting (nit′ing), *n.* **1.** the act of a person or thing that knits. **2.** the act of forming a fabric by looping a continuous yarn. **3.** knitted work. [KNIT + -ING[1]]

knit′ting nee′dle, an instrument for knitting by hand, consisting of a straight, slender rod of steel, plastic, etc., tapered to points at both ends, or tapered at one end with a knob at the other.

knit·wear (nit′wâr′), *n.* clothing made of knitted fabric. [KNIT + WEAR]

knives (nīvz), *n.* pl. of **knife.**

knob (nob), *n., v.,* **knobbed, knob·bing.** —*n.* **1.** a projecting part, usually rounded, forming the handle of a door, drawer, or the like. **2.** a rounded lump or protuberance on the surface or at the end of something, as a knot on a tree trunk, a pimple on the skin, etc. **3.** *Archit.* an ornamental boss, as of carved work. **4.** a rounded hill, mountain, or elevation on a ridge. —*v.t.* **5.** to produce a knob or knobs on. **6.** to furnish with a knob or knobs. **7.** (in stone cutting) to knock off (excess stone) preparatory to dressing; knobble; skiffle. [ME *knobbe* < MLG] —**knob′like′,** *adj.*

knob·ble (nob′əl), *v.t.,* **-bled, -bling.** **1.** to knob (excess stone). **2.** *Metall.* to treat (semi-refined puddled iron) on a hearth before shingling to produce wrought iron. [ME; see KNOB, -LE] —**knob·bler** (nob′lər), *n.*

knob′bling roll′ (nob′ling), *Metalworking.* a roll for a rolling mill, having a series of regularly shaped projections and depressions on its face.

knob·by (nob′ē), *adj.,* **-bi·er, -bi·est.** **1.** full of knobs: *the knobby trunk of a tree.* **2.** like a knob. [KNOB + -Y[1]] —**knob′bi·ness,** *n.*

knob′ cel′ery, celeriac.

knob′cone pine′ (nob′kōn′), a pine, *Pinus attenuata,* of the Pacific coast of the U.S., bearing cones with knoblike scales. [KNOB + CONE]

knob·ker·rie (nob′ker′ē), *n.* a short, heavy stick or club with a knob on one end, used by South African natives for striking and throwing. [< SAfrD *knopkiri,* equiv. to *knop* KNOB + Hottentot *kiri, kirri* stick, club]

knob′ latch′, a latch having a spring bolt controlled by a knob on one or both sides.

knob′ lock′, a lock having a spring bolt moved by a knob or knobs, and a dead bolt moved by a key.

knock (nok), *v.i.* **1.** to strike a sounding blow with the fist, knuckles, or anything hard, esp. on a door, window, or the like, as in seeking admittance, calling attention, giving a signal, etc.: *Knock twice and ask for Louie.* **2.** to make a pounding or rattling noise: *The engine of our car is knocking badly.* **3.** *Informal.* to engage in trivial or carping criticism. **4.** to strike in collision; bump: *He knocked into a table.* **5.** *Cards.* to end a game, as in knock rummy, by laying down a hand in which those cards not included in sets total less than a specific amount. —*v.t.* **6.** to give a sounding or forcible blow to; hit; strike; beat. **7.** to drive, force, or render by a blow or blows: *to knock a man senseless.* **8.** to make by striking a blow or blows: *to knock a hole in the door.* **9.** to strike (a thing) against something else. **10.** *Informal.* to criticize, esp. in a carping manner: *He's always knocking everything.* **11.** *Brit. Slang.* to astound; impress greatly. **12. knock around** or **about,** *Slang.* **a.** to wander aimlessly or idly. **b.** to loiter; loaf. **c.** to mistreat (someone), esp. physically: *As children they had been knocked around by a succession of foster parents.* **13. knock down, a.** to signify the sale of an article at auction by a blow of the hammer or mallet. **b.** *Com.* to take apart for facility in handling. **c.** *Slang.* to embezzle money from one's employer. **d.** *Slang.* to receive, as a salary or a scholastic grade; earn: *He knocks down about 12 grand a year.* **e.** *Informal.* to lower the price of; reduce: *The storekeeper decided to knock down his remaining winter stock.* **f.** to cause (a sailing vessel) to heel, as by a gust of wind, to such a degree that it cannot right itself. **14. knock it off,** *Slang.* stop it (usually used to halt noise or a commotion, fight, or argument). **15. knock off,** *Slang.* **a.** to cease activity, esp. work. **b.** to dispose of; finish. **c.** to murder; kill. **d.** to die. **e.** to get rid of; reduce. **f.** to disable or defeat. **g.** to commit a robbery at; steal from: *The gang knocked off a gas station and two stores.* **h.** *Naut.* to blow the head (of a sailing vessel) off the wind. **16. knock (oneself) out,** to exert (oneself) to the limit; exhaust; deplete. **17. knock out, a.** to defeat (an opponent) in a boxing match by striking him such a blow that he is unable to rise within the specified time. **b.** *Slang.* to produce quickly or efficiently. **c.** to damage or destroy: *The explosion knocked out the power for several hours.* **d.** to knock (a pitcher) out of the box. **18. knock out of the box,** *Baseball.* to cause a pitcher to be removed from the box because he has permitted too many hits. Also, **knock out. 19. knock over, a.** to strike (someone or something) from an erect to a prone position: *to knock over a lamp.* **b.** to distress; overcome: *When the announcement came we were completely knocked over.* **c.** *Slang.* to commit a robbery: *an expert who had already knocked over five banks.* **20. knock together,** to make or construct in a hurry or with little attention to detail: *He could knock together some furniture if the present pieces are not adequate.* **21. knock up, a.** to damage; mar: *The children knocked up the new table.* **b.** to injure; wound: *He was afraid to come home from school all knocked up again.* **c.** *Brit. Informal.* to wake up; rouse: *He knocked us up before dawn.* **d.** *Slang.* to make pregnant. —*n.* **22.** the act or sound of knocking. **23.** a rap, as at a door. **24.** a blow or thump. **25.** *Informal.* an adverse criticism. **26.** the noise resulting from faulty combustion or from incorrect functioning of some part of an internal-combustion engine. **27.** *Cricket.* an innings. **28.** *Brit. Slang.* **a.** one of a combination of dealers who bid together, rather than against each other, at an auction, and later resell the purchases among themselves. **b.** an auction at which this is done. **c.** a sale of merchandise recently obtained by a dealer at an auction. [ME *knokke(n),* var. of *knoken,* OE *cnocian, cnucian;* c. Icel *knoka* to thump, knock] —**knock′less,** *adj.*
—**Syn. 1.** See **strike.**

knock·a·bout (nok′ə bout′), *n.* **1.** *Naut.* any of various fore-and-aft-rigged sailing vessels having a single jib bent to a stay from the stemhead, no bowsprit being used: usually rigged as a sloop. **2.** *Australian.* an itinerant farm hand or ranch hand; an itinerant handyman. **3.** something designed or suitable for rough or casual use, as a sturdy jacket, a secondhand car, etc. **4.** *Brit. Archaic.* wanderer. —*adj.* **5.** suitable for rough use, as a garment: *Weekends were usually spent exploring the rough countryside in knockabout jackets and jeans.* **6.** characterized by knocking about; rough; boisterous. **7.** slapstick: *knockabout comedy.* **8.** shiftless; aimless: *He's a knockabout kind of hobo.* [n., adj. use of v. phrase *knock about*]

knock·down (nok′doun′), *adj.* **1.** capable of knocking something down; overwhelming; irresistible: *a knockdown blow.* **2.** constructed in separate parts that can readily be taken apart for easy storage, shipping, etc.: *a knockdown shelter; a knockdown workbench.* —*n.* **3.** a knockdown object. **4.** act of knocking down, esp. by a blow. **5.** that which fells or overwhelms. **6.** reduction or lowering, as in price or number: *The store offered a knockdown of 15 percent to its own employees.* **7.** *Slang.* an introduction, esp. to a person: *He gave me a real knockdown to the company.* **8.** *Naut.* the capsizing of a small boat as a result of a strong gust of wind. [adj., n. use of v. phrase *knock down*]

knock-down-drag-out (nok′doun′drag′out′), *adj.* marked by unrelenting violence: *a knock-down-drag-out fight.* Also, **knock′-down′, drag′-out′; knock′-down′-and-drag′-out′.** [adj. use of v. phrases *knock down* and *drag out*]

knocked-down (nokt′doun′), *adj. Com.* composed of parts or units ready to be assembled: *knocked-down furniture.*

knock·er (nok′ər), *n.* **1.** one who or that which knocks. **2.** a hinged knob, bar, etc., on a door, for use in knocking. **3.** *Informal.* a persistent and carping critic; faultfinder. **4.** *Slang (vulgar).* a female breast. **5. on the knocker,** *Brit. Slang.* canvassing or selling door-to-door. [ME; see KNOCK, -ER[1]]

knock-knee (nok′nē′), *n.* **1.** inward curvature of the legs, causing the knees to knock together in walking. **2. knock-knees,** the knees of a person whose legs have such curvature. —**knock′-kneed′,** *adj.*

knock·out (nok′out′), *n.* **1.** the act of knocking out. **2.** the state or fact of being knocked out. **3.** a knockout blow. **4.** *Informal.* a person or thing overwhelmingly successful or attractive. **5.** *Mach.* a device for knocking something loose, as finished work from a lathe chuck. **6.** a panel in a casing, can, or box, esp. of metal or plastic, so designed that it can readily be removed, as by punching, hammering, or cutting, to provide an opening into the interior: *a knockout in a junction box.* —*adj.* **7.** that knocks out: *the knockout punch.* [n., adj. use of v. phrase *knock out*]

knock′out drops′, *Slang.* chloral hydrate or any similar drug put in a drink secretly to make the drinker unconscious.

knock′ rum′my, *Cards.* a variety of rummy for two to six players, in which a player can end a game by laying down a hand with any number of points in cards not included in sets.

knock·wurst (nok′wûrst, -wŏŏrst), *n.* knackwurst.

knoll[1] (nōl), *n.* a small, rounded hill or eminence; hillock. [ME *cnol,* OE *cnoll;* c. Norw *knoll* hillock; akin to D *knol* turnip, Icel *knollur,* G *Knollen,* Dan *knold* tuber] —**knoll′y,** *adj.*

knoll[2] (nōl), *Archaic.* —*v.t.* **1.** to ring or toll a bell for; announce by tolling. **2.** to ring or toll (a bell). —*v.i.* **3.** to sound, as a bell; ring. **4.** to sound a knell. —*n.* **5.** a stroke of a bell in ringing or tolling. [ME; var. of KNELL] —**knoll′er,** *n.*

Knoop′ scale′ (nōōp), a scale of hardness based on the indentation made in the material to be tested by a diamond point. [named after F. *Knoop,* 20th-century American chemist]

knop (nop), *n.* a small knob or similar rounded protuberance. [ME; OE *cnop;* c. D *knop,* G *Knopf*]

knorr (nôr), *n.* a medieval ship of northern Europe having a single sail and used for cargo. [< OIcel *knörr* merchant ship; cf. OE *cnear* small ship]

knosp (nosp), *n.* a budlike ornament. [< G *Knospe* bud; akin to KNOP]

Knos·sos (nos′əs), *n.* a ruined city on N central Crete; capital of the ancient Minoan civilization. Also, **Cnossus, Gnossus.** —**Knos·si·an** (nos′ē ən), *adj.*

knot[1] (not), *n., v.,* **knot·ted, knot·ting.** —*n.* **1.** an interlacing, twining, looping, etc., of a cord, rope, or the like, drawn tight into a knob or lump, for fastening, binding, or connecting two cords together or a cord to something else. **2.** a piece of ribbon or similar material tied or folded upon itself and used or worn as an ornament. **3.** a group or cluster of persons or things: *a knot of spectators; a knot of trees.* **4.** *Anat., Zool.* a protuberance or swelling on or in a part or process, as in a muscle. **5.** a protuberance in the tissue of a plant; an excrescence on a stem, branch, or root; a node or joint in a stem. esp. when of swollen form. **6.** the hard, cross-grained mass of wood at the place where a branch joins the trunk of a tree. **7.** a part of this mass showing in a piece of lumber, wood panel, etc. **8.** any of various diseases of trees characterized by the formation of an excrescence, knob, or gnarl. **9.** *Naut.* **a.** a unit of speed equal to one nautical mile or about 1.15 statute miles per hour. **b.** a unit of 47 feet 3 inches on a log line, marked off by knots. **c.** (loosely) a nautical mile. **10.** an involved, intricate, or difficult matter; complicated problem. **11.** a bond or tie: *the knot of matrimony.* **12. tie the knot,** *Informal.* to marry: *They will tie the knot in November.* —*v.t.* **13.** to tie in a knot or knots; form a knot or knots in. **14.** to secure or fasten by a knot. **15.** to form protuberances, bosses, or knobs in; make knotty. —*v.i.* **16.** to become tied or tangled in a knot or knots. **17.** to form knots or joints. [ME *knot(te),* OE *cnotta;* c. D *knot,* G *knoten* to KNIT] —**knot′less,** *adj.* —**knot′like′,** *adj.*
—**Syn. 3.** company, band, crew, gang, crowd. **5.** lump, knob, gnarl. **10.** perplexity, puzzle, conundrum.

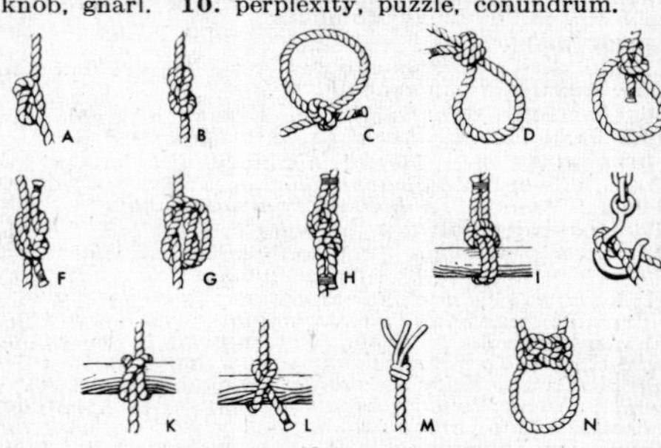

Knots
A, Overhand knot; B, Figure of eight; C, Slip knot; D, Loop knot; E, Bowline; F, Square knot; G, Granny's knot; H, Carrick bend; I, Fisherman's bend; J, Blackwall hitch; K, Clove hitch; L, Half hitch; M, Matthew Walker; N, Prolonge knot

knot[2] (not), *n.* either of two large sandpipers, *Calidris canatus* or *C. tenuirostris,* that breed in the Arctic and winter in the Southern Hemisphere. [?]

knot·grass (not′gras′, -gräs′), *n.* **1.** a polygonaceous weed, *Polygonum aviculare,* having nodes in its stems. **2.** any of certain other species of this genus. [KNOT[1] + GRASS]

knot·hole (not′hōl′), *n.* a hole in a board or plank formed by the falling out of a knot or a portion of a knot. [KNOT[1] + HOLE]

knot·root (not′rōōt′, -rŏŏt′), *n.* See **Chinese artichoke.** [KNOT[1] + ROOT[1]]

knot′ stitch′, a stitch that produces a knot on the fabric surface, made by twining the thread about the needle.

knot·ted (not′id), *adj.* **1.** having knots; knotty. **2.** *Bot.* having many nodes or nodelike swellings; gnarled. **3.** *Zool.* having one or more swellings; nodose. [ME *cnotted.* See KNOT[1], -ED[3]]

knot·ter (not′ər), *n.* **1.** one who or that which ties knots. **2.** a device that ties knots in thread during the manufacture of yarn. **3.** one who or that which takes out or removes knots. [KNOT[1] + -ER[1]]

knot·ting (not′ing), *n.* a decorative, lacelike pattern produced by interlacing and knotting various yarns, as in crocheting or embroidery. [KNOT[1] + -ING[1]]

knot·ty (not′ē), *adj.,* **-ti·er, -ti·est.** **1.** having knots; full of knots: *a knotty piece of pine.* **2.** involved, intricate, or difficult: *a knotty situation.* [late ME; early ME *cnotti.* See KNOT[1], -Y[1]] —**knot′ti·ly,** *adv.* —**knot′ti·ness,** *n.*
—**Syn. 2.** complex, complicated.

knot′ty rhat′any. See under **rhatany** (def. 1).

knot·weed (not′wēd′), *n.* any of several knotty-stemmed, polygonaceous plants of the genus, *Polygonum,* as *P. maritimum* **(seaside knotweed),** a glaucous herb of sandy soils. [KNOT[1] + WEED[1]]

knout (nout), *n.* **1.** a whip having a lash of leather thongs, formerly used in Russia for flogging criminals. —*v.t.* **2.** to flog with the knout. [< F < Russ *knut* < Scand; cf. Icel *knūtr* knot]

know[1] (nō), *v.,* **knew, known, know·ing,** *n.* —*v.t.* **1.** to perceive or understand as fact or truth; to apprehend clearly and with certainty: *I know the problem fully.* **2.** to have established or fixed in the mind or memory: *to know a poem by heart; to know the route to a destination.* **3.** to be cognizant or aware of; be acquainted with (a thing, place, person, etc.), as by sight, experience, or report: *to know French; to know the mayor.* **4.** to understand from experience or attainment (usually fol. by *how* before an infinitive): *to know how to make something.* **5.** to be able to distinguish, as one from another: *to know right from wrong.* **6.** *Archaic.* to have sexual intercourse with. —*v.i.* **7.** to have knowledge, or clear and certain perception, as of fact or truth. **8.** to be cognizant or aware, as of some fact, circumstance, or occurrence; have information, as about something. **9. know the ropes,** *Informal.* to understand or be familiar with the particulars of a subject or business: *He knew the ropes better than anyone in the trade.* —*n.* **10.** the fact or state of knowing; knowledge. **11. in the know,** *Informal.* possessing inside information. [ME *knowe(n), knawe(n),* OE *gecnāwan;* c. OHG *-cnāhan,* Icel *knā* to know how, can; akin to L *(g)nōvī* I know, Gk *gignṓskein,* etc. See GNOSTIC] —**know′er,** *n.*
—**Syn. 1.** KNOW, COMPREHEND, UNDERSTAND imply being aware of meanings. To KNOW is to be aware of something as a fact or truth: *He knows the basic facts of the subject. I know that he agrees with me.* To COMPREHEND is to know something thoroughly and to perceive its relationships to certain other ideas, facts, etc. To UNDER-

STAND is to be fully aware not only of the meaning of something but also its implications: *I could comprehend all he said, but did not understand that he was joking.*

know[2] (nō, nou), *n. Scot. and North Eng.* knoll[1].

know·a·ble (nō′ə bəl), *adj.* capable of being known. [KNOW[1] + -ABLE] —**know′a·ble·ness, know′a·bil′i·ty,** *n.*

know-all (nō′ôl′), *n. Informal.* a know-it-all.

knowe (nou, nō), *n. Scot. and North Eng.* knoll[1]. Also, **know.**

know-how (nō′hou′), *n.* knowledge of how to do something; faculty or skill for a particular activity: *Designing a computer requires a lot of know-how.* [n. use of v. phrase *know how*]

know·ing (nō′ing), *adj.* **1.** shrewd, sharp, or astute. **2.** affecting, implying, or deliberately revealing shrewd knowledge of secret or private information: *a knowing glance.* **3.** that knows; having knowledge or information; intelligent; wise. **4.** conscious; intentional; deliberate. [late ME *knawynge* (earlier *knowende, knawande*). See KNOW[1], -ING[2]] —**know′ing·ly,** *adv.* —**know′ing·ness,** *n.*

know-it-all (nō′it ôl′), *Informal.* —*n.* **1.** a person who acts as though he knows everything and who ignores or dismisses the comments and suggestions of others as inconsequential, as unnecessary, or as already having been considered and rejected. —*adj.* **2.** of or characteristic of a know-it-all.

knowl·edge (nol′ij), *n.* **1.** acquaintance with facts, truths, or principles, as from study or investigation; general erudition: *a little knowledge of many things.* **2.** familiarity or conversance, as with a particular subject, branch of learning, etc.: *A knowledge of physics was necessary for the job.* **3.** acquaintance or familiarity gained by sight, experience, or report: *a knowledge of human nature.* **4.** fact or state of knowing; perception of fact or truth; clear and certain mental apprehension. **5.** awareness, as of a fact or circumstance: *She was pleased by their knowledge of her good fortune.* **6.** that which is or may be known; information: *To the best of my knowledge, she never arrived.* **7.** the body of truths or facts accumulated by mankind in the course of time: *Man's knowledge of the origin of the universe is largely theoretical.* **8.** the sum of what is known: *Knowledge of the true situation is limited.* **9.** *Archaic.* sexual intercourse. Cf. **carnal knowledge. 10. to one's knowledge, a.** according to one's certain knowledge. **b.** (with a negative) according to the information available to one: *To my knowledge he hasn't been here.* [ME *knouleche,* OE *cnāwlǣc* acknowledgement, equiv. to *cnāw(an)* (to) KNOW[1] + *-lǣc,* akin to OE *lāc* play, c. Icel (-)*leikr*] —**know′ledge·less,** *adj.*

—**Syn. 1.** enlightenment. See **information. 4.** understanding, discernment, comprehension, judgment. **6.** learning, lore, erudition, scholarship; wisdom, science.

knowl·edge·a·ble (nol′i jə bəl), *adj.* possessing or exhibiting knowledge, insight, or understanding; intelligent; well-informed; discerning; perceptive. Also, **knowl′edg·a·ble.** [KNOWLEDGE + -ABLE] —**knowl′edge·a·ble·ness, knowl′edg·a·ble·ness,** *n.* —**knowl′edge·a·bly, knowl′edg·a·bly,** *adv.*

known (nōn), *v.* **1.** pp. of **know.** —*n.* **2.** a known quantity.

know-noth·ing (nō′nuth′ing), *n.* **1.** an ignorant or totally uninformed person; ignoramus. **2.** an agnostic. **3.** (*caps.*) *U.S. Hist.* a member of a political party (**American party** or **Know′-Noth′ing par′ty**) prominent from 1853 to 1856, whose aim was to keep control of the government in the hands of native-born citizens: so called because members originally professed ignorance of the party's activities. **4.** a person whose anti-intellectualism, xenophobia, and other illiberal traits and political attitudes recall the Know-Nothings. —*adj.* **5.** grossly ignorant; totally uninformed. **6.** agnostic. **7.** (*caps.*) of or pertaining to the Know-Nothings. **8.** of or pertaining to a political know-nothing. —**know′-noth′ing·ism,** *n.*

known′ quan′tity, *Math.* a quantity whose value is given: in algebra, frequently represented by a letter from the first part of the alphabet, as *a, b,* or *c.*

Knox (noks), *n.* **1. (William) Frank(lin),** 1874–1944, U.S. publisher and government official. **2. Henry,** 1750–1806, American Revolutionary general: 1st U.S. Secretary of War 1785–94. **3. John,** c1510–72, Scottish religious reformer and historian. **4. Phi·lan·der Chase** (fi lan′dər), 1853–1921, U.S. lawyer and politician: Secretary of State 1909–13. **5.** a town in NW Indiana. 3458 (1960). **6. Fort.** See **Fort Knox.**

Knox·ville (noks′vil), *n.* **1.** a city in E Tennessee, on the Tennessee River. 111,827 (1960). **2.** a town in central Iowa. 7817 (1960). **3.** a town in central Illinois. 2560 (1960).

KNP, *Chess.* king's knight's pawn.

Knt., Knight.

knuck·le (nuk′əl), *n., v.,* **-led, -ling.** —*n.* **1.** a joint of a finger, esp. one of the joints at the roots of the fingers. **2.** the rounded prominence of such a joint when the finger is bent. **3.** a joint of meat, consisting of the parts about the carpal or tarsal joint of a quadruped. **4.** an angle or protrusion at the intersection of two members or surfaces, as in the timbers of a ship or in a roof. **5.** See **brass knuckles. 6.** a cylindrical projecting part on a hinge, through which an axis or pin passes; the joint of a hinge. **7.** (in a wire mesh) a bend in a wire crossing another wire. **8.** (on a chair arm) one of the ridges left at the front end by longitudinal flutes carved to accommodate the fingers. **9.** *Naut.* a pronounced edge formed by a change in the form of the shell of a hull, esp. between the upper, nearly vertical portion of a fantail stern and the lower portion. —*v.t.* **10.** *Marbles.* to shoot (a marble) from the thumb and forefinger. **11. knuckle down, a.** *Informal.* to apply oneself vigorously and earnestly; become serious: *Just knuckle down for an hour or so and finish.* **b.** Also, **knuckle under.** to submit, yield. [ME *knokel* (akin to D *kneukel,* G *Knöchel*), dim. of a word represented by D *knok,* G *Knochen* bone; see -LE] —**knuck′ly,** *adj.*

knuck′le ball′, *Baseball.* a slow pitch that moves erratically toward home plate, usually delivered by holding the ball between the thumb and the knuckles of the first joints of the first two or three fingers.

knuck·le·bone (nuk′əl bōn′), *n.* **1.** (in man) a bone forming a knuckle of a finger. **2.** (in quadrupeds) a bone homologous with a wrist, ankle, or finger bone of man, or its knobbed end. [KNUCKLE + BONE[1]]

knuck·le-dust·er (nuk′əl dus′tər), *n.* See **brass knuckles.**

knuck·le·head (nuk′əl hed′), *n. Informal.* a stupid, bumbling, inept person. [KNUCKLE + HEAD] —**knuck′le·head′ed,** *adj.*

knuck′le joint′, **1.** a joint forming a knuckle. **2.** *Mach.* a joint between two parts allowing movement in one plane only.

knuck·ler (nuk′lər), *n. Baseball Slang.* See **knuckle ball.** [KNUCKLE + -ER[1]]

Knud·sen (no͞od′sən; *Dan.* kno͞o′sən), *n.* **William S.** (*Signius Wilhelm Paul Knudsen*), 1879–1948, U.S. industrialist, born in Denmark.

Knud′sen effect′, *Thermodynamics.* the different pressures of two gases in containers connected by a capillary tube when the temperatures in the containers are unequal. [named after M. H. C. *Knudsen* (1871–1949), Danish physicist]

knull·ing (nul′ing), *n. Archit.* a convex molding having a series of members separated by indentations, as a bead and reel. Also, **knurling, nulling.** [var. of KNURLING]

knur (nûr), *n.* a knotty or hard protuberance or growth, as on a tree. [ME *knorre, knor;* c. MLG, MD, MHG *knorre*]

knurl (nûrl), *n.* **1.** a small ridge or bead, esp. one of a series, as on a button for decoration or on the edge of a thumbscrew to assist in obtaining a firm grip. **2.** a knur. —*v.t.* **3.** to make knurls or ridges on. Also, **nurl.** [var. of *knurle.* See KNUR, -LE]

knurled (nûrld), *adj.* **1.** having small ridges on the edge or surface; milled. **2.** having knurls or knots; gnarled. [KNURL + -ED[3]]

knurl·ing (nûr′ling), *n.* **1.** a series of knurls, as on a knob. **2.** *Archit.* knulling. [KNURL + -ING[1]]

knurl′ toe′, *Furniture.* See **French foot** (def. 1).

knurl·y (nûr′lē), *adj.,* **knurl·i·er, knurl·i·est.** having knurls or knots; gnarled. [KNURL + -Y[1]]

Knut (kə no͞ot′, -nyo͞ot′), *n.* Canute.

K.O., *pl.* **K.O.'s.** *Boxing.* knockout. Also, **k.o., KO**

ko·a (kō′ə), *n.* **1.** an acacia, *Acacia koa,* of the Hawaiian Islands, characterized by spreading branches and gray bark. **2.** the hard, red or golden-brown wood of this tree, used for making furniture. [< Hawaiian]

ko·a·la (kō ä′lə), *n.* a sluggish, tailless, gray, furry, arboreal marsupial, *Phascolarctos cinereus,* of Australia. [< native Austral]

ko·an (kō′än), *n., pl.* **-ans, -an.** *Zen.* a nonsensical question to a student for which an answer is demanded, the stress of meditation on the question often being illuminating. Cf. **mondo.** [< Jap, equiv. to *kō* public + *an* proposal, design]

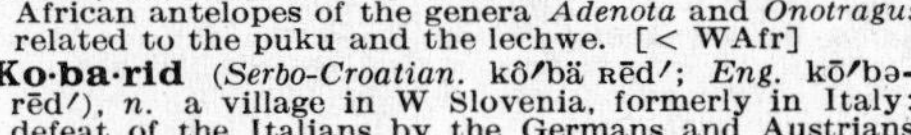

Koalas (Length 2½ ft.)

kob (kob, kōb), *n.* any of several African antelopes of the genera *Adenota* and *Onotragus,* related to the puku and the lechwe. [< WAfr]

Ko·ba·rid (*Serbo-Croatian.* kô′bä rēd′; *Eng.* kō′bə-rēd′), *n.* a village in W Slovenia, formerly in Italy: defeat of the Italians by the Germans and Austrians 1917. Italian, **Caporetto.**

Ko·be (kō′bē; *Jap.* kô′be′), *n.* a seaport on S Honshu, in S Japan. 1,195,152 (1964).

Kö·ben·havn (kœ′bən houn′), *n.* Danish name of **Copenhagen.**

Ko·blenz (kō′blents), *n.* Coblenz.

ko·bold (kō′bold, -bōld), *n.* (in German folklore) **1.** a kind of spirit or goblin, often mischievous, that haunts houses. **2.** a spirit that haunts mines or other underground places. [< G]

Koch (kōkh), *n.* **Ro·bert** (rō′bert), 1843–1910, German bacteriologist and physician: Nobel prize 1905.

Ko·cher (kō′kər; *Ger.* kō′khər), *n.* **E·mil The·o·dor** (ā′mil tā′ō dōr′), 1841–1917, Swiss physiologist, pathologist, and surgeon: Nobel prize 1909.

Ko·chi (kō′chē; *Jap.* kô′chē′), *n.* a seaport on central Shikoku, in SW Japan. 224,900 (1964).

Ko·da·chrome (kō′də krōm′), *n. Trademark.* **1.** a color photograph. **2.** a process of color photography.

Ko·dak (kō′dak), *n., v.,* **-daked, -dak·ing.** —*n.* **1.** *Trademark.* a portable camera introduced by George Eastman in 1888, using a roll of film and intended for taking snapshots. —*v.t., v.i.* **2.** (*l.c.*) to photograph with a Kodak. —**ko′dak·er,** *n.*

Ko·dá·ly (kō dī′, -dä′ē; *Hung.* kō′dä yᵊ), *n.* **Zol·tán** (zôl′tän), 1882–1967, Hungarian composer.

Ko·di·ak (kō′dē ak′), *n.* **1.** an island in the N Pacific, near the base of the Alaska Peninsula. 100 mi. long. **2.** a town on this island. 2628 (1960). **3.** See **Kodiak bear.**

Ko′diak bear′, a large, brown bear, *Ursus middendorffi,* found along the coast of Alaska and British Columbia, that grows to a length of nine feet. Also, **Kadiak bear.** Also called **Kodiak.**

ko·do·gu (kō dō′go͞o; *Jap.* kô dô′go͝o), *n., pl.* **-gu.** the complete set of mounts for a Japanese sword or knife, excepting the tsuba. [< Jap, equiv. to *ko* small + *dogu* implements]

Ko·dok (kō′dok), *n.* modern name of **Fashoda.**

kOe, kilo-oersted; kilo-oersteds.

ko·el (kō′əl), *n.* any of several cuckoos of the genus *Eudynamys,* of India, the Malay Archipelago, and Australia. [< Hindi < Skt *kokila*]

Koest·ler (kest′lər; *Hung.* kœst′ler), *n.* **Ar·thur** (är′thər; *Hung.* or′to͝or), 1905–87, Hungarian novelist, critic, and journalist.

K. of C., Knights of Columbus.

Koff·ka (kôf′kä), *n.* **Kurt** (ko͝ort), 1886–1941, German psychologist in the U.S.

K. of P., Knights of Pythias.

Ko·fu (kô′fo͞o), *n.* a city on S Honshu, in central Japan. 169,128 (1964).

ko·gai (kō gī′; *Jap.* kô gī′), *n., pl.* **-gai.** an ornamental pin carried in a sheath in the scabbard of a wakizashi or katana. [< Jap: bodkin]

Ko·hel·eth (kō hel′eth), *n.* the book of Ecclesiastes. [< Heb *qōheleth* counselor]

Ko·hen (kô hän′; *Eng.* kō′hän, kō′ən, koin), *n., pl.* **Ko·ha·nim** (kô hä nēm′), *Eng.* **Ko·hens.** *Hebrew.* a member of the Jewish priestly class, descended from Aaron, having sacrificial, ministerial, and other sacred functions from Aaronic times to about the 1st century A.D. and now having essentially honorific religious duties and prerogatives. Also, **Cohen.**

Ko·hi·ma (kō′hē mä′), *n.* a town in and the capital of Nagaland, in E India. 7200 (1961).

Koh·i·noor (kō′ə no͝or′), *n.* an Indian diamond weighing 106 carats; now part of the British crown jewels. [< Pers *kōhinūr,* lit., mountain (*kōh*) of (*i*) light (*nūr*)]

Kohl (kōl), *n.* **Hel·mut** (hel′mo͝ot), born 1930, German political leader: chancellor of West Germany (1982–90); chancellor of Germany since 1990.

kohl (kōl), *n.* a powder, as finely powdered antimony sulfide, used in the East to darken the eyelids, eyebrows, etc.

Köh·ler (kœ′lər), *n.* **Wolf·gang** (vôlf′gäng), 1887–1967, German psychologist.

kohl·ra·bi (kōl rä′bē, kōl′rä′-), *n., pl.* **-bies.** a brassicaceous plant, *Brassica oleracea gongylodes,* whose stem above ground swells into an edible bulblike formation. [< G < It *cavolrape* (pl. of *cavolrapa,* lit., stalk or cabbage turnip), with G *Kohl* cabbage for It *cavol-.* See COLE, RAPE[2]]

Kohlrabi

koil·o·nych·i·a (koi′lō nik′ē ə), *n. Med.* an abnormal condition in which the outer surfaces of the nails are concave; spoon nail. [< Gk *koîl(os)* hollow + *onych-* (s. of *ónyx* nail; see ONYX) + -IA]

koi·ne (koi nā′), *n.* **the koine,** an amalgam of Greek dialects, chiefly Attic and Ionic, that replaced the Classical Greek dialects in the Hellenistic period and flourished under the Roman Empire. [< Gk *koinḗ* (*diálektos*) common (dialect); see CENO-[2]]

Ko·kand (ko känt′), *n.* a city in NE Uzbekistan, in the SW Soviet Union in Asia: formerly the center of a powerful khanate. 117,000 (est. 1962).

ko·kan·ee (kō kan′ē), *n.* any of several lacustrine sockeye salmons. [? after the *Kokanee,* a stream in British Columbia]

ko·ka·ta·na (kō′kə tä′nə; *Jap.* kô′kä tä′nä), *n., pl.* **-na.** kozuka (def. 2). [< Jap, equiv. to *ko* small + *katana* sword]

Kok·ka (kôk′kä), *adj.* of or pertaining to the branch of Shinto recognized as the official state religion of Japan; jinja. Cf. **Shuha.** [< Jap]

Kok·ko·la (kôk′kô lä), *n.* a seaport in E Finland, on the Gulf of Bothnia. 18,989 (est. 1965).

ko·ko (kō′kō), *n., pl.* **-kos.** lebbek (def. 2). [var. of *kokko* < ?]

Ko·ko·mo (kō′kə mō′), *n.* a city in central Indiana. 47,197 (1960).

Ko·ko Nor (kō′kō′ nôr′), **1.** a lake in W China, in Chinghai province. 23 sq. mi. **2.** Chinghai.

Ko·kosch·ka (kō kôsh′kä), *n.* **Os·kar** (ôs′kär), 1886–1980, Austrian painter and dramatist.

kok-sa·ghyz (kōk′sə gēz′), *n.* a dandelion, *Taraxacum kok-saghyz,* of central Asia, having fleshy roots that yield a rubberlike latex. Also called **Russian dandelion.** [< Russ *kok-sagyz* < Turkic (Kazak) *kok-sagiz,* lit., root gum]

ko·ku (kō′ko͞o; *Jap.* kô′ko͝o), *n., pl.* **-ku.** a Japanese unit of dry measure equivalent to 5.12 bushels. [< Jap: lit., measure]

Ko·ku·ra (kô′ko͝o rä′), *n.* a seaport on N Kyushu, in SW Japan. 286,474 (1964).

ko·la (kō′lə), *n.* **1.** See **kola nut. 2.** an extract prepared from it. **3.** the tree producing it. **4.** cola[1]. Also, **cola.** [appar. var. of Mandingo *kolo*]

Ko·la (kō′lä), *n.* **1.** Also, **Ko′la Penin′sula.** a peninsula in the NW Soviet Union in Europe, between the White and Barents seas. **2.** Also, **Cola.** a boy's given name.

ko·lac·ky (kə lä′chē, -kē), *n., pl.* **-ky.** a sweet bun filled with jam or pulped fruit. Also, **ko·lach** (kō′läch). [< Czech *koláč*]

ko′la nut′, a brownish seed, about the size of a chestnut, produced by a sterculiaceous tree, *Cola nitida,* of western tropical Africa, the West Indies, and Brazil, and containing both caffein and theobromine; formerly used as a stimulant in soft drinks.

Ko·lar′ Gold′ Fields′ (kō lär′), a city in SE Mysore, in S India: rich mining district. 146,811 (1961).

Kol·be (kôl′bə), *n.* **Ge·org** (gā ôrk′), 1877–1947, German sculptor.

Kol·chak (kol chäk′), *n.* **A·le·ksan·dr Va·si·lye·vich** (ä le ksän′dər vä sē′lyə vich), 1874–1920, Russian counterrevolutionary and admiral.

Kol·de·wey (kôl′də vī′), *n.* **Ro·bert** (rob′ərt; *Ger.* rō′bert), 1855–1925, German architect and archaeologist.

Kol′ha·pur′ and Dec′can States′ (kōl′hä po͝or′), a group of former princely states in W India: incorporated into Bombay state in 1948; now part of Gujarat and Maharashtra states.

Ko·li (kō′lē), *n., pl.* **-lis,** (*esp. collectively*) **-li.** a people of low caste in northern India.

Ko·li·ma (*Russ.* ko li mä′), *n.* Kolyma.

ko·lin·sky (kə lin′skē), *n., pl.* **-skies. 1.** an Asian mink, *Mustela siberica,* having buff or tawny fur. **2.** the fur of such an animal. [< Russ *kolinski* pertaining to KOLA]

kol·khoz (kol khôz′), *n.* (in the U.S.S.R.) a collective farm. [< Russ, equiv. to *kol(lektivnoe)* COLLECTIVE + *khoz(yaistvo)* household, farm]

Koll·witz (kôl′vits), *n.* **Kä·the** (ke′tə), 1867–1945, German graphic artist and sculptress.

Köln (kœln), *n.* German name of **Cologne.**

Kol Ni·dre (kôl nē drā′; *Eng.* kōl′ nid′rə, -rā, kōl′), *Judaism.* a liturgical prayer for recitation at the beginning of the service on the eve of Yom Kippur asking that all unfulfilled vows to God be nullified and all transgressions forgiven. [< Aram *kōl* all + *nidhrē* vows, promises]

ko·lo (kō′lō), *n., pl.* **-los.** a Serbian folk dance performed by a group arranged in a circle, with the soloists in the center. [< Serbo-Croatian < OSlav: wheel]

Ko·lom·na (ko lôm′nä), *n.* a city in the W RSFSR, in the central Soviet Union in Europe, SE of Moscow. 125,000 (est. 1962).

Ko·lozs·vár (kô′lōzh vär′), *n.* Hungarian name of **Cluj.**

Kol·we·zi (kōl wez′ē), *n.* a city in S Zaire. 47,772 (est. 1958).

Ko·ly·ma (ko li mä′), *n.* a river in the NE Soviet Union in Asia, flowing NE to the Arctic Ocean. 1000 mi. long. Also, **Kolima.**

Kolyma′ Range′, a mountain range in NE Siberia.

ko·mat·ik (kō mat′ik), *Chiefly Canadian.* an Eskimo sled made by binding crossbars to wooden runners with rawhide. [< Eskimo (Labrador dial.)]

Ko·mi (kō′mē), *n.* Zyrian.

Ko′mi Auton′omous Repub′lic (kō′mē), an autonomous republic in the NW Russian Federation in Europe. 1,118,000; 145,221 sq. mi. *Cap.:* Syktyvkar.

Kom·in·tern (kom′in tûrn′), *n.* Comintern.

Kom·mu·narsk (kom mo͞o närsk′), *n.* a city in the E Ukraine, in the Soviet Union. 110,000 (est. 1962).

Ko·mo′do drag′on (kə mō′dō), a monitor lizard, *Varanus komodoensis,* of Komodo and adjacent Indonesian islands, that grows to a length of 10 feet: the largest lizard in the world. Also called **dragon lizard, giant lizard, Komo′do liz′ard.**

Ko·mon·dor (kom′ən dôr′), *n., pl.* **-dors, -dor·ok** (-dôr′ək, -dôr′-). one of a Hungarian breed of large dogs having a long, matted, white coat, used for herding sheep and as a watchdog. [< Hung]

Kom·so·mol (kom′sə môl′, kom′sə môl′), *n.* **1.** a communist organization in the Soviet Union for youths 16 years of age and older. **2.** a member of this organization. Cf. **Octobrist, Pioneer.** [< Russ, short for *Kommunisticheskii Soyuz Molodezhi* Communist Union of Youth]

Kom·so·molsk (kom so môlsk′), *n.* a city in the E RSFSR, in the E Soviet Union in Asia, on the Amur River. 192,000 (est. 1962).

Ko·mu·ra (kô′mo͞o rä′), *n.* **Marquis Ju·ta·ro** (jo͞o′tä rō′), 1855–1911, Japanese statesman and diplomat.

ko·na (kō′nə), *n.* a southwesterly winter wind in Hawaii, often strong and bringing rain, associated with a kona cyclone. [< Hawaiian]

ko′na cy′clone, a slow-moving cyclone occurring during the winter over the subtropical Pacific Ocean. Also called **ko′na storm′.**

ko·nak (kō näk′), *n.* (in Turkey) a large, usually official residence. [< Turk: lit., stopping-place (for the night, on a journey)]

Ko·na·kri (*Fr.* kō na krē′), *n.* Conakry.

Ko·na·rak (kō nä′rək), *n.* a village in E Orissa, in E India: site of the famous Black Pagoda. Also, **Kanarak.**

Ko·ner (kō′nər), *n.* **Pauline,** born 1912?, U.S. dancer and choreographer.

Ko·nev (kô′nyəf), *n.* **I·van Ste·pa·no·vich** (i vän′ stepä′no vich), 1897–1973, Russian general and politician.

Kon·ia (kōn′yä), *n.* Konya.

Ko·nig (kō′nig), *n.* a crater in the third quadrant of the face of the moon: about 14 miles in diameter.

Kö·nig·grätz (kœ′niḵh grets′), *n.* a town in NW Czechoslovakia, on the Elbe River: Austrians defeated by Prussians in Battle of Sadowa 1866. 55,136 (1961). Czech, **Hradec Králové.**

Kö·nigs·berg (kœ′niḵhs berḵh′; *Eng.* kō′nigz bûrg′), *n.* German name of **Kaliningrad.**

Kö·nigs·hüt·te (kœ′niḵhs hy′tə), *n.* German name of **Chorzów.**

ko·nim·e·ter (kō nim′i tər), *n.* an instrument for measuring the amount of dust in the air. [< Gk *kóni(s)* dust + -METER]

ko·ni·ol·o·gy (kō′nē ol′ə jē), *n.* the study of atmospheric dust and other impurities suspended in the air, as germs, pollen, etc. Also, **coniology.** [< Gk *kóni(s)* dust + -o- + -LOGY]

Ko·no·ye (kô′nô ye′), *n.* **Prince Fu·mi·ma·ro** (fo͞o′mē mä′rō), 1891–1945, Japanese statesman: premier 1937–39, 1940–41.

Kon·rad (kon′rad), *n.* a boy's given name. Also, **Conrad.**

Kon·stanz (kôn′stänts), *n.* German name of **Constance.**

kon·ta·ki·on (kôn tä′kē ôn; *Eng.* kon tä′kē on′), *n., pl.* **-ki·a** (-kē ä; *Eng.* -kē ə). *Gk. Orth. Ch.* a short hymn honoring a saint. Also, **contakion.** [< eccl. Gk, special use of LGk *kontákion* scroll, equiv. to *kontak-* (s. of *kontáx*) pole + *-ion* dim. suffix]

Kon·ya (kôn′yä), *n.* a city in S Turkey, S of Ankara. 157,801 (1965). Also, **Kon′ia.** Ancient, **Iconium.**

Koo (ko͞o), *n.* **(Vi·kyuin) Wellington** (wē′gyin′), (*Ku Wei-chün*), born 1887, Chinese diplomat and statesman.

koo·doo (ko͞o′do͞o), *n., pl.* **-doos.** kudu.

kook (ko͞ok), *n. Slang.* **1.** an unusual, peculiar, or foolish person. **2.** an insane person. [? alter. of CUCKOO]

kook·a·bur·ra (ko͝ok′ə bûr′ə), *n.* an Australian kingfisher, *Dacelo gigas,* having a loud, harsh cry that resembles laughter. Also called **laughing jackass.** [< native Austral]

kook·y (ko͞o′kē), *adj.,* **kook·i·er, kook·i·est.** *Slang.* of or pertaining to a kook. Also, **kook′ie.** [KOOK + -Y¹]

koo·ra·jong (ko͝or′ə jong′), *n.* kurrajong.

Koord (kûrd, ko͝ord), *n.* a Kurd.

Koo·te·nay (ko͞ot′ənā′), *n.* a river flowing from SW Canada through NW Montana and N Idaho, swinging back into Canada to the Columbia River. 400 mi. long. Also, **Koo′te·nai′, Kutenay, Kutenai.**

Koo′tenay Lake′, a lake in W Canada, in S British Columbia. 64 mi. long.

kop (kop), *n.* (in South Africa) a hill. [< SAfrD: lit., head, hence high or top part. See COP²]

kop., kopeck.

ko·peck (kō′pek), *n.* an aluminum-bronze coin of Russia, the Soviet Union, and its successor states, the 100th part of a ruble. Also, **ko′pek, copeck.** [< Russ *kopéĭka,* equiv. to *kop′ë* lance, spear + *-ka* dim. suffix: so called from the lance with which the figure on the coin was armed]

Ko·peisk (ko pāsk′), *n.* a city in the SW RSFSR, in the W Soviet Union in Asia, near the Urals. 168,000 (est. 1962). Also, **Ko·peysk′.**

kopf·ring (kôpf′ring), *n.* a metal ring welded to the nose of a bomb to reduce its penetration in earth or water. [< G, equiv. to *Kopf* head + *Ring* band, RING¹]

koph (kôf), *n.* **1.** the 19th letter of the Hebrew alphabet. **2.** the uvular stop consonant sound represented by this letter. [< Heb *qoph*]

ko·pis (kō′pis), *n.* a curved, double-edged sword of ancient Egypt and Greece. Also called **machaira, machera.** [< Gk *kopís* cleaver, sword]

Kop·it (kop′it), *n.* **Arthur,** born 1937, U.S. playwright.

kop·je (kop′ē), *n.* (in South Africa) a small hill. [< SAfrD, equiv. to *kop* KOP + *-je* dim. suffix]

Kop′lik's spots′ (kop′liks), (in measles) small pale spots with reddish rims that appear on the lips and mucous membranes inside the cheeks before the skin eruption takes place. [named after Henry *Koplik* (1858–1927), American pediatrician]

kor (kōr, kôr), *n.* homer². [< Heb]

ko·rad·ji (kô rä′jē), *n. Australian.* boyla. Also, **coraji.** [< native Austral]

Ko·rah (kōr′ə, kôr′ə), *n.* a Levite who led a rebellion against Moses and Aaron. Num. 16. Also, **Core.**

Ko·ran (kō rän′, -ran′, kô-), *n.* the sacred text of Islam, divided into 114 suras, believed to have been dictated to Muhammad by Gabriel and regarded by Muslims as the foundation of law, religion, culture, and politics. Also, **Quran.** [< Ar *qur'ān* book, reading, akin to *qara'a* to read, recite] —**Ko·ran·ic** (kō ran′ik, kō-), *adj.*

Kor·do·fan (kôr′dō fän′), *n.* a province in the central Sudan. 1,761,968 (1956); ab. 147,000 sq. mi. *Cap.:* El Obeid.

Kor·do·fan·i·an (kôr′də fan′ē ən), *n.* a subfamily of Niger-Kordofanian that comprises about 30 languages spoken in southern Kordofan. [KORDOFAN + -IAN]

ko·re (kōr′ē, kôr′ē; kōr′ā, kôr′ā), *n., pl.* **ko·rai** (kōr′ī, kôr′ī). **1.** *Gk. Antiq.* a sculptured representation of a young woman, esp. one produced prior to the 5th century B.C. **2.** (*cap.*) *Class. Myth.* Cora (def. 1). [< Gk *kórē* girl]

Ko·re·a (kə rē′ə, kō-), *n.* a former country in E Asia, on a peninsula SE of Manchuria and between the Sea of Japan and the Yellow Sea: a kingdom prior to 1910; under Japanese rule 1910–45; now divided at 38° N into North Korea and South Korea. Outbreak of Korean War June 25, 1950 led to UN aid in defense of South Korea. *Cap.:* Seoul. Cf. **North Korea, South Korea.** Japanese, **Chosen.**

Ko·re·an (kō rē′ən, kō-), *adj.* **1.** of Korea, its inhabitants, or their language. —*n.* **2.** a native of Korea. **3.** the language of Korea. [KORE(A) + -AN]

Kore′an azal′ea, a semi-evergreen shrub, *Azalea yedoensis,* of eastern Asia, having leaves which are dark green above and paler beneath, and purple-spotted, reddish flowers.

Kore′an lawn′ grass′, a creeping grass, *Zoysia japonica,* of Japan and China, having purplish spikelets and rootstalks that send up numerous tough, wiry shoots. Also called **Japanese lawn grass.**

Kore′an War′, the war, begun on June 25, 1950, between North Korea aided by Communist China and South Korea aided by the United Nations: truce signed July 27, 1953.

Kore′a Strait′, a strait between Korea and Japan, connecting the Sea of Japan and the East China Sea. 120 mi. long.

Ko·ren (kōr′ən, kôr′-), *n.* a girl's given name.

Ko·ri·deth·i·an·us (kôr′i deth′ē an′əs, -ā′nəs), *n.* the Greek uncial codex, dating from the 8th or 9th century A.D., that contains the text of the Gospels. Cf. **codex** (def. 2). [named after *Korideth,* Anatolia, whence it came; see -IAN]

Korn·berg (kôrn′bərg), *n.* **Arthur,** born 1918, U.S. biochemist: Nobel prize for medicine 1959.

Korn·gold (kôrn′gōld′; *Ger.* kôrn′gôlt′), *n.* **E·rich Wolf·gang** (er′ik wo͝olf′gang; *Ger.* ā′riḵh vôlf′gäng), 1897–1957, Austrian composer, conductor, and pianist in the U.S.

ko·ro·na (kōr′ə nə, kôr′-), *n.* **1.** Also, **krone.** a former silver coin and monetary unit of Austria, equal to 100 hellers: discontinued after 1923. **2.** koruna. [var. of KRONE²]

Kor·o·seal (kôr′ə sēl′, kor′-), *Trademark.* any of a group of strong, durable, elastic, vinyl-coated fabrics, used for insulation, linings, and coatings, in the manufacture of inflatable devices, etc.

Kort′ noz′zle (kôrt), *Naut.* a cylindrical fitting around a propeller, tapered inward toward the stern to increase thrust and maneuverability.

ko·ru·na (kôr′ə nä′), *n., pl.* **ko·ru·ny** (kôr′ə nē), **ko·run** (kôr′o͞on), **ko·ru·nas.** an aluminum bronze coin and monetary unit of the Czech Republic, equal to 100 halers. *Abbr.:* Kčs. Also, **korona.** [< Czech < L *corōna* a crown, wreath; see CORONA]

Ko·rzyb·ski (kôr zip′skē; *Pol.* kô zhip′skē), *n.* **Alfred (Hab·dank Skar·bek)** (hab′dangk skär′bek; *Pol.* häp′dängk skär′bek), 1879–1950, U.S. writer on general semantics, born in Poland.

kos (kōs), *n., pl.* **kos.** (in India) a unit of land distance of various lengths from 1 to 3 miles. Also, **coss.** [< Hindi < Skt *krośa*]

Kos (kos, kôs), *n.* one of the Greek Dodecanese Islands in the SE Aegean Sea, off the SW coast of Turkey. 19,076 (1951); 111 sq. mi. Also, **Cos.** Italian, **Coo.**

Kos·ci·us·ko (kos′ē us′kō; *also for 1 Pol.* kôsh cho͞osh′-ko), *n.* **1. Thaddeus** (*Tadeusz Andrzej Bonawentura Kościuszko*), 1746–1817, Polish patriot: general in the American Revolutionary army. **2. Mount,** the highest mountain in Australia, in SE New South Wales. **3.** a town in central Mississippi. 6800 (1960).

ko·sha (kō′shə), *n. Hinduism.* any of the five layers of physical and mental being composing the personal self, Atman being within the innermost layer. [< Skt]

ko·sher (kō′shər), *adj.* **1.** *Judaism.* **a.** fit or allowed to be eaten or used, according to the dietary or ceremonial laws: *kosher meat; kosher dishes; a kosher tallith.* **b.** adhering to the laws governing such fitness: *a kosher restaurant.* **2.** *Informal.* **a.** genuine; authentic. **b.** proper; legitimate. **3. keep kosher,** to adhere to dietary laws of Judaism. —*n.* **4.** *Informal.* kosher food: *Let's eat kosher tonight.* —*v.t.* **5.** *Judaism.* to make kosher: *to kosher meat by salting.* Also, **kasher.** [< Yiddish < Heb *kāshēr* right, fit]

Ko·shu (kō′sho͞o′), *n.* Japanese name of **Kwangju.**

Ko·ši·ce (kô′shi tse), *n.* a city in SE Slovakia. 202,368. Hungarian, **Kassa.**

ko·so (kō′sō), *n., pl.* **-sos.** *Pharm.* brayera. [var. of KUSSO]

Kos·sel (kôs′əl), *n.* **Al·brecht** (äl′breḵht), 1853–1927, German chemist: Nobel prize for medicine 1910.

Kos·suth (kos′o͞oth; *Hung.* kô′sho͞ot), *n.* **1. Fer·enc** (fer′ents), 1841–1914, Hungarian statesman. **2.** his father, **La·jos** (lo′yōsh), 1802–94, Hungarian patriot, statesman, and writer.

Kos·te·la·netz (kos′tə lä′nits), *n.* **An·dré** (än′drā), born 1901, U.S. orchestra conductor and pianist, born in Russia.

Kos·ti (kôs′tē), *n.* a city in E Sudan, on the White Nile. 22,688 (1956).

Ko·stro·ma (ko stro mä′), *n.* a city in the W RSFSR, in the central Soviet Union in Europe, NE of Moscow, on the Volga. 198,000 (est. 1964).

Ko·sy·gin (ko sē′gin), *n.* **A·lek·sei Ni·ko·la·ye·vich** (ä lek sā′ ni ko lä′yə vich), 1904–80, Russian politician: premier of the U.S.S.R. 1964–80.

Ko·ta Bha·ru (kō′tə bär′o͞o), a seaport in N Kelantan, in Malaysia, on the SE Malay Peninsula. 38,103 (1957). Also, **Ko′ta Bah′ru.**

ko·to (kō′tō; *Jap.* kô′tô′), *n., pl.* **-tos,** *Jap.* **-to.** a Japanese musical instrument having numerous strings that are stretched over a convex wooden sounding board and are plucked with a plectrum. [< Jap]

ko·tow (kō′tou′, -tou′), *v.i., n.* kowtow. —**ko′tow′·er,** *n.*

kot·ta·bos (kot′ə bos′), *n., pl.* **-boi** (-boi′). **1.** (in ancient Greece) any of several games characterized by the hurling of wine dregs from a cup into or upon a given object, as into a floating cup in order to sink it or upon the pans of a suspended balance in order to cause a pan to strike the object set below. **2.** a similar game, in which wine dregs were hurled at a saucerlike float in order to sink it. [< Gk]

kot′tabos ka·tak′tos (kə tak′təs), kottabos. [< Gk, equiv. to *kóttabos* KOTTABOS + *kataktós* brought down (*kat-* KAT- + *ak-,* var. s. of *ágein* to bring, + *-tos* ptp. suffix)]

kot·wal (kōt′wäl), *n. Anglo-Indian.* a native police officer. Also, **cotwal.** [< Hindi *koṭwāl*]

kot·wa·li (kōt′wä lē), *n. Anglo-Indian.* a police station. Also, **kot′wa·lee.** [< Hindi *kotwālī*]

Kot·ze·bue (kôt′sə bo͞o′), *n.* **Au·gust Frie·drich Ferdi·nand von** (ou′go͝ost frē′driḵh fer′di nänt′ fən), 1761–1819, German dramatist.

kou·mis (ko͞o′mis), *n.* kumiss. Also, **kou′miss, kou′myss.**

kou·prey (ko͞o′prā), *n., pl.* **-preys,** (*esp. collectively*) **-prey.** a wild ox, *Bibos* (*Novibos*) *Sauveli,* of Laos and Cambodia, having a blackish-brown body with white markings on the back and feet. Also called **gray ox.** [from native Cambodian word]

kour·bash (ko͝or′bash), *n., v.t.* kurbash.

kou·ros (ko͝or′ōs), *n., pl.* **kou·roi** (ko͝or′oi). *Gk. Antiq.* a sculptured representation of a young man, esp. one produced prior to the 5th century B.C. [< Gk, var. of *kóros* boy; cf. *kórē* girl]

Kous·se·vitz·ky (ko͞o′sə vit′skē), *n.* **Serge** (sârzh), (*Sergei Alexandrovich Koussevitsky*), 1874–1951, Russian orchestra conductor in the U.S.

kous·so (ko͞o′sō), *n., pl.* **-sos.** *Pharm.* brayera. [var. of KUSSO]

Ko·va·lev·sky (kov′ə lef′skē, -lev′-), *n.* **So·nia** (sōn′yə), 1850–91, Russian mathematician.

Kov·no (kôv′no), *n.* Russian name of **Kaunas.**

Kov·rov (kov rôf′), *n.* a city in the W RSFSR, in the central Soviet Union in Europe, ENE of Moscow. 105,000 (est. 1962).

Ko·weit (kō wāt′), *n.* Kuwait.

Kow·loon (kou′lo͞on′), *n.* **1.** a peninsula in SE China, opposite Hong Kong island: a part of the Hong Kong colony. 1,000,000 (est. 1954); 3 sq. mi. **2.** a seaport on this peninsula.

kow·tow (kou′tou′, -tou′, kō′-), *v.i.* **1.** to touch the forehead to the ground while kneeling, as an act of worship, reverence, apology, etc., esp. in former Chinese custom. **2.** to act in an obsequious manner; show servile deference. —*n.* **3.** the act of kowtowing. Also, **kotow.** [< Chin (Mandarin) *k'o-t'ou,* lit., knock (one's) head] —**kow′tow′er,** *n.*

Ko·za·ni (kô zä′nē), *n.* a city in central Greece. 21,537 (1961). Also, **Ko·zá′ne.**

Ko·zhi·kode (kō′zhi kōd′), *n.* Malayalam name of **Calicut.**

Koz·lov (koz lôf′), *n.* **Frol R(o·ma·no·vich)** (frôl romä′no vich), 1908–65, Russian government official.

ko·zu·ka (kō zo͞o′kə; *Jap.* kô zo͞o′kä), *n., pl.* **-ka.** **1.** a detachable dagger blade made of a plate of steel and a plate of iron welded together and sharpened with a bevel on the iron face, used with an elaborately decorated handle, and worn mainly with the wakizashi. **2.** Also called **ko-katana.** this blade with its handle. [< Jap: lit., small hilt]

KP, *Chess.* king's pawn.

K.P., **1.** *Mil.* See **kitchen police. 2.** Knight of the Order of St. Patrick. **3.** Knights of Pythias.

kpc, kiloparsec; kiloparsecs.

Kr, *Chem.* krypton.

KR, *Chess.* king's rook.

Kr., **1.** (in Sweden and the Faroe Islands) krona; kronor. **2.** (in Iceland) króna; krónur. **3.** (in Denmark and Norway) krone; kroner.

kr., **1.** kreutzer. **2.** krona; kronor. **3.** króna; krónur. **4.** krone; kroner.

Kra (krä), *n.* **Isthmus of,** the narrowest part of the Malay Peninsula, between the Bay of Bengal and the Gulf of Siam. 35 mi. wide.

kraal (kräl), *n.* **1.** a village of South African natives, usually surrounded by a stockade or the like and often

CONCISE ETYMOLOGY KEY: <, descended or derived from; >, whence; b., blend of, blended; c., cognate with; deriv., derivative; equiv., equivalent; imit., imitative; m., modification of; obl., oblique; r., replacing; s., stem; sp., spelling; translation; ?, origin unknown, perhaps; *, hypothetical. See the full key inside the front cover.

having a central space for livestock. 2. the kraal as a social unit. 3. an enclosure for cattle and other domestic animals in southern Africa. —*v.t.* 4. to shut up in a kraal, as cattle. Also, **craal.** [< SAfrD < Pg *curral* pen; see CORRAL]

K-ra·di·a·tion (kā′rā′dē ā′shən), *n.* *Physics.* See under **K-line.**

Krae·pe·lin (kre′pə lēn′), *n.* **E·mil** (ā′mēl), 1856–1926, German psychiatrist.

Krafft (kraft, kräft), *n.* a crater in the second quadrant of the face of the moon: about 30 miles in diameter.

Krafft-E·bing (kraft′eb′ing, kräft′-; *Ger.* kräft′ā′-bing), *n.* **Rich·ard** (rich′ərd; *Ger.* riᴋʜ′ärt), **Baron von,** 1840–1902, German neurologist and author of works on mental disease.

kraft (kraft, kräft), *n.* a strong, usually brown paper processed from wood pulp and used for bags and as wrapping paper. [< G: lit., strength]

kraft′ proc′ess. See **sulfate process.**

Krag′-Jor′gen·sen ri′fle (kräg′yôr′gən sən, krag′-), a Danish bolt-action .30-caliber rifle, used by the U.S. Army between 1894 and 1904. [named after O. *Krag* and E. *Jörgensen,* the Norwegian inventors]

krait (krīt), *n.* any of several extremely venomous elapid snakes of the genus *Bungarus,* of southeastern Asia and the Malay Archipelago. [< Hindi *karait*]

Krak (kräk), *n.* Kerak.

Kra·ka·tau (krä′kə tou′), *n.* a small volcanic island in Indonesia, between Java and Sumatra: violent eruption 1883. Also, **Kra′ka·tao′, Kra·ka·to·a** (krä′kə-tō′ə).

Kra·kau (krä′kou), *n.* German name of **Cracow.**

kra·ken (krä′kən), *n.* (*often cap.*) a legendary sea-monster causing large whirlpools off the coast of Norway. [< Norw]

Kra·ków (krä′ko͝of), *n.* Polish name of **Cracow.**

kra·ko·wi·ak (krə kō′vē ak′), *n.* a lively Polish folk dance in duple meter with syncopated accents. Also, **cracovienne.** [< Pol, after Kraków]

Kra·ma·torsk (krä mä tôrsk′), *n.* a city in the E Ukraine, in the S Soviet Union in Europe. 126,000 (est. 1962).

Kra·mer (krā′mər), *n.* **John Albert (Jack),** born 1921, U.S. tennis player.

kran (krän), *n.* a former silver coin of Iran. [< Pers *qrān*]

Kra·nach (*Ger.* krä′näᴋʜ), *n.* Cranach.

Kras·no·dar (kräs′no där′), *n.* 1. a territory of the RSFSR, in the S Soviet Union in Europe. 3,766,000 (1959); 34,200 sq. mi. 2. Formerly, **Ekaterinodar.** a port in and the capital of this territory, on the Kuban River, near the Sea of Azov. 377,000 (est. 1964).

Kras·no·yarsk (kräs′no yärsk′), *n.* 1. a territory of the RSFSR, in the central Soviet Union in Asia. 2,614,-000 (1959); 827,507 sq. mi. 2. a town in and the capital of this territory, on the Yenisei River. 542,000 (1965).

Kras·ny (kräs′ni), *n.* Russian name of **Kyzyl.**

kra·ter (krā′tər), *n.* *Gk. and Rom. Antiq.* a mixing bowl characterized by a wide neck and body with two handles projecting vertically from the juncture of the neck and body, used to mix wine and water. Also, **crater.** Cf. **kelebe.** [< Gk: mixing bowl; see CRATER]

K ration, *U.S. Army.* one of the emergency field rations used when other rations are not available. [K for Ancel *Keys* (b. 1904), American physiologist]

krau·ro·sis (krô rō′sis), *n.* *Med.* atrophy and shrinkage of the skin, esp. of the vulva. [< Gk *kraur(ós)* dry, brittle + -OSIS] —**krau·rot·ic** (krô rot′ik), *adj.*

Kraus (krous), *n.* **Karl** (kärl), 1874–1936, Austrian writer and editor.

Krauss (krous; *Ger.* krous), *n.* **Cle·mens** (klā′mens), 1893–1954, Austrian conductor and pianist.

Kraut (krout), *n.* (*often l.c.*) *Disparaging.* a German. [< G (*Sauer*)*kraut* pickled (sour) cabbage]

Krebs (kreps; *Eng.* krebz), *n.* **Hans A·dolf** (häns ä′-dôlf; *Eng.* hanz ad′ôlf, ā′dôlf), born 1900, German biochemist in England: Nobel prize for medicine 1953.

Kre·feld (krā′feld; *Ger.* krā′felt′), *n.* a city in W North Rhine-Westphalia, in W West Germany, NW of Cologne. 216,900 (1963). Also, **Crefeld.**

Kreis·ler (krīs′lər), *n.* **Fritz** (frits), 1875–1962, Austrian violinist and composer in the U.S.

Krem·en·chug (krem′en cho͞ok′), *n.* a city in the central Ukraine, in the SW Soviet Union in Europe, on the Dnieper River. 100,000 (est. 1962).

Krem·lin (krem′lin), *n.* 1. the executive branch of the government of the Soviet Union, esp. in regard to its foreign affairs. 2. **the Kremlin,** the citadel of Moscow, including within its walls the chief office of the Soviet government. 3. (*l.c.*) the citadel of any Russian city or town. [earlier *Kremelien* < G (now obs.) < Russ *kreml′* fortress (< Tatar) + G *-in* fem. suffix; r. 17th-century *Kremelina,* Latinization of G *Kremelin*]

Krem·lin·ol·o·gy (krem′li nol′ə jē), *n.* the study of the government of the Soviet Union, esp. the study of those factors that govern its foreign affairs. [Kremlin + -o- + -logy] —**Krem·lin·ol·o·gist** (krem′li nol′ə jist), *n.*

Krems (krems), *n.* a city in NE Austria, on the Danube. 20,353 (1958).

Kře·nek (*Czech.* krzhe′nek), *n.* **Ernst** (ernst), born 1900, U.S. composer, born in Austria.

kre·pis (krē′pis), *n.* crepidoma. [var. of CREPIS]

krep·lach (krep′läᴋʜ, -läᴋʜ), *n.* (*construed as sing. or pl.*) turnovers or pockets of noodle dough filled with any of several mixtures, as with kasha or chopped chicken livers, usually boiled, and served in soup. Also, **kreplech** (krep′ləᴋʜ). [< Yiddish, var. of *kreplech,* pl. of *krepel,* equiv. to dial. G *Kräppel* fritter; akin to G *Krapfen* apple-fritter]

kreut·zer (kroit′sər), *n.* 1. any of various former minor coins issued by German states. 2. a former copper coin of Austria, the 100th part of a florin. [< G *Kreuzer,* equiv. to *Kreuz* CROSS (orig. the device on the coin) + *-er* -ER[1]]

Kreut·zer (kroit′sər; *Fr.* krœ tser′), *n.* **Ro·dolphe** (rô dôlf′), 1766–1831, French violinist.

Kreut′zer So·na′ta, a sonata for violin and piano-forte (1803, Op. 47) by Ludwig van Beethoven.

Kreut′zer So·na′ta, The, a novel (1890) by Leo Tolstoy.

Kreym·borg (krām′bôrg), *n.* **Alfred,** 1883–1966, U.S. poet, playwright, and critic.

Krieg (krēᴋʜ; *Eng.* krēg), *n.,* *pl.* **Krie·ge** (krē′gə), *Eng.* **Kriegs.** *German.* war.

Krie·ger (krē′gər), *n.* a crater in the second quadrant of the face of the moon: about 13 miles in diameter.

krieg·spiel (krēg′spēl′), *n.* 1. (*sometimes cap.*) a game using small figures and counters that represent troops, ships, etc., played on a map or miniature battlefield, developed for teaching military tactics to officers. 2. a form of a game of chess in which each player sees only his own pieces on a board in front of him, having to remember his opponent's moves as told to him by a referee who maintains a third board on which the play of both players is shown. [< G: war's game. See KREIG, -s[1], SPELL[3]]

Kriem·hild (krēm′hilt), *n.* (in the *Nibelungenlied*) the wife of Siegfried and the sister of Gunther. She kills Gunther and Hagen in revenge for the murder of Siegfried: corresponds to Gudrun in Scandinavian legends.

krill (kril), *n., pl.* **krill.** any of the small, pelagic, shrimplike crustaceans of the family *Euphausiidae,* used as food by certain whales. [< Norw *kril* young fry (of fish)]

krim·mer (krim′ər), *n.* a lambskin from the Crimean region, dressed as a fur, with wool in loose soft curls and usually whitish or pale gray. Also, **crimmer.** [< G, equiv. to *Krim* CRIMEA + *-er* -ER[1]]

Krips (krips), *n.* **Jo·sef** (yō′zef), born 1902, Austrian orchestra conductor.

kris (krēs), *n.* creese.

Krish·na (krish′nə), *n.* 1. *Hinduism.* an avatar of Vishnu, and one of the most popular of Indian deities, who appears in the *Bhagavad-Gita* as the teacher of Arjuna. 2. a boy's given name. [< Skt: lit., black, dark]

Krish′na Men′on (men′ən), **Ven·ga·lil Krish·nan** (ven gä′lēl krish′nən), born 1897, Indian politician and statesman: Minister of Defense 1957–62.

Kriss Krin·gle (kris′ kring′gəl). See **Santa Claus.** [< G *Christkindl* little Christ child, equiv. to *Christ* CHRIST + *kind* CHILD + *-l* dim. suffix]

Kris·tian·sand (kris′chən sand′; *Norw.* kris′tyän-sän′), *n.* a seaport in S Norway. 25,815 (est. 1959). Formerly, **Christiansand.**

Kris·tin (kris′tən), *n.* a girl's given name, form of **Christine.**

Kri·ta Yu·ga (krit′ə yo͝og′ə), *Hinduism.* See **Satya Yuga.** [< Skt *kṛtayuga,* equiv. to *kṛta* best throw of four at dice + *yuga* YOKE[1]]

Kri·voi Rog (kri voi′ rôg′), a city in the SE Ukraine, in the SW Soviet Union in Europe. 448,000 (est. 1962).

kri·vu (krē′vo͞o), *n.* crivetz.

Kroe·ber (krō′bər), *n.* **Alfred Louis,** 1876–1960, American anthropologist.

Krogh (krôg), *n.* **(Schack) Au·guste (Steen·berg)** (shäk ou′go͞ost stēn′barg), 1874–1949, Danish physiologist: Nobel prize for medicine 1920.

Kró·lew·ska Hu·ta (*Pol.* kro͞o lef′skä ho͞o′tä), former name of **Chorzów.**

kro·na (krō′nə), *n., pl.* **-nor** (-nôr). 1. a silver and copper coin and monetary unit of Sweden, equal to 100 öre and equivalent to about .20 of a U.S. dollar. *Abbr.:* Kr., kr. 2. the monetary unit of the Faeroe Islands, equal to 100 öre and equivalent to about .145 of a U.S. dollar. *Abbr.:* Kr., kr. [< Sw < ML *corōna;* see KRONA]

kró·na (krō′nə), *n., pl.* **kró·nur** (krō′nər). a copper coin and monetary unit of Iceland, equal to 100 aurar and equivalent to about .14 of a U.S. dollar. *Abbr.:* Kr., kr. [< Icel < ML *corōna* gold coin (so called because it bore the imprint of a crown); see CROWN]

Kro·nach (*Ger.* krō′näᴋʜ), *n.* Cranach.

kro·ne[1] (krō′nə), *n., pl.* **-ner** (-nər). 1. an aluminum bronze coin and monetary unit of Denmark, equal to 100 öre and equivalent to about .15 of a U.S. dollar. *Abbr.:* Kr., kr. 2. a cupronickel coin and monetary unit of Norway, equal to 100 öre and equivalent to about .14 of a U.S. dollar. *Abbr.:* Kr., kr. [< Dan, Norw < MLG < ML *corōna;* see KRONA]

kro·ne[2] (krō′nə), *n., pl.* **-nen** (-nən). 1. a former gold coin of Germany, equal to 10 marks. 2. korona (def. 1). [< G; see KRONE[1]]

Kro·neck·er (krō′nek ər; *Ger.* krō′nek ər), *n.* **Le·o·pold** (lē′ə pōld′; *Ger.* lā′ō pôlt′), 1823–91, German mathematician.

Kro′necker del′ta, *Math.* a function of two variables, *i* and *j,* which equals one when the variables have the same value, $i = j$, and equals zero when the variables have different values, $i \neq j$. Symbol: δ^i_j. [named after Leopold Kronecker]

Kro·nos (krō′nos), *n.* Cronus.

Kron·stadt (kron shtät′ *for 1;* krōn′shtät *for 2*), *n.* 1. a seaport in the NW RSFSR, in the NW Soviet Union in Europe, on an island in the Gulf of Finland, W of Leningrad: naval base. 59,000 (1959). 2. German name of **Brasov.**

kroon (kro͞on), *n., pl.* **kroons, kroon·i** (kro͞o′nē). a former aluminum bronze coin and monetary unit of Estonia, equal to 100 marks or senti. [< Estonian *kron* < Sw *krona* KRONA]

Kro·pot·kin (krō pot′kin, krə-; *Russ.* kro pôt′kin), *n.* **Prince Pë·ter A·le·kse·e·vich** (pyō′tər ä′le kse′yə-vich), 1842–1921, Russian geographer, author, and anarchist.

KRP, *Chess.* king's rook's pawn.

krs, kurus.

Kru·ger (kro͞o′gər; *Du.* kry′ᴋʜər), *n.* **Ste·pha·nus Jo·han·nes Paul·us** (ste fä′nœs yō hä′nəs pō′lœs), ("*Oom Paul*"), 1825–1904, South African statesman: president of the Transvaal 1883–1900. —**Kru′ger·ite′,** *n., adj.*

Kru·gers·dorp (kro͞o′gərz dôrp′; *Du.* kry′ᴋʜərs-dôrp′), *n.* a city in S Transvaal, in the NE Republic of South Africa, SW of Johannesburg. 89,493 with suburbs (1960).

krul·ler (krul′ər), *n.* cruller.

krum·horn (krum′hôrn′), *n.* cromorne.

Krumm·holz (kro͝om′hōlts), *n., pl.* **-holz.** a forest of stunted trees near the timber line on a mountain. Also called **elfinwood.** [< G, equiv. to *krumm* crooked (OHG *krumb;* see CROMORNE) + *Holz* wood; see HOLT]

Krupp (krup; *Ger.* kro͝op), *n.* **Al·fred** (al′frid; *Ger.* äl′frät), 1812–87, German manufacturer of armaments.

Krup·ska·ya (kro͞op′skä yä), *n.* **Na·dezh·da Kon·stan·ti·nov·na** (nä dezh′dä kôn′stän tē′nov nä), 1869–1939, Russian social worker and wife of Nikolai Lenin.

Kru·sen·stern (kro͞o′zən stûrn′), *n.* a walled plain in the fourth quadrant of the face of the moon: about 34 miles in diameter.

Krutch (kro͞och), *n.* **Joseph Wood,** born 1893, U.S. drama and social critic, biographer, naturalist, and teacher.

Kry·lon (krī′lon), *Trademark.* a plastic coating, applied as a liquid, that forms a protective film: used on blueprints, paintings, etc.

kryo-, var. of **cryo-.**

kryp·ton (krip′ton), *n.* *Chem.* an inert, monatomic gaseous element, present in very small amounts in the atmosphere: used in high-power, tungsten-filament light bulbs. *Symbol:* Kr; *at. wt.:* 83.80; *at. no.:* 36; *weight of one liter at 0°C and 760 mm. pressure:* 3.708g. [< Gk, neut. of *kryptós* hidden, secret; see CRYPT]

K-se·ries (kā′sēr′ēz), *n.* *Physics.* See under **K-line.**

Kshat·ri·ya (kshat′rē ə), *n.* a member of the Hindu royal and warrior caste above the Vaisyas and below the Brahmans. Cf. **Brahman, Harijan, Sudra, untouchable** (def. 5), **Vaisya.** [< Skt: lit., ruling, ruler]

K-shell (kā′shel′), *n.* *Physics.* the first shell of electrons surrounding the nucleus of an atom and containing, when filled, two electrons having principal quantum number one. Cf. **L-shell, M-shell, N-shell.**

ksi, one thousand pounds per square inch. [*k,* repr. *kilo-* thousand + *s*(*quare*) *i*(*nch*)]

Kt, *Chess.* knight.

Kt., Knight.

kt., 1. karat. 2. kiloton. 3. knot.

K.T., 1. Knights Templars. 2. Knight of the Order of the Thistle.

Kt. Bach., knight bachelor.

K-truss (kā′trus′), *n.* a truss having in each panel two diagonals running from the ends of one post to the center of the adjacent post, the arrangement being symmetrical about the center of the truss.

Kua·la Lum·pur (kwä′lə lo͝om po͝or′), a city in and the capital of Malaysia, in the SW Malay Peninsula: also the capital of Selangor state. 316,230 (1957).

Kuang·chou (gwäng′jō′), *n.* Chinese name of **Canton.** Also, **Kwangchow.**

Kuan·tan (kwän′tän), *n.* a seaport in E Pahang, in Malaysia, on the SE Malay Peninsula. 23,025 (1957).

Ku·ban (ko͞o ban′; *Russ.* ko͞o bän′yə), *n.* a river in the Soviet Union in Europe, flowing NW from the Caucasus Mountains to the Black and the Azov seas. 512 mi. long. Ancient, **Hypanis.**

Ku·ban·go (ko͞o bäng′gō), *n.* Okovanggo.

Ku·be·lík (ko͞o′be lēk; *Eng.* ko͞ob′ə lik), *n.* 1. **Jan** (yon), 1880–1940, Czech violinist and composer in Hungary. 2. his son, **(Jeronym) Rafael,** born 1914, Czech conductor.

Ku·blai Khan (ko͞o′blī kän′), 1216–94, khan c1260–94: founder of the Mongol dynasty in China (grandson of Genghis Khan). Also, **Ku′bi·lai Khan′** (ko͞o′bi lī′).

Ku·bla Khan (ko͞o′blə kän′), 1. (*italics.*) a poetic fragment (1816) by Coleridge. 2. See **Kublai Khan.**

ku·chen (ko͞o′ᴋʜən), *n.* a yeast-raised coffee cake, usually including fruit. [< G: cake]

Ku·ching (ko͞o′ching), *n.* a seaport in SW Sarawak, in E Malaysia: capital of the former colony of Sarawak. 50,579 (1960).

ku·dos (ko͞o′dōz, -dōs, -dos, kyo͞o′-) *n.* (*construed as sing.*) glory; renown; praise; approval: *He received kudos from everyone on his performance.* [irreg. transliteration of Gk *kŷdos*]

Kud·run (ko͝od′ro͞on), *n.* Gudrun.

ku·du (ko͞o′do͞o), *n.* a large African antelope, *Strepsiceros strepsiceros,* the male of which has large corkscrewlike horns. Also, **koodoo.** [< Hottentot]

Kudu (5 ft. high at shoulder; horns 4 to 5 ft.; length 9 ft.)

kud′zu vine′ (ko͝od′zo͞o), a leguminous, climbing vine, *Pueraria lobata,* of China and Japan, having tuberous, starchy roots and stems that yield a useful fiber; also grown for forage. Also called **kud′zu.** [< Jap, after *Kuzu,* the name of a village whose production of this vine was originally considered the best]

Kuen·lun (ko͝on′lo͞on′), *n.* Kunlun.

Ku·fa (ko͞o′fə, -fa), *n.* a town in central Iraq: former seat of Abbassid caliphate; Muslim pilgrimage center. Aso, **Al Kufa.**

Ku·fic (ko͞o′fik, kyo͞o′-), *adj.* 1. of or pertaining to Kufa or its inhabitants. 2. noting or pertaining to the characters of the Arabic alphabet used in the writing of the original Koran, in the time of Muhammad. —*n.* 3. the Kufic alphabet. Also, **Cufic.** [Kuf(a) + -ic]

ku·fi·yeh (kə fē′ə), *n.* kaffiyeh. Also, **kuf·fi′eh.**

ku·gel (ko͞o′gəl, ko͝og′əl), *n.* *Jewish Cookery.* a baked casserole resembling a soufflé or pudding. [special use of G *Kugel* ball; see CUDGEL]

Kuhn (ko͞on), *n.* 1. **Rich·ard** (rich′ərd; *Ger.* riᴋʜ′ärt), 1900–1967, German chemist, born in Austria: declined 1938 Nobel prize at insistence of Nazi government. 2. **Walt,** 1877?–1949, U.S. painter.

Kuh·nau (ko͞o′nou), *n.* **Jo·hann** (yō′hän), 1660–1722, German clavier composer, organist, and author.

Kui·by·shev (kwē′bi shef′; *Russ.* ko͞o′i bi shef′), *n.* a port in the RSFSR, in the SE Soviet Union in Europe, on the Volga. 950,000 (est. 1965). Formerly, **Samara.**

Ku-Klux (ko͞o′kluks′, kyo͞o′-), *n.* 1. See **Ku Klux Klan.** 2. any member of that organization.

Ku Klux·er (ko͞o′ kluk′sər, kyo͞o′), a member of a Ku Klux Klan. Also called **Ku′ Klux′ Klan′ner.** [Ku Klux (Klan) + -er[1]]

Ku′ Klux′ism (kluk′siz əm), the doctrines, theories, and practices of the Ku Klux Klan. Also, **Ku′ Klux′-er·y** (kluk′sə rē). [Ku Klux (Klan) + -ism]

Ku Klux Klan (kluks′ klan′), 1. a secret organization in the southern U.S., active for several years after the Civil War, which aimed to suppress the newly acquired powers of the Negroes and to oppose carpetbaggers from the North, and was responsible for many lawless and violent proceedings. **2.** Official name, **Knights of the Ku Klux Klan.** a secret organization inspired by the former, founded in 1915 and active in the southern and other parts of the U.S., and professing Americanism as its object. Also called **Ku′ Klux′.** [*Ku Klux* (? < Gk *kýklos* circle, assembly) + *klan*, sp. var. of CLAN]

kuk·ri (ko͝ok′rē), *n.* a large knife used for hunting and combat purposes by the Nepalese Gurkhas having a heavy curved blade sharp on the concave side. [< Hindi *kukrī*]

Kuk·su (ko͝ok′so͞o), *adj.* of, pertaining to, or characteristic of, a religious cult among Indians of central California. [?]

ku·lak (ko͝o läk′, ko͞o′läk), *n.* (in Russia) **1.** a comparatively wealthy peasant who employed hired labor or possessed farm machinery. **2.** (before the revolution of 1917) a prosperous, ruthless, and stingy merchant or village usurer. [< Russ: fist, tight-fisted person]

Kul·la (ko͞ol′ä), *n.* the Sumerian and Akkadian god of bricks.

Kul·ler·vo (ko͞o′lər vô′), *n.* (in the *Kalevala*) a slave who, after a series of tragic misadventures, commits suicide.

Kulp·mont (kulp′mont), *n.* a town in central Pennsylvania. 4288 (1960).

Kul·tur (*Ger.* ko͝ol to͞or′), *n.* **1.** culture as a social force causing evolutionary development resulting in higher forms of civilization. **2.** a civilization characteristic of a time or a people. [< G < L *cultūr(a)* CULTURE]

Kul·tur·kampf (*Ger.* ko͝ol to͞or′ kämpf′), *n.* the conflict between the German imperial government and the Roman Catholic Church from 1872 or 1873 until 1886, chiefly over the control of educational and ecclesiastical appointments. [< G: culture struggle, equiv. to *Kultur* KULTUR + *Kampf* battle, struggle (c. OE *camp*) < LL *camp(us)* battle, battlefield (L: field); see CAMP[1]]

Kul·tur·kreis (*Ger.* ko͝ol to͞or′krīs′), *n., pl.* **-krei·se** (-krī′zə). *Anthropol.* a complex of related cultural traits regarded as the nucleus from which subsequent cultures developed. [< G, equiv. to *Kultur* KULTUR + *Kreis* circle]

Ku·lun (ko͞o′lo͞on′), *n.* Chinese name of **Ulan Bator.**

Ku·ma·mo·to (ko͞o′mə mō′tō; *Jap.* ko͞o′mä mô′tô), *n.* a city on W central Kyushu, in SW Japan. 405,488 (1964).

Ku·mas·i (ko͝o mä′sē), *n.* a city in and the capital of Ashanti district, in S Ghana. 190,362 (1960).

ku·miss (ko͞o′mis), *n.* **1.** fermented mare's or camel's milk, used as a beverage by Asian nomads. **2.** a similar drink prepared from other milk, esp. that of the cow, and used for dietetic and medicinal purposes. Also, **koumis, koumiss, koumyss.** [< Russ *kumys* < Tatar *kumyz*]

küm·mel (kim′əl; *Ger.* kʏm′əl), *n.* **1.** a colorless cordial or liqueur flavored with cumin, caraway seeds, etc., made esp. in the Baltic area. **2.** Leyden cheese containing caraway seeds. **3.** (*cap., italics.*) *German.* caraway seed. [< G; OHG *kumil*, appar. dissimilated var. of *kumin* CUMIN]

Kum·mer (ko͝om′ər; *Ger.* ko͝om′ər), *n.* **Ernst E·du·ard** (ûrnst ed′wərd; *Ger.* ernst ā′do͞o ärt′), 1810–93, German mathematician.

kum·mer·bund (kum′ər bund′), *n.* cummerbund.

kum·quat (kum′kwot), *n.* **1.** a small, round or oblong citrus fruit having a sweet rind and acid pulp, used chiefly for preserves. **2.** any of several rutaceous shrubs of the genus *Fortunella*, native to China and cultivated in Japan, Florida, California, etc., bearing this fruit. Also, **cumquat.** [< Chin (Cantonese) *kam kwat* gold orange]

Kun (ko͝on), *n.* **Bé·la** (bā′lo), 1885–1937, Hungarian Communist leader.

kun·da·li·ni (ko͝on′də li nē), *n.* *Yoga.* a spiritual power said to be located at the base of the spine and liberated through the cakras. [< Hindi]

Kung (ko͝ong), *n., pl.* **Kungs,** (*esp. collectively*) **Kung.** a member of a Bushman people of the Kalahari desert basin of southern Africa. [var. of *Qung*, tribal name]

Kung (ko͝ong, go͝ong), *n.* **H. H.** (*K'ung Hsiang-hsi*), 1881–1967, Chinese financier and statesman.

K'ung Ch'iu (ko͝ong′ chyo͞o′), personal name of **Confucius.**

K'ung Fu-tzü (ko͝ong′ fo͞o′dzü′), Chinese name of **Confucius.** Also, **K'ung′ Fu′-tse′.**

Ku·ni·yo·shi (ko͞o′nē yō′shē; *Jap.* ko͞o′nē yô′shē), *n.* **Ya·su·o** (yä so͞o′ō), 1893–1953, U.S. painter, born in Japan.

Kun·lun (ko͝on′lo͞on′), *n.* a mountain range in China, bordering on the N edge of the Tibetan plateau and extending W across central China: highest peak, 25,000 ft. Also, **Kuenlun.**

Kun·ming (ko͝on′ming′), *n.* a city in and the capital of Yünnan province, in SW China: an important transshipment point on the Burma Road in World War II. 880,000 (est. 1957). Also called **Yünnan.**

Ku·now·sky (kə nou′skē), *n.* a walled plain in the second quadrant of the face of the moon: about 11 miles in diameter.

Kunst·lied (*Ger.* ko͝onst′lēt′), *n., pl.* **-lie·der** (*Ger.* -lē′dər). an art song, esp. as distinguished from a folk song. [< G, equiv. to *Kunst* art (OHG: skill, ability) + *Lied* song]

Kun·tse·vo (ko͞on′sə vō′; *Russ.* ko͞on′tsi və), *n.* a former city in the W Russian Federation in Europe, incorporated into Moscow 1962.

kunz·ite (ko͝onts′īt), *n.* a transparent lilac variety of spodumene, used as a gem. [named after G. F. *Kunz* (1856–1932), American expert in precious stones; see -ITE[1]]

Kuo·min·tang (kwō′min′tang′, -täng′; *Chin.* gwô′-min′däng′), *n.* the main political party of the Republic of China, founded chiefly by Sun Yat-sen in 1911 and led after 1925 by Chiang Kai-shek; the dominant party in mainland China until 1948. [< Chin (Mandarin dial.): National People's Party, equiv. to *kuo* nation + *min* people + *tang* party; see TANG, TONG[2]]

Kuo·pio (kwô′pyô), *n.* a city in central Finland. 51,051 (est. 1965).

Ku·prin (ko͞o′prin; *Russ.* ko͝o prēn′), *n.* **A·le·xan·der I·va·no·vich** (ä′le ksän′dər i vä′no vich), 1870–1938 Russian novelist and short-story writer.

Kur (ko͝or), *n.* (in Sumerian mythology) the world of the dead.

Ku·ra (ko͝o rä′), *n.* a river flowing from NE Turkey, through the Georgian and Azerbaijan republics of the Soviet Union, SE to the Caspian Sea. 950 mi. long.

kur·bash (ko͝or′bash), *n.* **1.** a whip with leather thongs, formerly used in Turkey, Egypt, etc. —*v.t.* **2.** to whip with a kurbash. Also, **kourbash.** [< Ar *qurbāsh* << Turk *kirbaç* whip]

Kurd (kûrd; *Pers.* ko͞ord), *n.* a member of an Islamic people speaking an Iranian language and dwelling chiefly in Kurdistan. —**Kurd′ish,** *adj., n.*

Kurd·ish (kûr′dish, ko͝or′-), *adj.* **1.** of or pertaining to the Kurds or their language. **2.** of or pertaining to Kurdistan, its people, or their language. —*n.* **3.** the language of the Kurds, an Iranian language. [KURD + -ISH[1]]

Kur·di·stan (kûr′di stan′; *Pers.* ko͞or′di stän′), *n.* **1.** a mountain and plateau region in SE Turkey, NW Iran, and N Iraq: inhabited largely by Kurds. 74,000 sq. mi. **2.** any of several rugs woven by the Kurds of Turkey or Iran.

Ku·re (ko͞o′re), *n.* a seaport on SW Honshu, in SW Japan. 225,722 (1964).

Kurg (ko͝org), *n.* Coorg.

Kur·gan (ko͝or gän′), *n.* a city in the S RSFSR, in the W Soviet Union in Asia, near the Ural Mountains. 191,000 (est. 1964).

ku·ri·ka·ta (kə rē′kə tä′; *Jap.* ko͝o rē′kä tä′), *n., pl.* **-ta.** a small projecting mount on a Japanese scabbard, for reinforcing the opening of the kogai and for preventing the sword from slipping down behind the sash, into which it is thrust when worn. [< Jap, equiv. to *kuri* chestnut + *kata* shape, pattern]

Ku′rile Is′lands (ko͝or′il, ko͝o rēl′), a chain of small islands off the NE coast of Asia, extending from N Japan to the S tip of Kamchatka: renounced by Japan in 1945; under Soviet administration. Also, **Ku′ril Is′lands.** Japanese, **Chishima.**

Kur·land (ko͝or′lənd), *n.* Courland.

kurn (kûrn), *n.* *Scot. and North Eng.* kirn[2].

Ku·ro·ki (ko͞o′ro kē′), *n.* **Ta·me·sa·da** (tä′me sä′dä), **Count,** (*Tamemoto Kuroki*), 1844–1923, Japanese general.

Ku·ro·pat·kin (ko͞o′ro pät′kin), *n.* **A·le·ksei Ni·ko·la·e·vich** (ä′le ksā′ ni′ko lä′yə vich), 1848–1925, Russian general.

Ku·ro·shi·o (ko͝o rō′shē ō′; *Jap.* ko͝o rô′shē ô′), *n.* See **Japan Current.** [< Jap: black stream]

kuro′shio exten′sion, a warm ocean current flowing eastward across the northern Pacific Ocean at about latitude 35°N.

kuro′shio sys′tem, the system of currents in the North Pacific ocean comprised chiefly of the kuroshio, the kuroshio extension, and the North Pacific current.

kur·ra·jong (kûr′ə jong′), *n.* a bottle tree, *Brachychiton populneum*, of Australia, having showy yellowish-white, bell-shaped flowers, grown as an ornamental. Also, **koorajong, currajong, currijong.** [< native Austral]

Kur·saal (ko͞or′zäl), *n., pl.* **Kur·sä·le** (ko͞or sā′lə). *German.* a public hall for visitors at a spa or health resort. [lit., treatment hall]

kürsch (*Ger.* kʏrsh), *n.* a fur used in German heraldry, represented as brown and shaggy. [< G *Kürsch* fur]

Kursk (ko͝orsk), *n.* a city in the W RSFSR, in the central Soviet Union in Europe. 240,000 (est. 1964).

Kurt (kûrt), *n.* a boy's given name. Also, **Curt.**

kur·ta (kûr′tə), *n.* a long, collarless shirt worn by men in India. [< Hindi]

kur·to·sis (kûr tō′sis), *n.* *Statistics.* the state or quality of flatness or peakedness of the curve describing a frequency distribution in the region about its mode. [< Gk *kýrtōsis* curvature. See CYRTO-, -SIS]

ku·rus (ko͝o ro͞osh′), *n., pl.* **-rus.** a bronze coin of Turkey, the 100th part of a lira, equivalent to about .001 of a U.S. dollar; piaster. [< Turk *kuruş*]

Ku·rus (ko͝or′o͞oz), *n.* (*construed as pl.*) Kauravas.

Ku·ru·su (ko͝o ro͞o′so͞o), *n.* **Sa·bu·ro** (sä bo͞o′rô), 1888–1954, Japanese diplomat.

Kusch (ko͝osh), *n.* **Po·ly·karp** (pol′i kärp′; *Ger.* pō′lʏ-kärp′), born 1911, U.S. physicist, born in Germany: Nobel prize 1955.

Kush (ko͝osh), *n.* Cush.

kus·so (ko͝os′ō, kus′ō), *n., pl.* **-sos.** *Pharm.* brayera. [< Cushitic *kosso*]

Ku·sta·nai (ko͝o stä nī′), *n.* a city in N Kazakstan, in the Soviet Union in Asia. 108,000 (est. 1964).

Ku·ta·i·si (ko͝o tä ē′si), *n.* a city in W Georgia, in the S Soviet Union in Europe. 141,000 (est. 1962). Also, **Ku·ta·is** (ko͝o tīs′; *Russ.* ko͝o tä ēs′).

Kutch (kuch), *n.* Cutch.

kut·cha (kuch′ə), *adj.* *Anglo-Indian.* crude, imperfect, or temporary. Also, **cutcha, kacha, kachcha.** [< Hindi *kaccā*]

Ku·te·nai (ko͞ot′ənā′, -ənē′), *n.* **1.** a member of an American Indian people of British Columbia, Montana, and Idaho. **2.** the language of the Kutenai Indians. **3.** Kootenay. Also, **Ku′te·nay′.**

Ku·tu·zov (ko͝o to͞o′zof), *n.* **Mi·kha·il I·la·ri·o·no·vich** (mi khä ēl′ i lä′ri o nô′vich), **Prince of Smolensk,** 1745–1813, Russian field marshal and diplomat.

Kutz·town (ko͝ots′toun′), *n.* a town in central Pennsylvania. 3312 (1960).

ku·vasz (ko͝ov′äs, ko͞o′väs), *n., pl.* **ku·va·szok** (ko͝ov′ä sôk′, ko͞o′vä-). one of a Hungarian breed of large dogs having a short, slightly wavy, white coat, used for herding sheep and as a watchdog. [< Hung < Turk *kavas* guard < Ar *qawwās* bowman]

Ku·wait (ko͝o wāt′, -wīt′), *n.* **1.** a state in NE Arabia, on the NW coast of the Persian Gulf: formerly a British protectorate. 467,789 (1965); ab. 8000 sq. mi. **2.** a seaport in and the capital of this state. 99,633 (1965). Also, **Koweit.**

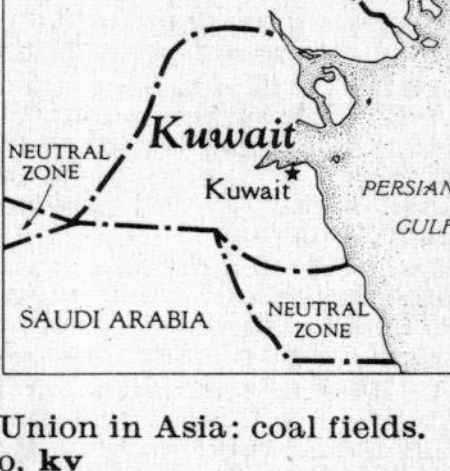

Ku·wai·ti (ko͝o wā′tē, -wī′-), *n.* **1.** a native or inhabitant of Kuwait. —*adj.* **2.** of, pertaining to, or characteristic of Kuwait or its inhabitants. [< Ar *kuwaytīy*, deriv. of *Kuwayt* KUWAIT]

Kuyp (*Du.* koip), *n.* **Ael·bert** (*Du.* äl′bərt). See **Cuyp, Aelbert.**

Kuz·netsk′ Ba′sin (ko͝oz netsk′), an industrial region in the S Soviet Union in Asia: coal fields.

kV, kilovolt; kilovolts. Also, **kv**

K.V., *Music. Köchel-Verzeichnis*, the chronological listing of Mozart's works (used with a number to identify a specific work).

kVA, kilovolt-ampere; kilovolt-amperes. Also, **kva**

kVAH, kilovolt-ampere-hour. Also, **kvah**

kVAr, kilovar; kilovars. Also, **kvar**

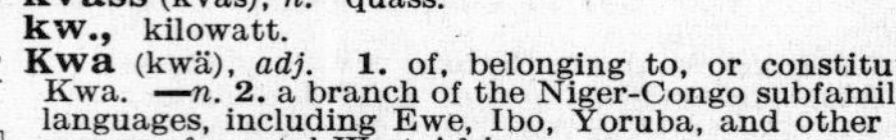

kvass (kväs), *n.* quass.

kw., kilowatt.

Kwa (kwä), *adj.* **1.** of, belonging to, or constituting Kwa. —*n.* **2.** a branch of the Niger-Congo subfamily of languages, including Ewe, Ibo, Yoruba, and other languages of coastal West Africa.

kwai·ken (kwī ken′), *n., pl.* **-ken.** a curved knife formerly used by Japanese women to commit suicide. [< Jap, equiv. to *kwai* pocket + *ken* dagger]

Kwa·ki·u·tl (kwä′kē o͞ot′əl), *n.* **1.** a member of an American Indian people of Vancouver Island and the adjacent British Columbian coast. **2.** the language of the Kwakiutl, a Wakashan language.

Kwang·chow (gwäng′jō′), *n.* Chinese name of **Canton.**

Kwang·cho·wan (kwäng′chō′wän′, kwang′-; *Chin.* gwäng′jō′wän′), *n.* a territory on the SW coast of Kwangtung province, in S China: leased to France 1898–1945. ab. 250,000, ab. 190 sq. mi.

Kwang·ju (gwäng′jo͞o′), *n.* a city in SW South Korea. 314,420 (1960). Japanese, **Koshu.**

Kwang·si-Chuwang (kwäng′sē′chwäng′, kwang′-; *Chin.* gwäng′sē′jwäng′), *n.* an administrative division in S China. 19,390,000 (est. 1957); 85,096 sq. mi. *Cap.:* Nanning. Official name, **Kwang′si′-Chuang′ Auton′omous Re′gion.**

Kwang·tung (kwäng′to͝ong′, kwang′-; *Chin.* gwäng′do͝ong′), *n.* **1.** a province in SE China. 37,960,000 (est. 1957); 89,344 sq. mi. *Cap.:* Canton. **2.** Kwantung.

Kwan·tung (kwän′to͝ong′, kwan′-; *Chin.* gwän′do͝ong′), *n.* a territory in NE China at the tip of Liaotung Peninsula, Manchuria: leased to Japan 1905–45; part of Shantung province.

Kwan-yin (kwän′yin′), *n.* *Buddhism.* one of the Chinese female Boddhisattvas, noted for her kindness, often considered an aspect of Avaloketesvara.

kwar·tje (kwär′chə, -tyə), *n.* a silver 25-cent piece of the Netherlands, equivalent to about .07 of a U.S. dollar. [< D < L *quartār(ius)*; see QUARTER]

kwash·i·or·kor (kwash′ē ôr′kôr, -kər, kwä′shē-), *n.* *Pathol.* a nutritional disease of infants and children, occurring chiefly in Africa, associated with a heavy corn diet and the resultant lack of protein, and characterized by edema, potbelly, and changes in skin pigmentation. [from native Ghanaian word]

Kwei·chow (kwā′chou′, -chō′; *Chin.* gwā′jō′), *n.* **1.** a province in S China. 16,890,000 (est. 1957); 67,181 sq. mi. *Cap.:* Kweiyang. **2.** Fengkieh.

Kwei·hwa·ting (gwā′hwä′ting′), *n.* former name of **Kweisui.**

Kwei·lin (kwā′lin′; *Chin.* gwā′lin′), *n.* a city in the Kwangsi-Chuang region, in S China. 145,000 (est. 1957).

Kwei·sui (kwā′swā′; *Chin.* gwā′swā′), *n.* a city in Inner Mongolia, in N China: formerly the capital of Suiyüan province. 140,000 (est. 1957). Formerly, **Kweihwating.**

Kwei·yang (kwā′yäng′, -yang′; *Chin.* gwā′yäng′), *n.* a city in and the capital of Kweichow province, in S China. 504,000 (est. 1957).

kWh, kilowatt-hour. Also, **kwhr, K.W.H.**

Ky., Kentucky.

ky·ack (kī′ak), *n.* kayak.

Ky·ack (kī′ak), *n.* a type of packsack which consists of two connected sacks and which is hung on either side of a packsaddle. [?]

ky·ak (kī′ak), *n.* kayak.

ky·an·ise (kī′ə nīz′), *v.t.,* **-ised, -is·ing.** *Chiefly Brit.* kyanize.

ky·a·nite (kī′ə nīt′), *n.* cyanite.

ky·an·ize (kī′ə nīz′), *v.t.,* **-ized, -iz·ing.** to treat (wood) against decay with a solution of mercuric chloride. Also, *esp. Brit.,* **kyanise.** [named after J. H. *Kyan* (1774–1850), Irish developer of the process; see -IZE]

kyat (kyät, kē ät′), *n.* a cupronickel coin and monetary unit of Burma, equal to 100 pyas, and equivalent to about .21 of a U.S. dollar. [< Burmese]

ky·a·thos (kī′ə thos′), *n., pl.* **-thoi** (-thoi′). *Gk. and Rom. Antiq.* a cup in the shape of a deep bowl set on a foot, often having a high voluted or serpentine handle rising from the brim and terminating immediately above the juncture of the body and the stem: used for ladling wine into drinking cups. Also, **cyathus.** [< Gk]

Kyd (kid), *n.* **Thomas,** 1558–94, English dramatist. Also, **Kid.**

kyle (kīl), *n.* *Scot.* a narrow channel of water between two islands or between an island and the mainland; a strait or sound. [< Gael *caoil* (gen. of *caol*) strait, sound (n. use of *caol* narrow)]
Kyle (kīl), *n.* a boy's or girl's given name.
ky·lie (kī′lē), *n.*, *pl.* **-lies.** *Australian.* boomerang. Also, **kiley.** [< native Austral]
ky·lix (kī′liks, kil′iks), *n.*, *pl.* **ky·li·kes** (kī′lə kēz′, kil′ə-). *Gk. and Rom. Antiq.* a cup in the shape of a shallow bowl having two horizontal handles projecting from the sides, often set upon a stem terminating in a foot: used as a drinking vessel. Also, **cylix.** [< Gk: cup]
kymo-, var. of **cymo-:** *kymograph.*
ky·mo·graph (kī′mə graf′, -gräf′), *n.* **1.** an instrument for measuring and graphically recording variations in fluid pressure, as those of the human pulse. **2.** an instrument measuring the angular oscillations of an airplane in flight, with respect to axes fixed in space. Also, **cymograph.** [KYMO- + -GRAPH] —**ky·mo·graph·ic** (kī′mə graf′ik), *adj.*
Kym·ric (kim′rik), *adj.*, *n.* Cymric.
Kym·ry (kim′rē), *n.pl.* Cymry.
Kyn·e·wulf (kin′ə wo͝olf), *n.* Cynewulf.
Kyo·ga (kyō′gə), *n.* **Lake,** a lake in central Uganda. ab. 1000 sq. mi. Also, **Lake Kioga.**
ky·oo·dle (kī o͞od′ᵊl), *v.i.*, **-dled, -dling.** *Chiefly Dial.* to bark or yelp noisily or foolishly; yap. [imit.]
Kyo·to (kē ō′tō; *Jap.* kyô′tô), *n.* a city on S Honshu, in central Japan: the capital of Japan A.D. 784–1868. 1,337,228 (1964). Also, **Kioto.**
ky·pho·sco·li·o·sis (kī′fō skō′lē ō′sis, -skol′ē-), *n.* *Pathol.* a condition in which the spinal column is convex both backward and sideways. [< Gk *kyphó(s)* humpbacked + SCOLIOSIS] —**ky·pho·sco·li·ot·ic** (kī′fō skō′lē ot′ik), *adj.*
ky·pho·sis (kī fō′sis), *n.* *Pathol.* a curvature of the spine, convex backward. [< Gk *kýphōsis* a hunched state; see -OSIS] —**ky·phot·ic** (kī fot′ik), *adj.*
Kyr·gyz·stan (kir′gi stän′), *n.* official name of **Kirghizia.**
Kyr·i·a·le (kir′ē ä′lā), *n.* a liturgical book containing the text and musical notations for parts of the ordinary of the Mass. [< NL, equiv. to *Kyri(e)* (see KYRIE ELEISON) + *-āle* -AL²]
Kyr·i·e e·le·i·son (*Rom. Cath. Ch.*, *Angl. Ch.* kir′ē-ā′ e lā′i sôn′, -son′, -sən; *Gk. Orth. Ch.* kē′rē e ele′i-sôn), **1.** (*italics.*) the brief petition "Lord, have mercy," used in various offices of the Greek Orthodox Church and of the Roman Catholic Church. **2.** the brief response or petition in services in the Anglican Church, beginning with the words, "Lord, have mercy upon us." **3.** Also called **Kyr′i·e′.** a musical setting of either of these. [ME *kyrieleyson* < LL *Kyrie, eleīson* < LGk *Kýrie, eléēson* Lord, have mercy]
kyte (kīt), *n.* *Scot. and North Eng.* the paunch; stomach; belly. Also, **kite.** [? < Scand; cf. Icel *kȳta* stomach of the blenny]
kythe (kīth), *v.t.*, *v.i.*, **kythed, kyth·ing.** *Scot. and North Eng.* kithe.
Ky·the·ra (kē′thē rä′), *n.* Greek name of **Cerigo.**
ky·toon (kī to͞on′), *n.* *Meteorol.* a captive balloon, combining the features of a balloon and kite, used to maintain meteorological instruments at a fixed height. [KITE + (BALL)OON]
Kyu·shu (kē o͞o′sho͞o; *Jap.* kyo͞o′sho͞o), *n.* an island in SW Japan. 12,903,076 (1960); 15,750 sq. mi. Also, **Kiushu.**
Ky·zyl (ki zil′), *n.* a city in and the capital of the Tuva Autonomous Republic, in the S Russian Federation in Asia. 71,000. Russian, **Krasny.**
Ky·zyl Kum (ki zil′ ko͞om′), a desert in S Asia, SE of the Aral Sea, in the Soviet Union in Asia. ab. 90,000 sq. mi. Also, **Kizil Kum, Qizil Qum.**

L

L, l (el), *n., pl.* **L's or Ls, l's or ls.** **1.** the 12th letter of the English alphabet, a consonant. **2.** any spoken sound represented by the letter *L* or *l*, as in *let, dull, cradle*, etc. **3.** something having the shape of an L. **4.** a written or printed representation of the letter *L* or *l*. **5.** a device, as a printer's type, for reproducing the letter *L* or *l*.

L (el), *n., pl.* **L's** or **Ls.** *Informal.* an elevated railroad.

L (el), *n., pl.* **L's** or **Ls.** ell[1].

L, *pl.* **L's.** **1.** elevated railroad. **2.** ell. **3.** Large. **4.** Latin. **5.** *Physics.* length. **6.** *Mil.* liaison (used in designations of U.S. Army light aircraft). **7.** pound. [< L *libra*] **8.** *Geodesy.* (terrestrial) longitude. **9.** *Theat.* stage left.

L, **1.** lambert; lamberts. **2.** large. **3.** Latin. **4.** left. **5.** length. **6.** *Brit.* pound; pounds. [< L *libra*] **7.** *Geodesy.* (terrestrial) longitude. **8.** *Theat.* stage left.

L, **1.** the 12th in order or in a series, or, if *I* is omitted, the 11th. **2.** (*sometimes l.c.*) the Roman numeral for 50. Cf. **Roman numerals.** **3.** *Elect.* inductance. **4.** *Physics.* See **kinetic potential.**

l, **1.** large. **2.** liter; liters. **3.** lumen.

L., **1.** Lady. **2.** Lake. **3.** large. **4.** Latin. **5.** latitude. **6.** law. **7.** left. **8.** lempira; lempiras. **9.** leu; lei. **10.** lev; leva. **11.** book. [< L *liber*] **12.** Liberal. **13.** lira. **14.** place. [< L *locus*] **15.** Lord. **16.** Low. **17.** *Theat.* stage left. **18.** lumen.

l., **1.** large. **2.** latitude. **3.** law. **4.** leaf. **5.** league. **6.** left. **7.** length. **8.** *pl.* **ll.,** line. **9.** link. **10.** lira; lire; liras. **11.** liter. **12.** lumen.

L-, **1.** Also, **l-.** *Chem.* levo-. **2.** *U.S. Mil.* (in designations of light aircraft) liaison: *L-15.*

la[1] (lä), *n., Music.* **1.** the syllable used for the sixth tone of a diatonic scale. **2.** (in the fixed system of solmization) the tone A. Cf. **sol-fa** (def. 1). [see GAMUT]

la[2] (lô, lä), *interj.* (used as an exclamation of wonder, surprise, etc.): *La, Sir, how you do go on!* [ME, OE; weak var. of OE *lā*, LO]

La, *Chem.* lanthanum.

La., Louisiana.

L.A., **1.** Latin America. **2.** Law Agent. **3.** Library Association. **4.** Local Agent. **5.** Los Angeles.

laa·ger (lä′gər), *South African.* —*n.* **1.** a camp or encampment, esp. within a circle of wagons. —*v.t., v.i.* **2.** to arrange or encamp in a laager. Also, **lager.** [< SAfrD, var. of *lager;* c. G *Lager* camp. See LAIR[1]]

Laa·land (lô′län), *n.* an island in SE Denmark, S of Zealand. 83,170 (1960); 495 sq. mi. Also, **Lolland.**

lab (lab), *n.* laboratory. [by shortening]

Lab., **1.** Laborite. **2.** Labrador.

lab., **1.** labor. **2.** laboratory. **3.** laborer.

La·ban (lā′bən), *n.* the brother of Rebekah and the father-in-law of Jacob. Gen. 24:29; 29:16–30.

lab·a·rum (lab′ər əm), *n., pl.* **-a·ra** (-ər ə). **1.** an ecclesiastical standard or banner, as for carrying in procession. **2.** the military standard of Constantine the Great and later Christian emperors of Rome, bearing Christian symbols. [< LL < ?]

Lab·da·cus (lab′də kəs), *n. Class. Myth.* a Theban king who was the father of Laius and the grandfather of Oedipus.

lab·da·num (lab′də nəm), *n.* a resinous juice that exudes from various rockroses of the genus *Cistus:* used in perfumery, fumigating substances, medicinal plasters, etc. Also, **ladanum.** [earlier *lapdanum* < ML, for L *lādanum* < Gk *lā́danon*, akin to *lḗdon* rockrose < Sem]

La·be (lä′be), *n.* Czech name of the **Elbe.**

lab·e·fac·tion (lab′ə fak′shən), *n.* a shaking or weakening; overthrow; downfall. [< LL *labefactiōn-* (s. of *labefactiō*), equiv. to *labefact*(*us*) (ptp. of *labefacere* to loosen) + *-iōn-* -ION]

la·bel (lā′bəl), *n., v.,* **-beled, -bel·ing** or (*esp. Brit.*) **-belled, -bel·ling.** —*n.* **1.** a slip of paper or other material, marked or inscribed, for affixing to something to indicate its nature, ownership, destination, etc. **2.** a short word or phrase descriptive of a person, group, intellectual movement, etc. **3.** *Archit.* a molding or dripstone over a door or window, esp. one which extends horizontally across the top of the opening and vertically downward for a certain distance at the sides. **4.** a trademark, esp. of a manufacturer of phonograph records: *She records under a new label.* **5.** *Heraldry.* a narrow horizontal strip with a number of downward extensions of rectangular or dovetail form, usually placed in chief as the cadency mark of an eldest son. **6.** *Obs.* a strip or narrow piece of anything. —*v.t.* **7.** to affix a label to; mark with a label. **8.** to designate or describe by or on a label: *The bottle was labeled poison.* **9.** to put in a certain class; classify. [ME < MF: ribbon, perh. < Gmc. See LAP[1]] —**la′bel·er;** *esp. Brit.,* **la′bel·ler,** *n.*

La Belle Dame Sans Mer·ci (*Fr.* la bel dam sän mer sē′), a ballad (1819) by Keats.

la·bel·lum (lə bel′əm), *n., pl.* **-bel·la** (-bel′ə). *Bot.* the division of the corolla of an orchidaceous plant which differs more or less markedly from the other divisions, often forming the most conspicuous part. [< L, dim. of *labrum* lip] —**la·bel′loid,** *adj.*

la·bi·a (lā′bē ə), *n.* pl. of **labium.**

la·bi·al (lā′bē əl), *adj.* **1.** of, pertaining to, or resembling a labium. **2.** *Music.* having the tones produced by the impact of a stream of air on a sharp liplike edge, as in a flute or the flue pipes of an organ. **3.** of or pertaining to the lips. **4.** *Phonet.* involving lip articulation, as *p, v, m, w*, or a rounded vowel. —*n. Phonet.* **5.** any labial consonant, esp. a bilabial. **6.** any labial sound. [< ML *labiāl*(*is*). See LABIUM, -AL[1]] —**la′bi·al′i·ty,** *n.* —**la′bi·al·ly,** *adv.*

la·bi·al·ise (lā′bē ə līz′), *v.t.,* **-ised, -is·ing.** *Chiefly Brit.* labialize. —**la′bi·al·i·sa′tion,** *n.*

la·bi·al·ism (lā′bē ə liz′əm), *n. Phonet.* **1.** a quality characterized by labial articulation. **2.** the tendency, sometimes habitual, to make sounds labial, as pronouncing the *l* in *love* as a *w*-like sound. [LABIAL + -ISM]

la·bi·al·ize (lā′bē ə līz′), *v.t.,* **-ized, -iz·ing.** *Phonet.* to give a labial character to (a sound), for example, to round (a vowel). Also, *esp. Brit.,* **labialise.** [LABIAL + -IZE] —**la′bi·al·i·za′tion,** *n.*

la·bi·al·ized (lā′bē ə līzd′), *adj. Phonet.* pronounced with secondary labial articulation. Also, *esp. Brit.,* **la′bi·al·ised′.** [LABIALIZE + -ED[2]]

la·bi·a ma·jo·ra (lā′bē ə mə jōr′ə, -jôr′ə), *sing.* **la·bi·um ma·jus** (lā′bē əm mā′jəs). *Anat.* the outer folds of skin of the external female genitalia. [< NL: greater lips]

la·bi·a mi·no·ra (lā′bē ə mi nōr′ə, -nôr′ə), *sing.* **la·bi·um mi·nus** (lā′bē əm mī′nəs). *Anat.* the inner folds of skin of the external female genitalia. [< NL: lesser lips]

la·bi·ate (lā′bē āt′, -it), *adj.* **1.** having parts which are shaped or arranged like lips; lipped. **2.** *Bot.* **a.** belonging to the *Labiatae* (or *Menthaceae*, formerly *Lamiaceae*), the mint family of plants, most of which have bilabiate corollas. **b.** two-lipped; bilabiate: said of a gamopetalous corolla or gamosepalous calyx. —*n.* **3.** a labiate plant. [< NL *labiāt*(*us*). See LABIUM, -ATE[1]]

La·biche (la bēsh′), *n.* **Eu·gène Ma·rin** (œ zhen′ ma ran′), 1815–88, French dramatist.

la·bile (lā′bil *or, esp. Brit.,* -bīl), *adj.* apt to lapse or change; unstable. [late ME *labyl* < LL *lābil*(*is*), equiv. to L *lāb*(*ī*) (to) slip + *-ilis* -ILE] —**la·bil·i·ty** (lə bil′i tē), *n.*

la·bi·lize (lā′bə līz′), *v.t.,* **-lized, -liz·ing.** to cause to become labile. [LABILE + -IZE] —**la′bi·li·za′tion,** *n.*

labio-, a learned borrowing from Latin meaning "lip," used in the formation of compound words: *labiodental.* [comb. form repr. L *labium*]

la·bi·o·den·tal (lā′bē ō den′tᵊl), *Phonet.* —*adj.* **1.** articulated with the lower lip touching the upper front teeth, as *f* or *v*, or, rarely, with the upper lip touching the lower front teeth. —*n.* **2.** a labiodental speech sound. [LABIO- + DENTAL]

la·bi·o·gres·sion (lā′bē ō gresh′ən), *n. Dentistry.* location of the anterior teeth forward of their natural position. [LABIO- + L *gress*(*us*) (ptp. of *gradī* to step, pace, walk) + -ION]

la·bi·o·na·sal (lā′bē ō nā′zəl), *Phonet.* —*adj.* **1.** articulated with the lips and given resonance in the nasal cavity, as *m*. —*n.* **2.** a labionasal sound. [LABIO- + NASAL[1]]

la·bi·o·ve·lar (lā′bē ō vē′lər), *Phonet.* —*adj.* **1.** pronounced with simultaneous bilabial and velar articulations, as *w*. —*n.* **2.** a labiovelar speech sound. [LABIO- + VELAR]

la·bi·o·ve·lar·ise (lā′bē ō vē′lə rīz′), *v.t., v.i.,* **-ised, -is·ing.** *Chiefly Brit.* labiovelarize. —**la′bi·o·ve′lar·i·sa′tion,** *n.*

la·bi·o·ve·lar·ize (lā′bē ō vē′lə rīz′), *v.t., v.i.,* **-ized, -iz·ing.** *Phonet.* to make or become labiovelar. [LABIOVELAR + -IZE] —**la′bi·o·ve′lar·i·za′tion,** *n.*

la·bi·um (lā′bē əm), *n., pl.* **-bi·a** (-bē ə). **1.** a lip or liplike part. **2.** *Anat.* **a.** a lip or lip-shaped structure or part. **b.** any of the folds of skin bordering the vulva. **3.** *Bot.* the lower lip of a bilabiate corolla. **4.** *Entomol.* the posterior unpaired member of the mouth parts of an insect, formed by the united second maxillae. [< L: lip, akin to *lambere* to lick, LAP[3]. See LABRUM, LIP]

lab·lab (lab′lab′), *n.* See **hyacinth bean.** [< Ar]

La Bo·hème (lä′ bō em′; *Fr.* la bô em′), an opera (1896) by Giacomo Puccini.

la·bor (lā′bər), *n.* **1.** productive activity, esp. for the sake of economic gain. **2.** the body of persons engaged in such activity, esp. those working for wages. **3.** this body of persons considered as a class (distinguished from *management* and *capital*). **4.** work, esp. of a hard or fatiguing kind; toil. **5.** a job or task done or to be done: *the 12 labors of Hercules.* **6.** the pangs and efforts of childbirth; travail. **7.** the period during which these pains and efforts occur. —*v.i.* **8.** to perform labor; exert one's powers of body or mind; work; toil. **9.** to strive, as toward a goal; work hard (often fol. by *for*): *to labor for peace.* **10.** to act, behave, or function at a disadvantage (usually fol. by *under*): *to labor under a misapprehension.* **11.** to be in travail or childbirth. **12.** to roll or pitch heavily, as a ship. —*v.t.* **13.** to develop in excessive detail; elaborate: *Don't labor the point.* **14.** to burden or tire: *to labor the reader with unnecessary detail.* **15.** *Archaic.* to work or till (soil or the like). Also, *esp. Brit.,* **labour.** [ME *labour* < MF < L *labōr-* (s. of *labor*) work] —**la′bor·ing·ly,** *adv.* —**la′bor·less,** *adj.*
—**Syn. 2.** working men, working class. **4.** exertion. See **work. 6.** parturition, delivery. **8.** drudge. **11.** suffer. **13.** overdo. —**Ant. 1, 4,** idleness; leisure. **1, 4, 8.** rest.

La′bor and So′cialist Interna′tional, a socialist association, formed in Hamburg in 1923, uniting the Second International and the Vienna International. Cf. **international** (def. 6).

la·bo·ra·re est o·ra·re (lä′bō rä′re est ō rä′re; *Eng.* lab′ō rā′rē est ō rā′rē, lab′ō râr′ē est ō râr′ē). *Latin.* to work is to pray.

lab·o·ra·to·ry (lab′rə tōr′ē, -tôr′ē, lab′ər ə-; *Brit.* lə bor′ə tə rē, -ə trē), *n., pl.* **-ries,** *adj.* —*n.* **1.** a building or part of a building equipped to conduct scientific experiments, tests, investigations, etc., or to manufacture chemicals, medicines, or the like. **2.** any place, situation, set of conditions, or the like, conducive to experimentation, investigation, observation, etc.; anything suggestive of a scientific laboratory. —*adj.* **3.** serving a function in a laboratory. **4.** relating to techniques of work in a laboratory: *laboratory methods; laboratory research.* [< ML *labōrātōri*(*um*) workshop, equiv. to L *labōrāt*(*us*) (ptp. of *labōrāre;* see LABOR) + *-ōrium* -ORY[2]] —**lab′o·ra·to′ri·al,** *adj.* —**lab′o·ra·to′ri·al·ly,** *adv.* —**lab′o·ra·to′ri·an,** *n.*

lab′oratory school′, a school maintained by a college or university for the training of student teachers.

la′bor camp′, **1.** Also called **slave labor camp.** a penal colony where inmates are forced to work. **2.** a camp for the shelter of migratory farm workers.

La′bor Day′, (in most States of the U.S. and in Canada) a legal holiday, commonly the first Monday in September, in honor of labor.

la·bored (lā′bərd), *adj.* **1.** not easy; with difficulty; heavy: *labored breathing.* **2.** exhibiting a great deal of effort; lacking grace, fluency, or spontaneity: *a labored*

style. Also, *esp. Brit.,* **laboured.** [LABOR + -ED²] —**la′bored·ly,** *adv.* —**la′bored·ness,** *n.*
—**Syn. 2.** overdone, ornate, unnatural, stiff. See **elaborate.** —**Ant. 1.** simple, easy. **2.** plain, natural.

la·bor·er (lā′bər ər), *n.* **1.** one engaged in work which requires bodily strength rather than skill or training: *a laborer in the field.* **2.** one who labors. Also, *esp. Brit.,* **labourer.** [ME; see LABOR, -ER¹]

la′bor force′, **1.** a group of workers who are employed by a particular company, corporation, etc. **2.** the total number of people who are either employed or available for employment: *The nation boasts a large labor force.* **3.** (in the U.S.) the body of people who are at least 14 years old and are either employed or available for employment.

la·bo·ri·ous (lə bôr′ē əs, -bōr′-), *adj.* **1.** requiring much labor, exertion, or perseverance: *a laborious undertaking.* **2.** characterized by or requiring extreme care and much attention to detail: *laborious research.* **3.** characterized by or exhibiting excessive effort, dullness, and lack of spontaneity; labored: *a strained, laborious plot.* **4.** given to or diligent in labor: *a careful, laborious craftsman.* [ME < L *labōriōs(us).* See LABOR, -IOUS] —**la·bo′ri·ous·ly,** *adv.* —**la·bo′ri·ous·ness,** *n.*
—**Syn. 1.** toilsome, arduous, onerous, burdensome, difficult, hard, tiresome, wearisome, fatiguing. **4.** hard-working, industrious, assiduous, sedulous, painstaking.

La·bor·ism (lā′bə riz′əm), *n.* **1.** a political theory favoring the dominance of labor in the economic and political life of a country. **2.** the doctrines and programs of the Labour party. Also, *esp. Brit.,* **Labourism.** [LABOR + -ISM] —**la′bor·is′tic,** *adj.*

La·bor·ite (lā′bə rīt′), *n.* a member of a group or political party promoting the interests of labor. [LABOR + -ITE¹]

La′bor-Man′age·ment Rela′tions Act′ (lā′bər man′ij mənt). See **Taft-Hartley Act.**

la′bor mar′ket, the available supply of labor considered with reference to the demand for it.

la′bor move′ment, **1.** labor unions collectively: *The labor movement supported the bill.* **2.** the complex of organizations and individuals supporting and advocating improved conditions for labor: *There was increasing dissension within the labor movement.* **3.** the effort of organized labor and its supporters to bring about improved conditions for the worker, as through collective bargaining: *Their activities proved more harmful than helpful to the labor movement.*

la′bor of love′, work done for the sake of enjoyment rather than for material rewards: *He coached amateur baseball teams as a labor of love.*

la·bor om·ni·a vin·cit (lä′bôr ôm′nē ä′ wiŋ′kit; *Eng.* lā′bôr om′nē ə vin′sit), *Latin.* work conquers all: motto of Oklahoma.

la′bor pains′, the increasingly frequent and intense discomfort experienced by the mother prior to giving birth, caused by uterine contractions.

la′bor rela′tions, the manner of conducting operations between management and labor, esp. on the part of a business organization with respect to the demands of its labor force: *The firm had excellent labor relations and therefore few work stoppages.*

la·bor-sav·ing (lā′bər sā′viŋ), *adj.* made to reduce or replace labor: *a labor-saving device.* Also, *esp. Brit.,* **labour-saving.**

la′bors of Her′cules, *Class. Myth.* the 12 extraordinary feats performed by Hercules for his cousin Eurystheus in order to gain immortality. They are the slaying of the Nemean lion, the killing of the Hydra, the capture of the Erymanthian boar, the capture of the Cerynean stag, the driving away of the Stymphalian birds, the cleansing of the Augean stables, the capture of the Cretan bull, the capture of the mares of Diomedes, the seizing of the girdle of Hippolyte, the abduction of the cattle of Geryon, the stealing of the golden apples of the Hesperides, and the fetching of Cerberus from Hades.

la′bor spy′, an employee who spies on union activities for management.

la′bor un′ion, an organization of wage earners or salaried employees for mutual aid and protection and for dealing collectively with employers; trade union.

la·bour (lā′bər), *n., v.i., v.t. Chiefly Brit.* labor. —**la′bour·ing·ly,** *adv.* —**la′bour·less,** *adj.*

La′bour Day′, *Brit.* Labor Day, celebrated on May 1, in Britain and some parts of the Commonwealth, but on the first Monday in September in Canada, Australia, and New Zealand.

la·boured (lā′bərd), *adj. Chiefly Brit.* labored. —**la′boured·ly,** *adv.* —**la′boured·ness,** *n.*

la·bour·er (lā′bər ər), *n. Chiefly Brit.* laborer.

la′bour exchange′, *Brit.* **1.** a building or part of a building housing union offices and meeting halls. **2.** an employment agency. **3.** (formerly) an organized cooperative of farmers or laborers, for the exchange or sale of their products.

La′bour Exchange′, (in Britain) a government agency that helps the unemployed find work, pays unemployment compensation, compiles unemployment statistics, etc.

La·bour·ism (lā′bə riz′əm), *n. Chiefly Brit.* Laborism.

La·bour·ite (lā′bə rīt′), *n.* a member or supporter of the Labour party. Also, **La′bour·ist.**

La′bour par′ty, a political party in Great Britain, formed in 1900 from various socialist and labor groups and taking its present name in 1906, characterized chiefly by the promotion of labor interests, of gradual socialization of key industries, and of broad social reforms.

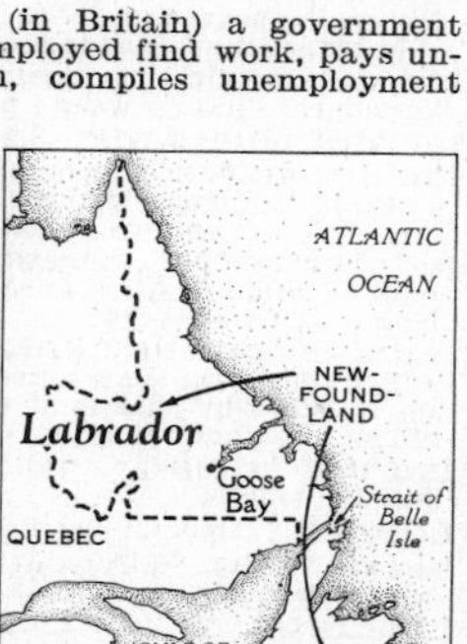

la·bour-sav·ing (lā′bər sā′viŋ), *adj. Chiefly Brit.* labor-saving.

Lab·ra·dor (lab′rə dôr′), *n.* **1.** a peninsula in NE North America surrounded by Hudson Bay, the Atlantic, and the Gulf of St. Lawrence, containing the Canadian provinces of Newfoundland and Quebec. 510,000 sq. mi. **2.** the portion of Newfoundland in the E part of the peninsula. 13,534 (1961); ab. 120,000 sq. mi.

Lab′rador Cur′rent, a cold ocean current flowing S along the Labrador coast through Davis Strait to the Grand Banks where it divides, the E branch joining the North Atlantic Current and the W branch flowing into the Gulf of St. Lawrence.

Lab′rador duck′, an extinct sea duck, *Camptorhynchus labradorius,* of northern North America, having black and white plumage.

Lab·ra·dor·e·an (lab′rə dôr′ē ən), *adj.* **1.** of or pertaining to Labrador. **2.** noting or pertaining to the Pleistocene ice located mainly E of Hudson Bay. Also, **Lab′ra·dor′i·an.** [LABRADOR + *-ean,* var. of -IAN]

lab·ra·dor·ite (lab′rə dô rīt′, lab′rə dôr′īt), *n.* a mineral of the plagioclase feldspar group, often characterized by a brilliant change of colors with blue and green most common. [named after LABRADOR, where first discovered; see -ITE¹] —**lab·ra·dor·it·ic** (lab′rə dô rit′ik), *adj.*

Lab′rador retriev′er, one of a breed of retrievers having a short, thick, oily, solid black or golden coat, raised originally in Newfoundland. See illus. under **retriever.**

Lab′rador tea′, a North American bog shrub, *Ledum groenlandicum,* having white flowers and evergreen leaves.

la·bret (lā′bret), *n.* an ornament worn in a pierced hole in the lip by some primitive peoples. [< L *labr(um)* lip + -ET]

la·brid (lā′brid, lab′rid), *n.* **1.** any of numerous fishes of the family *Labridae,* comprising the wrasses, the tautog, the cunner, etc. —*adj.* **2.** belonging or pertaining to the family *Labridae.* [< NL *Labrid(ae),* equiv. to L *labr(us)* (see LABROID) + *-idae* -ID²]

lab·roid (lab′roid), *adj., n.* labrid. [< L *labr(us)* a kind of fish (? akin to LABRUM¹) + -OID]

la·brum¹ (lā′brəm, lab′rəm), *n., pl.* **la·bra** (lā′brə, lab′rə). **1.** a lip or liplike part. **2.** *Zool.* **a.** the anterior, unpaired member of the mouth parts of an arthropod, projecting in front of the mouth. **b.** the outer margin of the aperture of a shell of a gastropod. **3.** *Anat.* a ring of cartilage about the edge of a joint surface of a bone. [< L: lip; akin to LABIUM]

la·brum² (lā′brəm), *n., pl.* **-bra** (-brə). *Archaeol.* an ornamented bathtub of ancient Rome. [< L: lit., basin]

La Bru·yère (LA BRY YER′), **Jean de** (zhäN də), 1645–96, French moralist and author, esp. of satire.

La·bu·an (lä′bōō än′), *n.* an island off the NW coast of Sabah: formerly part of the colony of British North Borneo, and one of the Straits Settlements: now part of the federation of Malaysia. 9253 (est. 1947); 35 sq. mi.

la·bur·num (lə bûr′nəm), *n.* any of several small, leguminous trees of the genus *Laburnum,* having pendulous racemes of yellow flowers, esp. *L. anagyroides,* of Europe. [< NL, special use of L *labernum* golden chain]

lab·y·rinth (lab′ə rinth), *n.* **1.** an intricate combination of passages in which it is difficult to find one's way or to reach the exit. **2.** a maze of paths bordered by high hedges, as in a park or garden. **3.** a mazelike pattern inlaid in the pavement of a church. **4.** a complicated or tortuous arrangement, as of streets, buildings, etc. **5.** any confusingly intricate state of things or events; a bewildering complex. **6.** (*cap.*) *Class. Myth.* a vast maze built in Crete by Daedalus, at the command of King Minos, to house the Minotaur. **7.** *Anat.* **a.** the internal ear, consisting of a bony portion (**bon′y lab′yrinth**) and a membranous portion (**mem′branous lab′yrinth**). **b.** the aggregate of air chambers in the ethmoid bone, between the eye and the upper part of the nose. **8.** a loudspeaker enclosure with air chambers at the rear for absorbing sound waves radiating in one direction so as to prevent their interference with waves radiated in another direction. [< L *labyrinth(us)* < Gk *labýrinthos;* r. ME *laborintus* < ML]

lab′yrinth fish′, any of several fresh-water fishes of the order *Labyrinthi,* found in southeastern Asia and Africa, having a labyrinthine structure above each gill chamber enabling them to breathe air while out of water.

lab·y·rin·thine (lab′ə rin′thin, -thēn), *adj.* **1.** of, pertaining to, or resembling a labyrinth. **2.** intricate; complicated; tortuous: *He wandered helplessly through the labyrinthine byways of modern literature.* Also, **lab·y·rin·thi·an** (lab′ə rin′thē ən), **lab′y·rin′thic.** [LABYRINTH + -INE¹] —**lab′y·rin′thi·cal·ly,** *adv.*

lab·y·rin·thi·tis (lab′ə rin thī′tis), *n. Pathol.* inflammation of the inner ear, or labyrinth, characterized by dizziness, nausea, and visual disturbances. Also called **otitis interna.** [< NL; see LABYRINTH, -ITIS]

lac¹ (lak), *n.* a resinous substance deposited on the twigs of various trees in southern Asia by the female of the lac insect: used in the manufacture of varnishes, sealing wax, etc., and in the production of a red coloring matter. Cf. **shellac** (defs. 1, 2). [< Hindi *lākh* < < Skt *lākshā*]

lac² (läk), *n.* (in India) **1.** the sum of 100,000, esp. of rupees. The usual punctuation for sums of Indian money above a lac is with a comma after the number of lacs: Rs. 30,52,000 (i.e., 30 lacs and 52,000) instead of 3,052,000. **2.** an indefinitely large number. Also, **lakh.** [< Hindi *lākh* < < Skt *lākshā*]

lac³ (lak), *n.* (in prescriptions) milk. [< L]

LAC, leading aircraftsman.

La·caille (lä kī′, lə-; *Fr* LA kä′yᵊ), *n.* a crater in the fourth quadrant of the face of the moon: about 35 miles in diameter.

La Ca·sa de Ber·nar·da Al·ba (*Sp.* lä kä′sä the ber när′thä äl′vä). See **House of Bernarda Alba, The.**

Lac′ca·dive Is′lands (lak′ə dīv′), a group of islands and coral reefs in the Arabian Sea, off the SW coast of India: a part of Madras province. 24,108 (1961): ab. 80 sq. mi.

lac·co·lith (lak′ə lith), *n. Geol.* a mass of igneous rock formed from lava which when rising from below did not find its way to the surface but spread out laterally into a lenticular body, thereby causing the overlying strata to bulge upward. Also, **lac·co·lite** (lak′ə līt′). [< Gk *lákko(s)* pond + -LITH] —**lac′co·lith′ic, lac·co·lit·ic** (lak′ə lit′ik), *adj.*

lace (lās), *n., v.,* **laced, lac·ing.** —*n.* **1.** a netlike ornamental fabric made of threads by hand or machine. **2.** a cord or string for holding or drawing together, as when passed through holes in opposite edges. **3.** ornamental cord or braid, esp. of gold or silver, used to decorate uniforms, hats, etc. **4.** a small amount of liquor added to food or drink. —*v.t.* **5.** to fasten, draw together, or compress by or as if by means of a lace. **6.** to pass (a cord, leather strip, etc.), as through holes. **7.** to compress the waist of (a person) by drawing tight the laces of a corset, or the like. **8.** to adorn or trim with lace. **9.** to interlace or intertwine. **10.** *Informal.* to lash, beat, or thrash. **11.** to mark or streak, as with color. **12.** to add a small amount of liquor to (food or drink): *He took his coffee laced with brandy.* —*v.i.* **13.** to be fastened with a lace: *These shoes lace up the side.* **14.** to attack physically or verbally (often fol. by *into*): *The teacher laced into his students for not studying.* [ME *las* < OF *laz, las* < L *laqueus* noose] —**lace′less,** *adj.* —**lace′like′,** *adj.* —**lac′er,** *n.*

lace·bark (lās′bärk′), *n.* **1.** a West Indian tree, *Lagetta lintearia,* the inner bark of which yields a lacelike material. **2.** a malvaceous tree, *Hoheria populnea,* of New Zealand. [LACE + BARK²]

lace′ bug′, any of several hemipterous insects of the family *Tingidae,* characterized by a lacy pattern of ridges on the head, thorax, and wings, and feeding on the leaves of oak, birch, sycamore, etc.

Lac·e·dae·mon (las′i dē′mən), *n.* **1.** Sparta (def. 1). **2.** the son of Zeus and Taÿgete and the legendary founder of the city of Sparta.

Lac·e·dae·mo·ni·an (las′i di mō′nē ən), *adj.* **1.** of or pertaining to ancient Sparta; Spartan. —*n.* **2.** a native or inhabitant of ancient Sparta; a Spartan. [LACEDAEMON + -IAN]

lace-fern (lās′fûrn′), *n.* a small, tufted fern, *Cheilanthes gracillima,* having dark-brown stalks and fronds about four inches long.

lace′ glass′, glass in a filigree pattern.

La Cei·ba (lä sā′bä), a seaport in N Honduras. 24,863 (1961).

lace-leaf (lās′lēf′), *n., pl.* **-leaves.** a submerged aquatic plant, *Aponogeton fenestralis,* of Madagascar, having broad leaves consisting only of veins which float just beneath the surface, and tiny white flowers. Also called **lattice-leaf.**

La Ce·les·ti·na (*Sp.* lä the′les tē′nä, se′-), (*Comedia de Calisto y Melibea*) a novel in dramatic form (1499), the major portion of which was written by Fernando de Rojas. Also called **The Tragicomedy of Calisto and Melibea.**

lace·mak·ing (lās′mā′kiŋ), *n.* the art, act, or process of making lace. [LACE + MAKING]

lace′ piece′, *Naut.* a timber fayed to the back of a figurehead to steady it. Also called **lacing.**

lace′ pil′low, pillow (def. 3).

lac·er·ate (*v.* las′ə rāt′; *adj.* las′ə rāt′, -ər it), *v.,* **-at·ed, -at·ing,** *adj.* —*v.t.* **1.** to tear roughly; mangle: *to lacerate the flesh.* **2.** to distress or torture mentally or emotionally; wound deeply; pain greatly: *to lacerate the soul.* —*adj.* **3.** lacerated. [< L *lacerāt(us)* (ptp. of *lacerāre* to tear up), deriv. of *lacer* mangled; see -ATE¹] —**lac·er·a·bil·i·ty** (las′ər ə bil′i tē), *n.* —**lac′er·a·ble,** *adj.* —**lac·er·a·tive** (las′ə rā′tiv, -ər ə tiv), *adj.*
—**Syn. 1.** rend. See **maim.**

lac·er·at·ed (las′ə rā′tid), *adj.* **1.** mangled; jagged; torn. **2.** pained; wounded; tortured: *lacerated sensibilities.* **3.** *Bot., Zool.* having the edge variously cut as if torn into irregular segments, as a leaf. [LACERATE + -ED²]

lac·er·a·tion (las′ə rā′shən), *n.* **1.** act of lacerating. **2.** the result of lacerating; a rough, jagged tear. [< L *lacerātiōn-* (s. of *lacerātiō*). See LACERATE, -ION]

la·cer·na (lə sûr′nə, lä kär′nə), *n., pl.* **-nas, -nae** (-nē nī). (in ancient Rome) a short mantle, sometimes hooded, worn over the toga. [< L]

La·cer·ta (lə sûr′tə), *n., gen.* **-tae** (-tē). *Astron.* the Lizard, a northern constellation between Cepheus and Pegasus. [< L: lizard]

la·cer·tid (lə sûr′tid), *n.* **1.** any of numerous Old World lizards of the family *Lacertidae.* —*adj.* **2.** belonging or pertaining to the *Lacertidae* family of lizards. [< NL *Lacertid(ae).* See LACERTA, -ID²]

lac·er·til·i·an (las′ər til′ē ən, -til′yən), *adj.* **1.** belonging or pertaining to the suborder *Lacertilia,* comprising the lizards. —*n.* **2.** a lacertilian reptile. Also, **la·cer·tian** (lə sûr′shən, -shē ən). [< NL *Lacertili(a)* (L *Lacert(a)* LACERTA + *-ilia,* neut. pl. of *-ilis* -ILE) + -AN]

lace-vine (lās′vīn′), *n.* See **silver-lace vine.**

lace·wing (lās′wiŋ′), *n.* any of several neuropterous insects of the family *Chrysopidae,* having delicate, lacelike wings and golden or copper-colored eyes, the larvae of which are predaceous on aphids. [LACE + WING]

lace·wood (lās′wŏŏd′), *n.* the quartersawed wood of the sycamore tree. [LACE + WOOD¹]

lace·work (lās′wûrk′), *n.* lace (def. 1). [LACE + WORK]

Lac·ey (lā′sē), *n.* a town in W Washington. 6630 (1960).

La Chaise (LA shez′), **Père Fran·çois d'Aix de** (FRäN SWA′ de də), 1624–1709, French Roman Catholic priest: confessor to Louis XIV.

La·chaise (lə shez′; *Fr.* LA shez′), *n.* **Gas·ton** (gas′tən; *Fr.* GA STôN′), 1882–1935, U.S. sculptor, born in France.

La Char·treuse de Parme (*Fr.* LA SHAR TRŒZ′ də PARM′). See **Charterhouse of Parma, The.**

lach·es (lach′iz), *n.* (*construed as sing.*) *Law.* failure to do a thing at the proper time, esp. such delay as will bar a party from bringing a legal proceeding. [ME *lachesse* < AF, var. of MF *laschesse,* deriv. of OF *lasche* slack (< Gmc); see -ICE]

Lach·e·sis (lach′i sis), *n. Class. Myth.* the Fate who determines the length of the thread of life. [< L < Gk, personification of *láchesis* destiny, equiv. to *lache(in)* (to) happen by lot + *-sis* -SIS]

La·chish (lā′kish), *n.* a Canaanite city captured by Joshua: now an archaeological site in Israel.

Lach·ry·ma Chris·ti (lak′rə mə kris′tē), **1.** a table wine produced from grapes grown near Vesuvius, in Italy. **2.** a medium dry, sparkling wine produced in the Piedmont region of Italy. Also, **Lacrima Christi.** [< L: lit., the tears of Christ]

lach·ry·mal (lak′rə məl), *adj.* **1.** of or pertaining to tears; producing tears. **2.** characterized by tears; indicative of weeping. **3.** *Anat.* lacrimal (def. 2). —*n.* **4.** Also called **lach′rymal bone′.** *Anat.* See **lacrimal bone. 5.** lachrymatory (def. 2). [< ML *lachrymālis*, var. of *lacrimālis*, equiv. to L *lacrim(a)* tear (OL *dacruma*; akin to Gk *dákry*) + *-ālis* -AL¹]

lach·ry·ma·tor (lak′rə mā′tər), *n.* *Chem.* a substance that causes the shedding of tears; tear gas. Also, **lacrimator.** [< ML *lacrimātor*, equiv. to L *lacrimāt(us)* (see LACHRYMATORY) + *-or* -OR²]

lach·ry·ma·to·ry (lak′rə mə tōr′ē, -tôr′ē), *adj.*, *n.*, *pl.* **-ries.** —*adj.* **1.** of, pertaining to, or causing the shedding of tears. —*n.* **2.** Also called **lachrymal.** a small, narrow-necked vase found in ancient Roman tombs, formerly thought to have been used for containing the tears of bereaved friends. Also, **lacrimatory.** [< ML *lachrymātōri(um)* (n.), *lachrymātōri(us)* (adj.), equiv. to L *lacrimāt(us)* (ptp. of *lacrimāre* to weep, deriv. of *lacrima* tear; see LACHRYMAL) + *-ōrium*, *-us* -ORY¹]

lach·ry·mose (lak′rə mōs′), *adj.* **1.** given to shedding tears; tearful: *He was, in his youth, a rather lachrymose fellow.* **2.** suggestive of or tending to cause tears; mournful. [< L *lacrimōs(us)*, equiv. to *lacrim(a)* tear + *-ōsus* -OSE¹] —**lach′ry·mose′ly,** *adv.* —**lach·ry·mos·i·ty** (lak′rə mos′i tē), *n.*

La Chute (*Fr.* lȧ shyt′). See **Fall, The.**

lac·ing (lā′sing), *n.* **1.** act of one who or that which laces. **2.** a lace used for fastening, as a shoe or corset lace. **3.** a trimming of lace or braid. **4.** a small amount of liquor added to food or drink. **5.** *Naut.* **a.** any light line for fastening a sail, awning, or other cloth. **b.** See **lace piece. 6.** a beating or thrashing. **7.** *Building Trades, Engineering* any member or members, as a batten plate or steel bars, uniting the angles or flanges of a composite girder, column, or strut. **8.** Also called **lac′ing course′.** *Masonry.* **a.** a course of brick in a wall of rubble. **b.** a bond course in a rowlock arch. [ME; see LACE, -ING¹]

la·cin·i·ate (lə sin′ē āt′, -it), *adj.* *Bot., Zool.* cut into narrow, irregular lobes; slashed; jagged. [< NL *lacini(a)* (special use of L *lacinia* lappet) + -ATE¹]

Laciniate leaf

lac′ in′sect (lak), a scale insect, *Laccifer lacca*, of southeast Asia, the female of which secretes lac.

lack (lak), *n.* **1.** deficiency or absence of something needed, desirable, or customary: *lack of money or skill.* **2.** something missing or needed: *After he left, they really felt the lack.* —*v.t.* **3.** to be without or deficient in: *to lack ability; to lack confidence; to lack the necessities of life.* **4.** to fall short in respect of: *The vote lacks three of being a majority.* —*v.i.* **5.** to be absent, as something needed or desirable: *Three votes are lacking to make a majority.* **6. lack in,** to be short of or deficient in: *What he lacks in brains, he makes up for in brawn.* [ME *lak*; c. MLG *lak*, MD *lac* deficiency; akin to Icel *lakr* deficient]
—**Syn. 1.** dearth, scarcity, paucity, shortcoming, deficit, insufficiency. **1, 3.** want, need. —**Ant. 1.** surplus.

lack·a·dai·si·cal (lak′ə dā′zi kəl), *adj.* **1.** without vigor or determination; listless; lethargic: *They pursued their goals in a lackadaisical manner.* **2.** lazy; indolent: *He is a lackadaisical fellow.* [*lackadais(y)* (var. of LACKADAY) + -ICAL] —**lack′a·dai′si·cal·ly,** *adv.* —**lack′a·dai′si·cal·ness,** *n.*

lack·a·day (lak′ə dā′), *interj.* *Archaic.* (used as an expression of regret, sorrow, dismay, or disapproval.) [alter. of *alack the day*]

Lack·a·wan·na (lak′ə won′ə), *n.* a city in W New York, on Lake Erie, near Buffalo. 29,564 (1960).

lack·er (lak′ər), *n.*, *v.t.* lacquer. —**lack′er·er,** *n.*

lack·ey (lak′ē), *n.*, *pl.* **-eys,** *v.*, **-eyed, -ey·ing.** —*n.* **1.** a footman or liveried manservant. **2.** a servile follower. —*v.t.* **3.** to attend as a lackey does. Also, **lacquey.** [< MF *laquais*, perh. < Catalan *lacayo*, *alacayo* < ?]

lack·ing (lak′ing), *prep.* **1.** being without; wanting; less: *Lacking equipment, we couldn't continue climbing the mountain.* —*adj.* **2.** wanting; deficient: *He was found lacking in stamina.* [LACK + -ING²]

lack·lus·ter (lak′lus′tər), *adj.* **1.** lacking brilliance, radiance, liveliness, etc.; dull or vapid: *a lackluster existence; a lackluster stare; lackluster eyes; a lackluster color.* —*n.* **2.** a lack of brilliance or vitality. Also, *esp. Brit.,* **lack′lus′tre.** [LACK + LUSTER¹]

La·clos (lȧ klō′), *n.* **Pierre Am·broise Fran·çois Cho·der·los de** (pyer äN brwaz′ fräN swȧ′ shô der-lō′ də), 1741–1803 French general and writer.

La Co·mé·die Hu·maine (*Fr.* lȧ kô mā dē y men′). See **Human Comedy, The.**

La Con·di·tion Hu·maine (*Fr.* lȧ kôN dē syôN y-men′). See **Man's Fate.**

La·co·ni·a (lə kō′nē ə), *n.* an ancient country in the S part of Greece. *Cap.:* Sparta. —**La·co′ni·an,** *adj.*, *n.*

la·con·ic (lə kon′ik), *adj.* using few words; expressing much in few words; concise: *a laconic remark; a laconic reply.* [< L *lacōnic(us)* < Gk *lakōnik(ós)* Laconian, equiv. to *Lákōn* a Laconian + *-ikos* -IC] —**la·con′i·cal·ly,** *adv.*
—**Syn.** brief, pithy, terse; succinct. —**Ant.** voluble.

la·con·i·cal (lə kon′i kəl), *adj.* *Archaic.* laconic. [< L *lacōnic(us)* (see LACONIC) + -AL¹]

la·con·i·cum (lə kon′i kəm), *n.*, *pl.* **-ca** (-kə). the sudatorium of an ancient Roman bath. [< L: sweating-room, n. use of neut. of *Lacōnicus* Laconian (see LACONIC); the sweat bath was a Spartan custom]

lac·o·nism (lak′ə niz′əm), *n.* **1.** laconic brevity. **2.** a laconic utterance or sentence. Also, **la·con·i·cism** (lə-kon′i siz′əm). [< Gk *lakōnism(ós)*, n. answering to *lakōnízein* to favor or ape the Spartans. See LACONIC, -ISM]

La Co·ru·ña (lä′ kô ro͞o′nyä), a seaport in NW Spain. 169,750 (est. 1960). Also called **Coruña, Corunna.**

lac·quer (lak′ər), *n.* **1.** a protective coating consisting of a resin, cellulose ester, or both, dissolved in a volatile solvent, sometimes with pigment added. **2.** any of various resinous varnishes, esp. a resinous varnish obtained from a Japanese tree, *Rhus verniciflua*, used to produce a highly polished, lustrous surface on wood or the like. **3.** Also called **lac′quer ware′.** ware, esp. of wood, coated with such a varnish, and often inlaid: *They collected fine old lacquers, vases, and other items from the Orient.* —*v.t.* **4.** to coat with lacquer. **5.** to cover, as with facile or fluent words, explanations, etc.; obscure the faults of; gloss; smooth (often fol. by *over*): *The cunning speech tended to lacquer over the terrible conditions. He lacquered the inanity of his thought with clever phrases.* Also, **lacker.** [earlier *leckar*, *laker* < OPg *lacre*, *lacar*, unexplained var. of *laca* < Ar *lakk* < Pers *lāk* LAC¹] —**lac′quer·er,** *n.*

lac·quey (lak′ē), *n.*, *pl.* **-queys,** *v.t.*, **-queyed, -quey·ing.** lackey.

La Cres·cent (lə kres′ənt), a town in SE Minnesota. 2624 (1960).

La·cre·telle (lȧ krə tel′), *n.* **Jacques de** (zhäk də), born 1888, French novelist.

Lac·ri·ma Chris·ti (lak′rə mə kris′tē). See **Lachryma Christi.**

lac·ri·mal (lak′rə məl), *adj.* **1.** lachrymal (defs. 1, 2). **2.** Also, **lachrymal.** *Anat.* of, pertaining to, or situated near the organs that secrete tears. —*n.* **3.** See **lacrimal bone.** [var. of LACHRYMAL]

A, Lacrimal gland
B, Lacrimal ducts
C, Lacrimal sac
D, Nasolacrimal duct

lac′rimal bone′, *Anat.* a small, thin, membrane bone forming the front part of the inner wall of each orbit. See diag. under **skull.** Also called **lachrymal, lacrimal.**

lac′rimal duct′, *Anat.* either of two small ducts extending from the inner corner of each eyelid to the lacrimal sac.

lac′rimal gland′, *Anat.* either of two tear-secreting glands situated in the upper outer angle of the orbit.

lac′rimal sac′, *Anat.* the dilated upper portion of the nasolacrimal duct which receives tears from the lacrimal ducts.

lac·ri·ma·tor (lak′rə mā′tər), *n.* lachrymator.

lac·ri·ma·to·ry (lak′rə mə tōr′ē, -tôr′ē), *adj.*, *n.*, *pl.* **-ries.** lachrymatory.

La·croix (lə krō′), *n.* a crater in the third quadrant of the face of the moon: about 20 miles in diameter.

La Crosse (lə krôs′, kros′), a city in W Wisconsin, on the Mississippi River. 47,575 (1960).

la·crosse (lə krôs′, -kros′), *n.* a game, originated by Indians of North America, in which two 10-member teams attempt to send a small ball into each other's netted goal, each player being equipped with a crosse or stick at the end of which is a netted pocket for catching, carrying, or throwing the ball. [< CanF: lit., the crook (stick used in the game). See CROSSE]

Lacrosse racquet

lact-, var. of **lacto-** before a vowel: *lactalbumin.*

lac·tal·bu·min (lak′tal byo͞o′min), *n.* *Biochem.* the simple protein of milk, resembling serum albumin, obtained from whey, used in the preparation of certain foods and in adhesives and varnishes. [LACT- + ALBUMIN]

lac·tam (lak′tam), *n.* *Chem.* any of a group of cyclic amides characterized by the –NH–CO– group, derived from aminocarboxylic acids by the intramolecular elimination of water from the amino and carboxylic groups. [LACT(ONE) + AM(IDE)]

lac·ta·ry (lak′tə rē), *adj.* *Rare.* of, pertaining to, or of the nature of milk. [< L *lactāri(us)* milk-giving. See LACT-, -ARY]

lac·tase (lak′tās), *n.* *Biochem.* an enzyme capable of hydrolyzing lactose into glucose and galactose. [LACT- + -ASE]

lac·tate¹ (lak′tāt), *n.* *Chem.* an ester or salt of lactic acid. [LACT- + -ATE²]

lac·tate² (lak′tāt), *v.i.*, **-tat·ed, -tat·ing.** to produce milk. [< L *lactāt(us)*, ptp. of *lactāre* to suckle. See LACT-, -ATE¹]

lac·ta·tion (lak tā′shən), *n.* **1.** the secretion or formation of milk. **2.** the period of milk production. [< LL *lactātiōn-* (s. of *lactātiō*) a giving suck. See LACTATE², -ION] —**lac·ta′tion·al,** *adj.* —**lac·ta′tion·al·ly,** *adv.*

lac·te·al (lak′tē əl), *adj.* **1.** pertaining to, consisting of, or resembling milk; milky. **2.** *Anat.* conveying or containing chyle. —*n.* **3.** *Anat.* any of the minute lymphatic vessels which convey chyle from the small intestine to the thoracic duct. [< L *lacte(us)* milky (see LACT-, -EOUS) + -AL¹] —**lac′te·al·ly,** *adv.*

lac·te·ous (lak′tē əs), *adj.* *Archaic.* milky; of the color of milk. [< L *lacte(us)* (see LACTEAL) + -OUS]

lac·tes·cent (lak tes′ənt), *adj.* **1.** becoming or being milky. **2.** *Bot., Entomol.* secreting or producing a milky juice. [< L *lactēscent-* (s. of *lactēscēns*) turning to milk, prp. of *lactēscere.* See LACT-, -ESCENT] —**lac·tes′cense, lac·tes′cen·cy,** *n.*

lacti-, var. of **lacto-:** *lactiferous.*

lac·tic (lak′tik), *adj.* of, pertaining to, or obtained from milk. [LACT- + -IC]

lac′tic ac′id, *Biochem.* a colorless or yellowish, syrupy, water-soluble liquid, $CH_3CHOHCOOH$, found in sour milk, prepared usually by fermentation of cornstarch, molasses, potatoes, etc., or synthesized: used chiefly in dyeing and textile printing, in food, and in medicine.

lac·tif·er·ous (lak tif′ər əs), *adj.* **1.** producing or secreting milk: *lactiferous glands; lactiferous animals.* **2.** conveying milk or a milky fluid: *lactiferous ducts.* [< L *lactifer* milk-bearing (see LACTI-, -FER) + -OUS] —**lac·tif′er·ous·ness,** *n.*

lacto-, a learned borrowing from Latin meaning "milk," used in the formation of compound words (*lactometer*); specialized in chemical terminology to mean "lactate," or "lactic acid." Also, **lact-, lacti-.** [comb. form repr. L *lact-* (s. of *lac*)]

lac·to·ba·cil·lus (lak′tō bə sil′əs), *n.*, *pl.* **-cil·li** (-sil′ī). *Bacteriol.* any long, slender, rod-shaped, aerobic bacterium of the genus *Lactobacillus*, which produces large amounts of lactic acid in the fermentation of carbohydrates, esp. in milk. [< NL; see LACTO-, BACILLUS]

lac·to·fla·vin (lak′tō flā′vin, lak′tō flā′-), *n.* *Biochem.* riboflavin. [LACTO- + -FLAVIN]

lac·to·gen (lak′tə jin, -jen′), *n.* *Biochem.* luteotropin. [LACTO- + -GEN] —**lac·to·gen·ic** (lak′tə jen′ik), *adj.*

lac′togen′ic hor′mone, *Biochem.* luteotropin.

lac·tom·e·ter (lak tom′i tər), *n.* an instrument for determining the specific gravity of milk. [LACTO- + -METER]

lac·tone (lak′tōn), *n.* *Chem.* any of a group of internal esters derived from hydroxy acids. [LACT- + -ONE] —**lac·ton·ic** (lak ton′ik), *adj.*

lac·to·nize (lak′tō nīz′), *v.t.*, *v.i.*, **-nized, -niz·ing.** to change into a lactone. [LACTONE + -IZE] —**lac′to·ni·za′tion,** *n.*

lac·to·pro·tein (lak′tō prō′tēn, -prō′tē in), *n.* any protein existing in milk. [LACTO- + PROTEIN]

lac·to·scope (lak′tə skōp′), *n.* an optical device for determining the amount of cream in milk. [LACTO- + -SCOPE]

lac·tose (lak′tōs), *n.* **1.** *Biochem.* a disaccharide, $C_{12}H_{22}O_{11}$, present in milk, that upon hydrolysis yields glucose and galactose. **2.** a white, crystalline, sweet, water-soluble commercial form of this compound, obtained from whey and used in infant feedings, in confections and other foods, in bacteriological media, and in pharmacy as a diluent and excipient. Also called **milk sugar, sugar of milk.** [LACT- + -OSE²]

La Cum·bre (*Sp.* lä ko͞om′bre). See **Uspallata Pass.**

la·cu·na (lə kyo͞o′nə), *n.*, *pl.* **-nae** (-nē), **-nas.** **1.** a gap or missing part, as in a manuscript, rational argument, or the like; hiatus. **2.** *Anat.* one of the numerous minute cavities in the substance of bone, supposed to contain nucleate cells. **3.** *Bot.* an air space in the cellular tissue of plants. [< L: ditch, pit, hole, gap, deficiency, akin to *lacus* vat, lake. See LAGOON]

la·cu·nal (lə kyo͞on′əl), *adj.* **1.** of or pertaining to a lacuna. **2.** having lacunae. Also, **lac·u·nar·y** (lak′yo͞o-ner′ē, lə kyo͞o′nə rē). [LACUN(A) + -AL¹]

la·cu·nar (lə kyo͞o′nər), *n.*, *pl.* **la·cu·nars, lac·u·nar·i·a** (lak′yə nâr′ē ə), *adj.* —*n.* **1.** *Archit.* **a.** a coffered vault, ceiling, or soffit. **b.** coffer (def. 4). —*adj.* **2.** lacunal. [LACUN(A) + -AR¹]

lac·u·nar·is (lak′yə nâr′is), *adj.* (not in technical use) lacunosis. [< L; see LACUNA, -AR¹]

la·cu·nose (lə kyo͞o′nōs), *adj.* full of or having lacunae. [< L *lacūnōs(us)* full of holes or gaps. See LACUNA, -OSE¹] —**lac·u·nos·i·ty** (lak′yo͞o nos′i tē), *n.*

lac·u·no·sis (lak′yə nō′sis), *adj.* *Meteorol.* (of a cloud) characterized by rounded spaces between the elements. [< L *lacūnōs(us)* LACUNOSE + -SIS]

la·cu·nule (lə kyo͞o′nyo͞ol), *n.* a small lacuna. [LACUN(A) + -ULE]

La·cus Mor·tis (lā′kəs môr′tis), a dark plain in the first quadrant of the face of the moon: about 7500 square miles. Also called **Lake of Death.**

La·cus So·lis (lak′əs sō′lis), an area in the southern hemisphere of Mars.

La′cus Som·ni·o·rum (som′nē ōr′əm, -ôr′-), a dark plain in the first quadrant of the face of the moon: about 11,000 square miles. Also called **Lake of Dreams, Lake of the Sleepers.**

la·cus·trine (lə kus′trin), *adj.* **1.** of or pertaining to a lake. **2.** living or growing in lakes, as various animals and plants. **3.** formed at the bottom or along the shore of lakes, as geological strata. [< It *lacustr(e)* of lakes + -INE¹]

LACW, leading aircraftswoman.

lac·y (lā′sē), *adj.*, **lac·i·er, lac·i·est.** of or resembling lace; lacelike. [LACE + -Y¹] —**lac′i·ly,** *adv.* —**lac′i·ness,** *n.*

La·cy (lā′sē), *n.* a boy's given name.

lad (lad), *n.* **1.** a boy or youth. **2.** *Informal.* a familiar or affectionate term of address for a man; chap. [ME *ladde*, OE *Ladda* (nickname) < ?] —**lad′dish,** *adj.* —**lad′hood,** *n.*

La Dame aux Ca·mé·lias (*Fr.* lȧ dȧm ō kȧ mā-lyȧ′). See **Lady of the Camelias, The.**

lad·a·num (lad′ənəm), *n.* labdanum.

Ladd (lad), *n.* a boy's given name.

lad·der (lad′ər), *n.* **1.** a structure of wood, metal, or rope, commonly consisting of two sidepieces between which a series of bars or rungs are set at suitable distances, forming a means of climbing up or down. **2.** something resembling a ladder. **3.** a means of rising, as to eminence: *ladder of success.* **4.** a graded series of stages or levels in status; a hierarchical order of position or rank: *He was high on the political and social ladders.* **5.** *Chiefly Brit.* a run in a stocking: *Her stocking had a ladder in it.* —*v.t.* **6.** to climb or mount by means of a ladder: *to ladder a wall.* **7.** to furnish with a ladder or ladders: *to ladder a water tower.* **8.** *Chiefly Brit.* to cause a run in (a stocking): *She laddered her stocking when she bent down.* —*v.i.* **9.** *Chiefly Brit.* to get a run, as in a stocking: *Her stockings laddered an hour after she put them on.* **10.** to gain in popularity or importance: *He laddered to the top of his profession.* [ME *laddre*, OE *hlǣder*; c. G *Leiter*, D *leer* (also *ladder* < Fris); akin to Goth *hleithra* tent; orig. something that slopes. See LEAN¹] —**lad′der·less,** *adj.* —**lad′der·like′, lad′der·y,** *adj.*

lad′der back′, a chair back having a number of horizontal slats between uprights.

lad′der com′pany. See **hook-and-ladder company.**

lad·der·man (lad′ər mən, -man′), *n.*, *pl.* **-men** (-mən, -men′). a fireman who is a member of a hook-and-ladder company. [LADDER + MAN¹]

lad′der stitch′, an embroidery stitch in which crossbars at equal distances are produced between two solid ridges of raised work.

lad′der tour′nament, *Sports.* a tournament in which the entrants are listed by name and rank, advancement being by means of challenging and defeating an entrant ranked one or two places higher.

lad′der track′, a railroad track linking a series of parallel tracks.

lad′der truck′. See **hook and ladder.**

lad·der·way (lad′ər wā′), *n.* *Mining.* a vertical manway with ladders. [LADDER + WAY]

lad·die (lad′ē), *n.* *Chiefly Scot.* a young lad; boy. [LAD + -IE]

lade (lād), *v.*, **lad·ed, lad·en** or **lad·ed, lad·ing.** —*v.t.* **1.** to put (something) on or in, as a burden, load, cargo, etc.; load. **2.** to load oppressively; burden (used chiefly in the passive): *laden with responsibilities.* **3.** to fill or cover abundantly (used chiefly in the passive): *trees laden with fruit; a man laden with honors.* **4.** to lift or

CONCISE ETYMOLOGY KEY: <, descended or derived from; >, whence; b., blend of, blended; c., cognate with; deriv., derivative; equiv., equivalent; imit., imitative; m., modification of; obl., oblique; r., replacing; s., stem; sp., spelling; trans., translation; ?, origin unknown, perhaps; *, hypothetical. See the full key inside the front cover.

throw in or out, as a fluid, with a ladle or other utensil. —*v.i.* **5.** to take on a load. **6.** to lade a liquid. [ME *lade(n)*, OE *hladan* to load, draw up (water); c. D *laden*, G *laden*, Icel *hlatha* to load. Cf. LADLE] —**lad′er,** *n.*

lad·en (lād′ən), *adj.* **1.** burdened; loaded down. —*v.t.* **2.** to lade. [LADE + -EN³]

la-di-da (lä′dē dä′), *Informal.* —*interj.* **1.** (used as an expression of derision directed at affected gentility, pretentious refinement, or the like.) —*adj.* **2.** affected; pretentious; foppish: *a la-di-da manner.* —*n.* **3.** a person who affects gentility or exaggerates refinement. **4.** behavior characterized by affected or exaggerated gentility. Also, **la′-de-da′, lah-di-dah.** [in derisive imitation of affected, pseudo-elevated speech]

La′dies Aid′, a local organization of women who raise money for the church at which they worship.

La′dies Auxil′iary, an association whose members are usually the wives of members of an association with which it is affiliated.

La′dies′ Day′, a special day set aside, either occasionally or regularly, on which women are invited to participate in a certain activity at a greatly reduced fee or at no cost: *Friday was Ladies' Day at the ball park, and they had to pay only a dime to get in.*

la·dies-in-wait·ing (lā′dēz in wā′ting), *n.* pl. of **lady-in-waiting.**

la′dies′ man′, a man who strives especially to please women and to attract their attention and admiration: *She had the bad sense to marry a ladies' man.* Also, **lady's man.**

la′dies′ room′, a public lavatory for women. Also called **powder room, women's room.**

la·dies′-to·bac·co (lā′dēz tə bak′ō), *n., pl.* **-cos, -coes.** See **pussy's toe.**

La·din (lə dēn′), *n.* **1.** a Rhaeto-Romanic dialect of the southern Tyrol. **2.** a dialect of Romansh spoken in the Inn River valley of Grisons canton, Switzerland. **3.** a person who speaks Ladin. [< Romansh < L *Latīnus* LATIN]

lad·ing (lā′ding), *n.* **1.** act of lading. **2.** that with which something is laden; load; freight; cargo. [LADE + -ING¹]

La·di·no (lə dē′nō; *Sp.* lä dē′nō), *n., pl.* **-nos** (-nōz; *Sp.* -nōs) for 2. **1.** the Spanish dialect of the Sephardic Jews, written in the Hebrew script. **2.** (in Spanish America) a mestizo. [< Sp < L *Latīnus* LATIN. See LADIN]

Ladi′no clo′ver, a variety of white clover, *Trifolium repens giganteum*, used for pasture and hay.

Lad·is·laus (lad′is lôs′), *n.* **Saint,** c1040–95, king of Hungary 1077–95. Also, **Lad·is·las** (lad′is ləs, -läs′).

la·dle (lād′əl), *n., v.,* **-dled, -dling.** —*n.* **1.** a long-handled utensil with a cup-shaped bowl for dipping or conveying liquids. **2.** *Metall.* a bucketlike, refractory-lined container for transferring molten metal. —*v.t.* **3.** to dip or convey with or as with a ladle: *He was in the kitchen ladling soup into the plates.* [ME *ladel*, OE *hlædel.* See LADE, -LE] —**la′dler,** *n.*

la·dle·ful (lād′əl fo͝ol′), *n., pl.* **-fuls.** the amount that fills a ladle. [late ME *ladelful.* See LADLE, -FUL]

La·do·ga (lä′do gä′, -də-), *n.* **Lake,** a lake in the NW Soviet Union in Europe, NE of Leningrad: largest lake in Europe. 7000 sq. mi.

La·don (lād′ən), *n. Class. Myth.* a dragon having 100 heads and guarding the garden of the Hesperides. It was killed by Hercules.

la·drone (lə drōn′), *n. Southwest U.S.* a thief. Also, **la·dron′.** [< Sp *ladrōn* < L *latrōn-* (s. of *latrō*) mercenary, bandit]

Ladrone′ Is′lands (lə drōn′), former name of **Mariana Islands.** Also called **La·drones** (lə drōnz′; *Sp.* la thrō′nes).

La·due (lə do͞o′, -dyo͞o′), *n.* a town in E Missouri. 9466 (1960).

la·dy (lā′dē), *n., pl.* **-dies,** *adj.* —*n.* **1.** a woman of good family or social position, or of good breeding, refinement, etc. **2.** a polite term for any woman. **3.** any woman; female: *a cleaning lady.* **4.** wife: *The ambassador and his lady arrived late.* **5.** (*cap.*) (in Great Britain) the proper title of any woman whose husband is higher in rank than baronet or knight, or who is the daughter of a nobleman not lower than an earl, although the title is given by courtesy also to the wives of baronets and knights. **6.** a woman who has proprietary rights or authority, as over a manor; a female feudal superior. Cf. **lord** (def. 3). **7.** (*cap.*) the Virgin Mary. **8.** a woman who is the object of chivalrous devotion. **9.** (*usually cap.*) *Archaic.* **a.** an attribute or abstraction personified as a woman; a designation of an allegorical figure as feminine: *Lady Fortune; Lady Virtue.* **b.** a title prefixed to the name of a goddess: *Lady Diana.* —*adj.* **10.** being a lady: *a lady reporter.* **11.** of a lady; ladylike. [ME; earlier *lavedi*, OE *hlǣfdīge*, ? orig. meaning loaf-kneader, equiv. to *hlāf* LOAF + *dīge*, var. of *dǣge* kneader (see DOUGH), c. Icel *deigja* maid] —**la′dy·hood′,** *n.* —**la′dy·ish,** *adj.* —**la′dy·ish·ly,** *adv.* —**la′dy·ish·ness,** *n.* —**la′dy·less,** *adj.*

—**Syn. 1.** See **woman.**

La′dy Bal′timore cake′, a white layer cake using only the beaten whites of eggs and spread with a fruit-nut filling consisting of raisins, figs, walnuts or pecans, and sometimes candied cherries. Cf. **Lord Baltimore cake.**

La′dy Banks′ rose′. See **Banks' rose.**

la′dy·bird bee′tle (lā′dē bûrd′), ladybug. Also called **la′dy·bird′.** [LADY (uninflected poss. case) Virgin Mary + BIRD; i.e. (our) Lady's bird]

La′dy Boun′tiful, 1. a wealthy lady in George Farquhar's *The Beaux' Stratagem*, noted for her kindness and generosity. **2.** a woman of noteworthy generosity or charity: *In her later years she became a Lady Bountiful.*

la·dy·bug (lā′dē bug′), *n.* any of numerous, often brightly colored beetles of the family *Coccinellidae*, feeding chiefly on aphids and other small insects, but including several forms that feed on plants. Also called **la′dy bee′tle, lady-bird beetle.** [LADY + BUG¹]

Ladybug, *Hippodamia convergens* (Length ¼ in.)

La′dy chap′el, a chapel dedicated to the Virgin Mary, attached to a church, and generally behind the high altar at the extremity of the apse. [ME (*oure*) *lady chapell*]

La′dy Chat′ter·ley's Lov′er (chat′ər lēz), a novel (1928) by D. H. Lawrence.

la′dy crab′, a brightly speckled swimming crab, *Ovalipes ocellatus*, found on sandy beaches along the Atlantic coast of the U.S. Also called **calico crab.**

La′dy Day′, 1. annunciation (def. 3). **2.** one of various days celebrated in honor of the Virgin Mary. **3.** *Brit.* the spring quarter day, when quarterly rents and accounts are due. Cf. **quarter day.** [ME *oure lady day*]

la′dy fern′, a fern, *Athyrium Filix-femina*, having delicate, feathery fronds.

la·dy·fin·ger (lā′dē fing′gər), *n.* a small, finger-shaped sponge cake. [LADY + FINGER]

la·dy·fish (lā′dē fish′) *n., pl.* (*esp. collectively*) **-fish,** (*esp. referring to two or more kinds or species*) **-fish·es. 1.** Also called **tenpounder.** a game fish, *Elops saurus*, found in warm seas, closely related to but smaller than the tarpon. **2.** bonefish. [LADY + FISH]

La′dy in the Chair′, *Astron.* the constellation Cassiopeia.

la·dy-in-wait·ing (lā′dē in wā′ting), *n., pl.* **la·dies-in-wait·ing.** a lady who is in attendance upon a queen or princess.

la·dy-kill·er (lā′dē kil′ər), *n. Informal.* a man who fascinates or is especially attractive to women, in fact or by reputation. —**la′dy-kill′ing,** *n., adj.*

la·dy·kin (lā′dē kin), *n.* (often used as a term of endearment) a little lady. [LADY + -KIN]

la·dy·like (lā′dē līk′), *adj.* **1.** like a lady. **2.** befitting a lady: *in a ladylike manner.* [LADY + -LIKE] —**la′dy·like′ness,** *n.*

la·dy·love (lā′dē luv′), *n.* a beloved lady; sweetheart or mistress. [LADY + LOVE]

la′dy of pleas′ure, a prostitute.

La′dy of the Camel′lias, The, a novel (1848) and play (1852) by Alexandre Dumas fils. French, **La Dame aux Camélias.**

la′dy of the eve′ning, a prostitute.

la′dy of the house′, the housewife or mistress of a house or apartment (usually prec. by *the*).

La′dy of the Lake′, The, a narrative poem (1810) by Sir Walter Scott.

la·dy-of-the-night (lā′dē əv thə nīt′), *n., pl.* **la·dies-of-the-night.** a shrub, *Brunfelsia americana*, of tropical America, having berrylike, yellow fruit and fragrant, white flowers. Also called **Franciscan nightshade.**

la·dy·ship (lā′dē ship′), *n.* **1.** (*often cap.*) the form used in speaking of or to a woman having the title of *Lady* (usually prec. by *her* or *your*). **2.** the rank of a lady. [ME; see LADY, -SHIP]

la′dy's maid′, a maid who is a lady's personal attendant, as in dressing.

la′dy's man′. See **ladies' man.**

la·dy's-man·tle (lā′dēz man′təl), *n.* any rosaceous herb of the genus *Alchemilla*, as *A. vulgaris*, having grayish, lobed leaves and tight clusters of greenish-yellow flowers.

La·dy·smith (lā′dē smith′), *n.* **1.** a city in W Natal, in the E Republic of South Africa: besieged by Boers 1889–1900. 16,413 (est. 1960). **2.** a town in N Wisconsin. 3584 (1960).

La′dy's Not′ for Burn′ing, The, a verse play (1948) by Christopher Fry.

la·dy's-slip·per (lā′dēz slip′ər), *n.* **1.** any orchid of the genus *Cypripedium*, the flowers of which have a protruding labellum somewhat resembling a slipper. **2.** any of several other related plants having similar flowers, as of the genera *Paphiopedilum, Phragmipedium,* and *Selenipedium.* Also, **la′dy-slip′per.**

Lady's-slipper, *Cypripedium reginae*

la·dy's-smock (lā′dēz smok′), *n.* a cruciferous plant, *Cardamine pratensis*, having white or purple flowers. Also called **milkmaid.**

la·dy's-this·tle (lā′dēz this′əl), *n.* an herb, *Silybum Marianum*, of the Mediterranean region, having glossy, spiny leaves and purplish-red flower heads nearly 2½ inches wide. Also called **holy thistle, milk thistle.**

la·dy's-thumb (lā′dēz thum′), *n.* a smartweed, *Polygonum Persicaria*, having pink or purplish flowers and a dark spot on the leaves resembling a thumbprint.

la·dy's-tress·es (lā′dēz tres′iz), *n., pl.* **la·dy's-tress·es.** (*construed as sing. or pl.*) any orchid of the genus *Spiranthes.*

La′dy Wash′ington gera′nium. See **show geranium.** [named after Martha WASHINGTON]

La′dy Win′der·mere's Fan′ (win′dər mērz′), a comedy (1892) by Oscar Wilde.

La·e (lä′ā, lā′ē), *n.* a seaport in E Territory of New Guinea: used as a major supply base by the Japanese in World War II. 70,516 (est. 1961).

Lae·laps (lē′laps), *n. Class. Myth.* a hound fated to capture what it pursued, borrowed from Cephalus by Amphitryon to chase a vixen fated to escape anything pursuing it. The hound was petrified, with the vixen, by the gods to solve the inherent dilemma.

Laemm·le (lem′lē), *n.* **Carl,** 1867–1939, U.S. producer of motion pictures, born in Germany.

La·ën·nec (lä nek′), *n.* **Re·né Thé·o·phile Hya·cinthe** (rə nā′ tā ô fēl′ yȧ sant′), 1781–1826, French physician who invented the stethoscope.

La·er·tes (lā ûr′tēz), *n. Class. Myth.* the father of Odysseus.

La·er·ti·a·des (lā′ər tī′ə dēz′), *n.* (in the *Odyssey*) an epithet of Odysseus, meaning "son of Laertes."

Laes·tryg·o·nes (les trig′ə nēz′), *n.pl., sing.* **Laes·try·gon** (les′trə gon′). *Class. Myth.* giant cannibals encountered by Odysseus on his return to Ithaca. Also called **Laes·try·go·ni·ans** (les′tri gō′nē ənz).

Lae·tar′e Sun′day (lē târ′ē), the fourth Sunday of Lent when the introit begins with "*Laetare Jerusalem*" (Rejoice ye, Jerusalem). Also called **Mid-Lent Sunday.**

Lae·ti·tia (lə tish′ə, -tē′shə), *n.* a girl's given name. Also, **Latitia, Letitia.**

la·e·trile (lā′ə tril′), *n.* a controversial drug prepared from the pits of apricots or peaches, claimed to cure cancer.

lae·vo (lē′vō), *adj.* levorotatory. [by shortening]

laevo-, var. of **levo-.**

lae·vo·gy·rate (lē′vō jī′rāt), *adj.* levogyrate.

lae·vo·ro·ta·tion (lē′vō rō tā′shən), *n.* levorotation.

lae·vo·ro·ta·to·ry (lē′vō rō′tə tôr′ē, -tōr′ē), *adj.* levorotatory.

LaF, Louisiana French.

La Farge (lə färzh′, färj′), **1. John,** 1835–1910, U.S. painter, stained-glass designer, and writer. **2. Oliver Hazard Perry** ("*Oliver II*"), 1901–63, U.S. novelist and anthropologist.

La Fa·yette (laf′ē et′, lä′fē-, -fā-; *for 1 also Fr.* lȧ fȧ yet′), **1. Ma·rie Ma·de·leine Pioche de la Vergne** (mȧ rē′ mȧdᵊ len′ pyôsh də lȧ ver′nyᵊ), **Comtesse de,** 1634–93, French novelist. **2.** a town in NW Georgia. 5588 (1960).

La·fa·yette (laf′ē et′, lä′fē-, -fā-; *for 1 also Fr.* lȧ fȧ-yet′), *n.* **1. Ma·rie Jo·seph Paul Yves Roch Gil·bert du Mo·tier** (mȧ rē′ zhô zef′ pôl ēv rôk zhēl ber′ dy mô tyā′), **Marquis de.** Also, **La Fayette.** 1757–1834, French soldier, statesman, and liberal leader, who served in the American Revolutionary Army and took a leading part in the French revolutions of 1789 and 1830. **2.** a city in W Indiana, on the Wabash River. 42,330 (1960). **3.** a city in S Louisiana. 40,400 (1960). **4.** a town in W California. 7114 (1960). **5.** a town in central Colorado. 2612 (1960). **6.** a town in E Alabama. 2605 (1960). **7.** a boy's given name.

Lafayette′ Southwest′, a town in S Louisiana. 6682 (1960).

Laf·ca′di·o's Adven′tures (läf kä′dē ōz′), a novel (1914) by André Gide. Also called **The Vatican Swindle.** French, **Les Caves du Vatican.**

La Fe·ri·a (lə fēr′ē ə), a town in S Texas. 3047 (1960).

La·fitte (lä fēt′), *n.* **Jean** (zhäN), c1780–c1825, French privateer in the Americas. Also, **Laf·fite′.**

La Folle de Chail·lot (*Fr.* lȧ fôl də shȧ yō′). See **Madwoman of Chaillot, The.**

La Fol·lette (lə fol′it), **1. Robert Marion,** 1855–1925, U.S. political leader: U.S. Senator 1906–25. **2.** a town in NE Tennessee. 6204 (1960).

La Fon·taine (*Fr.* lȧ fôN ten′), **1. Hen·ri** (*Fr.* äN-rē′), 1854–1943, Belgian statesman: Nobel peace prize 1913. **2. Jean de** (zhäN də), 1621–95, French poet and fabulist.

La Fres·naye (lȧ fre nā′), **Ro·ger de** (rô zhā′ də), 1885–1925, French painter.

lag¹ (lag), *v.,* **lagged, lag·ging,** *n.* —*v.i.* **1.** to fall behind; fail to maintain a desired pace or to keep up: *After five minutes of hard running, some of them began to lag.* **2.** to move or develop slowly, as toward a goal or objective, or in relation to an associated factor (often fol. by *behind*): *to lag behind in production.* **3.** to delay or fail in reaching full development: *The plant lags regularly in making its quota. Business is lagging critically in that sector.* **4.** to hang back; linger; delay: *The old friends lagged because they wanted to talk some more.* **5.** to decrease, wane, or flag gradually, as in intensity: *Interest lags in such matters.* **6.** *Marbles.* to throw one's shooting marble toward a line (**lag line**) on the ground in order to decide on the order of play. **7.** *Billiards, Pool.* string (def. 14b). —*v.t.* **8.** *Obs.* to cause to lag. —*n.* **9.** a lagging or falling behind; retardation. **10.** one who lags behind, is the last to arrive, etc. **11.** an interval or lapse of time: *There was a developmental lag in the diffusion of ideas.* **12.** *Mech.* the amount of retardation of some motion. **13.** *Elect.* the retardation of one alternating quantity, as current, with respect to another related alternating quantity, as voltage, often expressed in electrical degrees. **14.** *Marbles, Billiards.* the act of lagging. [< Scand; cf. Norw *lagga* to go slowly]

—**Syn. 1.** loiter, linger. **9.** slowing, slowdown. —**Ant. 1.** hasten.

lag² (lag), *v.,* **lagged, lag·ging,** *n. Slang.* —*v.t.* **1.** to send to penal servitude; imprison. —*n.* **2.** a convict or ex-convict. **3.** a term of penal servitude; prison sentence. [?]

lag³ (lag), *n., v.,* **lagged, lag·ging.** —*n.* **1.** one of the staves or strips which form the periphery of a wooden drum, the casing of a steam cylinder, or the like. **2.** *Masonry.* a crosspiece between ribs in a centering. —*v.t.* **3.** to cover with insulation, as a steam boiler, to prevent radiation of heat. [< Scand; cf. Sw *lagg* stave]

lag·an (lag′ən), *n. Law.* anything sunk in the sea, but attached to a buoy or the like so that it may be recovered. Also, **ligan.** [< ML *lagan(um)* right to own wreckage washed up from the sea, perh. < Gmc]

La·gash (lā′gash), *n.* an ancient Sumerian city between the Tigris and Euphrates rivers, at the modern village of Telloh in SE Iraq: a palace, statuary, and inscribed clay tablets unearthed here.

lag′ bolt′, a heavy wood screw, esp. a lag screw.

Lag b'O·mer (läg bō′mər), a Jewish festival celebrated on the 18th day of the month of Iyar, being the 33rd day of the Omer, in commemoration chiefly of the martyrdom of the Jewish scholar Akiba ben Joseph (A.D. c50–132) and the bravery of the Jewish commander Simon Bar Cocheba (died A.D. 135) in an unsuccessful revolt against the Romans. [< Heb, equiv. to *lag* 33rd + *'omer* period from Passover (2nd day) to Shabuoth, special use of *'omer* OMER]

lag·en (lag′ən), *n. Scot. and North Eng.* laggin.

la·ge·na (lə jē′nə), *n., pl.* **-nae** (-nē). *Zool.* an outpocketing of the saccule of birds, reptiles, and bony fishes corresponding to the cochlear duct of mammals. [< NL, special use of L *lagēna* flask, flagon; c. Gk *lágȳnos*]

la·gen·i·form (lə jen′ə fôrm′), *adj. Bot., Zool.* shaped like a flask; having an enlarged base tapering to a narrow neck. [LAGEN(A) + -I- + -FORM]

la·ger¹ (lä′gər, lô′-), *n.* a beer stored from six weeks to six months before use. Also called **la′ger beer′.** [short for *lager beer*, half adoption, half trans. of G *Lagerbier.* See LAIR¹, BEER]

la·ger² (lä′gər), *n., v.t., v.i. South African.* laager.

La·ger·kvist (lä′gər kvist′), *n.* **Pär** (pär), 1891–1974, Swedish novelist, poet, and essayist: Nobel prize 1951.

La·ger·löf (lä′gər lœf′), *n.* **Sel·ma** (**Ot·ti·li·a·na Lo·vi·sa**) (sel′mä ôt′ti lē ä′nä lo͞o′vi sä′), 1858–1940. Swedish novelist and poet: Nobel prize 1909.

lag·gard (lag′ərd), *n.* **1.** one who or that which lags; lingerer; loiterer: *It was a group composed of laggards, none of whom could be counted on.* —*adj.* **2.** moving, developing, or responding slowly; sluggish; dilatory; backward. [LAG¹ + -ARD] —**lag′gard·ness,** *n.*

lag·gard·ly (lag′ərd lē), *adv.* **1.** in the manner of a laggard. —*adj.* **2.** of, pertaining to, characteristic of, or being a laggard: *He behaved in a laggardly fashion.* [LAGGARD + -LY]

lag·gen (lag′ən), *n. Scot. and North Eng.* laggin.

lag·gen-gird (lag′ən gûrd′; *Scot.* lag′ən gird′), *n. Scot. and North Eng.* **1.** the bottom hoop securing the staves of a tub or barrel. **2. cast a laggen-gird,** to sire an illegitimate child.

lag·ger¹ (lag′ər), *n.* a laggard. [LAG¹ + -ER¹]

lag·ger² (lag′ər), *n. Slang.* a convict or ex-convict. [LAG² + -ER¹]

lag·gin (lag′ən), *n. Scot. and North Eng.* **1.** Usually, **laggins.** the staves at the bottom of a barrel, cask, or other hooped vessel. **2.** the inner angle of a wooden dish, formed by the meeting of the sides and bottom. Also, **lagen, laggen, leglen.** [*lagg* (< Scand; cf. Icel *lögg* chime) + *-in,* var. of -ING¹]

lag·ging¹ (lag′ing), *n.* **1.** act of lagging behind. —*adj.* **2.** lingering; loitering; slow and dragging: *lagging steps.* [LAG¹ + -ING¹] —**lag′ging·ly,** *adv.*

lag·ging² (lag′ing), *n.* **1.** act of covering a boiler, oil tank, etc., with heat-insulating material. **2.** the covering formed. **3.** the material used. **4.** a number of boards or the like joined together side by side to line an excavation. **5.** *Masonry.* a number of lags, taken as a whole. [LAG³ + -ING¹]

La·ghou·at (lä gwät′), *n.* a city in N Algeria. 11,058 (1954).

La Gio·con·da (*It.* lä′ jô kôn′dä). **1.** See **Mona Lisa. 2.** See **Gioconda, La** (def. 2).

lag′ line′. See under **lag¹** (def. 6).

-lagnia, a learned borrowing from Greek, where it meant "coition," used in the formation of compound words: *algolagnia.* [comb. form repr. Gk *lagneía* coition, lust]

la·gniappe (lan yap′, lan′yap), *n.* **1.** *Chiefly Southern Louisiana and Southeast Texas.* something given with a purchase to a customer, by way of compliment or for good measure. **2.** a gratuity or tip. Also, **la·gnappe′.** [< LaF < AmerSp *la ñapa* the addition, equiv. to *la* fem. definite article + *ñapa,* var. of *yapa* < Quechua]

lag·o·morph (lag′ə môrf′), *n.* any mammal of the order *Lagomorpha,* resembling the rodents but having two pairs of upper incisors, and comprising the hares, rabbits, and pikas, formerly classified as a suborder of rodents. [< NL *Lagomorph(a)* name of the order, equiv. to Gk *lagṓ(s)* hare + *morph(ḗ)* -MORPH + L *-a* neut. pl. suffix] —**lag′o·mor′phic, lag′o·mor′phous,** *adj.*

Lag·o·mor·pha (lag′ə môr′fə), *n.* the order comprising the lagomorphs. [< NL: LAGOMORPH]

la·goon (lə go͞on′), *n.* **1.** an area of shallow water separated from the sea by low banks. **2.** any small, pondlike body of water, esp. one communicating with a larger body of water. Also, **lagune.** [earlier *laguna* (sing.), *lagune* (pl.) < It < L *lacūna* ditch, pool, akin to *lacus* basin, lake] —**la·goon′al,** *adj.*

Lagoon′ Is′lands. See **Ellice Islands.**

La·gos (lä′gōs, lā′gos), *n.* a seaport in and the capital of Nigeria, in the SW part. 665,246 (1963); 24 sq. mi.

La Grande (lə grand′), *n.* a town in NE Oregon. 9014 (1960).

La Grange (lə grānj′), **1.** a city in W Georgia. 23,632 (1960). **2.** a city in NE Illinois, near Chicago. 15,285 (1960). **3.** a town in central Texas. 3623 (1960).

La·grange (lə grānj′; *Fr.* LA GRÄNZH′), *n.* **1. Jo·seph Louis** (zhô zef′ lwē), **Comte,** 1736–1813, French mathematician and astronomer. **2.** a walled plain in the third quadrant of the face of the moon: about 100 miles in diameter.

Lagrange′ mul′tipliers, *Math.* unknowns introduced into differential equations for finding maximum and minimum values by Lagrange's method.

Lagrange′'s meth′od, *Math.* a procedure for finding maximum and minimum values of a function of several variables when the variables are restricted by additional conditions. [named after J. L. LAGRANGE]

Lagrange′ the′orem, *Math.* the theorem that the order of each subgroup of a finite group is a factor of the order of the group. [named after J. L. LAGRANGE]

La·gran′gi·an func′tion (lə gran′jē ən), *Physics.* See **kinetic potential.** [named after J. L. LAGRANGE; see -IAN]

La Gran·ja (*Sp.* lä gräng′hä). See under **San Ildefonso.**

lag′ screw′, a heavy wood screw having a square or hexagonal head driven by a wrench. Also called **coach screw.** See illus. under **screw.**

Lag·ting (läg′ting′), *n.* Storting. Also, **Lag′thing′.** [< Scand; cf. Norw *lagting,* Icel *lagthing.* See LAW¹, THING²]

La Guai·ra (lä gwī′rä), a seaport in N Venezuela: the port of Caracas. 16,279 (1951).

La Guar·di·a (lə gwär′dē ə), **Fi·o·rel·lo H(enry)** (fē′ə rel′ō), 1882–1947, U.S. lawyer, political reformer, and government administrator: mayor of New York City 1933–45.

La·guerre (lä gâr′; *Fr.* LA GER′), *n.* **Ed·mond-Ni·co·las** (ed môn′nē kô lä′), 1834–86, French mathematician.

Laguerre′ equa′tion, *Math.* a differential equation of the form, $x\frac{d^2y}{dx^2} + (1-x)\frac{dy}{dx} + ny = 0$, where *n* is any nonnegative integer. [named after E.-N. LAGUERRE]

La·gu′na Beach′ (lə go͞o′nə), a town in S California. 9288 (1960).

la·gune (lə go͞on′), *n.* lagoon.

La Ha·bra (lə hä′brə), a city in SW California, near Los Angeles. 25,136 (1960).

La·hai·na (lə hī′nə, lä hī′nä), *n.* a town on W Maui, in central Hawaii. 3423 (1960).

la·har (lä′här), *n. Geol.* **1.** a landslide of water-saturated volcanic debris on the side of a volcano. **2.** the deposit left by such a landslide. [< Javanese]

lah-di-dah (lä′dē dä′), *interj., adj., n.* la-di-da.

La Hogue (LA ôg′), a roadstead off the NW coast of France; naval battle, 1692. Also, **La Hougue** (LA o͞og′).

La·ho·ma (lə hō′mə), *n.* a girl's given name.

La·hore (lə hōr′, -hôr′), *n.* a city in and the capital of West Pakistan province, in the NE part, in Pakistan. 1,297,000 (est. 1961).

Lahore′ par′ty, *Islam.* See under **Ahmadiya.**

lai (lā), *n.* (in medieval French literature) **1.** a narrative poem written in octosyllabic couplets and dealing with tales of adventure and romance. **2.** a lyric poem, often a love poem, having great metrical variety and designed to be sung to a popular melody. [< F, OF. See LAY⁴]

Lai·bach (lī′bäкн), *n.* German name of **Ljubljana.**

la·ic (lā′ik), *adj.* **1.** Also, **la′i·cal.** lay; secular. —*n.* **2.** layman. [< LL *lāic(us)* < Gk *lāïkós* of the people, equiv. to *lā(ós)* people + *-ikos* -IC] —**la′i·cal·ly,** *adv.*

la·i·cise (lā′i sīz′), *v.t.,* **-cised, -cis·ing.** *Chiefly Brit.* laicize. —**la·i·ci·sa·tion** (lā′i si zā′shən), *n.*

la·i·cism (lā′i siz′əm), *n.* the nonclerical, or secular, control of political and social institutions in a society (distinguished from *clericalism*). [LAIC + -ISM]

la·i·cize (lā′i sīz′), *v.t.,* **-cized, -ciz·ing.** to deprive of clerical character; secularize: *to laicize a school; to laicize the office of headmaster.* Also, *esp. Brit.,* **laicise.** [LAIC + -IZE] —**la·i·ci·za·tion** (lā′i si zā′shən), *n.*

laid (lād), *v.* pt. and pp. of **lay¹.**

laid-back (lād′bak′), *adj. Slang.* **1.** relaxed and unhurried: *a laid-back style of music.* **2.** feeling no social or moral pressure; carefree: *a laid-back way of living.*

laid′ deck′, *Shipbuilding.* a wooden deck having planking laid parallel to the sides of the hull so as to follow the curves toward the ends of the vessel. Also called **swept deck.** Cf. **straight deck.**

laid′ pa′per, paper with fine parallel and cross lines produced in manufacturing. Cf. **wove paper.**

laigh (lāкн), *Scot.* —*adj., adv.* **1.** low¹. —*n.* **2.** a small valley or hollow. [ME *lawch.* See LOW¹]

lain (lān), *v.* pp. of **lie².**

lair¹ (lâr), *n.* **1.** a den or resting place of a wild animal: *The cougar retired to its lair.* **2.** a secluded or hidden place, esp. a secret retreat or base of operations; a hideout or hideaway: *a pirate's lair.* **3.** *Brit.* a place in which to lie or rest; a bed. —*v.t.* **4.** to place in a lair. **5.** to serve as a lair for. —*v.i.* **6.** to go to, lie in, or have a lair. [ME *leir,* OE *leger;* c. D, OHG *leger* bed, camp; akin to LIE²]

lair² (lâr), *n.* **1.** *Brit. Dial.* mud; mire. —*v.i.* **2.** *Scot.* to sink or stick in mud or mire. [v. use of ME *lair* clay, mire < Scand; cf. Icel *leir* clay, LOAM]

lair³ (lâr), *n. Chiefly Scot.* lore; learning. [ME (north) *lare,* OE *lār* LORE]

laird (lârd; *Scot.* lārd), *n. Scot.* a landed proprietor. [ME *laverd,* northern form of *loverd* LORD] —**laird′ly,** *adj.* —**laird′ship′,** *n.*

Laird (lârd), *n.* **Melvin R(obert),** born 1922, U.S. political leader: Secretary of Defense 1969–73.

lais·ser-al·ler (le sā A lā′), *n. French.* unchecked freedom or ease; unrestraint; looseness: *He spoke with much too much* laisser-aller. Also, **lais·sez-al·ler** (le sā A lā′). [lit., allow to go]

lais·sez faire (les′ā fâr′; *Fr.* le sā fer′), **1.** the theory or system of government that upholds the autonomous character of the economic order, believing that government should intervene as little as possible in the direction of economic affairs. **2.** the practice or doctrine of noninterference in the affairs of others, esp. with reference to individual conduct or freedom of action. Also, **lais′ser faire′.** [< F: lit., allow to act]

lais·sez-faire (les′ā fâr′; *Fr.* le sā fer′), *adj.* of, pertaining to, or conforming to the principles or practices of laissez faire. Also, **lais′ser-faire′.** —**lais′sez-faire′ism,** *n.*

lais·sez-pas·ser (le sā pä sā′), *n., pl.* **-ser.** *French.* permit; pass, esp. one issued in lieu of a passport: *He received a* laissez-passer *enabling him to leave the country.* [lit., allow to pass]

lai·tance (lāt′ᵊns), *n.* a milky deposit on the surface of new cement or concrete, caused by too much water, excessive vibration, etc. [special use of F *laitance* milt, equiv. to *lait* milk (< L *lact-,* s. of *lac*) + *-ance* -ANCE]

lait d'a·mandes (le dA mänd′), *French.* See **almond milk.**

laith (lāth), *Scot.* —*adj.* **1.** loath. —*v.t.* **2.** loathe.

la·i·ty (lā′i tē), *n.* **1.** the body of religious worshipers, as distinguished from the clergy. **2.** the people outside of a particular profession, as distinguished from those belonging to it; those lacking professional knowledge of a specific subject. [LAY³ + -ITY]

La·ius (lā′əs, lā′ē əs), *n.* a king of Thebes, the husband of Jocasta and father of Oedipus: unwittingly killed by Oedipus.

Laj·oi·e (lash′ə wā′), *n.* **Napoleon** ("*Nap*"), 1875–1959, U.S. baseball player.

La Jun·ta (lə hun′tə), a town in SE Colorado. 8026 (1960).

lake¹ (lāk), *n.* **1.** a body of fresh or salt water of considerable size, surrounded by land. **2.** some similar body of water or other liquid. [ME; OE *lacu* stream, pool, pond (c. G *Lache* pool, bog); r. early ME *lac* < OF < L *lac(us)* vat, tank, pool, lake]

lake² (lāk), *n.* **1.** any of various pigments prepared from animal, vegetable, or coal-tar coloring matters by chemical or other union with metallic compounds. **2.** a red pigment prepared from lac or cochineal by combination with a metallic compound. [var. of LAC¹]

Lake (lāk), *n.* **Simon,** 1866–1945, U.S. engineer and naval architect.

Lake′ Ar′al. See **Aral Sea.**

Lake′ Ar′thur, a town in SW Louisiana. 3541 (1960).

Lake′ Bluff′, a town in NE Illinois. 3464 (1960).

lake′ breeze′, a thermally produced wind blowing during the day from the surface of a large lake to the shore, caused by the difference in the rates of heating of the surfaces of the lake and of the land. Cf. **sea breeze.**

Lake′ Car′mel, a town in SE New York. 2735 (1960).

Lake′ Charles′, a city in SW Louisiana. 63,392 (1960).

Lake′ Cit′y, 1. a town in central South Carolina. 6059 (1960). **2.** a town in SE Minnesota. 3494 (1960).

Lake′ Dis′trict, a mountainous region in NW England containing many lakes. Also, **Lake′ Coun′try.**

lake′ dwell′er, an inhabitant of a lake dwelling.

lake′ dwell′ing, a dwelling, esp. of prehistoric times, built on piles or other support over the water of a lake.

Lake′ For′est, a city in NE Illinois, N of Chicago, on Lake Michigan. 10,687 (1960).

lake·front (lāk′frunt′), *n.* the land along the edge of a lake: *Property along the lakefront is more expensive every year.* Also called **lakeshore.** [LAKE¹ + FRONT]

Lake′ Gene′va, a town in SE Wisconsin. 4929 (1960).

lake′ her′ring, a cisco or whitefish, esp. *Coregonus artedii,* of the Great Lakes.

Lake·hurst (lāk′hûrst), *n.* **1.** a borough in central New Jersey: naval air station; dirigible hangar. 2780 (1960). **2.** a town in E New Jersey. 2780 (1960).

Lake′ Isle′ of In′nis·free, The (in′is frē′), a poem (1893) by W. B. Yeats.

Lake′ Jack′son, a town in S Texas. 9651 (1960).

Lake·land (lāk′lənd), *n.* a city in central Florida. 41,350 (1960).

Lake′land ter′rier, one of a breed of small, slender terriers, raised originally in northwestern England for hunting foxes.

Lake′ Mills′, a town in S Wisconsin. 2951 (1960).

Lake′ Mo′hawk, a town in NW New Jersey. 4647 (1960).

Lake·more (lāk′mōr, -môr), *n.* a town in NE Ohio. 2765 (1960).

Lake′ of the Woods′, a lake in S Canada and the N United States, between N Minnesota and Ontario and Manitoba provinces. 1485 sq. mi.

Lake′ O′ri·on (ōr′ē ən, ôr′-), a town in SE Michigan. 2698 (1960).

Lake′ Park′, a town in SE Florida. 3589 (1960).

Lake′ Plac′id, a town in NE New York, in the Adirondack Mountains: resort. 2998 (1960).

Lake′ Po′ets, the poets Wordsworth, Coleridge, and Southey: so called from their residence in the Lake District. Also called **Lake School.**

lake·port (lāk′pōrt′, -pôrt′), *n.* a port city located on the shore of a lake, esp. one of the Great Lakes. [LAKE¹ + PORT¹]

Lake′ Prov′idence, a town in NE Louisiana. 5781 (1960).

lak·er (lā′kər), *n.* **1.** a person closely associated with a lake, as a resident, visitor, or worker. **2.** (*cap.*) one of the Lake poets. **3.** a fish found in lakes or caught in a lake, esp. the lake trout. **4.** a vessel designed for navigating on lakes, esp. the Great Lakes. [LAKE¹ + -ER¹]

Lake′ Ronkon′koma, a town on central Long Island, in SE New York. 4841 (1960).

lake′ salm′on. See **landlocked salmon.**

Lake′ School′. See **Lake Poets.**

lake·shore (lāk′shōr′, -shôr′), *n.* lakefront. [LAKE¹ + SHORE¹]

lake′ stur′geon, a sturgeon, *Acipenser fulvescens,* of the Great Lakes and Mississippi and St. Lawrence rivers.

Lake′ Success′, a town on Long Island, in SE New York: temporary United Nations headquarters 1946–51. 2954 (1960).

lake′ trout′, a large, fork-tailed trout, *Salvelinus namaycush,* found in the lakes of Canada and the northern U.S., used for food.

Lake·view (lāk′vyo͞o′), *n.* **1.** a town in SE Texas. 3849 (1960). **2.** a town in S Oregon. 3260 (1960).

Lake′ Vil′lage, a town in SE Arkansas. 2998 (1960).

Lake·ville (lāk′vil), *n.* a town in NE Ohio. 4181 (1960).

Lake′ Wales′, a town in central Florida. 8346 (1960).

lake′ white′fish, a whitefish, *Coregonus clupeaformis,* found in the Great Lakes and north to Alaska, used for food.

Lake·wood (lāk′wo͝od′), *n.* **1.** a city in SW California, near Los Angeles. 67,126 (1960). **2.** a city in NE Ohio, on Lake Erie, near Cleveland. 66,154 (1960). **3.** a town in central Colorado, near Denver. 19,338 (1960). **4.** a town in E New Jersey. 13,004 (1960). **5.** a town in W New York. 3933 (1960).

Lake′ Worth′, a city in SE Florida. 20,758 (1960).

Lake′ Worth′ Vil′lage, a town in N Texas. 3833 (1960).

Lake′ Zu′rich, a town in NE Illinois. 3458 (1960).

lakh (lak), *n.* lac².

la·kin (lā′kin), *n.* **1.** Also, **lak·ing** (lā′kin, -king). *Brit. Dial.* a toy; plaything. **2.** *Obs.* ladykin. [late ME *laken* for **ladyken* little lady. See LADY, -KIN]

Lak·mé (läk′mā; *Fr.* lAk mā′), *n.* an opera (1883) by Clément Delibes.

Laksh·mi (lukshʹmē), *n.* the Hindu goddess of fortune.

lak·y¹ (lā′kē), *adj.,* **lak·i·er, lak·i·est.** of, pertaining to, or resembling a lake. [LAKE¹ + -Y¹]

lak·y² (lā′kē), *adj.* of the color of a lake pigment. [LAKE² + -Y¹]

La·la (lā′lə), *n.* a girl's given name.

La·lande (lə land′), *n.* a walled plain in the fourth quadrant of the face of the moon: about 14 miles in diameter.

la·la·pa·loo·za (lol′ə pə lo͞o′zə), *n.* lollapalooza. Also, **lal′la·pa·loo′za.**

-lalia, a combining form denoting a speech defect of a type specified by the preceding element: *echolalia.* [< NL, comb. form repr. Gk *laliá* talking, chatter, equiv. to *lal(eîn)* (to) chatter, babble + *-ia* -IA]

La Lí·ne·a (lä lē′ne ä), a seaport in S Spain, near Gibraltar. 60,379 (1960).

La·li·ta (lə lē′tə), *n.* a girl's given name.

lall (lal), *v.i. Phonet.* to make imperfect *l-* or *r-*sounds, or both, often by substituting a *w-*like sound for *r* or *l* or a *y-*like sound for *l.* [imit.; see LALLATION]

Lal·lan (lal′ən), *adj. Scot.* belonging to the Lowlands of Scotland. [var. of LOWLAND]

Lal·lans (lal′ənz), *n.pl.* **1.** the Lowlands of Scotland. **2.** the inhabitants of the Scottish Lowlands. **3.** (*construed as sing.*) the literary form of the English dialect of the Scottish Lowlands, representing a compromise among the several spoken subdialects.

lal·la·tion (la lā′shən), *n. Phonet.* a speech defect in which *l* is pronounced instead of *r,* or in which an *l-*sound is mispronounced. Cf. **lambdacism.** [< L *lallā(re)* (to) sing lalla or lullaby + -TION]

L'Al·le·gro (lä lā′grō, la-), *n.* a poem (1632) by John Milton. Cf. **Il Penseroso.**

CONCISE ETYMOLOGY KEY: <, descended or derived from; >, whence; b., blend of, blended; c., cognate with; deriv., derivative; equiv., equivalent; imit., imitative; m., modification of; obl., oblique; r., replacing; s., stem; sp., spelling; trans., translation; ?, origin unknown, perhaps; *, hypothetical. See the full key inside the front cover.

Lal·ly (lă/lē), *n., pl.* **-lies.** *Trademark.* See **Lally column.**

Lal′ly col′umn, *Trademark.* a tubular steel column, usually filled with concrete.

lal·ly·gag (lol′ē gag′), *v.i.,* **-gagged, -gag·ging.** *Informal.* **1.** to idle; loaf. **2.** to indulge in kisses and caresses; make love; neck. Also, **lollygag.** [?]

La·lo (lȧ lō′), *n.* **(Vic·tor An·toine) É·douard** (vēk-tôr′ äɴ twȧɴ′ ā dwȧr′), 1823–92, French composer.

lalo-, a combining form referring to speech: *lalophobia.* [< NL, comb. form repr. Gk *lálos* talkative, chattering; see -LALIA]

la·lop·a·thy (la lop′ə thē), *n., pl.* **-thies.** *Pathol.* any defect of speech. [LALO- + -PATHY]

lal·o·pho·bi·a (lal′ə fō′bē ə), *n. Psychiatry.* an abnormal fear of speaking. [LALO- + -PHOBIA]

lal·o·ple·gi·a (lal′ə plē′jē ə), *n. Pathol.* paralysis of the speech organs in which the tongue is not affected. [LALO- + -PLEGIA]

La·lu (lal′o͞o), *n.* a boy's given name.

lam[1] (lam), *v.,* **lammed, lam·ming.** *Slang.* —*v.t.* **1.** to beat; thrash. —*v.i.* **2.** to beat; strike; thrash (usually fol. by *out* or *into*). [< Scand; cf. Icel *lamdi,* past tense of *lemja* to beat, akin to LAME[1]]

lam[2] (lam), *n., v.,* **lammed, lam·ming.** *Slang.* —*n.* **1.** a quick escape; flight. **2. on the lam,** escaping, fleeing, or hiding, esp. from the police: *Not one of his old friends would have anything to do with him now that he was on the lam.* **3. take it on the lam,** to flee or escape in great haste: *The swindler took it on the lam and was never heard from again.* —*v.i.* **4.** to run away quickly; escape; flee: *I'm going to lam out of here as soon as I've finished.* [special use of LAM[1]. Cf. *beat it* be off]

lām (läm), *n.* the 23rd letter of the Arabic alphabet. [< Ar; (see LAMBDA]

Lam., Lamentations.

lam., laminated.

la·ma (lä′mə), *n.* a priest or monk in Lamaism. [< Tibetan *blama* (*b-* is silent)]

La·ma·ism (lä′mə iz′əm), *n.* the Buddhism of Tibet and Mongolia, a Mahayana form including non-Buddhist Indian elements as well as elements of the preexisting Bön shamanism. Cf. **Red Hats, Yellow Hats.** [LAMA + -ISM] —**La′ma·ist,** *n.* —**La′ma·is′tic,** *adj.*

La Man·cha (lä män′chä), a plateau region in central Spain.

La Ma·no Ne·ra (lä mä′nô ne′rä), *Italian.* See **Black Hand** (def. 1a).

La·mar (lə mär′), *n.* **1. Joseph R.,** 1857–1916, U.S. jurist: associate justice of the U.S. Supreme Court 1911–16. **2. Lucius Quin·tus Cin·cin·nat·us** (kwin′təs sin′sə nat′əs, -nā′təs), 1825–93, U.S. politician and jurist: associate justice of the U.S. Supreme Court 1888–93. **3.** a town in SE Colorado. 7369 (1960). **4.** a town in SW Missouri. 3608 (1960). **5.** a boy's given name.

La·marck (lə märk′; *Fr.* lȧ mȧrk′), *n.* **Jean Bap·tiste Pierre An·toine de Mo·net de** (zhäɴ bȧ tēst′ pyer äɴ twȧɴ′ də mô ne′ də), 1744–1829, French naturalist: pioneer in the field of comparative anatomy.

La·marck·i·an (lə mär′kē ən), *adj.* **1.** of or pertaining to Jean de Lamarck or his theory of organic evolution. —*n.* **2.** one who holds this theory. [LAMARCK + -IAN]

La·marck·ism (lə mär′kiz əm), *n.* the Lamarckian theory that characters acquired by habit, use, disuse, or adaptations to changes in environment may be inherited. [LAMARCK + -ISM]

La·mar·tine (lȧ mȧr tēn′), *n.* **Al·phonse Ma·rie Louis de Prat de** (al fôɴs′ mȧ rē′ lwē də prȧ də), 1790–1869, French poet, historian, and statesman.

La·mas (lä′mäs), *n.* **Car·los Sa·a·ve·dra** (kär′lôs sä′ä ve′drä). See **Saavedra Lamas, Carlos.**

la·ma·ser·y (lä′mə ser′ē), *n., pl.* **-ser·ies.** a monastery of lamas. [< F *lamaserie.* See LAMA, SERAI]

La·maze′ technique′ (lə mäz′), psychoprophylaxis. [named after Fernand *Lamaze,* 20th-century French physician, its originator.]

lamb (lam), *n.* **1.** a young sheep. **2.** the meat of a young sheep. **3.** one who is gentle, meek, innocent, etc.: *I hated to speak harshly to her, for she is such a lamb.* **4.** one who is easily cheated, esp. an inexperienced speculator. **5. the Lamb,** Christ. —*v.i.* **6.** to give birth to a lamb. [ME, OE; c. D *lam,* G *Lamm,* Icel, Goth *lamb;* akin to Gk *élaphos* deer. See also ELK]

Lamb (lam), *n.* **1. Charles** ("*Elia*"), 1775–1834, English essayist and critic. **2. Mary Ann,** 1764–1847, English author who wrote in collaboration with her brother Charles Lamb. **3. William, 2nd Viscount Melbourne,** 1779–1848, English statesman: prime minister 1834, 1835–41. **4. Willis E(ugene), Jr.,** born 1913, U.S. physicist: Nobel prize 1955.

lam·baste (lam bāst′), *v.t.,* **-bast·ed, -bast·ing.** *Informal.* **1.** to beat or whip severely. **2.** to reprimand or berate harshly; censure; excoriate. Also, **lam·bast′.** [appar. LAM[1] + BASTE[3]]

lamb·da (lam′də), *n.* **1.** the 11th letter of the Greek alphabet (Λ, λ). **2.** the consonant sound represented by this letter. [< Gk < Sem; see LAMED]

lamb·da·cism (lam′də siz′əm), *n. Phonet.* excessive use of the sound *l,* its misarticulation, or its substitution for the sound *r.* Cf. **lallation.** [< LL *lambdacism(us)* < Gk *lambdakismós.* See LAMBDA, -AC, -ISM]

lamb·doid (lam′doid), *adj.* having the shape of the Greek capital lambda. Also, **lamb·doi′dal.** [< NL *lambdoīd(ēs)* < Gk *lambdoeidēs.* See LAMBDA, -OID]

lambdoi′dal su′ture, *Anat.* the suture between the occipital and two parietal bones of the skull.

lam·ben·cy (lam′bən sē), *n., pl.* **-cies.** **1.** the quality of being lambent. **2.** that which is lambent. [LAMB(ENT) + -ENCY]

lam·bent (lam′bənt), *adj.* **1.** running or moving lightly over a surface: *lambent tongues of flame.* **2.** dealing lightly and gracefully with a subject; brilliantly playful: *lambent wit.* **3.** softly bright or radiant: *a lambent light.* [< L *lambent-* (s. of *lambēns*) lapping, prp. of *lambere* to lick, wash (said of water or fire); akin to LAP[2]; see -ENT] —**lam′bent·ly,** *adv.*

lam·bert (lam′bərt), *n. Optics.* the centimeter-gram-second unit of luminance or brightness, equivalent to .32 candles per square centimeter, and equal to the brightness of a perfectly-diffusing surface emitting or reflecting one lumen per square centimeter. *Abbr.:* L [named after J. H. LAMBERT]

Lam·bert (lam′bərt; *for 2 also Ger.* läm′bert), *n.* **1. Constant,** 1905–51, English composer and conductor. **2. Jo·hann Hein·rich** (yō′hän hīn′riкн), 1728–77, German scientist and mathematician. **3.** a walled plain in the second quadrant of the face of the moon: about 18 miles in diameter. **4.** a boy's given name.

Lam′bert confor′mal projec′tion, *Cartog.* a conformal projection in which meridians are represented as straight lines converging toward the nearest pole and parallels as arc segments of concentric circles. [named after J. H. LAMBERT]

Lam·bert·ville (lam′bərt vil′), *n.* a town in W New Jersey. 4269 (1960).

Lam·beth (lam′bith), *n.* a borough of S London, England. 223,162 (1961).

Lam′beth Con′ference, a convention of the bishops of the Anglican communion, held about every 10 years at Lambeth Palace to confer but not to define doctrine or to legislate on ecclesiastical matters.

Lam′beth degree′, *Anglican Ch.* an honorary degree conferred by the archbishop of Canterbury in divinity, arts, law, medicine, or music.

Lam′beth Pal′ace, the official residence of the archbishop of Canterbury, in S London.

Lam′beth walk′, a spirited ballroom dance popular, esp. in England, in the late 1930's.

lamb·kill (lam′kil′), *n.* See **sheep laurel.** [LAMB + KILL[1]; so called because poisonous to sheep]

lamb·kin (lam′kin), *n.* **1.** a little lamb. **2.** one who is young and innocent, esp. a small child. [ME *lambkyn.* See LAMB, -KIN]

lamb·like (lam′līk′), *adj.* like a lamb; gentle; meek. [LAMB + -LIKE]

Lamb′ of God′, Christ. [ME]

lam·boy (lam′boi′), *n.* a tonlet. [?]

lam·bre·quin (lam′brə kin, lam′bər-), *n.* **1.** a woven fabric worn over a helmet in medieval times to protect it from heat, rust, and sword blows. **2.** a curtain or drapery covering the upper part of an opening, as a door or window, or suspended from a shelf. **3.** *Heraldry.* mantling. **4.** a band of decoration near the top of the body of a vase. [< F, MF < MFlem *lamperkijn, dim. of *lamper* kind of crepe, crepe-veil (akin to LAP[1]); see -KIN]

lamb's′ ears′, *pl.* **lamb's ears.** a hardy, perennial herb, *Stachys lanata,* of the Caucasus and Iran, having small, purple flowers in dense whorls.

lamb·skin (lam′skin′), *n.* **1.** the skin of a lamb, esp. when dressed with its wool, and used for clothing. **2.** leather made from such skin. **3.** parchment made from such skin. [ME; see LAMB, SKIN]

lamb's-quar·ters (lamz′kwôr′tərz), *n., pl.* **-ters.** the pigweed, *Chenopodium album.*

lamb's′ tongue′, *Archit.* a molding having a deep, symmetrical profile ending in a narrow edge, as in a sash bar.

lamb's′ wool′, **1.** a soft, virgin wool possessing superior spinning qualities, shorn from a seven-month-old lamb. **2.** a fabric made from this wool.

lame[1] (lām), *adj.,* **lam·er, lam·est,** *v.,* **lamed, lam·ing.** —*adj.* **1.** crippled or physically disabled, as a person or animal, esp. in the foot or leg so as to limp or walk with difficulty. **2.** impaired or disabled through defect or injury: *His arm was lame.* **3.** weak; inadequate; clumsy: *a lame excuse.* —*v.t.* **4.** to make lame or defective. [ME; OE *lama;* c. D *lam,* G *lahm,* Icel *lami;* akin to Lith *lúomas*] —**lame′ly,** *adv.* —**lame′ness,** *n.*

lame[2] (lām; *Fr.* lȧm), *n., pl.* **lames** (lāmz; *Fr.* lȧm). *Armor.* any of a number of thin, overlapping plates composing a piece of plate armor, as a fauld, tasset, gauntlet, etc. [< MF < L *lāmina* a thin piece or plate]

la·mé (la mā′; *Fr.* lȧ mā′), *n.* an ornamental fabric in which metallic threads are woven with silk, wool, rayon, or cotton. [< F, equiv. to *lame* LAME[2] + *-é* < L *-ātus* -ATE[1]]

lame·brain (lām′brān′), *n. Slang.* a dunce; booby; fool. [LAME[1] + BRAIN]

La·mech (lā′mik), *n.* the son of Enoch, and the father of Jabal, Jubal, and Tubal-cain. Gen. 4:18.

la·med (lä′mid), *n.* **1.** the 12th letter of the Hebrew alphabet. **2.** the consonant sound represented by this letter. [< Heb; see LAMBDA]

lame′ duck′, **1.** *U.S. Informal.* an elected official, esp. a Congressman, who is completing his term in office after an election in which he has failed to be reelected. **2.** *Informal.* one who or that which is disabled, helpless, ineffective, or inefficient. **3.** *Slang.* a person who has lost a great deal of money in speculations on the stock market.

Lame′ Duck′ Amend′ment, the 20th amendment to the Constitution of the U.S., which abolished the December to March session (**lame′-duck′ ses′sion**) of those Congressmen defeated for reelection in November.

la·mel·la (lə mel′ə), *n., pl.* **-mel·lae** (-mel′ē), **-mel·las.** **1.** a thin plate, scale, membrane, or layer, as of bone, tissue, cell walls, etc. **2.** *Bot.* **a.** an erect scale or blade inserted at the junction of the claw and limb in some corollas and forming a part of their corona or crown. **b.** gill[1]. **c.** (in mosses) a thin sheet of cells standing up along the midrib of a leaf. **3.** *Building Trades.* a member of wood, metal, or reinforced concrete, joined in a criss-cross pattern with other lamellae to form a vault. **4.** *Ophthalm. Rare.* a small disk of gelatin and glycerin mixed with a medicinal substance, used as a medicament for the eyes. [< L, dim. of *lāmina* LAME[2]]

la·mel·lar (lə mel′ər, lam′ə lər), *adj.* **1.** referring to a lamella or lamellae. **2.** lamellate. **3.** noting a type of armor composed of small plates or lames laced together. **4.** *Math.* conservative (def. 7). [LAMELL(A) + -AR[1]] —**la·mel′lar·ly,** *adv.*

lamel′la roof′, a vaulted roof composed of lamellae.

lam·el·late (lam′ə lāt′, -lit; lə mel′āt, -it), *adj.* **1.** composed of or having lamellae. **2.** flat; platelike. Also, **lam′el·lat′ed, lamellose.** [< NL *lamellāt(us).* See LAMELLA, -ATE[1]] —**lam′el·late′ly,** *adv.*

lamelli-, a combining form of **lamella:** *lamelliform.*

la·mel·li·branch (lə mel′ə braŋk′), *n.* **1.** a mollusk of the class *Pelecypoda* (*Lamellibranchiata*); a pelecypod. —*adj.* **2.** pelecypod. Also, **la·mel·li·bran·chi·ate** (lə-mel′ə braŋ′kē āt′, -it). [< NL *Lāmellibranch(ia).* See LAMELLI-, -BRANCHIA]

la·mel·li·corn (lə mel′ə kôrn′), *Entomol.* —*adj.* **1.** having antennae with lamellate terminal segments, as beetles of the group *Lamellicornia,* including the scarabaeids and stag beetles. **2.** (of an antenna) having lamellate terminal segments. —*n.* **3.** a lamellicorn beetle. [< NL *lāmellicorn(is),* equiv. to *lāmelli-* LAMELLI- + L *-cornis* horned (*corn(ū)* a horn + *-is* adj. suffix)]

la·mel·li·form (lə mel′ə fôrm′), *adj.* shaped like a lamella; platelike; scalelike. [LAMELLI- + -FORM]

la·mel·li·ros·tral (lə mel′ə ros′trəl), *adj. Ornith.* having a beak equipped with thin plates or lamellae for straining water and mud from food, as the ducks, geese, swans, and flamingoes. Also, **la·mel·li·ros·trate** (lə-mel′ə ros′trāt). [< NL *lāmellirostr(is)* + -AL[1]. See LAMELLI-, ROSTRAL]

la·mel·lose (lə mel′ōs, lam′ə lōs′), *adj.* lamellate. [LAMELL(A) + -OSE[1]] —**lam·el·los·i·ty** (lam′ə los′i tē), *n.*

la·ment (lə ment′), *v.t.* **1.** to feel or express sorrow or regret for; mourn for or over: *to lament his absence; to lament one's folly.* —*v.i.* **2.** to feel, show, or express grief, sorrow, or regret; mourn deeply. [< L *lāment(ārī),* deriv. of n.]
—*n.* **3.** an expression of grief or sorrow. **4.** a formal expression of sorrow or mourning, esp. in verse or song; an elegy or dirge. [< L *lāment(um)* plaint] —**la·ment′er,** *n.* —**la·ment′ing·ly,** *adv.*
—**Syn. 1.** bewail, bemoan, deplore. **2.** grieve, weep. **3.** lamentation, moan, wail. **4.** monody, threnody.
—**Ant. 2.** rejoice.

lam·en·ta·ble (lam′ən tə bəl, lə men′tə-), *adj.* **1.** that is to be lamented; regrettable; unfortunate; deplorable: *a lamentable occurrence; a lamentable decision.* **2.** *Rare.* mournful. [late ME < L *lāmentābil(is),* equiv. to *lāment(ārī)* (see LAMENT) + *-ābilis* -ABLE] —**lam′en·ta·ble·ness,** *n.* —**lam′en·ta·bly,** *adv.*

lam·en·ta·tion (lam′ən tā′shən), *n.* **1.** act of lamenting or expressing grief. **2.** a lament. **3. Lamentations,** (*construed as sing.*) a book of the Bible, traditionally ascribed to Jeremiah. [< L *lāmentātiōn-* (s. of *lāmentātiō*), equiv. to *lāmentāt(us)* (ptp. of *lāmentārī;* see LAMENT) + *-iōn-* -ION; r. ME *lamentacioun* < AF]

la·ment·ed (lə men′tid), *adj.* mourned for, as one who is dead: *the late lamented Grady.* [LAMENT + -ED[2]] —**la·ment′ed·ly,** *adv.*

La Me·sa (lä mā′sə), a city in SW California. 30,441 (1960).

la·mi·a (lā′mē ə), *n., pl.* **-mi·as, mi·ae** (-mē ē′) for 1, 2. **1.** *Class. Myth.* one of a class of fabulous monsters, commonly represented with the head and breast of a woman and the body of a serpent, said to allure youths and children in order to suck their blood. **2.** a vampire; a female demon. **3.** (*cap., italics.*) a narrative poem (1819) by John Keats. [ME < L < Gk *lámia* a female man-eater]

la·mi·a·ceous (lā′mē ā′shəs), *adj.* belonging to the *Labiatae* (or *Menthaceae,* formerly *Lamiaceae*) or mint family of plants. [< NL *Lāmi(um)* genus name (special use of L *lāmium* dead nettle) + -ACEOUS]

lam·i·na (lam′ə nə), *n., pl.* **-nae** (-nē′), **-nas.** **1.** a thin plate, scale, or layer. **2.** a layer or coat lying over another, as the plates of minerals, bones, etc. **3.** *Bot.* the blade or expanded portion of a leaf. [< L; see LAME[2]]

lam·i·na·ble (lam′ə nə bəl), *adj.* capable of being laminated. [LAMIN(ATE) + -ABLE]

lam·i·nar (lam′ə nər), *adj.* composed of, or arranged in, laminae. Also, **lam·i·nar·y** (lam′ə ner′ē), **lam′i·nal.** [LAMIN(A) + -AR[1]]

lam′inar flow′, *Hydraulics, Mech.* the flow of a viscous fluid in which particles of the fluid move in parallel layers, each of which has a constant velocity but is in motion relative to its neighboring layers.

lam·i·na·ri·a·ceous (lam′ə ner′ē ā′shəs), *adj.* belonging or pertaining to the family *Laminariaceae,* comprising the kelps. [< NL *Lāminārі(a)* genus name (see LAMINA, -ARIA) + -ACEOUS]

lam·i·nate (*v.* lam′ə nāt′; *adj., n.* lam′ə nāt′, -nit), *v.,* **-nat·ed, -nat·ing,** *adj., n.* —*v.t.* **1.** to separate or split into thin layers. **2.** to form (metal) into a thin plate, as by beating or rolling. **3.** to construct by placing layer upon layer. **4.** to cover or overlay with laminae. —*v.i.* **5.** to split into thin layers. —*adj.* **6.** Also, **laminous.** composed of or having a lamina or laminae. —*n.* **7.** a laminated product; lamination. [< NL *lāmināt(us).* See LAMINA, -ATE[1]] —**lam′i·na′tor,** *n.*

lam·i·nat·ed (lam′ə nā′tid), *adj.* **1.** formed of or set in thin layers or laminae. **2.** made or constructed of a succession of layers: *laminated wood.* [LAMINATE + -ED[2]]

lam·i·na·tion (lam′ə nā′shən), *n.* **1.** act or process of laminating; state of being laminated. **2.** laminated structure; arrangement in thin layers. **3.** a lamina. [LAMINATE + -ION]

lam·i·ni·tis (lam′ə nī′tis), *n. Vet. Pathol.* inflammation of sensitive laminae in the hoof of a horse, caused by overwork, overfeeding, etc. [< NL; see LAMINA, -ITIS]

lam·i·nose (lam′ə nōs′), *adj.* laminate; laminar. [LAMIN(A) + -OSE[1]]

lam·i·nous (lam′ə nəs), *adj.* laminate; laminose. [LAMIN(A) + -OUS]

lam·is·ter (lam′i stər), *n. Slang.* lamster.

Lam·mas (lam′əs), *n.* **1.** a former festival held in England on August 1, in which bread made from the first harvest of corn was blessed. **2.** *Hist.* a festival (**Feast′ of St. Pe′ter's Chains′**) observed by Roman Catholics on August 1, in memory of St. Peter's imprisonment and his miraculous deliverance. Also called **Lam′mas Day′.** [ME *Lammesse,* OE *hlāmmæsse, hlāfmæsse.* See LOAF, -MAS]

Lam·mas·tide (lam′əs tīd′), *n.* the season of Lammas. [ME; see LAMMAS, TIDE[1]]

lam·mer·gei·er (lam′ər gī′ər), *n.* the largest European bird of prey, *Gypaëtus barbatus,* having a 9–10-foot wingspread, ranging in the mountains from southern Europe to China, having black feathers hanging from below the bill like a mustache. Also, **lam′mer·gey′er, lam′mer·ge′ir.** Also called **bearded vulture.** [< G *Lämmergeier,* lit., lambs' vulture (from its preying on lambs), equiv. to *Lämmer,* pl. of *Lamm* LAMB + *Geier* vulture, c. D *gier*]

La·mont (lə mont′), *n.* **1.** a town in central California. 6177 (1960). **2.** a walled plain in the first quadrant of the face of the moon: about 46 miles in diameter. **3.** a boy's given name.

La·mou·reux (lȧ mo͞o rœ′), *n.* **Charles** (sharl), 1834–99, French violinist and conductor.

lamp (lamp), *n.* **1.** any of various devices furnishing artificial light, as by gas or electricity. **2.** a vessel for containing an inflammable liquid, as oil, which is burned at a wick as a means of illumination. **3.** a source of intellectual or spiritual light: *the lamp of learning.* **4.** any of various devices furnishing heat, ultraviolet, or other radiation: *an infrared lamp.* **5.** *Archaic.* a celestial body that gives off light, as the moon or a star. **6.** *Archaic.* a torch. **7. lamps,** *Slang.* the eyes. **8. smell of the lamp,** to give evidence of laborious study or effort: *His dissertation smells of the lamp.* —*v.t.* **9.** *Slang.* to look at; eye. [ME *lampe* < OF < LL **lampa* < Gk *lámpē* torch, lamp, akin to *lampás* lamp, *lámpein* to shine] —**lamp′less,** *adj.*

lam·pad (lam′pad), *n.* lamp or candlestick. [< Gk *lampad-* (s. of *lampás*) lamp; see LAMP]

lam·pa·daire (lam′pə dâr′, läm′-), *n.* a pedestal of the Empire period for a lamp or candelabrum. [< F < ML *lampadār(ium).* See LAMPAD, -ARY]

Lam·pang (lam′päng′), *n.* a city in NW Thailand. 25,000 (est. 1961).

lam·pas[1] (lam′pəs), *n.* *Vet. Pathol.* congestion of the mucous membrane of the hard palate of horses. Also **lampers.** [< MF: disease of horses, OF: disease (of men) with great thirst as symptom]

lam·pas[2] (lam′pəs), *n.* an elaborately embellished fabric woven with a double warp and one or more picks. [ME *lawmpas* < MFlem *lampers,* var. of *lamper* kind of crepe; see LAMBREQUIN]

Lam·pas·as (lam pas′əs), *n.* a town in central Texas. 5061 (1960).

lamp·black (lamp′blak′), *n.* a fine black pigment consisting of almost pure carbon collected as soot from the smoke of burning oil, gas, etc. [LAMP + BLACK]

lamp′ cage′, *Naut.* a metal framework in which signal lamps are hoisted.

Lam·pe·du·sa (läm′pi do͞o′zä), *n.* an island in the Mediterranean, between Tunisia and Malta: belonging to Italy.

lam′per eel′ (lam′pər), lamprey.

lam·pers (lam′pərz), *n.* (*construed as sing.*) *Vet. Pathol.* lampas[1].

Lam·pe·ti·a (lam pē′shē ə), *n.* (in the *Odyssey*) a daughter of Helius and the nymph Neaera, who informed her father of the theft of his cattle by Odysseus' men.

lam·pi·on (lam′pē ən), *n.* a small lamp, esp. an oil lamp, formerly very popular as a source of illumination. [< F < It *lampione* carriage or street light, aug. of *lampa* LAMP]

lamp·light (lamp′līt′), *n.* the light shed by a lamp. [LAMP + LIGHT[1]]

lamp·light·er (lamp′lī′tər), *n.* **1.** one who lights street lamps. **2.** a contrivance for lighting lamps. [LAMP + LIGHTER]

lam·poon (lam po͞on′), *n.* **1.** a sharp, often virulent satire directed against an individual, a social institution, a government, etc.; a work of literature, art, or the like, ridiculing severely the character or behavior of a person, society, etc. —*v.t.* **2.** to mock or ridicule in a lampoon: *The play lampooned several persons of importance in the government.* [< F *lampon,* said to be n. use of *lampons* let us guzzle (from a drinking song), impv. of *lamper,* nasalized var. of *laper* to lap up < Gmc; see LAP[3]] —**lam·poon′er, lam·poon′ist,** *n.* —**lam·poon′er·y,** *n.* —**Syn. 1.** See **satire.**

lamp·post (lamp′pōst′), *n.* a post, usually of iron, supporting a lamp which lights a street, park, etc. [LAMP + POST[1]]

lam·prey (lam′prē), *n., pl.* **-preys.** any eellike, marine or fresh-water fish of the group *Hyperoartia,* having undeveloped eyes and a circular, suctorial mouth with horny teeth for boring into the flesh of other fishes to feed on their blood. Also called **lam′prey eel′, lamper eel.** [ME *lampreye* < AF **lampreie* (OF *lamproie*) < LL *lamprēda;* r. OE *lamprede* < ML *lampreda*]

Lamprey, *Petromyzon marinus* (Length 21 in.)

lam·proph·o·ny (lam prof′ə nē), *n.* *Phonet.* loudness and clarity of voice. Also, **lam·pro·pho·ni·a** (lam′prə fō′nē ə). [< Gk *lamprophōnía,* equiv. to *lamprophōn(os)* clear of voice (*lampró(s)* clear, distinct + *-phonos* -PHONOUS) + *-ia* -Y[3]; see -PHONY] —**lam·pro·phon·ic** (lam′prə fon′ik), *adj.*

lam·pro·phyre (lam′prə fīᵊr′), *n.* *Mineral.* any dark dike rock the dark minerals of which occur both as phenocrysts and as groundmass. [*lampro-* (< Gk *lamprós* clear) + -PHYRE] —**lam·pro·phyr·ic** (lam′prə fir′ik), *adj.*

lamp·shade (lamp′shād′), *n.* a shade, usually translucent or opaque, for shielding the glare of a light source in a lamp or for directing the light over a particular area. [LAMP + SHADE]

lamp′ shell′, any of several brachiopods. [so called because its shape was thought to resemble that of an ancient Roman oil lamp]

lamp′ trim′mer, a seaman responsible for keeping the oil lamps of a vessel burning brightly, esp. the deck and navigation lamps.

lamp·work·ing (lamp′wûr′king), *n.* the method or process of producing articles made of glass tubes or rods formed or shaped while softened by the flame of a lamp or blast lamp. [LAMP + WORKING] —**lamp′work′er,** *n.*

lam·py·rid (lam′pə rid), *n.* **1.** any of several insects of the family *Lampyridae,* comprising the fireflies. —*adj.* **2.** belonging or pertaining to the family *Lampyridae.* [< NL *Lampyrid(ae)* glowworm family, equiv. to *Lampyr(is)* typical genus (<Gk: glowworm; see LAMP) + *-idae* -ID[2]]

lam·ster (lam′stər), *n.* *Slang.* a fugitive from the law. Also, **lamister.** [LAM[2] + -STER]

La·mus (lā′məs), *n.* *Class. Myth.* **1.** a son of Hercules and Omphale. **2.** the king of a people who attacked 11 ships of Odysseus and devoured their crews.

La·my's′ the′orem (lä mēz′), *Physics.* the theorem that for a particle in equilibrium under the action of three forces, the ratios of each force to the sine of the angle between the lines of application of the other two forces are equal.

Lan·a (lan′ə, lä′nə), *n.* a girl's given name, form of **Helen.**

la·na·i (lä nä′ē, lə nī′), *n., pl.* **-na·is.** *Hawaiian.* a veranda.

La·na·i (lä nä′ē, lə nī′), *n.* an island in central Hawaii. 2115 (1960); 141 sq. mi.

Lan·ark (lan′ərk), *n.* a county in S Scotland. 1,626,317 (1961); 898 sq. mi. *Co. seat:* Lanark. Also called **Lan·ark·shire** (lan′ərk shēr′, -shər).

la·nate (lā′nāt), *adj.* woolly; covered with something resembling wool. Also, **lanose.** [< L *lānāt(us)* woolly, equiv. to *lān(a)* wool + *-ātus* -ATE[1]]

La Nau·sée (*Fr.* LA nō zā′), nausea (def. 4).

Lan·ca·shire (lang′kə shēr′, -shər), *n.* a county in NW England. 5,131,646 (1961); 1878 sq. mi. *Co. seat:* Lancaster. Also called **Lancaster.**

Lan′cashire chair′, *Eng. Furniture.* a chair similar to a Windsor chair, having a rush seat and a back formed of spindles.

Lan′cashire hearth′, a furnace for converting pig iron into wrought iron, having a water-cooled hearth on which the iron is puddled under an air blast.

Lan·cas·ter (lang′kə stər; *for 3, 5–10 also* lang′kas tər), *n.* **1.** the English royal family which reigned 1399–1461, descended from John of Gaunt (Duke of Lancaster), and which included Henry IV, Henry V, and Henry VI. Cf. **York** (def. 1). **2.** a member of this family. **3.** a city in SE Pennsylvania. 61,055 (1960). **4.** a city in and the county seat of Lancashire, in NW England. 48,887 (1961). **5.** a city in central Ohio. 29,916 (1960). **6.** a town in S California. 26,012 (1960). **7.** a town in N South Carolina. 7999 (1960). **8.** a town in N Texas. 7501 (1960). **9.** a town in SW Wisconsin. 3703 (1960). **10.** a town in central Kentucky. 3021 (1960). **11.** Lancashire.

Lan′caster Mills′, a town in N South Carolina. 3274 (1960).

Lan·cas·tri·an (lang kas′trē ən), *adj.* **1.** of or pertaining to the royal family of Lancaster. —*n.* **2.** an adherent or member of the house of Lancaster, esp. in the Wars of the Roses. **3.** a native or resident of Lancashire or Lancaster. [LANCAST(E)R + -IAN]

lance[1] (lans, läns), *n., v.,* **lanced, lanc·ing.** —*n.* **1.** a long, shafted weapon with a metal head, used by mounted soldiers in charging. **2.** a soldier armed with this weapon; lancer. **3.** an implement resembling the weapon, as a spear for killing a harpooned whale. **4.** a lancet. **5.** See **oxygen lance. 6.** *Mach.* **a.** a tube having a nozzle for cleaning furnace walls and other inaccessible surfaces with air, water, or steam. **b.** a pipe for directing oxygen onto a heated metal object in order to burn a hole in it, the lance also being consumed so as to add to the heat. —*v.t.* **7.** to open with or as if with a lancet. **8.** to cut through (concrete or the like) with an oxygen lance. [ME *launce* < OF *lance* < L *lancea*] —**lance′like′,** *adj.*

lance[2] (lans, läns), *n.* See **sand lance.** [? special use of LANCE[1], from its shape]

Lance (lans), *n.* a boy's given name.

lance′ cor′poral, 1. *U.S. Marine Corps.* an enlisted man ranking between private first class and corporal. **2.** *Brit. Mil.* **a.** a corporal of the lowest rank. **b.** (formerly) a private acting as corporal without increased pay. [earlier *lancepesade* < MF *lancepessade* lowest ranking grade of noncommissioned officer < It *lancia spezzata* superior soldier, lit., broken LANCE[1] (from having shivered many lances, i.e., fought well in many battles)]

Lanceolate Leaf

lance·let (lans′lit, läns′-), *n.* any small, fishlike, chordate animal of the subphylum *Cephalochordata,* having a notochord in the slender, elongated body pointed at each end. [LANCE[2] + -LET]

Lan·ce·lot (lan′sə lət, -lot′, län′-), *n.* **1.** Also, **Launcelot.** *Arthurian Romance,* the greatest of Arthur's knights and the lover of Queen Guinevere. **2.** a boy's given name.

lance′ of cour′tesy, a lance having a blunt head to prevent a jouster's causing serious injury to an opponent.

lan·ce·o·late (lan′sē ə lāt′, -lit), *adj.* **1.** shaped like the head of a lance. **2.** narrow, and tapering toward the apex or sometimes at the base, as a leaf. [< L *lanceolāt(us)* armed with a small lance, equiv. to *lanceol(a)* small lance (*lance(a)* LANCE[1] + *-ola* dim. suffix) + *-ātus* -ATE[1]] —**lan′ce·o·late′ly,** *adv.*

lance·pod (lans′pod′), *n.* any tropical, leguminous tree or shrub of the genus *Lonchocarpus* as *L. Nicou* and *L. Urucu,* the roots of which yield rotenone. [LANCE[1] + POD[1]]

lanc·er (lan′sər, län′-), *n.* a mounted soldier armed with a lance. [< MF *lancier.* See LANCE[1], -ER[2]]

lance′ rest′, a support for a couched lance, fixed to the breastplate of a suit of armor. See diag. under **armor.**

lanc·ers (lan′sərz, län′-), *n.* (*construed as sing.*) **1.** a set of quadrilles danced in sequence. **2.** music for such a set of dances. [pl. of LANCER]

lance′ ser′geant, *Brit. Mil.* **1.** a sergeant of the lowest rank. **2.** (formerly) a corporal appointed to act as sergeant, without increase in pay; an acting sergeant.

lan·cet (lan′sit, län′-), *n.* **1.** a small surgical instrument, usually sharp-pointed and two-edged, for letting blood, opening abscesses, etc. **2.** *Archit.* **a.** a lancet arch. **b.** a lancet window. [late ME *lancette* < MF. See LANCE[1], -ET]

lan′cet arch′, *Archit.* an arch having a head that is acutely pointed.

lan′cet clock′, a mantel clock having a case formed like an acutely pointed arch.

lan·cet·ed (lan′si tid, län′-), *adj.* having lancet-headed openings. [LANCET + -ED[3]]

lan·cet·fish (lan′sit fish′, län′-), *n., pl.* (*esp. collectively*) **-fish,** (*esp. referring to two or more kinds or species*) **-fish·es.** any large, marine fish of the genus *Alepisaurus,* having daggerlike teeth. [LANCET + FISH]

lan′cet win′dow, *Archit.* a high, narrow window terminating in a lancet arch.

lance·wood (lans′wo͝od′, läns′-), *n.* **1.** the tough, elastic wood of any of various trees, as *Oxandra lanceolata,* of tropical America, used for carriage shafts, cabinetwork, etc. **2.** a tree which yields it. [LANCE[1] + WOOD[1]]

Lan·chow (län′jō′), *n.* a city in and the capital of Kansu, in N China, on the Hwang Ho. 699,000 (est. 1957).

lan·ci·form (lan′sə fôrm′), *adj.* shaped like a lance: *a church with lanciform windows.* [LANCE[1] + -I- + -FORM]

lan·ci·nate (lan′sə nāt′), *v.t.,* **-nat·ed, -nat·ing.** to stab or pierce. [< L *lancināt(us)* torn to pieces, ptp. of *lancināre,* akin to *lanius* butcher, *lacer* torn; see -ATE[1]] —**lan′ci·na′tion,** *n.*

land (land), *n.* **1.** any part of the earth's surface not covered by a body of water: *Land was sighted from the crow's nest.* **2.** the part of the earth's surface occupied by continents and islands: *on land or at sea.* **3.** an area of ground with reference to its nature or composition: *arable land; The land hereabouts is mostly shale.* **4.** an area or areas of ground with specific boundaries: *to buy land in Florida.* **5.** rural or farming areas, as contrasted with the town or city: *They left the land in large numbers during the war.* **6.** *Law.* **a.** any part of the earth's surface which can be owned as property, and everything annexed to it, whether by nature or by the hand of man. **b.** any legal interest held in land. **7.** *Econ.* natural resources as a factor of production. **8.** a part of the surface of the earth marked off by natural or political boundaries or the like; a region or country; *They came from many lands.* **9.** the people of a country: a nation: *The land was in a turmoil; pestilence throughout the land.* **10.** a realm or domain: *the land of the living.* **11.** a surface between furrows, as on a millstone or on the interior of a rifle barrel. **12.** *Scot.* a tenement house. **13. see how the land lies,** to investigate in advance; inform oneself of the facts of a situation before acting: *We have been reading everything available on that country to see how the land lies before we decide to move.* Cf. **lay of the land.** —*v.t.* **14.** to bring to or set on land: *to land passengers or goods from a ship; to land an airplane.* **15.** to bring into or cause to arrive in any place, position, or condition: *His behavior will land him in jail.* **16.** *Informal,* to catch or capture; gain; win: *to land a man; to land a job.* **17.** *Angling.* to bring (a fish) to land, or into a boat, etc., as with a hook or a net. —*v.i.* **18.** to come to land or shore: *The boat lands at Cherbourg.* **19.** to go or come ashore from a ship or boat. **20.** to alight upon a surface, as the ground, a body of water, or the like: *to land on both feet; The plane landed.* **21.** to hit or strike the ground, as from a height: *The ball landed at the far side of the court.* **22.** to strike and come to rest on a surface or in something: *It landed in the lake. It landed on the couch.* **23.** to come to rest or arrive in any place, position or condition (sometimes fol. by *up*): *to land in trouble; to land up 40 miles from home.* **24. land on,** *Informal.* to reprimand; criticize: *His mother landed on him for coming home so late.* **25. land on one's feet,** to emerge without harm from a situation that is risky or governed largely by chance: *I've been in a few scrapes, but I've always landed on my feet.* Also, *fall on one's feet.* [ME, OE; c. D, G, Icel, Goth *land;* akin to Ir *lann,* Welsh *llan* church (orig. enclosure). Breton *lann* heath. See LAWN[1]] —**land′like′,** *adj.*

Land (land), *n.* **Edwin Herbert,** born 1909, U.S. inventor and businessman.

-land, a combining form of **land:** *hinterland; lowland.*

land′ a′gent, 1. a person or firm engaged at a commission to obtain grants of public lands or to negotiate the buying and selling of private lands between two or more parties. **2.** a government official in charge of the management of public lands. **3.** *Brit.* the steward of an estate.

lan·dau (lan′dô, -dou), *n.* **1.** a four-wheeled, two-seated carriage with a top made in two parts which may be let down or folded back. **2.** a sedanlike automobile with a short convertible back. [after *Landau,* town in Germany where first made]

Landau

Lan·dau (län dou′), *n.* **Lev Da·vi·do·vich** (lef dä vē′do vich), 1908–68, Russian scientist: Nobel prize for physics 1962.

lan·dau·let (lan′dô let′), *n.* an automobile having a convertible top for the back seat, with the front seat either roofed or open. Also, **lan′dau·lette′.** [LANDAU + -LET]

land′ bank′, a banking association that engages in the financing of transactions in real property, esp. in agricultural land.

land′ board′, *U.S. Naut.* any of a number of boards laid to protect wooden decking while cargo is being loaded or unloaded.

land′ breeze′, a coastal breeze blowing at night from land to sea, caused by the difference in the rate of cooling of their respective surfaces. Also called **land wind.** Cf. **lake breeze, sea breeze.**

land′ crab′, any of several crabs, esp. of the family *Gecarcinidae,* that live chiefly upon land, returning to the sea to breed.

land·ed (lan′did), *adj.* **1.** owning land: *a landed proprietor.* **2.** consisting of land: *landed property.* [ME; OE *(ge)landod.* See LAND, -ED[3]]

Lan·der (lan′dər), *n.* a town in central Wyoming. 4182 (1960).

Landes (länd), *n.* a department in SW France. 260,495 (1962); 3615 sq. mi. *Cap.:* Mont-de-Marsan.

land·fall (land′fôl′), *n.* **1.** an approach to or sighting of land. **2.** the land sighted or reached. **3.** a landslide. [LAND + FALL]

land′fall light′, *Navig.* See **making light.**

land′fall mark′, *Navig.* any visual navigational aid, conspicuous at a great distance, that indicates the approach to a harbor or estuary from the sea.

land′ fast′, *Naut.* any secure object on shore to which a vessel can be moored.

land-grab·ber (land′grab′ər), *n.* a person who seizes land or landed property illegally or underhandedly.

land′ grant′, a tract of land given by the government, as for colleges, railroads, etc.

land′-grant col′lege (land′grant′, -gränt′), *U.S.* a college or university (**land′-grant univer′sity**) entitled to support from the federal government under the provisions of the Morrill Acts.

land·grave (land′grāv′), *n.* **1.** (in medieval Germany) a count having jurisdiction over a large territory. **2.** (*usually cap.*) the title of certain German princes. [< MLG; see GRAF, MARGRAVE, REEVE[1]]

land·gra·vi·ate (land grā′vē it, -āt′), *n.* the office, jurisdiction, or territory of a landgrave. [< ML *landgraviāt(us).* See LANDGRAVE (ML *landgravius*), -ATE[1]]

land·gra·vine (land′grə vēn′), *n.* **1.** the wife of a landgrave. **2.** a woman of the rank of a landgrave. [< D *landgravin,* fem. of *landgraaf* LANDGRAVE]

land·hold·er (land′hōl′dər), *n.* a holder, owner, or occupant of land. [late ME; see LAND, HOLDER] —**land′hold′ing,** *adj., n.*

land·ing (lan′ding), *n.* **1.** act of one who or that which lands: *The pilot brought his plane in for a landing.* **2.** a place where persons or goods are landed, as from a ship: *The boat moored at the landing, and we disembarked.* **3.** *Archit.* **a.** the floor at the head or foot of a flight of stairs. **b.** a platform between flights of stairs. **4.** *Shipbuilding.* **a.** the overlap of two plates or planks, as in a clinker-built shell. **b.** the distance between the center of a rivet hole and the edge of the plate or shape into which it is cut. [late ME; see LAND, -ING[1]]

land′ing card′, *Naut.* **1.** an identification card issued to a passenger landing from a vessel. **2.** a card issued to a seaman in a foreign port permitting him to go ashore.

land′ing clerk′, a representative of a shipping line who boards its incoming passenger ships to give passengers information and advice.

land′ing craft′, *Navy.* any of various flat-bottomed vessels designed to move troops and equipment close to shore.

land′ing edge′, *Shipbuilding.* an edge of a plate or plank that is overlapped by an adjoining plate or plank as seen from outside the hull of a vessel, above the deck, or on the side of a bulkhead opposite to that on which the stiffeners are placed. Cf. **sight edge.**

land′ing field′, an area of land cleared for the landing and take-off of aircraft.

land′ing flap′, a flap in the under surface of the trailing edge of an aircraft wing, capable of being moved downward to increase either lift or drag or both, as for landing. Cf. **split flap** (def. 1).

land′ing force′, *Mil.* the ground forces of an amphibious task force that effect the assault landing in an amphibious operation.

land′ing gear′, the wheels, floats, etc., of an aircraft, upon which it moves on ground or water.

land′ing net′, *Angling.* a small, bag-shaped net with a handle at the mouth, for scooping a hooked fish out of the water and bringing it to shore or into a boat.

land′ing par′ty, a component of a ship's company detached for special duty ashore.

land′ing ship′, *Navy.* any of various ships designed for transporting troops and heavy equipment in amphibious warfare, capable of making assault landings directly onto a beach.

land′ing stage′, a floating platform used as a wharf.

land′ing strake′, *Shipbuilding.* the next strake of planking in an open boat below the sheer strake.

land′ing strip′, **1.** a runway, esp. the part that an aircraft touches during landing or take-off. **2.** a runway auxiliary to the regularly used runways of an airfield.

land′ing tee′. See **wind tee.**

land·ing-wait·er (lan′ding wā′tər), *n.* landwaiter.

Lan·di·ni (län dē′nē), *n.* **Fran·ces·co** (fʀän ches′kō), c1325–97, Italian organist and composer. Also, **Lan·di·no** (län dē′nô).

Landi′ni ca′dence, *Music.* a melodic cadential formula, associated esp. with the Ars Nova music of Francesco Landini, progressing from the tonic to the leading tone, then to the submediant and back to the tonic.

Landini cadence

Lan·dis (lan′dis), *n.* **Ken·e·saw Mountain** (ken′i sô′), 1866–1944, U.S. jurist: first commissioner of baseball 1920–44.

land·la·dy (land′lā′dē), *n., pl.* **-dies.** **1.** a woman who owns and leases apartments to others. **2.** a woman who owns or runs an inn, lodging house, or boarding house. **3.** a woman who owns and leases land, buildings, etc. [LAND + LADY]

land′ lane′, *Naut.* (in an ice floe) an opening that leads toward a shore. Also called **land′ lead′** (lēd).

länd·ler (lent′lər), *n., pl.* **-ler, -lers.** **1.** an Austrian and southern German folk dance in moderately slow triple meter, antecedent to the waltz. **2. a.** music for this dance. **b.** a piano or orchestral composition patterned after such music. [< G: lit., something connected with *Landl* (lit., little land) popular name of Upper Austria, where the dance first won vogue]

land·less (land′lis), *adj.* without landed property or ownership of land: *a landless noble; a people who were landless.* [OE *landlēas.* See LAND, -LESS] —**land′less·ness,** *n.*

land·locked (land′lokt′), *adj.* **1.** shut in completely, or almost completely, by land: *a landlocked bay.* **2.** not having access to the sea: *a landlocked country.* **3.** living in waters shut off from the sea, as some fish. [LAND + LOCK[1] + -ED[2]]

land′locked salm′on, a variety of the Atlantic Ocean salmon, *Salmo salar,* confined to the fresh-water lakes of New England and adjacent areas of Canada.

land·lop·er (land′lō′pər), *n.* a wanderer, vagrant, or adventurer. Also, **land·loup·er** (land′lou′pər, -lo͞o′pər). [< MD: lit., land-runner. See LAND, LOPE, -ER[1]]

land·lord (land′lôrd′), *n.* **1.** one who owns and leases apartments to others. **2.** the master of an inn, lodging house, etc. **3.** one who owns and leases land, buildings, etc. **4.** a landowner. [ME; OE *landhlāford.* See LAND, LORD] —**land′lord′ly,** *adj.* —**land′lord′ry,** *n.* —**land′lord′ship′,** *n.*

land·lord·ism (land′lôr diz′əm), *n.* the practice under which a person owns property and leases it to others for occupancy or cultivation. [LANDLORD + -ISM]

land·lub·ber (land′lub′ər), *n.* *Naut.* a landsman or raw seaman. [LAND + LUBBER] —**land′lub′ber·ish,** *adj.* —**land′lub′ber·ly, land′lub′bing,** *adj.*

land·man (land′mən), *n., pl.* **-men.** **1.** landsman (def. 1). **2.** leaseman (def. 1). [ME; OE *landmann.* See LAND, MAN[1]]

land·mark (land′märk′), *n.* **1.** a prominent or conspicuous object on land that serves as a guide, esp. to ships at sea or to travelers on a road; a distinguishing landscape feature marking a site or location. **2.** a prominent or distinguishing feature, part, event, etc. **3.** something used to mark the boundary of land. [OE *landmearc.* See LAND, MARK[1]]

land′ meas′ure, **1.** any system of measurement for measuring land. **2.** a unit or a series of units of measurement used in land measure.

land′ mine′, *Mil.* **1.** an explosive charge concealed just under the surface of the ground or of a roadway, designed to be detonated by pressure, proximity of a vehicle or person, etc. **2.** See **aerial mine** (def. 2). **3.** a shaft dug under enemy lines and filled with explosives for blowing a gap in the enemy defenses.

Lan·do (län′dō), *n.* died A.D. 914, pope 913–914. Also, **Landus.**

Land′ of Beu′lah, (in Bunyan's *Pilgrim's Progress*) the peaceful land in which the pilgrim awaits the call to the Celestial City.

land′ of′fice, a government office for the transaction of business relating to public lands.

land′-of·fice busi′ness (land′ô′fis, -of′is), *U.S. Informal.* a lively, booming, expanding, or very profitable business.

land′ of milk′ and hon′ey, **1.** a land of unusual fertility and abundance. **2.** the blessings of heaven. **3.** Israel. Also, **Land′ of Milk′ and Hon′ey.**

land′ of Nod′ (nod), the mythical land of sleep: *Mother read the children a bedtime story to hasten them to the land of Nod.* [pun on *Land of Nod* (Gen. 4:16); see NOD]

Land′ of Prom′ise. See **Promised Land.**

Land′ of the Mid′night Sun′, **1.** any of those countries containing land within the Arctic Circle where there is a midnight sun in midsummer, esp. Norway, Sweden, or Finland. **2.** Lapland.

Land′ of the Ris′ing Sun′, *Informal.* Japan.

Lan·don (lan′dən), *n.* **1. Alfred Moss·man** (môs′mən, mos′-), 1887–1987, U.S. politician. **2.** a boy's given name, form of **Langdon.**

Lan·dor (lan′dər, -dôr), *n.* **1. Walter Savage,** 1775–1864, English poet and prose writer. **2.** a boy's given name.

land·own·er (land′ō′nər), *n.* an owner or proprietor of land. [LAND + OWNER] —**land′own′er·ship′,** *n.* —**land′own′ing,** *n., adj.*

Lan·dow·ska (lan dôf′skə; *Pol.* län dôf′skä), *n.* **Wan·da** (won′də; *Pol.* vän′dä), 1879–1959, Polish harpsichordist, in the U.S. after 1940.

land′ pat′ent, *U.S.* an official document by which title to a portion of public land is conveyed from the government.

land′ plas′ter, finely ground gypsum, used chiefly as a fertilizer.

land-poor (land′po͝or′), *adj.* in need of ready money while owning much unremunerative land.

land′ pow′er, **1.** a nation having an important and powerful army. **2.** military power on land.

land′ rail′. See **corn crake.**

land′ reform′, any program, esp. when undertaken by a national government, involving the redistribution of large holdings of agricultural land among the landless.

Lan′drum-Grif′fin Act′ (lan′drəm grif′in), an act of Congress in 1959 outlawing secondary boycotts, requiring public disclosure of the financial records of unions, and guaranteeing the use of secret ballots in union voting.

land·scape (land′skāp′), *n., v.,* **-scaped, -scap·ing.** —*n.* **1.** a section or portion of rural scenery, usually extensive, that may be seen from a single viewpoint. **2.** a picture representing natural inland or coastal scenery. **3.** *Fine Arts.* the category of subject matter in which natural scenery is represented. **4.** *Obs.* a panoramic view of scenery; vista. —*v.t.* **5.** to improve the landscape of. **6.** to improve the appearance of (an area of land, a highway, etc.), as by planting trees, shrubs, or grass, or altering the contours of the ground. —*v.i.* **7.** to do landscape gardening as a profession. [earlier *landscap, landskip* < MD *lantscap;* c. OE *landsceap, landscipe;* akin to G *Landschaft.* See LAND, -SHIP]

land′scape ar′chitecture, the art of arranging or modifying the features of a landscape, an urban area, etc., to secure beautiful or advantageous effects. —**land′scape ar′chitect.**

land′scape gar′dening, the art of arranging trees, shrubbery, paths, fountains, etc., to produce picturesque effects. —**land′scape gar′dener.**

land·scap·er (land′skā′pər), *n.* a gardener who does landscaping. [LANDSCAPE + -ER[1]]

land·scap·ist (land′skā′pist), *n.* one who paints landscapes. [LANDSCAPE + -IST]

Land·seer (land′sēr, -syər), *n.* **Sir Edwin Henry,** 1802–73, English painter, esp. of animals.

Land's′ End′, the SW tip of England.

land·side (land′sīd′), *n.* the part of a plow consisting of a sidepiece opposite the moldboard, for guiding the plow and resisting the side pressure caused by the turning of the furrow. [LAND + SIDE[1]]

land·skip (land′skip′), *n.* *Archaic.* landscape.

lands·knecht (*Ger.* länts′knekнt′), *n.* a European mercenary foot soldier of the 16th century, armed with a pike or halberd. Also, **lansquenet.** [< G; see LANSQUENET]

land·slide (land′slīd′), *n., v.,* **-slid, -slid** or **-slid·den, -slid·ing.** —*n.* **1.** the downward falling or sliding of a mass of soil, detritus, or rock, on or from a steep slope. **2.** the mass itself. **3.** an election in which a particular candidate or party receives an overwhelming mass or majority of votes: *the 1936 landslide for Roosevelt.* **4.** any overwhelming victory: *She won the bake-off by a landslide.* —*v.i.* **5.** to come down in or as a landslide. **6.** to win an election by an overwhelming majority. Also called, *esp. Brit.,* **land·slip** (land′slip′) (for defs. 1, 2). [LAND + SLIDE]

Lands·mal (länts′môl), *n.* *Norwegian.* Nynorsk. Formerly, **Lands′maal.** Also, **lands′maal.**

lands·man (landz′mən), *n., pl.* **-men.** **1.** Also, **landman.** a person who lives or works on land. **2.** *Naut.* **a.** a sailor on his first voyage. **b.** an inexperienced seaman, rated below an ordinary seaman. [LAND + 'S[1] + MAN[1]]

lands·man (länts′mən), *n., pl.* **-leit** (-līt), *Eng.* **-men.** *Yiddish.* **1.** a person from the same town, geographical area, region, etc., as another; compatriot. **2.** a Jewish compatriot.

lands·man·shaft (länts′mən shäft′), *n., pl.* **-shaf·ten** (-shäf′tən). *Yiddish.* a fraternal organization made up of immigrants from the same region.

Land·stei·ner (land′stī′nər; *Ger.* länt′shtī′nəʀ), *n.* **Karl** (kärl; *Ger.* kärl), 1868–1943, Austrian pathologist in the U.S.: Nobel prize 1930.

Lands·ting (läns′ting′), *n.* (formerly) the upper house of the Danish parliament. Also, **Lands·thing** (läns′ting). Cf. **Rigsdag.** [< Dan, equiv. to *lands,* poss. of *land* LAND + *t(h)ing* THING[2]. See LAGTHING]

Land·sturm (*Ger.* länt′shto͝orm′), *n.* (in certain European countries). **1.** a general draft of people in time of war. **2.** the force so called out or subject to such call, consisting of all men capable of bearing arms and not in the army, navy, or Landwehr. [< G: lit., land storm]

Land·tag (*Ger.* länt′täкн′), *n.* *Hist.* the legislature of certain states in Germany. [< G: lit., land parliament. See DAY, DIET[2]]

Lan·dus (lan′dəs), *n.* Lando.

land·wait·er (land′wā′tər), *n.* a British customs officer who enforces import-export regulations, collects import duties, etc. [LAND + WAITER]

land·ward (land′wərd), *adv.* **1.** Also, **land′wards.** toward the land or interior. —*adj.* **2.** lying, facing, or tending toward the land or away from the coast. **3.** being in the direction of the land: *a landward breeze.* [late ME; see LAND, -WARD]

Land·wehr (länt′vāʀ′), *n.* (in Germany, Austria, etc.) the part of the organized military forces of a nation that has completed a certain amount of compulsory training, and whose continuous service is required only in time of war. [< G: lit., land defense; see WEIR]

land′ wind′ (wind). See **land breeze.**

lane[1] (lān), *n.* **1.** a narrow way or passage between hedges, fences, walls, or houses. **2.** any narrow or well-defined passage, track, channel, or course. **3.** a fixed route pursued by ocean steamers or airplanes. **4.** a part of a highway wide enough to accommodate one vehicle. **5.** (in a running or swimming race) the marked-off space or path within which a competitor must remain during the course of a race. **6.** See **bowling alley** (def. 1). [ME, OE; c. D *laan* avenue, Icel *lön* row of houses, hayrick]
—**Syn. 1.** alley. See **path.**

lane[2] (lān), *Scot.*—*adj.* **1. lone.** —*n.* **2. by his lane.** See **lonesome** (def. 4).

Lane (lān), *n.* a boy's given name.

La·nett (lə net′), *n.* a town in E Alabama. 7674 (1960).

Lan·franc (lan′frangk), *n.* 1005?–89, Italian Roman Catholic prelate and scholar in England: archbishop of Canterbury 1070–89.

lang (lang), *adj., n., adv.* *Scot. and North Eng.* long[1].

Lang (lang), *n.* **1. Andrew,** 1844–1912, Scottish poet, prose writer, and scholar. **2. Cos·mo Gordon** (koz′mō), 1864–1945, English clergyman: archbishop of Canterbury 1928–42. **3. Fritz,** born 1890, U.S. motion-picture director and producer, born in Austria. **4.** a boy's given name.

lang., language.

Lang·dale (lang′dāl), *n.* a town in E Alabama. 2528 (1960).

Lang·don (lang′dən), *n.* a boy's given name.

Lang·e (läng′ə), *n.* **Chris·tian Lou·is** (kʀis′tyän lo͞o′ē, -is), 1869–1938, Norwegian historian: Nobel peace prize 1921.

lan·geel (lang′gēl), *n.* *Australian.* leangle.

Lang·er (lang′ər), *n.* **Susanne (Knauth)** (knout), born 1895, U.S. philosopher.

Lang′han's lay′er (läng′hänz, -häns), *Embryol.* cytotrophoblast. [named after Theodor *Langhans* (1839–1915), German pathologist]

lan·giel (lang′gēl), *n.* *Australian.* leangle.

Lang·land (lang′lənd), *n.* **William,** 1332?–c1400, English poet. Also, **Langley.**

lang·lauf (läng′louf′), *n.* cross-country skiing. [< G: lit., long run. See LONG, LOPE, LEAP]

lang·lauf·er (läng′loi′fər), *n., pl.* **-läuf·er, -läuf·ers.** a participant in cross-country skiing. [< G; see LANGLAUF, -ER[1]]

lang′ lay′ (lang), *Ropemaking.* a wire rope in which the lays of the strands and of their component wires are the same. [*lang.* (var. of ALONG) + LAY[1]]

Lang·ley (lang′lē), *n.* **1. Edmund of.** See **York, Edmund of Langley, 1st Duke of.** **2. Samuel Pier·pont** (pēr′pont), 1834–1906, U.S. astronomer, physicist, and pioneer in aeronautics. **3. William.** See **Langland, William.**

Lang·muir (lang′myo͝or), *n.* **Irving,** 1881–1957, U.S. chemist: Nobel prize for chemistry 1932.

Lan·go·bard (lang′gə bärd′), *n.* Lombard (def. 2). [< L *Langobardī* (pl.), Latinized form of Germanic tribal name; c. OE *Longbeardan*]

Lan·go·bar·dic (lang′gə bär′dik), *adj.* **1.** Lombard (def. 3). —*n.* **2.** a West Germanic language, the language of the ancient Lombards. [LANGOBARD + -IC]

lan·grage (lang′grij), *n.* a kind of shot consisting of bolts, nails, etc., fastened together or enclosed in a case, formerly used for damaging sails and rigging in battles at sea. Also, **lan′gridge.** [?]

Lan·gre·nus (lan grē′nəs), *n.* a walled plain in the fourth quadrant of the face of the moon: about 85 miles in diameter.

Lan·gre·o (läng gʀe′ô), *n.* a city in N Spain. 65,399 (1955).

lang·sat (läng′sät), *n.* **1.** a meliaceous tree, *Lansium domesticum,* of the East Indies. **2.** the yellowish, tart, edible fruit of this tree. Also, **lang·set** (läng′set), **lansa, lansat, lanseh.** [< Malay]

Langs·ton (lang′stən), *n.* a boy's given name.

lang·syne (lang′zīn′, -sīn′), *Scot.* —*adv.* **1.** long since; long ago. —*n.* **2.** time long past. [LANG + SYNE]

Lang·ton (lang′tən), *n.* **Stephen,** c1165–1228, English theologian, historian, and poet: archbishop of Canterbury.

Lang·try (lang′trē), *n.* **Lil·lie** (lil′ē), (*Emily Charlotte Le Breton*) ("*the Jersey Lily*"), 1852–1929, English actress.

lan·guage (lang′gwij), *n.* **1.** the body of words and systems for their use common to a people who are of the same community or nation, the same geographical area, or the same cultural tradition: *the two languages of Belgium; a Bantu language; the French language; the Yiddish language.* **2.** communication by voice in the distinctively human manner, using arbitrary, auditory symbols in conventional ways with conventional meanings. **3.** the system of linguistic signs or symbols considered in the abstract (opposed to *speech*). **4.** any set or system of such symbols as used in a more or less uniform fashion by a number of people, who are thus enabled to communicate intelligibly with one another. **5.** any system of formalized symbols, signs, gestures, or the like, used or conceived as a means of communicating thought, emotion, etc.: *the language of mathematics; the language of love.* **6.** the means of communication used by animals: *the language of birds.* **7.** communication of meaning in any way: *the language of flowers; the language of art.* **8.** linguistics. **9.** the speech or phraseology peculiar to a class, profession, etc. **10.** a particular manner of verbal expression: *in his own language; flowery language; formal language.* **11.** diction or style of writing: *the language of poetry; the stilted language of official documents.* **12.** *Archaic.* faculty or power of speech. **13.** a nation or people considered in terms of their speech. [ME < AF, var. sp. of *langage* < LL **linguāticum.* See LINGUA, -AGE]
—Syn. 2. See **speech. 4, 9.** tongue; terminology; lingo, lingua franca. LANGUAGE, DIALECT, JARGON, VERNACULAR refer to patterns of vocabulary, syntax, and usage characteristic of communities of various sizes and types. LANGUAGE is applied to the general pattern of a people or race: *the English language.* DIALECT is applied to certain forms or varieties of a language, often those which provincial communities or special groups retain (or develop) even after a standard has been established: *Scottish dialect.* A JARGON is either an artificial pattern used by a particular (usually occupational) group within a community or a special pattern created for communication in business or trade between members of the groups speaking different languages: *the jargon of the theater; the Chinook jargon.* A VERNACULAR is the authentic natural pattern of speech, now usually on the informal level, used by persons indigenous to a certain community, large or small.

lan′guage arts′, the skills, including reading, composition, speech, spelling, dramatics, etc., taught in elementary and secondary schools to give students a thorough proficiency in using the English language.

langued (langd), *adj. Heraldry.* (of a beast) represented with the tongue of a different tincture from that of the body: *a lion's head argent langued azure.* [< AF *langue* tongue (< L *lingua*) + -ED[3]]

langue de boeuf (*Fr.* läng də bœf′), *pl.* **langues de boeuf** (*Fr.* läng də bœf′). See **ox-tongue partisan.** [< F: lit., ox tongue]

Langue·doc (läng dôk′), *n.* a former province in S France. *Cap.:* Toulouse. **—Langue·do·cian** (lang dō′shən, lang′gwə dō′shən), *adj., n.*

langue d'oc (läng dôk′), the Romance language of medieval southern France. [< F: language of *oc,* yes < L *hoc* (*ille fecit*) this (he did)]

langue d'oïl (läng dô ēl′, dô′ē, doil), the Romance language of medieval northern France. [< F: language of *oïl,* yes < L *hoc ille* (*fecit*) this he (did)]

lan·guet (lang′gwet), *n.* any of various small tongue-shaped parts, processes, or projections. [late ME < MF *languete,* dim. of *langue* tongue; see -ET]

lan·guette (lang′gwet), *n. Music.* a thin plate fastened to the mouth of certain organ pipes. [var. of LANGUET]

lan·guid (lang′gwid), *adj.* **1.** drooping or flagging from weakness or fatigue; faint. **2.** lacking in vigor or vitality; slack: *a languid manner.* **3.** lacking in spirit or interest; indifferent. [< L *languid*(*us*) faint. See LANGUISH, -ID[4]] **—lan′guid·ly,** *adv.* **—lan′guid·ness,** *n.*
—Syn. 1. weak, feeble, weary, exhausted, debilitated. **2.** listless, spiritless. **3.** inactive, inert, sluggish, torpid. **—Ant. 1.** vigorous. **2.** active, energetic.

lan·guish (lang′gwish), *v.i.* **1.** to be or become weak or feeble; droop; fade. **2.** to lose vigor and vitality. **3.** to undergo neglect: *to languish in prison for 10 years.* **4.** to pine with desire or longing. **5.** to assume an expression of tender, sentimental melancholy. **—n. 6.** act of languishing. **7.** a tender, melancholy look or expression. [ME < MF *languiss-,* long s. of *languir* < L *languēre* to languish; see -ISH[2]] **—lan′guish·er,** *n.*

lan·guish·ing (lang′gwi shing), *adj.* **1.** becoming languid, in any way. **2.** expressive of languor; indicating tender, sentimental melancholy: *a languishing sigh.* **3.** lingering: *a languishing death.* [ME; see LANGUISH, -ING[2]] **—lan′guish·ing·ly,** *adv.*

lan·guish·ment (lang′gwish mənt), *n. Archaic.* **1.** act or state of languishing. **2.** a languishing expression.

lan·guor (lang′gər), *n.* **1.** physical weakness or faintness. **2.** lack of energy or vitality; sluggishness. **3.** lack of spirit; listlessness. **4.** emotional softness or tenderness. **5.** soothing or oppressive stillness. [< L (see LANGUISH, -OR[1]); r. ME *langour* sickness, woe < OF]

lan·guor·ous (lang′gər əs), *adj.* **1.** characterized by languor; languid. **2.** inducing languor: *languorous fragrance.* [LANGUOR + -OUS; r. late ME *langorous* woeful, adj. of *langour* woe] **—lan′guor·ous·ly,** *adv.*

lan·gur (lung gōōr′), *n.* any of several slender, long-tailed monkeys of the genus *Presbytis,* of Asia, feeding on leaves, fruits, and seeds. Also called **leaf monkey.** [< Hindi; akin to Skt *lāngūlin* having a tail]

lani-, a learned borrowing from Latin meaning "wool," used in the formation of compound words: *laniferous.* [< LL, comb. form of *lāna* wool; akin to Gk *lēnos* wool]

lan·iard (lan′yərd), *n.* lanyard.

la·ni·ar·y (lā′nē er′ē, lan′ē-), *adj.* **1.** (of teeth) adapted for tearing. **—n. 2.** a laniary tooth; a canine of dagger-like shape. [< L *laniāri*(*us*) of a butcher, equiv. to *lani*(*us*) butcher + *-ārius* -ARY]

La·nier (lə nēr′), *n.* **Sidney,** 1842–81, U.S. poet and literary scholar.

la·nif·er·ous (lə nif′ər əs), *adj.* wool-bearing. Also called **la·nig·er·ous** (lə nij′ər əs). [< L *lānifer* wool-bearing (see LANI-, -FER) + -OUS; see -FEROUS]

La·ni·kai (lä′nē kī′), *n.* a town adjoining Kailua, on SE Oahu, in Hawaii. With Kailua, 25,622 (1960).

Lan·i·tal (lan′i tal′), *n. Trademark.* a casein derivative chemically similar to wool, used similarly.

lank (langk), *adj.* **1.** (of hair) straight and limp; without spring or curl. **2.** (of plants) unduly long and slender: *lank grass; lank, leafless trees.* **3.** lean; gaunt; thin. [ME *lanc,* OE *hlanc;* akin to OHG *hlanca* loin, side. See FLANK] **—lank′ly,** *adv.* **—lank′ness,** *n.*

Lan·kes·ter (lang′ki stər, -kes tər), *n.* **Sir Edwin Ray,** 1847–1929, English zoologist and writer.

lank·y (lang′kē), *adj.,* **lank·i·er, lank·i·est.** ungracefully thin and rawboned; bony; gaunt: *a tall, lanky man.* [LANK + -Y[1]] **—lank′i·ly,** *adv.* **—lank′i·ness,** *n.*

lan·ner (lan′ər), *n.* **1.** a falcon, *Falco biarmicus,* of southern Europe, northern Africa, and southern Asia. **2.** *Falconry.* the female of this bird. [late ME *laner* < MF *lanier* kind of falcon, lit., wool weaver (< L *lānārius;* see LANIARY), a term of abuse in early Middle Ages, applied especially to sluggards, laggards, and cowards, and so to the lanner, slow in flight and thought to be cowardly]

lan·ner·et (lan′ə ret′), *n. Falconry.* the male lanner, which is smaller than the female. [late ME *lanret* < MF *laneret.* See LANNER, -ET]

Lan·ny (lan′ē), *n.* a boy's given name, form of **Lenny.**

lan·o·lin (lan′əlin), *n.* a fatty substance, extracted from wool, used in ointments. Also, **lan·o·line** (lan′əlin, -əlēn′). Also called **wool fat.** [< L *lān*(*a*) wool + -OL[2] + -IN[2]] **—lan·o·lat·ed** (lan′əlā′tid), *adj.*

la·nose (lā′nōs), *adj.* lanate. [< L *lānōs*(*us*). See LANI-, -OSE[1]] **—la·nos·i·ty** (lā nos′i tē), *n.*

La Nou·velle Hé·lo·ïse (*Fr.* la nōō vel ā lô ēz′), (*Julie, ou la Nouvelle Héloïse*) a novel (1761) by J. J. Rousseau.

lan·sa (lan′sə), *n.* langsat. Also, **lan·sat** (lan′sət), **lan·seh** (lan′sə).

Lans·berg (lanz′bârg), *n.* a walled plain in the third quadrant and extending into the second quadrant of the face of the moon: about 29 miles in diameter.

Lans·ford (lans′fərd, lanz′-), *n.* a town in E Pennsylvania. 5958 (1960).

Lan·sing (lan′sing), *n.* **1. Robert,** 1864–1928, U.S. lawyer and statesman: Secretary of State 1915–20. **2.** a city in and the capital of Michigan, in the S part. 107,807 (1960). **3.** a city in NE Illinois, near Chicago. 18,098 (1960).

lans·que·net (lans′kə net′), *n.* landsknecht.

lan·ta·na (lan tā′nə, -tä′-), *n.* any of several chiefly tropical, verbenaceous plants of the genus *Lantana,* certain species of which, as *L. Camara,* are cultivated for their aromatic yellow and orange, or blue and violet flowers. [< NL, special use of dial. It *lantana* wayfaring tree]

Lan·tan·a (lan tan′ə), *n.* a town in SE Florida. 5021 (1960).

lan·tern (lan′tərn), *n.* **1.** a transparent or translucent case for enclosing a light and protecting it from the wind, rain, etc. **2.** the chamber at the top of a lighthouse, surrounding the light. **3.** See **magic lantern. 4.** *Archit.* **a.** a tall, more or less open construction admitting light to an enclosed area below. **b.** any light, decorative structure of relatively small size crowning a roof, dome, etc. **c.** Also called **femerell.** an open-sided structure on a roof to let out smoke or to assist ventilation. **5.** a light, usually over the entrance to an elevator on each floor of a multi-story building, that signals the approach of the elevator. [ME *lanterne* < L *lanterna* < Gk *lampt*(*ḗr*) lamp, light + L (*iuc*)*erna* lamp]

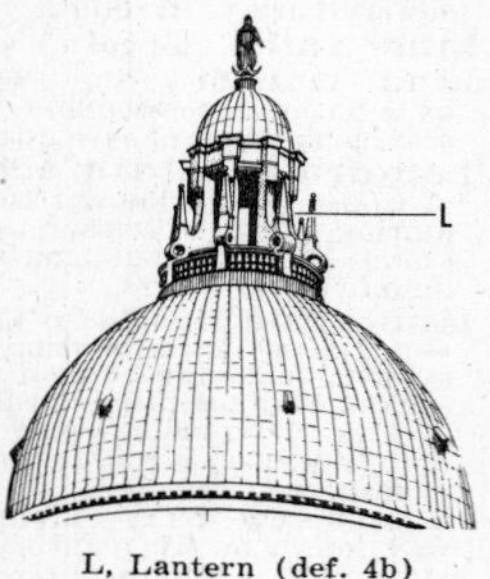

L. Lantern (def. 4b)

lan′tern clock′, an English bracket clock of the late 16th and 17th centuries, having a brass case with corner columns supporting pierced crestings on the sides and front. Also called **birdcage clock.**

lan·tern-fish (lan′tərn fish′), *n., pl.* (*esp. collectively*) **-fish,** (*esp. referring to two or more kinds or species*) **-fish·es.** any of several small, deep-sea fishes of the family *Myctophidae,* having rows of luminous organs along each side, certain species of which migrate to the surface at night. [LANTERN + FISH]

lan′tern fly′, any of several tropical, homopterous insects of the family *Fulgoridae,* formerly thought to be luminescent.

lan′tern gear′, a gear mechanism including a lantern wheel.

lan′tern jaw′, a long, thin jaw. [so called from the fancied resemblance of the face to the shape of a lantern]

lan·tern-jawed (lan′tərn jôd′), *adj.* having a lantern jaw.

lan′tern keg′, *Naut.* (formerly, in whaling) a keg of provisions placed in a boat for use if the boat became separated from the ship for a long time.

lan′tern ring′, *Mach.* gland[2] (def. 1).

lan′tern slide′, a slide or transparency in a slide projector or magic lantern.

lan′tern tree′, a tree, *Crinodendron hookerianum,* of Chile, having leathery leaves and urn-shaped deep-crimson flowers with petals curving in at the tip.

lan′tern wheel′, a wheel, used like a pinion, consisting essentially of two parallel disks or heads whose peripheries are connected by a series of bars which engage with the teeth of another wheel. Also called **lan′tern pin′ion.**

lan·tha·nide (lan′thə nīd′, -nid), *n. Chem.* one of the rare-earth elements of atomic number 57–71, inclusive. [LANTHAN(UM) + -IDE]

lan·tha·num (lan′thə nəm), *n. Chem.* a rare-earth, trivalent, metallic element, allied to aluminum, found in certain rare minerals, as monazite. *Symbol:* La; *at. wt.:* 138.91; *at. no.:* 57; *sp. gr.:* 6.15 at 20°C. [< NL, equiv. to *lanthan-* (< Gk *lanthán*(*ein*) (to) lurk unseen) + *-um,* var. of *-ium* -IUM]

lant·horn (lant′hôrn′, lan′tərn), *n. Archaic.* lantern.

Lan·tsang (län′tsäng′), *n.* Chinese name of **Mekong.**

la·nu·gi·nose (lə nōō′jə nōs′, -nyōō′-), *adj.* **1.** covered with lanugo, or soft, downy hairs. **2.** of the nature of down; downy. Also, **la·nu·gi·nous** (lə nōō′jə nəs, -nyōō′-). [< L *lānūginōs*(*us*) downy, woolly, equiv. to *lānūgin-* (s. of *lānūgo;* see LANUGO) + *-ōsus* -OSE[1]] **—la·nu·gi·nous·ness** (lə nōō′jə nəs nis, -nyōō′-), *n.*

la·nu·go (lə nōō′gō, -nyōō′-), *n., pl.* **-gos.** *Biol.* a coat of delicate, downy hairs, esp. that with which the human fetus or a newborn infant is covered. [< L: woolliness, down, deriv. of *lāna* wool]

lan·yard (lan′yərd), *n.* **1.** *Naut.* a short rope or wire rove through deadeyes to hold and tauten standing rigging. **2.** any of various small cords or ropes for securing or suspending something, as a whistle about the neck, a knife from one's belt, etc. **3.** *Mil.* a cord with a small hook at one end, used in firing certain kinds of cannon. **4.** *U.S. Mil.* **a.** a colored, single-strand cord worn around the left shoulder by a member of a military unit awarded a foreign decoration. **b.** a white cord worn around the right shoulder, as by a military policeman, and secured to the butt of a pistol. Also, **laniard.** [b. late ME *lanyer* (< MF *laniere* thong, equiv. to *lasne* noose + *-iere* -ER[2]) and YARD[1]]

Lao (lou), *n.* a language of Laos and northern Thailand that belongs to the Thai group of languages.

La·oag (lä wäg′), *n.* a seaport on NW Luzon, in the N Philippines. 22,218 (1948).

La·oc·o·ön (lā ok′ō on′), *n.* **1.** *Class. Myth.* a priest of Apollo at Troy who warned the Trojans against the Trojan Horse, and who, with his two sons, was killed by serpents sent by Athena or Apollo. **2.** (*italics*) a late 2nd century B.C. representation in marble of Laocoon and his sons struggling with the serpents: attributed to Agesander, Athenodorus, and Polydorus of Rhodes. Also, **La·oc′o·ön′.**

La·od·a·mas (lā od′ə məs), *n. Class. Myth.* **1.** a son of Eteocles who defended Thebes against the Epigoni, killed Aegialeus, and was killed by Alcmaeon. **2.** (in the *Odyssey*) the son of Alcinous who, not recognizing Odysseus, challenged him to athletic contests when Odysseus landed in Phaeacia.

La·od·a·mi·a (lā od′ə mī′ə), *n. Class. Myth.* **1.** a daughter of Acastus who committed suicide so that she could join her husband, Protesilaus, in the underworld. **2.** (in the *Iliad*) the mother, by Zeus, of Sarpedon.

La·od·i·ce (lā od′i sē′), *n.* (in the *Iliad*) a daughter of Priam and Hecuba who chose to be swallowed up by the earth rather than live as a Greek concubine.

La·od·i·ce·a (lā od′i sē′ə, lā′ə di sē′ə), *n.* ancient name of **Latakia.**

La·od·i·ce·an (lā od′i sē′ən, lā′ə di sē′ən), *adj.* **1.** lukewarm or indifferent, esp. in religion, as were the early Christians of Laodicea. **—n. 2.** a person who is lukewarm or indifferent, esp. in religion. [LAODICE(A) + -AN]

La·od·o·cus (lā od′ə kəs), *n. Class. Myth.* a son of Apollo and Phthia who was killed by Aetolus.

Laoigh·is (lā′ish), *n.* a county in Leinster, in the central Republic of Ireland. 45,069 (1961); 623 sq. mi. *County seat:* Port Laoighise. Also called **Leix.**

La·om·e·don (lā om′i don′), *n. Class. Myth.* a king of Troy and the father of Priam, for whom the walls of Troy were built by Apollo and Poseidon.

Laon (läɴ), *n.* a town in and the capital of Aisne, in N France, E of Paris. 27,268 (1962).

La·os (lä′ōs, lā′os; *Fr.* la ôs′), *n.* a country in SE Asia: formerly part of French Indochina. 1,925,000 (est. 1963); 91,500 sq. mi. *Cap.:* Vientiane. **—La·o·tian** (lā ō′shən), *n.*

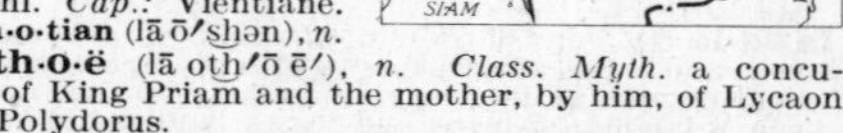

La·oth·o·ë (lā oth′ō ē′), *n. Class. Myth.* a concubine of King Priam and the mother, by him, of Lycaon and Polydorus.

Lao-tzu (lou′dzu′), *n.* **1.** (*Li Erh*) 6th century B.C., Chinese philosopher: reputed founder of Taoism. **2.** (*italics*) See **Tao Te Ching.** Also, **Lao-tse** (lou′dzu′).

lap[1] (lap), *n.* **1.** the front part of the human body from the waist to the knees when in a sitting position. **2.** the part of the clothing that lies on the front portion of the body from the waist to the knees when one sits. **3.** a place or environment of rest or nurture: *living in the lap of luxury.* **4.** a metaphorical area of responsibility, care, charge, or control: *They dropped the problem right in his lap. The outcome is in the lap of the gods.* **5.** a hollow place, as a hollow among hills. **6.** the front part of a skirt, esp. as held up to contain something. **7.** a loose border or fold. **8.** a part of a garment that extends over another: *the front lap of a coat.* [ME *lappe,* OE *læppa;* c. D *lap;* akin to G *lappen,* Icel *leppr* rag, patch]

lap[2] (lap), *v.,* **lapped, lap·ping,** *n.* **—v.t. 1.** to fold over or about something; wrap or wind around something: *to lap a bandage around one's head.* **2.** to enwrap in something; wrap up; clothe. **3.** to envelop or enfold: *lapped in luxury.* **4.** to lay (something) partly over something underneath; lay (things) together, one partly over another; overlap. **5.** to lie partly over (something underneath). **6.** to get a lap or more ahead of (a competitor) in racing. **7.** to cut or polish with a lap. **8.** to join, as by scarfing, to form a single piece with the same dimensions throughout. **9.** to change (cotton, wool, etc.) into a compressed layer or sheet. **—v.i. 10.** to fold or wind around something. **11.** to lie partly over or alongside of something else. **12.** to lie upon and extend beyond a thing; overlap. **13.** to extend beyond a limit. **—n. 14.** the act of lapping. **15.** the amount of material required to go around a thing once. **16.** a complete circuit of a course in racing or walking for exercise: *The track has four laps to the mile.* **17.** an overlapping part. **18.** the extent or amount of overlapping. **19.** a rotating wheel or disk holding an abrasive or polishing powder on its surface, used for gems, cutlery, etc. **20.** a compressed layer or sheet of cotton, wool, or other fibrous material usually wound on an iron rod or rolled into a cylindrical form for further processing during carding. [ME *lappe*(*n*) (to) fold, wrap; c. D *lappen* to patch, mend; akin to LAP[1]]

lap[3] (lap), *v.,* **lapped, lap·ping,** *n.* **—v.t. 1.** (of water) to wash against or beat upon (something) with a light, slapping or splashing sound: *Waves lapped the shoreline.* **2.** to take in (liquid) with the tongue; lick in (often fol. by *up*): *The dog was thirsty and lapped up the water.* —*v.i.* **3.** to wash or move in small waves with a light, slapping or splashing sound: *The water lapped gently against the mooring.* **4.** to take up liquid with the tongue; lick up a liquid. **5. lap up, a.** *Informal.* to receive enthusiastically: *The audience lapped up his monologue.* **b.** to eat or drink: *The cat lapped up her milk and looked for more.* —*n.* **6.** the act of lapping liquid. **7.** the lapping of water against something. **8.** the sound of this: *the quiet lap of the sea on the rocks.* **9.** something lapped up, as liquid food for dogs. [ME *lappe,* unexplained var. of *lape,* OE *lapian;* c. MLG *lapen,* OHG *laffan;* akin to L *lambere,* Gk *láptein* to lick, lap]

lap[4] (lap), *v. Dial.* pt. of **leap.**

la·pac·tic (lə pak′tik), *Med.* —*adj.* **1.** purgative; cathartic. —*n.* **2.** a lapactic agent; purgative. [< Gk *lapaktik(ós)* laxative, equiv. to *lapak-* (verbid s. of *lapássein* to evacuate) + *-tikos* -TIC]

lapar-, var. of **laparo-** before a vowel: *laparectomy.*

lap·a·rec·to·my (lap′ə rek′tə mē), *n. Surg.* excision of strips of the abdominal wall and suturing of the wounds so as to correct laxity of the abdominal muscles. [LAPAR- + -ECTOMY]

laparo-, a learned borrowing from Greek, where it meant "flank," used in the formation of compound words to denote the abdominal wall: *laparotomy.* Also, *esp. before a vowel,* **lapar-.** [comb. form repr. Gk *lapárā* flank (lit., soft part), n. use of fem. of *laparós* soft]

lap·ar·o·tome (lap′ər ə tōm′), *n. Surg.* a cutting instrument for performing a laparotomy. [LAPARO- + -TOME]

lap·a·rot·o·mize (lap′ə rot′ə mīz′), *v.t.,* **-mized, -miz·ing.** *Surg.* to perform a laparotomy on. [LAPAROTOM(Y) + -IZE] —**lap′a·rot′o·mist,** *n.*

lap·a·rot·o·my (lap′ə rot′ə mē), *n., pl.* **-mies. 1.** *Surg.* incision into the loin. **2.** Also called **celiotomy.** incision into the abdominal cavity through any point in the abdominal wall. Also called **ventrotomy.** [LAPARO- + -TOMY]

La Paz (lä päs′; *Eng.* lə päz′), **1.** a city in W Bolivia: seat of the government; Sucre is the nominal capital. 352,912 (est. 1962); ab. 12,000 ft. above sea level. **2.** a city in SE Lower California, in NW Mexico. 13,081 (1950).

lap·board (lap′bōrd′, -bôrd′), *n.* a thin, flat board to be held on the lap for use as a table or desk. [LAP[1] + BOARD]

lap′ dissolve′, dissolve (def. 17).

lap′ dog′, a small pet dog.

lap′ dove′tail joint′. See **half-blind joint.**

La·peer (lə pēr′), *n.* a town in E Michigan. 6160 (1960).

la·pel (lə pel′), *n.* a part of a garment folded back on the breast, esp. a continuation of a coat collar. [dim. of LAP[1]; see -LE] —**la·pelled′,** *adj.*

lapel′ mike′, a small microphone that may be clipped to the speaker's lapel, pocket, or the like. Also called **lap microphone.**

La Pé·rouse (lä pā ro͞oz′), **Jean Fran·çois de Ga·laup** (zhäN fräN swä′ də gä lō′), 1741–88, French naval officer and explorer.

La Peste (*Fr.* lä pest′). See **Plague, The.**

Lap·ey·rouse (lap′ə ro͞os′), *n.* a walled plain in the fourth quadrant of the face of the moon: about 51 miles in diameter.

lap·ful (lap′fo͝ol), *n., pl.* **-fuls.** as much as the lap can hold. [LAP[1] + -FUL]

Laph·ri·a (laf′rē ə), *n. Class. Myth.* an epithet of Artemis.

La·phys·ti·us (lə fis′tē əs), *n. Class. Myth.* an epithet of Zeus. [< Gk *laphýstios* gluttonous]

lap·i·dar·y (lap′i der′ē), *n., pl.* **-dar·ies,** *adj.* —*n.* **1.** Also, **lap·i·dist** (lap′i dist). a workman who cuts, polishes, and engraves precious stones. **2.** the art of cutting, polishing, and engraving precious stones. **3.** an old book on the lore of gems. **4.** Also, **la·pid·ar·ist** (lə pid′ər ist). an expert in or connoisseur of precious stones and of the art or techniques used in cutting and engraving them. —*adj.* **5.** of or pertaining to the cutting or engraving of precious stones. **6.** characterized by an exactitude and extreme refinement that suggests gem cutting: *a lapidary style; lapidary verse.* **7.** of, pertaining to, or suggestive of inscriptions on stone monuments. [ME *lapidarie* (n.) < L *lapidāri(us)* of stone (adj.) stone-cutter (n.), equiv. to *lapid-* (s. of *lapis*) stone + *-ārius* -ARY]

lap·i·date (lap′i dāt′), *v.t.,* **-dat·ed, -dat·ing. 1.** to pelt with stones. **2.** to stone to death. [< L *lapidāt(us)* stoned, ptp. of *lapidāre.* See LAPIDARY, -ATE[1]] —**lap′i·da′tion,** *n.*

la·pid·i·fy (lə pid′ə fī′), *v.t., v.i.,* **-fied, -fy·ing.** *Archaic.* to turn into stone. [*lapidi(fication)* petrifaction (see LAPIDARY, -I-, -FICATION) + -FY] —**lap·i·dif·ic** (lap′i dif′ik), **lap′i·dif′i·cal,** *adj.* —**la·pid′i·fi·ca′tion,** *n.*

la·pil·lus (lə pil′əs), *n., pl.* **-pil·li** (-pil′ī). a stony particle ejected from a volcano, esp. a round one less than an inch in diameter. [< L: little stone, pebble, dim. of *lapis* stone]

lap·in (lap′in; *Fr.* lä paN′), *n., pl.* **lap·ins** (lap′inz; *Fr.* lä paN′). **1.** a rabbit. **2.** its fur. [< F, MF < ?]

la·pis (lā′pis, lap′is), *n., pl.* **lap·i·des** (lap′i dēz′). *Latin.* stone: used in Latin names for minerals, gems, etc.

lap·is laz·u·li (lap′is laz′o͝o lē, -lī′, laz′yo͝o-, lazh′o͝o-), **1.** a deep-blue mineral composed mainly of lazurite with smaller quantities of other minerals, used mainly as a gem or as a pigment. **2.** a sky-blue color; azure. Also called **lap′is, lazuli.** [ME < ML, equiv. to L *lapis* a stone + ML *lazulī,* gen. of *lazulum* lapis lazuli; see AZURE]

Lap·ith (lap′ith), *n., pl.* **Lap·i·thae** (lap′ə thē′), **Lap·iths.** *Class. Myth.* a member of a Thessalian people who were defeated in a war provoked by drunken centaurs at the wedding of the Lapith king Pirithoüs.

lap′ joint′, 1. Also called **plain lap.** a joint, as between two pieces of metal or timber, in which the pieces overlap without any change in form. **2.** any of various joints between two members, as timbers, in which an end or section of one is partly cut away to be overlapped by an end or section of the other, often so that flush surfaces result. —**lap′-joint′ed,** *adj.*

La·place (lä pläs′), *n.* **1. Pierre Si·mon** (pyer sē môN′), 1749–1827, French astronomer and mathematician. **2.** a town in SE Louisiana. 3541 (1960).

Laplace′ equa′tion, *Math.* the second-order partial differential equation indicating that the Laplace operator operating on a given function results in zero. Cf. **harmonic** (def. 4c).

Laplace′ op′erator, *Math.* an operator that upon operating on a function of several variables results in the sum of the partial derivatives of second order with respect to each variable. *Symbol:* ∇^2 Also called **Laplacian.** [named after P. S. LAPLACE]

Laplace′ trans′form, *Math.* a new function, $f(x)$, obtained from a given function, $g(x)$, by the formula $f(x) = \int_0^\infty e^{-xt}\,g(t)dt.$ [named after P. S. LAPLACE]

La·plac·i·an (lä plä′sē ən, -plā′shən), *n. Math.* **1.** See **Laplace operator. 2.** the function produced by applying the operator to a given function. [named after P. S. LAPLACE; see -IAN]

Lap·land (lap′land′), *n.* a region in N Norway, N Sweden, N Finland, and the Kola Peninsula of the NW Soviet Union in Europe: inhabited by Lapps.

La Pla·ta (lä plä′tä), **1.** a seaport in E Argentina. 406,000 (est. 1965). **2.** See **Rio de la Plata.**

lap′ link′, a chain link for joining two lengths of chain, having a split in one end so that it can be opened to receive other links and then closed again. Also called **monkey link.**

lap′ mi′crophone. See **lapel mike.**

La Porte (lə pōrt′, pôrt′), **1.** a city in NW Indiana. 21,157 (1960). **2.** a town in S Texas. 4512 (1960).

La Porte E·troite (*Fr.* lä pôrt ā trwät′). See **Strait is the Gate.**

Lapp (lap), *n.* **1.** Also called **Lap·land·er** (lap′lan′dər, -lən-). a member of a Finnic people of northern Norway, Sweden, Finland, and adjacent regions. **2.** Also called **Lappish.** any of the languages of the Lapps, closely related to Finnish. [< Sw]

lap·page (lap′ij), *n. Law.* an overlapping of part or all of a piece of land claimed by one person on land claimed by another. [LAP[2] + -AGE]

Lap·peen·ran·ta (läp′pen rän tä), *n.* a city in SE Finland. 23,733 (est. 1965).

lap·per[1] (lap′ər), *n.* one who or that which laps liquid. [LAP[3] + -ER[1]]

lap·per[2] (lap′ər), *v.i. Scot. and North Eng.* to clabber; curdle. [ME *lopir* to curdle < Scand; cf. Icel *hleypa* to make (milk) curdle, *hleypir* rennet]

lap·pet (lap′it), *n.* **1.** a small lap, flap, or loosely hanging part, esp. of a garment or headdress. See illus. under **miter. 2.** a projecting, lobelike structure in certain invertebrate animals. **3.** *Ornith.* a wattle or other fleshy process on a bird's head. **4.** *Textiles.* **a.** a rack or bar containing needles, situated at the front of the reed, and used in the production of figured patterns. **b.** an ornamented fabric produced by lappet weaving. [LAP[1] + -ET] —**lap′pet·ed,** *adj.*

lap′pet weav′ing, weaving into which an embroidered pattern produced by additional warp threads has been introduced with the aid of a lappet.

Lap·pish (lap′ish), *n.* **1.** Lapp (def. 2). —*adj.* **2.** Also, **Lap′pic.** of, pertaining to, or characteristic of Lapland or the Lapps. [LAPP + -ISH[1]]

L'A·près-mi·di d'un Faune (*Fr.* lä pre mē dē′ dœN fōn′), a poem (1876) by Mallarmé, source of Debussy's *Prélude à l'Après-midi d'un Faune* (1892–94). English, **The Afternoon of a Faun.**

La Prin·cesse de Clèves (*Fr.* lä praN ses də klev′), a novel (1678) by Mme. de La Fayette.

lap′ robe′, a fur robe, blanket, or the like, to cover the lap and legs of a person, esp. when riding in an automobile, carriage, etc.

laps·a·ble (lap′sə bəl), *adj.* liable to lapse. Also, **laps·ible.** [LAPSE + -ABLE]

lapse (laps), *n., v.,* **lapsed, laps·ing.** —*n.* **1.** an accidental or temporary decline from an expected or accepted condition or state; a temporary falling or slipping from a previous standard: *a lapse of principle; a lapse of justice.* **2.** a slip or error, often of a trivial sort; failure: *There were occasional lapses in his treatment of the material. He had a lapse of memory.* **3.** an interval or passage of time; an elapsed period: *There was a lapse of 10 minutes before the program resumed.* **4.** a moral fall, as from rectitude. **5.** a fall or decline to a lower grade, condition, or degree: *a lapse into savagery.* **6.** *Law.* the termination of a right or privilege through neglect to exercise it or through failure of some contingency. **7.** a falling into disuse: *a lapse of a custom.* **8.** *Insurance.* discontinuance of coverage resulting from nonpayment of a premium; termination of a policy. **9.** *Meteorol.* See **lapse rate. 10.** the act of falling, slipping, sliding, etc., slowly or by degrees. **11.** *Archaic.* a gentle, downward flow, as of water. —*v.i.* **12.** to fall from a previous standard; fail to maintain a normative level: *Toward the end of the book the author lapsed into bad prose. After the removal of social strictures, a community might easily lapse into savagery.* **13.** *Law.* to become void, as a legacy to one who dies before the testator. **14.** *Insurance.* to cease being in force; terminate: *The policy will lapse after 30 days.* **15.** to fall, slip, or sink; subside: *to lapse into silence.* **16.** to fall spiritually, as an apostate: *to lapse from grace.* **17.** to deviate or abandon principles, beliefs, etc.: *to lapse into heresy.* **18.** to fall into disuse: *The custom lapsed after a period of time.* **19.** to pass away, as time; elapse. [< L *laps(us)* an error, slipping, falling, u-stem (4th-decl.) deriv. of *lapsus,* ptp. of *lābī* to slide, slip, fall, make mistakes] —**laps′er,** *n.*

lapse′ rate′, *Meteorol.* the rate of decrease of atmospheric temperature with increase of elevation vertically above a given location.

Lap·sey (lap′sē), *n.* a boy's given name.

lap·si·ble (lap′sə bəl), *adj.* lapsable. [LAPSE + -IBLE]

lap·strake (lap′strāk′), *adj.* **1.** noting a hull having a shell each strake of which overlaps that below; clinker-built. —*n.* **2.** a vessel built with a lapstrake hull. [LAP[2] + STRAKE]

lap·sus (lap′səs; *Lat.* läp′so͞os), *n.* a slip or lapse. [< L]

lap·sus ca·la·mi (läp′so͞os kä′lä mē′; *Eng.* lap′səs kal′ə mī′), *Latin.* a slip of the pen.

lap·sus lin·guae (läp′so͞os liNG′gwī; *Eng.* lap′səs liNG′gwē), *Latin.* a slip of the tongue.

lap·sus me·mo·ri·ae (läp′so͞os me mō′rē ī′; *Eng.* lap′səs me mōr′ē ē′, -môr′-), *Latin.* a lapse of memory.

Lap′tev Sea′ (läp′tef), an arm of the Arctic Ocean N of the Soviet Union in Asia, between Taimyr Peninsula and the New Siberian Islands. Also called **Nordenskjöld Sea.**

La Puen·te (lä pwen′tā), a city in SW California, E of Los Angeles. 24,723 (1960).

La·pu·ta (lə pyo͞o′tə), *n.* an imaginary flying island in Swift's *Gulliver's Travels,* the inhabitants of which engaged in a variety of ridiculous projects and pseudoscientific experiments. —**La·pu′tan,** *adj.*

lap·wing (lap′wiNG′), *n.* **1.** a large, Old World plover, *Vanellus vanellus,* having a long, slender, upcurved crest, an erratic, flapping flight, and a shrill cry. **2.** any of several similar, related plovers. [ME, var. (by assoc. with WING) of *lapwinke,* OE *hlēapwince* plover. See LEAP, WINK]

la·que·us (lā′kwē əs, lak′wē-), *n., pl.* **la·que·i** (lā′kwē ī′, -kwē ē′, lak′wē ī′, -wē ē′). *Anat. Rare.* lemniscus. [< L: noose]

L'Aq·ui·la (lä′kwē lä), *n.* Aquila.

lar (lär), *n., pl.* **lar·es** (lâr′ēz, lā′rēz), **lars** (lärz). *Rom. Religion.* any of the lares. [< L]

La·raine (lə rān′), *n.* a girl's given name.

Lar·a·mie (lar′ə mē), *n.* **1.** a city in SE Wyoming. 17,520 (1960). **2. Fort.** See **Fort Laramie.**

Lar′amie Range′, a mountain range in N Colorado and SE Wyoming. Highest peak, Laramie Peak, 9020 ft.

la·rar·i·um (lə râr′ē əm), *n., pl.* **-rar·i·a** (-râr′ē ə). (in an ancient Roman home) a shrine for the lares. [< LL; see LARES, -ARY]

Lar·baud (lär bō′), *n.* **Va·lé·ry** (vä lā rē′), 1881–1957, French novelist, critic, and translator.

lar·board (lär′bōrd′, -bôrd′; *Naut.* lär′bərd), *Naut. Obs.* —*n.* **1.** port[2] (def. 1). —*adj.* **2.** port[2] (defs. 2, 3). [ME *laddeborde* (? lit., loading side; see LADE, BOARD); later *larborde* (by analogy with *starboard*)]

lar·ce·ner (lär′sə nər), *n.* a person who commits larceny. Also, **lar′ce·nist.** [LARCEN(Y) + -ER[1]]

lar·ce·nous (lär′sə nəs), *adj.* **1.** of, resembling, or characteristic of larceny. **2.** guilty of larceny. [LARCEN(Y) + -OUS] —**lar′ce·nous·ly,** *adv.*

lar·ce·ny (lär′sə nē), *n., pl.* **-nies.** *Law.* the wrongful taking and carrying away of the personal goods of another from his possession with intent to convert them to the taker's own use. Cf. **grand larceny, petty larceny.** [late ME < AF *larcin* theft (< L *latrōcin(ium)* robbery, equiv. to *latrōcin(ārī)* (to) rob, orig. serve as mercenary soldier (deriv. of *latrō* hired soldier, robber) + *-ium* -IUM) + -Y[3]]

larch (lärch), *n.* **1.** any coniferous tree of the genus *Larix,* yielding a tough durable wood. **2.** the wood of such a tree. [earlier *larche* < MHG << L *laric-* (s. of *larix*) larch] —**larch′en,** *adj.*

Larch·mont (lärch′mont), *n.* a town in SE New York. 6789 (1960).

larch′ saw′fly, a red and black sawfly, *Pristiphora erichsonii,* the larvae of which infest and feed on the leaves of larch.

lard (lärd), *n.* **1.** the rendered fat of hogs, esp. the internal fat of the abdomen. —*v.t.* **2.** to apply lard or grease to. **3.** to prepare or enrich (lean meat, chicken, etc.) with pork or fat, esp. with lardons. **4.** to intersperse with something for improvement or ornamentation: *a literary work larded with mythological allusions.* [ME (v.), late ME (n.) < MF *larder* (v.), *lard* (n.) < L *lār(i)dum* bacon fat; akin to Gk *lārīnos* fat] —**lard′like′,** *adj.*

lar·da·ceous (lär dā′shəs), *adj.* lardlike; fatty. [LARD + -ACEOUS]

lar·der (lär′dər), *n.* a room or place where food is kept; pantry. [ME < AF (equiv. to OF *lardier*). See LARD, -ER[2]]

lar′der bee′tle, a black beetle, *Dermestes lardarius,* the larvae of which feed on dried meats, hides, furs, etc.

Lard·ner (lärd′nər), *n.* **Ring(gold Wil·mer)** (riNG′gōld′ wil′mər), 1885–1933, U.S. short-story writer and journalist.

lard′ oil′, a colorless or yellowish oil expressed from lard, used chiefly as a lubricant for cutting tools.

lar·don (lär′dən), *n.* a strip of fat used in larding, esp. as drawn through the substance of meat, chicken, etc., with a kind of needle or pin. Also, **lar·doon** (lär do͞on′). [late ME *lardun* < MF *lardon* piece of pork, equiv. to *lard* LARD + *-on* n. suffix]

lard·y (lär′dē), *adj.,* **lard·i·er, lard·i·est. 1.** like or consisting of lard: *lardy pastry.* **2.** fat or becoming fat: *the woman's lardy figure.* [LARD + -Y[1]]

lar·dy-dar·dy (lär′dē där′dē), *adj. Chiefly Brit. Slang.* characterized by excessive elegance. [imit.]

La·re·do (lə rā′dō), *n.* a city in S Texas, on the Rio Grande. 60,678 (1960).

Lar·en·ta·li·a (lar′ən tā′lē ə, -tāl′yə), *n.* (*sometimes construed as pl.*) (in ancient Rome) an annual festival in honor of Acca Larentia.

lar·es (lâr′ēz, lā′rēz), *n.pl., sing.* **lar** (lär). *Rom. Religion.* the spirits who, if propitiated, watched over the house or community to which they belonged. Cf. **penates.** [< L]

lar′es and pena′tes, 1. *Rom. Religion.* the benevolent spirits and gods of the household. **2.** the cherished possessions of a family or household.

lar·gan·do (lär gän′dō; *It.* lär gän′dô), *adj. Music.* allargando. [< It, prp. of *largare* < LL *largāre* to make broad; see LARGE]

large (lärj), *adj.,* **larg·er, larg·est,** *n., adv.* —*adj.* **1.** of more than average size, quantity, degree, etc.; exceeding that which is common to a kind or class; big; great: *a large house; a large number; in large measure; to a large extent.* **2.** on a great scale: *a large producer of kitchen equipment.* **3.** of great scope or range; extensive; broad: *His interest is large enough to encompass a wide variety of subjects.* **4.** grand or pompous: *a man given to*

large, bombastic talk. 5. (of a map, model, etc.) representing the features of the original with features of its own that are relatively large so that great detail may be shown. 6. *Obs.* generous; bountiful; lavish. 7. *Obs.* a. unrestrained in the use of language; gross; improper. b. unrestrained in behavior or manner; uninhibited. 8. *Naut.* (of the wind) blowing in a favorable direction; free. —*n.* 9. *Music.* the longest note in mensural notation. 10. *Obs.* generosity; bounty. 11. **at large,** a. free from restraint or confinement; at liberty: *The murderer is still at large.* b. to a considerable extent; at length: *to treat a subject at large.* c. as a whole; in general: *the country at large.* d. Also, **at-large.** representing the whole of a state, district, or body rather than one division or part of it: *a congressman at large.* 12. **in large,** on a large scale; from a broad point of view: *a problem seen in large.* Also, **in the large.** —*adv.* 13. *Naut.* with the wind free or abaft the beam so that all sails draw fully. [ME < OF < L *larga,* fem. of *largus* ample, generous] —**large′ness,** *n.*
—**Syn. 1.** huge, enormous, immense, gigantic, colossal; massive; vast. See **great.** —**Ant. 1.** small.

large′ cal′orie, calorie (def. 1a).

large′ cane′. See under **cane** (def. 5).

large′ cran′berry. See under **cranberry** (def. 1).

large-heart·ed (lärj′här′tid), *adj.* having or showing generosity. —**large′-heart′ed·ness,** *n.*

large′ intes′tine, intestine (def. 3).

large-leaved cu′cumber tree′ (lärj′lēvd′), a round-headed tree, *Magnolia macrophylla,* of the southeastern U.S., having soft-hairy leaves from one to three feet long, fragrant, cup-shaped, creamy-white flowers with a purplish base which are from 10 to 12 inches wide, and rose-colored, round fruit.

large·ly (lärj′lē), *adv.* 1. to a great extent; in great part; generally; chiefly: *It depends largely on his willingness to cooperate. That is largely incorrect.* 2. in great quantity; much. [ME; see LARGE, -LY]

large-mind·ed (lärj′mīn′did), *adj.* having or showing tolerant views or liberal ideas; broad-minded. —**large′-mind′ed·ly,** *adv.* —**large′-mind′ed·ness,** *n.*

large-mouth bass (lärj′mouth′ bas′), a North American, fresh-water game fish, *Micropterus salmoides,* blackish-green above and lighter below, having the lower jaw extending beyond the eye. Cf. **smallmouth bass.** See illus. under **bass.** [LARGE + MOUTH]

large′ per′iwinkle. See under **periwinkle.**

large-scale (lärj′skāl′), *adj.* 1. very extensive; of great scope: *a large-scale treatment of the topic.* 2. made to a large scale: *a large-scale map.*

lar·gess (lär jes′, lär′jis), *n.* 1. generous bestowal of gifts. 2. the gift or gifts, as of money, so bestowed. 3. *Obs.* generosity; liberality. Also, **lar·gesse′.** [ME *largesse* < OF < LL **largitia* generosity. See LARGE, -ICE]

Large′ White′, a strain of large Yorkshire hogs.

lar·ghet·to (lär get′ō), *adj., n., pl.* **-ghet·tos.** *Music.* —*adj.* 1. somewhat slow; not so slow as largo, but usually slower than andante. —*n.* 2. a larghetto movement. [< It, dim. of *largo* LARGO]

larg·ish (lär′jish), *adj.* rather large. [LARGE + -ISH[1]]

lar·go (lär′gō), *adj., n., pl.* **-gos.** *Music.* —*adj.* 1. slow; in a broad, dignified style. —*n.* 2. a largo movement. [< It; see LARGE]

Lar·go (lär′gō), *n.* a town in W Florida. 5302 (1960).

lar·i·at (lar′ē ət), *n.* 1. a long, noosed rope used to catch horses, cattle, or other livestock; lasso. 2. a rope used to picket grazing animals. [< Sp *la reata* the RIATA]

La·ri·na (lə rē′nə), *n.* a girl's given name, form of **Laraine.** Also, **La·rine** (lə rēn′).

lar·ine (lar′in), *adj.* 1. characteristic of or resembling a gull. 2. of or pertaining to the suborder *Lari,* family *Laridae,* comprising the gulls. [< NL *Larin(ae)* name of the subfamily, equiv. to *Lar(us)* genus name (< Gk *láros* a sea bird, a kind of gull) + *-inae* -INE[1]]

La Rio·ja (lä ryō′hä), a city in W Argentina. 39,728 (est. 1965).

La·ris·sa (lə ris′ə; *Gk.* lä′rē sä), *n.* a city in E Thessaly, in E Greece. 55,733 (1961). Also, **La′ri·sa.**

la·rith·mics (lə rith′miks), *n.* (*construed as sing.*) the study of quantitative relations in population aggregates. [< Gk *lā(ós)* the people + *(a)rithmós* number + -ICS] —**la·rith′mic,** *adj.*

lar′ix·in′ic ac′id (lâr′ik sin′ik, lâr′-), *Chem.* maltol. [< NL *Larix* (*decidua*) genus of larch tree + IN[2] + -IC]

lark[1] (lärk), *n.* 1. any of numerous, chiefly Old World, oscine birds, of the family *Alaudidae,* characterized by an unusually long, straight hind claw, esp. the skylark, *Alauda arvensis.* 2. any of various similar birds of other families, as the meadowlark and titlark. [ME *larke,* OE *lāwerce;* c. G *Lerche,* D *leeuwerik,* Icel *lǽvirki*]

lark[2] (lärk), *n.* 1. a merry, carefree adventure; frolic. 2. innocent or good-natured mischief; prank. —*v.i.* 3. to have fun; frolic; romp. 4. to behave mischievously; play pranks. 5. *Fox Hunting.* (of a rider) to take jumps unnecessarily: *He tired his horse by larking on the way home.* [?] —**lark′er,** *n.* —**lark′i·ness, lark′ish·ness,** *n.* —**lark′ing·ly,** *adv.* —**lark′ish, lark′y,** *adj.* —**lark′ish·ly,** *adv.* —**lark′some,** *adj.*

lark′ bun′ting, a finch, *Calamospiza melanocorys,* of the western U.S., the male of which is black with a large, white patch on each wing.

lark′ spar′row, a North American sparrow, *Chondestes grammacus,* having brownish and white plumage.

lark·spur (lärk′spûr′), *n.* any plant of the genus *Delphinium,* characterized by the spur-shaped formation of the calyx and petals. [LARK[1] + SPUR]

Rocket larkspur, *Delphinium ajacis*

Lark·spur (lärk′spûr′), *n.* a town in W California. 5710 (1960).

Larks·ville (lärks′vil), *n.* a town in central Pennsylvania. 4390 (1960).

Lar′mor preces′sion (lär′môr), *Physics.* the precession of charged particles, as electrons, placed in a magnetic field, the frequency of the precession (**Lar′mor fre′quency**) being equal to the electronic charge times the strength of the magnetic field divided by 4π times the mass. [named after Sir Joseph *Larmor* (1857–1942), English mathematician]

Lar′mor the′orem, *Physics.* the theorem that an electron subjected only to the force exerted by the nucleus about which it is moving will undergo Larmor precession but no other change in motion when placed in a magnetic field.

Lar·ned (lär′nid), *n.* a town in central Kansas. 5001 (1960).

La Roche·fou·cauld (lᴀ rōsh fōō kō′), **Fran·çois** (fʀäɴ swᴀ′), **6th Duc de,** 1613–80, French moralist and composer of epigrams and maxims.

La Ro·chelle (lᴀ rō shel′), a seaport in and the capital of Charente Maritime, in W France; besieged while a Huguenot stronghold 1627–29. 68,445 (1962).

La·rose (lə rōz′), *n.* a town in SE Louisiana. 2796 (1960).

La·rousse (lᴀ rōōs′), *n.* **Pierre A·tha·nase** (pyeʀ ᴀ tᴀ näz′), 1817–75, French grammarian, lexicographer, and encyclopedist.

Lar·ri·gan (lar′ə gən), *n. U.S. and Canada.* a knee-high boot of oiled leather with a moccasin foot, worn by lumbermen and trappers. [?]

lar·ri·kin (lar′ə kin), *Australian Slang.* —*n.* 1. a street rowdy; hoodlum. —*adj.* 2. disorderly; rowdy. [?] —**lar′ri·kin·ism,** *n.*

lar·rup (lar′əp), *v.t.,* **-ruped, -rup·ing.** *Dial.* to beat or thrash. [? < D *larpen* to thresh with flails] —**lar′rup·er,** *n.*

lar·ry (lar′ē), *n., pl.* **-ries.** a hoe with a perforated blade for mixing mortar or plaster. [? special use of LARRY]

Lar·ry (lar′ē), *n.* a boy's given name, form of **Lawrence, Laurence, Laurance.**

Lars (lärz; *Swed., Nor.* läʀs), *n.* a boy's given name, form of **Lawrence.**

Lar·sa (lär′sə), *n.* an ancient Sumerian city in southern Iraq: archaeological site.

l-ar·te·re·nol (el′är tēr′ə nōl′, -nôl′, -nol′), *n. Biochem.* levarterenol.

lar·um (lar′əm), *n.* alarum.

lar·va (lär′və), *n., pl.* **-vae** (-vē). 1. *Entomol.* the immature, wingless, feeding stage of an insect that undergoes complete metamorphosis. 2. any animal in an analogous immature form. 3. the young of any invertebrate animal. 4. **larvae,** *Rom. Antiq.* malignant ghosts, as lemures. [< NL special use of L *larva* a ghost, specter, mask, skeleton; akin to LARES]

lar·val (lär′vəl), *adj.* 1. of, pertaining to, or in the form of a larva. 2. Also, **lar·vate** (lär′vāt). *Pathol.* (of disease) masked; not clearly defined. [< L *larvāl(is).* See LARVA, -AL[1]]

lar′va mi′grans, *Vet. Pathol.* See **creeping eruption.** [< NL: lit., migrating larva]

lar·vi·cide (lär′vi sīd′), *n.* an agent for killing larvae. [LARV(A) + -I- + -CIDE] —**lar′vi·cid′al,** *adj.*

lar·vip·a·rous (lär vip′ər əs), *adj. Zool.* producing larvae, as certain insects and mollusks. [LARV(A) + -I- + -PAROUS]

lar·viv·o·rous (lär viv′ər əs), *adj.* larva-eating. [LARV(A) + -I- + -VOROUS]

laryng-, var. of **laryngo-** before a vowel: *laryngectomy.*

la·ryn·ge·al (lə rin′jē əl, -jəl, lar′ən jē′əl), *adj.* 1. of, pertaining to, or located in the larynx. 2. *Phonet.* articulated in the larynx. —*n.* 3. *Phonet.* a laryngeal sound. Also, **la·ryn·gal** (lə ring′gəl). [< NL *larynge(us)* of, pertaining to the larynx (see LARYNG-, -EOUS) + -AL[1]] —**la·ryn′ge·al·ly,** *adv.*

lar·yn·gec·to·mee (lar′ən jek′tə mē′), *n.* a person upon whom a laryngectomy has been performed. [LARYNGECTOM(Y) + -EE]

lar·yn·gec·to·mize (lar′ən jek′tə mīz′), *v.t.,* **-mized, -miz·ing.** *Surg.* to perform a laryngectomy on. [LARYNGECTOM(Y) + -IZE]

lar·yn·gec·to·my (lar′ən jek′tə mē), *n., pl.* **-mies.** *Surg.* excision of part or all of the larynx. [LARYNG- + -ECTOMY]

lar·yn·gi·tis (lar′ən jī′tis), *n. Pathol.* inflammation of the larynx. [LARYNG- + -ITIS] —**lar·yn·git·ic** (lar′ən jit′ik), *adj.*

laryngo-, a combining form of **larynx:** *laryngotomy.* Also, *esp. before a vowel,* **laryng-.** [comb. form repr. NL, Gk *lárynx* (s. *laryng-*) LARYNX; see -O-]

lar·yn·gol·o·gy (lar′ing gol′ə jē), *n.* the branch of medicine dealing with the larynx. [LARYNGO- + -LOGY] —**la·ryn·go·log·i·cal** (lə ring′gə loj′i kəl), **la·ryn·go·log′ic,** *adj.* —**lar′yn·gol′o·gist,** *n.*

la·ryn·go·pha·ryn·ge·al (lə ring′gō fə rin′jē əl, -jəl, -far′in jē′əl), *adj.* of, pertaining to, or involving the larynx and pharynx. [LARYNGO- + PHARYNGEAL]

la·ryn·go·phar·ynx (lə ring′gō far′ingks), *n., pl.* **-pha·ryn·ges** (-fə rin′jēz), **-phar·ynx·es.** *Anat.* the lower part of the pharynx, behind the larynx. [LARYNGO- + PHARYNX]

la·ryn·go·scope (lə ring′gə skōp′), *n. Med.* an apparatus for examining the larynx. [LARYNGO- + -SCOPE] —**la·ryn·go·scop·ic** (lə ring′gə skop′ik), **la·ryn′go·scop′i·cal,** *adj.* —**la·ryn′go·scop′i·cal·ly,** *adv.* —**lar·yn·gos·co·pist** (lar′ing gos′kə pist), *n.*

lar·yn·gos·co·py (lar′ing gos′kə pē), *n., pl.* **-pies.** *Med.* an examination by means of a laryngoscope. [LARYNGO- + -SCOPY]

lar·yn·got·o·my (lar′ing got′ə mē), *n., pl.* **-mies.** *Surg.* incision of the larynx. [LARYNGO- + -TOMY]

la·ryn·go·tra·che·al (lə ring′gō trā′kē əl), *adj.* of, pertaining to, or involving the larynx and trachea. [LARYNGO- + TRACHEAL]

Human larynx (Section) A, Epiglottis; B, Hyoid bone; C, Thyroid cartilage; D, Esophagus; E, Cricoid cartilage; F, Trachea

lar·ynx (lar′ingks), *n., pl.* **la·ryn·ges** (lə rin′jēz), **lar·ynx·es.** 1. *Anat.* a. a muscular and cartilaginous structure lined with mucous membrane at the upper part of the trachea in man, in which the vocal cords are located. 2. *Zool.* a. a similar vocal organ in other mammals. b. a corresponding structure in certain lower animals. [< NL < Gk: the throat, gullet, larynx]

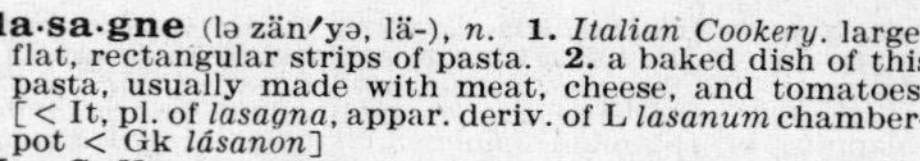

la·sa·gne (lə zän′yə, lä-), *n.* 1. *Italian Cookery.* large, flat, rectangular strips of pasta. 2. a baked dish of this pasta, usually made with meat, cheese, and tomatoes. [< It, pl. of *lasagna,* appar. deriv. of L *lasanum* chamber-pot < Gk *lásanon*]

La Salle (lə sal′; *Fr.* lᴀ sᴀl′), **(Re·né) Ro·bert Ca·ve·lier** (ʀə nā′ ʀō beʀ′ kᴀ və lyā′), **Sieur de,** 1643–87, French explorer of North America.

Las An·i·mas (las an′ə məs), a town in SE Colorado. 3402 (1960).

las·car (las′kər), *n.* 1. an East Indian sailor. 2. *Anglo-Indian.* an artilleryman. Also, **lashkar.** [< Pg *laschar,* short for *lasquarin* soldier < Urdu *lashkarī* < Pers, equiv. to *lashkar* army + *-ī* suffix of appurtenance]

Las Ca·sas (läs kä′säs), **Bar·to·lo·mé de** (bär tô′lô me′ de), 1474–1566, Spanish Dominican missionary and historian in the Americas.

Las·caux′ Cave′ (lᴀs kō′), a cave in Lascaux, France, containing prehistoric wall drawings and wall paintings probably of the Aurignacian culture.

las·civ·i·ous (lə siv′ē əs), *adj.* 1. inclined to lustfulness; wanton; lewd: *a lascivious, girl-chasing old man.* 2. arousing sexual desire: *lascivious behavior; lascivious photographs.* 3. indicating sexual interest or expressive of lust or lewdness: *a lascivious smirk; a lascivious gesture.* [< L *lascīvi(a)* playfulness, wantonness (*lascīv(us)* playful, wanton + *-ia* -IA) + -OUS] —**las·civ′i·ous·ly,** *adv.* —**las·civ′i·ous·ness,** *n.*

Las Cru·ces (läs krōō′sis), a city in S New Mexico, on the Rio Grande. 29,367 (1960).

lase (lāz), *v.i.,* **lased, las·ing.** *Optics.* (of a crystal) to be suitable for use as a laser. [back formation from LASER]

la·ser (lā′zər), *n.* See **optical maser.** [*l(ight) a(mplification by) s(timulated) e(mission of) r(adiation)*]

La Se·re·na (lä se ʀe′nä), a seaport in central Chile. 37,618 (1951).

lash[1] (lash), *n.* 1. the flexible part of a whip; the piece of cord or the like forming the extremity of a whip. 2. a swift stroke or blow, with a whip or the like, given as a punishment: *He was sentenced to 20 lashes.* 3. something that goads or pains in a manner compared to that of a whip: *They suffered under the constant lash of his sharp tongue.* 4. a swift dashing or sweeping movement; a switch: *a lash of an animal's tail.* 5. a violent beating or impact, as of waves, rain, etc., against something. 6. an eyelash. 7. Also called **neck cord.** a cord or a series of cords for lifting the warp in weaving a figured fabric. —*v.t.* 8. to strike or beat, usually with a whip or something slender and flexible. 9. to beat violently or sharply against: *The rain lashed the trees.* 10. to drive by or as if by strokes of a whip: *He lashed them on to further effort.* 11. to attack severely with words: *She lashed the students with harsh criticism.* 12. to dash, fling, or switch suddenly and swiftly: *The crocodile lashed its tail furiously.* —*v.i.* 13. to strike vigorously at someone or something, as with a weapon, whip, or the like (often fol. by *out*): *He lashed wildly at his attackers.* 14. to attack or reprove someone with harsh words (often fol. by *out*): *The article lashed out at social injustice.* 15. to move suddenly and swiftly; rush, dash, or flash: *The coiled snake lashed suddenly.* 16. *Chiefly Brit.* to spend money lavishly or foolishly (usually fol. by *out*). [ME *lasshe,* perh. imit.] —**lash′er,** *n.* —**lash′ing·ly,** *adv.* —**lash′less,** *adj.*

lash[2] (lash), *v.t.* to bind or fasten with a rope, cord, or the like. [late ME *lasschyn* < MD *lasschen* to patch, sew together, scarf (timber); akin to G *Lasche* flap, latchet] —**lash′er,** *n.* —**lash′ing·ly,** *adv.*

lash′ and car′ry, *Naut.* to awaken, get out of one's hammock, and prepare for duty.

lashed (lasht), *adj.* having lashes or eyelashes, esp. of a specified kind or description (usually used in combination): *a long-lashed beauty.* [LASH[1] + -ED[3]]

lash·ing[1] (lash′ing), *n.* 1. the act of one who or that which lashes. 2. a whipping with or as if with a lash. 3. a severe scolding; tongue-lashing. [LASH[1] + -ING[1]]

lash·ing[2] (lash′ing), *n.* 1. a binding or fastening with a rope or the like. 2. the rope or the like used. [LASH[2] + -ING[1]]

lash·ings (lash′ingz), *n.pl. Chiefly Brit. Informal.* an abundance; plenty (usually fol. by *of*): *lashings of fresh strawberries.* [pl. of LASHING[1]; see LASH[1], def. 16]

Lash·io (läsh′yō), *n.* a town in N Burma, NE of Mandalay: the SW terminus of the Burma Road. ab. 5000.

lash·kar (lash′kər), *n.* lascar.

Lash·kar (lush′kər), *n.* a part of Gwalior city in N India. 241,577 urban community (1951).

lash′ line′, a rope or cord for lashing together the edges of two flats or other pieces of theatrical scenery.

lash′ rail′, *Naut.* a rail, solidly fixed to the bulwarks of a vessel, to which objects on deck can be lashed.

Las·ker (läs′kəʀ), *n.* **E·ma·nu·el** (ā mä′nōō el), 1868–1941, German chess player, mathematician, and author.

Las·ki (las′kē), *n.* **Harold Joseph,** 1893–1950, English political scientist and writer.

Las Me·ni·nas (*Sp.* läs me nē′näs). See **Maids of Honor.**

La Soi·rée a·vec Mon·sieur Teste (*Fr.* lᴀ swᴀ ʀā ᴀ vek mə syœ test′). See **Evening With Mr. Teste, An.**

Las Pal·mas (läs päl′mäs), a seaport on NE Gran Canaria, in the central Canary Islands. 193,984 (est. 1960).

La Spe·zia (lä spe′tsyä), a seaport in NW Italy, on the Ligurian Sea: naval base. 121,191 (1961).

lass (las), *n.* 1. a girl or young woman, esp. one who is unmarried. 2. a female sweetheart: *a young lad and his lass.* [ME *lasse;* < ?]

Las·sa (lä′sə, -sä), *n.* Lhasa.

Las·salle (lə sal′; *Ger.* lä säl′), *n.* **Fer·di·nand** (fûr′dᵊnand′; *Ger.* feʀ′di nänt′), 1825–64, German socialist and writer.

Las·sell (lä sel′), *n.* a crater in the third quadrant of the face of the moon: about 14 miles in diameter.

Las′sen Peak′ (las′ən), an active volcano in N California, in the S Cascade Range. 10,465 ft. Also called **Mount Lassen.**

Las′sen Volcan′ic Na′tional Park′, a national park in N California, in the S Cascade Range, including Lassen Peak. 163 sq. mi.

las·sie (las′ē), *n.* a young girl; lass. [LASS + -IE]

Las·sie (las′ē), *n.* a girl's given name. Also, **Las′se.**

las·si·tude (las′i to͞od′, -tyo͞od′), *n.* **1.** weariness of body or mind from strain, oppressive climate, etc.; languor. **2.** a condition of indolent indifference: *He abandoned himself to the pleasant lassitude of the warm summer afternoon.* [< L *lassitūdō* weariness, equiv. to *lass(us)* weary + *-i-* -I- + *-tūdō* -TUDE]

las·so (las′ō, la so͞o′), *n., pl.* **-sos, -soes,** *v.,* **-soed, -so·ing.** —*n.* **1.** a long rope or line of hide or other material with a running noose at one end, used for roping horses, cattle, etc.; lariat. —*v.t.* **2.** to catch with a lasso. [< Sp *lazo* < L *laqueus* bond; see LACE] —**las′so·er,** *n.*

last[1] (last, läst), *adj. a superl. of* **late** *with* **later** *as compar.* **1.** occurring or coming after all others, as in time, order, or place: *the last line on a page.* **2.** most recent; next before the present; latest: *last week; last Friday.* **3.** being the only remaining: *one's last dollar; the last outpost; a last chance.* **4.** final: *in his last hours.* **5.** conclusive; definitive: *He is determined to have the last word in the argument.* **6.** utmost; extreme: *the last degree of delight.* **7.** coming after all others in importance. **8.** coming after all others in suitability or likelihood: *He is the last person we'd want to represent us.* **9.** *Eccles.* (of the sacraments of penance, viaticum, or extreme unction) extreme or final: administered to a person dying or in danger of dying. **10.** individual; single: *The lecture won't start until every last person is seated.* —*adv.* **11.** after all others: *He arrived last at the party.* **12.** on the most recent occasion: *When last seen, the suspect was wearing a checked suit.* **13.** in the end; finally; in conclusion. —*n.* **14.** one who or that which is last. **15.** a final appearance or mention: *We've seen the last of her. That's the last we'll hear of it.* **16.** the end or conclusion: *We are going on vacation the last of September.* **17. at last,** after a lengthy pause or delay: *He was lost in thought for several minutes, but at last he spoke.* **18. at long last,** after much annoying or troublesome delay: *The ship docked at long last.* **19. breathe one's last,** to die: *He was nearly 90 when he breathed his last.* [ME *last, latst,* syncopated var. of *latest,* OE *latest, lætest,* superl. of *læt,* LATE]

—**Syn. 1.** LAST, FINAL, ULTIMATE refer to what comes as an ending. That which is LAST comes or stands after all others in a stated series or succession; LAST may refer to objects or activities: *a seat in the last row.* That which is FINAL comes at the end, or serves to end or terminate, admitting of nothing further; FINAL is rarely used of objects: *to make a final attempt.* That which is ULTIMATE (literally, most remote) is the last that can be reached, as in progression or regression, experience, or a course of investigation: *ultimate truths.*

—**Usage.** As can be seen from the inflected forms above, LAST is properly a superlative form of LATE, with LATER and, formerly, LATTER as comparatives. Therefore, English speakers who insist on precision maintain that LATTER should be used only to refer to the second of two items, with LAST being confined to the final item in a list of three or more. (LATER is not used in this sense in modern English.) *Of the two choices, I prefer the latter. John, George, and James were her sons, and she obviously favored the last.* See **comparative, superlative.**

last[2] (last, läst), *v.i.* **1.** to go on or continue in time: *The festival lasted three weeks.* **2.** to continue unexpended or unexhausted; be enough: *We'll enjoy ourselves while our money lasts.* **3.** to continue in force, vigor, effectiveness, etc.: *Only the strongest runners can last for the whole course.* **4.** to continue or remain in usable condition for a reasonable period of time: *They were handsome shoes but they didn't last.* —*v.t.* **5.** to continue to survive for the duration of (often fol. by *out*): *They lasted the war in Switzerland. Occasional food packages helped them last out the famine.* [ME *lasten,* OE *lǣstan* to follow, (lit., go in the tracks of), perform, continue, last; c. G *leisten* to follow, Goth *laistjan.* See LAST[3]] —**Syn. 1.** See **continue.**

last[3] (last, läst), *n.* **1.** a wooden or metal model of the human foot on which boots or shoes are shaped or repaired. **2. stick to one's last,** to keep to that work, field, etc., in which one is competent or skilled. —*v.t.* **3.** to shape on or fit to a last. [ME; OE *lǣste;* c. G *Leisten;* akin to OE *lāst,* Goth *laists* track] —**last′er,** *n.*

last[4] (last, läst), *n.* any of various large units of weight or capacity, varying in amount in different localities and for different commodities, often equivalent to 4000 pounds. [ME; OE *hlæst;* c. D *last* G *Last* load: akin to LADE]

last[5] (last, läst), *n. Naut.* miter (def. 6).

Last′ Days′ of Pompe′ii, The, a historical novel (1834) by Edward Bulwer-Lytton.

last-ditch (last′dich′, läst′-), *adj.* **1.** made in a final, desperate effort to avoid calamity: *a last-ditch attempt to avert war.* **2.** fought with every resource at one's command: *a last-ditch battle for the pennant.* [LAST[1] + DITCH] —**last′-ditch′er,** *n.*

Las·tex (las′teks), *n. Trademark.* a yarn made from a core of latex rubber covered with fabric strands.

last-in, first-out (last′in′ fûrst′out′, läst′-), an inventory plan based on the assumption that materials constituting manufacturing costs should be carried on the books at their current market price. *Abbr.:* LIFO Cf. **first-in, first-out.**

last·ing (las′ting, lä′sting), *adj.* **1.** that lasts; enduring; permanent; durable: *a lasting friendship.* —*n.* **2.** a strong, durable, closely woven fabric for shoe uppers, coverings on buttons, etc. [ME (adj.) (n. use for material is later). See LAST[2], -ING[2], -ING[1]] —**last′ing·ly,** *adv.* —**last′ing·ness,** *n.*

Last′ Judg′ment, judgment (def. 8).

last·ly (last′lē, läst′-), *adv.* in conclusion; in the last place; finally. [ME *lestely.* See LAST[1], -LY]

last′ mile′, the distance walked by a condemned man from his cell to the place of execution.

last′ name′, surname (def. 1).

Last′ of the Mohi′cans, The, a major historical novel (1826) by James Fenimore Cooper. Cf. **Leather-Stocking Tales.**

last′ post′, See under **post**[2] (def. 7).

last′ quar′ter, *Astron.* the instant, approximately one week after a full moon, when half of the moon's disk is illuminated by the sun. See diag. under **moon.**

last′ straw′, the last of a succession of irritations that strains one's patience to the limit: *The service in this garage has been bad before, but this is the last straw.* [after the proverb "It is the *last straw* that breaks the camel's back."]

Last′ Sup′per, 1. the supper of Jesus and His disciples on the eve of His Crucifixion. Cf. **Lord's Supper** (def. 1). **2.** a work of art representing this. **3.** (*italics.*) **The,** a mural (1495–98) by Leonardo da Vinci.

last′ word′, 1. the closing remark, as in an argument: *He succeeded in having the last word.* **2.** a final or definitive work, statement, etc.: *This paper is the last word on the treatment of the disease.* **3.** *Informal.* the latest, most modern thing: *Casual hairdos will be the last word this season.*

Las Ve·gas (läs vā′gəs), **1.** a city in SE Nevada. 64,405 (1960). **2.** a city in central New Mexico. 13,818 (1960).

La Sym·pho·nie Pas·to·rale (*Fr.* lȧ saN fô nē pȧs tô rȧl′). See **Pastoral Symphony, The.**

lat (lät), *n., pl.* **lats, la·ti** (lä′tē). a former silver coin of Latvia, equal to 100 santimi. [< Lettish *lats,* equiv. to *Lat(vija)* Latvia + *-s* nom. sing. n. ending]

lāt (lät), *n. Archit.* (in India) a monolithic stamba. [< Hindi]

Lat., Latin.

lat., latitude.

la·tah (lä′tə), *n.* a pattern of neurotic behavior found chiefly among Malays and characterized by the compulsive imitation of the actions and words of others. Also, **la′ta.** [< Malay]

Lat·a·ki·a (lat′ə kē′ə *or, esp. for 1,* lä′tä kē′ä), *n.* **1.** a seaport in NW Syria. 72,378 (1962). Ancient, **Laodicea. 2.** a variety of Turkish tobacco.

latch (lach), *n.* **1.** a device for holding a door, gate, or the like, closed, consisting basically of a bar falling or sliding into a catch, groove, hole, etc. —*v.t.* **2.** to close or fasten with a latch. —*v.i.* **3.** to close tightly so that the latch is secured: *The door won't latch.* **4. latch onto,** *Informal.* **a.** to take possession of; obtain; get. **b.** to acquire understanding of; comprehend. **c.** to attach oneself to; join in with: *She latched onto another man within a year after her husband's death.* [ME *lacche(n),* OE *lǣccan* to take hold of, catch, seize; akin to Gk *lázesthai* to take]

latch·et (lach′it), *n. Archaic.* a strap or lace used to fasten a shoe. [ME *lachet* < MF, dial. var. of *lacet.* See LACE, -ET]

latch·ing (lach′ing), *n.* any of the loops by which a bonnet is attached to a sail. [ME; see LATCH, -ING[1]]

latch·key (lach′kē′), *n., pl.* **-keys.** a key for drawing back or releasing a latch, esp. on an outer door. [LATCH + KEY[1]]

latch·string (lach′string′), *n.* a string passed through a hole in a door, for raising the latch from the outside. [LATCH + STRING]

late (lāt), *adj.,* **lat·er** or **lat·ter, lat·est** or **last,** *adv.* **lat·er, lat·est.** —*adj.* **1.** occurring, coming, or being after the usual or proper time: *late frosts; a late spring.* **2.** continued until after the usual time or hour; protracted: *a late session.* **3.** coming toward the end of day or well into the night: *a late hour.* **4.** belonging to the time just before the present moment; most recent: *They were reading a late bulletin that had come in.* **5.** immediately preceding the present one: *the late attorney general.* **6.** recently deceased: *the late Mr. Phipps.* **7.** occurring at an advanced stage in life: *a late marriage.* **8.** belonging to an advanced period or stage in the history or development of something: *the late phase of feudalism.* **9. of late,** lately; recently: *The days have been getting warmer of late.* —*adv.* **10.** after the usual or proper time, or after delay: *to arrive late.* **11.** until after the usual time or hour; until an advanced hour, esp. of the night: *to work late.* **12.** at or to an advanced time, period, or stage: *The flowers keep their blossoms late in warm climates.* **13.** recently but no longer: *a man late of Chicago, now living in Philadelphia.* [ME; OE *læt* slow, late; c. G *lass* slothful, Icel *latr,* Goth *lats,* L *lassus* tired] —**late′ness,** *n.*

—**Syn. 1.** tardy; slow, dilatory; delayed, belated. **5.** former.

late′ blight′, *Plant Pathol.* a disease of plants, esp. potatoes, celery, etc., characterized by spotting, blighting, and withering or decay of the entire plant, caused by any of several fungi, as *Phytophthora infestans* or *Septoria apii.*

late·com·er (lāt′kum′ər), *n.* one who arrives late: *The latecomers were seated after the overture.* [LATE + COMER]

lat·ed (lā′tid), *adj. Literary.* belated. [LATE + -ED[2]]

la·teen (la tēn′, lə-), *adj.* pertaining to or having a lateen sail or sails. [< F *(voile) latine* Latin (sail)]

la·teen-rigged (la tēn′rigd′, lə-), *adj.* having lateen sails.

lateen′ sail′, a triangular sail set on a long sloping yard, used esp. on the Mediterranean Sea.

Lateen sail

Late′ George′ Ap′ley, The (ap′lē), a novel (1937) by J. P. Marquand.

Late′ Greek′, the Greek of the early Byzantine Empire and of patristic literature, from about A.D. 300 to 700.

Late′ Lat′in, the Latin of the late Western Roman Empire and of patristic literature, from about A.D. 300 to 700.

late·ly (lāt′lē), *adv.* of late; recently; not long since: *He has lately started going to the country.* [ME; see LATE, -LY]

la·ten·cy (lāt′ən sē), *n.* **1.** the state of being latent. **2.** *Computer Technol.* the time required to locate the first bit or character in a storage location, expressed as access time minus word time. **3.** See **latent period.** [LAT(ENT) + -ENCY]

la′tency pe′riod, *Psychoanal.* the stage of personality development, extending from about 4 or 5 years of age to the beginning of puberty, during which sexual urges appear to lie dormant.

La Tène (*Fr.* lȧ ten′), **1.** *Archaeol.* designating the period or culture of the late Iron Age typified by the structural remains, swords, tools, utensils, etc., found at La Tène. Cf. **Hallstattan. 2.** a shallow area at the E end of the Lake of Neuchâtel, Switzerland, where these remains were found.

la·ten·si·fy (lā ten′sə fī′), *v.t.,* **-fied, -fy·ing.** *Photog.* to increase the developability of (the latent image on a film or plate) after exposure. [LAT(ENT) + (IN)TENSIFY, modeled on *latensification,* b. LATENT and INTENSIFICATION] —**la·ten·si·fi·ca·tion** (lā ten′sə fə kā′shən), *n.*

la·tent (lāt′ənt), *adj.* **1.** present but not visible, apparent, or actualized; existing as potential: *latent ability; latent brutality; latent resources.* **2.** *Pathol.* (of an infectious agent or disease) remaining in a resting or hidden phase; dormant. **3.** *Psychol.* existing in concealed or dormant form but potentially able to achieve expression: *a latent emotion; latent powers.* **4.** *Bot.* (of buds that are not externally manifest) dormant or undeveloped. [< L *latent-* (s. of *latēns*) lying hidden, prp. of *latēre;* see -ENT] —**la′tent·ly,** *adv.*

—**Syn. 1.** dormant, quiescent, veiled. LATENT, POTENTIAL refer to powers or possibilities existing but hidden or not yet actualized. LATENT emphasizes the hidden character or the dormancy of what is named: *latent qualities, defects, diseases.* That which is POTENTIAL exists in an as yet undeveloped state, but is thought of as capable of coming into full being or activity at some future time: *potential genius, tragedy.* POTENTIAL may be applied also to tangibles: *High-tension wires are a potential source of danger.* —**Ant. 1.** open, active; kinetic.

la′tent con′tent, *Psychoanal.* the hidden meaning of a dream, discoverable by analysis of the content of the dream.

la′tent heat′, *Physics.* heat absorbed or radiated during a change of phase at constant temperature and pressure. Cf. **heat of fusion, heat of vaporization.**

la′tent pe′riod, 1. *Pathol.* the period that elapses before the presence of a disease is manifested by symptoms. **2.** *Physiol.* the lag between stimulus and reaction. Also called **latency.**

la′tent strabis′mus, *Ophthalm.* the tendency, controllable by muscular effort, for one or both eyes to exhibit strabismus.

lat·er·al (lat′ər əl), *adj.* **1.** of or pertaining to the side; situated at, proceeding from, or directed to a side: *a lateral view.* **2.** *Phonet.* articulated so that the breath passes on either or both sides of the tongue, as *l.* —*n.* **3.** a lateral part or extension, as a branch or shoot. **4.** *Mining.* a small drift off to the side of a principal one. **5.** *Phonet.* a lateral speech sound. **6.** *Football.* See **lateral pass.** —*v.i.* **7.** *Football.* to throw a lateral pass. [< L *laterāl(is)* of the side, equiv. to *later-* (s. of *latus*) side + *-ālis* -AL[1]] —**lat′er·al·ly,** *adv.*

lat′eral canal′, 1. a canal running parallel to a stream that is inconvenient or impossible to navigate. **2.** one of a number of irrigation canals distributing water from a main canal.

lat′eral chain′, *Chem.* See **side chain.**

lat′eral fis′sure, *Anat.* the fissure separating the frontal, temporal, and parietal lobes of the cerebrum. Also called **fissure of Sylvius, Sylvian fissure.**

lat·e·ral·i·ty (lat′ə ral′i tē), *n.* **1.** the use of one hand in preference to the other. Cf. **handedness. 2.** the dominance or superior development of one side of the body. [LATERAL + -ITY]

lat′eral line′, the line, or system of lines, of sensory structures along the head and sides of fishes and amphibians, by which the animal is believed to detect water current and pressure changes and vibrations.

lat′eral lisp′, *Phonet.* See under **lisp** (def. 2).

lat′eral magnifica′tion, *Optics.* the ratio of the height of the image to the height of the object in a lens or other optical system. Also called **transverse magnification.**

lat′eral mer′istem, meristem located along the sides of a part, as a stem or root.

lat′eral moraine′, a moraine formed at the side of a glacier.

lat′eral pass′, *Football.* a pass thrown parallel to the goal line or backward from the position of the passer.

lat′eral plane′, *Naval Archit.* the area represented by the submerged portion of the midship fore-and-aft section of a hull, measured along with the area represented by the submerged area of any centerboard, leeboard, or the like, and divided over the submerged area of the transverse midship section to obtain a factor revealing the lateral resistance of the vessel.

lat′eral resist′ance, *Naval Archit.* resistance to sidewise motion caused by wind pressure, supplied by the immersed portion of a hull of a vessel and sometimes by a projecting keel, centerboard, leeboard, or the like.

lat′eral sys′tem, a system of coding navigational aids by shape, color, and number, according to the side of a channel they occupy and their relative position along that side. Cf. **cardinal system.**

lat′eral tan′gent arc′. See **arc of Lowitz.**

Lat·er·an (lat′ər ən), *n.* the church of St. John Lateran, the cathedral church of the city of Rome; the church of the pope as bishop of Rome.

Lat′eran Coun′cil, *Rom. Cath. Ch.* any of the five ecumenical councils (1123, 1139, 1179, 1215, 1512–17) held in the Lateran Palace.

Lat′eran Pal′ace, a palace in Rome used as the papal residence from the 4th century A.D. to the removal of the papal court to Avignon, rebuilt in 1586, and now a museum for classical and Christian antiques.

Lat′er Han′, the Han dynasty after the interregnum A.D. 9–25. Cf. **Han** (def. 1), **Earlier Han.**

lat·er·i·grade (lat′ər ə grād′), *adj.* having a sideways manner of moving, as a crab. [*lateri-* (comb. form of L *latus,* s. *later-*) side, flank + -GRADE]

lat·er·ite (lat′ə rīt′), *n. Geol.* **1.** a reddish ferruginous soil formed in tropical regions by the decomposition of the underlying rocks. **2.** a similar soil formed of materials deposited by water. **3.** any soil produced by the decomposition of the rocks beneath it. [< L *later* brick, tile + -ITE[1]] —**lat·er·it·ic** (lat′ə rit′ik), *adj.*

lat·er·i·tious (lat′ə rish′əs), *adj.* of the color of brick; brick-red. Also, **lat′er·i′ceous.** [< L *laterīti(us)* of brick. See LATERITE, -ITIOUS]

lat·est (lā′tist), *adj. a superl. of* **late** *with* **later** *as compar.* **1.** coming after all others; occurring last. **2.** most recent; current: *latest fashions.* **3. at the latest,** not any later than (a specified time): *Be at the airport by 7 o'clock at the latest.* **4. the latest,** the most recent advance, development, disclosure, etc.: *Have you heard the latest about the Joneses? This is the latest in phonographs.* [late ME; see LATE, -EST]

late′ wood′, summerwood.

la·tex (lā′teks), *n., pl.* **lat·i·ces** (lat′i sēz′), **la·tex·es. 1.** a milky liquid in certain plants, as milkweeds, euphorbias, poppies, the plants yielding India rubber, etc., which coagulates on exposure to air. **2.** *Chem.* any emulsion in water of finely divided particles of synthetic rubber or plastic. [< NL, special use of L *latex* something liquid]

lath (lath, läth), *n., pl.* **laths** (lat͟hz, laths, lät͟hz, läths), *v.* —*n.* **1.** a thin, narrow strip of wood, used with other strips to form latticework, a backing for plaster or stucco, a support for slates and other roofing materials, etc. **2.** a number of such strips. **3.** work consisting of such strips. **4.** wire mesh or the like used in place of wooden laths as a backing for plasterwork. **5.** a thin, narrow, flat piece of wood used for any purpose. —*v.t.* **6.** to cover or line with laths. [ME *la(th)the;* r. ME *latt,* OE *lætt;* c. G *Latte,* D *lat*] —**lath′like′,** *adj.*

lathe (lāt͟h), *n., v.,* **lathed, lath·ing.** —*n.* **1.** a machine for use in working metal, wood, etc., which holds the material and rotates it about a horizontal axis against a tool that shapes it. **2.** batten³. —*v.t.* **3.** to cut, shape, or otherwise treat on a lathe. [late ME *lath* stand < Scand; cf. D *-lad* lathe, Icel *hlath* stack, c. OE *hlæd* heap, mound]

Lathe
A, Headstock; B, Tool rest; C, Tailstock; D, Motor

la·thee (lä′tē), *n. Anglo-Indian.* lathi.

lath·er¹ (lat͟h′ər), *n.* **1.** foam or froth made by soap stirred or rubbed in water, as by a brush used in shaving or by hands in washing. **2.** foam or froth formed in profuse sweating, as on a horse. **3.** *Informal.* a state of excitement, agitation, nervous tension, or the like: *He worked up a lather over trifles.* —*v.i.* **4.** to form a lather: *a soap that lathers well.* **5.** to become covered with lather, as a horse. —*v.t.* **6.** to apply lather to; cover with lather: *He lathered his face before shaving.* **7.** *Informal.* to beat or whip. [ME; OE *lēathor* soap; c. Icel *lauthr* (now *löthur*) lather, foam] —**lath′er·er,** *n.*

lath·er² (lat͟h′ər, lä′t͟hər), *n.* a workman who puts up laths. [LATH + -ER¹]

lath·er·y (lat͟h′ə rē), *adj.* consisting of, covered with, or capable of producing lather. [LATHER¹ + -Y¹]

la·thi (lä′tē), *n. Anglo-Indian.* a heavy pole or stick, esp. one used as a club by police. Also, **lathee.** [< Hindi *lāṭhī*]

lath·ing (lath′ing, lä′thing), *n.* **1.** the act or process of applying lath. **2.** a quantity of lath in place. **3.** material used as lath. Also called **lath·work** (lath′wûrk′, läth′-) (for defs. 1, 2). [LATH + -ING¹]

lath′ing ham′mer, a hatchet having a small hammer face for trimming and nailing wooden lath. Also called **lath′ing hatch′et.**

lath·y (lath′ē, lä′thē), *adj.,* **lath·i·er, lath·i·est.** lathlike; long and thin. [LATH + -Y¹]

la·ti (lä′tē), *n.* a pl. of **lat.**

lat·i·ces (lat′i sēz′), *n.* a pl. of **latex.**

lat·i·cif·er·ous (lat′i sif′ər əs), *adj. Bot.* bearing or containing latex. [< L *latici-* (s. of *latex; see* LATEX) + -FEROUS]

lat·i·fun·di·um (lat′ə fun′dē əm), *n., pl.* **-di·a** (-dē ə). *Rom. Hist.* a great estate. [< L, equiv. to *lāt(us)* wide, broad + *-i-* -I- + *fund(us)* a piece of land, farm, estate + *-ium* -IUM]

Lat·i·mer (lat′ə mər), *n.* **Hugh,** c1470–1555, English Protestant Reformation bishop, reformer, and martyr.

Lat·in (lat′ᵊn, -in), *n.* **1.** an Italic language spoken in ancient Rome, fixed in the 2nd or 1st century B.C., and established as the official language of the Roman Empire. **2.** one of the forms of literary Latin, as Medieval Latin, Late Latin, Biblical Latin, Liturgical Latin, or of nonclassical Latin, as Vulgar Latin. **3.** a native or inhabitant of Latium; an ancient Roman. **4.** a member of any of the Latin peoples. **5.** *Rare.* a member of the Latin Church; a Roman Catholic, as distinguished from a member of the Greek Church. —*adj.* **6.** denoting or pertaining to those peoples, as the Italians, French, Spanish, Portuguese, Rumanians, etc., using languages derived from that of ancient Rome, esp. the peoples of Central and South America: *a meeting of the Latin republics.* **7.** of or pertaining to the Latin Church. **8.** of or pertaining to Latium or its inhabitants. **9.** noting or pertaining to the alphabetical script derived from the Etruscan alphabet used from about the 7th century B.C. for the writing of Latin, and since adopted, with modifications and additions of letters such as *w,* by English, French, Turkish, and many other languages. [ME, OE < L *Latīn(us).* See LATIUM, -INE¹]

Lat′in Amer′ica, the part of the American continents south of the United States in which Romance languages are officially spoken. —**Lat′in-A·mer′i·can,** *n., adj.* —**Lat′in Amer′ican.**

Lat·in·ate (lat′ᵊnāt′), *adj.* of, like, pertaining to, or derived from Latin: *his pedantic, Latinate style of writing.* [LATIN + -ATE¹]

Lat′in Church′, the Roman Catholic Church, esp. the branch of this church that employs Liturgical Latin in its liturgy.

Lat′in cross′, an upright or vertical bar crossed near the top by a shorter horizontal bar. See illus. under **cross.**

La·tin·ic (lə tin′ik), *adj.* **1.** of or pertaining to the Latin language or the ancient Latin-speaking peoples. **2.** of or pertaining to the modern Latin peoples or nations. [LATIN + -IC]

Lat·in·ise (lat′ᵊnīz′), *v.t., v.i.,* **-ised, -is·ing.** *Chiefly Brit.* Latinize. —**Lat′in·i·sa′tion,** *n.*

Lat·in·ism (lat′ᵊniz′əm), *n.* a mode of expression imitative of Latin. [< ML *latinism(us).* See LATIN, -ISM]

Lat·in·ist (lat′ᵊnist), *n.* a specialist in Latin. [< ML *latīnist(a).* See LATIN, -IST]

La·tin·i·ty (lə tin′i tē), *n.* **1.** knowledge or use of the Latin language: *bemoaned the lack of Latinity among today's scholars.* **2.** Latin style or idiom. [< L *latīnitās* Latin style. See LATIN, -ITY]

Lat·in·ize (lat′ᵊnīz′), *v.,* **-ized, -iz·ing.** —*v.t.* **1.** to cause to conform to the customs, traditions, beliefs, etc., of the Latins or the Latin Church. **2.** to intermix with Latin elements. **3.** to translate into Latin. —*v.i.* **4.** to use words and phrases from Latin: *He Latinizes frequently in his poetry.* Also, *esp. Brit.,* **Latinise.** [< LL *latīnīz(āre)* (to) translate into Latin. See LATIN, -IZE] —**Lat′in·i·za′tion,** *n.*

La·ti·no (la tē′nō), *n.* an American citizen or resident of Latin-American or Spanish-speaking descent.

Lat′in Quar′ter, the quarter of Paris on the south side of the Seine, frequented for centuries by students and artists.

Lat′in Rite′, **1.** Also called **Roman liturgy, Roman rite.** the forms of worship and liturgy expressed in Liturgical Latin in the Roman Catholic Church in the West. **2.** See **Latin Church.**

Lat′in school′, a secondary school emphasizing instruction in Latin and Greek.

Lat′in square′, *Math.* a square array of numbers, letters, etc., in which each item appears exactly once in each row and column: used in statistical analysis.

La·ti·nus (lə tī′nəs), *n. Rom. Legend.* the father of Lavinia and king of Latium at the time of the arrival of Aeneas.

lat·ish (lā′tish), *adj.* somewhat late. [LATE + -ISH¹]

la·tis·si·mus dor·si (lə tis′ə məs dôr′sī), *pl.* **la·tis·si·mi dor·si** (lə tis′ə mī′ dôr′sī). *Anat.* a broad, flat muscle on each side of the lower part of the back, the action of which draws the arm backward and downward, and rotates the front of the arm toward the body. [< NL; lit., the broadest (muscle) of the back]

La·ti·tia (lə tish′ə, -tē′shə), *n.* a girl's given name. Also, **Laetitia, Letitia.**

lat·i·tude (lat′i to͞od′, -tyo͞od′), *n.* **1.** *Geog.* **a.** the angular distance north or south from the equator of a point on the earth's surface, measured on the meridian of the point. **b.** a place or region as marked by this distance. **2.** freedom from narrow restrictions; permitted freedom of action, opinion, etc.: *He allowed his children a fair amount of latitude in their social life.* **3.** *Astron.* **a.** See **celestial latitude. b.** See **galactic latitude. 4.** *Photog.* the ability of an emulsion to record the brightness values of a subject in their true proportion to one another, expressed as the ratio of the amount of brightness in the darkest possible value to the amount of brightness in the brightest: *a latitude of 1 to 128.* [ME < L *lātitūdō* breadth, equiv. to *lāt(us)* broad + *-i-* -I- + *-tūdō* -TUDE]
—**Syn. 2.** extent, liberty, indulgence. See **range.**

lat·i·tu·di·nal (lat′i to͞od′ᵊnᵊl, -tyo͞od′-), *adj.* of or pertaining to latitude. [< L *lātitūdin-* (s. of *lātitūdō*) LATITUDE + -AL¹] —**lat′i·tu′di·nal·ly,** *adv.*

lat·i·tu·di·nar·i·an (lat′i to͞od′ᵊnâr′ē ən, -tyo͞od′-), *adj.* **1.** allowing or characterized by latitude in opinion or conduct, esp. in religious views. —*n.* **2.** one who is latitudinarian in opinion or conduct. **3.** *Anglican Ch.* one of the churchmen in the 17th century who maintained the wisdom of the episcopal form of government and ritual but denied that they possessed divine origin and authority. [< L *lātitūdin-* (see LATITUDINAL) + -ARIAN] —**lat′i·tu′di·nar′i·an·ism,** *n.*

lat·i·tu·di·nous (lat′i to͞od′ᵊnəs, -tyo͞od′-), *adj.* having latitude, scope, range, breadth, etc., esp. of ideas, interests, interpretations, or the like: *a Renaissance man of latitudinous outlook.* [< L *lātitūdin-* (see LATITUDINAL) + -OUS]

La·ti·um (lā′shē əm), *n.* a country in ancient Italy, SE of Rome.

lat·ke (lät′kə), *n. Jewish Cookery.* a pancake, esp. one made with grated potato. [< Yiddish < Russ *latka*]

La·to·na (lə tō′nə), *n.* **1.** the goddess Leto as identified in Roman mythology. **2.** a girl's given name.

La Tor·tue (lᴀ tôr tʏ′). French name of **Tortuga.**

La Tour (lä to͝or′; *Fr.* lᴀ to͞or′), **Georges de** (zhôrzh də), 1593–1652, French painter.

La Trappe (lᴀ trap′), an abbey in Normandy, France, at which the Trappist order was founded.

La Tra·vi·a·ta (lä trä′vē ä′tə; *It.* lä trä vyä′tä). See **Traviata, La.**

la·treu·tic (la tro͞o′tik), *adj. Rare.* of or pertaining to latria. Also, **la·treu′ti·cal.** [< Gk *latreutik(ós)* of divine service, equiv. to *latreú(ein)* (to) serve (see LATRIA) + *-tikos* -TIC]

la·tri·a (lə trī′ə), *n. Rom. Cath. Theol.* the supreme worship, which may be offered to God only. Cf. **dulia, hyperdulia.** [< LL < Gk *latreía* service, worship, akin to *látris* hired servant; see -IA]

la·trine (lə trēn′), *n.* a toilet or something used as a toilet, as a trench in the earth, esp. one in a military camp, a barracks, or in a military bivouac area. [< F < L *lātrīna,* short for *lavātrīna* place for washing, deriv. of *lavāre* to wash]

La·trobe (lə trōb′), *n.* **Benjamin Henry,** 1764–1820, U.S. architect and engineer, born in England.

-latry, an element occurring in loan words from Greek meaning "worship" (*idolatry*); on this model, used in the formation of compound words (*bardolatry*). [< Gk *-latria.* See LATRIA, -Y³]

lat·ten (lat′ᵊn), *n.* **1.** a brasslike alloy commonly made in thin sheets and formerly much used for church utensils. **2.** tin plate. **3.** any metal in thin sheets. [ME *lato(u)n* < MF *laton* copper-zinc alloy << Ar *lāṭūn* < Turkic; cf. Turk *altin* gold]

lat·ter (lat′ər), *adj.* **1.** being the second mentioned of two (distinguished from *former*): *I prefer the latter proposition to the former.* **2.** more advanced in time; later: *in these latter days of human progress.* **3.** near or comparatively near to the end: *the latter part of the century.* **4.** *Obs.* last; final. [ME *latt(e)re,* OE *lætra,* comp. of *læt* LATE]
—**Usage.** See **last¹.**

lat·ter-day (lat′ər dā′), *adj.* **1.** of a later or following period: *latter-day pioneers.* **2.** of the present period or time; modern: *the latter-day problems of our society.* [LATTER + DAY]

Lat′ter-day Saint′, a Mormon.

lat·ter·ly (lat′ər lē), *adv.* **1.** of late; lately: *He has been latterly finding much to keep himself busy.* **2.** in a later or subsequent part of a period: *Her father was an artist and latterly became a patron of the arts.* [LATTER + -LY]

lat·ter·most (lat′ər mōst′, -məst), *adj.* latest; last. [LATTER + -MOST]

lat·tice (lat′is), *n., v.,* **-ticed, -tic·ing.** —*n.* **1.** a structure of crossed wooden or metal strips usually arranged to form a diagonal pattern of open spaces between the strips. **2.** a window, gate, or the like, consisting of such a structure. **3.** *Physics.* the structure of fissionable and nonfissionable materials geometrically arranged within a nuclear reactor. **4.** Also called **Bravais space lattice, crystal lattice, space lattice.** *Crystall.* an arrangement in space of isolated points (**lat′tice points′**) in a regular pattern, showing the positions of atoms, molecules, or ions in the structure of a crystal. **5.** *Math.* a partially ordered set in which every subset containing exactly two elements has a greatest lower bound or intersection and a least upper bound or union. Cf. **partially ordered set.** —*v.t.* **6.** to furnish with a lattice or latticework. **7.** to form into or arrange like latticework. [ME *latis* < MF *lattis,* deriv. of *latte* lath < Gmc; see LATH] —**lat′tice·like′,** *adj.*

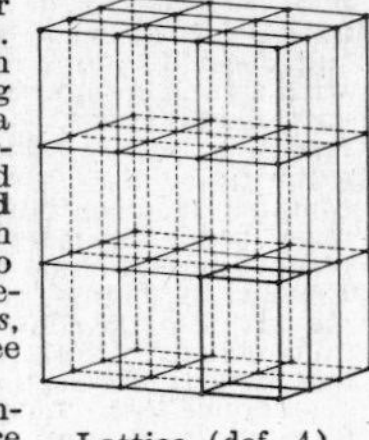

Lattice (def. 4)

lat′tice bridge′, a bridge constructed on the pattern of a lattice truss.

lat·ticed (lat′ist), *adj.* **1.** having a lattice or latticework. **2.** *Biol.* clathrate. [LATTICE + -ED³]

lat′tice gird′er, a trusslike girder having the upper and lower chords connected by latticing.

lat·tice-leaf (lat′is lēf′), *n., pl.* **-leaves.** lace-leaf.

lat′tice truss′, a truss having crisscrossed diagonals between chords.

lat·tice·work (lat′is wûrk′), *n.* **1.** work consisting of crossed strips usually arranged in a diagonal pattern of open spaces. **2.** a lattice. [LATTICE + WORK]

lat·tic·ing (lat′i sing), *n.* **1.** the act or process of furnishing with or making latticework. **2.** latticework. **3.** (in a composite column, girder, or strut) lacing consisting of crisscross strips of wood, iron, or steel. [LATTICE + -ING¹]

lat·ti·ci·nio (lat′i chēn′yō), *n., pl.* **-ci·ni** (-chē′nē). an opaque, white glass first produced in Venice during the Renaissance, often used in thread form to decorate clear glass pieces. [< It < LL *lacticīnium* food prepared with milk; see LACT-]

la·tus rec·tum (lā′təs rek′təm), *pl.* **la·ter·a rec·ta** (lā′tər ə rek′tə). *Geom.* the chord perpendicular to the principal axis and passing through a focus of an ellipse, parabola, or hyperbola. [< NL: lit., straight side]

Lat·vi·a (lat′vē ə, lät′-), *n.* a republic in N Europe, on the Baltic, S of Estonia, an independent state 1918–40; annexed by the Soviet Union 1940; regained independence 1991. 2,681,000; 25,395 sq. mi. *Cap.:* Riga. Latvian, **Lat·vi·ja** (lät′vi yä′).

Lat·vi·an (lat′vē ən), *adj.* **1.** of or pertaining to Latvia, its inhabitants, or their language. —*n.* **2.** a native or inhabitant of Latvia. **3.** Lettish (def. 2). [LATVI(A) + -AN]

laud (lôd), *v.t.* **1.** to praise; extol. [ME *laude* < L *laudāre* to praise, deriv. of *laus* (s. *laud-*) praise]
—*n.* **2.** a song or hymn of praise. **3. lauds,** (*construed as sing. or pl.*) *Eccles.* a canonical hour, marked esp. by psalms of praise, usually recited with matins. [ME *laude,* back formation from *laudes* (pl.) < eccl. L, special use of pl. of L *laus* praise] —**laud′er, lau·da·tor** (lô′dā tər), *n.*
—**Syn. 1.** applaud, celebrate, honor.
—**Ant. 1.** censure.

Laud (lôd), *n.* **William,** 1573–1645, archbishop of Canterbury and opponent of Puritanism: executed for treason.

laud·a·ble (lô′də bəl), *adj.* **1.** praiseworthy or commendable: *a laudable idea.* **2.** *Med. Obs.* healthy; wholesome; not noxious. [late ME < L *laudābil(is).* See LAUD, -ABLE] —**laud′a·bil′i·ty, laud′a·ble·ness,** *n.* —**laud′a·bly,** *adv.*

lau·da·num (lôd′ᵊnəm, lôd′nəm), *n.* **1.** a tincture of opium. **2.** *Obs.* any preparation in which opium is the chief ingredient. [orig. ML var. of LADANUM; arbitrarily used by Paracelsus to name a remedy based on opium]

lau·da·tion (lô dā′shən), *n.* an act or instance of lauding; tribute. [late ME *laudacion* < L *laudātiōn-* (s. of *laudātiō*) a praising, equiv. to *laudāt(us)* praised (ptp. of *laudāre* to LAUD) + *-iōn-* -ION]

laud·a·to·ry (lô′də tôr′ē, -tōr′ē), *adj.* containing or expressing praise: *overwhelmed by the speaker's laudatory remarks.* Also, **laud′a·tive.** [< LL *laudātōri(us).* See LAUDATION, -ORY¹] —**laud′a·to′ri·ly,** *adv.*

Lau·der (lô′dər), *n.* **Sir Harry** (*Harry MacLennan*), 1870–1950, Scottish balladeer and composer.

Laud·i·an (lô′dē ən), *adj.* **1.** of or pertaining to Archbishop Laud or his beliefs, esp. that the Church of England preserves more fully than the Roman Catholic Church the faith and practices of the primitive church and that kings rule by divine right. **2.** noting or pertaining to a style of English Gothic architecture of the early 17th century, characterized by a mixture of medieval and Renaissance motifs, attributed to the influence of the policies of Archbishop Laud. —*n.* **3.** a supporter of Archbishop Laud or of Laudianism. [LAUD + -IAN]

Laud·i·an·ism (lô′dē ə niz′əm), *n.* the policies and practices of Archbishop Laud or his supporters. [LAUDIAN + -ISM]

Laud·i·an·us (lô′dē an′əs, -ā′nəs), *n.* the uncial codex, dating from the 6th or 7th century A.D., that contains portions of the Acts of the Apostles, in Greek and Latin, on facing pages. Cf. **codex** (def. 2). [< NL; see LAUDIAN]

Lau·e (lou′ə), *n.* **Max The·o·dor Fe·lix von** (mäks tā′ō dōr′ fā′liks fən), 1879–1960, German physicist: Nobel prize 1914.

Lau·en·burg (lou′ən bûrg′), *n.* a region in Schleswig-Holstein, in N West Germany: duchy under German rulers 1260–1689; later part of Prussia.

laugh (laf, läf), *v.i.* **1.** to express emotion, as mirth, pleasure, derision, or nervousness, with an audible, vocal expulsion of air from the lungs that can range from a loud burst of sound to a series of quiet chuckles and is usually accompanied by characteristic facial and bodily movements. **2.** to experience the emotion so expressed: *He laughed inwardly at the scene.* **3.** to produce a sound resembling human laughter: *A coyote laughed in the night. They listened to the laughing brook.* —*v.t.* **4.** to drive, put, bring, etc., by or with laughter (often fol. by *out, away, down,* etc.): *They laughed him out of town. We laughed away our troubles.* **5.** to utter with laughter: *He laughed his consent.* **6. laugh at, a.** to make fun of; deride; ridicule: *They were laughing at him, not along with him.* **b.** to show apathy or indifference to; reject: *Industry to a great extent still laughs at the idea that women can be successful as engineers.* **c.** to find sympathetic amusement in: *We can learn to laugh a little at even our most serious foibles.* **7. laugh in** or **up one's sleeve.** See **sleeve** (def. 4). **8. laugh off,** to ridicule or dismiss as absurd: *He had received threats but laughed them off as the work of a crank.* **9. laugh on the other** or **wrong side of one's face** or **mouth,** to be disappointed or depressed; be on the verge of tears: *He'll laugh on the other side of his mouth when somebody finally plays a practical joke on him.* **10. laugh out of court,** to dismiss or depreciate by means of ridicule: *His violent protests were laughed out of court by the others.* —*n.* **11.** the act or sound of laughing; laughter. **12.** an expression of mirth, derision, etc., by laughing. **13. have the last laugh on,** to prove ultimately successful after a seeming defeat: *She smiled slyly, because she knew she would yet have the last laugh on them.* [ME *laughe(n),* OE *hlæhan* (Anglian); c. D, G *lachen,* Goth *hlahjan,* Icel *hlæja*] —**laugh′er,** *n.*

—**Syn. 1.** chortle, cackle, cachinnate, hawhaw, guffaw, roar; giggle, snicker, snigger, titter. **11.** LAUGH, CHUCKLE, GRIN, SMILE refer to methods of expressing mirth, appreciation of humor, etc. A LAUGH may be a sudden, voiceless exhalation, but is usually an audible sound, either soft or loud: *a hearty laugh.* CHUCKLE suggests a barely audible series of sounds expressing private amusement or satisfaction: *a delighted chuckle.* A SMILE is a (usually pleasant) lighting up of the face and an upward curving of the corners of the lips (which may or may not be open); it may express amusement or mere recognition, friendliness, etc.: *a courteous smile.* A GRIN, in which the teeth are usually visible, is like an exaggerated smile, less controlled in expressing the feelings: *a friendly grin.*

laugh·a·ble (laf′ə bəl, lä′fə-), *adj.* such as to excite laughter; funny; amusing; ludicrous. [LAUGH + -ABLE] —**laugh′a·ble·ness,** *n.* —**laugh′a·bly,** *adv.*
—**Syn.** humorous, droll, comical, farcical, ridiculous; risible. See **funny.** —**Ant.** sad, melancholy.

laugh·ing (laf′ing, lä′fing), *n.* **1.** laughter. —*adj.* **2.** that laughs or is given to laughter: *a laughing child; a laughing audience.* **3.** uttering sounds like human laughter, as some birds. **4.** suggesting laughter by brightness, color, sound, etc.: *a laughing stream; laughing flowers.* **5.** laughable: *The increase in crime is no laughing matter.* [ME; see LAUGH, -ING[1], -ING[2]] —**laugh′ing·ly,** *adv.*

laugh′ing gas′. See **nitrous oxide.**

laugh′ing gull′, a North American gull, *Larus atricilla,* having a high, laughlike call.

laugh′ing hye′na. See **spotted hyena.**

laugh′ing jack′ass, kookaburra. [so called because of its loud braying sound]

laugh·ing·stock (laf′ing stok′, lä′fing-), *n.* an object of ridicule; the butt of a joke or the like: *Their lavender and green house made them the laughingstock of the whole town.* [LAUGHING + STOCK]

laugh·ter (laf′tər, läf′-), *n.* **1.** the action or sound of laughing. **2.** an experiencing of the emotion expressed by laughing: *inward laughter.* **3.** an expression or appearance of merriment or amusement. **4.** *Archaic.* an object of laughter; subject or matter for amusement. [ME; OE *hleahtor;* c. OHG *lahtar,* Icel *lātr;* see LAUGH] —**laugh′ter·less,** *adj.*

Laugh·ton (lôt′ən), *n.* **Charles,** 1899–1962, U.S. actor, born in England.

lau lau (lou′ lou′), *Polynesian Cookery.* meat and fish wrapped in or covered with leaves and steamed or roasted. Also, **lau′lau′.** [< Hawaiian]

lau·mont·ite (lō mon′tīt), *n.* a mineral of the zeolite group, chiefly hydrated silicate of aluminum and calcium. [named after F. P. N. G. de *Laumont* (1747–1834), French mineralogist who discovered it; see -ITE[1]]

launce (lans, läns), *n.* See **sand lance.** [var. of LANCE[2]]

Laun·ce·lot (lan′sə lət, -lot′, län′-), *n.* *Arthurian Romance.* Lancelot (def. 1).

Laun·ces·ton (lôn′ses′tən, län′-), *n.* a city on N Tasmania. 38,118, with suburbs 56,721 (1961).

launch[1] (lônch, länch), *n.* **1.** a heavy open or half-decked boat propelled by oars or by an engine. **2.** a large utility boat carried by a warship. [< Sp *lancha* < Pg: pinnace < Malay *lanchāran* speedboat, deriv. of *lanchār* speed, speedy]

launch[2] (lônch, länch), *v.t.* **1.** to set (a small vessel) in the water. **2.** to float (a newly constructed vessel) usually by allowing it to slide down inclined ways into the water. **3.** to start on a course, career, etc. **4.** to set going: *to launch a scheme.* **5.** to send forth; start off forcefully: *The submarine launched its torpedoes and dived rapidly.* **6.** to throw; hurl: *to launch a spear.* —*v.i.* **7.** to burst out or plunge boldly or directly into action, speech, etc. **8.** to start out or forth; push out or put forth on the water. —*n.* **9.** the act of launching. [late ME *launche* < AF *lanch(er)* < LL *lanceāre* to wield a lance; see LANCE[1]] —**launch′a·ble,** *adj.* —**launch′er,** *n.*

launch′ pad′, *Rocketry.* a platform, usually of reinforced concrete, from which a rocket is launched. Also called **launch′ing pad′, pad.**

laun·der (lôn′dər, län′-), *v.t.* **1.** to wash (clothes, linens, etc.). **2.** to wash and iron (clothes). —*v.i.* **3.** to wash laundry. **4.** to undergo washing and ironing: *The shirt didn't launder well.* —*n.* **5.** (in ore dressing) a passage carrying products of intermediate grade and residue in water suspension. **6.** *Metall.* a channel for conveying molten steel to a ladle. [syncopated var. of ME *lavendere* washer of linen < MF *lavandier(e)* < ML *lavandārius* (masc.), *lavandāria* (fem.), equiv. to L *lavand-* (ger. s. of *lavāre* to wash) + *-ārius, -āria* -ER[2]) —**laun·der·a·bil′i·ty,** *n.* —**laun′der·a·ble,** *adj.* —**laun′der·er,** *n.*

laun·der·ette (lôn′də ret′, län′-, lôn′də ret′, län′-), *n.* Laundromat. [formerly trademark]

laun·dress (lôn′dris, län′-), *n.* a woman whose occupation is the washing and ironing of clothes, linens, etc. [obs. *launder* washer (see LAUNDER) + -ESS]

Laun·dro·mat (lôn′drə mat′, län′-), *n.* *Trademark.* a commercial laundry having coin-operated, automatic machines for the washing and drying of clothes, linens, etc.

laun·dry (lôn′drē, län′-), *n., pl.* **-dries. 1.** articles of clothes, linens, etc., to be washed. **2.** a business establishment where clothes, linens, etc., are laundered. **3.** a room or area, as in a home, apartment building, etc., reserved for doing the family wash. [ME *lavandrie* < MF *lavanderie.* See LAUNDER, -Y[3]]

laun′dry·man (lôn′drē man′, län′-), *n., pl.* **-men. 1.** one who works in or operates a laundry. **2.** a man who collects and delivers laundry. [LAUNDRY + -MAN[1]]

laun·dry·wom·an (lôn′drē wo͝om′ən, län′-), *n., pl.* **-wom·en.** laundress. [LAUNDRY + WOMAN]

lau·ra (läv′rä; *Eng.* lä′vrə), *n.* *Gk. Orth. Ch.* a monastery consisting formerly of a group of cells or huts for monks who met together for meals and worship. [< Gk: lane, alley]

Lau·ra (lôr′ə), *n.* a girl's given name.

lau·ra·ceous (lô rā′shəs), *adj.* belonging to the *Lauraceae,* or laurel family of plants. [< NL *Laur(us)* genus name (special use of L *laurus* bay-tree) + -ACEOUS]

laur·al·de·hyde (lô ral′də hīd′, lo-), *n.* *Chem.* See **lauric aldehyde.** [LAUR(IC) + ALDEHYDE]

Lau·ra·lee (lôr′ə lē′, lôr′ə lē′), *n.* a girl's given name.

Laur·a·sia (lô rā′zhə, -shə), *n.* *Geol.* a hypothetical land mass in the Northern Hemisphere near the end of the Paleozoic that separated to form North America and Eurasia. Cf. **Gondwana.** [b. LAUR(ENTIAN) (def. 2) and (EUR)ASIA]

lau·rate (lôr′āt, lär′-), *n.* *Chem.* a salt or ester of lauric acid. [LAUR(IC) + -ATE[2]]

lau·re·ate (lôr′ē it), *adj.* **1.** crowned or decked with laurel as a mark of honor. **2.** having special distinction or recognition in a field: *the laureate scribe; the laureate men of science.* **3.** deserving or having special recognition for achievement, as for poetry (often used immediately after the noun that is modified): *poet laureate; conjurer laureate.* **4.** consisting of or resembling laurel, as a wreath, crown, etc. —*n.* **5.** one who has been honored for achieving distinction in a particular field. **6.** See **poet laureate.** [< L *laureāt(us)* crowned with laurel, equiv. to *laure(us)* of laurel (*laur(us)* bay-tree + *-eus* -EOUS) + *-ātus* -ATE[1]] —**lau′re·ate·ship′,** *n.*

Lau·reen (lô rēn′), *n.* a girl's given name, form of **Laura.** Also, **Lau·re·na** (lô rē′nə), **Laurene′.**

lau·rel (lôr′əl, lor′-), *n., v.,* **-reled, -rel·ing** or (*esp. Brit.*) **-relled, -rel·ling.** —*n.* **1.** a small, evergreen, lauraceous tree, *Laurus nobilis,* of Europe. **2.** any tree of the genus *Laurus.* **3.** any of various similar trees or shrubs, as the mountain laurel or the great rhododendron. **4.** the foliage of the true laurel as an emblem of victory or distinction. **5.** a branch or wreath of laurel foliage. **6.** Usually, **laurels.** honor won, as for achievement in a field, activity, etc. **7. look to one's laurels,** to be alert to the possibility of being excelled: *New developments in the industry are forcing long-established firms to look to their laurels.* **8. rest on one's laurels,** to be content with one's present honors, achievements, etc.: *He retired at the peak of his career and is resting on his laurels.* —*v.t.* **9.** to adorn or wreathe with laurel. **10.** to honor with marks of distinction. [dissimilated var. of ME *laurer,* earlier *lorer* < OF *lorier* bay-tree, equiv. to *lor* bay, laurel (< L *laurus*) + *-ier* -ER[2]]

Lau·rel (lôr′əl, lor′-), *n.* **1. Stan** (*Arthur Stanley Jefferson*), 1890–1965, U.S. motion-picture actor and comedian, born in England. **2.** a city in SE Mississippi. 27,889 (1960). **3.** a town in central Maryland. 8503 (1960). **4.** a town in S Montana. 4601 (1960). **5.** a town in SW Delaware. 2709 (1960). **6.** a girl's given name.

lau′rel cher′ry, a tree, *Laurocerasus caroliniana,* of the southeastern U.S., having small, milky-white flowers and black, shiny fruit. Also called **cherry laurel, mock orange, wild orange.**

lau′rel oak′, 1. an oak, *Quercus laurifolia,* of the southeastern U.S. **2.** See **shingle oak.**

lau·rence (lôr′əns, lor′-), *n.* a shimmering effect seen over a hot surface, such as a pavement or roadway, on a clear and calm day, caused by the irregular refraction of light. Cf. **scintillation** (def. 4). [special use of proper name]

Lau·rence (lôr′əns, lor′-), *n.* a boy's given name, form of **Lawrence.** Also, **Lorence.**

Lau·ren·cin (lō rän san′), *n.* **Ma·rie** (ma rē′), 1885–1956, French painter, lithographer, and stage designer.

Lau·rens (lôr′ənz, lor′-), *n.* a town in central South Carolina. 9598 (1960).

Lau·ren·tian (lô ren′shən), *adj.* **1.** of or pertaining to the St. Lawrence River. **2.** *Geol.* noting or pertaining to the granite intrusions and orogeny in Canada around the Great Lakes during the Archeozoic. [< L *Laurenti(us)* Lawrence (orig. adj., equiv. to *Laurent(ēs)* men of *Lavinium* + *-ius* -IOUS) + -AN]

Lauren′tian Moun′tains, a range of low mountains in E Canada, between the St. Lawrence River and Hudson Bay. Also called **Lau·ren′tians.**

Lau′ren·tides Park′ (lôr′ən tīdz′, lor′-; *Fr.* lō-rän tēd′), a national park in SE Canada, in Quebec province between the St. Lawrence and Lake St. John.

Lau·ren·ti·us (lô ren′shē əs, -shəs), *n.* **Saint.** See **Lawrence, Saint.**

Laurent′ se′ries (lô rent′; *Fr.* lō rän′), *Math.* a power series in which the negative as well as the positive powers appear. [named after Hermann *Laurent* (1841–1908), French mathematician]

Laurent′s′ the′orem, *Math.* the theorem that a function that is analytic on an annulus can be represented by a Laurent series on the annulus.

Lau·ret·ta (lô ret′ə), *n.* a girl's given name, form of **Laurel.** Also, **Lau·rette** (lô ret′).

lau·ric (lôr′ik, lor′-), *adj.* *Chem.* of or derived from lauric acid. [< L *laur(us)* laurel + -IC]

lau′ric ac′id, *Chem.* a white, crystalline, water-insoluble powder, $CH_3(CH_2)_{10}COOH$, a fatty acid occurring as the glyceride in many vegetable fats, esp. coconut oil and laurel oil: used chiefly in the manufacture of soaps, detergents, cosmetics, and lauryl alcohol.

lau′ric al′dehyde, *Chem.* a colorless, extremely alcohol-soluble liquid having a strong floral odor, $CH_3(CH_2)_{10}CHO$, used chiefly in perfumery. Also, **lauryl aldehyde.** Also called **lauraldehyde, dodecanal, dodecyl aldehyde.**

Lau·rie (lôr′ē), *n.* **1.** a boy's given name, form of **Lawrence. 2.** a girl's given name, form of **Laura.**

Lau·ri·er (lôr′ē ā′; *Fr.* lō ryā′), *n.* **Sir Wil·frid** (wil′frid; *Fr.* wēl frēd′), 1841–1919, Canadian statesman: prime minister 1896–1911.

Lau·rin·burg (lôr′in bûrg′, lor′in-), *n.* a town in S North Carolina. 8242 (1960).

Lau·ris·sa (lô ris′ə), *n.* a girl's given name, form of **Laura.**

lau·rite (lôr′īt, lor′-), *n.* a very rare mineral, ruthenium sulfide, RuS_2, with some osmium, occurring in minute, iron-black crystals or grains. [named by its finder (F. Wöhler, 1800–82, German chemist) after Mrs. *Laura* Joy; see -ITE[1]]

Lau·ri·um (lô′rē əm, lor′ē-), *n.* a town in NW Michigan, in the Upper Peninsula. 3058 (1960).

lau·ro·yl (lôr′ō il, lor′-), *adj.* *Chem.* containing the lauroyl group. Also, **lauryl.** [LAUR(IC) + -O- + -YL]

lau′royl group′, *Chem.* the monovalent group, $CH_3(CH_2)_{10}CO–$, derived from lauric acid. Also called **lau′royl rad′ical.**

lau·rus·ti·nus (lôr′ə stī′nəs), *n.* an evergreen, caprifoliaceous shrub, *Viburnum Tinus,* of southern Europe, having white or pinkish flowers. [< NL, formerly *Laurus Tīnus* (L *laurus* laurel + *tīnus* a plant, perh. laurustinus]

lau′ryl al′cohol (lôr′il, lor′-), *Chem.* a compound that, depending upon purity, is either a crystalline solid or colorless liquid, $CH_3(CH_2)_{10}CH_2OH$, obtained by the reduction of fatty acids of coconut oil: used chiefly in the manufacture of synthetic detergents. [LAUR(IC) + -YL]

lau′ryl al′dehyde, *Chem.* See **lauric aldehyde.**

Lau·sanne (lō zan′; *Fr.* lō zan′), *n.* a city in and the capital of Vaud, in W Switzerland, on the Lake of Geneva. 135,800 (est. 1964).

laus De·o (lôs dē′ō, lous dā′ō), *Latin.* praise (be) to God.

laut·en·cla·vi·cym·bal (lout′ən klä′vē tsēm′bəl), *n.* a harpsichord with strings of gut rather than metal. [< G: lit., lute-clavichord. See LUTE, CLAVICHORD, CYMBAL]

lau′ter tub′ (lou′tər), *Brewing.* a tank for draining off and filtering the wort from grain mash. [< G *lauter:* clear, unmixed]

Lau·tré·a·mont (lō trā a môn′), *n.* **Comte de** (*Isidore Lucien Ducasse*), 1846–70, French poet, born in Uruguay.

Lau·trec (lō trek′), *n.* See **Toulouse-Lautrec, Henri.**

lau·wine (lô′win; *Ger.* lou vē′nə), *n.* lawine.

la·va (lä′və, lav′ə), *n.* **1.** the molten or fluid rock that issues from a volcano or volcanic vent. **2.** the substance formed when this solidifies, occurring in many varieties differing greatly in structure and constitution. [< It, orig. Neapolitan dial.: avalanche < L *lābēs* a sliding down, falling, akin to *lābī* to slide]

la·va·bo (lə vā′bō, -vä′-), *n., pl.* **-boes.** *Eccles.* **1.** the ritual washing of the celebrant's hands after the offertory in the Mass, accompanied in the Roman rite by the recitation of Psalm 26:6–12 or, in the Douay Version, Psalm 25:6–12. **2.** the passage recited. **3.** the small towel or the basin used. **4.** (in many medieval monasteries) a large stone basin equipped with a number of small orifices through which water flowed, used for the performance of ablutions. [< L: I shall wash]

La·va·da (lə vā′də), *n.* a girl's given name.

lav·age (lə väzh′, lav′ij; *Fr.* la vazh′), *n., pl.* **lav·a·ges** (lə vä′zhiz, lav′i jiz; *Fr.* la vazh′). **1.** a washing. **2.** *Med.* **a.** cleansing by injection or the like. **b.** the washing out of the stomach. [< F: lit., a washing, equiv. to *lav(er)* (to) wash (< L *lavāre*) + *-age* -AGE]

La·val (la val′), *n.* **1. Pierre** (pyer), 1883–1945, French lawyer and politician: premier 1931–32, 1935–36; premier of the Vichy government 1942–44: executed for treason 1945. **2.** a city in and the capital of Mayenne, in W France. 43,196 (1962).

la·va-la·va (lä′və lä′və), *n.* the principal garment for both sexes in Polynesia, esp. in Samoa, consisting of a piece of printed cloth worn as a loincloth or skirt. Also called **pareu.** [< Samoan: clothing]

lav·a·liere (lav′ə lēr′, lä′və-), *n.* an ornamental pendant, usually jeweled, worn on a chain around the neck. Also, **lav′a·lier′, la·val·lière** (*Fr.* la va lyer′). [after the Duchesse de *La Vallière* (1644–1710), one of the mistresses of Louis XIV]

La Valse des To·re·a·dors (*Fr.* la vals dā tô rā a-dôr′). See **Waltz of the Toreadors.**

L'A·vare (*Fr.* la var′). See **Miser, The.**

lav·a·ret (lav′ə ret′, -ər it), *n.* a whitefish, *Coregonus lavaretus,* found in the lakes of central Europe. [< F]

La·va·ter (lä′vä tər, lä vä′tər), *n.* **Jo·hann Kas·par** (yō′hän käs′pär), 1741–1801, Swiss poet, theologian, and physiognomist.

la·va·tion (la vā′shən, lā-, lə-), *n.* the process of washing. [< L *lavātiōn-* (s. of *lavātiō*) a washing, equiv. to *lavāt(us)* washed (ptp. of *lavāre*) + *-iōn-* -ION] —**la·va′tion·al,** *adj.*

lav·a·to·ry (lav′ə tôr′ē, -tōr′ē), *n., pl.* **-ries. 1.** a room fitted with equipment for washing the hands and face and usually with toilet facilities. **2.** a bowl or basin with running water for washing or bathing purposes. **3.** any place where washing is done. **4.** a toilet; water-closet. [ME *lavatorie* < LL *lavātōri(um)* washing-place. See LAVATION, -ARY]

lave[1] (lāv), *v.,* **laved, lav·ing.** —*v.t.* **1.** to wash; bathe. **2.** (of a river, sea, etc.) to flow along, against, or past; wash. **3.** *Literary.* to ladle; pour or dip with a ladle. —*v.i.* **4.** *Archaic.* to bathe. [ME *lave(n),* OE *lafian* to pour water on, wash, perh. < L *lavāre* to wash]

lave[2] (lāv), *n.* *Scot.* the remainder; the rest. [ME; OE *lāf;* c. OHG *leiba,* Icel *leif,* Goth *laiba;* akin to LEAVE[1]]

lave[3] (lāv), *adj.* *Brit. Obs.* (of ears) large and drooping. [special use of LAVE[1]]

la·ve·che (lä ve′che), *n.* leveche.

la·veer (lə vēr′), *v.i.* *Naut. Archaic.* to beat to windward. [< MD *lavere(n)* < MF *loveer,* deriv. of *lof* windward < early D; see LUFF]

lav·en·der (lav′ən dər), *n.* **1.** pale bluish purple. **2.** any Old World, menthaceous herb or shrub of the genus *Lavandula,* esp. *L. officinalis,* having spikes of fragrant, pale purple flowers. **3.** the dried flowers or other parts of this plant placed among linen, clothes, etc., for scent or as a preservative. **4.** Also called **lav′ender wa′ter.** toilet water, shaving lotion, or the like, made with a solution of oil of lavender. [ME *lavendre* < AF < ML *lavendula,* var. of *livendula,* nasalized var. of **lividula* a plant livid in color. See LIVID, -ULE]

lav′ender cot′ton, a silvery-gray, evergreen, woody, perennial herb, *Santolina Chamaecyparissus,* of southern Europe, having yellow flower heads.

la·ver[1] (lā′vər), *n.* **1.** *Old Testament.* a large basin upon a foot or pedestal in the court of the Hebrew tabernacle and subsequently in the temple, containing water for the ablutions of the priests and for the washing of the sacrifices in the temple service. **2.** *Eccles.* the font or water of baptism. **3.** any spiritually cleansing agency. **4.** *Archaic.* **a.** a basin, bowl, or cistern to wash in. **b.** any bowl or pan for water. [ME *lavo(u)r* < MF *laveoir* < LL *lavatōr(ium)* LAVATORY]

la·ver[2] (lā′vər), *n.* any of several edible seaweeds, esp. of the genus *Porphyra.* [< NL, special use of L *laver* a water plant]

La·ve·ran (LAV ə RÄN′), *n.* **Charles Louis Al·phonse** (shärl lwē al fôns′), 1845–1922, French physician and bacteriologist: Nobel prize for medicine 1907.

La Vé·ren·drye (*Fr.* la vā rän drē′), **Pierre Gaul·tier de Va·renne** (*Fr.* pyer gō tyā′ də va ren′), **Sieur de,** 1685–1749, Canadian explorer of North America.

La·vern (lə vûrn′), *n.* **1.** Also, **La·ver·na** (lə vûr′nə). a girl's given name, form of **Verna. 2.** a boy's given name, form of **Vernon.** Also, **La·Vern′, La·verne′.**

La Verne (lə vûrn′), a town in S California. 6516 (1960).

lav·er·ock (lav′ər ək, lāv′rək), *n.* *Chiefly Scot.* a lark, esp. a skylark. Also, **lavrock.** [ME *laverok,* OE *lāwerce* LARK[1]]

La Vi·da Es Sue·ño (*Sp.* lä bē′thä es swe′nyô). See **Life Is a Dream.**

La·vin·i·a (lə vin′ē ə), *n.* **1.** *Rom. Legend.* the daughter of Latinus and second wife of Aeneas. **2.** a girl's given name.

lav·ish (lav′ish), *adj.* **1.** using or giving in great amounts; prodigal (often fol. by *of*): *lavish of his time; lavish of affection.* **2.** expended, bestowed, or occurring in profusion; unlimited: *lavish spending.* —*v.t.* **3.** to expend or give in great amounts or without limit: *to lavish favors on a person.* [late ME *lavas* profusion (n.), profuse (adj.) < MF *lavasse* downpour of rain, deriv. of *laver* to wash < L *lavāre*] —**lav′ish·er,** *n.* —**lav′ish·ly,** *adv.* —**lav′ish·ment,** *n.* —**lav′ish·ness,** *n.*

—**Syn. 1, 2.** unstinted, extravagant, excessive, wasteful, improvident; generous, openhanded. LAVISH, PRODIGAL, PROFUSE refer to that which exists in abundance and is poured out copiously. LAVISH suggests (sometimes excessive) generosity and openhandedness: *lavish hospitality, much too lavish.* PRODIGAL suggests wastefulness, improvidence, and reckless impatience of restraint: *a prodigal extravagance.* PROFUSE emphasizes abundance, but may suggest overemotionalism, exaggeration, or the like: *profuse thanks, compliments, apologies.* **3.** heap, pour; waste, squander, dissipate. —**Ant. 1, 2.** niggardly.

La·voi·sier (la vwa zyā′), *n.* **1. An·toine Lau·rent** (än twan′ lō rän′), 1743–94, French scientist: pioneer in the field of chemistry. **2.** a crater in the second quadrant of the face of the moon: about 40 miles in diameter.

La·vonne (lə von′), *n.* a girl's given name.

lav·rock (lav′rək), *n.* *Chiefly Scot.* laverock.

law[1] (lô), *n.* **1.** the principles and regulations established by a government and applicable to a people, whether in the form of legislation or of custom and policies recognized and enforced by judicial decision. **2.** any written or positive rule or collection of rules prescribed under the authority of the state or nation, as by the people in its constitution. Cf. **bylaw, statute law. 3.** the controlling influence of such rules; the condition of society brought about by their observance: *maintaining law and order.* **4.** a system or collection of such rules. **5.** the department of knowledge concerned with these rules; jurisprudence: *to study law.* **6.** the body of such rules concerned with a particular subject or derived from a particular source: *commercial law.* **7.** an act of the supreme legislative body of a state or nation, as distinguished from the constitution. **8.** the principles applied in the courts of common law, as distinguished from equity. **9.** the profession that deals with law and legal procedure: *to practice law.* **10.** legal action; litigation: *to go to law.* **11.** an agent or agency acting to enforce the law: *the long arm of the law; The law arrived at the scene soon after the alarm was given.* **12.** any rule or injunction that must be obeyed: *Having a good breakfast was an absolute law in the household.* **13.** a rule or principle of proper conduct sanctioned by man's conscience, concepts of natural justice, or the will of a deity: *a moral law.* **14.** a rule or manner of behavior that is instinctive or spontaneous: *the law of self-preservation.* **15.** (in philosophy, science, etc.) **a.** a statement of a relation or sequence of phenomena invariable under the same conditions. **b.** a mathematical rule. **16.** a principle based on the predictable consequences of an act, condition, etc.: *the law of supply and demand; the law of diminishing returns.* **17.** a rule, principle, or convention regarded as governing the structure or the relationship of an element in the structure of something, as of a language, work of art, etc.: *the laws of playwriting; the laws of grammar.* **18.** a commandment or a revelation from God. **19.** (*sometimes cap.*) a divinely appointed order or system. **20. the Law.** See **Law of Moses. 21.** the Pentateuch, containing the Mosaic dispensations, or system of rules and ordinances, and forming the first of the three Jewish divisions of the Old Testament. Cf. **Hagiographa, Prophets. 22.** the preceptive part of the Bible, esp. of the New Testament, in contradistinction to its promises: *the law of Christ.* **23.** *Brit. Sports.* an allowance of time or distance given a quarry or competitor in a race, as the head start given a fox before the hounds are set after it. **24. be a law to or unto oneself,** to follow one's own inclinations, rules of behavior, etc.; act independently or unconventionally, esp. without regard for established mores. **25. lay down the law, a.** to state one's views authoritatively. **b.** to give a command in an imperious manner: *The foreman laid down the law to the workmen.* **26. take the law into one's own hands,** to attempt to obtain justice as one sees fit without recourse to the usual legal processes: *When the murderer was not found, the husband of the victim vowed to take the law into his own hands.* —*v.t.* **27.** *Brit.* (formerly) to expeditate (an animal). [ME *law, lagh,* OE *lagu* < Scand; cf. Icel *lag* layer, pl. *lög* law, lit., that which is laid down; akin to LAY[1], LIE[2]] —**law′like′,** *adj.*

law[2] (lô), *adj., adv., n.* *Obs.* low[1].

law[3] (lô), *v.i., v.t., n.* *Obs.* low[2].

law[4] (lô), *interj.* *Dial.* (used as an exclamation expressing astonishment.)

Law (lô), *n.* **1. Andrew Bon·ar** (bon′ər), 1858–1923, English statesman, born in Canada: prime minister 1922–23. **2. John,** 1671–1729, Scottish financier. **3. William,** 1686–1761, English clergyman and devotional writer.

law-a·bid·ing (lô′ə bī′ding), *adj.* abiding by or keeping the law; obedient to law: *law-abiding citizens.* —**law′-a·bid′ing·ness,** *n.*

law·book (lô′bo͝ok′), *n.* a book consisting or treating of laws, legal issues, or cases that have been adjudicated. [ME *lagheboc.* See LAW[1], BOOK]

law·break·er (lô′brā′kər), *n.* one who breaks or violates the law. [ME *lawbreker;* r. OE *lahbreca.* See LAW[1], BREAKER[1]] —**law′break′ing,** *n., adj.*

law′ court′, a court of law, esp. one that administers justice on the basis of the rules and practices of the common law.

Lawes (lôz), *n.* **1. Henry** ("*Harry*"), 1596–1662, English composer. **2. Lewis E(dward),** 1883–1947, U.S. penologist.

law′ French′, the legal jargon of England, now extinct except in phrases: originally a dialect of Old French.

law·ful (lô′fəl), *adj.* **1.** allowed or permitted by law; not contrary to law: *a lawful enterprise.* **2.** appointed or recognized by law; legally qualified: *a lawful king.* **3.** recognized or sanctioned by law; legitimate: *a lawful marriage; a lawful heir.* **4.** acting or living according to the law; law-abiding: *a lawful man; a lawful community.* [ME *laghful.* See LAW[1], -FUL] —**law′ful·ly,** *adv.* —**law′ful·ness,** *n.*

—**Syn. 1.** legal. **3.** licit.

law·giv·er (lô′giv′ər), *n.* one who promulgates a law or a code of laws. [ME *lawe givere.* See LAW[1], GIVER] —**law′giv′ing,** *n., adj.*

law-hand (lô′hand′), *n.* a style of handwriting used in old legal documents, esp. in England. [LAW[1] + HAND]

la·wine (lô′win; *Ger.* lä vē′nə), *n.* an avalanche. Also, **lauwine.** [< G << LL *lābīna;* cf. L *lābī* to fall down, slip, slide]

law·ing (lô′ing), *n.* *Scot.* a bill, esp. for food or drink in a tavern. [obs. Scot *law* bill, ME (dial.) *lagh* < ON *lag* price, tax, proper place + -ING[1]]

law·less (lô′lis), *adj.* **1.** contrary to or without regard for the law: *lawless violence.* **2.** being without law; uncontrolled by a law; unbridled; unruly; unrestrained: *lawless passion.* **3.** illegal: *bootleggers' lawless activity.* [ME *laweles.* See LAW[1], -LESS] —**law′less·ly,** *adv.* —**law′less·ness,** *n.*

law·mak·er (lô′mā′kər), *n.* one who makes or enacts law; legislator. [ME *lawe maker.* See LAW[1], MAKER] —**law′mak′ing,** *n., adj.*

law·man (lô′man′, -mən), *n., pl.* **-men** (-men′, -mən). an officer of the law, as a sheriff or policeman. [ME *laweman,* earlier *lageman,* OE *lahmann.* See LAW[1], MAN]

Law·man (lô′mən), *n.* Layamon.

law′ mer′chant, the principles and rules, drawn chiefly from custom, determining the rights and obligations of commercial transactions; commercial law.

lawn[1] (lôn, län), *n.* **1.** a stretch of grass-covered land, esp. one closely mowed, as near a house, on an estate, in a park, etc. **2.** *Archaic.* a glade. [ME *launde* < MF *lande* glade < Celt; cf. Breton *lann* heath. See LAND] —**lawn′y,** *adj.*

lawn[2] (lôn, län), *n.* a thin or sheer linen or cotton fabric, either plain or printed. [late ME *lawnd, laun,* perh. named after LAON, where linen-making once flourished] —**lawn′y,** *adj.*

lawn′ bowl′ing, a game played with wooden balls on a level, closely mowed green having a slight bias, the object being to roll one's ball as near as possible to a smaller white ball at the other end of the green. Also called **bowls, bowling on the green.** Cf. **bowl**[2] (def. 2), **bowling green, jack**[1] (def. 7), **rink** (def. 5).

Lawn·dale (lôn′dāl′), *n.* a city in SW California, near Los Angeles. 21,740 (1960).

lawn′ mow′er, a machine for cutting grass.

lawn′ par′ty. See **garden party.**

lawn′ sleeves′, 1. the sleeves of lawn of an Anglican bishop. **2.** the office of an Anglican bishop. **3.** an Anglican bishop or bishops.

lawn′ ten′nis, tennis, esp. when played on a grass court.

law′ of ac′tion and reac′tion, *Physics.* third law of motion. See under **law of motion.**

law′ of ad′ditive pres′sures, *Physics, Chem.* See **Dalton's law.**

law′ of av′erages, a statistical principle formulated by Jacques Bernoulli to show a more or less predictable ratio between the number of random trials of an event and its occurrences.

law′ of conserva′tion of an′gular momen′tum, *Physics.* See **conservation of angular momentum.**

law′ of conserva′tion of charge′, *Physics.* See **conservation of charge.**

law′ of conserva′tion of en′ergy, *Physics.* See **conservation of energy.**

law′ of conserva′tion of lin′ear momen′tum, *Physics.* See **conservation of linear momentum.**

law′ of conserva′tion of mass′, *Physics.* See **conservation of mass.**

law′ of contradic′tion, *Logic.* the law that a proposition cannot be both true and false or that a thing cannot both have and not have a given property.

law′ of co′sines, *Math.* **1.** a plane trigonometric equation in which the square of a side of a plane triangle is equal to the sum of the squares of the other two sides minus twice the product of the other sides multiplied by the cosine of the angle between them. **2.** a spherical trigonometric equation in which the cosine of an arc of a spherical triangle equals the sum of the product of the cosines of the other two arcs added to the product of the sines of the other two arcs multiplied by the cosine of the angle between them. **3.** a spherical trigonometric equation in which the cosine of an angle of a spherical triangle is equal to the negative of the product of the cosines of the other two angles added to the product of the sines of the other two angles multiplied by the cosine of the included arc.

law′ of def′inite composi′tion, 1. *Chem.* the statement that in a pure compound the elements are always combined in fixed proportions by weight. **2.** *Logic.* the law that either a proposition or its denial must be true.

law′ of dimin′ishing mar′ginal util′ity, *Econ.* the law that for a single consumer the marginal utility of a commodity diminishes for each additional unit of the commodity consumed.

law′ of exclud′ed mid′dle, *Logic.* the principle that if one of a pair of contradictory statements is considered false the other must be considered true.

law′ of expo′nents, *Math.* the theorem stating the elementary properties of exponents, as the property that the product of the same bases, each raised to an exponent, is equal to the base raised to the sum of the exponents: $x^a \cdot x^b = x^{a+b}$.

law′ of gravita′tion, *Physics.* the law that all bodies and particles in the universe are subject to gravitation. Also called **Newton's law of gravitation.**

law′ of iden′tity, *Logic.* the law that any proposition implies itself.

law′ of large′ num′bers, *Math.* the theorem in probability theory that the number of successes increases as the number of experiments increases and approximates the probability times the number of experiments for a large number of experiments.

law′ of Malus′, *Optics.* See **Malus' law.**

law′ of mass′ ac′tion, *Chem.* the statement that the velocity of a chemical reaction is proportional to the concentrations of the reacting substances.

Law′ of Mo′ses, the Pentateuch or Torah.

law′ of mo′tion, *Physics.* one of three laws of classical mechanics, either the law that a body remains at rest or in motion with a constant velocity unless an external force acts on the body (**first law of motion**), the law that the sum of the forces acting on a body is equal to the product of the mass of the body and the acceleration produced by the forces, with motion in the direction of the resultant of the forces (**second law of motion**), or the law that for every force acting on a body, the body exerts a force having equal magnitude and the opposite direction along the same line of action as the original force (**third law of motion**). Also called **Newton's law of motion.**

law′ of mul′tiple propor′tion, *Chem.* the statement that where two elements can combine to form more than one compound, the ratio by weight of one element to a given weight of the second is usually a small whole number.

law′ of na′tions, 1. See **international law. 2.** (in Roman use) the body of rules applicable to the relations between nations.

law′ of par′simony, *Philos.* a principle according to which an explanation of a thing or event is made with the fewest possible assumptions. Cf. **Occam's razor.**

law′ of par′tial pres′sures, *Physics, Chem.* See **Dalton's law.**

law′ of reflec′tion, the principle that a ray of light, radar pulse, or the like, is reflected from a smooth surface with the angle of reflection equal to the angle of incidence, the incident ray, the reflected ray, and the normal to the surface at the point of incidence all lying in the same plane.

law′ of refrac′tion, the principle that for a ray, radar pulse, or the like, that is incident on the interface of two media, the ratio of the sine of the angle of incidence to the sine of the angle of refraction is equal to the ratio of the velocity of the ray in the first medium to the velocity in the second medium and the incident ray, refracted ray, and normal to the surface at the point of incidence all lie in the same plane.

law′ of sines′, *Math.* **1.** a plane trigonometric equation in which the ratio of a side of a plane triangle to the sine of the opposite angle is the same for all three sides. **2.** a spherical trigonometric equation in which the ratio of the sine of an arc of a spherical triangle to the sine of the opposite angle is the same for all three arcs.

law′ of the jun′gle, a system or mode of action in which the fittest survive, presumably as animals in nature or as human beings whose activity is not regulated by the laws of civilization.

law′ of the mean′, *Math.* See **mean value theorem.**

Law′ of the Medes′ and the Per′sians, unalterable law.

law′ of thermodynam′ics, 1. any of three principles variously stated in equivalent forms, being the principle that the change of energy of a thermodynamic system is equal to the heat transferred minus the work done (**first law of thermodynamics**), the principle that no isolated process is possible in which heat is absorbed from a reservoir at a single temperature and converted completely into mechanical work (**second law of thermodynamics**), and the principle that it is impossible to reduce the temperature of a system to absolute zero in a finite number of operations (**third law of thermodynamics**). **2.** See **zeroth law of thermodynamics.**

law′ of thought′, any of the three basic laws of traditional logic, including the law of contradiction, the law of excluded middle, and the law of identity.

law′ of trichot′omy, *Math.* an axiom that an integer is either zero, positive, or negative, often applied to an algebraic system with a set of positive elements.

Law·rence (lôr′əns, lor′-), *n.* **1. D(avid) H(erbert),** 1885–1930, English novelist. **2. Ernest O(rlando),** 1901–58, U.S. physicist: inventor of the cyclotron; Nobel prize 1939. **3. Gertrude,** 1901?–52, English actress. **4. James,** 1781–1813, U.S. naval officer in the War of 1812. **5. Saint.** Also, **Lorenzo.** died A.D. 258?, early church martyr. Latin, **Lau·ren·ti·us** (lō ren′shē əs). **6. Sir Thomas,** 1769–1830, English painter. **7. T(homas) E(dward)** (*T. E. Shaw*) ("*Lawrence of Arabia*"), 1888–1935, English archaeologist, soldier, and writer. **8.** a city in NE Massachusetts, on the Merrimack River. 70,933 (1960). **9.** a city in E Kansas, on the Kansas River. 32,858 (1960). **10.** a town on SW Long Island, in SE New York. 5907 (1960). **11.** Also, **Laurence, Lorence, Loren, Lorin.** a boy's given name.

Law·rence·burg (lôr′əns bûrg′, lor′-), *n.* **1.** a town in S Tennessee. 8042 (1960). **2.** a town in SE Indiana. 5004 (1960). **3.** a town in central Kentucky. 2523 (1960).

Law′rence frame′, a gilded frame for a circular or oval painting, having a rectangular exterior form.

Law′rence Park′, a town in NW Pennsylvania. 4403 (1960).

Law·rence·ville (lôr′əns vil, lor′-), *n.* **1.** a town in SE Illinois. 5492 (1960). **2.** a town in central Georgia. 3804 (1960).

Law·ren·cian (lô ren′chən), *adj.* **1.** of, pertaining to, or characteristic of D. H. Lawrence, his works, or his philosophy. —*n.* **2.** one who studies the works of D. H. Lawrence. **3.** an advocate or adherent of the philosophy of D. H. Lawrence. [LAWRENCE + -IAN]

law·ren·ci·um (lô ren′sē əm, lo-), *n.* *Chem.* a synthetic, radioactive, metallic element. *Symbol:* Lw; *at. no.:* 103. [*Lawrence* Radiation Laboratory, Berkeley, California + -IUM]

Law·son (lô′sən), *n.* **Robert,** 1892–1957, U.S. illustrator and author, esp. of children's books.

law·suit (lô′so͞ot′), *n.* a suit at law; a prosecution of a claim in a court of law; an action. [LAW¹ + SUIT]

Law·ton (lôt′ᵊn), *n.* a city in SW Oklahoma. 61,697 (1960).

law·yer (lô′yər, loi′ər), *n.* **1.** a person whose profession is to conduct lawsuits for clients in a court of law and to advise or act for clients in other legal matters. **2.** *New Testament.* an interpreter of the Mosaic Law. Luke 14:3. **3.** a burbot: so called from the beardlike barbel. [ME *lawyere.* See LAW¹, -IER] —**law′yer·like′, law′yer·ly,** *adj.*

law′yer ref′erence, *Law.* reference to a layman of a suitable lawyer, made by a bar association.

lax (laks), *adj.* **1.** lacking in strictness or severity; careless or negligent: *lax morals; a lax attitude toward discipline.* **2.** not rigidly exact or precise; vague: *lax ideas of a subject.* **3.** loose or slack; not tense, rigid, or firm: *a lax cord; a lax handshake.* **4.** open or not retentive, as the bowels. **5.** (of a person) having the bowels unduly open. **6.** open or not compact; having a loosely cohering structure; porous: *lax tissue; lax texture.* **7.** *Phonet.* (of a vowel) articulated with relatively relaxed tongue muscles. Cf. **tense**¹ (def. 4). [late ME < L *lax(us)* loose, slack, wide] —**lax′ly,** *adv.* —**lax′ness,** *n.*

lax·a·tion (lak sā′shən), *n.* **1.** a loosening or relaxing. **2.** the state of being loosened or relaxed. **3.** a bowel movement. [ME *laxacion* < L *laxātiōn-* (s. of *laxātiō*) a loosening, equiv. to *laxāt(us)* loosened (ptp. of *laxāre;* see LAX) + *-iōn-* -ION]

lax·a·tive (lak′sə tiv), *n.* **1.** a medicine or agent for relieving constipation. —*adj.* **2.** of, pertaining to, or constituting a laxative; purgative. **3.** *Archaic.* **a.** (of the bowels) subject to looseness. **b.** (of a disease) characterized by looseness of the bowels. [< ML *laxātīv(us)* loosening (see LAXATION, -IVE); ME *laxatif* < MF] —**lax′a·tive·ly,** *adv.* —**lax′a·tive·ness,** *n.*

lax·i·ty (lak′si tē), *n.* the state or quality of being lax; looseness. [< L *laxitās* wideness, openness. See LAX, -ITY]

Lax·ness (läks′nes), *n.* **Hall·dór Kil·jan** (häl′dōr kil′yän), born 1902, Icelandic writer: Nobel prize 1955.

lay¹ (lā), *v.,* **laid** or, for 8, **layed; lay·ing;** *n.* —*v.t.* **1.** to put or place in a horizontal position or position of rest; set down: *to lay a book on a desk.* **2.** to beat down, as from an erect position; strike or throw to the ground: *One punch laid him low. The summer storm laid the grain flat.* **3.** to place before a person or bring to a person's notice or consideration: *He laid his case before the commission.* **4.** to present, bring forward, or prefer, as a claim, charge, etc. **5.** to impute, attribute, or ascribe: *to lay blame on someone.* **6.** to bury: *They laid him to rest.* **7.** to bring forth and deposit (an egg or eggs). **8.** to deposit as a wager; stake: *He layed $10 on the horse.* **9.** to bet (someone): *I'll lay you ten to one that he wins.* **10.** to place, set, or cause to be in a particular situation, state, or condition: *The failure of his crops laid him in debt.* **11.** to impose as a burden, duty, penalty, or the like: *to lay an embargo on shipments of oil.* **12.** to set, place, or apply (often fol. by *to* or *on*): *to lay hands on a child.* **13.** to set (a trap). **14.** to place or locate: *The scene is laid in France. The story is laid in a tropical setting.* **15.** to dispose or place in proper position or in an orderly fashion: *to lay bricks.* **16.** to place in position on or along a surface: *to lay a pipeline; to lay a superhighway.* **17.** to place dinner service on (a table); set. **18.** to place on or over a surface, as paint; cover or spread with something else. **19.** to devise or arrange, as a plan. **20.** to bring (a stick, lash, etc.) down, as on a person, in inflicting punishment. **21.** to smooth down or make even: *to lay the nap of cloth.* **22.** to form by twisting strands together, as a rope. **23.** to allay, appease, or suppress: *to lay a person's doubts at rest.* **24.** to cause to subside: *laying the clouds of dust with a spray of water.* **25.** *Naut.* to move or turn into a certain position or direction. **26.** to aim a cannon in a specified direction at a specified elevation. **27.** to put (dogs) on a scent. **28.** *Slang.* to have sexual intercourse with.
—*v.i.* **29.** to lay eggs. **30.** to wager or bet. **31.** to deal or aim blows vigorously (usually fol. by *on, at, about,* etc.). **32.** to apply oneself vigorously. **33.** *Dial.* to plan or scheme (often fol. by *out*). **34.** *Naut.* to take up a specified position, direction, etc.: *to lay aloft; to lay close to the wind.* **35.** *Nonstandard.* lie². **36. lay aboard,** *Naut.* (formerly, of a fighting vessel) to come alongside (another fighting vessel) in order to board it. **37. lay about one, a.** to strike blows in every direction. **b.** to proceed to do; set about. **38. lay a course, a.** *Naut.* to sail in the desired direction without tacking. **b.** to proceed according to a plan. **39. lay aside, a.** to abandon; reject: *They laid aside their childish pastimes and behaved as adults.* **b.** to save for use at a later time; store: *If you lay aside a stated sum every month, you will soon have enough for a trip.* **40. lay away, a.** to reserve for later use; save. **b.** to hold merchandise pending final payment or request for delivery: *I plan to lay away a winter coat.* **c.** to bury: *They laid him away in the tomb.* **41. lay by, a.** to put away for future use; store; save: *He had managed to lay by some money for college from his earnings as a newspaperboy.* **b.** *Naut.* (of a sailing vessel) to come to a standstill; heave to; lay to. **42. lay close,** *Naut.* (of a sailing vessel) to sail close to the wind. **43. lay down, a.** to give up; yield: *to lay down one's arms.* **b.** to stock; store: *to lay down wine.* **c.** to assert firmly; state authoritatively: *to lay down certain rigid rules.* **d.** to ordain; prescribe: *to lay down rules of conduct.* **e.** *Shipbuilding.* to draw at full size (the lines of a hull), as on the floor of a mold loft; lay off; loft. **44. lay for,** *Slang.* to wait for in order to attack or surprise; lie in wait for: *The police are laying for him.* **45. lay in,** to store away for future use: *We laid in a supply of canned goods.* **46. lay into,** *Slang.* to attack physically or verbally; assail: *He laid into the opposition with fiery words.* **47. lay it on,** *Informal.* to exaggerate in one's speech or actions, esp. to engage in exaggerated flattery or reproof: *She was glad to be told what a fine cook she was, but they didn't have to lay it on so much.* Also, **lay it on thick, lay it on with a trowel. 48. lay low.** See **low**¹ (defs. 44). **49. lay off, a.** to dismiss an employee, esp. temporarily because of slack business. **b.** to put aside. **c.** *Slang.* to stop annoying or teasing; cease: *Lay off the complaining! Lay off me, will you?* **d.** to mark off; measure; plot. **e.** *Naut.* to sail away from. **f.** *Naut.* to remain stationary at a distance from; lie off. **g.** *Shipbuilding.* See **lay**¹ (def. 43e). **50. lay on, a.** to cover with; apply: *to lay on a coat of wax.* **b.** to strike blows at; attack violently: *When the mob became unruly, the police began to lay on.* **c.** *Naut.* to sail toward. **d.** *Naut.* to row (an oar) with a full stroke. **e.** *Brit. Informal.* to provide as a gift, bonus, or treat; give; treat: *The owners laid on a Christmas dinner for the employees.* **51. lay oneself open,** to expose oneself to unfavorable comment or criticism: *He was careful not to lay himself open to charges of partiality.* **52. lay oneself out,** *Informal.* to try one's best; make a great effort: *They laid themselves out to see that the reception would be a success.* **53. lay out, a.** to extend at length. **b.** to spread out in order; arrange; prepare. **c.** to ready (a corpse) for burial. **d.** *Informal.* to spend or contribute (money). **e.** *Slang.* to knock (someone) unconscious; strike down. **f.** to plan; plot; design. **g.** to make a layout of. **54. lay out on,** *Naut.* to row (an oar) with a full or increased stroke. **55. lay over, a.** to be postponed until action may be taken: *The vote will have to be laid over until next week.* **b.** to make a stop, as during a trip: *We will have to lay over in Lyons on our way to the Riviera.* **56. lay siege to.** See **siege** (def. 8). **57. lay to, a.** *Naut.* to check the motion of (a ship). **b.** *Naut.* to put (a ship) in a dock or other place of safety. **c.** to attack vigorously. **d.** to put forth effort; apply oneself. **58. lay up, a.** to put away for future use; store up. **b.** to cause to be confined to bed or to be kept indoors; make ill; disable. **c.** *Naut.* to retire (a vessel) from active use. **d.** *Naut.* (of a vessel) to be retired from active use. **e.** to construct (a masonry structure): *The masons laid the outer walls up in Flemish bond.* **59. lay up for,** *Naut.* to shape a course towards.
—*n.* **60.** the way or position in which a thing is laid or lies: *the lay of the south pasture.* **61.** *Ropemaking.* the quality of a fiber rope characterized by the degree of twist, the angles formed by the strands, and the fibers in the strands. **62.** a share of the profits or the catch of a whaling or fishing voyage, distributed to officers and crew. **63.** batten³ (defs. 1, 2). **64.** *Slang.* **a.** a partner in sexual intercourse. **b.** an instance of sexual intercourse. [ME *laye(n), legge(n),* OE *lecgan* (causative of *licgan* to LIE²); c. D *leggen,* G *legen,* Icel *legja,* Goth *lagjan*]
—**Syn. 1.** deposit. See **put, lie**². **23, 24.** calm, still, quiet.

lay² (lā), *v.* pt. of **lie**².

lay³ (lā), *adj.* **1.** belonging to, pertaining to, or performed by the people or laity, as distinguished from the clergy: *a lay sermon.* **2.** not belonging to, connected with, or proceeding from a profession, esp. the law or medicine. [ME < MF *lai* < eccl. L *lāic(us)* LAIC]

lay⁴ (lā), *n.* **1.** a short narrative or other poem, esp. one to be sung. **2.** a song. [ME *lai* < OF < Gmc; cf. OHG *leih* song, c. Goth *laiks* dance, OE *lāc,* Icel *leikr* play]

lay⁵ (lā), *n.* **1.** (on a loom) a movable frame that contains the shuttles, the race plate, and the reed, and that by its oscillating motion beats the filling yarn into place. **2.** any movable part of a loom. [var. of LATHE]

La·ya·mon (lā′ə mən, lī′yə-), *n.* fl. c1200, English poet and chronicler. Also called **Lawman.**

lay′ an′alyst, a psychoanalyst who does not have a medical degree.

Layard (lârd, lā′ərd), *n.* **Sir Aus·ten Henry** (ô′stən), 1817–94, English archaeologist, writer, and diplomat.

lay′a·way plan′ (lā′ə wā′), a method of purchasing by which the purchaser reserves an article with a down payment and claims it only after paying the full balance. [adj. use of v. phrase *lay away*]

lay′ bap′tism, *Eccles.* baptism administered by a layman.

lay′ board′, *Shipbuilding.* See **hog piece.**

lay′ boat′, *Naut.* a boat anchored for some specific purpose, as to serve as a marker.

lay′ broth′er, a man who has taken religious vows and habit but is employed by his order chiefly in manual labor.

lay-by (lā′bī′), *n.* **1.** *Brit.* (on a road or railroad) a place beside the main road or track where vehicles may wait. **2.** *Naut.* a mooring place in a narrow river or canal, formed to one side so as to leave the channel free. [n. use of v. phrase *lay by*]

lay′ clerk′. See **lay vicar.**

lay′ day′, **1.** *Com.* one of a certain number of days allowed by a charter party for loading or unloading a vessel without demurrage. **2.** *Naut.* a day in which a vessel is delayed in port. [LAY¹ + DAY]

lay·down (lā′doun′), *n.* *Bridge.* **1.** a hand held by a declarer that is or can be played with all cards exposed because no action by the opponents can prevent him from taking the number of tricks necessary to make his contract. **2.** an unbeatable contract that can so easily be made that a declarer can or does play his hand with all cards exposed. [n. use of v. phrase *lay down*]

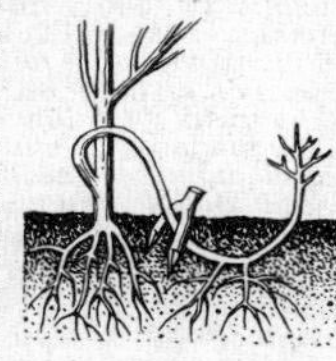
Layer (def. 4)

lay·er (lā′ər), *n.* **1.** a thickness of some material laid on or spread over a surface: *a layer of soot on the windowsill; two layers of paint.* **2.** bed; stratum: *alternating layers of basalt and sandstone.* **3.** one who or that which lays. **4.** *Hort.* **a.** a shoot or twig that is induced to root while still attached to the living stock, as by bending and covering with soil. **b.** a plant so propagated. **5.** *Ropemaking.* a machine for laying rope or cable. —*v.t.* **6.** to make a layer of. **7.** *Hort.* to propagate by layers. [ME *leyer, legger.* See LAY¹, -ER¹]

lay·er·age (lā′ər ij), *n.* *Hort.* a method of propagating plants by causing their shoots to take root while still attached to the parent plant. [LAYER + -AGE]

lay′er board′. See **lear board.**

lay′er cake′, a cake made in layers, with a cream, jelly, or other filling between them.

lay·er-out (lā′ər out′), *n., pl.* **lay·ers-out.** *Shipbuilding.* one who indicates on plates and shapes how they will be formed. [n. use of v. phrase *lay out*]

lay·ette (lā et′), *n.* an outfit of clothing, toilet articles, etc., for a newborn child. [< F; MF *laiete* small coffer, equiv. to *laie* chest (< MD *laeye,* var. of *lade;* akin to LADE) + *-ete* -ETTE]

lay′ fig′ure, 1. a jointed model of the human body, usually of wood, from which artists work in the absence of a living model. **2.** a similar figure used in shops to display costumes. **3.** a person of no importance, individuality, distinction, etc.; nonentity. [*lay,* abstracted from obs. *lay(man)* < D *leeman,* lit., joint-man (*le(d)e-* joint, c. OE, ME *lith* limb + *man* MAN¹)]

lay′ing on′ of hands′, 1. *Theol.* a rite in which the cleric places his hands on the head of one being confirmed, ordained, or the like. **2.** (in divine healing) the placing of the hands of the healer upon the person to be cured.

lay′ interme′diary, *Law.* a layman who interposes himself between a lawyer and client to prevent the existence of a direct relationship between them.

lay·man (lā′mən), *n., pl.* **-men.** one of the laity; one who is not a clergyman or who is not a member of a specified profession, as of law, medicine, etc. [late ME; see LAY³, MAN¹]

lay·off (lā′ôf′, -of′), *n.* **1.** the act of laying off, as workers. **2.** an interval of enforced unemployment. [n. use of v. phrase *lay off*]

lay′ of the land′, the general state or condition of affairs under consideration; the facts of a situation: *We asked a few questions to get the lay of the land.* Also, *esp. Brit.,* **lie of the land.**

Lay′ of the Last′ Min′strel, The, a verse narrative (1805) by Sir Walter Scott.

lay·out (lā′out′), *n.* **1.** a laying or spreading out. **2.** an arrangement or plan: *We objected to the layout of the house.* **3.** a plan or sketch of a page of a newspaper, magazine, etc., or of an advertisement indicating the arrangement and relationship of the parts, as of type, artwork, or the like. **4.** (in advertising, publishing, etc.) the art, technique, process, or occupation of making layouts: *an expert in layout; a course in layout; a new job in layout.* **5.** *Journalism.* spread (def. 32). **6.** *Informal.* a place, as of residence or business, and the things that go with it; a setup: *a fancy layout with a swimming pool and a two-car garage.* **7.** *Informal.* a display or spread, as of dishes at a meal. **8.** a collection or set of tools, implements, or the like. **9.** *Cards.* an arrangement of cards dealt according to a given pattern, as in solitaire. **10.** *Sports.* **a.** (in fancy diving) a dive in which the body is straight. **b.** (in tumbling) a position in which the body is extended and the back is arched. Cf. **pike**⁷ (def. 2), **tuck**¹ (def. 12b). [n. use of v. phrase *lay out*]

lay·o·ver (lā′ō′vər), *n.* stopover. [n. use of v. phrase *lay over*]

lay′ read′er, *Anglican Ch.* a layman authorized by a bishop to conduct certain parts of a service.

lay′ sis′ter, a woman who has taken religious vows and habit but is employed in her order chiefly in manual labor.

lay·stall (lā′stôl′), *n.* *Brit.* a place where refuse and dung are put. [LAY¹ + STALL¹]

Lay·ton (lāt′ᵊn), *n.* a town in N Utah. 9027 (1960).

lay-up (lā′up′), *n.* *Basketball.* a shot with one hand from a point close to the basket, in which a player shoots the ball usually off the backboard.

lay·up (lā′up′), *n.* the operation of assembling veneers for pressing into plywood. [n. use of v. phase *lay up*]

lay′ vic′ar, *Ch. of Eng.* a lay officer in a cathedral who performs those parts of a service not reserved to the priests. Also called **clerk vicar, lay clerk, secular vicar.**

lay·wom·an (lā′wo͝om′ən), *n., pl.* **-wom·en.** a female member of the laity. [LAY³ + WOMAN]

laz·ar (laz′ər; *more formally* lā′zər), *n.* a person infected with a loathsome disease, esp. a leper. [ME < ML *lazar(us)* leper, special use of LL *Lazarus* LAZARUS] —**laz′ar·like′,** *adj.*

laz·a·ret·to (laz′ə ret′ō), *n., pl.* **-tos. 1.** a hospital for those affected with contagious or loathsome diseases, as for lepers. **2.** a building or a ship set apart for quarantine purposes. **3.** Also called **glory hole.** *Naut.* a small storeroom within the hull of a vessel, esp. one at the extreme stern. Also, **laz·a·ret, laz·a·rette** (laz′ə ret′). [< It *lazareto* (Venetian dial.) < *l(azzaro)* LAZAR + *(N)azareto* popular name of a hospital maintained in Venice by the Church of Santa Maria di Nazaret]

La·za·ri·llo de Tor·mes (lä′thä rē′lyō the tôr′mes), a picaresque romance (1554) of unknown authorship.

Laz·a·rist (laz′ər ist), *n.* *Rom. Cath. Ch.* Vincentian (def. 1). [after the College of St. *Lazare,* Paris, a former Vincentian center]

Laz·a·rus (laz′ər əs), *n.* **1.** the diseased beggar in the parable of the rich man and the beggar. Luke 16:19–31. **2.** a brother of Mary and Martha whom Jesus raised from the dead. John 11:1–44; 12:1–18. **3. Emma,** 1849–87, U.S. poet. **4.** (*italics*) a short story (1906) by Andreyev. [< LL < Gk *Lázaros* < Heb *El'āzār* Eleazar (one God has helped)]

laze (lāz), *v.,* **lazed, laz·ing,** *n.* —*v.i.* **1.** to idle or lounge lazily. —*v.t.* **2.** to pass (time, life, etc.) lazily (usually fol. by *away*). —*n.* **3.** a period of ease or indolence: *a quiet laze in the hammock.* [back formation from LAZY]

La·zear (lə zēr′), *n.* **Jesse William,** 1866–1900, U.S. physician and bacteriologist.

laz·u·li (laz′o͞o lē, -lī′, laz′yo͞o-, lazh′o͞o-), *n.* See **lapis lazuli.**

laz·u·line (laz′ə lēn′, -lin′, laz′yə-, lazh′ə-), *adj.* having the color of lapis lazuli. [LAZUL(I) + -INE¹]

laz·u·lite (laz′ə līt′, laz′yə-, lazh′ə-), *n.* an azure-blue mineral, hydrous magnesium iron aluminum phosphate,

$(FeMg)Al_2P_2O_8(OH)_2$. [< ML *lāzul(um)* azure, LAPIS LAZULI + -ITE[1]] —**laz·u·lit·ic** (laz′yə lit′ik), *adj.*

laz·u·rite (laz′ə rīt′, lazh′yə-, lazh′ə-), *n.* a mineral, sodium aluminum silicate and sulfide, $Na_5Al_3Si_3O_{12}S_3$, occurring in deep-blue crystals, used for ornamental purposes. [< ML *lāzur* AZURE + -ITE[1]]

la·zy (lā′zē), *adj.*, **la·zi·er, la·zi·est.** **1.** having an aversion to work or effort; indolent. **2.** causing idleness or indolence: *a hot, lazy afternoon.* **3.** slow-moving; sluggish: *a lazy stream.* **4.** (of a livestock brand) placed on its side instead of upright. [?] —**la′zi·ly,** *adv.* —**la′zi·ness,** *n.* —**la′zy·ish,** *adj.*
—**Syn. 1.** slothful. See **idle. 3.** inert, inactive, torpid.
—**Ant. 1.** industrious. **3.** quick.

la·zy·bones (lā′zē bōnz′), *n.* (*usually construed as sing.*) *Informal.* a lazy person. [LAZY + BONE[1] + -S[3]]

la′zy guy′, *Naut.* a rope or light tackle for keeping a boom from swinging.

la′zy hal′yard, *Naut.* a temporary halyard of light or old line, used in port so that the regular halyard can be preserved.

la′zy Su′san, a large, revolving tray for food, condiments, etc., placed at the center of a dining table.

la′zy tack′, *Naut.* **1.** either of the lines attached to the clews of a course so that the weather clew can be held down until a tackle is fitted. **2.** a running bight passing around a stay and attached to the tack of a fore-and-aft topsail set flying in order to keep it from blowing free.

la′zy tongs′, extensible tongs for grasping objects at a distance, consisting of a series of pairs of crossing pieces, each pair pivoted together in the middle and connected with the next pair at the extremities.

Lazy tongs

lb., *pl.* **lbs., lb.** pound. [< L *libra*, pl. *librae*]

L.B., 1. landing barge. **2.** light bomber. **3.** bachelor of letters; bachelor of literature. [< L *Litterārum Baccalaureus*; *Līterārum Baccalaureus*] **4.** local board.

lb. ap., *Pharm.* pound apothecary's.

L bar. See **angle iron** (def. 2). Also called **L beam.**

lb. av., pound avoirdupois.

lbf, pound-force.

LBJ, Lyndon Baines Johnson.

L.B.P., *Naut.* See **length between perpendiculars.**

lb. t., pound troy.

LC, landing craft.

L.C., Library of Congress.

l.c., 1. left center. **2.** letter of credit. **3.** in the place cited. [< L *locō citātō*] **4.** *Print.* lower case.

L/C, letter of credit. Also, **l/c**

l.c.a., lower-case alphabet.

LCD, a method of displaying readings continuously on digital watches, calculators, etc., using a liquid-crystal film, sealed between glass plates, that changes its optical properties when a current is applied. [L(IQUID)-C(RYSTAL) D(ISPLAY)]

L.C.D., lowest common denominator. Also, **l.c.d.**

L.C.F., lowest common factor. Also, **l.c.f.**

LCI, *U.S. Mil. and Navy.* a type of landing craft used in World War II and designed principally for carrying personnel and landing them on beaches. [*L(anding) C(raft) I(nfantry)*]

L.C.L., *Com.* less than carload lot. Also, **l.c.l.**

LCM, landing craft, mechanized.

L.C.M., least common multiple. Also, **l.c.m.**

LCT, *U.S. Mil. and Navy.* a type of landing craft used in World War II and designed for landing tanks and other vehicles on beaches. [*L(anding) C(raft), T(ank)*]

LCVP, landing craft, vehicle and personnel.

LD, 1. praise (be) to God. [< L *laus Deō*] **2.** lethal dose. **3.** long distance. **4.** Low Dutch.

Ld., 1. limited. **2.** lord.

L.D., Low Dutch.

L-dopa (el′ dō′pə, el′ do′pä), *n.* a drug for reversing the crippling effects of Parkinson's disease. [*L-(3, 4) d(ihydr)o(xy)p(henyl)a(lanine)*]

Ldp., 1. ladyship. **2.** lordship.

L.D.S., 1. Latter-day Saints. **2.** praise (be) to God forever. [< L *laus Deō semper*] **3.** Licentiate in Dental Surgery.

-le, 1. a suffix of verbs having a frequentative force: *dazzle; twinkle.* **2.** a suffix of adjectives formed originally on verbal stems and having the sense of "apt to": *brittle.* **3.** a noun suffix having originally a diminutive meaning: *bramble.* **4.** a noun suffix indicating agent or instrument: *beadle; bridle; thimble.* [ME *-len*, OE *-lian* (v.); ME *-el*, OE *-ol* (adj.); ME *-el*, OE *-il* (dim.); ME *-el*, OE *-ol*, *-ul* (agent)]

l.e., *Football.* left end.

lea[1] (lē, lā), *n.* **1.** a tract of open ground, esp. grassland; a meadow. **2.** land used for a few years for pasture or for growing hay, then plowed over and replaced by another crop. **3.** a crop of hay on tillable land. —*adj.* **4.** untilled; fallow. Also, **ley.** [ME *lege, lei*, OE *lēah*; c. OHG *lōh*, Flem *loo* (as in *Waterloo*), L *lūcus*]

lea[2] (lē), *n.* **1.** a measure of yarn of varying quantity, for wool usually 80 yards, cotton and silk 120 yards, linen 300 yards. **2.** *Textiles.* **a.** a unit length used to ascertain the linear density of yarns. **b.** a count or number representing units of linear measure per pound in linen or cotton yarn: *a 20-lea yarn.* [? back formation from ME *lese*, var. of LEASH]

Le·a (lē′ə), *n.* a girl's given name, form of **Leah** or **Lee.**

lea., 1. league. **2.** leather.

leach[1] (lēch), *v.t.* **1.** to cause (water or other liquid) to percolate through something. **2.** to remove soluble constituents from (ashes, soil, etc.) by percolation. —*v.i.* **3.** (of ashes, soil, etc.) to undergo the action of percolating water. **4.** to percolate, as water. —*n.* **5.** a leaching. **6.** the material leached. **7.** a vessel for use in leaching. [unexplained var. of obs. *letch* to wet (whence dial. *letch* bog), OE *leccan*, causative of LEAK] —**leach′a·bil′i·ty,** *n.* —**leach′a·ble,** *adj.* —**leach′er,** *n.*

leach[2] (lēch), *n.* *Naut.* leech[3].

leach·y (lē′chē), *adj.*, **leach·i·er, leach·i·est.** allowing water to percolate through, as sandy or rocky soil; porous. [LEACH[1] + -Y[1]]

Lea·cock (lē′kok), *n.* **Stephen (Butler),** 1869–1944, Canadian humorist and economist.

lead[1] (lēd), *v.*, **led, lead·ing,** *n.*, *adj.* —*v.t.* **1.** to take or conduct on the way; go before or with to show the way: *to lead a group on a cross-country hike.* **2.** to conduct by holding and guiding: *to lead a horse by a rope.* **3.** to influence or induce; cause: *Subsequent events led him to reconsider his position.* **4.** to guide in direction, course, action, opinion, etc.; bring: *You can lead him around to your point of view if you are shrewd with him.* **5.** to conduct or bring (water, wire, etc.) in a particular course. **6.** (of a road, passage, etc.) to serve to bring (a person) to a place: *The first street on the left will lead you to Andrews Place.* **7.** to take or bring: *The prisoners were led in to the warden's office.* **8.** to command or direct (an army or other large organization): *He led the Allied forces during the war.* **9.** to go at the head of or in advance of (a procession, list, body, etc.); proceed first in: *The chief will lead the parade.* **10.** to be superior to; have the advantage over: *The first baseman leads his teammates in runs batted in.* **11.** to have top position or first place in: *Iowa leads the nation in corn production.* **12.** to have the directing or principal part in: *He led a peace movement in the late 1930's.* **13.** to act as leader of (an orchestra, band, etc.); conduct. **14.** to go through or pass (time, life, etc.): *to lead a dreary existence; to lead a full life.* **15.** *Cards.* to begin a round, game, etc., with (a card or suit specified). **16.** to aim and fire a firearm or cannon ahead of (a moving target) in order to allow for the travel of the target while the bullet or shell is reaching it. **17.** *Football.* to throw a lead pass to (an intended receiver): *The quarterback led the left end.*
—*v.i.* **18.** to act as a guide; show the way: *You lead, we'll follow.* **19.** to afford passage to a place: *That path leads directly to his house.* **20.** to go first; be in advance: *The band will lead and the audience will follow.* **21.** to result in; tend toward (usually fol. by *to*): *The incident led to his resignation. One remark often leads to another.* **22.** to take the directing or principal part. **23.** to take the offensive: *The contender led with a right to the body.* **24.** *Cards.* to make the first play. **25.** to be led or submit to being led, as a horse: *A properly trained horse will lead easily.* **26.** *Baseball.* (of a base runner) to leave a base before the delivery of a pitch in order to reach the next base more quickly (often fol. by *away*). **27. lead off, a.** to take the initiative; begin. **b.** *Baseball.* to be the first player in the batting order or the first batter in an inning. **28. lead on,** to induce to continue a course of action that will probably end unfavorably; mislead: *She led him on to think that she would eventually accept his proposal of marriage.* **29. lead out, a.** to make a beginning. **b.** to escort a partner to begin a dance: *He led her out and they began a rumba.* **30. lead someone a chase** or **dance,** to cause someone difficulty by forcing him to do irksome or unnecessary things: *My search for the out-of-print book led me a chase through several libraries and bookstores.* **31. lead the way.** See **way** (def. 35). **32. lead up to, a.** to prepare the way for. **b.** to approach (a subject, disclosure, etc.) gradually or evasively: *I could tell by her allusions that she was leading up to something.*
—*n.* **33.** the first or foremost place; position in advance of others: *He took the lead in the race.* **34.** the extent of such advance: *He had a lead of four lengths.* **35.** one who or that which leads. **36.** a leash. **37.** a guide or indication of a road, course, method, etc., to follow. **38.** precedence; example; leadership: *They followed the lead of the capital in their fashions.* **39.** *Theat.* **a.** the principal part in a play. **b.** the person who plays it. **40.** *Cards.* **a.** the act or right of playing first, as in a round. **b.** the card, suit, etc., so played. **41.** *Journalism.* a short summary serving as an introduction to a news story, article, or other copy. **42.** *Elect.* an often flexible and insulated single conductor, as a wire, used in connections between pieces of electric apparatus. **43.** act of taking the offensive. **44.** *Naut.* **a.** the direction of a rope, wire, or chain. **b.** Also called **leader.** any of various devices for guiding a running rope. **45.** *Naval Archit.* the distance between the center of lateral resistance and the center of effort of a sailing vessel, usually expressed decimally as a fraction of the water-line length. **46.** an open channel through a field of ice. **47.** *Mining.* **a.** a lode. **b.** an auriferous deposit in an old river bed. **48.** the act of aiming a gun ahead of a moving target. **49.** the distance ahead of a moving target that a gun must be aimed in order to score a direct hit. **50.** *Baseball.* an act or instance of leading. **51.** *Manège.* (of a horse at a canter or gallop) the foreleg which consistently extends beyond and strikes the ground ahead of the other foreleg: *The horse is cantering on the left lead.*
—*adj.* **52.** most important; first: *lead editorial; lead elephant.* **53.** *Football.* (of a forward pass) thrown ahead of the intended receiver so as to allow him to catch it while running. **54.** *Baseball.* (of a base runner) nearest to scoring: *They forced the lead runner at third base on an attempted sacrifice.* [ME *lede(n)*, OE *lǣdan* (causative of *līthan* to go, travel); c. D *leiden*, G *leiten*, Icel *leitha*]
—**Syn. 1.** escort, precede. See **guide. 3.** persuade, convince. **10.** excel, outstrip, surpass. **33.** head, vanguard.
—**Ant. 1.** follow.

lead[2] (led), *n.* **1.** *Chem.* a heavy, comparatively soft, malleable, bluish-gray metal, sometimes found in its natural state but usually combined as a sulfide, esp. in galena. *Symbol:* Pb; *at. wt.:* 207.19; *at. no.:* 82; *sp. gr.:* 11.34 at 20°C. **2.** something made of this metal or of one of its alloys. **3.** a plummet or mass of lead suspended by a line, as for taking soundings. **4.** bullets collectively; shot. **5.** black lead or graphite. **6.** a small stick of graphite, as used in pencils. **7.** Also, **leading.** *Print.* a thin strip of type metal or brass less than type-high, used for increasing the space between lines of type. **8.** a grooved bar of lead or came in which sections of glass are set, as in stained-glass windows. **9. leads,** *Brit.* a roof, esp. one that is shallow or flat, covered with lead. **10.** See **white lead. 11. heave the lead,** *Naut.* to take a sounding with a lead. —*v.t.* **12.** to cover, line, weight, treat, or impregnate with lead or one of its compounds. **13.** *Print.* to insert leads between the lines of. **14.** to fix (window glass) in position with leads. —*adj.* **15.** made of or containing lead: *lead toys; a lead pipe; lead oxide; a lead compound.* [ME *lede*, OE *lēad*; c. D *lood*, G *Lot* plummet] —**lead′less,** *adj.*
—**Syn. 3.** weight, plumb.

Lead (lēd), *n.* a town in W South Dakota. 6211 (1960).

lead′ ac′etate (led), *Chem.* a white, crystalline, water-soluble, poisonous solid, $Pb(C_2H_3O_2)_2 \cdot 3H_2O$, used chiefly as a mordant in dyeing and printing textiles and as a drier in paints and varnishes. Also called **sugar of lead.**

lead′ ar′senate (led), *Chem.* a white, crystalline, water-insoluble, highly poisonous powder, $PbHAsO_4$, used as an insecticide.

Lead·bel·ly (led′bel′ē), *n.* See **Ledbetter, Huddie.**

lead′ block′ (lēd), *Naut.* any block that alters the direction of a rope; fairlead. Also called **leading block.**

lead′ col′ic (led), *Pathol.* See **painter's colic.**

lead·en (led′ən), *adj.* **1.** heavy or hard to lift or move: *a leaden weight; leaden feet.* **2.** dull, spiritless, or gloomy, as in mood, thought, etc.: *the leaden lines of prose in his book; a leaden atmosphere.* **3.** of a dull gray color: *leaden skies.* **4.** oppressive; heavy: *a leaden silence.* **5.** sluggish; listless: *He moved at a leaden pace.* **6.** of poor quality or little value: *a leaden age.* **7.** made or consisting of lead. —*v.t.* **8.** to make leaden, sluggish, dull, etc.: *Fatigue had leadened his brain and step.* [ME *leden*, OE *lēaden.* See LEAD[2], -EN[2]] —**lead′en·ly,** *adv.* —**lead′en·ness,** *n.*

lead·er (lē′dər), *n.* **1.** one who or that which leads. **2.** a guiding or directing head, as of an army, movement, political group, etc. **3.** a duct for conveying warm air from a hot-air furnace to a register or stack. **4.** *Music.* **a.** a conductor or director, as of an orchestra, band, or chorus. **b.** the player at the head of the first violins in an orchestra, the principal cornetist in a band, or the principal soprano in a chorus, to whom any incidental solos are usually assigned. **5.** a horse harnessed at the front of a team. **6.** *Journalism.* See **leading article. 7.** a featured article of trade, esp. one offered at a low price to attract customers. Cf. **loss leader. 8.** a pipe for conveying rain water downward, as from a roof; downspout. **9.** *Naut.* lead[1] (def. 44b). **10. leaders,** *Print.* a row of dots or a short line to lead the eye across a space. **11.** *Angling.* **a.** a length of nylon, silkworm gut, wire, or the like, to which the lure or hook is attached. **b.** the net used to direct fish into a weir, pound, etc. **12.** *Mining.* a thin vein of ore connected with a large vein. **13.** blank film or tape at the beginning of a length of film or magnetic tape, used for threading a motion-picture camera, tape recorder, etc. Cf. **trailer** (def. 6). [ME *leder(e).* See LEAD[1], -ER[1]] —**lead′er·less,** *adj.*

lead′er block′, *Naut.* See **lead block.**

lead′er ca′ble, *Naut.* a submarine cable laid along a channel and emitting signals received by vessels in such a way that they can follow the cable under conditions of poor visibility.

lead′er head′, a boxlike head of a downspout connected to a gutter.

lead·er·ship (lē′dər ship′), *n.* **1.** the position or function of a leader: *He managed to maintain his leadership of the party despite heavy opposition.* **2.** ability to lead: *He displayed leadership potential.* **3.** an act or instance of leading: *They prospered under his leadership.* **4.** the leaders of a group: *The union leadership agreed to arbitrate.* [LEADER + -SHIP]

lead′ glass′ (led), glass containing lead oxide.

lead′ glaze′ (led), *Ceram.* a siliceous glaze containing lead oxide as a flux.

lead-in (lēd′in′), *n.* **1.** *Radio, Television.* the connection between an antenna and a transmitter or receiving set. **2.** *Radio, Television.* the portion of a program or script that precedes or introduces a commercial. —*adj.* **3.** (of a conductor) carrying input to an electric or electronic device or circuit, esp. from an antenna. [n., adj. use of v. phrase *lead in*]

lead·ing[1] (lē′ding), *adj.* **1.** chief; principal; most important; foremost: *He was a leading figure in industry.* **2.** coming in advance of others; first: *He rode in the leading car.* **3.** directing, guiding. —*n.* **4.** the act of one who or that which leads. [ME (n.); see LEAD[1], -ING[2], -ING[1]] —**lead′ing·ly,** *adv.*
—**Syn. 3, 4.** ruling, governing.

lead·ing[2] (led′ing), *n.* **1.** a covering or framing of lead: *the leading of a stained-glass window.* **2.** *Print.* lead[2] (def. 7). [late ME; see LEAD[2], -ING[1]]

lead′ing ar′ticle (lē′ding), *Journalism.* **1.** the most important news story in a newspaper. **2.** *Brit.* the principal editorial in a newspaper. Also called **leader.**

lead′ing block′ (lē′ding). See **lead block.**

lead′ing coeffi′cient (lē′ding), *Math.* the coefficient of the term of highest degree in a given polynomial. *5 is the leading coefficient in* $5x^3 + 3x^2 - 2x + 1$.

lead′ing edge′ (lē′ding), *Aeron.* the edge of an airfoil or propeller blade facing the direction of motion.

lead′ing la′dy (lē′ding), an actress who plays the principal female role in a motion picture or play.

lead′ing light′ (lē′ding), **1.** *Naut.* See **range light** (def. 1). **2.** an important or influential person: *a leading light of the community.*

lead′ing man′ (lē′ding), an actor who plays the principal male role in a motion picture or play.

lead′ing mark′ (lē′ding), *Navig.* either of two conspicuous objects regarded as points on a line (**lead′ing line′**) upon which a vessel can sail a safe course.

lead′ing ques′tion (lē′ding), a question so worded as to suggest the proper or desired answer.

lead′ing strings′ (lē′ding), **1.** strings for leading and supporting a child learning to walk. **2.** excessively restraining guidance: *His mother tried to keep him in leading strings, but he finally married and moved away.*

lead′ing tone′ (lē′ding), *Music.* the seventh degree of the scale. Also called **lead′ing note′.**

lead·ing wind (lē′ding wind′), *Naut.* a wind abeam or on the quarter, esp. one strong enough to be a good sailing wind.

lead′ line′ (led), *Naut.* a line by which a lead is lowered into the water to take soundings: in deep-sea practice, divided into levels one fathom apart, variously treated as marks and deeps. [ME *leede lyne*]

lead′ monox′ide (led), *Chem.* litharge.

lead-off (lēd′ôf′, -of′), *adj.* leading off or beginning: *the lead-off item on the agenda.* [adj. use of v. phrase *lead off*]

lead·off (lēd′ôf′, -of′), *n.* **1.** an act that starts something; start; beginning. **2.** *Baseball.* the player who is first in the batting order or who is first to bat in an inning. [n. use of v. phrase *lead off*]

lead′ ox′ide (led), **1.** litharge. **2.** any oxide of lead, as red lead.

lead′ pen′cil (led), a writing or drawing implement made of graphite in a wooden or metal holder.

lead′-pipe cinch′ (led′pīp′), *Slang.* **1.** an absolute certainty: *It's a lead-pipe cinch he'll be there.* **2.** something very easy to accomplish: *Getting him elected will be a lead-pipe cinch.*

lead·plant (led′plant′, -plänt′), *n.* a North American, leguminous shrub, *Amorpha canescens*, the leaves and twigs of which have a gray cast. [LEAD[2] + PLANT]

lead′ poi′soning (led), **1.** *Pathol.* **a.** an acute toxic condition produced by absorption of lead into the body through skin contact, ingestion, or inhalation, occurring chiefly in children from mouthing toys or furnishings coated with lead paint, and characterized by convulsions and coma. **b.** Also called **plumbism, saturnism.** a chronic form of this condition, occurring chiefly in adults whose work involves contact with lead products, characterized by anemia, constipation, and abdominal pain. **2.** *Slang.* death or injury inflicted by a bullet or shot.

lead′ screw′ (lēd), (on a lathe) a rotating horizontal screw for moving the tool carriage along the work at a constant rate.

lead′ sheet′ (lēd), a copy of a song containing the melody line, sometimes along with the lyrics and the notations indicating the harmonic structure.

leads·man (ledz′mən), *n., pl.* **-men.** a seaman who sounds with a lead line. [LEAD[2] + 'S[1] + MAN]

lead′ tetraeth′yl (led), *Chem.* tetraethyllead.

lead′ time′ (lēd), the period of time between the planning and completed manufacture of a product.

lead′ track′ (lēd), a track connecting a railroad yard or facility with a main line or running track.

Lead·ville (led′vil), *n.* a town in central Colorado. 4008 (1960).

lead′ white′ (led), a poisonous pigment used in painting, consisting of basic lead carbonate and characterized chiefly by a fugitive white color, covering power, and tough, flexible film-forming properties. Also called **Cremnitz white, flake white.**

lead·wort (led′wûrt), *n.* any plumbaginaceous herb or shrub of the genus *Plumbago*, having spikes of blue, white, or red flowers. [LEAD[2] + WORT[2]]

lead·y (led′ē), *adj.,* **lead·i·er, lead·i·est.** like lead; leaden. [ME *leedy.* See LEAD[2], -Y[1]]

leaf (lēf), *n., pl.* **leaves** (lēvz), *v.* —*n.* **1.** one of the expanded, usually green organs borne by the stem of a plant. **2.** any similar or corresponding lateral outgrowth of a stem. **3.** a petal: *a rose leaf.* **4.** leaves collectively; foliage. **5.** *Bibliog.* a unit generally comprising two printed pages of a book, one on each side, but also applied to blank or illustrated pages. **6.** a thin sheet of metal: *silver leaf.* **7.** a lamina or layer. **8.** a sliding, hinged, or detachable flat part, as of a door, table top, etc. **9.** one of two sections of a drawbridge. **10.** a single strip of metal in a leaf spring. **11.** a tooth of a small gear wheel, as of a pinion. **12.** one single moving section of a drawbridge or bascule bridge. **13.** See **leaf fat.** **14.** *Textiles.* shaft (def. 14). **15. in leaf,** covered with foliage; having leaves: *the pale green tint of the woods newly in leaf.* **16. take a leaf out of** or **from someone's book,** to follow someone's example; imitate: *European countries that took a leaf out of American industry's book are now doing very well for themselves.* **17. turn over a new leaf,** to begin anew; make a fresh start: *Every New Year's we make resolutions to turn over a new leaf.* —*v.i.* **18.** to put forth leaves. **19.** *U.S.* to turn pages quickly (usually fol. by *through*): *to leaf through a book.* —*v.t.* **20.** to thumb or turn, as the pages of a book or magazine, in a casual or cursory inspection of the contents. [ME *leef,* OE *lēaf;* c. D *loof,* G *Laub,* Icel *lauf,* Goth *laufs*] —**leaf′like′,** *adj.*

A B C

Leaf of willow *Salix cordata* A, Blade B, Petiole C, Stipule

Leaf (lēf), *n.* **Mun·ro** (mun rō′), born 1905, U.S. author and illustrator of books for children.

leaf·age (lē′fij), *n.* foliage. [LEAF + -AGE]

leaf′ bee′tle, any of numerous, often brightly colored beetles of the family *Chrysomelidae,* that feed on the leaves of plants, the larvae of which infest the roots, stem, and leaves.

leaf·bird (lēf′bûrd′), *n.* any of several greenish, passerine birds of the genus *Chloropsis,* of Asia, related to the bulbuls, and often kept as pets. [LEAF + BIRD]

leaf′ blight′, *Plant Pathol.* **1.** a symptom or phase of many diseases of plants, characterized by necrotic spots or streaks on the leaves, accompanied by seed rot and seedling blight. **2.** any disease so characterized.

leaf′ blotch′, *Plant Pathol.* **1.** a symptom or phase of certain diseases of plants, characterized by necrotic discoloration of the leaves. **2.** any disease so characterized.

leaf′ bud′. See under **bud**[1] (def. 1a).

leaf′ bug′. See **plant bug.**

leaf′ cor′al, a red alga, *Bossea Orbigniana,* found on the Pacific coast of the U.S., having calcified, flattened, jointed stems.

leaf′-cut·ting ant′ (lēf′kut′ing), any of several tropical American ants of the genus *Atta* that cut and chew bits of leaves and flowers into a mash which they use to cultivate a fungus garden.

leaf′-cutting bee′, any of the bees of the family *Megachilidae* that cut circular pieces from leaves or flowers to line their nests.

leafed (lēft), *adj.* having leaves. [LEAF + -ED[2]]

leaf′ fat′, a layer of fat, esp. that about the kidneys of a hog.

leaf·hop·per (lēf′hop′ər), *n.* any of numerous leaping, homopterous insects of the family *Cicadellidae,* that suck plant juices, many being serious crop pests. [LEAF + HOPPER]

leaf′ in′sect, any of several orthopterous insects of the family *Phasmatidae,* of southern Asia and the East Indies, having a body that resembles a leaf in color and form. Also called **walking leaf.**

leaf′ lard′, lard prepared from the leaf fat of the hog.

leaf·less (lēf′lis), *adj.* without leaves. [LEAF + -LESS] —**leaf′less·ness,** *n.*

leaf·let (lēf′lit), *n.* **1.** a small flat or folded sheet of printed matter, as for distribution. **2.** one of the separate blades or divisions of a compound leaf. **3.** a small leaflike part or structure. **4.** a small or young leaf. [LEAF + -LET]

leaf′ min′er, the larva of any of numerous insects, as moths of the family *Gracilariidae,* that live in and feed on the parenchyma of leaves.

leaf′ mold′, a layer of soil or a compost consisting chiefly of decayed vegetable matter, esp. leaves.

leaf′ mon′key, langur.

leaf′ mus′tard. See under **mustard** (def. 2).

leaf′-nosed bat′ (lēf′nōzd′), any of various New and Old World bats, as of the families *Phyllostomatidae, Rhinolophidae,* and *Hipposideridae,* having a leaflike flap of skin at the tip of the nose.

leaf′ roll′, *Plant Pathol.* a disease of plants, esp. potatoes, characterized by upward rolling of the leaflets, chlorosis, stunting, and necrosis of the phloem, caused by a virus.

leaf′ roll′er, any of several insects, esp. moths of the family *Tortricidae,* the larvae of which form a nest by rolling and tying leaves with spun silk.

leaf′ rust′, *Plant Pathol.* a disease of cereals and other grasses, characterized by rust-colored pustules of spores on the affected leaf blades and sheaths and caused by any of several rust fungi of the genus *Puccinia.*

leaf′ scald′, *Plant Pathol.* a disease of plants, characterized by irregular, bleached areas on the leaves and defoliation and caused by any of several bacteria or fungi.

leaf′ spot′, *Plant Pathol.* **1.** a limited, often circular, discolored, diseased area on a leaf, usually including a central region of necrosis. **2.** any disease so characterized.

leaf′ spring′, a long, narrow, multiple spring composed of several layers of spring metal bracketed together. See illus. under **spring.**

leaf·stalk (lēf′stôk′), *n.* petiole (def. 1). [LEAF + STALK[1]]

leaf′ war′bler, any of several small, greenish or brownish, Old World warblers of the genus *Phylloscopus,* that feed on insects among the leaves of trees.

leaf·y (lē′fē), *adj.,* **leaf·i·er, leaf·i·est.** **1.** having large amounts of, covered with, or consisting of leaves or foliage: *the leafy woods.* **2.** leaflike; foliaceous. [LEAF + -Y[1]] —**leaf′i·ness,** *n.*

league[1] (lēg), *n., v.,* **leagued, lea·guing.** —*n.* **1.** a covenant or compact made between persons, parties, states, etc., for the maintenance or promotion of common interests or for mutual assistance or service. **2.** the aggregation of persons, parties, states, etc., associated in such a covenant or compact; confederacy. **3.** an association of individuals having a common goal: *The League of Women Voters held their meeting last week.* **4.** group; class; category: *He just simply isn't in your league.* **5.** a group of athletic teams organized to promote mutual interests and to compete chiefly among themselves: *a bowling league.* **6.** *Sports.* **a.** See **major league. b.** See **minor league.** **7. in league,** having a compact or agreement; united; allied: *The neighbors were in league to keep the streets safe for their children.* —*v.t.* **8.** to unite in a league; combine. [earlier *leage* < It *lega,* back formation from *legare* < L *ligāre* to bind; r. late ME *ligg* < MF *ligue* < It *liga,* var. of *lega*]
—**Syn. 1.** See **alliance. 2.** combination, coalition.

league[2] (lēg), *n.* **1.** a unit of distance, varying at different periods and in different countries, in English-speaking countries usually estimated roughly at three miles. **2.** a square league, as a unit of land measure. [ME *lege leuge* < LL *leuga,* var. of *leuca* < Celt; r. OE *lēowa* < Celt]

League′ Cit′y, a town in S Texas. 2622 (1960).

League′ of Na′tions, the organization of nations of the world to promote world peace and cooperation that was created by the Treaty of Versailles (1919) and dissolved, April 1946, by action of its 21st assembly.

lea·guer[1] (lē′gər), *Archaic.* —*v.t.* **1.** to besiege. —*n.* **2.** a siege. [< D *leger* bed, camp. See LAIR[1], LAAGER]

lea·guer[2] (lē′gər), *n.* a member of a league. [LEAGUE[1] + -ER[1]]

Le·ah (lē′ə), *n.* **1.** Also, *Douay Bible,* **Lia.** the first wife of Jacob. Gen. 29:23–26. **2.** Also, **Lea.** a girl's given name.

Lea·hy (lā′hē), *n.* **William Daniel,** 1875–1959, U.S. admiral and diplomat.

leak (lēk), *n.* **1.** an unintended hole, crack, or the like, through which water, air, light, etc., enters or escapes: *a leak in a garden hose; a leak in a blackout curtain.* **2.** any means of unintended entrance or escape. **3.** *Elect.* the loss of current from a conductor, usually resulting from poor insulation. **4.** an act of leaking. —*v.i.* **5.** to let water, air, light, etc., enter or escape, as through an unintended hole, crack, or the like: *The roof leaks.* **6.** to pass in or out in this manner, as water, air, light, etc.: *gas leaking from a pipe.* **7.** to transpire or become known undesignedly (usually fol. by *out*): *The news leaked out.* —*v.t.* **8.** to let (water, air, light, etc.) enter or escape: *This camera leaks light.* **9.** to allow to become known, as information given out covertly: *to leak the news of the ambassador's visit.* [ME *leke(n)* < Scand; cf. Icel *leka* to drip, leak; akin to D *lek,* obs. G *lech* leaky. See LEACH[1]] —**leak′er,** *n.* —**leak′less,** *adj.*

leak·age (lē′kij), *n.* **1.** an act of leaking; leak. **2.** something that leaks in or out. **3.** the amount that leaks in or out. **4.** *Com.* an allowance for loss by leaking. **5.** *Physics, Elect.* the loss of all or part of a useful agent, as of the electric current that flows through an insulator (**leak′age cur′rent**) or of the magnetic flux that passes outside useful flux circuits (**leak′age flux′**). [LEAK + -AGE]

leak·ance (lē′kəns), *n.* *Elect.* the reciprocal of the resistance of insulation. [LEAK + -ANCE]

Leaks·ville (lēks′vil), *n.* a town in N North Carolina. 6427 (1960).

Lea·key (lē′kē), *n.* **Louis Seymour Bazett,** born 1903, British archaeologist and anthropologist.

leak·y (lē′kē), *adj.,* **leak·i·er, leak·i·est.** **1.** allowing water, gas, etc., to leak in or out: *a leaky boat; a leaky container.* **2.** *Archaic.* unreliable: *a leaky memory; a leaky tongue.* [LEAK + -Y[1]] —**leak′i·ness,** *n.*

leal (lēl), *adj.* *Scot.* loyal; true. [ME *leel* < OF < L *lēgālis* LEGAL; see LOYAL] —**leal′ly,** *adv.* —**le·al·ty** (lē′əl tē), *n.*

lean[1] (lēn), *v.,* **leaned** or (*esp. Brit.*) **leant; lean·ing;** *n.* —*v.i.* **1.** to incline or bend from a vertical position: *She leaned over the balustrade and shouted to the men downstairs.* **2.** to incline, as in a particular direction; slant: *The post leans to the left. The building leaned sharply before renovation.* **3.** to incline in feeling, opinion, action, etc.: *to lean toward socialism.* **4.** to rest against or on something for support: *to lean against a wall.* **5.** to depend or rely: *to lean on empty promises.* —*v.t.* **6.** to incline or bend: *He leaned his head forward.* **7.** to cause to lean or rest; prop: *to lean a chair against the railing.* **8. lean over backward,** to go to great lengths to compensate for something: *He leans over backward in his efforts to prove he is unprejudiced.* —*n.* **9.** the act of leaning; inclination: *The tower has a pronounced lean.* [ME *lene(n),* OE *hleonian, hlinian;* c. G. *lehnen;* akin to L *clīnāre* to incline]

lean[2] (lēn), *adj.* **1.** (of persons or animals) without much flesh; not plump or fat; thin: *lean cattle.* **2.** (of meat) containing little or no fat. **3.** lacking in richness, fullness, quantity, etc.; poor: *a lean diet; lean years.* **4.** (of paint) having more pigment than oil. Cf. **fat** (def. 5). **5.** *Naut.* (of a bow) having fine lines; sharp. —*n.* **6.** the part of flesh that consists of muscle rather than fat. **7.** the lean part of anything. **8.** *Typesetting.* matter that is difficult to set because of complexity or intermixed fonts. Cf. **fat** (def. 25). [ME *lene,* OE *hlǣne*] —**lean′ly,** *adv.* —**lean′ness,** *n.*
—**Syn. 1.** skinny, lank, lanky, emaciated. See **thin. 3.** sparse, barren, unfruitful, jejune. —**Ant. 1, 2.** fat. **3.** fruitful.

Le·an·der (lē an′dər), *n.* *Class. Myth.* a youth who was the lover of Hero.

lean·er (lē′nər), *n.* **1.** one who or that which leans. **2.** *Horseshoes.* a thrown horseshoe that leans against the stake. [LEAN[1] + -ER[1]]

lean-faced (lēn′fāst′), *adj.* having a thin face.

lean·gle (ling′gəl, lē ang′gəl), *n.* *Australian.* an aboriginal war club or bludgeon. Also, **langeel, langiel.** [< native Austral]

lean·ing (lē′ning), *n.* inclination; tendency: *strong literary leanings.* [late ME *leninge,* OE *hlining.* See LEAN[1], -ING[1]]
—**Syn.** bent, propensity, proclivity, bias, penchant.

Lean′ing Tow′er of Pi′sa, The, a round, marble campanile in Pisa, Italy, begun by Bonanno in 1174 and now 16½ feet out of the perpendicular in its height of 179 feet.

lean′ limbed′, having lean, gaunt arms and legs.

Le·an·na (lē an′ə), *n.* a girl's given name.

leant (lent), *v.* *Chiefly Brit.* a pp. and pt. of **lean**[1].

lean-to (lēn′to͞o′), *n., pl.* **-tos.** **1.** a shack or shed supported at one side by trees or posts and having an inclined roof. **2.** a roof of a single pitch with the higher end abutting a wall or larger building. See illus. under **roof.** **3.** a structure with such a roof. [n. use of v. phrase *lean to*]

Lea·o (lē′ō), *n.* a boy's given name, form of **Leo.**

leap (lēp), *v.,* **leaped** or **leapt, leap·ing,** *n.* —*v.i.* **1.** to spring through the air from one point or position to another; jump: *to leap over a ditch.* **2.** to move quickly and lightly: *to leap aside.* **3.** to pass, come, rise, etc., as if with a jump: *to leap to a conclusion.* —*v.t.* **4.** to jump over: *to leap a fence.* **5.** to pass over as if by a jump: *to leap the Atlantic in a jet.* **6.** to cause to leap. —*n.* **7.** a spring, jump, or bound; a light, springing movement. **8.** the amount of space cleared in a leap; distance jumped. **9.** a place leaped or to be leaped over or from. **10.** an abrupt transition: *a successful leap from piano class to concert hall.* **11.** a sudden and decisive increase: *a leap in the company's profits.* **12. by leaps and bounds,** very rapidly: *We are progressing by leaps and bounds.* **13. leap in the dark,** an action of which the consequences are unknown: *The experiment was a leap in the dark.* [ME *lepe(n),* OE *hlēapan* to leap, run; c. G *laufen,* Icel *hlaupa,* Goth *hlaupan*]
—**Syn. 1.** bound. See **jump.**

leap·er (lē′pər), *n.* **1.** one who leaps. **2.** *Naut.* lipper. [ME; OE *hlēapere.* See LEAP, -ER[1]]

leap·frog (lēp′frog′, -frôg′), *n., v.t.,* **-frogged, -frog·ging.** —*n.* **1.** a game in which players take turns in leaping over another player bent over from the waist. —*v.t.* **2.** to jump over (a person or thing) in or as if in leapfrog: to move or advance (something) by leaping in this manner over intervening obstacles. [LEAP + FROG[1]] —**leap′frog′ger,** *n.*

leapt (lept, lēpt), *v.* a pt. and pp. of **leap.**

leap′ year′, **1.** (in the Gregorian calendar) a year that contains 366 days, with February 29 as an additional day added to offset the difference between the common year (365 days) and the astronomical year (365¼ days): occurring every fourth year, with the exception of centenary years not divisible by 400. **2.** a year containing an extra day in any calendar. Cf. **common year.** [ME *lepe yere*]

lear (lēr), *n.* *Scot. and North Eng.* learning; instruction; a lesson. [late ME *lere* lesson, n. use of *lere* to teach, OE *lǣran;* c. D *leren,* G *lehren,* Goth *laisjan;* akin to LORE]

Lear (lēr), *n.* **1. Edward,** 1812–88, English writer. **2.** (*italics.*) See **King Lear.**

lear′ board′, (on a sloping roof) a board laid next to the gutter to receive the turned-up edge of the metal lining. Also called **layer board.**

Le·ar·chus (lē är′kəs), *n.* *Class. Myth.* a son of Athamas and Ino who was killed by his father in a fit of madness.

lea′ rig′ (lē, lā), *Brit. Dial.* **1.** a ridge of grass or land left unplowed in a field. **2.** a ridge of grass marking the boundary around a cultivated field. [OE *lǣghrycg* lit., fallow ridge, equiv. to *lǣg-* (ME *leye,* modern *lea* adj. untilled) + *hrycg* back, spine, RIDGE]

learn (lûrn), *v.,* **learned** (lûrnd) or **learnt; learn·ing.** —*v.t.* **1.** to acquire knowledge of or skill in by study, instruction, or experience: *to learn French.* **2.** to become informed of or acquainted with; ascertain: *to learn the truth.* **3.** to memorize: *He learned the poem so he could recite it at the dinner.* **4.** to gain (a habit, mannerism, etc.) by experience, exposure to example, or the like; acquire: *He learned patience from his father.* **5.** *Nonstandard.* to instruct in; teach: *I'll learn him a thing or two.* —*v.i.* **6.** to acquire knowledge or skill: *to learn rapidly.* **7.** to become informed (usually fol. by *of*): *to learn of an accident.* [ME *lerne(n),* OE *leornian* to learn, read, ponder, akin to *lesan* to glean (c. G *lernen* to learn, *lesen* to read). See LEAR] —**learn′a·ble,** *adj.* —**learn′er,** *n.*
—**Syn. 1.** LEARN, ASCERTAIN, DETECT, DISCOVER imply adding to one's store of facts. To LEARN is to add to one's knowledge or information: *to learn a language.* To ASCERTAIN is to verify facts by inquiry or analysis: *to ascertain the truth about an event.* To DETECT implies becoming aware of something which had been obscure, secret, or concealed: *to detect a flaw in reasoning.* To

DISCOVER is also used with objective clauses as a synonym of LEARN in order to suggest that the new information acquired is surprising to the learner: *I discovered that she had been married before.*

learn·ed (lûr′nid), *adj.* **1.** having much knowledge; scholarly: *a group of learned men.* **2.** connected or involved with the pursuit of knowledge, esp. of a scholarly nature: *a learned society; a learned journal.* **3.** of or showing learning: *He was learned in the ways of the world.* [ME *lerned.* See LEARN, -ED[2]] —**learn′ed·ly,** *adv.* —**learn′ed·ness,** *n.*

learn′ed profes′sion, one of the three vocations of theology, law, and medicine, commonly held to require highly advanced learning, high principles, etc. Cf. **profession** (def. 1).

learn·ing (lûr′ning), *n.* **1.** knowledge acquired by systematic study in any field or fields of scholarly application. **2.** the act or process of acquiring knowledge or skill. **3.** *Psychol.* the modification of behavior through practice, training, or experience. [ME *lerning,* OE *leornung.* See LEARN, -ING[1]]
—**Syn. 1.** LEARNING, ERUDITION, LORE, SCHOLARSHIP refer to knowledge existing or acquired. LEARNING is knowledge acquired by systematic study, as of literature, history, or science: *a body of learning; fond of literary learning.* ERUDITION suggests a thorough, formal, and profound sort of knowledge obtained by extensive research; it is esp. applied to knowledge in fields other than those of mathematics and physical sciences: *a man of vast erudition in languages.* LORE is accumulated knowledge in a particular field, esp. of a curious, anecdotal, or traditional nature; the word is now somewhat poetic: *nature lore; gypsy lore.* SCHOLARSHIP is the formalized learning which is taught in schools, esp. as actively employed by one trying to master some field of knowledge or extend its bounds: *high standards of scholarship in history.*

learnt (lûrnt), *v.* a pt. and pp. of **learn.**

Lea·roy (lē′roi, lə roi′), *n.* a boy's given name. Also, **Leroy, Leeroy.**

lear·y (lēr′ē), *adj.* leery[2].

lease[1] (lēs), *n., v.,* **leased, leas·ing.** —*n.* **1.** a contract renting land, buildings, etc., to another; a contract or instrument conveying property to another for a specified period or for a period determinable at the will of either lessor or lessee in consideration of rent or other compensation. **2.** the property leased. **3.** the period of time for which it is made: *a five-year lease.* **4. a new lease on life,** a chance to improve one's circumstances or to live more happily because of some good fortune: *Plastic surgery has given many persons a new lease on life.* —*v.t.* **5.** to grant the temporary possession or use of (lands, tenements, etc.) to another, usually for compensation at a fixed rate; let: *She planned to lease her apartment for the year she was gone.* **6.** to take or hold by lease: *He leased the farm from the old count.* —*v.i.* **7.** to grant a lease; let or rent: *to lease at a lower rental.* [late ME *les* < AF (equiv. to OF *lais,* now *legs* legacy), back formation from *lesser* to lease, lit., let go (equiv. to OF *laissier*) < L *laxāre* to release, let go. See LAX] —**leas′a·ble,** *adj.* —**lease′less,** *adj.* —**leas′er,** *n.*
—**Syn. 5, 6.** rent, charter, hire.

lease[2] (lēs), *n. Textiles.* **1.** a system for keeping the warp in position and under control by alternately crossing the warp yarn over and under the lease rods. **2.** the order of drawing in the warp ends. [ME *lese* length or coil of thread, var. of *lesh* LEASH]

lease·back (lēs′bak′), *n.* the disposal of a building, land, or the like, to a buyer under special arrangements for simultaneously leasing it on a long-term basis to the original seller, usually with an option to renew the lease. Also called **sale and leaseback.** [n. use of v. phrase *lease back*]

lease·hold (lēs′hōld′), *n.* **1.** a land interest acquired under a lease. —*adj.* **2.** held by lease. [LEASE[1] + HOLD[1]]

lease·hold·er (lēs′hōl′dər), *n.* a tenant under a lease. [LEASE[1] + HOLDER]

lease·man (lēs′mən), *n., pl.* **-men. 1.** Also called **landman.** one who leases land and obtains the rights to its use, esp. oil-drilling rights. **2.** one who leases land from property owners with the intention of erecting advertising billboards on it. [LEASE[1] + MAN[1]]

lease-pur·chase (lēs′pûr′chəs), *n.* **1.** the continuing use of goods, as office equipment, under a lease for a stipulated period with option for the lessee to buy them on favorable terms, as with the rental charges already paid credited toward the purchase price. **2.** *U.S.* a contract under which the government purchases real property by equal annual payments of rent over a term of 10 to 25 years, stipulating that upon expiration of the term the government will obtain title to the real property and construct or remodel federal buildings. —*adj.* **3.** of or pertaining to lease-purchase.

lease′ rod′, a rod or bar between the whip roll and the harness on a loom for keeping the warp in place.

leash (lēsh), *n.* **1.** a thong or line for holding a dog or other animal in check; a lead. **2.** check; curb; restraint: *to keep one's temper in leash; a tight leash on one's subordinates.* **3.** *Hunting.* a brace and a half, as of foxes. —*v.t.* **4.** to secure or hold in or as in a leash; control: *to leash water power for industrial use.* **5.** to bind together by or as if by a leash; connect; link; associate. [ME *lesh,* var. of *lece, lese* < OF *laisse.* See LEASE[1]]

leas·ing (lē′zing), *n. Archaic.* lying; falsehood. [ME *lesing,* OE *lēasung,* verbid of *lēasian* to tell lies, deriv. of *lēas* false. See -LESS, -ING[1]]

least (lēst), *adj., a superl. of* **little** *with* **less** *or* **lesser** *as compar.* **1.** smallest in size, amount, degree, etc.; slightest: *He walked the least distance of all.* **2.** lowest in consideration or importance. —*n.* **3.** something that is least; the least amount, quantity, degree, etc. **4. at least, a.** at the lowest estimate or figure: *The repairs will cost at least $100.* **b.** at any rate; in any case: *At least he has an alternative.* Also, **at the least. 5. not in the least,** not in the smallest degree; not at all: *I am not in the least concerned about the outcome of the World Series.* —*adv.* **6.** *superl. of* **little** *with* **less** *as compar.* to the smallest extent, amount, or degree: *That's the least important of all. He talks least.* [ME *leest(e),* OE *lǣst,* superl. of *lǣs(sa)* LESS]

least′ bit′tern. See under **bittern**[1] (def. 2).

least′ com′mon denom′inator, *Math.* the smallest number that is a common denominator of a given set of fractions. Also called **lowest common denominator.**

least′ com′mon mul′tiple. See **lowest common multiple.**

least′ fly′catcher, a small flycatcher, *Empidonax minimus,* of eastern North America. Also called **chebec.**

least′ kil′lifish, a poeciliid fish, *Heterandria formosa,* found in coastal swamps from South Carolina to Florida, which feeds on mosquito larvae.

least′ sand′piper, a small, American sandpiper, *Erolia minutilla,* related to the stints of Europe.

least′ shrew′, a brownish shrew, *Cryptotis parva,* found in grassy regions of the eastern U.S., that grows to a length of about three inches.

least′ signif′icant dig′it, the digit farthest to the right in a number. *Abbr.:* LSD Cf. **most significant digit.**

least′ squares′, *Statistics.* a method of determining constants from observations by minimizing squares of residuals between observations and their theoretical expected values.

least′ up′per bound′, *Math.* an upper bound that is less than or equal to all the upper bounds of a particular set. *3* is the least upper bound of the set consisting of *1, 2, 3. Abbr.:* lub Also called **supremum.** Cf. **bound**[3] (def. 4), **greatest lower bound, lower bound, upper bound.**

least·ways (lēst′wāz′), *adv. Dial.* at least; at any rate; in any event. [ME *leest weye.* See LEAST, -WAYS]

least′ wea′sel, a weasel, *Mustela rixosa,* found in northern regions, that grows to a length of about six inches. Also called **pygmy weasel.**

least·wise (lēst′wīz′), *adv. Informal.* at least; at any rate. Also, **least·ways.** [LEAST + -WISE]

leath·er (leth′ər), *n.* **1.** the skin of animals prepared for use by tanning or a similar process designed to preserve it against decay and to make it pliable or supple when dry. **2.** some article or appliance made of this material. **3.** See **stirrup leather.** —*adj.* **4.** pertaining to, made of, or resembling leather: *leather processing; leather upholstery.* —*v.t.* **5.** to cover or furnish with leather. **6.** *Informal.* to beat with a leather strap. [ME *lether,* OE *lether-* (in compounds); c. D, G *leder,* Icel *lethr,* Ir *leathar*]

leath′er·back tur′tle (leth′ər bak′), a sea turtle, *Dermochelys coriacea,* having a leathery skin covering its shell, reaching a length of over eight feet and weighing over a thousand pounds: the largest living sea turtle. Also called **leath′er·back′.** [LEATHER + BACK[1]]

Leath·er·ette (leth′ə ret′), *n. Trademark.* material constructed of paper or cloth and finished to simulate the grain, color, and texture of leather, used in the manufacture of luggage, novelty items, bookbindings, etc.

leath·er·fish (leth′ər fish′), *n., pl.* **-fish·es,** (*esp. collectively*) **-fish.** a filefish. [LEATHER + FISH]

leath·er·flow·er (leth′ər flou′ər), *n.* any of several plants of the genus *Clematis,* esp. *C. Viorna,* of the eastern U.S., having purplish flowers with thick, leathery sepals. [LEATHER + FLOWER]

leath·er-hard (leth′ər härd′), *adj.* (of ceramic clay) moist but not sufficiently so to be plastic.

leath·er·jack·et (leth′ər jak′it), *n.* **1.** Also called **leath′er jack′.** any of several carangid fishes having narrow, linear scales embedded in the skin at various angles, esp. *Oligoplites saurus,* found in tropical American waters. **2.** *Australian.* a pancake or other dough fried over a campfire by bushmen. **3.** the grub of the crane fly. [LEATHER + JACKET]

leath·er·leaf (leth′ər lēf′), *n., pl.* **-leaves.** an evergreen, ericaceous shrub, *Chamaedaphne calyculata,* having leathery leaves, found in bogs in the North Temperate Zone. [LEATHER + LEAF]

leath·er-lunged (leth′ər lungd′), *adj. Informal.* speaking or capable of speaking in a loud, resonant voice, esp. for prolonged periods: *The leather-lunged senator carried on the filibuster for 18 hours.*

leath·ern (leth′ərn), *adj.* **1.** made of leather. **2.** resembling leather. [ME, OE *lether(e)n.* See LEATHER, -EN[2]]

leath·er·neck (leth′ər nek′), *n. Slang.* a U.S. marine. [from the leather-lined collar of original Marine uniform, mid-19th century]

Leath·er·oid (leth′ə roid′), *n. Trademark.* an imitation leather product consisting of chemically treated and vulcanized paper or other vegetable fiber.

leath′er star′, a starfish, *Dermasterias imbricata,* of the western coast of North America, having the body covered by a thick, leathery skin.

Leath′er-Stock·ing Tales′ (leth′ər stok′ing), a series of historical novels by James Fenimore Cooper, comprising *The Pioneers, The Last of the Mohicans, The Prairie, The Pathfinder,* and *The Deerslayer.*

leath·er·wood (leth′ər wŏŏd′), *n.* an American shrub, *Dirca palustris,* having a tough bark. Also called **moosewood.** [LEATHER + WOOD[1]]

leath·er·work (leth′ər wûrk′), *n.* **1.** work or decoration done in leather. **2.** an article or articles made of leather. [LEATHER + WORK]

leath·er·work·er (leth′ər wûr′kər), *n.* a person whose trade is working in leather. [LEATHER + WORKER]

leath·er·y (leth′ə rē), *adj.* like leather; tough and flexible. [LEATHER + -Y[1]] —**leath′er·i·ness,** *n.*

leave[1] (lēv), *v.,* **left, leav·ing.** —*v.t.* **1.** to go away from, depart from, or quit, as a place, a person, or a thing: *to leave a room; to leave the house; to leave a job.* **2.** to let stay or be as specified: *to leave a door unlocked.* **3.** to let (a person or animal) remain in a position to do something without interference: *Leave the puppy alone. We left him to his work.* **4.** to stop or abandon: *He left drinking for nearly two years. He left writing that passage for another day. He left music to study law.* **5.** to let (a thing) remain for action or decision: *He left the details to his lawyer.* **6.** to disregard; neglect: *We will leave this for the moment and concentrate on the major problem.* **7.** to exclude; fail to make part of something; omit (often fol. by *out* or *off*): *to leave out information in a report; to leave a name off a list.* **8.** to allow to remain in the same place, condition, etc.: *There is plenty of work left.* **9.** to let remain or have remaining behind after going, disappearing, ceasing, etc.: *The wound left a scar.* **10.** to have remaining after death: *He leaves a widow.* **11.** to give for use after one's death or departure: *to leave money in a will.* **12.** to give in charge: *to leave a parcel with the porter.* **13.** to have as a remainder after subtraction: *2 from 4 leaves 2.* —*v.i.* **14.** to go away, depart, or set out: *We leave for Europe tomorrow.* **15. leave in,** *Bridge.* to make no further bid after a bid, double, or redouble, esp. by one's partner. **16. leave off, a.** to desist from; stop; abandon. **b.** to stop using or wearing: *It had stopped raining, so we left off our coats.* **17. leave out,** to omit; exclude: *She left out an important detail in her account. He always fights, so we left him out of the game.* [ME *leve(n),* OE *lǣfan* (causative formation from root in *lāf* remainder); c. OHG *leiban* (cf. G *bleiben* to remain), Icel *leifa,* Goth *-laibjan*] —**leav′er,** *n.*
—**Syn. 1.** vacate; abandon, forsake, desert; relinquish. **4.** forbear, cease, renounce. See **let**[1]. **6.** ignore, forget. **11.** bequeath, will; devise, transmit. —**Ant. 1.** join. **14.** arrive.

leave[2] (lēv), *n.* **1.** permission to do something: *to beg leave to go elsewhere.* **2.** permission to be absent, as from duty: *to be on leave.* **3.** the time this permission lasts: *30 days' leave.* **4.** a parting; departure; farewell: *He took his leave before the formal ceremonies began. He took leave of her after dinner.* **5.** *Foundry.* draft (def. 17). **6.** *Bowling.* the pin or pins in upright position after the bowl of the first ball. [ME *leve,* OE *lēaf.* See FURLOUGH]
—**Syn. 1–3.** liberty. **2, 3.** vacation, furlough.

leave[3] (lēv), *v.i.,* **leaved, leav·ing.** to put forth leaves; leaf. [ME *levi,* OE **lēafian,* deriv. of *lēaf* LEAF]

leaved (lēvd), *adj.* **1.** having leaves; leafed. **2.** *Heraldry.* represented as having leaves: *a lily leaved and slipped proper.* [ME *leved.* See LEAVE[3], -ED[2]]

leav·en (lev′ən), *n.* **1.** a mass of fermenting dough reserved for producing fermentation in a new batch of dough. **2.** an agent or element that acts in or upon something to produce a gradual change or modification: *the leaven of wit in his writing.* —*v.t.* **3.** to produce bubbles of gas in (dough or batter) by means of any of a variety of leavening agents. **4.** to permeate with an altering or transforming influence. [ME *levain* < MF < L *levāmen* that which raises (the spirits), equiv. to *levā(re)* (to) raise + *-men* suffix of result] —**leav′en·less,** *adj.*
—**Syn. 4.** infect, lighten, enliven.

leav·en·ing (lev′ə ning), *n.* **1.** an agent used to produce fermentation in dough or batter; leaven. **2.** an additional element or quality that alters or modifies something. [LEAVEN + -ING[1]]

Leav·en·worth (lev′ən wûrth′, -wərth), *n.* **1.** a city in NE Kansas. 22,052 (1960). **2.** a federal and military prison there.

leave′ of ab′sence, 1. permission to be absent from duty, employment, service, etc.; leave. **2.** the length of time granted in such permission: *a two-year leave of absence.*

leaves (lēvz), *n.* pl. of **leaf.**

Leaves′ of Grass′, a book of poems (first edition, 1855; final edition, 1891–92) by Walt Whitman.

leave-tak·ing (lēv′tā′king), *n.* a saying farewell; a parting or good-by; departure: *His leave-taking was brief.* [ME]

leav·ing (lē′ving), *n.* **1.** something that is left; residue. **2. leavings,** remains; refuse. [ME *leving.* See LEAVE[1], -ING[1]]

Lea·vis (lē′vis), *n.* **F(rank) R(aymond),** born 1895, English critic and teacher.

leav·y (lē′vē), *adj.,* **leav·i·er, leav·i·est.** *Archaic.* leafy. [late ME *levy.* See LEAF, -Y[1]]

Lea·wood (lē′wŏŏd′), *n.* a town in E Kansas. 7466 (1960).

Le Bal des Vo·leurs (*Fr.* lə bal dā vô lœr′). See **Thieves' Carnival.**

Leb·a·nese (leb′ə nēz′, -nēs′), *adj., n., pl.* **-nese.** —*adj.* **1.** of or pertaining to Lebanon or its natives or inhabitants. —*n.* **2.** a native or inhabitant of Lebanon. [LEBAN(ON) + -ESE]

Leb·a·non (leb′ə nən), *n.* **1.** a republic at the E end of the Mediterranean, N of Israel. 2,200,000 (est. 1965); 3927 sq. mi. *Cap.:* Beirut. **2.** a city in SE Pennsylvania. 30,045 (1960). **3.** a town in central Indiana. 9523 (1960). **4.** a town in W New Hampshire. 9299 (1960). **5.** a town in central Missouri. 8220 (1960). **6.** a town in SW Ohio. 5993 (1960). **7.** a town in W Oregon. 5858 (1960). **8.** a town in central Kentucky. 4813 (1960). **9.** a town in SW Illinois. 2863 (1960).

Leb′anon Moun′tains, a mountain range extending the length of Lebanon, in the central part. Highest peak, 10,049 ft.

Le Ba·teau Iv·re (*Fr.* lə ba tō ē′vrᵊ), a poem (1871) by Rimbaud. English, **The Drunken Boat.**

leb·bek (leb′ek), *n.* **1.** Also called **leb′bek tree′.** a leguminous tree, *Albizzia Lebbek,* of tropical Asia and Australia, having pinnate leaves and greenish-yellow flowers. **2.** Also called **koko.** the hard, durable wood of this tree, used in the construction of buildings. [?]

Le·bens·raum (lā′bəns roum′, -bənz-), *n.* additional territory desired by a nation, as for the expansion of trade. [< G: space for living]

le·bes (lē′bēz), *n., pl.* **-bes.** *Gk. and Rom. Antiq.* a wine bowl having an oval body without handles and with a rounded base. [< L < Gk: kettle, cauldron]

Le·besgue (lə beg′), *n.* **Hen·ri Lé·on** (äN rē′ lā ôN′), 1875–1941, French mathematician.

Lebesgue′ in′tegral, *Math.* an integral obtained by application of the theory of measure and more general than the Riemann integral. [named after H. L. LEBESGUE]

leb·ku·chen (lāb′kōō kən; *Ger.* lāp′kōō′KHən), *n., pl.* **-chen.** *German Cookery.* a hard, chewy or brittle Christmas cooky, usually flavored with honey and spices and containing nuts and citron. [< G; MHG *lebekuoche.* See LOAF[1], CAKE]

Le Bour·geois Gen·til·homme (*Fr.* lə bōōr zhwa zhäN tē yôm′), a comedy (1670) by Molière.

Le Bour·get (lə bōōr zhā′; *Fr.* lə bōōr zhe′), a suburb of Paris: airport.

Le·brun (lə brœN′), *n.* **1. Al·bert** (al ber′), 1871–1950, president of France 1932–40. **2. Charles** (sharl). Also, **Le Brun.** 1619–90, French painter. **3. Mme. Vigée-.** See **Vigée-Lebrun, Marie Anne Elisabeth.**

Lec·ce (let′che), *n.* a city in SE Italy: ancient Greek and Roman city; noted for its baroque architecture. 75,439 (1961).

le·cha·te·lier·ite (lə shät′əlēr′īt), *n.* a mineral, an amorphous form of silica formed by the fusion by heat of silica and found in fulgurites. [< F, named after H.-L. *Le Châtelier* (1850–1936), French chemist; see -ITE¹]

Le Cha′te·lier prin′ciple (lə shät′əl yā′), *Physics.* the law that if a constraint is applied to a system in equilibrium, the system adjusts to a new equilibrium that tends to counteract the constraint. [see LECHATELIERITE]

le·cha·yim (lə кнä′yim, -кнä yēm′), *n. Hebrew.* lehayim.

Lech·e·a·tes (lek′ē ā′tēz), *n. Class. Myth.* an epithet of Zeus, meaning "in childbed."

lech·er (lech′ər), *n.* **1.** a man given to excessive sexual indulgence. —*v.i.* **2.** to engage in lechery. [ME *lech(o)ur* < OF *lecheor* glutton, libertine, equiv. to *lech(ier)* (to) lick (< Gmc; cf. OHG *leccōn* to LICK) + *-eor* -OR²]

lech·er·ous (lech′ər əs), *adj.* **1.** given to or characterized by lechery: *a lecherous old man.* **2.** erotically suggestive; inciting to lust: *lecherous photographs.* [ME < MF *lechereus.* See LECHER, -OUS] —**lech′er·ous·ly,** *adv.* —**lech′er·ous·ness,** *n.*

lech′er wires′ (lek′ər), *Electronics.* parallel wires of such length and terminations that the system will resonate, producing standing waves, if the frequency of the excitation is correct. [named after E. *Lecher* (d. 1926), Austrian physicist]

lech·er·y (lech′ə rē), *n., pl.* **-er·ies. 1.** free or excessive indulgence of sexual desire. **2.** a lecherous act. [ME *lecherie* < OF. See LECHER, -Y³]

lech′o·sos o′pal (lek′ə sōs′), a variety of opal having a deep-green play of color. [*lechosos* < Sp *lechoso* milky, equiv. to *leche* milk (< L *lact-*; see LACT-) + *-oso* (< L *-ōsus* -OUS)]

lech·u·guil·la (lech′ə gē′ə; *Sp.* le′chōō gē′yä), *n., pl.* **-guil·las** (-gē′əz; *Sp.* -gē′yäs). a semi-desert plant, *Agave lecheguilla,* of Mexico, grown as an ornamental. [< Sp, dim. of *lechuga* LETTUCE]

le·chwe (lēch′wē), *n.* an African antelope, *Onotragus leche,* related to the waterbuck, inhabiting wet, grassy plains. [< Bantu]

Le Cid (*Fr.* lə sēd′), **1.** a drama (1636) by Corneille. **2.** an opera (1885) by Jules Massenet.

lec·i·thal (les′ə thəl), *adj. Embryol.* having a yolk, as certain eggs or ova. Also, **lec·i·thic** (les′ə thik). [< Gk *lékith(os)* egg yolk + -AL¹] —**lec·i·thal·i·ty** (les′i thal′i tē), *n.*

lec·i·thin (les′ə thin), *n.* **1.** *Biochem.* any of a group of yellow-brown fatty substances, occurring in animal and plant tissues and egg yolk, composed of units of choline, phosphoric acid, fatty acids, and glycerol. **2.** a commercial form of this substance, obtained chiefly from soybeans, corn, and egg yolk, used in candies, foods, cosmetics, and inks. [< Gk *lékith(os)* egg yolk + -IN²]

le·cith·i·nase (lə sith′ə nās′), *n. Biochem.* an enzyme that catalyzes the hydrolysis of lecithin. [LECITHIN + -ASE]

lec·i·thoid (les′ə thoid′), *adj. Biochem.* pertaining to or resembling lecithin. [< Gk *lékith(os)* egg yolk + -OID]

Leck·y (lek′ē), *n.* **William Edward Hart·pole** (härt′pōl), 1838–1903, Irish essayist and historian.

Le Comte de Mon·te-Cris·to (*Fr.* lə kôɴt də môɴ tə krē′stō). See **Count of Monte Cristo, The.**

Le·conte de Lisle (lə kôɴt də lēl′), **Charles Ma·rie** (sharl ma rē′), 1818–94, French poet.

Le Cor·bu·sier (*Fr.* lə kôr by zyā′), (*Charles Édouard Jeanneret*), 1887–1965, Swiss architect in France.

Le Crac (lə kräk′), former name of **Kerak.**

Le Creu·sot (lə krœ zō′), a city in E central France. 33,779 (1962).

lect., 1. lecture. **2.** lecturer.

lec·tern (lek′tərn), *n.* **1.** a reading desk in a church on which the Bible rests and from which the lessons are read during the church service. **2.** a desk or stand with a slanted top, used to hold a book, manuscript, etc., at the proper height for a reader, lecturer, etc. [ME *lettorne* < MF *letrun,* var. of *letrin* < ML *lect(ō)rīn(um),* n. use of neut. of *lectōrīnus.* See LECTOR, -INE¹]

lec·tion (lek′shən), *n.* **1.** a version of a passage in a particular copy or edition of a text; a variant reading: *Much critical discussion has revolved around the lections in the writings of Henry James.* **2.** a portion of sacred writing read in a divine service; lesson; pericope. [< L *lectiōn-* (s. of *lectiō*) a reading, equiv. to *lect(us)* chosen, read (ptp. of *legere;* c. Gk *légein* to speak) + *-iōn* -ION]

lec·tion·ar·y (lek′shə ner′ē), *n., pl.* **-ar·ies.** a book or a list of lections for reading in a divine service. [< eccl. L *lectiōnāri(um).* See LECTION, -ARY]

lec·tor (lek′tər), *n.* **1.** a lecturer in a college or university. **2.** *Rom. Cath. Ch.* **a.** a member of the next to lowest-ranking of the minor orders. **b.** the order itself. Cf. **acolyte** (def. 2), **exorcist** (def. 2), **ostiary** (def. 1). [late ME < L: a reader. See LECTION, -OR²] —**lec·tor·ate** (lek′tər it, -tə rāt′), **lec′tor·ship′,** *n.*

lec·ture (lek′chər), *n., v.,* **-tured, -tur·ing.** —*n.* **1.** a discourse read or delivered before an audience, esp. for instruction or to set forth some subject: *a lecture on Picasso's paintings.* **2.** a speech of warning or reproof as to conduct; a long, tedious reprimand. —*v.i.* **3.** to give a lecture or series of lectures: *He spent the year lecturing at various ladies' clubs on the island.* —*v.t.* **4.** to deliver a lecture to or before; instruct by lectures. **5.** to rebuke or reprimand at some length: *He lectured the child regularly but with little effect.* [late ME < L *lectūra* a reading. See LECTION, -URE] —**Syn. 1.** address, talk, paper, speech. **4.** address, teach. **5.** admonish; hector.

lec·tur·er (lek′chər ər), *n.* **1.** one who lectures. **2.** an academic rank given in American colleges to a teacher ranking below assistant professor. [LECTURE + -ER¹]

lec·ture·ship (lek′chər ship′), *n.* the office of lecturer. [LECTURE + -SHIP]

Le·cuo·na (lə kwō′nə; *Sp.* le kwō′nä), *n.* **Er·nes·to** (er nes′tō), 1896–1963, Cuban composer.

lec·y·thus (les′ə thəs), *n., pl.* **-thi** (-thī′). lekythos. —**lec′y·thoid′,** *adj.*

led (led), *v.* pt. and pp. of **lead¹.**

LED, a semiconductor diode that emits light when energized by a pulse of current: used in electronic equipment, and esp. for displaying readings on digital watches, calculators, etc. [L(IGHT)-E(MITTING) D(IODE)]

Le·da (lē′də), *n.* **1.** *Class. Myth.* the mother, by her husband Tyndareus, of Castor and Clytemnestra and, by Zeus in the form of a swan, of Pollux and Helen. **2.** a girl's given name.

Le′da and the Swan′, a poem (1925) by W. B. Yeats.

Led·bet·ter (led′bet ər), *n.* **Hud·die** (hud′ē), ("*Leadbelly*"), 1885?–1949, U.S. folk singer.

Le·der·berg (lā′dər bûrg′), *n.* **Joshua,** born 1925, U.S. scientist: Nobel prize for medicine 1958.

le·der·ho·sen (lā′dər hō′zən), *n.pl.* short leather pants worn esp. in Bavaria. [< G, pl. of *Lederhose,* equiv. to *Leder* LEATHER + *Hose* trousers]

ledge (lej), *n., v.,* **ledged, ledg·ing.** —*n.* **1.** any relatively narrow, projecting part, as a horizontal, shelflike projection on the façade of a building or a raised edge on a tray. **2.** a more or less flat shelf of rock protruding from a cliff or slope. **3.** a reef, ridge, or line of rocks in the sea or other body of water. **4.** *Mining.* **a.** a layer or mass of rock underground. **b.** a lode or vein. **5.** *Carpentry.* a member similar to but larger than a cleat. **6.** *Shipbuilding.* a minor transverse deck beam running between regular deck beams to form part of a coaming. Cf. **headledge.** —*v.t.* **7.** to assemble (a door or the like) with ledges. [ME *legge,* OE *lecg,* appar. the cross-bar of a weapon, akin to *lecgan* to LAY¹] —**ledge′less,** *adj.*

ledge′ment ta′ble (lej′mənt), a stringcourse, esp. one at the top of an earth table. [ME *legement.* See LEDGE, -MENT]

ledg·er (lej′ər), *n.* **1.** *Bookkeeping.* an account book of final entry, containing all the accounts. **2.** *Building Trades.* **a.** a horizontal timber fastened to the vertical uprights of a scaffold, to support the putlogs. **b.** ribbon (def. 7). **3.** a flat slab of stone laid over a grave or tomb. **4.** Also, **leger.** *Angling.* **a.** See **ledger bait. b.** See **ledger line** (def. 1). **c.** See **ledger tackle.** [ME *legger* (book). See LEDGE, -ER¹]

ledg′er bait′, *Angling.* bait so set on a line that the bait rests on the bottom, below the sinker.

ledg′er beam′, a reinforced-concrete beam having projecting ledges for receiving the ends of joists or the like.

ledg′er board′, 1. a horizontal board, as in a fence. **2.** *Carpentry.* ribbon (def. 7).

ledg′er line′, 1. *Angling.* a line so set that both the bait and sinker rest on the bottom. **2.** *Music.* See **leger line.**

ledg′er pa′per, a foldable paper with a smooth finish.

ledg′er plate′, *Carpentry.* **1.** a strip of wood laid flat across the tops of studding as a support for joists. **2.** See **ledger strip.**

ledg′er strip′, *Carpentry.* a piece attached to the face of a beam at the bottom as a support for the ends of joists.

ledg′er tack′le, *Angling.* tackle so set that both the bait and sinker rest on the bottom of the water.

ledge′ stone′, stratified rock used as a building stone.

ledg·y (lej′ē), *adj.,* **ledg·i·er, ledg·i·est.** having ledges. [LEDGE + -Y¹]

Le·doux (lə dōō′), *n.* **Claude-Ni·co·las** (klōd nē kō-lä′), 1736–1806, French architect.

lee¹ (lē), *n.* **1.** shelter: *The lee of the rock gave us some protection against the storm.* **2.** the side or part that is sheltered or turned away from the wind: *We erected our huts under the lee of the mountain.* **3.** *Chiefly Naut.* the quarter or region toward which the wind blows. **4. by the lee,** *Naut.* accidentally against what should be the lee side of a sail or sails: *Careless steering brought the wind by the lee.* **5. under the lee,** *Naut.* to leeward. —*adj.* **6.** *Chiefly Naut.* pertaining to, situated in, or moving toward the quarter or region toward which the wind blows (opposed to *weather*). [ME; OE *hlēo(w)* shelter; c. Icel *hlȳ*]

lee² (lē), *n.* Usually, **lees.** the insoluble matter that settles from a liquid, esp. from wine; sediment; dregs. [ME *lie* < MF < ML *lia,* prob. < Celt; cf. Ir *lige* bed, akin to OE *gelege* bed. See LIE²]

Lee (lē), *n.* **1. Ann,** 1736–84, British mystic: founder of Shaker sect in U.S. **2. Charles,** 1731–82, American Revolutionary general, born in England. **3. Doris Emrick** (em′rik), born 1905, U.S. painter. **4. Fitz·hugh** (fits′hyōō), 1835–1905, U.S. general and statesman (grandson of Henry Lee; nephew of Robert E. Lee). **5. Francis Light·foot** (līt′fŏŏt′), 1734–97, American Revolutionary statesman (brother of Richard H. Lee). **6. Gypsy Rose** (*Rose Louise Hovick*), 1914–70, U.S. entertainer. **7. Henry** ("*Light-Horse Harry*"), 1756–1818, American Revolutionary general (father of Robert E. Lee). **8. Kuan Yew** (kwän′yōō′), born 1923, Singapore political leader: prime minister since 1959. **9. Richard Henry,** 1732–94, American Revolutionary statesman (brother of Francis L. Lee). **10. Robert E(dward),** 1807–70, U.S. soldier and educator: Confederate general in the American Civil War (son of Henry Lee). **11. Sir Sidney,** 1859–1926, English biographer and critic. **12. Tsung-Dao** (dzŏŏng′dou′), born 1926, U.S. physicist born in China: Nobel prize 1957. **13.** a town in W Massachusetts. 3078 (1960). **14.** a walled plain in the third quadrant of the face of the moon: about 28 miles in diameter. **15.** Also, **Leigh.** a boy's or girl's given name.

lee·board (lē′bōrd′, -bôrd′), *n. Naut.* either of two broad, flat objects attached to the sides of a sailing vessel amidships, the one on the lee side being lowered into the water to prevent the vessel from making leeway. [late ME; see LEE¹, BOARD]

Leech *Hirudo medicinalis* (length 5 to 6 in.)

leech¹ (lēch), *n.* **1.** any bloodsucking or carnivorous aquatic or terrestrial worm of the class *Hirudinea,* certain fresh-water species of which were formerly much used in medicine for bloodletting. **2.** an instrument used for drawing blood. **3.** a person who clings to another for personal gain, esp. without giving anything in return, and usually with the implication of exhausting the other's resources; parasite. —*v.t.* **4.** to cling to and feed upon or drain, as a leech: *They leeched him until his entire fortune was exhausted.* **5.** *Archaic.* to cure; heal. —*v.i.* **6.** to hang on to a person in the manner of a leech: *She leeched on to him for dear life.* [ME *leche,* OE *lǣce;* r. (by confusion with LEECH², def. 2) ME *liche,* OE *lȳce;* c. MD *lieke;* akin to OE *lūcan* to pull out, MHG *liechen* to pull] —**leech′like′,** *adj.* —**Syn. 3.** bloodsucker; extortioner; sponger.

leech² (lēch), *v.t.* **1.** to apply leeches to, so as to bleed. —*n.* **2.** *Archaic.* a physician. [ME *leche,* OE *lǣce;* c. OS *lāki,* OHG *lāchi,* Goth *lēkeis;* akin to Icel *lǣknir*]

leech³ (lēch), *n. Naut.* **1.** either of the lateral edges of a square sail. **2.** the after edge of a fore-and-aft sail. Also, **leach.** See diag. under **sail.** [late ME *lek, leche, lyche;* akin to D *lijk* leech, Icel *līk* leech line]

Leech·burg (lēch′bûrg), *n.* a town in central Pennsylvania. 3545 (1960).

leech′ line′, *Naut.* a line for hauling the middle of a leech of a square sail up to the yard. Cf. **leech rope.**

leech′ rope′, *Naut.* a boltrope along a leech.

Leeds (lēdz), *n.* **1.** a city in central Yorkshire, in N England. 510,579 (1961). **2.** a town in central Alabama. 6162 (1960).

lee·fang (lē′fang), *n. Naut.* **1.** a rope for holding the clew of a jib temporarily while a bonnet is being attached. **2.** See **deck horse.** Also, **lee′fange.** [LEE¹ + FANG¹]

lee′ gauge′, *Naut.* See under **gauge** (def. 17).

Lee·grant (lē′grant′), *n.* a boy's given name.

leek (lēk), *n.* **1.** a liliaceous plant, *Allium Porrum,* allied to the onion, having a cylindrical bulb and leaves used in cookery. **2.** any of various allied species. [ME; OE *lēac;* c. G *Lauch,* Icel *laukr*]

Leek, *Allium porrum* (Height 2 ft. or more)

leek-green (lēk′grēn′), *adj.* dull bluish green.

leer¹ (lēr), *v.i.* **1.** to look with a sideways or oblique glance, esp. suggestive of lascivious interest or sly and malicious intention: *They leaned back in their chairs, leering at the girls as they passed.* —*n.* **2.** a lascivious or sly look. [perh. v. use of obs. *leer* cheek, ME *leor,* OE *hlēor;* c. Icel *hlȳr*] —**leer′ing·ly,** *adv.*

leer² (lēr), *adj. Brit. Dial.* **1.** having no burden or load. **2.** faint for lack of food; hungry. [ME *lere,* OE *gelǣr;* c. G *leer* empty]

leer³ (lēr), *n.* lehr.

Lee·roy (lē′roi, lə roi′), *n.* a boy's given name. Also, **Learoy, Leroy.**

leer·y¹ (lēr′ē), *adj.,* **leer·i·er, leer·i·est. 1.** wary, suspicious (usually fol. by *of*). **2.** *Archaic.* knowing; alert. [LEER¹ + -Y¹] —**leer′i·ly,** *adv.* —**leer′i·ness,** *n.*

leer·y² (lēr′ē), *adj.,* **leer·i·er, leer·i·est.** leer². Also, **leary.** [LEER² + -Y¹]

lees (lēz), *n.* pl. of **lee².**

Lees·burg (lēz′bûrg), *n.* a town in N Virginia. 2869 (1960).

lee′ shore′, 1. a shore toward which the wind blows. **2. on a lee shore,** in difficulty or danger: *They found themselves on a lee shore with little hope of escape.*

Lees′ Sum′mit (lēz), a town in W Missouri. 8267 (1960).

Lees·ville (lēz′vil), *n.* a town in W Louisiana. 4689 (1960).

leet (lēt), *n. Brit. Obs.* **1.** a special annual or semiannual court in which the lords of certain manors had jurisdiction over local disputes. **2.** the area over which this jurisdiction extended, including the manor itself and, sometimes, nearby counties or shires. [late ME *lete* meeting (of law-court), OE *gelǣte* meeting (of roads), lit., course together (whence AF *lete,* AL *leta*); cf. *wætergelǣt* watercourse]

lee′ tide′, a tidal current running in the direction toward which the wind is blowing. Also, **lee′ward tide′.**

Lee·to·ni·a (li tō′nē ə, -tōn′yə), *n.* a town in E Ohio. 2543 (1960).

Lee·u·war·den (lā′y wär′dən), *n.* a city in the N Netherlands. 85,386 (1962).

Lee·u·wen·hoek (lā′vən hŏŏk′; *Du.* lā′y wən hōōk′), *n.* **An·ton van** (än′tôn vän), 1632–1723, Dutch naturalist and microscopist.

lee·ward (lē′wərd; *Naut.* lōō′ərd), *adj.* **1.** pertaining to, situated in, or moving toward the quarter toward which the wind blows (opposed to *windward*). —*n.* **2.** the lee side; the point or quarter toward which the wind blows. —*adv.* **3.** toward the lee. [LEE¹ + -WARD] —**lee′ward·ly,** *adv.*

Lee′ward Is′lands (lē′wərd), **1.** a group of islands in the N Lesser Antilles of the West Indies, extending from Puerto Rico SE to Martinique. **2.** a former British colony in the E West Indies, consisting of Antigua, Barbuda, St. Kitts, Nevis, Anguilla, Montserrat, and the British Virgin Islands. 130,493 (1960); 413 sq. mi.

lee′ wave′. See **mountain wave.**

lee·way (lē′wā′), *n.* **1.** *Naut.* the amount or angle of the drift of a vessel to leeward from its heading. **2.** *Aeron.* the amount a plane is blown off its normal course by cross winds. **3.** extra time, space, materials, or the like, within which to operate: *With 10 minutes' leeway we can catch the train.* **4.** a degree of freedom of action or thought: *His instructions gave him plenty of leeway.* [LEE¹ + WAY]

left¹ (left), *adj.* **1.** of, pertaining to, or belonging to the side of a person or thing that is turned toward the west when the subject is facing north (opposed to *right*). **2.** of or belonging to the political left. **3.** *Math.* pertaining to an element of a set which has a given property when written on the left of an element or set of elements of the set: *a left identity, as 1 in 1 · x = x.* —*n.* **4.** the left side or something that is on the left side. **5.** a left-hand turn: *Make a left at the next corner.* **6.** (*usually cap.*) *Govt.* **a.** the part of a legislative assembly, esp. in continental Europe, that is situated on the left side of the presiding officer and that is customarily assigned to members of the legislature who hold more radical and socialistic views than the rest of the members. **b.** the members of such an assembly who sit on the left. **7. the Left, a.** the complex of individuals or organized groups advocating liberal reform or revolutionary change in the social, political, or economic order, usually on behalf of greater personal freedom or improved social conditions. **b.** the position held by these people. Cf. **right** (def. 32a, b). **c.** See **left wing. 8.** *Boxing.* a blow delivered by the left hand. **9.** *Baseball.* See **left field** (def. 1). —*adv.* **10.** toward the left: *She moved left on entering the room.* [ME *left, lift, luft,* OE *left* idle, dial. var. of *lyft-* (in *lyftādl* palsy); c. D, LG *lucht;* akin to ME *libbe* (modern dial. *lib*) to castrate, c. D, LG *lubben*]

left² (left), *v.* **1.** pt. and pp. of **leave¹**. **2. get left,** *Slang.* **a.** to be left stranded. **b.** to miss an opportunity, objective, etc.

Left′ Bank′, a part of Paris, France, on the S bank of the Seine: frequented by artists, writers, and students. Cf. **Right Bank.**

left′-eyed floun′der (left′īd′), any of several flatfishes of the family *Bothidae*, having both eyes on the left side of the head. Also, **left′eye floun′der.**

left′ field′, **1.** *Baseball.* **a.** the area of the outfield to the left of center field, as viewed from home plate. **b.** the position of the player covering this area. **2. out in left field,** *Slang.* completely mistaken; wrong: *Don't listen to him, he's out in left field.*

left′ field′er, *Baseball.* the player whose position is left field.

left-hand (left′hand′), *adj.* **1.** on or to the left. **2.** of, for, or with the left hand. [ME *left hande*]

left′-hand buoy′, *Navig.* a distinctive buoy marking the side of a channel regarded as the left or port side.

left′-hand dag′ger. See **main gauche.**

left-hand·ed (left′han′did), *adj.* **1.** having the left hand more serviceable than the right; preferably using the left hand: *a left-handed pitcher.* **2.** adapted to or performed by the left hand: *a left-handed punch; a left-handed tool.* **3.** situated on the side of the left hand. **4.** *Mach.* **a.** rotating counterclockwise. **b.** noting a helical, or spiral, member, as a gear tooth or screw thread, that twists counterclockwise as it recedes from an observer. **5.** *Building Trades.* **a.** (of a door) having the hinges on the left when seen from the exterior of the building, room, closet, etc., to which the doorway leads. **b.** (of a casement sash) having the hinges on the left when seen from inside the window. **6.** ambiguous or doubtful: *a left-handed compliment.* **7.** clumsy or awkward. **8.** of, pertaining to, or issuing from a morganatic marriage: so called from the custom, in morganatic marriage ceremonies, of having the bridegroom give his left hand to the bride. —*adv.* **9.** with the left hand: *He writes left-handed.* **10.** toward the left hand; in a counterclockwise direction: *The strands of the rope are laid left-handed.* [LEFT¹ + HANDED] —**left′-hand′ed·ly,** *adv.* —**left′-hand′ed·ness,** *n.*

left-hand·er (left′han′dər, -han′-), *n.* **1.** one who is left-handed, esp. a baseball pitcher who throws with his left hand. **2.** *Informal.* a slap or punch delivered with the left hand. [LEFT-HAND + -ER¹]

left·ist (lef′tist), *n.* **1.** a member of the Left or a person sympathizing with its views. —*adj.* **2.** of, pertaining to, characteristic of, or advocated by the Left. Also, **Left′ist.** [LEFT¹ + -IST] —**left′ism,** *n.*

left-laid (left′lād′), *adj.* noting a rope, strand, etc., laid in a left-handed, or counterclockwise, direction as one looks away along it (opposed to *right-laid*).

left′-lug′gage of′fice (left′lug′ij), *Brit.* a checkroom for baggage.

left·o·ver (left′ō′vər), *n.* **1.** something left or remaining from a larger amount; remainder. **2.** a remnant of food, as from a meal. —*adj.* **3.** being left or remaining, as an unused portion or amount: *leftover meat loaf; leftover merchandise.* [n. use of v. phrase; see LEFT²]

left′ stage′. See **stage left.**

left·ward (left′wərd), *adv.* **1.** Also, **left′wards.** toward or on the left. —*adj.* **2.** situated on the left. **3.** directed toward the left. [late ME; see LEFT¹, -WARD] —**left′ward·ly,** *adv.*

left′ wing′, **1.** members of a socialistic or radical political party, or those favoring extensive political reform. **2.** such a party or a group of such parties. **3.** the part of a political or social organization advocating a liberal or radical position. —**left′wing′,** *adj.* —**left′-wing′er,** *n.*

left·y¹ (lef′tē), *n., pl.* **left·ies.** *Informal.* a left-handed person. [LEFT¹ + -Y²]

left·y² (lef′tē), *Informal.* —*adj.* **1.** left-handed. —*adv.* **2.** with the left hand; in a left-handed manner: *He bats lefty.* [LEFT¹ + -Y¹]

leg (leg), *n., v.,* **legged, leg·ging.** —*n.* **1.** one of the two lower limbs of a biped, as man, or one of the paired limbs of a quadruped, as a dog, that support and move the body. **2.** *Anat.* the lower limb of man from the knee to the ankle. **3.** something resembling or suggesting a leg in use, position, or appearance. **4.** the part of a garment that covers the leg: *the leg of a stocking; trouser leg.* **5.** one of usually several, relatively tall, slender supports for a piece of furniture. **6.** one of the sides of a forked object, as of a compass or pair of dividers. **7.** one of the sides of a triangle other than the base or hypotenuse. **8.** a timber, bar, or the like, serving to prop or shore up a structure. **9.** one of the flanges of an angle iron. **10.** one of the distinct portions of any course: *the last leg of a trip.* **11.** *Naut.* **a.** one of the series of straight runs that make up the zigzag course of a sailing ship. **b.** one straight or nearly straight part of a multiple-sided course in a sailing race. **12.** *Sports.* **a.** one of a designated number of contests that must be successfully completed in order to determine the winner. **b.** one of the stretches or sections of a relay race. **13.** *Cricket.* **a.** the part of the field to the left of and behind the batsman as he faces the bowler or to the right of and behind him if he is left-handed. **b.** the fielder playing this part of the field. **c.** the position of this fielder. **14.** *Elect.* a component or branch of a circuit, network, antenna, etc. **15.** *Radio and Television.* a connecting link between stations in a network, as the microwave relays used in transmitting a show from one geographical area to another. **16. give a leg up,** to give assistance; help to advance: *She was grateful to her aunt for having given her a leg up when she needed it.* **17. not have a leg to stand on,** to lack a valid basis for one's argument or attitude: *Without evidence, the prosecutor doesn't have a leg to stand on.* **18. on one's** or **its last legs,** just short of exhaustion, breakdown, failure, etc.: *The aristocracy was on its last legs. Our car is on its last legs.* **19. pull one's leg, a.** to make fun of; tease. **b.** to deceive; trick: *He loves to kid people, so be careful that he doesn't pull your leg.* **20. shake a leg,** *Slang.* **a.** to hurry up. **b.** to dance: *Let's step out on the dance floor and shake a leg.* **21. stretch one's legs,** to take a walk; get some needed exercise after prolonged sitting: *He got up during the intermission to stretch his legs.* —*v.t.* **22.** to move or propel (a boat) with the legs: *They legged the boat through the tunnel.* **23. leg it,** *Informal.* to walk rapidly or run: *We'd better leg it or we'll be late for class.* **24. leg up,** to help (someone) to mount a horse. [ME < Scand; cf. Icel *leggr*] —**leg′less,** *adj.* —**leg′like′,** *adj.*

leg., **1.** legal. **2.** legate. **3.** legato. **4.** legend. **5.** legislative. **6.** legislature.

leg·a·cy (leg′ə sē), *n., pl.* **-cies. 1.** *Law.* a gift of property, esp. personal property, as money, by will; a bequest. **2.** anything handed down from the past, as from an ancestor or predecessor: *the legacy of ancient Rome.* **3.** *Obs.* the office, function, or commission of a legate. [ME *legacie* office of a deputy or legate < ML *lēgātia.* See LEGATE, -Y³]
—**Syn. 2.** inheritance.

le·gal (lē′gəl), *adj.* **1.** permitted by law; lawful: *Such acts are not legal.* **2.** of or pertaining to law; connected with the law or its administration: *the legal profession.* **3.** appointed, established, or authorized by law; deriving authority from law. **4.** recognized by law rather than by equity. **5.** of, pertaining to, or characteristic of the profession of law or of lawyers: *a legal mind.* **6.** *Theol.* **a.** of or pertaining to the Mosaic Law. **b.** of or pertaining to the doctrine that salvation is gained by good works rather than through free grace. —*n.* **7. legals,** authorized investments that may be made by fiduciaries, as savings banks, trustees, etc. [< L *lēgāl(is)* of the law, equiv. to *lēg-* (s. of *lex*) law + *-ālis* -AL¹] —**le′gal·ly,** *adv.*
—**Syn. 3.** licit, legitimate, sanctioned.

le′gal aid′, free legal service to a person or persons unable to pay for it.

le′gal aid′ soci′ety, an organization providing free help in legal guidance and service to persons who cannot afford a lawyer. Also called **le′gal aid′ associa′tion.**

le′gal cap′, *U.S.* ruled writing paper, usually measuring 8x13½ inches, with the fold at the top, for use by lawyers.

le′gal chem′istry. See **forensic chemistry.**

le′gal geol′ogy, the branch of geology dealing with legal questions arising with relation to mines or the like.

le′gal hol′iday, a holiday established by law and limited as to the amount of work and official business that may be conducted.

le·gal·ise (lē′gə līz′), *v.t.,* **-ised, -is·ing.** *Chiefly Brit.* legalize. —**le′gal·i·sa′tion,** *n.*

le·gal·ism (lē′gə liz′əm), *n.* **1.** strict adherence, or the principle of strict adherence, to law or prescription, esp. to the letter rather than the spirit. **2.** *Theol.* **a.** the doctrine that salvation is gained through good works. **b.** the judging of conduct in terms of adherence to precise laws. **3.** (*cap.*) (in Chinese philosophy) the principles and practices of a school of political theorists advocating strict legal control over all activities, a system of rewards and punishments uniform for all classes, and an absolute monarchy. [LEGAL + -ISM] —**le′gal·ist,** *n.* —**le′gal·is′tic,** *adj.* —**le′gal·is′ti·cal·ly,** *adv.*

le·gal·i·ty (lē gal′i tē), *n., pl.* **-ties. 1.** the state or quality of being in conformity with the law; lawfulness. **2.** attachment to or observance of law. **3.** *Theol.* reliance on good works for salvation rather than on free grace. [late ME *legalite* < ML *lēgālitās.* See LEGAL, -ITY]

le·gal·ize (lē′gə līz′), *v.t.,* **-ized, -iz·ing.** to make legal; authorize. Also, *esp. Brit.,* **legalise.** [LEGAL + -IZE] —**le′gal·i·za′tion,** *n.*

Le Gal·lienne (lə gal′yən, -gal yen′), **1. Eva,** born 1899, U.S. actress and producer, born in England. **2.** her father, **Richard,** 1866–1947, English writer.

le′gal med′icine. See **forensic medicine.**

le′gal reserve′, the amount of cash assets that a bank, insurance company, etc., are required by law to set aside as reserves.

le′gal separa′tion. See **judicial separation.**

le′gal ten′der, currency that may be lawfully tendered or offered in payment of money debts and that may not be refused by creditors.

le′gal weight′, the weight of merchandise itself plus that of its immediate wrapping material but not of the outside shipping container: used esp. in some Latin-American countries for the purpose of assessing import duties.

leg′ art′, *Slang.* cheesecake.

Le·gas·pi (lə gas′pē; *Sp.* le gäs′pē), *n.* a seaport on SE Luzon, in the Philippines. 98,410 (est. 1960). Formerly, **Albay.**

leg·ate (leg′it), *n.* **1.** an ecclesiastic delegated by the pope as his representative. **2.** *Rom. Hist.* **a.** an assistant to a general or to a consul or magistrate, in the government of any army or a province; a commander of a legion. **b.** a provincial governor of senatorial rank appointed by the emperor. **3.** an envoy or emissary. [early ME *legat* < L *lēgāt(us)* deputy (orig. masc. ptp. of *lēgāre* to depute), equiv. to *lēg-* (s. of *lex*) law + *-ātus* -ATE¹] —**leg′ate·ship′,** *n.*

leg·a·tee (leg′ə tē′), *n.* one to whom a legacy is bequeathed. [< L *lēgāt(us)* deputed, bequeathed (see LEGATE) + -EE]

leg·a·tine (leg′ə tin, -tīn′), *adj.* of, pertaining to, or authorized by a legate. [< ML *lēgātīn(us).* See LEGATE, -INE¹]

le·ga·tion (li gā′shən), *n.* **1.** a diplomatic minister and his staff when the minister is not of ambassadorial rank. **2.** the official headquarters of a diplomatic minister. **3.** the office or position of a legate; mission. [late ME *legacion* < L *lēgātiōn-* (s. of *lēgātiō*) embassy. See LEGATE, -ION] —**le·ga·tion·ar·y** (li gā′shə ner′ē), *adj.*

le·ga·to (lə gä′tō; *It.* le gä′tô), *adj. Music.* smooth and connected; without breaks between the successive tones. Cf. **staccato.** [< It, ptp. of *legare* < L *ligāre* to bind]

le·ga·tor (li gā′tər, leg′ə tôr′), *n.* one who bequeaths; a testator. [< L: one who bequeaths. See LEGATE, -OR²] —**leg·a·to·ri·al** (leg′ə tôr′ē əl, -tōr′-), *adj.*

Le·gaz·pi (le gäs′pē), *n.* **Mi·guel Lóp·ez de** (mē gel′ lô′peth de, lô′pes). See **López de Legazpi.**

leg-break (leg′brāk′), *n.* *Cricket.* a ball deviating to the off side from the leg side when bowled.

leg′ bye′, *Cricket.* a run or bye scored on a bowled ball that ricochets off any part of the batsman's body except the hand.

leg′ drop′, *Theat.* a narrow scenery flat or drop, often used in a pair to form an inverted U.

leg·end (lej′ənd), *n.* **1.** a nonhistorical or unverifiable story handed down by tradition from earlier times and popularly accepted as historical. **2.** the body of stories of this kind, esp. as they relate to a particular people, group, or clan: *a popular hero in American legend.* **3.** an inscription, esp. on a coat of arms, on a monument, under a picture, or the like. **4.** a table on a map, chart, or the like, listing and explaining the symbols used. Cf. **key¹** (def. 4). **5.** *Numis.* inscription (def. 8). **6.** a collection of stories about an admirable person. **7.** one who is the center of such stories: *She became a legend in her own lifetime.* **8.** *Obs.* a story on the life of a saint, esp. one stressing the miraculous or unrecorded deeds of the saint. **9.** *Obs.* a collection of such stories or stories like them. [ME *legende* collection of saints' lives < ML *legenda,* so called because appointed to be read on respective saints' days, lit., lesson to be read, n. use of fem. of L *legendus,* ger. of *legere* to read]
—**Syn. 1.** LEGEND, FABLE, MYTH refer to fictitious stories, usually handed down by tradition (although some fables are modern). LEGEND, originally denoting a story concerning the life of a saint, is applied to any fictitious story, sometimes involving the supernatural, and usually concerned with a real person, place, or other subject: *the legend of St. Andrew.* A FABLE is specifically a fictitious story (often with animals or inanimate things as speakers or actors) designed to teach a moral: *a fable about industrious bees.* A MYTH is one of a class of stories, usually concerning gods, semi-divine heroes, etc., current since primitive times, the purpose of which is to attempt to explain some belief or natural phenomenon: *the Greek myth about Demeter.* —**Ant. 1.** fact.

Le·gen·da Au·re·a (lə jen′də ôr′ē ə), a 13th-century hagiology compiled by Jacobus de Voragine (1230–98): primary source for Caxton's *Golden Legend.* Also called **Golden Legend.**

leg·end·ar·y (lej′ən der′ē), *adj., n., pl.* **-ar·ies.** —*adj.* **1.** of, pertaining to, or of the nature of a legend or legends. **2.** celebrated or described in legend: *a legendary hero.* —*n.* **3.** a collection of legends. [ML *legendāri(us).* See LEGEND, -ARY] —**leg′end·ar′i·ly,** *adv.*
—**Syn. 1.** heroic, marvelous, supernatural, strange, superhuman.

leg·end·ist (lej′ən dist), *n.* one who writes or compiles legends. [LEGEND + -IST]

leg·end·ize (lej′ən dīz′), *v.t.,* **-ized, -iz·ing.** to make a legend of: *Devoted followers legendized his birth.* [LEGEND + -IZE]

Leg′end of Good′ Wom′en, The, a cycle of narrative poems (1386–87?) by Geoffrey Chaucer.

Leg′end of Sleep′y Hol′low, The, a short story (1820) by Washington Irving.

Leg′end of the True′ Cross′, a fresco cycle (1452?–59?) painted by Piero della Francesca.

Le·gen·dre (lə zhän′dər, -zhänd′; *Fr.* lə zhäɴ′drᵊ), *n.* **1. A·dri·en Ma·rie** (A drē aɴ′ mA rē′), 1752–1833, French mathematician. **2.** a walled plain in the fourth quadrant of the face of the moon: about 46 miles in diameter.

Legen′dre equa′tion, *Math.* a differential equation of the form, $(1-x^2)\frac{d^2y}{dx^2}-2x\frac{dy}{dx}+a(a+1)y=0$, where a is an arbitrary constant. [named after A. M. LEGENDRE]

Legen′dre polyno′mial, *Math.* a polynomial solution of the Legendre equation.

leg·end·ry (lej′ən drē), *n.* legends collectively. [LEGEND + -RY]

leg·er (lej′ər), *n.* *Angling.* ledger (def. 4).

Lé·ger (lā zhā′), *n.* **1. A·lex·is Saint-Lé·ger** (A lek sē′ saɴ lā zhā′), (*St.-John Perse*), born 1887, French poet and diplomat: Nobel prize for literature 1960. **2. Fer·nand** (fer näɴ′), 1881–1955, French artist.

leg·er·de·main (lej′ər də mān′), *n.* **1.** skill in or practice of feats of magic, jugglery, or other arts involving a dexterous manipulation of the hands; sleight of hand. **2.** trickery; deception. **3.** any artful trick. [earlier *leger de main* < MF, lit., light of hand; r. late ME *lygarde-de-mayne,* etc., alter. of MF form] —**leg′er·de·main′ist,** *n.*

le·ger·i·ty (lə jer′i tē), *n.* physical or mental quickness; nimbleness; agility. [< MF *legerete,* equiv. to *leger* (< LL *leviārius;* see LEVITY, -ARY) + *-ete* -ITY]
—**Syn.** lightness, grace, alacrity, celerity.

L, Leger lines

leg′er line′ (lej′ər), *Music.* a short line added when necessary above or below the staff to increase the range of the staff. Also, **ledger line.**

le·ges (lē′jēz; *Lat.* le′ges), *n.* pl. of **lex.**

leg·ged (leg′id, legd), *adj.* **1.** having a specified number or kind of legs (often used in combination): *two-legged; long-legged.* **2.** fitted with legs: *a legged desk.* [late ME; see LEG, -ED¹]

leg·ging (leg′ing), *n.* **1.** a covering for the leg, usually extending from the ankle to the knee but sometimes higher, worn by soldiers, riders, workmen, etc. Cf. **chaps, gaiter, puttee. 2. leggings, a.** close-fitting trousers, usually with shoulder straps and extending over the instep, worn outdoors in the winter by children, often with a matching coat or jacket. **b.** the pants of a two-piece snowsuit. Also, **leg·gin** (leg′in). [LEG + -ING¹] —**leg′ginged,** *adj.*

leg·gy (leg′ē), *adj.,* **-gi·er, -gi·est. 1.** having awkwardly long legs. **2.** having long, attractively shaped legs: *a gorgeous, leggy blonde.* **3.** of, pertaining to, or characterized by showing the legs: *a leggy stage show.* [LEG + -Y¹] —**leg′gi·ness,** *n.*

leg·har·ness (leg′här′nis), *n.* armor for the leg, sometimes including that for the foot. [ME; see LEG, HARNESS]

leg′ hit′, *Cricket.* a hit made into leg.

Leg·horn (leg′hôrn′ *for 1–3;* leg′ərn, -hôrn′ *for 4*), *n.* **1.** Italian, **Livorno.** a seaport in W Italy on the Ligurian Sea. 159,973 (1961). **2.** a fine, smooth, plaited straw. **3.** (*l.c.*) a hat made of such straw, often having a broad, soft brim. **4.** one of a Mediterranean breed of chickens that are prolific layers of white-shelled eggs.

leg·i·bil·i·ty (lej′ə bil′i tē), *n.* **1.** Also, **leg′i·ble·ness.** the state or quality of being legible. **2.** Also called **visibility.** *Typography.* the quality of type that affects the perceptibility of a word, line, or paragraph of printed matter. Cf. **readability** (def. 2). [LEGIBLE + -ITY]

leg·i·ble (lej′ə bəl), *adj.* **1.** capable of being read or deciphered, esp. with ease, as writing or printing. **2.** capable of being discerned or distinguished: *Anger was legible in his looks and behavior.* [< LL *legibil(is).* See LEGEND, -IBLE] —**leg′i·bly,** *adv.*

le·gion (lē′jən), *n.* **1.** (in ancient Rome) an infantry brigade numbering from 3000 to 6000 men, and usually combined with from 300 to 700 cavalry. **2.** a military or semimilitary unit. **3. the Legion. a.** See **American Legion. b.** See **foreign legion** (def. 2). **4.** any large body of armed men. **5.** any great host or multitude of persons or things. [< L *legiōn-* (s. of *legiō*) picked body of soldiers, equiv. to *leg(ere)* (to) gather, choose, read, etc. + *-iōn-* -ION; r. ME *legi(o)un* < OF]

le·gion·ar·y (lē′jə ner′ē), *adj., n., pl.* **-ar·ies.** —*adj.* **1.** of, pertaining to, or belonging to a legion. **2.** constituting a legion or legions. —*n.* **3.** *Hist.* a soldier of a legion. **4.** *Brit.* a member of the British Legion. Cf. **legionnaire** (def. 1). **5.** legionnaire (def. 2). [< L *legiōnāri(us).* See LEGION, -ARY]

le′gionary ant′. See **army ant.**

le·gion·naire (lē′jə nâr′), *n.* **1.** (*often cap.*) a member of the American Legion. **2.** a member of any legion; legionary.* [< F; see LEGIONARY]

Le′gion of Hon′or, a French order of distinction instituted in 1802 by Napoleon with membership being granted for meritorious civil or military services. [trans. of F *Légion d'honneur*]

Le′gion of Mer′it, *Mil.* a decoration ranking below the Silver Star and above the Distinguished Flying Cross, awarded to U.S. and foreign military personnel for exceptionally meritorious conduct in the performance of outstanding services to the United States.

Legis., Legislature.

leg·is·late (lej′is lāt′), *v.,* **-lat·ed, -lat·ing.** —*v.i.* **1.** to exercise the function of legislation; make or enact laws. —*v.t.* **2.** to create or control by legislation: *attempts to legislate morality.* [back formation from LEGISLATION, LEGISLATOR]

leg·is·la·tion (lej′is lā′shən), *n.* **1.** the act of making or enacting laws. **2.** a law or a body of laws enacted. [< LL *lēgislātiōn-* (s. of *lēgislātiō*), equiv. to L phrase *lēgis lātiō* the bringing (i.e., proposing) of a law, equiv. to *lēgis* (gen. of *lēx* law) + *lātiō* a bringing; see RELATION]

leg·is·la·tive (lej′is lā′tiv), *adj.* **1.** having the function of making laws: *a legislative body.* **2.** of or pertaining to the enactment of laws: *legislative proceedings; legislative power.* **3.** pertaining to a legislature: *a legislative recess.* **4.** enacted or ordained by legislation or a legislature: *legislative ruling; legislative remedy.* —*n.* **5.** legislature. [LEGISLAT(ION) + -IVE] —**leg′is·la′tive·ly,** *adv.*

Leg′islative Assem′bly, *Fr. Hist.* the legislature of France 1791–92.

leg·is·la·tor (lej′is lā′tər), *n.* **1.** one who gives or makes laws. **2.** a member of a legislative body. [< L phrase *lēgis lātor* a law's bringer (i.e., proposer), equiv. to *lēgis* (gen. of *lēx* law) + *lātor* bringer (*lāt(us),* ptp. of *ferre* to bring + *-or* -OR²)] —**leg′is·la′tor·ship′,** *n.*

leg·is·la·to·ri·al (lej′is lə tōr′ē əl, -tôr′-), *adj.* of or pertaining to a legislator, legislature, or legislation; legislative. [LEGISLATOR + -IAL]

leg·is·la·trix (lej′is lā′triks), *n., pl.* **leg·is·la·trix·es, leg·is·la·tri·ces** (lej′is lā′tri sēz′, -lə trī′sēz). a woman member of a legislature. Also, **leg·is·la·tress** (lej′is-lā′tris, lej′is lā′-). [LEGISLA(TOR) + -TRIX]

leg·is·la·ture (lej′is lā′chər), *n.* **1.** a deliberative body of persons, usually elective, who are empowered to make, change, or repeal the laws of a country or state; the branch of government invested with the power to make laws, as distinguished from the executive and judicial branches of government. **2.** *U.S.* the legislative branch of a State government: *State legislatures are generally bicameral.* [LEGISLAT(OR) + -URE]

le·gist (lē′jist), *n.* one versed in law. [late ME < ML *lēgista.* See LEGAL, -IST]

le·git (lə jit′), *Slang.* —*adj.* **1.** legitimate; truthful. —*n.* **2.** the legitimate theater or stage. [shortened form]

leg·i·tim (lej′i tim), *n.* *Roman and Civil Law, Scots Law.* the part of an estate that children or other close relatives can claim against the decedent's testament. [< L *lēgitim(a)* (*pars*) the lawful (part), equiv. to *lēgi-* (s. of *lēx* law) + *-tima,* fem. of *-timus,* var. of *-tumus* adj. suffix]

le·git·i·ma·cy (li jit′ə mə sē), *n.* the state or quality of being legitimate. [LEGITIM(ATE) + -ACY]

le·git·i·mate (*adj., n.* li jit′ə mit; *v.* li jit′ə māt′), *adj., v.,* **-mat·ed, -mat·ing,** *n.* —*adj.* **1.** according to law; lawful: *the property's legitimate owner.* **2.** in accordance with established rules, principles, or standards. **3.** born in wedlock or of parents legally married: *legitimate children.* **4.** in accordance with the laws of reasoning; logically inferable; logical: *a legitimate conclusion.* **5.** resting on or ruling by the principle of hereditary right: *a legitimate sovereign.* **6.** not spurious or unjustified; genuine: *It was a legitimate complaint.* **7.** of the normal or regular type or kind. **8.** *Theat.* of or pertaining to professionally produced stage plays, as distinguished from burlesque, vaudeville, television, motion pictures, etc.: *legitimate drama.* —*v.t.* **9.** to make lawful or legal; pronounce or state as lawful: *Parliament legitimated his accession to the throne.* **10.** to establish as lawfully born: *His bastard children were afterward legitimated by law.* **11.** to show or declare to be legitimate or proper: *He was under obligation to legitimate his commission.* **12.** to justify; sanction or authorize: *His behavior was legitimated by custom.* —*n.* **13. the legitimate,** the legitimate theater or drama. **14.** one who is established as being legitimate. [< ML *lēgitimāt(us)* made lawful (ptp. of *lēgitimāre*). See LEGITIM, -ATE¹] —**le·git′i·mate·ly,** *adv.* —**le·git′i·mate·ness,** *n.* —**le·git′i·ma′tion,** *n.*
—**Syn. 1.** legal, licit. **2.** sanctioned. **4.** valid. **9.** legalize. —**Ant. 1.** illegitimate.

le·git·i·ma·tise (li jit′ə mə tīz′), *v.t.,* **-tised, -tis·ing.** *Chiefly Brit.* legitimatize.

le·git·i·ma·tize (li jit′ə mə tīz′), *v.t.,* **-tized, -tiz·ing.** to make legitimate. [LEGITIMATE + -IZE]

le·git·i·mise (li jit′ə mīz′), *v.t.,* **-mised, -mis·ing.** *Chiefly Brit.* legitimize. —**le·git′i·mi·sa′tion,** *n.*

le·git·i·mist (li jit′ə mist), *n.* **1.** a supporter of legitimate authority, esp. of a claim to a throne based on direct descent. —*adj.* **2.** Also, **le·git′i·mis′tic.** of, pertaining to, or supporting legitimate authority. [< L *lēgitim(us)* lawful (see LEGITIM) + -IST, modeled on F *lēgitimiste*] —**le·git′i·mism,** *n.*

le·git·i·mize (li jit′ə mīz′), *v.t.,* **-mized, -miz·ing.** to make legitimate. Also, *esp. Brit.,* **legitimise.** [< L *lēgitim(us)* (see LEGITIM) + -IZE] —**le·git′i·mi·za′tion,** *n.*

leg·len (leg′lin), *n.* *Scot. and North Eng.* **1.** laggin. **2.** a milk pail. [? < Scand; cf. Icel *legillinn* the keg, equiv to *legill* keg (<< L; see LAGENA) + *-inn* the]

leg·man (leg′man′, -mən), *n., pl.* **-men** (-men′, -mən). **1.** a person employed to transact business outside an office, esp. on behalf of one whose responsibilities require his presence in the office. **2.** *Journalism.* a reporter who gathers information by visiting news sources or by being present at events. Cf. **district man.** [LEG + MAN¹]

Leg·ni·ca (leg nē′tsä), *n.* Polish name of **Liegnitz.**

leg-of-mut·ton (leg′ə mut′ən, -əv-), *adj.* having the triangular shape of a leg of mutton: *a dress with leg-of-mutton sleeves.* Also, **leg′-o′-mut′ton.**

leg′-of-mut′ton sail′, *Naut.* a jib-headed sail, esp. a mainsail.

leg′-of-mut′ton spank′er, *Naut.* See **mutton spanker.**

leg-pull (leg′po͝ol′), *n.* an amusing hoax, practical joke, or the like: *The entire story was a hilarious leg-pull.* —**leg′-pull′er,** *n.*

Le·grand (lə grand′), *n.* a boy's given name.

Le·gree (li grē′), *n.* **Simon.** See **Simon Legree.**

leg·room (leg′ro͞om′, -ro͝om′), *n.* space sufficient for a person to keep his legs in a comfortable position: *Some of the new theaters provide hardly enough legroom for a three-year-old.* [LEG + ROOM]

leg′ stump′, *Cricket.* either of the outside stumps at which the batsman takes his position. Cf. **middle stump, off stump.**

Le·guí·a (le gē′ä), *n.* **Au·gus·to Ber·nar·di·no** (ou-go͞os′tô ber′när dē′nô), 1863–1932, president of Peru 1908–12, 1919–30.

leg·ume (leg′yo͞om, li gyo͞om′), *n.* **1.** any plant of the family *Leguminosae,* esp. those used for feed, food, or as a soil-improving crop. **2.** the pod or seed vessel of such a plant, being usually dehiscent by both sutures and thus dividing into two parts or valves. **3.** any table vegetable of the family *Leguminosae.* [< F *légume* vegetable < L *legūmen* plant with seed-pods, deriv. of *legere* to gather]

le·gu·min (li gyo͞o′mən), *n.* *Biochem.* a protein resembling casein, obtained from the seeds of leguminous and other plants. [LEGUME + -IN²]

le·gu·mi·nous (li gyo͞o′mə nəs), *adj.* **1.** pertaining to, of the nature of, or bearing legumes. **2.** belonging or pertaining to the *Leguminosae,* an order or family regarded as comprising the legume-bearing plants, and sometimes subdivided into the bean, senna, and mimosa families. [< L *legūmin-* (s. of *legūmen;* see LEGUME) + -OUS]

leg·work (leg′wûrk′), *n.* work or research involving extensive walking or moving about, as in gathering data for a story, a legal action, etc. [LEG + WORK]

Le·hár (lā′här; *Hung.* le′här), *n.* **Franz** (fränts), 1870–1948, Hungarian composer of operettas.

Le Ha·vre (lə hä′vrə, -vər; *Fr.* lə ᴀ′vʀᵊ), a seaport in N France, at the mouth of the Seine. 184,133 (1962). Also called **Havre.**

le·ha·yim (lə ᴋʜä′yim), *n.* *Hebrew.* a toast used by Jews in drinking to a person's health or well-being. Also, **lechayim.** [lit., to life]

Le·hi (lē′hī), *n.* a town in central Utah. 4377 (1960).

Le·high (lē′hī), *n.* a river in E Pennsylvania, flowing SW and SE into the Delaware River. 103 mi. long.

Le·high·ton (lē hīt′ən), *n.* a town in E Pennsylvania. 6318 (1960).

Leh·man (lē′mən, lā′-), *n.* **Herbert H(enry),** 1878–1963, U.S. banker and statesman: director of UNRRA 1943–46.

Leh·mann (lā′mən; *for 1, 2 also Ger.* lā′män), *n.* **1. Lil·li** (lil′ē), 1848–1929, German operatic soprano. **2. Lot·te** (lô′tə), born 1888, German operatic soprano in the U.S. **3.** a crater in the third quadrant of the face of the moon: about 28 miles in diameter.

Lehm·bruck (läm′bro͝ok; *Eng.* lem′bro͝ok, läm′-), *n.* **Wil·helm** (vil′helm), 1881–1919, German sculptor.

lehr (lēr, lâr), *n.* an oven used to anneal glass. Also, **leer.** [< G *Lehr, Leer* model]

le·hu·a (lā ho͞o′ä), *n.* **1.** a tree, *Metrosideros polymorpha,* of the Pacific islands, yielding a hard wood. **2.** the bright-red, corymbose flower of this tree: the State flower of Hawaii. [< Hawaiian]

le·i¹ (lā′ē, lā), *n., pl.* **le·is.** (in the Hawaiian Islands) a wreath of flowers, leaves, etc., for the neck or head. [< Hawaiian]

lei² (lā), *n.* pl. of **leu.**

Leib·niz (līb′nits; *Ger.* līp′nits), *n.* **Gott·fried Wil·helm von** (*Ger.* gôt′frēt vil′helm fən), 1646–1716, German philosopher, writer, and mathematician. Also, **Leib′nitz.** —**Leib·niz·i·an, Leib·nitz·i·an** (līb nit′sē-ən), *adj., n.* —**Leib·niz′i·an·ism, Leib·nitz′i·an·ism,** *n.*

Leices·ter (les′tər), *n.* **1. 1st Earl of.** See **Dudley, Robert. 2.** a city in and the county seat of Leicestershire, in central England. 273,298 (1961). **3.** Leicestershire. **4.** one of an English breed of large sheep, noted for its coarse, long wool and large yield of mutton. **5.** a boy's given name, form of **Lester.**

Leices·ter·shire (les′tər shēr′, -shər), *n.* a county in central England. 682,196 (1961); 832 sq. mi. *Co. seat:* Leicester. Also called **Leicester.**

Lei·den (līd′ən), *n.* a city in the W Netherlands. 96,440 (est. 1960).

Lei·den des Jung·en Wer·ther, Die (*Ger.* dē līd′-ən des yo͝ong′ən ver′tər). See **Sorrows of Werther.**

Leif (lēf, lāf), *n.* a boy's given name.

Leigh (lē), *n.* a boy's or girl's given name. Also, **Lee.**

Leigh-Mal·lo·ry (lē′mal′ə rē), *n.* **Sir Traf·ford Leigh** (traf′ərd lē), 1892–1942, British Air Force officer.

Leigh·ton (lāt′ən), *n.* **1. Frederick** (*Baron Leighton of Stretton*), 1830–96, English painter and sculptor. **2.** a boy's given name.

Lei·la (lē′lə, lā′-), *n.* a girl's given name.

Leins·dorf (līnz′dôrf; *Ger.* līns′dôrf), *n.* **E·rich** (er′ik; *Ger.* ā′ʀɪᴋʜ), born 1912, U.S. orchestra conductor, born in Austria.

Lein·ster (len′stər), *n.* a province in the E Republic of Ireland. 1,332,149 (1961); 7576 sq. mi.

lei·o·my·o·ma (lī′ō mī ō′mə), *n., pl.* **-mas, -ma·ta** (-mə tə). *Pathol.* a tumor composed of nonstriated muscular tissue. Cf. **rhabdomyoma.** [< Gk *leîo(s)* smooth + MYOMA] —**lei·o·my·om·a·tous** (lī′ō mī om′-ə təs, -ō′mə təs), *adj.*

Leip·zig (līp′sig, -sik; *Ger.* līp′tsɪᴋʜ), *n.* a city in S East Germany. 595,203 (est. 1964). Also, **Leip·sic**

leish·ma·ni·a (lēsh mā′nē ə), *n.* any parasitic flagellate protozoan of the genus *Leishmania,* occurring in vertebrates in an oval or spherical, nonflagellate form, and in invertebrates in an elongated, flagellated form. [< NL, named after Gen. Sir W. B. *Leishman* (1865–1926), Scottish bacteriologist; see -IA] —**leish·ma′ni·al, leish·man·ic** (lēsh man′ik), **leish·ma′ni·oid′,** *adj.*

leish·man·i·a·sis (lēsh′mə nī′ə sis, lish′-), *n.* *Pathol.* any infection caused by a protozoan of the genus *Leishmania.* Also, **leish·ma·ni·o·sis** (lēsh mā′nē ō′sis, -man′ē-, lish-). Cf. **kala-azar.** [LEISHMAN(IA) + -IASIS]

leis·ter (lē′stər), *n.* **1.** a spearlike implement having three or more prongs, for use in spearing fish. —*v.t.* **2.** to spear (fish) with a leister. [< Scand; cf. Icel *ljōstr* salmon-spear, akin to *ljōsta* to strike]

lei·sure (lē′zhər, lezh′ər), *n.* **1.** freedom from the demands of work or duty: *He enjoyed a life of leisure.* **2.** free or unoccupied time: *He had the leisure in which to follow his interests.* **3.** unhurried ease: *a work written with leisure and grace.* **4. at leisure, a.** with free or unrestricted time. **b.** without haste; slowly. **c.** out of work; unemployed: *Because of the failure of the magazine, many experienced editors are now at leisure.* **5. at one's leisure,** when one has free time; at one's convenience: *Take this book and read it at your leisure.* —*adj.* **6.** free or unoccupied: *leisure hours.* **7.** having leisure: *the leisure class.* **8.** (of clothing) suitable to or adapted for wear during leisure; casual: *a leisure jacket.* [ME *leisir* < OF, n. use of inf. < L *licēre* to be permitted] —**lei′-sur·a·ble,** *adj.* —**lei′sure·less,** *adj.*

lei·sured (lē′zhərd, lezh′ərd), *adj.* **1.** having leisure: *the leisured classes.* **2.** characterized by leisure; leisurely; unhurried: *the leisured manner of her walk.* [LEISURE + -ED³]

lei·sure·ly (lē′zhər lē, lezh′ər-), *adj.* **1.** acting, proceeding, or done without haste; deliberate: *a leisurely conversation.* **2.** showing or suggesting ample leisure; unhurried: *a leisurely manner.* —*adv.* **3.** in a leisurely manner; without haste: *to travel leisurely.* [late ME *laiserly* (adv.). See LEISURE, -LY] —**lei′sure·li·ness,** *n.*
—**Syn. 1.** See **slow.**

Leitch·field (lich′fēld′), *n.* a town in central Kentucky. 2982 (1960).

Leith (lēth), *n.* a seaport in SE Scotland, on the Firth of Forth: now part of Edinburgh.

leit·mo·tif (līt′mō tēf′), *n.* a motif or theme associated throughout a music drama with a particular person, situation, or idea. [< G: leading motive]

Le·i·tus (lē′i təs), *n.* (in the *Iliad*) the only Boeotian chief to return home safely from the siege of Troy.

Leix (lāks), *n.* Laoighis.

Le Jeune (*Fr.* lə zhœn′), **Claude** (klōd), **(Claudin),** 1530?–1600?, Flemish composer.

Le·jeune (lə jo͞on′, -zhœn′), *n.* **John Ar·cher** (är′-chər), 1867–1942, U.S. Marine Corps general.

Le Juif Er·rant (*Fr.* lə zhwē fe ʀäɴ′). See **Wandering Jew, The.**

lek (lek), *n.* a zinc coin and monetary unit of Albania, equal to 100 qintars, equivalent to about .02 of a U.S. dollar. [< Albanian]

Lek (lek), *n.* a river in the central Netherlands, flowing W to the Meuse River; the N branch of the lower Rhine. 40 mi. long.

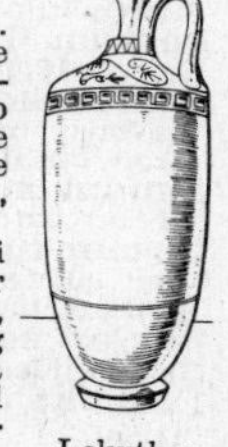
Lekythos

lek·a·ne (lek′ə nē), *n., pl.* **-nai** (-nī′). *Gk. and Rom. Antiq.* a bowl having a large ovoid body set on a short stem terminating in a foot, a lid, and usually two loop handles projecting vertically from the shoulder: used chiefly for various feminine articles. [< Gk *lekánē,* akin to *lékos* dish, plate, pot]

lek·y·thos (lek′ə thos′), *n., pl.* **-thoi** (-thoi′). *Gk. and Rom. Antiq.* an oil jar having an ellipsoidal body, narrow neck, flanged mouth, curved handle extending from below the lip to the shoulder, and a narrow base terminating in a foot: used chiefly for ointments. Also, **lecythus, lekythus.** Cf. **alabastron, aryballos, askos.** [< Gk]

lek·y·thus (lek′ə thəs), *n., pl.* **-thi** (-thī′). lekythos.

Le·la (lē′lə), *n.* a girl's given name.

Le·land (lē′lənd), *n.* **1.** a town in W Mississippi. 6295 (1960). **2.** a boy's given name.

Le·ly (lē′lē; *Du.* lā′lē), *n.* **Sir Pe·ter** (pē′tər; *Du.* pā′tər), (*Pieter van der Faes*), 1618–80, Dutch painter in England.

LEM (lem), Lunar Excursion Module.

Le·maî·tre (lə me′tʀᵊ), *n.* **Fran·çois É·lie Jules** (fʀäɴ swA′ ā lē′ zhyl), 1853–1915, French critic and dramatist.

lem·an (lem′ən, lē′mən), *n.* *Archaic.* **1.** a sweetheart; beloved. **2.** a mistress. [ME *lemman,* earlier *leofman.* See LIEF, MAN¹]

Le·man (lē′mən), *n.* **Lake.** See **Geneva, Lake of.**

Le Mans (lə mäɴ′), a city in and the capital of Sarthe, in NW France: auto racing. 136,083 (1962).

Le Mars (lə märz′), a town in NW Iowa. 6767 (1960).

Le·mass (lə mas′), *n.* **Seán Francis** (shôn), born 1899, prime minister of Ireland since 1959.

Lem·berg (lem′berk′; *Eng.* lem′bûrg), *n.* German name of **Lwów.**

Le·mes·sus (lə mes′əs), *n.* ancient name of **Limassol.**

Le Mi·san·thrope (*Fr.* lə mē zäɴ tʀôp′), a comedy, (1666) by Molière.

lem·ma¹ (lem′ə), *n., pl.* **lem·mas, lem·ma·ta** (lem′ə tə). **1.** a subsidiary proposition introduced in proving some other proposition; a helping theorem. **2.** an argument, theme, or subject. **3.** the heading of a gloss, annotation, etc. [< L: theme, title, epigram < Gk *lêmma,* lit., premise, akin to *lambánein* to take (for granted), receive]

lem·ma² (lem′ə), *n., pl.* **lem·mas, lem·ma·ta** (lem′ə tə). *Bot.* a bract in a grass spikelet just below the pistil and stamens. [< Gk *lémma* shell, husk, akin to *lépein* to peel]

lem·ming (lem′ing), *n.* any of various small, mouselike rodents of the genera *Lemmus, Myopus,*

Brown lemming, *Lemmus trimucronatus* (Length to 6½ in.)

and *Dicrostonyx*, of far northern regions, as *L. lemmus*, of Norway, Sweden, etc. [< Norw; c. Icel *læmingi* lemming, *læmingr* loon; akin to Goth *laian* to revile, Icel *lā* to blame, L *lātrāre* to bark. See LAMENT]

Lem·min·käi·nen (lem′in-kai′nen), *n.* (in the *Kalevala*) a young, jovial hero who has many adventures in which he is sometimes helped by his mother.

lem·nis·cate (lem nis′kit, lem′-nis·kāt′, -kit), *n.* *Geom.* a plane curve generated by the locus of the point at which a variable tangent to a rectangular hyperbola intersects a perpendicular from the center to the tangent. Equation: $r^2=2a^2\cos\theta$. Also called **Bernoulli's lemniscate.** [< L *lemniscāt(us)* adorned with ribbons. See LEMNISCUS, -ATE[1]]

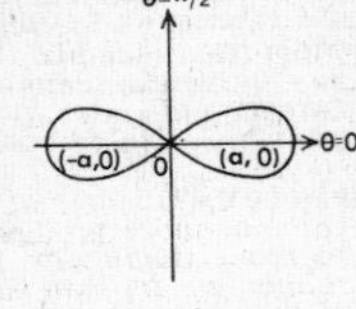

Lemniscate

lem·nis·cus (lem nis′kəs), *n., pl.* **-nis·ci** (-nis′ī, -nis′kē). *Anat.* a band of fibers, esp. of white nerve fibers in the brain. Also called **fillet, laqueus.** [< NL, special use of L *lēmniscus* pendent ribbon < Gk *lēmnískos* ribbon]

Lem·ni·tzer (lem′nit sər), *n.* **Ly·man Louis** (lī′mən), born 1899, U.S. army officer; chairman Joint Chiefs of Staff 1960–63; supreme allied commander NATO since 1963.

Lem·nos (lem′nos, -nōs; *Gk.* lēm′nôs), *n.* a Greek island in the NE Aegean. 24,016 (1951); 186 sq. mi. *Cap.:* Kastro. —**Lem·ni·an** (lem′nē ən), *adj., n.*

lem·on (lem′ən), *n.* **1.** the yellowish, acid fruit of a subtropical, rutaceous tree, *Citrus Limon.* **2.** the tree itself. **3.** clear, light yellow color. **4.** *Informal.* one who or that which proves to be inferior or unsatisfactory; a dud: *His car turned out to be a lemon.* —*adj* **5.** made of or with lemon, or having the color, taste, or odor of lemon. [< ML *lemōn(ium)*; r. late ME *lymon* < ML *līmō*, s. *līmōn-* << Pers *līmū, līmūn*] —**lem′on·ish,** *adj.* —**lem′on·like′, lem′on·y,** *adj.*

lem·on·ade (lem′ə nād′), *n.* a beverage consisting of lemon juice, sweetener, and water, sometimes carbonated. [LEMON + -ADE[1], modeled on F *limonade* or Sp *limonada*]

lem′onade su′mac, a semi-desert plant, *Agave lecheguilla,* of Mexico, grown as an ornamental.

lem′on balm′. See under **balm** (def. 5).

lem′on day′ lil′y, an herb, *Hemerocallis flava,* of eastern Asia, having yellow flowers on weak, arching stalks.

lem′on drop′, a lemon-flavored lozenge.

lem·on·fish (lem′ən fish′), *n., pl.* **-fish·es,** (*esp. collectively*) **-fish.** *Southern U.S.* the cobia. [LEMON + FISH]

lem′on gera′nium, a garden geranium, *Pelargonium Limoneum,* having lemon-scented leaves.

lem′on grass′, any of several lemon-scented grasses of the genus *Cymbopogon,* esp. *C. citratus,* of tropical regions, and *C. flexuosus,* of the East Indies, yielding lemon-grass oil.

lem′on-grass oil′ (lem′ən gras′, -gräs′), a yellowish to brownish oil distilled from the leaves of the lemon grasses *Cymbopogon citratus* and *C. flexuosus,* used chiefly in perfumery.

Lem′on Grove′, a town in SW California, near San Diego 19,348 (1960).

lem′on kal′i (kal′ē, kā′lē), *Brit.* an artificially flavored carbonated lemon drink; lemon soda pop. [*kali,* obs. for *kalium;* see ALKALI]

lem′on mint′, an annual herb, *Monarda citriodora,* of the central U.S., having white or pinkish flowers.

Le·mon·nier (lə mōn′yā), *n.* a walled plain in the first quadrant of the face of the moon: about 33 miles in diameter.

lem′on squash′, *Brit.* lemon soda; a soft drink of lemon juice and soda water.

Le·mont (lə mont′), *n.* a town in NE Illinois. 3397 (1960).

lem′on verbe′na, a verbena, *Lippia citriodora,* having long, slender leaves with a lemonlike fragrance. Also called **citronalis.**

lem′on vine′. See **Barbados gooseberry** (def. 1).

Le·moore (lə mōr′, -môr′), *n.* a town in central California. 2561 (1960).

Le Morte d'Ar·thur (lə môrt′ där′thər), a compilation and translation of French Arthurian romances by Sir Thomas Malory, printed by Caxton in 1485. Also, **Le Morte′ Dar′thur.**

Le·moyne (lə moin′), *n.* a town in central Pennsylvania. 4662 (1960).

Lem′pert opera′tion (lem′pərt), *Surg.* fenestration (def. 3c). Also, **Lem′pert's opera′tion.** [named after Julius *Lempert* (b. 1890), American otologist who devised it]

lem·pi·ra (lem pē′rə), *n.* a paper money and monetary unit of Honduras, equal to 100 centavos and equivalent to .50 of a U.S. dollar. *Abbr.:* L. [< AmerSp, after *Lempira,* Indian chief]

Lem·u·el (lem′yo͞o əl), *n.* a boy's given name.

le·mur (lē′mər), *n.* any of various small, arboreal, chiefly nocturnal mammals, esp of the genus *Lemur,* allied to the monkeys, usually having a foxlike face and woolly fur, and found chiefly in Madagascar. [< NL, special use of L *lemurēs* (pl.) ghosts, specters] —**le′mur·like′,** *adj.*

Lemur, *Lemur catta* (Length 3½ ft.)

Le·mu·ra·li·a (lem′yə rā′lē ə, -rāl′yə), *n.* (*sometimes construed as pl.*) the annual festival in ancient Rome in which the lemures were exorcised from houses. Also, **Le·mu·ri·a** (le myo͞or′ē ə).

lem·u·res (lem′yə rēz′; *Lat.* lem′o͞o res′), *n.pl.* *Rom. Religion.* the ghosts of the dead of a family, considered as troublesome unless exorcised or propitiated; larvae. [< L; see LEMUR]

lem·u·roid (lem′yə roid′), *adj.* **1.** lemurlike; of the lemur kind. —*n.* **2.** a lemur. [< NL *Lemuroid(ea).* See LEMUR, -OID]

Len (len), *n.* a boy's given name, form of **Leonard.**

Le·na (lē′nə; *Russ.* le′nä), *n.* **1.** a river in the S Soviet Union in Asia, flowing from Lake Baikal through the Yakutsk Republic into the Arctic Ocean. 2800 mi. long. **2.** a girl's given name.

Le·nae·a (lə nē′ə), *n.* (*sometimes construed as pl.*) one of the festivals in ancient Athens composing the Dionysia, celebrated at the beginning of February, and comprising a public banquet followed by dramatic performances.

Le·nae·us (lə nē′əs), *n.* *Class. Myth.* an epithet of Dionysus, as god of the wine press. [deriv. of *lēnós* wine vat, wine press]

Le Nain (lə naN′), **An·toine** (äN twaN′), (*"the Elder"*), 1588?–1648, and his two brothers **Louis** (lwē), (*"the Roman"*), 1593?–1648, and **Ma·thieu** (ma tyœ′), 1607–77, French painters.

Len·a·pe (len′ə pē, lə nä′pē), *n., pl.* **-pes,** (*esp. collectively*) **-pe.** Delaware (defs. 4, 5). [< Algonquian (Delaware): lit., person]

Le·nard (lā′närt; *Eng.* lā′närd), *n.* **Phi·lipp** (fē′lip), 1862–1947, German physicist, born in Czechoslovakia: Nobel prize 1905.

Le′nard rays′, *Electronics.* the cathode rays emitted into the atmosphere through the window of a Lenard tube.

Le′nard tube′, *Electronics.* a cathode ray tube having at the end opposite the cathode a window of thin glass or metal allowing cathode rays to pass out into the atmosphere. [named after P. LENARD]

Len·ca (leng′kə), *n., pl.* **-cas,** (*esp. collectively*) **-ca.** a member of an Indian people of El Salvador and central Honduras.

Len·clos (län klō′), *n.* **Anne** (än, AN), (*Ninon de Lenclos*), 1620–1705?, French courtesan and wit.

lend (lend), *v.,* **lent, lend·ing.** —*v.t.* **1.** to give the temporary use of (money) for a consideration. **2.** to grant the use of (something) with the understanding that it or its equivalent will be returned. **3.** to furnish or impart: *Distance lends enchantment to the view.* **4.** to give or contribute obligingly or helpfully: *to lend one's aid to a cause.* **5.** to adapt (oneself or itself) to something: *The building should lend itself to remodeling.* —*v.i.* **6.** to make a loan or loans. [ME *lende* (orig. past tense), var. of *lene,* OE *lǣnan* (c. D *lenen,* G *lehnen,* Icel *lāna*), deriv. of *lǣn* loan; c. G *Lehnen,* Icel *lān.* See LOAN[1]] —**lend′er,** *n.*

lend·a·ble (len′də bəl), *adj.* reserved or at hand for purposes of lending: *lendable stock; lendable money.* [LEND + -ABLE]

lend′ing li′brary, a small library that is maintained by a commercial establishment, as a drugstore, and is comprised largely of current books which are lent to customers for a minimal daily fee. Also called **circulating library, rental library.**

lend-lease (lend′lēs′), *n., v.,* **-leased, -leas·ing.** —*n.* (during World War II) **1.** the matériel and services supplied by the U.S. to its allies under the provisions of the Lend-Lease Act, through its agency (**Lend′-Lease′ Administra′tion**). —*v.t.* **2.** to supply (matériel or services) as authorized by the Lend-Lease Act.

Lend′-Lease′ Act′, an act of Congress (1941) authorizing the U.S. government to supply matériel and services to its allies in World War II, with the provision that such aid be repaid in kind after the war.

L'En·fant (län fän′), *n.* **Pierre Charles** (pyer sharl), 1754–1825, U.S. engineer, architect, and soldier; born in France: designer of Washington, D.C.

length (lengkth, length), *n.* **1.** the linear extent of anything as measured from end to end: *the length of a river.* **2.** the measure of the greatest dimension of a plane or solid figure. **3.** extent from beginning to end of a series, enumeration, account, book, etc.: *a government report 300 pages in length.* **4.** extent in time; duration: *the length of a battle.* **5.** a distance determined by the extent of something specified: *He stood nearly a car's length away from me. Hold the picture at arm's length.* **6.** a piece or portion of a certain or a known extent: *a length of rope.* **7.** the quality or state of being long rather than short: *a journey remarkable for its length.* **8.** the extent to which one would go in pursuing something: *He went to great lengths to get what he wanted.* **9.** a large extent or expanse of something. **10.** the measure from end to end of a horse, boat, etc., as a unit of distance in racing: *The horse won by two lengths.* **11.** *Clothing.* the extent of a garment from top to bottom as related to a specified point on the wearer's body, the floor, or to a garment used as a standard of measurement (usually used in combination): *an ankle-length gown; a floor-length negligee; a three-quarter-length coat.* **12.** *Pros., Phonet.* **a.** (of a vowel or syllable) quantity, whether long or short. **b.** the quality of vowels. **13.** *Bridge.* the possession of four or more than four cards in a given suit. **14.** *Theat. Archaic.* forty-two lines of an acting part. **15. at length, a.** in or to the full extent; completely. **b.** after a time; finally: *At length there was a step forward in the negotiations.* **16. go to any lengths,** to disregard any impediment that could prevent one from accomplishing one's purpose: *He would go to any lengths to get his own way.* **17. keep at arm's length.** See **arm**[1] (def. 15). [ME *length(e),* OE *length(u);* c. D *lengte,* Icel *lengd.* See LONG[1], -TH[1]]
—**Syn. 1.** span, stretch, reach, scope. measure.

length′ between′ perpendic′ulars, *Naut.* the length of a hull between the forward and after perpendicular. *Abbr.:* L.B.P., Length B.P. Cf. **perpendicular** (def. 10).

length·en (lengk′thən, leng′-), *v.t.* **1.** to make greater in length. —*v.i.* **2.** to become greater in length; grow long. [LENGTH + -EN[1]] —**length′en·er,** *n.*
—**Syn. 1.** elongate, draw out. LENGTHEN, EXTEND, STRETCH, PROLONG, PROTRACT agree in the idea of making longer. To LENGTHEN is to make longer, either in a material or an immaterial sense: *to lengthen a dress.* To EXTEND is to lengthen beyond some original point or so as to reach a certain point: *to extend a railway line by a hundred miles.* To STRETCH is primarily to lengthen by drawing or tension: *to stretch a rubber band.* Both PROLONG and PROTRACT mean esp. to lengthen in time, and therefore apply to intangibles. To PROLONG is to continue beyond the desired, estimated, or allotted time: *to prolong an interview.* To PROTRACT is to draw out to undue length or to be slow in coming to a conclusion: *to protract a discussion.* —**Ant. 1.** shorten.

length′ o′ver all′, *Naut.* the entire length of a vessel. *Abbr.:* L.O.A.

length·ways (lengkth′wāz′, length′-), *adv., adj.* lengthwise. [LENGTH + -WAYS]

length·wise (lengkth′wīz′, length′-), *adv., adj.* in the direction of the length. [LENGTH + -WISE]

length·y (lengk′thē, leng′-), *adj.,* **length·i·er, length·i·est. 1.** having or being of great length; very long: *a lengthy journey.* **2.** tediously verbose: *Don't make your speech lengthy.* [LENGTH + -Y[1]] —**length′i·ly,** *adv.* —**length′i·ness,** *n.*

le·ni·en·cy (lē′nē ən sē, lēn′yən-), *n., pl.* **-cies. 1.** the quality or state of being lenient. **2.** a lenient act. Also, **le′ni·ence.** [LENI(ENT) + -ENCY]

le·ni·ent (lē′nē ənt, lēn′yənt), *adj.* **1.** gently tolerant; permissive; indulgent: *He tended to be lenient toward the children. More lenient laws encouraged greater freedom of expression.* **2.** *Archaic.* softening, soothing, or alleviative. [< L *lēnient-* (s. of *lēniēns*) softening, alleviating, soothing, prp. of *lēnīre.* See LENIS, -ENT] —**le′ni·ent·ly,** *adv.*
—**Syn. 1.** easy, forbearing, tender. —**Ant. 1.** harsh.

Len·in (len′in), *n.* **Ni·ko·lai** (ni ko lī′) or **Vla·di·mir Il·yich** (vlä de′mir il yēch′), (*Vladimir Ilyich Ulyanov*), 1870–1924, Russian revolutionary leader: Soviet premier 1918–24.

Le·ni·na·kan (le′ni nä kän′), *n.* a city in NW Armenia, in the SW Soviet Union in Europe. 117,000 (est. 1962). Formerly, **Aleksandropol.**

Len·in·grad (len′in grad′; *Russ.* le′nin grät′), *n.* a seaport in the NW RSFSR, in the NW Soviet Union in Europe, on the Gulf of Finland, off the Baltic Sea: founded 1703 by Peter the Great; capital of the Russian Empire 1712–1917. 3,636,000 (1965). Formerly, **St. Petersburg** (1703–1914); **Petrograd** (1914–24).

Len·in·ism (len′i niz′əm), *n.* the form of Communism as taught by Nikolai Lenin, with emphasis on the dictatorship of the proletariat. [LENIN + -ISM]

Len·in·ist (len′in ist), *adj.* **1.** of or pertaining to Nikolai Lenin or to Leninism. —*n.* **2.** an advocate or supporter of Lenin or Leninism. Also, **Len·in·ite** (len′init′). [LENIN + -IST]

Len·insk-Kuz·nets·ki (len′insk ko͞oz nets′ki), *n.* a city in the S RSFSR, in the W Soviet Union in Asia. 140,000 (est. 1962). Also, **Leninsk-Kuznetskiy.**

le·nis (lē′nis, lā′-), *adj., n., pl.* **le·nes** (lē′nēz, lā′-). *Phonet.* —*adj.* **1.** pronounced with relatively weak muscular tension and breath pressure, resulting in weak sound effect in stressed or unstressed position. *b, d, g, j, v, th, z,* and *zh* are lenis as compared with *p, t, k, ch, f, th, s,* and *sh,* which are fortis. Cf. **fortis** (def. 1). —*n.* **2.** a lenis consonant. [< L: soft, mild, gentle, calm]

le·nit·ic (li nit′ik), *adj.* lentic. [*lenit-* (as in LENITION, LENITIVE, etc.) + -IC]

le·ni·tion (li nish′ən), *n.* *Phonet.* a weakening of the articulation of a consonant often leading to radical sound changes and even to loss of the sound, as the *l*-sound of *talk, palm,* etc. [< L *lēnīt(us)* softened (ptp. of *lēnīre;* see LENIS, -ITE[2]) + -ION]

len·i·tive (len′i tiv), *adj.* **1.** softening, soothing, or mitigating, as medicines or applications. **2.** mildly laxative. —*n.* **3.** a lenitive medicine or application; a mild laxative. **4.** *Archaic.* anything that softens or soothes. [< ML *lēnītīv(us).* See LENITION, -IVE]

len·i·ty (len′i tē), *n., pl.* **-ties. 1.** the quality or state of being mild or gentle, as toward others. **2.** a lenient act. [< L *lēnitās.* See LENIS, -TY[2]]

Len·nie (len′ē), *n.* a boy's given name, form of **Leonard.** Also, **Lenny.**

Len·nox (len′əks), *n.* **1.** a town in SW California, near Los Angeles. 31,224 (1960). **2.** a boy's given name.

Len·ny (len′ē), *n.* a boy's given name, form of **Leonard.** Also, **Lennie.**

le·no (lē′nō), *n., pl.* **-nos,** *adj.* —*n.* **1.** Also called **le′no weave′, gauze weave.** a weave structure in which paired warp yarns are intertwined in a series of figure eights and filling yarn is passed through each of the interstices so formed, producing a firm, open mesh. **2.** any fabric in this weave —*adj.* **3.** made in leno weave. [? Anglicized var. of F *linon* lawn, deriv. of *lin* linen (< L *līnum* flax)]

Le Noeud de Vi·pères (*Fr.* lə nœ də vē per′). See **Viper's Tangle, The.**

Le·noir (lə nwar′), *n.* **Jean Jo·seph É·tienne** (zhäN zhō zef′ ā tyen′), 1822–1900, French inventor.

Le·noir′ Cit′y (lə nōr′, -nôr′), a town in E Tennessee. 4979 (1960).

Le·nore (lə nōr′, -nôr′), *n.* a girl's given name. Also, **Le·no·ra** (lə nōr′ə, -nôr′ə), **Leonora, Leonore.**

Le·nô·tre (lə nō′trᵊ), *n.* **An·dré** (äN drā′), 1613–1700, French architect and landscape designer.

Len·ox (len′əks), *n.* a town in W Massachusetts, in the Berkshire Hills: site of a former estate (**Tanglewood**) where summer music festivals are held annually. 4253 (1960).

lens (lenz), *n., pl.* **lens·es. 1.** a piece of transparent substance, usually glass, having two opposite surfaces either both curved or one curved and one plane, used in changing the convergence of light rays, as for magnification, or in correcting defects of vision. **2.** a combination of such pieces. **3.** some analogous device, as for affecting sound waves, electromagnetic radiation, or streams of electrons. **4.** *Anat.* the crystalline lens-shaped body that focuses light rays in the eye. [< NL, special use of L *lēns* a lentil (from its shape); see LENTIL] —**lens′less,** *adj.* —**lens′like′,** *adj.*

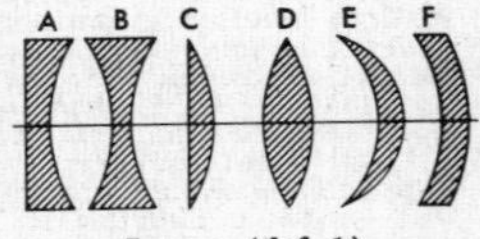

Lenses (def. 1) A, Plano-concave; B, Biconcave (concavo-concave); C, Plano-convex; D, Biconvex (convexo-convex); E, The meniscus (converging concavo-convex, converging meniscus); F, Concavo-convex

lens·man (lenz′mən), *n., pl.* **-men.** *Informal.* a photographer. [LENS + MAN[1]]

lens′ tur′ret, *Photog.* a rotating device on a camera for bringing any of several lenses in front of the shutter.

lent (lent), *v.* pt. and pp. of **lend.**

Lent (lent), *n.* (in the Christian religion) an annual season of fasting and penitence in preparation for Easter, beginning on Ash Wednesday and lasting 40 weekdays to Easter, observed by Roman Catholic, Anglican, and certain other churches. [ME *lente(n)*, OE *len(c)ten*, var. of *lengten* spring, Lent, lit., lengthening (of daylight hours); c. D *lente*, G *Lenz* spring]

-lent, an element occurring in adjectives borrowed from Latin, where it meant "full of": *pestilent.* [< L *-lent(us)*]

len·ta·men·te (len′tə men′tā; *It.* len′tä men′te), *adv. Music.* slowly (used as a musical direction). [< It, equiv. to *lenta-* (see LENTO) + *-mente* adv. suffix < L *menti-* (s. of *mēns*) mind]

len·tan·do (len tän′dō; *It.* len tän′dō), *adj.* becoming slower (used as a musical direction). [< It, prp. of *lentare* to become slow; see LENTO]

Lent·en (len′tən), *adj.* **1.** of, pertaining to, or suitable for Lent. **2.** suggesting Lent, as in austerity, frugality, or rigorousness. Also, **lent′en.** [ME; OE *lengten.* See LENT, -EN[2]]

Lent′en rose′, a perennial herb, *Helleborus orientalis,* of Asia Minor, having showy white or pinkish-green flowers.

Len·thi·el (len′thē əl), *n.* a boy's given name.

len·tic (len′tik), *adj.* pertaining to or living in still water. Also, **lenitic.** [< L *lent(us)* slow, motionless + -IC]

len·ti·cel (len′ti sel′), *n. Bot.* a body of cells formed on the periderm of a stem, appearing on the surface of the plant as a lens-shaped spot, and serving as a pore. [< NL *lenticell(a)*, dim. of L *lenticula* little lentil, equiv. to *lenti-* (s. of *lēns*; see LENS) + *-cula* -CULE] —**len·ti·cel·late** (len′ti sel′it), *adj.*

len·ti·cle (len′ti kəl), *n.* **1.** a window in a clock case revealing the motion of the pendulum bob. **2.** *Photog.* a tiny convex lens forming part of a pattern of such lenses impressed on the surface of a film. [< L *lenticula* little lentil. See LENTICEL]

len·tic·u·lar (len tik′yə lər), *adj.* **1.** of or pertaining to a lens. **2.** biconvex; convexo-convex. **3.** resembling the seed of a lentil in form; lentil-shaped. [< L *lenticulār(is)* lentillike, equiv. to *lenticul(a)* (see LENTICEL) + *-āris* -AR[1]] —**len·tic′u·lar·ly,** *adv.*

lentic′ular cloud′, a very smooth, round or oval, lens-shaped cloud that is often seen, singly or stacked in groups, near a mountain ridge.

len·tic·u·lar·is (len tik′yə lâr′is), *adj. Meteorol.* (of a cloud) having the shape of a lens. [< NL: LENTICULAR]

lentic′ular proc′ess, *Photog.* a method for producing images with a three-dimensional effect by photographing on lenticulated film.

lentic′ular truss′, a truss, used esp. for bridges, having at the ends uprights from which a suspension chain depends and against which a metal or wooden arch abuts, the load being divided between them in such a way that the tendency of the suspension cable to pull inwards toward the center is balanced by the tendency of the arch to thrust outwards toward the ends.

len·tic·u·late (len tik′yə lāt′), *v.t.,* **-lat·ed, -lat·ing.** *Photog.* to impress lenticles on the surface of (film). [< L *lenticul(a)* (see LENTICEL) + -ATE[1]]

len·tig·i·nous (len tij′ə nəs), *adj.* **1.** of or pertaining to a lentigo. **2.** *Bot., Zool.* covered with minute dots; freckled; speckled. Also, **len·tig·i·nose** (len tij′ə nōs′). [< L *lentiginōs(us)* freckled, equiv. to *lentigin-* (s. of *lentīgō*) LENTIGO + *-ōsus* -OUS]

len·ti·go (len tī′gō), *n., pl.* **-tig·i·nes** (-tij′ə nēz′). *Med.* a freckle. [< L, equiv. to *lenti-* (var. of *lenti-*, s. of *lēns* lentil) + *-go,* as in LUMBAGO]

len·til (len′til, -tᵊl), *n.* **1.** an annual, fabaceous plant, *Lens culinaris,* having flattened, biconvex seeds used as food. **2.** the seed itself. [ME < OF *lentille* < LL **lenticula* for L *lenticula* little lentil. See LENTICEL]

len′til cut′, *Jewelry.* a cabochon cut in which the upper and lower portions of the stone are identical.

len·tis·si·mo (len tis′ə mō′; *It.* len tēs′sē mō′), *Music.* —*adj.* **1.** very slow. —*adv.* **2.** very slowly. [< It, superl. of *lento* LENTO]

len·to (len′tō; *It.* len′tô), *Music.* —*adj.* **1.** slow; —*adv.* **2.** slowly. [< It < L *lentus* slow]

len·toid (len′toid), *adj.* **1.** having the shape of a biconvex lens. —*n.* **2.** a lentoid body. [< L *lent-* (s. of *lēns*) lentil (see LENS) + -OID]

Le·o (lē′ō), *n., gen.* **Le·o·nis** (lē ō′nis) for 1. **1.** *Astron.* the Lion, a zodiacal constellation between Virgo and Cancer, containing the bright star Regulus. **2.** *Astrol.* the fifth sign of the zodiac. See illus. under **zodiac. 3.** a boy's given name.

Le·o I (lē′ō; *It.* le′ô), **Saint,** ("*Leo the Great*"), A.D. c390–461, Italian ecclesiastic: pope 440–461.

Leo II, Saint, died A.D. 683, Sicilian ecclesiastic: pope 682–683.

Leo III, 1. Saint, A.D. c750–816, Italian ecclesiastic: pope 795–816. **2.** ("*the Isaurian*"), A.D. c680–741, Eastern Roman emperor 717–741.

Leo IV, Saint, died A.D. 855, Italian ecclesiastic: pope 847–855.

Leo V, fl. 10th century A.D., Italian ecclesiastic: pope 903.

Leo VI, pope A.D. 928.

Leo VII, died A.D. 939, Italian ecclesiastic: pope 936–939.

Leo VIII, died A.D. 965, Italian ecclesiastic: pope 963–965.

Leo IX, Saint (*Bruno*), 1002–54, German ecclesiastic: pope 1049–54.

Leo X, (*Giovanni de'Medici*), 1475–1521, Italian ecclesiastic: pope 1513–21 (son of Lorenzo de'Medici).

Leo XI, (*Alessandro de'Medici*), 1535–1605, Italian ecclesiastic: pope 1605.

Leo XII, (*Annibale Francesco della Genga*), 1760–1829, Italian ecclesiastic: pope 1823–29.

Leo XIII, (*Giovanni Vincenzo Pecci*), 1810–1903, Italian ecclesiastic: pope 1878–1903.

Lé·o·ca·dia (*Fr.* lā ō kä dyä′), *n.* See **Time Remembered.**

Le·o·dis (lē ō′dis), *n.* a boy's given name.

Le·of·ric (lē of′rik), *n.* died 1057, earl of Mercia c1030–57 (husband of Lady Godiva). Latin, **Leuricus.**

Le·o Mi·nor (lē′ō mī′nər), *gen.* **Le·o·nis Mi·no·ris** (lē ō′nis mi nôr′is, -nōr′-). *Astron.* the Little Lion, a northern constellation between Leo and Ursa Major.

Leom·in·ster (lem′in stər), *n.* a city in N Massachusetts. 27,929 (1960).

Le·on (lē′on), *n.* a boy's given name.

Le·ón (le ôn′), *n.* **1.** a province in NW Spain: formerly a kingdom. 598,700 (est. 1960); 5936 sq. mi. **2.** the capital of this province. 71,697 (est. 1960). **3.** a city in W Guanajuato, in central Mexico. 226,245 (1960). **4.** a city in W Nicaragua: the former capital. 48,541 (est. 1959).

Leon·ard (len′ərd), *n.* **1. William El·ler·y (Channing)** (el′ə rē), 1876–1944, U.S. poet, essayist, and teacher. **2.** a boy's given name.

Le·o·nar·desque (lē′ə när desk′), *adj.* of, pertaining to, or suggesting Leonardo da Vinci or the style of his paintings. [LEONARD(O) + -ESQUE]

Le·o·nar·do da Vin·ci (lē′ə när′dō də vin′chē; *It.* le′ô när′dô dä vēn′chē). See **Vinci, Leonardo da.**

Le·on·ca·val·lo (le ôn′kä väl′lô), *n.* **Rug·gie·ro** (rōōd je′rô), 1858–1919, Italian operatic composer and librettist.

Le·o·ni (le ô′ne; *Eng.* lā ō′nē), *n.* **Ra·úl** (rä ōōl′), born 1905, Venezuelan statesman: president 1964–69.

Le·o·ni·a (lē ō′nē ə, -ōn′yə), *n.* a town in NE New Jersey. 8384 (1960).

Le·o·nid (lē′ə nid), *n., pl.* **Le·o·nids, Le·on·i·des** (lē on′i dēz′). *Astron.* any of a shower of meteors occurring around November 15 and appearing to radiate from a point in the constellation Leo. [back formation from NL *Leōnidēs* (pl.), equiv. to L *Leōn-* (s. of *Leō*) LEO + *-idēs* pl. suffix; see -ID[1]]

Le·on·i·das (lē on′i dəs), *n.* **1.** died 480 B.C., Greek hero: king of Sparta 489?–480. **2.** a boy's given name.

Le·o·nie (lē′ə nē), *n.* a girl's given name.

le·o·nine (lē′ə nīn′), *adj.* **1.** of or pertaining to the lion. **2.** resembling or suggestive of a lion. [ME *leonyn* < L *leōnīn(us)* lionlike, equiv. to *leōn-* (s. of *leō*) + *-īnus* -INE[1]]

Le·o·no·ra (lē′ə nôr′ə, -nōr′ə), *n.* a girl's given name. Also, **Lenora, Lenore, Le·o·nore** (lē′ə nôr′, -nōr′).

Le·o·nov (le ô′nof), *n.* **Le·o·nid Mak·si·mo·vich** (le o nēt′ mäk sē′mo vich), born 1899, Russian writer.

Le·on·te·us (lē on′tē əs, -tōōs, -tyōōs), *n.* (in the *Iliad*) one of Helen's early suitors and a leader of the Greek forces at Troy.

leop·ard (lep′ərd), *n.* **1.** a large, ferocious, spotted Asian or African carnivore, *Panthera pardus,* of the cat family, usually tawny with black markings; the Old World panther. **2.** the fur or pelt of this animal. **3.** any of various related cats resembling this animal. **4.** *Heraldry.* a lion represented from the side as walking, usually with one forepaw raised, and looking toward the spectator; a lion passant gardant. **5.** *Numis.* **a.** an Anglo-Gallic gold coin issued by Edward III, equal to half a florin, bearing the figure of a leopard. **b.** a silver Anglo-Gallic coin issued by Henry V. [ME < LL *leōpard(us)* < LGk *leópardos,* syncopated var. of *leontópardos,* equiv. to *leonto-* (s. of *léōn*) lion + *párdos* PARD[1]]

Leopard, *Panthera pardus* (About 2½ ft. high at shoulder; total length 7½ ft.; tail 3 ft.)

leop·ard·ess (lep′ər dis), *n.* a female leopard. [LEOPARD + -ESS]

leop′ard frog′, a common green frog, *Rana pipiens,* of North America, having oval, white-edged, dark spots on the back.

Le·o·par·di (le′ô pär′dē), *n.* **Count Gia·co·mo** (jä′kô-mô), 1798–1837, Italian poet.

leop′ard lil′y, a bulbous herb, *Lilium pardalinum,* of California, having drooping, purple-spotted, orange-red flowers with a yellow base and recurved petal tips, growing from six to eight feet high.

leop′ard liz′ard, a long-tailed iguanid lizard, *Crotaphytus (Gambelia) wislizeni,* of the western U.S. and northern Mexico, having the body marked with spots and bars of dark or light brown or black.

leop′ard moth′, a moth, *Zeuzera pyrina,* having white wings spotted with black and larvae that bore into the wood of various trees and shrubs.

leop·ard's-bane (lep′ərdz bān′), *n.* any composite herb of the genus *Doronicum,* of Europe and Asia, having alternate, usually clasping leaves and heads of yellow flowers.

leop′ard seal′, a yellowish-gray seal, *Hydrurga leptonyx,* of the Antarctic, having the body marked with black spots.

Le·o·pold (lē′ə pōld′), *n.* a boy's given name.

Leopold I, 1. 1640–1705, king of Hungary 1655–1705; emperor of the Holy Roman Empire 1658–1705. **2.** 1790–1865, king of Belgium 1831–65.

Leopold II, 1. 1747–92, emperor of the Holy Roman Empire 1790–92 (son of Francis I; brother of Joseph II and Marie Antoinette). **2.** 1835–1909, king of Belgium 1865–1909 (son of Leopold I of Belgium).

Leopold III, born 1901, king of Belgium 1934–51 (son of Albert I).

Lé·o·pold·ville (lē′ə pōld vil′, lā′-; *Fr.* lā ô pôld vēl′), *n.* former name of **Kinshasa.** Also, **Le·o·pold·ville** (lē′ə pōld vil′, lā′-).

Le·os (lē′os), *n. Class. Myth.* **1.** a herald who warned Theseus of an impending attack on Athens. **2.** a son of Orpheus who sacrificed his three daughters to end a famine.

le·o·tard (lē′ə tärd′), *n.* a skin-tight, one-piece garment for the torso, having a high or low neck, long or short sleeves, and a lower portion resembling either briefs or tights, worn by acrobats, dancers, etc. Cf. **tights.** [named after J. *Léotard,* 19th-century French gymnast]

Le·o·tine (lē′ə tīn′), *n.* a girl's given name. Also, **Le′o·tyne′.**

Le·pan·to (li pan′tō; *It.* le′pän tô), *n.* **1.** a seaport in W Greece, on the Lepanto Strait: Turkish seapower destroyed here 1571. **2. Gulf of.** See **Corinth, Gulf of. 3. Strait of.** Also called **Rion Strait.** a strait between the Ionian Sea and the Gulf of Corinth. 1 mi. wide.

Le·paute (lə pōt′), *n.* a crater in the third quadrant of the face of the moon: about 13 miles in diameter.

lep·er (lep′ər), *n.* a person affected with leprosy. [ME *lepre* leprosy < L *lepra* < Gk, n. use of fem. of *leprós* scaly, akin to *lépos* scale, *lépein* to peel]

lep′er house′, a hospital for lepers; leprosarium.

Le Pe·tit Prince (*Fr.* lə pə tē PRANS′). See **Little Prince, The.**

lepido-, a learned borrowing from Greek meaning "scale," used in the formation of compound words: *lepidopteron.* [< Gk, comb. form repr. *lepís* (gen., *lepídos*) scale. See LEPER]

le·pid·o·lite (li pid′ə līt′, lep′i dᵊlīt′), *n.* a mineral of the mica group, potassium lithium aluminum silicate, commonly occurring in lilac, rose-colored, or whitish scaly masses: an ore of lithium. [LEPIDO- + -LITE]

Lep·i·dop·ter·a (lep′i dop′tər ə), *n.pl.* the order comprising the lepidopterous insects. [< NL; pl. of LEPIDOPTERON]

lep·i·dop·ter·an (lep′i dop′tər ən), *adj.* **1.** lepidopterous. —*n.* **2.** a lepidopterous insect. [LEPIDOPTER(A) + -AN]

lep·i·dop·ter·ol·o·gy (lep′i dop′tə rol′ə jē), *n.* the branch of zoology dealing with butterflies and moths. [LEPIDOPTER(A) + -O- + -LOGY] —**lep·i·dop·te·ro·log·i·cal** (lep′i dop′tər ə loj′i kəl), *adj.* —**lep·i·dop·ter·ist** (lep′i dop′tər ist), *n.*

lep·i·dop·ter·on (lep′i dop′tər ən), *n., pl.* **-ter·a** (-tər ə). any lepidopterous insect. [< NL, equiv. to *lepido-* LEPIDO- + Gk *pterón* wing]

lep·i·dop·ter·ous (lep′i dop′tər əs), *adj.* belonging or pertaining to the *Lepidoptera,* an order of insects comprising the butterflies, moths, and skippers, that in the adult state have four membranous wings more or less covered with small scales. Also, **lep′i·dop′ter·al.** [LEPIDOPTER(A) + -OUS]

lep·i·do·si·ren (lep′i dō sī′rən), *n.* a lungfish, *Lepidosiren paradoxa,* found in the Amazon, having an eel-shaped body. [< NL; see LEPIDO-, SIREN]

lep·i·dote (lep′i dōt′), *adj. Bot.* covered with scurfy scales or scaly spots. [< NL *lepidōt(us)* < Gk *lepidōtós* scaly, equiv. to *lepidō-* (verbid s. of *lepidoûn* to make scaly; see LEPIDO-) + *-tos* verbid suffix]

Lep·i·dus (lep′i dəs), *n.* **Marcus Ae·mil·i·us** (ē mil′ē-əs), died 13 B.C., Roman politician: member of the second triumvirate.

Le·pon′tine Alps′ (li pon′tin), a central range of the Alps in S Switzerland and N Italy. Highest peak, Mt. Leone, 11,684 ft.

lep·o·rid (lep′ə rid), *n., pl.* **le·por·i·dae** (li pôr′i dē′, -por′-), *adj.* —*n.* **1.** an animal of the family *Leporidae,* comprising the rabbits and hares. —*adj.* **2.** belonging or pertaining to the family *Leporidae.* [< NL *Leporid(ae)* family name, equiv. to *Lepor-* (s. of *Lepus* genus name, L *lepus* hare) + *-idae* -ID[4]]

lep·o·ride (lep′ə rid, -rīd′, -rēd′), *n.* a Belgian hare formerly believed to be a hybrid of the European rabbit and hare. [< F; see LEPORID]

lep·o·rine (lep′ə rīn′, -rin), *adj. Zool.* of, pertaining to, or resembling a rabbit or hare. [< L *leporīn(us)*, equiv. to *lepor-* (s. of *lepus*) hare + *-īnus* -INE[1]]

lep·re·chaun (lep′rə kôn′, -kon′), *n. Irish Folklore.* a pygmy, sprite, or goblin. [< Ir *leipreachān,* MIr *luchrupān,* OIr *luchorpān,* equiv. to *lu* small + *corp* body (< L *corpus*) + *-ān* dim. suffix]

lep·rol·o·gy (le prol′ə jē), *n.* the branch of medical science that deals with the study and treatment of leprosy. [< LL *lepr(a)* leprosy (see LEPER) + -O- + -LOGY] —**lep·rol′o·gist,** *n.*

lep·ro·sar·i·um (lep′rə sâr′ē əm), *n., pl.* **-sar·i·a** (-sâr′ē ə). a hospital for the treatment of leprosy. [< ML; see LEPROUS, -ARY]

lep·rose (lep′rōs), *adj.* leprous. [< LL *leprōs(us)* LEPROUS]

lep·ro·sy (lep′rə sē), *n. Pathol.* a mildly infectious disease caused by an organism, *Mycobacterium leprae,* and variously characterized by ulcerations, tubercular nodules, spots of pigmentary excess or deficit, loss of fingers and toes, anesthesia in certain nerve regions, etc. Also called **Hansen's disease.** [? < ML *leprōsi(a)* (recorded only as synonym for LEPROSARIUM) < Gk *léprōs(is)* leprosy + *-ia* -Y[3]]

lep·rot·ic (le prot′ik), *adj. Pathol.* of or noting the disease leprosy; leprous. [LEPRO(SY) + -TIC]

lep·rous (lep′rəs), *adj.* **1.** *Pathol.* affected with leprosy. **2.** of or resembling leprosy. **3.** *Bot., Zool.* covered with scales. [ME *lepr(o)us* < LL *leprōs(us).* See LEPER, -OUS] —**lep′rous·ly,** *adv.* —**lep′rous·ness,** *n.*

Lep·si·us (lep′sē ōōs′), *n.* **Karl Rich·ard** (kärl RIKH′ärt), 1810–84, German philologist and Egyptologist.

-lepsy, a learned borrowing from Greek meaning "seizure," used in the formation of compound words: *epilepsy.* [comb. form repr. NL *-lēpsia* < Gk *-lēpsia,* equiv. to *lēps(is)* a seizure (*lēp-* verbid s. of *lambánein* to seize + *-sis* -SIS) + *-ia* -Y[3]]

lepto-, a learned borrowing from Greek meaning "thin," "fine," "slight," used in the formation of compound words: *leptophyllous.* [< Gk *lepto-,* comb. form of *leptós* thin, slight, fine, lit., stripped, equiv. to *lép(ein)* (to) strip + *-tos* verbid suffix]

lep·to·dac·ty·lous (lep′tə dak′tᵊləs), *adj.* having slender toes. [LEPTO- + *-dactylous* toed; see -DACTYL, -OUS]

lep·to·kurt·ic (lep′tō kûr′tik), *adj. Statistics.* **1.** (of a frequency distribution) being more concentrated about the mean than the corresponding normal distribution. **2.** (of a frequency distribution curve) having a high, narrow concentration about the mode. [LEPTO- + Gk *kyrt(ós)* swelling + -IC]

lep·to·kur·to·sis (lep′tō kûr tō′sis), *n. Statistics.* the state of being leptokurtic. [< NL; see LEPTOKURTIC, -OSIS]

lep·ton (lep′ton), *n., pl.* **-ta** (-tə). **1.** a money of account of modern Greece, the 100th part of a drachma, equivalent to about .0003 of a U.S. dollar. **2.** *Physics.* an elementary particle that is an electron, positron, neutrino, antineutrino, or mu-meson. [< Gk *leptón* (*nómisma*) a small (coin), n. use of neut. of *leptós* small; see LEPTO-]

lep·to·phyl·lous (lep′tō fil′əs), *adj.* having long, slender leaves. [LEPTO- + -PHYLLOUS]

lep·to·pro·so·pic (lep′tō prə sō′pik, -sop′ik), *adj. Anthropol.* having a relatively narrow face. [LEPTO- + Gk *prósop(on)* face (*prós* before + *ōp-,* s. of *ōps,* eye, face + *-on* neut. suffix) + -IC] —**lep·to·pros·o·py** (lep′tə-pros′ə pē), *n.*

lep·tor·rhine (lep′tə rīn′, -rin), *adj. Anthropol.* having a narrow and high-bridged nose. [LEPTO- + *-rhine;* see RHINO-] —**lep′tor·rhi′ny,** *n.*

lep·to·some (lep′tə sōm′), *n.* a person of asthenic build. [LEPTO- + -SOME³] —**lep′to·so′mic, lep·to·so·mat·ic** (lep′tō sə mat′ik), *adj.*

lep·to·spi·ra (lep′tə spī′rə), *n., pl.* **-rae** (-rē), **-ras.** *Bacteriol.* any of several spirally shaped, aerobic bacteria of the genus *Leptospira,* certain species of which are pathogenic for man. [LEPTO- + L *spīra* coil; see SPIRE²] —**lep′to·spi′ral,** *adj.*

lep·to·spi·ro·sis (lep′tō spī rō′sis), *n. Pathol., Vet. Pathol.* a spirochetal disease occurring esp. in man and dogs and also in swine, cattle, and horses. Cf. **canicola fever, canine leptospirosis, Weil's disease.** [< NL; see LEPTOSPIRA, -OSIS]

Lep·us (lep′əs, lē′pəs), *n., gen.* **Lep·o·ris** (lep′ər is). *Astron.* the Hare, a small southern constellation south of Orion. [< L]

Le Puy (lə pwē′), a city in and the capital of Haute-Loire, in central France: cathedral. 28,007 (1962).

Ler (ler), *n. Irish Myth.* the personification of the sea and the father of Manannan: corresponds to the Welsh Llyr. Also, **Lir.**

Lé·ri·da (le′rē thä), *n.* a city in NE Spain. 66,847 (est. 1963)

Ler·mon·tov (leʀ′mon tôf′), *n.* **Mi·kha·il Yur·i·e·vich** (mi кнä ēl′ yo͞or′yə vich), 1814–41, Russian poet and novelist.

Ler·na (lûr′nə), *n.* a marshy region near Argos, Greece: the legendary abode of the Hydra slain by Hercules. Also, **Ler·ne** (lûr′nē).

Ler·nae·a (lər nē′ə), *n. Class. Myth.* Demeter: so called because of mysteries celebrated in her honor at Lerna.

Ler·nae·an (lər nē′ən), *adj.* of or pertaining to Lerna. Also, **Ler·ne′an.** [LERNA + *-e-* connecting vowel + -AN]

Ler·ner (lûr′nər), *n.* **Alan Jay,** born 1918, U.S. lyricist and librettist.

le roi est mort, vive le roi (lə ʀwa e môʀ′, vēv lə ʀwa′), *French.* the king is dead, long live the king!

le roi le veut (lə ʀwa lə vœ′), *French.* the king wills it.

Le·ros (lē′ros), *n.* one of the Dodecanese Islands, off the SW coast of Turkey. ab. 6200; 21 sq. mi.

Le Rouge et le Noir (*Fr.* lə ʀo͞ozh ā lə nwaʀ′). See **Red and the Black, The.**

Le·roy (lə roi′, lē′roi), *n.* , a boy's given name. Also, **Learoy, Leeroy, Le Roy.**

Le Roy (lə roi′, lē′ roi), **1.** a town in W New York. 4662 (1960). **2.** Also, **Leroy.** a boy's given name.

Ler·wick (lûr′wik, ler′-, ler′ik), *n.* a city in the Shetland Islands, N of Scotland. 5538 (1951).

Le Sage (lə sazh′), **A·lain Re·né** (a laɴ′ rə nā′), 1668–1747, French novelist and dramatist. Also, **Le·sage′.**

Les·bi·an (lez′bē ən), *adj.* **1.** of or pertaining to Lesbos. **2.** (*l.c.*) of, pertaining to, or characteristic of lesbianism. **3.** erotic; so called from the reputed character of the ancient inhabitants of Lesbos and the tone of their poetry. —*n.* **4.** an inhabitant of Lesbos. **5.** (*usually l.c.*) a female homosexual. [< L *Lesbi(us)* (< Gk *Lésbios* Lesbian, equiv. to *Lésb(os)* LESBOS + *-ios* adj. suffix) + -AN]

Les′bian cyma′tium. See **cyma reversa.** Also, **Les′bian cy′ma.**

les·bi·an·ism (lez′bē ə niz′əm), *n.* homosexual relations between women. [LESBIAN + -ISM]

Les′bian leaf′. See **water leaf** (def. 2).

Les′bian ode′, *Pros.* See **Horatian ode.**

Les·bos (lez′bos, -bōs; *Gk.* lez′vôs), *n.* Mytilene (def. 1).

Les Caves du Va·ti·can (*Fr.* lā kav dʏ va tē kän′). See **Lafcadio's Adventures.**

Les Cayes (lā kā′; *Fr.* lā ka′yᵊ), a seaport on the SW coast of Haiti. 12,621 (1957). Also called **Cayes.** Formerly, **Aux Cayes.**

Les Cé·li·ba·taires (*Fr.* lā sā lē ba teʀ′). See **Perish in Their Pride.**

Les Chants de Mal·do·ror (*Fr.* lā shäɴ də mal dô-ʀôʀ′), a prose poem by Lautréamont, first published in part in 1868 and afterward in full in 1890.

les·che (les′kē), *n.* an arcade or other public place in ancient Greece. [< Gk *lésche* (place for) conversation, akin to *légein* to speak]

Le·sche·tiz·ky (lesh′ə tit′skē), *n.* **The·o·dor** (tā′-ə dôr′, -dôr′, thē′-), 1830–1915, Polish pianist and composer.

lese′ maj′esty (lēz), **1.** Also, **leze majesty.** *Law.* any crime or offense against the sovereign power in a state, esp. one against the dignity of a ruler. **2.** an attack on any custom, institution, belief, etc., held sacred or revered by numbers of people: *Her speech against Mother's Day was criticized as lese majesty.* Also, **lèse′ maj′esty.** [< F *lèse-majesté* < L *laesa mājestās,* lit., injured greatness. See LESION, MAJESTY]

Les En·fants Ter·ri·bles (*Fr.* lā zäɴ fäɴ te ʀē′blᵊ), a novel (1929) by Jean Cocteau.

Les Fleurs du Mal (*Fr.* lā flœʀ dʏ mal′). See **Flowers of Evil.**

Les Faux-Mon·na·yeurs (*Fr.* lā fō mô ne yœʀ′). See **Counterfeiters, The.**

Les Gueux (lā gœ′), **1.** a league of Dutch and Flemish patriots, composed chiefly of nobles and formed in 1566 to resist the introduction of the Spanish Inquisition into the Netherlands. **2.** (later) any of various Dutch or Flemish partisan groups organized to gain independence for the Netherlands from Spain. [< F: lit., the beggars]

Les Halles (lā al′), the large, central, wholesale food market area of Paris, France.

Les Il·lu·mi·na·tions (*Fr.* lā zē lʏ mē nä syôɴ′), a series of poems (1871–75?) by Rimbaud.

le·sion (lē′zhən), *n.* **1.** an injury; hurt; wound. **2.** *Pathol.* any localized, abnormal structural change in the body. **3.** *Plant Pathol.* any localized, defined area of diseased tissue, as a spot, canker, blister, scab, etc. [late ME < LL *laesiōn-* (s. of *laesiō*) injury (L: attack), equiv. to L *laes(us)* harmed (ptp. of *laedere*) + *-iōn-* -ION]

Les·ley (les′lē; *Brit.* lez′-), *n.* a boy's or girl's given name. Also, **Leslie.**

Les Liai·sons Dan·ge·reuses (*Fr.* lā lye zôɴ däɴzhᵊ ʀœz′), an epistolary novel (1782) by Pierre Choderlos de Laclos.

Les·lie (les′lē; *Brit.* lez′-), *n.* a boy's or girl's given name. Also, **Lesley.**

Les Mi·sé·ra·bles (*Fr.* lā mē zā ʀa′blᵊ), a novel (1862) by Victor Hugo.

Le·so·tho (le sō′thō), *n.* a monarchy in S Africa: formerly a British protectorate; gained independence 1966; member of the Commonwealth of Nations. 729,000 (est. 1964); 11,716 sq. mi. *Cap.:* Maseru. Formerly, **Basutoland.**

Le Sou·lier de Sa·tin (*Fr.* lə so͞o lyā də sa taɴ′). See **Satin Slipper, The.**

les·pe·de·za (les′pi dē′zə), *n.* any leguminous shrub or herb of the genus *Lespedeza,* having trifoliolate leaves and lavender flowers, grown for forage, soil improvement, etc. [< NL, named after V. M. de *Zespedez* (misread as *Lespedez*), 18th-century Spanish governor of Florida]

L'Es·prit des Lois (*Fr.* les pʀē dā lwä′). See **Spirit of Laws, The.**

less (les), *adv., a compar. of* **little** *with* **least** *as superl.* **1.** to a smaller extent, amount, or degree: *less exact.* **2.** most certainly not (often prec. by *much* or *still*): *He could barely pay for his own lodging, much less for that of his friend.* **3.** in any way different; other: *He is nothing less than a thief.* **4. less than,** by far short of being; not in the least; hardly at all: *The job is less than perfect.* —*adj., a compar. of* **little** *with* **least** *as superl.* **5.** smaller in size, amount, degree, etc.; not so large, great, or much: *less speed.* **6.** lower in consideration, dignity, or importance: *no less a person than the manager.* **7.** fewer. —*n.* **8.** a smaller amount or quantity. —*prep.* **9.** minus; without: *a year less two days.* [ME; OE *lǣs(sa)*; c. OFris *lēs(sa).* See LEAST] —**Syn. 5.** See **fewer, small.** —**Usage. 5.** See **fewer.**

-less, an adjective suffix meaning "without" (*childless; peerless*), and in adjectives derived from verbs, indicating failure or inability to perform or be performed (*resistless; countless*). [ME *-les,* OE *-lēas,* special use of *lēas* free from, without, false; c. Icel *lauss,* G *los,* LOOSE]

les·see (le sē′), *n.* one to whom a lease is granted. [late ME < AF. See LEASE¹, -EE] —**les·see′ship,** *n.*

less·en (les′ən), *v.i.* **1.** to become less. —*v.t.* **2.** to make less; reduce. **3.** *Archaic.* to represent as less; depreciate; disparage. [late ME (see LESS, -EN¹), r. ME *lasnen,* equiv. to *lasse* (var. of *lesse* LESS) + *-nen* -EN¹] —**Syn. 1, 2.** decrease, diminish, abate. —**Ant. 1, 2.** increase.

Les·seps (les′əps; *Fr.* le seps′), *n.* **Fer·di·nand Ma·rie, Vi·comte de** (feʀ dē näɴ′ ma ʀē′, vē kôɴ də), 1805–94, French engineer and diplomat: promoter of the Suez Canal.

less·er (les′ər), *adj., a compar. of* **little** *with* **least** *as superl.* **1.** less; smaller, as in size, amount, importance, etc.: *a lesser evil.* **2.** being the smaller or less important of two. [ME *lasser, lesser.* See LESS, -ER⁴]

Less′er Antil′les. See under **Antilles.**

less′er Bai′ram. See under **Bairam.**

Less′er Bear′, *Astron.* the constellation Ursa Minor.

Less′er Diony′sia, (in ancient Attica) the wine feasts, processions, and dramatic performances composing one of the festivals of the Dionysia, held in the middle of December. Also called **Rural Dionysia.**

Less′er Dog′, *Astron.* the constellation Canis Minor.

less′er doxol′ogy. See **Gloria Patri.**

less′er Ion′ic. See under **Ionic** (def. 2).

less′er multan′gular bone. See under **multangulum.**

less′er omen′tum, *Anat.* an omentum attached to the stomach, part of the duodenum, and part of the liver and supporting the hepatic vessels. Also called **gastrohepatic omentum.** Cf. **greater omentum.**

less′er pan′da, panda (def. 1).

Less′er Sanhed′rin, Sanhedrin (def. 2).

Less′er Sun′da Is′lands. See under **Sunda Islands.**

less′er wee′ver. See under **weever.**

less′er win′tergreen, a low, perennial herb, *Pyrola elliptica,* of North America, having thin, dull, olive-green leaves and greenish-white, fragrant, waxy flowers in loose clusters.

less′er yel′lowlegs. See under **yellowlegs.**

Les·sing (les′ing), *n.* **Gott·hold E·phra·im** (gôt′hôlt ā′fʀä im), 1729–81, German critic and dramatist.

les·son (les′ən), *n.* **1.** a part of a book or the like, as an exercise, a text, or dictated matter, assigned a pupil for study: *The lesson for today is on page 22. He worked assiduously at his music lesson.* **2.** a section into which a course of study is divided, esp. a single, continuous session of formal instruction in a subject, usually lasting one hour: *The manual was broken down into 50 lessons. He gave lessons in French for a living.* **3.** something to be learned or studied: *They learned well the lessons of the past.* **4.** a useful piece of practical wisdom acquired by experience or study: *That slight adventure certainly taught him a lesson.* **5.** something from which one learns or should learn; an instructive example: *This should serve as a lesson to you.* **6.** a reproof or punishment intended to teach one better ways. **7.** a portion of Scripture or other sacred writing read or appointed to be read at a divine service; lection; pericope. —*v.t.* **8.** to teach; give a lesson to: *He lessoned him in the subtle art of persuasion.* **9.** to admonish or reprove. [ME *lesso(u)n* < OF *leçon* < L *lectiōn-* (s. of *lectiō*) LECTION]

les·sor (les′ôr, le sôr′), *n.* one who grants a lease. [late ME *lesso(u)r* < AF. See LEASE¹, -OR²]

lest (lest), *conj.* **1.** for fear that; so that (one) should not (used negatively to introduce a clause expressive of an action or occurrence requiring caution): *He kept his notes by his side, lest faulty memory lead him astray.* **2.** that (used after words expressing fear, danger, etc.): *There was danger lest the plan become known.* [ME *leste,* late OE *the lǣste,* earlier *thȳ lǣs the* lest (lit., whereby less that; *the* is the relative particle)]

les·te (les′tā; *Sp.* les′te), *n.* a hot, dry, dusty wind that blows from Morocco to Madeira and the Canary Islands. [< Sp: east (wind)]

Les·ter (les′tər), *n.* a boy's given name.

les·to·bi·o·sis (les′tō bī ō′sis), *n., pl.* **-ses** (-sēz). cleptobiosis characterized by furtive thievery. [< NL < Gk *lēist(ḗs)* robber + *-o-* -O- + *-biosis* -BIOSIS] —**les·to·bi·ot·ic** (les′tō bī ot′ik), *adj.*

Les Trois Mous·que·taires (*Fr.* lā tʀwä mo͞os kə-teʀ′). See **Three Musketeers, The.**

le style, c'est l'homme (lə stēl′, se lôm′), *French.* the style is the man.

Le Sueur (lə so͞or′), a town in S Minnesota. 3310 (1960).

les·ya (lesh′yä), *n. Jainism.* any of six possible colors given to the monad, which is the individual soul, by its karma and is lighter or darker according to the proportion of good or evil included in the karma. [< Skt: light]

let¹ (let), *v.,* **let, let·ting,** *n.* —*v.t.* **1.** to allow or permit: *Let me do that for you.* **2.** to allow to pass, go, or come: *The maid let us into the house.* **3.** to grant the occupancy or use of (land, buildings, rooms, space, etc., or movable property) for rent or hire (sometimes fol. by *out*). **4.** to contract for performance: *to let work to a carpenter.* **5.** to cause or make: *to let one know the truth.* **6.** used in the imperative as an auxiliary expressive of a request, command, warning, suggestion, etc.: *Let me see. Let us go. Let them just try it!* —*v.i.* **7.** to admit of being rented or leased: *The apartment lets for $100 per week.* **8.** *Aeron.* (of an airplane) to descend from a higher to a lower altitude preparatory to making an approach and landing or a similar maneuver. **9. let alone.** See **alone** (def. 5). **10. let be,** to refrain from bothering or interfering with; let alone: *Please let me be for the rest of the afternoon.* **11. let down, a.** to disappoint; fail. **b.** to betray; desert. **c.** to slacken; abate: *We were too near success to let down in our efforts.* **12. let go.** See **go** (def. 75). **13. let in, a.** to admit. **b.** to involve (a person) in without his knowledge or permission: *to let someone in for a loss.* **c.** to insert into the surface of a wall or the like as a permanent addition: *to let a plaque into a wall.* **d.** Also, **let in on.** to share a secret with; permit to participate in. **14. let off, a.** to release by exploding. **b.** to free from duty or responsibility; excuse. **c.** to allow to go with little or no punishment; pardon: *The judge let off the youthful offender with a reprimand.* **15. let on,** *Informal.* **a.** to allow to be known; reveal: *She was terrified at the prospect, but didn't let on.* **b.** to pretend: *They let on that they didn't care about not being invited, but I could tell that they were hurt.* **16. let out, a.** to divulge; make known. **b.** to release from confinement, restraint, etc. **c.** to enlarge (a garment). **d.** to terminate; be finished; end: *When does the university let out for the summer?* **e.** to make (a let-out fur or pelt). **17. let someone have it,** *Informal.* to do injury to, as by striking, shooting, or upbraiding: *The gunman threatened to let the teller have it if he didn't move fast.* **18. let up,** *Informal.* **a.** to slacken; abate: *It is forecast that this heat wave will let up by the beginning of next week.* **b.** to cease; stop: *The rain let up for a few hours.* **19. let up on,** *Informal.* to treat less severely; be more lenient with: *He refused to let up on the boy until his school grades improved.* —*n.* **20.** *Brit.* a lease. [ME *lete(n),* OE *lǣtan*; c. D *laten,* G *lassen,* Icel *lāta,* Goth *lētan*; akin to Gk *lēdein* to be weary, L *lassus* tired. See LATE] —**Syn. 1.** See **allow. 1, 5.** suffer, grant. LET, LEAVE, although not synonyms, are often confused, LEAVE being the one used more frequently in both meanings. A further confusion of the verb LEAVE with the noun LEAVE may have helped to perpetuate the misuse. (The noun LEAVE, meaning "permission," might readily be associated with LET, whose most common meaning is "permit" or "allow." The verb LEAVE, however, does not have a meaning of "permit" or "allow"; its most common meaning is "to go away from.") In the constructions in which the confusion arises, it should be noted that, although either verb can take a nominal object (*Let John leave home.*), only LET can take the infinitive (with *to* not expressed: *let fly; let go*). In certain idiomatic expressions, the two verbs are used in parallel constructions, but the meanings differ widely: LET it out means "allow it to escape" (as the breath), but LEAVE it out means "omit it" (as a sentence). LET him alone means "allow him to be without interference" (don't bother him), and although purists insist that LEAVE him alone means "go away, so that he will be alone," the facts of usage show that this construction means "don't bother him" as frequently as it does "go away," if not more frequently. At best, the two appear in entirely ambiguous contexts. **3.** lease, rent, sublet, hire. —**Ant. 1.** prevent.

let² (let), *n., v.,* **let, let·ting.** —*n.* **1.** (in tennis, badminton, etc.) any play that is voided and must be replayed, esp. a service that hits the net and drops into the proper part of the opponent's court. **2.** *Archaic.* a hindrance or obstruction; an impediment or obstacle: *to act without let or inquiry.* —*v.t.* **3.** *Archaic.* to hinder; stand in the way of. [ME *lette(n),* OE *lettan* (deriv. of *læt* slow, tardy, LATE); c. Icel *letja* to hinder]

-let, a diminutive suffix attached to nouns: *ringlet; frontlet; bracelet.* [ME *-let, -lette* < MF *-elet,* equiv. to *-el* (< L *-āle,* neut. of *-ālis* -AL¹ (see BRACELET); or < L *-ellus,* dim. suffix; see CHAPLET) + *-et* -ET]

Le·ta (lē′tə), *n.* a girl's given name, form of **Latona.**

l'é·tat, c'est moi (lā ta′, se mwa′), *French.* I am the state (attributed to Louis XIV).

letch (lech), *n. Slang.* **1.** a lecherous craving. **2.** a lecher. **3.** a strong liking, as for automobiles, golf, or other objects or activities. [? alter. and back formation from LECHER]

let·down (let′doun′), *n.* **1.** a decrease in volume, force, energy, etc.: *a letdown in sales; a letdown in production; a general letdown of social barriers.* **2.** disillusionment or disappointment: *The job was a letdown.* **3.** depression; deflation: *He felt a terrible letdown at the end of the play.* **4.** *Aeron.* the descent of an aircraft from a higher to a lower altitude preparatory to making an approach and landing, a target run, etc. [n. use of v. phrase *let down*]

Le·tha (lē′thə), *n.* a girl's given name.

le·thal (lē′thəl), *adj.* **1.** of, pertaining to, or causing death; deadly; fatal: *a lethal weapon; a lethal dose.* **2.** made to cause death: *a lethal chamber; a lethal attack.* [< L *lēthāl(is),* deriv. of *lēthum* death (*-h-* by confusion with Gk *lḗthē* oblivion); see -AL¹] —**le·thal′i·ty,** *n.* —**le′thal·ly,** *adv.* —**Syn. 1.** See **fatal.**

le′thal gene′, *Genetics.* a gene that under certain conditions causes the death of an organism. Also called **le′thal fac′tor.**

le·thar·gic (lə thär′jik), *adj.* **1.** of, pertaining to, or affected with lethargy; drowsy; sluggish. **2.** producing lethargy. Also, **le·thar′gi·cal.** [< L *lēthargic(us)* < Gk *lēthargikós* (see LETHARGY, -IC); r. ME *litargik*] —**le·thar′gi·cal·ly,** *adv.*

lethar′gic encephali′tis, *Pathol.* See **sleeping sickness** (def. 2).

leth·ar·gise (leth′ər jīz′), *v.t.*, **-gised, -gis·ing.** *Chiefly Brit.* lethargize.

leth·ar·gize (leth′ər jīz′), *v.t.*, **-gized, -giz·ing.** to make lethargic; stupefy. [LETHARG(Y) + -IZE]

leth·ar·gy (leth′ər jē), *n., pl.* **-gies. 1.** the quality or state of being drowsy and dull or of having the faculties and energies suspended; apathetic or sluggish inactivity. **2.** *Pathol.* an abnormal state or a disorder characterized by overpowering drowsiness or sleep. [< LL *lēthargīa* < Gk *lēthargía*, equiv. to *lēthárg(os)* drowsy + *-ia* -Y[3] (see LETHE, -ALGIA); r. ME *litargie* < ML *lītargīa* < MGk (in which *ē* had the value *ī*)]

Leth·bridge (leth′brij′), *n.* a city in S Alberta, in SW Canada. 35,454 (1961).

Le·the (lē′thē), *n.* **1.** *Class. Myth.* a river in Hades whose water caused forgetfulness of the past in those who drank of it. **2.** forgetfulness; oblivion. [< L < Gk, special use of *lḗthē* forgetfulness, akin to *lanthánesthai* to forget] —**Le·the·an** (li thē′ən, lē′thē ən), **Le′thied,** *adj.*

le·thif·er·ous (li thif′ər əs), *adj.* *Archaic.* lethal. [< L *lēthifer* (*lēthi-*, comb. form of *lēthum* death (see LETHAL) + *-fer* bearing) + -OUS; see -FEROUS]

Le·ti·tia (li tish′ə, -tē′shə), *n.* a girl's given name. Also, **Laetitia, Latitia.**

Le·to (lē′tō), *n.* *Class. Myth.* the mother by Zeus of Apollo and Artemis.

l'é·toile du nord (lā twal′ dy nôr′), *French.* the star of the north: motto of Minnesota.

Le Tou·quet (lə to͞o kā′), a town in N France, on the English Channel, near Boulogne: seaside summer resort; airport. 4064 (1962).

let-out (let′out′), *adj.* (of fur) processed by cutting parallel diagonal slashes into the pelt and sewing the slashed edges together to lengthen the pelt and to improve the appearance of the fur. [adj. use of v. phrase *let out*]

le tout en·sem·ble (lə to͞o tän sän′blᵊ), *French.* the whole (taken or considered) together.

L'É·tran·ger (*Fr.* lā trän zhā′). See **Stranger, The.**

let's (lets), contraction of *let us.*

Lett (let), *n.* **1.** one of a people living on or near the eastern coast of the Baltic Sea and being related to the Lithuanians. **2.** Lettish (def. 2).

Lett., Lettish.

let·ted (let′id), *v.* a pt. and pp. of **let**[2].

let·ter[1] (let′ər), *n.* **1.** a communication in writing or printing addressed to a person or a number of persons. **2.** one of the marks or signs conventionally used in writing and printing to represent speech sounds; an alphabetic character. **3.** a piece of printing type bearing such a mark or character. **4.** a particular style of type. **5.** such types collectively. **6.** actual terms or wording, as distinct from implied meaning or intent (opposed to *spirit*): *the letter of the law.* **7. letters,** (*construed as sing. or pl.*) **a.** literature in general. **b.** the profession of literature: *a man of letters.* **c.** learning; knowledge, esp. of literature. **8.** an emblem consisting of the initial or monogram of a school, awarded to a student for outstanding performance, esp. in athletics. **9. to the letter, a.** with strict adherence to the actual wording or literal interpretation: *keeping to the letter of the law.* **b.** to the last particular; precisely: *His orders were carried out to the letter.* —*v.t.* **10.** to mark or write with letters; inscribe. —*v.i.* **11.** to receive a letter in an interscholastic or intercollegiate activity, esp. a sport: *He lettered in track at Harvard.* [ME, var. of *lettre* < OF < L *littera* alphabetic character, in pl., epistle, literature] —**let′ter·er,** *n.* —**let′ter·less,** *adj.*
—**Syn. 7.** See **literature.**

let·ter[2] (let′ər), *n.* *Chiefly Brit.* one who lets, esp. one who rents out property. [LET[1] + -ER[1]]

Letter, The, a painting (1666) by Jan Vermeer.

let′ter box′, *Chiefly Brit.* mailbox.

let·ter-card (let′ər kärd′), *n.* *Brit.* a large postal card, with gummed edges, that can be folded lengthwise and sealed with the message inside.

let′ter car′rier, a postman.

let′ter drop′, (in a door or partition) a metal piece with a slot through which letters can be pushed.

let·tered (let′ərd), *adj.* **1.** educated or learned. **2.** of, pertaining to, or characterized by learning or literary culture. **3.** marked with or as if with letters. [ME; see LETTER[1], -ED[3]]

let·ter·gram (let′ər gram′), *n.* a telegram sent at a reduced rate, as a day letter or night letter. [LETTER[1] + (TELE)GRAM]

let·ter·head (let′ər hed′), *n.* **1.** a printed heading on stationery, esp. one giving the name and address of a business concern, an institution, etc. **2.** a sheet of paper with such a heading. [LETTER[1] + HEAD]

let·ter·ing (let′ər ing), *n.* **1.** the act or process of inscribing with or making letters. **2.** the letters themselves. [LETTER[1] + -ING[1]]

let·ter·man (let′ər man′, -mən), *n., pl.* **-men.** one who has won a letter in an interscholastic or intercollegiate activity, esp. a sport. [LETTER[1] + MAN[1]]

let′ter of advice′, 1. a notification from a consignor to a consignee giving specific information as to a shipment, the name of the carrier, the date shipped, etc. **2.** *Com.* a document from the drawer notifying the drawee that a bill of exchange has been drawn.

let′ter of cred′it, 1. an order issued by a banker allowing a person named to draw money to a specified amount from correspondents of the issuer. **2.** an instrument issued by a banker authorizing a person named to make drafts upon the issuer up to an amount specified.

let′ter of marque′, license or commission granted by a state to a private citizen to capture and confiscate the merchant ships of another nation. Also, **let′ters of marque′.** Also called **let′ter of marque′ and repris′al, let′ters of marque′ and repris′al.**

let·ter-per·fect (let′ər pûr′fikt), *adj.* **1.** knowing one's part, lesson, or the like, perfectly. **2.** verbatim; precise or exact.

let·ter·press (let′ər pres′), *n.* **1.** matter printed from letters or type in relief, rather than from intaglio plates or planographically. **2.** *Chiefly Brit.* printed text or reading matter, as distinguished from illustrations. —*adv.* **3.** by letterpress: *The circular should be printed letterpress, not offset.* —*adj.* **4.** set in letterpress: *letterpress work.* [LETTER[1] + PRESS[1]]

let′ters of administra′tion, *Law.* an instrument issued by a court or public official authorizing an administrator to take control of and dispose of the estate of a deceased person.

let′ters of cre′dence, credentials issued to a diplomat or other governmental representative for presentation to the country to which he is sent. Also, **let′ter of cre′dence.** Also called **let′ters creden′tial.**

let·ter·space (let′ər spās′), *v.t.*, **-spaced, -spac·ing.** *Print.* to space out (the letters of a word or line) for balance or emphasis. [LETTER[1] + SPACE]

let′ters pat′ent, *Law.* a written or printed instrument issued by a sovereign power, conferring upon a patentee some right, as the exclusive right to make, use, and sell his invention for a limited time.

let′ters testamen′tary, *Law.* an instrument issued by a court or public official authorizing an executor to take control of and dispose of the estate of a deceased person.

Let·tic (let′ik), *adj.* of or pertaining to the Letts or their language. [LETT + -IC]

Let·tice (let′is), *n.* a girl's given name, form of **Laetitia.**

Let·tie (let′ē), *n.* a girl's given name, form of **Laetitia.** Also, **Letty.**

Let·tish (let′ish), *adj.* **1.** of or pertaining to the Letts or their language. —*n.* **2.** Also, **Latvian, Lett.** the Baltic language of Latvia. [LETT + -ISH[1]]

let·tre de ca·chet (le′trᵊ də ka shε′), *pl.* ***let·tres de ca·chet*** (le′trᵊ də ka shε′). *French.* a letter under the seal of the sovereign, esp. one ordering imprisonment, frequently without trial.

let·tre de change (le′trᵊ də shänzh′), *pl.* ***let·tres de change*** (le′trᵊ də shänzh′). *French.* See **bill of exchange.**

let·tre de cré·ance (le′trᵊ də krā äns′), *pl.* ***let·tres de cré·ance*** (le′trᵊ də krā äns′). *French.* See **letter of credit.**

let·tuce (let′is), *n.* **1.** an annual herb, *Lactuca sativa*, occurring in many varieties and having succulent leaves used for salads. **2.** any species of *Lactuca*. **3.** *Slang.* paper money; cash. [ME *letuse*, appar. < OF *laitues*, pl. of *laitue* < L *lactūca* a lettuce, perh. orig. fem. of *lactūcus* milky (the *-ū-* of which is unexplained); see LACTIC]

Let·ty (let′ē), *n.* a girl's given name, form of **Laetitia.** Also, **Lettie.**

let·up (let′up′), *n.* *Informal.* cessation; pause; relief. [n. use of v. phrase *let up*]

le·u (le′o͞o), *n., pl.* **lei** (lā). a coin and monetary unit of Rumania, equal to 100 bani and equivalent to about .083 of a U.S. dollar. *Abbr.:* L. Also, **ley.** [< Rumanian: lit., LION]

leuc-, var. of **leuco-** before a vowel: *leucemia.* Also, **leuk-.**

Leu·cae·us (lo͞o sē′əs), *n.* *Class. Myth.* an epithet of Zeus, meaning "of the white poplar."

Leu·cas (lo͞o′kəs), *n.* Levkas.

Leu·ce (lo͞o′sē), *n.* *Class. Myth.* a nymph changed into a white poplar tree as a protection against the pursuing Pluto.

leu·ce·mi·a (lo͞o sē′mē ə), *n.* *Pathol.* leukemia. —**leu·ce′mic,** *adj.*

leu·cine (lo͞o′sēn, -sin), *n.* *Chem.* a white, crystalline, water-soluble amino acid, $(CH_3)_2CHCH_2CH(NH_2)$-COOH, obtained by the decomposition of proteins and made synthetically: essential in the nutrition of man and animals. [LEUC- + -INE[1]]

Leu·cip·pe (lo͞o sip′ē), *n.* *Class. Myth.* **1.** a daughter of Minyas of Orchomenus. **2.** a daughter of Thestor. **3.** the mother of Teuthras.

Leu·cip·pi·des (lo͞o sip′i dēz′), *n.pl.* *Class. Myth.* Phoebe and Hilaira, the daughters of Leucippus.

Leu·cip·pus (lo͞o sip′əs), *n.* *Class. Myth.* **1.** a youth who disguised himself as a girl to be near Daphne and was killed by Daphne and her companions when his disguise was discovered. **2.** the son of Gorgophone and Perieres who fathered the Leucippides.

leu·cite (lo͞o′sīt), *n.* a whitish or grayish mineral, potassium aluminum silicate, $KAlSi_2O_6$, found in alkali volcanic rocks. [< G *Leukit.* See LEUCO-, -ITE[1]] —**leu·cit·ic** (lo͞o sit′ik), *adj.*

leu·ci·tite (lo͞o′si tīt′), *n.* a fine-grained rock formed of leucite and pyroxene. [LEUCITE + -ITE[1]]

leuco-, a learned borrowing from Greek meaning "white," used in the formation of compound words: *leucocyte.* Also, **leuc-, leuk-, leuko-.** [< Gk *leuko-*, comb. form of *leukós* white; akin to L *lūx* LIGHT[1]]

leu′co base′ (lo͞o′kō), *Chem.* a noncolored or slightly colored compound that is produced by reducing a dye and is readily oxidized to regenerate the dye.

leu·co·blast (lo͞o′kə blast′), *n.* leukoblast.

leu·co·ci·din (lo͞o′kə sīd′ᵊn), *n.* leukocidin.

leu·co·crat·ic (lo͞o′kə krat′ik), *adj.* *Geol.* (of a rock) composed mainly of light-colored minerals. [LEUCO- + -CRAT + -IC]

leu·co·cyte (lo͞o′kə sīt′), *n.* leukocyte.

leu·co·cy·the·mi·a (lo͞o′kō sī thē′mē ə), *n.* *Pathol.* leukemia. Also, **leu′co·cy·thae′mi·a.** [< NL *leucocythaemia.* See LEUCOCYTE, -HEMIA] —**leu′co·cy·the′mic, leu′co·cy·thae′mic,** *adj.*

leu·co·cyt·ic (lo͞o′kə sit′ik), *adj.* leukocytic.

leu·co·cy·to·sis (lo͞o′kō sī tō′sis), *n.* *Physiol., Pathol.* leukocytosis. —**leu·co·cy·tot·ic** (lo͞o′kō sī tot′ik), *adj.*

leu·co·der·ma (lo͞o′kə dûr′mə), *n.* *Pathol.* vitiligo. Also, **leukoderma.** [< NL; see LEUCO-, DERMA]

leu·co·line (lo͞o′kə lēn′, -lin), *n.* *Chem.* quinoline. [LEUC- + -OL[1] + -INE[2]]

leu·co·ma (lo͞o kō′mə), *n.* *Pathol.* leukoma.

leu·co·ma·ine (lo͞o kō′mə ēn′, -in, lo͞o′kə mān′), *n.* *Biochem.* any of a class of poisonous nitrogenous substances normally produced in a living animal body through metabolism. [LEUCO- + (PTO)MAINE]

leu·con (lo͞o′kon), *n.* *Zool.* a type of sponge having a thick body wall with a highly branched canal system leading into the spongocoel. Cf. **ascon, sycon.** [< NL < Gk *leukón*, n. use of neut. of *leukós* white]

Leu·con (lo͞o′kon), *n.* *Class. Myth.* a son of Athamas and Nephele who died because of his father's crimes.

leu·co·noid (lo͞o′kə noid′), *adj.* pertaining to or resembling a leucon. [LEUCON + -OID]

leu·co·nos·toc (lo͞o′kə nos′tok), *n.* *Bacteriol.* any of several usually spherical bacteria of the genus *Leuconostoc*, found in milk and in plant juices. [LEUCO- + NOSTOC]

leu·co·pe·ni·a (lo͞o′kə pē′nē ə), *n.* *Med.* leukopenia.

Leu·co·phry·ne (lo͞o′kə frī′nē), *n.* *Class. Myth.* an epithet of Artemis referring to her temple in the town of Leucophrys, Asia Minor.

leu·co·plast (lo͞o′kə plast′), *n.* *Bot.* one of the colorless bodies found within the protoplasm of vegetable cells, serving as points around which starch forms. [LEUCO- + -PLAST]

leu·co·poi·e·sis (lo͞o′kō poi ē′sis), *n.* leukopoiesis. —**leu·co·poi·et·ic** (lo͞o′kō poi et′ik), *adj.*

leu·cor·rhe·a (lo͞o′kə rē′ə), *n.* *Pathol.* leukorrhea. Also, **leu′cor·rhoe′a.** —**leu′cor·rhe′al, leu′cor·rhoe′al,** *adj.*

leu·co·sis (lo͞o kō′sis), *n.* *Vet. Pathol.* leukosis. —**leu·cot·ic** (lo͞o kot′ik), *adj.*

leu·co·stic·te (lo͞o′kə stik′tē), *n.* any bird of the genus *Leucosticte*, comprising the rosy finches. [< NL, genus name < Gk *leuko-* LEUCO- + *stiktḗ*, fem. of *stiktós* pricked, spotted, equiv. to *stik-* (verbid s. of *stízein* to prick) + *-tos* verbid adj. suffix]

leu·co·tax·ine (lo͞o′kə tak′sēn, -sin), *n.* *Biochem.* leukotaxine. Also, **leu·co·tax·in** (lo͞o′kə tak′sin).

Leu·coth·e·a (lo͞o koth′ē ə), *n.* *Class. Myth.* a sea goddess, the deified Ino, who gave Odysseus a veil as a float after a storm had destroyed his raft. Also, **Leukothea.** [< Gk: lit., the white goddess]

Leu·coth·o·ë (lo͞o koth′ō ē′), *n.* *Class. Myth.* a Babylonian princess who was changed into a fragrant plant by Apollo.

leu·co·tome (lo͞o′kə tōm′), *n.* *Surg.* an instrument for dissecting the white matter of the brain, consisting of a cannula containing a slender rotating blade. [LEUCO- + -TOME]

leu·cot·o·my (lo͞o kot′ə mē), *n., pl.* **-mies.** *Surg.* lobotomy. [LEUCO- + -TOMY]

Leuc·tra (lo͞ok′trə), *n.* a town in ancient Greece, in Boeotia: Thebans defeated Spartans here 371 B.C.

Leu·cus (lo͞o′kəs), *n.* *Class. Myth.* **1.** a Cretan who usurped the throne of King Idomeneus. **2.** (in the *Iliad*) a brave companion of Odysseus who was killed by Antiphus in the Trojan War.

leud (lo͞od), *n., pl.* **leuds, leu·des** (lo͞o′dēz). a feudal vassal or tenant. [< ML *leud(ēs)* (pl.) < Gmc; cf. OE *lēode*, G *Leute* people]

leuk-, var. of **leuko-** before a vowel.

Leu·kas (lo͞o′kəs), *n.* Levkas.

leu·ke·mi·a (lo͞o kē′mē ə), *n.* *Pathol.* an almost uniformly fatal cancerous disease characterized by excessive production of white blood cells, usually in greatly increased numbers in the blood, and accompanied by often severe anemia and enlargement and hyperactivity of the spleen and lymphatic glands. Also, **leu·kae′mi·a, leucemia.** Also called **leukocythemia, leucocythemia, leucocythaemia.** [var. of NL *leuchaemia.* See LEUCO-, -HEMIA] —**leu·ke′mic, leu·kae′mic,** *adj.*

leu·ke·mid (lo͞o kē′mid), *n.* any cutaneous lesion that occurs in leukemia. [LEUKEM(IA) + -ID[1]]

leu·ke·moid (lo͞o kē′moid), *adj.* resembling the symptoms of leukemia. [LEUKEM(IA) + -OID]

leuko-, var. of **leuco-.** Also, *esp. before a vowel,* **leuk-.**

leu·ko·blast (lo͞o′kə blast′), *n.* *Anat.* an immature leukocyte. Also, **leucoblast.** [LEUKO- + -BLAST] —**leu′ko·blas′tic,** *adj.*

leu·ko·ci·din (lo͞o′kə sīd′ᵊn, lo͞o′kə sīd′-), *n.* *Bacteriol.* a coccoid substance that destroys leukocytes. Also, **leucocidin.** [LEUKO- + -CIDE + -IN[1]]

leu·ko·cyte (lo͞o′kə sīt′), *n.* *Anat.* one of the white or colorless nucleate cells of the blood that are sometimes found in the tissues and that help maintain immunity to infection and resistance against bacteria and other foreign particles. Also, **leucocyte.** [LEUKO- + -CYTE]

leu·ko·cy·the·mi·a (lo͞o′kō sī thē′mē ə), *n.* *Pathol.* leukemia. [< NL *leucocythaemia.* See LEUKOCYTE, -HEMIA]

leu·ko·cyt·ic (lo͞o′kə sit′ik), *adj.* **1.** of or pertaining to leukocytes. **2.** characterized by an excess of leukocytes. Also, **leucocytic.** [LEUKOCYTE + -IC]

leu·ko·cy·to·pe·ni·a (lo͞o′kə sī′tə pē′nē ə), *n.* *Med.* leukopenia. [< NL; see LEUKOCYTE, LEUKOPENIA]

leu·ko·cy·to·sis (lo͞o′kō sī tō′sis), *n.* *Physiol., Pathol.* the presence of an increased number of leukocytes in the blood, esp. when temporary, as in infection, and not due to leukemia. Also, **leucocytosis.** [< NL; see LEUKOCYTE, -OSIS] —**leu·kocy·tot·ic** (lo͞o′kə sī tot′ik), *adj.*

leu·ko·der·ma (lo͞o′kə dûr′mə), *n.* *Pathol.* vitiligo. Also, **leucoderma.** [< NL; see LEUKO-, DERMA]

leu·ko·ma (lo͞o kō′mə), *n.* *Pathol.* a dense, white opacity of the cornea. Also, **leucoma.** [< NL *leucoma.* See LEUKO-, -OMA]

leu·ko·pe·de·sis (lo͞o′kō pi dē′sis), *n.* an outward flow of leukocytes through a blood-vessel wall. [< NL; see LEUKO-, PEDESIS]

leu·ko·pe·ni·a (lo͞o′kə pē′nē ə), *n.* *Med.* a decrease in the number of leukocytes in the blood. Also, **leucopenia.** Also called **leukocytopenia.** [< NL *leucopenia*, equiv. to *leuco-* LEUKO- + Gk *penía* poverty, akin to *pénesthai* to be poor, toil; see -IA] —**leu′ko·pe′nic,** *adj.*

leu·ko·poi·e·sis (lo͞o′kō poi ē′sis), *n.* the formation and development of leukocytes. Also, **leucopoiesis.** [< NL *leucopoiesis.* See LEUKO-, -POIESIS] —**leu·ko·poi·et·ic** (lo͞o′kō poi et′ik), *adj.*

leu·kor·rhe·a (lo͞o′kə rē′ə), *n.* *Pathol.* a whitish discharge from the female genital organs. Also, **leu′kor·rhoe′a, leucorrhea, leucorrhoea.** [< NL *leucorrhea.* See LEUKO-, -RRHEA] —**leu′kor·rhe′al, leu′kor·rhoe′al,** *adj.*

leu·ko·sis (lo͞o kō′sis), *n.* *Vet. Pathol.* any of several diseases occurring chiefly in chickens, involving proliferation of the leukocytes and characterized by paralysis, blindness, formation of tumors in the internal organs, and bone calcification. Also, **leucosis.** Also called **fowl leukosis, avian leukosis.** [< NL *leucosis* < Gk *leúkōsis.* See LEUKO-, -OSIS]

leu·ko·tax·ine (lo͞o′kə tak′sēn, -sin), *n.* *Biochem.* a crystalline polypeptide that is found in injured tissue and inflammatory exudates and serves to increase the permeability of capillaries and to stimulate leukopedesis. Also, **leu·ko·tax·in** (lo͞o′kə tak′sin), **leucotaxine, leucotaxin.** [LEUKO- + -TAX(IS) + -INE[1]]

CONCISE PRONUNCIATION KEY: act, āble, dâre, ärt; ebb, ēqual; if, īce; hot, ōver, ôrder, oil, bo͝ok, o͞oze, out; up, ûrge; chief; sing; shoe; thin, that; zh as in *measure.* ə = *a* as in *alone*, *e* as in *system*, *i* as in *easily*, *o* as in *gallop*, *u* as in *circus*; ᵊ as in *button* (but′ᵊn), *fire* (fīᵊr), *cradle* (krād′ᵊl). See the full key inside the front cover.

Leu·koth·e·a (lo͞o koth′ē ə), *n. Class. Myth.* Leucothea.
leu·kot·o·my (lo͞o kot′ə mē), *n., pl.* **-mies.** *Surg.* lobotomy. [LEUKO- + -TOMY]
Leu·ri·cus (lo͞o rī′kəs; *Lat.* le o͞o′ri ko͞os′), *n.* Leofric.
Leu·tze (loit′sə), *n.* **E·ma·nu·el Gott·lieb** (i man′yo͞o əl got′lēb; *Ger.* ā mä′no͞o el gôt′lēp), 1816–68, German painter in the U.S.
lev (lef), *n., pl.* **lev·a** (lev′ə). a coin and monetary unit of Bulgaria, equal to 100 stotinki and equivalent to about .855 of a U.S. dollar. *Abbr.:* L., LV. [< Bulg: lit., lion, OBulg *lĭvŭ*, prob. < OHG *lewo* < L *leo*]
lev-, var. of **levo-** before a vowel: *levulose.*
Lev., Leviticus.
le·vade (lə väd′), *n. Dressage.* a movement in which the horse first lowers his body on increasingly bent hocks then sits on his hind hooves while keeping his forelegs raised and drawn in. [< G < F *lev(er)* (to) raise + *-ade* -ADE[1]]
Le·val·loi·si·an (lev′ə loi′zē ən, -zhən), *adj.* of, pertaining to, or characteristic of a distinctive Middle Paleolithic cultural tradition noted for its technique of producing flint cutting tools by preparing the core before striking off the flakes. Also, **Le·val·lois** (lə val′wä). [LEVALLOIS(-PERRET) + -IAN]
Le·val·lois-Per·ret (lə val wä′pe re′), *n.* a suburb of Paris, in N France, on the Seine. 61,962 (1962).
le·vant (li vant′), *v.i. Brit. Slang.* to default or flee a gambling debt; welsh. [? < Sp *levant(ar)* (to) lift (cf. *levantar el campo* to break camp, leave), freq. of *levar* < L *levāre*] —**le·vant′er,** *n.*
Le·vant (li vant′), *n.* **1.** the lands bordering the E shores of the Mediterranean and Aegean seas, esp. Syria, Lebanon, and Israel. **2.** Also called **Levant morocco.** a superior grade of morocco having a large and prominent grain, originally made in the Levant. **3.** levanter. [late ME *levaunt* < MF *levant,* n. use (with reference to rising sun) of prp. of *lever* to raise (*se lever* to rise). See LEVER]
Levant′ dol′lar, a silver coin, either a Maria Theresa thaler or an imitation of one, formerly used for trade with Abyssinia, Eritrea, Aden, etc. Imitations bear the date 1780 regardless of the year of minting. Also called **Levant thaler.**
le·vant·er (li van′tər), *n.* **1.** a strong easterly wind, accompanied by overcast or rainy weather, that blows in the western Mediterranean, esp. in the Strait of Gibraltar and on the eastern coast of Spain. **2.** a strong easterly wind in the E Mediterranean. [LEVANT + -ER[1]]
le·van·ter·a (lā′vän târ′ə; *It.* le′vän te′rä), *n.* a steady east wind of the Adriatic often accompanied by overcast. [< It; see LEVANT]
Le·van·tine (lev′ən tīn′, -tēn′, li van′tin, -tīn), *adj.* **1.** of or pertaining to the Levant. —*n.* **2.** a native of the Levant. [LEVANT + -INE[1]] —**Lev′an·tin′ism,** *n.*
Levant′ moroc′co, Levant (def. 2).
le·van·to (li van′tō, -vän′-; *Sp.* le vän′tô), *n.* a hot wind that blows from the southeast in the Canary Islands. [< Sp; see LEVANT]
Levant′ red′. See **Adrianople red.**
Levant′ sto′rax. See under **storax** (def. 2).
Levant′ tha′ler. See **Levant dollar.**
Levant′ worm′seed. See under **wormseed** (def. 1).
lev·ar·te·re·nol (lev′är tēr′ə nōl′, -nôl′, -nol′, -ter′-), *n.* **1.** *Biochem.* a hormone, $C_6H_3(OH)_2CH(OH)CH_2NH_2$ occurring in the adrenal gland, that causes vasoconstriction. **2.** *Pharm.* a commercial form of this compound, used as its bitartrate in treating shock. Also called **l-arterenol, l-noradrenaline, l-norepinephrine.** [LEV(OROTATORY) + ARTERENOL]
le·va·tor (li vā′tər, -tôr), *n., pl.* **lev·a·to·res** (lev′ə tôr′ēz, -tōr′-). **1.** *Anat.* a muscle that raises a part of the body. **2.** *Surg.* an instrument used to raise a depressed part of the skull. [< NL, special use of ML *levātor* one who raises (levies) recruits or taxes, equiv. to L *levāt(us)* raised (ptp. of *levāre*) + *-or* -OR[2]]
Le Vau (lə vō′), **Louis** (lwē), 1612–70, French architect.
le·ve·che (le ve′che; *Eng.* li vā′chā), *n. Spanish.* a sirocco, esp. one that blows on the southeastern coast of Spain and a short distance inland. Also, **laveche.**
lev·ee[1] (lev′ē), *n., v.,* **lev·eed, lev·ee·ing.** —*n.* **1.** *Phys. Geog.* **a.** an embankment designed to prevent the flooding of a river. **b.** See **natural levee. 2.** *Agric.* one of the small continuous ridges surrounding fields that are to be irrigated. **3.** *Hist.* a landing place for vessels; a quay. —*v.t.* **4.** to furnish with a levee: *to levee a treacherous stream.* [< F *levée* < ML *levāta* embankment, n. use of fem. ptp. of L *levāre* to raise, orig. lighten, akin to *levis* light, not heavy]
lev·ee[2] (lev′ē, le vē′), *n.* **1.** (in Great Britain) a public court assembly, held in the early afternoon, at which men only are received. **2.** a reception, usually in someone's honor: *a presidential levee at the White House.* **3.** *Hist.* a reception of visitors held on rising from bed, as formerly by a royal or other personage. [< F *levé,* var. sp. of *lever* rising (n. use of inf.) < L *levāre* to raise (oneself); see LEVEE[1]]
lev·el (lev′əl), *adj., n., v.,* **-eled, -el·ing** or (*esp. Brit.*) **-elled, -el·ling,** *adv.* —*adj.* **1.** having no part higher than another; having an even surface. **2.** being in a plane parallel to the plane of the horizon; horizontal. **3.** equal, as one thing with another or two or more things with one another. **4.** even, equable, or uniform. **5.** mentally well-balanced: *to keep a level head in a crisis.* **6. one's level best,** *Informal.* one's very best; one's utmost: *We tried our level best to drive there in three hours, but there was an unexpected detour.* —*n.* **7.** a device used for determining or adjusting something to a horizontal surface. **8.** See **spirit level. 9.** *Survey.* **a.** Also called **surveyor's level.** an instrument for observing levels, having a sighting device, usually telescopic, and capable of being made precisely horizontal. **b.** an observation made with this instrument. **10.** an imaginary line or surface everywhere at right angles to the plumb line. **11.** the horizontal line or plane in which anything is situated, with regard to its elevation. **12.** a horizontal position or condition. **13.** an extent of land approximately horizontal and unbroken by irregularities. **14.** a level or flat surface. **15.** a position with respect to a given or specified height: *The water rose to a level of 30 feet. It will seek its own level.* **16.** a position or plane in a graded scale of values; status; rank: *His acting was on the level of an amateur. They consorted only with those on their own social level.* **17.** an extent, measure, or degree of achievement: *Her level of knowledge was pretty high.* **18. find one's** or **one's own level,** to attain the place or position merited by one's abilities or achievements: *After coming up through the ranks, he found his level as one of the directors of the firm.* **19. on the level,** *Slang.* honest; sincere; reliable: *Is this information on the level?* —*v.t.* **20.** to make (a surface) level or even: *to level ground before building.* **21.** to raise or lower to a particular level or position. **22.** to bring (something) to the level of the ground: *They leveled the trees to make way for the new highway.* **23.** *Informal.* to knock down (a person): *He leveled his opponent with one blow.* **24.** to make (two or more things) equal, as in status, condition, etc.: *Contemporary social processes often seem to level the various classes and obscure traditional social distinctions.* **25.** to make even or uniform, as coloring. **26.** to aim or point (a weapon, criticism, etc.) at a mark or objective: *He leveled his criticism at the nation as a whole.* **27.** *Survey.* to find the relative elevation of different points in (land), as with a level. **28.** *Archaic.* to turn (one's eyes) in a particular direction. —*v.i.* **29.** to bring things or persons to a common level. **30.** to aim a weapon, criticism, etc., at a mark or objective. **31.** *Survey.* **a.** to take a level. **b.** to use a leveling instrument. **32.** *Aeron.* to fly parallel to the ground, usually just before landing (usually fol. by *off*). **33.** *Slang.* to tell the truth (often fol. by *with*): *You're not leveling with me about your trip to Chicago.* **34.** *Obs.* to direct the mind, purpose, etc., at something. —*adv.* **35.** *Obs.* in a level, direct, or even way or line. [ME, var. of *livel* (n.) < MF < LL *lībell(um), r. L lībellā plummet line, level, dim. of *lībra* balance, scales, water level, pound (12 oz.)] —**lev′el·ly,** *adv.* —**lev′el·ness,** *n.*
—**Syn. 1, 2.** flush. LEVEL, EVEN, FLAT, SMOOTH suggest a uniform surface without marked unevenness. That which is LEVEL is parallel to the horizon: *a level surface; A billiard table must be level.* FLAT is applied to any plane surface free from marked irregularities: *a flat roof.* With reference to land or country, FLAT connotes lowness or unattractiveness; LEVEL does not suggest anything derogatory. That which is EVEN is free from irregularities, though not necessarily level or plane: *an even land surface with no hills.* SMOOTH suggests a high degree of evenness in any surface, esp. to the touch and sometimes to the sight: *as smooth as silk.* **20.** smooth, flatten. **22.** raze, demolish, destroy. **24.** equalize. **26.** direct. —**Ant. 1.** uneven. **2.** vertical.
lev′el cross′ing, *Brit.* See **grade crossing.**
lev′el curve′. See **contour line.**
lev·el·er (lev′ə lər), *n.* one who or that which levels. Also, *esp. Brit.,* **leveller.** [LEVEL + -ER[1]]
lev·el-head·ed (lev′əl hed′id), *adj.* having common sense and sound judgment. —**lev′el-head′ed·ness,** *n.*
lev′eling rod′, *Survey.* rod (def. 17).
lev′el in′strument, *Survey.* a hand level consisting of a spirit level observed opposite a horizontal cross hair.
lev·el·ler (lev′ə lər), *n.* **1.** *Chiefly Brit.* leveler (def. 1). **2.** *Brit.* **a.** (*usually cap.*) (during the British Civil War) a member of the Parliamentary army advocating constitutional reforms, equal rights, and separation of church and state. **b.** a member of the Whiteboys. **3.** (*cap.*) *Eng. Hist.* a member of a group comprised chiefly of former Parliamentarians advocating universal suffrage, a written constitution, and religious tolerance. [LEVEL + -ER[1]]
lev′el line′. See **contour line.**
lev·el-off (lev′əl ôf′, -of′), *n. Aeron.* the maneuver of bringing an aircraft into a horizontal flying position after an ascent or descent. [n. use of v. phrase *level off*]
Le·ven (lē′vən), *n.* **Loch,** a lake in E Scotland: ruins of a castle in which Mary Queen of Scots was imprisoned.
lev·er (lev′ər, lē′vər), *n.* **1.** a bar or rigid body used to lift weight and operating on the principle that force or power applied at one point to lift a resistive weight or force at a second point tends to rotate the bar in opposite directions about a fixed axis or fulcrum. **2.** *Mach.* any rigid bar, straight or bent, that oscillates about a pivot and acts with other parts in the manner of a lever. **3.** *Horol.* the pallet of an escapement. —*v.t., v.i.* **4.** to move with or apply a lever: *to lever a rock; to lever mightily and to no avail.* [ME *levere, levour* for *lever < OF levier < LL *levār(ius) (recorded in ML), lit., lifter, equiv. to L *lev-* (base of *levis* light, *levāre* to lighten, lift up) + *-ārius* -ER[2]] —**lev′er·like′,** *adj.*
Le·ver (lē′vər), *n.* **Charles James** (*"Cornelius O'Dowd"*), 1806–72, Irish novelist and essayist.
lev′er ac′tion, a rifle action in which the extracting and ejecting of the shell case and the recocking of the weapon are accomplished by a hand-operated lever arm in front of the trigger housing.
lev·er-ac·tion (lev′ər ak′shən, lē′vər-), *adj.* (of a rifle) having a lever action.
lev·er·age (lev′ər ij, lē′vər ij), *n.* **1.** the action of a lever. **2.** the mechanical advantage or power gained by using a lever. **3.** power of action: *He was unable to gain much leverage, and as a result failed to get what he wanted.* [LEVER + -AGE]
lev′er escape′ment, *Horol.* an escapement in which a pivoted lever, made to oscillate by the escape wheel, engages a balance staff and causes it to oscillate.

Lever escapement
A, Impulse roller; B, Notch; C, Lever; D, Ruby pin; E, Safety roller; F, Crescent; G, Fork; H, Guard pin; J, Pallets; K, Escape wheel

lev·er·et (lev′ər it), *n.* a young hare. [late ME < MF *levrete,* dim. of *levre* < L *lepor(em),* acc. of *lepus* hare; see -ET]
Lev·er·ett (lev′ər it), *n.* a boy's given name.
Le·ver·hulme (lē′vər hyo͞om′), *n.* **Viscount** (*William Hesketh Lever*), 1851–1925, English manufacturer.
Le·ver·ri·er (lə ver′ē ā′; *for 1 also Fr.* lə ve ryā′), *n.* **1. Ur·bain Jean Jo·seph** (yr ban′ zhän zhō zef′), French astronomer. **2.** a crater in the second quadrant of the face of the moon: about 11 miles in diameter.
lev′er tum′bler, a flat metal tumbler in a lock.
Le·vi (lē′vī; *for 5 also* lē′vē), *n.* **1.** a son of Jacob and Leah. Gen. 29:34. **2.** one of the 12 tribes of Israel. **3.** a Levite. **4. Rabbi.** See **Rabbi Levi. 5.** Also, **Levy.** a boy's given name.
Le·vi (le′vē), *n.* **Car·lo** (kär′lô), born 1902, Italian painter and writer.
lev·i·a·ble (lev′ē ə bəl), *adj.* **1.** that may be levied. **2.** liable or subject to a levy. [late ME *levyable.* See LEVY, -ABLE]
le·vi·a·than (li vī′ə thən), *n.* **1.** *Bible.* a sea monster, possibly the crocodile. **2.** any huge marine animal, as the whale. **3.** anything of immense size and power, as a huge, ocean-going ship. **4.** (*cap., italics.*) a philosophical work (1651) by Thomas Hobbes dealing with the political organization of society. [ME *levyathan* < LL *leviathan* << Heb *liwyāthān*]
lev·i·er (lev′ē ər), *n.* one who levies. [late ME *levyer.* See LEVY, -ER[1]]
lev·i·gate (lev′ə gāt′), *v.,* **-gat·ed, -gat·ing,** *adj.* —*v.t.* **1.** to rub, grind, or reduce to a fine powder, as in a mortar, with or without the addition of a liquid. **2.** *Chem.* to make a homogeneous mixture of, as gels. **3.** to prepare (the surface of a lithographic stone) by grinding with a steel disk and an abrasive. —*adj.* **4.** *Bot.* having a smooth, glossy surface; glabrous. [< L *lēvigāt(us)* smoothed (ptp. of *lēvigāre;* see -ATE[1]), akin to *lēvis* smooth] —**lev′i·ga′tion,** *n.* —**lev′i·ga′tor,** *n.*
lev·in (lev′in), *n. Archaic.* lightning. [ME *levene,* OE *lēafne, var. of *lēamne; c. Goth *lauhmuni;* akin to L *lūmen* light]
Le·vi·na (lə vē′nə), *n.* a girl's given name.
Le·vine (lə vēn′), *n.* **Jack,** born 1915, U.S. painter.
lev·i·rate (lev′ər it, -ə rāt′, lē′vər it, -və rāt′), *n.* the custom of marriage by a man with his brother's widow, such marriage required among Jews in Biblical times if the brothers lived together and the deceased was childless. Deut. 25:5–10. [< L *lēvir* husband's brother (akin to Gk *daēr,* Skt *dēvar,* OE *tācor*) + -ATE[1]] —**lev·i·rat·ic** (lev′ə rat′ik, lē′və-), **lev′i·rat′i·cal,** *adj.*
Le·vis (lē′vīz), *n. Trademark.* close-fitting, heavy trousers made of denim or denimlike material that have a low waistline and are reinforced with copper rivets at the strain points. Cf. **blue jeans.**
Levit., Leviticus.
lev·i·tate (lev′i tāt′), *v.,* **-tat·ed, -tat·ing.** —*v.i.* **1.** to rise or float in the air, esp. as a result of a supernatural power that overcomes gravity. —*v.t.* **2.** to cause to rise or float in the air. [LEVIT(Y) + -ATE[1], modeled on *gravitate*] —**lev′i·ta′tor,** *n.*
lev·i·ta·tion (lev′i tā′shən), *n.* **1.** the act or phenomenon of levitating. **2.** (chiefly among spiritualists) the alleged phenomenon of bodies heavier than air being by spiritual means rendered buoyant in the atmosphere. [LEVITATE + -ION] —**lev′i·ta′tion·al,** *adj.* —**lev′i·ta′tive,** *adj.*
Le·vite (lē′vīt), *n.* **1.** a member of the tribe of Levi. **2.** a descendant of Levi, esp. one appointed to assist the priests in the temple or tabernacle. [ME < LL *lēvīt(a)* < Gk *leuítēs* Levite, equiv. to *Leuí* (< Heb *Lēvī* Levi, Levite) + *-tēs* member, associate]
lev·i·ter (lev′i tər), *adv.* (in prescriptions) lightly. [<L]
Le·vit·i·cal (li vit′i kəl), *adj.* **1.** of or pertaining to the Levites. **2.** of or pertaining to Leviticus or the law (**Levit′ical law′**) contained in Leviticus. [< LL *Lēvitic(us)* (see LEVITICUS) + -AL[1]] —**Le·vit′i·cal·ly,** *adv.*
Le·vit·i·cus (li vit′ə kəs), *n.* the third book of the Bible, containing laws relating to the priests and Levites and to the forms of Jewish ceremonial observance. [< LL *Lēviticus* (*liber*) Levitical (book) < Gk *Leuïtikós.* See LEVITE, -IC]
Lev·it·town (lev′it toun′), *n.* a town on W Long Island, in SE New York. 65,276 (1960).
lev·i·ty (lev′i tē), *n., pl.* **-ties.** **1.** lightness of mind, character, or behavior; lack of proper seriousness or earnestness. **2.** an instance or exhibition of this. **3.** fickleness. **4.** lightness in weight. [< L *levitās* lightness, frivolity, equiv. to *levi(s)* light + *-tās* -TY[2]]
—**Syn. 1, 2.** frivolity, flippancy, triviality, giddiness.
Lev·kas (lef käs′), *n.* an island in the Ionian group, off the W coast of Greece. 37,752 (1951); 114 sq. mi. Also, **Leucas, Leukas.** Italian, **Santa Maura.**
le·vo (lē′vō), *adj. Chem.* levorotatory. Also, **laevo.** [by shortening]
levo-, a combining form meaning "left," often used to denote a substance which rotates the plane of polarized light to the left: *levoglucose; levorotation.* Also, **laevo-, lev-.** [repr. L *laevus* left, on the left]
le·vo·glu·cose (lē′və glo͞o′kōs), *n. Chem.* See under **glucose** (def. 1). [LEVO- + GLUCOSE]
le·vo·gy·rate (lē′və jī′rāt), *adj. Optics, Chem.* levorotatory. Also, **laevogyrate, le·vo·gyre** (lē′vō jīər′). [LEVO- + GYRATE]
Lev·o·phed (lev′ō fed′), *n. Pharm., Trademark.* levarterenol (def. 2).
le·vo·ro·ta·tion (lē′vō rō tā′shən), *n. Optics, Crystall.* a turning to the left of the plane of polarization. Also, **laevorotation.** [LEVO- + ROTATION]
le·vo·ro·ta·to·ry (lē′və rō′tə tôr′ē, -tōr′ē), *adj. Optics, Crystall.* turning to the left, as the rotation to the left of the plane of polarization of light in certain crystals and compounds; levogyrate. Also, **laevorotatory, le·vo·ro·ta·ry** (lē′vō rō′tə rē). [LEVO- + ROTATORY]
lev′u·lin′ic ac′id (lev′yə lin′ik, lev′-), *Chem.* a white or colorless, water-soluble solid, $CH_3CO(CH_2)_2COOH$, produced by the hydrolysis of cane sugar, starch, or cellulose; used chiefly in the organic synthesis of nylon, plastics, and pharmaceuticals. [LEVUL(OSE) + -IN[2] + -IC]
lev·u·lose (lev′yə lōs′), *n. Chem.* fructose. [LEV- + -ULE + -OSE[2]]
lev·y (lev′ē), *n., pl.* **lev·ies,** *v.,* **lev·ied, lev·y·ing.** —*n.* **1.** a raising or collecting, as of money or troops, by authority or force. **2.** one who or that which is raised or collected in this manner, as a body of troops or a tax. —*v.t.* **3.** to make a levy of; collect (taxes, contributions, etc.). **4.** to impose (a tax): *to levy a duty on imports.* **5.** to conscript or enlist (troops) for service: *Fighting men were levied by local princes during periods of crisis.* **6.** to start or make (war). —*v.i.* **7.** to make a levy. **8.** *Law.* to seize or attach property by judicial order. [late ME

levee < MF, n. use of fem. ptp. of *lever* to raise < L *levāre*, akin to *levis* light]

Le·vy (lē′vē, -vī), *n.* a boy's given name. Also, **Levi.**

lev′y en masse′, a mass rising of citizens not organized into military units, for defense of a country threatened with invasion. Also, **lev′y in mass′.** [modeled on F *levée en masse*]

Lew (lo͞o), *n.* a boy's given name, form of **Lewis, Llewellyn,** or **Louis.**

lewd (lo͞od), *adj.* **1.** inclined to, characterized by, or inciting to lust or lechery. **2.** obscene or indecent, as language, songs, etc. **3.** *Obs.* **a.** low or vulgar. **b.** base or vile, esp. of a person. **c.** bad, worthless, or poor, esp. of a thing. [ME *leud, lewed*, OE *lǣwed* lay, unlearned] —**lewd′ly,** *adv.* —**lewd′ness,** *n.*

Lew·es (lo͞o′is), *n.* **1. George Henry,** 1817–78, English writer and critic. **2.** a city in central Sussex, in SE England: battle 1264. 13,637 (1961). **3.** a town in SE Delaware. 3025 (1960).

lew·is (lo͞o′is), *n.* a device for lifting a dressed stone, consisting of a number of pieces fitting together to fill a dovetailed recess cut into the stone. Also called **lewis iron, lewisson.** [named after its inventor]

Lewis

Lew·is (lo͞o′is), *n.* **1. C(ecil) Day,** 1904–72, British poet: poet laureate after 1968. **2. C(live) S(ta·ples)** (stā′pəlz), ("*Clive Hamilton*"), 1898–1963, English novelist and essayist. **3. Gilbert Newton,** 1875–1946, U. S. chemist. **4. Isaac Newton,** 1858–1931, U.S. soldier and inventor. **5. John (Aaron),** born 1920, U.S. jazz pianist, composer, and musical director. **6. John L(lewellyn),** 1880–1969, U.S. labor leader. **7. Matthew Gregory** ("*Monk Lewis*"), 1775–1809, English novelist, dramatist, and poet. **8. Mer·i·weth·er** (mer′i weth′ər), 1774–1809, U.S. explorer: leader of the Lewis and Clark expedition 1804–06. **9. Sinclair,** 1885–1951, U.S. novelist, playwright, and journalist: Nobel prize 1930. **10. (Percy) Wynd·ham** (win′dəm), 1884–1957, English novelist, essayist, and painter; born in the U.S.

Lew′is ac′id, *Chem.* any substance capable of forming a covalent bond with a base by accepting a pair of electrons from it. [named after G. N. LEWIS]

Lew′is base′, *Chem.* any substance capable of forming a covalent bond with an acid by transferring a pair of electrons to it. [named after G. N. LEWIS]

lew′is bolt′, *Building Trades.* an anchor bolt having a conical base around which concrete or lead is poured to hold it.

Lew·is·burg (lo͞o′is bûrg′), *n.* **1.** a town in central Tennessee. 6338 (1960). **2.** a town in central Pennsylvania. 5523 (1960).

Lew′is gun′, a light, air-cooled machine gun with a circular magazine, designed to be operated by one man. Also called **Lew′is automat′ic, Lew′is machine′ gun′.** [named after I. N. LEWIS]

lew′is i′ron, lewis.

lew·is·ite (lo͞o′i sīt′), *n.* a chemical-warfare agent, ClCH=CHAsCl$_2$, characterized by its vesicant action. [named after Winford Lee *Lewis* (1878–1943), American chemist who developed it; see -ITE¹]

Lew′is Moun′tains, a mountain range in the NW United States and W Canada, in W Montana and Alberta province: part of the Rocky Mountains.

Lew·i·sohn (lo͞o′i sən, -zən, -sōn′), *n.* **Lud·wig** (lud′wig), 1882?–1955, U.S. novelist and critic, born in Germany.

lew·is·son (lo͞o′i sən), *n.* lewis.

Lew·is·ton (lo͞o′i stən), *n.* **1.** a city in SW Maine, on the Androscoggin River. 40,804 (1960). **2.** a city in W Idaho. 12,691 (1960). **3.** a town in central Montana. 7408 (1960). **4.** a town in W New York. 3320 (1960). **5.** a town in central Illinois. 2603 (1960).

Lew′iston Or′chards, a town in W Idaho. 9680 (1960).

Lew·is·ville (lo͞o′is vil′), *n.* a town in N Texas. 3956 (1960).

Lew′is with Har′ris, the northernmost island of the Hebrides, in NW Scotland. 26,466 (1951); 825 sq. mi.

lex (leks), *n.*, *pl.* **le·ges** (lē′jēz; *Lat.* le′ges). law¹. [< L]

lex., **1.** lexical. **2.** lexicon.

Lex·ell (l (lek′səl), *n.* a walled plain in the third quadrant of the face of the moon: about 40 miles in diameter.

lex·i·cal (lek′si kəl), *adj.* **1.** of or pertaining to the words or vocabulary of a language, esp. as contrasted with its grammatical and syntactical aspects. **2.** of, pertaining to, or of the nature of a lexicon. [LEXIC(ON) + -AL¹] —**lex′i·cal′i·ty,** *n.* —**lex′i·cal·ly,** *adv.*

lex′ical mean′ing, the meaning of a base morpheme. Cf. **grammatical meaning.**

lexicog., **1.** lexicographer. **2.** lexicographical. **3.** lexicography.

lex·i·cog·ra·pher (lek′sə kog′rə fər), *n.* a writer or compiler of a dictionary. [< LGk *lexikográph(os)* (see LEXICON, -GRAPH) + -ER¹]

lex·i·cog·ra·phy (lek′sə kog′rə fē), *n.* the writing or compiling of dictionaries. [LEXICO(N) + -GRAPHY] —**lex·i·co·graph·ic** (lek′sə kō graf′ik, -sə kə-), **lex′i·co·graph′i·cal,** *adj.* —**lex′i·co·graph′i·cal·ly,** *adv.*

lex·i·col·o·gist (lek′sə kol′ə jist), *n.* one who compiles and studies the meaning of words and of idiomatic combinations of words. [LEXICOLOG(Y) + -IST]

lex·i·col·o·gy (lek′sə kol′ə jē), *n.* the study of the meaning of words and of idiomatic combinations of words. [LEXICO(N) + -LOGY] —**lex·i·co·log·i·cal** (lek′sə kə loj′i kəl), **lex′i·co·log′ic,** *adj.*

lex·i·con (lek′sə kon′, -kən), *n.*, *pl.* **lex·i·ca** (lek′sə kə), **lex·i·cons.** **1.** a wordbook or dictionary, esp. of Greek, Latin, or Hebrew. **2.** the vocabulary of a particular language, field, social class, person, etc. **3.** inventory or record: *unparalleled in the lexicon of human relations.* **4.** *Ling.* **a.** the total inventory of morphemes in a given language. **b.** the inventory of base morphemes plus their combinations with derivational morphemes. [< ML < MGk, Gk *lexikón*, n. use of neut. of *lexikós* of words, equiv. to *léx(is)* speech, word (verbid of *légein* to speak) + *-ikos* -IC]

lex·i·co·sta·tis·tics (lek′sə kō stə tis′tiks), *n.* (*construed as sing.*) *Ling.* the statistical study of the vocabulary of a language or languages for historical purposes. Cf. **glottochronology.** [LEXICO(N) + STATISTICS] —**lex′i·co·sta·tis′tic, lex′i·co·sta·tis′ti·cal,** *adj.*

Lex·ing·ton (lek′sing tən), *n.* **1.** a town in E Massachusetts, NW of Boston: first battle of American Revolution fought here April 19, 1775. 27,691 (1960). **2.** a city in N Kentucky. 62,810 (1960). **3.** a city in central North Carolina. 16,093 (1960). **4.** a town in W Virginia. 7537 (1960). **5.** a town in central Nebraska. 5572 (1960). **6.** a town in central Missouri. 4845 (1960). **7.** a town in W Tennessee. 3943 (1960). **8.** a town in central Mississippi. 2839 (1960).

Lex′ington Park′, a town in S Maryland. 7039 (1960).

lex lo·ci (leks lō′sī, -kē), *Law.* the law of a place. [< L]

lex non scrip·ta (leks non skrip′tə, nōn), *Law.* unwritten law; common law. [< L]

lex scrip·ta (leks skrip′tə), *Law.* written law; statute law. [< L]

lex ta·li·o·nis (leks tal′ē ō′nis), the principle or law of retaliation that a punishment inflicted should correspond in degree and kind to the offense of the wrongdoer, as an eye for an eye, a tooth for a tooth. Also called **talion.** [< L: law of talion]

ley¹ (lā, lē), *n.* lea¹.

ley² (lā), *n.* leu.

ley³ (lā), *n.* a pewter containing about 80 percent tin and 20 percent lead. [aph. var. of obs. *aley* ALLOY]

Ley·den (līd′ən), *n.* **1. Lu·cas van** (lo͞o′käs vän), (*Lucas Hugensz*), 1489?–1533. Dutch painter and engraver. **2.** Leiden. **3.** a Dutch cheese similar to Edam, often flavored with caraway seeds, cumin, cinnamon, or cloves.

Ley′den jar′, *Elect.* a device for storing electric charge, consisting essentially of a glass jar lined inside and outside, for about two thirds of its height, with tinfoil. [so called because invented in LEYDEN]

Ley′dig cell′ (lī′dig), *Anat.* any of the interstitial cells of the testes believed to produce certain internal secretions. Also, **Ley′dig's cell′.** [named after F. von *Leydig* (1821–1908), German physiologist]

Ley·te (lā′tē; *Sp.* lā′te), *n.* an island in the central Philippines: focal point of the U.S. invasion of the Philippines 1944. 1,146,000 (est. 1965); 3085 sq. mi.

Ley·ton (lāt′ən), *n.* a city in SE England, near London. 93,857 (1961).

leze′ maj′esty (lēz), *Law.* See **lese majesty** (def. 1).

lf, See **low frequency.**

lf., *Baseball.* left fielder.

L. F. Ball, a crater in the first quadrant of the face of the moon: about 40 miles in diameter.

LG, Low German. Also, **L.G.**

lg., **1.** large. **2.** long.

l.g., *Football.* left guard.

L. Ger., **1.** Low German. **2.** Low Germanic.

LGk., Late Greek. Also **L.Gk., LGk**

l-glu·cose (el′glo͞o′kōs), *n.* *Chem.* See under **glucose** (def. 1). [L(EVOROTATORY) + GLUCOSE]

lgth., length.

lg. tn., long ton.

LH, *Biochem.* See **ICSH.**

l.h., left hand. Also, **L.H.**

Lha·sa (lä′sə, -sä, las′ə), *n.* a city in and the capital of Tibet, in the SE part: sacred city of Lamaism. 25,000 (est. 1950); ab. 12,000 ft. above sea level. Also, **Lassa.**

Lha′sa ap′so (ap′sō), *pl.* **Lhasa apsos.** one of a breed of small terriers having a long, heavy coat, raised in Tibet as watchdogs. [*apso* < Tibetan: terrier]

l.h.b., *Football.* left halfback.

L.H.D., **1.** Doctor of Humane Letters. **2.** Doctor of Humanities. [< L *Litterārum Humāniōrum Doctor*]

L′-head en′gine (el′hed′), an internal-combustion engine having the intake and exhaust valves arranged in a chamber along one side of the pistons.

Lhe·vinne (lā vēn′), *n.* **Jo·sef** (jō′zəf), 1874–1944, Russian pianist.

L'Hos·pi·tal (lō pē tal′; *Eng.* lō′pi tal′), *n.* **Guil·laume Fran·çois An·toine de** (gē yōm′ fräN swa′ äN twan′ də), 1661–1704, French mathematician. Also, **L'Hô·pi·tal′.**

L'Hospital's′ rule′, *Math.* the theorem that for the quotient of two functions satisfying certain conditions on a given closed interval, each having infinite limit or zero as limit at a given point, the limit of the quotient at the given point is equal to the limit of the quotient of the derivatives of each function. [named after G. F. A. L'HOSPITAL]

li¹ (lē), *n.* *Music.* the solmization syllable used for the semitone between the sixth and seventh degrees of a scale. [alter. of LA¹]

li² (lē), *n.*, *pl.* **li.** a Chinese unit of distance, equivalent to about one third of a mile. [< Chin]

li³ (lē), *n.* (in Chinese philosophy) the etiquette traditionally prescribed for individuals or groups of people in a given situation. [< Chin: decorum]

Li, *Chem.* lithium.

li, link; links.

L.I., **1.** *Brit.* light infantry. **2.** Long Island.

Li·a (lī′ə), *n.* *Douay Bible.* Leah (def. 1).

li·a·bil·i·ty (lī′ə bil′i tē), *n.*, *pl.* **-ties.** **1. liabilities, a.** moneys owed; debts or pecuniary obligations (opposed to *assets*). **b.** *Accounting.* liabilities as detailed on a balance sheet, esp. in relation to assets and capital. **2.** something disadvantageous. **3.** Also, **li′a·ble·ness.** the state or quality of being liable: *liability to disease.* [*liabil-* (comb. form of LIABLE; see -ABLE) + -ITY]

liabil′ity insur′ance, insurance covering the insured against losses arising from injury or damage to another person or property.

liabil′ity lim′it, the highest amount that a liability insurer will pay on a single claim.

li·a·ble (lī′ə bəl), *adj.* **1.** subject, exposed, or open to something possible or likely, esp. something undesirable. **2.** under legal obligation; responsible or answerable. [< AF *li(er)* (to) bind (< L *ligāre*) + -ABLE] —**Syn. 1.** See **likely. 2.** obliged, accountable.

li·ai·son (lē′ā zôN′, lē′ə zon′, -zən; lē ā′zən, -zon; *Fr.* lye zôN′), *n.*, *pl.* **-sons** (-zôNz′, -zonz′, -zənz, -zonz; *Fr.* -zôN′). **1.** *Mil., Navy.* the contact maintained between units in order to ensure concerted action. **2.** a similar connection or relation maintained between the units of any organization. **3.** an illicit, intimate relationship between a man and a woman. **4.** *Cookery.* a thickening, as of beaten eggs and cream, for sauces, soups, etc. **5.** *Phonet.* a speech-sound redistribution, occurring esp. in French, in which the primary phonetic feature of an otherwise silent final consonant is articulated as the initial sound of a following syllable that begins with a vowel or with a silent *h*, as the *z*- and *n*-sounds in *Je suis un homme* (zhə swē zœ nôm′). [< F, OF < L *ligātiōn-* (s. of *ligātiō*) a binding. See LIGATURE, -ION]

Liai·sons Dange·reuses, Les (*Fr.* lā lye zôN′ däNzhə rœz′). See **Les Liaisons Dangereuses.**

Lia·kou·ra (*Gk.* lyä′ko͞o rä), *n.* modern name of Mount Parnassus.

li·a·na (lē ä′nə, -an′ə), *n.* a climbing plant or vine. Also, **li·ane** (lē än′). [earlier *liannes* (pl.), appar. misspelling of F *lianes*, pl. of *liane*, deriv. of *lier* to bind; the current form is learned] —**li·a′noid,** *adj.*

liang (lyäng, lyang), *n.*, *pl.* **liang, liangs.** a Chinese unit of weight, equal to $\frac{1}{16}$ catty, and equivalent to about $1\frac{1}{3}$ ounce. Also called **tael, haikwan tael.** [< Chin]

Liao (lyou), *n.* a river in NE China, flowing through S Manchuria into the Gulf of Liaotung. 700 mi. long.

Liao·ning (lyou′ning′), *n.* a province in S Manchuria, in NE China. 24,090,000 (est. 1957); 58,301 sq. mi. *Cap.:* Shenyang. Formerly, **Fengtien.**

Liao·peh (lyou′bā′), *n.* a former province in Manchuria, in NE China. 47,612 sq. mi.

Liao·tung (lyou′do͝ong′), *n.* **1.** a peninsula in Manchuria, in NE China, extending S into the Yellow Sea. **2. Gulf of,** a gulf W of this peninsula.

Liao·yang (lyou′yäng′), *n.* a city in S Manchuria, in NE China, SW of Mukden. 135,000 (est. 1957).

li·ar (lī′ər), *n.* one who tells lies. [ME *lier*, OE *lēogere* (north). See LIE¹, -AR¹]

li·ard (lē är′; *Fr.* lē AR′), *n.*, *pl.* **li·ards** (lē ärz′; *Fr.* lē AR′). a former silver coin of France, the fourth part of a sol, issued from the 15th century to 1793 and made from copper after 1650. [named after G. *Liard*, 15th-century French minter]

Li·ard (lē′ärd, lē ärd′, -är′), *n.* a river in W Canada, flowing from S Yukon through N British Columbia and the Northwest Territories into the Mackenzie River. 550 mi. long.

Li·as (lī′əs), *n.* *Stratig.* the lowermost main part of the European Jurassic. [late ME *lyas* a kind of limestone < MF *liois*, prob. akin to *lie* dregs. See LEE²] —**Li·as·sic** (lī as′ik), *adj.*

lib (lib), *n.* *Informal.* liberation, esp. as a social reform: *women's lib; gay lib.* [by shortening]

Lib., Liberal.

lib., **1.** book. [< L *liber*] **2.** librarian. **3.** library.

li·ba·tion (lī bā′shən), *n.* **1.** a pouring out of wine or other liquid in honor of a deity. **2.** the liquid poured out. **3.** *Often Facetious.* **a.** an intoxicating beverage, as wine, esp. when drunk in ceremonial or celebrative situations. **b.** an act or instance of drinking such a beverage. [ME *libacio(u)n* < L *lībātiōn-* (s. of *lībātiō*) a drink offering, equiv. to *lībāt(us)* poured (ptp. of *lībāre*; c. Gk *leíbein*) + *-iōn-* -ION] —**li·ba′tion·al, li·ba′tion·ar′y,** *adj.*

Li·ba·tion-Bear·ers, The (lī bā′shən bâr′ərz), Choëphori.

Li·bau (lē′bou), *n.* German name of **Liepāja.**

Li·ba·va (li bä′vä), *n.* Russian name of **Liepāja.**

Lib·by (lib′ē), *n.* **1. Willard Frank,** born 1908, U.S. chemist: Nobel prize 1960. **2.** a town in NW Montana. 2828 (1960). **3.** a girl's given name, form of **Elizabeth.**

li·bec·cio (li bet′chō; *Eng.* li bech′ē ō′), *n.* *Italian.* a southwest wind, esp. one that blows in northern Corsica.

li·bel (lī′bəl), *n.*, *v.*, **-beled, -bel·ing** or (*esp. Brit.*) **-belled, -bel·ling.** —*n.* **1.** *Law.* **a.** defamation by written or printed words, pictures, or in any form other than by spoken words or gestures. **b.** the crime of publishing it. **c.** a formal written declaration or statement, as one containing the allegations of a plaintiff or the grounds of a charge. **2.** anything that is defamatory or that maliciously or damagingly misrepresents. —*v.t.* **3.** to publish a libel against. **4.** to misrepresent damagingly. **5.** to institute suit against by a libel, as in an admiralty court. [ME: little book, formal document, esp. plaintiff's statement < L *libell(us)*, dim. of *liber* book]

li·bel·ant (lī′bə lənt), *n.* *Law.* one who libels, or institutes suit. Also, *esp. Brit.*, **li′bel·lant.** [LIBEL + -ANT]

li·bel·ee (lī′bə lē′), *n.* *Law.* one against whom a libel instituting a suit has been filed; the respondent. Also, *esp. Brit.*, **li′bel·lee′.** [LIBEL + -EE]

li·bel·er (lī′bə lər), *n.* one who libels; one who publishes a libel assailing another. Also, *esp. Brit.*, **li′bel·ler.** [LIBEL + -ER¹]

li·bel·ous (lī′bə ləs), *adj.* containing, constituting, or involving a libel; maliciously defamatory. Also, *esp. Brit.*, **li′bel·lous.** [LIBEL + -OUS] —**li′bel·ous·ly;** *esp. Brit.*, **li′bel·lous·ly,** *adv.*

li·ber¹ (lī′bər), *n.* *Bot.* phloem. [< L: bark]

li·ber² (lī′bər; *Lat.* li′bER), *n.*, *pl.* **li·bri** (lī′brī; *Lat.* li′brē), **li·bers.** a book of public records, as deeds, birth certificates, etc. [< L: book, orig. bark; see LIBER¹]

Li·ber (lī′bər), *n.* an ancient Italian god of wine and vineyards, in later times identified with Bacchus.

Lib·er·a (lib′ər ə), *n.* an ancient Italian goddess of wine, vineyards, and fertility and the wife of Liber, in later times identified with Persephone.

lib·er·al (lib′ər əl, lib′rəl), *adj.* **1.** favorable to progress or reform, as in religious or political affairs. **2.** (*often cap.*) noting or pertaining to a political party advocating measures of progressive political reform. **3.** of or pertaining to representational forms of government rather than aristocracies and monarchies. **4.** of, pertaining to, based on, or advocating liberalism. **5.** favorable to

or in accord with concepts of maximum individual freedom possible, esp. as guaranteed by law and secured by governmental protection of civil liberties. **6.** favoring or permitting freedom of action, esp. with respect to matters of personal belief or expression: *The government followed a liberal policy toward the country's artists and writers.* **7.** free from prejudice or bigotry; tolerant: *a liberal attitude toward religion.* **8.** open-minded or tolerant, esp. free of or not bound by traditional or conventional ideas, values, etc. **9.** characterized by generosity and willingness to give in large amounts: *a liberal patron; a liberal donor.* **10.** given freely or abundantly: *a liberal donation.* **11.** not strict or rigorous; free; not literal: *a liberal interpretation of a rule.* **12.** of, pertaining to, or befitting a freeman. —*n.* **13.** a person of liberal principles or views, esp. in religion or politics. **14.** (*often cap.*) a member of a liberal party in politics, esp. of the Liberal party in Great Britain. [ME < L *līberāl(is)* of freedom, befitting the free, equiv. to *līber* free + *-ālis* -AL¹] —**lib′er·al·ly,** *adv.* —**lib′er·al·ness,** *n.*
—**Syn. 1.** progressive. **7.** broad-minded, unprejudiced. **9.** generous, beneficent, charitable, open-handed, munificent, unstinting, lavish. **10.** See **ample.** —**Ant. 1.** reactionary. **7.** intolerant. **9, 10.** niggardly.

lib′eral arts′, the course of instruction at a college granting an academic degree, comprising the arts, natural sciences, social sciences, and humanities. [trans. of L *artēs līberālēs* work befitting a free man]

lib′eral educa′tion, an education based primarily on the liberal arts and intended to provide maximum opportunities for self-expression or self-fulfillment.

Li·ber·a·li·a (lib′ə rā′lē ə, -rāl′yə), *n.* (*sometimes construed as pl.*) an ancient Roman festival held annually in honor of Liber and Libera.

lib·er·al·ise (lib′ər ə līz′, lib′rə-), *v.t., v.i.,* **-ised, -is·ing.** *Chiefly Brit.* liberalize. —**lib′er·al·i·sa′tion,** *n.* —**lib′er·al·is′er,** *n.*

lib·er·al·ism (lib′ər ə liz′əm, lib′rə-), *n.* **1.** the quality or state of being liberal, as in behavior, attitude, etc. **2.** (*sometimes cap.*) the principles and practices of a liberal party in politics. **3.** a political or social philosophy advocating the freedom of the individual, parliamentary systems of government, nonviolent modification of political, social, or economic institutions to assure unrestricted development in all spheres of human endeavor, and governmental guarantees of individual rights and civil liberties. **4.** a movement in modern Protestantism which emphasizes freedom from tradition and authority, the adjustment of religious beliefs to scientific conceptions, and the spiritual capacities of men. [LIBERAL + -ISM] —**lib′er·al·ist,** *n., adj.* —**lib′er·al·is′tic,** *adj.*

lib·er·al·i·ty (lib′ə ral′i tē), *n., pl.* **-ties. 1.** the quality or condition of being liberal in giving; generosity; bounty. **2.** a liberal gift. **3.** breadth of mind. **4.** broadness or fullness, as of proportions, physical attributes, etc. **5.** liberalism. [ME *liberalite* < L *līberālitās.* See LIBERAL, -ITY]

lib·er·al·ize (lib′ər ə līz′, lib′rə-), *v.t., v.i.,* **-ized, -iz·ing.** to make or become liberal. Also, *esp. Brit.,* **liberalise.** [LIBERAL + -IZE] —**lib′er·al·i·za′tion,** *n.* —**lib′er·al·iz′er,** *n.*

Lib′eral par′ty, a political party in Great Britain, formed about 1830 as a fusion of Whigs and Radicals and constituting one of the dominant British parties in the 19th and early part of the 20th centuries when its advocacy of electoral reform and improvement of the conditions of the working classes gained it much popular support.

lib·er·ate (lib′ə rāt′), *v.t.,* **-at·ed, -at·ing. 1.** to set free, as from bondage; release. **2.** to disengage; set free from combination, as a gas. **3.** *U.S. Army Slang.* to steal: *We liberated three cars and a consignment of cigarettes.* [< L *līberāt(us)* freed (ptp. of *līberāre*). See LIBERAL, -ATE¹] —**lib′er·a′tion,** *n.* —**lib′er·a′tive, lib·er·a·to·ry** (lib′ər ə tôr′ē, -tōr′ē), *adj.* —**lib′er·a′tor,** *n.*
—**Syn. 1.** deliver, unfetter, disenthrall, loose. See **release.** —**Ant. 1.** imprison; enthrall.

Lib·er·a·tor (lib′ə rā′tər), *n.* a four-engined heavy bomber widely used over Europe and the Mediterranean by the U.S. Army Air Force in World War II. *Symbol:* B-24 [< L; see LIBERATE, -OR²]

Li·be·rec (li′be rets), *n.* a city in the NW Czech Republic. 104,000. German, **Reichenberg.**

Li·be·ri·a (lī bēr′ē ə), *n.* a republic in W Africa: founded by freed American slaves 1822. 1,016,443 (1962); ab. 43,000 sq. mi. *Cap.:* Monrovia. —**Li·be′ri·an,** *adj., n.*

Li·be·ri·us (lī bēr′ē əs), *n.* died A.D. 366, pope 352–366.

lib·er·tar·i·an (lib′ər târ′ē ən), *n.* **1.** one who advocates liberty, esp. with regard to thought or conduct. **2.** one who maintains the doctrine of free will (opposed to *necessitarian*). —*adj.* **3.** advocating liberty or conforming to principles of liberty. **4.** maintaining the doctrine of free will. [LIBERT(Y) + -ARIAN] —**lib′er·tar′i·an·ism,** *n.*

Li·ber·tas (li bûr′təs), *n.* the ancient Roman personification of liberty.

li·ber·té, é·ga·li·té, fra·ter·ni·té (lē bɛʀ tā′, ā ga lē tā′, fʀa tɛʀ nē tā′), *French.* Liberty, Equality, Fraternity: motto of the French Revolution.

li·ber·ti·cide (li bûr′ti sīd′), *n.* **1.** destruction of liberty. **2.** one who destroys liberty. [LIBERTY + -CIDE] —**li·ber′ti·cid′al,** *adj.*

lib·er·tin·age (lib′ər tē′nij, -tin ij), *n.* libertine conduct, esp. in sexual or religious matters. [LIBERTINE + -AGE]

lib·er·tine (lib′ər tēn′, -tin), *n.* **1.** one who is morally or sexually unrestrained, esp. a dissolute man; a profligate; rake. **2.** one freed from slavery in ancient Rome. **3.** a freethinker in religious matters. —*adj.* **4.** free of moral, esp. sexual, restraint; dissolute; licentious. **5.** freethinking in religious matters. **6.** *Archaic.* unrestrained; uncontrolled. [ME *libertyn* < L *lībertīn(us)* of a freedman (adj.), freedman (n.), equiv. to *lībert(us)* freedman (*lībert(ās)* LIBERTY + *-us* masc. n. suffix) + *-īnus* -INE¹]
—**Syn. 1.** roué, debauchee, lecher, sensualist. **4.** amoral, sensual, lascivious, lewd. —**Ant. 1.** prude.

lib·er·tin·ism (lib′ər tē niz′əm, -ti-), *n.* libertine practices or habits of life; disregard of authority or convention in sexual or religious matters. [LIBERTINE + -ISM]

lib·er·ty (lib′ər tē), *n., pl.* **-ties. 1.** freedom from arbitrary or despotic government or control. **2.** freedom from external or foreign rule; independence. **3.** freedom from control, interference, obligation, restriction, hampering conditions, etc.; power or right of doing, thinking, speaking, etc., according to choice. **4.** freedom from captivity, confinement, or physical restraint: *The prisoner soon regained his liberty.* **5.** leave granted to a sailor, esp. in the navy, to go ashore. **6.** freedom or right to frequent or use a place: *The visitors were given the liberty of the city.* **7.** unwarranted or impertinent freedom in action or speech, or a form or instance of it: *to take liberties.* **8.** a female figure personifying freedom from despotism. **9. at liberty, a.** free from captivity or restraint. **b.** unemployed; out of work. **c.** free to do or be as specified: *You are at liberty to leave at any time during the meeting.* [ME *liberte* < L *lībertās,* equiv. to *līber* free + *-tās* -TY²]
—**Syn. 4.** liberation. See **freedom. 6.** franchise, permission, license, privilege, immunity.

Lib·er·ty (lib′ər tē), *n.* **1.** a town in W Missouri. 8909 (1960). **2.** a town in E Texas. 6127 (1960). **3.** a town in SE New York. 4704 (1960). **4.** a town in SW Pennsylvania. 3624 (1960). **5.** a town in NW South Carolina. 2567 (1960). **6.** a girl's given name.

Lib′erty Bell′, the bell of Independence Hall, rung on July 8, 1776 to proclaim the signing of the Declaration of Independence; since then a national symbol of liberty.

Lib′erty bond′, a single Liberty loan bond.

lib′erty cap′, a soft, conical cap given to a freed slave in ancient Rome at manumission of his servitude, used as a symbol of liberty, esp. since the 18th century. Cf. **Phrygian cap.**

Lib′erty Is′land, a small island in upper New York Bay: site of the Statue of Liberty. Formerly, **Bedloe's Island.**

Lib′erty loan′, any of the five bond issues of the U.S. government floated in World War I.

lib′erty of speech′. See **freedom of speech.**

lib′erty of the press′. See **freedom of the press.**

Lib′erty par′ty, *U.S. Hist.* the first antislavery political party, organized in 1839 and merged with the Free Soil party in 1848.

Lib′erty ship′, a slow cargo ship built during World War II, having a capacity of about 11,000 deadweight tons.

Lib·er·ty·ville (lib′ər tē vil′), *n.* a town in NE Illinois. 8560 (1960).

Li·bia (lē′byä), *n.* Italian name of **Libya.**

li·bid·i·nous (li bid′ənəs), *adj.* **1.** of, pertaining to, or characteristic of the libido. **2.** full of lust; lustful; lewd. [late ME *lybydynous* < L *libīdinōs(us)* willful, lustful, equiv. to *libīdin-* (s. of *libīdō*) LIBIDO + *-ōsus* -OUS] —**li·bid′i·nous·ly,** *adv.* —**li·bid′i·nous·ness,** *n.*

li·bi·do (li bē′dō, -bī′dō), *n.* **1.** *Psychoanal.* all of the instinctual energies and desires that are derived from the id. **2.** the sexual instinct. [< L: desire, willfulness, lust, akin to *libēre* to like] —**li·bid·i·nal** (li bid′ənəl), *adj.* —**li·bid′i·nal·ly,** *adv.*

li·bra¹ (lī′brə), *n., pl.* **-brae** (-brē). the ancient Roman pound (containing 5053 grains). [< L]

li·bra² (lē′brä), *n., pl.* **-bras.** sol³ (def. 2). [< Sp < L]

Li·bra (lī′brə, lē′-), *n., gen.* **-brae** (-brē) for 1. **1.** *Astron.* the Balance, a zodiacal constellation between Virgo and Serpens. **2.** *Astrol.* the seventh sign of the zodiac. See illus. under **zodiac.** [< L: lit., pair of scales]

li·brar·i·an (lī brâr′ē ən), *n.* **1.** a person trained in library science and engaged in library service. **2.** an officer in charge of a library. **3.** a person who is in charge of any specialized body of literature, as a collection of musical scores. [LIBRARY + -AN]

li·brar·i·an·ship (lī brâr′ē ən ship′), *n.* **1.** a profession concerned with organizing collections of books and related materials in libraries and servicing these resources to readers and others. **2.** the position or duties of a librarian. [LIBRARIAN + -SHIP]

li·brar·y (lī′brer′ē, -brə rē, -brē), *n., pl.* **-brar·ies. 1.** a place set apart to contain books and other material for reading, study, or reference, as a room, set of rooms, or building where books may be read or borrowed. **2.** a public body organizing and maintaining such an establishment: *the Library of Congress.* **3.** a commercial establishment lending books for a fixed charge; a rental library. **4.** a collection of manuscripts, publications, and other materials for reading, study, or reference. **5.** a collection of any materials for study and enjoyment, as films, musical recordings, maps, etc. **6.** a series of books of similar character or alike in size, binding, etc., issued by a single publishing house. **7.** canon¹ (def. 10). **8.** *Computer Technol.* a collection of standard programs, routines, and subroutines available for solving a variety of computer problems. **9.** *Brit.* a ticket agency for theaters. [ME *librarie* < ML *librāria,* n. use of fem. of L *librārius* (adj.) of books, equiv. to *liber* book + *-ārius* -ARY]

li′brary bind′ing, **1.** a tough, durable cloth binding for books. Cf. **edition binding. 2.** the production of books that are bound with library binding.

li′brary card′, a card issued by a circulating library to individuals entitling them to borrow books and sometimes containing a record of the dates a book was borrowed and returned. Also called **borrower's card.**

Li′brary of Con′gress, the national library of the U.S. in Washington, D.C., established by Congress in 1800 for service to its members. It now also serves government agencies, other libraries, and the public.

Li′brary of Con′gress classifica′tion, *Library Science.* a system for classifying books and other materials, using for its notation both letters of the alphabet and numerals to allow for expansion.

li′brary paste′, a white, smooth paste for paper and lightweight cardboard.

li′brary sci′ence, the study of the organization and administration of a library and of its technical, informational, and reference services.

li′brary steps′, a folding stepladder, esp. one folding into another piece of furniture, as a table or chair.

li′brary ta′ble, *Brit.* a large pedestal writing table or desk.

li·brate (lī′brāt), *v.i.,* **-brat·ed, -brat·ing. 1.** to oscillate or move from side to side or between two points. **2.** to remain poised or balanced. [< L *librāt(us)* balanced, poised, ptp. of *librāre.* See LIBRA, -ATE¹]

li·bra·tion (lī brā′shən), *n.* *Astron.* a real or apparent oscillatory motion, esp. of the moon. [< L *lībrātiōn-* (s. of *lībrātiō*) a balancing. See LIBRATE, -ION] —**li·bra′tion·al,** *adj.*

li·bra·to·ry (lī′brə tôr′ē, -tōr′ē), *adj.* oscillatory. [LIBRATE + -ORY¹]

li·bret·tist (li bret′ist), *n.* the writer of a libretto. [< It *librettist(a).* See LIBRETTO, -IST]

li·bret·to (li bret′ō), *n., pl.* **-bret·tos, -bret·ti** (-bret′ē). **1.** the text or words of an opera or similar extended musical composition. **2.** a book or booklet containing such a text. [< It, dim of *libro* book < L *liber;* see -ET]

Li·bre·ville (*Fr.* lē′bre vēl′), *n.* a port in and the capital of Gabon, in the W part, on the Gulf of Guinea. 31,027 (1961).

li·bri (lī′brī; *Lat.* li′brē), *n.* pl. of **liber**².

li·bri·form (lī′brə fôrm′), *adj.* *Bot.* having the form of or resembling liber or phloem. [LIB(E)R¹ + -I- + -FORM]

Lib·ri·um (lib′rē əm), *n.* *Pharm., Trademark.* chlordiazepoxide.

Lib·y·a (lib′ē ə), *n.* **1.** *Anc. Geog.* the part of N Africa W of Egypt. **2.** Italian, **Libia.** a constitutional monarchy in N Africa between Tunisia and the United Arab Republic. 1,559,399 (1964); 679,400 sq. mi. *Capitals:* Tripoli and Benghazi.

Lib·y·an (lib′ē ən), *adj.* **1.** of or pertaining to Libya or its inhabitants. —*n.* **2.** a native or inhabitant of Libya. **3.** a Berber language of ancient Libya. [LIBY(A) + -AN]

Lib′yan Des′ert, a desert in N Africa, in E Libya, W United Arab Republic, and NW Sudan, W of the Nile: part of the Sahara. ab. 650,000 sq. mi.

lice (līs), *n.* pl. of **louse.**

li·cence (lī′səns), *n., v.t.,* **-cenced, -cenc·ing.** license. —**li′cence·a·ble,** *adj.*

li·cense (lī′səns), *n., v.,* **-censed, -cens·ing.** —*n.* **1.** permission to do or not to do something. **2.** formal permission from a constituted authority to do something, as to carry on some business, profession, etc. **3.** a certificate of such permission; an official permit: *a driver's license.* **4.** intentional deviation from rule, convention, or fact, as for the sake of literary or artistic effect: *poetic license.* **5.** exceptional freedom allowed in a special situation. **6.** excessive or undue freedom or liberty. **7.** licentiousness. **8.** the legal right to use a patent owned by another. **9.** *Naut.* a document issued to a U.S. vessel, other than a barge or the like, of less than 20 tons gross and more than 5 tons gross that is engaged in fishing, in trade along the U.S. coast, on U.S. inland waters, or on the Great Lakes, or that is operating as a yacht along the U.S. coast or between the U.S. and foreign countries. —*v.t.* **10.** to grant authoritative permission or license to. **11.** *Naut.* to document (a U.S. vessel) with a license. [ME *licence* < MF < ML *licentia* authorization, L: freedom, equiv. to *licent-* (s. of *licēns,* prp. of *licēre* to be allowed) + *-ia* -IA; see -ENCE] —**li′cense·less,** *adj.* —**li′cens·er;** *esp. Law,* **li′cen·sor,** *n.*

li·cen·see (lī′sən sē′), *n.* one to whom a license is granted or issued. Also, **li′cen·cee′.** [LICENSE + -EE]

li′cense plate′, a plate or tag, usually of metal, bearing evidence of official registration and permission, as for the use of an automobile, the keeping of a pet, etc.

li·cen·ti·ate (lī sen′shē it, -āt′), *n.* **1.** one who has received a license, as from a university, to practice an art or profession. **2.** the holder of a certain university degree intermediate between that of bachelor and that of doctor, now confined chiefly to certain continental European universities. [< ML *licentiāt(us)* authorized (person), ptp. of *licentiāre.* See LICENSE, -ATE¹] —**li·cen′ti·ate·ship′,** *n.* —**li·cen′ti·a′tion,** *n.*

li·cen·tious (lī sen′shəs), *adj.* **1.** sexually unrestrained; lascivious; libertine; lewd. **2.** unrestrained by law or morality; lawless; immoral. **3.** going beyond customary or proper bounds or limits; disregarding rules. [< L *licentiōs(us)* arbitrary. See LICENSE, -OUS] —**li·cen′tious·ly,** *adv.* —**li·cen′tious·ness,** *n.*
—**Syn. 2.** abandoned, profligate. —**Ant. 2.** lawful, restrained.

li·cet (lē′ket; *Eng.* lī′set), *Latin.* it is allowed.

Li·ce·tus (li sē′təs), *n.* a walled plain in the fourth quadrant of the face of the moon: about 46 miles in diameter.

lich (lich), *n.* *Brit. Obs.* **1.** the body; the trunk. **2.** a dead body; corpse. Also, **lych.** [ME *liche* body (alive or dead), OE *līc;* c. D *lijk,* G *Leiche,* Icel *līk,* Goth *leik.* See LIKE¹]

Li·chas (lī′kəs), *n.* *Class. Myth.* **1.** a herald who in innocence delivered a poisoned robe to Hercules and was turned to stone. **2.** a Spartan who sought the bones of Orestes.

li·chee (lē′chē′), *n.* litchi.

li·chen (lī′kən), *n.* **1.** any compound, thallophytic plant of the group *Lichenes* that is composed of a fungus in symbiotic union with an alga and has a greenish, gray, yellow, brown, or blackish thallus growing in leaflike, crustlike, or branching forms on rocks, trees, etc. **2.** *Pathol.* any of various eruptive skin diseases. —*v.t.* **3.** to cover with or as with lichens. [< L < Gk *leichēn*] —**li′chen·like′,** *adj.*

li·chen′ic ac′id (lī ken′ik), *Chem.* See **fumaric acid.** [LICHEN + -IC]

li·chen·i·fi·ca·tion (lī ken′ə fə kā′shən), *n.* *Med.* **1.** a leathery hardening of the skin, usually caused by chronic irritation. **2.** a patch of skin so hardened. [LICHEN + -I- + -FICATION]

li·chen·in (lī′kə nin), *n.* *Chem.* a white, gelatinous, polysaccharide starch, $(C_6H_{10}O_5)_n$, obtained from various mosses. [LICHEN + -IN²]

li·chen·ise (lī′kə nīz′), *v.t.,* **-ised, -is·ing.** *Chiefly Brit.* lichenize.

li·chen·ism (lī′kə niz′əm), *n.* the symbiosis between algae and fungi that enables them to become lichens. [LICHEN + -ISM]

li·chen·ize (lī′kə nīz′), *v.t.*, **-ized, -iz·ing.** to cover with lichen. Also, *esp. Brit.*, **lichenise.** [LICHEN + -IZE]

li·chen·oid (lī′kə noid′), *adj.* resembling lichen; lichenlike. [LICHEN + -OID]

li·chen·ol·o·gy (lī′kə nol′ə jē), *n.* the branch of botany dealing with lichens. [LICHEN + -O- + LOGY] —**li·chen·o·log·ic** (lī′kə nō loj′ik), **li′chen·o·log′i·cal,** *adj.* —**li′chen·ol′o·gist,** *n.*

li·chen·ous (lī′kə nəs), *adj.* **1.** of, pertaining to, or resembling a lichen. **2.** covered with lichens. Also, **li·chen·ose** (lī′kə nōs′). [LICHEN + -OUS]

Lich·field (lich′fēld′), *n.* a town in SE Staffordshire, in central England, N of Birmingham: birthplace of Samuel Johnson. 14,077 (1961).

lich′ gate′, (esp. in England) a roofed gate to a churchyard under which a bier is set down to await the coming of the clergyman. Also, **lych gate.** Also called **resurrection gate.**

li·chi (lē′chē), *n., pl.* **-chis.** litchi.

lich′ stone′, a stone on which to rest a coffin momentarily at the entrance to a cemetery.

licht (likʜt), *n., adj., v.t., v.i., adv. Scot.* light[1]. [ME (Scot sp.), early ME *leo(c)ht*, OE *lēoht* LIGHT[1]] —**licht′ly,** *adv.*

Lich·ten·berg (lik′tən bûrg′), *n.* a crater in the second quadrant of the face of the moon: about 12 miles in diameter.

lic·it (lis′it), *adj.* legal; lawful; permitted. [< L *licit(us)* permitted (ptp. of *licēre*); r. late ME *licite* < MF; see -ITE[2]] —**lic′it·ly,** *adv.*

lick (lik), *v.t.* **1.** to pass the tongue over the surface of (often fol. by *up, off, from,* etc.). **2.** to make, or cause to become, by stroking with the tongue: *to lick a plate clean.* **3.** (of waves, flames, etc.) to pass or play lightly over: *The flame licked the base of the tree trunk.* **4.** *Informal.* **a.** to smite, esp. as a punishment; beat; thrash; whip. **b.** to overcome, as in a fight; defeat. **c.** to outdo or surpass. **5. lick into shape,** *Informal.* to bring to completion or perfection through discipline, hard work, etc.: *They needed another rehearsal to lick the production into shape.* **6. lick someone's boots.** See **boot**[1] (def. 19). **7. lick the dust.** See **dust** (def. 15). —*n.* **8.** a stroke of the tongue over something. **9.** as much as can be taken up by one stroke of the tongue: *a lick of an ice cream cone.* **10.** See **salt lick. 11.** *Informal.* **a.** a blow. **b.** a brief, brisk burst of activity or energy. **c.** a quick pace or clip; speed. **12.** *Jazz.* an improvisational figure in swing music. **13. lick and a promise,** a hasty and perfunctory manner of doing something: *She didn't have time to clean thoroughly, but gave the room a lick and a promise.* [ME *licke(n)*, OE *liccian*; c. D *likk*, G *lecken*; akin to Goth *(bi)laigon*, L *lingere*, Gk *leíchein* to lick (up)] —**lick′er,** *n.*
—**Syn. 11a.** thwack, thump, rap, slap, cuff, buffet.

Lick (lik), *n.* a ring formation in the first quadrant of the face of the moon: about 21 miles in diameter.

lick·er-in (lik′ər in′), *n.* a roller on a carding machine, esp. the roller that opens the stock as it is fed into the card and transfers the fibers to the main cylinder. Also called **taker-in.** [n. use of v. phrase *lick in*]

lick·er·ish (lik′ər ish), *adj. Archaic.* **1.** fond of and eager for choice food. **2.** greedy; longing. **3.** lustful; lecherous. Also, **liquorish.** [ME *liker(ous)* pleasing to the taste, lit., to a licker (see LICK, -ER[1]) + -ISH[1]] —**lick′er·ish·ly,** *adv.* —**lick′er·ish·ness,** *n.*

lick·e·ty-split (lik′i tē split′), *adv. Informal.* at great speed; rapidly: *to travel lickety-split.* [? dial. *licket* rag (for wiping in haste, with one lick) + -Y[1] + SPLIT, as in *split second*]

lick·ing (lik′ing), *n.* **1.** *Informal.* **a.** a beating or thrashing. **b.** a reversal or disappointment; setback. **2.** the act of one who or that which licks. [ME; see LICK, -ING[1]]

lick·spit·tle (lik′spit′əl), *n.* a contemptible, fawning person; a flatterer or toady. Also, **lick′spit′.** [LICK + SPITTLE]

lic·o·rice (lik′ə ris, -ər ish, lik′rish), *n.* **1.** a leguminous plant, *Glycyrrhiza glabra,* of Europe and Asia. **2.** the sweet-tasting, dried root of this plant or an extract made from it, used in medicine, confectionery, etc. **3.** any of various related or similar plants. Also, **liquorice.** [ME *lycorys* < AF < LL *liquirītia* for L *glycyrrhiza* < Gk *glykýrriza* sweetroot (plant), equiv. to *glyký(s)* sweet + *rhiza* root; see -IA]

lic′orice stick′, *Slang.* a clarinet.

lic·tor (lik′tər), *n.* (in ancient Rome) one of a body of attendants on certain magistrates, who preceded them carrying the fasces. [< L] —**lic·to·ri·an** (lik tōr′ē ən, -tôr′-), *adj.*

Li·cym·ni·us (lī sim′nē əs), *n. Class. Myth.* a son of Electryon and Midea and the uncle of Hercules.

lid (lid), *n.* **1.** a movable piece, whether separate or hinged, for closing the opening, usually at the top, of a jar, trunk, etc.; a movable cover. **2.** an eyelid. **3.** (in mosses) **a.** the cover of the capsule; operculum. **b.** the upper section of a pyxidium. **4.** *Mining.* cap[1] (def. 8). **5.** *Slang.* a hat. **6.** *Informal.* a restraint, ceiling, or curb, as on prices, news, etc. **7. blow the lid off,** *Slang.* to expose to public view, esp. to reveal something scandalous, illegal, etc.: *A series of editorials blew the lid off the widespread graft-taking of public building inspectors.* **8. flip one's lid,** *Slang.* to lose control, esp. to laugh or rage hysterically: *He nearly flipped his lid over the way they damaged his car.* [ME; OE *hlid*; c. D, G *lid*, Icel *hlith*] —**lid′ded,** *adj.*

Lid·del Hart (lid′əl härt′), **Basil Henry,** born 1895, English military authority and writer.

Lid·di·ard (lid′ē ərd), *n.* a walled plain in the first quadrant of the face of the moon: about 100 miles in diameter.

Lid·die (lid′ē) *n.* a girl's given name, form of **Lydia.** Also, **Lidie.**

li·di·a (lid′ē ə; *Sp.* lē′dyä), *n. pl.* **li·dias** (lid′ē əz; *Sp.* lē′dyäs). (in bullfighting) one section of a corrida, comprising the action that takes place from the entrance of the bull to the time it is killed and dragged from the arena by mules. [< Sp: bullfight]

Li·di·ce (li′dyi tse; *Eng.* lē′də chā′, lid′ə sē), *n.* a village in the W Czech Republic: suffered a ruthless reprisal by the Nazis in 1942 for the assassination of a high Nazi official. 509.

Lid·ie (lid′ē), *n.* a girl's given name, form of **Lydia.**

lid·less (lid′lis), *adj.* **1.** (of objects) without a lid. **2.** (of eyes) without or as if without lids. **3.** vigilant: *a lidless guard for public morals.* [LID + -LESS]

Li·do (lē′dō; *It.* lē′dô), *n.* a chain of sandy islands in NE Italy, between the Lagoon of Venice and the Adriatic: resort.

lie[1] (lī), *n., v.,* **lied, ly·ing.** —*n.* **1.** a false statement made with deliberate intent to deceive; an intentional untruth; a falsehood. **2.** something intended or serving to convey a false impression; imposture: *His wig was a lie that deceived no one.* **3.** the charge or accusation of lying; a flat contradiction: *He flung the lie back at his accusers.* **4. give the lie to, a.** to charge with lying; contradict. **b.** to prove or imply the falsity of; belie: *His work gives the lie to his claims of experience.* —*v.i.* **5.** to speak falsely or utter untruth knowingly, as with intent to deceive. **6.** to express what is false, or convey a false impression. [ME; OE *lyge*; c. G *Lüge*, Icel *lygi*; akin to Goth *liugn*]
—*v.t.* **7.** to bring, take, put, etc., by lying (often used reflexively): *to lie oneself out of a difficulty; accustomed to lying his way out of difficulties.* **8. lie in one's throat** or **teeth,** to lie grossly or maliciously: *If she told you exactly the opposite of what she told me, she must be lying in her teeth.* [ME *lie(n)*, OE *lēogan*; c. G *lügen*, Icel *ljúga*, Goth *liugan*]
—**Syn. 1.** prevarication, falsification. See **falsehood. 5.** prevaricate, fib. —**Ant. 1.** truth.

lie[2] (lī), *v.,* **lay, lain, ly·ing,** *n.* —*v.i.* **1.** to be in a recumbent or prostrate position, as on a bed or the ground; recline. **2.** to be buried in a particular spot: *Their ancestors lie in the family plot.* **3.** (of objects) to rest in a horizontal position: *The book lies on the table.* **4.** to be or remain in a position or state of inactivity, subjection, restraint, concealment, etc.: *to lie in ambush.* **5.** to rest, press, or weigh (usually fol. by *on* or *upon*): *These things lie upon my mind.* **6.** to depend (usually fol. by *on* or *upon*). **7.** to be found, or be located in a particular area or place: *The fault lies here.* **8.** to be placed or situated: *land lying along the coast.* **9.** to be stretched out or extended: *the broad plain that lies before us.* **10.** to consist or be grounded (usually fol. by *in*): *The real remedy lies in education.* **11.** to be in or have a specified direction: *The trail from here lies to the west.* **12.** *Law.* to be sustainable or admissible, as an action or appeal. **13.** *Archaic.* to lodge; stay the night; sojourn. **14. lie by, a.** to pause for rest; stop (activities, work, etc.) temporarily. **b.** to lie unused: *Ever since the last member of the family died, the old house has lain by.* **15. lie down,** to assume a prostrate position, as for the purpose of resting. **16. lie down on the job,** *Informal.* to do less than one could or should do; shirk one's obligations: *When the work was going very slowly, we were suspected of lying down on the job.* **17. lie in,** to be confined in childbed: *Women nowadays generally do not lie in for long periods of time.* **18. lie low.** See **low**[1] (def. 45). **19. lie over,** to be postponed for action at some future time: *The other business on the agenda will have to lie over until the next meeting.* **20. lie to,** *Naut.* (of a ship) to lie comparatively stationary, usually with the head as near the wind as possible. **21. lie with, a.** to be the duty or function of: *The decision in this matter lies with him.* **b.** *Archaic.* to have sexual intercourse with. **22. take lying down,** *Informal.* to yield without objection or resistance: *I refuse to take such an insult lying down.* —*n.* **23.** manner of lying; the relative position or direction in which something lies. **24.** the haunt or covert of an animal. **25.** *Golf.* the position of the ball relative to how easy or how difficult it is to play. [ME *lie(n)*, *liggen*, OE *licgan*; c. G *liegen*, D *liggen*, Icel *liggja*, Goth *ligan*]
—**Syn. 1.** LIE, LAY, often confused, are not synonyms. LIE, meaning to recline or rest, does not require an object. Its principal parts, too, are irregular, and are therefore distinctive. LAY (originally *to cause to lie*) with its forms *laid, have laid, laying,* etc., means to put or place. If "put" or "place" can be substituted in a contemplated sentence, the verb to use is LAY. Moreover, since one must always "put" or "place" *something,* the verb LAY is used only when there is a grammatical object to complete the sense. (It should be noticed, however, that the past tense of LIE is also spelled LAY.) **23.** place, location, site. —**Ant. 1, 3.** stand.

Lie (lē), *n.* **1. Jonas,** 1880–1940, U.S. painter, born in Norway. **2. (Ma·ri·us) So·phus** (mä′rē o͝os sō′fo͝os), 1842–99, Norwegian mathematician. **3. Tryg·ve Halv·dan** (trig′və häl′dän; *Nor.* trʏg′və häl′dän), born 1896, Norwegian statesman: secretary-general of the United Nations 1946–53.

lie-a·bed (lī′ə bed′), *n.* a person who remains in bed until a relatively late hour.

Lie·ber·mann (*Ger.* lē′bər män′), *n.* **1. Max** (mäks), 1847–1935, German painter and etcher. **2. Rolf** (rolf), born 1910, Swiss composer.

lieb·frau·milch (lēb′frou milk′, lēp′-; *Ger.* lēp′frou-mĭlkʜ′), *n.* a white wine produced chiefly in the region of Hesse in West Germany. [< G, named after *Liebfrauenstift* convent of the Virgin, religious establishment in Worms, where the wine was first made; see MILK (G *Milch*)]

Lie·big (lē′biкʜ), *n.* **Jus·tus** (yo͞os′to͝os), **Baron von** (fən), 1803–73, German chemist.

Lieb·knecht (lēp′knekʜt), *n.* **1. Karl** (kärl), 1871–1919, German socialist leader. **2.** his father, **Wil·helm** (vil′helm), 1826–1900, German journalist and political leader.

lie-by (lī′bī), *n., pl.* **-bys.** *Brit.* **1.** a railroad siding. **2.** a paved section alongside a highway for automobiles in need of emergency repairs. [n. use of v. phrase *lie by*]

Liech·ten·stein (lik′tən stīn′; *Ger.* likʜ′tən-shtīn′), *n.* a small principality in central Europe between Austria and Switzerland. 16,628 (1960); 65 sq. mi. *Cap.:* Vaduz.

lied (lēd; *Ger.* lēt), *n., pl.* **lied·er** (lē′dər; *Ger.* lē′dər). a German song, lyric, or ballad. [< G]

Lie·der·kranz (lē′dər kränts′, -krants′), *n.* **1.** *Trademark.* a strong, soft milk cheese with a creamy center, made in small rectangular blocks. **2.** a German choral society or singing club, esp. of men. [< G: garland of songs]

lie′ detec′tor, an instrument for recording impulses due to changes in certain body activities, as blood pressure, pulse, breathing, and perspiration, the results of which may be interpreted to indicate the truth or falsity of a person's answers under questioning.

lie-down (lī′doun′), *n. Chiefly Brit.* a nap. [n. use of v. phrase *lie down*]

lief (lēf), *adv.* **1.** gladly; willingly. —*adj. Archaic.* **2.** willing; desirous. **3.** dear; beloved; treasured. [ME *leef*, OE *lēof*; c. D *lief*, G *lieb*, Icel *ljúfr*, Goth *liufs*; akin to LOVE] —**lief′ly,** *adv.*

liege (lēj), *n.* **1.** a feudal lord entitled to allegiance and service. **2.** a feudal vassal or subject. —*adj.* **3.** owing allegiance and service to a feudal lord. **4.** pertaining to the relation between a feudal vassal and his lord. **5.** loyal; faithful: *the liege adherents of a cause.* [ME *li(e)ge* < OF << Gmc **lēt-* vassal + L *-icus* -IC; cf. ML *lētī* barbarians allowed to settle on Roman land (< Gmc; ? akin to LET[1]), *laeticus* for **lēticus*, deriv. of *lētus*]

Li·ège (lē āzh′; *Fr.* lyezh), *n.* **1.** a city in E Belgium, on the Meuse River: one of the first cities attacked in World War I. 155,898 (est. 1964). **2.** a province in E Belgium. 1,012,826 (est. 1964); 1521 sq. mi. *Cap.:* Liège. Also, **Liége.** Flemish, **Luik.**

liege·man (lēj′mən), *n., pl.* **-men. 1.** a vassal; subject. **2.** a faithful follower. [ME; see LIEGE, MAN[1]]

Lieg·nitz (lēg′nits), *n.* a city in SW Poland: formerly in Germany. 69,000 (est. 1963). Polish, **Legnica.**

Lie′ group′ (lē), *Math.* a topological group that is a manifold.

lien[1] (lēn, lē′ən), *n.* a legal right to hold property or to have it sold or applied for payment of a claim. [< MF << L *ligāmen* tie, bandage, equiv. to *ligā(re)* (to) tie + *-men* n. suffix of result] —**lien′a·ble,** *adj.*

li·en[2] (lī′ən, -en), *n. Anat.* the spleen. [< L *liēn* SPLEEN] —**li·e·nal** (lī ēn′əl, lī′ə nəl), *adj.*

li·en·ec·to·my (lī′ə nek′tə mē), *n., pl.* **-mies.** *Surg.* splenectomy. [LIEN[2] + -ECTOMY]

li·en·i·tis (lī′ə nī′tis), *n. Pathol.* inflammation of the spleen; splenitis. [LIEN[2] + -ITIS]

li·en·ter·y (lī′ən ter′ē), *n. Pathol.* a form of diarrhea in which the food is discharged undigested or only partly digested. [< ML *lienteria* < Gk *leientería*, lit., smoothbowelness, equiv. to *lei(os)* smooth + *-enteria*, as in *dysentería* DYSENTERY] —**li′en·ter′ic,** *adj.*

lie′ of the land′, *Chiefly Brit.* See **lay of the land.**

Lie·pā·ja (lye′pä yä), *n.* a seaport in W Latvia, in the W Soviet Union in Europe, on the Baltic. 90,000 (1959). German, **Libau.** Russian, **Libava.**

li·er (lī′ər), *n.* one who or that which lies, as in wait or in ambush. [LIE[2] + -ER[1]]

li·erne (lē ûrn′), *n. Archit.* an ornamental vaulting rib other than one springing from a pier or a ridge rib. [< F: lit., binding timber, equiv. to *li(er)* (to) bind (< L *ligāre*) + *-erne* < ?]

Lies·tal (lēs′täl), *n.* a town in and the capital of Basel-Land, in NW Switzerland. 10,262 (1960).

Li·e·tu·va (lē′ə to͞o′vä), *n.* Lithuanian name of **Lithuania.**

lieu (lo͞o), *n.* **1.** *Archaic.* place; stead. **2. in lieu of,** instead of: *He gave us an I.O.U. in lieu of cash.* [< MF; r. ME *liue* < OF *liu* < L *locus* place; see LOCUS]

Lieut., lieutenant.

Lieut. Col., lieutenant colonel.

Lieut. Comdr., lieutenant commander.

lieu·ten·an·cy (lo͞o ten′ən sē), *n., pl.* **-cies. 1.** the office, authority, incumbency, or jurisdiction of a lieutenant. **2.** lieutenants collectively. [late ME *lieutenauncie.* See LIEUTENANT, -ANCY]

lieu·ten·ant (lo͞o ten′ənt; *in Brit. use, except in the navy,* lef ten′ənt), *n.* **1.** *Mil.* **a.** See **first lieutenant. b.** See **second lieutenant. 2.** *Navy.* a commissioned officer ranking between lieutenant junior grade and lieutenant commander. **3.** one who holds an office, civil or military, in subordination to a superior for whom he acts: *If he can't attend, he will send his lieutenant.* [ME < MF, n. use of adj. phrase *lieu tenant* place-holding. See LOCUM TENENS, LIEU, TENANT]

lieuten′ant colo′nel, *Mil.* a commissioned officer ranking next below a colonel and next above a major.

lieuten′ant comman′der, *Navy.* an officer next in rank below a commander and next above a lieutenant senior grade.

lieuten′ant gen′eral, *Mil.* an officer ranking next below a general and next above a major general.

lieuten′ant gov′ernor, 1. *U.S.* a State officer next in rank to the governor, whose place he takes in case of the latter's absence, disability, or death. **2.** *Brit.* a deputy governor.

lieuten′ant jun′ior grade′, *U.S. Navy.* a commissioned officer ranking above an ensign and below a lieutenant.

lieve (lēv), *adv. Dial.* lief.

Li·far (lyi fär′yə), *n.* **Ser·ge** (ser ge′), born 1905, Russian ballet dancer and choreographer.

life (līf), *n., pl.* **lives,** *adj.* —*n.* **1.** the condition that distinguishes animals and plants from inorganic objects and dead organisms, being manifested by growth through metabolism, reproduction, and the power of adaptation to environment through changes originating internally. **2.** the sum of the distinguishing phenomena of plants and animals, esp. metabolism, growth, reproduction, and adaptation to environment. **3.** the animate existence or term of animate existence of an individual: *to risk one's life; a short life and a merry one.* **4.** a corresponding state, existence, or principle of existence conceived of as belonging to the soul: *eternal life.* **5.** the general or universal condition of human existence: *Too bad, but life is like that.* **6.** any specified period of animate existence: *a man in middle life.* **7.** the term of existence, activity, or effectiveness of something inanimate, as a machine, lease, play, etc.: *The life of the car may be 10 years.* **8.** a living being: *several lives were lost.* **9.** living things collectively, whether animals or plants: *the hope of discovering life on other planets; insect life.* **10.** a particular aspect of existence: *He enjoys an active physical life even though he is now ninety-one.* **11.** the course of existence or sum of experiences and actions that constitute a person's existence: *His business has been his entire life.* **12.** a biography: *a life of Churchill.* **13.** animation; liveliness: *a speech full of life.* **14.** resilience; elasticity. **15.** that which makes or keeps something alive; the vivifying or quickening principle: *The life of the treaty has been an increase of mutual understanding and respect.*

16. a mode or manner of existence, as in the world of affairs, society, etc.: *So far her business life has not overlapped her social life.* **17.** the term or extent of authority, popularity, approval, etc.: *the life of the committee; the life of a best seller.* **18.** a prison sentence covering the remaining portion of the offender's animate existence: *The judge gave him life.* **19.** a person who is considered by another to be as precious as life: *She was my love and my life.* **20.** one who or that which enlivens: *the life of the party.* **21.** effervescence or sparkle, as of wines. **22.** pungency or strong, sharp flavor, as of substances when fresh or in good condition. **23.** nature or any of the forms of nature as the model or subject of a work of art: *drawn from life.* **24.** *Baseball.* another chance allowed a batter to bat, as when he reaches a base on a misplay by a fielder. **25.** (in English pool) one of a limited number of shots allowed a player: *Each pool player has three lives at the beginning of the game.* **26. as large as life,** actually; indeed: *There he stood, as large as life.* Also, **as big as life. 27. come to life, a.** to recover consciousness. **b.** to display animation and vigor: *The evening passed, but somehow the party never came to life.* **c.** to appear lifelike: *The characters of the beloved novel came to life on the screen.* **28. for dear life,** with desperate energy or speed: *We ran for dear life, with the dogs at our heels.* Also, **for one's life. 29. for the life of one,** as hard as one tries; even with the utmost effort: *He can't understand it for the life of him.* **30. not on your life,** *Informal.* absolutely not; by no means: *Will I stand for such a thing? Not on your life!* **31. take one's life in one's hands,** knowingly to risk death: *We were warned that we were taking our lives in our hands by going through that swampy area.* **32. to the life,** in perfect imitation; exactly: *The portrait characterized him to the life.*
—*adj.* **33.** for or lasting a lifetime; lifelong: *a life membership in a club; life imprisonment.* **34.** of or pertaining to animate existence: *the life force; life functions.* **35.** working from nature: *a life drawing.* [ME; OE *līf*; c. D *lijf*, G *Leib* body, Icel *līf* life, body; akin to LIVE¹]
—Syn. 13. vivacity, sprightliness, vigor, vitality, verve, spirit, activity, energy. **—Ant. 3.** death. **13.** inertia.

life-and-death (līf′ən deth′), *adj.* ending with the possible death of one of the participants; vital: *The cobra was engaged in a life-and-death struggle with the mongoose.* Also, **life-or-death.**

life′ annu′ity, *Insurance.* any annuity that is contingent upon the survival of the annuitant or annuitants, esp. an annuity that terminates with the death of a single annuitant.

life′ ar′row, *Naut.* an arrowlike projectile for carrying a line for use in maritime rescue operations.

life′ belt′, a beltlike life preserver.

life·blood (līf′blud′), *n.* **1.** the blood, considered as essential to maintain life: *to spill one's lifeblood in war.* **2.** the element that vivifies or animates anything: *Agriculture is the lifeblood of the people.* [LIFE + BLOOD]

life·boat (līf′bōt′), *n.* **1.** a double-ended ship's boat, constructed, mounted, and provisioned so as to be readily able to rescue and maintain persons from a sinking vessel. **2.** a similarly constructed boa used by shore-based rescue services. [LIFE + BOAT]

life·boat·man (līf′bōt′mən), *n., pl.* **-men.** a seaman qualified to take charge of a lifeboat or life raft. [LIFEBOAT + MAN¹]

life′ buoy′, any of variously formed buoyant devices for supporting a person fallen into the water until he can be recovered.

life′ car′, a watertight container used in marine rescue operations, suspended from a hawser and hauled back and forth between a stranded or wrecked vessel and the shore. Also called **ark, safety car.**

life′ cy′cle, *Biol.* the continuous sequence of changes undergone by an organism from one primary form to the development of the same form again.

life′ expect′ancy, the probable life span of an individual or class of persons determined statistically, affected by such factors as heredity, physical condition, nutrition, occupation, etc.

life′ float′, a ring-shaped float of balsa wood or metal tubing, having a grating or network at the center, for rescuing a number of survivors from a foundered vessel.

life·ful (līf′fəl), *adj.* full of life; lively. [ME *lifful.* See LIFE, -FUL]

life-giv·ing (līf′giv′ing), *adj.* imparting, or having the ability to impart, life or vitality; invigorating; vitalizing: *life-giving love and praise.* —**life′-giv′er,** *n.*

life·guard (līf′gärd′), *n.* a person employed, as at a beach or pool, to protect bathers from drowning or other accident. [LIFE + GUARD]

Life′ Guards′, (in Britain) a cavalry regiment forming part of the ceremonial guard of the monarch. Cf. **household cavalry.**

life′ his′tory, *Biol.* **1.** the series of living phenomena exhibited by an organism in the course of its development from inception to death. **2.** See **life cycle.**

life′ insur′ance, insurance providing for payment of a sum of money to a named beneficiary upon the death of the policyholder or to the policyholder should he reach a specified age.

Life′ Is a Dream′, a drama in verse (1635) by Pedro Calderón de la Barca. Spanish, **La Vida Es Sueño.**

life′ jack′et, a sleeveless jacket of buoyant or inflatable construction, for supporting the wearer in deep water and preventing him from drowning. Also called **life vest,** *Brit.,* **air jacket.**

life·less (līf′lis), *adj.* **1.** not endowed with life; inanimate: *lifeless matter.* **2.** destitute of living things: *a lifeless planet.* **3.** deprived of life; dead: *a battlefield strewn with lifeless bodies.* **4.** without animation, liveliness, or spirit; dull; colorless; torpid: *a lifeless performance of a play.* **5.** insensible, as one in a faint. [ME *lifles,* OE *līflēas.* See LIFE, -LESS] —**life′less·ly,** *adv.* —**life′less·ness,** *n.*
—Syn. 1. inorganic. **3.** defunct. See **dead. 4.** inactive, inert, passive; sluggish; spiritless. **—Ant. 1, 3.** living. **4.** lively.

life·like (līf′līk′), *adj.* resembling or simulating real life: *a lifelike bust.* [LIFE + -LIKE] —**life′like′ness,** *n.*

life′ line′, **1.** a line, fired across a vessel, by means of which a hawser for a breeches buoy may be hauled aboard. **2.** a line or rope for saving life, as one attached to a lifeboat. **3.** any of various lines running above the decks, spars, etc., of a vessel to give seamen something to grasp when there is danger of falling or being washed away. **4.** a wire safety rope supported by stanchions about 18 to 30 inches above the deck at the rails of a yacht. **5.** the line by which a diver is lowered and raised. **6.** any of several anchored lines used by swimmers for support. **7.** a route over which supplies must be sent to sustain an area otherwise isolated: *The snow storm cut off the village's life line to the city.* **8.** assistance at a critical time.

life·long (līf′lông′, -long′), *adj.* lasting or continuing through life: *lifelong regret.* [LIFE + LONG¹ (adv.)]

life′ mask′, a cast of the face of a living person. Cf. **death mask.**

life′ net′, a strong net or the like held by firemen or others to catch persons jumping from a burning building.

life′ of Ri′ley, *Slang.* an easy or enjoyable mode of life: *Since getting that promotion, he's led the life of Riley.* [perh. after the Reilly mentioned in the title of some song or songs popular around 1900 ("The Best of the House Is None Too Good for Reilly")]

Life′ of Sam′uel John′son, The, a biography (1791) by James Boswell.

Life′ on the Mississip′pi, an autobiographical narrative (1883) by Mark Twain.

life-or-death (līf′ər deth′), *adj.* life-and-death.

life′ plant′, See **air plant** (def. 2).

life′ preserv′er, **1.** a buoyant jacket, belt, or other like device for saving persons in the water from sinking and drowning. **2.** *Brit. Slang.* a weapon, esp. a short stick with a weighted head; blackjack.

lif·er (lī′fər), *n. Slang.* a person sentenced to or serving a term of life imprisonment. [LIFE + -ER¹]

life′ raft′, a raft for use in emergencies, as when a ship must be abandoned.

life′ rock′et, a rocket for carrying a line between a wrecked or stranded vessel and the shore.

life·sav·er (līf′sā′vər), *n.* **1.** a person who rescues another from danger of death, esp. from drowning. **2.** *Chiefly Brit.* a lifeguard. **3.** *Informal.* one who or that which saves a person, as from a difficult situation, critical moment, or the like: *That money was a lifesaver.* [LIFE + SAVER] —**life′sav′ing,** *adj., n.*

Life′saving Serv′ice, a private organization or government agency for general marine rescue operations.

life′ sen′tence, a sentence condemning a convicted felon to spend the rest of his life in prison. Cf. **death sentence.**

life-size (līf′sīz′), *adj.* of the natural size of an object in life; of the size of a living original: *a life-size picture; a life-size statue.* Also, **life′-sized′.**

life′ span′, **1.** the longest period over which the life of any plant or animal organism or species may extend, according to the available biological knowledge concerning it. **2.** the longevity of an individual.

life′ style′, a person's typical approach to living, including moral attitudes, preferred entertainment, fads, fashions, etc. Also, **life·style** (līf′stīl′).

life′ ta′ble, *Insurance.* See **mortality table.**

life·time (līf′tīm′), *n.* **1.** the time that the life of someone or something continues; the term of a life: *peace within our lifetime.* —*adj.* **2.** for the duration of a person's life: *He has a lifetime subscription to the magazine.* [ME *liftime.* See LIFE, TIME]

life′ vest′, See **life jacket.**

life·work (līf′wûrk′), *n.* the complete or principal work, labor, or task of a lifetime. [LIFE + WORK]

LIFO (lī′fō). See **last-in, first-out.**

lift (lift), *v.t.* **1.** to move or bring (something) upward from the ground or other support to some higher position; hoist. **2.** to raise or direct upward: *He lifted his arm in a gesture of farewell; to lift one's head.* **3.** to remove or rescind by an official act, as a ban, curfew, or tax: *a court decision to lift the ban on the book.* **4.** to stop or put an end to (a boycott, blockade, etc.): *The citizenry will have to conserve food and water until the siege against the city is lifted.* **5.** to hold up or display on high. **6.** to raise in rank, condition, estimation, etc.; elevate or exalt (sometimes used reflexively): *His first book lifted him from obscurity. By hard work they lifted themselves from poverty.* **7.** to make audible or louder, as the voice or something voiced: *The congregation lifted their voices in song.* **8.** to plagiarize: *Whole passages had been lifted from the book.* **9.** *Slang.* to steal, as goods or money, esp. from a store. **10.** airlift (def. 5). **11.** to remove (plants and tubers) from the ground as after harvest or for transplanting. **12.** *Horol.* (of an escape wheel) to move (a pallet) by moving along its outer, oblique face. **13.** *U.S.* to pay off (a mortgage, promissory note, etc.). **14.** *Golf.* to pick up (the ball), as to move it from an unplayable lie. **15.** to perform a face lifting on. **16.** *Shipbuilding.* **a.** to transfer (measurements and the like) from a drawing, model, etc., to a piece being built. **b.** to form (a templet) according to a drawing, model, etc. **17.** to cease temporarily from directing (fire or bombardment) on an objective or area: *They lifted the fire when the infantry began to advance.* **18.** *Fox Hunting.* to take (hounds) from the line of a fox to where it has just been seen.
—*v.i.* **19.** to go up; give to upward pressure: *The box is too heavy to lift. The lid won't lift.* **20.** to pull or strain upward in the effort to lift something: *to lift at a heavy weight.* **21.** to move upward or rise; rise and disperse, as clouds, fog, etc. **22.** to rise to view above the horizon when approached, as land seen from the sea.
—*n.* **23.** the act of lifting or raising, or of rising: *the lift of a hand.* **24.** the distance that anything rises or is raised: *a lift of 20 feet per second; a lift of 20 feet between canal locks.* **25.** a lifting or raising force: *A kite depends on the wind to act as its lift.* **26.** the weight, load, or quantity lifted. **27.** an act or instance of helping to climb or mount: *He gave her a lift onto the wagon.* **28.** a ride in a vehicle, esp. one given to a pedestrian: *Can you give me a lift across town?* **29.** a feeling of exaltation or uplift: *Their visit gave me quite a lift.* **30.** a device or apparatus for lifting: *a hydraulic lift.* **31.** *Skiing.* **a.** See **ski lift. b.** See **chair lift. 32.** *Chiefly Brit.* **a.** an elevator. **b.** any device used to lift or elevate, as a dumbwaiter, hoist, or the like. **33.** a rise or elevation of ground: *a sudden lift toward the top of the hill.* **34.** *Aeron.* the component of the aerodynamic force exerted by the air on an airfoil, having a direction perpendicular to the direction of motion and causing an aircraft to stay aloft. **35.** *Naut.* **a.** the capacity of a cargo ship measured in dead-weight tons. **b.** See **topping lift. 36.** one of the layers of leather forming the heel of a boot or shoe. **37.** *Mining.* the slice or thickness of ore mined in one operation. **38.** *Building Trades.* the height of the quantity of concrete poured into a form at one time. **39.** *Naval Archit.* any of the horizontal planks forming a type of half model (**lift′ mod′el),** able to be removed and measured as a guide to laying out the water lines of the vessel at full scale. **40.** *Typesetting.* fat (def. 25). **41.** *Print.* the quantity of paper loaded into or removed from a press or other printing machine at one time. **42.** *Horol.* **a.** the displacement of a pallet by an escape wheel which has been unlocked. **b.** the angle through which the pallet passes when so displaced. **43.** airlift (defs. 1–3). [ME *lifte(n)* < Scand; cf. Icel *lypta,* c. G *lüften,* lit., to take aloft; see LOFT] —**lift′a·ble,** *adj.* —**lift′er,** *n.*
—Syn. 1. elevate. See **raise. —Ant. 1.** lower.

lift′ bolt′, *Naut.* an eyebolt, as on a yardarm, to which a topping lift is secured.

lift′-drag′ ra′tio (lift′drag′), *Aeron.* the ratio of the lift to the drag of an airfoil.

lift′ing sail′, *Naut.* a sail that when filled tends to raise the hull of a vessel (opposed to *driving sail*).

lift-off (lift′ôf′, -of′), *n. Aeron., Rocketry.* **1.** the action of an aircraft in becoming airborne or of a rocket in rising from its launching site under its own power. **2.** the instant when such action occurs. [n. use of v. phrase *lift off*]

lift′-off hinge′. See **loose-joint hinge.**

lift′ pump′, a pump that merely lifts or raises a liquid (distinguished from *force pump*).

lift-slab (lift′slab′), *adj.* noting or pertaining to a technique of constructing multi-story buildings in which all horizontal slabs are cast at ground level and, when ready, are raised into position by hydraulic jacks.

lift′ truck′, a dolly or truck for lifting and moving esp. palletized loads.

lig·a·ment (lig′ə mənt), *n.* **1.** *Anat.* a band of tissue, usually white and fibrous, serving to connect bones, hold organs in place, etc. **2.** a tie or bond: *The desire for freedom is a ligament uniting all peoples.* [< ML *ligāmentum* ligament, L: band, equiv. to *ligā(re)* (to) tie + *-mentum* -MENT]

lig·a·men·tous (lig′ə men′təs), *adj.* pertaining to, of the nature of, or forming a ligament. Also, **lig·a·men·tal** (lig′ə men′tᵊl), **lig·a·men·ta·ry** (lig′ə men′tə rē). [LIGAMENT + -OUS] —**lig′a·men′tous·ly,** *adv.*

lig·a·men·tum (lig′ə men′təm), *n., pl.* **-ta** (-tə). *Anat.* ligament.

li·gan (lī′gən), *n. Law.* lagan.

li·gate (lī′gāt), *v.t.,* **-gat·ed, -gat·ing.** to bind with or as with a ligature; tie up (a bleeding artery or the like). [< L *ligāt(us)* tied, bound (ptp. of *ligāre*); see -ATE¹]

li·ga·tion (lī gā′shən), *n.* **1.** the act of ligating, esp. of surgically tying up a bleeding artery. **2.** anything that binds or ties up; ligature. [< LL *ligātiōn-* (s. of *ligātiō*), equiv. to L *ligāt(us)* (see LIGATE) + *-iōn-* -ION] —**lig·a·tive** (lig′ə tiv), *adj.*

lig·a·ture (lig′ə chər, -cho͝or′), *n., v.,* **-tured, -tur·ing.** —*n.* **1.** the act of binding or tying up: *The ligature of the artery was done with skill and expertness.* **2.** anything that serves for binding or tying up, as a band, bandage, or cord. **3.** a tie or bond: *the ligature of mutual need that bound them together.* **4.** *Print., Writing.* a stroke or bar connecting two letters. **5.** *Print.* a character or type combining two or more letters, as ﬁ, ﬄ. **6.** *Music.* **a.** slur. **b.** a group of notes connected by a slur. **c.** a metal band for securing the reed of a clarinet or saxophone to the mouthpiece. **7.** *Surg.* a thread or wire for constriction of blood vessels or for removing tumors by strangulation. —*v.t.* **8.** to bind with a ligature; tie up; ligate. [late ME < LL *ligātūra.* See LIGATE, -URE]

li·geance (lī′jəns, lē′-), *n.* **1.** *Chiefly Law.* the territory subject to a sovereign or liege lord. **2.** *Archaic.* allegiance. [ME < MF; see LIEGE, -ANCE]

Li·ge·ia (lī jē′ə), *n.* a short story (1838) by Edgar Allan Poe.

li·ger (lī′gər), *n.* the offspring of a male lion and a female tiger. [LI(ON) + TI(GER)]

light¹ (līt), *n., adj., v.,* **light·ed** or **lit, light·ing.** —*n.* **1.** that which makes things visible or affords illumination: *All colors depend on light.* **2.** *Physics.* **a.** Also called **luminous energy, radiant energy.** electromagnetic radiation to which the organs of sight react, ranging in wavelength from about 4000 to 7700 angstrom units and propagated at a speed of about 186,300 miles per second. It is considered variously as a wave, corpuscular, or quantum phenomenon. **b.** a similar form of radiant energy which does not affect the retina, as ultraviolet or infrared rays. **3.** the sensation produced by stimulation of the organs of sight. **4.** an illuminating agent or source, as the sun, a lamp, or a beacon. **5.** the radiance or illumination from a particular source: *the light of a candle.* **6.** the illumination from the sun; daylight: *We awoke at the first light.* **7.** daybreak or dawn: *when light appeared in the east.* **8.** daytime: *Summer has more hours of light.* **9.** a measure or supply of light; illumination: *The wall cuts off our light.* **10.** a particular light or illumination in which an object seen takes on a certain appearance: *viewing the portrait in dim light.* **11.** *Art.* **a.** the effect of light falling on an object or scene as represented in a picture. **b.** one of the brightest parts of a picture. **12.** the aspect in which a thing appears or is regarded: *Try to look at the situation in a more cheerful light.* **13.** a gleam or sparkle, as in the eyes. **14.** a means of igniting, as a spark, flame, match, or the like: *Could you give me a light?* **15.** the state of being visible, exposed to view, or revealed to public notice or knowledge; limelight: *Stardom has placed her in the light.* **16.** *Archit.* **a.** Also called **day.** one compartment of a window or window sash. **b.** a window, esp. a small one. **17.** mental or spiritual illumination or enlightenment: *the light of truth.* **18. lights,** the information, ideas, or mental capacities possessed: *to act according to one's lights.* **19.** a person who is an illuminating or shining example; luminary: *He became one of the leading lights of Restoration drama.* **20.** a lighthouse. **21.** a traffic light: *Don't cross till the light changes.* **22.** *Archaic.* the eyesight. **23. bring to light,** to discover or reveal: *The excavations brought to light the remnants of an ancient civilization.*

24. come to light, to be discovered; be revealed: *Some previously undiscovered letters have lately come to light.* **25. hide one's light under a bushel,** to obscure or suppress one's talents. **26. in a good** (or **bad**) **light,** under favorable (or unfavorable) circumstances: *She worshiped him, but then she'd only seen him in a good light.* **27. in the light of,** taking into account; considering: *It was necessary to review the decision in the light of recent developments.* **28. see the light, a.** to come into being. **b.** to be made public. **c.** to begin to accept or understand a point of view one formerly opposed: *Her father was opposed to her attending an out-of-town college, but he finally saw the light.* **29. shed** or **throw light on,** to clarify; clear up: *His deathbed confession threw light on a mystery of long standing.* **30. stand in one's own light,** to damage one's reputation or chances for success through imprudent behavior: *Through such a scandal during his term of office he has unquestionably stood in his own light.* —*adj.* **31.** having light or illumination; well-lighted: *the lightest room in the entire house.* **32.** pale, whitish, or not deep or dark in color: *a light blue.* —*v.t.* **33.** to set burning, as a candle, lamp, fire, match, cigarette, etc.; kindle; ignite. **34.** to turn or switch on (an electric light): *One flick of the master switch lights all the lamps in the room.* **35.** to give light to; furnish with light or illumination: *A huge rose window lights the nave of the church. The room is lighted by two large chandeliers.* **36.** to make (an area or object) bright with or as with light (often fol. by *up*): *Hundreds of candles lighted up the ballroom.* **37.** to cause (the face, surroundings, etc.) to brighten, esp. with joy, animation, or the like (often fol. by *up*): *A smile lit up her face. Her presence lighted up the room.* **38.** to guide or conduct with a light: *a candle to light you to bed.* —*v.i.* **39.** to take fire or become kindled: *The damp wood refused to light.* **40.** to ignite a cigar, cigarette, or pipe for purposes of smoking (usually fol. by *up*): *He took out a pipe and lighted up before speaking.* **41.** to become bright, as with light or color (often fol. by *up*): *The sky lights up at sunset.* **42.** to brighten with animation or joy, as the face, eyes, etc. (often fol. by *up*). [ME; OE *lēoht;* c. D *licht*, G *Licht*, Goth *liuhath;* akin to Icel *ljōs*, L *lūx*, Gk *leukós*] —**light′ful,** *adj.* —**light′ful·ly,** *adv.*

light[2] (līt), *adj.* **1.** of little weight; not heavy: *a light load.* **2.** of little weight in proportion to bulk; of low specific gravity: *a light metal.* **3.** of less than the usual or average weight: *light clothing.* **4.** weighing less than the proper or standard amount: *to be caught using light weights in trade.* **5.** of small amount, force, intensity, etc.: *light trading on the stock market; a light rain; light sleep.* **6.** using or applying little or slight pressure or force: *The child sat petting the puppy with light, gentle strokes.* **7.** not distinct; faint: *The writing on the page had become light and hard to read.* **8.** easy to endure, deal with, or perform; not difficult or burdensome: *She has been given some light duties.* **9.** not very profound, serious, or heavy; amusing or entertaining: *light reading.* **10.** of little importance or consequence; trivial: *The loss of his job was no light matter.* **11.** easily digested: *light food.* **12.** not heavy or strong: *For luncheon I prefer a light wine.* **13.** spongy or well leavened, as bread. **14.** (of soil) containing much sand; porous or crumbly. **15.** slender or delicate in form or appearance: *a light, graceful figure.* **16.** airy or buoyant in movement: *When she dances, she's as light as a feather.* **17.** nimble or agile: *light fingers; light on one's feet.* **18.** free from trouble, sorrow, or worry; carefree: *a light heart.* **19.** cheerful; gay: *a light laugh.* **20.** characterized by lack of proper seriousness; frivolous: *light conduct.* **21.** sexually wanton; promiscuous; loose: *light women.* **22.** easily swayed; changeable; volatile: *a heart light of love; His is a life of a man light of purpose.* **23.** dizzy; slightly delirious: *She gets light on one martini.* **24.** *Mil.* lightly armed or equipped: *light infantry.* **25.** having little or no cargo, encumbrance, or the like; not burdened: *a light freighter drawing little water.* **26.** adapted by small weight or slight build for small loads or swift movement: *The grocer bought a light truck for deliveries.* **27.** *Naut.* noting any sail of light canvas set only in moderate or calm weather, as a royal, skysail, studdingsail, gaff topsail, spinnaker, etc. **28.** (of wind) having a speed up to seven miles per hour. Cf. **light air, light breeze. 29.** *Phonet.* **a.** having a less than normally strong pronunciation, as of a vowel or syllable. **b.** (of *l*-sounds) resembling a front vowel in quality; clear: *French* l *is lighter than English* l. **30.** *Poker.* being in debt to the pot: *He's light ten chips.* **31. make light of,** to treat as unimportant or trivial: *They made light of their achievements.* —*adv.* **32.** lightly: *to travel light.* **33.** with no load or cargo hauled or carried: *a locomotive running light to its roundhouse.* [ME; OE *lēoht*, *līht;* c. D *licht*, G *leicht*, Icel *lēttr*, Goth *leihts*]
—**Syn. 7.** indistinct; faded. **10.** trifling, inconsiderable. **18.** cheery, happy. **20.** flighty. **22.** light-hearted, giddy. —**Ant. 1.** heavy. **9.** deep.

light[3] (līt), *v.i.*, **light·ed** or **lit, light·ing. 1.** to get down or descend, as from a horse or a vehicle. **2.** to come to rest, as on a spot or thing; fall or settle upon; land: *The bird lighted on the branch. My eye lighted on some friends in the crowd:* **3.** to come by chance, happen, or hit (usually fol. by *on* or *upon*): *to light on a clue; to light on an ideal picnic spot.* **4.** to fall, as a stroke, weapon, vengeance, choice, etc., on a place or person: *The choice lighted upon our candidate.* **5. light into,** *Informal.* to make a physical or verbal attack on: *He would light into anyone with the slightest provocation.* **6. light out,** *Slang.* to leave quickly; depart hurriedly: *He lighted out of here as fast as his legs would carry him.* [ME *lihte(n)*, OE *līhtan* to make light, relieve of a weight; see LIGHT[2]]

light′ adapta′tion, *Ophthalm.* the reflex adaptation of the eye to bright light, consisting of an increase in the number of functioning cones, accompanied by a decrease in the number of functioning rods (opposed to *dark adaptation*).

light′ air′, *Meteorol.* (on the Beaufort scale) a wind of 1–3 miles per hour.

light′ and shade′ sur′face. See **surface of light and shade.**

light-armed (līt′ärmd′), *adj.* carrying light weapons: *light-armed troops.*

light′ artil′lery, *Mil.* **1.** guns and howitzers of small caliber. **2.** *U.S.* guns and howitzers of caliber up to and including 105 millimeters. Cf. **heavy artillery** (def. 2), **medium artillery.**

light-beard·ed (līt′bēr′did), *adj.* **1.** having a beard that is light in color. **2.** having a beard that is not heavy or thick.

light·boat (līt′bōt′), *n.* a small, unattended vessel carrying a light for use as a navigational aid. [LIGHT[1] + BOAT]

light′ bomb′er, *Mil.* a small airplane designed to carry light bomb loads relatively short distances, esp. one having a gross loaded weight of less than 100,000 pounds. Cf. **heavy bomber, medium bomber.**

light′ box′, a boxlike object having a uniformly lighted surface, as of ground glass, against which films or transparencies can be held for examination.

light′ breeze′, *Meteorol.* (on the Beaufort scale) a wind of 4–7 miles per hour. Cf. **breeze**[1] (def. 2).

light′ bridge′, *Theat.* See under **bridge**[1] (def. 18a).

light′ bulb′, an incandescent bulb.

light′ colo′nel, *U.S. Mil. Slang.* a lieutenant colonel.

light′ cream′, sweet cream with less butterfat than heavy cream.

light′ cruis′er, a naval cruiser having six-inch guns as its main armament. Cf. **heavy cruiser.**

light′ displace′ment, *Naut.* the weight of a vessel with all its permanent equipment, excluding the weight of cargo, persons, ballast, dunnage, and fuel, but usually including the weight of permanent ballast and water used to operate steam machinery. Also called **light weight.**

light′ draft′, *Naut.* the draft of a vessel at its light displacement.

light·en[1] (līt′ən), *v.i.* **1.** to become lighter or less dark; brighten: *The sky lightened after the storm.* **2.** to flash as or like lightning (often used impersonally with *it* as subject): *It thundered and lightened for hours.* **3.** to brighten or light up, as the eyes, features, etc.: *Her face lightened when she heard the good news.* **4.** *Archaic.* to shine, gleam, or be bright: *steel blades lightening in the sun.* —*v.t.* **5.** to give light to; illuminate: *A full moon lightened the road.* **6.** to brighten (the eyes, features, etc.): *A large smile lightened his face.* **7.** to make lighter or less dark: *Add white to lighten the paint.* **8.** *Obs.* enlighten. **9.** *Obs.* to flash or emit like lightning (usually fol. by *out, forth,* or *down*): *eyes that lightened forth implacable hatred.* [ME; see LIGHT[1], -EN[1]] —**light′en·er,** *n.*

light·en[2] (līt′ən), *v.t.* **1.** to make lighter in weight: *to lighten the load on a donkey's back.* **2.** to lessen the load of or upon: *to lighten a cargo ship.* **3.** to make less burdensome or oppressive; mitigate: *to lighten taxes; to lighten someone's cares.* **4.** to cheer or gladden: *Such news lightens my heart.* —*v.i.* **5.** to become less severe, stringent, or harsh; ease up: *Border inspections have lightened recently.* **6.** to become less heavy, cumbersome, burdensome, oppressive, etc.: *His worries seem to have lightened somewhat.* **7.** to become less gloomy; perk up: *People's spirits usually lighten when spring arrives.* [ME; see LIGHT[2], -EN[1]]
—**Syn. 3.** ease, lessen, reduce. —**Ant. 3.** aggravate.

light·en·ing (līt′ən ing), *n. Med.* the descent of the uterus into the pelvic cavity, occurring toward the end of pregnancy, changing the contour of the abdomen and facilitating breathing. [LIGHTEN[2] + -ING[1]]

light′ening hole′, *Building Trades, Shipbuilding.* a hole left by the cutting away of metal from the web of a metal structural member to lessen its weight.

light·er[1] (lī′tər), *n.* one who or that which lights or ignites. **2.** a mechanical device used in lighting cigars, cigarettes, or pipes for smoking. [LIGHT[1], -ER[1]]

light·er[2] (lī′tər), *n.* **1.** a vessel, commonly an unpowered, flat-bottomed barge, used in lightening or unloading and in loading ships, or in transporting goods for short distances. —*v.t.* **2.** to convey in or as in a lighter. [late ME < MD *lichter (recorded in 16th century). See LIGHT[2], -ER[1]]

light·er·age (lī′tər ij), *n.* **1.** the use of lighters in loading and unloading ships and in transporting goods for short distances. **2.** a fee paid for lighter service. [late ME; see LIGHTER[2], -AGE]

light·er·man (lī′tər mən), *n., pl.* **-men.** a person who navigates a lighter; bargeman. [LIGHTER[2] + MAN[1]]

light·er-than-air (lī′tər than âr′), *adj. Aeron.* **1.** of lower specific gravity than the air, as balloons or dirigibles. **2.** of or pertaining to lighter-than-air craft.

light·face (līt′fās′), *Print.* —*n.* **1.** a type characterized by thin lines. —*adj.* **2.** (of printed matter) set in lightface. Cf. **boldface.** [LIGHT[2] + FACE] —**light·faced** (līt′fāst′), *adj.*

This is a sample of lightface.

light·fast (līt′fast′, -fäst′), *adj.* not affected by light, esp. sunlight; colorfast. [LIGHT[1] + FAST[1]] —**light′fast′ness,** *n.*

light-fin·gered (līt′fing′gərd), *adj.* having nimble fingers, esp. in picking pockets; inclined to pilfer or steal; thievish; dishonest.

light-foot·ed (līt′fo͝ot′id), *adj.* stepping lightly or nimbly; light of foot; nimble. [late ME *lyght foted*] —**light′-foot′ed·ly,** *adv.* —**light′-foot′ed·ness,** *n.*

light-hand·ed (līt′han′did), *adj.* **1.** having a light touch; handling things delicately and deftly. **2.** having the hands lightly or only slightly encumbered, as with parcels or bundles. **3.** short-handed. [ME *lyghte handyd*] —**light′-hand′ed·ly,** *adv.* —**light′-hand′ed·ness,** *n.*

light·head (līt′hed′), *n. Archaic.* a person who is frivolous; a light-headed person. [LIGHT[2] + HEAD]

light-head·ed (līt′hed′id), *adj.* **1.** having or showing a frivolous or volatile disposition; thoughtless: *light-headed persons.* **2.** giddy, dizzy, or delirious: *After two drinks she begins to feel light-headed.* —**light′-head′ed·ly,** *adv.* —**light′-head′ed·ness,** *n.*

light-heart·ed (līt′här′tid), *adj.* carefree; cheerful; gay; debonair: *We all loved her infectious, light-hearted laugh.* Also, **light′heart′ed.** [late ME *ligt-herted*] —**light′-heart′ed·ly, light′heart′ed·ly,** *adv.* —**light′-heart′ed·ness, light′heart′ed·ness,** *n.*
—**Syn.** cheery, joyous, joyful, blithe, happy, glad, merry, jovial, jocund. —**Ant.** cheerless, melancholy, gloomy.

light′ heav′yweight, a boxer or other contestant intermediate in weight between a middleweight and a heavyweight, esp. a professional boxer weighing up to 175 pounds.

light′ horse′, cavalry carrying light arms and equipment.

Light′-Horse′ Har′ry (līt′hôrs′), epithet of Henry Lee.

light-horse·man (līt′hôrs′mən), *n., pl.* **-men.** a light-armed cavalry soldier. [LIGHT HORSE + MAN[1]]

light·house (līt′hous′), *n., pl.* **-hous·es** (-hou′ziz). **1.** a tower or other structure displaying a light or lights for the guidance of mariners. **2.** Also called **light tower, sidelight castle, sidelight tower.** either of two cylindrical metal towers placed forward on the forecastle of the main deck of a vessel, esp. a sailing vessel, to house the port and starboard running lights. [LIGHT[1] + HOUSE]

Lighthouse (def. 1)

light′house clock′, an American mantel clock of the early 19th century, having the dial and works exposed beneath a glass dome on a tapered, cylindrical body.

light′house cof′feepot, a coffeepot of the late 17th and 18th centuries, having a tapering, circular body with a domed lid.

light′house tube′, *Electronics,* a vacuum tube with the electrodes arranged in parallel layers closely spaced, giving a relatively high-power output at high frequencies. Also called **disk-seal tube, megatron.**

Light′ in Au′gust, a novel (1932) by William Faulkner.

light·ing (lī′ting), *n.* **1.** the act of igniting or illuminating: *the lighting of many candles; the annual lighting of the Christmas tree.* **2.** the arrangement of lights to achieve particular effects: *to work out the lighting for one's living room.* **3.** an effect achieved by the arrangement of lights: *Several critics praised the lighting of the play.* **4.** the science, theory, or method of achieving particular effects by the use of lights: *At the Yale Drama School he majored in lighting.* **5.** the way light falls upon a face, object, etc., esp. in a picture. [ME *lightinge*, OE *lihting*. See LIGHT[1], -ING[1]]

light·ish[1] (lī′tish), *adj.* rather light in color. [LIGHT[1] + -ISH[1]]

light·ish[2] (lī′tish), *adj.* rather light in weight. [LIGHT[2] + -ISH[1]]

light·less (līt′lis), *adj.* **1.** without light or lights; receiving no light; dark. **2.** giving no light. [ME *lihtles*, OE *lēohtlēas*. See LIGHT[1], -LESS] —**light′less·ness,** *n.*

light′ line′, *Naut.* the line or level to which a vessel sinks when fully supplied with fuel and ballast but without cargo. Also called **light′ load′ line′.**

light·ly (līt′lē), *adv.* **1.** with little weight, force, intensity, etc.: *to press lightly on a door bell.* **2.** to but a small amount or degree; slightly: *lightly fried eggs.* **3.** easily; without trouble or effort: *Lightly come, lightly go.* **4.** cheerfully; without complaining: *to take bad news lightly.* **5.** frivolously; flippantly: *to behave lightly.* **6.** without due consideration or reason (often used negatively): *an offer not to be refused lightly.* **7.** nimbly; quickly: *to leap lightly aside.* **8.** with a lack of concern; indifferently; slightingly: *to think lightly of one's achievements.* **9.** airily; buoyantly: *flags floating lightly.* [ME *lightli*, OE *lēohtlīce*. See LIGHT[2], -LY]

light′ machine′ gun′, *Mil.* any air-cooled machine gun having a caliber not greater than .30 inch.

light′ meat′. See **white meat** (defs. 1, 2).

light′ me′ter. See **exposure meter.**

light-mind·ed (līt′mīn′did), *adj.* having or showing a lack of serious purpose, attitude, etc.; characterized by levity; frivolous; trifling: *to be in a light-minded mood.* —**light′-mind′ed·ly,** *adv.* —**light′-mind′ed·ness,** *n.*

light′ min′eral, *Geol.* any rock-forming mineral that has a specific gravity of less than 2.8 and is generally light in color. Cf. **dark mineral.**

light′ min′eral oil′, *Chem.* See under **mineral oil.**

light·ness[1] (līt′nis), *n.* **1.** the state or quality of being light or illuminated. **2.** thin or pale coloration. **3.** the relative degree to which an object reflects light, esp. light of complementary or nearly complementary colors. [ME *lightnes*, OE *līhtnes*. See LIGHT[1], -NESS]

light·ness[2] (līt′nis), *n.* **1.** the state or quality of being light in weight: *the amazing lightness of the new metal.* **2.** the quality of being agile, nimble, or graceful. **3.** lack of pressure or burdensomeness. **4.** gaiety of manner, speech, style, etc.; cheerfulness: *His lightness was just what the party needed.* **5.** lack of seriousness; levity in actions, thoughts, or speech: *That kind of lightness seemed out of place.* [ME *lightnesse*. See LIGHT[2], -NESS]
—**Syn. 2.** agility, grace, nimbleness, sprightliness.

light·ning (līt′ning), *n., v.,* **-ninged, -ning,** *adj.* —*n.* **1.** a luminous, electric discharge in the atmosphere caused by the electric-charge separation produced in cumulonimbus, or thunderstorm, clouds. —*v.i.* **2.** to emit a flash or flashes of lightning (often used impersonally with *it* as subject): *If it starts to lightning, we'd better go inside.* —*adj.* **3.** of, pertaining to, or resembling lightning, esp. in regard to speed of movement: *lightning flashes; lightning speed.* [ME, var. of lightening. See LIGHTEN[1], -ING[1]]

light′ning arrest′er, *Elect.* a device for preventing damage to radio, telephonic, or other electric equipment from lightning or other high-voltage currents, using spark gaps to carry the current to the ground without passing through the device. Also called **arrester.**

light′ning bug′, firefly.

light′ning rod′, a rodlike conductor installed to divert lightning away from a structure by providing a direct path to the ground.

light-o'-love (līt′ə luv′), *n.* a woman inconstant in love; wanton. Also, **light-of-love** (līt′ə luv′).

light′ op′era, operetta.

light′ quan′tum, *Physics.* photon.

lights (līts), *n.pl.* the lungs, esp. of sheep, pigs, etc. [ME *lihte*, *lightes*, n. use of *liht* LIGHT[2]]

light·ship (līt′ship′), *n.* a ship anchored in a specific location and displaying a light or lights for the guidance of mariners. [LIGHT[1] + SHIP]

light·some[1] (līt′səm), *adj.* **1.** light, esp. in form, appearance, or movement; airy; buoyant; agile; nimble; graceful. **2.** cheerful; gay; light-hearted. **3.** frivolous; changeable. [late ME *lyghtesum* (c. MHG *līhtsam*). See LIGHT[2], -SOME[1]] —**light′some·ly,** *adv.* —**light′some·ness,** *n.*

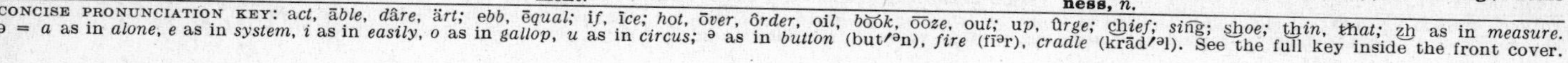
CONCISE PRONUNCIATION KEY: *act, āble, dâre, ärt; ebb, ēqual; if, īce; hot, ōver, ôrder, oil, bo͝ok, o͞oze, out; up, ûrge; chief; sing; shoe; thin, that; zh as in measure.* ə = *a* as in *alone*, *e* as in *system*, *i* as in *easily*, *o* as in *gallop*, *u* as in *circus*; ə as in *button* (but′ən), *fire* (fīər), *cradle* (krād′əl). See the full key inside the front cover.

light·some[2] (līt′səm), *adj.* **1.** emitting or reflecting light; luminous. **2.** well-lighted; illuminated; bright. [late ME *lyghtesum.* See LIGHT[1], -SOME[1]] —**light′some·ly,** *adv.* —**light′some·ness,** *n.*

lights′ out′, *Chiefly Mil.* a signal, usually by drum or bugle, that all or certain camp or barracks lights are to be extinguished for the night.

light-struck (līt′struk′), *adj.* *Photog.* (of a film or the like) injured by accidental exposure to light.

light′ tow′er, *Naut.* lighthouse (def. 2).

light′ valve′, *Elect.* a light-transmitting device having transmissions that vary in accordance with an electric input, such as voltage, current, an electron beam, etc., used chiefly for recording sound on motion-picture film.

light′ verse′, verse that is written to entertain, amuse, or please, usually by the perfection of subtlety of its form rather than by its profundity or seriousness.

light′ weight′, *Naut.* See **light displacement.**

light·weight (līt′wāt′), *adj.* **1.** light in weight. **2.** being lighter in weight, texture, etc., than another item or object of identical use, quality, or function: *a lightweight topcoat; a lightweight alloy for ship construction.* **3.** without seriousness of purpose; trivial or trifling: *acceptable as lightweight reading.* **4.** of or pertaining to a lightweight: *He's the new lightweight contender.* **5.** (of a horse, esp. a hunter) able to carry up to 165 pounds. —*n.* **6.** a person of less than average weight. **7.** *Informal.* a person who, because of a weak character, inferior intelligence, or the like, is of little influence, importance, or effect. **8.** a boxer or other contestant intermediate in weight between a featherweight and a welterweight, esp. a professional boxer weighing up to 135 pounds. [LIGHT[2] + WEIGHT]

light·wood (līt′wo͝od′), *n.* *Southern U.S.* **1.** wood used in lighting a fire; kindling. **2.** resinous pine wood. **3.** See **black acacia.** [LIGHT[1] + WOOD[1]]

light-year (līt′yēr′, -yēr′), *n.* *Astron.* the distance traversed by light in one mean solar year, about 5,880,000,000,000 miles: used as a unit in measuring stellar distances. *Abbr.:* lt-yr [LIGHT[1] + YEAR]

lign-, var. of **ligni-** before a vowel: *lignite.*

lign·al·oes (lī nal′ōz, lig-), *n.* (*construed as sing.*) agalloch. [ME *ligne aloes* < ML *lignum aloēs* wood of the aloe. See LIGNI, ALOE]

ligne (lēn; *Fr.* lēn′yə), *n., pl.* **lignes** (lēnz; *Fr.* lēn′yə). **1.** (in Swiss watchmaking) a unit equal to 0.0888 inch or 2.2558 millimeters, divided into 12 douziemes: used mainly to gauge the thickness of a movement. **2.** line[1] (def. 46). [< F: LINE[1]]

lig·ne·ous (lig′nē əs), *adj.* of the nature of or resembling wood; woody. [< L *ligneus* of wood. See LIGN-, -EOUS]

ligni-, a learned borrowing from Latin meaning "wood," used in the formation of compound words: *ligniform.* Also, **lign-, ligno-.** [< L, comb. form repr. *lignum* wood]

lig·nic·o·lous (lig nik′ə ləs), *adj.* *Bot.* growing on or in wood, as certain mosses, lichens, or fungi. [LIGNI- + -COLOUS]

lig·ni·form (lig′nə fôrm′), *adj.* having the form of wood; resembling wood, as a variety of asbestos. [LIGNI- + -FORM]

lig·ni·fy (lig′nə fī′), *v.,* **-fied, -fy·ing.** —*v.t.* **1.** to convert into wood; cause to become woody. —*v.i.* **2.** to become wood or woody. [LIGNI- + -FY] —**lig′ni·fi·ca′tion,** *n.*

lig·nin (lig′nin), *n.* **1.** *Bot.* an organic substance that, with cellulose, forms the chief part of woody tissue. **2.** *Papermaking.* impure matter found in wood pulp. [LIGN- + -IN[2]]

lig·nite (lig′nīt), *n.* an imperfectly formed coal, usually dark-brown and often having a distinct woody texture; brown coal. [LIGN- + -ITE[1]] —**lig·nit·ic** (lig nit′ik), *adj.*

lig′nite wax′. See **montan wax.**

lig·niv·or·ous (lig niv′ər əs), *adj.* xylophagous. [LIGNI- + -VOROUS]

ligno-, var. of **ligni-:** *lignocellulose.*

lig·no·cel·lu·lose (lig′nō sel′yə lōs′), *n.* *Bot.* any of various compounds of lignin and cellulose comprising the essential part of woody cell walls. [LIGNO- + CELLULOSE] —**lig·no·cel·lu·los·ic** (lig′nō sel′yə los′ik), *adj.*

lig·num vi·tae (lig′nəm vī′tē), **1.** the hard, extremely heavy wood of either of two species of guaiacum, *Guaiacum officinale* or *G. sanctum,* used in making pulleys, rulers, etc., and formerly thought to have great medicinal powers. **2.** either tree. **3.** any of various other trees yielding a similar hard wood. [< NL, LL, name of the tree, lit., wood of life]

Lig·o·nier (lig′ə nēr′), *n.* a town in NE Indiana. 2595 (1960).

lig·ro·in (lig′rō in), *n.* a flammable mixture of hydrocarbons that boils at from 60°C to 110°C, obtained from petroleum by distillation and used as a solvent. Also, **lig′ro·ine.** [?]

lig·u·la (lig′yə lə), *n., pl.* **-lae** (-lē′), **-las. 1.** *Bot., Zool.* a tonguelike or strap-shaped part or organ. **2.** *Bot.* ligule. [< NL, special use of L *li(n)gula* spoon, shoe-strap, equiv. to *ling(ere)* (to) lick up + *-ula* -ULE] —**lig′u·lar,** *adj.* —**lig′u·loid′,** *adj.*

lig·u·late (lig′yə lit, -lāt′), *adj.* **1.** having or forming a ligula. **2.** having the shape of a strap. Also, **lig·u·lat·ed** (lig′yə lā′tid). [LIGUL(A) + -ATE[1]]

lig·ule (lig′yo͞ol), *n.* *Bot.* **1.** a thin, membranous outgrowth from the base of the blade of most grasses. **2.** a strap-shaped corolla, as in the ray flowers of the head of certain composite plants. [< L *ligul(a)*; see LIGULA]

lig·ure (lig′yo͞or), *n.* a precious stone, probably the jacinth. Ex. 28:19. [ME *ligury* < LL *ligūri(us)* < LGk *ligýrion* a kind of precious stone]

A, Ligule of a grass section; B, Stem; C, Leaf blade; D, Leaf sheath

Li·gu·ri·a (li gyo͞or′ē ə), *n.* a region in NW Italy. 1,717,630 (1961); 2099 sq. mi.

Li·gu·ri·an (li gyo͞or′ē ən), *n.* **1.** an apparently Indo-European language used in ancient times along the NW coast of the Ligurian Sea. —*adj.* **2.** of or pertaining to Liguria or its inhabitants. [LIGURI(A) + -AN]

Ligu′rian bell′flower, a trailing, garden plant, *Campanula isophylla,* of Italy, having numerous, pale-blue, bell-shaped flowers.

Ligu′rian Repub′lic, *Hist.* the republic in NW Italy set up by Napoleon in 1797, incorporated into France in 1805, and united with the Kingdom of Sardinia in 1814.

Ligu′rian Sea′, a part of the Mediterranean between Corsica and the NW coast of Italy.

Li Hsüeh (lē′ s͟hye′), *Chinese.* See **School of Law.**

Li·hu·e (lē ho͞o′ā), *n.* a town on E Kauai, in NW Hawaii. 3908 (1960).

Li Hung-chang (lē′ ho͞ong′jäng′), 1823–1901, Chinese statesman.

lik·a·ble (lī′kə bəl), *adj.* readily or easily liked; pleasing: *a likable girl; a quality that is likable.* Also, **likeable.** [LIKE[2] + -ABLE] —**lik′a·ble·ness, lik′a·bil′i·ty,** *n.*

like[1] (līk), *adj.,* (*Poetic*) **lik·er, lik·est,** *prep., adv., conj., n., v.,* **liked, lik·ing.** —*adj.* **1.** of the same form, appearance, kind, character, amount, etc.: *I cannot cite a like instance.* **2.** corresponding or agreeing in general or in some noticeable respect; similar; analogous: *drawing, painting, and like arts.* **3.** bearing resemblance. **4.** *Dial.* likely: *'Tis like that he's gone mad. It's like to happen again.* **5.** *Dial.* about: *The poor chap seemed like to run away.* **6. something like,** *Informal.* something approaching or approximating: *It looked something like this.* —*prep.* **7.** in like manner with; similarly to; in the manner characteristic of: *He works like a beaver.* **8.** resembling (someone or something): *He is just like his father. Your necklace is just like mine.* **9.** characteristic of: *It would be like him to forget our appointment.* **10.** as if there is promise of; indicative of: *It looks like rain.* **11.** as if someone or something gives promise of being: *He looks like a good prospect for the job.* **12.** disposed or inclined to (usually prec. by *feel*): *to feel like going to bed.* **13.** similar or comparable to: *There is nothing like a cold drink of water when one is thirsty. What was he like?* **14.** (used correlatively to indicate similarity through relationship): *like father, like son.* **15.** (used to establish an intensifying, often facetious, comparison): *sleeping like a log; running like a bat out of hell.* **16.** *Nonstandard.* as; such as: *There are numerous hobbies you might enjoy, like photography or painting.* **17. like anything,** *Informal.* very much; extremely; with great intensity: *The maid wanted like anything to try on her mistress's clothes.* —*adv.* **18.** nearly; closely; approximately: *She's more like 30 than 25.* **19.** *Informal.* likely or probably (usually fol. by *enough*): *like enough; like as not.* **20.** *Nonstandard.* **a.** as it were; in a way; somehow: *There was this old lady with her face all wrinkled like.* **b.** to a degree; more or less: *standing against the wall, looking very tough like.* —*conj. Nonstandard.* **21.** in the same way as; just as; as: *It happened like you might expect it would.* **22.** as if: *He acted like he was afraid.* —*n.* **23.** a like person or thing, or like persons or things; counterpart, match, or equal (usually prec. by a possessive adjective or *the*): *No one has seen his like in a long time. Like attracts like.* **24.** kind; sort; type (usually prec. by a possessive adjective): *I despise moochers and their like.* **25. the like,** something of a similar nature: *They grow oranges, lemons, and the like.* **26. the like** or **likes of,** someone or something like; the equal of: *I've never seen the like of it anywhere.* —*v.i.* **27. like to** or **liked to,** *Nonstandard.* was on the verge of or came close to (doing something): *She liked to have had a fit. The poor kid like to froze. I like to died from laughing.* [ME; OE *gelīc,* c. D *gelijk,* G *gleich,* Icel *(g)līkr,* Goth *galeiks* like, lit., of the same body or form. See Y-, LICH] —**lik′er,** *n.*

—**Usage. 21, 22.** The use of LIKE in place of AS is universally condemned by teachers and editors, notwithstanding its wide currency, especially in advertising slogans. *Do as I say, not as I do* does not admit of LIKE instead of AS. In an occasional idiomatic phrase, it is somewhat less offensive when substituted for AS IF (*He raced down the street like crazy*), but this example is clearly colloquial and not likely to be found in any but the most informal written contexts.

like[2] (līk), *v.,* **liked, lik·ing,** *n.* —*v.t.* **1.** to take pleasure in; find agreeable or congenial to one's taste: *We all liked the concert.* **2.** to regard with favor, or have a kindly or friendly feeling for (a person, group, etc.); find attractive: *His parents like me, and I like them.* —*v.i.* **3.** to feel inclined; wish: *Come whenever you like.* **4.** *Archaic.* to suit the tastes or wishes; please. —*n.* **5.** Usually, **likes.** a favorable feeling; preference: *likes and dislikes.* [ME *like(n),* OE *līcian;* c. D *lijken,* Icel *līka;* see LIKE[1]]

-like, a suffixal use of **like**[1] in the formation of adjectives (*childlike; lifelike*), sometimes hyphenated.
—**Syn.** See **-ish**[1].

like·a·ble (lī′kə bəl), *adj.* likable. —**like′a·ble·ness, like′a·bil′i·ty,** *n.*

like·li·hood (līk′lē ho͝od′), *n.* **1.** the state of being likely or probable; probability. **2.** a probability or chance of something: *There is a strong likelihood of his succeeding.* **3.** *Archaic.* indication of a favorable end; promise. Also, **like′li·ness.** [ME *liklihood.* See LIKELY, -HOOD]

like·ly (līk′lē), *adj.,* **-li·er, -li·est,** *adv.* —*adj.* **1.** probably or apparently destined (usually fol. by an infinitive): *a thing not likely to happen.* **2.** seeming like truth, fact, or certainty; reasonably to be believed or expected: *a likely story.* **3.** apparently suitable; seeming to fulfill requirements or expectations: *a likely spot to build on; a likely place to dig a well.* **4.** showing promise of achievement or excellence; promising: *a fine, likely young man.* —*adv.* **5.** probably: *We will likely stay home this evening.* [ME < Scand; cf. Icel *līkligr.* See LIKE[1], -LY]

—**Syn. 1.** LIKELY, APT, LIABLE are not alike in indicating probability; though APT is used colloquially, and LIABLE, mistakenly, in this sense. LIKELY is the only one of these words which means "probable" or "to be expected": *It is likely to rain today.* APT refers to a natural bent or inclination; if something is natural and easy, it is often probable; hence APT comes to be associated with LIKELY and to be used informally as a substitute for it: *He is apt at drawing. He is apt to do well at drawing.* LIABLE should not be used to mean "probable." When used with an infinitive, it may remind one of LIKELY: *He is liable to be arrested.* But the true meaning, susceptibility to something unpleasant, or exposure to risk, becomes evident when it is used with a prepositional phrase: *He is liable to arrest. The machine is liable to error.* **3.** appropriate.

like-mind·ed (līk′mīn′did), *adj.* having a similar or identical opinion, purpose, etc. [LIKE[1] + -MINDED] —**like′-mind′ed·ly,** *adv.* —**like′-mind′ed·ness,** *n.*

lik·en (lī′kən), *v.t.* to represent as like; compare: *to liken someone to a weasel.* [ME *liknen.* See LIKE[1], -EN[1]]

like·ness (līk′nis), *n.* **1.** a representation, picture, or image, esp. a portrait: *to draw a good likeness of someone.* **2.** the semblance or appearance of something; guise: *to assume the likeness of a swan.* **3.** the state or fact of being like: *I can't get over your likeness to my friend.* [ME *liknesse,* OE *līcnes,* var. of *gelīcnes.* See ALIKE, -NESS]
—**Syn. 2.** shape, form. **3.** resemblance, similitude.

like·wise (līk′wīz′), *adv.* **1.** moreover; in addition; also; too: *She is likewise our social chairman.* **2.** in like manner; in the same way; similarly: *I'm tempted to do likewise.* [late ME; earlier *in like wise* in a like way. See LIKE[1], WISE[2]]

li·kin (lē′kēn′), *n.* (formerly in China) a provincial duty imposed on articles of trade that are in transit. [< Chin *li* 1/1000 of an ounce + *kin* money]

lik·ing (lī′king), *n.* **1.** preference, inclination, or favor: *to show a liking for privacy.* **2.** pleasure or taste: *much to his liking.* **3.** the state or feeling of a person who likes. [ME; OE *līcung.* See LIKE[2], -ING[1]]
—**Syn. 1.** leaning, propensity, predilection, partiality, fondness, affection. —**Ant. 1.** antipathy.

lik·ker (lik′ər), *n.* *Eye Dial.* liquor.

li·la (lē′lä), *n.* *Hinduism.* creation, seen as the playful activity of a god. [< Skt *līlā* play, sport, diversion]

Li·la (lī′lə), *n.* a girl's given name, form of **Leila.**

li·lac (lī′lək), *n.* **1.** any oleaceous shrub of the genus *Syringa,* as *S. vulgaris,* having large clusters of fragrant purple or white flowers: the State flower of New Hampshire. **2.** pale reddish purple. —*adj.* **3.** having the color lilac. [< Sp < Ar *līlak* < Pers, assimilated var. of *nīlak* bluish, equiv. to *nīl* blue, indigo (< Skt *nīla*) + *-ak* suffix of appurtenance; cf. -ISH[1]]

Li·lac (lī′lək), *n.* a girl's given name.

li·la·ceous (lī lā′s͟həs), *adj.* of or approaching the color lilac. [LILAC + -EOUS]

Lil·i (lil′ē), *n.* a girl's given name. Also, **Lilli, Lilly, Lily.**

lil·i·a·ceous (lil′ē ā′s͟həs), *adj.* **1.** of or like the lily. **2.** belonging to the *Liliaceae,* or lily family of plants. [< LL *liliāceus.* See LILY, -ACEOUS]

Lil·i·an (lil′ē ən), *n.* a girl's given name. Also, **Lillian, Lilyan.**

Lil·i·bel (lil′i bel′), *n.* a girl's given name. Also, **Lil′i·bell′, Lil′i·belle′, Lilybelle.**

L'Île de Pin·gouins (*Fr.* lēl də paN gwaN′). See **Penguin Island.**

lil·ied (lil′ēd), *adj.* **1.** abounding in lilies. **2.** *Archaic.* lilylike; white. [LILY + -ED[3]]

Lil·i·en·thal (lil′ē ən thôl′ *for 1;* lē′lē ən täl′ *for 2*), *n.* **1. David E(ly),** born 1899, U.S. public administrator. **2. Ot·to** (ôt′ō), 1848–96, German aeronautical engineer and inventor.

Lil·ith (lil′ith), *n.* **1.** *Semitic Myth.* a female demon dwelling in deserted places and attacking children. **2.** *Jewish Folklore.* Adam's first wife, before Eve was created.

Li·li·u·o·ka·la·ni (lē lē′o͞o ō kä lä′nē), *n.* **Lydia Ka·me·ke·ha** (kä′me ke′hä), 1838–1917, last queen of the Hawaiian Islands 1891–93.

Lil·i·us (lil′ē əs), *n.* a walled plain in the fourth quadrant of the face of the moon: about 32 miles in diameter.

Lille (lēl), *n.* a city in and the capital of Nord, in N France. 199,033 (1962). Formerly, **Lisle.**

Lil·li (lil′ē), *n.* a girl's given name. Also, **Lili, Lilly, Lily.**

Lil·li·an (lil′ē ən), *n.* a girl's given name. Also, **Lilian, Lilyan.**

Lil·li·bul·le·ro (lil′ē bə lēr′ō), *n.* **1.** a part of the refrain to a song deriding the Irish Roman Catholics, popular in England during and after the revolution of 1688. **2.** the song, or the tune to which it was sung.

Lil·lie (lil′ē), *n.* **Beatrice,** born 1898, English actress, born in Canada.

Lil·li·put (lil′i put′, -pət), *n.* an imaginary country inhabited by tiny people, described in Swift's *Gulliver's Travels.*

Lil·li·pu·tian (lil′i pyo͞o′s͟hən), *adj.* **1.** extremely small; diminutive. —*n.* **2.** an inhabitant of Lilliput. **3.** a very small person. **4.** a person who is narrow or petty in outlook. [LILLIPUT + -IAN]

Lil·lo (lil′ō), *n.* **George,** 1693?–1739, English dramatist.

Lil·ly (lil′ē), *n.* a girl's given name. Also, **Lili, Lilli, Lily.**

Li·long·we (li lông′wā), *n.* a city in SW Malawi. 6660 (est. 1956).

lilt (lilt), *n.* **1.** rhythmic swing or cadence. **2.** a lilting song or tune. —*v.i., v.t.* **3.** to sing or play in a light, tripping, or rhythmic manner. [ME *lulte;* ? akin to D *lul* pipe, *lullen* to lull]

lil·y (lil′ē), *n., pl.* **lil·ies,** *adj.* —*n.* **1.** any scaly-bulbed herb of the genus *Lilium,* having showy, funnel-shaped or bell-shaped flowers. **2.** the flower or the bulb of such a plant. **3.** any of various related or similar plants or their flowers, as the mariposa lily or the calla lily. **4.** fleur-de-lis, esp. as the symbol of France. **5.** *Bowling Slang.* a split in which the five, seven, and ten pins remain standing. —*adj.* **6.** white as a lily: *her lily hands.* **7.** delicately fair: *a lily maiden.* **8.** pure; unsullied: *the lily truth.* **9.** pale; fragile; weak. [ME, OE *lilie* < L *līli(um)* < Gk *leírion*] —**lil′y·like′,** *adj.*

Lil·y (lil′e), *n.* a girl's given name. Also, **Lili.**

Lil·yan (lil′yən), *n.* a girl's given name. Also, **Lilian, Lillian.**

Lil·y·belle (lil′i bel′), *n.* a girl's given name. Also, **Lilibel, Lilibell, Lilibelle.**

lil′y i′ron, a harpoon whose head may be detached.

lil′y leek′, a large herb, *Allium Moly,* of southern Europe, having showy, yellow flowers, grown as an ornamental.

lil·y-liv·ered (lil′ē liv′ərd), *adj.* weak in courage; cowardly. [LILY + LIVER[1] + -ED[3]]

lil′y of the val′ley, *pl.* **lilies of the valley.** a stemless herb, *Convallaria majalis,* having a raceme of drooping, bell-shaped, fragrant, white flowers.

lil′y pad′, the large, floating leaf of a water lily.

lil·y-trot·ter (lil′ē trot′ər), *n.* jacana.

lil·y-white (*adj.* lil′ē hwīt′, -wīt′; *n.* lil′ē hwīt′, -wīt′), *adj.* **1.** white as a lily: *She has the softest, lily-white skin.* **2.** pure; untouched by corruption or imperfection;

above reproach: *He tries to pass himself off as some sort of lily-white saint, but he's not.* **3.** designating or pertaining to any faction or group opposing the inclusion of Negroes in political life. **—*n.* 4.** a member of a lily-white organization, esp. a member of a former faction of the Republican party in the South opposed to the inclusion of Negroes in the party or in political life in general. [ME *lylie-whyt*]

Li·ma (lē′mə; *Sp.* lē̆ma *for 1;* lī′mə *for 2*), *n.* **1.** a city in and the capital of Peru, near the Pacific coast. 1,920,745 (1961). **2.** a city in NW Ohio. 51,037 (1960).

Li·ma (lē′mə), *n.* a word used in communications to represent the letter *L.*

li′ma bean′ (lī′mə), **1.** a bean, *Phaseolus limensis,* having a broad, flat, edible seed. **2.** the seed, used for food. [after LIMA, PERU]

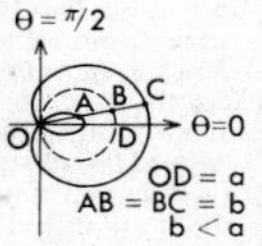

lim·a·cine (lim′ə sīn′, -sin, lī′mə-), *adj.* pertaining to or resembling a slug; sluglike. [< L *līmāc-* (s. of *līmāx*) slug snail + -INE¹]

lim·a·çon (lim′ə son′), *n. Geom.* a plane curve generated by the locus of a point on a line at a fixed distance from the point of intersection of the line with a fixed circle, as the line revolves about a point on the circumference of the circle. Equation: $r = a\cos\theta + b$. Also called **Pascal's limaçon.** [< F: lit., snail, OF, deriv. of *limaz* < L *līmācem,* acc. of *līmāx* snail, slug]

θ = π/2
θ = 0
OD = a
AB = BC = b
b < a

Limaçon

Li·mas·sol (lim′ə sôl′), *n.* a seaport in S Cyprus: Phoenician ruins. 43,561 (1960). Also, **Limmasol.** Ancient, **Lemessus.**

limb¹ (lim), *n.* **1.** a part or member of an animal body distinct from the head and trunk, as a leg, arm, or wing: *the lower limbs; artificial limbs.* **2.** a large or main branch of a tree. **3.** a projecting part or member: *the four limbs of a cross.* **4.** a person or thing regarded as a part, member, branch, offshoot, or scion of something: *a limb of the central committee.* **5.** *Archery.* the upper or lower part of a bow. **6.** *Informal.* an imp, young scamp, or mischievous child. **7. out on a limb,** *U.S. Informal.* in a dangerous or compromising situation; vulnerable: *The company overextended itself and was soon out on a limb.* [ME, OE *lim;* akin to Icel *limr* foliage, *limr* limb, *līmi* rod, L *līmus* aslant, *līmen* threshold] **—limbed** (limd), *adj.* **—limb′less,** *adj.*
—Syn. 1. extremity. See **member. 2.** See **branch.**

limb² (lim), *n.* **1.** *Astron.* the edge of the disk of the sun, a moon, or a planet. **2.** the graduated edge of a quadrant or similar instrument. **3.** *Bot.* **a.** the upper spreading part of a gamopetalous corolla. **b.** the expanded portion of a petal, sepal, or leaf. [< L *limb(us);* see LIMBUS², LIMBO]

lim·bate (lim′bāt), *adj. Bot., Zool.* bordered, as a flower in which one color is surrounded by an edging of another. [< LL *limbāt(us)* bordered, edged. See LIMB², -ATE¹]

lim·ber¹ (lim′bər), *adj.* **1.** bending readily; flexible; pliant. **2.** characterized by ease in bending the body; supple; lithe. **—*v.i.* 3.** to make oneself limber (usually fol. by *up*): *to limber up before the game.* **—*v.t.* 4.** to make (something) limber (usually fol. by *up*): *She tried to limber up her wits before the exam.* [? akin to LIMB¹] **—lim′ber·ly,** *adv.* **—lim′ber·ness,** *n.*
—Syn. 1. pliable. See **flexible. —Ant. 1.** rigid, unbending. **1, 2.** stiff.

lim·ber² (lim′bər), *Mil.* **—*n.* 1.** a two-wheeled vehicle, originally pulled by four or six horses, behind which is towed a field gun or caisson. **—*v.t.* 2.** to attach the limber to (a gun) in preparation for moving away (sometimes fol. by *up*). **—*v.i.* 3.** to attach a limber to a gun (usually fol. by *up*). [late ME *lymo(u)r* pole of a vehicle. See LIMB¹, -ER¹]

lim·ber³ (lim′bər), *n.* Usually, **limbers.** *Naut.* a passage or gutter in which seepage collects to be pumped away, located on each side of a central keelson; bilge. [? < F *lumière* hole, light < L *lūmināria* windows (i.e., openings admitting light). See LUMEN, -AR²]

lim′ber hole′, *Naut.* any of a series of holes pierced through a frame or floor to allow the passage of accumulated moisture.

lim·ber·neck (lim′bər nek′), *n. Vet. Pathol.* a highly fatal infection of botulism affecting birds, esp. chickens and ducks, caused by ingestion of the toxin produced by the organism *Clostridium botulinum,* and characterized by weakness of the neck muscles and refusal to eat. [LIMBER¹ + NECK]

lim′ber pine′, a pine, *Pinus flexis,* of western North America, having light, soft wood used locally for railroad ties, poles, fuel, etc. Also called **Rocky Mountain white pine.**

lim·bic (lim′bik), *adj.* pertaining to or of the nature of a limbus or border; marginal. [LIMB(US)¹ + -IC]

lim·bo¹ (lim′bō), *n., pl.* **-bos. 1.** (*often cap.*) a supposed region on the border of hell or heaven, serving as the abode after death of unbaptized infants **(lim′bo of in′fants)** and of the righteous who died before the coming of Christ **(lim′bo of the fa′thers** or **lim′bo of the pa′triarchs). 2.** a place or state of oblivion to which persons or things are regarded as being relegated when cast aside, forgotten, past, or out of date: *My hopes of yore are in the limbo of lost dreams.* **3.** a place or state of imprisonment or confinement. **4.** a state of being or place midway between two extremes. [ME, abstracted from ML phrase *in limbo* on hell's border (L: on the edge), equiv. to *in* on + *limbō,* abl. of *limbus* edge, border (L), place bordering on hell (ML)]

lim·bo² (lim′bō), *n., pl.* **-bos.** a dance of West Indian origin in which the dancer bends backward and moves with a shuffling step under a horizontal bar that is lowered after each successive pass. [? var. of LIMBER²; see BANJO]

Lim·bourg (*Fr.* laN bo͞or′), *n.* See under **Limburg.**

Lim·burg (lim′bûrg; *Du.* lim′bœrkh), *n.* a medieval duchy in W Europe: now divided into a province in the SE Netherlands **(Limburg)** and a province in NE Belgium **(Limbourg).**

Lim·burg·er (lim′bûr′gər), *n.* a variety of soft cheese of strong odor and flavor. Also called **Lim′burger cheese′, Lim′burg cheese′.** [after LIMBURG; see -ER¹]

lim·bus¹ (lim′bəs), *n., pl.* **-bi** (-bī). limbo¹. [< ML]

lim·bus² (lim′bəs), *n., pl.* **-bi** (-bī). *Anat., Zool.* a border, edge, or limb. [< NL, L]

lime¹ (līm), *n., v.,* **limed, lim·ing. —*n.* 1.** Also called **burnt lime, calcium oxide, caustic lime, calx, quicklime.** a white or grayish-white, odorless, lumpy, very slightly water-soluble solid, CaO, that when combined with water forms calcium hydroxide **(slaked lime),** obtained from calcium carbonate, limestone, or oyster shells: used chiefly in mortars, plasters, and cements, in bleaching powder **(chlorinated lime),** and in the manufacture of steel, paper, glass, and various chemicals of calcium. **2.** a calcium compound for improving crops grown in soils deficient in lime. **3.** birdlime. **—*v.t.* 4.** to treat (soil) with lime or compounds of calcium. **5.** to smear (twigs, branches, etc.) with birdlime. **6.** to catch with or as with birdlime. **7.** to paint or cover (a surface) with a composition of lime and water; whitewash: *Government buildings were freshly limed by the native workers.* [ME, OE *līm;* c. D *lijm,* G *Leim,* Icel *līm* glue, L *līmus* slime; akin to LOAM] **—lime′less,** *adj.* **—lime′like′,** *adj.*

lime² (līm), *n.* **1.** the small, greenish-yellow, acid fruit of a tropical tree, *Citrus aurantifolia,* allied to the lemon. **2.** the tree that bears this fruit. [< Sp *lima* < Ar *līmah, līm* citrus fruit] **—lime′less,** *adj.* **—lime′like′,** *adj.*

lime³ (līm), *n.* a linden. [unexplained var. of obs. *line, lind,* ME, OE *lind.* See LINDEN]

lime⁴ (līm), *n. Informal.* limelight. [shortened form]

lime·ade (līm′ād′), *n.* a beverage consisting of lime juice, a sweetener, and plain or carbonated water. [LIME² + -ADE¹]

lime′ burn′er, a person who makes lime by burning or calcining limestone, shells, etc.

Lime·house (līm′hous′), *n.* a district in the East End of London, England, notorious for its squalor.

lime′ hy′drate. See **slaked lime.**

lime·kiln (līm′kil′, -kiln′), *n.* a kiln or furnace for making lime by calcining limestone or shells. [ME *limkilne.* See LIME¹, KILN]

lime·light (līm′līt′), *n.* **1.** *Theat.* **a.** (formerly) a lighting unit for spotlighting the front of the stage, producing illumination by means of a flame of mixed gases directed at a cylinder of lime and having a special lens for concentrating the light in a strong beam. **b.** the light so produced. **c.** *Chiefly Brit.* a lighting unit, esp. a spotlight. **2.** the light of public notice, interest, observation, or notoriety: *He has long held the limelight in the musical world. She seems fond of the limelight.* [LIME¹ + LIGHT¹] **—lime′light′er,** *n.*

lime′ lin′iment, *Pharm.* See **carron oil.**

li·men (lī′mən), *n., pl.* **li·mens, lim·i·na** (lim′ə nə). *Psychol.* threshold (def. 4). [< L]

Lim·e·ni·a (lim′ə nī′ə), *n. Class. Myth.* an epithet of Aphrodite, meaning "of the harbor."

lime·quat (līm′kwot′), *n.* **1.** a hybrid citrus tree produced by crossing the lime and the kumquat. **2.** the tart, pale yellow fruit of this tree. [LIME² + (KUM)QUAT]

lim·er·ick (lim′ər ik), *n.* a kind of humorous verse of five lines, in which the first and second lines rhyme with the fifth line, and the shorter third line rhymes with the shorter fourth. [after LIMERICK: said to go back to social gatherings where the group sang "Will you come up to Limerick?" after each set of verses, extemporized in turn by the members of the party]

Lim·er·ick (lim′ər ik), *n.* **1.** a county in N Munster, in the SW Republic of Ireland. 133,339 (1961); 1037 sq. mi. **2.** its county seat: a seaport at the head of the Shannon estuary. 50,786 (1961). **3.** *Angling.* a fishhook having a sharp bend below the barb.

li·mes (lī′mēs), *n., pl.* **lim·i·tes** (lim′i tēz′). **1.** a boundary, esp. the fortified border or frontier of a country. **2.** (*cap.*) See **Siegfried line. 3.** an ancient Roman frontier fortification. [< L; see LIMIT]

lime·stone (līm′stōn′), *n.* any stone consisting wholly or mainly of calcium carbonate: some varieties suitable for burning into lime. [LIME¹ + STONE]

lime·sul·fur (līm′sul′fər), *n. Chem.* a mixture of lime and sulfur that has been boiled in water: used in powdered form or in aqueous solution as an insecticide, a fungicide, a sheep dip. Also, **lime′sul′phur.** [LIME¹ + SULFUR]

lime′ tree′, a linden or basswood.

lime′ twig′, 1. a twig smeared with birdlime to catch birds. **2.** a snare or trap. [late ME]

lime·wa·ter (līm′wô′tər, -wot′ər), *n.* **1.** an aqueous solution of slaked lime, used in medicine, antacids, lotions, and to absorb carbon dioxide from the air. **2.** water containing naturally an unusual amount of calcium carbonate or calcium sulfate. [LIME¹ + WATER]

lime·wood (līm′wo͝od′), *n.* the wood of a linden. [LIME³ + WOOD¹]

lim·ey (lī′mē), *n., pl.* **-eys,** *adj. Slang.* **—*n.* 1.** a British sailor. **2.** an Englishman. **3.** a British ship. **—*adj.* 4.** British. [short for *lime-juicer* British sailor, so called because required by law to drink lime juice to ward off scurvy; see -Y²]

li·mic·o·line (lī mik′ə līn′, -lin), *adj.* shore-inhabiting; of or pertaining to numerous birds of the families *Charadriidae,* comprising the plovers, and *Scolopacidae,* comprising the sandpipers. [< LL *līmicol(a)* mud-dweller + -INE¹; see LIME¹, -COLINE]

li·mic·o·lous (lī mik′ə ləs), *adj.* dwelling in mud or muddy regions. [< LL *līmicol(a)* mud-dweller + -OUS; see LIME¹, -COLOUS]

lim·i·nal (lim′ə nᵊl, lī′mə-), *adj. Psychol.* of, pertaining to, or situated at the limen. [< L *līmin-* (s. of *līmen*) threshold + -AL¹]

lim·it (lim′it), *n.* **1.** the final or furthest bound or point as to extent, amount, continuance, procedure, etc.: *the limit of his experience; the limit of vision.* **2.** a boundary or bound, as of a country, tract, district, etc. **3. limits,** the premises or region enclosed within boundaries: *We found them on school limits after hours.* **4.** *Math.* **a.** a number such that the value of a given function remains arbitrarily close to this number when the independent variable is sufficiently close to a specified point or is sufficiently large. The limit of $1/x$ is zero as x approaches infinity; the limit of $(x-1)^2$ is zero as x approaches 1. **b.** a number such that the absolute value of the difference between terms of a given sequence and the number approaches zero as the index of the terms increases to infinity. **c.** one of two numbers affixed to the integration symbol for a definite integral, indicating the interval or region over which the integration is taking place and substituted in a primitive, if one exists, to evaluate the integral. **5.** *Games.* the maximum sum by which a bet may be raised at any one time. **6. the limit,** *Informal.* something or someone that exasperates, delights, etc., to an extreme or intolerable degree: *She has made errors before, but this is the limit. His antics are the limit.* **—*v.t.* 7.** to restrict by or as by establishing limits (usually fol. by *to*): *Please limit questions to 25 words.* **8.** to confine or keep within limits: *to limit one's ability to act; to limit expenditures.* **9.** *Law.* to fix or assign definitely or specifically. [ME *lymyt* < L *līmit-* (s. of *līmes*) boundary, path between fields] **—lim′it·a·ble,** *adj.* **—lim′it·a·ble·ness,** *n.* **—lim′it·er,** *n.*
—Syn. 2. confine, frontier, border. **8.** restrain, bound.

lim·i·tar·y (lim′i ter′ē), *adj.* **1.** of, pertaining to, or serving as a limit. **2.** *Archaic.* subject to limits; limited. [< L *līmitāri(s)* on the border. See LIMIT, -ARY]

lim·i·ta·tion (lim′i tā′shən), *n.* **1.** that which limits; a limit or bound; restriction: *an arms limitation; a limitation on imports.* **2.** a limiting condition; restrictive weakness; inability; lack of capacity: *He knows his limitations as a writer.* **3.** the act of limiting. **4.** the quality or state of being limited. **5.** *Law.* the assignment, as by statute, of a period of time within which an action must be brought, or the period of time assigned: *a statute of limitations.* [ME *lymytacion* < L *līmitātiōn-* (s. of *līmitātiō*) a bounding, equiv. to *līmitāt(us)* bounded (ptp. of *līmitāre;* see LIMIT, -ATE¹) + *-iōn-* -ION]

lim·i·ta·tive (lim′i tā′tiv), *adj.* limiting; restrictive. [< ML *līmitātīv(us).* See LIMITATION, -IVE]

lim·it·ed (lim′i tid), *adj.* **1.** confined within limits; restricted or circumscribed: *a limited space; limited resources.* **2.** restricted with reference to governing powers by limitations prescribed in laws and in a constitution: *a limited government.* **3.** characterized by an inability to think imaginatively or independently; lacking scope; narrow: *a rather limited intelligence.* **4.** *Chiefly Brit.* **a.** responsible for the debts of a company only to a specified amount proportionate to the percentage of stock held. **b.** (of a business firm) owned by stockholders, each having a restricted liability for the company's debts. **c.** (*usually cap.*) incorporated; Inc. *Abbr.:* Ltd. **5.** (of railroad trains, buses, etc.) making only a limited number of stops en route. **—*n.* 6.** *U.S.* a limited train, bus, etc. [LIMIT + -ED²] **—lim′it·ed·ly,** *adv.* **—lim′it·ed·ness,** *n.*

lim′ited com′pany, *Brit.* a company in which the shareholders cannot be assessed for debts of the company beyond the sum they still have invested in the company. Also called **limited-liability company.**

lim′ited divorce′, *Law.* See **judicial separation.**

lim′ited edi′tion, an edition of a book limited to a specified number of copies.

lim′ited liabil′ity, a liability restricted by law or contract, as the liability of owners of shares in a corporation or limited company or that of a special partner.

lim′ited mon′archy, a monarchy that is limited by laws and a constitution.

lim′ited part′ner. See **special partner.**

lim′ited part′nership, a partnership formed by at least one general partner and at least one special partner. Also called **special partnership.** Cf. **general partnership.**

lim′ited pay′ment insur′ance, life insurance in which premiums are paid over a limited period of time, as 20 or 30 years.

lim′ited pol′icy, *Insurance.* a policy which covers only certain types of losses within an area of risks.

lim·it·er (lim′i tər), *n.* **1.** someone or something that limits. **2.** *Electronics.* a device for limiting the amplitude of a frequency-modulated signal to a certain value in order to remove amplitude modulation. [LIMIT + -ER¹; r. ME *limitour* see -OR²]

lim·it·ing (lim′i ting), *adj.* **1.** serving to restrict or restrain; confining. **2.** *Gram.* of the nature of a limiting adjective or a restrictive clause. [LIMIT + -ING²]

lim′iting ad′jective, *Gram.* **1.** (in English and some other languages) one of a small group of adjectives that modify the nouns to which they are applied by restricting rather than describing or qualifying. *This, some,* and *certain* are limiting adjectives. **2.** an adjective, as *few* or *other,* that in English follows determiners and precedes descriptive adjectives: *a few red apples.*

lim·it·less (lim′it lis), *adj.* without limit; boundless: *limitless ambition; limitless space.* [LIMIT + -LESS] **—lim′it·less·ly,** *adv.* **—lim′it·less·ness,** *n.*

lim′it of proportional′ity, *Physics.* See **elastic limit.**

lim′it of resolu′tion, *Optics.* the capacity of an optical system to resolve point objects as separate images. The human eye can accommodate a limit of resolution of approximately .1 millimeter, or 1 inch of arc, corresponding to a capacity to resolve two points one inch apart at a distance of 100 yards.

lim′it point′, *Math.* See **accumulation point.**

lim′it switch′, a switch automatically cutting off current to an electric motor when an object moved by it, as an elevator, has passed a given point.

Lim·ma·sol (lim′ə sôl′), *n.* Limassol.

lim·mer (lim′ər), *n. Scot. and North Eng.* **1.** a woman of loose morals; strumpet. **2.** *Obs.* a worthless, unprincipled man; scoundrel; rogue. [late ME (Scot); see LIMB¹ (def. 6; ME *develes lim* limb of Satan), -ER¹]

L'Im·mo·ra·liste (*Fr.* lē mô RA lēst′). See **Immoralist, The.**

limn (lim), *v.t. Archaic.* **1.** to represent in drawing or painting. **2.** to portray in words; describe. [late ME *lymne,* var. of ME *lumine* to illuminate (manuscripts), aph. var. of *enlumine* < MF *enluminer* < L *inlūmināre* to embellish, lit., light up; see ILLUMINATE]

Lim·nae·a (lim nē′ə), *n. Class. Myth.* an epithet of Artemis, meaning "of the lake."

lim·ner (lim′nər), *n.* a painter, esp. a portrait painter. [ME *limnour.* See LIMN, -ER¹]

lim·net·ic (lim net′ik), *adj.* pertaining to or living in the open water of a fresh-water pond or lake. [< Gk *limnēt(ēs)* marsh-dwelling (*límnē* pool, marsh + *-tēs* inhabiting) + -IC]

lim·nol·o·gy (lim nol′ə jē), *n.* the scientific study of bodies of fresh water, as lakes and ponds, with reference to their physical, geographical, biological, and other features. [*limno-* (comb. form repr. Gk *límnē* pool, marsh) + -LOGY] **—lim·no·log·i·cal** (lim′nᵊloj′i kəl), **lim′no·log′ic,** *adj.* **—lim′no·log′i·cal·ly,** *adv.* **—lim·nol′o·gist,** *n.*

Lim·no·ri·a (lim nōr′ē ə, -nôr′-), *n. Class. Myth.* one of the Nereids.

Li·moges (li mōzh′; *Fr.* lē mōzh′), *n.* **1.** a city in and the capital of Haute Vienne, in S central France. 120,596 (1962). **2.** Also called **Limoges′ ware′.** a type of fine porcelain manufactured at Limoges.

Li·mon (lī′mən), *n. Class. Myth.* a son of Tegeates and Maera who killed his brother, Scephrus, believing that Scephrus had informed against him to Apollo.

Li·món (lē môn′), *n.* **1. Jo·sé** (hô se′), born 1908, Mexican dancer in U.S. **2.** Also called **Puerto Limón.** a seaport in E Costa Rica. 18,000 (est. 1963).

lim·o·nene (lim′ə nēn′), *n. Chem.* a liquid terpene, $C_{10}H_{16}$, occurring in two optically different forms, the dextrorotatory form being present in the essential oils of lemon, orange, etc., and the levorotatory form in Douglas fir needle oil. [< NL *Limon(um)* lemon + -ENE]

li·mo·nite (lī′mə nīt′), *n.* an important iron ore, a hydrated ferric oxide, varying in color from dark brown to yellow. Also called **bog-iron ore, brown hematite.** [< Gk *leimṓn* meadow + -ITE[1]] —**li·mo·nit·ic** (lī′mə nit′ik), *adj.*

Li·mou·sin (lē mōō zan′), *n.* a former province in central France.

lim·ou·sine (lim′ə zēn′, lim′ə zēn′), *n.* **1.** an automobile having a permanently enclosed compartment for from three to five persons, the roof of which projects forward over the driver's seat in front. **2.** any large, luxurious automobile. **3.** a large sedan or small bus, esp. one for transporting passengers to and from an airport, between train stations, etc. [< F: kind of motorcar, special use of *limousine* long cloak, so called because worn by the shepherds of LIMOUSIN]

limp[1] (limp), *v.i.* **1.** to walk with a labored, jerky movement, as when lame. **2.** to proceed in a lame, faltering, or labored manner: *His writing limps from one cliché to another. The old car limped along at a snail's pace.* **3.** to progress with great difficulty; make little or no advance: *a people suffering under an economy that limps along at a level just above total bankruptcy.* —*n.* **4.** a lame movement or gait: *The accident left him with a slight limp.* [back formation from obs. *limphault*, OE *lemphealt* limping (see HALT[2]); akin to MHG *limpfen* to limp] —**limp′er,** *n.* —**limp′ing·ly,** *adv.*

limp[2] (limp), *adj.* **1.** lacking stiffness or firmness, as of substance, fiber, structure, or bodily frame: *a limp body.* **2.** lacking vitality; tired; fatigued: *Limp with exhaustion, he dropped into the nearest chair.* **3.** without proper firmness, force, energy, etc., as of character: *limp, spiritless prose.* [? < Scand; cf. Icel *limpa* slackness, *limpilegur* soft, *limpfast* to become flabby] —**limp′ly,** *adv.* —**limp′ness,** *n.*
—**Syn. 1.** flabby, flaccid, soft, loppy. **2, 3.** feeble, weak.

lim·pet (lim′pit), *n.* any of various marine gastropods with a low conical shell open beneath, found adhering to rocks, used for bait and sometimes for food. [ME *lempet*, OE *lempedu*, nasalized var. of **lepedu* < L *lepada*, acc. of *lepas* < Gk *lepás* limpet]

lim·pid (lim′pid), *adj.* **1.** clear, transparent, or pellucid, as water, crystal, air, etc.: *We could see to the very bottom of the limpid pool.* **2.** free from obscurity; lucid: *a limpid style.* **3.** completely calm; without distress or worry: *a limpid, emotionless existence.* [< L *limpid(us)* clear. See LYMPH, -ID[4]] —**lim·pid′i·ty, lim′pid·ness,** *n.* —**lim′pid·ly,** *adv.*

limp·kin (limp′kin), *n.* a large, loud-voiced, wading bird, *Aramus guarauna*, intermediate in size and character between the cranes and the rails, of the warmer regions of America. [LIMP[1] + -KIN; so called because of its jerky walk]

Lim·po·po (lim pō′pō), *n.* a river in S Africa, flowing from the Republic of South Africa, through S Mozambique into the Indian Ocean. 1000 mi. long. Also called **Crocodile River.**

limp·sy (limp′sē), *adj. Dial.* flimsy; limp; weak; lazy; flaccid. Also, **limp′sey, lim·sy** (lim′sē). [LIMP[2] + *-sy* adj. suffix]

lim·u·loid (lim′yə loid′), *adj.* **1.** resembling or pertaining to a horseshoe crab, esp. of the genus *Limulus.* —*n.* **2.** See **horseshoe crab.** [LIMUL(US) + -OID]

lim·u·lus (lim′yə ləs), *n., pl.* **-li** (-lī′). a crab of the genus *Limulus*; a horseshoe crab. [< NL *Līmulus* name of the genus, special use of L *līmulus*, dim. of *līmus* sidelong; see -ULE]

lim·y (lī′mē), *adj.,* **lim·i·er, lim·i·est. 1.** consisting of, containing, or like lime. **2.** smeared with birdlime. [LIME[1] + -Y[1]] —**lim′i·ness,** *n.*

lin (lin), *n.* linn.

Lin (lin), *n.* a girl's given name, form of **Caroline** or **Carolyn.** Also, **Lynn, Lynne.**

lin., 1. lineal. **2.** linear. **3.** liniment.

Li·na (lē′nə), *n.* a girl's given name.

Lin·a·cre (lin′ə kər), *n.* **Thomas,** 1460?–1524, English humanist and physician.

lin·age (lī′nij), *n.* **1.** the number of printed lines, esp. agate lines, covered by a magazine article, newspaper advertisement, etc. **2.** the amount charged, paid, or received per printed line, as of a magazine article, short story, or the like. **3.** *Archaic.* alignment. Also, **lineage.** [LINE[1] + -AGE]

lin·al·o·ol (li nal′ō ōl′, -ôl′, -ol′, lin′ə lōōl′), *n. Chem.* a colorless, unsaturated terpene liquid alcohol $(CH_3)_2$-$C{-}CHCH_2CH_2C(CH_3)OHCH{-}CH_2$, having a fragrance similar to that of bergamot oil, obtained from several essential oils: used in perfumery. Also, **lin·a·lol** (lin′ə lōl′, -lôl′, -lol′). [< MexSp *lináloe* a fragrant Mexican wood (see LIGNALOES) + -OL[1]]

lin′a·lyl ac′etate (lin′ə lil, -lēl′), *Chem.* a colorless, water-insoluble liquid, $CH_3COOC_{10}H_{17}$, having a pleasant odor: used chiefly in perfumes, cosmetics, toilet water, and soap. [LINAL(OOL) + -YL]

Li·na·res (lē nä′res), *n.* a city in S Spain. 56,154 (1955).

li·na·rite (lī′nə rīt′, li när′īt), *n.* a mineral, complex basic sulfate of lead and copper, having a deep blue color resembling that of azurite. [named after LINAR(ES), where found; see -ITE[1]]

Linc (liŋk), *n.* a boy's given name, form of **Lincoln.**

linch (linch), *n. Brit.* lynch[2].

linch·pin (linch′pin′), *n.* a pin inserted through the end of an axletree to keep the wheel on. [unexplained alter. of ME *lynspin*, equiv. to *lyns*, OE *lynis* axle-pin (c. G *Lünse*) + *pin* PIN]

Lin·coln (liŋ′kən), *n.* **1. Abraham,** 1809–65, 16th president of the U.S. 1861–65. **2. Benjamin,** 1733–1810, American Revolutionary general. **3.** a city in and the capital of Nebraska, in the SE part. 128,521 (1960). **4.** a city in and the county seat of Lincolnshire, in E central England. 77,065 (1961). **5.** a city in central Illinois. 16,890 (1960). **6.** a town in central Maine. 3616 (1960). **7.** a town in central California. 3197 (1960). **8.** Lincolnshire. **9.** one of an English breed of large mutton sheep, noted for its heavy fleece of coarse, long wool. **10.** a boy's given name.

Lin·coln·esque (liŋ′kə nesk′), *adj.* like or characteristic of Abraham Lincoln. [LINCOLN + -ESQUE]

Lin′coln green′, 1. an olive-green color. **2.** *Brit. Obs.* a forester's outfit, perhaps of bright green: *clad in Lincoln green.* [so called from the color of a fabric originally made in LINCOLN, England]

Lin′coln Heights′, 1. a town in central Ohio. 8004 (1960). **2.** a town in SW Ohio. 7798 (1960).

Lin·coln·i·an (liŋ kō′nē ən), *adj.* of or pertaining to Abraham Lincoln or his political principles. [LINCOLN + -IAN]

Lin·coln·i·an·a (liŋ kō′nē an′ə, -ä′nə, liŋ′kə-), *n.pl.* material pertaining to Abraham Lincoln, as objects, writings, anecdotes, etc. [LINCOLN + -IANA]

Lin′coln Park′, 1. a city in SE Michigan. 53,933 (1960). **2.** a town in N New Jersey. 6048 (1960). **3.** a town in SE New York. 2707 (1960).

Lin′coln's Birth′day, February 12, a legal holiday in many states of the U.S., in honor of the birth of Abraham Lincoln.

Lin·coln·shire (liŋ′kən shēr′, -shər), *n.* a county in E England. 743,383 (1961); 2663 sq. mi. *Co. seat:* Lincoln. Also called **Lincoln.**

Lin′coln's Inn′. See under **Inns of Court** (def. 1).

Lin′coln's spar′row, a North American sparrow, *Melospiza lincolnii*, having a buff breast with black streaks. [named (by Audubon) after Thomas *Lincoln* (d. 1883)]

Lin·coln·ton (liŋ′kən tən), *n.* a town in central North Carolina. 5699 (1960).

Lind (lind), *n.* **Jenny** (*Johanna Maria Lind Goldschmidt*) (*"The Swedish Nightingale"*), 1820–87, Swedish soprano.

Lin·da (lin′də), *n.* a girl's given name. Also, **Lynda.**

lin·dane (lin′dān), *n. Chem.* a white, crystalline, water-insoluble powder, $C_6H_6Cl_6$, the gamma isomer of benzene hexachloride: used chiefly as an insecticide and weed-killer. [named after T. van der *Linden*, 20th-century Dutch chemist; see -ANE]

Lind·bergh (lind′bûrg, lin′-), *n.* **Charles Augustus,** born 1902, U.S. aviator: made the first solo, nonstop, transatlantic flight 1927.

Lin·de·löf (lin′də lof′, -lôf′, -lœf′), *adj.* of or pertaining to a topological space having the property that every cover consisting of open sets has a subcover consisting of a countable number of subsets. [named after Ernst *Lindelöf*]

lin·den (lin′dən), *n.* **1.** any tree of the genus *Tilia*, as *T. americana* **(American linden)** or *T. europaea* **(European linden),** having fragrant yellowish-white flowers and cordate leaves, grown as an ornamental or shade tree. **2.** the soft, light, white wood of any of these trees, used for making furniture and in the construction of houses, boxes, etc. [n. use of obs. ME, OE *linden* (adj.) of the lime tree. See LIME[3], -EN[2]]

Lin·den (lin′dən), *n.* **1.** a city in NE New Jersey, near Newark. 39,931 (1960). **2.** a town in W Alabama. 2516 (1960).

Lin·de·nau (lin′də nou′), *n.* a crater in the fourth quadrant of the face of the moon: about 32 miles in diameter.

Lin·den·hurst (lin′dən hûrst′), *n.* a city on central Long Island, in SE New York. 20,905 (1960).

Lin·den·wold (lin′dən wōld′), *n.* a town in SW New Jersey. 7335 (1960).

Lind·es·nes (lin′dis nes′), *n.* a cape at the S tip of Norway, on the North Sea. Also called **The Naze.**

Lin·di (lin′dē), *n.* a seaport in SE Tanzania. 10,315 (1957).

Lind·ley (lind′lē, lin′-), *n.* **1. John,** 1799–1865, English botanist. **2.** a boy's given name.

Lin·don (lin′dən), *n.* a boy's given name. Also, **Lyndon.**

Lind·say (lind′zē, lin′-), *n.* **1. Howard,** 1889–1968, U.S. playwright, producer, and actor. **2. John V(liet)** (vlēt), born 1921, U.S. political leader: mayor of New York City since 1966. **3. (Nicholas) Va·chel** (vā′chəl), 1879–1931, U.S. poet. **4.** a town in central California. 5397 (1960). **5.** a town in central Oklahoma. 4258 (1960).

Linds·borg (linz′bôrg), *n.* a town in central Kansas. 2609 (1960).

Lind·sey (lind′zē, lin′-), *n.* **1. Ben(jamin Barr)** (bär), 1869–1943, U.S. jurist and authority on juvenile delinquency. **2.** Also, **Lind′say.** a boy's given name.

lin·dy (lin′dē), *n., pl.* **-dies,** *v.,* **-died, -dy·ing.** —*n.* **1.** Also called **lin′dy hop′.** an energetic jitterbug dance. —*v.i.* **2.** to dance the lindy. [prob. from nickname of Charles A. LINDBERGH]

Lin·dy (lin′dē), *n.* a girl's given name, form of **Linda.**

Lin·dy·beth (lin′dē beth′), *n.* a girl's given name.

Lin·dy·lou (lin′dē lōō′, lin′dē lōō′), *n.* a girl's given name.

line[1] (līn), *n., v.,* **lined, lin·ing.** —*n.* **1.** a mark or stroke long in proportion to its breadth, made with a pen, pencil, tool, etc., on a surface: *Draw two lines down the page.* **2.** *Math.* a continuous extent of length, straight or curved, without breadth or thickness; the trace of a moving point. **3.** something resembling a traced line, as a band of color, a seam, a furrow, etc.: *lines of stratification in rock.* **4.** a furrow or wrinkle on the face, neck, etc.: *a new face cream guaranteed to erase lines.* **5.** something arranged along a line, esp. a straight line; a row or series: *a line of trees.* **6.** a number of persons standing one behind the other and waiting their turns at or for something; queue. **7.** a row of written or printed letters, words, etc.: *a page of 30 lines.* **8.** banner (def. 7). **9.** a verse of poetry: *A line in iambic pentameter contains five feet.* **10.** Usually, **lines.** a speech given an actor in a play; the spoken words of an actor's part, or of a drama, musical comedy, etc.: *One of his best lines was cut. The hero forgot his lines. Who has the next line?* **11.** a short written message: *a line from a friend; to drop someone a line.* **12.** an indication of demarcation; boundary; limit: *to draw a line between right and wrong.* **13.** a course of action, procedure, thought, policy, etc.: *to vote along party lines; to mouth the Communist party line.* **14.** a piece of pertinent information (usually fol. by *on*): *I've got a line on a good used car. Try to get a line on that new fellow she's dating.* **15.** a course of direction; route: *the line of march.* **16.** a series of generations of persons, animals, or plants descended from a common ancestor: *a line of kings; a line of thoroughbred horses.* **17.** *Slang.* a mode of conversation, esp. one that is glib or exaggerated in order to impress or influence another person: *He really handed her a line about his rich relatives.* **18. lines, a.** outline or contour: *a ship of fine lines.* **b.** plan of construction, action, or procedure: *two books written along the same lines.* **c.** *Informal.* a certificate of marriage. **d.** *Rare.* one's lot or portion: *to endure the hard lines of poverty.* **19.** a department of activity; a kind of occupation or business: *What line is he in?* **20.** a transportation company: *The steamship line is advertising inexpensive tours.* **21.** a system of public conveyances, as buses, steamers, etc., plying regularly between places and over specified routes. **22.** *Elect.* **a.** a wire circuit connecting two or more pieces of electric apparatus, esp. the wire or wires connecting points or stations in a telegraph or telephone system, or the system itself. **b.** maxwell. **23.** *Television.* one scanning line. **24.** *Fine Arts.* **a.** a mark made by a pencil, brush, crayon, etc., that serves to define the contours of a shape, or to form hatching, and that constitutes a primary element in the formal structure of a work of art. **b.** the edge of a shape. **25.** a straight line drawn from an observed object to the fovea of the eye: *line of vision; line of sight.* **26.** a circle of the terrestrial or celestial sphere: *the equinoctial line.* **27. the line,** *Geog.* the equator. **28.** a stock of commercial goods of the same general class but having a range of styles, sizes, prices, or quality: *The salesman said his new line of women's shoes was very popular.* **29.** *Insurance.* **a.** a class or type of insurance: *casualty line.* **b.** the amount of insurance written for a particular risk. **30.** *Law.* a limit defining one estate from another; the outline or boundary of a piece of real estate. **31.** *Bridge.* a line on a score sheet that separates points scored toward game **(below the line)** from points scored by setting a contract, having honors, etc. **(above the line). 32.** *Music.* any of the straight, horizontal, parallel strokes of the staff, or one placed above or below the staff. **33.** *Mil.* **a.** a defensive position or front. **b.** a series of fortifications: *the Maginot line.* **34.** Usually, **lines.** a distribution of troops, sentries, etc., for the defense of a position or for an attack: *within the enemy's lines.* **35.** (formerly) an arrangement of troops of an army or of ships of a fleet as drawn up for battle: *line of battle.* **36.** a body or formation of troops or ships drawn up abreast (distinguished from *column*). **37.** the body of military personnel comprising the combatant forces of an army, as distinguished from the supply services and staff corps. **38.** the class of officers serving with combatant units or warships. **39.** that part of an administrative organization consisting of persons actively engaged on a given project. Cf. **staff**[1] (def. 8). **40.** (formerly) the regular forces of an army or navy. **41.** a thread, string, cord, rope, or the like. **42.** a strong cord or slender rope. **43.** a clothesline: *Are the things on the line dry yet?* **44.** a cord, wire, or the like, used for measuring or as a guide. **45.** *Naut.* a pipe or hose: *a steam line.* **46.** Also, **ligne.** a unit, 1/40 inch, for measuring the diameter of buttons. **47.** *Angling.* a length of nylon, silk, linen, cord, etc., to which are attached the leader, hook, sinker, float, etc. **48.** *Football.* **a.** either of the two front rows of opposing players lined up opposite each other on the line of scrimmage: *a strong line.* **b.** See **line of scrimmage. 49.** *Fencing.* any of the four divisions of the portion of a fencer's body on which a touch can be scored, taken as an area of attack or defense. **50.** *Textiles.* the longer and preferred flax or hemp fibers. Cf. **tow**[2] (def. 2). **51.** *Fox Hunting.* the trail of scent left by a fox. **52.** a unit of length equivalent to 1/12 inch. **53. all along the line,** in every detail; entirely: *This report has proved inaccurate all along the line.* **54. bring, come,** or **get into line, a.** to become or cause to become straight, as in a row: *The members of the marching band got into line. The riders brought their mounts into line.* **b.** to conform or cause to conform or agree: *He was persuaded to come into line with the party policy. He finally succeeded in bringing his opponents into line with his own views.* **55. draw the line,** to impose a restriction; limit: *They would draw the line at murder.* **56. give line,** *Survey.* (of a lineman) to mark the position of a survey mark so that it can be observed from a distance. **57. go up in one's lines,** *U.S. Theat.* to forget one's part. Also, *Brit.,* **go up on one's lines. 58. hard lines,** *Brit. Informal.* bad luck; a hard lot. **59. hold the line,** to maintain the status quo, esp. in order to forestall unfavorable developments: *The cost-of-living index held the line last month. We're trying to hold the line on prices.* **60. in line, a.** in alignment; straight. **b.** in conformity or agreement. **c.** in control (of one's conduct): *He could never seem to keep his temper in line.* **61. in line of duty,** in the execution of the duties belonging to some occupation, esp. with regard to the responsibility for life and death: *a policeman who met his death in line of duty.* Also, **in the line of duty. 62. lay it on the line,** *Slang.* **a.** to give money; pay. **b.** to give the required information; speak directly or frankly: *I'm going to stop beating about the bush and lay it on the line with you.* **63. on a line,** *Baseball.* (of a batted or thrown ball) through the air in an approximately straight line from the point of impact or delivery: *hit on a line between third and short; thrown in on a line from the center fielder.* **64. on line,** *Survey.* on a survey line. **65. out of line, a.** not in a straight line. **b.** *Slang.* in disagreement with what is accepted or practiced. **c.** *Slang.* impertinent; presumptuous: *That last remark was out of line.* **66. read between the lines,** to comprehend the unexpressed but implied meaning of something said or written: *Her letter sounded cheerful enough, but I read a certain sadness between the lines.* **67. take line,** *Survey.* (of a lineman) to place a range pole or the like according to the directions of a transitman. **68. toe the line** or **mark, a.** to conform strictly to a rule, command, etc. **b.** to shoulder responsibilities; do one's duty: *Because he was new and*

wanted to do a good job, he tried hard to toe the line.
—*v.i.* **69.** to take a position in a line; range (often fol. by *up*): *to line up before the start of a parade.* **70.** *Baseball.* **a.** to hit a line drive. **b.** to line out.
—*v.t.* **71.** to bring into a line, or into line with others (often fol. by *up*): *Line up your men, corporal! Line up the target in your sights.* **72.** to secure; make available; get hold of (usually fol. by *up*): *We have to line up a speaker for the banquet; to line up evidence for a legal case.* **73.** to delineate with or as with lines; draw: *to line the silhouette of a person's head.* **74.** to mark with a line or lines: *to line paper for writing.* **75.** to sketch verbally or in writing; outline (often fol. by *out*): *We followed the plan he had lined out.* **76.** to arrange a line along: *to line a coast with colonies.* **77.** to form a line along: *People lined the streets. Trees lined the drive.* **78.** to apply liner to (the eyes). **79.** *Archaic.* to measure or test with a line. **80. line out, a.** *Baseball, Softball.* to be put out by hitting a line drive caught on the fly by a player of the opposing team. **b.** to execute or perform: *He lined out a few songs upon request.* [ME, OE: cord, rope, stroke, mark, row, guiding rule < L *līnea,* n. use of fem. of *līneus* flaxen, equiv to *līn(um)* flax (see LINE²) + *-eus* -EOUS] —**lin′a·ble, line′a·ble,** *adj.* —**line′less,** *adj.* —**line′like′,** *adj.*

line² (līn), *v.,* **lined, lin·ing,** *n.* —*v.t.* **1.** to cover the inner side of: *I used blue silk to line the dress.* **2.** to provide with a layer of material applied to the inner side: *to line a coat with silk.* **3.** to serve to cover: *Velvet draperies lined the walls of the chamber.* **4.** to furnish or fill: *a purse well lined with questionable profits.* **5.** to reinforce the back of a book with glued fabric, paper, vellum, etc. —*n.* **6.** a thickness of glue, as between two veneers in a sheet of plywood. [ME *lyne(n),* deriv. of *line* flax, linen, OE *līn* < L *līnum* flax]

lin·e·age¹ (lin′ē ij), *n.* **1.** lineal descent from an ancestor; ancestry or extraction: *She could trace her lineage back several centuries.* **2.** the line of descendants of a particular ancestor; family; race. [LINE(AL) + -AGE; r. ME *linage* < AF; OF *lignage* < LL **līneāticum.* See LINE¹, -AGE]
—**Syn. 1.** pedigree, parentage, derivation; genealogy. **2.** tribe, clan.

line·age² (lī′nij), *n.* linage.

lin·e·al (lin′ē əl), *adj.* **1.** being in the direct line, as a descendant, ancestor, etc., or in a direct line, as descent, succession, etc. **2.** of or transmitted by lineal descent. **3.** linear. [late ME < LL *līneāl(is).* See LINE¹, -AL¹] —**lin′e·al·ly,** *adv.*

lin·e·a·ment (lin′ē ə mənt), *n.* **1.** Often, **lineaments.** a feature or detail of a face, body, or figure, considered with respect to its outline or contour: *She carefully examined every lineament of her face. His fine lineaments made him the very image of his father.* **2.** Usually, **lineaments.** distinguishing features; distinctive characteristics: *The lineaments of the time made him despair.* [< L *līneāment(um)* a stroke, pl., features, equiv. to *līneā(re)* (to) draw a line (see LINE¹) + *-mentum* -MENT] —**lin·e·a·men·tal** (lin′ē ə men′təl), *adj.* —**lin′e·a·men·ta′tion,** *n.*

lin·e·ar (lin′ē ər), *adj.* **1.** extended or arranged in a line: *a linear series.* **2.** involving measurement in one dimension only; pertaining to length: *linear measure.* **3.** pertaining to or represented by lines: *linear dimensions.* **4.** consisting of or using lines: *linear design.* **5.** of or pertaining to the characteristics of a work of art in which forms and rhythms are defined chiefly in terms of line. **6.** having the form of or resembling a line: *linear nebulae.* **7.** *Math.* **a.** consisting of, involving, or describable by terms of the first degree: *a linear equation.* **b.** having the same effect on a sum as on each of the summands: *a linear operation.* **8.** threadlike; narrow and elongated: *a linear leaf.* [< L *līneār(is)* of, belonging to lines. See LINE¹, -AR¹] —**lin′e·ar·ly,** *adv.*

Linear leaf

Linear A, an ancient system of writing, not yet deciphered, inscribed on clay tablets, pottery, and other objects found at Minoan sites on Crete and other Greek islands.

lin′ear accel′erator, *Physics.* an accelerator in which particles are propelled in straight paths by the use of alternating electric voltages so placed that the particles receive increasing increments of energy.

lin′ear al′gebra, *Math.* See under **algebra** (def. 2).

Linear B, an ancient system of writing representing a very early form of Greek, deciphered by Michael Ventris chiefly from clay tablets found at Knossos on Crete and at Pylos.

lin′ear combina′tion, *Math.* a polynomial in several variables, all of which are raised to the first power.

lin′ear depend′ence, *Math.* the property of a set of elements, often vectors, in which multiplying each element and adding the resulting quantities results in zero for some set of scalars not all equal to zero. Cf. **linear independence.**

lin′ear differen′tial equa′tion, *Math.* an equation involving derivatives in which the dependent variables and all the derivatives appearing in the equation are raised to the first power.

lin′ear frac′tional transforma′tion, *Math.* See **Möbius transformation.**

lin′ear func′tional, *Math.* a function having scalar values, the domain being a linear space and having the properties that the function of the sum of two elements is equal to the sum of the functional values of the two elements, and the function of a scalar times an element of the space is equal to the scalar times the functional value of the element.

lin′ear graph′, *Math.* graph (def. 2b).

lin′ear independ′ence, *Math.* the property of a set of elements, often vectors, in which multiplying each element of the set by a scalar chosen from some particular set of scalars and adding the resulting quantities gives zero only if all the chosen scalars were zero. Cf. **linear dependence.**

lin·e·ar·ise (lin′ē ə rīz′), *v.t.,* **-ised, -is·ing.** *Chiefly Brit.* linearize. —**lin′e·ar·i·sa′tion,** *n.*

lin·e·ar·i·ty (lin′ē ar′i tē), *n., pl.* **-ties. 1.** the property, quality, or state of being linear. **2.** *Television.* the accuracy with which the shapes in a televised image are reproduced on the screen of a receiving set. **3.** *Electronics.* the measure of the extent to which a certain response is directly proportional to the applied excitation. [LINEAR + -ITY]

lin·e·ar·ize (lin′ē ə rīz′), *v.t.,* **-ized, -iz·ing.** to make linear; give linear form to. Also, *esp. Brit.,* **linearise.** [LINEAR + -IZE] —**lin′e·ar·i·za′tion,** *n.*

lin′early or′dered set′, *Math.* See **totally ordered set.**

lin′ear man′ifold, *Math.* subspace (def. 2).

lin′ear meas′ure, 1. any system of measurement for measuring length. **2.** any unit of measurement used in linear measure, as the inch, foot, meter, etc.

lin′ear perspec′tive, a mathematical system for representing three-dimensional objects and space on a two-dimensional surface by means of intersecting lines that are drawn vertically and horizontally and that radiate from one point (**one-point perspective**), two points (**two-point perspective**), or several points on a horizon line as perceived by a viewer imagined in an arbitrarily fixed position. See diag. under **perspective.**

lin′ear polariza′tion, *Optics.* See **plane polarization.**

lin′ear pro′gramming, *Math.* any of several methods for finding where a given linear function of several nonnegative variables assumes an extreme value and for determining the extreme value, the variable usually being subjected to constraints in the form of linear equalities or inequalities.

lin′ear space′, *Math.* See **vector space.**

lin′ear transforma′tion, *Math.* a map from one vector space to a vector space having the same field of scalars, with the properties that the map of the sum of two vectors is the sum of the maps of the vectors and the map of a scalar times a vector equals the scalar times the map of the vector. Also called **lin′ear op′erator.**

lin·e·ate (lin′ē it, -āt′), *adj.* marked with lines, esp. lengthwise, parallel lines; striped. Also, **lin′e·at′ed.** [< L *līneāt(us)* lined, made straight, ptp. of *līneāre.* See LINEAMENT, -ATE¹]

lin·e·a·tion (lin′ē ā′shən), *n.* **1.** the act of marking with or tracing by lines. **2.** a division into lines. **3.** an outline or delineation. **4.** an arrangement or group of lines. [ME *lyneacion* < LL *līneātiōn-* (s. of *līneātiō*) the drawing of a line. See LINEATE, -ION]

line·back·er (līn′bak′ər), *n. Football.* **1.** a player on defense who takes a position close behind the linemen. **2.** the position played by this player. [LINE¹ + BACKER]

line·bred (līn′bred′), *adj.* produced by linebreeding. [LINE¹ + BRED]

line·breed·ing (līn′brē′ding), *n. Genetics.* a form of inbreeding directed toward keeping the offspring closely related to a superior ancestor. [LINE¹ + BREEDING]

line-cast·ing (līn′kas′ting, -käs′ting), *n. Print.* the casting of an entire line of type in a slug. —**line′ cast′er.**

line′ cop′y, *Print.* a document, drawing, or the like, consisting of two tones, as black and white, without intermediate gradations. Cf. **halftone** (def. 1).

line′ cut′, *Print.* an engraving consisting only of lines or areas that are solid black or white. Cf. **halftone** (def. 2).

line′ draw′ing, a drawing done exclusively in line, providing gradations in tone entirely through variations in width and density.

line′ drive′, *Baseball.* a ball batted in the air that describes little or no arc in flight and usually travels with great speed. Also called **liner.**

line′ drop′, *Elect.* the decrease in voltage between two points on an electric line, often caused by resistance or leakage along the line.

line′ engrav′ing, 1. a technique of engraving in which all effects are produced by variations in the width and density of lines incised with a burin. **2.** a metal plate so engraved. **3.** a print or picture made from it. —**line′ engrav′er.**

line′ gale′. See **equinoctial storm.**

line′ gauge′, a printer's ruler, usually marked off in points, picas, agates, and inches, and sometimes also in centimeters.

line′ in′tegral, *Math.* the limit, as the norm of the partition of a given curve approaches zero, of the sum of the product of the length of the arcs in the partition times the value of the function at some point on each arc.

line·man (līn′mən), *n., pl.* **-men. 1.** Also, **linesman.** a man who installs or repairs telephone, telegraph, or other wires. **2.** *Survey.* a person who marks the positions of a survey mark with a range pole or the like. **3.** *Football.* one of the players in the line, as a center, guard, tackle, or end. [LINE¹ + MAN¹]

lin·en (lin′ən), *n.* **1.** fabric woven from flax yarns. **2.** Often, **linens.** clothing, bedding, etc., made of linen cloth or a more common substitute, as cotton. **3.** yarn made of flax fiber. **4.** thread made of flax yarns. **5. wash one's dirty linen in public,** to discuss in public one's personal scandals or domestic difficulties. —*adj.* **6.** made of linen. [ME *lin(n)en* (n., adj.), OE *linnen, līnen* (adj.) made of flax, equiv. to *līn* flax (< L *līnum*) + *-en* -EN²] —**lin′en·y,** *adj.*

lin′en clos′et, a closet in which sheets, towels, table linen, etc., are kept.

lin′en drap′er, *Brit.* a drygoods merchant.

lin·en·fold (lin′ən fōld′), *n.* an ornamental motif resembling folded linen, carved on paneling. Also called **lin′en pat′tern.** [LINEN + FOLD¹]

lin′en pan′el, a panel carved with a linenfold.

lin′en pa′per, paper made from pure linen or from substitutes which produce a similar paper finish.

line′ of ap′sides, *Astron.* the line connecting the two apsides of an eccentric orbit, being coincident with the major axis of the orbit. Also called **apse line.**

line′ of bat′tle, *Mil., Navy.* a line formed by troops or ships for delivering or receiving an attack.

line′-of-bat′tle ship′ (līn′əv bat′əl). See **ship of the line.**

line′ of cred′it. See **credit line** (def. 2).

line′ of′ficer, *Mil.* an officer serving with combatant units or warships, as distinguished from a staff officer, supply officer, etc.

line′ of fire′, the straight horizontal line from the muzzle of a weapon in the direction of the axis of the bore, just prior to firing.

line′ of force′, *Physics.* an imaginary line or curve in a field of force, as an electric field, such that the direction of the line at any point is that of the force in the field at that point. Also called **field line.**

line′ of induc′tion, *Physics Obs.* a line of force in a magnetic field.

line′ of posi′tion, *Navig.* a line connecting all the possible positions of a vessel or aircraft, as determined by a single observation. Also called **position line.**

line′ of scrim′mage, *Football.* an imaginary line parallel to the goal lines that passes from one sideline to the other through the point of the football closest to the goal line of each team.

line′ of sight′, 1. Also called **line′ of sight′ing.** an imaginary straight line running through the perfectly aligned sights of a firearm. **2.** *Astron.* an imaginary line from an observer to a celestial body, coincident with the path traveled by light rays received from the body. **3.** *Radio.* a straight line connecting two points sufficiently high and near one another so that the line is entirely above the surface of the earth. **4.** *Ophthalm.* See **line of vision.**

line′ of site′, *Mil.* a straight line from the muzzle of an artillery gun to its target.

line′ of vi′sion, *Ophthalm.* a straight line that connects the fovea centralis of an eye with the point focused on.

lin·e·o·late (lin′ē ə lāt′), *adj. Zool., Bot.* marked with minute lines; finely lineate. Also, **lin′e·o·lat′ed.** [< L *līneol(a)* (dim. of *līnea* LINE¹) + -ATE¹]

lin·er¹ (lī′nər), *n.* **1.** one of a commercial line of steamships or airplanes. **2.** one who or that which traces by or marks with lines. **3.** *Baseball.* See **line drive. 4.** a cosmetic, esp. a grease pencil or other preparation used to outline or highlight the eyes. **5.** *Obs.* See **ship of the line.** [LINE¹ + -ER¹]

lin·er² (lī′nər), *n.* **1.** one who fits or provides linings. **2.** something serving as a lining. **3.** a protective covering, usually of cardboard, for a phonograph record or records; album; jacket: *A leading music critic did the notes on the liner.* [LINE² + -ER¹]

lines·man (līnz′mən), *n., pl.* **-men. 1.** lineman (def. 1). **2.** *Sports.* **a.** an official, as in tennis and soccer, who assists the referee. **b.** *Football.* an official who marks the distances gained and lost in the progress of play and otherwise assists the referee and field judge. [LINE¹ + -'S¹ + MAN¹]

line′ space′, (on a typewriter) the horizontal space provided for a line of typing.

line′ spec′trum, *Physics.* an optical spectrum, usually characteristic of an excited atom, in which the lines of the spectrum are clustered in defined, separated groups, the groups corresponding to quanta of radiated energy. Cf. **continuous spectrum.**

lines′ plan′, *Naval Archit.* a set of scale drawings defining the hull form of a vessel, comprising a body plan, a half-breadth plan, and a sheer plan, usually made to molded dimensions and showing water lines, stations, diagonals, and bow and buttock lines. Also called **lines′ draw′ing.**

line′ squall′, (not in technical use) a squall advancing along a front that forms a more or less definite line.

line′ storm′. See **equinoctial storm.**

Li·net·ta (li net′ə), *n.* a girl's given name. Also, **Linnet, Linnete, Lynette.**

line-up (līn′up′), *n.* **1.** a particular order or disposition of persons or things as lined up or drawn up for action, inspection, etc. **2.** the persons or things themselves: *a suspect identified in a police line-up.* **3.** *Sports.* the list of the participating players in a game together with their positions: *to announce the starting line-up of a game.* **4.** an organization of people, companies, etc., for some common purpose: *a line-up of support for the new tax bill.* Also, **line′up′.** [n. use of v. phrase *line up*]

line′ vec′tor, *Math.* See **sliding vector.**

line′ volt′age, *Elect.* the voltage supplied by a power line, measured at the point of use.

line·y (lī′nē), *adj.,* **lin·i·er, lin·i·est.** liny.

lin ft, linear foot.

ling¹ (ling), *n., pl.* (*esp. collectively*) **ling,** (*esp. referring to two or more kinds or species*) **lings. 1.** an elongated, marine, gadoid food fish, *Molva molva,* found in Greenland and northern Europe. **2.** the burbot. **3.** any of various other elongated food fishes. [ME *ling, lenge;* c. D *leng;* akin to Icel *langa;* so called from its length. See LONG¹]

ling² (ling), *n.* the heather, *Calluna vulgaris.* [ME *lyng* < Scand; cf. Icel *lyng*]

-ling¹, a suffix of nouns, often pejorative, denoting one concerned with (*hireling; underling*), or diminutive (*princeling; duckling*). [ME, OE; c. G *-ling,* Icel *-lingr,* Goth *-lings;* orig. *-l-* (OE *-la,* hypocoristic suffix) + *-ing* -ING¹]

-ling², an adverbial suffix expressing direction, position, state, etc.: *darkling; sideling.* [ME, OE; adv. use of gradational var. *lang* LONG¹]

ling., linguistics.

lin·ga (ling′gə), *n.* **1.** *Sanskrit Gram.* the masculine gender. **2.** (in popular Hinduism) a phallus, symbol of Siva. Also, **lin·gam** (ling′gəm). Cf. **yoni.** [< Skt, s. of *lingam* mark, token, penis]

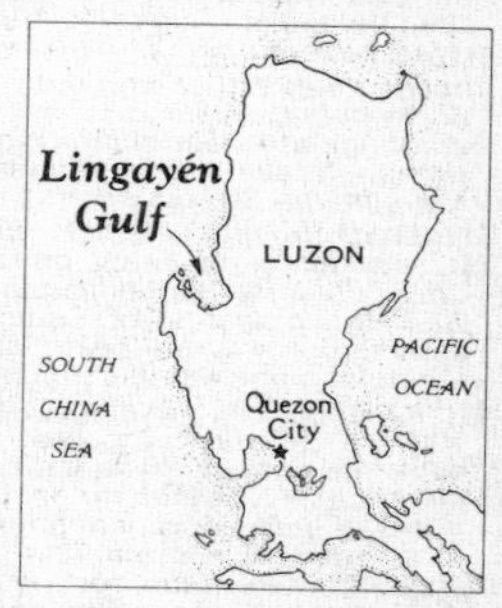

Lin·ga·yat (ling gä′yit), *n. Hinduism.* a member of the Lingayata cult. [< Kanarese *lingāyata;* see LINGA]

Lin·ga·ya·ta (ling gä′yə tə), *n. Hinduism.* a Saiva cult emphasizing devotion and faith. Also called **Vira Saiva.** [< Kanarese; akin to Skt *linga* LINGA]

Lin·ga·yén′ Gulf′ (ling′gä yen′), a gulf in the Philippines, on the NW coast of Luzon.

ling·cod (ling′kod′), *n., pl.* **-cods,** (*esp. collectively*) **-cod.** a large-mouthed game fish, *Ophiodon elongatus,* found in the North Pacific, related to the greenling. Also, **ling′ cod′.** Also called **cultus.** [LING¹ + COD¹]

lin·ger (ling′gər), *v.i.* **1.** to remain or stay on in a place longer than is usual or expected, as if from reluctance to leave it: *We lingered awhile after the party.* **2.** to remain alive; continue or persist, although slowly dying or tending to cease, disappear, etc.: *She lingered only a few months after the heart attack. Such practices still linger among the older natives.* **3.** to dwell in contemplation, thought, or enjoyment: *to linger over the beauty of a poem.* **4.** to be tardy in action; delay; dawdle: *to linger in discharging one's duties.* **5.** to walk slowly; saunter along. —*v.t.* **6.** to pass (time, life, etc.) in a leisurely or a tedious manner (usually fol. by *away* or *out*): *We lingered away the whole summer at the beach. He lingered out his last years in utter solitude.* **7.** *Archaic.* to drag out or protract. [ME *lenger* to dwell, remain (somewhere), freq. of *lengen*, OE *lengan* to delay, prolong, lit., lengthen. See LONG¹, -ER⁶] —**lin′ger·er,** *n.* —**lin′ger·ing·ly,** *adv.*
—**Syn. 1, 4.** tarry. **1, 5.** loiter.

lin·ge·rie (län′zhə rā′, lan′zhə rē′, -jə-; *Fr.* lanzhᵊ rē′), *n.* **1.** underwear, sleepwear, and the like, of linen, cotton, silk, rayon, lace, etc., worn by women. **2.** *Archaic.* linen goods in general. —*adj.* **3.** having the qualities of lingerie; being lacy or frilly. [< F, equiv. to MF *linge* linen (< L *līneus* of flax; see LINE¹) + *-erie* -ERY]

lin·go¹ (ling′gō), *n., pl.* **-goes.** *Informal.* **1.** language or speech, esp. if strange or foreign. **2.** the specialized language or speech peculiar to a particular field, group, class, etc.; terminology. **3.** the language or speech peculiar to a particular individual. [< Lingua Franca < It *lin(gua)* tongue (<L) + Pr *(len)go* tongue < L *lingua*; see LINGUA]
—**Syn. 2.** cant, argot, patois, slang, jargon.

lin·go² (ling′gō), *n., pl.* **-goes.** lingoe.

lin·goe (ling′gō), *n.* **1.** a metal weight attached to the cords of a Jacquard harness, for lowering the warp threads after they have been raised and for keeping the harness cords taut. **2.** the same object attached to a drawloom. Also, **lingo.** [prob. < F *lingot* INGOT]

ling·on·ber·ry (ling′ən ber′ē), *n., pl.* **-ries.** the cowberry, *Vaccinium Vitis-Idaea.* [< Sw *lingon* mountain cranberry + BERRY]

-lings, var. of **-ling².** [ME *-linges.* See -LING², -S¹]

lin·gua (ling′gwə), *n., pl.* **-guae** (-gwē). the tongue or a part like a tongue. [< L]

lin′gua fran′ca (frang′kə), *pl.* **lingua francas, lin·guae fran·cae** (ling′gwē fran′sē). **1.** any language that is widely used as a means of communication among speakers of other languages. **2.** (*cap.*) the Italian-Provençal jargon formerly widely used in eastern Mediterranean ports. [< It: lit., Frankish tongue]

lin′gua ge·ral′ (zhə räl′), (*often caps.*) a lingua franca based on Tupí and spoken in the Amazon basin of South America. [< Pg: general language]

lin·gual (ling′gwəl), *adj.* **1.** of or pertaining to the tongue or some tonguelike part. **2.** pertaining to languages. **3.** *Phonet.* articulated with the aid of the tongue, esp. the tip of the tongue, as *d, n, s,* or *r.* —*n.* **4.** *Phonet.* a lingual sound. [< ML *linguāl(is).* See LINGUA, -AL¹] —**lin′gual·ly,** *adv.*

lin′gual protru′sion lisp′, *Phonet.* See under **lisp** (def. 2).

lin·gui·form (ling′gwə fôrm′), *adj.* tongue-shaped. [< L *lingu(a)* tongue + -I- + -FORM]

lin·gui·ni (ling gwē′nē), *n.* *Italian Cookery.* a type of pasta in long, slender, flat pieces. [< It, pl. of *linguino*, dim. of *lingua* tongue; see -INE¹]

lin·guist (ling′gwist), *n.* **1.** a person who is skilled in several languages; polyglot. **2.** a specialist in linguistics. [< L *lingu(a)* tongue + -IST]

lin·guis·tic (ling gwis′tik), *adj.* **1.** of or belonging to language: *linguistic change.* **2.** of or pertaining to linguistics. [LINGUIST + -IC] —**lin·guis′ti·cal·ly,** *adv.*

lin·guis·ti·cal (ling gwis′ti kəl), *adj.* (not in technical use) linguistic. [LINGUISTIC + -AL¹]

linguis′tic at′las. See **dialect atlas.**

linguis′tic form′, any meaningful unit of speech, as a sentence, phrase, word, suffix, etc.

linguis′tic geog′raphy. See **dialect geography.** —**linguis′tic geog′rapher.**

lin·guis·ti·cian (ling′gwi stish′ən), *n.* *Rare.* linguist (def. 2). [LINGUISTIC + -IAN]

lin·guis·tics (ling gwis′tiks), *n.* (*construed as sing.*) the science of language, including phonetics, phonology, morphology, and syntax and often divided into historical linguistics and descriptive linguistics. [see LINGUISTIC, -ICS]

linguis′tic stock′, **1.** a parent language and all its derived dialects and languages. **2.** the people speaking any of these dialects or languages.

lin·gu·late (ling′gyə lāt′), *adj.* formed like a tongue; ligulate. Also, **lin′gu·lat′ed.** [< L *lingulāt(us)* tongue-shaped, equiv. to *lingul(a)* (dim. of *lingua* tongue; see -ULE) + *-ātus* -ATE¹]

lin·i·ment (lin′ə mənt), *n.* a liquid preparation, usually oily, for rubbing on or applying to the skin, as for sprains, bruises, etc. [late ME *lynyment* < LL *linīmentum* ointment, equiv. to *linī(re)* (var. of *linere* to smear) + *-mentum* -MENT]

li·nin (lī′nin), *n.* *Biol.* the substance forming the netlike structure which connects the chromatin granules in the nucleus of a cell. [< L *līn(um)* flax + -IN²]

lin·ing¹ (lī′ning), *n.* **1.** that with which something is lined; a layer of material on the inner side of something. **2.** *Bookbinding.* the material used to strengthen the back of a book after the sheets have been folded, backed, and sewed. **3.** the act or process of lining something. [late ME *lynyng.* See LINE², -ING¹]

lin·ing² (lī′ning), *n.* **1.** the act or process of lining. **2.** the act of marking or ornamenting a surface with lines. **3.** a design or ornamentation composed of lines. **4.** *Print.* a system of designing type so that all characters of the same point size, regardless of font, will align with one another. [LINE¹ + -ING¹]

link¹ (lingk), *n.* **1.** one of the rings or separate pieces of which a chain is composed. **2.** anything serving to connect one part or thing with another; a bond or tie: *The locket was a link with the past.* **3.** a ring, loop, or the like: *a link of hair.* **4.** any of a number of sausages in a chain. **5.** a unit in a communications system, as a radio relay station, a television booster station, etc. **6.** a cuff link: *He's wearing a beautiful pair of ruby links.* **7.** *Survey., Civ. Eng.* **a.** (in a surveyor's chain) a unit of length equal to 7.92 inches. **b.** one of 100 rods or loops of equal length forming a surveyor's or engineer's chain. **8.** *Chem.* bond¹ (def. 15). **9.** *Elect.* See **fuse link. 10.** *Mach.* a rigid, movable piece or rod, connected with other parts by means of pivots or the like, for the purpose of transmitting motion. **11.** *Typography.* the connecting line between the bowl and tail of a *g.* —*v.t., v.i.* **12.** to join by or as by a link or links; unite (often fol. by *up*): *The new bridge will link the island to the mainland. The company will soon link up with a hotel chain.* [late ME *link(e)* < ODan *lænkia* chain; c. Icel *hlekkr* link (pl., chain), OE *hlence* coat of chain mail, akin to G *Gelenk* joint]
—**Syn. 2.** connection, connective, copula. **12.** bond, connect, league, conjoin, fasten, bind, tie, pin.

link² (lingk), *n.* a torch, esp. of tow and pitch. [? special use of LINK¹; the torches so called may have been made of strands twisted together in chainlike form]

link·age (ling′kij), *n.* **1.** the act of linking; state or manner of being linked. **2.** a system of links. **3.** *Genetics.* an association between two or more genes located on the same chromosome which tends to cause the characters determined by these genes to be inherited as an inseparable unit. **4.** *Mach.* an assembly of four or more rods for transmitting motion, usually in the same plane or in parallel planes. Cf. **space linkage. 5.** any of various mathematical or drawing devices consisting of a combination of bars or pieces pivoted together so as to turn about one another, usually in parallel planes. **6.** *Elect.* a quantity associated with the magnetic flux in a coil or circuit, equal to the product of the number of lines of magnetic flux times the number of turns in the coil or circuit. [LINK¹ + -AGE]

link′age group′, *Genetics.* a group of genes in a chromosome that tend to be inherited as a unit.

link·boy (lingk′boi′), *n.* (formerly) a boy hired to carry a torch for a pedestrian on dark streets. [LINK² + BOY]

linked (lingkt), *adj.* *Genetics.* (of a gene) exhibiting linkage. [late ME; see LINK¹, -ED²]

linked′ rhyme′, *Pros.* a rhyme in which the end of one rhyming line together with the first sound of the next line forms a rhyme with the end of the other rhyming line, as in *Some birds fly / Towards the night.*

linked′ verse′, *Pros.* a Japanese verse form in which stanzas of three lines alternating with stanzas of two lines are composed by two or more poets in alternation. Also called **renga.**

link·ing r, *Phonet.* the *r*-sound as reintroduced into an utterance by speakers of an *r*-dropping dialect when postvocalic *r* becomes intervocalic, as in the pronunciation (fär′ə wā′) for *far away* by a speaker who would ordinarily pronounce *far* as (fä).

link′ing verb′, a copulative verb.

link·man (lingk′mən), *n., pl.* **-men.** linkboy. [LINK² + MAN¹]

link′ mo′tion, (in a steam engine) a valve gear using a moving link that acts with other parts, as rods from eccentrics, to determine the position of the valve at any phase of the cycle of revolution and thereby to determine whether the engine is run forward or in reverse.

Lin·kö·ping (lēn′chœ′pēng), *n.* a city in S Sweden. 70,691 (1965).

links (lingks), *n.pl.* See **golf course.** [ME *lynkys* slopes, OE *hlincas*, pl. of *hlinc* rising ground, equiv. to *hlin(ian)* (to) lean, bend (akin to Gk *klīnein* to cause to slope) + *-k* suffix]

Link′ train′er, *Aeron., Trademark.* a ground training device used in instrument-flight training.

link·work (lingk′wûrk′), *n.* **1.** something composed of links, as a chain. **2.** a linkage. **3.** *Mach.* a mechanism or device in which motion is transmitted by links. [LINK¹ + WORK]

Lin·lith·gow (lin lith′gō), *n.* former name of **West Lothian.**

linn (lin), *n.* *Chiefly Scot.* **1.** a cascade of water in a watercourse, esp. a waterfall or torrent of rushing water in a river or stream. **2.** a pool of water, esp. at the foot of a waterfall. **3.** a steep ravine or precipice. Also, **lin.** [OE *hlynn* torrent, lit., something noisy + ScotGael *linne* (Ir *linn*, Welsh *llyn*) pool]

Lin·nae·us (li nē′əs), *n.* **Car·o·lus** (kar′ə ləs), (*Carl von Linné*), 1707–78. Swedish botanist.

Lin·né (li nā′), *n.* a crater in the first quadrant of the face of the moon: about 5 miles in diameter.

Lin·ne·an (li nē′ən), *adj.* **1.** of or pertaining to Linnaeus, who established the binomial system of scientific nomenclature. **2.** noting or pertaining to a former system of botanical classification introduced by him, based mainly on the number or characteristics of the stamens and pistils. Also, **Lin·nae′an.** [LINNAE(US) + -AN]

lin·net (lin′it), *n.* **1.** a small, Old World, fringilline songbird, *Carduelis cannabina.* **2.** any of various related birds, as the house finch. [OE *līnete*, short for *līnetwige* linnet; see LINTWHITE]

Lin·net (lin′it, li net′), *n.* a girl's given name. Also, **Linetta, Lin′nete, Lynette.**

lin′net hole′, a small hole joining a glassmaking furnace to the arch.

li·no·cut (lī′nə kut′), *n.* **1.** a cut made from a design cut into linoleum mounted on a block of wood. **2.** a print made from such a cut. [LINO(TYPE) + CUT]

lin·o·le·ic (lin′ᵊ lē′ik, li nō′lē ik), *adj.* *Chem.* of or derived from linoleic acid. [< Gk *lín(on)* flax + OLEIC]

lin′ole′ic ac′id, *Chem.* an unsaturated fatty acid, $C_{17}H_{31}COOH$, occurring as a glyceride in drying oils, as in linseed oil. Also, **li·no′lic ac′id** (lə nō′lik).

li·no·le·um (li nō′lē əm), *n.* a floor covering formed by coating burlap or canvas with linseed oil, powdered cork, and rosin, and adding pigments to create the desired colors and patterns. [< L *līn(um)* flax, linen + *oleum* oil; formerly trademark]

lino′leum block′, a piece of thick, soft, cork linoleum often mounted on a block of wood, incised or carved in relief with a design, pattern, or pictorial motif, and used in making prints.

Lin·o·type (lī′nə tīp′), *n., v.,* **-typed, -typ·ing.** —*n.* **1.** *Trademark.* a typesetting machine that casts solid lines of type from brass dies, or matrices, which are selected automatically by actuating a keyboard. —*v.t., v.i.* **2.** (*l.c.*) *Print.* to typeset on such a machine. —**lin′o·typ′er, lin′o·typ′ist,** *n.*

Lin Piao (lin′ byou′), born 1908, Chinese marshal and communist leader; defense minister since 1959.

Lins (lēns), *n.* a city in E Brazil. 32,384 (1960).

lin·sang (lin′sang), *n.* any of several catlike carnivores of the genera *Prionodon* (or *Linsang*), of the East Indies, or *Poina*, of Africa, having retractile claws and a long tail. [< Malay]

lin·seed (lin′sēd′), *n.* flaxseed. [ME *linsed*, OE *linsǣd.* See LINE², SEED]

lin′seed cake′, a cake or a mass made by expressing the oil from linseed, used chiefly as feed for cattle.

lin′seed meal′, ground linseed cake.

lin′seed oil′, a drying oil obtained by pressing flaxseed, used in making paints, printing inks, linoleum, etc.

lin·sey (lin′zē), *n., pl.* **-seys.** linsey-woolsey.

lin·sey-wool·sey (lin′zē wo͝ol′zē), *n., pl.* **-seys. 1.** a coarse fabric woven from linen warp and coarse wool filling. **2.** any mixture that is incongruous or of poor quality; jumble: *That last speech was a linsey-woolsey of stale metaphor.* Also called **linsey.** [ME *lynsy wolsye*, lit., linen cloth, wool cloth, equiv. to *lyn* (OE *līn*; see LINEN) + *-sy*, var. of *say* cloth (< OF *saie*; akin to ML *sagia* kind of weave, L *sagum* cloak) + *wol* WOOL + *-sye*, var. of *say*]

lin·stock (lin′stok′), *n.* a staff with one end forked to hold a match, formerly used in firing cannon. [earlier *lyntstock* < D *lontstok* match-stick, with LINT r. *lont*]

lint (lint), *n.* **1.** staple cotton fiber used to make yarn. **2.** minute shreds or ravelings of yarn; bits of thread. **3.** cotton waste produced by the ginning process. **4.** a soft material for dressing wounds, procured by scraping or otherwise treating linen cloth. [ME, var. of *linnet*, OE *līnet-* flax (or flax-field) in *līnetwige* LINTWHITE] —**lint′less,** *adj.*

lin·tel (lin′tᵊl), *n.* a horizontal architectural member supporting the weight above an opening such as a window or a door. Also, *Brit.,* **lin′tol.** [ME *lyntel* < MF *lintel*, assimilated var. of **linter* < LL **līmitāris* of the boundary (taken as synonym of *līmināris* of the threshold). See LIMIT, -AR¹]

lint·er (lin′tər), *n.* **1. linters,** short cotton fibers that stick to seeds after a first ginning. **2.** a machine which removes lint from cloth. [LINT + -ER¹]

Lin·ton (lin′tᵊn), *n.* **1.** a town in SW Indiana. 5736 (1960). **2.** a boy's given name.

lint·white (lint′hwīt′, -wīt′), *n.* *Chiefly Scot.* the linnet, *Carduelis cannabina.* [*lint* (syncopated var. of LINNET) + WHITE; r. OE *līnetwige* linnet, lit., flax (or flax-field) trouble-maker, so called because the bird pecks out and eats flaxseed, equiv. to *līnet-* (< ML *līnētum* flax-field) + *-wige*, fem. of *wiga* fighter]

lint·y (lin′tē), *adj.,* **lint·i·er, lint·i·est. 1.** full of or covered with lint: *This blue suit gets linty much too quickly.* **2.** like lint: *linty bits on his coat.* [LINT + -Y¹]

Li·nus (lī′nəs), *n.* **1.** *Class. Myth.* **a.** a musician and poet, the inventor of melody and rhythm, of whom various stories are told: often identified, through his untimely death, with the harvesting or withering of crops and vegetation. **b.** Also called **Li′nus song′.** a dirge: originally sung in W Asia to mourn the death of crops being harvested, later sung to mourn the death of Linus or that of Adonis. **2.** a boy's given name.

Li·nus (lī′nəs), *n.* **Saint,** died A.D. 76?, pope 67?–76?.

L'In·vi·ta·tion au Châ·teau (*Fr.* lan vē tä syôn ō shä tō′). See **Ring Round the Moon.**

Lin·wood (lin′wo͝od′), *n.* a town in SE New Jersey. 3847 (1960).

lin·y (lī′nē), *adj.,* **lin·i·er, lin·i·est. 1.** full of or marked with lines. **2.** resembling lines; linelike. Also, **liney.** [LINE¹ + -Y¹]

li·nyph·i·id (li nif′ē id), *n.* **1.** a spider of the family *Linyphiidae*, comprising the sheet-web spiders. —*adj.* **2.** belonging or pertaining to the family *Linyphiidae.* [< NL *Linyphiid(ae)* < Gk *linyph(os)* linen-weaver + NL *-idae*; see -ID²]

Lin·yu (lin′yo͞o′), *n.* a city in NE China, on the Gulf of Liaotung: strategically located at the E end of the Great Wall. 35,000 (est. 1957). Formerly, **Shanhaikwan.**

Lin Yu·tang (lin′ yo͞o′täng′), (*Lin Yü-t'ang*) born 1895, Chinese author and philologist in the U.S.

Linz (lints), *n.* a port in N Austria, on the Danube River. 196,206 (1961).

Lin·zer torte (lin′zər tôrt′), *pl.* **Lin·zer tortes.** (*sometimes l.c.*) a sweet pastry, often made with powdered nuts, having a filling of red jam and a lattice crust. [< G: lit., Linz torte]

Liod (lyōd), *n.* (in the *Volsunga Saga*) the wife of Volsung and mother of Sigmund and Signy. Also, **Hliod, Ljod.**

li·on (lī′ən), *n.* **1.** a large, grayish-tan cat, *Panthera leo*, native in Africa and southern Asia, the male of which usually has a mane. **2.** this animal as the national emblem of Great Britain. **3.** a man of great strength, courage, etc. **4.** a person of note or celebrity who is much sought after. **5.** *Brit.* an object of interest or note. **6.** (*cap.*) *Astron., Astrol.* the constellation or sign of Leo. **7.** (*cap.*) a member of any one of the internationally affiliated service clubs (**Interna′tional Associa′tion of Li′ons Clubs′**) founded in 1917 and dedicated to promoting responsible citizenship, sound government, and community, national, and international welfare. **8.** *Numis.* **a.** a silver, Anglo-Gallic denier, issued during the reign of Henry III, bearing the figure of a lion. **b.** a gold coin of Scotland, issued c1400–1589, bearing the figure of a lion. **c.** any of various other coins bearing the figure of a lion. **d.** hardhead². **9. beard the lion in his den,** to confront someone in his own familiar surroundings in order to settle a dispute. **10. twist the lion's tail,** to tax the patience of or provoke Great Britain. [ME < OF, var. of *leon* < L *leōn-* (s. of *leō*) < Gk *léōn*; r. ME, OE *leo* < L] —**li′on·esque′,** *adj.* —**li′on·like′, li′on·ly,** *adj.*

Lion and lioness (3½ ft. high at shoulder; total length 9 ft.; tail to 3 ft.)

li·on·cel (lī′ən sel′), *n.* *Heraldry.* a lion: so called when three or more are displayed on an escutcheon. [< MF, dim. of *lion* LION]

Li·o·nel (lī′ə nəl), *n.* a boy's given name, form of **Leon.**

li·on·ess (lī′ə nis), *n.* a female lion. [ME *liones, leonesse* < MF *lion(n)esse.* See LION, -ESS]

li·on·et (lī′ə net′), *n.* a young or small lion. [< MF; see LION, -ET]

li·on·fish (lī′ən fish′), *n., pl.* **-fish·es,** (*esp. collectively*) **-fish. 1.** a scorpionfish of the genus *Pterois,* esp. *P. volitans,* found in the Indo-Pacific region, having large pectoral fins and long, separated, highly poisonous dorsal spines. **2.** an Atlantic scorpionfish, *Scorpaena grandicornis.* [LION + FISH]

li·on·heart (lī′ən härt′), *n.* a person of great courage and bravery. [LION + HEART]

li·on·heart·ed (lī′ən här′tid), *adj.* courageous; brave. [LION + HEARTED] —**li′on·heart′ed·ly,** *adv.* —**li′on·heart′ed·ness,** *n.*

li·on·ise (lī′ə nīz′), *v.t., v.i.,* **-ised, -is·ing.** *Chiefly Brit.* lionize. —**li′on·i·sa′tion,** *n.* —**li′on·is′er,** *n.*

li·on·ize (lī′ə nīz′), *v.,* **-ized, -iz·ing.** —*v.t.* **1.** to treat (a person) as a celebrity: *They lionize the strangest people at those parties.* **2.** *Brit.* to visit or exhibit the objects of interest of (a place). —*v.i.* **3.** *Brit.* to visit the objects of interest of a place. **4.** to pursue celebrities or seek their company: *She was quite shameless about her attempts to lionize.* [LION + -IZE] —**li′on·i·za′tion,** *n.* —**li′on·iz′er,** *n.*

Li·ons (lī′ənz), *n.* **Gulf of,** a wide bay of the Mediterranean off the coast of S France. Also, **Gulf′ of the Li′ons.** French, **Golfe du Lion.**

li′on's share′, the largest share; a disproportionate portion: *The eldest son received the lion's share of the estate.* [prob. after Aesop's fable in which the lion claimed all the spoils of a hunt]

Li·ou (lē′ō), *n.* a boy's given name, form of **Leo.**

Liou·ville (lyōō vēl′; *Eng.* lē′ōō vil′), *n.* **Jo·seph** (zhô zef′; *Eng.* jō′zəf, -səf), 1809–82, French mathematician.

Liouville's′ the′orem, *Math.* the theorem that every function of a complex variable, bounded and differentiable for all finite values of the variable, is a constant function. [named after Joseph LIOUVILLE]

lip (lip), *n., adj., v.,* **lipped, lip·ping.** —*n.* **1.** either of the two fleshy parts or folds forming the margins of the mouth and functioning in speech. **2.** Usually, **lips.** these parts as organs of speech: *The rumor went from lip to lip. I heard it from his own lips.* **3.** *Slang.* impudent talk: *Don't give me any of your lip.* **4.** a liplike part or structure, esp. of anatomy. **5.** *Bot.* either of the two parts into which the corolla or calyx of certain plants, esp. of the mint family, is divided. **6.** *Zool.* **a.** a labium. **b.** the outer or the inner margin of the aperture of a gastropod's shell. **7.** *Music.* the position and arrangement of lips and tongue in playing a wind instrument: *He has the greatest lip of any jazz trumpeter I've heard.* **8.** a projecting edge on a container or other hollow object: *the lip of a pitcher; the lip of a bell.* **9.** any edge or rim. **10.** the edge of an opening or cavity, as of a canyon or a wound: *We ventured to the very lip of the crater.* **11.** the cutting edge of a tool. **12.** the blade, at the end of an auger, which cuts the chip after it has been circumscribed by the spur. **13.** (in a twist drill) the cutting edge at the bottom of each flute. **14. bite one's lip** or **tongue,** to repress one's anger or other emotions: *He wanted to return the insult, but bit his lip in order to avoid a scene.* **15. button one's lip,** *Slang.* to keep silent, esp., to refrain from revealing information: *They told him to button his lip if he didn't want trouble.* Also, **button up. 16. hang on the lips of,** to listen to very attentively: *The members of the women's club hung on the lips of the visiting lecturer.* **17. keep a stiff upper lip,** to face misfortune bravely and resolutely: *Throughout the crisis they kept a stiff upper lip.* **18. smack one's lips,** to indicate one's keen enjoyment of: *We smacked our lips over the delicious wine.* —*adj.* **19.** of or pertaining to the lips or a lip: *lip pomade; lip rouge.* **20.** pertaining to, characterized by, or made with the lips: *to read lip movements.* **21.** superficial or insincere: *to offer lip praise.* —*v.t.* **22.** to touch with the lips. **23.** *Golf.* to hit the ball over the rim of (the hole). **24.** to utter, esp. softly. **25.** *Archaic.* to kiss. —*v.i.* **26.** to use the lips in playing a musical wind instrument. [ME *lip(pe),* OE *lippa;* c. D *lip,* G *Lippe;* akin to Norw *lepe,* L *labium, labrum*] —**lip′less,** *adj.* —**lip′like′,** *adj.*

lip-, var. of **lipo-**[1] before a vowel: *lipectomy.*

Lip′a·ri Is′lands (lip′ə rē; *It.* lē′pä rē), a group of volcanic islands N of Sicily, belonging to Italy. 11,799 (1951); 44 sq. mi.

li·pase (lī′pās, lip′ās), *n.* *Biochem.* any of a class of enzymes that break down fats, produced by the liver, pancreas, and other digestive organs or by certain plants. [LIP- + -ASE]

Lip·chitz (lip′shits), *n.* **Jacques** (zhäk), born 1891, U.S. sculptor, born in Lithuania.

li·pec·to·my (li pek′tə mē), *n., pl.* **-mies.** *Surg.* an operation for removal of superficial fat, usually a pendulous abdominal apron of fat, in obese persons. [LIP- + -ECTOMY]

li·pe·mi·a (li pē′mē ə), *n.* *Med.* excessive amounts of fat and fatty substances in the blood; hyperlipemia. Also, **li·pae·mi·a.** [< NL *lipaemia.* See LIP-, -EMIA] —**li·pe′mic, li·pae′mic,** *adj.*

Li·petsk (lē′petsk), *n.* a city in the W RSFSR, in the central Soviet Union in Europe, SSE of Moscow. 218,000 (est. 1964).

li·pid (lī′pid, lip′id), *n.* *Biochem.* any of a group of organic compounds that are greasy to the touch, insoluble in water, and soluble in alcohol, ether, and other fat solvents. Lipids comprise the fats and other esters with analogous properties and constitute, with proteins and carbohydrates, the chief structural components of living cells. Also, **li·pide** (lī′pīd, -pid, lip′īd, -id), **lip·in** (lip′in), **lipoid.** [LIP- + -ID[3]]

Lip·iz·za·ner (lip′it sä′nər), *n.* Lippizaner.

Lip·mann (lip′mən), *n.* **Fritz Albert,** born 1899, U.S. biochemist, born in Germany: Nobel prize for medicine 1953.

lip′ mold′ing, *Furniture.* a bead surrounding the opening of a drawer.

Li Po (lē′ pō′; *Chin.* lē′ bô′), A.D. 701?–762, Chinese poet of the Tang dynasty. Also called **Li Tai Po.**

lipo-[1], a learned borrowing from Greek meaning "fat," used in the formation of compound words: *lipolysis.* Also, *esp. before a vowel,* **lip-.** [comb. form repr. Gk *lípos* fat]

lipo-[2], a learned borrowing from Greek meaning "lacking," "leaving," used in the formation of compound words: *lipography.* [comb. form of *lip-,* weak s. of *leípein* to leave, be lacking; see -O-]

lip·o·ca·ic (lip′ə kā′ik), *n.* *Biochem.* a lipotropic substance occurring in the pancreas. [LIPO-[1] + Gk *kaí(ein)* (to) burn + -IC]

lip·o·chrome (lip′ə krōm′), *n.* *Biochem.* any of the naturally occurring pigments that contain a lipid, as carotene. [LIPO-[1] + -CHROME] —**lip′o·chro′mic,** *adj.*

lip·o·cyte (lip′ə sīt′), *n.* *Anat.* See **fat cell.**

lip·o·gram (lip′ə gram′), *n.* a written work composed of words chosen so as to avoid the use of one or more specific alphabetic characters. [< Gk *lipográmm(atos)* wanting a letter. See LIPO-[2], -GRAM[1]] —**lip·o·gram·mat·ic** (lip′ō grə mat′ik, lī′pō-), *adj.* —**lip·o·gram·ma·tism** (lip′ə gram′ə tiz′əm, lī′pə-), *n.* —**lip′o·gram′ma·tist,** *n.*

li·pog·ra·phy (li pog′rə fē, lī-), *n.* unintentional omission in writing, as of a letter or syllable. [LIPO-[2] + -GRAPHY] —**lip·o·graph·ic** (lip′ə graf′ik, lī′pə-), *adj.*

lip·oid (lip′oid, lī′poid), *adj.* **1.** Also, **lip·oi′dal.** fatty; resembling fat. —*n.* **2.** a fat or fatlike substance, as lecithin, wax, etc. **3.** lipid. [LIP- + -OID]

li·pol·y·sis (li pol′i sis), *n.* *Chem.* the hydrolysis of fats into fatty acids and glycerol, as by lipase. [< NL; see LIPO-[1], -LYSIS] —**lip·o·lit·ic** (lip′ə lit′ik), *adj.*

li·po·ma (li pō′mə), *n., pl.* **-mas, -ma·ta** (-mə tə). *Pathol.* a tumor made up of fat tissue. Also called **fatty tumor.** [< NL; see LIP-, -OMA] —**li·pom·a·tous** (li pom′ə təs), *adj.*

lip·o·pex·i·a (lip′ə pek′sē ə), *n.* *Biochem.* the storage of fat in the body. Also called **adipopexia, adipopexis.** [< NL; see LIPO-[1], -PEXY] —**lip·o·pec·tic** (lip′ə pek′tik, lī′pə-), *adj.*

lip·o·phil·ic (lip′ə fil′ik), *adj.* *Physical Chem.* **1.** having a strong affinity for lipids. **2.** promoting the dissolvability or absorbability of lipids. [LIPO-[1] + -PHILIC]

lip·o·pro·tein (lip′ə prō′tēn, -tē in, lī′pə-), *n.* *Biochem.* any of the class of proteins that contain a lipid combined with a simple protein. [LIPO-[1] + PROTEIN]

lip·o·suc·tion (lip′ə suk′shən, lī′pə-), *n.* the surgical withdrawal of excess fat from local areas under the skin by means of a small incision and vacuum suctioning.

lip·o·trop·ic (lip′ə trop′ik, -trō′pik, lī′pə-), *adj.* *Chem., Biochem.* having an affinity for lipids and thus preventing or correcting the excess accumulation of fat in the liver. [LIPO-[1] + -TROPIC] —**li·pot·ro·pism** (li po′trə piz′əm), *n.*

Lip·pe (lip′ə), *n.* a former state in NW Germany: now part of North Rhine-Westphalia, in West Germany.

lipped (lipt), *adj.* **1.** having lips or a lip. **2.** *Bot.* labiate. [ME; see LIP, -ED[3]]

lip·pen (lip′ən), *Chiefly Scot.* —*v.t.* **1.** to trust (a person). **2.** to entrust (something) to a person. —*v.i.* **3.** to have confidence, faith, or trust. [early ME *lipn(i)en*]

lip·per (lip′ər), *n.* *Naut.* **1.** a slightly rough surface on a body of water. **2.** spray from small waves. Also called **leaper.** [n. use of dial. *lipper* to ripple. See LAP[3], -ER[6]]

Lip·per·shey (lip′ər shā′), *n.* a crater in the third quadrant of the face of the moon: about 4 miles in diameter.

Lip·pi (lip′ē; *It.* lēp′pē), *n.* **Fi·lip·pi·no** (fil′ə pē′nō; *It.* fē′lēp pē′nō), 1457–1504, and his father, **Fra Filip·po** (frä fi lip′ō; *It.* frä fē lēp′pô) or **Fra Lip·po** (frä lip′ō; *It.* frä lēp′pô), 1406?–69, Italian painters.

Lip·pi·zan·er (lip′it sä′nər), *n.* one of a breed of finely shaped, gray horses developed at the Austrian Imperial Stud at Lippiza and used generally in dressage exhibitions. Also, **Lipizzaner, Lip·piz·za·na** (lip′it sä′nə), **Lip′piz·zan′er.**

Lipp·mann (lip′mən; *also Fr.* lēp MAN′ *for 1*), *n.* **1. Ga·bri·el** (GA brē el′), 1845–1921, French physicist: Nobel prize 1908. **2. Walter,** born 1889, U.S. journalist and author.

Lip·pold (lip′ōld), *n.* **Richard,** born 1915, U.S. sculptor.

lip-read (lip′rēd′), *v.,* **-read** (-red′), **-read·ing.** —*v.t.* **1.** to comprehend spoken words by watching the movements of a speaker's lips. —*v.i.* **2.** to read lips.

lip′ read′ing, the reading or understanding, as by a deaf person, of the movements of another's lips when forming words. Cf. **speech reading.** —**lip′ read′er.**

Lip′schitz condi′tion (lip′shits), *Math.* the property of a function on a closed interval such that the absolute value of the difference in functional values at any two points in the interval is less than a constant times the absolute value of the difference of the points raised to some positive power *m,* called the order. Also called **Hölder condition.** [named after Rudolf *Lipschitz* (1832–1903), German mathematician]

Lips·comb (lips′kəm), *n.* a town in central Alabama. 2811 (1960).

lip′ serv′ice, insincere profession of devotion or good will; service by words only: *He paid only lip service to the dictator.* —**lip′ serv′er.**

lip·stick (lip′stik′), *n.* a crayonlike oil-based cosmetic used in coloring the lips, usually in a tubular container.

Lip·ton (lip′tən), *n.* **Sir Thomas John·stone** (jon′stən, -sən), 1850–1931, Scottish merchant and yachtsman.

liq., **1.** liquid. **2.** liquor. **3.** (in prescriptions) solution.

li·quate (lī′kwāt), *v.,* **-quat·ed, -quat·ing.** *Metall.* —*v.t.* **1.** to heat (an alloy or mixture) sufficiently to melt the more fusible matter and thus to separate it from the rest, as in the refining of tin. —*v.i.* **2.** to become separated by such a fusion (often fol. by *out*). [< L *liquāt(us)* liquefied, ptp. of *liquāre.* See LIQUID, -ATE[1]] —**li·qua·tion** (lī kwā′shən, -zhən), *n.*

liq·ue·fa·cient (lik′wə fā′shənt), *n.* that which liquefies or promotes liquefaction. [< L *liquefacient-* (s. of *liquefaciēns* liquefying, prp. of *liquefacere*), equiv. to *lique-* (s. of *liquēre* to be liquid) + *facient-* FACIENT]

liq·ue·fac·tion (lik′wə fak′shən), *n.* **1.** the act or process of liquefying or making liquid. **2.** the state of being liquefied. [< LL *liquefactiōn-* (s. of *liquefactiō*) a melting, equiv. to L *liquefact(us)* melted (ptp. of *liquefacere;* see LIQUEFACIENT) + *-iōn-* -ION] —**liq′ue·fac′tive,** *adj.*

liq′uefied petro′leum gas′, a gas liquefied by compression, consisting of flammable hydrocarbons, as propane and butane, obtained as a by-product from the refining of petroleum or from natural gas: used chiefly as a domestic fuel in rural areas, as an industrial and motor fuel, and in organic synthesis, esp. of synthetic rubber. Also called **bottled gas, compressed petroleum gas, LPG, LP gas.**

liq·ue·fy (lik′wə fī′), *v.t., v.i.,* **-fied, -fy·ing.** to make or become liquid. [late ME *lyqyfye* < L *lique(facere)* to **melt** (see LIQUEFACIENT); see -FY] —**liq′ue·fi′a·ble,** *adj.* —**liq′ue·fi′er,** *n.*

—**Syn.** melt, fuse, dissolve, thaw; condense. —**Ant.** solidify; evaporate.

li·ques·cent (li kwes′ənt), *adj.* **1.** becoming liquid; melting. **2.** tending toward a liquid state. [< L *liquescent-* (s. of *liquescēns*) melting, prp. of *liquescere.* See LIQUID, -ESCENT] —**li·ques′cence,** *n.*

li·queur (li kûr′ *or, esp. Brit.,* -kyŏŏr′; *Fr.* lē kœʀ′), *n.* any of a class of alcoholic liquors, usually strong, sweet, and highly flavored, as chartreuse or curaçao; cordial. [< F; see LIQUOR]

liq·uid (lik′wid), *adj.* **1.** composed of molecules which move freely among themselves but do not tend to separate like those of gases; neither gaseous nor solid. **2.** of, pertaining to, or consisting of, liquids: *a liquid diet.* **3.** flowing like water. **4.** clear, transparent, or bright: *liquid eyes.* **5.** (of sounds, tones, etc.) smooth; agreeable; flowing freely: *the liquid voice of a trained orator.* **6.** (of movements, gestures, etc.) graceful; smooth; free and unconstricted: *the ballerina's liquid arabesques.* **7.** in cash or readily convertible into cash without significant loss of principal: *liquid assets.* **8.** *Phonet.* identified with or being either *r* or *l.* —*n.* **9.** a liquid substance. **10.** *Phonet.* either *r* or *l.* [ME *liquyd* < L *liquid(us),* equiv. to *liqu(ēre)* (to) be liquid + *-idus* -ID[4]] —**liq′uid·ly,** *adv.* —**liq′uid·ness,** *n.*

—**Syn.** LIQUID, FLUID agree in referring to that which is not solid. LIQUID commonly refers to substances such as water, oil, alcohol, and the like, which are neither solids nor gases: *Water ceases to be a liquid when it is frozen or turned to steam.* FLUID is applied to anything that flows, whether liquid or gaseous: *Pipes can carry fluids from place to place.*

liq′uid air′, a pale-blue, intensely cold liquid, obtained by the compression and cooling of air: used as a source of oxygen, nitrogen, and inert gases, and as a refrigerant.

liq·uid·am·bar (lik′wid am′bər), *n.* **1.** any tree of the genus *Liquidambar,* having maplelike, star-shaped leaves, and globose, spiny fruit. Cf. **sweet gum. 2.** the fragrant, yellowish, balsamic liquid exuded by this tree, used in medicine. Cf. **storax** (def. 2). [< NL; genus name. See LIQUID, AMBER]

liq·ui·date (lik′wi dāt′), *v.,* **-dat·ed, -dat·ing.** —*v.t.* **1.** to settle or pay (a debt): *to liquidate a claim.* **2.** to reduce (accounts) to order; determine the amount of (indebtedness or damages). **3.** to convert into cash. **4.** to get rid of, esp. by killing: *to liquidate the enemies of the regime.* **5.** to break up, abolish, or do away with: *to liquidate a partnership.* —*v.i.* **6.** to liquidate debts or accounts; go into liquidation. [< LL *liquidāt(us)* made clear or liquid, ptp. of *liquidāre.* See LIQUID, -ATE[1]]

liq·ui·da·tion (lik′wi dā′shən), *n.* **1.** the process of realizing upon assets and of discharging liabilities in concluding the affairs of a business, estate, etc. **2.** the process of converting securities or commodities into cash. **3.** the state of being liquidated: *an estate in liquidation.* [LIQUIDATE + -ION]

liq·ui·da·tor (lik′wi dā′tər), *n.* **1.** a person who liquidates assets, esp. one authorized to do so by a court of law. **2.** an official appointed by a court of law to direct the liquidation of a business. [LIQUIDATE + -OR[2]]

liq′uid com′pass, *Navig.* See **wet compass.**

liq′uid crys′tal, a liquid having certain crystalline characteristics, esp. different optical properties in different directions.

liq′uid fire′, flaming petroleum or the like as employed against an enemy in warfare.

liq′uid glass′. See **sodium silicate.**

liq′uid gold′, a suspension of finely divided gold in a vegetable oil, used chiefly for gilding ceramic ware.

liq·uid·ise (lik′wi dīz′), *v.t.,* **-ised, -is·ing.** *Chiefly Brit.* liquidize.

li·quid·i·ty (li kwid′i tē), *n.* **1.** a liquid state or quality. **2.** *Com.* the ability or ease with which assets can be converted into cash. [< L *liquiditās.* See LIQUID, -ITY]

liquid′ity pref′erence, (in Keynesian economics) the degree of individual preference for cash over less liquid assets.

liq·uid·ize (lik′wi dīz′), *v.t.,* **-ized, -iz·ing. 1.** to make liquid; liquefy. **2.** to stimulate; give facility to: *a thought that liquidizes the imagination.* **3.** to cause (a sound) to be full, round, mellifluous, etc. Also, *esp. Brit.,* **liquidise.** [LIQUID + -IZE]

liq′uid meas′ure, the system of units of capacity ordinarily used in measuring liquid commodities, as milk, oil, etc.: 4 gills = 1 pint; 2 pints = 1 quart; 4 quarts = 1 gallon.

liq′uid ox′ygen, a clear, pale-blue liquid obtained by compressing oxygen and then cooling it below its boiling point: used chiefly as an oxidizer in liquid rocket propellants. Also called **lox.**

liq′uid petro′latum. See **mineral oil.**

liq′uid sto′rax. See under **storax** (def. 2).

liq·ui·dus (lik′wi dəs), *n.* *Physical Chem.* the portion of a temperature composition diagram which consists of the curve connecting the temperatures at which a liquid solution is in equilibrium with its vapor and with the solid solution, and therefore connects freezing temperatures of liquid solutions. Cf. **solidus**[2]. [< L; see LIQUID]

liq·uor (lik′ər *or, for 3,* lik′wôr), *n.* **1.** a distilled or spirituous beverage, as brandy or whiskey, as distinguished from a fermented beverage, as wine or beer. **2.** any liquid substance, as broth from cooked meats, vegetables, etc. **3.** *Pharm.* solution (def. 6). **4.** a solution of a substance, esp. a concentrated one used in the industrial arts. —*v.t.* **5.** *Informal.* to furnish or ply with liquor to drink (often fol. by *up*). —*v.i.* **6.** *Informal.* to drink large quantities of liquor (often fol. by *up*). [< L a liquid, orig. liquidity (*liqu(ēre)* (to) be liquid + *-or* -OR[1]); r. ME *lic(o)ur* < OF < L *liquōrem,* acc. of *liquor*] —**liq′uor·y,** *adj.*

liq·uo·rice[1] (lik′ə ris, -ə rish, lik′rish), *n.* licorice.

liq·uo·rice[2] (lik′ə ris), *adj.* lickerish.

liq′uorice all′sorts (ôl′sôrts′), *Chiefly Brit.* variously shaped licorice or licorice-centered, sugar-coated candies.

Lir (lēr), *n.* Ler.

li·ra (lēr′ə; *It.* lē′rä), *n., pl.* **li·re** (lēr′ā; *It.* lē′re), **li·ras.** **1.** an aluminum coin and monetary unit of Italy, equal to 100 centesimi and equivalent to about .0016 of a U.S. dollar. *Abbr.:* L., Lit. **2.** a silver, bronze, or chrome steel coin and monetary unit of Turkey, equal to 100 kurus and equivalent to about .11 of a U.S. dollar; equal to 100 piasters before 1933; Turkish pound. *Abbr.:* TL. [< It < OPr *lieura* < L *lībra* pound]

li·ra da brac·cio (lēr′ə də brä′chō, -chē ō′; *It.* lē′rä dä brät′chō), *pl.* **li·ras da brac·cio,** *It.* **li·re da brac·cio** (lē′re dä brät′chō). a many-stringed musical instrument of the 15th and 16th centuries, played with a bow and used for polyphonic improvisation. [< It: lyre for the arm]

li·rel·la (li rel′ə, lī-), *n. Bot.* the elongated, narrow apothecium of certain lichens. [< NL, dim. of L *līra* a ridge, furrow]

li·rel·late (li rel′āt, lī-), *adj.* of, pertaining to, or resembling a lirella. [LIRELL(A) + -ATE[1]]

lir·i·o·den·dron (lir′ē ō den′drən), *n., pl.* **-drons, -dra** (-drə). any magnoliaceous tree of the genus *Liriodendron.* Cf. **tulip tree.** [< NL *Līriodendron* name of the genus < Gk *leíro(n)* lily + *déndron* -DENDRON]

lir·i·pipe (lir′ə pīp′), *n.* **1.** the tail or pendent part at the back of a hood, as in the 14th- and 15th-century French costume. **2.** a scarf or tippet; hood. [< ML *liripip(ium)*]

Li·sa (lē′sə, -zə), *n.* a girl's given name, form of **Elizabeth.**

Li-sao (*Chin.* lē′sou′), *n.* a poem (c320 B.C.) by Ch'ü Yüan.

Lis·bon (liz′bən), *n.* **1.** a seaport in and the capital of Portugal, in the SW part, on the Tagus estuary. 802,230 (1960). Portuguese, **Lis·bo·a** (lēzh bô′ə). **2.** a town in E Ohio. 3579 (1960).

Lis′bon Falls′, a town in SW Maine. 2640 (1960).

Li·se (lē′sə, -zə), *n.* a girl's given name, form of **Elizabeth.**

Li·se·lot·te (lē′sə lot′ē, -lot′ə, -zə-), *n.* a girl's given name.

Li Shih-min (*Chin.* lē′ shœ′mēn′). See **T'ai Tsung.**

lisle (līl), *n.* **1.** knit goods, as gloves or hose, made of lisle thread. **2.** See **lisle thread.** —*adj.* **3.** made of lisle thread. [after LISLE, France, where first made]

Lisle (lēl *for 1–3;* līl *for 4*), *n.* **1.** See **Leconte de Lisle. 2.** See **Rouget de Lisle. 3.** former name of **Lille. 4.** a town in NE Illinois. 4219 (1960).

lisle′ thread′, a fine, high-twisted and hard-twisted cotton thread, at least two-ply, used esp. for hosiery. Also called **lisle.**

lisp (lisp), *n.* **1.** a speech defect consisting in pronouncing *s* and *z* like or nearly like the *th*-sounds of *thin* and *this,* respectively. **2.** *Phonet.* any unconventional articulation of the sibilants, as the pronunciation of *s* and *z* with the tongue between the teeth (**lingual protrusion lisp**), close to or touching the upper front teeth (**dental lisp**), or raised so that the breath is emitted laterally (**lateral lisp**). **3.** the act, habit, or sound of lisping. —*v.t., v.i.* **4.** to pronounce or speak with a lisp. [ME *wlispen, lipsen,* OE *(ā)wlyspian;* akin to D *lisp(el)en,* G *lispeln,* Norw *leipsa*] —**lisp′er,** *n.* —**lisp′ing·ly,** *adv.*

lis pen·dens (lis pen′denz), *Law.* **1.** a pending suit listed on the court docket. **2.** the rule placing property involved in litigation under the court's jurisdiction. **3.** the principle that the filing of a suit constitutes notice of the claim asserted. [< L]

Lis′sa·jous fig′ure (lē′sə zhōō′, lē′sə zhōō′), *Physics.* the series of plane curves traced by an object executing two mutually perpendicular harmonic motions, forming a distinct pattern when the ratio of the frequencies of the motions is a ratio of small integers. [named after Jules A. *Lissajous* (1822–80), French physicist]

lis·some (lis′əm), *adj.* **1.** lithesome or lithe, esp. of body; limber; supple; flexible. **2.** agile or active. Also, **lis′som.** [var. of LITHESOME] —**lis′some·ly, lis′·som·ly,** *adv.* —**lis′some·ness, lis′som·ness,** *n.*
—**Ant. 1.** rigid. **2.** clumsy.

lis·sot·ri·chous (li so′trə kəs), *adj. Anthropol.* having straight hair. [< Gk *lissó(s)* smooth (c. *leios, lispos*) + *trich-* (s. of *thríx*) hair + -OUS]

list[1] (list), *n.* **1.** a series of names or other items written or printed together in a meaningful grouping or sequence so as to constitute a record. **2.** See **list price. 3.** a complete record of stocks handled by a stock exchange. —*v.t.* **4.** to set down together in a list; make a list of: *to list the membership of a society for a brochure.* **5.** to enter in a list with others: *Do you want to list him among the life members?* **6.** to register a security on a stock exchange so that it may be traded there. **7.** *Archaic.* enlist. —*v.i.* **8.** to be offered for sale, as in a catalogue, at a specified price: *This radio lists at $34.98.* **9.** *Archaic.* enlist. [special use of LIST[2] (roll of names, perh. orig. of contestants in the LISTS); cf. F *liste* < It *lista* roll of names, earlier, band, strip (e.g., of paper), border < OHG (G *Leiste*)]
—**Syn. 1.** register. LIST, CATALOGUE, INVENTORY, ROLL, SCHEDULE imply a definite arrangement of items. LIST denotes a series of names, items, or figures arranged in a row or rows: *a list of groceries.* CATALOGUE adds the idea of alphabetical or other orderly arrangement, and, often, descriptive particulars and details: *a library catalogue.* An INVENTORY is a detailed descriptive list of property, stock, goods, or the like made for legal or business purposes: *a store inventory.* A ROLL is a list of names of members of some defined group often used to ascertain their presence or absence: *a class roll.* A SCHEDULE is a methodical (esp. official) list, often indicating the time or sequence of certain events: *a train schedule.* **4.** record, catalog. **5.** enroll.

list[2] (list), *n.* **1.** a border or bordering strip, usually of cloth. **2.** a selvage. **3.** selvages collectively. **4.** a strip of cloth or other material. **5.** a strip or band of any kind. **6.** a stripe of color. **7.** a division of the hair or beard. **8.** one of the ridges or furrows of earth made by a lister. **9.** a strip of material, as bark or sapwood, to be trimmed from a board. **10.** fillet (def. 6a). **11.** *Metall.* (on tin plate) a solidified accumulation of molten tin on the edge of the plate that was placed lowest after leaving the tin-plating bath. —*adj.* **12.** made of selvages or strips of cloth. —*v.t.* **13.** to produce furrows and ridges on (land) with a lister. **14.** to prepare (ground) for planting by making ridges and furrows. **15.** to cut away a narrow strip of wood from the edge of (a stave, plank, etc.). **16.** *Metall.* to remove the list from (tin plate) by remelting it in molten tin and wiping it off. **17.** *Obs.* to apply a border or edge to. [ME *lista,* OE *līst* border; c. D *lijst,* G *Leiste* (OHG *līsta*)]

list[3] (list), *n.* **1.** a careening, or leaning to one side, as of a ship. —*v.i.* **2.** (of a vessel) to incline to one side; careen: *The ship listed to starboard.* —*v.t.* **3.** to cause (a vessel) to incline to one side: *The shifting of the cargo listed the ship to starboard.* [?]

list[4] (list), *Archaic.* —*v.t.* **1.** to be pleasing to; please. **2.** to like or desire. —*v.i.* **3.** to like; wish; choose. [ME *liste(n), luste(n),* OE *(ge)lystan* to please; c. G *gelüsten,* Icel *lysta,* akin to Goth *luston* to desire. See LUST]

list[5] (list), *Archaic.* —*v.i.* **1.** to listen. —*v.t.* **2.** to listen to. [ME *liste(n),* OE *hlystan* to listen, hear; c. Sw *lysta;* akin to Icel *hlusta* to listen; deriv. of *hlyst* hearing, akin to Icel *hlyst* meatus. See LISTEN]

List (list), *n.* **Frie·drich** (frē′drik), 1789–1846, U.S. political economist and journalist, born in Germany.

list·ed (lis′tid), *adj.* **1.** (of a security) admitted to trading privileges on a stock exchange. **2.** (of a telephone, telephone number, or telephone subscriber's name and address) represented in a telephone book. [LIST[1] + -ED[2]]

lis·tel (lis′t**ə**l), *n. Archit.* a narrow list or fillet. [< F < It *listello,* dim. of *lista* band, LIST[2]]

lis·ten (lis′ən), *v.i.* **1.** to give attention with the ear; attend closely for the purpose of hearing; give ear. **2.** to pay attention; heed; obey (often fol. by *to*): *Children don't always listen to their parents. I've told him repeatedly, but he doesn't listen.* **3.** to wait attentively for a sound (usually fol. by *for*): *She found herself unconsciously listening for the children's voices, as they returned from school.* **4.** *Slang.* to convey a particular impression to the hearer; sound: *The new recording doesn't listen as well as the old one.* **5. listen in,** to overhear a conversation or communication, esp. by telephone or radio; eavesdrop: *She was on a party line and suspected that someone was listening in.* —*v.t.* **6.** *Archaic.* to give ear to; hear. [ME *lis(t)ne(n),* OE *hlysnan;* c. MHG *lüsenen,* Sw *lyssna;* akin to LIST[5]] —**lis′ten·er,** *n.*
—**Syn. 1.** See **hear.**

lis′tening post′, 1. *Mil.* a post or position, as in advance of a defensive line, established for the purpose of listening to detect the enemy's movements. **2.** any concealed position maintained to obtain information: *The government had listening posts to keep informed of revolutionary activities.* **3.** any foreign country or city viewed as a source of intelligence about an enemy or rival nation or one that is a potential enemy.

list·er[1] (lis′tər), *n.* **1.** Also called **lister plow.** a plow with a double moldboard, used to prepare the ground for planting by producing furrows and ridges. **2.** Also called **lister planter, list′er drill′.** a lister plow fitted with attachments for dropping and covering seeds. [LIST[2] + -ER[1]]

list·er[2] (lis′tər), *n.* a person who makes or compiles a list, esp. an appraiser, assessor, or the like. [LIST[1] + -ER[1]]

Lis·ter (lis′tər), *n.* **Joseph, 1st Baron Lister of Lyme Re·gis** (lim rē′jis), 1827–1912, English surgeon: founder of modern antiseptic surgery.

lis·ter·el·lo·sis (lis′tər ə lō′sis), *n., pl.* **-ses** (-sēz). *Vet. Pathol.* listeriosis. [< NL *listerell(a)* (named after Joseph LISTER) + -OSIS]

lis·te·ri·a (li stēr′ē ə), *n. Bacteriol.* any of several rod-shaped, aerobic, parasitic bacteria of the genus *Listeria,* pathogenic for man and animals. [< NL, named after J. LISTER; see -IA]

lis·te·ri·a·sis (lis′tə rē′ə sis), *n., pl.* **-ses** (-sēz′). *Vet. Pathol.* listeriosis.

lis·te·ri·o·sis (li stēr′ē ō′sis), *n., pl.* **-ses** (-sēz). *Vet. Pathol.* a disease of wild and domestic mammals, birds, and occasionally of man, characterized by lack of control of movement, paralysis, fever, and monocytosis, caused by a bacterium, *Listeria monocytogenes.* [LISTERI(A) + -OSIS]

Lis·ter·ise (lis′tə rīz′), *v.t.,* **-ised, -is·ing.** *Chiefly Brit.* Listerize.

Lis·ter·ism (lis′tə riz′əm), *n.* an antiseptic method introduced by Lister, involving the spraying of the parts under operation with a carbolic acid solution. [LISTER + -ISM]

Lis·ter·ize (lis′tə rīz′), *v.t.,* **-ized, -iz·ing.** to treat (a patient, disease, etc.) using the methods of Lister. Also, *esp. Brit.,* **Listerise.** [LISTER + -IZE]

list′er plant′er, lister[1] (def. 2).

list′er plow′, lister[1] (def. 1).

l'is·tes·so tem·po (lē stes′ō tem′pō; *It.* lē stes′sô tem′pô), (of a musical passage or section following a change in time signature) at the same tempo as before. [< It]

list·ing[1] (lis′ting), *n.* **1.** the act of compiling a list: *Don't begin the listing until you've verified the membership.* **2.** the fact of being included in a list: *Does the telephone company charge for a listing in the telephone book?* **3.** a list; record; catalogue. [LIST[1] + -ING[1]]

list·ing[2] (lis′ting), *n.* material, as bark or sapwood, that is trimmed from a board. [late ME; see LIST[2], -ING[1]]

list·less (list′lis), *adj.* feeling no inclination toward or interest in anything; languid; spiritless; indifferent: *a listless mood; a listless handshake.* [late ME *lystles.* See LIST[4], -LESS] —**list′less·ly,** *adv.*

list·less·ness (list′lis nis), *n.* the quality or state of being listless; languid inattention; indifference; spiritlessness. [LISTLESS + -NESS]
—**Syn.** heedlessness. See **indifference.**

list′ pot′, a bath of molten tin in which tin plate is listed.

list′ price′, *Com.* the price given by a wholesaler from which a trade discount is computed.

lists (lists), *n.* (*construed as sing. or pl.*) **1.** an enclosed arena for a tilting contest. **2.** the barriers enclosing this arena. **3.** any place or scene of combat, competition, controversy, etc. **4. enter the lists,** to involve oneself in a conflict or contest: *to enter the lists against the protective tariff.* [ME *listes,* pl. of *liste* LIST[2]]

Liszt (list), *n.* **Franz** (fränts), 1811–86, Hungarian composer and pianist. —**Liszt′i·an,** *adj.*

lit[1] (lit), *v.* **1.** a pt. and pp. of **light**[1]. —*adj.* **2.** *Slang.* under the influence of liquor or narcotics; intoxicated.

lit[2] (lit), *n.* litas.

lit[3] (lit), *v.* a pt. and pp. of **light**[3].

Lit., lira; lire.

lit., **1.** liter; liters. **2.** literal. **3.** literally. **4.** literary. **5.** literature.

Li·tae (lī′tē), *n.pl. Class. Myth.* the daughters of Zeus who personify prayer.

Li Tai Po (*Chin.* lē′ tī′ bô′). See **Li Po.**

lit·a·ny (lit′ə nē), *n., pl.* **-nies. 1.** a ceremonial or liturgical form of prayer consisting of a series of invocations or supplications with responses which are the same for a number in succession. **2. the Litany,** the supplication in this form in the *Book of Common Prayer.* **3.** a recitation or recital which resembles a litany. **4.** a prolonged or monotonous account: *We heard the whole litany of her complaints.* [< LL *litanīa* < eccl. Gk *litaneía* litany, Gk: an entreating, equiv. to *litan-* (s. of *litaínein,* var. of *litaneúein* to pray) + *-eia* -Y[3]; r. ME *letanie,* OE *letanīa* < ML]

li·tas (lē′täs), *n., pl.* **-tai** (-tā), **-tu** (-tōō). a former silver coin and monetary unit of Lithuania, equal to 100 centu. Also, **lit.** [< Lith]

Lit.B., Bachelor of Letters; Bachelor of Literature. [< L *Lit(t)erārum Baccalaureus*]

Litch·field (lich′fēld′), *n.* **1.** a town in central Illinois. 7330 (1960). **2.** a town in W Connecticut. 6264 (1960). **3.** a town in central Minnesota. 5078 (1960).

li·tchi (lē′chē), *n., pl.* **-tchis. 1.** the fruit of a Chinese, sapindaceous tree, *Litchi chinensis,* consisting of a thin, brittle shell enclosing a sweet, jellylike pulp and a single seed. **2.** the tree itself. Also, **lichee, lichi.** [< Chin *li chih*]

li′tchi nut′, the brownish, dried litchi fruit.

Lit.D., Doctor of Letters; Doctor of Literature. [< L *Lit(t)erārum Doctor*]

lit de jus·tice (lē də zhys tēs′), *French.* **1.** the sofa upon which the king of France sat when holding formal sessions of the parliament. **2.** such a session. [lit., bed of justice]

-lite, a word element used in the names of minerals or fossils: *aerolite; chrysolite.* Cf. **-lith.** [< F, simplified of *-lithe* < Gk *líthos* stone; similarly G *-lit,* earlier *-lith*]

li·ter (lē′tər), *n. Metric System.* a unit of capacity redefined in 1964 by a reduction of 28 parts in a million to be exactly equal to one cubic decimeter. It is equivalent to 1.0567 U.S. liquid quarts. *Abbr.:* l, lit. Also, *esp. Brit.,* **litre.** [< F *litre,* back formation from *litron* an old measure of capacity, deriv. (with *-on* suffix) of LL *litra* < Gk *lítra* pound]

lit·er·a·cy (lit′ər ə sē), *n.* **1.** the quality or state of being literate, esp. the ability to read and write. **2.** possession of education: *to question someone's literacy.* [LITER(ATE) + -ACY]

lit′eracy test′, an examination to determine whether a person meets the literacy requirements for voting, serving in the armed forces, etc.; a test of one's ability to read and write.

lit·er·al (lit′ər əl), *adj.* **1.** following the words of the original very closely and exactly: *a literal translation of Goethe.* **2.** (of persons) tending to construe words in the strict sense or in an unimaginative way; matter-of-fact; prosaic. **3.** in accordance with, involving, or being the primary or strict meaning of the word or words; not figurative or metaphorical: *the literal meaning of a word.* **4.** true to fact; not exaggerated; actual or factual: *a literal statement of conditions.* **5.** being actually such, without exaggeration or inaccuracy: *the literal extermination of a city.* **6.** of or pertaining to the letters of the alphabet. **7.** of the nature of letters. **8.** expressed by letters. **9.** affecting a letter or letters: *a literal error.* [ME < LL *litterāl(is)* of letters. See LETTER, -AL[1]] —**lit′er·al·ness,** *n.*

lit·er·al·ise (lit′ər ə līz′), *v.t.,* **-ised, -is·ing.** *Chiefly Brit.* literalize. —**lit′er·al·i·sa′tion,** *n.* —**lit′er·al·is′er,** *n.*

lit·er·al·ism (lit′ər ə liz′əm), *n.* **1.** adherence to the exact letter or the literal sense, as in translation or interpretation: *to interpret the Bible with uncompromising literalism.* **2.** a peculiarity of expression resulting from this: *The work is studded with these obtuse literalisms.* **3.** exact representation or portrayal, without idealization, as in art or literature: *a literalism more appropriate to journalism than to the novel.* [LITERAL + -ISM] —**lit′er·al·ist,** *n.* —**lit′er·al·is′tic,** *adj.* —**lit′er·al·is′ti·cal·ly,** *adv.*

lit·er·al·i·ty (lit′ə ral′i tē), *n., pl.* **-ties. 1.** the quality or state of being literal; literalness. **2.** a literal interpretation. [LITERAL + -ITY]

lit·er·al·ize (lit′ər ə līz′), *v.t.,* **-ized, -iz·ing.** to make literal; interpret literally. Also, *esp. Brit.,* **literalise.** [LITERAL + -IZE] —**lit′er·al·i·za′tion,** *n.* —**lit′er·al·iz′er,** *n.*

lit·er·al·ly (lit′ər ə lē), *adv.* **1.** in a literal manner; word for word: *to translate literally.* **2.** in the literal or strict sense: *What does the word mean literally?* **3.** actually; without exaggeration or inaccuracy: *The city was literally destroyed.* [LITERAL + -LY]

lit·er·al-mind·ed (lit′ər əl mīn′did), *adj.* unimaginative; prosaic; matter-of-fact.

lit·er·ar·y (lit′ə rer′ē), *adj.* **1.** pertaining to or of the nature of books and writings, esp. those classed as literature: *literary history.* **2.** versed in or acquainted with literature; well-read. **3.** engaged in or having the profession of writing: *a literary man.* **4.** characterized by an excessive or affected display of learning; stilted; pedantic. **5.** preferring books to actual experience; bookish. [< L *litterāri(us), litterārius* of reading and writing. See LETTER, -ARY] —**lit′er·ar′i·ly,** *adv.* —**lit′er·ar′i·ness,** *n.*

lit·er·ate (lit′ər it), *adj.* **1.** able to read and write. **2.** having an education; educated. **3.** having or showing knowledge of literature, writing, etc.; literary; well-read. **4.** characterized by skill, lucidity, polish, or the like: *His writing is always literate, but the style is cold and clinical.* —*n.* **5.** a person who can read and write. **6.** a learned person. [late ME < L *literāt(us), litterātus* learned, scholarly. See LETTER, -ATE[1]] —**lit′er·ate·ly,** *adv.*

lit·e·ra·ti (lit′ə rä′tē, -rā′tī), *n.pl.* persons of scholarly or literary attainments; intellectuals; intelligentsia. [< L *literāti* learned, scholarly people, n. use of pl. of *literātus.* See LITERATE]

lit·e·ra·tim (lit′ə rā′tim), *adv.* letter for letter; literally. [< ML, a formation based on L *literā(tus)* (see LITERATE), with adv. suffix *-tim*]

lit·er·a·tor (lit′ə rā′tər), *n.* littérateur. [< L: an (inferior) grammarian. See LITERATE, -OR[2]]

lit·er·a·ture (lit′ər ə chər, -chŏŏr′, li′trə-), *n.* **1.** writings in which expression and form, in connection with ideas of permanent and universal interest, are characteristic or essential features, as poetry, romance, history, biography, essays, etc. **2.** the entire body of writings of a specific language, period, people, etc.: *the literature of England; medieval literature.* **3.** the writings dealing with a particular subject: *the literature of ornithology.* **4.** the profession of a writer or author. **5.** literary work or production. **6.** any kind of printed material, as circulars, leaflets, or handbills: *We wrote for literature on various brands of steel shelving.* **7.** *Archaic.* polite learning; literary culture; appreciation of letters and books. [late ME *litterature* < L *litterātūra* grammar. See LITERATE, -URE]

—Syn. 1. LITERATURE, BELLES-LETTRES, LETTERS refer to artistic writings worthy of being remembered. In the broadest sense, LITERATURE includes any type of writings on any subject: *the literature of medicine;* usually, however, it means the body of artistic writings of a country or period which are characterized by beauty of expression and form and by universality of intellectual and emotional appeal: *English literature of the 16th century.* BELLES-LETTRES is a more specific term for writings of a light, elegant, or excessively refined character: *His talent is not for scholarship but for belles-lettres.* LETTERS (rare today outside of certain fixed phrases) refers to literature as a domain of study or creation: *a man of letters.*

lith (lith), *n. Brit. Dial.* **1.** an arm or leg; limb. **2.** a joint, as of the finger: *He ached in every lith and limb.* **3.** a segment, as of an orange. [ME, OE; c. D, OHG *lid,* Icel *lithr,* Goth *lithus* limb, member; akin to G *Glied*]

lith-, var. of **litho-** before a vowel: *lithic.*

-lith, a noun termination meaning "stone" (*acrolith; megalith; paleolith*); sometimes occurring in words that are variant forms of *-lite* (*batholith; laccolith*). Cf. **-lite.** [see LITHO-]

Lith., **1.** Lithuania. **2.** Also, **Lith** Lithuanian.

lith., **1.** lithograph. **2.** lithography. Also, **litho., lithog.**

lith·arge (lith′ärj, li thärj′), *n.* a yellowish or reddish, odorless, heavy, earthy, water-insoluble, poisonous solid, PbO, used chiefly in the manufacture of storage batteries, pottery, lead glass, paints, enamels, and inks. Also called **lead monoxide, plumbous oxide.** Cf. **red lead.** [late ME (r. ME *litarge*) < MF *lit(h)arge,* apocopated var. of *litargire* < L *lithargyrus* < Gk *lithárgyros* spume of silver, equiv. to *lith-* LITH- + *árgyros* silver]

lithe (lī*th*), *adj.,* **lith·er, lith·est.** bending readily; pliant; limber; supple; flexible. Also, **lithe′some.** [ME *lith(e),* OE *līthe;* c. OLG *līthi,* G *lind* mild, L *lentus* slow] **—lithe′ly,** *adv.* **—lithe′ness,** *n.*

li·the·mi·a (li thē′mē ə), *n. Med.* the presence of an excessive amount of uric acid in the blood. Also, **li·thae′mi·a.** Also called **uricacidemia.** [< NL *lithaemia.* See LITH-, -EMIA] **—li·the′mic, li·thae′mic,** *adj.*

lith·i·a (lith′ē ə, lith′yə), *n.* a white oxide of lithium, Li_2O. [< NL; see LITH-, -IA]

li·thi·a·sis (li thī′ə sis), *n. Pathol.* the formation or presence of stony concretions, as calculi, in the body. [< NL < Gk; see LITH-, -IASIS]

lith′ia wa′ter, a mineral water, natural or artificial, containing lithium salts.

lith·ic (lith′ik), *adj.* **1.** pertaining to or consisting of stone. **2.** *Pathol.* pertaining to stony concretions, or calculi, formed within the body, esp. in the bladder. **3.** *Chem.* of, pertaining to, or containing lithium. [< Gk *lithik(ós)* of stone. See LITH-, -IC] **—lith′i·cal·ly,** *adv.*

-lithic, an adjectival suffix identical with **lithic,** used esp. in archaeology: *paleolithic.*

lith′ic ac′id, *Chem.* See **uric acid.**

lith·i·um (lith′ē əm), *n. Chem.* a soft, silver-white metallic element, the lightest of all metals, occurring combined in certain minerals. *Symbol:* Li; *at. wt.:* 6.939; *at. no.:* 3; *sp. gr.:* 0.53 at 20°C. [< NL; see LITH-, -IUM]

lith′ium alu′minum hy′dride, *Chem.* a white powder, $LiAlH_4$, used chiefly as a chemical reducing agent, esp. in pharmaceutical and perfume manufacturing.

lith′ium chlo′ride, *Chem.* a white, water-soluble, deliquescent, crystalline solid, LiCl, used chiefly in the manufacture of mineral water, esp. lithia water, and as a flux in metallurgy.

lith′ium flu′oride, *Chem.* a fine, white, slightly water-soluble powder, LiF, used chiefly in the manufacture of ceramics.

lith′ium ste′arate, *Chem.* a white, crystalline, slightly water-soluble powder, $CH_3(CH_2)_{16}COOLi$, used chiefly in cosmetics, in plastics, and as a lubricant in powder metallurgy.

lith·o (lith′ō), *n., pl.* **lith·os,** *adj., v.,* **lith·oed, lith·o·ing.** **—n. 1.** lithography. **2.** lithograph. **—adj. 3.** lithographic. **—v.t. 4.** to lithograph. [shortened form]

litho-, a learned borrowing from Greek meaning "stone," used in the formation of compound words: *lithography; lithonephrotomy.* Also, *esp. before a vowel,* **lith-.** [< Gk, comb. form of *líthos*]

litho., **1.** lithograph. **2.** lithography. Also, **lith., lithog.**

lith·o·graph (lith′ə graf′, -gräf′), *n.* **1.** a print produced by lithography. **—v.t. 2.** to produce or copy by lithography. [back formation from LITHOGRAPHY]

li·thog·ra·pher (li thog′rə fər), *n.* a person who works at lithography. [LITHOGRAPH(Y) + -ER¹]

li·thog·ra·phy (li thog′rə fē), *n.* **1.** the art or process of producing a picture, writing, or the like, on a flat, specially prepared stone, with some greasy or oily substance, and of taking ink impressions from this as in ordinary printing. **2.** a similar process in which a substance other than stone, as aluminum or zinc, is used. Cf. **offset** (def. 7). [< NL *lithographia.* See LITHO-, -GRAPHY] **—lith·o·graph·ic** (lith′ə graf′ik), **lith′o·graph′i·cal,** *adj.* **—lith′o·graph′i·cal·ly,** *adv.*

lith·oid (lith′oid), *adj.* resembling stone; stonelike. Also, **li·thoi′dal.** [< Gk *lithoeid(ḗs).* See LITH-, -OID]

lithol., lithology.

li·thol·a·pax·y (li thol′ə pak′sē, lith′əl ə-), *n. Surg.* a procedure for crushing a urinary calculus within the bladder and washing out the fragments. [LITHO- + Gk *lápax(is)* an emptying (*lapak-,* verbal s. of *lapássein* to empty + *-sis* -SIS) + -Y³]

li·thol·o·gy (li thol′ə jē), *n.* **1.** the science dealing with the mineral composition and structure of rocks, esp. with such characters of structure as can be studied without high magnification. Cf. **petrography. 2.** *Med.* the science treating of calculi in the human body. [LITHO- + -LOGY] **—lith·o·log·ic** (lith′ə loj′ik), **lith′o·log′i·cal,** *adj.* **—lith′o·log′i·cal·ly,** *adv.*

lith·o·marge (lith′ə märj′), *n.* kaolin in compact, massive, usually impure form. [< NL *lithomarga* stone marl, equiv. to *litho-* LITHO- + L *marga* marl]

lith·o·me·te·or (lith′ə mē′tē ər), *n. Meteorol.* a mass of small particles of solid matter suspended in the atmosphere, as dust, haze, etc. Cf. **hydrometeor.** [LITHO- + METEOR]

lith·o·ne·phrot·o·my (lith′ō ni frot′ə mē), *n., pl.* **-mies.** *Surg.* an incision into the kidney for removal of calculi. [LITHO- + NEPHROTOMY]

lith·o·phane (lith′ə fān′), *n.* a transparency made of thin porcelain or bone china having an intaglio design. [LITHO- + -PHANE]

lith·o·phile (lith′ə fīl′), *Geol.* **—adj. 1.** (of a chemical element in the earth) having an affinity for the rocks in the earth's crust. **—n. 2.** a lithophile element. [LITHO- + -PHILE]

lith·o·phone (lith′ə fōn′), *n.* a Chinese stone chime consisting of 16 stone slabs hung in two rows and struck with a hammer. [LITHO- + -PHONE]

lith·o·phyte (lith′ə fīt′), *n.* **1.** *Zool.* a polyp with a hard or stony structure, as a coral. **2.** *Bot.* any plant growing on the surface of rocks. [LITHO- + -PHYTE] **—lith·o·phyt·ic** (lith′ə fit′ik), *adj.*

lith·o·pone (lith′ə pōn′), *n.* a white pigment consisting of zinc sulfide, barium sulfate, and some zinc oxide, used as a pigment and filler in the manufacture of paints, inks, leather, paper, linoleum, and face powders. [LITHO- + Gk *pón(os)* a work, structure]

lith·o·print (lith′ə print′), *v.t., v.i.* **1.** to lithograph. **—n. 2.** printed matter produced by lithography. [LITHO- + PRINT] **—lith′o·print′er,** *n.*

lith·o·sere (lith′ə sēr′), *n. Ecol.* a sere originating on rock. [LITHO- + SERE²]

lith·o·sol (lith′ə sôl′, -sol′), *n.* a group of shallow soils lacking well-defined horizons, esp. an entisol consisting of partially weathered rock fragments, usually on steep slopes. [LITHO- + -SOL]

lith·o·sphere (lith′ə sfēr′), *n.* the crust of the earth.

li·thot·o·my (li thot′ə mē), *n., pl.* **-mies.** *Surg.* the operation or art of cutting for stone in the urinary bladder. [< LL *lithotomia* < Gk *lithotomía.* See LITHO-, -TOMY] **—lith·o·tom·ic** (lith′ə tom′ik), **lith′o·tom′i·cal,** *adj.* **—li·thot′o·mist,** *n.*

lith·o·trite (lith′ə trīt′), *n. Surg.* an instrument for performing lithotrity. [back formation from LITHOTRITY; see -ITE¹]

li·thot·ri·ty (li tho′tri tē), *n., pl.* **-ties.** *Surg.* the operation of crushing stone in the urinary bladder into particles that may be voided. [LITHO- + L *trīt(us)* rubbed, ground, crushed (ptp. of *terere*) + -Y³; see -ITY] **—li·thot′ri·tist,** *n.*

Lith·u·a·ni·a (lith′o͞o ā′nē ə), *n.* a republic in N Europe, on the Baltic: an independent state 1918–40; annexed by the Soviet Union 1940; regained independence 1991. 3,690,000; 25,174 sq. mi. *Cap.:* Vilnius. Lithuanian, **Lietuva.** **—Lith·u·an·ic** (lith′o͞o an′ik), *adj., n.*

Lith·u·a·ni·an (lith′o͞o ā′nē ən), *adj.* **1.** of or pertaining to Lithuania, its inhabitants, or their language. **—n. 2.** a native or inhabitant of Lithuania. **3.** a Baltic language, the official language of Lithuania.

lith·u·re·sis (lith′yə rē′sis), *n. Pathol.* the passage of gravel in the urine. [< NL < Gk *líth(os)* LITH- + *oúrēsis* urination, equiv. to *ourē-* (verbid s. of *ourein* to urinate; see URO-¹) + *-sis* -SIS]

li·thu·ri·a (li thyo͝or′ē ə), *n. Med.* the presence of an excessive amount of uric acid in the urine. [< NL; see LITH-, -URIA]

lith·y (lī′*th*ē), *adj. Archaic.* lithe; supple; flexible. [ME *lethi,* OE *lithig,* akin to D, G *ledig* empty, Icel *lithugr* free, nimble]

lit·i·ga·ble (lit′ə gə bəl), *adj.* subject to litigation. [< L *lītigā(re)* (to) go to law (see LITIGATE) + -BLE]

lit·i·gant (lit′ə gənt), *n.* **1.** a person engaged in a lawsuit. **—adj. 2.** litigating; engaged in a lawsuit. [< L *lītigant-* (s. of *lītigāns* going to law, prp. of *lītigāre*), equiv. to *līt-* (s. of *līs*) a lawsuit + *-ig-* (comb. form of *agere* to carry on) + *-ant-* -ANT]

lit·i·gate (lit′ə gāt′), *v.,* **-gat·ed, -gat·ing.** **—v.t. 1.** to make the subject of a lawsuit; contest at law. **2.** *Archaic.* to dispute (a point, assertion, etc.). **—v.i. 3.** to carry on a lawsuit. [< L *lītigāt(us)* (ptp. of *lītigāre*). See LITIGANT, -ATE¹] **—lit′i·ga′tor,** *n.*

lit·i·ga·tion (lit′ə gā′shən), *n.* **1.** the act or process of litigating: *a matter that is still in litigation.* **2.** a lawsuit.

li·ti·gious (li tij′əs), *adj.* **1.** of or pertaining to litigation. **2.** excessively inclined to litigate: *a litigious person.* **3.** inclined to dispute or disagree; argumentative. [ME < L *lītigiōs(us)* contentious, equiv. to *lītigi(um)* a quarrel (see LITIGANT, -IUM) + *-ōsus* -OUS] **—li·ti′gious·ly,** *adv.* **—li·ti′gious·ness, li·ti·gi·os·i·ty** (li tij′ē os′i tē), *n.*

—Syn. 3. contentious, disputatious, quarrelsome.

Lit·itz (lit′its), *n.* a town in SE Pennsylvania. 5987 (1960).

lit·mus (lit′məs), *n.* a blue coloring matter obtained from certain lichens, esp. *Roccella tinctoria.* In alkaline solution litmus turns blue, in acid solution, red: widely used as an indicator. [earlier *lytmos* < Scand; cf. Icel *litmosi* dye-moss (*lit-* color, dye + *mosi* moss), *litunarmosi* lichen for dyeing, *mosa* to dye with moss. The unique form *lygtmose* (1502) may reflect MD *lijcmoes* litmus]

lit′mus pa′per, a strip of paper impregnated with litmus, used as an indicator.

lit·o·ral (lit′ər əl), *adj.* littoral.

li·to·tes (lī′tə tēz′, -tō-, lit′ə-, lī tō′tēz), *n., pl.* **-tes.** *Rhet.* understatement, esp. that in which an affirmative is expressed by the negative of its contrary, as in "not bad at all." Cf. **hyperbole.** [< NL < Gk *litótēs* a diminution, deriv. of *litós* plain, small, meager]

li·tre (lē′tər), *n. Chiefly Brit.* liter.

Litt. B., Bachelor of Letters; Bachelor of Literature. [< L *Lit(t)erārum Baccalaureus*]

Litt. D., Doctor of Letters; Doctor of Literature. [< L *Lit(t)erārum Doctor*]

lit·ten (lit′ən), *adj. Archaic.* lighted.

lit·ter (lit′ər), *n.* **1.** objects strewn or scattered about; scattered rubbish. **2.** a condition of disorder or untidiness: *We were appalled at the litter of the room.* **3.** a number of young brought forth at one birth. **4.** a framework of canvas stretched between two parallel bars, for the transportation of a sick or wounded person. **5.** a vehicle carried by men or animals, consisting of a bed or couch, often covered and curtained, suspended between shafts. **6.** straw, hay, or the like, used as bedding for animals, as protection for plants, etc. **7.** the layer of slightly decomposed organic material on the surface of the floor of the forest. **—v.t. 8.** to strew (a place) with scattered objects, rubbish, etc.: *to be fined for littering the sidewalk.* **9.** to scatter (objects) in disorder: *They littered their toys from one end of the playroom to the other.* **10.** to be strewn about (a place) in disorder (often fol. by *up*): *Dirty clothes littered up the room. Bits of paper littered the floor.* **11.** to give birth to (young), as a multiparous animal. **12.** to supply (an animal) with litter for a bed. **13.** to use (straw, hay, etc.) for litter. **14.** to cover (a floor or other area) with straw, hay, etc., for litter. **—v.i. 15.** to give birth to a litter: *The cat had littered in the closet.* **16.** to strew objects about: *If you litter, you may be fined.* [ME *litere* bed, litter < AF, equiv. to OF *litiere* (ML *lectāria*) < L *lect(us)* bed + *-āria* fem. of *-ārius* -ER²]

—Syn. 2. clutter, untidiness. **3.** See **brood. 4.** stretcher. **8.** mess (up). **9.** disarrange, derange.

lit·te·rae hu·ma·ni·o·res (lit′ə rē′ hyo͞o man′ē ôr′ēz, -ōr′ēz), the humanities as a field of study. [< ML: lit., more humane letters]

lit·té·ra·teur (lit′ər ə tûr′; *Fr.* lē tā RA tœR′), *n., pl.* **-teurs** (-tûrz′; *Fr.* -tœR′). a writer of literary works. Also, **lit′te·ra·teur′.** [< F; see LITERATOR]

lit·te·ra·tim (lit′ə rā′tim), *adv. Obs.* literatim.

lit·ter·bug (lit′ər bug′), *n.* a person who litters public thoroughfares, buildings, etc., with wastepaper or other refuse. [LITTER + BUG]

lit·ter·y (lit′ə rē), *adj.* of, pertaining to, or covered with litter; untidy. [LITTER + -Y¹]

lit·tle (lit′əl), *adj.,* **less** or **less·er, least** or **lit·tler, lit·tlest;** *adv.,* **less, least;** *n.* **—adj. 1.** small in size; not big; not large; tiny: *a little girl.* **2.** short in duration; not extensive; short; brief: *a little while.* **3.** small in number: *a little group of artists.* **4.** small in amount or degree; not much: *little hope.* **5.** of a certain amount; appreciable (usually prec. by *a*): *We're having a little difficulty.* **6.** being such on a small scale: *little farmers.* **7.** not strong, forceful, or loud; weak: *a little voice.* **8.** small in consideration, importance, position, affluence, etc.: *little discomforts; tax reductions to help the little fellow.* **9.** mean, narrow, or illiberal: *a little mind.* **10.** endearingly small or considered as such: *Bless your little heart!* **11.** amusingly small or so considered: *a funny little way of laughing.* **12.** contemptibly small, petty, mean, etc., or so considered: *filthy little tricks.* **—adv. 13.** not at all (used before a verb): *He little knows what awaits him.* **14.** in only a small amount or degree; not much; slightly: *a little known work of art; little better than a previous effort.* **15.** seldom; rarely; infrequently: *We see each other very little.* **—n. 16.** something not very appreciable; a small amount, quantity, or degree: *They did little to make him comfortable. If you want some ice cream, there's a little in the refrigerator.* **17.** a short distance: *It's down the road a little.* **18.** a short time: *Stay here for a little.* **19. in little,** on a small scale: *a replica in little of Independence Hall.* **20. little by little,** slowly by degrees; gradually: *The water level rose little by little.* **21. make little of, a.** belittle: *to make little of one's troubles.* **b.** to understand or interpret only slightly: *He made little of the old Slavonic text.* **22. not a little,** to a great extent; very much; considerably: *It tired me not a little to stand for three hours.* **23. think little of,** to treat casually; regard as trivial: *They think little of driving 50 miles to see a movie.* [ME, OE *lȳtel* (*lȳt* few, small + *-el* dim. suffix), c. D *luttel,* OHG *luzzil*] **—lit·tlish** (lit′əlish, lit′lish), *adj.* **—lit′tle·ness,** *n.*

—Syn. 1–4. tiny, teeny, wee. LITTLE, DIMINUTIVE, MINUTE, SMALL refer to that which is not large or significant. LITTLE (the opposite of *big*) is very general, covering size, extent, number, quantity, amount, duration, or degree: *a little boy; a little time.* SMALL (the opposite of *large* and of *great*) can many times be used interchangeably with LITTLE, but is especially applied to what is limited or below the average in size: *small oranges.* DIMINUTIVE denotes (usually physical) size that is much less than the average or ordinary; it may suggest delicacy: *the baby's diminutive fingers; diminutive in size but autocratic in manner.* MINUTE suggests that which is so tiny it is difficult to discern, or that which implies attentiveness to the smallest details: *a minute quantity, examination.*

Lit′tle Ab′aco. See under **Abaco.**

Lit′tle Alli′ance, *Europ. Hist.* an economic and military alliance (1920) between Czechoslovakia and Yugoslavia, who were joined the following year by Rumania, formed as a counterbalance to the informal alliance that existed between Austria, Germany, Hungary, and Italy.

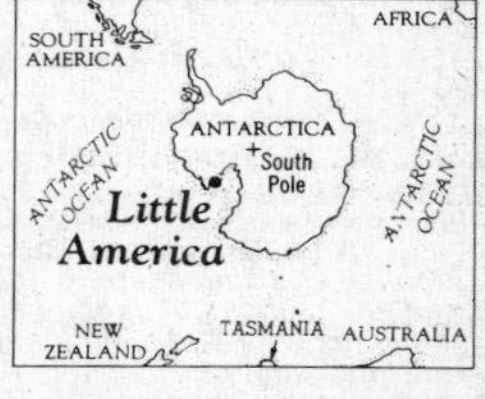

Lit′tle Amer′ica, a base in the Antarctic, on the Bay of Whales, S of the Ross Sea: established by Adm. Richard E. Byrd in 1929; used for later Antarctic expeditions.

lit′tle auk′, the dovekie, *Plautus alle.*

Lit′tle Bear′, *Astron.* the constellation Ursa Minor.

Lit′tle Belt′ Moun′tains, a range of the Rocky Mountains, in central Montana.

Lit′tle Big′horn, a river flowing N from N Wyoming to S Montana into the Bighorn River: General Custer defeated near here by Indians 1876. 80 mi. long. Also called **Little Horn.**

lit′tle black′ ant′, a widely distributed ant, *Monomorium minimum,* sometimes found as a household pest.

lit′tle blue′ her′on, a small heron. *Florida caerulea,* of the warmer parts of the Western Hemisphere, having bluish-gray plumage.

lit′tle broth′er, *Naut.* a smaller hurricane following a major one.

lit′tle casi′no, *Casino.* the two of spades.

Lit′tle Chute′, a town in E Wisconsin. 5099 (1960).

Lit′tle Cor′poral, epithet of Napoleon I.

Lit′tle Dae′dala. See under **Daedala.**

Lit′tle Di′omede. See under **Diomede Islands.**

Lit′tle Dip′per, *Astron.* dipper (def. 3b).

Lit′tle Dog′, *Astron.* the constellation Canis Minor.

lit′tle e′gret. See under **egret** (def. 1).

Lit′tle Eng′lander, an Englander who believes the best interests of Britain are served by attention to Britain itself and that the former Empire should be made completely self-sufficient. —**Lit′tle Eng′landism.**

Lit′tle En′trance, *Eastern Ch.* the solemn procession in which the book of the Gospels is carried through the nave of the church and into the bema. Cf. **Great Entrance.**

Lit′tle Falls′, **1.** a town in NE New Jersey. 9730 (1960). **2.** a town in central New York. 8935 (1960). **3.** a town in central Minnesota. 7551 (1960).

Lit′tle Fer′ry, a town in NE New Jersey. 6175 (1960).

Lit·tle·field (lit′əl fēld′), *n.* a town in NW Texas. 7236 (1960).

lit′tle fin′ger, the finger farthest from the thumb, the smallest of the five fingers.

Lit′tle Fox′, *Astron.* the constellation Vulpecula.

Lit′tle Fox′es, The, a play (1939) by Lillian Hellman.

Lit′tle Gid′ding (gid′ing), a poem (1942) by T. S. Eliot. Cf. **Four Quartets.**

lit′tle gull′, a small, Old World gull, *Larus minutus.*

Lit′tle Horn′. See **Little Bighorn.**

Lit′tle Horse′, *Astron.* the constellation Equuleus.

lit′tle hours′, *Rom. Cath. Ch.* the hours of prime, tierce, sext, and nones, and sometimes also vespers and complin.

lit′tle Joe′, a cast of four in craps.

Lit′tle John′, a big, powerful yeoman who was a member of Robin Hood's band.

Lit′tle League′, a baseball league consisting of teams whose players are not over 12 years of age, usually sponsored by a business, fraternal, or other such organization. Cf. **Pony League.** —**Lit′tle Lea′guer.**

Lit′tle Li′on, *Astron.* the constellation Leo Minor.

Lit′tle Lord′ Faunt′le·roy (fônt′lə roi′), a novel (1886) by Frances H. Burnett.

lit′tle Mar′y, *Brit. Informal.* the stomach.

Lit′tle Men′, a novel (1871) by Louisa May Alcott.

lit·tle·neck (lit′əl nek′), *n.* the quahog clam, *Venus mercenaria,* when young and small. [named after *Littleneck* Bay, N.Y., where it was once plentiful]

lit′tle of′fice, (*sometimes caps.*) *Rom. Cath. Ch.* an office similar to but shorter than the divine office, in honor of a saint, a mystery, or, esp., of the Virgin Mary.

lit′tle owl′, a small, European owl, *Athene noctua,* having variegated brown and white plumage.

lit′tle peo′ple, **1.** (in folklore) small, imaginary beings, as elves, fairies, leprechauns, etc. **2.** the common people, esp. workmen, small merchants, or the like, whose lot is obscurity.

Lit′tle Prince′, The, an allegorical fantasy (1943) by Antoine de Saint-Exupéry French, **Le Petit Prince.**

Lit′tle Rhod′y (rō′dē), Rhode Island (used as a nickname).

Lit′tle Rock′, a city in and the capital of Arkansas, in the central part, on the Arkansas River. 107,813 (1960).

Lit′tle Rus′sia, a region in the SW Soviet Union in Europe, consisting mainly of the Ukraine but sometimes considered as including adjacent areas.

Lit′tle Rus′sian, **1.** a member of a division of the Russian people dwelling in southern and southwestern Soviet Union in Europe and in adjoining regions. Cf. **Ruthenian.** **2.** Ukrainian (def. 3).

Lit′tle Sea′. See **Mare Parvum.**

Lit′tle Sil′ver, a town in E New Jersey. 5202 (1960).

lit′tle slam′, *Bridge.* the winning of twelve of the thirteen tricks of a deal. Also called **small slam.** Cf. **grand slam** (def. 1).

lit′tle spot′ted cat′, a small tiger cat, *Felis tigrina,* of tropical America.

Little St. Bernard. See **St. Bernard, Little.**

Lit·tles·town (lit′əlz toun′), *n.* a town in S Pennsylvania. 2756 (1960).

lit′tle the′ater, **1.** noncommercial drama, usually of an experimental nature and directed at a limited audience. **2.** a small theater, producing plays whose effectiveness would be lost in larger houses. **3.** amateur theatricals.

lit′tle toe′, the fifth, outermost, and smallest digit of the foot.

Lit·tle·ton (lit′əl tən), *n.* **1. Sir Thomas,** c1407–1481, English jurist and author. **2.** a town in NW New Hampshire. 3355 (1960).

Lit′tle Wom′en, a novel (1868) by Louisa May Alcott.

Lit′tle Zimbab′we. See under **Zimbabwe.**

Litt.M., Master of Letters.

lit·to·ral (lit′ər əl), *adj.* **1.** pertaining to the shore of a lake, sea, or ocean. —*n.* **2.** a littoral region. Also, **litoral.** [< L *littorālis,* var. of *lītorālis* of the shore, equiv. to *lītor-* (s. of *lītus*) shore + *-ālis* -AL[1]]

Lit·tré (lē trā′), *n.* **Max·i·mi·lien Paul É·mile** (mak sē mē lyan′ pôl ā mēl′), 1801–88, French lexicographer and philosopher.

Lit·trow (li′trō), *n.* a crater in the first quadrant of the face of the moon: about 22 miles in diameter.

li·tu (lē′to͞o), *n.* a pl. of **litas.**

li·tur·gi·cal (li tûr′ji kəl), *adj.* **1.** of or pertaining to public worship. **2.** having to do with liturgies or forms of public worship. **3.** of or pertaining to the liturgy or Eucharistic service. **4.** of or pertaining to liturgics. Also, **li·tur′gic.** [< LL *litūrgic(us)* < LGk *leitourgikós* ministering (*leitourg(ós)* minister + *-ikos* -IC; see LITURGY) + -AL[1]] —**li·tur′gi·cal·ly,** *adv.*

litur′gical east′, *Eccles.* the direction toward which the chief altars of certain churches are oriented, and toward which most of the congregation in the nave faces. In theory it is toward the east, but in practice it may be in any direction.

Litur′gical Lat′in, the Latin characteristic of the liturgies of the Western Church.

litur′gical north′, *Eccles.* the direction to the left when facing the liturgical east.

litur′gical south′, *Eccles.* the direction to the right when facing the liturgical east.

litur′gical west′, *Eccles.* the direction opposite the liturgical east.

li·tur·gics (li tûr′jiks), *n.* (*construed as sing.*) **1.** the science or art of conducting public worship. **2.** the study of liturgies. [pl. of *liturgic* < LL *litūrgicus* liturgical; see -ICS]

li·tur·gi·ol·o·gy (li tûr′jē ol′ə jē), *n.* liturgics. [LITURGY + -OLOGY] —**li·tur·gi·o·log·i·cal** (li tûr′jē ə loj′i kəl), *adj.* —**li·tur′gi·ol′o·gist,** *n.*

lit·ur·gist (lit′ər jist), *n.* **1.** an authority on liturgies. **2.** a compiler of a liturgy or liturgies. **3.** a person who uses or favors the use of a liturgy. [LITURG(Y) + -IST] —**lit′ur·gism,** *n.* —**lit′ur·gis′tic,** *adj.*

lit·ur·gy (lit′ər jē), *n., pl.* **-gies. 1.** a form of public worship; ritual. **2.** a collection of formularies for public worship. **3.** a particular arrangement of services. **4.** a particular form or type of the Eucharistic service. **5.** the service of the Eucharist, esp. this service **(Divine Liturgy)** in the Eastern Church. [< eccl. L *litūrgia* < Gk *leitourgía* public service, eccl. Gk, Eucharist, equiv. to *leitourg(ós)* minister + *-ia* -Y[3]]

lit·u·us (lit′yo͞o əs), *n., pl.* **lit·u·i** (lit′yo͞o ī′). **1.** *Geom.* a polar curve generated by the locus of a point moving so that the square of its radius vector varies inversely as the angle the radius vector makes with the polar axis. Equation: $\theta r^2 = a$. **2.** (in ancient Rome) a crook-shaped staff used by augurs for divination. [< L: crooked staff, crosier]

Lituus (def. 1)

Lit·vi·nov (lit vē′nof), *n.* **Ma·ksim Ma·ksi·mo·vich** (mä ksēm′ mä′ksi mô′vich), 1876–1951, Russian communist leader and statesman.

Lit·y·er·ses (lit′ē ûr′sēz), *n.* *Class. Myth.* an illegitimate son of King Midas who challenged visitors to reaping contests and then murdered the losers.

litz′ wire′ (lits), *Elect.* a wire used as a conductor of alternating current, composed of a number of insulated strands woven together to reduce skin effect. [half adaptation, half translation of G *Litzendraht* wire made up of strands, equiv. to *Litze* (< L *līcium* thread) + *Draht* wire]

Liu Pang (lyo͞o′ bäng′), 247–195 B.C., Chinese emperor: founder of the Han dynasty 202 B.C.

Liu Shao-chi (lyo͞o′ shou′chē′), born 1898, chairman of the People's Republic of China 1959–66.

liv·a·ble (liv′ə bəl), *adj.* **1.** suitable for living in; habitable; comfortable: *a livable old barn of a house.* **2.** that can be lived with; companionable (often used in combination with *with*): *polite and charming but not altogether livable-with.* **3.** worth living; endurable: *She needed something to make life more livable.* Also, **liveable.** [LIVE[1] + -ABLE] —**liv′a·ble·ness, liv′a·bil′i·ty,** *n.*

live[1] (liv), *v.,* **lived** (livd), **liv·ing.** —*v.i.* **1.** to have life, as an animal or plant; be alive; be capable of vital functions. **2.** to continue to have life; remain alive: *to live to a ripe old age.* **3.** to continue in existence, operation, memory, etc.; last: *a book that lives in my memory.* **4.** to maintain life; rely for maintenance: *to live on one's income.* **5.** to feed or subsist (usually fol. by *on* or *upon*): *to live on rice.* **6.** to dwell or reside (usually fol. by *in, at,* etc.): *to live in a cottage; to live at the boardinghouse.* **7.** to pass life in a specified manner: *They lived happily ever after.* **8.** to direct or regulate one's life: *to live by the golden rule.* **9.** to experience or enjoy life to the full: *At 40 she was just beginning to live.* **10.** to cohabit (usually fol. by *with*). **11.** to escape destruction or remain afloat, as a ship, aircraft, or the like. —*v.t.* **12.** to pass (life): *to live a life of ease.* **13.** to represent or exhibit in one's life: *to live a lie; to live one's philosophy.* **14. live down,** to live so as to allow (a scandal, disgrace, etc.) to be forgotten or forgiven: *After his release from prison, he vowed to live down his crimes.* **15. live high,** to live sumptuously, luxuriously, etc.: *In Mexico they were able to live high on a moderate income.* **16. live high off the hog.** See **hog** (def. 10). **17. live in** or **out,** to reside at or away from the place of one's employment, esp. as a domestic servant: *Their butler, cook, and chauffeur live in, but the two maids live out.* **18. live it up,** *Informal.* to live in an extravagant, wild, or carefree manner: *He started living it up after he got out of the Army.* **19. live up to,** to live in accordance with some ideal or standard; come up to expectation: *He never lived up to his father's vision of him.* **20. live well, a.** to live comfortably. **b.** to live virtuously: *He died a peaceful death after having lived well all his days.* [ME *live(n),* OE *lifian, libban;* c. D *leven,* G *leben,* Icel *lifa,* Goth *liban*]

live[2] (līv), *adj.* **liv·er, liv·est** for 4–9, *adv.* —*adj.* **1.** being in life; living; alive: *live animals.* **2.** of, pertaining to, or during the life of a living being: *the animal's live weight.* **3.** characterized by or indicating the presence of living creatures: *the live sounds of the forest.* **4.** full of life, energy, or activity: *His approach in any business dealing is live and fresh.* **5.** *Informal.* (of a person) energetic; alert; up-to-date (sometimes used facetiously): *The club members are a really live bunch.* **6.** *Chiefly U.S.* of current interest or importance, as a question or issue; controversial; unsettled: *a live problem.* **7.** burning or glowing, as a coal. **8.** vivid or bright, as color. **9.** having resilience or bounce: *a live tennis ball.* **10.** being highly resonant or reverberant, as an auditorium, concert hall, or the like. **11.** being in play, as a baseball, football, etc. **12.** loaded or unexploded, as a cartridge or shell: *live ammunition.* **13.** Also, **alive.** *Elect.* electrically connected to a source of potential difference, or electrically charged so as to have a potential different from that of earth: *a live wire.* **14.** moving or imparting motion; powered: *the live head on a lathe.* **15.** still in use, or to be used, as type set up or copy for printing. **16.** (of a radio or television program) broadcast or televised at the moment it is being presented at the studio. **17.** made up of actual persons: *to perform before a live audience.* **18. live one,** *U.S. Slang.* **a.** a person who spends money readily. **b.** a person easily imposed upon or made the dupe of others. —*adv.* **19.** (of a radio or television program) at the moment of its happening or being performed; not on tape or by prerecording: *brought to you live from New York.* [aph. var. of ALIVE, used attributively] —**live′ness,** *n.*

live·a·ble (liv′ə bəl), *adj.* livable. —**live′a·ble·ness, live′a·bil′i·ty,** *n.*

live·bear·er (līv′bâr′ər), *n.* any viviparous fish of the family *Poeciliidae,* often kept in home aquariums. [LIVE[2] + BEARER]

live′ cen′ter (līv). See under **center** (def. 16a).

lived (līvd), *adj.* having life, a life, or lives, as specified (usually used in combination): *a many-lived cat.* [ME; see LIVE[1], -ED[3]]

live-for·ev·er (liv′fər ev′ər), *n.* an orpine. [LIVE[1] + FOREVER]

live·li·hood (līv′lē ho͝od′), *n.* a means of maintaining life; maintenance; living: *to gain a livelihood as a tenant farmer.* [earlier *liveliod,* metathetic var. of ME *livlod,* OE *līf(ge)lād* life-course (see LIFE, LODE, LOAD); current form influenced by obs. *livelihood* liveliness]
—**Syn.** sustenance, subsistence. See **living.**

live′ load′ (līv). See under **load** (def. 10).

live·long (liv′lông′, -long′), *adj.* (of time) whole or entire, esp. when tediously long, slow in passing, etc.: *We played checkers the livelong day. They stayed with us the livelong summer.* [alter. (by assoc. with LIVE[1]) of earlier *leeve long,* ME *leve longe* dear long. See LIEF, LONG[1]]

live·ly (līv′lē), *adj.,* **-li·er, -li·est,** *adv.* —*adj.* **1.** full or suggestive of life or vital energy; active, vigorous, or brisk: *a lively discussion.* **2.** animated, spirited, vivacious, or sprightly: *a lively tune.* **3.** eventful, stirring, or exciting: *The opposition gave us a lively time.* **4.** strong, keen, or distinct: *a lively recollection.* **5.** striking, telling, or effective, as an expression or instance. **6.** vivid or bright, as color or light: *She was dressed in a lively pink.* **7.** sparkling, as wines. **8.** fresh or invigorating, as air: *a lively breeze.* **9.** rebounding quickly; springing back; resilient: *lively materials.* **10.** (of a baseball) likely to travel a great distance when hit: *a lively ball that lost us the game.* **11.** bustling with activity; astir: *The market place was lively with vendors of all descriptions.* **12.** riding the sea buoyantly, as a ship. —*adv.* **13.** with activity, vigor, or animation; briskly: *to step lively.* [ME; OE *līflīc* vital. See LIFE, -LY] —**live′li·ly,** *adv.* —**live′li·ness,** *n.*
—**Syn. 1.** alert, spry, nimble, agile, quick, peart. **2.** gay, buoyant. **4.** forceful, clear. **6.** brilliant, clear, glowing.
—**Ant. 1.** inactive, torpid. **2.** dull. **4.** weak. **6.** dim.

liv·en (lī′vən), *v.t.* **1.** to put life into; rouse; cheer (often fol. by *up*): *What can we do to liven up the party?* —*v.i.* **2.** to become more lively; brighten (usually fol. by *up*): *If this party doesn't liven up soon let's leave.* [aph. var. of ENLIVEN] —**liv′en·er,** *n.*

Li·ven·za (lē ven′tsä), *n.* a river in NE Italy, flowing SE to the Adriatic. 70 mi. long.

live′ oak′ (līv), **1.** an evergreen oak, *Quercus virginiana,* of the southern U.S.: the State tree of Georgia. **2.** any of various related trees. **3.** the hard, durable wood of any of these trees.

Live′ Oak′ (līv), **1.** a town in N Florida. 6544 (1960). **2.** a town in central California. 3518 (1960).

live′ park′ing (līv), the parking of an automobile or other vehicle, with its operator in attendance.

liv·er[1] (liv′ər), *n.* **1.** *Anat.* a large, reddish-brown, glandular organ located in the upper right side of the abdominal cavity, divided by fissures into five lobes, and functioning in the secretion of bile and various metabolic processes. **2.** an organ in other animals similar to the human liver, often used as food. **3.** a diseased condition of the liver: *The doctor says it's just a touch of liver.* **4.** a reddish-brown color. **5.** a rubberlike, irreversible thickening suspension occurring in paint, ink, etc., due to a chemical reaction between a colloidal pigment and a vehicle or as a result of polymerization of the vehicle. —*adj.* **6.** of the color liver. —*v.i.* **7.** (of paint, ink, etc.) to undergo irreversible thickening. [ME; OE *lifer,* c. D *lever,* G *Leber,* Icel *lifr,* akin to Gk *liparós* fat] —**liv′er·less,** *adj.*

liv·er[2] (liv′ər), *n.* **1.** a person who lives in a manner specified: *He was always a high liver.* **2.** a dweller or resident; inhabitant: *a liver in cities.* [LIVE[1] + -ER[1]]

liv·er[3] (lī′vər), *adj.* comparative of **live**[2]. [LIVE[2] + -ER[4]]

liv·er·ber·ry (liv′ər ber′ē), *n., pl.* **-ries. 1.** a low, perennial herb, *Disporum lanuginosum,* of eastern North America, having greenish-yellow flowers and fleshy, red berries. **2.** the fruit itself. [LIVER[1] + BERRY]

liv′er chest′nut (liv′ər), chestnut (def. 9).

liv′er ex′tract (liv′ər), an extract of mammalian liver, esp. hog or beef, for treating pernicious anemia.

liv′er fluke′ (liv′ər), any of various trematodes, as *Fasciola hepatica,* parasitic in the liver and bile ducts of man and domestic animals.

liv′er fluke′ disease′ (liv′ər), *Vet. Pathol.* liver-rot.

liv·er·ied (liv′ə rēd, liv′rēd), *adj.* clad in livery, as servants: *a liveried footman.* [LIVERY + -ED[3]]

liv·er·ish (liv′ər ish), *adj.* **1.** resembling liver, esp. in color. **2.** having one's liver out of order. **3.** bilious; disagreeable; crabbed; melancholy: *to have a liverish disposition.* [LIVER[1] + -ISH[1]] —**liv′er·ish·ness,** *n.*

liv·er·leaf (liv′ər lēf′), *n., pl.* **-leaves.** a hepatica. [LIVER[1] + LEAF]

Liv·er·more (liv′ər mōr′, -môr′), *n.* a city in W California. 16,058 (1960).

Liv′ermore Falls′, a town in SW Maine. 2882 (1960).

liv′er of sul′fur. See **sulfurated potash.**

Liv·er·pool (liv′ər po͞ol′), *n.* **1.** a seaport in SW Lancashire, in W England, on the Mersey estuary. 747,490 (1961). **2.** a town in central New York. 3487 (1960).

Liv′erpool house′, *Naut.* a midship superstructure extending from side to side of a sailing vessel to provide a bridge deck.

Liv·er·pud·li·an (liv′ər pud′lē ən), *n.* a native or inhabitant of Liverpool, England. [*Liverpuddle* (jocular alter. of LIVERPOOL) + -IAN]

liv·er-rot (liv′ər rot′), *n.* *Vet. Pathol.* a disease chiefly of sheep and cattle, characterized by sluggishness, weight loss, and local damage to the liver and caused by a trematode infection, liver fluke. Also called **distomatosis, fascioliasis, liver fluke disease.**

liv′er spots′, *Pathol.* a form of chloasma in which irregularly shaped light-brown spots occur on the skin.

liv·er·wort (liv′ər wûrt′), *n.* any mosslike or thalloid, cryptogamic plant of the class *Hepaticae,* growing chiefly on damp ground, in water, or on tree trunks. [ME; late OE *liferwyrt.* See LIVER[1], WORT[2]]

liv·er·wurst (liv′ər wûrst′, -wŏŏrst′), *n.* a sausage made with a large percentage of liver, esp. one made with pork liver and pork meat. [half trans., half adoption of G *Leberwurst*]

liv·er·y[1] (liv′ə rē, liv′rē), *n., pl.* **-er·ies. 1.** a distinctive dress, badge, or device formerly provided by someone of rank or title for his retainers, as in time of war. **2.** a uniform worn by servants. **3.** distinctive attire worn by an official, a member of a company or guild, etc. **4.** Also called **liv′ery com′pany.** *Brit.* a guild or company of the City of London entitled to wear such livery. **5.** characteristic dress, garb, or outward appearance: *the green livery of summer.* **6.** the keep, feeding, stabling, etc., of horses for pay. **7.** *U.S.* a livery stable. **8.** *Law.* an ancient method of conveying a freehold by formal delivery of possession. [ME *livere* < AF, equiv. to OF *livree* allowance (of food, clothing, etc.), n. use of fem. ptp. of *livrer* to give over < L *līberāre;* see LIBERATE]

liv·er·y[2] (liv′ə rē), *adj.* liverish. [LIVER[1] + -Y[1]]

liv′ery col′ors, *Heraldry.* the principal tinctures of a coat of arms, usually one color and one metal, used for liveries, standards, etc.

liv′ery cup′board, a cupboard with pierced doors, formerly used as a storage place for food. Also called **almoner's cupboard.**

liv·er·y·man (liv′ə rē mən, liv′rē-), *n., pl.* **-men. 1.** a keeper of or an employee in a livery stable. **2.** *Brit.* a freeman of the City of London, entitled to wear the livery of the ancient guild or city district to which he belongs and to vote in the election of Lord Mayor, chamberlain, and other municipal and honorary officers. **3.** *Obs.* a person in livery, esp. a servant. [LIVERY + MAN[1]]

liv′ery sta′ble, a stable where horses and vehicles are cared for or let out for pay.

lives (līvz), *n.* pl. of **life.**

Lives′ of the Po′ets, The, a collection (1779–81), by Samuel Johnson, of biographical and critical essays on 52 English poets.

live′ spin′dle (līv). See under **spindle** (def. 5).

live′ steam′ (līv), **1.** steam fresh from the boiler and at full pressure. **2.** steam which has performed no work or only part of its work.

live·stock (līv′stok′), *n.* (*construed as sing. or pl.*) the horses, cattle, sheep, and other useful animals kept or raised on a farm or ranch. [LIVE[2] + STOCK]

live′ wire′ (līv), *Slang.* an energetic, alert person.

Liv·i·a (liv′ē ə), *n.* a girl's given name, form of **Olivia.**

liv·id (liv′id), *adj.* **1.** having a discolored, bluish appearance due to a bruise, congestion of blood vessels, strangulation, etc., as the face, flesh, hands, or nails. **2.** dull blue; dark, grayish blue. **3.** feeling or appearing as though strangulated due to a strong emotion such as fear, rage, or the like. **4.** enraged: *Willful stupidity makes me absolutely livid.* **5.** deathly pale; ashen: *Fear turned his cheeks livid for a moment.* [< L *līvidus* black and blue, equiv. to *līv(ere)* (to) be livid (akin to Welsh *lliw* color) + *-idus* -ID[4]] —**liv′id·ly,** *adv.* —**liv′id·ness, li·vid′i·ty,** *n.*

liv·ing (liv′ing), *adj.* **1.** having life; being alive; not dead: *living persons.* **2.** in actual existence or use: *living languages.* **3.** active; strong: *a living faith.* **4.** burning or glowing, as a coal. **5.** flowing freely, as water. **6.** lifelike; true to life, as a picture, narrative, etc. **7.** of or pertaining to living persons: *within living memory.* **8.** pertaining to or sufficient for living: *living conditions; a living wage.* **9.** in its natural state and place; native: *living rock.* **10.** very; absolute (used as an intensifier): *to scare the living daylights out of someone.* —*n.* **11.** act or condition of one who or that which lives: *Living is very expensive these days.* **12.** a particular manner or course of life: *austere living; luxurious living.* **13.** the means of maintaining life; livelihood: *to earn one's living.* **14.** *Brit.* the benefice of a clergyman. **15.** (*construed as pl.*) living persons collectively (usually prec. by *the*): *glad to be among the living.* [ME *lyvynge,* earlier *liviende* (adj.), OE *lifgende* (adj.). See LIVE[1], -ING[2], -ING[1]] —**liv′ing·ly,** *adv.* —**liv′ing·ness,** *n.*

—**Syn. 1.** live, quick. **2.** extant, surviving. **3.** lively, vigorous. **13.** sustenance, subsistence. LIVING, LIVELIHOOD, MAINTENANCE, SUPPORT refer, directly or indirectly, to what is earned or spent for subsistence. LIVING and LIVELIHOOD (a somewhat more formal word), both refer to what one earns to keep (oneself) alive, but are seldom interchangeable within the same phrase: *to earn one's living; to seek one's livelihood.* "To make a living" suggests making just enough to keep alive, and is particularly frequent in the negative: *You cannot make a living out of that.* "To make a livelihood out of something" suggests rather making a business of it: *to make a livelihood out of trapping foxes.* MAINTENANCE and SUPPORT refer usually to what is spent for the living of another: *to provide for the maintenance or support of someone.* MAINTENANCE occasionally refers to the allowance itself provided for livelihood: *They are entitled to a maintenance from this estate.* —**Ant. 1.** dead.

liv′ing death′, a life completely devoid of joy; a wretched existence: *He found the steaming jungle a living death.*

liv′ing pic′ture. See **tableau vivant.**

liv′ing room′, a room used, esp. by a family, for varied individual and shared social activities; parlor.

Liv·ing·ston (liv′ing stən), *n.* **1. Robert R.,** 1746–1813, U.S. statesman and jurist. **2.** a town in NE New Jersey. 23,124 (1960). **3.** a town in S Montana. 8229 (1960). **4.** a town in E Texas. 3398 (1960). **5.** a town in N Tennessee. 2817 (1960).

Liv·ing·stone (liv′ing stən), *n.* **1. David,** 1813–73, Scottish missionary and explorer in Africa. **2.** a town in SW Zambia, on the Zambesi River, near Victoria Falls: the former capital. 35,400 (est. 1964).

liv′ing wage′, a wage on which it is possible for a wage earner to live according to minimum customary standards.

Li·vo·ni·a (li vō′nē ə), *n.* **1.** a former Russian province on the Baltic: now part of the Latvian and Estonian republics of the Soviet Union. **2.** a city in SE Michigan, near Detroit. 66,702 (1960). —**Li·vo′ni·an,** *adj., n.*

Li·vor·no (lē vôr′nô), *n.* Italian name of **Leghorn.**

Li·vra·men·to (lē′vrə meɴ′tŏŏ), *n.* a city in S Brazil. 29,099 (1960).

li·vre (lē′vər; *Fr.* lē′vrᵊ), *n., pl.* **-vres** (-vərz; *Fr.* -vrᵊ). a former money of account and group of coins of France, issued in coin form first in gold, then in silver, finally in copper, and discontinued in 1794. [< MF, OF < L *lībra* balance, pound]

Liv·y (liv′ē), *n.* (*Titus Livius*) 59 B.C.–A.D. 17, Roman historian.

li·wan (lē′wän), *n.* **1.** an arcade in the courtyard of a mosque. **2.** (in an Islamic house) a raised floor area supporting the mattress of a divan.

lix·iv·i·ate (lik siv′ē āt′), *v.t.,* **-at·ed, -at·ing.** to treat with a solvent; leach. [LIXIVI(UM) + -ATE[1]] —**lix·iv′i·a′tion,** *n.*

lix·iv·i·um (lik siv′ē əm), *n., pl.* **lix·iv·i·ums, lix·iv·i·a** (lik siv′ē ə). **1.** the solution, containing alkaline salts, obtained by leaching wood ashes with water; lye. **2.** any solution obtained by leaching. [< L *lixīvium* lye, n. use of neut. of *lixīvius* made into lye, equiv. to *lix* ashes, lye + *-īvius,* var. of *-īvus* -IVE]

Li Yüan (lē′ yyän′), (*Kao Tsu*), A.D. 565–635, Chinese emperor 618–27: founder of the Tang dynasty.

Liz (liz), *n.* a girl's given name, form of **Elizabeth.**

li·za (lī′zə), *n.* a mullet, *Mugil liza,* found chiefly in the tropical Atlantic Ocean. [< Sp]

Li·za (lī′zə), *n.* a girl's given name, form of **Elizabeth.**

liz·ard (liz′ərd), *n.* **1.** any of numerous reptiles of the suborder *Lacertilia* (*Sauria*), typically having a moderately elongate body, a tapering tail, and two pairs of legs, comprising terrestrial, fossorial, arboreal, and aquatic species. **2.** any of various reptiles resembling a lizard, as a dinosaur or crocodile. **3.** leather made from the skin of the lizard, used for shoes, purses, etc. **4.** (*cap.*) *Astron.* the constellation Lacerta. **5.** See **lounge lizard. 6.** *Naut.* a pennant used as a leader for running rigging, having a thimble or bull's-eye. **7. The Lizard.** See **Lizard Head.** [ME *liserd,* var. of *lesard(e)* < MF *lesard* (masc.) *lesarde* (fem.) < L *lacertus, lacerta*]

Fence lizard,
Sceloperus undulatus
(length 4 to 7¼ in.)

liz·ard·fish (liz′ərd fish′), *n., pl.* (*esp. collectively*) **-fish,** (*esp. referring to two or more kinds or species*) **-fish·es.** any of several large-mouthed fishes of the family *Synodontidae,* having a lizardlike head. [LIZARD + FISH]

Liz′ard Head′, a promontory in SW Cornwall, in SW England: the southernmost point in England. Also called **The Lizard.**

liz·ard's-tail (liz′ərdz tāl′), *n.* either of two marsh herbs of the genus *Saururus,* esp. *S. cernuus,* of North America, having spikes of fragrant, white flowers.

Liz·beth (liz′beth′, -bəth), *n.* a girl's given name, form of **Elizabeth.**

liz·zie (liz′ē), *n.* See **tin lizzie.**

Liz·zy (liz′ē), *n.* a girl's given name, form of **Elizabeth.** Also, **Liz′zie.**

Ljod (lyōth), *n.* Liod.

Lju·blja·na (lo͞o′blē ä′nə; *Serbo-Croatian.* lyo͞o′blyä-nä), *n.* a city in and the capital of Slovenia. 305,211. German, **Laibach.**

'll, 1. contraction of *will: I'll answer the phone. He'll pay the check. What'll we do?* **2.** *Informal.* contraction of *till*[1]: *Wait'll he comes.*

LL, 1. Late Latin. **2.** Low Latin. Also, **L.L.**

ll., lines.

l.l., 1. in the place quoted. [< L *loco laudato*] **2.** loose-leaf.

lla·ma (lä′mə), *n.* **1.** a woolly-haired, South American ruminant of the genus *Lama,* believed to be a domesticated variety of the guanaco. **2.** the fine, soft fleece of the llama, combined with the wool for coating. [< Sp < Kechua]

Llama,
Lama guanicoe
(4 ft. high at
shoulder; length
4 to 5 ft.)

Llan·el·ly (la nel′ē; *Welsh.* hla-ne′hlē), *n.* a seaport in S Wales. 29,994 (1961).

lla·no (lä′nō; *Sp.* yä′nô), *n., pl.* **-nos** (-nōz; *Sp.* -nôs). (in Spanish America) an extensive grassy plain with few trees. [< Sp: a plain < L *plānus* PLAIN[1]]

Llan·o (lä′nō, lan′ō), *n.* a town in central Texas. 2656 (1960).

Lla·no Es·ta·ca·do (lä′nō es′tə kä′dō, lan′ō), a large plateau in the SW United States, in W Texas and SE New Mexico: cattle-grazing region. 1000–5000 ft. above sea level. Also called **Staked Plain.**

L. Lat., 1. Late Latin. **2.** Low Latin.

LL.B., Bachelor of Laws. [< L *Legum Baccalaureus*]

LL.D., Doctor of Laws. [< L *Legum Doctor*]

Llew·el·lyn (lo͞o el′in), *n.* **1. Richard** (*Richard David Vivian Llewellyn Lloyd*), born 1907?, Welsh novelist. **2.** a boy's given name.

Llew Llaw Gyf·fes (hlī′ hlou′ gœ′fes), *Welsh Legend.* the son of Gwydion and Arianhrod, provided with a name, weapons, and a wife through the magic and trickery of Gwydion in spite of the curses of Arianhrod. [< Welsh: lit., lion with the steady hand]

L-line (el′līn′), *n.* *Physics.* one of a series of lines (**L-series**) in the x-ray spectrum of an atom corresponding to radiation (**L-radiation**) caused by the transition of an electron to the L-shell.

LL.M., Master of Laws. [< L *Legum Magister*]

Lloyd (loid; *for 1 also Welsh* hloid), *n.* **1.** *Welsh Legend.* a magician who, to avenge his friend Gwawl upon Pryderi, the son of Pwyll, cast various spells upon Pryderi and his estate. **2. Harold (Clay·ton)** (klāt′ᵊn), born 1894, U.S. actor. **3. (John) Sel·wyn (Brooke)** (sel′win), born 1904, British statesman. **4.** Also, **Loyde.** a boy's given name.

Lloyd′ George′, David, 1st Earl of Du·for (do͞o′vôr), 1863–1945, British statesman: prime minister 1916–22.

Lloyd′ Har′bor, a town on N Long Island, in SE New York. 2521 (1960).

Lloyd's (loidz), *n.* an association of English insurance underwriters, founded in London about 1688, originally engaged in underwriting only marine risks but now also issuing policies on almost every type of insurance. [named after Edward *Lloyd,* owner of a London coffee house that was frequented by insurers against sea risk]

Lloyd's′ List′, a daily newspaper, published by Lloyd's, devoted to shipping news.

Lloyd's′ Reg′ister, a publication, issued annually by Lloyd's, consisting of a list of all of the world's seagoing vessels and including such information as their age, tonnage, and classification.

Llud (hlyd), *n.* *Welsh Legend.* a king of Britain who rid his kingdom of three plagues and was famous for his generosity: sometimes regarded as a god. Also, **Ludd, Nudd.**

Llyr (hlyr), *n.* *Welsh Legend.* the father of Manawydan: corresponds to the Irish Ler.

LM (lem), Lunar Module.

lm, lumen; lumens.

L.M., 1. Licentiate in Medicine. **2.** Licentiate in Midwifery. **3.** Lord Mayor.

lm/ft², lumens per square foot.

lm-hr, lumen-hour; lumen-hours.

lm/m², lumens per square meter.

LMT, Local Mean Time.

lm/W, lumen per watt.

ln, *Math.* See **natural logarithm.** [*l*(*ogarithm*) *n*(*atural*)]

LNG, liquefied natural gas.

l-nor·ep·i·neph·rine (el′nôr′ep ə nef′rin), *n.* levarterenol. Also called **l-nor·ad·ren·al·ine** (el′nôr′ə-dren′ᵊlin, -ᵊlēn′). [L(EVARTERENOL) + NOR- + EPINEPHRINE]

lo (lō), *interj.* look; see; behold. [ME; OE *lā* oh! ah!; c. Goth *laian,* Icel *lā* blame]

L.O.A., *Naut.* See **length over all.**

loach (lōch), *n.* any of several slender, European and Asian fishes of the family *Cobitidae* and related families, having several barbels around the mouth. [ME *loche* < MF]

load (lōd), *n.* **1.** that which is laid on or placed in anything for conveyance. **2.** the quantity that can be or usually is carried, as in a cart. **3.** this quantity taken as a unit of measure or weight (usually used in combination): *carload; wagonload.* **4.** the quantity borne or sustained by something: *a tree weighed down by its load of fruit.* **5.** something that weighs down or oppresses like a burden: *The responsibility of supporting two families has been a heavy load for him to carry.* **6.** the amount of work assigned to or to be done by a person, department, machine, or mechanical system: *to assign each employee his work load for the month.* **7.** the charge for a firearm. **8. loads,** *Informal.* a great quantity or number: *loads of fun; loads of people.* **9.** the weight supported by a structure or part. **10.** *Engineering.* any of the forces which a structure is calculated to oppose, comprising any unmoving and unvarying force (**dead load**), any load from wind or earthquake, and any other moving or temporary force (**live load**). **11.** *Elect.* **a.** the power delivered by a generator, motor, power station, or transformer (often followed by *on*). **b.** a device that receives power. **12.** *Mech.* the external resistance overcome by an engine, dynamo, or the like, under given conditions, measured and expressed in terms of the power required. **13.** *Slang.* a sufficient amount of liquor drunk to cause intoxication; drunkenness: *He's got a load on tonight.* **14. get a load of,** *Slang.* **a.** to look at; observe. **b.** to listen to with interest: *Did you get a load of what she said?* —*v.t.* **15.** to put a load on or in; fill: *to load a cart; to load a washing machine.* **16.** to supply abundantly or excessively with something (often fol. by *down*): *They loaded us down with gifts.* **17.** to weigh down, burden, or oppress (often fol. by *down, with, on,* etc.): *to feel loaded down with responsibilities; to load oneself with obligations; to load duties on one's assistant.* **18.** to add to the weight of, often fraudulently: *The silver candlesticks were loaded with lead.* **19.** *Insurance.* to increase (the net premium) by adding charges, as for expenses. **20.** to take on as a load: *a vessel loading coal.* **21.** to insert a charge, projectile, etc., into (a firearm). **22.** to add additional or prejudicial meaning to (a statement, question, etc.): *The attorney kept loading his questions in the hope of getting the sort of reply he wanted.* **23.** to overcharge (a word, expression, etc.) with extraneous values of emotion, sentiment, or the like: *the automatic rush of emotion that loads any reference to home, flag, mother, or man's best friend.* **24.** to weight (dice) so that they will fall with particular faces upward. **25.** *Baseball.* to have or put runners at first, second, and third bases at the same time: *They loaded the bases with two out in the bottom of the eighth inning.* **26.** *Photog.* to place film, sensitized paper, etc., into (a camera, cartridge, etc.) for exposure. **27.** *Fine Arts.* **a.** to place a large amount of pigment on (a brush) **b.** to apply a thick layer of pigment to (a canvas). **28.** *Metalworking.* **a.** (of metal being deep-drawn) to become welded to (the drawing tool). **b.** (of material being ground) to fill the depressions in the surface of (a grinding wheel). **c.** (in powder metallurgy) to fill the cavity of (a die). **29.** *Elect.* to add (a power-absorbing device) to an electric circuit. —*v.i.* **30.** to put on or take on a load, as of passengers, goods, etc.: *The bus usually loads at the side door.* **31.** to load a firearm. **32.** to enter a carrier or conveyance (usually fol. by *into*): *The campers loaded into the buses.* **33.** to become loaded: *The ship loaded with people in only 15 minutes.* **34. load the dice,** to place someone or something in a favorable or unfavorable position; affect or influence the result: *Lack of sufficient education loaded the dice against him as a candidate for the job. He uses his great wealth to load the dice in his favor.* —*adv.* **35. loads,** *Informal.* very much; a great deal: *Thanks loads. It would help loads if you sent money.* [ME *lode;* orig. the same word as LODE (OE *lād* way, course, carrying) but associated with LADE] —**load′er,** *n.* —**load′less,** *adj.*

—**Syn. 5.** onus, weight, encumbrance. LOAD, BURDEN referred originally to something placed on a person or animal or put into a vehicle for conveyance; LOAD has still retained this concrete meaning; BURDEN has lost it, except in such fixed phrases as: *beast of burden,* and *a ship of 1500 tons burden* (carrying capacity). Both words have come to be used figuratively to refer to duties, cares, etc., that are oppressively heavy, and this is now the main meaning of BURDEN: *You have taken a load off my mind. Some children are a burden.* **15.** lade. **17.** weight, encumber. —**Ant. 17.** disburden.

load′ displace′ment, *Naut.* the weight, in long tons, of a cargo vessel loaded so that the summer load line touches the surface of the water.

load′ draft′, *Naut.* the draft of a vessel at load displacement.

load·ed (lō′did), *adj.* **1.** bearing a load; full: *a loaded bus; a loaded suitcase.* **2.** containing ammunition or an explosive charge: *a loaded rifle; a loaded cigar.* **3.** (of a word, statement, or argument) fraught with emotional or associative significance that hinders rational or unprejudiced consideration of the terms involved in a discourse. **4.** (of dice) fraudulently weighted so as to increase the chances of certain combinations to face up when the dice are thrown. **5.** *Slang.* very intoxicated; drunk. **6.** *Slang.* having a great deal of money; very wealthy. [LOAD + -ED²]

load′ fac′tor, *Elect.* the ratio of the average load over a designated period of time to the peak load occurring in that period.

load·ing (lō′ding), *n.* **1.** the act of one who or that which loads. **2.** that with which something is loaded; load; burden; charge. **3.** *Elect.* the process of adding reactance to a telephone circuit, radio antenna, etc. **4.** *Aeron.* the ratio of the gross weight of an airplane to engine power (**power loading**), wing span (**span loading**), or wing area (**wing loading**). **5.** *Insurance.* an addition to the net premium, to cover expenses and allow a margin for contingencies and profit. [LOAD + -ING¹]

load′ing coil′, *Elect.* an inductance coil used to improve the characteristics of a transmission line.

load′ line′, *Naut.* **1.** Also called **Plimsoll line.** any of various lines marked on the sides of a cargo vessel to indicate the depth to which a vessel may be immersed under certain conditions, as time of year, part of the world, presence of salt or fresh water, construction of the hull, and type of cargo carried. Cf. **freeboard** (def. 1). **2.** the line made by the surface of the water on the hull of a loaded ship.

Load line
AB, Official load line set by American Bureau of Shipping; TF, Tropical, fresh water; F, Fresh water; T, Tropical; S, Summer; W, Winter; WNA, Winter, North Atlantic

load′-line disk′ (lōd′līn′), *Naut.* a mark painted as one of the load-line marks on the side of an ocean-going vessel, consisting of a circle crossed by a horizontal line, symbolizing the load line of the vessel at load displacement, as well as the initials of the authority assigning the load lines of the vessel.

load′-line mark′, *Naut.* any of various marks by which the allowable loading and the load line at load displacement are established for a merchant vessel; a load line or load-line disk. Also called **Plimsoll mark.**

load·star (lōd′stär′), *n.* lodestar.

load·stone (lōd′stōn′), *n.* **1.** a variety of magnetite which possesses magnetic polarity and attracts iron. **2.** a piece of this serving as a magnet. **3.** something that attracts. Also, **lodestone.** [*load* LODE + STONE]

loaf¹ (lōf), *n., pl.* **loaves** (lōvz). **1.** a portion of bread or cake baked in a mass of definite form. **2.** a shaped or molded mass of food, as of sugar, chopped meat, etc.: *a veal loaf.* **3.** *Brit.* **a.** the rounded head of a cabbage, lettuce, etc. **b.** *Slang.* one's head or brains: *Use your loaf.* [ME *lo(o)f,* OE *hlāf* loaf, bread; c. G *Laib,* Icel *hleifr,* Goth *hlaifs*]

loaf² (lōf), *v.i.* **1.** to lounge or saunter lazily and idly: *We loafed for hours along the water's edge.* **2.** to idle away time: *He figured the pool hall was as good a place as any in which to loaf.* —*v.t.* **3.** to pass (time) by idling (usually fol. by *away*): *to loaf one's life away.* [? back formation from LOAFER]

loaf·er (lō′fər), *n.* **1.** a person who loafs; a lazy person; idler. **2.** a casual, moccasinlike, slip-on shoe. [? short for *landloafer,* appar. var. of *landloper* vagabond (< MD; see LAND, LOPE), with *-f-* from its G synonym *Landläufer*] —**loaf′er·ish,** *adj.*

lo·a·i·a·sis (lō′ə ī′ə sis), *n.* *Pathol.* loiasis.

loam (lōm), *n.* **1.** a rich, friable soil containing a relatively equal mixture of sand and silt and a somewhat smaller proportion of clay. **2.** a mixture of clay, sand, straw, etc., used in making molds for founding and in plastering walls, stopping holes, etc. **3.** *Archaic.* earth or soil. **4.** *Obs.* clay or clayey earth. —*v.t.* **5.** to cover or stop with loam. [late ME *lome,* ME *lam(e),* OE *lām;* c. D *leem,* G *Lehm* loam, clay; akin to LIME¹] —**loam′i·ness,** *n.* —**loam′less,** *adj.* —**loam′y,** *adj.*

loan¹ (lōn), *n.* **1.** the act of lending; a grant of the temporary use of something: *the loan of a book.* **2.** something lent or furnished on condition of being returned, esp. a sum of money lent at interest. **3.** the temporary service of a person furnished by his superior to another: *He's on loan to another movie studio for two films.* —*v.t.* **4.** to make a loan of; lend: *Will you loan me your umbrella?* **5.** to lend (money) at interest. —*v.i.* **6.** to make a loan or loans; lend. [ME *lon(e), lan(e),* OE *lān* < Scand; cf. Icel *lān;* r. its cognate, OE *lǣn* loan, grant, c. D *leen,* G *Lehn*] —**loan′a·ble,** *adj.* —**loan′er,** *n.*

loan² (lōn), *n.* *Scot.* **1.** a country lane; secondary road. **2.** an uncultivated plot of farmland, as used for milking cows. Also, **loan·in** (lō′nin). [ME, OE *lone* LANE]

loan·blend (lōn′blend′), *n.* a compound word or expression consisting of both native and foreign elements. [LOAN¹ + BLEND]

Lo·an·da (lō än′də), *n.* Luanda.

loan′ of′fice, **1.** an office for making loans or receiving payments on loans. **2.** a pawnbroker's shop. **3.** a public office for receiving subscriptions to a government loan.

loan′ shark′, *Informal.* a person who lends money at excessive rates of interest; usurer.

loan·shift (lōn′shift′), *n.* **1.** *Ling.* change or extension of the meaning of a word through the influence of a foreign word, as in the application of the meaning of *profession* to *calling* through the influence of Latin *vocātio.* **2.** a word created by loanshift. [LOAN¹ + SHIFT]

loan′ transla′tion, **1.** the process whereby a compound word or expression is created by literal translation of each of the elements of a compound word or expression in another language, as *marriage of convenience* from French *mariage de convenance.* Cf. **calque. 2.** a word or expression so created.

loan′ val′ue, *Insurance.* the highest amount of money that can be borrowed against on a life-insurance policy, based on the cash value of the policy.

loan′ word′, a word in one language that has been borrowed or taken over from another language, as *wine,* taken into Old English from Latin, or *blitz,* taken into Modern English from German. [trans. of G *Lehnwort*]

loath (lōth, lōth), *adj.* unwilling; reluctant; disinclined; averse: *to be loath to admit a mistake.* Also, **loth.** [ME *loth, lath,* OE *lāth* hostile, hateful; c. D *leed,* G *leid* sorry, Icel *leithr* hateful] —**loath′ness,** *n.*
—**Syn.** See **reluctant.** —**Ant.** eager.

loathe (lōth), *v.t.,* **loathed, loath·ing.** to feel disgust or intense aversion for; abhor: *I loathe people who spread malicious gossip. Most of all, I loathe mashed yellow turnips.* [ME *loth(i)en, lath(i)en,* OE *lāthiān,* deriv. of *lāth* LOATH] —**loath′er,** *n.*
—**Syn.** detest, abominate, hate. —**Ant.** like.

loath·ful (lōth′fəl), *adj.* **1.** *Scot.* bashful; reluctant. **2.** *Rare.* hateful; loathsome. [late ME *lothfull.* See LOATH, -FUL]

loath·ing (lō′thing), *n.* strong dislike mingled with disgust; intense aversion. [ME *lathynge.* See LOATHE, -ING¹] —**loath′ing·ly,** *adv.*
—**Syn.** abhorrence; hatred. See **aversion.**

loath·ly¹ (lōth′lē, lōth′-), *adv.* reluctantly; unwillingly. [late ME *lothely,* early ME *lothliche,* OE *lāthlīce.* See LOATH, -LY (adv. suffix)]

loath·ly² (lōth′lē, lōth′-), *adj.* *Archaic.* loathsome; hideous; repulsive. [ME *loothly,* OE *lāthlīc.* See LOATH, -LY (adj. suffix)]

loath·some (lōth′səm, lōth′-), *adj.* such as to excite loathing; hateful; disgusting; revolting; repulsive: *A loathsome little man called each day.* [ME *lothsom.* See LOATH, -SOME¹] —**loath′some·ly,** *adv.* —**loath′some·ness,** *n.*
—**Syn.** offensive, repellent, detestable, abhorrent, abominable. —**Ant.** attractive.

loaves (lōvz), *n.* pl. of **loaf¹.**

lob¹ (lob), *v.,* **lobbed, lob·bing,** *n.* —*v.t.* **1.** *Tennis.* to hit (a ball) in a high arc to the back of the opponent's court. **2.** *Cricket.* to bowl (the ball) with a slow underhand motion. **3.** to fire (a missile, as a shell) in a high trajectory so that it drops onto a target. —*v.i.* **4.** *Tennis.* to lob a ball. —*n.* **5.** *Tennis.* a ball hit in a high arc to the back of the opponent's court. **6.** *Cricket.* a ball bowled with a slow underhand motion. **7.** *Brit. Dial.* a slow, heavy, dull-witted person. [orig. v.: to behave like a *lobbe* bumpkin, clumsy person (ME, pollack; OE, spider; basic sense, something pendulous); c. MLG, MD *lobbe* dangling part, stockfish, etc.] —**lob′ber,** *n.*

lob² (lob), *n.* lobworm.

Lo·ba·chev·sky (lō′bə chef′skē; *Russ.* lo bä chef′ski), *n.* **Ni·ko·lai I·va·no·vich** (nē ko lī′ ē vä′no vich), 1793–1856, Russian mathematician.

lo·bar (lō′bər, -bär), *adj.* of or pertaining to a lobe, as of the lungs. [< NL *lobār(is).* See LOBE, -AR¹]

lo′bar pneumo′nia, *Pathol.* pneumonia (def. 2).

lo·bate (lō′bāt), *adj.* **1.** having a lobe or lobes; lobed. **2.** having the form of a lobe. **3.** *Ornith.* noting or pertaining to a foot in which the individual toes have membranous flaps along the sides. Also, **lo′bat·ed.** [< NL *lobāt(us).* See LOBE, -ATE¹] —**lo′bate·ly,** *adv.*

lo·ba·tion (lō bā′shən), *n.* **1.** lobate formation. **2.** a lobe. [LOBATE + -ION]

lob·by (lob′ē), *n., pl.* **-bies,** *v.,* **-bied, -by·ing.** —*n.* **1.** a corridor, vestibule, or entrance hall, as in a public building, often serving as an anteroom; foyer. **2.** a group of persons who conduct a campaign to influence members of a legislature to vote according to the group's special interest. —*v.i.* **3.** to frequent the lobby of a legislative chamber to influence the members. **4.** to solicit or try to influence the votes of members of a legislative body. —*v.t.* **5.** to influence (legislators), or urge or procure the passage of (a bill), by lobbying. [< ML *lobia, laubia* covered way < OHG **laubia* (later *lauba*) arbor, deriv. of *laub* LEAF] —**lob′by·er,** *n.*

lob·by·ism (lob′ē iz′əm), *n.* *U.S.* **1.** the system of lobbying. **2.** the practices of those who lobby. [LOBBY + -ISM] —**lob′by·ist,** *n.*

lobe (lōb), *n.* **1.** a roundish projection or division, as of an organ, a leaf, etc. **2.** the soft, pendulous, lower part of the external ear. See diag. under **ear.** [< LL *lobus* < Gk *lobós,* akin to L *legula* lobe of the ear]

lo·bec·to·my (lō bek′tə mē), *n., pl.* **-mies.** *Surg.* excision of a lobe of an organ or gland. [LOBE + -ECTOMY]

lobed (lōbd), *adj.* **1.** having a lobe or lobes; lobate. **2.** *Bot.* (of a leaf) having lobes or divisions extending less than halfway to the middle of the base. [LOBE + -ED³]

lo·bel·ia (lō bēl′yə), *n.* any herbaceous or woody plant of the genus *Lobelia,* having blue, red, yellow, or white flowers. [< NL; named after Matthias de *Lobel* (1538–1616), Flemish botanist, physician to James I of England; see -IA]

lo·be·li·a·ceous (lō bē′lē ā′shəs), *adj.* belonging to the *Lobeliaceae,* or lobelia family of plants. [< NL *Lobeli(aceae)* name of family (*Lobelia* type genus + -ACEAE) + -ACEOUS]

lo·be·line (lō′bə lēn′, -lin, lō bē′lēn, -lin), *n.* *Pharm.* a crystalline, poisonous alkaloid, $C_{22}H_{27}NO_2$, obtained by extraction from lobelia: used chiefly in the form of its sulfate or hydrochloride as a respiratory stimulant, and because of its nicotinelike pharmacological action as an agent to discourage tobacco smoking. [LOBEL(IA) + -INE³]

Lo·bi·to (lo͞o bē′to͞o, lo͞o bē′tō), *n.* a seaport in W Angola. 31,630 (est. 1955).

lob·lol·ly (lob′lol′ē), *n., pl.* **-lies. 1.** a pine, *Pinus Taeda,* of the southern U.S. **2.** the wood of this tree. **3.** *Dial.* a mire; mudhole. **4.** *Dial.* a thick gruel. Also called **lob′lolly pine′** (for defs. 1, 2). [short for *loblolly pine* swamp pine, special use of nautical term *loblolly* thick gruel, whence also the American sense mudhole; see LOBSCOUSE]

lob′lolly bay′, an evergreen tree, *Gordonia Lasianthus,* having fragrant, long-stalked, white flowers from two to three inches wide and egg-shaped fruit. Also called **tan bay.**

lob′lolly boy′, *Obs.* an attendant who assists the surgeon on board a ship.

lo·bo (lō′bō), *n., pl.* **-bos.** the gray or timber wolf of the western U.S. [< Sp < L *lupus* wolf]

lo·bo·lo (lō′bə lə), *n., pl.* **-los.** a bride price, typically of cattle, paid to a bride's father among Bantu-speaking tribes of southern Africa. Also, **lo′bo·la.** [< a Bantu dial.]

lo·bose (lō′bōs), *adj.* *Zool.* having broad, thick pseudopodia, as certain amoeboid protozoans. [< NL *lobōs(us).* See LOBE, -OSE]

lo·bot·o·my (lō bot′ə mē, lə-), *n., pl.* **-mies.** *Surgery.* the cutting into or across a lobe of the brain, usually of the cerebrum, to alter brain function, esp. in the treatment of mental disorders. Also called **leucotomy, leukotomy.** [Gk *lobó(s)* lobe + -TOMY]

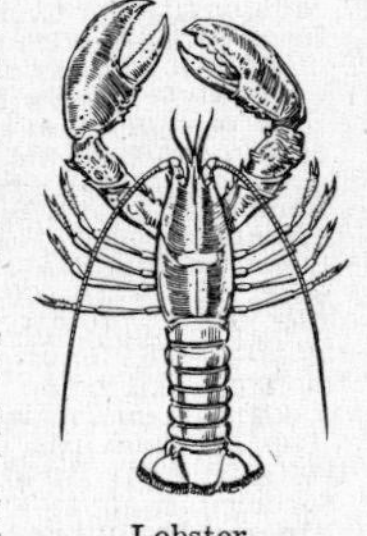
Lobster, *Homarus americanus* (Length 8 to 12 in.)

lob·scouse (lob′skous), *n.* *Naut.* a stew of meat, potatoes, onions, ship biscuit, etc. Also, **lob·scourse** (lob′skōrs, -skôrs). [cf. G *Labskaus* > Norw *lapskaus,* Dan *labskous*]

lob·ster (lob′stər), *n., pl.* (*esp. collectively*) **-ster,** (*esp. referring to two or more kinds or species*) **-sters. 1.** any of various large, edible, marine, stalk-eyed decapod crustaceans of the family *Homaridae,* esp. of the genus *Homarus.* **2.** See **spiny lobster. 3.** any of various similar crustaceans, as certain crayfishes. [ME *lopster,* OE *loppestre,* lit., spidery creature (*loppe* spider + *-stre* -STER), so called because marked by many projecting parts. See LOP¹]

lob·ster·ing (lob′stər ing), *n.* the act or process of capturing lobsters. [LOBSTER + -ING¹]

lob′ster New′burg, (*sometimes l.c.*) lobster cooked in a thick seasoned cream sauce made with sherry or brandy. Also, **lob′ster New′burgh.** Also called **lob′ster à la New′burg, lob′ster à la New′burgh.** [*Newburg* < ?]

lob′ster pot′, a trap, typically made of wooden slats, for catching lobsters.

lob′ster roll′, lobster salad served on a frankfurter roll or the like.

lob′ster-tail hel′met (lob′stər tāl′), *Armor.* a burgonet fitted with a long, articulated tail of lames for protecting the nape of the neck, worn by cavalry in the 17th century.

lob′ster ther′midor, cooked lobster meat placed back in the shell with a cream sauce, sprinkled with grated cheese and melted butter, and browned in the oven. [named by Napoleon after the month it was first served to him; see THERMIDOR]

lob′ster trick′, dogwatch (def. 2). Also called **lob′ster shift′.**

lob·stick (lob′stik′), *n.* *Canadian.* lopstick.

lob′ular pneumo′nia, *Pathol.* bronchopneumonia. [LOBULE + -AR¹]

lob′ular pump′, a blower or pump displacing air or liquid by means of rotors having meshing lobes which act as a seal at their place of mesh. Also called **gear pump.**

lob·u·late (lob′yə lit, -lāt′), *adj.* consisting of, divided into, or having lobes. Also, **lob′u·lat′ed.** [LOBULE + -ATE¹] —**lob′u·la′tion,** *n.*

lob·ule (lob′yo͞ol), *n.* **1.** a small lobe. **2.** a subdivision of a lobe. [< NL *lobul(us).* See LOBE, -ULE] —**lob·u·lar** (lob′yə lər), *adj.*

lob·u·lus (lob′yə ləs), *n., pl.* **-li** (-lī′). *Anat.* a lobule. [< NL; see LOBULE]

lo·bus (lō′bəs), *n., pl.* **-bi** (-bī). *Anat.* a lobe. [< NL; see LOBE]

lob·worm (lob′wûrm′), *n.* the lungworm. Also called **lob.** [dial. *lob,* earlier *lobbe,* orig., something pendulous (see LOB¹) + WORM]

lo·ca (lō′kə), *n.* a pl. of **locus.**

lo·cal (lō′kəl), *adj.* **1.** pertaining to or characterized by place or position in space. **2.** pertaining to, characteristic of, or restricted to a particular place or particular places: *a local custom.* **3.** pertaining to a town or a small district rather than the entire state or country: *local transportation; a local saying.* **4.** pertaining to or affecting a particular part or particular parts, as of a physical system, organism, or the like: *a local disease.* **5.** *Med.* (of anesthesia or an anesthetic) affecting a particular part or area of the body without loss of consciousness. **6.** stopping at all stations: *a local train.* —*n.* **7.** a local train, bus, etc. **8.** a newspaper item of local interest. **9.** a local branch of a union, fraternity, etc. **10.** Often, **locals. a.** a local person or resident: *primarily of interest to locals.* **b.** a local athletic team: *the locals versus the state champions.* **11.** Also called **lo′cal stamp′.** stamp (def. 22). **12.** *Brit. Informal.* a neighborhood pub or tavern. [late ME < LL *locāl(is).* See LOCUS, -AL¹] —**lo′cal·ness,** *n.*

lo′cal col′or, **1.** distinctive characteristics or peculiarities of a place or period as represented in literature, drama, etc., or as observed in reality. **2.** *Fine Arts.* the natural color of a particular object as it appears in normal light.

lo·cale (lō kal′, -käl′), *n.* **1.** a place or locality, esp. with reference to events or circumstances connected with it: *to move to a warmer locale.* **2.** the scene or setting, as of a play, motion picture, or the like: *The locale is a small Kansas town just before World War I.* [earlier *local* < F: n. use of adj. See LOCAL]
—**Syn. 1.** location, site, spot.

lo′cal gov′ernment, the administration of the local affairs of a town or district by its inhabitants, rather than by the state or country at large.

lo·cal·ise (lō′kə līz′), *v.t., v.i.,* **-ised, -is·ing.** *Chiefly Brit.* localize. —**lo′cal·is′a·ble,** *adj.* —**lo′cal·i·sa′tion,** *n.* —**lo′cal·is′er,** *n.*

lo·cal·ism (lō′kə liz′əm), *n.* **1.** a manner of speaking, pronunciation, usage, or inflection that is peculiar to one locality. **2.** a local custom. **3.** attachment to a particular locality. **4.** excessive devotion to and promotion of the interests of a particular locality; sectionalism. [LOCAL + -ISM] —**lo′cal·ist,** *n.* —**lo′cal·is′tic,** *adj.*

lo·cal·i·ty (lō kal′i tē), *n., pl.* **-ties. 1.** a place, spot, or district, with or without reference to things or persons in it: *They moved to another locality.* **2.** the place in which a thing is or occurs: *the locality where the incident took place.* **3.** the state or fact of being local or having a location: *the locality which every material object must have.* [< LL *locālitās.* See LOCAL, -ITY]

lo·cal·ize (lō′kə līz′), *v.,* **-ized, -iz·ing.** —*v.t.* **1.** to make local; fix in, or assign or restrict to, a particular place, locality, etc. —*v.i.* **2.** to gather or collect in one locality. Also, *esp. Brit.,* **localise.** [LOCAL + -IZE] —**lo′cal·iz′a·ble,** *adj.* —**lo′cal·i·za′tion,** *n.* —**lo′cal·iz′er,** *n.*

lo·cal·ly (lō′kə lē), *adv.* **1.** in a particular place, area, location, etc. **2.** with regard to place. **3.** in a local respect: *Not much interest is taken in the contest locally.* [late ME *localliche.* See LOCAL, -LY]

lo′cally compact′ space′, *Math.* a topological space in which each point has a neighborhood that is compact.

lo′cally Euclid′ean space′, *Math.* a topological space in which each point has a neighborhood that is homeomorphic to an open set in a Euclidean space of specified dimension.

lo′cally fi′nite set′, *Math.* a collection of sets in a topological space in which each point of the space has a neighborhood that intersects a finite number of sets of the collection.

lo′cal max′imum, *Math.* maximum (def. 2a).

lo′cal min′imum, *Math.* minimum (def. 4a).

lo′cal op′tion, a right of choice exercised by a minor political division, esp. as to allowing the sale of liquor.

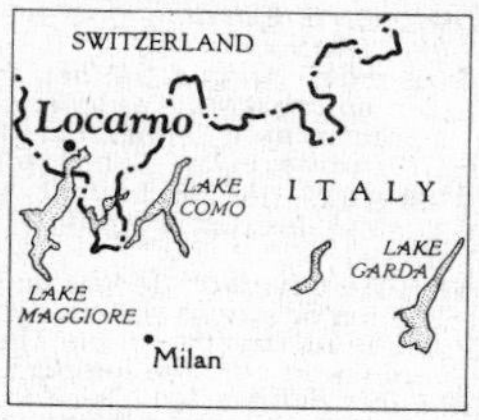

lo′cal wind′ (wind), one of a number of winds that are influenced predominantly by the topographic features of a relatively small region.

Lo·car·no (*It.* lô kär′nô), *n.* a town in S Switzerland, on Lake Maggiore: Locarno Pact 1925. 14,700 (est. 1959).

lo·cate (lō′kāt, lō kāt′), *v.,* **-cat·ed, -cat·ing.** —*v.t.* **1.** to discover the place or location of: *to locate a leak in a pipe.* **2.** to set, fix, or establish in a position, situation, or locality; place; settle: *to locate one's European headquarters in Paris.* **3.** *U.S.* to survey and enter a claim to a tract of land; take up or take possession of land. **4.** to assign or ascribe a particular location to (something), as by knowledge or opinion: *Many scholars locate the Garden of Eden in Babylonia.* —*v.i.* **5.** to establish oneself, one's business, or one's residence in a place; settle. [< L *locāt(us)* placed, ptp. of *locāre.* See LOCUS, -ATE[1]] —**lo′cat·a·ble,** *adj.* —**lo′cat·er,** *n.*

lo·ca·tion (lō kā′shən), *n.* **1.** a place of settlement or residence: *This town is a good location for a young doctor.* **2.** a place or situation occupied: *a house in a fine location.* **3.** a tract of land located, or of designated situation or limits: *a mining location.* **4.** (in an electronic computer) any position on a register or memory device capable of storing one machine word. **5.** *Motion Pictures.* a place, outside of the studio, affording a suitable environment for filming a particular movie, scene, etc. (usually prec. by *on*): *They're filming most of the action on location.* **6.** the act of locating; state of being located. **7.** *Civil Law.* a letting or renting. [< L *locātiōn-* (s. of *locātiō*) a placing. See LOCATE, -ION]

loc·a·tive (lok′ə tiv), *Gram.* —*adj.* **1.** (in certain inflected languages) noting a case whose distinctive function is to indicate place in or at which, as Latin *domī* "at home." —*n.* **2.** the locative case. **3.** a word in that case. [LOCATE + -IVE, modeled on *vocative*]

lo·ca·tor (lō′kā tər, lō kā′tər), *n.* *U.S.* a person who fixes the boundaries of land or a mining claim. [< L *locāt(or)* a contractor. See LOCATE, -OR[2]]

loc. cit. (lok′ sit′), in the place cited. [< L *locō citātō*]

loch (lok, lokH), *n.* *Scot.* **1.** a lake. **2.** a partially landlocked or protected bay; a narrow arm of the sea. [< Gael; r. ME *louch,* OE *luh* lake, pond < OWelsh *luch* (Welsh *llwch*) < OIr. See LOUGH]

Loch·a′ber ax′ (lo KHä′bər; *Eng.* lo kä′bər), a Scottish battle-ax of the 16th century, having a tall cleaver-like blade with a hook at its upper end. [after *Lochaber,* Scotland]

loche (lōch), *n.* the North American burbot. [< CanF, F: loach]

lo·chi·a (lō′kē ə, lok′ē ə), *n., pl.* **-chi·a.** *Med.* the liquid discharge from the uterus after childbirth. [< NL < Gk, n. use of neut. pl. of *lóchios* of childbirth, equiv. to *lóch(os)* childbirth + *-ios* -IOUS] —**lo′chi·al** (lō′kē əl), *adj.*

Lo·chi·a (lō kī′ə, lō′kē ə), *n.* *Class. Myth.* Artemis: so called because she protected women in childbirth. [< Gk *Locheía,* substantive use of fem. of *locheios* of, belonging to childbirth]

Loch·in·var (lok′in vär′, lokH′-), *n.* **1.** the hero of a ballad included in the narrative poem *Marmion* (1808) by Sir Walter Scott. **2.** a romantic suitor.

Loch′ Ra′ven (lok), a town in central Maryland, near Baltimore. 23,278 (1960).

loch·us (lok′əs), *n., pl.* **loch·i** (lok′ī). (in ancient Greece) a subdivision of an army. [< Gk *lóchos* ambush, men that form the ambush, body of troops]

lo·ci (lō′sī), *n.* pl. of **locus.**

lock[1] (lok), *n.* **1.** a device for securing a door, gate, lid, drawer, or the like, in position when closed, consisting of a bolt or system of bolts propelled and withdrawn by a mechanism operated by a key, dial, etc. **2.** any device or part for stopping temporarily the motion of a mechanism. **3.** a contrivance for fastening or securing something. **4.** (in a firearm) **a.** the mechanism that explodes the charge; gunlock. **b.** safety (def. 4). **5.** an enclosed chamber in a canal, dam, etc., with gates at each end, for raising or lowering vessels from one level to another by admitting or releasing water. **6.** an air lock or decompression chamber. **7.** *Wrestling.* any of various holds, esp. a hold secured on the arm, leg, or head: *arm lock; leg lock; head lock.* **8.** *Horol.* (in an escapement) the overlap between a tooth of an escape wheel and the surface of the pallet locking it. **9.** *Metalworking.* a projection or recess in the mating face of a forging die. **10. lock, stock, and barrel,** completely; entirely; including every part, no matter how small or insignificant: *We bought the whole company from him, lock, stock, and barrel.* **11. under lock and key,** in a safe place; securely locked up: *The documents were under lock and key.* —*v.t.* **12.** to fasten or secure (a door, window, building, etc.) by the operation of a lock or locks (sometimes fol. by *up*): *Don't forget to lock up the store.* **13.** to shut in a place fastened by a lock or locks, as for security or restraint (often fol. by *up*): *to lock up a prisoner.* **14.** to make fast or immovable by or as by a lock: *He locked the steering wheel on his car.* **15.** to make fast or immovable, as by engaging parts: *to lock the wheels of a wagon before starting downhill.* **16.** to join or unite firmly by interlinking or intertwining: *to lock arms.* **17.** to hold fast in an embrace: *She was locked in his arms.* **18.** to move (a ship) by means of a lock or locks, as in a canal. **19.** to furnish with locks, as a canal. —*v.i.* **20.** to become locked: *This door locks with a key.* **21.** to become fastened, fixed, or interlocked: *gears that lock into place.* **22.** to go or pass by means of a lock or locks, as a vessel. **23.** to construct locks in waterways. **24. lock horns,** to come into conflict; clash: *They locked horns on the subject of foreign policy in the East; to lock horns with a political opponent.* **25. lock off,** to enclose (a waterway) with a lock. **26. lock out, a.** to keep out by or as by a lock. **b.** to subject (employees) to a lockout. **27. lock up, a.** *Print.* to make (type) immovable in a chase by securing the quoins. **b.** to fasten or secure with a lock or locks. **c.** to fasten or fix firmly, as by engaging parts. [ME; OE *loc* fastening, bar; c. MLG *lok,* OHG *loh,* Icel *lok* lock, Goth *-luk* in *usluk* opening; akin to OE *lūcan* to shut] —**lock′a·ble,** *adj.* —**lock′less,** *adj.*

lock[2] (lok), *n.* **1.** a tress or portion of hair. **2. locks, a.** the hair of the head. **b.** short wool of inferior quality, as that obtained in small clumps from the legs. **3.** a flock or small portion of wool, cotton, flax, etc. [ME *locke,* OE *locc* lock of hair, c. Icel *lokkr,* D *lok* curl, G *Locke*]

Lock (lok), *n.* a boy's or girl's given name. Also, **Locke.**

lock·age (lok′ij), *n.* **1.** the construction, use, or operation of locks, as in a canal or stream. **2.** passage through a lock or locks. **3.** a toll paid for such passage. [LOCK[1] + -AGE]

lock′ bay′, a broadened section of a canal before the gates of a lock.

lock·box (lok′boks′), *n.* **1.** a strongbox. **2.** a rented post-office box equipped with a lock. [LOCK[1] + BOX[1]]

Locke (lok), *n.* **1. Al·ain Le·Roy** (al′in lə roi′, lē′roi), 1886–1954, U.S. educator and author. **2. David Ross** ("*Petroleum V. Nasby*"), 1833–88, U.S. humorist and journalist. **3. John,** 1632–1704, English philosopher. **4.** Also, **Lock.** a boy's or girl's given name.

Lock·e·an (lok′ē ən), *n.* **1.** an adherent of the philosophy of Locke. —*adj.* **2.** of, pertaining to, or resembling the philosophy of Locke. [John LOCKE + -AN] —**Lock′e·an·ism, Lock′i·an·ism,** *n.*

lock·er (lok′ər), *n.* **1.** a chest, drawer, compartment, closet, or the like, that may be locked. **2.** *Naut.* a chest or compartment in which to stow things. **3.** a refrigerated compartment, as in a locker plant, that may be rented for storing frozen foods. **4.** one who or that which locks. [late ME *loker.* See LOCK[1], -ER[1]]

Lock·er-Lamp·son (lok′ər lam′sən), *n.* **Frederick** (*Frederick Locker*), 1821–95, English poet.

lock′er plant′, an establishment for storing food under refrigeration, containing lockers for renting to individual users.

lock′er room′, a room containing lockers, as in a gymnasium, factory, school, etc., usually for the temporary storage and safekeeping of clothing and other personal belongings.

lock·et (lok′it), *n.* **1.** a small case for a miniature portrait, a lock of hair, or other keepsake, usually worn on a necklace. **2.** the uppermost mount of a scabbard. [ME *lokat* cross-bar in a framework < AF *loquet,* dim. of *loc* latch < ME. See LOCK[1], -ET]

Lock·ett (lok′it, lo ket′), *n.* a girl's given name, form of **Locke.**

Lock·hart (lok′härt, *for 1 also* lok′ərt), *n.* **1. John Gibson,** 1794–1854, Scottish biographer and novelist. **2.** a town in central Texas. 6084 (1960).

Lock·ie (lok′ē), *n.* a boy's or girl's given name, form of **Locke.** Also, **Locky.**

lock′ing gaunt′let, *Armor.* See **close gauntlet.**

lock′ing piece′, *Horol.* (in a striking train) a hooked part, rising and falling on a locking plate and arresting the rotation of the plate after the proper number of strokes.

lock′ing plate′, *Horol.* a narrow wheel geared to a striking train or other mechanism and having a notched rim engaging with another mechanism permitting it to rotate through a specific arc.

lock·jaw (lok′jô′), *n.* *Pathol.* tetanus in which the jaws become firmly locked together; trismus. [LOCK[1] + JAW]

Lock·land (lok′lənd), *n.* a town in SW Ohio. 5292 (1960).

lock′ nut′, *Mach.* **1.** a nut specially constructed to prevent its coming loose, usually having a means of providing extra friction between itself and the screw. **2.** Also called **jam nut.** a thin supplementary nut screwed down upon a regular nut to prevent its loosening. Also, **lock′nut′.**

lock·out (lok′out′), *n.* the closing of a business or wholesale dismissal of employees by the employer because the employees refuse to accept his terms or because the employer refuses to operate on terms set by a union. [LOCK[1] + OUT]

Lock·port (lok′pōrt′, -pôrt′), *n.* **1.** a city in W New York, on the New York State Barge Canal 26,443 (1960). **2.** a town in NE Illinois. 7560 (1960).

lock′ rail′, the rail of a door that meets the shutting stile at the level of the lock.

lock′ seam′, a joint between two pieces of sheet metal, made by folding up the overlapping edges against each other, then folding them over in the same direction a number of times.

Locks′ley Hall′ (loks′lē), a narrative poem (1842) by Tennyson.

lock·smith (lok′smith′), *n.* one who makes or mends locks. [ME *lokismith.* See LOCK[1], SMITH] —**lock′smith′er·y,** *n.* —**lock′smith′ing,** *n.*

lock′ step′, a mode of marching in very close file, in which the leg of each person moves with and closely behind the corresponding leg of the person ahead.

lock′ stitch′, a sewing-machine stitch in which two threads are locked together at small intervals.

lock·up (lok′up′), *n.* **1.** a jail. **2.** the act of locking up. **3.** *Print.* **a.** the entire body of type and cuts locked up in a chase preparatory to printing or platemaking. **b.** the act or procedure of locking up type and cuts in a chase. **4.** *Brit. Informal.* a rented locker, storage space, or garage. [n. use of v. phrase; see LOCK[1] (v.), UP]

lock′ wash′er, a washer placed under a nut on a bolt or screw, so made as to prevent the nut from shaking loose.

Lock·y (lok′ē), *n.* a boy's or girl's given name, form of **Locke.** Also, **Lockie.**

Lock·yer (lok′yər), *n.* **1. Sir Joseph Norman,** 1836–1920, English astronomer and author. **2.** a crater in the fourth quadrant of the face of the moon: about 30 miles in diameter.

lo·co (lō′kō), *n., pl.* **-cos,** *v.,* **-coed, -co·ing,** *adj.* —*n.* **1.** locoweed. **2.** *Slang.* an insane person; maniac. **3.** *Vet. Pathol.* locoism. —*v.t.* **4.** to poison with locoweed. **5.** *Slang.* to cause to be crazy. —*adj.* **6.** *Slang.* out of one's mind; insane; crazy. [< Sp: insane]

loco-, a learned borrowing from Latin used, with the meaning "from place to place," in the formation of compound words: *locomobile.* [comb. form repr. L *locō,* abl. of *locus* place]

lo·co ci·ta·to (lō′kō ki tä′tō; *Eng.* lō′kō sī tā′tō, -tä′-). *Latin.* See **loc. cit.**

Lo·co·fo·co (lō′kō fō′kō), *n.* **1.** (*sometimes l.c.*) *U.S.* a member of the radical faction of the New York City Democrats, organized in 1835 to oppose the conservative members of the party. **2.** (*l.c.*) a friction match or cigar developed in the 19th century, ignited by rubbing against any hard, dry surface. [special use of *locofoco* (cigar), self-lighting, rhyming compound appar. based on LOCO(MOTIVE), taken to mean self-moving; *-foco,* alter. of It *fuoco* fire < L *focus* fireplace]

Lo·co·fo·co·ism (lō′kō fō′kō iz′əm), *n.* (*sometimes l.c.*) the doctrines of the Locofocos. [LOCOFOCO + -ISM]

lo·co·ism (lō′kō iz′əm), *n.* *Vet. Pathol.* a disease chiefly of sheep, horses, and cattle, caused by the eating of locoweed and characterized by weakness, impaired vision, irregular behavior, and paralysis. Also called **loco, lo′co disease′.** [LOCO + -ISM]

lo·co·mo·bile (lō′kə mō′bəl, -bēl), *adj.* **1.** automotive; self-propelling. —*n.* **2.** a self-propelled vehicle, traction engine, or the like. [LOCO- + MOBILE] —**lo·co·mo·bil·i·ty** (lō′kə mō bil′i tē), *n.*

lo·co·mo·tion (lō′kə mō′shən), *n.* the act or power of moving from place to place. [LOCO- + MOTION]

lo·co·mo·tive (lō′kə mō′tiv), *n.* **1.** *Railroads.* a self-propelled vehicle for pulling trains. **2.** an organized group cheer, usually led by a cheerleader, as at a football or basketball game, that begins slowly and progressively increases in speed in such a way as to suggest a steam locomotive. **3.** *Archaic.* any self-propelled vehicle. —*adj.* **4.** moving or traveling by means of its own mechanism or powers. **5.** serving to produce such movement; adapted for or used in locomotion: *locomotive organs.* **6.** of or pertaining to locomotives: *a locomotive engineer.* **7.** of, pertaining to, or aiding in locomotion or movement from place to place: *the locomotive powers of most animals.* **8.** having the power of locomotion: *an animal that is locomotive at birth.* [LOCO- + MOTIVE (adj.)] —**lo′co·mo′tive·ly,** *adv.* —**lo′co·mo′tive·ness, lo′co·mo·tiv′i·ty,** *n.*

lo·co·mo·tor (lō′kə mō′tər), *adj.* **1.** Also, **lo′co·mo′to·ry.** of, pertaining to, or affecting locomotion. —*n.* **2.** one who or that which is capable of locomotion. [LOCO- + MOTOR]

locomo′tor atax′ia, *Pathol.* See **tabes dorsalis.**

lo·co·pri·mo ci·ta·to (lō′kō prē′mō ki tä′tō; *Eng.* lō′kō prī′mō sī tā′tō, -tä′-). *Latin.* See **loc. primo cit.**

lo·co su·pra ci·ta·to (lō′kō sōō′prä ki tä′tō; *Eng.* lō′kō sōō′prə sī tā′tō, -tä′-). *Latin.* See **l.s.c.**

lo·co·weed (lō′kō wēd′), *n.* any of various fabaceous plants of the genera *Astragalus* and *Oxytropis,* of the southwestern U.S., causing locoism in sheep, horses, etc. [LOCO- + WEED[1]]

loc. primo cit. (lok′ prī′mō sit′), in the place first cited. [< L *locō prīmō citātō*]

Lo′crian A′jax, *Class. Myth.* Ajax (def. 2).

Lo·cris (lō′kris), *n.* either of two districts in the central part of ancient Greece. —**Lo′cri·an,** *n., adj.*

Lo·crus (lō′krəs), *n.* *Class. Myth.* the eponymous king of the Locrians.

loc·u·lar (lok′yə lər), *adj.* *Biol.* having one or more loculi, chambers, or cells. [< NL *loculār(is)* kept in boxes. See LOCULUS, -AR[1]]

loc·u·late (lok′yə lāt′, -lit), *adj.* *Bot.* having one or more loculi. Also, **loc′u·lat′ed.** [LOCUL(US) + -ATE[1]] —**loc′u·la′tion,** *n.*

loc·ule (lok′yōōl), *n.* *Chiefly Bot.* loculus.

loc·u·li·cid·al (lok′yə li sīd′əl), *adj.* *Bot.* (of a capsule) dehiscing lengthwise so as to divide each loculus into two parts. [LOCU-L(US) + -I- + -CIDAL] —**loc′u·li·cid′al·ly,** *adv.*

loc·u·lus (lok′yə ləs), *n., pl.* **-li** (-lī′). **1.** *Biol., Anat.* a small compartment or chamber; cell. **2.** *Bot.* **a.** the cell of a carpel in which the seed is located. **b.** the cell of an anther in which the pollen is located. **3.** *Eccles.* a compartment in an altar, where relics are kept. **4.** a recess in an ancient catacomb or tomb, where a body or cinerary urn was placed. [< NL, special use of L *loculus,* dim. of *locus* place; see -ULE]

A, Loculicidal dehiscence in capsule of lily; B, Transverse section

lo·cum (lō′kəm), *n.* *Brit. Informal.* See **locum tenens.**

lo·cum te·nens (lō′kəm tē′nenz, ten′inz), *pl.* **lo·cum te·nen·tes** (lō′kəm tə nen′tēz). *Chiefly Brit.* a temporary substitute, esp. for a clergyman or doctor. Also called **locum.** [< ML: holding the place] —**lo·cum-te·nen·cy** (lō′kəm tē′nən sē, -ten′ən-), *n.*

lo·cus (lō′kəs), *n., pl.* **-ci** (sī), **-ca** (-kə). **1.** a place; locality. **2.** *Math.* the set of all points, lines, or surfaces which satisfies a given requirement. **3.** *Genetics.* the chromosomal position of a gene as determined by its linear order relative to the other genes on that chromosome. [< L; OL *stlocus* a place, akin to Gk *stéllein* to set up, Skt *sthalami* I stand. See STAND, STALL]

lo·cus clas·si·cus (lō′kōōs kläs′si kōōs′; *Eng.* lō′kəs klas′ə kəs), *pl.* **lo·ci clas·si·ci** (lō′kē kläs′si kē′; *Eng.* lō′sī klas′i sī′). *Latin.* classical source: a passage commonly cited to illustrate or explain a subject.

lo·cus in quo (lō′kōōs in kwō′; *Eng.* lō′kəs in kwō′), *Latin.* the place in which.

lo·cus si·gil·li (lō′kōōs sē gēl′lē; *Eng.* lō′kəs si jil′ī), *pl.* **lo·ci si·gil·li** (lō′sī si jil′ī). *Latin.* See **L.S.** (def. 3).

lo·cust (lō′kəst), *n.* **1.** Also called **short-horned grasshopper.** any of several grasshoppers of the family *Acrididae,* having short antennae and commonly migrating in swarms that strip the vegetation from large areas. **2.** any of various cicadas, as the seventeen-year locust. **3.** an American, fabaceous tree, *Robinia Pseudo-Acacia,* having thorny branches and white flowers. **4.** the durable wood of this tree. **5.** any of various other trees, as the carob and the honey locust. [ME < L *locusta* grasshopper] —**lo′cust-like′,** *adj.*

lo·cus·ta (lō kus′tə), *n., pl.* **-tae** (-tē). *Bot.* the spikelet of grasses. [< NL, special use of L *locusta* grasshopper] —**lo·cus′tal,** *adj.*

lo·cu·tion (lō kyōō′shən), *n.* **1.** a particular form of expression; phrase, expression, or idiom. **2.** a style of speech or verbal expression; phraseology. [< L *locūtiōn-* (s. of *locūtiō*) (style of) speech, equiv. to *locūt(us)* spoken (ptp. of *loquī*) + *-iōn-* -ION]

lo·cu·to·ri·um (lō′kyōō tôr′ē əm, -tôr′-, lok′yōō-), *n., pl.* **-to·ri·a** (-tôr′ē ə, -tôr′-). parlor (def. 3). Also, **locutory.** [< ML; see LOCUTION, -ORIUM]

loc·u·to·ry (lok′yə tôr′ē, -tôr′ē), *n., pl.* **-ries.** locutorium.

lode (lōd), *n.* **1.** a veinlike deposit, usually metalliferous. **2.** any body of ore set off from adjacent rock formations. [ME; OE *lād* way, course, carrying; c. Icel *leith* way, route, OHG *leita* procession. See LOAD, LEAD[1]]

lo·den (lōd′ən), *n.* **1.** a thick, heavily fulled, waterproof fabric, used in cold climates. **2.** Also called **lo′den green′.** the deep olive-green color of this fabric. [< G; OHG *lodo;* cf. OE *lotha* cloak, OIcel *lothi* fur cloak, *lothinn* shaggy]

lode·star (lōd′stär′), *n.* **1.** a star that shows the way. **2.** Polaris. **3.** something that serves as a guide or on which the attention is fixed. Also, **loadstar.** [ME *loode sterre.* See LODE, STAR]

lode·stone (lōd′stōn′), *n.* loadstone.

lodge (loj), *n., v.,* **lodged, lodg·ing.** —*n.* **1.** a small, slight, or crude shelter or habitation, as of boughs, poles, skins, earth, rough boards, or the like; a cabin or hut. **2.** a house used as a temporary abode, as in the hunting season. **3.** a summer cottage. **4.** a house or cottage, as in a park or on an estate, occupied by a gatekeeper, caretaker, gardener, or the like. **5.** a resort hotel. **6.** the main building of a camp, resort hotel, or the like. **7.** the meeting place of a branch of a secret society. **8.** the members composing the branch: *The lodge is planning a picnic.* **9.** the home of a college head or master at Cambridge University, England. **10.** an American Indian dwelling. **11.** the den of an animal or group of animals, esp. beavers. —*v.i.* **12.** to have a habitation or quarters, esp. temporarily, as in a hotel, inn, etc.: *We lodged that night in a tourist home.* **13.** to live in rented quarters in another's house: *He lodged with an Irish family during his school days.* **14.** to be fixed, implanted, or caught in a place or position: *a cough drop that lodged in his throat.* —*v.t.* **15.** to furnish with a habitation or quarters, esp. temporarily: *Can you lodge us for the night?* **16.** to furnish with a room or rooms in one's house for payment; have as a lodger: *a boarding house that lodges oil workers.* **17.** to serve as a habitation, shelter, or dwelling for; shelter; harbor: *The chateau will lodge the ambassador during his stay.* **18.** to put or deposit, as in a place, for storage or keeping: *to lodge one's valuables in a hotel safe.* **19.** to bring or send into a particular place or position: *to lodge a bullet in one's heart.* **20.** to house or contain: *the spinal canal which lodges and protects the spinal cord.* **21.** to vest (power, authority, etc.). **22.** to lay (information, a complaint, etc.) before a court or other authority. **23.** to beat down or lay flat, as vegetation in a storm: *A sudden hail had lodged the crops.* **24.** to track (a deer) to its lair. [ME *logge* < OF *loge* < OHG. See LOBBY] —**lodge′a·ble,** *adj.*
—**Syn. 1.** See **cottage. 7.** club, association, society. **15.** house, quarter. **18.** place, set, plant, settle.

Lodge (loj), *n.* **1. Henry Cabot,** 1850–1924, U.S. statesman and author: senator 1893–1924. **2.** his grandson, **Henry Cabot, Jr.,** born 1902, U.S. journalist, statesman, and diplomat: ambassador to the United Nations 1953–60; ambassador to South Vietnam 1963–64 and since 1965. **3. Sir Oliver Joseph,** 1851–1940, English physicist and writer. **4. Thomas,** 1558?–1625, English poet and dramatist.

lodged (lojd), *adj.* *Heraldry.* (of a deer or the like), represented as lying down: *a stag lodged.* [LODGE + -ED[2]]

lodg·er (loj′ər), *n.* a person who lives in rented quarters in another's house. [ME *loger.* See LODGE, -ER[1]]

lodg·ing (loj′ing), *n.* **1.** accommodation in a house, esp. in rooms for rent: *to furnish board and lodging.* **2.** a temporary place to stay; temporary quarters. **3. lodgings, a.** a room or rooms rented for residence in another's house. **b.** *Brit.* the rooms of a university student who lives neither on campus nor with his family. **4.** the act of lodging. [LODGE + -ING[1]]

lodg′ing house′, a house in which lodgings are let, esp. a house other than an inn or hotel.

lodg′ing knee′, *Shipbuilding.* a knee reinforcing a hull horizontally, as at the ends of deck beams. Also called **bosom knee.**

lodg·ment (loj′mənt), *n.* **1.** the act of lodging; state of being lodged. **2.** something lodged or deposited. **3.** *Mil.* a position or foothold gained from an enemy, or an intrenchment made upon it. **4.** a lodging place; lodgings. Also, *esp. Brit.,* **lodge′ment.** [< MF *logement.* See LODGE, -MENT]

Lo·di (lō′dē *for 1;* lō′dī *for 2, 3*), *n.* **1.** a town in N Italy, SE of Milan: Napoleon's defeat of the Austrians 1796. 38,321 (1961). **2.** a city in NE New Jersey. 23,502 (1960). **3.** a city in central California, near Sacramento. 22,229 (1960).

lod·i·cule (lod′ə kyōōl′), *n.* *Bot.* one of the specialized scales at the base of the ovary of certain grass flowers. [< L *lōdīcula,* dim. of *lōdix* (s., *lōdīc-*) coverlet; see -ULE]

Łódź (lōōj), *n.* a city in central Poland, SW of Warsaw. 730,000 (est. 1963). Russian, **Lodz** (lôdz).

loe (lōō), *n., v.t., v.i.,* **loed, loe·ing.** *Scot.* love.

Loeb (lōb; *Ger.* lœb), *n.* **Jacques** (zhäk), 1859–1924, German physiologist and experimental biologist in the U.S.

Loef·fler (lef′lər), *n.* **Charles Martin Tor·nov** (tôr′nof), 1861–1935, U.S. violinist and composer, born in France.

loel·ling·ite (lel′ing īt′), *n.* *Mineral.* löllingite.

lo·ess (lō′es, les, lus; *Ger.* lœs), *n.* a loamy deposit formed by wind, usually yellowish and calcareous, common in the Mississippi valley and in Europe and Asia. [< G *löss,* coined 1823 by von Leonhard on basis of Alemannic *lösch* loose, light, akin to G *lösen* to loosen, deriv. of *los* LOOSE] —**lo·ess′i·al, lo·ess′al,** *adj.*

Loewe (lō), *n.* **Frederick,** born 1904, U.S. composer, born in Austria.

Loe·wi (lō′ē; *Ger.* lœ′vē), *n.* **Ot·to** (ot′ō; *Ger.* ôt′ō), 1873–1961, German pharmacologist in the U.S.: Nobel prize for medicine 1936.

Loe·wy (lō′ē), *n.* **Raymond Fer·nand** (fər nand′), born 1893, U.S. industrial designer, born in France.

Löff·ler (lœf′lər), *n.* **Frie·drich Au·gust Jo·han·nes** (frē′drikh ou′gōōst yō hä′nəs), 1852–1915, German bacteriologist.

Lofn (lôf′vən), *n.* *Scand. Myth.* a goddess to whom Odin gave permission to unite in marriage those who had been forbidden to wed.

Lo′fo·ten Is′lands (lō′fōōt′ən), a group of islands NW of and belonging to Norway: rich fishing grounds. 30,000 (est. 1945); 474 sq. mi.

loft (lôft, loft), *n.* **1.** a room or the like within a sloping roof. **2.** a gallery or upper level in a church, hall, etc., designed for a special purpose: *a choir loft.* **3.** a hayloft. **4.** an upper story of a warehouse, mercantile building, or factory, esp. of buildings designed for small, light industries. **5.** *Golf.* **a.** the slope of the face of the head of a club backward from the vertical, tending to drive the ball upward. **b.** the act of lofting. **c.** a lofting stroke. **6.** the resiliency of wool. **7.** to store in a loft. **8.** to hit or throw aloft: *He lofted a fly ball into center field.* —*v.t.* **9.** *Golf.* **a.** to slant the face of (a club). **b.** to hit (a golf ball) into the air or over an obstacle. **c.** to clear (an obstacle) in this manner. **10.** *Shipbuilding.* to form or describe (the lines of a hull) at full size, as in a mold loft; lay off. **11.** *Archaic.* to provide (a house, barn, etc.) with a loft. —*v.i.* **12.** to hit or throw something aloft, esp. a ball. **13.** to go high into the air when hit, as a ball. [ME *lofte,* late OE *loft* < Scand; cf. Icel *lopt* upper chamber or region, the air, sky. See LIFT] —**loft′less,** *adj.*

Loft·ing (lôf′ting, lof′-), *n.* **Hugh,** 1886–1947, U.S. author of books for children, born in England.

loft′ing i′ron, *Golf.* a club whose head has a sloped face, for lofting the ball. Also called **loft′er.**

lofts·man (lôfts′mən, lofts′-), *n., pl.* **-men.** *Shipbuilding.* a person who prepares molds and patterns. [LOFT + 's[1] + MAN[1]]

loft·y (lôf′tē, lof′-), *adj.,* **loft·i·er, loft·i·est. 1.** extending high in the air; of imposing height; towering: *lofty mountains.* **2.** exalted in rank, dignity, or character. **3.** elevated in style or sentiment, as writings, speech, etc. **4.** haughty; proud; consciously superior or dignified: *to treat someone in a lofty manner.* **5.** *Naut.* noting a rig of a sailing vessel having extraordinarily high masts. [late ME; see LOFT, -Y[1]] —**loft′i·ly,** *adv.* —**loft′i·ness,** *n.*
—**Syn. 1.** elevated. See **high. 3.** sublime. **4.** arrogant. —**Ant. 2.** lowly. **4.** humble.

log[1] (lôg, log), *n., v.,* **logged, log·ging.** —*n.* **1.** an unhewn portion or length of the trunk or of a large limb of a felled tree. **2.** something inert, heavy, or senseless: *to sleep like a log.* **3.** *Naut.* any of various devices for determining the speed of a vessel, as a chip log or patent log. **4.** any of various records, made in rough or finished form, concerning a trip made by a vessel or aircraft and dealing with particulars of navigation, weather, engine performance, discipline, and other pertinent details; logbook. **5.** *Motion Pictures.* an account describing or denoting each shot as it is taken, written down during production and referred to in editing the film. **6.** a register of the operation of a machine. **7.** a record kept during the drilling of a well, esp. of the geological formations penetrated. **8.** *Radio and Television.* a written account of everything transmitted by a station or network. —*v.t.* **9.** to cut (trees) into logs: *to log pine trees for fuel.* **10.** to cut down the trees or timber on (land): *We logged the entire area in a week.* **11.** to enter in a log; compile; amass; keep a record of: *to log a day's events.* **12.** to make (a certain speed), as a ship or airplane: *We are logging 18 knots.* **13.** to travel for (a certain distance or a certain amount of time), according to the record of a log: *We logged 30 miles the first day. He has logged 10,000 hours flying time.* —*v.i.* **14.** to cut down trees and get out logs from the forest for timber: *to log for a living.* [ME *logge,* var. of *lugge* pole, limb of tree, now dial.; cf. obs. *logget* pole. See LUGSAIL] —**log′gish,** *adj.*

log[2] (lôg, log), *n.* logarithm.

log-, var. of **logo-** before a vowel: *logarithm.*

-log, var. of **-logue:** *analog.*

log, logarithm.

log., logic.

lo·gan (lō′gən), *n.* pokelogan.

Lo·gan (lō′gən), *n.* **1. Joshua,** born 1908, U.S. playwright, director, and producer. **2. Mount,** a mountain in Canada, in the Mount Elias Mountains: second highest peak in North America. 19,850 ft. **3.** a city in N Utah. 18,731 (1960). **4.** a town in central Ohio. 6417 (1960). **5.** a town in SW West Virginia. 4185 (1960). **6.** a boy's given name.

lo·gan·ber·ry (lō′gən ber′ē), *n., pl.* **-ries. 1.** the large, dark-red, acid fruit of a plant, *Rubus loganobaccus.* **2.** the plant itself. [named after James H. *Logan* (1841–1928), American horticulturist who first bred it; see BERRY]

lo·ga·ni·a·ceous (lō gā′nē ā′shəs), *adj.* belonging to the *Loganiaceae,* a family of herbs, shrubs, and trees of tropical and subtropical regions, including the nux vomica tree and other plants with poisonous properties. [< NL *Logani(a)* the typical genus (named after James *Logan,* 1674–1751, Irish-American botanist) + -ACEOUS]

Lo·gans·port (lō′gənz pôrt′, -pōrt′), *n.* a city in N Indiana, on the Wabash River. 21,106 (1960).

log′an stone′ (log′ən). See **rocking stone.** [var. of LOGGING STONE]

log·a·oe·dic (lôg′ə ē′dik, log′ə-), *Pros.* —*adj.* **1.** composed of dactyls and trochees or of anapests and iambs, producing a movement somewhat suggestive of prose. —*n.* **2.** a logaoedic verse. [< LL *logaoedic(us)* < Gk *logaoidikós.* See LOGO-, ODE, -IC]

log·a·rithm (lôg′ə rith′əm, -rith′-, log′ə-), *n.* *Math.* the exponent of the power to which a base number must be raised to equal a given number: *2 is the logarithm of 100 to the base 10. Symbol:* log. [< NL *logarithm(us)* < Gk *lóg(os)* LOG- + *arithmós* number; see ARITHMETIC]

log·a·rith·mic (lôg′ə rith′mik, -rith′-, log′ə-), *adj.* *Math.* **1.** pertaining to a logarithm or logarithms. **2.** (of an equation) having a logarithm as one or more of its unknowns. **3.** (of a function) **a.** pertaining to the function $y = \log x$. **b.** expressible by means of logarithms. Also, **log′a·rith′mi·cal.** [LOGARITHM + -IC] —**log′a·rith′mi·cal·ly,** *adv.*

log·book (lôg′bŏŏk′, log′-), *n.* a book in which details of a trip made by a vessel or aircraft are recorded; log. [LOG[1] + BOOK]

log′ canoe′, a small, narrow boat, used for fishing and oystering on Chesapeake Bay, having a hull composed wholly or mainly of hewn logs, a centerboard, and one or two masts with leg-of-mutton sails and a jib.

log′ chip′, *Naut.* the wooden chip of a chip log, for holding the end of the log line. Also, **log′chip′, log ship, logship.**

loge (lōzh), *n.* **1.** a small enclosure; booth. **2.** a box in a theater or opera house. **3.** (in a theater) the front section of the lowest balcony, separated from the back section by an aisle or railing or both. **4.** (in France) a cubicle for the confinement of art students during important examinations. **5. en loge,** (of an art student) working on a project for examination purposes, without access to books, advice, or help of any kind. [< F; see LODGE]

log′gan stone′ (log′ən). See **rocking stone.** [var. of LOGGING STONE]

log·ger[1] (lô′gər, log′ər), *n.* **1.** a person who cuts trees into suitable lengths after the trees have been felled. **2.** a tractor used in logging. **3.** a machine for loading logs. Cf. **lumberman.** [LOG[1] + -ER[1]]

log·ger[2] (lô′gər, log′ər), *adj.* *Scot.* **1.** heavy or thick. **2.** thick-headed; stupid. [back formation from LOGGERHEAD]

log·ger·head (lô′gər hed′, log′ər-), *n.* **1.** a thick-headed or stupid person; blockhead. **2.** Also called **log′gerhead tur′tle.** a sea turtle, *Caretta caretta,* having a large head. **3.** See **loggerhead shrike. 4.** a ball or bulb of iron with a long handle, used, after being heated, to melt tar, heat liquids, etc. **5.** a rounded post, in the stern of a whaleboat, around which the harpoon line is passed. **6.** a circular inkwell having a broad, flat base. **7. at loggerheads,** engaged in dispute; quarreling: *They were at loggerheads over the distribution of funds.* [logger block of wood (first recorded in 18th century) + HEAD] —**log′ger·head′ed,** *adj.*

log′gerhead shrike′, a common, North American shrike, *Lanius ludovicianus,* gray above and white below with a black tail, facial mask, and wings.

log·gia (loj′ə, lô′jē ə; *It.* lôd′jä), *n., pl.* **-gias,** *It.* **-gie** (-je). **1.** a gallery or arcade open to the air on at least one side. **2.** a space within the body of a building but open to the air on one side, serving as an open-air room or as an entrance porch. [< It; see LODGE]

Loggia

log·ging (lô′ging, log′ing), *n.* **1.** the process, work, or business of cutting down trees and transporting the logs to sawmills. **2.** *Naut.* a deduction from the pay of a seaman, made as a fine or forfeit and recorded in the log book of the vessel. [LOG[1] + -ING[1]]

log′ging stone′. See **rocking stone.** [? dial. *log* to rock + -ING[2]]

Lo·gi (lô′gē, lō′-), *n.* *Scand. Myth.* a man, a personification of fire, who defeated Loki in an eating contest.

lo·gi·a (lô′gē ə, -jē ə, log′ē ə), *n.* a pl. of **logion.**

log·ic (loj′ik), *n.* **1.** the science which investigates the principles governing correct or reliable inference. **2.** a particular method of reasoning or argumentation: *We were unable to follow his logic.* **3.** the system or principles of reasoning applicable to any branch of knowledge or study. **4.** reason or sound judgment, as in utterances or actions: *There wasn't much logic in her move.* **5.** convincing forcefulness: *the irresistible logic of facts.* [ME *logik* < L *logica,* n. use of neut. pl. (in ML taken as fem. sing.) of Gk *logikós* of speech or reason. See LOGO-, -IC] —**log′ic·less,** *adj.*

-logic, an element used in the formation of adjectives corresponding to nouns ending in *-logy: analogic.* [< Gk *-logikós.* See LOGIC]

log·i·cal (loj′i kəl), *adj.* **1.** according to or agreeing with the principles of logic: *a logical inference.* **2.** reasoning in accordance with the principles of logic, as a person, the mind, etc.: *a logical man; logical thinking.* **3.** reasonable; reasonably to be expected: *War was the logical consequence of such threats.* **4.** of or pertaining to logic. [< ML *logicāl(is).* See LOGIC, -AL[1]] —**log·i·cal·i·ty** (loj′i kal′i tē), **log′i·cal·ness,** *n.* —**log′i·cal·ly,** *adv.*
—**Syn. 1, 3.** valid. —**Ant. 1–3.** unreasonable.

-logical, an element used in the formation of adjectives corresponding to nouns with stems ending in *-logy: analogical.* Cf. **-logic.** [< Gk, adj. word-element *-logikos* (see LOGIC) + -AL[1]]

log′ical construc′tion, *Logic, Philos.* anything referred to by an incomplete symbol capable of contextual definition.

log′ical pos′itivism, a contemporary philosophical movement that stresses the function of philosophy as a method of criticizing and analyzing science and that rejects all transcendental metaphysics, statements of fact being held to be meaningful only if they have verifiable consequences in experience and statements of logic, mathematics, or philosophy itself, deriving their validity from the rules of language. Also called **log′ical empir′icism.**

log′ical sum′, union (def. 10a).

log′ical syn′tax, syntactics.

lo·gi·cian (lō jish′ən), *n.* a person who is skilled in logic. [LOGIC + -IAN; r. ME *logicien* < MF]

log·i·cise (loj′i sīz′), *v.t., v.i.,* **-cised, -cis·ing.** *Chiefly Brit.* logicize.

lo·gi·cize (loj′i sīz′), *v.*, **-cized, -ciz·ing.** —*v.t.* **1.** to make logical; give logical form to: *to logicize a sequence of events.* —*v.i.* **2.** to employ logic: *One could not logicize about such a happening.* [LOGIC + -IZE]

lo·gi·on (lō′gē on′, -jē-, log′ē-), *n., pl.* **lo·gi·a** (lō′gē ə, -jē ə, log′ē ə), **lo·gi·ons. 1.** a traditional saying or maxim, as of a religious teacher. **2.** (*sometimes cap.*) *Biblical Criticism.* **a.** a saying of Jesus, esp. one contained in collections supposed to have been among the sources of the present Gospels. **b.** a saying included among the agrapha. [< Gk *lógion* saying, oracle, neut. of *lógios* skilled in words, eloquent. See LOG(O)-, -IOUS]

lo·gis·tic[1] (lō jis′tik), *adj.* of or pertaining to logistics. Also, **lo·gis′ti·cal.** [back formation from LOGISTICS] —**lo·gis′ti·cal·ly,** *adv.*

lo·gis·tic[2] (lō jis′tik), *n.* (*sometimes pl.*) **1.** symbolic logic. **2.** *Archaic.* mathematical calculation. —*adj.* **3.** of or pertaining to logistic. [< F *logistique* < LL *logisticus* of computation < Gk *logistikós* skilled in calculation, rational = *logist(ḗs)* calculator, reasoner (< *logízein* to reckon < *lógos* word, reason) + *-ikos* -IC]

lo·gis·ti·cian[1] (lō′ji stish′ən), *n.* an expert in logistics. [LOGISTIC(S) + -IAN]

lo·gis·ti·cian[2] (lō′ji stish′ən), *n.* a person who is skilled in symbolic logic. [LOGISTIC[3] + -IAN]

lo·gis·tics (lō jis′tiks), *n.* (*construed as sing. or pl.*) the branch of military science and operations dealing with the procurement, supply, and maintenance of equipment, with the movement, evacuation, and hospitalization of personnel, with the provision of facilities and services, and with related matters. [< F *logistique* quartermaster's work, equiv. to *log(er)* (to) LODGE, be quartered (said of troops) + *-istique* -ISTIC; see -ICS]

log·jam (lôg′jam′, log′-), *n.* **1.** an immovable tangle of logs, as in a river during a drive. **2.** any similar blockage: *There was a logjam in Congress, and the bill died in committee.* [LOG[1] + JAM[1]]

log′ line′, *Navig.* the line by which a log or patent log is streamed.

log-log (lôg′lôg′, log′log′), *n.* **1.** the logarithm of a logarithm. —*adj.* **2.** of or pertaining to a device, graph, etc., using log-logs.

lo·go (lô′gō, log′ō), *n.* *Print.* logotype. [by shortening]

logo-, an element appearing in loan words from Greek, where it meant "word," "speech," (*logography*); on this model, used in the formation of new compound words (*logotype*). Also, *esp. before a vowel,* **log-.** Cf. **-log, -logic, -logical, -logue, -logy.** [< Gk *logo-,* comb. form of *lógos*]

log·o·gram (lô′gə gram′, log′ə-), *n.* a conventional, abbreviated symbol for a frequently recurring word or phrase, as & for *and.* Also called **log·o·graph** (lô′gə-graf′, -gräf′, log′ə-). [LOGO- + -GRAM[1]] —**log′o·gram·mat·ic** (lô′gə grə mat′ik, log′ə-), *adj.* —**log′o·gram·mat′i·cal·ly,** *adv.*

log·o·graph·ic (lô′gə graf′ik, log′ə-), *adj.* **1.** of, pertaining to, or using logograms: *logographic writing.* **2.** of or pertaining to logography. [< Gk *logographik(ós).* See LOGO-, -GRAPHIC] —**log′o·graph′i·cal·ly.** *adv.*

lo·gog·ra·phy (lō gog′rə fē), *n.* **1.** printing with logotypes. **2.** a method of longhand reporting, each of several reporters in succession taking down a few words. [< Gk *logographía* speech writing. See LOGO-, -GRAPHY] —**lo·gog′ra·pher,** *n.*

log·o·griph (lô′gə grif, log′ə-), *n.* **1.** an anagram, or a puzzle involving anagrams. **2.** a puzzle in which a certain word, and other words formed from any or all of its letters, must be guessed from indications given in a set of verse. [LOGO- + Gk *grîph(os)* a fishing basket, riddle] —**log′o·griph′ic,** *adj.*

lo·gom·a·chy (lō gom′ə kē), *n., pl.* **-chies. 1.** a dispute about or concerning words. **2.** a contention or debate marked by the reckless or incorrect use of words; a meaningless battle of words. **3.** a game played with cards, each bearing one letter, with which words are formed. [< Gk *logomachía.* See LOGO-, -MACHY] —**log·o·mach·ic** (log′ə mak′ik), **log′o·mach′i·cal,** *adj.* —**lo·gom′a·chist, log′o·mach′,** *n.*

log·o·pe·dics (lô′gə pē′diks, log′ə-), *n.* (*construed as sing.*) *Pathol.* the science that deals with the study and treatment of speech defects. Also, **log·o·pe·di·a** (lô′gə-pē′dē ə, log′ə-). [LOGO- + (ORTHO)PEDICS] —**log′o·pe′dic,** *adj.*

log·or·rhe·a (lô′gə rē′ə, log′ə-), *n.* pathologically incoherent, repetitious speech. [LOGO- + -RRHEA] —**log′-or·rhe′ic,** *adj.*

lo·gos (lō′gos, -gōs, log′os), *n.* **1.** (*often cap.*) *Philos.* the rational principle that governs and develops the universe. **2.** *Theol.* the divine word or reason incarnate in Jesus Christ. John 1:1–14. [< Gk: a word, saying, speech, discourse, thought, proportion, ratio, reckoning, akin to *légein* to speak]

log·o·type (lô′gə tīp′, log′ə-), *n.* **1.** a single piece of type bearing two or more uncombined letters, a syllable, or a word. **2.** a trademark or company name or device. **3.** nameplate (def. 2). Also called **logo.** [LOGO- + TYPE] —**log′o·typ′y,** *n.*

log·perch (lôg′pûrch′, log′-), *n., pl.* **-perch·es,** (*esp. collectively*) **-perch.** a darter, *Percina caprodes,* found in eastern North American lakes and streams, having a piglike snout. [LOG[1] + PERCH[2]]

log′ reel′, *Naut.* a reel from which the line of a log chip runs.

log·roll (lôg′rōl′, log′-), *Chiefly U.S.* —*v.t.* **1.** to procure the passage of (a bill) by logrolling. —*v.i.* **2.** to engage in political logrolling. [back formation from *logrolling*] —**log′roll′er,** *n.*

log·roll·ing (lôg′rō′ling, log′-), *n.* **1.** *Chiefly U.S.* the exchange of backing or favors, esp. by legislators for mutual political gain. **2.** the action of rolling logs to a particular place. **3.** the action of rotating a log rapidly in the water, esp. as a competitive sport; birling. [LOG[1] + ROLLING]

Lo·gro·ño (lô grô′nyô), *n.* a city in N Spain. 63,781 (est. 1963).

log′ ship′, *Naut.* See **log chip.** Also, **log′ship′.**

-logue, a combining form denoting a specified kind of discourse, spoken or written: *analogue; monologue; travelogue.* Also, **-log.** [< F; r. ME *-loge* < L *-logus* < Gk *-logos.* See LOGOS]

log·way (lôg′wā′, log′-), *n.* gangway (def. 7). [LOG[1] + WAY]

log·wood (lôg′wo͝od′, log′-), *n.* **1.** the heavy, brownish-red heartwood of a West Indian and Central American, caesalpiniaceous tree, *Haematoxylon campechianum,* used in dyeing. **2.** the tree itself. Also called **campeachy wood.** [LOG[1] + WOOD[1]]

lo·gy (lō′gē), *adj.,* **-gi·er, -gi·est.** physically or mentally lacking vitality; sluggish; dull; lethargic. [? < D *log* heavy, dull + -Y[1]] —**lo′gi·ly,** *adv.* —**lo′gi·ness,** **log′gi·ness,** *n.*

-logy, **1.** a combining form used in the names of sciences or bodies of knowledge: *paleontology; theology.* **2.** a termination of nouns referring to writing, discourses, collections, etc.: *trilogy; martyrology.* [ME *-logie* < L *-logia* < Gk *-logia.* See -LOGUE, -Y[3]]

Lo·hen·grin (lō′ən grin, -grēn′), *n.* **1.** *German Legend.* the son of Parzival, and a knight of the Holy Grail. **2.** (*italics.*) a romantic opera (composed, 1846–48; première, 1850) by Richard Wagner.

Lohr·mann (lôr′mən), *n.* a crater in the third quadrant of the face of the moon: about 28 miles in diameter.

Loh·se (lō′zə), *n.* a crater in the fourth quadrant of the face of the moon: about 27 miles in diameter.

lo·i·a·sis (lō ī′ə sis), *n.* *Pathol.* infestation with the parasitic eye worm, *Loa loa,* of the subcutaneous tissues and orbit: endemic in West Africa. Also, **loaiasis.** [< NL, equiv. to *Lo(a)* + *-iasis* -IASIS]

loin (loin), *n.* **1.** Usually, **loins.** the part or parts of the body of man or of a quadruped animal on either side of the spinal column, between the false ribs and hipbone. **2.** a cut of meat from this region of an animal, esp. a portion including the vertebrae of such parts. **3. loins,** *Chiefly Literary.* the parts of the body which should be clothed or girded, or which are regarded as the seat of physical strength and generative power. **4. gird up one's loins,** to prepare oneself for a test of one's readiness, strength, or endurance: *He girded up his loins to face his competitor.* [ME *loyne* < MF *lo(i)gne,* perh. < LL **lumbea,* n. use of fem. of **lumbeus* of the loins, equiv. to L *lumb(us)* loin + *-eus* -EOUS]

loin·cloth (loin′klôth′, -kloth′), *n.* a piece of cloth worn around the loins or hips, esp. by primitive inhabitants of tropical regions as the sole item of clothing. [LOIN + CLOTH]

Loire (lwar), *n.* **1.** a river in France, flowing S into the Atlantic: the longest river in France. 625 mi. long. **2.** a department in central France. 696,348 (1962); 1853 sq. mi. *Cap.:* St.-Étienne.

Loire-At·lan·tique (lwar at län tēk′), *n.* a department in NW France. 803,372 (1962); 2695 sq. mi. *Cap.:* Nantes. Formerly, **Loire-Inférieure.**

Loire-In·fé·rieure (lwar an fā ryœr′), *n.* former name of **Loire-Atlantique.**

Loi·ret (lwa re′), *n.* a department in central France. 389,854 (1962); 2630 sq. mi. *Cap.:* Orléans.

Loir-et-Cher (lwa rā sher′), *n.* a department in central France. 250,741 (1962); 2479 sq. mi. *Cap.:* Blois.

Lo·is (lō′is), *n.* a girl's given name.

loi·ter (loi′tər), *v.i.* **1.** to linger aimlessly or as if aimlessly in or about a place: *We noticed several young boys loitering around the building last night.* **2.** to move in a slow, idle manner; make purposeless stops in the course of a trip, journey, errand, etc.: *to loiter along.* **3.** to waste time or dawdle over work: *Each night he loiters over his homework until one or two in the morning.* —*v.t.* **4.** to pass (time) in an idle or aimless manner (usually fol. by *away*): *to loiter away the afternoon in daydreaming.* [late ME *loytre, lotere,* perh. < MD *loteren,* D *leuteren,* freq. of a verb akin to OE *lūtian* to lurk; see -ER[6]] —**loi′ter·er,** *n.* —**loi′ter·ing·ly,** *adv.*

—**Syn. 1.** LOITER, DALLY, DAWDLE, IDLE imply moving or acting slowly, stopping for unimportant reasons, and in general wasting time. To LOITER is to linger aimlessly: *to loiter until late.* To DALLY is to loiter indecisively or to delay sportively as if free from care or responsibility: *to dally on the way home.* To DAWDLE is to saunter, stopping often, and taking a great deal of time, or to fritter away time working in a half-hearted way: *to dawdle over a task.* To IDLE is to move slowly and aimlessly, or to spend a great deal of time doing nothing: *to idle away the hours.* **1–4.** loaf. **2, 3.** delay, tarry.

Lo·ja (lô′hä), *n.* a city in S Ecuador. 26,000 (est. 1959).

lo·ka·ca·ra (lō′kä kä′rə), *n.* *Hinduism.* an action in accordance with socially accepted rules. Cf. **shastracara.** [< Skt *lokācāra* world custom]

Lo·ka·ya·ta (lō kä′yə tə), *n.* a materialistic school of philosophers in India that opposed Hinduism by regarding only matter as real, sense data as the only source of knowledge, and the gratification of the appetites as the only good. [< Skt *lokāyata,* lit., world-stretching]

Lo·ka·ya·ti·ka (lō′kə yä′ti kə), *n.* a member of the Lokayata school. Also called **Charvaka.** [< Skt, equiv. to *lokāyat(a)* LOKAYATA + *-ika* agent suffix]

Lo·ki (lō′kē), *n.* *Scand. Myth.* a god of fire and the father of Fenir, Hel, and the Midgard serpent, often the companion of the Aesir but often harmful to them: the god who caused the death of Balder. [< Icel]

Lo·la (lō′lə), *n.* a girl's given name, form of **Charlotte** or **Dolores.**

Lo·li·ta (lō lē′tə), *n.* a girl's given name, form of **Charlotte** or **Dolores.** Also, **Lo·le′ta.**

loll (lol), *v.i.* **1.** to recline or lean in a relaxed or indolent manner; lounge: *to loll on a sofa.* **2.** to hang loosely or droopingly; dangle: *The dog stood in the heat with his tongue lolling out of his mouth.* —*v.t.* **3.** to allow to hang, droop, or dangle. —*n.* *Archaic.* **4.** the act of lolling. **5.** one who or that which lolls. [ME *lolle, lulle* (? imit.); cf. MD *lollen* doze, sit over the fire] —**loll′er,** *n.* —**loll′ing·ly,** *adv.*

Lol·land (lol′ənd; *Dan.* lô′län), *n.* Laaland.

lol·la·pa·loo·za (lol′ə pə lo͞o′zə), *n.* *Slang.* an extraordinary or unusual thing, person, or event; an exceptional example of something. Also, **lol′la·pa·loo′sa, lalapalooza, lallapalooza.** [?]

Lol·lard (lol′ərd), *n.* an English or Scottish follower of the religious teachings of John Wycliffe from the 14th to the 16th centuries. [ME < MD *lollaerd* mumbler (of prayers), deriv. of *lollen* to mumble, hum. See LULL, -ARD] —**Lol′lard·y, Lol′lard·ry, Lol′lard·ism,** *n.*

löl·ling·ite (lel′ing īt′), *n.* a mineral, iron arsenide, $FeAs_2$, occurring in steel-gray prismatic crystals. Also, **loellingite, lol′ling·ite′.** [named after *Lölling,* town in Austria near the find; see -ITE]

lol·li·pop (lol′ē pop′), *n.* a kind of taffy or hard candy stuck on the end of a stick made of paper or wood. Also, **lol′ly·pop′.** [? dial. *lolly* tongue + POP[1]]

lol·lop (lol′əp), *v.i.* **1.** *Brit. Dial.* to loll; lounge. **2.** to move forward with a bounding or leaping motion. [extended var. of LOLL; *-op* perh. to bring out contrast (in meaning) with GALLOP]

lol·ly (lol′ē), *n., pl.* **-lies. 1.** lollipop. **2.** *Brit. Informal.* **a.** a piece of candy, esp. hard candy. **b.** a treat. **c.** a small bribe or gratuity. **d.** money. [shortening of LOLLYPOP]

lol·ly·gag (lol′ē gag′), *v.i.,* **-gagged, -gag·ging.** lallygag.

lo·ma (lō′mə), *n.* *Chiefly Southwestern U.S.* a hill or ridge having a broad top. [< Sp, akin to *lomo* back, ridge, LOIN]

Lo·max (lō′maks), *n.* **John Avery,** 1867–1948, and his son, **Alan,** born 1915, U.S. folklorists.

Lom·bard (lom′bərd, -bärd, lum′-), *n.* **1.** a native or inhabitant of Lombardy. **2.** a member of an ancient Germanic tribe that settled in N Italy. —*adj.* **3.** Also, **Lom·bar′dic.** of or pertaining to the Lombards or Lombardy.

Lom·bard (lom′bərd, -bärd, lum′-; *Fr.* lôn bar′ *for 1;* lom′bärd *for 2*), *n.* **1. Peter** (*Petrus Lombardus*), c1100–64?, Italian theologian: bishop of Paris 1159–64?. **2.** a city in NE Illinois, near Chicago. 22,561 (1960).

Lom′bard Street′, a street in London, England: a financial center.

Lom·bard·y (lom′bər-dē, lum′-), *n.* a region and former kingdom in N Italy. 7,390,492 (1961); 9190 sq. mi.

Lom′bardy pop′lar, a poplar, *Populus nigra italica,* having a columnar, fastigiate manner of growth.

Lom·bok (lom bok′), *n.* an island in Indonesia, E of Java. 1,297,523 (est. 1961); 1826 sq. mi.

Lom·bro′si·an school′ (lom brō′zē ən), a school of criminology, holding the theories and employing the methods developed by Cesare Lombroso. [LOMBROS(O) + -IAN]

Lom·bro·so (lom brō′sō; *It.* lôm brô′sô), *n.* **Ce·sa·re** (che′zä re′), 1836–1909, Italian physician and criminologist.

Lo·mé (lô mā′), *n.* a seaport in and the capital of Togo, on the Gulf of Guinea. 80,000 (est. 1962).

lo·ment (lō′ment), *n.* *Bot.* a legume which is contracted in the spaces between the seeds, and breaks at maturity into one-seeded indehiscent joints. [late ME *lomente* < L *lōment(um)* LOMENTUM] —**lo′ment·like′,** *adj.*

lo·men·ta·ceous (lō′mən tā′shəs), *adj.* *Bot.* resembling a loment; lomentlike. [LOMENT + -ACEOUS]

lo·men·tum (lō men′təm), *n., pl.* **-ta** (-tə). *Bot.* loment. [< NL, special use of L *lōmentum* bean meal, face cream made of loment, equiv. to *lō(tus)* washed (var. of *lautus,* ptp. of *lavāre;* see LAVE[1]) + *-mentum* -MENT]

Lo·mond (lō′mənd), *n.* **Loch,** a lake in W Scotland. 23 mi. long; 27 sq. mi.

lon., longitude.

Lon·don (lun′dən), *n.* **1. Jack,** 1876–1916, U.S. short-story writer and novelist. **2.** a metropolis in SE England, on the Thames: capital of the United Kingdom and the British Commonwealth. **3. City of,** an old city in the central part of the County of London: the ancient nucleus of the modern metropolis. 5400; 1 sq. mi. **4. County of,** an administrative county comprising the City of London and the 28 metropolitan boroughs. 117 sq. mi. **5. Greater,** Also **Greater London Council.** an urban area comprising the city of London and 32 metropolitan boroughs. 7,111,500; 609 sq. mi. **6.** a city in S Ontario, in SE Canada. 169,569 (1961). **7.** a town in central Ohio. 6379 (1960). **8.** a town in SE Kentucky. 4035 (1960).

Lon′don broil′, a broiled flank steak, crosscut into thin slices for serving.

Lon′don brown′, carbuncle (def. 3).

Lon′don Com′pany, a company, chartered in England in 1606 to establish colonies in America, that founded Jamestown, Virginia, in 1607.

Lon·don·der·ry (lun′dən der′ē), *n.* **1.** a county in N Northern Ireland. 111,536 (1961); 804 sq. mi. **2.** its county seat: a seaport. 53,762 (1961). Also called **Derry.**

Lon·don·er (lun′də nər), *n.* a native or inhabitant of London. [LONDON + -ER[1]]

Lon·don·esque (lun′də nesk′), *adj.* **1.** resembling or characteristic of London, England. **2.** resembling or characteristic of the writings of Jack London. [LONDON + -ESQUE]

Lon′don forc′es, *Physics, Chem.* forces between atoms or molecules which are related to the physical rather than the chemical properties of the molecules and which are attractive when the particles are in the lowest energy state.

Lon·don·ish (lun′də nish), *adj.* suggesting, characteristic of, or resembling London, England. [LONDON + -ISH[1]]

Lon′don plane′, a tall, hardy, widely spreading tree, *Platanus acerifolia,* of North America, having bristly clusters of fruit.

Lon′don pride′, a perennial herb, *Saxifraga umbrosa,* of Europe, having small, pink-spotted, white flowers. Also called **St. Patrick's cabbage.**

Lon·don·y (lun′də nē), *adj.* having characteristics suggestive of London, England. [LONDON + -Y[1]]

Lon·dres (lon′dres), *n.* a cylindrically shaped cigar of medium to large size. [< Sp *londrés* Havana cigar, special use of *Londres* London (cigars for the British market)]

Lon·dri·na (lônn drē′nə), *n.* a city in E Brazil. 77,382 (1960).

lone (lōn), *adj.* **1.** being alone; without company or accompaniment; solitary; unaccompanied: *a lone traveler.* **2.** standing by itself or apart; isolated: *a lone house*

in the valley. **3.** sole; single: *That company constitutes our lone competitor in the field.* **4.** *Poetic.* lonely; unfrequented. **5.** without companionship; lonesome. **6.** unmarried or widowed. [ME; aph. var of ALONE, used attributively] —**lone′ness,** *n.*
—Syn. 2. separate, separated, secluded.

lone′ hand′, **1.** *Cards.* **a.** a person who holds a hand so strong that he can play a deal without the hand of his partner. **b.** the hand played by such a person. **2.** someone who deliberately conducts his affairs without the advice or assistance of others: *He was always a lone hand in investment circles.* **3.** a stand or action taken independently: *a country that played a lone hand in the trade negotiations.*

lone·ly (lōn′lē), *adj.*, **-li·er, -li·est.** **1.** lone; solitary; without company; companionless. **2.** destitute of sympathetic or friendly companionship or relationships: *a lonely exile.* **3.** remote from cities, towns, or other places of human habitation; desolate; unfrequented: *a lonely road.* **4.** standing apart; isolated: *a lonely tower.* **5.** affected with, characterized by, or causing a depressing feeling of being alone; lonesome: *a lonely heart.* [LONE + -LY] —**lone′li·ly,** *adv.* —**lone′li·ness, lone′li·hood′,** *n.*

lone′ly end′, *Football.* an offensive end who lines up far outside of a tackle on each play, usually without entering the huddle. Also called **lone′some end′.**

lon·er (lō′nər), *n.* a person who remains alone or avoids the company of others: *As a child he was always a loner.* [LONE + -ER[1]]

lone·some (lōn′səm), *adj.* **1.** depressed or sad because of the lack of friends, companionship, etc.; lonely: *to feel lonesome.* **2.** attended with or causing such a state of feeling: *a lonesome evening at home.* **3.** lonely in situation; remote, desolate, or isolated: *a lonesome road.* —*n.* **4. on** or **by one's lonesome,** Also, *Scot.*, **by his lane.** *Informal.* alone: *She went walking by her lonesome.* [LONE + -SOME[1]] —**lone′some·ly,** *adv.* —**lone′some·ness,** *n.*

Lone′ Star′ State′, Texas (used as a nickname).

lone′ wolf′, *Informal.* one who chooses to live, act, or work alone.

Lo·ney (lō′nē), *n.* a boy's given name.

long[1] (lông, long), *adj.* **long·er** (lông′gər, long′-), **long·est** (lông′gist, long′-), *n.*, *adv.* —*adj.* **1.** having considerable extent in space: *a long distance; a long automobile.* **2.** having considerable duration: *a long conversation; to wait a long while.* **3.** extending, lasting, or totaling a number of specified units: *eight miles long; eight hours long; eight pages long.* **4.** containing many items or units: *a long list; a long line of ancestors.* **5.** requiring a considerable time to relate, read, etc.: *a long novel.* **6.** extending beyond normal or moderate limits: *a long, boring speech.* **7.** experienced as passing slowly, because of the tedium or unpleasantness involved: *long years of study.* **8.** reaching well into the past: *a long memory.* **9.** the longer of two or the longest of several: *He must have taken the long way home. A stretcher is a brick with the long side exposed.* **10.** taking a long time; slow: *He's awfully long getting here.* **11.** forward-looking or considering all aspects; broad: *to take a long view of life.* **12.** intense; thorough; concentrated: *a long look at one's past mistakes.* **13.** having an ample supply or endowment of something (often fol. by *on*): *to be long on advice; He's long on brains.* **14.** having a considerable time to run, as a promissory note. **15.** *Chiefly Law.* distant or remote in time: *a long date.* **16.** extending relatively far: *a man with a long reach; the long arm of the law.* **17.** being higher or taller than usual: *long casement windows.* **18.** being against great odds; unlikely: *a long chance.* **19.** (of beverages) mixed or diluted with soda, seltzer, etc.: *highballs, collinses, and other long drinks.* **20.** (of the head or skull) of more than ordinary length from front to back. **21.** *Phonet.* **a.** lasting a relatively long time: *"Feed" has a longer sound than "feet" or "fit."* **b.** belonging to a class of sounds considered as usually longer in duration than another class, as the vowel of *bought* as compared to that of *but.* **c.** having the sound of the vowels in, conventionally, *mate, meet, mote,* and *moot,* and, popularly, in *mite* and *mute.* **d.** (in many languages) serving as a distinctive feature of phonemes, as the *ah* in German *Bahn* in contrast with the *a* in *Bann,* or the *tt* in Italian *fatto* in contrast with the *t* in *fato* (opposed to *short*). Cf. **distinctive feature.** **22.** *Pros.* (of a syllable in quantitative verse) lasting a relatively longer time than a short syllable. **23.** *Finance.* **a.** owning some commodity or stock. **b.** depending for profit on a rise in prices. **24.** *Gambling.* **a.** of an exceptionally large difference in proportional amounts on an event: *long odds.* **b.** of or pertaining to the large number in the odds in betting. **25.** *Ceram.* (of clay) very plastic; fat.
—*n.* **26.** a long time: *They haven't been gone for long. Will it take long?* **27.** something that is long: *The signal was two longs and a short.* **28.** a size of garment designed for men who are taller than average. **29.** a garment, as a suit or overcoat, in this size: *The regulars, the shorts, and the longs are hung separately.* **30.** *Finance.* a person who invests in stocks or commodities with the expectation of a rise in prices; a bull. **31.** *Music.* longa. **32. before long,** soon: *We should have news of her whereabouts before long.* **33. the long and the short of,** the point or gist of; substance of: *The long and the short of it is that they will be forced to sell all their holdings.* Also, **the long and short of.**
—*adv.* **34.** for or through a great extent of space or, esp., time: *a reform long advocated.* **35.** for or throughout a specified extent, esp. of time: *How long did he stay?* **36.** used elliptically in referring to the length of an absence, delay, etc.: *Don't be long. Will we be long?* **37.** throughout a specified period of time (usually used to emphasize a preceding noun): *It's been muggy all summer long.* **38.** at a point of time far distant from the time indicated: *long before.* **39. as long as.** See **as**[1] (def. 20). [ME *longe,* OE *lang, long;* c. D and G *lang,* Icel *langr,* Goth *langs,* L *longus*] —**long′ly,** *adv.* —**long′ness,** *n.*
—Syn. 1. lengthy, extensive. **2, 4.** protracted, prolonged, extended. **6.** overlong, wordy, prolix; tedious, boring.

long[2] (lông, long), *v.i.* to have an earnest or strong desire; yearn: *to long for spring; to long to return home.* [ME *longen,* OE *langian* grow longer, yearn after, summon; see LONG[1]]

long[3] (lông, long), *v.i.* **1.** *Archaic.* to be suitable or fitting. **2.** *Obs.* to be the possession of. [ME *longen,* OE *langian* to belong, deriv. of *gelang* belonging to, dependent on; see ALONG]

Long (lông, long), *n.* **1. Crawford Wil·liam·son** (wil′yəm sən), 1815–78, U.S. surgeon. **2. Hu·ey Pierce** (hyōō′ē), 1893–1935, U.S. politician. **3. Stephen Har·riman,** 1784–1864, U.S. army officer and explorer.

long., longitude.

lon·ga (long′gə), *n.* *Music.* the second longest note in medieval mensural notation. Also, **long.** [< L, fem. of *longus* LONG]

long′ account′, *Finance.* the account of a customer who buys securities or commodities on margin.

lon·gan (long′gən), *n.* **1.** the small, one-seeded, greenish-brown, pleasant-tasting fruit of the large, evergreen, sapindaceous tree, *Euphoria Longan,* native to China and allied to the litchi. **2.** the tree itself. Also, **lungan.** [< NL *longan(um)* < Chin *lung-yen* dragon's eye]

long′-and-short′ work′ (lông′ən shôrt′, long′-), *Masonry.* an arrangement of rectangular quoins or jambstones set alternately vertically and horizontally.

lon·ga·nim·i·ty (long′gə nim′i tē), *n.* patient endurance of hardship or injuries; fortitude; forbearance; long-suffering. [late ME *longanimyte* < LL *longanimitās* patience, equiv. to *longanimi(s)* patient (*long(us)* long + *anim(us)* spirit + *-is* adj. suffix) + *-tās* -TY[2]] —**lon·gan·a·mous** (long gan′ə məs), *adj.*

long′ arm′, manhelper.

Long′ Beach′, **1.** a city in SW California, S of Los Angeles: a seaside resort. 344,168 (1960). **2.** a city on SW Long Island, in SE New York. 26,473 (1960). **3.** a town in SE Mississippi. 4770 (1960).

long·beard (lông′bērd′, long′-), *n.* bellarmine. [LONG[1] + BEARD]

long·boat (lông′bōt′, long′-), *n.* *Naut.* the largest boat formerly carried by a sailing vessel. [LONG[1] + BOAT]

long·bow (lông′bō′, long′-), *n.* **1.** a large bow drawn by hand, as that used by English archers from the 12th to the 16th centuries. **2. draw the longbow,** to exaggerate in telling stories; overstate something: *He's sure to draw the longbow on the size of his catch of fish.* [LONG[1] + BOW[2]]

Long′ Branch′, a city in E New Jersey: seaside resort. 26,228 (1960).

long′ card′, *Chiefly Bridge.* a card of a suit that remains in a hand after all outstanding cards of the suit have been drawn.

long′ clam′. See **soft-shell clam.**

long·cloth (lông′klôth′, long′kloth′), *n.* a fine, white, cotton cloth, high-texture and plain-woven; high-grade muslin. [LONG[1] + CLOTH]

long′ cross′, *Heraldry.* See **Latin cross.**

Long′ Day's′ Jour′ney Into Night′, a play (1956) by Eugene O'Neill.

long′ dis′tance, telephone service between distant points. —**long′-dis′tance,** *adj.*

long′ divi′sion, *Math.* division, usually by a number of two or more digits, in which each step of the process is written down.

long′ doz′en, a dozen plus one; thirteen; baker's dozen.

long-drawn (lông′drôn′, long′-), *adj.* **1.** drawn out; prolonged: *a long-drawn narrative.* **2.** *Rare.* of great length; long: *the long-drawn line of soldiers.* Also, **long-drawn-out** (lông′drôn′out′, long′-).

longe (lunj, lonj), *n.*, *v.*, **longed, longe·ing.** —*n.* **1.** a long rope used to guide a horse during training or exercise. —*v.t.* **2.** to train or exercise (a horse) by use of a longe. Also, **lunge.** [< F, OF: n. use of *longe* < L *longa,* fem. of *longus* long]

long′-eared owl′ (lông′ērd′, long′-), a mottled, gray owl, *Asio otus,* of the Northern Hemisphere, having a long tuft of feathers on each side of the head.

lon·ge·ron (lon′jər ən), *n.* *Aeron.* a main longitudinal brace or support on an airplane. [< F: side-piece, equiv. to *longer* to skirt + *-on* n. suffix]

long′ ess′ (es). See **long s.**

lon·gev·i·ty (lon jev′i tē), *n.* **1.** long life; great duration of life: *That branch of the family has never enjoyed longevity.* **2.** the length or duration of life: *research in human longevity.* **3.** length of service, tenure, etc.; seniority: *promotions based on longevity.* [< L *longaevitās.* See LONGEV(OUS), -ITY]

lon·ge·vous (lon jē′vəs), *adj.* long-lived; living to a great age. [< L *longaevus* aged, equiv. to *long(us)* long + *aev(um)* age + *-us* -OUS]

long′ face′, an unhappy or troubled expression: *He's been walking around with a long face ever since he failed the examination.*

long-faced (lông′fāst′, long′-), *adj.* **1.** having an unhappy or gloomy expression; glum. **2.** having a face longer than the usual.

long′ fake′, *Naut.* a fake in which a rope is laid down in a series of lengths side-by-side in the direction in which the rope is hauled. Also called **long′-flaked coil′** (lông′flākt′, long′-). Cf. **French fake.**

Long·fel·low (lông′fel′ō, long′-), *n.* **Henry Wads·worth** (wodz′wərth), 1807–82, U.S. poet.

Long·ford (lông′fərd, long′-), *n.* a county in Leinster, in the N Republic of Ireland. 30,642 (1961); 403 sq. mi. *Co. seat:* Longford.

long′ gal′lery, a large gallery, found esp. in the uppermost stories of Elizabethan and Jacobean manor houses, used as a family room and as a promenade.

long′ game′, **1.** the aspect of golf considered in relation to the ability of a player to hit shots, esp. drives, for distance. Cf. **short game** (def. 1). **2.** a card game in which all cards in the pack are dealt before play. Cf. **short game** (def. 2).

long′ green′, *Slang.* paper money; cash.

long·hair (lông′hâr′, long′-), *Informal.* —*n.* **1.** *Sometimes Disparaging.* an intellectual. **2.** a person, usually gifted, who is very interested in or devoted to the arts, esp. a performer, composer, or lover of classical music. —*adj.* **3.** Also, **long′-haired′.** of or characteristic of a longhair or his taste. [LONG[1] + HAIR]

long·hand (lông′hand′, long′-), *n.* **1.** writing of the ordinary kind, in which words are written out in full. —*adj.* **2.** using longhand: *longhand writing.* **3.** written in longhand: *a longhand account of the meeting.*

long·head (lông′hed′, long′-), *n.* *Anthropol.* **1.** a dolichocephalic person. **2.** a head with a low cephalic index. [LONG[1] + HEAD]

long-head·ed (lông′hed′id, long′-), *adj.* **1.** *Anthropol.* dolichocephalic. **2.** of great discernment or foresight; far-seeing or shrewd. Also, **long′head′ed.** —**long′-head′ed·ly, long′head′ed·ly,** *adv.* —**long′-head′ed·ness, long′head′ed·ness,** *n.*

long′ horn′, a moist Cheddar of cylindrical shape, weighing about 12 pounds.

Long·horn (lông′hôrn′, long′-), *n.* **1.** one of a nearly extinct English breed of beef cattle having long horns. **2.** (*l.c.*) See **Texas longhorn.** **3.** (*l.c.*) See **long-horned beetle.** **4.** *Slang.* a Texan. [LONG[1] + HORN]

long′-horned bee′tle (lông′hôrnd′, long′-), any of numerous, often brightly colored beetles of the family *Cerambycidae,* usually with long antennae, the larvae of which bore into the wood of living or decaying trees. Also called **longhorn.**

long′-horned grass′hopper, any of numerous insects of the family *Tettigoniidae,* having long, thread-like antennae and well-developed stridulating organs on the forewings of the male.

long′ horse′, *Gymnastics.* a cylindrical, leather-covered block that has one end upturned and narrowed and is mounted in horizontal position on one or two vertical, adjustable posts set in a steel frame, for use chiefly in vaulting. Cf. **side horse.**

long′ house′, **1.** a communal dwelling of the Iroquois and various other American Indian peoples, consisting of a wooden, bark-covered framework often as much as 100 feet in length. **2.** (*caps.*) the league of the Iroquois.

long′ hun′dredweight, a hundredweight of 112 pounds, the usual hundredweight in Great Britain, but now rare in the U.S.

longi-, a learned borrowing from Latin meaning "long," used in the formation of compound words: *longicorn.* [< L, comb. form of *longus* long; see -I-]

lon·gi·cau·dal (lon′ji kôd′əl), *adj.* *Rare.* having a long tail; macrutous. Also, **lon·gi·cau·date** (lon′ji kô′dāt). [LONGI- + CAUDAL]

lon·gi·corn (lon′ji kôrn′), *Entomol.* —*adj.* **1.** having long antennae. **2.** belonging or pertaining to the *Cerambycidae,* comprising the long-horned beetles. —*n.* **3.** See **long-horned beetle.** [< NL *longicorn(is)* long-horned, equiv. to *longi-* LONGI- + *corn(ū)* horn + *-is* adj. suffix]

long·ies (lông′ēz, long′-), *n.* (*construed as pl.*) **1.** long underwear. **2.** long pants made for boys. [pl. of *longie* (LONG[1] + -IE)]

long·ing (lông′ing, long′-), *n.* **1.** prolonged, unceasing, or earnest desire: *a life filled with longing* **2.** an instance of this: *a sudden longing to see old friends.* —*adj.* **3.** having or characterized by prolonged or earnest desire: *a longing look.* [LONG[2] + -ING[1]] —**long′ing·ly,** *adv.* —**long′ing·ness,** *n.*
—Syn. 1. aspiration. See **desire.** **—Ant. 1.** apathy.

Lon·gi·nus (lon jī′nəs), *n.* **Dionysius Cas·sius** (kash′əs), A.D. 213?–273, Greek philosopher and rhetorician. —**Lon·gin·e·an** (lon jin′ē ən), *adj.*

long′ i′ron, *Golf.* a club, as a driving iron, midiron, or mid-mashie, with a long shaft and an iron head the face of which has little slope, for hitting long, low shots. Cf. **short iron.**

long·ish (lông′ish, long′-), *adj.* somewhat long. [LONG[1] + -ISH[1]]

Long′ Is′land, an island in SE New York: the boroughs of Brooklyn and Queens of New York City are located at its W end. 118 mi. long; 12–20 mi. wide; 1682 sq. mi.

Long′ Is′land Sound′, an arm of the Atlantic between Connecticut and Long Island. 110 mi. long.

lon·gi·tude (lon′ji tōōd′, -tyōōd′), *n.* **1.** *Geog.* angular distance east or west on the earth's surface, measured by the angle contained between the meridian of a particular place and some prime meridian, as that of Greenwich, England, and expressed either in degrees or by some corresponding difference in time. **2.** *Astron.* **a.** See **celestial longitude.** **b.** See **galactic longitude.** [< L *longitūdō* length. See LONGI-, -TUDE]

lon′gitude by account′, *Navig.* the longitude of the position of a vessel as estimated by dead reckoning.

lon·gi·tu·di·nal (lon′ji tōōd′ənəl, -tyōōd′-), *adj.* **1.** of or pertaining to longitude or length: *longitudinal measurement.* **2.** *Zool.* pertaining to or extending along the long axis of the body, or the direction from front to back, or head to tail. **3.** extending in the direction of the length of a thing; running lengthwise: *a thin, longitudinal stripe.* —*n.* **4.** a longitudinal framing member, as in the hull of a ship. [< L *longitūdin-* (s. of *longitūdō*) length + -AL[1]] —**lon′gi·tu′di·nal·ly,** *adv.*

longitu′dinal coeffi′cient, *Naval Archit.* the ratio of the immersed volume of a hull to the product obtained by multiplying its length on the water line by the immersed area of the midship transverse section, all assuming a given depth of immersion of the hull. Also called **cylindrical coefficient, prismatic coefficient.**

longitu′dinal fram′ing, *Naval Archit.* See **Isherwood framing.**

longitu′dinal magnifica′tion, *Optics.* the amount of displacement of an image of an object along a given axis for a small longitudinal displacement of the object.

longitu′dinal sec′tion, the representation of an object as it would appear if cut by the vertical plane passing through the longest axis of the object.

longitu′dinal wave′, *Physics.* a wave in which the direction of displacement is the same as the direction of propagation, as a sound wave. Cf. **transverse wave.**

long′ johns′, *Slang.* long underwear.

long′ jump′, *Chiefly Brit.* See **broad jump.**

Long′ Lake′, a town in NE Illinois. 3502 (1960).

long′leaf pine′ (lông′lēf′, long′-), *n.* **1.** an American pine, *Pinus palustris,* valued as a source of turpentine and for its timber. **2.** the wood of this tree.

long-limbed (lông′limd′, long′-), *adj.* having long, slender arms and legs: *a long-limbed youth.*

long-lived (lông′līvd′, -livd′, long′-), *adj.* **1.** having a long life, existence, or duration: *a long-lived man; long-lived fame.* **2.** (of an object) lasting or functioning a long time: *a long-lived building; a long-lived car.* [late ME *longe lyved;* see LONG[1], -LIVED] —**long′-lived′ness,** *n.*

long′ meas′ure. See **linear measure.**

long′ moss′. See **Spanish moss.**

Lon·go·bard (long′gō bärd′, -gə-), *n.* Lombard (def. 2).

Lon·go·mon·ta·nus (long′gō mon tä′nəs, -tā′-, long′-), *n.* a walled plain in the third quadrant of the face of the moon: about 90 miles in diameter.

Long′ Par′liament, *Eng. Hist.* the Parliament which assembled November 3, 1640, was expelled by Cromwell in 1653, reconvened in 1659, and was dissolved in 1660.

long′ pig′, (among the Maori and Polynesian peoples) human flesh eaten by cannibals.

long-play·ing (lông′plā′ing, long′-), *adj.* of or pertaining to disk records devised to be played at 33⅓ revolutions per minute.

long′ poop′er (po͞o′pər), *Naut.* a merchant ship having the poop deck brought forward to the bridge house to serve as a weather deck.

long′ prim′er, *Print.* a 12-point type.

long-range (lông′rānj′, long′-), *adj.* **1.** designed to fire a long distance: *a long-range gun.* **2.** allowing for or extending into the more distant future: *a long-range outlook; long-range plans.*

long′ ri′fle. See **Kentucky rifle.**

long′ rod′, *Survey.* See **high rod.**

long s (es), a style of the letter *s*, formerly common in handwriting and as a type character. Also, **long ess.**

long·ship (lông′ship′, long′-), *n.* a medieval ship used in northern Europe esp. by the Norse, having a narrow, open hull, a single square sail, and a large number of oars, which provided most of the propulsion. [LONG[1] + SHIP]

long·shore (lông′shôr′, -shōr′, long′-), *adj.* existing, found, or employed along the shore, esp. at or near a seaport: *longshore jobs; longshore current.* [aph. var. of *alongshore*]

long·shore·man (lông′shôr′mən, -shōr′-, -shôr′-, -shōr′-, long′-), *n., pl.* **-men.** a man employed on the wharves of a port, as in loading and unloading vessels. [LONGSHORE + MAN[1]]

long′ shot′, **1.** a selection that has very little chance of winning: *He decided to put his money on a long shot.* **2.** an attempt or undertaking that offers much, but in which there is little chance for success. **3.** *Motion Pictures, Television.* a camera shot taken at a relatively great distance from the subject and permitting a broad view of a scene. Cf. **close-up** (def. 2), **medium shot. 4. by a long shot,** by any means; by a measurable degree: *They haven't finished by a long shot.*

long-sight·ed (lông′sī′tid, long′-), *adj.* **1.** farsighted; hypermetropic. **2.** having great foresight; foreseeing remote results. —**long′-sight′ed·ness,** *n.*

long·sleev·er (lông′slē′vər, long′-), *n.* *Australian.* **1.** about ¾ pint of beer. **2.** any tall glass. [LONG[1] + SLEEVE + -ER[1]]

long·some (lông′səm, long′-), *adj.* tiresomely long; protracted so as to weary or cause boredom. [ME, OE *longsum, langsum.* See LONG[1], -SOME[1]] —**long′some·ly,** *adv.* —**long′some·ness,** *n.*

Longs′ Peak′ (lôngz, longz), a peak in N Colorado, in the Rocky Mountain National Park. 14,255 ft.

long′ splice′, a splice for forming a united rope narrow enough to pass through a block, made by unlaying the ends of two ropes for a considerable distance, overlapping the strands so as to make pairs of one strand from each rope, unlaying one of each pair, twisting the other strand into its place in the united rope, and tucking the yarns of the unlaid strand separately into place. Cf. **short splice.** See illus. under **splice.**

long·spur (lông′spûr′, long′-), *n.* any of several fringilline birds of the genera *Calcarius* and *Rhynchophanes,* of tundra or prairie regions of North America, characterized by a long, spurlike hind claw on each foot. [LONG[1] + SPUR]

long·stand·ing (lông′stan′ding, long′-), *adj.* existing or occurring for a long time: *a longstanding feud.* [LONG[1] + STANDING]

long-stemmed (lông′stemd′, long′-), *adj.* **1.** having a long stem or stems: *one dozen long-stemmed American Beauty roses.* **2.** long-legged and slender: *The chorus line was full of long-stemmed beauties.*

Long·street (lông′strēt′, long′-), *n.* **James,** 1821–1904, Confederate general in the U.S. Civil War.

long-suf·fer·ance (lông′suf′ər əns, long′-), *n.* *Archaic.* long-suffering.

long-suf·fer·ing (lông′suf′ər ing, long′-), *adj.* **1.** enduring injury or provocation long and patiently: *the long-suffering poor of the world.* —*n.* **2.** long and patient endurance of injury or trouble: *She has borne years of long-suffering and privation because of her husband's illness.* —**long′-suf′fer·ing·ly,** *adv.*

long′ suit′, *Cards.* **1.** the suit in which the most cards are held in a hand. **2.** *Bridge.* a suit in which four or more cards are held in a hand. **3.** the quality, activity, endeavor, etc., in which one excels: *Diligence is his long suit.*

long′ sweet′ening, *Chiefly Southern and Midland U.S.* liquid sweetening, as maple syrup, molasses, or sorghum.

long-term (lông′tûrm′, long′-), *adj.* **1.** covering a relatively long period of time: *a long-term lease.* **2.** maturing over a relatively long period of time: *a long-term loan.*

long′-term bond′, a bond not maturing for several years or more.

long′ tom′, **1.** *Army Slang.* a large field gun, usually the 155-millimeter gun. **2.** a long heavy cannon formerly carried by small naval vessels. [LONG[1] + TOM]

long′ ton′. See under **ton**[1] (def. 1). *Abbr.:* L/T

long-tongued (lông′tungd′, long′-), *adj.* talking too much or too openly, esp. of private or confidential matters; chattering; gossipy: *She is the most long-tongued individual I have ever known.*

long′ topgal′lant mast′, *Naut.* a single spar fitted above a topmast to carry topgallants, a royal, and all sails above. Also called **pole topgallant mast.**

lon·gueur (lông gûr′, long-; *Fr.* lôn gœr′), *n., pl.* **-gueurs** (-gûrz′; *Fr.* -gœr′). a long and boring passage in a literary work, drama, musical composition, or the like: *The longueurs in this book make it almost unreadable.* [< F: lit., length]

long′ vaca′tion, *Brit.* the summer vacation given in the law courts and universities.

Long·view (lông′vyo͞o′, long′-), *n.* **1.** a city in NE Texas. 40,050 (1960). **2.** a city in SW Washington, on the Columbia. 23,349 (1960). **3.** a town in central North Carolina. 2997 (1960).

Long′ Voy′age Home′, The, a play (1917) by Eugene O'Neill. Cf. **Glencairn Cycle.**

long-waist·ed (lông′wā′stid, long′-), *adj.* of more than average length between the shoulders and waistline; having a low waistline. Cf. **short-waisted.**

long·wall (lông′wôl′, long′-), *adj.* *Mining.* noting or pertaining to a means of extracting coal or other minerals in an underground mine from a continuous face, the roof before the face being supported at intervals by piers of waste. Cf. **room-and-pillar.** [LONG[1] + WALL]

long′ wave′, **1.** *Elect.* an electromagnetic wave over 60 meters in length. **2.** See **L wave.** —**long′-wave′,** *adj.*

long·ways (lông′wāz′, long′-), *adv.* **1.** *Dancing.* in two long lines with the couples facing each other: *to perform a country dance longways.* **2.** longwise. —*adj.* **3.** longwise. [LONG[1] + -WAYS]

long-wind·ed (lông′win′did, long′-), *adj.* **1.** talking or writing at tedious length, as persons: *How one despises these long-winded after-dinner speakers.* **2.** continued to a tedious length in speech or writing: *another of his long-winded election speeches; a dull, long-winded novel.* **3.** able to breathe deeply; not tiring easily. —**long′-wind′ed·ly,** *adv.* —**long′-wind′ed·ness,** *n.*

long·wise (lông′wīz′, long′-), *adj., adv.* lengthwise. [LONG[1] + -WISE]

Long·worth (lông′wûrth, long′-), *n.* **Nicholas,** 1869–1931, U.S. politician: Speaker of the House 1925–31.

Lon·i (lon′ē), *n.* a girl's given name, form of **Lona.** Also, **Lon′ie.**

Lon·nie (lon′ē), *n.* a boy's given name, form of **Lon** or **Alonzo.** Also, **Lon′ny.**

Lönn·rot (len′rot, -ro͞ot; *Fin.* lœn′Rôt), *n.* **E·lias** (e′lyäs), 1802–84, Finnish scholar and editor.

Lons-le-Sau·nier (lôN lə sō nyā′), *n.* a city in and the capital of Jura, in E France. 18,752 (1962).

Lon·zo (lon′zō), *n.* a boy's given name, form of **Alonzo.** Also, **Lon·zie** (lon′zē).

loo[1] (lo͞o), *n., pl.* **loos,** *v.,* **looed, loo·ing.** —*n.* **1.** a game at cards in which forfeits are paid into a pool. **2.** the forfeit or sum paid into the pool. **3.** the fact of being looed. —*v.t.* **4.** to subject to a forfeit at loo. [short for *lanterloo* < D *lanterlu* < F *lantur(e)lu,* special use of meaningless refrain of an old song]

loo[2] (lo͞o), *n., pl.* **loos,** *v.t., v.i.,* **looed, loo·ing.** *Scot.* love. [? var. of *lew* shelter, OE *hlēow*]

loo[3] (lo͞o), *n.* *Brit. Informal.* toilet.

loo·by (lo͞o′bē), *n., pl.* **-bies.** an awkward fellow, esp. one who is lazy or stupid; lout; lubber. [ME *loby.* See LOB[1], LUBBER]

loof[1] (lo͞of), *n.* *Scot. and North Eng.* the palm of the hand. [ME *lofe* < Scand; cf. Icel *lōfi,* c. Goth *lōfa*]

loof[2] (lo͞of), *n.* *Naut.* **1.** the tapering of a hull toward the stern. **2.** Also, **luff.** *Obs.* the broad after part of the bows of a vessel. **3.** *Obs.* luff (def. 1) [special uses of LOOF[1]]

loo·fa (lo͞o′fə), *n.* luffa.

Loo·goo·tee (lə gō′tē), *n.* a town in SW Indiana. 2858 (1960).

loo·ie (lo͞o′ē), *n.* *Slang.* a lieutenant of the armed forces. Also, **loo′ey, louie.** [LIEU(TENANT) + -IE]

look (lo͝ok), *v.i.* **1.** to set one's eyes upon something or in some direction in order to see: *He looked toward the western horizon to see if he could spot the returning planes.* **2.** to glance or gaze in a manner specified: *to look questioningly at a person.* **3.** to use the sight in seeking, searching, examining, watching, etc.: *to look through the papers.* **4.** to tend, as in bearing or significance: *Conditions look toward war.* **5.** to appear or seem to the eye as specified: *to look pale.* **6.** to seem to the mind: *The case looks promising.* **7.** to direct the mental regard or attention: *to look at the facts.* **8.** to have an outlook or afford a view: *The window looks upon the street.* **9.** to face or front: *The house looks to the east.* —*v.t.* **10.** to give (someone) a look: *He looked me straight in the eye.* **11.** to have an appearance appropriate to or befitting (something): *She looked her years. The actor looked his part.* **12.** to try to find; seek (usually fol. by *up*): *We looked his phone number up in the directory. Look it up in the library.* **13.** to express or suggest by looks: *to look one's annoyance at a person.* **14.** to view, inspect, or examine (often fol. by *over*): *He looked the place over.* **15.** to appear to be; look like: *He looked a perfect fool, coming to the party a day late.* **16.** *Archaic.* to bring, put, etc., by looks. **17. look after, a.** to follow with the eye, as someone or something moving away: *She looked after him as he walked toward the train station.* **b.** to pay attention to; concern oneself with: *to look after one's own interests.* **c.** to take care of; minister to: *to look after a child.* **18. look back,** to review past events; return in thought: *Looking back on our school days, it seems as if they were a century ago.* **19. look daggers,** to look at someone with a furious, menacing expression: *She was looking daggers at her husband as he prattled obliviously on.* **20. look down on** or **upon,** to regard with scorn or disdain; have contempt for: *They look down on all foreigners.* **21. look down one's nose at,** to regard with an overbearing attitude of superiority, disdain, or censure: *I can't stand the way she looks down her nose at people who have not had her advantages.* **22. look for, a.** to seek; search for: *Columbus was looking for a shorter route to the East when he discovered America.* **b.** to anticipate; expect: *I'll be looking for you at the reception.* **23. look forward to,** to anticipate with eagerness or pleasure: *I always look forward to your visits.* **24. look in, a.** Also, **look into.** to look briefly inside of: *Look in the jar and tell me if any cookies are left.* **b.** Also, **look in on.** to visit (a person, place, etc.) briefly: *I'll stop by and look in some day next week. The doctor looks in on his patients in the morning.* **25. look into,** to inquire into; investigate; examine: *The auditors are looking into the records to find the cause of the discrepancy.* **26. look on** or **upon, a.** to be a spectator; watch: *The crowd looked on as the police herded the troublemakers into patrol wagons.* **b.** to consider; regard: *They look upon gambling as sinful.* **27. look out, a.** to look to the outside, as from a window or a place of observation: *From her window, she could look out over the bustling city to the hills beyond.* **b.** to be on guard: *to look out for trouble.* **c.** to take watchful care; be concerned about: *He has to look out for his health.* **d.** to afford a view; face: *The room looks out on the garden.* **28. look sharp, a.** to be alert and quick: *If you want to get ahead, you must learn to look sharp.* **b.** Also, *Brit.,* **look slippy.** to hurry: *You'd better look sharp! It's getting late.* **29. look over,** to examine, esp. briefly or superficially: *Will you please look over my paper before I submit it?* **30. look to, a.** to direct one's glance or gaze to: *If you look to your left, you can see the Empire State Building.* **b.** to give attention to: *Look to your own affairs and stay out of mine!* **c.** to direct one's expectations or hopes to: *We look to the day when world peace will be a reality.* **d.** to regard with expectation and anticipation: *We look to the future and greater advances in science and technology.* **e.** to depend or rely on: *the increasing number of countries that look to America to protect them from Communist aggression.* **31. look up, a.** to direct the eyes upward; raise one's glance: *The other guests looked up as she entered the room.* **b.** *Informal.* to become better or more prosperous; improve: *Business is looking up.* **c.** to search for, as an item of information, in a reference book or the like: *Look up the answer in the encyclopedia.* **d.** to seek out, esp. to visit: *to look up an old friend.* **e.** *Naut.* (of a sailing vessel) to head more nearly in the direction of its destination after a favoring change of wind. **32. look up to,** to regard with admiration or respect; esteem: *A boy needs a father he can look up to.* —*n.* **33.** the act of looking: *a look of inquiry.* **34.** a visual search or examination. **35.** the way in which a person or thing appears to the eye or to the mind; aspect: *He has the look of an honest man. The material of that tablecloth has a cheap look.* **36.** an expressive glance: *to give someone a sharp look.* **37. looks,** general aspect; appearance: *to like the looks of a place; to be blessed with good looks.* [ME *lōk(i)en,* OE *lōcian;* c. MD *lœken,* akin to dial. G *lugen* to look out]
—**Syn. 1.** See **watch. 6.** See **seem. 34.** gaze, glance. **35.** appearance, air.

look-a·like (lo͝ok′ə līk′), *n.* a person who or thing that looks like or closely resembles another; double. [n. use of v. phrase *look alike*]

look-down (lo͝ok′doun′), *n.* the appearance of paper when inspected under reflected light. Cf. **look-through.** [n. use of v. phrase *look down*]

look·down (lo͝ok′doun′), *n.* a silvery carangid fish of the genus *Selene,* esp. *S. vomer,* found in the Atlantic Ocean, having a compressed body and eyes placed high on the truncated forehead. [n. use of v. phrase *look down*]

look·er (lo͝ok′ər), *n.* **1.** a person who looks. **2.** *Slang.* a very good looking person, esp. a woman. [LOOK + -ER[1]]

look·er-on (lo͝ok′ər on′), *n., pl.* **look·ers-on.** a person who looks on; spectator. [n. use of v. phrase *look on;* see -ER[1]]

Look′ Home′ward, An′gel, a novel (1929) by Thomas Wolfe.

look-in (lo͝ok′in′), *n.* **1.** a brief glance. **2.** a short visit. [n. use of v. phrase *look in*]

Look′ing Back′ward, a utopian novel (1888) by Edward Bellamy.

look·ing-glass (lo͝ok′ing glas′, -gläs′), *n.* **1.** a mirror made of glass with a metallic or amalgam backing. **2.** the glass used in a mirror. **3.** anything used as a mirror, as highly polished metal or a reflecting surface.

look·out (lo͝ok′out′), *n.* **1.** the act of looking out or keeping watch. **2.** a watch kept, as for something that may come or happen. **3.** a person or group stationed or employed to keep such a watch. **4.** a station or place from which a watch is kept. **5.** *Chiefly Brit.* view; prospect; outlook: *The lookout from the summit was breath-taking. The business lookout is far from optimistic.* **6.** *Informal.* an object of care or concern: *That's not my lookout.* **7.** *Building Trades.* **a.** Also called **tail, tailpiece.** a piece, as a cantilever or the projecting end of a rafter, supporting eaves or a bargeboard beyond the outside of a building. **b.** tailpiece (def. 4). [n. use of v. phrase *look out*]

Look′out Moun′tain, a mountain ridge in Georgia, Tennessee, and Alabama: a battle of the Civil War fought here, near Chattanooga, Tennessee 1863; highest point, 2126 ft.

look-see (lo͝ok′sē′), *n.* *Slang.* a visual survey; look; inspection: *He came over to have a look-see.* [n. use of impv. sequence LOOK, SEE[1]]

look-through (lo͝ok′thro͞o′), *n.* the opacity and texture of paper when inspected by transmitted light. Also called **see-through.** Cf. **look-down.** [n. use of v. phrase *look through*]

loo·kum (lo͞o′kəm), *n.* a small roof or penthouse for sheltering a hoist or the like. [*lew* shelter (OE *hlēow*) + *-kum* (< ?). See LEE[1]]

look-up (lo͝ok′up′), *n.* the automatic search conducted by a digital computer in referring to its storage: *a table look-up.* [n. use of v. phrase *look up*]

look·y (lo͝ok′ē), *interj.* look; look here: *Looky here now, young man!* Also, **look′ee.** [alter. of impv. *look ye!*]

loom[1] (lo͞om), *n.* **1.** a hand-operated or power-driven apparatus for weaving fabrics, containing harnesses, lay, reed, shuttles, treadles, etc. **2.** the art or the process of weaving. **3.** the part of an oar between the blade and the handle. —*v.t.* **4.** to weave (something) on a loom. [ME *lome,* OE *gelōma* tool, implement. See HEIRLOOM]

loom[2] (lo͞om), *v.i.* **1.** to appear indistinctly; come into view in indistinct and enlarged form: *The mountainous island loomed on the horizon. Through the haze a freighter suddenly loomed on our starboard bow.* **2.** to rise before the vision with an appearance of great or portentous size: *As we turned the corner, a skyscraper loomed in front of us.* **3.** to assume form as an impending event: *The convention looms as a political battle.* —*n.* **4.** a looming appearance, as of something seen indistinctly at a distance or through a fog: *the loom of a moraine directly in their path.* [?]

loom[3] (lo͞om), *n.* *Brit. Dial.* **1.** loon[1]. **2.** a guillemot or murre. [< Scand; cf. Icel *lōmr,* Sw *lom*]

L.O.O.M., Loyal Order of Moose.

loom·ing (lo͞o′ming), *n.* a mirage in which objects below the horizon seem to be raised above their true positions. [LOOM[2] + -ING[1]]

loon[1] (lo͞on), *n.* any of several large, short-tailed, web-footed, fish-eating diving birds of the genus *Gavia*, of the Northern Hemisphere. [var. of LOOM[3]]

loon[2] (lo͞on), *n.* a worthless, sorry, lazy, or stupid fellow. [late ME *lowen* < Scand; cf. Icel *lūinn* beaten, beat (ptp. of *lȳja* to beat), *lūalag* base conduct]

loon·ey (lo͞o′nē), *adj.* **loon·i·er, loon·i·est,** *n., pl.* **loon·ies.** loony.

loon·y (lo͞o′nē), *adj.*, **loon·i·er, loon·i·est,** *n., pl.* **loon·ies.** *Slang.* —*adj.* **1.** lunatic; insane. **2.** extremely or senselessly foolish. —*n.* **3.** a lunatic. Also, **looney, luny.** [LUN(ATIC) + -Y[2]] —**loon′i·ness,** *n.*

loon′y bin′, *Slang.* an insane asylum or the mental ward of a hospital.

loop[1] (lo͞op), *n.* **1.** a portion of a cord, ribbon, etc., folded or doubled upon itself so as to leave an opening between the parts. **2.** anything shaped more or less like a loop, as a line drawn on paper, a part of a letter, a part of a path, a line of motion, etc. **3.** a curved piece or a ring of metal, wood, or the like, used for the insertion of something, as a handle, etc. **4.** *Aeron.* a maneuver executed by an airplane in such a manner that the airplane describes a closed curve in a vertical plane. **5.** a circular area at the end of a trolley line, railroad line, etc., where cars turn around. **6.** an arm of a cloverleaf where traffic may turn off or onto a main road or highway. **7.** *Physics.* the part of a vibrating string, column of air or other medium, etc., between two adjacent nodes. **8.** *Elect.* a closed electric or magnetic circuit. **9.** *Computer Technol.* **a.** reiteration of a set of instructions in a routine or program. **b.** a routine or program consisting of a set of iterative instructions. **10.** a wire, usually of platinum, one end of which is curved to form a loop, used for transferring microorganisms from one medium to another. **11.** a sand bar that encloses or nearly encloses a body of water. **12.** *Figure Skating.* a school figure in which a skater traces a large half circle, a small oval within its arc, and another large half circle to complete the figure while remaining on the same skating edge. **13. the Loop,** the main business district of Chicago. —*v.t.* **14.** to form into a loop or loops. **15.** to make a loop or loops in. **16.** to enfold or encircle in or with something arranged in a loop: *He looped the rope around the steer's horns.* **17.** to fasten by forming into a loop, or by means of something formed into a loop (often fol. by *up*): *to loop up the new draperies.* **18.** to cause (a missile or projectile) to trace a looping or loop-like trajectory through the air: *The rebels looped several homemade bombs into the building.* **19.** to fly (an airplane) in a loop or series of loops. **20.** to construct a closed electric or magnetic circuit. —*v.i.* **21.** to make or form a loop or loops: *The river loops around the two counties.* **22.** to move by forming loops, as a measuring worm. **23.** to trace a looping or looplike path through the air: *The fly ball looped high in the air.* **24.** to perform a loop or series of loops in an airplane. [late ME *loupe;* perh. < Gael *lub* loop, bend]

loop[2] (lo͞op), *n.* *Archaic.* a small or narrow opening, as in a wall; loophole. [ME *loupe* window; cf. MD *lūpen* peep, peer]

loop[3] (lo͞op), *n.* *Metalworking.* a hot bloom of pasty consistency, to be worked under a hammer or in rolls. [< F *loupe* (whence also G *Luppe*), special use of *loupe* wen, knob, gnarl < Gmc. See LOUPE]

loop′ back′. See **bow back.**

looped (lo͞opt), *adj.* *Slang.* drunk; inebriated. [LOOP[1] + -ED[2]]

loop·er (lo͞o′pər), *n.* **1.** one who or that which loops something or forms loops. **2.** measuringworm. **3.** the thread holder in a sewing machine using two threads. **4.** *Baseball.* blooper (def. 3a). [LOOP[1] + -ER[1]]

loop·hole (lo͞op′hōl′), *n., v.,* **-holed, -hol·ing.** —*n.* **1.** a small or narrow opening, as in a wall, for looking through, for admitting light and air, or, particularly in a fortification, for the discharge of missiles against an enemy outside. See illus. under **battlement. 2.** an opening or aperture. **3.** a means of escape or evasion; a means or opportunity of evading a rule, law, etc.: *The defense attorney kept trying to find some loophole in the prosecution's case. There are a number of loopholes in the tax laws whereby large corporations can save money.* —*v.t.* **4.** to furnish with loopholes. [LOOP[2] + HOLE]

loop′hole frame′, a frame in the opening of a wall enclosing a window and some other opening or openings.

loop′ing mill′, *Metalworking.* a rolling mill for bar stock, wire, and the like, having the successive stands side by side so that the metal forms a loop in passing from stand to stand.

loop′ knot′, a knot made by doubling over a line at its end and tying both thicknesses into a square knot in such a way as to leave a loop. Also called **open hand knot.** See illus. under **knot.**

loop′ of Hen′le (hen′lē), *Anat.* the part of a nephron between the proximal and distal convoluted tubules that extends, in a loop, from the cortex into the medulla of the kidney. Also called **Henle's loop.** [named after F. G. J. *Henle* (1809–85), German pathologist]

loop′ stitch′, *Sewing.* any stitch, as the chain stitch, that uses loops in the pattern or process of working.

loop-the-loop (lo͞op′thə lo͞op′), *n.* **1.** an airplane maneuver in which a plane, starting upward, makes one complete vertical loop. **2.** a ride in an amusement park that simulates this maneuver.

loop′ win′dow, a tall, narrow window.

loop·y (lo͞o′pē), *adj.* **loop·i·er, loop·i·est. 1.** full of loops. **2.** *Informal.* eccentric; pixilated; dotty. **3.** *Informal.* befuddled or confused, esp. due to intoxication. **4.** *Scot.* crafty; sly. [LOOP[1] + -Y[1]]

Loos (lōs), *n.* **1. A·dolf** (ā′dolf; *Ger.* ä′dôlf), 1870–1933, Austrian architect and writer. **2. Anita,** born 1893, U.S. writer.

loose (lo͞os), *adj.,* **loos·er, loos·est,** *adv., v.* **loosed, loos·ing.** —*adj.* **1.** free from anything that binds or restrains; unfettered: *At night one often sees a few loose cats prowling around ash cans or in alleyways.* **2.** free or released from fastening or attachment: *a loose end.* **3.** uncombined, as a chemical element. **4.** not bound together, as papers or flowers: *to wear one's hair loose.* **5.** not put up in a package or other container: *loose mushrooms.* **6.** available for disposal; unemployed; unappropriated: *loose funds.* **7.** lacking in reticence or power of restraint: *a loose tongue.* **8.** lax, as the bowels. **9.** free from moral restraint; lax in principle or conduct: *He is known for his loose business practices.* **10.** sexually promiscuous or wanton; unchaste: *a loose woman.* **11.** not firm, taut, or rigid: *a loose tooth; a loose rein.* **12.** relaxed or limber in nature: *He runs with a loose, open stride.* **13.** not fitting closely or tightly: *a loose sweater.* **14.** not close or compact in structure or arrangement; having spaces between the parts; open: *a loose weave.* **15.** having few restraining factors between associated constituents and allowing ample freedom for independent action: *a loose federation of city states.* **16.** (of earth, soil, etc.) not cohering: *loose sand.* **17.** not strict, exact, or precise: *loose thinking; a loose interpretation of the law.* **18.** *Sports.* **a.** having the players on a team positioned at fairly wide intervals, as in a football formation. **b.** (of a ball, hockey puck, etc.) not in the possession of either team; out of player control. **19. on the loose, a.** free; unconfined, as, esp., an escaped convict, circus animal, etc. **b.** *Informal.* unrestrained; dissolute: *a woman on the loose.*
—*adv.* **20.** in a loose manner; loosely (usually used in combination): *loose-fitting; loose-flowing.* **21. break loose,** to free oneself; escape: *The circus train became derailed, and many of the animals broke loose.* **22. cast loose, a.** to loosen or unfasten, as a vessel from a mooring. **b.** to send forth; set adrift or free: *He was cast loose at an early age to make his own way in the world.* **23. cut loose, a.** to release from domination or control. **b.** to become free, independent, etc. **c.** to abandon restraint: *After the rodeo they headed into town to cut loose on their winnings.* **24. let loose, a.** to free or become free. **b.** to yield; give way: *The guardrail let loose and we very nearly plunged over the edge.* **25. turn loose, a.** to release, as from confinement. **b.** to relieve of restraint: *The kindergarten teacher turned the children loose to do finger painting.*
—*v.t.* **26.** to let loose; free from bonds or restraint. **27.** to release, as from constraint, obligation, penalty, etc. **28.** *Chiefly Naut.* to set free from fastening or attachment: *loose a boat from its moorings.* **29.** to unfasten, undo, or untie, as a bond, fetter, or knot. **30.** to shoot; let fly: *to loose missiles at the invaders.* **31.** to make less tight; slacken or relax. **32.** to render less firmly fixed; lessen an attachment; loosen.
—*v.i.* **33.** to let go a hold. **34.** to hoist anchor; get under way. **35.** to shoot or let fly an arrow, bullet, etc. (often fol. by *off*): *to loose off at a flock of ducks.* **36.** *Obs.* to become loose; loosen. [ME *los, loos* < Scand; cf. Icel *lauss* loose, free, empty; c. OE *lēas* (see -LESS), D, G *los* loose, free] —**loose′ly,** *adv.* —**loose′ness,** *n.*
—**Syn. 1.** unbound, untied, unrestricted, unconfined. **10.** libertine, dissolute, licentious. **17.** vague, general, indefinite. **26.** loosen, unbind. **27.** liberate. **31.** ease. —**Ant. 1.** bound. **10.** chaste. **31.** tighten.

loose′ end′, 1. a part or piece left hanging, unattached, or unused: *Remind me to tack down that loose end on the stairway carpet.* **2.** an unsettled detail, as of a business matter: *The arrangements for the meeting have been made, except for a few loose ends.* **3. at loose ends, a.** in an uncertain or unsettled situation or position: *Ever since leaving the company he's been at loose ends.* **b.** undecided with regard to one's immediate plans: *He felt at loose ends, so he went for a walk.* Also, **at a loose end.**

loose-fit·ting (lo͞os′fit′ing), *adj.* (of a garment) fitting loosely; not following the contours of the body. Cf. **close-fitting.**

loose-foot·ed (lo͞os′fo͝ot′id), *adj.* *Naut.* (of a fore-and-aft sail) not having the foot bent to a boom.

loose-joint·ed (lo͞os′join′tid), *adj.* **1.** having loose joints. **2.** loosely built or framed; badly put together. **3.** having or marked by easy, free movement; limber.

loose′-joint hinge′ (lo͞os′joint′), a hinge having a knuckle formed from half of each flap, and with the upper half removable from the pin. Also called **heave-off hinge, lift-off hinge.**

loose-leaf (lo͞os′lēf′), *adj.* (of a book, notebook, etc.) consisting of individual leaves held in a binder (**loose′-leaf bind′er**) in such a way as to allow their removal without tearing.

loose-limbed (lo͞os′limd′), *adj.* having supple arms and legs: *a loose-limbed athlete.*

loos·en (lo͞o′sən), *v.t.* **1.** to unfasten or undo, as a bond or fetter. **2.** to make less tight; slacken or relax: *to loosen one's grasp.* **3.** to make less firmly fixed in place: *to loosen a tooth.* **4.** to let loose or set free from bonds, restraint, or constraint. **5.** to make less close or compact in structure or arrangement. **6.** to make less dense or coherent: *to loosen the soil in a garden.* **7.** to relieve (the bowels) of their constipated condition. **8.** to relax in strictness or severity, as restraint or discipline: *to loosen restrictions on trade.* —*v.i.* **9.** to become loose or looser (sometimes fol. by *up*): *His hold on the children loosened as they got older. Your shoes will loosen up with wear.* [ME *loosne.* See LOOSE, -EN[1]] —**loos′en·er,** *n.*

loose′ sen′tence, a sentence that does not end with the completion of its main clause, but continues with one or more subordinate clauses or other modifiers. Cf. **periodic sentence.**

loose′ smut′, *Plant Pathol.* a disease of cereal grasses, characterized by uncovered, powdery masses of spores which replace the affected heads, caused by smut fungi of the genus *Ustilago.*

loose·strife (lo͞os′strīf′), *n.* **1.** any of several primulaceous plants of the genus *Lysimachia,* as *L. vulgaris* (**yellow loosestrife**), having yellow flowers, or *L. quadrifolia* (**whorled loosestrife**), having leaves in whorls of four or five. **2.** any of several lythraceous herbs of the genus *Lythrum,* as *L. Salicaria* (**purple loosestrife**), having purple flowers. [LOOSE (V.) + STRIFE, mistranslation of L *lysimachia* (< Gk; see LYSI-, -MACHY), plant said to be named after a certain *Lysimakhos;* see -IA]

loose-tongued (lo͞os′tungd′), *adj.* unrestrained or irresponsible in speech; given to gossiping or chattering. [LOOSE + TONGUE + -ED[3]]

loot[1] (lo͞ot), *n.* **1.** spoils or plunder taken by pillaging, as in war. **2.** anything taken by dishonesty, force, stealth, etc.: *a burglar's loot.* **3.** *Informal.* a collection of valuable objects: *The children shouted and laughed as they opened their Christmas loot.* **4.** *Slang.* money: *You'll have a fine time spending all that loot.* **5.** act of looting or plundering: *to take part in the loot of a conquered city.* —*v.t.* **6.** to carry off or take (something) as loot: *to loot a nation's art treasures.* **7.** to despoil by taking loot; plunder or pillage (a city, house, etc.), as in war. **8.** to rob, as by burglary, corrupt practice in public office, etc.: *conspiring to loot the public treasury.* —*v.i.* **9.** to take loot; plunder: *The conquerors looted and robbed throughout the entire country.* [< Hindi *lūt,* akin to Skt *lo(p)tra* booty] —**loot′er,** *n.*
—**Syn. 1.** booty. **7.** sack, ransack.

loot[2] (lo͞ot), *v.* *Scot.* pt. of **let**[1]. [< ?]

lop[1] (lop), *v.,* **lopped, lop·ping,** *n.* —*v.t.* **1.** to cut off (branches, twigs, etc.) from a tree or other plant. **2.** to cut off (the head, limbs, etc.) from a person. **3.** to cut off the branches, twigs, etc., of (a tree or other plant). **4.** to eliminate unnecessary or excess parts of: *We had to lop off whole pages of the report before presenting it to the committee.* **5.** *Archaic.* to cut off the head, limbs, etc., of (a person). —*v.i.* **6.** to cut off branches, twigs, etc., as of a tree. **7.** to remove parts by or as by cutting. —*n.* **8.** parts or a part lopped off. **9.** (of trees) the smaller branches and twigs not useful as timber. [late ME *loppe* n. (def. 8), etymologically identified with OE *loppe* spider, both objects being marked by many projecting parts. See LOBSTER]

lop[2] (lop), *v.,* **lopped, lop·ping,** *adj.* —*v.i.* **1.** to hang loosely or limply; droop. **2.** to sway, move, or go in a drooping or heavy, awkward way. **3.** to move in short, quick leaps: *a rabbit lopping through the garden.* —*v.t.* **4.** to let hang or droop: *He lopped his arms at his sides in utter exhaustion.* —*adj.* **5.** hanging down limply or droopingly: *a rabbit with lop ears.* [v. use of obs. *lop* spider or *lop* dangling part of a tree (see LOP[1]); lit., to behave like a *lop,* i.e., to dangle, hang loosely. See LOB[1]]

Lo·pat·ni·kov (lō pat′ni kôf′; *Russ.* lo pät′ni kôf′), *n.* **Ni·co·lai Lvo·vich** (nē ko lī′ lvô′vich), born 1903, U.S. composer, born in Russia. Also, **Lo·pat′ni·koff′.**

lope (lōp), *v.,* **loped, lop·ing,** *n.* —*v.i.* **1.** to move or run with bounding steps, as a quadruped, or with a long, easy stride, as a person. **2.** to canter leisurely with a rather long, easy stride, as a horse. —*v.t.* **3.** to cause to lope, as a horse. —*n.* **4.** the act or the gait of loping. **5.** a long, easy stride. [< D *lopen* to run, c. G *laufen* to run, Icel *hlaupa* to jump. See LEAP]

lop-eared (lop′ērd′), *adj.* having ears that lop or hang down.

Lo·pe de Ve·ga (lō′pā də vā′gə; *Sp.* lô′pe the ve′gä). See **Vega, Lope de.**

lop·er (lō′pər), *n.* **1.** one who or that which lopes, as a horse with a loping gait. **2.** Also called **draw runner, draw slip.** *Furniture.* either of two runners coming forward to support a hinged leaf, as the slant front of a desk. [LOPE + -ER[1]]

Ló·pez (lō′pez; *Sp.* lô′pes), *n.* **Os·val·do** (ôs väl′dō), (*Osvaldo López Arellano*), born 1921, Honduran air force colonel: president of Honduras since 1963.

Ló·pez de A·ya·la (lô′peth the ä yä′lä), **Pe·dro** (pe′thrō), 1332–1407, Spanish writer and statesman.

Ló·pez de Le·gaz·pe (lô′peth the le gäth′pe, lô′pes the le gäs′pe), **Mi·guel** (mē gel′), 1510?–1572, Spanish conqueror and colonizer of the Philippines 1565: founder of Manila 1571. Also, **Ló′pez de Le·gas′pi** (le gäs′pē).

Ló·pez Ma·te·os (lô′pes mä te′ôs), **A·dol·fo** (ä thôl′fō), born 1910, Mexican lawyer and politician: president of Mexico 1958–64.

Ló·pez y Fuen·tes (lô′pes ē fwen′tes), **Gre·go·rio** (gre gô′ryô), born 1895, Mexican writer.

loph·o·branch (lof′ə brangk′, lō′fə-), *adj.* **1.** belonging or pertaining to the *Lophobranchii,* the group of fishes comprising the pipefishes, sea horses, snipefishes, trumpetfishes, etc. —*n.* **2.** a lophobranch fish. [< NL *Lophobranch(ii)* name of the group < Gk *lóph(os)* crest, tuft + *bránchi(a)* BRANCHIA + L -ī nom. pl. n. suffix] —**loph·o·bran·chi·ate** (lof′ə brang′kē it, -āt′, lō′fə-), *adj., n.*

loph·o·dont (lof′ə dont′, lō′fə-), *adj.* having molar teeth with crowns in the form of transverse ridges. Cf. **bunodont.** [< Gk *lóph(os)* a crest, tuft + -ODONT]

loph·o·phore (lof′ə fōr′, -fôr′, lō′fə-), *n.* **1.** the ring of ciliated tentacles encircling the mouth of a bryozoan or phoronid. **2.** a similar organ in a brachiopod, composed of two ciliated, spirally coiled tentacles. [< Gk *lópho(s)* a crest, ridge + -PHORE] —**lo·phoph·o·ral** (lə fof′ər əl), *adj.*

lop·o·lith (lop′ə lith), *n.* *Geol.* a mass of igneous rock similar to a laccolith but concave downward rather than upward. [< Gk *lopó(s)* shell, husk + -LITH]

lop·per[1] (lop′ər), *n.* one who or that which lops. [LOP[1] + -ER[1]]

lop·per[2] (lop′ər), *v.i., v.t.* *Scot. and North Central U.S.* (esp. of milk) to curdle or coagulate. [ME *lopir* (v.), equiv. to *lop-* (< Scand; cf. Icel *hlaup* coagulation) + *-ir,* var. of -ER[6]]

lop·py (lop′ē), *adj.* **-pi·er, pi·est.** lopping; hanging limply: *awkward, loppy arms.* [LOP[2] + -Y[1]]
—**Syn.** flabby, flaccid, drooping. —**Ant.** erect.

lop·seed (lop′sēd′), *n.* a weedy herb, *Phryma Leptostachya,* of Asia and North America. [LOP[2] + SEED]

lop·sid·ed (lop′sī′did), *adj.* **1.** lopping or inclining to one side. **2.** heavier, larger, or more developed on one side than on the other; unevenly balanced; unsymmetrical. [LOP[2] + SIDED] —**lop′sid′ed·ly,** *adv.* —**lop′sid′ed·ness,** *n.*

lop·stick (lop′stik′), *n.* *Canadian.* a tree trimmed of all but its topmost branches to serve as a landmark or marker. Also, **lobstick.** [LOP[1] + STICK[1]]

loq., loquitur.

lo·qua·cious (lō kwā′shəs), *adj.* **1.** talking or disposed to talk much or freely; talkative; chattering; babbling; garrulous: *Under the influence of the drug, she became extremely loquacious.* **2.** characterized by or showing a disposition toward excessive talk; wordy: *easily the most loquacious play of the season.* [LOQUACI(TY) + -OUS] —**lo·qua′cious·ly,** *adv.* —**lo·qua′cious·ness,** *n.*
—**Syn. 1.** verbose, voluble, wordy. See **talkative.**

lo·quac·i·ty (lō kwas′i tē), *n., pl.* **-ties. 1.** the state of being loquacious; talkativeness; garrulity. **2.** an instance of talkativeness or garrulity; a loquacious flow of talk: *Her sudden loquacities have become very tiresome.* [< L *loquācitās* talkativeness, equiv. to *loquāci-* (s. of *loquāx*) talkative + *-tās* -TY[2]]

lo·quat (lō′kwot, -kwat), *n.* **1.** a small, evergreen, malaceous tree, *Eriobotrya japonica,* native to China and Japan, but cultivated elsewhere for ornament and for its yellow, plumlike fruit. **2.** the fruit itself. [< Chin (Cantonese) *lō-kwat,* lit., rush orange]

lo·qui·tur (lō′kwi to͞or′; *Eng.* lok′wi tər), *Latin.* he speaks; she speaks.

Lo·ra (lōr′ə, lôr′ə), *n.* a girl's given name, form of **Laura.**

Lo·rain (lō rān′, lô-), *n.* a port in N Ohio, on Lake Erie. 68,932 (1960).

Lo·raine (lə rān′, lō-, lô-), *n.* a girl's given name, form of **Lorraine.**

lo·ral[1] (lōr′əl, lôr′-), *adj.* of or pertaining to lore, knowledge, learning, etc. [LORE[1] + -AL[1]]

lo·ral[2] (lōr′əl, lôr′-), *adj. Zool.* of or pertaining to a lore. [LORE[2] + -AL[1]]

Lo·ral (lōr′əl, lôr′-), *n.* a boy's given name.

lo·ran (lōr′ən, lôr′-), *n.* a device by which a navigator can locate his position by determining the time displacement between radio signals from two known stations. [*lo(ng) ra(nge) n(avigation)*]

Lor·ca (lôr′kə; *Sp.* lôr′kä), *n.* **1.** See **García Lorca. 2.** a city in SE Spain. 71,757 (est. 1956).

lord (lôrd), *n.* **1.** a person who has dominion over others; a master, chief, or ruler. **2.** a person who exercises authority from property rights; an owner or possessor of land, houses, etc. **3.** a person who is a leader or has great influence in his chosen profession: *the lords of the theatrical world; one of the great lords of banking.* **4.** a feudal superior; the proprietor of a manor. **5.** a titled nobleman or peer; a person whose ordinary appellation contains by courtesy the title *Lord* or some higher title. **6. Lords,** the Lords Spiritual and Lords Temporal comprising the House of Lords. **7.** (*cap.*) *Brit.* **a.** the title of certain high officials (used with some other title or the like): *Lord Mayor of London.* **b.** the formally polite title of a bishop: *Lord Bishop of Durham.* **c.** the title informally substituted for marquis, earl, viscount, etc., as in the use of *Lord Kitchener* for *Earl Kitchener.* **8.** (*cap.*) the Supreme Being; God; Jehovah. **9.** (*cap.*) the Saviour, Jesus Christ. **10.** *Astrol.* a planet having dominating influence. —*interj.* **11.** (*often cap.*) (used in exclamatory phrases to express surprise, elation, etc.): *Lord, what a beautiful day!* —*v.i.* **12.** to play the lord; assume airs of importance and authority; behave arrogantly or dictatorially; domineer (usually fol. by *it*): *to lord it over someone.* [ME *lord, loverd,* OE *hlāford, hlāfweard,* lit., loaf-keeper. See LOAF[1], WARD] —**lord′like′,** *adj.*

Lord′ Bal′timore cake′, a yellow layer cake, using only the yolks of eggs and having a fruit-nut filling consisting of pecans, almonds, maraschino cherries, and macaroon crumbs. Cf. **Lady Baltimore cake.**

Lord′ Chan′cellor, the highest judicial officer of the British crown: law adviser of the ministry, keeper of the great seal, presiding officer in the House of Lords, etc. Also called **Lord′ High′ Chan′cellor.**

Lord′ Chief′ Jus′tice, the presiding judge of Britain's High Court of Justice, the superior court of record for both criminal and civil cases.

Lord′ Haw′-Haw (hô′hô′). See **Joyce, William.**

Lord′ Howe′ Is′land, an island in the S Pacific, E of Australia: a dependency of New South Wales. 249 (1961); 5 sq. mi.

lord·ing (lôr′ding), *n. Archaic.* **1.** lord. **2.** Often, **lordings.** lords; sirs; gentlemen (often used as a term of address). [ME; OE *hlāfording* prince, lit., offspring of a lord, equiv. to *hlāford* LORD + *-ing* patronymic suffix]

lord-in-wait·ing (lôrd′in wā′ting), *n., pl.* **lords-in-wait·ing.** a nobleman in attendance on a British monarch or the Prince of Wales.

Lord′ Jim′, a novel (1900) by Joseph Conrad.

lord·less (lôrd′lis), *adj.* having no lord. [ME *lordles,* OE *hlāfordlēas.* See LORD, -LESS]

Lord′ Lieuten′ant, *Brit.* **1.** the title of various high officials holding authority deputed from a sovereign. **2.** (formerly) the viceroy in Ireland. —**Lord′ Lieuten′ancy,** *n.*

lord·ling (lôrd′ling), *n.* a young or unimportant lord; petty or insignificant lord. [ME; see LORD, -LING[1]]

lord·ly (lôrd′lē), *adj.,* **-li·er, -li·est,** *adv.* —*adj.* **1.** suitable for a lord, as trappings, ceremonies, etc.; grand or magnificent. **2.** insolently imperious; haughty; arrogant; overbearing: *lordly contempt.* **3.** of or pertaining to a lord or lords. **4.** having the character or attributes of a lord. **5.** befitting a lord, as actions: *elegant, lordly manners.* —*adv.* **6.** Also, **lord′lily.** in the manner of a lord. [ME; OE *hlāfordlīc.* See LORD, -LY] —**lord′li·ness,** *n.*

—**Syn. 1.** majestic, regal, dignified, noble, lofty. **2.** domineering. —**Ant. 2.** meek.

Lord′ May′or, (in Britain) the mayor of certain cities or the chief municipal officer of certain boroughs: *Lord Mayor of London; Lord Mayor of York.*

Lord′ of hosts′, Jehovah; God. Also, **Lord′ of Hosts′.**

Lord′ of Misrule′, (in England) a person formerly chosen to direct the Christmas revels and sports.

lor·do·sis (lôr dō′sis), *n. Pathol.* forward curvature of the spine. [< NL < Gk: lit., a bending back, equiv. to *lord(ós)* bent backwards + *-ōsis* -OSIS] —**lor·dot·ic** (lôr dot′ik), *adj.*

Lord′ Protec′tor, protector (def. 2b).

Lord′ Pro′vost, the chief magistrate of any of certain large cities in Scotland.

lords-and-la·dies (lôrdz′ən lā′dēz), *n., pl.* **-la·dies.** cuckoopint.

Lords·burg (lôrdz′bûrg), *n.* a town in SW New Mexico. 3436 (1960).

Lord's′ day′, the, Sunday.

lord·ship (lôrd′ship), *n.* **1.** (*often cap.*) a British term of respect used when speaking of or to judges or certain noblemen (usually prec. by *his* or *your*). **2.** the state or dignity of a lord. **3.** *Hist.* **a.** the authority or power of a lord. **b.** the domain of a lord. [ME; OE *hlāfordscipe.* See LORD, -SHIP]

Lord′ Spir′itual, *pl.* **Lords Spiritual.** a bishop or archbishop belonging to the House of Lords. Cf. **Lord Temporal.** [late ME]

Lord's′ Prayer′, the, the prayer given by Jesus to His disciples, and beginning with the words *Our Father.* Matt. 6:9–13; Luke 11:2–4.

Lord's′ Sup′per, the, 1. the sacrament in commemoration of the Last Supper; Communion; Mass; Eucharist. **2.** See **Last Supper.**

Lord's′ ta′ble, the. See **communion table.**

Lord′ Tem′poral, *pl.* **Lords Temporal.** a member of the House of Lords who is not a member of the clergy. Cf. **Lord Spiritual.** [late ME]

lore[1] (lōr, lôr), *n.* **1.** the body of knowledge, esp. of a traditional, anecdotal, or popular nature, on a particular subject: *the lore of herbs.* **2.** learning, knowledge, or erudition. **3.** *Archaic.* **a.** the process or act of teaching; instruction. **b.** that which is taught; lesson. [ME; OE *lār;* c. D *leer,* G *Lehre* teaching. See LEARN] —**lore′less,** *adj.*

—**Syn. 1.** wisdom. See **learning.**

lore[2] (lōr, lôr), *n. Zool.* the space between the eye and the bill of a bird, or a corresponding space in other animals, as serpents. [< NL *lōr(um),* special use of L *lōrum* thong, strap]

Lo·re (lōr′ə, lôr′ə), *n.* a girl's given name.

Lor·e·lei (lôr′ə lī′; *Ger.* lō′ʀə lī′), *n.* **1.** a quasi-legendary nymph of the Rhine who lured sailors to shipwreck on her rock by singing: a creation of Klemens Brentano in a poem of 1800. **2.** a girl's given name. [< G, var. of *Lurlei,* cliff overlooking Rhine river, thought to be abode of a nymph]

Lo·rel·la (lō rel′ə, lô-), *n.* a girl's given name, form of **Laura.** Also, **Lo·relle** (lō rel′, lô-).

Lo·ren (lōr′ən, lôr′-), *n.* a boy's given name, form of **Lawrence.** Also, **Lorin.**

Lo·re·na (lō rē′nə, lô-), *n.* a girl's given name. Also, **Lorna.**

Lo·rence (lōr′əns, lôr′-), *n.* a boy's given name, form of **Laurence.**

Lo·rentz (lōr′ents, lôr′-; *Du.* lō′ʀents), *n.* **Hen·drik An·toon** (hen′drik än′tōn), 1853–1928, Dutch physicist: Nobel prize 1902.

Lo′rentz-Fitz·Ger′ald contrac′tion (lōr′ents-fits jer′əld, lôr′-), *Physics.* See **FitzGerald contraction.**

Lo′rentz transforma′tion, *Physics.* one of a series of equations in the special theory of relativity that relate position and time in two frames of reference moving uniformly with respect to each other, usually at speeds near the speed of light. Cf. **Galilean transformation.** [named after Hendrik LORENTZ]

Lo·renz (lōr′ənz, lôr′-; *Ger.* lō′ʀents), *n.* **A·dolf** (ä′dolf; *Ger.* ä′dôlf), 1854–1946, Austrian orthopedic surgeon.

Lo·ren·zet·ti (lôr′ən zet′ē; *It.* lô′ʀen dzet′tē), *n.* **Am·bro·gio** (äm brô′jô), c1319–48, and his brother, **Pie·tro** (pye′trô), c1305–48, Italian painters.

Lo·ren·zo (lō ren′zō, lô-), *n.* **Saint.** See **Lawrence, Saint.**

Lo·re·stan (lōr′i stän′, -stan′, lôr′-), *n.* Luristan.

Lo·ret·ta (lō ret′ə, lô-), *n.* a girl's given name, form of **Laura.** Also, **Lo·rette** (lō ret′, lô-).

lor·gnette (lôrn yet′), *n.* **1.** a pair of eyeglasses mounted on a handle. **2.** a pair of opera glasses held in the hand by a handle. [< F, deriv. of *lorgner* to eye furtively; see -ETTE]

lor·gnon (*Fr.* lôr nyôɴ′), *n., pl.* **-gnons** (*Fr.* -nyôɴ′). **1.** an eyeglass or a pair of eyeglasses. **2.** See **opera glasses.** [< F: *lorgn(er)* (see LORGNETTE) + *-on* n. suffix]

lo·ri·ca (lō rī′kə, lô-, lə-), *n., pl.* **-cae** (-sē, -kē). **1.** *Zool.* a hard protective case or sheath, as the protective coverings secreted by certain infusorians. **2.** a cuirass or corselet, originally of leather. [def. 1: < NL, special use of L *lōrīca* corselet (orig. of leather), akin to *lōrum* thong; def. 2: < L]

lor·i·cate (lôr′ə kāt′, -kit, lor′-), *adj. Zool.* covered with a lorica. Also, **lor′i·cat′ed.** [< L *lōrīcāt(us).* See LORICA, -ATE[1]] —**lor′i·ca′tion,** *n.*

Lo·rient (lô ʀyäɴ′), *n.* a seaport in NW France, on the Bay of Biscay. 63,924 (1962).

lor·i·keet (lôr′ə kēt′, lor′-, lôr′ə kēt′, lor′-), *n.* any of various small lories. [LORY + (PARRA)KEET]

lor·i·mer (lôr′ə mər), *n.* a craftsman who makes hardware for harnesses and riding habits, as bits, spurs, etc. Also, **lor·i·ner** (lôr′ə nər). [ME < LL *lōrām(entum)* thong (L *lōrum* reins, thong + *-mentum* -MENT) + ME *-er* -ER[1]]

Lo·rin (lōr′in, lôr′-), *n.* a boy's given name, form of **Lawrence.** Also, **Loren.**

Lo·ring (lōr′ing, lôr′-), *n.* a boy's given name.

lo·ris (lōr′is, lôr′-), *n., pl.* **-ris. 1.** Also called **slender loris.** a small, slender, tailless, large-eyed, nocturnal lemur, *Loris gracilis,* of southern India and Ceylon. **2.** Also called **slow loris.** a similar but stockier lemur of the genus *Nycticebus,* of southeastern Asia. [< NL < D *loeris* booby (now obs.), earlier *loerisch* clownish, equiv. to *loer* stupid person (< F *lourd* < L *lūridus* LURID) + *-isch* -ISH[1]]

lorn (lôrn), *adj.* **1.** *Poetic.* forsaken, desolate, bereft, or forlorn. **2.** *Obs.* lost, ruined, or undone. [ME; OE *loren,* ptp. of *-lēosan* LOSE (recorded in compounds)] —**lorn′ness,** *n.*

Lor·na (lôr′nə), *n.* a girl's given name. Also, **Lorena.**

Lor·raine (lō rān′, lô-; *Fr.* lô ʀen′), *n.* **1. Claude.** Also, **Lorrain.** (*Claude Gelée*), 1600–82, French painter. **2.** a medieval kingdom in W Europe along the Moselle, Meuse, and Rhine rivers. **3.** a region in NE France, once included in this kingdom: a former province. Cf. **Alsace-Lorraine. 4.** a girl's given name.

Lorraine′ cross′. See **cross of Lorraine.**

Lor·rie (lôr′ē), *n.* a girl's given name, form of **Laura.**

lor·ry (lôr′ē, lor′ē), *n., pl.* **-ries. 1.** *Brit.* a motor truck, esp. a large one. **2.** any of various vehicles or cars running on rails, as for transporting material in a mine or factory. **3.** a long, low, horse-drawn wagon without sides, common in England. [akin to dial. *lurry* pull, drag, lug]

Lo·rus (lōr′əs, lôr′-), *n.* a boy's given name.

lo·ry (lōr′ē, lôr′ē), *n., pl.* **-ries.** any of several small, usually brilliantly colored, Australasian parrots having the tongue bordered with a brushlike fringe for feeding on nectar and fruit juices. [< D, var. of *lori, loeri* < Malay *lūrī,* dial. var. of *nūrī*]

los·a·ble (lo͞o′zə bəl), *adj.* that may be lost. [LOSE + -ABLE] —**los′a·ble·ness,** *n.*

Los Al·a·mi·tos (lôs al′ə mē′tōs, los), a town in S California. 4312 (1960).

Los Al·a·mos (lôs al′ə mōs′, los), a town in central New Mexico: atomic research center. 12,584 (1960).

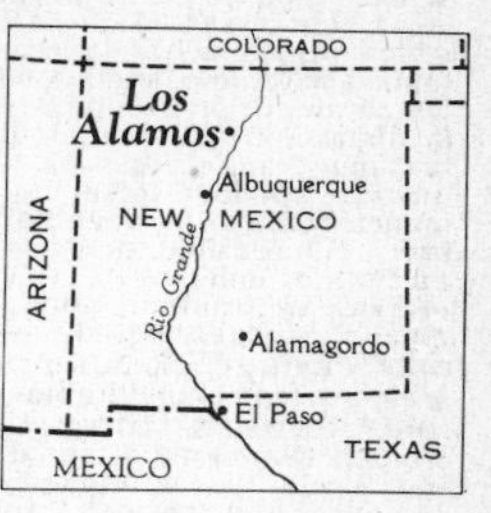

Los Al′tos Hills′ (lôs al′təs, los), a town in W California. 3412 (1960).

Los An·ge·le·no (lôs an′jə lē′nō, los), an inhabitant or native of Los Angeles. Also called **Los An·ge·le·an** (lôs an′jə-lē′ən, los).

Los An·ge·les (lôs an′jə ləs, -lēz′, los *or, often,* lôs ang′gə ləs, -lēz′, los), a seaport in SW California. 2,966,763; with suburbs, 6,977,000; 452 sq. mi.

Los Ba·nos (lôs ban′əs, los), a town in central California. 5272 (1960).

lose (lo͞oz), *v.,* **lost, los·ing.** —*v.t.* **1.** to come to be without (something in one's possession or care), through accident, theft, etc., so that there is no hope of recovery: *I'm sure I've merely misplaced my hat, not lost it.* **2.** to fail inadvertently to retain (something) in such a way that it cannot be immediately recovered: *I just lost a dime under this sofa.* **3.** to suffer the deprivation of: *to lose one's job; to lose one's life.* **4.** to be bereaved of by death: *to lose a sister.* **5.** to fail to keep, preserve, or maintain: *to lose one's balance; to lose one's figure.* **6.** to give up; forfeit the possession of: *to lose a fortune at the gaming table.* **7.** to cease to have, esp. as a result of will power, mastery, or the like: *to lose one's fear of the dark.* **8.** to bring to destruction or ruin (usually used passively): *Ship and crew were lost.* **9.** to have slip from sight, hearing, attention, etc.: *to lose a face in a crowd.* **10.** to stray from or become ignorant of (one's way, directions, etc.): *He lost his bearings in the strange city and had to take a cab back to his hotel.* **11.** to leave far behind in a pursuit, race, etc.; outstrip: *He managed to lose the other runners on the final lap of the race.* **12.** to use to no purpose; waste: *to lose time in waiting.* **13.** to fail to have, get, catch, etc.; miss: *to lose a bargain.* **14.** to fail to win (a prize, stake, etc.): *to lose a bet.* **15.** to be defeated in (a game, lawsuit, battle, etc.): *He has lost very few cases in his career as a lawyer.* **16.** to cause the loss of: *The delay lost the battle for them.* **17.** to let (oneself) go astray, miss the way, etc.: *We lost ourselves in the woods.* **18.** to allow (oneself) to become absorbed or engrossed in something and oblivious to all else: *I had lost myself in thought.* **19.** (of a physician) to fail to preserve the life of (a patient). **20.** (of a woman) to fail to be delivered of (a live baby) because of miscarriage, complications in childbirth, etc. —*v.i.* **21.** to suffer loss: *to lose on a contract.* **22.** to suffer defeat or fail to win, as in a contest, race, game, or the like: *We played well but we lost. He had often loved and invariably lost.* **23.** to depreciate in effectiveness or in some other essential quality: *a classic that loses in translation.* **24. lose face.** See **face** (def. 27). **25. lose out,** *Informal.* to suffer defeat or loss; fail to obtain something desired: *He got through the preliminaries but lost out in the finals.* [ME *losen,* OE *-lēosan,* r. ME *lesen,* OE *-lēosan* (cf. CHOOSE r. *chese*); c. G *(ver)lieren,* Goth *(fra)liusan* to lose. See LOSS]

lo·sel (lō′zəl, lo͞o′-, loz′əl), *Archaic.* —*n.* **1.** a worthless person; scoundrel. —*adj.* **2.** worthless or useless. [ME: lit., one who is lost, equiv. to *los-* (ptp. s. of LOSE) + *-el* n. suffix of personalization]

los·er (lo͞o′zər), *n.* **1.** a person, team, nation, etc., that loses: *The visiting team was the loser in three out of five games in the series.* **2.** *Informal.* **a.** a person who has been convicted of a misdemeanor or, esp., a felony: *a two-time loser.* **b.** a person who has failed at an activity, as a business or social endeavor, career, etc.: *He's a three-time loser at marriage.* **3.** *Slang.* someone or something that is marked by consistently bad quality, performance, etc.: *Don't bother to see that film; it's a real loser. That girl he dated last weekend was such a loser.* [LOSE + -ER[1]]

Los Ga·tos (lôs gat′əs, los), a town in W California. 9036 (1960).

los·ing (lo͞o′zing), *adj.* **1.** that loses. —*n.* **2. losings,** losses. [LOSE + -ING[2], -ING[1]] —**los′ing·ly,** *adv.*

los′ing haz′ard. See under **hazard** (def. 10).

Los Mo·chis (lôs mô′chēs, los), a city in W Mexico. 21,491 (1960).

loss (lôs, los), *n.* **1.** detriment or disadvantage from failure to keep, have, or get: *to bear the loss of a robbery.* **2.** that which is lost: *The loss from the robbery amounted to a week's salary for all employees.* **3.** an amount or number lost: *The loss of life increased each day.* **4.** the state of being deprived of or of being without something that one has had: *to suffer the loss of one's friends.* **5.** the accidental or inadvertent losing of something dropped, misplaced, stolen, etc.: *to discover the loss of a document.* **6.** a losing by defeat; failure to win: *the loss of a bet.* **7.** failure to make good use of something, as time; waste. **8.** failure to preserve or maintain: *loss of engine speed at high altitudes.* **9.** destruction or ruin: *the loss of a ship by fire.* **10.** a thing or a number of related things that are lost or destroyed to some extent: *Most buildings in the burned district were a total loss.* **11.** *Mil.* **a.** the losing of soldiers by death, capture, etc. **b.** Often, **losses.** the number of soldiers so lost. **12.** *Insurance.* occurrence of an event, as death or damage of property, for which the insurer makes indemnity under the terms of a policy. **13.** *Elect.* a measure of the power lost in a system, as by conversion to heat, expressed as a relation between power input and power output, as the ratio of or difference between the two quantities. **14. at a loss, a.** at less than cost; at a financial loss. **b.** in a state of bewilderment or uncertainty; perplexed: *We were completely at a loss for an answer to the problem.* [ME; OE *los* destruction; c. Icel *los* breaking up. See LOSE, LOOSE]

—**Syn. 4.** privation, deprivation. —**Ant. 1.** gain.

loss′ lead′er, a popular article which is sold at a loss for the purpose of attracting trade to a retail store. Cf. **leader** (def. 6).

loss′ ra′tio, *Insurance.* the ratio of the losses paid or accrued by an insurer to premiums earned, usually for a period of one year.

lost (lôst, lost), *adj.* **1.** no longer possessed or retained: *lost friends.* **2.** no longer to be found: *lost articles.* **3.** having gone astray or missed the way; bewildered as to place, direction, etc.: *Several lost children were reported.* **4.** not used to good purpose, as opportunities, time, labor, etc.; wasted: *a lost advantage.* **5.** being that which someone has failed to win: *a lost prize.* **6.** attended with defeat: *a lost battle.* **7.** destroyed or ruined: *lost ships.* **8.** preoccupied; rapt: *He seems lost in thought.* **9.** distracted; distraught; desperate; hopeless: *His eyes had that frantic, lost look of a man who is trapped and afraid.* **10. lost to, a.** no longer belonging to. **b.** no longer possible or open to: *The opportunity was lost to him.* **c.** insensible to: *lost to all sense of duty.* —*v.* **11.** pt. and pp. of **lose.**

—**Syn. 1.** forfeited, gone, missing. **3.** confused, perplexed. **4.** squandered. —**Ant. 1.** found.

lost′ cause′, a cause that has been defeated or for which defeat is inevitable.

Lost′ Genera′tion, 1. the generation of men and women who came of age during or immediately following World War I: viewed, as a result of their war experiences and the social upheaval of the time, as having found themselves without cultural or emotional stability. **2.** a group of American writers of this generation, including Ernest Hemingway, F. Scott Fitzgerald, and John Dos Passos.

lost′ mo′tion, *Mach.* **1.** motion of a machine or mechanism, esp. a reciprocating one, during which no useful work is performed. **2.** motion between parts in an assembly due to manufacturing tolerances, adjustments, slip, or wear.

Lost′ Ple′iad. See under **Pleiades** (def. 1).

lost′ riv′er, a river that flows into an underground passage or sinkhole.

lost′ tribes′, the members of the 10 tribes of ancient Israel who were taken into captivity in 722 B.C. by Sargon II and are believed never to have returned to Palestine.

lost′-wax′ proc′ess (lôst′waks′, lost′-), *Foundry.* a process of casting in which a refractory mold is built up around a pattern of wax and then baked so as to melt and drain off the wax; investment casting. Also called **cire perdue.** [trans. of F *cire perdue*]

lot (lot), *n., v.,* **lot·ted, lot·ting,** *adv.* —*n.* **1.** one of a set of objects, as straws, pebbles, etc., drawn or thrown from a container to decide a question or choice by chance. **2.** the casting or drawing of such objects as a method of deciding something: *to choose a person by lot.* **3.** the decision or choice made by such a method. **4.** allotted share or portion: *to receive one's lot of an inheritance.* **5.** the portion in life assigned by fate or Providence; one's fate, fortune, or destiny: *Her lot had not been a happy one.* **6.** a distinct portion or piece of land: *a building lot.* **7.** a piece of land forming a part of a district, city, or other community. **8.** *Motion Pictures.* the site of a motion picture being filmed, esp. a studio. **9.** a distinct portion or parcel of anything, as of merchandise: *The furniture was to be auctioned off in 20 lots.* **10.** a number of things or persons collectively: *What shall we do with this lot of recruits?* **11.** *Informal.* kind of person; sort: *He's a bad lot.* **12.** Often, **lots.** *Informal.* a great many or a great deal: *a lot of books; lots of money.* **13.** *Chiefly Brit.* a tax or duty. **14. cast** or **cast in one's lot with,** to ally oneself with; share the life and fortunes of: *She had cast in her lot with the bohemian element.* **15. draw** or **cast lots,** to settle a question by the use of lots: *They drew lots to see who would go first.* **16. the lot,** *Informal.* the constituents of a class, group, etc., taken as a whole: *He dismissed the lot of them as hypocrites.* —*v.t.* **17.** to divide or distribute by lot (sometimes fol. by *out*): *to lot furniture for sale; to lot out apples by the basketful.* **18.** to assign to one as his lot; allot. **19.** to divide into lots, as land. **20.** *Obs.* to cast or draw lots for. —*v.i.* **21.** to draw lots. —*adv.* **22.** Often, **lots.** *Informal.* a great deal; greatly: *Thanks a lot for the ride. I care lots about my family.* [ME; OE *hlot;* c. D *lot,* Icel *hlutr;* akin to OE *hlīet,* G *Los,* Icel *hlaut,* Goth *hlauts*] —**lot′ter,** *n.*

—**Syn. 4.** part, quota. **7.** plot, parcel. **10.** group, crowd, gang.

Lot (lot), *n.* the nephew of Abraham. His wife was changed into a pillar of salt for looking back during their flight from Sodom. Gen. 13:1–12,19.

Lot (lôt), *n.* **1.** a river in S France, flowing W to the Garonne. 300 mi. long. **2.** a department in S France. 149,929 (1962); 2018 sq. mi. *Cap.:* Cahors.

lot., (in prescriptions) a lotion. [< L *lōtio*]

lo·ta (lō′tə), *n.* (in India) a small vessel for water, usually of brass or copper and round in shape. Also, **lo′tah.** [< Hindi *lotā*]

L'O·tage (*Fr.* lô tȧzh′). See **Hostage, The.**

lote (lōt), *n.* *Archaic.* lotus. [< L *lōtus*]

lote′ bush′. See **Texas jujube.**

Lot-et-Ga·ronne (lô tā gȧ rôn′), *n.* a department in SW France. 275,028 (1962); 2079 sq. mi. *Cap.:* Agen.

loth (lōth, lōth), *adj.* loath.

Lo·tha (lō′thə), *n.* a girl's given name.

Lo·thair I (lō thâr′, -târ′), A.D. 795?–855, king of Germany 840–843; emperor of the Holy Roman Empire 840–855 (son of Louis I).

Lothair II, (*"the Saxon"*), c1070–1137, king of Germany and emperor of the Holy Roman Empire 1125–37.

Lo·thar·i·o (lō thâr′ē ō′), *n., pl.* **-thar·i·os. 1.** (*sometimes l.c.*) a charming man who seduces and deceives women; libertine; rake. **2.** a young seducer in Nicholas Rowe's tragedy *The Fair Penitent* (1703).

Lo·thi·ans (lō′thē ənz, -thē-), *n.pl.* **The,** the three counties in SW Scotland: East Lothian, Midlothian, West Lothian.

loth·ly (lōth′lē, lōth′-), *adv.* *Rare.* loathly[1].

loth·some (lōth′səm, lōth′-), *adj.* *Obs.* loathsome.

Lo·ti (lô tē′), *n.* **Pierre** (pyer), (*Louis Marie Julien Viaud*), 1850–1923, French novelist.

lo·tic (lō′tik), *adj.* pertaining to or living in flowing water. [< L *lōt*(*us*) a washing, bathing (see LOMENTUM) + -IC]

lo·tion (lō′shən), *n.* **1.** *Pharm.* a liquid, usually aqueous or sometimes alcoholic preparation containing insoluble material in the form of a suspension or emulsion, intended for external application without rubbing, in such skin conditions as itching, infection, allergy, pain, or the like. **2.** a liquid cosmetic, usually containing agents for soothing or softening the skin, esp. that of the face or hands: *after-shave lotion; hand lotion.* [< L *lōtiōn-* (s. of *lōtiō*) a washing. See LOTIC, -ION]

Lo·tis (lō′tis), *n.* *Class. Myth.* a nymph who was changed into a lotus tree.

lo·toph·a·gi (lə tof′ə jī′), *n.pl.* *Class. Myth.* lotus-eaters. [< L < Gk *Lōtophágoi.* See LOTUS-EATER]

lot·ter·y (lot′ə rē), *n., pl.* **-ter·ies. 1.** a gambling game or method of raising money, as for some public, charitable purpose, in which a large number of tickets are sold and a drawing is held for certain prizes. **2.** any scheme for the distribution of prizes by chance. **3.** any happening or process that is or appears to be determined by chance: *the defeatist attitude that life is a lottery.* [< MD *loterije* (whence also F *loterie*). See LOT, -ERY]

Lot·tie (lot′ē), *n.* a girl's given name, form of **Charlotte.** Also, **Lot·ta** (lot′ə), **Lot′ty.**

lot·to (lot′ō), *n.* a game of chance in which a leader draws numbered disks at random from a stock and the players cover the corresponding numbers on their cards, the winner being the first to cover five in a row. [< It < Gmc; see LOT]

lo·tus (lō′təs), *n., pl.* **-tus·es. 1.** a plant believed to be a jujube or elm, referred to in Greek legend as yielding a fruit which induced a state of dreamy and contented forgetfulness in those who ate it. **2.** the fruit itself. **3.** any aquatic, nymphaceous plant of the genus *Nelumbo,* having shieldlike leaves and showy, solitary flowers usually projecting above the water. **4.** any of several water lilies of the genus *Nymphaea.* **5.** a decorative motif derived from such a plant and used widely in ancient art, as on the capitals of Egyptian columns. **6.** any shrubby, leguminous herb of the genus *Lotus,* having red, pink, or white flowers. Also, **lo′tos.** [< L < Gk *lōtós* the lotus plant]

Lotus (def. 5)

Lo·tus (lō′təs), *n.* a girl's given name.

lo·tus-eat·er (lō′təs ē′tər), *n.* **1.** *Class. Myth.* a member of a people whom Odysseus found existing in a state of languorous forgetfulness induced by their eating of the fruit of the legendary lotus; one of the lotophagi. **2.** one who leads a life of dreamy, indolent ease, indifferent to the busy world; daydreamer. [sing. of *lotus-eaters,* trans. of Gk *Lōtophágoi,* n. use of masc. pl. of *lōtophágos* lotus-eating. See LOTUS, -PHAGOUS]

Lo′tus of the Good′ Law′, *Buddhism.* Saddharma-Pundarika. Also called **Lo′tus of the True′ Law′.**

Lo·tze (lōt′sə; *Ger.* lō′tsə), *n.* **Ru·dolf Her·mann** (ro͞o′dolf hûr′mən; *Ger.* ro͞o′dôlf her′män), 1817–1881, German philosopher.

Lou (lo͞o), *n.* **1.** a boy's given name, form of **Louis. 2.** a girl's given name, form of **Louise.**

loud (loud), *adj.* **1.** striking strongly upon the organs of hearing, as sound, noise, the voice, etc.; strongly audible: *loud talking; loud thunder.* **2.** making, emitting, or uttering strongly audible sounds: *a quartet of loud trombones.* **3.** full of sound or noise; resounding: *They conversed in loud whispers.* **4.** clamorous, vociferous, or blatant: *a loud party; a loud demonstration.* **5.** emphatic or insistent: *to be loud in one's praises; a loud denial.* **6.** garish, conspicuous, or ostentatious, as colors, dress, the wearer of garish dress, etc.: *to have a penchant for loud ties; to be known as a loud dresser.* **7.** obtrusively vulgar, as manners, persons, etc. **8.** strong or offensive in smell. —*adv.* **9.** loudly. [ME; OE *hlūd;* c. D *luid,* G *laut;* akin to Gk *klytós* famous] —**loud′ly,** *adv.* —**loud′ness,** *n.*

—**Syn. 1.** resounding; deafening; stentorian. LOUD, NOISY describe a strongly audible sound or sounds. LOUD means characterized by a full, powerful sound or sounds, which make a strong impression on the organs of hearing: *a loud voice, laugh, report.* NOISY refers to a series of sounds, and suggests clamor and discordance, or persistence in making loud sounds which are disturbing and annoying: *a noisy crowd.* **6.** gaudy, flashy, showy. —**Ant. 1.** quiet.

loud·en (loud′ən), *v.t., v.i.* to make or become loud. [LOUD + -EN[1]]

loud·ish (lou′dish), *adj.* somewhat loud. [LOUD + -ISH[1]]

loud·mouth (loud′mouth′), *n., pl.* **-mouths** (-mouthz′). loud-mouth.

loud-mouth (loud′mouth′), *n., pl.* **-mouths** (-mouthz′). a person who brags, gossips, or otherwise speaks foolishly or indiscreetly. Also, **loud′mouth′.**

loud-mouthed (loud′moutht′, -moutht′), *adj.* loud of voice or utterance; vociferous. Also, **loud′mouthed′.**

Lou·don (loud′ən), *n.* a town in E Tennessee. 3812 (1960).

Lou·don·ville (loud′ən vil′), *n.* a town in central Ohio. 2611 (1960).

loud′ ped′al, *Music.* See **damper pedal.**

loud·speak·er (loud′spē′kər), *n.* any of various electronic devices by which speech, music, etc., can be intensified and made audible throughout a room, hall, or the like. [LOUD + SPEAKER]

Lou·el·la (lo͞o el′ə), *n.* a girl's given name.

lough (lok, lokh), *n.* *Irish Eng.* **1.** a lake. **2.** a partially landlocked or protected bay; a narrow arm of the sea. Cf. **loch.** [Anglo-Irish sp. of Ir *loch* lake; ME *lough* (south), equiv. to *louch* (north). See LOCH]

Lou·hi (lō′hi), *n.* *Finnish Legend.* a sorceress, the mistress of Pohjola and an enemy of the Finns, eventually defeated by Vainamoinen.

lou·ie (lo͞o′ē), *n.* looie.

Lou·ie (lo͞o′ē), *n.* a boy's given name, form of **Louis.**

lou·is (lo͞o′ē; *Fr.* lwē), *n., pl.* **lou·is** (lo͞o′ēz; *Fr.* lwē). See **louis d'or.**

Lou·is (lo͞o′is *or, for 2,* lo͞o′ē), *n.* **1. Joe** (*Joseph Louis Barrow*), 1914–81, U.S. boxer: world heavyweight champion 1937–49. **2.** a boy's given name.

Lou·is I (lo͞o′ē, lo͞o′is; *Fr.* lwē), (*"le Débonaire"; "the Pious"*) A.D. 788–840, king of France and Germany 814–840; emperor of the Holy Roman Empire 814–840 (son of Charlemagne).

Louis II, (*"the German"*) A.D. 804–876 (son of Louis I). German, **Ludwig II.**

Louis II de Bourbon. See **Condé.**

Louis IV, (*"the Bavarian"*) 1287?–1347, king of Germany and emperor of the Holy Roman Empire 1314–47.

Louis V, (*"le Fainéant"*) A.D. 967?–987, king of France 986–987: last Carolingian to rule France.

Louis IX, Saint, 1214?–70, king of France 1226–70.

Louis XI, 1423–83, king of France 1461–83 (son of Charles VII).

Louis XII, (*"the Father of the People"*) 1462–1515, king of France 1498–1515.

Louis XIII, 1601–43, king of France 1610–43 (son of Henry IV of Navarre).

Louis XIV, (*"the Great"; "the Sun King"*) 1638–1715, king of France 1643–1715 (son of Louis XIII).

Louis XV, 1710–74, king of France 1715–74.

Louis XVI, 1754-93, king of France 1774–92 (grandson of Louis XV and husband of Marie Antoinette).

Louis XVII, (*"Louis Charles of France"*) 1785–95, titular king of France 1793–95 (son of Louis XVI).

Louis XVIII, (*Louis Xavier Stanislas*) 1755–1824, king of France 1814–15, 1815–24 (brother of Louis XVI).

Lou·is·burg (lo͞o′is bûrg′), *n.* **1.** a seaport on SE Cape Breton Island, Nova Scotia, in SE Canada: French fortress captured by British 1745, 1758. 1417 (1961). **2.** a town in central North Carolina. 2862 (1960).

lou·is d'or (lo͞o′ē dôr′; *Fr.* lwē dôr′), *pl.* **lou·is d'or** (lo͞o′ēz dôr′; *Fr.* lwē dôr′). a former gold coin of France, issued from 1640 to 1795; pistole. Also called **louis.** [< F: lit., louis of gold]

Lou·ise (lo͞o ēz′), *n.* **1. Lake,** a glacial lake in W Canada, in SW Alberta in the Canadian Rockies: resort. 5670 ft. above sea level. **2.** Also, **Lou·i·sa** (lo͞o ē′zə). a girl's given name.

Lou·ise (lo͞o ēz′), *n.* an opera (1900) by Gustave Charpentier.

Lou·i·sette (lo͞o′ē zet′), *n.* a girl's given name, form of **Louise.**

Lou′is heel′ (lo͞o′ē), a French heel of medium height, flared out or widened at the base, used on women's shoes. [after LOUIS XV]

Lou·i·si·an·a (lo͞o ē′zē an′ə, lo͞o′ə zē-, lo͞o′ē-), *n.* **1.** a State in the S United States. 3,257,022 (1960); 48,522 sq. mi. *Cap.:* Baton Rouge. *Abbr.:* La. **2.** a town in E Missouri. 4286 (1960). —**Lou·i′si·an′an, Lou·i′si·an′i·an,** *adj., n.*

Loui′sian′a French′, French as spoken in Louisiana.

Loui′sian′a her′on, an American heron, *Hydranassa tricolor,* dark bluish-gray above and white below.

Loui′sian′a Pur′chase, the territory that the United States purchased from France in 1803 for $15,000,000, extending from the Mississippi River to the Rocky Mountains and from the Gulf of Mexico to Canada.

Loui′sian′a tan′ager. See **western tanager.**

Lou′is Napo′leon (lo͞o′ē, lo͞o′is; *Fr.* lwē). See **Napoleon III.**

Lou′is Philippe′, (*"Citizen King"*) 1773–1850, king of France 1830–48.

Lou′is Qua·torze′ (kə tôrz′; *Fr.* kȧ tôrz′), noting or pertaining to the style of architecture, furnishings, and decoration prevailing in France in the late 17th century, characterized by increasingly classicizing tendencies, by the influence of official and academic control over all the arts, and by an emphasis on dignity rather than comfort. Cf. **Régence.**

Lou′is Quinze′ (kanz; *Fr.* kanz), noting or pertaining to the Rococo style of architecture, furnishings, and decoration prevailing in France in the early and mid-18th century, characterized by fantasy, lightness, elegance, and comfort.

Lou′is Seize′ (sez), noting or pertaining to the style of architecture, furnishings, and decoration prevailing in France at the end of the 18th century, continuing the lightness of the Louis Quinze period with a stricter adherence to classical models.

Lou′is Treize′ (trez; *Fr.* trez), noting or pertaining to the style of architecture, furnishings, and decoration prevailing in France in the early 17th century, characterized by a gradual transition from the free invention and composition of the Renaissance to the classicism of the Louis Quatorze period.

Lou·is·ville (lo͞o′ē vil′), *n.* **1.** a port in N Kentucky, on the Ohio River: Kentucky Derby. 390,639 (1960). **2.** a town in central Ohio. 5116 (1960). **3.** a town in central Mississippi. 5066 (1960). —**Lou·is·vill·ian** (lo͞o′ē-vil′yən), *n.*

loun (lo͞on), *n.* *Scot.* loon[2].

lounge (lounj), *v.,* **lounged, loung·ing,** *n.* —*v.i.* **1.** to pass time idly and indolently. **2.** to recline indolently; loll: *We lounged in the sun all afternoon.* **3.** to go or move in a leisurely, indolent manner; saunter (usually fol. by *around, along, off,* etc.). —*v.t.* **4.** to pass (time) in lounging (usually fol. by *away* or *out*): *to lounge away the afternoon at the seashore.* —*n.* **5.** a sofa for reclining, sometimes backless, having a headrest at one end. **6.** a place for sitting, waiting, smoking, etc., esp. a large public room, as in a hotel, theater, air terminal, or the like. **7.** a place or section on a train, plane, or ship having various club or social facilities. **8.** a cocktail lounge. **9.** *Archaic.* the act or a period of lounging. **10.** *Archaic.* a lounging gait. [?] —**loung′er,** *n.* —**loung′y,** *adj.*

lounge′ liz′ard, *Slang.* a foppish man who idles about the lounges of bars, cafes, hotels, etc., with or in search of women, esp. women who are willing to support him. Also called **lizard.**

lounge′ suit′, *Chiefly Brit.* a man's suit, as opposed to formal attire.

loung·ing (loun′jing), *adj.* **1.** (of a garment) worn for leisure, as at home: *lounging robe; lounging jacket.* **2.** lacking energy or vigor; relaxed. [LOUNGE + -ING[2]] —**loung′ing·ly,** *adv.*

Louns·bur·y (lounz′ber′ē, -bə rē), *n.* **Thomas Raynes·ford** (rānz′fərd), 1838–1915, U.S. linguist and educator.

loup[1] (lo͞o), *n.* a cloth mask, often of silk, which covers only half the face. [< F: lit., wolf < L *lupus*]

loup[2] (loup, lōp, lo͞op), *Scot.* —*v.i.* **1.** to leap; jump; spring. —*v.t.* **2.** to leap or jump at, over, or into (something). [ME *loupe* < Scand; cf. Icel *hloupa, hlaupa,* c. OE *hlēapan* to LEAP]

loup·cer·vier (lo͞o/ser vyā/), *n., pl.* **-viers,** (*esp. collectively*) **-vier.** a Canada lynx, *Lynx canadensis.* [< CanF, F: lynx < L *lupus cervarius,* lit., wolf like a deer. See LUPUS, CERVINE, -ER[2]]

loupe (lo͞op), *n.* any of several varieties of magnifying glasses, used by jewelers and watchmakers, of from 2 to 20 power and intended to fit in the eye socket, to be attached to spectacles, or to be held in the hand. [< F < Gmc; see LOB[1]]

loup-ga·rou (lo͞o GA RO͞O/; *Eng.* lo͞o/gə ro͞o/), *n., pl.* **loups-ga·rous** (lo͞o GA RO͞O/; *Eng.* lo͞o/gə ro͞oz/). *French.* a werewolf; lycanthrope.

loup/ing ill/ (lou/piṅg, lō/-, lo͞o/-), *Vet. Pathol.* an acute, virus-induced infectious disease of sheep, affecting the nervous system and transmitted by a tick that also attacks man. [late ME *lowpynge* leaping (see LOUP[2], -ING[2])

lour (lour, lou/ər), *v.i., n.* lower[2].

Lourdes (lo͝ord, lo͝ordz; *Fr.* lo͞oRd), *n.* a city in SW France: shrine. 16,376 (1962).

Lou·ren·ço Mar·ques (lō ren/sō mär/kes, lō-; *Port.* lō RENN/so͞o mäR/kezh), a seaport in and the capital of Mozambique, on Delagoa Bay. 78,530 (1960).

lour·ing (lour/iṅg, lou/ər-), *adj.* lowering. —**lour/ing·ly,** *adv.* —**lour/ing·ness,** *n.*

lour·y (lour/ē, lou/ə rē), *adj.* lowery.

louse (lous), *n., pl.* **lice** (līs) for 1, 2, 3, **lous·es** for 4, *v.* —*n.* **1.** any small, wingless insect of the order *Anoplura* **(sucking louse),** parasitic on man and other mammals and having mouthparts adapted for sucking, as *Pediculus humanus* **(body louse** or **head louse)** and *Phthirius pubis* **(crab louse). 2.** any insect of the order *Mallophaga* **(bird louse, biting louse,** or **chewing louse),** parasitic on birds and mammals, having mouthparts adapted for biting. **3.** See **plant louse. 4.** *Slang.* a contemptible person, esp. an unethical one. —*v.t.* **5.** to delouse. **6. louse up,** *Slang.* to spoil; botch; make a mess of: *Miscasting loused up the entire movie.* [ME *lows(e), lous(e),* OE *lūs,* pl. *lȳs;* c. D *luis,* G *Laus,* Icel *lūs*]

Body louse (Length 1/8 in.)

louse·wort (lous/wûrt/), *n.* any scrophulariaceous herb of the genus *Pedicularis,* as the wood betony, formerly supposed to cause lice in sheep feeding on it. [LOUSE + WORT[2]]

lous·y (lou/zē), *adj.,* **lous·i·er, lous·i·est. 1.** infested with lice. **2.** *Informal.* **a.** mean or contemptible: *That was a lousy thing to do.* **b.** wretchedly bad; miserable: *He did a lousy job. I feel lousy.* **3. lousy with,** *Slang.* well supplied with: *He's lousy with money.* [ME *lousi.* See LOUSE, -Y[1]] —**lous/i·ly,** *adv.* —**lous/i·ness,** *n.*

lout[1] (lout), *n.* **1.** an awkward, stupid person; clumsy, ill-mannered boor; oaf. —*v.t.* **2.** *Obs.* to flout; treat with contempt; scorn. [? special use of LOUT[2]]

lout[2] (lout), *v.t., v.i. Archaic.* to bend or stoop; bow in respect or courtesy. [ME *louten,* OE *lūtan;* c. Icel *lūta;* akin to LITTLE]

Louth (lout͟h), *n.* a county in Leinster province, in the NE Republic of Ireland. 67,378 (1961); 317 sq. mi. *Co. seat:* Dunkalk.

lout·ish (lou/tish), *adj.* like or characteristic of a lout; awkward; clumsy; boorish. [LOUT[1] + -ISH[1]] —**lout/ish·ly,** *adv.* —**lout/ish·ness,** *n.*
—**Syn.** churlish, uncouth, vulgar, coarse.

lou·troph·o·ros (lo͞o trof/ə ros/), *n., pl.* **-roi** (-roi/). *Gk. and Rom. Antiq.* a water jar, characterized by an elongated neck and flaring mouth, used to carry water for the marriage bath and set on the tomb of a person who had been unmarried. [< Gk: lit., bringing water for the bath, equiv. to *loutrō(n)* bath + *-phoros* -PHOROUS]

Lou·vain (*Fr.* lo͞o VAN/), *n.* a city in central Belgium. 32,441 (est. 1964).

lou·var (lo͞o/vär), *n.* a red-finned, deep-sea, tropical fish, *Luvarus imperialis,* having the vent at the base of the pectoral fin. [appar. a Frenchified sp. of NL *Luvarus* genus name < dial. It (Sicilian) *luvaru*]

lou·ver (lo͞o/vər), *n.* **1.** any of a series of narrow openings framed at their longer edges with slanting, overlapping fins or slats. **2.** a fin or slat framing such an opening. **3.** a ventilating turret or lantern, as on the roof of a medieval building. **4.** any of a system of slits formed in the hood of an automobile, the door of a metal locker, etc., used esp. for ventilation. **5.** a door, window, or the like, having adjustable glass louvers. [ME *lover* < MF *louv(i)er*] —**lou/vered,** *adj.*

L, Louver

lou/ver board/, one of a series of overlapping, sloping boards used as louvers in an opening, so arranged as to admit air but to exclude rain or cut off visibility from the outside.

Lou·ver·tie (lo͞o/vûr tē), *n.* a girl's given name.

L'Ou·ver·ture (*Fr.* lo͞o veR tyR/), *n.* See **Toussaint L'Ouverture.**

Lou·vre (lo͞o/vRə), *n.* a building in Paris, France: formerly a royal palace; since 1793 a national museum.

Louys (lwē), *n.* **Pierre** (pyeR), 1870–1925, French poet and novelist.

lov·a·ble (luv/ə bəl), *adj.* of such a nature as to attract love; deserving love; amiable; engaging. Also, **loveable.** [ME *lufabyll.* See LOVE, -ABLE] —**lov/a·bil/i·ty, lov/a·ble·ness,** *n.* —**lov/a·bly,** *adv.*
—**Syn.** dear, tender, warm, affectionate.

lov·age (luv/ij), *n.* a European, apiaceous herb, *Levisticum officinale,* cultivated in gardens. [ME *loveache* < AF *luvesche* (by assoc. with *ache* celery < L *apium*) < OE *lufes(ti)ce* (by syncope) < ML *levistica* r. LL *levisticum,* alter. of L *ligusticum* lovage, n. use of neut. of *Ligusticus* Ligurian; see -AGE]

love (luv), *n., v.,* **loved, lov·ing.** —*n.* **1.** the profoundly tender or passionate affection for a person of the opposite sex. **2.** a feeling of warm personal attachment or deep affection, as for a parent, child, or friend. **3.** sexual passion or desire, or its gratification. **4.** a person toward whom love is felt; beloved person; sweetheart. **5.** (used in direct address as a term of endearment, affection, or the like): *Would you like to see a movie, love?* **6.** a love affair; amour. **7.** (*cap.*) a personification of sexual affection, as Eros or Cupid. **8.** affectionate concern for the well-being of others: *a love of little children; the love of one's neighbor.* **9.** strong predilection or liking for anything: *her love of books.* **10.** the object or thing so liked: *The theater was her great love.* **11.** the benevolent affection of God for His creatures, or the reverent affection due from them to God. **12.** *Chiefly Tennis.* a score of zero; nothing. **13.** a word formerly used in communications to represent the letter L. **14. for love, a.** out of affection or liking; for pleasure. **b.** without compensation; gratuitously: *He took care of the poor for love.* **15. for the love of,** in consideration of; for the sake of: *For the love of mercy, stop that noise.* **16. in love (with),** feeling deep affection or passion for (a person, idea, occupation, etc.); enamored of: *in love with life; in love with one's work.* **17. make love, a.** to embrace and kiss as lovers. **b.** to engage in sexual intercourse. **18. no love lost,** dislike; animosity: *There was no love lost between the two brothers.* [ME; OE *lufu;* c. OFris *luve,* OHG *luba,* Goth *lubō*]
—*v.t.* **19.** to have love or affection for: *All her pupils love her.* **20.** to have a profoundly tender or passionate affection for (a person of the opposite sex). **21.** to have a strong liking for; take great pleasure in: *to love music; She loves to go dancing.* **22.** to need or require; benefit greatly from: *Plants love sunlight.* **23.** to make love to; have sexual intercourse with. —*v.i.* **24.** to have love or affection, esp. for one of the opposite sex. [ME *lov(i)en,* OE *lufian;* c. OFris *luvia,* OHG *lubōn* to love, L *lubēre* (later *libēre*) to please; akin to LIEF]
—**Syn. 1.** tenderness, fondness, predilection, warmth, passion, adoration. **1, 2.** LOVE, AFFECTION, DEVOTION all mean a deep and enduring emotional regard, usually for another person. LOVE may apply to various kinds of regard: the charity of the Creator, reverent adoration toward God or toward a person, the relation of parent and child, the regard of friends for each other, romantic feelings for one of the opposite sex, etc. AFFECTION is a fondness for persons of either sex, that is enduring and tender, but calm. DEVOTION is an intense love and steadfast, enduring loyalty to a person; it may also imply consecration to a cause. **2.** liking, inclination, regard, friendliness. **19.** like. **20.** adore, adulate, worship.
—**Ant. 1, 2.** hatred, dislike. **19, 20.** detest, hate.

Love (luv), *n.* a boy's or girl's given name.

love·a·ble (luv/ə bəl), *adj.* lovable. —**love/a·bil/i·ty, love/a·ble·ness,** *n.* —**love/a·bly,** *adv.*

love/ affair/, 1. a romantic relationship or episode between lovers; an amour. **2.** an active enthusiasm for something: *my love affair with sailing.*

love/ ap/ple, 1. (formerly) the tomato. **2.** a tropical, tender, annual plant, *Solanum aculeatissimum,* having prickly leaves, small, nodding, white flowers, and red, tomatolike fruit. [cf. F *pomme d'amour,* G *Liebesapfel*]

love/ ar/rows, fine needles of rutile crystals embedded in quartz. Also called **flèches d'amour, Cupid's arrows.**

love·bird (luv/bûrd/), *n.* **1.** any of various small parrots, esp. of the genus *Agapornis,* of Africa, noted for the affection shown one another and often kept as pets. **2. lovebirds,** *Informal.* a pair of lovers, esp. a married couple who display close mutual affection and concern. [LOVE + BIRD]

love/ chest/, a Pennsylvania Dutch chest incised or painted with the initials of a bride and groom for presentation to them.

love-en·tan·gle (luv/en taṅ/gəl), *n.* the stonecrop, *Sedum acre.* Also, **love/-en·tan/gled.**

love/ feast/, 1. (among the early Christians) a meal eaten in token of brotherly love and charity. **2.** a rite in imitation of this, practiced by a number of modern denominations; a fellowship meal. **3.** a banquet or gathering of persons to promote good feeling, restore friendly relations, honor a special guest, etc.

Love/ for Love/, a comedy (1695) by William Congreve.

love/ game/, *Tennis.* a game in which one's opponent fails to win a point.

love·grass (luv/gras/, -gräs/), *n.* any grass of the genus *Eragrostis,* as *E. curvula* **(weeping lovegrass)** and *E. trichodes* **(sand lovegrass),** cultivated as forage and ground cover. [LOVE + GRASS]

love-in-a-mist (luv/in ə mist/), *n.* a ranunculaceous plant, *Nigella damascena,* having feathery dissected leaves and whitish or blue flowers. Also called **devil-in-the-bush.**

love-in-i·dle·ness (luv/in īd/əl nis), *n.* the wild pansy, *Viola tricolor.*

love/ knot/, a knot of ribbon as a token of love. [ME *love knotte*]

Love·lace (luv/lās/), *n.* **Richard,** 1618–56, English poet.

Love·land (luv/lənd), *n.* **1.** a town in N Colorado. 9734 (1960). **2.** a town in SW Ohio. 5008 (1960).

love·less (luv/lis), *adj.* **1.** devoid of or unattended with love: *a loveless marriage.* **2.** feeling no love. **3.** receiving no love. [ME *loveles.* See LOVE, -LESS] —**love/less·ly,** *adv.* —**love/less·ness,** *n.*

love-lies-bleed·ing (luv/līz/blē/diṅg), *n.* an amaranth, esp. *Amaranthus caudatus,* having spikes of crimson flowers.

Lov·ell (lov/əl), *n.* **1. Sir Alfred Charles Bernard,** born 1931, British astronomer. **2.** a boy's given name.

love·lock (luv/lok/), *n.* **1.** any lock of hair hanging or worn separately from the rest of the hair. **2.** (formerly) a long, flowing lock or curl dressed separately from the rest of the hair, worn by courtiers. [LOVE + LOCK[2]]

love·lorn (luv/lôrn/), *adj.* being without love; forsaken by one's lover. [LOVE + LORN] —**love/lorn/ness,** *n.*

love·ly (luv/lē), *adj.,* **-li·er, -li·est,** *n., pl.* **-lies.** —*adj.* **1.** charmingly or exquisitely beautiful: *a lovely flower.* **2.** having a beauty that appeals to the heart as well as to the eye, as a person, a face, etc. **3.** *Informal.* delightful; highly pleasing: *to have a lovely time.* **4.** of a great moral or spiritual beauty: *She is endowed with a lovely character.* —*n.* **5.** *Informal.* a pretty woman, esp. a show girl, model, or the like. —*adv.* **6.** *Colloq.* very well; splendidly: *This skirt and blouse go lovely together. The kids behaved lovely at the party.* [ME *luvelich,* OE *luflic* amiable. See LOVE, -LY] —**love/li·ly,** *adv.* —**love/li·ness,** *n.*

love-mak·ing (luv/mā/kiṅg), *n.* **1.** the act of courting or wooing. **2.** sexual intercourse. [late ME; see LOVE, MAKING]

love/ match/, a marriage entered into for love alone.

love/ po/tion, a potion believed to arouse love or sexual passion toward a specified person, esp. the person administering it.

lov·er (luv/ər), *n.* **1.** a person who is in love, esp. a man in love with a woman. **2.** a man amorously involved with a woman not his wife; paramour. **3. lovers,** a man and woman in love with each other or having a love affair. **4.** a person who has a strong predilection or liking for something, as specified: *a lover of music.* **5.** a person who loves, esp. a person who has or shows affectionate regard for others: *a lover of mankind.* [ME; see LOVE, -ER[1]] —**lov/er·less,** *adj.* —**lov/er·like/,** *adj.*

Lov·er (luv/ər), *n.* **Samuel,** 1797–1868, Irish novelist, painter, and songwriter.

lov·er·ly (luv/ər lē), *adj., adv.* like, characteristic of, or in the manner of a lover; loverlike. [LOVER + -LY]

lov/ers' lane/, a secluded walkway, as in a park, sought out by lovers for its privacy.

lov/er's leap/, 1. a high area, as on a cliff, from which frustrated or grieving lovers jump to their death. **2.** *Backgammon.* a player's move from ace point to twelve point in one roll of the dice.

love/ seat/, an upholstered seat for two persons. Also called **courting chair.**

love/ set/, *Tennis.* a set in which one's opponent fails to win a game.

love·sick (luv/sik/), *adj.* **1.** languishing with love: *a trying, lovesick adolescent.* **2.** expressive of such languishing: *an anonymous, lovesick note.* [LOVE + SICK[1]] —**love/sick/ness,** *n.*

Love's/ La/bour's Lost/, a comedy (1594–95?) by Shakespeare.

love·some (luv/səm), *adj. Archaic.* **1.** inspiring love because beautiful; lovely; lovable. **2.** amorous; loving. [ME *lovesom,* OE *lufsum.* See LOVE, -SOME[1]]

Love/ Song/ of J./ Al/fred Pru/frock, The, a poem (1917) by T. S. Eliot.

Loves/ Park/, a town in N Illinois. 9086 (1960).

love/ vine/, dodder[2].

Lov·ie (luv/ē), *n.* a girl's given name.

lov·ing (luv/iṅg), *adj.* feeling or showing love; affectionate; fond: *loving glances.* [ME *lovyng,* r. *lovende,* OE *lufiende.* See LOVE, -ING[2]] —**lov/ing·ly,** *adv.* —**lov/ing·ness,** *n.*

lov/ing cup/, 1. a large cup, as of silver, usually with two or more handles, given as a prize, award, token of esteem or affection, etc. **2.** a wine cup, usually of large size with several handles, passed from one person to another, as at a farewell gathering, homecoming, etc.

lov·ing-kind·ness (luv/iṅg kīnd/nis), *n.* kindness motivated by affectionate regard.

Lov·ing·ton (luv/iṅg tən), *n.* a town in SE New Mexico. 9660 (1960).

low[1] (lō), *adj.* **1.** situated or occurring not far above the ground, floor, or base: *a low shelf.* **2.** of small extent upward; not high or tall: *A low wall surrounds the property.* **3.** not far above the horizon, as a heavenly body: *The moon was low in the sky.* **4.** lying or being below the general level: *low ground.* **5.** designating or pertaining to regions near sea level or the sea as opposed to highland or inland regions: *low countries.* **6.** bending or passing far downward; deep: *a low bow; a low swoop over a bomber target.* **7.** (of a garment) low-necked; décolleté: *The dress she wore was outrageously low.* **8.** rising but slightly from a surface: *a low relief on a frieze.* **9.** of less than average or normal height or depth, as a liquid, stream, etc.: *The river is often low this time of year.* **10.** lacking in strength or vigor; feeble; weak: *to feel low and listless.* **11.** providing little nourishment or strength, as a diet. **12.** of small amount, degree, force, intensity, etc.: *a low number; low visibility; a generator with a low output; a low flame.* **13.** indicated or represented by a low number: *A low latitude is one relatively near the equator.* **14.** assigning or attributing little worth, value, excellence, or the like: *a low estimate of a new book.* **15.** indicating something inferior or below an acceptable standard: *to receive low marks in school; special classes for children with low intelligence; people in the low income bracket.* **16.** containing a relatively small amount: *a diet low in starches.* **17.** nearing depletion; not adequately supplied: *low on funds; Our stock of towels is low.* **18.** depressed or dejected: *low spirits.* **19.** far down in the scale of rank or estimation; humble: *low birth.* **20.** of inferior quality or character: *a low grade of fabric; a low type of intellect.* **21.** lacking in dignity or elevation, as of thought or expression. **22.** mean, base, or disreputable: *a low trick; to consort with low companions.* **23.** coarse or vulgar: *entertainment of a low sort.* **24.** *Boxing.* struck or delivered below a contestant's belt. **25.** *Biol.* having a relatively simple structure; not complex in organization. **26.** *Music.* produced by relatively slow vibrations, as sounds; grave in pitch. **27.** soft; subdued; not loud: *a low murmur.* **28.** indicating the bottom or the point farthest down: *He felt it was the low point in his creative life.* **29.** prostrate or dead: *Many were low after the battle.* **30.** *Chiefly Brit.* holding to Low Church principles and practices. **31.** *Phonet.* (of a vowel) articulated with a relatively large opening above the tongue, as the vowels of *hat, hut, hot, ought,* etc. Cf. **high** (def. 23). **32.** *Auto.* of, pertaining to, or operating at the gear transmission ratio at which the drive shaft moves at the lowest speed with relation to the speed of the engine crankshaft, used esp. for temporarily overcoming the weight or inertia of the vehicle; first: *low gear.* **33.** *Baseball.* (of a pitched ball) passing the plate at a level below that of the batter's knees: *a curve, low and inside.* **34.** *Cards.* having less value than other cards: *a low card.* **35.** *Metall.* having a relatively small amount of a specified constituent (usually used in combination): *low-carbon steel.*
—*adv.* **36.** in or to a low position, point, degree, etc.: *The raiders crouched low in the bushes.* **37.** near the ground, floor, or base; not aloft: *The plane was flying low for a commercial airliner.* **38.** in or to a humble or abject state: *Some live low while others live high. She swore she would bring him low.* **39.** in or to a condi-

tion of depletion, prostration, or death: *The gas in the tank is running low; a severe illness that brought him low.* **40.** at comparatively small cost; cheaply: *to buy something low and sell it high.* **41.** at or to a low pitch, volume, intensity, etc.: *to sing low; to turn the radio low; lights turned down low.* **42.** in a low tone; softly; quietly: *to speak low.* **43.** *Archaic.* far down in time; late. **44. lay low, a.** to overpower or kill: *to lay one's attackers low.* **b.** *Slang.* to lie low. **45. lie low, a.** to conceal oneself: *He had to lie low for a while.* **b.** to keep one's intentions concealed; bide one's time: *Until the merger is concluded, you would do best to lie low on drawing up any new contracts.* Also, *Informal,* **lay low.**
—*n.* **46.** that which is low, as ground, prices, etc.: *numerous marshy lows in the forest; the recent low in the stock market.* **47.** *Auto.* low gear; first gear: *She shifted directly from low into high.* **48.** *Meteorol.* an atmospheric low-pressure system; cyclone. Cf. **high** (def. 40). **49.** *Cards.* **a.** the lowest trump card. **b.** a card of small value, or of lower value than other cards. **c.** the lowest score in a game. **d.** a player having such a score. **50.** a point of deepest decline, vulgarity, etc.: *a new low in tastelessness.* [ME *lowe, lohe,* earlier *lāh* < Scand; cf. Icel *lāgr;* c. D *laag;* akin to LIE[2]] —**low′ish,** *adj.* —**low′ness,** *n.*
—**Syn. 10.** exhausted, sinking, expiring, dying. **18.** dispirited, unhappy, sad. **19.** lowly, meek, obscure. **21.** unbecoming, disgraceful. **22.** ignoble, degraded, servile. **23.** rude, crude. See **mean**[2]. **26.** deep. **27.** quiet. —**Ant. 1–3.** high. **19.** lofty.

low[2] (lō), *v.i.* **1.** to utter the sound characteristic of cattle; moo. —*v.t.* **2.** to utter by or as by lowing. —*n.* **3.** the act or the sound of lowing: *the low of a distant herd.* [ME *lowen,* OE *hlōwan;* c. D *loeien,* OHG *hluoen,* OS *hlōian;* akin to Icel *Hlōi* proper name (lit., bellower, shouter), L *calāre* to call out]

low[3] (lō), *v.i. Brit. Dial.* **1.** to burn; blaze. **2.** (of a person) to feel strong emotions; glow with excitement. Also, **lowe.** [ME < Scand; cf. Icel *loga* to flame, *log* a flame, akin to G *lohen* (v.), *Lohe* (n.), L *lūcēre* (v.), *lūx* (n.)]

Low (lō), *n.* **1. David,** 1891–1963, English political cartoonist, born in New Zealand. **2. Juliette,** 1860–1927, founder of Girl Scouts in the U.S.

Low′ Archipel′ago. See **Tuamotu Archipelago.**

low′ ar′ea, *Meteorol.* a region where the atmospheric pressure is lower than that of the surrounding regions: *the low area in the central part of a cyclone.*

low·ball (lō′bôl′), *n. Cards.* a game of draw poker in which the player having the lowest-ranking hand wins the pot. [LOW[1] + BALL[1]]

low′ beam′, an automobile headlight beam providing short-range illumination of a road and intended chiefly for use in driving in cities, towns, etc. Cf. **high beam.**

Lowboy (18th century)

low·born (lō′bôrn′), *adj.* of humble birth. [ME *lohiboren.* See LOW[1], BORN]

low·boy (lō′boi′), *n. U.S. Furniture.* a low chest of drawers on short legs, resembling the lower part of a highboy. [LOW[1] + BOY]

low′ brass′, an alloy of about 80 percent copper and 20 percent zinc, with traces of lead and iron.

low·bred (lō′bred′), *adj.* characterized by or characteristic of low or vulgar breeding; ill-bred; coarse. [LOW[1] + BRED]
—**Syn.** unrefined, coarse, rude. —**Ant.** noble.

low·brow (*n.* lō′brou′; *adj.* lō′brou′), *Informal.* —*n.* **1.** a person who is unconcerned, uninvolved, or uneducated in intellectual activities or pursuits. —*adj.* **2.** being a lowbrow: *that lowbrow idiot.* **3.** of, pertaining or proper to a lowbrow: *lowbrow entertainment.* [LOW[1] + BROW] —**low′brow′ism,** *n.*

low′ bunt′, *Naut.* a small bunt on a furled sail, tapering gradually toward the ends of the yard. Also called **rolling bunt.**

low′bush blue′berry (lō′bo͝osh′), a shrub, *Vaccinium angustifolium,* of eastern North America, having small, white flowers and blue-black fruit. [LOW[1] + BUSH[1]]

low′ camp′. See under **camp**[2] (def. 1).

Low′ Church′, pertaining or belonging to a party in the Anglican Church emphasizing evangelicalism and laying little stress on the sacraments, church rituals, and church authority. Cf. **High Church, Broad Church.**

Low′ Church′man, a person who advocates or follows Low Church practices.

low′ com′edy, comedy which depends on physical action, broadly humorous or farcical situations, and often bawdy jokes. Cf. **high comedy.** —**low′ come′dian.**

low-cost (lō′kôst′, -kost′), *adj.* able to be purchased or acquired at relatively little cost: *low-cost life insurance; low-cost housing.*

Low′ Coun′tries, the lowland region near the North Sea, forming the lower basin of the Rhine, Meuse, and Scheldt rivers, divided in the Middle Ages into numerous small states: corresponding to modern Belgium, Luxembourg, and the Netherlands. —**low′-coun′try,** *adj.*

low-down (*n.* lō′doun′; *adj.* lō′doun′), *Informal.* —*n.* **1.** Also, **low′down′.** the unadorned facts; the truth; inside information (usually prec. by *the*): *We gave them the low-down on the new housing project.* —*adj.* **2.** contemptible; base; mean: *That was a low-down trick to pull.* **3.** low, esp. socially or morally; degraded. [LOW[1] + DOWN[1]]

lowe (lō), *v.i.* **lowed, low·ing.** *Brit. Dial.* low[3].

Low·ell (lō′əl), *n.* **1. Ab·bott Lawrence** (ab′ət), 1856–1943, political scientist and educator: president of Harvard University 1909–33. **2.** his sister, **Amy,** 1874–1925, U.S. poet and critic. **3. James Russell,** 1819–91, U.S. poet, essayist, and diplomat. **4. Percival,** 1855–1916, U.S. astronomer and author (brother of Abbott Lawrence Lowell and Amy Lowell). **5. Robert,** born 1917, U.S. poet. **6.** a city in NE Massachusetts, on the Merrimack River. 92,107 (1960). **7.** a town in S North Carolina. 2784 (1960). **8.** a town in SW Michigan. 2545 (1960). **9.** a boy's given name.

low′-en′er·gy fis′sion (lō′en′ər jē), *Physics.* fission induced by a low-energy particle.

low·er[1] (lō′ər), *v.t.* **1.** to cause to descend; let down: *to lower a flag.* **2.** to make lower in height or level: *to lower the water in a canal.* **3.** to reduce in amount, price, degree, force, etc. **4.** to make less loud, as the voice. **5.** to bring down in rank or estimation; degrade; humble; abase (oneself), as by some sacrifice of dignity: *I would not lower myself to do such a thing.* **6.** *Music.* to make lower in pitch; flatten. —*v.i.* **7.** to become lower, grow less, or diminish, as in amount, intensity, degree, etc.: *The brook begins to lower in early summer. Stock prices rise and lower constantly.* **8.** to descend; sink: *the sun lowering in the west.* —*adj.* **9.** comparative of **low**[1]. **10.** (*often cap.*) *Stratig.* noting an early division of a period, system, or the like: *the lower Devonian.* —*n.* **11.** a denture for the lower jaw. **12.** a lower berth. [orig. comp. of LOW[1] (adj.)] —**low′er·a·ble,** *adj.*
—**Syn. 1.** drop, depress. **3.** decrease, diminish, lessen. **4.** soften. **5.** humiliate, dishonor, disgrace, debase. —**Ant. 3.** raise, increase. **5.** elevate, honor.

low·er[2] (lou′ər, lour), *v.i.* **1.** to be dark and threatening, as the sky or the weather. **2.** to frown, scowl, or look sullen; glower: *I can't stand the way he lowers at people when he's annoyed.* —*n.* **3.** a dark, threatening appearance, as of the sky, weather, etc. **4.** a frown or scowl. Also, **lour.** [ME *lour* (n.), *loure* (v.) to frown, LURK; akin to G *lauern,* D *loeren*]
—**Syn. 1.** darken, threaten.

Low·er (lou′ər), *n.* a crater in the first quadrant of the face of the moon: about 50 miles in diameter.

low′er ap′sis. See under **apsis.**

Low′er Aus′tria (lō′ər), a province in NE Austria. 1,371,911 (1961); 7092 sq. mi.

low′er bound′ (lō′ər), *Math.* an element less than or equal to all the elements in a given set: *The numbers 0 and 1 are lower bounds of the set consisting of 1, 2, and 3.* Cf. **bound**[3] (def. 4), **greatest lower bound, least upper bound, upper bound.**

Low′er Bur′ma. See under **Burma.**

Low′er Califor′nia, a narrow peninsula in NW Mexico between the Gulf of California and the Pacific, forming two territories of Mexico. 604,346 (1960); 55,634 sq. mi. *Capitals:* Mexicali (Northern Territory) and La Paz (Southern Territory). Spanish, **Baja California.**

Low′er Can′ada, former name of Quebec province 1791–1841.

Low′er Carbonif′erous, *Geol.* Mississippian (defs. 2, 4).

low′er case′ (lō′ər), *Print.* See under **case**[2] (def. 8). Cf. **upper case.**

low·er-case (lō′ər kās′), *adj., v.,* **-cased, -cas·ing,** *n.* —*adj.* **1.** (of an alphabetical letter) of a particular form often different from and smaller than its corresponding capital letter, and occurring after the initial letter of a proper name, of the first word in a sentence, etc., as a, b, q, r. **2.** *Print.* pertaining to or belonging in the lower case. See **case**[2] (def. 8). —*v.t.* **3.** to print or write with a lower-case letter or letters. —*n.* **4.** a lower-case letter. Cf. **upper-case.**

low′er-case al′phabet, *Print.* (in automatic typesetting) a unit, consisting of the length of the entire minuscule alphabet, set solid, of a specified type size and font, used as a measure in fitting copy. The specification for Teletypesetter-wire copy calls for a line 11 picas long to result from setting in a font having a lower-case alphabet of 118 points. *Abbr.:* l.c.a.

low′er cham′ber. See **lower house.**

Low′er Chinook′, an extinct Chinookan language that was spoken by tribes on both banks of the Columbia River estuary.

low·er·class·man (lō′ər klas′mən, -kläs′-), *n., pl.* **-men.** underclassman. [LOWER[1] + CLASS + MAN[1]]

low′er crit′icism, a form of Biblical criticism having as its object the reconstruction of the original texts of the books of the Bible. Also called **textual criticism.** Cf. **higher criticism.**

low′er deck′, *Naut.* **1.** the lowermost deck in a hull having two or three decks. **2.** the deck next above the lowermost, or orlop, deck in a hull having four or more decks.

Low′er Depths′, The, a play (1902) by Maxim Gorki.

Low′er E′gypt. See under **Egypt.**

low′er hold′, *Naut.* the lowermost hold space in a hull having 'tween decks or a shelter deck.

low′er house′, one of two branches of a legislature, generally more representative and with more members than the upper branch.

low·er·ing (lou′ər ing, lour′ing), *adj.* **1.** dark and threatening, as the sky, clouds, weather, etc.; overcast; gloomy: *lowering skies.* **2.** frowning or sullen, as the face, gaze, etc.; scowling; angry. Also, **louring.** [ME *louring.* See LOWER[2], -ING[2]] —**low′er·ing·ly,** *adv.*

Low′er Lakes′, (*sometimes l.c.*) *Chiefly Canadian.* Lakes Erie and Ontario, the southernmost Great Lakes.

low′er mast′, *Naut.* the lowermost spar of a compound mast, stepped in the hull of a vessel and carrying a topmast and any other upper spars.

Low′er Mer′i·on (mer′ē ən), a town in SE Pennsylvania, near Philadelphia. 59,420 (1960).

Low′er Mich′igan, the southern part of Michigan, S of the Strait of Mackinac. Also called **Low′er Penin′sula.**

low·er·most (lō′ər mōst′ *or, esp. Brit.,* -məst), *adj.* lowest. [LOWER[1] + -MOST]

Low′er Palat′inate, Palatinate (def. 1).

Low′er Sax′ony, a state in N West Germany. 6,761,000 (1963); 18,294 sq. mi. *Cap.:* Hanover. German, **Niedersachsen.**

low′er school′, a school that is preparatory to one on a more advanced level.

low′er semicontin′uous func′tion, *Math.* (at a given point) a function for which all functional values at points in a neighborhood of the given point are greater than the difference of the functional value at the given point and an arbitrarily selected small number. Cf. **upper semicontinuous function.**

low′er world′, **1.** *Class. Myth.* the regions of the dead, conceived of as lying beneath the surface of the earth; Hades; the underworld. **2.** the earth, as distinguished from the heavenly bodies or from heaven.

low·er·y (lou′ə rē, lour′ē), *adj.* gloomy; forbidding; threatening; dark: *a lowery sky.* Also, **loury.** [earlier *lowry.* See LOWER[2], -Y[1]]

Lowes (lōz), *n.* **John Livingston,** 1867–1945, U.S. scholar, critic, and teacher.

low′est com′mon denom′inator, *Math.* See **least common denominator.**

low′est com′mon mul′tiple, *Math.* the smallest number that is a common multiple of a given set of numbers. Also called **least common multiple.**

Lowes·toft (lōs′tôft, -toft, -təf), *n.* a seaport in NE Suffolk, in E England: famous for a type of china. 45,687 (1961).

low′ explo′sive, a relatively slow-burning explosive, usually set off by heat or friction, used for propelling charges in guns or for ordinary blasting.

low′ fre′quency, *Radio.* any frequency between 30 and 300 kilocycles per second. *Abbr.:* LF —**low′-fre′quen·cy,** *adj.*

low′ ful′ham. See under **fulham.**

Low′ Ger′man, **1.** the West Germanic languages not included in the High German group, as English, Dutch, Flemish, Plattdeutsch, etc. Cf. **High German** (def. 1). **2.** Plattdeutsch.

low-grade (lō′grād′), *adj.* of an inferior quality, worth, value, etc.: *The mine yields low-grade silver ore.* [LOW[1] + GRADE]

low′ ground′, Often, **low grounds.** *Southern U.S.* bottom (def. 4).

low′ hur′dles, *Track.* a race in which runners leap over hurdles two feet six inches high. Cf. **high hurdles.**

Lo′witz arc′ (lō′vits). See **arc of Lowitz.**

low-key (lō′kē′), *adj.* of reduced intensity; restrained; understated. Also, **low′-keyed′.**

Lowl (lō′əl), *n.* a boy's given name, form of **Lowell.**

low·land (lō′lənd), *n.* **1.** land which is low or level, with respect to the adjacent country. **2. the Lowlands,** a low, level region in S, central, and E Scotland. —*adj.* **3.** of, pertaining to, or characteristic of a lowland or lowlands. **4.** (*cap.*) of, pertaining to, or characteristic of the Lowlands of Scotland or the speech of this area. [LOW[1] + LAND]

Low·land·er (lō′lən dər, -lan′-), *n.* **1.** a native of the Lowlands. **2.** (*l.c.*) an inhabitant of a lowland or lowlands. [LOWLAND + -ER[1]]

low′land white′ fir′. See **grand fir.** Also called **low′land fir′.**

Low′ Lat′in, any form of nonclassical Latin, as Late Latin, Vulgar Latin, or Medieval Latin.

low·life (lō′līf′), *n., pl.* **-lifes.** *Slang.* a despicable person; degenerate. [LOW[1] + LIFE]

low·li·head (lō′lē hed′), *n. Archaic.* lowly state; lowliness. [late ME *lowliheed.* See LOWLY, -HEAD]

low·ly (lō′lē), *adj.,* **-li·er, -li·est,** *adv.* —*adj.* **1.** humble in station, condition, or nature: *a lowly cottage.* **2.** low in growth or position. **3.** humble in spirit; meek. —*adv.* **4.** in a low position, manner, or degree: *a lowly placed shelf; a lowly behaved person.* **5.** in a lowly manner; humbly: *to kneel lowly in receiving a blessing.* **6.** in a quiet voice; softly: *to converse lowly.* [ME; see LOW[1], -LY] —**low′li·ly,** *adv.* —**low′li·ness,** *n.*
—**Syn. 3.** modest.

Low′ Mass′, a Mass that is said, and not sung, by the celebrant, who is assisted by one server, and which has less ceremonial form than a High Mass, using no music or choir. Cf. **High Mass.**

low′ mill′ing, a process for making flour in which the grain is ground once and then bolted. Cf. **high milling.**

low-mind·ed (lō′mīn′did), *adj.* having or showing a low, coarse, or vulgar mind. —**low′-mind′ed·ly,** *adv.* —**low′-mind′ed·ness,** *n.*

lown[1] (loun), *adj., n., v.t., v.i. Dial.* calm; quiet. [ME *lown* (v.), late ME *lowne* (adj.) < Scand; cf. Icel *lygna* to become calm, *lognast ūt af* to die away, *logn* a calm, *lygn* calm]

lown[2] (lo͞on), *n. Scot.* loon[2].

Lowndes (loundz), *n.* **William Thomas,** 1798–1843, English bibliographer.

low-necked (lō′nekt′), *adj.* (of a garment) cut low so as to leave the neck and shoulders exposed; décolleté.

low′ pitch′, *Music.* See **diapason normal pitch.**

low-pitched (lō′picht′), *adj.* **1.** pitched in a low register or key: *a low-pitched aria for the basso.* **2.** produced by slow vibrations; relatively grave in pitch or soft in sound: *a low-pitched whistle.* **3.** (of a roof) having a low proportion of vertical to lateral dimensions.

low-pres·sure (lō′presh′ər), *adj.* **1.** having or involving a low or below-normal pressure, as steam, water, or the like. **2.** without vigor or persistence; lacking in forcefulness or aggressiveness: *a low-pressure campaign that failed dismally.* **3.** quietly persuasive; subtle; indirect: *Customers appreciated his low-pressure manner.*

low′ relief′, bas-relief.

Low·ry (lou′rē), *n.* a boy's given name, form of **Lawrence.**

lowse (*adj., adv.* lōs; *v.* lōz), *adj.* **lows·er, lows·est,** *adv., v.* **lowsed, lows·ing.** *Brit. Dial.* loose.

low′side win′dow (lō′sīd′), (in medieval English churches) a window set low in the outside wall, permitting the interior to be seen from the outside. Also, **low′ side′ win′dow.** Also called **lychnoscope.** [LOW[1] + SIDE[1]]

low-spir·it·ed (lō′spir′i tid), *adj.* depressed; dejected: *He is feeling rather low-spirited today.* —**low′-spir′it·ed·ly,** *adv.* —**low′-spir′it·ed·ness,** *n.*

Low′ Sun′day, the first Sunday after Easter.

low-ten·sion (lō′ten′shən), *adj. Elect.* subjected to, or capable of operating under, relatively low voltage: *low-tension wire.*

low-test (lō′test′), *adj.* (of gasoline) boiling at a comparatively high temperature.

low′ tide′, **1.** a tide at low water. **2.** the time of low water. **3.** the lowest point of decline of anything: *His spirits were at low tide.*

Low·ville (lou′vil), *n.* a town in central New York. 3616 (1960).

low-vol·tage (lō′vōl′tij), *adj.* noting or pertaining to an electric system with an operating voltage under 750 volts.

low′ wa′ter, water at its lowest level, as in a river. —**low′-wa′ter,** *adj.*

low′-wa′ter mark′ (lō′wô′tər, -wot′ər), **1.** the lowest point reached by a low tide. **2.** something indicating the bottom of a decline; the lowest or least admirable level that has been reached by something: *the low-water mark of political chicanery.*

low′ wine′, Often, **low wines.** *Distilling.* the weak spirits obtained from the first distillation; the result of the first run of the still from the fermented mash.

lox[1] (loks), *n.* a kind of smoked salmon, often eaten with cream cheese on a bagel. [< Yiddish *laks*, var. of G *Lachs* salmon; c. OE *leax*, Icel *lax*]

lox[2] (loks), *n.* **1.** See **liquid oxygen.** —*v.t.* **2.** to supply (a rocket) with this fuel. [*l(iquid) ox(ygen)*]

Lox·i·as (lok′sē əs), *n. Class. Myth.* an epithet of Apollo, meaning "ambiguous," in reference to the difficulty men had in interpreting his oracles.

lox·o·dont (lok′sə dont′), *adj.* **1.** having molar teeth with shallow depressions between the ridges. —*n.* **2.** a loxodont animal; an elephant. [< Gk *lox(ós)* oblique + -ODONT]

lox·o·drome (lok′sə drōm′), *n.* See **rhumb line.** [back formation from LOXODROMIC]

lox·o·drom·ic (lok′sə drom′ik), *adj.* **1.** noting, pertaining to, or according to loxodromes or rhumb lines. **2.** noting or pertaining to a map projection, as Mercator's projection, in which rhumb lines appear as straight lines. Also, **lox′o·drom′i·cal.** [< Gk *loxó(s)* slanting + *dromik(ós)* of a course; see -DROME, -IC] —**lox′o·drom′i·cal·ly,** *adv.*

lox·o·drom·ics (lok′sə drom′iks), *n.* (*construed as sing.*) the technique of navigating according to loxodromes or rhumb lines. Also, **lox·od·ro·my** (lok sod′rə mē). [see LOXIDROMIC, -ICS]

Loy (loi), *n.* a girl's given name.

loy·al (loi′əl), *adj.* **1.** faithful to one's allegiance, as to a sovereign, government, or state: *a loyal subject.* **2.** faithful to one's oath, commitments, or obligations: *to be loyal to a vow.* **3.** faithful to any leader, party, or cause, or to any person or thing conceived as deserving fidelity or imposing obligations: *a loyal friend.* **4.** characterized by or showing faithfulness to commitments, vows, allegiance, obligations, etc.: *loyal conduct.* [< MF, OF *loial, le(i)al* < L *lēgālis* LEGAL] —**loy′al·ly,** *adv.* —**loy′al·ness,** *n.* —**Syn. 1.** patriotic. **2.** See **faithful.** —**Ant. 1.** faithless, treacherous.

loy·al·ist (loi′ə list), *n.* **1.** a person who is loyal; a supporter of the sovereign or of the existing government, esp. in time of revolt. **2.** (*sometimes cap.*) a person who remained loyal to the British during the American Revolution; Tory. **3.** (*cap.*) an adherent of the republic during the Spanish Civil War. [LOYAL + -IST] —**loy′al·ism,** *n.*

loy·al·ty (loi′əl tē), *n., pl.* **-ties. 1.** the state or quality of being loyal; faithfulness to commitments or obligations. **2.** faithful adherence to a sovereign or government, or to a leader, cause, or the like. **3.** an example or instance of faithfulness, adherence, or the like: *a man with fierce loyalties.* [late ME *loyaltee* < MF *loialte.* See LOYAL, -TY[2]]
—**Syn. 2.** fealty, devotion, constancy. LOYALTY, ALLEGIANCE, FIDELITY all imply a sense of duty or of devoted attachment to something or someone. LOYALTY connotes sentiment and the feeling of devotion which one holds for one's country, creed, family, friends, etc. ALLEGIANCE applies particularly to a citizen's duty to his country, or, by extension, one's obligation to support a party, cause, leader, etc. FIDELITY implies unwavering devotion and allegiance to a person, principle, etc. —**Ant. 1, 2.** faithlessness.

Loyce (lois), *n.* a girl's given name, form of **Lois.**

Loyde (loid), *n.* a boy's given name. Also, **Lloyd.**

Loy·o·la (loi ō′lə), *n.* **Saint Ignatius** (*Iñigo López de Loyola*), 1491–1556, Spanish soldier and ecclesiastic: founder of the Society of Jesus.

loz·enge (loz′inj), *n.* **1.** a small flavored confection of sugar or syrup, often medicated, originally diamond-shaped. **2.** *Geom.* a four-sided equilateral figure whose opposing angles are equal; diamond. **3.** *Heraldry.* **a.** a diamond-shaped charge. **b.** a diamond-shaped shield bearing the arms of a woman. [ME *losenge* < MF, OF, appar. < Gaulish **lausa* flat stone + Gmc *-inga* suffix of appurtenance]

loz·eng·y (loz′ən jē), *adj. Heraldry.* divided into lozenges of alternating tinctures: *lozengy or and gules.* [LOZENGE + -Y[1]]

Lo·zère (lô zer′), *n.* a department in S France. 81,868 (1962); 2000 sq. mi. *Cap.:* Mende.

LP, *pl.* **LPs, LP's.** *Trademark.* a phonograph record designed to be played at 33⅓ revolutions per minute; a long-playing record. Also, **L-P**

L.P., 1. long primer. **2.** low pressure. Also, **l.p.**

LPG., See **liquefied petroleum gas.** Also, **LP gas.**

L.P.S., Lord Privy Seal.

lpW, lumen per watt; lumens per watt. Also, **l.p.w., L.P.W.**

L.R., Lloyd's Register.

L-ra·di·a·tion (el′rā′dē ā′shən), *n. Physics.* See under **L-line.**

LRBM, long-range ballistic missile.

L.S., 1. Licentiate in Surgery. **2.** Linnaean Society. **3.** the place of the seal, as on a document. [< L *locus sigilli*]

l.s., See **L.S.** (def. 3).

l.s.c., in the place mentioned above. [< L *locō suprā citātō*]

LSD, 1. *U.S. Navy.* a sea-going, amphibious vessel capable of carrying and launching assault landing craft from a large, inner compartment that can be flooded and of making emergency repairs at sea to smaller vessels. [*l(anding) s(hip) d(eck)*] **2.** Also called **LSD-25, lysergic acid diethylamide.** *Pharm.* a crystalline solid, $C_{15}H_{15}N_2CON(C_2H_5)_2$, the diethyl amide of lysergic acid, that produces temporary hallucinations and a schizophrenic psychotic state: used in medical research of mental disorders. **3.** See **least significant digit.**

L.S.D., pounds, shillings, and pence. Also, **£.s.d., l.s.d.** [< L *librae, solidi, denarii*]

L-se·ries (el′sēr′ēz), *n. Physics.* See under **L-line.**

L-shell (el′shel′), *n. Physics.* the second shell of electrons surrounding the nucleus of an atom and containing, when filled, eight electrons having principal quantum number two. Cf. **K-shell, M-shell, N-shell.**

L sill, *Carpentry.* a sill for a building frame composed of a plate resting on the basement wall and a header or joist at the outer edge of the plate, the studs resting either on the plate with the header or joist let in or on a soleplate laid over the rough floor.

LSM, *U.S. Mil. and Navy.* a type of landing ship slightly more than 200 feet long. [*l(anding) s(hip) m(edium)*]

L.S.S., Lifesaving Service.

LST, an ocean-going military vessel, used by amphibious forces for landing troops and heavy equipment on beaches. [*l(anding) s(hip) t(ank)*]

l.s.t., local standard time.

Lt., lieutenant.

l.t., 1. *Football.* left tackle. **2.** local time. **3.** long ton.

Lt. Col., Lieutenant Colonel.

Lt. Comdr., Lieutenant Commander. Also, **Lt. Com.**

Ltd., limited (def. 3). Also, **ltd.**

Lt. Gen., Lieutenant General.

Lt. Gov., Lieutenant Governor.

L.Th., Licentiate in Theology.

Lt. Inf., *Mil.* light infantry.

lt-yr, light-year; light-years.

Lu (lo͞o), *n.* a boy's or girl's given name, form of **Lou.**

Lu, *Chem.* lutetium.

Lu·a·la·ba (lo͞o′ä lä′bä), *n.* a river in the SE Republic of the Congo: a headstream of the Congo River. 400 mi. long.

Lu·a·lu·a·le·i-Ma·i·li (lo͞o′ä lo͞o′ä le′ē mä ē′lē), *n.* a town on W Oahu, in central Hawaii. 5045 (1960).

Lu·an·da (lo͞o an′də), *n.* a seaport in and the capital of Angola, in SW Africa. 224,540 with suburbs (1960). Also, **Loanda.** Also called **São Paulo de Luanda.**

Luang Pra·bang (lwäng′ prä bäng′), *n.* a city in N Laos, on the Mekong River: royal capital. 18,000 (est. 1957). Cf. **Vientiane.**

Lu·anne (lo͞o an′), *n.* a girl's given name.

lu·au (lo͞o ou′, lo͞o′ou), *n.* **1.** a feast of Hawaiian food, usually accompanied by Hawaiian entertainment. **2.** a cooked dish of taro leaves, usually prepared with coconut cream and octopus or chicken. [< Hawaiian *lu'au*]

lub, *Math.* See **least upper bound.**

Lu·bang′ Is′lands (lo͞o bäng′), a group of islands in the NW Philippines, located NW of Mindoro. 15,000 (est. 1962); 98 sq. mi.

lub·ber (lub′ər), *n.* **1.** a big, clumsy, stupid person; lout; worthless idler. **2.** *Naut.* an awkward or unskilled seaman; landlubber. —*adj.* **3.** clumsy; stupid; lubberly. —*v.i.* **4.** to behave like a lubber, esp. in the handling of a boat. [ME *lobre.* See LOB[1], -ER[1]]

lub′ber line′, *Naut.* any line made as a reference mark in the bowl of a fixed compass, esp. a line indicating the precise forward direction from the pivot of the compass card.

lub·ber·ly (lub′ər lē), *adj.* **1.** of or resembling a lubber. —*adv.* **2.** in a lubberly manner. [LUBBER + -LY] —**lub′ber·li·ness,** *n.*

lub′ber's hole′, *Naut.* (in a top on a mast) an open space through which a sailor may pass instead of climbing out on the futtock shrouds.

lub′ber's knot′, *Naut.* an improperly made reef or square knot, likely to slip loose. Also called **granny, granny knot, granny's knot, granny's bend.**

lub′ber's line′, *Navig.* a reference mark on a compass or other navigational instrument, indicating the heading of a vessel. Also, **lub′ber line′.** Also called **lub′ber's mark′, lub′ber's point′.**

Lub·bock (lub′ək), *n.* **1. Sir John, 1st Baron Avebury,** 1834–1913, English author, natural scientist, and statesman. **2.** a city in NW Texas. 128,691 (1960). **3.** a crater in the fourth quadrant of the face of the moon: about 8 miles in diameter.

lube (lo͞ob), *n. Informal.* **1.** lubricant. **2.** an application of a lubricant, as to a vehicle. [short form]

Lü·beck (ly′bek), *n.* a seaport in N West Germany: important Baltic port in the medieval Hanseatic League. 236,600 (1963). See map under **Hanseatic League.**

Lu·bin·iez·ky (lo͞o′bin yet′skē), *n.* a walled plain in the third quadrant of the face of the moon: about 24 miles in diameter.

Lu·bitsch (lo͞o′bich), *n.* **Ernst** (ûrnst; *Ger.* ernst), 1892–1947, German motion-picture director and producer, in the U.S. after 1922.

Lüb·ke (lyp′kə), *n.* **Hein·rich** (hīn′riḵh), born 1894, German statesman: president of West Germany since 1959. Also, **Luebke.**

Lu·blin (lyo͞o′blin), *n.* a city in E Poland. 194,000 (est. 1963). Russian, **Lyublin.**

lu·bra (lo͞o′brə), *n. Australian.* a female aborigine. [< native Austral]

lu·bric (lo͞o′brik), *adj. Archaic.* lubricous. [late ME *lubrik* < L *lūbric(us)* slippery, smooth, ML: lewd]

lu·bri·cant (lo͞o′brə kənt), *n.* **1.** a substance, as oil, grease, etc., for lessening friction, esp. in the working parts of a mechanism. —*adj.* **2.** capable of lubricating; used to lubricate. [< L *lūbricant-* (s. of *lūbricāns*) making slippery, prp. of *lūbricāre.* See LUBRIC, -ANT]

lu·bri·cate (lo͞o′brə kāt′), *v.,* **-cat·ed, -cat·ing.** —*v.t.* **1.** to apply some oily or greasy substance to (a machine, parts of a mechanism, etc.) in order to diminish friction; oil or grease (something). **2.** to make slippery or smooth; apply a lubricant to: *to lubricate one's hands with a lotion.* **3.** to smooth over, make viable, or the like, as some human relationship, as if through the use of a lubricant: *to lubricate the friction between enemies.* **4.** *Slang.* to provide with intoxicating drinks. —*v.i.* **5.** to act as a lubricant. **6.** to apply a lubricant to something: *When it's time to lubricate, try this oil.* **7.** *Slang.* to drink or become drunk. [< L *lūbricāt(us)* made slippery, ptp. of *lūbricāre.* See LUBRIC, -ATE[1]] —**lu′bri·ca′tion,** *n.* —**lu′bri·ca′tion·al,** *adj.* —**lu′bri·ca′tive,** *adj.* —**lu·bri·ca·to·ry** (lo͞o′brə kə tôr′ē, -tōr′ē, -kā′tə rē), *adj.*

lu·bri·ca·tor (lo͞o′brə kā′tər), *n.* a person or a device that lubricates. [LUBRICATE + -OR[2]]

lu·bri·cious (lo͞o brish′əs), *adj.* lubricous. [LUBRIC + -IOUS] —**lu·bri′cious·ly,** *adv.*

lu·bric·i·ty (lo͞o bris′i tē), *n.* **1.** oily smoothness, as of a surface; slipperiness. **2.** ability to lubricate; capacity for lubrication: *the wonderful lubricity of this new oil.* **3.** instability; shiftiness; fleetingness: *the lubricity of fame and fortune.* **4.** lewdness; wantonness; lustfulness: lasciviousness; salaciousness. **5.** something that arouses lasciviousness, esp. pornography. [late ME *lubrycyte* lewdness < ML *lubricitās* lechery, LL: slipperiness. See LUBRIC, -ITY]

lu·bri·cous (lo͞o′brə kəs), *adj.* **1.** (of a surface, coating, etc.) having an oily smoothness; slippery. **2.** unstable; uncertain; shifty. **3.** sexually wanton; lewd; lecherous; salacious. Also, **lubricious.** [< L *lūbricus* slippery, LL: unstable]
—**Syn. 2.** unsteady, wavering, undependable. **3.** lascivious, lustful, libidinous, concupiscent, impure, pornographic, obscene, filthy.

Lu·bum·ba·shi (lo͞o bo͝om′bä shē), *n.* a city in the S Democratic Republic of the Congo. 183,711 (est. 1959). Formerly, **Elisabethville.**

Lu·can (lo͞o′kən), *n.* (*Marcus Annaeus Lucanus*) A.D. 39–65, Roman poet, born in Spain.

Lu·ca·ni·a (lo͞o kā′nē ə), *n.* **1.** an ancient region in S Italy, NW of the Gulf of Taranto. **2.** a modern region in S Italy, comprising most of the ancient region. 648,085 (1961); 3856 sq. mi. Italian, **Basilicata.**

lu·carne (lo͞o kärn′), *n. Rare.* a dormer window. [< F; r. *lucane* < MF; orig. of both F forms obscure]

Lu·cas (lo͞o′kəs), *n.* a boy's given name, form of **Luke.**

Lu·cas van Ley·den (lo͞o′käs vän līd′ən), (*Lucas Hugensz*) 1494–1533, Dutch painter and engraver.

Luc·ca (lo͞ok′kä), *n.* a city in NW Italy, W of Florence. 85,940 (1961).

luce (lo͞os), *n.* **1.** a pike, esp. when fully grown. **2.** *Heraldry.* a stylized representation of a pike. [ME < MF *lus* pike < LL *lūcius*]

Luce (lo͞os), *n.* **1. Clare Boothe,** born 1903, U.S. writer and politician. **2. Henry Robinson,** 1898–1967, U.S. publisher and editor (husband of Clare Boothe Luce). **3.** a girl's given name, form of **Lucy.**

Lu·celle (lo͞o sel′), *n.* a girl's given name, form of **Lucia** or **Lucy.** Also, **Lucile, Lucille.**

lu·cent (lo͞o′sənt), *adj.* **1.** shining. **2.** translucent; clear. [< L *lūcent-* (s. of *lūcēns*) shining, prp. of *lūcēre.* See LUCID, -ENT] —**lu′cen·cy;** *Rare,* **lu′cence,** *n.* —**lu′cent·ly,** *adv.*

lu·cerne (lo͞o sûrn′), *n. Chiefly Brit.* alfalfa. Also, **lu·cern′.** [alter. (by assoc. with L *lucerna* lamp) of F *luzerne* < Pr *luzerno* glowworm (the plant was so called in allusion to its bright seeds); akin to OPr *luzerna* lamp < LL **lūcerna,* r. L *lucerna.* See LUCID]

Lu·cerne (lo͞o sûrn′; *Fr.* ly sern′), *n.* **1.** a canton in central Switzerland. 253,446 (1960); 576 sq. mi. **2.** the capital of this canton, on Lake of Lucerne. 72,600 (est. 1964). **3. Lake of.** Also called **Lake of the Four Forest Cantons.** a lake in central Switzerland. 24 mi. long; 44 sq. mi. German, **Luzern.**

lu·ces (lo͞o′sēz), *n.* pl. of **lux.**

Lu·cia (lo͞o′shə, -shē ə, -sē ə; *Ger.* lo͞o′tsē ä; *It.* lo͞o chē′ä), *n.* a girl's given name.

Lu·ci·a di Lam·mer·moor (lo͞o chē′ə dē lam′ər mo͝or′; *It.* lo͞o chē′ä dē läm′mer mo͝or′), an opera (1835) by Gaetano Donizetti, based on Sir Walter Scott's novel *The Bride of Lammermoor.*

Lu·cian (lo͞o′shən), *n.* **1.** A.D. 117–c180, Greek rhetorician and satirist. **2.** ("*Lucian of Antioch*"; "*Lucian the Martyr*") A.D. c240–312, theologian and Biblical critic, born at Samosata, in Syria. **3.** a boy's given name.

Lu·ci·anne (lo͞o′sē an′), *n.* a girl's given name.

lu·cid (lo͞o′sid), *adj.* **1.** shining or bright. **2.** clear; pellucid; transparent. **3.** easily understood; intelligible or comprehensible: *a lucid explanation.* **4.** characterized by clear perception or understanding; rational or sane: *There are a few lucid moments in his madness.* [< L *lūcid(us).* See LUX (L s. *lūc-*), -ID[4]] —**lu·cid′i·ty, lu′cid·ness,** *n.* —**lu′cid·ly,** *adv.*
—**Syn. 1.** radiant, luminous. **2.** limpid. **3.** plain, understandable, evident, obvious. **4.** sound, reasonable. —**Ant. 1.** dim. **2, 3.** obscure. **4.** irrational.

lu·ci·da (lo͞o′si də), *n., pl.* **-dae** (-dē′). *Astron.* the brightest star in a constellation. [< NL, special use of L *lūcida (stella)* bright (star), fem. of *lūcidus* LUCID]

Lu·ci·fer (lo͞o′sə fər), *n.* **1.** a proud, rebellious archangel, identified with Satan, who fell from heaven. **2.** the planet Venus when appearing as the morning star. **3.** (*l.c.*) See **friction match.** [< L: morning star, lit., light bringing, equiv. to *lūci-* (s. of *lūx*) light + *-fer* -FER]

lu·cif·er·ase (lo͞o sif′ə rās′), *n. Biochem.* an enzyme that is present in the luminous organs of fireflies and that produces luminosity when acting upon luciferin. [LUCIFER(IN) + -ASE]

lu·cif·er·in (lo͞o sif′ər in), *n. Biochem.* a pigment occurring in fireflies, luminous when acted upon by luciferase. [< L *lūcifer* (see LUCIFER) + -IN[2]]

lu′cifer match′. See **friction match.**

lu·cif·er·ous (lo͞o sif′ər əs), *adj.* bringing or giving light. [< L *lūcifer* (see LUCIFER) + -OUS]

Lu·cil·i·us (lo͞o sil′ē əs), *n.* **Ga·ius** (gā′əs), c180–102? B.C., Roman satirist.

Lu·cille (lo͞o sēl′), *n.* a girl's given name, form of **Lucia** or **Lucy.** Also, **Lucelle, Lu·cile′.**

Lu·ci·na (lo͞o sī′nə), *n.* the ancient Roman goddess of childbirth, sometimes associated with Juno or Diana. [< L, n. use of fem. of *lūcīnus* of light. See LUCID, -INE[1]]

Lu·cin·da (lo͞o sin′də), *n.* a girl's given name, form of **Lucy.**

Lu·cite (lo͞o′sīt), *n. Trademark.* any of a class of methyl methacrylate ester polymers, used chiefly as substitutes for glass.

Lu·cius (lo͞o′shəs), *n.* a boy's given name.

Lu·ci·us I (lo͞o′shē əs, -shəs), **Saint,** died A.D. 254, pope 253–254.

Lucius II, (*Gherardo Caccianemici dell' Orso*) died 1145, Italian ecclesiastic: pope 1144–45.

Lucius III, (*Ubaldo Allucingoli*) died 1185, Italian ecclesiastic: pope 1181–85.

luck (luk), *n.* **1.** the force that seems to operate for good or ill in a person's life, as in shaping circumstances, events, opportunities, etc.: *With my luck I'll probably get pneumonia.* **2.** good fortune; advantage or success, considered as the result of chance: *Wish me luck. He had no* *luck finding work.* **3.** a combination of circumstances, events, etc., operating by chance to bring good or ill to a person: *He had wonderful luck in all his ventures. She's had nothing but bad luck all year.* **4.** some object on which good fortune is supposed to depend: *This rabbit's foot is my luck.* **5. crowd one's luck,** *Informal.* to try to make too much of an opportunity. Also, **push one's luck. 6. down on one's luck,** in unfortunate circumstances; unlucky: *She hated to see her old friend so down on her luck.* **7. in luck,** lucky; fortunate: *We were in luck, for the bakery was still open.* **8. out of luck,** unlucky; unfortunate: *When it comes to getting theater tickets, we're usually out of luck.* [late ME < MD *luc;* akin to D *geluk,* G *Glück*]

luck·ie (luk′ē), *n. Scot.* lucky².

luck·i·ly (luk′ə lē), *adv.* by good luck; fortunately: *Luckily he had enough money to pay the bill.* [LUCKY + -LY]

luck·less (luk′lis), *adj.* having no luck; unfortunate; hapless; ill-fated; turning out or ending disastrously: *a luckless venture which ruined many of the investors.* [LUCK + -LESS] —**luck′less·ly,** *adv.* —**luck′less·ness,** *n.*

Luck·now (luk′nou), *n.* a city in S Uttar Pradesh, in N India: British were besieged (1857–58) during Sepoy Rebellion. 595,400 (1961).

luck·y¹ (luk′ē), *adj.,* **luck·i·er, luck·i·est. 1.** having or attended with good luck; fortunate: *That was my lucky day.* **2.** happening fortunately: *a lucky accident.* **3.** bringing or foretelling good luck, or supposed to do so: *a lucky penny.* [LUCK + -Y¹] —**luck′i·ness,** *n.*
—**Syn. 1.** favored. See **fortunate. 3.** auspicious, propitious, favorable. —**Ant. 1.** unfortunate.

luck·y² (luk′ē), *n., pl.* **luck·ies.** *Scot.* **1.** a familiar name applied to any elderly woman, esp. a grandmother; granny. **2.** a familiar name applied to any woman, as one's wife, a barmaid, etc. Also, **luckie.** [LUCK + -Y²]

Luck·y (luk′ē), *n.* a boy's or girl's given name.

lu·cra·tive (lo͞o′krə tiv), *adj.* profitable; moneymaking; remunerative: *a lucrative business; lucrative employment.* [< L *lucrātīv(us)* gainful, equiv. to *lucrāt(us)* profited (ptp. of *lucrārī;* see LUCRE) + *-īvus* -IVE; r. late ME *lucratif* < MF] —**lu′cra·tive·ly,** *adv.* —**lu′cra·tive·ness,** *n.*

lu·cre (lo͞o′kər), *n.* monetary reward or gain; money: *The tour netted her a pile of lucre.* [ME < L *lucr(um)* profit; akin to OE *lēan* reward, G *Lohn,* Goth, Icel *laun*]

Lu·cre·tia (lo͞o krē′shə, -shē ə), *n.* **1.** Also called **Lucrece** (lo͞o krēs′). *Rom. Legend.* a Roman woman whose suicide, after her rape by a son of Tarquin the Proud, led to the expulsion of the Tarquins and the establishment of the Roman republic. **2.** a girl's given name.

Lu·cre·tius (lo͞o krē′shəs), *n.* (*Titus Lucretius Carus*) 97?–54 B.C., Roman poet and philosopher. —**Lu·cre′tian,** *adj.*

Lu·cre·zi·a Bor·gia (lo͞o kret′sē ə bôr′jə, -krē′shə, bôr′zhə; *It.* lo͞o kre′tsyä bôʀ′jä), an opera (1833) by Gaetano Donizetti.

lu·cu·brate (lo͞o′kyo͞o brāt′), *v.i.,* **-brat·ed, -brat·ing. 1.** to work, write, or study laboriously, esp. at night. **2.** to write learnedly. [< L *lūcubrāt(us),* ptp. of *lūcubrāre* to work by artificial light. See LUCULENT, CANDELABRA, -ATE¹] —**lu′cu·bra′tor,** *n.* —**lu′cu·bra·to·ry,** *adj.*

lu·cu·bra·tion (lo͞o′kyo͞o brā′shən), *n.* **1.** laborious work, study, etc., esp. at night. **2.** the result of such activity, as a learned speech, dissertation, etc. **3.** Often, **lucubrations.** any literary effort, esp. of a pretentious or solemn nature. [< L *lūcubrātiōn-* (s. of *lūcubrātiō*) night-work. See LUCUBRATE, -ION]

lu·cu·lent (lo͞o′kyo͞o lənt), *adj.* **1.** clear or lucid, as explanations, interpretations, etc. **2.** convincing; cogent. [< L *lūculent(us)* bright, equiv. to *lūc-* (s. of *lūx*) light + *-ulentus* -ULENT] —**lu′cu·lent·ly,** *adv.*

Lu·cul·lus (lo͞o kul′əs), *n.* **Lucius Li·cin·i·us** (li sin′ē əs), c110–57? B.C., Roman general and epicure. —**Lu·cul′lan, Lu·cul·le·an** (lo͞o′kə lē′ən), **Lu·cul′li·an,** *adj.*

lu·cus a non lu·cen·do (lo͞o′ko͞os ä nōn lo͞o ken′dō; *Eng.* lo͞o′kəs ā non lo͞o sen′dō), *Latin.* an absurd conclusion, explanation, manner of reasoning, etc.; non sequitur; absurdity. [lit., grove from not giving light, i.e., a grove (*lūcus*) is so called because it does not shine (*lūcēre*), an illustration of the etymological procedure (mentioned by Quintilian) of deriving a word from another having a contrary sense]

Lu·cy (lo͞o′sē), *n.* a girl's given name. Also, **Luci.**

Lu′cy Ston′er (stō′nər), a person who advocates the retention of the maiden name by married women. Cf. **Stone** (def. 4). [*Lucy* STONE + -ER¹]

Ludd (*Welsh.* lʏᴛʜ), *n.* Llud.

Lud·dite (lud′īt), *n.* a member of any of various bands of workmen in England (1811–16) organized to destroy manufacturing machinery, under the belief that its use diminished employment. [after Ned *Ludd,* 18th-century Leicestershire worker who originated the idea; see -ITE¹] —**Lud′dism, Lud′dit·ism,** *n.*

Lu·den·dorff (lo͞od′ᵊn dôrf′), *n.* **E·rich Frie·drich Wil·helm von** (ā′ʀɪᴋʜ frē′dʀɪᴋʜ vil′helm fən), 1865–1937, German general.

Lü·der·itz (lʏ′dər its), *n.* a seaport in SW South-West Africa: diamond-mining center. 3925 (1951).

Lu·dhi·a·na (lo͞o′dē ä′nä), *n.* a city in central Punjab, in N India. 244,000 (1961).

lu·di·crous (lo͞o′də krəs), *adj.* causing laughter; provoking or deserving derision; amusingly absurd; ridiculous; comical; laughable: *a ludicrous incident.* [< L *lūdicrus* sportive, equiv. to *lūdicr(um)* a show, public games (*lūdi-,* s. of *lūdere* to play, + *-crum* n. suffix of instrument or result) + *-us* -OUS] —**lu′di·crous·ly,** *adv.* —**lu′di·crous·ness,** *n.*
—**Syn.** farcical. See **funny.** —**Ant.** solemn, serious, tragic.

Lu·die (lo͞o′dē), *n.* a girl's given name.

Lud·ing·ton (lud′ing tən), *n.* a town in W Michigan. 9421 (1960).

Lud·low (lud′lō), *n.* **1.** a town in S Shropshire, in W England: agricultural market center. 6774 (1961). **2.** a town in N Kentucky. 6233 (1960).

Lud·low (lud′lō), *n. Typesetting, Trademark.* a machine for casting slugs from matrices handset in a composing stick.

Lud·wig (lud′wig; *Ger.* lo͞ot′vɪᴋʜ, lo͞od′-), *n.* **1. E·mil** (ā′mēl), (*Emil Cohn*), 1881–1948, German biographer. **2.** a boy's given name.

Ludwig II, German name of **Louis II.**

Lud·wigs·ha·fen (lo͞ot′vɪᴋʜs hä′fən, lo͞od′-), *n.* a city in W West Germany, on the Rhine opposite Mannheim. 171,500 (1963).

Lueb·ke (lʏp′kə), *n.* **Hein·rich** (hīn′ʀɪᴋʜ). See **Lübke, Heinrich.**

Lu·el·la (lo͞o el′ə), *n.* a girl's given name.

Luen·ing (lo͞o′ning), *n.* **Otto,** born 1900, U.S. composer, conductor, and flutist.

lu·es (lo͞o′ēz), *n. Pathol.* syphilis. [< NL, special use of L *lues* contagious disease]

lu·et·ic (lo͞o et′ik), *adj. Pathol.* syphilitic. [LUE(S) + -TIC] —**lu·et′i·cal·ly,** *adv.*

luff (luf), *n. Naut.* **1.** the forward edge of a fore-and-aft sail. See diag. under **sail. 2.** *Obs.* loof (def. 2). —*v.i.* **3.** to bring the head of a sailing vessel closer to or directly into the wind, with sails shaking. **4.** (of a sail) to shake from being set too close to the wind: *The sail luffed as we put about for port.* **5.** to raise or lower the outer end of the boom of a crane or derrick so as to move its load horizontally. —*v.t.* **6.** to set (the helm of a vessel) in such a way as to bring the head of the vessel into the wind. **7.** to raise or lower the outer end of (the boom of a crane or derrick). **8. luff alee!** *Naut.* See **hard** (def. 48). [ME *lof, loof* some kind of steering gear < OD (unrecorded), later D *loef* tholepin (of tiller); akin to Goth *lōfa,* Icel *lōfi* palm of the hand, OHG *lappo* palm of the hand, blade of a rudder]

luf·fa (luf′ə), *n.* **1.** Also called **dishcloth gourd, rag gourd. a.** the fruit of any cucurbitaceous plant of the genus *Luffa.* **b.** a plant bearing this fruit. **2.** Also called **vegetable sponge.** the fibrous interior of the dried fruit, used as a sponge. Also, **loofa, loofah.** [< NL, name of genus < Ar *lūf*]

luff′ on luff′, *Naut.* a tackle composed of one luff attached to the fall of another. Also called **luff′ upon luff′.**

luff′ tack′le, *Naut.* a tackle composed of a fall rove through a double block and a single block and fastened to the single block, giving a mechanical advantage of three or four, neglecting friction, depending on which is the standing and which is the running block. See diag. under **tackle.**

Luf·kin (luf′kin), *n.* a city in E Texas. 17,641 (1960).

Luft·waf·fe (lo͞oft′väf′ə), *n. German.* (under the Nazis) the German air force. [lit., air weapon]

lug¹ (lug), *v.,* **lugged, lug·ging,** *n.* —*v.t.* **1.** to pull along or carry with force or effort: *to lug a suitcase upstairs.* **2.** *Informal.* to introduce or interject in a forced, inappropriate, or irrelevant manner: *to lug personalities into a discussion of philosophy.* **3.** (of a sailing vessel) to carry an excessive amount of (sail) for the conditions prevailing. —*v.i.* **4.** to pull; tug. —*n.* **5.** an act or instance of lugging; a forcible pull; haul. **6.** a wooden box for transporting fruit or vegetables. **7.** *Slang.* a request for or exaction of money, as for political purposes: *They put the lug on him at the office.* [ME *lugge(n)* < Scand; cf. Norw *lugge,* Sw *lugga* to pull by the hair]

lug² (lug), *n.* **1.** a projecting piece by which anything is held or supported. **2.** *Masonry.* either of the ends of a lug sill. **3.** *Carpentry.* (in a double-hung window) one of a pair of projections extending downward from the ends of the meeting rail of the upper sash. **4.** a leather loop hanging down from a saddle, through which a shaft is passed for support. **5.** *Shipbuilding.* clip² (def. 6). **6.** *Slang.* **a.** an awkward, clumsy fellow. **b.** a blockhead. **c.** an average man; guy. [< Scand; cf. Norw, Sw *lugg* forelock. See LUG¹]

lug³ (lug), *n.* lugsail. [by shortening]

lug⁴ (lug), *n.* lugworm. [? special use of LUG²]

Lug (lo͞oᴋʜ), *n.* an ancient Irish god, probably a solar deity, appearing in a number of legends.

Lu·gan·da (lo͞o gan′də, -gän′-), *n.* a Bantu language of Uganda. Also called **Ganda.**

Lu·gansk (lo͞o gänsk′), *n.* a city in the E Ukraine, in the S Soviet Union in Europe. 323,000 (est. 1964). Formerly, **Voroshilovgrad.**

luge (lo͞ozh), *n.* a one-man or two-man sled for coasting or racing down a chute, used esp. in Europe. [< dial. F]

Lu·ger (lo͞o′gər), *n. Trademark.* an automatic pistol of 9-millimeter caliber, made in Germany.

lug′ fore′sail, *Naut.* a gaff foresail having no boom or sometimes a partial boom.

lug·gage (lug′ij), *n.* suitcases, trunks, valises, etc.; baggage. [LUG¹ + -AGE] —**lug′gage·less,** *adj.*

lug′gage tan′, the color generally used for leather luggage, varying from light, yellowish tan to dark brown.

lug·ger (lug′ər), *n. Naut.* a small vessel lug-rigged on two or three masts. [LUG(SAIL) + -ER¹]

lug′ger top′sail, *Naut.* a fore-and-aft topsail used above a lugsail.

lug·gie (lug′ē, lo͞og′ē, lo͞o′gē), *n. Scot.* any wooden vessel with a lug, or handle, as a mug, a pail, or a dish with a handle on the side. [LUG² + -IE]

Lug·nas·ad (*Irish Gaelic.* lo͞o′nə sə), *n.* a feast formerly held in Ireland on the first of August.

lug′ nut′, a large nut fitting over a heavy bolt, used esp. in attaching a wheel to an automobile.

Lu·go (lo͞o′gō), *n.* a city in NW Spain. 59,368 (1963).

Lu·go·nes (lo͞o gô′nes), *n.* **Le·o·pol·do** (le′ō pôl′dō), 1874–1938, Argentine poet and diplomat.

lug′ pad′, padeye.

lug-rigged (lug′rigd′), *adj. Naut.* rigged with a lugsail or lugsails.

lug·sail (lug′sāl′; *Naut.* lug′səl), *n. Naut.* a quadrilateral sail bent upon a yard that crosses the mast obliquely. See diag. under **sail.** Also called **lug.** [ME *lugge* pole (now dial.) + SAIL]

lug′ sill′, *Building Trades.* a sill that has its ends built into the masonry. Cf. **slip sill.**

lug′ top′sail, *Naut.* See under **jackyard.**

lu·gu·bri·ous (lo͞o go͞o′brē əs, -gyo͞o′-), *adj.* mournful, dismal, gloomy, or the like, esp. in an affected, exaggerated, or unrelieved manner: *lugubrious tones of voice; a lugubrious expression.* [< L *lūgubri(s)* mournful (akin to *lūgēre* to mourn) + -OUS] —**lu·gu′bri·ous·ly,** *adv.* —**lu·gu′bri·ous·ness, lu·gu·bri·os·i·ty** (lə go͞o′brē os′i tē, -gyo͞o′-), *n.*
—**Syn.** sorrowful, melancholy. —**Ant.** cheerful.

lug·worm (lug′wûrm′), *n.* any burrowing, marine annelid of the genus *Arenicola,* having tufted gills, found in the sand and used as bait for fishing. Also called **lug.** [LUG⁴ + WORM]

lug′ wrench′, a wrench for loosening or tightening lug nuts.

Lu Hsün (lo͞o′ shʏn′), (*Chou Shu-jên*) 1881–1936, Chinese writer.

Luik (loik, lo͞ok), *n.* Flemish name of **Liège.**

Lu·kacs (lo͞o′käch), *n.* **George,** born 1885, Hungarian literary critic. Hungarian, **György Lu·kács** (dyœʀ′dyᵊ lo͞o′käch).

Lu·kan (lo͞o′kən), *adj.* of or pertaining to the Evangelist Luke or to the third Gospel, traditionally believed to have been written by him. [LUKE + -AN]

Lu·kas (lo͞o′kəs), *n.* **Paul,** born 1895, U.S. actor, born in Hungary.

Luke (lo͞ok), *n.* **1.** an early Christian disciple and companion of Paul, a physician and probably a gentile: traditionally believed to be the author of the Gospel of St. Luke and the Acts. **2.** the third Gospel. **3.** a boy's given name.

luke·warm (lo͞ok′wôrm′), *adj.* **1.** moderately warm; tepid. **2.** having or showing little ardor or zeal; indifferent: *lukewarm applause.* [ME *lukewarme* tepid, equiv. to *luke* tepid (*lew,* OE *gehlēow* tepid + *k-* suffix) + *warme* WARM] —**luke′warm′ly,** *adv.* —**luke′warm′ness, luke′warmth′,** *n.*

Luks (luks), *n.* **George Benjamin,** 1867–1933, U.S. painter.

Lu·la (lo͞o′lə), *n.* a girl's given name, form of **Louise.**

lu·lab (lo͞o läb′), *n., pl.* **lu·la·bim** (lo͞o lä bēm′), **lu·labs.** *Judaism.* a palm branch for use with the ethrog during the Sukkoth festival service. Also, **lulav.** [< Heb *lūlābh*]

lu·lav (lo͞o′lôv, -ləv), *n., pl.* **lu·lav·im** (lo͞o′lô vēm′, -lə-), **lu·lavs.** *Judaism.* lulab.

Lu·le·å (lo͞o′le ô′), *n.* a seaport in NE Sweden, on the Gulf of Bothnia. 33,983 (1965).

Lu·lie (lo͞o′lē), *n.* a girl's given name, form of **Louise.** Also, **Lu′li.**

Lu·ling (lo͞o′ling), *n.* a town in central Texas. 4412 (1960).

lull (lul), *v.t.* **1.** to put to sleep or rest by soothing means: *to lull a child by singing.* **2.** to soothe or quiet. **3.** to give or lead to feel a false sense of safety; cause to be less alert, aware, or watchful. —*v.i.* **4.** to quiet down, let up, or subside: *furious activity that finally lulled.* —*n.* **5.** a lulled condition; a temporary quiet or stillness: *a lull in a storm.* **6.** a soothing sound: *the lull of falling waters.* **7.** a pacified or stupefied condition: *The drug had put him in a lull.* [ME *lulle(n),* perh. imit.; cf. Sw *lulla,* G *lullen,* L *lallāre* to sing lullaby] —**lull′er,** *n.* —**lull′ing·ly,** *adv.*

lull·a·by (lul′ə bī′), *n., pl.* **-bies,** *v.,* **-bied, -by·ing.** —*n.* **1.** a song used to lull a child to sleep; cradlesong. **2.** any lulling song. —*v.t.* **3.** to lull with or as with a lullaby. [late ME interj. *lulla! + by!*]

Lul·ly (lo͞o′lē, *Fr.* lʏ lē′ *for 1;* lul′ē *for 2*), *n.* **1.** *Italian,* **Lul·li** (lo͞ol′lē). **Jean Bap·tiste** (zhäɴ bᴀ tēst′), 1632–87, French composer, esp. of operas and ballets, born in Italy. **2.** Catalan, **Lull** (lo͞ol). **Raymond** or **Ra·món** (rä môn′), ("*Doctor Illuminatus*"), 1235?–1315, Spanish theologian, philosopher, and author.

lu·lu¹ (lo͞o′lo͞o), *n.* **1.** *Slang.* any remarkable or outstanding person or thing: *Our new secretary is a lulu.* **2.** (*cap.*) a girl's given name, form of **Louise.** [slang sense, after the proper name]

lu·lu² (lo͞o′lo͞o), *n. Slang.* **1.** a tax-free allowance granted to some members of the legislative body in certain States, usually in recognition of a legislator's seniority, position as head of an important committee, etc. **2.** such an allowance granted by a governor to a legislator in return for a political favor. [special use of LULU¹]

Lu·lua·bourg (lo͞ol′wä bo͞or′), *n.* a city in central Democratic Republic of the Congo. 115,049 (est. 1959).

lumb-, var. of **lumbo-** before a vowel: *lumbar.*

lum·ba·go (lum bā′gō), *n. Pathol.* pain in the lower, or lumbar, region of the back or loins, esp. chronic or recurring pain. [< LL, deriv. of *lumbus* the loin]

lum·bar (lum′bər, -bär), *adj.* **1.** of or pertaining to the loin or loins. —*n.* **2.** a lumbar vertebra, artery, or the like. See illus. under **spinal column.** [< NL *lumbār(is).* See LUMB-, -AR¹]

lum·ber¹ (lum′bər), *n.* **1.** *U.S., Canadian.* timber sawed or split into planks, boards, etc. **2.** miscellaneous useless articles that are stored away. —*v.i.* **3.** *U.S., Canadian.* to cut timber and prepare it for market. **4.** to become useless or to be stored away as useless. —*v.t.* **5.** *U.S., Canadian.* to convert (a specified amount, area, etc.) into lumber: *We lumbered more than a million acres last year. The company will lumber the south forest next month.* **6.** to heap together in disorder. **7.** to fill up or obstruct with miscellaneous useless articles; encumber. [orig. n. use of LUMBER²; i.e., useless goods that weigh one down, impede one's movements] —**lum′ber·er,** *n.* —**lum′ber·less,** *adj.* —**lum′ber·ly,** *adv.*

lum·ber² (lum′bər), *v.i.* **1.** to move clumsily or heavily, esp. from great or ponderous bulk: *a fat man lumbering down the walk.* **2.** *Obs.* to make a rumbling noise. [ME *lomere(n);* cf. dial. Sw *lomra* to resound, *loma* to walk heavily]

lum·ber·ing¹ (lum′bər ing), *n. U.S., Canadian.* the trade or business of cutting and preparing timber. [LUMBER¹ + -ING¹]

lum·ber·ing² (lum′bər ing), *adj.* **1.** moving clumsily or heavily; awkward. **2.** *Obs.* moving along with a rumbling noise. [LUMBER² + -ING²] —**lum′ber·ing·ly,** *adv.* —**lum′ber·ing·ness,** *n.*

lum·ber·jack (lum′bər jak′), *n.* **1.** *U.S., Canadian.* a person who works at lumbering. **2.** See **lumber jacket. 3.** *Canadian.* See **Canada jay.** [LUMBER¹ + JACK¹]

lum′ber jack′et, a short, straight, wool plaid jacket or coat, for informal wear, usually belted and having patch pockets. Also called **lumberjack.**

lum·ber·man (lum′bər mən), *n., pl.* **-men. 1.** a person who deals in lumber. **2.** a person who cuts and prepares timber. Cf. **logger.** [LUMBER¹ + MAN¹]

lum·ber·mill (lum′bər mil′), *n.* a mill for dressing logs and lumber. [LUMBER¹ + MILL¹]

lum′ber room′, *Brit.* a room in a house used for storing odds-and-ends, esp. old furniture.

Lum·ber·ton (lum′bər tən), *n.* a city in S North Carolina. 15,305 (1960).

lum·ber·yard (lum′bər yärd′), *n. U.S., Canadian.* a yard where lumber is stored for sale. [LUMBER¹ + YARD²]

lumbo-, a learned borrowing from Latin meaning "loin," used in the formation of compound words: *lumbosacral.* Also, *esp. before a vowel,* **lumb-.** [comb. form repr. L *lumbus* loin; see -o-]

lum·bo·sa·cral (lum′bō sā′krəl), *adj. Anat.* of, pertaining to, or involving the lumbar and sacral regions or parts. [LUMBO- + SACRAL]

lum·bri·cal (lum′bri kəl), *n. Anat.* any of four wormlike muscles in the palm of the hand and in the sole of the foot. [< NL *lumbricāl(is),* lit., pertaining to a worm, equiv. to L *lumbrīc(us)* maw-worm, earthworm + *-ālis* -AL[1]]

lum·bri·ca·lis (lum′brə kā′lis), *n., pl.* **-les** (-lēz). *Anat.* lumbrical. [< NL]

lum·bri·coid (lum′brə koid′), *adj.* resembling an earthworm. [< NL *lumbricoid(es).* See LUMBRICAL, -OID]

lu·men (lo͞o′mən), *n., pl.* **-mi·na** (-mə nə). **1.** *Optics.* the unit of luminous flux, equal to the luminous flux emitted in a unit solid angle by a point source of one-candle intensity. *Abbr.:* lm **2.** *Anat.* the canal, duct, or cavity of a tubular organ. **3.** *Bot.* (of a cell) the cavity which the cell walls enclose. [< NL, special uses of L *lūmen* light, window]

Lu·men (lo͞o′mən), *n.* a boy's given name.

lu·men-hour (lo͞o′mən our′, -ou′ər), *n. Optics.* a unit of luminous energy, equal to that emitted in one hour by a light source emitting a luminous flux of one lumen. *Abbr.:* lm-hr

Lu·mière (ly myer′), *n.* **Au·guste Ma·rie Louis Ni·co·las** (ō gyst′ ma rē′ lwē nē kô lä′), 1862–1954, and his brother, **Louis Jean** (lwē zhäN), 1864–1948, French chemists and manufacturers of photographic materials: inventors of a motion-picture camera (1895) and a process of color photography.

Lu·mi·nal (lo͞o′mə nᵊl), *n. Pharm., Trademark.* phenobarbital.

lu·mi·nance (lo͞o′mə nəns), *n.* **1.** the state or quality of being luminous. **2.** Also called **luminosity.** the quality or condition of radiating or reflecting light: *the blinding luminance of the sun.* **3.** *Optics.* the quantitative measure of brightness of a light source or an illuminated surface, equal to luminous flux per unit solid angle emitted per unit projected area of its surface. [< L *lūmin-* (s. of *lūmen*) light + -ANCE]

lu·mi·nar·y (lo͞o′mə ner′ē), *n., pl.* **-nar·ies,** *adj.* —*n.* **1.** a celestial body, as the sun or moon. **2.** a body, object, etc., that gives light. **3.** a person of intellectual or moral eminence, esp. a person who has attained eminence in his field or is an inspiration to others; a leading light: *one of the luminaries in the field of medical science; a Hollywood luminary.* **4.** (loosely) any famous person; celebrity: *trying to glimpse some of the theatrical luminaries at the party.* —*adj.* **5.** of, pertaining to, or characterized by light. [late ME *luminarye* < ML *lūminăria* lamp (fem. sing.), L: windows (neut. pl.). See LUMEN, -ARY]

lu·mine (lo͞o′min), *v.t.* **-mined, -min·ing.** *Obs.* to illumine. [ME *lumine(n),* aph. var. of *enlumine(n)* to ILLUMINE. See LIMN]

lu·mi·nesce (lo͞o′mə nes′), *v.i.,* **-nesced, -nesc·ing.** to exhibit luminescence. [back formation from LUMINESCENT]

lu·mi·nes·cence (lo͞o′mə nes′əns), *n.* **1.** the emission of light not caused by incandescence and occurring at a temperature below that of incandescent bodies. **2.** the light produced by such an emission. [< L *lūmin-* (see LUMEN) + -ESCENCE]

lu·mi·nes·cent (lo͞o′mə nes′ənt), *adj.* characterized by or pertaining to luminescence. [< L *lūmin-* (see LUMEN) + -ESCENT]

lu·mi·nif·er·ous (lo͞o′mə nif′ər əs), *adj.* producing light: *the luminiferous properties of a gas.* [< L *lūmin-* (see LUMEN) + -I- + -FEROUS]

lu·mi·no·phore (lo͞o′mə nə fōr′, -fôr′), *n. Physics, Chem.* a molecule or group of molecules that emits light when illuminated. Also, **lu′mi·no·phor′.** [< L *lūmin-* (see LUMEN) + -O- + -PHORE]

lu·mi·nos·i·ty (lo͞o′mə nos′i tē), *n., pl.* **-ties. 1.** luminance (def. 2). **2.** the quality of being intellectually brilliant, enlightened, inspired, etc.: *The luminosity of his poetry is unequaled.* **3.** something luminous: *This new play appears as a luminosity in an otherwise drab season on Broadway.* **4.** *Astron.* the brightness of a star in comparison with that of the sun: the luminosity of Sirius expressed as 23 indicates an intrinsic brightness 23 times as great as that of the sun. [< L *lūminōs(us)* LUMINOUS + -ITY]

lu·mi·nous (lo͞o′mə nəs), *adj.* **1.** radiating or reflecting light; shining; bright. **2.** lighted up or illuminated; well-lighted: *The ballroom was luminous with the light from a thousand candles.* **3.** brilliant intellectually; enlightened or enlightening, as a writer or his writings: *a luminous concept; luminous prose.* **4.** clear; readily intelligible: *a concise, luminous report.* [< L *lūminōsus.* See LUMEN, -OUS] —**lu′mi·nous·ly,** *adv.* —**lu′mi·nous·ness,** *n.*

—**Syn. 1.** lucid, radiant, resplendent, brilliant. **3.** bright, intelligent. **4.** understandable, perspicuous, lucid. —**Ant. 1, 2.** dark. **3.** stupid. **4.** obscure.

lu′minous emit′tance, *Optics.* luminous flux emitted per unit area.

lu′minous en′ergy, light[1] (def. 2a).

lu′minous flux′, *Optics.* the rate of transmission of luminous energy: expressed in lumens.

lu′minous flux′ den′sity, luminous flux per unit of cross-sectional area.

lu′minous inten′sity, *Optics.* the luminous flux in lumens emitted per unit solid angle by a light source, measured in candles.

lu′minous range′, *Navig.* the distance at which a certain light, as that of a lighthouse, is visible in clear weather, disregarding interference from obstructions and from the curvature of the earth and depending on the power of the light.

lu·mis·ter·ol (lo͞o mis′tə rôl′, -rōl′), *n. Biochem.* a water-insoluble compound, $C_{28}H_{44}O$, produced by the irradiation of ergosterol. [< L *lumi(n)-* (see LUMEN) + STEROL]

lum·mox (lum′əks), *n. Informal.* a clumsy, stupid person. [?]

lump[1] (lump), *n.* **1.** a piece or mass of solid matter without regular shape or of no particular shape. **2.** a protuberance or swelling: *a blow that raised a lump on his head.* **3.** an aggregation, collection, or mass; clump: *All the articles were piled in a great lump.* **4.** Also called **lump of sugar.** a small cube of granulated sugar, usually oblong, designed for sweetening hot coffee, tea, etc.: *How many lumps in your coffee, Jack?* **5.** majority; plurality; multitude: *The great lump of voters are still undecided.* **6.** *Informal.* a heavy, clumsy, and usually stupid person. **7. get** or **take one's lumps,** to receive or endure deserved or undeserved hardship, punishment, criticism, etc. **8. in the lump,** as a whole; taken together: *In the lump they were interesting people.* —*adj.* **9.** in the form of a lump or lumps: *lump sugar.* **10.** made up of a number of items taken together; not separated or considered separately: *The royalties were paid in a lump sum.* —*v.t.* **11.** to unite into one aggregation, collection, or mass (often fol. by *together*): *We lumped the reds and blues together. We lumped the old things with the new.* **12.** to deal with, handle, consider, etc., in the lump or mass: *She tends to lump disparate matters indiscriminately.* **13.** to make into a lump or lumps: *to lump dough before shaping it into loaves.* **14.** to raise into or cover with lumps: *a plow lumping the moist earth; golf balls lumping his pockets.* —*v.i.* **15.** to form or raise a lump or lumps: *If it starts to lump, take it off the fire.* **16.** to move heavily and awkwardly: *The big oaf lumped along beside me.* [ME *lumpe, lomp(e);* c. early D *lompe* piece, Dan *lump(e)* lump, dial. Norw *lump* block] —**lump′ing·ly,** *adv.*

lump[2] (lump), *v.t. Informal.* to put up with; resign oneself to; accept and endure: *If you don't like it, you can lump it.* [?]

lum·pen (lum′pən), *adj.* of or pertaining to disfranchised and uprooted individuals or groups, esp. those who have lost status in their class: *The marginal members of the middle class suffer heavily during a depression and often become part of the lumpen bourgeoisie.* [< G *Lumpen-,* comb. form of *Lump* ragamuffin and *Lumpen* rag, as in *Lumpenproletariat*]

lump·er (lum′pər), *n.* a laborer employed to load and unload vessels in port; dock-walloper; longshoreman. [LUMP[1] + -ER[1]]

lump·fish (lump′fish′), *n., pl.* (*esp. collectively*) **-fish,** (*esp. referring to two or more kinds or species*) **-fish·es.** any of several thick-bodied, sluggish fishes of the family *Cyclopteridae,* found in northern seas, having the pelvic fins modified and united into a sucking disk, esp. *Cyclopterus lumpus,* of the North Atlantic. [LUMP[1] + FISH]

lump·ish (lum′pish), *adj.* **1.** like a lump. **2.** having a heavy appearance; moving clumsily. **3.** having a sluggish mind; unresponsive; dull; stupid. [ME *lumpisch.* See LUMP[1], -ISH[1]] —**lump′ish·ly,** *adv.* —**lump′ish·ness,** *n.*

lump·suck·er (lump′suk′ər), *n.* any of several fishes of the lumpfish family. [obs. *lump* LUMPFISH + SUCKER]

lump·y (lum′pē), *adj.,* **lump·i·er, lump·i·est. 1.** full of lumps: *lumpy gravy.* **2.** covered with lumps, as a surface. **3.** heavy or clumsy, as in movement, style, or the like; crude: *to have a lumpy gait; a lumpy narrative.* **4.** (of water) rough or choppy. [LUMP[1] + -Y[1]] —**lump′i·ly,** *adv.* —**lump′i·ness,** *n.*

lump′y jaw′, *Pathol., Vet. Pathol.* actinomycosis.

Lu·mum·ba (lo͞o mo͝om′bə), *n.* **Pa·trice (Em·er·gy)** (pə trēs′ em′er zhē′), 1925–61, African political leader: premier of the Republic of the Congo 1960–61.

Lu·na (lo͞o′nə), *n.* **1.** the ancient Roman goddess personifying the moon, sometimes identified with Diana. **2.** (in alchemy) silver. **3.** (*l.c.*) Also, **lunette.** *Eccles.* the crescent-shaped receptacle within the monstrance, for holding the consecrated Host in an upright position. [< L: moon]

lu·na·cy (lo͞o′nə sē), *n., pl.* **-cies. 1.** intermittent insanity, formerly believed to be related to phases of the moon. **2.** any form of insanity, sometimes not including idiocy. **3.** extreme foolishness or an instance of it: *Her decision to resign was sheer lunacy.* **4.** *Law.* unsoundness of mind sufficient to incapacitate one for civil transactions. [LUNA(TIC) + -CY]

—**Syn. 2.** derangement, dementia; craziness, madness, mania, aberration. **3.** folly, stupidity. —**Ant. 1, 2.** rationality, sanity.

lu′na moth′, a large, pale-green, American moth, *Actias luna,* having purple-brown markings, lunate spots, and long tails. Also, **Lu′na moth′.**

lu·nar (lo͞o′nər), *adj.* **1.** of or pertaining to the moon: *the lunar orbit.* **2.** measured by the moon's revolutions: *a lunar month.* **3.** resembling the moon; round or crescent-shaped. **4.** of or pertaining to silver. —*n.* **5.** a lunar observation taken for purposes of navigation or mapping. [< L *lūnār(is)* of the moon. See LUNA, -AR[1]]

lu′nar caus′tic, *Med., Chem.* silver nitrate, $AgNO_3$, esp. in a sticklike mold, used to cauterize tissues.

lu′nar cy′cle. See **Metonic cycle.**

lu′nar day′, a division of time that is equal to the elapsed time between two consecutive returns of the same terrestrial meridian to the moon.

lu′nar dis′tance, *Navig.* the observed angle between the moon and another celestial body.

lu′nar eclipse′. See under **eclipse** (def. 1a).

lu·nar·i·an (lo͞o nâr′ē ən), *n.* **1.** a being supposedly inhabiting the moon. **2.** *Rare.* a selenographer. [< L *lūnāri(s)* LUNAR + -AN]

lu′nar month′. See under **month** (def. 5).

lu′nar rain′bow, moonbow.

lu′nar year′, year (def. 4a).

lu·nate (lo͞o′nāt), *adj.* **1.** Also, **lu′nat·ed.** crescent-shaped. —*n.* **2.** *Anat.* the second bone from the thumb side of the proximal row of bones of the carpus. **3.** *Archaeol.* any ancient crescent-shaped implement. [< L *lūnāt(us)* crescent-shaped. See LUNA, -ATE[1]] —**lu′nate·ly,** *adv.*

lu·na·tic (lo͞o′nə tik), *n.* **1.** an insane person. **2.** a person whose actions and manner are marked by extreme eccentricity or recklessness. **3.** *Law.* a person legally declared to be of unsound mind and who therefore is not held capable or responsible before the law. —*adj.* **4.** insane; demented; crazy. **5.** characteristic or suggestive of lunacy; wildly or recklessly foolish: *his lunatic handling of responsibilities.* **6.** designated for or used by the insane: *a lunatic asylum.* **7.** gaily or lightheartedly mad, frivolous, eccentric, etc.: *She has a lunatic charm that is quite engaging.* Also, **lu·nat·i·cal** (lo͞o nat′i kəl) (for defs. 4, 5, 7). [ME *lunatik* < OF *lunatique* < LL *lūnātic(us)* moonstruck. See LUNA, -ATIC] —**lu·nat′i·cal·ly,** *adv.*

lu′natic fringe′, members on the periphery of any group, esp. political, social, or religious, who hold extreme or fanatical views not subscribed to by the majority of members.

lu·na·tion (lo͞o nā′shən), *n.* the period of time from one new moon to the next (about 29½ days); a lunar month. [ME *lunacyon* < ML *lūnātiōn-* (s. of *lūnātiō*). See LUNA, -ATION]

lunch (lunch), *n.* **1.** a light meal between breakfast and dinner; luncheon. **2.** any light meal or snack: *a box lunch; picnic lunch.* **3.** an establishment which prepares and sells meals; lunchroom: *Let's eat at the dairy lunch.* —*v.i.* **4.** to eat lunch: *We lunched quite late today.* —*v.t.* **5.** to provide lunch for: *They lunched us in regal fashion.* [short for LUNCHEON] —**lunch′er,** *n.* —**lunch′less,** *adj.*

lunch·eon (lun′chən), *n.* lunch, esp. a formal lunch held in connection with a club meeting, convention, or other special occasion: *We met at the alumni luncheon.* [dissimilated var. of *nuncheon* (now dial.), ME *none(s)-chench* noon drink, equiv. to *none* NOON + *schench,* OE *scenc* a drink, cup, akin to OE *scencan* to pour out, give drink, c. D, G *schenken*] —**lunch′eon·less,** *adj.*

lunch·eon·ette (lun′chə net′), *n.* a lunchroom or restaurant where light meals are served. [LUNCHEON + -ETTE]

lunch′eon meat′, any of various sausages or molded loaf meats, usually sliced and served cold, as in sandwiches or as garnishes for salads.

Lunch′eon on the Grass′. See **Déjeuner sur l'Herbe.**

lunch·hook (lunch′ho͝ok′), *n. Slang.* a light anchor for mooring a small yacht for a short time. [LUNCH + HOOK]

lunch·room (lunch′ro͞om′, -ro͝om′), *n.* a restaurant that specializes in serving light meals. [LUNCH + ROOM]

lunch·time (lunch′tīm′), *n.* a period set aside for eating lunch or the period of an hour or so, beginning roughly at noon, during which lunch is commonly eaten. [LUNCH + TIME]

Lund·berg (lund′bərg), *n.* **George A(ndrew),** born 1895, U.S. sociologist and author.

Lun·dy (lun′dē), *n.* a boy's given name.

Lun′dy's Lane′, a road near Niagara Falls, in Ontario, Canada: battle between the British and Americans in 1814.

lune[1] (lo͞on), *n.* **1.** anything shaped like a crescent or a half moon. **2.** a crescent-shaped figure bounded by two arcs of circles, either on a plane or a spherical surface. [< L *lūna* moon]

lune[2] (lo͞on), *n. Falconry. Rare.* a line for securing a hawk. [late ME, var. of *loyn* < MF *loigne* LONGE]

lunes (lo͞onz), *n.* (*construed as pl.*) fits of madness. [< F, MF, pl. of *lune* caprice < ML *lūna* fit of lunacy, special use of L *lūna* moon; cf. G *Laune*]

Lu·net·ta (lo͞o net′ə), *n.* a girl's given name.

lu·nette (lo͞o net′), *n.* **1.** any of various objects or spaces of crescentlike or semicircular outline or section. **2.** *Archit.* (in the plane of a wall) an area enframed by an arch or vault. **3.** a painting, sculpture, or window filling such an area. **4.** *Fort.* a work consisting of a salient angle with two flanks and an open gorge. **5.** *Ordn.* a towing ring in the trail plate of a towed vehicle, as a gun carriage. **6.** *Eccles.* Luna (def. 3). [< F, dim. of *lune* moon < L *lūna;* see -ETTE]

Lu·né·ville (ly nā vēl′), *n.* a city in NE France, W of Strasbourg: treaty between France and Austria 1801. 24,463 (1962).

lung (lung), *n.* **1.** either of the two saclike respiratory organs in the thorax of man and the higher vertebrates. **2.** an analogous organ in certain invertebrates, as arachnids, terrestrial gastropods, etc. **3. at the top of one's lungs,** as loudly as possible; with full voice: *The baby cried at the top of his lungs.* [ME *lunge(n),* OE *lungen;* c. G *Lunge;* akin to LIGHT[2], LIGHTS]

Lungs (Human)
A, Larynx; B, Trachea; C, Bronchi; D, Ramifications of bronchial tubes

lun·gan (lung′gən), *n.* longan.

lung′ book′. See **book lung.**

lunge[1] (lunj), *n., v.,* **lunged, lung·ing.** —*n.* **1.** a sudden forward thrust, as with a sword or knife; stab. **2.** any sudden forward movement; plunge. —*v.i.* **3.** to make a lunge or thrust; move with a lunge. —*v.t.* **4.** to thrust (something) forward; cause to move with a lunge: *lunging his finger accusingly.* [earlier *longe* for F *allonge* (n.; misheard as *a longe*), *allonger* (v.) to lengthen, extend, deliver (blows) << LL *ēlongāre* to elongate]

lunge[2] (lunj), *n., v.,* **lunged, lung·ing.** longe. [var. of *longe* < F; see LONGE, LUNE[2]]

lun·gee (lo͞ong′gē), *n.* lungi.

lun·geous (lun′jəs), *adj. Brit. Dial.* (of a person) violent; rough. [LUNGE[1] + -OUS]

lung·er (lung′ər), *n. Slang.* a person who has chronic lung disease, esp. tuberculosis. [LUNG + -ER[1]]

lung·fish (lung′fish′), *n., pl.* (*esp. collectively*) **-fish,** (*esp. referring to two or more kinds or species*) **-fish·es.** any fish of the group *Dipnoi,* having a functional, lunglike air bladder as well as gills. [LUNG + FISH]

lung′ fluke′, any of various trematodes, as *Paragonimus westermanni,* parasitic in the lungs of man and other mammals.

lun·gi (lo͞ong′gē), *n.* **1.** a cloth used as a turban, scarf, etc., in India, Pakistan, and Burma. **2.** a loincloth worn by men in India. Also, **lungee, lungyi.** [< Hindi *lungī* < Pers]

Lung·ki (lo͞ong′kē′), *n.* Changchowfu.

lung·worm (lung′wûrm′), *n.* **1.** any nematode worm of the superfamily *Metastrongylidae,* parasitic in the lungs of various mammals. **2.** a nematode worm of the genus *Rhabdias,* parasitic in the lungs of reptiles and amphibians. [LUNG + WORM]

lung·wort (lung′wûrt′), *n.* **1.** a European, boraginaceous plant, *Pulmonaria officinalis,* having blue flowers. **2.** a related American plant, *Mertensia virginica,* having blue flowers. [LUNG + WORT[2]]

lun·gyi (lo͞ong′gē, -jē), *n., pl.* **-gyis.** lungi.

luni-, a learned borrowing from Latin meaning "moon," used in the formation of compound words: *lunitidal.* [comb. form repr. L *lūna* moon; see -I-]

Lu·nik (lo͞o′nik), *n.* one of a series of lunar probes fired by the Soviet Union. [< Russ *lun(a)* moon + *-ik* dim. suffix]

l'u·nion fait la force (lʏ nyôɴ′ fe lᴀ fôʀs′), *French.* union makes strength: motto of Belgium.

lu·ni·so·lar (lo͞o′ni sō′lər), *adj.* pertaining to or based upon the relations or joint action of the moon and the sun. [LUNI- + SOLAR¹]

luniso′lar preces′sion, *Astron.* the principal component of the precession of the equinoxes, produced by the gravitational attraction of the sun and the moon on the equatorial bulge of the earth.

lu·ni·tid·al (lo͞o′ni tīd′əl), *adj.* pertaining to the part of the tidal movement dependent upon the moon. [LUNI- + TIDAL]

lu′nitid′al in′terval, the period of time between the moon's transit and the next high lunar tide.

lunk·head (luŋk′hed′), *n. Slang.* a dull or stupid person; blockhead. Also called **lunk.** [*lunk* (unexplained) + HEAD] —**lunk′head′ed,** *adj.*

lunt (lunt, lo͞ont), *Scot.* —*n.* **1.** a match or torch; the flame used to light a fire. **2.** smoke or steam, esp. smoke from a tobacco pipe. —*v.i.* **3.** to emit smoke or steam. **4.** to smoke a pipe. —*v.t.* **5.** to kindle (a fire). **6.** to light (a pipe, torch, etc.). **7.** to smoke (a pipe). [< D *lont* match, rag; akin to MLG *lunte* match, wick]

Lunt (lunt), *n.* **Alfred,** born 1893, U.S. actor (husband of Lynn Fontanne).

lu·nu·la (lo͞o′nyə lə), *n., pl.* **-lae** (-lē′). something shaped like a narrow crescent, as the small, white area at the base of the human fingernail. Also, **lu·nule** (lo͞o′nyo͞ol). [< L, dim. of *lūna* moon; see -ULE]

lu·nu·lar (lo͞o′nyə lər), *adj.* crescent-shaped: *lunular markings.* [LUNUL(A) + -AR¹]

lu·nu·late (lo͞o′nyə lāt′), *adj.* **1.** having lunular markings. **2.** crescent-shaped. Also, **lu′nu·lat′ed.** [LUNUL(A) + -ATE¹]

lun·y (lo͞o′nē), *adj.,* **lun·i·er, lun·i·est,** *n., pl.* **lun·ies.** loony.

Lun Yü (*Ch.* lo͞on′ yʏ′). See **Analects of Confucius, The.**

Lupe (lo͞op), *n.* a girl's given name.

Lu·per·ca·li·a (lo͞o′pər kā′lē ə, -kāl′yə), *n., pl.* **-li·a, -li·as.** (*sometimes construed as pl.*) an ancient Roman festival held annually in honor of Lupercus. [< L, neut. pl. of *Lupercālis* of LUPERCUS; see -AL¹] —**Lu′per·ca′li·an,** *adj.*

Lu·per·cus (lo͞o pûr′kəs), *n.* **1.** an ancient Roman fertility god, often identified with Faunus or Pan. **2.** a priest of this god.

lu·pine¹ (lo͞o′pin), *n.* any leguminous plant of the genus *Lupinus,* as *L. albus* (**white lupine**), of Europe, bearing edible seeds, or *L. perennis,* of the eastern U.S., having blue, pink, or white flowers. [ME < L *lupīn(us)* or *lupīn(um)* plant name, n. use of masc. or neut. of *lupīnus* (adj.) LUPINE²]

lu·pine² (lo͞o′pīn), *adj.* **1.** pertaining to or resembling the wolf. **2.** related to the wolf. **3.** savage; ravenous; predatory. [< L *lupīn(us)* of a wolf, equiv. to *lup(us)* wolf + *-īnus* -INE¹]

lu·po·ma (lo͞o pō′mə), *n. Pathol.* any of the tubercles occurring in lupus vulgaris. [< NL; see LUPUS, -OMA]

lu·pu·lin (lo͞o′pyə lin), *n.* the glandular hairs of the hop, *Humulus Lupulus,* used in medicine. [< NL *lupul(us)* (dim. of L *lupus* the hop plant; see -ULE) + -IN²]

lu·pu·lone (lo͞o′pyə lōn′), *n. Pharm.* a white or yellow, slightly water-soluble, crystalline solid, $C_{26}H_{38}O_4$, obtained from lupulin: used chiefly as a fungicide and as a bactericide. [< NL *lupul(us)* (see LUPULIN) + -ONE]

lu·pus (lo͞o′pəs), *n. Pathol.* See **lupus vulgaris.** [< ML (medical), special use of L *lupus* wolf] —**lu′pous,** *adj.*

Lu·pus (lo͞o′pəs), *n., gen.* **-pi** (-pī). *Astron.* the Wolf, a southern constellation between Centaurus and Norma. [< L]

lu′pus er·y·the·ma·to′sus (er′ə thē′mə tō′səs, -them′ə-), *Pathol.* a usually chronic disease of unknown cause, occasionally affecting internal organs, characterized by red, scaly patches on the skin. [< medical L: erythematous lupus]

lu′pus vul·ga′ris (vul gâr′əs), *Pathol.* tuberculosis of the skin characterized by brownish nodular tubercles, usually about the nose and ears. Also called **lupus.** [< medical L: vulgar lupus]

Lu·ra (lo͞or′ə), *n.* a girl's given name.

Lu·ray (lo͞o rā′), *n.* a town in N Virginia: site of Luray Caverns. 3014 (1960).

Lur·çat (lʏʀ sᴀ′), *n.* **Jean** (zhäɴ), 1892–1966, French painter and tapestry designer.

lurch¹ (lûrch), *n.* **1.** an act or instance of swaying abruptly. **2.** a sudden tip or roll to one side, as of a ship or a staggering person. **3.** an awkward, swaying or staggering motion or gait. —*v.i.* **4.** (of a ship) to roll or pitch suddenly. **5.** to make a lurch; move with lurches; stagger: *The wounded man lurched across the room at his assailant.* [?] —**lurch′ing·ly,** *adv.*

lurch² (lûrch), *n.* **1.** a situation at the close of various games in which the loser scores nothing or is far behind his opponent. **2. leave in the lurch,** to leave in an uncomfortable or desperate situation; desert (someone) in time of trouble: *His secretary left him in the lurch at the peak of the busy season.* [< MF *lourche* a game, n. use of *lourche* (adj.) discomfited < HG; cf. MHG *lurz* left (hand), OE *belyrtan* to deceive]

lurch³ (lûrch), *v.t.* **1.** *Archaic.* to do out of; defraud; cheat. **2.** *Obs.* to acquire through underhanded means; steal; filch. —*v.i.* **3.** *Brit. Dial.* to lurk near a place; prowl. —*n.* **4.** *Archaic.* the act of lurching or state of watchfulness. [late ME *lorche(n),* appar. var. of *lurken* to LURK]

lurch·er (lûr′chər), *n.* **1.** a crossbred dog used esp. by poachers. **2.** *Archaic.* a person who lurks or prowls; a petty thief; poacher. [LURCH³ + -ER¹]

lur·dan (lûr′dən), *Archaic.* —*n.* **1.** a lazy, stupid, loutish fellow. —*adj.* **2.** lazy; stupid; worthless. [ME < MF *lourdin* dullard, equiv. to *lourd* heavy, dull (<< L *lūridus* LURID) + *-in* < L *-īnus* -INE¹]

lure (lo͞or), *n., v.,* **lured, lur·ing.** —*n.* **1.** anything that attracts, entices, or allures. **2.** the power of attracting or enticing. **3.** a decoy; live or esp. artificial bait used in angling or trapping. **4.** *Falconry.* a feathered decoy for attracting a hawk, swung at the end of a long line and sometimes baited with raw meat. **5.** a flap or tassel dangling from the dorsal fin of pediculate fish. **6. in lure,** *Heraldry.* noting a pair of wings joined with the tips downward (opposed to *a vol*). —*v.t.* **7.** to attract; entice; tempt; invite; allure. **8.** to draw, as by a lure or decoy. [ME < MF, OF *loire* < Gmc; cf. G *Luder* bait] —**lure′ment,** *n.* —**lur′er,** *n.* —**lur′ing·ly,** *adv.*
—**Syn. 1.** temptation. **7.** seduce. —**Ant. 7.** repel.

lu·rid (lo͞or′id), *adj.* **1.** lighted or shining with an unnatural, fiery glow; wildly or garishly red: *a lurid sunset.* **2.** glaringly vivid or sensational: *the typically lurid tales of pulp magazines.* **3.** gruesome; horrible; revolting: *the lurid details of an accident.* **4.** terrible in fiery intensity, fierce passion, or wild unrestraint: *lurid crimes.* **5.** wan, pallid, or ghastly in hue; livid. [< L *lūrid(us)* somber, equiv. to *lūr(ēre)* (to) be yellow + *-idus* -ID⁴] —**lu′rid·ly,** *adv.* —**lu′rid·ness,** *n.*
—**Syn. 5.** lowering, dismal, pale, murky. —**Ant. 4.** mild.

Lu·ri·stan (lo͞or′i stän′, -stan′), *n.* a mountainous region in W Iran. Also, **Lorestan.**

lurk (lûrk), *v.i.* **1.** to lie or wait in concealment, as a person in ambush; remain in or around a place secretly or furtively. **2.** to go furtively; slink; steal. **3.** to exist unperceived or unsuspected. [ME *lurken,* freq. of LOWER²; cf. Norw *lurka* to sneak away] —**lurk′er,** *n.* —**lurk′ing·ly,** *adv.*
—**Syn. 1.** LURK, SKULK, SNEAK, PROWL suggest avoiding observation, often because of a sinister purpose. To LURK is to lie in wait for someone or to hide about a place, often without motion, for periods of time. SKULK suggests cowardliness and stealth of movement. SNEAK emphasizes the attempt to avoid being seen. It has connotations of slinking and of an abject meanness of manner, whether there exists a sinister intent or the desire to avoid punishment for some misdeed. PROWL implies the definite purpose of seeking for prey; it suggests continuous action in roaming or wandering, slowly and quietly but watchfully, as a cat that is hunting mice.

Lur·lei (lo͞or′lī), *n. Rare.* Lorelei.

Lur·line (lûr′lēn, -līn), *n.* a girl's given name.

Lur·ton (lûr′tᵊn), *n.* a boy's given name.

Lu·sa·ka (lo͞o sä′kə), *n.* a city in and the capital of Zambia, in the central part. 122,300 (est. 1964).

Lu·sa·ti·a (lo͞o sā′shē ə, -shə), *n.* a region in E East Germany and SW Poland, between the Elbe and Oder rivers.

Lu·sa·tian (lo͞o sā′shən), *n.* **1.** a native or inhabitant of Lusatia. **2.** Sorbian (def. 2). —*adj.* **3.** of or pertaining to Lusatia, its people, or their language. [LUSATI(A) + -AN]

lus·cious (lush′əs), *adj.* **1.** highly pleasing to the taste or smell: *luscious peaches.* **2.** sweet to the senses or the mind: *the luscious, ornate style of his poetry.* **3.** richly adorned; luxurious; extremely attractive: *luscious furnishings.* **4.** arousing physical, or sexual, desire; voluptuous: *The heroine was a luscious blonde.* **5.** *Archaic.* sweet to excess; cloying. [late ME *lucius,* unexplained var. of *licius,* aph. var. of DELICIOUS] —**lus′cious·ly,** *adv.* —**lus′cious·ness,** *n.*
—**Syn. 1.** delectable, palatable. See **delicious.** —**Ant. 1.** disgusting, unpalatable.

lush¹ (lush), *adj.* **1.** (of vegetation, plants, grasses, etc.) luxuriant; succulent; tender and juicy. **2.** characterized by luxuriant vegetation: *a lush valley.* **3.** characterized by abundance, luxuriousness, opulence, etc.: *He held the interview in the lush surroundings of his own home.* [late ME *lusch* slack; akin to OE *lysu* bad, *lēas* lax, MLG *lasch* slack, Icel *löskr* weak, Goth *lasiws* weak] —**lush′ly,** *adv.* —**lush′ness,** *n.*
—**Syn. 1.** luxurious, fresh. —**Ant. 1.** withered, stale.

lush² (lush), *Slang.* —*n.* **1.** a person who drinks excessive amounts of intoxicants habitually; drunkard; alcoholic; sot. **2.** intoxicating liquor. —*v.i.* **3.** to drink liquor. —*v.t.* **4.** to drink (liquor). [?]

lush·y¹ (lush′ē), *adj.,* **lush·i·er, lush·i·est.** lush¹. [LUSH¹ + -Y¹]

lush·y² (lush′ē), *adj.,* **lush·i·er, lush·i·est.** *Slang.* drunk; tipsy. [LUSH² + -Y¹]

Lu·si·a (lo͞o sī′ə), *n. Class. Myth.* an epithet of Demeter, meaning "bather," in reference to a ritual bath she took after being raped by Poseidon.

Lu·si·ta·ni·a (lo͞o′si tā′nē ə), *n.* **1.** (*italics*) a British luxury liner sunk by a German submarine in the North Atlantic on May 7, 1915: one of the events leading to U.S. entry into World War I. **2.** an ancient region and Roman province in the Iberian Peninsula, corresponding generally to modern Portugal. —**Lu′si·ta′ni·an,** *adj., n.*

lust (lust), *n.* **1.** sexual desire or appetite. **2.** uncontrolled or illicit sexual desire or appetite; lecherousness. **3.** a passionate or overmastering desire (usually fol. by *for*): *a lust for power.* **4.** ardent enthusiasm; zest; relish: *an enviable lust for life.* **5.** *Obs.* **a.** pleasure or delight. **b.** desire; inclination; wish. —*v.i.* **6.** to have strong sexual desire. **7.** to have a passionate yearning or desire; have a strong or excessive craving (often fol. by *for* or *after*). [ME *luste,* OE *lust;* c. D, G *lust* pleasure, desire; akin to Icel *lyst* desire; see LIST⁴]

lus·ter¹ (lus′tər), *n.* **1.** the state or quality of shining by reflecting light; glitter, sparkle, sheen, or gloss: *the luster of satin.* **2.** a substance, as a coating or polish, used to impart sheen or gloss. **3.** radiant or luminous brightness; brilliance; radiance. **4.** radiance of beauty, excellence, merit, distinction, or glory: *achievements that add luster to one's name.* **5.** a shining object, esp. one used for decoration, as a cut-glass pendant, ornament, or the like. **6.** a chandelier, candleholder, etc., ornamented with cut-glass pendants. **7.** any natural or synthetic fabric with a lustrous finish. **8.** Also called **metallic luster.** an iridescent metallic film produced on the surface of a ceramic glaze. **9.** *Mineral.* the nature of a mineral surface with respect to its reflective qualities: *greasy luster.* —*v.t.* **10.** to finish (fur, cloth, pottery, etc.) with a luster or gloss. —*v.i.* **11.** to be or become lustrous. Also, *esp. Brit.,* **lustre.** [< MF *lustre* < OIt *lustro,* akin to *lustrare* < L *lūstrāre* to illumine, purify. See LUSTRUM] —**lus′ter·less,** *adj.*
—**Syn. 1.** See **polish.** —**Ant. 1.** dullness.

lus·ter² (lus′tər), *n.* lustrum (def. 1). Also, *esp. Brit.,* **lustre.** [ME *lustre* < L *lūstrum.* See LUSTRUM]

lus·ter³ (lus′tər), *n.* a person who lusts: *a luster after power.* [LUST + -ER¹]

lus·tered (lus′tərd), *adj.* having or finished with a luster. Also, *esp. Brit.,* **lustred.** [LUSTER¹ + -ED³]

lus·ter·er (lus′tər ər), *n.* a person who puts a lustrous finish or gloss on textiles. [LUSTER¹ + -ER¹]

lus·ter·ing (lus′tər iŋ), *n.* the treatment of fabrics by chemical or mechanical means in order to increase their property to reflect light. Also, *esp. Brit.,* **lustring.** [LUSTER¹ + -ING¹]

lus·ter·ware (lus′tər wâr′), *n.* ceramic ware covered with a luster. Also, *esp. Brit.,* **lustreware.** [LUSTER¹ + WARE¹]

lust·ful (lust′fəl), *adj.* **1.** full of or motivated by lust, greed, or the like: *He was an emperor lustful of power. We looked at the food with lustful eyes.* **2.** having lewd desires; lecherous; libidinous. **3.** *Archaic.* lusty. [ME, OE; see LUST, -FUL] —**lust′ful·ly,** *adv.* —**lust′ful·ness,** *n.*

lust·i·hood (lus′tē ho͝od′), *n. Archaic.* lustiness; vigor. [LUSTY + -HOOD]

lus·tral (lus′trəl), *adj.* **1.** of, pertaining to, or employed in the lustrum, or rite of purification. **2.** occurring every five years; quinquennial. [< L *lūstrāl(is).* See LUSTRUM, -AL¹]

lus·trate (lus′trāt), *v.t.,* **-trat·ed, -trat·ing.** to purify by a propitiatory offering or other ceremonial method. [< L *lūstrāt(us)* purified, illumined, ptp. of *lūstrāre.* See LUSTER¹, -ATE¹] —**lus·tra′tion,** *n.* —**lus·tra·tive** (lus′trə tiv), *adj.*

lus·tre¹ (lus′tər), *n., v.t., v.i.,* **-tred, -tring.** *Chiefly Brit.* luster¹. —**lus′tre·less,** *adj.*

lus·tre² (lus′tər), *n. Chiefly Brit.* luster².

lus·tred (lus′tərd), *adj. Chiefly Brit.* lustered.

lus·tre·ware (lus′tər wâr′), *n. Chiefly Brit.* lusterware.

lus·tring (lus′triŋ), *n. Chiefly Brit.* lustering.

lus·trous (lus′trəs), *adj.* **1.** having luster; shining; luminous: *lustrous silk; lustrous eyes.* **2.** brilliant; splendid; resplendent; glamorous; illustrious. [LUST(E)R¹ + -OUS] —**lus′trous·ly,** *adv.* —**lus′trous·ness,** *n.*
—**Syn. 1.** gleaming, radiant, glowing, shimmering. **2.** refulgent, dazzling, gorgeous.

lus·trum (lus′trəm), *n., pl.* **-trums, -tra** (-trə). **1.** Also, **luster;** *esp. Brit.,* **lustre.** a period of five years. **2.** *Rom. Hist.* a lustration or ceremonial purification of the people, performed every five years, after the taking of the census. [< L, akin to *luere* to atone for, avert by expiation (lit., get rid of by washing), *lavāre* to LAVE¹]

lust·y (lus′tē), *adj.,* **lust·i·er, lust·i·est.** **1.** full of or characterized by healthy vigor. **2.** hearty, as a meal or the like. [ME; see LUST, -Y¹] —**lust′i·ly,** *adv.* —**lust′i·ness,** *n.*
—**Syn. 1.** robust, strong, sturdy, stout. —**Ant. 1.** feeble, weak.

lu·sus na·tu·rae (lo͞o′səs nə to͝or′ē, -tyo͝or′ē), a deformed person or thing; freak. [< L: a jest of nature]

lu·tan·ist (lo͞ot′ᵊnist), *n.* a person who plays the lute. Also, **lutenist.** [< ML *lūtānist(a),* deriv. of *lūtāna* lute; see -IST]

Lutch·er (luch′ər), *n.* a town in central Louisiana. 3274 (1960).

Lut′ Des′ert (lo͞ot), Dasht-i-Lut.

lute¹ (lo͞ot), *n., v.,* **lut·ed, lut·ing.** —*n.* **1.** a stringed musical instrument having a long, fretted neck and a hollow, typically pear-shaped body with a vaulted back. —*v.i.* **2.** to play a lute. —*v.t.* **3.** to perform (music) on a lute: *a man skilled at luting Elizabethan ballads.* **4.** to express (a feeling, mood, etc.) by means of a lute: *The minstrel eloquently luted his melancholy.* [ME < MF, OF < OPr *laut* < Ar *al 'ūd,* lit., the wood]

Lute

lute² (lo͞ot), *n., v.,* **lut·ed, lut·ing.** —*n.* **1.** luting. —*v.t.* **2.** to seal or cement with luting. [late ME < ML *lutum,* special use of L *lutum* mud, clay]

lute³ (lo͞ot), *n., v.,* **lut·ed, lut·ing.** —*n.* **1.** a paving tool for spreading and smoothing concrete, consisting of a straightedge mounted transversely on a long handle. —*v.t.* **2.** to spread and smooth (concrete in a pavement) with a lute. [< D *loet*]

lu·te·al (lo͞o′tē əl), *adj.* of, pertaining to, or involving the corpus luteum. [< L *lūte(us)* kind of yellow (see LUTEOUS) + -AL¹]

lu·te·ci·um (lo͞o tē′shē əm), *n. Chem.* lutetium.

lu·te·in (lo͞o′tē in), *n. Biochem.* **1.** Also called **xanthophyll.** a yellow-red, water-insoluble, crystalline, carotenoid alcohol, $C_{40}H_{56}O_2$, found in the petals of marigold and certain other flowers, egg yolk, algae, and corpora lutea: used chiefly in the biochemical study of the carotenoids. **2.** a preparation consisting of dried and powdered corpora lutea from hogs. [< L *lūte(um)* yolk of an egg (n. use of neut. of *lūteus* yellow; see LUTEOUS) + -IN²]

lu·te·in·ize (lo͞o′tē ə nīz′), *v.,* **-ized, -iz·ing.** —*v.t.* **1.** to produce corpora lutea in. —*v.i.* **2.** to undergo transformation into corpora lutea. [LUTEIN + -IZE] —**lu′te·in·i·za′tion,** *n.*

lu′teinizing hor′mone, *Biochem.* See **ICSH.**

lu·te·nist (lo͞ot′ᵊnist), *n.* lutanist.

luteo-, a learned borrowing from Latin meaning "golden yellow," used in the formation of compound words: *luteotropin.* [comb. form repr. L *lūte(us);* see -O-]

lu·te·o·lin (lo͞o′tē ə lin), *n. Chem.* a yellow coloring substance, $C_{15}H_{10}O_6$, obtained from the weed *Reseda Luteola:* used in dyeing silk and, formerly, in medicine. [< NL (*Reseda*) *Lūteol(a),* fem. of L *lūteolus* yellowish (dim. of *lūteus* yellow; see LUTEOUS) + -IN²]

lu·te·o·trop·ic (lo͞o′tē ə trop′ik), *adj.* affecting the corpus luteum. Also, **lu·te·o·troph·ic** (lo͞o′tē ə trof′ik, -trō′fik). [LUTEO- + -TROPIC]

lu·te·o·tro·pin (lo͞o′tē ə trō′pin), *n.* **1.** *Biochem.* an anterior pituitary hormone that, in mammals, regulates the production of progesterone by the corpus luteum and stimulates lactation of the mammary glands and, in birds, stimulates the activity of the crop glands. **2.** *Pharm.* a commercial form of this substance, obtained from the pituitary glands of oxen, sheep, and swine and used chiefly to induce lactation and in the treatment of uterine bleeding. Also, **lu·te·o·tro·phin** (lo͞o/tē ə trō/-fin). Also called **adenohypophyseal luteotropin, anterior pituitary luteotropin, lactogen, lactogenic hormone, lu/teotrop/ic hor/mone, prolactin, mammotropin.** [LUTEOTROP(IC) + -IN²]

lu·te·ous (lo͞o/tē əs), *adj.* (of yellow) having a light to medium greenish tinge. [< L *lūteus* golden-yellow, lit., *lūtum*-colored, equiv. to *lūt(um)* yellowweed + *-eus* -EOUS]

lute/ stern/, *Naut.* a transom stern used on small boats, having an open after extension for breaking up seas coming from astern.

lute·string (lo͞ot/string/), *n.* **1.** a silk fabric of high sheen, formerly used in the manufacture of dresses. **2.** a narrow ribbon finished with a high gloss. [by folk etymology < F *lustrine* < It *lustrino.* See LUSTER¹, -INE¹]

Lu·te/tia Pa·ris·i·o/rum (lo͞o tē/shə pə riz/ē ôr/-əm, -ōr/-), *n.* an ancient name of **Paris.**

lu·te·ti·um (lo͞o tē/shē əm), *n. Chem.* a rare-earth, trivalent, metallic element. *Symbol:* Lu; *at. wt.:* 174.97; *at. no.:* 71. Also, **lutecium.** [< L *Lūtēt(ia)* Paris + -IUM]

Luth., Lutheran.

Lu·ther (lo͞o/thər; *Ger.* lo͞ot/ər), *n.* **1. Mar·tin** (mär/-tən; *Ger.* mär/tēn), 1483–1546, German theologian and author: leader, in Germany, of the Protestant Reformation. **2.** a crater in the first quadrant of the face of the moon: about 8 miles in diameter. **3.** a boy's given name.

Lu·ther·an (lo͞o/thər ən), *adj.* **1.** of or pertaining to Luther, adhering to his doctrines, or belonging to one of the Protestant churches that bear his name. —*n.* **2.** a follower of Luther, or an adherent of his doctrines; a member of the Lutheran Church. [LUTHER + -AN] —**Lu/ther·an·ism, Lu/ther·ism** (lo͞o/thə riz/əm), *n.*

lu·thern (lo͞o/thərn), *n. Rare.* a dormer window. [? alter. of LUCARNE]

Lu·thu·li (lo͞o to͞o/lē, -tyo͞o/-), *n.* **Albert John,** 1898–1967, African leader in the Republic of South Africa and former Zulu chief: Nobel peace prize 1960.

Lu/tine bell/ (lo͞o/tēn), the salvaged bell from the wrecked British warship *Lutine,* hung in the insurance office of Lloyd's of London and traditionally rung before announcements of ships overdue or lost at sea.

lut·ing (lo͞o/ting), *n.* any of various readily molded substances for sealing joints, cementing objects together, or waterproofing surfaces. [ME *lute* (< ML *lutāre* to coat, stop, seal; see LUTE²) + -ING¹]

lut·ist (lo͞o/tist), *n.* **1.** a lute player; lutanist. **2.** a maker of lutes. [LUTE¹ + -IST]

lu·tose (lo͞o/tōs), *adj.* covered with a powdery substance resembling mud, as certain insects. [< L *lutōs(us)* muddy, equiv. to *lut(um)* mud + *-ōsus* -OSE¹]

Lu·tu·am·i·an (lo͞o/to͞o am/ē ən), *n., pl.* **-ans,** (*esp. collectively*) **-an.** a member of a group of American Indian peoples including the Modoc and the Klamath.

Lut·yens (luch/ənz, lut/yənz), *n.* **Sir Edwin Landseer,** 1869–1944, English architect.

Lüt·zen (lʏt/sən), *n.* a town in S East Germany, WSW of Leipzig: site of Gustavus Adolphus' victory over Wallenstein in 1632 and Napoleon's victory over the Russians in 1813.

Lüt/zow-Holm Bay/ (lʏ/tsôf hōlm/), *n.* an inlet of the Indian Ocean on the coast of Antarctica between Queen Maud Land and Enderby Land.

Lu·verne (lo͞o vûrn/), *n.* a town in SW Minnesota. 4249 (1960).

Lu/-Wang/ school/ (lo͞o/wäng/), *Philos.* See **School of Mind.** [after *Lu* Chin-yüan and *Wang* Shou-jen, two members of the group]

Lu·wi·an (lo͞o/ē ən), *n.* **1.** an extinct ancient Anatolian language written in cuneiform. —*adj.* **2.** of or pertaining to Luwian. [*Luwi* nation of ancient Asia Minor + -AN]

lux (luks), *n., pl.* **lu·ces** (lo͞o/sēz). *Optics.* a unit of illumination, equivalent to .0929 foot-candle and equal to the illumination produced by luminous flux of one lumen falling perpendicularly on a surface one meter square. *Abbr.:* lx Also called **meter-candle.** [< L: light]

Lux., Luxembourg.

lux·ate (luk/sāt), *v.t.,* **-at·ed, -at·ing.** to put out of joint; dislocate: *The accident luxated the left shoulder.* [< L *luxāt(us)* put out of joint (ptp. of *luxāre*), equiv. to *lux(us)* dislocated (c. Gk *loxós* oblique) + *-ātus* -ATE¹] —**lux·a/tion,** *n.*

luxe (lo͝oks, luks; *Fr.* lʏks), *n.* luxury; elegance; sumptuousness: *hotel accommodations that provided luxe at reasonable rates.* Cf. **deluxe.** [< F < L *lux(us)* excess]

Lux·em·bourg (luk/səm bûrg/; *Fr.* lʏk sän-bo͞or/), *n.* **1.** a grand duchy between Germany, France, and Belgium. 313,089 (1960); 999 sq. mi. **2.** a city in and the capital of this grand duchy. 70,652 (1960). **3.** a province in SE Belgium: formerly a part of the grand duchy of Luxembourg. 218,784 (est. 1960); 1706 sq. mi. *Cap.:* Arlon.

Lux·em·burg (luk/səm bûrg/; *Ger.* lo͝ok/səm bo͝orkh/), *n.* **1. Ro·sa** (rō/zə; *Ger.* rō/zä), ("*Red Rosa*"), 1870–1919, German socialist agitator, born in Poland. **2.** Luxembourg.

Lux·or (luk/sôr), *n.* a town in Upper Egypt, in the S United Arab Republic, on the Nile: ruins of ancient Thebes. ab. 15,000.

lux·u·ri·ance (lug zho͝or/ē əns, luk sho͝or/-), *n.* the condition of being luxuriant; luxuriant growth or productiveness; rich abundance; lushness. [LUXURI(ANT) + -ANCE]

lux·u·ri·ant (lug zho͝or/ē ənt, luk sho͝or/-), *adj.* **1.** abundant or exuberant in growth, as vegetation. **2.** producing abundantly, as soil; fertile; productive: *to settle in luxuriant country.* **3.** richly abundant, profuse, or superabundant. **4.** florid, as imagery or ornamentation; lacking in restraint. [< L *luxuriant-* (s. of *luxuriāns*), prp. of *luxuriāre* to be rank. See LUXURY, -ANT] —**lux·u/ri·ant·ly,** *adv.*
—**Syn. 1.** lush, teeming. **2.** fruitful, prolific. **3.** copious.

lux·u·ri·ate (lug zho͝or/ē āt/, luk sho͝or/-), *v.i.,* **-at·ed, -at·ing. 1.** to enjoy oneself without stint; indulge in luxury; revel: *to luxuriate in newly acquired leisure.* **2.** to grow fully or abundantly; thrive: *The plants luxuriated in the new soil.* **3.** to take great delight; find keen pleasure: *a person who luxuriated in flattery; a mind that luxuriates in paradox.* [< L *luxuriāt(us),* ptp. of *luxuriāre.* See LUXURIANT, -ATE¹] —**lux·u/ri·a/tion,** *n.*

lux·u·ri·ous (lug zho͝or/ē əs, luk sho͝or/-), *adj.* **1.** characterized by luxury; ministering or conducive to luxury: *a luxurious hotel.* **2.** given to or loving luxury; wanting or requiring what is choice, expensive, or the like: *a person with luxurious tastes.* **3.** given to pleasure, esp. of the senses; voluptuous: *She has indulged herself too long in luxurious tears.* **4.** present or occurring in great abundance, rich profusion, etc.; opulent: *a luxurious harvest; music of luxurious beauty.* **5.** excessively ornate; overelaborate: *luxurious prose that overwhelmed the slender story.* [< L *luxuriōs(us).* See LUXURY, -OUS] —**lux·u/ri·ous·ly,** *adv.* —**lux·u/ri·ous·ness,** *n.*
—**Syn. 1.** rich, sumptuous. **2.** epicurean. **3.** sensual, self-indulgent. —**Ant. 1.** squalid.

lux·u·ry (luk/shə rē, lug/zhə-), *n., pl.* **-ries. 1.** a material object, service, etc., conducive to sumptuous living, usually a delicacy, elegance, or refinement of living rather than a necessity: *Gold cufflinks were a luxury not allowed for in his budget.* **2.** free or habitual indulgence in or enjoyment of comforts and pleasures in addition to those necessary for a reasonable standard of well-being: *a life of luxury.* **3.** a means of ministering to such indulgence or enjoyment: *the luxury of hothouse grapes all winter.* **4.** a pleasure out of the ordinary allowed to oneself: *the luxury of an extra cupcake at tea.* **5.** a foolish or worthless form of self-indulgence: *the luxury of self-pity.* **6.** *Archaic.* lasciviousness; lechery. —*adj.* **7.** of, pertaining to, or affording luxury or luxuries: *a luxury hotel.* [ME *luxurie* < L *luxuria* rankness, luxuriance, equiv. to *luxur-* (comb. form of *luxus* extravagance) + *-ia* -Y³]

Lu·zern (lo͞o tsern/), *n.* German name of **Lucerne.**

Lu·zerne (lo͞o zûrn/), *n.* a town in central Pennsylvania. 5118 (1960).

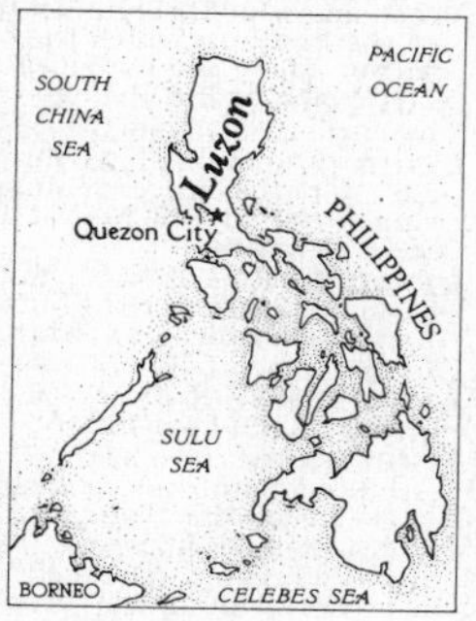

Lu·zon (lo͞o zon/; *Sp.* lo͞o sôn/), *n.* the chief island of the Philippines, in the N part of the group. 12,000,000 (est. 1960); 40,420 sq. mi. *Cap.:* Manila.

LV., lev.

lv., 1. leave; leaves. **2.** livre; livres.

Lw, *Chem.* Lawrencium.

l/w, lumen per watt; lumens per watt.

L wave, an earthquake wave that travels around the earth's surface and is usually the third conspicuous wave to reach a seismograph. Also called **long wave.** Cf. **P wave, S wave.**

L.W.L., length (at) water line.

l.w.m., low water mark.

Lwoff (lwôf), *n.* **An·dré** (än drā/), born 1912, French microbiologist: Nobel Prize for medicine 1965.

lwop, leave without pay.

Lwów (*Pol.* lvo͞of), *n.* a city in W Ukraine, in the SW Soviet Union in Europe: formerly in Poland. 487,000 (est. 1964). German, **Lemberg.** Russian, **Lvov** (lvôf). Ukrainian, **Lwiw** (lvēf).

lwp, leave with pay.

lx, lux; luces.

LXX, Septuagint.

-ly, 1. a suffix forming adverbs from adjectives: *gladly; gradually; secondly.* **2.** a suffix meaning "every," attached to certain nouns denoting units of time: *hourly; daily.* **3.** an adjective suffix meaning "-like": *saintly; manly.* [ME *-li, -lich(e),* OE *-līce* (*-līc* adj. suffix + *-e* adv. suffix); in the sense of -like: ME *-li, -ly, -lich(e),* OE *-līc* (c. G *-lich*), suffixal use of *(ge)līc* LIKE¹]
—**Syn. 3.** See **-ish¹.**

Ly·ae·us (lī ē/əs), *n. Class. Myth.* an epithet of Dionysus, meaning "loosener," in reference to his ability to free men from care.

Ly·all (lī/əl), *n.* a boy's given name. Also, **Lyle.**

Ly·all·pur (lī/əl po͝or/), *n.* a city in NE West Pakistan province, in Pakistan. 425,248 (1961).

ly·am-hound (lī/əm hound/), *n. Archaic.* a bloodhound. Also, **lyme-hound.** [late ME *lyame* leash (< MF *liem* << L *ligāmen* a band, tie, equiv. to *ligā(re)* (to) tie + *-men* n. suffix) + HOUND¹]

ly·ard (lī/ərd), *adj. Brit. Dial.* streaked or spotted with gray or white. Also, **ly·art** (lī/ərt). [ME < MF, OF *liart*]

Lyau·tey (lyō te/), *n.* **Louis Hu·bert Gon·zalve** (lwē ʏ ber/ gôn zalv/), 1854–1934, French marshal: resident general of Morocco 1912–16, 1917–25.

Ly·cae·us (lī sē/əs), *n. Class. Myth.* an epithet of Zeus, meaning "wolfish."

ly·can·thrope (lī/kən thrōp/, lī kan/thrōp), *n.* **1.** a person affected with lycanthropy. **2.** a werewolf or alien spirit in the physical form of a bloodthirsty wolf. [< Gk *lykánthrōp(os)* wolf-man, equiv. to *lýk(os)* wolf + *ánthrōpos* man]

ly·can·thro·py (lī kan/thrə pē), *n.* **1.** a kind of insanity in which the victim imagines himself to be a wolf or other wild beast. **2.** the supposed or fabled assumption of the form of a wolf by a human being. [< Gk *lykanthrōpía.* See LYCANTHROPE, -Y³] —**ly·can·throp·ic** (lī/kən throp/ik), *adj.*

Ly·ca·on (lī kā/on, -ən), *n. Class. Myth.* an Arcadian king transformed into a wolf for presuming to test the divinity of Zeus.

Lyc·a·o·ni·a (lik/ā ō/nē ə, -ōn/yə, lī/kā-), *n.* an ancient country in S Asia Minor: later a Roman province.

ly·cée (lē sā/), *n., pl.* **-cées** (-sāz/; *Fr.* -sā/). a secondary school, esp. in France, maintained by the state. [< F < L *lycēum* LYCEUM]

ly·ce·um (lī sē/əm), *n.* **1.** *U.S.* an institution for popular education providing discussions, lectures, concerts, etc. **2.** a building, hall, or the like, devoted to instruction by lectures or to public discussions, meetings, etc. **3.** (*cap.*) a gymnasium where Aristotle taught, in ancient Athens. **4.** (*cap.*) the Aristotelian, or Peripatetic, school of philosophy. **5.** a lycée. [< L < Gk *Lýkeion* place in Athens, so named from the neighboring temple of Apollo; n. use of neut. of *lýkeios,* epithet of Apollo, variously explained]

lych (lich), *n. Brit. Obs.* lich.

lych/ gate/. See **lich gate.**

lych·nis (lik/nis), *n.* any showy-flowered, caryophyllaceous plant of the genus *Lychnis.* Cf. **rose campion, scarlet lychnis.** [< L < Gk *lychnís* red flower, akin to *lýchnos* lamp]

lych·no·scope (lik/nə skōp/), *n.* See **lowside window.** [< Gk *lýchn(os)* lamp + -o- + -SCOPE] —**lych·no·scop·ic** (lik/nə skop/ik), *adj.*

Ly·ci·a (lish/ē ə), *n.* an ancient country in SW Asia Minor: later a Roman province.

Ly·ci·an (lish/ē ən), *adj.* **1.** of or pertaining to Lycia. —*n.* **2.** an inhabitant of Lycia. **3.** an Anatolian language of Lycia, written in a form of the Greek alphabet. [LYCI(A) + -AN]

Lyc·i·das (lis/i dəs), *n.* an elegy (1637) by John Milton in memory of his college friend Edward King.

ly·cine (lī/sēn), *n. Chem.* betaine. [< Gk *lýk(ion)* boxthorn + -INE²]

Ly·co·me·des (lī/kə mē/dēz), *n. Class. Myth.* a king of Scyrus who pushed Theseus over a cliff.

Ly·con (lī/kon), *n.* (in the *Iliad*) a Trojan warrior slain by Peneleus.

Ly·co·phron (lī/kə fron/), *n.* (in the *Iliad*) a Greek who committed a murder, took sanctuary with Telamonian Ajax, accompanied him to Troy, and was killed there by Hector.

ly·co·po·di·um (lī/kə pō/dē əm), *n.* any erect or creeping, mosslike, evergreen plant of the genus *Lycopodium,* as the club moss or ground pine. Also, **locopod.** [< L < Gk *lýk(os)* wolf + *-podion* -PODIUM]

ly·co·sid (lī kō/sid), *n.* **1.** a spider of the family *Lycosidae,* comprising the wolf spiders. —*adj.* **2.** belonging or pertaining to the family *Lycosidae.* [< NL *Lycosid(ae),* equiv. to *Lycos(a)* type genus (< Gk *lýkos* wolf) *-idae* -ID²]

Ly·co·ther·ses (lī/kə thûr/sēz), *n. Class. Myth.* a king of Illyria who was murdered by his wife, Agave.

Ly·cur·gus (lī kûr/gəs), *n.* **1.** fl. 9th century B.C., Spartan lawgiver. **2.** *Class. Myth.* a king of Thrace whose opposition to the worship of Dionysus was punished when, in a fit of madness, he killed Dryas, his son.

Ly·cus (lī/kəs), *n. Class. Myth.* **1.** a son of King Pandion and Pylia who succeeded Sarpedon as king of Cilicia. **2.** a king in Mysia who earned the gratitude and military assistance of Hercules by hospitably entertaining him. **3.** the husband of Dirce and the uncle of Antiope who was killed by Antiope's sons. **4.** a son of Lycus and Dirce whose murder of Creon was avenged by Hercules.

lydd·ite (lid/īt), *n. Chem.* a high explosive consisting chiefly of picric acid. [named after *Lydd,* borough in SE England near the site where it was first tested; see -ITE¹]

Lyd·gate (lid/gāt/, -git), *n.* **John,** c1370–1451?, English monk, poet, and translator.

Lyd·i·a (lid/ē ə), *n.* **1.** an ancient kingdom in W Asia Minor: under Croesus, a wealthy empire including most of Asia Minor. **2.** a girl's given name.

Lyd·i·an (lid/ē ən), *adj.* **1.** of or pertaining to Lydia. **2.** (of music) softly or sensuously sweet; voluptuous. —*n.* **3.** an inhabitant of Lydia. **4.** an Anatolian language of Lydia, written in a modified Greek alphabet. [LYDI(A) + -AN]

Lyd/ian mode/, *Music.* an authentic church mode represented on the white keys of a keyboard instrument by an ascending scale from F to F.

lye (lī), *n. Chem.* **1.** a highly concentrated, aqueous solution of potassium hydroxide or sodium hydroxide. **2.** any solution resulting from leaching, percolation, or the like. [ME *lie, ley,* OE *lēag;* c. D *loog,* G *Lauge* lye, Icel *laug* warm bath. See LAVE¹]

Ly·ell (lī/əl), *n.* **1. Sir Charles,** 1797–1875, English geologist. **2.** a walled plain in the first quadrant of the face of the moon: about 26 miles in diameter.

ly·gae·id (lī jē/id, lī/jē id), *n.* **1.** See **lygaeid bug.** —*adj.* **2.** belonging or pertaining to the family *Lygaeidae.* [< NL *Lygaeid(ae),* equiv. to *Lygae(us)* type genus (< Gk *lýgaios* murky) + *-idae* -ID²]

lygae/id bug/, any of numerous, often brightly marked hemipterous insects of the family *Lygaeidae,* which feed on the juices of plants in both the larval and adult stages.

Ly·go·des·ma (lī/gə des/mə), *n. Class. Myth.* an epithet of Artemis, meaning "willow-bound," referring to an image of her that was supported by willow branches.

ly·ing¹ (lī/ing), *n.* **1.** the telling of lies; untruthfulness. —*adj.* **2.** telling lies; being deliberately untruthful; mendacious; false: *a lying report.* [ME; see LIE¹, -ING¹, -ING²] —**ly/ing·ly,** *adv.*
—**Syn. 1.** falsehood, falsity, mendacity, prevarication. **2.** deceptive, misleading, fallacious; sham, counterfeit.
—**Ant. 1.** truth. **2.** true, candid.

ly·ing² (lī/ing), *v.* ppr. of **lie².** —**ly/ing·ly,** *adv.*

ly·ing-in (lī/ing in/), *n., pl.* **lyings-in, lying-ins,** *adj.* —*n.* **1.** the state of being in childbed; confinement. —*adj.* **2.** pertaining to or providing facilities for childbirth: *a lying-in hospital.* [late ME *lyynge in.* See LIE², -ING¹, IN]

Ly·kens (lī/kənz), *n.* a town in central Pennsylvania. 2527 (1960).

Lyle (līl), *n.* a boy's given name. Also, **Lyall.**

Lyl·y (lil/ē), *n.* **John,** 1554?–1606, English writer of romances and plays.

Ly·man (lī/mən), *n.* a boy's given name.

lyme-hound (līm/hound/), *n.* lyam-hound.

lymph (limf), *n.* **1.** *Anat., Physiol.* a clear yellowish, slightly alkaline, coagulable fluid, containing white blood cells in a liquid resembling blood plasma, that is derived from the tissues of the body and conveyed to the blood stream by the lymphatic vessels. **2.** *Archaic.* the sap of a plant. **3.** *Archaic.* a stream or spring of clear, pure water. [< L *lymph(a)* water, earlier **limpa* (see LIMPID); pseudo-Gk form, by assoc. with *nympha* < Gk *nýmphē* NYMPH]

lymph-, var. of **lympho-** before a vowel: *lymphoma.*

lym·phad (lim′fad), *n. Archaic.* a galley having a single mast: represented in heraldry as having a single yard. [< ScotGael *longfhada* galley, equiv. to *long* ship + *fada* long]

lym·phad·e·ni·tis (lim fad′ᵊnī′tis, lim′fə dᵊnī′-), *n. Pathol.* inflammation of a lymphatic gland. [LYMPH- + ADEN- + -ITIS]

lym·phad·e·no·ma (lim fad′ᵊnō′mə, lim′fə dᵊnō′-), *n., pl.* **-mas, -ma·ta** (-mə tə). *Pathol.* an enlarged lymph node. [LYMPH- + ADEN- + -OMA]

lymphangi-, a combining form denoting the lymphatic vessels: *lymphangioma.* [< NL *lymphangion.* See LYMPHO-, ANGIO-]

lym·phan·gi·al (lim fan′jē əl), *adj.* pertaining to the lymphatic vessels. [LYMPHANGI- + -AL¹]

lym·phan·gi·o·ma (lim fan′jē ō′mə), *n., pl.* **-mas, -ma·ta** (-mə tə). *Pathol.* a benign neoplasm composed of dilated and newly formed lymph vessels. [< NL; see LYMPHANGI-, -OMA] **—lym·phan·gi·om·a·tous** (lim-fan′jē om′ə təs), *adj.*

lym·phan·gi·tis (lim′fan jī′tis), *n., pl.* **-git·i·des** (-jit′i dēz′). *Pathol.* inflammation of the lymphatic vessels. Also, **lym·phan·gi·i·tis** (lim fan′jē ī′tis). [LYMPHANG(I)- + -ITIS]

lym·phat·ic (lim fat′ik), *adj.* **1.** pertaining to, containing, or conveying lymph. **2.** (of persons) having the characteristics, as flabbiness or sluggishness, formerly believed to be due to an excess of lymph in the system. —*n.* **3.** a lymphatic vessel. [< NL *lymphāticus*). See LYMPH-, -ATIC] **—lym·phat′i·cal·ly,** *adv.*

lymphato-, a combining form of **lymphatic:** *lymphatolysis.*

lym·pha·tol·y·sis (lim′fə tol′i sis), *n. Pathol.* destruction of lymphatic vessels or of lymphoid tissue. [NL; see LYMPHATO-, -LYSIS] **—lym·pha·to·lyt·ic** (lim′fə-tᵊlit′ik), *adj.*

lymph′ cell′, a lymphocyte. Also called **lymph′ cor′puscle.**

lymph′ gland′, any of the glandlike masses of tissue in the lymphatic vessels containing cells that become lymphocytes. Also called **lymph′ node′, lymphat′ic gland′.**

lympho-, a combining form of **lymph:** *lymphocyte.* Also, *esp. before a vowel,* **lymph-.**

lym·pho·blast (lim′fə blast′), *n. Anat.* an immature lymphocyte. [LYMPHO- + -BLAST] **—lym′pho·blas′tic,** *adj.*

lym·pho·cyte (lim′fə sīt′), *n. Anat.* a leukocyte, formed in lymphoid tissue, having a large, spherical nucleus surrounded by a thin layer of nongranular cytoplasm. [LYMPHO- + -CYTE] **—lym·pho·cyt·ic** (lim′fə sit′ik), *adj.*

lym·pho·cy·to·sis (lim′fə sī tō′sis), *n. Pathol.* an abnormal increase in the number of lymphocytes in the blood. [LYMPHOCYTE + -OSIS] **—lym·pho·cy·tot·ic** (lim′fō sī tot′ik), *adj.*

lym·pho·gran·u·lo·ma (lim′fə gran′yə lō′mə), *n., pl.* **-mas, -ma·ta** (-mə tə). *Pathol.* **1.** any of certain diseases characterized by granulomatous lesions of lymph nodes. **2.** Also called **lym′phogranulo′ma in·gui·na′le** (iŋ′gwə nā′lē, -na′-, -nā′-), **lym′phogranulo′ma ve·ne′re·um** (və nēr′ē əm), a venereal form of lymphogranuloma, caused by a filterable virus and characterized initially by a lesion on the genitals. **3.** *Obs.* See **Hodgkin's disease.** [LYMPHO- + GRANULOMA]

lym·phoid (lim′foid), *adj.* **1.** of, pertaining to, or resembling lymph. **2.** of or pertaining to the tissue (**lym′-phoid tis′sue**) that occurs esp. in the lymph glands, thymus, tonsils, and spleen and produces lymphocytes. [LYMPH- + -OID]

lym′phoid cell′, *Anat.* a cell in the lymph glands which produces leukocytes.

lym·phoid·o·cyte (lim foi′də sīt′), *n.* hemocytoblast. [LYMPHOID + -O- + -CYTE]

lym·pho·ma (lim fō′mə), *n. Pathol.* a tumor arising from any of the cellular elements of lymph nodes. [< NL; see LYMPH-, -OMA] **—lym·pho′ma·toid′,** *adj.*

lym·pho·pe·ni·a (lim′fō pē′nē ə, -pēn′yə), *n. Pathol.* a reduction in the number of lymphocytes in the blood. [< NL; see LYMPHO-, -PENIA]

lym·pho·sar·co·ma (lim′fō sär kō′mə), *n. Pathol.* a malignant neoplasm in lymphatic tissue, caused by the growth of abnormal lymphocytes. [< NL; see LYMPHO-, SARCOMA]

Lyn·brook (lin′bro͝ok′), *n.* a city on W Long Island, in SE New York. 19,881 (1960).

lyn·ce·an (lin sē′ən), *adj.* **1.** of or pertaining to a lynx; lynxlike. **2.** lynx-eyed; sharp-sighted. [< L *lynce(us)* sharp-sighted (< Gk *lýnkeios* lynxlike, equiv. to *lynk-,* s. of *lýnx* LYNX + *-eios* -EOUS) + -AN]

lynch¹ (linch), *v.t.* to hang, burn, or otherwise kill (a person) by mob action and without legal authority, as for some offense known or presumed to have been committed. [v. use of *lynch* in LYNCH LAW] **—lynch′er,** *n.* **—Syn.** See **hang.**

lynch² (linch), *n. Brit.* a strip of unplowed land marking the boundary between two fields. Also called **lyn·chet** (lin′chit). [earlier *linch,* var. of *link;* see LINKS]

Lynch (linch), *n.* a town in SE Kentucky. 3810 (1960).

Lynch·burg (linch′bûrg), *n.* a city in central Virginia. 54,790 (1960).

lynch·ing (lin′chiŋ), *n.* the act or an instance of a mob's killing of a person, esp. by hanging, as if in performance of execution for a crime; a murder by a mob. [LYNCH¹ + -ING¹]

lynch′ law′, the administration of summary punishment, esp. death, upon an actual or reputed offender by private persons acting in concert without authority of law. [orig. *Lynch's law;* perhaps named after the author, Captain William *Lynch* (1742–1820) of Virginia]

Lyn·da (lin′də), *n.* a girl's given name. Also, **Linda.**

Lyn·den (lin′dən), *n.* a town in NW Washington. 2542 (1960).

Lynd·hurst (lind′hûrst), *n.* **1.** a town in NE New Jersey. 21,867 (1960). **2.** a city in NE Ohio, near Cleveland. 16,805 (1960).

Lyn·don (lin′dən), *n.* a boy's given name. Also, **Lindon.**

Lyn·do·ra (lin dōr′ə, -dôr′-), *n.* **1.** a town in W Pennsylvania. 3232 (1960). **2.** a girl's given name.

Ly·nen (lē′nen), *n.* **Fe·o·dor** (fā ō′dôr), born 1911, German biochemist: Nobel prize in medicine 1964.

Lyn·ette (li net′), *n.* a girl's given name. Also, **Linetta, Linnet, Linnete.**

Lyn·gi (lyŋ′gē), *n.* (in the *Volsunga Saga*) a rival of Sigmund for Hiordis who kills Sigmund and is killed by Sigurd.

Lynn (lin), *n.* **1.** a seaport in E Massachusetts, on Massachusetts Bay. 94,478 (1960). **2.** a boy's given name, form of **Lincoln, Lindberg,** or **Linton. 3.** Also, **Lynne.** a girl's given name, form of **Caroline** or **Carolyn.** Also, **Lin** (for defs. 2, 3).

Lynn′ Gar′dens, a town in NE Tennessee. 5261 (1960).

Lynn′ Ha′ven, a town in NW Florida. 3078 (1960).

Lyn·wood (lin′wo͝od′), *n.* a city in SW California. 31,614 (1960).

Canada lynx, *Lynx canadensis* (Length to 3½ ft.)

lynx (liŋks), *n., pl.* **lynx·es,** (*esp. collectively*) **lynx** for 1, *gen.* **Lyn·cis** (lin′sis) for 2. **1.** any of several wildcats of the genus *Lynx,* having long limbs, a short tail, and usually tufted ears, esp. *L. canadensis* **(Canada lynx),** of Canada and the northern U.S., having grayish-brown fur marked with white. **2.** (*cap.*) *Astron.* a northern constellation between Ursa Major and Auriga. [ME < L < Gk *lýnx*] **—lynx′like′,** *adj.*

lynx-eyed (liŋks′īd′), *adj.* sharp-sighted.

ly·o·crat·ic (lī′ə krat′ik), *adj. Physical Chem.* noting a colloid owing its stability to the affinity of its particles for the liquid in which they are dispersed. Cf. **electrocratic.** [*lyo-* (see LYOPHILIC) + -CRATIC]

ly·ol·y·sis (lī ol′i sis), *n. Chem.* solvolysis. [*lyo-* (see LYOPHILIC) + -LYSIS] **—ly·o·lyt·ic** (lī′ə lit′ik), *adj.*

Ly·on (lī′ən *for 1;* lyôN *for 2*), *n.* **1. Mary,** 1797–1849, U.S. pioneer in providing advanced education for women: founder of Mount Holyoke College. **2.** French name of **Lyons.**

Ly′on bean′ (lī′ən), a vine, *Stizolobium niveum,* of southern Asia and the Philippines, having showy clusters of white flowers and white-hairy pods. [named after W. S. *Lyon* (d. 1916), American botanist]

Ly·on·nais (lē ô ne′), *n.* a former province in E France. Also, **Ly·o·nais′.**

ly·on·naise (lī′ə nāz′; *Fr.* lē ô nez′), *adj.* (of food, esp. fried potatoes) cooked with pieces of onion. [< F *(à la) Lyonnaise* (fem. adj.) in the manner of *Lyons*]

Ly·on·nesse (lī′ə nes′), *n. Arthurian Romance.* the mythical region where Sir Tristram was born, located near Cornwall in SW England and supposed to have been submerged by the sea.

Ly′on Of′fice of Arms′ (lī′ən), *Scot Heraldry.* See **Heralds' Office.** Also called **Ly′on Of′fice.** [obs. *lyon* lion]

Ly·ons (lī′ənz), *n.* **1. Joseph Aloysius,** 1879–1939, Australian statesman: prime minister 1932–39. **2.** French, **Lyon.** a city in and the capital of Rhone, in E France at the confluence of the Rhone and Saône rivers. 535,784 (1962). **3.** a town in NE Illinois. 9936 (1960). **4.** a town in W New York. 4673 (1960). **5.** a town in central Kansas. 4592 (1960). **6.** a town in central Georgia. 3219 (1960).

ly·o·phil·ic (lī′ə fil′ik), *adj. Physical Chem.* noting a colloid the particles of which have a strong affinity for the liquid in which they are dispersed. [*lyo-* (comb. form repr. Gk *lýein* to loose, dissolve, set free; see -O-) + -PHILIC]

ly·oph·i·lize (lī of′ə līz′), *v.t.,* **-lized, -liz·ing.** *Biochem.* (of tissue, blood, serum, or the like) to dry by freezing in a high vacuum. [LYOPHIL(IC) + -IZE] **—ly·oph′i·li·za′tion,** *n.*

ly·o·pho·bic (lī′ə fō′bik, -fob′ik), *adj. Physical Chem.* noting a colloid the particles of which have little or no affinity for the liquid in which they are dispersed. [*lyo-* (see LYOPHILIC) + -PHOBIC]

ly·o·trop·ic (lī′ə trop′ik), *adj. Physical Chem.* noting any series of ions, salts, or radicals arranged in descending order relative to the magnitude of their effect on a given solvent. [*lyo-* (see LYOPHILIC) + -TROPIC]

Ly·ra (lī′rə), *n., gen.* **-rae** (-rē) for 1. **1.** *Astron.* the Lyre, a northern constellation between Cygnus and Hercules, containing the bright star Vega. **2.** a girl's given name.

Lyre

ly·rate (lī′rāt, -rit), *adj.* **1.** *Bot.* (of a pinnate leaf) divided transversely into several lobes, the smallest at the base. **2.** *Zool.* lyre shaped, as the tail of certain birds. Also, **ly′rat·ed.** [< NL *lyrāt(us).* See LYRE, -ATE¹] **—ly′rate·ly,** *adv.*

lyre (līᵊr), *n.* **1.** a musical instrument of ancient Greece consisting of a soundbox made typically from a turtle shell, with two curved arms connected by a yoke from which strings are stretched to the body, used esp. to accompany singing and recitation. **2.** (*cap.*) *Astron.* the constellation Lyra. [ME *lire* < L *lyra* < Gk *lýra*]

lyre′ back′, a back of a chair or the like having a pierced splat in the form of a lyre, often with metal rods representing strings.

lyre·bird (līᵊr′bûrd′), *n.* an Australian passerine bird of the genus *Menura,* the male of which has a long tail which is lyrate when spread. [LYRE + BIRD]

Lyrebird, *Menura novaehollandiae* (Length 3 ft.; tail feathers 2 ft.)

lyre′-form so′fa (līᵊr′fôrm′), a sofa of the early 19th century having a front rail curving upward and outward at either end to form arms and terminating in a downward scroll.

lyre′ snake′, any of several mildly venomous colubrid snakes of the genus *Trimorphodon,* found in rocky deserts of North and Central America, having fangs in the rear of the upper jaw and a lyre-shaped marking on the head.

lyr·ic (lir′ik), *adj.* Also, **lyr′i·cal. 1.** (of poetry) having the form and musical quality of a song, and esp. the character of a songlike outpouring of the poet's own thoughts and feelings, as distinguished from epic and dramatic poetry. **2.** pertaining to or writing such poetry: *a lyric poet.* **3.** characterized by or expressing spontaneous, direct feeling: *a lyric outburst of song.* **4.** pertaining to, rendered by, or employing singing. **5.** pertaining, adapted, or sung to the lyre, or composing poems to be sung to the lyre: *ancient Greek lyric odes.* **6.** (of a voice) relatively light of volume and modest in range, most suited for graceful, cantabile melody: *a lyric soprano.* **7.** (of style, manner, etc.) rapturous, effusive, or undisciplined: *lyric outpourings from a newshen's typewriter.* —*n.* **8.** a lyric poem. **9.** Often, **lyrics.** the words of a song. [< L *lyric(us)* < Gk *lyrikós.* See LYRE, -IC] **—lyr′i·cal·ly,** *adv.* **—lyr′i·cal·ness,** *n.*

Lyr′ical Bal′lads, a collection of poetry (1798) by Wordsworth and Coleridge.

lyr·i·cise (lir′i sīz′), *v.i., v.t.,* **-cised, -cis·ing.** *Chiefly Brit.* lyricize. **—lyr′i·ci·sa′tion,** *n.*

lyr·i·cism (lir′i siz′əm), *n.* **1.** lyric character or style, as in poetry. **2.** lyric outpouring of feeling; enthusiasm, esp. when unrestrained or exaggerated. [LYRIC + -ISM]

lyr·i·cist (lir′i sist), *n.* **1.** a person who writes the words for songs. **2.** a lyric poet. [LYRIC + -IST]

lyr·i·cize (lir′i sīz′), *v.,* **-cized, -ciz·ing.** —*v.i.* **1.** to write lyrics. **2.** to sing the lyrics of a song. **3.** to write lyrically or in a lyric style. —*v.t.* **4.** to put into lyric form; treat in a lyric style: *to lyricize the landing of the Pilgrim Fathers.* Also, *esp. Brit.,* **lyricise.** [LYRIC + -IZE] **—lyr′i·ci·za′tion,** *n.*

ly·ri·form (lī′rə fôrm′), *adj.* shaped like a lyre. [< F *lyriforme.* See LYRE, -I-, -FORM]

lyr·ism (lir′iz əm *for 1;* līᵊr′iz əm *for 2*), *n.* **1.** lyricism. **2.** *Rare.* the playing of the lyre or any other lyric performance, as the singing of songs. [< Gk *lyrism(ós).* See LYRE, -ISM]

lyr·ist (līᵊr′ist *for 1;* lir′ist *for 2*), *n.* **1.** a person who plays the lyre or who sings and accompanies himself on the lyre. **2.** a lyric poet. [< L *lyrist(es)* < Gk *lyristḗs.* See LYRE, -IST]

Ly·rus (lī′rəs), *n. Class. Myth.* a son of Aphrodite and Anchises.

Lys (lēs), *n.* a river in W Europe, in N France and W Belgium, flowing NE into the Scheldt River at Ghent. 120 mi. long.

lys-, a learned borrowing from Greek meaning "loosening," "decomposition," used in the formation of compound words: *lysin.* Also, **lysi-, lyso-.** Cf. **-lyse, -lysis, -lyte.** [< Gk; see LYSIS]

Ly·san·der (lī san′dər), *n.* died 395 B.C., Spartan naval commander and statesman.

Ly·san·dra (li san′drə, lī-), *n.* a girl's given name.

lyse (līs), *v.,* **lysed, lys·ing.** *Immunol., Biochem.* —*v.t.* **1.** to cause dissolution or destruction of cells by lysins. —*v.i.* **2.** to undergo lysis. [back formation from LYSIN OR LYSIS]

-lyse, *esp. Brit.,* var. of **-lyze.**

Ly·sen·ko (li seŋ′kō; *Russ.* li sen′ko), *n.* **Tro·fim De·ni·so·vich** (tʀo fēm′ de nē′so vich), born 1898, Russian biologist and agronomist.

Ly·sen·ko·ism (li seŋ′kō iz′əm), *n.* a genetic doctrine formulated by Lysenko and asserting that heredity is not based on chromosomes and genes and that acquired characters are inherited. [named after T. D. LYSENKO; see -ISM]

ly·ser·gic ac·id (li sûr′jik, lī-), *Chem.* a crystalline solid, $C_{15}H_{15}N_2COOH$, obtained from ergot or synthesized: used in the synthesis of LSD. [LYS- + ERG(OT) + -IC]

lyser′gic ac′id dieth′ylamide, *Pharm.* See **LSD** (def. 2).

lysi-, var. of **lys-:** *lysimeter.*

Lys·i·as (lis′ē əs), *n.* c450–c380 B.C., Athenian orator.

Ly·sim·a·chus (lī sim′ə kəs), *n.* 361?–281 B.C., Macedonian general: king of Thrace 306–281.

ly·sim·e·ter (lī sim′i tər), *n.* an instrument for determining the amount of water-soluble matter in soil. [LYSI- + -METER]

ly·sin (lī′sin), *n. Immunol., Biochem.* an antibody causing the disintegration of erythrocytes or bacterial cells. [LYS- + -IN²]

ly·sine (lī′sēn, -sin), *n. Biochem.* a crystalline, basic, amino acid, $H_2N(CH_2)_4CH(NH_2)COOH$, produced chiefly from many proteins by hydrolysis, essential in the nutrition of man and animals. [LYS- + -INE²]

Ly·sip·pe (lī sip′ē), *n. Class. Myth.* a daughter of Antia and Proetus who was driven mad.

Ly·sip·pus (lī sip′əs), *n.* fl. c360–c320 B.C., Greek sculptor.

ly·sis (lī′sis), *n.* **1.** *Immunol., Biochem.* the dissolution or destruction of cells by lysins. **2.** *Med.* the gradual recession of a disease (distinguished from a crisis, in which the change is abrupt). [< NL < Gk *lýsis* a loosening, equiv. to *lý(ein)* (to) loose, release + *-sis* -SIS]

-lysis, an element of Greek origin, occurring esp. in scientific terms, denoting a breaking down, loosening, decomposition, etc.: *analysis; electrolysis; paralysis.* [< Gk; see LYSIS]

Ly·sis·tra·ta (lis′i strä′tə, lī sis′trə tə), *n.* a comedy (411 B.C.) by Aristophanes.

lyso-, var. of **lys-.**

Ly·sol (lī′sōl, -sôl, -sol), *n. Trademark.* a clear, brown, oily solution of cresols in soap, used as a disinfectant and antiseptic.

ly·so·zyme (lī′sə zīm′), *n. Biochem.* a bacteriolytic enzyme that serves as an antiseptic, found in tears, leukocytes, mucus, egg albumin, and certain plants. [LYSO- + (EN)ZYME]

lysso-, a learned borrowing from Greek meaning "madness," used in the formation of compound words: *lyssophobia.* [< Gk, comb. form repr. *lýssa* rage, rabies, madness]

lys·so·pho·bi·a (lis′ə fō′bē ə), *n. Psychiatry.* an obsessive fear of going insane. [LYSSO- + -PHOBIA]

-lyte[1], an element denoting something subjected to a certain process (indicated by a noun ending in *-lysis*): *electrolyte.* [< Gk *lyt(ós)* loosable, soluble, verbid of *lýein* to loose, dissolve; c. L *luere* to loose]

-lyte[2], var. of **-lite.**

lyth·ra·ceous (lith rā′shəs, lī thrā′-), *adj.* belonging to the *Lythraceae*, or loosestrife family of plants. [< NL *Lythr(um)* plant genus (< Gk *lýthron* gore, bloody gore) + -ACEOUS]

lyt·ic (lit′ik), *adj.* of, noting, or pertaining to lysis or a lysin. [< Gk *lytik(ós)* able to loosen. See -LYTE[1], -IC]

-lytic, a termination of adjectives corresponding to nouns in **-lysis:** *analytic; paralytic.* [see LYTIC]

Ly·tle (lit′əl), *n.* a boy's given name.

lyt·ta (lit′ə), *n., pl.* **lyt·tas, lyt·tae** (lit′ē). a long, wormlike cartilage in the tongue of the dog and other carnivorous animals. [< NL < Gk, Attic var. of *lýssa* rage, rabies; so named because cartilage was thought to be a parasite causing rabies]

Lyt·ton (lit′ən), *n.* **1. Edward George Earle Lytton Bulwer-, 1st Baron Lytton of Kneb·worth** (neb′wərt), 1803–73, English novelist, dramatist, and politician. **2.** his son, **Edward Robert Bulwer Lytton, 1st Earl Lytton** ("*Owen Meredith*"), 1831–91, English statesman and poet.

Lyu·ber·tsy (lyo͞o ber′tsi), *n.* a city in the W RSFSR, in the central part of the Soviet Union in Europe, SE of Moscow. 100,000 (est. 1961).

Lyu·blin (lyo͞o′blin), *n.* Russian name of **Lublin.**

-lyze, a word element used to form verbs from nouns with stems in **-lysis:** *catalyze.* Also, *esp. Brit.*, **-lyse.** [LY(SIS) + -(I)ZE]

M

M, m (em), *n., pl.* **M's** or **Ms, m's** or **ms. 1.** the thirteenth letter of the English alphabet, a consonant. **2.** any spoken sound represented by the letter *M* or *m*, as in *my, summer, him,* etc. **3.** something having the shape of an M. **4.** a written or printed representation of the letter *M* or *m*. **5.** a device, as a printer's type, for reproducing the letter *M* or *m*. **6.** *Print.* em.

m-, meta-.

M'-, Mac.

M, 1. Medieval. **2.** medium. **3.** Middle.

M, 1. the 13th in order or in a series, or, when *I* is omitted, the 12th. **2.** (*sometimes l.c.*) the Roman numeral for 1000. Cf. **Roman numerals.**

m, 1. medieval. **2.** medium. **3.** meter; meters. **4.** middle.

M., 1. Majesty. **2.** Manitoba. **3.** markka. **4.** Marquis. **5.** Medicine. **6.** Medium. **7.** Meridian. **8.** noon. [< L *meridies*] **9.** Monday. **10.** *pl.* **MM.** Monsieur. **11.** mountain.

m., 1. male. **2.** mark² (def. 1). **3.** married. **4.** masculine. **5.** *Mech.* mass. **6.** medium. **7.** noon. [< L *meridies*] **8.** meter. **9.** middle. **10.** mile. **11.** minim. **12.** minute. **13.** (in prescriptions) mix. [< L *misce*] **14.** modification of. **15.** modulus. **16.** molar. **17.** month. **18.** morning. **19.** mouth.

M-1 (em′wun′), *n., pl.* **M-1's. 1.** Also called **Garand rifle, M-1 rifle.** a semiautomatic, gas-operated, clip-fed rifle, with a .30 caliber and a weight of 8.56 pounds: the standard U.S. Army rifle in World War II and in the Korean War. **2.** *U.S. Mil.* the first production model of any item of military equipment.

M-14 (em′fôr′tēn′, -fôr′-), *n., pl.* **M-14's.** a fully automatic, gas-operated, .30 caliber rifle developed from the M-1: replaced the M-1 as the standard U.S. Army combat rifle.

M-16 (em′siks′tēn′), *n., pl.* **M-16's.** a light-weight, fully automatic rifle shooting a small-caliber bullet at an extremely high velocity: a U.S. Army combat weapon for mobile units and jungle fighting.

ma (mä), *n. Informal.* mother. [shortened var. of MAMA]

MA, *Psychol.* mental age.

Ma, *Chem.* masurium.

mA, milliampere; milliamperes.

mÅ, milliangstrom; milliangstroms.

M.A., 1. Master of Arts. [< L *Magister Artium*] **2.** *Psychol.* mental age. **3.** Military Academy. **4.** Mountain Artillery.

MAA, master-at-arms.

MAAG, Military Assistance Advisory Group.

ma'am (mam, mäm; *unstressed* məm), *n.* **1.** *Informal.* madam. **2.** (in Britain) a term used in addressing the Queen or a royal princess.

M.A.Arch., Master of Arts in Architecture.

Ma·a·rib (mä ä rēb′; *Eng.* mär′iv), *n. Hebrew.* the religious service celebrated by Jews daily in the evening. Also, **Ma·a·riv** (mä ä rēv′; *Eng.* mär′iv). Cf. **Minhah, Shaharith.** [lit., prayers]

Maar·ten (mär′tᵊn), *n.* a boy's given name.

Maas (mäs), *n.* Dutch name of the **Meuse.**

Maas·tricht (mäs′trikht), *n.* a city in the SE Netherlands, on the Maas River. 90,202 (est. 1960). Also, **Maestricht.**

Ma·at (mə ät′, mā′ət), *n. Egyptian Religion.* the goddess personifying law and righteousness.

Mab (mab), *n.* **1.** See **Queen Mab. 2.** a girl's given name.

Mab·i·no·gi·on, The (mab′ə nō′gē ən), a collection of medieval Welsh romances which were translated (1838–49) by Lady Charlotte Guest.

Ma·bel (mā′bəl), *n.* a girl's given name, form of **Amabel.** Also, **Ma·belle** (mā bel′, mā′bel), **Ma′ble.**

Ma·ble·ton (mā′bəl tən), *n.* a town in NW Georgia. 7127 (1960).

Ma·buse (*Fr.* ma byz′), *n.* **Jan** (*Flemish.* yän), (*Jan Gossaert* or *Gossart*), 1478?–1533?, Flemish painter.

mac¹ (mak), *n.* (*often cap.*) *U.S. Informal.* fellow; bud (a familiar term of address to a man or boy whose name is not known to the speaker). [special use of MAC]

mac² (mak), *n. Brit. Informal.* mackintosh. [shortened form]

Mac (mak), *n.* a boy's given name. Also, **Mack.**

Mac, a prefix found in many family names of Irish or Scottish Gaelic origin. Also, **Mc-, M'-, M'-.** [< Gael *mac* name prefix meaning son of, OIr *macc* son; c. Welsh *mab*, OWelsh *map*, Cornish *mab*]

Mac., Maccabees.

M.Ac., Master of Accountancy.

ma·ca·bre (mə kab′rə, -käb′), *adj.* **1.** gruesome; horrible; grim; ghastly. **2.** of, pertaining to, dealing with, or representing death, esp. its grimmer or uglier aspect. **3.** of or suggestive of the allegorical dance of death. Also, **ma·ca′ber.** [< F; r. late ME (*daunce of*) *Machabree* < MF (*danse*) *Macabré* for *Macabé* < LL *Maccabaeus* MACCABAEUS]

ma·ca·co (mə kä′kō, -kā′-), *n., pl.* **-cos. 1.** any of several lemurs, as *Lemur macaco.* **2.** *Obs.* macaque. [< Pg: monkey < an Afr language; see MACAQUE]

mac·ad·am (mə kad′əm), *n.* **1.** a macadamized road or pavement. **2.** the broken stone used in making such a road. [named after J. L. *McAdam* (1756–1836), Scottish inventor]

mac·a·da·mi·a (mak′ə dā′mē ə), *n.* **1.** any Australian tree of the genus *Macadamia*, esp. *M. ternifolia*, having whorled leaves and white flowers. **2.** Also called **macada′mia nut′.** the edible, hard-shelled seed of this tree. Also called **Queensland nut.** [< NL, named after J. *Macadam* (d. 1865), Australian chemist; see -IA]

mac·ad·am·ise (mə kad′ə mīz′), *v.t.,* **-ised, -is·ing.** *Chiefly Brit.* macadamize. **—mac·ad′am·i·sa′tion,** *n.*

mac·ad·am·ize (mə kad′ə mīz′), *v.t.,* **-ized, -iz·ing.** to pave by laying and compacting successive layers of broken stone. [MACADAM + -IZE] **—mac·ad′am·i·za′tion,** *n.*

CHINA
Canton
HONG KONG
Macao
SOUTH CHINA SEA

Ma·cao (mə kou′), *n.* **1.** a Portuguese overseas territory in S China, in the delta of the Chu-Kiang River and including two small adjacent islands. 215,000 (est. 1959); 6 sq. mi. **2.** the seaport and capital of this territory. 161,252 (1960). Portuguese, **Macáu.**

Ma·ca·pá (mə kə pä′), *n.* a city in and the capital of Amapá, in NE Brazil, at the mouth of the Amazon. 28,845 (1960).

Ma·ca·pa·gal (mä′kä pä gäl′), *n.* **Di·os·da·do** (dē′ôs dä′dō), born 1910, Philippine statesman: president 1961–65.

ma·caque (mə käk′), *n.* any monkey of the genus *Macaca*, chiefly found in Asia, characterized by cheek pouches and, usually, a short tail. [< F < Pg *macaco* monkey. See MACACO]

Macaque, *Macaca philippinensis* (Total length 5½ ft.; tail 2 ft.)

Mac·a·reus (mak′ə rōōs′), *n. Class. Myth.* a son of Aeolus and Encrete.

mac·a·ro·ni (mak′ə rō′nē), *n., pl.* **-nis, -nies. 1.** a pasta prepared from wheat flour, in the form of dried, hollow tubes. **2.** an English dandy of the 18th century who affected Continental mannerisms. Also, **maccaroni.** [earlier *maccaroni* < dial. It, pl. of *maccarone* (It *maccherone*). See MACAROON]

mac·a·ron·ic (mak′ə ron′ik), *adj.* **1.** composed of or characterized by Latin words mixed with vernacular words or non-Latin words terminated in Latin endings. **2.** composed of a mixture of languages. **3.** mixed; jumbled. **—***n.* **4. macaronics,** macaronic language. **5.** a macaronic verse or other piece of writing. [< ML *macarōnic(us)* < dial. It *maccarone* MACARONI + L *-icus* -IC] **—mac′a·ron′i·cal·ly,** *adv.*

mac·a·roon (mak′ə rōōn′), *n.* a drop cooky made of egg whites, sugar, usually almond paste or coconut, and sometimes a little flour. [< MF *macaron* < dial. It *maccarone* cake or biscuit made of ground almonds; see MACARONI]

Mac·Ar·thur (mək är′thər, mə kär′-), *n.* **Douglas,** 1880–1964, U.S. general.

Ma·cart′ney rose′ (mə kärt′nē), a trailing or climbing, evergreen rose, *Rosa bracteata*, of China, having shiny leaves and solitary, white flowers nearly three inches wide. [named after George, 1st Earl *Macartney* (1737–1806), British diplomat]

Ma·cas·sar (mə kas′ər), *n.* **1.** a seaport on SW Celebes, in central Indonesia. 367,882 with suburbs (est. 1961). **2. Strait of,** a strait between Borneo and Celebes: naval engagement between the Allies and the Japanese 1942. Dutch, **Makassar.**

Macas′sar oil′, 1. an oil derived from materials said to be obtained from Macassar, formerly used as a hairdressing. **2.** a similar oil or preparation for the hair.

Ma·cáu (mə kou′), *n.* Portuguese name of **Macao.**

Ma·cau·lay (mə kô′lē), *n.* **1. Dame Rose,** c1885–1958, English poet and novelist. **2. Thomas Bab·ing·ton** (bab′ing tən), **1st Baron,** 1800–59, English historian, author, and statesman. **—Ma·cau′lay·an,** *adj.* **—Ma·cau′lay·ism,** *n.*

ma·caw (mə kô′), *n.* any of various large, long-tailed parrots, chiefly of the genus *Ara*, of tropical and subtropical America, noted for their brilliant plumage and harsh voice. [< Pg *macoa* parrot, perh. < Tupi-Guarani *macaú(ba)* macaw palm (< Arawak *maco(ya)* + Tupi-Guarani *úba* tree); possibly brought into Brazilian Indian tongues by African slaves]

Macaw, *Ara macao* (Length 3 ft.)

Mac·beth (mək beth′, mak-), *n.* **1.** died 1057, king of Scotland 1040–57. **2.** (*italics*) a tragedy (1606?) by Shakespeare.

Macc., Maccabees.

Mac·ca·bae·us (mak′ə bē′əs), *n.* **Judas** or **Je·hu·dah** (jə hōō′də), (*"the Hammer"*), died 160 B.C., Judean patriot: military leader 166–160 (son of Mattathias).

Mac·ca·be·an (mak′ə bē′ən), *adj.* of or pertaining to the Maccabees or Judas Maccabaeus. [MACCABE(ES) + -AN]

Mac·ca·bees (mak′ə bēz′), *n.* **1.** (*construed as pl.*) the members of the Hasmonean family of Jewish leaders and rulers comprising the sons of Mattathias and their descendants and reigning in Judea from 167? to 37 B.C., esp. Judas Maccabaeus and his brothers, who defeated the Syrians under Antiochus IV in 165? and rededicated the Temple in Jerusalem. **2.** Also, *Douay Bible,* **Machabees.** (*construed as sing.*) either of two books of the Apocrypha, I Maccabees or II Maccabees, that contain the history of the Maccabees.

mac·ca·boy (mak′ə boi′), *n.* a kind of snuff, usually rose-scented. Also, **mac′co·boy′.** [earlier *Maca(u)ba(o)* < F *macouba* a kind of aromatic tobacco; special use of *Macouba* place in northern Martinique, where made]

mac·ca·ro·ni (mak′ə rō′nē), *n., pl.* **-nis, -nies.** macaroni.

Mac·clen·ny (mə klen′ē), *n.* a town in N Florida. 2671 (1960).

Mac·don·ald (mək don′əld), *n.* **1. George,** 1824–1905, Scottish novelist and poet. **2. Sir John Alexander,** 1815–91, Canadian statesman, born in Scotland: 1st prime minister 1867–73, 1878–91.

Mac·Don·ald (mək don′əld), *n.* **James Ramsay,** 1866–1937, British statesman and labor leader: prime minister 1924, 1929–35.

Mac·Don·ough (mək don′ə), *n.* **Thomas,** 1783–1825, U.S. naval officer: defeated British on Lake Champlain 1814.

Mac·Dow·ell (mək dou′əl), *n.* **Edward Alexander,** 1861–1908, U.S. composer and pianist.

mace[1] (mās), *n.* **1.** a clublike weapon of war, often with a flanged or spiked metal head, used chiefly in the Middle Ages. **2.** a ceremonial staff carried before or by certain officials as a symbol of office. **3.** macebearer. **4.** *Billiards.* a light stick with a flat head, formerly used at times instead of a cue. **5.** (*cap.*) *U.S.* a surface-to-surface, pilotless nuclear aircraft. [ME < OF (cf. F *masse*) large mallet < VL **mattea;* akin to L *matteola* kind of mallet, Skt *matya* harrow]

mace[2] (mās), *n.* a spice ground from the layer between a nutmeg shell and its outer husk, resembling nutmeg in flavor.

Mace (mās), *n.* a nonlethal spray containing purified tear gas and chemical solvents which temporarily incapacitate a person by causing eye and skin irritations: used esp. as a means of subduing rioters. Also called **Chemical Mace.** [after MACE, a trademark]

mace·bear·er (mās′bâr′ər), *n.* an official, as of a city or legislative body, who carries the ceremonial mace before dignitaries. [MACE[1] + BEARER]

Maced., Macedonia.

mac·é·doine (mas′i dwän′; *Fr.* ma sā dwan′), *n., pl.* **mac·é·doines** (mas′i dwänz′; *Fr.* ma sā dwan′). **1.** a mixture of vegetables or fruits, often served as a salad. **2.** a medley. [F, special use of *Macédoine* MACEDONIA, prob. an allusion to the racial variety of the region]

Mac·e·do·ni·a (mas′i dō′nē ə, -dōn′yə), *n.* **1.** also, **Mac·e·don** (mas′i don′). an ancient kingdom in the Balkan Peninsula, in SE Europe: now a region including parts of Greece, the republic of Macedonia, and Bulgaria. **2.** a republic in SE Europe: formerly part of Yugoslavia. 2,040,000; 9928 sq. mi. *Cap.:* Skopje.

Mac·e·do·ni·an (mas′i dō′nē ən), *n.* **1.** a Slavic language of modern Macedonia. **2.** an extinct language of ancient Macedonia, an Indo-European language of uncertain relationship within the Indo-European language family. —*adj.* **3.** of, pertaining to, or characteristic of ancient Macedonia. **4.** of, pertaining to, or characteristic of modern Macedonia, its inhabitants, or their language. [MACEDONI(A) + -AN]

Ma·ceió (mä′sā ô′), *n.* a seaport in and the capital of Alagoas, in E Brazil. 161,863 (1960).

mac·er (mā′sər), *n.* **1.** macebearer. **2.** (in Scotland) an officer who attends the Court of Session and carries out its orders.

mac·er·ate (mas′ə rāt′), *v.,* **-at·ed, -at·ing.** —*v.t.* **1.** to soften or separate (a substance) into parts by steeping in a liquid. **2.** to soften or decompose (food) by the action of a solvent. **3.** to cause to grow thin. —*v.i.* **4.** to undergo maceration. **5.** to become thin; waste away. [< L *mācerāt(us)* made soft, weakened, steeped (ptp. of *mācerāre*), equiv. to *māc-* make soft or tender + *-er-* freq. suffix + *-ātus* -ATE[1]] —**mac′er·at′er, mac′er·a′tor,** *n.* —**mac′er·a′tive,** *adj.* —**mac′er·a′tion,** *n.*

mac·far·lane (mək fär′lin), *n.* (*sometimes cap.*) an overcoat with an attached cape and two slits in front near the waist. Also, **Mac·Far′lane.** [special use of surname *MacFarlane*]

mach., **1.** machine. **2.** machinery. **3.** machinist.

Mach (mäk, mak; *Ger.* mäkh), *n.* **1. Ernst** (ernst), 1838–1916, Austrian physicist, psychologist, and philosopher. **2.** Also, **mach.** See **Mach number.**

Mach·a·bees (mak′ə bēz′), *n.* *Douay Bible.* Maccabees (def. 2).

Ma·cha·do de As·sis (mä shä′dŏŏ di ä sēs′), **Jo·a·quim Ma·ri·a** (zhŏŏ ä kim′ mä rē′ä), 1839–1908, Brazilian writer.

Ma·cha·do y Mo·ra·les (mä chä′thō ē mō rä′les), **Ge·rar·do** (he rär′thō), 1871–1939, president of Cuba 1925–33.

Ma·cha·do y Ru·iz (mä chä′thō ē rōō ēth′), **An·to·nio** (än tō′nyō), 1875–1939, Spanish writer.

Ma·chae·rus (mə kēr′əs), *n.* *Class. Myth.* a Phocian who killed Neoptolemus.

ma·chai·ra (mə kī′rə), *n.* kopis. Also, **ma·che·ra** (mə kâr′ə, -kēr′ə). [< Gk: large knife, dagger, deriv. of *máchē* battle]

Ma·cha·on (mə kā′on), *n.* (in the *Iliad*) a son of Asclepius who was famed as a healer and who served as physician of the Greeks in the Trojan War.

Ma·chaut (*Fr.* ma shō′), *n.* **Guil·laume de** (*Fr.* gē yōm′ də). See **Guillaume de Machaut.** Also, **Ma·chault′.**

Mach·en (mak′ən), *n.* **Arthur,** 1863–1947, Welsh novelist and essayist.

ma chère (ma sher′), *French.* (referring to a woman or girl) my dear. Cf. **mon cher.**

ma·chet·e (mə shet′ē, -chet′ē; *Sp.* mä che′te), *n., pl.* **-chet·es** (-shet′ēz, -chet′ēz; *Sp.* -che′tes). **1.** a large heavy knife used esp. in Latin-American countries as a tool in cutting sugar cane and clearing underbrush or as a weapon. **2.** a tarpon, *Elops affinis,* found in the eastern Pacific Ocean, having an elongated, compressed body. [< Sp, equiv. to *mach(o)* mallet (see MACE[1]) + *-ete* n. suffix]

Machete

Mach·i·a·vel·li (mak′ē ə vel′ē; *It.* mä′kyä vel′lē), *n.* **Nic·co·lò di Ber·nar·do** (nēk′kō lô′ dē ber när′dō), 1469–1527, Italian statesman, political philosopher, and author.

Mach·i·a·vel·li·an (mak′ē ə vel′ē ən), *adj.* **1.** of, like, or befitting Machiavelli: *Machiavellian astuteness.* **2.** being or acting in accordance with the principles of government analyzed in Machiavelli's *The Prince,* in which political expediency is placed above morality and the use of craft and deceit to maintain the authority and carry out the policies of a ruler is described. **3.** characterized by subtle or unscrupulous cunning, deception, or dishonesty: *He resorted to Machiavellian tactics in order to get ahead.* —*n.* **4.** a follower of the principles analyzed or described in *The Prince,* esp. with reference to techniques of political manipulation. Also, **Mach′i·a·vel′i·an.** [MACHIAVELLI + -AN] —**Mach′i·a·vel′li·an·ism, Mach′i·a·vel′lism,** *n.* —**Mach′i·a·vel′li·an·ly,** *adv.*

ma·chic·o·late (mə chik′ə lāt′), *v.t.,* **-lat·ed, -lat·ing.** to provide with machicolations. [< ML *machico(l)lāt(us)* furnished with machicolations, ptp. of *machico(l)lāre,* Latinization of MF *machecoller,* equiv. to *mache-* chew, crush (OF *ma(s)cher* < LL *masticāre;* see MASTICATE) + *coller* to flow, run < L *cōlāre* to filter]

ma·chic·o·lat·ed (mə chik′ə lā′tid), *adj.* provided with, or given the form of, machicolations. [MACHICOLATE + -ED[2]]

ma·chic·o·la·tion (mə chik′ə lā′shən), *n.* *Archit.* **1.** an opening in the floor between the corbels of a projecting gallery or parapet, as on a wall or in the vault of a passage, through which missiles, molten lead, etc., might be cast upon an enemy beneath. **2.** a projecting gallery or parapet with such openings. [MACHICOLATE + -ION]

ma·chin·a·ble (mə shē′nə bəl), *adj.* (of a material) capable of being cut with machine tools. Also, **ma·chine′a·ble.** Cf. **free-machining.** [MACHINE + -ABLE] —**ma·chin′a·bil′i·ty,** *n.*

mach·i·nate (mak′ə nāt′), *v.,* **-nat·ed, -nat·ing.** to contrive or devise, esp. artfully or with evil purpose: *to machinate the overthrow of the government.* [< L *māchināt(us)* skillfully contrived, adjusted, ptp. of *māchinārī.* See MACHINE, -ATE[1]] —**mach′i·na′tor,** *n.*

mach·i·na·tion (mak′ə nā′shən), *n.* **1.** the act, an instance, or the process of machinating. **2.** Usually, **machinations.** crafty schemes; plots; intrigues. [< L *māchinātiōn-* (s. of *māchinātiō*). See MACHINATE, -ION] —**Syn. 2.** stratagem, complot, device.

ma·chine (mə shēn′), *n., v.,* **-chined, -chin·ing.** —*n.* **1.** an apparatus consisting of interrelated parts with separate functions, used in the performance of some kind of work: *a sewing machine.* **2.** a mechanical apparatus or contrivance; a mechanism. **3.** something operated by a mechanical apparatus, as an automobile or airplane. **4.** *Mech.* **a.** a device that transmits or modifies force or motion. **b.** Also called **simple machine.** any of six or more elementary mechanisms, as the lever, wheel and axle, pulley, screw, wedge, and inclined plane. **c.** Also called **complex machine.** a combination of simple machines. **5.** any of various contrivances, esp. those formerly used in the theater, for producing stage effects. **6.** some agency, personage, incident, or other feature introduced for effect into a literary composition. **7.** any complex agency or operating system: *the machine of government.* **8.** an organized group of persons that conducts or controls the activities of a political party or other organization: *He heads the Democratic machine in our city.* **9.** one who or that which acts in a mechanical or automatic manner: *Routine work had turned her into a machine.* —*v.t.* **10.** to make, prepare, or finish with a machine. [< F < L *māchina* < Doric Gk *māchanā́* pulley, akin to *mâchos* contrivance] —**ma·chine′less,** *adj.* —**ma·chine′like′,** *adj.* —**ma·chine′ly,** *adv.*

machine′ bolt′, a threaded fastener, used with a nut for connecting metal parts, having a thread diameter of about ¼ inch or more and a square or hexagonal head for tightening by a wrench. Cf. **cap screw, machine screw, stove bolt.** See illus. under **bolt**[1].

machine′ gun′, a small arm operated by a mechanism, able to deliver a rapid and continuous fire of bullets as long as the trigger is pressed.

ma·chine-gun (mə shēn′gun′), *v.t.,* **-gunned, -gun·ning.** to shoot at, using a machine gun: *to machine-gun a crowd.* —**machine′ gun′ner.**

machine′ lan′guage, *Computer Technol.* the coding system for letters, numbers, and instructions that assigns actual storage locations and requires no translation by the computer for operation.

machine′ pis′tol, a fully automatic pistol; submachine gun. Also called **burp gun.**

machine′ ri′fle. See **automatic rifle.**

ma·chin·er·y (mə shē′nə rē), *n., pl.* **-er·ies.** **1.** an assemblage of machines or mechanical apparatuses: *the machinery of a factory.* **2.** the parts of a machine, collectively: *the machinery of a watch.* **3.** a group of contrivances for producing stage effects. **4.** the group or aggregate of literary machines, esp. those of supernatural agency (**epic machinery**) in an epic poem. **5.** any system by which action is maintained: *the machinery of government.* [MACHINE + -ERY]

machine′ screw′, a threaded fastener, either used with a nut or driven into a tapped hole, usually having a diameter of about ¼ inch or less and a slotted head for tightening by a screwdriver. Cf. **cap screw, machine bolt.**

machine′ shop′, a workshop in which metal and other substances are cut, shaped, etc., by machine tools.

machine′ tool′, a power-operated machine, as a lathe, used for general cutting and shaping of metal. —**ma·chine′-tooled′,** *adj.*

machine′ word′, *Computer Technol.* a standard unit consisting of a fixed number of bits treated as a single entity by a computer.

ma·chin·ist (mə shē′nist), *n.* **1.** one who operates machinery, esp. a highly trained, skilled operator of machine tools. **2.** one who makes and repairs machines. **3.** *U.S. Navy.* a warrant officer whose duty is to assist the engineering officer in the engine room. [MACHINE + -IST]

ma·chis·mo (mä chiz′mō), *n.* (in Hispanic cultures) maleness or virility; male domination. [< Sp *macho* male, he-man]

Mach·me·ter (mäk′mē′tər, mak′-), *n.* *Aeron.* a device that indicates airspeed relative to the speed of sound. [MACH + -METER]

Mach′ num′ber, a number indicating the ratio of the speed of an object through a medium to the speed of sound in the medium. *Abbr.:* M Also, **mach′ num′ber.** Also called **Mach, mach.**

Mach·pe·lah (mak pē′lä), *n.* the site of a cave, probably in the ancient city of Hebron, where Abraham, Sarah, Rebekah, Isaac, Jacob, and Leah were buried. Gen. 23:19; 25:9; 49:30; 50:13.

ma·chree (mə krē′, mə khrē′), *n.* *Irish Eng.* dear: *mother machree.* [< Ir *mo croidhe,* lit., my heart]

Ma·chu Pic·chu (mä′chōō pēk′chōō), the site of an ancient Incan and pre-Incan city, about 7000 feet above sea level in the Andes, in S central Peru.

-machy, a learned borrowing from Greek meaning "fighting," used in the formation of compound words: *logomachy.* [< Gk *-machia,* equiv. to *mách(ē)* battle + *-ia* -Y[3]]

mach·zor (mäkh zôr′; *Eng.* mäkh′zôr, -zôr, -zər), *n., pl.* **mach·zo·rim** (mäkh zō rēm′), *Eng.* **mach·zors.** *Hebrew.* mahzor.

mac·in·tosh (mak′in tosh′), *n.* mackintosh.

Mac·in·tosh (mak′in tosh′), *n.* **Charles,** 1766–1843, Scottish chemist, inventor, and manufacturer.

Mac·I·ver (mək ī′vər, mə kī′-), *n.* **1. Loren,** born 1909, U.S. painter. **2. Robert Morrison,** 1882–1970, U.S. sociologist, born in Scotland.

Mack (mak), *n.* **1. Con·nie** (kon′ē), (*Cornelius McGillicuddy*), 1862–1956, U.S. baseball player and manager. **2.** Also, **Mac.** a boy's given name.

Mac·kay (mə kī′), *n.* a seaport in E Australia. 16,809 (1961).

Ma·cke (mä′kə), *n.* **Au·gust** (ou′gŏŏst), 1887–1914, German painter.

Mack·en·sen (mäk′ən zən), *n.* **Au·gust von** (ou′gŏŏst fən), 1849–1945, German field marshal.

Mac·ken·zie (mə ken′zē), *n.* **1. Sir Alexander,** 1764–1820, Scottish explorer in Canada. **2. Alexander,** 1822–92, Canadian statesman, born in Scotland: prime minister 1873–78. **3. William Lyon,** 1795–1861, Canadian political leader and journalist, born in Scotland. **4.** a river in NW Canada, flowing NW from the Great Slave Lake to the Arctic Ocean. 1120 mi. long; with tributaries 2525 mi. long. **5.** a district in the SW Northwest Territories of Canada. 527,490 sq. mi.

mack·er·el (mak′ər əl, mak′rəl), *n., pl.* (*esp. collectively*) **-el,** (*esp. referring to two or more kinds or species*) **-els.** **1.** a swift food fish, *Scomber scombrus,* found in the North Atlantic, having wavy cross markings on the back. **2.** See **Spanish mackerel.** **3.** any of various similar fishes, as the Atka mackerel. [ME *makerel* < OF, perh. same word as MF *maquerel* pimp < MD *makelare* broker (by metathesis), equiv. to *makel(en)* (to) bring together + *-are* -ER[1]]

mack′erel gull′, *Dial.* tern[1].

mack′erel sky′, **1.** a sky spotted with small, white, fleecy clouds. **2.** an extensive group of cirrocumulus or altocumulus clouds, esp. when well-marked in their arrangement.

Mack·i·nac (mak′ə nô′), *n.* **1. Straits of,** a strait between the peninsulas of Upper Michigan and Lower Michigan, connecting Lakes Huron and Michigan. **2.** Also, **Mack′inac Is′land.** an island in Lake Huron at the entrance of this strait. 942 (1960); 3 mi. long. **3.** a town on this island.

mack·i·naw (mak′ə nô′), *n.* See **Mackinaw coat.** [sp. var. of MACKINAC] —**mack′i·nawed′,** *adj.*

Mack′inaw blan′ket, a thick blanket, often woven with bars of color, formerly much used in the northern and western U.S. by Indians, lumbermen, etc.

Mack′inaw boat′, a flat-bottomed boat with sharp prow and square stern, propelled by oars and sometimes sails, as used on the upper Great Lakes.

Mack′inaw coat′, a short coat of a thick, blanketlike, commonly plaid, woolen material. Also called **mackinaw.**

Mack′inaw trout′. See **lake trout.**

mack·in·tosh (mak′in tosh′), *n.* **1.** a raincoat made of cloth rendered waterproof by India rubber. **2.** such cloth. **3.** any raincoat. Also, **macintosh.** [named after Charles *Macintosh* (1766–1843), its inventor] —**mack′in·toshed′,** *adj.*

Mack·in·tosh (mak′in tosh′), *n.* **Charles Ren·nie** (ren′ē), 1868–1928, Scottish architect and designer.

mack·le (mak′əl), *n., v.,* **-led, -ling.** —*n.* **1.** a blur in printing, as from a double impression. —*v.t., v.i.* **2.** to blur, as from a double impression in printing. Also, **macule.** [var. of earlier *macle, makle,* late ME *macule* spot, blemish < L *macula.* See MACULA]

Mac·lar·en (mə klar′ən), *n.* **I·an** (ē′ən, ī′ən). See **Watson, John.**

Mac·lau·rin (mək lôr′in, mə klô′-; *for 1 also Scot.* mäk lô′rin), *n.* **1. Colin,** 1698–1746, Scottish mathematician. **2.** a crater in the fourth quadrant of the face of the moon: about 30 miles in diameter.

Maclau′rin se′ries, *Math.* a Taylor series in which the reference point is zero. [named after C. MACLAURIN]

ma·cle (mak′əl), *n.* *Crystall. Obs.* a twin. [< F < L *macula.* See MACULA]

Mac·lear (mə klēr′), *n.* a walled plain in the first quadrant of the face of the moon: about 12 miles in diameter.

ma·cled (mak′əld), *adj.* *Armor.* (of mail) formed of diamond-shaped metal plates sewed to a flexible backing. [MACLE + -ED[3]]

Mac·Leish (mək lēsh′, mə klēsh′), *n.* **Archibald,** born 1892, U.S. poet and dramatist.

Mac·leod (mə kloud′), *n.* **1. Fiona.** See **Sharp, William.** **2. John James Rick·ard** (rik′ərd), 1876–1935, Scottish physiologist: Nobel prize for medicine 1923.

Mac·Ma·hon (mak ma ôn′), *n.* **Ma·rie Ed·mé Pa·trice Mau·rice** (ma rē′ ed mā′ pa trēs′ mō rēs′), **Count de** (*Duke of Magenta*), 1808–93, president of France 1873–79.

Mac·Man·us (mək man′əs), *n.* **Seu·mas** (shā′məs), 1869–1960, Irish poet and short-story writer.

Mac·Mil·lan (mək mil′ən), *n.* **Donald Bax·ter** (bak′stər), 1874–1970, U.S. arctic explorer.

Mac·mil·lan (mək mil′ən), *n.* **Harold,** born 1894, British statesman: prime minister 1957–63.

Mac·Mon·nies (mək mun′ēz), *n.* **Frederick William,** 1863–1937, U.S. sculptor.

mac·nab′ cy′press (mək nab′), a hardy, bushy tree, *Cupressus macnabiana*, of the western coast of the U.S. Also called **Shasta cypress, white cedar.** [after James *MacNab* (d. 1878), Scottish botanist]

ma·co (mä′kō), *n.* an Egyptian cotton, much used in the manufacture of hosiery and undergarments. [after *Mako* Bey 19th-century Egyptian officer]

ma·co·ma (mə kō′mə), *n.* any marine bivalve mollusk of the genus *Macoma*, having a glossy, thin, usually white shell. [< NL]

Ma·con (mā′kən), *n.* **1. Nathaniel,** 1758–1837, U.S. politician: Speaker of the House 1801–07. **2.** a city in central Georgia. 69,764 (1960).

Mâ·con (mä kôɴ′), *n.* **1.** a city in and the capital of Saône-et-Loire, in E central France. 27,669 (1962). **2.** a Burgundy wine from the Mâcon district.

Mac·pher·son (mək fûr′sən), *n.* **James,** 1736–96, Scottish author and translator.

Mac·quar·ie (mə kwôr′ē, -kwor′ē), *n.* a river in SE Australia, in New South Wales, flowing NW to the Darling River. 750 mi. long.

mac·ra·mé (mak′rə mā′), *n.* a hand-knotted garment, trimming, or fringe, usually in a geometrical pattern. Also called **mac′ramé lace′.** [< F < It *macramè* kind of fringe on hand towels < Turk *makrama* napkin, face towel < Ar *migrama* embroidered veil]

Mac·rea·dy (mə krē′dē), *n.* **William Charles,** 1793–1873, English actor.

macro-, a learned borrowing from Greek meaning "large," "long," "great," "excessive," used in the formation of compound words, contrasting with *micro-*: *macrocosm; macrofossil; macrograph; macroscopic.* Also, *esp. before a vowel,* **macr-.** [< Gk *makro-*, comb. form of *makrós*; c. L *macer* lean; see MEAGER]

mac·ro·bi·ot·ic (mak′rō bī ot′ik), *adj.* **1.** long-lived. **2.** lengthening the life span. **3.** of or consisting primarily of grains and vegetables whose use is said to give long life: *a macrobiotic diet.* **4.** of, pertaining to, or serving macrobiotic food: *macrobiotic cooking; a macrobiotic restaurant.* [MACRO- + BIOTIC] —**mac′ro·bi·ot′i·cal·ly,** *adv.*

mac·ro·bi·ot·ics (mak′rō bī ot′iks), *n.* (*construed as sing.*) the art of lengthening life, esp. by a vegetarian diet.

Ma·cro·bi·us (mə krō′bē əs), *n.* a walled plain in the first quadrant of the face of the moon: about 42 miles in diameter.

mac·ro·car·pous (mak′rō kär′pəs), *adj.* having large fruit. [< NL (*Cupressus*) *macrocarp(a)* evergreen species (see MACRO-, -CARPOUS) + -OUS]

mac·ro·ce·phal·ic (mak′rō sə fal′ik), *adj.* *Craniom.* being or having a skull with a large cranial capacity. Also, **mac·ro·ceph·a·lous** (mak′rō sef′ə ləs). [< Gk *makroképhal(os)* large-headed (see MACRO-, -CEPHALIC) + -IC] —**mac·ro·ceph·a·ly** (mak′rō sef′ə lē), *n.*

mac·ro·ceph·a·lus (mak′rō sef′ə ləs), *n., pl.* **-li** (-lī′). **1.** a person with a macrocephalic skull. **2.** a macrocephalic skull. [< NL < Gk *makroképhalos.* See MACRO-, -CEPHALOUS]

mac·ro·cli·mate (mak′rə klī′mit), *n.* the general climate of a large area, as of a continent or country. Cf. **microclimate.** [MACRO- + CLIMATE] —**mac·ro·cli·mat·ic** (mak′rō klī mat′ik), *adj.* —**mac′ro·cli·mat′i·cal·ly,** *adv.*

mac·ro·cli·ma·tol·o·gy (mak′rō klī′mə tol′ə jē), *n.* the study of the climatic conditions of a large area. Cf. **macrometeorology, microclimatology.** [MACRO- + CLIMATOLOGY]

mac·ro·cosm (mak′rə koz′əm), *n.* **1.** the great world or universe; the universe considered as a whole (opposed to *microcosm*). **2.** the total or entire complex structure of something: *the macrocosm of war.* **3.** a representation of a smaller unit or entity by a larger one, presumably of a similar structure. [< F *macrocosme* < ML *macrocosm(us).* See MACRO-, COSMOS] —**mac′ro·cos′mic,** *adj.* —**mac′ro·cos′mi·cal·ly,** *adv.*

mac·ro·cy·clic (mak′rō sī′klik, -sik′lik), *adj.* *Chem.* having a ring structure consisting of more than 12 atoms. [MACRO- + CYCLIC]

mac·ro·cyst (mak′rə sist′), *n.* *Bot.* a large cyst or spore case, esp. the encysted, resting plasmodium of a slime mold. [MACRO- + CYST]

mac·ro·cyte (mak′rə sīt′), *n.* *Pathol.* an abnormally large red blood cell. [MACRO- + -CYTE] —**mac′ro·cyt·ic** (mak′rə sit′ik), *adj.*

mac′rocyt′ic ane′mia, *Pathol.* an anemia characterized by predominance of macrocytes.

mac·ro·dome (mak′rə dōm′), *n.* *Crystall.* a dome the faces of which are parallel to the greater lateral axis. Cf. **brachydome.** [MACRO- + DOME]

mac·ro·dont (mak′rə dont′), *adj.* having abnormally large teeth; megadont; megadontic. Also, **mac′ro·don′tic.** [MACR- + -ODONT]

mac·ro·don·tia (mak′rə don′shə, -shē ə), *n.* abnormally large teeth. Also, **mac′ro·dont′ism.** Also called **megadontia, megadontism, megadonty.** [< NL; see MACRODONT, -IA]

mac·ro·e·co·nom·ics (mak′rō ē′kə nom′iks, -ek′ə-), *n.* (*construed as sing.*) the branch of economics dealing with the broad and general aspects of an economy, as the relationship between the income and investments of a country as a whole. Cf. **microeconomics.** [MACRO- + ECONOMICS] —**mac′ro·e′co·nom′ic,** *adj.*

mac·ro·etch (mak′rō ech′), *v.t.* to etch deeply into the surface of (a metal). [MACRO- + ETCH]

mac·ro·fos·sil (mak′rō fos′il), *n.* a fossil large enough to be studied and identified without the use of a microscope. Cf. **microfossil.** [MACRO- + FOSSIL]

mac·ro·gam·ete (mak′rō gam′ēt, -gə mēt′), *n.* *Biol.* (in heterogamous reproduction) the larger and usually female of a pair of conjugating gametes. [MACRO- + GAMETE]

mac·ro·graph (mak′rə graf′, -gräf′), *n.* a representation of an object that is of the same size as or larger than the object. [MACRO- + -GRAPH]

ma·crog·ra·phy (mə krog′rə fē), *n.* **1.** examination or study of an object with the naked eye (opposed to *micrography*). **2.** markedly or excessively large handwriting. [MACRO- + -GRAPHY] —**mac·ro·graph·ic** (mak′rə graf′ik), *adj.*

mac·ro·lec·i·thal (mak′rō les′ə thəl), *adj.* *Embryol.* megalecithal. [MACRO- + LECITHAL]

mac·ro·lin·guis·tics (mak′rō ling gwis′tiks), *n.* (*construed as sing.*) *Ling.* the field of study dealing with language in the broadest sense. [MACRO- + LINGUISTICS] —**mac′ro·lin·guis′tic,** *adj.* —**mac′ro·lin·guis′ti·cal·ly,** *adv.*

mac·ro·lith (mak′rə lith′), *n.* *Archaeol.* a stone tool, about one foot long. [MACRO- + -LITH]

mac·ro·me·te·or·ol·o·gy (mak′rō mē′tē ə rol′ə jē), *n.* the study of large-scale atmospheric phenomena, as the general circulation of the air, global weather conditions, etc. Cf. **macroclimatology, mesometeorology, micrometeorology.** [MACRO- + METEOROLOGY] —**mac·ro·me·te·or·o·log·i·cal** (mak′rō mē′tē ər ə loj′i kəl), *adj.*

mac·ro·mol·e·cule (mak′rə mol′ə kyōōl′), *n.* *Chem.* a very large molecule, as a colloidal particle, protein, or esp. a polymer, composed of hundreds or thousands of atoms. Also, **mac·ro·mole** (mak′rə mōl′). [MACRO- + MOLECULE] —**mac·ro·mo·lec·u·lar** (mak′rō mə lek′yə lər), *adj.*

ma·cron (mā′kron, mak′ron), *n.* a horizontal line used as a diacritic over a vowel to indicate that it has a long sound, as in *fate* (fāt). [< Gk *makrón*, n. use of neut. of *makrós* long. See MACRO-]

mac·ro·nu·cle·ate (mak′rō nōō′klē it, -āt′, -nyōō′-), *adj.* having a macronucleus. [MACRONUCLE(US) + -ATE[1]]

mac·ro·nu·cle·us (mak′rə nōō′klē əs, -nyōō′-), *n.* *Zool.* the larger of the two nuclei of a ciliate. Cf. **micronucleus.** [< NL; see MACRO-, NUCLEUS] —**mac′ro·nu′cle·ar,** *adj.*

mac·ro·phage (mak′rə fāj′), *n.* *Anat.* a large, amoeboid, phagocytic blood cell in connective tissue. [< NL *macrophag(us).* See MACRO-, -PHAGE] —**mac·ro·phag·ic** (mak′rə faj′ik), *adj.*

mac·ro·phyl·lous (mak′rō fil′əs), *adj.* *Bot.* having large leaves. [MACRO- + -PHYLLOUS]

mac·ro·phys·ics (mak′rə fiz′iks), *n.* (*construed as sing.*) the branch of physics that deals with physical objects large enough to be observed and treated directly. [MACRO- + PHYSICS]

mac·rop·o·dous (ma krop′ə dəs), *adj.* *Bot.* **1.** (of a leaf) having a long stalk. **2.** (of an embryo) having an enlarged hypocotyl. [MACRO- + -PODOUS]

ma·crop·si·a (ma krop′sē ə), *n.* *Ophthalm.* a defect of vision in which objects appear to be larger than their actual size. Also, **ma·cro·pi·a** (ma krō′pē ə), **mac·rop·sy** (mak′rop sē). Also called **megalopsia, megalopia.** Cf. **micropsia.** [< NL; see MACR-, -OPSIS, -IA]

ma·crop·ter·ous (ma krop′tər əs), *adj.* *Zool.* having large wings or fins. [< Gk *makrópteros* long-winged. See MACRO-, -PTEROUS] —**ma·crop′ter·y,** *n.*

ma·crop·tic (ma krop′tik), *adj.* *Ophthalm.* pertaining to or having macropsia. [MACR- + OPTIC]

mac·ro·scop·ic (mak′rə skop′ik), *adj.* visible to the naked eye. Cf. **microscopic** (def. 1). [MACRO- + -SCOPE + -IC] —**mac′ro·scop′i·cal·ly,** *adv.*

mac·ro·seg·ment (mak′rō seg′mənt), *n.* a stretch of speech preceded and followed but not interrupted by a pause. Cf. **microsegment.** [MACRO- + SEGMENT]

mac·ro·spo·ran·gi·um (mak′rō spə ran′jē əm), *n., pl.* **-gi·a** (-jē ə). *Bot.* megasporangium. [MACRO- + SPORANGIUM]

mac·ro·spore (mak′rə spôr′, -spōr′), *n.* *Bot.* megaspore. [MACRO- + -SPORE] —**mac·ro·spor·ic** (mak′rə spôr′ik, -spor′-), *adj.*

mac·ro·sto·mi·a (mak′rə stō′mē ə), *n.* *Med.* the state of having an abnormally large mouth. [< NL; see MACRO-, STOMA, -IA] —**mac·ro·stom·a·tous** (mak′rə stom′ə təs, -stō′mə-), *adj.*

mac·ro·struc·ture (mak′rō struk′chər), *n.* the gross structure of a metal, as made visible to the naked eye by deep etching. [MACRO- + STRUCTURE]

mac·ro·sty·lous (mak′rō stī′ləs), *adj.* *Bot.* having long styles. Cf. **mesostylous, microstylous.** [MACRO- + STYLE + -OUS]

ma·cru·ran (mə krŏŏr′ən), *adj.* **1.** belonging or pertaining to the suborder *Macrura*, comprising the lobsters, crayfishes, shrimps, and prawns. —*n.* **2.** a macruran crustacean. [< NL *macrūr(a)* (pl.) (see MACR-, -UR[2]) + -AN]

ma·cru·rous (mə krŏŏr′əs), *adj.* *Zool.* long-tailed, as a lobster (opposed to *brachyurous*). [< NL *macrūr(a)* (see MACRURAN) + -OUS]

mac·u·la (mak′yə lə), *n., pl.* **-lae** (-lē′). **1.** a spot or blotch, esp. on one's skin; macule. **2.** *Ophthalm.* **a.** a corneal opacity of moderate density. **b.** Also called **mac′ula lu′tea.** the retinal area of maximal visual acuity surrounding the fovea centralis. [late ME < L: spot, blemish] —**mac′u·lar,** *adj.*

mac·u·late (*v.* mak′yə lāt′; *adj.* mak′yə lit), *v.,* **-lat·ed, -lat·ing,** *adj.* —*v.t.* **1.** to mark with a spot or spots; stain. **2.** to sully or pollute. —*adj.* **3.** spotted; stained. **4.** defiled or impure. [late ME < L *maculāt(us)* spotted, stained (ptp. of *maculāre*). See MACULA, -ATE[1]]

mac·u·la·tion (mak′yə lā′shən), *n.* **1.** act of spotting. **2.** a spotted condition. **3.** a marking of spots, as on an animal. **4.** a disfiguring spot or stain. **5.** defilement. [late ME *maculacion* < L *maculātiōn-* (s. of *maculātiō*). See MACULATE, -ION]

mac·ule (mak′yōōl), *n., v.,* **-uled, -ul·ing.** —*n.* **1.** mackle. **2.** macula. —*v.t., v.i.* **3.** mackle. [late ME; see MACKLE]

ma·cum·ba (mə kŏŏm′bə), *n.* **1.** a Brazilian cult incorporating the use of fetishes and sorcery and deriving largely from African practices. **2.** the Brazilian dance or music derived from macumba. [< Pg]

ma·cush·la (mə kŏŏsh′lə), *n.* *Irish.* darling. [< Ir Gael *mo cuishle*, lit., my blood]

mad (mad), *adj.,* **mad·der, mad·dest,** *v.,* **mad·ded, mad·ding,** *n.* —*adj.* **1.** mentally disturbed or deranged; insane; demented. **2.** enraged or irritated; angry: *She was mad at him for forgetting her birthday.* **3.** (of wind, storms, etc.) furious in violence: *A mad gale swept across the channel.* **4.** (of animals) **a.** abnormally furious: *a mad bull.* **b.** affected with rabies; rabid: *a mad dog.* **5.** wildly excited; frantic: *mad haste.* **6.** extremely foolish or unwise; imprudent; irrational: *a mad scheme to invade France.* **7.** overcome by desire, eagerness, enthusiasm, etc.; excessively or uncontrollably fond; infatuated: *She is mad about him.* **8.** wildly gay or merry; enjoyably hilarious: *to have a mad time at the Mardi gras.* **9. like mad,** *Slang.* with great haste, impulsiveness, energy, or enthusiasm: *She ran like mad to catch the bus.* **10. mad as a hatter,** completely mad: *Oh, he's absolutely insane, mad as a hatter, I tell you. Can you imagine, he wanted to fly to San Francisco for dinner.* —*v.t.* **11.** *Archaic.* to make mad. —*v.i.* **12.** *Archaic.* to be, become, or act mad. —*n.* **13.** a period or spell of anger or ill temper: *The last time he had a mad on, it lasted for days.* [ME; OE *gemǣd(e)d* maddened, ptp. of **gemǣdan*, akin to *gemād* mad, foolish, c. OS *gemēd*, OHG *gimeit* foolish]
—**Syn. 1.** lunatic, maniacal, crazed, crazy. **2.** furious, exasperated, raging, wrathful, irate. **5.** frenzied. **6.** ill-advised; unsafe, dangerous, perilous. MAD, CRAZY, INSANE are used to characterize wildly impractical or foolish ideas, actions, etc. MAD suggests senselessness and excess: *The scheme of buying the bridge was absolutely mad.* In informal usage, CRAZY suggests recklessness and impracticality: *a crazy young couple.* INSANE is used with some opprobrium to express unsoundness and possible harmfulness: *The new traffic system is simply insane.* —**Ant. 6.** sensible, practical; sound, safe.
—**Usage. 2.** Careful speakers and writers of English object to the use of MAD to mean "irritated, angry, annoyed." Their objections are in vain on semantic grounds, because MAD is widely used with this meaning by educated *speakers.* But on the grounds of style, these critics may be justified, since educated *writers* will avoid such a vague, general term and cleave to one that is more precisely expressive.

Mad., Madam.

Madag., Madagascar.

Mad·a·gas·car (mad′ə gas′kər), *n.* an island republic in the Indian Ocean, about 240 mi. off the SE coast of Africa: formerly a French colony; now an independent member of the French Community. 6,180,000 (est. 1964); 227,800 sq. mi. *Cap.:* Tananarive. Official name, **Malagasy Republic.** —**Mad′a·gas′can,** *n., adj.*

Mad′agas′car jas′mine, a twining, woody vine, *Stephanotis floribunda*, of Madagascar, having waxy-white, fragrant flowers. Also called **wax flower.**

Mad′agas′car per′iwinkle. See **Cape periwinkle.**

Mad·a·lyn (mad′ᵊlin), *n.* a girl's given name, form of **Magdalen.** Also, **Mad′a·lynne, Madelaine, Madeleine, Madelene, Madeline, Madlyn, Madlynne.**

mad·am (mad′əm), *n.* **1.** a polite term of address to a woman, originally used only to a woman of rank or authority: *Madam Chairman; May I help you, madam?* **2.** the woman in charge of a household: *Is madam at home?* **3.** the woman in charge of a brothel. [ME *madame* < OF, orig. *ma dame* my lady; see DAME]

mad·ame (mad′əm; mə dam′, -däm′, ma-; *Fr.* MA-DAM′), *n., pl.* **mes·dames** (mā dam′, -däm′; *Fr.* me DAM′). a conventional title of respect used in speaking to or of a married woman, esp. one of rank, who is not of American or British origin: *Madame De Gaulle; Mesdames Callas and Sutherland. Abbr.:* Mme. [< F; see MADAM]

Mad′ame Bo′vary, a novel (1857) by Gustave Flaubert.

Mad′ame But′terfly, an opera (1904) by Giacomo Puccini. Also, **Ma·da′ma But′terfly** (mə dam′ə, -däm′ə), **Mad′am But′terfly, Mme. Butterfly.**

Ma·dang (mä′däng), *n.* a seaport on the N coast of New Guinea, in the Territory of New Guinea. 6130 (est. 1958).

Ma·da·ria·ga (mä′thä ryä′gä), *n.* **Sal·va·dor de** (säl′vä thōr′ the), (*Salvador de Madariaga y Rojo*), 1886–1978, Spanish diplomat, historian, and writer in England.

Mad·a·was·ka (mad′ə wos′kə), *n.* a town in N Maine. 4035 (1960).

mad·cap (mad′kap′), *adj.* **1.** wildly impulsive; reckless; rash: *a madcap scheme.* —*n.* **2.** a madcap person, esp. a girl. [MAD + CAP[1]]

mad·den (mad′ᵊn), *v.t.* **1.** to make mad or insane. **2.** to infuriate: *The delays maddened him.* —*v.i.* **3.** to become mad; act as if mad; rage: *He maddened at the thought of how he had been betrayed.* [MAD + -EN[1]]
—**Syn. 2.** provoke, enrage, anger, inflame; exasperate, irritate, vex, annoy. —**Ant. 2.** calm, mollify.

mad·den·ing (mad′ᵊning), *adj.* **1.** driving to madness or frenzy: *a maddening thirst.* **2.** infuriating; exasperating: *his maddening indifference to my pleas.* **3.** raging; furious: *a maddening wind.* [MADDEN + -ING[2]] —**mad′den·ing·ly,** *adv.* —**mad′den·ing·ness,** *n.*

mad·der[1] (mad′ər), *n.* **1.** any rubiaceous plant of the genus *Rubia*, esp. a climbing herb, *R. tinctorum*, of Europe, having panicles of small, yellowish flowers. **2.** the root of this plant, used in dyeing. **3.** the dye or coloring matter itself. **4.** a color produced by such a dye. [ME *mad(d)er*, OE *mæd(e)re*; c. Icel *madhra*, OHG *matara*]

mad·der[2] (mad′ər), *adj.* comparative of **mad.**

mad′der lake′, 1. a strong purple-red color. **2.** a pigment of this color formerly obtained from the madder root, characterized chiefly by lack of permanence. Cf. **rose madder.**

mad·dest (mad′ist), *adj.* superlative of **mad.**

mad·ding (mad′ing), *adj.* **1.** mad; acting madly or senselessly; frenzied: *Let us leave this madding town.* **2.** making mad: *a madding grief.* [mad (ME *maden*, OE *gemǣdan* to hurt, drive mad) + -ING[2]]

mad·dish (mad′ish), *adj.* somewhat mad. [MAD + -ISH[1]]

mad′-dog skull′cap (mad′dôg′, -dog′), *Bot.* a North American skullcap, *Scutellaria lateriflora.* [so called because of former use as antispasmodic]

made (mād), *v.* **1.** pt. and pp. of **make.** —*adj.* **2.** produced by making, preparing, etc., in a particular way (often used in combination): *hand-made garments.* **3.** artificially produced: *made fur.* **4.** invented or made-up: *to tell made stories about oneself.* **5.** assured of success or fortune: *a made man.*

Ma·dei·ra (mə dēr′ə, -der′ə; *Port.* mä de′ʀə), *n.* **1.** a group of five islands off the NW coast of Africa, belonging to Portugal. 269,769 (1950); 308 sq. mi. *Cap.:* Funchal. **2.** the chief island of this group. 266,990 (1950); 286 sq. mi. **3.** (*often l.c.*) a rich, strong white wine, resembling sherry, made there. **4.** a river in W Brazil flowing NE to the Amazon: chief tributary of the Amazon. 2100 mi. long. **5.** a town in SW Ohio. 6744 (1960).

Madei′ra to′paz, citrine (def. 2).

Ma·dei·ra-vine (mə-dēr′ə vīn′), *n.* a vine, *Boussingaultia baselloides*, of tropical America, having small, white, fragrant flowers. Also called **mignonette-vine.**

Mad·e·leine (mad′ᵊlin; *Fr.* mᴀdᵊ len′), *n.* a girl's given name, form of **Magdalen.** Also, **Madalyn, Madalynne, Mad′e·laine, Mad′e·lene, Mad′e·line, Madlyn, Madlynne.**

made′ mast′, *Naut.* a wooden mast formed of several shaped, longitudinal pieces joined together. Also called **built-up mast.**

mad·e·moi·selle (mad′ə mə zel′, mad′mwə-; *Fr.* mᴀd mwᴀ zel′), *n., pl.* **mad·e·moi·selles** (mad′ə mə-zelz′, mad′mwə-), **mes·de·moi·selles** (mā′də mə zel′, mād′mwə zel′; *Fr.* mād mwᴀ zel′). **1.** title of respect used in speaking to or of a girl or unmarried woman who is not of American or British origin: *Mademoiselle Lafitte; Mademoiselle Schumann. Abbr.:* Mlle. **2.** See **silver perch** (def. 1). [< F; OF *ma damoisele* my noble young lady; see MADAME, DAMSEL]

Ma·de·moi·selle de Mau·pin (*Fr.* mᴀd mwᴀ zel′ də mō pᴀɴ′), a novel (1835) by Théophile Gautier.

Ma·de·moi·selle Fi·fi (*Fr.* mᴀd mwᴀ zel′ fē fē′), a short story (1882) by Guy de Maupassant.

Ma·der·no (mä deʀ′nô), *n.* **Car·lo** (kär′lô), 1556–1629, Italian architect.

Ma·de·ro (mä ᵺe′ʀō), *n.* **Fran·cis·co In·da·le·cio** (frän sēs′kô ēn′dä le′syô), 1873–1913, Mexican revolutionary and political leader: president 1911–13.

made-to-meas·ure (mād′tə mezh′ər), *adj.* (of a garment, shoes, etc.) made in accordance with individual measurements. Cf. **ready-to-wear.**

made-to-or·der (mād′to͞o ôr′dər, -tə-), *adj.* made in or as if in accordance with individual specifications or requirements: *a made-to-order suit; lucky to find a made-to-order house.* Cf. **ready-to-wear.**

made-up (mād′up′), *adj.* **1.** concocted; invented: *a made-up story.* **2.** being in make-up; wearing facial cosmetics: *We can't begin the play until you're made-up.* **3.** put together; finished.

Madge (maj), *n.* a girl's given name, form of **Margaret.**

mad·house (mad′hous′), *n., pl.* **-hous·es** (-hou′ziz). **1.** a hospital for mentally disturbed persons; an insane asylum. **2.** a wild, confused, and often noisy place, set of circumstances, etc. [MAD + HOUSE]

Madh·ya Bha·rat (mud′yə bä′rut, -rət), a former state of central India; now included in Madhya Pradesh.

Madh·ya·mi·ka (mäd yu′mi kə), *n.* *Buddhism.* a school of philosophy, of A.D. c200, which attempted a reconciliation with Hinayana from a Mahayana position. [< Skt]

Madh·ya Pra·desh (mud′yə prə dāsh′, prä′desh), a state in central India. 32,372,408 (1961); 171,201 sq. mi. *Cap.:* Bhopal.

Ma·di·an (mā′dē ən), *n.* *Douay Bible.* Midian.

Ma·dill (mə dil′), *n.* a town in S Oklahoma. 3084 (1960).

Mad·i·son (mad′i sən), *n.* **1. Dol·ly** or **Dol·ley** (dol′ē), (*Dorothea Payne*), 1768–1849, wife of James Madison. **2. James,** 1751–1836, 4th president of the U.S. 1809–17. **3.** a city in and the capital of Wisconsin, in the S part. 126,706 (1960). **4.** a city in NE New Jersey. 15,122 (1960). **5.** a town in SW Illinois. 6861 (1960). **6.** a town in SE South Dakota. 5420 (1960). **7.** a town in N Florida. 3239 (1960). **8.** a town in central Maine. 2761 (1960). **9.** a town in central Georgia. 2680 (1960). **10.** a dance in which the participants stand side by side in a line while one person, acting as leader, calls out various steps, each letter of the word "Madison" signaling a specific step.

Mad′ison Av′enue, a street in New York City on which are concentrated the offices of many advertising and public relations firms and that has become a symbol of their attitudes, methods, etc.

Mad·i·son·ville (mad′i sən vil′), *n.* a city in W Kentucky. 13,110 (1960).

Mäd·ler (mad′lər), *n.* a crater in the fourth quadrant of the face of the moon: about 20 miles in diameter.

mad·ly (mad′lē), *adv.* **1.** insanely or wildly: *The old witch cackled madly.* **2.** with desperate haste or intensity; furiously: *They worked madly to fix the bridge.* **3.** foolishly: *They lived madly, wasting all their money.* [ME; see MAD, -LY]

Mad·lyn (mad′lin), *n.* a girl's given name, form of **Magdalen.** Also, **Madalyn, Madalynne, Madelaine, Madeleine, Madelene, Madeline, Mad′lynne.**

Madm., Madam.

mad·man (mad′man′, -mən), *n., pl.* **-men** (-men′, -mən). an insane man; lunatic; maniac. [ME *madd man.* See MAD, MAN¹]

mad′ mon′ey, *Slang.* **1.** a small sum of money carried by a woman or girl on a date to enable her to reach home alone in case she and her escort separate. **2.** such a sum kept in reserve by a woman for an emergency or for minor expenses.

mad·ness (mad′nis), *n.* **1.** state of being mad; insanity. **2.** rabies. **3.** senseless folly: *It is sheer madness to speak as you do.* **4.** frenzy; rage. **5.** intense excitement or enthusiasm: *the madness of balletomanes.* [ME *maddnesse.* See MAD, -NESS]

Ma·doe·ra (mä do͞o′rä), *n.* Dutch name of **Madura.**

Ma·don·na (mə don′ə), *n.* **1.** the Virgin Mary (usually prec. by *the*). **2.** a picture or statue representing the Virgin Mary. **3.** (*l.c.*) *Archaic.* an Italian title of formal address to a woman [< It: my lady]

Madon′na and Child′, *Fine Arts.* a representation of the Virgin Mary holding the infant Jesus.

Madon′na lil′y, a lily, *Lilium candidum*, having pure white flowers. Also called **Annunciation lily.**

Mad·ra (mä′drə), *n.* a girl's given name.

mad·ras (mad′rəs, mə dras′, -dräs′), *n.* **1.** a light cotton fabric with cords set at intervals or with woven stripes or figures, often of another color, for shirts, dresses, jackets, etc. **2.** a thin curtain fabric of a light, gauzelike weave with figures of heavier yarns. **3.** a large, brightly colored kerchief, of silk or cotton, often used for turbans. —*adj.* **4.** made of or resembling madras. [after MADRAS]

Ma·dras (mə dras′, -dräs′), *n.* **1.** a large state in S India: formerly a presidency; boundaries readjusted on a linguistic basis 1956. 33,686,953 (1961); 50,110 sq. mi. **2.** a seaport in and the capital of this state, in the NE part, on the Bay of Bengal. 1,729,100 (1961).

Madras′ States′, a former agency of British India, including the native states of Cochin, Travancore, and Pudukottai: now included in Madras state.

Madras′ thorn′, guamachil.

ma·dre (mä′ᵺre; *Eng.* mä′drā), *n., pl.* **-dres** (-ᵺres; *Eng.* -drāz). *Spanish.* mother.

Ma·dre de Dios (mä′ᵺre ᵺe dyôs′), a river in Peru and Bolivia, flowing E to the Beni River. 900 mi. long.

mad·re·pore (mad′rə pōr′, -pôr′), *n.* any true or stony coral of the order *Madreporaria*, forming reefs or islands in tropical seas. [< F *madrépore* reef-building coral < It *madrepora*, equiv. to *madre* mother (< L *māter*) + *-pora* for *poro* < Gk *pôros* kind of stone] —**mad·re·por·ic** (mad′rə pôr′ik, -por′-), **mad·re·po·rit·ic** (mad′rə pə rit′ik, mə drep′ə-), **mad·re·po·ri·an** (mad′rə pōr′ē ən, -pôr′-), *adj.*

mad·re·por·ite (mad′rə pōr′it, -pôr′-, mə drep′ə-rīt′), *n.* the sievelike plate in certain echinoderms, through which water passes into the vascular system. [MADREPORE + -ITE¹]

Ma·drid (mə drid′; *Sp.* mä ᵺreᵺ′), *n.* a city in and the capital of Spain, in the central part. 2,443,152 (est. 1963). —**Mad·ri·le·ni·an** (mä′drə lē′nē ən, -lēn′-yən), *adj., n.*

mad·ri·gal (mad′rə gəl), *n.* **1.** a lyric poem suitable for being set to music, usually short and often of amatory character, esp. fashionable in the 16th century and later, in Italy, France, England, etc. **2.** a part song without instrumental accompaniment, usually for five or six voices, and making abundant use of contrapuntal imitation. **3.** any part song. **4.** any song. [< It *madrigale* < ML *mātricāle* something simple, n. use of neut. of LL *mātricālis*, lit., of the womb. See MATRIX, -AL¹] —**mad′ri·gal·esque′,** *adj.* —**mad·ri·gal·i·an** (mad′rə gal′ē ən, -gal′yən, -gā′lē ən), *adj.*

mad·ri·gal·ist (mad′rə gə list), *n.* a composer or a singer of madrigals. [MADRIGAL + -IST]

mad·ri·lène (mad′rə len′, -lān′; *Fr.* mᴀ dʀē len′), *n.* a consommé flavored with tomato, frequently jellied and served cold. [< F (*consommé*) *madrilène*, lit., Madrid consommé]

ma·dro·ño (mə drōn′yō), *n., pl.* **-ños.** an evergreen, ericaceous tree or shrub, *Arbutus Menziesii*, of western North America, yielding a hard wood, having a smooth bark, and bearing a yellow, edible berry. Also, **ma·dro·ña** (mə drōn′yə), **ma·dro·ne** (mə drō′nə). Also called **Pacific madrone.** [< Sp]

mad′ stag′gers, *Vet. Pathol.* stagger (def. 13).

mad·tom (mad′tom′), *n.* any of several tadpolelike, fresh-water catfishes of the genus *Shilbeodes*, found in the central and eastern U.S., having a poisonous pectoral spine. [MAD + TOM]

Ma·du·ra (mə do͞or′ä *for 1;* maj′o͞o rə *for 2*), *n.* **1.** Dutch, **Madoera.** an island in Indonesia, off the NE coast of Java. 51,637,072 with Java (est. 1955); 2112 sq. mi. **2.** Also, **Ma·du·rai** (mad′yo͞o rī′). a city in S Madras, in S India. 424,800 (1961).

ma·du·ro (mə do͞or′ō), *adj.* (of cigars) strong and darkly colored. [< Sp < L *mātūrus* ripe]

mad·wo·man (mad′wo͝om′ən), *n., pl.* **-wom·en.** an insane woman. [MAD + WOMAN]

Mad′woman of Chail·lot′, The (shä yō′), a satirical comedy (1945) by Jean Giraudoux. French, **La Folle de Chaillot.**

mad·wort (mad′wûrt′), *n.* **1.** any of several plants, as the gold-of-pleasure. **2.** a boraginaceous plant, *Asperugo procumbens.* [MAD + WORT²]

mae¹ (mā), *adj., n., adv.* *Scot.* more. [ME (north), OE *mā*; c. G *mehr*, Icel *meir*, Goth *mais.* See MORE]

mae² (ma, mā), *v.i.,* **maed, mae·ing,** *n.* *Brit. Dial.* baa. [imit.]

Mae (mā), *n.* a girl's given name. Also, **Mai, May.**

M.A.E., **1.** Master of Aeronautical Engineering. **2.** Master of Art Education. **3.** Master of Arts in Education.

Mae·an·der (mē an′dər), *n.* ancient name of the **Menderes.** Also, **Meander.**

Ma·e·ba·shi (mä′e bä′shē), *n.* a city in the central part of Honshu, in central Japan. 190,000 (est. 1963).

Mae·belle (mā bel′, mā′bel), *n.* a girl's given name. Also, **Maybelle.**

Mae·ce·nas (mē sē′nəs, mī-), *n.* **1. Gaius Cil·ni·us** (sil′nē əs), c70–8 B.C., Roman statesman: friend and patron of Horace and Vergil. **2.** a generous patron or supporter, esp. of art, music, literature, etc.

M.A.Ed., Master of Arts in Education.

Mael (māl), *n.* *Irish Myth.* a son of Ronan, unjustly killed by him.

Mae·ly (mā′lē), *n.* a girl's given name.

Mael·strom (māl′strəm), *n.* **1.** a famous whirlpool off the NW coast of Norway. **2.** (*l.c.*) any large, powerful, or violent whirlpool. **3.** (*l.c.*) a restless, disordered, or tumultuous state of affairs: *the maelstrom of early morning traffic.* [< early D *maelstroom* (now *maalstroom*), lit., grinding stream. See MEAL², STREAM]

mae·nad (mē′nad), *n.* **1.** bacchante. **2.** any frenzied or raging woman. Also, **menad.** [< L *Maenad-* (s. of *Maenas*) < Gk: madwoman] —**mae·nad′ic,** *adj.* —**mae′nad·ism,** *n.*

Maen·a·lus (men′ə ləs, mēn′ə-), *n.* *Class. Myth.* a son of Lycaon.

Mae·on (mē′on), *n.* *Class. Myth.* a Theban who was among 50 warriors instructed to ambush Tydeus and was the only one of them who was not slain.

Mae·ra (mēr′ə), *n.* *Class. Myth.* **1.** Hecuba, after being changed into a dog for blinding Polymnestor. **2.** a daughter of Atlas and the wife of Tegeates. **3.** a hound belonging to Icarius.

M.Aero.E., Master of Aeronautical Engineering.

Ma·e·stà′ Al′tar (mī stä′; *It.* mä es tä′), a polyptych (1308?–11?) painted by Duccio for the Siena Cathedral, representing the Madonna and Child enthroned among saints and angels as well as numerous scenes from the lives of Christ and the Virgin.

ma·es·to·so (mī stō′sō; *It.* mä′es tô′sô), *adj., adv.* with majesty; stately (used as a musical direction). [< It: stately, majestic, equiv. to *maest(à)* (< L *mājestās* MAJESTY) + *-oso* -OSE¹]

Maes·tricht (*Du.* mäs′tʀɪᴋʜt), *n.* Maastricht.

maes·tro (mī′strō; *It.* mä es′tʀō), *n., pl.* **maes·tros,** *It.* **ma·es·tri** (mä es′tʀē). **1.** an eminent composer, teacher, or conductor of music: *Toscanini, Monteux, and other great maestros.* **2.** (*cap.*) a title of respect used in addressing or referring to such a person. **3.** a master of any art: *the maestros of poetry.* [< It: master]

Mae·ter·linck (mā′tər lingk′; *Fr.* mᴀ teʀ lᴀɴ′; *Du.* mä′teʀ lingk′), *n.* **Comte Mau·rice** (*Fr.* mō ʀēs′), 1862–1947, Belgian poet, dramatist, and essayist: Nobel prize 1911. —**Mae′ter·linck′i·an,** *adj.*

Mae′ West′, **1.** an inflatable yellow or orange life jacket for emergency use, esp. by sailors or by airplane pilots in flights over water. **2.** *U.S. Naut.* See **parachute spinnaker.** [named after *Mae* WEST, American actress]

Maf·e·king (mä′fə king′), *n.* a town in N Republic of South Africa: former administrative seat of Bechuanaland; besieged for 217 days by Boers 1899–1900. 6965 (1951).

maf·fick (maf′ik), *v.i.* *Brit. Informal.* to celebrate with extravagant public demonstrations. [back formation from MAFEKING; the relief of the besieged city was joyously celebrated in London] —**maf′fick·er,** *n.*

Ma·fi·a (mä′fē ə; *It.* mä′fē ä), *n.* **1.** a secret organization of persons, mostly of Sicilian and Italian origin, allegedly engaged in smuggling, racketeering, trafficking in narcotics, and other criminal activities in the U.S. and elsewhere. **2.** (in Sicily) **a.** (*l.c.*) a popular spirit of hostility to legal restraint and to the law, often manifesting itself in criminal acts. **b.** a 19th-century secret society, similar to the Camorra in Naples, which acted in this spirit. Also, **Maf′fi·a.** [< It (Sicilian) *mafia* boldness; perh. < Ar *mahyah* boasting]

maf·ic (maf′ik), *adj.* *Geol.* of or pertaining to rocks rich in iron, magnesium, or other dark minerals. Cf. **felsic.** [MA(GNESIUM) + L *f(errum)* iron + -IC]

ma foi (mᴀ fwᴀ′), *French.* my word! really! [lit.: my faith]

maf·tir (mäf tēʀ′, mäf′tēʀ), *n.* *Hebrew.* **1.** the concluding section of the portion of the Torah chanted or read in a Jewish service on the Sabbath and festivals. **2.** the person who recites the blessings before and after the chanting or reading of this section and often chants or reads the Haftarah. [lit., dismisser]

mag¹ (mag), *n.* *Brit. Slang.* a halfpenny. [?]

mag² (mag), *n.* *Informal.* magazine. [shortened form]

mag³ (mag), *n., v.,* **magged, mag·ging.** *Brit. Dial.* —*n.* **1.** a magpie. **2.** talk; chatter. —*v.i.* **3.** to talk idly; chatter. [shortened form of MAGPIE]

Mag (mag), *n.* a girl's given name, form of **Margaret.**

mag., **1.** magazine. **2.** magnetism. **3.** magnitude. **4.** (in prescriptions) large. [< L *magnus*]

Ma·ga·lla·nes (*Sp.* mä′gä yä′nes), *n.* See **Punta Arenas.**

Ma·gan·gué (mä′gäng ge′), *n.* a city in NW Colombia. 17,114 (1951).

mag·a·zine (mag′ə zēn′, mag′ə zēn′), *n.* **1.** *Publishing.* **a.** a publication that is issued periodically, usually bound in a paper cover, and typically containing stories, essays, poems, etc., by many writers and often photographs and drawings, frequently specializing in a particular subject or area, as hobbies, news, or sports. **2.** a room or place for keeping gunpowder and other explosives, as in a fort or on a warship. **3.** a building or place for keeping military stores, as arms, ammunition, provisions, etc. **4.** a metal receptacle for a number of cartridges, inserted into certain types of automatic weapons and when empty removed and replaced by a full receptacle in order to continue firing. **5.** *Photog.* cartridge (def. 4). **6.** a supply chamber, as in a stove. **7.** a storehouse; warehouse. **8.** a collection of war munitions. [< F *magasin* < It *magazzino* storehouse < Ar *makhāzin*, pl. of *makhzan* storehouse] —**mag′a·zin′ish, mag′a·zin′y,** *adj.*

magazine′ sec′tion. See **roto section.**

mag·a·zin·ist (mag′ə zē′nist), *n.* a person engaged in magazine work, esp. as a writer. [MAGAZINE + -IST] —**mag′a·zin′ism,** *n.*

Mag·da (mag′də; *Ger.* mäg′dä), *n.* a girl's given name, German form of **Magdalen.**

Mag·da·la (mag′də lə), *n.* an ancient town in Palestine, W of the Sea of Galilee: supposed home of Mary Magdalene.

Mag·da·le·na (mag′də lā′nə, -lē′-; *for 1 also Sp.* mäg′ᵺä le′nä), *n.* **1.** a river in SW Colombia, flowing N to the Caribbean. 1060 mi. long.

Mag′dale′na Bay′, a bay in NW Mexico, on the SW coast of Lower California. 17 mi. long; 12 mi. wide.

Mag·da·lene (mag′də lēn′, mag′də lē′nē), *n.* **1. the.** See **Mary Magdalene. 2.** (*l.c.*) a reformed prostitute. **3.** Also, **Magdalena, Mag·da·lenne** (mag′də lən, -len′). a girl's given name. Also, **Mag·da·len** (mag′də lən).

Mag·da·le·ni·an (mag′də lē′nē ən), *adj.* noting the period or culture in the Old World Stone Age in which Cro-Magnon man reached his highest level of industry and art. [< F *Magdalénien*, equiv. to *Magdalen-* (Latinization of *La Madeleine*, prehistoric station in Southwestern France) + *-ien* -IAN]

Mag·de·burg (mag′də bûrg′; *Ger.* mäg′də bo͝orᴋ′), *n.* the capital of Saxony-Anhalt, in central Germany. 290,579.

Mag′deburg hem′isphere, *Physics.* one of a pair of hemispherical cups from which air can be evacuated when they are placed together: used to demonstrate the force of air pressure.

mage (māj), *n. Archaic.* a magician. [ME < MF < L *mag(us).* See MAGUS]

M.Ag.Ec., Master of Agricultural Economics.

M.Ag.Ed., Master of Agricultural Education.

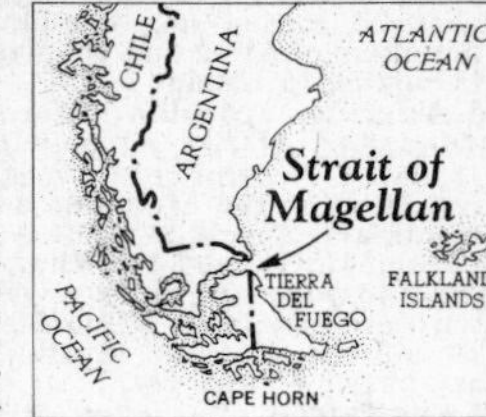

Mag·el·hanz (mag′əl-hänz′), *n.* a crater in the fourth quadrant of the face of the moon: about 25 miles in diameter.

Ma·gel·lan (mə jel′ən), *n.* **1. Ferdinand,** c1480–1521, Portuguese navigator: discoverer of the Straits of Magellan 1520 and the Philippines 1521. **2. Strait of,** a strait near the S tip of South America between the mainland of Chile and Tierra del Fuego and other islands, connecting the Atlantic and the Pacific. 360 mi. long. 2½–17 mi. wide.

Magel′lan bar′berry, an evergreen shrub, *Berberis buxifolia,* of southern Chile, having prickle-tipped leaves, dark-purple fruit, and orange-yellow flowers.

Mag·el·lan·ic (maj′ə lan′ik), *adj.* pertaining to or named after Ferdinand Magellan. [MAGELLAN + -IC]

Mag′ellan′ic cloud′, *Astron.* either of two irregular galactic clusters in the southern heavens that are the nearest independent star system to the Milky Way.

Ma·gen Da·vid (mä gān′ dä vēd′, mô′gən dô′vid), *Judaism.* See **Star of David.** [< Heb: lit., Shield of David]

ma·gen·ta (mə jen′tə), *n.* **1.** fuchsin. **2.** reddish purple. [named after MAGENTA; discovered the year of the battle]

Ma·gen·ta (mə jen′tə), *n.* a town in N Italy, W of Milan: the French and Sardinians defeated the Austrians here 1859. 18,533 (1961).

Mag·gie (mag′ē), *n.* a girl's given name, form of **Margaret.**

Mag·gie (mag′ē), *n.* (*Maggie: A Girl of the Streets*) a novel (1893) by Stephen Crane.

Mag·gio·re (mə jôr′ē, -jôr′ē; *It.* mäd jô′re), *n.* **Lake,** a lake in N Italy and S Switzerland. 83 sq. mi.

mag·got (mag′ət), *n.* **1.** a soft-bodied, legless larva of certain dipterous insects. **2.** an odd fancy; whim. [ME *magot, magat,* unexplained var. of *maddock,* early ME *mathek* < Scand; cf. Icel *mathkr,* Dan *maddik* maggot; akin to OE *matha, mathu* grub, maggot, OHG *mado* maggot]

mag·got·y (mag′ə tē), *adj.* **1.** infested with maggots, as food. **2.** having queer notions; full of whims. [MAGGOT + -Y¹]

Ma·gi (mā′jī), *n.pl., sing.* **-gus** (-gəs). **1.** (*sometimes l.c.*) the three wise men who paid homage to the infant Jesus. Matt. 2:1–12. **2.** the class of Zoroastrian priests in ancient Media and Persia, reputed to possess supernatural powers. **3.** (*l.c.*) astrologers. Cf. **Magus** (def. 2). [pl. of MAGUS] —**Ma·gi·an** (mā′jē ən), *adj.*

mag·ic (maj′ik), *n.* **1.** the art of producing a desired effect or result through the use of various techniques, as incantation, that presumably assure human control of supernatural agencies or the forces of nature. Cf. **contagious magic, imitative magic, sympathetic magic. 2.** the exercise of this art: *Magic, it was believed, could drive illness from the body.* **3.** the effects produced: *the magic of recovery.* **4.** power or influence exerted through this art: *a wizard of great magic.* **5.** any extraordinary or irresistible influence, charm, power, etc.: *the magic in a great name; the magic of music; the magic of spring.* **6.** the art of causing illusions as entertainment by the use of sleight of hand, deceptive devices, etc.; legerdemain; conjuring: *to pull a rabbit out of a hat by magic.* —*adj.* **7.** employed in magic: *magic spells; magic dances; magic rites.* **8.** mysteriously enchanting: *magic beauty.* **9.** of, pertaining to, or due to magic. **10.** producing the effects of magic; like magic: *The cosmetics produced a magic transformation in her appearance.* [ME *magik(e)* witchcraft < LL *magica,* L *magicē* < Gk *magikḗ,* n. use of fem. of *magikós.* See MAGUS, -IC]

—**Syn. 1.** enchantment. MAGIC, NECROMANCY, SORCERY, WITCHCRAFT imply producing results through mysterious influences or unexplained powers. MAGIC may have glamorous and attractive connotations; the other terms suggest the harmful and sinister. MAGIC is an art of using some occult force of nature: *Fifty years ago television would have seemed to be magic.* NECROMANCY is an art of prediction, supposedly because of communicating with the dead (it is called "the black art," because Greek *nekro,* dead, was confused with Latin *niger,* black): *Necromancy led to violating graves.* SORCERY, originally divination by casting lots, came to mean supernatural knowledge gained through the aid of evil spirits, and often used for evil ends: *spells and charms used in sorcery.* WITCHCRAFT esp. suggests a malign kind of magic, often used against innocent victims: *Those accused of witchcraft were executed.*

mag·i·cal (maj′i kəl), *adj.* magic: *a magical night; a voice that was magical in its range.* [MAGIC + -AL¹]

mag·i·cal·ly (maj′ik lē), *adv.* in a magical way or manner. [MAGICAL + -LY]

Mag′ic Flute′, The, an opera (1791) by Wolfgang Amadeus Mozart. German, **Die Zauberflöte.**

ma·gi·cian (mə jish′ən), *n.* **1.** a person who is skilled in magic. **2.** an entertainer who is skilled in causing illusion by sleight of hand, deceptive devices, etc.; conjurer. [MAGIC + -IAN; r. ME *magicien* < MF]

—**Syn. 1.** sorcerer, necromancer, enchanter, wizard.

mag′ic lan′tern, a device having an enclosed lamp and a lenslike opening for projecting and magnifying images mounted on slides or films.

Mag′ic Moun′tain, The, a novel (1924) by Thomas Mann. German, **Der Zauberberg.**

mag′ic num′ber, *Physics.* the atomic number or neutron number of an exceptionally stable nuclide.

10	3	8
5	7	9
6	11	4

Magic square

mag′ic square′, a square containing integers arranged in an equal number of rows and columns so that the sum of the integers in any row, column, or diagonal is the same.

Ma·gin·da·na·o (mä gēn′dä nä′ō, mə gin′də nou′, mə gin′də nou′), *n., pl.* **-na·os,** (*esp. collectively*) **-na·o. 1.** a member of a Moro people of Mindanao in the Philippines. **2.** the Malayo-Polynesian language of the Magindanao.

Ma′gi·not line′ (mazh′ə nō′; *Fr.* mA zhē nō′), a zone of French fortifications erected along the French-German border in the years preceding World War II. [named after André *Maginot* (1877–1932), French minister of war]

Mag·i·nus (maj′ə nəs), *n.* a walled plain in the third quadrant of the face of the moon: about 110 miles in diameter.

mag·is·te·ri·al (maj′i stēr′ē əl), *adj.* **1.** of, pertaining to, or befitting a master; authoritative; weighty; of importance or consequence: *a magisterial pronouncement by the director of the board.* **2.** imperious; domineering: *a magisterial tone of command.* **3.** of or befitting a magistrate or his office: *The judge spoke with magisterial gravity.* **4.** of the rank of a magistrate: *magisterial standing.* [< ML *magisteriāl(is)* of control, equiv. to L *magisteri(um)* control, mastery (see MAGISTERY) + *-ālis* -AL¹] —**mag′is·te′ri·al·ly,** *adv.* —**mag′is·te′ri·al·ness,** *n.*

mag·is·te·ri·um (maj′i stēr′ē əm), *n. Rom. Cath. Ch.* the authority and power of the church to teach religious truth. [< L: MAGISTERY]

Ma·gis·ter Lu·di (mä′gis tər lōō′dē), a novel (1943) by Hermann Hesse.

mag·is·ter·y (maj′i ster′ē, -stə rē), *n., pl.* **-ter·ies. 1.** an agency or substance, as in alchemy, to which faculties of healing, transformation, etc., are ascribed. **2.** mastership. [< L *magisteri(um),* equiv. to *magister* MASTER + *-ium* -Y³]

mag·is·tra·cy (maj′i strə sē), *n., pl.* **-cies. 1.** the office or function of a magistrate. **2.** a body of magistrates. **3.** the district under a magistrate. Also, **mag·is·tra·ture** (maj′i strā′chər). [MAGISTRA(TE) + -CY]

mag·is·tral (maj′i strəl), *adj.* **1.** *Pharm.* prescribed or prepared for a particular occasion, as a remedy. Cf. **officinal** (def. 1). **2.** *Fort.* principal. **3.** *Rare.* magisterial. —*n.* **4.** See **magistral line.** [< L *magistrāl(is)* of a master, equiv. to *magist(e)r* MASTER + *-ālis* -AL¹] —**mag′is·tral′i·ty,** *n.* —**mag′is·tral·ly, mag·is·trat·i·cal·ly** (maj′i strat′ik lē), *adv.*

mag′istral line′, *Fort.* the line from which the position of the other lines of fieldworks is determined.

mag·is·trate (maj′i strāt′, -strit), *n.* **1.** a civil officer charged with the administration of the law. **2.** a minor judicial officer, as a justice of the peace or a police justice, having jurisdiction to try minor criminal cases and to conduct preliminary examinations of persons charged with serious crimes. [ME *magistrat* < L *magistrāt(us)* magistracy, magistrate, equiv. to *magist(e)r* MASTER + *-ātus* -ATE¹] —**mag′is·trate′ship,** *n.*

Mag·le·mo·se·an (mag′lə mō′sē ən, -shən, -zhən), *adj.* of, pertaining to, or characteristic of a Mesolithic culture of northern Europe. Also, **Mag′le·mo′si·an.** [*Maglemose* site of Mesolithic station in Denmark + -AN]

mag·ma (mag′mə), *n., pl.* **-mas, -ma·ta** (-mə tə). **1.** any crude mixture of finely divided mineral or organic matter. **2.** *Geol.* molten material beneath or within the earth's crust, from which igneous rock is formed. **3.** *Chem., Pharm.* a paste composed of solid and liquid matter. [< L: dregs, leavings < Gk: kneaded mass, salve, equiv. to *mag-* (base of *mássein* to knead, press) + *-ma* n. suffix of result] —**mag·mat·ic** (mag mat′ik), *adj.* —**mag′ma·tism,** *n.*

magn-, var. of **magni-** before a vowel: *magnanimous.*

Mag·na (mag′nə), *n.* a town in N Utah. 6442 (1960).

Mag·na Char·ta (mag′nə kär′tə), **1.** the "great charter" of English liberties, forced from King John by the English barons, and sealed at Runnymede, June 15, 1215. **2.** any fundamental constitution or law guaranteeing rights: *a Magna Charta of racial equality.* Also, **Mag′na Car′ta.** [< ML]

mag·na cum lau·de (mäg′nə kŏŏm lou′dā, -də, -dē; mag′nə kum lô′dē), with great praise: used in diplomas to grant the next-to-highest of three special honors for grades above the average. Cf. **cum laude, summa cum laude.** [< L]

mag·na est ve·ri·tas, et prae·va·le·bit (mäg′nä est we′ri täs′, et prī′wä le′bit; *Eng.* mag′nə est ver′i tas′, et prē′və lē′bit), *Latin.* truth is great and will prevail.

Mag·na Grae·ci·a (mag′nə grē′shē ə; *Lat.* mäg′nä grī′ki ä′), the ancient colonial cities and settlements of Greece in S Italy.

mag·na·li·um (mag nā′lē əm), *n.* an alloy of magnesium and aluminum, sometimes also containing copper, nickel, tin, and lead. [MAG(NESIUM) + AL(UMINUM) + -IUM]

Mag·na Ma·ter (mäg′nə mä′ter), *Rom. Religion.* Cybele; Ops; Rhea. [< L: great mother]

mag·na·nim·i·ty (mag′nə nim′i tē), *n., pl.* **-ties. 1.** quality of being magnanimous. **2.** a magnanimous act. [ME *magnanimite* < L *magnanimitās.* See MAGNANIMOUS, -ITY]

mag·nan·i·mous (mag nan′ə məs), *adj.* **1.** generous in forgiving an insult or injury; free from petty resentfulness or vindictiveness: *to be magnanimous toward one's enemies.* **2.** high-minded; noble: *a magnanimous king.* **3.** proceeding from or revealing nobility of mind, character, etc: *a magnanimous love of justice.* [< L *magnanimus* great-souled, equiv. to *magn(us)* MAGN- + *anim(us)* spirit, soul, mind + *-us* -OUS] —**mag·nan′i·mous·ly,** *adv.* —**mag·nan′i·mous·ness,** *n.*

—**Syn. 1.** big, liberal, unspiteful. **2.** See **noble. 3.** elevated, lofty.

mag·nate (mag′nāt, -nit), *n.* **1.** a person of great influence, importance, or standing in a particular enterprise, field of business, etc.: *a railroad magnate.* **2.** a person of eminence or distinction in any field: *literary magnates.* **3.** a member of the former upper house in either the Polish or Hungarian parliament. [back formation from ME *magnates* (pl.) < LL, equiv. to L *magn(us)* MAGN- + *-ātēs,* pl. of *-ās* n. suffix] —**mag′nate·ship′,** *n.*

mag·ne·sia (mag nē′zhə, shə), *n.* a white, tasteless substance, magnesium oxide, MgO, used in medicine as an antacid and laxative. Cf. **milk of magnesia.** [ME < ML < Gk (*hē*) *Magnēsíē* (*líthos*) (the stone) of MAGNESIA] —**mag·ne′sian, mag·ne·sic** (mag nē′sik), **mag·ne′sial,** *adj.*

Mag·ne·si·a (mag nē′shē ə, -zhē ə), *n.* ancient name of **Manisa.**

mag·ne·site (mag′ni sīt′), *n.* a mineral, magnesium carbonate, $MgCO_3$, having a characteristic conchoidal fracture and usually occurring in white masses. [MAGNES(IA) + -ITE¹; cf. F *magnésite*]

mag·ne·si·um (mag nē′zē əm, -zhəm, -shē əm), *n. Chem.* a light, ductile, silver-white metallic element which burns with a dazzling white light, used in lightweight alloys, flares, fireworks, in the manufacture of flash bulbs, optical mirrors, and precision instruments, and as a zinc substitute in batteries. *Symbol:* Mg; *at. wt.:* 24.312; *at. no.:* 12; *sp. gr.:* 1.74 at 20°C. [< NL; see MAGNESIA, -IUM]

magne′sium ar′senate, *Chem.* a white, when pure, water-insoluble powder, $Mg_3(AsO_4)_2 \cdot xH_2O$, used chiefly as an insecticide.

magne′sium diox′ide, *Chem.* See **magnesium peroxide.**

magne′sium hydrox′ide, *Chem.* a white, crystalline, slightly water-soluble powder, $Mg(OH)_2$, used chiefly in medicine as an antacid and as a laxative.

magnes′ium light′, the strongly actinic white light produced when magnesium is burned: used in photography, signaling, pyrotechnics, etc.

magne′sium ox′ide, *Chem.* magnesia.

magne′sium perox′ide, *Chem.* a white, tasteless, water-insoluble powder, MgO_2, used as an antiseptic and as an oxidizing and bleaching agent. Also called **magnesium dioxide.**

magne′sium sul′fate, *Chem.* a white, water-soluble salt, $MgSO_4$, used chiefly in medicine and in the processing of leather and textiles. Cf. **epsom salt.**

magne′sium trisil′icate, *Chem.* a white, fine, odorless and tasteless powder, $2MgO \cdot 3SiO_2 \cdot nH_2O$, used industrially to absorb odors and decolorize and, pharmaceutically, as an antacid.

mag·net (mag′nit), *n.* **1.** a body, as a piece of iron or steel, that possesses the property of attracting certain substances, as iron. **2.** a loadstone. **3.** a thing or person that attracts, as by some inherent power or charm: *The actress found herself the magnet of attention.* [late ME *magnete* < L *magnēta* < Gk, acc. of *mágnēs,* short for *ho Mágnēs líthos* the stone of Magnesia]

magnet-, var. of **magneto-** before some vowels: *magneton.*

mag·net·ic (mag net′ik), *adj.* **1.** of or pertaining to a magnet or magnetism. **2.** having the properties of a magnet. **3.** capable of being magnetized or attracted by a magnet. **4.** pertaining to the magnetic field of the earth: *the magnetic equator.* **5.** exerting a strong attractive power or charm: *a magnetic personality.* **6.** noting or pertaining to various bearings and measurements as indicated by a magnetic compass: *magnetic amplitude; magnetic course; magnetic meridian.* Also, **mag·net′i·cal.** [< LL *magnēticus*]. See MAGNET, -IC] —**mag·net′i·cal·ly,** *adv.*

magnet′ic ax′is, *Physics.* a straight line connecting and extending through the poles of a magnet.

magnet′ic bear′ing, *Navig.* the bearing of a point relative to that of the nearest magnetic pole.

magnet′ic chart′, a chart showing the magnetic properties of a portion of the earth's surface, giving isogonal lines and often isoclinal and isodynamic lines.

magnet′ic cir′cuit, *Physics.* the closed path described by the lines of force of a magnetic field.

magnet′ic coeffi′cient, *Navig.* any of various factors affecting the sensitivity of a ship's magnetic compass as a result of its construction or environment.

magnet′ic com′pass, a compass having a magnetized needle generally in line with the magnetic poles of the earth.

magnet′ic concentra′tion, beneficiation of crushed ore in which a magnetic mineral is separated from the gangue by means of a magnetic field.

magnet′ic core′, **1.** *Computer Technol.* core¹ (def. 13). **2.** *Elect.* core¹ (def. 3).

magnet′ic course′, *Navig.* a course whose bearing is given relative to the magnetic meridian of the area. Cf. **compass course, true course.**

magnet′ic declina′tion, *Navig.* variation (def. 8).

magnet′ic dip′, dip (def. 30).

magnet′ic drum′, *Computer Technol.* a revolving cylinder in a computer, having a magnetized surface on which information can be stored as small polarized spots.

magnet′ic equa′tor. See **aclinic line.**

magnet′ic field′, a condition of space in the vicinity of a magnetic or current-carrying substance, manifesting itself as a force on a moving charge or magnetic pole within that space.

magnet′ic flux′, *Physics.* the total number of lines of induction through a given cross section of a surface, expressed in maxwells or webers.

magnet′ic flux′ den′sity, *Physics.* See **magnetic induction.**

magnet′ic force′, *Physics.* the force of attraction or repulsion exerted by a magnetic field upon a magnetic pole, electric charge, etc., placed in the region of the field.

magnet′ic induc′tion, *Physics.* a vector quantity used as a measure of a magnetic field, directly proportional to the force on a moving conductor in the field and inversely proportional to the product of the charge on the conductor and the velocity of the conductor. *Symbol:* B Also called **magnetic flux density.**

magnet′ic merid′ian, a line on the earth's surface, passing in the direction of the horizontal component of the earth's magnetic field.

magnet′ic mine′, *Navy.* a large mine moored underwater and set off by any disturbance of its magnetic field, as by the metal hull of a ship. Cf. **acoustic mine, contact mine.**

magnet′ic mo′ment, *Physics.* a quantity associated with a given magnet, equal to the product of the pole strength and length of the magnet and having the property that its product with the field intensity of a uniform magnetic field gives the torque tending to move the magnet parallel to the lines of force of the magnet; a vector quantity having the property that its vector product with the magnetic-field vector of a magnetic field equals the torque acting on a given electric current, magnet, or the like, in the magnetic field.

magnet′ic nee′dle, a slender magnetized steel rod which, when adjusted to swing in a horizontal plane, as in a compass, indicates the direction of the earth's magnetic fields or the approximate position of north and south.

magnet′ic north′, north as indicated by a magnetic compass, differing in most places from true north.

magnet′ic pick′up, a phonograph pickup in which the vibrations of the stylus cause variations in or motions of a coil in a magnetic field which produces corresponding variations in an electrical voltage. Cf. **crystal pickup.**

magnet′ic pole′, **1.** the region of a magnet towards which the lines of induction converge **(south pole)** or from which the lines of induction diverge **(north pole).** **2.** either of the two points on the earth's surface where the dipping needle of a compass stands vertical, one in the arctic, the other in the antarctic. See maps under **North Pole, South Pole.**

magnet′ic poten′tial, *Elect.* a scalar quantity, analogous to the electric potential, defined at each point in a given magnetic field to be equal to the work done in bringing a unit north pole from infinity to the point. Also called **magnetic scalar potential.**

magnet′ic pul′ley, *Metall.* a magnetic device for separating metal from sand, refuse, etc.

magnet′ic quan′tum num′ber, *Physics.* the quantum number that designates the component of the orbital angular momentum in a fixed direction and that can assume all integral values between and including the orbital quantum number and the negative of the orbital quantum number.

magnet′ic record′er, a device that records sound on magnetic tape, wire, etc.

magnet′ic record′ing, the process of recording sound or other data on magnetic tape, wire, belts, etc.

magnet′ic roast′ing, *Metall.* roasting of a nonmagnetic ore to render it magnetic so that it can be separated from gangue by means of a magnetic field.

magnet′ic rota′tion, *Optics.* See **Faraday effect.**

mag·net·ics (mag net′iks), *n.* (*construed as sing.*) the science of magnetism. [see MAGNETIC, -ICS]

magnet′ic sca′lar poten′tial. See **magnetic potential.**

magnet′ic storm′, a temporary disturbance of the earth's magnetic field, induced by radiation and streams of charged particles from the sun.

magnet′ic tape′, a ribbon of material, usually with a plastic base, coated on one side **(single tape)** or both sides **(double tape)** with a substance containing iron oxide, to make it sensitive to impulses from an electromagnet. Also called **electromagnetic tape, tape.**

magnet′ic varia′tion, *Navig.* variation (def. 8).

mag·net·ise (mag′ni tīz′), *v.t.*, **-ised, -is·ing.** *Chiefly Brit.* magnetize. —**mag′net·i·sa′tion,** *n.* —**mag′net·is′er,** *n.*

mag·net·ism (mag′ni tiz′əm), *n.* **1.** the properties of attraction possessed by magnets; the molecular properties common to magnets. **2.** the agency producing magnetic phenomena. **3.** the science dealing with magnetic phenomena. **4.** magnetic or attractive power or charm: *Women succumbed to the magnetism of his smile.* [< NL *magnētism(us).* See MAGNET, -ISM]

mag·net·ite (mag′ni tīt′), *n.* a very common black iron oxide, Fe_3O_4, that is strongly attracted by magnets: an important iron ore. [MAGNET + -ITE[1]; cf. G *Magnetit*]

mag·net·iz·a·ble (mag′ni tī′zə bəl), *adj.* susceptible to magnetization. [MAGNETIZE + -ABLE] —**mag′ne·tiz′a·bil′i·ty,** *n.*

mag·net·ize (mag′ni tīz′), *v.t.*, **-ized, -iz·ing.** **1.** to make a magnet of or impart the properties of a magnet to. **2.** to exert an attracting or compelling influence upon: *The evangelist's voice magnetized his listeners.* **3.** *Archaic.* to mesmerize. Also, *esp. Brit.,* **magnetise.** [MAGNET + -IZE] —**mag′net·i·za′tion,** *n.* —**mag′net·iz′er,** *n.*

mag·ne·to (mag nē′tō), *n., pl.* **-tos.** *Elect.* a small electric generator with an armature that rotates in a magnetic field provided by permanent magnets, as a hand-operated generator for telephone signaling. Also called **magnetoelectric generator, magnetogenerator.** [short for MAGNETOELECTRIC GENERATOR]

magneto-, a combining form of **magnetic, magnetism:** *magnetochemistry.* Also, *esp. before a vowel,* **magnet-.**

mag·ne·to·cal·or′ic effect′ (mag nē′tō kə lôr′ik, -lor′-), *Physics.* an increase or decrease of the temperature of a thermally isolated magnetic substance accompanying an increase or decrease in the intensity of a magnetic field. [MAGNETO- + CALORIC]

mag·ne·to·chem·is·try (mag nē′tō kem′i strē), *n.* the study of magnetic and chemical phenomena in their relation to one another. [MAGNETO- + CHEMISTRY] —**mag·ne′to·chem′i·cal,** *adj.*

mag·ne·to·e·lec·tric (mag nē′tō i lek′trik), *adj.* of or pertaining to the induction of electric current or electromotive force by means of permanent magnets. Also, **mag·ne′to·e·lec′tri·cal.** [MAGNETO- + ELECTRIC]

magne′toelec′tric gen′erator, magneto.

mag·ne·to·e·lec·tric·i·ty (mag nē′tō i lek tris′i tē, -ē′lek-), *n.* electricity developed by the action of magnets. [MAGNETO- + ELECTRICITY]

mag·ne·to·gen·er·a·tor (mag nē′tō jen′ə rā′tər), *n.* magneto. [MAGNETO- + GENERATOR]

mag·ne·to·graph (mag nē′tə graf′, -gräf′), *n.* a recording magnetometer, used esp. for recording variations in the earth's magnetic field. [MAGNETO- + GRAPH] —**mag·ne·to·graph·ic** (mag nē′tə graf′ik), *adj.*

mag·ne·to·hy·dro·dy·nam·ic (mag nē′tō hī′drō dī nam′ik, -di-), *adj.* *Physics.* of or pertaining to the phenomena associated with the motion of an electrically conducting fluid, as liquid metal or ionized gas, in a magnetic field. [MAGNETO- + HYDRODYNAMIC] —**mag·ne′to·hy′dro·dy·nam′ic,** *adj.* —**mag·ne′to·hy′dro·dy·nam′i·cal·ly,** *adv.*

mag·ne·to·hy·dro·dy·nam·ics (mag nē′tō hī′drō dī nam′iks, -di-), *n.* **1.** Also called **hydromagnetics.** (*construed as sing.*) *Physics.* the branch of physics that deals with magnetohydrodynamic phenomena. **2.** See **MHD.** [MAGNETO- + HYDRODYNAMICS]

mag·ne·to·me·chan′i·cal ra′tio (mag nē′tō mə kan′i kəl), *Physics.* the ratio of the angular momentum of a rotating charged particle to its magnetic moment; the reciprocal of the gyromagnetic ratio. [MAGNETO- + MECHANICAL]

mag·ne·tom·e·ter (mag′ni tom′i tər), *n.* an instrument for measuring the intensity of a magnetic field, esp. the earth's magnetic field. [MAGNETO- + -METER] —**mag·ne·to·met·ric** (mag′nē tō me′trik), *adj.* —**mag′ne·tom′e·try,** *n.*

mag·ne·to·mo·tive (mag nē′tō mō′tiv), *adj.* producing magnetic effects. [MAGNETO- + MOTIVE]

magne′tomo′tive force′, *Elect.* the force which gives rise to a magnetic field, equal to the product of magnetic flux and reluctance.

mag·ne·ton (mag′ni ton′), *n.* *Physics.* a unit of magnetic moment, used in measuring the magnetic moment of atomic and subatomic particles. Cf. **Bohr magneton, nuclear magneton.** [MAGNET- + -ON[1]]

mag·ne·to·op·tic (mag nē′tō op′tik), *adj.* pertaining to the effect of magnetism upon the propagation of light. [MAGNETO- + OPTIC] —**mag·ne′to·op′ti·cal·ly,** *adv.*

mag·ne·to·op·tics (mag nē′tō op′tiks), *n.* (*construed as sing.*) *Physics.* the branch of physics that deals with magnetooptic phenomena. [MAGNETO- + OPTICS]

mag·ne·to·scope (mag nē′tə skōp′), *n.* *Physics.* (no longer current) a device for detecting and measuring magnetic force. [MAGNETO- + -SCOPE]

mag·ne·to·stat·ics (mag nē′tō stat′iks), *n.* (*construed as sing.*) the branch of magnetics that deals with magnetic fields that do not vary with time **(magne′tostat′ic fields′).** [MAGNETO- + STATICS]

mag·ne·to·stric·tion (mag nē′tō strik′shən), *n.* *Physics.* a change in dimensions exhibited by ferromagnetic materials when subjected to a magnetic field. [MAGNETO- + (CON)STRICTION] —**mag·ne·to·stric·tive** (mag nē′tə strik′tiv), *adj.*

mag·ne·to·ther·mo·e·lec·tric·i·ty (mag nē′tō thûr′mō i lek tris′i tē, -ē′lek-), *n.* *Physics.* thermoelectricity induced or affected by a magnetic field. [MAGNETO- + THERMOELECTRICITY]

mag·ne·tron (mag′ni tron′), *n.* *Electronics.* a two-element vacuum tube in which the flow of electrons is under the influence of an external magnetic field, used to generate extremely short radio waves. [MAGNE(T) + (ELEC)TRON]

magni-, an element appearing in loan words from Latin, where it meant "large," "great": *magnify.* Also, *esp. before a vowel,* **magn-.** [< L, comb. form of *magnus*]

mag·nif·ic (mag nif′ik), *adj.* *Archaic.* **1.** magnificent; imposing. **2.** grandiose; pompous. Also, **mag·nif′i·cal.** [< L *magnific(us)* grand (see MAGNI-, -FIC); r. late ME *magnyfyque* < MF] —**mag·nif′i·cal·ly,** *adv.*

Mag·nif·i·cat (mag nif′ə kat′, mäg nif′ə kät′, män yif′-), *n.* **1.** (*italics.*) the hymn of the Virgin Mary in Luke, 1:46–55, beginning "My soul doth magnify the Lord," used as a canticle at evensong or vespers. **2.** a musical setting for this. [ME < L: (it) magnifies (from the first word of the hymn)]

mag·ni·fi·ca·tion (mag′nə fə kā′shən), *n.* **1.** act of magnifying; state of being magnified. **2.** the power to magnify. **3.** a magnified copy or reproduction. [< LL *magnificātiōn-* (s. of *magnificātiō*). See MAGNIFIC, -ATION]

mag·nif·i·cence (mag nif′i səns), *n.* **1.** quality or state of being magnificent; splendor; grandeur; impressiveness; sublimity: *the magnificence of lofty trees.* **2.** impressiveness of surroundings: *the magnificence of Versailles.* [ME < L *magnificentia,* equiv. to *magnific(us)* MAGNIFIC + *-entia* -ENCE]
—**Syn. 1.** sumptuousness, pomp, state, majesty. **2.** luxury, luxuriousness, brilliance. —**Ant. 1, 2.** squalor, poverty.

mag·nif·i·cent (mag nif′i sənt), *adj.* **1.** making a splendid appearance or show; of surpassing beauty, size, etc.: *a magnificent cathedral.* **2.** extraordinarily fine; superb: *a magnificent opportunity.* **3.** noble; sublime: *a magnificent poem.* **4.** (*usually cap.*) (now used only as a title) great; grand: *Lorenzo the Magnificent.* **5.** lavishly munificent; extravagant: *a magnificent inheritance.* [< MF < L *magnificent-* (recorded in comp., superl., and other forms) for *magnificus.* See MAGNIFIC] —**mag·nif′i·cent·ly,** *adv.* —**mag·nif′i·cent·ness,** *n.*
—**Syn. 1, 2.** luxurious, lavish; exquisite; showy. MAGNIFICENT, GORGEOUS, SPLENDID, SUPERB are terms of high admiration and all are used informally in weak exaggeration. That which is MAGNIFICENT is beautiful, princely, grand, or ostentatious: *a magnificent display of paintings.* That which is GORGEOUS moves one to admiration by the richness and (often colorful) variety of its effects: *a gorgeous array of handsome gifts.* That which is SPLENDID is dazzling or impressive in its brilliance, radiance, or excellence: *splendid jewels; a splendid body of scholars.* That which is SUPERB is above others in, or is of the highest degree of, excellence or elegance (less often, today, of grandeur): *a superb rendition of a song; superb wines.* —**Ant. 1.** modest; squalid, poor.

Magnif′icent Am′ber·sons, The (am′bər sənz), a novel (1918) by Booth Tarkington.

magnif′icent ri′fle bird′. See under **rifle bird.**

mag·nif·i·co (mag nif′ə kō′), *n., pl.* **-coes.** **1.** a Venetian grandee. **2.** any grandee or great personage. [< It (adj.) < L *magnificus.* See MAGNIFIC]

mag·ni·fy (mag′nə fī′), *v.,* **-fied, -fy·ing.** —*v.t.* **1.** to increase the apparent size of, as a lens does. **2.** to make greater in actual size; enlarge: *to magnify a drawing in preparing for a fresco.* **3.** to cause to seem greater or more important; attribute too much importance to; exaggerate: *to magnify one's difficulties.* **4.** to make more exciting; intensify; dramatize; heighten: *The playwright magnified the conflict to get his point across.* **5.** *Archaic.* to extol; praise: *to magnify the Lord.* —*v.i.* **6.** to increase or be able to increase the apparent or actual size of an object, as a lens does. [ME *magnifie(n)* < L *magnific(āre).* See MAGNI-, -FY] —**mag′ni·fi′a·ble,** *adj.* —**mag′ni·fi′er,** *n.*
—**Syn. 2.** augment, increase, amplify. **3.** overstate. —**Ant. 1, 2.** reduce. **3.** minimize.

mag′nifying glass′, a lens that produces an enlarged image of an object.

mag·nil·o·quent (mag nil′ə kwənt), *adj.* speaking or expressed in a lofty or grandiose style; pompous; bombastic; boastful. [back formation from L *magniloquentia* elevated language, equiv. to *magniloqu(us)* speaking grandly (*magni-* MAGNI- + *loqu(ī)* (to) speak + *-us* adj. suffix) + *-entia* -ENCE] —**mag·nil′o·quence,** *n.* —**mag·nil′o·quent·ly,** *adv.*

mag·nip·o·tent (mag nip′ə tənt), *adj.* *Rare.* having great power. [< ML *magnipotent-* (s. of *magnipotēns*). See MAGNI-, POTENT[1]] —**mag·nip′o·tence,** *adj.*

mag·nis·o·nant (mag nis′ə nənt), *adj.* *Archaic.* high-sounding. [< LL *magnisonant-* (s. of *magnisonāns*). See MAGNI-, SONANT]

Mag·ni·to·gorsk (mäg ni to gôrsk′), *n.* a city in the W RSFSR, in the W Soviet Union in Asia, on the Ural River, near the boundary between Europe and Asia. 333,000 (est. 1962).

mag·ni·tude (mag′ni to͞od′, -tyo͞od′), *n.* **1.** size; extent; dimensions: *to determine the magnitude of an angle.* **2.** great amount, importance, etc.: *affairs of magnitude; a harvest of magnitude.* **3.** greatness; great size: *The magnitude of the loss ruined the business completely.* **4.** moral greatness: *magnitude of mind.* **5.** *Astron.* **a.** Also called **visual magnitude, apparent magnitude.** the brightness of a star or other celestial body as viewed by the unaided eye and expressed by a mathematical ratio of 2.512: a star of the first magnitude is approximately 2½ times as bright as one of the second magnitude and 100 times brighter than one of the fifth magnitude. Only stars of the sixth magnitude or brighter may be seen with the unaided eye. **b.** See **absolute magnitude.** **6.** *Math.* a number characteristic of a quantity and forming a basis for comparison with similar quantities, as length. **7. of the first magnitude,** of utmost or major importance: *an artist of the first magnitude.* [ME < L *magnitūdō.* See MAGNI-, -TUDE] —**mag·ni·tu·di·nous** (mag′ni to͞od′ᵊnəs, -tyo͞od′-), *adj.*

mag·no·lia (mag nōl′yə, -nō′lē ə), *n.* **1.** any shrub or tree of the genus *Magnolia,* having large, usually fragrant flowers and an aromatic bark, much cultivated for ornament. **2.** the blossom of any such shrub or tree, as of the evergreen magnolia tree: the state flower of Louisiana and Mississippi. [< NL, named after Pierre *Magnol* (1638–1715), French botanist; see -IA]

Mag·no·lia (mag nōl′yə, -nō′lē ə), *n.* **1.** a town in SW New Jersey. 4199 (1960). **2.** a girl's given name.

mag·no·li·a·ceous (mag nō′lē ā′shəs), *adj.* belonging to the *Magnoliaceae,* or magnolia family of plants, including the magnolias, the tulip trees, etc. [MAGNOLI(A) + -ACEOUS]

Magno′lia State′, Mississippi (used as a nickname).

magno′lia war′bler, a black and yellow wood warbler, *Dendroica magnolia,* of North America.

mag·num (mag′nəm), *n.* **1.** a large bottle for wine or spirits, containing about 50 ounces. **2.** a magnum cartridge or firearm. —*adj.* **3.** (of a cartridge) equipped with a larger charge than other cartridges of the same size. [< L: large; great]

mag′num o′pus, a great work, esp. the chief work of a writer or artist: Remembrance of Things Past *is Proust's magnum opus.* [< L]

Mag′nus effect′ (mag′nəs), *Mech.* the thrust on a cylinder rotating about its axis while in motion in a fluid, the thrust being perpendicular to the relative motion of the cylinder in the fluid. [named after Heinrich G. *Magnus* (1802–70), German scientist]

Mag′nus hitch′, a knot similar to a clove hitch but taking one more turn around the object to which the line is being bent; rolling hitch. [see MAGNUS EFFECT]

Black-billed magpie, *Pica pica* (Length 18 in.)

Ma·gog (mā′gog), *n.* a people descended from Japheth. Gen. 10:2; Ezek. 38, 39. Cf. **Gog and Magog.**

mag·pie (mag′pī′), *n.* **1.** either of two corvine birds, *Pica pica* **(black-billed magpie),** of Eurasia and North America, or *P. nuttalli* **(yellow-billed magpie),** of California, having long, graduated tails, black-and-white plumage, and noisy, mischievous habits. **2.** any of several related corvine birds. **3.** any of several black-and-white birds not related to the true magpies, as *Gymnorhina tibicen,* of Australia. **4.** an incessantly talkative person; noisy chatterer; chatterbox. [*Mag* Margaret + PIE[2]]

mag′pie goose′, a black-and-white gooselike bird, *Anseranas semipalmatus,* of Australia, believed to be the most primitive waterfowl in existence.

M. Agr., Master of Agriculture.

Ma·gritte (*Fr.* MA grēt′), *n.* **Re·né** (*Fr.* Rə nā′), 1898–1967, Belgian painter.

Mag·say·say (mäg sī′sī), *n.* **Ra·món** (rä mōn′; *Sp.* Rä-mōn′), 1907–57, Philippine statesman: president 1953–57.

mag·uey (mag′wā, mə gā′; *Sp.* mä ge′ē), *n.* **1.** any of several amaryllidaceous plants of the genus *Agave,* esp. *A. Cantala,* or of the related genus *Furcraea.* **2.** the fiber from these plants. [< Sp < Taino]

Ma·gus (mā′gəs), *n., pl.* **-gi** (-jī). **1.** (*sometimes l.c.*) one of the Magi. **2.** (*l.c.*) one who is learned or skilled in astrology, magic, sorcery, and the like. **3.** a Zoroastrian priest. Cf. **Magi** (def. 2). [< L < Gk *mágos* < OPers *magus* seer, wizard. See MAGIC]

Mag·yar (mag′yär; *Hung.* mo′dyoR), *n.* **1.** a member of the ethnic group, of the Finno-Ugric stock, which forms the predominant element of the population of Hungary. **2.** Hungarian (def. 3). —*adj.* **3.** of or pertaining to the Magyars or their language; Hungarian.

Mag·yar·ize (mag′yä rīz′), *v.t.,* **-ized, -iz·ing.** to put under the domination or influence of Magyars. [MAGYAR + -IZE] —**Mag′yar·i·za′tion,** *n.*

Ma·gyar·or·szág (mo′dyoR ôR′säg), *n.* Hungarian name of **Hungary.**

Ma·ha·ba·li·pur·am (mə hä′bə lē po͝or′əm), *n.* a village in NE Madras, in SE India: Hindu temples; early Dravidian architecture. Also, **Ma·ha′ba·li·pur′, Mamallapuram.**

Ma·ha·bha·ra·ta (mə hä′bär′ə tə), *n.* an epic poem of India, one of the *Puranas,* dealing mainly with the conflict between the Pandavas and the Kauravas, with many digressions; includes the *Bhagavad-Gita.* Also, **Ma·ha·bha·ra·tum** (mə hä′bär′ə təm). [< Skt, equiv. to *mahā-* great + *Bhārata* descendant of a king or tribe named Bharata]

Ma·ha·de·va (mə hä′dā′və), *n.* *Hinduism.* a name of Siva. [< Skt: great god, equiv. to *mahā-* great + *deva* god. See DEITY]

Ma·ha·la (mə hä′lə), *n.* a girl's given name.

ma·hal′a mat′ (mə hal′ə), a prostrate evergreen shrub, *Ceanothus prostratus*, of the Pacific Coast of the U.S., having wedge-shaped, spiny-edged leaves and blue flowers. [< AmerInd *mahala* woman; so called from its use by Indian women in weaving]

ma·ha·leb (mä′hə leb′), *n.* a cherry, *Prunus Mahaleb*, introduced into the U.S. from Eurasia, used as a stock in grafting cherries. Also called **ma′haleb cher′ry, St. Lucie cherry.** [< Ar]

Ma·hal·ia (mə hāl′yə), *n.* a girl's given name, form of **Mahala.** Also, **Mahalie.**

Ma·ha·lie (mə hā′lē), *n.* a girl's given name, form of **Mahala.** Also, **Mahalia.**

Ma·hal·la el Ku·bra (mə hal′ə el ko͞o′brə), a city in the N United Arab Republic, in the Nile delta. 198,900 (est. 1962).

Ma·ha·ma·ya (mə hä′mä′yə), *n.* *Hinduism.* maya (def. 4). [< Skt, equiv. to *mahā-* great + *māyā* MAYA]

Ma·han (mə han′), *n.* **Alfred Thay·er** (thā′ər), 1840–1914, U.S. naval officer and writer on naval history.

Ma′ha·noy Cit′y (mä′hə noi′), a town in central Pennsylvania. 8536 (1960).

ma·ha·ra·jah (mä′hə rä′jə; *Hind.* mə hä′RÄ′jə), *n.* the title of a ruling prince in India, esp. of one of the major states. Also, **ma′ha·ra′ja.** [< Hindi *mahārājā* great king, equiv. to *mahā-* great + *rājā* RAJAH]

ma·ha·ra·nee (mä′hə rä′nē; *Hind.* mə hä′RÄ′nē), *n.* **1.** the wife of a maharajah. **2.** an Indian princess who is sovereign in her own right. Also, **ma′ha·ra′ni.** [< Hindi *mahārānī* great queen, equiv. to *mahā-* great + *rānī* RANEE]

Ma·ha·rash·tra (mä′hə räsh′trə; *Hind.* mə hä′RÄSH′trə), *n.* a state in SW India. 39,553,718 (1961); 118,903 sq. mi. *Cap.:* Bombay.

Ma·ha·sa·ma·dhi (mə hä′sə mä′dē), *n.* *Hinduism, Buddhism.* the highest state of samadhi. [< Skt, equiv. to *mahā-* great + *samādhi* SAMADHI]

ma·hat·ma (mə hät′mə, -hat′-), *n.* **1.** a Brahman sage. **2.** (*chiefly in India*) a person who is held in the highest esteem for his wisdom and saintliness. **3.** (in Theosophy) a great sage who has renounced further spiritual development in order to aid those who are less advanced. [< Skt *mahātma(n)* high-souled, magnanimous, equiv. to *mah(ā)-* great + *ātmān* ATMAN] —**ma·hat′ma·ism,** *n.*

Mahat′ma Gan′dhi. See **Gandhi, Mohandas Karamchand.**

Ma·ha·vi·ra (mə hä′vēr′ə), *n.* Vardhamana.

Ma·ha·ya·na (mä′hə yä′nə; *Hind.* mə hä′yä′nə), *n.* one of the two great schools of Buddhism, formerly prevalent in China, Tibet, and Japan, characterized by eclecticism and a general belief in a common search for salvation, sometimes thought to be attainable through faith alone. Cf. **Bodhisattva, Hinayana.** [< Skt, equiv. to *mahā-* great + *yāna* vehicle] —**ma·ha·ya·nist** (mä′hə yä′nist), *n.*

Mah·di (mä′dē), *n., pl.* **-dis. 1.** (in Muslim, esp. Shiite, usage) the title of an expected spiritual and temporal ruler destined to establish a reign of righteousness throughout the world. **2.** any of various claimants of this title, esp. Muhammad Ahmed, who set up in the Egyptian Sudan an independent government which lasted until 1898. [< Ar *mahdīy* he who is guided] —**Mah·dism** (mä′diz əm), *n.* —**Mah′dist,** *n.*

Ma·hen·dra (mä hen drä′), *n.* (*Mahendra Bir Bikram Shah Deva*) born 1920, king of Nepal since 1955.

Ma·hi·can (mə hē′kən), *n., pl.* **-cans,** (*esp. collectively*) **-can. 1.** a tribe or confederacy of North American Indians of Algonquian speech, centralized formerly in the upper Hudson valley. **2.** an Indian of this confederacy. **3.** Mohegan (def. 1). Also, **Mohican.** [< AmerInd (Algonquian): lit., wolf]

mah-jongg (mä′jông′, -jŏng′, -zhông′, -zhŏng′), *n.* **1.** a game of Chinese origin usually played by four persons with 144 dominolike pieces or tiles marked in suits, counters, and dice, the object being to build a winning combination of pieces. —*v.i.* **2.** to win a game of mah-jongg. Also, **mah′-jong′.** [formerly trademark]

Mah·ler (mä′lər), *n.* **Gus·tav** (go͝os′täf), 1860–1911, Austrian composer and conductor, born in Bohemia.

Mah·lon (mä′lən, mä′-), *n.* a boy's given name.

mahl·stick (mäl′stik′, môl′-), *n.* a painter's stick, held in one hand as a support for the other, which holds the brush. Also, **maulstick.** [< D *maalstok*, lit., paint-stick. See MOLE[1], STOCK]

Mahl·ya and Mahl·ya·nag (mäl′yə; mäl yä′nəg), *Zoroastrianism.* See **Masya and Masyanag.**

Mah·mud II (mä mo͞od′), 1785–1839, sultan of Turkey 1809–39.

Mah·mud of Ghaz·ni (mə mo͞od′ əv guz′nē), A.D. 971?–1030, Muslim Amir of Ghazni 997–1030.

ma·hog·a·ny (mə hog′ə nē), *n., pl.* **-nies,** *adj.* —*n.* **1.** any of several tropical American, meliaceous trees, esp. *Swietenia Mahogoni* and *S. macrophylla*, yielding a hard, reddish-brown wood used for making furniture. **2.** the wood itself. **3.** any of various related or similar trees, or their wood. **4.** a reddish-brown color. —*adj.* **5.** pertaining to or made of mahogany. **6.** of the color mahogany. [? < some non-Carib WInd tongue]

Ma·hom·et (mə hom′it), *n.* Muhammad. Also, **Ma·hom·ed** (mə hom′id).

Ma·hom·e·tan (mə hom′i tᵊn), *n., adj.* Muslim. [MAHOMET + -AN] —**Ma·hom′et·an·ism,** *n.*

Ma·hon (mə ho͞on′, -hōn′), *n.* a boy's given name.

Ma·hón (mä ôn′), *n.* a seaport on E Minorca, in the Balearic Islands. 15,732 (1950).

Ma·hound (mə hound′, -ho͞ond′), *n.* **1.** *Archaic.* Muhammad. **2.** *Scot.* Satan; the devil. [early ME *Mahun, Mahum* < OF, short for MAHOMET; *-d* by assoc. with HOUND[1]]

ma·hout (mə hout′), *n.* the keeper or driver of an elephant, esp. in India and the East Indies. [< Hindi *mahāut*, var. of *mahāvat*]

Mah·rat·ta (mə rat′ə), *n.* a member of a Hindu people inhabiting central and western India. Also, **Maratha.**

Mahrat′ta Confed′eracy, a loose league of states in central and western India, broken up in 1818.

Mah·rat·ti (mə rat′ē), *n.* Marathi.

Mäh·ren (me′Rən), *n.* German name of **Moravia.**

Mäh·risch-Os·trau (me′Rish ôs′tRou), *n.* German name of **Moravská Ostrava.**

ma·hua (mä′hwä), *n.* any of several sapotaceous trees of the genus *Madhuca*, of India, the Malay Peninsula, and southeastern Asia, esp. *M. latifolia*, the flowers of which are used, fresh or dried, for food or are fermented to prepare an intoxicating drink. Also, **ma′hwa, mohwa, mowra, mowrah.** [< Hindi *mahūā* << Skt *madhūka* tree-name, equiv. to *madhu* sweet + *-ka* n. suffix]

mah·zor (mäKH zôR′; *Eng.* mäKH′zôr, -zôr), *n., pl.* **mah·zo·rim** (mäKH′zô Rēm′), *Eng.* **mah·zors.** *Hebrew.* a Jewish prayer book designed for use on festivals and holy days. Also, **machzor.** Cf. **siddur.**

Mai (mā), *n.* a girl's given name. Also, **Mae, May.**

Ma·ia (mā′yə, mī′ə), *n.* **1.** *Class. Myth.* the eldest of the Pleiades and the mother of Hermes by Zeus. **2.** a girl's given name.

maid (mād), *n.* **1.** a girl; young unmarried woman. **2.** a female servant. **3.** *Rare.* a spinster; old maid. **4.** *Archaic.* a virgin. [apocopated var. of MAIDEN] —**Syn. 1.** lass; maiden.

mai·dan (mī dän′), *n.* *Anglo-Indian.* an open area or space in or near a town, often used as a market place or parade ground. [< Hindi *maidān*]

Mai·da·nek (mīd′ᵊnek′, mī de′nek), *n.* a Nazi concentration camp in E Poland.

maid·en (mād′ᵊn), *n.* **1.** a girl; young unmarried woman; maid: *village maidens and lads.* **2.** an instrument resembling the guillotine, formerly used in Scotland for beheading criminals. **3.** *Cricket.* See **maiden over. 4.** a maiden horse. **5.** a maiden race. —*adj.* **6.** of, pertaining to, or befitting a girl or unmarried woman: *Her maiden name is shorter than her married name.* **7.** unmarried: *a maiden lady.* **8.** made, tried, appearing, etc., for the first time: *maiden flight.* **9.** virgin. **10.** (of a horse) never having won a race or a prize. **11.** (of a prize or a race) offered for or open only to maiden horses. **12.** untried, as a knight, soldier, or weapon. [ME; OE *mægden*, equiv. to *mægd* (c. Goth *magaths*, G *Magd*) + *-en* -EN[5]] —**maid′en·ish,** *adj.* —**maid′en·ship′,** *n.* —**maid′ish,** *adj.* —**maid′ish·ness,** *n.* —**Syn. 1.** virgin.

Maid′en Cas′tle, an ancient fortification in Dorsetshire, England, first erected c250 B.C. over the remains of Neolithic and Bronze Age settlements of c2000–c1500 B.C.

maid·en·hair (mād′ᵊn hâr′), *n.* any fern of the genus *Adiantum*, the cultivated species of which have fine, glossy stalks and delicate, finely divided fronds. [ME; see MAIDEN, HAIR]

maid′enhair spleen′wort, an evergreen fern, *Asplenium Trichomanes*, found throughout woody areas of the North Temperate Zone, having thickly clustered fronds.

maid·en·hair-tree (mād′ᵊn hâr′trē′), *n.* ginkgo.

maid·en·hair-vine (mād′ᵊn hâr′vīn′), *n.* See **wire vine.**

maid·en·head (mād′ᵊn hed′), *n.* **1.** maidenhood; virginity. **2.** the hymen. [ME *maidenhed.* See MAIDEN, -HEAD]

maid·en·hood (mād′ᵊn ho͝od′), *n.* the state or time of being a maiden; virginity. Also called **maidhood.** [ME; OE *mægdenhād.* See MAIDEN, -HOOD]

maid·en·ly (mād′ᵊn lē), *adj.* **1.** pertaining to a maiden: *maidenly years.* **2.** characteristic of or befitting a maiden: *maidenly behavior; a maidenly blush.* [ME; see MAIDEN, -LY] —**maid′en·li·ness,** *n.*

maid′en name′, a woman's surname before marriage.

maid′en o′ver, *Cricket.* an over in which no runs are made.

maid′en pink′, a turf-forming plant, *Dianthus deltoides*, found from western Europe to eastern Asia, having red or pink flowers. Also called **meadow pink, spink.**

maid·en's-tears (mād′ᵊnz tērz′, -terz′), *n., pl.* **-tears.** See **bladder campion.**

maid·en's-wreath (mād′ᵊnz rēth′), *n., pl.* **-wreaths** (-rēthz′). a perennial herb, *Francoa ramosa*, of California, having crinkled leaves and showy spikes of white flowers often two feet long. Also called **bridal wreath.**

maid′en voy′age, *Naut.* the first voyage of a vessel after its acceptance by the owners from the builders.

maid·hood (mād′ho͝od′), *n.* maidenhood.

maid-in-wait·ing (mād′in wā′ting), *n., pl.* **maids-in-wait·ing.** an unmarried woman who acts as an attendant to a queen or princess; a lady-in-waiting.

Maid′ Mar′ian, 1. Queen of the May, one of the characters in the old morris dance. **2.** See **morris dance. 3.** Robin Hood's sweetheart.

maid′ of hon′or, 1. the chief unmarried attendant of a bride. **2.** an unmarried woman, usually of noble birth, attendant on a queen or princess.

Maid′ of Or′leans. See **Joan of Arc.**

maid·ser·vant (mād′sûr′vənt), *n.* a female servant. [MAID + SERVANT]

Maids′ of Hon′or, The, a painting (1656) by Diego Velázquez. Also called **Las Meninas.**

Maid·stone (mād′stōn′, -stən), *n.* a city in and the county seat of Kent, in SE England. 59,761 (1961).

Mai·du·gu·ri (mī do͞o′go͞o rē), *n.* a city in NE Nigeria. 139,965 (1963).

Mai·er (mī′ər), *adj.* *Naval Archit.* noting a form of hull design intended to minimize the resistance of water to the immersed body of the hull, resulting in a bow with a long, sweeping forefoot and a middle body having steep, diagonal bilges at an angle parallel to that of any transverse section of the immersed portions of the bow and stern. [named after its German inventor]

ma·ieu·tic (mā yo͞o′tik), *adj.* noting the method used by Socrates in bringing forth knowledge in the mind of a person by interrogation and insistence on close and logical reasoning. [< Gk *maieutik(ós)* of, pertaining to midwifery, equiv. to *maieú(esthai)* (to) serve as a midwife (akin to *maia* midwife) + *-tikos* -TIC]

mai·gre (mā′gər; *Fr.* me′gRᵊ), *adj.* containing neither flesh nor its juices, as food permissible on days of religious abstinence. [< F; see MEAGER]

mai·hem (mā′hem), *n.* mayhem.

mail[1] (māl), *n.* **1.** letters, packages, etc., that are sent or delivered by means of the post office: *Storms delayed delivery of the mail.* **2.** a single collection of such letters, packages, etc., as sent or delivered: *to open one's mail; to find a bill in the mail; The mail for England was put on board the ship.* **3.** Also, **mails.** the system, usually operated by the national government, for sending or delivering letters, packages, etc.; postal system: *to communicate by mail.* **4.** a train, boat, person, etc., as a carrier of postal matter. —*adj.* **5.** of or pertaining to mail: *mail delivery.* —*v.t.* **6.** to send by mail; place in a post office or mailbox for transmission. [ME *male* < OF *malle* < Gmc; cf. OHG *mal(a)ha* satchel, bag]

mail[2] (māl), *n.* **1.** flexible armor of interlinked rings. **2.** (loosely) any flexible armor, as one having a protective exterior of scales or small plates. **3.** *Textiles.* an oval piece of metal pierced with a hole through which the warp ends are threaded, serving as an eyelet on a heddle or esp. on the harness cords of a Jacquard loom. —*v.t.* **4.** to clothe or arm with mail. [ME *maille* one of the rings of which armor was composed < OF < L *macula* spot, mesh of a net] —**mail′less,** *adj.*

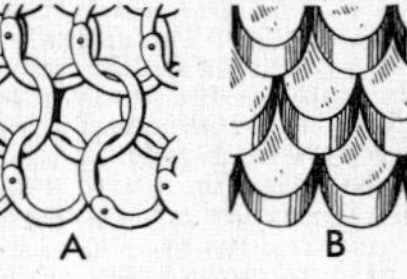

Mail[2]
A, (Def. 1); B, (Def. 2)

mail[3] (māl), *n.* *Scot.* monetary payment or tribute, esp. rent or tax. Also, **maill.** [ME (north) *mal(e)*, OE *māl* agreement < Scand; cf. Icel *māl* agreement, speech, c. OE *mǣl* speech]

mail·a·ble (mā′lə bəl), *adj.* legally acceptable as mail. [MAIL[1] + -ABLE] —**mail′a·bil′i·ty,** *n.*

mail·bag (māl′bag′), *n.* **1.** a large bag used by mailmen for carrying mail, usually equipped with a strap fitting over the shoulder. **2.** a large bag or pouch used in transporting mail in bulk from general post offices to branch offices, from city to city, etc. [MAIL[1] + BAG]

mail·boat (māl′bōt′), *n.* a boat for carrying mail. Also, **mail′ boat′.** [MAIL[1] + BOAT]

mail·box (māl′boks′), *n.* **1.** a public box in which mail is placed for delivery by the post office. **2.** a private box, as at a home, into which mail is delivered by the mailman. Also called **postbox.** [MAIL[1] + BOX[1]]

mail′ car′, a railroad car for carrying mail.

mail·catch·er (māl′kach′ər), *n.* *Railroads.* a device on a mail car that, while the train is moving, picks up mailbags suspended beside the track. [MAIL[1] + CATCHER]

mail-cheeked (māl′chēkt′), *adj.* (of certain fishes) having the cheeks crossed with a bony plate.

mailed (māld), *adj.* clad or armed with mail: *a mailed knight.* [ME; see MAIL[2], -ED[2]]

mailed′ fist′, 1. superior force, esp. when presented as a threat: *The country showed its mailed fist in negotiations.* **2.** brutal or naked power, esp. coercive force: *the mailed fist hidden in the velvet glove.*

mail·er (mā′lər), *n.* **1.** a person who mails or prepares material for mailing. **2.** See **mailing machine. 3.** *Archaic.* a mailboat. [MAIL[1] + -ER[1]]

Mail·er (mā′lər), *n.* **Norman,** born 1923, U.S. writer.

mail′ flag′, *Naut.* **1.** a flag of the International Code of Signals symbolizing the letter Y, flown alone by a vessel to indicate that it is carrying mail: a square flag with red and yellow diagonal stripes. **2.** any of various other flags, or a pennant, indicating that a vessel is carrying mail.

mail·ing (mā′ling), *n.* *Scot.* **1.** a rented farm. **2.** the rent paid by a tenant farmer. [late ME; see MAIL[3], -ING[1]]

mail′ing machine′, a machine that prepares mail for sending, as by addressing, stamping, weighing, etc. Also called **mailer.**

mail′ing tube′, an elongated cylinder of cardboard, used for mailing rolled-up papers, magazines, etc.

maill (māl), *n.* *Scot.* mail[3].

Mail·lart (mA yAR′), *n.* **Ro·bert** (Rô beR′), 1872–1940, Swiss engineer.

Mail·lol (mA yôl′), *n.* **A·ris·tide** (A Rēs tēd′), 1861–1944, French sculptor.

mail·lot (mä yō′, ma-; *Fr.* mA yō′), *n., pl.* **mail·lots** (mä yōz′; *Fr.* mA yō′). **1.** tights worn by dancers, acrobats, etc. **2.** a close-fitting, one-piece bathing suit for women. **3.** a close-fitting knitted shirt, esp. a pullover. [< F: bathing costume, tights, swaddling clothes, var. of earlier *maillol*, deriv. of *maille* MAIL[2]]

mail·man (māl′man′), *n., pl.* **-men.** a man, usually employed by the post office, who delivers mail; postman. [MAIL[1] + MAN]

mail′ or′der, *Com.* an order received or shipped through the mail.

mail′-order house′, a firm that conducts all or most of its business through orders received and merchandise shipped through the mail, and which supplies its customers with catalogs, circulars, etc.

Mai·lyn (mā lin′), *n.* a girl's given name.

maim (mām), *v.t.* **1.** to deprive of the use of some part of the body by wounding or the like; cripple: *The explosion maimed him for life.* **2.** to impair; make essentially defective: *The editors maimed the essay beyond recognition.* —*n. Obs.* **3.** a physical injury, esp. a loss of a limb. **4.** an injury or defect; blemish; lack. [ME *mayme*, deriv. of *mayme* MAYHEM] —**maimed′ness,** *n.* —**maim′er,** *n.*
—**Syn. 1.** MAIM, LACERATE, MANGLE, MUTILATE indicate the infliction of painful and severe injuries on the body. To MAIM is to injure by giving a disabling wound, or by depriving a person of one or more members or their use: *maimed in an accident.* To LACERATE is to inflict severe cuts and tears on the flesh or skin: *to wound and lacerate an arm.* To MANGLE is to chop undiscriminatingly or to crush or rend by blows or pressure, as if by machinery: *bodies mangled in a train wreck.* To MUTILATE is to injure the completeness or beauty of a body, esp. by cutting off an important member: *to mutilate a statue, a tree, a person.* **2.** injure, disable, deface, mar.

Mai·mon·i·des (mī mon′i dēz′), *n.* (*Moses ben Maimon*) ("*RaMBaM*") 1135–1204, Jewish scholastic philosopher and rabbi, born in Spain: one of the major theologians of Judaism. —**Mai·mon′i·de′an,** *adj., n.*

main[1] (mān), *adj.* **1.** chief; principal; leading; most important: *the main office; the main features of a plan.* **2.** sheer; utmost, as strength, force, etc.: *to lift a stone* by *main force.* **3.** of or pertaining to a broad expanse: *main sea.* **4.** *Gram.* syntactically independent; capable of use in isolation. In *I walked out when the bell rang, I walked out* is the main clause. Cf. **dependent** (def. 4), **independent** (def. 12). **5.** *Naut.* **a.** of or pertaining to a mainmast. **b.** noting or pertaining to a sail, yard, boom, etc., or to any rigging belonging to a main lower mast or to some upper mast of a mainmast. **c.** noting any stay running aft and upward to the head of a main lower mast or of some specified upper mast of a mainmast: *main topmast stay.* **6.** *Obs.* having or exerting great strength or force; mighty. **7.** *Obs.* highranking. **8.** *Obs.* having momentous or important results; essential. **—*n.*** **9.** a principal pipe or duct in a system used to distribute water, gas, etc. **10.** strength; force; violent effort: *to struggle with might and main.* **11.** the chief or principal part or point: *The main of their investments was lost during the war.* **12.** *Literary.* the open ocean; high sea: *the bounding main.* **13.** the mainland. **14. in the main,** for the most part; chiefly: *In the main, the essay was dull reading.* [< ME *meyn,* OE *mægen* strength, power; c. Icel *megin* strength] **—Syn. 1.** cardinal, prime, paramount, primary, capital. **2.** pure, direct. **9.** conduit. **10.** power, might. **—Ant. 1.** secondary, least. **10.** weakness.

main[2] (mān), *n.* a cockfighting match. [? special use of MAIN[1]; cf. *main chance*]

Main (mān; *also for 1 Ger.* mīn), *n.* **1.** a river in central and W Germany, flowing W from the Bohemian Forest into the Rhine at Mainz, in West Germany. 305 mi. long. **2.** a crater in the first quadrant of the face of the moon, in the libration area and near the North Pole: about 30 miles in diameter.

main′ bod′y, *Naut.* the hull, as distinguished from the rest of a vessel.

main′ brace′, *Naut.* a brace leading to a main yard.

main′ chance′, an opportunity offering the greatest gain: *Being ambitious, he always had an eye for the main chance.*

main′ clause′, *Gram.* a clause that can stand alone as a sentence, containing a subject, a predicate of a finite verb, and sometimes a direct object, as *I was there* in the sentence *I was there when he arrived.* Cf. **subordinate clause.**

main′ course′, *Naut.* a square mainsail.

main′ deck′, **1.** *Naut.* the uppermost weatherproof deck, running the full length of a vessel. **2.** (on a Great Lakes ore boat) a partial deck at the level of the tops of the side tanks.

main-de-fer (man′də-fer′), *n.* *Armor.* manifer.

main′ diag′onal, *Math.* See under **diagonal** (def. 9).

main′ drag′, *Slang.* the main street of a city or town; main stem: *Broadway is New York's main drag.*

Maine (mān), *n.* **1.** a State in the NE United States, on the Atlantic coast. 969,265 (1960); 33,215 sq. mi. *Cap.:* Augusta. *Abbr.:* Me. **2.** a former province in NW France. *Cap.:* Le Mans. **3.** (*italics*) a U.S. battleship blown up in the harbor of Havana, Cuba, on February 15, 1898.

Maine-et-Loire (me′nā lwar′), *n.* a department in W France. 556,272 (1962); 2787 sq. mi. *Cap.:* Angers.

Main·er (mā′nər), *n.* a native or inhabitant of the State of Maine.

main·frame (mān′frām′), *n.* *Computer Technol.* a large high-speed computer with greater storage capacity than a minicomputer, often serving as the central unit in a system of smaller computers. [MAIN[1] + FRAME]

main gauche (maN gōsh′), a dagger of the 16th and 17th centuries, held in the left hand in dueling and used to parry the sword of an opponent. Also called **left-hand dagger.** [< F: lit., left hand]

main·land (mān′land′, -lənd), *n.* the principal land of a country, region, etc., as distinguished from adjacent islands: *the mainland of Greece.* [ME; see MAIN[1], LAND] **—main′land′er,** *n.*

Main·land (mān′land′, -lənd), *n.* **1.** the largest of the Shetland Islands. 15,172 (1951); ab. 200 sq. mi. **2.** Pomona (def. 3).

main′ line′, **1.** a through railroad route; a principal line of a railroad as contrasted with a branch or secondary line. **2.** *Slang.* **a.** a prominent and readily accessible vein of the body that may be used for a narcotic's injection. **b.** the act of mainlining.

Main′ Line′, a fashionable residential district west of Philadelphia.

main·line (mān′līn′, -līn′), *v.i.,* **-lined, -lin·ing.** *Slang.* to inject a narcotic, esp. heroin, directly into the vein. [v. use of MAIN LINE] **—main′lin′er,** *n.*

main·ly (mān′lē), *adv.* **1.** chiefly; principally; for the most part; in the main; to the greatest extent: *Our success was due mainly to his efforts. The audience consisted mainly of students.* **2.** *Obs.* greatly; abundantly. [ME *maynliche, maynly.* See MAIN[1], -LY]

main·mast (mān′mast′, -mäst′; *Naut.* mān′məst), *n.* *Naut.* **1.** the second mast from forward in any vessel having two or more masts, except for a yawl, ketch, or dandy. See illus. under **quarter deck. 2.** the larger forward mast of a yawl, ketch, or dandy. **3.** the sole mast of any of various vessels, as sloops or cutters. [MAIN[1] + MAST[1]]

main·our (mā′nər), *n.* *Old Eng. Law.* a stolen article found on the person of or near the thief: *to be taken with the mainour.* Also, **manner.** [ME < AF *mainoure* (OF *manoeuvre* hand labor); see MANEUVER]

mains (mānz), *n.* (*construed as sing.*) *Brit. Dial.* the main or home farm of a manor, as where the owner lives; manse. [pl. of *main,* aph. var. of ME *demain* DEMESNE]

main·sail (mān′sāl′; *Naut.* mān′səl), *n.* *Naut.* the lowermost sail on a mainmast. [ME; see MAIN[1] + SAIL]

main·sheet (mān′shēt′), *n.* *Naut.* a sheet of a mainsail. [ME; see MAIN[1], SHEET[1]]

main·spring (mān′spring′), *n.* **1.** the principal spring in a mechanism, as in a watch. **2.** the chief motive power; the impelling cause: *Desire for fame is the mainspring of his behavior.* [MAIN[1] + SPRING]

main·stay (mān′stā′), *n.* **1.** *Naut.* the stay that secures the mainmast forward. **2.** one who or that which acts as a chief support or part: *Coffee is the mainstay of the country's economy.* [ME; see MAIN[1], STAY[2]]

main′ stem′, *Slang.* the main street of a city or town; the main drag.

main·stream (mān′strēm′), *n.* **1.** the principal or dominant course, tendency, or trend: *the mainstream of our nation's history.* **2.** a river having tributaries. **—*adj.*** **3.** of, pertaining to, or characteristic of jazz falling historically between Dixieland and modern jazz; specifically, swing music. Cf. **traditional** (def. 4). [MAIN[1] + STREAM]

Main′ Street′, a novel (1920) by Sinclair Lewis.

main·tain (mān tān′), *v.t.* **1.** to keep in existence or continuance; preserve; retain: *to maintain good relations with Canada.* **2.** to keep in due condition, operation, or force; keep unimpaired: *to maintain order; to maintain public highways.* **3.** to keep in a specified state, position, etc.: *to maintain a correct posture.* **4.** to affirm; assert; declare: *He maintained that the country was going downhill.* **5.** to support in speech or argument, as a statement, proposition, etc. **6.** to keep or hold against attack: *to maintain one's ground.* **7.** to provide for the upkeep or support of; carry the expenses of: *He has to maintain a large family on a small salary.* [ME *mainteine(n)* < OF *mainten(ir)* < LL *manūtenēre,* L *manū tenēre,* lit., to hold in hand, equiv. to *manū,* abl. of *manus* hand (see MANUAL) + *tenēre* to hold (see TENET)] **—main·tain′a·ble,** *adj.* **—main·tain′er,** *n.* **—Syn. 1.** keep up, continue. **4.** aver, asseverate, state, hold, allege. **5.** uphold, defend, vindicate, justify. **7.** See **support. —Ant. 1.** discontinue. **5.** contradict.

maintain′ing pow′er, *Horol.* a mechanism for maintaining a constant force on the going train of a timepiece as it is being wound.

main·tain·or (mān tā′nər), *n.* *Law.* one guilty of maintenance. [ME *meyntenour* < AF. See MAINTAIN, -OR[2]]

main·te·nance (mān′tᵊnəns), *n.* **1.** act of maintaining: *The apartment was too expensive for easy maintenance.* **2.** state of being maintained: *The maintenance of friendly relations with England has always been important.* **3.** means of upkeep, support, or subsistence; livelihood: *The widow was left with sufficient maintenance.* **4.** *Law.* an officious meddling in a suit in which the meddler has no interest, by assisting either party with means to prosecute or defend it. [ME *maintenaunce* < MF *maintenance.* See MAINTAIN, -ANCE] **—Syn. 3.** See **living.**

main′tenance and cure′, *Law.* the right of an injured seaman to support and medical treatment.

main′tenance of mem′bership, an arrangement or agreement between an employer and a labor union by which employees who are members of the union at the time the agreement is made, or who subsequently join, must either remain members until the agreement expires, or be discharged.

Main·te·non (maNtᵊ nôN′), *n.* **Marquise de** (*Françoise d'Aubigné*), 1635–1719, second wife of Louis XIV.

main·top (mān′top′), *n.* *Naut.* a platform at the head of the lower mainmast. [ME; see MAIN[1], TOP[1]]

main-top·gal·lant (mān′top gal′ənt; *Naut.* mān′tə-gal′ənt), *n.* the main-topgallantmast, its sail, or its yard. See illus. under **sail.**

main-top·gal·lant·mast (mān′top gal′ənt mast′, -mäst′; *Naut.* mān′tə gal′ənt məst), *n.* *Naut.* the mast next above the main-topmast.

main-top·mast (mān′top′mast′, -mäst′; *Naut.* mān′-top′məst), *n.* *Naut.* the mast next above the main lower mast.

main-top·sail (mān′top′sāl′; *Naut.* mān′top′səl), *n.* *Naut.* a topsail set on the mainmast.

main′-top′sail schoon′er, *Naut.* a two-masted or three-masted schooner having square topsails on the foremast and mainmast: a jackass brig or jackass bark. Also called **two-topsail schooner.**

Main′-Trav′elled Roads′ (mān′trav′əld), a collection of short stories (1891) by Hamlin Garland.

main′-try′sail rig′ (mān′trī′səl, -sāl′), *Naut.* See **wishbone rig.**

main′ yard′, *Naut.* a yard for a square mainsail.

Mainz (mīnts), *n.* a port in W West Germany, at the confluence of the Rhine and Main rivers. 139,400 (1963). French, **Mayence.**

Mainz′ Psal′ter, a book printed by Johannes Gutenberg: thought by some to be the first book printed from movable type.

ma·iol·i·ca (mə yol′ə kə), *n.* majolica.

mair (mār), *adj., n., adv.* *Scot. and North Eng.* more.

Mai·sie (mā′zē), *n.* a girl's given name, Scottish form of **Margaret.**

Mai·son de Mo·lière, La (*Fr.* lȧ me zôN′ də mô-lyer′). See **Comédie Française.**

mai·son de san·té (me zôN də sāN tā′), *pl.* **mai·sons de san·té** (me zôN də saN tā′). *French.* a private hospital or sanitarium for the sick or insane. [lit., house of health]

mai·son·ette (mā′zə net′), *n.* *Chiefly Brit.* a small apartment, esp. part of a private house rented as an apartment. Also, **mai′son·nette′.** [< F, OF, equiv. to *maison* house (see MANSION) + *-ette* -ETTE]

maist (māst), *adj., n., adv.* *Scot. and North Eng.* most.

mai·thu·na (mī′tōō nə), *n.* *Hinduism.* sexual intercourse, when regarded as taboo.

Mait·land (māt′lənd), *n.* **1. Fredrick William,** 1850–1906, English jurist and legal historian. **2.** a town in central Florida. 3570 (1960).

maî·tre d′ (mā′tər dē′, mā′trə-), *pl.* **maî·tre d's.** *Informal.* See **maître d'hôtel** (defs. 1–3).

maî·tre de bal·let (*Fr.* me′trᵊ də bȧ lā′), *pl.* **maî·tres de bal·let** (me′trᵊ də bȧ lā′). See **ballet master.** [< F: master of ballet]

maî·tre d'hô·tel (mā′tər dō tel′, mā′trə; *Fr.* me′trᵊ dō tel′), *pl.* **mai·tres d'hô·tel** (mā′tərz dō-tel′, mā′trəz; *Fr.* me′trᵊ dō tel′). **1.** a steward or butler. **2.** a headwaiter. **3.** the owner or manager of a hotel. **4.** *Cookery.* a sauce of melted butter, minced parsley, and lemon juice or vinegar. [< F: master of (the) hotel]

maize (māz), *n.* **1.** (chiefly in British and technical usage) corn[1] (def. 1). **2.** a pale yellow resembling the color of corn. **—*adj.*** **3.** of the color of maize. [< Sp *maíz* < Hispaniolan Taino *mahís*]

maize′ oil′. See **corn oil.**

Maj., Major.

Ma·jes·ta (mə jes′tə), *n.* a girl's given name.

ma·jes·tic (mə jes′tik), *adj.* characterized by or possessing majesty; of lofty dignity or imposing aspect; stately; grand: *the majestic Alps.* Also, **ma·jes′ti·cal.** [MAJEST(Y) + -IC] **—ma·jes′ti·cal·ly,** *adv.* **—Syn.** august, splendid, magnificent, regal, royal, kingly, imperial, noble, lofty. **—Ant.** base, mean.

maj·es·ty (maj′i stē), *n., pl.* **-ties. 1.** regal, lofty, or stately dignity; imposing character; grandeur: *majesty of bearing.* **2.** supreme greatness or authority; sovereignty: *All paid tribute to the majesty of Rome.* **3.** a royal personage, or royal personages collectively: *The royal wedding was attended by the majesties of Europe.* **4.** (*usually cap.*) a title used when speaking of or to a sovereign (usually prec. by *his, her,* or *your*): *His Majesty's Navy; Will your Majesty hear our petitions?* **5. Christ in Majesty,** a representation of Christ as ruler of the universe. [ME *majeste* < MF < L *mājestāt-* (s. of *mājestās*) sovereignty, greatness, grandeur, equiv. to **mājes-* (akin to *mājus;* see MAJOR) + *-tāt-* -TY[2]]

Maj. Gen., Major General.

ma·jol·i·ca (mə jol′ə kə, mə yol′-), *n.* **1.** Italian earthenware covered with an opaque glaze of tin oxide and usually highly decorated. **2.** any earthenware having an opaque glaze of tin oxide; faience; delft. Also, **maiolica.** [earlier *maiolica* < It < ML, var. of LL *Mājorica* MAJORCA, where it was made]

ma·jor (mā′jər), *n.* **1.** *Mil.* a commissioned officer ranking next below a lieutenant colonel and next above a captain. **2.** one of superior rank, ability, etc., in a specified class: *Minors outnumber majors in most fields of endeavor.* **3.** a subject or field of study chosen by a student to represent his principal interest and upon which he concentrates a large share of his efforts: *History was his major at college.* **4.** a person of full legal age (opposed to *minor*). **5.** *Music.* a major interval, chord, scale, etc. **6. the majors,** *Sports.* the major leagues: *He coached in the majors as well as in the minors.* **—*adj.*** **7.** greater, as in size, amount, extent, importance, rank, etc.: *the major part of the town.* **8.** great, as in rank or importance: *a major question; a major artist.* **9.** of or pertaining to the majority: *the major opinion.* **10.** of or full legal age. **11.** *Music.* **a.** (of an interval) being between the tonic and the second, third, sixth, and seventh degrees of a major scale: *the major third; the major sixth.* **b.** (of a chord) having a major third between the root and the note next above it. **12.** (*cap.*) (of one of two male students in an English public school who have the same surname) being the elder or higher in standing: *Hobbes Major is not of a scientific bent.* **13.** pertaining to the subject in which a student takes most of his courses: *His major field is English history.* **—*v.i.*** **14.** to follow a major course of study: *He is majoring in the physical sciences.* [< L, comp. of *magnus* great; r. ME *majour* < AF] **—Syn. 8.** See **capital**[1].

Ma·jor (mā′jər), *n.* a boy's given name.

ma′jor ax′is, *Math.* the axis of an ellipse which passes through the two foci.

Ma′jor Bar′bara, a comedy (1905) by G. B. Shaw.

Ma·jor·ca (mə jôr′kə, -yôr′-), *n.* a Spanish island in the W Mediterranean: the largest of the Balearic Islands. 328,000 (est. 1954); 1405 sq. mi. *Cap.:* Palma. Spanish, **Mallorca. —Ma·jor′can,** *adj., n.*

ma·jor-do·mo (mā′jər dō′mō), *n., pl.* **-mos. 1.** a man in charge of a great household, as that of a sovereign; a chief steward. **2.** a steward or butler. [< Sp *mayordomo* < LL *mājordomūs* head of the house, equiv. to *major* MAJOR + *domūs,* gen. of *domus* house; see DOME]

ma′jor el′ement, *Geol.* any chemical found in great quantity in the rocks of the earth's crust. Cf. **minor element** (def. 1).

ma·jor·ette (mā′jə ret′), *n.* See **drum majorette.** [(DRUM) MAJOR + -ETTE]

ma′jor gen′eral, *Mil.* an officer ranking next below a lieutenant general and next above a brigadier general. **—ma′jor-gen′er·al·cy, ma′jor-gen′er·al·ship′,** *n.*

ma·jor·i·ty (mə jôr′i tē, -jor′-), *n., pl.* **-ties. 1.** the greater part or number; the number larger than half the total, as opposed to the minority: *the majority of mankind.* **2.** a number of voters or votes, jurors, or others in agreement, constituting more than half of the total number. **3.** the amount by which the greater number, as of votes, surpasses the remainder (distinguished from *plurality*). **4.** the party or faction with the majority vote: *The Democratic party is the majority.* **5.** the state or time of being of full legal age: *to attain one's majority.* **6.** the military rank or office of a major. **7. join the majority** or **the great majority,** to die. [< ML *mājoritās.* See MAJOR, -ITY]

ma′jor key′, *Music.* a key whose essential harmony is based on the major scale. Also called **major mode.**

ma′jor league′, **1.** either of the two main professional baseball leagues in the U.S. **2.** a league of corresponding stature in certain other sports, as ice hockey, football, or basketball.

ma·jor-lea·guer (mā′jər lē′gər), *n.* a member of a major-league team. [MAJOR LEAGUE + -ER[1]]

ma′jor mode′, *Music.* **1.** See **major scale. 2.** See **major key.**

ma′jor or′der, *Rom. Cath. Ch.* the degree or grade of priesthood, diaconate, or subdiaconate. Cf. **minor order.**

ma′jor pen′alty, *Ice Hockey.* a penalty consisting of the removal of a player for five minutes from play, no substitute for the player being permitted. Cf. **minor penalty.**

ma′jor piece′, *Chess.* a queen or rook.

ma′jor plan′et, *Astron.* planet (def. 1a).

ma′jor prem′ise, *Logic.* See under **syllogism** (def. 1).

Ma′jor Proph′ets, Isaiah, Jeremiah, and Ezekiel. Cf. **Minor Prophets.**

ma′jor scale′, *Music.* a scale consisting of a series of whole steps except for half steps between the third and fourth and seventh and eighth degrees. Also called **major mode.** See illus. under **scale.**

ma′jor suit′, *Bridge.* hearts or spades, esp. with reference to their higher point values. Cf. **minor suit.**

ma′jor ten′ace, *Bridge, Whist.* the ace and queen of a suit held by one player. Cf. **minor tenace, tenace.**

ma′jor term′, *Logic.* See under **syllogism** (def. 1).

ma′jor tri′ad, *Music.* a triad consisting in root position of a root tone with a major third and a perfect fifth above.

Ma·jun·ga (mə jung′gə), *n.* a seaport on W Madagascar. 34,119 (1960).

ma·jus·cule (mə jus′kyo͞ol, maj′ə skyo͞ol′), *adj.* **1.** (of letters) capital. **2.** large, as either capital or uncial letters. **3.** written in such letters (opposed to *minuscule*). —*n.* **4.** a majuscule letter. [< L *mājuscula* (*littera*) a somewhat bigger (letter), equiv. to *mājus-*, s. of *mājor* MAJOR + *-cula* -CULE] —**ma·jus′cu·lar,** *adj.*

Ma·ka·lu (muk′ə lo͞o′), *n.* a mountain in the Himalayas, on the boundary between Nepal and Tibet. 27,790 ft.

Ma·kar·i·os III (mə kar′ē əs, -ōs′; *Gk.* mä kä′rē ôs), (*Michael Christedoulos Mouskos*) 1913–77, Cypriote statesman and Greek Orthodox prelate: archbishop and patriarch of Cyprus 1950–77; president 1960–77 (in exile 1974).

Ma·kas·sar (mə käs′ər), *n.* Dutch name of **Macassar.**

make[1] (māk), *v.,* **made, mak·ing,** *n.* —*v.t.* **1.** to bring into existence by shaping or changing material, combining parts, etc.: *to make a dress; to make a chair; to make a work of art.* **2.** to produce; cause to exist; bring about: *to make trouble; to make war.* **3.** to cause to be or become; render: *to make someone happy.* **4.** to appoint or name: *The President made him his special envoy.* **5.** to put in the proper condition or state, as for use; fix; prepare: *to make a meal.* **6.** to bring into a certain form: *to make bricks out of clay.* **7.** to convert from one state, condition, category, etc., to another: *to make a virtue of one's vices.* **8.** to cause, induce, or compel: *to make a horse jump a barrier.* **9.** to give rise to; occasion: *It's not worth making a fuss over such a trifle.* **10.** to produce, earn, or win for oneself: *to make a good salary; to make one's fortune in oil.* **11.** to write or compose, as a poem. **12.** to draw up, as a legal document: *to make a will.* **13.** to do; effect: *to make a bargain.* **14.** to establish or enact; put into existence: *to make laws.* **15.** to become by development; prove to be: *He will make a good lawyer.* **16.** to form in the mind, as a judgment, estimate, etc. **17.** to judge or interpret, as to the truth, nature, meaning, etc. (often fol. by *of*): *What do you make of it?* **18.** to estimate; reckon: *to make the distance at ten miles.* **19.** to bring together separate parts so as to produce a whole; compose; form: *to make a matched set.* **20.** to bring to; bring up the total to: *two plus two makes four; to make an even dozen.* **21.** to serve as: *to make good reading.* **22.** to be sufficient to constitute; be adequate to: *That makes a good answer!* **23.** to assure the success or fortune of. **24.** to deliver, utter, or put forth: *to make a stirring speech.* **25.** to go or travel at a particular speed: *to make 60 miles an hour.* **26.** to arrive at or reach: *The ship made port on Friday.* **27.** to arrive in time for: *to make the first show.* **28.** *Informal.* to arrive in time to be a passenger on (a plane, boat, bus, or train): *If you hurry, you can make the next flight.* **29.** *Informal.* to gain or acquire a position within: *He made the big time.* **30.** to receive mention or appear in or on: *to make the front page.* **31.** to gain recognition or honor by winning a place or being chosen for inclusion in or on: *The novel made the list of the 50 best books of the year. He made the all-American team three years in a row.* **32.** *Slang.* to persuade to have sexual intercourse with; seduce. **33.** *Cards.* **a.** to name (the trump). **b.** to take a trick with (a card). **c.** *Bridge.* to fulfill or achieve (a contract or bid). **d.** to shuffle (the cards). **34.** to earn, as a score: *make a home run.* **35.** to close (an electric circuit). —*v.i.* **36.** to cause oneself, or something understood, to be as specified: *to make sure.* **37.** to show oneself to be or seem in action or behavior (usually fol. by an adjective): *to make merry.* **38.** *Informal.* to direct or pursue a course; move; go: *to make for home.* **39.** to be made, as specified: *This toy stove makes easily: just fold on the dotted lines.* **40.** to rise, as the tide, water in a ship, etc. **41. make a board,** *Naut.* to sail on a certain tack, as in headreaching. **42. make a good board,** *Naut.* to advance well to windward when sailing close-hauled. **43. make a half board,** *Naut.* to luff until nearly halted, then to fill away on the same tack. **44. make a play for,** to try to get: *He made a play for his buddy's girl. They made a play for control of the cotton market, and almost got it.* **45. make as if** or **as though,** *Informal.* to act as if; pretend: *We will make as if to leave, then come back and surprise him with a party and presents.* **46. make away with, a.** to get rid of: *The cat made away with the mice in the attic.* **b.** to steal: *The clerk made away with the cash and checks.* **c.** to destroy; kill: *He made away with his enemies.* **d.** to consume completely: *The boys made away with the contents of the refrigerator.* **47. make believe,** to pretend; imagine: *The little girl dressed in her mother's old evening gown and made believe she was Cinderella at the ball.* **48. make bold** or **so bold,** to have the temerity; be so rash; dare: *May I make so bold as to suggest that you insert a comma at this point?* **49. make book,** *Slang.* **a.** to take bets and give odds. **b.** to make a business of this. **50. make colors,** *Naut.* to hoist an ensign, as on board a warship. **51. make do,** to function, manage, or operate, usually on a deprivation level with minimal requirements: *During the war we had no butter or coffee, so we had to make do without them.* **52. make fast,** *Naut.* to fasten or secure. **53. make for, a.** to go toward; approach. **b.** to lunge at; attack. **c.** to help to promote or maintain: *This incident will not make for better understanding between the warring factions.* **54. make foul water,** *Naut.* to eddy and discolor shallow water under a boat by the motion of the hull, propellers, paddles, etc. **55. make good, a.** to provide restitution or reparation for: *The bank teller made good the shortage and was given a light sentence.* **b.** to succeed: *Talent and education are necessary to make good in some fields.* **c.** to fulfill: *He made good on his promise to take her to the opera.* **d.** *Navig.* to compute (a course) allowing for leeway and compass deviation. **56. make good weather,** *Naut.* (of a vessel) to ride easily in a heavy sea. **57. make heavy weather, a.** *Naut.* to roll and pitch in heavy seas. **b.** to progress laboriously; struggle, esp. to struggle needlessly: *I am making heavy weather with my income tax return.* **58. make her number,** *Naut.* (of a vessel) to announce its official number with a hoist of code flags. **59. make it,** *Informal.* **a.** to achieve a specific goal: *to make it to the train; to make it through college.* **b.** to succeed in general: *You don't have to worry, he'll make it: he's got a rich daddy.* **60. make it so,** *Naut.* strike the ship's bell accordingly: said by the officer of the watch when the hour is announced. **61. make like,** *Slang.* to try or pretend to be like; imitate: *In her black velvet gown she was making like a femme fatale.* **62. make off, a.** to run away; depart hastily: *The only witness to the accident made off before the police arrived.* **b.** *Naut.* to stand off from a coast, esp. a lee shore. **63. make off with,** to carry away; steal: *While the family was away for the summer, thieves made off with many of their valuables.* **64. make one's number,** *Naut. Slang.* to present oneself, as at an interview. **65. make out, a.** to write out or complete, as a bill, check, etc. **b.** to establish; prove. **c.** to decipher; discern. **d.** to imply, suggest, or impute: *He made me out to be a liar.* **e.** *Informal.* to manage; succeed: *How are you making out in your new job?* **f.** *Slang.* to engage in kissing and caressing; neck. **66. make out with,** (of a man) to persuade (a woman) to have sexual intercourse; make. **67. make over, a.** to remodel; alter: *to make over a dress; make over a page.* **b.** to transfer the title of (property); convey: *The old lady made over her property to her children and moved to Florida.* **68. make sail,** *Naut.* **a.** to set sails. **b.** to brace the yards of a ship that has been hove to in order to make headway. **69. make time.** See **time** (def. 43). **70. make up, a.** (of parts) to constitute; form. **b.** to put together; construct; compile. **c.** to concoct; invent. **d.** Also, **make up for.** to compensate for; make good. **e.** to complete. **f.** to put in order; arrange. **g.** to conclude; decide. **h.** to settle amicably, as differences. **i.** to become reconciled, as after a quarrel. **j.** *Print.* to arrange set type, illustrations, etc., into columns or pages. **k.** to dress in appropriate costume and apply cosmetics for a part on the stage. **l.** to apply cosmetics. **m.** to adjust or balance, as accounts; prepare, as statements. **n.** *Educ.* to repeat (a course or examination that one has failed). **o.** *Educ.* to take an examination which one had been unable to take when first given, usually because of absence. **p.** to specify and indicate the make-up of (columns, pages, etc., of matter to be printed). **71. make up to, a.** *Informal.* to try to become friendly with; fawn on. **b.** to make advances to; flirt with: *He makes up to every new girl in the office.* **72. make water, a.** to urinate. **b.** *Naut.* (of a hull) to leak. **73. make with,** *Slang.* **a.** to operate; use: *Let's make with the feet.* **b.** to bring about; produce: *He makes with the big ideas, but can't follow through.* —*n.* **74.** style or manner of being made; form; build. **75.** production with reference to the maker: *our own make.* **76.** disposition; character; nature. **77.** act or process of making. **78.** quantity made; output. **79.** *Cards.* act of naming the trump, or the suit named as trump. **80.** *Elect.* the closing of an electric circuit. **81.** *Jewelry.* the excellence of a polished diamond with regard to proportion, symmetry, and finish. **82. on the make,** *Informal.* **a.** seeking to improve one's social or financial position at the expense of others or of principle. **b.** increasing; advancing. **c.** *Slang.* seeking amorous relations: *The park was swarming with sailors on the make.* [ME *make(n),* OE *macian;* c. LG, D *maken,* G *machen*] —**mak′a·ble,** *adj.*
—**Syn. 1.** form; build; produce; fabricate, create, fashion, mold. MAKE, CONSTRUCT, MANUFACTURE mean to produce, to put into definite form, or to put parts together to make a whole. MAKE is the general term: *Bees make wax.* CONSTRUCT, more formal, means to put parts together, usually according to a plan or design: *to construct a building.* MANUFACTURE usually refers to producing something from material that requires conversion from one state or condition to another, now almost entirely by means of machinery in a relatively complex process: *to manufacture automobiles by the assembly of different parts.* The term is also often used contemptuously of unimaginative or hackneyed works of art with the implication that the work was produced mechanically, and is used abstractly with the idea of denying genuineness: *to manufacture an excuse.* **7.** transform, change, turn. **8.** force. **10.** get, gain, acquire, obtain, secure, procure. **13.** perform, execute. **15.** accomplish. **18.** judge, gauge. **74.** shape, structure, construction, constitution. **75.** brand. —**Ant. 1.** destroy.

make[2] (māk), *n. Brit. Dial.* **1.** one's peer or equal. **2.** one's spouse, mate, consort, or lover. **3.** a friend; companion. [ME *mak, make,* OE *gemaca.* See MATCH[2]]

make-and-break (māk′ən brāk′), *adj.* noting or pertaining to a device, operated by an electric current, for automatically opening or closing a circuit once it has been closed or opened by a mechanical springlike device: a common application is the ordinary doorbell.

make-be·lieve (māk′bi lēv′), *n.* **1.** pretense; feigning; sham: *the make-believe of little girls playing house together.* **2.** a pretender; one who pretends: *The dancer was a make-believe, not a genuine talent.* —*adj.* **3.** pretended; feigned; sham; made-up; unreal: *a make-believe world of fantasy.*

Ma·ke·ev·ka (*Russ.* mä ke′yəf kä′), *n.* Makeyevka.

make·fast (māk′fast′, -fäst′), *n. Naut.* any structure to which a vessel is tied up, as a bollard, buoy, etc. [n. use of v. phrase *make fast*]

make·less (māk′lis), *adj. Dial.* having no mate or match. [ME; see MAKE[2], -LESS]

make-or-break (māk′ər brāk′), *adj.* either completely successful or utterly disastrous: *a make-or-break fiscal policy.*

make-peace (māk′pēs′), *n.* a peacemaker. [n. use of v. phrase *make peace*]

mak·er (mā′kər), *n.* **1.** one who makes. **2.** (*cap.*) God. **3.** the party executing a legal instrument, esp. a promissory note. **4.** *Cards.* the one who first names the successful bid. **5.** *Archaic.* a poet. **6. go to** or **meet one's Maker,** to die: *He found the world intolerable and prayed that he might soon meet his Maker.* [ME; see MAKE[1], -ER[1]]

make-read·y (māk′red′ē), *n.* the process of preparing a form for printing by overlays or underlays to equalize the impression. [n. use of v. phrase *make ready*]

mak′er's mark′, the personal mark of a goldsmith or silversmith, struck on pieces coming from his shop.

make·shift (māk′shift′), *n.* **1.** a temporary expedient or substitute: *Boxes were a handy makeshift while the chairs were being painted.* —*adj.* **2.** Also, **make′shift′y.** serving as, or of the nature of, a makeshift. [n., adj. use of v. phrase *make shift*] —**make′shift′ness,** *n.* —**Syn. 1.** contrivance, jury rig. **2.** emergency, temporary, improvised, jury, ersatz.

make-up (māk′up′), *n.* **1.** facial cosmetics, as lipstick, powder, etc., used by women to enhance their features. **2.** cosmetics used on other parts of the body, as to make the skin appear darker, cover birthmarks, etc. **3.** the application of cosmetics: *She spends hours on her make-up.* **4.** the ensemble or effect created by such application: *Her make-up is too showy.* **5.** the total ensemble consisting of cosmetics, costumes, etc., used by an actor for a particular role, or by a performer in television, night clubs, etc. **6.** the manner of being made up or put together; composition: *the make-up of a team; the make-up of a situation.* **7.** physical or mental constitution: *the make-up of an athlete; the defective make-up of a criminal.* **8.** the art, technique, or process of making up, as pages in a publication: *Make-up is his specialty, but he's also been a crack reporter.* **9.** the appearance of a page, book, or the like, resulting from the disposition and the variation in size and style of the printed elements: *The make-up would be helped by a picture in this corner.* **10.** *Journalism.* a characteristic, identifiable appearance, esp. of a newspaper, resulting from a consistent approach to the organization of elements on a page: *That paper's make-up is as stodgy as its editorial policy.* **11.** *Print.* the arrangement of set type, cuts, etc., into columns or pages. **12.** (in education) an examination taken in substitution for an examination which one failed to pass or from which one was absent. Also, **make′up′.** [n. use of v. phrase *make up*]

make·weight (māk′wāt′), *n.* **1.** something put in a scale to complete a required weight. **2.** anything added to supply a lack. [MAKE[1] + WEIGHT]

make-work (māk′wûrk′), *n.* unnecessary work invented to keep workers from being idle. [n. use of v. phrase *make work*]

Ma·ke·yev·ka (mä ke′yəf kä′), *n.* a city in the SE Ukraine, in the SW Soviet Union in Europe, N of the Sea of Azov. 358,000 (1959). Also, **Makeevka.**

Ma·khach·ka·la (mə käch′kə lä′; *Russ.* mä khäch′kä lä′), *n.* a seaport in the W RSFSR, in the S Soviet Union in Europe, on the Caspian Sea. 119,000 (1959).

ma·ki·mo·no (mä′kē mô′nô; *Eng.* mä′kə mō′nō, -nə, mak′ə-), *n., pl.* **-no,** *Eng.* **-nos.** *Japanese.* a horizontal hand scroll containing either text or a painting, intended to be viewed as it is unrolled. Cf. **kakemono.** [lit., scroll-thing]

mak·ing (mā′king), *n.* **1.** act of one who or that which makes: *The making of a violin requires great skill.* **2.** structure; constitution; make-up. **3.** means or cause of success or advancement: *to be the making of someone.* **4.** Usually, **makings.** capacity or potential: *He has the makings of a first-rate officer.* **5. makings,** material of which something may be made: *the makings of a cigarette; the makings of a house.* **6.** something made. **7.** the quantity made: *a making of butter.* **8. in the making,** in the process of being made; developing; growing: *Our space scientists see history in the making.* [ME; OE *macung.* See MAKE[1], -ING[1]]

mak′ing light′, *Navig.* a light or beacon intended to be seen before any other lights by vessels approaching land. Also called **landfall light.**

Mak·kah (mak′kə, -kä), *n.* Mecca. (def. 1).

mak·luk (mak′luk), *n.* a large seal, esp. the bearded seal. [< Eskimo *muklok*]

ma·ko (mä′kō), *n., pl.* **-kos.** a powerful mackerel shark, *Isurus oxyrinchus,* found in the Atlantic and Pacific oceans. Also called **ma′ko shark′.** [< Maori]

mak·soo·rah (mäk so͝or′ə), *n.* (in a mosque) a screen or partition enclosing an area for prayer or a tomb. [< Ar]

Mak′su·tov tel′escope (mak′so͞o tôf′, -tof′), a reflecting telescope in which coma and spherical aberration are reduced to a minimum by a combination of a spherical mirror and a meniscus lens placed inside the radius of curvature of the mirror. [named after D. *Maksutov* (born 1896), Russian scientist]

mal-, a prefix meaning "bad," "wrongful," "ill," occurring originally in loan words from French (*malapert*); on this model, used in the formation of other words (*malfunction; malcontent*). Cf. **male-.** [ME < OF, repr. *mal,* adv. (<< L *male* badly, ill), or *mal,* adj. (<< L *malus* bad)]

Mal., **1.** Malachi. **2.** Malayan.

Mal′a·bar Coast′ (mal′ə bär′), a region along the entire SW coast of India, extending from the Arabian Sea inland to the Western Ghats. Also called **Malabar.**

Mal′abar gourd′, a climbing vine, *Cucurbita ficifolia,* of eastern Asia, having bell-shaped, yellow flowers and roundish or oblong, smooth, white-striped, green fruit with black seeds, grown as an ornamental.

Mal′abar night′shade, any of several Asian vines of the genus *Basella,* having succulent leaves and red or white flowers, cultivated as a potherb in the tropics and as an ornamental plant in temperate regions.

mal·ab·sorp·tion (mal′ab sôrp′shən, -zôrp′-), *n. Pathol.* faulty absorption of nutritive material from the intestine. [MAL- + ABSORPTION]

Ma·lac·ca (mə lak′ə), *n.* **1.** a state in Malaysia, on the SW Malay Peninsula: formerly a part of the British Straits Settlements and of the Federation of Malaya. 361,162 (est. 1963); 640 sq. mi. **2.** a seaport in and the capital of this state. 69,848 (1957). **3.** **Strait of,** a strait between Sumatra and the Malay Peninsula. 35–185 mi. wide. —**Ma·lac′can,** *adj., n.*

Malac′ca cane′, a cane or walking stick made of the brown, often mottled or clouded stem of an East Indian rattan palm, *Calamus Scipionum.*

ma·la·ceous (mə lā′shəs), *adj.* belonging to the *Malaceae,* or apple family of plants, comprising the apple, pear, quince, medlar, loquat, hawthorn, etc. [< L *mā-l(um)* apple (c. Gk *mâlon,* var. of *mêlon*) + -ACEOUS]

Mal·a·chi (mal′ə kī′), *n.* **1.** a Minor Prophet of the 5th century B.C. **2.** the book of the Bible bearing his name. Also, *Douay Bible,* **Mal·a·chi·as** (mal′ə kī′əs).

mal·a·chite (mal′ə kīt′), *n.* **1.** a green mineral, basic copper carbonate, $Cu_2CO_3(OH)_2$, an ore of copper, used for making ornamental articles. **2.** a ceramic ware made in imitation of this. [< Gk *malách(ē)* MALLOW + -ITE[1]; r. ME *melochites* < L *molochītēs* < Gk *molōch(ē)* mallow]

ma·la·cia (mə lā′shə, -shē ə, -sē ə), *n. Pathol.* **1.** softening, or loss of consistency, of an organ or tissue. **2.** an abnormal craving for highly spiced foods. [< NL < Gk *malakía* softness, tenderness, weakness. See MALACO-, -IA] —**mal·a·coid** (mal′ə koid′), *adj.* —**mal·a·cot·ic** (mal′ə kot′ik), *adj.*

malaco-, a learned borrowing from Greek, where it meant "soft," used in the formation of compound words: *malacopterygian.* [< Gk *malako-,* comb. form of *malakós*]

mal·a·col·o·gy (mal′ə kol′ə jē), *n.* the science dealing with the study of mollusks. [< F *malacologie,* syncopated var. of *malacozoologie.* See MALACO-, ZOOLOGY] —**mal·a·co·log·i·cal** (mal′ə kə loj′i kəl), *adj.* —**mal′a·col′o·gist,** *n.*

mal·a·coph·i·lous (mal′ə kof′ə ləs), *adj.* (of a flower) adapted to pollination by snails. [MALACO- + -PHILOUS]

mal·a·cop·te·ryg·i·an (mal′ə kop′tə rij′ē ən), *adj.* belonging or pertaining to the *Malacopterygii* (*Malacopteri*), a division of soft-finned, teleost fishes. [< NL *Malacopterygi(i)* (MALACO- + Gk *pteryg-,* s. of *ptéryx* wing, fin + L *-ii* masc. pl. ending) + -AN]

mal·a·cos·tra·can (mal′ə kos′trə kən), *adj.* **1.** belonging or pertaining to the subclass *Malacostraca,* which includes the lobsters, shrimps, crabs, etc. —*n.* **2.** a malacostracan crustacean. [< NL *Malacostrac(a)* order of crustacea (< Gk *malakóstrakos* soft-shelled; see MALACO-, OSTRACIZE) + -AN]

mal·ad·ap·ta·tion (mal′ad əp tā′shən), *n.* incomplete or faulty adaptation: *a maladaptation to the demands of modern society.* [MAL- + ADAPTATION]

mal·a·dapt·ed (mal′ə dap′tid), *adj.* poorly suited or adapted to a particular condition or set of circumstances: *Trite, maladapted speeches won't help the campaign.* [MAL- + ADAPTED]

mal·a·dap·tive (mal′ə dap′tiv), *adj.* of, pertaining to, or characterized by maladaptation: *The maladaptive behavior of slum children was difficult to correct.* [MAL- + ADAPTIVE]

mal·ad·just·ed (mal′ə jus′tid), *adj.* badly or unsatisfactorily adjusted, esp. in relationship to one's circumstances, environment, etc.: *The urban ethos tends to produce an increase in maladjusted individuals.* [MAL- + ADJUSTED]

mal·ad·just·ment (mal′ə just′mənt), *n.* bad or unsatisfactory adjustment. [MAL- + ADJUSTMENT]

mal·ad·min·is·ter (mal′əd min′i stər), *v.t.* to manage badly or inefficiently: *Though not a fool, the mayor was a bungler who maladministered his affairs.* [MAL- + ADMINISTER] —**mal′ad·min′is·tra′tion,** *n.* —**mal′ad·min′is·tra′tor,** *n.*

mal·a·droit (mal′ə droit′), *adj.* lacking in adroitness; unskillful; awkward; bungling; tactless: *to handle a situation in a very maladroit way.* [< F, MF; see MAL-, ADROIT] —**mal′a·droit′ly,** *adv.* —**mal′a·droit′ness,** *n.* —**Syn.** clumsy, inept; gauche.

mal·a·dy (mal′ə dē), *n., pl.* **-dies.** **1.** any disorder or disease of the body, esp. one that is chronic or deep-seated: *Arthritis can be a lifelong malady.* **2.** any undesirable or disordered condition: *social maladies; a malady of the spirit.* [ME *maladie* < OF, equiv. to *malade* sick (< LL *male habitus,* lit., ill-conditioned) + *-ie* -Y[3]] —**Syn. 1.** illness, sickness, affliction, complaint, ailment, indisposition. See **disease.**

ma·la fi·de (mä′lä fē′de; *Eng.* mā′lə fī′dē), *Latin.* in bad faith; not genuine.

ma·la fi·des (mä′lä fē′des; *Eng.* mā′lə fī′dēz), *Latin.* bad faith; intent to cheat or deceive. Cf. **bona fides.**

Mal·a·ga (mal′ə gə), *n.* **1.** a strong, sweet dessert wine with a pronounced muscat grape flavor, produced in Málaga, Spain. **2.** any of the grapes grown in or exported from Málaga.

Mál·a·ga (mal′ə gə; *Sp.* mä′lä gä′), *n.* **1.** a province in S Spain, in Andalusia. 775,167 (1960); 2813 sq. mi. **2.** a seaport in S Spain, on the Mediterranean. 324,949 (1965).

Mal·a·gas·y (mal′ə gas′ē), *n., pl.* **-gas·y, -gas·ies** for 1. **1.** a native of the Malagasy Republic. **2.** the Malayo-Polynesian language of Madagascar.

Malagas′y Repub′lic, official name of **Madagascar.** French, **République Malgache.**

ma·la·gue·na (mal′ə gān′yə *or, often,* -gwān′-; *Sp.* mä′lä ge′nyä), *n., pl.* **-gue·nas** (-gān′yəz *or, often,* -gwān′-; *Sp.* -ge′nyäs). a Spanish dance similar to the fandango, originating in Málaga. [< Sp *malagueña* (fem.) of MÁLAGA]

ma·laise (ma lāz′; *Fr.* MA lez′), *n.* **1.** a condition of general bodily weakness or discomfort, often marking the onset of a disease. **2.** an unfocused feeling of mental uneasiness or discomfort: *Repression of feelings generally produces a malaise that destroys the chance of happiness or satisfaction.* [< F, OF; see MAL-, EASE]

Ma·la·kal (mal′ə kal′), *n.* a city in E Sudan, on the White Nile. 9680 (1960).

Mal·a·mud (mal′ə məd, -mo͝od′), *n.* **Bernard,** born 1914, U.S. novelist and short-story writer.

mal·a·mute (mal′ə myo͞ot′), *n.* (*sometimes cap.*) See **Alaskan malamute.** Also, **malemute.** [var. of *Malemute,* Eskimo tribe that bred the dogs]

Ma·lan (mä län′), *n.* **Daniel Fran·çois** (frän swä′), 1874–1959, South African editor and political leader: prime minister 1948–54.

mal·an·ders (mal′ən dərz), *n.* (*construed as sing.*) *Vet. Pathol.* a dry, scabby or scurfy eruption or scratch behind the knee in a horse's foreleg. Also, **mallanders, mallenders.** Cf. **sallenders.** [late ME *malawnder* < MF *malander* < L *malandria* blister on a horse's neck]

Ma·lang (mä läng′), *n.* a city on E Java, in S Indonesia. 341,452 (1961).

ma·lan·ga (mə lang′gə), *n.* a thick, fleshy-leaved herb, *Xanthosoma atrovirens,* of South America, having leaves from two to three feet long and nearly two feet wide. Also called **West Indian kale.** [< AmerSp]

Ma·lan·je (mə lan′jə), *n.* a city in N Angola. 12,815 (est. 1955). Also, **Ma·lan·ge** (mə lan′jə).

mal·a·pert (mal′ə pûrt′), *Archaic.* —*adj.* **1.** unbecomingly bold or saucy. —*n.* **2.** a malapert person. [late ME: insolent < MF: unskillful. See MAL-, PERT] —**mal′a·pert′ly,** *adv.* —**mal′a·pert′ness,** *n.*

mal·ap·por·tioned (mal′ə pôr′shənd, -pôr′-), *adj.* (of a state or other political unit) poorly apportioned, esp. divided, organized, or structured in a manner that prevents large sections of a population from having equitable representation in a legislative body. [MAL- + APPORTIONED] —**mal′ap·por′tion·ment,** *n.*

Mal·a·prop (mal′ə prop′), *n.* **Mrs.,** a character in Sheridan's *The Rivals* (1775), noted for her misapplication of words.

mal·a·prop·ism (mal′ə prop iz′əm), *n.* **1.** act or habit of misusing words ridiculously, esp. by the confusion of words that are similar in sound. **2.** an instance of this, as in "Lead the way and we'll precede." [MALAPROP + -ISM]

mal·ap·ro·pos (mal′ap rə pō′), *adj.* **1.** inappropriate; out of place; inopportune; untimely: *a malapropos remark.* —*adv.* **2.** inappropriately; inopportunely. [< F *mal à propos* badly (suited) to the purpose]

ma·lar (mā′lər), *Anat.* —*adj.* **1.** of or pertaining to the cheek or zygomatic bone. —*n.* **2.** Also, **ma′lar bone′.** See **zygomatic bone.** [< NL *mālār(is)* of, pertaining to the cheek, equiv. to L *māl(a)* cheek, jaw + *-āris* -AR[1]]

Mä·lar (mā′lər, -lär), *n.* **Lake,** a lake in S Sweden, extending W from Stockholm toward the Baltic Sea. 440 sq. mi. Swedish, **Mä·lar·en** (me′lä ren).

ma·lar·i·a (mə lâr′ē ə), *n.* **1.** *Pathol.* any of a group of diseases, usually intermittent or remittent, characterized by attacks of chills, fever, and sweating: formerly supposed to be due to swamp exhalations but now known to be caused by five or more species of parasitic protozoans, which are transferred to the human bloodstream by mosquitoes of the genus *Anopheles* and which occupy and destroy the red blood corpuscles. **2.** *Archaic.* unwholesome or poisonous air. [< It, contr. of *mala aria* bad air] —**ma·lar′i·al, ma·lar′i·an, ma·lar′i·ous,** *adj.*

ma·lar·key (mə lär′kē), *n. Informal.* speech or writing designed to obscure, mislead, or impress; bunkum: *The claims were just a lot of malarkey.* [?]

mal·as·sim·i·la·tion (mal′ə sim′ə lā′shən), *n. Pathol.* imperfect assimilation or nutrition. [MAL- + ASSIMILATION]

mal·ate (mal′āt, mā′lāt), *n. Chem.* a salt or ester of malic acid. [MAL(IC) + -ATE[2]]

Mal·a·thi·on (mal′ə thī′on), *n. Chem., Trademark.* a yellow liquid, $C_{10}H_{19}O_6PS_2$, used as an insecticide.

Ma·la·tya (mä′lä tyä′), *n.* a city in central Turkey. 105,207 (1965). Ancient, **Melitene.**

Ma·la·wi (mä lä′wē), *n.* a republic in SE Africa, on the W and S shores of Lake Nyasa: formerly a British protectorate and part of the Federation of Rhodesia and Nyasaland; gained independence July 6, 1964; a member of the British Commonwealth of Nations. 3,753,000 (est. 1963); 49,177 sq. mi. *Cap.:* Zomba. Formerly, **Nyasaland.**

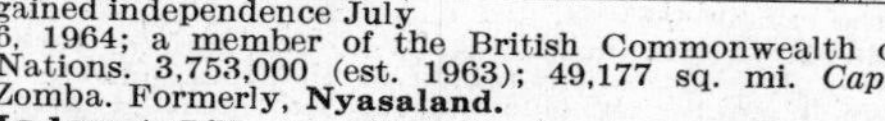

Ma·lay (mā′lā, mə lā′), *adj.* **1.** of or pertaining to the Malays or their country or language. **2.** of, pertaining to, or characteristic of a racially intermixed, brown-skinned people of the Malay Peninsula who are marked generally by short stature, roundish skull, moderate prognathism, and wavy to straight black hair; Malayo-Indonesian. —*n.* **3.** a member of the dominant people of the Malay Peninsula and adjacent islands. **4.** a Malayo-Polynesian language widespread in the East Indies as a language of commerce and serving as the first language of a large population in the Malay peninsula.

Ma·lay·a (mə lā′ə), *n.* **1.** See **Malay Peninsula.** **2.** **Federation of.** Formerly, **Malay States, Malay′an Un′ion.** a former federation of 11 states in the S Malay Peninsula: a British protectorate 1948–57; now forms part of the federation of Malaysia. 50,690 sq. mi. *Cap.:* Kuala Lumpur. Cf. **Malaysia** (def. 1).

Mal·a·ya·lam (mal′ə yä′ləm), *n.* a Dravidian language spoken in extreme southwestern India.

Ma·lay·an (mə lā′ən), *adj.* **1.** Malay. —*n.* **2.** a Malay. **3.** (no longer current) Indonesian (def. 3). [MALAY + -AN]

Malay′an cam′phor, borneol.

Ma′lay Archipel′ago, an extensive island group in the Indian and Pacific oceans, SE of Asia: including Sumatra, the Moluccas, Borneo, the Philippines, Celebes, and Timor. Also called **Malaysia.**

Malayo-, a combining form of **Malay.**

Ma·lay·o-In·do·ne·sian (mə lā′ō in′də nē′zhən, -shən, -dō-), *adj.* Malay (def. 2).

Ma·lay·o-Pol·y·ne·sian (mə lā′ō pol′ə nē′zhən, -shən), *adj.* **1.** of or belonging to a family of languages including those of the indigenous inhabitants of most of Oceania, the Philippines, Formosa, the East Indies, the Malay Peninsula, and Madagascar; Austronesian. —*n.* **2.** Also called **Austronesian.** the family of Malayo-Polynesian languages.

Ma′lay Penin′sula, a peninsula in SE Asia, consisting of the Federation of Malaya and the S part of Thailand. Also called **Malaya.**

Ma·lay·sia (mə lā′zhə, -shə), *n.* **1.** an independent federation of SE Asia, comprising the former British territories of Malaya, Sabah, Sarawak, and, formerly, Singapore: member of the British Commonwealth of Nations. 9,137,000 (est. 1964); 126,310 sq. mi. *Cap.:* Kuala Lumpur. **2.** See **Malay Archipelago.**

Ma·lay·sian (mə lā′zhən, -shən), *n.* **1.** a native of Malaysia. **2.** Indonesian (def. 1). **3.** Malay (def. 3). —*adj.* **4.** of, pertaining to, or characteristic of Malaysia or its inhabitants. [MALAYSI(A) + -AN]

Ma′lay States′, former name of the Federation of Malaya.

Mal·colm (mal′kəm), *n.* a boy's given name. Also, **Mal′com.**

mal·con·tent (mal′kən tent′), *adj.* **1.** not happy about currently prevailing conditions or circumstances; discontented; dissatisfied: *He is malcontent with the present state of literature.* **2.** dissatisfied with the existing government, administration, system, etc. —*n.* **3.** a malcontent person. [< MF, OF; see MAL-, CONTENT[2]] —**mal′con·tent′ed·ly,** *adv.* —**mal′con·tent′ed·ness,** *n.*

M.A.L.D., Master of Arts in Law and Diplomacy.

mal de mer (mal də mer′), *French.* seasickness.

Mal·den (môl′dən), *n.* **1.** a city in E Massachusetts, near Boston. 57,676 (1960). **2.** a town in SE Missouri. 5007 (1960).

Mal′dive Is′lands (mal′dīv), a group of about 2000 islands constituting an independent republic in the Indian Ocean, SW of Ceylon: British protectorate 1887–1965. 101,000 (est. 1966); 115 sq. mi. *Cap.:* Malé.

mal du pa·ys (mal dʏ pā ē′), *French.* homesickness.

male (māl), *adj.* **1.** of or belonging to the sex that begets young by fertilizing the female. **2.** pertaining to or characteristic of this sex; masculine: *His male instincts were aroused by her perfume.* **3.** composed of males: *a male choir.* **4.** *Bot.* **a.** designating or pertaining to any reproductive structure producing or containing elements that bring about the fertilization of the female element. **b.** (of seed plants) staminate. **5.** *Mach.* noting a part, thread, etc., fitting into a corresponding female part. —*n.* **6.** a person of the male sex; a man or boy. **7.** any animal of male sex. **8.** *Bot.* a staminate plant. [ME < MF *ma(s)le* < L *mascul(us).* See MASCULINE] —**male′ness,** *n.*

—**Syn. 1.** MALE, MASCULINE, VIRILE are descriptive of one belonging to the paternal sex. MALE always refers to sex, whether of human beings, animals, or plants: *Male animals are often larger than the females.* MASCULINE applies to the qualities that properly characterize the male sex: *a masculine love of sports.* The term may be applied to women, also, in either of two ways. It usually suggests some incongruity (as, *a masculine appearance*), but it may be used with complimentary or ambivalent implications: *She has a masculine mind.* VIRILE is a strong and comprehensive term, which formerly emphasized obvious maleness, but now usually implies the vigor, health, and force of mature manhood: *a virile opponent.* **2.** manly. —**Ant. 1.** female.

Ma·lé (mä′lē), *n.* a city in and the capital of the Maldive Islands. 8515 (1963).

male-, a prefix meaning "evil," occurring in loan words from Latin: *malediction.* Cf. **mal-.** [< L; see MAL-]

ma·le·ate (mə lē′it), *n. Chem.* a salt or ester of maleic acid. [MALE(IC ACID) + -ATE[2]]

male·ber·ry (māl′ber′ē, -bə rē), *n., pl.* **-ries.** See **swamp andromeda.** [< L *māl(us)* apple tree + BERRY]

Male·branche (mal brānsh′), *n.* **Ni·co·las de** (nē kô lä′ də), 1638–1715, French philosopher.

mal·e·dict (mal′i dikt), *adj. Archaic.* accursed. [< L *maledict(us)* abused, slandered (LL: accursed), ptp. of *maledīcere.* See MALEDICTION]

mal·e·dic·tion (mal′i dik′shən), *n.* **1.** a curse; the utterance of a curse; imprecation. **2.** slander. [late ME *malediccion* < L *maledictiōn-* (s. of *maledictiō*) slander (LL: curse). See MALE-, DICTION] —**mal′e·dic′tive, mal·e·dic·to·ry** (mal′i dik′tə rē), *adj.*

—**Syn. 1.** damning, execration. —**Ant. 1.** benediction.

ma·lee (mä′lē), *n. Anglo-Indian.* mali.

mal·e·fac·tion (mal′ə fak′shən), *n.* an evil deed; crime; wrongdoing. [MALEFACT(OR) + -ION]

mal·e·fac·tor (mal′ə fak′tər), *n.* **1.** a person who violates the law; criminal. **2.** a person who does evil, esp. toward another: *People who waste our time are malefactors, however unwitting.* Also, *referring to a woman,* **mal·e·fac·tress** (mal′ə fak′tris). [late ME *malefactour* < L *malefactor,* equiv. to *malefact(um)* evil deed (see MALE-, FACT) + *-or* -OR[2]]

—**Syn. 1.** felon, culprit. **2.** offender. —**Ant. 1, 2.** benefactor.

male′ fern′, a fern, *Dryopteris Filix-mas,* of Europe and North America, that yields aspidium.

ma·lef·ic (mə lef′ik), *adj.* productive of evil; malign; doing harm; baneful: *a malefic spell.* [< L *maleficus*) evil-doing, wicked. See MALE-, -FIC]

ma·lef·i·cence (mə lef′i səns), *n.* **1.** the doing of evil or harm: *the maleficence of thieves.* **2.** maleficent or harmful character: *the maleficence of a slum environment.* [< L *maleficentia.* See MALEFIC, -ENCE]

ma·lef·i·cent (mə lef′i sənt), *adj.* doing evil or harm; harmfully malicious: *maleficent destroyers of reputations.* [back formation from L *maleficentia* MALEFICENCE; see -ENT]

ma·le′ic ac′id (mə lē′ik), *Chem.* a colorless, crystalline, water-soluble solid, HOOCCH=CHCOOH, isomeric with fumaric acid, having an astringent, repulsive taste and faint acidulous odor: used in the manufacture of synthetic resins, the dyeing and finishing of textiles, and as a preservative for fats and oils. [< F *maléique*, alter. of *malique* MALIC]

mal·e·mute (mal′ə myōōt′), *n.* (*sometimes cap.*) See **Alaskan malamute.**

Ma·len·kov (mä′lən kôf′; *Russ.* mä len kôf′), *n.* **Ge·or·gi Ma·xi·mi·lia·no·vich** (gā ôr′gi mä′ksi milyä′no vich), born 1902, Russian political leader: premier of the Soviet Union 1953–55.

mal·en·ten·du (mal än tän dy′), *adj.*, *n.*, *pl.* **-dus** (-dy′). *French.* —*adj.* **1.** misunderstood; misapprehended. —*n.* **2.** a misunderstanding; mistake.

ma·lev·o·lence (mə lev′ə ləns), *n.* state or feeling of being malevolent; ill will; malice; hatred. [< L *malevolentia* (see MALEVOLENT, -ENCE); r. late ME *malivolence* < MF]
—**Syn.** maliciousness, spite, spitefulness, grudge, venom. MALEVOLENCE, MALIGNITY, RANCOR suggest the wishing of harm to others. MALEVOLENCE is a smoldering ill will: *a vindictive malevolence in his expression.* MALIGNITY is a deep-seated and virulent disposition to injure; it is more dangerous than MALEVOLENCE, because it is not only more completely concealed but it often instigates harmful acts: *The malignity of his nature was shocking.* RANCOR is a lasting, corrosive, and implacable hatred and resentment.

ma·lev·o·lent (mə lev′ə lənt), *adj.* **1.** wishing evil to another or others; showing ill will; ill-disposed; vindictive; malicious: *His failures made him malevolent toward the successful.* **2.** evil; harmful; injurious: *He had malevolent inclinations to destroy the happiness of others.* **3.** *Astrol.* evil or malign in influence. [< L *malevolent-* (s. of *malevolēns*) ill-disposed, spiteful, equiv. to *male-* MALE- + *volent-* (s. of *volēns*) wishing, prp. of *velle;* see WILL[1], -ENT] —**ma·lev′o·lent·ly,** *adv.*

mal·fea·sance (mal fē′zəns), *n.* *Law.* the performance by a public official of an act that is legally unjustified, harmful or contrary to law; wrongdoing (used esp. of an act in violation of a public trust). Cf. **misfeasance** (def. 2), **nonfeasance.** [earlier *malefeasance.* See MALE-, FEASANCE] —**mal·fea′sant,** *adj.*, *n.*

mal·for·ma·tion (mal′fôr mā′shən), *n.* faulty or anomalous formation or structure, esp. in a living body: *malformation of the teeth.* [MAL- + FORMATION]

mal·formed (mal fôrmd′), *adj.* faultily formed. [MAL- + FORMED]

mal·func·tion (mal fungk′shən), *n.* **1.** failure to function properly: *a malfunction of the liver.* —*v.i.* **2.** to fail to function properly. [MAL- + FUNCTION]

mal·gré (mal grā′), *prep.* *French.* despite.

mal·gré lui (mal grā lwē′), *French.* in spite of himself; despite his action or intent: *He is likable* malgré lui.

Mal·herbe (mal erb′), *n.* **Fran·çois de** (frän swa′ də), 1555–1628, French poet and critic.

ma·li (mä′lē), *n.* *Anglo-Indian.* a native boy or man employed as a household gardener. Also, **malee, malie.** [< Hindi *mālī* < Skt *mālika*]

Ma·li (mä′lē), *n.* **Republic of,** a republic in W Africa: a member of the French Community; formerly a territory of France. 4,394,000 (est. 1963); 463,500 sq. mi. *Cap.:* Bamako. Formerly, **French Sudan.**

Ma·li·bran (mä′li brän′; *Fr.* mä lē brän′; *Sp.* mä′lē vrän′), *n.* **Ma·ri·a Fe·li·ci·ta** (*Sp.* mä rē′ä fe′lē thē′tä), 1808–36, mezzo-contralto, born in France.

mal·ic (mal′ik, mā′lik), *adj.* **1.** pertaining to or derived from apples. **2.** *Chem.* of or derived from malic acid. [< F *malique* < L *māl(um)* apple + F *-ique* -IC]

mal′ic ac′id, *Chem.* a colorless, crystalline, water-soluble solid, $HOOCCH_2CH(OH)COOH$, occurring in apples and other fruits, and as an intermediate in animal metabolism.

mal·ice (mal′is), *n.* **1.** desire to inflict injury or suffering on another, esp. when based on deep-seated meanness: *the malice and spite of a lifelong enemy.* **2.** *Law.* evil intent on the part of one who commits a wrongful act injurious to others. [ME < OF < L *malitia.* See MAL-, -ICE]
—**Syn. 1.** ill will, spite, spitefulness; animosity, enmity; malevolence; venom, hate, hatred; bitterness, rancor. See **grudge.** —**Ant. 1.** benevolence, good will.

mal′ice afore′thought, *Law.* a predetermination to commit an unlawful act without just cause or provocation (applied chiefly to cases of first-degree murder). Also called **mal′ice prepense′.**

ma·li·cious (mə lish′əs), *adj.* **1.** full of, characterized by, or showing malice; malevolent; spiteful: *malicious gossip.* **2.** *Law.* motivated by vicious, wanton, or mischievous purposes. [ME *malicius* < OF < L *malitiōs(us).* See MALICE, -OUS] —**ma·li′cious·ly,** *adv.* —**ma·li′cious·ness,** *n.*

ma·lie (mä′lē), *n.* *Anglo-Indian.* mali.

ma·lign (mə līn′), *v.t.* **1.** to speak harmful untruths about; speak evil of; slander; defame: *to malign an honorable man.* —*adj.* **2.** evil in effect; pernicious; baleful; injurious: *The gloomy house had a malign influence upon his spirits.* **3.** having or showing an evil disposition; malevolent; malicious. [ME *maligne* < MF < L *malign(us).* See MAL-, BENIGN] —**ma·lign′er,** *n.* —**ma·lign′ly,** *adv.*
—**Syn. 1.** libel, calumniate; disparage; revile, abuse, vilify. **2.** baneful. —**Ant. 1.** praise.

ma·lig·nan·cy (mə lig′nən sē), *n.*, *pl.* **-cies. 1.** quality or condition of being malignant: *the malignancy of a bad climate.* **2.** malignant character, behavior, action, or the like: *the malignancies of war.* Also, **ma·lig′nance.** [MALIGN(ANT) + -ANCY]

ma·lig·nant (mə lig′nənt), *adj.* **1.** disposed to cause harm, suffering, or distress deliberately; feeling or showing ill will or hatred: *He seemed to be dogged by a malignant destiny.* **2.** very dangerous; harmful in influence or effect. **3.** *Pathol.* deadly; tending to produce death, as a disease, tumor, etc. [< LL *malignant-* (s. of *malignāns*), prp. of *malignāre* to act maliciously. See MALIGN, -ANT] —**ma·lig′nant·ly,** *adv.*
—**Syn. 1.** spiteful, malevolent. **2.** perilous, hurtful, pernicious. —**Ant. 1-3.** benign.

malig′nant hyperten′sion, *Pathol.* abnormally high blood pressure that suddenly occurs and rapidly progresses, causing damage to blood vessels in the kidneys, the eyes, etc.

ma·lig·ni·ty (mə lig′ni tē), *n.*, *pl.* **-ties. 1.** state or character of being malign; malevolence; intense ill will; spite. **2.** a malignant feeling, action, etc. [ME *malignitee* < L *malignitās.* See MALIGN, -ITY]
—**Syn. 1.** See **malevolence.**

ma·li·hi·ni (mä′lē hē′nē), *n.*, *pl.* **-hi·nis.** *Hawaiian.* a newcomer to Hawaii.

Ma·lin·da (mə lin′də), *n.* a girl's given name. Also, **Melinda.**

Ma·lines (ma lēn′; *Eng.* mə lēnz′), *n.* French name of **Mechlin.**

ma·lines (mə lēn′; *Fr.* ma lēn′), *n.* **1.** Also, **ma·line′.** a delicate net resembling tulle, originally made by hand in the town of Mechlin, Belgium. **2.** See **Mechlin lace.** [after MALINES]

ma·lin·ger (mə ling′gər), *v.i.* to pretend illness, esp. in order to avoid duty, work, etc. [< F *malingre* sickly, ailing, equiv. to *mal* bad(ly) + OF *heingre* haggard (perh. < Gmc)] —**ma·lin′ger·er,** *n.*

Ma·li·nov·sky (mä′li nôf′ski), *n.* **Ro·di·on Ya·kov·le·vich** (rô′dē on yä′kov le vich), 1898–1967, Russian army officer: minister of defense of the U.S.S.R. since 1957.

Ma·li·now·ski (mä′li nôf′skē), *n.* **Bro·ni·slaw Kas·per** (brô nē′släf käs′pər), 1884–1942, Polish anthropologist in the U.S.

Ma·li·pie·ro (mä′lē pye′rô), *n.* **Gian Fran·ces·co** (jän frän che′skô), born 1882, Italian composer.

mal·i·son (mal′i zən, -sən), *n.* *Archaic.* a curse. [ME *maliso(u)n* < OF *maleison* < L *maledictiōn-* (s. of *maledictiō*) MALEDICTION]

mal·kin (mô′kin, môl′-, mal′-), *n.* *Brit. Dial.* **1.** an untidy or lewd woman; slattern. **2.** a maid, female servant, or any woman of the lower class. **3.** a scarecrow, ragged puppet, or grotesque effigy. **4.** a mop, esp. one made from a bundle of rags and used to clean out a baker's oven. **5.** a cat. **6.** a hare. Also, **mawkin.** [ME: lit., little Molly, equiv. to *Mal,* var. of *Molly* Mary; see -KIN]

mall (môl, mäl, mal), *n.* **1.** a large area, usually lined with shade trees and shrubbery, used as a public walk or promenade. **2.** a strip of land, usually planted or paved, separating lanes of opposite traffic on highways, boulevards, etc. **3.** the mallet used in the game of pall-mall. **4.** the game of pall-mall. **5.** the place or alley where pall-mall was played. **6.** maul. —*v.t.* **7.** to maul. [contr. of PALL-MALL]

mal·lan·ders (mal′ən dərz), *n.* (*construed as sing.*) *Vet. Pathol.* malanders.

mal·lard (mal′ərd), *n.*, *pl.* **-lards,** (*esp. collectively*) **-lard. 1.** a common, almost cosmopolitan, wild duck, *Anas platyrhynchos,* from which the domestic ducks descended. **2.** a male of this species. [ME < MF, OF *mallart,* ? < OHG *Madelhart,* thought to be name given to duck as character in fable]

Mallard (Length 2 ft.)

Mal·lar·mé (ma lar mā′), *n.* **Sté·phane** (stā fan′), 1842–1898, French poet.

mal·le·a·ble (mal′ē ə bəl), *adj.* **1.** capable of being extended or shaped by hammering or by pressure from rollers. **2.** adaptable or tractable: *the malleable mind of a child.* [ME *malliable* < ML *malleābil(is),* equiv. to *malle(āre)* (to) hammer (deriv. of L *malleus* hammer) + *-ābilis* -ABLE] —**mal′le·a·bil′i·ty, mal′le·a·ble·ness,** *n.*

mal′leable cast′ i′ron, white cast iron that has been malleablized.

mal′leable i′ron, 1. See **malleable cast iron. 2.** *U.S.* See **wrought iron.**

mal·le·a·blize (mal′ē ə blīz′), *v.t.*, **-blized, -bliz·ing.** to make (white cast iron) malleable by annealing it so that the carbon is transformed to graphite or removed completely. [MALLEABLE + -IZE]

mal·le·ate (mal′ē āt′), *v.t.*, **-at·ed, -at·ing.** to beat or shape with a hammer, as in metalworking. [< LL *malleāt(us)* wrought with a hammer, equiv. to L *malle(us)* hammer + *-ātus* -ATE[1]] —**mal′le·a′tion,** *n.*

Mal·le Bab·be (mä′lə bä′bə; *Du.* mä′le bä′be), a painting (c1650) by Frans Hals.

mal·lee (mal′ē), *n.* **1.** any of various dwarf Australian eucalyptuses, as *Eucalyptus dumosa* and *E. oleosa,* which sometimes form large tracts of brushwood. **2.** the brushwood itself. [< native Austral]

mal·le·muck (mal′ə muk′), *n.* *Dial.* any of various oceanic birds, as the fulmar or albatross. [< D *mallemok,* equiv. to *malle,* var. of *mal* foolish + *mok* < Norw *måk* MEW[2]]

mal·len·ders (mal′ən dərz), *n.* (*construed as sing.*) *Vet. Pathol.* malanders.

mal·le·o·lar (mə lē′ə lər), *adj.* *Anat.* pertaining to a malleolus. [MALLEOL(US) + -AR[1]]

mal·le·o·lus (mə lē′ə ləs), *n.*, *pl.* **-li** (-lī′). *Anat.* the bony protuberance on either side of the ankle, at the lower end of the fibula or of the tibula. [< L: small hammer, mallet, equiv. to *malle(us)* hammer + *-olus* dim. suffix]

mal·let (mal′it), *n.* **1.** a hammerlike tool with a head commonly of wood but occasionally of rawhide, plastic, etc., used for driving any tool with a wooden handle, as a chisel. **2.** the wooden implement used to strike the balls in croquet. **3.** *Polo.* the long-handled stick, or club, used to drive the ball. [late ME *maillet* < MF, equiv. to *mail* MAUL + *-et* -ET]

A, Mallet; B, Stone cutter's mallet

Mal·let (mal′it), *n.* a crater in the fourth quadrant of the face of the moon: about 28 miles in diameter.

mal·le·us (mal′ē əs), *n.*, *pl.* **mal·le·i** (mal′ē ī′). *Anat.* the outermost of a chain of three small bones in the middle ear of man and other mammals. Cf. **incus** (def. 1), **stapes.** See diag. under **ear.** [< L: hammer]

Mal·lia (mäl yä′), *n.* a town in E Crete: site of an excavated Minoan palace.

Ma·llor·ca (mä lyôr′kä, -yôr′-; *Eng.* mä yôr′kə), *n.* Spanish name of **Majorca.**

Mal·lo·ry (mal′ə rē), *n.* **Stephen Russell,** 1813?–73, U.S. lawyer and politician.

mal·low (mal′ō), *n.* **1.** any herb of the genus *Malva,* having angularly lobed or dissected leaves and purple, pink, or white flowers. **2.** any malvaceous plant, as the marsh mallow. [ME *malue,* OE *mealwe* < L *malva*]

mal′low rose′, a rose mallow of the genus *Hibiscus.*

malm (mäm), *n.* **1.** a kind of soft, friable limestone. **2.** a chalk-bearing soil of the southeastern part of England. **3.** an artificial mixture of chalk and clay for making into bricks. [ME *malme,* OE *mealm-* (in *mealmiht* sandy, *mealmstān* sandstone); c. Goth *malma* sand, Icel *malmr* metal (in granular form); akin to OS, OHG *melm* dust. See MEAL[2]]

Mal·mé·dy (mal mā dē′), *n.* See **Eupen and Malmédy.**

Malmes·bur·y (mämz′ber ē, -bə rē), *n.* **William of.** See **William of Malmesbury.**

Malm·ö (mal′mō; *Swed.* mälm′œ′), *n.* a seaport in S Sweden, on the sound opposite Copenhagen, Denmark. 245,565 (1965).

malm·sey (mäm′zē), *n.* a strong, sweet wine with a strong flavor, originally made in Greece, but now in Madeira. [late ME *malmesye* < MLG << *Monemvasia* Greek town where it was originally produced]

mal·nu·tri·tion (mal′nōō trish′ən, -nyōō-), *n.* lack of proper nutrition; inadequate or unbalanced nutrition. [MAL- + NUTRITION]

mal·oc·clu·sion (mal′ə klōō′zhən), *n.* *Dentistry.* faulty occlusion; irregular contact of opposing teeth in the upper and lower jaws. [MAL- + OCCLUSION] —**mal′oc·clud′ed,** *adj.*

mal·o·dor (mal ō′dər), *n.* an unpleasant or offensive odor; stench. [MAL- + ODOR]

mal·o·dor·ous (mal ō′dər əs), *adj.* having an unpleasant or offensive odor; smelling bad: *a malodorous swamp.* [MAL- + ODOROUS] —**mal·o′dor·ous·ly,** *adv.* —**mal·o′dor·ous·ness,** *n.*

Ma·lone (mə lōn′), *n.* **1. Edmond,** 1741–1812, Irish literary critic and Shakespearean scholar. **2.** a town in N New York. 8737 (1960).

ma·lo·nic (mə lō′nik, -lon′ik), *adj.* *Chem.* of or derived from malonic acid; propanedioic. [< F *malonique,* alter. of *malique* MALIC]

malo′nic ac′id, *Chem.* a white, crystalline, water-soluble, dibasic acid, $CH_2(COOH)_2$, easily decomposed by heat: used chiefly as an intermediate in the synthesis of barbiturates.

malo′nic es′ter, *Chem.* See **ethyl malonate.**

mal·o·nyl (mal′ə nil, -nēl′), *adj.* *Chem.* containing the malonyl group. [MALON(IC) + -YL]

mal′onyl group′, *Chem.* the bivalent group, $-OCCH_2CO-$, derived from malonic acid. Also called **mal′onyl rad′ical.**

mal·o·nyl·u·re·a (mal′ə nil yōō rē′ə, -yōōr′ē ə, -nēl-), *n.* *Chem.* See **barbituric acid.** [MALONYL + UREA]

Mal·o·ry (mal′ə rē), *n.* **Sir Thomas,** c1400–71, English author.

mal·pa·is (mäl′pä ēs′), *n.* *Southern U.S.* an extensive area covered with basaltic lava. [< Sp *mal país* bad country]

Mal·pert (mäl′pərt), *n.* a walled plain in the third quadrant of the face of the moon, in the libration area and near the South Pole: about 35 miles in diameter.

Mal·pi·ghi (mäl pē′gē), *n.* **Mar·cel·lo** (mär chel′lô), 1628–94, Italian anatomist. —**Mal·pigh·i·an** (mal pig′ē ən), *adj.*

mal·pigh·i·a·ceous (mal pig′ē ā′shəs), *adj.* belonging or pertaining to the *Malpighiaceae,* a large family of tropical plants, certain of which are cultivated for ornamental purposes. [< NL *Malpighi(a)* the typical genus (named after MALPIGHI) + -ACEOUS]

Malpigh′ian cor′puscle, *Anat.* **1.** Also called **Malpigh′ian bod′y.** the structure at the beginning of a vertebrate nephron, consisting of a glomerulus and its surrounding Bowman's capsule. **2.** a compact aggregation of lymphoid tissue surrounding an arteriole in the spleen.

Malpigh′ian lay′er, *Anat.* the deep, germinative layer of the epidermis.

Malpigh′ian tube′, one of a group of long, slender excretory tubules at the anterior end of the hindgut in insects and other terrestrial arthropods. Also called **Malpigh′ian tu′bule, Malpigh′ian ves′sel.**

Malpigh′ian tuft′, glomerulus (def. 2).

mal·po·si·tion (mal′pə zish′ən), *n.* *Pathol.* faulty or wrong position, esp. of a part or organ of the body or of a fetus in the uterus. [MAL- + POSITION]

mal·prac·tice (mal prak′tis), *n.* **1.** failure of a professional person to render proper services through reprehensible ignorance or negligence, or through criminal intent, esp. when injury or loss follows: *the malpractice of a physician.* **2.** any improper, negligent practice; misconduct or misuse: *the malpractice of those in positions of influence; the malpractice of language.* [MAL- + PRACTICE] —**mal·prac·ti·tion·er** (mal′prak tish′ə nər), *n.*

Mal·raux (mal rō′), *n.* **An·dré** (än drā′), born 1901, French novelist, critic, and politician.

M.A.L.S., 1. Master of Arts in Liberal Studies. **2.** Master of Arts in Library Science.

malt (môlt), *n.* **1.** germinated grain, usually barley, used in brewing and distilling. **2.** a beverage, as beer or ale, produced from malt by fermentation. **3.** whisky, as Scotch, that is distilled entirely from malted barley. **4.** See **malted milk** (def. 2). —*v.t.* **5.** to convert (grain) into malt. **6.** to treat or mix with malt, malt extract, etc. **7.** to make (liquor) with malt. —*v.i.* **8.** to become malt. **9.** to produce malt from grain. [ME; OE *mealt;* c. Icel *malt,* G *Malz;* akin to MELT]

Mal·ta (môl′tə), *n.* **1.** an island in the Mediterranean between Sicily and Africa: British naval station. 302,144 (est. 1962); 95 sq. mi. **2.** a former British colony consisting of this island and two small adjacent islands: now an independent sovereign state and a member of the British Commonwealth. 329,326 (est. 1962); 122 sq. mi. *Cap.:* Valletta.

Mal′ta fe′ver, *Pathol.* brucellosis.

malt·ase (môl′tās), *n. Biochem.* an enzyme that converts maltose into dextrose and causes similar cleavage of many other glucosides. [MALT + -ASE]

malt·ed (môl′tid), *n.* See **malted milk.** [MALT + -ED[3]]

malt′ed milk′, **1.** a soluble powder made of dehydrated milk and malted cereals. **2.** a beverage made by dissolving this powder, usually in milk, often with ice cream and flavoring added.

Mal·tese (môl tēz′, -tēs′), *adj., n., pl.* **-tese.** —*adj.* **1.** of or pertaining to Malta, its people, or their language. —*n.* **2.** a native or inhabitant of Malta. **3.** the Arabic dialect spoken in Malta. [MALT(A) + -ESE]

Mal′tese cat′, a bluish-gray variety of the domestic cat.

Mal′tese cross′, **1.** a cross having four equal arms that expand in width outward. See illus. under **cross. 2.** See **scarlet lychnis.**

Mal′tese dog′, one of a breed of toy dogs having a long, straight, silky, white coat.

malt′ ex′tract, a sweet, gummy substance derived from an infusion of malt.

mal·tha (mal′thə), *n.* **1.** a liquid bitumen used in ancient times as a mortar or waterproofing agent. **2.** any of various natural mixtures of hydrocarbons, as ozocerite. **3.** a viscous mineral liquid or semiliquid bitumen; a mineral tar. [< Gk: mixed wax and pitch; r. late ME *malthe*]

mal·thene (mal′thēn), *n. Chem.* petrolene. [MALTH(A) + -ENE]

Mal·thon (mal′thən), *n.* a boy's given name.

Mal·thus (mal′thəs), *n.* **Thomas Robert,** 1766–1834, English economist and clergyman.

Mal·thu·si·an (mal thōō′zē ən), *adj.* **1.** of or pertaining to the theories of T. R. Malthus, which state that population tends to increase faster, at a geometrical ratio, than the means of subsistence, which increases at an arithmetical ratio, and that this will result in an inadequate supply of the goods supporting life, unless war, famine, or disease reduce the population, or the increase of population is checked by sexual restraint. —*n.* **2.** a follower of Malthus. [MALTHUS + -IAN] —**Mal·thu′si·an·ism,** *n.*

malt′ liq′uor, an alcoholic beverage, as beer, fermented from malt.

malt·ol (môl′tōl, -tôl, -tol), *n. Chem.* a crystalline compound, $C_6H_6O_3$, obtained from larch bark, pine needles, chicory, or roasted malt, used for enhancing flavors and aromas, as in foods, wines, and perfumes. Also called **larixinic acid.** [MALT + -OL[1]]

malt·ose (môl′tōs), *n. Chem.* a white, crystalline, water-soluble sugar, $C_{12}H_{22}O_{11}·H_2O$, formed by the action of diatase, esp. from malt, on starch: used chiefly as a nutrient, as a sweetener, and in culture media. Also called **malt′ sug′ar, mal·to·bi·ose** (môl′tō bī′ōs). [MALT + -OSE[2]]

mal·treat (mal trēt′), *v.t.* to treat badly; handle roughly; abuse: *to maltreat a prisoner.* [earlier *maltrait* < F *maltrait(er).* See MAL-, TREAT] —**mal·treat′er,** *n.* —**mal·treat′ment,** *n.*
—**Syn.** mistreat, injure.

malt·ster (môlt′stər), *n.* a maker of or dealer in malt. [ME *malt(e)stere.* See MALT, -STER]

malt·y (môl′tē), *adj.,* **malt·i·er, malt·i·est.** of, like, or containing malt. [MALT + -Y[1]] —**malt′i·ness,** *n.*

Ma·lus′ law′ (mə lōōs′; *Fr.* MA LYS′), *Optics.* the law that the intensity of a beam of plane-polarized light after passing through a rotatable polarizer varies as the square of the cosine of the angle through which the polarizer is rotated from the position that gives maximum intensity. Also called **law of Malus, Malus′ co′sine-squared law′** (kō′sīn skwârd′). [named after E. L. *Malus* (1775–1812), French physicist]

Mal·va (mal′və), *n.* a girl's given name.

mal·va·ceous (mal vā′shəs), *adj.* belonging to the *Malvaceae,* or mallow family of plants, comprising the abutilon, althea, hollyhock, okra, cotton plant, etc. [< L *malvāceus.* See MALLOW, -ACEOUS]

mal·va·si·a (mal′və sē′ə), *n.* a sweet grape from which malmsey wine is made. [< It, for *Monemvasia.* See MALMSEY] —**mal′va·si′an,** *adj.*

Mal·vern (môl′vərn, mô′- *for 1;* mal′vərn *for 2*), *n.* **1.** an urban area in W Worcestershire, in W England, SW of Birmingham: comprises several small towns; mineral springs. 24,373 (1961). **2.** a town in central Arkansas. 9566 (1960).

Mal·verne (mal′vərn), *n.* a town on SW Long Island, in SE New York. 9968 (1960).

Mal′vern Hill′ (mal′vərn), a plateau in E Virginia, SE of Richmond: battle 1862.

Mal′vern Hills′ (môl′vərn, mô′-), a range of hills in W England, between Worchestershire and Herefordshire: highest point, 1395 ft.

mal·ver·sa·tion (mal′vər sā′shən), *n. Chiefly Law.* improper or corrupt behavior in office, esp. in public office. [< MF, equiv. to *malvers(er)* (to) embezzle (< L *male versārī* to behave badly; see MAL-, REVERSE) + *-ation* -ATION]

Mal·vine (mal′vīn, -vēn), *n.* a girl's given name. Also, **Mal·vi·na** (mal vī′nə, -vē′-).

mal·voi·sie (mal′voi zē, -və-), *n.* **1.** malmsey wine. **2.** the malvasia grape. [< F; r. ME *malvesie* < MF < It *malvasia.* See MALMSEY]

ma·ma (mä′mə, mə mä′), *n. Informal.* mamma[1].

Ma·mal·la·pur·am (mə mä′lə pōōr′əm), *n.* Mahabalipuram.

Ma·mar·o·neck (mə mar′ə nek′), *n.* a city in SE New York. 17,673 (1960).

ma′ma's boy′. See **mother's boy.**

mam·ba (mäm′bä), *n.* any of several long, slender, arboreal snakes of the genus *Dendroaspis,* of central and southern Africa, the bite of which often causes death. [< SAfr (Kaffir) *m'namba*]

mam·bo (mäm′bō), *n., pl.* **-bos,** *v.* —*n.* **1.** a fast ballroom dance of Haitian origin, rhythmically similar to the rumba and cha-cha but having a more complex pattern of steps. —*v.i.* **2.** to dance the mambo. [prob. < Creole of Hispaniola]

Mame (mām), *n.* a girl's given name. Also, **Mayme.**

Mam·e·luke (mam′ə lōōk′), *n.* **1.** a member of a military class, originally composed of slaves, that seized control of the Egyptian sultanate in 1250, ruled until 1517, and remained powerful until massacred or dispersed by Mehemet Ali in 1811. **2.** (*l.c.*) (in Muslim countries) a slave. [< Ar *mamlūk,* lit., slave, n. use of ptp. of *malaka* to possess]

Ma·mers (mā′mərz), *n. Rom. Legend.* Mars.

ma·mey (mä mā′, -mē′), *n.* mammee.

Ma·mie (mā′mē), *n.* a girl's given name, form of **Mary.**

mam·ma[1] (mä′mə, mə mä′), *n.* **1.** *Informal.* mother. **2.** *Slang.* a sexually attractive, usually mature woman. Also, **mama.** [nursery word based on baby's meaningless syllable *ma* in repetitive babbling. Cf. F *maman,* L *mamma,* Gk *mâmmē,* Russ, Lith *mama*]

mam·ma[2] (mam′ə), *n., pl.* **mam·mae** (mam′ē) for 1; **mam·ma** for 2. **1.** *Anat., Zool.* the organ, characteristic of mammals, which in the female secretes milk; a breast or udder. **2.** (*construed as pl.*) hanging, breastlike protuberances on the under surface of a cloud. [< L: breast, teat (whence OE *mamme* teat). See MAMMA[1]]

mam·mal (mam′əl), *n.* any vertebrate of the class *Mammalia* that feeds its young with milk from the female mammary glands, that has the body more or less covered with hair, and that, with the exception of the monotremes, brings forth living young rather than eggs. [back formation from MAMMALIA] —**mam′mal-like′,** *adj.*

Mam·ma·li·a (mə mā′lē ə, -māl′yə), *n.* the class comprising the mammals. [< NL, n. use of neut. pl. of LL *mammālis* of the breast. See MAMMA[2], -AL[1]]

mam·ma·li·an (mə mā′lē ən, -māl′yən), *n.* **1.** an animal of the class *Mammalia;* mammal. —*adj.* **2.** belonging or pertaining to the class *Mammalia;* characteristic of mammals. [MAMMALI(A) + -AN] —**mam·mal·i·ty** (mə mal′i tē), *n.*

mam·mal·o·gy (mə mal′ə jē), *n.* the science dealing with mammals. [MAMMAL + -LOGY] —**mam·ma·log·i·cal** (mam′ə loj′i kəl), *adj.* —**mam·mal′o·gist,** *n.*

mam·ma·ry (mam′ə rē), *adj. Anat., Zool.* of or pertaining to the mamma or breast; mammalike. [MAMM(A)[2] + -ARY]

mam′ma's boy′. See **mother's boy.**

mam·ma·to·cu·mu·lus (mə mā′tō kyōō′myə ləs), *n., pl.* **-lus.** *Meteorol. Obs.* mamma[2] (def. 2). [< NL, equiv. to L *mammāt(us)* of, like the breast (*mamm(a)* MAMMA[2] + *-ātus* -ATE[1]) + *-o-* -O- + *cumulus* CUMULUS]

mam·mec·to·my (mə mek′tə mē), *n., pl.* **-mies.** *Surg.* mastectomy [MAMM(A)[2] + -ECTOMY]

mam·mee (ma mā′, -mē′), *n.* **1.** a tall, tropical American tree, *Mammea americana,* having thick, glossy leaves and white flowers. **2.** the usually round, edible fruit of this tree, having a russet-colored rind and yellow, juicy flesh. **3.** the sapodilla. **4.** See **marmalade tree.** Also, **mamey.** Also called **mammee′ ap′ple** (for defs. 1, 2). [< Sp *mamey,* perh. < Taino]

mam·mer (mam′ər), *v.i. Brit. Dial.* **1.** to stammer; mutter; falter. **2.** to hesitate; be undecided; waver in determination. [late ME *mamere.* See MUMBLE, -ER[6]]

mam·met (mam′it), *n.* maumet.

mam·mif·er·ous (ma mif′ər əs), *adj.* having mammae; mammalian. [MAMM(A)[2] + -I- + -FEROUS]

mam·mil·la (ma mil′ə), *n., pl.* **-mil·lae** (-mil′ē). **1.** *Anat.* the nipple of the mamma, or breast. **2.** any nipplelike process or protuberance. [< L: breast, teat, dim. of *mamma* MAMMA[2]]

mam·mil·lar·y (mam′ə ler′ē), *adj.* of, pertaining to, or resembling a mammilla [MAMMILL(A) + -ARY]

mam·mil·late (mam′ə lāt′), *adj.* having a mammilla or mammillae. Also, **mam′mil·lat′ed.** [< LL *mammillāt(us).* See MAMMILLA, -ATE[1]] —**mam′mil·la′tion,** *n.*

mam·mock (mam′ək), *Brit. Dial.* —*n.* **1.** a fragment; scrap. —*v.t.* **2.** to break, tear, or cut into fragments; shred. [?]

mam·mo·gram (mam′ə gram′), *n.* an x-ray photograph obtained by mammography. [MAMM(A)[2] + -O- + -GRAM]

mam·mog·ra·phy (ma mog′rə fē), *n.* x-ray photography of the breast, esp. for early detection of cancer. [MAMM(A)[2] + -O- + -GRAPHY] —**mam·mo·graph·ic** (mam′ə graf′ik), *adj.*

mam·mon (mam′ən), *n.* **1.** *New Testament.* riches or material wealth. Matt. 6:24; Luke 16:9,11,13. **2.** (*cap.*) a personification of riches as an evil spirit or deity. [ME *mammona* < LL < Gk *mam(m)ōnâs* < Aram *māmōnā* riches] —**mam′mon·ish,** *adj.*

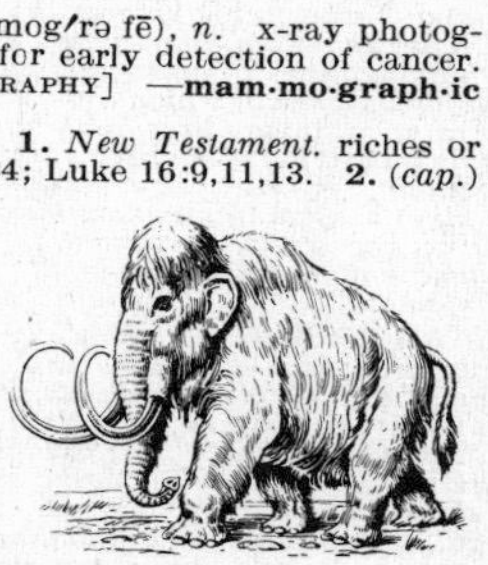

mam·mon·ism (mam′ə niz′əm), *n.* the greedy pursuit of riches. [MAMMON + -ISM] —**mam′mon·ist, mam′mon·ite′,** *n.* —**mam′mon·is′tic,** *adj.*

Mammoth, *Mammuthus primigenius* (9 ft. high at shoulder; tusks to 16 ft.)

mam·moth (mam′əth), *n.* **1.** any large, elephantlike mammal of the extinct genus *Mammuthus,* from the Pleistocene epoch, having a hairy skin and ridged molar teeth. —*adj.* **2.** huge; enormous; immensely large: *a mammoth organization for selling magazines.* [< Russ *mamot*]
—**Syn. 2.** See **gigantic.**

Mam′moth Cave′, a large limestone cavern in central Kentucky: noted for its onyx formations; now included in Mammoth Cave National Park. 79 sq. mi.

mam·mo·tro·pin (mam′ō trō′pin), *n. Biochem.* luteotropin. [MAMM(A)[2] + -O- + -TROPE + -IN[2]]

mam·mu·la (mam′yə lə), *n., pl.* **-lae** (-lē′). *Zool.* a small nipplelike process or protuberance, as the spinneret of a spider. [< L: little breast. See MAMMA[2], -ULE]

mam·my (mam′ē), *n., pl.* **-mies. 1.** *Informal.* mother. **2.** a Negro woman engaged as a nurse to white children or as a servant to a white family. **3.** *Offensive.* any Negro woman. [MAMM(A)[1] + -Y[2]]

mam′my chair′, *Naut. Slang.* a slinglike device for raising or lowering passengers to and from ships anchored away from the shore in a heavy swell.

ma·mon·cil·lo (mä′mən sē′ō; *Sp.* mä′môn sē′yô), *n., pl.* **-cil·los** (-sē′ōz; *Sp.* -sē′yôs). the genip, *Melicocca bijuga.* [< AmerSp, dim. of *mamón,* ? < Venezuelan native name]

Ma·mo·ré (mä′mô RĀ′), *n.* a river in Bolivia, flowing N to the Beni River on the border of Brazil to form the Madeira River. 700 mi. long.

ma·mo·ri ka·ta·na (mä mōr′ē kə tä′nə, -môr′ē; *Jap.* mä mô′RE kä tä′nä), *pl.* **ma·mo·ri ka·ta·na.** a sword covered with brocaded silk, worn by a son of a samurai until five years old. [< Jap]

Ma·mou (mä mōō′), *n.* a town in central Louisiana. 2978 (1960).

Ma'mun, al- (al′mä mōōn′, -ma-), (*abu-al-'Abbās 'Abdullāh*) A.D. 786–833, caliph of Baghdad 813–833 (son of Harun al-Rashid). Also, **al-Mamoun.**

Ma·mu·ri·us (mə mōōr′ē əs), *n. Rom. Legend.* a smith who made 11 copies of the Ancile, to prevent thieves from recognizing the original.

mam·zer (mom′zər), *n.* **1.** *Slang.* bastard (def. 3a). **2.** a child born of a marriage forbidden in Judaism. Also, **momser, momzer.** [< Yiddish (slang sense) < Heb *mamzēr* (LL *mamzer* rabbinical sense)]

man[1] (man), *n., pl.* **men,** *v.,* **manned, man·ning.** —*n.* **1.** an adult male person, as distinguished from a boy or woman. **2.** an individual, *Homo sapiens,* at the highest level of animal development, characterized esp. by a highly developed brain and the ability to reason abstractly and form articulate speech. **3.** the human individual as representing the species; the human race; mankind: *Man hopes for peace, but he prepares for war.* **4.** a human being; a person (usually used in contexts in which sexual distinctions are not relevant): *When the audience smelled the smoke, it was every man for himself.* **5.** an individual; someone; one (usually prec. by *a*): *to give a man a chance.* **6.** a husband: *man and wife.* **7.** a male follower, subordinate, or employee: *officers and men of the army.* **8.** a male having typically manly qualities or virtues: *Be a man. The army will make a man of you.* **9.** a male servant; a valet. **10.** a term of familiar address to a man; fellow: *Now, now, my good man, please calm down.* **11.** *Slang.* a term of address to a man or woman: *Hey, man, don't you dig that music?* **12.** *Slang.* (used as an interjection to express astonishment, enthusiasm, etc.): *Man! Listen to him blow that horn!* **13.** one of the pieces used in playing certain games, as chess or checkers. **14.** *Hist.* a liegeman; vassal. **15.** *Obs.* manly character or courage. **16. as one man,** in complete accord; unanimously: *They arose as one man to protest the verdict.* **17. be one's own man, a.** to be free from restrictions or control; be independent: *Now that he has a business he is his own man.* **b.** to be in complete command of one's faculties: *After a refreshing nap he was again his own man.* **18. man and boy,** ever since childhood: *He's been working that farm, man and boy, for more than 50 years.* **19. the man,** *Slang.* a person's employer (used esp. by a Negro in referring to a white employer). **20. to a man,** with no exception; everyone; all: *To a man, the members of the team did their best.* [ME; OE *man(n);* c. Goth *manna,* G *Mann,* D *man,* Icel *mathr*] —*v.t.* **21.** to furnish with men, as for service or defense. **22.** to take one's place for service, as at a gun, post, etc.: *to man the ramparts.* **23.** to strengthen, fortify, or brace: *to man oneself for the dangers ahead.* **24.** *Falconry.* to accustom (a hawk) to the presence of men. —*interj.* **25.** *Slang.* an expression of surprise, enthusiasm, or other strong feeling: *Man, what a ball game!* [ME *manne(n),* OE *mannian*] —**man′less,** *adj.* —**man′less·ly,** *adv.* —**man′less·ness,** *n.* —**man′ness,** *n.*

man[2] (män, man; *unstressed* mən), *aux. v. Scot.* maun.

Man (man), *n.* **Isle of,** an island of the British Isles, in the Irish Sea. 48,151 (1961); 227 sq. mi. *Cap.:* Douglas.

-man, a combining form of **man:** *layman; postman.*

Man., 1. Manila. **2.** Manitoba.

man., manual.

ma·na (mä′nä), *n. Anthropol.* a generalized, supernatural force or power, which may be concentrated in objects or persons. [< Polynesian, Melanesian]

Man·a (man′ā), *n.* Mannai.

man′ about town′, a socially active, sophisticated man who frequents fashionable nightclubs, theaters, restaurants, etc.; playboy.

Man·a·bo·zho (man′ə bō′zhō), *n.* the trickster and culture hero of the Ottawa, Chippewa, Potawatomi, and other Central Algonquian tribes.

man·a·cle (man′ə kəl), *n., v.,* **-cled, -cling.** —*n.* **1.** a shackle for the hand; handcuff. **2.** Usually, **manacles.** restraints; checks. —*v.t.* **3.** to handcuff; fetter. **4.** to hamper; restrain: *He was manacled by his inhibitions.* [ME, var. of *manicle* < MF: handcuff < L *manicula* a small hand. See MANUS, -I-, -CLE]

Ma·na·do (mä nä′dō), *n.* Menado.

man·age (man′ij), *v.,* **-aged, -ag·ing.** —*v.t.* **1.** to bring about; succeed in accomplishing: *He managed to see the governor.* **2.** to take charge or care of: *to manage an estate.* **3.** to dominate or influence (a person) by tact, address, or artifice: *She manages the child with exemplary skill.* **4.** to handle, direct, govern, or control in action or use: *He managed the boat efficiently. He managed the plot of the story with inventiveness.* **5.** to wield (a weapon, tool, etc.). **6.** to contrive to bring about, succeed in accomplishing, etc., usually despite hardship or difficulty: *Somehow we must manage the suppression of our baser instincts. He lives well, but I can't understand how he manages it on such a small income.* **7.** to handle or train (a horse) in the exercises of the manège. **8.** *Archaic.* to use sparingly or with judgment, as health, money, etc.; husband. —*v.i.* **9.** to conduct business, commercial affairs, etc.; be in charge: *Who will manage while the boss is away?* **10.** to continue to function, progress, or succeed, usually despite hardship or difficulty; get along: *How will she manage with her husband gone? People thought we would go bankrupt, but we managed.* [earlier *manege* < It *manegg(iare)* (to) handle, train (horses), deriv. of *mano* < L *manus* hand] —**Syn. 1.** arrange, contrive. **4.** guide, conduct, regulate, engineer. See **rule. 5.** handle, manipulate.

man·age·a·ble (man′i jə bəl), *adj.* that can be managed; governable; contrivable; tractable. [MANAGE + -ABLE] —**man′age·a·bil′i·ty, man′age·a·ble·ness,** *n.* —**man′age·a·bly,** *adv.*

man′aged cur′rency, a currency whose value is established and maintained by deliberate governmental action working through national and international financial institutions, in contrast to the quasi-automatic gold standard.

man·age·ment (man′ij mənt), *n.* **1.** act or manner of managing; handling, direction, or control: *a poor management.* **2.** skill in managing; executive ability: *great management and tact.* **3.** the person or persons controlling and directing the affairs of an institution, business, etc.: *a shop labeled, "Under New Management."* **4.** executives collectively, considered as a class (distinguished from *labor*). [MANAGE + -MENT] —**man·age·men·tal** (man′ij men′tᵊl), *adj.*
—**Syn. 1.** regulation, administration; superintendence, care, charge, conduct, guidance, treatment.

man·ag·er (man′i jər), *n.* **1.** a person who manages: *the manager of our track team.* **2.** a person charged with the control or direction of an institution, business, or the like. **3.** a person who controls and manipulates resources and expenditures, as of a household. [MANAGE + -ER[1]] —**man′ag·er·ship′,** *n.*
—**Syn. 1.** administrator, executive, superintendent, supervisor; boss.

man·ag·er·ess (man′i jər is; *Brit.* man′i jə res′), *n.* *Chiefly Brit.* a female manager. [MANAGER + -ESS]

man·a·ge·ri·al (man′i jēr′ē əl), *adj.* pertaining to management or a manager: *managerial functions; the managerial class of society.* [MANAGER + -IAL] —**man′a·ge′ri·al·ly,** *adv.*

man′aging ed′itor, an editor responsible for the editorial functions of a newspaper, magazine, book publishing company, and the like. *Abbr.:* M.E., m.e.

Ma·na·gua (mä nä′gwä), *n.* **1. Lake,** a lake in W Nicaragua. 390 sq. mi. **2.** a city in and the capital of Nicaragua, in the W part, on Lake Managua: almost totally destroyed by an earthquake 1931. 234,600 (1963).

man·ak (man′ak), *n.* a wooden ball fitted with hooks and attached to a rope, used by Eskimos to secure and haul in seals killed offshore. [< Eskimo]

Ma·na·ka·ra (mä′nä kä′rä), *n.* a city on E Madagascar. 12,297 (1960).

man·a·kin (man′ə kin), *n.* **1.** any of several small, songless, passerine birds of the family *Pipridae,* of the warmer parts of America, having usually brilliantly colored plumage. **2.** manikin. [var. of MANIKIN]

Ma·na·la (mä′nə lə), *n.* Tuonela.

Ma·na·ma (*Pers.* ma na′mə, -ma), *n.* a city in and the capital of the Bahrein Islands, on N Bahrein. ab. 28,000. Also called **Al Manamah.**

ma·ña·na (mä nyä′nä; *Eng.* mə nyä′nə), *Spanish.* —*n.* tomorrow; the (indefinite) future. —*adv.* **2.** tomorrow; in the (indefinite) future.

Man′ and Su′perman, a comedy (1903) by G. B. Shaw.

Ma·nan·ja·ry (mä′nän zhär′ē), *n.* a city on E Madagascar. 13,582 (1960).

Ma·nan·nan (mä′nə nän′, man′ə nan′), *n.* *Irish Myth.* the god of the sea and son of Ler.

Ma·náos (mä nous′), *n.* a port in and the capital of Amazonas, in N Brazil, on the Río Negro near its confluence with the Amazon: ab. 1000 mi. from the Atlantic but accessible to some ocean trade. 154,040 (1960). Also, **Manaus.**

man·as (man′əs, mun′-), *n.* *Hinduism, Buddhism.* the rational faculty of the mind. [< Skt: judgment, respect] —**ma·nas·ic** (mə nas′ik), *adj.*

Man·a·squan (man′ə skwon′), *n.* a town in E New Jersey. 4022 (1960).

Ma·nas·sas (mə nas′əs), *n.* a town in NE Virginia: battles of Bull Run 1861, 1862. 3555 (1960).

Manas′sas Park′, a town in N Virginia. 8385 (1960).

Ma·nas·seh (mə nas′ə), *n.* **1.** the first son of Joseph. Gen. 41:51. **2.** the tribe of Israel traditionally descended from him. Gen. 48:14–19. **3.** a king of Judah of the 7th century B.C. II Kings 21. Also, *Douay Bible,* **Ma·nas·ses** (mə nas′ēz).

Ma·nas·site (mə nas′īt), *n.* a member of the tribe of Manasseh. [MANASS(EH) + -ITE[1]]

Ma·nat (mä nät′), *n.* a pre-Islamic Arabian goddess personifying fortune, sometimes considered to be a daughter of Allah.

man-at-arms (man′ət ärmz′), *n., pl.* **men-at-arms. 1.** a soldier. **2.** a heavily armed soldier on horseback.

man·a·tee (man′ə tē′, man′ə tē′), *n.* any of several herbivorous, gregarious sirenians of the genus *Trichechus,* of West Indian, Floridian, and Gulf Coast waters, having two flippers in front and a spoon-shaped tail. [< Sp *manatí* < Carib, but assoc. with L *manātus* provided with hands] —**man·a·toid** (man′ə toid′), *adj.*

Manatee, *Trichechus manatus* (Length 8 to 13 ft.)

Ma·naus (mä nous′), *n.* Manáos.

ma·nav·el·ins (mə nav′ə linz), *n.pl.* *Naut. Slang.* miscellaneous pieces of gear and material. Also, **ma·nav′il·ins.** [?]

Man·a·wy·dan (man′ə wœ′thən; *Eng.* man′ə wid′ən), *n.* *Welsh Legend.* a brother of Bran, Evnissyen, and Branwen, and the second husband of Rhiannon. He rescued Pryderi from enchantments cast upon him by Lloyd.

man·bote (man′bōt), *n.* *Old Eng. Law.* a sum of money paid to a lord whose vassal was murdered. [OE *manbōt.* See MAN[1], BOOT[2]]

manche (mänch), *n.* *Heraldry.* a conventional representation of a sleeve with a flaring end, used as a charge. Also, **maunche, maunch.** [ME < MF < L *manicae* (pl.) long sleeves, gloves, handcuffs, deriv. of *manus* hand. See MANACLE]

Manche (mänsh), *n.* a department in NW France. 446,878 (1962); 2476 sq. mi. *Cap.:* Saint-Lô.

Man·ches·ter (man′ches′tər, -chi stər), *n.* **1.** a city in SE Lancashire, in NW England: connected with the Mersey estuary by a ship canal (35½ mi. long). 661,041 (1961). **2.** a city in S New Hampshire. 88,282 (1960). **3.** a town in central Connecticut. 42,102 (1960). **4.** a town in E Iowa. 4402 (1960). **5.** a town in W Georgia. 4115 (1960). **6.** a town in central Tennessee. 3930 (1960).

Man′chester School′, a school of economists in England in the first half of the 19th century, devoted to free trade and the repeal of the Corn Laws, led by Richard Cobden and John Bright.

Man′chester ter′rier, one of a breed of slender terriers having a short, glossy, black-and-tan coat, raised originally in Manchester, England.

man·chet (man′chit), *n.* **1.** *Archaic.* a kind of white bread made from the finest flour. **2.** *Chiefly Dial.* a piece or small loaf of such bread. [late ME *manchete*]

man·chette (män shet′), *n.* armpad. [< F; dim. of MANCHE]

man-child (man′chīld′), *n., pl.* **men-chil·dren.** a male child; boy; son.

man·chi·neel (man′chə nēl′), *n.* a tropical American, euphorbiaceous tree or shrub, *Hippomane Mancinella,* having a milky, highly caustic, poisonous sap. [earlier *mançanilla* < Sp *manzanilla,* dim. of *manzana* apple << L (*māla*) *Matiāna* (apples) of *Matius* (1st century B.C.), Roman author of a cooking manual]

Man·chu (man chōō′), *n., pl.* **-chus,** (*esp. collectively*) **-chu,** *adj.* —*n.* **1.** a member of a Mongolian people of Manchuria who conquered China in the 17th century and established a dynasty there (**Manchu′ dy′nasty** or **Ch′ing** 1644–1912). **2.** a Tungusic language spoken by the Manchus. —*adj.* **3.** of or pertaining to the Manchus, their country, or their language.

Man·chu·kuo (man′chōō′kwō′; *Chin.* män′jō′kwō′), *n.* a former country (1932–45) in E Asia, under Japanese control: included Manchuria and parts of Inner Mongolia; now a part of China. Also, **Man′chou′kuo′.**

Man·chu·ri·a (man chŏŏr′ē ə), *n.* a region in NE China: formerly comprising nine provinces of that country; ancestral home of the Manchus. ab. 413,000 sq. mi. —**Man·chu′ri·an,** *adj., n.*

man·ci·ple (man′sə pəl), *n.* an officer or steward of a monastery, college, etc., authorized to purchase provisions. [ME < ML *mancipius* buyer, agent, peddler (r. L *manceps,* lit., one who takes (something) in hand) + OF *manciple,* var. of *mancipe* < L *mancip(ium)* a purchase, possession, slave]

Man·cu·ni·an (man kyōō′nē ən, -kyōōn′yən), *n.* **1.** a native or resident of Manchester, England. —*adj.* **2.** of, pertaining to, or characteristic of Manchester, England, or its natives or residents. [< ML *Mancuni(um)* MANCHESTER + -AN]

-mancy, a combining form meaning "divination": *necromancy.* [ME *-manci(e), -mancy(e)* < OF *-mancie* < L *-mantia* < Gk *manteia* divination. See MANTIC, -Y[3]]

man·da·ca·ru (män′də kə rōō′), *n.* a woody-trunked cactus, *Cereus Jamacaru,* having sharp spines and large, white flowers that are green on the outside. [?]

Man·dae·an (man dē′ən), *n.* **1.** a member of an ancient Gnostic sect extant in Iraq. **2.** the Aramaic language of the Mandaean sacred books. —*adj.* **3.** of or pertaining to the Mandaeans. Also, **Mandean.** [< Mandaean *mandayy(ā)* Gnostics (lit., the knowing ones) + -AN] —**Man·dae′an·ism,** *n.*

man·da·la (mun′dᵊlə), *n.* **1.** *Oriental Art.* a schematized representation of the cosmos, chiefly characterized by a concentric organization of geometric shapes, each of which contains an image of a deity or an attribute of a deity. **2.** (in Jungian psychology) a symbol representing the effort to reunify the self. [< Skt *maṇḍala* circle]

Man·da·lay (man′dᵊlā′, man′dᵊlā′), *n.* a city in central Burma, on the Irrawaddy River: the former capital of Upper Burma. 212,873 (est. 1963).

man·da·mus (man dā′məs), *n., pl.* **-mus·es,** *v.* —*n.* **1.** *Law.* a writ from a superior court to an inferior court, or to an officer, a corporation, etc., commanding that a specified thing be done. —*v.t.* **2.** *Informal.* to intimidate or serve with such writ. [< L: we command]

Man·dan (man′dan, -dən), *n.* **1.** a member of a Siouan people of North Dakota. **2.** the Siouan language of the Mandan Indians.

Man·dan (man′dən), *n.* a city in S North Dakota, near Bismarck. 10,525 (1960).

man·da·rin (man′də rin), *n.* **1.** (in the Chinese Empire) a member of any of the nine ranks of public officials, each distinguished by a particular kind of button worn on the cap. **2.** (*cap.*) the standard Chinese language. **3.** (*cap.*) the north China language, esp. that of Peking. **4.** the flattish, yellow to reddish-orange, loose-skinned fruit of a Chinese citrus tree, *Citrus reticulata,* cultivated in many varieties. **5.** the tree itself. Also called **mandarin orange** (for defs. 4, 5). [< pidgin English < Pg *mandarim,* alter. of Skt *mantrin* councilor, deriv. of *mantra* counsel; akin to MIND]

man′darin col′lar, a narrow, stand-up collar, not quite meeting at the front.

man′darin duck′, a crested, Asian duck, *Aix galericulata,* having variegated purple, green, chestnut, and white plumage.

man′darin or′ange, mandarin (defs. 4, 5).

man·da·tar·y (man′də ter′ē), *n., pl.* **-tar·ies.** a person or nation holding a mandate. Also, **mandatory.** [< LL *mandātāri(us)* one to whom a charge is given. See MANDATE, -ARY]

man·date (*n.* man′dāt, -dit; *v.* man′dāt), *n., v.,* **-dat·ed, -dat·ing.** —*n.* **1.** (in the League of Nations) a commission given to a nation to administer the government and affairs of a former Turkish territory or German colony. **2.** a mandated territory or colony. **3.** *Politics.* a command or authorization to act in a particular way on a public issue given by the electorate to its representative: *The President had a clear mandate to end the war.* **4.** a command from a superior court or official to an inferior one. **5.** an authoritative order or command: *a royal mandate.* **6.** *Rom. Cath. Ch.* an order issued by the pope, esp. one commanding the preferment of a certain person to a benefice. **7.** *Roman and Civil Law.* a contract by which one engages gratuitously to perform services for another. **8.** (in modern civil law) any contract by which a person undertakes to perform services for another. **9.** *Roman Law.* an order or decree by the emperor, esp. to governors of provinces. —*v.t.* **10.** to consign (a territory, colony, etc.) to the charge of a particular nation under a mandate. [< L *mandāt(um),* n. use of neut. of *mandātus,* ptp. of *mandāre* to commission, lit., to give into (someone's) hand. See MANUS, DATE[1]]
—**Syn. 5.** fiat, decree, injunction, edict, ruling.

man·da·tor (man dā′tər), *n.* one who gives a mandate. [< LL; see MANDATE, -OR[2]]

man·da·to·ry (man′də tōr′ē, -tôr′ē), *adj., n., pl.* **-ries.** —*adj.* **1.** pertaining to, of the nature of, or containing a command. **2.** authoritatively ordered; obligatory: *A reply to this letter is mandatory.* **3.** *Law.* permitting no option: *a mandatory clause.* **4.** having received a mandate, as a nation. —*n.* **5.** mandatary. [< LL *mandātōri(us).* See MANDATE, -ORY[1]] —**man′da·to′ri·ly,** *adv.*

man-day (man′dā′), *n., pl.* **man-days.** work done by one man in one working day.

Man·de (män′dā), *n.* a branch of Niger-Congo, comprising languages spoken in the upper Niger and Senegal drainage basins and in the coastland to the west of these basins. Also called **Mandingo.**

Man·de·an (man dē′ən), *n., adj.* Mandaean.

Man·del (man′dᵊl, man del′), *n.* a boy's given name.

man·del′ic ac′id (man del′ik, -dē′lik), *Chem.* any of three stereoisomeric acids having the formula $C_6H_5CHOHCOOH$, esp. dl-mandelic acid, a white, crystalline, slightly water-soluble solid obtainable from amygdalin: used chiefly in medicine as an antiseptic. Also called **amygdalic acid.** [< G *Mandel* almond + -IC]

Man·de·ville (man′də vil), *n.* **1. Bernard de** (də), c1670–1733, English physician and satirist, born in Holland. **2. Sir John,** died 1372, English compiler: ostensibly the author of a 14th-century book of travels.

man·di·ble (man′də bəl), *n.* **1.** the bone of the lower jaw. **2.** (in birds) **a.** the lower part of the bill. **b. mandibles,** the upper and lower parts of the bill. **3.** (in arthropods) one of the first pair of mouthpart appendages, typically a jawlike biting organ, but styliform or setiform in piercing and sucking species. [< LL *mandibula* jaw, equiv. to *mandi-* (s. of *mandere* to chew) + *-bula* n. suffix of means]

Mandible (def. 1)

man·dib·u·lar (man dib′yə lər), *adj.* pertaining to or of the nature of a mandible. [< LL *mandibul(a)* MANDIBLE + -AR[1]]

man·dib·u·late (man dib′yə lit, -lāt′), *adj.* **1.** having mandibles. —*n.* **2.** a mandibulate insect, as a beetle. [< NL *mandibulāt(us)* having mandibles. See MANDIBLE, -ATE[1]]

man·dil·ion (man dil′yən), *n.* **1.** a short cloak, with full hanging sleeves, often open or slit under the arms, worn by soldiers in the 16th and 17th centuries. **2.** a similar garment without sleeves, worn by servants in the 16th and 17th centuries. [< MF, dim. of *mandil* cloak << L *mantell(um)* cloak]

Man·din·go (man ding′gō), *n., pl.* **-gos, -goes,** *adj.* —*n.* **1.** a member of any of a number of Negro peoples forming an extensive linguistic group in western Africa. **2.** Mande. —*adj.* **3.** of or pertaining to the Mandingos or their language.

man·di·o·ca (man′dē ō′kə, män′-), *n.* the cassava, *Manihot esculenta.* [< Sp, Pg < Tupi]

man·di·ra (mun′dər ə), *n.* a Hindu temple. [< Skt *mandirā* palace, temple]

man·do·lin (man′dᵊlin, man′dᵊlin′), *n.* a musical instrument with a pear-shaped wooden body (smaller than that of the lute) and a fretted neck, usually having metal strings plucked with a plectrum. [< It *mandolin(o),* dim. of *mandola,* var. of *mandora,* alter. of *pandora* BANDORE] —**man′do·lin′ist,** *n.*

Mandolin

man·dor·la (män′dôr lä′, -dôr-; *It.* män′dôr lä′), *n., pl.* **-las,** *It.* **-le** (-le′). *Fine Arts.* an almond-shaped area or space, esp. a schematic aureole containing a representation of a sacred personage. [< It: ALMOND]

man·drag·o·ra (man drag′ər ə, man′drə gōr′ə, -gôr′ə), *n.* **1.** mandrake (def. 1). **2.** a mandrake root. [ME, OE < LL; L *mandragoras* < Gk]

man·drake (man′drāk, -drik), *n.* **1.** a narcotic, short-stemmed, European, solanaceous herb, *Mandragora officinarum,* having a fleshy, often forked root thought to resemble a human form. **2.** *U.S.* the May apple. [ME, var. of *mandrage* (short for MANDRAGORA), taken (by folk etymology) as MAN[1] + DRAKE[2]]

man·drel (man′drəl), *n.* **1.** *Mach.* a shaft or bar the end of which is inserted into a workpiece to hold it during machining. **2.** the driving spindle in the headstock of a lathe. **3.** a spindle on which a circular saw or grinding wheel rotates. Also, **man′dril.** [? akin to F *mandrin*]

man·drill (man′dril), *n.* a large, ferocious-looking baboon, *Papio sphinx*, of W Africa, the male of which has the face marked with blue and scarlet and the muzzle ribbed. [MAN[1] + DRILL[4]]

Mandrill (20 in. high at shoulder; length 3 ft.)

man·du·cate (man′jo͞o kāt′), *v.t.*, **-cat·ed, -cat·ing.** *Archaic.* to chew; masticate; eat. [< L *mandūcāt(us)* chewed, eaten (ptp. of *mandūcāre*), deriv. of *mandūcus* glutton; see -ATE[1]] —**man·du·ca·ble** (man′jə kə bəl), *adj.* —**man′du·ca′tion,** *n.* —**man·du·ca·to·ry** (man′jo͞o kə tôr′ē, -tōr′ē), *adj.*

man·dy·as (män dē′äs; *Eng.* man dē′əs, man′dē əs), *n., pl.* **-dy·ai** (-dē′e), *Eng.* **-dy·as·es.** *Gk. Orth. Ch.* **1.** a short, black cloak, worn by monks. **2.** a mantle, usually purple, worn by bishops. [< Gk]

mane (mān), *n.* the long hair growing on the back of or about the neck and neighboring parts of some animals, as the horse, lion, etc. [ME; OE *manu;* c. Icel *mön*, G *Mähne*, D *manen*] —**mane′less,** *adj.*

man-eat·er (man′ē′tər), *n.* **1.** a human cannibal. **2.** an animal, esp. a tiger, lion, or shark, that eats or is said to eat human flesh. **3.** See **great white shark.**

man-eat·ing (man′ē′ting), *adj.* feeding on or having an appetite for human flesh: *a man-eating tiger.*

maned (mānd), *adj.* having a mane. [MANE + -ED[3]]

maned′ wolf′, a South American wild dog, *Chrysocyon jubatus*, having a shaggy, reddish coat and long ears and legs.

ma·nège (ma nezh′, -nāzh′), *n.* **1.** the art of training and riding horses. **2.** the action or movements of a trained horse. **3.** a school for training horses and teaching horsemanship. Also, **ma·nege′.** [< F < It *maneggio;* see MANAGE]

man′ en′gine, *Mining Obs.* a device for moving miners from one level to another, consisting of a series of small platforms mounted on a vertical reciprocating shaft, and a similar series fixed to a wall, so that after each rise or fall of the shaft a moving platform is beside a fixed one.

ma·nent (mä′nent), *v.i.* (they) remain (used as a stage direction to indicate that the characters named are to remain onstage). [< L]

ma·nes (mā′nēz; *Lat.* mä′nes), *n.* **1.** (*construed as pl.*) *Rom. Religion.* the souls of the dead; shades. **2.** (*construed as sing.*) the spirit or shade of a particular dead person. Also, **Ma′nes.** [< L: lit., the good ones; akin to OL *mānus* good]

Ma·nes (mā′nēz), *n.* A.D. 216?–276?, Persian prophet: founder of Manicheanism. Also called **Manicheus, Mani.**

ma·net (mä′net), *v.i.* (he or she) remains (used as a stage direction to indicate that a named character is to remain onstage). [< L]

Ma·net (ma nā′; *Fr.* MA ne′), *n.* **É·dou·ard** (ā dwar′), 1832–83, French painter.

Man·e·tho (man′ə thō′), *n.* fl. c250 B.C., Egyptian high priest of Heliopolis: author of a history of Egypt.

ma·neu·ver (mə no͞o′vər), *n., v.,* **-vered, -ver·ing.** —*n.* **1.** a planned and regulated movement or evolution of troops, war vessels, etc. **2. maneuvers,** a series of tactical exercises usually carried out in the field by large bodies of troops in imitation of war. **3.** an adroit move, skillful proceeding, etc., esp. as characterized by craftiness: *political maneuvers.* —*v.t.* **4.** to change the position of (troops, vessels, etc.) by a maneuver. **5.** to bring, put, drive, or make by maneuvers: *He maneuvered his way into the confidence of the enemy.* **6.** to manipulate or manage with skill or adroitness: *to maneuver a conversation.* **7.** *Naut.* to steer (a vessel) on several different headings in close succession. —*v.i.* **8.** to perform a maneuver or maneuvers. **9.** to scheme; intrigue. Also, **manoeuvre.** [< F *manoeuvre*, MF *manuevre* hand work, deriv. of OF *manuvrer* < L *manū operāre* to do handwork, equiv. to *manū* (abl. of *manus* hand) + *operāre* to work (see OPERATE)] —**ma·neu′ver·a·ble,** *adj.* —**ma·neu′ver·a·bil′i·ty,** *n.* —**ma·neu′ver·er,** *n.* —**Syn. 3.** stratagem, ruse, artifice; procedure, scheme, plot, plan. **6.** handle, finesse. **9.** plot, plan.

man′-for-man′ defense′ (man′fər man′), *Sports.* See **man-to-man defense.**

Man·fred (man′frid), *n.* a dramatic poem (1817) by Byron.

man′ Fri′day, a male administrative assistant with diverse duties. [after character in *Robinson Crusoe*]

man·ful (man′fəl), *adj.* having or showing manly spirit; resolute; bold; courageous. [ME; see MAN[1], -FUL] —**man′ful·ly,** *adv.* —**man′ful·ness,** *n.* —**Syn.** See **manly.**

man·ga·bey (mang′gə bā′), *n., pl.* **-beys.** any of several slender, long-tailed monkeys of the genus *Cercocebus*, found in forests of Africa. [after *Mangabey*, Madagascar]

mangan-, var. of **mangano-** before a vowel: *manganic.*

man·ga·nate (mang′gə nāt′), *n.* *Chem.* a salt of manganic acid, as potassium manganate, K_2MnO_4. [MANGAN(ESE) + -ATE[2]]

man·ga·nese (mang′gə nēs′, -nēz′), *n.* *Chem.* a hard, brittle, grayish-white, metallic element, an oxide of which, MnO_2 **(man′ganese diox′ide),** is a valuable oxidizing agent: used chiefly as an alloying agent in steel to give it toughness. *Symbol:* Mn; *at. wt.:* 54.938; *at. no.:* 25; *sp. gr.:* 7.2 at 20°C. [< F *manganèse* < It *manganese*, metathetic var. of ML *magnesia* MAGNESIA]

man′ganese bronze′, an alloy that is about 55 percent copper, 40 percent zinc, and up to 3.5 percent manganese.

man′ganese spar′, rhodonite or rhodochrosite.

man′ganese steel′, any of various steels containing manganese, esp. one that is up to 14 percent manganese, used in work involving heavy strains and impacts.

man′ganese sul′fate, *Chem.* See **manganous sulfate.**

man′ganese vi′olet, 1. a moderate to strong purple color. **2.** a pigment used in painting, consisting of manganese ammonium phosphate and characterized chiefly by its purple color and permanence in oils and tempera. Also called **Nuremberg violet, Nürnberg violet.**

mangani-, var. of **mangano-:** *manganiferous.*

man·gan·ic (man gan′ik), *adj.* *Chem.* of or containing manganese, esp. in the trivalent state. [MANGAN- + -IC]

mangan′ic ac′id, *Chem.* a hypothetical acid, H_2MnO_4, occurring only in the form of its salts and in solution.

man·ga·nif·er·ous (mang′gə nif′ər əs), *adj.* *Mineral.* containing manganese. [MANGANI- + -FEROUS]

Man·ga·nin (mang′gə nin), *n.* *Trademark.* an alloy of copper, manganese, and nickel, having various electrical applications.

man·ga·nite (mang′gə nīt′), *n.* **1.** a gray to black mineral, hydrous manganese oxide, MnO(OH); gray manganese ore. **2.** *Chem.* any of a series of salts containing tetravalent manganese and derived from either of two acids, H_4MnO_4 or H_2MnO_3. [MANGAN- + -ITE[1]]

mangano-, a combining form of **manganese:** *manganophyllite.* Also, **mangan-, mangani-.** [< G *Mangan* manganese + -o-]

man·ga·no·phyl·lite (mang′gə nō fil′īt), *n.* *Mineral.* a bronze-colored variety of biotite containing manganese; manganiferous phyllite. [< G *Manganophyll* (see MANGANO-, -PHYLL) + -ITE[1]]

man·ga·nous (mang′gə nəs, man gan′əs), *adj.* *Chem.* containing bivalent manganese. [MANGAN- + -OUS]

man′ganous sul′fate, *Chem.* a pink, water-soluble, usually tetrahydrate salt, $MnSO_4·4H_2O$, used chiefly in fertilizers, paints, and varnishes. Also called **manganese sulfate.**

mange (mānj), *n.* *Vet. Pathol.* any of various skin diseases caused by parasitic mites, affecting animals and sometimes man and characterized by loss of hair and scabby eruptions. [late ME *manjewe* itch < MF *mangeue* an eating, itch, deriv. of *mangier* to eat; see MANGER]

man·gel-wur·zel (mang′gəl wûr′zəl), *n.* *Chiefly Brit.* a variety of the beet *Beta vulgaris*, cultivated as food for livestock. Also, **mangold-wurzel.** Also called **man′gel, mangold.** [< G, var. of *Mangoldwurzel* (*Mangold* beet + *Wurzel* root)]

man·ger (mān′jər), *n.* **1.** a box or trough from which horses or cattle eat. **2.** *Naut.* **a.** a space at the bow of a vessel, having a partition for confining water entering at the hawseholes until it can be drained. **b.** a sunken bottom in a chain locker, covered by a grating and used to collect water from the anchor chain. [ME < MF *maingeure*, deriv. of *mangier* to eat < L *mandūcāre* to chew, eat. See MANDUCATE]

man·gey (mān′jē), *adj.*, **-gi·er, -gi·est.** mangy.

man·gle[1] (mang′gəl), *v.t.*, **-gled, -gling. 1.** to cut, slash, or crush so as to disfigure: *the corpse of a warrior mangled in battle.* **2.** to spoil; ruin; mar badly: *to mangle a text by careless typesetting.* [late ME < AF *mangler*, perh. dissimilated var. of OF *mangonner* to mangle; akin to MANGONEL] —**man′gler,** *n.* —**Syn. 1.** See **maim. 2.** deface; destroy.

man·gle[2] (mang′gəl), *n., v.,* **-gled, -gling.** —*n.* **1.** a machine for smoothing or pressing cloth, household linen, etc., by means of rollers. —*v.t.* **2.** to smooth with a mangle. **3.** *Metalworking.* to squeeze (metal plates) between rollers. [< D *mangel* < LL *mangan(um)* (by dissimilation). See MANGONEL]

man·go (mang′gō), *n., pl.* **-goes, -gos. 1.** the oblong, slightly acid fruit of a tropical, anacardiaceous tree, *Mangifera indica*, eaten ripe, or preserved or pickled. **2.** the tree itself. [< Pg *manga* < Malay *manggā* < Tamil *mān-kāy* fruit (*kāy*) of mango tree (*mān*)]

man·gold-wur·zel (mang′gōld wûr′zəl, -gəld-), *n.* mangel-wurzel. Also called **man′gold.**

man·go·nel (mang′gə nel′), *n.* any of various former military engines for throwing large stones and darts. [ME < OF (dim.), deriv. of LL *manganum* < Gk *mánganon* engine of war]

man·go-squash (mang′gō skwosh′), *n.* the chayote.

man·go·steen (mang′gə stēn′), *n.* **1.** the juicy, edible fruit of an East Indian tree, *Garcinia Mangostana.* **2.** the tree itself. [< Malay *mangustan*]

man·grove (mang′grōv, man′-), *n.* **1.** any tropical tree or shrub of the genus *Rhizophora*, the species of which are mostly low trees noted for a copious development of interlacing adventitious roots above the ground. **2.** any of various similar plants. [alter. of earlier *mangrow* < Pg *mangue* (by folk etymology) << Taino]

man′grove snap′per. See **gray snapper.**

Mang·rum (mang′grəm), *n.* **Lloyd,** born 1914, U.S. golf player.

Man·gum (mang′gəm), *n.* a town in SW Oklahoma. 3950 (1960).

man·gy (mān′jē), *adj.*, **-gi·er, -gi·est. 1.** having, caused by, or like the mange. **2.** contemptible; mean: *a mangy trick.* **3.** squalid; shabby: *a mangy little suburb.* Also, **mangey.** [MANGE + -Y[1]] —**man′gi·ly,** *adv.* —**man′gi·ness,** *n.*

man·han·dle (man′han′dəl, man han′dəl), *v.t.*, **-dled, -dling. 1.** to handle roughly. **2.** to move by human strength, without the use of mechanical appliances. [MAN[1] + HANDLE]

Man·hat·tan (man hat′ən, *esp. for 1, 2,* mən-), *n.* **1.** Also called **Man·hat′tan Is′land.** an island in New York City between the Hudson, East, and Harlem rivers. 13½ mi. long; 2½ mi. greatest width; 22¼ sq. mi. **2.** a borough of New York City approximately coextensive with Manhattan Island: chief business district of the city: 1,698,281 (1960). **3.** a city in NE Kansas, on the Kansas River. 22,993 (1960). **4.** a cocktail of whiskey and sweet vermouth, usually made with a dash of bitters and served with a maraschino cherry.

Manhat′tan Beach′, a city in SW California, SW of Los Angeles. 33,934 (1960).

Manhat′tan clam′ chow′der, a chowder made from clams, salt pork, tomatoes, and other vegetables. Cf. **New England clam chowder.**

Manhat′tan Dis′trict, the code name for the large-scale project that developed the first atomic bomb.

Man·hat·tan·ite (man hat′nīt′), *n.* a native or inhabitant of the borough of Manhattan. [MANHATTAN + -ITE[1]]

Man·heim (man′hīm), *n.* a town in SE Pennsylvania. 4790 (1960).

man·help·er (man′hel′pər), *n.* a long pole for holding a paintbrush, used in painting areas otherwise out of reach. Also called **long arm, striker.** [MAN[1] + HELPER]

man·hole (man′hōl′), *n.* a hole, usually with a cover, through which a man may enter a sewer, drain, steam boiler, etc. [MAN[1] + HOLE]

man·hood (man′ho͝od), *n.* **1.** state of being a man or adult male person. **2.** manly qualities: *He proved his manhood in the war.* **3.** men collectively. **4.** state of being human. [ME; see MAN[1], -HOOD]

man-hour (man′our′, -ou′ər), *n.* an hour of work by one man, used as an industrial time unit. *Abbr.:* man-hr

man·hunt (man′hunt′), *n.* **1.** an intensive search for a criminal, suspect, escaped convict, etc., as by the law enforcement agencies of a country. **2.** any intensive search for a man. [MAN[1] + HUNT] —**man′ hunt′er.**

Ma·ni (mä′nē), *n.* Manes.

ma·ni·a (mā′nē ə, mān′yə), *n.* **1.** excessive excitement or enthusiasm; craze: *She has a mania for bizarre cocktails.* **2.** *Psychiatry.* a form of insanity characterized by great excitement, with or without delusions, and in its acute stage by great violence. [late ME < L < Gk: madness; akin to MAENAD, MIND]

Ma·ni·a (mā′nē ə, män′yə), *n.* **1.** an ancient Roman goddess of the dead. **2.** Also, **Manya.** a girl's given name.

-mania, a combining form of **mania** (*megalomania*); extended to mean exaggerated desire or love for (*bibliomania*).

ma·ni·ac (mā′nē ak′), *n.* **1.** a raving or violently insane person; madman; lunatic. —*adj.* **2.** raving with madness; mad. [< ML *maniac(us)* of, pertaining to madness. See MANIA, -AC]

ma·ni·a·cal (mə nī′ə kəl), *adj.* of or pertaining to mania or a maniac. [MANIAC + -AL[1]] —**ma·ni′a·cal·ly,** *adv.*

man·ic (man′ik, mā′nik), *adj.* pertaining to or affected by mania. [< Gk *manik(ós)* inclined to madness. See MANIA, -IC]

man·ic-de·pres·sive (man′ik di pres′iv), *Psychiatry.* —*adj.* **1.** having a mental disorder marked by alternating extremes of excitement and depression. —*n.* **2.** a person suffering from this disorder.

Man·i·che·an (man′ə kē′ən), *n.* **1.** Also, **Man·i·chee** (man′ə kē′). an adherent of the dualistic religious system of Manes, a combination of Gnostic Christianity, Buddhism, Zoroastrianism, and various other elements, with a basic doctrine of a conflict between light and dark, matter being regarded as dark and evil. —*adj.* **2.** of or pertaining to the Manicheans or their doctrines. Also, **Man′i·chae′an.** [ME *Manichee* (< LL *Manichae(us)* < LGk *Manichaîos* of Manes) + -AN] —**Man′i·che′an·ism, Man′i·che′ism, Man′i·chae′an·ism, Man′i·chae′ism,** *n.*

Man·i·che·us (man′ə kē′əs), *n.* Manes.

ma·ni·cot·ti (man′ə kot′ē; *It.* mä′nē kôt′tē), *n.* *Italian Cookery.* a dish consisting of large, flat noodles stuffed with a mild cheese and baked in a tomato sauce. [< It: muffs, pl. of *manicotto*]

man·i·cure (man′ə kyo͝or′), *n., v.,* **-cured, -cur·ing.** —*n.* **1.** a professional treatment of the hands and fingernails, as for removing cuticle, trimming and shaping nails, etc. **2.** a manicurist. —*v.t., v.i.* **3.** to take care of (the hands and fingernails); apply manicure treatment to. [< F < L *mani-* (comb. form of *manus* hand) + *cūra* care]

man·i·cur·ist (man′ə kyo͝or′ist), *n.* a person, esp. a woman, who provides manicures. [MANICURE + -IST]

man·i·fer (man′ə fer′, -fər), *n.* *Armor.* a gauntlet for protecting the left hand when holding the reins of a horse. Also, **main-de-fer.** [alter. of MF *main-de-fer* hand of iron]

man·i·fest (man′ə fest′), *adj.* **1.** readily perceived by the eye or the understanding; evident; obvious; apparent; plain: *a manifest error.* **2.** *Psychoanal.* of or pertaining to conscious feelings, ideas, and impulses that contain repressed psychic material: *the manifest content of a dream as opposed to the latent content which it conceals.* —*v.t.* **3.** to make manifest to the eye or the understanding; show plainly: *He manifested his approval with a hearty laugh.* **4.** to prove; put beyond doubt or question: *The evidence manifests the guilt of the defendant.* **5.** to record in a ship's manifest. —*n.* **6.** a list of the cargo carried by a vessel, made for the use of various agents and officials at the ports of destination. **7.** a list of goods transported by land. **8.** a list of the cargo or passengers carried on an airplane. [ME < L *manifest(us)*, var. of *manufestus* evident, lit., struck with the hand. See MANUS, INFEST] —**man′i·fest′a·ble,** *adj.* —**man′i·fest′er,** *n.* —**man′i·fest′ly,** *adv.* —**man′i·fest′ness,** *n.* —**Syn. 1.** clear, distinct, unmistakable, patent, open, palpable, visible, conspicuous. **3.** reveal, disclose, evince, evidence, demonstrate, declare, express. See **display.** —**Ant. 1.** obscure. **3.** conceal.

man·i·fes·tant (man′ə fes′tənt), *n.* one who initiates or participates in a public demonstration. [< L *manifestant-* (s. of *manifestāns*), prp. of *manifestāre* to MANIFEST; see -ANT]

man·i·fes·ta·tion (man′ə fe stā′shən), *n.* **1.** act of manifesting. **2.** state of being manifested. **3.** a means of manifesting; indication: *At first there was no manifestation of the disease.* **4.** a public demonstration, as for political effect. **5.** *Spiritualism.* a materialization. [< LL *manifestātiōn-* (s. of *manifestātiō*). See MANIFEST, -ATION]

man·i·fes·ta·tive (man′ə fes′tə tiv), *adj.* manifesting; showing clearly or conclusively. [< ML *manifestātīv(us)*, equiv. to L *manifestāt(us)* (see MANIFEST, -ATE)[1] + *-īvus* -IVE] —**man′i·fes′ta·tive·ly,** *adv.*

man′ifest con′tent, *Psychoanal.* the images or happenings in a dream.

Man′ifest Des′tiny, the belief or doctrine, held chiefly in the middle and latter part of the 19th century, that it is the destiny of the U.S. to expand its territory over the whole of North America and to extend and enhance its political, social, and economic influences.

man·i·fes·to (man′ə fes′tō), *n., pl.* **-toes.** a public declaration of intentions, opinions, objectives, or motives, as when issued by a government, sovereign, or organization. [< It; see MANIFEST]

man·i·fold (man′ə fōld′), *adj.* **1.** of many kinds; numerous and varied: *manifold duties.* **2.** having many different parts, elements, features, forms, etc.: *a manifold program for social reform.* **3.** doing or operating several things at once. **4.** (of paper business forms) made up of a number of sheets interleaved with carbon paper. —*n.* **5.** something having many different parts or features: *Marriage is a manifold of duties.* **6.** a copy or facsimile, as of something written, such as is made by manifolding. **7.** any thin, inexpensive paper for making carbon copies on a typewriter. **8.** *Mach.* a chamber having several outlets through which a liquid or gas is distributed or gathered. **9.** *Philos.* (in Kantian epistemology) the totality of discrete items of experience as presented to the mind; the constituents of a sensory experience. **10.** *Math.* a topological space that is connected and locally Euclidean. Cf. **locally Euclidean space.** —*v.t.* **11.** to make copies of, as with carbon paper. [ME; OE *manigf(e)ald.* See MANY, -FOLD] —**man′i·fold′ly,** *adv.* —**man′i·fold′ness,** *n.*
—**Syn. 1.** various, multitudinous. See **many. 2.** varied, divers, multifarious. —**Ant. 1.** simple, single.

man·i·fold·er (man′ə fōl′dər), *n.* a machine for making manifolds or copies, as of writing. [MANIFOLD + -ER[1]]

man·i·form (man′ə fôrm′), *adj.* shaped like a hand. [< NL *maniform(is)* hand-shaped. See MANUS, -I-, -FORM]

man·i·kin (man′ə kin), *n.* **1.** a little man; a dwarf; pygmy. **2.** mannequin. **3.** a model of the human body for teaching anatomy, demonstrating surgical operations, etc. Also, **manakin, mannikin.** [< D *manneken,* dim. of *man* MAN[1]. See -KIN, MANNEQUIN]

Ma·nil·a (mə nil′ə), *n.* **1.** a seaport in and the capital of the Philippines, on S Luzon. 1,339,000 (est. 1965). Cf. **Quezon City. 2.** See **Manila hemp. 3.** See **Manila paper.**

Manil′a Bay′, a bay in the Philippines, in W Luzon Island: the American fleet under Admiral Dewey defeated the Spanish fleet 1898.

manil′a grass′, a compact, turf-forming grass, *Zoysia Matrella,* of southeastern Asia, having stiff leaves and flowering spikelets.

Manil′a hemp′, a fibrous material obtained from the leaves of the abacá, *Musa textilis,* used for making ropes, fabrics, etc. Also called **Manila, manilla.**

Manil′a pa′per, 1. strong, light-brown or buff paper, originally made from Manila hemp but now also from wood pulp substitutes and various other fibers. **2.** any paper resembling Manila paper. Also called **Manila, manilla.**

Manil′a rope′, rope made from Manila hemp.

Manil′a tam′arind, guamachil.

Ma·nil·i·us (mə nil′ē əs), *n.* a crater in the first quadrant of the face of the moon: about 25 miles in diameter.

ma·nil·la (mə nil′ə), *n.* **1.** See **Manila hemp. 2.** See **Manila paper.**

ma·nille (mə nil′), *n. Cards.* the second highest trump in certain card games, as the seven of trumps in omber or nine of trumps in klaberjass. Also, **menel.** [alter. of Sp *malilla,* dim. of obs. *mala,* n. fem. use of *malo* bad < L *malus*]

man′ in the street′, the ordinary man; the average citizen: *a newspaper written for the man in the street.*

man·i·oc (man′ē ok′, mā′nē-), *n.* cassava. [< Tupi *man(d)ioca;* r. *manihot* < MF < Guarani *man(d)io*]

man·i·ple (man′ə pəl), *n.* **1.** (in ancient Rome) a subdivision of a legion, consisting of 60 or 120 men. **2.** *Eccles.* one of the Eucharistic vestments, consisting of an ornamental band or strip worn on the left arm near the wrist. See illus. under **chasuble.** [< ML *manipul(us)* sudarium, L: infantry company, lit., handful, equiv. to *mani-* (comb. form of *manus* hand) + *-pulus* full]

ma·nip·u·lar (mə nip′yə lər), *adj.* **1.** of or pertaining to the Roman maniple. **2.** of or pertaining to manipulation. —*n.* **3.** a soldier belonging to a maniple. [< L *manipulār(is).* See MANIPLE, -AR[1]]

ma·nip·u·late (mə nip′yə lāt′), *v.t.,* **-lat·ed, -lat·ing. 1.** to handle, manage, or use, esp. with skill, in some process of treatment or performance: *to manipulate a tractor.* **2.** to manage or influence by artful skill: *to manipulate a person; to manipulate stocks.* **3.** to adapt or change (accounts, figures, etc.) to suit one's purpose or advantage. [back formation from MANIPULATION] —**ma·nip′u·lat′a·ble, ma·nip·u·la·ble** (mə nip′yə ləbəl), *adj.* —**ma·nip·u·la·tive** (mə nip′yə lā′tiv, -yə lə-tiv), *adj.* —**ma·nip′u·la′tive·ly,** *adv.* —**ma·nip·u·la·to·ry** (mə nip′yə lə tōr′ē, -tôr′ē), *adj.*
—**Syn. 2, 3.** juggle, falsify.

ma·nip·u·la·tion (mə nip′yə lā′shən), *n.* **1.** skillful or artful management. **2.** act of manipulating. **3.** state or fact of being manipulated. [< F, equiv. to *manipule* handful (of grains, etc.; see MANIPLE) + *-ation* -ATION]

ma·nip·u·la·tor (mə nip′yə lā′tər), *n.* **1.** one who manipulates. **2.** a mechanical device for handling small objects or materials in conditions not permitting the immediate presence of workers. [MANIPULATE + -OR[2]]

Ma·ni·pur (mun′i po͝or′), *n.* a union territory in NE India between Assam and Burma. 780,037 (1961); 8620 sq. mi. *Cap.:* Imphal.

Ma·ni·sa (mä′ni sä′), *n.* a city in W Turkey, near the Aegean: Roman defeat of Antiochus the Great 190 B.C. 48,484 (1955). Ancient, **Magnesia.**

ma·nism (mā′niz əm, mä′-), *n.* worship of, and attempted communication with, the spirits of ancestors. [MAN(ES) + -ISM] —**ma·nis′tic,** *adj.*

Man·is·tee (man′i stē′, man′i stē′), *n.* a town in NW Michigan. 8324 (1960).

Man·is·tique (man′i stēk′, man′i stēk′), *n.* a town in NW Michigan, in the Upper Peninsula. 4875 (1960).

man·it (man′it), *n.* man-minute. [by syncope]

Man·i·to·ba (man′i tō′bə), *n.* **1.** a province in central Canada. 921,686 (1961); 246,512 sq. mi. *Cap.:* Winnipeg. **2. Lake,** a lake in the S part of this province. 120 mi. long; 1817 sq. mi. —**Man′i·to′ban,** *adj., n.*

man·i·tou (man′i to͞o′), *n., pl.* **-tous,** (*esp. collectively*) **-tou.** (among the Algonquian Indians) a supernatural being that controls nature; a spirit, deity, or object that possesses supernatural power. Also, **man·i·to** (man′i tō′), **man·i·tu** (man′i to͞o′). [< Algonquian; cf. Ojibwa *manito* spirit, god]

Man·i·tou·lin (man′i to͞o′lin), *n.* an island in N Lake Huron belonging to Canada. 80 mi. long. Also called **Manitou′lin Is′land.**

Man′i·tou Springs′ (man′i to͞o′), a town in central Colorado. 3626 (1960).

Man·i·to·woc (man′i tə wok′), *n.* a port in E Wisconsin, on Lake Michigan. 32,275 (1960).

Ma·ni·za·les (mä′nē sä′les), *n.* a city in W Colombia. 186,910 (est. 1964).

man·jak (man′jak), *n.* See **glance pitch.** Also, **man·jack.** [< Carib]

Man·ju·sri (mun′jo͞osh rē′), *n. Buddhism.* a Bodhisattva personifying wisdom.

Man·ka·to (man kā′tō), *n.* a city in S Minnesota, on the Minnesota River. 23,797 (1960).

Man·kie·wicz (mang′kə wits), *n.* **Joseph L(eo),** born 1909, U.S. motion-picture director, producer, and writer.

man·kind (man′kīnd′ *for 1;* man′kīnd′ *for 2*), *n.* **1.** the human race; human beings collectively. **2.** men, as distinguished from women. [ME; see MAN[1], KIND[2]]

man·lift (man′lift′), *n.* an endless belt having handles and straps for lifting people from one level to another. [MAN[1] + LIFT]

man·like (man′līk′), *adj.* **1.** resembling a man. **2.** belonging or proper to a man; manly: *manlike fortitude.* [late ME; see MAN[1], -LIKE] —**man′like′ly,** *adv.* —**man′like′ness,** *n.*

man′ lock′, an air lock serving as a decompression chamber for workmen.

man·ly (man′lē), *adj.,* **-li·er, -li·est,** *adv.* —*adj.* **1.** having the qualities usually considered desirable in a man; strong; brave; honorable; resolute; virile. **2.** pertaining to or befitting a man: *manly sports.* —*adv.* **3.** *Archaic.* in a manly manner. [ME (adj., adv.); OE *manlīce* (adv.). See MAN[1], -LY] —**man′li·ness,** *n.*
—**Syn. 1.** masculine, male. MANLY, MANFUL, MANNISH mean possessing the qualities of a man. MANLY implies possession of the most valuable or desirable qualities a man can have, as dignity, honesty, directness, etc., in opposition to servility, insincerity, underhandedness, etc.: *A manly foe is better than a weak friend.* It also connotes courage, strength, and fortitude: *manly determination to face what comes.* MANFUL stresses the reference to courage, strength, and industry: *manful resistance.* MANNISH applies to that which resembles man: *a boy with a mannish voice.* Applied to a woman, the term is derogatory, suggesting the aberrant possession of masculine characteristics: *a mannish girl; a mannish stride.* —**Ant. 1.** feminine; weak, cowardly.

Man·ly (man′lē), *n.* a boy's given name.

man-made (man′mād′), *adj.* **1.** produced, formed, or made by man. **2.** produced artificially; not resulting from natural processes. **3.** *Textiles.* **a.** (of a fiber) manufactured synthetically from a cellulosic or noncellulosic base; produced chemically. **b.** (of a fabric or garment) constructed of man-made fibers.

man-min·ute (man′min′it), *n.* work done by one man in one minute.

Mann (män, man *for 1, 3;* man *for 2, 4*), *n.* **1. Heinrich** (hin′rik; *Ger.* hin′rikh), 1871–1950, German novelist and dramatist, in the U.S. after 1940 (brother of Thomas Mann). **2. Horace,** 1796–1859, U.S. educational reformer: instrumental in establishing the first normal school in the U.S. 1839. **3. Thom·as** (tom′əs; *Ger.* tō′mäs), 1875–1955, German novelist and critic, in the U.S. after 1937: Nobel prize 1929. **4.** a boy's given name.

man·na (man′ə), *n.* **1.** the food miraculously supplied to the Israelites in the wilderness. Ex. 16:14–36. **2.** divine or spiritual food. **3.** anything likened to the manna of the Israelites: *The unexpected money was manna.* **4.** the exudation of the ash *Fraxinus Ornus* and related plants; source of mannitol. [ME, OE < LL < Gk < Heb *mān*]

Mann′ Act′ (man), *U.S.* an act of Congress in 1910 making it a federal offense to aid or participate in the transportation of a woman from one State to another for immoral purposes. Also called **White Slave Act.**

Man·nae·an (ma nē′ən), *adj.* **1.** of or pertaining to the ancient kingdom of Mannai or its inhabitants. —*n.* **2.** a native or inhabitant of Mannai. [MANNAI + -AN]

man′na grass′, any aquatic or marsh grass of the genus *Glyceria,* of Europe, Asia, and North America.

Man·nai (man′ā), *n.* an ancient kingdom in Iran, in Kurdistan. Also, **Mana, Minni.**

man′na li′chen, *Bot.* any of several crustose lichens of the genus *Lecanora,* esp. *L. esculenta,* found in the African and Arabian deserts, used for food by man and animals.

man·nan (man′an, -ən), *n. Biochem.* any of the class of hexosans, found in the ivory nut, carob bean, and the like, that yield mannose upon hydrolysis. [MANN(OSE) + -AN]

man′na sug′ar, mannitol.

man·ne·quin (man′ə kin), *n.* **1.** a person employed to wear clothing to exhibit to customers; a clothes model. **2.** a styled and three-dimensional representation of the human form used in window displays, as of clothing. **3.** a wooden figure or model of the human figure used by tailors, dress designers, etc., for fitting or making clothes. **4.** See **lay figure** (def. 1). Also, **manikin.** [< F < D *mannekijn, manneken;* see MANIKIN]

man·ner[1] (man′ər), *n.* **1.** way of doing, being done, or happening; mode of action, occurrence, etc.: *What is the best manner of peeling onions?* **2.** characteristic or customary way of doing: *houses built in the Mexican manner.* **3. manners, a.** the prevailing customs, ways of living, and the like, of a people, class, period, etc.: *The novels of Jane Austen are concerned with the manners of her time.* **b.** ways of behaving with reference to polite standards: *She has lovely manners.* **c.** good or polite ways of behaving: *Have you no manners?* **4.** a person's outward bearing; way of addressing and treating others: *She has a charming manner in speaking to her guests.* **5.** air of distinction: *That old gentleman had quite a manner.* **6.** (*construed as pl.*) kind; sort: *All manner of things were happening.* **7.** characteristic style in art, literature, or the like: *verses in the manner of Spenser.* **8.** mannered style; mannerism: *Exuberance in art often gives way to manner.* **9.** *Obs.* **a.** nature; character. **b.** guise; fashion. **10. by all manner of means,** by all means; certainly: *If you would care to join us, please do, by all manner of means.* **11. by no manner of means,** by no means; certainly not: *She was by no manner of means an unattractive girl.* **12. in a manner,** so to speak; after a fashion; somewhat. **13. in a manner of speaking,** in a way; as it were; so to speak: *We were, in a manner of speaking, babes in the woods.* **14. to the manner born, a.** accustomed by birth to a high position: *He was a gentleman to the manner born.* **b.** used to a particular custom from birth. [ME *manere* < AF; OF *maniere* << LL *manuāria,* fem. of *manuārius* of, pertaining to the hand. See MANUS, -ER[2]]
—**Syn. 1.** method. **2.** mode, fashion, style; habit, custom. **4.** demeanor, deportment. MANNER, AIR, BEARING all refer to one's outward aspect or behavior. MANNER applies to a distinctive mode of behavior, or social attitude toward others, etc.: *a gracious manner.* AIR applies to outward appearance insofar as this is distinctive or indicative: *an air of martyrdom.* AIRS imply affectation: *to put on airs.* BEARING applies esp. to carriage: *a noble bearing.*

man·ner[2] (man′ər), *n. Old Eng. Law.* mainour.

man·nered (man′ərd), *adj.* **1.** having manners as specified (usually used in combination): *ill-mannered people.* **2.** having mannerisms; affected: *a mannered walk.* [ME *manered.* See MANNER[1], -ED[3]]

Man·ner·heim (mä′nər hām′), *n.* **Baron Carl Gus·taf E·mil von** (kärl go͝os′täf ā′mēl fən), 1867–1951, Finnish soldier and statesman.

Man′nerheim line′, a zone of Finnish fortification erected along part of the border between Finland and Russia before the Finno-Russian War. [named after Baron von MANNERHEIM]

man·ner·ism (man′ə riz′əm), *n.* **1.** marked or excessive adherence to an unusual or a particular manner, esp. if affected: *Natural courtesy is a world apart from snobbish mannerism.* **2.** (*usually cap.*) a style in the fine arts developed principally in Europe during the 16th century, chiefly characterized by a complex perspectival system, elongation of forms, strained gestures or poses of figures, and intense, often strident color. **3.** a habitual or characteristic manner, mode, or way of doing something; distinctive quality or style, as in behavior, speech, etc.: *They copied his literary mannerisms, but failed to get his ebullience. Each of us has his own peculiarities, or mannerisms, of speech or bearing.* [MANNER[1] + -ISM] —**man′ner·ist,** *n.* —**man′ner·is′tic,** *adj.* —**man′ner·is′ti·cal·ly,** *adv.*

man·ner·less (man′ər lis), *adj.* without good manners; discourteous; impolite. [ME *manerles.* See MANNER[1], -LESS] —**man′ner·less·ness,** *n.*

man·ner·ly (man′ər lē), *adj.* **1.** having or showing good manners; courteous; polite. —*adv.* **2.** with good manners; courteously; politely. [ME *manerly.* See MANNER[1], -LY] —**man′ner·li·ness,** *n.*

Man·ners (man′ərz), *n.* a crater in the first quadrant of the face of the moon: about 10 miles in diameter.

Man·nes (man′is), *n.* **Leopold Damrosch,** 1899–1964, U.S. composer and chemist.

Mann·heim (man′hīm; *Ger.* män′hīm), *n.* **1. Karl** (kärl; *Ger.* kärl), 1893–1947, German sociologist. **2.** a city in SW West Germany, on the Rhine. 321,100 (1963).

Mann′heim gold′, a brass alloy used to imitate gold; red brass.

Mann′heim School′, a group of musicians of the mid-18th century in Mannheim, Germany, notable for developing a style of orchestral composition and performance directly antecedent to and influential on the classical style of Haydn and Mozart.

Man·nie (man′ē), *n.* a boy's given name, form of **Emanuel.** Also, **Manny.**

man·ni·kin (man′ə kin), *n.* **1.** manikin. **2.** any of several estrildine finches of the genus *Lonchura,* of Asia, Australia, and the Pacific islands, often kept as pets. [var. of MANIKIN]

Man·ning (man′ing), *n.* **1. Henry Edward,** 1808–92, English prelate and ecclesiastical writer: cardinal 1875–92. **2.** a town in central South Carolina. 3917 (1960).

Man·ning·ton (man′ing tən), *n.* a town in N West Virginia. 2996 (1960).

man·nish (man′ish), *adj.* **1.** (of a woman or her behavior, attributes, etc.) resembling, characteristic of, natural to, or appropriate for a man: *She has a mannish voice. She is a mannish old lady.* **2.** resembling a man, as in size, manner, etc.: *a mannish youth.* **3.** imitating a man or something associated with a man: *a mannish shirt; a mannish hair style.* [ME; see MAN[1], -ISH[1]] —**man′nish·ly,** *adv.* —**man′nish·ness,** *n.*
—**Syn. 1, 2.** See **manly.**

man·nite (man′īt), *n.* mannitol. [MANN(OSE) + -ITE[1]]

man·ni·tol (man′i tōl′, -tôl′, -tol′), *n. Chem.* a white, crystalline, sweetish, water-soluble, carbohydrate alcohol, $HOCH_2(CHOH)_4CH_2OH$, occurring in three optically different forms, the common one being found in the manna of the ash *Fraxinus Ornus* and in other plants: used chiefly in the manufacture of resins, electrolytic condensers for radios, plasticizers, and mannitol hexanitrate, and as a pill excipient. [MANNITE + -OL[1]]

man′nitol hexani′trate, *Chem., Pharm.* a colorless, crystalline, water-insoluble, explosive solid, $C_6H_8(ONO_2)_6$, used as a fulminating agent in percussion caps, and in the treatment of hypertension and coronary insufficiency. Also called **nitromannitol, nitromannite.**

man·nose (man′ōs), *n. Chem.* a hexose, $C_6H_{12}O_6$, obtained from the hydrolysis of the ivory nut, and yielding mannitol upon reduction. [MANN(A) + -OSE[2]]

Man·ny (man′ē), *n.* a boy's given name, form of **Emanuel.** Also, **Mannie.**

Ma·no·ah (mə nō′ə), *n.* the father of Samson. Judges 13. Also, *Douay Bible,* **Manue.**

ma·noeu·vre (mə no͞o′vər), *n., v.t., v.i.,* **-vred, -vring.** maneuver.

Man′ of Des′tiny, epithet of Napoleon I.

Man′ of Gal′ilee, Jesus.

man′ of God′, 1. a saint, prophet, etc. **2.** a clergyman.

Man′ of Prop′erty, The, a novel (1906) by John Galsworthy. Cf. **Forsyte Saga, The.**

Man′ of Sor′rows, (in Christian exegesis) an appellation of Jesus Christ as the suffering Savior. Isa. 53:3.

man′ of straw′. See **straw man.**

man′ of the cloth′, a clergyman or other ecclesiastic.

man-of-the-earth (man′əv t͟hē ûrth′, -ûrth′), *n., pl.* **men-of-the-earth, man-of-the-earths.** a morning-glory, *Ipomoea pandurata,* of eastern North America, having a very large, tuberous root. Also called **manroot, wild potato, wild sweet potato.**

man′ of the house′, the male head of a household.

man′ of the world′, a worldly, sophisticated man; a man who is widely experienced in the ways of people: *The ambassador was an able, cosmopolitan man of the world.*

man-of-war (man′əv wôr′), *n., pl.* **men-of-war. 1.** a warship. **2.** See **Portuguese man-of-war.**

man′-of-war′ fish′, a small, tropical fish, *Nomeus gronovii,* commonly found living among the tentacles of the Portuguese man-of-war.

Ma·no·le·te (mä′nô le′te), *n.* (*Manuel Laureano Rodríguez y Sánchez*) 1917–47, Spanish matador.

ma·nom·e·ter (mə nom′i tər), *n.* an instrument for measuring the pressure of a fluid, consisting of a tube filled with a liquid so that the level of the liquid is determined by the fluid pressure and the height of the liquid may be read from a scale. [< F *manomètre,* equiv. to *mano* (< Gk *manós* loose, rare, sparse) + *-mètre* -METER] —**man·o·met·ric** (man′ə me′trik), **man′o·met′ri·cal,** *adj.* —**man′o·met′ri·cal·ly,** *adv.* —**ma·nom′e·try,** *n.*

Ma·non (mᴀ nôɴ′), *n.* an opera (1884) by Jules Massenet.

Ma·no Ne·ra, La (lä mä′nô ne′rä), *Italian.* See **Black Hand** (def. 1a).

man′ on horse′back, a military figure who presents himself as the savior of the country during a period of crisis and either assumes or threatens to assume dictatorial powers.

Ma·non Les·caut (mᴀ nôɴ les kō′), **1.** a novel (1731) by Marcel Prévost. **2.** an opera (1893) by Giacomo Puccini.

Ma·no·no (mä nō′nō), *n.* a city in the E Republic of the Congo. 28,465 (est. 1954).

man·or (man′ər), *n.* **1.** (in England) a landed estate or territorial unit, originally of the nature of a feudal lordship, consisting of a lord's demesne and of lands within which he has the right to exercise certain privileges, exact certain fees, etc. **2.** any similar territorial unit in medieval Europe, as a feudal estate. **3.** the mansion of a lord with the land belonging to it. **4.** the main house or mansion on an estate, plantation, etc. [ME *maner* < OF *manoir,* n. use of *manoir* to remain, dwell < L *manēre* to remain; see MANSION] —**ma·no·ri·al** (mə nōr′ē əl, -nôr′-), *adj.*

Man·or·ha·ven (man′ər hā′vən), *n.* a town on NW Long Island, in SE New York. 3566 (1960).

man′or house′, the house of the lord of a manor. Also called **mansion.**

ma·no·ri·al·ism (mə nōr′ē ə liz′əm, -nôr′-), *n.* the manorial organization, or its principles and practices in the Middle Ages; manorial system. [MANORIAL + -ISM]

ma·no·ri·al·ize (mə nōr′ē ə līz′, -nôr′-), *v.t.,* **-ized, -iz·ing.** to bring under manorialism. [MANORIAL + -IZE]

mano′rial sys′tem, manorialism.

man′-o′-war′ bird′ (man′ə wôr′). See **frigate bird.**

man′ pow′er, 1. the power supplied by the physical exertions of a man or men: *an ancient building constructed entirely by man power.* **2.** a unit of power, assumed to be equal to the rate at which a man can do mechanical work, and commonly taken as 1/10 horsepower. **3.** rate of work in terms of this unit. **4.** manpower.

man·pow·er (man′pou′ər), *n.* power in terms of men available or required: *the manpower of an army.* [MAN¹ + POWER]

manque (mäɴk), *n. French.* the numbers 1 to 18 in roulette: *douze: rouge, pair, et manque.* Cf. **passe.** [lit., lack]

man·qué (mäɴ kā′; *Eng.* mäng kā′), *adj. French.* having failed, missed, or fallen short, esp. because of circumstances or a defect of character; unsuccessful; unfulfilled: *He was little more than a poet* manqué.

man·root (man′ro͞ot′, -ro͝ot′), *n.* man-of-the-earth. [MAN¹ + ROOT¹]

man·rope (man′rōp′), *n. Naut.* a rope placed at the side of a gangway, ladder, or the like, to serve as a rail. [MAN¹ + ROPE]

man·sard (man′särd), *n.* **1.** Also called **man′sard roof′.** a form of curb roof the lower slope of which approaches the vertical and usually contains dormer windows, while the upper slope is nearly flat. **2.** the story under such a roof. See illus. under **roof.** [< F *mansarde,* named after N. F. MANSART]

Man·sart (mäɴ sᴀʀ′; *Eng.* man′särt), *n.* **1. Jules Har·douin** (zhʏl ᴀʀ dwaɴ′), (*Jules Hardouin*), 1646–1708, French architect: chief architectural director for Louis XIV. **2.** his grand-uncle, **(Ni·co·las) Fran·çois** (nē kô lä′ fʀäɴ swᴀ′), 1598–1666, French architect. Also, **Man·sard** (mäɴ sᴀʀ′; *Eng.* man′särd).

man's′ best′ friend′, *Facetious.* a dog, esp. as a pet.

manse (mans), *n.* **1.** the house and land occupied by a minister or parson. **2.** *Obs.* the dwelling of a landholder; mansion. [ME *manss* < ML *māns(us)* a farm, dwelling, n. use of ptp. of L *manēre* to dwell. See REMAIN]

man·serv·ant (man′sûr′vənt), *n., pl.* **men·serv·ants.** a male servant, esp. a valet. [MAN¹ + SERVANT]

Man's′ Fate′, a novel (1933) by André Malraux. French, **La Condition Humaine.**

Mans·field (manz′fēld), *n.* **1. Katherine** (*Kathleen Beauchamp Murry*), 1888–1923, English short-story writer. **2. Richard,** 1857–1907, U.S. actor, born in Germany. **3.** a city in W Nottinghamshire, in central England. 53,222 (1961). **4.** a city in N Ohio. 47,325 (1960). **5. Mount,** a mountain in N Vermont: highest peak of the Green Mountains. 4393 ft. **6.** a town in NW Louisiana. 5839 (1960). **7.** a town in SE Massachusetts. 4674 (1960). **8.** a town in N Pennsylvania. 2678 (1960).

Mans′field Park′, a novel (1814) by Jane Austen.

Mans′field Southeast′, a town in central Ohio. 2961 (1960).

man·sion (man′shən), *n.* **1.** a very large, impressive, or stately residence. **2.** See **manor house. 3.** Often, **mansions.** *Brit.* See **apartment house. 4.** *Oriental and Medieval Astron.* each of 28 divisions of the ecliptic occupied by the moon on successive days. **5.** *Archaic.* a place of abode, as in John 14:2. [ME < L *mānsiōn-* (s. of *mānsiō*) an abiding, abode. See MANSE, -ION]

man-sized (man′sīzd′), *adj. Informal.* large; big; of a kind or size fit for a man: *a man-sized undertaking; a man-sized bite of food.* Also, **man′-size′.**

man·slaugh·ter (man′slô′tər), *n.* **1.** the killing of a human being by another; homicide. **2.** *Law.* the killing of a human being unlawfully but without malice aforethought. [ME; see MAN¹, SLAUGHTER]

man·slay·er (man′slā′ər), *n.* one who kills a human being. [ME *manslaer.* See MAN¹, SLAYER] —**man′slay′ing,** *n., adj.*

Man·son (man′sən), *n.* **1. Sir Patrick,** 1844–1922, Scottish physician. **2.** a boy's given name.

Man spricht deutsch (män′ shpʀɪкнт′ doich′), *German.* German is spoken (here).

man·steal·ing (man′stē′ling), *n.* act of kidnaping. [MAN¹ + STEALING]

man·stop·per (man′stop′ər), *n. Mil. Slang.* a bullet striking with sufficient impact to knock down a charging soldier. [MAN¹ + STOPPER]

man·stop·ping (man′stop′ing), *adj. Mil.* of, pertaining to, or characteristic of a manstopper. [MAN¹ + STOPPING]

man·sue·tude (man′swi to͞od′, -tyo͞od′), *n.* mildness; gentleness: *the mansuetude of Christian love.* [ME < L *mansuētūdō* tameness, mildness, equiv. to *mansuēt(us)* tamed, gentle, lit., accustomed to the (guiding) hand (*man(us)* hand + *suētus,* ptp. of *suēscere* to grow accustomed) + *-ūdō* abstract n. suffix; see -TUDE]

Man·sur, al- (al′man so͝or′), (*′Abdullāh al-Mansūr*) A.D. 712?–775, Arab caliph 754–775: founder of Baghdad 764.

Man·sû·ra (man so͝or′ə; *Arab.* mon so͞o′rä), *n.* See **El Mansûra.**

man·ta (man′tə; *Sp.* män′tä), *n., pl.* **-tas** (-təz; *Sp.* -täs). **1.** (in Spain and Spanish America) a cloak or wrap. **2.** the type of blanket or cloth used on a horse or mule. **3.** *Mil.* a movable shelter formerly used to protect besiegers. **4.** See **manta ray.** [< Sp < Pr: blanket. See MANTLE]

Man·ta (män′tä, -tə), *n.* a seaport in W Ecuador, on Manta Bay. 19,021 (1950).

Man′ta Bay′, an inlet of the Pacific, on the W coast of Ecuador.

man-tai·lored (man′tā′lərd), *adj.* (of women's clothing) tailored in the manner and with the details of men's clothing. Cf. **dressmaker** (def. 2).

man·ta·pa (mun′tə pə), *n.* a porch or vestibule of a Brahman temple. Also, **man′tap·pa.** Also called **chaori.** [< Hindi]

man′ta ray′, a huge, tropical ray, reaching a width of 20 feet and having earlike flaps on each side of the head.

man·teau (man′tō, man tō′; *Fr.* mäɴ tō′), *n., pl.* **-teaus** (-tōz, -tōz′), *Fr.* **-teaux** (-tō′). *Obs.* a mantle or cloak, esp. one worn by women. [< F; see MANTLE]

Man·te·ca (man tē′kə), *n.* a town in central California. 8242 (1960).

Man·te·gna (män te′nyä), *n.* **An·dre·a** (än dʀe′ä), 1431–1506, Italian painter and engraver.

man·tel (man′tᵊl), *n.* **1.** a construction framing the opening of a fireplace and usually covering part of the chimney breast in a more or less decorative manner. **2.** Also called **mantelshelf.** a shelf above a fireplace opening. Also, **mantle.** Also called **mantelpiece, mantlepiece.** [late ME *mantell* mantelet; var. of MANTLE]

man·tel·et (man′tᵊlet′, mant′lit), *n.* **1.** a short mantle. **2.** Also, **mantlet.** *Mil.* **a.** manta (def. 3). **b.** any of various bulletproof shelters or screens. [ME < MF; see MANTLE, -ET]

Man·tell (man tel′, man′tel), *n.* **Robert Bruce,** 1854–1928, U.S. actor, born in Scotland.

man·tel·let·ta (man′tᵊlet′ə), *n. Rom. Cath. Ch.* a silk or woolen sleeveless vestment reaching to the knees, worn by cardinals, bishops, and other prelates. [< It, prob. < ML *mantelletum,* dim. of L *mantellum* MANTLE]

man·tel·lo·ne (man′tᵊlō′nē), *n. Rom. Cath. Ch.* a purple mantle extending to the ankles, worn over the cassock by lesser prelates of the papal court. [< It, aug. of *mantello* MANTLE]

man·tel·piece (man′tᵊl pēs′), *n.* mantel. [MANTEL + PIECE]

man·tel·shelf (man′tᵊl shelf′), *n., pl.* **-shelves.** mantel (def. 2). [MANTEL + SHELF]

man·tel·tree (man′tᵊl trē′), *n.* **1.** a wooden or stone lintel over the opening of a fireplace. **2.** a masonry arch used in place of such a lintel. Also, **mantletree.** [late ME; see MANTEL, TREE]

Man′ That Corrupt′ed Had′ley·burg, The (had′lē bûrg′), a short story (1900) by Mark Twain.

Mantilla

man·tic (man′tik), *adj.* **1.** of or pertaining to divination. **2.** having the power of divination. [< Gk *mantik(ós)* of, for a soothsayer, prophetic. See MANTIS, -IC] —**man′ti·cal·ly,** *adv.*

-mantic, a combining form of **mantic,** used in the formation of adjectives corresponding to nouns with stems in *-mancy: necromantic.*

man·tid (man′tid), *n.* mantis. [MANT(IS) + -ID²]

man·til·la (man til′ə, -tē′ə), *n.* **1.** a silk or lace head scarf arranged over a high comb and falling over the back and shoulders, worn in Spain, Mexico, etc. **2.** a short mantle or light cape. [< Sp; dim. of MANTA]

Man·ti·ne·a (man′tə nē′ə), *n.* an ancient city in S Greece, in Arcadia: battles 362 B.C., 223 B.C.

man·tis (man′tis), *n., pl.* **-tis·es, -tes** (-tēz). any of several predaceous insects of the order *Mantidae,* having a long prothorax and typically holding the forelegs in an upraised position as if in prayer. Also, **mantid.** Also called **praying mantis, praying mantid.** [< NL < Gk: prophet, kind of insect; akin to MANIA]

Mantis, *Mantis religiosa* (Length 2 in.)

man·tis·pid (man tis′pid), *n.* any neuropterous, mantislike insect of the family *Mantispidae,* the larvae of which are parasites in the nests of spiders or wasps. [< NL *Mantispid(ae)* family of insects, equiv. to *Mantis p(agana)* genus name (see MANTIS, PAGAN) + *-idae* -ID²]

man·tis·sa (man tis′ə), *n. Math.* the decimal part of a common logarithm. Cf. **characteristic** (def. 3a). [< L, var. of *mantīsa* makeweight, said to be from Etruscan]

man′tis shrimp′, any stomatopod crustacean having a pair of appendages modified for grasping prey and resembling those of a mantis.

Man·tius (man′shəs), *n. Class. Myth.* a son of Melampus and the father of Clitus.

man·tle (man′tᵊl), *n., v.,* **-tled, -tling.** —*n.* **1.** a loose, sleeveless cloak. **2.** something that covers, envelops, or conceals: *the mantle of darkness.* **3.** *Zool.* a single or paired outgrowth of the body wall that lines the inner surface of the valves of the shell in mollusks and brachiopods. **4.** a chemically prepared, incombustible network hood for a gas jet, kerosene wick, etc., which, when the jet or wick is lighted, becomes incandescent and gives off a brilliant light. **5.** *Ornith.* the back, scapular, and inner wing plumage, esp. when of the same color. **6.** Also called **man·tle·piece** (man′tᵊl-pēs′). mantel. **7.** *Metall.* a continuous beam set on a ring of columns and supporting the upper brickwork of a blast furnace in such a way that the brickwork of the hearth and bosh may be readily replaced. **8.** *Geol.* the portion of the earth, about 1800 miles thick, between the crust and the core. Cf. **crust** (def. 6), **core**¹ (def. 11). —*v.t.* **9.** to cover with or as with a mantle; envelop; conceal. —*v.i.* **10.** to spread like a mantle, as a blush over the face. **11.** to flush; blush. **12.** (of a hawk) to spread out one wing and then the other over the corresponding outstretched leg. **13.** to be or become covered with a coating, as a liquid; foam: *The champagne mantled in the glass.* [ME *mantel,* OE *mæntel* < L *mantell(um),* dim. of *mantum* cloak]

Man·tle (man′tᵊl), *n.* **1. Mickey (Charles),** born 1931, U.S. baseball player. **2. (Robert) Burns,** 1873–1948, U.S. journalist.

man′tle rock′, *Phys. Geog.* the layer of disintegrated and decomposed rock fragments, including soil, just above the solid rock of the earth's crust; regolith.

mant·let (mant′lit), *n. Mil.* mantelet (def. 2).

man·tle·tree (man′tᵊl trē′), *n.* manteltree.

man·tling (mant′ling), *n. Heraldry.* a decorative piece of cloth represented as hanging from a torse so as to cover the sides and rear of a helmet and often so as to frame the escutcheon below. Also called **lambrequin.** [MANTLE + -ING¹]

Man·to (man′tō), *n. Class. Myth.* a daughter of Tiresias who, like her father, had prophetic powers.

man-to-man (man′tə man′), *adj.* characterized by directness, openness, etc.: *He had a man-to-man talk with his son about sex.*

man′-to-man′ defense′, *Sports.* a method of defense, esp. in basketball and football, in which each member of the defensive team is designated to guard a particular member of the offensive team. Also called **man-for-man defense.** Cf. **zone defense.**

Man·toux′ test′ (man to͞o′, man′to͞o; *Fr.* mäɴ-to͞o′), *Med.* a test for tuberculosis in which a hypersensitive reaction to an intracutaneous injection of tuberculin indicates a tubercular condition, either healed or active, remote or recent. [named after C. *Mantoux* (b. 1877), French physician]

man·tra (man′trə, mun′-), *n. Hinduism.* a word or formula to be recited or sung. Also, **man·tram** (man′-trəm, mun′-). [< Skt: speech] —**man′tric,** *adj.*

man·trap (man′trap′), *n.* **1.** a trap for catching a man, esp. one who trespasses. **2.** *Informal.* an especially seductive woman.

man·tu·a (man′cho͞o ə), *n.* **1.** a loose gown formerly worn by women. **2.** a mantle. [var. of MANTEAU, by assoc. with MANTUA]

Man·tu·a (man′cho͞o ə), *n.* a city in E Lombardy, in N Italy: birthplace of Vergil. 61,580 (1961). Italian, **Man·to·va** (män′tô vä). —**Man′tu·an,** *adj., n.*

Man·u (man′o͞o), *n. Hindu Legend.* the progenitor and lawgiver of the human race.

Ma·nu′a Is′lands (mä no͞o′ä, mə no͞o′ə), a group of three small islands in the E part of American Samoa. 2695 (1960).

man·u·al (man′yo͞o əl), *adj.* **1.** of or pertaining to the hand or hands: *manual deformities.* **2.** done, worked, etc., by the hand or hands: *a manual gearshift.* **3.** involving or using human power, energy, etc.: *manual labor.* **4.** of the nature of a manual or handbook: *manual instructions.* —*n.* **5.** a small book, esp. one giving information or instructions: *a manual of golf.* **6.** *Mil.* prescribed drill in handling a rifle: *the manual of arms.* **7.** *Music.* a keyboard, esp. one of several belonging to a pipe organ. [< L *manuāl(is)* (adj.), *manuāle* (n.) (something) that can be held in the hand (*manu(s)* hand + *-ālis, -āle* -AL¹); r. late ME *manuel* < MF] —**man′u·al·ly,** *adv.*

man′ual train′ing, training in the various manual arts and crafts, esp. woodworking.

ma·nu′bi·al col′umn (mə no͞o′bē əl, -nyo͞o′-), **1.** a triumphal column decorated with spoils of the enemy. **2.** any triumphal or memorial column. [< L *manubiāl(is),* equiv. to *manubi(ae)* spoils of war + *-ālis* -AL¹]

ma·nu·bri·um (mə no͞o′brē əm, -nyo͞o′-), *n., pl.* **-bri·a** (-brē ə), **-bri·ums. 1.** *Anat., Zool.* a segment, bone, cell, etc., resembling a handle. **2.** *Anat.* **a.** the uppermost of the three portions of the sternum. Cf. **gladiolus**

(def. 2), **xiphisternum. b.** the long process of the malleus. [< NL, L: a handle. See MANUS] **—ma·nu′bri·al,** *adj.*

man·u·code (man′yə kōd′), *n.* any of various birds of paradise of the New Guinea region, having dark, metallic plumage. [< F < NL *manucod(iata)* < Malay *mānuq dēwāta* bird of the gods]

man·u·duc·tion (man′yə duk′shən), *n.* **1.** act of directing or guiding. **2.** a means of direction, introduction, or guidance. [< ML *manūductiōn-* (s. of *manūductiō*) a leading by the hand. See MANUS, REDUCTION] **—man′u·duc′tive, man′u·duc′to·ry,** *adj.*

Ma·nu·e (mə nyo͞o′ē), *n. Douay Bible.* Manoah.

Man·u·el (man′yo͞o əl), *n.* a boy's given name, form of **Emanuel.**

manuf., **1.** manufacture. **2.** manufacturer. **3.** manufacturing.

man·u·fac·to·ry (man′yə fak′tə rē), *n., pl.* **-ries.** *Archaic.* a factory. [obs. *manufact* hand-made (< LL *manūfact(us)*; see MANUS, FACT) + -ORY²]

man·u·fac·ture (man′yə fak′chər), *n., v.,* **-tured, -tur·ing.** **—n. 1.** the making of goods or wares by manual labor or by machinery, esp. on a large scale: *the manufacture of television sets.* **2.** the making of anything: *the manufacture of body cells.* **3.** the thing or material manufactured: *Plastic is an important manufacture.* **—v.t. 4.** to make or produce by hand or machinery, esp. on a large scale. **5.** to make anything. **6.** to work up (material) into form for use: *to manufacture cotton.* **7.** to invent fictitiously; fabricate; concoct: *to manufacture an account of the incident.* **8.** to produce in a mechanical way without inspiration or originality: *to manufacture poetry.* [obs. *manufact* (see MANUFACTORY) + -URE] **—man′u·fac′tur·a·ble,** *adj.* **—man′u·fac′tur·al,** *adj.*

—Syn. 4. build. MANUFACTURE, ASSEMBLE, FABRICATE apply to processes in industry. MANUFACTURE, originally to make by hand, now means to make by machine or by industrial process: *to manufacture rubber tires.* To ASSEMBLE is to fit together the manufactured parts of something mechanical: *to assemble an automobile.* To FABRICATE is to construct or build by fitting standardized parts together: *to fabricate houses.* See **make. 7.** compose. **—Ant. 4.** destroy.

man·u·fac·tur·er (man′yə fak′chər ər), *n.* **1.** one who owns or runs a manufacturing plant. **2.** one who manufactures. [MANUFACTURE + -ER¹]

manufac′turer's a′gent, an agent representing one or more manufacturers in selling related but noncompeting goods, usually on a commission basis and in a particular territory.

man·u·mis·sion (man′yə mish′ən), *n.* act of manumitting. [late ME < L *manūmissiōn-* (s. of *manūmissiō*). See MANUMIT, MISSION]

man·u·mit (man′yə mit′), *v.t.,* **-mit·ted, -mit·ting.** to release from slavery or servitude. [late ME < L *manūmitt(ere),* earlier *manū ēmittere* to send away from (one's) hand, i.e., to set free. See MANUS, EMIT] **—man′u·mit′ter,** *n.*

ma·nure (mə no͝or′, -nyo͝or′), *n., v.,* **-nured, -nur·ing.** **—n. 1.** any natural or artificial substance for fertilizing the soil. **2.** excrement, esp. of animals, or other refuse used as fertilizer. **—v.t. 3.** to treat (land) with fertilizing matter; apply manure to. [late ME *manour* (v.) < MF *manouvrer* to do manual work. See MANEUVER] **—ma·nur′er,** *n.* **—ma·nu′ri·al,** *adj.* **—ma·nu′ri·al·ly,** *adv.*

ma·nus (mā′nəs), *n., pl.* **-nus. 1.** *Anat., Zool.* the distal segment of the forelimb of a vertebrate, including the carpus and the forefoot or hand. **2.** *Roman Law.* power over persons, as that of the husband over the wife. [< L: hand]

Ma·nus (mä′no͞os), *n., pl.* **-nus.** a member of a people living on the island of Manus, in the Admiralty Islands.

man·u·script (man′yə skript′), *n.* **1.** a book, document, letter, etc., written by hand. **2.** an author's copy of his work, written by hand or typewriter, that is used as the basis for typesetting. **3.** writing, as distinguished from print. **—adj. 4.** written by hand or typed. [< ML *manūscript(um)* something written by hand, equiv. to L *manū* by hand (abl. of *manus*) + *scriptum* written; see SCRIPT] **—man′u·script′al,** *adj.*

Ma·nu·ti·us (mə no͞o′shē əs, -nyo͞o′-), *n.* **Al·dus** (ôl′dəs, al′-), (*Teobaldo Mannucci* or *Manuzio*), 1450–1515, Italian printer and classical scholar.

man·ward (man′wərd), *adv.* **1.** Also, **man′wards.** toward man: *The church directed its attention manward as well as heavenward.* **—adj. 2.** directed toward man. [late ME; see MAN¹, -WARD]

man·way (man′wā′), *n.* a passage in a mine intended for the use of miners only. [MAN¹ + WAY]

Man′ Who Came′ to Din′ner, The, a comedy (1939) by George S. Kaufman and Moss Hart.

man·wise (man′wīz′), *adv.* in the manner of a man. [MAN¹ + -WISE]

Manx (mangks), *adj.* **1.** of or pertaining to the Isle of Man, its inhabitants, or their language. **—n. 2.** (*construed as pl.*) the inhabitants of the Isle of Man. **3.** the Gaelic of the Isle of Man, virtually extinct. [metathetic and syncopated form of earlier *Manisk(e)* (< Scand; cf. Icel *manskr* of the Isle of Man), equiv. to *man* MAN¹ + *-sk* -ISH¹]

Manx cat

manx′ cat′, a tailless variety of the domestic cat.

Manx·man (mangks′mən), *n., pl.* **-men.** a native or inhabitant of the Isle of Man. [MANX + -MAN]

man·y (men′ē), *adj.,* **more, most,** *n., pron.* **—adj. 1.** constituting or forming a large number: *many people.* **2.** being one of a large number (usually fol. by *a* or *an*): *Many a day it rained.* **—n. 3.** a great or considerable number: *Many were there; the rights of the many.* **—pron. 4.** many persons or things: *Many of us disagree with her ideas.* **5. one too many,** excessive; unnecessary; unwanted: *That drink is one too many. I feel that I am one too many in this company.* **6. one too many for,** superior to in force, strength, etc.; overwhelming: *The obstacles were one too many for him.* **7. the many,** the majority; the multitude: *the attitudes of the many.* [ME *mani, meni,* OE *manig, menig;* akin to OS, OHG *manag, menig,* Goth *managș,* Dan *mange*]

—Syn. 1. multifarious, multitudinous, myriad; divers, sundry, various. MANY, INNUMERABLE, MANIFOLD, NUMEROUS imply the presence or succession of a large number of units. MANY is a popular and common word for this idea: *many times.* NUMEROUS, a more formal word, refers to a great number, or to containing very many units: *letters too numerous to mention.* INNUMERABLE denotes number that is beyond count, or, more loosely, what is extremely difficult to count: *the innumerable stars in the sky.* MANIFOLD implies not only that the number is large but also that there is variety or complexity. **—Ant. 1.** few, single.

Man·y (man′ē), *n.* a town in W Louisiana. 3164 (1960).

Man·ya (mon′yə), *n.* a girl's given name, Polish form of **Mary.** Also, **Mania.**

man-year (man′yēr′), *n.* the amount of work done by one man in a year consisting of a standard number of man-days.

man·y-one (men′ē wun′; *usually read as* men′ē tə wun′), *adj. Logic, Math.* (of a relation) having the property that each element is assigned to only one element but that many elements may be assigned to the same element.

Man·yō·shū (män yô′shŏŏ), *n.* a collection of Japanese poetry compiled in the 8th century A.D. Also called **Collection of Ten Thousand Leaves.**

man·y·plies (men′ē plīz′), *n.* (*construed as sing.*) *Zool.* the omasum: so called from the many plies or folds of its membrane. [MANY + *plies,* pl. of PLY²]

man·y-sid·ed (men′ē sī′did), *adj.* **1.** having many sides. **2.** having many aspects: *a many-sided question.* **3.** having many interests, qualities, accomplishments, etc.; versatile: *The typical man of the Renaissance was many-sided.* **—man′y-sid′ed·ness,** *n.*

man·y-val·ued (men′ē val′yo͞od), *adj. Math.* (of a function) having the property that some elements in the domain have more than one image point; multiple-valued. Cf. **single-valued.**

man·za·nil·la (man′zə nēl′yə, -nē′ə), *n.* a pale, very dry sherry from Spain. [< Sp; see MANCHINEEL]

Man·za·nil·lo (män′sä nē′yô), *n.* a seaport in SE Cuba. 36,295 (1953).

man·za·ni·ta (man′zə nē′tə), *n.* **1.** any ericaceous shrub of the genus *Arctostaphylos,* of the western U.S. **2.** the fruit of one of these shrubs. [< Sp, dim. of *manzana* apple]

Man·zo·ni (män dzô′nē), *n.* **A·les·san·dro (Fran·ces·co Tom·ma·so An·to·nio)** (ä′les sän′drô frän ches′kô tôm mä′zô än tô′nyô), 1785–1873, Italian novelist, poet, and dramatist.

Man·zù (män zo͞o′), *n.* **Gia·co·mo** (jä′kô mô), born 1908, Italian sculptor.

Ma·o·ri (mä′ō rē, -ô rē, mou′rē, mä′rē), *n., pl.* **-ris,** (*esp. collectively*) **-ri,** *adj.* **—n. 1.** a member of a brown-skinned Polynesian people of New Zealand. **2.** a Polynesian language, the language of the Maoris. **—adj. 3.** of or pertaining to the Maoris or their language.

Mao Tse-tung (mou′ dzu′do͝ong′; *Eng.* mou′ dzə do͝ong′, tsə to͝ong′), 1893–1976, Chinese Communist leader: chairman of the People's Republic of China 1949–59; chairman of the Chinese Communist party 1943–1976. Also *Pinyin,* **Mao′ Ze·dong′.**

map (map), *n., v.,* **mapped, map·ping.** **—n. 1.** a drawing or representation, usually on a flat surface, of part or all of the surface of the earth or of some other heavenly body, of the heavens, etc., indicating a specific group of features, as land masses, countries, planets, etc., in terms of their relative size and position: *a map of Canada.* **2.** a maplike delineation or representation of anything: *The old man's face is a map of time.* **3.** *Math.* function (def. 4a). **4.** *Slang.* the face: *Wipe that smile off that ugly map of yours.* **5. off the map,** out of existence; into oblivion: *Whole cities were wiped off the map.* **6. put on the map,** to bring into the public eye; make known: *The discovery of gold put our town on the map.* **—v.t. 7.** to represent or delineate on or as on a map. **8.** to sketch or plan (often fol. by *out*): *to map out a new career.* [< ML *mapp(a)* (*mundī*) map (of the world); special use of L *mappa* napkin] **—map′pa·ble,** *adj.*

—Syn. 1. plan, outline, diagram. MAP, CHART, GRAPH refer to representations of surfaces, areas, or facts. MAP most commonly refers to a representation of the surface of the earth or a section of it, or an area of the sky: *a map of England.* A CHART may be an outline map with symbols conveying information superimposed on it, a map designed esp. for navigators on water or in the air, a diagram, or a table giving information in an orderly form: *a chart of the shoals off a coast.* A GRAPH may be a diagram representing a set of interrelated facts by means of dots or lines on a coordinate background; or it may use small figures (people, animals, machines, etc.) appropriate to the facts being represented, each figure standing for a specific number in statistics being given: *a graph of the rise in population from 1900 to 1940.*

Map (map), *n.* **Walter,** c1140–1209?, Welsh ecclesiastic, poet, and satirist. Also, **Mapes** (māps, mā′pēz).

ma·ple (mā′pəl), *n.* **1.** any of numerous trees or shrubs of the genus *Acer,* species of which are grown as shade or ornamental trees, for timber, or for sap. **2.** the wood of any such tree. **3.** *Bowling Slang.* pin (def. 10). [ME *mapel,* OE *mapul-,* in *mapultrēow, mapulder* mapletree, c. OS *mapulder*] **—ma′ple·like′,** *adj.*

Ma′ple Heights′, a city in NE Ohio, near Cleveland. 31,667 (1960).

ma′ple-leaved vibur′num (mā′pəl lēvd′), the dockmackie.

ma′ple sug′ar, a yellowish-brown sugar produced by boiling down maple syrup.

ma′ple syr′up, **1.** a syrup produced by partially boiling down the sap of the sugar maple or of any of several other maple trees. **2.** a commercial variety of such syrup, often mixed with cane sugar or some other sweetening agent.

Ma·ple·wood (mā′pəl wo͝od′), *n.* **1.** a town in NE New Jersey. 23,977 (1960). **2.** a city in SE Minnesota, near St. Paul. 18,519 (1960).

Map·pah (mä pä′), *n.* a body of Ashkenazic-oriented commentaries on the *Shulhan Aruk,* written by the Polish Talmudic scholar Moses Isserles (c1520–72) and incorporated by him into the code. Cf. **Shulhan Aruk.**

map·ping (map′ing), *n.* **1.** act of one who maps. **2.** *Math.* function (def. 4a). [MAP + -ING¹]

map′ tur′tle, any of several aquatic turtles of the genus *Graptemys,* as *G. geographica,* of the eastern and central U.S., usually having yellow stripes on the head and neck.

ma·quette (ma ket′, mə-), *n.* a small model or study in three dimensions for either a sculptural or an architectural project. [< F < It *macchietta,* dim. of *macchia* a sketch, complex of lines < L *macula* mesh, spot]

ma·qui (mä′kē), *n.* an evergreen shrub, *Aristotelia Macqui,* of Chile, having greenish-white flowers and purple berries, grown as an ornamental in S California. [< Sp < Mapuche]

ma·quis (mä kē′; *Fr.* MA kē′), *n., pl.* **-quis** (-kē′). (*often cap.*) a member of the French underground movement resisting the Nazis in World War II. [< F, special use of *maquis, makis* wild, bushy land (Corsican dial.) < It *macchie,* pl. of *macchia* a thicket < L *macula* spot]

Ma·quo·ke·ta (mə kō′kə tə), *n.* a town in E Iowa. 5909 (1960).

mar (mär), *v.t.,* **marred, mar·ring. 1.** to damage or spoil to a certain extent; render less perfect, attractive, useful, etc.; impair: *That billboard mars the view. The holiday was marred by bad weather. His character is marred by selfishness.* **2.** to disfigure; deface: *The painting was marred by cracks.* [ME *merre(n),* OE *merran* to hinder, waste; c. OS *merrian,* OHG *merren* to hinder, Icel *merja* to bruise, Goth *marzjan* to offend]

—Syn. 1, 2. flaw, injure; blot. MAR, DEFACE, DISFIGURE, DEFORM agree in applying to some form of injury. MAR is general, but usually refers to an external or surface injury, if it is a physical one: *The table top was marred by dents and scratches.* DEFACE refers to a surface injury which may be temporary or easily repaired: *a tablecloth defaced by penciled notations.* DISFIGURE applies to external injury of a more permanent and serious kind: *A birthmark disfigured one side of his face.* DEFORM suggests that something has been distorted or internally injured so severely as to change its normal form or qualities, or else that some fault has interfered with its proper development: *deformed by an accident which had crippled him; to deform feet by binding them.* **—Ant. 1, 2.** enhance, adorn.

Mar., March.

mar., **1.** maritime. **2.** married.

M.A.R., Master of Arts in Religion.

Ma·ra (mär′ə), *n.* **1.** *Hindu Myth.* the god of death, sometimes seen as one aspect of a god whose other aspect is Kama, or erotic desire. **2.** a girl's given name, form of **Mary.**

mar·a·bou (mar′ə bo͞o′), *n.* **1.** any of three large storks of the genus *Leptoptilus,* as *L. crumeniferus,* of Africa, *L. javanicus,* of the East Indies, and *L. dubius,* the adjutant stork, having under the wings and tail soft, downy feathers that are used in millinery and for making a furlike trimming or material. **2.** one of the feathers. **3.** the trimming or material made of the feathers. Also, **marabout.** [< F *marabout,* lit., MARABOUT]

Marabou, *Leptoptilus crumeniferus* (Length 5 ft.)

mar·a·bout (mar′ə bo͞ot′, -bo͞o′), *n.* **1.** *Islam.* **a.** a hermit or holy man, esp. in N Africa, often credited with supernatural powers. **b.** the tomb or shrine of such a man. **2.** marabou. [< F < Pg *marabuto* < Ar *murābiṭ*] **—mar′a·bout′ism,** *n.*

ma·rac·a (mə rä′kə, -rak′ə), *n.* a gourd or a gourd-shaped rattle filled with seeds or pebbles and used, often in a pair, as a rhythm instrument. [< Pg < Tupi]

Lake Maracaibo

Mar·a·cai·bo (mar′ə kī′bō; *Sp.* mä′rä kī′vô), *n.* **1.** a seaport in NW Venezuela. 358,875 (est. 1955). **2. Gulf of,** a gulf on the NW coast of Venezuela. **3. Lake,** a lake in NW Venezuela, an extension of the Gulf of Maracaibo. 100 mi. long; 75 mi. wide.

Mar·a·can·da (mar′ə kan′də), *n.* ancient name of **Samarkand.**

mar·age (mär′āj′), *v.t.,* **-aged, -ag·ing.** to treat (steel containing 18 to 25 percent nickel and other alloying elements), in order to improve strength and ductility, by heating and quenching to form martensite, then aging for a specified time at a temperature similar to that used in tempering. [named after Adolf *Martens* (1850–1914), German metallurgist; see -AGE]

Ma·ra·jó (mä′rä zhô′), *n.* an island in N Brazil, at the mouth of the Amazon. 19,000 sq. mi.

Ma·ral·di (mə ral′dē), *n.* a walled plain in the first quadrant of the face of the moon: about 23 miles in diameter.

Ma·ra·line (mär′ə lēn′, -līn′), *n.* a girl's given name. Also, **Ma·ra·li·na** (mär′ə lē′nə, -lī′nə).

mar·a·nath·a (mar′ə nath′ə), *interj.* O Lord, come: used as an invocation in I Cor. 16:22. [< Gk < Aram]

Ma·ra·nhão (mä′rə nyouN′), *n.* a state in NE Brazil. 2,492,139 (1960); 125,312 sq. mi. *Cap.:* São Luiz.

Ma·ra·ñón (mä′rä nyôn′), *n.* a river in Peru, flowing N and then E, joining the Ucayali to form the Amazon. 1000 mi. long.

ma·ras·ca (mə ras′kə), *n.* a wild cherry, *Prunus Cerasus Marasca,* yielding a small, bitter fruit, from which maraschino is made. [< It, aph. var. of *amarasca,* deriv. of *amaro* < L *amārus* bitter]

mar·a·schi·no (mar′ə skē′nō, -shē′-), *n.* a cordial or liqueur distilled from marascas. [< It; see MARASCA, -INE¹]

mar′aschi′no cher′ry, a cherry cooked in colored syrup and flavored with imitation maraschino, used to garnish desserts, cocktails, etc.

CONCISE ETYMOLOGY KEY: <, descended or derived from; >, whence; b., blend of, blended; c., cognate with; deriv., derivative; equiv., equivalent; imit., imitative; m., modification of; obl., oblique; r., replacing; s., stem; sp., spelling; trans., translation; ?, origin unknown, perhaps; *, hypothetical. See the full key inside the front cover.

ma·ras·mus (mə raz′məs), *n. Pathol.* gradual loss of flesh and strength from no apparent cause, occurring chiefly in infants. [< NL < Gk *marasmós* a wasting away, akin to *maraínein* to weaken, waste away] —**ma·ras′mic,** *adj.* —**ma·ras′moid,** *adj.*

Ma·rat (ma ra′), *n.* **Jean Paul** (zhäN pôl), 1743–93, French politician and journalist: leader in the French Revolution; assassinated by Charlotte Corday d'Armont.

Ma·ra·tha (mə rä′tə), *n.* Mahratta.

Ma·ra·thi (mə rä′tē, -rat′ē), *n.* an Indic language of Bombay and vicinity. Also, **Mahratti.**

mar·a·thon (mar′ə thon′, -thən), *n.* **1.** any long-distance race. **2.** a foot race on a course measuring 26 miles 385 yards. **3.** any long contest with endurance as the primary factor: *a dance marathon.* [allusion to Pheidippides' 26-mile run from *Marathon* to Athens to carry news of the Greek victory over the Persians] —**mar′a·thon′er,** *n.*

Mar·a·thon (mar′ə-thon′), *n.* **1.** a plain in SE Greece, in Attica: the Athenians defeated the Persians here 490 B.C. **2.** an ancient village that is near this plain. **3.** *Class. Myth.* a son of Epopeus and the father of Corinthus.

Mar·a·tho·ni·an (mar′ə thō′nē ən), *adj.* **1.** of or pertaining to Marathon. —*n.* **2.** a native or inhabitant of Marathon. [MARATHON + -IAN]

Mar′atho′nian bull′, *Class. Myth.* See **Cretan bull.**

ma·raud (mə rôd′), *v.i.* **1.** to rove in quest of plunder; make a raid for booty: *We heard that freebooters were marauding all across the country.* —*v.t.* **2.** to raid for plunder (often used passively): *At the war's end the country had been marauded by returning bands of soldiers.* —*n.* **3.** *Archaic.* act of marauding. [< F *maraud(er)*, deriv. of *maraud* rogue, vagabond] —**ma·raud′er,** *n.* —**Syn. 1, 2.** invade, attack; ravage, harry.

ma·raud·ing (mə rô′ding), *adj.* **1.** engaged in raiding for plunder, esp. roving about and ravaging an area: *marauding bands of outlaws.* **2.** undertaken for plunder: *a marauding raid.* [MARAUD + -ING²]

mar·a·ve·di (mar′ə vā′dē), *n., pl.* **-dis. 1.** a former gold coin issued by the Moors in Spain. **2.** a former minor copper coin of Spain, discontinued in 1848. [< Sp *maravedí* < Ar *Murābiṭīn* relating to the Almoravides, Moorish dynasty (11th-12th centuries), pl. of *Murābiṭ*; see MARABOUT]

mar·bel·ize (mär′bə līz′), *v.t.,* **-ized, -iz·ing.** marble. —**mar′bel·i·za′tion,** *n.*

mar·ble (mär′bəl), *n., adj., v.,* **-bled, -bling.** —*n.* **1.** limestone in a more or less crystalline state and capable of taking a high polish, occurring in a wide range of colors and variegations and used in sculpture and architecture. **2.** a variety of this stone: *Carrara marble.* **3.** a piece of this stone: *the fallen marbles of Roman ruins.* **4.** a work of art carved in marble: *Renaissance marbles.* **5.** a marbled appearance or pattern; marbling: *The woodwork had a greenish marble.* **6.** something resembling marble in hardness, coldness, smoothness, etc.: *a brow of marble.* **7.** something lacking in warmth or feeling. **8.** a little ball made of stone, baked clay, glass, porcelain, agate, or steel, esp. for use in games. **9. marbles,** (*construed as sing.*) a game for children in which a marble is propelled by the thumb to hit other marbles, so as to drive them out of a circle drawn or scratched on the ground. **10. marbles,** *Slang.* normal rational faculty; wits; common sense: *to lose one's marbles; to be born without one's marbles.* —*adj.* **11.** consisting of marble. **12.** like marble, as in hardness, coldness, smoothness, etc. **13.** lacking in warmth, compassion, or sympathy: *marble heart.* **14.** of variegated or mottled color. —*v.t.* **15.** to color or stain like variegated marble. **16.** to apply a decorative pattern to (paper, the edges of a book, etc.) by transferring oil pigments floating on water. [ME *marbel*, dissimilated var. of OE *marmel* (in *marmelstān* marble stone) < L *marmor* < Gk *mármaros*, akin to *marmaírein* to sparkle] —**mar′bler,** *n.*

Mar·ble (mär′bəl), *n.* **Alice,** born 1913, U.S. tennis player.

mar′ble cake′, a loaf cake given a marblelike appearance by the incomplete mixing of dark and light batters.

Mar′ble Faun′, The, a novel (1860) by Nathaniel Hawthorne.

Mar·ble·head (mär′bəl hed′, mär′bəl hed′), *n.* a resort in NE Massachusetts: yachting. 18,521 (1960).

mar·ble·ize (mär′bə līz′), *v.t.,* **-ized, -iz·ing.** marble. [MARBLE + -IZE] —**mar′ble·i·za′tion,** *n.*

mar·bling (mär′bling), *n.* **1.** act, process, or art of coloring or staining in imitation of variegated marble. **2.** an appearance like that of variegated marble. **3.** *Bookbinding.* marblelike decoration on the paper edges, lining, or binding boards of a book. [MARBLE + -ING¹]

mar·bly (mär′blē), *adj.* like marble in appearance, hardness, coldness, etc. [late ME; see MARBLE, -Y¹]

Mar·burg (mär′bo͝orkh; *Eng.* mär′bûrg), *n.* **1.** a city in central West Germany. 47,800 (1963). **2.** German name of **Maribor.**

marc (märk; *Fr.* mar), *n.* **1.** the grapes contained in the wine press and the residue, as skins and pips, remaining after the juice is expressed. **2.** (in France) the brandy distilled from grape pomace. **3.** *Pharm.* the residue that remains following the extraction of active principles from a vegetable drug by means of a solvent. [< MF, akin to *marcher* to tread; see MARCH¹]

Marc (märk; *for 1 also Ger.* märk), *n.* **1. Franz** (fränts), 1880–1916, German painter. **2.** Also, **Mark.** a boy's given name, form of **Marcus.**

Mar·can (mär′kən), *adj.* of, pertaining to, or characteristic of St. Mark or of the second Gospel. Also, **Markan.**

Marc·an·ton·i·o (mär′kan tō′nē ō′), *n.* See **Raimondi, Marcantonio.**

Marc′ An′tony (märk). See **Antony, Mark.**

mar·ca·site (mär′kə sīt′), *n.* **1.** a common mineral, iron disulfide, FeS_2, chemically similar to pyrite but crystallizing in the orthorhombic system; white iron pyrites. **2.** (formerly) any of the crystallized forms of iron pyrites, much used in the 18th century for ornaments. **3.** a specimen or ornament of this substance. [late ME *markasit* < ML *marcasīta*, equiv. to *marcas-* (< ?) + *-īta* -ITE¹] —**mar·ca·sit·i·cal** (mär′kə sit′i-kəl), *adj.*

mar·ca·to (mär kä′tō; *It.* mär kä′tô), *adj.* (of notes or chords in a musical score) strongly accented. [< It: marked]

Mar·ceau (mär sō′; *Fr.* mar sō′), *n.* **Mar·cel** (mär-sel′; *Fr.* mar sel′), born 1923, French actor and pantomimist.

mar·cel (mär sel′), *v.,* **-celled, -cel·ling,** *n.* —*v.t.* **1.** to wave (the hair) by means of special irons, producing the effect of regular, continuous waves (**marcel′ waves′**). —*n.* **2.** a marcelling. **3.** a marcelled condition. [named after *Marcel* Grateau (1852–1936), French hairdresser who originated it] —**mar·cel′ler,** *n.*

Mar·cel (mär sel′; *Fr.* mar sel′), *n.* **1. Ga·bri·el** (ga bre el′), born 1887, French philosopher, dramatist, and critic. **2.** a boy's given name.

Mar·ce·line (mär′sə lēn′), *n.* a town in central Missouri. 2872 (1960).

mar·cel·la (mär sel′ə), *n.* a cotton or linen fabric constructed in twill weave, used in the manufacture of vests, mats, etc. [alter. of MARSEILLES]

Mar·cel·la (mär sel′ə), *n.* a girl's given name. Also, **Mar·celle** (mär sel′), **Marcile, Marcille.**

Mar·cel·lette (mär′sə let′), *n.* a girl's given name.

Mar·cel·li·na (mär′sə lē′nə), *n.* a girl's given name, form of **Marcella.** Also, **Mar·cel·line** (mär′sə lēn′).

Mar·cel·li·nus (mär′sə lī′nəs), *n.* **Saint,** died A.D. 304, pope 296–304.

Mar·cel·lo (mär chel′lô), *n.* **Be·ne·det·to** (be′ne-det′tô), 1686–1739, Italian composer.

Mar·cel·lus (mär sel′əs), *n.* **Marcus Claudius,** 268?–208 B.C., Roman general and consul.

Marcellus I, Saint, died A.D. 309, pope 308–309.

Marcellus II, (*Marcello Cervini*) 1501–55, Italian ecclesiastic: pope 1555.

mar·ces·cent (mär ses′ənt), *adj. Bot.* withering but not falling off, as a part of a plant. [< L *marcēscent-* (s. of *marcēscēns*) beginning to wither (prp. of *marcēscere*), equiv. to *marc(ēre)* (to) wither + *-ēscent-* -ESCENT] —**mar·ces′cence,** *n.*

march¹ (märch), *v.i.* **1.** to walk with regular and measured tread, as soldiers; advance in step in an organized body. **2.** to walk in a stately or deliberate manner. **3.** to go forward; advance; proceed: *It's time to start marching if we are to get our work finished.* —*v.t.* **4.** to cause to march. —*n.* **5.** act or course of marching. **6.** the distance covered in a single period of marching. **7.** advance; forward movement: *the march of science.* **8.** a piece of music with a rhythm suited to accompany marching. **9. on the march,** moving ahead; advancing: *Automation is on the march.* **10. steal a march on,** to gain an advantage over, esp. secretly or slyly. [< MF *march(i)er*, OF *marchier* to tread < ?]

march² (märch), *n.* **1.** a tract of land along a border of a country; frontier. **2. marches,** the border districts between England and Scotland, or England and Wales. —*v.i.* **3.** to touch at the border; border. [ME *marche*, OE *(ge)mearc*, *gem(i)erce* boundary + OF *marche* < Gmc; cf. Goth *marka* boundary]

March (märch), *n.* the third month of the year, containing 31 days. [ME *March(e)* < AF *Marche;* r. OE *Martius* < L, short for *Martius mēnsis* month of Mars (*Marti-*, s. of *Mars*, + *-us* adj. suffix)]

March (märch *for 1, 2;* märkh *for 3*), *n.* **1. Frederic** (*Frederick McIntyre Bickel*), born 1897, U.S. actor. **2. Pey·ton Con·way** (pāt′ən kon′wā), 1864–1955, U.S. army officer. **3.** German name of the **Morava.**

March., Marchioness.

M.Arch., Master of Architecture.

Mar·che (mär′ke), *n.* **Le,** Italian name of **The Marches.**

M.Arch.E., Master of Architectural Engineering.

Mär·chen (mer′khən), *n., pl.* **-chen.** *German.* fairy story; folk tale.

march·er¹ (mär′chər), *n.* one who marches on foot: *a line of marchers.* [MARCH¹ + -ER¹]

march·er² (mär′chər), *n. Hist.* an inhabitant of, or an officer or lord having jurisdiction over, a march or border territory. [late ME; see MARCH², -ER¹]

March·es (mär′chiz), *n.* **The,** a region in central Italy, bordering the Adriatic. 1,347,234 (1961); 3743 sq. mi. Italian, **Le Marche.**

mar·che·sa (mär ke′zä), *n., pl.* **-se** (-zē). **1.** an Italian noblewoman, equivalent in rank to a marchioness. **2.** the wife or widow of a marchese. [< It; fem. of MARCHESE]

mar·che·se (mär ke′ze), *n., pl.* **-si** (-zē). an Italian nobleman, equivalent in rank to a marquis. [< It; see MARQUIS]

Mar·chesh·van (mär hezh′vən; *Heb.* mär khesh-vän′), *n.* Heshvan.

Mar·chette (mär shet′), *n.* a girl's given name, form of **Marcia.**

March′ fly′, any of several dipterous insects of the family *Bibionidae* that appear during spring and early summer.

march′ing or′ders, *Mil.* orders to begin a march or other troop-movement.

mar·chion·ess (mär′shə nis, mär′shə nes′), *n.* **1.** the wife or widow of a marquis. **2.** a lady holding in her own right the rank equal to that of a marquis. [< ML *marchiōnissa*, equiv. to *marchiōn-* (s. of *marchiō*) MARQUIS (lit., man of the border; see MARCH²) + *-issa* -ESS]

march·land (märch′land′, -lənd), *n.* borderland. [MARCH² + LAND]

march-or·der (märch′ôr′dər), *v.t. Mil.* to prepare (personnel, arms, and equipment) for a march.

march·pane (märch′pān′), *n.* marzipan. [< F, dial. var. of *massepain*, *marcepain* < It *marzapane*, orig. sugar-candy box < Ar *mauṭabān* glazed vessel]

march-past (märch′past′, -päst′), *n.* a parade or procession, esp. of troops past a reviewing stand. [n. use of v. phrase *march past*]

Mar·cia (mär′shə), *n.* a girl's given name.

Mar·cian (mär′shən), *n.* A.D. 392?–457, emperor of the Eastern Roman Empire 450–457. Also, **Mar·ci·a·nus** (mär′shē ā′nəs, mär′sē-).

Mar·ci·a·no (mär′sē ä′nō, -an′ō), *n.* **Rocky** (*Rocco Francis Marchegiano*), born 1924, U.S. boxer: world heavyweight champion 1952–56.

Mar·cie (mär′sē), *n.* a girl's given name, form of **Marcia.** Also, **Marcy.**

Mar·cile (mär sēl′), *n.* a girl's given name. Also, **Marcella, Mar·cille′, Marcelle.**

Mar·cion (mär′shən, -shē ən, -sē ən), *n.* A.D. c100–c160, Christian Gnostic.

Mar·cion·ism (mär′shə niz′əm), *n.* the doctrines and principles of the Marcionites. [MARCION + -ISM]

Mar·cion·ite (mär′shə nīt′), *n.* **1.** a member of a Gnostic ascetic sect that flourished from the 2nd to 7th century A.D. and that rejected the Old Testament and denied the incarnation of God in Christ. —*adj.* **2.** of or pertaining to the Marcionites or their doctrines. Also, **Mar′cion·ist.** [< LL *Marciōnīta*. See MARCION, -ITE¹]

Mar·co·man·ni (mär′kō man′ī), *n.* (*construed as pl.*) an ancient Germanic people who lived in central Europe. —**Mar·co·man·nic** (mär′kō man′ik), *adj.*

Mar·co·ni (mär kō′nē; *It.* mär kô′nē), *n.* **1. Gu·gliel·mo** (go͞o lyel′mô), **Marchese,** 1874–1937, Italian electrical engineer and inventor, esp. in the field of wireless telegraphy: Nobel prize for physics 1909. —*adj.* **2.** (*sometimes l.c.*) pertaining to or noting the system of wireless telegraphy invented by Guglielmo Marconi.

mar·co·ni·gram (mär kō′nə gram′), *n. Rare.* a radiogram. [MARCONI + -GRAM¹]

mar·co·ni·graph (mär kō′nə graf′, -gräf′), *n.* the wireless telegraph of Guglielmo Marconi. [MARCONI + -GRAPH]

Marco′ni mast′, *Naut.* **1.** an elaborately stayed mast. **2.** *Obs.* a mast for a radio antenna.

Marco′ni rig′, *Naut.* a rig of triangular sails for a yacht. Also called **Bermuda rig, Bermudan rig, Bermudian rig.**

Mar·co Po·lo (mär′kō pō′lō). See **Polo, Marco.**

Mar·cos (mär′kōs), *n.* **Ferdinand E(d·ra·lin)** (ed′rə-lin), born 1917, Philippine political leader: president 1965–86.

Mar·cus (mär′kəs), *n.* **1. Saint.** Also, **Mark.** died A.D. 336, pope 336. **2.** a boy's given name.

Mar′cus Au·re′li·us (ô rē′lē əs, ô rēl′yəs), (*Marcus Annius Verus*) A.D. 121–180, Stoic philosopher and writer: emperor of Rome 161–180. Also called **Mar′cus Aure′lius An·to·ni′nus** (an′tə nī′nəs).

Mar·cy (mär′sē), *n.* **1. Mount,** a mountain in NE New York: highest peak of the Adirondack Mountains, 5344 ft. **2.** a girl's given name, form of **Marcia.**

Mar del Pla·ta (mär′ thel plä′tä), a city in E Argentina: seaside resort. 141,886 (est. 1958).

Mar·di gras (mär′dē grä′, grä′), the day before Lent, celebrated in some cities, as New Orleans and Paris, as a day of carnival and merrymaking; Shrove Tuesday. [< F: lit., fat Tuesday]

Mar·do·chai (mär′də kī′), *n. Douay Bible.* Mordecai (def. 1).

Mar·duk (mär′do͝ok), *n. Babylonian Religion.* the chief of the Babylonian deities. Also, **Merodach.** Also called **Baal Merodach.**

mare¹ (mâr), *n.* a fully mature female horse or other equine animal. [ME, var. of *mere*, OE *m(i)ere;* c. Icel *merr*, D *merrie*, G *Mähre;* akin to OE *mearh*, Icel *marr*, Ir *marc* horse. See MARSHAL]

mare² (mâr), *n. Obs.* nightmare (def. 3). [ME, OE; c. G *Mahre*, Icel *mara*. See NIGHTMARE]

ma·re³ (mär′ā, mâr′ē), *n., pl.* **ma·ri·a** (mär′ē ə, mâr′-). *Astron.* any of the several large, dark plains on the moon, believed by Galileo to be seas when he first saw them through a telescope. [< L: sea]

Mar.E., Marine Engineer.

Ma′re Acidal′ium (mär′ā, mâr′ē), an area in the northern hemisphere of Mars, appearing as a dark region when viewed telescopically from the earth.

Ma′re Aesta′tis (mär′ā, mâr′ē), a dark plain in the third quadrant of the face of the moon: about 600 square miles. Also called **Summer Sea.**

Ma′re An′guis (mär′ā, mâr′ē), a dark plain in the first quadrant of the face of the moon: about 1800 square miles. Also called **Serpent Sea.**

Ma′re Austral′e (mär′ā, mâr′ē), **1.** Also called **Southern Sea.** a dark plain in the fourth quadrant of the face of the moon: about 60,000 square miles. **2.** an area near the south pole of Mars, appearing as a dark region when viewed telescopically from the earth.

Ma′re Autum′ni (mär′ā, mâr′ē), a dark plain in the third quadrant of the face of the moon: about 2300 square miles. Also called **Autumn Sea.**

Ma′re Bo′reum (mär′ā, mâr′ē), an area near the north pole of Mars, appearing as a dark region when viewed telescopically from the earth.

Ma′re Chro′nium (mär′ā, mâr′ē), an area in the southern hemisphere of Mars, appearing as a dark region when viewed telescopically from the earth.

Ma′re Cimmer′ium (mär′ā, mâr′ē), an area in the southern hemisphere of Mars, appearing as a dark region when viewed telescopically from the earth.

ma·re clau·sum (mâr′ē klô′səm; *Lat.* mä′re klou′-so͝om), a body of navigable water under the sole jurisdiction of a nation. [< L: closed sea]

Ma′re Cog′nitum (mär′ā, mâr′ē), an area in the third quadrant of the face of the moon: formerly part of Mare Nubium; renamed after being photographed by Ranger VII on July 28, 1964.

Ma′re Cri′sium (mär′ā, mâr′ē), a dark plain in the first quadrant of the face of the moon: about 66,000 square miles. Also called **Sea of Crises.**

Ma′re Desider′ii (mär′ā, mâr′ē), a dark plain in the averted hemisphere or far side of the moon.

Ma′re Erythrae′um (mär′ā, mâr′ē), an area in the southern hemisphere of Mars, appearing as a dark region when viewed telescopically from the earth.

Ma′re Fecundita′tis (mär′ā, mâr′ē), a dark plain in the fourth quadrant and extending into the first quadrant of the face of the moon: about 160,000 square miles. Also called **Sea of Fertility, Sea of Plenty.**

Ma′re Frigo′ris (mär′ā, mâr′ē), a dark plain in the northern hemisphere, in the first and second quadrants of the face of the moon: about 55 miles wide at its narrowest width and 750 miles long: about 67,000 square miles. Also called **Sea of Cold.**

Ma/re Hie/mis (mär/ā, mâr/ē), a dark area in the third quadrant of the face of the moon. Also called **Winter Sea.**

Ma/re Humboldtia/num (mär/ā, mâr/ē), a dark plain in the first quadrant of the face of the moon: about 20,000 square miles. Also called **Humboldt's Sea.**

Ma/re Hu/morum (mär/ā, mâr/ē), a dark plain in the third quadrant of the face of the moon: about 45,000 square miles. Also called **Sea of Moisture.**

Ma/re Im/brium (mär/ā, mâr/ē), a dark plain in the second quadrant of the face of the moon: about 340,000 square miles. Also called **Sea of Showers, Sea of Rains.**

Ma/re Incogni/to (mär/ā, mâr/ē), a dark plain in the averted hemisphere or far side of the moon, extending into the libration area of the first quadrant of the face of the moon. Also called **Unknown Sea.**

Mare/ Is/land (mâr), an island in the N part of San Francisco Bay, California: U.S. navy yard.

mar·e·kan·ite (mar/ə kə nīt/), *n.* a rhyolitic perlite occurring in weathered, rounded pebbles. [named after *Marekana* river in eastern Siberia; see -ITE[1]]

Ma·rel·da (mə rel/də), *n.* a girl's given name.

ma·re li·be·rum (mâr/ē lib/ər əm; *Lat.* mä/RE lē/be-RŏŏM/), a body of navigable water to which all nations have unrestricted access. [< L: free sea]

Ma/re Mar/ginis (mär/ā, mâr/ē), a dark plain in the first quadrant and in the libration area of the face of the moon: about 60,000 square miles. Also called **Border Sea.**

ma·rem·ma (mə rem/ə), *n., pl.* **-rem·me** (-rem/ē). **1.** a marshy region near the seashore, esp. in Italy. **2.** the miasma associated with such a region. [< It < L *maritima,* fem. of *maritimus* MARITIME]

Ma/re Mos/coviae (mär/ā, mâr/ē), a dark plain in the averted hemisphere or far side of the moon: about 27,000 square miles. Also called **Moscow Sea.**

Ma/re Necta/ris (mär/ā, mâr/ē), a dark plain in the fourth quadrant of the face of the moon: about 26,000 square miles. Also called **Sea of Nectar.**

Ma·ren·go (mə reng/gō; *for 1 also It.* mä RENG/gô), *n., pl.* **-gos** for 3, *adj.* **—n. 1.** a village in Piedmont, in NW Italy: Napoleon defeated the Austrians 1800. 2034 (1961). **2.** a town in N Illinois. 3568 (1960). **3.** a former gold coin of Italy, issued by Napoleon after the battle of Marengo. **—adj. 4.** (*sometimes l.c.*) (of food) browned in oil and cooked with tomatoes, garlic, wine, and often mushrooms and brandy.

ma·re nos·trum (mä/RE nōs/tRŏŏm; *Eng.* mâr/ē nos/trəm), *Latin.* our sea, esp. the Mediterranean to the ancient Romans.

Ma/re No/vum (mär/ā, mâr/ē), a dark plain in the first quadrant and in the libration area of the face of the moon. Also called **New Sea.**

Ma/re Nu/bium (mär/ā, mâr/ē), a dark plain in the third quadrant of the face of the moon: about 95,000 square miles. Also called **Sea of Clouds.**

mar·e·o·graph (mar/ē ə graf/, -gräf/), *n.* marigraph.

Ma/re Orienta/lis (mär/ā, mâr/ē), a dark plain in the third quadrant and in the libration area of the face of the moon. Also called **Eastern Sea.**

Ma/re Par/vum (mär/ā, mâr/ē), a dark plain in the third quadrant of the face of the moon. Also called **Little Sea.**

Ma/re Serenita/tis (mär/ā, mâr/ē), a dark plain in the first quadrant of the face of the moon: about 120,000 square miles. Also called **Sea of Serenity.**

Ma/re Sire/num (mär/ā, mâr/ē), an area in the southern hemisphere of Mars, appearing as a dark region when viewed telescopically from the earth.

Ma/re Smyth/ii (mär/ā, mâr/ē), a dark plain in the first quadrant and extending into the fourth quadrant of the face of the moon, in the libration area: about 63,000 square miles. Also called **Smyth's Sea.**

mare's-nest (mârz/nest/), *n.* **1.** something imagined to be an extraordinary discovery but proving to be a delusion or a hoax: *the mare's-nests of early navigators.* **2.** an extremely confused, entangled, or disordered place, situation, etc.: *As he has just moved in, his apartment is a mare's-nest.*

mares/ of Diome/des, *Class. Myth.* wild mares owned by Diomedes, a Thracian king, who fed them on human flesh; captured by Hercules in fulfillment of one of his labors.

Ma/re Spu/mans (mär/ā, mâr/ē), a dark plain in the first quadrant of the face of the moon: about 3,800 square miles. Also called **Foaming Sea.**

mare's-tail (mârz/tāl/), *n.* **1.** an erect, aquatic, Old World plant, *Hippuris vulgaris,* having crowded whorls of narrow, hairlike leaves. **2.** a cirrus cloud resembling a horse's tail.

Ma/re Stru/ve (mär/ā, mâr/ē). See **Struve.**

Ma·ret·ta (mə ret/ə), *n.* a girl's given name, form of **Margaret** or **Marietta.** Also, **Ma·rette** (mə ret/).

Ma/re Tranquillita/tis (mär/ā, mâr/ē), a dark plain in the first quadrant of the face of the moon: about 110,000 square miles. Also called **Sea of Tranquillity.**

Ma/re Tyrrhe/num (mär/ā, mâr/ē), a dark area in the southern hemisphere of Mars, appearing as a dark region when viewed telescopically from the earth.

Ma/re Unda/rum (mär/ā, mâr/ē), a dark plain in the first quadrant of the face of the moon: about 4800 square miles. Also called **Sea of Waves.**

Ma/re Vapo/rum (mär/ā, mâr/ē), a dark plain in the first quadrant and near the center of the face of the moon: about 39,000 square miles. Also called **Sea of Vapors.**

Ma/re Ver/is (mär/ā, mâr/ē), a dark plain in the third quadrant of the face of the moon. Also called **Spring Sea.**

ma·rez·zo (mə ret/zō), *n.* an imitation marble composed of Keene's cement, fiber, and coloring matter.

Mar·fa (mär/fə), *n.* a town in W Texas. 2799 (1960).

marg., **1.** margin. **2.** marginal.

mar·ga (mär/gə), *n.* *Hinduism.* any of the three ways to salvation, which are those of devotion to certain gods (**bhakti-marga**), of study (**jnana-marga**), and of actions (**karma-marga**). [< Skt: path]

Mar·ga·ret (mär/gə rit, -grit), *n.* a girl's given name. Also, **Mar·ga·re·ta** (mär/gə rē/tə, -rēt/ə), **Mar·ga·ret·ta** (mär/gə ret/ə, -rē/tə), **Mar·ga·rete** (mär/gə rēt/), **Mar·ga·rette** (mär/gə ret/).

Mar/garet of An/jou, 1430–82, queen of Henry VI of England.

Mar/garet of Navarre/, 1492–1549, queen of Navarre 1544–49: patroness of literature, authoress of stories, and poet. Also called **Mar/garet of An·gou·lême/** (äng/gŏŏ lem/; *Fr.* äN gōō lem/).

Mar/garet of Valois/, (*"Queen Margot"*) 1533–1615, 1st wife of Henry IV of France: queen of Navarre; patroness of science and literature (daughter of Henry II of France and Catherine de' Medici). Also called **Mar/garet of France/.**

Mar/garet Rose/, born 1930, English princess (daughter of George VI; sister of Elizabeth II).

mar·gar/ic ac/id (mär gar/ik, -gär/-), *Chem.* a colorless, crystalline, water-insoluble, fatty acid, $CH_3(CH_2)_{15}COOH$, resembling stearic acid, obtained from lichens or synthetically. [< Gk *márgar(on)* pearl + -IC]

mar·ga·rine (mär/jər in, -jə rēn/, märj/rin), *n.* **1.** a butterlike product made of refined vegetable oils, sometimes blended with animal fats, and emulsified, usually with milk. **2.** oleomargarine. Also, **mar·ga·rin** (mär/jər in, märj/rin). [MARGAR(IC) + -INE[2]]

mar·ga·ri·ta·ceous (mär/gər i tā/shəs), *adj.* resembling mother-of-pearl; pearly. [< NL *margarītāceus.* See MARGARITE, -ACEOUS]

mar·ga·rite (mär/gə rīt/), *n.* **1.** a mineral, hydrated aluminum calcium silicate, $H_2CaAl_4Si_2O_{12}$, occurring in monoclinic crystals having a gray, pink, or yellowish color. **2.** an aggregate of small, rudimentary crystals resembling minute globules in a row. **3.** *Obs.* a pearl. [ME < L *margarīta* < Gk *margarī́tēs,* equiv. to *márgar(on)* pearl + *-ītēs* -ITE[1]]

mar·gate (mär/gāt, -git), *n.* *Ichthyol.* an edible grunt, *Haemulon album,* found from Florida to Brazil. [perh. after MARGATE]

Mar·gate (mär/gāt), *n.* a city in E Kent, in SE England: seaside resort. 45,780 (1961).

Mar/gate Cit/y, a town in S New Jersey. 9474 (1960).

Mar·gaux (*Fr.* MAR gō/), *n.* a dry red claret from the parish of Margaux in the Bordeaux region.

mar·gay (mär/gā), *n.* a small tiger cat, *Felis tigrina,* of tropical America. [< F, alter. of *margaia* < Pg *maracajá* < Tupi *mbaracaiá*]

marge[1] (märj), *n.* *Archaic.* margin; edge. [< MF < L *margō;* see MARGIN]

marge[2] (märj), *n.* *Chiefly Brit. Informal.* margarine. [shortened form]

Marge (märj), *n.* a girl's given name, form of **Margaret.**

mar·gent (mär/jənt), *n.* *Archaic.* margin. [late ME *margente,* alter. of MARGIN]

Mar·ger·y (mär/jə rē), *n.* a girl's given name, form of **Margaret.**

Mar·ghe·ri·ta (mär/gə rē/tə; *It.* mär/ge RĒ/tä), *n.* a girl's given name, Italian form of **Margaret.**

Mar·gie (mär/jē), *n.* a girl's given name, form of **Margaret.**

mar·gin (mär/jin), *n.* **1.** a border or edge. **2.** the space around the printed or written matter on a page. **3.** a limit in condition, capacity, etc., beyond or below which something ceases to exist, be desirable, or be possible: *the margin of endurance; the margin of sanity.* **4.** an amount allowed or available beyond what is actually necessary: *to allow a margin for error; a margin for unforeseen expenses.* **5.** *Finance.* **a.** security, as a percentage in money, deposited with a broker as a provision against loss on transactions on behalf of his principal. **b.** the amount representing the customer's investment or equity in such an account. **6.** the difference between the amount of a loan and the market value of the collateral pledged as security for it. **7.** *Com.* the difference between the cost and the selling price. **8.** *Econ.* the point at which the return from economic activity barely covers the cost of production, and below which production is unprofitable. **—v.t. 9.** to provide with a margin or border. **10.** to furnish with marginal notes, as a document. **11.** to enter in the margin, as of a book. **12.** *Finance.* to deposit a margin upon. [ME < L *margin-* (s. of *margō*) border; akin to MARCH[2]]
—Syn. 1. rim, verge, brink. See **edge. 3.** confine, bound. **—Ant. 1.** center.

mar·gin·al (mär/jə nəl), *adj.* **1.** pertaining to a margin. **2.** situated on the border or edge. **3.** at the outer or lower limits; minimal for requirements; almost insufficient: *marginal subsistence; marginal ability.* **4.** written or printed in the margin of a page: *a marginal note.* **5.** marked by contact with two or more different groups, the cultural values and traits of which have not been completely accepted. **6.** *Econ.* **a.** selling goods at a price which just equals the additional cost of producing the last unit supplied. **b.** of or pertaining to goods produced and marketed at margin: *marginal profits.* [< ML *margināl(is)* of, pertaining to an edge. See MARGIN, -AL[1]] **—mar/gin·al/i·ty,** *n.* **—mar/gin·al·ly,** *adv.*

mar·gi·na·li·a (mär/jə nā/lē ə, -nāl/yə), *n.pl.* marginal notes. [< NL, n. use of neut. pl. of ML *margin-ālis* MARGINAL]

mar/ginal man/, *Sociol.* a person who lives on the margins of two cultural groups without feeling identified with either group.

mar/ginal sea/, water that lies alongside a state, falls under its authority, and extends about 3½ statute miles from the coast.

mar/ginal util/ity, *Econ.* the extra utility or satisfaction derived by a consumer from the consumption of the last unit of a commodity.

mar·gin·ate (mär/jə nāt/), *adj., v.,* **-at·ed, -at·ing.** **—adj.** Also, **mar/gin·at/ed. 1.** having a margin. **2.** *Entomol.* having the margin of a distinct color: *marginate with purple.* **—v.t. 3.** to furnish with a margin; border. [< L *margināt(us)* furnished with a border, bordered, ptp. of *margināre.* See MARGIN, -ATE[1]] **—mar/gin·a/tion,** *n.*

mar·gi·nis (mär/gə nis) *n.* **Mare.** See **Mare Marginis.**

mar/gin line/, **1.** *Naval Archit.* an imaginary line used in making calculations regarding the flooding of hulls, running fore-and-aft three inches below the upper surface of the bulkhead deck at the side. **2.** *Naut.* the line along which the planking on a transom-sterned vessel terminates aft.

mar/gin plank/, *Naut.* a plank forming a border for wooden decking. Also called **waterway plank.**

Mar·got (mär/gō, -gət), *n.* a girl's given name.

Mar·gra·jean (mär/grə jēn/), *n.* a girl's given name.

mar·gra·vate (mär/grə vāt/), *n.* the province or territory of a margrave. Also, **mar·gra·vi·ate** (mär-grā/vē āt/). [MARGRAVE + -ATE[1]]

mar·grave (mär/grāv), *n.* **1.** the hereditary title of the rulers of certain states. **2.** *Hist.* a hereditary German title, equivalent to marquis. **3.** (originally) a German military governor of a mark, or border province. [earlier *marcgrave* < MD, equiv. to *marc* border (c. MARCH[2]) + *grave* count (c. REEVE[1])] **—mar·gra/vi·al,** *adj.*

mar·gra·vine (mär/grə vēn/), *n.* the wife of a margrave. [earlier *margravinne* < MD *marcgravinne,* equiv. to *marcgrave* MARGRAVE + *-inne* fem. n. suffix]

mar·gue·rite (mär/gə rēt/), *n.* **1.** Also called **Paris daisy.** the European daisy, *Bellis perennis.* **2.** any of several daisylike flowers, esp. *Chrysanthemum frutescens,* cultivated for its numerous white-rayed, yellow-centered flowers. [< F: daisy, pearl < L *margarīta* pearl < Gk; see MARGARITE]

Mar·gue·rite (mär/gə rēt/; *Fr.* MAR gə RĒT/), *n.* a girl's given name, form of **Margaret.**

mar-hawk (mär/hôk/), *n.* *Falconry.* a falconer who trains or handles his birds badly. [MAR + HAWK[1]]

Mar·hesh·van (mär hesh/vən; *Heb.* mäR KHESH-vän/), *n.* Heshvan.

Ma·ri·a (mə rē/ə, -rī/ə; *Du., Ger., It., Sp.* mä RĒ/ä), *n.* a girl's given name, form of **Mary.**

Ma·ri·a de Me·di·ci (*It.* mä rē/ä de me/dē chē). See **Marie de Médicis.**

ma·riage de con·ve·nance (MA RYAZH/ də kôN-və näNS/), *French.* See **marriage of convenience.**

ma·ri·a·lite (mə rē/ə līt/, mar/ē ə-), *n.* *Mineral.* a member of the scapolite group, rich in sodium and containing no calcium. [< G *Marialit;* named after *Marie* Rose, wife of Gerhard vom Rath, 19th-century German mineralogist; see -LITE]

Ma·ri·a Lu·i·sa (*Ger.* mä RĒ/ä lōō ē/sä). See **Marie Louise.**

Mar·i·am (mâr/ē əm), *n.* a girl's given name, form of **Mary.**

Mar·i·an (mâr/ē ən *or, for 6,* mar/-), *adj.* **1.** of or pertaining to the Virgin Mary. **2.** of or pertaining to some other Mary, as Mary Tudor of England or Mary, Queen of Scots. **—n. 3.** one who has a particular devotion to the Virgin Mary. **4.** an adherent or defender of Mary, Queen of Scots. **5.** a crater in the second quadrant of the face of the moon: about 25 miles in diameter. **6.** a girl's given name, form of **Mary.** [MARY + -AN]

Mar·i·a/na Is/lands (mâr/ē an/ə, mar/-; *Sp.* mä/RĒ ä/nä), a group of 15 small islands in the Pacific, E of the Philippines: except Guam, formerly mandated to Japan; now under U.S. trusteeship. 43,105 (est. 1955); 453 sq. mi. Also called **Marianas.** Formerly, **Ladrone Islands, Ladrones.**

Ma·ri·a·na·o (mä/rē ä nä/ô), *n.* a city in NW Cuba, a part of Havana.

Mar·i·an·na (mâr/ē an/ə, mar/-), *n.* **1.** a town in NW Florida. 7152 (1960). **2.** a town in E Arkansas. 5134 (1960). **3.** a girl's given name.

Mar·i·anne (mâr/ē an/, mar/-), *n.* **1.** the French Republic, personified as a woman. **2.** Also, **Maryanne.** a girl's given name.

Ma·ri·án·ské Láz·ně (mä/ryän ske läz/nye), Czech name of **Marienbad.**

Ma·ri·a The·re·sa (mə rē/ə tə rē/sə, -zə, mə rī/ə), 1717–80, archduchess of Austria; queen of Hungary and Bohemia 1740–80 (wife of Francis I; mother of Joseph II, Leopold II, Marie Antoinette). German, **Ma·ri·a The·re·si·a** (mä rē/ä te rā/zē ä).

Mari/a There/sa tha/ler, a former silver coin of Austria, issued between 1740 and 1780 and used or imitated for trade with Ethiopia and other countries; Levant dollar. Also called **Mari/a There/sa dol/lar.**

Mari/a tree/. See **calaba tree.**

Ma/ri Auton/omous Repub/lic (mär/ē; *Russ.* mu RYĒ/), an autonomous republic in the Russian Federation in Europe. 750,000; 8994 sq. mi. *Cap.:* Ioshkar-Ola.

Mar·i·bel (mâr/ē bel/), *n.* a girl's given name. Also, **Mar/i·belle/, Marybelle.**

Ma·ri·bor (mär/i bôr/), *n.* a city in N Slovenia, on the Drava River. 185,699. German, **Marburg.**

Ma·ri·ca (mə rē/kə), *n.* a deity worshiped in ancient Rome, sometimes as a goddess of marshes. Also called **Dea Marica.**

Ma·rie (mə rē/), *n.* **1.** (*Marie Alexandra Victoria of Saxe-Coburg*) 1875–1938, queen of Rumania 1914–27. **2.** a girl's given name, French form of **Mary.**

Ma·rie An·toi·nette (mə rē/ an/twə net/; *Fr.* MA-RĒ/ äN TWA NET/), (*Josèphe Jeanne Marie Antoinette*) 1755–93, queen of France 1774–93: wife of Louis XVI; executed in the French Revolution (daughter of Maria Theresa; sister of Joseph II, Leopold II).

Ma·rie/ Byrd/ Land/ (mə rē/ bûrd/), a part of Antarctica, SE of the Ross Sea: discovered and explored by Adm. Richard E. Byrd.

Ma·rie de France (MA RĒ/ də fRäNS/), fl. 12th century, French poet in England.

Ma·rie de Mé·di·cis (MA RĒ/ də mā dē sēs/), 1573–1642, queen of Henry IV of France: regent 1610–17. Italian, **Maria de Medici.**

Ma·rie Ga·lante (*Fr.* MA RĒ GA läNt/), an island in the E West Indies: a dependency of Guadeloupe. 16,037 (1954); 58 sq. mi.

Ma·ri·e·hamn (mä rē/ə hä/mən), *n.* a seaport on S Åland Island, in the Baltic. 7722 (est. 1965).

Ma·rie Lou·ise (mə rē/ lōō ēz/; *Fr.* MA RĒ/ lwēz/), 1791–1847, 2nd wife of Napoleon I: empress of France;

duchess of Parma 1816–31 (daughter of Francis I of Austria; mother of Napoleon II). German, **Maria Luisa.**

Ma·rie·mont (mə rē′mont), *n.* a town in SW Ohio. 4120 (1960).

Ma·ri·en·bad (mâr′ē ən bad′, mar′-; *Ger.* mä RĒ′ən-bät′), *n.* a spa and resort town in W Bohemia, in the W Czech Republic. 18,510. Czech, **Mariánské Lázně.**

Mar·i·et·ta (mâr′ē et′ə; *for 3 also It.* mä′RE et′tä), *n.* **1.** a city in NW Georgia. 25,565 (1960). **2.** a city in SE Ohio, on the Ohio River. 16,847 (1960). **3.** Also, **Mar·i·ett** (mâr′ē et′). a girl's given name, form of **Mary.**

Mar′iet′ta East′, a town in central Georgia. 4535 (1960).

Ma·riette (mᴀ ryet′), *n.* **Au·guste É·dou·ard** (ō-gʏsᴛ′ ā dwᴀʀ′), 1821–81, French Egyptologist.

Mar·i·fran·ces (mâr′ē fran′sis), *n.* a girl's given name. Also, **Maryfrances.**

Mar·i·gene (mâr′ə jēn′), *n.* a girl's given name.

mar·i·gold (mar′ə gōld′), *n.* **1.** any of several chiefly golden-flowered, composite plants, esp. of the genus *Tagetes*, as *T. erecta*, having strong-scented foliage. **2.** any of several other, unrelated plants, esp. of the genus *Calendula*, as *C. officinalis*, the pot marigold. [ME; see MARY (the Virgin), GOLD]

Mar·i·gold (mar′ə gōld′), *n.* a girl's given name.

mar′igold win′dow. See **wheel window.**

mar·i·gram (mar′ə gram′), *n.* a graphic representation from a marigraph. [< L *mari-* (comb. form of *mare* sea) + -GRAM[1]]

mar·i·graph (mar′ə graf′, -gräf′), *n.* a device that automatically registers the rise and fall of the tide. Also, **mareograph.** [< L *mari-* (comb. form of *mare* sea) + -GRAPH] —**mar·i·graph·ic** (mar′ə graf′ik), *adj.*

ma·ri·jua·na (mar′ə wä′nə, -hwä′-, mär′-), *n.* **1.** the Indian hemp, *Cannabis sativa.* **2.** its dried leaves and flowers, used in cigarettes as a narcotic. Also, **ma′ri·hua′na.** [< MexSp *marihuana*]

Mar·i·lee (mâr′ē lē′, mâr′i lē′), *n.* a girl's given name. Also, **Merilee, Marylee.**

Mar·i·lyn (mar′ə lin), *n.* a girl's given name, form of **Mary.** Also, **Mar′i·lynne, Marylyn, Marylynne.**

ma·rim·ba (mə rim′bə), *n.* a musical instrument, originating in Africa but popularized and modified in Central America, consisting of a set of graduated wooden bars, often with resonators beneath to reinforce the sound, struck with mallets. [< WAfr]

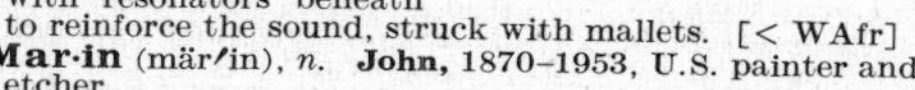

Marimba

Mar·in (mär′in), *n.* **John,** 1870–1953, U.S. painter and etcher.

ma·ri·na (mə rē′nə), *n.* a boat basin offering dockage and other service for small craft. [< It, Sp, n. use of fem. of *marino* < L *marīnus* MARINE]

Ma·ri·na (mə rē′nə), *n.* **1.** a town in W California. 3310 (1960). **2.** a girl's given name.

mar·i·nade (*n.* mar′ə nād′; *v.* mar′ə nād′), *n., v.,* **-nad·ed, -nad·ing.** —*n.* **1.** a seasoned liquid, usually of vinegar or wine with oil, herbs, spices, etc., in which meat, fish, vegetables, etc., are steeped before cooking. **2.** meat or fish steeped in it. —*v.t.* **3.** to marinate. [< F < Sp *marinada.* See MARINATE, -ADE[1]]

ma·ri·na·ra (mär′ə när′ə, mar′ə nar′ə), *n.* **1.** *Italian Cookery.* a highly seasoned sauce of tomatoes, garlic, and spices. —*adj.* **2.** garnished or served with marinara: *shrimps marinara.* [< It; see MARINATE]

mar·i·nate (mar′ə nāt′), *v.t.,* **-nat·ed, -nat·ing.** to let stand in a seasoned vinegar-oil mixture; marinade. [prob. < It *marinato,* ptp. of *marinare* to pickle. See MARINE, -ATE[1]] —**mar′i·na′tion,** *n.*

Ma·rin·du·que (*Sp.* mä′rin do͞o′ke), *n.* an island of the Philippines, between Luzon and Mindora islands. 107,150 (est. 1960); 347 sq. mi.

ma·rine (mə rēn′), *adj.* **1.** of or pertaining to the sea; existing in or produced by the sea: *marine vegetation.* **2.** pertaining to navigation or shipping; nautical; naval; maritime. **3.** serving on shipboard, as soldiers. **4.** of or belonging to the marines. **5.** adapted for use at sea: *a marine barometer.* —*n.* **6.** a member of the U.S. Marine Corps. **7.** one of a class of naval troops serving both on shipboard and on land. **8.** seagoing vessels collectively, esp. with reference to nationality or class; shipping in general. **9.** a picture with a marine subject. **10.** naval affairs, or the department of a government, as in France, having to do with such affairs. **11. tell it or that to the marines!** I don't believe your story. I refuse to be fooled. [ME *maryne* < MF *marin* (fem. *marine*) < L *marīn(us)* of the sea, deriv. of *mare* sea; see -INE[1]]

marine′ barom′eter, a barometer for use on shipboard, esp. one mounted in gimbals and having a tube of mercury with a narrow area for damping the surge caused by the motion of the vessel.

marine′ belt′. See **territorial waters.**

Marine′ Cit′y, a town in E Michigan. 4404 (1960).

Marine′ Corps′, a division of the U.S. Department of the Navy, usually employed in amphibious landing operations and trained, organized, and equipped as soldiers.

marine′ engineer′, an officer who operates, maintains, and repairs the machinery of a ship.

marine′ engineer′ing, the branch of mechanical engineering that deals with the design, construction, installation, operation, and repair of the machinery of vessels.

marine′ glue′, a tarlike composition for coating the seams of a planked deck after calking.

marine′ insur′ance, 1. See **ocean marine insurance. 2.** See **inland marine insurance.**

marine′ i′vy, a vine, *Cissus incisa,* of the southern U.S., having three leaflets or three-lobed leaves and black fruit.

marine′ league′, a unit of three nautical miles.

mar·i·ner (mar′ə nər), *n.* **1.** one who directs or assists in the navigation of a ship; seaman; sailor. **2.** (*cap.*) *U.S.* one of a series of unmanned spacecraft for flights to Mars and Venus. [ME < AF; OF *marinier.* See MARINE, -ER[2]] —**Syn. 1.** seafarer. See **sailor.**

marine′ rail′way, a railway having a rolling cradle for hauling vessels out of water onto land and returning them. Also called **slipway.**

mar′iner's com′pass, 1. a compass used for navigational purposes, consisting of a pivoted compass card in a gimbal-mounted, nonferrous metal bowl. **2.** (*cap.*) *Astron.* compass (def. 8a).

marine′ superintend′ent, one who is responsible for the maintenance of the vessels of a shipping line, for their docking and the handling of cargo, and for the hiring of men for deck departments. Also called **port captain, port superintendent.**

Ma·ri·net·ti (mar′ə net′ē; *It.* mä′RE net′tē), *n.* **E·mi·lio Fi·lip·po Tom·ma·so** (e mē′lyô fē lēp′pô tôm mä′zô), 1876–1944, Italian writer.

Ma·ri·ni (mə rē′nē; *It.* mä RE′nē), *n.* **1. Giam·bat·tis·ta** (jäm′bät tēs′tä). Also, **Ma·ri·no** (mə rē′nō; *It.* mä RE′nô). ("*il Cavalier Marino*") 1569–1625, Italian poet. **2. Ma·ri·no** (mə rē nō; *It.* mä RE′nô), born 1901, Italian sculptor and painter.

Mar·i·nus (mar′ə nəs), *n.* a crater in the fourth quadrant of the face of the moon: about 30 miles in diameter.

Ma·ri·nus I (mə rī′nəs), died A.D. 884, pope 882–884. Also called **Martin II.**

Marinus II, died A.D. 946, pope 942–946. Also called **Martin III.**

Ma·ri·o (mär′ē ō′, mar′-; *It.* mä′ʀyô), *n.* a boy's given name.

Mar·i·ol·a·try (mâr′ē ol′ə trē), *n.* **1.** excessive and proscribed veneration of the Virgin Mary, esp. in forms appropriate to God. **2.** veneration of women. [MARY + -O- + -LATRY] —**Mar′i·ol′a·ter,** *n.* —**Mar′i·ol′a·trous,** *adj.*

Mar·i·ol·o·gist (mâr′ē ol′ə jist), *n.* a student of Mariology. [MARIOLOG(Y) + -IST]

Mar·i·ol·o·gy (mâr′ē ol′ə jē), *n.* **1.** the body of belief, doctrine, and opinion concerning the Virgin Mary. **2.** the study of the person and nature of the Virgin Mary, esp. in reference to her role in the incarnation of God in Christ. [MARY + -O- + -LOGY]

Mar·i·on (mar′ē ən, mâr′-), *n.* **1. Francis,** 1732?–95, American Revolutionary general. **2.** a city in central Indiana. 37,854 (1960). **3.** a city in central Ohio. 37,079 (1960). **4.** a town in E South Carolina. 7174 (1960). **5.** a town in central Alabama. 3807 (1960). **6.** a town in W North Carolina. 3345 (1960). **7.** a boy's or girl's given name.

mar·i·on·ette (mar′ē ə net′), *n.* a puppet manipulated from above by strings attached to its jointed limbs. [< F *marionnette,* equiv. to *Marion* (dim. of *Marie* Mary) + *-ette* -ETTE]

Mar·i·otte's′ law′ (mar′ē ots′, mar′ē ots′), *Thermodynamics.* See **Boyle's law.** [named after Edme *Mariotte* (d. 1684), French physicist]

mar·i·po′sa lil′y (mar′ə pō′sə, -zə), any liliaceous plant of the genus *Calochortus,* of the western U.S. and Mexico, having tuliplike flowers of various colors. Also called **mar·i·po′sa, maripo′sa tu′lip.** [< Sp *mariposa* butterfly, moth; so named because blooms were likened to butterflies]

Ma·ris (mär′is *or, for 2,* mar′-), *n.* **1.** (in the *Iliad*) a companion of Sarpedon in the Trojan War. **2.** Also, **Meris.** a girl's given name.

mar·ish (mar′ish), *Archaic.* —*n.* **1.** a marsh. —*adj.* **2.** marshy. [ME *mareis* < MF < Gmc. See MORASS, MARSH]

Mar·i·sol (mar′i sol′), *n.* (*Marisol Escubar*) born 1930, Venezuelan artist, in U.S. since 1950.

Mar·ist (mâr′ist), *n.* *Rom. Cath. Ch.* a member of a religious order founded in Lyons, France, in 1816 for missionary and educational work in the name of the Virgin Mary. [< F *Mariste.* See MARY, -IST]

Ma·ri·tain (mᴀ RE tᴀɴ′), *n.* **Jacques** (zhäk), born 1882, French philosopher and diplomat.

mar·i·tal (mar′i tᵊl), **1.** of or pertaining to marriage; conjugal; connubial; matrimonial: *marital discord.* **2.** *Archaic.* of or pertaining to a husband. [< L *marītāl(is)* of married people, deriv. of *marītus* of marriage. See MARRY[1], -AL[1]] —**mar′i·tal·ly,** *adv.*

mar·i·time (mar′i tīm′), *adj.* **1.** connected with the sea in relation to navigation, shipping, etc.: *maritime law.* **2.** of or pertaining to the sea: *a maritime civilization.* **3.** bordering on the sea: *maritime provinces.* **4.** living near or in the sea: *maritime plants.* **5.** characteristic of a seaman; nautical: *maritime ability.* [< L *maritim(us)* pertaining to the sea, equiv. to *mari-* (s. of *mare* sea) + *-timus* adj. suffix]

Mar′itime Alps′, a range of the Alps in SE France and NW Italy.

mar′itime belt′, *Law.* the part of the sea that is within the jurisdiction of the bordering states.

Mar′itime Prov′inces, the Canadian provinces of Nova Scotia, New Brunswick, and Prince Edward Island.

Ma·ri·tsa (mä′RE tsä′), *n.* a river in S Europe, flowing from S Bulgaria along the boundary between Greece and European Turkey and into the Aegean. 300 mi. long.

Ma·ri·u·pol (*Russ.* mä′RE o͞o′pol′yᵊ), *n.* former name of **Zhdanov.**

Mar·i·us (mâr′ē əs), *n.* **1. Gaius,** c155–86 B.C., Roman general and consul: opponent of Lucius Cornelius Sulla. **2.** a crater in the second quadrant of the face of the moon: about 26 miles in diameter.

Ma·ri·vaux (mᴀ RE vō′), *n.* **Pierre Car·let de Cham·blain de** (pyeʀ kᴀʀ le′ də shäɴ blaɴ′ də), 1688–1763, French novelist and dramatist.

mar·jo·ram (mär′jər əm), *n.* any of several mints of the genera *Origanum* and *Marjorana,* as pot marjoram and sweet marjoram. [ME *majorane* < ML *majorana,* var. of *majoraca,* alter. of L *amāracus* < Gk *amārakos* majoram]

Mar·jo·ry (mär′jə rē), *n.* a girl's given name, form of **Margaret.** Also, **Mar′jo·rie.**

mark[1] (märk), *n.* **1.** a visible impression or trace upon something, as a line, cut, dent, stain, bruise, etc.: *a small mark on his arm.* **2.** a badge, brand, or other visible sign assumed or imposed: *a mark of rank.* **3.** a symbol used in writing or printing: *a punctuation mark.* **4.** a sign, usually an X or cross, made instead of a signature by someone who does not know how to write his name. **5.** an affixed or impressed device, symbol, inscription, etc., serving to give information, identify, indicate origin or ownership, attest to character or comparative merit, or the like, as a trademark. **6.** a sign, token, or indication: *to bow as a mark of respect.* **7.** a symbol used in rating conduct, proficiency, attainment, etc., as of pupils in a school: *good marks; bad marks.* **8.** something serving as an indication of position, as a landmark. **9.** a recognized or required standard of quality, accomplishment, etc.; norm: *His dissertation was below the mark.* **10.** distinction or importance; repute; note: *a man of mark.* **11.** a distinctive trait or characteristic: *the usual marks of a gentleman.* **12.** (*usually cap.*) *Mil.* a designation for an item of military equipment in production, used in combination with a numeral to indicate the order of adoption, and often abbreviated: *a Mark-4 tank; an M-1 rifle.* **13.** an object aimed at; target: *to aim at the mark.* **14.** an object or end desired or striven for; goal. **15.** an object of derision, scorn, hostile schemes, swindling, or the like: *He was an easy mark.* **16.** *Track.* the starting line. **17.** *Boxing.* the middle of the stomach. **18.** *Lawn Bowling.* jack[1] (def. 7). **19.** *Bowling.* a strike or spare. **20.** *Naut.* any of the distinctively marked points on a deep-sea lead line, occurring at levels of 2, 3, 5, 7, 10, 13, 15, 17, and 20 fathoms above the lead. Cf. **deep** (def. 31). **21.** a tract of land that was held in common by a primitive or medieval community of freemen in Germany. **22.** *Archaic or Hist.* a boundary; frontier. **23. beside the mark,** not pertinent; irrelevant: *Her criticism is beside the mark, and I would like to see the prpduction for myself.* **24. bless** or **save the mark!** (used as an exclamation of disapproval, contempt, impatience, etc.) Also, **God bless** or **save the mark! 25. make one's mark,** to attain success; achieve one's ambition: *As a young man he had set out to make his mark as a writer.* **26. on your mark** or **marks!** (in calling the start of a race) take your places: *On your mark! Get set! Go!* Also, **get ready!, ready! 27. wide of the mark,** inaccurate or irrelevant: *My first guess was wide of the mark.* —*v.t.* **28.** to be a distinguishing feature of: *a day marked by rain.* **29.** to put a mark or marks on: *to mark a wall with stains.* **30.** to furnish with figures, signs, tags, etc., to indicate price, quality, brand name, or the like: *We marked all the books with price tags.* **31.** to trace or form by or as by marks (often fol. by *out*): *to mark out a plan of attack.* **32.** to indicate or designate by or as by marks: *to mark passages to be memorized.* **33.** to single out; destine (often fol. by *out*): *to be marked out for promotion.* **34.** to record, as a score. **35.** to make manifest: *to mark approval with a nod.* **36.** to give heed or attention to: *Mark my words!* **37.** to notice or observe: *to mark a change in a condition.* —*v.i.* **38.** to take notice; give attention; consider. **39. mark down,** to reduce the price of: *These towels have been marked down.* **40. mark off,** to mark the proper dimensions or boundaries of; separate: *We marked off the limits of our lot with stakes.* **41. mark time.** See **time** (def. 41). **42. mark up, a.** to mark with notations or symbols. **b.** to fix the selling price of (an article) by adding the seller's expenses and desired profit to cost: *Those dresses have been marked up 50 percent.* [ME; OE *mearc* mark, sign, banner, dividing line, borderland; c. Icel *mörk* forest (orig. borderland), unit of weight, Goth *marka* boundary, borderland, G *Mark* borderland, unit of weight, L *margō* MARGIN]
—**Syn. 10.** eminence, consequence. **11.** feature, stamp, print. **14.** purpose, objective. **32.** identify, label, tag. **35, 36.** note. **37.** eye, regard, spot.

mark[2] (märk), *n.* **1.** the monetary unit of Germany since 1871: originally a silver coin. Cf. **Deutsche mark, ostmark, reichsmark. 2.** the markka of Finland. **3.** Also, **merk.** a former silver coin of Scotland, equal to 13s. 4d. **4.** a former money of account of England, equal to 13s. 4d. **5.** a former coin of Estonia, the 1/100th part of a kroon: replaced by the sent after 1927. **6.** a former European unit of weight, esp. for gold and silver, generally equal to 8 ounces. [ME; OE *marc* unit of weight < ML *marca* < Gmc; see MARK[1]]

Mark (märk), *n.* **1.** one of the four Evangelists: traditionally believed to be the author of the second Gospel. **2.** the second Gospel: *the Gospel of St. Mark.* **3.** Marcus. **4. King,** *Arthurian Romance.* ruler of Cornwall, husband of Iseult and uncle of Sir Tristram. **5.** Also, **Marc.** a boy's given name, form of **Marcus.**

Mar·kan (mär′kən), *adj.* Marcan.

Mark An·to·ny (märk an′tə nē). See **Antony, Mark.**

mark·down (märk′doun′), *n.* **1.** a reduction in price, usually to encourage buying. **2.** the amount by which a price is reduced. [n. use of v. phrase *mark down*]

marked (märkt), *adj.* **1.** strikingly noticeable; conspicuous: *with marked success.* **2.** watched as an object of suspicion or vengeance: *a marked man.* **3.** having a mark or marks: *beautifully marked birds; to read the marked pages.* **4.** *Ling.* **a.** characterized by the presence of a feature that distinguishes the members of a minimal pair, as in /târ/ and /dâr/; the second is the marked member because the distinguishing feature is voice in the first phoneme. Cf. **unmarked** (def. 2a). **b.** characterized by a marker. [OE *gemearcodan.* See MARK[1], -ED[2]] —**mark·ed·ly** (mär′kid lē), *adv.* —**mark′ed·ness,** *n.*

Marked′ Tree′, a town in NE Arkansas. 3216 (1960).

mark·er (mär′kər), *n.* **1.** one who or that which marks. **2.** something used as a mark or indication, as a bookmark, tombstone, etc. **3.** one who records the scores, points, etc., as in a game or contest. **4.** a counter used in card playing. **5.** *Ling.* **a.** an element of a construction, as a coordinating conjunction, which is not a part of either immediate constituent. **b.** a constituent that determines the function of a construction. **6.** a small radio beacon, automatically operated, used for local navigation of vessels. [MARK[1] + -ER[1]]

mark·er-off (mär′kər ôf′, -of′), *n., pl.* **mark·ers-off.** *Shipbuilding.* a person who marks plates to indicate how they will be punched for rivet holes. [n. use of v. phrase *mark off*]

mar·ket (mär′kit), *n.* **1.** a meeting of people for selling and buying. **2.** the assemblage of people at such a meeting. **3.** an open place or a covered building where buyers and sellers convene for the sale of goods; a market place. **4.** a store for the sale of food: *a meat market.* **5.** trade or traffic, esp. as regards a particular commodity: *the market in cotton.* **6.** a body of persons carrying on extensive transactions in a specified commodity: *the cotton market; the arms and munitions market.* **7.** the field of trade or business: *the best shoes in the market.* **8.** demand for a commodity: *an unprecedented market for leather.* **9.** a body of persons of a specific region where anything is or may be sold: *a car that will appeal to the foreign market.* **10.** current price or value: *a rising market.* **11. at the market,** at the prevailing price in the open market. **12. in the market for,** ready to buy; seeking to buy: *I am in the market for a motor scooter.* **13. on the market,** for sale; available: *Fresh asparagus will be on the market this week.* —*v.i.* **14.** to buy or sell in a market; deal. —*v.t.* **15.** to carry or send to market for disposal: *to market produce many miles.* **16.** to dispose of in a market; sell. [ME, late OE < VL *marcāt(us),* L *mercātus* trading, traffic, market] —**mar′ket·er,** *n.*

mar·ket·a·ble (mär′ki tə bəl), *adj.* **1.** readily salable. **2.** of or pertaining to selling or buying: *marketable values; marketable areas.* [MARKET + -ABLE] —**mar′ket·a·bil′i·ty, mar′ket·a·ble·ness,** *n.* —**mar′ket·a·bly,** *adv.*

mar′ket anal′ysis, *Com.* the process of determining factors, conditions, and characteristics of a market. —**mar′ket an′alyst.**

mar′ket boat′, **1.** a boat that transfers fish from a fishing fleet to a market on shore. **2.** a boat for carrying produce to market. **3.** a boat assigned to bring provisions to a ship.

mar′ket crab′, an edible, reddish-brown crab, *Cancer magister,* of the Pacific coast of the U.S.

mar′ket gar′den, **1.** a garden or farm for growing vegetables to be shipped esp. to local or nearby markets. Cf. **truck farm. 2.** *Brit.* See **truck farm.** —**mar′ket gar′dener.** —**mar′ket gar′dening.**

mar·ket·ing (mär′ki ting), *n.* **1.** the act of buying or selling in a market. **2.** the total of activities by which transfer of title or possession of goods from seller to buyer is effected, including advertising, shipping, storing, and selling. [MARKET + -ING¹]

mar′ket let′ter, a publication containing information concerning market conditions, expectations, etc., esp. one produced by a securities brokerage firm or other financial organization.

mar′ket or′der, an order to purchase or sell at the current market price.

mar·ket·place (mär′kit plās′), *n.* **1.** an open area or a building where goods are offered for sale, often by many independent merchants. **2.** the commerical world; the realm of business, trade, and economics. **3.** the commercial world considered as a place where ideas, thoughts, artistic creations, etc., compete for recognition. Also, **mar′ket place′.** [ME; see MARKET, PLACE]

mar′ket price′, the price at which a commodity, security, or service is selling in the open market. Also called **market value.**

mar′ket research′, the gathering and studying of data relating to consumer preferences, purchasing power, etc., esp. preliminary to introducing a product on the market.

mar′ket town′, a town where a market is held. [late ME]

mar′ket val′ue, **1.** the value of a business, property, etc., in terms of what it can be sold for on the open market; current value (distinguished from *book value*). **2.** See **market price.**

Mar·ke·vich (mär kā′vich; *Russ.* mär ke′vich), *n.* **I·gor** (ē′gôr y°), born 1912, Russian composer and conductor.

Mark·ham (mär′kəm), *n.* **1. (Charles) Edwin,** 1852–1940, U.S. poet. **2. Mount,** a mountain in Antarctica, SW of the Ross Sea. 15,100 ft. **3.** a boy's given name.

mar·khoor (mär′ko͝or), *n., pl.* **-khoors,** (*esp. collectively*) **-khoor.** markhor.

mar·khor (mär′kôr), *n., pl.* **-khors,** (*esp. collectively*) **-khor.** a wild goat, *Capra falconeri,* found in mountainous regions from Afghanistan to India, having compressed, spiral horns and long, shaggy hair. Also, **markhoor.** [< Pers, equiv. to *mār* snake + *-khōr* eating]

mark·ing (mär′king), *n.* **1.** a mark, or a number or pattern of marks: *birds with colorful markings.* **2.** act of one who or that which marks: *the marking of papers.* [ME; see MARK¹, -ING¹]

mark′ing gage′, *Carpentry.* any of various adjustable tools for marking a line parallel to a straight edge against which the tool is moved.

mark·ka (märk′kä), *n., pl.* **-kaa** (-kä). a cupronickel or bronze coin and monetary unit of Finland, equal to 100 pennia and equivalent to about .31 of a U.S. dollar; finmark. *Abbr.:* F.M.K., M. [< Finn; see MARK²]

Mar·ko·va (mär kō′və), *n.* **Alicia,** born 1910, English ballet dancer.

Mar′kov chain′ (mär′kôf), *Statistics.* a Markov process restricted to discrete random events or to discontinuous time sequences.

Mar′kov proc′ess, *Statistics.* a process in which future values of a random variable are statistically determined by present events and dependent only on the event immediately preceding.

Marks (märks), *n.* a town in NW Mississippi. 2572 (1960).

marks·man (märks′mən), *n., pl.* **-men. 1.** one skilled in shooting at a mark; one who shoots well. **2.** *U.S. Army,* the lowest qualification at target practice. [MARK¹ + 's¹ + MAN¹] —**marks′man·ship′,** *n.*

Marks·ville (märks′vil), *n.* a town in central Louisiana. 4257 (1960).

marks·wom·an (märks′wo͝om′ən), *n., pl.* **-wom·en.** a woman skilled at marksmanship. [MARK¹ + 's¹ + WOMAN]

mark·up (märk′up′), *n.* **1.** *Commerce.* **a.** the amount or percentage of the final selling price of an article that represents the difference between the cost to the seller and the final selling price. **b.** the amount or percentage of the cost to the seller that is added to form the final selling price. **2.** a detailed instruction, usually written on a manuscript to be typeset, concerning style of type, make-up of pages, and the like. [n. use of v. phrase *mark up*]

marl¹ (märl), *n.* **1.** a friable earthy deposit consisting of clay and calcium carbonate, used esp. as a fertilizer for soils deficient in lime. **2.** *Archaic.* earth. —*v.t.* **3.** to fertilize with marl. [ME *marle* < MFlem < OF < LL *margila,* dim. of L *marga*] —**mar·la·cious** (mär lā′shəs), **marl′y,** *adj.*

marl² (märl), *v.t. Naut.* to wind (a rope) with marline, every turn being secured by a hitch. [late ME *marlyn* to tie; akin to OE *mārels* cable. See MOOR²]

Mar·la (mär′lə), *n.* a girl's given name, form of **Mary.**

marl·ber·ry (märl′ber′ē, -bə rē), *n., pl.* **-ries.** a shrub or small tree, *Ardisia paniculata,* of southern Florida, having oblong leaves, white flowers, and shiny, black fruit. [dial. *marl* (contr. of MARBLE) + BERRY]

Marl·bor·o (märl′bûr ō, -bur ō), *n.* a city in E Massachusetts. 18,819 (1960).

Marl·bor·ough (märl′bûr ō, -bur ō, *or, for 1,* -brə, môl′-), *n.* **1. John Churchill, 1st Duke of.** See **Churchill, John, 1st Duke of Marlborough. 2.** Marlboro.

Marl′borough leg′, *Furniture.* a tapered leg having a square section.

marled (märld), *adj.* fertilized with marl. [MARL¹ + -ED³]

Mar·leigh (mär′lē), *n.* a girl's given name.

Mar·lene (mär lēn′, -lā′nə), *n.* a girl's given name, form of **Madeleine.** Also, **Mar·leen, Mar·leene** (mär-lēn′), **Mar·le·na** (mär lā′nə).

mar·lin¹ (mär′lin), *n., pl.* (*esp. collectively*) **-lin,** (*esp. referring to two or more kinds or species*) **-lins.** any large, salt-water game fish of the genus *Makaira,* having the upper jaw elongated into a spearlike structure. [short for MARLINESPIKE]

mar·lin² (mär′lin), *n.* marline.

Mar·lin (mär′lin), *n.* **1.** a town in central Texas. 6918 (1960). **2.** a boy's given name.

mar·line (mär′lin), *n. Naut.* small stuff of two fiber strands, sometimes tarred, laid up left-handed. Also, **marlin, mar·ling** (mär′ling). [late ME *marlyne.* See MARL², LINE¹]

mar·line·spike (mär′lin spīk′), *n. Naut.* a pointed iron implement used in separating the strands of rope in splicing, marling, etc. Also, **mar′lin·spike′, mar·ling·spike** (mär′ling spīk′). [orig. *marling spike.* See MARL², SPIKE]

mar′linespike sea′manship, the art or practice of handling and caring for fiber or wire rope and of making knots, splices, seizings, etc.

mar·lin·suck·er (mär′lin suk′ər), *n.* a remora, *Rhombochirus* (or *Remora*) *osteochir,* which attaches itself to marlins and other large fishes. [MARLIN¹ + SUCKER]

marl·ite (mär′līt), *n.* a variety of marl resistant to the action of the air. [MARL¹ + -ITE¹] —**mar·lit·ic** (mär lit′ik), *adj.*

Mar·lon (mär′lən), *n.* a boy's given name.

Mar·lo·vi·an (mär lō′vē ən), *adj.* of, pertaining to, or characteristic of Christopher Marlowe or his writings, esp. his plays. [MARLOWE (Latinization with *-v-* substitution) + -IAN]

Mar·low (mär′lō), *n.* a town in S Oklahoma. 4027 (1960).

Mar·lowe (mär′lō), *n.* **1. Christopher,** 1564–93, English dramatist and poet. **2. Julia** (*Sarah Frances Frost Sothern*), 1866–1950, U.S. actress born in England (wife of E. H. Sothern).

Mar·ma·duke (mär′mə do͞ok′, -dyo͞ok′), *n.* a boy's given name.

mar·ma·lade (mär′mə lād′, mär′mə lād′), *n.* a jellylike preserve in which small pieces of fruit and fruit rind, as of oranges, lemons, etc., are suspended. [< Pg *marmelada* quince jam, deriv. of *marmelo* quince < L *melimēlum* a kind of apple < Gk *melímēlon* (*méli* honey + *mēlon* a fruit); see -ADE¹]

mar′malade tree′, a sapotaceous tree, *Calocarpum Sapota,* of tropical America, yielding a durable wood resembling mahogany and bearing a fruit used for preserves.

Mar·ma·ra (mär′mər ə), *n.* **Sea of,** a sea in NW Turkey, between European and Asian Turkey, connected with the Black Sea by the Bosporus, and with the Aegean by the Dardanelles. 4300 sq. mi. Also, **Marmo·ra** (mär′mər ə, mär môr′ə, -môr′ə).

Mar·max (mär′maks), *n. Class. Myth.* a suitor of Hippodamia who was murdered by her father, Oenomaus.

Mar.Mech.E., Marine Mechanical Engineer.

Mar·met (mär′mit), *n.* a town in W West Virginia. 2500 (1960).

mar·mite (mär′mīt, mär mēt′), *n.* a metal or earthenware cooking pot with a cover, usually large and often having legs. [< F]

Mar·mo·la·da (mär′mô lä′dä), *n.* a mountain in N Italy: highest peak of the Dolomite Alps, 11,020 ft.

mar·mo·re·al (mär môr′ē əl, -mōr′-), *adj.* of or like marble: *skin of marmoreal smoothness.* Also, **mar·mo′re·an.** [< L *marmore(us)* made of marble (see MARBLE, -EOUS) + -AL¹] —**mar·mo′re·al·ly,** *adv.*

Marmoset, *Callithrix jacchus* (Total length 21 in.; tail 11½ in.)

mar·mo·set (mär′mə zet′), *n.* any of several small, squirrellike, South and Central American monkeys of the genera *Callithrix, Leontocebus,* etc., having soft fur and a long, nonprehensile tail. [ME *marmuset* < MF *marmouse* grotesque image]

mar·mot (mär′mət), *n.* **1.** any bushy-tailed, stocky rodent of the genus *Marmota,* as the woodchuck. **2.** any of certain related animals, as the prairie dogs. [< F *marmotte*]

Marmot, *Marmota caligata* (Total length 2½ ft.; tail 10 in.)

Marne (märn; *Fr.* marn), *n.* **1.** a river in NE France, flowing W to the Seine near Paris: battles 1914, 1918, 1944. 325 mi. long. **2.** a department in N France. 442,195 (1962); 3168 sq. mi. *Cap.:* Châlons-sur-Marne.

Ma·ro (mā′rō), *n.* (in the *Odyssey*) a priest of Apollo spared by Odysseus. In gratitude, he gave Odysseus several casks of powerful wine.

Ma·roc (ma rôk′), *n.* French name of **Morocco.**

mar·o·cain (mar′ə-kān′, mar′ə kān′), *n.* a crepe fabric made of silk, wool, or rayon, or a combination of these fibers, and distinguished by a strong rib effect, used in the manufacture of dresses and women's suits; a heavy Canton crepe. Also called **crepe marocain.** [< F (*crêpe*) *marocain* Moroccan (crepe)]

Mar·on (mar′ən), *n.* a boy's given name.

Mar·o·nite (mar′ə nīt′), *n.* a member of a body of Uniats living chiefly in Lebanon, who maintain a Syriac liturgy and a married clergy, and who are governed by the patriarch of Antioch. [< LL *Marōnīta,* named after St. Maron, 4th-century monk, founder of the sect; see -ITE¹]

ma·roon¹ (mə ro͞on′), *adj.* **1.** dark brownish-red. **2.** *Chiefly Brit.* **a.** a loudly exploding firework consisting of a cardboard container filled with gunpowder. **b.** a similar firework used as a danger or warning signal, as by railway brakemen. [< F *marron* < It *marrone* chestnut]

ma·roon² (mə ro͞on′), *v.t.* **1.** to put ashore and leave on a desolate island or coast by way of punishment, as was done by buccaneers. **2.** to isolate as if on a desolate island: *Having lost all his money, he was marooned in the strange city.* —*n.* **3.** any of a group of Negroes, descended from fugitive slaves of the 17th and 18th centuries, living in the West Indies and Guiana, esp. in mountainous areas. **4.** one who is marooned: *Crusoe lived for years as a maroon.* [< AmerSp (*ci*)*marrón* wild; first used in reference to domestic animals which escaped into the woods; later, to fugitive slaves]

ma·ror (mä rôr′), *n. Hebrew.* a serving of horseradish or other bitter-tasting herb or condiment that is eaten at the Seder meal on Passover. Also, **moror.**

Ma·ros (mo′rôsh), *n.* Hungarian name of **Mures.**

ma·rou·flage (mär′ə fläzh′, mär′ə fläzh′), *n.* **1.** a method of attaching a canvas to a wall through adhesion, accomplished by coating the surface with white lead mixed with oil. **2.** a cloth backing for openwork, as on a piece of furniture. [< F, deriv. of *maroufler* to attach canvas to a surface with *maroufle* strong glue; see -AGE]

Mar·pes·sa (mär pes′ə), *n. Class. Myth.* a Greek maiden who, being permitted to choose between Apollo and his rival, a mortal named Idas, chose to marry Idas.

mar·plot (mär′plot′), *n.* one who mars or defeats a plot, design, or project by officious interference: *Her constant worry made her a marplot of everybody's plans for an enjoyable vacation.* [MAR + PLOT¹]

Marq., **1.** Marquess. **2.** Marquis.

Mar·quand (mär kwond′), *n.* **J(ohn) P(hillips),** 1893–1960, U.S. novelist and short-story writer.

marque (märk), *n.* **1.** See **letter of marque. 2.** *Obs.* seizure by way of reprisal or retaliation. [ME *mark* < MF < Pr *marca* seizure by warrant (orig. token) < Gmc; see MARK¹]

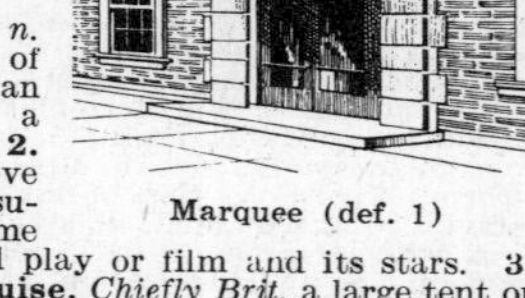

Marquee (def. 1)

mar·quee (mär kē′), *n.* **1.** a rooflike shelter, as of glass, projecting above an outer door and over a sidewalk or a terrace. **2.** a similar projection above a theater entrance, usually containing the name of a currently featured play or film and its stars. **3.** Also, **marquess, marquise.** *Chiefly Brit.* a large tent or tentlike shelter with open sides, esp. one for temporary use in entertainments, receptions, etc. [assumed sing. of MARQUISE, taken as pl.]

Mar·que·san (mär kā′zən, -sən), *n.* **1.** a Polynesian native of the Marquesas Islands. **2.** the Malayo-Polynesian language of the Marquesas Islands. —*adj.* **3.** of, pertaining to, or characteristic of the Marquesas Islands, the Marquesans, or their language. [MARQUES(AS ISLANDS) + -AN]

Mar·que′sas Is′lands (mär kā′zəz, -səz, -səs), a group of French islands in the S Pacific. 4170 (1960); 480 sq. mi.

mar·quess (mär′kwis), *n. Chiefly Brit.* **1.** marquee (def. 3). **2.** marquis.

mar·que·try (mär′ki trē), *n., pl.* **-tries.** inlaid work of variously colored woods or other materials, esp. in furniture. Also, **mar·que·te·rie** (mär′ki trē). [< MF *marqueterie* inlaid work, equiv. to *marquet(er)** (to) speckle, spot, inlay (lit., make marks < Gmc; see MARK¹) + *-erie* -ERY]

Mar·quette (mär ket′; *for 1 also Fr.* mar ket′), *n.* **1. Jacques** (zhäk), ("*Père Marquette*"), 1637–75, French Jesuit missionary and explorer in America. **2.** a city in N Michigan, on Lake Superior. 19,824 (1960).

mar·quis (mär′kwis, mär kē′; *Fr.* mar kē′), *n., pl.* **-quis·es, -quis** (-kēz′; *Fr.* -kē′). a nobleman ranking next below a duke and above an earl or count. Also, *esp. Brit.,* **marquess.** [ME *markis* < MF *marquis* < It *marchese* < Pr *marques;* r. ME *marchis* < MF. See MARCH², -ESE]

Mar·quis (mär′kwis), *n.* **Don(ald Robert Perry),** 1878–1937, U.S. novelist, playwright, and poet.

mar·quis·ate (mär′kwi zit), *n.* **1.** the rank of a marquis. **2.** the territory ruled by a marquis or a margrave. [MARQUIS + -ATE¹, modeled on F *marquisat*, It *marchesato*]

mar·quise (mär kēz′; *Fr.* MAR kēz′), *n., pl.* **-quis·es** (-kē′ziz; *Fr.* -kēz′). **1.** the wife or widow of a marquis. **2.** a lady holding the rank equal to that of a marquis. **3.** a gem, esp. a diamond, having the form of a low, pointed oval with many facets. Cf. **navette. 4.** (*often construed as pl.*) *Chiefly Brit.* marquee (def. 3). **5.** Also called **marquise′ chair′.** *Fr. Furniture.* a wide bergère. [< F; fem. of MARQUIS]

mar·qui·sette (mär′ki zet′, -kwi-), *n.* a lightweight open fabric of leno weave in cotton, rayon, silk, or nylon. [< F, dim. of *marquise.* See MARQUISE, -ETTE]

Mar′quis of Queens′ber·ry rules′ (kwēnz′-ber′ē, -bə rē), *Boxing.* a set of basic rules for modern boxing, requiring among the main provisions the use of gloves instead of bare knuckles, the 10-second count for a knockout, etc.: named after Sir John Sholto Douglas (1844–1900), 8th Marquis of Queensberry, an English sportsman who originated the rules in 1867. Also called **Queensberry rules.**

Mar·ra·kech (mə rä′kesh, mar′ə kesh′), *n.* a city in W Morocco: former capital of Southern Sultanate. 243,134 (1960). Also, **Mar·ra′kesh.** Also called **Morocco.**

mar′ram grass′ (mar′əm), a grass, *Ammophila arenaria,* having matted, creeping rhizomes, grown on sandy shores of Europe, North America, and Australia to bind the sand. Also called **mar′ram.** [< Scand]

Mar·ran·ism (mə rä′niz əm), *n.* the practices, principles, or condition characteristic of the Marranos. Also, **Mar·ra·no·ism** (mə rä′nō iz′əm). [MARRAN(O) + -ISM]

Mar·ra·no (mə rä′nō), *n., pl.* **-nos.** a Spanish or Portuguese Jew who was converted to Christianity during the late Middle Ages, esp. one who was converted under duress or social pressure and often adhered to Judaism in secret. [< Sp: lit., pig, from the Jewish law forbidding the eating of pork]

mar·riage (mar′ij), *n.* **1.** the social institution under which a man and woman establish their decision to live as husband and wife by legal commitments, religious ceremonies, etc. **2.** state, condition, or relationship of being married; wedlock: *a happy marriage.* **3.** the legal or religious ceremony that formalizes the decision of a man and woman to live as husband and wife, including the accompanying social festivities: *to officiate at a marriage.* **4.** any close or intimate association or union: *the marriage of form and content.* **5.** *Cards.* a meld of the king and queen of a suit, as in pinochle. Cf. **royal marriage. 6.** *Obs.* the formal declaration or contract by which act a man and a woman join in wedlock. [ME *mariage* < OF < VL **marītātic(um)* the wedded state. See MARRY¹, -AGE]

—Syn. 3. matrimony. MARRIAGE, WEDDING, NUPTIALS are terms for the ceremony uniting couples in wedlock. MARRIAGE is the simple and usual term, without implications as to circumstances and without emotional connotations: *to announce the marriage of a daughter.* WEDDING has strong emotional, even sentimental, connotations, and suggests the accompanying festivities, whether elaborate or simple: *a beautiful wedding; a reception after the wedding.* NUPTIALS is a formal and lofty word applied to the ceremony and attendant social events; it does not have emotional connotations but strongly implies surroundings characteristic of wealth, rank, pomp, and grandeur: *royal nuptials.* It appears frequently on newspaper society pages chiefly as a result of the attempt to avoid continual repetition of MARRIAGE and WEDDING. **4.** alliance, confederation; weld, junction. **—Ant. 1.** divorce.

mar·riage·a·ble (mar′i jə bəl), *adj.* **1.** suitable for marriage: *The wealthy young man was considered eminently marriageable.* **2.** of an age suitable for marriage: *a marriageable daughter.* [MARRIAGE + -ABLE] **—mar′riage·a·bil′i·ty, mar′riage·a·ble·ness,** *n.*

Mar·riage-à-la-Mode (mar′ij ä lə mōd′, -al ə-), *n.* a comedy (1694) by John Dryden.

mar′riage of conven′ience, a marriage for some advantage or expediency, esp. one for the sake of money or social position.

Mar′riage of Fig′a·ro, The (fig′ə rō′), an opera (1786) by Wolfgang Amadeus Mozart. Italian, **Le Nozze di Figaro.**

mar′riage por′tion, dowry.

mar·ried (mar′ēd), *adj.* **1.** united in wedlock; wedded: *married couples.* **2.** of or pertaining to marriage or married persons; connubial; conjugal: *married happiness.* [ME; see MARRY¹, -ED²] **—mar′ried·ly,** *adv.*

mar′ried print′, *Chiefly Brit.* a completed motion-picture print containing images and a synchronized sound track.

mar·ron (mar′ən, mə rōn′; *Fr.* MA RÔN′), *n.* a chestnut, esp. as used in cookery: candied or preserved in syrup. [< F; see MAROON¹]

mar·rons gla·cés (*Fr.* MA RÔN′ GLA SĀ′), chestnuts glazed or coated with sugar eaten as a confection; candied chestnuts. [< F]

mar·row¹ (mar′ō), *n.* **1.** a soft, fatty, vascular tissue in the interior cavities of bones. **2.** the inmost or essential part: *to pierce to the marrow of a problem.* **3.** strength or vitality: *Fear took the marrow out of him.* **4.** rich and nutritious food. [ME *mar(o)we,* OE *mearg;* c. D *merg,* G *Mark,* Icel *mergr*] **—mar′row·ish,** *adj.* **—mar′row-less,** *adj.* **—mar′row·y,** *adj.*

mar·row² (mar′ō; *Scot.* MAR′ə), *n.* *Scot. and North Eng.* **1.** a partner; fellow worker. **2.** a spouse; helpmate. **3.** a companion; close friend. [late ME *marwe* fellow worker, partner, perh. < Scand; cf. Icel *margr* friendly, lit., many]

mar·row·bone (mar′ō bōn′), **1.** a bone containing edible marrow. **2. marrowbones,** *Facetious.* the knees. [ME; see MARROW¹, BONE¹]

mar·row·fat (mar′ō fat′), *n.* **1.** a large-seeded variety of pea. **2.** the seed itself. [MARROW¹ + FAT]

mar′row squash′, any of several squashes having a smooth surface, an oblong shape, and a hard rind.

Mar·rue·cos (mär RWE′kôs), *n.* Spanish name of **Morocco.**

mar·ry¹ (mar′ē), *v.,* **-ried, -ry·ing.** **—***v.t.* **1.** to take as a husband or wife; take in marriage: *Susan married Ed.* **2.** to perform the marriage ceremonies for (two people who wish to be husband and wife); join in wedlock: *The minister married Susan and Ed.* **3.** to give in marriage (often fol. by *off*): *Her father married Susan off to Ed.* **4.** to unite intimately: *Common interests marry the two countries.* **5.** *Naut.* **a.** to lay together (the unlaid strands of two ropes) to be spliced. **b.** to seize (two ropes) together end to end for use as a single line. **c.** to seize (parallel ropes) together at intervals. **—***v.i.* **6.** to take a husband or wife; wed. [ME *marie(n)* < OF *marie(r)* < L *marītāre* to wed, deriv. of *marītus* conjugal, akin to *mās* male (person)] **—mar′ri·er,** *n.*

mar·ry² (mar′ē), *interj.* *Archaic.* (used as an exclamation of surprise, astonishment, etc.) [euphemistic var. of MARY (the Virgin)]

Mar·ry·at (mar′ē ət), *n.* **Frederick,** 1792–1848, English naval officer and novelist.

Mars (märz), *n.* **1.** the ancient Roman god of war, identified with the Greek god Ares. **2.** *Astron.* the planet fourth in order from the sun, having a diameter of 4230 miles, a mean distance from the sun of 142,000,000 miles, a period of revolution of 686.9 days, and two satellites. **—***adj.* **3.** (*often l.c.*) of or pertaining to any of various pigments used in painting that are artificially made from an iron oxide base: *Mars color; Mars pigments.*

Mar·sa·la (mär sä′lə; *It.* mär sä′lä), *n.* **1.** a seaport in W Sicily. 81,426 (1961). **2.** a sweet, dark, fortified wine made near there.

Mars′ brown′, **1.** a medium brown color. **2.** a brown pigment used in painting, artificially made from an iron oxide base and characterized by strong film-forming properties and permanence.

marse (märs), *n.* *Southern U.S.* (used chiefly in representation of southern Negro speech) master. Also, **mars, massa.**

Mar·seil·laise (mär′sə lāz′, -sā ez′; *Fr.* MAR se yez′), *n.* the French national anthem, written in 1792 by Rouget de Lisle, and originally entitled *Chant de guerre pour l'armée du Rhin.*

mar·seilles (mär sālz′), *n.* a thick cotton fabric woven in figures or stripes with an embossed effect, chiefly for bedspreads and other coverings. [after MARSEILLES]

Mar·seilles (mär sā′; *older* mär sālz′), *n.* **1.** French, **Mar·seille** (MAR se′yᵊ). a seaport in and the capital of Bouches-du-Rhône department, in SE France. 783,738 (1962). **2.** a town in N Illinois. 4347 (1960).

marsh (märsh), *n.* a tract of low wet land, often treeless and periodically inundated: characterized by grasses, sedges, cattails, and rushes. [ME *mershe,* OE *mer(i)sc* (c. G *Marsch*). See MERE², -ISH¹] **—marsh′like′,** *adj.*

Marsh (märsh), *n.* **Reginald,** 1898–1954, U.S. painter and illustrator.

Mar·sha (mär′shə), *n.* a girl's given name, form of **Marcia.**

mar·shal (mär′shəl), *n., v.,* **-shaled, -shal·ing** or (*esp. Brit.*) **-shalled, -shal·ling.** **—***n.* **1.** a military officer of the highest rank, as in the French and some other armies. Cf. **field marshal. 2.** an administrative officer of a U.S. judicial district who performs duties similar to those of a sheriff. **3.** a court officer serving processes, attending court, giving personal attention to the judges, etc. **4.** the police officer in some communities. **5.** a higher officer of a royal household or court. **6.** a person charged with the arrangement or regulation of ceremonies, parades, etc. **—***v.t.* **7.** to arrange in proper order; set out in an orderly manner; arrange clearly: *to marshal facts; to marshal one's arguments.* **8.** to array, as for battle. **9.** to usher or lead: *Their host marshaled them into the room.* **10.** *Heraldry.* to combine (two or more coats of arms) on a single escutcheon. [ME *marshal,* syncopated var. of *mareschal* < OF < Gmc; cf. OHG *marahscalh* groom, equiv. to *marah* horse (see MARE¹) + *scalh* servant, c. OE *scealc*] **—mar′shal·cy, mar′shal·ship′,** *n.* **—mar′shal·er;** *esp. Brit.,* **mar′shal·ler,** *n.*
—Syn. 7. order, dispose; convoke. See **gather. —Ant. 7.** scatter.

Mar·shall (mär′shəl), *n.* **1. Alfred,** 1842–1924, English economist. **2. George Cat·lett** (kat′lit), 1880–1959, U.S. general and statesman: Secretary of State 1947–49; Nobel peace prize 1953. **3. John,** 1755–1835, U.S. jurist and statesman: Chief Justice of the U.S. 1801–35. **4. Thomas Riley,** 1854–1925, vice-president of the U.S. 1913–21. **5. Thur·good** (thûr′go͝od), born 1908, U.S. jurist. **6.** a city in NE Texas. 23,846 (1960). **7.** a town in central Missouri. 9572 (1960). **8.** a town in S Michigan. 6736 (1960). **9.** a town in SW Minnesota. 6681 (1960). **10.** a town in E Illinois. 3270 (1960). **11.** Also, **Mar′shal.** a boy's given name.

Mar·shall·ese (mär′shə lēz′, -lēs′), *n., pl.* **-ese,** *adj.* **—***n.* **1.** a native or inhabitant of the Marshall Islands, esp. a member of a Micronesian people native to the Marshall Islands. **2.** the Malayo-Polynesian language of the Marshall Islands. **—***adj.* **3.** of or pertaining to the Marshall Islands, their inhabitants, or their language. [MARSHALL (ISLANDS) + -ESE]

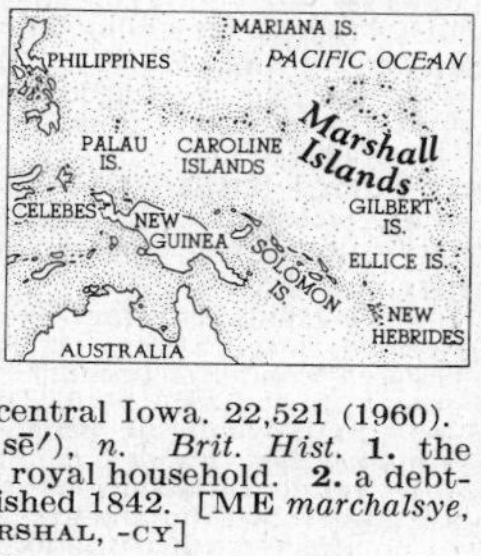

Mar′shall Is′lands, a group of 24 atolls in the N Pacific: formerly mandated to Japan; now under U.S. trusteeship. 14,907 (1960); 74 sq. mi.

Mar′shall Plan′. See **European Recovery Program.**

Mar·shall·town (mär′shəl toun′), *n.* a city in central Iowa. 22,521 (1960).

Mar·shal·sea (mär′shəl sē′), *n.* *Brit. Hist.* **1.** the court of the marshal of the royal household. **2.** a debtors' prison in London, abolished 1842. [ME *marchalsye,* var. of *marschalcie.* See MARSHAL, -CY]

marsh′ buck′, sitatunga.

marsh′ cress′, any annual or biennial cress of the genus *Rorippa,* esp. *R. islandica,* that grows in marshy areas in North America and Eurasia.

marsh′ deer′, a large South American deer, *Blastocerus dichotomus,* that lives in forests near rivers and swamps.

marsh′ el′der, **1.** *U.S.* any of various composite plants of the genus *Iva,* as *I. frutescens,* which grows in salt marshes. **2.** See **cranberry tree.**

marsh′ gas′, a gaseous decomposition product of organic matter, consisting primarily of methane.

marsh′ har′rier, *Ornith.* an Old World harrier, *Circus aeruginosus,* having reddish-brown plumage above and a grayish tail.

marsh′ hawk′, an American hawk, *Circus cyaneus hudsonius,* which frequents marshes and meadows, feeding on frogs, snakes, etc.

marsh′ hen′, any of various rails or raillike birds.

marsh·land (märsh′land′), *n.* a region, area, district, etc., characterized by marshes, swamps, bogs, or the like. [ME *mershland,* OE *merscland.* See MARSH, LAND]

marsh′ mal′low, **1.** an Old World mallow, *Althaea officinalis,* having pink flowers, found in marshy places. **2.** the rose mallow, *Hibiscus Moscheutos.* Also called **sweetweed.** [ME *marshmalue,* OE *merscmealwe.* See MARSH, MALLOW]

marsh·mal·low (märsh′mel′ō, -mal′ō), *n.* **1.** a sweetened paste or confection made from the mucilaginous root of the marsh mallow. **2.** a similar confection containing gum arabic or gelatin, sugar, corn syrup, and flavoring. [see MARSH MALLOW] **—marsh′mal′low·y,** *adj.*

marsh′ mar′igold, a yellow-flowered, ranunculaceous plant, *Caltha palustris,* growing in marshes and meadows; cowslip.

marsh′ tre′foil. See **buck bean.**

marsh′ wren′, either of two American wrens, *Telmatodytes palustris* (**long′-billed marsh′ wren′**) or *Cistothorus platensis* (**short′-billed marsh′ wren′**), that inhabit marshes.

marsh·y (mär′shē), *adj.,* **marsh·i·er, marsh·i·est. 1.** soft and wet, as a marsh; boggy. **2.** pertaining to a marsh. **3.** consisting of or constituting a marsh, bog, swamp, or the like. [ME *mershi.* See MARSH, -Y¹] **—marsh′i·ness,** *n.*

Mar·si·lid (mär′sə lid), *n.* *Pharm., Trademark.* iproniazid.

Mar·sil′i·us of Pad′u·a (mär sil′ē əs), c1280–1343?, Italian scholar and political theorist. Italian, **Mar·si·glio de·i Mai·nar·di·ni** (mär sē′lyô de′ē mī′när dē′nē).

mar·si·po·branch (mär′sə pō braŋk′), *adj.* **1.** belonging to the *Marsipobrachii* or *Cyclostomata,* a group or class of vertebrates comprising the cyclostomes. **—***n.* **2.** a marsipobranch fish. [back formation from NL *Marsipobranchia* a class of vertebrates < Gk *mársipo(s)* bag, pouch (see MARSUPIUM) + *bránchia* gills]

Mars′ red′, **1.** a deep red-orange color. **2.** a red pigment used in painting, artificially made from an iron oxide base and characterized by strong film-forming properties and permanence.

Mars·ton (mär′stən), *n.* **John,** c1575–1634, English dramatist and satirical poet.

Mars′ton Moor′, a former moor in NE England, west of York: Cromwell's victory over the Royalists 1644.

mar·su·pi·al (mär so͞o′pē əl), *adj.* **1.** pertaining to, resembling, or having a marsupium. **2.** of or pertaining to the marsupials. **—***n.* **3.** any viviparous, nonplacental mammal of the order *Marsupialia,* comprising the opossums, kangaroos, wombats, bandicoots, etc., most of which have a marsupium containing the mammary glands and serving as a receptacle for the young. [< NL *marsupiāl(is)* pertaining to a pouch. See MARSUPIUM, -AL¹]

Mar·su·pi·a·li·a (mär so͞o′pē ā′lē ə), *n.* the order comprising the marsupials. [< NL, n. use of neut. pl. of *marsupiālis* MARSUPIAL]

mar·su·pi·al·ise (mär so͞o′pē ə līz′), *v.t.,* **-ised, -is·ing.** *Chiefly Brit.* marsupialize.

mar·su·pi·al·i·za·tion (mär so͞o′pē ə li zā′shən), *n.* *Surg.* an operation in which a cyst is opened, its contents emptied, and its borders sutured to the edges of the incision, for healing. [MARSUPIALIZE + -ATION]

mar·su·pi·al·ize (mär so͞o′pē ə līz′), *v.t.,* **-ized, -iz·ing.** *Surg.* to perform a marsupialization on. Also, *esp. Brit.,* **marsupialise.** [MARSUPIAL + -IZE]

marsu′pial mole′, a burrowing Australian marsupial of the genus *Notoryctes,* resembling a common mole in form and behavior. Also called **pouched mole.**

marsu′pial wolf′, a thylacine. Also called **marsu′pial ti′ger.**

mar·su·pi·um (mär so͞o′pē əm), *n., pl.* **-pi·a** (-pē ə). the pouch or fold of skin on the abdomen of a female marsupial. [< NL, var. of L *marsuppium* pouch, purse < Gk *marsýpion,* dim. of *mársip(os)* a bag, pouch]

Mars′ vi′olet, **1.** a dark, grayish purple color. **2.** a purple pigment used in painting, artificially made from an iron oxide base and characterized by strong film-forming properties and permanence.

Mar·sy·as (mär′sē əs), *n.* *Class. Myth.* a satyr who lost in a flute-playing competition with Apollo and was flayed alive as a penalty.

Mars′ yel′low, **1.** a medium to deep orange-yellow color. **2.** a yellow pigment used in painting, artificially made from an iron hydroxide base and characterized by strong film-forming properties and permanence.

mart¹ (märt), *n.* **1.** market place; trading center; trade center. **2.** *Archaic.* a fair. [late ME < MD, var. of *markt* MARKET]

mart² (märt), *n.* *Scot. and North Eng.* a cow or ox fattened for slaughter. [ME < ScotGael]

Mar·ta (mär′tə; *It.* mär′tä), *n.* a girl's given name.

Mar·ta·ban (mär′tə bän′), *n.* **Gulf of,** an inlet of the Bay of Bengal, in Burma.

Mar′ta·gon lil′y (mär′tə gən). See **Turk's-cap lily.** [< Turk *martagān* turban]

mar·tel (mär′tel, mär tel′), *n.* a hammerlike, shafted weapon having a head with a point at one end and a blunt face at the other. Also called **mar·tel-de-fer** (mär′-tel də fer′, mär tel′-). [late ME < MF < LL *martel-l(us),* var. of L *marcellus,* dim. of *marcus* hammer]

Mar·tel (mär tel′; *Fr.* MAR tel′), *n.* **Charles.** See **Charles Martel.**

mar·te·lé (mär′tᵊlā′; *Fr.* MARTᵊ lā′), *adj.* *Music.* martellato. [< F: hammered]

mar·tel·la·to (mär′tᵊlä′tō; *It.* mär′tel lä′tô), *adj.* (of notes or chords in a musical score) heavily accented and detached. [< It: hammered, ptp. of *martellare.* See MARTEL, -ATE¹]

Mar·tel′lo tow′er (mär tel′ō), *Fort.* a circular, towerlike fort with guns on the top. Also, **martel′lo tow′er.** Also called **martel′lo, Martel′lo.** [named after Cape *Mortella,* Corsica, where a tower of this kind was taken by British forces in 1794]

mar·tem·per (mär′tem pər), *v.t. Metall.* to quench (austenitic steel) at a temperature slightly above or below that at which martensite begins to form, then allowing it to cool slowly to room temperature, thereby hardening it and minimizing its tendency to crack. [MAR(TENSITE) + TEMPER]

Marten, *Martes americana* (Total length about 2½ ft.; tail 9 in.)

mar·ten (mär′tᵊn, -tin), *n., pl.* **-tens,** (*esp. collectively*) **-ten. 1.** any of several slender, chiefly arboreal carnivores of the genus *Martes,* found in northern forests, having a long, glossy coat and bushy tail. **2.** the fur of such an animal, generally a dark brown. [< MLG, equiv. to *mart* marten (c. OE *mearth*) + *-en* -EN⁵; r. late ME *martren* < MF *martrine* marten fur, n. use of fem. of *martrin* pertaining to a marten, equiv. to *martre* marten (< Gmc; cf. G *marder*) + *-in* -IN¹]

mar·tens·ite (mär′ten zīt′), *n. Metall.* a metastable microconstituent of any of various alloys, produced by undercooling sufficiently below the normal transformation temperature, esp. a hard, brittle product of the decomposition of austenite, produced in this way. [named after Adolf *Martens* (d. 1914), German metallurgist; see -ITE¹] —**mar·ten·sit·ic** (mär′ten zit′ik), *adj.*

Marth (märth), *n.* a crater in the third quadrant of the face of the moon: about 3 miles in diameter.

Mar·tha (mär′thə), *n.* **1.** the sister of Mary and Lazarus. Luke 10:38–42; John 11:1–44. **2.** a girl's given name.

Mar′tha's Vine′yard, an island off SE Massachusetts: summer resort. 5763 (1960); 108¾ sq. mi.

Mar′tha Wash′ington chair′, a chair of the 18th century having a high upholstered back, a low upholstered seat, and short arms resting on incurvate supports.

Mar′tha Wash′ington mir′ror. See **Constitution mirror.**

Mar′tha Wash′ington ta′ble, a sewing table of the 18th century having an oval top that may be lifted, and a central compartment of drawers with semicircular bins at each end.

Mar·tí (mär tē′), *n.* **Jo·sé** (hô se′), 1853–1895, Cuban patriot and writer.

mar·tial (mär′shəl), *adj.* **1.** inclined or disposed to war; warlike; brave: *The ancient Romans were a martial people.* **2.** pertaining to or connected with the army and navy. **3.** pertaining to or appropriate for war: *martial music.* **4.** characteristic of or befitting a warrior: *a martial stride.* [ME < L *Mārtiāl(is)* of, belonging to Mars, equiv. to *Mārti-* (s. of *Mārs*) + *-ālis* -AL¹] —**mar′tial·ism,** *n.* —**mar′tial·ist,** *n.* —**mar′tial·ly,** *adv.* —**mar′tial·ness,** *n.*
—**Syn. 2.** military, soldierly.

Mar·tial (mär′shəl), *n.* (*Marcus Valerius Martialis*) A.D. 43?–104?, Roman epigrammatist, born in Spain.

mar′tial law′, the law imposed upon an area by state or national military forces when civil authority has broken down.

Mar·tian (mär′shən), *adj.* **1.** pertaining to the planet Mars. —*n.* **2.** a supposed inhabitant of the planet Mars. [< L *Mārti(us)* of, belonging to Mars (see MARCH) + -AN]

mar·tin (mär′tᵊn, -tin), *n.* any of several swallows. Cf. **house martin, purple martin.** [named after St. MARTIN of Tours, supposedly because it comes north in March (Mar's month; L *Martīnus* is a dim. of *Mars*) and goes south at Martinmas or thereafter]

Mar·tin (mär′tᵊn, -tin), *n.* **1. Ar·cher John Porter** (är′chər), born 1910, English biochemist: Nobel prize 1952. **2. Frank,** born 1890, Swiss composer. **3. Glenn Luther,** 1886–1955, U.S. airplane designer and manufacturer. **4. Homer Dodge,** 1836–97, U.S. painter. **5. Joseph W(illiam) Jr.,** born 1884, U.S. political leader and publisher: Speaker of the House 1947–49, 1953–55. **6. Saint,** A.D. 316?–397, French prelate: bishop of Tours 370?–397. **7.** a town in NW Tennessee. 4750 (1960). **8.** a boy's given name.

Martin I, Saint, died A.D. 655, Italian ecclesiastic: pope 649–655.

Martin II. See **Marinus I.**

Martin III. See **Marinus II.**

Martin IV, (*Simon de Brie* or *Simon de Brion*) c1210–85, French ecclesiastic: pope 1281–85.

Martin V, (*Oddone Colonna*) 1368–1431, Italian ecclesiastic: pope 1417–31.

Mar·ti·na (mär tē′nə), *n.* a girl's given name. Also, **Mar·tine** (mär tēn′).

Mar·tin du Gard (MAR TAN′ DY GAR′), **Ro·ger** (rô zhā′), 1881–1958, French novelist: Nobel prize 1937.

Mar·ti·neau (mär′ti nō′, -tᵊnō′), *n.* **1. Harriet,** 1802–76, English novelist and economist. **2.** her brother, **James,** 1805–1900, English theologian and philosopher.

Mar·ti·nel·li (mär′tᵊnel′ē; *It.* mär′tē nel′lē), *n.* **Gio·van·ni** (jē′ə vä′nē; *It.* jô vän′nē), born 1885, U.S. operatic tenor, born in Italy.

mar·ti·net¹ (mär′tᵊnet′, mär′tᵊnet′), *n.* a strict disciplinarian, esp. a military one. [named after General Jean *Martinet* (d. 1672), French inventor of a system of drill] —**mar′ti·net′ish,** *adj.* —**mar′ti·net′ism,** *n.*

mar·ti·net² (mär′tᵊnet′, mär′tᵊnet′), *n.* martnet.

Mar·ti·nez (mär tē′nis), *n.* a town in W California. 9604 (1960).

Marti′nez East′, a town in W California. 3958 (1960).

Mar·ti·nez Ru·iz (mär tē′neth ROO ēth′), **Jo·sé** (hô se′). See **Azorín.**

Mar·ti·nez Zu·vi·rí·a (mär tē′nes sōō′vē RĒ′ä), **Gus·ta·vo** (gōōs tä′vô), ("*Hugo Wast*"), born 1883, Argentine writer.

mar·tin·gale (mär′tᵊn gāl′), *n.* **1.** Also called **standing martingale.** part of the tack or harness of a horse, consisting of a strap that fastens to the girth, passes between the forelegs and through a loop in the neckstrap or hame, and fastens to the noseband: used to steady or hold down the horse's head. See illus. under **harness. 2.** Also called **running martingale.** a similar device that divides at the chest into two branches, each ending in a ring through which the reins pass. **3.** *Naut.* **a.** a stay from the end of a jib boom or spike bowsprit to some part of a martingale boom. **b.** See **martingale boom. 4.** a system of gambling in which the stakes are doubled or otherwise raised after each loss. [< MF < ?]

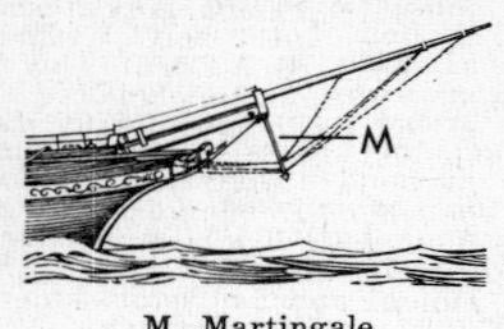

M, Martingale (def. 3a)

mar′tingale back′rope, *Naut.* any of a number of stays leading from the bottom of a martingale boom to the bow at each side. Also called **backrope, gaub line, gob line, gob rope.**

mar′tingale boom′, *Naut.* a strut extending downward at the end of a bowsprit, or part of the way along a spike bowsprit, and stayed in place by martingales and martingale backstays, the whole reinforcing the jib boom or bowsprit against the upward pull of headstays. Also called **martingale, dolphin striker.**

mar·ti·ni (mär tē′nē), *n., pl.* **-nis.** a cocktail made with gin or vodka and dry vermouth, usually served with an olive or a twist of lemon peel. [appar. special use of the name *Martini*]

Mar·ti·ni (mär tē′nē; *It.* mär tē′nē), *n.* **Si·mo·ne** (sē-mô′ne), 1283–1344, Italian painter.

Mar·ti·nique (mär′tᵊnēk′), *n.* an island in the E West Indies; a department of France. 275,000 (est. 1960); 425 sq. mi. *Cap.:* Fort-de-France. —**Mar·ti·ni·can** (mär′tᵊnē′kən), *n.*

Mar·tin·mas (mär′tᵊn məs, -tin-), *n.* a church festival, November 11, in honor of St. Martin. [ME *Martinmasse.* See Saint MARTIN, -MAS]

Mar·ti·non (MAR tē nôN′), *n.* **Jean** (zhäN), born 1910, French violinist, conductor, and composer.

Mar·tins·burg (mär′tᵊnz bûrg′, -tinz-), *n.* a city in NE West Virginia. 15,179 (1960).

Mar·tins·ville (mär′tᵊnz vil′, -tinz-), *n.* **1.** a city in S Virginia. 18,798 (1960). **2.** a town in central Indiana. 7525 (1960).

Mar·ti·nu (mär′tyi nōō′), *n.* **Bo·hu·slav** (bô′hōō släf′), 1890–1959, Czech composer.

mart·let (märt′lit), *n.* **1.** *Brit. Dial.* a house martin. **2.** *Heraldry.* a representation of a swallow close and without legs, used esp. as the cadency mark of a fourth son. [< MF *martelet,* var. of *martinet,* dim. of *martin* MARTIN]

mart·net (märt′net′), *n. Naut.* an arrangement of lines formerly used for gathering up a leech of a sail. Also, **martinet.** [?]

Mar·ton (mär′tᵊn), *n.* a boy's given name, form of **Martin.**

mar·tyr (mär′tər), *n.* **1.** one who willingly suffers death rather than renounce his religion. **2.** one who is put to death or endures great suffering on behalf of any belief, principle, or cause: *a martyr to the cause of social justice.* **3.** one who undergoes severe or constant suffering: *a martyr to severe headaches.* **4.** a person who seeks sympathy or attention by pretending to or exaggerating pain, deprivation, etc. [ME *martire(n),* OE *martyrian,* deriv. of n.]
—*v.t.* **5.** to put to death as a martyr. **6.** to make a martyr of. **7.** to torment or torture. [ME *marter,* OE *martyr* < LL < LGk, var. of Gk *mártys* a witness] —**mar′tyr·ish,** *adj.* —**mar′tyr·ly,** *adv., adj.*

mar·tyr·dom (mär′tər dəm), *n.* **1.** the condition, sufferings, or death of a martyr. **2.** extreme suffering; torment. [ME *martirdom,* OE *martyrdōm.* See MARTYR, -DOM]

mar·tyr·ise (mär′tə rīz′), *v.t.,* **-ised, -is·ing.** *Chiefly Brit.* martyrize. —**mar′tyr·i·sa′tion,** *n.*

mar·tyr·i·um (mär tir′ē əm), *n., pl.* **-tyr·i·a** (-tir′ē ə). **1.** a place where the relics of a martyr are kept. **2.** a church built above the tomb of a martyr or in honor of a martyr. [< LL; see MARTYRY]

mar·tyr·ize (mär′tə rīz′), *v.t.,* **-ized, -iz·ing. 1.** to make a martyr of: *The ancient Romans martyrized many Christians.* **2.** to torment. Also, *esp. Brit.,* **martyrise.** [ME *martirize(n)* < ML *martyriz(āre).* See MARTYR, -IZE] —**mar′tyr·i·za′tion,** *n.*

mar·tyr·ol·o·gy (mär′tə rol′ə jē), *n., pl.* **-gies. 1.** the branch of knowledge dealing with the lives of martyrs. **2.** an account or history of martyrs. **3.** such histories collectively. **4.** a list of martyrs. [< ML *martyrologi(um)* history of martyrs < LGk *martyrológion.* See MARTYR, -O-, -LOGY] —**mar·tyr·o·log·i·cal** (mär′tər ə-loj′i kəl), **mar′tyr·o·log′ic,** *adj.* —**mar′tyr·ol′o·gist,** *n.*

mar·tyr·y (mär′tə rē), *n., pl.* **-tyr·ies.** a shrine, chapel, or the like, erected in honor of a martyr. [< eccl. L *martyri(um)* martyrdom, martyr's grave < Gk *martýrion.* See MARTYR, -Y³]

ma·ru′mi kum′quat (mə rōō′mē). See **round kumquat.** [*marumi* < Jap, equiv. to *maru* circle + *mi* fruit]

Marv (märv), *n.* a boy's given name, form of **Marvin.**

mar·vel (mär′vəl), *n., v.,* **-veled, -vel·ing** or (*esp. Brit.*) **-velled, -vel·ling.** —*n.* **1.** something that arouses wonder, admiration, or astonishment; a wonderful thing; a wonder or prodigy: *The new bridge is a marvel of grace.* **2.** *Archaic.* the feeling of wonder; astonishment. —*v.t.* **3.** to wonder at (usually fol. by a clause as object): *I marvel that you were able to succeed against such odds.* **4.** to wonder or be curious about (usually fol. by a clause as object): *A child marvels that the stars can be.* —*v.i.* **5.** to be affected with wonder, as at something surprising or extraordinary: *I marvel at your courage.* [ME *mervel* < OF *merveil(l)e* < LL *mīrābilia* marvels, n. use of neut. pl. of L *mīrābilis* marvelous. See ADMIRABLE] —**mar′vel·ment,** *n.*

Mar·vell (mär′vəl), *n.* **Andrew,** 1621–78, English poet and satirist.

Mar·vel·la (mär vel′ə), *n.* a girl's given name.

mar·vel-of-Pe·ru (mär′vəl əv pə rōō′), *n.* the four-o'clock, *Mirabilis Jalapa.*

mar·vel·ous (mär′və ləs), *adj.* **1.** such as to arouse wonder, admiration, or astonishment; surprising; extraordinary. **2.** superb; excellent; great: *That was a marvelous show.* **3.** improbable or incredible: *the marvelous events of Greek myth.* Also, *esp. Brit.,* **mar′vel·lous.** [ME *merve(il)lous* < MF *merveilleus.* See MARVEL, -OUS] —**mar′vel·ous·ly;** *esp. Brit.,* **mar′vel·lous·ly,** *adv.* —**mar′vel·ous·ness;** *esp. Brit.,* **mar′vel·lous·ness,** *n.*
—**Syn. 1.** wondrous, amazing, miraculous. **2.** wonderful. **3.** unbelievable. —**Ant. 1.** commonplace. **2.** terrible.

mar·ver (mär′vər), *n.* **1.** a hard, flat surface of stone, wood, or metal, on which a mass of molten glass is rolled and shaped in glassmaking. —*v.t.* **2.** to roll (glass) on a marver. [< F *marbre* MARBLE]

Mar·vin (mär′vin), *n.* a boy's given name. Also, **Mervin, Mervyn.**

Mar·war (mär′wär), *n.* Jodhpur (def. 1).

Marx (märks; *Ger.* märks), *n.* **Karl (Hein·rich)** (kärl hīn′rik; *Ger.* kärl hīn′rɪкн), 1818–83, German economist, philosopher, and socialist.

Marx·i·an (märk′sē ən), *adj.* of or pertaining to Karl Marx or his theories. [MARX + -IAN] —**Marx′i·an·ism,** *n.*

Marx·ism (märk′siz əm), *n.* the system of thought developed by Karl Marx, along with Friedrich Engels, esp. the doctrine that the state throughout history has been a device for the exploitation of the masses by a dominant class, that class struggle has been the main agency of historical change, and that the capitalist system, containing from the first the seeds of its own decay, will inevitably, after the period of the dictatorship of the proletariat, be superseded by a socialist order and a classless society. [MARX + -ISM]

Marx·ist (märk′sist), *n.* **1.** an adherent of Karl Marx or his theories. —*adj.* **2.** of Karl Marx or his theories. [MARX + -IST]

mar·y (mâr′ē), *n., pl.* **mar·ys, mar·ies.** *Australian.* a female aborigine. [special use of name MARY]

Mar·y (mâr′ē), *n.* **1.** Also called **Virgin Mary, Saint Mary.** the mother of Jesus. **2.** the sister of Lazarus and Martha. Luke 10:38–42; John 11:1,2. **3.** *Douay Bible.* Miriam. (def. 1). **4.** (*Princess Victoria Mary of Teck*) 1867–1953, Queen of England 1910–36 (wife of George V). **5.** a girl's given name. [ME *Marie,* OE *Maria* < L < Gk < Heb *Miryām*]

Mary I, ("*Bloody Mary*") 1516–58, queen of England 1553–58 (wife of Philip II of Spain; daughter of Henry VIII). Also called **Mary Tudor.**

Mary II, 1662–94, queen of England 1689–94: joint ruler with her husband William III (daughter of James II).

Mar·ya (mär′yə), *n.* a girl's given name, form of **Mary.**

Mar·y·ann (mâr′ē an′), *n.* a girl's given name. Also, **Marianne, Mar′y·anne′.**

Mar·y·belle (mâr′ē bel′), *n.* a girl's given name. Also, **Maribel, Maribelle.**

Mar·y·beth (mâr′ē beth′, mâr′ē beth′), *n.* a girl's given name.

Mar·y·bob (mâr′ē bob′), *n.* a girl's given name.

Mar·y·bor·ough (mâr′ē bûr′ō, -bur′ō, -bər e, -brə), *n.* a seaport in E Australia. 19,350 (est. 1963).

Mar·y·el·len (mâr′ē el′ən), *n.* a girl's given name.

Mar·y·fran·ces (mâr′ē fran′sis), *n.* a girl's given name. Also, **Marifrances.**

Mar′y Jane′, *Trademark.* a young girl's low-heeled shoe of patent leather having across the instep a single strap that fastens at the side.

Mar·y·jo (mâr′ē jō′), *n.* a girl's given name.

Mar·y·kay (mâr′ē kā′), *n.* a girl's given name.

Mar·y·land (mer′ə-lənd), *n.* a State in the E United States, on the Atlantic coast. 3,100,689 (1960); 10,577 sq. mi. *Cap.:* Annapolis. *Abbr.:* Md.

Mar′yland yel′low-throat. See under **yellowthroat.**

Mar·y·lee (mâr′ē lē′, mâr′i lē′), *n.* a girl's given name. Also, **Marilee, Merilee.**

Mar·y·lou (mâr′ē lōō′), *n.* a girl's given name.

Mar·y·lyn (mâr′ə lin, mar′-), *n.* a girl's given name, form of **Mary.** Also, **Marilyn, Marilynne, Mar′y·lynne.**

Mar′y Mag′dalene, Mary of Magdala: traditionally identified with the repentant woman whom Jesus forgave. Luke 7:37–50.

Mar·y·ruth (mâr′ē rōōth′), *n.* a girl's given name.

Mar′y Stu′art (stōō′ərt, styōō′-), 1542–87, queen of Scotland 1542–67: beheaded for plotting to assassinate her cousin Queen Elizabeth I. Also called **Mar′y, Queen′ of Scots′.**

Mar·ys·ville (mâr′ēz vil′), *n.* **1.** a town in central California. 9553 (1960). **2.** a town in central Ohio. 4952 (1960). **3.** a town in NE Kansas. 4143 (1960). **4.** a town in E Michigan. 4065 (1960). **5.** a town in NW Washington. 3117 (1960). **6.** a town in central Pennsylvania. 2580 (1960).

Mar′y Tu′dor. See **Mary I.**

Mar·y·ville (mâr′ē vil′), *n.* a town in NW Missouri. 7807 (1960).

mar·zi·pan (mär′zə pan′), *n.* a confection made of almonds reduced to a paste with sugar and often molded into various forms, usually diminutive fruits and vegetables. Also called **marchpane.** [< G < It *marzapane.* See MARCHPANE]

-mas, a combining form of **Mass,** occurring in certain names of holidays and Christian feasts: *Michaelmas.*

mas., masculine.

Ma·sac·cio (mä sät′chô; *Eng.* mə sä′chē ō′), *n.* (*Tommaso Guidi*) 1401–28?, Italian painter.

Mas·a·chi·ka (mas′ə chē′kə), *n.* a boy's given name.

Ma·sai (mə sī′), *n., pl.* **-sais,** (*esp. collectively*) **-sai.** a member of an African people inhabiting the highlands of Kenya and Tanganyika and having a largely pastoral economy and a society based on the patrilineal clan.

Ma·sa·ryk (mas′ə rik; *Czech.* mä′sä rik), *n.* **1. Jan** (yän), 1886–1948, Czech statesman (son of Tomáš). **2. To·máš Gar·rigue** (tô′mäsh gə rēg′), 1850–1937, Czech statesman: 1st president of Czechoslovakia 1918–35.

Mas·ba·te (mäs bä′te), *n.* one of the central islands of the Philippines. 263,550 (est. 1960); 1262 sq. mi.

masc., masculine.

Mas·ca·gni (mäs kä′nyē), *n.* **Pie·tro** (pye′trô), 1863–1945, Italian operatic composer.

mas·car·a (ma skar′ə), *n.* a substance used as a cosmetic to color the eyelashes and sometimes the eyebrows. [< Sp: mask; see MASQUERADE]

mas·ca·rene′ grass′ (mas′kə rēn′), a creeping grass, *Zoysia tenuifolia,* of California, having fine leaves and shoots that make good turf. [after the *Mascarene* Islands, east of Madagascar]

mas·ca·ron (mas′kə ron′), *n. Archit.* mask (def. 10). [< F < It *mascherone,* aug. of *maschera* MASK]

mas·cle (mas′kəl), *n. Heraldry.* a lozenge represented as having a lozenge-shaped hole at the center. [ME *mascle,* deriv. of *mask* (now dial.), var. of MESH; see -LE]

mas·con (mas′kon′), *n.* a massive concentration of heavy material beneath the surface of the moon, caused by the uneven gravity field of the moon. [MAS(S) + CON(CENTRATION)]

mas·cot (mas′kət, -kot), *n.* a person, animal, or thing supposed to bring good luck: *The Navy mascot is a goat.* [< F *mascotte* < Pr *mascoto* talisman, charm, dim. of *masco* witch < ML *mascus* ghost. See MASK]

mas·cu·line (mas′kyə lin), *adj.* **1.** having the qualities or characteristics of a man; manly; virile; strong; bold: *a deep, masculine voice.* **2.** pertaining to or characteristic of a man or men: *masculine attire.* **3.** *Gram.* noting or pertaining to the gender of Latin, Greek, German, French, Spanish, Hebrew, etc., which has among its members most nouns referring to males, as well as other nouns, as Spanish *dedo,* "finger," German *Bleistift,* "pencil." **4.** (of a woman) mannish. —*n. Gram.* **5.** the masculine gender. **6.** a noun or other element in or marking that gender. [ME *masculin* < L *masculīn(us),* equiv. to *mascul(us)* male (*mās* male + *-culus* -CULE) + *-īnus* -INE[1]] —**mas′cu·line·ly,** *adv.* —**mas′cu·lin′i·ty, mas′cu·line·ness,** *n.*
—**Syn. 1.** See **male.**

mas′culine caesu′ra, *Pros.* a caesura occurring immediately after a stressed or a long syllable.

mas′culine rhyme′, *Pros.* a rhyme of but a single stressed syllable, as in *disdain, complain.*

mas·cu·lin·ise (mas′kyə lə nīz′), *v.t.,* **-ised, -is·ing.** *Chiefly Brit.* masculinize. —**mas′cu·lin·i·sa′tion,** *n.*

mas·cu·lin·ize (mas′kyə lə nīz′), *v.t.,* **-ized, -iz·ing.** *Med.* to produce certain male secondary sex characteristics in (a female). [MASCULINE + -IZE] —**mas′cu·lin·i·za′tion,** *n.*

Mase·field (mās′fēld′, māz′-), *n.* **John,** 1878–1967, English poet, playwright, novelist, and critic: poet laureate 1930–67.

ma·ser (mā′zər), *n.* a device for amplifying electrical impulses by stimulated emission of radiation. [*m(icrowave) a(mplification by) s(timulated) e(mission of) r(adiation)*]

Mas·e·ru (maz′ə ro͞o′), *n.* a town in and the capital of Lesotho, in the NW part. ab. 10,000.

mash (mash), *n.* **1.** a soft, pulpy mass. **2.** pulpy condition. **3.** a mess of boiled grain, bran, meal, etc., fed warm to horses and cattle. **4.** crushed malt or meal of grain mixed with hot water to form wort. **5.** *Brit. Slang.* mashed potatoes. **6.** *Slang.* **a.** a flirtation or infatuation. **b.** a flirt; sweetheart; lover. —*v.t.* **7.** to crush: *He mashed his thumb with a hammer.* **8.** to reduce to a soft, pulpy mass, as by heating or pressure, esp. in the preparation of food. **9.** to mix (crushed malt or meal of grain) with hot water to form wort. **10.** *Slang.* to flirt with; court the affections of. [ME; OE *mǣsc-, masc-* (in compounds); c. G *Maische*]

Ma·shar·brum (mush′ər bro͞om′), *n.* a mountain in N India, in the Himalayas. 25,660 ft. Also, **Ma′sher·brum′.**

mash·er (mash′ər), *n.* **1.** one who or that which mashes. **2.** *Slang.* a man who makes advances, esp. to women he does not know, with a view to physical intimacy. [MASH + -ER[1]]

mash·gi·ach (mäsh gē′äkh), *n., pl.* **mash·gi·chim** (mäsh gē khēm′). *Hebrew.* mashgiah.

mash·gi·ah (mäsh gē′äkh), *n., pl.* **mash·gi·him** (mäsh gē khēm′). *Hebrew.* an inspector appointed by a board of Orthodox rabbis to guard against any violation of the Jewish dietary laws in food processing plants, meat markets, etc., where food presumed to be kosher is prepared or served for public consumption. Also, **mashgiach.**

Mash·had (mash had′), *n.* Persian name of **Meshed.**

mash·ie (mash′ē), *n. Golf.* a club with an iron head, the face of which has more slope than a mashie iron but less slope than a mashie niblick. Also, **mashy.** Also called **number five iron.** [perh. < F *massue* club < VL **matteuca,* equiv. to **matte(a)* MACE[1] + *-uca,* n. use of fem. of L *-ūcus* suffix of appurtenance]

mash′ie i′ron, *Golf.* a club with an iron head, the face of which has more slope than a mid-mashie but less slope than a mashie. Also called **number four iron.**

mash′ie nib′lick, *Golf.* a club with an iron head the face of which has more slope than a mashie but less slope than a pitcher. Also called **number six iron.**

mash·lam (mash′ləm), *n. Brit. Dial.* maslin.

ma·shre·bee·yah (mä′shri bē′ə), *n.* meshrebeeyeh. Also, **ma′shre·bee′yeh.**

mash·y (mash′ē), *n., pl.* **mash·ies.** *Golf.* mashie.

Mas·i·nis·sa (mas′ə nis′ə), *n.* 238–149 B.C., king of Numidia 210–149. Also, **Massinissa.**

mas·jid (mus′jid), *n. Arabic.* a mosque. Also, **musjid.**

mask (mask, mäsk), *n.* **1.** a covering for all or part of the face, usually worn to conceal one's identity; false face: *Halloween masks.* **2.** Also called **swim mask.** a device consisting typically of a transparent glass or plastic panel fitted into a flexible rubber gasket that fits snugly around the eyes, over the cheeks, and usually over the nose: used by skin divers. **3.** a piece of cloth, silk, or plastic material covering the face of an actor to symbolize the character he represents: used in Greek and Roman drama and in some modern plays. **4.** anything that disguises or conceals; a disguise; a pretense: *His politeness is a mask for a fundamentally malicious personality.* **5.** a person wearing a mask; a masker. **6.** a masquerade or revel. **7.** masque (defs. 1, 2). **8.** a likeness of a face, as one molded on the face in plaster. Cf. **death mask, life mask. 9.** the face or head, as of a fox. **10.** a representation of a face or head, generally grotesque, used as an ornament. **11.** a covering of wire, gauze, etc., to protect the face, as from splinters, dust, a pitched ball, etc. **12.** See **gas mask. 13.** *Fort.* a screen, as of earth or brush, for concealing or protecting a battery or any military operation. **14.** any protective covering, as paper, cardboard, plastic, or the like, used for masking an area of something, as of a photograph, window, etc. **15.** the dark shading on the muzzle of certain dogs. **16.** Also called **braker, shield.** *Shipbuilding.* a sliding timber construction braced against the stern of a hull being launched to keep it from entering the water too rapidly. —*v.t.* **17.** to disguise; conceal; hide; dissemble: *to mask one's intentions.* **18.** to cover with a mask. **19.** to cover or shield a part of (a design, picture, etc.) in order to prevent reproduction or to protect the surface from the colors used, as in working with an air brush or in painting. **20.** *Fort.* to conceal (a battery or any military operation) from the enemy. **21.** to hinder, as an army, from conducting an operation. —*v.i.* **22.** to put on a mask; disguise oneself. [< MF *masque* < ML *mascus, masco* ghost, *masca* witch < ?] —**mask′like′,** *adj.*
—**Syn. 6.** mummery. **17.** veil, screen, cloak, shroud, cover.

mas·ka·longe (mas′kə lonj′), *n., pl.* **-long·es,** (*esp. collectively*) **-longe.** muskellunge.

mas·ka·nonge (mas′kə nonj′), *n., pl.* **-nong·es,** (*esp. collectively*) **-nonge.** muskellunge.

masked (maskt, mäskt), *adj.* **1.** employing or wearing a mask or masks: *a masked burglar; masked actors.* **2.** disguised; concealed; hidden: *masked treachery; masked forces.* **3.** *Bot.* personate[2] (def. 1). **4.** *Zool.* having markings that resemble a mask. [MASK + -ED[3]]

masked′ ball′, a ball at which masks are worn.

Mas·ke·lyne (mas′kə līn′), *n.* a crater in the first quadrant of the face of the moon: about 19 miles in diameter.

mask·er (mas′kər, mä′skər), *n.* one who masks; one who takes part in a masque. Also, **masquer.** [MASK + -ER[1]]

Mas·kil (mäs′kēl), *n., pl.* **Mas·ki·lim** (mäs kē lēm′). *Judaism.* an advocate or supporter of the Haskalah. [< Heb: enlightened] —**Mas·kil·ic** (mä skil′ik), *adj.*

mask′ing piece′, *Theat.* a flat, curtain, or other piece of scenery for concealing a part of a stage from the audience.

mask′ing tape′, an adhesive tape used for defining margins, protecting surfaces, etc., as when painting illustrations.

mas·ki·nonge (mas′kə nonj′), *n., pl.* **-nong·es,** (*esp. collectively*) **-nonge.** muskellunge.

mas·lin (maz′lin), *n. Brit. Dial.* **1.** a mixture of different grains, flours, or meals, esp. rye mixed with wheat. **2.** bread made from such a mixture of grains. **3.** a mixture; medley. Also called **mashlam.** [ME *mastlyoun* < MF *mesteillon,* deriv. of *mesteil* mixture < VL **mixtilium.* See MIXED, -ILE]

mas·och·ism (mas′ə kiz′əm, maz′-), *n.* **1.** *Psychiatry.* the condition in which sexual gratification depends on suffering, physical pain, and humiliation. **2.** gratification gained from pain, deprivation, etc., inflicted or imposed on oneself, either as a result of one's own actions or the actions of others, esp. the tendency to seek this form of gratification. **3.** the act of turning one's destructive tendencies inward or upon oneself. **4.** the tendency to find pleasure in self-denial, submissiveness, etc. [named after L. von SACHER-MASOCH, who described it; see -ISM] —**mas′och·ist,** *n.* —**mas′och·is′tic,** *adj.* —**mas′och·is′ti·cal·ly,** *adv.*

ma·son (mā′sən), *n.* **1.** one whose trade is building with units of various natural or artificial mineral products, as stones, bricks, cinder blocks, tiles, etc., usually with the use of mortar or cement as a bonding agent. **2.** one who dresses stones or bricks. **3.** (*often cap.*) a Freemason. —*v.t.* **4.** to construct of or strengthen with masonry. [ME < OF *maçon* < Frankish **makjo,* deriv. of **makan* to MAKE[1]]

Ma·son (mā′sən), *n.* **1. Charles,** 1730–87, English astronomer. **2. George,** 1725–92, American statesman. **3.** a town in SW Ohio. 4727 (1960). **4.** a crater in the first quadrant of the face of the moon: about 15 miles in diameter. **5.** a town in central Michigan. 4522 (1960). **6.** a boy's given name.

ma′son bee′, any of numerous solitary bees, as of the family *Megachilidae,* that construct nests of clay.

Ma′son Cit′y, a city in N Iowa. 30,642 (1960).

Ma′son-Dix′on line′ (mā′sən dik′sən), the boundary between Pennsylvania and Maryland, partly surveyed by Charles Mason and Jeremiah Dixon between 1763 and 1767, popularly considered before the extinction of slavery as a line of demarcation between free and slave States. Also, **Ma′son and Dix′on line′.**

ma·son·ic (mə son′ik), *adj.* (*often cap.*) pertaining to or characteristic of Freemasons or Freemasonry. [MASON + -IC] —**ma·son′i·cal·ly,** *adv.*

Ma·son·ite (mā′sə nīt′), *Trademark.* a wood-fiber material, pressed in sheets, and used for partitions, insulation, etc.

Ma′son jar′, a glass jar with an airtight screw top, much used in home canning. [named after John L. *Mason,* 19th-century American who patented it in 1857]

ma·son·ry (mā′sən rē), *n., pl.* **-ries. 1.** the art or occupation of a mason. **2.** work constructed by a mason, esp. stonework: *the crumbling masonry of ancient walls.* **3.** (*often cap.*) Freemasonry. [ME *masonerie* < MF *maçonnerie.* See MASON, -ERY]

Ma·son·town (mā′sən toun′), *n.* a town in SW Pennsylvania. 4730 (1960).

ma′son wasp′, any of several solitary wasps, as *Rygchium dorsale,* that construct nests of mud or clay.

Ma·so·rah (mə sōr′ə, -sôr′ə), *n.* a collection of critical and explanatory notes on the Hebrew text of the Old Testament, compiled from the 7th? to 10th centuries A.D. and traditionally accepted as an authoritative exegetic guide, chiefly in matters of pronunciation and grammar. Also, **Ma·so′ra, Massorah, Massora.** [< Heb: tradition]

Mas·o·rete (mas′ə rēt′), *n.* **1.** one of the writers or compilers of the Masorah. **2.** one versed in the Masorah. Also, **Massorete, Mas·o·rite** (mas′ə rīt′). [earlier *mas(s)oreth* < Heb *māsōreth*]

Mas·o·ret·ic (mas′ə ret′ik), *adj.* of or pertaining to the Masorah or the Masoretes. Also, **Mas′o·ret′i·cal, Massoretic, Massoretical.** [MASORETE + -IC]

Mas·pe·ro (mas pə rō′), *n.* **Sir Gas·ton Ca·mille Charles** (gas tôN′ ka mē′yə sharl), 1846–1916, French Egyptologist.

mas. pil., (in prescriptions) a pill mass. [< L *massa pilulāris*]

Mas·qat (mus kat′), *n.* Arabic name of **Muscat.**

masque (mask, mäsk), *n.* **1.** a form of aristocratic entertainment in England in the 16th and 17th centuries, originally consisting of pantomime and dancing but later including dialogue and song, presented in elaborate productions given by amateur and professional actors. **2.** a dramatic composition for such entertainment. **3.** a masquerade; revel. Also, **mask** for defs. 1, 2. [var. of MASK]

Masque′ of the Red′ Death′, The, a short story (1842) by Edgar Allan Poe.

mas·quer (mas′kər, mä′skər), *n.* masker.

mas·quer·ade (mas′kə rād′), *n., v.,* **-ad·ed, -ad·ing.** —*n.* **1.** a party, dance, or other festive gathering of persons wearing masks and other disguises, and often elegant, historical, or fantastic costumes. **2.** disguise such as is worn at such an assembly: *to appear in masquerade.* **3.** false outward show; disguise; pretense: *a hypocrite's masquerade of virtue.* **4.** a going about under false pretenses: *a rich man's masquerade as a beggar.* —*v.i.* **5.** to go about under false pretenses or a false character; assume the character of; give oneself out to be: *to masquerade as a former Russian count.* **6.** to disguise oneself. **7.** to take part in a masquerade. [earlier *masquerada* < Sp *mascarada,* equiv. to *mascar(a)* mask (<< Gmc; cf. OE *mæscre* mesh) + *-ada* -ADE[1]] —**mas′quer·ad′er,** *n.*

mass (mas), *n.* **1.** a body of coherent matter, usually of indefinite shape and often of considerable size: *a mass of dough.* **2.** a collection of incoherent particles, parts, or objects regarded as forming one body: *a mass of sand.* **3.** aggregate; whole (usually prec. by *in the*): *The valley, in the mass, is extremely fertile.* **4.** a considerable assemblage, number, or quantity: *a mass of errors; a mass of troops.* **5.** *Fine Arts.* **a.** *Painting.* an expanse of color or tone that defines form or shape in general outline rather than in detail. **b.** a shape or three-dimensional volume that has or gives the illusion of having weight, density, and bulk. **6.** the main body, bulk, or greater part of anything: *the great mass of American products.* **7.** bulk, size, or massiveness: *towers of great mass and strength.* **8.** *Physics.* a fundamental property of a body, giving a measure of the acceleration the body will have when a given force is applied, usually considered constant and a measure of the matter in the body although mass varies with the velocity of the body. **9.** *Pharm.* a preparation of thick, pasty consistency, from which pills are made. **10. the masses,** the great body of the common people; the working classes or lower social orders. —*v.i.* **11.** to come together in or form a mass or masses: *The clouds are massing in the west.* —*v.t.* **12.** to gather into or dispose in a mass or masses; assemble: *The houses are massed in blocks.* **13. mass in,** *Fine Arts.* to sketch or indicate (forms, colors, etc.) in a broad or generalized manner rather than in detail. [ME *masse* < L *massa* mass < Gk *māza* barley cake, akin to *mássein* to knead] —**mass·ed·ly** (mas′id lē, mast′lē), *adv.*
—**Syn. 2.** aggregate, assemblage, heap, congeries. **4.** collection, accumulation, pile, conglomeration. **6.** majority. **7.** magnitude, dimension. See **size**[1]. **10.** proletariat, plebeians. **12.** collect, marshal, amass, aggregate. —**Ant. 12.** disperse.

Mass (mas), *n.* **1.** the celebration of the Eucharist. Cf. **High Mass, Low Mass. 2.** (*sometimes l.c.*) a musical setting of certain parts of this service, as the Kyrie eleison, Gloria, Credo, Sanctus, Benedictus, and Agnus Dei. [ME *masse,* OE *mæsse* < VL *messa,* L *missa,* orig. application of Latin term is uncertain]

Mass., Massachusetts.

mas·sa (mas′ə), *n.* marse.

Mas·sa (mäs′sä), *n.* a city in W Italy, near the Ligurian Sea: important marble industry. 55,626 (1959).

Mas·sa·chu·set (mas′ə cho͞o′sit), *n., pl.* **-sets,** (*esp. collectively*) **-set. 1.** a member of an Algonquian Indian people. **2.** the extinct Algonquian language of the Massachuset and Wampanoag Indians. Also, **Massachusetts.** [< Algonquian: lit., at or about the biggish hill]

Mas·sa·chu·setts (mas′ə cho͞o′sits), *n.* **1.** a State in the NE United States, on the Atlantic coast. 5,148,578 (1960); 8257 sq. mi. *Cap.:* Boston. *Abbr.:* Mass. **2.** Massachuset.

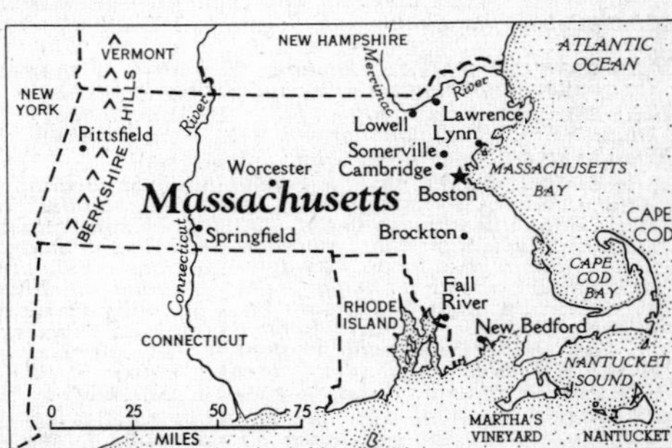

Mas′sachu′setts bal′lot, a ballot on which the candidates, with their party designations, are listed alphabetically in columns under the office for which they were nominated. Cf. **Indiana ballot, office-block ballot.**

Mas′sachu′setts Bay′, an inlet of the Atlantic, off the E coast of Massachusetts.

Mas′sachu′setts Bay′ Com′pany, a company, chartered in England in 1629 to establish a colony on Massachusetts Bay, that founded Boston in 1630.

mas·sa·cre (mas′ə kər), *n., v.,* **-cred, -cring.** —*n.* **1.** the unnecessary, indiscriminate killing of a number of human beings, as in barbarous warfare or persecution, or for revenge or plunder. **2.** a general slaughter, as of persons, animals, etc.: *the massacre of millions during the war.* —*v.t.* **3.** to kill indiscriminately, esp. a large number of persons. [< MF, deriv. of OF *macecler* to butcher, deriv. of *mache-col* butcher, equiv. to *mach(er)* (to) smash (see MASH) + *col* neck (< L *collum*); also influenced by *masselier* butcher < L *macellār(ius)*] —**mas′sa·crer** (mas′ə krər), *n.*
—**Syn. 1, 2.** carnage, extermination, butchery, genocide. **3.** slay. See **slaughter.**

Mas′sacre of Chi′os, The, a painting (1822–24) by Eugène Delacroix.

mas·sage (mə säzh′, -säj′ *or, esp. Brit.,* mas′äzh), *n., v.,* **-saged, -sag·ing.** —*n.* **1.** act or art of treating the body by rubbing, kneading, or the like, to stimulate circulation, increase suppleness, etc. —*v.t.* **2.** to treat by massage. [< F, equiv. to *mass(er)* (to) massage (< Ar *massa* to handle) + *-age* -AGE] —**mas·sag′er, mas·sag′ist,** *n.*

Mas·sa·pe·qua (mas′ə pē′kwə), *n.* a town on SW Long Island, in SE New York. 32,900 (1960).

Mas′sape′qua Park′, a city on SW Long Island, in SE New York. 19,904 (1960).

mas·sa·sau·ga (mas′ə sô′gə), *n.* a small rattlesnake, *Sistrurus catenus,* ranging from the Great Lakes to the Mexican border. [irreg. after *Missisauga* river, Ontario, Canada]

Mas·sa·soit (mas′ə soit′), *n.* c1580–1661, North American Indian leader: sachem of the Wampanoag tribe; negotiator of peace treaty with the Pilgrim Fathers 1621 (father of King Philip).

Mas·sa·ua (mäs sä′wä), *n.* a seaport in E Eritrea, in N Ethiopia, on the Red Sea. 26,627 (est. 1956).

Mass′ book′, missal (def. 1).

mass′ de′fect, *Physics.* the amount by which the mass of an atomic nucleus is less than the sum of the masses of its constituent particles, being the mass equivalent of the energy released in the formation of the nucleus. Cf. **binding energy.**

mas·sé (ma sā′ *or, esp. Brit.,* mas′ē), *n. Billiards.* a stroke made by hitting the cue ball with the cue held almost or quite perpendicular to the table. Also called **massé′ shot′.** [< F: lit., hammered, i.e., struck from above, straight down, equiv. to *masse* sledge hammer (OF *mace;* see MACE¹) + *-é* -EE]

Mas·se·na (mə sē′nə), *n.* a city in N New York, on the St. Lawrence River. 15,478 (1960).

Mas·sé·na (MA sā NA′), *n.* **1. An·dré** (äN drā′), **duc de Ri·vo·li** (*Fr.* RĒ vô lē′; *It.* RĒ′vô lē) and **Prince d'Ess·ling** (des′ling), 1758–1817, French marshal under Napoleon I.

mass′-en′er·gy equa′tion (mas′en′ər jē), *Physics.* the equation, $E = mc^2$, formulated by Albert Einstein, expressing the equivalence between mass and energy, where E is energy, m is mass, and c is the velocity of light.

Mas·se·net (mas′ə nā′; *Fr.* MAS^ə ne′), *n.* **Jules É·mile Fré·dé·ric** (zhyl ā mēl′ frā dā rēk′), 1842–1912, French composer.

mas·se·ter (ma sē′tər), *n. Anat.* a short, thick, masticatory muscle, the action of which assists in closing the jaws by raising the mandible or lower jaw. [< NL < Gk *masētḗr* a chewer, equiv. to *mas(âsthai)* (to) chew + *-e-* connecting vowel + *-ter* agentive suffix] —**mas·se·ter·ic** (mas′i ter′ik), *adj.*

mas·seur (mə sûr′; *Fr.* MA sœR′), *n., pl.* **-seurs** (-sûrz′; *Fr.* -sœR′). a man who provides massage as a profession or occupation. [< F; see MASSAGE, -OR²]

mas·seuse (mə so͞os′, -so͞oz′; *Fr.* MA sœz′), *n., pl.* **-seus·es** (-so͞o′siz, -so͞o′ziz; *Fr.* -sœz′). a woman who provides massage as a profession or occupation. [< F; fem. of MASSEUR]

Mas·sey (mas′ē), *n.* **1. Raymond,** born 1896, U.S. actor and producer, born in Canada. **2.** his brother, **Vincent,** 1887–1967, Canadian statesman: governor general 1952–59. **3. William Ferguson,** 1856–1925, New Zealand statesman, born in Ireland: prime minister 1912–25.

mas·si·cot (mas′ə kot′), *n.* monoxide of lead, PbO, in the form of a yellow powder, used as a pigment and drier. Also, **mas′si·cot·ite′.** [< F < It *massicotto* < Sp *mazacote* soda ash, mortar, alter. of Ar *shabb kubṭī* coptic alum]

mas·sif (mas′if; *Fr.* MA sēf′), *n.* **1.** a compact portion of a mountain range, containing one or more summits. **2.** a large elevated block of old complex rocks resistant to both erosion and crustal folding. **3.** a band or zone of the earth's crust raised or depressed as a unit and bounded by faults. [< F, n. use of *massif* MASSIVE]

Mass·if Cen·tral (MA sēf′ säN tRAl′), a great plateau and the chief water divide of France, in the central part.

Mas·sil·lon (mas′ə lon′), *n.* a city in NE Ohio. 31,236 (1960).

Mas·sine (mä sēn′), *n.* **Lé·o·nide** (lā ô nēd′), born 1896, U.S. ballet dancer and choreographer, born in Russia.

Mas·sin·ger (mas′ən jər), *n.* **Philip,** 1583–1640, English dramatist: collaborated with John Fletcher.

Mas·si·nis·a (mas′ə nis′ə), *n.* Masinissa.

mas·sive (mas′iv), *adj.* **1.** consisting of or forming a large mass; bulky and heavy: *a massive bundle.* **2.** large, as the head or forehead. **3.** solid or substantial; great or imposing: *massive erudition.* **4.** *Mineral.* having no outward crystal form, although sometimes crystalline in internal structure. **5.** *Geol.* homogeneous. **6.** *Med.* **a.** affecting a large, continuous mass of bodily tissue: *a massive collapse of the lung.* **b.** of or pertaining to a larger than usual amount of medication: *a massive dose.* [late ME (see MASS, -IVE); r. ME *massif* < MF] —**mas′sive·ly,** *adv.* —**mas′sive·ness, mas·siv′i·ty,** *n.*

mass·less (mas′lis), *adj.* pertaining to an elementary particle having zero rest mass, as a photon. [MASS + -LESS] —**mass′less·ness,** *n.*

mass′ man′, a hypothetical common man, esp. one held to be typical of a mass society, to be characterized by the absence of unique values or distinct personality traits, to lack a sense of personal or social responsibility, and to be readily manipulated by the techniques developed by mass media.

mass′ me′dia, media¹ (def. 2).

mass′ meet′ing, a large or general assembly to discuss or hear discussed some matter of common interest.

mass′ move′ment, 1. a movement through space involving large numbers of people: *mass movement of troops.* **2.** *Sociol.* a loosely organized effort by a large number of people, esp. those not forming part of the elite of a given society, to bring about pervasive changes in existing social, economic, or political institutions, frequently characterized by charismatic leadership.

mass′ noun′, *Gram.* a noun that typically refers to an indefinitely divisible substance or an abstract notion, and that in English cannot be used, in such a sense, with the indefinite article or in the plural, as *water, air, happiness.* Cf. **count noun.**

mass′ num′ber, *Physics.* the integer nearest in value to the atomic weight of an atom and equal to the number of nucleons in the nucleus of the atom. *Symbol:* A

Mass′ Observa′tion, *Brit., Trademark.* a specific method of polling and judging public opinion by a combination of personal interviews, surveys, and the examination of diaries and other personal documents. *Abbr.:* M.O.

Mas′son disk′ (mas′ən), a white disk on which a series of concentric gray circles appear to vanish intermittently when the disk is rotated, used for testing the fluctuation of attention and the visual threshhold of an individual.

Mas·so·rah (mə sôr′ə, -sōr′ə), *n.* Masorah. Also, **Mas·so′ra.**

Mas·so·rete (mas′ə rēt′), *n.* Masorete.

Mas·so·ret·ic (mas′ə ret′ik), *adj.* Masoretic. Also, **Mas′so·ret′i·cal.**

mas·so·ther·a·py (mas′ō ther′ə pē), *n. Med.* treatment by massage. [MASS(AGE) + -O- + THERAPY] —**mas′so·ther′a·pist,** *n.*

mass-pro·duce (mas′prə do͞os′, -dyo͞os′), *v.t.,* **-duced, -duc·ing.** to produce or manufacture goods in large quantities, esp. by machinery. —**mass′-pro·duc′er,** *n.*

mass′ produc′tion, the production or manufacture of goods in large quantities, esp. by machinery.

mass′ soci′ety, 1. general society, esp. relating to a large geographical area or to broad social units. **2.** *Sociol.* a society whose members are characterized by having segmentalized, impersonal relations, a high degree of physical and social mobility, a spectator relation to events, and a pronounced tendency to conform to external popular norms.

mass′ spec′trograph, *Physics.* a mass spectroscope for recording a mass spectrum on a photographic plate.

mass′ spectrom′eter, *Physics.* a device for identifying the various kinds of particles present in a given substance, by ionizing the particles and subjecting a beam of the ionized particles to an electric or magnetic field such that the field deflects the particles in angles directly proportional to the masses of the particles.

mass′ spec′troscope, *Physics.* an instrument used to determine the masses of small, electrically charged particles. —**mass′ spectros′copy.**

mass′ spec′trum, *Physics.* a spectrum of charged particles, arranged in accordance with their masses or mass-to-charge ratios.

mass·y (mas′ē), *adj.,* **mass·i·er, mass·i·est.** massive. [ME; see MASS, -Y¹] —**mass′i·ness,** *n.*

Mas·sys (mä′sīs), *n.* **Quen·tin** (kven′tin; *Eng.* kwen′tᵊn), 1466?–1530, Flemish painter. Also, **Matsys, Metsys.**

mast¹ (mast, mäst), *n.* **1.** *Naut.* **a.** a spar or structure rising above the hull and upper portions of a vessel to hold sails, spars, rigging, booms, signals, etc., at some point on the fore-and-aft line, as a foremast or mainmast. **b.** any of a number of individual spars composing such a structure, as a topmast supported on trestletrees at the head of a lower mast. **c.** any of various portions of a single spar which are beside particular sails, as a topgallant mast and royal mast formed as a single spar. **2.** Also called **pillar.** the upright support of a jib crane. **3.** any upright pole, as a support for an aerial, a post in certain cranes, etc. **4. before the mast,** *Naut.* as an unlicensed seaman: *He served several years before the mast.* —*v.t.* **5.** to provide with a mast or masts. [ME; OE *mæst;* c. G *Mast;* akin to L *mālus* pole] —**mast′less,** *adj.* —**mast′like′,** *adj.*

mast² (mast, mäst), *n.* the fruit of the oak and beech or other forest trees, used as food for hogs and other animals. [ME; OE *mæst;* c. G *Mast;* akin to MEAT]

mast-, var. of **masto-** before a vowel: *mastectomy.*

mas·ta·ba (mas′tə bə), *n.* **1.** an ancient Egyptian tomb, rectangular in plan, with sloping sides and a flat roof. **2.** (in Islamic countries) a fixed bench, esp. one of stone. Also, **mas′ta·bah.** [< Ar: bench]

mas·tax (mas′taks), *n.* the muscular pharynx of a rotifer, containing a masticatory apparatus. [< NL < Gk: mouth, jaws, akin to *masâsthai* to chew]

mast′ ball′, *Naut.* an ornamental ball forming the truck of a mast.

mast′ band′, *Naut.* a hoop of metal around a mast, used as a reinforcement or as an object for attaching stays, tackles, etc.

mast′ bed′, *Naut.* a construction in a wooden deck around the opening for a mast.

mast′ clamp′, *Naut.* **1.** a pierced slab of hardwood built into the deck structure of a small vessel to receive the force of the mast, which is fitted tightly through it. **2.** Also called **mast hasp.** a metal collar fitted to a thwart of a small boat to steady a mast.

mast′ cloth′, *Naut.* **1.** Also called **mast lining.** a partial lining sewed to the back of a square sail to prevent chafing from contact with the mast. **2.** Also called **mast′ cov′er.** a cloth covering part of a mast to protect it against smoke from a funnel.

mas·tec·to·my (ma stek′tə mē), *n., pl.* **-mies.** *Surg.* the operation of removing the breast or mamma. Also called **mammectomy.** [MAST- + -ECTOMY]

mas·ter (mas′tər, mä′stər), *n.* **1.** a person with the ability or power to use, control, or dispose of something: *a master of six languages.* **2.** an employer of workmen or servants. **3.** one who commands a merchant vessel; captain. **4.** the male head of a household. **5.** an owner of a slave, animal, etc.: *The master beat the dog.* **6.** a presiding officer. **7.** *Chiefly Brit.* a male teacher, tutor, or schoolmaster. **8.** a person whose teachings one accepts or follows: *a master of Zen.* **9. the Master,** Jesus Christ. **10.** a victor or conqueror. **11.** a workman qualified to teach apprentices and to carry on his trade independently. **12.** a man eminently skilled in something, as an occupation, art, or science: *an old master in the conjurer's art.* **13.** a title given to a bridge or chess player who has won or placed in a certain number of officially recognized tournaments. **14.** one holding this title. **15.** an officer of the court to whom some or all of the issues in a case may be referred for the purpose of taking testimony and making a report to the court. **16.** *Educ.* a person who has been awarded a master's degree. **17.** a boy or young man (used chiefly as a term of address). **18.** Also called **matrix.** something to be mechanically reproduced. **19.** a device for controlling another device operating in a similar way. Cf. **slave** (def. 5). **20.** Also called **master matrix.** the matrix made from an original disk recording, from which other disks may be cast. **21.** Also called **master film.** *Photog.* a film, usually a negative, used primarily for making large quantities of prints. **22.** (*usually cap.*) See **master of foxhounds. 23.** *Archaic.* a work of art produced by a master. —*adj.* **24.** being master; exercising mastery. **25.** chief or principal: *the master bedroom.* **26.** directing or controlling: *a master cylinder.* **27.** dominating or predominant: *a master play.* **28.** being a master carrying on his trade independently, rather than a workman employed by another: *a master plumber.* **29.** being a master of some occupation, art, etc.; eminently skilled: *a master diplomat; a master pianist.* **30.** characteristic of a master; showing mastery: *a master stroke.* —*v.t.* **31.** to conquer or subdue; reduce to subjection: *Caesar mastered Gaul.* **32.** to rule or direct as master: *to master a crew.* **33.** to make oneself master of; become an adept in: *to master a language.* [ME *maistre, maister,* OE *magister* < L; akin to *magnus* great] —**mas′ter·dom,** *n.* —**mas′ter·hood′,** *n.* —**mas′ter·less,** *adj.*
—**Syn. 1.** adept, expert. **26.** main, leading, primary, prime, cardinal. **30.** adept, expert, skillful. **31.** subjugate, overcome, overpower. **32.** govern, manage.

mas′ter al′loy, *Metall.* an alloy rich in certain elements, used in small quantities as an additive to melts of alloyed metal.

mas·ter-at-arms (mas′tər ət ärmz′, mä′stər-), *n., pl.* **mas·ters-at-arms. 1.** *Navy.* a petty officer who has various duties, such as keeping order on the ship, taking charge of prisoners, etc. **2.** an officer of a fraternal organization, veterans' society, or the like, empowered to maintain order, exclude unauthorized persons, etc.

mas′ter build′er, 1. a building contractor. **2.** an architect.

Mas′ter Build′er, The, a play (1892) by Ibsen.

mas′ter film′, master (def. 21).

mas·ter·ful (mas′tər fəl, mä′stər-), *adj.* **1.** having or showing the qualities of a master; authoritative; domineering; self-willed; imperious: *a masterful general.* **2.** showing mastery or skill; masterly: *Horowitz gave a masterful performance.* [ME; see MASTER, -FUL] —**mas′ter·ful·ly,** *adv.* —**mas′ter·ful·ness,** *n.*
—**Syn. 1.** peremptory. **2.** consummate, supreme; adept, expert, skilled, skillful, matchless.

mas′ter hand′, 1. an expert: *He was a master hand at diplomacy.* **2.** great expertness: *to show a master hand.*

mas′ter key′, a key that will open a number of locks, the proper keys of which are not interchangeable.

mas·ter·ly (mas′tər lē, mä′stər-), *adj.* **1.** like or befitting a master, as in skill or art; worthy of a master; very skillful: *a masterly presentation of a difficult subject.* —*adv.* **2.** in a masterly manner. [ME *maisterly.* See MASTER, -LY] —**mas′ter·li·ness,** *n.*

mas′ter ma′son, 1. (*often caps.*) a Freemason who has reached the third degree. **2.** an expert mason.

mas′ter ma′trix, master (def. 20).

mas′ter mechan′ic, a mechanic, esp. one who is thoroughly skilled, in charge of other mechanics.

mas·ter·mind (mas′tər mīnd′, mä′stər-), *v.t.* **1.** to plan and direct activities skillfully: *Two colonels had masterminded the revolt.* —*n.* **2.** a person who originates or is primarily responsible for the execution of a particular idea, project, or the like: *the masterminds of company policy.* [MASTER + MIND]

Mas′ter of Arts′, 1. a master's degree usually in a specific branch of the humanities or social sciences. **2.** a person who has been awarded this degree. *Abbr.:* A.M., M.A. [late ME]

Mas′ter of Bal·lan·trae′, The (bal′ən trā′), a novel (1889) by Robert Louis Stevenson.

mas′ter of cer′emonies, a person who directs the entertainment at a party, dinner, or the like.

mas′ter of fox′hounds, the person responsible for the conduct of a hunt and to whom all members of the hunt and its staff are responsible. *Abbr.:* M.F.H.

Mas′ter of Sci′ence, 1. a master's degree given usually in a specific branch of the natural sciences, mathematics, or technology. **2.** a person who has been awarded this degree. *Abbr.:* M.S., M.Sc., S.M., Sc.M.

mas·ter·piece (mas′tər pēs′, mä′stər-), *n.* **1.** one's most excellent production, as in an art; one's best work: *the masterpiece of a painter.* **2.** any production of masterly skill: *a masterpiece of improvisation.* **3.** a consummate example of skill or excellence of any kind: *Her cake was a masterpiece.* **4.** a piece made by a journeyman or other craftsman aspiring to the rank of master in a guild or other craft organization as a proof of his competence. [MASTER + PIECE, modeled on D *meesterstuk,* G *Meisterstück*]

mas′ter point′, a point awarded to a bridge player who has won or placed in an officially recognized tournament.

mas′ter race′, a race or nation, as the German during the Nazi period, whose members consider themselves superior to all other peoples and therefore justified in conquering and ruling them.

Mas·ters (mas′tərz, mä′stərz), *n.* **Edgar Lee,** 1869–1950, U.S. poet and novelist.

mas′ter's degree′, a degree awarded by a graduate school or department, usually to a person who has completed at least one year of graduate study. Also called **mas′ter's.**

mas′ter ser′geant, 1. *Army, Air Force, Marine Corps.* a noncommissioned officer ranking next to the highest noncommissioned officer. 2. *U.S. Air Force.* a noncommissioned officer of one of the three top enlisted grades.

mas·ter·ship (mas′tər ship′, mä′stər-), *n.* 1. the office, function, or authority of a master. 2. control; command: *to have mastership over one's desires.* 3. mastery, as of a subject. 4. masterly skill or knowledge: *He played with the mastership of a devoted musician.* [ME; see MASTER, -SHIP]

mas·ter·sing·er (mas′tər siŋ′ər, mä′stər-), *n.* Meistersinger (def. 1).

mas′ter-slave′ manip′ulator (mas′tər slāv′, mä′stər-), any of various devices, guided by the hand of the operator, for imitating the motions and tactile sensitivity of the human hand to a greater or lesser extent: used in situations in which direct handling of the objects or materials involved would be dangerous or impossible.

Mas′ter spoon′, an Apostle spoon having a figure of Christ.

mas′ter stroke′, a masterly action or achievement; an extremely skillful or effective action: *War was avoided by a master stroke of statesmanship.*

mas·ter·work (mas′tər wûrk′, mä′stər-), *n.* masterpiece. [MASTER + WORK]

mas′ter work′man, 1. a workman in charge. 2. one who is master of his craft.

mas·ter·wort (mas′tər wûrt′, mä′stər-), *n.* a perennial herb, *Astrantia major,* of Europe, having pinkish-rose or white flower clusters with purplish bracts beneath. [MASTER + WORT[2]]

mas·ter·y (mas′tə rē, mä′stə-), *n., pl.* **-ter·ies.** 1. state of being master; power of command or control. 2. command or grasp, as of a subject: *a mastery of Italian.* 3. victory: *mastery over one's enemies.* 4. act of mastering. 5. expert skill or knowledge: *They appealed to his mastery for help in solving their problem.* [MASTER + -Y[3]; r. ME *maistre* < OF]

mast′ fun′nel, *Naut.* a fitting on certain upper masts that are housed within hollow lower ones when not in use to hold the standing rigging of the upper mast: remains on the cap of the lower mast when the upper mast is housed. Also called **jack.**

mast′ hasp′, *Naut.* See **mast clamp** (def. 2).

mast·head (mast′hed′, mäst′-), *n.* 1. *Naut.* **a.** the head of a mast. **b.** (loosely) the uppermost point of a mast. 2. Also called **flag.** a statement printed in all issues of a newspaper, magazine, or the like, usually on the editorial page, giving the publication's name, the names of the owner and staff, etc. 3. nameplate (def. 2). —*v.t. Naut.* 4. to hoist a yard to the fullest extent. 5. to hoist to the truck of a mast, as a flag. 6. to send to the upper end of a mast as a punishment. —*adj.* 7. *Naut.* run up to the head of a mast: *masthead rig.* [MAST[1] + HEAD]

mast′ hoop′, *Naut.* 1. Also called **mast ring.** any of a number of rings of wood or metal, sliding on a mast and holding the luff of a fore-and-aft sail. 2. a metal hoop for strengthening a made mast; mast band.

mast′ house′, *Naut.* 1. a deckhouse built around a mast as a platform for cargo-handling machinery, gear, and controls. 2. Also called **masting house.** (formerly) a towerlike crane for stepping and removing masts from vessels. 3. a building in which masts are made.

mas·tic (mas′tik), *n.* 1. Also, **mas·ti·che** (mas′ti kē), **mastix.** Also called **pistachia galls.** an aromatic, astringent resin obtained from a small anacardiaceous evergreen tree, *Pistacia Lentiscus,* native to the Mediterranean region: used in making varnish. 2. any similar resin, esp. one yielded by other trees of the same genus. 3. a tree yielding a mastic, esp. *Pistacia Lentiscus.* 4. *Building Trades.* **a.** any of various preparations containing bituminous materials and used as an adhesive or seal. **b.** a pasty form of cement used for filling holes in masonry or plaster. [ME *mastyk* < L *masticha* < Gk *mastíchē* chewing-gum, akin to *mastichân* to gnash the teeth]

mas·ti·cate (mas′tə kāt′), *v.t., v.i.,* **-cat·ed, -cat·ing.** 1. to chew. 2. to reduce to a pulp by crushing or kneading, as rubber. [< LL *masticāt(us)* chewed, ptp. of *masticāre.* See MASTIC, -ATE[1]] —**mas·ti·ca·ble** (mas′tə kə bəl), *adj.* —**mas′ti·ca′tion,** *n.* —**mas′ti·ca′tor,** *n.*

mas·ti·ca·to·ry (mas′tə kə tôr′ē, -tōr′ē), *adj., n., pl.* **-ries.** —*adj.* 1. of, pertaining to, or used in or for mastication. —*n.* 2. *Pharm.* a medicinal substance to be chewed, as to promote the secretion of saliva. [< NL *masticātōri(us).* See MASTICATE, -ORY[1]]

Mas′tic Beach′ (mas′tik), a town on SE Long Island, in SE New York. 3035 (1960).

Mas′tic Shir′ley, a town on SE Long Island, in SE New York. 3397 (1960).

mas′tic tree′, a pepper tree, *Schinus molle.*

mas·tiff (mas′tif, mä′stif), *n.* one of a breed of large, powerful, short-haired dogs having an apricot, fawn, or brindled coat. [ME *mastif* << VL *mansuētivus,* equiv. to L *mansuēt(us)* tamed (see MANSUETUDE) + *-īvus* -IVE. Cf. OF *mastin* mastiff]

Mastiff
(30 in. high at shoulder)

mas·tig·i·um (ma stij′ē əm), *n., pl.* **mas·tig·i·a** (ma stij′ē ə). an extensible, lashlike, anal organ in certain caterpillars. [< NL < Gk *mástigion,* dim. of *mástix* whip]

Mas·ti·goph·o·ra (mas′tə gof′ər ə), *n.* the class comprising the flagellates. [< NL (neut. pl.) < Gk *mastigophóros.* See MASTIGIUM, -PHOROUS]

mas·ti·goph·o·ran (mas′tə gof′ər ən), *n.* 1. Also, **mas·ti·go·phore** (mas′tə gə fōr′, -fôr′). a protozoan of the class *Mastigophora (Flagellata),* comprising the flagellates. —*adj.* 2. Also, **mas·ti·goph′o·rous.** belonging or pertaining to the *Mastigophora.* [MASTIGOPHOR(A) + -AN]

mast·ing (mas′tiŋ, mä′stiŋ), *n. Naut.* 1. the technique of locating masts in sailing vessels with regard to their form, size, and service. 2. act or process of placing masts in vessels. 3. the masts of a vessel, taken as a whole. [MAST[1] + -ING[1]]

mast′ing house′, *Naut.* See **mast house** (def. 2).

mas·ti·tis (ma stī′tis), *n.* 1. *Pathol.* inflammation of the breast. 2. *Vet. Pathol.* inflammation of the udder, esp. of cows; garget. [MAST- + -ITIS] —**ma·stit·ic** (ma stit′ik), *adj.*

mas·tix (mas′tiks), *n.* mastic (def. 1).

mast′ lin′ing, *Naut.* See **mast cloth** (def. 1).

masto-, a learned borrowing from Greek meaning "breast," used in the formation of compound words: *mastopathy.* Also, *esp. before a vowel,* **mast-.** [comb. form repr. Gk *mastós* breast]

mas·to·car·ci·no·ma (mas′tō kär′sə nō′mə), *n., pl.* **-mas, -ma·ta** (-mə tə). *Pathol.* carcinoma of the breast. [MASTO- + CARCINOMA]

Mastodon,
Mammut americanum
(7 to 9½ ft. high at shoulder)

mas·to·don (mas′tə don′), *n.* 1. any large, elephantlike mammal of the genera *Mammut, Mastodon,* etc., from the Oligocene and Pleistocene epochs, having conical projections on the molar teeth. 2. a person of immense size, power, influence, etc.: *Alexander the Great was one of the mastodons of the ancient world.* [< NL < Gk *mast(ós)* breast + *odṓn* tooth] —**mas′to·don′ic,** *adj.*

mas·toid (mas′toid), *adj.* 1. resembling a breast or nipple. 2. denoting the nipplelike process of the temporal bone behind the ear. 3. of or pertaining to the mastoid process. —*n.* 4. the mastoid process. [< NL *mastoīd(ēs)* < Gk *mastoeidḗs.* See MAST-, -OID]

mas·toid·ec·to·my (mas′toi dek′tə mē), *n., pl.* **-mies.** *Surg.* the removal of part of a mastoid bone, usually for draining an infection. [MASTOID + -ECTOMY]

mas·toid·i·tis (mas′toi dī′tis), *n. Pathol.* inflammation of the mastoid process of the temporal bone of the skull. [MASTOID + -ITIS]

mas·to·pa·ri·e·tal (mas′tō pə rī′i təl), *adj. Anat.* of, pertaining to, or involving the mastoid process of the temporal bone and the parietal bone. [MASTO- + PARIETAL]

mas·top·a·thy (ma stop′ə thē), *n., pl.* **-thies.** *Pathol.* any disease of the breast. Also, **mazopathy.** [MASTO- + -PATHY]

mas·to·pex·y (mas′tə pek′sē), *n. Surg.* fixation of a pendulous breast. [MASTO- + -PEXY]

mast′ part′ner, a fitting on the deck of a vessel through which a mast is stepped.

mast′ ring′, *Naut.* See **mast hoop** (def. 1).

mast′ track′, *Naut.* a railway for guiding objects up and down a mast, as the parrels of yards or the hanks on the luff of a sail.

mas·tur·bate (mas′tər bāt′), *v.,* **-bat·ed, -bat·ing.** —*v.i.* 1. to engage in masturbation. —*v.t.* 2. to practice masturbation upon. [< L *masturbāt(us)* engaged in masturbation, ptp. of *masturbārī* < ?] —**mas′tur·ba′tor,** *n.*

mas·tur·ba·tion (mas′tər bā′shən), *n.* 1. the stimulation or manipulation of one's own genitals resulting in an orgasm; sexual self-gratification. 2. the stimulation, other than by coitus, of another's genitals resulting in an orgasm. [MASTURBATE + -ION] —**mas·tur·bat·ic** (mas′tər bat′ik), *adj.* —**mas′tur·ba′tion·al,** *adj.* —**mas·tur·ba·to·ry** (mas′tər bə tōr′ē, -tôr′ē), *adj.*

Ma·su·ri·a (mə zŏŏr′ē ə), *n.* a region in NE Poland, formerly in East Prussia, Germany: German defeat of Russians 1914–15. German, **Ma·su·ren** (mä zōō′rən).

ma·su·ri·um (mə sŏŏr′ē əm), *n. Chem.* (formerly) technetium. *Symbol:* Ma [< NL, named after MASURIA, where the element was first found; see -IUM]

Ma·su·ry (mazh′ə rē), *n.* a town in NE Ohio. 2512 (1960).

Mas·ya and Mas·ya·nag (mäsh′yə; mäsh yä′nəg), *Zoroastrianism.* (in the Avesta) the first couple, man and woman, created by Ahura Mazda from a rhubarb plant grown from the seed of Gayomart. Also called **Mahlya and Mahlyanag.**

mat[1] (mat), *n., v.,* **mat·ted, mat·ting.** —*n.* 1. a usually square or rectangular piece of fabric made of plaited or woven rushes, straw, hemp, or similar fiber, or of some other pliant material, as rubber, used as a protective covering on a floor or other surface, to wipe the shoes on, etc. 2. a smaller piece of material, often ornamental, set under a dish of food, a lamp, vase, etc. 3. *Sports.* **a.** the padded canvas covering the entire floor of a wrestling ring, for protecting the contestants from injury when thrown. **b.** a thick pad placed on the floor for the protection of tumblers and others engaged in gymnastic sports. 4. a thickly growing or thick and tangled mass, as of hair, weeds, etc. 5. a sack made of matting, as for coffee or sugar. 6. a slablike footing of concrete, esp. one for an entire building. 7. a heavy mesh reinforcement for a concrete slab. —*v.t.* 8. to cover with or as with mats or matting. 9. to form into a mat, as by interweaving. —*v.i.* 10. to become entangled; form tangled masses. [ME, OE *matte* << LL *matta* mat of rushes < Sem (Punic)] —**mat′less,** *adj.*

mat[2] (mat), *n., v.,* **mat·ted, mat·ting.** —*n.* 1. a piece of cardboard or other material placed over or under a drawing, painting, photograph, etc., to serve as a frame or provide a border between the picture and the frame. —*v.t.* 2. to provide (a picture) with a mat. [special use of MAT[3] + MAT[1]]

mat[3] (mat), *adj., n., v.,* **mat·ted, mat·ting.** —*adj.* 1. lusterless and dull in surface: *mat paint; a mat complexion.* —*n.* 2. a dull or dead surface, without luster, produced on metals, as gold or silver, by a special operation. 3. a tool for producing it. —*v.t.* 4. to finish with a mat surface. Also, **matt, matte.** [earlier *matte* < G *matt* < ML *matt(us)* stupid, downcast; orig. disputed]

mat[4] (mat), *n. Print.* 1. the intaglio, usually of papier-mâché, impressed from type or a cut, from which a stereotype plate is cast. 2. *Informal.* matrix (def. 8). [shortened form of MATRIX]

mat., 1. matins. 2. maturity.

M.A.T., 1. Master of Arts for Teachers. 2. Master of Arts in Teaching.

Mat·a·be·le (mat′ə bē′lē), *n., pl.* **-les,** (*esp. collectively*) **-le.** a member of a Bantu-speaking people of Southern Rhodesia and formerly of the Transvaal. Also called **Ndebele.**

Ma·ta·di (mə tä′dē), *n.* a seaport in the W Republic of the Congo, near the mouth of the Congo River. 59,184 (est. 1958).

mat·a·dor (mat′ə dôr′), *n.* 1. the bullfighter who kills the bull in a bullfight; a torero. 2. one of the principal cards in skat and certain other games. 3. (*cap.*) *U.S.* a surface-to-surface, pilotless aircraft. [< Sp < L *mactātor* slayer, deriv. of *mactāre* to kill; see -ATE[1], -OR[2]]

Ma·ta Ha·ri (mä′tə här′ē, mat′ə har′ē), (*Gertrud Margarete Zelle*) 1876–1917, Dutch dancer in France: executed as a spy by the French.

Mat·a·mo·ros (mat′ə mōr′əs, -môr′-; *Sp.* mä′tä mô′rôs), *n.* a seaport in NE Mexico, on the Rio Grande opposite Brownsville, Texas. 45,737 (1950).

Ma·tane (mə tan′; *Fr.* MA TAN′), *n.* a city in E Quebec, in SE Canada, on the St. Lawrence River. 9190 (1961).

Mat·a·nus·ka (mat′ə nōō′skə), *n.* 1. a river in S Alaska flowing SW to Cook Inlet. 90 mi. long. 2. a village in the valley of this river, NE of Anchorage: site of federal experiment in rural resettlement in 1935.

Ma·tan·zas (mə tan′zəs; *Sp.* mä tän′säs), *n.* a seaport on the NW coast of Cuba. 67,558 (1953).

Mat·a·pan (mat′ə pan′), *n.* **Cape,** a cape in S Greece, at the S tip of the Peloponnesus.

ma′ta·ra dia′mond (mä′tər ə, mat′-). See **matura diamond.** Also, **Ma′tara dia′mond.**

Mat·a·wan (mat′ə won′), *n.* a town in E New Jersey. 5097 (1960).

mat′ bean′, a low, trailing, annual herb, *Phaseolus aconitifolius,* of India, having yellow flowers grown for forage and the edible, black-mottled gray seeds. Also called **moth bean.** [*mat* < Marathi *maṭh* mat bean]

match[1] (mach), *n.* 1. a short, slender piece of wood or other material tipped with a chemical substance which produces fire when rubbed on a rough or chemically prepared surface. 2. a wick, cord, or the like, prepared to burn at an even rate, used to fire cannon, gunpowder, etc. [ME *macche* wick < MF *meiche,* OF *mesche* < VL **mesca* lamp wick, metathetic var. of L *myxa* < Gk: mucus, nostril, nozzle of a lamp]

match[2] (mach), *n.* 1. a person or thing that equals or resembles another in some respect. 2. a person or thing that is an exact counterpart of another: *In habits, tastes, and appearance he is his father's match.* 3. one able to cope with another as an equal: *to meet one's match.* 4. a corresponding or suitably associated pair: *The blue hat and green scarf were not a good match.* 5. *Chiefly Brit.* a contest or game. 6. an engagement for a contest or game. 7. a person considered with regard to suitability as a partner in marriage: *a good match.* 8. a matrimonial compact or alliance: *Their parents did not approve of the match.* —*v.t.* 9. to equal; be equal to: *My talent does not match his.* 10. to be the match or counterpart of: *The color of the skirt does not match that of the coat.* 11. to cause to correspond; adapt: *to match one's actions to one's beliefs.* 12. to fit together, as two things: *to match the pieces of a puzzle.* 13. to fit (boards) together, side by side or end to end, with a tongue-and-groove or rabbeted joint. 14. to procure or produce an equal to: *Try though he did, he could not match his first success.* 15. to place in opposition or conflict: *I matched my wits against his strength.* 16. to provide with an adversary or competitor of equal power: *The teams were well matched.* 17. to encounter as an adversary with equal power. 18. to prove a match for. 19. to unite in marriage; procure a matrimonial alliance for. —*v.i.* 20. to be equal or suitable: *Our talents match.* 21. to correspond; be of corresponding size, shape, color, pattern, etc.: *These gloves do not match.* 22. to ally oneself in marriage: *He matched well.* [ME *macche,* OE *gemæcca* mate, fellow] —**match′a·ble,** *adj.* —**match′er,** *n.*

match·board (mach′bōrd′, -bôrd′), *n.* a board having a tongue formed on one edge and a groove of the same dimensions cut into the other, used with similar boards to compose floors, dados, etc. [MATCH[2] + BOARD]

match·board·ing (mach′bōr′diŋ, -bôr′-), *n.* 1. a construction of matchboards. 2. a quantity of matchboards. [MATCHBOARD + -ING[1]]

match·book (mach′bŏŏk′), *n.* a small cardboard folder into which several rows of paper matches are stapled. [MATCH[1] + BOOK]

match·box (mach′boks′), *n.* a small box, usually of cardboard, for matches. [MATCH[1] + BOX[1]]

matched′ or′der, *Stock Exchange.* an order placed with a broker to buy a specified stock at a price above the market price with the intention of immediately selling the stock through another broker at the same price. It is designed to give the appearance of active trading in the stock.

match·less (mach′lis), *adj.* having no equal; peerless; unequaled; incomparable: *matchless courage.* [MATCH[2] + -LESS] —**match′less·ly,** *adv.* —**match′less·ness,** *n.*

match·lock (mach′lok′), *n.* 1. an old form of gunlock in which the priming was ignited by a slow match. 2. a hand gun, usually a musket, with such a lock. [MATCH[1] + LOCK[1]]

match·mak·er[1] (mach′mā′kər), *n.* 1. a person who arranges or tries to arrange marriages by introducing possible mates. 2. a person who arranges matches for athletic contests, esp. prizefights and wrestling matches. [MATCH[2] + MAKER] —**match′mak′ing,** *n., adj.*

match·mak·er[2] (mach′mā′kər), *n.* one who makes matches for burning. [MATCH[1] + MAKER] —**match′mak′ing,** *n., adj.*

match·mark (mach′märk′), *n.* 1. a mark put on each of two objects belonging together, as machine parts, in order that they may be matched during assembly. —*v.t.* 2. to put a matchmark on. [MATCH[2] + MARK[1]]

match′ plate′, *Foundry.* a plate on which patterns are set to be molded.

match′ play′, *Golf.* play in which the score is reckoned by counting the holes won by each side. Cf. **medal play.** —**match′ play′er.**

match point (mach′ point′ *for 1;* mach′ point′ *for 2*), **1.** (in tennis, squash, handball, etc.) the point that if won by the side would enable him or his side to win the match. **2.** *Duplicate Bridge.* a scoring unit consisting of one point awarded to a partnership for each opposing partnership whose score they better on a hand and of one-half point for each opposing partnership whose score they equal.

match·wood (mach′wo͝od′), *n.* **1.** wood suitable for matches. **2.** splinters: *to reduce something to matchwood.* [MATCH[1] + WOOD[1]]

mate[1] (māt), *n., v.,* **mat·ed, mat·ing.** —*n.* **1.** one of a pair: *I can't find the mate to this glove.* **2.** a counterpart. **3.** husband or wife; spouse. **4.** one of a pair of mated animals. **5.** a habitual associate; fellow worker; comrade; partner (often used in combination): *classmate; roommate; messmate.* **6.** *Naut.* **a.** See **first mate. b.** any of a number of officers of varying degrees of rank subordinate to the master of a merchant vessel. **7.** an assistant to a warrant officer or other functionary on a ship. **8.** *Archaic.* an equal in reputation; peer; match. **9.** a gear, rack, or worm engaging with another gear or worm. —*v.t.* **10.** to join as a mate or as mates. **11.** to match or marry. **12.** to bring (animals) together for breeding purposes. **13.** to join or associate suitably, as one thing with another: *to mate thought with daring action.* **14.** to treat as comparable, as one thing with another: *Can modern achievements be mated with those of the past?* —*v.i.* **15.** to associate as a mate or as mates. **16.** to marry. **17.** (of animals) to pair for the purpose of breeding. **18.** (of animals) to copulate. **19.** (of a gear, rack, or worm) to engage with another gear or worm; mesh. **20.** *Archaic.* to consort; keep company. [ME < MLG; r. ME *mette,* OE *gemetta* messmate, guest. See MEAT] —**mate′less,** *adj.* —**mate′ship,** *n.*

mate[2] (māt), *n., v.t.,* **mat·ed, mat·ing,** *interj. Chess.* checkmate (def. 1). [ME *mat* defeated (adj.), defeat (n.) << Pers: helpless. See CHECKMATE]

ma·te[3] (mä′tā, mat′ā), *n.* maté.

ma·té (mä′tā, mat′ā), *n.* **1.** a shrub or small tree, *Ilex paraguariensis,* of Brazil. **2.** a tealike South American beverage made from the leaves of a species of holly. Also, **mate.** [< Sp: lit., vessel in which the herb is steeped < Quechua *mati* calabash]

Mat.E., Materials Engineer.

mat·e·las·sé (mät′əlä sā′; *Fr.* matᵊ lä sā′), *n.* an embossed, compound fabric woven on a dobby or Jacquard loom. Also, **mat′e·las·se′, mat′el·las·se′.** [< F, ptp. of *matelasser* to quilt, deriv. of *matelas* MATTRESS]

mate·lot (mat′lō, mat′əlō′), *n. Brit. Slang.* a sailor. Also, **mate′low.** [< F << MD *mattenoot* bed-companion, equiv. to *matte* MAT[1] + *noot,* c. OE *genēat* companion, akin to NEAT[2]]

mat·e·lote (mat′əlōt′; *Fr.* matᵊlôt′), *n.* a highly seasoned fish stew made with white or red wine. [< F, special fem. use of *matelot* MATELOT]

ma·ter (mā′tər), *n., pl.* **-ters, -tres** (-trēz). **1.** *Brit. Informal.* mother. **2.** the backing holding the movable parts of an astrolabe. [< L]

ma·ter do·lo·ro·sa (mä′ter dō′lō rō′sä; *Eng.* mā′tər dō′lō rō′sə, -lō-), *Latin.* **1.** the sorrowful mother. **2.** (*caps.*) the mother of Christ sorrowing for her son.

Ma·ter et Ma·gis·tra (mä′ter et mä′ji strä′), *Latin.* Mother and Teacher (opening words and the title of an encyclical by Pope John XXIII, issued in 1961, on contemporary topics as birth control and underdeveloped nations).

ma·ter·fa·mil·i·as (mā′tər fə mil′ē əs), *n.* the mother of a family. [< L; cf. PATERFAMILIAS]

ma·te·ri·al (mə tēr′ē əl), *n.* **1.** the substance or substances of which a thing is made or composed: *Stone is a durable material.* **2.** any constituent element of a thing: *Gold is a common material in jewelry.* **3.** anything that serves as crude or raw matter to be used or developed: *Wood pulp is the raw material from which paper is made.* **4.** a group of related facts, ideas, or data that may serve as the basis for some integrated work, as a novel, sociological report, survey, etc.: *to gather material for a history of North Carolina.* **5.** a textile fabric: *material for a dress.* **6. materials,** the articles or apparatus needed to make or do something: *writing materials.* —*adj.* **7.** formed or consisting of matter; physical; corporeal: *the material world.* **8.** relating to, concerned with, or involving matter: *material force.* **9.** pertaining to or characterized by an undue interest in corporeal things; unspiritual: *a gross, material love of gain.* **10.** pertaining to the physical rather than the spiritual or intellectual aspect of things: *material comforts.* **11.** of substantial import; of much consequence; important: *Your support will make a material difference in the success of our program.* **12.** pertinent or essential (usually fol. by *to*): *evidence material to our lawsuit.* **13.** *Law.* likely to influence the determination of a case: *material evidence.* **14.** *Philos.* of or pertaining to matter as distinguished from form. [ME < LL *māteriāl(is)* of, belonging to matter. See MATTER, -AL[1]] —**ma·te′ri·al·ness,** *n.*
—**Syn. 1.** See **matter. 11.** essential, vital. —**Ant. 7.** incorporeal. **11.** unimportant.

mate′rial cause′, *Aristotelianism.* See under **cause** (def. 8b).

mate′rial cul′ture, *Sociol.* the aggregate of physical objects or artifacts used by a society. Cf. **nonmaterial culture.**

ma·te·ri·al·ise (mə tēr′ē ə līz′), *v.t., v.i.,* **-ised, -is·ing.** *Chiefly Brit.* materialize. —**ma·te′ri·al·i·sa′tion,** *n.* —**ma·te′ri·al·is′er,** *n.*

ma·te·ri·al·ism (mə tēr′ē ə liz′əm), *n.* **1.** the philosophical theory that regards matter and its motions as constituting the universe, and all phenomena, including those of mind, as due to material agencies. **2.** *Ethics.* egoism (def. 3). **3.** attention to or emphasis on material objects, needs, and considerations, with a disinterest in or rejection of spiritual values. [< NL *māteriālism(us).* See MATERIAL, -ISM]

ma·te·ri·al·ist (mə tēr′ē ə list), *n.* **1.** an adherent of philosophical materialism. **2.** one who is markedly more concerned with material things than with spiritual values. [< NL *māteriālista.* See MATERIAL, -IST] —**ma·te′ri·al·is′tic,** *adj.* —**ma·te′ri·al·is′ti·cal·ly,** *adv.*

ma·te·ri·al·i·ty (mə tēr′ē al′i tē), *n., pl.* **-ties** for 2. **1.** material nature or quality. **2.** something material. [< ML *māteriālitās.* See MATERIAL, -ITY]

ma·te·ri·al·ize (mə tēr′ē ə līz′), *v.,* **-ized, -iz·ing.** —*v.t.* **1.** to give material form to; realize: *to materialize an ambition.* **2.** to invest with material attributes: *to materialize abstract ideas with metaphors.* **3.** to make physically perceptible; cause (a spirit or the like) to appear in bodily form. **4.** to render materialistic. —*v.i.* **5.** to assume material or bodily form; become corporeal: *The ghost materialized before Hamlet.* **6.** to come into perceptible existence; appear; become actual fact; be realized or carried out: *Our plans never materialized.* Also, *esp. Brit.,* **materialise.** [MATERIAL + -IZE] —**ma·te′ri·al·i·za′tion,** *n.* —**ma·te′ri·al·iz′er,** *n.*

ma·te·ri·al·ly (mə tēr′ē ə lē), *adv.* **1.** to an important degree; considerably: *His work didn't help materially.* **2.** with reference to matter or material things and conditions; physically: *Because of the storm, it was materially impossible for me to go.* **3.** *Philos.* with regard to matter or substance as distinguished from form. [MATERIAL + -LY]

mate′rials han′dling, the loading, unloading, and transportation of goods.

ma·te·ri·a med·i·ca (mə tēr′ē ə med′ə kə), **1.** the remedial substances employed in medicine. **2.** Also called **pharmacognosy.** the science dealing with the sources, physical characteristics, uses, and doses of drugs. [< ML: medical material]

ma·té·ri·el (mə tēr′ē el′), *n.* **1.** the aggregate of things used or needed in any business, undertaking, or operation (distinguished from *personnel*). **2.** *Mil.* arms, ammunition, and equipment in general. Also, **ma·te′ri·el′.** [< F; see MATERIAL]

Ma′ter Matu′ta (mā′tər), Matuta.

ma·ter·nal (mə tûr′nᵊl), *adj.* **1.** of, pertaining to, having the qualities of, or befitting a mother: *maternal instincts.* **2.** derived from a mother. **3.** related through a mother: *his maternal aunt.* [late ME < ML *māternāl(is),* equiv. to L *mātern(us)* (*māter* mother + *-nus* adj. suffix) + *-ālis* -AL[1]] —**ma·ter′nal·ism,** *n.* —**ma·ter′nal·is′tic,** *adj.* —**ma·ter′nal·ly,** *adv.*

ma·ter·nal·ise (mə tûr′nᵊlīz′), *v.t.,* **-ised, -is·ing.** *Chiefly Brit.* maternalize.

ma·ter·nal·ize (mə tûr′nᵊlīz′), *v.t.,* **-ized, -iz·ing.** to make maternal. [MATERNAL + -IZE]

ma·ter·ni·ty (mə tûr′ni tē), *n.* **1.** state of being a mother; motherhood. **2.** motherliness. —*adj.* **3.** of, pertaining to, or for the period in which a woman is pregnant or has just given birth to a child: *maternity clothes; a maternity hospital; maternity leave.* [< ML *māternitās,* equiv. to L *mātern(us)* (see MATERNAL) + *-itās* -ITY]

Ma′ter Tur·ri·ta (to͝o rē′tə), *Rom. Religion.* Cybele.

mate·y[1] (mā′tē), *n., pl.* **mate·ys.** *Chiefly Brit. Informal.* comrade; chum; buddy. [MATE[1] + -Y[2]] —**mate′y·ness, mat′i·ness,** *n.*

mate·y[2] (mā′tē), *adj. Chiefly Brit. Informal.* sociable; friendly: *a matey chat.* [MATE[1] + -Y[1]]

math[1] (math), *n. Informal.* mathematics. [shortened form]

math[2] (math), *n. Brit. Dial.* **1.** a mowing. **2.** the crop mowed. [OE *mǣth;* c. G *Mahd*]

math[3] (muth), *n.* an order of Hindu monks. Also, **ma·tha** (muth′ə). [< Hindi < Skt *maṭha* hut]

math., **1.** mathematical. **2.** mathematics.

math·e·mat·i·cal (math′ə mat′i kəl), *adj.* **1.** of, pertaining to, or of the nature of mathematics: *mathematical truth.* **2.** employed in the operations of mathematics: *mathematical instruments.* **3.** having the exactness or precision of mathematics: *The birds flew in a mathematical formation.* Also, **math′e·mat′ic.** [< L *mathēmatic(a ars)* MATHEMATICS + -AL[1]] —**math′e·mat′i·cal·ly,** *adv.*

mathemat′ical expecta′tion, **1.** *Math.* the product of the probability of the occurrence of an event and the value associated with the occurrence of a given event. **2.** *Statistics.* the summation or integration over all values of a variate, of the product of the variate and its probability or its probability density.

mathemat′ical induc′tion, induction (def. 3).

mathemat′ical log′ic, a modern development of formal logic employing a special notation or symbolism capable of manipulation in accordance with precise rules. Also called **symbolic logic.**

math·e·ma·ti·cian (math′ə mə tish′ən), *n.* an expert in mathematics. [late ME *mathematicion* (? misspelling). See MATHEMATICS, -IAN]

math·e·mat·ics (math′ə mat′iks), *n.* **1.** (*construed as sing.*) the systematic treatment of magnitude, relationships between figures and forms, and relations between quantities expressed symbolically. **2.** (*construed as sing. or pl.*) mathematical procedures, operations, or properties. [n. use of *mathematic* < L *mathēmatic(a ars)* < Gk *mathēmatikḕ* (*téchnē*) scientific (craft), equiv. to *mathēmat-* (s. of *máthēma*) science, knowledge + *-ikē,* fem. of *-ikos* -IC]

Math·er (math′ər, math′-), *n.* **1. Cotton,** 1663–1728, American clergyman and author. **2.** his father **Increase,** 1639–1723, American clergyman and author.

Math·ew·son (math′yo͞o sən), *n.* **Christopher** ("Christy"), 1880–1925, U.S. baseball player.

Ma·thi·as (mə thī′əs), *n.* **Robert Bruce** (*Bob*), born 1930, U.S. athlete.

Ma·thil·de (mə til′də; *Fr.* ma tēld′; *Ger.* mä til′də), *n.* a girl's given name, French or German form of **Matilda.**

Math·is (math′is), *n.* a town in S Texas. 6075 (1960).

Ma·this der Ma·ler (*Ger.* mä tēs′ der mä′lər), a symphony (1934) and opera (1938) by Paul Hindemith.

math·na·vi (math nä′vē, mäth′nä vē′), *n.* a poem of Arabic origin in rhyming couplets. [special use of (THE) MATHNAVI]

Math·na·vi, The (math nä′vē, mäth′nä vē′), a long poem (13th century) in rhymed couplets by Rūmī.

Math·ol·w·ych (math ol′ō ikh), *n.* a legendary king of Ireland and the husband of Branwen.

Ma·thu·ra (mut′o͝o rə), *n.* a city in W Uttar Pradesh, in N India: Hindu shrine and holy city: reputed birthplace of Krishna. 123,096 (est. 1964). Formerly, **Muttra.**

Ma·thu·sa·la (mə tho͞o′sə lə), *n. Douay Bible.* Methuselah (def. 1).

ma·til·da (mə til′də), *n. Australian.* swag. [special use of proper name *Matilda*]

Ma·til·da (mə til′də; *Ital.* mä tēl′dä), *n.* a girl's given name. Also, **Ma·til·de** (mə til′də; *Fr.* ma tēld′; *Ital.* mä tēl′de).

Ma·til′i·ja pop′py (mə til′ə hä′), a tree poppy, *Romneya coulteri,* of California and Mexico, having thin, paperlike leaves and solitary, white flowers nearly six inches wide. [after the *Matilija* Canyon, Ventura County, California]

mat·in (mat′ᵊn, mat′in), *n.* **1. matins.** Also, *esp. Brit.,* **mattins.** (*usually construed as sing.*) *Eccles.* **a.** the first of the seven canonical hours. **b.** the service for it, properly beginning at midnight, but sometimes beginning at daybreak. **c.** Also called **Morning Prayer.** the service of public prayer, said in the morning, in the Anglican Church. **2.** a morning song, as of birds. —*adj.* **3.** Also, **mat′in·al.** pertaining to the morning or to matins. [ME *matyn* (pl. *matines*) < OF *matin* < L *mātūtīn(us)* MATUTINAL]

Ma·ti·na (mə tē′nə; *It.* mä tē′nä), *n.* a girl's given name.

mat·i·née (mat′ᵊnā′; *esp. Brit.,* mat′ᵊnā′), *n.* an entertainment, esp. a dramatic or musical performance, held in the daytime, usually in the afternoon. Also, **mat′i·nee′.** [< F: morning. See MATIN]

matinée′ i′dol, a male actor, esp. a leading man, idolized by female audiences.

mat·ing (mā′ting), *n.* an instance or act of pairing or matching. [ME; see MATE[1], -ING[1]]

Ma·tin′i·cus boat′ (mə tin′ə kəs), a small boat, used for fishing and lobstering off the coast of Maine, having a sloop rig with a removable mast and retractable bowsprit and a hull with a centerboard. [?]

Ma·tisse (ma tēs′), *n.* **Hen·ri** (äN rē′), 1869–1954, French painter.

Ma·to Gros·so (mä′to͞o grô′so͞o; *Eng.* mat′ə grō′sō), **1.** a plateau in SW Brazil. **2.** a state in SW Brazil. 910,262 (1960); 475,378 sq. mi. *Cap.:* Cuiabá. Also, **Matto Grosso.**

Ma·tra·li·a (mə trā′lē ə), *n., pl.* **-li·a, -li·as.** (*sometimes construed as pl.*) an annual festival of ancient Rome celebrated by women in honor of Matuta. [< L *Mātrālia* (*festa*) (festival) of *Māter Mātūta* (goddess of dawn); *mātrālia,* neut. pl. of *mātrālis* pertaining to a mother. See MATER, -AL[1]]

mat·rass (mat′rəs), *n. Chem. Obs.* **1.** a rounded, long-necked, glass vessel, used for distilling and dissolving substances. **2.** a small glass closed at one end. Also, **mattrass.** [< F *matras,* ? < Ar *maṭrah* leather bottle]

matri-, a learned borrowing from Latin meaning "mother," used in the formation of compound words: *matrilineal.* [< L, comb. form of *māter* MOTHER]

ma·tri·arch (mā′trē ärk′), *n.* a woman holding a position analogous to that of a patriarch, as in a family or tribe. [MATRI- + -ARCH] —**ma′tri·ar′chal, ma′tri·ar′chic,** *adj.* —**ma′tri·ar′chal·ism,** *n.*

ma·tri·ar·chate (mā′trē är′kit, -kāt), *n.* **1.** a matriarchal system or community. **2.** a social order believed to have preceded patriarchal tribal society in the early period of human communal life, embodying rule by the mothers, or by all adult women. [MATRIARCH + -ATE[1]]

ma·tri·ar·chy (mā′trē är′kē), *n., pl.* **-chies.** the matriarchal system; a form of social organization, as in certain primitive tribes, in which the mother is head of the family, and in which descent is reckoned in the female line, the children belonging to the mother's clan. [MATRI- + -ARCHY]

ma·tri·ces (mā′tri sēz′, ma′tri-), *n.* a pl. of **matrix.**

ma·tri·cide (ma′tri sīd′, mā′-), *n.* **1.** act of killing one's mother. **2.** one who kills his mother. [< L *mātricīd(ium), mātricīd(a).* See MATRI-, -CIDE] —**mat′ri·cid′al,** *adj.*

ma·tric·u·lant (mə trik′yə lənt), *n.* one who matriculates; a candidate for matriculation. [< LL *mātrīcul(a)* list (dim. of *mātrīx* list; see MATRIX, -ULA) + -ANT]

ma·tric·u·late (*v.* mə trik′yə lāt′; *n.* mə trik′yə lit), *v.,* **-lat·ed, -lat·ing,** *n.* —*v.t.* **1.** to enroll, or admit to membership and privileges by enrolling, esp. in a college or university. **2.** to register (a coat of arms), used esp. in Scottish heraldry. —*v.i.* **3.** to be matriculated. —*n.* **4.** one who has been matriculated. [< ML *mātrīculāt(us)* keeper, lit., person listed (for some specific duty), equiv. to *mātrīcul(a)* list (see MATRICULANT) + *-ātus* -ATE[1]] —**ma·tric′u·la′tion,** *n.* —**ma·tric′u·la′tor,** *n.*

mat·ri·lat·er·al (ma′trə lat′ər əl, mā′-), *adj.* related through the mother, as to a maternal uncle. Cf. **patrilateral.** [MATRI- + LATERAL] —**mat′ri·lat′er·al·ly,** *adv.*

mat·ri·lin·e·age (ma′trə lin′ē ij, mā′-), *n.* lineal descent traced through the female line. [MATRI- + LINEAGE[1]]

mat·ri·lin·e·al (ma′trə lin′ē əl, mā′-), *adj.* inheriting or determining descent through the female line. Also, **mat′ri·lin′e·ar.** Cf. **patrilineal.** [MATRI- + LINEAL] —**mat′ri·lin′e·al·ly, mat′ri·lin′e·ar·ly,** *adv.*

mat·ri·lin·y (ma′trə lin′ē, -lī′nē, mā′-), *n., pl.* **-lin·ies.** the tracing of descent through the mother's line of a family. [MATRILIN(EAL) + -Y[3]]

mat·ri·lo·cal (ma′trə lō′kəl, mā′-), *adj. Anthropol.* of or pertaining to residence with the family or tribe of one's wife: *matrilocal customs.* Cf. **patrilocal.** [MATRI- + LOCAL] —**mat′ri·lo·cal′i·ty,** *n.*

mat·ri·mo·ni·al (ma′trə mō′nē əl), *adj.* of or pertaining to matrimony; marital; nuptial; connubial; conjugal. [< LL *mātrimōniāl(is).* See MATRIMONY, -AL[1]] —**mat′ri·mo′ni·al·ly,** *adv.*
—**Syn.** married, wedded.

mat·ri·mo·ny (ma′trə mō′nē), *n., pl.* **-nies.** **1.** the rite, ceremony, or sacrament of marriage. **2.** the state of marriage; wedlock. [ME < L *mātrimōni(um)* wedlock. See MATRI-, -MONY]

mat′rimony vine′, any solanaceous plant of the genus *Lycium,* species of which are cultivated for their foliage, flowers, and berries. Also called **boxthorn.**

mat·ri·po·tes·tal (ma′trē pō tes′tᵊl, mā′-), *adj. Anthropol.* of or pertaining to the authority exercised by a mother or a mother's blood relatives. [MATRI- + *potestal* < L *potest(ās)* power + -AL[1]]

ma·trix (mā′triks, ma′-), *n., pl.* **ma·tri·ces** (mā′tri sēz′, ma′-), **ma·trix·es.** **1.** that which gives origin or form to a thing, or which serves to enclose it: *Rome was the matrix of Western civilization.* **2.** *Anat.* a formative part, as the corium beneath a nail. **3.** *Biol.* the intercellular substance of a tissue. **4.** the fine-grained portion of a rock in which coarser crystals or rock fragments are embedded. **5.** fine material, as cement, in which lumps of coarser material, as of an aggregate, are embedded. **6.** *Mining.* gangue. **7.** *Metall.* a crystalline phase in an alloy in which other phases are embedded. **8.** *Print.* a mold for casting type faces. **9.** master (def. 18). **10.** (in a press or stamping machine) a multiple die or perforated block on which the material to be formed is placed. **11.** *Math.* the rectangular arrangement into rows and columns of the elements of a set or sets. **12.** a mold made by electroforming from a disk recording, from which other disks may be pressed. **13.** (in the circuit of an electronic computer) an array of components and parts, as relays, tubes, transistors, diodes, magnetic storage cores, etc., for translating from one code to another. **14.** *Archaic.* the womb. [< L: female beast kept for breeding (LL: register, orig. of such beasts), womb, parent stem (of plants), deriv. of *māter* mother]

ma·tron (mā′trən), *n.* **1.** a married woman, esp. a mature one with children, or one who has an established social position. **2.** a woman who has charge of the domestic affairs of a hospital, prison, or other institution. **3.** a woman serving as a guard, warden, or attendant for women or girls, as in a female prison. [ME *matrone* < L *mātrōna* wife, lady, deriv. of *māter* mother] —**ma·tron·al** (mā′trə nᵊl, ma′-), *adj.* —**ma′tron·hood′, ma′tron·ship′,** *n.*

ma·tron·age (mā′trə nij, ma′-), *n.* **1.** state of being a matron. **2.** guardianship by a matron. **3.** matrons collectively. [MATRON + -AGE]

Ma·tron·al·i·a (mā′trə nā′lē ə, -nāl′yə, ma′-), *n., pl.* **-al·i·a, -al·i·as.** (*sometimes construed as pl.*) an annual festival of ancient Rome held by matrons in honor of Juno. [< L *Mātrōnālia* (*festa*), neut. pl. of *mātrōnālis* of, belonging to a married woman. See MATRON, -AL[1]]

ma·tron·ize (mā′trə nīz′), *v.,* **-ized, -iz·ing.** —*v.t.* **1.** to cause to become matronly; act as, or fulfill the role of, matron: *The bride was soon matronized by the responsibilities of marriage.* **2.** to serve as a matron to; chaperon. —*v.i.* **3.** to become a matron. [MATRON + -IZE]

ma·tron·ly (mā′trən lē), *adj.* **1.** of, pertaining to, or having the characteristics of a matron; maturely dignified and socially respected. **2.** characteristic of or suitable for a matron: *a matronly insistence upon good behavior.* [MATRON + -LY] —**ma′tron·li·ness,** *n.*

ma′tron of hon′or, a married woman acting as the principal attendant of the bride at a wedding.

mat·ro·nym·ic (ma′trə nim′ik), *adj.* metronymic.

MATS (mats), *n.* Military Air Transport Service.

mat·su (mat′so͞o), *n.* a pine, *Pinus Massoniana,* of Japan, yielding a wood used in making furniture, the construction of houses, etc. [< Jap]

Ma·tsu (mat so͞o′, mat′so͞o; *Chin.* mä′dzo͞o), *n.* an island off the SE coast of China, in the East China Sea: remained with Nationalist China after the Communist conquest of the mainland. 11,002 (est. 1956); 17 sq. mi. Cf. **Quemoy.**

Ma·tsu·o·ka (mä′tso͝o ô′kä), *n.* **Yo·su·ke** (yô so͞o′ke), 1880–1946, Japanese statesman.

Ma·tsu·ya·ma (mä′tso͝o yä′mä), *n.* a seaport on NW Shikoku, in SW Japan. 238,514 (1960).

Mat·sys (mät′sīs), *n.* **Quentin.** See **Massys, Quentin.**

matt (mat), *adj., n., v.t.* mat[3].

Matt (mat), *n.* a boy's given name, form of **Matthew.**

Matt., Matthew.

Mat·ta·thi·as (mat′ə thī′əs), *n.* died 167? B.C., Jewish priest in Judea (father of Judas Maccabaeus).

matte[1] (mat), *adj., n., v.,* **mat·ted, mat·ting.** —*adj.* **1.** (of paper) having a dull surface. Cf. **glossy** (def. 3), **semimat. 2.** mat[3] (def. 1). —*n.* **3.** *Metall.* an unfinished metallic product of the smelting of certain sulfide ores, esp. those of copper. **4.** mat[3] (defs. 2, 3). —*v.t.* **5.** mat[3] (def. 4). [< F < G *matt* MAT[3]]

matte[2] (mat), *n.* *Mining.* a mass of timber caved beneath overburden so as to cushion the fall of the overburden and separate it from mineral to be extracted beneath. [< G; akin to MAT[1]]

mat·ted[1] (mat′id), *adj.* **1.** covered with a dense growth or a tangled mass: *a garden matted with weeds.* **2.** covered with mats or matting. **3.** formed into a mat; entangled in a thick mass: *matted hair.* **4.** formed of mats, or of plaited or woven material. [MAT[1] + -ED[2]] —**mat′ted·ly,** *adv.* —**mat′ted·ness,** *n.*

mat·ted[2] (mat′id), *adj.* having a dull finish; matte. [MAT[3] + -ED[2]]

Mat·te·ot·ti (mät′te ôt′tē), *n.* **Gia·co·mo** (jä′kô mô), 1885–1924, Italian socialist leader.

mat·ter (mat′ər), *n.* **1.** the substance or substances of which any physical object consists or is composed: *the matter of which the earth is made.* **2.** physical or corporeal substance in general, whether solid, liquid, or gaseous, esp. as distinguished from incorporeal substance, as spirit or mind, or from qualities, actions, and the like. **3.** that which occupies space. **4.** a particular kind of substance: *coloring matter.* **5.** a substance discharged by a living body, esp. pus. **6.** the material or substance of a discourse, book, etc., often as distinguished from the form. **7.** something written or printed: *printed matter.* **8.** a situation, state, affair, or business: *a trivial matter.* **9.** an amount or extent reckoned approximately: *a matter of 10 miles.* **10.** something of consequence: *matter for serious thought.* **11.** importance or significance: *decisions of little matter.* **12.** difficulty; trouble (usually prec. by *the*): *There is something the matter.* **13.** ground, reason, or cause: *a matter for complaint.* **14.** *Philos.* **a.** that which by integrative organization forms chemical substances and living things. **b.** *Aristotelianism.* that which relates to form as potentiality does to actuality. **15.** *Law.* statement or allegation. **16.** *Print.* **a.** material for work; copy. **b.** type set up. **17. a matter of life and death,** something of vital importance: *He told the telephone operator that his call was a matter of life and death.* **18. as a matter of fact,** in reality; actually; truthfully: *As a matter of fact, there is no substance to that rumor.* **19. for that matter,** as far as that is concerned; as for that: *For that matter, you are no better qualified to judge than I.* Also, **for the matter of that. 20. no matter,** it is unimportant; it makes no difference: *No matter. This string will do as well as any other.* —*v.i.* **21.** to be of importance; signify: *It matters little.* **22.** *Pathol.* to suppurate. [ME *mater,* back formation from early ME *materie* < L *māteria* stuff, matter, wood of trees] —**mat′ter·ful,** *adj.* —**mat′ter·less,** *adj.*

—**Syn. 1.** MATTER, MATERIAL, STUFF, SUBSTANCE refer to that of which physical objects are composed (though all these terms are also used abstractly). MATTER, as distinct from mind and spirit, is a broad word which applies to anything perceived, or known to be occupying space: *solid matter; gaseous matter.* MATERIAL usually means some definite kind, quality, or quantity of matter, esp. as intended for use: *woolen material; a house built of good materials.* STUFF, a less technical word, with approximately the same meanings as MATERIAL, is characterized by being on an informal level when it refers to physical objects (*Dynamite is queer stuff*), and on a literary or poetic one when it is used abstractly (*the stuff that dreams are made on*). SUBSTANCE is the matter that composes a thing, thought of in relation to its essential properties: *a sticky substance.* **6.** subject, topic. **8.** question. **10.** concern. **11.** moment. **21.** count.

Mat·ter·horn (mat′ər hôrn′), *n.* a mountain on the border of Switzerland and Italy, in the Pennine Alps. 14,780 ft. French, **Mont Cervin.**

mat′ter in deed′, *Law.* a fact or statement that can be proved or established by a deed or specialty.

mat′ter of course′, something that follows in logical or customary sequence or that is treated as such: *These unexpected setbacks would have crushed a weaker-willed individual, but he met them as a matter of course. After such reprisals, war followed as a matter of course.*

mat·ter-of-course (mat′ər əv kōrs′, -kôrs′), *adj.* **1.** occurring or proceeding in or as if in the natural course of things; expected or inevitable: *After his brilliant work, his success was matter-of-course.* **2.** accepting things as occurring in their natural course, or characterized by an acceptance of things as such: *to be matter-of-course in confronting the difficulties of existence; a gay, matter-of-course manner.*

mat′ter of fact′, **1.** *Law.* a statement or allegation to be judged on the basis of the evidence. **2.** something of a factual nature, as an actual occurrence.

mat·ter-of-fact (mat′ər əv fakt′), *adj.* adhering strictly to fact; not imaginative; prosaic; dry; commonplace: *a matter-of-fact account of the rally.* —**mat′ter-of-fact′ly,** *adv.* —**mat′ter-of-fact′ness,** *n.*

mat′ter of law′, *Law.* an issue or matter to be determined according to the relevant principles of law.

mat′ter of rec′ord, *Law.* a fact or statement that appears on the record of a court and that can be proved or established by producing such record.

Matte·son (mat′sən), *n.* a town in NE Illinois. 3225 (1960).

Mat·thew (math′yo͞o), *n.* **1.** one of the four Evangelists, a customs collector from Capernaum, summoned to be one of the 12 apostles. Matt. 9:9–13. **2.** the first Gospel: *the Gospel of St. Matthew.* **3.** a boy's given name.

Mat′thew of Par′is, c1200–59, English chronicler. Also called **Mat′thew Par′is.**

Mat·thews (math′yo͞oz), *n.* **(James) Bran·der** (bran′dər), 1852–1929, U.S. writer and educator.

Mat′thew Walk′er, a knot formed on the end of a rope by partly unlaying the strands and tying them in a certain way. See illus. under **knot.** [after a proper name]

Mat·thi·as (mə thī′əs), *n.* **1.** a disciple chosen to take the place of Judas Iscariot as one of the apostles. Acts 1:23–26. **2.** Also, **Mat·thy′as.** a boy's given name, form of **Matthew.**

Mat·tie (mat′ē), *n.* a boy's or girl's given name. Also, **Matty.**

mat·ting[1] (mat′ing), *n.* **1.** a coarse fabric of rushes, grass, straw, hemp, or the like, used for covering floors, wrapping, etc. **2.** material for mats. [MAT[1] + -ING[1]]

mat·ting[2] (mat′ing), *n.* a dull, slightly roughened surface, free from polish, produced by the use of a mat. [MAT[3] + -ING[1]]

mat·tins (mat′ənz, -inz), *n.* (*usually construed as sing.*) *Chiefly Brit.* matin (def. 1).

mat·tock (mat′ək), *n.* an instrument for loosening the soil in digging, shaped like a pickax, but having one end broad instead of pointed. [ME *mattok,* OE *mattuc*]

Mat·to Gros·so (mat′ə grō′sō; *Port.* mä′tô̂ grô′-sô). See **Mato Grosso.**

mat·toid (mat′oid), *n.* *Rare.* a person of abnormal mentality bordering on insanity. [< It *mattoide* slightly mad, equiv. to *matt(o)* mad (< ML *mattus* foolish; see MAT[3]) + *-oide* -OID]

Mat·toon (mə to͞on′), *n.* a city in E Illinois. 19,088 (1960).

mat·trass (ma′trəs), *n.* *Chem.* matrass.

mat·tress (ma′tris), *n.* **1.** a large pad for supporting the reclining body, used as or on a bed, consisting of a quilted or similarly fastened case, usually of heavy cloth, that contains hair, straw, cotton, foam rubber, etc., or a framework of metal springs. **2.** a mat woven of brush, poles, or similar material, used to prevent erosion of the surface of dikes, jetties, embankments, dams, etc. **3.** a layer of concrete placed on bare ground, as to provide a footing; mat. [ME *materas* < OF < It *materass(o)* < Ar (*al-*) *maṭrah* (the) mat, cushion]

Mat·ty (mat′ē), *n.* a boy's or girl's given name. Also, **Mattie.**

ma·tu·ra dia′mond (mä′tər ə, mat′-), *Jewelry.* a zircon heat-treated to render it colorless; not a true diamond. Also, **matara diamond.** [after *Matura,* town in Ceylon]

mat·u·rate (mach′o͝o rāt′, mat′yo͝o-), *v.i.,* **-rat·ed, -rat·ing. 1.** *Pathol.* to suppurate. **2.** to mature. [< L *mātūrāt(us)* grown ripe, brought to maturity, ptp. of *mātūrāre.* See MATURE, -ATE[1]] —**ma·tur·a·tive** (mə-cho͝or′ə tiv, mach′o͝o rā′-, mat′yo͝o-), *adj.*

mat·u·ra·tion (mach′o͝o rā′shən, mat′yo͝o-), *n.* **1.** act or process of maturating. **2.** *Biol.* the second phase of gametogenesis, resulting in the production of mature eggs and sperms from oogonia and spermatogonia. [< medical L *mātūrātiōn-* (s. of *mātūrātiō*). See MATURATE -ION] —**mat′u·ra′tion·al,** *adj.*

ma·ture (mə to͝or′, -tyo͝or′, -cho͝or′), *adj., v.,* **-tured, -tur·ing.** —*adj.* **1.** complete in natural growth or development, as plant and animal forms. **2.** ripe, as fruit, or fully aged, as cheese, wine, etc. **3.** fully developed in body or mind, as a person: *a mature woman.* **4.** pertaining to or characteristic of full development: *a mature appearance; fruit with a mature softness.* **5.** completed, perfected, or elaborated in full by the mind: *mature plans.* **6.** *Finance.* having reached the limit of its time; having become payable or due, as a note. **7.** *Med.* **a.** having attained definitive form or function, as by maturation of an epithelium from a basal layer. **b.** having attained the end stage of a normal or abnormal biological process: *a mature boil.* **8.** *Phys. Geog.* (of topographical features) exhibiting the stage of maximum stream development, as in the process of erosion of a land surface. —*v.t.* **9.** to make mature; ripen, as fruit, cheese, etc. **10.** to bring to full development: *His hard experiences in the city matured him.* **11.** to complete or perfect: *He matured the novel by constant revision.* —*v.i.* **12.** to become mature; ripen, as fruit, cheese, etc. **13.** to come to full development: *Our plans have not yet matured.* **14.** *Finance.* to become due, as a note. [late ME < L *mātūr(us)* ripe, timely, early; akin to MANES] —**ma·ture′ly,** *adv.* —**ma·ture′ment,** *n.* —**ma·ture′ness,** *n.* —**ma·tur′er,** *n.*

—**Syn. 1, 3.** aged, grown, adult. **2.** See **ripe. 5.** ready, prepared. **9, 11.** age, develop. —**Ant. 1, 3.** childish, raw, green, young.

Ma·tu·rín (mä′to͞o rēn′), *n.* a city in NE Venezuela. 42,000 (1951).

ma·tu·ri·ty (mə to͝or′i tē, -tyo͝or′-, -cho͝or′-), *n.* **1.** state of being mature; ripeness: *the maturity of fruit; the plays of Shakespeare's maturity.* **2.** full development; perfected condition: *maturity of judgement; to bring a plan to maturity.* **3.** *Finance.* **a.** state of being due. **b.** the time when a note or bill of exchange becomes due. [ME *maturite* < L *mātūritās* ripeness. See MATURE, -ITY]

Ma·tu·ta (mə to͞o′tə, -tyo͞o′-), *n.* an ancient Roman goddess of childbirth and sometimes of the dawn, harbors, and the sea, associated with Leucothea. Also called **Mater Matuta.**

ma·tu·ti·nal (mə to͞ot′ᵊnᵊl, -tyo͞ot′-), *adj.* pertaining to or occurring in the morning; early in the day. [< LL *mātūtīnāl(is)* of, belonging to the morning, early, equiv. to L *mātūtīn(us)* of the morning (*Mātūt(a)* goddess of dawn + *-īnus* pertaining to) + *-ālis* -AL[1]] —**ma·tu′ti·nal·ly,** *adv.*

mat·zah (mät′sə), *n., pl.* **mat·zoth** (mät′sōt), **mat·zahs.** matzo.

mat·zo (mät′sə, -sō), *n., pl.* **mat·zoth** (mät′sōt), **mat·zos** (mät′səz, -sōs). **1.** unleavened bread in the form of large crackers, typically square and corrugated, eaten by Jews during Passover. **2.** one of these crackers. Also, **matzah.** [< Yiddish *matse* < Heb *maṣṣāh*]

mat′zo meal′, ground matzoth.

Mau·beuge (mō bœzh′), *n.* a city in N France, on the Sambre River, near the Belgian border. 27,287 (1962).

maud (môd), *n.* **1.** a gray woolen plaid worn by shepherds and others in S Scotland. **2.** a rug or wrap of like material, used as a traveling robe, steamer rug, etc. [? apocopated var. of *maldy* a coarse gray woolen cloth]

Maud (môd), *n.* a girl's given name, form of **Matilda.** Also, **Maude.**

Maud (môd), *n.* a poem (1855), by Tennyson, in the form of a dramatic monologue.

Maud·ie (mô′dē), *n.* a girl's given name, form of **Maud.** Also, **Maud′y, Maud′ye.**

maud·lin (môd′lin), *adj.* **1.** tearfully or weakly emotional; mawkishly sentimental: *a maudlin story of a little orphan and her lost doggy.* **2.** mawkishly drunk or pertaining to mawkish drunkenness. [special use of *Maudlin,* ME *Maudelen* << LL *Magdalene* < Gk *Magdalēnḗ* Mary Magdalene, portrayed in art as a weeping penitent] —**maud′lin·ism,** *n.* —**maud′lin·ly,** *adv.* —**maud′lin·ness,** *n.*

Mauds·lay (môdz′lē), *n.* **Henry,** 1771–1831, English mechanical engineer.

Maugham (môm), *n.* **W(illiam) Som·er·set** (sum′ər-set′, -sit), 1874–1965, English novelist, dramatist, and short-story writer.

mau·gre (mô′gər), *prep.* *Archaic.* in spite of; notwithstanding. Also, **mau′ger.** [ME < MF: lit., spite, ill-will, equiv. to *mau-* MAL- + *gre* GREE[2]]

Ma·u·i (mä′o͞o ē′, mou′ē), *n.* an island in central Hawaii. 40,103 (1950); 728 sq. mi.

mau·kin (mô′kin), *n.* *Brit. Dial.* malkin.

maul (môl), *n.* **1.** a heavy hammer, as for driving piles. **2.** *Archaic.* a heavy club or mace. [ME *malle* < OF *mail* mallet, hammer < L *malle(us)* hammer] —*v.t.* **3.** to handle or use roughly: *The book was badly mauled by its borrowers.* **4.** to injure by a rough beating, shoving, or the like; bruise: *to be mauled by a crowd.* **5.** *U.S.* to split with a maul and wedge, as a wooden rail. Also, **mall.** [ME *malle(n)* < OF *maill(ier),* deriv. of n.] —**maul′er,** *n.*

Maul·din (môl′din), *n.* **William Henry** (*Bill*), born 1921, U.S. cartoonist.

Maul·main (môl mān′, môl-), *n.* Moulmein.

maul·stick (môl′stik′), *n.* mahlstick.

maul·vi (moul′vē), *n.* (in India) an expert in Islamic law: used esp. as a term of respectful address among native Muslims. Also, **molvi, moolvee, moolvi, moulvi.** [< Hindi *maulvī* < Ar *mawlawī*]

Ma·u·man (mä o͞o′mən), *n.* *Douay Bible.* Mehuman.

Mau Mau (mou′ mou′), *pl.* **Mau Maus,** (*esp. collectively*) **Mau Mau.** a member of a revolutionary society in Kenya, established in the early 1950's, that consisted chiefly of Kikuyu tribesmen and that engaged in terrorist activities in an attempt to drive out the European settlers and to give government control to the native Kenyans. [< Kikuyu]

Mau·mee (mô mē′, mô′mē), *n.* a river in E Indiana and W Ohio, flowing NE to Lake Erie, at Toledo. 175 mi. long.

mau·met (mô′mit), *n.* **1.** *Brit. Dial.* **a.** a doll, puppet, scarecrow, or any other figure built to resemble a human being. **b.** *Disparaging.* a person who seems to have the mind of a doll or puppet. **2.** *Obs.* an idol; a false god. [ME < OF *mahommet* idol, special use of *Mahommet* MOHAMMED, whose image was thought to be an object of worship] —**mau′met·ry,** *n.*

maun (män, môn), *auxiliary v. Scot.* must. Also, **man.** [ME *man* < Scand; cf. Icel *man* must, shall, will]

Mau·na Ke·a (mou′nə kā′ə, mô′nə kē′ə), an extinct volcano on the island of Hawaii. 13,784 ft.

Mau·na Lo·a (mou′nə lō′ə, mô′nə), an active volcano on the island of Hawaii. 13,680 ft.

maunche (mänch), *n. Heraldry.* manche. Also, **maunch.**

maund (mônd), *n.* a unit of weight in India and other parts of Asia, varying greatly according to locality: in India, from about 25 to 82.286 pounds (the latter being the government maund). [< Hindi *man* < Skt *manā*]

maun·der (môn′dər), *v.i.* **1.** to talk in a rambling, foolish, or meaningless way. **2.** to move, go, or act in an aimless, confused manner: *He maundered through life without a single ambition.* [?] —**maun′der·er,** *n.*

maund·y (môn′dē), *n.* **1.** the ceremony of washing the feet of the poor, esp. commemorating Jesus' washing of His disciples' feet on Maundy Thursday. **2.** Also called **maund′y mon′ey.** money distributed as alms in conjunction with the ceremony of maundy or on Maundy Thursday. [ME *maunde* < OF *mande* < L *mandāt(um)* command, mandate (from the opening phrase *novum mandātum* (Vulgate) of Jesus' words to the disciples after he had washed their feet). See MANDATE]

Maun′dy Thurs′day, the Thursday of Holy Week, commemorating Jesus' Last Supper and His washing of the disciples' feet upon that day.

Mau·pas·sant (mō′pə sänt′; *Fr.* mō pA sän′), *n.* **(Hen·ri Re·né Al·bert) Guy de** (äN Rē′ Rə nā′ Al bεR′ gē də), 1850–93, French short-story writer and novelist.

Mau·ra (môr′ə), *n.* a girl's given name, Irish form of **Mary.**

Mau·reen (mô rēn′), *n.* a girl's given name, Irish form of **Mary.** Also, **Mau·rene′, Mau·rine′.**

Mau·re·ta·ni·a (môr′i tā′nē ə), *n.* an ancient kingdom in NW Africa: it included the territory that is modern Morocco and part of Algeria. Also, **Mauritania.** —**Mau′re·ta′ni·an,** *adj., n.*

Mau·riac (mô RyäK′), *n.* **Fran·çois** (fRäN swA′), born 1885, French novelist: Nobel prize 1952.

Mau·rice (môr′is, mor′-, mô rēs′; *for 3 also Fr.* mō Rēs′), *n.* **1.** German, **Moritz.** 1521–53, German general: elector of Saxony 1547–53. **2. of Nassau,** 1567–1625, Dutch statesman. **3.** a boy's given name.

Mau·rist (môr′ist), *n.* a member of the Benedictine "Congregation of St. Maur," founded in France in 1618, distinguished for its scholarship and literary works: suppressed during the French Revolution. [St. *Maur* 6th-century French monk and disciple of St. Benedict + -IST]

Mau·ri·ta·ni·a (môr′i tā′nē ə), *n.* **1.** Official name, **Islamic Republic of Mauritania.** a republic in W Africa, largely in the Sahara Desert: formerly a French colony; now an independent member of the French Community. 780,000 (est. 1963); 418,120 sq. mi. *Cap.:* Nouakchott. **2.** Mauretania. —**Mau′ri·ta′ni·an,** *adj., n.*

Mau·ri·tius (mô rish′əs, -rish′ē əs), *n.* **1.** an island in the Indian Ocean, E of Madagascar. 681,619 (1962); 720 sq. mi. **2.** a republic consisting of this island and dependencies, formerly a British colony. 701,019 (1962); 809 sq. mi. *Cap.:* Port Louis. Formerly, **Ile de France.** —**Mau·ri′tian,** *adj.*

Mauri′tius hemp′. See **giant lily.**

Mau·ro (mär′ō), *n.* **Fra.** See **Fra Mauro.**

Mau·rois (mô RwA′), *n.* **An·dré** (äN dRā′), (*Émile Salomon Wilhelm Herzog*), 1885–1967, French biographer and novelist.

Mau·ry (môr′ē, mor′ē *for 1, 3;* mou′rē *for 2*), *n.* **1. Matthew Fon·taine** (fon tān′, fon′tān), 1806–73, U.S. naval officer and scientist. **2.** a walled plain in the first quadrant of the face of the moon: about 12 miles in diameter.

Mau·ry·a (mour′ē ə), *n.* a member of an ancient Indian people who united northern India and established an empire 322–184 B.C. —**Mau′ry·an,** *adj.*

Mau·ser (mou′zər), *n.* **Peter Paul,** 1838–1914, and his brother, **Wilhelm,** 1834–82, German inventors of firearms.

mau·so·le·um (mô′sə lē′əm, -zə-), *n., pl.* **-le·ums, -le·a** (-lē ə). **1.** a stately and magnificent tomb. **2.** (*cap.*) the tomb erected at Halicarnassus in Asia Minor in 350? B.C. Cf. **Seven Wonders of the World.** [< L < Gk *mausōleîon* the tomb of Mausolus, king of Caria] —**mau′so·le′an,** *adj.*

Maus·ton (mô′stən), *n.* a town in central Wisconsin. 3531 (1960).

mauve (mōv), *n.* **1.** pale bluish purple. **2.** a purple dye obtained from aniline, discovered in 1856; the first of the coal-tar dyes. —*adj.* **3.** of the color of mauve: *a mauve dress.* [< F: lit., mallow < L *malva* MALLOW]

mauve′ dec′ade, the 1890's as a social and cultural period, characterized by prosperity and complacency.

mav·er·ick (mav′ər ik, mav′rik), *n.* **1.** *Southwestern U.S.* an unbranded calf, cow, or steer, esp. an unbranded calf that is separated from its mother. **2.** a dissenter, as an intellectual, an artist, or a politician, who takes an independent stand apart from his associates. [named after Samuel A. *Maverick* (1803–70), Texas pioneer who neglected to brand his cattle]

ma·vin (mā′vən), *n.* an expert, esp. in everyday matters. Also, **ma′ven.** [< Yiddish < Heb: connoisseur]

ma·vis (mā′vis), *n. Brit. Chiefly Poetic.* a song thrush. [ME *mavys* thrush < MF *mauvis* < ?]

Ma·vis (mā′vis), *n.* a girl's given name.

Ma·vors (mā′vôrs), *n. Rom. Religion.* Mars.

ma·vour·neen (mə vŏŏr′nēn, -vôr′-, -vōr′-), *n. Irish English.* darling; dear. Also, **ma·vour′nin.** [< Ir *mo mhuirnīn*]

maw[1] (mô), *n.* **1.** the mouth, throat, or gullet of an animal, esp. a carnivorous mammal. **2.** the crop or craw of a fowl. **3.** the stomach, esp. that of an animal. **4.** a cavernous opening that resembles the jaws of an animal: *the gaping maw of hell.* **5.** the symbolic or theoretical center of a voracious hunger or appetite of any kind: *the ravenous maw of Death.* [ME *mawe,* OE *maga;* c. D *maag,* G *Magen,* Icel *magi*]

maw[2] (mô), *n. Dial.* mother. [var. of MA]

maw·kin (mô′kin), *n.* malkin.

mawk·ish (mô′kish), *adj.* **1.** having a faint sickly flavor; slightly nauseating; insipid. **2.** characterized by sickly sentimentality; feebly emotional. [obs. *mawk* maggot (late ME < Scand; cf. Icel *mathkr* maggot) + -ISH[1]. See MAGGOT] —**mawk′ish·ly,** *adv.* —**mawk′ish·ness,** *n.*

Maw·son (mô′sən), *n.* **Sir Douglas,** 1882–1958, Australian antarctic explorer, born in England.

Max (maks), *n.* a boy's given name, form of **Maximilian.**

max., maximum.

Maxilla (def. 1)

max·i (mak′sē), *n.* **1.** maxiskirt. —*adj.* **2.** of the length of a maxiskirt. [by shortening]

Max·ie (mak′sē), *n.* a boy's given name, form of **Max.** Also, **Maxy.**

max·il·la (mak sil′ə), *n., pl.* **max·il·lae** (mak sil′ē). **1.** a jaw or jawbone, esp. the upper. **2.** one of the paired appendages immediately behind the mandibles of arthropods. [< NL, special use of L *maxilla* lower jaw, dim. of *māla* (earlier **maxla*) upper jaw, cheekbone]

max·il·lar·y (mak′sə ler′ē, mak sil′ə rē), *adj., n., pl.* **-lar·ies.** —*adj.* **1.** of or pertaining to a jaw, jawbone, or maxilla. —*n.* **2.** a maxilla or maxillary bone. [< L *maxillār(is)* of, belonging to the jaw. See MAXILLA, -ARY]

max·il·li·ped (mak sil′ə ped′), *n.* one member of the three pairs of appendages situated immediately behind the maxillae of crustaceans. [MAXILL(A)- + -I- + -PED] —**max′il·li·ped′a·ry,** *adj.*

max·im (mak′sim), *n.* **1.** an expression of a general truth or principle, esp. an aphoristic or sententious one: *the maxims of La Rochefoucauld.* **2.** a principle of conduct: *It was his maxim never to give a sucker an even break.* [ME *maxime* << ML *maxima* (orig. in phrase *maxima prōpositiō* axiom, lit., greatest proposition), fem. of L *maximus,* superl. of *magnus* great; see MUCH] —**Syn. 1.** aphorism, saying, adage, apothegm. See **proverb.**

Max·im (mak′sim), *n.* **1. Hiram Percy,** 1869–1936, U.S. inventor. **2.** his father, **Sir Hiram Stevens,** 1840–1916, English inventor, born in the U.S. **3. Hudson,** 1853–1927, U.S. inventor and explosives expert (brother of Sir Hiram Stevens Maxim).

Max·im (*Fr.* mAk sēm′; *Russ.* mä ksem′), *n.* a boy's given name, form of **Maximilian.**

max·i·ma (mak′sə mə), *n.* a pl. of **maximum.**

max·i·mal (mak′sə məl), *adj.* of or being a maximum; greatest possible; highest. [MAXIM(UM) + -AL[1]] —**max′i·mal·ly,** *adv.*

max′imal ide′al, *Math.* an ideal in a ring which is not included in any other ideal except the ring itself.

Max·i·mal·ist (mak′sə mə list), *n.* a member of an extremist group or faction of socialists. Cf. **Minimalist.** [MAXIMAL + -IST]

Max·imes (*Fr.* mAk sēm′), *n.* (*Réflexions ou sentences et maximes morales*) a collection of paradoxical, cynical maxims and gnomic reflections (1665) by La Rochefoucauld.

Max′im gun′, an early single-barreled, water-cooled machine gun cocked by the force of its own recoil.

Max·i·mil·ian (mak′sə mil′yən), *n.* **1.** 1832–67, archduke of Austria: emperor of Mexico 1864–67. **2.** Also, **Max, Maxim.** a boy's given name.

Maximilian I, 1459–1519, emperor of the Holy Roman Empire 1493–1519.

Maximilian II, 1527–76, emperor of the Holy Roman Empire 1564–76.

Max′imil′ian ar′mor, full plate armor of the early 16th century, representing a combination of Italian and German styles and characterized by extensive use of fluting for lightness and strength.

max·i·min (mak′sə min), *n.* a strategy of game theory employed to maximize a player's minimum possible gain. Cf. **minimax.** [MAXI(MUM) + MIN(IMUM)]

max·i·mise (mak′sə mīz′), *v.t.,* **-mised, -mis·ing.** *Chiefly Brit.* maximize. —**max′i·mi·sa′tion, max′i·ma′tion,** *n.* —**max′i·mis′er,** *n.*

max·im·ite (mak′sə mīt′), *n. Chem.* a powerful explosive consisting primarily of picric acid. [named after Hudson MAXIM; see -ITE[1]]

max·i·mize (mak′sə mīz′), *v.t.,* **-mized, -miz·ing.** to increase to the greatest possible amount or degree: *He maximized his importance in the program, minimizing the contributions of the rest.* Also, *esp. Brit.,* **maximise.** [MAXIM(UM) + -IZE] —**max′i·mi·za′tion, max′i·ma′tion,** *n.* —**max′i·miz′er,** *n.*

max·i·mum (mak′sə məm), *n., pl.* **-mums, -ma** (-mə), *adj.* —*n.* **1.** the greatest quantity or amount possible, assignable, allowable, etc.; the highest amount, value, or degree attained or recorded (opposed to *minimum*): *They increased the speed of the car to the maximum.* **2.** *Math.* **a.** Also called **relative maximum, local maximum.** the value of a function at a certain point in its domain, which is greater than or equal to the values at all other points in the immediate vicinity of the point. Cf. **absolute maximum. b.** the point in the domain at which a maximum occurs. —*adj.* **3.** that is a maximum; greatest possible; highest: *maximum satisfaction.* **4.** pertaining to a maximum or maximums. [< L, n. use of neut. of *maximus,* superl. of *magnus* great, large] —**max′i·mum·ly,** *adv.*

max′imum like′lihood estima′tion, *Statistics.* a method of estimating population characteristics from a sample by choosing the values of the parameters which will maximize the probability of getting the particular sample actually obtained from the population.

max′imum prin′ciple, *Math.* the theorem that a function of a complex variable that is analytic in a domain and on its boundary attains its maximum absolute value on the boundary. Also called **max′imum mod′ulus prin′ciple.**

max′imum thermom′eter, a thermometer designed to show the highest temperature recorded between resettings. Cf. **minimum thermometer.**

Max·ine (mak sēn′, mak′sēn), *n.* a girl's given name.

max·i·skirt (mak′sē skûrt′), *n.* a long skirt or skirt part, as of a coat, dress, etc., ending below the middle of the calf but above the ankle. Also, **maxi.** [MAXI(MUM) + SKIRT; modeled on MINISKIRT]

Max Mül·ler (maks mul′ər; *Ger.* mäks mʏ′lər), **Fried·rich** (frē′drik; *Ger.* fʀē′dʀɪkh). See **Müller, Friedrich Max.**

max·well (maks′wəl, -wel), *n. Elect.* the centimeter-gram-second unit of magnetic flux, equal to the magnetic flux through one square centimeter normal to a magnetic field of one gauss. *Abbr.:* Mx Also called **line.** [named after J. C. MAXWELL]

Max·well (maks′wəl, -wel), *n.* **1. Elsa,** 1883–1963, U.S. professional hostess and author. **2. James Clerk** (klärk), 1831–79, Scottish physicist. **3.** a boy's given name.

Max′well-Boltz′mann statis′tics (maks′wəl-bôlts′män, -mən, -wel), *Physics.* statistics for classical physics, based on the assumption that in a given physical system consisting of indistinguishable particles and regions, all possible arrangements of the particles in the various regions have equal probability. [named after J. C. MAXWELL and Ludwig BOLTZMANN]

Max′well de′mon, *Physics.* a hypothetical agent or device of arbitrarily small mass that is considered selectively to admit or block the passage of individual molecules from one compartment to another according to their speed, constituting a violation of the second law of thermodynamics. [named after J. C. MAXWELL]

Max·y (mak′sē), *n.* a boy's given name, form of **Max.** Also, **Maxie.**

may[1] (mā), *v., pres. sing. 1st pers.* **may,** *2nd* **may** or (*Archaic*) **may·est** or **mayst,** *3rd* **may;** *pres. pl.* **may;** *past* **might. 1.** (used to express wish or prayer): *May you live long.* **2.** (used to express contingency, esp. in clauses indicating condition, concession, purpose, result, etc.): *I may be wrong, but I think you would be wise to go. Times may change, but human nature stays the same.* **3.** (used to express possibility, opportunity, or permission): *It may rain. You may enter.* **4.** *Archaic.* (used to express ability or power.) [OE *mæg,* 1st and 3rd pers. sing. pres. ind. of *magan,* c. G *mögen*] —**Syn. 3.** See **can**[1].

may[2] (mā), *n. Archaic.* a maiden.

May (mā), *n.* **1.** the fifth month of the year, containing 31 days. **2.** the early part of one's life, esp. the prime: *a young woman in her May.* **3.** the festivities of May Day. **4.** (*l.c.*) *Brit.* the hawthorn. **5.** Also, **Mae, Mai.** a girl's given name. —*v.i.* **6.** (*l.c.*) to gather flowers in the spring: *when we were maying.* [ME; OE *Maius* < L, short for *Maius mēnsis* Maia's month]

May (mā), *n.* **Cape,** a cape at the SE tip of New Jersey, on Delaware Bay.

ma·ya (mä′yä, -yə), *n. Hinduism.* **1.** the power, as of a god, to produce illusions. **2.** the production of an illusion. **3.** (in Vedantic philosophy) the illusion of the reality of sensory experience and of the experienced qualities and attributes of oneself. **4.** (*cap.*) Also called **Mahamaya.** a goddess personifying the power that creates phenomena. [< Skt] —**ma′yan,** *adj.*

Ma·ya (mä′yə), *n., pl.* **-yas,** (*esp. collectively*) **-ya. 1.** a member of an Amerindian people of Yucatán who had attained a relatively high pre-Columbian civilization. **2.** the historical and modern language of the Mayas, of Mayan stock.

Ma·ya·güez (mä′yä gwes′), *n.* a seaport in W Puerto Rico. 50,147 (1960).

Ma·ya·kov·ski (mä yä kôf′ski), *n.* **Vla·di·mir Vla·di·mi·ro·vich** (vlä dē′mir vlä dē′mi ro vich), 1893–1930, Russian poet. Also, **Ma·ya·kov′sky.**

Ma·yan (mä′yən), *adj.* **1.** of or pertaining to the Mayas. —*n.* **2.** a member of the Mayan tribe. **3.** a linguistic stock of southern Mexico, Guatemala, and British Honduras, including Maya and Quiche, and probably related to Penutian. [MAY(A) + -AN]

May′ ap′ple, 1. a perennial, American herb, *Podophyllum peltatum,* bearing an edible, yellowish, egg-shaped fruit. **2.** the fruit itself. Also called **Indian apple.**

may·be (mā′bē), *adv.* perhaps; possibly: *Maybe I'll go too.* [late ME *may be,* short for *it may be*]

May·beck (mā′bek), *n.* **Bernard,** 1862–1957 U. S. architect.

May′ bee′tle. See **June bug** (def. 1).

May-blob (mā′blob′), *n.* See **marsh marigold.**

May′ Day′, the first day of May, long celebrated with various festivities, as the crowning of the May queen, dancing around the Maypole, and, in recent years, often marked by labor parades and political demonstrations. [late ME] —**May′-day′,** *adj.*

May·day (mā′dā′), *n.* the international radiotelephone distress signal, used by ships and aircraft. [< pseudo-F *m'aidez* help me]

Ma·yence (mA yäNs′), *n.* French name of **Mainz.**

Ma·yenne (mA yen′), *n.* a department in W France. 250,030 (1962); 2012 sq. mi. *Cap.:* Laval.

Ma·yer (mā′ər *for 1;* mī′ər *for 2*), *n.* **1. Louis B(urt)** (bûrt), 1885–1957, U.S. motion-picture producer, born in Russia. **2. Maria Goep·pert** (gō′pərt), born 1906, U.S. physicist, born in Poland: Nobel prize 1963.

may·est (mā′ist), *v. Archaic.* 2nd pers. sing. pres. indic. of **may.**

May·fair (mā′fâr′), *n.* a fashionable locality in London, England, E of Hyde Park.

may′fair tan′. See **sun tan** (def. 2). [after MAYFAIR]

May·field (mā′fēld′), *n.* a town in SW Ohio. 2747 (1960).

may·fish (mā′fish′), *n., pl.* **-fish·es,** (*esp. collectively*) **-fish.** See **striped killifish.** [MAY + FISH]

May·flow·er (mā′flou′ər), *n.* **1.** (*italics.*) the ship in which the Pilgrim Fathers sailed from Southampton to the New World in 1620. **2.** any of various plants that blossom in May, as the trailing arbutus, hepatica, or anemone in the U.S., and the hawthorn or cowslip in England. [MAY + FLOWER]

May′flower com′pact, an agreement to establish a government, entered into by the Pilgrims in the cabin of the *Mayflower* on November 11, 1620.

Mayfly, *Hexagenia limbata* (Body length 1 in.)

May′ fly′, *Angling.* an artificial fly made to resemble the mayfly.

may·fly (mā′flī′), *n., pl.* **-flies.** **1.** any insect of the order *Ephemeroptera,* having delicate, membranous wings with the front pair much larger than the rear and having an aquatic larval stage and a brief, terrestrial adult stage. **2.** *Angling.* an artificial fly made to resemble this insect. Also, **May′ fly′.** [MAY + FLY²]

may·hap (mā′hap′, mā′hap′), *adv.* perhaps. [short for *it may hap*]

may·hap·pen (mā′hap′ən), *adv.* *Chiefly Dial.* mayhap. [short for *it may happen*]

may·hem (mā′hem, mā′əm), *n.* *Law.* the crime of willfully inflicting a bodily injury on another so as to make him less able to defend himself or, under modern statutes, so as to cripple or mutilate him. Also, **maihem.** [ME *maheym, maim* < AF *mahem,* etc. < Gmc; akin to MHG *meidem* gelding, Icel *meitha* to injure. See MAIM]

May·ing (mā′ing), *n.* the celebration of May Day. [late ME; see MAY, -ING¹]

Mayme (mām), *n.* a girl's given name, form of **Mary.** Also, **Mame.**

May·nard (mā′nərd), *n.* **1.** a town in central Massachusetts. 7695 (1960). **2.** a boy's given name.

May·net (mā′nit), *n.* a girl's given name.

may·n't (mā′ənt, mānt), contraction of *may not.*

May·o (mā′ō), *n.* **1. Charles Horace,** 1865–1939, and his brother **William James,** 1861–1939, U.S. surgeons. **2.** a county in NW Connaught province, in the NW Republic of Ireland. 123,330 (1961); 2084 sq. mi. *Co. seat:* Castlebar.

Ma·yon (mä yōn′), *n.* an active volcano in the Philippines, on SE Luzon Island. 7926 ft.

may·on·naise (mā′ə nāz′, mā′ə nāz′), *n.* a thick dressing of egg yolks, vinegar or lemon juice, seasonings, and oil, used for salads, sandwiches, vegetable dishes, etc. [< F, equiv. to *mayon* (? var. of *Mahón,* town in Minorca) + *-aise* -ESE]

may·or (mā′ər, mâr), *n.* **1.** the chief executive official of a city, village, or town. **2.** the chief magistrate of a city or borough. [< ML *māior,* sp. var. of *mājor* MAJOR; r. ME *mer, mair* < OF *maire*] —**may′or·al,** *adj.* —**may′or·ship′,** *n.*

may·or·al·ty (mā′ər əl tē, mâr′əl-), *n., pl.* **-ties.** the office or tenure of a mayor. [alter. of ME *mairaltee* < MF *mairalte.* See MAYOR, -AL¹, -TY²]

may·or·ess (mā′ər is, mâr′is), *n.* **1.** a woman mayor. **2.** *Brit.* a woman chosen by the mayor to be a town's first lady, usually the mayor's wife, daughter, sister, etc. [MAYOR + -ESS; r. ME *meyresse*]

May′or of Cas′ter·bridge, The (kas′tər brij′), a novel (1886) by Thomas Hardy.

Ma·yotte (*Fr.* MA yôt′), *n.* one of the Comoro Islands, in the Indian Ocean, NW of Madagascar. 23,000 (est. 1960); 143 sq. mi.

May·pole (mā′pōl′), *n.* (*often l.c.*) a high pole, decorated with flowers and ribbons, around which revelers dance or engage in sports during May Day celebrations. [MAY + POLE¹]

may·pop (mā′pop′), *n.* **1.** the edible fruit of a passion flower, *Passiflora incarnata,* of the southern U.S. **2.** the plant itself. [? repr. a Virginia var. of Algonquian *maracock*]

May′ queen′, a girl or young woman crowned with flowers and honored as queen in the sports of May Day.

Mays (māz), *n.* **Willie (Howard),** born 1931, U.S. baseball player.

mayst (māst), *v.* *Archaic.* 2nd pers. sing. pres. indic. of **may.**

Mays·ville (māz′vil), *n.* a town in NE Kentucky. 8484 (1960).

May·time (mā′tīm′), *n.* the month of May. Also called **May·tide** (mā′tīd′). [MAY + TIME]

may′ tree′, *Brit.* the hawthorn.

May·ville (mā′vil), *n.* a town in central Wisconsin. 3607 (1960).

may·weed (mā′wēd′), *n.* a composite herb, *Anthemis Cotula,* native to Europe and Asia but naturalized in North America, having pungent, rank-scented foliage and flower heads with a yellow disk and white rays. [obs. *may(th)* mayweed (OE *mægtha*) + WEED¹]

May′ wine′, a punch consisting typically of Alsatian, Moselle, or Rhine wine, flavored with woodruff.

May·wood (mā′wo͝od′), *n.* a city in NE Illinois, near Chicago. 27,330 (1960).

ma·zae·di·um (mə zē′dē əm, ma-), *n., pl.* **-di·a** (-dē ə). (in certain lichens) a fructification composed of paraphyses and a powdery mass of ascospores. [< NL < Gk *mâz(a)* mass + L *aed(ēs)* building + *-ium* -IUM]

ma·zal tov (mä′zəl tôv′, tôf′, tov′). See **mazel tov.**

maz·ard (maz′ərd), *n.* **1.** *Archaic.* **a.** head. **b.** face. **2.** *Obs.* a mazer. [MAZ(ER) + -ARD]

Maz·a·rin (maz′ə rin, maz′ə rēn′; *Fr.* MA ZA RAN′), *n.* **Jules** (jo͞olz; *Fr.* zhYl), (*Giulio Mazarini*), 1602–61, French cardinal and statesman, born in Italy: chief minister of Louis XIV 1642–61.

ma·za·rine (maz′ə rēn′, maz′ə rēn′, -rin), *n.* a silver strainer fitting over a meat dish and used for draining the water from boiled fish. [< F, ? after Cardinal MAZARIN]

Ma·zar-i-Sha·rif (mä zär′ē shä rēf′), *n.* a city in N Afghanistan. 50,000 (est. 1964).

Maz·a·tec·a (maz′ə tek′ə, -tä′kə), *n., pl.* **-tec·as,** (*esp. collectively*) **-tec·a.** a member of a people of Guerrero, Puebla, and Oaxaca, in Mexico.

Ma·zat·lán (mä′sät län′), *n.* a seaport in S Sinaloa, in W Mexico. 75,751 (1960).

Maz·da (maz′də), *n.* *Zoroastrianism.* See **Ahura Mazda.**

Maz·da·ism (maz′də iz′əm), *n.* Zoroastrianism. [MAZDA + -ISM]

maz·door (məz do͝or′), *n.* *Anglo-Indian.* a coolie; laborer. Also, **maz·dur′.** [< Hindi *mazdūr*]

maze (māz), *n., v.,* **mazed, maz·ing.** —*n.* **1.** a confusing network of intercommunicating paths or passages; a labyrinth. **2.** a state of bewilderment, confusion, or perplexity: *His petition was lost in a maze of bureaucratic red tape.* **3.** a winding movement, as in dancing. —*v.t.* **4.** *Chiefly Dial.* to stupefy or daze. [ME *mase,* aph. var. of *amase(n)* (to) AMAZE] —**maz·ed·ly** (mā′zid lē, mā′zid-), *adv.* —**mazed′ness,** *n.* —**maze′like′,** *adj.*

ma·ze·ga·ne (mä ze′gä ne′), *n.* a Japanese decorative metal technique in which shakudo and shibuichi are melted and allowed to cool so as to produce a mottled effect, used esp. for sword mounts. [< Jap]

ma·zel tov (mä′zel tôv, tôf′, tov′), an expression of congratulations and best wishes, used chiefly by Jews on an occasion of success or good fortune. Also, **mazal tov.** [< Heb; lit., good luck]

ma·zer (mā′zər), *n.* a large metal drinking bowl or cup, formerly of wood. [early ME: kind of wood (prob. maple), OE *mæser-* (in adj. *mæseren,* equiv. to *mæser* maple + *-en* -EN²); c. Icel *mösurr* maple, MHG *maser* maple, drinking cup]

ma·zo·path·i·a (mā′zō path′ē ə), *n.* *Pathol.* any disease of the placenta. Also, **mazopathy.** [< NL, equiv. to *mazo-* (comb. form of *māza* placenta < Gk *mâza* barley-cake) + *-pathia* -PATHY]

ma·zop·a·thy (mā zop′ə thē), *n.* *Pathol.* **1.** mazopathia. **2.** mastopathy.

ma·zu·ma (mə zo͞o′mə), *n.* *Slang.* money. [< Yiddish *mezumen* < Heb *mezūmān* set, fixed]

ma·zur·ka (mə zûr′kə, -zo͝or′-), *n.* **1.** a lively Polish dance in moderately quick triple meter. **2.** music for, or in the rhythm of, this dance. Also, **ma·zour′ka.** [< Pol, equiv. to *Mazur* Mazovia (district in northern Poland) + *-ka* suffix of appurtenance]

Ma·zu·rov (mä zo͞o′rof), *n.* **Ki·ril Tro·fi·mo·vich** (ki rēl′ tro fē′mo vich), born 1914, Russian government official: alternate member of the Presidium.

ma·zy (mā′zē), *adj.,* **-zi·er, -zi·est.** full of confusing turns, passages, etc.; like a maze; labyrinthine: *mazy paths and streams.* [MAZE + -Y¹] —**ma′zi·ly,** *adv.* —**ma′zi·ness,** *n.*

maz·zard (maz′ərd), *n.* a wild sweet cherry, *Prunus avium,* used as a rootstock for cultivated varieties of cherries. [earlier *mazer;* cf. obs. *mazers* spots, MEASLES]

Maz·zi·ni (mät tsē′nē, mäd dzē′-; *Eng.* mat sē′nē, mad zē′-), *n.* **Giu·sep·pe** (jo͞o zep′pe), 1805–72, Italian patriot and revolutionary. —**Maz·zi·ni·an** (mät zē′nē ən, mäs dē′-), *adj., n.*

mb, **1.** millibar; millibars. **2.** millibarn; millibarns.

M.B., *Chiefly Brit.* Bachelor of Medicine. [< L *Medicinae Baccalaureus*]

M'Ba (əmbä), *n.* **Lé·on** (le ôN′), 1902–67, African statesman: president of Gabon 1961–67.

M.B.A., Master of Business Administration.

Mban·da·ka (əmbän′dä kä), *n.* a city in W Zaire. 37,587 (est. 1958). Formerly, **Coquilhatville.**

M.B.E., Member of the Order of the British Empire.

Mbm, one thousand feet, board measure.

Mboy·a (əmboi′ə), *n.* **Tom** (*Thomas Joseph Mboya*), 1930–69, African political leader in Kenya.

Mc-, var. of **Mac-.** Also, **Mᶜ-.**

MC, **1.** Marine Corps. **2.** Medical Corps. **3.** Member of Congress.

Mc, **1.** megacurie; megacuries. **2.** megacycle. **3.** megacycles per second.

mC, millicoulomb; millicoulombs.

mc, **1.** megacycle. **2.** millicurie; millicuries. **3.** millicycle.

M.C., **1.** Master Commandant. **2.** Master of Ceremonies. **3.** Medical Corps. **4.** Member of Congress. **5.** Member of Council. **6.** *Brit.* Military Cross.

Mc·A·doo (mak′ə do͞o′), *n.* **1. William Gibbs,** 1863–1941, U.S. lawyer and statesman: Secretary of the Treasury 1913–18. **2.** a town in central Pennsylvania. 3560 (1960).

Mc·Al·es·ter (mə kal′i stər), *n.* a city in E Oklahoma. 17,419 (1960).

Mc·Al·len (mə kal′ən), *n.* a city in S Texas, on the Rio Grande. 32,728 (1960).

Mc·Ca·mey (mə kā′mē), *n.* a town in W Texas. 3375 (1960).

Mc·Car′ran-Wal′ter Act′ (mə kar′ən wôl′tər), *U.S.* the Immigration and Nationality Act enacted by Congress in 1952 that removed racial barriers to immigration and empowered the Department of Justice to deport immigrants or naturalized citizens who have engaged in subversive activities.

Mc·Car·thy (mə kär′thē), *n.* **1. Joseph R(aymond)** (*Joe*), 1909–57, U.S. politician. **2. Mary (Therese),** born 1912, U.S. writer.

Mc·Car·thy·ism (mə kär′thē iz′əm), *n.* **1.** the practice of making accusations of disloyalty, esp. of pro-Communist activity, in many instances unsupported by proof or based on slight, doubtful, or irrelevant evidence. **2.** unfairness in investigative technique. **3.** persistent search for and exposure of disloyalty, esp. in government office. [J. R. MCCARTHY + -ISM]

Mc·Clel·lan (mə klel′ən), *n.* **George Brin·ton** (brin′tən, -tᵊn), 1826–85, Union general in the U.S. Civil War.

Mc·Cloy (mə kloi′), *n.* **John Jay,** born 1895, U.S. lawyer, banker, and government official.

Mc·Clure (mə klo͝or′), *n.* **1. Samuel Sidney,** 1857–1949, U.S. editor and publisher, born in Ireland. **2.** a crater in the fourth quadrant of the face of the moon: about 15 miles in diameter.

Mc·Cone (mə kōn′), *n.* **John Alex,** born 1902, U.S. government official: director of the CIA 1961–65.

Mc·Cook (mə ko͝ok′), *n.* a city in S Nebraska. 8301 (1960).

Mc·Cor·mack (mə kôr′mik), *n.* **1. John,** 1884–1945, U.S. tenor, born in Ireland. **2. John William,** 1891–1980, U.S. politician: Speaker of the House 1962–70.

Mc·Cor·mick (mə kôr′mik), *n.* **1. Cyrus Hall,** 1809–84, U.S. inventor, esp. of harvesting machinery. **2. Robert Rutherford,** 1880–1955, U.S. newspaper publisher.

Mc·Coy (mə koi′), *n.* the genuine thing or person as promised, stated, or implied (usually prec. by *the* or *the real*): *Those other paintings are copies, but this one is the McCoy.* [said to refer to a U.S. pugilist, Kid *McCoy,* distinguishing him from an obscure or inferior boxer of the same name]

Mc·Crae (mə krā′), *n.* **John,** 1872–1918, Canadian physician, soldier, and poet.

Mc·Cul·lers (mə kul′ərz), *n.* **Car·son** (kär′sən), 1917–1967, U.S. novelist and short-story writer.

Mc·Don·ald (mək don′ᵊld), *n.* **1. David John,** 1902–79, U.S. labor leader: president of the United Steelworkers of America 1952–65. **2.** a town in SW Pennsylvania. 3141 (1960). **3.** a town in NE Ohio. 2727 (1960).

Mc·Doug·all (mək do͞o′gəl), *n.* **William,** 1871–1938, U.S. psychologist and writer, born in England.

Mc·Dow·ell (mək dou′əl), *n.* **1. Ephraim,** 1771–1830, U.S. surgeon. **2. Irvin,** 1818–85, Union general in the U.S. Civil War.

M.C.E., Master of Civil Engineering.

Mcf, one thousand cubic feet.

Mc·Far·land (mək fär′lənd), *n.* a town in central California. 3686 (1960).

Mcfd, thousands of cubic feet per day.

Mc·Fee (mək fē′), *n.* **William,** 1881–1966, English writer.

mcg, microgram.

Mc·Gehee (mə gē′), *n.* a town in SE Arkansas. 4448 (1960).

Mc·Graw (mə grô′), *n.* **John Joseph,** 1873–1934, U.S. baseball player and manager.

Mc·Greg·or (mə greg′ər), *n.* a town in central Texas. 4642 (1960).

Mc·Guf·fey (mə guf′ē), *n.* **William Holmes,** 1800–73, U.S. educator: editor of the *Eclectic Readers.*

M.Ch.E., Master of Chemical Engineering.

Mc·Hen·ry (mək hen′rē, mə ken′-), *n.* **1.** a town in NE Illinois. 3336 (1960). **2. Fort.** See **Fort McHenry.**

MCi, megacurie; megacuries.

mCi, millicurie; millicuries.

Mc·In·tire (mak′in tīᵊr′), *n.* **Samuel,** 1757–1811, U.S. architect and wood carver.

Mc·In·tosh (mak′in tosh′), *n.* **1.** a variety of red apple that ripens in early autumn. **2.** the tree bearing this fruit. [named after John *McIntosh* of Ontario, Canada, who first cultivated it (1796)]

Mc·In·tyre (mak′in tīᵊr′), *n.* **James Francis Aloysius,** 1886–1979, U.S. Roman Catholic clergyman: cardinal 1953; archbishop of Los Angeles 1948–70.

M.C.J., Master of Comparative Jurisprudence.

Mc·Kees·port (mə kēz′pôrt′, -pōrt′), *n.* a city in SW Pennsylvania, near Pittsburgh. 45,489 (1960).

Mc·Ken·na (mə ken′ə), *n.* **Sio·bhan** (shə vôn′), born 1923, Irish actress.

Mc·Ken·zie (mə ken′zē), *n.* **1. Robert Tait** (tāt), 1867–1938, Canadian physician, educator, sculptor. **2.** a town in NW Tennessee. 3780 (1960).

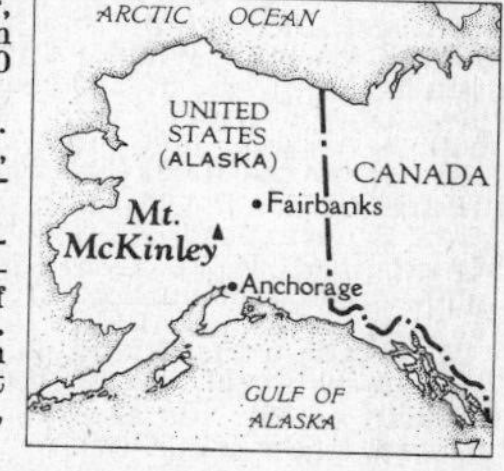

Mc·Kim (mə kim′), *n.* **Charles Fol·len** (fol′ən), 1847–1909, U.S. architect.

Mc·Kin·ley (mə kin′lē), *n.* **1. William,** 1843–1901, 25th president of the U.S. 1897–1901. **2. Mount,** a mountain in central Alaska: highest peak in North America, 20,300 ft.

Mc·Kis·sick (mə kis′ik), *n.* **Floyd Bix·ler** (biks′lər), born 1922, U.S. lawyer and civil-rights leader: chairman of Congress of Racial Equality 1963–68.

Mc·Ku·en (mə kyo͞o′ən), *n.* **Rod,** born 1933, U.S. poet and songwriter.

M.C.L., **1.** Master of Civil Law. **2.** Master of Comparative Law.

Mc·Leans·bor·o (mə klānz′bûr ō, -bur ō), *n.* a town in SE Illinois. 2951 (1960).

Mc·Leod′ gauge′ (mə kloud′), *Physical Chem.* a device for determining very low gas pressures by manometrically measuring the pressure of a sample after its compression to a known fraction of its original volume. [named after Herbert *McLeod* (1841–1932), English chemist]

Mc·Lu·han (mə klo͞o′ən), *n.* **Marshall,** 1911–80, Canadian cultural historian and mass-communications theorist.

Mc·Mas·ter (mək mas′tər, -mä′stər), *n.* **John Bach,** 1852–1932, U.S. historian and educator.

Mc·Mech·en (mək mek′ən), *n.* a town in NW West Virginia. 2999 (1960).

Mc·Mil·lan (mək mil′ən), *n.* **Edwin Mat·ti·son** (mat′i sən), born 1907, U.S. educator and physicist: Nobel prize for chemistry 1951.

Mc·Minn·ville (mək min′vil), *n.* **1.** a town in central Tennessee. 9013 (1960). **2.** a town in NW Oregon. 7656 (1960).

Mc·Mur′do Sound′ (mək mûr′dō), an inlet of Ross Sea, in Antarctica, N of Victoria Land.

Mc·Nair (mək nâr′), *n.* **Lesley James,** 1883–1944, U.S. army officer.

Mc·Na·ma·ra (mak′nə mar′ə), *n.* **Robert Strange,** born 1916, U.S. business executive and government official: Secretary of Defense 1961–68.

Mc·Naugh·ton (mək nôt′ən), *n.* **Andrew George Lat·ta** (lat′ə), 1887–1966, Canadian army officer, statesman, diplomat, and scientist.

Mc·Nutt (mək nut′), *n.* **Paul Vo·ries** (vōr′ēz, vôr′-), 1891–1955, U.S. diplomat and government official.

M.C.P., Master of City Planning.

Mc·Pher·son (mək fûr′sən, -fēr′-), *n.* a town in central Kansas. 9996 (1960).

M.C.R., Master of Comparative Religion.

Mc·Rae (mə krā′), *n.* a town in central Georgia. 2738 (1960).

Mc·Rey·nolds (mək ren′əldz), *n.* **James Clark,** 1862–1946, U.S. jurist: associate justice of the U.S. Supreme Court 1914–41.

Mc/s, megacycle per second.

Mc·Sher·rys·town (mək sher′ēz toun′), *n.* a town in S Pennsylvania. 2839 (1960).

Mc·Teague (mək tēg′), *n.* a novel (1899) by Frank Norris.

MD, Middle Dutch. Also, **MD.**

Md, *Chem.* mendelevium.

Md., Maryland.

M/D, months after date. Also, **M/d, m/d**

M.D., **1.** Doctor of Medicine. [< L *Medicinae Doctor*] **2.** Middle Dutch.

MDAP, Mutual Defense Assistance Program.

M-day (em′dā′), *n.* *Mil.* mobilization day: a day assumed by the Department of Defense as the first day of mobilization, used by the military for planning purposes.

M.Des., Master of Design.

Mdlle., *pl.* **Mdlles.** Mademoiselle. Also, **Mdlle**

Mdm., *pl.* **Mdms.** Madam.

Mdme., *pl.* **Mdmes.** Madame.

MDR, Minimum Daily Requirement.

mdse., merchandise.

me (mē), *pron.* **1.** the objective case of **I:** *They asked me to the party.* **2.** the dative case of **I:** *Give me your hand.* **3.** *Informal.* (used instead of the pronoun *my* in gerundive constructions): *Did you hear about me getting promoted?* [ME *me,* OE *mē* (dat. sing.); c. D *mij, mir;* akin to L *mē* (acc.)]

—Usage. 3. This sense of ME has been labeled *Informal* because in traditional grammar a gerund, being considered syntactically identical to a noun, requires modification by the genitive form of the noun or pronoun preceding it. Hence, traditional grammarians will insist on constructions like: *She likes my* (rather than *me*) *singing her to sleep.* This is true of all pronominal constructions (HIS, HER, ITS, OUR, THEIR, and YOUR), as well as of noun-gerund combinations (*He hates the carpenter's making so much noise*). However, many good writers and speakers do not invariably follow the tradition. Indeed, there are situations in which the genitive form is not possible (*There is little hope of this coming about*) or, at the very least, would be awkward (*She disliked the father and son tracking up the rug*). These situations, however, are exceptions; in careful speech and particularly in careful writing the genitive case preceding a gerund is more common than the objective case.

ME, Middle English.

Me, *Chem.* methyl.

Me., Maine.

M.E., **1.** (*often l.c.*) See **managing editor. 2.** Master of Education. **3.** Master of Engineering. **4.** Mechanical Engineer. **5.** Methodist Episcopal. **6.** Middle English. **7.** Mining Engineer.

M.E.A., Master of Engineering Administration.

mea·con (mē′kən), *v.t.* to give false signals to (electronic navigational equipment), as by means of a radio transmitter. [M(ISLEAD) + (B)EACON]

me·a cul·pa (me′ä kōōl′pä; *Eng.* mē′ə kul′pə), *Latin.* through my fault; my fault.

mead[1] (mēd), *n.* **1.** an alcoholic liquor made by fermenting honey and water. **2.** any of various nonalcoholic beverages. [ME *mede,* OE *medu;* c. D *mee,* G *met,* Icel *mjöthr* mead, Skt *madhu* honey, Gk *méthy* wine]

mead[2] (mēd), *n.* *Archaic.* meadow. [ME *mede,* OE *mǣd.* See MEADOW]

Mead (mēd), *n.* **1. George Herbert,** 1863–1931, U.S. philosopher and author. **2. Margaret,** 1901–78, U.S. anthropologist. **3. Lake,** a lake in NW Arizona and SE Nevada, formed by Boulder Dam: largest artificial lake in the world. 115 mi. long; 227 sq. mi.

Meade (mēd), *n.* **George Gordon,** 1815–72, Union general in the U.S. Civil War.

mead·ow (med′ō), *n.* **1.** a tract of grassland used for pasture or serving as a hayfield. **2.** a tract of grassland in an upland area near the timber line. [ME *medwe,* OE *mǣdw-,* in inflectional forms of *mǣd* MEAD[2]; akin to G *Matte*] **—mead′ow·less,** *adj.*

mead′ow bird′, the bobolink.

mead·ow-brown (med′ō broun′), *n.* any of several satyr butterflies, as *Hipparchia janira.*

mead′ow fes′cue, a perennial, European fescue, *Festuca elatior,* grown for pasture in North America.

mead′ow grass′, any grass of the genus *Poa,* esp. *P. pratensis,* the Kentucky bluegrass.

mead·ow·lark (med′ō lärk′), *n.* any of several American songbirds of the genus *Sturnella,* of the family *Icteridae,* esp. *S. magna* (**east′ern mead′owlark**), and *S. neglecta* (**west′ern mead′owlark**), having a brownish and black back and wings and a yellow breast, noted for their clear, tuneful song. [MEADOW + LARK[1]]

Western meadowlark, *Sturnella neglecta* (Length 9 in.)

mead′ow lil′y, a lily, *Lilium canadense,* of eastern North America, having nodding, orange-yellow or red flowers.

mead′ow mouse′, any of numerous short-tailed rodents of the genus *Microtus* and allied genera, found chiefly in fields and meadows of the temperate Northern Hemisphere. Also called **meadow vole.**

mead′ow mush′room. See under **mushroom** (def. 2).

mead′ow pars′nip, any perennial, umbelliferous plant of the genus *Thaspium,* of North America, having yellow or purple flowers.

mead′ow pink′. See **maiden pink.**

mead′ow rue′, a ranunculaceous plant of the genus *Thalictrum,* having leaves resembling those of rue, esp. *T. dioicum,* of North America. Also called **early meadow rue, silverweed.**

mead′ow saf′fron. See **autumn crocus.**

mead′ow sal′sify, a European, biennial, weedy herb, *Tragopogon pratensis,* naturalized in North America, having yellow flowers. Also called **star-of-Jerusalem.**

mead·ow·sweet (med′ō swēt′), *n.* **1.** any rosaceous plant of the genus *Spiraea,* esp. *S. latifolia,* having white or pink flowers. **2.** any plant of the closely related genus *Filipendula* (or *Ulmaria*). [MEADOW + SWEET]

mead′ow vole′. See **meadow mouse.**

mead·ow·y (med′ō ē), *adj.* pertaining to, resembling, or consisting of meadow. [MEADOW + -Y[1]]

Mead·ville (mēd′vil), *n.* a city in NW Pennsylvania. 16,671 (1960).

mea·ger (mē′gər), *adj.* **1.** deficient in quantity or quality; lacking fullness or richness; poor; scanty; inadequate: *a meager salary; meager fare; a meager harvest.* **2.** having little flesh; lean; thin: *a body meager with hunger.* **3.** maigre. Also, *esp. Brit.,* **mea′gre.** [ME *megre* < OF *maigre* < L *macer* lean] **—mea′ger·ly;** *esp. Brit.,* **mea′gre·ly,** *adv.* **—mea′ger·ness;** *esp. Brit.,* **mea′gre·ness,** *n.*

—Syn. 1. See **scanty. 2.** gaunt, spare, skinny.

meal[1] (mēl), *n.* **1.** one of the regular occasions during the day when food is taken, as breakfast, lunch, or supper. **2.** the food served or eaten at such occasions. [ME; OE *mǣl* measure, fixed time, occasion, meal; c. G *Mal* time, *Mahl* meal, ON *māl,* Goth *mēl* time, hour] **—meal′less,** *adj.*

meal[2] (mēl), *n.* **1.** the edible part of any grain, usually excluding wheat, or pulse ground to a coarse powder and unbolted. **2.** *U.S.* coarse, unbolted grain, corn meal, or Indian meal. **3.** any ground or powdery substance, as of nuts or seeds, resembling this. [ME *mele,* OE *melu;* c. G *Mehl,* D *meel,* Icel *mjöl;* akin to Goth *malan,* L *molere* to grind. See MILL[1]] **—meal′less,** *adj.*

-meal, a native English combining form, now largely obsolete, denoting a fixed measure at a time: *piecemeal.* [ME *-mele,* OE *-mǣlum,* comb. form repr. *mǣl* MEAL[1]]

meal·ie (mē′lē), *n.* (in Africa) **1. mealies,** corn[1] (def. 1a). **2.** an ear of corn. [< SAfrD *mielie* < Pg *milho* maize, millet < L *milium* MILLET]

meal′ tick′et, 1. a ticket that entitles the bearer to meals in a specified restaurant, esp. when meals purchased in this manner are offered at reduced rates. **2.** *Slang.* someone upon whom one is dependent for one's income or livelihood: *She is a selfish woman who looks upon her husband only as a meal ticket.* **3.** *Slang.* something, as an object or ability possessed by a person, that is necessary to his livelihood: *A radio announcer's voice is his meal ticket.* **4.** *Slang.* a person who can be relied upon to do well or to do what is expected of him.

meal·time (mēl′tīm′), *n.* the usual time for a meal. [ME *meeltyme.* See MEAL[1], TIME]

meal·worm (mēl′wûrm′), *n.* the larva of any of several darkling beetles of the genus *Tenebrio,* which infests granaries and is used as food for birds and animals. [MEAL[2] + WORM]

meal·y (mē′lē), *adj.,* **meal·i·er, meal·i·est. 1.** having the qualities of meal; powdery; soft, dry, and crumbly: *mealy potatoes; a mealy stone.* **2.** of the nature of or containing meal; farinaceous: *baked fish with a mealy crust.* **3.** covered with or as with meal or powder: *flowers mealy with their pollen.* **4.** colored as if flecked with meal; spotty: *horses with mealy hides.* **5.** pale, as the complexion; sallow. **6.** mealy-mouthed. [MEAL[2] + -Y[1]] **—meal′i·ness,** *n.*

meal′y bell′wort, a slender, perennial herb, *Uvularia perfoliata,* of eastern North America, having pale-yellow, bell-shaped flowers. Also called **mohawkweed.**

meal·y·bug (mē′lē bug′), *n.* any of several scalelike, homopterous insects of the family *Pseudococcidae* that are covered with a powdery, waxy secretion. [MEALY + BUG[1]]

meal·y-mouthed (mē′lē mouthd′, -moutht′), *adj.* avoiding the use of direct and plain language, as from timidity, excessive delicacy, or hypocrisy; inclined to mince words; insincere or compromising. **—meal·y-mouth·ed·ly** (mē′lē mou′thid lē, -thid-, -moutht′-), *adv.* **—meal′y-mouth′ed·ness,** *n.*

mean[1] (mēn), *v.,* **meant, mean·ing.** **—***v.t.* **1.** to have in mind as one's purpose or intention; intend: *I mean to talk to him about the show.* **2.** to intend for a particular purpose, destination, etc.: *They were meant for each other.* **3.** to intend to express or indicate: *What do you mean by "liberal"?* **4.** to have as its sense or signification; signify: *The word "liberal" means many things to many people.* **5.** to bring, cause, or produce as a result: *This bonus means that we can take a trip to Florida.* **6.** to have (certain intentions) toward a person: *He means you no good.* **7.** to have the value of; assume the importance of: *Money means everything to him. His mother means the world to him.* **—***v.i.* **8.** to be minded or disposed; have intentions: *Beware, she means ill, despite her solicitous manner.* **9. mean well,** to have good intentions; try to be kind or helpful: *Her constant queries about your health must be tiresome, but I'm sure she means well.* [ME *mene(n),* OE *mǣnan;* c. G *meinen,* D *meenen*]

—Syn. 1. contemplate. See **intend. 2.** destine, foreordain. **4.** denote, indicate; import, imply, connote.

mean[2] (mēn), *adj.* **1.** inferior in grade, quality, or character: *a mean scholar.* **2.** low in station, rank, or dignity: *mean servitors.* **3.** of little importance or consequence: *mean, daily gossip.* **4.** unimposing or shabby: *a mean abode.* **5.** small-minded or ignoble: *mean motives.* **6.** penurious, stingy, or miserly: *a man who is mean about money.* **7.** offensive, selfish, or unaccommodating; nasty; malicious: *When he drinks he is mean and insulting.* **8.** *Informal.* small, humiliated, or ashamed: *You should feel mean for being so stingy.* **9.** *Informal.* in poor physical condition. **10.** *Informal.* troublesome or vicious, as a horse. **11.** *Slang.* skillful or impressive: *He blows a mean trumpet.* [ME *mene,* aph. var. of *imene,* OE *gemǣne;* c. G *gemein,* D *gemeen* common, Goth *gemains* in common]

—Syn. 2. common, humble; undignified, plebeian. **3.** inconsequent, insignificant, petty, paltry, little, poor, wretched. **4.** squalid, poor. **5.** contemptible, despicable. MEAN, LOW, BASE, SORDID, and VILE all refer to ignoble characteristics worthy of dislike, contempt, or disgust. MEAN suggests pettiness and small-mindedness: *to take a mean advantage.* LOW suggests coarseness and vulgarity: *low company.* BASE suggests selfish cowardice or moral depravity: *base motives.* SORDID suggests a wretched uncleanness, or sometimes an avariciousness without dignity or moral scruples: *a sordid slum; sordid gain.* VILE suggests disgusting foulness or repulsiveness: *vile insinuation; a vile creature.* **6.** niggardly, close, tight, parsimonious, illiberal, ungenerous, selfish.

mean[3] (mēn), *n.* **1.** Usually, **means.** (*often construed as sing.*) an agency, instrument, or method used to attain an end: *The telephone is a means of communication.* **2. means, a.** available resources, esp. money: *to live beyond one's means.* **b.** considerable financial resources; riches: *a man of means.* **3.** something intermediate; that which is midway between two extremes: *to seek a mean between cynicism and blind faith.* **4.** *Math.* **a.** a quantity having a value intermediate between the values of other quantities; an average, esp. the arithmetic mean. **b.** either the second or third term in a proportion of four terms. **5.** *Statistics.* See **expected value.** Cf. **arithmetic mean, geometric mean, harmonic mean. 6.** *Logic.* the middle term in a syllogism. **7. by all means, a.** at any cost; without fail. **b.** (in emphasis) certainly: *Go, by all means.* **8. by means of,** with the help of; by the agency of; through: *We crossed the stream by means of a log placed from bank to bank.* **9. by no means,** in no way; not at all: *a thing by no means certain.* **10. not by any means,** not in any way; not at all: *We were not surprised at the news by any means.* **—***adj.* **11.** occupying a middle position or an intermediate place, as in kind, quality, degree, time, etc.: *a mean speed; a mean course; a mean intelligence.* [ME *mene* < MF *meen,* var. of *meien* < L *mediān(us);* see MEDIAN]

mean′ anom′aly, *Astron.* the anomaly of a mean planet; the angular distance of the planet from perihelion or aphelion.

me·an·der (mē an′dər), *v.i.* **1.** to proceed by a winding or indirect course: *The stream meandered along the valley.* **2.** to wander aimlessly; ramble: *The talk meandered on.* **—***v.t.* **3.** *Survey.* to define the margin of (a body of water) with a meander line. **—***n.* **4.** Usually, **meanders.** turnings or windings; a winding path or course. **5.** a circuitous movement or journey. **6.** an intricate variety of fret or fretwork. [< L *maeander* < Gk *maíandros* a winding, special use of *Maíandros,* the Menderes river, noted for its winding course] **—me·an′der·er,** *n.* **—me·an′der·ing·ly,** *adv.*

Me·an·der (mē an′dər), *n.* ancient name of the **Menderes.** Also, **Maeander.**

mean′der line′, *Survey.* a zigzag traverse made to define the approximate margin of a natural body of water.

mean′ devia′tion, *Statistics.* a measure of dispersion, computed by taking the arithmetic mean of the absolute values of the deviations of the functional values from some central value, usually the mean or median. Also called **average deviation.**

mean′ dis′tance, *Astron.* the arithmetic mean of the greatest and least distances of a planet from the sun, used in stating the size of an orbit; the semimajor axis.

me·an·drous (mē an′drəs), *adj.* winding; rambling. [MEAND(E)R + -OUS]

mean′ free′ path′, *Physics, Chem.* (in a collection of moving particles) the average distance that a particle travels between successive collisions with other particles.

mean·ie (mē′nē), *n.* meany.

mean·ing (mē′ning), *n.* **1.** that which is intended to be, or actually is, expressed or indicated; signification; import: *the three meanings of a word.* **2.** the end, purpose, or significance of something: *What is the meaning of life? What is the meaning of this intrusion?* **3.** *Ling.* **a.** the nonlinguistic cultural correlate, reference, or denotation of a linguistic form; expression. **b.** linguistic content (opposed to *expression*). **—***adj.* **4.** intentioned (usually used in combination): *She's a well-meaning person.* **5.** full of significance; expressive: *a meaning look.* [ME (n.); see MEAN[1], -ING[1], -ING[2]] **—mean′ing·ly,** *adv.* **—mean′ing·ness,** *n.*

—Syn. 1. tenor, gist, drift, trend. MEANING, PURPORT, SENSE, SIGNIFICANCE denote that which is expressed or indicated by something. MEANING is the general word denoting that which is intended to be or actually is expressed or indicated: *the meaning of a word or glance.* SENSE may be used to denote a particular meaning (among others) of a word or phrase: *The word is frequently used in this sense.* SENSE may also be used loosely to refer to intelligible meaning: *There's no sense in what he says.* SIGNIFICANCE refers particularly to a meaning that is implied rather than expressed: *the significance of her glance;* or to a meaning the importance of which may not be easy to perceive immediately: *The real significance of his words was not grasped at the time.* PURPORT is mainly limited to the meaning of a formal document, speech, important conversation, etc., and refers to the gist of something fairly complicated: *the purport of his letter to the editor.* **5.** See **expressive.**

mean·ing·ful (mē′ning fəl), *adj.* full of meaning, significance, or value; significant: *a meaningful wink; a meaningful decision.* [MEANING + -FUL] **—mean′ing·ful·ly,** *adv.* **—mean′ing·ful·ness,** *n.*

mean·ing·less (mē′ning lis), *adj.* without meaning, significance, or value; purposeless; insignificant: *a meaningless reply; a meaningless existence.* [MEANING + -LESS] **—mean′ing·less·ly,** *adv.* **—mean′ing·less·ness,** *n.*

mean′ lat′itude. See **middle latitude.**

mean′ line′, *Print.* an imaginary x-high line. Also called **x-line.**

mean·ly[1] (mēn′lē), *adv.* **1.** in a poor, lowly, or humble manner. **2.** in a base, contemptible, or shabby manner. **3.** in a stingy, miserly manner. [MEAN[2] + -LY]

mean·ly[2] (mēn′lē), *adv.* *Obs.* moderately. [ME; see MEAN[3], -LY]

mean·ness (mēn′nis), *n.* **1.** state or quality of being mean. **2.** a mean act: *to answer meannesses with forgiveness.* [MEAN[2] + -NESS]

mean′ noon′, *Astron.* the moment when the mean sun's center crosses the meridian.

mean′ plan′et, *Astron.* a hypothetical planet that coincides with a real planet when the real planet is at perihelion and that moves in an orbit at a constant velocity equal to the mean velocity of the real planet.

Means′ grass′ (mēnz). See **Johnson grass.** [? from proper name *Means*]

mean′ so′lar day′, day (def. 3a).

mean′ so′lar time′, *Astron.* time measured by the hour angle of the mean sun. Also called **mean′ time′.**

mean·spir·it·ed (mēn′spir′i tid), *adj.* petty; small-minded; ungenerous: *a meanspirited man, unwilling to* *forgive.* [MEAN² + SPIRITED] **—mean′spir′it·ed·ly,** *adv.* **—mean′spir′it·ed·ness,** *n.*

means′ test′, **1.** *Brit.* an inquiry into the income of a person who receives unemployment relief. **2.** any investigation into the financial position of a person applying for aid from public funds.

mean′ sun′, *Astron.* an imaginary sun moving uniformly in the celestial equator and taking the same time to make its annual circuit as the true sun does in the ecliptic.

meant (ment), *v.* pt. and pp. of **mean¹.**

mean·time (mēn′tīm′), *n.* **1.** the intervening time: *Death awaits, but in the meantime, live.* **—***adv.* **2.** in the intervening time; during the interval. **3.** at the same time: *Meantime, the others were back home enjoying themselves.* [ME; see MEAN³, TIME]

mean′time screw′, *Horol.* See **quarter screw.**

mean′tone sys′tem (mēn′tōn′), *Music.* a system for tuning keyboard instruments, used before the development of tuning by equal temperament and considered practical only for tonalities of not more than two sharps or flats. [MEAN³ + TONE]

mean′ val′ue, *Math.* the ratio of the integral of a given function over a closed interval to the length of the interval.

mean′ val′ue the′orem, *Math.* the theorem that for a function continuous on a closed interval and differentiable on the corresponding open interval, there is a point in the interval such that the difference in functional values at the endpoints is equal to the derivative evaluated at the particular point and multiplied by the difference in the endpoints. Also called **law of the mean, theorem of the mean.**

mean·while (mēn′hwīl′, -wīl′), *n., adv.* meantime. [ME; see MEAN³, WHILE]

mean·y (mē′nē), *n., pl.* **mean·ies.** *Informal.* a small-minded, malicious person: *The children said their teacher was an old meany.* Also, **meanie.** [MEAN² + -Y²]

Mean·y (mē′nē), *n.* **George,** 1894–1980, U.S. labor leader: 3rd president of the AFL 1952–55; 1st president of the AFL-CIO 1955–79.

mear (mēr), *n.* *Brit. Dial.* mere³.

meas., measure.

mea·sle (mē′zəl), *n.* sing. of **measles** (def. 3).

mea·sled (mē′zəld), *adj.* (of swine or other livestock) affected with measles. [ME *meseled.* See MEASLES, -ED³]

mea·sles (mē′zəlz), *n.* **1.** (*construed as sing. or pl.*) *Pathol.* **a.** an acute infectious disease occurring mostly in children, characterized by catarrhal and febrile symptoms and an eruption of small red spots; rubeola. **b.** any of certain other eruptive diseases. Cf. **German measles.** **2.** *Vet. Pathol.* a disease in swine and other animals caused by the larvae of certain tapeworms of the genus *Taenia.* **3.** (*construed as pl.*) the larvae which cause measles in swine and other animals, and which upon maturation produce trichinosis in man. [ME *mesels,* mutated var. of *maseles* (pl.); c. D *maselen* (pl.), MD *masel;* akin to G *Masern* measles, pl. of *Maser* speck]

mea·sly (mē′zlē), *adj.,* **-sli·er, -sli·est.** **1.** infected with measles, as an animal or its flesh. **2.** pertaining to or resembling measles. **3.** *Informal.* **a.** wretchedly poor or unsatisfactory: *a measly performance.* **b.** very little or small: *a measly share.* [MEASL(ES) + -Y¹]

meas·ur·a·ble (mezh′ər ə bəl), *adj.* that may be measured. [ME *mesurable* < MF < LL *mensūrābil(is)* that can be measured. See MEASURE, -ABLE] **—meas′ur·a·bil′i·ty, meas′ur·a·ble·ness,** *n.* **—meas′ur·a·bly,** *adv.*

meas·ure (mezh′ər), *n., v.,* **-ured, -ur·ing.** **—***n.* **1.** act or process of ascertaining the extent, dimensions, quantity, etc., of something, esp. by comparison with a standard; measurement: *A measure of the field was promptly made.* **2.** size, dimensions, quantity, etc., as thus ascertained: *to take the measure of a thing.* **3.** an instrument, as a graduated rod or a vessel of standard capacity, for measuring. **4.** a unit or standard of measurement. **5.** a definite or known quantity measured out: *to drink a measure of wine.* **6.** a system of measurement. **7.** any standard of comparison, estimation, or judgment. **8.** a quantity, degree, or proportion. **9.** a moderate amount: *to live with a measure of enjoyment.* **10.** a limit, or an extent or degree not to be exceeded: *to know no measure.* **11.** reasonable bounds or limits: *a civilized sense of measure.* **12.** a legislative bill or enactment: *The senate passed the new measure.* **13.** Usually, **measures.** actions or procedures intended as a means to an end: *to take measures to avert suspicion.* **14.** a short rhythmical movement or arrangement, as in poetry or music. **15.** a particular kind of such arrangement. **16.** a metrical unit. **17.** an air or melody. **18.** the music contained between two bar lines; bar. **19.** a slow, dignified dance. **20.** *Print.* the width, measured in ems or picas, to which a column or page of printed matter is set: *wide or narrow measure; full measure.* **21. measures,** *Geol.* beds; strata. **22.** *Math.* an abstraction of the property of length; a set function assigning to each set of a collection of sets a value, usually having the properties of sigma finiteness and finite additivity, the functional value of the whole collection being greater than zero. **23. beyond measure,** too much to be reckoned; immeasurably; extremely: *The suffering that they endured was beyond measure.* **24. for good measure,** as an extra: *In addition to dessert, they served chocolates and fruit for good measure.* **25. have** or **take one's measure,** to judge or assess someone's character, capabilities, etc.; size up: *During their conversation she was taking his measure as a prospective husband for her daughter.* **26. in a measure,** to some extent or degree: *He is right in a measure.* **—***v.t.* **27.** to ascertain the extent, dimensions, quantity, capacity, etc., of, esp. by comparison with a standard: *to measure boundaries.* **28.** to mark off or deal out by way of measurement (often fol. by *off* or *out*): *to measure out martinis.* **29.** to estimate the relative amount, value, etc., of, by comparison with some standard: *to measure the importance of an issue.* **30.** to judge or appraise by comparison with something or someone else: *to measure Shakespeare against Racine.* **31.** to serve as the measure of: *Her sacrifices measure the degree of her love.* **32.** to adjust or proportion: *to measure a portion to one's liking.* **33.** to bring into comparison or competition: *to measure one's strength with another's.* **34.** to travel over; traverse: *to measure a room with great strides.* **—***v.i.* **35.** to take measurements. **36.** to admit of measurement. **37.** to be of a specified measure. **38. measure one's length,** to fall or be knocked down; fall flat: *He missed a step in the dark and measured his length at the bottom.* **39. measure swords, a.** to test one's preparedness for a contest or encounter. **b.** to battle with swords. **c.** to fight, compete, etc.: *The producer of the poorly reviewed show decided to measure swords with the critics.* **40. measure up, a.** to reach a certain standard: *The exhibition didn't measure up to last year's.* **b.** to be capable or qualified: *As an administrator he couldn't quite measure up.* [ME *mesure* < MF < L *mensūra,* equiv. to *mēns(us)* (ptp. of *mētīrī* to measure, mete) + *-ūra* -URE] **—meas′ur·er,** *n.*

M M

M, Measure (def. 18)

meas·ured (mezh′ərd), *adj.* **1.** ascertained or apportioned by measure. **2.** accurately regulated or proportioned. **3.** regular or uniform, as in movement; rhythmical: *to walk with measured strides.* **4.** deliberate and restrained; careful; well-weighed; well-considered: *measured language; measured terms.* **5.** in the form of meter or verse; metrical. [ME; see MEASURE, -ED²] **—meas′ured·ly,** *adv.* **—meas′ured·ness,** *n.*

Meas′ure for Meas′ure, a comedy (1604) by Shakespeare.

meas·ure·less (mezh′ər lis), *adj.* without limits or bounds; unlimited; immeasurable: *a measureless distance; measureless contempt.* [ME *measureles.* See MEASURE, -LESS] **—meas′ure·less·ly,** *adv.* **—meas′ure·less·ness,** *n.*
—Syn. boundless, unbounded, limitless, vast, infinite, immense.

meas·ure·ment (mezh′ər mənt), *n.* **1.** act of measuring. **2.** a measured dimension. **3.** extent, size, etc., ascertained by measuring. **4.** a system of measuring or measures: *liquid measurement.* [MEASURE + -MENT]

meas′urement ton′. See under **ton¹** (def. 5).

meas′ure ze′ro, *Math.* the property of a set of points for which, given any small number, there exists a set of intervals such that each point of the given set is contained in at least one of the intervals and such that, essentially, the combined length of the intervals is less than the small number.

meas′uring cup′, a graduated cup, often of glass or plastic, used esp. in cooking for measuring ingredients and usually having a capacity of one or two cups.

meas·ur·ing·worm (mezh′ər ing wûrm′), *n.* the larva of any geometrid moth, which progresses by bringing the rear end of the body forward and then advancing the front end. Also called **inchworm, looper, spanworm.** [MEASURING + WORM]

meat (mēt), *n.* **1.** the flesh of animals as used for food. **2.** food in general: *meat and drink.* **3.** the edible part of anything, as a fruit, nut, etc. **4.** the principal meal: *to say grace before meat.* **5.** the essential point or part of an argument, literary work, etc.; gist; crux: *a problem full of meat.* [ME, OE *mete;* c. Icel *matr,* Goth *mats,* OHG *maz* food] **—meat′less,** *adj.*

meat·ball (mēt′bôl′), *n.* **1.** chopped meat, esp. beef, molded or shaped into a ball before cooking. **2.** *Slang.* an awkward, clumsy, and stupid person. [MEAT + BALL¹]

Meath (mēth, mēth), *n.* a county in Leinster, in the E Republic of Ireland. 65,106 (1961); 902 sq. mi. *Co. seat:* Trim.

meat·head (mēt′hed′), *n.* *Slang.* blockhead; dunce; fool. [MEAT + HEAD]

meat·i·ness (mē′tē nis), *n.* the condition or quality of being meaty. [MEATY + -NESS]

meat·man (mēt′man′), *n., pl.* **-men.** a dealer in meat; butcher. [MEAT + MAN¹]

meat′ tea′, *Brit.* See **high tea.**

me·a·tus (mē ā′təs), *n., pl.* **-tus·es, -tus.** *Anat.* an opening or foramen, esp. in a bone or bony structure, as the opening of the ear, nose, etc. [< L: course, channel (4th decl.), deriv. of ptp. s. of *meāre* to go] **—me·a′tal,** *adj.*

meat·y (mē′tē), *adj.,* **meat·i·er, meat·i·est.** **1.** of or like meat. **2.** abounding in meat. **3.** rich in matter; full of substance; pithy: *a meaty argument.* [MEAT + -Y¹] **—meat′i·ly,** *adv.*

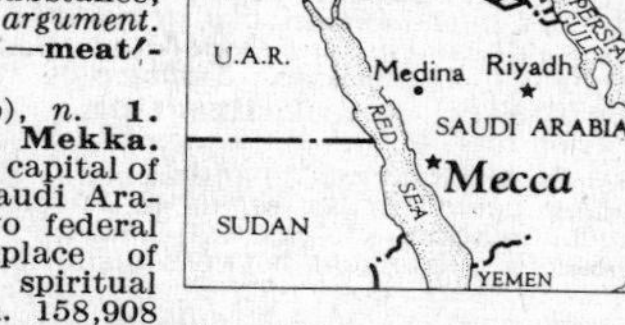

Mec·ca (mek′ə), *n.* **1.** Also, **Makkah, Mekka.** a city in and the capital of Hejaz, in W Saudi Arabia: one of two federal capitals; birthplace of Mohammed; spiritual center of Islam. 158,908 (1963). **2.** (*often l.c.*) any place that many people visit or hope to visit: *The President's birthplace is a mecca for his admirers.* **—Mec′can,** *adj., n.*

Mec′ca bal′sam. See **balm of Gilead** (def. 2).

mech., **1.** mechanical. **2.** mechanics. **3.** mechanism.

Me·cha·ne·us (mə kā′nē əs, -nōōs, -nyōōs), *n.* *Class. Myth.* an epithet of Zeus, meaning "contriver."

me·chan·ic (mə kan′ik), *n.* **1.** a skilled worker with tools, machines, equipment, etc. **2.** a person who repairs machinery, motors, etc. **3.** *Slang.* a person skilled in the dishonest handling of cards, dice, or other objects used in games of chance. [< L *mēchanic(us)* a mechanic < Gk *mēchanikós,* equiv. to *mēchan(ḗ)* machine + *-ikos* -IC]
—Syn. 1. craftsman, artisan. **2.** repairman, machinist.

me·chan·i·cal (mə kan′i kəl), *adj.* **1.** having to do with machinery: *a mechanical failure.* **2.** being a machine, or including machinery: *a mechanical toy.* **3.** caused by or derived from machinery: *mechanical propulsion.* **4.** using machine parts only: *mechanical, hydraulic, or compressed-air brakes.* **5.** brought about by friction, abrasion, etc.: *a mechanical bond between stones; mechanical erosion.* **6.** pertaining to the design or contrivance of tools or machinery: *a mechanical genius.* **7.** working with tools or machinery: *the mechanical trades.* **8.** pertaining to the use or comprehension of tools, machinery, or the like: *mechanical ability.* **9.** produced by such means. **10.** acting or performed without spontaneity spirit, individuality, etc.: *a mechanical performance of* Hamlet. **11.** habitual; routine; automatic: *Practice that step until it becomes mechanical.* **12.** belonging or pertaining to the subject matter of mechanics. **13.** pertaining to, or controlled or effected by, physical forces. **14.** (of a philosopher or philosophical theory) explaining phenomena as due to mechanical action or the material forces of the universe. **15.** subordinating the spiritual to the material; materialistic. **—***n.* **16.** *Print.* a sheet of stiff paper on which has been pasted artwork, type proofs, or both for making a printing plate; paste-up. [late ME *mechanicall* < L *mēchanic(us)* MECHANIC; see -AL¹] **—me·chan′i·cal·ly,** *adv.* **—me·chan′i·cal·ness, me·chan′i·cal′i·ty,** *n.*

mechan′ical advan′tage, *Mech.* the ratio of the output force doing the work of a mechanism to the input force applied to the mechanism.

mechan′ical ap′titude, a person's ability or relative propensity for using and understanding machinery, tools, etc.

mechan′ical draw′ing, drawing, as of machinery, done with the aid of rulers, scales, compasses, etc.

mechan′ical engineer′, an engineer who specializes in mechanical engineering.

mechan′ical engineer′ing, the branch of engineering dealing with the design and production of machinery.

mechan′ical equiv′alent of heat′, (in any system of physical units) the number of units of work or energy equal to one unit of heat, as 4.1858 joules or 4.1858×10^7 ergs equals one small calorie.

mechan′ical imped′ance, *Physics.* impedance (def. 2).

mechan′ical met′allurgy, the branch of metallurgy dealing with the response of metals to applied forces.

mechan′ical pen′cil, a pencil for holding lead that can be extended or withdrawn by mechanical means, as by a screw.

mechan′ical scan′ning, **1.** *Electronics.* a technique for varying the sector covered by a transmitting or receiving antenna by rotating it. **2.** *Television.* a technique, formerly used in televising, for scanning by means of a scanning disk. Cf. **electrical scanning.**

mechan′ical suspen′sion. See under **suspension** (def. 7).

mechan′ical twin′, *Metall.* a crystalline twin formed by the strain set up by an applied force.

mech·a·ni·cian (mek′ə nish′ən), *n.* a person skilled in constructing, working, or repairing machines. [MECHANIC + -IAN]

me·chan·ics (mə kan′iks), *n.* **1.** (*construed as sing.*) the science that deals with the action of forces on bodies and with motion, comprised of kinetics, statics, and kinematics. **2.** (*construed as sing.*) the theoretical and practical application of this science to machinery, mechanical appliances, etc. **3.** (*usually construed as pl.*) the technical aspect or working part; mechanism; structure. **4.** (*usually construed as pl.*) routine methods, procedures, or details: *the mechanics of running an office.* [see MECHANIC, -ICS]

Me·chan·ics·burg (mə kan′iks bûrg′), *n.* a town in central Pennsylvania. 8123 (1960).

mechan′ic's lien′, a lien secured on property, as an automobile, building, or the like, by the contractor who has repaired or built it, in order to ensure payment for his labor and materials.

Me·chan·ics·ville (mə kan′iks vil′), *n.* a village in E Virginia, near Richmond: Civil War battle 1862.

Me·chan·ic·ville (mə kan′ik vil′), *n.* a town in E New York. 6831 (1960).

mech·a·nise (mek′ə nīz′), *v.t.,* **-nised, -nis·ing.** *Chiefly Brit.* mechanize. **—mech′a·ni·sa′tion,** *n.* **—mech′a·nis′er,** *n.*

mech·an·ism (mek′ə niz′əm), *n.* **1.** an assembly of moving parts performing a complete functional motion, often being part of a large machine; linkage. **2.** the agency or means by which an effect is produced or a purpose is accomplished. **3.** machinery or mechanical appliances in general. **4.** the structure or arrangement of parts of a machine or similar device, or of anything analogous. **5.** the mechanical part of something; any mechanical device: *the mechanism of a clock.* **6.** routine methods or procedures; mechanics: *the mechanism of government.* **7.** mechanical execution, as in painting or music; technique. **8.** the theory that everything in the universe is produced by matter in motion; materialism. Cf. **dynamism** (def. 1), **vitalism** (def. 1). **9.** *Philos., Biol.* a natural process interpreted as machinelike or as explicable in terms of Newtonian physics. **10.** *Psychoanal.* (used as an analogy drawn from mechanics) the operation and interaction of psychological forces. [< NL *mēchanism(us),* equiv. to Gk *mēchan(ḗ)* machine + *-ismos* -ISM] **—mech′a·nis′mic,** *adj.*

mech·a·nist (mek′ə nist), *n.* **1.** a person who believes in the theory of mechanism. **2.** *Rare.* a mechanician. [MECHAN(IC) + -IST]

mech·a·nis·tic (mek′ə nis′tik), *adj.* **1.** of or pertaining to the theory of mechanism or to mechanists. **2.** of or pertaining to mechanics. [MECHANIST + -IC] **—mech′a·nis′ti·cal·ly,** *adv.*

mech·a·nize (mek′ə nīz′), *v.t.,* **-nized, -niz·ing.** **1.** to make mechanical. **2.** to operate or perform by or as if by machinery. **3.** to introduce machinery into (an industry, enterprise, etc.), esp. in order to replace manual labor. **4.** *Mil.* to equip with tanks and other track-laying vehicles. Also, *esp. Brit.*, **mechanise.** [MECHAN(IC) + -IZE] —**mech′a·ni·za′tion,** *n.* —**mech′a·niz′er,** *n.*

mech·a·no·mor·phism (mek′ə nō môr′fiz əm), *n.* *Philos.* the doctrine that the universe is fully explicable in mechanistic terms. [MECHAN(IC) + -O- + MORPHISM] —**mech′a·no·mor′phic,** *adj.* —**mech′a·no·mor′phi·cal·ly,** *adv.*

mech·a·no·ther·a·py (mek′ə nō ther′ə pē), *n.* *Obs.* curative treatment by mechanical means. [MECHAN(IC) + -O- + THERAPY] —**mech′a·no·ther′a·pist,** *n.*

Mech·i·tar·ist (mek′i tär′ist), *n.* Mekhitarist.

me·chi·tzah (mə KHē tsä′), *n.*, *pl.* **-chi·tzoth** (-KHē tsôt′). *Hebrew.* mehitzah.

Mech·lin (mek′lin), *n.* **1.** French, **Malines.** Flemish, **Mech·e·len** (meKH′ə lən). a city in N Belgium. 64,015 (est. 1959). **2.** See **Mechlin lace.**

Mech′lin lace′, **1.** a bobbin lace with raised cord, originally made in Mechlin. **2.** a similar lace made by machine. Also called **Mechlin, malines.** [after MECHLIN]

Mech·ni·kov (mech nē kôf′), *n.* **É·lie** (ā lē′). See **Metchnikoff, Élie.**

me·cism (mē′siz əm), *n.* *Pathol.* abnormal prolongation of one or more parts of the body. [< Gk *mêk(os)* length + -ISM]

Me·cis·te·us (mi sis′tē əs, -to͞os, -tyo͞os), *n.* *Class. Myth.* a brother of Adrastus, sometimes mentioned as one of the Seven against Thebes.

Meck·len·burg (mek′lən bûrg′; *Ger.* mek′lən-bo͝ork′, mā′klən-), *n.* a former state in NE Germany, formed in 1934 from two states (**Mecklenburg-Schwerin** and **Mecklenburg-Strelitz**).

Meck·len·burg-Schwe·rin (mek′lən bûrg′shwer′-ən; *Ger.* mek′lən bo͝ork′shvä ʀēn′, mā′klən-), *n.* See under **Mecklenburg.**

Meck·len·burg-Stre·litz (mek′lən bûrg′shtrā′lits; *Ger.* mek′lən bo͝ork′shtrā′lits, mā′klən-), *n.* See under **Mecklenburg.**

mec·li·zine (mek′li zēn′), *n.* *Pharm.* a compound, $C_{25}H_{27}ClN_2$, used in the form of its hydrochloride to prevent nausea of motion sickness, pregnancy, etc. [ME(THYLBENZENE) + C(H)L(ORO)-² + -I- + (PIPERA)ZINE]

me·com·e·ter (mə kom′i tər), *n.* *Med.* a caliperlike instrument for measuring the length of newborn infants. [< Gk *mêko(s)* length + -METER]

me·co·ni·um (mə kō′nē əm), *n.* the first fecal excretion of a newborn child, composed chiefly of bile, mucus, and epithelial cells. [< L < Gk *mēkṓnion*, dim. of *mḗkon* poppy]

med., **1.** medical. **2.** medicine. **3.** medieval. **4.** medium.

M.Ed., Master of Education.

Me·da (mē′də), *n.* *Class. Myth.* the wife of King Idomeneus who took Leucus as her lover when she suspected her husband of planning to bring a concubine back from Troy.

mé·dail·lon (mā dA yôN′), *n.* *French.* a portion of food cut or served in a round or oval shape: *médaillon de veau.* Also, **me·dail·lon′.** [lit., medallion]

me·da·ka (mi dak′ə), *n.* a small, Japanese killifish, *Oryzias latipes*, common in rice fields, often kept in aquariums. [< Jap]

med·al (med′əl), *n.*, *v.*, **-aled, -al·ing** or (*esp. Brit.*) **-alled, -al·ling.** —*n.* **1.** a flat piece of metal, often a disk but sometimes a cross, star, or other form, usually decorated with a ribbon and bearing an inscription or design, issued to commemorate a person, action, or event, or given as a reward for bravery, merit, or the like: *a gold medal for the best orator.* —*v.t.* **2.** to decorate or honor with a medal. [earlier *medaille* < MF < It *medaglia* copper coin worth a halfpenny < VL **medalia*, var. (by dissimilation) of LL *mediālia*, neut. pl. of *mediālis* MEDIAL]

Med′al for Free′dom, a medal awarded by the U.S. to a civilian or a member of the armed forces of a friendly nation for the performance of some meritorious act or service.

Med′al for Mer′it, a medal awarded by the U.S. to a civilian for distinguished service to the country.

med·al·ist (med′əlist), *n.* **1.** a designer, engraver, or maker of medals. **2.** a person to whom a medal has been awarded. **3.** (in a golf tournament) the player having the lowest score in a qualifying round scored by strokes. Also, *esp. Brit.*, **med′al·list.** [< F *médailliste* < It *medaglista.* See MEDAL, -IST]

me·dal·lic (mə dal′ik), *adj.* of or pertaining to medals. [MEDAL + -IC]

me·dal·lion (mə dal′yən), *n.* **1.** a large medal. **2.** *Archit.* **a.** a tablet, usually rounded, often bearing objects represented in relief. **b.** a member in a decorative design resembling a panel. [< F *médaillon* < It *medaglione*, aug. of *medaglia* MEDAL]

Med′al of Hon′or, *U.S.* the nation's highest military decoration, awarded in the name of Congress to a soldier, sailor, airman, or marine who, in action involving actual combat with an enemy, distinguishes himself conspicuously, at the risk of life, by gallantry and intrepidity above and beyond the call of duty.

med′al play′, *Golf.* play in which the score is reckoned by counting the strokes taken to complete the round. Also called **stroke play.** Cf. **match play.**

Me·dan (me dän′), *n.* a city in NE Sumatra, in W Indonesia. 624,000 (est. 1972).

Med·a·war (med′ə wər), *n.* **Peter Brian,** born 1915, English zoologist and anatomist, born in Brazil: Nobel prize for medicine 1960.

med·dle (med′əl), *v.i.*, **-dled, -dling.** to involve oneself in a matter without right or invitation; interfere officiously and unwantedly. [ME *medle(n)* < MF *medler*, var. of OF *mes(d)ler* < LL **misculāre* to mix, deriv. of *misculus*, var. of L *miscellus* mixed] —**med′dler,** *n.* —**med′dling·ly,** *adv.*

med·dle·some (med′əl səm), *adj.* given to meddling; interfering; officious. [MEDDLE + -SOME¹] —**med′dle·some·ly,** *adv.* —**med′dle·some·ness,** *n.*
—**Syn.** intrusive. See **curious.**

Mede (mēd), *n.* a native or inhabitant of Media. [ME *Medis* (pl.), OE *Mēdas* < L *Mēdī* < Gk *Mêdoi* (pl.), *Mêdos* (sing.) < OPers *Māda*]

Me·de·a (mi dē′ə), *n.* **1.** *Gk. Legend.* a sorceress, daughter of Aeëtes, King of Colchis, and wife of Jason, whom she assisted in obtaining the Golden Fleece. **2.** (*italics.*) a tragedy (431 B.C.) by Euripides.

Me·del·lín (me the yēn′), *n.* a city in W Colombia. 1,400,000 (est. 1970).

Me·de·us (mē′dē əs), *n.* *Class. Myth.* a son of Medea and Aegeus who fled to Asia with his mother.

Med·ford (med′fərd), *n.* **1.** a city in E Massachusetts, near Boston. 64,971 (1960). **2.** a city in SW Oregon. 24,425 (1960). **3.** a town in central Wisconsin. 3260 (1960).

Med′ford Lakes′, a town in central New Jersey. 2876 (1960).

medi-, an element occurring in loan words from Latin, where it meant "middle": *mediate.* Also, **medio-.** [comb. form of L *medius* MID¹]

me·di·a¹ (mē′dē ə), *n.* **1.** a pl. of **medium. 2. the media.** Also called **mass media.** the means of communication, as radio and television, newspapers, magazines, etc., that reach very large numbers of people: *His speech will be covered by the media.* —*adj.* **3.** pertaining to or concerned with such means: *a job in media research.*

me·di·a² (mē′dē ə), *n.*, *pl.* **-di·ae** (-dē ē′). **1.** *Gk. Grammar.* a voiced plosive, as β, δ, γ. **2.** *Anat.* the middle layer of an artery or lymphatic vessel. **3.** *Entomol.* a longitudinal vein in the middle portion of the wing of an insect. [< LL (grammar sense only), n. use of fem. sing. of L *medius* MID¹]

Me·di·a (mē′dē ə), *n.* **1.** an ancient country in W Asia, S of the Caspian Sea, corresponding generally to NW Iran. *Cap.:* Ecbatana. **2.** a town in SE Pennsylvania. 5803 (1960).

Me′dia Atropate′ne, an ancient region in NW Iran, formerly a part of Media. Also called **Atropatene.**

me·di·a·cy (mē′dē ə sē), *n.* state of being mediate. [MEDIA(TE) + -CY]

me·di·ad (mē′dē ad′), *adv.* *Anat., Zool.* toward the middle line or plane. [MEDI- + L *ad* to, toward]

me·di·ae·val (mē′dē ē′vəl, med′ē-, mid′ē-, mid ē′vəl), *adj.* medieval. —**me′di·ae′val·ism,** *n.* —**me′di·ae′val·ist,** *n.*

me·di·al (mē′dē əl), *adj.* **1.** situated in or pertaining to the middle; median; intermediate. **2.** pertaining to a mean or average; average. **3.** ordinary. **4.** *Phonet.* within a word or syllable; neither initial nor final, as the *t*, *a*, and *n* in *stand.* **5.** *Entomol.* pertaining to, involving, or situated near the media. **6.** *Phonet.* media² (def. 1). [< LL *mediāl(is)* middle. See MEDI-, -AL¹] —**me′di·al·ly,** *adv.*

me·di·an (mē′dē ən), *adj.* **1.** noting or pertaining to a plane dividing something into two equal parts, esp. one dividing an animal into right and left halves. **2.** situated in or pertaining to the middle; medial. —*n.* **3.** *Arith., Statistics.* the middle number in a given sequence of numbers, taken as the average of the two middle numbers when the sequence has an even number of numbers: *4 is the median of 1, 3, 4, 8, 9.* **4.** *Geom.* a straight line from a vertex of a triangle to the midpoint of the opposite side. [< L *mediān(us)* that is in the middle, middle. See MEDI-, -AN] —**me′di·an·ly,** *adv.*

Me·di·an (mē′dē ən), *adj.* **1.** of or pertaining to Media, the Medes, or their language. —*n.* **2.** a Mede. **3.** the Iranian language of ancient Media, contemporaneous with Old Persian. [MEDI(A) + -AN]

me′dian strip′, a space, often landscaped, dividing opposing traffic on a highway. Also called **me′dial strip′.**

me·di·ant (mē′dē ənt), *n.* the third degree of a major or minor musical scale. [< It *mediante* < LL *mediant-* (s. of *mediāns*), prp. of *mediāre* to be in the middle. See MEDI-, -ANT]

me·di·as·ti·num (mē′dē a stī′nəm), *n.*, *pl.* **-as·ti·na** (-a stī′nə). *Anat.* **1.** a median septum or partition between two parts of an organ, or paired cavities of the body. **2.** the partition separating the right and left thoracic cavities, formed of the two inner pleural walls, and, in man, comprising all the viscera of the thorax except the lungs. [< medieval L, neut. of ML *mediastī-n(us)* medial, L: drudge (n.), equiv. to *medias-* mid + *-tīnus* adj., n. suffix] —**me′di·as·ti′nal,** *adj.*

me·di·ate (*v.* mē′dē āt′; *adj.* mē′dē it), *v.*, **-at·ed, -at·ing,** *adj.* —*v.t.* **1.** to bring about (an agreement, peace, etc.) as an intermediary between parties by compromise, reconciliation, removal of misunderstanding, etc. **2.** to settle (disputes, strikes, etc.) as an intermediary between parties; reconcile. **3.** to effect (a result) or convey (a message, gift, etc.) by or as by an intermediary. —*v.i.* **4.** to act between parties to effect an agreement, compromise, or reconciliation. **5.** to occupy an intermediate place or position. —*adj.* **6.** acting through, dependent on, or involving an intermediate agency; not direct or immediate. [ME < LL *mediāt(us)* divided in the middle, ptp. of *mediāre.* See MEDI-, -ATE¹] —**me′di·ate·ly,** *adv.* —**me′di·ate·ness,** *n.*
—**Syn. 1, 2.** arbitrate. **4.** intercede, interpose.

me′diated generaliza′tion, *Psychol.* generalization (def. 4c).

me·di·a·tion (mē′dē ā′shən), *n.* **1.** action in mediating between parties, as to effect an agreement or reconciliation. **2.** *Internat. Law.* an attempt to effect a peaceful settlement between disputing nations through the friendly good offices of another power. [ME *mediacioun* < ML *mediātiōn-* (s. of *mediātiō*). See MEDIATE, -ION]
—**Syn. 1.** MEDIATION, ARBITRATION designate processes for bringing about agreement or reconciliation between opponents in a dispute. MEDIATION implies deliberation that results in solutions that may or may not be accepted by the contending parties: *Mediation settled the strike.* ARBITRATION involves a more formal deliberation, it being understood that the results will be binding on the contending parties: *The strike was settled only after arbitration.*

me·di·a·tise (mē′dē ə tīz′), *v.t.*, **-tised, -tis·ing.** *Chiefly Brit.* mediatize. —**me′di·a·ti·sa′tion,** *n.*

me·di·a·tive (mē′dē ā′tiv, -ə tiv), *adj.* mediating; mediatory. [MEDIATE + -IVE]

me·di·a·tize (mē′dē ə tīz′), *v.t.*, **-tized, -tiz·ing.** to annex (a principality) to another state, while allowing certain rights to its former sovereign. Also, *esp. Brit.*, **mediatise.** [MEDIATE + -IZE, modeled on G *mediatisieren*] —**me′di·a·ti·za′tion,** *n.*

me·di·a·tor (mē′dē ā′tər), *n.* a person who mediates, esp. between parties at variance. [< LL (see MEDIATE, -OR²); r. ME *mediatour* < AF] —**me′di·a′tor·ship′,** *n.*

me·di·a·to·ri·al (mē′dē ə tôr′ē əl, -tōr′-), *adj.* of, pertaining to, or characteristic of a mediator. [MEDIATOR + -IAL]

me·di·a·to·ry (mē′dē ə tôr′ē, -tōr′ē), *adj.* **1.** pertaining to mediation. **2.** having the function of mediating. [< LL *mediātōri(us).* See MEDIATE, -ORY¹]

me·di·a·tress (mē′dē ā′tris), *n.* a female mediator. Also, **me′di·a′trice, mediatrix.** [MEDIAT(O)R + -ESS]

me·di·a·trix (mē′dē ā′triks), *n.*, *pl.* **-a·tri·ces** (-ə trī′sēz, -ā′tri sēz′), **-a·trix·es.** mediatress. [late ME < L; fem. of MEDIATOR; see -TRIX]

med·ic¹ (med′ik), *n.* *Slang.* a doctor, medical student, or medical corpsman. [shortened form of MEDICAL]

med·ic² (med′ik), *n.* any fabaceous plant of the genus *Medicago.* Also, **medick.** Cf. **alfalfa, bur clover.** [< L *mēdica* < Gk (*póa*) *Mēdikḗ*, lit., Median (grass)]

med·i·ca·ble (med′ə kə bəl), *adj.* susceptible of medical treatment; curable. [< L *medicābil(is)* healing, curative. See MEDIC¹, -ABLE] —**med′i·ca·bly,** *adv.*

Med·i·caid (med′ə kād′), *n.* *U.S.* a government program, financed by federal, state, and local funds, of hospitalization and medical insurance for persons of all ages within certain income limits. Cf. **Medicare.** [MEDIC(AL) + AID]

med·i·cal (med′i kəl), *adj.* **1.** of or pertaining to the science or practice of medicine: *medical knowledge; medical history.* **2.** curative; medicinal; therapeutic: *medical properties.* [< ML *medicālis*, equiv. to L *medic(us)* medical (adj.), physician (n.) (deriv. of *medērī* to heal; see -IC) + *-ālis* -AL¹] —**med′i·cal·ly,** *adv.*

med′ical exam′iner, **1.** a physician or other person trained in medicine who is appointed by a city, county, or the like, to perform autopsies on the bodies of persons supposed to have died from unnatural causes and to investigate the cause and circumstances of such deaths. **2.** a physician retained by an insurance company, industrial firm, or the like, to give medical examinations to its clients or employees.

med′ical jurispru′dence. See **forensic medicine.**

Med′ical Lake′, a town in E Washington. 4765 (1960).

me·dic·a·ment (mə dik′ə mənt, med′ə kə-), *n.* a healing substance; medicine; remedy. [< L *medicāment(um)* remedy, physic, equiv. to *medicā(rī)* (to) cure + *-mentum* -MENT. See MEDICATE] —**med·i·ca·men·tal** (med′ə kə men′təl), **med′i·ca·men′tous,** *adj.*

Med·i·care (med′ə kâr′), *n.* *U.S.* a federal program of hospitalization insurance and voluntary medical insurance for persons aged 65 and over. Also, **med′i·care′.** Cf. **Medicaid.** [MEDI(CAL) + CARE]

med·i·cate (med′ə kāt′), *v.t.*, **-cat·ed, -cat·ing.** **1.** to treat with medicine or medicaments. **2.** to impregnate with a medicine. [< L *medicāt(us)* medicated (ptp. of *medicāre*), healed (ptp. of *medicārī*). See MEDIC¹, -ATE¹]

med·i·ca·tion (med′ə kā′shən), *n.* **1.** the use or application of medicine. **2.** a medicinal substance; medicament. [< L *medicātiōn-* (s. of *medicātiō*). See MEDICATE, -ION]

med·i·ca·tive (med′ə kā′tiv), *adj.* medicinal. [< ML *medicātīv(us).* See MEDICATE, -IVE]

med·i·ca·tor (med′ə kā′tər), *n.* **1.** an instrument for applying medicaments. **2.** *Obs.* one who prescribes or prepares medicines. [MEDICATE + -OR²]

Med·i·ci (med′i chē; *It.* me′dē chē), *n.* **1. Catherine de′.** See **Catherine de Médicis. 2. Cos·mo** (kôz′mô) or **Co·si·mo, de′** (kô′zē mô de), ("*the Elder*"), 1389–1464, Italian banker, statesman, and patron of art and literature. **3. Cosmo** or **Cosimo, de′** ("*the Great*"), 1519–74, duke of Florence and first grand duke of Tuscany. **4. Gio·van·ni de′** (jô vän′nē de). See **Leo X. 5. Giu·lio de′** (jo͞o′lyô de). See **Clement VII. 6. Lo·ren·zo de′** (lô ʀen′tsô de), ("*Lorenzo the Magnificent*"), 1449–92, poet and patron of the arts and literature: ruler of Florence 1478–92 (father of Leo X). **7. Ma·ri·a de′** (mə rē′ə de; *It.* mä ʀē′ä de). See **Marie de Médicis.** —**Med·i·ce·an** (med′i sē′ən, -chē′ən), *adj.*

me·dic·i·na·ble (mə dis′ə nə bəl), *adj.* medicinal. [ME < MF. See MEDICINE, -ABLE]

me·dic·i·nal (mə dis′ə nəl), *adj.* of, pertaining to, or having the properties of a medicine; curative; remedial: *medicinal properties; medicinal substances.* [ME < L *medicīnāl(is).* See MEDICINE, -AL¹] —**me·dic′i·nal·ly,** *adv.*

med·i·cine (med′i sin *or, esp. Brit.*, med′sin), *n.*, *v.*, **-cined, -cin·ing.** —*n.* **1.** any substance or substances used in treating disease or illness; medicament; remedy. **2.** the art or science of restoring or preserving health or due physical condition, as by means of drugs, surgical operations or appliances, manipulations, etc.: often divided into medicine proper, surgery, and obstetrics. **3.** the art or science of treating disease with drugs or curative substances, as distinguished from surgery and obstetrics. **4.** the medical profession. **5.** any object or practice regarded by savages as of magical efficacy, whether for good or evil: *That man is bad medicine.* **6. give someone a dose** or **taste of his own medicine,** to repay or punish a person for an injury by use of his own methods: *He came an hour late for their date to give her a taste of her own medicine.* **7. take one's medicine,** to undergo or accept punishment, esp. as the result of one's own actions: *He took his medicine like a man.* —*v.t.* **8.** to administer medicine to. [ME *medicin* < L *medicīna* (*ars*) the healing (art), fem. of *medicīnus* pertaining to a physician. See MEDIC¹, -INE¹]
—**Syn. 1.** medication, drug; pharmaceutical; physic.

med′icine ball′, a large, solid, heavy, leather-covered ball, thrown from one person to another for exercise.

Med′icine Bow′ Range′ (bō), a range of the Rocky Mountains, in Wyoming and Colorado. Highest peak, Elk Mountain, 11,162 ft.

Med′icine Hat′, a city in SE Alberta, in SW Canada. 24,484 (1961).

med′icine lodge′, **1.** a structure used for various ceremonials of the North American Indians. **2.** (*caps.*) the most important religious society among the Central Algonquian tribes of North America.

Med′icine Lodge′, a town in S Kansas. 3072 (1960).

med′icine man′, **1.** (among American Indians and other aboriginal peoples) a man supposed to possess mysterious or supernatural powers. **2.** a salesman of patent medicine, esp. before 1900, presenting a medicine show to attract customers.

med′icine show′, a traveling troupe that offers entertainment to attract customers for the patent medicines or purported cures proffered for sale.

med·ick (med′ik), *n.* medic[2].

med·i·co (med′ə kō′), *n., pl.* **-cos.** *Slang.* a doctor. [< Sp *médico,* It *medico* < L *medicus* physician; see MEDIC[1]]

medico-, a combining form meaning "medical": *medicolegal.* [comb. form repr. L *medicus* of, pertaining to healing; see MEDICAL]

med·i·co·chi·rur·gi·cal (med′ə kō kī rûr′ji kəl), *adj.* **1.** pertaining to medicine and surgery. **2.** *Archaic.* consisting of both physicians and surgeons. [MEDICO- + CHIRURGICAL]

med·i·co·le·gal (med′ə kō lē′gəl), *adj.* pertaining to medicine and law, or to medical jurisprudence. [MEDICO- + LEGAL]

me·di·e·val (mē′dē ē′vəl, med′ē-, mid′ē-, mid ē′vəl), *adj.* of or pertaining to, characteristic of, or in the style of the Middle Ages: *medieval architecture.* Also, **mediaeval.** Cf. **Middle Ages.** [earlier *mediaeval* < NL *medi(um) aev(um)* the middle age + -AL[1]. See MEDIUM, AGE] —**me′di·e′val·ly,** *adv.*

Medie′val Greek′, the Greek language of the Middle Ages, usually dated A.D. 700 to 1500. Also called **Middle Greek.** *Abbr.:* MGk.

me·di·e·val·ism (mē′dē ē′və liz′əm, med′ē-, mid′ē-, mid ē′və-), *n.* **1.** the spirit, practices, or methods of the Middle Ages. **2.** devotion to or adoption of medieval ideals or practices. **3.** a medieval belief, practice, or the like. Also, **mediaevalism.** [MEDIEVAL + -ISM]

me·di·e·val·ist (mē′dē ē′və list, med′ē-, mid′ē-, mid ē′və-), *n.* **1.** an expert in medieval history, literature, philosophy, etc. **2.** a person who is greatly attracted to the art, culture, spirit, etc., of the Middle Ages. Also, **mediaevalist.** [MEDIEVAL + -IST]

Medie′val Lat′in, the Latin language of the literature of the Middle Ages (usually dated A.D. 700 to 1500), including many Latinized words from other languages. *Abbr.:* ML Also called **Middle Latin.**

Me·di·i (mā′dē ē′), *n.* **Sinus.** See **Sinus Medii.**

Me·dill (mə dil′), *n.* **Joseph,** 1823–99, U.S. journalist.

Me·di·na (mə dē′nə *for 1;* mə dī′nə *for 2, 3*), *n.* **1.** a city in W Saudi Arabia, where Muhammad was first accepted as the supreme Prophet from Allah and where his tomb is located. 71,998 (1963). **2.** a town in N Ohio. 8235 (1960). **3.** a town in W New York. 6681 (1960).

medio-, var. of **medi-.**

me·di·o·cre (mē′dē ō′kər, mē′dē ō′kər), *adj.* of only ordinary or moderate quality; neither good nor bad; barely adequate; rather poor or inferior: *a mediocre biography of Napoleon.* [< MF < L *mediocr(is)* in a middle state, lit., at middle height, equiv. to *medi-* MEDI- + OL *ocris* rugged mountain, c. Gk *ókris,* akin to *ákros* apex]
—**Syn.** average, commonplace. —**Ant.** superior.

me·di·o·cris (mē′dē ō′kris), *adj.* *Meteorol.* (of a cloud) of medium height and often lacking in distinctive summit. [< NL: MEDIOCRE]

me·di·oc·ri·ty (mē′dē ok′ri tē), *n., pl.* **-ties.** **1.** the state or quality of being mediocre. **2.** mediocre ability or accomplishment. **3.** a person of but moderate ability. [late ME *mediocrite* < MF *mediocrite* < L *mediocritāt-* (s. of *mediocritās*) a middle state, moderation. See MEDIOCRE, -ITY]

Medit., Mediterranean.

med·i·tate (med′i tāt′), *v.,* **-tat·ed, -tat·ing.** —*v.t.* **1.** to consider as something to be done or effected; intend; purpose: *to meditate revenge.* —*v.i.* **2.** to engage in thought or contemplation; reflect. [< L *meditāt(us),* ptp. of *meditārī*] —**med′i·tat′ing·ly,** *adv.* —**med′i·ta′tor,** *n.*
—**Syn. 1.** contemplate, plan, devise, contrive. **2.** ponder, muse; ruminate; cogitate, study, think.

med·i·ta·tion (med′i tā′shən), *n.* **1.** act of meditating. **2.** continued or extended thought; reflection; contemplation. [< L *meditātiōn-* (s. of *meditātiō*) a thinking over (see MEDITATE, -ION); r. ME *meditacioun* < AF]

med·i·ta·tive (med′i tā′tiv), *adj.* given to, characterized by, or indicative of meditation; contemplative. [< LL *meditātīv(us).* See MEDITATE, -IVE] —**med′i·ta′tive·ly,** *adv.* —**med′i·ta′tive·ness,** *n.*
—**Syn.** thoughtful. See **pensive.**

Med·i·ter·ra·ne·an (med′i tə rā′nē ən), *n.* **1.** See **Mediterranean Sea.** **2.** a person whose physical characteristics are considered typical of the peoples native to or inhabiting the Mediterranean area. —*adj.* **3.** pertaining to, situated on or near, or dwelling about the Mediterranean Sea. **4.** of or belonging to a Caucasoid subrace distributed chiefly in the areas surrounding the Mediterranean Sea. **5.** surrounded or nearly surrounded by land. [< L *mediterrāne(us)* midland, inland (see MEDI-, TERRA, -AN, -EOUS) + -AN]

Med′iterra′nean fe′ver, *Pathol.* brucellosis.

Med′iterra′nean fruit′ fly′. See under **fruit fly** (def. 1).

Med′iterra′nean Sea′, a sea surrounded by Africa, Europe, and Asia. 2400 mi. long; 1,145,000 sq. mi.; greatest known depth 14,436 ft. Also called **Mediterranean.**

me·di·um (mē′dē əm), *n., pl.* **-di·a** (-dē ə) for 1–9, **-di·ums** for 1–10, *adj.* —*n.* **1.** a middle state or condition; mean. **2.** something intermediate in nature or degree. **3.** an intervening substance, as air, through which a force acts or an effect is produced. **4.** the element that is the natural habitat of an organism. **5.** surrounding objects, conditions, or influences; environment. **6.** an agency, means, or instrument: *Newspapers are a popular advertising medium.* **7.** *Biol.* the substance in which specimens are displayed or preserved. **8.** Also called **culture medium.** *Bacteriol.* a liquid or solidified nutrient material suitable for the cultivation of microorganisms. **9.** *Fine Arts.* **a.** *Painting.* a liquid with which pigments are mixed. **b.** the material or technique with which an artist works: *graphic medium; sculpture as a medium of artistic expression.* **10.** a person serving, or conceived of as serving, as an instrument through which another personality or a supernatural agency is alleged to manifest itself: *a spiritualistic medium.* **11.** a size of printing paper, 18½ x 23½ inches in England, 18 x 23 to 19 x 25 inches in America. **12.** *Chiefly Brit.* a size of drawing or writing paper, 17½ x 22 inches. **13. in medium,** *Motion Pictures.* with the principal actors in the middle distance: *The scene was shot in medium.* —*adj.* **14.** about halfway between extremes, as of degree, quality, size, etc.: *Cook over medium heat. He is of medium height.* [< L: the middle, neut. of *medius* middle. See MID[1]]
—**Syn. 14.** average, mean, middling, mediocre.

me′dium artil′lery, *U.S. Mil.* guns and howitzers of more than 105-millimeter and less than 155-millimeter caliber, sometimes including the 155-millimeter howitzers. Cf. **heavy artillery** (def. 2), **light artillery** (def. 2).

me′dium bomb′er, *Mil.* a moderately large airplane capable of carrying large bomb loads for moderate distances at medium altitudes, esp. one having a gross loaded weight of 100,000 to 250,000 pounds. Cf. **heavy bomber, light bomber.**

me′dium fre′quency, *Radio.* any frequency between 300 and 3,000 kilohertz. *Abbr.:* MF

me·di·um·is·tic (mē′dē ə mis′tik), *adj.* pertaining to a spiritualistic medium. [MEDIUM + -ISTIC]

me′dium octa′vo, a size of book, about 6 x 9½ inches, untrimmed. *Abbr.:* medium 8vo

me′dium of exchange′, anything generally accepted as representing a standard of value and exchangeable for goods or services.

me′dium quar′to, *Chiefly Brit.* a size of book, about 9½ x 12 inches, untrimmed. *Abbr.:* medium 4to

me′dium shot′, *Motion Pictures, Television.* a camera shot taken at a medium distance from the subject to permit some of the background to be seen. Cf. **close-up** (def. 2), **long shot** (def. 3).

me·di·um-sized (mē′dē əm sīzd′), *adj.* neither very large nor very small: *a medium-sized house.*

me·di·us (mē′dē əs), *n., pl.* **-di·i** (-dē ī′). *Anat.* the middle finger. [< L: middle]

med·lar (med′lər), *n.* **1.** a small, malaceous tree, *Mespilus germanica,* the fruit of which resembles a crab apple and is not edible until the early stages of decay. **2.** any of certain other malaceous trees. **3.** the fruit of any of these trees. [ME *medler* < MF: medlar tree, equiv. to *medle* (var. of *mesle* the fruit < L *mespil(um)* < Gk *méspilon*) + *-er* -ER[2]]

med·ley (med′lē), *n., pl.* **-leys,** *adj.* —*n.* **1.** a mixture, esp. of heterogeneous elements; a jumble. **2.** a piece of music combining airs or passages from various sources. —*adj.* **3.** *Archaic.* mixed; mingled. [ME *medlee* < MF, n. use of fem. of ptp. of *medler* to mix, fight; see MEDDLE]

med′ley re′lay, **1.** *Track.* a relay race in which each member of a team usually runs an unequal portion of the total distance. Cf. **distance medley, sprint medley.** **2.** *Swimming.* a relay race in which no member of a team uses the same stroke as another. Cf. **individual medley.**

Mé·doc (mā dok′; *Fr.* mā dôk′), *n.* **1.** a wine-growing region in Gironde, in SW France. **2.** a claret wine produced there.

Me·don (mēd′ən), *n.* **1.** (in the *Odyssey*) a herald who warned Penelope that her suitors were conspiring against Telemachus. **2.** (in the *Iliad*) the illegitimate son of Oileus and Rhene, slain in the Trojan War by Æneas.

Med.Sc.D., Doctor of Medical Science.

me·dul·la (mi dul′ə), *n., pl.* **-dul·las, -dul·lae** (-dul′ē). **1.** *Anat.* **a.** the marrow of the bones. **b.** the soft, marrowlike center of an organ, as the kidney, adrenal gland, etc. **c.** See **medulla oblongata.** **2.** *Bot.* the pith of plants. [< L: marrow, innermost part, equiv. to *med(ius)* middle + *-ulla* dim. suffix]

medul′la oblonga′ta, *pl.* **medulla oblongatas, medullae oblongatae.** *Anat.* the lowest or hindmost part of the brain, continuous with the spinal cord. See diag. under **brain.** [< NL: the long medulla]

med·ul·lar·y (med′əler′ē, mej′ə ler′ē, mi dul′ə rē), *adj.* pertaining to, consisting of, or resembling the medulla of an organ or the medulla oblongata. [< LL *medullār(is)* situated in the marrow. See MEDULLA, -ARY]

med′ullary ray′, *Bot.* (in the stems of exogenous plants) one of the vertical bands or plates of parenchymatous tissue that radiate between the pith and the bark.

med′ullary sheath′, **1.** *Bot.* a narrow zone made up of the innermost layer of woody tissue immediately surrounding the pith in plants. **2.** *Anat.* See **myelin sheath.**

med·ul·lat·ed (med′əlā′tid, mej′ə lā′-, mi dul′ā tid), *adj.* *Anat.* myelinated. [MEDULL(A) + -ATE[1] + -ED[2]]

med·ul·la·tion (med′əlā′shən, mej′ə lā′-), *n.* *Biol.* the formation of a medullary sheath about a nerve fiber. [MEDULL(A) + -ATION]

med·ul·li·za·tion (med′əli zā′shən, mej′ə li-, mi-dul′i-), *n.* *Pathol.* conversion of bone into marrow, as in osteitis. [MEDULL(A) + -IZE + -ATION]

me·du·sa (mə dōō′sə, -zə, -dyōō′-), *n., pl.* **-sas, -sae** (-sē, -zē). *Zool.* a jellyfish. [special use of MEDUSA, alluding to the Gorgon's snaky locks] —**me·du·soid** (mə dōō′soid, -dyōō′-), *adj.*

Me·du·sa (mə dōō′sə, -zə, -dyōō′-), *n., pl.* **-sas.** *Class. Myth.* the only mortal of the three Gorgons. She was killed by Perseus, and her head was mounted upon the aegis of Zeus and Athena. [< L < Gk *Médousa,* special use of *médousa,* fem. of *médōn* ruler]

me·du·sa·fish (mə dōō′sə fish′, -zə-, -dyōō′-), *n., pl.* **-fish·es,** (*esp. collectively*) **-fish.** a stromateid fish, *Icichthys lockingtoni,* found in the deep waters off the coast of California, living as a commensal in and about medusas. [MEDUSA + FISH]

me·du·san (mə dōō′sən, -zən, -dyōō′-), *adj.* **1.** pertaining to a medusa or jellyfish. —*n.* **2.** a medusa or jellyfish. [MEDUS(A) + -AN]

meek (mēk), *adj.* **1.** humbly patient or submissive, as under provocation from others. **2.** overly patient or submissive; spiritless; tame. **3.** *Obs.* gentle; kind. [ME *meke, meoc* < Scand; cf. Icel *mjūkr* soft, mild, meek; akin to obs. D *muik,* Goth *mūka-* soft] —**meek′ly,** *adv.* —**meek′ness,** *n.*
—**Syn. 1.** forebearing; yielding, docile; unassuming; pacific, calm, soft. See **gentle.**

Meer (mēr; *Du.* mār), *n.* **Jan van der** (yän vän dər). See **Vermeer, Jan.** Also called **Meer van Delft** (vän delft′).

meer·schaum (mēr′shəm, -shôm, -shoum), *n.* **1.** a mineral, hydrous magnesium silicate, $H_4Mg_2Si_3O_{10}$, occurring in white, claylike masses, used for ornamental carvings, for pipe bowls, etc.; sepiolite. **2.** a tobacco pipe with the bowl made of this substance. [< G: lit., sea foam]

Mee·rut (mēr′ət), *n.* a city in W Uttar Pradesh, in N India. 200,500 (1961).

meet[1] (mēt), *v.,* **met, meet·ing,** *n.* —*v.t.* **1.** to recognize as being present; encounter: *I would meet him on the street at unexpected moments.* **2.** to notice, as by chance or in passing: *I met few travelers on the road.* **3.** to become or to make oneself acquainted with: *I have already met Miss Quill.* **4.** to join at an appointed place or time: *Meet me in St. Louis.* **5.** to join at an expected place of arrival: *to meet guests at one's front door; to meet a train.* **6.** to come to or before (one's notice, or a means of noticing, as the eyes or ears): *A peculiar sight met my eyes.* **7.** to come into the company of (a person, group, etc.) in dealings, conference, etc. **8.** to face, eye, etc., directly or without avoidance. **9.** to come into physical contact or collision: *The two cars met each other head-on.* **10.** to encounter in opposition, conflict, or contest: *Harvard meets Yale next week in football.* **11.** to oppose: *to meet charges with countercharges.* **12.** to cope or deal effectively with (an objection, difficulty, etc.). **13.** to satisfy (needs, obligations, demands, etc.): *He could not meet his bills.* **14.** to come into conformity with (wishes, expectations, views, etc.). **15.** to encounter in experience: *to meet hostility.* —*v.i.* **16.** to come together, face to face, or into company: *We met on the street.* **17.** to assemble for action or conference, as a committee, legislature, society, etc. **18.** to become personally acquainted. **19.** to come into contact or form a junction, as lines, planes, areas, etc.: *The two lines meet to form an angle.* **20.** to be conjoined or united. **21.** to concur or agree. **22.** to come together in opposition or conflict, as adversaries, hostile forces, etc. **23. meet halfway, a.** to concede in part, as to the demands of an opposing faction; make concessions, as to another person: *Despite their differences, the union and the company finally agreed to meet halfway and settle their dispute.* **b.** to anticipate another's actions and conduct oneself accordingly: *Whenever she asked for anything he'd meet her halfway.* **24. meet with, a.** to come across; encounter: *to meet with opposition.* **b.** to experience; undergo; receive: *The visitors met with courtesy during their stay.* **25. well met,** *Archaic.* welcome. —*n.* **26.** an assembly, as of persons and hounds for a hunt, swimmers or runners for a race or series of races, etc.: *a track meet.* **27.** those assembled. **28.** the place of such an assembling. **29.** *Math.* intersection (def. 3a). [ME *mete(n),* OE *(ge)mētan;* c. Icel *moeta,* OLG *mōtian.* See MOOT[1]] —**meet′er,** *n.*
—**Syn. 8.** confront. **9.** join, connect, intersect, cross, converge, unite. **13.** settle; discharge, fulfill, answer. **17.** collect. **26.** contest, competition. —**Ant. 13.** repudiate. **17.** adjourn, scatter. **19.** diverge.

meet[2] (mēt), *adj.* suitable; fitting; proper: *It was meet that we should make merry.* [ME *mete,* repr. OE (dial.); r. OE *gemæte* suitable, c. G *gemäss* conformable] —**meet′ness,** *n.* —**Syn.** apt, appropriate.

meet·ing (mē′ting), *n.* **1.** act of coming together: *a chance meeting in the park; a meeting of minds.* **2.** an assembly of persons for a specific purpose: *a medical meeting.* **3.** the body of persons present at an assembly: *to read a report to the meeting.* **4.** a hostile encounter; a duel. **5.** an assembly for religious worship, esp. of Quakers. **6.** See **meeting house.** **7.** a place or point of contact; junction; union: *the meeting of two roads; the meeting of the waters.* [ME; see MEET[1], -ING[1]]

meet′ing house′, **1.** a house or building for religious worship. **2.** a house of worship for Quakers.

meet′ing post′, a chamfered timber at the outer edge of a lock gate, fitting against the meeting post of another lock gate. Also called **miter post.**

meet′ing rail′, (in a double-hung window) the rail of each sash that meets a rail of the other when the window is closed.

meet·ly (mēt′lē), *adv.* suitably; fittingly; properly; in a seemly manner. [ME; see MEET[2], -LY]

Me·fi·tis (mə fī′tis), *n.* an ancient Roman goddess who prevented pestilential winds. Also, **Mephitis.**

Meg (meg), *n.* a girl's given name, form of **Margaret.**

meg, *Elect.* megohm; megohms.

mega-, a learned borrowing from Greek meaning "large," "great" (*megalith*); specialized in physics to mean 1,000,000 times a given unit (*megahertz*). Also, *esp. before a vowel,* **meg-.** Cf. **megalo-.** [comb. form repr. Gk *mégas* large, great, vast, powerful]

meg·a·bit (meg′ə bit′), *n.* *Computer Technol.* **1.** 1024 kilobits, or 1,048,576 bits. **2.** (loosely) one million bits.

meg·a·buck (meg′ə buk′), *n.* *Slang.* one million dollars. [MEGA- + BUCK[1]]

meg·a·byte (meg′ə bīt), *n.* *Computer Technol.* **1.** 1024 kilobytes, or 1,048,576 bytes. **2.** (loosely) one million bytes.

meg·a·ce·phal·ic (meg′ə sə fal′ik), *adj.* **1.** *Craniom.* having a skull with a large cranial capacity or one exceeding the mean. Cf. **microcephalic** (def. 1). **2.** large-headed. Also, **meg·a·ceph·a·lous** (meg′ə sef′ə ləs). [MEGA- + CEPHALIC] —**meg′a·ceph′a·ly,** *n.*

meg·a·cit·y (meg′ə sit′ē), *n., pl.* **-cit·ies.** a city having a population of 1,000,000 or more. [MEGA- + CITY]

meg·a·cu·rie (meg′ə kyŏŏr′ē, -kyŏŏ rē′), *n.* one million curies. *Abbr.:* Mc, MCi. [MEGA- + CURIE]

meg·a·cy·cle (meg′ə sī′kəl), *n.* a unit, equal to one million cycles per second; megahertz. The term megahertz is now preferred in technical use. *Abbr.:* Mc, mc [MEGA- + CYCLE]

meg·a·dont (meg′ə dont′), *adj.* macrodont. Also, **meg′a·don′tic.** [MEGA- + -(O)DONT]

meg·a·don·tia (meg′ə don′shə, -shē ə), *n.* macrodontia. Also, **meg′a·don′tism, meg′a·don′ty.** [< NL; see MEGA-, -ODONT, -IA]

Me·gae·ra (mə jēr′ə), *n.* *Class. Myth.* one of the Furies.

meg·a·ga·mete (meg′ə gə mēt′, -gam′ēt), *n.* macrogamete. [MEGA- + GAMETE]

meg·a·hertz (meg′ə hûrts′), *n., pl.* **-hertz, -hertz·es.** *Elect.* a unit of frequency, equal to one million cycles per second. *Abbr.:* MHz [MEGA- + HERTZ]

meg·a·joule (meg′ə joul′, -jōōl′), *n.* *Physics.* a unit of work or energy: one million joules. [MEGA- + JOULE]

meg·a·kar·y·o·blast (meg′ə kar′ē ə blast′), *n.* *Anat.* an immature megakaryocyte. [MEGA- + KARYO- + -BLAST]

meg·a·kar·y·o·cyte (meg′ə kar′ē ə sīt′), *n.* *Anat.* a large cell having a lobulate nucleus in bone marrow, regarded as the source of blood platelets. [MEGA- + KARYO- + -CYTE] —**meg·a·kar·y·o·cyt·ic** (meg′ə kar′ē ə sit′ik), *adj.*

megal-, var. of **megalo-** before a vowel: *megalopsia.*

meg·a·lec·i·thal (meg′ə les′ə thəl), *adj.* *Embryol.* having a large amount of yolk, as certain eggs or ova. [MEGA- + LECITHAL]

Meg·a·le·sia (meg′ə lē′zhə, -shə, -sē ə), *n.* (*sometimes construed as pl.*) an ancient Roman festival in honor of the Magna Mater. Also called **Meg′ale′sian Games′.** [< L, short for *megalēsia* (*lūdī*) Megalesian (games), deriv. of *megalē* the great (< Gk), surname of the Magna Mater]

-megalia, var. of **-megaly:** *cardiomegalia.*

meg·a·lith (meg′ə lith), *n.* *Archaeol.* a stone of great size, esp. in ancient construction work, as the Cyclopean masonry, or in primitive monumental remains, as menhirs, dolmens, cromlechs, etc. [MEGA- + -LITH] —**meg′a·lith′ic,** *adj.*

megalo-, a learned borrowing from Greek indicating bigness, exaggeration, extravagance: *megalomania.* Also, *esp. before a vowel,* **megal-.** Cf. **mega-.** [< Gk, comb. form of *megal-* (s. of *mégas*) great, large]

meg·a·lo·car·di·a (meg′ə lō kär′dē ə), *n.* *Pathol.* hypertrophy of the heart. [MEGALO- + CARDIA]

meg·a·lo·ce·phal·ic (meg′ə lō sə fal′ik), *adj.* megacephalic. Also, **meg·a·lo·ceph·a·lous** (meg′ə lō sef′ə ləs). [MEGALO- + CEPHALIC] —**meg′a·lo·ceph′a·ly, meg·a·lo·ce·pha·li·a** (meg′ə lō sə fā′lē ə, -fāl′yə), *n.*

meg·a·lo·ma·ni·a (meg′ə lō mā′nē ə), *n.* **1.** *Psychiatry.* a form of mental illness marked by delusions of greatness, wealth, etc. **2.** an obsession with doing extravagant or grand things. [MEGALO- + -MANIA]

meg·a·lo·ma·ni·ac (meg′ə lō mā′nē ak′), *n.* a person afflicted with megalomania. [MEGALO- + MANIAC] —**meg·a·lo·ma·ni·a·cal** (meg′ə lō mə nī′ə kəl), *adj.*

meg·a·lop·o·lis (meg′ə lop′ə lis), *n.* an urban region, esp. one consisting of several large cities and suburbs that adjoin each other. Also, **megapolis.** [MEGALO- + POLIS]

meg·a·lo·pol·i·tan (meg′ə lō pol′i tən), *adj.* **1.** of, pertaining to, or characteristic of a megalopolis. —*n.* **2.** an inhabitant of a megalopolis. [from MEGALOPOLIS, modeled after *metropolis: metropolitan*] —**meg′a·lo·pol′i·tan·ism,** *n.*

meg·a·lop·si·a (meg′ə lop′sē ə), *n.* *Ophthalm.* macropsia. Also, **meg·a·lop·i·a** (meg′ə lop′ē ə). [MEGAL- + -OPSIA]

meg·a·lo·saur (meg′ə lə sôr′), *n.* any gigantic carnivorous dinosaur of the genus *Megalosaurus.* [< NL *megalosaur*(*us*). See MEGALO-, -SAUR] —**meg′a·lo·sau′ri·an,** *adj., n.*

-megaly, a suffix indicating enlargement: *cardiomegaly.* Also, **-megalia.** [< NL *-megalia.* See MEGALO-, -Y[3]]

Meg·a·me·de (meg′ə mē′dē), *n.* *Class. Myth.* the wife of King Thespius and the mother of his 50 daughters.

meg·a·me·ter (meg′ə mē′tər), *n.* *Metric System.* a unit of measure equal to one million meters. Also, **meg′a·me′tre.** [MEGA- + -METER]

Me·gan·thro·pus (mə gan′thrə pəs, meg′an thrō′pəs), *n.* a proposed genus of extinct, late Lower Pleistocene primates based on two large lower jaws found in Java, and believed to be either Australopithecine or human. [< NL; see MEGA-, ANTHROPO-]

Meg·a·pen·thes (meg′ə pen′thēz), *n.* *Class. Myth.* **1.** a son of King Proetus who succeeded his father and exchanged kingdoms with Perseus. **2.** an illegitimate son of Menelaus and a slave.

meg·a·phone (meg′ə fōn′), *n.* a device for magnifying sound or for directing it in increased volume, usually in the form of a large, funnel-shaped instrument: used in addressing a large audience out of doors or in calling to someone at a distance. Cf. **bull horn.** [MEGA- + -PHONE] —**meg·a·phon·ic** (meg′ə fon′ik), *adj.* —**meg′a·phon′i·cal·ly,** *adv.*

meg·a·pod (meg′ə pod′), *adj.* having large feet. [MEGA- + -POD]

meg·a·pode (meg′ə pōd′), *n.* any of several large-footed, gallinaceous birds of the family *Megapodiidae,* of Australia. [< NL *Megapod*(*ius*) genus of bird. See MEGA-, -POD]

me·gap·o·lis (mə gap′ə lis), *n.* megalopolis. [MEGA- + -POLIS]

Meg·a·ra (meg′ər ə), *n.* **1.** a city in ancient Greece: the chief city of Megaris. **2.** *Class. Myth.* a daughter of Creon whose children were slain by her husband, Hercules, in a fit of madness. —**Me·gar·i·an, Me·gar·e·an** (mə gar′ē ən, me-), **Me·gar·ic,** *adj.*

meg·a·rad (meg′ə rad′), *n.* *Physics.* a unit of absorbed radiation dose, equal to one million rads. [MEGA- + RAD]

Meg·a·ris (meg′ər is), *n.* a district in ancient Greece, between the Gulf of Corinth and Saronic Gulf.

meg·a·ron (meg′ə ron′), *n., pl.* **-a·ra** (-ər ə), **-a·rons.** (in pre-Hellenic Greek architecture) a building or semi-independent unit of a building, generally used as a living apartment and typically having a square or broadly rectangular principal chamber with a porch, often of columns in antis, and sometimes an antichamber or other small compartments. Cf. **hairpin megaron.** [< Gk: great hall, equiv. to *mega-* MEGA- + *-ron* n. suffix of place]

Meg·a·rus (meg′ər əs), *n.* *Class. Myth.* a son of Zeus who fled to the safety of Mount Gerania during the flood that Zeus sent to punish mankind.

meg·a·scope (meg′ə skōp′), *n.* *Rare.* a camera for making enlargements. [MEGA- + -SCOPE] —**meg·a·scop·ic** (meg′ə skop′ik), *adj.* —**meg′a·scop′i·cal·ly,** *adv.*

meg·a·spo·ran·gi·um (meg′ə spō ran′jē əm, -spô-), *n., pl.* **-gi·a** (-jē ə). *Bot.* a sporangium containing megaspores. [MEGA- + SPORANGIUM]

meg·a·spore (meg′ə spōr′, -spôr′), *n.* *Bot.* **1.** the larger of the two kinds of spores produced by some pteridophytes. **2.** the embryo sac of a flowering plant. [MEGA- + SPORE] —**meg′a·spor′ic,** *adj.*

meg·a·spo·ro·phyll (meg′ə spōr′ə fil, -spôr′-), *n.* *Bot.* a sporophyll producing megasporangia only. [MEGA- + SPOROPHYLL]

me·gass (mə gas′, -gäs′), *n.* bagasse. Also, **me·gasse′.** [unexplained var.]

Megathere,
Genus *Megatherium*
(Length 20 ft.)

meg·a·there (meg′ə thēr′), *n.* any of the huge, slothlike animals of the extinct genus *Megatherium.* [< NL *megatherium*(*ium*), equiv. to Gk *megá-* MEGA- + *thērion* wild beast]

meg·a·therm (meg′ə thûrm′), *n.* a plant requiring a constant high temperature and abundant moisture for growth. [MEGA- + THERM] —**meg′a·ther′mic, meg′a·ther′mal,** *adj.*

meg·a·ton (meg′ə tun′), *n.* **1.** one million tons. **2.** an explosive force equal to that of one million tons of TNT (used especially in reference to an atom or hydrogen bomb). *Abbr.:* MT [MEGA- + TON[1]] —**meg·a·ton·ic** (meg′ə ton′ik), *adj.*

meg·a·tron (meg′ə tron′), *n.* *Electronics.* See **lighthouse tube.** [MEGA- + -TRON]

meg·a·volt (meg′ə vōlt′), *n.* *Elect.* a unit of electromotive force, equal to one million volts. *Abbr.:* MV, Mv [MEGA- + VOLT]

meg·a·volt-am·pere (meg′ə vōlt′am′pēr, -am pēr′), *n.* one million volt-amperes. *Abbr.:* MVA, Mva

meg·a·watt (meg′ə wot′), *n.* *Elect.* a unit of power, equal to one million watts. *Abbr.:* Mw [MEGA- + WATT]

meg·a·watt-hour (meg′ə wot′our′, -ou′ər), *n.* a unit of energy equal to one million watt-hours. *Abbr.:* MWh, Mwhr

Me·ges (mē′jēz), *n.* (in the *Iliad*) a nephew of Odysseus who commanded the Epeans in the Trojan War.

meg·ger (meg′ər), *n.* *Elect. Slang.* megohmmeter. [formerly trademark]

Me·gid·do (mə gid′ō), *n.* an ancient city in N Israel, on the plain of Esdraelon: site of many battles; often identified with the Biblical Armageddon.

me·gil·lah (mə gil′ə; *for 1 also Heb.* mə gē lä′), *n., pl.* **-gil·lahs** for 1, **-gil·loth** for 2. **1.** *Slang.* a lengthy, detailed explanation or account: *Just give me the facts, not a whole megillah.* **2.** (*italics*) *Hebrew.* a scroll, esp. one containing the Book of Esther or of Ecclesiastes, the Song of Solomon, the Book of Ruth, or the Book of Lamentations.

meg·ohm (meg′ōm′), *n.* *Elect.* a unit of resistance, equal to one million ohms. *Abbr.:* meg, MΩ [MEG- + OHM]

meg·ohm·me·ter (meg′ōm mē′tər), *n.* *Elect.* an instrument for measuring large resistances, esp. the resistance of insulation. [MEGOHM + -METER]

me·grim (mē′grim), *n.* **1. megrims,** low spirits; the blues. **2.** *Archaic.* a whim or caprice. **3.** *Obs.* migraine. [ME *mygrame* a type of headache < MF *migraine* (by misreading, *in* taken as *m*); see MIGRAINE]

Me·hem·et A·li (mi hem′et ä lē′, ä′lē, mā′met), 1769–1849, viceroy of Egypt 1805–48. Also, **Mohammed Ali.**

Me·hit·a·bel (mə hit′ə bəl), *n.* a girl's given name. Also, **Me·het·a·bel** (mə het′ə bəl).

me·hi·tzah (mə ḵʜē tsä′), *n., pl.* **-hit·zoth** (-ḵʜē tsôt′). *Hebrew.* a curtain or other barrier that serves as a partition between the women's and the men's sections in Orthodox Jewish synagogues. Also, **mechitzah.**

Mé·hul (mā ʏl′), *n.* **É·tienne Ni·co·las** (ā tyen′ nē kô lä′) (or **Étienne Hen·ri**) (äɴ ʀē′), 1763–1817, French composer.

Me·hu·man (mi hyo͞o′mən), *n.* one of the seven eunuchs who served in the court of King Ahasuerus. Esther 1:10. Also, *Douay Bible,* **Mauman.**

Meigh·en (mē′ən), *n.* **Arthur,** 1874–1960, Canadian statesman: prime minister 1920–21, 1926.

Meigs (megz), *n.* **Fort.** See **Fort Meigs.**

Mei·ji (mā′jē′), *n.* *Japanese Hist.* the designation of the period of the reign of Emperor Mutsuhito from 1867 to 1912. [< Jap: lit., enlightened peace]

Meil·hac (me yak′), *n.* **Hen·ri** (äɴ ʀē′), 1831–97, French dramatist: collaborator with Ludovic Halévy.

Mei·lich·i·us (mī lik′ē əs), *n.* *Class. Myth.* an epithet of Zeus, meaning "gracious."

Mei′ners Oaks′ (mī′nərz), a town in S California. 3513 (1960).

Mein Kampf (mīn kämpf′), the autobiography (1925–27) of Adolf Hitler, setting forth his political philosophy and his plan for German conquest.

mein·y (mā′nē), *n., pl.* **mein·ies.** **1.** *Scot. Archaic.* a multitude; crowd. **2.** *Archaic.* a group or suite of attendants, followers; dependents, etc. Also, **mein′ie.** [ME *meynee* household < OF *meyne, mesnie, mesnede* < LL **mansiōnāta.* See MANSION, -ATE[1]]

mei·o·nite (mī′ə nīt′), *n.* *Mineral.* a member of the scapolite group, rich in calcium and containing no sodium. [< Gk *meiōn* less + -ITE[1]; cf. F *méionite*]

mei·o·phyl·ly (mī′ə fil′ē), *n.* *Bot.* reduction in the usual number of leaves in a whorl, owing to suppression of some of the leaves. [< Gk *meiō*(*n*) less + -PHYLL + -Y[3]]

mei·o·sis (mī ō′sis), *n.* **1.** *Biol.* the maturation process of gametes, consisting of chromosome conjugation and two cell divisions, in the course of which the diploid chromosome number becomes reduced to the haploid. **2.** *Rhet.* **a.** belittlement. **b.** expressive understatement, esp. litotes. [< Gk: a lessening, equiv. to *mei*(*oûn*) (to) lessen (deriv. of *meiōn* less) + *-ōsis* -OSIS] —**mei·ot·ic** (mī ot′ik), *adj.*

Me·ir (mī′ər, mā ēr′), *n.* **Gol·da** (gōl′də), 1898–1978, Israeli political leader, born in Russia: premier 1969–74.

Meis·sen (mī′sən), *n.* a city in SE East Germany, on the Elbe River: famous for fine porcelain. 49,900 (est. 1955).

Meis′sen por′celain. See **Dresden china.**

Meis·so·nier (me sô nyā′), *n.* **Jean Louis Er·nest** (zhäɴ lwē er nest′), 1815–91, French painter.

Meis·ter·sing·er (mī′stər sing′ər, -zing′-), *n., pl.* **-sing·er, -sing·ers** for 1. **1.** Also, **mastersinger.** a member of one of the guilds, chiefly of workingmen, established during the 14th, 15th, and 16th centuries in the principal cities of Germany, for the cultivation of poetry and music. **2.** (*italics.*) **Die** (dē), an opera (1867) by Richard Wagner. [< G: master singer]

Meit·ner (mīt′nər), *n.* **Li·se** (lē′zə), 1878–1968, Austrian nuclear physicist.

mei′wa kum′quat (mā′wä), an evergreen shrub or small tree, *Fortunella crassifolia,* of China, having thick leaves and small, egg-shaped citrus fruit. [*meiwa* < Chin]

Mé·ji·co (me′hē kô), *n.* Spanish name of **Mexico.**

Mek′er burn′er (mek′ər), *Chem.* a gas burner similar to the Bunsen burner but producing a hotter flame by virtue of having at its mouth a metal screen to allow a more intimate mixture of air and gas. [named after George *Meker,* 20th-century chemist, its inventor]

Mekh·i·tar·ist (mek′i tär′ist), *n.* *Rom. Cath. Ch.* a member of an order of Armenian monks founded in Constantinople in the 18th century and following the rule of St. Benedict. Also **Mechitarist.** [named after Peter M. *Mekhitar* (1676–1749), Armenian religious reformer; see -IST]

Mek·ka (mek′ə), *n.* Mecca. (def. 1).

Mek·nès (mek nes′), *n.* a city in N Morocco: former capital of Morocco. 175,943 (1960).

Me·kong (mā′kong′; *Thai.* mä kông′), *n.* a river whose source is in SW China, flowing SE along most of the boundary between Thailand and Laos to the South China Sea. 2600 mi. long. Chinese, **Lantsang.**

Me′kong Del′ta, the delta of the Mekong River in South Vietnam.

mel[1] (mel), *n.* (in prescriptions) honey. [< L]

mel[2] (mel), *n.* a unit of pitch, equal to the difference in pitch between a standard tone of 1000 cycles per second and a tone, which, in a listener's judgment, has $^{999}/_{1000}$ the pitch of the standard tone. [abstracted from MELODY]

Mel (mel), *n.* a boy's given name, form of **Melvin.**

me·la (mā′lä), *n.* (in India) **1.** a religious fair, esp. one held in connection with a festival. **2.** a throng of people. [< Hindi < Skt *melā* assembly, company]

me·lae·na (mi lē′nə), *n.* *Med.* melena. —**me·lae′nic,** *adj.*

Me·lae·nis (mə lē′nis), *n.* *Class. Myth.* an epithet of Aphrodite, meaning "black."

me·la·med (mə lä mäd′; *Eng.* mə lä′mid), *n., pl.* **-lam·dim** (-läm dēm′; *Eng.* -läm′dim). *Hebrew.* a teacher in a Jewish school, esp. in Europe, who instructs children of elementary school age in Hebrew, the Bible, and prayers in the Jewish liturgy. Also, **melammed.** [lit., teacher]

mel·a·mine (mel′ə mēn′, mel′ə mēn′), *n.* **1.** *Chem.* a white, crystalline, slightly water-soluble solid, $C_3N_3(NH_2)_3$, used chiefly in organic synthesis and in the manufacture of resins, esp. melamine resins. **2.** any of the melamine resins. [< G *Melamin,* deriv. of *Melam* distillate of ammonium thiocyanate (arbitrary coinage, but *-am* repr. AMMONIUM); see -INE[2]]

mel′amine res′in, *Chem.* any of the class of thermosetting resins formed by the interaction of melamine and formaldehyde: used chiefly as adhesives for laminated materials and as coatings for paper, plastics, and textiles.

me·lam·med (mə lä mäd′; *Eng.* mə lä′mid), *n., pl.* **-lamm·dim** (-läm dēm′; *Eng.* -läm′dim). *Hebrew.* melamed.

Me·lam·pus (mə lam′pəs), *n.* *Class. Myth.* the first seer and healer. His ears were licked by serpents he had raised, enabling him to understand the speech and wisdom of animals.

melan-, var. of **melano-** before a vowel: *melanism.*

mel·an·cho·li·a (mel′ən kō′lē ə, -kōl′yə), *n.* *Psychiatry.* mental disease characterized by great depression of spirits and gloomy forebodings. [< LL; see MELANCHOLY]

mel·an·cho·li·ac (mel′ən kō′lē ak′), *adj.* **1.** affected with melancholia. —*n.* **2.** one affected with melancholia. [MELANCHOLI(A) + -AC]

mel·an·chol·ic (mel′ən kol′ik), *adj.* **1.** disposed to or affected with melancholy; gloomy. **2.** pertaining to melancholia. [ME *melancolik* < L *melancholic*(*us*) < Gk *melancholikós.* See MELANCHOLY, -IC] —**mel′an·chol′i·cal·ly,** *adv.*

mel·an·chol·y (mel′ən kol′ē), *n., pl.* **-chol·ies,** *adj.* —*n.* **1.** a gloomy state of mind, esp. when habitual or prolonged; depression. **2.** sober thoughtfulness; pensiveness. **3.** *Archaic.* **a.** condition of having too much black bile. **b.** the bile itself. —*adj.* **4.** affected with, characterized by, or showing melancholy; mournful; depressed: *a melancholy mood.* **5.** causing melancholy or sadness; saddening: *a melancholy occasion.* **6.** soberly thoughtful; pensive. [ME *melancolie* < LL *melancholia* < Gk: black bile] —**mel′an·chol′i·ly,** *adv.* —**mel′an·chol′i·ness,** *n.*

—**Syn. 1.** sadness, dejection, despondency; hypochondria. **2.** seriousness. **4.** gloomy, despondent, blue, dispirited, sorrowful, dismal, doleful, glum, downcast. See **sad. 6.** serious. —**Ant. 1.** cheer, happiness. **5.** happy.

Me·lanch·thon (mə langk′thən; *Ger.* mä längkʜ′tôn), *n.* **Phil·ipp** (fil′ip; *Ger.* fē′lip), (*Philipp Schwarzert*), 1497–1560, German Protestant reformer. Also, **Me·lanc·thon** (mə lan′thən; *Ger.* mä län′tôn).

Mel·a·ne·sia (mel′ə nē′zhə, -shə), *n.* one of the three principal divisions of Oceania, comprising the island groups in the S Pacific NE of Australia.

Mel·a·ne·sian (mel′ə nē′zhən, -shən), *adj.* **1.** of or pertaining to Melanesia, its inhabitants, or their languages. —*n.* **2.** a member of any of the dark-skinned, frizzy-haired peoples inhabiting Melanesia. **3.** the

Malayo-Polynesian languages of Melanesia, taken collectively. [MELANESI(A) + -AN]

Melane′sian Pidg′in Eng′lish, a former name of **Neo-Melanesian.**

mé·lange (*Fr.* mā läɴzh′), *n., pl.* **-langes** (*Fr.* -läɴzh′). a mixture; medley. [< F; see MELL, MEDLEY]

me·lan·ic (mə lan′ik), *adj.* **1.** *Pathol.* melanotic. **2.** of or pertaining to melanism. [MELAN- + -IC]

Mel·a·nie (mel′ə nē), *n.* a girl's given name.

mel·a·nif·er·ous (mel′ə nif′ər əs), *adj.* containing melanin, as hair. [MELAN- + -I- + -FEROUS]

mel·a·nin (mel′ə nin), *n. Biochem.* the dark pigment in the body of man and certain animals, as that occurring in the hair, epidermis, etc., of colored races, or one produced in certain diseases. [MELAN- + -IN[2]] —**mel′a·nin·like′,** *adj.*

Me·la·ni·on (mə lā′nē ən), *n. Class. Myth.* a youth of Arcadia, usually identified with Hippomenes as the successful suitor of Atalanta.

Mel·a·nip·pe (mel′ə nip′ē), *n. Class. Myth.* **1.** an Amazon queen who was a daughter of Ares. **2.** a foal born to Euippe: Poseidon transformed the foal into a human girl, Arne.

Mel·a·nip·pus (mel′ə nip′əs), *n. Class. Myth.* **1.** a son of Theseus and Perigune. **2.** a Theban who killed Tydeus in the battle of the Seven against Thebes and who was, in turn, slain by Amphiaraus. **3.** (in the *Iliad*) a son of Hicetaon, slain by Antilochus. **4.** a youth who impiously made love to Comaetho in the temple of Artemis.

mel·a·nism (mel′ə niz′əm), *n.* **1.** *Ethnol.* the condition of having a high amount of dark or black pigment granules in the skin, hair, and eyes of a human being. Cf. **melanin. 2.** *Zool.* the condition in which an unusually high concentration of dark or black pigment occurs in the skin, plumage, or pelage of an animal. [MELAN- + -ISM] —**mel′a·nis′tic,** *adj.*

mel·a·nite (mel′ə nīt′), *n. Mineral.* a deep black variety of andradite garnet. [MELAN- + -ITE[1]] —**mel·a·nit·ic** (mel′ə nit′ik), *adj.*

melano-, a learned borrowing from Greek meaning "black," used in the formation of compound words: *melanocyte.* Also, *esp. before a vowel,* **melan-.** [< Gk, comb. form of *mélas*]

mel·a·noch·ro·i (mel′ə nok′rō ī′), *n.pl.* (*often cap.*) light-complexioned Caucasians with dark hair. [< NL < Gk **melánōchroi* black-pale ones, equiv. to *melan-* MELAN- + *-ōchroi,* pl. of *ōchrós* pale] —**mel·a·noch·roid** (mel′ə nok′roid), **mel·a·no·chro·ic** (mel′ə nō krō′ik), *adj.*

mel·a·no·cyte (mel′ə nə sīt′, mə lan′ə-), *n. Anat.* a cell producing and containing melanin. [MELANO- + -CYTE]

mel′a·no·cyte-stim·u·lat·ing hor′mone (mel′ə nə sīt′stim′yə lā′tiŋg, mə lan′ə-), *Biochem.* See **MSH.**

mel·an·o·derm (mel′ə nə dûrm′, mə lan′ə-), *n.* a person with dark pigmentation of the skin. [MELANO- + -DERM]

mel·a·noid (mel′ə noid′), *adj.* **1.** of or characterized by melanosis. **2.** resembling melanin; darkish. [MELAN- + -OID]

mel·a·no·ma (mel′ə nō′mə), *n., pl.* **-mas, -ma·ta** (-mə tə). *Pathol.* a darkly pigmented tumor, esp. of the skin or eye, of cells containing melanin. [MELAN- + -OMA]

mel·a·no·sis (mel′ə nō′sis), *n. Pathol.* **1.** abnormal deposition or development of black or dark pigment in the tissues. **2.** a discoloration caused by this. [< NL < LGk *melánōsis* a becoming black. See MELAN-, -OSIS]

mel·a·no·sper·mous (mel′ə nō spûr′məs, mə lan′ō-), *adj.* having dark spores, as certain seaweeds. [MELANO- + -SPERM + -OUS]

mel·a·not·ic (mel′ə not′ik), *adj. Pathol.* of or affected with melanosis. Also, **melanic.** [MELAN- + -OTIC]

Me·lan·tha (mə lan′thə), *n.* a girl's given name.

mel·an·tha·ceous (mel′ən thā′shəs), *adj.* belonging to the *Melanthaceae,* a family of bulbless plants related to and sometimes classified in the lily family, comprising the bellwort, white hellebore, etc. [< NL *Melanth(ium)* name of typical genus (< Gk *mél(as)* black + *ánth(os)* flower + *-ion,* neut. of *-ios* -IOUS) + -ACEOUS]

Me·lan·thi·us (mə lan′thē əs), *n.* (in the *Odyssey*) a goatherd of Odysseus who curried favor with the suitors of Penelope and was quartered and thrown to the dogs when Odysseus returned to Ithaca.

Me·lan·tho (mə lan′thō), *n.* (in the *Odyssey*) a handmaid of Penelope who became the mistress of Eurymachus: she mocked Odysseus on his return and was killed for her faithlessness.

Me·lan·thus (mə lan′thəs), *n. Class. Myth.* a descendant of Neleus who was king of Messenia and who became king of Athens when he was ousted from his kingdom by the Dorians.

mel·a·phyre (mel′ə fīər′), *n. Obs.* any of various dark-colored igneous rocks of porphyritic texture. [< F *mélaphyre,* equiv. to *méla-* (< Gk *méla(s)* black) + *(por)phyre* PORPHYRY]

Mel·as (mel′əs), *n. Class. Myth.* a son of Phrixus and Chalciope.

mel·a·to·nin (mel′ə tō′nin), *n. Biochem.* a hormone, $C_{13}H_{16}O_2N_2$, produced by the pineal gland of cattle, and found by experiment to lighten the skin color of certain frogs and toads. [< Gk *méla(s)* black + TONE + -IN[2]]

mel·a·xu·ma (mel′ə ko͞o′mə, -ə zo͞o′-, -ək so͞o′-), *n. Plant Pathol.* a disease of trees, esp. walnuts, characterized by an inky-black liquid oozing from the affected twigs, branches, and trunk, and by bark cankers, caused by any of several fungi, as *Dothiorella gregaria.* Also called **black sap.** [< NL, irreg. < Gk *méla(s)* black + *chýma* fluid (with *x-* r. Gk *ch-*)]

Mel·ba (mel′bə), *n.* **1. (Dame) Nellie** (*Helen Porter Mitchell Armstrong*), 1861–1931, Australian operatic soprano. **2.** a girl's given name, form of **Malva.**

Mel′ba sauce′, a clear raspberry sauce, used esp. as a dessert topping. [named after Nellie MELBA]

Mel′ba toast′, narrow slices of thin, crisp toast. [named after Nellie MELBA]

Mel·bourne (mel′bərn), *n.* **1. 2nd Viscount.** See **Lamb, William. 2.** a seaport in and the capital of Victoria, in SE Australia. 1,911,895 (1961). **3.** a city on the E coast of Florida. 11,982 (1960). —**Mel·bur·ni·an** (mel bûr′nē ən), *n., adj.*

Mel·chers (mel′chərz), *n.* **Gar·i** (gâr′ē), 1860–1932, U.S. painter.

Mel·chi·a·des (mel kī′ə dēz′), *n.* **Saint,** died A.D. 314, pope 310–314. Also, **Miltiades.**

Mel·chior (mel′kyôr, mel′kē ôr′), *n.* **Lau·ritz (Leb·recht Hom·mel)** (lou′rits, lôr′its; *Dan.* lou′rits lib′REKHT hom′el), born 1890, U.S. operatic tenor, born in Denmark.

Mel·chite (mel′kīt), *n.* **1.** a Christian in Egypt and Syria who accepted the definition of faith adopted by the Council of Chalcedon in A.D. 451. —*adj.* **2.** of or pertaining to the Melchites. Also, **Melkite.** [< ML *Melchīta* < MGk *Melchī́tēs* royalist, equiv. to *melch-* king (< Sem) + *-ītēs* -ITE[1]]

Mel·chiz·e·dek (mel kiz′i dek′), *n.* **1.** Also, *Douay Bible,* **Mel·chis′e·dech′.** a priest and king of Salem. Gen. 14:18. **2.** the higher order of priests in the Mormon Church.

meld[1] (meld), *Cards.* —*v.t., v.i.* **1.** to announce and display (a counting combination of cards in the hand) for a score. —*n.* **2.** act of melding. **3.** any combination of cards to be melded. [< G *melde(n)* (to) announce; akin to OE *meldian,* etc.]

meld[2] (meld), *v.t., v.i.* to merge; blend. [MEL(T + WEL)D]

meld·er (mel′dər), *n. Scot.* the quantity of meal ground at one time; the yield of meal from a crop or specific amount of grain. [late ME *meltyre* < Scand; cf. Icel *meldr* grain or meal in the mill]

Mel·e·a·ger (mel′ē ā′jər), *n.* **1.** fl. 1st century B.C., Greek epigrammatist. **2.** *Gk. Legend.* the heroic son of Althea, an Argonaut, and the slayer of the Calydonian boar. It had been prophesied to his mother that as long as a certain brand remained unburnt, Meleager would live. After he killed his uncles in an argument over the boar, Althea threw the brand into the fire, killing her son.

Mel·e·ag·ri·des (mel′ē ag′ri dēz′), *n.pl. Class. Myth.* the sisters of Meleager of Calydon who were changed into guinea hens by Artemis in order to relieve their grief over the death of their brother.

Mel·e·cent (mel′i sənt), *n.* a girl's given name. Also, **Milicent, Millecent, Millicent.**

me·lee[1] (mā′lā, mā lā′, mel′ā), *n.* **1.** a confused, general, hand-to-hand fight. **2.** confusion; turmoil; jumble: *the melee of Christmas shopping.* Also, **mê′lée.** [< F *mêlée.* See MEDLEY]

me·lee[2] (mā′lā, mā lā′), *n.* a group of diamonds, each weighing less than .25 carat. [?]

me·le·na (mə lē′nə), *n. Med.* the discharge of black, tarry, bloody stools, usually resulting from a hemorrhage in the alimentary tract. Also, **melaena.** [< NL < Gk *mélaina,* fem. of *mélas* black]

M.El.Eng., Master of Electrical Engineering.

Mel·e·te (mel′i tē), *n. Class. Myth.* one of the original three Muses, the Muse of meditation. [< Gk *melétē* care, attention]

mel·e·tin (mel′i tin), *n. Chem.* quercetin.

me·lez·i·tose (mə lez′i tōs′), *n. Biochem.* a crystalline, trisaccharide dihydrate, $C_{18}H_{32}O_{16}·2H_2O$, composed of one molecule of fructose and two of glucose, that first yields glucose and turanose upon hydrolysis: obtained from the sap of jack pine, larch, Douglas fir, and other trees. [< F, b. *mélèze* larch + *(mél)itose* MELITOSE]

-melia, an element indicating a specified condition of the limbs: *phocomelia.* [< NL, comb. form repr. Gk *mélos* limb; see -IA]

me·li·a·ceous (mē′lē ā′shəs), *adj.* belonging to the *Meliaceae,* a family of trees and shrubs comprising the azedarach, mahogany, Spanish cedar, etc. [< NL *Meli(a)* name of genus (< Gk: ash) + -ACEOUS]

Me·li·ad (mē′lē əd), *n. Class. Myth.* a nymph of fruit trees or of flocks.

Me·li·ae (mē′lē ē′), *n.pl. Class. Myth.* the nymphs born from the blood of Uranus at the time of his mutilation by Cronus; the nymphs of ash trees. [< Gk *meliai,* deriv. of *melía* manna, ash]

Mel·i·boe·a (mel′ə bē′ə), *n. Class. Myth.* a maiden who, forbidden to marry Alexis, tried to leap to her death from a housetop but survived to marry him.

mel·ic (mel′ik), *adj.* **1.** intended to be sung. **2.** noting or pertaining to the more elaborate form of Greek lyric poetry, as distinguished from iambic and elegiac poetry. [< Gk *melik(ós),* equiv. to *mél(os)* limb, song + *-ikos* -IC]

Mel·i·cer·tes (mel′i sûr′tēz), *n. Class. Myth.* a son of Athamas and Ino who was changed into the sea god Palaemon when his father, in a fit of madness, tried to kill him.

Mel′ic Nymphs′, (mel′ik), *Class. Myth.* Meliae.

Mel·i·ë (mel′ē ē′), *n. Class. Myth.* a nymph who was the mother, by Poseidon, of Amycus.

mel·i·lite (mel′ə līt′), *n.* a mineral group, chiefly of sodium, calcium, and aluminum silicates, occurring in igneous rocks. [< NL *melilith(us),* equiv. to Gk *méli* honey (see MEL[1]) + *líthos* -LITE]

Me·lil·la (mā lēl′yä), *n.* a seaport belonging to Spain on the NE coast of Morocco, in NW Africa. 79,056 (1961).

mel·i·lot (mel′ə lot′), *n.* any cloverlike, fabaceous herb of the genus *Melilotus.* [ME *mellilot* < L *melilōt(os)* < Gk *melílōtos* a clover, equiv. to *méli* honey + *lōtós* LOTUS]

Me·lin·da (mə lin′də), *n.* a girl's given name. Also, **Malinda.**

mel·i·nite (mel′ə nīt′), *n. Chem.* a high explosive containing picric acid. [< F *mélinite* < Gk *mḗlin(os)* (deriv. of *mêlon* apple); see -ITE[1]]

mel·io·rate (mēl′yə rāt′, mē′lē ə-), *v.t., v.i.,* **-rat·ed, -rat·ing.** ameliorate. [< L *meliōrāt(us)* made better, improved (ptp. of *meliōrāre*), equiv. to *melior-* (s. of *melior*) better + *-ātus* -ATE[1]] —**mel·io·ra·ble** (mēl′yər ə bəl, mē′lē ər ə-), *adj.* —**mel·io·ra·tive** (mēl′yə rā′tiv, -yər ə tiv, mē′lē ə rā′-, -ər ə-), *adj.* —**mel′io·ra′tor,** *n.*

mel·io·ra·tion (mēl′yə rā′shən, mē′lē ə-), *n.* **1.** *Historical Ling.* semantic change in a word to a more approved or more respectable meaning. Cf. **pejoration** (def. 2). **2.** amelioration. [< LL *meliōrātiōn-* (s. of *meliōrātiō*), equiv. to *meliōrāt(us)* (see MELIORATE) + *-iōn-* -ION]

mel·io·rism (mēl′yə riz′əm, mē′lē ə-), *n.* the doctrine that the world tends to become better, or may be made better by human effort. [< L *melior* better + -ISM] —**mel′io·rist,** *n., adj.* —**mel′io·ris′tic,** *adj.*

mel·ior·i·ty (mēl yôr′i tē, -yor′-, mē′lē ôr′-, -or′-), *n.* superiority. [< ML *meliōritās,* equiv. to L *meliōr-* (s. of *melior*) better + *-itās* -ITY]

me·lis·ma (mi liz′mə), *n., pl.* **-mas, -ma·ta** (-mə tə). *Music.* an ornamental phrase of several notes sung to one syllable of text, as in plainsong. [< Gk: song, tune. See MELODY, -ISM] —**mel·is·mat·ic** (mel′iz-mat′ik), *adj.*

Me·lis·sa (mə lis′ə), *n.* **1.** *Class. Myth.* the sister of Amalthea who nourished the infant Zeus with honey. **2.** Also, **Me·lis·sie, Me·lis·sy** (mə lis′ē). a girl's given name. [< Gk *mélissa* bee]

Me·lis·se·us (mə lis′ē əs, -lis′o͞os), *n. Class. Myth.* a Cretan king who fathered Adrastea and Ida.

Mel·i·te·ne (mel′i tē′nē), *n.* ancient name of **Malatya.**

Me·li·to·pol (mel′ə tô′pəl; *Russ.* me li tô′pol), *n.* a city in the SE Ukraine, in the SW Soviet Union in Europe, NW of the Sea of Azov: battles 1941, 1943. 104,000 (est. 1962).

mel·i·tose (mel′i tōs′), *n. Chem.* raffinose. [MEL[1] + -I- + -t- (connective) + -OSE[2]]

mel·i·tri·ose (mel′i trī′ōs), *n. Chem.* raffinose. [MEL[1] + -I- + TRI- + -OSE[2]]

Me·lit·ta (mə lit′ə), *n.* a girl's given name.

Mel·kite (mel′kīt), *n., adj.* Melchite.

mell[1] (mel), *Brit. Dial.* —*v.t.* **1.** to blend; mix; meld. —*v.i.* **2.** to meddle; concern oneself. [ME *melle(n)* < MF *meller(r),* var. of *mesler;* see MEDDLE]

mell[2] (mel), *Scot. and North Eng.* —*n.* **1.** a heavy hammer; mallet. —*v.t.* **2.** to beat with a mallet; to hammer. [ME; see MALL]

mel·ler (mel′ər), *n. Slang.* melodrama (def. 1). [by shortening and alter.]

Mel·lers (mel′ərz), *n.* **Wilfrid Howard,** born 1914, English musicologist and composer.

mel·lif·er·ous (mə lif′ər əs), *adj.* yielding or producing honey. [< L *mellifer* honey-bearing (*melli-,* s. of *mel* honey, + *-fer* -FER) + -OUS]

mel·lif·lu·ent (mə lif′lo͞o ənt), *adj.* mellifluous. [< LL *mellifluent-* (s. of *mellifluēns*), equiv. to L *melli-* (s. of *mel*) honey + *fluent-* FLUENT] —**mel·lif′lu·ence,** *n.* —**mel·lif′lu·ent·ly,** *adv.*

mel·lif·lu·ous (mə lif′lo͞o əs), *adj.* **1.** sweetly or smoothly flowing; sweet-sounding: *a mellifluous voice; mellifluous tones.* **2.** flowing with honey; sweetened with or as with honey. [< LL *mellifluus,* equiv. to L *melli-* (s. of *mel*) honey + *-flu(ere)* (to) flow + *-us* -OUS] —**mel·lif′lu·ous·ly,** *adv.* —**mel·lif′lu·ous·ness,** *n.*

mel·lite (mel′īt), *n. Pharm.* a pharmaceutical containing honey. Also, **mellitum.** [< NL *mellites.* See MEL[1], -ITE[1]]

mel·li·tum (mə lī′təm), *n., pl.* **-li·ta** (-lī′tə). *Pharm.* mellite. [< NL]

Mel·lon (mel′ən), *n.* **Andrew William,** 1855–1937, U.S. financier: Secretary of the Treasury 1921–32.

mel·low (mel′ō), *adj.* **1.** soft and full-flavored from ripeness, as fruit. **2.** well-matured, as wines. **3.** softened, toned down, or improved, as by aging or ripening. **4.** soft and rich, as sound, tones, color, light, etc. **5.** genial; jovial. **6.** friably or loamy, as soil. **7.** *Informal.* mildly intoxicated; tipsy. —*v.t., v.i.* **8.** to make or become mellow; soften by aging or ripening. [late ME *mel(o)we,* alter. of ME *meruw,* OE *meru* soft (? by dissimilation, in phrase *meruw fruit*)] —**mel′low·ly,** *adv.* —**mel′low·ness,** *n.*

—**Syn. 1.** See **ripe. 5.** good-natured. **8.** develop, mature, improve. —**Ant. 1.** immature, raw, green. **4.** harsh.

Me·lo (mā′lō; *Sp.* me′lō), *n.* a city in NE Uruguay. 36,000 (est. 1954).

me·lo·de·on (mə lō′dē ən), *n.* **1.** a small reed organ. **2.** a kind of accordion. Also, **melodion.** [< G, formed on *Melodie* melody]

me·lo·di·a (mə lō′dē ə), *n.* an eight-foot wooden flue-pipe stop organ resembling the clarabella in tone. [special use of LL *melōdia* MELODY]

me·lod·ic (mə lod′ik), *adj.* **1.** melodious. **2.** pertaining to melody as distinguished from harmony and rhythm. [< LL *melōdic(us)* < Gk *melōidikós.* See MELODY, -IC] —**me·lod′i·cal·ly,** *adv.*

melod′ic mi′nor scale′, *Music.* See **minor scale** (def. 2).

me·lod·ics (mə lod′iks), *n.* (*construed as sing.*) the branch of musical science concerned with the pitch and succession of tones. [see MELODIC, -ICS]

Mel·o·die (mel′ə dē), *n.* a girl's given name. Also, **Melody, Melodye.**

me·lo·di·on (mə lō′dē ən), *n.* melodeon.

me·lo·di·ous (mə lō′dē əs), *adj.* **1.** of the nature of or characterized by melody; tuneful. **2.** producing melody; sweet-sounding; musical. [ME < ML *melōdiōs(us).* See MELODY, -OUS] —**me·lo′di·ous·ness,** *n.*

mel·o·dise (mel′ə dīz′), *v.t., v.i.,* **-dised, -dis·ing.** *Chiefly Brit.* melodize. —**mel′o·dis′er,** *n.*

mel·o·dist (mel′ə dist), *n.* a composer or a singer of melodies. [MELOD(Y) + -IST]

mel·o·dize (mel′ə dīz′), *v.,* **-dized, -diz·ing.** —*v.t.* **1.** to make melodious. —*v.i.* **2.** to make melody. **3.** to blend melodiously. Also, *esp. Brit.,* **melodise.** [MELOD(Y) + -IZE] —**mel′o·diz′er,** *n.*

mel·o·dra·ma (mel′ə drä′mə, -dram′ə), *n.* **1.** a play form that does not observe the dramatic laws of cause and effect and that intensifies sentiment and exaggerates emotion. **2.** (in the 17th, 18th, and early 19th centuries) a romantic dramatic composition with music interspersed. [< F *mélodrame,* equiv. to *mélo-* (< Gk *mélo(s)* song) + *drame* DRAMA] —**mel·o·dram·a·tist** (mel′ə dram′ə tist, -drä′mə-), *n.*

mel·o·dra·mat·ic (mel′ə drə mat′ik), *adj.* **1.** of, like, or befitting melodrama; sentimental and exaggerated. —*n.* **2. melodramatics,** melodramatic writing or behavior. [MELODRAMA + -TIC] —**mel′o·dra·mat′i·cal·ly,** *adv.*

mel·o·dram·a·tise (mel′ə dram′ə tīz′, -drä′mə-), *v.t.,* **-tised, -tis·ing.** *Chiefly Brit.* melodramatize.

mel·o·dram·a·tize (mel′ə dram′ə tīz′, -drä′mə-), *v.t.,* **-tized, -tiz·ing. 1.** to make melodramatic. **2.** to turn (a novel, story, etc.) into a melodrama. [MELODRAMA + *-t-* connective -IZE]

mel·o·dy (mel′ə dē), *n., pl.* **-dies.** **1.** musical sounds in agreeable succession or arrangement. **2.** *Music.* **a.** the succession of single tones in musical compositions, as distinguished from harmony and rhythm. **b.** the principal part in a harmonic composition; the air. **c.** a rhythmical succession of single tones producing a distinct musical phrase or idea. **3.** a poem suitable for singing. **4.** intonation, as of a segment of connected speech. [ME *melodie* < eccl. L *melōdia* < Gk *melōidía* (choral) singing, equiv. to *mel-* (see MELIC) + *-ōid-* (see ODE) + *-ia* -Y³] —**mel′o·dy·less,** *adj.*
—**Syn. 1.** See **harmony. 2.** tune, song, descant, theme.

Mel·o·dy (mel′ə dē), *n.* a girl's given name. Also, **Melodie, Mel′o·dye.**

mel·oid (mel′oid), *n.* **1.** a beetle of the family *Meloidae,* comprising the blister beetles. —*adj.* **2.** belonging or pertaining to the family *Meloidae.* [< NL *Meloid(ae)* name of typical genus, equiv. to *Melo(ē)* a beetle + *-idae* -ID²]

mel·o·lon·thine (mel′ə lon′thin, -thin), *n.* **1.** any of several scarabaeid beetles of the subfamily *Melolonthinae,* comprising the June bugs, chafers, etc. —*adj.* **2.** belonging or pertaining to the family *Melolonthinae.* [< Gk *mēlolónth(ē)* a kind of beetle or cockchafer + -INE¹]

mel·on (mel′ən), *n.* **1.** the fruit of any of various cucurbitaceous plants, as the muskmelon or watermelon. **2.** medium crimson or deep pink. **3.** *Slang.* a large extra dividend to be distributed to stockholders: *Profits zoomed so in the last quarter that the corporation cut a nice melon.* Cf. **plum**¹ (def. 10). [ME < LL *mēlōn-* (s. of *mēlō*), short for *mēlopepō* < Gk *mēlopépōn* apple-shaped melon, equiv. to *mēlo(n)* apple + *pépōn* PEPO]

mel·on·bulb (mel′ən bulb′), *n. Furniture.* a large, bulbous turning, sometimes with surface carving, found esp. on the legs and posts of Elizabethan and Jacobean furniture.

mel′on foot′, *Eng. Furniture.* a bun foot having vertical channels.

mel′on pear′, pepino (def. 2).

mel′on seed′, a small, broad, shallow boat for sailing or rowing, formerly used by hunters in various bays and marshes along the coast of New Jersey.

mel′on shrub′, pepino.

mel·os (mel′os, -ōs, mē′los, -lōs), *n.* the succession of musical tones constituting a melody. [< Gk: song, tune]

Me·los (mē′los, -lōs, mel′os, -ōs; *Gk.* me′lôs), *n.* a Greek island in the Cyclades, in the SW Aegean: statue, *Venus de Milo,* found here 1820. 5586 (1951); 51 sq. mi. Also, **Milo, Milos.** —**Me·li·an** (mē′lē ən, mēl′yən), *adj., n.*

Mel·pom·e·ne (mel pom′ə nē′), *n. Class. Myth.* the Muse of tragedy. [< L < Gk, special use of fem. of prp. of *mélpesthai* to sing]

Mel·rose (mel′rōz), *n.* **1.** a city in E Massachusetts, near Boston. 29,619 (1960). **2.** a village in SE Scotland, on the Tweed River: ruins of a famous abbey.

Mel′rose Park′, a city in NE Illinois, near Chicago. 22,291 (1960).

melt¹ (melt), *v.,* **melt·ed, melt·ed** or **mol·ten, melt·ing,** *n.* —*v.i.* **1.** to become liquefied by heat, as ice, snow, butter, metal, etc. **2.** to become liquid; dissolve: *Let the cough drop melt in your mouth.* **3.** to pass, dwindle, or fade gradually (often fol. by *away*): *His fortune slowly melted away.* **4.** to pass, change, or blend gradually (often fol. by *into*): *Night melted into day.* **5.** to become softened in feeling by pity, sympathy, love, or the like: *The tyrant's heart would not melt.* **6.** *Obs.* to be subdued or overwhelmed by sorrow, dismay, etc. —*v.t.* **7.** to reduce to a liquid state by heat; fuse: *Fire melts ice.* **8.** to cause to pass away or fade. **9.** to cause to pass, change, or blend gradually. **10.** to soften in feeling, as a person, the heart, etc.: *Nothing could melt that tyrant's heart.* —*n.* **11.** act or process of melting; state of being melted. **12.** that which is melted. **13.** a quantity melted at one time. [ME *melte(n),* OE *meltan* (v.i.), *m(i)elten* (v.t.) to melt, digest; c. Icel *melta* to digest, Gk *méldein* to melt] —**melt′a·bil′i·ty,** *n.* —**melt′a·ble,** *adj.* —**melt′ing·ly,** *adv.* —**melt′ing·ness,** *n.*
—**Syn. 1.** MELT, DISSOLVE, FUSE, THAW imply reducing a solid substance to a liquid state. To MELT is to bring a solid to a liquid condition by the agency of heat: *to melt butter.* DISSOLVE, though sometimes used interchangeably with MELT, applies to a different process, depending upon the fact that certain solids, placed in certain liquids, distribute their particles throughout the liquids: *A greater number of solids can be dissolved in water and in alcohol than in any other liquids.* To FUSE is to subject the solid (usually a metal) to a very high temperature; it applies esp. to melting or blending metals together: *Bell metal is made by fusing copper and tin.* To THAW is to reduce a frozen substance (whose ordinary condition is liquid) to a liquid or semiliquid by raising its temperature above the freezing point: *Sunshine will thaw ice in a lake.* **4.** dwindle. **10.** gentle, mollify, relax. —**Ant. 1.** freeze. **2.** solidify, crystallize.

melt² (melt), *n.* the spleen, esp. that of a cow, pig, etc. Also, **milt.** [var. of MILT]

melt·age (mel′tij), *n.* the amount melted or the result of melting. [MELT + -AGE]

melt·down (melt′doun′), *n.* the melting of a significant portion of a nuclear-reactor core due to inadequate cooling of the fuel elements, potentially resulting in escape of radiation. [n. use of v. phrase *melt down*]

melt·er (mel′tər), *n.* **1.** one who or that which melts. **2.** a man in charge of a group of open-hearth furnaces. [MELT + -ER¹]

melt′ing point′, *Physical Chem.* the temperature at which a solid substance melts or fuses.

melt′ing pot′, **1.** a pot in which metals or other substances are melted or fused. **2.** a country, locality, or situation in which a blending of races and cultures is taking place.

mel·ton (mel′tᵊn), *n.* a smooth, heavy woolen cloth, for overcoats, hunting jackets, etc. [after *Melton* Mowbray, town in Leicestershire, England]

melt·wa·ter (melt′wô′tər, -wot′ər), *n.* water from melted snow or ice. [MELT + WATER]

Me·lun (mə lœɴ′), *n.* a city in and the capital of Seine-et-Marne, in N France. 28,796 (1962).

Me·lun·geon (mə lun′jən), *n.* a member of a people of mixed Caucasian, Negroid, and American Indian ancestry living in the southern Appalachians.

Mel·us (mel′əs), *n. Class. Myth.* the son of Cinyras of Cyprus whose grief at the death of Adonis so touched Aphrodite that she changed him into an apple tree.

Mel·ville (mel′vil), *n.* **1. Herman,** 1819–91, U.S. novelist. **2.** a boy's given name.

Mel′ville Is′land, an island in the Arctic Ocean, N of Canada: belonging to Canada. 200 mi. long; 130 mi. wide.

Mel′ville Penin′sula, a peninsula in N Canada, SE of the Gulf of Boothia. 250 mi. long.

Mel·vin (mel′vin), *n.* a boy's given name. Also, **Mel′vyn.**

mem (mem), *n.* **1.** the 13th letter of the Hebrew alphabet. **2.** the consonant sound represented by this letter. [< Heb: lit., water]

mem., **1.** member. **2.** memoir. **3.** memorandum.

mem·ber (mem′bər), *n.* **1.** each of the persons composing a society, party, community, or other body. **2.** *Govt.* **a.** a member of Congress, esp. of the House of Representatives. **b.** a member of the British Parliament, esp. of the House of Commons. **c.** any member of a legislative body. **3.** a part or organ of an animal body; a limb, as a leg, arm, or wing. **4.** a constituent part of any structural or composite whole, as a subordinate architectural feature of a building or the like. **5.** *Math.* **a.** either side of an equation. **b.** an element of a set. [ME *membre* < L *membr(um)*] —**mem′ber·less,** *adj.*
—**Syn. 3, 4.** MEMBER, LIMB refer to an integral part of a larger body. MEMBER is the general term applied to any integral part or vital organ of an organized animal body, or, more widely, to any integral or distinguishable constituent part of a whole which is considered as organic: *a member of a façade; The nose, tongue, and arms are members of the body.* LIMB, which once, like MEMBER, referred to any organ of the body, is now restricted to the legs and arms (particularly of human beings), and is secondarily applied to the branches of a tree. It has such figurative uses as a *limb of Satan,* or a *limb of the law.* The Victorian "limb" as a prudish euphemism for "leg" stimulated further humorous use of the word. **4.** element, portion.

Mem′ber of the Wed′ding, The, a novel (1946) and play (1950) by Carson McCullers.

mem·ber·ship (mem′bər ship′), *n.* **1.** state of being a member, as of a society, club, etc. **2.** the status of a member. **3.** the total number of members belonging to an organization, society, etc. [MEMBER + -SHIP]

mem·brane (mem′brān), *n. Biol.* **1.** a thin, pliable sheet or layer of animal or vegetable tissue, serving to line an organ, connect parts, etc. **2.** the thin, limiting covering of a cell or cell part. [earlier *membraan* parchment < L *membrāna.* See MEMBER, -ANE] —**mem′brane·less,** *adj.*

mem′brane bone′, a bone that develops from membranous tissue. Cf. **cartilage bone.**

mem·bra·no·phone (mem brā′nə fōn′), *n.* any musical instrument, as a drum, in which the sound is produced by striking, rubbing, or blowing against a membrane stretched over a frame. [MEMBRANE + -O- + -PHONE] —**mem·bra·no·phon·ic** (mem brā′nə fon′ik), *adj.*

mem·bra·nous (mem′brə nəs), *adj.* **1.** consisting of, of the nature of, or resembling membrane. **2.** characterized by the formation of a membrane. Also, **mem·bra·na·ceous** (mem′brə nā′shəs). [MEMBRANE + -OUS; cf. F *membraneux*] —**mem′bra·nous·ly,** *adv.*

mem′branous lab′yrinth. See under **labyrinth** (def. 7)

Me·mel (mā′məl, mem′əl), *n.* **1.** a seaport in NW Lithuania, in the W Soviet Union in Europe. 89,000 (1959). **2.** a territory including this seaport: ceded to Germany by Lithuania 1939; incorporated into the Soviet Union 1945. 933 sq. mi. **3.** the lower course of the Niemen River. Cf. **Niemen.** Lithuanian, **Klaipeda** (for defs. 1, 2).

me·men·to (mə men′tō), *n., pl.* **-tos, -toes. 1.** something that serves as a reminder of what is past or gone. **2.** anything serving as a reminder or warning. **3.** (*cap., italics*) *Rom. Cath. Ch.* either of two prayers in the canon of the Mass, one for persons living and the other for persons dead. [< L *mementō,* impv. of *meminisse* to remember]

me·men·to mo·ri (mə men′tō mōr′ī, môr′ī, mōr′ē, môr′ē), *pl.* **memento mori** for 2. **1.** (*italics*) *Latin.* remember that thou must die. **2.** an object, as a skull or the like, serving as a reminder of death.

Mem·ling (mem′ling), *n.* **Hans** (häns), c1430–94?, German painter of the Flemish school. Also, **Mem·linc** (mem′lingk).

Mem·non (mem′non), *n.* **1. Colossus of,** (in ancient Egypt) a colossal statue near Thebes said to produce a musical sound when the rays of the early morning sun struck it. Cf. **Vocal Memnon. 2.** *Class. Myth.* an Oriental or Ethiopian hero slain by Achilles in the Trojan War. —**Mem·no·ni·an** (mem nō′nē ən), *adj.*

Mem·no·ni·a (mem nō′nē ə), *n.* an area in the southern hemisphere of Mars, appearing as a light region when viewed telescopically from the earth.

Mem·non·i·des (mem non′i dēz′), *n.pl. Class. Myth.* the companions of Memnon who were changed into birds because of grief for their king. They gathered at Memnon's tomb annually, to fight and to lament.

mem·o (mem′ō), *n., pl.* **mem·os.** *Informal.* memorandum. [by shortening]

mem·oir (mem′wär, -wôr), *n.* **1. memoirs, a.** records of facts or events in connection with a particular subject, historical period, etc., as known to the writer or gathered from special sources. **b.** records of one's life and experiences. **c.** a collection of reports made to a scientific or other learned society. **2.** a biography. [< F *mémoire* < L *memoria;* see MEMORY]

Mé·moires d'Ou·tre-tombe (*Fr.* mā mwar dōō-trᵊ tōnb′), an autobiographical work (1849–50) by Chateaubriand.

mem·o·ra·bil·i·a (mem′ər ə bil′ē ə, -bil′yə), *n.pl., sing.* **-o·rab·i·le** (-ə rab′ə lē). matters or events worthy to be remembered; points worthy of note. [< L: things to be remembered, neut. pl. of *memorābilis* MEMORABLE]

mem·o·ra·ble (mem′ər ə bəl), *adj.* **1.** worthy to be remembered; notable: *a memorable speech.* **2.** easy to be remembered. [late ME < L *memorābil(is)* worth mentioning, equiv. to *memorā(re)* (to) mention + *-bilis* -BLE] —**mem′o·ra·bil′i·ty, mem′o·ra·ble·ness,** *n.* —**mem′o·ra·bly,** *adv.*

mem·o·ran·dum (mem′ə ran′dəm), *n., pl.* **-dums, -da** (-də). **1.** a note designating something to be remembered, esp. something to be done or acted upon in the future; reminder. **2.** a record or written statement of something. **3.** *Informal.* a message, esp. one sent between two or more employees of the same company, concerning company business: *an interoffice memorandum.* **4.** *Law.* a writing, usually informal, containing the terms of a transaction. **5.** *Diplomacy.* a summary of the state of a question, the reasons for a decision agreed on, etc. **6.** a document transferring title to goods but authorizing the return of the goods to the seller at the option of the buyer. [< L: something to be noted, neut. of *memorandus* notable, orig. gerundive of *memorāre* to mention, tell]

me·mo·ri·al (mə mōr′ē əl, -môr′-), *n.* **1.** something designed to preserve the memory of a person, event, etc., as a monument, a periodic observance, etc. **2.** a written statement of facts presented to a sovereign, a legislative body, etc., as the ground of, or expressed in the form of, a petition or remonstrance. —*adj.* **3.** preserving the memory of a person or thing; commemorative: *memorial services.* **4.** of or pertaining to the memory. [ME < LL *memoriāle,* n. use of neut. of L *memoriālis* for memoranda. See MEMORY, -AL¹] —**me·mo′ri·al·ly,** *adv.*

Memo′rial Day′, *U.S.* **1.** Also called **Decoration Day.** a day, May 30, set aside in most States for observances in memory of dead servicemen of all wars. **2.** any of several days, as April 26, May 10, or June 3, similarly observed in various Southern States.

me·mo·ri·al·ise (mə mōr′ē ə līz′, -môr′-), *v.t.,* **-ised, -is·ing.** *Chiefly Brit.* memorialize. —**me·mo′ri·al·i·sa′tion,** *n.* —**me·mo′ri·al·is′er,** *n.*

me·mo·ri·al·ist (mə mōr′ē ə list, -môr′-), *n.* **1.** a person who writes memorials. **2.** a person who writes memoirs. [MEMORIAL + -IST]

me·mo·ri·al·ize (mə mōr′ē ə līz′, -môr′-), *v.t.,* **-ized, -iz·ing. 1.** to commemorate. **2.** to present a memorial to. Also, *esp. Brit.,* **memorialise.** [MEMORIAL + -IZE] —**me·mo′ri·al·i·za′tion,** *n.* —**me·mo′ri·al·iz′er,** *n.*

memo′rial park′, cemetery.

memo′rial rose′, a prostrate or trailing rose, *Rosa wichuraiana,* of eastern Asia, having strong, hooked prickles and white, fragrant flowers nearly two inches wide.

mem·o·ried (mem′ə rēd), *adj.* **1.** having a memory (usually used in combination): *short-memoried; well-memoried.* **2.** filled with memories: *a quiet, memoried town.* [MEMORY + -ED³]

me·mo·ri·ter (mə mōr′i tər, -ter, -môr′-), *adv.* **1.** by heart; by memory. —*adj.* **2.** involving or requiring memorization: *the memoriter aspects of a college course.* [< L, equiv. to *memori-* (s. of *memor*) mindful of + *-ter* adv. suffix]

mem·o·rize (mem′ə rīz′), *v.t.,* **-rized, -riz·ing.** to commit to memory; learn by heart: *to memorize a poem.* [MEMOR(Y) + -IZE] —**mem′o·riz′a·ble,** *adj.* —**mem′o·ri·za′tion,** *n.* —**mem′o·riz′er,** *n.*

mem·o·ry (mem′ə rē), *n., pl.* **-ries. 1.** the mental capacity or faculty of retaining and reviving impressions, or of recalling or recognizing previous experiences. **2.** this faculty as possessed by a particular individual: *to have a good memory.* **3.** act or fact of retaining mental impressions; remembrance; recollection: *to draw from memory.* **4.** the length of time over which recollection extends: *a time within the memory of living men.* **5.** a mental impression retained; a recollection: *one's earliest memories.* **6.** the reputation of a person or thing, esp. after death; fame: *a ruler of beloved memory.* **7.** state or fact of being remembered. **8.** a person or thing remembered. **9.** commemorative remembrance; commemoration: *a monument in memory of Columbus.* **10.** the ability of certain materials to return to an original shape after deformation. **11.** Also called **storage.** *Computer Technol.* **a.** the capacity of a computer to store information subject to recall. **b.** the components of the computer, in which such information is stored. **12.** *Rhet.* the step in the classical preparation of a speech in which the wording is memorized. **13.** *Cards.* concentration (def. 7). [ME *memorie* < L *memoria,* equiv. to *memor* remembering + *-ia* -Y³]

mem′ory verse′, a verse or passage from the Bible to be memorized, esp. by members of a Sunday School.

Mem·phi·an (mem′fē ən), *n.* **1.** a native or inhabitant of the ancient Egyptian city of Memphis. **2.** Egyptian (def. 3). **3.** a native or resident of Memphis, Tennessee. [MEMPHI(S) + -AN]

Mem·phis (mem′fis), *n.* **1.** a port in SW Tennessee, on the Mississippi. 497,524 (1960). **2.** a ruined city in Upper Egypt, on the Nile, S of Cairo: the ancient capital of Egypt. **3.** a town in NW Texas. 3332 (1960).

Mem·phite (mem′fīt), *adj.* **1.** Also, **Mem·phit·ic** (mem fit′ik). of or pertaining to the ancient Egyptian city of Memphis. —*n.* **2.** Memphian (def. 1). [<< Gk *Memphī́tēs* inhabitant of Memphis; see -ITE¹]

Mem·phre·ma·gog (mem′frē mā′gog), *n.* **Lake,** a lake on the boundary between the U.S. and Canada, between N Vermont and S Quebec. 30 mi. long.

mem·sa·hib (mem′sä′ib, -ēb, -sä′hib, -hēb), *n.* (in India) a native's term of respect for a European lady. [< Hindi, equiv. to *mem* (< E MA'AM) + *sāhib* master]

men (men), *n.* pl. of **man.**

Me·na (mē′nə), *n.* a town in W Arkansas. 4388 (1960).

men·ace (men′is), *n., v.,* **-aced, -ac·ing.** —*n.* **1.** something that threatens to cause evil, harm, injury, etc.; a threat: *The garbage is a menace to health.* —*v.t.* **2.** to utter or direct a threat against; threaten. **3.** to serve as a probable threat to; imperil. [late ME < MF < L *minācia,* equiv. to *mināc-* (s. of *mināx*) jutting out, threatening + *-ia* -IA] —**men′ac·er,** *n.* —**men′ac·ing·ly,** *adv.*

men·ac·me (mə nak′mē, mē nak′-), *n. Physiol.* the part of a female's life during which menstruation occurs. [< Gk *mēn* month + ACME]

me·nad (mē′nad), *n.* maenad. —**me·nad′ic,** *adj.*

Me·na·do (me nä′dō), *n.* a seaport on NE Celebes, in NE Indonesia. 127,614 (1961). Also, **Manado.**

Me·naech·mi (mi nek′mē; *Lat.* me nīk′mē), *n.* a comedy (c200 B.C.) by Plautus.

mé·nage (mā näzh′; *Fr.* mā nazh′), *n., pl.* **-nages** (-nä′zhiz; *Fr.* -nazh′). **1.** a domestic establishment; household. **2.** housekeeping. Also, **me·nage′.** [< F << VL *mansiōnāticum. See MANSION, -AGE]

mé·nage à trois (mā nazh a trwä′), *French.* a domestic arrangement involving a married couple and the lover of one of them, in which all three occupy the same household. [lit., household of three]

CONCISE ETYMOLOGY KEY: <, descended or derived from; >, whence; b., blend of, blended; c., cognate with; deriv., derivative; equiv., equivalent; imit., imitative; m., modification of; obl., oblique; r., replacing; s., stem; sp., spelling; trans., translation; ?, origin unknown, perhaps; *, hypothetical. See the full key inside the front cover.

me·nag·er·ie (mə naj′ə rē, -nazh′-), *n.* **1.** a collection of wild or strange animals, esp. for exhibition. **2.** a place where they are kept or exhibited. [< F: lit., housekeeping. See MÉNAGE, -ERY]

Men′ai Strait′ (men′ī), a strait between Anglesey island and the mainland of NW Wales. 14 mi. long.

Me·nam (me näm′), *n.* a river in N Thailand, flowing S to the Gulf of Siam. 150 mi. long. Also called **Chao Phraya, Nam.**

Me·nan·der (mə nan′dər), *n.* 342?–291 B.C., Greek writer of comedies.

men·ar·che (mə när′kē, me-), *n.* *Physiol.* the first menstrual period; the establishment of menstruation. [< Gk *mēn* month + *archē* beginning] —**men·ar′che·al, men·ar′chi·al,** *adj.*

Me·nash·a (mə nash′ə), *n.* a city in E Wisconsin. 14,647 (1960).

me·nat (mā′nät), *n.* an amulet worn by certain Egyptians in ancient times to secure divine protection and to insure fertility. [< Egypt *mnit*]

men·chil·dren (men′chil′drən, -drin), *n.* pl. of **man-child.**

Men·ci·us (men′shē əs), *n.* c380–289 B.C., Chinese philosopher. Also called **Mêng-tzŭ, Meng-tse.**

Menck·en (meng′kən), *n.* **H(enry) L(ouis),** 1880–1956, U.S. author, editor, and critic. —**Menck·e·ni·an** (meng kē′nē ən), *adj., n.*

mend (mend), *v.t.* **1.** to make (something broken, worn, torn, or otherwise damaged) whole, sound, or usable by repairing: *to mend clothes.* **2.** to remove or correct defects or errors in. **3.** to remove or correct. **4.** to set right; make better; improve: *to mend matters.* —*v.i.* **5.** to progress toward recovery, as a sick person. **6.** to improve, as conditions, affairs, etc. **7. mend sail,** *Naut.* to refurl sails that have been badly furled; mend the furl. **8. mend the furl,** *Naut.* to mend sail. —*n.* **9.** act of mending; repair or improvement. **10.** a mended place. **11. on the mend, a.** recovering from an illness. **b.** improving in general, as a state of affairs: *The breach between father and son is on the mend.* [aph. var. of AMEND] —**mend′a·ble,** *adj.*
—**Syn. 1.** fix, restore, retouch. MEND, DARN, PATCH mean to repair something and thus renew its usefulness. MEND is an informal and general expression which emphasizes the idea of making whole something damaged: *to mend a broken dish, a tear in an apron.* DARN and PATCH are more specific, referring particularly to repairing holes or rents. To DARN is to repair by means of stitches interwoven with one another: *to darn stockings.* To PATCH is to cover a hole or rent (usually) with a piece or pieces of similar material and to secure the edges of these; it implies a more temporary or makeshift repair than the others: *to patch the knees of trousers, a rubber tire.* **2.** rectify, amend, emend. **4.** ameliorate, meliorate. **5.** heal, recover, amend. —**Ant. 1.** ruin, destroy. **5.** die, sicken.

men·da·cious (men dā′shəs), *adj.* **1.** false or untrue: *a mendacious report.* **2.** lying; untruthful; dishonest: *a mendacious person.* [< L *mendāci-* (see MENDACITY) + -OUS] —**men·da′cious·ly,** *adv.* —**men·da′cious·ness,** *n.*
—**Ant. 1, 2.** veracious.

men·dac·i·ty (men das′i tē), *n., pl.* **-ties** for 2. **1.** quality of being mendacious; untruthfulness; tendency to lie. **2.** an instance of lying; falsehood. [< LL *mendācitās* falsehood, equiv. to L *mendāci-* (s. of *mendāx*) given to lying, false + *-tās* -TY²]

Men·del (men′dᵊl), *n.* **1. Gre·gor Jo·hann** (greg′ər yō′hän; *Ger.* grā′gôr yō′hän), 1822–84, Austrian monk and botanist. **2.** a boy's given name, form of **Mandel.**

Men·de·le·ev (men′dᵊlā′əf; *Russ.* men′də le′yəf), *n.* **Dmi·tri I·va·no·vich** (dmē′tri i vä′no vich), 1834–1907, Russian chemist: helped develop the periodic law. Also, **Men′de·le′yev, Men′de·lej′eff.**

Men′dele′ev's law′, *Chem.* See **periodic law** (def. 2).

men·de·le·vi·um (men′dᵊlē′vē əm), *n.* *Chem.* a synthetic, radioactive element. *Symbol:* Md, Mv; *at. no.:* 101. [named after D. I. MENDELEEV; see -IUM]

Men·de·li·an (men dē′lē ən, -dēl′yən), *adj.* **1.** of or pertaining to Gregor Mendel or to his laws of heredity. —*n.* **2.** a follower of Gregor Mendel; one who accepts Mendelism. [MENDEL + -IAN]

Men·del·ism (men′dᵊliz′əm), *n.* the theories of heredity advanced by Gregor Mendel. Also, **Men·de·li·an·ism** (men dē′lē ə niz′əm). [MENDEL + -ISM]

Men′del's laws′, *Genetics.* the basic principles of heredity discovered by Gregor Mendel, showing that alternative hereditary factors of hybrids exhibit a clean-cut separation or segregation from one another and that different pairs of hereditary traits are independently sorted from each other.

Men·del·sohn (men′dᵊl sən; *Ger.* men′dəl zōn′), *n.* **E·rich** (ā′rikh), 1887–1953, German architect in England and in the U.S.

Men·dels·sohn (men′dᵊl sən; *Ger.* men′dəl zōn′), *n.* **1. Fe·lix** (fē′liks; *Ger.* fā′liks), (*Jacob Ludwig Felix Mendelssohn-Bartholdy*), 1809–47, German composer. **2.** his grandfather **Mo·ses** (mō′ziz, -zis; *Ger.* mō′zes), 1729–86, German philosopher.

mend·er (men′dər), *n.* **1.** one who or that which mends. **2.** a piece of sheet metal that has been imperfectly tinned but which may be retinned to an acceptable standard. [ME; see MEND, -ER¹]

Men·de·res (men′de res′), *n.* **1. Ad·nan** (äd′nän), 1899–1961, Turkish political leader: premier 1950–60. **2.** Ancient, **Maeander, Meander.** a river in W Asia Minor, flowing into the Aegean near Samos. 240 mi. long. **3.** Ancient, **Scamander.** a river in NW Asia Minor, flowing across the Trojan plain into the Dardanelles. 60 mi. long.

Men·dès-France (men′dis frans′, -fräns′; *Fr.* mäɴ des fräɴs′), *n.* **Pierre** (pyer), 1907–82, French statesman and economist: premier 1954–55.

men·di·cant (men′də kənt), *adj.* **1.** begging; practicing begging; living on alms. **2.** pertaining to or characteristic of a beggar. —*n.* **3.** a person who lives by begging; a beggar. **4.** a mendicant friar. [late ME < L *mendicant-* (s. of *mendicāns*) begging (prp. of *mendicāre*), equiv. to *mendic(us)* beggarly, needy + *-ant-* -ANT] —**men′di·can·cy,** *n.*

men·dic·i·ty (men dis′i tē), *n.* **1.** the practice of begging. **2.** the condition of life of a beggar. [late ME *mendicite* < L *mendīcitās* beggary, equiv. to *mendīc(us)* needy, beggarly + *-itās* -ITY]

Mend′ing Wall′, a poem (1914) by Robert Frost.

Men·do·ci·no (men′də sē′nō), *n.* **Cape,** a cape in NW California: the westernmost point in California.

Men·do·ta (men dō′tə), *n.* **1.** a town in N Illinois. 6154 (1960). **2. Lake,** a lake in S Wisconsin, in N Madison. ab. 15 sq. mi.

Mendo′ta Heights′, a town in SE Minnesota. 5028 (1960).

Men·do·za (men dō′zə; *Sp.* men dô′sä *or, for 1,* -thä), *n.* **1. Pe·dro de** (pe′thrô the), about 1487–1537, Spanish soldier and explorer: founder of the first colony of Buenos Aires 1536?. **2.** a city in W central Argentina. 194,921 (est. 1965).

me·nel (mə nel′), *n.* manille.

Men·e·la·us (men′ᵊlā′əs), *n.* **1.** *Class. Myth.* a king of Sparta, the husband of Helen and brother of Agamemnon, to whom he appealed for an army against Troy in order to recover Helen from her abductor, Paris. **2.** a crater in the first quadrant of the face of the moon: about 20 miles in diameter.

Men·e·lik II (men′ᵊlik), 1844–1913, emperor of Ethiopia 1889–1913.

me·ne, me·ne, tek·el, u·phar·sin (mē′nē, mē′nē, tek′əl, yōō fär′sin), *Aramaic.* numbered, numbered, weighed, divided: the miraculous writing on the wall interpreted by Daniel as foretelling the destruction of Belshazzar and his kingdom. Dan. 5:25–31.

Me·nén·dez de A·vi·lés (me nen′deth the ä′vē-les′), **Pe·dro** (pe′thrô), 1519–74, Spanish admiral and colonizer: founder of St. Augustine, Florida, 1565.

Me·nep·tah (me′nep tä′), *n.* Merneptah.

Me·nes (mē′nēz), *n.* fl. c3200 B.C., 1st king of Egypt: founder of the 1st dynasty.

Me·nes·the·us (mə nes′thē əs, -thōōs), *n.* *Class. Myth.* a regent of Athens and a rejected suitor of Helen who assisted Menelaus by leading 50 ships against Troy in the Trojan War.

Me·nes·thi·us (mə nes′thē əs), *n.* (in the *Iliad*) a son of Areïthoüs who assisted the Greeks at Troy and was killed by Paris.

men·folk (men′fōk′), *n.pl.* men, esp. those belonging to a family or community: *The menfolk are all out haying.* Also, **men′folks′.** [MEN + FOLK]

M.Eng., Master of Engineering.

Meng·er (meng′ər), *n.* **Karl** (kärl), 1840–1921, Austrian economist.

Meng·tze (mung′dzu′), *n.* a city in SE Yünnan, in SW China. ab. 200,000. Also, **Meng′tseu′, Meng′tsu′, Meng′-tzu′.**

Mêng-tzŭ (mung′dzu′), *n.* Mencius. Also, **Meng′-tse′.**

men·ha·den (men hād′ᵊn), *n., pl.* **-den.** any marine clupeoid fish of the genus *Brevoortia*, esp. *B. tyrannus*, resembling a shad but with a more compressed body, found along the eastern coast of the U.S., and used for making oil and fertilizer. [< Algonquian; cf. Narraganset *munnawhatteaûg*, lit., fertilizer]

menha′den boat′, a motor vessel used by menhaden fishers along the coast of the Middle Atlantic and Southern States.

men·hir (men′hir), *n.* *Archaeol.* an upright monumental stone, standing either alone or with others, as in a cromlech, found chiefly in Cornwall. [< Breton phrase *men hir*, equiv. to *men* stone + *hir* long]

me·ni·al (mē′nē əl, mēn′yəl), *adj.* **1.** pertaining or proper to domestic servants. **2.** servile; degrading: *a menial occupation.* —*n.* **3.** a domestic servant. **4.** a servile person. [ME *meynyal* < AF *me(i)nial.* See MEINY, -AL¹] —**me′ni·al·ly,** *adv.*
—**Syn. 2.** fawning. See **servile. 3.** attendant, flunky, underling, hireling, lackey. —**Ant. 2.** proud, dignified.

Mé·nière's′ syn′drome (mān yârz′), *Pathol.* a disease of the labyrinth of the ear, characterized by deafness, ringing in the ears, dizziness, nausea, and vomiting. Also called **Ménière's′ disease′.** [named after Prosper *Ménière* (1799–1862), French physician]

me·nin·ges (mi nin′jēz), *n.pl., sing.* **me·ninx** (mē′ningks). *Anat.* the three membranes investing the brain and spinal cord. Cf. **arachnoid** (def. 6), **dura mater, pia mater.** [< NL < Gk, pl. of *mēninx* membrane] —**me·nin·ge·al** (mi nin′jē əl), *adj.*

men·in·gi·tis (men′in jī′tis), *n.* *Pathol.* inflammation of the meninges, esp. of the pia mater and arachnoid. [< NL; see MENINGES, -ITIS] —**men·in·git·ic** (men′in jit′ik), *adj.*

me·nin·go·coc·cus (mə ning′gō kok′əs), *n., pl.* **-coc·ci** (-kok′sī). *Bacteriol.* a reniform or spherical bacterium, *Neisseria meningitidis*, that causes cerebrospinal meningitis. [< NL; see MENINGES, -O-, COCCUS] —**me·nin′go·coc′cal, me·nin·go·coc·cic** (mə ning′gō kok′ik, -kok′sik), *adj.*

Me·nip·pe (mə nip′ē), *n.* *Class. Myth.* a daughter of Orion who, with her sister Metioche, offered herself as a sacrifice to end a plague in Boeotia.

A B

Menisci (def. 3)
A, Concave, containing water;
B, Convex, containing mercury

me·nis·co·cy·to·sis (mə nis′kō-sī tō′sis), *n.* *Pathol.* See **sickle cell anemia.** [MENISC(US) + -O- + CYTOSIS]

me·nis·cus (mi nis′kəs), *n., pl.* **-nis·ci** (-nis′ī), **-nis·cus·es. 1.** a crescent or a crescent-shaped body. **2.** *Optics.* a lens with a crescent-shaped section; a concavo-convex or convexo-concave lens. See diag. under **lens. 3.** the convex or concave upper surface of a column of liquid, the curvature of which is caused by surface tension. **4.** *Anat.* a disk of cartilage between the articulating ends of the bones in a joint. [< NL < Gk *mēniskos* crescent, dim. of *mēnē* moon] —**me·nis·coid** (mi nis′koid), *adj.*

men·i·sper·ma·ceous (men′i spər mā′shəs), *adj.* belonging to the *Menispermaceae*, a family of chiefly woody, climbing plants. [< NL *Menisperm(um)* the typical genus, moonseed (< Gk *mēnē* moon + *spérma* seed) + -ACEOUS]

Men·ku·re (men kōō′re), *n.* Mycerinus.

Men′lo Park′ (men′lō), **1.** a city in W California, near San Francisco. 26,957 (1960). **2.** a village in central New Jersey, SE of Plainfield: site of Thomas Edison's laboratory, 1876–87.

Men·ning·er (men′ing ər), *n.* **Karl Augustus,** born 1893, and his brother **William Claire,** 1899–1966, U.S. psychiatrists.

Men·non·ite (men′ə nīt′), *n.* a member of an evangelical Protestant sect, originating in Europe in the 16th century, that opposes infant baptism, practices baptism of believers only, restricts marriage to members of the denomination, and is noted for simplicity of living and plain dress. [< G *Mennonit;* named after *Menno* Simons (1492–1559), Frisian religious leader; see -ITE¹] —**Men′no·nit′ism,** *n.*

me·no (mā′nō; *It.* me′nô), *adv.* *Music.* less. [< It < L *minus* less]

meno-, a learned borrowing from Greek, where it meant "month," used with reference to menstruation in the formation of compound words: *menopause.* [< Gk *mēno-*, comb. form of *mēn* month]

Me·nod·i·ce (mə nod′i sē′), *n.* *Class. Myth.* a nymph who was the mother, by Thiodamas, of Hylas.

Me·noe·ce·us (mə nē′sē əs, -sōōs), *n.* *Class. Myth.* **1.** a descendant of the Sparti and the father of Jocasta and Creon who sacrificed himself to end a plague in Thebes. **2.** the son of Creon of Thebes who took his own life because of the prophecy that the Seven against Thebes would fail only if a descendant of the Sparti sacrificed himself.

Me·noe·tes (mə nē′tēz), *n.* *Class. Myth.* a cowherd who tended the cattle of Hades on Erythea.

Me·noe·ti·us (mə nē′shē əs), *n.* *Class. Myth.* **1.** a Titan, the brother of Prometheus, Epimetheus, and Atlas. **2.** one of the Argonauts and the father of Patroclus.

me·nol·o·gy (mi nol′ə jē), *n., pl.* **-gies. 1.** a calendar of the months. **2.** a record or account, as of saints, arranged in the order of a calendar. [< NL *mēnologi(um)* < LGk *mēnológion.* See MENO-, -LOGY]

Me·nom′i·nee white′fish (mə nom′ə nē). See **round whitefish.**

Me·nom′o·nee Falls′ (mə nom′ə nē), a city in SE Wisconsin, NW of Milwaukee. 18,276 (1960).

Me·nom·o·nie (mə nom′ə nē), *n.* a town in W Wisconsin. 8624 (1960).

me·no mos·so (mā′nō mô′sō; *It.* me′nô môs′sô), *adj., adv.* *Music.* less rapidly; slower. [< It]

men·o·pause (men′ə pôz′), *n.* *Physiol.* the period of permanent cessation of menstruation, usually occurring between the ages of 45 and 50. [< F *ménopause.* See MENO-, PAUSE] —**men′o·pau′sic, men′o·pau′sal,** *adj.*

men·o·pha·ni·a (men′ə fā′nē ə), *n.* *Med.* the first show of menstruation at puberty. [MENO- + *-phania* appearance, equiv. to Gk *phaín(ein)* (to) appear + -IA]

me·nor·ah (mə nōr′ə, -nôr′ə), *n.* **1.** a candelabrum having nine branches, for use on the Jewish festival of Hanukkah. **2.** a candelabrum having seven branches (as used in the Biblical tabernacle or the Temple in Jerusalem), or any number of branches (as used in modern synagogues). [< Heb: lit., lampstand]

Menorah

Me·nor·ca (me nôr′kä), *n.* Spanish name of **Minorca.**

men·or·rha·gi·a (men′ə rā′jē ə, -jə), *n.* *Pathol.* excessive menstrual discharge. [MENO- + -RRHAGIA] —**men·or·rhag·ic** (men′ə raj′ik), *adj.*

me·nos·che·sis (mə nos′ki sis, men′ə skē′sis), *n.* *Pathol.* suppression of menstruation. [MENO- + Gk *schésis* state, condition]

men·o·stax·is (men′ə stak′sis), *n.* *Pathol.* an abnormally prolonged period of menstruation. [MENO- + Gk *stáxis* dropping, dripping (of blood)]

Me·not·ti (mə not′ē; *It.* me nôt′tē), *n.* **Gian Car·lo** (jän kär′lō; *It.* jän kär′lô), born 1911, U.S. composer, born in Italy.

men·sa (men′sə), *n., pl.* **-sas, -sae** (-sē) for 1, *gen.* **-sae** for 2. **1.** Also called **altar slab, altar stone.** the flat stone forming the top of the altar in a Roman Catholic church. **2.** (*cap.*) *Astron.* the Table, a southern constellation near Octans. [< L: table]

men·sal¹ (men′səl), *adj.* monthly. [< L *mens(is)* month + -AL¹]

men·sal² (men′səl), *adj.* **1.** of, pertaining to, or used at the table. **2.** *Rom. Cath. Ch.* (of a benefice, church, etc.) set aside for the maintenance of a priest or bishop, esp. for his board. [< L *mensāl(is)* of, pertaining to a table. See MENSA, -AL¹]

mense (mens), *n., v.,* **mensed, mens·ing.** *Brit. Dial.* —*n.* **1.** propriety; discretion. —*v.t.* **2.** to adorn; bring honor to; grace. [var. (north) of *mensk*, ME *menske* courtesy, honor < Scand; cf. Icel *menska* humanity, c. OE *mennisc*u, lit., the human state; akin to G *Mensch.* See MAN¹, -ISH¹] —**mense′ful,** *adj.* —**mense′less,** *adj.*

men·ser·vants (men′sûr′vənts), *n.* pl. of **manservant.**

men·ses (men′sēz), *n.* (*construed as sing. or pl.*) *Physiol.* the periodic flow of blood and mucosal tissue from the uterus. [< L, pl. of *mensis* month]

Men·she·vik (men′shə vik; *Russ.* men′she vēk′), *n., pl.* **-viks, -vik·i** (-vik′ē, -vē′kē; *Russ.* -vi kē′). (in Russia) a member of the Social Democratic party in opposition to the Bolsheviks and advocating gradual development of full socialism through parliamentary government and cooperation with bourgeois parties: absorbed into the Communist party formed in 1918. Also, **men′she·vik.** [< Russ: minority, equiv. to *men′she* less + *-vik* n. suffix] —**Men·she·vism, men·she·vism** (men′shə viz′əm), *n.* —**Men′she·vist, men′she·vist,** *adj.*

men's′ room′, a public lavatory for men. Also called **men's′ lounge′, gentleman's lounge, gentleman's room.**

mens sa·na in cor·po·re sa·no (mens sä′nä in kôr′pō re′ sä′nō; *Eng.* menz sā′nō in kôr′pə rē′ sā′nō), *Latin.* a sound mind in a sound body.

men·stru·al (men′strōō əl, -strəl), *adj.* **1.** of or pertaining to menstruation or to the menses. **2.** monthly. [ME *menstruall* < L *mēnstruāl(is)* having monthly courses, equiv. to *mēnstru(a)* monthly courses (n. use of neut. pl. of *mēnstruus* monthly) + *-ālis* -AL[1]

men·stru·ate (men′stro͞o āt′), *v.i.*, **-at·ed, -at·ing.** to undergo menstruation. [v. use of ME *menstruate* menstruous < LL *mēnstruāt(us)*, equiv. to *mēnstru(a)* monthly courses (see MENSTRUAL) + *-ātus* -ATE[1]]

men·stru·a·tion (men′stro͞o ā′shən), *n.* **1.** the act of periodically discharging blood and mucosal tissue from the uterus, occurring approximately monthly from puberty to menopause. **2.** the period of menstruating. [MENSTRUATE + -ION]

men·stru·ous (men′stro͞o əs), *adj.* pertaining to menstruation. [< L *mēnstruus* monthly; see -OUS]

men·stru·um (men′stro͞o əm), *n., pl.* **-stru·ums, -stru·a** (-stro͞o ə). a solvent. [special use of ME *menstruum* monthly period < ML (in L only pl. *mēnstrua* occurs). See MENSTRUAL]

men·sur·a·ble (men′shər ə bəl), *adj.* measurable. [< LL *mēnsūrābil(is)*, equiv. to *mēnsūrā(re)* (to) MEASURE + *-bilis* -BLE] —**men′sur·a·bil′i·ty,** *n.*

men·su·ral (men′shər əl), *adj.* pertaining to measure. [< LL *mēnsūrāl(is)*, equiv. to L *mēnsur(a)* MEASURE + *-ālis* -AL[1]]

men′sural mu′sic, polyphonic music of the 13th century in which each note has a strictly determined value.

men′sural nota′tion, a system of musical notation of the 13th to the late 16th centuries, marked by the use of note symbols such as the longa and brevis, the absence of bar lines and ties, and the equivalence in value of one note to either two or three of the next smaller degree.

men·su·ra·tion (men′shə rā′shən), *n.* **1.** the branch of geometry that deals with the measurement of length, area, or volume. **2.** act or process of measuring. [< LL *mēnsūrātiōn-* (s. of *mēnsūrātiō*) a measuring. See MEASURE, -ATION] —**men′su·ra′tion·al,** *adj.*

men·su·ra·tive (men′shə rā′tiv, -shər ə tiv), *adj.* adapted for or concerned with measuring. [MENSURAT(ION) + -IVE]

-ment, a suffix of nouns, often concrete, denoting an action or resulting state (*abridgment; refreshment*), a product (*fragment*), or means (*ornament*). [< F < L *-ment(um)*, suffix forming nouns, usually from verbs]

men·tal[1] (men′tᵊl), *adj.* **1.** of or pertaining to the mind: *a mental weakness; a mental state.* **2.** characterized by a disorder of the mind: *mental patient; mental illness.* **3.** providing care for persons with disordered minds, emotions, etc.: *mental hospital.* **4.** performed by or existing in the mind: *mental arithmetic.* **5.** pertaining to intellectuals. **6.** *Informal.* slightly daft; out of one's mind: *The way she behaves you'd think she was mental.* [late ME < LL *mentāl(is)*, equiv. to L *ment-* (s. of *mēns*) mind + *-ālis* -AL[1]]

men·tal[2] (men′tᵊl), *adj.* of or pertaining to the chin. [< L *ment(um)* the chin + -AL[1]]

men′tal age′, *Psychol.* the level of native mental ability or capacity of an individual, usually as determined by an intelligence test, in relation to the chronological age of the average individual at this level: *a ten-year-old child with the mental age of a twelve-year-old; a mental age of 12.* Cf. **achievement age.**

men′tal defi′ciency, *Psychol.* lack of some mental power or powers associated with normal intellectual development, resulting in an inability of the individual to function fully or adequately in everyday life; feeblemindedness. Mental deficiency includes all types of idiocy, imbecility, and moronism.

men′tal disease′, any of the various forms of insanity or severe neurosis. Also called **men′tal disor′der, men′tal ill′ness.**

men′tal dynam′ics. See under **metapsychology** (def. 2).

men′tal econ′omy. See under **metapsychology** (def. 2).

men′tal heal′ing, the healing of a physical ailment or disorder by mental concentration or suggestion. —**men′tal heal′er.**

men·tal·ism (men′tᵊliz′əm), *n.* the doctrine that objects of knowledge have no existence except in the mind of the perceiver. [MENTAL[1] + -ISM] —**men′tal·is′tic,** *adj.* —**men′tal·is′ti·cal·ly,** *adv.*

men·tal·ist (men′tᵊlist), *n.* **1.** a person who believes in or advocates mentalism. **2.** a mind reader. [MENTAL[1] + -IST]

men·tal·i·ty (men tal′i tē), *n., pl.* **-ties.** mental capacity or endowment; intellectual character; mind: *She was of average mentality.* [MENTAL[1] + -ITY]

men·tal·ly (men′tᵊlē), *adv.* **1.** in or with the mind or intellect; intellectually. **2.** with regard to the mind. [MENTAL[1] + -LY]

men′tal retarda′tion. See **mental deficiency.**

men′tal topog′raphy. See under **metapsychology** (def. 2).

Men·tes (men′tēz), *n.* (in the *Odyssey*) a captain of the Taphians. Athena assumed his form when she urged Telemachus to search for Odysseus.

men·tha·ceous (men thā′shəs), *adj.* belonging to the *Menthaceae* (usually included in the *Labiatae*) or mint family of plants, comprising the horsemint, peppermint, pennyroyal, savory, etc. [< L *menth(a)* MINT[1] + -ACEOUS]

Men·the (men′thē), *n.* Minthe.

men·thene (men′thēn), *n.* *Chem.* **1.** any of several isomeric, monocyclic terpenes having the formula $C_{10}H_{18}$. **2.** a colorless, liquid terpene, $C_{10}H_{18}$, found in certain essential oils and prepared from menthol. [< NL *Menth(a)* (see MINT[1]) + -ENE]

men·thol (men′thōl, -thôl, -thol), *n.* *Chem., Pharm.* a colorless, crystalline, slightly water-soluble alcohol, $CH_3C_6H_9(C_3H_7)OH$, obtained from peppermint oil or synthesized: used chiefly in perfumes, confections, liqueurs, and in medicine for colds and nasal disorders because of its cooling effect on mucous membranes. Also called **hexahydrothymol, peppermint camphor.** [< NL *Menth(a)* (see MINT[1]) + -OL[1]]

men·tho·lat·ed (men′thə lā′tid), *adj.* **1.** covered or treated with menthol. **2.** saturated with or containing menthol. [MENTHOL + -ATE[1] + -ED[3]]

men·ti·cide (men′ti sīd′), *n.* the systematic effort to undermine and destroy a person's values and beliefs, as by the use of prolonged interrogation, drugs, torture, etc., and to induce radically different ideas. [< L *ment-* (s. of *mēns*) mind + -I- + -CIDE]

men·tion (men′shən), *v.t.* **1.** to refer briefly to; refer to by name incidentally; name, specify, or speak of. **2.** to cite formally for a meritorious act or achievement: *He was mentioned in the newspapers for his contributions to the community.* **3. not to mention,** in addition to; without mentioning: *We were served a sumptuous entree, not to mention the other courses.* —*n.* **4.** a direct or incidental reference; a mentioning: *to make mention of a place.* **5.** formal recognition for a meritorious act or achievement: *His entry in the science competition won him an honorable mention.* [< L *mentiōn-* (s. of *mentiō*) a calling to mind, a touching upon (see MENTAL[1], -ION); r. ME *mencioun* < AF] —**men′tion·a·ble,** *adj.* —**men′tion·er,** *n.*
—**Syn. 1.** indicate, allude to. **4.** allusion, notice.

Men·ton (men tōn′; *Fr.* mäɴ tôɴ′), *n.* a city in SE France, on the Mediterranean: winter resort. 20,069 (1962). Italian, **Men·to·ne** (men tô′ne).

men·ton·nière (men′tən yâr′; *Fr.* mäɴ tô nyeʀ′), *n., pl.* **-ton·nières** (-tən yârz′; *Fr.* -tô nyeʀ′). *Armor.* any of various plate pieces for protecting the lower part of the face, as a beaver. [< F, equiv. to *menton* chin + *-ière*; see -ARY]

Men·tor (men′tər), *n.* **1.** (in the *Odyssey*) a loyal adviser of Odysseus entrusted with the care and education of Telemachus. **2.** (*l.c.*) a wise and trusted counselor. —**men′tor·ship′,** *n.*

Men·tor (men′tər), *n.* a town in NE Ohio. 4354 (1960).

Men·tor-on-the-Lake-Vil·lage (men′tər on thə lāk′vil′ij), *n.* a town in NE Ohio. 3290 (1960).

men·u (men′yo͞o, mā′nyo͞o), *n.* **1.** a list of the dishes that can or will be served at a meal; bill of fare. **2.** the dishes served. [< F: detailed list, n. use of *menu* small, detailed < L *minūt(us)* MINUTE[2]]

Me·nu·hin (men′yo͞o in), *n.* **Ye·hu·di** (yə ho͞o′dē), born 1916, U.S. violinist.

me·nui·se·rie (mə nwēzᵊ ʀē′), *n., pl.* **-ries** (-ʀē′). *French.* the work or craft of a *menuisier.*

me·nui·sier (mə nwē zyā′), *n., pl.* **-siers** (-zyā′). *French.* a person who makes furniture and joinery from solid wood.

me·nu·ki (me no͞o′kē), *n.pl.* a pair of ornaments on the sides of the hilt of a Japanese sword or knife. [< Jap, equiv. to *me* eye, hole + *nuki* piercer]

men·yie (men′yē), *n.* *Scot. Archaic.* meiny (def. 1).

Men·zies (men′zēz), *n.* **Robert Gordon,** born 1894, Australian statesman: prime minister 1939–41 and 1946–1966.

me·ow (mē ou′, myou), *n.* **1.** the sound a cat makes. —*v.i.* **2.** to make such a sound. Also, **miaow, miaou, miaul.** [imit.]

M.E.P., Master of Engineering Physics.

M.E.P.A., Master of Engineering and Public Administration.

me·per·i·dine (mə per′i dēn′, -din), *n.* *Pharm.* a narcotic compound, $C_2H_5OOCC(C_6H_5)CH_2CH_2N(CH_3)CH_2CH_2$, used in the form of its hydrochloride as an analgesic and sedative. [ME(THYL) + PI)PERIDINE]

Me·phib·o·sheth (mə fib′ə sheth′), *n.* a son of Jonathan, and the grandson of Saul. II Sam 4:4. Also, *Douay Bible,* **Miphiboseth.**

Meph·i·stoph·e·les (mef′i stof′ə lēz′), *n.* *Medieval Demonology.* one of the seven chief devils. Also, **Me·phis·to** (mə fis′tō). —**Meph·is·to·phe·li·an, Meph·is·to·phe·le·an** (mef′i stō fē′lē ən), *adj.*

me·phit·ic (mə fit′ik), *adj.* **1.** offensive to the smell. **2.** noxious; pestilential; poisonous. [< LL *mephītic(us)*. See MEPHITIS, -IC] —**me·phit′i·cal·ly,** *adv.*

me·phi·tis (mə fī′tis), *n.* **1.** a noxious or pestilential exhalation from the earth, as poison gas. **2.** any noisome or poisonous stench. **3.** (*cap.*) Mefitis. [< L < Oscan *mefītis*]

me·pro·ba·mate (mə prō′bə māt′, mep′rō bam′āt), *n.* *Pharm.* a white powder, $CH_3(C_3H_7)C(CH_2OOCNH_2)_2$, used in medicine chiefly as a tranquilizer for treating anxiety, tension, and skeletal muscle spasm. [ME(THYL) + PRO(PYL + CAR)BAMATE]

meq., milliequivalent.

Meq·uon (mek′won), *n.* a town in E Wisconsin. 8543 (1960).

-mer, *Chem.* a combining form denoting a member of a particular group: *isomer.* Cf. **-mere, -merous.** [comb. form repr. Gk *méros* part, portion]

mer., **1.** meridian. **2.** meridional.

mer·bro·min (mər brō′min), *n.* *Pharm.* an iridescent green, water-soluble powder, $C_{20}H_8Br_2HgNa_2O_6$, that forms a red solution when dissolved in water: used as an antiseptic and as a germicide. [MER(CURIC) + BROM(O) + -IN[2]]

merc., **1.** mercantile. **2.** mercurial. **3.** mercury.

Mer·ca (mer′kä), *n.* a city in S Somalia. 59,300 (1956).

mer·can·tile (mûr′kən tēl′, -tīl′, -til), *adj.* **1.** of or pertaining to merchants or trade; commercial. **2.** engaged in trade or commerce: *a mercantile nation.* **3.** *Econ.* of or pertaining to the mercantile system. [< F < It: pertaining to merchants, equiv. to *mercant(e)* merchant (< L *mercant-,* s. of *mercāns* buyer, n. use of prp. of *mercārī* to buy) + *-ile* -ILE]
—**Syn. 1.** See **commercial.**

mer′cantile a′gency, *Rare.* See **commercial agency.**

mer′cantile pa′per, *Rare.* See **commercial paper.**

mer′cantile sys′tem, *Econ.* a system of political and economic policy, evolving with the modern national state and seeking to secure a nation's political and economic supremacy in its rivalry with other states. According to this system, money was regarded as a store of wealth, and the goal of a state was the accumulation of precious metals, by exporting the largest possible quantity of its products and importing as little as possible, thus establishing a favorable balance of trade.

mer·can·til·ism (mûr′kən ti liz′əm, -tē-, -tī-), *n.* **1.** the mercantile spirit. **2.** See **mercantile system.** [< F *mercantilisme.* See MERCANTILE, -ISM] —**mer′can·til·ist,** *n., adj.*

mer·cap·tan (mər kap′tan), *n.* *Chem.* **1.** any of a class of sulfur-containing compounds having the type formula RSH, in which R represents a radical, and having an extremely offensive, garlicklike odor. **2.** Also called **ethanethiol, ethyl mercaptan, thioethyl alcohol.** a colorless, slightly water-soluble, flammable liquid, CH_3CH_2SH, having a characteristic penetrating odor. [< L, short for phrase *corpus mercurium captāns* a body capturing quicksilver]

mer·cap·tide (mər kap′tīd), *n.* *Chem.* a metallic salt of a mercaptan. [MERCAPT(AN) + -IDE]

mer·cap·to (mər kap′tō), *adj.* *Chem.* containing the mercapto group; sulfhydryl; thiol. [MERCAPT(AN) + -O-]

mercap′to group′, *Chem.* the univalent group, –SH. Also called **mercap′to rad′ical.**

mer·cap·to·pu·rine (mər kap′tō pyo͝or′ēn), *n.* *Pharm.* a yellow, crystalline, water-insoluble powder, $C_5H_4N_4S$, used in the treatment of leukemia; 6-mercaptopurine. [MERCAPTO + PURINE]

Mer·cast (mûr′kast′, -käst′), *n.* a broadcasting system used by U.S. agencies to deliver messages to government-operated vessels. [? *Mer(chant Marine broad)cast*]

Mer·ca·tor (mər kā′tər; *for 1 also Flem.* mɛʀ kä′tôʀ), *n.* **1. Ger·har·dus** (jər här′dəs), (*Gerhard Kremer*), 1512–94, Flemish cartographer and geographer. **2.** a walled plain in the third quadrant of the face of the moon: about 28 miles in diameter. —*adj.* **3.** noting, pertaining to, or according to the principles of a Mercator projection: *a Mercator chart.*

Merca′tor projec′tion, *Cartog.* a conformal projection on which any rhumb line is represented as a straight line, used chiefly in navigation, though the scale varies notably with latitude and areal size, and the shapes of large areas are greatly distorted. Also, **Merca′tor's projec′tion.**

Merca′tor sail′ing, *Navig.* sailing according to rhumb lines, which appear as straight lines on a Mercator chart.

Merca′tor track′, *Navig.* a line appearing straight on a Mercator chart; rhumb line.

Mer·ced (mər sed′), *n.* a city in central California. 20,068 (1960).

Mer·ce·des (mər sā′dēz, -sē′-, mûr′si dēz′; *Sp.* meʀ the′des, -se′-), *n.* a girl's given name.

mer·ce·nar·y (mûr′sə ner′ē), *adj., n., pl.* **-nar·ies.** —*adj.* **1.** working or acting merely for money or other reward; venal. **2.** hired: now only of soldiers serving in a foreign army. —*n.* **3.** a professional soldier serving in a foreign army. **4.** any hireling. [ME *mercenarie* < L *mercēnāri(us)* hireling (n.), hired, paid (adj.), equiv. to *mercēd-* (s. of *mercēs* wages, akin to *merx* goods) + *-ārius* -ARY] —**mer·ce·nar·i·ly** (mûr′sə nâr′ə lē, mûr′sə ner′-), *adv.* —**mer′ce·nar′i·ness,** *n.*
—**Syn. 1.** grasping; acquisitive, avaricious, covetous.
—**Ant. 1.** generous.

mer·cer (mûr′sər), *n.* *Chiefly Brit.* a dealer in textile fabrics. [early ME < AF; OF *mercier* merchant, equiv. to *merci-* (< L, s. of *merx* goods) + *-er* -ER[2]]

Mer·cer (mûr′sər), *n.* a town in W Pennsylvania. 2800 (1960).

mer·cer·ize (mûr′sə rīz′), *v.t.,* **-ized, -iz·ing.** to treat (cotton yarns or fabric) with caustic alkali under tension, in order to increase its strength, luster, and affinity for dye. [named after John *Mercer* (1791–1866), English calico printer, the patentee (1850) of the process; see -IZE] —**mer′cer·i·za′tion,** *n.* —**mer′cer·iz′er,** *n.*

mer·cer·y (mûr′sə rē), *n., pl.* **-cer·ies.** *Brit.* **1.** a mercer's shop. **2.** mercers' wares. [ME *mercerie* < OF. See MERCER, -Y[3]]

mer·chan·dise (*n.* mûr′chən dīz′, -dīs′; *v.* mûr′chən dīz′), *n., v.,* **-dised, -dis·ing.** —*n.* **1.** goods, esp. manufactured goods; commodities. **2.** the manufactured goods bought and sold in any business. **3.** the stock of goods in a store. —*v.i.* **4.** to carry on trade. —*v.t.* **5.** to buy and sell; deal in; trade. **6.** to plan for and promote the sales of. [ME *marchandise* < OF. See MERCHANT, -ICE] —**mer′chan·dis′er,** *n.*

mer·chan·dis·ing (mûr′chən dī′zing), *n.* the planning and promotion of sales by presenting a product to the right market at the proper time, by carrying out organized, skillful advertising, using attractive displays, etc. Also called **mer′chandise plan′ning.** [ME; see MERCHANDISE, -ING[1]]

mer·chan·dize (*n.* mûr′chən dīz′, -dīs′; *v.* mûr′chən dīz′), *n., v.i., v.t.,* **-dized, -diz·ing.** merchandise. —**mer′chan·diz′er,** *n.*

mer·chant (mûr′chənt), *n.* **1.** a person who buys and sells commodities for profit; dealer; trader. **2.** a storekeeper; retailer. **3.** *Chiefly Brit.* a wholesaler. —*adj.* **4.** pertaining to or used for trade or commerce: *a merchant ship.* **5.** pertaining to the merchant marine. [ME *marchant* < OF *marcheant* < LL **mercātant-* (s. of *mercātāns*), prp. of **mercātāre,* freq. of L *mercārī* to trade, deriv. of *merx* goods] —**mer′chant·like′,** *adj.*

mer·chant·a·ble (mûr′chən tə bəl), *adj.* marketable: *merchantable war-surplus goods.* [ME *marchandabull.* See MERCHANT, -ABLE] —**mer′chant·a·ble·ness,** *n.*

mer′chant bank′, *Brit. Finance.* a private banking firm engaged chiefly in accepting bills of exchange in foreign trade and investing in new issues of securities.

mer′chant guild′, a medieval guild composed of merchants.

mer·chant·man (mûr′chənt mən), *n., pl.* **-men.** a trading vessel. [ME *marchandman.* See MERCHANT, MAN[1]]

mer′chant marine′, **1.** the vessels of a nation that are engaged in commerce. **2.** the officers and crews of such vessels.

Mer′chant of Ven′ice, The, a comedy (1596?) by Shakespeare.

mer′chant prince′, a very wealthy or influential merchant.

Mer·chant·ville (mûr′chənt vil′), *n.* a town in SW New Jersey. 4075 (1960).

mer·ci (mɛʀ sē′), *interj.* *French.* thank you.

Mer·ci·a (mûr′shē ə, -shə), *n.* **1.** an early English kingdom in central Britain. **2.** a girl's given name.

mer·ci beau·coup (mɛʀ sē′ bō ko͞o′), *French.* thank you very much.

Mer·cier (*Fr.* mɛʀ syā′), *n.* **Dé·si·ré Jo·seph** (dā zē ʀā′ zhō zef′), 1851–1926, Belgian cardinal and patriot.

mer·ci·ful (mûr′si fəl), *adj.* full of mercy; characterized by or exercising mercy; compassionate: *a merciful God.* [ME; see MERCY, -FUL] —**mer′ci·ful·ly,** *adv.* —**mer′ci·ful·ness,** *n.*
—**Syn.** kind, clement, lenient, forgiving, benignant, tender, sympathetic. —**Ant.** cruel, relentless.

mer·ci·less (mûr′si lis), *adj.* without mercy; pitiless: *a merciless king.* [ME *mercyles.* See MERCY, -LESS] —**mer′ci·less·ly,** *adv.* —**mer′ci·less·ness,** *n.*
—**Syn.** cruel, hard, relentless, unrelenting, fell, unsympathetic, inexorable. —**Ant.** compassionate.

mercur-, a combining form of **mercury:** *mercuric.* Also, **mercuro-.**

mer·cu·rate (mûr′kyə rāt′), *n., v.,* **-rat·ed, -rat·ing.** *Chem.* —*n.* **1.** Also, **mercuriate.** any salt in which bivalent mercury is part of a complex anion. —*v.t.* **2.** to introduce mercury into (an organic compound); treat with mercury. [MERCUR- + -ATE²] —**mer′cu·ra′tion,** *n.*

mer·cu·ri·al (mər kyŏŏr′ē əl), *adj.* **1.** pertaining to, containing, or caused by the metal mercury. **2.** (*cap.*) of or pertaining to the god Mercury. **3.** (*cap.*) of or pertaining to the planet Mercury. **4.** active; lively; sprightly; volatile: *The guests enjoyed his mercurial gaiety.* **5.** changeable; fickle; flighty; erratic: *a mercurial nature.* —*n.* **6.** *Pharm.* a preparation of mercury used as a drug. [< L *mercuriāl(is)* of, pertaining to the god or planet Mercury. See MERCURY, -AL¹] —**mer·cu′ri·al·ness, mer·cu′ri·al′i·ty,** *n.*
—**Syn. 4.** spirited. **5.** inconstant, indecisive. —**Ant. 4.** phlegmatic. **5.** constant, steady.

mercu′rial barom′eter. See **mercury barometer.**

mer·cu·ri·al·ise (mər kyŏŏr′ē ə līz′), *v.t.,* **-ised, -is·ing.** *Chiefly Brit.* mercurialize. —**mer·cu′ri·al·i·sa′tion,** *n.*

mer·cu·ri·al·ism (mər kyŏŏr′ē ə liz′əm), *n.* *Pathol.* poisoning by mercury. [MERCURIAL + -ISM]

mer·cu·ri·al·ize (mər kyŏŏr′ē ə līz′), *v.t.,* **-ized, -iz·ing. 1.** to make mercurial, esp. in temperament: *The bright lights and music mercurialized her spirits.* **2.** to treat or impregnate with mercury or one of its compounds. Also, *esp. Brit.,* **mercurialise.** [MERCURIAL + -IZE] —**mer·cu′ri·al·i·za′tion,** *n.*

mer·cu·ri·ate (mər kyŏŏr′ē it, -āt′), *n.* *Chem.* mercurate (def. 1).

mer·cu·ric (mər kyŏŏr′ik), *adj.* *Chem.* of or containing mercury, esp. in the bivalent state. [MERCUR- + -IC]

mercu′ric chlo′ride, *Chem.* a white, crystalline, water-soluble, strongly acrid, highly poisonous solid, $HgCl_2$, prepared by sublimation of chlorine with mercury, and used chiefly as an antiseptic. Also called **mercury bichloride, corrosive mercury chloride, corrosive sublimate.**

mercu′ric ox′ide, *Chem.* a slightly crystalline, water-soluble, poisonous compound, HgO, occurring as a coarse, orange-red powder (**red mercuric oxide**) or as a fine, orange-yellow powder (**yellow mercuric oxide**): used chiefly as a pigment in paints and as an antiseptic in pharmaceuticals.

mercu′ric sub·sul′fate (sub sul′fāt), *Chem.* a lemon-yellow, water-insoluble, poisonous powder, $Hg(HgO)_2SO_4$, used chiefly in medicine. Also called **turpeth, turpeth mineral.**

mercu′ric sul′fide, *Chem.* a crystalline, water-insoluble, poisonous compound, HgS, occurring as a coarse, black powder (**black mercuric sulfide**) or as a fine, bright-scarlet powder (**red mercuric sulfide**): used chiefly as a pigment and a source of the free metal. Also, **mercury sulfide.**

mer·cu·ri·fy (mər kyŏŏr′ə fī′), *v.t.,* **-fied, -fy·ing.** to mix with mercury; amalgamate. [MERCUR- + -IFY]

Mer·cu·ri·us (mər kyŏŏr′ē əs), *n.* a walled plain in the first quadrant of the face of the moon: about 25 miles in diameter.

mer·cu·rize (mûr′kyə rīz′), *v.t.,* **-rized, -riz·ing.** mercurate (def. 2). [MERCUR- + -IZE] —**mer′cu·ri·za′tion,** *n.*

mercuro-, var. of **mercur-:** *Mercurochrome.*

Mer·cu·ro·chrome (mər kyŏŏr′ə krōm′), *n.* *Pharm., Trademark.* merbromin.

mer·cu·rous (mər kyŏŏr′əs, mûr′kyər əs), *adj.* *Chem.* containing univalent mercury, Hg^{+1} or Hg_2^{+2}. [MERCUR- + -OUS]

mercu′rous chlo′ride, *Pharm.* calomel.

mer·cu·ry (mûr′kyə rē), *n., pl.* **-ries. 1.** *Chem.* a heavy, silver-white, metallic element, noted for its fluidity at ordinary temperatures: used in barometers, thermometers, pesticides, pharmaceutical preparations, reflecting surfaces of mirrors, dental fillings, in certain switches, lamps, and other electric apparatus, and as a laboratory catalyst; quicksilver. *Symbol:* Hg; *at. wt.:* 200.59; *at. no.:* 80; *sp. gr.:* 13.546 at 20°C; *freezing point:* −38.9°C; *boiling point:* 357°C. **2.** *Pharm.* this metal, used in medicine, in the form of various organic and inorganic compounds, usually for skin infections. **3.** (*cap.*) the ancient Roman god who served as messenger of the gods and was also the god of commerce, thievery, eloquence, and science, identified with the Greek god Hermes. **4.** (*cap.*) *Astron.* the planet nearest the sun, having a diameter of 3000 miles, a mean distance from the sun of 36,000,000 miles, a period of revolution of 88 days, and having no satellites: it is the smallest planet in the solar system. **5.** a messenger; carrier of news. **6.** any euphorbiaceous herb of the genus *Mercurialis,* esp. the poisonous, weedy *M. perennis.* **7.** Good-King-Henry. **8.** (*cap.*) *U.S.* a one-man spacecraft launched by an Atlas booster and weighing approximately 4000 pounds. Cf. **Project Mercury.** [ME *Mercurie* < ML, L *Mercurius,* akin to *merx* goods]

Mercury

mer′cury arc′, *Elect.* a bluish-green electric arc that has passed through a mercury vapor cathode.

mer′cury barom′eter, a barometer in which the weight of a column of mercury in a glass tube with a sealed top is balanced against that of the atmosphere pressing on an exposed cistern of mercury at the base of the mercury column, the height of the column varying with atmospheric pressure. Also called **mercurial barometer.** Cf. **aneroid barometer.**

mer′cury bichlo′ride, *Chem.* See **mercuric chloride.**

mer′cury chlo′ride, 1. *Chem.* See **mercuric chloride. 2.** calomel.

mer′cury dichlo′ride, *Chem.* See **mercuric chloride.**

mer′cury ful′minate, *Chem.* a gray, crystalline solid, $Hg(CNO)_2$, used chiefly in the manufacture of commercial and military detonators.

mer′cury mass′, *Pharm.* **1.** See **blue mass** (def. 1). **2.** See **blue pill** (def. 1).

mer′cury perchlo′ride, *Chem.* See **mercuric chloride.**

mer′cury sul′fide, *Chem.* See **mercuric sulfide.**

mer′cu·ry-va′por lamp′ (mûr′kyə rē vā′pər), *Elect.* a lamp producing a light with a high actinic and ultraviolet content by means of an electric arc in mercury vapor.

mer·cy (mûr′sē), *n., pl.* **-cies** for 4, 5. **1.** compassionate or kindly forbearance shown toward an offender, an enemy, or other person in one's power; compassion, pity, or benevolence: *Have mercy on the poor sinner.* **2.** the disposition to be merciful: *an adversary wholly without mercy.* **3.** the discretionary power of a judge to pardon or to mitigate punishment, esp. to send to prison rather than invoke the death penalty. **4.** an act of kindness, compassion, or favor: *She has performed countless small mercies for her friends and neighbors.* **5.** *Dial.* that which gives evidence of divine favor; blessing: *It was just a mercy we had our seat belts on when it happened.* **6. at the mercy of,** subject to; entirely in the power of: *They were at the mercy of their captors.* Also, **at one's mercy.** [ME *merci* < OF, earlier *mercit* < L *mercēd-* (s. of *mercēs*) wages, deriv. of *merx* goods]
—**Syn. 1.** forgiveness, indulgence, clemency, leniency, lenity, consideration, tenderness, mildness. —**Ant. 1.** cruelty.

Mer·cy (mûr′sē), *n.* a girl's given name.

mer′cy kill′ing, euthanasia (def. 1).

mer′cy seat′, *Bible.* **1.** the gold covering on the ark of the covenant, regarded as the resting place of God. Ex. 25:17–22. **2.** the throne of God.

mer′cy stroke′. See **coup de grace.**

mer·div·or·ous (mər div′ər əs), *adj.* coprophagous. [< L *merd(a)* dung + -I- + -VOROUS]

mere¹ (mēr), *adj., superl.* **mer·est. 1.** being nothing more nor better than what is specified: *He is still a mere child.* **2.** *Obs.* pure and unmixed, as of wine, a people, a language, etc. **3.** *Obs.* fully as much as what is specified; completely fulfilled or developed; absolute. [ME < L *mer(us)* pure, unmixed, mere]
—**Syn. 1.** MERE, BARE imply a scant sufficiency. They are often interchangeable, but MERE frequently means no more than (enough). BARE suggests scarcely as much as (enough). Thus *a mere livelihood* means enough to live on but no more; *a bare livelihood* means scarcely enough to live on. —**Ant. 1.** abundant.

mere² (mēr), *n.* **1.** *Chiefly Brit. Dial.* a lake or pond. **2.** *Obs.* any body of sea water. [ME, OE; c. G *Meer,* Icel *marr,* Goth *marei,* Ir *muir,* L *mare*]

mere³ (mēr), *n.* *Brit. Dial.* a boundary or boundary marker. Also, **mear.** [ME; OE *(ge)mǣre;* c. Icel *mæri;* akin to L *mūrus* wall, rim]

-mere, a learned borrowing from Greek meaning "part," used in the formation of compound words: *blastomere.* Cf. **-mer, -merous.** [comb. form repr. Gk *méros*]

Mer·e·dith (mer′i dith), *n.* **1. George,** 1828–1909, English novelist and poet. **2. Owen,** pen name of Edward Robert Bulwer Lytton. **3.** Also, **Mer′e·dyth.** a boy's or girl's given name.

mere·ly (mēr′lē), *adv.* **1.** only as specified, and nothing more; simply: *merely a matter of form.* **2.** *Obs.* without admixture; purely: *not mixedly but merely true and good.* **3.** *Obs.* altogether; entirely: *His love is merely mine.* [MERE¹ + -LY]

mer·en·gue (mə reng′gā; *Sp.* me reng′ge), *n., pl.* **-gues** (-gāz; *Sp.* -ges), *v.,* **-gued, -gu·ing.** —*n.* **1.** a ballroom dance of Dominican and Haitian origin, characterized by a stiff-legged, limping step. —*v.i.* **2.** to dance the merengue. Also, **méringue.** [< AmerSp]

me·rese (mā rēz′, -rēs′), *n.* (on a stemmed glass) a flat, sharp-edged knop joining the stem to the bowl or foot. Also called **collar.** [?]

mer·e·tri·cious (mer′i trish′əs), *adj.* **1.** alluring by a show of flashy or vulgar attractions; showily attractive; tawdry. **2.** based on pretense, deception, or insincerity. **3.** of, pertaining to, or characteristic of a prostitute. [< L *meretrīcius,* of, pertaining to harlots, equiv. to *meretrīci-* (s. of *meretrīx* harlot, lit., earner, equiv. to *mere-,* s. of *merēre* to earn, + *-trix* -TRIX) + *-us* -OUS] —**mer′e·tri′cious·ly,** *adv.* —**mer′e·tri′cious·ness,** *n.*
—**Syn. 1.** showy, gaudy. **2.** spurious, sham, false. —**Ant. 2.** genuine.

mer·gan·ser (mər gan′sər), *n., pl.* **-sers,** (*esp. collectively*) **-ser.** any of several fish-eating diving ducks of the subfamily *Merginae,* having a narrow bill hooked at the tip and serrated at the edges. [< NL, equiv. to L *merg(us)* diver, a kind of water-bird + *anser* goose]

merge (mûrj), *v.,* **merged, merg·ing.** —*v.t.* **1.** to cause to combine or coalesce; unite. **2.** to combine, blend, or unite gradually so as to blur the individuality of (often fol. by *in* or *into*): *They voted to merge the two branch offices into a single unit.* —*v.i.* **3.** to become combined, united, swallowed up, or absorbed; lose identity by uniting or blending (often fol. by *in* or *into*): *This stream merges into the river up ahead.* **4.** to combine or unite into a single enterprise, organization, body, etc.: *The two firms merged last year.* [< L *merge(re)* (to) dip, immerse, plunge into water] —**mer′gence,** *n.*
—**Syn. 1, 2, 3.** amalgamate, consolidate.

Mer·gen·tha·ler (mûr′gən thô′lər; *Ger.* mer′gən tä′lər), *n.* **Ott·mar** (ot′mär; *Ger.* ôt′mär), 1854–99, U.S. inventor of the Linotype, born in Germany.

merg·er (mûr′jər), *n.* **1.** a statutory combination of two or more corporations by the transfer of the properties to one surviving corporation. **2.** any combination of two or more business enterprises into a single enterprise. **3.** the act or an instance of merging. [MERGE + -ER¹]

Mer·gui (mûr gwē′), *n.* a seaport in S Burma, on the Andaman Sea. 33,697 (1953).

mer·i·carp (mer′ə kärp′), *n.* *Bot.* one of the carpels of a schizocarp. [*meri-* (comb. form of Gk *merís* part, portion) + -CARP]

mer·i·da (mer′i də), *n.* See **sun tan** (def. 2). [appar. after MÉRIDA, Mexico]

Mé·ri·da (me′rē thä′), *n.* **1.** a city in and the capital of Yucatán, in SE Mexico. 177,405 (1960). **2.** a city in W Venezuela. 34,143 (est. 1955).

Mer·i·den (mer′i dᵊn), *n.* a city in central Connecticut. 51,850 (1960).

me·rid·i·an (mə rid′ē ən), *n.* **1.** *Geog.* **a.** a great circle of the earth passing through the poles and any given point on the earth's surface. **b.** the half of such a circle included between the poles. **2.** *Astron.* the great circle of the celestial sphere which passes through its poles and the observer's zenith. **3.** a point or period of highest development, greatest prosperity, or the like. —*adj.* **4.** of or pertaining to a meridian. **5.** of or pertaining to midday or noon: *the meridian hour.* **6.** pertaining to a period of greatest prosperity, splendor, elevation, etc.; culminating. [ME < L *merīdiān(us)* of noon, equiv. to *merīdi(ēs)* midday (dissimilated var. of *medīdiēs,* orig. *medi-,* comb. form of *medius* MID¹ + *diēs* day) + *-ānus* -AN]

Me·rid·i·an (mə rid′ē ən), *n.* a city in E Mississippi. 49,374 (1960).

merid′ian an′gle, *Astron.* the angle measured eastward or westward through 180°, between the celestial meridian of an observer and the hour circle of a celestial body. Cf. **hour angle.**

merid′ian cir′cle, *Astron.* a transit instrument provided with a graduated vertical scale, used to measure the declinations of heavenly bodies and to determine the time of meridian transits. Also called **circle, transit circle, transit instrument.**

Mer·i·di·a·ni·i (mer′i dē ä′nē ē′), *n.* **Sinus.** See **Sinus Meridianii.**

mé·ri·di·enne (mə rid′ē en′, mə rid′ē en′; *Fr.* mā rē dyen′), *n., pl.* **mé·ri·di·ennes** (mə rid′ē enz′, mə rid′ē enz′; *Fr.* mā rē dyen′). *Fr. Furniture.* a short day bed of the Empire period, having ends of unequal height connected by a back with a sloping top. [< F, special use of fem. of *méridien* MERIDIAN (adj.)]

me·rid·i·o·nal (mə rid′ē ə nᵊl), *adj.* **1.** of, pertaining to, or resembling a meridian. **2.** characteristic of the south or people inhabiting the south, esp. of France. **3.** southern; southerly. —*n.* **4.** an inhabitant of the south, esp. the south of France. [ME < LL *merīdiōnā-l(is)* southern, an irreg. formation. See MERIDIAN, -AL¹] —**me·rid′i·o·nal·ly,** *adv.*

Mer·i·lee (mer′i lē′), *n.* a girl's given name. Also, **Marilee, Marylee.**

Mé·ri·mée (mā rē mā′), *n.* **Pros·per** (prô sper′), 1803–70, French short-story writer, novelist, and essayist.

me·ringue (mə rang′), *n.* **1.** a delicate, frothy mixture made with beaten egg whites and sugar or hot syrup, and browned, used as a topping for pies, pastry, etc. **2.** a pastry or pastry shell made by baking such a mixture, sometimes filled with fruit, whipped cream, etc. [< F]

mé·ringue (mā rang′; *Fr.* mā RANG′), *n., pl.* **-ringues** (-rangz′; *Fr.* -RANG′), *v.i.,* **-ringued, -ring·ing.** merengue.

me·ri·no (mə rē′nō), *n., pl.* **-nos,** *adj.* —*n.* **1.** (*cap.*) one of a breed of sheep, raised originally in Spain, valued for its fine wool. **2.** wool from such sheep. **3.** a knitted fabric of wool or wool and cotton. —*adj.* **4.** made of merino wool, yarn, or cloth. [< Sp < L *(ariēs) mājōrīn(us)* (male sheep) of the larger sort. See MAJOR, -INE¹]

Merino, *Ovis aries* (2 ft. high at shoulder)

Meri′no Vil′lage, a town in S Massachusetts. 3099 (1960).

Me·ri·o·nes (mə rī′ə nēz′), *n.* (in the *Iliad*) a skillful archer who aided the Greek forces in the Trojan War.

Mer·i·on·eth·shire (mer′ē on′ith shēr′, -shər), *n.* a county in N Wales. 39,007 (1961); 660 sq. mi. *Co. seat:* Dolgelly. Also called **Mer′i·on′eth.**

Mer·is (mer′is), *n.* a girl's given name. Also, **Maris.**

Me·rise (mə rēs′), *n.* a girl's given name.

mer·i·sis (mer′i sis), *n.* *Biol.* growth, esp. growth resulting from cell division. Cf. **auxesis.** [< Gk *meri-* (comb. form of *merís* part, portion) + -SIS]

mer·i·stem (mer′i stem′), *n.* *Bot.* embryonic tissue; undifferentiated, growing, actively dividing cells. [< Gk *meristó(s)* divided, distribute (verbid of *merízein* to divide into parts, deriv. of *merís,* part, share) + *-em,* var. of -EME]

mer·i·ste·mat·ic (mer′i stə mat′ik), *adj.* *Bot.* consisting of or having the properties of meristem. [MERISTEM + -ATE¹ + -IC] —**mer′i·ste·mat′i·cal·ly,** *adv.*

me·ris·tic (mə ris′tik), *adj.* *Biol.* of, pertaining to, or divided into segments or somites. [< Gk *meristik(ós)* of division. See MERISTEM, -IC]

mer·it (mer′it), *n.* **1.** claim to commendation; excellence; worth. **2.** something that entitles a reward or commendation; a commendable quality, act, etc.: *The book's only merit is its sincerity.* **3. merits,** the intrinsic right and wrong of a matter, as a law case, unobscured by procedural details, technicalities, personal feelings, etc.: *The case will be decided on its merits alone.* **4.** Often, **merits.** the state or fact of deserving; desert: *to treat someone according to his merits.* **5.** *Rom. Cath. Ch.* worthiness of spiritual reward, acquired by righteous acts made under the influence of grace. **6.** *Obs.* that which is deserved, whether good or bad. —*v.t.* **7.** to be worthy of; deserve. —*v.i.* **8.** *Chiefly Theol.* to acquire merit. [ME < L *merit(um)* act worthy of praise (or blame), n. use of *meritus* earned, ptp. of *merēre*] —**mer′it·less,** *adj.*
—**Syn. 1.** value, credit. MERIT, DESERT, WORTH refer to the quality in a person, action, or thing which entitles recognition, esp. favorable recognition. MERIT is usually the excellence which entitles to praise: *a man of great merit.* DESERT is the quality which entitles one to a just reward: *according to his deserts.* WORTH is always

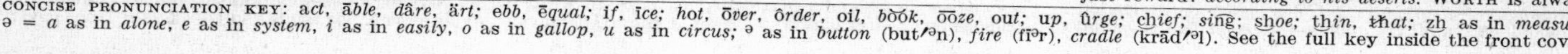

used in a favorable sense and signifies inherent value or goodness: *The worth of his contribution is incalculable.*

mer·it·ed (mer′i tid), *adj.* deserved. [MERIT + -ED[2]] —**mer′it·ed·ly,** *adv.*

mer·i·to·ri·ous (mer′i tōr′ē əs, -tôr′-), *adj.* possessing merit; deserving praise, reward, esteem, etc.; praiseworthy: *to receive a gift for meritorious service to one's employer.* [late ME < L *meritōrius* on hire. See MERIT, -ORY[1], -OUS] —**mer′i·to′ri·ous·ly,** *adv.* —**mer′i·to′ri·ous·ness,** *n.*

mer′it sys′tem, (in the U.S. civil service) a system or practice in which persons are hired or promoted on the basis of ability rather than patronage.

merk (merk), *n.* *Scot.* mark[2] (def. 3).

mer·kin (mûr′kən), *n.* false hair for the female pudenda. [?]

merle[1] (mûrl), *n.* *Chiefly Scot.* the blackbird, *Turdus merula.* Also, **merl.** [late ME < MF < L *merul(us), merula* ousel, blackbird]

merle[2] (mûrl), *adj.* **1.** of the color bluish-gray mottled with black, esp. of the coat of a dog. —*n.* **2.** the color merle. [?]

Merle (mûrl), *n.* a boy's or girl's given name.

mer·lin (mûr′lin), *n.* **1.** a small, bold, European falcon, *Falco columbarius aesalon.* **2.** *Falconry.* the pigeon hawk. [ME *merlioun* < AF *merilun,* OF *esmerillon,* aug. of *esmeril* < Gmc; akin to G *Schmerl,* Icel *smyrill*]

Mer·lin (mûr′lin), *n.* **1.** *Arthurian Romance.* a venerable magician and seer. **2.** a boy's given name.

mer·lon (mûr′lən), *n.* (in a battlement) the solid part between two crenels. See illus. under **battlement.** [< F < It *merlone,* aug. of *merlo* (in pl., *merli* battlements) < ?]

mer·maid (mûr′mād′), *n.* **1.** an imaginary female marine creature, having the head, torso, and arms of a woman and the tail of a fish. **2.** a highly-skilled girl swimmer, as a member of a swimming team. [ME *mermayde.* See MERE[2], MAID]

mer′maid's purse′, the horny or leathery egg case of certain cartilaginous fishes, as skates.

Mer′maid Tav′ern, an inn once located on Bread Street, Cheapside, in the heart of old London: a meeting place and informal club for Elizabethan playwrights and poets.

mer′maid weed′, any of several North American, aquatic herbs of the genus *Proserpinaca.*

mer·man (mûr′man′), *n., pl.* **-men.** **1.** an imaginary male marine creature, having the head, torso, and arms of a man and the tail of a fish. **2.** a highly-skilled male swimmer, as a member of a swimming team. [ME; see MERE[2] MAN[1]]

Mer·mer·us (mûr′mər əs), *n.* *Class. Myth.* a son of Jason and Medea.

Mer·nep·tah (mer′nep tä′, mər nep′tä), *n.* king of ancient Egypt c1225–c1215 B.C. (son of Ramses II). Also, **Meneptah.**

mero-, a learned borrowing from Greek meaning "part," "partial," used in the formation of compound words: *merogony.* [< Gk *méros* part]

mer·o·blas·tic (mer′ə blas′tik), *adj.* *Embryol.* (of certain eggs) undergoing partial cleavage. Cf. **holoblastic.** [MERO- + -BLAST + -IC] —**mer′o·blas′ti·cal·ly,** *adv.*

Mer·o·dach (mer′ə däk′), *n.* Marduk.

Mé·rode′ Al′tarpiece, The (mā rōd′), a triptych (c1425) painted by the Master of Flémalle.

Mer·o·ë (mer′ō ē′), *n.* a ruined city in Sudan, on the Nile, NE of Khartoum: a capital of ancient Ethiopia.

me·rog·o·ny (mə rog′ə nē), *n.* *Embryol.* the development of egg fragments. [MERO- + -GONY] —**mer·o·gon·ic** (mer′ə gon′ik), **me·rog′o·nous,** *adj.*

mer·o·mor·phic (mer′ə môr′fik), *adj.* *Math.* of or pertaining to a function that is analytic, except for poles, in a given domain. [MERO- + -MORPHIC]

me·ro·pi·a (mə rō′pē ə), *n.* *Ophthalm.* partial blindness. [MERO- + -OPIA]

Me·rops (mē′rops), *n.* **1.** (in the *Iliad*) a Percosian augur who foresaw and unsuccessfully tried to prevent the death of his sons in the Trojan War. **2.** *Class. Myth.* the husband of Clymene and the stepfather of Phaëthon.

me·ros (mē′ros), *n.* (in the Doric order) a flat surface between two channels of a triglyph. [< Gk *mērós* generally, leg-bone, lit., thigh]

-merous a suffix meaning "having parts (of a specified number or type)," "partite": *dimerous.* Cf. **-mer, -mere.** [< Gk *méros* part, portion, share; see -OUS]

Mer·o·vin·gi·an (mer′ə vin′jē ən, -jən), *adj.* **1.** of or pertaining to the Frankish dynasty established by Clovis, which reigned in Gaul and Germany from about A.D. 500 to 751. —*n.* **2.** a member or supporter of the Merovingian dynasty. [< F *mérovingien,* equiv. to *méroving-* (< ML < Gmc; cf. OE *Merewīowing* offspring of *Merewīg,* grandfather of Clovis) + *-ien* -IAN]

mer·o·zo·ite (mer′ə zō′it), *n.* (in the asexual reproduction of certain sporozoans) a cell developed from a schizont which parasitizes an erythrocyte in the host. [MERO- + ZO- + -ITE[1]]

Mer·ri·am (mer′ē əm), *n.* a town in E Kansas. 5084 (1960).

Mer·rick (mer′ik), *n.* a town on SW Long Island, in SE New York. 18,789 (1960).

Mer·rill (mer′əl), *n.* **1.** a town in central Wisconsin. 9451 (1960). **2.** a boy's given name.

Mer′rill's Maraud′ers, the U.S. soldiers under the command of Brig. Gen. Frank Merrill during World War II, noted esp. for their skill at jungle fighting in the China-Burma-India theater. Also called **Mer′rill's Raid′ers.**

Mer·ri·ly (mer′ə lē), *n.* a girl's given name, form of **Merry.**

Mer·ri·lyn (mer′ə lin), *n.* a girl's given name.

Mer·ri·mac (mer′ə mak′), *n.* the first ironclad warship: used by the Confederates in a battle against the *Monitor* in 1862.

Mer·ri·mack (mer′ə mak′), *n.* a river in central New Hampshire and NE Massachusetts, flowing S and NE to the Atlantic. 110 mi. long.

mer·ri·ment (mer′i mənt), *n.* **1.** merry gaiety; mirth; hilarity; laughter. **2.** *Obs.* a cause of mirth; a jest, entertainment, etc. [MERRY + -MENT]
—**Syn. 1.** See **mirth.** —**Ant. 1.** misery, melancholy.

Mer′ritt Is′land (mer′it), a town in E Florida. 3554 (1960).

mer·ry (mer′ē), *adj.,* **mer·ri·er, mer·ri·est.** **1.** full of cheerfulness or gaiety; joyous in disposition or spirit: *a merry little man.* **2.** laughingly gay; mirthful; festively joyous; hilarious: *a merry time at the party.* **3.** *Archaic.* causing happiness; pleasant; delightful. **4. make merry, a.** to be gay or festive: *The New Year's revelers were making merry in the ballroom.* **b.** to make fun of; ridicule: *The unthinking children made merry of the boy who had no shoes.* [ME *meri(e), myrie, murie,* OE *myr(i)ge, mer(i)ge* pleasant, delightful] —**mer′ri·ly,** *adv.* —**mer′ri·ness,** *n.*
—**Syn. 1.** happy, blithe, blithesome, frolicsome, cheery, glad. See **gay. 2.** jolly, jovial, gleeful. —**Ant. 1.** sad. **2.** solemn.

Mer·ry (mer′ē), *n.* a girl's given name.

mer·ry-an·drew (mer′ē an′drōō), *n.* a clown; buffoon. [MERRY + *Andrew,* the name]

mer·ry-go-round (mer′ē gō round′), *n.* **1.** Also called **carousel, carrousel.** (in amusement parks, carnivals, etc.) a revolving, circular platform fitted with wooden horses or other animals on which a person may ride, usually to the accompaniment of music. **2.** a rapid whirl; a busy round, as of social life, business affairs, etc.

mer·ry·mak·er (mer′ē mā′kər), *n.* a person who gaily or enthusiastically takes part in some festive or merry celebration. [MERRY + MAKER]

mer·ry·mak·ing (mer′ē mā′king), *n.* **1.** the act of taking part gaily or enthusiastically in some festive or merry celebration. **2.** a merry festivity; revel. —*adj.* **3.** producing mirth; gay; festive. [MERRY + MAKING]

mer·ry·thought (mer′ē thôt′), *n.* *Chiefly Brit.* the wishbone or furcula of a fowl. [so called from the custom of two persons pulling the bone until it breaks; the person holding the longer (sometimes shorter) piece will supposedly marry first or will be granted a wish at the time]

Mer′ry Wives′ of Wind′sor, The, a comedy (1598–1602?) by Shakespeare.

Mer·se·ni·us (mûr sē′nē əs), *n.* a walled plain in the third quadrant of the face of the moon: about 45 miles in diameter.

Mer·senne (mər sen′; *Fr.* mer sen′), *n.* **Ma·rin** (ma ran′), 1588–1648, French mathematician.

Mersenne′ num′ber, *Math.* a number of the form, $2^p - 1$, where *p* is a prime number. [named after M. MERSENNE]

Mer·sey (mûr′zē), *n.* a river in W England, flowing W from Derbyshire to the Irish Sea. 70 mi. long.

Mer·thi·o·late (mər thī′ə lāt′), *n.* *Pharm., Trademark.* thimerosal.

Mer·thyr Tyd·fil (mûr′thər tid′vil; *Welsh* mur′thər tud′vil), a city in SE Wales. 59,008 (1961).

Mer·ton (mûr′tən), *n.* **Thomas,** born 1915, U.S. poet and religious writer, born in France.

Mer·vin (mûr′vin), *n.* a boy's given name. Also, **Marvin, Mer′vyn.**

Mer·win (mûr′win), *n.* a boy's given name. Also, **Mer′wyn.**

Mer·yl (mer′əl), *n.* a girl's given name, form of **Merle.**

mes-, var. of **meso-** before some vowels: *mesencephalon.*

me·sa (mā′sə; *Sp.* me′sä), *n.* a land formation having a relatively flat top and steep rock walls: common in arid and semiarid parts of the SW United States and Mexico. [< Sp: table < L *mēnsa*]

Me·sa (mā′sə), *n.* a city in central Arizona, near Phoenix. 33,772 (1960).

mes·ail (mes′āl), *n.* *Armor.* a pivoted piece on a helmet between a visor and a beaver. Also, **mezail.** [prob. << OF *muçaille* concealment, deriv. of *mucier* to conceal; cf. Norman dial. *mucher* to hide]

mé·sal·li·ance (mā′zə lī′əns, mā zal′ē əns; *Fr.* mā zal yäns′), *n., pl.* **mé·sal·li·anc·es** (mā′zə lī′ən sis, mā zal′ē ən sis; *Fr.* mā zal yäns′). a marriage with a social inferior; misalliance. [< F; see MIS-, ALLIANCE]

mes·arch (mez′ärk, mes′-, mē′zärk, -särk), *adj.* **1.** *Bot.* having the metaxylem develop on both sides of the protoxylem. **2.** *Ecol.* (of a sere) originating in a mesic habitat. [MES- + -ARCH]

Me·sa Ver·de (mā′sə vûrd′; *Sp.* me′sä ber′the), a national park in SW Colorado: ruins of cliff dwellings. 80 sq. mi.

mes·cal (me skal′), *n.* **1.** either of two species of cactus, *Lophophora Williamsii* or *L. Lewinni,* of Texas and northern Mexico. **2.** an intoxicating beverage distilled from the fermented juice of certain species of agave. **3.** any agave yielding this spirit. [< AmerSp < Nahuatl *mexcalli* mescal, equiv. to *me(tl)* maguey + *(i)xcalli* stew]

mescal′ bean′, an evergreen shrub or small tree, *Sophora secundiflora,* of the southwestern U.S. and northern Mexico, having fragrant, violet-blue flowers.

mescal′ but′tons, the dried, buttonlike tops of a mescal of the genus *Lophophora,* used as a stimulant, esp. by the Indians during religious ceremonies; peyote.

mes·ca·line (mes′kə lēn′, -lin), *n.* *Pharm.* a white water-soluble, crystalline powder, $C_{11}H_{17}NO_3$, obtained from mescal buttons, used in experimental psychology to produce hallucinations; peyote. Also, **mezcaline.** [MESCAL + -INE[2]]

mes·dames (mā däm′, -dam′; *Fr.* mā dam′), *n.* pl. of **madame.**

mes·de·moi·selles (mā′də mə zel′, mād′mwə zel′; *Fr.* mād mwa zel′), *n.* pl. of **mademoiselle.**

me·seems (mē sēmz′), *v. impers.; pt.* **me·seemed.** *Archaic.* it seems to me. [ME + *seems,* 3rd pers. sing. pres. indic. of SEEM]

mes·en·ceph·a·lon (mes′en sef′ə lon′, mez′-), *n., pl.* **-la** (-lə), **-lons.** the midbrain. [MES- + ENCEPHALON] —**mes·en·ce·phal·ic** (mes′en sə fal′ik), *adj.*

mes·en·chyme (mes′eng kim, mez′-), *n.* *Embryol.* an aggregation of cells of mesodermal origin that are capable of developing into connective tissues, blood, and lymphatic and blood vessels. [var. of *mesenchyma* < NL < Gk, equiv. to *mes-* MES- + *énchyma* infusion] —**mes·en·chy·mal** (mes eng′kə məl), **mes·en·chym·a·tous** (mes′eng kim′ə təs), *adj.*

mes·en·ter·i·tis (mes′ən tə rī′tis, mez′-, mes en′tə-), *n.* *Pathol.* inflammation of the mesentery. [MES- + ENTERITIS]

mes·en·ter·on (mes en′tə ron′, mez-), *n., pl.* **-ter·a** (-tər ə). *Obs.* midgut. [MES- + ENTERON] —**mes·en′ter·on′ic,** *adj.*

mes·en·ter·y (mes′ən ter′ē, mez′-), *n., pl.* **-ter·ies.** *Anat.* the membrane, consisting of a double layer of peritoneum, that invests the intestines, attaching them to the posterior wall of the abdomen, maintaining them in position in the abdominal cavity, and supplying them with blood vessels, nerves, and lymphatics, esp. the part of this membrane investing the jejunum and ileum. [< NL *mesenteri(um)* < Gk *mesentérion* (equiv. to *mes-* MES- + *entérion,* neut. of *entérios* of the bowel); see ENTERON] —**mes′en·ter′ic,** *adj.*

mesh (mesh), *n.* **1.** one of the open spaces between the lines or ropes of a net. **2. meshes, a.** the threads that bind such spaces. **b.** the means of catching or holding fast: *to be caught in the meshes of the law.* **3.** an interwoven or intertwined structure; network. **4.** *Mach.* the engagement of gear teeth. **5.** any knit, woven, or knotted fabric of open texture. **6.** any arrangement of interlocking metal links or wires with evenly-spaced, uniform small openings between, as used in jewelry, sieves, etc. **7.** *Elect.* a set of branches that forms a closed path in a network so that removal of a branch results in an open path. **8.** *Metall.* a designation of a given fineness of powder used in powder metallurgy in terms of the number of the finest screen through which almost all the particles will pass: *This powder is 200 mesh.* —*v.t.* **9.** to catch or entangle in or as in a net; enmesh. **10.** to form with meshes, as a net. **11.** *Mach.* to engage, as gear teeth. **12.** to cause to match, coordinate, or interlock. —*v.i.* **13.** to become enmeshed. **14.** *Mach.* to become or be engaged, as the teeth of one gear with those of another. **15.** to match, coordinate, or interlock. [appar. back formation from OE *mǣscre* mesh; akin to OHG *māsca,* etc.]

Me·shach (mē′shak), *n.* a companion of Daniel. Cf. **Shadrach.**

Me′sha Ste′le (mē′shə). See **Moabite Stone.**

Me·shed (me shed′), *n.* a city in NE Iran: Muslim shrine. 312,186 (est. 1963). Persian, **Mashhad.**

mesh′ knot′. See **sheet bend.**

mesh·re·bee·yeh (mesh′rə bē′yə), *n.* (in Islamic countries) an oriel screened by latticework. Also, **mashrebeeyah, mashrebeeyeh.** [< Ar *mashrabīyyah*]

me·shu·ga (mə shōōg′ə), *adj.* *Slang.* crazy; insane. Also, **me·shug·ga.** [< Heb *meshuggā‘*]

me·shu·gaas (mi shōō gäs′, mish′ə-), *n.* *Slang.* foolishness; nonsense. Also, **me·shug·gaas′.** [< Yiddish < Heb *meshuggā‘*]

me·shu·ga·na (mə shōōg′ə nə), *n.* *Slang.* a crazy person. Also, **me·shug′ga·na.** [deriv. of MESHUGA]

mesh·work (mesh′wûrk′), *n.* meshed work; network. [MESH + WORK]

mesh·y (mesh′ē), *adj.,* **mesh·i·er, mesh·i·est.** formed with meshes; meshed. [MESH + -Y[1]]

me·si·al (mē′zē əl, -sē-, mez′ē əl, mes′-), *adj.* **1.** medial. **2.** *Dentistry.* directed toward the sagittal plane or midline of the face, along the dental arch. Cf. **buccal** (def. 3), **distal** (def. 2). [MES- + -IAL] —**me′si·al·ly, me′sal·ly,** *adv.*

me·sic (mez′ik, mes′-, mē′zik, -sik), *adj.* of, pertaining to, or adapted to an environment having a balanced supply of moisture. [MES- + -IC] —**mes′i·cal·ly,** *adv.*

me·sit·y·lene (mi sit′əlēn′, mes′itəlēn′), *n.* *Chem.* a colorless, liquid, aromatic hydrocarbon, $C_6H_3(CH_3)_3$, occurring naturally in coal tar and prepared from acetone: used chiefly as a chemical intermediate. [MESITYL + -ENE]

mes′i·tyl ox′ide (mez′i til, mes′-), *Chem.* an oily, colorless liquid, $(CH_3)_2C{=}CHCOCH_3$, having a honeylike odor: used chiefly as a solvent and in the manufacture of synthetic organic compounds. Also called **isopropylideneacetone, methylisobutenyl ketone.** [*mesityl* < NL *mesīt(a)* (< Gk *mesítēs* mediator, gobetween, equiv. to *mes-* MES- + *-ītēs* -ITE[1]) + -YL]

Mes·mer (mez′mər; *Ger.* mes′mər), *n.* **Franz** (frants, franz; *Ger.* fränts) or **Frie·drich An·ton** (frē′drik an′tən, -ton; *Ger.* frē′drikh än′tōn), 1733–1815, Austrian physician.

mes·mer·ic (mez mer′ik, mes-), *adj.* **1.** produced by mesmerism; hypnotic. **2.** compelling; fascinating. [*mesmer* (see MESMERISM) + -IC] —**mes·mer′i·cal·ly,** *adv.*

mes·mer·ise (mez′mə rīz′), *v.t.,* **-ised, -is·ing.** *Chiefly Brit.* mesmerize. —**mes′mer·i·sa′tion,** *n.* —**mes′mer·is′er,** *n.*

mes·mer·ism (mez′mə riz′əm, mes′-), *n.* **1.** hypnosis as induced by F.A. Mesmer through animal magnetism. **2.** hypnotism. **3.** a compelling attraction; fascination. [MESMER + -ISM] —**mes′mer·ist,** *n.*

mes·mer·ize (mez′mə rīz′, mes′-), *v.t.,* **-ized, -iz·ing.** **1.** to hypnotize. **2.** to spellbind; fascinate. **3.** to compel by fascination. Also, *esp. Brit.,* **mesmerise.** [*mesmer* (see MESMERISM) + -IZE] —**mes′mer·i·za′tion,** *n.* —**mes′mer·iz′er,** *n.*

mesn·al·ty (mēn′əl tē), *n.* *Law.* the estate of a mesne lord. [< legal AF *me(s)nalte,* equiv. to *mesnal* (see MESNE, -AL[1]) + *-te* -TY[2]]

mesne (mēn), *adj.* *Law.* intermediate or intervening. [< legal AF, sp. var. of *meen* MEAN[3]]

mesne′ lord′, (in old English law) an intermediate feudal lord; the tenant of a chief lord and a lord to his own tenants.

meso-, a learned borrowing from Greek meaning "middle," used in the formation of compound words: *mesocephalic.* Also, **mes-.** [comb. form repr. Gk *mésos* middle, in the middle; akin to L *medius*]

Mes·o·a·mer·i·ca (mez′ō ə mer′i kə, mes′-, mē′zō-, -sō-), *n.* *Chiefly Archaeol.* See **Central America.** [MESO- + AMERICA] —**Mes′o·a·mer′i·can,** *adj., n.*

mes·o·ap·pen·dix (mez′ō ə pen′diks, mes′-, mē′zō-, -sō-), *n., pl.* **-dix·es, -di·ces** (-di sēz′). *Anat.* the mesentery of the vermiform appendix. [MESO- + APPENDIX] —**mes·o·ap·pen·di·ceal** (mez′ō ap′ən dish′əl, -ə pen′di sē′əl, mes′-, mē′zō-, -sō-), *adj.*

mes·o·blast (mez′ə blast′, mes′-, mē′zə-, -sə-), *n.* *Embryol.* **1.** the mesoderm. **2.** the primordial middle layer of a young embryo before the segregation of the germ layers, capable of becoming the mesoderm. [MESO- + -BLAST] —**mes′o·blas′tic,** *adj.*

mes·o·car·di·um (mez′ə kär′dē əm, mes′-, mē′zə-, -sə-), *n., pl.* **-di·a** (-dē ə). *Embryol.* the double layer of splanchnic mesoderm supporting the embryonic heart. [MESO- + NL *cardium;* see CARDIO-]

mes·o·carp (mez′ə kärp′, mes′-, mē′zə-, -sə-), *n. Bot.* the middle layer of pericarp, as the fleshy part of certain fruits. See diag. under **pericarp.** [MESO- + -CARP]

mes·o·ce·cum (mez′ə sē′kəm, mes′-, mē′zə-, -sə-), *n., pl.* **-ca** (-kə). *Anat.* the mesentery of the cecum. [MESO- + CECUM] —**mes·o·ce·cal** (mez′ə sē′kəl, mes′-, mē′zə-, -sə-), *adj.*

mes·o·ce·phal·ic (mez′ō sə fal′ik, mes′-, mē′zō-, -sō-), *adj. Cephalom.* having a head with a cephalic index between that of dolichocephaly and brachycephaly. [MESO- + CEPHALIC] —**mes·o·ceph·al** (mez′ə sef′əl, mes′-, mē′zə-, -sə-), *n.* —**mes′o·ceph′al·y,** *n.*

mes·o·co·lon (mez′ə kō′lən, mes′-, mē′zə-, -sə-), *n., pl.* **-lons, -la** (-lə). *Anat.* the mesentery of the colon. [MESO- + COLON[2]]

mes·o·cra·nic (mez′ə krā′nik, mes′-, mē′zə-, -sə-), *adj. Craniom.* having a skull with a cranial index between that of dolichocranic and brachycranic skulls. [MESO- + CRAN(IUM) + -IC]

mes·o·crat·ic (mez′ə krat′ik, mes′-, mē′zə-, -sə-), *adj. Geol.* composed of light and dark minerals in nearly equal amounts. [MESO- + -CRAT + -IC]

mes·o·derm (mez′ə dûrm′, mes′-, mē′zə-, -sə-), *n. Embryol.* the middle germ layer of a metazoan embryo. [MESO- + -DERM] —**mes′o·der′mal, mes′o·der′mic,** *adj.*

mes·o·dont (mez′ə dont′, mes′-, mē′zə-, -sə-), *adj.* having medium-sized teeth. Also, **mes′o·don′tic.** [MES- + -ODONT]

mes·o·dont·ism (mez′ə don′tiz əm, mes′-, mē′zə-, -sə-), *n.* the condition of having medium-sized teeth. Also, **mes′o·don′ty.** [MESODONT + -ISM]

mes·o·gas·tri·um (mez′ə gas′trē əm, mes′-, mē′zə-, -sə-), *n., pl.* **-tri·a** (-trē ə). *Anat.* the mesentery of the embryonic stomach. [< NL, equiv. to *meso-* MESO- + Gk *gastḗr* belly + NL *-ium* -IUM] —**mes′o·gas′tric,** *adj.*

mes·o·gle·a (mez′ə glē′ə, mes′-, mē′zə-, -sə-), *n.* the noncellular, gelatinous material between the inner and outer body walls of a coelenterate or sponge. Also, **mes′o·gloe′a.** [< NL, equiv. to *meso-* MESO- + Gk *gloía* glue] —**mes′o·gle′al, mes′o·gloe′al,** *adj.*

me·sog·na·thous (mi zog′nə thəs, -sog′-), *adj. Anthropol.* **1.** having medium, slightly protruding jaws. **2.** having a moderate or intermediate gnathic index of from 98 to 103. Also, **mes·og·nath·ic** (mez′og nath′ik, mes′-, mē′zog-, -sog-). [MESO- + -GNATHOUS] —**me·sog′na·thism, me·sog′na·thy,** *n.*

mes·o·lec·i·thal (mez′ə les′ə thəl, mes′-, mē′zə-, -sə-), *adj. Embryol.* centrolecithal. [MESO- + LECITHAL]

mes·o·lite (mez′ə līt′, mes′-, mē′zə-, -sə-), *n.* a mineral variety of the zeolite group, intermediate in chemical composition between natrolite and scolecite. [MESO- + -LITE]

Mes·o·lith·ic (mez′ə lith′ik, mes′-, mē′zə-, -sə-), *adj.* of, pertaining to, or characteristic of a transitional period of the Stone Age intermediate between the Paleolithic and the Neolithic periods; Epipaleolithic. [MESO- + -LITHIC]

Me·so·lon·ghi (*Gk.* me′sô lông′gē), *n.* Missolonghi.

mes·o·me·te·or·ol·o·gy (mez′ō mē′tē ə rol′ə jē, mes′-, mē′zō-, -sō-), *n.* the study of atmospheric phenomena of relatively small size, as thunderstorms, tornadoes, etc., and of the detailed structure of larger disturbances. Cf. **macrometeorology, micrometeorology.** [MESO- + METEOROLOGY] —**mes·o·me·te·or·o·log·i·cal** (mez′ō mē′tē ər ə loj′i kəl, mes′-, mē′zə-, -sə-), *adj.*

mes·o·morph (mez′ə môrf′, mes′-, mē′zə-, -sə-), *n. Psychol.* a person of the mesomorphic type. [MESO- + -MORPH]

mes·o·mor·phic (mez′ə môr′fik, mes′-, mē′zə-, -sə-), *adj.* **1.** *Physical Chem.* pertaining to or existing in an intermediate state, as a liquid crystal in the nematic or smectic state. **2.** *Psychol.* having or pertaining to a muscular or sturdy body build characterized by the relative prominence of structures developed from the embryonic mesoderm (contrasted with *ectomorphic, endomorphic*). [MESO- + -MORPHIC] —**mes′o·mor′phism,** *n.* —**mes′o·mor′phy,** *n.*

me·son[1] (mē′zon, -son, mez′on, mes′-), *n. Physics.* any of several elementary particles having a mass intermediate between that of an electron and a proton, either a negative or a positive charge, and a spin of ½ or 0. Also called **mesotron. Cf. mu meson, pi meson.** [MES- + -ON[1]]

me·son[2] (mes′on, mē′son), *n.* the plane dividing a bilaterally symmetric body into symmetric halves. [< NL < Gk *mḗson* middle, neut. of *mésos*]

mes·o·neph·ros (mez′ə nef′ros, mes′-, mē′zə-, -sə-), *n., pl.* **-roi** (-roi). *Embryol.* one of the three embryonic excretory organs of vertebrates, becoming the functional kidney of fishes and amphibians and becoming part of the epididymis in higher vertebrates. Cf. **metanephros, pronephros.** [< NL, equiv. to *meso-* MESO- + Gk *nephrós* kidney] —**mes′o·neph′ric,** *adj.*

mes·o·pause (mez′ə pôz′, mes′-, mē′zə-, -sə-), *n. Meteorol.* the boundary or transition zone between the mesosphere and the ionosphere. [MESO- + PAUSE]

mes·o·peak (mez′ə pēk′, mes′-, mē′zə-, -sə-), *n.* the level of maximum temperature in the mesosphere, at an altitude of about 30 miles. [MESO(SPHERE) + PEAK[1]]

mes·o·phile (mez′ə fīl′, -fil, mes′-, mē′zə-, -sə-), *Bacteriol.* —*adj.* **1.** mesophilic. —*n.* **2.** a mesophilic bacterium. [MESO- + -PHILE]

mes·o·phil·ic (mez′ə fil′ik, mes′-, mē′zə-, -sə-), *adj.* (of bacteria) growing best at moderate temperatures, between 25° and 40°C. Also, **mesophile, me·soph·i·lous** (mi zof′ə ləs, -sof′-). [MESOPHILE + -IC]

mes·o·phyll (mez′ə fil, mes′-, mē′zə-, -sə-), *n. Bot.* the parenchyma, usually containing chlorophyll, which forms the interior parts of a leaf. [MESO- + -PHYLL] —**mes′o·phyl′lic, mes′o·phyl′lous,** *adj.*

mes·o·phyte (mez′ə fīt′, mes′-, mē′zə-, -sə-), *n.* a plant growing under conditions of well-balanced moisture supply. [MESO- + -PHYTE] —**mes·o·phyt·ic** (mez′ə fit′ik, mes′-, mē′zə-, -sə-), *adj.*

Mes·o·po·ta·mi·a (mes′ə pə tā′mē ə), *n.* an ancient country in Asia between the Tigris and Euphrates rivers. The modern republic of Iraq includes much of this region. —**Mes′o·po·ta′mi·an,** *adj., n.*

mes·o·rec·tum (mez′ə rek′təm, mes′-, mē′zə-, -sə-), *n., pl.* **-tums, -ta** (-tə). *Anat.* the mesentery of the rectum. [MESO- + RECTUM]

mes·or·rhine (mez′ə rīn′, -rin, mes′-, mē′zə-, -sə-), *adj. Anthropol.* having a moderately broad and high-bridged nose. [MESO- + RHIN-] —**mes′or·rhi′ny,** *n.*

mes·o·sphere (mez′ə sfēr′, mes′-, mē′zə-, -sə-), *n.* **1.** (in the classification of the earth's atmosphere by chemical properties) the region between the ionosphere and the exosphere, extending from about 250–650 miles above the surface of the earth. **2.** (in the classification of the earth's atmosphere by thermal properties) the region between the stratosphere and the thermosphere, extending from about 20–50 miles above the surface of the earth. [MESO- + -SPHERE] —**mes·o·spher·ic** (mez′ə sfer′ik, mes′-, mē′zə-, -sə-), *adj.*

mes·o·sty·lous (mez′ə stī′ləs, mes′-, mē′zə-, -sə-), *adj. Bot.* having styles intermediate in length. Cf. **macrostylous, microstylous.** [MESO- + STYLE + -OUS]

mes·o·the·li·um (mez′ə thē′lē əm, mes′-, mē′zə-, -sə-), *n., pl.* **-li·a** (-lē ə). *Anat., Embryol.* epithelium of mesodermal origin, which lines the body cavities. [MESO- + (EPI)THELIUM] —**mes′o·the′li·al,** *adj.*

mes·o·tho·rax (mez′ə thôr′aks, -thōr′-, mes′-, mē′zə-, -sə-), *n., pl.* **-tho·rax·es, -tho·ra·ces** (-thôr′ə sēz′, -thōr′-). the middle segment of the three divisions of the thorax of an insect, bearing the second pair of legs and the first pair of wings. [MESO- + THORAX] —**mes·o·tho·rac·ic** (mez′ə thō ras′ik, -thô-, mes′-, mē′zə-, -sə-), *adj.*

mes·o·tho·ri·um (mez′ə thôr′ē əm, -thōr′-, mes′-, mē′zə-, -sə-), *n. Chem.* any of two radioactive isotopes formed from thorium minerals, either of radium (**mesothorium I**): *at. no.:* 88; *at. wt.:* 228, *half life:* 6.7 years; or of actinium (**mesothorium II**): *at. no.:* 89; *at. wt.:* 228; *half life:* 6.2 hrs. *Symbol:* Ms-Th [MESO- + THORIUM]

mes·o·tron (mez′ə tron′, mes′-, mē′zə-, -sə-), *n. Physics.* meson[1]. [MESO- + (ELEC)TRON] —**mes′o·tron′ic,** *adj.*

mes·o·var·i·um (mez′ə vâr′ē əm, mes′-, mē′zə-, -sə-), *n., pl.* **-var·i·a** (-vâr′ē ə). *Anat.* the mesentery of the ovary. [MES- + OVARIUM]

Mes·o·zo·ic (mez′ə zō′ik, mes′-, mē′zə-, -sə-), *Geol.* —*adj.* **1.** noting or pertaining to an era occurring between 70,000,000 and 220,000,000 years ago, characterized by the appearance of flowering plants and by the appearance and extinction of dinosaurs. See table under **era.** —*n.* **2.** the Mesozoic era or group of systems. [MESO- + ZO- + -IC]

mes·quite (me skēt′, mes′kēt), *n.* **1.** a mimosaceous tree or shrub, *Prosopis glandulosa,* of the southwestern U.S. and Mexico, that bears beanlike pods, which are rich in sugar and are used for fodder. **2.** any plant of the genus *Prosopis.* Also, **mes·quit′.** [< AmerSp *mezquite* < Nahuatl *mizquitl*]

Mes·quite (me skēt′, mi-), *n.* a city in NE Texas, E of Dallas. 27,526 (1960).

mess (mes), *n.* **1.** a dirty or untidy condition: *The room was in a mess.* **2.** a state of embarrassing confusion: *His affairs are in a mess.* **3.** an unpleasant or difficult situation: *He got into a mess driving without a license.* **4.** a dirty or untidy mass, litter, or jumble: *a mess of papers.* **5.** a group regularly taking meals together. **6.** the meal so taken. **7.** See **mess hall. 8.** *Naval.* messroom. **9.** a quantity of food sufficient for a dish or a single occasion: *to pick a mess of sweet corn for dinner.* **10.** a sloppy or unappetizing preparation of food. **11.** a dish or quantity of soft or liquid food: *to cook up a nice mess of pottage.* **12.** *Informal.* a person whose life or affairs are in a state of confusion, esp. a person with a confused or disorganized moral or psychological outlook. —*v.t.* **13.** to make dirty or untidy (often fol. by *up*): *Don't mess up my clean floor.* **14.** to make a mess or muddle of (affairs, responsibilities, etc.) (often fol. by *up*): *They messed up the whole deal.* **15.** to supply with meals, as military personnel. —*v.i.* **16.** to eat in company, esp. as a member of a mess. **17.** to make a dirty or untidy mess. **18. mess around** or **about, a.** *Informal.* to busy oneself without purpose or plan; work half-heartedly; putter. **b.** *Slang.* to waste time; loaf. **c.** *Slang.* to involve or associate (oneself) with, esp. for immoral or unethical purposes: *His wife accused him of messing around with gamblers.* **19. mess in** or **with,** to intervene officiously; meddle: *You'll get no thanks for messing in the affairs of others.* [ME *mes* < OF < LL *miss(um)* what is sent (put on the table), n. use of neut. of ptp. of L *mittere* to send] —**Syn. 2.** muddle, farrago, hodgepodge. **3.** predicament, plight, muddle, pickle. **14.** confuse, mix up. —**Ant. 1.** tidiness. **2.** order. **14.** arrange.

mes·sage (mes′ij), *n.* **1.** a communication containing some information, advice, request, or the like, sent by messenger, radio, telephone, or other means. **2.** an official communication, as from a chief executive to a legislative body: *the President's message to Congress.* **3.** the inspired utterance of a prophet or sage. **4.** (in automated information and data processing) one or more words taken as a unit. **5.** (the point, moral, or meaning of a gesture, utterance, novel, motion picture, musical composition, etc.: *The new play is short on humor and long on message.* [ME < OF < LL **missātic(um),* equiv. to L *miss(us)* sent (ptp. of *mittere* to send) + *-āticum* -AGE]

mes′sage cen′ter, *Mil.* an office handling the incoming and outgoing messages, mail, etc., of a base.

Mes·sal·a (mə sal′ə), *n.* a walled plain in the first quadrant of the face of the moon: about 77 miles in diameter.

Mes·sa·lian (mi sāl′yən, -sā′lē ən), *n.* Euchite. [< LGk *Messaliān(ós)* < Syrian *meṣalyānā* given to prayer]

Mes·sa·li·na (mes′ə lī′nə), *n.* **Valeria,** died A.D. 48, 3rd wife of Claudius I.

mes·sa·line (mes′ə lēn′, mes′ə lēn′), *n.* a thin, soft silk with a twill or satin weave. [< F]

mes·san (mes′ən), *n. Scot.* a lap dog; small pet dog. Also, **messin.** [< ScotGael *measan,* dim. of *meas* pet]

Mes·sa·pic (mə sā′pik, -sap′ik), *n.* a dialect of Illyrian that was spoken in what is now SE Italy and written with an alphabet derived from that of Greek. Also, **Mes·sa·pi·an** (mi sā′pē ən). [< L *Messap(ii)* inhabitants of *Messapia* + -IC]

mess′ call′, *Mil.* a bugle call for mess.

Mes·sei·gneurs (*Fr.* mā se nyœr′), *n.* (*sometimes l.c.*) pl. of **Monseigneur.**

Mes·se·ne (me sē′nē), *n.* **1.** an ancient city in the SW Peloponnesus; capital of ancient Messenia. **2.** *Class. Myth.* the wife of Polycaon, for whom Messenia was named.

mes·sen·ger (mes′ən jər), *n.* **1.** a person who bears a message or goes on an errand, esp. as a matter of duty or business. **2.** a person employed to convey official dispatches or to go on other official or special errands: *a bank messenger.* **3.** *Naut.* **a.** a rope or chain made into an endless belt to pull on an anchor cable or to drive machinery from some power source, as a capstan or winch. **b.** a light line by which a heavier line, as a hawser, can be pulled across a gap between a vessel and a pier, a buoy, another vessel, etc. **4.** *Oceanog.* a brass weight sent down a line to actuate a Nansen bottle or other oceanographic instrument. **5.** *Archaic.* a herald or harbinger. [ME *messager, messangere* < OF *messagier.* See MESSAGE, -ER[2]] —**Syn. 1.** bearer, courier. **5.** forerunner.

Mes·se·ni·a (mə sē′nē ə -sēn′yə), *n.* a division of ancient Greece, in the SW Peloponnesus: an important center of Mycenaean culture.

Mes·ser·schmitt (mes′ər shmit′), *n.* any of several types of fighter aircraft extensively used by the German air force in World War II, esp. the ME-109. [named after Willy *Messerschmitt* (born 1898), German aircraft designer]

mess′ gear′. See **mess kit.**

mess′ hall′, a place in which a group eats regularly, esp. a dining hall in a military camp, post, etc.

Mes·siaen (mes yäN′), *n.* **O·li·vier Eu·gène Prosper Charles** (ô lē vyā′ œ zhen′ prô sper′ sharl), born 1908, French composer and organist.

Mes·si·ah (mi sī′ə), *n.* **1.** the promised and expected deliverer of the Jewish people. **2.** Jesus Christ, regarded by Christians as fulfilling this promise and expectation. John 4:25, 26. **3.** (*usually l.c.*) any expected deliverer. **4.** (*usually l.c.*) a zealous leader of some cause or project. **5.** (*italics.*) an oratorio (1742) by George Frederick Handel. Also, *Douay Bible,* **Mes·si·as** (mi sī′əs) (for defs. 1, 2). [< Heb *māshīaḥ* anointed] —**Mes·si′ah·ship′,** *n.* —**Mes·si·an·ic** (mes′ē an′ik), *adj.* —**Mes′si·an′i·cal·ly,** *adv.*

Mes·si·dor (me sē dôr), *n.* (in the French Revolutionary calendar) the 10th month of the year, extending from June 19 to July 18. [< F < L *messi(s)* harvest + Gk *dōr(on)* gift]

Mes·sier (me syā′), *n.* **1. Charles** (sharl), 1730–1817, French astronomer. **2.** a crater in the fourth quadrant of the face of the moon: about 9 miles in diameter.

mes·sieurs (mes′ərz; *Fr.* me syœ′), *n.* pl. of **monsieur.**

mess·i·ly (mes′ə lē), *adv.* in a messy manner. [MESSY + -LY]

mes·sin (mes′ən), *n. Scot.* messan.

Mes·si·na (mi sē′nə), *n.* **1.** a seaport in NE Sicily: totally destroyed by an earthquake 1908. 251,423 (1961). **2. Strait of,** a strait between Sicily and Italy. 2½ mi. wide.

Mes·sines (*Fr.* me sēn′), *n.* a village in W Belgium, near Ypres: battles 1914, 1917.

mess′ jack′et, a short, tailless jacket extending to just below the waist, used for semiformal occasions and now esp. as part of the uniform of waiters, bellboys, etc.

mess′ kit′, 1. a portable metal dish, often with several divided compartments and a lid, and accompanying eating utensils, esp. one carried by a soldier in the field. **2.** a metal kit in which these utensils are packed. Also called **mess gear.**

mess·man (mes′mən), *n., pl.* **-men.** *Naval.* an enlisted man who serves in the messroom. [MESS + MAN[1]]

mess·mate (mes′māt′), *n.* a person, esp. a friend, who is a member of a group regularly taking meals together, as in an army camp. [MESS + MATE[1]]

mess·room (mes′ro͞om′, -ro͝om′), *n. Naval.* a dining room aboard ship or at a naval base. [MESS + ROOM]

Messrs. (mes′ ərz), pl. of **Mr.**

mes·suage (mes′wij), *n. Law.* a dwelling house with its adjacent buildings and the lands appropriated to the use of the household. [ME < AF, misreading (*n* taken as *u*) of OF *mesnage* MÉNAGE]

mess·y (mes′ē), *adj.,* **mess·i·er, mess·i·est. 1.** characterized by a dirty, untidy, or confused condition: *a messy room.* **2.** causing a mess: *a messy experiment in chemistry; messy work.* **3.** embarrassing, difficult, or unpleasant: *a messy political situation.* **4.** *Informal.* characterized by a confused moral or psychological outlook [MESS + -Y[1]] —**mess′i·ness,** *n.*

mes·tee (me stē′), *n.* mustee.

Mes·thles (mes′thlēz), *n.* (in the *Iliad*) a commander of the Maeonian allies of Troy.

mes·ti·zo (me stē′zō, mi-), *n., pl.* **-zos, -zoes. 1.** a person of mixed blood. **2.** (in Spanish America) a person of mixed Spanish and Amerindian blood. **3.** a person of European and East Indian, Negro, or Malay blood. **4.** a person who is of mixed Philippine and foreign ancestry. Also, *referring to a woman,* **mes·ti·za** (me stē′zə, mi-). [< Sp, n. use of adj. *mestizo* mixed < LL *mixtīcius* of mixed race]

Mes·tor (mes′tôr), *n. Class. Myth.* a son of Perseus and Andromeda.

Meš·tro·vić (mesh′trə vich; *Serbo-Croatian.* mesh′-trô vich′), *n.* **I·van** (ī′vən; *Serbo-Croatian.* ē′vän), 1883–1962, Yugoslav sculptor, in the U.S. after 1946.

met (met), *v.* pt. and pp. of **meet**[1].

met-, var. of **meta-** before a vowel: *metempirical.*

met., **1.** metaphor. **2.** metaphysics. **3.** metropolitan.

me·ta[1] (mē′tə), *n., pl.* **-tae** (-tē). (in ancient Rome) a column or post, or a group of columns or posts, placed at each end of a race track to mark the turning places. [< L]

met·a[2] (met′ə), *adj. Chem.* pertaining to or occupying two positions in the benzene ring that are separated by one carbon atom. Cf. **ortho, para**[2]. [separate use of META-]

Me·ta (mē′tə), *n.* a girl's given name.

meta-, **1.** a learned borrowing from Greek meaning "after," "along with," "beyond," "among," "behind," and often denoting change, used in the formation of compound words: *metacarpus; metagenesis; metalinguistics.* **2.** *Chem.* **a.** (of acids, salts, or their organic derivatives) a combining form denoting the least hydrated of a series: *meta-antimonic,* $HSbO_3$; *meta-antimonous,* $HSbO_2$. Cf. **ortho-, pyro-.** **b.** a combining form designating the meta position in the benzene ring. *Abbr.:* m-. Cf. **ortho-, para-**[1]. Also, *esp. before a vowel,* **met-.** [< Gk, prefix and prep.; c. OE *mid* with, G *mit,* Goth *mith*]

met·a·bi·o·sis (met′ə bī ō′sis), *n. Biol.* a mode of living in which one organism is dependent on another for preparation of an environment in which it can live. [META- + -BIOSIS] —**met·a·bi·ot·ic** (met′ə-bī ot′ik), *adj.* —**met′a·bi·ot′i·cal·ly,** *adv.*

met·a·bol·ic (met′ə bol′ik), *adj.* **1.** of, pertaining to, or affected by metabolism. **2.** undergoing metamorphosis. [< Gk *metabolik(ós)* changeable, equiv. to *metabol(ḗ)* (see METABOLISM) + *-ikos* -IC] —**met′a·bol′i·cal·ly,** *adv.*

met′abol′ic heat′, *Physiol.* See **animal heat.**

me·tab·o·lise (mə tab′ə līz′), *v.t.,* **-lised, -lis·ing.** *Chiefly Brit.* metabolize.

me·tab·o·lism (mə tab′ə liz′əm), *n. Biol., Physiol.* the sum of the physical and chemical processes in an organism by which protoplasm is produced, maintained, and destroyed, and by which energy is made available for its functioning. Cf. **anabolism, catabolism.** [< Gk *metabol(ḗ)* transition + -ISM; see METABOLOUS]

me·tab·o·lite (mə tab′ə līt′), *n. Biol., Physiol.* a product of metabolic action. [METABOL(ISM) + -ITE[1]]

me·tab·o·lize (mə tab′ə līz′), *v.t.,* **-lized, -liz·ing.** to subject to metabolism; change by metabolism. Also, *esp. Brit.,* **metabolise.** [METABOL(ISM) + -IZE] —**me·tab′o·liz′a·bil′i·ty,** *n.* —**me·tab′o·liz′a·ble,** *adj.*

me·tab·o·lous (mə tab′ə ləs), *adj.* metabolic (def. 2). [< Gk *metabólos* changeable, akin to *metabállein* to change, equiv. to *meta-* META- + *bállein* to throw]

Met·a·bus (met′ə bəs), *n. Rom. Legend.* the father of Camilla.

met·a·car·pal (met′ə kär′pəl), *adj.* **1.** of or pertaining to the metacarpus. —*n.* **2.** a metacarpal bone. [META- + CARPAL]

met·a·car·pus (met′ə kär′pəs), *n., pl.* **-pi** (-pī). *Anat.* the part of a hand or forelimb, esp. of its bony structure, included between the wrist, or carpus, and the fingers, or phalanges. See diag. under **skeleton.** [< NL (see META-, CARPUS), r. *metacarpium* < Gk *metakárpion*]

M, Metacenter of a boat; G, Center of gravity; B, Center of buoyancy; B′, Center of buoyancy when boat is displaced

met·a·cen·ter (met′ə sen′tər), *n. Naval Archit.* the intersection between two vertical lines, one through the center of buoyancy of a hull in equilibrium, the other through the center of buoyancy when the hull is inclined slightly to one side or toward one end: the distance of this intersection above the center of gravity is an indication of the initial stability of the hull. Also, *esp. Brit.,* **met·a·cen·tre.** [< F *métacentre.* See -META, CENTER] —**met′a·cen′tric,** *adj.* —**met·a·cen·tric·i·ty** (met′ə sen tris′i tē), *n.*

met′acen′tric height′, *Naval Archit.* the distance between the center of gravity and the metacenter of a floating body, as of a vessel.

metacen′tric stabil′ity, *Naval Archit.* See **initial stability.**

met·a·chro·ma·tism (met′ə krō′mə tiz′əm), *n.* change of color, esp. that due to variation in the temperature of a body. [META- + CHROMAT- + -ISM] —**met·a·chro·mat·ic** (met′ə krō mat′ik, -krə-), *adj.*

me·tach·ro·nal (mə tak′rə nəl), *adj. Zool.* of or pertaining to a wave of rhythmic beat, esp. to a wave of muscular contraction passing over the body surface of certain animals by means of which locomotion is accomplished. [META- + CHRON- + -AL[1]]

met·a·cin·na·bar (met′ə sin′ə bär′), *n. Mineral.* a polymorph of cinnabar, black mercuric sulfide, HgS. [META- + CINNABAR]

Met·a·com·et (met′ə kom′it), *n.* See **Philip, King.**

met·a·cryst (met′ə krist′), *n. Geol.* a crystal formed by recrystallization of minerals in a metamorphic rock. [META- + (PHENO)CRYST]

met·a·gal·ax·y (met′ə gal′ək sē), *n., pl.* **-ax·ies.** *Astron.* the complete system of galaxies; the Milky Way and all the surrounding galaxies [META- + GALAXY] —**met·a·ga·lac·tic** (met′ə gə lak′tik), *adj.*

met·age (mē′tij), *n.* **1.** the official measurement of contents or weight. **2.** the charge for such measurement. [METE[1] + -AGE]

met·a·gen·e·sis (met′ə jen′i sis), *n. Biol.* reproduction characterized by the alternation of a sexual generation and a generation which reproduces asexually. [META- + GENESIS] —**met·a·ge·net·ic** (met′ə jə-net′ik), **met′a·gen′ic,** *adj.* —**met′a·ge·net′i·cal·ly,** *adv.*

me·tag·na·thous (mə tag′nə thəs), *adj. Ornith.* having the tips of the mandibles crossed, as the crossbills. [META- + GNATHOUS] —**me·tag′na·thism,** *n.*

met·a·in·fec·tive (met′ə in fek′tiv), *adj. Med.* occurring after an infection, as a fever in a patient convalescing from an infectious disease. [META- + INFECTIVE]

met·al (met′əl), *n., v.,* **-aled, -al·ing** or (*esp. Brit.*) **-alled, -al·ling.** —*n.* **1.** any of a class of elementary substances, as gold, silver, copper, etc., all of which are crystalline when solid and many of which are characterized by opacity, ductility, conductivity, and a peculiar luster when freshly fractured. **2.** *Chem.* **a.** such a substance in its pure state, as distinguished from alloys. **b.** an element yielding positively charged ions in aqueous solutions of its salts. **3.** an alloy or mixture composed wholly or partly of such substances. **4.** formative material; mettle. **5.** *Print.* **a.** See **type metal.** **b.** the state of being set in type. **6.** *Brit.* broken stone used for roads or railroad-track ballast. **7.** molten glass in the pot or melting tank. **8.** *Heraldry.* either of the tinctures or or argent, represented respectively by gold or yellow, and silver or white. —*v.t.* **9.** to furnish or cover with metal. **10.** *Brit.* to pave or surface (a road) with broken stone. [ME (< OF) < L *metall(um)* quarry, metal < Gk *métallon* mine, quarry, metal] —**met′al·like′,** *adj.*

metal., **1.** metallurgical. **2.** metallurgy.

met·a·lan·guage (met′ə laŋ′gwij), *n.* any language or symbolic system used to discuss, describe, or analyze another language or symbolic system. [META- + LANGUAGE]

met·a·lep·sis (met′əlep′sis), *n., pl.* **-ses** (-sēz). *Rhet.* the use of metonymy to replace a word already used figuratively. [< L < Gk, akin to *metalambánein* to substitute, equiv. to *meta-* META- + *lambánein* to take] —**met′a·lep′tic, met′a·lep′ti·cal,** *adj.* —**met′a·lep′ti·cal·ly,** *adv.*

met′al-free phthalocy′anine (met′əl frē′), *Chem.* phthalocyanine (def. 1).

met·a·lin·guis·tic (met′ə liŋ gwis′tik), *adj. Ling.* noting or pertaining to metalinguistics or a metalanguage. [META- + LINGUISTIC]

met·a·lin·guis·tics (met′ə liŋ gwis′tiks), *n.* (*construed as sing.*) **1.** the study of the relation between languages and the other cultural systems they refer to. **2.** the study of features accompanying and incidental to speech that are not generally considered to be a part of language, as facial expression, gestures, etc. [META- + LINGUISTICS] —**met′a·lin·guis′ti·cal·ly,** *adv.*

met·al·ist (met′əlist), *n.* **1.** a person who works with metals. **2.** a person who advocates the use of metallic money exclusively, instead of paper money. Also, **metallist.** [METAL + -IST]

met·al·ize (met′əlīz′), *v.t.,* **-ized, -iz·ing.** to make metallic; give the characteristics of metal to. Also, **metallize.** [METAL + -IZE] —**met′al·i·za′tion,** *n.*

metall-, var. of **metallo-** esp. before a vowel: *metallurgy.*

metall., metallurgy.

met′al lath′, **1.** any of various meshlike laths of metal for plastering. **2.** nondecorative interior metalwork for supporting lighting fixtures, dropped ceilings, etc. —**met′al lath′er.**

met·alled (met′əld), *adj. Brit.* (of a road) paved; surfaced. [METAL + -ED[2]]

metalli-, a combining form of Latin origin meaning "metal": *metalliferous.* [< L, comb. form of *metallum*]

me·tal·lic (mə tal′ik), *adj.* **1.** of, pertaining to, or consisting of metal. **2.** of the nature of metal, as in luster, resonance, hardness, etc.: *metallic green; a harsh metallic sound.* **3.** *Chem.* **a.** (of a metal element) being in the free or uncombined state: *metallic iron.* **b.** containing or yielding metal. [< L *metallic(us)* < Gk *metallikós* of, for mines. See METAL, -IC] —**me·tal′li·cal·ly,** *adv.* —**met·al·lic·i·ty** (met′əlis′i tē), **met·al·le·i·ty** (met′əlē′i tē), *n.*

me·tal·li·cize (mə tal′i sīz′), *v.t.,* **-cized, -ciz·ing.** to make (a telephone line or the like) thoroughly metallic by replacing a ground return with another wire. [METALLIC + -IZE]

metal′lic lus′ter, *Ceram.* luster[1] (def. 8).

metal′lic soap′, *Chem.* any usually water-insoluble salt formed by the interaction of a fatty acid and a metal, esp. lead or aluminum: used chiefly as a drier in paints and varnishes and for waterproofing textiles.

metal′lic wood′-bor′ing bee′tle (wŏŏd′bōr′iŋ, -bôr′-), any of numerous metallic green, blue, copper, or black beetles of the family *Buprestidae,* the larvae of which bore into the wood of living, decaying, or dead trees.

met·al·lif·er·ous (met′əlif′ər əs), *adj.* containing or yielding metal. [< L *metallifer* (see METALLI-, -FER) + -OUS]

met·al·line (met′əlin, -əlīn′), *adj.* **1.** metallic. **2.** containing one or more metals or metallic salts. [ME *mettaline* < ML *metallīn(us)* of metal. See METAL, -INE[1]]

met·al·lise (met′əlīz′), *v.t.,* **-lised, -lis·ing.** *Chiefly Brit.* metallize. —**met′al·li·sa′tion,** *n.*

met·al·list (met′əlist), *n.* metalist.

met·al·lize (met′əlīz′), *v.t.,* **-lized, -liz·ing.** metalize. Also, *esp. Brit.,* **metallise.** —**met′al·li·za′tion,** *n.*

metallo-, a combining form of Greek origin meaning "metal": *metallography.* Also, *esp. before a vowel,* **metall-.** [< Gk, comb. form of *métallon*]

me·tal·lo·graph (mə tal′ə graf′, -gräf′), *n.* a microscope for observing the microstructure of metals. [METALLO- + -GRAPH]

met·al·log·ra·phy (met′əlog′rə fē), *n.* **1.** the microscopic study of the structure of metals and alloys. **2.** an art or process that is similar to lithography but in which metallic plates are substituted for stones. [< NL *metallographia.* See METALLO-, -GRAPHY] —**met′al·log′ra·pher, met′al·log′ra·phist,** *n.* —**met·al·lo·graph·ic** (mə tal′ə graf′ik), **me·tal′lo·graph′i·cal,** *adj.*

met·al·loid (met′əloid′), *n.* **1.** a nonmetal. **2.** an element which is both metallic and nonmetallic, as arsenic, silicon, or bismuth. —*adj.* **3.** of or pertaining to a metalloid. **4.** resembling both a metal and a nonmetal. [METALL- + -OID]

me·tal·lo·phone (mə tal′ə fōn′), *n.* any musical instrument consisting of a graduated series of metal bars which may either be struck by hammers operated manually or used with a keyboard. [METALLO- + -PHONE]

me·tal·lo·ther·a·py (mə tal′ō ther′ə pē), *n. Med.* therapy by the use of metals or their salts. [METALLO- + THERAPY]

Met′al Lum′ber, *Trademark.* sheet metal pressed and welded together to form joists and studding.

met·al·lur·gy (met′əlûr′jē *or, esp. Brit.,* mə tal′ər jē), *n.* **1.** the technique or science of separating metals from their ores. **2.** the technique or science of making and compounding alloys. **3.** the technique or science of working or heat-treating metals so as to give them certain desired shapes or properties. [< NL *metallurgia* < Gk *metallourgós* working in metals, mines. See METALL-, -URGY] —**met′al·lur′gic, met′al·lur′gi·cal,** *adj.* —**met′al·lur′gi·cal·ly,** *adv.* —**met·al·lur·gist** (met′əlûr′jist, mə tal′ər jist), *n.*

met′al paste′-up, *Print.* a method for making up a form for printing in which engravings mounted on blocks are positioned on and pasted to a metal base.

met·al·smith (met′əl smith′), *n.* a person skilled in fashioning articles of metal. [METAL + SMITH]

met·al·ware (met′əl wâr′), *n.* work of metal, esp. utensils, flatware, etc. [METAL + WARE[1]]

met′al wood′, a structural material consisting of a sheet of metal glued between two veneers or of a veneer glued between two sheets of metal.

met·al·work·ing (met′əl wûr′kiŋ), *n.* the act or technique of making metal objects. [METAL + WORKING]

met·a·math·e·mat·ics (met′ə math′ə mat′iks), *n.* (*construed as sing.*) the logical analysis of the fundamental concepts of mathematics, as number, function, etc. [META- + MATHEMATICS] —**met′a·math′e·mat′i·cal,** *adj.* —**met·a·math·e·ma·ti·cian** (met′ə-math′ə mə tish′ən), *n.*

met·a·mer (met′ə mər), *n. Chem.* a compound exhibiting metamerism with one or more other compounds. [META- + -MER]

met·a·mere (met′ə mēr′), *n* a somite. [META- + -MERE]

met·a·mer·ic (met′ə mer′ik), *adj.* **1.** Also, **me·tam·er·al** (mə tam′ər əl). *Zool.* **a.** consisting of metameres. **b.** pertaining to metamerism. **2.** *Chem.* of, pertaining to, or characteristic of metamerism. [METAMERE + -IC] —**met′a·mer′i·cal·ly,** *adv.*

me·tam·er·ism (mə tam′ə riz′əm), *n.* **1.** *Zool.* **a.** division into metameres, the developmental process of somite formation. **b.** existence in a metameric state. **2.** *Chem.* isomerism resulting from the attachment of different groups to the same atom, as C_2H_5-NHC_2H_5 and $CH_3NHC_3H_7$. [METAMERE + -ISM]

met·a·mor·phic (met′ə môr′fik), *adj.* **1.** pertaining to or characterized by change of form, or metamorphosis. **2.** *Geol.* pertaining to or exhibiting structural change or metamorphism. [META- + -MORPHIC]

met′amor′phic cy′cle, *Geol.* the cycle of transformation of rock materials in which magmas cool into igneous rocks that erode and become sediments that are compressed into sedimentary rocks which may eventually be transformed into metamorphic rocks or remelted into magma.

met·a·mor·phism (met′ə môr′fiz əm), *n.* **1.** metamorphosis. **2.** *Geol.* a change in the structure or constitution of a rock due to natural agencies, as pressure and heat, esp. when the rock becomes harder and more completely crystalline. [META- + -MORPHISM]

met·a·mor·phose (met′ə môr′fōz, -fōs), *v.,* **-phosed, -phos·ing.** —*v.t.* **1.** to change the form or nature of; transform. **2.** to subject to metamorphosis or metamorphism. —*v.i.* **3.** to undergo or be capable of undergoing a change in form or nature. [back formation from METAMORPHOSIS] —**Syn. 1.** mutate, transmute.

Met·a·mor·pho·ses (met′ə môr′fə sēz′), *n.* a series of mythological tales or legends in verse (A.D. 7–8) by Ovid.

met·a·mor·pho·sis (met′ə môr′fə sis), *n., pl.* **-ses** (-sēz′). **1.** a complete change of form, structure, or substance, as transformation by magic or witchcraft. **2.** any complete change in appearance, character, circumstances, etc. **3.** a form resulting from any such change. **4.** *Zool.* a change or successive changes of form during the postembryonic or embryonic growth of an animal by which it is adapted to a new or special environment or way of living: *the metamorphosis of tadpoles into frogs.* **5.** *Pathol.* **a.** a type of alteration or degeneration in which tissues are changed: *fatty metamorphosis of the liver.* **b.** the resultant form. **6.** *Bot.* the structural or functional modification of a plant organ or structure during its development. [< L < Gk: transformation. See META-, -MORPH, -OSIS] —**Syn. 2.** mutation, transmutation. —**Ant. 1, 2.** stasis.

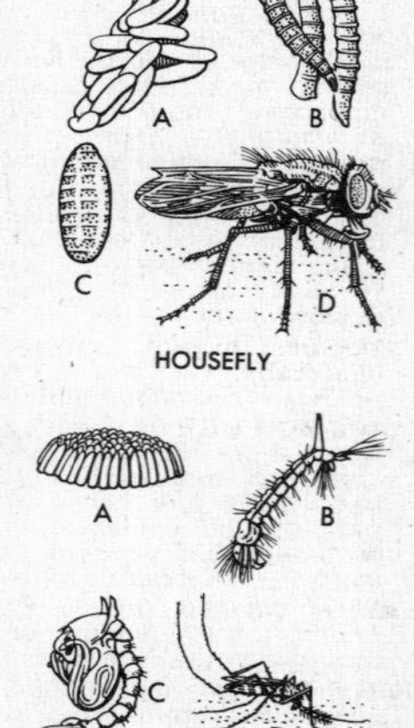

Metamorphosis (def. 4)
A, Eggs; B, Larva; C, Pupa; D, Adult

Met′amor′phosis, The, a short story (1937) by Franz Kafka. German, **Die Verwandlung.**

met·a·mor·phous (met′ə môr′fəs), *adj.* metamorphic. [META- + -MORPHOUS]

met·a·neph·ros (met′ə nef′ros), *n., pl.* **-roi** (-roi). *Embryol.* one of the three embryonic excretory organs of higher vertebrates, becoming the permanent and functional kidney. Cf. **mesonephros, pronephros.** [< NL < Gk *meta-* META- + *nephrós* kidney] —**met′a·neph′ric, met·a·ne·phrit·ic** (met′ə nə frit′ik), *adj.*

Met·a·ni·ra (met′ə nī′rə), *n. Class. Myth.* the wife of Celeus and the mother of Abas, Demophoön, and Triptolemus.

CONCISE ETYMOLOGY KEY: <, descended or derived from; >, whence; b., blend of, blended; c., cognate with; deriv., derivative; equiv., equivalent; imit., imitative; m., modification of; obl., oblique; r., replacing; s., stem; sp., spelling; trans., translation; ?, origin unknown, perhaps; *, hypothetical. See the full key inside the front cover.

met·a·ni·tro·phe·nol (met′ə nī′trə fē′nōl, -nôl, -nol), *n.* See under **nitrophenol** (def. 2).

metaph., 1. metaphysical. 2. metaphysics.

met·a·phase (met′ə fāz′), *n.* *Biol.* the stage in mitosis in which the duplicated chromosomes lie on the equatorial plane of the spindle. [META- + PHASE]

Met·a·phen (met′ə fen′), *n.* *Pharm., Trademark.* nitromersol.

met·a·phor (met′ə fôr′, -fər), *n.* the application of a word or phrase to an object or concept which it does not literally denote, in order to suggest comparison with another object or concept, as in "A mighty fortress is our God." Cf. **mixed metaphor, simile** (def. 1). [< L *metaphora* < Gk: a transfer, akin to *metaphérein* to transfer. See META-, -PHORE] —**met·a·phor·i·cal** (met′ə fôr′i kəl, -for′-), **met′a·phor′ic,** *adj.* —**met′a·phor′i·cal·ly,** *adv.* —**met′a·phor′i·cal·ness,** *n.*

met·a·phos·phate (met′ə fos′fāt), *n.* *Chem.* a salt or ester of metaphosphoric acid. [META- + PHOSPHATE]

met′a·phos·phor′ic ac′id (met′ə fos fôr′ik, -for′-), *Chem.* an acid, HPO_3, derived from phosphorous pentoxide, and containing the smallest amount of water of the phosphoric acids. Cf. **phosphoric acid.** [META- + PHOSPHORIC]

met·a·phrase (met′ə frāz′), *n., v.,* **-phrased, -phras·ing.** —*n.* 1. a translation. —*v.t.* 2. to translate, esp. literally. 3. to change the phrasing or literary form of. [< Gk *metáphras(is)* a paraphrasing, change of phrasing. See META-, PHRASE]

met·a·phrast (met′ə frast′), *n.* a person who translates or changes a literary work from one form to another, as prose into verse. [MGk *metaphrást(ēs)* one who translates, akin to *metaphrázein* to translate] —**met′a·phras′tic, met′a·phras′ti·cal,** *adj.* —**met′a·phras′ti·cal·ly,** *adv.*

metaphys., metaphysics.

met·a·phys·ic (met′ə fiz′ik), *n.* 1. metaphysics. 2. *Obs.* a metaphysician. [ME *methaphesik* < ML *metaphysica* (neut. pl.); see METAPHYSICS]

met·a·phys·i·cal (met′ə fiz′i kəl), *adj.* 1. pertaining to or of the nature of metaphysics. 2. *Philos.* a. concerned with abstract thought or subjects, as existence, causality, truth, etc. b. concerned with first principles and ultimate grounds, as being, time, or substance. 3. highly abstract or abstruse. 4. designating or pertaining to the poetry of an early group of 17th-century English poets, notably John Donne, whose characteristic style is highly intellectual and philosophical and features intensive use of ingenious conceits and turns of wit. 5. *Archaic.* imaginary. [ME < ML *metaphysicāl(is).* See METAPHYSIC, -AL[1]] —**met′a·phys′i·cal·ly,** *adv.*

met·a·phy·si·cian (met′ə fi zish′ən), *n.* a person who is versed in metaphysics. Also, **met·a·phys·i·cist** (met′ə fiz′i sist). [prob. < MF *metaphysicien,* equiv. to *metaphysique* METAPHYSIC + *-ien* -IAN]

met·a·phys·ics (met′ə fiz′iks), *n.* (*construed as sing*) 1. the branch of philosophy that treats of first principles, includes ontology and cosmology, and is always intimately connected with an epistemology. 2. philosophy, esp. in its more abstruse branches. 3. (*cap., italics.*) a treatise (4th century B.C.) by Aristotle, dealing with first principles, the relation of universals to particulars, and the teleological doctrine of causation. [< ML *metaphysic(a)* < MGk (*tà*) *metaphysiká* (neut. pl.), Gk *tà metà tà physiká* the (works) after the physics; with reference to the arrangement of Aristotle's writings]

met·a·phyte (met′ə fīt′), *n.* *Bot.* a multicellular plant. [META- + -PHYTE] —**met·a·phyt·ic** (met′ə fit′ik), *adj.*

met·a·pla·sia (met′ə plā′zhə, -zhē ə), *n.* *Physiol.* transformation of one type of tissue into another. [META- + -PLASIA]

met·a·plasm (met′ə plaz′əm), *n.* 1. *Biol.* the nonliving matter or inclusions, as starch, pigments, etc., in the protoplasm of a cell. 2. *Gram.* a. a change in the structure of a word or sentence made by adding, removing, or transposing the sounds or words of which it is composed or the letters that represent them. b. the formation of oblique cases from a stem other than that of the nominative. [< L *metaplasm(us)* a grammatical change, irregularity < Gk *metaplasmós* reforming, remodeling, deriv. of *metaplássein* to mould differently, remodel. See META-, -PLASM] —**met′a·plas′mic,** *adj.*

met·ap·neus·tic (met′ap nōō′stik, -nyōō′-), *adj.* *Entomol.* having only the last pair of abdominal spiracles open, as the tracheal system of certain insect larvae. [META- + Gk *pneustik(ós)* of breathing]

met·a·pro·tein (met′ə prō′tēn, -tē in), *n.* *Biochem.* a hydrolytic derivative of protein, insoluble in water but soluble in dilute acids or alkalies. [META- + PROTEIN]

met·a·psy·chol·o·gy (met′ə sī kol′ə jē), *n.* *Psychol.* 1. speculative thought dealing systematically with concepts extending beyond the limits of psychology as an empirical science. 2. (in psychoanalytic theory) the conception of mental processes as subsumed under three major categories representing causal relations **(mental dynamics),** structural placement **(mental topography),** and functional value **(mental economy).** [META- + PSYCHOLOGY] —**met·a·psy·cho·log·i·cal** (met′ə sī′kə loj′i kəl), *adj.*

met·a·scope (met′ə skōp′), *n.* a device for converting infrared radiation into visible light. [META- + -SCOPE]

met·a·so·ma·tism (met′ə sō′mə tiz′əm), *n.* *Geol.* 1. the series of processes whereby minerals or rocks are replaced by others of different chemical composition as a result of the introduction of material, usually in very hot aqueous solutions, from sources external to the formation undergoing change. 2. replacement (def. 3). Also, **met·a·so·ma·to·sis** (met′ə sō′mə tō′sis). [META- + SOMAT- + -ISM] —**met·a·so·mat·ic** (met′ə sō mat′ik), *adj.*

me·ta·sta·ble (met′ə stā′bəl, met′ə stā′-), *adj.* 1. *Metall.* chemically unstable in the absence of certain conditions that would induce stability, but not liable to spontaneous transformation. 2. *Physics, Chem.* pertaining to a body or system existing at an energy level above that of a more stable state and requiring the addition of a small amount of energy to induce a transition to the more stable state. [META- + STABLE[2]] —**met·a·sta·bil·i·ty** (met′ə stə bil′i tē), *n.*

met′asta′ble state′, *Physics, Chem.* an excited energy level of relatively long duration of an atom, body, or system.

Me·ta·sta·sio (me′tä stä′zyô), *n.* (*Pietro Antonio Domenico Bonaventura Trapassi*) 1698–1782, Italian poet and dramatist.

me·tas·ta·sis (mə tas′tə sis), *n., pl.* **-ses** (-sēz′). 1. *Pathol.* a. the transference of disease-producing organisms or of malignant or cancerous cells to other parts of the body by way of the blood vessels, lymphatics, or membranous surfaces. b. the condition produced by this. 2. transformation (def. 2). 3. *Rhet.* a rapid transition, as from one subject to another. 4. *Physics.* a change in position or orbit of an elementary particle. [< Gk: a changing. See META-, STASIS] —**met·a·stat·ic** (met′ə stat′ik), *adj.* —**met′a·stat′i·cal·ly,** *adv.*

me·tas·ta·size (mə tas′tə sīz′), *v.i.,* **-sized, -siz·ing.** *Pathol.* (of malignant cells or disease-producing organisms) to spread to other parts of the body by way of the blood vessels, lymphatics, or membranous surfaces. [METASTAS(IS) + -IZE]

met·a·tar·sal (met′ə tär′səl), *adj.* 1. of or pertaining to the metatarsus. —*n.* 2. a bone in the metatarsus. [META- + TARSAL] —**met′a·tar′sal·ly,** *adv.*

met·a·tar·sus (met′ə tär′səs), *n., pl.* **-si** (-sī). *Anat., Zool.* the part of a foot or hind limb, esp. its bony structure, included between the tarsus and the toes or phalanges. See diag. under **skeleton.** [< NL; see META-, TARSUS]

met·a·the·ri·an (met′ə thēr′ē ən), *adj.* 1. belonging or pertaining to the group *Metatheria,* comprising the marsupial mammals. —*n.* 2. a metatherian animal. [< NL *Metathēri(a)* name of the group (< Gk *meta-* META- + *thēria,* pl. of *thērion* animal) + -AN]

me·tath·e·sis (mə tath′i sis), *n., pl.* **-ses** (-sēz′). 1. the transposition of letters, syllables, or sounds in a word. 2. *Chem.* See **double decomposition.** [< L: transposition of letters of a word < Gk *metáthesis* transposition. See META-, THESIS] —**met·a·thet·ic** (met′ə thet′ik), **met′a·thet′i·cal,** *adj.*

me·tath·e·sise (mə tath′i sīz′), *v.i., v.t.,* **-sised, -sis·ing.** *Chiefly Brit.* metathesize.

me·tath·e·size (mə tath′i sīz′), *v.i., v.t.,* **-sized, -siz·ing.** to undergo or cause to undergo metathesis. [METATHES(IS) + -IZE]

met·a·tho·rax (met′ə thôr′aks, -thōr′-), *n., pl.* **-tho·rax·es, -tho·ra·ces** (-thôr′ə sēz′, -thōr′-). the posterior division of the thorax of an insect, bearing the third pair of legs and the second pair of wings. [META- + THORAX] —**met·a·tho·rac·ic** (met′ə thō ras′ik, -thô-), *adj.*

met·a·tol·u·i·dine (met′ə tə lōō′i dēn′, -din), *n.* *Chem.* a colorless, slightly water-soluble liquid, $CH_3C_6H_4NH_2$, the meta isomer of toluidine, used in the manufacture of dyes and other organic compounds.

met·a·troph·ic (met′ə trof′ik, -trō′fik), *adj.* requiring dead organic matter for food; saprophytic. [META- + TROPHIC] —**met·a·troph** (met′ə trof′, -trōf′), *n.* —**me·tat·ro·phy** (mə ta′trə fē), *n.*

Me·tax·a (mə tak′sə; *Gk.* me′tä ksä′), *n.* *Trademark.* a strong, dark brandy from Greece.

Me·ta·xas (mə tak′səs; *Gk.* me′tä ksäs′), *n.* **Jo·an·nes** (yô ä′nyes), 1871–1941, Greek general and political leader: dictator 1936–40.

met·a·xy·lem (met′ə zī′lem), *n.* *Bot.* the part of the primary xylem which is the last to be formed, usually having weblike or pitted surfaces. [META- + XYLEM]

mé·ta·yage (met′ə yäzh′, mā′tə-), *n.* the system of agriculture based on the use of métayers. [< F; see MÉTAYER, -AGE]

mé·ta·yer (met′ə yā′, mā′tə-), *n.* a person who tills land and receives a share of the harvest, the tools, seed, etc., being furnished by the landlord. [< F < ML *mediētār(ius),* equiv. to *mediet(ās)* (see MOIETY) + *-ārius* -ARY]

Met·a·zo·a (met′ə zō′ə), *n.* a zoological division comprising the multicellular animals. [META- + -ZOA] —**met′a·zo′an,** *adj., n.* —**met′a·zo′ic, met′a·zo′al,** *adj.*

Met′calfe bean′ (met′kaf′, -käf′), a trailing perennial herb, *Phaseolus metcalfei,* of southwestern North America, having a large, fleshy root, reddish-purple flowers, and brownish-black seeds. [named after J.K. *Metcalfe,* 19th-century American who first cultivated it in America]

Metch·ni·koff (mech nē kôf′), *n.* **É·lie** (ā lē′), 1845–1916, Russian zoologist and bacteriologist in France: Nobel prize for medicine 1908. Russian, **Mechnikov.**

mete[1] (mēt), *v.t.,* **met·ed, met·ing.** 1. to distribute or apportion by measure; allot (usually fol. by *out*): *to mete out punishment.* 2. *Archaic.* to measure. [ME; OE *metan;* c. D *meten,* Icel *meta,* Goth *mitan,* G *messen* to measure, Gk *médesthai* to ponder]
—**Syn.** 1. dole, deal, measure, parcel.

mete[2] (mēt), *n.* 1. a limiting mark. 2. a limit or boundary. [late ME < MF < L *mēta* goal-mark, turning post]
—**Syn.** 2. bound.

Met.E., metallurgical engineer.

met·em·pir·i·cal (met′em pir′i kəl), *adj.* 1. beyond or outside the field of experience. 2. of or pertaining to metempirics. [MET- + EMPIRICAL] —**met′em·pir′i·cal·ly,** *adv.*

met·em·pir·ics (met′em pir′iks), *n.* (*construed as sing.*) the philosophy dealing with the existence of things outside, or beyond, experience. [see METEMPIRIC, -ICS] —**met′em·pir′i·cist,** *n.*

me·tem·psy·cho·sis (mə tem′sə kō′sis, -temp′-, met′əm sī-), *n., pl.* **-ses** (-sēz). 1. the passage of the soul from one body to another. 2. the rebirth of the soul at death in another body of either human or animal form. [< L < Gk] —**met·em·psy·chic** (met′əm sī′kik), **me·tem′psy·cho′sic, me·tem′psy·cho′si·cal,** *adj.*

met·en·ceph·a·lon (met′en sef′ə lon′), *n., pl.* **-lons, -la** (-lə). *Anat.* the anterior section of the hindbrain, comprising the cerebellum and pons. [MET- + ENCEPHALON] —**met·en·ce·phal·ic** (met′en sə fal′ik), *adj.*

me·te·or (mē′tē ər), *n.* 1. a meteoroid or meteorite. 2. a transient fiery streak in the sky produced by a meteoroid passing through the earth's atmosphere; a shooting star or bolide. 3. *Informal.* any person or object that moves, progresses, becomes famous, etc., with spectacular speed. 4. *Obs.* any atmospheric phenomenon, as hail, a typhoon, etc. [< ML *meteor(um)* < Gk *meteōron* meteor, a thing in the air, n. use of neut. of *meteōros* raised in the air, equiv. to *met-* MET- + *eōr-* (var. s. of *aeírein* to raise) + *-os* adj. suffix] —**me′te·or·like′,** *adj.*

meteor., 1. meteorological. 2. meteorology.

Me′teor Cra′ter. See **Crater Mound.**

me·te·or·ic (mē′tē ôr′ik, -or′-), *adj.* 1. of, pertaining to, or like a meteor or meteors. 2. consisting of meteors: *a meteoric shower.* 3. resembling a meteor in transient brilliance, suddenness of appearance, swiftness, etc.: *a meteoric career.* 4. of the atmosphere; meteorological. [< ML *meteoric(us).* See METEOR, -IC] —**me′te·or′i·cal·ly,** *adv.*

me′teor′ic show′er, *Astron.* See **meteor shower.**

me·te·or·ite (mē′tē ə rīt′), *n.* 1. a mass of stone or metal that has reached the earth from outer space; a fallen meteoroid. 2. a meteoroid. [METEOR + -ITE[1]] —**me·te·or·it·ic** (mē′tē ə rit′ik), **me′te·or·it′i·cal, me·te·or·it·al** (mē′tē ə rīt′əl), *adj.*

me·te·or·it·ics (mē′tē ə rit′iks), *n.* (*construed as sing.*) *Astron.* the science that deals with meteors. [METEORITE + -ICS] —**me·te·or·it·i·cist** (mē′tē ə rit′i sist), *n.*

me·te·or·o·gram (mē′tē ôr′ə gram′, -or′-, mē′tē-ər ə-), *n.* *Meteorol.* 1. a record made by a meteorograph. 2. a diagram or chart representing the pattern of recurrence of two or more meteorological phenomena over a period of time as observed at a given weather station or group of stations. [METEORO(LOGY) + -GRAM[1]]

me·te·or·o·graph (mē′tē ôr′ə graf′, -gräf′, -or′-, mē′tē ər ə-), *n.* an instrument for automatically recording various meteorological conditions, as of barometric pressure, temperature, etc., at the same time. [METEORO(LOGY) + -GRAPH] —**me·te·or·o·graph·ic** (mē′tē ôr′ə graf′ik, -or′-, mē′tē ər ə-), *adj.* —**me·te·o·rog·ra·phy** (mē′tē ə rog′rə fē), *n.*

me·te·or·oid (mē′tē ə roid′), *n.* *Astron.* any of the small bodies, often remnants of comets, traveling through space: when such a body enters the earth's atmosphere it is heated to luminosity and becomes a meteor. [METEOR + -OID]

meteorol., 1. meteorological. 2. meteorology.

me·te·or·o·log·i·cal (mē′tē ər ə loj′i kəl), *adj.* pertaining to meteorology or to phenomena of the atmosphere or weather. Also, **me′te·or·o·log′ic.** [< Gk *meteōrologik(ós)* pertaining to celestial phenomena (see METEOROLOGY, -IC) + -AL[1]] —**me′te·or·o·log′i·cal·ly,** *adv.*

me·te·or·ol·o·gy (mē′tē ə rol′ə jē), *n.* 1. the science dealing with the atmosphere and its phenomena, including weather and climate. 2. the atmospheric conditions and weather of an area. [< Gk *meteōrologia* a treatise on the heavenly bodies. See METEOR, -O-, -LOGY] —**me′te·or·ol′o·gist,** *n.*

me·te·or·o·path·o·log·ic (mē′tē ər ə path′ə loj′ik, -tē ôr′ə-, -or′ə-), *adj.* *Pathol.* of or pertaining to the harmful effect of climatic conditions on health. [METEORO(LOGY) + PATHOLOG(Y) + -IC]

me′teor show′er, *Astron.* the profusion of meteors observed when the earth passes through a meteor swarm. Also, **meteoric shower.**

me′teor swarm′, *Astron.* any large number of meteoroids moving in parallel paths. Cf. **meteor shower.**

me·ter[1] (mē′tər), *n.* the fundamental unit of length in the metric system, equivalent to 39.37 U.S. inches, originally intended to be, and being very nearly, equal to one ten-millionth of the distance from the equator to the pole measured on a meridian: defined from 1889 to 1960 as the distance between two lines on a platinum-iridium bar (the "International Prototype Meter") preserved at the International Bureau of Weights and Measures near Paris, and now defined as 1,650,763.73 wavelengths of the orange-red radiation of krypton 86 under specified conditions. *Abbr.:* m Also, *esp. Brit.,* **metre.** [< F *mètre* < Gk *métron* measure]

me·ter[2] (mē′tər), *n.* 1. *Pros.* a. poetic measure; arrangement of words in regularly measured, patterned, or rhythmic lines or verses. b. a particular form of such arrangement, depending on both the kind and the number of feet constituting the verse (usually used in combination): *iambic trimeter.* 2. *Music.* a. the rhythmic element as measured by division into parts of equal time value. b. the unit of measurement, in terms of number of beats, adopted for a given piece of music. Cf. **measure** (def. 18). Also, *esp. Brit.,* **metre.** [ME *metir, metur,* OE *mēter* < L *metr(um)* poetic meter, verse < Gk *métron* measure; r. ME *metre* < MF]

me·ter[3] (mē′tər), *n.* 1. an instrument for measuring, esp. one that automatically measures and records the quantity of a substance, as of gas, water, or electricity, passing through or actuating it. —*v.t.* 2. to measure by means of a meter. [ME; see METE[1], -ER[1]]

Me·ter (mē′tər), *n.* *Class. Myth.* an epithet of Athena, meaning "mother."

-meter, a learned borrowing from Latin and Greek meaning "measure," used in the names of instruments measuring quantity, extent, degree, etc.: *altimeter; barometer.* Cf. **-metry.** [< NL *-metrum* < Gk. See METER[1]]

me·ter·age (mē′tər ij), *n.* 1. the practice of measuring; measurement. 2. a sum or price charged for measurement. [METER[3] + -AGE]

me·ter-can·dle (mē′tər kan′dəl), *n.* lux.

me·ter-can·dle-sec·ond (mē′tər kan′dəl sek′ənd), *n.* a unit of light-exposure equivalent to one lux for one second.

me·ter-kil·o·gram-sec·ond (mē′tər kil′ə gram′-sek′ənd), *adj.* of or pertaining to the system of units in which the meter, kilogram, and second are the principal units of length, mass, and time. *Abbr.:* mks, m.k.s., MKS

metes′ and bounds′ (mēts), the boundaries or limits of a piece of land. [trans. of AF *metes et boundes.* See METE[2], BOUND[3]]

meth-, a combining form of **methyl:** *methenamine.*

Meth., Methodist.

meth·a·ce·tin (meth′ə sēt′ən), *n.* *Pharm.* a white, crystalline, water-insoluble powder, the para isomer of $CH_3OC_6H_4NHCOCH_3$, used for relieving pain and reducing or preventing fever. Also called **acetanisidine.** [METH- + ACET- + -IN[2]]

meth·ac·ry·late (meth ak′rə lāt′), *n.* *Chem.* an ester or salt derived from methacrylic acid. [METH- + ACRYL + -ATE[2]]

methac′rylate res′in, *Chem.* an acrylic resin formed by polymerizing the esters or amides of methacrylic acid.

meth′a·cryl′ic ac′id (meth′ə kril′ik, meth′-), *Chem.* a colorless, liquid acid, $CH_2{=}C(CH_3)COOH$, produced synthetically, whose methyl ester, methyl methacrylate, polymerizes to yield a clear plastic. Cf. **Lucite, plexiglass.** [METH- + ACRYLIC]

meth·a·done (meth′ə dōn′), *n. Pharm.* a synthetic narcotic drug, $(C_6H_5)_2C(COC_2H_5)CH_2CH(CH_3)N(CH_3)_2$, slightly more potent than morphine, used usually in the form of its hydrochloride for relieving pain. Also, **meth·a·don** (meth′ə don′). [METH(Y) + A(MINO) + D(IPHENYL) + (HEPTAN)ONE]

met·hae·mo·glo·bin (met hē′mə glō′bin, -hem′ə-, -hē′mə glō′-, -hem′ə-), *n.* methemoglobin.

meth·a·nal (meth′ə nal′), *n. Chem.* formaldehyde. [METHANE + -AL[3]]

meth·a·na·tion (meth′ə nā′shən), *n. Chem.* the process of converting a mixture, as of hydrogen and carbon monoxide, into methane. [METHANE + -ATION]

meth·ane (meth′ān), *n. Chem.* a colorless, odorless, flammable gas, CH_4, the main constituent of marsh gas and the firedamp of coal mines, obtained commercially from natural gas: the first member of the methane, or alkane, series of hydrocarbons. [METH- + -ANE]

meth′ane se′ries, *Chem.* See **alkane series.**

meth·a·nol (meth′ə nōl′, -nôl′, -nol′), *n. Chem.* See **methyl alcohol.** [METHANE + -OL[1]]

meth·an·the·line (me than′thə lēn′), *n. Pharm.* a compound, $C_{21}H_{26}BrNO_3$, used in the form of its bromide in the treatment of excessive sweating and salivation, peptic ulcer, stomach cramps, and other conditions resulting from nerve dysfunction. [METH- + (X)ANTH- + -E(NE) + (CARBONY)L + -INE[2]]

Meth·e·drine (meth′ə drēn′, -drin), *n. Trademark.* a stimulating drug similar in its effects to amphetamine.

me·theg·lin (mə theg′lin), *n.* a variety of spiced mead. [< Welsh *meddyglyn*, equiv. to *meddyg* healing (< L *medicus*; see MEDICAL) + *llyn* liquor]

met·he·mo·glo·bin (met hē′mə glō′bin, -hem′ə-, -hē′mə glō′-, -hem′ə-), *n. Biochem.* a brownish compound of oxygen and hemoglobin, formed in the blood, as by the use of certain drugs. Also, **methaemoglobin.** Also called **ferrihemoglobin, hemiglobin.** [MET- + HEMOGLOBIN]

me·the·na·mine (me thē′nə mēn′, -min), *n. Chem.* hexamethylenetetramine. [METH- + -ENE + AMINE]

meth·e·nyl (meth′ə nil), *adj. Chem.* methylidyne. [METH- + -EN(E) + -YL]

me·thinks (mi thingks′), *v. impers.; pt.* **me·thought.** *Archaic.* it seems to me. [ME *me thinketh*, OE *me thyncth.* See ME, THINK[2]]

me·thi·o·nine (me thī′ə nēn′, -nin), *n. Biochem.* an amino acid, $CH_3SCH_2CH_2CH(NH_2)COOH$, found in casein, wool, and other proteins or prepared synthetically: used as a supplement to a high-protein diet in the prevention and treatment of certain liver diseases. [METH- + THIONINE]

meth·od (meth′əd), *n.* **1.** a manner or mode of procedure, esp. an orderly, logical, or systematic way of instruction, inquiry, presentation, etc.: *an effective method of teaching algebra.* **2.** a way of doing something, esp. in accordance with a definite plan: *There are three possible methods of doing this.* **3.** order or system in doing anything: *to work with method.* **4.** orderly or systematic arrangement, sequence, or the like. **5. the Method.** Also called **Stanislavski Method, Stanislavski System.** a theory and technique of acting in which the performer identifies with the character to be portrayed and renders the part in a naturalistic, nondeclamatory, and highly individualized manner. —*adj.* **6.** (*usually cap.*) of, pertaining to, or employing the Method: *Method actor; Method acting.* [< L *method(us)* < Gk *méthodos* systematic course, equiv. to *met-* META- + *hodós* way, road] —**meth′od·less,** *adj.*

—**Syn. 1.** means, technique. METHOD, MODE, WAY imply a manner in which a thing is done or in which it happens. METHOD refers to a settled kind of procedure, usually according to a definite, established, logical, or systematic plan: *the open-hearth method of making steel; one method of solving a problem.* MODE is a more formal word which implies a customary or characteristic fashion of doing something: *Kangaroos have a peculiar mode of carrying their young.* WAY, a word in popular use for the general idea, is equivalent to various more specific words: *someone's way* (manner) *of walking; the best way* (method) *of rapid calculating; the way* (mode) *of holding a pen.* **4.** disposition.

me·thod·i·cal (mə thod′i kəl), *adj.* **1.** performed, disposed, or acting in a systematic way; systematic; orderly: *a methodical person.* **2.** painstaking, esp. slow and painstaking. Also, **me·thod′ic.** [*methodic* (< L *methodicus* < Gk *methodikós*; see METHOD, -IC) + -AL[1]] —**me·thod′i·cal·ly,** *adv.* —**me·thod′i·cal·ness,** *n.* —**Syn. 1.** See **orderly.**

meth·od·ise (meth′ə dīz′), *v.t.,* **-ised, -is·ing.** *Chiefly Brit.* methodize. —**meth′od·is′er,** *n.*

Meth·od·ism (meth′ə diz′əm), *n.* **1.** the doctrines, polity, beliefs, and methods of worship of the Methodists. **2.** (*l.c.*) *Rare.* the act or practice of working, proceeding, etc., according to some method or system. **3.** (*l.c.*) *Rare.* an excessive use of or preoccupation with methods, systems, or the like. [METHOD + -ISM]

Meth·od·ist (meth′ə dist), *n.* **1.** a member of the largest Christian denomination which grew out of the revival of religion led by John Wesley: stresses both personal and social morality and has an Arminian doctrine and, in the U.S., a modified episcopal polity. **2.** (*l.c.*) *Rare.* a person who uses methods or a particular method, esp. habitually or excessively. —*adj.* **3.** Also, **Meth′od·is′tic, Meth′od·is′ti·cal.** of or pertaining to the Methodists or Methodism. [METHOD + -IST] —**Meth′od·is′ti·cal·ly,** *adv.*

Me·tho·di·us (mə thō′dē əs), *n.* **Saint** (*Apostle of the Slavs*), A.D. c825–885, Greek missionary in Moravia (brother of Saint Cyril).

meth·od·ize (meth′ə dīz′), *v.t.,* **-ized, -iz·ing.** **1.** to reduce (something) to a method. **2.** to arrange (something) according to a method. Also, *esp. Brit.,* **methodise.** [METHOD + -IZE] —**meth′od·iz′er,** *n.*

meth·od·ol·o·gy (meth′ə dol′ə jē), *n., pl.* **-gies.** **1.** a set or system of methods, principles, and rules for regulating a given discipline, as in the arts or sciences. **2.** *Logic.* the study of the principles underlying the organization of the various sciences and the conduct of scientific inquiry. **3.** *Educ.* a branch of pedagogics dealing with analysis and evaluation of subjects to be taught and of the methods of teaching them. [< NL *methodologia.* See METHOD, -O-, -LOGY] —**meth·od·o·log·i·cal** (meth′ə də loj′i kəl), *adj.* —**meth′od·o·log′i·cal·ly,** *adv.* —**meth′od·ol′o·gist,** *n.*

me·thought (mi thôt′), *v.* pt. of **methinks.**

meth·ox·ide (meth ok′sīd, -sid), *n. Chem.* methylate (def. 1). [METH- + OXIDE]

me·thox·y (mə thok′sē), *adj. Chem.* containing the methoxy group. Also, **meth·ox·yl** (mə thok′sil). [METH- + OXY-[2]]

methoxy-, a combining form representing the methoxy group: *methoxychlor.*

me·thox·y·ben·zene (mə thok′sē ben′zēn, -ben zēn′), *n. Chem.* anisole. [METHOXY- + BENZENE]

me·thox·y·chlor (mə thok′si klōr′, -klôr′), *n. Chem.* a white, crystalline, water-insoluble solid, $Cl_3CCH(C_6H_4OCH_3)_2$, used as an insecticide. Also called **DMDT, methoxy DDT.** [METHOXY- + CHLOR-[1]]

methoxy DDT, methoxychlor.

methox′y group′, *Chem.* the univalent group, CH_3O–. Also called **methox′y rad′ical.**

Me·thu·en (mə thōō′ən), *n.* a town in NE Massachusetts, near Lawrence. 28,114 (1960).

Me·thu·se·lah (mə thōō′zə lə, -thōōz′lə), *n.* **1.** Also, *Douay Bible,* **Mathusala.** a patriarch, said to have lived 969 years. Gen. 5:27. **2.** a wine bottle holding 6½ quarts.

meth·yl (meth′əl), *adj. Chem.* containing the methyl group. [METH- + -YL] —**me·thyl·ic** (me thil′ik, mə-), *adj.*

methyl-, a combining form indicating the presence of the methyl group: *methylamine.*

meth′yl ac′etate, *Chem.* a colorless, flammable, volatile liquid, CH_3COOCH_3, the methyl ester of acetic acid, having a fragrant odor: used chiefly as a solvent.

meth′yl·a·ce′tic ac′id (meth′əl ə sē′tik, -ə set′ik), *Chem.* See **propionic acid.** [METHYL- + ACETIC ACID]

meth·yl·al (meth′ə lal′, meth′ə lal′), *n. Chem.* a colorless, flammable, volatile liquid, $CH_3OCH_2OCH_3$, having a chloroformlike odor: used chiefly as a solvent, in perfumery, and in organic synthesis. Also called **dimethoxymethane, formal.** [METHYL- + -AL[3]]

meth′yl al′cohol, *Chem.* a colorless, volatile, water-soluble, poisonous liquid, CH_3OH, obtained by the destructive distillation of wood or the incomplete oxidation of natural gas, or produced synthetically from carbon monoxide and hydrogen: used chiefly as a solvent, a fuel, and an automobile antifreeze and in the synthesis of formaldehyde. Also called **methanol, wood alcohol, wood spirit.**

meth·yl·a·mine (meth′ə lə mēn′, -əl am′in), *n. Chem.* any of three derivatives of ammonia in which one or all of the hydrogen atoms are replaced by methyl groups, esp. a gas, CH_3NH_2, with an ammonialike odor, the simplest alkyl derivative of ammonia and, like the latter, forming a series of salts. Also called **monomethylamine.** [METHYL- + AMINE]

meth·yl·ate (meth′ə lāt′), *n., v.,* **-at·ed, -at·ing.** *Chem.* —*n.* Also called **methoxide. 1.** any derivative of methyl alcohol, as sodium methylate, CH_3ONa. **2.** any compound containing the methyl group. —*v.t.* **3.** (in a compound) to replace one or more hydrogen atoms with the methyl group. **4.** to mix with methyl alcohol, as in the denaturation of ethyl alcohol. [METHYL- + -ATE[1]] —**meth′yl·a′tor,** *n.*

meth′ylated spir′its, ethyl alcohol denatured with methyl alcohol for the purpose of preventing its use as an alcoholic beverage. Also, **meth′ylated spir′it.**

meth·yl·a·tion (meth′ə lā′shən), *n. Chem.* the process of replacing a hydrogen atom with a methyl group. [METHYLATE + -ION]

meth·yl·ben·zene (meth′əl ben′zēn, -ben zēn′), *n. Chem.* toluene. [METHYL- + BENZENE]

meth′yl bro′mide, *Chem.* a colorless, poisonous gas, CH_3Br, used chiefly as a solvent, refrigerant, and fumigant and in organic synthesis. Also called **bromomethane.**

meth·yl·cat·e·chol (meth′əl kat′ə chōl′, -chôl′, -chol′, -shōl′, -shôl′, -shol′, -kōl′, -kôl′, -kol′), *n. Pharm.* guaiacol. [METHYL- + CATECHOL]

meth′yl chlo′ride, *Chem.* a colorless, poisonous gas, CH_3Cl, used chiefly as a refrigerant, as a local anesthetic, and as a methylating agent in organic synthesis. Also called **chloromethane.**

meth′yl chlorocar′bonate. See **methyl chloroformate.**

meth′yl chlo·ro·form′ate (klōr′ə fôr′mit, -māt, klôr′-), *Chem.* a colorless liquid, $ClCOOCH_3$, used chiefly in organic synthesis.

meth′yl cy′anide, *Chem.* acetonitrile.

meth·yl·cy·clo·hex·a·nol (meth′əl sī′klə hek′sə nōl′, -nôl′, -nol′), *n. Chem.* a colorless, aromatic, viscous liquid mixture, chiefly of the ortho and para forms of $CH_3C_6H_{10}OH$, derived from cresol by hydrogenation: used chiefly as a solvent for rubber, cellulose, esters, and phenols. [METHYL- + CYCLOHEXANE + -OL[1]]

meth·yl·ene (meth′ə lēn′), *adj. Chem.* containing the methylene group. [METHYL- + -ENE]

meth′ylene blue′, *Chem., Pharm.* a dark-green, crystalline, compound, $C_{16}H_{18}ClN_3S{\cdot}3H_2O$, that dissolves in water to form a deep-blue solution: used chiefly as a dye, as a bacteriological and biological stain, and as an antidote for cyanide poisoning. Also called **methylthionine chloride.**

meth′ylene chlo′ride, *Chem.* a colorless, volatile liquid, CH_2Cl_2, used chiefly as a solvent, as a refrigerant, and as a local anesthetic in dentistry. Also called **methylene dichloride, dichloromethane.**

meth′ylene dichlo′ride, *Chem.* See **methylene chloride.**

meth′ylene group′, *Chem.* the bivalent group, $>CH_2$, derived from methane. Also called **meth′ylene rad′ical.**

meth′yl eth′yl ke′tone, *Chem.* a colorless, flammable liquid, $CH_3COCH_2CH_3$, produced by synthesis or fermentation: used chiefly as a solvent, as a paint remover, and in the manufacture of plastics. Also called **ethyl methyl ketone, butanone.**

meth′yl for′mate, *Chem.* a colorless, water-soluble, flammable liquid, $HCOOCH_3$, used chiefly in organic synthesis and as a solvent.

meth·yl·gly·ox·al (meth′əl glī ok′sal, -səl), *n. Chem.* See **pyruvic aldehyde.** [METHYL- + *glyoxal,* equiv. to GLY(COL) + OXAL(IC ACID)]

meth′yl group′, *Chem.* the univalent group, CH_3–, derived from methane. Also called **meth′yl rad′ical.**

meth·yl·hep·te·none (meth′əl hep′tə nōn′), *n. Chem.* a colorless liquid, $(CH_3)_2C{=}CH(CH_2)_2COCH_3$, occurring in many essential oils and produced by synthesis: used in organic synthesis and in the manufacture of inexpensive perfumes. [METHYL- + HEPTENE + -ONE]

me·thyl·ic (me thil′ik), *adj.* of, pertaining to, or characteristic of the methyl group. [METHYL- + -IC]

me·thyl·i·dyne (me thil′i dīn′), *adj. Chem.* containing the methylidyne group; methenyl. [METHYL- + -IDE + (ALK)YNE]

methyl′idyne group′, *Chem.* the trivalent group, $\equiv CH$. Also called **methyl′idyne rad′ical.**

meth′yl·i·so·bu′te·nyl ke′tone (meth′əl ī′sō byōō′tᵊnil, meth′-), *Chem.* See **mesityl oxide.** [METHYL- + ISO- + BUTENE + -YL]

meth′yl isobu′tyl ke′tone, *Chem.* a colorless, slightly water-soluble, flammable liquid, $(CH_3)_2CHCH_2COCH_3$, having a pleasant odor: used as a solvent for nitrocellulose, gums, resins, fats, waxes, and oils. Also called **hexone.**

meth′yl lac′tate, *Chem.* a colorless liquid, $CH_3CHOHCOOCH_3$, soluble with water and most organic liquids: used chiefly as a solvent for cellulose acetate.

meth′yl methac′rylate, *Chem.* a colorless, volatile, flammable, water-insoluble, liquid, unsaturated ester, $CH_2{=}C(CH_3)COOCH_3$, which polymerizes readily to a clear plastic. Cf. **Lucite, plexiglas.**

meth′yl meth′ane, ethane.

meth·yl·naph·tha·lene (meth′əl naf′thə lēn′, -nap′-), *n. Chem.* a compound, $C_{10}H_7CH_3$, whose alpha isomer, a colorless liquid, is used in determining cetane numbers. Cf. **cetane number.** [METHYL- + NAPHTHALENE]

meth′yl o′leate, *Chem.* an oily, clear to amber, water-insoluble liquid, $CH_3(CH_2)_7CH{=}CH(CH_2)_7COOCH_3$, used chiefly as an intermediate for detergents, wetting agents, and emulsifiers.

meth′yl or′ange, *Chem.* an orange-yellow, slightly water-soluble powder, $(CH_3)_2NC_6H_4N{=}NC_6H_4SO_3Na$, used chiefly as an acid-base indicator. Also called **gold orange, helianthine B, orange III, tropaeolin D, tropeolin D.** Cf. **methyl red.**

meth·yl·par·a·ben (meth′əl par′ə ben′), *n. Chem.* a fine, white, needlelike substance, $HOC_6H_4COOCH_3$, used chiefly as a preservative in foods and pharmaceuticals. [METHYL- + PARA- + BEN(ZOIC ACID)]

meth′yl phe′nol, *Chem.* cresol.

meth′yl·phen′yl·car′bi·nyl ac′etate (meth′əl fen′əl kär′bə nil, -fēn′əl-, meth′-), *Chem.* a colorless, synthetic liquid, $CH_3COOCH(CH_3)C_6H_5$, having a strong floral odor and occurring in oil of gardenia: used chiefly in gardenia and lily perfumes. Also called **phenylmethylcarbinyl acetate, styralyl acetate.** [METHYL- + PHENYL + CARB- + -IN[2] + -YL]

meth′yl phen′yl e′ther, *Chem.* anisole.

meth′yl pro′pyl ke′tone, *Chem.* a colorless, slightly water-soluble liquid, $CH_3COC_3H_7$, used chiefly as a solvent, esp. in lacquers.

meth′yl red′, *Chem.* a water-insoluble solid occurring as a dark-red powder or violet crystals, $(CH_3)_2NC_6H_4N{=}NC_6H_4COOH$, used chiefly as an acid-base indicator. Cf. **methyl orange.**

meth′yl·ros·an′i·line chlo′ride (meth′əl rō zan′ə lin, -lin′, meth′-). See **gentian violet.** [METHYL- + ROSANILINE CHLORIDE]

meth′yl salic′ylate, *Chem.* a colorless, water-soluble liquid, $HOC_6H_4COOCH_3$, produced synthetically or by maceration and subsequent distillation from birch or gaultheria: used chiefly in perfumery and flavoring, and in medicine as a counterirritant in external preparations. Also called **betula oil, gaultheria oil, oil of wintergreen, sweet birch oil, wintergreen oil.**

meth′yl sty′ryl ke′tone (stī′ril, stir′əl), *Chem.* See **benzylidene acetone.** [STYR(ENE) + -YL]

meth′yl sul′fate, *Chem.* See **dimethyl sulfate.**

meth·yl·the·o·bro·mine (meth′əl thē′ə brō′mēn, -min, meth′-), *n. Chem.* caffeine. [METHYL- + THEOBROMINE]

meth·yl·thi′o·nine chlo′ride (meth′əl thī′ə nēn′, -nin), *Chem.* See **methylene blue.** [METHYL- + THIONINE]

meth·yl·tri·ni·tro·ben·zene (meth′əl trī nī′trō ben′zēn, -ben zēn′), *n. Chem.* See **TNT.** [METHYL- + TRI- + NITRO- + BENZENE]

meth·y·pry·lon (meth′i prī′lon), *n. Pharm.* an almost white, crystalline, bitter powder, $C_{10}H_{17}NO_2$, used as a sedative and hypnotic. [METHY(L)- + P(IPE)R(IDINE + DIETH)YL + *-on,* var. of -ONE]

met·ic (met′ik), *n.* an alien resident of an ancient Greek city who paid a tax to remain there. [< LL *metyc(us),* var. of *metoecus* < Gk *métoikos* emigrant, equiv. to *met-* MET- + *-oikos* dwelling]

me·tic·u·lous (mə tik′yə ləs), *adj.* extremely or excessively careful about minute details; finical: *to be meticulous about one's personal appearance.* [< L *meticulōs(us)* full of fear, fearful, equiv. to *meti-* for *metu-* (s. of *metus* fear) + *-cul(us)* -CULE + *-ōsus* -OUS] —**me·tic′u·lous·ly,** *adv.* —**me·tic′u·lous·ness, me·tic·u·los·i·ty** (mə tik′yə los′i tē), *n.*

—**Syn.** exact, precise, demanding, finicky. —**Ant.** careless.

mé·tier (mā′tyā, mā tyā′), *n.* **1.** a field of work; occupation, trade, or profession. **2.** a field of work or other activity in which one has special ability, training, etc.; forte. [< F << L *minister(ium)* MINISTRY]

mé·tif (mā tēf′), *n.* métis.

Me·ti·o·che (mi tī′ō kē′), *n. Class. Myth.* a daughter of Orion. Cf. **Menippe.**

Me·ti·on (mē′tē on′), *n. Class. Myth.* a son of King Erechtheus and Praxithea who died before he could carry out his threat to murder his brother Cecrops.

mé·tis (mā tēs′, -tē′), *n., pl.* **-tis** (-tēs′, -tēz′). **1.** any person of mixed ancestry. **2.** *Canadian.* a half-breed of white, esp. French, and Indian parentage. [< F, MF < LL *mixtīcius* of mixed blood]

Me·tis (mē′tis), *n. Class. Myth.* a Titaness, the daughter of Oceanus and Tethys and the mother of Athena by Zeus.

Me·tis·cus (mi tis′kəs), *n. Rom. Legend.* the charioteer of Turnus.

mé·tisse (mā tēs′), *n., pl.* **-tisses** (-tēs′, -tē′siz). **1.** a woman of mixed ancestry. **2.** *Canadian.* a female half-breed of white, esp. French, and Indian parentage. [< F; fem. of MÉTIS]

Me·ti·us (mā′tē əs, met′ē-), *n.* a crater in the fourth quadrant of the face of the moon: about 50 miles in diameter.

Me·tol (mē′tōl, -tôl, -tol), *n. Chem., Trademark.* a colorless, crystalline, water-soluble salt, $(HOC_6H_4NHCH_3)_2 \cdot H_2SO_4$, para-methylaminophenol sulfate, used chiefly as a photographic developer.

Me·ton (mē′ton), *n.* a walled plain in the first quadrant of the face of the moon: about 100 miles in diameter.

Me·ton′ic cy′cle (mi ton′ik), *Astron.* a cycle of 235 synodic months, very nearly equal to 19 years, after which the new moon occurs on the same day of the year as at the beginning of the cycle with perhaps a shift of one day, depending on the number of leap years in the cycle. [named after *Meton,* 5th-century B.C. Athenian astronomer; see -IC]

met·o·nym (met′ə nim), *n.* a word used in metonymy. [back formation from METONYMY]

met·o·nym·i·cal (met′ə nim′i kəl), *adj.* having the nature of metonymy. Also, **met′o·nym′ic.** [< Gk *metōnymik(ós)* (see METONYMY, -IC) + -AL[1]] —**met′o·nym′i·cal·ly,** *adv.*

me·ton·y·my (mi ton′ə mē), *n. Rhet.* the use of the name of one object or concept for that of another to which it is related, or of which it is a part, as "scepter" for "sovereignty," or "the bottle" for "strong drink," or "count heads (or noses)" for "count people." [< LL *metōnymia* < Gk: change of name, equiv. to *met-* MET- + *-ōnym-* (comb. form of *ónyma* name) + *-ia* -Y[3]]

me-too (mē′to͞o′), *adj.* characterized by or involving me-tooism: *a me-too campaign.* [from phrase *me too*]

me-too·ism (mē′to͞o′iz əm), *n.* the practice of advocating or adopting policies, attitudes, beliefs, tactics, etc., similar or identical to those which have proved successful for another, esp. a political rival. [ME-TOO + -ISM] —**me′-too′er,** *n.* —**me′-too′ist,** *adj., n.*

met·o·pe (met′ə pē′, -ōp), *n. Archit.* any of the square spaces, either decorated or plain, between triglyphs in the Doric frieze. Also called **intertriglyph.** [< Gk]

Met·o·pe (met′ə pē′), *n. Class. Myth.* the wife of Asopus, who bore him many children, among them Thebe, Aegina, and Salamis.

me·top·ic (mə top′ik), *adj. Anat.* of or pertaining to the forehead; frontal. [< Gk *métōp(on)* forehead + -IC]

metr-, var. of **metro-**[2] before a vowel: *metralgia.*

me·tral·gi·a (mi tral′jē ə), *n. Pathol.* pain in the uterus. [METR- + ALGIA]

Met·ra·zol (me′trə zōl′, -zôl′, -zol′), *n. Pharm., Trademark.* pentylenetetrazol.

me·tre (mē′tər), *n. Chiefly Brit.* meter.

met·ric[1] (me′trik), *adj.* **1.** pertaining to the meter or to the metric system. —*n.* **2.** *Math.* a nonnegative real-valued function having properties analogous to those of the distance between points on a real line, as the distance between two points being independent of the order of the points, the distance between two points being zero if, and only if, the two points coincide, and the distance between two points being less than or equal to the sum of the distances from each point to an arbitrary third point. [< F *métrique,* deriv. of *mètre* METER[1]; see -IC]

met·ric[2] (me′trik), *adj.* **1.** pertaining to distance: *metric geometry.* **2.** metrical. [< L *metric(us)* < Gk *metrikós* of, relating to measuring. See METER[2], -IC]

met·ri·cal (me′tri kəl), *adj.* **1.** pertaining to meter or poetic measure. **2.** composed in meter or verse. **3.** pertaining to measurement. Also, **metric.** [late ME < LL *metric(us)* (see METRIC[2]) + -AL[1]] —**met′ri·cal·ly,** *adv.* —**met·ri·cism** (me′tri siz′əm), **me·tric·i·ty** (me-tris′i tē, mi-), *n.*

met′ric cent′ner, centner (def. 2).

met′ric hun′dredweight, a unit of weight equivalent to 50 kilograms.

me·tri·cian (mi trish′ən), *n.* a metrist. [late ME *metricion.* See METRIC[2], -IAN]

met·ri·cise (me′tri sīz′), *v.t.,* **-cised, -cis·ing.** *Math. Chiefly Brit.* metricize.

met·ri·cize (me′tri sīz′), *v.t.,* **-cized, -ciz·ing.** *Math.* metrize. [METRIC[1] + -IZE]

met·rics (me′triks), *n.* (*construed as sing.*) **1.** the science of meter. **2.** the art of metrical composition. [see METRIC[2], -ICS]

met′ric space′, *Math.* a space with a metric defined on it.

met′ric sys′tem, a decimal system of weights and measures, adopted first in France but now widespread over the world, universally used in science, mandatory for use for all purposes in a large number of countries, and permitted for use in most (as in the U.S.). The basic units are the meter (39.37 inches) for length and the gram (15.432 grains) for mass or weight. Derived units are the liter (0.908 U.S. dry quart, or 1.0567 U.S. liquid quart) for capacity, being the volume of 1000 grams of water under specified conditions; the are (119.6 square yards) for area, being the area of a square 10 meters on a side; and the stere (35.315 cubic feet) for volume, being the volume of a cube 1 meter on a side, the term "stere," however, usually being used only in measuring firewood. Names for units larger and smaller than these are formed from the above names by the use of the following prefixes: kilo, 1000; hecto, 100; deca, 10; deci, 0.1; centi, 0.01; milli, 0.001. To these are often added: tera, one trillion; giga, one billion; mega, one million. With the addition of basic physical units it is now officially known by the French name Le Système International d'Unités (abbreviation **SI**) or in English as the International System of Units.

met′ric ton′, a unit of 1000 kilograms, equivalent to 2204.62 avoirdupois pounds.

met′ric topol′ogy, *Math.* a topology for a space in which open sets are defined in terms of a given metric.

me·trid·i·um (mə trid′ē əm), *n.* a genus of sea anemones common in cooler waters of the Northern Hemisphere. [< NL, n. use of Gk *mētrídios* having a womb, fruitful, deriv. of *mḗtra* womb]

met·ri·fy (me′trə fī′), *v.t.,* **-fied, -fy·ing.** to put into meter; compose in verse. [< F *métrifi(er)* < ML *metrificāre,* equiv. to *metri-* (comb. form of *metrum* METER[2]) + *-ficāre* -FY] —**met′ri·fi·ca′tion,** *n.* —**met′ri·fi′er,** *n.*

met·rise (mi trīz′, me′trīz), *v.t.,* **-rised, -ris·ing.** *Math. Chiefly Brit.* metrize. —**met·ris′a·ble,** *adj.* —**met′ri·sa′tion,** *n.*

met·rist (me′trist, mē′trist), *n.* a person who is skilled in the use of poetic meters. [< ML *metrist(a).* See METER[2], -IST]

me·tri·tis (mi trī′tis), *n. Pathol.* inflammation of the uterus. [< NL; see METR-, -ITIS]

met·rize (mi trīz′, me′trīz), *v.t.,* **-rized, -riz·ing.** *Math.* to find a metric for (a topological space for which the metric topology is the given topology). Also, **metricize;** *esp. Brit.,* **metricise, metrise.** [METR(IC) + -IZE] —**met·riz′able,** *adj.* —**met′ri·za′tion,** *n.*

met·ro (me′trō), *n., pl.* **-ros.** (*often cap.*) a European subway, esp. the Paris, France, subway system or one of its cars or trains. Also, **mé·tro** (*Fr.* mā trō′). [< F *métro,* short for *chemin de fer métropolitain* metropolitan railway]

metro-[1], a learned borrowing from Greek meaning "measure," used in the formation of compound words: *metronome.* [comb. form repr. Gk *métron* measure]

metro-[2], a learned borrowing from Greek meaning "uterus," used in the formation of compound words: *metrorrhagia.* Also, *esp. before a vowel,* **metr-.** [comb. form repr. Gk *mḗtra* womb]

me·trol·o·gy (mi trol′ə jē), *n., pl.* **-gies.** the science of measures and weights. [METRO-[1] + -LOGY] —**met′ro·log′i·cal** (me′trə loj′i-kəl), *adj.* —**met′ro·log′i·cal·ly,** *adv.* —**me·trol′o·gist,** *n.*

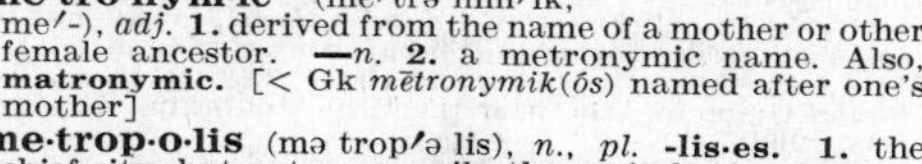

Metronome

met·ro·nome (me′trə nōm′), *n.* a mechanical or electrical instrument that makes repeated clicking sounds at an adjustable pace, used for marking rhythm, esp. in music. [METRO-[1] + Gk *nóm(os)* rule, law] —**met·ro·nom·ic** (me′trə nom′ik), **met′ro·nom′i·cal,** *adj.* —**met′ro·nom′i·cal·ly,** *adv.*

me·tro·nym·ic (mē′trə nim′ik, me′-), *adj.* **1.** derived from the name of a mother or other female ancestor. —*n.* **2.** a metronymic name. Also, **matronymic.** [< Gk *mētrōnymik(ós)* named after one's mother]

me·trop·o·lis (mə trop′ə lis), *n., pl.* **-lis·es. 1.** the chief city, but not necessarily the capital, of a country, state, or region. **2.** any large, busy city. **3.** a central or principal point, as of some activity. **4.** the mother city or parent state of a colony, esp. of an ancient Greek colony. **5.** the chief see of an ecclesiastical province. [< LL < Gk: a mother state or city]

Me·trop·o·lis (mə trop′ə lis), *n.* a town in S Illinois. 7339 (1960).

met·ro·pol·i·tan (me′trə pol′i tᵊn), *adj.* **1.** of, noting, or characteristic of a metropolis or its inhabitants, esp. in culture, sophistication, or in accepting and combining a wide variety of people, ideas, etc. **2.** pertaining to or constituting a mother country. **3.** pertaining to an ecclesiastical metropolis. —*n.* **4.** an inhabitant of a metropolis or chief city. **5.** a person who has the sophistication, fashionable taste, or other habits and manners associated with those who live in a metropolis. **6.** *Eastern Ch.* the head of an ecclesiastical province. **7.** an archbishop in the Church of England. **8.** *Rom. Cath. Ch.* an archbishop who has authority over one or more suffragan sees. **9.** a citizen of the mother city or parent state of a colony. [< LL *mētropolītān(us)* of, belonging to a metropolis < Gk *mētropolít(ēs)* (see METROPOLIS, -ITE[1]) + L *-ānus* -AN] —**met′ro·pol′i·tan·ism,** *n.*

me·tror·rha·gi·a (mē′trə rā′jē ə, -jə, me′-), *n. Pathol.* nonmenstrual discharge of blood from the uterus; uterine hemorrhage. [< NL; see METRO-[2], -RRHAGIA] —**me·tror·rhag·ic** (mē′trə raj′ik, me′-), *adj.*

me·tro·scope (mē′trə skōp′, me′-), *n. Med.* an instrument for examining the cavity of the uterus. [METRO-[2] + -SCOPE]

me·tro·tome (mē′trə tōm′, me′-), *n. Surg.* an instrument for incising the neck of the uterus. [METRO-[2] + -TOME]

-metry, a combining form denoting the process of measuring: *anthropometry; chronometry.* [< Gk *-metria* action, process of measuring, equiv. to *-metr(ēs)* measurer, deriv. of *métron* measure (see METER[1]) + *-ia* -Y[3]]

Met·sys (met′sīs), *n.* **Quen·tin** (*Flemish.* kven′tin; *Eng.* kwen′tᵊn). See **Massys, Quentin.**

Met·ter·nich (met′ər nɪkʜ; *Eng.* met′ər nik), *n.* **Prince Kle·mens Wen·zel Ne·po·muk Lo·thar von** (klā′mens ven′tsəl nā′pô mo͝ok lō′tär fən, lō tär′), 1773–1859, Austrian statesman and diplomat. —**Met′-ter·nich′i·an,** *adj.*

me·teur en scène (me tœʀ äɴ sen′), *pl.* **met·teurs en scène** (me tœʀ äɴ sen′). *French.* a director of a theatrical or cinematic production. [lit., he who puts (a production) on stage]

Met·tie (met′ē), *n.* a girl's given name, form of **Matilda** or **Martha.** Also, **Met′ty.**

met·tle (met′ᵊl), *n.* **1.** characteristic disposition or temperament: *Though differing in mettle, the two researchers worked well as a team; to try a man's mettle.* **2.** spirit; courage: *a man of mettle.* **3. on one's mettle,** in the position of being incited to do one's best: *The amount of the prize put them all on their mettle.* [var. of METAL]
—**Syn. 2.** valor, pluck, vigor, ardor, nerve, fiber.

met·tle·some (met′ᵊl səm), *adj.* spirited; courageous. [METTLE + -SOME[1]]

Me·tuch·en (mi tuch′ən), *n.* a city in NE New Jersey. 14,041 (1960).

Metz (mets; *Fr.* mes), *n.* a city in and the capital of Moselle, in NE France: fortress; battles 1870, 1918, 1940, 1944. 109,678 (1962).

me·um et tu·um (me′o͝om et to͞o′o͝om; *Eng.* mē′əm et to͞o′əm, -tyo͞o′-), *Latin.* mine and thine.

meu·nière (mən yâr′; *Fr.* mœ nyeʀ′), *adj.* (of food, esp. fish) dipped in flour, browned on both sides in butter, and sprinkled with lemon juice and parsley. [< F: lit., miller's wife (fem. of *meunier*)]

Meur·sault (mûr sō′; *Fr.* mœʀ sō′), *n.* a dry, white wine from the parish of Meursault in Burgundy.

Meurthe-et-Mo·selle (mœʀ tā mō zel′), *n.* a department in NE France. 678,078 (1962); 2038 sq. mi. *Cap.:* Nancy.

Meuse (myo͞oz; *Fr.* mœz), *n.* **1.** Dutch, **Maas.** a river in W Europe, flowing from NE France through E Belgium and S Netherlands into the North Sea. 575 mi. long. **2.** a department in NE France. 215,985 (1962); 2409 sq. mi. *Cap.:* Bar-le-Duc.

MeV (mev), *Physics.* million electron-volts. Also, **mev**

mew[1] (myo͞o), *n.* **1.** the sound a cat makes. —*v.i.* **2.** to make this sound. [imit.]

mew[2] (myo͞o), *n.* a sea gull, esp. the common gull, *Larus canus,* of Europe. [OE; c. G *Möwe*]

mew[3] (myo͞o), *n.* **1.** a cage for hawks, esp. while molting. **2.** a place of retirement or concealment. **3. mews,** (*usually construed as sing.*) *Chiefly Brit.* **a.** stables, carriage garages, and living quarters built around a yard, court, or street. **b.** the yard, court, or street lined by such buildings. —*v.t.* **4.** to shut up in or as in a mew; confine; conceal (often fol. by *up*). [ME *mue* < MF, akin to *muer* to molt. See MEW[4]]

mew[4] (myo͞o), *v.t., v.i.* to shed (feathers); to molt. [ME *mewe(n)* < OF *mue(r)* (to) molt < L *mūtāre* to change] —**mew′er,** *n.*

Me·war (me wär′), *n.* Udaipur (def. 2).

mewl (myo͞ol), *v.i.* to cry, as a baby, young child, or the like; whimper. [imit.] —**mewl′er,** *n.*

Mex., 1. Mexican. **2.** Mexico.

Me·xi·a (mə hā′ə), *n.* a town in central Texas. 6121 (1960).

Mex·i·cal·i (mek′sə kal′ē; *Sp.* me′hē kä′lē), *n.* a city in and the capital of Lower California, in NW Mexico, on the Mexican-U.S. border. 72,684 (1960).

Mex·i·can (mek′sə kən), *adj.* **1.** of or pertaining to Mexico or its people. —*n.* **2.** a native or inhabitant of Mexico. [< Sp *mexican(o).* See MEXICO, -AN]

Mex′ican ap′ple. See **white sapote.**

Mex′ican bamboo′, a hardy, perennial herb, *Polygonum cuspidatum,* of Japan, having small, greenish-white flowers.

Mex′ican bean′ bee′tle, a ladybird beetle, *Epilachna varivestis,* introduced into the U.S. from Mexico, that feeds on the foliage of the bean plant. Also called **bean beetle.**

Mex′ican blue′ palm′, a fan palm, *Erythea armata,* of California, having bluish-green, waxy leaves and fleshy fruit.

Mex′ican bush′ sage′, a low shrub, *Salvia leucantha,* of Mexico, having leaves that are covered with white, woolly hairs on the underside and showy, white flowers with lavender hairs.

Mex′ican fire′-plant′ (fīᵊr′plant′, -plänt′), a showy herb, *Euphorbia heterophylla,* found from the central U.S. to central South America, having red or mottled red and white bracts.

Mex′ican fire′-vine (fīᵊr′vīn′), a tender, herbaceous vine, *Senecio confusus,* of Mexico, having orange flowers that turn orange-red.

Mex′ican ground′ cher′ry, tomatillo.

Mex′ican hair′less, one of a breed of small, dogs having no hair at all except for a tuft on the top of the head and a little fuzz on the lower part of the tail.

Mex′ican hat′ dance′, 1. a dance performed by couples, consisting of eight measures during which the dancers kick out each foot alternately, followed by eight more measures during which they swing around with interlocking arms. **2.** a folk and courtship dance for a solo male around and on the brim of a Mexican straw hat.

Mex′ican i′vy. See **cup-and-saucer vine.**

Mex′ican jade′, Mexican onyx artificially colored green.

Mex′ican jump′ing bean′. See **jumping bean.**

Mex·i·ca·no (mek′sə kä′nō; *Sp.* me′hē kä′nô), *n. Informal.* the Nahuatl language. [< Sp: MEXICAN]

Mex′ican on′yx, *Mineral.* a translucent, banded variety of calcite, used for ornamental and decorative pieces. Also called **onyx marble.**

Mex′ican or′ange, an aromatic, evergreen shrub, *Choisya ternata,* of Mexico, having fragrant, white flowers, grown as an ornamental.

Mex′ican pop′py. See **prickly poppy.**

Mex′ican Span′ish, Spanish as used in Mexico.

Mex′ican tea′, a rank-smelling goosefoot, *Chenopodium ambrosioides,* of tropical America: a common weed in the U.S. Also called **American wormseed.**

Mex′ican War′, the war between the U.S. and Mexico, 1846–48.

Mex·i·co (mek′sə kō′), *n.* **1.** a republic in S North America. 34,625,903 (1960); 760,373 sq. mi. *Cap.:* Mexico City. **2.** a state in central Mexico 1,897,851 (1960); 8268 sq. mi. *Cap.:* Toluca. **3. Gulf of,** Mexican, **Gol·fo de Mé·xi·co** (gôl′fô the me′hē kô′). an arm of the Atlantic between the U.S., Cuba, and Mexico. 700,000 sq. mi.; greatest depth 12,714 ft. **4.** a town in NE Missouri. 12,889 (1960). **5.** a town in W Maine. 3951 (1960). Mexican, **Mé·xi·co** (me′hē kô′) (for defs. 1, 2). Spanish, **Méjico** (for defs. 1, 2).

Mex′ico Cit′y, a city in and the capital of Mexico, in the central part. 8,906,000; ab. 7400 ft. above sea level. Official name, **Mé·xi·co, Dis·tri·to Fe·de·ral** (me′hē kô′ dēs trē′tô fe the räl′).

MexSp, Mexican Spanish.

Mey·er (mī′ər), *n.* **1. Adolf,** 1866–1950, U.S. psychiatrist, born in Switzerland. **2. Albert (Gregory),** 1903–65, U.S. Roman Catholic clergyman. **3. Ju·li·us**

Lo·thar (jōōl′yəs lō′thär; *Ger.* yōō′lē ōōs lō′tär, lō tär′), 1830–95, German chemist. **4.** a boy's given name.

Mey·er·beer (mī′ər bēr′; *Ger.* mī′ər bār′), *n.* **Gia·co·mo** (jä′kō mō), (*Jakob Liebmann Beer*), 1791–1864, German composer.

Mey·er·hof (mī′ər hof′; *Ger.* mī′ər hōf′), *n.* **Otto** (ot′ō; *Ger.* ôt′ō), 1884–1951, German physiologist: Nobel prize for medicine 1922.

Mey·ers·dale (mī′ərz dāl′), *n.* a town in SW Pennsylvania. 2901 (1960).

Meyn·ell (men′əl), *n.* **Alice Christiana (Thompson),** 1850–1922, English poet and essayist.

mez·ail (mez′āl), *n.* *Armor.* mesail.

mé·zair (mā zâr′), *n.* *Dressage.* a movement in which the horse makes a series of short jumps forward while standing on its hind legs. [< F < It *mezzaria*, lit., middle gait]

mez·ca·line (mez′kə lēn′, -lin), *n.* *Pharm.* mescaline.

Me·zen·tius (mi zen′shəs), n. *Rom. Legend.* a notoriously cruel Etrurian king who was killed by Aeneas.

me·ze·re·on (mi zēr′ē on′), *n.* an Old World, thymelaeaceous shrub, *Daphne Mezereum*, cultivated for its fragrant purplish-pink flowers, which appear in early spring. [late ME *mizerion* < ML *mezereon* < Ar *māzaryūn*]

me·ze·re·um (mi zēr′ē əm), *n.* mezereon.

me·zu·za (mə zōōz′ə; *Heb.* mə zōō-zä′), *n., pl.* **-zas,** *Heb.* **-zu·zoth** (-zōō-zōt′). mezuzah.

me·zu·zah (mə zōōz′ə; *Heb.* mə zōō-zä′), *n., pl.* **-zahs,** *Heb.* **-zu·zoth** (-zōō zōt′). *Judaism.* a small case or tube, typically of metal or wood and with an aperture in front, that is traditionally attached by Jews to the doorpost of the home and that contains a piece of parchment inscribed on one side with verses 4–9 of Deut. 6 and 13–21 of Deut. 11, and on the other side with the word *Shaddai* (a name applied to God) and folded in the case or tube so that *Shaddai* is visible through the aperture. [< Heb: lit., doorpost]

Mezuzah

mez·za·nine (mez′ə nēn′, mez′ə nēn′), *n.* **1.** a low story between two other stories of greater height in a building, esp. when the low story and the one beneath it form part of one composition; an entresol. **2.** the lowest balcony or forward part of such a balcony in a theater. [< F < It *mezzanino*, equiv. to *mezzan(o)* middle (< L *mediānus* MEDIAN) + *-ino* dim. suffix]

mez·za vo·ce (met′sə vō′chā, mez′ə; *It.* med′dzä vô′che), with half the power of the voice (used as a musical direction). *Abbr.:* M.V. [< It]

mez·zo (met′sō, mez′ō; *It.* med′dzō), *adj.* middle; medium; half. [< It < L *medius* middle]

mez′zo for′te (fôr′tā; *It.* fôr′te), *Music.* somewhat softer than forte but louder than piano; moderately loud. [< It: lit., half loud]

mez′zo pia′no (pē ä′nō; *It.* pyä′nô), *Music.* somewhat louder than piano but softer than forte; moderately soft. [< It: lit., half soft]

mez·zo-re·lie·vo (met′sō ri lē′vō, mez′ō-), *n., pl.* **-vos** (-vōz). sculptured relief intermediate between high relief and bas-relief. Italian, **mezzo-rilievo.** [< It]

mez·zo-ri·lie·vo (med′dzō rē lye′vō; *Eng.* met′sō-ri lē′vō, mez′ō-), *n., pl.* **mez·zi-ri·lie·vi** (med′dzē rē-lye′vē; *Eng.* met′sē ri lē′vē, mez′ē-). *Italian.* mezzo-relievo.

mez·zo-so·pran·o (met′sō sə pran′ō, -prä′nō, mez′ō-), *n., pl.* **-pran·os, -pran·i** (-pran′ē, -prä′nē), *adj.* *Music.* —*n.* **1.** a voice or voice part intermediate in compass between soprano and contralto. **2.** a person having such a voice. —*adj.* **3.** of, pertaining to, characteristic of, or suitable to a mezzo-soprano. [< It]

mez′zo-sopran′o clef′, *Music.* a C clef locating middle C on the line next to the lowest line of the staff.

mez·zo·tint (met′sō tint′, mez′ō-), *n.* **1.** a method of engraving on copper or steel by burnishing or scraping away a uniformly roughened surface. **2.** a print produced by this method. —*v.t.* **3.** to engrave in mezzotint. [< It *mezzotinto* half-tint. See MEZZO, TINT[1]] —**mez′-zo·tint′er,** *n.*

MF, 1. See **medium frequency. 2.** Middle French.

mF, millifarad; millifarads. Also, **mf**

mf, 1. See **medium frequency. 2.** millifarad; millifarads.

mf., 1. *Music.* mezzo forte. **2.** microfarad.

M.F., 1. Master of Forestry. **2.** Middle French.

M.F.A., Master of Fine Arts.

mfd., 1. manufactured. **2.** microfarad.

mfg., manufacturing.

M.F.H., See **master of foxhounds.**

MFlem, Middle Flemish.

M.For., Master of Forestry.

mfr., 1. manufacture. **2.** *pl.* **mfrs.** manufacturer.

M.Fr., Middle French.

MFS, Modern Fiction Studies.

M.F.S., 1. Master of Food Science. **2.** Master of Foreign Service. **3.** Master of Foreign Study.

M.F.T., Master of Foreign Trade.

Mg, *Chem.* magnesium.

mg, milligram; milligrams.

mGal, milligal; milligals.

MGB, Soviet Ministry of State Security. [< R *Ministerstvo Gosudarstvennoi Bezopasnosti*]

mgd, millions of gallons per day.

M.Geol.E., Master of Geological Engineering.

MGk., Medieval Greek. Also, **MGk**

MGr., Medieval Greek.

mgr., 1. manager. **2.** Monseigneur. **3.** Monsignor. Also, **Mgr.**

mgt., management.

mH, millihenry. Also, **mh**

M.H., Medal of Honor.

M.H.A., Master in Hospital Administration; Master of Hospital Administration.

MHD, magnetohydrodynamics generation: a process for converting heat energy to electricity by using a magnetic coil around a duct to capture free electrons from a plasma, consisting of ionized gas heated to 2000–3000°C, being passed through the duct.

M.H.E., Master of Home Economics.

M.H.E.Ed., Master of Home Economics Education.

MHG, Middle High German. Also, **M.H.G.**

M.H.L., Master of Hebrew Literature.

mho (mō), *n., pl.* **mhos.** *Elect.* the meter-kilogram-second unit of electric conductance, equal to the conductance of a conductor in which a potential difference of one volt maintains a current of one ampere. Also called **reciprocal ohm.** [coined by Lord Kelvin, reversed sp. of OHM]

M.H.R., Member of the House of Representatives.

M.H.W., mean high water. Also, **m.h.w.**

mi (mē), *n.* *Music.* **1.** the syllable used for the third tone of a diatonic scale. **2.** (in the fixed system of solmization) the tone E. Cf. **sol-fa** (def. 1). [see GAMUT]

mi, mile; miles.

mi., 1. mile; miles. **2.** mill; mills.

M.I., 1. Military Intelligence. **2.** Mounted Infantry.

M.I.A., Master of International Affairs.

Mi·al (mī′əl), *n.* a boy's given name, form of **Michael.**

Mi·am·i (mī am′ē, -am′ə), *n., pl.* **-am·is** (*esp. collectively*) **-am·i. 1.** a member of a North American Indian tribe of the Algonquian family, formerly located in northern Indiana, southern Michigan, and possibly Illinois, now extinct as a tribe. **2.** their dialect of the Illinois language.

Mi·am·i (mī am′ē, -am′ə), *n.* **1.** a city in SE Florida: seaside winter resort. 346,931. **2.** Also called **Great Miami.** a river in W Ohio, flowing S into the Ohio River. 160 mi. long. **3.** a city in NE Oklahoma. 12,869 (1960). **4.** a town in central Arizona. 3350 (1960). —**Mi·am′i·an,** *n.*

mi·a·mi·a (mī′ə mī′ə), *n.* a temporary, hutlike shelter built by aboriginal tribes in Australia. [< native Austral]

Miam′i Beach′, a city in SE Florida on an island 2½ mi. across Biscayne Bay from Miami: seaside winter resort. 63,145 (1960).

Mi·am·is·burg (mī am′ēz bûrg′), *n.* a town in W Ohio. 9893 (1960).

Miam′i Shores′, a town in S Florida. 8865 (1960).

mi·aow (mē ou′, myou), *n., v.i.* meow. Also, **mi·aou′, mi·aul** (mē oul′, mē ôl′).

mi·as·ma (mī az′mə, mē-), *n., pl.* **-ma·ta** (-mə tə), **-mas. 1.** noxious exhalations from putrescent organic matter; poisonous effluvia or germs infecting the atmosphere. **2.** a dangerous, foreboding, or deathlike influence or atmosphere. [< NL < Gk: stain, pollution, akin to *miainein* to pollute, stain] —**mi·as′mal, mi·as·mat·ic** (mī′az mat′ik), **mi′as·mat′i·cal, mi·as′mic,** *adj.*

Mi·ass (mē äs′), *n.* a city in the S RSFSR, in the W Soviet Union in Asia, near the Ural Mountains. 109,000 (est. 1962).

mi·a·zine (mī′ə zēn′, -zin, mī az′ēn, -in), *n.* *Chem.* pyrimidine (def. 1). [M(ETA- + D)IAZINE]

mib (mib), *n.* *Chiefly Dial.* **1.** a playing marble, esp. one that is not used as a shooter. **2. mibs,** (*construed as sing.*) the game of marbles. [shortened var. of MARBLE]

Mic., Micah.

mi·ca (mī′kə), *n.* any member of a group of minerals, hydrous disilicates of aluminum with other bases, chiefly potassium, magnesium, iron, and lithium, that separate readily into thin, tough, often transparent, and usually elastic laminae; isinglass. [< L: crumb, morsel, grain] —**mi′ca·like′,** *adj.*

mi·ca·ceous (mī kā′shəs), *adj.* **1.** consisting of, containing, or resembling mica. **2.** of or pertaining to mica. [MIC(A) + -ACEOUS]

Mi·cah (mī′kə), *n.* **1.** a Minor Prophet of the 8th century B.C. **2.** a book of the Bible bearing his name. **3.** a boy's given name, form of **Michael.** Also, *Douay Bible,* **Micheas** (for defs. 1 and 2).

Mi·ca·jah (mī kā′yə), *n.* a boy's given name.

Mi·caw·ber (mi kô′bər), *n.* **Wilkins,** (in Dickens' *David Copperfield*) a persistently optimistic but improvident, chronically unlucky father of a family. —**Mi·caw′ber·ish,** *adj.* —**Mi·caw′ber·ism,** *n.*

mice (mīs), *n.* pl. of **mouse.**

mi·celle (mi sel′), *n.* **1.** *Physical Chem.* an electrically charged particle formed by an aggregate of molecules and occurring in certain colloidal electrolyte solutions, as those of soaps and detergents. **2.** *Biol.* one of the elemental, structural units of protoplasm. [< NL *micella,* equiv. to L *mic(a)* crumb, grain + *-ella* dim. suffix] —**mi·cel′lar,** *adj.* —**mi·cel′lar·ly,** *adv.*

Mich., 1. Michaelmas. **2.** Michigan.

Mi·chael (mī′kəl), *n.* **1.** a militant archangel. Dan. 10:13. **2.** Rumanian, **Mi·hai** (mē hī′). born 1921, king of Rumania 1927–30, 1940–47 (son of Carol II). **3.** (*italics*) a narrative poem (1800) by Wordsworth. **4.** a boy's given name.

Mi·chael·ann (mī′kəl an′), *n.* a girl's given name.

Mi·chae·lene (mī′kə lēn′), *n.* a girl's given name.

Michael VIII Pa·lae·ol·o·gus (pā′lē ol′ə gəs, pal′ē-), 1234–1282, Byzantine ruler 1259–82, first of the Palaeologus emperors.

Mich·ael·mas (mik′əl məs), *n.* *Chiefly Brit.* a festival celebrated on September 29 in honor of the archangel Michael. Also called **Mich′aelmas Day′.** [OE (*Sanct*) *Michaeles masse* (St.) Michael's mass]

Mich′aelmas dai′sy, *Brit.* an aster.

Mi·chal (mī′kəl), *n.* a daughter of Saul, who became the wife of David. I Sam. 14:49; 18:27. Also, *Douay Bible,* **Michol.**

Mi·chaux (mē shō′), *n.* **Hen·ri** (äN rē′), born 1899, French poet and painter, born in Belgium.

miche (mich), *v.i.,* **miched, mich·ing.** *Brit. Dial.* to lurk out of sight; withdraw from view. [ME *myche(n), michen* < OF *muchie(r)* (to) hide] —**mich′er,** *n.*

Mi·che·as (mī kē′əs), *n.* *Douay Bible.* Micah (defs. 1, 2).

Mi·chel·an·ge·lo (mī′kəl an′jə lō′, mik′əl-; *It.* mē′-kel än′je lô), *n.* (*Michelangelo Buonarroti*) 1475–1564, Italian sculptor, painter, architect, and poet.

Mi·chele (mi shel′), *n.* a girl's given name. Also, **Mi·chelle′.**

Mi·che·let (mēsh[ə] lā′), *n.* **Jules** (zhyl), 1798–1874, French historian

Mi·chel·son (mī′kəl sən), *n.* **Albert Abraham,** 1852–1931, U.S. physicist, born in Germany: Nobel prize 1907.

Mi′chel·son-Mor′ley exper′iment (mī′kəl sən-môr′lē), *Physics.* an experiment to determine the velocity of the earth through the hypothetical ether in space by comparing the velocities of two light rays, one in the direction of translation of the earth in the ether and the other at right angles to this direction, the result of the experiment being that the velocity could not be determined since the speed of light is constant in all directions in a given medium. [named after A. A. MICHELSON and Edward *Morley* (1838–1923), American chemist and physicist]

Mich·e·ner (mich′ə nər), *n.* **James A(lbert),** born 1907, U.S. novelist.

Mich·i·gan (mish′ə-gən), *n.* **1.** a State in the N central United States. 7,823,194 (1960; 58,216 sq. mi. *Cap.:* Lansing. *Abbr.:* Mich. **2. Lake,** a lake in the N central U.S., between Wisconsin and Michigan: one of the five Great Lakes. 22,400 sq. mi. **3.** a card game of the stops family, for three to eight players.

Mich′igan bank′roll, *Slang.* **1.** a roll of paper money in small denominations. **2.** a roll of counterfeit notes, paper money of small denomination, or of money-sized paper surrounded by a genuine note of large denomination. Also called **Mich′igan roll′.** [from slang meaning of *Michigan* deceptive]

Mich′igan Cen′ter, a town in S Michigan. 4611 (1960).

Mich′igan Cit′y, a port in NW Indiana, on Lake Michigan. 36,653 (1960).

Mich·i·gan·der (mish′ə gan′dər), *n.* a native or inhabitant of Michigan. Also called **Mich·i·gan·ite** (mish′ə gə nīt′). [b. MICHIGAN and GANDER, name first applied to Lewis Cass, governor of the Michigan Territory (1813–31)]

Mich·i·ga·ni·an (mish′ə gā′nē ən, -gan′ē-), *adj.* **1.** of, pertaining to, or characteristic of Michigan or its inhabitants. —*n.* **2.** a Michigander. [MICHIGAN + -IAN]

Mich′igan rum′my, *Cards.* a variety of five hundred rummy in which each player scores his melds as played.

Mi·cho·a·cán (mē′chō ä kän′), *n.* a state in SW Mexico. 1,862,568 (1960); 23,196 sq. mi. *Cap.:* Morelia.

Mi·chol (mī′kəl), *n.* *Douay Bible.* Michal.

Mick (mik), *n.* *Usually Offensive.* an Irishman. [from the name *Michael*]

Mick·ey (mik′ē), *n., pl.* **-eys,** *adj.* *Slang.* —*n.* **1.** Also called **Mick′ey Finn′.** a drink, usually of liquor, containing a drug, purgative, or the like, which renders the drinker helpless. **2.** (*often l.c.*) Also, **micky.** a potato, esp. a roasted Irish potato. —*adj.* **3.** (*sometimes l.c.*) See **mickey mouse.** [MICK + -EY[2]]

mick′ey mouse′, (*often caps.*) *Slang.* trite and commercially slick in character: *mickey mouse music.* [after the cartoon character created by Walt Disney]

Mic·kie·wicz (mits kye′vich), *n.* **A·dam** (ä′däm), 1798–1855, Polish poet.

mick·le (mik′əl), *adj.* *Archaic.* great; large; much. [ME *mikel* < Scand (cf. Icel *mykill*; r. ME *michel,* OE *micel* MUCH; c. OHG *mihil,* Goth *mikils,* akin to L *magnus,* Gk *mégas*]

mick·y (mik′ē), *n., pl.* **mick·ies.** (*sometimes cap.*) *Slang.* Mickey (def. 2).

Mic·mac (mik′mak), *n., pl.* **-macs,** (*esp. collectively*) **-mac** for 1. **1.** a member of a tribe of Algonquian Indians inhabiting the southern shores of the Gulf of St. Lawrence. **2.** the Algonquian language of these Indians.

mi·cra (mī′krə), *n.* a pl. of **micron.**

mi·cri·fy (mī′krə fī′), *v.t.,* **-fied, -fy·ing.** to make small or insignificant. [MICR- + -IFY]

micro-, a learned borrowing from Greek, where it meant "small" (*microcosm*), used to mean "enlarging (something small)" (*microphone*), as a combining form of **microscopic** (*microorganism*), and to represent a millionth part of a unit (*microgram*). Also, *esp. before a vowel,* **micr-.** [comb. form repr. Gk *mīkrós*]

mi·cro·aer·o·phile (mī′krō âr′ə fīl′), *n.* **1.** a microaerophilic organism. —*adj.* **2.** microaerophilic. [MICRO- + AERO- + -PHILE]

mi·cro·aer·o·phil·ic (mī′krō âr′ə fil′ik), *adj.* *Biol.* requiring only a small amount of free oxygen for growth. Also, **mi·cro·aer·oph·i·lous** (mī′krō â rof′ə-ləs), **microaerophile.** [MICROAEROPHILE + -IC] —**mi′cro·aer′o·phil′i·cal·ly,** *adv.*

mi·cro·am·me·ter (mī′krō am′mē tər), *n.* an instrument for measuring extremely small electric currents, calibrated in microamperes. [MICRO- + AMMETER]

mi·cro·am·pere (mī′krō am′pēr, -am pēr′), *n.* *Elect.* a unit of electric current, equal to one millionth of an ampere. *Symbol:* μA [MICRO- + AMPERE]

mi·cro·a·nal·y·sis (mī′krō ə nal′i sis), *n., pl.* **-ses** (-sēz′). *Chem.* the analysis of very small samples of substances. [MICRO- + ANALYSIS] —**mi·cro·an·a·lyst** (mī′krō an′əlist), *n.* —**mi·cro·an·a·lyt·i·cal** (mī′krō-an′əlit′i kəl), **mi′cro·an′a·lyt′ic,** *adj.*

mi·cro·ang·strom (mī′krō aŋ′strəm), *n.* one millionth of an angstrom. *Symbol:* μÅ [MICRO- + ANGSTROM]

mi·cro·bac·te·ri·um (mī′krō bak tēr′ē əm), *n., pl.* **-te·ri·a** (-tēr′ē ə). *Bacteriol.* any of several rod-shaped, thermoduric, saprophytic bacteria of the genus *Microbacterium,* found chiefly in dairy products. [MICRO- + BACTERIUM]

mi·cro·bal·ance (mī′krə bal′əns), *n.* *Chem.* a balance for weighing minute quantities of material. [MICRO- + BALANCE]

mi·cro·bar (mī′krə bär′), *n.* a centimeter-gram-second unit of pressure, equal to one millionth of a bar; one dyne per square centimeter. Also called **barye.** [MICRO- + BAR[1]]

mi·cro·bar·o·gram (mī′krə bär′ə gram′), *n. Meteorol.* a record made by a microbarograph. [MICRO- + BAROGRAM]

mi·cro·bar·o·graph (mī′krə bär′ə graf′, -gräf′), *n. Meteorol.* a barograph for recording minute fluctuations of atmospheric pressure. [MICRO- + BAROGRAPH]

mi·crobe (mī′krōb), *n.* a microorganism, esp. a pathogenic bacterium. [< F < Gk *mikro-* MICRO- + *bíos* life] —**mi·crobe·less,** *adj.* —**mi·cro′bi·al, mi·cro′bic, mi·cro′bi·an,** *adj.*

mi·cro·bi·cide (mī krō′bi sīd′), *n.* a substance or preparation for killing microbes. [MICROBE + -I- + -CIDE] —**mi·cro′bi·cid′al,** *adj.*

mi·cro·bi·ol·o·gy (mī′krō bī ol′ə jē), *n.* the science dealing with the structure, function, uses, etc., of microscopic organisms. [MICRO- + BIOLOGY] —**mi·cro·bi·o·log·i·cal** (mī′krō bī′ə loj′i kəl), **mi′cro·bi′o·log′ic,** *adj.* —**mi′cro·bi′o·log′i·cal·ly,** *adv.* —**mi′cro·bi·ol′o·gist,** *n.*

mi·cro·ce·phal·ic (mī′krō sə fal′ik), *adj.* **1.** *Craniom.* having a skull with a small cranial capacity. Cf. **megacephalic** (def. 1). **2.** *Pathol.* having an abnormally small skull. Also, **mi·cro·ceph·a·lous** (mī′krō sef′ə ləs). [< NL *microcephal(us).* See MICRO-, CEPHALIC] —**mi·cro·ce·pha·li·a** (mī′krō sə fā′lē ə, -fāl′yə), **mi·cro·ceph·a·lism** (mī′krō sef′ə liz′əm), **mi′cro·ceph′a·ly,** *n.*

mi·cro·chem·is·try (mī′krō kem′i strē), *n.* the branch of chemistry dealing with minute quantities of substances. [MICRO- + CHEMISTRY] —**mi·cro·chem·i·cal** (mī′krō kem′i kəl), *adj.*

mi·cro·chip (mī′krō chip′), *n. Electronics.* chip[1] (def. 7). [MICRO- + CHIP[1]]

Mi·cro·ci·o·na (mī′krə sī′ə nə), *n.* a genus of bright-red sponges of the Atlantic coast of North America and Europe, used in experiments on the dissociation and reintegration of sponge cells. [< NL < Gk *mīkro-* MICRO- + *kīōn* column]

mi·cro·cir·cuit (mī′krō sûr′kit), *n.* a compact electronic circuit whose miniaturized components form an inseparable unit, usually on a silicon chip. [MICRO- + CIRCUIT]

mi·cro·cli·mate (mī′krə klī′mit), *n.* the climate of a small area, as of confined spaces such as caves, houses, etc. **(cryptoclimate),** of plant communities, wooded areas, etc., or of urban communities. Cf. **macroclimate.** [MICRO- + CLIMATE] —**mi·cro·cli·mat·ic** (mī′krō klī mat′ik), *adj.* —**mi′cro·cli·mat′i·cal·ly,** *adv.*

mi·cro·cli·ma·tol·o·gy (mī′krō klī′mə tol′ə jē), *n.* the study of the local climatic conditions of a small area, esp. the analysis of climatic profiles of the lowest stratum of the atmosphere, as of confined spaces **(cryptoclimatology),** of plants and plant communities **(phytoclimatology),** or of urban communities. Cf. **macroclimatology, micrometeorology.** [MICRO- + CLIMATOLOGY] —**mi·cro·cli·ma·to·log·ic** (mī′krō klī′mə tᵊloj′ik), **mi′cro·cli′ma·to·log′i·cal,** *adj.* —**mi′cro·cli′ma·tol′o·gist,** *n.*

mi·cro·cline (mī′krə klīn′), *n.* a mineral of the feldspar group, potassium aluminum silicate, $KAlSi_3O_8$, identical in composition with orthoclase but having triclinic instead of monoclinic crystals, used in making porcelain. [MICRO- + Gk *klīn(ein)* (to) cause to lean, slant. See CLINIC]

mi·cro·coc·cus (mī′krə kok′əs), *n., pl.* **-coc·ci** (-kok′sī). *Bacteriol.* any spherical bacterium of the genus *Micrococcus,* occurring in irregular masses, many species of which are pigmented and are saprophytic or parasitic. [< NL; see MICRO-, COCCUS] —**mi′cro·coc′cal, mi·cro·coc·cic** (mī′krə kok′sik), *adj.*

mi·cro·com·put·er (mī′krō kəm pyōō′tər, mī′krō kəm pyōō′tər), *n.* a compact and inexpensive computer, relatively limited in capability and capacity, consisting of a microprocessor and other components of a computer, miniaturized where possible: now increasingly used in small business, by hobbyists, etc. [MICRO- + COMPUTER]

mi·cro·con·stit·u·ent (mī′krō kən stich′ōō ənt), *n.* a microscopically small constituent of a metal or alloy. [MICRO- + CONSTITUENT]

mi·cro·cop·y (mī′krə kop′ē), *n., pl.* **-cop·ies.** a greatly reduced photographic copy of a printed page or the like. [MICRO- + COPY]

mi·cro·cosm (mī′krə koz′əm), *n.* **1.** a little world; a world in miniature (opposed to *macrocosm*). **2.** anything that is regarded as a world in miniature. **3.** man, mankind, society, or the like, viewed as an epitome or miniature of the world or universe. Also called **mi·cro·cos·mos** (mī′krə koz′məs, -mōs). [late ME *microcosme* < ML *microcosm(us)* < Gk *mikròs kósmos* small world. See MICRO-, COSMOS] —**mi′cro·cos′mic, mi′cro·cos′mi·cal,** *adj.*

mi′cro·cos′mic salt′, *Chem.* See **sodium ammonium phosphate.**

mi·cro·cou·lomb (mī′krə kōō′lom), *n. Elect.* a unit of quantity of electricity, equal to one millionth of a coulomb. *Symbol:* μC [MICRO- + COULOMB]

mi·cro·crys·tal (mī′krə kris′tᵊl), *n.* a microscopic crystal. [MICRO- + CRYSTAL]

mi·cro·crys·tal·line (mī′krō kris′tᵊlin, -tᵊlīn′), *adj.* minutely crystalline; composed of microscopic crystals. [MICRO- + CRYSTALLINE] —**mi·cro·crys·tal·lin·i·ty** (mī′krō kris′tᵊlin′i tē), *n.*

mi·cro·cu·rie (mī′krə kyŏŏr′ē, mī′krō kyŏŏ rē′), *n. Physics, Chem.* a unit of radioactivity, equal to one millionth of a Curie; 3.70×10^4 disintegrations per second. *Symbol:* μCi, μc [MICRO- + CURIE]

mi·cro·cyte (mī′krə sīt′), *n.* **1.** a minute cell or corpuscle. **2.** *Pathol.* an abnormally small red blood cell, usually deficient in hemoglobin. [MICRO- + -CYTE] —**mi·cro·cyt·ic** (mī′krə sit′ik), *adj.*

mi·cro·den·si·tom·e·ter (mī′krō den′si tom′i tər), *n. Photog.* a densitometer for measuring the denseness of minute areas of photographic negatives. [MICRO- + DENSITOMETER]

mi·cro·de·tec·tor (mī′krō di tek′tər), *n.* **1.** an instrument measuring small quantities or changes. **2.** *Elect.* an extremely sensitive galvanometer. [MICRO- + DETECTOR]

mi·cro·dis·sec·tion (mī′krō di sek′shən), *n.* dissection performed under a microscope. [MICRO- + DISSECTION]

mi·cro·dis·til·la·tion (mī′krō dis′tᵊlā′shən), *n. Chem.* the distillation of minute quantities of material. [MICRO- + DISTILLATION]

mi·cro·dont (mī′krə dont′), *adj.* having abnormally small teeth. Also, **mi′cro·don′tic, mi′cro·don′tous.** [MICR- + -ODONT]

mi·cro·don·tia (mī′krə don′shə, -shē ə), *n.* the condition of having abnormally small teeth or an instance, or case, of it. Also, **mi·cro·dont·ism** (mī′krə don tiz′əm), **mi′cro·don′ty.** [< NL; see MICRODONT, -IA]

mi·cro·dyne (mī′krə dīn′), *n.* one millionth of a dyne. *Symbol:* μdyn [MICRO- + DYNE]

mi·cro·e·co·nom·ics (mī′krō ē′kə nom′iks, -ek′ə-), *n.* (*construed as sing.*) the branch of economics dealing with particular aspects of an economy, as the price-cost relationship of a firm. Cf. **macroeconomics.** [MICRO- + ECONOMICS] —**mi′cro·e′co·nom′ic,** *adj.*

mi·cro·e·lec·tron·ics (mī′krō i lek tron′iks, -ē′lek-), *n.* (*construed as sing.*) the technology dealing with the design, development, and construction of electronic systems utilizing extremely small elements, esp. solid-state devices employing microminiaturization. [MICRO- + ELECTRONICS] —**mi′cro·e·lec·tron′ic,** *adj.*

mi·cro·e·lec·tro·pho·re·sis (mī′krō i lek′trō fə rē′sis), *n. Chem.* any of several techniques for observing, by means of a microscope or an ultramicroscope, the electrophoresis of minute surface particles. [MICRO- + ELECTROPHORESIS] —**mi·cro·e·lec·tro·pho·ret·ic** (mī′krō i lek′trō fə ret′ik), *adj.*

mi·cro·el·e·ment (mī′krō el′ə mənt), *n. Biochem.* See **trace element.** [MICRO- + ELEMENT]

mi·cro·en·vi·ron·ment (mī′krō en vī′ərn mənt, -vī′-rən-), *n. Ecol.* the environment of a small area or of a particular organism in a community of plants and animals. [MICRO- + ENVIRONMENT] —**mi·cro·en·vi·ron·men·tal** (mī′krō en vī′ərn men′tᵊl, -vī′rən-), *adj.*

mi·cro·far·ad (mī′krə far′əd, -ad), *n. Elect.* a unit of capacitance, equal to one millionth of a farad. *Abbr.:* mf., mfd. *Symbol:* μF, μf [MICRO- + FARAD]

mi·cro·fiche (mī′krə fēsh′), *n.* a sheet of microfilm, in a form suitable for filing, containing a number of separate images. [MICRO- + F *fiche* small card]

mi·cro·film (mī′krə film′), *n.* **1.** a film bearing a miniature photographic copy of printed or other graphic matter, usually of a document, newspaper or book pages, etc., made for a library, archive, or the like. **2.** a film, esp. of motion-picture stock, on which microcopies are made. —*v.t.* **3.** to make a microfilm of. [MICRO- + FILM]

mi·cro·fos·sil (mī′krō fos′il), *n.* a fossil so small that it can be studied and identified only by means of a microscope. Cf. **macrofossil.** [MICRO- + FOSSIL]

mi·cro·gam·ete (mī′krō gam′ēt, -krō gə mēt′), *n. Biol.* (in heterogamous reproduction) the smaller and, usually, the male of two conjugating gametes. [MICRO- + GAMETE]

mi·crog·a·my (mī krog′ə mē), *n., pl.* **-mies.** (in certain protozoans and algae) syngamy in which the gametes are smaller than the asexual cells. [MICRO- + -GAMY]

mi·crog·li·a (mī krog′lē ə), *n. Anat.* a type of neuroglia in the central nervous system, consisting of small cells that are phagocytic under certain pathological conditions. [MICRO- + Gk *glía* glue] —**mi·crog′li·al,** *adj.*

mi·cro·gram[1] (mī′krə gram′), *n.* a unit of mass or weight equal to one millionth of a gram, used chiefly in microchemistry. *Symbol:* μg Also, *esp. Brit.,* **mi′cro·gramme′.** [MICRO- + -GRAM[2]]

mi·cro·gram[2] (mī′krə gram′), *n.* micrograph (def. 2). [MICRO- + -GRAM[1]]

mi·cro·graph (mī′krə graf′, -gräf′), *n.* **1.** an instrument for executing extremely minute writing or engraving. **2.** *Optics.* a photograph taken through a microscope or a drawing of an object as seen through a microscope. [MICRO- + -GRAPH]

mi·crog·ra·phy (mī krog′rə fē), *n.* **1.** the description or delineation of microscopic objects. **2.** examination or study with the microscope (opposed to *macrography*). **3.** the technique or practice of using the microscope. **4.** the art or practice of writing in very small characters. [MICRO- + -GRAPHY] —**mi·crog′ra·pher,** *n.* —**mi·cro·graph·ic** (mī′krə graf′ik), *adj.* —**mi′cro·graph′i·cal·ly,** *adv.*

mi·cro·groove (mī′krə grōōv′), *n.* **1.** (in a phonograph record) a needle groove much narrower than the conventional width, allowing more material to be included on a single record. **2.** a record with such grooves, esp. a long-playing record. [MICRO- + GROOVE]

mi·cro·hard·ness (mī′krō härd′nis), *n. Metall.* the hardness of a metal as measured by means of an indent made at a very slight pressure and covering a very small area. [MICRO- + HARDNESS]

mi·cro·hen·ry (mī′krə hen′rē), *n., pl.* **-ries, -rys.** *Elect.* a unit of inductance, equal to one millionth of a henry. *Symbol:* μH, μh [MICRO- + HENRY]

mi·crohm (mī′krōm′), *n. Elect.* a unit of resistance, equal to one millionth of an ohm. [MICR- + OHM]

mi·cro·im·age (mī′krō im′ij), *n.* a microreproduction.

mi·cro·inch (mī′krō inch′), *n.* a unit of length equal to one millionth of an inch. *Symbol:* μin [MICRO- + INCH]

mi·cro·in·jec·tion (mī′krō in jek′shən), *n. Biol.* injection performed under a microscope, esp. of a solution or transplant into a cell, tissue, or the like. [MICRO- + INJECTION]

mi·cro·lam·bert (mī′krə lam′bərt), *n. Optics.* a unit of luminance, equal to one millionth of a lambert. [MICRO- + LAMBERT]

mi·cro·lec·i·thal (mī′krə les′ə thəl), *adj. Embryol.* having a small amount of yolk, as certain eggs or ova. [MICRO- + LECITHAL]

mi·cro·lite (mī′krə līt′), *n.* **1.** *Mineral.* any microscopic crystal. **2.** a mineral, principally calcium pyrotantalate, $Ca_2Ta_2O_7$, usually including niobium, fluorine, and other impurities occurring in cubic crystals. [MICRO- + -LITE]

mi·cro·li·ter (mī′krə lē′tər), *n.* a unit of capacity equal to one millionth of a liter, used esp. in microchemistry. *Symbol:* μl Also, *esp. Brit.,* **mi′cro·li′tre.** [MICRO- + LITER]

mi·cro·lith (mī′krə lith), *n. Archaeol.* a tiny flint tool, usually triangular, found principally in Upper Paleolithic sites. [MICRO- + -LITH]

mi·cro·lith·ic (mī′krə lith′ik), *adj.* **1.** pertaining to or characterized by the use of microliths, as a people or culture. **2.** of the nature of or resembling a microlith, as a tool. [MICROLITH + -IC]

mi·crol·o·gy (mī krol′ə jē), *n.* excessive attention to petty details or distinctions. [< Gk *mikrología* minute discussion, frivolity. See MICRO-, -LOGY] —**mi·cro·log·i·cal** (mī′krə loj′i kəl), **mi′cro·log′ic,** *adj.* —**mi·crol′o·gist,** *n.*

mi·cro·lux (mī′krə luks′), *n. Optics.* a unit of illumination, equal to one millionth of a lux. [MICRO- + LUX]

mi·cro·me·te·or·ite (mī′krō mē′tē ə rīt′), *n. Astron.* a very small meteorite, usually one having a diameter of less than a millimeter. [MICRO- + METEORITE]

mi·cro·me·te·or·o·gram (mī′krō mē′tē ôr′ə gram′, -or′-, -mē′tē ər ə-), *n.* a record made by a micrometeorograph. [MICRO- + METEOROGRAM]

mi·cro·me·te·or·o·gragh (mī′krō mē′tē ôr′ə graf′, -gräf′, -or′-, -mē′tē ər ə-), *n.* a meteorograph adapted for use in aircraft. [MICRO- + METEOROGRAPH]

mi·cro·me·te·or·ol·o·gy (mī′krō mē′tē ə rol′ə jē), *n.* the study of local and small-scale atmospheric phenomena, usually confined to the physical and dynamic occurrences within a shallow stratum of air adjacent to the ground. Cf. **macrometeorology, mesometeorology, microclimatology.** [MICRO- + METEOROLOGY] —**mi·cro·me·te·or·o·log·i·cal** (mī′krō mē′tē ər ə loj′i kəl), *adj.*

mi·crom·e·ter (mī krom′i tər), *n.* **1.** any of various devices for measuring minute distances, angles, etc., as in connection with a telescope or microscope. **2.** See **micrometer caliper.** [MICRO- + -METER]

Micrometer

microm′eter cal′iper, a precision caliper with a spindle moved by a finely threaded screw, for the measurement of thicknesses and short lengths, commonly used by machinists for turning shafts or boring holes.

microm′eter drum′, a graduated head on a micrometer screw for the fine adjustment of the arm of a sextant.

microm′eter screw′, a screw with a very fine thread and a graduated head, used in micrometers or the like.

mi·crom·e·try (mī krom′i trē), *n.* the act or process of taking measurements with a micrometer. [MICRO- + -METRY] —**mi·cro·met·ri·cal** (mī′krə me′tri kəl), **mi′cro·met′ric,** *adj.* —**mi′cro·met′ri·cal·ly,** *adv.*

mi·cro·mho (mī′krə mō′), *n., pl.* **-mhos.** *Elect.* a unit of conductance, equal to one millionth of a mho. *Symbol:* μmho [MICRO- + MHO]

mi·cro·mi·cro·cu·rie (mī′krō mī′krō kyŏŏr′ē, -kyŏŏ-rē′), *n. Physics, Chem.* a unit of radioactivity, equal to one millionth of a microcurie; 3.70×10^{-2} disintegrations per second. [MICRO- + MICROCURIE]

mi·cro·mi·cro·far·ad (mī′krō mī′krō far′əd, -ad), *n. Elect.* one millionth of a microfarad. *Symbol:* μμf Also called **picofarad.** [MICRO- + MICROFARAD]

mi·cro·mi·cron (mī′krō mī′kron), *n., pl.* **-crons, -cra** (-krə). *Metric System.* one millionth of a micron. *Symbol:* μμ, mu mu Also called **picometer.** [MICRO- + MICRON]

mi·cro·mil·li·me·ter (mī′krō mil′ə mē′tər), *n. Metric System.* the millionth part of a millimeter. Also, *esp. Brit.,* **mi′cro·mil′li·me′tre.** Also called **nanometer.** [MICRO- + MILLIMETER]

mi·cro·min·i·a·ture (mī′krō min′ē ə chər, -min′ə-chər), *adj.* built on an extremely small scale, smaller than subminiature, esp. of electronic equipment with small solid-state components in the place of vacuum tubes. [MICRO- + MINIATURE]

mi·cro·min·i·a·tur·i·za·tion (mī′krō min′ē ə chər-i zā′shən), *n.* extreme miniaturization, esp. of electronic equipment smaller than subminiature and involving the substitution of solid-state components for vacuum tubes. [MICRO- + MINIATURIZATION]

mi·cro·min·i·a·tur·ize (mī′krō min′ē ə chə rīz′), *v.t.,* **-ized, -iz·ing.** (esp. of electronic equipment) to make extremely small; subject to microminiaturization. [MICRO- + MINIATURIZE]

mi·cro·mo·tion (mī′krə mō′shən), *n.* **1.** a motion, esp. a periodic one, of very short duration or length. **2.** (in time and motion study) the analysis of the time of a work performance in its basic subdivisions with the aid of a timing apparatus, motion-picture equipment, etc. [MICRO- + MOTION]

mi·cron (mī′kron), *n., pl.* **-crons, -cra** (-krə). **1.** *Metric System.* the millionth part of a meter. *Symbol:* μ, mu **2.** *Physical Chem.* a colloidal particle whose diameter is between .2 and 10 microns. Also, **mikron.** [< Gk *mīkron* small, little, neut. sing. of *mīkrós*]

mi·cro·ne·mous (mī′krə nē′məs), *adj. Bot., Zool.* having short filaments. [MICRO- + Gk *nêm(a)* thread + -OUS]

Mi·cro·ne·sia (mī′krə nē′zhə, -shə), *n.* one of the three principal divisions of Oceania, comprising the small Pacific islands N of the equator and E of the Philippines, whose main groups are the Mariana Islands, the Caroline Islands, and the Marshall Islands.

Mi·cro·ne·sian (mī′krə nē′zhən, -shən), *adj.* **1.** of or pertaining to Micronesia, its inhabitants, or their languages. —*n.* **2.** a native of Micronesia. **3.** the Malayo-Polynesian languages of Micronesia, taken collectively. [MICRONESI(A) + -AN]

mi·cro·nu·cle·ate (mī′krō nōō′klē it, -āt′, -nyōō′-), *adj.* having a micronucleus. [MICRONUCLE(US) + -ATE[1]]

mi·cro·nu·cle·us (mī′krō nōō′klē əs, -nyōō′-), *n., pl.* **-cle·i** (-klē ī′). *Zool.* the smaller of the two nuclei of a ciliate. Cf. **macronucleus.** [MICRO- + NUCLEUS] —**mi′cro·nu′cle·ar,** *adj.*

mi·cro·or·gan·ism (mī′krō ôr′gə niz′əm), *n.* a microscopic plant or animal. Also, **mi′cro-ör′gan·ism.** [MICRO- + ORGANISM] —**mi·cro·or·gan·ic, mi·cro·ör·gan·ic** (mī′krō ôr gan′ik), **mi′cro·or′gan·is′mal, mi′cro·ör′gan·is′mal,** *adj.*

mi·cro·pa·le·on·tol·o·gy (mī′krō pā′lē ən tol′ə jē, -pal′ē-), *n.* the branch of paleontology dealing with the study of microscopic fossils. [MICRO- + PALEONTOLOGY] —**mi·cro·pa·le·on·to·log·i·cal** (mī′krō pā′lē on′-tᵊloj′i kəl, -pal′ē-), **mi′cro·pa′le·on′to·log′ic,** *adj.* —**mi′cro·pa′le·on·tol′o·gist,** *n.*

mi·cro·par·a·site (mī′krō par′ə sīt′), *n.* a parasitic microorganism. [MICRO- + PARASITE] —**mi·cro·par·a·sit·ic** (mī′krō par′ə sit′ik), *adj.*

CONCISE PRONUNCIATION KEY: *act, āble, dâre, ärt; ebb, ēqual; if, īce; hot, ōver, ôrder, oil, bŏŏk, ōōze, out; up, ûrge; chief; sing; shoe; thin, that;* zh *as in measure.* ə = *a* as in *alone, e* as in *system, i* as in *easily, o* as in *gallop, u* as in *circus;* ᵊ as in *button* (but′ᵊn), *fire* (fīᵊr), *cradle* (krād′ᵊl). See the full key inside the front cover.

mi·cro·pa·thol·o·gy (mī′krō pə thol′ə jē), *n., pl.* **-gies.** the branch of pathology dealing with the microscopic study of changes that occur in tissues and cells during disease. [MICRO- + PATHOLOGY]

mi·cro·phage (mī′krə fāj′), *n. Anat.* a small phagocytic cell in blood or lymph, esp. a polymorphonuclear leukocyte. [MICRO- + -PHAGE]

mi·cro·phone (mī′krə fōn′), *n.* an instrument capable of transforming the air-pressure waves of sound into changes in electric currents or voltage, used in recording or transmitting sound. [MICRO- + -PHONE]

mi·cro·phon·ic (mī′krə fon′ik), *adj. Electronics.* tending to or capable of exhibiting microphonism. [MICRO- + PHONIC]

mi·cro·phon·ics (mī′krə fon′iks), *n.* (*construed as sing.*) *Electronics.* noise caused in an electronic circuit by microphonism. [MICRO- + PHONICS]

mi·cro·phon·ism (mī′krə fō′niz əm), *n. Electronics.* a usually undesirable property of some electronic circuits or components in which mechanical vibrations of a component affect the signal being transmitted through the circuit. [MICRO- + -PHONE + -ISM]

mi·cro·phot (mī′krə fot′, -fōt′), *n. Optics.* a unit of illumination equal to one millionth of a phot. [MICRO- + PHOT]

mi·cro·pho·to·graph (mī′krə fō′tə graf′, -gräf′), *n.* **1.** microfilm (def. 1). **2.** a small photograph requiring optical enlargement to render it visible in detail. **3.** a photomicrograph. [MICRO- + PHOTOGRAPH] —**mi·cro·pho·to·graph·ic** (mī′krə fō′tə graf′ik), *adj.* —**mi·cro·pho·tog·ra·phy** (mī′krō fə tog′rə fē), *n.*

mi·cro·pho·tom·e·ter (mī′krō fō tom′i tər), *n. Optics.* a photometer adapted for measuring the intensity of light emitted, transmitted, or reflected by minute objects. [MICRO- + PHOTOMETER] —**mi·cro·pho·to·met·ric** (mī′krō fō′tə me′trik), *adj.* —**mi′cro·pho′to·met′ri·cal·ly,** *adv.* —**mi′cro·pho·tom′e·try,** *n.*

mi·cro·phyl·lous (mī′krə fil′əs), *adj. Bot.* having small leaves. [MICRO- + -PHYLLOUS] —**mi′cro·phyll′,** *n.*

mi·cro·phys·ics (mī′krə fiz′iks), *n.* (*construed as sing.*) the branch of physics dealing with physical objects that are not large enough to be observed and treated directly, as elementary particles, atoms, and molecules. [MICRO- + PHYSICS] —**mi′cro·phys′i·cal,** *adj.*

mi·cro·phyte (mī′krə fīt′), *n.* a microscopic plant. [MICRO- + -PHYTE] —**mi·cro·phyt·ic** (mī′krə fit′ik), *adj.*

mi·cro·po·rous (mī′krə pōr′əs, -pôr′-), *adj.* composed of or having extremely small pores. [MICRO- + POROUS]

mi·cro·print (mī′krə print′), *n.* a microphotograph reproduced in print for reading by a magnifying device. [MICRO- + PRINT]

mi·cro·proc·es·sor (mī′krə pros′es ər *or, esp. Brit.,* prō′ses-; mī′krō pros′es ər *or, esp. Brit.,* -prō′ses-), *n. Computer Technol.* a miniaturized integrated circuit that performs all of the functions of a central processing unit. [MICRO- + PROCESS + -OR[2]]

mi·crop·si·a (mī krop′sē ə), *n. Ophthalm.* a defect of vision in which objects appear to be smaller than their actual size. Also, **mi·cro·pi·a** (mī krō′pē ə), **mi·crop·sy** (mī′krop sē). Cf. **macropsia.** [MICR- + -OPSIA] —**mi·crop·tic** (mī krop′tik), *adj.*

mi·cro·pyle (mī′krə pīl′), *n.* **1.** *Zool.* any minute opening in an ovum through which a spermatozoon can enter. See diag. under **orthotropous. 2.** *Bot.* the minute orifice or opening in the integuments of an ovule. [MICRO- + Gk *pýlē* gate] —**mi′cro·py′lar,** *adj.*

mi·cro·py·rom·e·ter (mī′krō pī rom′i tər), *n.* an optical pyrometer to measure the temperature of small glowing bodies. [MICRO- + PYROMETER]

mi·cro·read·er (mī′krō rē′dər), *n.* a device for projecting an enlarged image of a microfilm or microphotograph, esp. on a ground-glass screen. [MICRO- + READER]

mi·cro·re·pro·duc·tion (mī′krō rē′prə duk′shən), *n.* **1.** a photographic image too small to be read by the unaided eye. **2.** the technique of producing such images. [MICRO- + REPRODUCTION]

micros., microscopy

mi·cro·scope (mī′krə skōp′), *n.* **1.** an optical instrument having a magnifying lens or a combination of lenses for inspecting objects too small to be seen or too small to be seen distinctly and in detail by the naked eye. **2.** (*cap.*) *Astron.* the constellation Microscopium. [< NL *mīcroscop(ium).* See MICRO-, -SCOPE]

Microscope (Monocular) A, Eyepiece; B, Adjusting screw; C, Arm; D, Tube; E, Revolving eyepiece; F, Objective; G, Stage; H, Illuminating Mirror; I Stand

mi·cro·scop·ic (mī′krə skop′ik), *adj.* **1.** so small as to be invisible or indistinct without the use of the microscope: *microscopic organisms.* Cf. **macroscopic. 2.** very small; tiny. **3.** of, pertaining to, or involving a microscope: *microscopic investigation.* **4.** performing the function of or having the characteristics of a microscope: *Nothing in the painting escaped his microscopic study.* **5.** suggestive of the use of the microscope: *microscopic exactness.* Also, **mi′cro·scop′i·cal.** [MICROSCOPE + -IC]—**mi′cro·scop′i·cal·ly,** *adv.*

Mi·cro·sco·pi·um (mī′krə skō′pē əm), *n., gen.* **-pi·i** (-pē ī′). *Astron.* the Microscope, a small southern constellation south of Capricorn. [< NL]

mi·cros·co·py (mī kros′kə pē, mī′krə skō′pē), *n.* **1.** the use of the microscope. **2.** microscopic investigation. [MICROSCOPE + -Y[3]] —**mi·cros·co·pist** (mī kros′kə pist, mī′krə skō′pist), *n.*

mi·cro·sec·ond (mī′krə sek′ənd), *n. Metric System.* a unit of time equal to one millionth of a second. *Symbol:* μsec [MICRO- + SECOND[2]]

mi·cro·seg·ment (mī′krə seg′mənt), *n.* a stretch of speech preceded and followed but not interrupted by juncture. Cf. **macrosegment.** [MICRO- + SEGMENT]

mi·cro·seism (mī′krə sīz′əm, -səm), *n. Geol.* a feeble, recurrent vibration of the ground recorded by seismographs and believed to be due to an earthquake or a storm at sea. [MICRO- + SEISM] —**mi·cro·seis·mic** (mī′krə sīz′mik, -sīs′-), **mi′cro·seis′mi·cal,** *adj.*

mi·cro·sie·mens (mī′krə sē′mənz, -zē′-), *n.* one millionth of a siemens. *Symbol:* μs [MICRO- + SIEMENS]

mi·cro·some (mī′krə sōm′), *n. Biol.* a small inclusion, consisting of ribosomes and fragments of the endoplasmic reticulum, in the protoplasm of a cell. [MICRO- + -SOME[3]] —**mi′cro·so′mal, mi′cro·so′mi·al, mi′cro·so′mic,** *adj.*

mi·cro·spec·tro·pho·tom·e·ter (mī′krō spek′trə fō tom′i tər), *n. Optics.* a spectrophotometer for examining light emitted, transmitted, or reflected by minute objects. [MICRO- + SPECTROPHOTOMETER] —**mi·cro·spec·tro·pho·to·met·ric** (mī′krō spek′trō fō′tə me′trik), *adj.* —**mi′cro·spec′tro·pho·tom′e·try,** *n.*

mi·cro·spo·ran·gi·um (mī′krō spə ran′jē əm, -spô-), *n., pl.* **-gi·a** (-jē ə). *Bot.* a sporangium containing microspores. [MICRO- + SPORANGIUM]

mi·cro·spore (mī′krə spōr′, -spôr′), *n. Bot.* **1.** the smaller of two kinds of spores produced by some pteridophytes. **2.** a pollen grain. [MICRO- + SPORE] —**mi·cro·spor·ic** (mī′krə spōr′ik, -spor′-), **mi·cro·spor·ous** (mī′krə spōr′əs, -spôr′-, mī kros′pər əs), *adj.*

mi·cro·spo·ro·phyll (mī′krə spōr′ə fil, -spôr′-), *n. Bot.* a sporophyll bearing microsporangia. [MICRO- + SPOROPHYLL]

mi·cro·stat (mī′krə stat′), *n.* a negative of a microphotograph made directly from a negative by a copy camera. [MICRO- + -STAT]

mi·cro·steth·o·scope (mī′krə steth′ə skōp′), *n. Med.* a stethoscope containing an apparatus that greatly amplifies the sounds heard. [MICRO- + STETHOSCOPE]

mi·cro·stom·a·tous (mī′krə stom′ə təs, -stō′mə-), *adj.* having a very small mouth. Also, **mi·cros·to·mous** (mī kros′tə məs). [MICRO- + STOMATOUS]

mi·cro·stress (mī′krō stres′), *n. Metall.* a stress in the microscopic structure of a metal, as one caused by the distortion of space lattices. [MICRO- + STRESS]

mi·cro·struc·ture (mī′krō struk′chər), *n. Metall.* the structure of a metal or alloy as observed, after etching and polishing, under a high degree of magnification. [MICRO- + STRUCTURE]

mi·cro·sty·lous (mī′krə stī′ləs), *adj. Bot.* having short styles. Cf. **macrostylous, mesostylous.** [MICRO- + STYLE + -OUS]

mi·cro·sur·ger·y (mī′krō sûr′jə rē), *n.* the dissection of tissue or of individual cells under a microscope or a magnifying lens. [MICRO- + SURGERY]

mi·cro·switch (mī′krə swich′), *n.* a highly sensitive switch used in automatic-control devices. [MICRO- + SWITCH]

mi·cro·therm (mī′krə thûrm′), *n.* a plant requiring a minimum of heat for growth. [MICRO- + THERM] —**mi′cro·ther′mic,** *adj.*

mi·cro·tome (mī′krə tōm′), *n.* an instrument for cutting very thin sections, as of organic tissue, for microscopic examination. [MICRO- + -TOME]

mi·crot·o·my (mī krot′ə mē), *n., pl.* **-mies.** the cutting of very thin sections with the microtome. [MICRO- + -TOMY] —**mi·cro·tom·ic** (mī′krə tom′ik), **mi′cro·tom′i·cal,** *adj.* —**mi·crot′o·mist,** *n.*

mi·cro·tone (mī′krə tōn′), *n.* any musical interval smaller than a semitone, specifically, a quarter tone. [MICRO- + TONE] —**mi′cro·ton′al,** *adj.* —**mi′cro·to·nal′i·ty,** *n.* —**mi′cro·ton′al·ly,** *adv.*

mi·cro·volt (mī′krə vōlt′), *n. Elect.* a unit of electromotive force or potential difference equal to one millionth of a volt. *Symbol:* μV, μv [MICRO- + VOLT]

mi·cro·watt (mī′krō wot′), *n. Elect.* a unit of power equal to one millionth of a watt. *Symbol:* μW, μw [MICRO- + WATT]

mi·cro·wave (mī′krō wāv′), *n.* an electromagnetic wave of extremely high frequency, usually one having wavelength of from 1 mm. to 50 cm. [MICRO- + WAVE]

mi′crowave spectros′copy, *Physics.* the determination of those microwave frequencies of the microwave spectrum that are selectively absorbed by certain materials, providing information about atomic, molecular, and crystalline structure. —**mi′crowave spec′troscope.**

mi′crowave spec′trum, *Electronics.* a spectrum of electromagnetic radiations having wavelengths between 0.1 cm. and 30 cm.

mi·cro·zo·on (mī′krə zō′on, -ən), *n., pl.* **-zo·a** (-zō′ə). a microscopic animal, esp. a protozoan. [MICRO- + -ZOON]

mic·tu·rate (mik′chə rāt′), *v.i.,* **-rat·ed, -rat·ing.** to pass urine; urinate. [< L *mictur(īre)* (to) desire to make water (*mict(us),* ptp. of *mingere* to make water + *-ur-* desiderative suffix) + -ATE[1]]

mic·tu·ri·tion (mik′chə rish′ən), *n.* the act of passing urine; urination. [< L *micturī(re)* (to) desire to make water (see MICTURATE) + -TION]

mid[1] (mid), *adj.* **1.** being at or near the middle point of: *in mid autumn.* **2.** being or occupying a middle place or position: *in the mid nineties of the last century.* **3.** *Phonet.* (of a vowel) articulated with an opening above the tongue relatively intermediate between those for high and low: the vowels of *beet, bet,* and *hot* are respectively high, mid, and low. Cf. **high** (def. 23), **low** (def. 31). —*n.* **4.** *Archaic.* the middle. [ME, OE *midd;* c. OHG *mitti,* Icel *mithr,* Goth *midjis,* L *medius,* Gk *mésos,* Skt *madhya* middle]

mid[2] (mid), *prep.* amid. Also, **'mid.**

mid-, a combining form meaning "middle," "middle part of": *midday; mid-Victorian.* [ME, OE; see MID[1]]

Mid., Midshipman.

mid., middle.

M.I.D., Master of Industrial Design.

mid·af·ter·noon (mid′af′tər no͞on′, -äf′-), *n.* **1.** the part of the afternoon centering approximately on three o'clock; the period approximately halfway between noon and sunset. —*adj.* **2.** occurring, taking place, done, or pertaining to midafternoon. [MID- + AFTERNOON]

mid·air (mid âr′), *n.* any point in the air not contiguous with the earth or other solid surface: *to catch a ball in midair.* [MID- + AIR[1]]

Mi·das (mī′dəs), *n.* **1.** *Class. Myth.* a Phrygian king, son of Gordius, who was given by Dionysus the power of turning whatever he touched into gold. **2.** a man of great wealth or great moneymaking ability. **3.** an early-warning satellite for detecting and warning of enemy ballistic-missile launches.

mid·band (mid′band′), *n.* (in pewter work) a decorated band reinforcing a tankard at its middle. [MID- + BAND[2]]

mid·brain (mid′brān′), *n. Anat.* the mesencephalon, being the middle of the three primary divisions of the brain in the embryo of a vertebrate or the part of the adult brain derived from this tissue. [MID- + BRAIN]

mid·course (mid′kōrs′, -kôrs′), *n. Rocketry.* the portion of a ballistic trajectory between the end of powered flight and the beginning of the reentry phase. [MID- + COURSE]

mid·day (mid′dā′), *n.* **1.** the middle of the day; noon or the time around noon. —*adj.* **2.** of or pertaining to the middle part of the day. [ME; OE *middæg.* See MID-, DAY]

Mid·del·burg (mid′əl bûrg′), *n.* a city in the SW Netherlands. 23,231 (1962).

mid·den (mid′ən), *n.* **1.** *Brit. Dial.* a dunghill or refuse heap. **2.** See **kitchen midden.** [ME *midding* < Scand; cf. Dan *mödding,* equiv. to *mög* muck, dung + *dynge* heap, dunghill]

mid·dle (mid′əl), *adj., n., v.,* **-dled, -dling.** —*adj.* **1.** equally distant from the extremes or outer limits; central: *the middle point of a line; the middle singer in a trio.* **2.** intervening or intermediate: *the middle distance.* **3.** medium: *a man of middle size.* **4.** (*cap.*) (in the history of a language) intermediate between periods classified as Old and New or Modern: *Middle English.* **5.** *Gram.* (in some languages) noting a voice of verb inflection in which the subject is represented as acting on or for itself, in contrast to the active voice in which the subject acts, and the passive voice in which the subject is acted upon, as in Greek *'egrapsámēn* "I wrote for myself," *'égrapsa* "I wrote," *'egráphēn* "I was written." **6.** *Naut.* **a.** noting the spars, sails, or rigging of a middle mast. **b.** noting any fore-and-aft stay terminating at its upper end at the head of a lower middle mast or the head of some specified upper middle mast. **7.** (*often cap.*) *Stratig.* noting the division intermediate between the upper and lower divisions of a period, system, or the like: *the middle Devonian.* —*n.* **8.** the point, part, position, etc., equidistant from extremes or limits. **9.** the middle part of the human body, esp. the waist: *He gave him a punch in the middle.* **10.** a mean; something intermediate. **11.** (in farming) the ground between two rows of plants. —*v.t., v.i.* **12.** *Chiefly Naut.* to fold in half. [ME, OE *middel;* c. G *mittel;* akin to Icel *methal* among. See MID[1]]

—**Syn. 1.** equidistant, halfway, medial, midway. **8.** midpoint. MIDDLE, CENTER, MIDST indicate something from which two or more other things are (approximately or exactly) equally distant. MIDDLE denotes, literally or figuratively, the point or part equidistant from or intermediate between extremes or limits in space or in time (activity): *the middle of a road.* CENTER, a more precise word, is ordinarily applied to a point within circular, globular, or regular bodies, or wherever a similar exactness appears to exist: *the center of the earth;* it may also be used metaphorically (still suggesting the core of a sphere): *center of interest.* MIDST usually suggests that a person or thing is closely surrounded or encompassed on all sides, esp. by that which is thick or dense: *the midst o a storm.* —**Ant. 1.** extreme. **8.** extremity.

mid′dle age′, the period of human life between youth and old age, sometimes considered as the years between 45 and 65 or thereabout. [ME]

mid·dle-aged (mid′əl ājd′), *adj.* **1.** being of the age intermediate between youth and old age, roughly between 45 and 65. **2.** characteristic of or suitable for persons of this age. —**mid·dle-a·ged·ly** (mid′əl ā′jid lē, -ājd′-), *adv.* —**mid′dle-a′ged·ness,** *n.*

Mid′dle Ag′es, the time in European history between classical antiquity and the Italian Renaissance (from the late 5th century A.D. to about 1350): sometimes restricted to the later part of this period (after 1100) and sometimes extended to 1450 or 1500. [pl. of *Middle Age,* special use of phrase *middle age*]

Mid′dle Amer′ica, continental North America S of the U.S., comprising Mexico, Central America, and usually the West Indies. 65,912,144 (est. 1960); 1,060,118 sq. mi. —**Mid′dle Amer′ican.**

Mid′dle Atlan′tic States′, New York, New Jersey, and Pennsylvania. Also called **Middle States.**

mid′dle bod′y, *Naut.* the part of a ship's hull that has parallel or nearly parallel sides.

Mid·dle·bor·ough (mid′əl bûr′ō), *n.* a town in SE Massachusetts. 6003 (1960).

mid·dle·break·er (mid′əl brā′kər), *n.* lister (def 1). [MIDDLE + BREAKER[1]]

mid·dle·brow (mid′əl brou′), *n.* **1.** a person whose interests extend mainly to widely known aspects of culture; a person of conventional taste. **2.** a person who has intellectual pretensions but fears unconventional or not widely accepted literature, painting, and the like. [MIDDLE + BROW] —**mid′dle·brow′ism,** *n.*

Mid′dle·burg Heights′ (mid′əl bûrg′), a town in N Ohio. 7282 (1960).

Mid·dle·bur·y (mid′əl ber′ē, -bə rē), *n.* a town in W Vermont. 3688 (1960).

mid·dle·bust·er (mid′əl bus′tər), *n.* lister (def. 1). [MIDDLE + BUSTER]

middle C, *Music.* the note indicated by the first leger line above the bass staff and the first below the treble staff.

mid′dle class′, 1. *U.S.* a class of people intermediate between the classes of higher and lower social rank or standing; the largest social, economic, cultural, etc., class, having approximately average status, income, education, tastes, and the like. **2.** (in Great Britain) the class socially and conventionally intermediate between the aristocratic class and the laboring class. **3.** an intermediate class.

mid·dle-class (mid′əl klas′, -kläs′), *adj.* of, pertaining to, or characteristic of the middle class; bourgeois: *middle-class taste.*

Mid′dle Com′edy, Greek Attic comedy of the 4th century B.C. The few extant fragments are characterized chiefly by a realistic depiction of everyday life. Cf. **New Comedy, Old Comedy.**

Mid′dle Con′go, former name of the Republic of Congo.

mid′dle dis′tance, *Fine Arts.* the represented space between the foreground and background in paintings, drawings, etc. Also called **middle ground, middle plane.**

mid′dle ear′, *Anat.* the middle portion of the ear, consisting of the tympanic membrane and an air-filled chamber lined with mucous membrane, which contains the malleus, incus, and stapes. Cf. **ear** (def. 1). See diag. under **ear**.

Mid′dle East′, 1. the lands from the E shores of the Mediterranean and Aegean to India, taken collectively: the Near East with the exception of the Balkan States. 2. (formerly) the area including Iran, Afghanistan, India, Tibet, and Burma. —**Mid′dle East′ern.**

Mid′dle Em′pire. See **Middle Kingdom** (def. 1).

Mid′dle Eng′lish, the English language of the period c1150–c1475.

mid′dle fin′ger, the finger between the forefinger and the third finger.

Mid′dle Flem′ish, the Flemish language of the 14th, 15th, and 16th centuries.

Mid′dle French′, the French language of the 14th, 15th, and 16th centuries.

mid′dle game′, *Chess.* the stage between the opening and the end game, characterized by complicated moves by both opponents with pieces at full strength.

Mid′dle Greek′. See **Medieval Greek.**

mid′dle ground′, 1. See **middle distance.** 2. *Naut.* a length of comparatively shallow water having channels on both sides.

mid·dle·hand (mid′əl hand′), *n.* *Cards.* the player on the dealer's right in a game with three players. Cf. **endhand, forehand** (def. 7). [MIDDLE + HAND]

Mid′dle High′ Ger′man, the High German language of the period 1100–1500.

Mid′dle I′rish, the Irish language of the later Middle Ages.

Mid′dle King′dom, 1. Also called **Middle Empire.** the period in the history of ancient Egypt, c2000–1785 B.C., comprising the 11th to 14th dynasties. 2. *Hist.* **a.** the 18 inner provinces of China, taken collectively. **b.** (loosely) China. 3. the Chinese Empire: originally so called from its supposed location in the center of the earth. Cf. **New Kingdom, Old Kingdom.**

mid′dle lamel′la, *Bot.* the layer of cementing material, composed of pectates and similar substances, between the walls of adjacent cells.

Mid′dle Lat′in. See **Medieval Latin.**

mid′dle lat′itude, the latitude of the point that is midway between two parallels on the same side of the equator. Also called **mean latitude.**

Mid′dle Low′ Ger′man, Low German of the period 1100–1500.

mid·dle·man (mid′əl man′), *n., pl.* **-men.** 1. a person who plays an intermediate economic role between producer and consumer. 2. a business intermediary who distributes goods or securities to customers on his own account and at his own risk. 3. a person who acts as an intermediary. [MIDDLE + MAN[1]]

Mid·dle·march (mid′əl märch′), *n.* a novel (1871–72) by George Eliot.

mid′dle mast′, *Naut.* the third mast of a five-masted sailing vessel; mizzenmast.

mid·dle·most (mid′əl mōst′), *adj.* midmost. [ME *middelmast.* See MIDDLE, -MOST]

mid′dle name′, the part of a person's name occurring between the first and family names, as a second forename or a maternal surname.

mid·dle-of-the-road (mid′əl əv *th*ə rōd′), *adj.* not favoring any extreme position; moderate.

mid·dle-of-the-road·er (mid′əl əv *th*ə rō′dər), *n.* a person who advocates or follows a moderate or safe course, as in politics.

Mid′dle Paleolith′ic, *Anthropol.* (*sometimes l.c.*) See under **Paleolithic.** Also, **mid′dle Paleolith′ic.**

mid′dle pas′sage, *Hist.* the part of the Atlantic Ocean between the west coast of Africa and the West Indies: the longest part of the journey made by slave ships. Also, **Mid′dle Pas′sage.**

Mid′dle Path′, *Hinduism, Buddhism.* the conduct of life by a religious person in such a way as to avoid the extremes of luxury and asceticism.

Mid′dle Per′sian, the Persian language at a stage that begins c300 B.C. and includes Pahlavi (attested from the 3rd to the 7th centuries A.D.) as well as the West Iranian literatures (3rd–10th centuries A.D.) of religions carried outside Persia.

mid′dle plane′. See **middle distance.**

Mid·dle·port (mid′əl pōrt′, -pôrt′), *n.* a town in SE Ohio. 3373 (1960).

mid·dle·sail (mid′əl sāl′), *n.* *Naut.* the lowermost sail of a middle mast. [MIDDLE + SAIL]

Mid·dles·brough (mid′əlz brə), *n.* a seaport in NE England, on the Tees estuary. 157,308 (1961).

mid′dle school′, a scholastic division, esp. in a private school, including the upper elementary grades and leading to the final secondary grades.

Mid·dle·sex (mid′əl seks′), *n.* a county in SE England, bordering W and N London. 2,230,093 (1961); 232 sq. mi.

Mid′dle States′. See **Middle Atlantic States.**

mid′dle stay′sail, *Naut.* 1. a staysail set between a topmast staysail and a topgallant staysail. 2. a sail set on a stay from a topgallant masthead to the lower mast of the next mast forward.

mid′dle stump′, *Cricket.* the stump inside of the leg stump and the off stump; the second of the three stumps of a wicket.

Mid′dle Tem′ple, 1. See under **Inns of Court** (def. 1). 2. See under **temple**[1] (def. 10).

mid′dle term′. See under **syllogism** (def. 1).

Mid·dle·ton (mid′əl tən), *n.* 1. **Thomas,** c1570–1627, English dramatist. 2. a town in S Wisconsin. 4410 (1960).

mid·dle·tone (mid′əl tōn′), *n.* halftone (def. 1). [MIDDLE + TONE]

Mid·dle·town (mid′əl toun′), *n.* 1. a city in SW Ohio on the Miami River. 42,115 (1960). 2. a town in E New Jersey. 39,675 (1960). 3. a city in central Connecticut, on the Connecticut River. 33,250 (1960). 4. a town in E Pennsylvania. 26,894 (1960). 5. a city in SE New York. 23,475 (1960). 6. a town in N Kentucky. 2764 (1960).

mid′dle watch′, *Naut.* the watch from midnight until 4 A.M. Also called **graveyard watch, midwatch.**

mid·dle·weight (mid′əl wāt′), *n.* 1. a person of average weight. 2. a boxer or other contestant intermediate in weight between a welterweight and a light heavyweight, esp. a professional boxer weighing up to 160 pounds. —*adj.* 3. *Boxing.* of or pertaining to a middleweight or middleweights: *the middleweight division; the middleweight champion.* 4. (of a horse, esp. a hunter) able to carry up to 185 pounds. [MIDDLE + WEIGHT]

Mid′dle West′, the region of the United States bounded on the W by the Rocky Mountains, on the S by the Ohio River and the S extremities of Missouri and Kansas, and on the E, variously, by the Allegheny Mountains, the E border of Ohio, or the E border of Illinois. —**Mid′dle West′erner.**

Mid′dle West′ern, of or pertaining to the Middle West. Also called **Midwestern.**

Mid′dle White′, *Brit.* one of a strain of Yorkshire hogs of medium size.

mid·dling (mid′ling), *adj.* 1. medium in size, quality, grade, rank, etc.; moderately large, good, etc.: *Her cooking is only middling.* 2. *Dial.* in fairly good health: *He was poorly, but now he's middling.* —*adv.* 3. moderately; fairly. —*n.* 4. **middlings,** any of various products or commodities of intermediate quality, grade, size, etc., as the coarser particles of ground wheat mingled with bran. 5. Often, **middlings.** Also called **mid′dling meat′.** *Chiefly Southern and Midland U.S.* salt pork or smoked side meat. [late ME (north). See MID[1], -LING[2]] —**mid′dling·ly,** *adv.*

mid·dy (mid′ē), *n., pl.* **-dies.** 1. *Informal.* a midshipman. 2. See **middy blouse.** [MID(SHIPMAN) + -Y[2]]

mid′dy blouse′, any of various loose blouses with a sailor collar, often extending below the waistline to terminate in a broad band or fold, as worn by sailors, children, young girls, etc.

Mid·e·a (mid′ē ə), *n.* *Class. Myth.* the mother, by Electryon, of Licymnius.

Mid·field (mid′fēld′), *n.* a town in N central Alabama. 3556 (1960).

Mid·gard (mid′gärd), *n.* *Scand. Myth.* the abode of mankind, located between Niflheim and Muspelheim and connected with Asgard by the bridge Bifrost: formed from the body of Ymir. Also, **Mid·garth** (mid′gärth), **Mid·gar·dhr** (mid′gär′thər), **Mithgarth, Mithgarthr.** [< Icel *mithgarthr;* akin to OE *middangeard* the earth. See MID[1], GARTH]

Mid′gard ser′pent, *Scand. Myth.* a serpent, the child of Loki and Angerboda, who lies wrapped around the world, tail in mouth, and is destined to kill and to be killed by Thor at Ragnarok; Jormungandr.

midge (mij), *n.* 1. any of numerous minute dipterous insects, esp. of the family *Chironomidae,* somewhat resembling a mosquito. Cf. **gnat** (def. 1). 2. a tiny person. [ME *mygge,* OE *mycg(e);* c. G *Mücke,* Icel *mȳ;* akin to Gk *myia,* L *musca* fly]

midg·et (mij′it), *n.* 1. an extremely small person. 2. any animal or thing very small of its kind. —*adj.* 3. very small or of a class below the usual size. 4. being a miniature replica or model. [MIDGE + -ET] —**midg′et·ism,** *n.* —**Syn. 1.** See **dwarf.**

midg′et golf′. See **miniature golf.**

mid·gut (mid′gut′), *n.* *Embryol., Zool.* the middle part of the embryonic alimentary canal from which the intestines develop. Cf. **foregut, hindgut.** [MID- + GUT]

mid·i (mid′ē), *n.* 1. midiskirt. —*adj.* 2. of the length of a midiskirt. [by shortening]

Mi·di (mē dē′), *n.* 1. the south. 2. the south of France. [< F: lit., midday, equiv. to *mi-* half (< L *medius* MID[1]) + *-di* day (< L *diēs*)]

Mid·i·an (mid′ē ən), *n.* a son of Abraham and Keturah. Gen. 25:1–4. Also, *Douay Bible,* **Madian.**

Mid·i·an·ite (mid′ē ə nīt′), *n.* 1. a member of an ancient desert people of northwest Arabia near the Gulf of Aqaba, believed to have descended from Midian. —*adj.* 2. of or pertaining to the Midianites. [MIDIAN + -ITE[1]]

mid·i·nette (mid′ənet′; *Fr.* mē dē net′), *n., pl.* **-nettes** (-nets′; *Fr.* -net′). a Parisian salesgirl or seamstress. [< F: lit., little meal at noon, equiv. to *mi(di)* noon (see MIDI) + *dinette* (see DINE, -ETTE); the girls were so called because they had time for only a light meal at noon]

mid·i·ron (mid′ī′ərn), *n.* *Golf.* a club with an iron head the face of which has more slope than a driving iron but less slope than a mid-mashie. Also called **number two iron.** [MID- + IRON]

mid·i·skirt (mid′ē skûrt′), *n.* a long skirt or skirt part, as of a dress, coat, etc., ending at the middle of the calf. Also, **midi.** [*midi-* (alter. of MID-) + SKIRT; modeled on MINISKIRT]

mid·land (mid′lənd), *n.* 1. the middle or interior part of a country. 2. (*cap.*) the dialect of English spoken in the central part of England. 3. (*cap.*) the dialect of English spoken in the southern parts of Illinois, Indiana, Ohio, Pennsylvania, and New Jersey, and in West Virginia, Kentucky, and eastern Tennessee, and throughout the southern Appalachians. —*adj.* 4. in or of the midland; inland. 5. (*cap.*) of or pertaining to Midland. [MID- + LAND]

Mid·land (mid′lənd), *n.* 1. a city in W Texas. 62,625 (1960). 2. a city in central Michigan. 27,779 (1960). 3. a town in W Pennsylvania. 6425 (1960).

Mid′land Park′, a town in NE New Jersey. 7543 (1960).

Mid·lands (mid′ləndz), *n.pl.* the central part of England; the midland counties.

mid·leg (*n.* mid′leg′; *adv.* mid′leg′), *n.* 1. the middle part of the leg. 2. one of the second pair of legs of an insect. —*adv.* 3. at the middle of the leg. [MID- + LEG]

Mid′-Lent Sun′day (mid′lent′). See **Laetare Sunday.**

mid·line (mid′līn′), *n.* *Zool.* the median plane of the body of an animal. [MID- + LINE[1]]

Mid·lo·thi·an (mid lō′*th*ē ən), *n.* 1. Formerly, **Edinburgh.** a county in SE Scotland. 580,332 (1961); 366 sq. mi. *Co. seat:* Edinburgh. 2. a town in NE Illinois. 6605 (1960).

mid·mash·ie (mid′mash′ē), *n.* *Golf.* a club with an iron head the face of which has more slope than a midiron but less slope than a mashie iron. Also called **number three iron.** [MID- + MASHIE]

mid·morn·ing (mid′môr′ning), *n.* 1. the middle of the morning; the time around the midpoint between early morning and noon. —*adv.* 2. in the middle of the morning: *He usually arrives midmorning.* —*adj.* 3. occurring during, taking place, done in, or pertaining to the middle of the morning. [MID- + MORNING]

mid·most (mid′mōst′), *adj.* 1. being in the very middle; middlemost; middle. 2. being or occurring at or near the middle part or point of. —*adv.* 3. in the midmost part; in the midst. [MID- + -MOST; r. ME, OE *midmest*]

mid·night (mid′nīt′), *n.* 1. the middle of the night; twelve o'clock at night. —*adj.* 2. of or pertaining to midnight. 3. resembling midnight, as in darkness. 4. **burn the midnight oil,** to study or work far into the night: *After months of burning the midnight oil, he really needed a vacation.* [ME; OE *midniht.* See MID-, NIGHT] —**mid′night′ly,** *adj., adv.*

mid′night sun′, the sun visible at midnight in midsummer in arctic and antarctic regions.

mid·noon (mid′no͞on′), *n.* midday. [MID- + NOON]

mid′ off′, *Cricket.* 1. the position of a fielder on the off side of the wicket. 2. the fielder occupying this position. Also, **mid′-off′.** Also called **mid wicket off.**

mid′ on′, *Cricket.* 1. the position of a fielder on the on side of the wicket. 2. the fielder occupying this position. Also, **mid′-on′.** Also called **mid wicket on.**

mid·point (mid′point′), *n.* 1. a point at or near the middle of, or equidistant from, both ends, as of a line: *the midpoint of a boundary.* 2. *Geom.* the point on the line segment or the arc that is equidistant, when measured along the line or the arc, from both endpoints. 3. a point in time halfway between the beginning and the end, as of a process, event, situation, etc.: *the midpoint of the negotiations; the midpoint of a football game.* Also, **mid′-point′.** [MID- + POINT]

mid·rash (mid′räsh; *Heb.* mē dräsh′), *n., pl.* **mid·ra·shim** (mi drô′shim; *Heb.* mē drä shēm′), **mid·ra·shoth** (mi drô′shōs; *Heb.* mē drä shôt′). 1. an early Jewish interpretation of or commentary on a Biblical text, clarifying or expounding a point of law or developing or illustrating a moral principle. 2. (*cap.*) a collection of such interpretations or commentaries. [< Heb: explanation] —**mid·rash·ic** (mid rash′ik), *adj.*

mid·rib (mid′rib′), *n.* *Bot.* the central or middle rib of a leaf. [MID- + RIB[1]]

mid·riff (mid′rif), *n.* 1. the diaphragm of the human body. 2. the middle part of the body, between the chest and the waist. 3. the part of a dress or bodice, usually close-fitting, that covers this part of the body. 4. a garment that exposes this part of the body. —*adj.* 5. noting or pertaining to the middle part of the human body, the part of a garment that covers it, or a garment that exposes it. [ME *mydryf,* OE *midhrif,* equiv. to *midd* MID[1] + *hrif* belly, c. L *corpus* body]

M

M, Midrib

mid′-sag′it·tal plane′ (mid′saj′i təl), *Craniom., Cephalom.* a plane passing through the nasion at right angles to the biparionic or the bitragal plane when the skull or head is oriented in the Frankfurt horizontal.

mid·sec·tion (mid′sek′shən), *n.* 1. the middle section or part of anything. 2. *Informal.* the solar plexus; midriff: *a hard right to the midsection.* [MID- + SECTION]

mid·ship (mid′ship′), *adj.* in or belonging to the middle part of a ship. [MID- + SHIP]

mid·ship·man (mid′ship′mən, mid ship′-), *n., pl.* **-men.** 1. *U.S. Navy and Coast Guard.* **a.** a student officer attending a service academy. **b.** (*cap.*) the title and rank of such a student, below a warrant officer and above a master chief petty officer. 2. *Brit. Navy.* **a.** an officer of the rank held by young men immediately upon graduating from the government naval schools. **b.** (*cap.*) the title and rank of such a graduate. **c.** (formerly) one of a class of boys or young men who formed the group from which officers were chosen. 3. Also called **singingfish.** any of several toadfishes of the genus *Porichthys,* having many small luminous organs on the underside of the body and producing a hissing sound with the air bladder. [MIDSHIP + MAN[1]]

mid·ship·mite (mid′ship mīt′), *n.* *Slang.* a midshipman. [MIDSHIPM(AN) + -ITE[1], with pun on MITE[2]]

mid′ship oar′ (mid′ship′ ōr′, ôr′ *for 1;* mid′ship′ ōr′, ôr′ *for 2*), *Naut.* 1. the longest of the customary five oars of a whaleboat, amidships on the port side. 2. the seaman pulling this oar. Also called **waist oar.**

mid·ships (mid′ships′), *adv.* amidships.

midst[1] (midst), *n.* 1. the position of anything surrounded by other things or parts, or occurring in the middle of a period of time, course of action, etc. (usually prec. by *the*): *a familiar face in the midst of the crowd; in the midst of the performance.* 2. the middle point, part, or stage (usually prec. by *the*): *We arrived in the midst of a storm.* 3. **in our (your, their) midst,** in the midst of or among us (you, them): *To think there was a spy in our midst!* [ME *middes* (aph. var. of *amiddes* AMIDST) + excrescent *-t*]
—**Syn. 1, 2.** thick, core, heart. See **middle.** —**Ant. 1, 2.** edge, periphery.

midst[2] (midst), *prep.* amidst.

mid·stream (mid′strēm′), *n.* the middle of a stream. [ME *myddstreme.* See MID-, STREAM]

mid·sum·mer (mid′sum′ər, -sum′-), *n.* the middle of summer. [ME, OE *midsumer.* See MID[1], SUMMER[1]] —**mid′sum′mer·y,** *adj.*

Mid′summer Day′, *Chiefly Brit.* the saint's day of St. John the Baptist, celebrated on June 24, being one of the four quarter days in England. Also called **St. John's Day.** [late ME]

Mid′summer Eve′, *Chiefly Brit.* the evening preceding Midsummer Day: formerly believed to be a time when witches and other supernatural beings caused widespread mischief. Also called **Mid′summer Night′, St. John's Eve, St. John's Night.** [late ME]

mid′summer mad′ness, a temporary lapse into foolishness, senseless behavior, folly, etc., esp. during the summer: *His plan to become a beachcomber is midsummer madness.*

Mid′summer Night's′ Dream′, A, a comedy (1595?) by Shakespeare.

mid·term (mid′tûrm′), *n.* 1. the middle or halfway point of a term, as a school term, term of office, etc. 2. Often, **midterms.** *Informal.* an examination or series of examinations at the middle of a school term. —*adj.* 3.

pertaining to or occurring at or approximately at the middle of a term, as a school term, term of office, etc.: *a midterm recess; midterm elections.* [MID- + TERM]

mid·town (mid′toun′, -toun′), *adv.* **1.** to or in the part of a city or town between uptown and downtown: *to work midtown.* **2.** the major shopping or business district of a city or town. —*adj.* **3.** of, pertaining to, or situated in the middle part of a city or town: *a good midtown restaurant.* [MID- + TOWN]

Mid·vale (mid′vāl′), *n.* a town in N Utah. 5802 (1960).

mid-Vic·to·ri·an (mid′vik tôr′ē ən, -tôr′-), *adj.* **1.** of, pertaining to, or characteristic of the middle portion of the reign of Queen Victoria (reigned 1837–1901) in England: *mid-Victorian ideas; mid-Victorian writers.* —*n.* **2.** a person, as a writer, belonging to the mid-Victorian time. **3.** a person of mid-Victorian tastes, standards, ideas, etc. —**mid′-Vic·to′ri·an·ism,** *n.*

mid′wall′ col′umn (mid′wôl′), a column or the like carrying a wall overhanging it on both sides. Also called **mid′wall′ shaft′.** [MID- + WALL]

mid·watch (mid′woch′), *n.* *Naut.* See **middle watch.** [MID- + WATCH]

mid·way (*adv., adj.* mid′wā′; *n.* mid′wā′), *adv., adj.* **1.** in the middle of the way or distance; halfway. —*n.* **2.** a place or part situated midway. **3.** (*often cap.*) the place or way, as at a fair, carnival, or the like, on or along which side shows and similar amusements are located. **4.** the amusements, concessions, etc., located on or around this place or way. [ME *midwei,* OE *midweg.* See MID[1], WAY]

Mid·way (mid′wā′), *n.* **1.** several U.S. islets in the N Pacific, about 1200 mi. NW of Hawaii: Japanese defeated in a naval battle June, 1942. 2356 (1960); 2 sq. mi. **2.** an airport in Chicago.

Mid′way Park′, a town in E North Carolina. 4164 (1960).

mid·week (mid′wēk′), *n.* **1.** the middle of the week. **2.** (*cap.*) (among the Quakers) Wednesday. —*adj.* **3.** occurring or done in the middle of the week. **4.** of or pertaining to the middle of the week. [MID- + WEEK]

mid·week·ly (mid′wēk′lē), *adj.* **1.** midweek. —*adv.* **2.** in the middle of the week. [MIDWEEK + -LY]

Mid·west (mid′west′), *U.S.* —*n.* **1.** See **Middle West.** —*adj.* **2.** Also, **Mid·west′ern.** See **Middle Western.** [MID- + WEST] —**Mid′west′ern·er,** *n.*

Mid′west Cit′y, a city in central Oklahoma, near Oklahoma City. 36,058 (1960).

mid′ wick′et off′, *Cricket.* See **mid off.**

mid′ wick′et on′, *Cricket.* See **mid on.**

mid·wife (mid′wīf′), *n., pl.* **-wives** (-wīvz′). **1.** a woman who assists women in childbirth. **2.** one who or that which produces or aids in producing something. [ME *midwif;* OE *mid* with (c. G *mit,* Icel *meth,* Gk *metá*) + *wif* WIFE]

mid·wife·ry (mid′wī′fə rē, -wif′rē), *n.* the art or practice of assisting women in childbirth. [late ME; see MIDWIFE, -ERY]

mid·win·ter (mid′win′tər), *n.* **1.** the middle of winter. —*adj.* **2.** occurring in, of, or pertaining to the middle of the winter. [ME, OE; see MID[1], WINTER] —**mid′win′·try, mid′win′ter·ly,** *adj.*

mid·year (mid′yēr′), *n.* **1.** the middle of the year. **2.** Often, **midyears.** *Informal.* an examination or a series of examinations at the middle of a school year. —*adj.* **3.** of, pertaining to, or occurring in midyear: *midyear exams.* [MID- + YEAR]

M.I.E., **1.** Master of Industrial Engineering. **2.** Master of Irrigation Engineering.

Miel·zi·ner (mēl zē′nər), *n.* **Jo** (jō), born 1901, U.S. set designer, born in France.

mien (mēn), *n.* air, bearing, or aspect, as showing character, feeling, etc.: *a man of noble mien.* [prob. aph. var. of obs. *demean* bearing, n. use of DEMEAN[2]; spelt with *-ie-* to distinguish it from MEAN[2]]
—**Syn.** appearance, look; carriage.

Mies van der Ro·he (mēz′ van dər rō′ə, fän, mēs′), **Lud·wig** (lud′wig), born 1886, U.S. architect, born in Germany. Also, **Mi·ës van der Ro·he** (mē′əs van dər rō′ə, fän, mēz′, mēs′).

miff (mif), *Informal.* —*n.* **1.** petulant displeasure; a petty quarrel. —*v.t.* **2.** to give offense to; offend. [? imit. of exclamation of disgust; cf. G *muffen* to sulk]

miffed (mift), *adj.* put into an irritable mood, esp. by an offending incident: *I was miffed when they laughed at my new wig.* [MIFF + -ED[2]]

miff·y (mif′ē), *adj.,* **miff·i·er, miff·i·est.** *Informal.* touchy; inclined to take offense. [MIFF + -Y[1]]

mig (mig), *n.* *Chiefly Dial.* **1.** a playing marble, esp. one that is not used as a shooter. **2. migs,** (*construed as sing.*) the game of marbles. Also, **migg.** [? var. of MIB with *-g* from GAME]

Mig (mig), *n.* any of several Russian-built fighter aircraft, esp. the Mig-15, a jet used in the Korean War. [named after *Mi(koyan)* and *G(urevich),* Russian aircraft designers]

mig·gle (mig′əl), *n.* *Chiefly Dial.* **1.** a playing marble, esp. one that is not used as a shooter. **2. miggles,** (*construed as sing.*) the game of marbles. [? MIG + (MARB)LE]

might[1] (mīt), *v.* pt. of **may.**

might[2] (mīt), *n.* **1.** power or ability to do or accomplish; capacity. **2.** physical strength: *He swung with all his might.* **3.** superior power or strength; force: *the theory that might makes right.* **4. with might and main,** with all the vigor, force, or energy at one's command: *The sailors hauled in the rope with might and main.* [ME *myghte,* OE *miht, meaht;* c. G *macht,* Goth *mahts;* akin to MAY] —**might′less,** *adj.*
—**Syn. 1–3.** See **strength.** —**Ant. 1–3.** weakness.

might·i·ly (mīt′əlē), *adv.* **1.** in a mighty manner; powerfully; vigorously. **2.** to a great extent or degree; very much: *to desire something mightily.* [ME; OE *mihtiglice.* See MIGHTY, -LY]

might·y (mī′tē), *adj.,* **might·i·er, might·i·est. 1.** having, characterized by, or showing might or power: *mighty rulers.* **2.** of great size; huge: *a mighty oak.* **3.** great in amount, extent, degree, or importance; exceptional: *a mighty accomplishment.* —*adv.* **4.** *Informal.* very: *I'm mighty pleased.* [ME; OE *mihtig.* See MIGHT[2], -Y[1]] —**might′i·ness,** *n.*
—**Syn. 1.** strong, puissant. See **powerful. 2.** immense, enormous, tremendous, sizable. —**Ant. 1.** feeble. **2.** small.

mi·gnon (min yon′, -yun′, min′yon, -yon; *Fr.* mē nyôN′), *adj.* small and pretty; delicately pretty. Also, *referring to a woman,* **mi·gnonne** (min yon′, min′yon; *Fr.* mē nyôn′). [< F; see MINION]

Mi·gnon (min yon′, -yun′, min′yon, -yun), *n.* a girl's given name. Also, **Mi·gnonne′.**

Mi·gnon (mē nyôN′), *n.* an opera (1866) by Ambroise Thomas.

mi·gnon·ette (min′yə net′), *n.* **1.** a plant, *Reseda odorata,* common in gardens, having racemes of small, fragrant, greenish-white flowers with prominent reddish-yellow or brownish anthers. **2.** a grayish-green resembling the color of a reseda plant. [< F; see MIGNON, -ETTE]

Mi·gnon·ette (min′ yə net′; *Fr.* mē nyô net′), *n.* a girl's given name, form of **Mignon.**

mi·gnon·ette-vine (min′yə net′vīn′), *n.* Madeira-vine.

Mi·go·ni·tis (mī′gə nī′tis), *n.* *Class. Myth.* an epithet of Aphrodite, meaning "uniter."

mi·graine (mī′grān), *n.* a paroxysmal headache usually confined to one side of the head and often associated with nausea; hemicrania. [< F; see MEGRIM] —**mi·grain′oid,** *adj.* —**mi·grain′ous,** *adj.*

mi·grant (mī′grənt), *adj.* **1.** migrating; migratory. —*n.* **2.** one who or that which migrates, as a migratory worker. [< L *migrant-* (s. of *migrāns*), prp. of *migrāre.* See MIGRATE, -ANT]

mi·grate (mī′grāt), *v.i.* **-grat·ed, -grat·ing. 1.** to go from one country, region, or place of abode to settle in another. **2.** to pass periodically from one region to another, as certain birds, fishes, and animals: *The birds migrate southward in the winter.* **3.** (at British universities) to change or transfer from one college to another. [< L *migrāt(us)* changed, moved (ptp. of *migrāre*), equiv. to *migrā-* change abode + *-tus* ptp. suffix] —**mi′gra·tor,** *n.*
—**Syn. 1.** move, resettle. MIGRATE, EMIGRATE, IMMIGRATE are used of changing one's abode from one country or part of a country to another. To MIGRATE is to make such a move either once or repeatedly: *to migrate from Ireland to the United States.* To EMIGRATE is to leave a country, usually one's own (and take up residence in another): *Each year many people emigrate from Europe.* To IMMIGRATE is to enter and settle in a country not one's own: *There are many inducements to immigrate to South America.* MIGRATE is applied both to people or to animals that move from one region to another, esp. periodically; the other terms are generally applied to movements of men. —**Ant. 1.** remain.

mi·gra·tion (mī grā′shən), *n.* **1.** the act, process, or an instance of migrating: *the right of migration; the migration of birds.* **2.** a migratory movement: *preparations for the migration.* **3.** a number or body of persons or animals migrating together. **4.** *Chem.* a movement or change of position of atoms within a molecule. [< L *migrātion-* (s. of *migrātiō*). See MIGRATE, -ION] —**mi·gra′tion·al,** *adj.*

migra′tion of i′ons, *Chem.* the movement of ions toward an electrode during electrolysis.

mi·gra·tive (mī′grə tiv), *adj.* migratory. [MIGRATE + -IVE]

mi·gra·to·ry (mī′grə tôr′ē, -tôr′ē), *adj.* **1.** migrating. **2.** periodically migrating: *a migratory species.* **3.** pertaining to a migration: *migratory movements of birds.* **4.** roving; nomadic; wandering. [< NL *migrātōri(us).* See MIGRATE, -ORY[1]]

mi′gratory lo′cust, any of several locusts that migrate in great swarms, esp. *Locusta migratoria,* of Africa and Asia. Also called **mi′gratory grass′hopper.**

mig·ue·let (mig′ə let′), *n.* miquelet.

Mi·hai·lo·vić (*Serbo-Croatian* mi hī′lô vich), *n.* **Dra·ža** (*Serbo-Croatian* drä′zhä). See **Mikhailovitch, Draja.**

mih·rab (mēr′əb), *n.* (in a mosque) a niche or decorative panel designating the kiblah. [< Ar]

mi·ka·do (mi kä′dō), *n., pl.* **-dos. 1.** (*sometimes cap.*) a title of the emperor of Japan. **2.** (*cap., italics*) an operetta (1885) by Sir William S. Gilbert and Sir Arthur Sullivan. [< Jap, equiv. to *mi-* honorable + *kado* gate, door (of the imperial palace)]

Mi·kan (mī′kən, -kan), *n.* **George (Lawrence),** born 1922, U.S. basketball player.

mike[1] (mīk), *n.* **1.** *Informal.* a microphone. **2.** a word used in communications to represent the letter *M.* [short for MICRO-, used separately]

mike[2] (mīk), *n.* a forklike support for a light cannon on a sailing ship. [ME; ? < MD *micke* forked stick]

mike[3] (mīk), *n., v.,* **miked, mik·ing.** *Brit. Slang.* —*n.* **1.** loafing; idling; wasting time. —*v.i.* **2.** to loaf or waste time; idle. [?]

Mike (mīk), *n.* a boy's given name, form of **Michael.**

mike′ fright′, *Informal.* extreme nervousness experienced on speaking into a microphone, as on radio or television.

Mi·khai·lo·vitch (*Serbo-Croatian* mi khī′lô vich), *n.* **Dra·ja** (drä′zhä), 1893–1946, Yugoslav military leader. Also, **Draža Mihailović.**

Mi·ko·yan (mē ko yän′), *n.* **A·nas·tas I·va·no·vich** (ä näs täs′ i vä′no vich), born 1895, Russian government official: first deputy chairman of the Council of Ministers 1958–64; president of the Soviet Union 1964–65.

mi·kron (mī′kron), *n., pl.* **-krons, -kra** (-krə). micron.

mik·vah (mik vä′; *Eng.* mik′və), *n., pl.* **-voth** (-vôt′), *Eng.* **-vahs.** *Hebrew.* a public bathing establishment to which Orthodox Jews are traditionally required to go on certain occasions to cleanse and purify themselves. Also, **mik′veh.**

mil (mil), *n.* **1.** a unit of length equal to .001 of an inch, used in measuring the diameter of wires. **2.** a military unit of angular measurement equal to the angle subtended by 1/6400 of a circumference. **3.** (less accurately) the angle subtended by an arc equal to 1/1000 of the radius or distance. **4.** (used formerly in pharmaceutical prescriptions) milliliter or cubic centimeter. **5.** a former bronze coin of the mandate of Palestine, the thousandth part of a pound, equal to .001 of a British pound. [short for L *millēsimus* thousandth, equiv. to *mill(e)* thousand (see MILE) + *-ēsimus* ordinal suffix]

mil., **1.** military. **2.** militia.

mi·la·dy (mi lā′dē), *n., pl.* **-dies. 1.** an English noblewoman (often used as a term of address). **2.** a woman regarded as having fashionable or expensive tastes (used abstractly): *shoes to match milady's spring wardrobe.* Also, **mi·la′di.** [< F < E, contr. of phrase *my lady*]

mil·age (mī′lij), *n.* mileage.

Mi·lan (mi lan′, -län′ *for 1;* mī′lən *for 2–5;* mē′lan, -län *for 6*), *n.* **1.** Italian, **Mi·la·no** (mē lä′nô). a city in central Lombardy, in N Italy: cathedral. 1,580,978 (1961). **2.** a town in NW Tennessee. 5208 (1960). **3.** a town in SE Michigan. 3616 (1960). **4.** a town in NW Illinois. 3065 (1960). **5.** a town in W New Mexico. 2658 (1960). **6.** a boy's given name.

mil·a·naise (mil′ə nāz; *Fr.* mē lA nez′), *adj.* *French Cookery.* served with macaroni, or sometimes spaghetti, that has been flavored with tomatoes, mushrooms, shredded meat, etc.: *veal cutlets à la milanaise.* [< F, fem. of *milanais* of Milan]

Mil·an·ese (mil′ə nēz′, -nēs′), *n., pl.* **-ese,** *adj.* —*n.* **1.** a native or inhabitant of Milan, Italy. **2.** the Italian dialect spoken in Milan. **3.** (*l.c.*) *Textiles.* **a.** a run-resistant, warp-knitted fabric of silk, rayon, or nylon, used in the manufacture of women's apparel. **b.** a warp-knit structure in which two sets of threads are knitted in an interlocking series forming a crossed diagonal or diamond pattern. **c.** the machine that produces this knit structure. —*adj.* **4.** of, pertaining to, or characteristic of Milan, Italy, its inhabitants, or their dialect of Italian. **5.** *Italian Cookery.* **a.** (esp. of meats) coated with flour or bread crumbs and browned in hot oil or butter. **b.** (esp. of pasta) having a sauce of tomatoes, mushrooms, grated cheese, shredded meat, and truffles: *macaroni Milanese; spaghetti Milanese.* [< It; see MILAN, -ESE]

Mi·la·nov (mē′lä nôf′), *n.* **Zin·ka** (zing′kä) (*Zinka Kunc*), born 1906, Yugoslavian soprano, in the U.S.

Mi·laz·zo (mē lät′tsô), *n.* a seaport in NE Sicily, in Italy. 24,083 (1961).

Mil·bank (mil′bangk′), *n.* a town in NE South Dakota. 3500 (1960).

milch (milch), *adj.* (of a domestic animal) yielding milk; kept or suitable for milk production. [ME *milche,* OE *-milce* (in *thrimilcemōnath* May, lit., three-milch month). See MILK]

milch′ cow′, a cow that is raised for her milk rather than for beef.

milch′ glass′. See **milk glass.**

mild (mīld), *adj.* **1.** amiably gentle or temperate in feeling or behavior toward others. **2.** characterized by or showing such gentleness, as manners, speech, etc.: *a mild voice.* **3.** not cold, severe, or extreme, as air, weather, etc.: *mild breezes.* **4.** gentle or moderate in force or effect: *mild penalties.* **5.** soft; pleasant: *mild sunshine.* **6.** not sharp, pungent, or strong: *a mild flavor.* **7.** not acute, as disease: *a mild case of flu.* **8.** moderate in intensity, degree, or character: *mild regret.* **9.** *Brit. Dial.* comparatively soft and easily worked, as soil, wood, stone, etc. **10.** *Obs.* kind or gracious. [ME, OE *milde;* c. G *mild;* akin to Gk *malthakós* soft] —**mild′ly,** *adv.* —**mild′ness,** *n.*
—**Syn. 1.** soft, pleasant. See **gentle. 2.** placid, tranquil, calm. **3.** temperate, moderate, clement. **6.** bland. —**Ant. 1.** forceful. **3.** severe. **4.** harsh.

mild·en (mīl′dən), *v.t., v.i.* to make or become mild or milder. [MILD + -EN[1]]

mil·dew (mil′do͞o′, -dyo͞o′), *n.* **1.** *Plant Pathol.* a disease of plants, characterized by a cottony, usually whitish coating on the surface of affected parts, caused by any of various fungi. **2.** any of these fungi. **3.** any of similar coatings or discolorations, caused by fungi, as that which appears on cotton and linen fabrics, paper, leather, etc., when exposed to moisture. —*v.t., v.i.* **4.** to affect or become affected with mildew. [ME; OE *mildēaw,* equiv. to *mil-* honey (c. Goth *milith,* akin to L *mel,* Gk *méli,* etc.) + *dēaw* DEW] —**mil′dew′y,** *adj.*

mil·dew·proof (mil′do͞o pro͞of′, -dyo͞o-), *adj.* **1.** able to withstand or repel the effect of mildew. —*v.t.* **2.** to enable (fabric, paper, etc.) to withstand or repel the effect of mildew. [MILDEW + -PROOF]

mild′ mercu′rous chlo′ride, *Pharm.* calomel.

Mil·dred (mil′drid), *n.* a girl's given name.

mild′ sil′ver pro′tein, *Pharm.* a compound of silver and a protein, applied to mucous membranes as a mild antiseptic.

mild′ steel′, low-carbon steel, containing no more than 10.25 percent carbon.

mile (mīl), *n.* **1.** Also called **statute mile.** a unit of distance on land in English-speaking countries equal to 5280 feet, or 1760 yards. **2.** Also called **nautical mile, geographical mile,** or **sea mile.** a unit of distance officially fixed in Great Britain at 6080 feet and formerly fixed in the U.S. at 6080.20 feet, but now officially replaced in the U.S. by the international nautical mile. **3.** Also called **international nautical mile, international air mile.** a unit of distance in sea and air navigation equal to 1.852 kilometers, or 6076.1033 feet. **4.** any of various other units of distance or length at different periods and in different countries. Cf. **Roman mile, Swedish mile. 5.** a large gap, span, or distance: *He missed his target by a mile. Abbr.:* mi, mi. [ME; OE *mīl* < L *mīlia* (*passuum*) a thousand (paces)]

mile·age (mī′lij), *n.* **1.** the aggregate number of miles traveled over in a given time. **2.** length, extent, or distance in miles. **3.** an allowance for traveling expenses at a fixed rate per mile: *His mileage came to more than $90.* **4.** a fixed charge per mile, as for railroad transportation. **5.** See **mileage ticket. 6.** the number of miles or relative distance that a vehicle can travel on a quantity of fuel, often as compared with that traveled by other vehicles on the same quantity. **7.** the relative distance that a quantity of fuel will propel a vehicle: *Brand X costs more but delivers less mileage.* **8.** wear, use, advantage, or profit: *He had gotten a lot of mileage out of the old coat.* Also, **milage.** [MILE + -AGE]

mile′age tick′et, 1. a book (**mile′age book′**) or ticket containing coupons good for a certain number of miles of transportation at a fixed rate per mile. **2.** one of the coupons.

mile·post (mīl′pōst′), *n.* any of a series of posts set up to mark distance by miles, as along a highway or an individual post showing the distance to or from a place. [MILE + POST[1]]

mil·er (mī′lər), *n.* **1.** a participant in a one-mile race. **2.** an athlete who specializes in races of one mile. [MILE + -ER[1]]

Miles (mīlz), *n.* **1. Nelson Appleton,** 1839–1925, U.S. army officer. **2.** Also, **Myles.** a boy's given name.

Miles′ Cit′y, a town in SE Montana. 9665 (1960).

mi·les glo·ri·o·sus (mē′les glō′ʀē ō′sŏŏs; *Eng.* mī′lēz glôr′ē ō′səs, -glōr′-), *pl.* **mi·li·tes glo·ri·o·si** (mē′li-tes′ glō′ʀē ō′sē; *Eng.* mil′i tēz′ glôr′ē ō′sī, -glōr′-) for 1. **1.** *Latin.* a boastful soldier. **2.** (*caps.*) a comedy (206? B.C.) by Plautus.

Mi·le·sian (mi lē′zhən, -shən, mī-), *adj.* **1.** of or pertaining to Miletus. **2.** *Philos.* noting or pertaining to a school of philosophers of the late 7th to early 5th centuries B.C., including Thales, Anaximander, and Anaximenes, which was primarily concerned with the nature of matter and change. —*n.* **3.** a native of Miletus. [< L *Milēsi(us)* inhabitant of MILETUS + -AN]

Mi·le·sian (mi lē′shən, -shən, mī-), *n. Irish Legend.* **1.** any of the legendary race of people from Spain who invaded Ireland and defeated the Tuatha De Danann, and who were the ancestors of the present Irish people. **2.** (*sometimes l.c.*) an Irishman. —*adj.* **3.** (*sometimes l.c.*) Irish. [*Milesi(us)* (Latin form of Ir *Miled,* legendary Spanish king) + -AN]

mile·stone (mīl′stōn′), *n.* **1.** a stone functioning as a milepost. **2.** a significant event in the life, progress, development, or the like of a person, nation, etc.: *His getting the job was a milestone in his career.* [MILE + STONE]

Mi·le·tus (mī lē′təs), *n.* **1.** *Class. Myth.* a son of Apollo and Aria, and the father of Biblys and Caunus. **2.** an ancient city in Asia Minor, on the Aegean.

mil·foil (mil′foil′), *n.* yarrow (def. 1). [ME < OF < L *milifol(ium),* var. of *millefolium,* equiv. to *mille* thousand + *folium* leaf]

Mil·ford (mil′fərd), *n.* **1.** a city in S Connecticut, on Long Island Sound. 41,662 (1960). **2.** a town in E Delaware. 5795 (1960). **3.** a town in SE Michigan. 4323 (1960). **4.** a town in SW Ohio. 4131 (1960). **5.** a town in S New Hampshire. 3916 (1960). **6.** a boy's given name.

Mil′ford Ha′ven, 1. a bay in SW Wales. **2.** a seaport on the N side of this bay. 12,802 (1961).

Mi·lhaud (mē yō′), *n.* **Da·rius** (dA ʀYs′), born 1892, French composer, in U.S. since 1940.

mil·ia·ren·sis (mil′yə ren′sis), *n., pl.* **-ses** (-sēz). a silver coin of ancient Rome, introduced by Constantine I as the 14th part of a solidus. Under Justinian it became the 12th part. [< LL, deriv. of L *mille* thousand; see -ESE]

mil·i·ar·i·a (mil′ē âr′ē ə), *n. Pathol.* an inflammatory disease of the skin, located about the sweat glands, marked by the formation of vesicles or papules resembling millet seeds; prickly heat. [< NL, L, fem. of *miliārius* MILIARY]

mil·i·ar·y (mil′ē er′ē, mil′yə rē), *adj.* **1.** resembling a millet seed or seeds. **2.** *Pathol.* accompanied by papules or vesicles resembling millet seeds: *miliary fever.* [< L *miliāri(us)* of millet, equiv. to *mili(um)* millet + *-ārius* -ARY]

mil′iary tuberculo′sis, *Pathol.* tuberculosis in which the bacilli are spread by the blood from one point of infection, producing small tubercles in other parts of the body.

Mil·i·cent (mil′i sənt), *n.* a girl's given name. Also, **Melecent, Millecent, Millicent.**

Mi·lich·i·us (mə lēk′ē əs), *n.* a crater in the second quadrant of the face of the moon: about 8 miles in diameter.

mi·lieu (mil yōō′, mēl-; *Fr.* mē lyœ′), *n., pl.* **-lieus,** *Fr.* **-lieux** (-lyœ′). environment, medium, or condition: *a socially favorable milieu.* [< F, equiv. to *mi-* (< L *medius* middle; see MEDIUM) + *lieu* LIEU]
—**Syn.** background, sphere, surroundings, element.

milit., military.

mil·i·tant (mil′i tənt), *adj.* **1.** vigorously active, aggressive, or combative: *a militant group of reformers.* **2.** engaged in warfare; warring. —*n.* **3.** a militant person. **4.** a person engaged in warfare or strife. [late ME < L *mīlitant-* (s. of *mīlitāns*), prp. of *mīlitāre* to serve as a soldier. See MILITATE, -ANT] —**mil′i·tan·cy, mil′i·tant·ness,** *n.* —**mil′i·tant·ly,** *adv.*

mil·i·ta·rise (mil′i tə rīz′), *v.t.,* **-rised, -ris·ing.** *Chiefly Brit.* militarize. —**mil′i·ta·ri·sa′tion,** *n.*

mil·i·ta·rism (mil′i tə riz′əm), *n.* **1.** a strong military spirit or policy. **2.** the principle of maintaining a large military establishment. **3.** the tendency to regard military efficiency as the supreme ideal of the state, and to subordinate all other interests to those of the military. [< F *militarisme,* equiv. to *militar-* (< L *mīlitār(is)* MILITARY) + *-isme* -ISM]

mil·i·ta·rist (mil′i tər ist), *n.* **1.** a person imbued with militarism. **2.** a person skilled in the conduct of war and military affairs. [MILITAR(Y) + -IST] —**mil′i·ta·ris′tic,** *adj.* —**mil′i·ta·ris′ti·cal·ly,** *adv.*

mil·i·ta·rize (mil′i tə rīz′), *v.t.,* **-rized, -riz·ing. 1.** to equip with armed forces, military supplies, etc.; make military. **2.** to imbue with militarism. Also, *esp. Brit.,* **militarise.** [MILITAR(Y) + -IZE] —**mil′i·ta·ri·za′tion,** *n.*

mil·i·tar·y (mil′i ter′ē), *adj., n., pl.* **-tar·ies, -tar·y.** —*adj.* **1.** of, for, or pertaining to the army, armed forces, affairs of war, or a state of war: *military and naval strength; from civilian to military life; military preparedness.* **2.** of or pertaining to soldiers. **3.** befitting, characteristic of, or noting a soldier: *a military bearing.* **4.** following the life of a soldier: *a military career.* **5.** performed by soldiers: *military duty.* —*n.* **6.** the military establishment of a nation; the armed forces: *They complained that the military was growing more powerful.* **7.** military personnel, esp. commissioned officers, taken collectively: *representatives of the bar, the press, and the military.* [< L *mīlitāri(s),* equiv. to *mīlit-* (s. of *mīles*) soldier + *-āris* -ARY] —**mil·i·tar·i·ly** (mil′i târ′ə lē, mil′i ter′ə lē), *adv.* —**mil′i·tar′i·ness,** *n.*

mil′itary acad′emy, 1. a private school organized somewhat along the lines and following some of the procedures of military life. **2.** a school that trains men for military careers as army officers, usually as part of a college education. Also called **military school.**

mil′itary attaché′, the senior army officer on the staff of an ambassador or minister to a foreign country: in the U.S. his title is army attaché.

mil′itary brush′, one of a pair of matched hairbrushes having no handles, esp. for men and boys.

mil′itary gov′ernment, a government established in a defeated nation and administered by the military commander of the conquering nation.

mil′itary gov′ernor, the military officer in command of a military government.

mil′itary law′, the body of laws relating to the government of the armed forces; rules and regulations for the conduct of military personnel.

mil′itary march′, a brisk march, esp. one suitable for a military parade.

mil′itary mast′, (on a warship) a mast carrying various arrangements for observation, signaling, the mounting of small weapons, etc.

mil′itary pace′, a pace, equal to a single step, used to coordinate the marching of soldiers, equal in the U.S. to 2½ feet for quick time and 3 feet for double time.

mil′itary police′, soldiers who perform police duties within the army.

mil′itary school′. See **military academy.**

mil′itary sci′ence, 1. the study of the causative factors and tactical principles of warfare. **2.** an academic course dealing with these factors and principles.

mil′itary top′, an armored fighting top on a military mast.

mil·i·tate (mil′i tāt′), *v.i.,* **-tat·ed, -tat·ing. 1.** to operate against or in favor of; have effect or influence: *Every fact militated against his argument.* **2.** *Obs.* **a.** to be a soldier. **b.** to take part in warfare. **c.** to take a stand, as for a belief or movement. [< L *mīlitāt(us)* served as a soldier, taken part in warfare (ptp. of *mīlitāre*), equiv. to *mīlit-* (s. of *mīles*) soldier + *-ātus* -ATE[1]] —**mil′i·ta′tion,** *n.*

mi·li·tes glo·ri·o·si (mē′li tes′ glō′ʀē ō′sē; *Eng.* mil′i tēz′ glôr′ē ō′sī, glōr′-), *Latin.* pl. of **miles gloriosus.**

mi·li·tia (mi lish′ə), *n.* **1.** a body of men enrolled for military service, and called out periodically for drill and exercise but serving full time only in emergencies. **2.** *U.S.* all able-bodied males of each State between 18 and 45 years of age considered eligible for military service. **3.** a body of citizen soldiers as distinguished from professional soldiers. [< L: soldiery, equiv. to *mīlit-* (s. of *mīles*) soldier + *-ia* -IA]

mi·li·tia·man (mi lish′ə mən), *n., pl.* **-men.** a person serving in the militia. [MILITIA + MAN[1]]

mil·i·um (mil′ē əm), *n., pl.* **mil·i·a** (mil′ē ə). *Pathol.* a small white or yellowish nodule resembling a millet seed, produced in the skin by the retention of sebaceous secretion. [< NL, L: millet]

milk (milk), *n.* **1.** an opaque white or bluish-white liquid secreted by the mammary glands of female mammals, serving for the nourishment of their young. **2.** this liquid as secreted by cows, goats, or certain other animals and used by humans for food or as a source of butter, cheeses, etc. **3.** any liquid resembling this, as the liquid within a coconut, the juice or sap of certain plants, or various pharmaceutical preparations. **4. cry over spilt milk,** to lament what cannot be changed; express sorrow for past actions or events: *Crying over spilt milk will do you no good now.* —*v.t.* **5.** to press or draw milk by hand or machine from the udder of (a cow or other animal). **6.** to extract something from as if by milking. **7.** to drain strength, information, wealth, etc., from; exploit: *The gypsy milked her of all her savings.* —*v.i.* **8.** to yield milk, as a cow. **9.** to milk a cow or other animal. [ME; OE *milk* (Anglian); c. G *Milch,* Goth *miluks,* Icel *mjolk;* akin to L *mulgēre,* Gk *amélgein* to milk] —**milk′less,** *adj.*

milk-and-wa·ter (milk′ən wô′tər, -wot′ər), *adj.* weak or insipid; wishy-washy.

milk′ bar′, a simple, restaurantlike establishment, often with an open front, or a counter or booth where milk drinks, sandwiches, etc., are sold.

milk′ bench′. See **water bench.**

milk′ choc′olate, 1. chocolate that has been diluted with milk. **2.** a piece or bar of candy made of or coated with such chocolate.

milk·er (mil′kər), *n.* **1.** a person who milks. **2.** See **milking machine. 3.** a cow or other animal that gives milk. [MILK + -ER[1]]

milk′ fe′ver, 1. *Pathol.* fever coinciding with the beginning of lactation, formerly believed to be due to lactation but really due to infection. **2.** *Vet. Pathol.* an acute condition often affecting dairy cows immediately after calving, causing somnolence and paralysis.

milk·fish (milk′fish′), *n., pl.* **-fish·es,** (*esp. collectively*) **-fish.** a herringlike fish, *Chanos chanos,* found in southeastern Asia. [MILK + FISH, so called from its color]

milk′ glass′, an opaque white glass.

milk′ gra′vy, a gravy or sauce made from cooking fat, milk, flour, and seasonings.

milk′ing machine′, an electric machine for milking cows. Also called **milker.**

Milk′ing Short′horn, one of a breed of cattle developed from the Shorthorn for both beef and milk production.

milk′ing stool′, a low, three-legged stool with a flat seat in the shape of a half circle.

milk′ leg′, *Pathol.* a painful swelling of the leg, due to thrombosis of the large veins, occurring most frequently in connection with childbirth. Also called **white leg.**

milk-liv·ered (milk′liv′ərd), *adj.* cowardly; timid. [lit., with a liver that secretes milk instead of bile]

milk·maid (milk′mād′), *n.* **1.** a woman who milks cows or is employed in a dairy. **2.** lady's-smock. [MILK + MAID]

milk·man (milk′man′), *n., pl.* **-men.** a man who sells or delivers milk. [MILK + MAN[1]]

milk′ of al′monds. See **almond milk.**

milk′ of magne′sia, a milky white suspension in water of magnesium hydroxide, Mg $(OH)_2$, used as an antacid or laxative.

milk′ pow′der. See **dry milk.**

milk′ punch′, a beverage containing milk and alcoholic liquor with sugar, flavoring, etc.

milk′ purs′lane. See **flowering spurge.**

milk′ shake′, a frothy drink made of cold milk, flavoring, and usually ice cream, shaken together or blended in a mixer.

milk·shed (milk′shed′), *n.* a region producing milk for a specific community: *the St. Louis milkshed.* [MILK + SHED[1]]

milk′ sick′ness, *Pathol.* a disease of man, formerly common in some parts of the Middle West, caused by consuming milk from cattle that have been poisoned by eating certain kinds of snakeroot.

milk′ snake′, a brightly marked kingsnake, *Lampropeltis doliata,* of eastern North America. [so called because it is mistakenly believed to suck the milk from cows]

milk·sop (milk′sop′), *n.* an unmanly or effeminate man or youth. [MILK + SOP] —**milk′sop′ism,** *n.* —**milk′sop′py, milk′sop′ping,** *adj.*

milk′ sug′ar, lactose.

milk′ this′tle, lady's-thistle.

milk′ toast′, toast, usually buttered, served in hot milk with sugar or with salt and pepper.

milk-toast (milk′tōst′), *adj.* **1.** (of a man) easily dominated; extremely mild; ineffectual; namby-pamby; wishy-washy. —*n.* **2.** milquetoast.

milk′ tooth′, one of the temporary teeth of a mammal which are replaced by the permanent teeth. Also called **baby tooth, deciduous tooth.**

milk′ train′, *Slang.* a local train running through the early hours of the morning; owl train.

milk′ vetch′, 1. a European, fabaceous herb, *Astragalus Glycyphyllos,* believed to increase the secretion of milk in goats. **2.** any herb of certain allied genera.

milk·weed (milk′wēd′), *n.* **1.** any of several asclepiadaceous plants that secrete a milky juice or latex, esp. those of the genus *Asclepias,* as *A. syriaca.* **2.** any of various other plants having a milky juice, as certain spurges. [MILK + WEED[1]]

milk′weed bug′, any of several red and black lygaeid bugs, as *Oncopeltus fasciatus,* that feed on the juice of the milkweed.

milk′weed but′terfly, monarch (def. 4).

milk′weed tor′toise bee′tle. See under **tortoise beetle.**

milk-white (milk′hwīt′, -wīt′), *adj.* of a white or slightly blue-white color, as that of milk.

milk′ wil′low-herb (wil′ō ûrb′, -hûrb′), a perennial herb, *Lythrum alatum,* of North America, having solitary, purple flowers.

milk·wood (milk′wŏŏd′), *n.* any of various trees having a milky juice, as *Pseudomedia spuria,* of Jamaica. [MILK + WOOD[1]]

milk·wort (milk′wûrt′), *n.* **1.** any herb or shrub of the genus *Polygala,* formerly supposed to increase the secretion of milk. **2.** See **sea milkwort.** [MILK + WORT[2]]

milk·y (mil′kē), *adj.,* **milk·i·er, milk·i·est. 1.** of or like milk. **2.** white or whitish in color. **3.** giving a good supply of milk. **4.** meek, tame, or spiritless. [ME; see MILK, -Y[1]] —**milk′i·ly,** *adv.* —**milk′i·ness,** *n.*

milk′y disease′, a disease affecting Japanese beetle larvae, characterized by a milky appearance of the blood and caused by the bacteria *Bacillus popilliae* or *Bacillus lentimorbus.*

Milk′y Way′, *Astron.* the faintly luminous band stretching across the heavens, composed of innumerable stars too distant to be seen clearly with the naked eye; the galaxy containing the earth, sun, and solar system. [ME, trans. of L *via lactea*]

mill[1] (mil), *n.* **1.** a building or establishment, fitted with machinery, in which any of various mechanical operations or forms of manufacture is carried on: *a steel mill.* **2.** a building or establishment for converting grain into flour and other cereal products. **3.** a machine for grinding, crushing, or pulverizing any solid substance: *a coffee mill.* **4.** a steel roller for receiving and transferring an impressed design, as to a calico-printing cylinder or a banknote-printing plate. **5.** any of various machines which modify the shape or size of a workpiece by rotating tools or the work: *rolling mill.* **6.** any of various other apparatuses for working materials into due form or performing other mechanical operations. **7.** *Mach.* a cutter on a milling machine. **8.** a business establishment, institution, office, or the like, which dispenses products or services in an impersonal, routine, or perfunctory manner, esp. without due regard for propriety, individuality, or consequences: *They got the decree in an out-of-state divorce mill.* **9.** *Slang.* a boxing match or fist fight. **10. through the mill,** *Informal.* undergoing or having undergone severe difficulties, trials, etc., esp. with an effect on one's health, personality, or character: *He's really been through the mill since his wife's death.* —*v.t.* **11.** to grind, work, treat, or shape in or with a mill. **12.** *Coining.* **a.** to make a raised edge on (a coin or the like). **b.** to make narrow, radial grooves on the raised edge of (a coin or the like). **13.** to beat or stir, as to a froth: *to mill chocolate.* **14.** *Slang.* to beat or strike; fight; overcome. —*v.i.* **15.** to move around aimlessly or confusedly, as a herd of cattle (often fol. by *about* or *around*). **16.** *Slang.* to fight or box. [ME *mille,* OE *myl(e)n* < LL *molīna,* n. use of fem. of *molīnus* of a mill, equiv. to L *mol(a)* mill-(stone) + *-īnus* -INE[1]] —**mill′a·ble,** *adj.*

mill[2] (mil), *n.* a unit of monetary value equal to .001 of a U.S. dollar; one tenth of a cent: used in various times and places in the U.S. as a money of account, esp. in paying sales taxes. [short for L *mill(ēsimus)* thousandth; see MIL]

Mill (mil), *n.* **1. James,** 1773–1836, English philosopher, historian, and economist; born in Scotland. **2.** his son **John Stuart,** 1806–73, English philosopher and economist.

Mil·lais (mi lā′), *n.* **Sir John Everett,** 1829–96, English painter.

Mil·lard (mil′ərd), *n.* a boy's given name.

Mil·lay (mi lā′), *n.* **Edna St. Vincent** (*Mrs. Eugen Jan Boissevain*), 1892–1950, U.S. poet.

mill·board (mil′bōrd′, -bôrd′), *n. Bookbinding.* a strong, thick pasteboard used to make book covers. [MILL(ED) + BOARD]

Mill·brae (mil′brā), *n.* a city in W California, on San Francisco Bay. 15,873 (1960).

Mill·burn (mil′bərn), *n.* a town in NE New Jersey. 18,799 (1960).

mill·cake (mil′kāk′), *n.* See **linseed cake.** [MILL[1] + CAKE]

mill′ chis′el, a woodworking chisel having a blade more than eight inches long. Also called **millwright chisel.**

mill′ construc′tion, heavy, fire-resistant timber construction within masonry walls, all vertical communication being within masonry towers provided with fire doors. Also called **slow-burning construction.**

Mill·creek (mil′krēk′, -krik), *n.* a town in central Pennsylvania. 28,441 (1960).

mill·dam (mil′dam′), *n.* a dam built in a stream to furnish a head of water for turning a mill wheel. [ME; see MILL[1], DAM[1]]

Mil·le·cent (mil′i sənt), *n.* a girl's given name. Also, **Melecent, Milicent, Millicent.**

milled (mild), *v.* **1.** pt. and pp. of **mill**[1]. —*adj.* **2.** having undergone the operations of a mill. [MILL[1] + -ED[2]]

Mil·ledge·ville (mil′ij vil′), *n.* a city in central Georgia: State capital 1807–68. 11,117 (1960).

mil·le·fi·o·ri (mil′ə fē ôr′ē, -ōr′ē), *n.* decorative glass made by fusing multicolored glass canes together, cutting them crosswise, joining them into new groups, embedding the groups in transparent glass, and blowing the resultant mass into a desired shape. Also, **mil′le·fi·o′re.** [< It, equiv. to *mille* thousand (< L) + *fiori,* pl. of *fiore* < L *flōri-* (s. of *flōs*) FLOWER]

mille·fleur (mēl flûr′, -flŏŏr′; *Fr.* mēl flœr′), *adj.* having a background sprinkled with representations of flowers, as certain tapestries or pieces of glass work. [< F: lit., a thousand flowers]

Mil·len (mil′ən), *n.* a town in E Georgia. 3633 (1960).

mil·le·nar·i·an (mil′ə nâr′ē ən), *adj.* **1.** of or pertaining to a thousand, esp. the thousand years of the prophesied millennium. —*n.* **2.** a believer in the millennium. [MILLENARY + -AN]

mil·le·nar·y (mil′ə ner′ē), *adj., n., pl.* **-nar·ies.** —*adj.* **1.** consisting of or pertaining to a thousand, esp. a thousand years. **2.** pertaining to the millennium. —*n.* **3.** an aggregate of a thousand. **4.** millennium. **5.** millenarian. [< LL *millēnāri(us)* of a thousand, equiv. to *millēn(ī)* a thousand each (L *mill(e)* thousand + *-ēnī* distributive suffix) + *-ārius* -ARY]

mil·len·ni·al (mi len′ē əl), *adj.* **1.** of or pertaining to a millennium or the millennium. **2.** worthy or suggestive of the millennium. [MILLENNI(UM) + -AL[1]] —**mil·len′ni·al·ly,** *adv.*

Millen′nial Church′, the church of the Shakers.

mil·len·ni·um (mi len′ē əm), *n., pl.* **-ni·ums, -ni·a** (-nē ə). **1.** a period of 1,000 years. **2.** a thousandth anniversary. **3. the millennium,** the period of a thousand years during which Christ will reign on earth. Rev. 20:1–7. **4.** a period of general righteousness and happiness, esp. in the indefinite future. [< NL, equiv. to L *mill(e)* a thousand + *(bi)ennium* BIENNIUM]

mil·le·pede (mil′ə pēd′), *n.* millipede.

mil·le·pore (mil′ə pōr′, -pôr′), *n.* a coralline hydrozoan of the genus *Millipora,* having a smooth calcareous surface with many perforations. [< NL *millepora,* equiv. to *mille* thousand + *-pora* passage; see PORE[2]]

mill·er (mil′ər), *n.* **1.** a person who owns or operates a mill, esp. a grain mill. **2.** See **milling machine. 3.** any moth, esp. of the family *Noctuidae,* having wings that appear powdery. [ME *millere,* assimilated var. of *milnere,* equiv. to *miln* MILL[1] + *-ere* -ER[1]]

Mill·er (mil′ər), *n.* **1. Arthur,** born 1915, U.S. playwright and novelist. **2. Henry,** 1891–1980, U.S. novelist. **3. Joa·quin** (wä kēn′), *(Cincinnatus Heine Miller),* 1841–1913, U.S. poet. **4. Joe** *(Joseph* or *Josias Miller),* 1684–1738, English actor. **5. William,** 1782–1849, U.S. religious leader: founder of the Adventist Church. **6.** a boy's given name.

Mille·rand (mēl rän′), *n.* **A·le·xan·dre** (A lek sän′dr[ə]), 1859–1943, president of France 1920–24.

Mill′er in′dex, *Crystall.* one of three integers giving the orientation and position of the face of a crystal in terms of the reciprocals, in lowest terms, of the intercepts of the face with each axis of the crystal. [named after W. H. *Miller* (1801–80), British mineralogist]

mill·er·ite (mil′ə rīt′), *n.* a mineral, nickel sulfide, NiS, occurring in bronze-colored slender crystals: a minor ore of nickel. [see MILLER INDEX, -ITE[1]]

Mill·er·ite (mil′ə rīt′), *n.* a follower of William Miller, a U.S. preacher who taught that the Second Advent of Christ and the beginning of the millennium were to occur in 1843. [William MILLER + -ITE[1]]

Mil·lers·burg (mil′ərz bûrg′), *n.* **1.** a town in central Ohio. 3101 (1960). **2.** a town in central Pennsylvania. 2984 (1960).

mill·er's-thumb (mil′ərz thum′), *n.* any of several small, fresh-water sculpins of the genus *Cottus,* as *C. gobio,* of Europe. [ME; the fish is so called from its thumblike head]

Mil·lers·ville (mil′ərz vil′), *n.* a town in SE Pennsylvania. 3883 (1960).

mil·les·i·mal (mi les′ə məl), *adj.* **1.** thousandth. —*n.* **2.** a thousandth part. [< L *millēsim(us)* thousandth *(mille* thousand + *-ēsimus* ordinal suffix) + -AL[1]] —**mil·les′i·mal·ly,** *adv.*

mil·let (mil′it), *n.* **1.** a cereal grass, *Setaria italica,* extensively cultivated in the East and in southern Europe for its small seed, or grain, used as food for man and fowls, but in the U.S. grown chiefly for fodder. **2.** any of various related or similar grasses cultivated as grain plants or forage plants. **3.** the grain of any of these grasses. [ME *milet* < MF, equiv. to *mil* (< L *milium* millet) + *-et* -ET]

Mil·let (mi lā′; *for 2 also Fr.* mē le′), *n.* **1. Francis Davis,** 1846–1912, U.S. painter, illustrator, and journalist. **2. Jean Fran·çois** (zhän frän swa′), 1814–75, French painter.

mill′ hole′, *Mining.* See **draw hole.**

milli-, a learned borrowing from Latin meaning "thousand" *(millipede):* in the metric system, used to indicate one thousandth of the specified unit *(millimeter).* [< F < L, comb. form of *mille* thousand]

mil·li·am·me·ter (mil′ē am′mē tər), *n.* an instrument for measuring small electric currents, calibrated in milliamperes. [MILLIAM(PERE) + -METER]

mil·li·am·pere (mil′ē am′pēr), *n. Elect.* a unit of electric current equal to one thousandth of an ampere. *Abbr.:* mA [< F; see MILLI-, AMPERE]

mil·li·ang·strom (mil′ē aṅg′strəm), *n.* one thousandth of an angstrom. *Abbr.:* mÅ [MILLI- + ANGSTROM]

mil·liard (mil′yərd, -yärd), *n. Brit.* billion: one thousand millions. [< F; see MILLI-, -ARD]

mil·li·are (mil′ē âr′, -är′), *n. Metric System.* a unit of area equal to one thousandth of an are. [< F; see MILLI-, ARE[2]]

mil·li·ar·y (mil′ē er′ē), *adj.* **1.** of, pertaining to, or designating the ancient Roman mile of a thousand paces. **2.** marking a mile. [< L *milliāri(us)* having a thousand. See MILLI-, -ARY]

mil·li·bar (mil′ə bär′), *n.* a centimeter-gram-second of pressure equal to one thousandth of a bar or 1000 dynes per square centimeter, used to measure air pressure. *Abbr.:* mb [MILLI- + BAR[1]]

mil·li·barn (mil′ə bärn′), *n.* one thousandth of a barn. *Abbr.:* mb [MILLI- + BARN[2]]

Mil·li·cent (mil′i sənt), *n.* a girl's given name. Also, **Melecent, Milicent, Millecent.**

mil·li·cou·lomb (mil′ə ko͞o′lom, -ko͞o lom′), *Elect.* a unit of quantity of electricity equal to one thousandth of a coulomb. *Abbr.:* mC [MILLI- + COULOMB]

mil·li·cur·ie (mil′ə kyo͝or′ē, -kyo͝o rē′), *n. Physics, Chem.* a unit of radioactivity equal to one thousandth of a curie; 3.70×10^7 disintegrations per second. *Abbr.:* mCi, mc [MILLI- + CURIE]

Mil·lie (mil′ē), *n.* a girl's given name, form of **Millicent** or **Mildred.** Also, **Milly.**

mil·lieme (mēl yem′, mē yem′), *n.* any of the copper coins equal to the thousandth part of the pound, or the tenth part of the piaster, of Libya, Sudan, and the United Arab Republic. [< F *millième* << L *millēsim(us)* thousandth, equiv. to *mille* thousand + *-ēsimus* ordinal suffix]

mil·lier (mēl yā′), *n.* 1000 kilograms; a metric ton. Also called **tonneau.** [< F < L *milliār(ius).* See MILLI-, -IER]

mil·li·far·ad (mil′ə far′əd, -ad), *n. Elect.* a unit of capacitance, equal to one thousandth of a farad. *Abbr.:* mF, mf [MILLI- + FARAD]

mil·li·fold (mil′ə fōld′), *adj., adv. Obs.* thousandfold. [MILLI- + -FOLD]

mil·li·gal (mil′ə gal′), *n.* a unit of acceleration, equal to one thousandth of a gal; one thousandth of a centimeter per second per second. *Abbr.:* mGal [MILLI- + GAL[2]]

mil·li·gram (mil′ə gram′), *n. Metric System.* a unit of weight equal to one thousandth of a gram, and equivalent to 0.0154 grain. *Abbr.:* mg Also, *esp. Brit.,* **mil′li·gramme′.** [< F *milligramme.* See MILLI-, -GRAM[2]]

mil·li·gram-hour (mil′ə gram′our′, -ou′ər), *n. Radiotherapy.* a unit of measure for a dose of radium expressed as the amount of radiation received by exposure to one milligram of radium for one hour.

mil·li·hen·ry (mil′ə hen′rē), *n., pl.* **-ries, -rys.** *Elect.* a unit of inductance equal to one thousandth of a henry. *Abbr.:* mH, mh [MILLI- + HENRY]

Mil·li·kan (mil′ə kən), *n.* **Robert Andrews,** 1868–1953, U.S. physicist: Nobel prize 1923.

mil·li·lam·bert (mil′ə lam′bərt), *n. Optics.* a unit of luminance equal to one thousandth of a lambert. *Abbr.:* mL [MILLI- + LAMBERT]

mil·li·li·ter (mil′ə lē′tər), *n. Metric System.* a unit of capacity equal to one thousandth of a liter, and equivalent to 0.033815 fluid ounce, or 0.061025 cubic inch. *Abbr.:* ml Also, *esp. Brit.,* **mil′li·li′tre.** [< F *millilitre.* See MILLI-, LITER]

mil·li·lux (mil′ə luks′), *n. Optics.* a unit of illumination, equal to one thousandth of a lux. *Abbr.:* mlx [MILLI- + LUX]

mil·lime (mil′im, -ēm), *n.* an aluminum coin of Tunisia, the thousandth part of a dinar, equivalent to about .0024 of a U.S. dollar. [appar. alter. of F *millième* thousandth]

mil·li·me·ter (mil′ə mē′tər), *n. Metric System.* a unit of length equal to one thousandth of a meter and equivalent to 0.03937 inch. *Abbr.:* mm Also, *esp. Brit.,* **mil′le·me′tre.** [< F *millimètre.* See MILLI-, METER[1]] —**mil·li·met·ric** (mil′ə me′trik), *adj.*

mil·li·mho (mil′ə mō′), *n., pl.* **-mhos.** *Elect.* a unit of conductance equal to .001 mho. *Abbr.:* mmho [MILLI- + MHO]

mil·li·mi·cron (mil′ə mī′kron), *n., pl.* **-crons, -cra** (-krə). a unit of length equal to one thousandth of a micron. *Symbol:* mμ, m mu [MILLI- + MICRON]

mil·li·mole (mil′ə mōl′), *n.* one thousandth of a mole. *Abbr.:* mM [MILLI- + MOLE[4]]

mil·line (mil′līn′, mil līn′), *n.* **1.** one agate line of advertising one column in width appearing in one million copies of a periodical. **2.** Also called **mil′line rate′.** the charge or cost per milline. [MIL(LION) + LINE[1]]

mil·li·ner (mil′ə nər), *n.* a person who designs, makes, or sells hats for women. [var. of obs. *Milaner* native of Milan, dealer in goods from Milan; see -ER[1]]

mil·li·ner·y (mil′ə ner′ē, -nə rē), *n.* **1.** women's hats and other articles made or sold by milliners. **2.** the business or trade of a milliner. [MILLINER + -Y[3]]

mill·ing (mil′iṅg), *n.* **1.** the act or an instance of subjecting something to the operation of a mill. **2.** the act or process of producing plane or shaped surfaces with a milling machine. **3.** *Coining.* **a.** the act or process of making a raised edge on a coin or the like. **b.** the act or process of making narrow, radial grooves on such a raised edge. **c.** a number of grooves so made. **4.** *Slang.* a thrashing. [MILL[1] + -ING[1]]

mill′ing machine′, a machine tool for rotating a cutter to produce plane or formed surfaces on a workpiece, usually by moving the work past the cutter.

Mil·ling·ton (mil′iṅg tən), *n.* a town in SW Tennessee. 6059 (1960).

Mil·li·nock·et (mil′ə nok′it), *n.* a town in central Maine. 7318 (1960).

mil·li·ohm (mil′ē ōm′), *n. Elect.* a unit of resistance equal to one thousandth of an ohm. [MILLI- + OHM]

mil·lion (mil′yən), *n., pl.* **-lions,** *(as after a numeral)* **-lion,** *adj.* —*n.* **1.** a cardinal number, a thousand times one thousand. **2.** a symbol for this number, as 1,000,000 or M̄. **3.** the amount of a thousand thousand units of money, as pounds, dollars, or francs: *The three Dutch canvases fetched a cool million.* **4.** a very great number: *Don't interrupt now! I have a million things to do.* **5. the million,** the mass of the common people; the multitude: *music for the million.* —*adj.* **6.** amounting to one million in number. [ME < MF < early It *millione,* equiv. to *mille* thousand (< L) + *-one* aug. suffix]

mil·lion·aire (mil′yə nâr′), *n.* **1.** a person whose wealth amounts to a million or more in dollars, pounds, francs, or other currency. **2.** (loosely) any very rich person. Also, **mil′lion·naire′.** [< F *millionnaire,* equiv. to *million* MILLION + *-aire* -ARY] —**mil′lion·aire′dom,** *n.*

mil·lionth (mil′yənth), *adj.* **1.** coming last in a series of a million. **2.** being one of a million equal parts. —*n.* **3.** the millionth member of a series. **4.** a millionth part, esp. of one (1/1,000,000). [MILLION + -TH[2]]

mil·li·pede (mil′ə pēd′), *n.* any terrestrial arthropod of the class *Diplopoda,* having a cylindrical body composed of from 20 to over 100 segments, each with two pairs of legs. Also, **millepede.** [< L *millepeda* the wood louse, equiv. to *mille* thousand + *-peda* foot; see -PED]

Millipede, *Cambala annulata* (Length 1 in.)

mil·li·phot (mil′ə fot′, -fōt′), *n. Optics.* a unit of illumination equal to one thousandth of a phot. [MILLI- + PHOT]

mil·li·poise (mil′ə poiz′), *n.* a unit of viscosity equal to one thousandth of a poise. [MILLI- + POISE[2]]

mil·li·rem (mil′ə rem′), *n.* one thousandth of a rem. *Abbr.:* mrem [MILLI- + REM]

mil·li·roent·gen (mil′ə rent′gən, -jən, -runt′-), *n.* a unit of radiation equal to one thousandth of a roentgen. *Abbr.:* mR, mr [MILLI- + ROENTGEN]

mil·li·sec·ond (mil′i sek′ənd), *n.* one thousandth of a second. *Abbr.:* msec [MILLI- + SECOND[2]]

mil·li·sie·mens (mil′ə sē′mənz, -zē′-), *n.* one thousandth of a siemens. *Abbr.:* mS [MILLI- + SIEMENS]

mil·li·volt (mil′ə vōlt′), *n. Elect.* a unit of electromotive force equal to one thousandth of a volt. *Abbr.:* mV, mv [MILLI- + VOLT]

mil·li·watt (mil′ə wot′), *n.* a unit of power equal to one thousandth of a watt. *Abbr.:* mW, mw [MILLI- + WATT]

Mill′ on the Floss′, The, a novel (1860) by George Eliot.

mill′ out′let, a retail store that is owned or operated by a manufacturer for selling his goods directly to consumers. Also called **mill store.**

mill·pond (mil′pond′), *n.* a pond for supplying water to drive a mill wheel. [MILL[1] + POND]

mill·race (mil′rās′), *n.* **1.** the channel in which the current of water driving a mill wheel flows to the mill. **2.** the current itself. [MILL[1] + RACE[1]]

mill·rind (mil′rīnd′, -rind), *n.* rind[2]. [MILL[1] + RIND[2]]

mill-run (mil′run′), *adj.* being in the condition or state of having come from a mill, esp. unsorted as to quality: *mill-run carpets.*

mill·run (mil′run′), *n.* **1.** millrace. **2.** a test of the mineral content or quality of a rock or ore consisting of the actual milling of a sample. **3.** the mineral obtained by means of this test. [MILL[1] + RUN]

Mills (milz), *n.* **Robert,** 1781–1855, U.S. architect and engineer.

Mills′ grenade′ (milz), *Mil.* a type of high-explosive grenade weighing about 1.5 pounds. Also called **Mills′ bomb′.** [named after Sir W. *Mills* (1856–1932), its English inventor]

mill·stone (mil′stōn′), *n.* **1.** either of a pair of circular stones between which grain or another substance is ground, as in a mill. **2.** anything that grinds or crushes. **3.** any heavy mental or emotional burden (often used in the phrase *a millstone around one's neck*). Matt. 18:6. [ME *mylneston,* OE *mylenstān.* See MILL[1], STONE]

mill′ store′. See **mill outlet.**

mill·stream (mil′strēm′), *n.* the stream in a millrace. [MILL[1] + STREAM]

Mill·town (mil′toun′), *n.* a town in E New Jersey. 5435 (1960).

Mill·vale (mil′vāl′), *n.* a town in SW Pennsylvania. 6624 (1960).

Mill′ Val′ley, a town in W California, NW of San Francisco. 10,411 (1960).

Mill·ville (mil′vil), *n.* a city in S New Jersey. 19,096 (1960).

mill′ wheel′, a wheel, esp. a water wheel, for driving a mill. [ME *myln whele,* OE *mylenhwēol.* See MILL[1], WHEEL]

mill·work (mil′wûrk′), *n.* **1.** ready-made carpentry work from a mill. **2.** work done in a mill. **3.** profiled or finished woodwork: *The millwork of a hundred years ago was often made by hand.* Also, **mill′ work′.** [MILL[1] + WORK]

mill·wright (mil′rīt′), *n.* **1.** a person who erects the machinery of a mill. **2.** a person who designs and erects mills and mill machinery. [MILL[1] + WRIGHT]

mill′wright chis′el. See **mill chisel.**

Mil·ly (mil′ē), *n.* a girl's given name, form of **Milicent** or **Mildred.** Also, **Millie.**

Milne (miln), *n.* **A(lan) A(lexander),** 1882–1956, English novelist, playwright, and author of prose and verse for children.

Milne-Ed·wards (miln′ed′wərdz; *Fr.* mēl nā dwärs′), *n.* **Hen·ri** (än rē′), 1800–85, French zoologist.

Milne′ meth′od, *Math.* a numerical method, involving Simpson's rule, for solving a linear differential equation. [named after E. A. *Milne* (1896–1950), English astronomer and mathematician]

Mil·ner (mil′nər), *n.* **Alfred, 1st Viscount,** 1854–1925, British statesman and colonial administrator.

mi·lo (mī′lō), *n., pl.* **-los.** a grain sorghum having white, yellow, or pinkish seeds, grown chiefly in Africa, Asia, and the U.S. [< Bantu (Basutoland) *maili*]

Mi·lo (mī′lō; *for 1 also Gk.* mē′lô), *n.* **1.** Also, **Mi·los** *(Gk.* mē′lôs). Melos. **2.** a boy's given name.

mi′lo disease′, *Plant Pathol.* a disease of milo and other sorghums, characterized by root and stem rot, caused by a fungus, *Periconia circinata.*

mi·lord (mi lôrd′), *n.* an English nobleman (often used as a term of address). [< F < E, contr. of phrase *my lord*]

mi′lo root′ rot′, *Plant Pathol.* See **milo disease.**

mil·pa (mil′pə), *n.* (in certain tropical regions) a tract of land cleared from the jungle, usually by burning, farmed for a few seasons, and then abandoned. [< MexSp < Nahuatl, var. of phrase *milli pa* in cultivation]

Mil·pi·tas (mil pē′təs), *n.* a town in W California. 6572 (1960).

milque·toast (milk′tōst′), *n.* a very timid, spineless person, esp. a man who is easily dominated or intimidated: *a milquetoast who's afraid to ask for a raise.* [after Caspar *Milquetoast,* a character in *The Timid Soul,* comic strip by H. T. Webster, 20th-century American cartoonist]

M.I.L.R., Master of Industrial and Labor Relations.

mil·reis (mil′rās′; *Port.* mel rāsh′), *n., pl.* **-reis. 1.** a silver coin and former monetary unit of Brazil, equal to 1000 reis, discontinued in 1942. **2.** a gold coin and former monetary unit of Portugal, equal to 1000 reis, discontinued in 1910. [< Pg: a thousand reis. See MILLI-, REIS]

Mil·stein (mil′stīn), *n.* **Nathan,** born 1904, Russian violinist in the U.S.

milt (milt), *n.* **1.** the secretion of the male generative organs of fishes. **2.** the organs themselves. **3.** melt[2]. [ME *milte, milt,* OE *milte* spleen; c. G *Milz,* MD *milte* milt, spleen; akin to MELT[1]]

milt·er (mil′tər), *n.* a male fish in breeding time. [MILT + -ER[1]]

Mil·ti·a·des (mil tī′ə dēz′), *n.* **1.** c540–488? B.C., Athenian general. **2.** Melchiades.

Mil·ton (mil′tᵊn), *n.* **1. John,** 1608–74, English poet. **2.** a town in E Massachusetts, near Boston. 26,375 (1960). **3.** a town in central Pennsylvania. 7972 (1960). **4.** a town in NW Florida. 4108 (1960). **5.** a boy's given name.

Mil·ton·ic (mil ton′ik), *adj.* of or pertaining to the poet Milton or his writings. **2.** resembling Milton's majestic style. Also, **Mil·to·ni·an** (mil tō′nē ən). [MILTON + -IC]

Mil·town (mil′toun′), *n.* *Pharm., Trademark.* meprobamate.

Mil·wau·kee (mil wô′kē), *n.* a port in SE Wisconsin, on Lake Michigan. 741,324 (1960). —**Mil·wau′kee·an,** *n.*

Mil·wau·kie (mil wô′kē), *n.* a town in NW Oregon. 9099 (1960).

Mi·lyu·kov (mi′lyŏŏ kôf′), *n.* **Pa·vel Ni·ko·la·e·vich** (pä′vel ni ko lä′yə vich), 1859–1943, Russian statesman and historian.

mim (mim), *adj. Brit. Dial.* primly modest or demure. [? M(UM[2] + PR)IM]

mīm (mēm), *n.* the 24th letter of the Arabic alphabet. [< Ar]

Mi·mam·sa (mē mäm′sä), *n.* *Hinduism.* the study of the interpretation of the Vedas. [< Skt: lit., thinking, study]

Mi·mas (mī′mas), *n.* **1.** *Astron.* one of the nine satellites of Saturn. **2.** *Class. Myth.* one of the Gigantes, killed by Hercules. **3.** *Rom. Legend.* a companion of Aeneas, killed by Mezentius.

mim·bar (mim′bär), *n.* a pulpit in a mosque. [< Ar]

mime (mīm, mēm), *n., v.,* **mimed, mim·ing.** —*n.* **1.** the art or technique of portraying a character, mood, idea, or narration by gestures and bodily movements; pantomime. **2.** an actor who specializes in this art. **3.** an ancient Greek or Roman farce which depended for effect largely upon ludicrous actions and gestures. **4.** a player in such a farce. **5.** mimic (def. 4). **6.** a jester, clown, or comedian. —*v.t.* **7.** to mimic. —*v.i.* **8.** to play a part by mimicry, esp. without words. [OE *mīma* < L *mīmus* < Gk *mîmos* imitator, mime, akin to *mīmeîsthai* to copy, imitate] —**mim′er,** *n.*

Mim·e·o·graph (mim′ē ə graf′, -gräf′), *n.* **1.** *Trademark.* a printing device, commonly used in offices, in which a waxed paper stencil bearing text that has been cut by a typewriter, or text or a drawing done by hand with a stylus, is fastened to a drum which is inked on the inside so that the ink penetrates the cut areas and is deposited on a new sheet of paper with each revolution of the drum. —*v.t.* **2.** (*l.c.*) to make copies of (something) using a Mimeograph.

mi·me·sis (mi mē′sis, mī-), *n.* **1.** *Rhet.* imitation or reproduction of the supposed words of another, as in order to represent his character. **2.** *Biol.* imitation. **3.** *Zool.* mimicry. **4.** Also, **mimosis.** *Pathol.* **a.** the simulation, due to hysteria, of the symptoms of a disease. **b.** the simulation of the symptoms of one disease by another. [< Gk: imitation, equiv. to *mīmē-* (var. s. of *mīmeîsthai* to copy) + *-sis* -SIS]

mi·met·ic (mi met′ik, mī-), *adj.* **1.** characterized by, exhibiting, or of the nature of mimicry: *mimetic gestures.* **2.** mimic; make-believe. [< Gk *mīmētik(ós)* imitative, equiv. to *mīmē-* (see MIMESIS) + *-tikos* -TIC] —**mi·met′i·cal·ly,** *adv.*

mim·e·tite (mim′i tīt′, mī′mi-), *n.* a mineral, lead chloroarsenate, $Pb_5As_3O_{12}Cl$, occurring in yellow to brown prismatic crystals or globular masses: a minor ore of lead. [< Gk *mimēt(ḗs)* imitator (*mīmē-* imitate + *-tēs* agent suffix) + -ITE[1]]

Mim·i (mim′ē; *Fr.* mē mē′), *n.* a girl's given name.

mim·ic (mim′ik), *v.,* **-icked, -ick·ing,** *n., adj.* —*v.t.* **1.** to imitate or copy in action, speech, etc., often playfully or derisively. **2.** to imitate servilely or unintelligently; ape. **3.** to be an imitation of; simulate; resemble closely. —*n.* **4.** a person who is clever at or skilled in imitating or mimicking the voices and gestures of others, esp. as a professional entertainer. **5.** one who or that which imitates or mimics; an imitator or imitation. **6.** a performer in a mime. —*adj.* **7.** being merely an imitation or reproduction of the true thing, often on a smaller scale: *a mimic battle.* **8.** apt at or given to imitating; imitative; simulative. [< L *mīmic(us)* < Gk *mīmikós.* See MIME, -IC] —**mim′ick·er,** *n.* —**Syn. 1.** follow, mock; impersonate; simulate, counterfeit. **7.** mock, simulated.

mim·i·cal (mim′i kəl), *adj. Archaic.* mimic. [MIMIC + -AL[1]] —**mim′i·cal·ly,** *adv.*

mim·ic·ry (mim′ik rē), *n., pl.* **-ries. 1.** the act, practice, or art of mimicking. **2.** *Zool.* the close external resemblance, as if from imitation or simulation, of an animal to some different animal or to surrounding objects, esp. as serving for protection or concealment. **3.** an instance, performance, or result of mimicking. [MIMIC + -RY]

Mi·mir (mē′mir), *n. Scand. Myth.* the god of the open sea, whose head, cut off by the Vanir, was sent to Odin and was revived and kept as an oracle for the Aesir.

mi·mo·sa (mi mō′sə, -zə), *n.* any of numerous herbs, shrubs, or trees of the genus *Mimosa,* native to tropical or warm regions, having small flowers in globular heads or cylindrical spikes and often sensitive leaves. [< NL, equiv. to L *mīm(us)* MIME + *-ōsa,* fem. of *-ōsus* -OSE[1]]

mim·o·sa·ceous (mim′ə sā′shəs, mī′mə-), *adj.* belonging to the *Mimosaceae,* or mimosa family of plants, usually included in the family *Leguminosae.* [< NL *mīmōsāce(ae)* name of the family (see MIMOSA, -ACEAE) + -OUS]

mi·mo·sis (mi mō′sis), *n. Pathol.* mimesis (def. 4).

Mims (mimz), *n.* **Fort.** See **Fort Mims.**

min, minim; minims.

min., **1.** mineralogical. **2.** mineralogy. **3.** minim. **4.** minimum. **5.** mining. **6.** minor. **7.** minute; minutes.

mi·na[1] (mī′nə), *n., pl.* **-nae** (-nē), **-nas.** an ancient unit of weight and value equal to the sixtieth part of a talent. [< L < Gk *mnâ* < Sem; cf. Heb *māneh* mina]

mi·na[2] (mī′nə), *n.* myna.

Min·a (min′ə, mī′nə), *n.* a girl's given name, form of **Wilhelmina.**

mi·na·cious (mi nā′shəs), *adj.* menacing; threatening. [< L *mināci-* (s. of *minax*) overhanging, threatening + -OUS] —**mi·na′cious·ly,** *adv.* —**mi·na′cious·ness, mi·nac·i·ty** (mi nas′i tē), *n.*

mi·nah[1] (mī′nə), *n.* myna.

mi·nah[2] (mē′nä), *n.* *Indian Archit.* a memorial tower, as a stamba. [< Hindi, apocopated var. of *mīnāra;* see MINARET]

Mi·na·mo·to (mē′nä mō′tō), *n., pl.* **-to.** a member of a powerful family in Japan which ruled as shoguns, 1185–1219.

min·a·ret (min′ə ret′, min′ə-ret′), *n.* a lofty, often slender, tower or turret attached to a Muslim mosque, surrounded by or furnished with one or more balconies, from which the muezzin calls the people to prayer. [< Sp *minarete* < Ar *manārat* lighthouse, akin to *nār* fire] —**min′a·ret′ed,** *adj.*

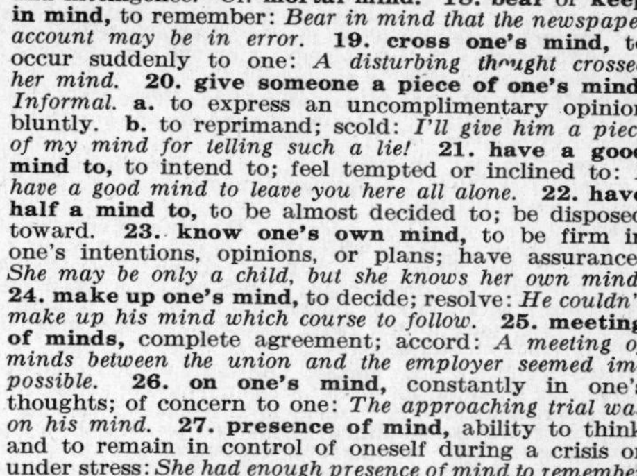

Minaret

Mi′nas Ba′sin (mī′nəs), a bay in E Canada, the easternmost arm of the Bay of Fundy, in N Nova Scotia: noted for its high tides.

Mi·nas de Rí·o·tin·to (mē′näs de ʀē′ō tēn′tō), a town in SW Spain: copper mines. 9060 (1950).

Mi·nas Ge·rais (mē′nəs zhi ʀīs′), a state in E Brazil. 8,886,000 (est. 1960); 224,701 sq. mi. *Cap.:* Belo Horizonte.

min·a·to·ry (min′ə tôr′ē, -tōr′ē), *adj.* menacing; threatening. Also, **min′a·to′ri·al.** [< LL *minātōri(us),* equiv. to L *mināt(us)* menaced (ptp. of *minārī* to threaten) + *-ōrius* -ORY[1]] —**min′a·to′ri·ly,** *adv.*

mince (mins), *v.,* **minced, minc·ing,** *n.* —*v.t.* **1.** to cut or chop into very small pieces. **2.** to subdivide minutely, as land, a topic for study, etc. **3.** to soften or moderate (one's words), esp. for the sake of decorum or courtesy. **4.** to perform or utter with affected elegance. —*v.i.* **5.** to walk or move with short, affectedly dainty steps. **6.** to act, behave, or speak with affected elegance. **7. not mince words** or **matters,** to speak directly and frankly; be blunt or outspoken: *He called us into his office, and he didn't mince words.* —*n.* **8.** something cut up very small; mincemeat. [ME *mince(n)* < MF *minc(i)er* < VL **minūtiāre* to mince; see MINUTE[2]]

mince·meat (mins′mēt′), *n.* **1.** a mixture composed of minced apples, suet, and sometimes meat, together with raisins, currants, candied citron, etc., for filling a pie (**mince′ pie′**). **2.** anything cut up very small, esp. meat. **3. make mincemeat of,** to destroy utterly: *His discoveries make mincemeat of earlier theories.* [MINCE + MEAT]

minc·er (min′sər), *n.* one who or that which minces. [MINCE + -ER[1]]

Min·chah (mēn ḵʜä′; *Eng.* min′ḵʜə), *n.* *Hebrew.* Minhah.

minc·ing (min′sing), *adj.* **1.** (of the gait or speech, behavior, etc.) affectedly dainty, nice, or elegant. **2.** walking, acting, or speaking in an affectedly nice or elegant manner. [MINCE + -ING[2]] —**minc′ing·ly,** *adv.*

mind (mīnd), *n.* **1.** (in a human or other conscious being) the element, part, substance, or process that reasons, thinks, feels, wills, perceives, judges, etc.: *the processes of the mind.* **2.** *Psychol.* the totality of conscious and unconscious mental processes and activities of the organism. **3.** intellect or understanding, as distinguished from the faculties of feeling and willing; intelligence. **4.** a particular instance of the intellect or intelligence, as in a person. **5.** a person considered with reference to intellectual power: *the greatest minds of the time.* **6.** intellectual power or ability. **7.** reason, sanity, or sound mental condition: *to lose one's mind.* **8.** a way of thinking and feeling; disposition; temper: *To my mind, it was a foolish mistake.* **9.** opinion or sentiments: *to change one's mind.* **10.** inclination or desire: *to be of a mind to listen.* **11.** purpose, intention, or will: *Let me know your mind in this matter before Tuesday.* **12.** psychic or spiritual being, as opposed to matter. **13.** a conscious or intelligent agency or being: *an awareness of a mind ordering the universe.* **14.** remembrance or recollection: *Former days were called to mind.* **15.** attention; thoughts: *He can't keep his mind on his studies. Maybe this will take your mind off your troubles.* **16.** *Rom. Cath. Ch.* a commemoration of a person's death, esp. by a Requiem Mass. Cf. **month's mind, year's mind. 17.** (*cap.*) Also called **Divine Mind.** *Christian Science.* the concept of the noncorporeal as the single source of life, substance, and intelligence. Cf. **mortal mind. 18. bear** or **keep in mind,** to remember: *Bear in mind that the newspaper account may be in error.* **19. cross one's mind,** to occur suddenly to one: *A disturbing thought crossed her mind.* **20. give someone a piece of one's mind,** *Informal.* **a.** to express an uncomplimentary opinion bluntly. **b.** to reprimand; scold: *I'll give him a piece of my mind for telling such a lie!* **21. have a good mind to,** to intend to; feel tempted or inclined to: *I have a good mind to leave you here all alone.* **22. have half a mind to,** to be almost decided to; be disposed toward. **23. know one's own mind,** to be firm in one's intentions, opinions, or plans; have assurance: *She may be only a child, but she knows her own mind.* **24. make up one's mind,** to decide; resolve: *He couldn't make up his mind which course to follow.* **25. meeting of minds,** complete agreement; accord: *A meeting of minds between the union and the employer seemed impossible.* **26. on one's mind,** constantly in one's thoughts; of concern to one: *The approaching trial was on his mind.* **27. presence of mind,** ability to think and to remain in control of oneself during a crisis or under stress: *She had enough presence of mind to remember the license plate of the speeding car.* **28. put in mind,** to cause to remember; remind: *The reunion put us in mind of our college days.* **29. to one's mind,** in accord with one's judgment or opinion: *To my mind, she'll always be an unpleasant person to deal with.* —*v.t.* **30.** to pay attention to, heed, or obey (a person, advice, instructions, etc.). **31.** to apply oneself or attend to: *to mind one's own business.* **32.** to look after; take care of; tend: *to mind the baby; Who's minding the store?* **33.** to be careful, cautious, or wary concerning: *Mind what you say.* **34.** to feel concern at; care about. **35.** to feel disturbed or inconvenienced by; object to (usually used in negative or interrogative constructions): *Would you mind handing me that book?* **36.** to regard as concerning oneself or as mattering: *Never mind his bluntness.* **37.** *Dial.* to perceive or notice. **38.** *Dial.* **a.** to remember. **b.** to remind. —*v.i.* **39.** to obey. **40.** to take notice, observe, or understand (used chiefly in the imperative): *Mind now, I want you home by twelve.* **41.** to be careful or wary. **42.** to care, feel concern, or object (often used in negative or interrogative constructions): *Mind if I go? Don't mind if I do.* **43.** to regard a thing as concerning oneself or as mattering: *You mustn't mind about their gossiping.* **44. never mind,** don't bother; it is of no concern: *Never mind—the broken glass will be easy to replace.* [ME *mynd(e),* OE *gemynd* commemoration; c. Goth *gamunds;* akin to L *mēns* mind]

—**Syn. 1.** reason. MIND, INTELLECT, INTELLIGENCE refer to mental equipment or qualities. MIND is that part of man which thinks, feels, and wills, as contrasted with body: *His mind was capable of grasping the significance of the problem.* INTELLECT is reasoning power as distinguished from feeling; it is often used in a general sense to characterize high mental ability: *to appeal to the intellect, rather than the emotions.* INTELLIGENCE is ability to learn and to understand; it is also mental alertness or quickness of understanding: *A dog has more intelligence than many other animals.* **6.** MIND, BRAIN, BRAINS may refer to mental capacity. MIND is the philosophical and general term for the center of mental activity, and is therefore used of intellectual powers: *a brilliant mind.* BRAIN is properly the physiological term for the organic structure which makes mental activity possible (*The brain is the center of the nervous system.*), but it is often applied, like mind, to intellectual capacity: *a fertile brain.* BRAINS is the anatomical word (*the brains of an animal used for food*), but, in popular usage, it is applied to intelligence (particularly of a shrewd, practical nature): *To run a business takes brains.* **10.** bent, leaning, proclivity, penchant; wish, liking. **11.** intent. **14.** memory. **30.** mark.

Min·da·na·o (min′dä nä′ō, -nou′; *Sp.* mēn′dä nä′ô), *n.* the second largest island of the Philippines, in the S part of the group. 3,174,810 (est. 1960); 36,537 sq. mi.

Min′dana′o Deep′, an area in the Pacific Ocean W of the Philippines: one of deepest points in any ocean.

mind′-bod′y prob′lem (mīnd′bod′ē), *Philos.* the problem of explaining the relation of the mind to the body.

mind′ deaf′ness, *Pathol.* See **word deafness.**

M.Ind.E., Master of Industrial Engineering.

mind·ed (mīn′did), *adj.* **1.** having a certain kind of mind (usually used in combination): *strong-minded.* **2.** inclined or disposed. [MIND + -ED[3]]

Min·del (min′dᵊl), *n. Geol.* the second stage of the glaciation of Eurasia during the Pleistocene. Cf. **Kansan** (def. 4). [after the *Mindel* river, Bavaria, Germany]

mind·er (mīn′dər), *n.* **1.** *Chiefly Brit.* a person who looks after or minds something (usually used in combination): *a baby-minder.* **2.** *Brit.* **a.** See **foster child. b.** *Archaic.* a pauper child placed with foster parents or in an orphanage, under the administration of the poor law. **c.** *Archaic.* a child living at home but sent to a woman or institution to be tended during the day while the parents work. [late ME *mendowre* one who remembers. See MIND, -ER[1]]

mind-ex·pand·ing (mīnd′ek span′ding), *adj.* (of a drug) causing changes in perception and thought processes; hallucinogenic.

mind·ful (mīnd′fəl), *adj.* attentive or careful (usually fol. by *of*): *mindful of one's responsibilities.* [ME *myndeful.* See MIND, -FUL] —**mind′ful·ly,** *adv.* —**mind′ful·ness,** *n.*

mind·less (mīnd′lis), *adj.* **1.** without intelligence; senseless. **2.** unmindful, careless, or heedless: *mindless of all dangers.* [ME *myndles,* OE *gemyndlēas.* See MIND, -LESS] —**mind′less·ly,** *adv.* —**mind′less·ness,** *n.*

Min·do·ro (min dôr′ō, -dōr′ō; *Sp.* mēn dô′ʀô), *n.* a central island of the Philippines. 209,360 (est. 1960); 3922 sq. mi.

mind′ read′er, a person professing the ability or power of mind reading, esp. as a professional entertainer.

mind′ read′ing, 1. the professed ability to discern the thoughts of others without the normal means of communication, esp. by means of an alleged preternatural power. 2. an alleged act or the practice of so discerning the thoughts of another.

mind's′ eye′, the hypothetical site of visual recollection or imagination: *In her mind's eye she saw the ancient city as it had been in Caesar's time.*

Mind·szen·ty (mind′sen tē), *n.* **Joseph** (*Joseph Pehm*), 1892–1975, Hungarian Roman Catholic clergyman: cardinal 1946.

mine[1] (mīn), *pron.* 1. a form of the possessive case of *I* used as a predicate adjective: *The yellow sweater is mine.* 2. that which belongs to me: *Mine is the car with the flat tire.* 3. *Archaic.* my (used before a word beginning with a vowel or a silent *h*, or following a noun): *mine eyes; lady mine.* [ME, OE *mīn*; c. Icel *mīn*, G *mein*, Goth *meina*; see ME]

mine[2] (mīn), *n., v.,* **mined, min·ing.** —*n.* 1. an excavation made in the earth for the purpose of extracting ores, precious stones, coal, etc. 2. a place where such minerals may be obtained, either by excavation or by washing the soil. 3. a natural deposit of such minerals. 4. an abundant source; store: *He has a mine of information about ships.* 5. a subterranean passage made to extend under an enemy's works or position, as for the purpose of securing access or of depositing explosives for blowing up a military position. 6. a passageway in the parenchyma of a leaf, made by certain insects. 7. a device containing a charge of explosive in a watertight casing, floating on or moored beneath the surface of the water for the purpose of blowing up an enemy vessel that strikes it or passes close by it. 8. a similar device used on land against personnel or vehicles; land mine. —*v.i.* 9. to dig in the earth for the purpose of extracting ores, coal, etc.; make a mine. 10. to extract ores, etc., from a mine. 11. to make subterranean passages. 12. to dig or lay mines, as in military operations. —*v.t.* 13. to dig in (earth, rock, etc.) in order to obtain ores, coal, etc. 14. to extract (ore, coal, etc.) from a mine. 15. to make subterranean passages in or under; burrow. 16. to make (passages, tunnels, etc.) by digging or burrowing. 17. to dig away or remove the foundations of. 18. to attack, ruin, or destroy by secret or slow methods. 19. to dig or lay military mines under: *to mine an enemy supply road.* [ME < MF, perh. back formation < OF *miniere* mine < ML *minera.* See MINERAL] —**min′a·ble, mine′a·ble,** *adj.*

Min.E., Mineral Engineer.

mine′ detec′tor, an electromagnetic device for locating buried or concealed land mines.

mine′ exam′iner. See **fire boss.**

mine·field (mīn′fēld′), *n. Mil., Naval.* an area of land or water throughout which explosive mines have been laid. [MINE[2] + FIELD]

mine·lay·er (mīn′lā′ər), *n.* a naval vessel equipped for laying mines in the water. [MINE[2] + LAYER]

Min·e·o·la (min′ē ō′lə), *n.* 1. a city on W Long Island, in SE New York. 20,519 (1960). 2. a town in NE Texas. 3810 (1960).

min·er (mī′nər), *n.* 1. a person who works in a mine, esp. a commercial mine producing coal or metallic ores. 2. (formerly) a person who digs or lays military mines. [MINE[2] + -ER[1]; r. ME *minour* < AF; see -OR[2]]

Min·er (mī′nər), *n.* a boy's given name. Also, **Minor.**

min·er·al (min′ər əl, min′rəl), *n.* 1. any of a class of substances occurring in nature, usually comprising inorganic substances, as quartz, feldspar, etc., of definite chemical composition and usually of definite crystal structure, but sometimes also including rocks formed by these substances as well as certain natural products of organic origin, as asphalt, coal, etc. 2. a substance obtained by mining; ore. 3. any substance that is neither animal nor vegetable. 4. **minerals,** *Brit.* See **mineral water.** —*adj.* 5. of the nature of a mineral; pertaining to a mineral or minerals. 6. containing or impregnated with a mineral or minerals. 7. neither animal nor vegetable; inorganic: *mineral matter.* [late ME < ML *minerāle* (n.), *minerālis* (adj.), equiv. to *miner(a)* mine, ore (< ?) + *-ālis* -AL[1]]

mineral., 1. mineralogical. 2. mineralogy.

min′eral char′coal, a fibrous substance resembling charcoal and having a high carbon content, often occurring in thin layers in bituminous coal. Also called **mother of coal.**

min·er·al·ise (min′ər ə līz′, min′rə-), *v.t., v.i.,* **-ised, -is·ing.** mineralize.

min·er·al·ize (min′ər ə līz′, min′rə-), *v.,* **-ized, -iz·ing.** —*v.t.* 1. to convert into a mineral substance. 2. to transform (a metal) into an ore. 3. to impregnate or supply with mineral substances. —*v.i.* 4. to study or collect the minerals of a region. Also, **mineralise.** [MINERAL + -IZE] —**min′er·al·i·za′tion,** *n.* —**min′er·al·iz′er,** *n.*

min′eral jel′ly, *Chem.* a gelatinous product made from petroleum, used to stabilize certain explosives.

min′eral king′dom, minerals collectively. Cf. **animal kingdom, plant kingdom.**

min·er·al·o·gist (min′ə rol′ə jist, -ral′ə-), *n.* a specialist in mineralogy. [MINERALOG(Y) + -IST]

min·er·al·o·gy (min′ə rol′ə jē, -ral′ə-), *n.* the science or study of minerals. [MINERA(L) + -LOGY] —**min·er·al·og·i·cal** (min′ər ə loj′i kəl), **min′er·al·og′ic,** *adj.* —**min′er·al·og′i·cal·ly,** *adv.*

min·er·al·oid (min′ər ə loid′), *n.* a mineral substance that does not have a definite chemical formula or crystal form. [MINERAL + -OID]

min′eral oil′, a colorless, oily, almost tasteless, water-insoluble liquid, usually of either a standard light density (**light mineral oil**) or a standard heavy density (**heavy mineral oil**), consisting of mixtures of hydrocarbons obtained from petroleum by distillation: used chiefly as a lubricant, in the manufacture of cosmetics, and in medicine as a laxative. Also called **liquid petrolatum.**

min′eral pitch′, asphalt.

min′eral spring′, a spring of water that contains a significant amount of dissolved minerals.

min′eral tar′, bitumen of the consistency of tar; maltha.

min′eral wa′ter, 1. water containing dissolved mineral salts or gases, esp. such water for medicinal use. 2. **mineral waters,** *Brit.* **a.** carbonated water; soda water. **b.** artificially flavored, bottled soft drinks; soda pop.

min′eral wax′, ozocerite.

min′eral wool′, a woollike material for heat and sound insulation, made by blowing steam or air through molten slag or rock. Also called **rock wool.**

min′er's ane′mia, *Pathol.* hookworm (def. 2).

min′er's di′al, *Mining.* dial (def. 5).

min′er's inch′, a unit of measure of water flow, varying with locality but often a flow equaling 1.5 cubic feet per minute.

min′er's let′tuce. See **winter purslane.**

Mi·ners·ville (mī′nərz vil′), *n.* a town in central Pennsylvania. 6606 (1960).

mine-run (mīn′run′), *n.* something that is run-of-the-mill, average, or undistinguished.

Mi·ner·va (mi nûr′və), *n.* 1. the ancient Roman goddess of wisdom and the arts, identified with the Greek goddess Athena. 2. a woman of great wisdom.

Mi·ner·va (mi nûr′və), *n.* a town in E Ohio. 3833 (1960).

min·e·stro·ne (min′i strō′nē; *It.* mē′ne strô′ne), *n. Italian Cookery.* a thick soup containing vegetables, chicken or meat, herbs, and bits of pasta, often served with Parmesan cheese. [< It, equiv. to *minestr(a)* kind of soup (lit., something served; see MINISTER) + *-one* aug. suffix]

mine·sweep·er (mīn′swē′pər), *n. Navy.* a vessel or ship used for dragging a body of water in order to remove enemy mines. [MINE[2] + SWEEPER] —**mine′-sweep′ing,** *n.*

mi·nette (mi net′), *n. Mineral.* an orthoclase biotite lamprophyre. [< G < F; see MINE[2], -ETTE]

min·e·ver (min′ə vər), *n.* miniver.

Ming (ming), *n.* 1. a dynasty in China, 1368–1644, marked by the restoration of traditional institutions and the development of the arts, esp. in porcelain, textiles, and painting. —*adj.* 2. of or pertaining to the Ming dynasty or to the art objects and forms developed during the Ming dynasty. 3. noting the fine porcelains produced in the Ming dynasty, esp. those produced by the imperial factory before 1620, noted for their brilliant, fine colors, chiefly underglaze or enamel on glaze, on a body of high quality.

min·gle (ming′gəl), *v.,* **-gled, -gling.** —*v.i.* 1. to become mixed, blended, or united. 2. to associate or mix in company. 3. to take part with others; participate. —*v.t.* 4. to mix or combine; put together in a mixture; blend. 5. to unite, join, or conjoin. 6. to associate in company: *a hostess who mingles diplomats with professional people.* 7. to form by mixing; compound; concoct. [ME *mengle,* freq. (with *-le* suffix) of *mengen,* OE *mengan* to mix; c. D, G *mengan*] —**min′gle·ment,** *n.* —**min′gler,** *n.*
—**Syn.** 4. commingle, intermingle, intermix. See **mix.**

Min′go Junc′tion (ming′gō), a town in E Ohio. 4987 (1960).

Min·gre·li·an (min grē′lē ən, ming-), *n.* a South Caucasian language spoken near the extreme eastern end of the Black Sea.

ming′ tree′ (ming), an artificially dwarfed tree resembling a bonsai. [? after MING]

min·gy (min′jē), *adj.,* **-gi·er, -gi·est.** mean and stingy; niggardly. [M(EAN[2] + ST)INGY[1]]

min·hag (mēn häg′; *Eng.* min′häg), *n., pl.* **min·ha·gim** (mēn hä gēm′; *Eng.* min hä′gim). *Hebrew.* a custom or procedure among Jews that is so firmly established as to have almost the binding force of law. [lit., custom] —**min·ha′gic,** *adj.*

Min·hah (mēn кнä′; *Eng.* min′кнə), *n. Hebrew, Judaism.* the daily religious service celebrated in the late afternoon. Also, **Minchah.** Cf. **Maarib Shaharith.**

Mi·nho (mē′nyŏŏ), *n.* a river in SW Europe, flowing SSW from NW Spain along the N boundary of Portugal into the Atlantic. 171 mi. long. Spanish, **Miño.**

Min·how (min′hō′), *n.* Foochow.

min·i (min′ē), *n.* 1. miniskirt. —*adj.* 2. of the length of a miniskirt. [by shortening]

mini-, a combining form of **miniature:** *miniskirt.*

min·i·a·ture (min′ē ə chər, min′ə chər), *n.* 1. a representation or image of something on a small or reduced scale. 2. a greatly reduced or abridged form. 3. a very small painting, esp. a portrait, on ivory, vellum, or the like. 4. the art of executing such a painting. 5. an illumination in an illuminated manuscript or book. 6. **in miniature,** in a reduced size; on a very small scale: *The children's rabbits and guinea pigs made the back porch a zoo in miniature.* —*adj.* 7. being, on, or represented on a very small scale; reduced. 8. being, of, or pertaining to a camera, photography, or a system of photography using 35-millimeter film. [< It *miniatura* < ML, equiv. to *miniāt(us)* rubricated, illuminated, L: colored with red lead (*mini(um)* MINIUM + *-ātus* -ATE[1]) + *-ūra* -URE]

min′iature cam′era, *Photog.* a small camera using 35-millimeter film.

min′iature golf′, a game or amusement modeled on golf and played with a putter and golf ball, in which each very short, grassless "hole" constitutes an obstacle course, consisting of wooden alleys, tunnels, bridges, etc., through which the ball must be driven to hole it. Also called **midget golf.**

min′iature photog′raphy, photography with a camera using 35-millimeter film.

min·i·a·tur·ize (min′ē ə chə rīz′, min′ə-), *v.t.,* **-ized, -iz·ing.** to make in extremely small size in order to keep volume or weight to a minimum: *to miniaturize transistors and other electronic equipment.* [MINIATURE + -IZE] —**min′i·a·tur·i·za′tion,** *n.*

min·i·cam (min′ə kam′), *n.* See **miniature camera.** Also, **min·i·cam·er·a** (min′ə kam′ər ə, -kam′rə). [MINI(ATURE) + CAM(ERA)]

min·i·com·put·er (min′ē kəm pyōō′tər), *n.* a computer with processing and storage capabilities smaller than those of a full-sized computer, used by small businesses, in manufacturing processes, scientific research, etc.

Min·ié ball′ (min′ē, min′ē ā′; *Fr.* mē nyā′), a conical bullet with a hollow base that expanded when fired, used in the 19th century. [named after C. E. *Minié* (1814–79), French officer who invented it]

min·i·fy (min′ə fī′), *v.t.,* **-fied, -fy·ing.** 1. to make less. 2. to minimize. [< L *min(us)* less + -IFY, modeled on *magnify*] —**min′i·fi·ca′tion,** *n.*

min·i·kin (min′ə kin), *n.* 1. a person who or object that is delicate or diminutive. 2. a printing type (about 3½ point). —*adj.* 3. delicate; dainty; mincing. [< MD *minneken,* equiv. to *minne* love + dim. suffix *-ken* -KIN]

min·im (min′əm), *n.* 1. the smallest unit of liquid measure, the sixtieth part of a fluid dram, roughly equivalent to one drop. *Symbol:* M, ♏ *Abbr.:* min, min. 2. *Music.* a note, formerly the shortest in use, but now equivalent in time value to one half of a semibreve; half note. See illus. under **note.** 3. the least quantity of anything. 4. something very small or insignificant. 5. (*cap.*) a member of a mendicant religious order founded in the 15th century by St. Francis of Paola. —*adj.* 6. smallest; very small. [late ME; as a musical term < ML *minima,* n. use of fem. of L *minimus* smallest, least; otherwise < ML, L *minimus.* See MINIMUM]

min·i·ma (min′ə mə), *n.* a pl. of **minimum.**

min·i·mal (min′ə məl), *adj.* 1. pertaining to or being a minimum. 2. least possible. 3. smallest; very small. [MINIM(UM) + -AL[1]] —**min′i·mal·ly,** *adv.*

Min·i·mal·ist (min′ə mə list), *n.* a member of a moderate group or faction of socialists. Cf. **Maximalist.** [MINIMAL + -IST]

min′imal pair′, *Ling.* a pair of words, as *pin* and *bin,* or *bet* and *bed,* differing only by one sound in the same position in each word, esp. when such a pair is taken as evidence for the existence of a phonological contrast between the two sounds.

min·i·max (min′ə maks′), *n.* a strategy of game theory employed to minimize a player's maximum possible loss. Cf. **maximin.** [MINI(MUM) + MAX(IMUM)]

min·i·mise (min′ə mīz′), *v.t.,* **-mised, -mis·ing.** *Chiefly Brit.* minimize. —**min′i·mi·sa′tion,** *n.* —**min′i·mis′er,** *n.*

min·i·mize (min′ə mīz′), *v.t.,* **-mized, -miz·ing.** 1. to reduce to the smallest possible amount or degree. 2. to represent at the lowest possible estimate; belittle. Also, *esp. Brit.,* **minimise.** [MINIM(UM) + -IZE] —**min′i·mi·za′tion,** *n.* —**min′i·miz′er,** *n.*

min·i·mum (min′ə məm), *n., pl.* **-mums, -ma** (-mə), *adj.* —*n.* 1. the least quantity or amount possible, assignable, allowable, etc. 2. the lowest amount, value, or degree attained or recorded (opposed to *maximum*). 3. an arbitrary amount set by a restaurant, night club, etc., as the least amount to be charged each person for food and drink. Cf. **cover charge.** 4. *Math.* **a.** Also called **relative minimum, local minimum.** the value of a function at a certain point in its domain, which is less than or equal to the values at all other points in the immediate vicinity of the point. Cf. **absolute minimum. b.** the point in the domain at which a minimum occurs. —*adj.* 5. noting or indicating a minimum. 6. least possible: *minimum risk.* 7. lowest: *a minimum rate.* 8. pertaining to a minimum or minimums. [< L, neut. of *minimus* smallest, least]

min′imum ac′cess pro′gramming, *Computer Technol.* a method of programming in which latency is reduced to a minimum. Also called **forced coding, min′imum la′tency pro′gramming, optimum programming.**

min′imum thermom′eter, a thermometer designed to show the lowest temperature recorded between resettings. Cf. **maximum thermometer.**

min′imum wage′, the lowest fixed wage that a government law or a union agreement makes payable to employees of a particular group.

min·i·mus (min′ə məs), *n., pl.* **-mi** (-mī′). 1. a being that is the smallest or least significant. 2. *Anat.* the little finger or toe. [< NL, L: lit., smallest]

min·ing (mī′ning), *n.* 1. the act, process, or industry of extracting ores, coal, etc., from mines. 2. the laying of explosive mines. [MINE[2] + -ING[1]]

Mining Eng., Mining Engineer.

min′ing engineer′ing, the branch of engineering dealing with the location and appraisal of mineral deposits and the laying out, equipment, and management of mines. —**min′ing engineer′.**

min·ion (min′yən), *n.* 1. a servile follower or subordinate of a person in power. 2. any favored or highly regarded person. 3. a minor official; subordinate authority. 4. *Print.* a 7-point type. —*adj.* 5. dainty; elegant; trim; pretty. [< MF *mignon,* r. OF *mignot* dainty < ?]

min′ion of the law′, a policeman.

min·i·se·ries (min′ē sēr′ēz), *n. pl.* **-ries.** 1. a short series of things, as events or presentations. 2. *Television.* a special program, dramatic presentation, etc., that is shown in three or more installments, often on successive evenings. Also, **min′i·se′ries.**

min·i·skirt (min′ē skûrt′), *n.* a very short skirt or skirt part, as of a coat, dress, etc., ending three or more inches above the knee. Also called **mini.** [MINI(ATURE) + SKIRT] —**min′i·skirt′ed,** *adj.*

min·is·ter (min′i stər), *n.* 1. a person authorized to conduct religious worship; clergyman; pastor. 2. a person authorized to administer sacraments, as at Mass. 3. (chiefly in Europe) a person appointed by or under the authority of a sovereign or executive head of a government to some high office of state, esp. to that of head of an administrative department: *the Minister of Finance.* 4. a diplomatic representative accredited by one government to another and ranking below an ambassador. Cf. **envoy**[1] (def. 1). 5. a person acting as the agent or instrument of another. —*v.t.* 6. to administer or apply. 7. *Archaic.* to furnish; supply. —*v.i.* 8. to perform the functions of a religious minister. 9. to give service, care, or aid; attend, as to wants, necessities, etc. 10. to contribute, as to comfort, happiness, etc. [< L: servant, equiv. to *minis-* less (var. of *minor*) + *-ter* n. suffix; r. ME *ministre* < OF]

min·is·te·ri·al (min′i stēr′ē əl), *adj.* 1. pertaining to the ministry of religion, or to a minister or clergyman. 2. (chiefly in Europe) pertaining to a ministry or minister of state. 3. pertaining to or invested with delegated executive authority. 4. of ministry or service. 5. serving as an instrument or means; instrumental. [< LL *ministeriāl(is),* equiv. to L *ministeri(um)* MINISTRY + *-ālis* -AL[1]] —**min′is·te′ri·al·ly,** *adv.*

min′ister plenipoten′tiary, plenipotentiary.

min′ister res′ident, *pl.* **ministers resident.** a diplomatic agent serving in a minor country and ranking next below an ambassador.

min′ister without′ portfo′lio, *pl.* **ministers without portfolios.** a member of a ministry who is not appointed to any specific department in a government.

min·is·trant (min′i strənt), *adj.* **1.** ministering. —*n.* **2.** a person who ministers. [< L *ministrant-* (s. of *ministrāns*) serving, prp. of *ministrāre*. See MINISTER, -ANT]

min·is·tra·tion (min′i strā′shən), *n.* **1.** the act of ministering care, aid, religious service, etc. **2.** an instance of this. [< L *ministrātiōn-* (s. of *ministrātiō*) service, equiv. to *ministrāt(us)* served (ptp. of *ministrāre*) + *-iōn-* -ION] —**min′is·tra′tive,** *adj.*

min·is·try (min′i strē), *n., pl.* **-tries. 1.** the service, functions, or profession of a minister of religion. **2.** the body or class of ministers of religion; clergy. **3.** the service, function, or office of a minister of state. **4.** the body of ministers of state. **5.** (*usually cap.*) any of the administrative departments of certain countries. **6.** (*usually cap.*) the building which houses such an administrative department. **7.** the term of office of a minister. **8.** the act or an instance of ministering; ministration; service. **9.** that which serves as an agency, instrument, or means. [ME < L *ministeri(um)*, equiv. to *minister* MINISTER + *-ium* -Y³]

min·i·track (min′i trak′), *n.* the procedure of tracing the orbit of an artificial satellite and of recording its signals by telemeter. [MINI(ATURE) + TRACK]

min·i·um (min′ē əm), *n.* See **red lead.** [ME < L: cinnabar, red lead < Iberian; cf. Basque *armineá* cinnabar]

min·i·ver (min′ə vər), *n.* **1.** (in the Middle Ages) a fur of white or spotted white and gray used for linings and trimmings. Cf. **vair** (def. 1). **2.** any white fur, particularly that of the ermine, used esp. on robes of state. Also, **minever.** [ME *meniver* < MF *menu vair* small VAIR; see MENU]

min·i·vet (min′ə vet′), *n.* any of several small, long-tailed cuckoo-shrikes of the genus *Pericrocotus*, having black and white or black and orange plumage. [?]

mink (miŋk), *n., pl.* **minks,** (*esp. collectively*) **mink. 1.** a semiaquatic weasellike animal of the genus *Mustela*, esp. the North American *M. vison*. **2.** the valuable fur of this animal, brownish in the natural state and having lustrous outside hairs and a thick, soft undercoat. **3.** a woman's coat, stole, etc., made of this fur. [late ME; akin to or < Sw *mänk*]

Mink, *Mustela vison* (Total length 2 ft.; tail to 9 in.)

mink·fish (miŋk′fish′), *n., pl.* **-fish·es,** (*esp. collectively*) **-fish.** *Ichthyol.* a drum, *Menticirrhus focaliger*, that is unable to produce sounds owing to its lack of an air bladder. [MINK + FISH]

Min·kow·ski (miŋ kôf′skē), *n.* **Her·mann** (hûr′mən; *Ger.* her′män), 1864–1909, German mathematician.

Minkow′ski world′, *Math.* a four-dimensional space in which the fourth coordinate is time and in which a single event is represented as a point. Also called **Minkow′ski u′niverse.** [named after H. MINKOWSKI]

Minn., Minnesota.

Min·na (min′ə), *n.* a girl's given name.

Min·ne·ap·o·lis (min′ē ap′ə lis), *n.* a city in SE Minnesota, on the Mississippi. 482,872 (1960). —**Min·ne·a·pol·i·tan** (min′ē ə pol′i tən), *n.*

min·ne·sing·er (min′i siŋ′ər), *n.* one of a class of German lyric poets and singers of the 12th, 13th and 14th centuries. [< G, equiv. to *Minne* love + *Singer* singer]

Min·ne·so·ta (min′i sō′tə), *n.* **1.** a State in the N central United States 3,413,864 (1960); 84,068 sq. mi. *Cap.:* St. Paul. *Abbr.:* Minn. **2.** a river flowing SE from the W border of Minnesota into the Mississippi near St. Paul. 332 mi. long. —**Min′ne·so′tan,** *adj., n.*

Min·ne·ton·ka (min′i toŋ′kə), *n.* a city in E Minnesota, near Minneapolis. 25,037 (1960).

Min·ne·wit (min′yo͞o it, -ə wit), *n.* **Peter.** See **Minuit, Peter.**

Min·ni (min′ē), *n., pl.* **-nis,** (*esp. collectively*) **-ni. 1.** an ancient people of Asia Minor. **2.** Mannai.

min·nie (min′ē), *n. Scot. and North Eng. Informal.* mother; mom. Also, **minny.** [pet var. of MITHER]

Min·nie (min′ē), *n.* a girl's given name.

min·nie·bush (min′ē bo͝osh′), *n.* a shrub, *Menziesia pilosa*, of the eastern U.S., having hairy leaves and bell-shaped, drooping, yellowish-white or pinkish flowers. [*minnie* (after Archibald *Menzies*, 1754–1842, Scottish botanist) + BUSH¹]

min·now (min′ō), *n., pl.* (*esp. referring to two or more kinds or species*) **-nows,** (*esp. collectively, Rare*) **-now** for 1, 2, 3. **1.** a small, European cyprinoid fish, *Phoxinus phoxinus*. **2.** any other fish of the family *Cyprinidae*, including the carps, goldfishes, daces, etc. **3.** any of various small, unrelated fishes. **4.** a person or thing that is comparatively small or insignificant. [ME *minwe*, OE **mynwe* (fem.), equiv. to *myne* (masc.); c. OHG *munewa* kind of fish]

min·ny (min′ē), *n., pl.* **-nies. 1.** *Dial.* minnow. **2.** *Scot. and North Eng.* minnie. [perh. **min* (OE *myne* minnow) + -Y²]

Mi·ño (mē′nyō), *n.* Spanish name of **Minho.**

Mi·no·an (mi nō′ən), *adj.* **1.** of or pertaining to the ancient civilization of the island of Crete, dating from about 3000 to 1100 B.C. —*n.* **2.** a native or inhabitant of ancient Crete. [MINO(S) + -AN]

mi·nor (mī′nər), *adj.* **1.** lesser, as in size, extent, or importance, or being or noting the lesser of two: *a minor share; minor faults.* **2.** not serious, important, dangerous, etc.: *a minor wound; a minor role in a play.* **3.** having low rank, status, position, etc.: *a minor official.* **4.** under legal age. **5.** (*cap.*) (of one of two male students in an English public school who have the same surname) being the younger or lower in standing: *Jackson Minor sits over here.* **6.** *Music.* **a.** of an interval) smaller by a chromatic half step than the corresponding major interval. **b.** (of a chord) having a minor third between the root and the note next above it. **7.** of or pertaining to the minority. **8.** *Educ.* of or pertaining to a field of study constituting a student's minor. —*n.* **9.** a person under legal age. **10.** a person of inferior rank or importance in a specified group, class, etc. **11.** *Educ.* **a.** a subject or a course of study pursued by a student, esp. a candidate for a degree, subordinately or supplementarily to a major or principal subject or course. **b.** a subject for which less credit than a major is granted in college or, occasionally, in high school. **12.** *Music.* a minor interval, chord, scale, etc. **13.** *Math.* the determinant of the matrix formed by crossing out the row and column containing a given element in a matrix. **14.** (*cap.*) See **Friar Minor. 15. the minors,** *Sports.* the minor leagues: *The pitcher spent three years in the minors before cracking the majors, in Baltimore.* —*v.i.* **16.** to follow a minor course of study: *He minored in Greek literature.* [ME < L: smaller, less; akin to Icel *minni* smaller, Goth *minniza* younger, Skt *mināti* lessens]
—**Syn. 1.** smaller, inferior, secondary, subordinate. **3.** petty, unimportant, small. **9.** child, adolescent.
—**Ant. 1.** major.

Mi·nor (mī′nər), *n.* a boy's given name. Also, **Miner.**

mi′nor ax′is, *Math.* the axis of an ellipse that is perpendicular to the major axis at a point equidistant from the foci.

Mi·nor·ca (mi nôr′kə), *n.* **1.** Spanish, **Menorca.** one of the Balearic Islands, in the W Mediterranean. 150,000. (est. 1964). 271 sq. mi. **2.** one of a Mediterranean breed of white-skinned chickens.

Mi·nor·can (mi nôr′kən), *adj.* **1.** of or pertaining to Minorca. —*n.* **2.** a native or inhabitant of Minorca. [MINORC(A) + -AN]

mi′nor can′on, a canon attached to a cathedral or collegiate church, though not necessarily a member of the chapter. Cf. **honorary canon.**

mi′nor coin′, a coin made of base metal. Cf. **subsidiary coin.**

mi′nor el′ement, 1. *Geol.* any chemical element found in small quantity in the rocks of the earth's crust. Cf. **major element. 2.** *Biochem.* See **trace element.**

Mi·nor·ite (mī′nə rīt′), *n.* See **Friar Minor.** [(*friars*) MINOR (< ML *frātrēs minōrēs*, lit., inferior brothers, a name emphasizing their humility); see -ITE¹]

mi·nor·i·ty (mi nôr′i tē, -nor′, -mī-), *n., pl.* **-ties,** *adj.* —*n.* **1.** the smaller part or number; a number, part, or amount forming less than half of the whole. **2.** a smaller party or group opposed to a majority, as in voting or other action. **3.** a group differing, esp. in race, religion, or ethnic background, from the majority of a population, esp. when the difference is obvious and causes or is likely to cause members to be treated unfairly. **4.** the state or period of being a minor or under legal age. —*adj.* **5.** of or pertaining to a minority or minorities. [< ML *minōritās*. See MINOR, -ITY]

minor′ity group′, minority (def. 3).

mi′nor key′, *Music.* a key or mode based on a minor scale.

mi′nor league′, *U.S.* any association of professional sports teams other than the acknowledged major leagues, esp. when the member teams are associated with or controlled by major-league teams which use them as training and proving teams for promising players. —**mi′nor-league′,** *adj.*

mi·nor-lea·guer (mī′nər lē′gər), *n.* **1.** a member of a minor-league team. **2.** a person whose skill or ability is suited only to a minor league or to a minor role in life. [MINOR LEAGUE + -ER¹]

mi′nor mode′, *Music.* **1.** See **minor scale. 2.** See **minor key.**

mi′nor or′der, *Rom. Cath. Ch.* the degree or grade of acolyte, exorcist, lector, or ostiary. Cf. **major order.**

mi′nor pen′alty, *Ice Hockey.* a penalty consisting of the removal of a player from play for two minutes, no substitute for the player being permitted. Cf. **major penalty.**

mi′nor piece′, *Chess.* a bishop or knight.

mi′nor plan′et, *Astron.* asteroid. (def. 1).

mi′nor prem′ise, *Logic.* See under **syllogism** (def. 1).

Mi′nor Proph′ets, Hosea, Joel, Amos, Obadiah, Jonah, Micah, Nahum, Habakkuk, Zephaniah, Haggai, Zechariah, and Malachi. Cf. **Major Prophets.**

mi′nor scale′, 1. Also called **harmonic minor scale.** a scale having half steps between the second and third, fifth and sixth, and seventh and eighth degrees, with whole steps for the other intervals. **2.** Also called **melodic minor scale.** a scale having the third degree lowered a half step when ascending, and the seventh, sixth, and third degrees lowered a half step when descending.

mi′nor sen′tence, *Gram.* any sentence that is not a true full sentence; a transformation by deletion from a full sentence.

mi′nor suit′, *Bridge.* diamonds or clubs. Cf. **major suit.**

mi′nor ten′ace, *Bridge, Whist.* the king and jack of a suit held by one player. Cf. **major tenace, tenace.**

mi′nor term′, *Logic.* See under **syllogism** (def. 1).

mi′nor tri′ad, *Music.* a triad consisting in root position of a root tone with a minor third and a perfect fifth above.

Mi·nos (mī′nəs, -nos), *n. Class. Myth.* a king of Crete, the son of Zeus and Europa and the husband of Pasiphaë: he ordered Daedalus to build the Labyrinth; after death, he was made a judge in Hades.

Mi·not (mī′nət), *n.* **1. George Rich·ards** (rich′ərdz), 1885–1950, U.S. physician: Nobel prize 1934. **2.** a city in N North Dakota. 30,604 (1960).

Min·o·taur (min′ə tôr′), *n.* **1.** *Class. Myth.* a monster, the offspring of Pasiphaë and the Cretan bull, that had the head of a bull on the body of a man: housed in the Cretan Labyrinth, it was fed on human flesh until Theseus, helped by Ariadne, killed it. **2.** any person or thing that devours or destroys. [< L *Mīnōtaur(us)* < Gk *Mīnṓtauros*, equiv. to *Mīnō(s)* MINOS + *taûros* bull]

Minsk (minsk; *Russ.* mēnsk), *n.* a city in and the capital of Byelorussia, in the W Soviet Union in Europe. 707,000 (1965).

min·ster (min′stər), *n. Chiefly Brit.* **1.** a church actually or originally connected with a monastic establishment. **2.** any large or important church, as a cathedral. [ME, OE *mynster* (c. G *Münster*) < VL **monister(ium)*, var. of L *monastērium* MONASTERY]

min·strel (min′strəl), *n.* **1.** one of a class of medieval musicians who sang or recited to the accompaniment of instruments. **2.** a musician, singer, or poet. **3.** one of a troupe of comedians, usually white men made up as Negroes, presenting songs, jokes, etc. [ME *ministrel* < OF < LL *ministeriāl(is)* servant (n. use of adj.); see MINISTERIAL]

min′strel show′, stage entertainment featuring comic dialogue, song, and dance in highly conventionalized patterns, performed by a troupe of actors in blackface comprising an interlocutor, two end men, and a chorus: developed in the U.S. in the early and mid-19th century.

min·strel·sy (min′strəl sē), *n.* **1.** the art or practice of a minstrel. **2.** minstrels' songs, ballads, etc.: *a collection of Scottish minstrelsy.* [ME *minstralcie* (cf. MF *menestralsie*). See MINSTREL, -CY]

mint¹ (mint), *n.* **1.** any aromatic, labiate herb of the genus *Mentha*, having opposite leaves and small, verticillate flowers, as the spearmint, peppermint, and horsemint. **2.** any plant of the mint family, *Labiatae*. **3.** a soft or hard confection, often shaped like a wafer, that is flavored with peppermint or other flavoring and sometimes served after lunch or dinner. **4.** any of various flavored hard candies packaged as a roll of small round wafers. —*adj.* **5.** made or flavored with mint: *mint tea.* [ME, OE *minte* (c. OHG *minza*) < L *ment(h)a* < Gk *mínthē*]

mint² (mint), *n.* **1.** a place where coins, paper currency, etc., are produced under government authority. **2.** a vast amount, esp. of money: *He made a mint in oil wells.* —*adj.* **3.** *Philately.* (of a stamp) as issued to the public, without having been used. **4.** unused or as if newly made and unused: *a book in mint condition.* —*v.t.* **5.** to make (coins, money, etc.) by stamping metal. **6.** to turn (metal) into coins: *to mint gold into sovereigns.* **7.** to make or fabricate as if by coining: *to mint words.* [ME *mynt*, OE *mynet* coin < L *monēta* coin, mint, after the temple of Juno *Monēta*, where Roman money was coined] —**mint′er,** *n.*

mint³ (mint), *Scot. and North Eng.* —*n.* **1.** intent; purpose. **2.** an attempt; try; effort. —*v.t.* **3.** to try (something); attempt. **4.** to take aim at (something) with a gun. **5.** to hit or strike at (someone or something). —*v.i.* **6.** to try; attempt. **7.** to take aim. [ME *minten*, OE (*ge*)*myntan* to intend; akin to MIND]

Min·ta (min′tə), *n.* a girl's given name.

mint·age (min′tij), *n.* **1.** the act or process of minting. **2.** the product or result of minting; coinage. **3.** the charge for or cost of minting or coining. **4.** the output of a mint. **5.** a stamp or character impressed. [MINT² + -AGE]

mint′ gera′nium, costmary.

Min·the (min′thē), *n. Class. Myth.* a nymph who was changed into a mint plant by Persephone to protect her from Hades. Also, **Menthe.**

mint′ ju′lep, a tall, frosted drink made with bourbon, sugar, and finely cracked ice and garnished with sprigs of mint.

mint′ sauce′, a sauce flavored with mint, often served with roast lamb.

mint·y (min′tē), *adj.,* **mint·i·er, mint·i·est.** having the flavor or aroma of mint. [MINT¹ + -Y¹]

min·ua·no (min wä′nō), *n., pl.* **-nos.** (in southern Brazil) a cold, southwest wind blowing from June to September. [after the *Minuanos*, an Indian tribe of Rio Grande]

Mi·nu·ci·us Fe·lix (mi no͞o′shē əs fē′liks, -shəs, -nyo͞o′-), **Marcus,** Roman writer of the 2nd century A.D. whose dialogue *Octavius* is the earliest known work of Latin-Christian literature.

min·u·end (min′yo͞o end′), *n. Arith.* a number from which another is subtracted. Cf. **subtrahend.** [< L *minuend(us)* (*numerus*) (the number) to be diminished or made smaller, (gerundive of *minuere*), equiv. to *minu-* (see MINUS) + *-endus* gerundive suffix]

min·u·et (min′yo͞o et′), *n.* **1.** a slow stately dance in triple meter, popular in the 17th and 18th centuries. **2.** a piece of music for such a dance or in its rhythm. [< F *menuet*, equiv. to *menu* small (see MENU) + *-et* -ET; so called from the shortness of the dancers' steps]

Min·u·it (min′yo͞o it), *n.* **Peter,** 1580–1638, Dutch colonial administrator in America: director general of the New Netherlands 1626–31. Also, **Minnewit.**

mi·nus (mī′nəs), *prep.* **1.** less by the subtraction of; decreased by: *ten minus six.* **2.** lacking or without: *a book minus its title page.* —*adj.* **3.** involving or noting subtraction. **4.** algebraically negative: *a minus quantity.* **5.** *Informal.* lacking or inferior; having negative or detracting qualities or characteristics. **6.** *Bot.* (in heterothallic fungi) designating, in the absence of morphological differentiation, one of the two strains of mycelia which must unite in the sexual process. —*n.* **7.** See **minus sign. 8.** a minus quantity. **9.** a deficiency or loss. [< L, neut. of *minor* less; see MINOR]

mi·nus·cule (min′ə skyo͞ol′, mi nus′kyo͞ol), *adj.* **1.** very small. **2.** (of letters or writing) small; not capital. **3.** written in such letters (opposed to *majuscule*). —*n.* **4.** a minuscule letter. **5.** a small cursive script developed in the 7th century A.D. from the uncial, which it afterward superseded. [< L *minuscul(us)* smallish. See MINUS, -CULE] —**mi·nus′cu·lar,** *adj.*

mi′nus sight′, *Survey.* a foresight used in leveling.

mi′nus sign′, *Arith.* the symbol (−) denoting subtraction or a negative quantity.

min·ute¹ (min′it), *n., v.,* **-ut·ed, -ut·ing,** *adj.* —*n.* **1.** the sixtieth part of an hour; sixty seconds. **2.** an indefinitely short space of time: *Wait a minute!* **3.** a point of time; instant; moment: *Come here this minute!* **4.** a

rough draft, as of a document. **5.** *Chiefly Brit.* a written summary, note, or memorandum. **6. minutes,** the official record of the proceedings at a meeting of a society, committee, or other group. **7.** *Geom.* the sixtieth part of a degree, often represented by the sign (′): *12°10′ is read as twelve degrees and ten minutes.* **8. minutes,** *Archit.* See under **diameter** (def. 5). **9. up to the minute,** modern; up-to-date: *This military installation is up to the minute.* —*v.t.* **10.** to time exactly, as movements, speed, etc. **11.** to make a draft of (a document or the like). **12.** to record in a memorandum; note down. **13.** to enter in the minutes of a society or other body. —*adj.* **14.** prepared in a very short time: *minute pudding.* [ME < ML *minūta,* n. use of fem. of *minūtus* MINUTE²]
—**Syn. 2.** jiffy, second. MINUTE, INSTANT, MOMENT refer to infinitesimal amounts of time. A MINUTE, properly denoting 60 seconds, is often used loosely for any very short space of time (and may be interchangeable with *second*): *just a minute.* An INSTANT is practically a point in time, with no duration, though it is also used to mean a perceptible amount of time: *not an instant's delay.* MOMENT denotes much the same as INSTANT, though with a somewhat greater sense of duration (but somewhat less than MINUTE): *It will take a moment.*

mi·nute² (mī no͞ot′, -nyo͞ot′, mi-), *adj.* **-nut·er, -nut·est. 1.** extremely small, as in size, amount, extent, or degree: *minute differences.* **2.** of minor importance; insignificant; trifling. **3.** attentive to or concerned with small details: *a minute examination.* [ME < L *minūt(us)* lessened, made smaller, hence, small (ptp. of *minuere*), equiv. to *minū-* (ptp. s.) + *-tus* ptp. suffix. See MINUS, MINOR] —**mi·nute′ness,** *n.*
—**Syn. 1.** tiny, infinitesimal, minuscule. See **little. 3.** detailed, exact, precise. —**Ant. 1.** large. **3.** rough, general.

min′ute gun′ (min′it), a cannon fired at intervals of a minute, esp. as a warning of distress or in a military funeral ceremony.

min′ute hand′ (min′it), the hand that indicates the minutes on a clock or watch.

min·ute·ly¹ (min′it lē), *adj.* **1.** occurring every minute. —*adv.* **2.** every minute; minute by minute. [MINUTE¹ + -LY]

mi·nute·ly² (mī no͞ot′lē, -nyo͞ot′-, mi-), *adv.* in a minute manner, form, or degree; in minute detail. [MINUTE² + -LY]

Min·ute·man (min′it man′), *n., pl.* **-men. 1.** (*sometimes l.c.*) one of a group of American militiamen just before and during the Revolutionary War who held themselves in readiness for instant military service. **2.** *U.S.* an intercontinental ballistic missile with three stages, powered by solid-propellant rocket engines. **3.** a member of a small, secret, ultraconservative organization formed into armed groups for the declared purpose of conducting guerrilla warfare against a communist invasion of the U.S. [MINUTE¹ + MAN¹]

min′ute steak′ (min′it), a thin piece of beefsteak that can be cooked quickly.

mi·nu·ti·a (mi no͞o′shē ə, -shə, -nyo͞o′-), *n., pl.* **-ti·ae** (-shē ē′). Usually, **minutiae.** small or trivial details; trifling circumstances or matters: *a thorough knowledge of the minutiae of his craft; an attorney who learns the minutiae of each case.* [< L: smallness, equiv. to *minūt(us)* MINUTE² + *-ia* -IA] —**mi·nu′ti·al,** *adj.*

minx (mingks), *n.* a pert, impudent, or flirtatious girl. [? < LG *minsk* man, impudent woman; c. G *Mensch;* see MANNISH] —**minx′ish,** *adj.*

Mi·ny·a·des (mə nī′ə dēz′), *n.pl.* *Class. Myth.* the daughters of Minyas who were driven mad by Dionysus as a punishment for refusing to take part in his revels.

min·yan (min yän′; *Eng.* min′yən), *n., pl.* **min·yan·im** (min′yə nēm′), *Eng.* **min·yans.** *Hebrew.* **1.** the number required to be present to enable the lawful conduct of a public Jewish service, being a minimum of 10 Jewish males over 13 years of age. **2.** such a group. [lit., number, reckoning]

Min·yans (min′yənz), *n.pl.* *Class. Myth.* the descendants of Minyas who inhabited Orchomenus in Boeotia and Iolcus in Thessaly. Also, **Min·yae** (min′yē).

Min·y·as (min′ē əs), *n.* *Class. Myth.* a king of Orchomenus, famed for his wealth.

Mi·o·cene (mī′ə sēn′), *Geol.* —*adj.* **1.** noting or pertaining to an epoch either of the Tertiary or Neogene period, occurring from 10 million to 25 million years ago and characterized by the presence of grazing mammals. See table under **era.** —*n.* **2.** the Miocene epoch or series. [*mio-* (< Gk *meîon* less) + -CENE]

Miöl·nir (myœl′nir), *n.* *Scand. Myth.* the hammer of Thor. Also, **Mioll′nir, Mjölnir, Mjöllnir, Mjolnir.** [< Icel; akin to Russ *molniya* lightning]

mi·o·sis (mī ō′sis), *n., pl.* **-ses** (-sēz). **1.** Also, **myosis.** *Med.* excessive constriction of the pupil of the eye, as a result of drugs, disease, or the like. Cf. **mydriasis. 2.** *Biol.* meiosis (def. 1). [var. of *myosis* < Gk *my(ein)* (to) shut (the eyes) + *-ōsis* -OSIS]

mi·ot·ic (mī ot′ik), *adj.* **1.** pertaining to or producing miosis. —*n.* **2.** a miotic drug. Also, **myotic.** [< NL; see MIOSIS, -TIC]

MIP, See **monthly investment plan.**

Mi·phib·o·seth (mi fib′ə seth′), *n.* *Douay Bible.* Mephibosheth.

miq·ue·let (mik′ə let′), *n.* **1.** (in the Peninsular War) a Spanish guerrilla who fought against the French. **2.** a soldier in any of several Spanish infantry regiments. **3.** a flintlock of a type developed in Spain. Also, **miguelet.** [< Catalan, equiv. to *Miquel* Michael + *-et* -ET]

Miq·ue·lon (mik′ə lon′; *Fr.* mēkə lôN′), *n.* See **St. Pierre and Miquelon.**

mir (mēr), *n., pl.* **mi·ri** (mē′rī). *Russian.* a Russian village commune. [lit., world, peace]

MIr., Middle Irish. Also, **M.Ir.**

Mi·ra (mī′rə), *n.* **1.** *Astron.* a bright variable star in the constellation Cetus, having an average period of 330 days: the first known variable star. **2.** Also, **Myra.** a girl's given name.

Mir·a·beau (mir′ə bō′; *Fr.* mē ra bō′), *n.* **Ho·no·ré Ga·bri·el Vic·tor Ri·que·ti** (ô nō rā′ ga brē el′ vēk tôr′ rēkə tē′), **Count de,** 1749–91, French Revolutionary statesman and orator.

mir·a·belle (mir′ə bel′, mir′ə bel′), *n.* a dry, white plum brandy from Alsace. [< F; MF *mirabolan* MYROBALAN by folk etym.]

mi·ra·bi·le dic·tu (mē rä′bi le′ dik′to͞o; *Eng.* mi rab′ə lē dik′to͞o, -tyo͞o), *Latin.* strange to say; marvelous to relate.

mi·ra·bi·li·a (mē′rä bil′i ä′; *Eng.* mir′ə bil′ē ə), *n.pl.* *Latin.* marvels; miracles. [lit., things to be wondered at]

mi·rab·i·lite (mi rab′ə līt′), *n.* a naturally occurring decahydrate form of sodium sulfate, $Na_2SO_4 \cdot 10H_2O$. Cf. **Glauber's salt.** [<(*sal*) *mirābil(is)* wonderful (salt) + *-ite*¹]

mi·ra·cid·i·um (mī′rə sid′ē əm), *n., pl.* **-cid·i·a** (-sid′ē ə). the larva that hatches from the egg of a trematode worm or fluke. [< NL < Gk *meirakídion* a youth, equiv. to *meirak-* (s. of *meirax*) boy, girl + *-idion* dim. suffix] —**mi′ra·cid′i·al,** *adj.*

mir·a·cle (mir′ə kəl), *n.* **1.** an effect or extraordinary event in the physical world which surpasses all known human or natural powers and is ascribed to a supernatural cause. **2.** such an effect or event manifesting or considered as a work of God. **3.** a wonder; marvel. **4.** a wonderful or surpassing example of some quality: *This machine is a miracle of efficiency.* **5.** See **miracle play.** [ME; late OE *miracul* < L *mīrācul(um),* equiv. to *mīrā(rī)* (to) wonder at + *-culum* -CLE]

mir′acle drug′. See **wonder drug.**

mir′acle man′, 1. a person who claims or is alleged to perform miracles. **2.** a person who performs or is capable of performing exceptional deeds, as from skill, talent, etc.: *a miracle man on skis.*

Miracle of St. Mark, The, a painting (1548) by Tintoretto.

mir′acle play′, a medieval dramatic form dealing with religious subjects such as Biblical stories or saints' lives, usually presented in a series or cycle by the craft guilds. Cf. **morality play, mystery play.**

mi·rac·u·lous (mi rak′yə ləs), *adj.* **1.** performed by or involving a supernatural power or agency: *a miraculous cure.* **2.** of the nature of a miracle; marvelous. **3.** having the power to work marvelous, outstanding, or unusual effects: *miraculous drugs.* [< ML *mīrāculōs(us),* equiv. to L *mīrācul(um)* MIRACLE + *-ōsus* -OUS] —**mi·rac′u·lous·ly,** *adv.* —**mi·rac′u·lous·ness,** *n.*
—**Syn. 2.** wonderful, extraordinary. MIRACULOUS, PRETERNATURAL, SUPERNATURAL refer to that which seems to transcend the laws of nature. MIRACULOUS usually refers to an individual event which apparently contravenes known laws governing the universe: *a miraculous answer; a miraculous success.* PRETERNATURAL suggests the possession of supernormal gifts or qualities: *Dogs have a preternatural sense of smell. Bats have a sense of hearing that is preternatural.* SUPERNATURAL suggests divine or superhuman properties: *supernatural aid in battle.* —**Ant. 1.** prosaic, commonplace. **2.** natural.

mir·a·dor (mir′ə dōr′, -dôr′), *n.* (in Spanish-speaking countries) any architectural feature, as a loggia, balcony, or oriel, affording a view of a landscape. [< Sp < Catalan, equiv. to *mira(r)* (to) look at (< L *mīrārī* to wonder at) + *-dor* agent suffix (< L *-tor*)]

Mi·ra·flo·res (mir′ə flōr′əs, -flôr′-; *Sp.* mē′rä flô′res), *n.pl.* the locks of the Panama Canal, near the Pacific entrance.

mi·rage (mi räzh′), *n.* **1.** an optical phenomenon by which reflected images of distant objects are seen, often inverted, caused when the air close to the ground is more dense than the air above. **2.** something illusory, without substance, or without a base in reality. [< F, equiv. to *(se) mir(er)* (to) look at (oneself), be reflected (< L *mīrārī* to wonder at) + *-age* -AGE]

Mi·raj (mēr′äj), *n.* *Islam.* a miraculous journey said to have been made by Muhammad from Mecca to Jerusalem, thence to heaven, and back again to Mecca. [< Ar]

Mi·ra Lo·ma (mēr′ə lō′mə), a town in S California. 3982 (1960).

Mir·a·mar (mir′ə mär′), *n.* a town in SE Florida. 5485 (1960).

Mi·ran·da (mi ran′də; *Sp.* mē rän′dä), *n.* **1. Fran·cis·co de** (fRän sēs′kô the), 1750–1816, Venezuelan revolutionist and patriot. **2.** *Astron.* one of the five satellites of Uranus. **3.** daughter of Prospero in Shakespeare's *The Tempest.* **4.** a girl's given name.

mire (mīər), *n., v.,* **mired, mir·ing.** —*n.* **1.** a section of wet, swampy ground; bog; marsh. **2.** ground of this kind, as wet, slimy soil of some depth, deep mud, etc. —*v.t.* **3.** to plunge and fix in mire; cause to stick fast in mire. **4.** to involve in difficulties. **5.** to soil with mire or filth; bespatter with mire. —*v.i.* **6.** to sink in mire or mud; stick. [ME < Scand; cf. Icel *mýrr* bog, c. OE *mēos* moss]

mire·poix (mir pwä′), *n.* **1.** a flavoring made from diced vegetables, seasonings, herbs, and sometimes meat, often placed in a pan to cook with meat or fish. **2.** finely chopped vegetables, as onions and carrots, sometimes with meat, often used as a bed for meat that is to be braised. Also, **mire·pois′.** [< F; said to have been named after C. P. G. F. de Lévis, duke of *Mirepoix,* 18th-century French diplomat]

Mir·i·am (mir′ē əm), *n.* **1.** Also, *Douay Bible,* **Mary.** the sister of Moses and Aaron. Num. 26:59. **2.** Also, **Miryam.** a girl's given name.

Mir·jam (mûr′jəm), *n.* a girl's given name.

mirk (mûrk), *n., adj.* murk.

mirk·y (mûr′kē), *adj.,* **mirk·i·er, mirk·i·est.** murky.

mir·li·ton (mûr′li ton′; *Fr.* mēr lē tôN′), *n., pl.* **mir·li·tons** (*Fr.* mēr lē tôN′). **1.** kazoo. **2.** chayote. [< F: lit., reed-pipe]

Mi·ró (mē rō′; *Sp.* mē rô′), *n.* **1. Ga·bri·el** (gä′bRē el′), 1879–1930, Spanish novelist, short-story writer, and essayist. **2. Jo·an** (hō än′), born 1893, Spanish painter.

mir·ror (mir′ər), *n.* **1.** a reflecting surface, originally of polished metal but now usually of glass with a silvery, metallic, or amalgam backing. **2.** such a surface set into a frame, attached to a handle, etc., for use in viewing oneself, as an ornament, etc. **3.** any reflecting surface, as the surface of calm water under certain lighting conditions. **4.** *Optics.* a surface that is either plane, concave, or convex and that reflects rays of light. **5.** something that gives a faithful representation, image, or idea of something else: *Gershwin's music was a mirror of the time.* **6.** a pattern for imitation; exemplar: *a man who was the mirror of fashion.* **7.** a glass, crystal, or the like, used by magicians, diviners, etc. —*v.t.* **8.** to reflect in or as in a mirror. **9.** to reflect as a mirror does. **10.** to be or give a faithful representation, image, or idea of: *Her views on politics mirror mine completely.* —*adj.* **11.** *Music.* (of a canon or fugue) capable of being played in retrograde or in inversion, as though read in a mirror placed beside or below the music. [ME *mirour* < OF *mireo(u)r,* equiv. to *mir-* (see MIRAGE) + *-eo(u)r* < L *-ātor;* see -OR²] —**mir′ror-like′,** *adj.*

mir′ror im′age, 1. an image of an object, plan, person, etc., as it would appear if viewed in a mirror, with right and left reversed. **2.** an object having a spatial arrangement that corresponds to that of another object except that the right-to-left sense on one object corresponds to the left-to-right sense on the other. **3.** a real or apparent arrangement of the parts of something such that it resembles a mirror reflection of the arrangement of similar parts in another thing. Also called **perverted image.**

mir·ror-writ·ing (mir′ər rī′ting), *n.* backward writing that resembles a mirror image of ordinary script.

mirth (mûrth), *n.* **1.** rejoicing; gaiety; jollity: *the excitement and mirth of the holiday season.* **2.** amusement or laughter: *He was unable to conceal his mirth.* [ME *mirthe,* OE *myrigth.* See MERRY, -TH¹]
—**Syn. 1, 2.** MIRTH, GLEE, HILARITY, MERRIMENT, JOLLITY, JOVIALITY refer to the gaiety characterizing people who are enjoying the companionship of others. MIRTH suggests spontaneous amusement or gaiety, manifested briefly in laughter: *uncontrolled outbursts of mirth.* GLEE suggests an effervescence of high spirits or exultation, often manifested in playful or ecstatic gestures; it may apply also to a malicious rejoicing over mishaps to others: *glee over the failure of a rival.* HILARITY implies noisy and boisterous mirth, often exceeding the limits of reason or propriety: *hilarity aroused by practical jokes.* MERRIMENT suggests fun, good spirits, and good nature rather than the kind of wit and sometimes artificial funmaking which cause hilarity: *The house resounded with music and sounds of merriment.* JOLLITY and JOVIALITY may refer either to a general atmosphere of mirthful festivity or to the corresponding traits of individuals. JOLLITY implies an atmosphere of easy and convivial gaiety, a more hearty merriment or a less boisterous hilarity: *The holiday was a time of jollity.* JOVIALITY implies a more masculine merriment generated by people who are hearty, generous, benevolent, and high-spirited: *the joviality of warm-hearted friends.* —**Ant. 1.** gloom.

mirth·ful (mûrth′fəl), *adj.* **1.** joyous; gay; jolly: *a mirthful laugh.* **2.** providing mirth; amusing: *a mirthful experience.* [ME; see MIRTH, -FUL] —**mirth′ful·ly,** *adv.* —**mirth′ful·ness,** *n.*

mirth·less (mûrth′lis), *adj.* without mirth; joyless; gloomy. [ME *myrtheles.* See MIRTH, -LESS] —**mirth′less·ly,** *adv.* —**mirth′less·ness,** *n.*

mir·y (mīər′ē), *adj.,* **mir·i·er, mir·i·est. 1.** of the nature of mire; swampy: *miry ground.* **2.** abounding in mire; muddy. **3.** covered or bespattered with mire. **4.** dirty; filthy. [ME; see MIRE, -Y¹] —**mir′i·ness,** *n.*

Mir·yam (mir′yəm), *n.* a girl's given name. Also, **Miriam.**

mir·za (mûr′zə; *Pers.* mēr′zä′), *n.* (in Persia, or Iran) **1.** a royal prince (placed after the name when used as a title). **2.** (a title of honor for men, prefixed to the name). [< Pers]

mis-¹, a prefix applied to various parts of speech, meaning "ill," "mistaken," "wrong," or simply negating: *mistrial; misprint; mistrust.* [ME; OE *mis(se)-;* c. G *miss-,* Goth *missa-* (see MISS¹); often r. ME *mes-* < OF < WGmc *mis(s)-*]

mis-², var. of **miso-** before some vowels: *misanthrope.*

M.I.S., Master of International Service.

mis·ad·dress (mis′ə dres′), *v.t.,* **-dressed** or **-drest, -dress·ing.** to address improperly or incorrectly: *to misaddress an instructor as professor.* [MIS-¹ + ADDRESS]

mis·ad·ven·ture (mis′əd ven′chər), *n.* **1.** an instance of bad fortune; mishap. **2.** bad fortune. [MIS-¹ + ADVENTURE; r. ME *mesaventure* < OF]
—**Syn. 1.** mischance, accident; disaster, calamity, catastrophe. **2.** misfortune. —**Ant. 2.** luck, fortune.

mis·ad·vise (mis′əd vīz′), *v.t.,* **-vised, -vis·ing.** to give bad or inappropriate advice to. [MIS-¹ + ADVISE] —**mis·ad·vice** (mis′əd vīs′), *n.*

mis·al·li·ance (mis′ə lī′əns), *n.* an improper alliance or association, esp. in marriage; mésalliance. [MIS-¹ + ALLIANCE, modeled on F *mésalliance*]

mis·al·ly (mis′ə lī′), *v.t.,* **-lied, -ly·ing.** to ally improperly or unsuitably. [MIS-¹ + ALLY]

mis·an·thrope (mis′ən thrōp′, miz′-), *n.* a hater of mankind. Also, **mis·an·thro·pist** (mis an′thrə pist, miz-). [< Gk *misánthrōp(os)* hating mankind, misanthropic. See MIS-², ANTHROPO-]

Mi·san·thrope, Le (*Fr.* lə mē zäN trôp′). See **Le Misanthrope.**

mis·an·throp·ic (mis′ən throp′ik, miz′-), *adj.* **1.** of, pertaining to, or characteristic of a misanthrope. **2.** resembling a misanthrope. Also, **mis′an·throp′i·cal.** [MISANTHROPE + -IC] —**mis′an·throp′i·cal·ly,** *adv.*

mis·an·thro·py (mis an′thrə pē, miz-), *n.* hatred, dislike, or distrust of mankind. [< Gk *mīsanthrōpía.* See MISANTHROPE, -Y³]

mis·ap·plied (mis′ə plīd′), *adj.* mistakenly applied; used wrongly. [MIS-¹ + APPLIED]

mis·ap·ply (mis′ə plī′), *v.t.,* **-plied, -ply·ing.** to make a wrong application or use of. [MIS-¹ + APPLY] —**mis′ap·pli′er,** *n.*

mis′ac·cused′, *adj.*
mis·act′, *v.i.*
mis′ad·apt′, *v.*
mis′ad·ap·ta′tion, *n.*
mis·add′, *v.*
mis′ad·ju′di·cat′ed, *adj.*
mis′ad·just′, *v.*
mis′ad·just′ed, *adj.*
mis′ad·just′ment, *n.*
mis′ad·min′is·tra′tion, *n.*
mis·aim′, *v., n.*
mis′a·lign′ment, *n.*
mis′al·le·ga′tion, *n.*
mis′al·lege′, *v.t.,* **-leged, -leg·ing.**
mis′al·lot′, *v.t.,* **-lot·ted, -lot·ting.**
mis′al·lot′ment, *n.*
mis·al′pha·bet·ize′, *v.t.,* **-ized, -iz·ing.**
mis′a·nal′y·sis, *n.*
mis·an′a·lyze′, *v.t.,* **-lyzed, -lyz·ing.**
mis′ap·pel·la′tion, *n.*
mis′ap·pend′ed, *adj.*

mis·ap·pre·hend (mis′ap ri hend′), *v.t.* to misunderstand. [MIS-[1] + APPREHEND] —**mis′ap·pre·hend′ing·ly,** *adv.*

mis·ap·pre·hen·sion (mis′ap ri hen′shən), *n.* misunderstanding. [MIS-[1] + APPREHENSION] —**mis′ap·pre·hen′sive,** *adj.* —**mis′ap·pre·hen′sive·ly,** *adv.* —**mis′ap·pre·hen′sive·ness,** *n.*

mis·ap·pro·pri·ate (mis′ə prō′prē āt′), *v.t.,* **-at·ed, -at·ing.** 1. to put to a wrong use. 2. to apply wrongfully or dishonestly, as funds entrusted to one's care. [MIS-[1] + APPROPRIATE] —**mis′ap·pro′pri·a′tion,** *n.*

mis·ar·range (mis′ə rānj′), *v.t.,* **-ranged, -rang·ing.** to arrange incorrectly or improperly: *to misarrange a file.* [MIS-[1] + ARRANGE] —**mis′ar·range′ment,** *n.*

mis·be·come (mis′bi kum′), *v.t.,* **-came, -come, -com·ing.** to be unsuitable, unbecoming, or unfit for. [MIS-[1] + BECOME]

mis·be·got·ten (mis′bi got′ən), *adj.* unlawfully or irregularly begotten; illegitimate. Also, **mis′be·got′.** [MIS-[1] + BEGOTTEN]

mis·be·have (mis′bi hāv′), *v.,* **-haved, -hav·ing.** —*v.i.* 1. to behave badly or improperly: *The children misbehaved during our visit.* —*v.t.* 2. to conduct (oneself) without regard for good manners or accepted moral standards (usually used reflexively): *Several of the guests reportedly misbehaved themselves.* [late ME; see MIS-[1], BEHAVE] —**mis′be·hav′er,** *n.*

mis·be·ha·vior (mis′bi hāv′yər), *n.* improper, inappropriate, or bad behavior. Also, *esp. Brit.,* **mis′be·hav′iour.** [ME; see MIS-[1], BEHAVIOR]

mis·be·lief (mis′bi lēf′), *n.* 1. erroneous belief; false opinion. 2. erroneous or unorthodox religious belief. [ME; see MIS-[1], BELIEF]

mis·be·lieve (mis′bi lēv′), *v.,* **-lieved, -liev·ing.** *Obs.* —*v.i.* 1. to believe wrongly; hold an erroneous belief. —*v.t.* 2. to disbelieve; doubt. [ME; see MIS-[1], BELIEVE] —**mis′be·liev′er,** *n.* —**mis′be·liev′ing·ly,** *adv.*

mis·be·stow (mis′bi stō′), *v.t.* to bestow mistakenly or improperly: *to misbestow one's affections.* [MIS-[1] + BESTOW]

mis·brand (mis brand′), *v.t.* 1. to brand or label erroneously. 2. to brand with a simulated trademark or trade name. [MIS-[1] + BRAND]

misc., 1. miscellaneous. 2. miscellany.

mis·cal·cu·late (mis kal′kyə lāt′), *v.t., v.i.,* **-lat·ed, -lat·ing.** to calculate or judge incorrectly: *to miscalculate the time required for a job.* [MIS-[1] + CALCULATE] —**mis′cal·cu·la′tion,** *n.* —**mis·cal′cu·la′tor,** *n.*

mis·call (mis kôl′), *v.t.* to call by a wrong name. [ME; see MIS-[1], CALL] —**mis·call′er,** *n.*

mis·car·riage (mis kar′ij), *n.* 1. failure to attain the just, right, or desired result: *a miscarriage of justice.* 2. failure of something sent, as a letter, to reach its destination. 3. the expulsion of a fetus before it is viable, esp. between the third and seventh months of pregnancy; abortion. 4. *Chiefly Brit.* transportation of goods not in accordance with the contract of shipment. [MIS-[1] + CARRIAGE]

mis·car·ry (mis kar′ē), *v.i.,* **-ried, -ry·ing.** 1. to fail to attain the right or desired end; be unsuccessful: *The plan miscarried.* 2. to go astray or be lost in transit, as a letter. 3. to have a miscarriage of a fetus. [ME *miscarien.* See MIS-[1], CARRY]

mis·cast (mis kast′, -käst′), *v.t.,* **-cast, -cast·ing.** 1. to select unsuitable actors for (a play, motion picture, or the like). 2. to allot a role to (an unsuitable actor). 3. to allot (a role) to an unsuitable actor. [MIS-[1] + CAST[1]]

Misc. Doc., miscellaneous document.

mis·ce (mis′ē, mēs), *v.* (in prescriptions) mix. [< L]

mis·ce·ge·na·tion (mis′i jə nā′shən, mi sej′ə-), *n.* 1. marriage or cohabitation between a man and woman of different races, esp., in the U.S., between a Negro and a white person. 2. interbreeding between members of different races. 3. the mixing or a mixture of races by interbreeding. [< L *misc(ēre)* (to) mix + *gen(us)* race, stock, species + -ATION] —**mis·ce·ge·net·ic** (mis′i jə net′ik, mi sej′ə-), *adj.*

mis·cel·la·ne·a (mis′ə lā′nē ə), *n.pl.* miscellaneous writings, papers, or objects. [< L: hash, hodge-podge, n. use of neut. pl. of *miscellāneus* MISCELLANEOUS]

mis·cel·la·ne·ous (mis′ə lā′nē əs), *adj.* 1. consisting of members or elements of different kinds: *a book of miscellaneous articles and essays.* 2. of mixed character: *a miscellaneous library; a miscellaneous house.* 3. having various qualities or aspects; dealing with various subjects: *a miscellaneous discussion.* [< L *miscellāneus* mixed, of all sorts, equiv. to *miscell(us)* mixed + *-āneus* -ANEOUS] —**mis·cel·la·ne·i·ty** (mis′ə lə nē′i tē), *n.* —**mis′cel·la′ne·ous·ly,** *adv.* —**mis′cel·la′ne·ous·ness,** *n.*
—**Syn.** 1. divers, varied. MISCELLANEOUS, INDISCRIMINATE, PROMISCUOUS refer to mixture and lack of order, and may imply lack of discernment or taste. MISCELLANEOUS emphasizes the idea of the mixture of things of different kinds or natures: *a miscellaneous assortment of furniture.* INDISCRIMINATE emphasizes lack of discrimination in choice (and consequent confusion): *indiscriminate praise.* PROMISCUOUS is even stronger than INDISCRIMINATE in its emphasis of complete absence of discrimination: *promiscuous in his friendships.* 2. heterogeneous, diversified.

mis·cel·la·ny (mis′ə lā′nē; *Brit.* mi sel′ə nē), *n., pl.* **-nies.** 1. a miscellaneous collection or group of various or unselected items. 2. a miscellaneous collection of literary compositions or pieces by several authors, dealing with various topics, assembled in a volume or book. 3. **miscellanies,** a miscellaneous collection of articles or entries, as in a book. [Anglicized var. of MISCELLANEA]

Mi·scha (mē′shə, mish′ə), *n.* a boy's given name, Russian form of **Michael.**

mis·chance (mis chans′, -chäns′), *n.* a mishap or misfortune. [MIS-[1] + CHANCE; r. ME *mescheance* < OF]

mis·chan·ter (mis chan′tər, mi shan′-), *n.* *Scot. and North Eng.* mishanter.

mis·chief (mis′chif), *n.* 1. harm or trouble, esp. as a result of an agent or cause. 2. an injury caused by a person or other agent, or an evil due to some cause. 3. a cause or source of harm, evil, or annoyance. 4. a vexatious or annoying action. 5. a tendency or disposition to tease, vex, or annoy. 6. conduct that playfully causes petty annoyance. 7. *Informal.* the devil. [ME *meschef* < OF, back formation from *meschever* to end badly, come to grief. See MIS-[1], ACHIEVE]
—**Syn.** 1. hurt. See **damage.** —**Ant.** 1. advantage.

mis·chief-mak·er (mis′chif mā′kər), *n.* a person who makes mischief; one who stirs up discord, as by talebearing. —**mis′chief-mak′ing,** *adj., n.*

mis·chie·vous (mis′chə vəs), *adj.* 1. harmful or injurious. 2. maliciously or playfully annoying, as persons, actions, etc. 3. fond of mischief, as children. 4. roguishly or slyly teasing, as a glance. [ME *mischevous* < AF *meschevous.* See MISCHIEF, -OUS] —**mis′chie·vous·ly,** *adv.* —**mis′chie·vous·ness,** *n.*

misch′ met′al (mish), an alloy composed mainly of rare earth elements in metallic form, the largest constituent being cerium. [< G *Mischmetall,* equiv. to *misch(en)* (to) MIX + *Metall* METAL]

mis·choose (mis chōōz′), *v.,* **-chose; -cho·sen** or (*Obs.*) **-chose; -choos·ing.** —*v.i.* 1. to make a wrong or improper choice. —*v.t.* 2. to choose wrongly or improperly. [MIS-[1] + CHOOSE; r. ME *mischesen*]

mis·ci·ble (mis′ə bəl), *adj.* capable of being mixed: *miscible ingredients.* [< L *misc(ēre)* (to) mix, mingle + -IBLE] —**mis′ci·bil′i·ty,** *n.*

mis·cite (mis sīt′), *v.t., v.i.,* **-cit·ed, -cit·ing.** to misquote. [MIS-[1] + CITE] —**mis′ci·ta′tion,** *n.*

mis·col·or (mis kul′ər), *v.t.* 1. to give a wrong color to. 2. to misrepresent: *She miscolored the facts.* [MIS-[1] + COLOR]

mis·con·ceive (mis′kən sēv′), *v.t., v.i.,* **-ceived, -ceiv·ing.** to conceive wrongly; misunderstand. [ME; see MIS-[1], CONCEIVE] —**mis′con·ceiv′er,** *n.*

mis·con·cep·tion (mis′kən sep′shən), *n.* an erroneous conception; mistaken notion. [MIS-[1] + CONCEPTION]

mis·con·duct (*n.* mis kon′dukt; *v.* mis′kən dukt′), *n.* 1. improper conduct; wrong behavior. 2. unlawful conduct by an official in regard to his office, or by a person in the administration of justice, such as a lawyer, witness, or juror. —*v.t.* 3. to mismanage. 4. to misbehave (oneself). [MIS-[1] + CONDUCT]

mis·con·struc·tion (mis′kən struk′shən), *n.* 1. wrong construction; misinterpretation: *to put a misconstruction upon an action.* 2. the act or an instance of misconstruing. [MIS-[1] + CONSTRUCTION]

mis·con·strue (mis′kən strōō′ *or, esp. Brit.,* mis kon′strōō), *v.t.,* **-strued, -stru·ing.** to misunderstand the meaning of; take in a wrong sense; misinterpret. [ME; see MIS-[1], CONSTRUE]
—**Syn.** misread, misapprehend, misjudge.

mis·cop·y (mis kop′ē), *v.,* **-cop·ied, -cop·y·ing,** *n., pl.* **-cop·ies.** —*v.t.* 1. to copy incorrectly: *to miscopy an address from the telephone directory.* —*n.* 2. an incorrect copy of something. [MIS-[1] + COPY]

mis·coun·sel (mis koun′səl), *v.t.,* **-seled, -sel·ing** or (*esp. Brit.*) **-selled, -sel·ling.** to advise wrongly. [ME; see MIS-[1], COUNSEL]

mis·count (mis kount′), *v.t., v.i.* 1. to count or calculate erroneously. —*n.* 2. an erroneous counting or miscalculation. [MIS-[1] + COUNT[1]; r. ME *mesconten* < MF *mesconter*]

mis·cre·ance (mis′krē əns), *n.* a wrong belief, misbelief, or false religious faith. [ME < MF *mescreance,* equiv. to *mes-* MIS-[1] + *creance* < VL **crēdentia* CREDENCE]

mis·cre·an·cy (mis′krē ən sē), *n.* 1. the state or condition of a miscreant; villainy. 2. *Archaic.* miscreance. [MISCREAN(T) + -CY]

mis·cre·ant (mis′krē ənt), *adj.* 1. depraved, villainous, or base. 2. misbelieving; holding a false or unorthodox religious belief. —*n.* 3. a vicious person; villain. 4. a misbelieving person, as a heretic or an infidel. [ME < MF *mescreant* unbelieving, equiv. to *mes-* MIS-[1] + *creant* < L *crēdent-* CREDENT]

mis·cre·ate (*v.* mis′krē āt′; *adj.* mis′krē it, -āt′), *v.,* **-at·ed, -at·ing,** *adj. Rare.* —*v.t., v.i.* 1. to create amiss or deformed. —*adj.* 2. miscreated. [MIS-[1] + CREATE] —**mis′cre·a′tion,** *n.* —**mis′cre·a′tive,** *adj.* —**mis′cre·a′tor,** *n.*

mis·cre·at·ed (mis′krē ā′tid), *adj.* wrongly created; misshapen; monstrous. [MIS-[1] + CREATED]

mis·cue[1] (mis kyōō′), *n., v.,* **-cued, -cu·ing.** —*n.* 1. *Sports.* a failure to execute a play, stroke, or maneuver properly; an error. —*v.i.* 2. to make a miscue. 3. *Theat.* to fail to answer one's cue or to answer another's cue. 4. *Baseball Slang.* to make an error. [MIS-[1] + CUE[1]]

mis·cue[2] (mis kyōō′), *n., v.,* **-cued, -cu·ing.** *Billiards, Pool.* —*n.* 1. a stroke in which the cue fails to make solid contact with the cue ball. —*v.i.* 2. to make a miscue. [MIS-[1] + CUE[2]]

mis·date (mis dāt′), *v.,* **-dat·ed, -dat·ing,** *n.* —*v.t.* 1. to assign or affix a wrong date to. —*n.* 2. a wrong date. [MIS-[1] + DATE[1]]

mis·deal (mis dēl′), *v.,* **-dealt, -deal·ing,** *n.* —*v.t., v.i.* 1. to deal wrongly, esp. to deal the wrong number at cards. —*n.* 2. *Cards.* a deal in which the wrong number of cards have been distributed or in which the cards were dealt in the wrong order or manner, necessitating a new deal and the cancellation of any points made on the hand, sometimes with a penalty to the dealer. [MIS-[1] + DEAL[1]] —**mis·deal′er,** *n.*

mis·deed (mis dēd′), *n.* an immoral or wicked deed. [ME *misdede,* OE *misdǣd.* See MIS-[1], DEED]

mis·deem (mis dēm′), *v.t., v.i.* to have a wrong opinion of; misjudge; mistake: *to misdeem someone's ability.* [ME *misdemen.* See MIS-[1], DEEM]

mis·de·mean (mis′di mēn′), *v.t. Rare.* to misbehave (oneself). [late ME; see MIS-[1], DEMEAN[2]]

mis·de·mean·ant (mis′di mē′nənt), *n.* 1. a person who is guilty of misbehavior. 2. *Law.* a person who has been convicted of a misdemeanor. [MISDEMEAN + -ANT]

mis·de·mean·or (mis′di mē′nər), *n.* 1. misbehavior or an instance of it. 2. *Law.* a criminal offense defined as less serious than a felony. Also, *esp. Brit.,* **mis′de·mean′our.** [MIS-[1] + DEMEANOR]
—**Syn.** 1. transgression, fault; offense.

mis·de·rive (mis′di rīv′), *v.t., v.i.,* **-rived, -riv·ing.** to derive wrongly; assign a wrong derivation to. [MIS-[1] + DERIVE]

mis·de·scribe (mis′di skrīb′), *v.t., v.i.,* **-scribed, -scrib·ing.** to describe incorrectly or falsely. [MIS-[1] + DESCRIBE] —**mis·de·scrip·tion** (mis′di skrip′shən), *n.* —**mis′de·scrip′tive,** *adj.*

mis·di·rect (mis′di rekt′), *v.t.* to direct or address wrongly: *to misdirect a person; to misdirect a letter.* [MIS-[1] + DIRECT]

mis·di·rec·tion (mis′di rek′shən), *n.* 1. a wrong direction, guidance, or instruction. 2. *Law.* an erroneous charge to the jury by a judge. [MIS-[1] + DIRECTION]

mis·do (mis dōō′), *v.,* **-did, -done, -do·ing.** —*v.t.* 1. to do wrongly; botch. —*v.i.* 2. *Obs.* to behave improperly. [ME *misdo(n),* OE *misdōn.* See MIS-[1], DO[1]] —**mis·do′er,** *n.*

mis·doubt (mis dout′), *v.t., v.i.* 1. to doubt or suspect. —*n.* 2. doubt or suspicion. [MIS-[1] + DOUBT]

mise (mēz, mīz), *n.* 1. a settlement or agreement. 2. *Law.* the issue in a proceeding instituted on a writ of right. [late ME < AF: a putting, setting down (e.g. of expenses), n. use of fem. of *mis* < L *miss(us)* sent, bestowed, ptp. of *mittere*]

mis·ease (mis ēz′), *n.* 1. *Archaic.* discomfort; distress; suffering. 2. *Obs.* poverty. [ME *misese* < OF *mesaise.* See MIS-[1], EASE]

mise en scène (mē zäN sen′), *French.* 1. the act or art of placing a play, scene, or the like, on the stage, with regard to the arrangement of actors, scenery, properties, technical equipment, etc. 2. the stage setting of a play. 3. surroundings; environment.

mis·em·ploy (mis′em ploi′), *v.t.* to employ wrongly or improperly; misuse. [MIS-[1] + EMPLOY] —**mis′em·ploy′ment,** *n.*

Mi·se·no (mē ze′nô), *n.* a cape in SW Italy, on the N shore of the Bay of Naples: ruins of ancient Misenum, a Roman naval station and resort.

Mi·se·nus (mī sē′nəs), *n.* *Rom. Legend.* a son of Aeolus who challenged the gods to a musical contest and was killed by them for his arrogance.

mi·ser (mī′zər), *n.* 1. a person who lives in wretched circumstances in order to save and hoard money. 2. a niggardly, avaricious person. 3. *Obs.* a wretched or unhappy person. [< L: wretched]
—**Syn.** 2. niggard, skinflint, tightwad, pinchpenny.

Miser, The, a comedy (1668) by Molière. French, **L'Avare.**

mis·er·a·ble (miz′ər ə bəl, miz′rə-), *adj.* 1. wretchedly unhappy, uneasy, or uncomfortable. 2. wretchedly poor, needy. 3. of wretched character or quality; contemptible. 4. attended with or causing misery: *a miserable existence.* 5. manifesting misery. 6. worthy of pity; deplorable: *a miserable failure.* [late ME < L *miserābil(is),* equiv. to *miserā(rī)* (to) pity (deriv. of *miser* wretched) + *-bilis* -BLE] —**mis′er·a·ble·ness,** *n.* —**mis′er·a·bly,** *adv.*
—**Syn.** 1. forlorn, disconsolate, doleful, distressed. See **wretched.** 2. destitute. 3. despicable, mean, low, abject. 6. pitiable, lamentable. —**Ant.** 1. happy. 2. wealthy. 3. good.

Mi·sé·ra·bles, Les (*Fr.* lā mē zä ʀᴀ′blᵊ). See **Les Misérables.**

Mis·e·re·re (miz′ə râr′ē, -rēr′ē), *n.* 1. the 51st Psalm, or the 50th in the Douay Bible. 2. a musical setting for it. 3. (*l.c.*) a prayer or expression of appeal for mercy. 4. (*l.c.*) misericord (def. 2). [< L: lit., have pity (impv.), first word of the psalm]

mis·er·i·cord (miz′ər ə kôrd′, mi zer′ə kôrd′), *n.* 1. a room in a monastery set apart for those monks permitted relaxation of the monastic rule. 2. a small projection on the underside of a hinged seat of a church stall, which, when the seat is lifted, gives support to a person standing in the stall. 3. a medieval dagger, used for the mercy stroke to a wounded foe. Also, **mis′er·i·corde′.** [ME *misericorde* < MF < L *misericordia* pity, equiv. to *misericord-* (s. of *misericors*) compassionate (*miseri-,* s. of *miserēre* to pity + *cor* heart) + *-ia* -Y[3]]

mis·er·i·cor·di·a (mis′er i kôr′dē ä′; *Eng.* miz′ər ə kôr′dē ə), *n.* *Latin.* compassion; mercy.

---

mis′ap·point′, *v.t.*
mis′ap·praise′, *v.t.,* **-praised, -prais·ing.**
mis′ar·tic′u·late′, *v.,* **-lat·ed, -lat·ing.**
mis′ar·tic′u·la′tion, *n.*
mis′as·sert′, *v.t.*
mis′as·ser′tion, *n.*
mis′as·sign′, *v.*
mis′as·sign′ment, *n.*
mis′au·thor·i·za′tion, *n.*
mis·au′thor·ize′, *v.t.,* **-ized, -iz·ing.**
mis′a·ver′, *v.t.,* **-verred, -ver·ring.**
mis′a·ward′, *v.t.*
mis·bill′, *v.t.*
mis·bind′, *v.,* **-bound, -bind·ing.**
mis·brew′, *v.t.*
mis·build′, *v.,* **-built, -build·ing.**
mis·but′toned, *adj.*
mis·cat′e·go·rize′, *v.t.,* **-rized, -riz·ing.**
mis·cat′e·go·rized′, *adj.*
mis·cen′sure, *v.,* **-sured, -sur·ing.**
mis·char′ac·ter·ize, *v.t.,* **-ized, -iz·ing.**
mis·charge′, *v.,* **-charged, -charg·ing.**
mis·claim′, *v.t.*
mis·class′, *v.*
mis′clas·si·fi·ca′tion, *n.*
mis·clas′si·fy′, *v.t.,* **-fied, -fy·ing.**
mis·coin′, *v.*
mis·coin′age, *n.*
mis′com·pu·ta′tion, *n.*
mis′com·pute′, *v.,* **-put·ed, -put·ing.**
mis′con·jec′ture, *v.,* **-tured, -tur·ing;** *n.*
mis·con′ju·gate′, *v.,* **-gat·ed, -gat·ing.**
mis·cul′ti·vat′ed, *adj.*
mis·cut′, *v.,* **-cut, -cut·ting.**
mis′de·fine′, *v.t.,* **-fined, -fin·ing.**
mis′de·liv′er, *v.t.*
mis′de·liv′er·y, *n., pl.* **-er·ies.**
mis·di′a·grammed′, *adj.*
mis·dic′tat·ed, *adj.*
mis′di·vide′, *v.,* **-vid·ed, -vid·ing.**
mis·draw′, *v.,* **-drew, -drawn, -draw·ing.**
mis·ed′it, *v.t.*
mis·ed′u·cate′, *v.t.,* **-cat·ed, -cat·ing.**
mis′ed·u·ca′tion, *n.*
mis·em′pha·sis, *n.*
mis·em′pha·size′, *v.t.,* **-sized, -siz·ing.**

CONCISE PRONUNCIATION KEY: act, āble, dâre, ärt; ebb, ēqual; if, īce; hot, ōver, ôrder, oil, bŏŏk, ōōze, out; up, ûrge; chief; sing; shoe; thin, that; zh as in measure.
ə = a as in *alone,* e as in *system,* i as in *easily,* o as in *gallop,* u as in *circus;* ᵊ as in button (butᵊn), fire (fīᵊr), cradle (krādᵊl). See the full key inside the front cover.

mis·er·ly (mī′zər lē), *adj.* of, like, or befitting a miser; penurious; niggardly. [MISER + -LY] —**mi′ser·li·ness,** *n.*
—**Syn.** cheap, stingy, parsimonious. —**Ant.** generous.

mis·er·y (miz′ə rē), *n., pl.* **-er·ies.** **1.** wretchedness of condition or circumstances. **2.** distress caused by need, privation, or poverty. **3.** great distress of mind; extreme unhappiness. **4.** a cause or source of distress. **5.** *Dial.* **a.** a pain: *a misery in my left side.* **b.** rheumatism. **c.** Often **miseries.** a case or period of despondency or gloom. [ME *miserie* < L *miseria,* equiv. to *miser* wretched + *-ia* -Y[3]]
—**Syn. 1.** tribulation, trial, suffering. **3.** grief, anguish, woe, torment, desolation. See **sorrow.** —**Ant. 3.** happiness.

mis·es·teem (mis′e stēm′), *v.t.* to fail to value or respect properly. [MIS-[1] + ESTEEM]

mis·es·ti·mate (*v.* mis es′tə māt′; *n.* mis es′tə mit), *v.,* **-mat·ed, -mat·ing,** *n.* —*v.t.* **1.** to estimate wrongly or inadequately. —*n.* **2.** a wrong estimate. [MIS-[1] + ESTIMATE] —**mis·es′ti·ma′tion,** *n.*

mis·fea·sance (mis fē′zəns), *n. Law.* **1.** wrong, actual or alleged, arising from or consisting of affirmative action. **2.** the wrongful performance of a normally lawful act; the wrongful and injurious exercise of lawful authority. Cf. **malfeasance, nonfeasance.** [< AF *mesfesance.* See MIS-[1], FEASANCE]

mis·fea·sor (mis fē′zər), *n. Law.* a person who is guilty of misfeasance. [< AF *mesfesor.* See MISFEASANCE, -OR[2]]

mis·fea·ture (mis fē′chər), *n. Archaic.* a distorted feature. [MIS-[1] + FEATURE] —**mis·fea′tured,** *adj.*

mis·file (mis fīl′), *v.t.,* **-filed, -fil·ing.** to file (papers, documents, records, etc.) incorrectly. [MIS-[1] + FILE[1]]

mis·fire (mis fīər′), *v.,* **-fired, -fir·ing,** *n.* —*v.i.* **1.** (of a rifle or gun or of a bullet or shell) to fail to fire or explode. **2.** to be misdirected; fail: *His criticisms completely misfired.* —*n.* **3.** (of a rifle or gun or of a bullet or shell) a failure to fire or explode or to fire or explode properly. [MIS-[1] + FIRE]

mis·fit (mis fit′; *for 2, 3 also* mis′fit), *v.,* **-fit·ted, -fit·ting,** *n.* —*v.t., v.i.* **1.** to fit badly. —*n.* **2.** a bad fit, as a garment that is too large or too small. **3.** a person who is not suitable or is unable to adjust to the circumstances of his particular situation: *a misfit in one's job.* [MIS-[1] + FIT[1]]

mis·for·tune (mis fôr′chən), *n.* **1.** adverse fortune; bad luck. **2.** an instance of this; mischance; mishap. [MIS-[1] + FORTUNE]
—**Syn. 2.** accident; disaster, calamity, catastrophe; reverse; blow. See **affliction.**

mis·give (mis giv′), *v.,* **-gave, -giv·en, -giv·ing.** —*v.t.* **1.** (of one's mind, heart, etc.) to give doubt or apprehension to. —*v.i.* **2.** to be apprehensive. [MIS-[1] + GIVE]

mis·giv·ing (mis giv′ing), *n.* a feeling of doubt, distrust, or apprehension. [MISGIVE + -ING[1]] —**mis·giv′ing·ly,** *adv.*
—**Syn.** suspicion, mistrust, hesitation. See **apprehension.**

mis·gov·ern (mis guv′ərn), *v.t.* to govern or manage badly. [late ME *misgoverne.* See MIS-[1], GOVERN] —**mis·gov′ern·ment, mis·gov′ern·ance,** *n.*

mis·guide (mis gīd′), *v.t.,* **-guid·ed, -guid·ing.** to direct wrongly; mislead. [MIS-[1] + GUIDE; r. ME *misgye(n);* see GUY[2]] —**mis·guid′ance,** *n.* —**mis·guid′er,** *n.*

mis·guid·ed (mis gī′did), *adj.* misled; mistaken: *a recipient of misguided charity.* [MISGUIDE + -ED[2]] —**mis·guid′ed·ly,** *adv.* —**mis·guid′ed·ness,** *n.*

mis·han·dle (mis han′dəl), *v.t.,* **-dled, -dling.** **1.** to handle badly; maltreat: *to mishandle a dog.* **2.** to manage badly: *to mishandle an estate.* [MIS-[1] + HANDLE]

mi·shan·ter (mi shan′tər), *n. Scot. and North Eng.* a misfortune; mishap. Also, **mischanter.** [MIS-[1] + *(h)anter,* ME *aunter,* var. of *aventure* ADVENTURE]

mis·hap (mis′hap, mis hap′), *n.* an unfortunate accident. [ME; see MIS-[1], HAP]

Mish·a·wa·ka (mish′ə wô′kə), *n.* a city in N Indiana, near South Bend. 33,361 (1960).

mis·hear (mis hēr′), *v.t.,* **-heard, -hear·ing.** to hear incorrectly or imperfectly: *to mishear a remark.* [ME *misheren,* OE *mishīeran.* See MIS-[1], HEAR]

mish·mash (mish′mash′, -mäsh′), *n.* a confused mess; hodgepodge; jumble. Also, **mish·mosh** (mish′mosh′). [late ME; gradational formation based on MASH]

Mish·na (mish′nə; *Heb.* mish nä′), *n., pl.* **Mish·na·yoth** (mish′nə yōt′; *Heb.* mish nä yôt′). Mishnah.

Mish·nah (mish′nə; *Heb.* mish nä′), *n., pl.* **Mish·na·yoth** (mish′nə yōt′; *Heb.* mish nä yôt′). *Judaism.* **1.** the section of the Talmud consisting of the collection of oral laws edited A.D. c200 by Rabbi Judah ha-Nasi. **2.** an article of this section. Also, **Mishna.** [< Heb: teaching by oral repetition] —**Mish·na·ic** (mish nā′ik), **Mish′nic, Mish′ni·cal,** *adj.*

mis·in·form (mis′in fôrm′), *v.t.* to give false or misleading information to. [ME *misenfourme(n).* See MIS-[1], INFORM] —**mis′in·form′ant, mis′in·form′er,** *n.* —**mis′in·form′a·tive,** *adj.* —**mis·in·for·ma·tion** (mis′in fər mā′shən), *n.*

mis·in·ter·pret (mis′in tûr′prit), *v.t.* to interpret, explain, or understand incorrectly. [MIS-[1] + INTERPRET] —**mis′in·ter′pret·a·ble,** *adj.* —**mis′in·ter′pre·ta′tion,** *n.* —**mis′in·ter′pret·er,** *n.*

mis·join·der (mis join′dər), *n. Law.* a joining in one suit or action of causes or of parties not permitted to be so joined. [MIS-[1] + JOINDER]

mis·judge (mis juj′), *v.t., v.i.,* **-judged, -judg·ing.** to judge, estimate, or value wrongly or unjustly. [MIS-[1] + JUDGE] —**mis·judg′er,** *n.* —**mis·judg′ing·ly,** *adv.* —**mis·judg′ment;** *esp. Brit.,* **mis·judge′ment,** *n.*

mis·know (mis nō′), *v.t.,* **-knew, -known, -know·ing.** to fail to understand or recognize: *to misknow the problem.* [ME *misknowe(n).* See MIS-[1], KNOW] —**mis·knowl·edge** (mis nol′ij), *n.*

Mis·kolc (mish′kôlts), *n.* a city in N Hungary. 143,364 (1960).

mis·la·bel (mis lā′bəl), *v.t.,* **-beled, -bel·ing** or (*esp. Brit.*) **-belled, -bel·ling.** to label wrongly or misleadingly: *to mislabel a bottle of medicine.* [MIS-[1] + LABEL]

mis·lay (mis lā′), *v.t.,* **-laid, -lay·ing.** **1.** to put in a place afterward forgotten. **2.** to lay or place wrongly; arrange or situate improperly: *A careless workman mislaid our kitchen linoleum.* [ME *misselaye(n).* See MIS-[1], LAY[1]] —**mis·lay′er,** *n.*

mis·lead (mis lēd′), *v.t.,* **-led, -lead·ing.** **1.** to lead or guide wrongly; lead astray. **2.** to lead into error of conduct, thought, or judgment. [ME *mislede(n),* OE *mislǣdan.* See MIS-[1], LEAD[1]] —**mis·lead′er,** *n.*
—**Syn. 1.** misguide, misdirect. **2.** delude, deceive.

mis·lead·ing (mis lē′ding), *adj.* deceptive; tending to mislead. [MISLEAD + -ING[2]] —**mis·lead′ing·ly,** *adv.* —**mis·lead′ing·ness,** *n.*

mis·leared (mis lērd′), *adj. Scot. and North Eng.* ill-mannered; rude; crude. [ptp. of *mislear,* ME *misleren,* OE *mislǣran* to teach amiss. See MIS-[1], LEARN]

mis·like (mis līk′), *v.t.,* **-liked, -lik·ing.** **1.** to dislike. **2.** *Archaic.* to displease. [ME *mislike(n),* OE *mislīcian.* See MIS-[1], LIKE[2]] —**mis·lik′er,** *n.*

mis·lo·cate (mis lō′kāt, mis′lō kāt′), *v.t.,* **-cat·ed, -cat·ing.** to misplace. [MIS-[1] + LOCATE] —**mis′lo·ca′tion,** *n.*

mis·man·age (mis man′ij), *v.t., v.i.,* **-aged, -ag·ing.** to manage incompetently or dishonestly: *to mismanage funds.* [MIS-[1] + MANAGE] —**mis·man′age·ment,** *n.* —**mis·man′ag·er,** *n.*

mis·mar·riage (mis mar′ij), *n.* an unsuitable or unhappy marriage. [MIS-[1] + MARRIAGE]

mis·match (mis mach′), *v.t.* **1.** to match badly or unsuitably. —*n.* **2.** a bad or unsatisfactory match. [MIS-[1] + MATCH[2]]

mis·mate (mis māt′), *v.t., v.i.,* **-mat·ed, -mat·ing.** to mate unsuitably or wrongly. [MIS-[1] + MATE[1]]

mis·move (mis mōōv′), *n.* a wrong or prohibited move, as in a game. [MIS-[1] + MOVE]

mis·name (mis nām′), *v.t.,* **-named, -nam·ing.** to call by a wrong name. [MIS-[1] + NAME]

mis·no·mer (mis nō′mər), *n.* **1.** a misapplied name or designation. **2.** an error in naming a person or thing. [late ME < AF, MF *mesnomer* to misname, equiv. to *mes-* MIS-[1] + *nomer* < L *nōmināre;* see NOMINATE]

miso-, a combining form referring to hate: *misogyny.* Also, **mis-.** [< Gk, comb. form of *mīsein* to hate, *mīsos* hatred]

mis·o·cai·ne·a (mis′ō kī′nē ə, -kā′-, mī′sō-), *n.* an abnormal aversion to anything new. [< NL; see MISO-, CAINO-, -IA]

mi·sog·a·my (mi sog′ə mē, mī-), *n.* hatred of marriage. [MISO- + -GAMY] —**mis·o·gam·ic** (mis′ə gam′ik, mī′sə-), *adj.* —**mi·sog′a·mist,** *n.*

mi·sog·y·ny (mi soj′ə nē, mī-), *n.* hatred of women. [< Gk *misogynía* hatred of women. See MISO-, GYN-, -Y[3]] —**mi·sog′y·nic, mi·sog′y·nous, mi·sog′y·nis′tic,** *adj.* —**mi·sog′y·nist,** *n.*

mi·sol·o·gy (mi sol′ə jē, mī-), *n.* distrust or hatred of reason or reasoning. [MISO- + -LOGY] —**mi·sol′o·gist,** *n.*

mis·o·ne·ism (mis′ō nē′iz əm, mī′sō-), *n.* hatred or dislike of what is new or represents change. [< It *misoneism(o).* See MISO-, NEO-, -ISM] —**mis′o·ne′ist,** *n.* —**mis′o·ne·is′tic,** *adj.*

mis·o·pe·di·a (mis′ō pē′dē ə, mī′sō-), *n.* hatred of children, esp. one's own. Also, **mis′o·pae′di·a.** [< NL; see MISO-, PED-[1], -IA] —**mis′o·pe′dist, mis′o·pae′dist,** *n.*

mis·pick (mis′pik′), *n.* **1.** a pick or filling yarn that has failed to interlace with the warp as a result of a mechanical defect in the loom. **2.** a defect in a fabric caused by such a pick or filling yarn. [MIS-[1] + PICK[3]]

mis·pick·el (mis′pik′əl), *n.* arsenopyrite. [< G]

mis·place (mis plās′), *v.t.,* **-placed, -plac·ing.** **1.** to put in a wrong or forgotten place. **2.** to place or bestow improperly, unsuitably, or unwisely: *to misplace one's trust.* [MIS-[1] + PLACE] —**mis·place′ment,** *n.*
—**Syn. 1.** mislay, lose. See **displace. 2.** misapply.

mis′placed mod′ifier, *Gram.* a word, phrase, or clause that modifies an unintended word because of its placement or construction in a sentence, as, *When a small boy* in *when a small boy, a girl is of little interest.* Cf. **dangling participle.**

mis·play (mis plā′), *Sports, Games.* —*n.* **1.** a wrong play. **2.** a play prohibited by the rules. —*v.t.* **3.** to make an error or incorrect play on or with; play wrongly: *The catcher misplayed the ball, allowing the base runner to score.* **4.** to make a play on or with (a card, chess piece, etc.) prohibited by the rules. [MIS-[1] + PLAY]

mis·plead (mis plēd′), *v.i., v.t.,* **-plead·ed** or **-plead** (-pled) or **-pled, -plead·ing.** to plead incorrectly. [MIS-[1] + PLEAD]

mis·plead·ing (mis plē′ding), *n. Law.* a mistake in pleading, as a misjoinder of parties, a misstatement of a cause of action, etc. [MIS-[1] + PLEADING]

mis·print (*n.* mis′print′, mis print′; *v.* mis print′), *n.* **1.** a mistake in printing, as an instance of printing a letter or word other than that intended. —*v.t.* **2.** to print incorrectly. [MIS-[1] + PRINT]

mis·prise (mis prīz′), *v.t.,* **-prised, -pris·ing.** misprize. —**mis·pris′er,** *n.*

mis·pri·sion[1] (mis prizh′ən), *n.* **1.** a wrongful action of commission, esp. of a public official. **2.** *Law.* any violation, esp. of an official duty. **3.** failure by a person not actively involved in the commission of treason, felony, or other crime, to prevent its commission or to report the crime to the proper authorities. [ME < AF, OF *mesprision,* equiv. to *mes-* MIS-[1] + *prision* < L *prēnsiōn-,* var of *prehēnsiōn-* (s. of *prehēnsiō*) PREHENSION]

mis·pri·sion[2] (mis prizh′ən), *n.* contempt or scorn. [MISPRISE + -ION]

mis·prize (mis prīz′), *v.t.,* **-prized, -priz·ing.** to despise; undervalue; slight; scorn. Also, **misprise.** [late ME *misprise* < MF *mesprisie(r),* equiv. to *mes-* MIS-[1] + *prisier* to PRIZE[2]] —**mis·priz′er,** *n.*

mis·pro·nounce (mis′prə nouns′), *v.t., v.i.,* **-nounced, -nounc·ing.** to pronounce incorrectly. [MIS-[1] + PRONOUNCE] —**mis′pro·nounc′er,** *n.* —**mis·pro·nun·ci·a·tion** (mis′prə nun′sē ā′shən), *n.*

mis·proud (mis proud′), *adj. Archaic.* unreasonably proud. [ME; see MIS-[1], PROUD]

mis·punc·tu·ate (mis pungk′chōō āt′), *v.t.,* **-at·ed, -at·ing.** to punctuate incorrectly. [MIS-[1] + PUNCTUATE] —**mis·punc′tu·a′tion,** *n.*

mis·quo·ta·tion (mis′kwō tā′shən), *n.* **1.** the act of misquoting. **2.** an instance or occasion of misquoting or of being misquoted. [MIS-[1] + QUOTATION]

mis·quote (mis kwōt′), *v.,* **-quot·ed, -quot·ing,** *n.* —*v.t., v.i.* **1.** to quote incorrectly. —*n.* **2.** a quotation that is incorrect. [MIS-[1] + QUOTE] —**mis·quot′er,** *n.*

mis·read (mis rēd′), *v.t.,* **-read** (red), **-read·ing.** to read wrongly; misinterpret. [OE *misrǣdan.* See MIS-[1], READ] —**mis·read′er,** *n.*

mis·reck·on (mis rek′ən), *v.t., v.i.* to reckon incorrectly; miscalculate. [MIS-[1] + RECKON]

mis·re·mem·ber (mis′ri mem′bər), *v.t., v.i.* **1.** to remember incorrectly. **2.** *Dial.* to fail to remember. [MIS-[1] + REMEMBER]

mis·re·port (mis′ri pōrt′, -pôrt′), *v.t.* **1.** to report incorrectly or falsely. —*n.* **2.** an incorrect or false report. [ME (n. and v.); see MIS-[1], REPORT] —**mis′re·port′er,** *n.*

mis·rep·re·sent (mis′rep ri zent′), *v.t.* **1.** to represent incorrectly, improperly, or falsely. **2.** to represent in an unsatisfactory manner: *Many tourists seriously misrepresent their country.* [MIS-[1] + REPRESENT] —**mis′rep·re·sen·ta′tion,** *n.* —**mis′rep·re·sen′ta·tive,** *adj.* —**mis′rep·re·sent′er,** *n.*

mis·rule (mis rōōl′), *n., v.,* **-ruled, -rul·ing.** —*n.* **1.** bad or unwise rule; misgovernment. **2.** disorder or lawless tumult. —*v.t.* **3.** to misgovern. [ME *misreulen* (v.), *misreule* (n.). See MIS-[1], RULE] —**mis·rul′er,** *n.*

mis·run (mis run′, mis′run′), *n. Foundry.* an incomplete casting the metal of which has solidified prematurely. [MIS-[1] + RUN]

miss[1] (mis), *v.t.* **1.** to fail to hit, light upon, meet, catch, receive, obtain, attain, accomplish, see, hear, etc.: *to miss a train.* **2.** to fail to perform, attend to, be present at, etc.: *to miss an appointment.* **3.** to perceive the absence or loss of, often with regret or longing: *to miss a friend.* **4.** to escape or avoid: *He just missed being caught.* **5.** to fail to perceive or understand: *to miss the point of a remark.* —*v.i.* **6.** to fail to hit, light upon, receive, or attain something. **7.** to fail of effect or success; be unsuccessful. **8. miss fire.** See **fire** (def. 24). —*n.* **9.** a failure to hit, meet, obtain, or accomplish something. **10.** an omission. [ME *missen,* OE *missan;* c. G *missen*]

miss[2] (mis), *n., pl.* **miss·es.** **1.** (*cap.*) the conventional title of respect for an unmarried woman, prefixed to the name or to the representational title: *Miss Kronvall; Miss Sweden.* **2.** (used, without a name or representational title, as a term of address to an unmarried woman): *Miss, does the Broadway bus stop here?* **3.** a young unmarried woman; girl: *a radiant miss of 18 or so.* **4. misses,** (*construed as sing. or pl.*) a range of even-numbered garment sizes, chiefly from 8–20, designed for women and girls of average build. [short for MISTRESS]

Miss., Mississippi.

miss., **1.** mission. **2.** missionary.

mis·sa (mēs′sä; *Eng.* mis′ə), *n. Latin.* Mass.

mis′ex·plained′, *adj.*
mis·fash′ion, *n.*
mis·fash′ioned, *adj.*
mis·field′, *v.*
mis·fo′cus, *v.,* **-cused, -cus·ing; -cussed, -cus·sing.**
mis·fo′cused, *adj.*
mis·fo′cussed, *adj.*
mis·form′, *v.*
mis′for·ma′tion, *n.*
mis·formed′, *adj.*
mis·frame′, *v.,* **-framed, -fram·ing.**
mis·gauge′, *v.t.,* **-gauged, -gaug·ing.**
mis·grade′, *v.,* **-grad·ed, -grad·ing.**
mis·grad′ed, *adj.*
mis·graft′, *v.*
mis′i·den′ti·fi·ca′tion, *n.*
mis′i·den′ti·fy′, *v.,* **-fied, -fy·ing.**
mis′in·fer′, *v.,* **-ferred, -fer·ring.**
mis·in′fer·ence, *n.*
mis′in·struct′, *v.t.*
mis′in·struc′tion, *n.*
mis′in·tend′, *v.*
mis′in·ten′tion, *n.*
mis·i′tem·ized′, *adj.*
mis·join′, *v.*
mis·learn′, *v.*
mis·make′, *v.,* **-made, -mak·ing.**
mis·meas′ure, *v.,* **-ured, -ur·ing.**
mis·mount′, *v.*
mis·nar′rate, *v.,* **-rat·ed, -rat·ing.**
mis·nav′i·gate′, *v.,* **-gat·ed, -gat·ing.**
mis′nav·i·ga′tion, *n.*
mis·num′ber, *v.*
mis·oc′cu·py′, *v.,* **-pied, -py·ing.**
mis·or′gan·i·za′tion, *n.*
mis·or′gan·ize, *v.,* **-ized, -iz·ing.**
mis·pack′aged, *adj.*
mis·packed′, *adj.*
mis·page′, *v.t.,* **-paged, -pag·ing.**
mis′pag·i·na′tion, *n.*
mis·parse′, *v.t.,* **-parsed, -pars·ing.**
mis·patch′, *v.t.*
mis′per·ceive′, *v.t.,* **-ceived, -ceiv·ing.**
mis′per·cep′tion, *n.*
mis′per·form′, *v.*
mis′per·form′ance, *n.*
mis·phrase′, *v.t.,* **-phrased, -phras·ing.**
mis·plant′, *v.t.*
mis·prac′tice, *n., v.,* **-ticed, -tic·ing.**
mis·prac′tise, *n., v.,* **-tised, -tis·ing.**
mis′pre·sent′, *v.t.*
mis·prin′ci·pled, *adj.*
mis′pro·duce′, *v.,* **-duced, -duc·ing.**
mis′pro·por′tion, *n.*
mis′pro·pos′al, *n.*
mis′pro·pose′, *v.,* **-posed, -pos·ing.**
mis′pro·voke′, *v.t.,* **-voked, -vok·ing.**
mis·pub′li·cized′, *adj.*
mis·pub′lished, *adj.*
mis·pur′chase, *v.t.,* **-chased, -chas·ing.**
mis·qual′i·fy′, *v.,* **-fied, -fy·ing.**
mis·rate′, *v.,* **-rat·ed, -rat·ing.**
mis′rec·ol·lect′, *v.*
mis′re·fer′, *v.,* **-ferred, -fer·ring.**
mis·ref′er·ence, *n.*
mis′re·flect′, *v.*
mis′re·form′, *v.*
mis·reg′u·late′, *v.t.,* **-lat·ed, -lat·ing.**
mis′re·hearse′, *v.,* **-hearsed, -hears·ing.**
mis′re·late′, *v.,* **-lat·ed, -lat·ing.**
mis′re·li′ance, *n.*
mis′re·ly′, *v.i.,* **-lied, -ly·ing.**
mis·ren′der, *v.t.*
mis′re·print′, *v.t.*
mis′re·ward′, *v.t.*
mis·rhymed′, *adj.*

mis·sal (mis′əl), *n.* **1.** (*sometimes cap.*) *Rom. Cath. Ch.* the book containing the prayers and rites used by the priest in celebrating Mass. **2.** any book of prayers or devotions. [ME < ML *missāle*, n. use of neut. of *missālis*, equiv. to *miss(a)* MASS + *-ālis* -AL[1]]

mis′sal stand′, a lectern for a missal, esp. one on an altar. Also called **altar stand.**

Mis·sa So·lem·nis (mis′ə sō lem′nis), Mass in D, Op. 123 (1818–23, published 1827) by Ludwig van Beethoven.

mis·say (mis sā′), *v.*, **-said, -say·ing.** *Archaic.* —*v.t.* **1.** to say or speak ill of; abuse; slander. **2.** to say wrongly. —*v.i.* **3.** to speak wrongly or incorrectly. [ME *misseye(n)*. See MIS-[1], SAY] —**mis·say′er,** *n.*

mis·seem (mis sēm′), *v.t.* *Archaic.* misbecome. [ME *misseme(n)*. See MIS-[1], SEEM]

mis′sel thrush′ (mis′əl). See **mistle thrush.**

mis·send (mis send′), *v.t.*, **-sent, -send·ing.** to send or forward, esp. mail, to the wrong place or person. [ME *missende(n)*. See MIS-[1], SEND]

mis·shape (mis shāp′), *v.t.*, **-shaped, -shaped** or **shap·en, -shap·ing.** to shape badly or wrongly; deform. [late ME; see MIS-[1], SHAPE]

mis·shap·en (mis shā′pən), *adj.* badly shaped; deformed: *a misshapen body.* [late ME, ptp. of MISSHAPE; see -EN[3]] —**mis·shap′en·ly,** *adv.* —**mis·shap′en·ness,** *n.*

mis·sile (mis′əl *or, esp. Brit.*, -īl), *n.* **1.** an object or weapon for throwing, hurling, or shooting, as a stone, bullet, arrow, etc. **2.** See **guided missile.** —*adj.* **3.** capable of being thrown, hurled, or shot, as from the hand, a gun, etc. **4.** used or designed for discharging missiles. [< L, neut. of *missilis*, equiv. to *miss(us)* sent, thrown (ptp. of *mittere*) + *-ilis* -ILE]

mis·sile·ry (mis′əl rē), *n.* the science of the construction and use of guided missiles. Also, **mis′sil·ry.** [MISSILE + -RY]

miss·ing (mis′ing), *adj.* lacking, absent, or not found: *to be missing in action; a missing person.* [MISS[1] + -ING[2]]

miss′ing link′, **1.** a hypothetical form of animal assumed to have constituted a connecting link between the anthropoid apes and man. **2.** something lacking for the completion of a series or sequence.

mis·sion (mish′ən), *n.* **1.** a group or committee of persons sent to a foreign country to conduct negotiations, establish relations, or the like. **2.** the business with which an agent, envoy, etc., is charged. **3.** *U.S.* a permanent diplomatic establishment abroad: *chief of mission.* **4.** *Mil.* an operational task, usually assigned by a higher headquarters: *a bombing mission; a mission to capture Hill 304.* **5.** a body of persons sent by a church to carry on religious work, esp. evangelization in foreign lands, and often to establish schools, hospitals, etc. **6.** an establishment of missionaries in a foreign land; a missionary post or station. **7.** a similar establishment in any region. **8.** the district assigned to a missionary priest. **9.** missionary duty or work. **10.** an organization for carrying on missionary work. **11. missions,** organized missionary work or activities in any country or region. **12.** a church or a region with a minister or priest who lives nearby but who is nonresident. **13.** a series of special religious services for increasing religious devotion and converting unbelievers: *to preach a mission.* **14.** an assigned or self-imposed duty or task. **15.** a sending or being sent for some duty or purpose. **16.** those sent. —*adj.* **17.** (*usually cap.*) noting or pertaining to a style of American furniture of the early 20th century, created in supposed imitation of the furnishings of the Spanish missions of California and characterized by the use of dark, stained wood, by heaviness, and by extreme plainness. Also called **foreign mission** (for defs. 3, 6). [< L *missiōn-* (s. of *missiō*) a sending off, equiv. to *miss(us)* sent (ptp. of *mittere*) + *-iōn-* -ION] —**mis′sion·al,** *adj.*

Mis·sion (mish′ən), *n.* a town in E Kansas. 4626 (1960).

mis·sion·ar·y (mish′ə ner′ē), *n.*, *pl.* **-ar·ies,** *adj.* —*n.* Also, **mis′sion·er. 1.** a person sent by a church into an area, esp. into a newly settled region or a foreign country, to carry on evangelism or other activities, as educational or hospital work. **2.** a person strongly in favor of a program, set of principles, etc., who attempts to persuade or convert others to his position. **3.** a person who is sent on a mission. —*adj.* **4.** pertaining to or connected with religious missions. **5.** engaged in such a mission, or devoted to work connected with missions. **6.** reflecting or prompted by the desire to persuade or convert others: *the missionary efforts of political fanatics; missionary zeal.* **7.** characteristic of a missionary. [< NL *missiōnāri(us)*. See MISSION, -ARY]

mis′sionary apos·tol′ic, *pl.* **missionaries apostolic.** *Rom. Cath. Ch.* an honorary title conferred by the pope on certain missionaries.

Mis′sionary Ridge′, a ridge in NW Georgia and SE Tennessee: Civil War battle 1863.

mis′sionary sales′·man, a representative of a manufacturer employed to call on wholesalers and retailers to promote the sale of a product.

Mis′sion Hills′, a town in E Kansas. 3621 (1960).

mis·sis (mis′iz, -is), *n.* **1.** *Informal.* wife: *I'll have to ask the missis.* **2.** *Dial.* the mistress of a household. Also, **missus.** [var. of MISTRESS]

miss·ish (mis′ish), *adj.* prim; affected; prudish. [MISS[2] + -ISH[1]] —**miss′ish·ness,** *n.*

Mis·sis·sip·pi (mis′i sip′ē), *n.* **1.** a State in the S United States. 2,178,141 (1960); 47,716 sq. mi. *Cap.:* Jackson. *Abbr.:* Miss. See map in preceding column. **2.** a river flowing S from N Minnesota to the Gulf of Mexico: the principal river of the U.S. 2470 mi. long; from the headwaters of the Missouri to the Gulf of Mexico 3988 mi. long.

Mis·sis·sip·pi·an (mis′i sip′ē ən), *adj.* **1.** of or pertaining to the State of Mississippi or the Mississippi River. **2.** *Geol.* noting or pertaining to a period of the Paleozoic era, occurring from about 300 million to 350 million years ago and characterized by the increase of land areas and the development of winged insects: sometimes considered an epoch of the Carboniferous period. See table under **era.** —*n.* **3.** a native or inhabitant of Mississippi. **4.** *Geol.* the Mississippian period or system. [MISSISSIPPI + -AN]

Mis′sissip′pi Cit′y, a town in SE Mississippi. 4169 (1960).

mis·sive (mis′iv), *n.* **1.** a written message; letter. —*adj.* **2.** sent or about to be sent, esp. as a letter from an official source. [late ME (*letter*) *missive* < ML (*littera*) *missīva* sent (letter), equiv. to L *miss(us)* sent (ptp. of *mittere*) + *-īva*, fem. of *-īvus* -IVE]

Miss′ Ju′lie, a play (1888) by Strindberg.

Miss′ Lone′ly·hearts (lōn′lē härts′), a satiric novel (1933) by Nathanael West.

Mis·so·lon·ghi (mis′ə lông′gē), *n.* a town in W Greece, on the Gulf of Patras: Byron died here 1824. 13,837 (1951). Also, **Mesolonghi.**

Mis·sou·la (mi zo͞o′lə), *n.* a city in W Montana. 27,090 (1960).

Missou′la Southwest′, a town in W Montana. 3817 (1960).

Mis·sour·i (mi zo͝or′ē, -zo͝or′ə), *n.*, *pl.* **-sour·is,** (*esp. collectively*) **-sour·i** for 3. **1.** a State in the central United States. 4,319,813 (1960); 69,674 sq. mi. *Cap.:* Jefferson City. *Abbr.:* Mo. **2.** a river flowing from SW Montana into the Mississippi N of St. Louis, Missouri. 2723 mi. long. **3.** a member of a North American Indian tribe belonging to the Siouan linguistic stock, located on the Missouri River in early historic times and now extinct as a tribe. **4. from Missouri,** *Informal.* unwilling to accept without proof; skeptical. —**Mis·sour′i·an,** *adj., n.*

Missour′i Com′promise, *U.S. Hist.* a proviso attached to a bill passed by Congress in 1820, by which slavery was to be excluded in any State formed from the Louisiana Territory north of latitude 36°30′N, except Missouri. Cf. **Kansas-Nebraska Act.**

Missour′i gourd′, calabazilla.

Missour′i meer′schaum, corncob (def. 2).

Missour′i Val′ley, a town in W Iowa. 3567 (1960).

mis·speak (mis spēk′), *v.t., v.i.*, **-spoke, -spok·en, -speak·ing.** to speak, utter, or pronounce incorrectly. [ME *misspeke(n)*. See MIS-[1], SPEAK (cf. OE *missprecan* to grumble)]

mis·spell (mis spel′), *v.t., v.i.*, **-spelled** or **-spelt, -spell·ing.** to spell incorrectly. [MIS-[1] + SPELL[1]]

mis·spend (mis spend′), *v.t.*, **-spent, -spend·ing.** to spend improperly; squander; waste. [ME *misspende(n)*. See MIS-[1], SPEND] —**mis·spend′er,** *n.*

mis·state (mis stāt′), *v.t.*, **-stat·ed, -stat·ing.** to state wrongly or misleadingly; make a wrong statement about. [MIS-[1] + STATE] —**mis·state′ment,** *n.* —**mis·stat′er,** *n.*

mis·step (mis step′), *n.* **1.** a wrong step. **2.** an error or slip in conduct. [MIS-[1] + STEP]

mis-strike (mis strīk′), *n.* *Numis.* a coin having the design stamped off center.

mis·sus (mis′əz, -əs), *n.* missis.

miss·y (mis′ē), *n., pl.* **miss·ies.** *Informal.* young miss; girl. [MISS[2] + -Y[2]]

mist (mist), *n.* **1.** a cloudlike aggregation of minute globules of water suspended in the atmosphere at or near the earth's surface. **2.** a cloud of particles resembling this: *a mist of dust; She sprayed a mist of perfume onto her handkerchief.* **3.** *Meteorol.* a very thin fog in which the horizontal visibility is greater than one kilometer; drizzle. **4.** something that dims, obscures, or blurs: *to dispel the mist of ignorance.* **5.** a haze before the eyes that dims the vision: *She waved farewell through a mist of tears.* **6.** a suspension of a liquid in a gas. —*v.i.* **7.** to become misty. **8.** to rain in very fine drops; drizzle (usually used impersonally with *it* as subject): *It was misting when they went out for lunch.* —*v.t.* **9.** to make misty. [ME, OE; c. D, LG, Sw *mist;* akin to Gk *omíchlē* fog, Skt *megha* cloud] —**mist′less,** *adj.* —**Syn. 1.** See **cloud.**

mist., (in prescriptions) a mixture. [< L *mistūra*]

mis·tak·a·ble (mi stā′kə bəl), *adj.* capable or liable to be mistaken or misunderstood. [MISTAKE + -ABLE] —**mis·tak′a·ble·ness,** *n.* —**mis·tak′a·bly,** *adv.*

mis·take (mi stāk′), *n., v.*, **-took, -tak·en, -tak·ing.** —*n.* **1.** an error in action, calculation, opinion, or judgment caused by poor reasoning, carelessness, insufficient information, etc. **2.** a misunderstanding or misconception. **3. and no mistake,** *Informal.* for certain; surely: *He's an honorable person, and no mistake.* —*v.t.* **4.** to regard or identify wrongly as something or someone else: *I mistook him for the mayor.* **5.** to understand, interpret, or evaluate wrongly; misunderstand. —*v.i.* **6.** to be in error. [ME < Scand; cf. Icel *mistaka* to take in error. See MIS-[1], TAKE] —**mis·tak′er,** *n.* —**mis·tak′ing·ly,** *adv.*
—**Syn. 1.** inaccuracy, erratum, fault, oversight. MISTAKE, BLUNDER, ERROR, SLIP refer to deviations from right, accuracy, correctness, or truth. A MISTAKE, grave or trivial, is caused by bad judgment or a disregard of rule or principle: *It was a mistake to argue.* A BLUNDER is a careless, stupid, or gross mistake in action or speech, suggesting awkwardness, heedlessness, or ignorance: *Through his blunder the message was lost.* An ERROR (often interchanged with MISTAKE) is an unintentional wandering or deviation from accuracy, or right conduct: *an error in addition.* A SLIP is usually a minor mistake made through haste or carelessness: *a slip of the tongue.* **5.** misconceive, misjudge, err. —**Ant. 2.** understanding.

mis·tak·en (mi stā′kən), *adj.* **1.** wrongly conceived, entertained, or done: *a mistaken notion.* **2.** erroneous; incorrect; wrong. **3.** having made a mistake; being in error. [ptp. of MISTAKE; see -EN[3]] —**mis·tak′en·ly,** *adv.* —**mis·tak′en·ness,** *n.*
—**Syn. 1.** inaccurate, misconceived.

Mis·tas·si·ni (mis′tə sē′nē), *n.* a lake in E Canada, in Quebec province. 840 sq. mi.

mist·bow (mist′bō′), *n.* fogbow. [MIST + BOW[2]]

mist·coat (mist′kōt′), *n.* (in house painting or interior decoration) a coat of thinner, sometimes pigmented, applied to a finish coat of paint to increase its luster. [MIST + COAT]

mis·teach (mis tēch′), *v.t.*, **-taught, -teach·ing.** to teach wrongly or badly. [ME *misteche(n)*, OE *mistǣcan.* See MIS-[1], TEACH] —**mis·teach′er,** *n.*

mis·ter (mis′tər), *n.* **1.** (*cap.*) the conventional title of respect for a man, prefixed to the name and to certain official designations (usually written as the abbreviation *Mr.*). **2.** *Informal.* sir (used in direct address and not followed by the name of the man addressed): *Mister, is this your umbrella? Watch it, mister!* **3.** the informal or social title used in addressing a military warrant officer or cadet or any naval officer below the rank of commander. **4.** *Informal.* husband: *You and the mister staying long?* —*v.t.* **5.** *Informal.* to address or speak of as "mister" or "Mr." [var. of MASTER]

mist·flow·er (mist′flou′ər), *n.* a North American, composite plant, *Eupatorium* (*Conoclinium*) *coelestinum*, having heads of blue flowers. [MIST + FLOWER]

mis·think (mis thingk′), *v.*, **-thought, -think·ing.** *Archaic.* —*v.i.* **1.** to think incorrectly or unfavorably. —*v.t.* **2.** to think unfavorably or ill of. [ME *misthenke(n)*. See MIS-[1], THINK[1]]

Mis·ti (mēs′tē), *n.* See **El Misti.**

mis·time (mis tīm′), *v.t.*, **-timed, -tim·ing.** to time badly; perform, say, propose, etc., at a bad or inappropriate time. [ME *mistime(n)*, OE *mistīmian.* See MIS-[1], TIME]

mis′tle thrush′ (mis′əl), a large, European thrush, *Turdus viscivorus*, that feeds on the berries of the mistletoe. Also called **missel thrush.** [obs. *mistle* (OE *mistel*) mistletoe]

mis·tle·toe (mis′əl tō′), *n.* **1.** a European plant, *Viscum album*, having yellowish flowers and white berries, growing parasitically on various trees, used in Christmas decorations. **2.** any of several other related, similar plants, as *Phoradendron flavescens*, of the U.S.: the State flower of Oklahoma. [ME *mistilto*, appar. back formation from OE *mistiltān* (*mistil* mistletoe, basil + *tān* twig), the *-n* being taken as pl. ending; c. Icel *mistilteinn*]

Mistletoe, *Phoradendron flavescens*

mis′tletoe cac′tus, a tropical, branched cactus, *Rhipsalis Cassytha*, having cylindrical stems and mistletoelike fruit.

mis·took (mi sto͝ok′), *v.* pt. of **mistake.**

mis·tral (mis′trəl, mi sträl′), *n.* a cold, dry, northerly wind common in southern France and neighboring regions. [< MF < Pr; OPr *maistral* < L *magistrāl(is)* MAGISTRAL]

Mis·tral (mē STRAL′ *for 1;* mēs träl′ *for 2*), *n.* **1. Fré·dé·ric** (frā dā rēk′), 1830–1914, French Provençal poet: Nobel prize 1904. **2. Ga·bri·e·la** (gä′vrē e′lä), (*Lucila Godoy Alcayaga*), 1889–1957, Chilean poet and educator: Nobel prize for literature 1945.

mis·trans·late (mis′trans lāt′, -tranz-, mis trans′lāt, -tranz′-), *v.t., v.i.*, **-lat·ed, -lat·ing.** to translate incorrectly. [MIS-[1] + TRANSLATE] —**mis′trans·la′tion,** *n.*

mis·treat (mis trēt′), *v.t.* to treat badly or abusively. [late ME *mistrete.* See MIS-[1], TREAT] —**mis·treat′ment,** *n.*

mis·tress (mis′tris), *n.* **1.** a woman who has authority, control, or power, esp. the female head of a household, institution, or other establishment. **2.** a woman employing, or in authority over, servants or attendants. **3.** a female owner, as of a slave, horse, dog, etc. **4.** a woman who has the power of controlling or disposing of something at pleasure: *mistress of a great fortune.* **5.** something regarded as feminine which has control or supremacy: *Great Britain, the mistress of the seas.* **6.** *Brit.* a female teacher; schoolmistress. **7.** a woman who has a continuing, illicit sexual relationship with one man, esp. a man who, in return for an exclusive and continuing liaison, provides her with financial support; paramour. **8.** *Archaic.* sweetheart. **9.** *Archaic.* (used as a term of address to a woman, esp. preceding the full name of an unmarried woman.) [ME *maistresse* < MF, OF, equiv. to *maistre* MASTER + *-esse* -ESS] —**mis′tressed,** *adj.* —**mis′tress·ship′,** *n.*

mis′tress of cer′emonies, a woman who acts as master of ceremonies.

mis·tri·al (mis trī′əl, -trīl′), *n.* *Law.* **1.** a trial terminated without conclusion on the merits of the case because of some error in the proceedings. **2.** an inconclusive trial, as where the jury cannot agree. [MIS-[1] + TRIAL]

mis·sam′ple, *v.*, **-pled, -pling.**
mis·seat′, *v.t.*
mis·ship′, *v.*, **-shipped, -ship·ping.**
mis·ship′ment, *n.*
mis·sing′, *v.*, **-sang, -sung.**
mis·sort′, *v.*
mis·sound′, *v.*
mis·space′, *v.t.*, **-spaced, -spac·ing.**
mis·start′, *v.*
mis·steer′, *v.*
mis·style′, *v.*, **-styled, -styl·ing.**
mis′sup·pose′, *v.*, **-posed, -pos·ing.**
mis′syl·lab′i·fi·ca′tion, *n.*
mis′syl·lab′i·fy, *v.t.*, **-fied, -fy·ing.**
mis·term′, *v.t.*
mis·thread′, *v.*
mis·throw′, *v.*, **-threw, -thrown, -throw·ing.**
mis·tilled′, *adj.*
mis·ti′tle, *v.t.*, **-tled, -tling.**
mis·trace′, *v.*, **-traced, -trac·ing.**
mis′tran·scribe′, *v.t.*, **-scribed, -scrib·ing.**
mis′tran·scrip′tion, *n.*

mis·trust (mis trust′), *n.* **1.** lack of trust or confidence; distrust. —*v.t.* **2.** to regard with mistrust; distrust. **3.** to suspect or surmise. —*v.i.* **4.** to be distrustful. [ME *mistruste(n).* See MIS-[1], TRUST] —**mis·trust′er,** *n.* —**mis·trust′ing·ly,** *adv.*

mis·trust·ful (mis trust′fəl), *adj.* full of mistrust; suspicious. [MISTRUST + -FUL] —**mis·trust′ful·ly,** *adv.* —**mis·trust′ful·ness,** *n.*

mis·tryst (mis trīst′), *v.t. Scot. and North Eng.* **1.** to fail to meet or to keep an appointment with (someone). **2.** to be confused or perplexed by (something). [MIS-[1] + TRYST]

Mists, *n.* **Marsh of.** See **Palus Nebularum.**

mist·y (mis′tē), *adj.,* **mist·i·er, mist·i·est. 1.** abounding in or clouded by mist. **2.** of the nature of or consisting of mist. **3.** appearing as if seen through mist; indistinct in form or outline. **4.** obscure; vague. [ME; OE *mistig.* See MIST, -Y[1]] —**mist′i·ly,** *adv.* —**mist′i·ness,** *n.*

mist·y-eyed (mis′tē īd′), *adj.* easily moved to the point of tears; sentimental: *a misty-eyed romantic.*

mis·un·der·stand (mis′un dər stand′), *v.t., v.i.,* **-stood, -stand·ing. 1.** to misinterpret, as words or actions. **2.** to understand wrongly; take (words, statements, etc.) in a wrong sense. [ME *misunderstande(n).* See MIS-[1], UNDERSTAND] —**mis′un·der·stand′er,** *n.*

mis·un·der·stand·ing (mis′un dər stan′ding), *n.* **1.** disagreement or dissension. **2.** failure to understand; mistake as to meaning. [late ME; see MIS-[1], UNDERSTANDING] —**mis′un·der·stand′ing·ly,** *adv.*
—**Syn. 1.** discord, difference, difficulty, quarrel. **2.** misapprehension, error, misconception. —**Ant. 1.** con cord.

mis·un·der·stood (mis′un dər stŏŏd′), *adj.* **1.** improperly interpreted. **2.** unappreciated.

mis·us·age (mis yōō′sij, -zij), *n.* **1.** wrong or improper usage, as of words. **2.** bad or abusive treatment. [MIS-[1] + USAGE]

mis·use (*n.* mis yōōs′; *v.* mis yōōz′), *n., v.,* **-used, -us·ing.** —*n.* **1.** wrong or improper use; misapplication. **2.** *Obs.* ill-usage. —*v.t.* **3.** to use wrongly or improperly; misapply. **4.** to treat abusively; maltreat. [ME; see MIS-[1], USE]

mis·us·er[1] (mis yōō′zər), *n. Law.* abuse of a right; unlawful use of an office, franchise, benefit, etc. [n. use of MF *mesuser* to MISUSE]

mis·us·er[2] (mis yōō′zər), *n.* a person who misuses. [MIS-[1] + USER]

mis·val·ue (mis val′yōō), *v.t.,* **-ued, -u·ing.** to value wrongly, esp. to undervalue. [MIS-[1] + VALUE]

mis·ven·ture (mis ven′chər), *n.* an unfortunate undertaking; misadventure. [MIS-[1] + VENTURE]

mis·word (mis wûrd′), *v.t.* to word incorrectly. [MIS-[1] + WORD]

mis·write (mis rīt′), *v.t.,* **-wrote, -writ·ten, -writ·ing.** to write incorrectly. [ME *miswrite(n),* OE *miswrītan.* See MIS-[1], WRITE]

Mi·tan·ni (mi tan′ē), *n.* the Hurrian kingdom in NW Mesopotamia in the 15th and 14th centuries B.C.

Mi·tan·ni·an (mi tan′ē ən), *n.* **1.** a native or inhabitant of the Mitanni kingdom. —*adj.* **2.** of or pertaining to the Mitannians or the Mitanni kingdom. [MITANNI + -AN]

Mit bren·nen·der Sor·ge (mit bren′ən dər zôr′gə), *German. With Burning Sorrow* (the opening words and title of an encyclical of Pope Pius XI issued in 1937 on the menace of Nazism).

mitch′ board′ (mich), *Naut.* a crutch, esp. one for a lowered mast. [*mitch* < ? (see MIKE[2])]

Mitch·ell (mich′əl), *n.* **1. John,** 1870–1919, U.S. labor leader. **2. Margaret,** 1900–49, U.S. novelist. **3. Maria,** 1818–89, U.S. astronomer. **4. Silas Weir** (wēr), 1829–1914, U.S. physician and novelist. **5. William,** 1879–1936, U.S. general: pioneer in the field of aviation. **6. Mount,** a mountain in W North Carolina: highest peak in the E United States, 6684 ft. **7.** a city in SE South Dakota. 12,555 (1960). **8.** a town in S Indiana. 3552 (1960). **9.** a walled plain in the first quadrant of the face of the moon: about 22 miles in diameter. **10.** a boy's given name, form of **Michael.**

mite[1] (mīt), *n.* any of numerous small or minute arachnids of the order *Acarina,* including species which are parasitic on animals and plants or which are free-living, feeding on decaying matter and stored foods. [ME *myte,* OE *mīte;* c. MD *mīte,* OHG *miza* midge]

mite[2] (mīt), *n.* **1.** a contribution that is small but is all that a person can afford. **2.** a very small sum of money. **3.** a coin of very small value. **4.** a very small object. **5.** a very small creature. —*adv.* **6.** to a small extent; somewhat (often prec. by *a*): *He's always been a mite selfish.* [ME *myte* < MD *mīte;* ult. identical with MITE[1]]

mi·ter (mī′tər), *n.* **1.** the official headdress of a bishop in the Western Church, in its modern form a tall cap with a top deeply cleft crosswise, the outline of the front and back resembling that of a pointed arch. **2.** the office or rank of a bishop; bishopric. **3.** *Judaism.* the official headdress of the high priest, bearing on the front a gold plate engraved with the words *Holiness to the Lord.* Ex. 28:36–38. **4.** a fillet worn by women of ancient Greece. **5.** an oblique surface formed on a piece of wood or the like so as to butt against an oblique surface on another piece to be joined with it. **6.** Also called **last.** *Naut.* the inclined seam connecting the two cloths of an angulated sail. —*v.t.* **7.** to bestow a miter upon, or raise to a rank entitled to it. **8.** to join with a miter joint. **9.** to cut to a miter. Also, *esp. Brit.,* **mitre.** [ME *mitre* < L *mitra* < Gk: turban, headdress]

A

Miter (def. 1)
A, Lappet

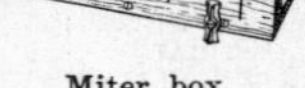

Miter box

mi′ter box′, *Carpentry.* any of various fixed or adjustable guides for a saw in making miters or cross cuts, esp. a troughlike box open at the ends and guiding the saw by slots in the opposite sides.

mi′ter box′ saw′. See **miter saw.**

mi·tered (mī′tərd), *adj.* **1.** shaped like a bishop's miter or having a miter-shaped apex. **2.** wearing, or entitled or privileged to wear, a miter. Also, *esp. Brit.,* **mitred.** [ME; see MITER, -ED[3]]

mi′tered jib′, *Naut.* a diagonal-cut jib. Also called **mi′ter jib′, patent-cut jib.**

mi′tered sail′, *Naut.* See **angulated sail.**

mi·ter·er (mī′tər ər), *n.* **1.** one who or that which miters. **2.** a machine or tool for making miters. [MITER + -ER[1]]

mi·ter·gate (mī′tər gāt′), *n.* (in a canal or the like) a lock gate having two leaves so made as to close at an angle pointing upstream. [MITER + GATE]

mi′ter gear′, either of a pair of bevel gears of equal size for driving shafts at right angles to each other.

Miter joint

mi′ter joint′, a joint, esp. a butt joint, between two pieces of wood or the like, meeting at an angle in which each of the butting surfaces is cut to an angle equal to half the angle of junction.

mi′ter post′. See **meeting post.**

mi′ter saw′, a backsaw used for cutting miters. Also called **miter box saw.**

mi′ter square′, *Carpentry.* an instrument for laying out miter joints, consisting of two straight edges joined at a 45° angle.

mi·ter·wort (mī′tər wûrt′), *n.* **1.** any saxifragaceous herb of the genus *Mitella,* having a capsule which resembles a bishop's miter. **2.** a low, loganiaceous plant, *Cynoctonum Mitreola,* of the southwestern U.S. Also, *esp. Brit.,* **mitrewort.** [MITER + WORT[2]]

Mit·ford (mit′fərd), *n.* **Mary Russell,** 1787–1855, English novelist, poet, playwright, and essayist.

mith·an (mith′ən), *n., pl.* **-an.** gayal. [< Assamese native name]

mith·er (mith′ər), *n. Scot. and North Eng.* mother.

Mith·gar·thr (mith′gär′thər), *n.* Midgard. Also, **Mith·garth** (mith′gärth).

Mith·rae·um (mi thrē′əm), *n., pl.* **Mith·rae·a** (mi thrē′ə), **Mith·rae·ums.** a temple of Mithras. [< NL < Gk *Mithraîon,* equiv. to *Mithr(âs)* MITHRAS + *-aion* suffix of place]

Mith·ra·ism (mith′rə iz′əm), *n.* an ancient Persian religion in which Mithras was worshipped, involving secret rituals to which only men were admitted: a major competitor of Christianity in the Roman empire during the 2nd and 3rd centuries A.D. Also, **Mith·ra·i·cism** (mith rā′i siz′əm). [MITHRA(S) + -ISM] —**Mith·ra·ic** (mith rā′ik), **Mith′ra·is′tic,** *adj.* —**Mith′ra·ist,** *n.*

Mith·ras (mith′ras), *n. Persian Myth.* the god of light and truth, later of the sun. Also, **Mith·ra** (mith′rə). [< L < Gk < OPers *Mithra*]

mith·ri·date (mith′ri dāt′), *n. Old Pharm.* a confection believed to contain an antidote to every poison. [earlier *mithridatum* < ML, var. of LL *mithridātium,* n. use of neut. of *Mithridātius,* equiv. to *Mithridāt(ēs)* MITHRIDATES VI + *-ius* -IOUS]

Mith·ri·da·tes VI (mith′ri dā′tēz), ("*the Great*") 132?–63 B.C., king of Pontus 120–63. Also called **Mith·rida′tes Eu′pa·tor** (yōō′pə tôr′).

mith·ri·da·tise (mith′ri dā′tīz), *v.t.,* **-tised, -tis·ing.** *Chiefly Brit.* mithridatize.

mith·ri·da·tism (mith′ri dā′tiz əm), *n.* the production of immunity against the action of a poison by taking the poison in gradually increased doses. [after MITHRIDATES (VI), said to have so immunized himself; see -ISM] —**mith·ri·dat·ic** (mith′ri dat′ik), *adj.*

mith·ri·da·tize (mith′ri dā′tīz), *v.t.,* **-tized, -tiz·ing.** to induce a state of mithridatism in (a person). Also, *esp. Brit.,* **mithridatise.** [MITHRIDAT(ISM) + -IZE]

mit·i·cide (mit′i sīd′), *n. Chem.* a substance or preparation for killing mites. [MITE[1] + -I- + -CIDE] —**mit′i·cid′al,** *adj.*

mit·i·gate (mit′ə gāt′), *v.,* **-gat·ed, -gat·ing.** —*v.t.* **1.** to lessen in force or intensity, as wrath, grief, harshness, pain, etc. **2.** to make less severe: *to mitigate a punishment.* **3.** *Rare.* to make (a person, one's state of mind, disposition, etc.) milder or more gentle; mollify; appease. —*v.i.* **4.** to become milder; lessen in severity. [< L *mītigāt(us)* calmed, softened, soothed (ptp. of *mītigāre*), equiv. to *mīt(is)* mild, soft, gentle + *-ig-* (var. of *ag-,* root of *agere* to make) + *-ātus* -ATE[1]] —**mit·i·ga·ble** (mit′ə gə bəl), *adj.* —**mit′i·gat′ed·ly,** *adv.* —**mit′i·ga′tion,** *n.* —**mit′i·ga′tive, mit·i·ga·to·ry** (mit′ə gə tōr′ē, -tôr′ē), *adj.* —**mit′i·ga′tor,** *n.*

mi·tis (mī′tis, mē′-), *n.* **1.** Also called **mi′tis met′al.** wrought iron melted and cast. —*adj.* **2.** noting or pertaining to mitis. [< L: soft; see MITIGATE]

Mit·nag·ged (mit nä gād′, mis-), *n., pl.* **Mit·nag·dim** (mit nag dēm′, mis-). *Judaism.* a Jew in central or eastern Europe in the 18th and 19th centuries who advocated an intellectual, legalistic approach to Judaism in opposition to the emotional, mystical approach of the Hasidim. Cf. **Hasid** (def. 1). [< Yiddish *misnaged,* NHeb *mithnaggēd,* Heb *mithnaggēd* opposing, opponent]

mi·to·chon·dri·on (mī′tə kon′drē ən, mit′ə-), *n., pl.* **-dri·a** (-drē ə). *Biol.* one of the minute, granular, rodlike or threadlike bodies occurring in the cytoplasm of cells and functioning in cellular metabolism. Also called **chondriosome.** [< Gk *míto(s)* a thread + *chondríon* small grain, equiv. to *chóndr(os)* grain, corn + *-ion* dim. suffix] —**mi′to·chon′dri·al,** *adj.*

mi·to·ko·ro·mo·no (mē tō′kō rō′mə nō′; *Jap.* mē tô′kô rô′mô nô′), *n., pl.* **-no.** a set of fittings for a Japanese sword, comprised of a kozuka, a kogai, and a pair of menuki. [< Jap, equiv. to *mi* three + *tokoro* places + *mono* items, objects]

mi·to·sis (mī tō′sis, mi-), *n. Biol.* the usual method of cell division, characterized typically by the resolving of the chromatin of the nucleus into a threadlike form, which separates into segments or chromosomes, each of which separates longitudinally into two parts, one part of each chromosome being retained in each of two new cells resulting from the original cell. [< Gk *mít(os)* a thread + -OSIS] —**mi·tot·ic** (mī tot′ik, mi-), *adj.* —**mi·tot′i·cal·ly,** *adv.*

mi·tra (mī′trə), *n. Bot.* **1.** the mitriform pileus of certain fungi. **2.** a galea. **3.** a spineless cactus, *Astrophytum myriostigma,* of Mexico, having brown-tipped, orange-yellow flowers. [< L: head-band; see MITER]

Mi·tra (mē′trə), *n. Hinduism.* the Vedic god of justice.

mi·trail·leur (mē trA yœr′), *n., pl.* **-trail·leurs** (-trA yœr′). *French.* a person who operates a machine gun.

mi·trail·leuse (mē trA yœz′), *n., pl.* **-trail·leuses** (-trA yœz′). *French.* a machine gun.

mi·tral (mī′trəl), *adj.* **1.** of or resembling a miter. **2.** *Anat.* of, pertaining to, or situated near a mitral valve. [MIT(E)R + -AL[1]]

mi′tral insuffi′ciency, *Pathol.* abnormal closure of the mitral valve resulting in regurgitation of blood into the atrium and leading to heart failure. Also called **mi′tral incom′petence.**

mi′tral steno′sis, *Pathol.* abnormal narrowing of the mitral valve usually resulting from disease, as rheumatic fever, and obstructing the free flow of blood from the atrium to the ventricle.

mi′tral valve′, *Anat.* the valve between the left atrium and ventricle of the heart, consisting of two triangular flaps of tissue, that prevents the blood from flowing back into the atrium. Also called **bicuspid valve.** Cf. **tricuspid valve.**

mi·tre (mī′tər), *n., v.t.,* **-tred, -tring.** *Chiefly Brit.* miter.

Mi·tre (mē′trā; *Sp.* mē′tre), *n.* **Bar·to·lo·mé** (bär′tô-lô me′), 1821–1906, Argentine soldier, statesman, and author: president of Argentina 1862–68.

Mit·re·pho·rus (mi trē′fər əs), *n. Class. Myth.* an epithet of Dionysus, meaning "headband-bearing."

mi·tre·wort (mī′tər wûrt′), *n. Chiefly Brit.* miterwort.

mi·tri·form (mī′trə fôrm′), *adj.* shaped like the miter of a bishop. [< NL *mitriform(is).* See MITER, -FORM]

Mi·tro·pou·los (mi trop′ə ləs; *Gk.* mē trô′pōō lôs), *n.* **Di·mi·tri** (di mē′trē; *Gk.* thē mē′trē), 1897–1960, Greek symphony orchestra conductor in the U.S.

Mit·scher (mich′ər), *n.* **Marc Andrew,** 1887–1947, U.S. naval officer and aviator.

mits·vah (mits vä′; *Eng.* mits′və), *n., pl.* **-voth** (-vôt′), *Eng.* **-vahs.** *Hebrew.* mitzvah.

mitt (mit), *n.* **1.** a long, fingerless glove extending to the elbow or beyond, worn by women. **2.** *Baseball.* **a.** a rounded glove with one internal section for the four fingers and another for the thumb and having the side next to the palm of the hand protected by a thick padding, used by catchers. **b.** a somewhat similar glove but with less padding and having sections for the thumb and one or two fingers, used by first basemen. Cf. **baseball glove. 3.** a mitten. **4.** *Slang.* a hand. [short for MITTEN]

mitt., (in prescriptions) send. [< L *mitte*]

mit·ta·tur (mi tā′tər), *v.* (in prescriptions) let it be sent. [< L]

Mit·tel·eu·ro·pa (mit′əl oi rō′pä), *n. German.* Central Europe; the continent of Europe under German domination: a concept of European politics prior to the end of World War I.

mit·ten (mit′ən), *n.* **1.** a hand covering enclosing the four fingers together and the thumb separately. **2.** mitt (def. 1). **3. mittens,** *Boxing Slang.* boxing gloves. **4. give** or **get the mitten,** *Informal.* to dismiss or be dismissed as a lover or suitor; jilt or be jilted. [ME *miteyn* < MF, OF *mitaine,* equiv. to *mite* mitten (< ?) + *-aine* -AN] —**mit′ten-like′,** *adj.*

mit′ten mon′ey, *Naut. Slang.* a supplementary charge for piloting in cold weather.

Mit·ter·rand (mētə rän; *Eng.* mē′tə rand′, mit′ə-), *n.* **Fran·çois** (frän swa′), born 1916, French political leader: president since 1981.

mit·ti·mus (mit′ə məs), *n., pl.* **-mus·es.** *Law.* **1.** a warrant of commitment to prison. **2.** a writ for removing a suit or a record from one court to another. [late ME < L: we send, first word of writ in Latin: see REMIT]

mitt. tal., (in prescriptions) send of such; send of this. [< L *mitte tālis*]

Mit·zi (mit′sē), *n.* a girl's given name. Also, **Mit′zie.**

mitz·vah (mits vä′; *Eng.* mits′və), *n., pl.* **-voth** (-vôt′), *Eng.* **-vahs.** *Hebrew.* **1.** any of the group of 613 commandments or precepts that are present in or derived from the Bible and that relate chiefly to the religious and moral conduct of Jews. **2.** a good or praiseworthy deed, as in conformity with the letter or spirit of a Biblical commandment. Also, **mitsvah.** [lit., commandment]

mix (miks), *v.,* **mixed** or **mixt, mix·ing,** *n.* —*v.t.* **1.** to put (substances, elements, things, etc.) together into one mass, collection, or assemblage, generally with a thorough blending of the constituents. **2.** to put together indiscriminately or confusedly (often fol. by *up*). **3.** to combine, unite, or join: *to mix business and pleasure.* **4.** to add as an element or ingredient: *to mix a little soda into the flour.* **5.** to form by combining ingredients: *to mix bread; to mix mortar.* **6.** to crossbreed. —*v.i.* **7.** to become mixed: *a paint that mixes easily with water.* **8.** to associate, as in company: *to mix with the other guests at a party.* **9.** to be crossbred, or of mixed breeding. **10.** *Boxing Slang.* to exchange blows vigorously and aggressively: *The crowd jeered as the fighters jabbed and clinched, refusing to mix.* **11. mix it up,** *Slang.* **a.** to engage in a quarrel. **b.** to fight with the fists. **12. mix up,** to confuse completely, esp. to mistake one person or thing for another: *The teacher was always mixing up the twins, to the amusement of the rest of us.* —*n.* **13.** the act or an instance of mixing. **14.** the result of mixing; mixture: *cement mix.* **15.** a commercially prepared blend of ingredients to which usually only a liquid must be added to make up the total of ingredients necessary or obtain the desired consistency: *a cake mix; muffin mix.* **16.** the proportion of ingredients in a mixture; formula: *a mix of two to one.* **17.** *Informal.* a mess or muddle. [late ME, back formation from *mixt* MIXED] —**mix′a·bil′i·ty, mix′a·ble·ness,** *n.* —**mix′a·ble, mix′i·ble,** *adj.*
—**Syn. 1, 7.** commingle, jumble, unite, amalgamate, fuse. MIX, BLEND, COMBINE, MINGLE concern the bringing of two or more things into more or less intimate

mis·tune′, *v.,* -tuned, -tun·ing. mis·tu′tor, *v.* mis·type′, *v.,* -typed, typ·ing. mis·typed′, *adj.* mis·un′ion, *n.* mis·wire′, *v.,* -wired, -wir·ing. mis·wor′ship, *v.,* -shiped or -shipped, -ship·ing or -ship·ping. mis·zone′, *v.,* -zoned, -zon·ing.

association. MIX is the general word for such association: *to mix fruit juices.* BLEND implies such a harmonious joining of two or more types of colors, feelings, etc., that the new product formed displays some of the qualities of each: *to blend fragrances or whiskeys.* COMBINE implies such a close or intimate union that distinction between the parts is lost: *to combine forces.* MINGLE usually suggests retained identity of the parts: *to mingle voices.* **7.** coalesce. **14.** concoction; formula.

mixed (mikst), *adj.* **1.** put together or formed by mixing. **2.** composed of different constituents or elements: *a mixed form of government.* **3.** of different kinds combined: *mixed nuts.* **4.** involving or comprised of persons of different sex, class, character, belief, religion, race, etc.: *mixed company; mixed neighborhood.* **5.** *Law.* involving more than one issue or aspect: *a mixed question of law and fact.* **6.** *Phonet.* (of a vowel) central. **7.** *Math.* (of partial derivatives) of second or higher order and involving differentiation with respect to more than one variable. **8.** (of trains) composed of both passenger and freight cars. **9.** *Logic.* containing quantifiers of unlike kind. **10. mixed up,** completely confused. [late ME *mixt* < L *mixt(us),* ptp. of *miscēre* to mingle. See MIX] —**mix·ed·ly** (mik′sid lē, mikst′lē), *adv.* —**mix′ed·ness,** *n.*

—**Syn. 1.** commingled. MIXED, MINGLED both refer to intimate association of two or more things. MIXED is generally applied to one noun, MINGLED commonly to two or more: *mixed feelings.*

mixed′ ac′id, *Chem.* any mixture of nitric acid and sulfuric acid, used as a nitrating agent in the manufacture of explosives, plastics, etc.

mixed′ bless′ing, an event or situation that, although generally favorable or advantageous, has one or more unfavorable or disadvantageous features.

mixed′ bud′. See under **bud**[1] (def. 1a).

mixed′ econ′omy, an economy in which there are elements of both public and private enterprise.

mixed′ four′some, a foursome of two teams, each comprised of a man and a woman.

mixed′ grill′, several kinds of broiled or grilled meats, and usually vegetables, served together, as a lamb chop, a pork sausage, a piece of liver, grilled tomatoes, and mushrooms.

mixed′ mar′riage, a marriage between persons of different religions or races.

mixed′ met′aphor, the use in the same expression of two or more metaphors which are incongruous or illogical when combined, as in "The president will put the ship of state on its feet."

mixed′ nerve′, *Anat.* a nerve composed of both sensory and motor fibers.

mixed′ num′ber, *Arith.* a number consisting of a whole number and a fraction, as 4½ or 4.5.

mix·er (mik′sər), *n.* **1.** one who or that which mixes. **2.** *Informal.* a person, with reference to his sociability: *He is a good mixer to have at a large party.* **3.** a kitchen utensil or an electrical appliance having one or more beaters and used in mixing, beating, blending, etc., foodstuffs. **4.** an electrical system, as in a broadcasting studio, providing for the blending, fading, substituting, etc., of sounds from various sources, as from microphones, recordings, etc. **5.** *Radio and Television.* a sound technician who operates the mixer in a studio. **6.** See **mixing faucet. 7.** *Metall.* a vessel for blending and storing molten pig iron from several blast furnaces. [MIX + -ER[1]]

mix′ing fau′cet, a single outlet for water from separately controlled hot-water and cold-water taps.

mix′ing ra′tio, the ratio of the mass of water vapor in the air to the mass of the dry air, a measure of atmospheric humidity. Cf. **absolute humidity, dew point, humidity, specific humidity.**

mix′ing valve′, a valve receiving water from both a hot-water and a cold-water line and controlling the relative amount of water admitted from each.

mix·ol·o·gist (mik sol′ə jist), *n. Facetious.* a person skilled in making cocktails and highballs, as a bartender. [MIXOLOG(Y) + -IST]

mix·ol·o·gy (mik sol′ə jē), *n. Facetious.* the art or skill of preparing mixed alcoholic beverages. [MIX + -O- + -LOGY]

mix′o·lyd′ian mode′ (mik′sə lid′ē ən, mik′-), *Music.* an authentic church mode represented on the white keys of a keyboard instrument by an ascending scale from G to G. [< Gk *mixolȳdi(os)* (*mixo-,* comb. form of *mîxis* a mingling + *Lȳdos* Lydian) + -AN]

mix·o·ploid (mik′sə ploid′), *n. Genetics.* an organism having an unequal number of chromosome sets in adjacent cells or tissues. [*mixo-* (< Gk, comb. form of *mîxis* a mingling) + *-ploid* < Gk *-pl(oos)* -fold (as in *tetraplóos* fourfold) + -OID] —**mix′o·ploi′dy,** *n.*

mixt (mikst), *v.* a pt. and pp. of **mix.**

Mix·tec (mēs′tek), *n., pl.* **-tecs,** (*esp. collectively*) **-tec** for 1. **1.** a member of an Amerindian people of Guerrero, Oaxaca, and Puebla, Mexico. **2.** the language spoken by this Indian tribe. Also, **Mixteco.** —**Mix·tec′an,** *adj., n.*

Mix·te·co (mēs tek′ō), *n., pl.* **-cos,** (*esp. collectively*) **-co.** Mixtec.

mix·ture (miks′chər), *n.* **1.** a product of mixing. **2.** any combination or blend of different elements, kinds, qualities, etc.: *a mixture of good and bad traits.* **3.** *Chem., Physics.* an aggregate of two or more substances which are not chemically united and which exist in no fixed proportion to each other. **4.** a fabric woven of yarns combining various colors: *a heather mixture.* **5.** the act of mixing or the state of being mixed. **6.** an added element or ingredient; admixture. [late ME < L *mixtūra,* equiv. to *mixt(us)* mixed + *-ūra* -URE]

—**Syn. 1.** blend, combination; compound. **2.** conglomeration, miscellany, jumble; medley; mélange, potpourri, hodgepodge.

mix-up (miks′up′), *n.* **1.** a confused state of things; muddle; tangle. **2.** *Informal.* a fight. [n. use of v. phrase *mix up*]

Mi·zar (mī′zär), *n. Astron.* a double star in the middle of the constellation Ursa Major.

Miz·ra·chi (miz rä′ḵʜē), *n.* **1.** an Israeli religious group organized in 1902 as a wing of the orthodox Zionist movement, chiefly devoted to furthering traditional Judaism. —*adj.* **2.** of or pertaining to the Mizrachi. Also, **Miz·ra′hi.** [< Heb *Mizrāhi,* lit., of the east]

miz·rah (miz ʀäḵʜ′), *n. Hebrew.* **1.** a decorative figure or picture, usually bearing an inscription, that is hung in homes on the eastern wall or in synagogues in front of the reading table when the worshiper is at prayer. **2.** the row of seats on each side of the Holy Ark in a synagogue. Also, **mizrach′.** [lit., east]

miz·zen (miz′ən), *Naut.* —*n.* **1.** a fore-and-aft sail set on a mizzenmast. Cf. **crossjack, spanker** (def. 1a). **2.** mizzenmast. —*adj.* **3.** of or pertaining to a mizzenmast. **4.** noting a sail, yard, boom, etc., or any rigging belonging to a mizzen lower mast or to some upper mast of a mizzenmast. **5.** noting any stay running aft and upward to the head of a mizzen lower mast or to some specified upper mast of a mizzen mast: *mizzen topmast stay.* Also, **miz′en.** [late ME *meson,* prob. < It *mezzana* < Ar *mazzān* mast]

miz·zen·mast (miz′ən mast′, -mäst′; *Naut.* miz′ən-məst), *n. Naut.* **1.** the third mast from forward in a vessel having three or more masts. See illus. under **quarter-deck. 2.** the after and shorter mast of a yawl, ketch, or dandy; jiggermast. Also, **miz′en·mast′.** [late ME *meson mast.* See MIZZEN, MAST[1]]

miz·zle[1] (miz′əl), *v.,* **-zled, -zling,** *n. Chiefly Dial.* —*v.t., v.i.* **1.** to rain in fine drops; drizzle; mist. —*n.* **2.** mist or drizzle. [late ME; c. Flem *mizzelen,* LG *miseln* to drizzle; akin to MD *misel* mist, dew, etc.]

miz·zle[2] (miz′əl), *v.i.,* **-zled, -zling.** *Brit. Slang.* to disappear suddenly; to slink away, decamp, or vanish. [?]

miz·zle[3] (miz′əl), *v.t.,* **-zled, -zling.** *Dial.* to confuse; muddle. [?]

M.J., Master of Journalism.

Mjöl·nir (myœl′nir), *n. Scand. Myth.* Miölnir. Also, **Mjöll′nir, Mjoll′nir.**

mk., *pl.* **mks.** mark[2] (def. 1).

MKS, meter-kilogram-second. Also, **mks, m.k.s.**

mkt., market.

ML, Medieval Latin. Also, **M.L.**

mL, millilambert; millilamberts.

ml, milliliter; milliliters.

ml., **1.** mail. **2.** milliliter.

M.L.A., **1.** Master of Landscape Architecture. **2.** Modern Language Association.

M.L.Arch., Master of Landscape Architecture.

MLB, Maritime Labor Board.

MLF, Multilateral Nuclear Force.

MLG., Middle Low German. Also, **M.L.G.**

M-line (em′līn′), *n. Physics.* one of a series of lines (**M-series**) in the x-ray spectrum of an atom corresponding to radiation (**M-radiation**) caused by the transition of an electron to the M-shell.

Mlle., *pl.* **Mlles.** Mademoiselle. Also, **Mlle**

M.L.S., Master of Library Science.

MLW, mean low water.

mlx, millilux; millilucis.

mM, millimole; millimoles.

mm, millimeter; millimeters.

MM., Messieurs.

mm., **1.** thousands. [< L *millia*] **2.** millimeter; millimeters.

M.M., **1.** Master Mason. **2.** Master Mechanic. **3.** Master of Music.

Mme., *pl.* **Mmes.** Madame.

M.M.E., **1.** Master of Mechanical Engineering. **2.** Master of Mining Engineering. **3.** Master of Music Education.

Mme. Butterfly. See **Madame Butterfly.**

M.Met.E., Master of Metallurgical Engineering.

mmf, *Elect.* micromicrofarad.

m.m.f., magnetomotive force.

mmfd, *Elect.* micromicrofarad.

M.Mgt.E., Master of Management Engineering.

mm Hg, millimeter of mercury.

mmho, millimho; millimhos.

MMRBM, *Rocketry.* mobile mid-range ballistic missile.

M.M.Sc., Master of Medical Science.

M.Mus., Master of Music.

M.Mus.Ed., Master of Music Education.

Mn, *Chem.* manganese.

M.N.A., Master of Nursing Administration.

M.N.A.S., Member of the National Academy of Sciences.

M.N.E., Master of Nuclear Engineering.

mne·me (nē′mē), *n.* **1.** *Psychol.* the retentive basis or basic principle in a mind or organism accounting for memory. **2.** (*cap.*) *Class. Myth.* the Muse of memory, one of the original three Muses. [< Gk *mnḗmē* memory; see MNEMONIC] —**mne·mic** (nē′mik), *adj.*

Mne·mon (nē′mən), *n. Class. Myth.* a companion of Achilles, slain by him when he failed to remind him never to kill a child of Apollo.

mne·mon·ic (nē mon′ik, ni-), *adj.* **1.** assisting or intended to assist the memory. **2.** pertaining to mnemonics or to memory. [< Gk *mnēmonik(ós)* of, relating to memory, equiv. to *mnēmon-* (s. of *mnḗmōn*) mindful + *-ikos* -IC] —**mne·mon′i·cal·ly,** *adv.*

mne·mon·ics (nē mon′iks, ni-), *n.* (*construed as sing.*) the art of improving or developing the memory. Also called **mne·mo·tech·nics** (nē′mō tek′niks). [see MNEMONIC, -ICS]

Mne·mos·y·ne (nē mos′ə nē′, -moz′-, ni-), *n.* the ancient Greek goddess of memory, a daughter of Uranus and Gaea and the mother by Zeus of the Muses. [< Gk: lit., memory, akin to *mnâsthai* to remember, *mnḗmōn* mindful]

-mnesia, a combining form denoting a certain type of memory: *paramnesia.* [comb. form abstracted from AMNESIA]

Mnes·i·cles (nes′ə klēz′), *n.* Greek architect of the 5th century B.C.

Mngr., Monsignor.

M.N.S., Master of Nutritional Science.

M.Nurs., Master of Nursing.

mo (mō), *n. Informal.* moment (def. 1). [by shortening]

Mo (mō), *n.* a boy's given name, form of **Morris** or **Moses.** Also, **Moe.**

-mo, a suffix occurring in a series of compounds that describe book sizes according to the number of leaves formed by the folding of a single sheet of paper: *sixteenmo.* [comb. form abstracted from DUODECIMO]

Mo, *Chem.* molybdenum.

Mo., **1.** Missouri. **2.** Monday.

mo., **1.** *pl.* **mos.** month. **2.** months.

M.O., **1.** mail order. **2.** manually operated. **3.** Medical Officer. **4.** method of working. [< L *modus operandi*] **5.** money order.

m.o., **1.** mail order. **2.** money order.

mo·a (mō′ə), *n.* any of several extinct, flightless birds of the family *Dinornithidae,* of New Zealand, related to the kiwis but resembling the ostrich. [< Maori]

Moa, *Dinornis maximus* (Height 10 ft.)

Mo·ab (mō′ab), *n.* **1** an ancient kingdom E of the Dead Sea, in what is now Jordan. See map under **Philistia. 2.** a town in E Utah. 4682 (1960).

Mo·ab·ite (mō′ə bīt′), *n.* **1.** an inhabitant or native of Moab. **2.** an extinct language of Moab, in the Canaanite group of Semitic languages. —*adj.* **3.** Also, **Mo·a·bit·ic** (mō′ə bit′ik). of or pertaining to the ancient kingdom of Moab, its people, or their language. Also, **Mo·a·bit·ish** (mō′ə bī′tish); *referring to a woman,* **Mo·a·bit·ess** (mō′ə bī′tis). [ME < L *Mōabīta* < Gk *Mōabítēs,* repr. Heb *mōābī.* See MOAB, -ITE[1]]

Mo′abite Stone′, a slab of black basalt bearing an inscription recording the victory of Mesha, the king of Moab, over the Israelites, about 860 B.C. Also called **Mesha Stele.**

moan (mōn), *n.* **1.** a prolonged, low, inarticulate sound uttered from or as if from physical or mental suffering. **2.** any similar sound: *the moan of the wind.* **3.** *Archaic.* complaint or lamentation. —*v.i.* **4.** to utter moans, as of pain or grief. **5.** (of the wind, sea, trees, etc.) to make any sound suggestive of such moans. —*v.t.* **6.** to utter (something) inarticulately or pitifully, as if in lamentation: *He moaned his response.* **7.** to lament or bemoan: *to moan one's fate.* [ME *mone, man(e),* OE **mān,* inferred from its deriv. *mǣnan* to mourn] —**moan′ful,** *adj.* —**moan′ful·ly,** *adv.* —**moan′ing·ly,** *adv.*

—**Syn. 1.** See **groan. 4.** grieve. **4, 7.** mourn. **7.** deplore.

moat (mōt), *Fort.* —*n.* **1.** a deep, wide trench, usually filled with water, surrounding a fortified place, as a town or a castle. —*v.t.* **2.** to surround with or as with a moat. [ME *mote* < OF: clod, mound, perh. < Gmc]

mob (mob), *n., adj., v.,* **mobbed, mob·bing.** —*n.* **1.** a disorderly or riotous crowd of people. **2.** a crowd bent on or engaged in lawless violence. **3.** *Sociol.* a group of persons stimulating one another to excitement and losing ordinary rational control over their activity. **4.** *Sometimes Disparaging.* any group or collection of persons, animals, or things. **5.** the mass of common people; the populace or multitude. **6.** a criminal gang: *John joined the mob when he was a kid.* —*adj.* **7.** of, pertaining to, or characteristic of a lawless, irrational, disorderly, or riotous crowd: *mob rule; mob instincts.* **8.** directed at or reflecting the lowest intellectual level of the common people: *mob appeal; the mob mentality.* —*v.t.* **9.** to crowd around noisily, as from curiosity or hostility: *Spectators mobbed the courtroom.* **10.** to attack violently or riotously: *The crowd mobbed the consulate.* **11.** *Fox Hunting.* to chop (a fox). [short for L *mōbile (vulgus)* the movable (i.e., changeable, inconstant) common people] —**mob′ber, mob′bist,** *n.* —**mob′bish,** *adj.* —**mob′bish·ly,** *adv.* —**mob′bish·ness,** *n.* —**mob′bism,** *n.*

mob·cap (mob′kap′), *n.* a large, full cap fitting down over the ears and frequently tying beneath the chin, formerly much worn indoors by women. [*mob* woman (? var. of *Mab* for *Mabel*) + CAP[1]]

mo·bile (mō′bəl *or, esp. for* 8, mō′bēl), *adj.* **1.** movable; capable of moving readily. **2.** *Mil.* permanently equipped with vehicles for transport. **3.** flowing freely, as a liquid. **4.** changeable or changing easily in expression, mood, purpose, etc., as the human face. **5.** quickly responding to impulses, emotions, etc., as the mind. **6.** *Sociol.* **a.** characterized by or permitting the mixing of social groups. **b.** characterized by or permitting individual progress from one social group to a higher one. **7.** of or pertaining to a mobile. —*n.* **8.** a piece of sculpture having delicately balanced units constructed of rods and sheets of metal or other material suspended in midair by wire or twine so that the individual parts can move independently, as when stirred by a breeze. Cf. **stabile** (def. 3). [< L, neut. of *mōbilis* movable, equiv. to *mō-* (ptp. s. of *movēre* to MOVE) + *-bilis* -BLE]

Mo·bile (mō bēl′), *n.* **1.** a seaport in SW Alabama at the mouth of the Mobile River. 202,779 (1960). **2.** a river in SW Alabama, formed by the confluence of the Alabama and Tombigbee rivers. 38 mi. long.

Mo′bile Bay′ (mō′bēl), a bay of the Gulf of Mexico, in SW Alabama: Civil War naval battle 1864. 36 mi. long; 8–18 mi. wide.

mo′bile home′, a large house trailer, designed for year-round living in one place.

mo′bile u′nit (mō′bəl), a vehicle supplied with the basic equipment or materials necessary for a particular purpose, as for televising on location, being used as an x-ray or inoculation clinic, etc.

mo·bi·lise (mō′bə līz′), *v.t., v.i.,* **-lised, -lis·ing.** *Chiefly Brit.* mobilize. —**mo′bi·lis′a·ble,** *adj.* —**mo′bi·li·sa′tion,** *n.* —**mo′bi·lis′er,** *n.*

mo·bil·i·ty (mō bil′i tē), *n.* **1.** the quality of being mobile. **2.** *Sociol.* the movement of people in a population, as from place to place, from job to job, or from one social class to another. [< L *mōbilitās.* See MOBILE, -ITY]

mo·bi·lize (mō′bə līz′), *v.,* **-lized, -liz·ing.** —*v.t.* **1.** to assemble or marshal (armed forces, military reserves, or civilian men of military age) into readiness for active service. **2.** to organize or adapt (industries, transportation facilities, etc.) for service to the government in time of war. **3.** to marshal, bring together, prepare (power, force, wealth, etc.) for action, esp. of a vigorous nature: *to mobilize one's energy for a task.* **4.** to increase or bring to a full stage of development: *to mobilize one's anger.* —*v.i.* **5.** to be or become assembled, organized, etc., as for war: *The troop mobilized for action.* Also, *esp. Brit.,* **mobilise.** [back formation from *mobilization.* See MOBILE, -IZATION] —**mo′bi·liz′a·ble,** *adj.* —**mo′bi·li·za′tion,** *n.* —**mo′bi·liz′er,** *n.*

Mö·bi·us (mœ′bē əs, mā′-, mē′-; *Ger.* mœ′bē o͝os), *n.* **Au·gust Fer·di·nand** (ou′go͝ost fer′di nänt′), 1790–1868, German mathematician. Also, **Moebius.**

Mö′bi·us strip′, *Geom.* a continuous, one-sided surface formed by twisting one end of a rectangular strip through 180° about the longitudinal axis of the strip and attaching this end to the other. [named after A. F. MÖBIUS]

Mö′bius transforma′tion, *Math.* a map of the complex plane to itself in which a point z is mapped to a point w by $w = (az + b)/(cz + d)$, where a, b, c, and d are complex numbers and $ad - bc$ does not equal zero. Also called **bilinear transformation, linear fractional transformation.** [see MÖBIUS STRIP]

mo·ble (mob′əl), *v.t.,* **-bled, -bling.** *Archaic.* to wrap the head of, as in a hood. [? var. of MUFFLE]

mob·oc·ra·cy (mob ok′rə sē), *n., pl.* **-cies.** **1.** political control by a mob; mob rule. **2.** the mob as a ruling class. [MOB + -O- + -CRACY] —**mob·o·crat** (mob′ə krat′), *n.* —**mob′o·crat′ic, mob′o·crat′i·cal,** *adj.*

Mo·bridge (mō′brij), *n.* a town in N South Dakota. 4391 (1960).

mob·ster (mob′stər), *n.* a member of a gang of criminals. [MOB + -STER]

Mo·by Dick (mō′bē dik′), a novel (1851) by Herman Melville.

moc (mok), *n. Informal.* moccasin. [shortened form]

Mo·çam·bi·que (mō′səm bē′kə), *n.* Portuguese name of **Mozambique.**

moc·ca·sin (mok′ə sin, -zən), *n.* **1.** a shoe made entirely of soft leather, as deerskin, worn originally by the American Indians. **2.** a hard-soled shoe or slipper resembling this. **3.** any of several snakes of the genus *Ancistrodon,* esp. the cottonmouth. [< Algonquian (Va.) *mockasin*]

moc′casin flow′er, **1.** the lady's-slipper. **2.** a cypripedium, *Cypripedium reginae,* of the U.S.

mo·cha (mō′kə), *n.* **1.** (*cap.*) a seaport in S Yemen. ab. 5000. **2.** a choice variety of coffee, originally coming from Mocha. **3.** a flavoring obtained from a coffee infusion or a combined infusion of chocolate and coffee. **4.** a brownish chocolate color. **5.** a glove leather, finer and thinner than doeskin, the best grades of which are made from Arabian goatskins.

Mo′cha ware′, a pottery ware of the late 18th through the early 20th centuries, ornamented with colored glaze worked into branchlike patterns by drops of a diffusing agent applied while the glaze is still wet.

Mo·chi·ca (mō che̲′kə), *adj.* of, pertaining to, or characteristic of an ancient culture that flourished on the northern coast of Peru. Also, **Mo·che** (mō′cha̲; *Sp.* mô′che).

mo·chi·la (mō che̲′lə; *Sp.* mô che̲′lä), *n.* a flap of leather on the seat of a saddle, used as a covering and sometimes as a base to which saddlebags are attached. [< Sp: lit., knapsack, deriv. of *mochil* errand boy < Basque *motxil,* dim. of *motil, mutil* boy, servant < L *mutilus* mutilated (from the custom of shaving boys' heads)]

mock (mok), *v.t.* **1.** to assail or treat with ridicule, contempt, or derision. **2.** to ridicule by mimicry of action or speech; mimic derisively. **3.** to mimic, imitate, or counterfeit. **4.** to dismiss; defy: *His actions mock convention.* **5.** to deceive, delude, or disappoint. —*v.i.* **6.** to use ridicule or derision; scoff; jeer (often fol. by *at*). **7. mock up,** to build a mock-up of. —*n.* **8.** a mocking or derisive action or speech; mockery or derision. **9.** something mocked or derided; an object of derision. **10.** an imitation. **11.** *Shipbuilding.* **a.** a hard pattern representing the surface of a plate with a warped form, upon which the plate is beaten to shape after furnacing. **b.** bed (def. 22). —*adj.* **12.** being an imitation, semblance, or counterfeit of: *a mock battle.* [late ME *mokke(n)* < MF *mocque(r)*] —**mock′a·ble,** *adj.* —**mock′er,** *n.* —**mock′ing·ly,** *adv.*
—**Syn. 1.** deride; taunt, flout, gibe; chaff, tease. See **ridicule. 5.** cheat, dupe, fool, mislead. **6.** ridicule; banter. **10.** sham, counterfeit, fake.

mock′ chick′en. See **city chicken.**

mock′ ep′ic, a long, humorous poem written in mock-heroic style.

mock·er·nut (mok′ər nut′), *n.* **1.** a North American hickory, *Carya tomentosa,* bearing a sweet, edible nut. **2.** the nut itself. Also called **mock′ernut hick′ory.** [MOCKER + NUT]

mock·er·y (mok′ə rē), *n., pl.* **-er·ies.** **1.** ridicule, contempt, or derision. **2.** a derisive action or speech. **3.** a subject or occasion of derision. **4.** an imitation, esp. of a ridiculous or unsatisfactory kind. **5.** a mocking pretense; travesty: *a mockery of justice.* **6.** something absurdly or offensively inadequate or unfitting. [ME *moquerie* < MF. See MOCK, -ERY]

mock-he·ro·ic (mok′hi rō′ik), *adj.* **1.** imitating or burlesquing that which is heroic, as in manner, character, or action: *mock-heroic dignity.* **2.** *Literature.* of or pertaining to a form of satire in which trivial subjects, characters, and events are treated in the ceremonious manner and with the elevated language and elaborate devices characteristic of the heroic style. —*n.* **3.** an imitation or burlesque of that which is heroic. —**mock′-he·ro′i·cal·ly,** *adv.*

mock·ing·bird (mok′ing bûrd′), *n.* **1.** any of several gray, black, and white songbirds of the genus *Mimus,* esp. *M. polyglottos,* of the southern U.S. and Mexico, noted for their ability to mimic the songs of other birds. **2.** any of various related or similar birds, as *Melanotis caerulescens* (**blue mockingbird**), of Mexico. [MOCKING + BIRD]

mock′ mold′, *Shipbuilding.* bed (def. 22).

mock′ moon′, paraselene.

mock′ or′ange, **1.** the syringa, *Philadelphus coronarius.* **2.** See **laurel cherry.**

mock′ pen′dulum, a false pendulum bob attached to the balances of certain timepieces and visible through a slot in the dial or case.

mock′ sun′, parhelion.

mock′ tur′tle soup′, a rich clear soup prepared to resemble turtle soup, made with a calf's head or other meat, seasonings, and often with wine.

mock-up (mok′up′), *n.* a model, often full-size, for study, testing, or teaching. [n. use of v. phrase *mock up*]

Moc·te·zu·ma (*Sp.* môk′te so͞o′mä), *n.* See Montezuma II.

mod (mod), *n.* (*sometimes cap.*) **1.** (formerly) a British teenager who strives to attain a sophisticated, aloof personality and affects an ultramodern version of Edwardian dress and manners. Cf. **rock**[2] (def. 13), **Teddy boy. 2.** a person who wears mod clothing. —*adj.* **3.** pertaining to a style of dress characterized by bold colors, patterns, and stripes. [short for MODERN]

mod., **1.** moderate. **2.** *Music.* moderato. **3.** modern.

mod·al (mōd′əl), *adj.* **1.** of or pertaining to mode, manner, or form. **2.** *Music.* **a.** pertaining to mode, as distinguished from key. **b.** based on a scale other than major or minor. **3.** *Gram.* noting or pertaining to mood. **4.** *Philos.* pertaining to a mode of a thing, as distinguished from one of its basic attributes or from its substance or matter. **5.** *Logic.* exhibiting or expressing some phase of modality. [< ML *modāl(is).* See MODE[1], -AL[1]] —**mod′al·ly,** *adv.*

mod′al auxil′iary, *Gram.* any of the group of English auxiliary verbs, including *can, dare, do, may, must, need, shall, will,* that are used with the base form of another verb to express distinctions of mood.

mo·dal·i·ty (mō dal′i tē), *n., pl.* **-ties.** **1.** the quality or state of being modal. **2.** a modal attribute or circumstance. **3.** Also called **mode.** *Logic.* the classification of propositions according to whether they are contingently true or false, possible, impossible, or necessary. **4.** *Med.* the application of a therapeutic agent, usually a physical therapeutic agent. **5.** one of the primary forms of sensation, as vision, touch, etc. [< ML *modālitās.* See MODAL, -ITY]

mode[1] (mōd), *n.* **1.** manner of acting or doing; method; way. **2.** the natural disposition or the manner of existence or action of anything; form: *Heat is a mode of motion.* **3.** *Philos.* **a.** appearance, form, or disposition taken by a thing, or by one of its essential properties or attributes. **b.** (in the philosophy of Spinoza) one of the nonessential qualifications of God, contingent upon other modes. Cf. **attribute** (def. 8). **4.** *Logic.* **a.** modality (def. 3). **b.** mood[2] (def. 2). **5.** *Music.* any of various arrangements of the diatonic tones of an octave, differing from one another in the order of the whole steps and half steps; scale. **6.** *Gram.* mood[2] (def. 1). **7.** *Statistics.* the value of the variate at which a relative or absolute maximum occurs in the frequency distribution of the variate. **8.** *Petrog.* the actual mineral composition of a rock, expressed in percentages by weight. [ME < L *mod(us)* manner]
—**Syn. 1.** See **method.**

mode[2] (mōd), *n.* **1.** customary or conventional usage in manners, dress, etc., esp. as observed by persons of fashion. **2.** a style or fashion: *He was much concerned to keep up with the latest mode.* **3.** a light gray or drab color. [< F < L *mod(us)* manner, measure]

mod·el (mod′əl), *n., adj., v.,* **-eled, -el·ing** or (*esp. Brit.*) **-elled, -el·ling.** —*n.* **1.** a standard or example for imitation or comparison. **2.** a representation, generally in miniature, to show the construction or serve as a copy of something. **3.** an image in clay, wax, or the like, to be reproduced in more durable material. **4.** a person or thing that serves as a subject for an artist, sculptor, writer, etc. **5.** a person whose profession is serving as a subject for artists. **6.** a person, esp. an attractive young woman, whose profession is posing with, wearing, using, or demonstrating a product to best display it to prospective customers, as at a fashion show, on a television commercial, or in an advertising photograph: *a couturier's model; She became a successful model and her face appeared on billboards all over the country.* **7.** a pattern or mode of structure or formation. **8.** a typical form or style. **9.** *Logic, Math.* a system of things and relations satisfying a set of axioms, so that the axioms can be interpreted as true statements about the system. **10.** *Zool.* an animal that is mimicked in form or color by another. —*adj.* **11.** serving as a model: *a model apartment.* **12.** worthy to serve as a model; exemplary: *a model student.* —*v.t.* **13.** to form or plan according to a model. **14.** to give shape or form to; fashion. **15.** to make a model or representation of. **16.** to fashion in clay, wax, or the like. **17.** to display to other persons or to prospective customers, esp. by wearing: *to model dresses; to model one's wedding gown.* —*v.i.* **18.** to make models. **19.** to produce designs in some plastic material. **20.** to assume a typical or natural appearance, as the parts of a drawing in progress. **21.** to serve or be employed as a model. [earlier *modell* < It *modell(o),* equiv. to *mod(o)* MODE[1] + *-ello* < L *-ellus* dim. suffix] —**mod′el·er;** *esp. Brit.,* **mod′el·ler,** *n.*
—**Syn. 1.** paragon; prototype, archetype, mold, original. See **ideal. 14.** design.

mod·el·ing (mod′əling), *n.* **1.** the act, art, or profession of one who models. **2.** the process of producing sculptured form with plastic material, as clay. **3.** the technique of rendering the illusion of volume on a two-dimensional surface by shading. **4.** the treatment of volume, as the turning of a form, in sculpture. Also, *esp. Brit.,* **mod′el·ling.** [MODEL + -ING[1]]

mo·dem (mō′dəm, -dem), *n. Computer Technol.* an electronic device, either built into a control unit or separate from it, that makes possible the transmission of data to or from a computer via telephone or other communication lines. [MO(DULATOR) + DEM(ODULATOR)]

Mo·de·na (mōd′ənə; *It.* mô′de nä), *n.* a city in N Italy, NW of Bologna. 139,496 (1961).

mod·er·ate (*adj., n.* mod′ər it, mod′rit; *v.* mod′ə rāt′), *adj., n., v.,* **-at·ed, -at·ing.** —*adj.* **1.** kept or keeping within reasonable or proper limits; not extreme, excessive, or intense: *a moderate drinker; a moderate request.* **2.** of medium quantity, extent, etc.: *a moderate income.* **3.** mediocre; fair: *moderate talent.* **4.** of or pertaining to moderates, as in politics or religion. —*n.* **5.** a person who is moderate in opinion or opposed to extreme views and actions, esp. in politics or religion. **6.** (*usually cap.*) a member of a political party advocating moderate reform. —*v.t.* **7.** to reduce the excessiveness of; make less violent, severe, intense, or rigorous: *to moderate the sharpness of one's words.* **8.** to preside over or at (a public forum, meeting, discussion, etc.). —*v.i.* **9.** to become less violent, severe, intense, or rigorous. **10.** to act as moderator; preside. [< L *moderāt(us)* restrained, controlled (ptp. of *moderārī*), equiv. to *moderā-* v. s. (see MODEST) + *-tus* ptp. suffix] —**mod′er·ate·ly,** *adv.* —**mod′er·ate·ness,** *n.*
—**Syn. 1.** reasonable, temperate, judicious, just, cool, steady, calm. **2.** average. **7.** meliorate, pacify, calm, mitigate, soften, mollify, temper, qualify, appease, abate, lessen, diminish, reduce. —**Ant. 4, 5.** radical.

mod′erate breeze′, *Meteorol.* (on the Beaufort scale) a wind of 13–18 miles per hour.

mod′erate gale′, *Meteorol.* (on the Beaufort scale) a wind of 32–38 miles per hour.

mod·er·a·tion (mod′ə rā′shən), *n.* **1.** the quality of being moderate; restraint; avoidance of extremes; temperance. **2. moderations,** *Brit.* the first public examinations at Oxford University for the B.A. degree in mathematics or in classics. **3.** the act of moderating. **4. in moderation,** without excess; moderately; temperately: *They were not averse to alcoholic beverages taken in moderation.* [ME *moderacion* < L *moderātiōn-* (s. of *moderātiō*). See MODERATE, -ION]

mod·e·ra·to (mod′ə rä′tō), *adj. Music.* moderate; in moderate time. [< It < L *moderātus* MODERATE]

mod·er·a·tor (mod′ə rā′tər), *n.* **1.** one who or that which moderates. **2.** a presiding officer, as at a public forum, a legislative body, or an ecclesiastical body in the Presbyterian Church. **3.** a radio or television performer who presides over a quiz show or panel discussion. **4.** *Physics.* a substance, as graphite or heavy water, used to slow down neutrons from the high speeds at which they are released in fission to lower speeds more efficient in causing fission. [ME < L; see MODERATE, -OR[2]] —**mod·er·a·to·ri·al** (mod′ər ə tôr′ē əl, -tōr′-), *adj.* —**mod′er·a′tor·ship′,** *n.*

mod·ern (mod′ərn), *adj.* **1.** of or pertaining to present and recent time; not ancient or remote: *modern city life.* **2.** of or pertaining to the historical period following the Middle Ages: *modern history.* **3.** of, pertaining to, or characteristic of contemporary styles of art, literature, music, etc., that reject traditionally accepted or sanctioned forms and emphasize individual experimentation and sensibility. **4.** characteristic of present and recent time; not antiquated or obsolete: *modern viewpoints.* **5.** *Typography.* noting or descriptive of a font of numerals in which the body aligns on the baseline, as **1234567890.** Cf. **old style** (def. 2). —*n.* **6.** a person of modern times. **7.** a person whose views and tastes are modern. **8.** *Print.* a type style differentiated from old style by heavy vertical strokes and straight serifs. [< LL *modern(us),* equiv. to L *mod(o), modō* lately, just now (orig. abl. sing. of *modus* MODE[1]) + *-ernus* adj. suffix of time] —**mod′ern·ly,** *adv.* —**mod′ern·ness,** *n.*
—**Syn. 1.** MODERN, RECENT, LATE apply to that which is near to or characteristic of the present as contrasted with any other time. MODERN is applied to those things which exist in the present age, esp. in contrast to those of a former age or an age long past; hence the word sometimes has the connotation of up-to-date and, thus, good: *modern ideas.* That which is RECENT is separated from the present or the time of action by only a short interval; it is new, fresh, and novel: *recent developments.* LATE may mean nearest to the present moment: *the late reports on the battle.*

mod′ern cut′, *Jewelry.* any of several modifications or combinations of the brilliant cut, step cut, or table cut, having the girdle outline often in some novel form. Also, **mod′erne cut′.**

mod′ern dance′, a form of contemporary theatrical and concert dance employing a special technique for developing the use of the entire body in movements expressive of abstract ideas.

Mod′ern Eng′lish, the English language since c1475. Also called **New English.**

Mod′ern French′, the French language since c1600.

Mod′ern Greek′, the Greek language since c1500. Also called **New Greek.**

Mod′ern He′brew, the living language of modern Israel, a revived form of ancient Hebrew.

Mod′ern Icelan′dic, the Icelandic language since c1550.

mod·ern·ise (mod′ər nīz′), *v.t., v.i.,* **-ised, -is·ing.** *Chiefly Brit.* modernize. —**mod′ern·i·sa′tion,** *n.* —**mod′ern·is′er,** *n.*

mod·ern·ism (mod′ər niz′əm), *n.* **1.** modern character, tendencies, or sympathy with what is modern. **2.** a modern usage or characteristic. **3.** (*cap.*) *Theol.* **a.** the movement in Roman Catholic thought which sought to interpret the teachings of the Church in the light of philosophic and scientific conceptions prevalent in the late 19th and early 20th centuries: condemned by Pope Pius X in 1907. **b.** the liberal theological tendency in Protestantism in the 20th century. [MODERN + -ISM]

mod·ern·ist (mod′ər nist), *n.* **1.** a person who follows or favors modern ways, tendencies, etc. **2.** a person who advocates the study of modern subjects in preference to ancient classics. **3.** an adherent of modernism in theological questions. —*adj.* **4.** of modernists or modernism. [MODERN + -IST]

mod·ern·is·tic (mod′ər nis′tik), *adj.* **1.** modern. **2.** of or pertaining to modernism or modernists. [MODERN + -ISTIC] —**mod′ern·is′ti·cal·ly,** *adv.*

mo·der·ni·ty (mo dûr′ni tē, mō-), *n., pl.* **-ties.** **1.** the quality of being modern. **2.** something modern. [MODERN + -ITY]

mod·ern·ize (mod′ər nīz′), *v.,* **-ized, -iz·ing.** —*v.t.* **1.** to make modern; give a new or modern character or appearance to: *to modernize one's ideas; to modernize a kitchen.* —*v.i.* **2.** to become modern; adopt modern ways, views, etc. Also, *esp. Brit.,* **modernise.** [MODERN(ISM) + -IZE] —**mod′ern·i·za′tion,** *n.* —**mod′ern·iz′er,** *n.*

mod′ern jazz′, any of various styles of jazz that have evolved since the early 1940's, and are marked generally by increasing harmonic and rhythmic complexity, a tendency to draw on classical forms and styles, and an increased use of written-out arrangements. Also called **progressive jazz.** Cf. **bop**[1], **cool jazz, hard bop, progressive jazz** (def. 1).

mod′ern lan′guage, one of the literary languages currently in use in Europe treated as a departmental course of study in a school, college, or university.

Mod/ern Per/sian, the Persian language since the Middle Persian stage.

mod·est (mod/ist), *adj.* **1.** having or showing a moderate or humble estimate of one's merits, importance, etc.; free from vanity, egotism, boastfulness, or great pretensions. **2.** free from ostentation or showy extravagance: *a modest house.* **3.** moderate. **4.** having or showing regard for the decencies of behavior, speech, dress, etc.; decent: *a modest neckline on a dress.* [< L *modest(us)* moderate, equiv. to *modes-* (*mod(us)* MODE[1] + *-es-*, var. of *-er-*; see MODERATE) + *-tus* adj. suffix] —**mod/est·ly,** *adv.*

—**Syn. 1.** retiring, unassuming. **1, 2.** unpretentious, unobtrusive. **4.** pure, virtuous. MODEST, DEMURE, PRUDISH imply conformity to propriety and decorum, and a distaste for anything coarse or loud. MODEST implies a becoming shyness, sobriety, and proper behavior: *a modest self-respecting person.* DEMURE implies a bashful, quiet simplicity, staidness, and decorum; but can also indicate an assumed or affected modesty: *a demure young chorus girl.* PRUDISH suggests an exaggeratedly self-conscious modesty or propriety in behavior or conversation of one who wishes to be thought of as easily shocked and who often is intolerant: *a prudish objection to a harmless remark.* —**Ant. 4.** bold, coarse.

Mo·des·ta (mō des/tə, mə-), *n.* a girl's given name, form of **Modesty.**

Mo·des·to (mə des/tō), *n.* a city in central California. 36,585 (1960).

mod·es·ty (mod/i stē), *n., pl.* **-ties. 1.** the quality of being modest; freedom from vanity, boastfulness, etc. **2.** regard for decency of behavior, speech, dress, etc. **3.** simplicity; moderation. [< L *modestia.* See MODEST, -Y[3]]

Mod·es·ty (mod/i stē), *n.* a girl's given name.

ModGk, Modern Greek. Also, **Mod. Gk., Mod. Gr.**

ModHeb, Modern Hebrew.

mod·i·cum (mod/ə kəm), *n.* a moderate or small quantity: *He hasn't even a modicum of common sense.* [late ME < L, neut. of *modicus* limited, measured. See MODE[1], -IC]

mod·i·fi·cand (mod/ə fə kand/), *n. Gram.* a word that is modified, or qualified, by another. In "red books," "books" is a modificand. [< L *modificand(um)* (a thing) to be measured or limited, neut. of ger. of *modificāre,* to MODIFY]

mod·i·fi·ca·tion (mod/ə fə kā/shən), *n.* **1.** the act or an instance of modifying. **2.** the state of being modified; partial alteration. **3.** a modified form; a variety. **4.** *Biol.* a change in a living organism acquired from its own activity or environment and not transmitted to its descendants. **5.** limitation or qualification. **6.** *Gram.* **a.** the use of a modifier in a construction, or of modifiers in a class of constructions or in a language. **b.** the meaning of a modifier, esp. as it affects the meaning of the word or other form modified: *Limitation is one kind of modification.* **c.** a change in the phonological shape of a morpheme, word, or other form when it functions as an element in a construction, as the change of *not* to *-n't* in *doesn't.* **d.** the feature of a construction resulting from such a change. **e.** an adjustment in the form of a word as it passes from one language to another. [< L *modificātiōn-* (s. of *modificātiō*), equiv. to *modificāt(us)* measured (ptp. of *modificāre;* see MODIFY) + *-iōn-* -ION]

mod·i·fi·ca·to·ry (mod/ə fə kā/tə rē), *adj.* modifying. Also, **mod/i·fi·ca/tive.** [< L *modificāt(us)* (see MODIFY) + -ORY[1]]

mod·i·fi·er (mod/ə fī/ər), *n.* **1.** one who or that which modifies. **2.** *Gram.* **a.** a word, phrase, or sentence element which limits or qualifies the sense of another word, phrase, or element in the same construction. **b.** the immediate constituent of an endocentric construction which is not the head. [MODIFY + -ER[1]]

mod·i·fy (mod/ə fī/), *v.,* **-fied, -fy·ing.** —*v.t.* **1.** to change somewhat the form or qualities of; alter partially: *to modify a design.* **2.** *Gram.* (of a word or phrase) to stand in a syntactically subordinate relation to (another word or phrase), usually with descriptive, limiting, or particularizing meaning; be a modifier. In *a good man, good* modifies *man.* **3.** to be the modifier or attribute of. **4.** to change (a vowel) by umlaut. **5.** to reduce in degree; moderate; qualify: *to modify one's statement.* —*v.i.* **6.** to be or become modified. [ME *modifie(n)* < MF *modifie(r)* < L *modificāre* to limit, measure. See MODE[1], -IFY] —**mod/i·fi/a·bil/i·ty, mod/i·fi/a·ble·ness,** *n.* —**mod/i·fi/a·ble,** *adj.*

—**Syn. 1.** vary, adjust, shape, reform. **5.** MODIFY, QUALIFY, TEMPER suggest altering an original statement, condition, or the like, so as to avoid anything excessive or extreme. To MODIFY is to alter in one or more particulars, generally in the direction of leniency or moderation: *to modify demands, rates.* To QUALIFY is to restrict or limit by exceptions or conditions: *to qualify one's praise, hopes.* To TEMPER is to alter the quality of something, generally so as to diminish its force or harshness: *to temper one's criticism with humor.*

Mo·di·glia·ni (mō dē/lē-ä/nē; *It.* mô/dē lyä/nē), *n.* **A·me·de·o** (ä/me de/ô), 1884–1920, Italian painter and sculptor in France.

mo·dil·lion (mō dil/yən, mə-), *n. Archit.* an ornamental cantilever beneath the corona or similar member of a cornice, stringcourse, etc. [< It *modiglione* < VL **mutiliōnem,* acc. of **mūtuliō.* See MUTULE, -ION]

Modillion

mo·di·o·lus (mō dī/ə ləs, mə-), *n., pl.* **-li** (-lī/). *Anat.* the central, conical axis around which the cochlea of the ear winds. [< NL, L: nave of a wheel (lit., small measure), equiv. to *modi(us)* a measure of grain (? deriv. of *modus* MODE[1]) + *-olus* dim. suffix] —**mo·di/o·lar,** *adj.*

mod·ish (mō/dish), *adj.* in accordance with the prevailing mode; fashionable; stylish. [MODE[2] + -ISH[1]] —**mod/ish·ly,** *adv.* —**mod/ish·ness,** *n.*

mo·diste (mō dēst/; *Fr.* mô dēst/), *n., pl.* **-distes** (-dēsts/; *Fr.* -dēst/). a maker of or dealer in articles of fashionable attire, esp. women's dresses, millinery, etc. [< F; see MODE[2], -IST]

Mo·djes·ka (mô jes/kə), *n.* **He·le·na** (hə lā/nə), (*Helena Opid Modrzejewska*), 1840–1909, Polish actress, in U.S. after 1876.

Mo·doc (mō/dok), *n., pl.* **-docs,** (*esp. collectively*) **-doc.** a member of an American Indian people belonging to the Lutuamian group and ranging from southern Oregon to northern California.

mo/dock wool/ (mō/dok). See **territory wool.** [special use of MODOC]

mod. praesc., (in prescriptions) in the manner prescribed; as directed. [< L *mōdō praescriptō*]

Mo·dred (mō/drid), *n. Arthurian Romance.* the nephew and treacherous killer of Arthur. Also, **Mordred.**

mod·u·lar (moj/ə lər, mod/yə-), *adj.* **1.** of or pertaining to a module or a modulus. **2.** composed of standardized units or sections for easy construction or flexible arrangement: *a modular home.* **3.** *Math.* (of a lattice) having the property that for any two elements with one less than the other, the union of the smaller element with the intersection of the larger element and any third element of the lattice is equal to the intersection of the larger element with the union of the smaller element and the third element. [< NL *modulār(is).* See MODULE, -AR[1]]

mod·u·late (moj/ə lāt/, mod/yə-), *v.,* **-lat·ed, -lat·ing.** —*v.t.* **1.** to regulate by or adjust to a certain measure or proportion; soften; tone down. **2.** to alter or adapt (the voice) according to the circumstances. **3.** *Music.* **a.** to attune to a certain pitch or key. **b.** to vary the volume of (tone). **4.** *Radio.* to cause the amplitude, frequency, phase, or intensity of (a carrier wave) to vary in accordance with a sound wave or other signal, the frequency of the signal wave usually being very much lower than that of the carrier: frequently applied to the application of sound-wave signals to a microphone to change the characteristic of a transmitted radio wave. —*v.i.* **5.** *Radio.* to modulate a carrier wave. **6.** *Music.* to pass from one key to another. [< L *modulāt(us)* measured, regulated (ptp. of *modulārī*). See MODULE, -ATE[1]] —**mod·u·la·bil·i·ty** (moj/ə lə bil/i tē, mod/yə-), *n.* —**mod/u·la/tive, mod·u·la·to·ry** (moj/ə lə tôr/ē, -tōr/ē, mod/yə-), *adj.*

mod·u·la·tion (moj/ə lā/shən, mod/yə-), *n.* **1.** the act of modulating. **2.** the state of being modulated. **3.** *Music.* transition from one key to another. **4.** *Gram.* **a.** the use of a particular distribution of stress or pitch in a construction, as the use of rising pitch on *here* in *John is here?* **b.** the feature of a construction resulting from such use. [ME *modulacion* < L *modulātiōn-* (s. of *modulātiō*) rhythmical measure. See MODULATE, -ION]

mod·u·la·tor (moj/ə lā/tər, mod/yə-), *n.* **1.** one who or that which modulates. **2.** *Radio.* a device for modulating a carrier wave. [< L; see MODULATE, -OR[2]]

mod·ule (moj/ōōl, mod/yōōl), *n.* **1.** a standard or unit for measuring. **2.** a selected unit of measure, ranging in size from a few inches to several feet, used as a basis for the planning and standardization of building materials. **3. diameters,** *Archit.* See under **diameter** (def. 5). **4.** *Math.* an Abelian group with a set of left or right operators forming a ring and that obeys the rule that the composition of two operators operating on an element of the group is equal to one operator operating on the value at the element of the other operator. Cf. **group with operators. 5.** a separable component, frequently one that is interchangeable with others, for assembly into units of differing size, complexity, or function. **6.** any of the individual, self-contained segments of a spacecraft, designed to perform a particular task in space: *a command module of the Apollo spacecraft; a lunar module.* [< L *modulus;* see MODULUS]

mod·u·lo (moj/ə lō/, mod/yə-), *adv. Math.* with respect to a modulus: *6 is congruent to 11, modulo 5.* [< NL, abl. of *modulus*]

mod·u·lus (moj/ə ləs, mod/yə-), *n., pl.* **-li** (lī). **1.** *Physics.* a coefficient pertaining to a physical property. **2.** *Math.* **a.** that number by which the logarithms in one system are multiplied to yield the logarithms in another. **b.** a quantity by which two given quantities can be divided to yield the same remainders. **c.** See **absolute value.** [< L: a little unit of measure; see MODE[1], -ULE]

mod/ulus of elastic/ity, *Physics.* any of several coefficients of elasticity of a body, expressing the ratio between a stress or force per unit area which acts to deform the body and the corresponding fractional deformation caused by the stress. Also called **coefficient of elasticity, elastic modulus.**

mod/ulus of rigid/ity, *Physics.* See **shear modulus.**

mod/ulus of vol/ume elastic/ity, *Physics.* See **bulk modulus.**

mo·dus o·pe·ran·di (mō/dōōs ō/pe rän/dē; *Eng.* mō/dəs op/ə ran/dī), *pl.* **mo·di o·pe·ran·di** (mō/dē ō/pe rän/dē; *Eng.* mō/dī op/ə ran/dī). *Latin.* mode of operating or working.

mo·dus vi·ven·di (mō/dōōs wē wen/dē; *Eng.* mō/dəs vi ven/dī), *pl.* **mo·di vi·ven·di** (mō/dē wē wen/dē; *Eng.* mō/dī vi ven/dī). **1.** (*italics*) *Latin.* manner of living. **2.** a temporary arrangement between persons or parties pending a settlement of matters in debate.

Moe (mō), *n.* a boy's given name, form of **Morris** or **Moses.** Also, **Mo.**

Moe·bi·us (mœ/bē əs, mā/-, mē/-), *n.* **August Ferdinand.** See **Möbius, August Ferdinand.**

Moe·rae (mē/rē), *n.pl. Class. Myth.* fate (def. 6).

Moe·rag·e·tes (mē raj/i tēz/), *n. Class. Myth.* an epithet of Apollo, meaning "guide of the Fates."

Moe·si·a (mē/shē ə), *n.* an ancient country in S Europe, S of the Danube and N of ancient Thrace and Macedonia: later a Roman province.

Moe·so·goth (mē/sō goth/, -sə-), *n.* one of the Christianized Goths who settled in Moesia in the 4th century A.D. [MOES(IA) + -O- + GOTH]

Moe·so·goth·ic (mē/sō goth/ik, -sə-), *adj.* of or pertaining to the Moesogoths or their language. [MOESOGOTH + -IC]

mo·fette (mō fet/; *Fr.* mô fet/), *n.* **1.** a noxious emanation, consisting chiefly of carbon dioxide, escaping from the earth in regions of nearly extinct volcanic activity. **2.** one of the openings or fissures from which this emanation issues. Also, **mof·fette/.** [< F < It (Neapolitan) *mofeta;* cf. dial. G *muffezen* to emit a rotten smell]

mog (mog), *v.,* **mogged, mog·ging.** *Dial.* —*v.i.* **1.** to move on, depart, or decamp (usually fol. by *off* or *on*). **2.** to walk or move along gently, slowly, and steadily. —*v.t.* **3.** to cause to go from one place to another. [? M(OVE + J)OG]

Mo·ga·di·scio (mog/ə dish/ē ō/, -dish/ō; *It.* mô/gä-dē/shō), *n.* a seaport in and the capital of the Somali Republic, in the S part. 120,649 (est. 1963). Also, **Mo·ga·di·shu** (mô/gä dē/shōō).

Mog·a·dor (mog/ə dōr/, -dôr/; *Fr.* mô gA dôR/), *n.* **1.** a seaport in W Morocco. 26,392 (1960). **2.** (*l.c.*) Also, **mog/a·dore/,** a ribbed fabric of silk or rayon warp and cotton or linen filling, used for neckties.

Mog·a·dore (mog/ə dōr/, -dôr/), *n.* a town in NE Ohio. 3851 (1960).

Mo·gen Da·vid (mô/gən dô/vid, dā/vid), *Judaism.* See **Star of David.**

mog·i·la·li·a (moj/ə lā/lē ə, -lāl/yə), *n. Pathol.* any speech defect, as stuttering or stammering. Also, **molilalia.** [< Gk *mogilál(os)* hardly talking (*mógi(s)* with difficulty + *lálos* babbling) + *-ia* -IA]

Mo·gi·lev (mō/gi lef/; *Russ.* mo gi lyôf/), *n.* a city in E Byelorussia, in the W Soviet Union in Europe, on the Dnieper. 151,000 (est. 1964).

mo·go (mō/gō), *n., pl.* **-gos.** *Australian.* a stone hatchet used by the aborigines. [< native Austral]

mo·go·te (mə gō/tē), *n.* **1.** a residual hillock of limestone, honeycombed with cavities between flat valleys. **2.** *Southwestern U.S.* a patch of thickly grown brush or dense shrubbery. [< AmerSp, Sp: knoll, stack of sheaves]

mo·gul (mō/gəl), *n.* a bump or mound of hard snow on a ski slope. [< Norw]

Mo·gul (mō/gul, -gəl, mō gul/), *n.* **1.** one of the Mongol conquerors of India who established an empire that lasted from 1526 to 1857, but held only nominal power after 1803. Cf. **Great Mogul. 2.** one of their descendants. **3.** (*l.c.*) an important, powerful, or influential person: *a mogul of the movie industry.* **4.** a Mongol or Mongolian. **5.** *Railroads.* a steam locomotive having a two-wheeled front truck, six driving wheels, and no rear truck. —*adj.* **6.** of or pertaining to the Moguls or their empire. [< Pers *Mugul* MONGOL]

mo·hair (mō/hâr/), *n.* **1.** the coat or fleece of an Angora goat. **2.** a fabric made of yarn from this fleece, in a plain weave for draperies and in a pile weave for upholstery. **3.** a garment made of this fabric. [var. (by folk etymology) of *mocayare* < It *moccaiaro* < Ar *mukhayyar,* lit., chosen, choice, ptp. of *khayyara* to choose]

Moham., Mohammedan.

Mo·ham·med (mō ham/id, -häm/-), *n.* Muhammad.

Mohammed II, ("*the Conqueror*") 1430–81, sultan of Turkey 1451–81: conqueror of Constantinople 1453.

Moham/med A·li/ (ä lē/, ä/lē), **1. Mau·la·na** (mō-lä/nə), 1878–1931, Indian journalist and political leader: advocate of Indian nationalization. **2.** See **Mehemet Ali.**

Mo·ham·med·an (mō ham/i dən), *adj.* **1.** of or pertaining to Muhammad or his religious system; Islamic; Muslim. —*n.* **2.** Muslim. [MOHAMMED + -AN]

Mo·ham·med·an·ism (mō ham/i dəniz/əm), *n.* the Muhammedan religion; Islam. [MOHAMMEDAN + -ISM]

Mo·ham·med·an·ize (mō ham/i dənīz/), *v.t.,* **-ized, -iz·ing.** Islamize. [MOHAMMEDAN + -IZE]

Mo·ham·med ibn-Ka·sim (mōō ham/id ib/ən kä/-sim, -hä/mid), fl. early 8th century A.D., Muslim conqueror of the Sind region in India. Also, **Moham/med ibn/-Qa/sim.**

Moham/med of Ghor/ (gōr, gôr), (*Mu'izz-ad-din*), died 1206, Muslim Sultan of Ghazni 1173–1206: established Muslim power in India. Also, **Muhammed Ghori.**

Moham/med Za·hir/ Shah/ (zä hēr/), born 1914, king of Afghanistan since 1933.

Mo·har·ram (mō har/əm), *n.* the first month of the Islamic calendar. Also, **Muharram.** [< Ar *muḥarram,* lit., holy]

Mo·ha·ve (mō hä/vē), *n., pl.* **-ves,** (*esp. collectively*) **-ve,** *adj.* —*n.* **1.** a member of a North American Indian tribe belonging to the Yuman linguistic family, formerly located in the Colorado River valley of Arizona and California. —*adj.* **2.** of or pertaining to the Mohave tribe. Also, **Mojave.**

Moha/ve Des/ert. See **Mojave Desert.**

Mo·hawk (mō/hôk), *n., pl.* **-hawks,** (*esp. collectively*) **-hawk. 1.** a member of a tribe of the most easterly of the Iroquois Five Nations, formerly resident along the Mohawk River, New York. **2.** the Iroquoian language of the Mohawk Indians. **3.** a river flowing E from central New York to the Hudson. 148 mi. long. **4.** a town in central New York. 3533 (1960).

mo·hawk·weed (mō/hôk wēd/), *n.* See **mealy bellwort.** [MOHAWK + WEED[1]]

Mo·he·gan (mō hē/gən), *n., pl.* **-gans,** (*esp. collectively*) **-gan. 1.** a member of a tribe of Algonquian-speaking North American Indians dwelling chiefly along the Thames River, Connecticut, in the 17th century. **2.** Mahican (defs. 1, 2).

mo·hel (mō hāl/, mō/hel; *Eng.* mō/əl, moi/-), *n., pl.* **mo·hal·im** (mō/hä lēm/), *Eng.* **mo·hels.** *Hebrew.* the person who performs the circumcision in the Jewish rite of circumcising a male child eight days after his birth.

Mo·hen·jo-Da·ro (mō hen/jō där/ō), *n.* an archaeological site in West Pakistan, near the Indus River: six successive ancient cities were built here.

Mo·hi·can (mō hē/kən), *n., pl.* **-cans,** (*esp. collectively*) **-can.** Mahican.

Mohi/can rig/, a rig used in the U.S. for sailing canoes, employing a sail **(Mohi/can sail/)** having the form of a balance lug with a stiffening batten.

Moh·ism (mō/iz əm), *n.* the doctrines of Mo-Tze, characterized by advocacy of universal love of mankind and government by an absolute monarch. [MO(-TZE) + hiatus-filling *-h-* + -ISM] —**Moh/ist,** *n., adj.*

Mo·hock (mō/hok), *n.* one of a group of aristocratic ruffians who attacked people at night on the streets of London in the early part of the 18th century. [var. of MOHAWK] —**Mo/hock·ism,** *n.*

Mo·hole (mō′hōl′), *n.* a hole bored through the earth's crust into the region below the Mohorovičić discontinuity, for geological research. [*Mo(horovičić)* (see MOHOROVIČIĆ DISCONTINUITY) + HOLE]

Mo·holy-Nagy (mō′hoi nod′y), *n.* **Lász·ló** (läs′lō) or **La·dis·laus** (lä′dis lous′), 1895–1946, Hungarian painter, designer, and photographer, in the U.S. after 1936.

Mo·ho·ro′vi·čić discontinu′ity (mō′hō rō′və-chich, -hō-), *Geol.* the discontinuity between the crust and the mantle of the earth, occurring at depths which average about 22 miles beneath the continents and about 6 miles beneath the ocean floor. Also, **Mo′ho.** [named after A. *Mohorovičić*, Yugoslav geologist]

Mohs′ scale′ (mōz), a scale of hardness used in mineralogy. Its degrees are: talc 1; gypsum 2; calcite 3; fluorite 4; apatite 5; feldspar 6; quartz 7; topaz 8; sapphire 9; diamond 10. *Abbr.:* MSH [named after F. *Mohs* (1773–1839), German mineralogist]

mo·hur (mō′hər), *n.* any of various gold coins of India, introduced in the 16th century by various Mogul princes and later used by the British as the standard gold coin of India. [earlier *muhr* < Urdu < Pers: seal, gold coin; akin to Skt *mudrā*]

moh·wa (mō′wə), *n.* mahua.

M.O.I., *Brit.* **1.** Ministry of Information. **2.** Ministry of the Interior.

moi·dore (moi′dōr, -dôr), *n.* a former gold coin of Portugal and Brazil. [< Pg *moeda de ouro* coin of gold < L *monēta dē aurō.* See MONEY, DE, OR[3]]

moi·e·ty (moi′i tē), *n., pl.* **-ties. 1.** a half. **2.** an indefinite portion. **3.** *Anthropol.* one of two units into which a tribe is divided on the basis of unilateral descent. [late ME *moite* < MF < L *medietāt-* (s. of *medietās*) the middle, equiv. to *medi(us)* mid + *-etāt-*, var. of *-itāt-* -ITY]

M.O.I.G., Master of Occupational Information and Guidance.

Moi·gno (moin′yō), *n.* a crater in the first quadrant of the face of the moon: about 20 miles in diameter.

moil (moil), *v.i.* **1.** to work hard; toil; drudge. —*n.* **2.** toil or drudgery. **3.** confusion, turmoil, or trouble. **4.** *Glassmaking.* a superfluous piece of glass formed during blowing and removed in the finishing operation. [ME *moille(n)* (to) make or get wet and muddy < MF *moillie(r)* < VL **molliāre*, deriv. of L *mollis* soft] —**moil′er,** *n.* —**moil′ing·ly,** *adv.*

Moi·na (moi′nə), *n.* a girl's given name. Also, **Moyna.**

Moi·ra (moi′rə), *n., pl.* **-rai** (-rī). *Class. Myth.* **1.** the personification of fate. **2.** Also, **Moirai.** fate (def. 6). **3.** a girl's given name.

moire (mwär, mōr, môr), *n.* any moiré fabric. [< F < MOHAIR]

moi·ré (mwä rā′, mōr′ā, môr′ā; *Fr.* MWA RĀ′), *adj.* **1.** (of silks and other fabrics) presenting a watery or wavelike effect. —*n.* **2.** a design pressed on silk, rayon, etc., by engraved rollers. **3.** any silk, rayon, etc., fabric with a watery or wavelike effect. **4.** *Print.* a smeared pattern of dots appearing in the print of process color. [< F; see MOIRE, -EE]

Moi·se·i·vich (moi sā′i vich), *n.* **Ben·no** (ben′ō), born 1890, English pianist, born in Russia. Also, **Moi·se′i·witsch.**

Moi·se·yev (moi se′yev, -yəf), *n.* **I·gor A·le·xan·dro·vich** (ē′gôr y ä le ksän′dro vich), born 1906, Russian dancer, choreographer, and ballet master.

Mois·san (MWA sän′), *n.* **Hen·ri** (äN rē′), 1852–1907, French chemist: Nobel prize 1906.

moist (moist), *adj.* **1.** moderately or slightly wet; damp. **2.** (of the eyes) tearful. **3.** accompanied by or connected with liquid or moisture. [ME *moiste* < MF; connected with L *mūcidus* MUCID] —**moist′ful,** *adj.* —**moist′less,** *adj.* —**moist′ly,** *adv.* —**moist′ness,** *n.* —**Syn. 1.** dank. See **damp.** —**Ant. 1, 2.** dry.

mois·ten (moi′sən), *v.t., v.i.* to make or become moist. [MOIST + -EN[1]] —**moist′en·er,** *n.*

mois·ture (mois′chər, moish′-), *n.* **1.** condensed or diffused liquid, esp. water. **2.** a small quantity of liquid, esp. water; enough liquid to moisten. [ME; see MOIST, -URE; cf. MF *moistour*] —**mois′ture·less,** *adj.*

mois·tur·ize (mois′chə rīz′, moish′-), *v.,* **-ized, -iz·ing.** —*v.t.* **1.** to impart or restore moisture to (something): *to moisturize one's skin with lotion; to moisturize air in a dry room.* —*v.i.* **2.** to make something moist; counteract a dry condition with moisture: *an air-conditioner that moisturizes as it cools; a skin cream that moisturizes while you sleep.* [MOISTURE + -IZE] —**mois′tur·iz′er,** *n.*

moit (moit), *n.* **1.** a foreign particle found in wool, as a burr, twig, seed, etc. —*v.t.* **2.** to remove moits from (wool). Also, **mote.** [orig. sp. var. (north) of MOTE[1], with silent *-i-*, which served only to mark the *o* long; but by sp. pron. *oi* now has its usual value]

moit·y (moi′tē), *adj.,* **moit·i·er, moit·i·est.** full of moits. Also, **motey.** [MOIT + -Y[1]]

mo·jar·ra (mō här′ə), *n.* any of several chiefly tropical, silvery fishes of the family *Gerridae*, having a protrusible mouth and grooves at the bases of the dorsal and anal fins into which the fins can be withdrawn. [< Sp: lit., point of a lance < Ar *muharrab* pointed, sharp, ptp. of *harrab* to sharpen]

Mo·ja·ve (mō hä′vē), *n., pl.* **-ves,** (*esp. collectively*) **-ve,** *adj.* Mohave.

Moja′ve Des′ert, a desert in S California: part of the Great Basin. ab. 13,500 sq. mi. Also, **Mohave Desert.**

Mo·ji (mô′jē′), *n.* a seaport on N Kyushu, in SW Japan. 152,081 (1964).

moke (mōk), *n.* **1.** *Disparaging.* a Negro. **2.** *Brit. Slang.* a donkey. **3.** *Australian Slang.* a poor-looking, inferior horse. [?]

Mo·ki (mō′kē), *n., pl.* **-kis,** (*esp. collectively*) **-ki.** Hopi (def. 1). Also, **Moqui.**

mok·ko (mō kō′; *Jap.* mô kô′), *n., pl.* **-ko.** a tsuba having four lobes. [< Jap]

Mok·po (mōk′pō), *n.* a seaport in SW South Korea. 129,650 (1960). Japanese, **Moppo.**

mo·ksha (mōk′shə), *n.* *Buddhism, Hinduism, Jainism.* freedom from the differentiated, temporal, and mortal world of ordinary experience. Also called **mukti.** [< Skt]

mol (mōl), *n.* *Chem.* mole[4].

mol., **1.** molecular. **2.** molecule.

mo·la (mō′lə), *n., pl.* (*esp. collectively*) **-la,** (*esp. referring to two or more kinds or species*) **-las.** any of several thin, silvery fishes of the family *Molidae*, found in tropical and temperate seas. Cf. **ocean sunfish.** [< L: millstone; so called from its shape]

mo·lal (mō′ləl), *adj.* *Chem.* **1.** noting or pertaining to gram-molecular weight. **2.** noting or pertaining to a solution containing one mole of solute per liter of solvent. [MOLE[4] + -AL[1]]

mo·lal·i·ty (mō lal′i tē), *n., pl.* **-ties.** *Chem.* the number of moles of solute per liter of solvent.

mo·lar[1] (mō′lər), *n.* **1.** Also called **mo′lar tooth′.** a tooth having a broad biting surface adapted for grinding, being one of twelve in man with three on each side of the upper and lower jaws. —*adj.* **2.** adapted for grinding, as teeth. **3.** pertaining to such teeth. [< L *molār(is)* grinder, short for (*dēns*) *molāris* grinding (tooth), equiv. to *mol(a)* millstone + *-āris* -AR[1]]

mo·lar[2] (mō′lər), *adj.* **1.** *Physics.* pertaining to a body of matter as a whole, as contrasted with molecular and atomic. **2.** *Chem.* pertaining to a solution containing one mole of solute per liter of solution. [< L *mōl(ēs)* a mass + -AR[1]]

mo·lar·i·ty (mō lar′i tē), *n.* *Chem.* the number of moles of solute per liter of solution. [MOLAR[2] + -ITY]

mo·las·ses (mə las′iz), *n.* any of various thick, dark-colored syrups produced during the refining of sugar or from sorghum. [< Pg *melaço* (< L *mellāceum* must, neut. of **mellāceus* honeylike, equiv. to *mell-*, s. of *mel* honey, + *-āceus* -ACEOUS) + *-es* pl. suffix]

mold[1] (mōld), *n.* **1.** a hollow form or matrix for giving a particular shape to something in a molten or plastic state. **2.** that on or about which something is formed or made. **3.** something formed in or on a mold: *a mold of jelly.* **4.** the shape imparted to a thing by a mold. **5.** shape or form. **6.** a prototype, example, or precursor. **7.** a distinctive nature, character, or type: *a person of a simple and unsophisticated mold.* **8.** *Shipbuilding.* **a.** a three-dimensional pattern for a furnaced plate. **b.** a templet for a frame. **9.** *Archit.* **a.** a molding. **b.** a group of moldings. —*v.t.* **10.** to work into a required shape or form; shape. **11.** to shape or form in or on a mold. **12.** *Foundry.* to form a mold of or from, in order to make a casting. **13.** to produce by or as if by shaping material; form. **14.** to have influence in forming: *to mold the character of a child; mold the taste of the public.* **15.** to ornament with moldings. Also, *esp. Brit.,* **mould.** [ME *molde* < OF *modle* < L *modul(us)* MODULE] —**mold′a·bil′i·ty,** *n.* —**mold′a·ble,** *adj.*

mold[2] (mōld), *n.* **1.** a growth of minute fungi forming on vegetable or animal matter, commonly as a downy or furry coating, and associated with decay. **2.** any of the fungi that produce such a growth. —*v.t., v.i.* **3.** to become or cause to become overgrown or covered with mold. Also, *esp. Brit.,* **mould.** [ME *mowlde*, appar. var. of *mowled*, ptp. of *moulen, mawlen*, c. dial. Dan *mugle* to grow moldy]

mold[3] (mōld), *n.* **1.** loose, friable earth, esp. when rich in organic matter and favorable to the growth of plants. **2.** *Brit. Dial.* ground; earth. Also, *esp. Brit.,* **mould.** [ME, OE *molde* earth, dust, ground; c. Goth *mulda* dust; akin to MEAL[2], MILL[1]]

Mol·dau (môl′dou, mōl′-), *n.* a river in Czechoslovakia, flowing N through the Bohemian Forest to the Elbe. 270 mi. long. Czech, **Vltava.**

Mol·da·vi·a (mol dā′vē ə, -vyə), *n.* **1.** a region in NE Rumania: formerly a principality that united with Wallachia to form Rumania. *Cap.:* Jassy. **2.** Official name, **Moldova.** Formerly, **Molda′vian So′viet So′cialist Repub′lic.** a republic in SE Europe: formed in 1940 from the former republic of Moldavia and the ceded Rumanian territory of Bessarabia. 4,341,000; 13,100 sq. mi. *Cap.:* Kishinev.

Mol·do·va (môl dō′və), *n.* **official name of Moldavia** (def. 2). —**Mol·do′van,** *adj., n.*

mol·da·vite (mol′də vīt′), *n.* a natural green glass found in Bohemia and thought to be of possible meteoritic origin. [MOLDAV(IA) + -ITE[1]]

mold-blown (mōld′blōn′), *adj.* blown-molded.

mold·board (mōld′bōrd′, -bôrd′), *n.* **1.** the curved metal plate in a plow, which turns over the earth from the furrow. **2.** a large blade mounted on the front of a bulldozer to push loose earth. **3.** a board forming one side or surface of a mold for concrete. Also, *esp. Brit.,* **mouldboard.** [MOLD[3] + BOARD]

mold′ed base′ line′, *Naval Archit.* a horizontal base line tangent to the lower edge of the midship floor above the keel.

mold′ed breadth′, *Naval Archit.* the extreme breadth of the framing of a vessel, excluding the thickness of the plating or planking.

mold′ed depth′, *Naval Archit.* the depth of a vessel at the broadest transverse section from the top of the keel to the upper side of the main deck beam at the side.

mold′ed displace′ment, *Naval Archit.* the displacement of a hull calculated so as to exclude the submerged volume of the shell planking or plating.

mold′ed draft′, *Naval Archit.* the vertical dimension of a hull between the molded base line and the designed summer water line. Also called **fairbody draft, rabbet draft.**

mold′ed form′, *Naval Archit.* the form of a hull as defined by the frames and assumed by the inner surface of the shell and deck planking or plating.

mold′ed line′, *Naval Archit.* a straight or curved datum line used in drawing or making patterns for the molded form of a hull.

mold·er[1] (mōl′dər), *v.i.* **1.** to turn to dust by natural decay; crumble; waste away: *a house that had been left to molder.* —*v.t.* **2.** to cause to molder. Also, *esp. Brit.,* **moulder.** [obs. *mold* to crumble (v. use of MOLD[3]) + -ER[6]]

mold·er[2] (mōl′dər), *n.* **1.** a person who molds; a maker of molds. **2.** *Print.* one of a set of electrotyped plates used only for making duplicate electrotypes. Also, *esp. Brit.,* **moulder.** [late ME; see MOLD[1], -ER[1]]

mold·ing (mōl′ding), *n.* **1.** the act or process of molding. **2.** something molded. **3.** (in architecture, furniture, etc.) **a.** any of various long, narrow, ornamental surfaces that are either continuous or discontinuous with uniform cross-sections for the full length and a strikingly modeled profile that casts strong shadows: used on frames, tables, etc., and certain architectural members, as cornices, stringcourses, or bases. **b.** a strip of wood, stone, etc., having such a surface. **4.** a strip of contoured wood or other material placed just below the juncture of a wall and a ceiling. Also, *esp. Brit.,* **moulding.** [ME; see MOLD[1], -ING[1]]

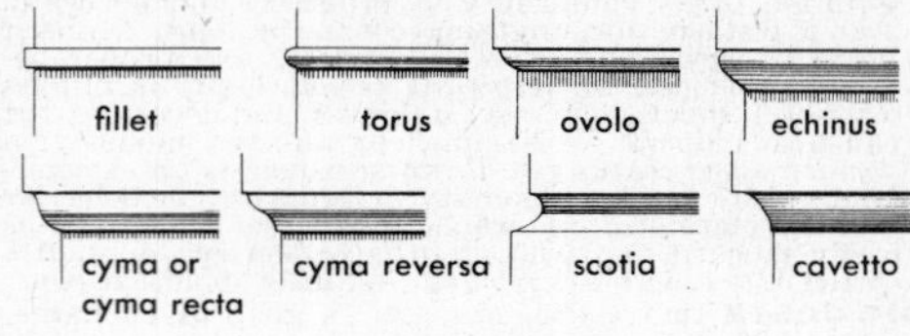

Moldings

mold′ing board′, a board upon which bread is kneaded, cookies prepared, etc.

mold′ing book′, *Shipbuilding.* a book giving the dimensions of the framing members for a hull, excluding the plates.

mold′ing plane′, *Carpentry.* a plane having a blade or a number of blades profiled to form moldings.

mold′ loft′, *Shipbuilding.* a broad, roofed area where molds and patterns are prepared.

mold·warp (mōld′wôrp′), *n.* the common European mole, *Talpa europaea.* [ME *moldwerp*, OE **moldweorp*, lit., earth-thrower (see MOLD[3], WARP); c. OS *moldwerp*, MHG *moltwerf*]

mold′ wash′, *Foundry.* a coating applied in liquid form to walls of a mold cavity.

mold·y (mōl′dē), *adj.,* **mold·i·er, mold·i·est. 1.** overgrown or covered with mold. **2.** musty, as from decay or age. Also, *esp. Brit.,* **mouldy.** [ME; see MOLD[2], -Y[1]] —**mold′i·ness,** *n.*

mole[1] (mōl), *n.* **1.** a small, congenital spot or blemish on the human skin, usually of a dark color, slightly elevated, and often hairy. **2.** a pigmented nevus. [ME; OE *māl*; c. OHG *meil* spot, Goth *mail* wrinkle]

mole[2] (mōl), *n.* any of various small insectivorous mammals, esp. of the family *Talpidae*, living chiefly underground, and having velvety fur, very small eyes, and strong, fossorial forefeet. [ME *molle*; akin to MD, MLG *mol*]

Mole, *Scalopus aquaticus* (Total length to 8 in.; tail to 1½ in.)

mole[3] (mōl), *n.* **1.** a massive structure, esp. of stone, set up in the water, as for a breakwater or a pier. **2.** an anchorage or harbor protected by such a structure. [< L *mōles* mass, dam, mole]

mole[4] (mōl), *n.* *Chem.* the molecular weight of a substance expressed in grams; gram molecule. Also, **mol.** [< G *Mol*, short for *Molekül* MOLECULE]

mole[5] (mōl), *n.* *Pathol.* a fleshy mass in the uterus formed by a hemorrhagic dead ovum. [< medical L *mola*, special use of *mola* millstone]

Mo·lech (mō′lek), *n.* Moloch (defs. 1, 2).

mole′ crab′, a burrowing crustacean of the genus *Emerita*, found on sandy ocean beaches of North America, having a distinctly curved carapace. Also called **sandbug.**

mole′ crick′et, any of several burrowing crickets of the family *Gryllotalpidae* that have fossorial forelegs and that feed on the roots of plants.

mo·lec·u·lar (mō lek′yə lər, mə-), *adj.* pertaining to, caused by, or consisting of molecules. [MOLECULE + -AR[1]] —**mo·lec′u·lar·ly,** *adv.*

molec′ular beam′, *Physics.* a stream of molecules which are freed from a substance, usually a salt, by evaporation and are then passed through a narrow slit for focusing, for investigating the properties of nuclei, atoms, and molecules. Also called **molec′ular ray′.**

molec′ular distilla′tion, *Chem.* a vacuum distillation in which the distillate travels so short a distance that it is condensed before it collides with other molecules.

molec′ular film′, *Physical Chem.* a film or layer one molecule thick. Also called **monolayer.**

molec′ular for′mula, *Chem.* a chemical formula that indicates the kinds of atoms and the number of each kind in a molecule of a compound. Cf. **empirical formula, structural formula.**

mo·lec·u·lar·i·ty (mō lek′yə lar′i tē, mə-), *n.* *Chem.* the number of molecules or atoms that participate in an elementary process. [MOLECULAR + -ITY]

molec′ular weight′, *Chem.* the average weight of a molecule of an element or compound measured in units once based on the weight of one hydrogen atom taken as the standard or on 1/16 the weight of an oxygen atom, but after 1961 based on 1/12 the weight of the carbon-12 atom; the sum of the atomic weights of all the atoms in a molecule. *Abbr.:* mol. wt.

mol·e·cule (mol′ə kyōōl′), *n.* **1.** *Chem., Physics.* the smallest physical unit of an element or compound, consisting of one or more like atoms in an element and two or more different atoms in a compound. **2.** a quantity of a substance, the weight of which, measured in any chosen unit, is numerically equal to the molecular weight; gram molecule. **3.** any very small particle: *They left not one molecule of steak for me.* [earlier *molecula* < NL, equiv. to L *mōle(s)* mass + *-cula* -CULE]

mole′ frac′tion, *Chem.* the ratio of the number of moles of a given component of a mixture to the total number of moles of all the components.

mole·hill (mōl′hil′), *n.* **1.** a small mound or ridge of earth raised up by moles burrowing under the ground. **2.** something insignificant, esp. a small obstacle or difficulty: *to make a mountain out of a molehill.* [late ME; see MOLE², HILL]

mole′ plow′, a plow typically having a pointed shoe at the end of a vertical support, for cutting a hollow drainage channel below the surface.

mole·skin (mōl′skin′), *n.* **1.** the soft, deep-gray, fragile fur of the mole. **2.** a stout, napped, twilled cotton fabric used for sportsmen's and laborers' clothing. **3. moleskins,** a garment, esp. trousers, of this fabric. [MOLE² + SKIN]

mo·lest (mə lest′), *v.t.* **1.** to bother, interfere with, or annoy. **2.** to make indecent sexual advances to. [ME *moleste(n)* < L *molest(āre)* (to) irk, deriv. of *molestus* irksome, equiv. to *molēs* mass, burden, trouble + *-tus* adj. suffix] **—mo·les·ta·tion** (mō′le-stā′shən, mol′e-), *n.* **—mo·lest′er,** *n.* **—mo·lest′ful,** *adj.*
—Syn. 1. harass, harry, disturb, trouble, plague, hector, torment. **2.** See **attack.**

mol·et (mol′it), *n.* mullet².

Mo·lière (mōl yâr′; *Fr.* mô lyer′), *n.* (*Jean Baptiste Poquelin*) 1622–73, French actor and playwright.

mol·i·la·li·a (mol′ə lā′lē ə, -lāl′yə), *n.* *Pathol.* mogilalia.

Mo·li·na (mō lē′nə, mə-; *Sp.* mô lē′nä), *n.* **1. Lu·is** (lo͞o ēs′), 1535–1600, Spanish Jesuit theologian. **2. Tirso de.** See **Tirso de Molina.**

mo·line (mō′lin, mō lin′), *adj.* *Heraldry.* (of a cross) having arms of equal length, split and curved back at the ends, used esp. as the cadency mark of an eighth son: *a cross moline.* See illus. under **cross.** [< AF **moliné,* equiv. to *molin* MILL¹ + *-é* -ED³]

Mo·line (mō lēn′), *n.* a city in NW Illinois, on the Mississippi. 42,705 (1960).

Moline′ A′cres, a town in E Missouri. 3132 (1960).

Mo·li·nism (mō′lə niz′əm, mol′ə-), *n.* the theological doctrine, formulated by Luis Molina, that the consent of the human will is necessary for divine grace to be effective. [MOLIN(A) + -ISM] **—Mo′li·nist,** *n.*

Mo·li·nos (mō lē′nōs; *Sp.* mô lē′nôs), *n.* **Mi·guel de** (mē gel′ de), c1640–c95, Spanish priest and mystic: chief exponent of quietism.

Mo·li·o·ne (mə lī′ə nē′), *n.* *Class. Myth.* the mother, by Poseidon, of Cteatus and Eurytus.

Mo·li·o·nes (mə lī′ə nēz′), *n.* *Class. Myth.* Cteatus and Eurytus, the twin sons of Molione, sometimes said to have been joined at the waist. They were fathered by Poseidon and reared by Actor.

moll (mol), *n.* *Slang.* **1.** Also called **gun moll.** a woman who is the girl friend or mistress of a gangster, thief, etc. **2.** a prostitute. [special use of MOLL]

moll (môl), *adj.* *German.* (in music) written in a minor key; minor.

Moll (mol), *n.* a girl's given name.

mol·lah (mō′lə), *n.* mullah.

Mol·len·do (mô yen′dô), *n.* a seaport in S Peru. 17,859 (est. 1957).

mol·les·cent (mə les′ənt), *adj.* softening or tending to soften. [< L *mollescent-* (s. of *mollescēns*) softening (prp. of *mollescere*), equiv. to *moll(is)* soft + *-escent-* -ESCENT] **—mol·les′cence,** *n.*

Mol·let (mō lā′; *Fr.* mô le′), *n.* **Guy** (gī; *Fr.* gē), born 1905, French political leader.

Moll′ Flan′ders, (*The Fortunes and Misfortunes of the Famous Moll Flanders*) a novel (1722) by Daniel Defoe.

Mol·lie (mol′ē), *n.* a girl's given name, form of **Mary** or **Milicent.** Also, **Molly.**

Mol′lier di′agram (môl′yā), *Thermodynamics.* a graph showing the enthalpy of a substance as a function of its entropy when some physical property of the substance, as temperature or pressure, is kept at a specified constant value. [named after Richard *Mollier* (d. 1935), German engineer]

mol·li·fy (mol′ə fī′), *v.t.*, **-fied, -fy·ing. 1.** to soften in feeling or temper, as a person; pacify; appease. **2.** to mitigate or reduce: *He mollified his demands after he understood the situation.* [ME *mollifie(n)* < MF *mollifie(r)* < LL *mollificāre,* equiv. to L *molli(s)* soft + *-ficāre* -FY] **—mol′li·fi·ca′tion,** *n.* **—mol′li·fi′er,** *n.* **—mol′li·fy′ing·ly,** *adv.* **—mol′li·fi′a·ble,** *adj.*

Mol·lus·ca (mə lus′kə), *n.* the phylum comprising the mollusks. [< NL, neut. pl. of L *molluscus* soft. See MOLLESCENT]

mol·lus·coid (mə lus′koid), *adj.* belonging or pertaining to the phylum *Molluscoidea,* in certain classifications comprising the bryozoans and brachiopods. [< NL *Molluscoid(ea).* See MOLLUSCA, -OID]

mol·lus·cum (mə lus′kəm), *n., pl.* **-ca** (-kə). *Pathol.* any of various skin conditions characterized by soft, rounded tumors. Cf. **molluscum contagiosum.** [< NL, L: fungus, n. use of neut. of *molluscus* soft. See MOLLESCENT] **—mol·lus′cous,** *adj.*

mollus′cum con·ta·gi·o′sum (kən tā′jē ō′səm), *Pathol.* an infectious form of molluscum, caused by a filterable virus. Also called **mollus′cum ep·i·the′li·ate** (ep′ə thē′lē āt′). [< NL: contagious molluscum]

mol·lusk (mol′əsk), *n.* any invertebrate of the phylum *Mollusca,* typically having a calcareous shell of one, two, or more pieces that wholly or partly enclose the soft, unsegmented body, including the chitons, snails, bivalves, squids, octopuses, etc. Also, **mol′lusc.** [< NL; see MOLLUSCA] **—mol·lus·can** (mə lus′kən), *adj., n.* **—mol′lusk·like′,** *adj.*

Moll′wei·de projec′tion (môl′vī də). See **homolographic projection.** [named after K. B. *Mollweide* (1774–1825), German astronomer and mathematician]

mol·ly (mol′ē), *n., pl.* **-lies.** any live-bearing, freshwater fish of the genus *Mollienisia,* often kept in aquariums. [shortened from NL *Mollienisia,* irreg. named after Count F.N. *Mollien* (1758–1850); see -IA]

Mol·ly (mol′ē), *n., pl.* **-lies.** *Trademark.* an expansion bolt having a split, sleevelike sheath threaded at one end so that when inserted snugly into masonry the turning of the bolt draws the ends of the sheath together, thus spreading the sides.

Mol·ly (mol′ē), *n.* a girl's given name, form of **Mary** or **Milicent.** Also, **Mollie.**

mol·ly·cod·dle (mol′ē kod′əl), *n., v.,* **-dled, -dling.** —*n.* **1.** a man or boy who is used to being coddled; a milksop. —*v.t., v.i.* **2.** to coddle; pamper. [MOLLY + CODDLE] **—mol′ly·cod′dler,** *n.*

Mol·ly Ma·guire (mol′ē mə gwīᵊr′), **1.** *Irish Hist.* a member of a secret terrorist society organized in 1843 to prevent evictions by the government: so called because the members disguised themselves as women. **2.** a member of a former secret association that terrorized the mine operators' agents in an effort to get relief from oppressive conditions in the anthracite coal-mining regions of Pennsylvania between 1865 and 1877.

Mol′ly Mil′ler, a blenny, *Blennius cristatus,* found in the Atlantic Ocean. [?]

Mol·nár (mōl′när; *Hung.* môl′när), *n.* **Fe·renc** (fe′-rents), 1878–1952, Hungarian playwright, novelist, and short-story writer.

Mo·loch (mō′lok, mol′ək), *n.* **1.** a deity, mentioned in the Bible, whose worship was marked by the burning of children offered as a propitiatory sacrifice by their own parents. II Kings 23:10; Jer. 32:35. **2.** anything conceived of as requiring appalling sacrifice: *the Moloch of war.* **3.** (*l.c.*) a spiny agamid lizard, *Moloch horridus,* of Australian deserts, that resembles the horned lizard. Also, **Molech** (for defs. 1, 2). [< LL *Moloch* (Vulgate) < Gk *Molóch* (Septuagint) < Heb *Mōlōkh,* var. of *melekh* king]

Mo·lo·ka·i (mō′lō kä′ē), *n.* an island in central Hawaii: leper colony. 4744 (1960); 259 sq. mi.

Mol·o·kan (mol′ə kän′), *n.* a member of an ascetic religious sect, founded in Russia in the 19th century by former Doukhobors, opposing sacraments and ritual and stressing the authority of the Bible. [< Russ *molok(o)* milk + -AN; ? so called because members of the sect were allowed to drink milk during Lent]

Mo·lor·chus (mə lôr′kəs), *n.* *Class. Myth.* a peasant whose son was killed by the Nemean lion.

Mo·los·sus (mə los′əs), *n.* *Class. Myth.* the son of Neoptolemus and Andromache.

Mo·lo·tov (mol′ə tôf′, -tof′, mōl′-; *Russ.* **mô′lo tof**), *n.* **1. Vya·che·slav Mi·khai·lo·vich** (vyä′che släf′ mi khī′lo vich), (*Vyacheslav Mikhailovich Skryabin*), 1890–1986, Russian statesman: commissar of foreign affairs 1939–49, 1953–56. **2. Perm.**

Mo′lotov cock′tail, a crude incendiary grenade consisting of a bottle filled with a flammable liquid and a saturated wick which is ignited before throwing: used originally for setting fire to enemy tanks. [named after V. M. MOLOTOV]

molt (mōlt), *v.i.* **1.** (of birds, insects, reptiles, etc.) to cast or shed the feathers, skin, or the like, that will be succeeded by a new growth. —*v.t.* **2.** to cast or shed (feathers, skin, etc.) in the process of renewal. —*n.* **3.** the act, process, or an instance of molting. **4.** that which is dropped in molting. Also, *esp. Brit.,* **moult.** [earlier *moult* (with analogical *-l-* as in *could*), ME *mouten,* OE *-mūtian* to change (in *bi-mūtian* to exchange for) < L *mūtāre* to change; see MUTATE] **—molt′er,** *n.*

mol·ten (mōl′tᵊn), *v.* **1.** a pp. of **melt.** —*adj.* **2.** liquefied by heat; in a state of fusion: *molten lead; molten lava.* **3.** produced by melting and casting: *a molten image.* [ME; old ptp. of MELT] **—mol′ten·ly,** *adv.*

Molt·ke (mōlt′kə), *n.* **1. Hel·muth Karl** (hel′mo͞ot kärl), 1800–91, Prussian field marshall: chief of staff 1858–88. **2.** his nephew, **Helmuth Jo·han·nes** (yō hä′-nəs), **Count von,** 1848–1916, German general: chief of staff 1906–14. **3.** a crater in the fourth quadrant of the face of the moon: about 3 miles in diameter.

mol·to (mōl′tō; *It.* môl′tō), *adv.* *Music.* very: *molto adagio; molto allegro.* [< It < L *multum,* adv. use of acc. sing. neut. of *multus* much]

Moluc′ca balm′ (mō luk′ə, mə-). See **Bells of Ireland.**

Mo·luc·cas (mō luk′əz, mə-), *n.* (*construed as pl.*) a group of islands in Indonesia, between Celebes and New Guinea. 797,000 (est. 1961); ab. 30,000 sq. mi. Also called **Mo·luc′ca Is′lands, Spice Islands.**

Mo·lus (mō′ləs), *n.* *Class. Myth.* a son of Ares and Demonice, father of Meriones.

mol·vi (mōl′vē), *n.* maulvi.

mol. wt., molecular weight.

mo·ly (mō′lē), *n., pl.* **-lies.** *Class. Myth.* an herb given to Odysseus by Hermes to counteract the spells of Circe. [< L < Gk]

mo·lyb·date (mə lib′dāt), *n.* *Chem.* a salt of any molybdic acid. [MOLYBD(IC) + -ATE²]

mo·lyb·de·nite (mə lib′də nīt′, mol′ib dē′nīt), *n.* a soft, graphitelike mineral, molybdenum sulfide, MoS_2, occurring in foliated masses or scales: the principal ore of molybdenum. [obs. *molybden(a)* MOLYBDENUM + -ITE¹]

mo·lyb·de·nous (mə lib′də nəs, mol′ib dē′nəs), *adj.* *Chem.* containing bivalent molybdenum. [MOLYBDEN(UM) + -OUS]

mo·lyb·de·num (mə lib′də nəm, mol′ib dē′nəm), *n.* *Chem.* a silver-white, high-melting metal element, used as an alloy with iron in making hard, high-speed cutting tools. *Symbol:* Mo; *at. wt.:* 95.94; *at. no.:* 42; *sp. gr.:* 10.2. [< NL, alter. of earlier *molybdēna* < L *molybdaena* < Gk *molýbdaina* galena, equiv. to *mólybd(os)* lead + *-aina* suffix of appurtenance]

molyb′denum triox′ide, *Chem.* a white, crystalline, sparingly water-soluble powder, MoO_3, used chiefly in the manufacture of molybdenum compounds. Also called **molybdic anhydride, molybdic oxide.**

mo·lyb·dic (mə lib′dik), *adj.* *Chem.* of or containing molybdenum, esp. in the trivalent or hexavalent states, as molybdic acid, H_2MoO_4. [MOLYBD(ENUM) + -IC]

molyb′dic anhy′dride, *Chem.* See **molybdenum trioxide.**

molyb′dic ox′ide, *Chem.* See **molybdenum trioxide.**

mo·lyb·dous (mə lib′dəs), *adj.* *Chem.* of or containing molybdenum, esp. in its lower valences. [MOLYBD(ENUM) + -OUS]

mom (mom), *n.* *Informal.* mother. [short for MOMMA]

Mom·ba·sa (mom bä′sä, -bas′ə), *n.* **1.** an island in S Kenya. **2.** a seaport on this island. 179,575 (1962).

mome (mōm), *n.* *Archaic.* a fool; blockhead. [?]

Mo·mence (mə mens′), *n.* a town in NE Illinois. 2949 (1960).

mo·ment (mō′mənt), *n.* **1.** an indefinitely short space of time; an instant: *I'll be with you in a moment.* **2.** the present or any other particular instant (usually prec. by *the*): *He is busy at the moment.* **3.** a definite period or stage, as in a course of events: *at this moment in history's progress.* **4.** importance or consequence: *a decision of great moment.* **5.** *Statistics.* the mean or expected value of the product formed by multiplying together a set of one or more variates or variables each to a specified power. **6.** *Philos.* **a.** an aspect of a thing. **b.** *Obs.* an essential or constituent factor. **7.** *Mech.* **a.** a tendency to produce motion, esp. about an axis. **b.** the product of a physical quantity and its perpendicular distance from an axis: *moment of area; moment of mass.* [ME < L *mōment(um)* motion, cause of motion, hence, influence, importance, equiv. to *mō-* (ptp. s. of *movēre* to MOVE) + *-mentum* -MENT]
—Syn. 1. second, jiffy, trice, flash, twinkling. See **minute**¹. **4.** significance, weight, gravity.

mo·men·tar·i·ly (mō′mən târ′ə lē, mō′mən ter′-), *adv.* **1.** for a moment: *to pause momentarily.* **2.** every moment; from moment to moment: *Our danger is increasing momentarily.* **3.** at any moment: *expected to occur momentarily.* [MOMENTARY + -LY]

mo·men·tar·y (mō′mən ter′ē), *adj.* **1.** lasting but a moment; very brief: *a momentary glimpse.* **2.** occurring at any moment: *to live in fear of momentary annihilation.* **3.** *Rare.* effective or recurring at every moment; constant. [< L *mōmentāri(us).* See MOMENT, -ARY] **—mo′-men·tar′i·ness,** *n.*

mo·ment·ly (mō′mənt lē), *adv.* **1.** every moment; from moment to moment. **2.** for a moment; momentarily. [MOMENT + -LY]

mo′ment of iner′tia, *Physics.* the sum of the products of the mass and the square of the perpendicular distance to the axis of rotation of each particle in a body rotating about an axis.

mo′ment of momen′tum, *Physics.* See **angular momentum.**

mo′ment of sail′, *Naval Archit.* the product of a given area of sail, taken as the maximum safe area, and the vertical distance from the center of effort and the center of lateral resistance.

mo′ment of stabil′ity, *Naval Archit.* See **righting moment.**

mo′ment of truth′, 1. the moment in a bullfight at which the matador is about to make the kill. **2.** the moment at which one's character, courage, skill, etc., is put to an extreme test; critical moment.

mo·men·tous (mō men′təs), *adj.* of great or far-reaching importance or consequence: *a momentous day in history.* [MOMENT + -OUS] **—mo·men′tous·ly,** *adv.* **—mo·men′tous·ness,** *n.*
—Syn. vital, critical, crucial, serious. See **heavy. —Ant.** trivial, trifling.

mo·men·tum (mō men′təm), *n., pl.* **-ta** (-tə), **-tums. 1.** force or speed of movement; impetus: *The car gained momentum as it began to go downhill.* **2.** *Mech.* a quantity expressing the motion of a body or system, equal to the product of the mass of a body and its velocity, and for a system equal to the vector sum of the products of mass and velocity of each particle in the system. **3.** *Philos.* moment (def. 6). [< L; see MOMENT]

mom·ism (mom′iz əm), *n.* (*sometimes cap.*) adulation of the mother and domination by a mother-image; excessive dependence on maternal care or protection, resulting in absence or loss of maturity and independence. [MOM + -ISM]

mom·ma (mom′ə), *n.* mama.

mom·me (mom′ē), *n., pl.* **mom·me.** a Japanese unit of weight equal to 3.75 grams. [< Jap]

Momm·sen (mom′sən; *Ger.* môm′zən), *n.* **The·o·dor** (tā′ō dôr′), 1817–1903, German classical historian: Nobel prize for literature 1902.

Mom·pós (môm pôs′), *n.* a city in NW Colombia, on the Magdalena. 9192 (1951).

Mom·po·u (mōm pō′o͞o), *n.* **Fe·de·ri·co** (fe′ṯhe rē′-kō), born 1893, Spanish composer.

mom·ser (mom′zər), *n.* mamzer. Also, **mom′zer.**

Mo·mus (mō′məs), *n., pl.* **-mus·es, -mi** (-mī) for 2. **1.** Also, **Mo·mos** (mō′mos). *Class. Myth.* the god of censure and ridicule. **2.** (*sometimes l.c.*) a faultfinder; a carping critic. [< L < Gk *Mômos,* special use of *mômos* blame, ridicule]

mon (mon), *n.* *Scot. and North Eng.* man.

Mon (mōn), *n.* an Austroasiatic language used chiefly in Burma in the vicinity of Moulmein.

mon-, var. of **mono-** before a vowel: *monacid.*

Mon., 1. Monday. **2.** Monsignor.

mon., 1. monastery. **2.** monetary.

Mo·na (mō′nə), *n.* a girl's given name.

Mon·a·ca (mon′ə kə), *n.* a town in W Pennsylvania. 8394 (1960).

mon·ac·e·tin (mon as′i tᵊn, -as′i tin), *n.* acetin. [MON- + ACETIN]

mon·a·chal (mon′ə kəl), *adj.* pertaining to or characteristic of monks or their life; monastic. [< ML *monachāl(is),* equiv. to LL *monach(us)* MONK + *-ālis* -AL¹]

mon·a·chism (mon′ə kiz′əm), *n.* monasticism. [< LL *monach(us)* MONK + -ISM] **—mon′a·chist,** *adj.*

mon·ac·id (mon as′id), *adj., n.* *Chem.* monoacid. **—mon′a·cid′ic,** *adj.*

mo·na·ci·llo (mon′ə sē′ō; *Sp.* mô′nä sē′yō), *n., pl.* **-cil·los** -sē′ōz; *Sp.* -sē′yôs). a low shrub, *Malvaviscus arboreus,* of tropical America, having scarlet flowers and berrylike fruit which is sticky when young. [< AmerSp, Sp: lit., altar-boy]

Mon·a·co (mon′ə kō′; *Fr.* mô na kō′; *It.* mō′nä kō′), *n.* **1.** a principality on the Mediterranean coast, bordering SE France. 22,297 (1961); ½ sq. mi. **2.** the capital of this principality. 1860 (1951).

mon·ad (mon′ad, mō′nad), *n.* **1.** *Biol.* **a.** any simple, single-celled organism. **b.** a certain type of small, flagellate, colorless, naked amoeboid with one to three flagella. **2.** *Chem.* an element, atom, or group having a valence of one. Cf. **dyad** (def. 3), **triad** (def. 2a). **3.** *Philos.* **a.** (in the metaphysics of Leibnitz) an unextended, indivisible, and indestructible entity that is the basic or ultimate constituent of the universe and a microcosm of it. **b.** (in the philosophy of Giordano Bruno) a basic and irreducible metaphysical unit that is spatially and psychically individuated. **c.** any basic metaphysical entity, esp. having an autonomous life. **4.** a single unit or entity. [< LL *monad-* (s. of *monas*) < Gk: unity. See MON-, -AD] —**mo·nad·ic** (mə nad′ik), **mo·nad′i·cal, mo·nad′al,** *adj.* —**mo·nad′i·cal·ly,** *adv.*

mon·a·del·phous (mon′ə del′fəs), *adj. Bot.* **1.** (of stamens) united into one bundle or set by their filaments. **2.** (of a plant or flower) having the stamens so united. [MON- + Gk *adelph(ós)* brother + -OUS]

Monadelphous flower of hollyhock, *Althaea rosea*

mon·a·des (mon′ə dēz′), *n.* pl. of **monas.**

mon·ad·ism (mon′ə diz′əm, mō′nad iz′əm), *n. Philos.* **1.** the doctrine of monads as ultimate units of being. **2.** (*sometimes cap.*) the philosophy of Leibnitz. Also, **mon·ad·ol·o·gy** (mon′ə dol′ə jē, mō′na dol′-). [MONAD + -ISM] —**mon′ad·is′tic,** *adj.*

mo·nad·nock (mə nad′nok), *n.* **1.** *Phys. Geog.* a residual hill or mountain standing well above the surface of a surrounding peneplain. **2.** (*cap.*) **Mount,** a mountain peak in SW New Hampshire. 3186 ft. [< AmerInd: (object) standing out, isolated]

Mon·a·ghan (mon′ə gən), *n.* a county in the NE Republic of Ireland. 47,088 (1961); 498 sq. mi. *Co. seat:* Monaghan.

Mon·a·hans (mon′ə hanz′), *n.* a town in W Texas. 8567 (1960).

Mo′na Li′sa (mō′nə lē′zə, lē′sə), a portrait (1503?–05?) by Leonardo da Vinci. Also called **La Gioconda.**

mo·nan·drous (mə nan′drəs), *adj.* **1.** having only one husband at a time. **2.** of or characterized by monandry. **3.** *Bot.* **a.** (of a flower) having only one stamen. **b.** (of a plant) having such flowers. [< Gk *mónandros.* See MON-, -ANDROUS]

Monandrous flower of mare's-tail, ***Hippuris vulgaris***

mo·nan·dry (mə nan′drē), *n.* the practice or condition of having but one husband at a time (distinguished from *polyandry*). [MONANDR(OUS) + -Y[3]]

mo·nan·thous (mə nan′thəs), *adj. Bot.* having one flower. [MON- + -ANTHOUS]

Mo′na Pas′sage (mō′nə; *Sp.* mō′nä), a strait between Hispaniola and Puerto Rico. 80 mi. wide.

mon·arch (mon′ərk), *n.* **1.** a hereditary sovereign with more or less limited powers, as a king, queen, emperor, etc. **2.** a sole and absolute ruler of a state. **3.** one who or that which holds a dominant position: *a monarch of international shipping.* **4.** Also called **milkweed butterfly.** a large, reddish-brown butterfly, *Danaus plexippus,* having black and white markings, the larvae of which feed on the leaves of milkweed. [late ME < LL *monarcha* < Gk *monárchēs* ruling alone]

mo·nar·chal (mə När′kəl), *adj.* **1.** pertaining to, characteristic of, or befitting a monarch: *monarchal pomp.* **2.** *Rare.* having the status of a monarch. Also, **mo·nar·chi·al** (mə när′kē əl). [MONARCH + -AL[1]] —**mo·nar′chal·ly,** *adv.*

Mo·nar·chi·an·ism (mə när′kē ə niz′əm), *n. Theol.* any of several doctrines of the Christian church in the 2nd and 3rd centuries A.D., emphasizing the unity of God by maintaining that the Father, the Son, and the Holy Ghost are three manifestations or aspects of God. [*monarchian* (< LL *monarchiān(us*); see MONARCHY, -AN) + -ISM] —**Mo·nar′chi·an,** *adj., n.* —**Mo·nar′chi·an·ist,** *adj.*

mo·nar·chi·cal (mə när′ki kəl), *adj.* **1.** of, like, or pertaining to a monarch or monarchy. **2.** characterized by or favoring monarchy. Also, **mo·nar′chic.** [< Gk *monarchik(ós)* (see MONARCH, -IC) + -AL[1]] —**mo·nar′chi·cal·ly,** *adv.*

mon·ar·chism (mon′ər kiz′əm), *n.* **1.** the principles of monarchy. **2.** advocacy of a monarch or monarchical rule. [MONARCH(Y) + -ISM; cf. F *monarchisme,* G *Monarchismus*] —**mon′ar·chist,** *n., adj.* —**mon′ar·chis′tic,** *adj.*

mon·ar·chy (mon′ər kē), *n., pl.* **-chies. 1.** a government or state in which the supreme power is actually or nominally lodged in a monarch. Cf. **absolute monarchy, limited monarchy. 2.** supreme power or sovereignty held by a single person. [ME *monarchie* < LL *monarchia* < Gk *monarchía.* See MONARCH, -Y[3]] —**Syn. 1.** See **kingdom.**

mo·nar·da (mə när′də), *n.* any aromatic, erect, labiate herb of the genus *Monarda,* of North America, including horsemint, Oswego tea, etc. [< NL, named after N. *Monardés* (1493–1588), Spanish botanist]

mon·as (mon′as, mō′nas), *n., pl.* **mon·a·des** (mon′ə dēz′). monad. [< LL < Gk, nom. sing. of *monad-* unity]

mon·as·ter·y (mon′ə ster′ē), *n., pl.* **-ter·ies. 1.** a house or place of residence occupied by a community of persons, esp. monks, living in seclusion under religious vows. **2.** the community of persons living in such a place. [ME < LL *monastēri(um)* < LGk *monastḗrion* monk house, orig. hermit's cell. See MONASTIC] —**mon·as·te·ri·al** (mon′ə stēr′ē əl), *adj.* —**Syn. 1.** convent, cloister; abbey, priory.

mo·nas·tic (mə nas′tik), *adj.* Also, **mo·nas′ti·cal. 1.** of or pertaining to monasteries: *a monastic library.* **2.** of, pertaining to, or characteristic of monks, their manner of life, or their devotion to religious rather than secular matters: *monastic vows of poverty, chastity, and obedience.* **3.** of, pertaining to, or characteristic of a secluded, dedicated, or harshly austere manner of living. —*n.* **4.** a member of a monastic community or order; a monk. [< ML *monastic(us)* < Gk *monastikós,* equiv. to *monast-* (verbid s. of *monázein* to be alone; see MON-) + *-ikos* -IC] —**mo·nas′ti·cal·ly,** *adv.*

mo·nas·ti·cism (mə nas′ti siz′əm), *n.* the monastic system, condition, or mode of life. [MONASTIC + -ISM]

Mo·na·stir (mô′nä stēr′), *n.* Turkish name of **Bitolj.**

mon·a·tom·ic (mon′ə tom′ik), *adj. Chem.* **1.** having one atom in the molecule. **2.** containing one replaceable atom or group. **3.** having a valence of one. Also, **monoatomic.** [MON- + ATOMIC] —**mon′a·tom′i·cal·ly,** *adv.*

mon·au·ral (mon ôr′əl), *adj.* **1.** monophonic (def. 2). **2.** of, pertaining to, or affecting one ear. [MON- + AURAL[2]] —**mon·au′ral·ly,** *adv.*

mon·ax·i·al (mon ak′sē əl), *adj. Bot.* **1.** uniaxial. **2.** having flowers that grow on the primary axis. [MON- + AXIAL]

mon·a·zite (mon′ə zīt′), *n.* a reddish- or yellowish-brown mineral, a phosphate of cerium and lanthanum, $(Ce,La)PO_4$: the principal ore of thorium. [< G *Monazit,* equiv. to *monaz-* (< Gk *monázein* to be alone; see MON-) + *-it* -ITE[1]]

Mön·chen-Glad·bach (mœn′кнən glät′bäкн), *n.* a city in W North Rhine-Westphalia, in W West Germany. 153,400 (1963). Formerly, **München-Gladbach.**

mon cher (môɴ sheʀ′), *French.* (referring to men) my dear. Cf. **ma chère.**

Monck (mungk), *n.* **George, 1st Duke of Albemarle and Earl of Torrington,** 1608–70, English general. Also, **Monk.**

Mon·clo·va (môṉg klō′vä), *n.* a city in NE Mexico. 23,870 (1962).

Monc·ton (mungk′tən), *n.* a city in SE New Brunswick, in E Canada. 43,840 (1961).

Mon·dale (mon′dāl′), *n.* **Walter F(rederick)** ("*Fritz*"), born 1928, 42nd vice-president of the U.S. 1977–81.

Mon·day (mun′dē, -dā), *n.* the second day of the week, following Sunday. [ME *Mone(n)day,* OE *mōn(an)dæg,* trans. of LL *lūnae diēs* moon's day]

Mon′day Conversa′tions, a collection of critical and biographical essays (1849–69) by Charles Augustin Sainte-Beuve. French, **Causeries du Lundi.**

Mon′day morn′ing quar′terback, *Informal.* a person who criticizes the actions or decisions of others after the fact, using hindsight to assess situations infallibly or to offer solutions to problems.

Mon′day morn′ing quar′terbacking, the criticism of others or the spurious solution of problems through hindsight.

Mon·days (mun′dēz, -dāz), *adv.* on Mondays.

monde (môɴd), *n. French.* the world; people; society.

mon·do (mon dō′), *n., pl.* **-dos.** *Zen.* a question to a student for which an immediate answer is demanded, the spontaneity of which is often illuminating. Cf. **koan.** [< Jap]

Mon·dri·an (môn′drē än′, mon′-), *n.* **Pie·t(er Cor·ne·lis)** (pē′tər kôr nā′lis), 1872–1944, Dutch painter. Dutch, **Mon·dri·aan** (mon′drē än′).

mo·ne·cious (mə nē′shəs, mō-), *adj.* monoecious.

Mo·nel′ met′al (mō nel′), *Trademark.* an alloy consisting mainly of nickel and copper.

mon·er·gism (mon′ər jiz′əm), *n. Theol.* the doctrine that the Holy Ghost acts independently of the human will in the work of regeneration. Cf. **synergism** (def. 1). [MON- + ERG + -ISM] —**mon′er·gist,** *n.* —**mon′er·gis′tic,** *adj.*

mo·ne·sia (mə nē′zhə), *n. Pharm.* a preparation extracted from the bark of a South American tree, *Pradosia lactescens,* and used chiefly as an astringent and as an expectorant. [< AmerSp]

Mo·nes·sen (mə nes′ən, mō-), *n.* a city in SW Pennsylvania, on the Monongahela River. 18,424 (1960).

Mo·net (mō nā′; *Fr.* mô ne′), *n.* **Claude** (klōd; *Fr.* klōd), 1840–1926, French painter.

Mo·ne·ta (mō nā′tə; *It.* mô ne′tä), *n.* **1. Er·ne·sto Te·o·do·ro** (eʀ ne′stô te′ô dô′ʀô), 1833–1918, Italian journalist: Nobel peace prize 1907. **2.** (in Roman religion) an epithet of Juno, meaning "adviser."

mon·e·tar·y (mon′i ter′ē, mun′-), *adj.* **1.** of or pertaining to the coinage or currency of a country. **2.** of or pertaining to money; pecuniary: *monetary as opposed to sentimental value.* [< LL *monētāri(us*). See MONEY, -ARY] —**mon·e·tar·i·ly** (mon′i târ′ə lē, mon′i ter′ə lē, mun′-, mun′-), *adv.* —**Syn. 1.** See **financial.**

mon′etary u′nit, the standard unit of value of the currency of a country, as the dollar in the U.S. and the franc in France.

mon·e·tise (mon′i tīz′, mun′-), *v.t.,* **-tised, -tis·ing.** *Chiefly Brit.* monetize. —**mon′e·ti·sa′tion,** *n.*

mon·e·tize (mon′i tīz′, mun′-), *v.t.,* **-tized, -tiz·ing. 1.** to legalize as money. **2.** to coin into money: *to monetize gold.* **3.** to give the character of money to. [< L *monēt(a)* MONEY + -IZE] —**mon′e·ti·za′tion,** *n.*

Mo·nett (mə net′), *n.* a town in SW Missouri. 5359 (1960).

mon·ey (mun′ē), *n., pl.* **mon·eys, mon·ies,** *adj.* —*n.* **1.** gold, silver, or other metal in pieces of convenient form stamped by public authority and issued as a medium of exchange and measure of value. **2.** See **paper money. 3.** any circulating medium of exchange, including coins, paper money, and demand deposits. **4.** any article or substance used as a medium of exchange, measure of wealth, or means of payment as checks on demand deposit, wampum, etc. **5.** a particular form or denomination of currency. **6.** See **money of account. 7.** property considered with reference to its pecuniary value. **8.** an amount or sum of money: *Can you lend me some money?* **9.** wealth considered in terms of money: *She was brought up with money.* **10. moneys** or **monies,** *Law.* pecuniary sums. **11.** pecuniary profit: *During that period everyone made money.* **12. for one's money,** *Informal.* with respect to one's opinion, choice, or wish: *For my money, there's nothing to be gained by waiting.* **13. in the money,** *Slang.* **a.** in possession of a great deal of money; affluent: *You can see he's in the money, look at all those clothes he buys.* **b.** first, second, or third place in a contest, esp. a horse or dog race. **14. make money,** to make a profit; become rich: *It is an interesting occupation, but you'll never make money at it.* —*adj.* **15.** having access to or controlling large sums of money or financial influence: *The Wall Street money men say the stock market will continue to rise.* **16.** having, spending, or requiring large sums of money: *I wanted to invest in the scheme, but it was a money proposition.* **17.** of or pertaining to money. **18.** used for carrying, keeping, or handling money: *Have you seen my little money purse?* [ME *moneie* < MF < L *monēta* MINT[2]] —**mon′ey·less,** *adj.* —**Syn. 1.** coin, cash, currency, specie, change. **7.** funds, capital, assets, wealth, riches.

mon·ey·bag (mun′ē bag′), *n.* **1.** a bag for money. **2. moneybags,** (*construed as sing.*) a wealthy person. [MONEY + BAG]

mon·ey·chang·er (mun′ē chān′jər), *n.* a person whose business is the exchange of currency at a fixed or official rate. [ME; see MONEY, CHANGER]

mon·eyed (mun′ēd), *adj.* **1.** having money; wealthy. **2.** consisting of or representing money: *moneyed interests.* [late ME; see MONEY, -ED[3]]

mon·ey·er (mun′ē ər), *n.* **1.** *Archaic.* one employed in the authorized coining of money. **2.** *Obs.* a money-lender or banker. [ME < OF *monier* < LL *monētār(ius)* (n. use of adj.); see MONETARY]

mon·ey·lend·er (mun′ē len′dər), *n.* one whose business it is to lend money at interest. [MONEY + LENDER]

mon·ey·mak·er (mun′ē mā′kər), *n.* **1.** one engaged in or successful at acquiring money. **2.** something that yields pecuniary profit. [late ME; see MONEY, MAKER]

mon·ey·mak·ing (mun′ē mā′king), *adj.* **1.** profitable: *a moneymaking scheme.* **2.** capable of making money: *the moneymaking part of the deal.* —*n.* **3.** the making of money. [MONEY + MAKING]

mon·ey·man (mun′ē man′), *n., pl.* **-men.** an investor; angel; backer. [MONEY + MAN[1]]

mon′ey of account′, a monetary denomination used in reckoning, esp. one not issued as a coin, as the U.S. mill.

mon′ey of neces′sity, temporary coinage, as siege pieces, issued in areas where regular coinage is unavailable: sometimes of unusual materials, as leather or wood.

mon′ey or′der, an order for the payment of money, as one issued by one bank or post office and payable at another.

mon′ey play′er, *Slang.* **1.** one who performs best under pressure, esp. in a competitive situation. **2.** a person skilled in gambling for large sums of money.

mon·ey·wort (mun′ē wûrt′), *n.* a creeping, primulaceous herb, *Lysimachia Nummularia,* having roundish leaves and yellow flowers. Also called **creeping Charlie, creeping Jennie.** [MONEY + WORT[2]]

mong (mung, mong), *n. Australian.* mongrel, esp. a mongrel dog. [shortened form]

Monge (mônzh *for 1;* mong, mong′gē *for 2*), *n.* **1. Gas·pard** (gas paʀ′), **Compte de Pé·luse** (pā lyz′), 1746–1818, French mathematician. **2.** a walled plain in the fourth quadrant of the face of the moon: about 24 miles in diameter.

mon·ger (mung′gər, mong′-), *n.* **1.** *Chiefly Brit.* a dealer in or trader of a commodity (usually used in combination): *cheesemonger; costermonger; fishmonger; ironmonger.* **2.** one who busies himself with something in a petty or contemptible way (usually used in combination): *a gossipmonger.* [ME, OE *mongere,* equiv. to *mong-* (< L *mango* salesman) + *-ere* -ER[1]; c. Icel, OHG *mangari*] —**mon′ger·ing,** *n., adj.*

mon·go (mong′gō), *n., pl.* **-gos.** mungo. Also, **mon′goe.**

Mon·gol (mong′gəl, -gol, -gōl, mon′-), *n.* **1.** a member of a pastoral people now living chiefly in Mongolia. **2.** a person having Mongoloid characteristics. **3.** any Mongolian language. **4.** (*often l.c.*) *Pathol.* a person affected with Mongolism. —*adj.* **5.** Mongolian. **6.** (*often l.c.*) *Pathol.* of, pertaining to, or characteristic of Mongolism.

Mon′gol Em′pire, an empire founded in the 12th century by Genghis Khan, which reached its greatest territorial extent in the 13th century, encompassing the larger part of Asia and extending westward to the Dnieper River in eastern Europe.

Mon·go·li·a (mong gō′lē ə, mon-), *n.* **1.** a region in Asia including Inner Mongolia of China, the Mongolian People's Republic, and the Tuva Autonomous Soviet Socialist Republic of the Soviet Union. **2. Inner.** Official name, **In′ner Mongo′lian Auton′omous Re′gion.** the S part of Mongolia, generally including the provinces of Jehol, Chahar, Suiyüan, and Ningsia: under China's control; boundaries subject to frequent change. **3. Outer,** former name of **Mongolian People's Republic.**

Mon·go·li·an (mong gō′lē ən, mon-), *adj.* **1.** pertaining to Mongolia. **2.** of or pertaining to the Mongol people of inner Asia. **3.** *Anthropol.* Mongoloid. **4.** (*often l.c.*) affected with Mongolism. **5.** of or pertaining to Mongolian, a branch of the Altaic family of languages. —*n.* **6.** a native or inhabitant of the Mongolian People's Republic. **7.** a native or inhabitant of Inner Mongolia. **8.** Also, **Mongolic.** a group of languages including Buriat, Khalkha, and several others, and constituting a branch of the Altaic family. **9.** any of the languages of this branch, esp. Khalkha. **10.** a member of the Mongoloid peoples of Asia. [MONGOLI(A) + -AN]

Mongo′lian fold′, epicanthus.

Mongo′lian id′iocy, (*often l.c.*) *Pathol.* Mongolism. —**Mongo′lian id′iot.**

Mon·go·li·an·ism (mong gō′lē ə niz′əm, mon-), *n.* (*often l.c.*) *Pathol.* Mongolism. [MONGOLIAN + -ISM]

Mongo′lian Peo′ple's Repub′lic, a republic in E central Asia, in N Mongolia. 909,600 (est. 1959); ab. 600,000 sq. mi. *Cap.:* Ulan Bator. Formerly, **Outer Mongolia.**

Mon·gol·ic (mong gol′ik, mon-), *adj.* **1.** Mongolian. —*n.* **2.** Mongolian (def. 8). [MONGOL + -IC]

Mon·gol·ism (mong′gə liz′əm, mon′-), *n.* (*often l.c.*) *Pathol.* abnormal condition of a child born with a wide, flattened skull, narrow, slanting eyes, and generally a

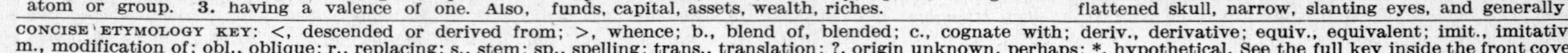
CONCISE ETYMOLOGY KEY: <, descended or derived from; >, whence; b., blend of, blended; c., cognate with; deriv., derivative; equiv., equivalent; imit., imitative; m., modification of; obl., oblique; r., replacing; s., stem; sp., spelling; trans., translation; ?, origin unknown, perhaps; *, hypothetical. See the full key inside the front cover.

mental deficiency. Now called **Down's syndrome.** [Mongol + -ism]

Mon·gol·oid (mong′gə loid′, mon′-), *adj.* **1.** resembling the Mongols. **2.** *Anthropol.* of, pertaining to, or characteristic of a racial division of mankind marked by yellowish complexion, prominent cheekbones, epicanthic folds about the eyes, straight black hair, small nose, and broad face, and including the Mongols, Manchus, Chinese, Koreans, Japanese, Annamese, Siamese, Burmese, Tibetans, and, to some extent, the Eskimos and the American Indians. **3.** (*often l.c.*) *Pathol.* of, pertaining to, or characteristic of Mongolism. —*n.* **4.** a member of a Mongoloid race. **5.** (*often l.c.*) *Pathol.* a person affected with Mongolism. [Mongol + -oid]

mon·goose (mong′gōōs′, mon′-), *n., pl.* **-goos·es.** **1.** a slender, ferretlike carnivore, *Herpestes edwardsii*, of India, that feeds on rodents, birds, eggs, etc., noted esp. for its ability to kill cobras and other venomous snakes. **2.** any of several other animals of this genus or related genera. [< Marathi *mangūs*]

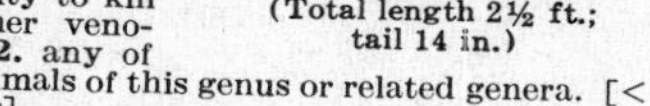

Mongoose
Herpestes edwardsii,
(Total length 2½ ft.;
tail 14 in.)

mon·grel (mung′grəl, mong′-), *n.* **1.** any animal or plant resulting from the crossing of different breeds or varieties. **2.** any cross between different things, esp. if inharmonious or indiscriminate. **3.** a dog of mixed or indeterminate breed. —*adj.* **4.** of mixed breed, race, origin, nature, etc.; of or like a mongrel. [obs. *mong* mixture (OE *gemang*) + -rel] —**mon′grel·ism, mon′grel·ness,** *n.* —**mon′grel·ly,** *adv.*
—**Syn. 1.** cross; half-breed. **3.** mutt. See **hybrid.** —**Ant. 1.** thoroughbred, purebred.

mon·grel·ise (mung′grə līz′, mong′-), *v.t.,* **-ised, -is·ing.** *Chiefly Brit.* mongrelize. —**mon′grel·i·sa′tion,** *n.* —**mon′grel·is′er,** *n.*

mon·grel·ize (mung′grə līz′, mong′-), *v.t.,* **-ized, -iz·ing.** **1.** to subject (a breed, race, etc.) to cross-breeding, esp. with a breed or race considered inferior. **2.** to mix the kinds, classes, types, characters, or sources of origin of (people, animals, or things). [mongrel + -ize] —**mon′grel·i·za′tion,** *n.* —**mon′grel·iz′er,** *n.*

mongst (mungst), *prep.* amongst. Also, **'mongst.**

Mon·gu (mong gōō′), *n.* a city in W Zambia. 3000 (est. 1961).

mo·ni·al (mō′nē əl), *n. Archaic.* a mullion. [earlier *muniall*, ME *moniel* < MF *moinel* < ?]

mon·ic (mon′ik), *adj. Math.* (of a polynomial) having the coefficient of the term of highest degree equal to 1. [mon- + -ic]

Mon·i·ca (mon′i kə), *n.* a girl's given name.

mon·ies (mun′ēz), *n.* a pl. of **money.**

mon·i·ker (mon′ə kər), *n. Slang.* a person's name, esp. a nickname. Also, **mon′ick·er.** [mono(gram + mar)ker]

Mo·nil·i·a (mə nil′ē ə), *n.* a genus of fungi of the class *Fungi Imperfecti*, having spherical or oval conidia in branched chains. [< NL, deriv. of L *monīl(e)* necklace; see -ia]

mo·nil·i·al (mə nil′ē əl), *adj.* pertaining to or caused by a fungus of the genus *Monilia.* [Monili(a) + -al[1]]

mo·nil·i·form (mō nil′ə fôrm′), *adj.* **1.** *Bot., Zool.* consisting of or characterized by a series of beadlike swellings alternating with contractions, as certain roots, stems, etc. **2.** resembling a string of beads in shape. [< L *monīli-* (s. of *monīle* necklace) + -form] —**mo·nil′i·form′ly,** *adv.*

Moniliform
fruits of
pagoda tree,
Saphora
japonica

mon·ish (mon′ish), *v.t. Archaic.* to admonish. [ME *monisshe(n)*, prob. aph. var. of *amonisshen* to admonish]

mon·ism (mon′iz əm, mō′niz əm), *n.* **1.** *Philos.* **a.** (in metaphysics) a theory that there is only one basic substance or principle as the ground of reality. Cf. **dualism** (def. 2), **pluralism** (def. 1a). **b.** a theory that reality consists of a single element. Cf. **pluralism** (def. 1b). **c.** (in epistemology) a theory that the object and datum of cognition are identical. **2.** the reduction of all processes, structures, concepts, etc., to a single governing principle; the theoretical explanation of everything in terms of one principle. **3.** the conception that there is one causal factor in history; the notion of a single element as primary determinant of individual behavior, social action, or institutional relations. [< G *Monismus*]. See mon-, -ism] —**mon′ist,** *n.* —**mo·nis·tic** (mə nis′tik, mō-), **mo·nis′ti·cal,** *adj.* —**mo·nis′ti·cal·ly,** *adv.*

mo·ni·tion (mō nish′ən, mə-), *n.* **1.** admonition; warning; caution. **2.** an official or legal notice. **3.** *Law.* a court order to a person, esp. one ordering him to appear and answer. **4.** a formal notice from a bishop requiring the amendment of an ecclesiastical offense. [late ME *monicio(u)n* < L *monitiōn-* (s. of *monitiō*) warning, equiv. to *monit(us)* warned (ptp. of *monēre*; see -ite) + *-iōn-* -ion]

mon·i·tor (mon′i tər), *n.* **1.** a pupil appointed to assist in the conduct of a class or school, as to help keep order. **2.** one who admonishes, esp. with reference to conduct. **3.** something that serves to remind or give warning. **4.** a device or arrangement for observing or recording the operation of a machine or system, esp. an automatic control system. **5.** an instrument for detecting dangerous gases, radiation, etc. **6.** *Naut.* **a.** a former U.S. steam-propelled, armored warship of very low freeboard, having one or more turrets and used for coastal defense. **b.** (*cap., italics*) the first of such vessels, used against the Confederate ironclad warship *Merrimac* at Hampton Roads, Virginia, in 1862. **7.** a raised construction straddling the ridge of a roof and having windows or louvers for lighting or ventilating a building, as a factory or warehouse. **8.** an articulated mounting for a nozzle, usually mechanically operated, which permits a stream of water to be played in any desired direction, as in fire fighting or hydraulic mining. **9.** Also called **giant.** (in hydraulic mining) a nozzle for dislodging and breaking up placer deposits with a jet of water. **10.** any of several large lizards of the family *Varanidae*, of Africa, southern Asia, the East Indies, and Australia, fabled to give warning of the presence of crocodiles. **11.** *Radio and Television.* a receiving apparatus, as a loudspeaker or Kinescope, used in a control room for monitoring transmission from a studio. —*v.t., v.i.* **12.** *Radio and Television.* **a.** to listen to (transmitted signals) on a receiving set in order to check the quality of the transmission. **b.** to view or listen to (a televised program, broadcast, or the like) for a specific purpose, as for determination of picture or audio quality, for purposes of censorship or propaganda analysis, etc. **13.** to observe, record, or detect an operation or condition with instruments that have no effect upon the operation or condition. **14.** to observe critically; oversee; supervise: *to monitor a group taking an examination.* [< L: prompter, adviser, equiv. to *monit(us)* reminded (ptp. of *monēre*; see -ite[2]) + *-or* -or[2]] —**mon′i·tor·ship′,** *n.*

mon·i·to·ri·al (mon′i tōr′ē əl, -tôr′-), *adj.* **1.** of or pertaining to a monitor. **2.** monitory. [monitory + -al[1]] —**mon′i·to′ri·al·ly,** *adv.*

mon·i·to·ry (mon′i tōr′ē, -tôr′ē), *adj., n., pl.* **-ries.** —*adj.* **1.** serving to admonish or warn; admonitory. **2.** giving monition. —*n.* **3.** Also called **mon′itory let′ter.** a letter, as one from a bishop, containing a monition. [< L *monitōri(us)* reminding, warning, equiv. to *monit(us)* (ptp.; see monitor) + *-ōrius* -ory[1]]

mon·i·tress (mon′i tris), *n.* **1.** a girl who helps keep order or assists a teacher in school. **2.** a girl or woman who admonishes, esp. with reference to conduct. [monit(o)r + -ess]

Mo·niz (mô nēsh′), *n.* **An·to·nio Ca·e·ta·no de A·bre·u Fre·i·re E·gas** (äɴn tô′nyŏŏ kä′ə tä′nŏŏ də ə brē′ŏŏ frā ē′rə ē′gəsh), 1874–1955, Portuguese neurosurgeon: Nobel prize 1949.

monk (mungk), *n.* **1.** (in Christianity) a man who has withdrawn from the world for religious reasons, esp. as a member of an order of cenobites living according to a particular rule and under vows of poverty, chastity, and obedience. **2.** a man who is a member of a monastic order within any religion: *a Buddhist monk.* **3.** *Print.* a dark area on a printed page caused by uneven inking of the plate or type. Cf. **friar** (def. 2). [ME; OE *munuc* < LL *monach(us)* < Gk *monachós* solitary (adj.), hermit (n.), equiv. to *món(os)* alone + *-achos* adj. suffix]
—**Syn. 1.** brother. Monk, friar refer to special male groups in the Roman Catholic Church whose lives are devoted to the service of the church. A monk is properly a member of a monastery, under a superior; he is bound by a vow of stability, and is a co-owner of the community property of the monastery. Since the Reformation, monk and friar have been used as if they were the same. A friar is, however, strictly speaking, a member of a mendicant order, whose members are not attached to a monastery and own no community property.

Monk (mungk), *n.* **1. The·lo·ni·ous** (thə lō′nē əs) **(Sphere),** 1918?–82, U.S. jazz pianist and composer. **2. George.** See **Monck, George.**

monk·er·y (mung′kə rē), *n., pl.* **-ies.** **1.** the mode of life, behavior, etc., of monks. **2. monkeries,** *Disparaging.* the practices, beliefs, etc., of monks. [monk + -ery]

mon·key (mung′kē), *n., pl.* **-keys,** *v.,* **-keyed, -key·ing.** —*n.* **1.** any mammal of the order *Primates*, including the guenons, macaques, langurs, capuchins, etc., but excluding man, the anthropoid apes, and, usually, the lemurs. **2.** the fur of certain species of such long-haired animals. **3.** a person likened to such an animal, as a mischievous child, a mimic, etc. **4.** any of various mechanical devices, as the ram of a pile driver. **5.** *Coal Mining.* a small passageway or opening. **6.** *U.S. Slang.* an addiction to narcotics. **7.** *Brit. Slang.* the sum of 500 pounds. **8.** *Australian Informal.* a sheep. **9.** a dance, deriving from the twist, in which the partners move their hands as if climbing a pole and jerk their heads back and forth. **10. have a monkey on one's back,** *U.S. Slang.* to be addicted to a narcotic drug. **11. have one's monkey up,** *Brit. Slang.* to be angry; be in a rage. **12. make a monkey out of,** to cause to appear ridiculous; make a fool of: *She made a monkey out of him in front of all his friends.* Also, **make a monkey of. 13. put someone's monkey up,** *Brit. Slang.* to enrage a person. —*v.i.* **14.** *Informal.* to play or trifle idly; fool (often fol. by *around* or *with*). —*v.t.* **15.** to imitate; ape; mimic. **16.** to mock. [appar. < LG; cf. MLG *Moneke* (name of son of Martin the Ape in the story of Reynard), equiv. to *mone-* (akin to obs. F *monne* she-ape, Sp, Pg *mono* ape) + *-ke* dim. suffix] —**mon′key·ish,** *adj.* —**mon′key·ish·ly,** *adv.* —**mon′key·ish·ness,** *n.*

Rhesus monkey,
Macaca mulatta
(Total length 2½ ft.;
tail 10 in.)

mon′key block′, *Naut.* a single block that swivels.

mon′key bread′, **1.** the gourdlike fruit of the baobab, eaten by monkeys. **2.** the tree itself.

mon′key bridge′, *Naut.* **1.** See **flying bridge. 2.** Also called **flying gangway.** a raised fore-and-aft catwalk permitting safe passage when the weather deck is washed by heavy seas.

mon′key busi′ness, *Slang.* **1.** improper or underhanded conduct: *He began to suspect monkey business when they didn't show up.* **2.** frivolous or mischievous behavior: *The teacher told them to cut out the monkey business and get down to work.*

mon′key dog′, affenpinscher.

mon′key-faced owl′ (mung′kē fāst′). See **barn owl.**

mon′key fist′. See **monkey's fist.**

mon′key flow′er, any scrophulariaceous plant of the genus *Mimulus*, as *M. cardinalis* **(scarlet monkey flower),** having spotted flowers that resemble a face.

mon′key fore′castle, *Naut.* a small forecastle, as an anchor deck.

mon′key fore′sail, *Naut.* a square foresail sometimes set flying on a sloop or schooner.

mon′key gaff′, *Naut.* a small, gafflike spar for supporting signals.

mon′key is′land, *Naut. Slang.* a flying bridge on top of a pilothouse or chart house.

mon′key jack′et, a short, close-fitting jacket or coat, formerly worn by sailors. [so called because like jacket worn by organ-grinder's monkey]

mon′key link′. See **lap link.**

mon′key nut′, *Chiefly Brit. Slang.* a peanut.

mon′key paw′. See **monkey's fist.**

mon′key pin′scher, affenpinscher.

mon′key pole′, *Theat. Brit.* a long pole having a hole at one end through which a line is drawn, used as a guide in lashing flats together.

mon′key poop′, *Naut.* a partial poop deck raised in the center of the quarter-deck of a sailing vessel.

mon·key·pot (mung′kē pot′), *n.* the woody, operculate seed vessel of any of certain large South American trees of the genus *Lecythis.* [so called because potlike in shape and big enough for a monkey to use]

mon′key puz′zle, a South American, coniferous tree, *Araucaria imbricata*, having candelabralike branches, stiff sharp leaves, and edible nuts. [? from intertwined state of its limbs]

mon′key rail′, *Naut.* a light rail fitted above an ordinary rail.

mon·key-rigged (mung′kē rigd′), *adj.* monkey-sparred.

mon′key's fist′, a ball-like knot used as an ornament or as a throwing weight at the end of a line. Also, **monkey fist.** Also called **monkey paw.** [so called from fancied resemblance]

mon·key·shine (mung′kē shīn′), *n.* Usually, **monkeyshines.** *Slang.* a trick or mischievous prank; a bit of monkey business. [monkey + shine]

mon′key spar′, *Naut.* an abnormally short spar.

mon·key-sparred (mung′kē spärd′), *adj. Naut.* lightly or meagerly rigged; monkey-rigged.

mon′key suit′, *Slang.* **1.** any uniform. **2.** a man's dress suit. [see monkey jacket]

mon′key tail′, *Naut.* **1.** any of various light or short ropes or lines. **2.** See **rudder horn.**

Mon′key Tri′al. See under **Scopes.**

mon′key wrench′, **1.** Also called, *esp. Brit.,* **spanner.** a wrench having an adjustable jaw permitting it to grasp nuts or the like of different sizes. **2.** *U.S.* something that interferes with functioning; an obstacle: *He threw a monkey wrench into our plans.*

Monkey wrench

monk·fish (mungk′fish′), *n., pl.* (*esp. collectively*) **-fish,** (*esp. referring to two or more kinds or species*) **-fish·es.** a goosefish. [? so called from its sea-bottom habitat, withdrawn from world]

Mon-Khmer (mōn′kmer′), *adj.* **1.** of or pertaining to a group of related languages that includes Mon, of Burma, and Khmer, the official language of Cambodia. —*n.* **2.** the Mon-Khmer languages collectively.

monk·hood (mungk′hŏŏd), *n.* **1.** the condition or profession of a monk. **2.** monks collectively. [late ME *monkehode*, OE *munuchade.* See monk, -hood]

monk·ish (mung′kish), *adj. Usually Derogatory.* of, pertaining to, characteristic of, or resembling a monk: *a monkish manner.* [monk + -ish[1]] —**monk′ish·ly,** *adv.* —**monk′ish·ness,** *n.*

monk's′ cloth′, a heavy cotton fabric in a basket weave, used for curtains, bedspreads, etc.

monks·hood (mungks′hŏŏd′), *n.* a plant of the genus *Aconitum*, esp. *A. Napellus*, the flowers of which have a large, hood-shaped sepal. [monk + -'s[1] + hood]

monk's′ pep′per tree′. See **chaste tree.**

Mon·mouth (mon′məth), *n.* **1. James Scott, Duke of,** 1649–85, illegitimate son of Charles II of England and pretender to the throne of James II. **2.** Monmouthshire. **3.** former name of **Freehold.**

Mon·mouth·shire (mon′məth shēr′, -shər), *n.* a county in E Wales. 443,689 (1961); 543 sq. mi. *Co seat:* Monmouth. Also called **Monmouth.**

Mon·net (mō nā′; *Fr.* mô ne′), *n.* **Jean** (zhäɴ), 1888–1979, French economist: originator of the European Common Market.

mon·ni·on (mon′ē ən), *n. Armor.* spaulder. [<< OF *moignon* stump (of a limb), hence, that which covers or protects it; akin to Sp *muñón* muscle of the arm]

mon·o[1] (mon′ō), *n. Informal.* infectious mononucleosis. [by shortening]

mon·o[2] (mon′ō), *n.* monaural (def. 1). [by shortening]

mono-, a learned borrowing from Greek meaning "alone," "single," "one" (*monogamy*); specialized in some scientific terms to denote a monomolecular thickness (*monolayer*), and adapted in chemistry to apply to compounds containing one atom of a particular element (*monohydrate*). Also, *esp. before a vowel,* **mon-.** [< Gk, comb. form of *mónos* alone, perh. akin to *mānós* thin]

mon·o·ac·e·tin (mon′ō as′i tin), *n. Chem.* acetin. [mono- + acetin]

mon·o·ac·id (mon′ō as′id, mon′ō as′id), *Chem.* —*adj.* Also, **monacidic. 1.** having one replaceable hydrogen atom or hydroxyl radical. **2.** capable of reacting with only one equivalent weight of an acid. —*n.* **3.** an acid having one replaceable hydrogen atom. Also, **monacid.** [mono- + acid]

mon·o·a·tom·ic (mon′ō ə tom′ik), *adj. Chem.* monatomic.

mon·o·ba·sic (mon′ə bā′sik), *adj.* **1.** *Chem.* (of an acid) containing one replaceable hydrogen atom. **2.** *Biol.* monotypic. [mono- + basic] —**mon·o·ba·sic·i·ty** (mon′ə bā sis′i tē), *n.*

monoba′sic so′dium phos′phate, *Chem.* See **sodium phosphate** (def. 1).

mon·o·bath (mon′ə bath′, -bäth′), *n. Photog.* a developer and fixer combined in the same solution. [mono- + bath[1]]

mon·o·blas·tic (mon′ə blas′tik), *adj.* having a single layer, as an embryo in the blastula stage. [mono- + -blast + -ic]

mon·o·ca·ble (mon′ə kā′bəl), *n.* an aerial ropeway having a single moving cable. [MONO- + CABLE]

mon·o·carp (mon′ə kärp′), *n.* *Bot.* a plant that dies after having once borne fruit. [MONO- + -CARP]

mon·o·car·pel·lar·y (mon′ə kär′pə ler′ē), *adj.* *Bot.* consisting of a single carpel. [MONO- + CARPELLARY]

mon·o·car·pic (mon′ə kär′pik), *adj.* *Bot.* producing fruit only once and then dying. [MONOCARP + -IC]

mon·o·car·pous (mon′ə kär′pəs), *adj.* *Bot.* **1.** having a gynoecium which forms only a single ovary. **2.** monocarpic. [MONO- + -CARPOUS]

Mo·noc·er·os (mə nos′ər əs), *n., gen.* **-noc·er·o·tis** (-nos′ə rō′tis). *Astron.* the Unicorn, a constellation south of Gemini and west of Orion.

mon·o·cha·si·um (mon′ə kā′zhē əm, -zhəm, -zē əm), *n., pl.* **-si·a** (-zhē ə, -zhə, -zē ə). *Bot.* a form of cymose inflorescence in which the main axis produces only a single branch. [< NL; see MONO-, DICHASIUM] —**mon′o·cha′si·al,** *adj.*

mon·o·chlo·ride (mon′ə klōr′īd, -klôr′-), *n.* *Chem.* a chloride containing one atom of chlorine with one atom of another element or with a group. [MONO- + CHLORIDE]

mon′ochlo·ro·a·ce′tic ac′id (mon′ə klōr′ō ə sē′tik, -ə set′ik, -klôr′-, mon′-), *Chem.* See **chloroacetic acid.** [MONO- + CHLOROACETIC ACID]

mon·o·chord (mon′ə kôrd′), *n.* an acoustical instrument dating from antiquity, consisting of an oblong wooden sounding box, usually with a single string, used for the mathematical determination of musical intervals. [ME *monocorde* < ML *monochord(um)* < Gk *monóchordon,* n. use of neut. of *monóchordos* with one string. See MONO-, CHORD[1]]

mon·o·chro·ic (mon′ə krō′ik), *adj.* of one color. [MONO- + -CHROIC]

mon·o·chro·mat (mon′ə krō′mat), *n.* *Ophthalm.* a person who has monochromatism. Also, **mon·o·chro·mate** (mon′ə krō′māt). [<< Gk *monochrōmat(os)* of one color. See MONOCHROME, CHROMATIC]

mon·o·chro·mat·ic (mon′ə krō mat′ik, -ō krə-), *adj.* **1.** of or having one color: *a monochromatic color scheme.* **2.** of, pertaining to, or having tones of one color in addition to the ground hue: *a monochromatic painting; monochromatic pottery decoration.* **3.** *Optics.* of, producing, or pertaining to one color or to a very limited range of wavelengths. **4.** *Ophthalm.* of or pertaining to monochromatism. [MONO- + CHROMATIC] —**mon′o·chro·mat′i·cal·ly,** *adv.* —**mon·o·chro·ma·tic·i·ty** (mon′ə krō′mə tis′i tē), *n.*

mon′ochromat′ic illu′minator, *Optics.* monochromator.

mon·o·chro·ma·tism (mon′ə krō′mə tiz′əm), *n.* **1.** a monochromatic quality: *the monochromatism of Southern Sung art.* **2.** *Ophthalm.* a defect of vision in which the retina fails to perceive color. Cf. **dichromatism** (def. 2), **trichromatism** (def. 3). Also, **mon·o·chro·ma·sia** (mon′ə krō mā′zhə, -zē ə, -shə, -shē ə). [MONO- + CHROMATISM]

mon·o·chro·ma·tor (mon′ə krō′mā tər), *n.* *Optics.* a spectroscope with a slit which can be moved across the spectrum so that a small portion of the spectrum can be isolated and viewed. Also called **monochromatic illuminator.** [MONOCHROMAT(IC + ILLUMINAT)OR]

mon·o·chrome (mon′ə krōm′), *n.* **1.** a painting or drawing in different shades of a single color. **2.** the art or technique of producing such a painting or drawing. **3.** the state or condition of being painted, decorated, etc., in shades of a single color. —*adj.* **4.** monochromatic (def. 2). [< ML *monochrōma.* See MONO-, -CHROME] —**mon′o·chro′mic, mon′o·chro′mi·cal,** *adj.* —**mon′o·chro′mi·cal·ly,** *adv.* —**mon′o·chrom′ist,** *n.* —**mon′o·chro′my,** *n.*

mon·o·cle (mon′ə kəl), *n.* an eyeglass for one eye. [< F < LL *monocul(us)* one-eyed, equiv. to *mon-* MON- + *oculus* eye] —**mon′o·cled,** *adj.*

mon·o·cli·nal (mon′ə klīn′əl), *Geol.* —*adj.* **1.** noting, pertaining to, or composed of strata dipping in only one direction. —*n.* **2.** monocline. [MONO- + Gk *klī́n(ein)* (to) incline + -AL[1]] —**mon′o·cli′nal·ly,** *adv.*

mon·o·cline (mon′ə klīn′), *n.* *Geol.* a monoclinal structure or fold. [back formation from MONOCLINAL]

mon·o·clin·ic (mon′ə klin′ik), *adj.* *Crystall.* noting or pertaining to crystallization in which the crystals have three unequal axes, with one oblique intersection. [MONO- + Gk *klī́n(ein)* (to) incline + -IC]

mon·o·cli·nous (mon′ə klī′nəs, mon′ə klī′nəs), *adj.* *Bot.* (of a plant, species, etc.) having both the stamens and pistils in the same flower. [MONO- + Gk *klī́n(ē)* bed + -OUS] —**mon′o·cli′nism,** *n.*

mon·o·coque (mon′ə kōk′, -kok′), *n.* *Aeron.* a type of fuselage construction in which the skin carries all or a major portion of the stresses on the fuselage. [< F, equiv. to *mono-* MONO- + *coque* shell < L *cocc(um)* < Gk *kókkos* core]

mon·o·cot (mon′ə kot′), *n.* a monocotyledon. Also, **mon·o·cot·yl** (mon′ə kot′əl). [shortened form]

mon·o·cot·y·le·don (mon′ə kot′əlēd′ən), *n.* an angiospermous plant of the subclass *Monocotyledoneae,* characterized by producing seeds with one cotyledon and an endogenous manner of growth. Cf. **dicotyledon.** [< NL; see MONO-, COTYLEDON]

mon·o·cot·y·le·don·ous (mon′ə kot′əlēd′ənəs), *adj.* belonging or pertaining to the *Monocotyledoneae,* characterized by having one cotyledon. [MONOCOTYLEDON + -OUS]

mo·noc·ra·cy (mō nok′rə sē, mə-), *n., pl.* **-cies.** government by a single person; autocracy. [MONO- + -CRACY; modeled on *aristocracy, democracy*] —**mon·o·crat·ic** (mon′ə krat′ik), *adj.*

mon·o·crat (mon′ə krat′), *n.* a person favoring monocracy. [< Gk *monokrat(ēs)* ruling alone. See MONO-, -CRAT]

mo·noc·u·lar (mə nok′yə lər), *adj.* **1.** having only one eye. **2.** of, pertaining to, intended for, or involving the use of only one eye: *a monocular microscope; monocular vision.* [< LL *monocul(us)* one-eyed (see MONOCLE) + -AR[1]] —**mo·noc′u·lar·ly,** *adv.*

mon·o·cul·ture (mon′ə kul′chər), *n.* *Agric.* the use of land for growing only one type of crop. [MONO- + CULTURE] —**mon′o·cul′tur·al,** *adj.*

mon·o·cy·cle (mon′ə sī′kəl), *n.* a one-wheeled vehicle. [MONO- + CYCLE]

mon·o·cy·clic (mon′ə sī′klik, -sik′lik), *adj.* **1.** having one cycle. **2.** *Bot.* arranged in a single whorl, as the parts of certain flowers. **3.** *Chem.* containing one ring. [MONO- + CYCLIC] —**mon′o·cy′cly,** *n.*

mon·o·cyte (mon′ə sīt′), *n.* *Anat.* a large, phagocytic leukocyte, formed in bone marrow and in the spleen, that has an oval or horseshoe-shaped nucleus. [MONO- + -CYTE] —**mon·o·cyt·ic** (mon′ə sit′ik), *adj.* —**mon′o·cy′toid,** *adj.*

Mo·nod (mō nō′), *n.* **Jacques** (zhäk), born 1910, French chemist: Nobel Prize 1965.

mon·o·dac·ty·lous (mon′ə dak′təl əs), *adj.* *Zool.* having only one digit or claw. Also, **mon′o·dac′tyl.** [< Gk *monodáktylos* one-fingered or toed. See MONO-, DACTYL, -OUS] —**mon′o·dac′tyl·ism, mon′o·dac′ty·ly,** *n.*

mo·nod·ic (mə nod′ik), *adj.* *Music.* of or relating to monody. [< Gk *monōidik(ós).* See MONODY, -IC] —**mo·nod′i·cal·ly,** *adv.*

mon·o·di·met·ric (mon′ō dī me′trik), *adj.* *Crystall.* tetragonal (def. 2). [MONO- + DIMETRIC]

mo·nod·o·mous (mə nod′ə məs), *adj.* living as a community in a single nest, as certain ant colonies. Cf. **polydomous.** [MONO- + Gk *dóm(os)* house + -OUS]

mon·o·dra·ma (mon′ə drä′mə, -dram′ə), *n.* a dramatic piece for a single performer. [MONO- + DRAMA] —**mon·o·dra·mat·ic** (mon′ə drə mat′ik), *adj.* —**mon′o·dram′a·tist,** *n.*

mon·o·dy (mon′ə dē), *n., pl.* **-dies.** **1.** a Greek ode sung by a single voice, as in a tragedy; lament. **2.** a poem in which one person laments another's death. **3.** *Music.* **a.** a style of composition in which one part or melody predominates; homophony, as distinguished from polyphony. **b.** a piece in this style. **c.** monophony (def. 1). [< LL *monōdia* < Gk *monōidía* a solo, equiv. to *monōid(ós)* singing alone (see MON-, ODE) + *-ia* -Y[3]] —**mon·o·dist** (mon′ə-dist), *n.*

A
B

Monoecious
Branch of walnut,
Juglans quadrangulata
A, Staminate flowers; B, Pistillate flowers

mo·noe·cious (mə nē′shəs), *adj.* **1.** *Biol.* having both male and female organs in the same individual; hermaphroditic. **2.** *Bot.* (of a plant, species, etc.) having the stamens and the pistils in separate flowers on the same plant. Also, **monecious, monoicous.** [MON- + Gk *oikí(on),* dim. of *oîkos* house + -OUS] —**mo·noe′cious·ly,** *adv.* —**mo·noe′cism** (mə nē′siz əm), **mo·noe′cy,** *n.*

mon·o·fil·a·ment (mon′ə fil′ə mənt), *n.* **1.** Also, **mon·o·fil** (mon′ə fil′). a single large filament of synthetic fiber. Cf. **multifilament** (def. 2). —*adj.* **2.** made of such a filament: *a monofilament fishing line.* [MONO- + FILAMENT]

mon·o·gam·ic (mon′ə gam′ik), *adj.* monogamous. [MONOGAM(Y) + -IC]

mo·nog·a·mist (mə nog′ə mist), *n.* one who practices or advocates monogamy. [MONOGAM(Y) + -IST] —**mo·nog′a·mis′tic,** *adj.*

mo·nog·a·mous (mə nog′ə məs), *adj.* **1.** practicing or advocating monogamy. **2.** pertaining to monogamy. Also, **monogamic.** [< LL *monogamus* < Gk *monógamos* marrying only once. See MONO-, -GAMY] —**mo·nog′a·mous·ly,** *adv.* —**mo·nog′a·mous·ness,** *n.*

mo·nog·a·my (mə nog′ə mē), *n.* **1.** marriage with only one person at a time. Cf. **bigamy, polygamy.** **2.** *Zool.* the practice of having only one mate. **3.** the practice of marrying only once during life. Cf. **deuterogamy, digamy.** [< LL *monogamia* < Gk. See MONO-, -GAMY]

mon·o·gen·e·sis (mon′ə jen′i sis), *n.* **1.** the hypothetical descent of the human race from a single pair. **2.** the hypothetical descent of all living things from a single cell. Also, **mo·nog·e·ny** (mə noj′ə nē). [MONO- + GENESIS]

mon·o·ge·net·ic (mon′ō jə net′ik), *adj.* **1.** of or pertaining to monogenesis. **2.** (of certain trematode worms) having only one generation in the life cycle, without an intermediate asexual generation. **3.** *Geol.* resulting from one genetic process. [MONO- + GENETIC]

mon·o·gen·ic (mon′ə jen′ik), *adj.* **1.** *Biol.* bearing either only males or only females. **2.** *Genetics.* pertaining to a character controlled by one pair of genes. [MONO- + -GEN or -GEN(Y) + -IC] —**mon′o·gen′i·cal·ly,** *adv.*

mo·nog·e·nism (mə noj′ə niz′əm), *n.* the theory that the human race has descended from a single pair or a single ancestral type. [MONO- + -GEN + -ISM] —**mo·nog′e·nist,** *n.* —**mo·nog′e·nis′tic,** *adj.*

mo·nog·e·nous (mə noj′ə nəs), *adj.* monogenetic. [MONO- + -GENOUS]

mon·o·glyc·er·ide (mon′ə glis′ə rīd′, -ər id), *n.* *Chem.* an ester obtained from glycerol by the esterification of one hydroxyl group with a fatty acid. Cf. **glyceride.** [MONO- + GLYCERIDE]

mon·o·gram (mon′ə gram′), *n.* a character consisting of two or more letters combined or interlaced, commonly one's initials, often printed on stationery, embroidered on clothing, etc. [< LL *monogram(ma)* < LGk. See MONO-, -GRAM[1]] —**mon·o·gram·mat·ic** (mon′ə grə mat′ik), **mon′o·gram·mat′i·cal, mon′o·gram′mic,** *adj.*

mon·o·graph (mon′ə graf′, -gräf′), *n.* **1.** a treatise on a particular subject, as a biographical study or study of the works of one artist. **2.** an account of a single thing or class of things, as of a species of animals or plants. **3.** a highly detailed and thoroughly documented study or paper written about a limited area of a subject or field of inquiry: *He checked the scholarly monographs on medieval pigments when researching his paper.* —*v.t.* **4.** to write a monograph about. [MONO- + -GRAPH] —**mo·nog·ra·pher** (mə nog′rə fər), **mo·nog′ra·phist,** *n.* —**mon·o·graph·ic** (mon′ə graf′ik), **mon′o·graph′i·cal,** *adj.* —**mon′o·graph′i·cal·ly,** *adv.*

mon·o·gy·noe·cial (mon′ō ji nē′shəl, -gi-), *adj.* (of a fruit) developing from a single pistil. [MONO- + GYNOECI(UM) + -AL[1]]

mo·nog·y·ny (mə noj′ə nē), *n.* the practice or condition of having only one wife at a time. Cf. **polygyny.** [MONO- + Gk *-gynia,* equiv. to *gyn(ē)* woman, wife + *-ia* -Y[3]] —**mo·nog′y·nous, mon·o·gyn·ic** (mon′ə jin′ik), **mon′o·gyn′i·ous,** *adj.* —**mo·nog′y·nist,** *n.*

mon·o·hy·drate (mon′ə hī′drāt), *n.* *Chem.* a hydrate that contains one molecule of water, as ammonium carbonate, $(NH_4)_2CO_3·H_2O$. [MONO- + HYDRATE] —**mon′o·hy′drat·ed,** *adj.*

mon·o·hy·dric (mon′ə hī′drik), *adj.* *Chem.* (esp. of alcohols and phenols) monohydroxy. [MONO- + HYDR-(OXYL) + -IC]

mon·o·hy·drox·y (mon′ə hī drok′sē), *adj.* *Chem.* (of a molecule) containing one hydroxyl group. [MONO- + HYDROXY]

mo·noi·cous (mə noi′kəs), *adj.* monoecious.

mon·oid (mon′oid), *n.* *Math.* groupoid. [MON- + -OID]

mon·o·ki·ni (mon′ə kē′nē), *n.* a woman's topless bathing suit. [MONO- + (BI)KINI]

mo·nol·a·try (mə nol′ə trē), *n.* the worship of but one god when other gods are recognized as existing. [MONO- + -LATRY] —**mo·nol·a·ter** (mə nol′ə tər), **mo·nol′a·trist,** *n.* —**mo·nol′a·trous,** *adj.*

mon·o·lay·er (mon′ə lā′ər), *n.* See **molecular film.** [MONO- + LAYER]

mon·o·lin·gual (mon′ə liŋ′gwəl), *adj.* using or able to speak only one language: *a monolingual country; monolingual tourists.* [MONO- + LINGUAL]

mon·o·lith (mon′ə lith), *n.* **1.** a single block or piece of stone of considerable size, esp. when used in architecture or sculpture. **2.** an obelisk, column, statue, etc., formed of a single block of stone. **3.** something resembling a huge block of stone, esp. in having a uniform, massive, or intractable quality or character: *There's a crack in the Communist monolith, as shown in the charges made by China against Russia.* [< LL *monolith(us)* < Gk *monólithos* made of one stone. See MONO-, -LITH] —**mon′o·lith′ism,** *n.*

mon·o·lith·ic (mon′ə lith′ik), *adj.* **1.** of or pertaining to a monolith. **2.** made of only one stone: *a monolithic column.* **3.** constructed of monoliths or huge blocks of stone: *the monolithic monuments of the New Stone Age.* **4.** characterized by massiveness, total uniformity, and intractability: *a monolithic society; a monolithic state.* [MONOLITH + -IC] —**mon′o·lith′i·cal·ly,** *adv.*

mon·o·logue (mon′ə lôg′, -log′), *n.* **1.** a prolonged talk or discourse by a single speaker. **2.** any composition, as a poem, in which a single person speaks alone. **3.** a part of a drama in which a single actor speaks alone. **4.** a form of dramatic entertainment by a single speaker. Also, **mon′o·log′.** [< F < Gk *monólog(os)* speaking alone, equiv. to *mono-* MONO- + *-log-* speech + *-os* adj. suffix] —**mon·o·log·ic** (mon′ə loj′ik), **mon′o·log′i·cal,** *adj.* —**mon·o·log·ist** (mon′ə lôg′ist, -log′-, mə nol′ə-jist), **mon·o·logu·ist** (mon′ə lôg′ist, -log′-), *n.*

mo·nol·o·gy (mə nol′ə jē), *n., pl.* **-gies.** **1.** the act or habit of soliloquizing. **2.** *Obs.* a monologue. [< Gk *monología.* See MONO-, -LOGY]

mon·o·ma·ni·a (mon′ə mā′nē ə, -mān′yə), *n.* **1.** partial insanity in which the psychotic thinking is confined to one idea or group of ideas. **2.** an exaggerated zeal for or interest in a single thing, idea, subject, or the like. [< NL; see MONO-, MANIA] —**mon·o·ma·ni·ac** (mon′ə-mā′nē ak′), *n.* —**mon·o·ma·ni·a·cal** (mon′ə mə nī′ə-kəl), *adj.*

mon·o·mer (mon′ə mər), *n.* *Chem.* a molecule of low molecular weight capable of reacting with identical or different molecules of low molecular weight to form a polymer. [MONO- + -MER] —**mon·o·mer·ic** (mon′ə-mer′ik), *adj.*

mo·nom·er·ous (mə nom′ər əs), *adj.* **1.** consisting of one part. **2.** *Bot.* (of flowers) having one member in each whorl. [< Gk *monomer(ḗs)* consisting of one part (*mono-* MONO- + *mér(os)* part + *-ēs* adj. suffix) + -OUS]

mon·o·me·tal·lic (mon′ō mə tal′ik), *adj.* **1.** of or using one metal. **2.** pertaining to monometallism. [MONO- + METALLIC]

mon·o·met·al·lism (mon′ə met′əliz′əm), *n.* **1.** the use of one metal only, as gold or silver, as a monetary standard. **2.** the doctrine or actions supporting such a standard. [MONO- + (BI)METALLISM] —**mon′o·met′al·list,** *n.*

mo·nom·e·ter (mə nom′i tər), *n.* *Pros.* a line of verse of one measure or foot. [< LL < Gk *monómetr(os),* equiv. to *mono-* MONO- + *métr(on)* METER[2] + *-os* adj. suffix] —**mon·o·met·ri·cal** (mon′ə me′tri kəl), **mon′o·met′ric,** *adj.*

mon·o·meth·yl·a·mine (mon′ə meth′əl ə mēn′, -meth′il′ə min), *n.* *Chem.* methylamine. [MONO- + METHYLAMINE]

mo·no·mi·al (mō nō′mē əl, mə-), *adj.* **1.** *Algebra.* **a.** consisting of one term only. **b.** (of a matrix) having exactly one non-zero term in each row and each column. **2.** *Biol.* noting or pertaining to a name which consists of a single word or term. —*n.* **3.** *Algebra.* a monomial expression or quantity. [MON- + (BIN)OMIAL]

mon·o·mo·lec·u·lar (mon′ō mə lek′yə lər), *adj.* **1.** noting or pertaining to a thickness of one molecule. **2.** having a thickness of one molecule. [MONO- + MOLECULAR] —**mon′o·mo·lec′u·lar·ly,** *adv.*

mon·o·mor·phic (mon′ə môr′fik), *adj.* **1.** *Biol.* having only one form. **2.** of the same or of an essentially similar type of structure. Also, **mon′o·mor′phous.** [MONO- + -MORPHIC]

mon·o·mor·phism (mon′ə môr′fiz əm), *n.* *Math.* a one-to-one homomorphism. [MONO- + -MORPHISM]

Mon′o·moy surf′boat (mon′ə moi′), a double-ended surfboat having rather full lines with high carrying capacity and seaworthiness, used by the U.S. Coast Guard. [after *Monomoy* Island, Massachusetts]

Mo·no·na (mə nō′nə), *n.* a town in S Wisconsin. 8178 (1960).

Mo·non·ga·he·la (mə noŋ′gə hē′lə), *n.* **1.** a river flowing from N West Virginia through SW Pennsylvania into the Ohio River. 128 mi. long. **2.** a town in SW Pennsylvania. 8388 (1960).

mon·o·nu·cle·ar (mon′ə nōō′klē ər, -nyōō′-), *adj.* **1.** having only one nucleus. **2.** *Chem.* (of hydrocarbons) monocyclic. [MONO- + NUCLEAR]

mon·o·nu·cle·o·sis (mon′ə nōō′klē ō′sis, -nyōō′-), *n.* *Pathol.* **1.** the presence of an abnormally large number of mononuclear leukocytes, or monocytes, in the blood. **2.** See **infectious mononucleosis.** [MONONUCLE(AR) + -OSIS]

mon·o·pet·al·ous (mon′ə pet′ᵊləs), *adj. Bot.* **1.** gamopetalous. **2.** having only one petal, as a corolla. [MONO- + PETALOUS]

mon·o·pha·gia (mon′ə fā′jə, -jē ə), *n. Med.* the eating of or craving for only one kind of food. [MONO- + Gk *-phagia* -PHAGY]

mo·noph·a·gous (mə nof′ə gəs), *adj.* (esp. of insects) feeding on only one kind of food. Cf. **oligophagous.** [MONO- + -PHAGOUS] —**mo·noph′a·gy,** *n.*

mon·o·pho·bi·a (mon′ə fō′bē ə), *n. Psychiatry.* an abnormal fear of being alone. [MONO- + -PHOBIA]

mon·o·phon·ic (mon′ə fon′ik), *adj.* **1.** *Music.* of or pertaining to monophony. **2.** Also, **monaural.** of or pertaining to a sound-reproducing system that produces a single output signal from one or more input signals. Cf. **stereophonic.** [MONOPHON(Y) + -IC]

mo·noph·o·ny (mə nof′ə nē), *n., pl.* **-nies. 1.** a musical style employing a single melodic line without accompaniment. **2.** monody (def. 3a). [MONO- + -PHONY]

mon·oph·thong (mon′əf thông′, -thong′), *n. Phonet.* a vowel of apparently unvarying quality. [< L Gk *monóphthong(os)* (n. use of adj.) with one sound, equiv. to *mono-* MONO- + *phthóngos* sound] —**mon·oph·thon·gal** (mon′əf thông′gəl, -thong′-), *adj.*

mon·oph·thong·ize (mon′əf thông īz′, -gīz′, -thong-), *v.,* **-ized, -iz·ing.** *Phonet.* —*v.t.* **1.** to change into or pronounce as a monophthong. —*v.i.* **2.** to become a monophthong. [MONOPHTHONG + -IZE] —**mon′oph·thong′i·za′tion,** *n.*

mon·o·phy·let·ic (mon′ō fī let′ik), *adj.* **1.** of or pertaining to a single tribe or stock. **2.** developed from a single ancestral type, as a group of animals. [MONO- + PHYLETIC] —**mon·o·phy·le·tism** (mon′ə fī′li tiz′əm, -fil′i-), **mon′o·phy′le·ty,** *n.*

mon·o·phyl·lous (mon′ə fil′əs), *adj. Bot.* **1.** consisting of one leaf, as a calyx. **2.** having only one leaf. [< Gk *monóphyllos.* See MONO-, -PHYLLOUS]

Mo·noph·y·site (mə nof′i sīt′), *n. Theol.* one who maintains that Christ has one nature, partly divine and partly human. Cf. **Dyophysite.** [< LL *monophysīta* < LGk *monophysī́tēs,* equiv. to Gk *mono-* MONO- + *phýs(is)* nature + *-ītēs* -ITE[1]] —**Mon·o·phy·sit·ic** (mon′ə fi sit′ik), *adj.* —**Mo·noph′y·sit′ism, Mo·noph′y·sism,** *n.*

mon·o·plane (mon′ə plān′), *n.* **1.** an airplane with a single sustaining wing. **2.** *Naut.* a planing craft the bottom of which is in an unbroken fore-and-aft line. [MONO- + PLANE[1]] —**mon′o·plan′ist,** *n.*

mon·o·ple·gi·a (mon′ə plē′jē ə, -plē′jə), *n. Pathol.* paralysis of only one extremity, muscle, or muscle area. [MONO- + -PLEGIA] —**mon·o·ple·gic** (mon′ə plē′jik, -plej′ik), *adj.*

mon·o·ploid (mon′ə ploid′), *Biol.* —*adj.* **1.** having the basic or haploid number of chromosomes. —*n.* **2.** a monoploid cell or organism. [MONO- + -PLOID]

mon·o·pode (mon′ə pōd′), *adj.* **1.** having only one foot. —*n.* **2.** a creature having only one foot. **3.** (*sometimes cap.*) one of a fabled race of men having only one foot. **4.** *Bot.* monopodium. [< LL *monopod(ius)* one-footed, equiv. to *monopod-* (< Gk; see MONO-, -POD) + *-ius* adj. suffix]

mon·o·po·di·um (mon′ə pō′dē əm), *n., pl.* **-di·a** (-dē ə). *Bot.* a single main axis which continues to extend at the apex in the original line of growth, giving off lateral branches beneath in acropetal succession. Cf. **sympodium.** [MONO- + -PODIUM] —**mon′o·po′di·al,** *adj.* —**mon′o·po′di·al·ly,** *adv.*

mo·nop·o·dy (mə nop′ə dē), *n., pl.* **-dies.** *Pros.* a measure consisting of one foot. [< Gk *monopodía.* See MONOPODE, -Y[3]] —**mon·o·pod·ic** (mon′ə pod′ik), *adj.*

mo·nop·o·lise (mə nop′ə līz′), *v.t.,* **-lised, -lis·ing.** *Chiefly Brit.* monopolize. —**mo·nop′o·li·sa′tion,** *n.* —**mo·nop′o·lis′er,** *n.*

mo·nop·o·lism (mə nop′ə liz′əm), *n.* the existence or prevalence of monopolies. [MONOPOL(Y) + -ISM]

mo·nop·o·list (mə nop′ə list), *n.* **1.** one who has a monopoly. **2.** an advocate of monopoly. [MONOPOL(Y) + -IST] —**mo·nop′o·lis′tic,** *adj.* —**mo·nop′o·lis′ti·cal·ly,** *adv.*

mo·nop·o·lize (mə nop′ə līz′), *v.t.,* **-lized, -liz·ing. 1.** to acquire, have, or exercise a monopoly of. **2.** to obtain exclusive possession of; keep entirely to oneself: *Her children monopolize her time.* Also, *esp. Brit.,* **monopolise.** [MONOPOL(Y) + -IZE] —**mo·nop′o·li·za′tion,** *n.* —**mo·nop′o·liz′er,** *n.*

mo·nop·o·ly (mə nop′ə lē), *n., pl.* **-lies. 1.** exclusive control of a commodity or service in a particular market, or a control that makes possible the manipulation of prices. Cf. **duopoly, oligopoly. 2.** an exclusive privilege to carry on a traffic or service, granted by a sovereign, state, etc. **3.** the exclusive possession or control of something. **4.** something that is the subject of such control, as a commodity, service, etc. **5.** a company or the like having such control. **6.** the market condition that exists when there is only one seller. [< L *monopōli(um)* < Gk *monopṓlion* right of exclusive sale, equiv. to *mono-* MONO- + *pōl(eîn)* (to) sell + *-ion* n. suffix] —**mo·nop′o·loid′,** *adj.*

Mo·nop·o·ly (mə nop′ə lē), *n. Trademark.* a board game in which a player attempts to gain a monopoly of real estate by advancing around the board and purchasing property, acquiring capital by collecting rent from other players whose pieces land on his property.

mon·o·pol·y·logue (mon′ə pol′i lôg′, -log′), *n.* a theatrical entertainment in which one performer plays several parts or characters. [MONO- + POLY- + *-logue,* as in *monologue, dialogue*]

mon·o·prot·ic (mon′ə prot′ik), *adj. Chem.* (of an acid) having one transferable proton. [MONO- + PROT(ON) + -IC]

mo·nop·so·ny (mə nop′sə nē), *n., pl.* **-nies.** the market condition which exists when there is one buyer. Cf. **duopsony, oligopsony.** [MON- + Gk *opsōní(a)* sutlery] —**mo·nop′so·nist,** *n.* —**mo·nop′so·nis′tic,** *adj.*

mo·nop·ter·al (mo nop′tər əl, mō-), *adj.* **1.** having the form of a monopteron. **2.** of or pertaining to a monopteron. [< L *monopter(os)* (see MONOPTERON) + -AL[1]]

mo·nop·te·ron (mo nop′tə ron′, mō-), *n., pl.* **-te·ra** (-tər ə). a classical building having a single outer colonnade surrounding a central structure or a courtyard. Also called **monopteros.** [< L, n. use of neut. of *monopteros* < Gk *mono-* MONO- + *-pteros* -PTEROUS]

mo·nop·te·ros (mo nop′tə ros′, mō-), *n., pl.* **-te·roi** (-tə roi′). monopteron.

mon·o·rail (mon′ə rāl′), *n.* **1.** a railroad, the rolling stock of which is balanced upon or suspended from one rail. **2.** the rail of such a railroad. [MONO- + RAIL[1]]

mon·o·rhi·nous (mon′ə rī′nəs), *adj. Zool.* having a single, median nostril, as the cyclostomes. Also, **mon′o·rhi′nal, mon′o·rhine′.** [MONO- + RHIN- + -OUS]

mon·o·rhyme (mon′ə rīm′), *n. Pros.* a poem or stanza in which all the lines rhyme with each other. [MONO- + RHYME]

mon·o·sac·cha·ride (mon′ə sak′ə rīd′, -ər id), *n. Chem.* a carbohydrate that does not hydrolyze, as glucose, fructose, ribose, or other simple sugar, occurring naturally or obtained by the hydrolysis of glycosides or polysaccharides. Also, **mon·o·sac·cha·rose** (mon′ə sak′ə rōs′). [MONO- + SACCHARIDE]

mon·o·scope (mon′ə skōp′), *n.* a cathode ray tube that provides a signal of a fixed pattern for testing television equipment. Also called **monotron, phasmajector.** [MONO- + -SCOPE]

mon·o·sep·al·ous (mon′ə sep′ə ləs), *adj. Bot.* **1.** gamosepalous. **2.** having only one sepal, as a calyx. [MONO- + -SEPALOUS]

mon·o·so·di·um (mon′ə sō′dē əm), *adj. Chem.* containing one atom of sodium. [MONO- + SODIUM]

monoso′dium glu′tamate, *Chem.* a white, crystalline, water-soluble powder, $HOOC(CH_2)_2CH(NH_2)$-COONa, used to intensify the flavor of foods. Also called **MSG, sodium glutamate.** Cf. **glutamic acid.**

mon·o·some (mon′ə sōm′), *n. Genetics.* a chromosome having no homologue, esp. an unpaired X chromosome; a monosomic individual. [MONO- + -SOME[3]]

mon·o·so·mic (mon′ə sō′mik), *adj. Genetics.* having one less than the usual diploid number of chromosomes. [MONOSOME + -IC]

mon·o·sper·mous (mon′ə spûr′məs), *adj. Bot.* having one seed. Also, **mon·o·sper′mal.** [< NL *monospermus.* See MONO-, SPERMOUS]

mon·o·sper·my (mon′ə spûr′mē), *n.* the fertilization of an ovum by only one spermatozoon. [MONO- + -SPERM + -Y[3]] —**mon′o·sper′mic,** *adj.*

mon·o·ste·a·rate (mon′ə stē′ə rāt′, -stēr′āt), *n. Chem.* a stearate containing one stearoyl group. [MONO- + STEARATE]

mon·o·stich (mon′ə stik′), *n.* **1.** a poem or epigram consisting of a single metrical line. **2.** a single line of poetry. [< LL *monostich(um)* < Gk *monóstichon,* n. use of neut. of *monóstichos* consisting of one line of verse. See MONO-, STICH] —**mon′o·stich′ic,** *adj.*

mon·o·stome (mon′ə stōm′), *adj.* having a single mouth, pore, or stoma. Also, **mo·nos·to·mous** (mə nos′tə məs). [MONO- + -STOME]

mo·nos·tro·phe (mə nos′trə fē, mon′ə strōf′), *n.* a poem in which all the strophes or stanzas are of the same metrical form. [< Gk *monóstroph(os)* consisting of one strophe. See MONO-, STROPHE]

mon·o·stroph·ic (mon′ə strof′ik, -strō′fik), *adj.* **1.** consisting of stanzas or strophes all having the same metrical structure. —*n.* **2. monostrophics,** monostrophic verses. [< Gk *monostrophik(ós).* See MONOSTROPHE, -IC]

mon·o·sty·lous (mon′ə stī′ləs), *adj. Bot.* having only one style. [MONO- + *-stylous;* see STYLE, -OUS]

mon·o·sub·sti·tut·ed (mon′ə sub′sti tōō′tid, -tyōō′-), *adj. Chem.* containing one substituent. [MONO- + SUBSTITUTED]

mon·o·syl·lab·ic (mon′ə si lab′ik), *adj.* **1.** having only one syllable, as the word *no.* **2.** having a vocabulary composed exclusively of monosyllables. **3.** using, composed of, or uttering monosyllables. [< ML *monosyllabic(us),* equiv. to LL *monosyllab(on)* monosyllable (< Gk, n. use of neut. of *monosýllabos* monosyllabic) + *-icus* -IC] —**mon′o·syl·lab′i·cal·ly,** *adv.* —**mon·o·syl·la·bic·i·ty** (mon′ə sil′ə bis′i tē), *n.*

mon·o·syl·la·bism (mon′ə sil′ə biz′əm), *n.* **1.** monosyllabic character. **2.** the use of monosyllables. [< LL *monosyllab(on)* monosyllable + -ISM]

mon·o·syl·la·ble (mon′ə sil′ə bəl), *n.* a word of one syllable, as *yes* or *no.* [MONO- + SYLLABLE]

mon·o·syl·lo·gism (mon′ə sil′ə jiz′əm), *n. Logic.* an argument consisting of one syllogism. [MONO- + SYLLOGISM]

mon·o·sym·met·ric (mon′ə si me′trik), *adj.* **1.** *Crystall.* monoclinic. **2.** *Biol., Bot.* zygomorphic. Also, **mon′o·sym·met′ri·cal.** [MONO- + SYMMETRIC] —**mon′o·sym·met′ri·cal·ly,** *adv.* —**mon·o·sym·met·ry** (mon′ə sim′i trē), *n.*

mon·o·symp·to·mat·ic (mon′ə simp′tə mat′ik), *adj. Med.* having a single distinct or dominant symptom. [MONO- + SYMPTOMATIC]

mon·o·the·ism (mon′ə thē iz′əm), *n.* the doctrine or belief that there is only one God. [MONO- + (POLY)THEISM] —**mon′o·the′ist,** *n., adj.* —**mon′o·the·is′tic, mon′o·the·is′ti·cal,** *adj.* —**mon′o·the·is′ti·cal·ly,** *adv.*

Mo·noth·e·lite (mə noth′ə līt′), *n. Theol.* one who maintains that Christ has a single theanthropic will. Cf. **Dyothelite.** [< ML *monothelīt(a)* < MGk *monothelḗtēs,* equiv. to Gk *mono-* MONO- + *thelētḗs* willer, equiv. to *thelē-* (var. s. of *thélein* to will) + *-tēs* agent suffix] —**Mo·noth·e·lit·ic** (mə noth′ə lit′ik), *adj.* —**Mo·noth·e·lit·ism** (mə noth′ə lī tiz′əm), **Mo·noth′e·lism,** *n.*

mon·o·tint (mon′ə tint′), *n.* monochrome. [MONO- + TINT[1]]

mon·o·to·nal (mon′ə tōn′ᵊl), *adj. Print.* having equal tone throughout, as sans-serif type. [MONOTONE[1] + -AL[1]]

mon·o·tone[1] (mon′ə tōn′), *n.* **1.** a vocal utterance or series of speech sounds in one unvaried tone of voice. **2.** a single tone without harmony or variation in pitch. **3.** recitation or singing of words in such a tone. **4.** a person who sings in such manner. **5.** sameness of style, as in composition or writing. [MONO- + TONE]

mon·o·tone[2] (mon′ə tōn′), *adj.* **1.** monotonous. **2.** consisting of or characterized by a uniform tone of one color: *a monotone drape.* **3.** *Math.* monotonic (def. 2). [< F *monotone* < LGk *monótono(s)* MONOTONOUS]

mon·o·ton·ic (mon′ə ton′ik), *adj.* **1.** of, pertaining to, or uttered in a monotone: *a monotonic delivery of a lecture.* **2.** *Math.* **a.** (of a function or of a particular set of values of a function) increasing or decreasing. **b.** (of an ordered system of sets) consisting of sets such that each set contains the preceding set or such that each set is contained in the preceding set. [MONOTONE[2] + -IC] —**mon′o·ton′i·cal·ly,** *adv.*

mo·not·o·nous (mə not′ᵊnəs), *adj.* **1.** lacking in variety; tiresomely uniform; unvarying: *the monotonous scenery of flat, barren land.* **2.** characterizing a sound continuing on one note. **3.** having very little inflection; limited to a narrow pitch range. [< LGk *monótonos.* See MONO-, TONE] —**mo·not′o·nous·ly,** *adv.* —**mo·not′o·nous·ness,** *n.*

—**Syn. 1.** tedious, humdrum, boring, dull. See **heavy.**

mo·not·o·ny (mə not′ᵊnē), *n.* **1.** wearisome uniformity or lack of variety, as in occupation, scenery, etc. **2.** the continuance of an unvarying sound; monotone. **3.** sameness of tone or pitch, as in speaking. [< LGk *monotonía,* equiv. to *monotón(os)* MONOTONOUS + *-ia* -Y[3]]

Mon·o·tre·ma·ta (mon′ə trem′ə tə, -trē′mə-), *n.* the order comprising the monotremes. [< NL, neut. pl. of *monotrēmatus;* see MONOTREMATOUS]

mon·o·trem·a·tous (mon′ə trem′ə təs, -trē′mə-), *adj.* of or pertaining to a monotreme. [< NL *monotrēmatus* one-holed, equiv. to *mono-* MONO- + *trēmat-* (< Gk, s. of *trêma* hole) + *-us* -OUS]

mon·o·treme (mon′ə trēm′), *n.* any oviparous animal of the *Monotremata,* the lowest order of mammals, comprising only the duckbill and the echidnas of Australia. [back formation from MONOTREMATA]

mo·not·ri·chate (mə no′trə kit), *adj.* (of bacteria) having a single flagellum at one pole. Also, **mo·not′ri·chous, mon·o·trich·ic** (mon′ə trik′ik). [MONO- + *trichate;* see TRICH-, -ATE[1]]

mon·o·tri·glyph (mon′ə trī′glif), *n.* (in the Doric order) any intercolumniation having one whole triglyph. [< LL *monotriglyph(us).* See MONO-, TRIGLYPH] —**mon′o·tri·glyph′ic,** *adj.*

mon·o·tron (mon′ə tron′), *n.* monoscope. [MONO- + -TRON]

mo·not·ro·py (mə no′trə pē), *n., pl.* **-pies.** *Crystall.* polymorphism that is irreversible. Cf. **enantiotropy.** [MONO- + -TROPY] —**mon·o·trop·ic** (mon′ə trop′ik), *adj.* —**mon′o·trop′i·cal·ly,** *adv.*

Mon·o·type (mon′ə tīp′), *n.* **1.** *Print., Trademark.* a machine for setting and casting type, consisting of a separate keyboard for producing a paper tape containing holes in a coded pattern so that when this tape is fed into the casting unit each code evokes a unique letter cast from hot metal by a special matrix. **2.** (*l.c.*) the only print made from a metal or glass plate on which a picture is painted in oil color, printing ink, or the like. **3.** (*l.c.*) the method of producing such a print. **4.** (*l.c.*) *Biol.* the only type of its group, as a single species constituting a genus. —**mon′o·typ′er,** *n.*

mon·o·typ·ic (mon′ə tip′ik), *adj.* **1.** having only one type. **2.** of the nature of a monotype. **3.** *Biol.* having only one representative, as a genus with a single species. [MONO- + TYPIC]

mon·o·va·lent (mon′ə vā′lənt), *adj.* **1.** *Chem.* univalent. **2.** *Bacteriol.* (of an immune serum) containing only one kind of antibody. [MONO- + -VALENT] —**mon′o·va′lence, mon′o·va′len·cy,** *n.*

mon·ox·ide (mon ok′sīd, mə nok′-), *n. Chem.* an oxide containing one oxygen atom in each molecule. [MON- + OXIDE]

mon·o·zy·got·ic (mon′ə zī got′ik), *adj.* enzygotic. Also, **mon·o·zy·gous** (mon′ə zī′gəs). [MONO- + ZYGOTIC]

Mon·roe (mən rō′), *n.* **1. Harriet,** 1861?–1936, U.S. editor and poet. **2. James,** 1758–1831, 5th president of the U.S. 1817–25. **3.** a city in N Louisiana. 52,219 (1960). **4.** a city in SE Michigan, on Lake Erie. 22,968 (1960). **5.** a town in S Wisconsin. 8050 (1960). **6.** a town in central Georgia. 6826 (1960). **7.** a town in SE New York. 3323 (1960). **8. Fort.** See **Fort Monroe. 9.** a boy's given name.

Monroe′ Doc′trine, the doctrine, based on statements contained in the message of President Monroe to Congress on December 2, 1823, that the attempt of any European power to control the destiny of a Spanish-American state would be looked upon as an expression of hostility toward the U.S., and that the American continents are closed to colonization by European countries.

Mon·roe·ville (mən rō′vil), *n.* **1.** a city in SW Pennsylvania, near Pittsburgh. 22,446 (1960). **2.** a town in SW Alabama. 3632 (1960).

Mon·ro·vi·a (mən rō′vē ə), *n.* **1.** a city in SW California. 27,079 (1960). **2.** a seaport in and the capital of Liberia, in W Africa. 80,992 (1962).

mons (monz), *n., pl.* **mon·tes** (mon′tēz). *Anat.* a rounded prominence of fatty tissue, covered with hair, over the pubic symphysis of the adult human. [< NL, L: mountain, hill; see MOUNT[2]]

Mons (môns), *n.* a city in Belgium. 26,988 (est. 1964).

Mons., Monsieur.

Mon·sar·rat (mon′sə rat′), *n.* **Nicholas,** born 1910, English novelist in Canada.

Mon·sei·gneur (môn se nyœr′), *n., pl.* **Mes·sei·gneurs** (mā se nyœr′). **1.** a French title of honor given to princes, bishops, and other persons of eminence. **2.** a person bearing this title. Also, **mon·sei·gneur′.** [< F: my lord; see SEIGNEUR]

mon·sieur (mə syœ′), *n., pl.* **mes·sieurs** (mes′ərz; *Fr.* mā syœ′). the conventional French title of respect and term of address for a man, corresponding to *Mr.* and to *Sir.* [< F: lit., my lord (orig. applied only to men of high station); see SIEUR]

Mon·si·gnor (mon sē′nyər; *It.* môn′sē nyôr′), *n., pl.* **Mon·si·gnors,** *It.* **Mon·si·gno·ri** (môn′sē nyô′rē). *Rom. Cath. Ch.* **1.** a title conferred upon certain prelates. **2.** a person bearing this title. Also, **mon·si′gnor, Monsignore.** [< It < F; see MONSEIGNEUR, SIGNOR]

Mon·si·gno·re (*It.* môn′sē nyô′re), *n., pl.* **Mon·si·gno·ri** (*It.* môn′sē nyô′rē). Monsignor.

mon·soon (mon sōōn′), *n.* **1.** the seasonal wind of the Indian Ocean and southern Asia, blowing from the southwest in summer and from the northeast in winter. **2.** (in India and nearby lands) the season during which the southwest monsoon blows, commonly marked by heavy rains; rainy season. **3.** any wind that changes directions with the seasons. **4.** any persistent wind established between water and adjoining land. [< D *monssoen* (now obs.) < Pg *monção,* earlier *moução* < Ar *mawsim* season] —**mon·soon′al,** *adj.*

mon′soon low′, the seasonal low found over most continents in summer and, to a lesser extent, over adjacent ocean areas in winter.

mon·ster (mon′stər), *n.* **1.** a fabled animal combining features of animal and human form or having the forms of various animals in combination, as a centaur, griffin, or sphinx. **2.** any creature so ugly or monstrous as to

frighten people. **3.** any animal or human grotesquely deviating from the normal shape, behavior, or character. **4.** anything unnatural or monstrous. **5.** *Biol.* an animal or plant of abnormal form or structure, as from marked malformation, the absence of certain parts or organs, etc. **6.** a person who excites horror by wickedness, cruelty, etc. **7.** any animal or thing of huge size. —*adj.* **8.** huge; enormous; monstrous: *a monster tree.* [ME *monstre* < L *monstr(um)*, orig. a portent, equiv. to *mon(ēre)* (to) warn + *-strum* n. suffix] —**mon′ster-like′,** *adj.*
—**Syn. 6.** fiend, brute, demon, devil, miscreant.

mon·strance (mon′strəns), *n.* *Rom. Cath. Ch.* a receptacle in which the consecrated Host is exposed for adoration. Also called **ostensorium, ostensory.** [ME < ML *monstrantia*, equiv. to *monstr(āre)* (to) show (see MUSTER) + *-antia* -ANCE]

mon·stros·i·ty (mon stros′i tē), *n., pl.* **-ties. 1.** the state or character of being monstrous. **2.** a monster or something monstrous. [< LL *monstrōsitās*, equiv. to L *monstrōs(us)* MONSTROUS + *-itās* -ITY]

mon·strous (mon′strəs), *adj.* **1.** frightful or hideous, esp. in appearance; extremely ugly. **2.** shocking or revolting; outrageous: *a monstrous plan to kill his family.* **3.** extraordinarily great; huge: *a monstrous sum of money.* **4.** deviating grotesquely from the natural or normal form or type: *a monstrous plant; a monstrous embryo.* **5.** having the nature or appearance of a fabulous monster. [late ME < L *monstrōs(us).* See MONSTER, -OUS] —**mon′strous·ly,** *adv.* —**mon′strous·ness,** *n.*
—**Syn. 1, 2.** horrible, atrocious. **3.** See **gigantic.**

mons ve·ne·ris (monz′ ven′ər is), *pl.* **mon·tes ve·ne·ris** (mon′tēz ven′ər is), *Anat.* the mons of the human female. [< NL: mons of Venus]

Mont., Montana.

mon·tage (mon täzh′; *Fr.* môɴ tȧzh′), *n., pl.* **-tag·es** (-täzh′iz; *Fr.* -tȧzh′). **1.** the technique of combining in a single photographic composition elements from various sources, as parts of different photographs, fragments of printing, etc., either to give the illusion that the elements belonged together originally or to allow each element to retain its separate identity as a means of adding interest or meaning to the composition. Cf. **collage** (def. 1). **2.** a photographic image produced by this technique. **3.** *Motion Pictures, Television.* **a.** juxtaposition or partial superimposition of several shots to form a single image. **b.** a technique of film editing in which this is used to present an idea or set of interconnected ideas. **4.** any combination of disparate elements that forms or is felt to form a unified whole, single image, etc. [< F, equiv. to *mont(er)* (to) MOUNT[1] + *-age* -AGE]

Mon·ta·gnac (*Fr.* môɴ tȧ nyȧk′), *n.* *Trademark.* a heavily fulled, napped, woolen fabric constructed in twill weave and used in the manufacture of overcoats.

Mon·ta·gnard (mon′tən yärd′, -yär′), *n., pl.* **-gnards,** (*esp. collectively*) **-gnard,** *adj.* —*n.* **1.** a member of an Athapaskan Indian tribe inhabiting the Canadian Rockies. **2.** (*sometimes l.c.*) a member of a dark-skinned people of mixed ethnic origins inhabiting the highland areas of both South and North Vietnam. —*adj.* **3.** (*sometimes l.c.*) of or pertaining to a Montagnard or Montagnards of either Canada or Vietnam.

Mon·ta·gu (mon′tə gyo͞o′), *n.* **1. Charles, 1st Earl of Halifax,** 1661–1715, British statesman: prime minister 1714–15. **2. Lady Mary Wort·ley** (wûrt′lē), (*Mary Pierrepont*), 1689–1762, English author.

Mon·ta·gue (mon′tə gyo͞o′), *n.* **1.** (in Shakespeare's *Romeo and Juliet*) the family name of Romeo. Cf. **Capulet. 2. William Pep·per·ell** (pep′ər əl), 1873–1953, U.S. philosopher. **3.** a boy's given name.

Mon·taigne (mon tān′; *Fr.* môɴ ten′yᵊ), *n.* **Mi·chel Ey·quem** (mē shel′ e kem′), **Seigneur de,** 1533–92, French essayist.

Mon·tal·vo (môn täl′vô), *n.* **Gar·ci·a Or·dó·ñez de** (gär thē′ä ôr thô′nyeth the), 15th-cent. Spanish writer.

Mon·tan·a (mon tan′ə), *n.* a State in the NW United States. 674,767 (1960); 147,138 sq. mi. *Cap.:* Helena. *Abbr.:* Mont. —**Mon·tan′an,** *adj., n.*

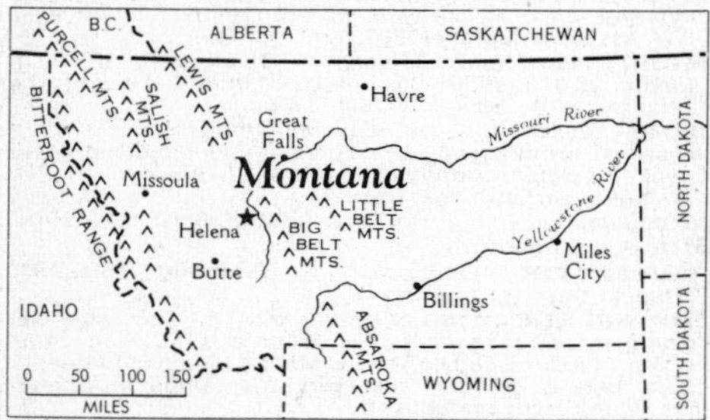

Mon·ta·nar·i (mon′tə när′ē), *n.* a walled plain in the third quadrant of the face of the moon: about 57 miles in diameter.

mon·tane (mon′tān), *Ecol.* —*adj.* **1.** pertaining to mountain conditions. —*n.* **2.** the lower vegetation belt on mountains. [< L *montān(us)*, equiv. to *mont-* (s. of *mōns*) MOUNT[2] + *-ānus* -ANE]

mon·ta·ni sem·per li·be·ri (mōn tä′nē sem′per lē′be rē; *Eng.* mon tā′ni sem′pər lib′ə rī′), *Latin.* mountaineers (are) always freemen: motto of W. Virginia.

mon′tan wax′ (mon′tan), a dark-brown bituminous wax extracted from lignite and peat: used chiefly in polishes and waxes for furniture, shoes, etc. Also called **lignite wax.** [< L *montān(us)* of a mountain (see MONTANE)]

Mon·tau·ban (môɴ tō bäɴ′), *n.* a city in and the capital of Tarn-et-Garonne, in S France, N of Toulouse. 43,401 (1962).

Mon′tauk Point′ (mon′tôk), the E end of Long Island, in SE New York.

Mont Blanc (môɴ bläɴ′), **1.** a mountain in SW Europe, between France and Italy: highest peak of the Alps, 15,781 ft. Italian, **Monte Bianco. 2.** a mountainous formation between the first and second quadrants of the face of the moon.

Mont·calm (mont käm′; *Fr.* môɴ kȧlm′), *n.* **Louis Jo·seph** (lwē zhô zef′), 1712–59, French general in Canada.

Mont Cer·vin (môɴ ser vaɴ′), French name of **Matterhorn.**

Mont·clair (mont clâr′), *n.* a city in NE New Jersey. 43,129 (1960).

Mont-de-Mar·san (môɴdᵊ mȧr säɴ′), *n.* a city in and the capital of Landes in SW France. 23,254 (1962).

mont-de-pié·té (môɴdᵊ pyā tā′), *n., pl.* **monts-de-pié·té** (môɴdᵊ pyā tā′). *French.* a public pawnbroking establishment for lending money on reasonable terms, esp. to the poor. [lit., mountain of pity]

mon·te (mon′tē, mōn′tā; *Sp.* môn′te), *n.* *Cards.* a gambling game played with a 40-card pack in which players bet that one of two layouts, each consisting of two cards drawn from either the top or bottom of the deck and turned face up, will be matched in suit by the next card turned up. Also called **mon′te bank′.** [< Sp: mountain, hence, heap (of cards); see MOUNT[2]]

Mon·te (mon′tē), *n.* a boy's given name. Also, **Monty.**

Mon·te·bel·lo (mon′tə bel′ō), *n.* a city in SW California, SE of Los Angeles. 32,097 (1960).

Mon·te Bian·co (môn′te byäng′kô), Italian name of **Mont Blanc.**

Mon·te Car·lo (mon′tē kär′lō; *It.* môn′te kär′lô), a town in Monaco principality, in SE France: gambling resort. 9430 (1951). See map under **Monaco.**

Mon·te Ca·se·ros (môn′te kä se′rôs), a city in NE Argentina, on the Uruguay River. 11,409 (1948).

Mon·te Cas·si·no (môn′te käs sē′nô), a monastery at Cassino: founded c A.D. 530 by St. Benedict and destroyed by Allied bombings in 1944.

Mon·te Cor·no (môn′te kôr′nô), a mountain in central Italy: highest peak in the Apennines, 9585 ft.

Mon·te·fia·sco·ne (môn′te fyäs kô′ne), *n.* a town in central Italy: wine-growing area. 12,054 (1961).

Mon·te′go Bay′ (mon tē′gō), a city on NW Jamaica: seaside resort. 21,300 (est. 1957).

mon·teith (mon tēth′), *n.* **1.** a large punch bowl, usually of silver, having a notched rim for suspending punch cups. **2.** Also called **bonnet glass.** a small stemless glass of the 18th century, having a bowl with a compoundly curved profile upon a broad foot. [said to have been named after *Monteith*, a Scot]

Mon·te·ne·gro (mon′tə nē′grō; *It.* môn′te ne′grô), *n.* a constituent republic of Yugoslavia, in the S part: formerly a kingdom. 485,000 (est. 1960); 5345 sq. mi. *Cap.:* Cetinje. —**Mon·te·ne·grin** (mon′tə nē′grin), *adj., n.*

Mon·te·rey (mon′tə rā′), *n.* **1.** a city in W California, on Monterey Bay: the capital of California until 1847. 22,618 (1960). **2.** Also called **jack cheese.** a mild, moist cheddar, made from whole, skimmed, or partially skimmed milk: first made in Monterey County, Calif.

Mon′terey Bay′, an inlet of the Pacific in W California. 26 mi. long.

Mon′terey cy′press, a tree, *Cupressus macrocarpa*, of southern California, being pyramid-shaped in youth, but spreading in age.

Mon′terey Park′, a city in SW California, E of Los Angeles. 37,821 (1960).

Mon′terey squid′ skiff′, a rowboat having a flat bottom, pronounced sheer, and sharp bow, used by Chinese squid fishermen on the coast of California.

Mon·te·rí·a (môn′te rē′ä), *n.* a city in N Colombia. 110,310 (est. 1964).

mon·te·ro (mon târ′ō; *Sp.* môn te′rô), *n., pl.* **-ros** (-rōz; *Sp.* -rôs). a huntsman's cap, round in shape and having a flap. [< Sp, special use of *montero* huntsman, lit., mountaineer, equiv. to *monte* MOUNT[2] + *-ero* -ER[2]]

Mon·ter·rey (mon′tə rā′; *Sp.* môn′ter rā′), *n.* a city in and the capital of Nuevo Leon, in NE Mexico: battle 1846. 600,609 (1960).

Mon·tes·pan (mon′tə span′; *Fr.* môn tes päɴ′), *n.* **Marquise de** (*Françoise Athénaïs de Rochechouart*), 1641–1707, mistress of Louis XIV of France.

Mon·tes·quieu (mon′te skyo͞o′; *Fr.* môɴ tes kyœ′), *n.* (*Charles Louis de Secondat, Baron de la Brède et de Montesquieu*) 1689–1755, French philosophical writer.

Mon·tes·so·ri (mon′ti sôr′ē, -sôr′ē; *It.* môn′tes sô′rē), *n.* **Ma·ri·a** (mə rē′ə; *It.* mä rē′ä), 1870–1952, Italian educator.

Montesso′ri meth′od, a system for training and instructing young children, of which the fundamental aim is self-education by the children themselves accompanied by special emphasis on the training of the senses. Also called **Montesso′ri sys′tem.** [named after Maria MONTESSORI]

Mon·teux (mon tœ′; *Fr.* môɴ tœ′), *n.* **Pierre** (pyer), 1875–1964, U.S. symphony orchestra conductor born in France.

Mon·te·val·lo (mon′tə val′ō), *n.* a town in central Alabama. 2755 (1960).

Mon·te·ver·di (mon′tə vâr′dē; *It.* môn′te ver′dē), *n.* **Clau·dio** (klou′dyô), 1567–1643, Italian composer.

Mon·te·vi·de·o (mon′tə vi dā′ō, -vid′ē ō′; *Sp.* môn′te vē the′ô *for 1;* mon′tə vid′ē ō′ *for 2*), *n.* **1.** a seaport in and the capital of Uruguay. 1,202,890 (1963). **2.** a town in SW Minnesota. 5693 (1960).

Mon·te Vis·ta (mon′tə vis′tə), a town in S Colorado. 3385 (1960).

Mon·te·zu·ma (mon′ti zo͞o′mə), *n.* a town in central Georgia. 3744 (1960).

Montezuma II, c1470–1520, last Aztec emperor of Mexico 1502–20. Also, **Moctezuma.**

Mon′tezu′ma cy′press, an evergreen tree, *Taxodium mucronatum*, found from central Mexico to Guatemala, having cones about 1½ inches long. Also called **ahuehuete.**

Mont·fort (mont′fərt; *Fr.* môɴ fôr′), *n.* **1. Si·mon de** (sē môɴ′ də), c1160–1218, French leader of the crusade against the Albigenses. **2.** his son **Simon de, Earl of Leicester,** 1208?–65, English soldier and statesman: leader of the Barons' War.

mont·gol·fi·er (mont gol′fē ər; *Fr.* môɴ gôl fyā′), *n.* *pl.* **-fi·ers** (-fē ərz; *Fr.* -fyā′). a balloon raised by air heated from a fire in the lower part. [named after Joseph and Jacques MONTGOLFIER]

Mont·gol·fi·er (mont gol′fē ər; *Fr.* môɴ gôl fyā′), *n.* **Jacques É·tienne** (zhäk ā tyen′), 1745–99, and his brother **Jo·seph Mi·chel** (zhô zef′ mē shel′), 1740–1810, French aeronauts: inventors of the first practical balloon 1783.

Mont·gom·er·y (mont gum′ə rē, -gum′rē), *n.* **1. Bernard Law, 1st Viscount Montgomery of Alamein** (*Monty*), born 1887, British field marshal: World War II commander of British 8th Army in Africa and Europe. **2. Richard,** 1736–75, American Revolutionary general. **3.** a city in and the capital of Alabama, in the central part, on the Alabama River. 134,393 (1960). **4.** a town in SW Ohio. 3075 (1960). **5.** a town in W West Virginia. 3000 (1960). **6.** Montgomeryshire. **7.** a boy's given name.

Mont·gom·er·y·shire (mont gum′ə rē shēr′, -shər), *n.* a county in central Wales. 44,228 (1961); 797 sq. mi. *Co. seat:* Montgomery. Also called **Montgomery.**

month (munth), *n.* **1.** Also called **solar month.** one twelfth of a solar or tropical year. **2.** Also called **calendar month.** any of the twelve parts, as January, February, etc., into which the calendar year is divided. **3.** the time from any day of one calendar month to the corresponding day of the next. **4.** a period of four weeks or 30 days. **5.** Also called **lunar month.** the period of a complete revolution of the moon around the earth, as the period between successive new moons **(synodic month)** or between successive conjunctions with a star **(sidereal month),** both equal to 29.531 days, or the period between successive perigees **(anomalistic month),** equal to 27.555 days, or the period between successive similar nodes **(nodical month** or **draconic month),** equal to 27.212 days. [ME; OE *mōnath;* c. OHG *mānōd*, Icel *mānathr.* See MOON]

Mon·ther·lant (môɴ ter läɴ′), *n.* **Hen·ry de** (äɴ rē′ də), born 1896, French author.

month·ly (munth′lē), *adj., n., pl.* **-lies,** *adv.* —*adj.* **1.** pertaining to a month, or to each month. **2.** done, happening, appearing, etc., once a month. **3.** continuing or lasting for a month. —*n.* **4.** a periodical published once a month. **5.** *Informal.* a menstrual period. —*adv.* **6.** once a month; by the month. [MONTH + -LY]

month′ly invest′ment plan′, (on the New York Stock Exchange) a plan by which investors may purchase listed stocks on monthly or quarterly installments.

month's′ mind′, *Rom. Cath. Ch.* a Requiem Mass said on the 30th day after a person's death or burial. [late ME *moneth mynde*]

mon·ti·cel·lite (mon′ti sel′īt, -chel′-), *n.* a mineral, silicate of magnesium and calcium, $CaMgSiO_4$, belonging to the olivine group and often occurring in contact metamorphosed limestones. [named after T. *Monticelli* (1758–1846), Italian mineralogist; see -ITE[1]]

Mon·ti·cel·lo (mon′ti sel′ō), *n.* **1.** the estate and residence of Thomas Jefferson, in central Virginia, near Charlottesville. **2.** a town in SE New York. 5222 (1960). **3.** a town in SE Arkansas. 4412 (1960). **4.** a town in NW Indiana. 4035 (1960). **5.** a town in central Illinois. 3219 (1960). **6.** a town in E Iowa. 3190 (1960). **7.** a town in S Kentucky. 2940 (1960).

mon·ti·cule (mon′tə kyo͞ol′), *n.* **1.** a small mountain, hill, or mound. **2.** a subordinate volcano cone. [< LL *monticul(us)*, equiv. to L *monti-* (s. of *mōns*) MOUNT[2] + *-culus* -CULE] —**mon·tic·u·late** (mon tik′yə lit), **mon·tic′u·lous,** *adj.*

mon·til·la (mon til′ə; *Sp.* môn tē′lyä), *n.* a dry, rather bitter wine of Spain. [after Montilla, Spanish town]

Mont·lu·çon (môɴ ly sôɴ′), *n.* a city in central France. 58,855 (1962).

Mont·mar·tre (môɴ mȧr′trᵊ), *n.* a hilly section in the N part of Paris, France: noted for its cafes and the artists who have frequented and lived in the area.

Mont·mo·ren·cy (mont′mə ren′sē; *Fr.* môɴ mô räɴ sē′), *n.* **Anne** (an; *Fr.* ȧn), **Duc de,** 1493–1567, French marshal: constable of France 1537.

mont·mo·ril·lon·ite (mont′mə ril′ə nīt′), *n.* any of a group of clay minerals characterized by the ability to expand when they absorb large quantities of water. [named after *Montmorillon*, France, where it was found; see -ITE[1]] —**mont·mo·ril·lon·it·ic** (mont′mə ril′ə nit′ik), *adj.*

Mon·tours·ville (mon to͝orz′vil), *n.* a town in central Pennsylvania. 5211 (1960).

Mont·par·nasse (môɴ pȧr nȧs′), *n.* a district in S Paris, France, on the left bank of the Seine: noted for its cafes and the artists and writers who have frequented and lived in the area.

Mont·pel·ier (mont pēl′yər), *n.* **1.** a city in and the capital of Vermont, in the central part. 8782 (1960). **2.** a town in NW Ohio. 4131 (1960). **3.** a town in SE Idaho. 3146 (1960).

Mont·pel·lier (môɴ pe lyā′), *n.* a city in and the capital of Herault, in S France, near the Mediterranean. 123,367 (1962).

Mon·tra·chet, Le (lə mōn′trä shā′, -trə-; *Fr.* lə môɴ tȧ shε′), a full-bodied white wine from Burgundy. [after a vineyard in Côte-d'Or, France]

Mont·re·al (mont′rē ôl′, mun′-), *n.* a seaport in S Quebec, in SE Canada, on an island in the St. Lawrence. 1,080,546. French, **Mont·ré·al** (môɴ rā ȧl′). —**Mont·re·al′er,** *n.*

Mon·treuil (môɴ trœ′yᵊ), *n.* a suburb of Paris, in N France. 92,316 (1962).

Mont·rose (mon trōz′), *n.* **1. James Graham, Marquis of,** 1612–50, Scottish supporter of Charles I. **2.** a town in W Colorado. 5044 (1960).

Mont-Saint-Mi·chel (môɴ saɴ mē shel′), *n.* a rocky islet near the coast in NW France, in an inlet of the Gulf of St. Malo: famous abbey and fortress. Also, **Mont Saint Michel.**

Mont-Saint-Mi·chel′ and Char′tres, (*A Study of Thirteenth-Century Unity*) a historical critique (1904) by Henry Adams.

Mont·ser·rat (mont′sə rat′; *for 2 also Sp.* mônt′ser-rät′), *n.* **1.** an island in the central Leeward Islands, in the E West Indies: a British colony. 12,200 (est. 1960); 32½ sq. mi. *Cap.:* Plymouth. **2.** a mountain in NE Spain, NW of Barcelona: the site of Montserrat Monastery. 4058 ft.

Mon·ty (mon′tē), *n.* a boy's given name. Also, **Monte.**

mon·u·ment (mon′yə mənt), *n.* **1.** something erected in memory of a person, event, etc., as a pillar, statue, or the like. **2.** any building, megalith, etc., surviving from a past age, and regarded as of historical or archaeological importance. **3.** any enduring evidence or notable example of something: *a monument to man's ingenuity.* **4.** an exemplar, model, or personification of some abstract quality, esp. when considered to be beyond question: *a monument of middle-class virtue.* **5.** a written tribute to a person, esp. after his death. **6.** an object, as a stone shaft, set in the ground to mark the boundaries of real estate or to mark a survey station. **7.** an area or a site of interest to the public, as being of historical significance, great natural beauty, etc., that is preserved and maintained by a government. **8.** a person considered as a heroic figure or of heroic proportions: *He became a monument in his lifetime.* **9.** *Obs.* a statue. **10.** *Obs.* a tomb; sepulcher. —*v.t.* **11.** to build a monument or monuments to; commemorate: *to monument the nation's war dead.* **12.** to build a monument on: *to monument a famous site.* [ME < L *monument(um),* equiv. to *monu-* (var. of *moni-*, comb. form of *monēre* to remind) + *-mentum* -MENT] —**mon′u·ment·less,** *adj.*

mon·u·men·tal (mon′yə men′tᵊl), *adj.* **1.** resembling a monument; massive or imposing. **2.** *Fine Arts.* having the quality of being larger than life; of heroic scale. **3.** of historical or enduring significance: *a monumental victory.* **4.** conspicuously great as in quantity, quality, extent, degree, etc.: *a monumental work; a monumental hangover.* **5.** of or pertaining to a monument or monuments. **6.** serving as a monument. [< LL *monumentāl(is).* See MONUMENT, -AL¹] —**mon′u·men′tal·ism,** *n.* —**mon′u·men·tal′i·ty,** *n.* —**mon′u·men′tal·ly,** *adv.*

mon·u·men·tal·ise (mon′yə men′tᵊlīz′), *v.t.*, **-ised, -is·ing.** *Chiefly Brit.* monumentalize.

mon·u·men·tal·ize (mon′yə men′tᵊlīz′), *v.t.*, **-ized, -iz·ing.** to establish an enduring memorial or record of. [MONUMENTAL + -IZE]

mon·y (mon′ē), *adj.*, *n.* *Scot. and North Eng.* many.

-mony, a noun suffix indicating result or condition (*parsimony*), but sometimes having the same function as **-ment.** [< L *-mōnia, -mōnium*]

Mon·za (mon′zə; *It.* môn′tsä), *n.* a city in N Italy, NNE of Milan. 85,065 (1961).

Mon·zam·ba·no (*Ger.* mōn′tsäm bä′nō), *n.* **Se·ve·ri·nus de** (*Ger.* zā′vā rē′no͝os de), pseudonym of Samuel von Pufendorf.

mon·zo·nite (mon′zə nīt′), *n.* any of a group of granular igneous rocks having approximately equal amounts of orthoclase and plagioclase feldspar, intermediate in composition between syenite and diorite. [< G *Monzonit,* named after *Monzoni,* mountain in Tyrol; see -ITE¹] —**mon·zo·nit·ic** (mon′zə nit′ik), *adj.*

moo (mo͞o), *v.*, **mooed, moo·ing,** *n.*, *pl.* **moos.** —*v.i.* **1.** to utter the characteristic sound of a cow; low. —*n.* **2.** a mooing sound. [imit.]

mooch (mo͞och), *Slang.* —*v.i.* **1.** to skulk or sneak. **2.** to loiter or wander about. —*v.t.* **3.** to borrow (a small item or amount) without any intention of returning or repaying it. **4.** to get or take without paying or at another's expense; sponge: *He always mooches cigarettes.* **5.** to beg. **6.** to steal. —*n.* **7.** Also, **mooch′er.** one who mooches. Also, **mouch.** [late ME, appar. var. of ME *michen* < OF *muchie(r)* (to) skulk, hide]

mood¹ (mo͞od), *n.* **1.** a state or quality of feeling at a particular time: *He certainly was in a mellow mood today.* **2.** a distinctive emotional quality or character: *The mood of the piece was gay and light.* **3.** a prevailing emotional tone or general attitude: *The President tried to gauge the mood of the country before proposing the bill.* **4.** frame of mind: *He was in a receptive mood.* **5. moods,** irregular and varying periods of sullenness or gloom. [ME; OE *mōd* mind, spirit; courage; c. G *Mut,* Goth *mōths* courage, Icel *mōthr* anger]
—**Syn. 1.** temper, humor, disposition, inclination.

mood² (mo͞od), *n.* **1.** *Gram.* **a.** a set of categories for which the verb is inflected in many languages, and which is typically used to indicate the syntactic relation of the clause in which the verb occurs to other clauses in the sentence, or the attitude of the speaker toward what he is saying, as certainty or uncertainty, wish or command, emphasis or hesitancy. **b.** a set of syntactic devices in some languages that is similar to this set in function or meaning, involving the use of auxiliary words, as *can, may, might.* **c.** any of the categories of these sets: *the Latin indicative, imperative, and subjunctive moods.* **2.** *Logic.* any of the various forms of valid syllogisms. Also called **mode.** [special use of MOOD¹ by influence of MODE¹]

mood′ mu′sic, music comprised chiefly of popular songs in lush orchestral arrangements, intended to induce in the listener a mood of languorous relaxation.

mood·y (mo͞o′dē), *adj.*, **mood·i·er, mood·i·est. 1.** given to gloomy or sullen moods; ill-humored. **2.** proceeding from or showing such a mood: *a moody silence.* **3.** expressing or exhibiting sharply varying moods; temperamental: *a moody person.* [ME *mody,* OE *mōdig.* See MOOD¹, -Y¹] —**mood′i·ly,** *adv.* —**mood′i·ness,** *n.*
—**Syn. 1.** sulky, morose, brooding; glowering.

Moo·dy (mo͞o′dē), *n.* **1. Dwight Ly·man** (lī′mən), 1837–99, U.S. evangelist. **2. William Vaughn** (vôn), 1869–1910, U.S. poet and playwright.

mool (mo͞ol), *n.* *Scot. and North Eng.* **1.** soft, crumbly soil rich in mold or humus. **2.** earth from or for a grave. **3.** a grave. [var. of MOLD³]

moo·la (mo͞o′lə), *n.* *Slang.* money. Also, **moo′lah.** [?]

mool·vee (mo͞ol′vē), *n.* maulvi. Also, **mool′vi.**

moon (mo͞on), *n.* **1.** the earth's natural satellite, orbiting the earth at a mean distance of 238,857 miles and having a diameter of 2160 miles. **2.** this body during a particular lunar month, or during a certain period of time, or at a certain point of time, regarded as a distinct object or entity. Cf. **full moon, half moon, new moon, old moon, waning moon, waxing moon.** See diag. in next col. **3.** a lunar month, or, in general, a month. **4.** any planetary satellite. **5.** something shaped like an orb or a crescent. **6.** a platy. **7. once in a blue moon,** rarely; seldom: *Such a chance comes once in a blue moon!* —*v.i.* *Informal.* **8.** to act or wander abstractedly or listlessly: *She was mooning about all day.* **9.** to sentimentalize or remember nostalgically: *She spent the day mooning about her lost love.* **10.** to gaze dreamily or sentimentally at something or someone: *They sat there mooning into each other's eyes as they planned their little house in the country.* —*v.t.* **11.** *Informal.* to spend (time) idly: *to moon the afternoon away.* **12.** to find by aid of the moon. [ME *mone,* OE *mōna;* c. OHG *māno,* Icel *māni,* Goth *mena,* Gk *mēnē* moon; akin to G *Mond* moon, L *mensis* month, Skt *māsa* moon, month] —**moon′less,** *adj.*

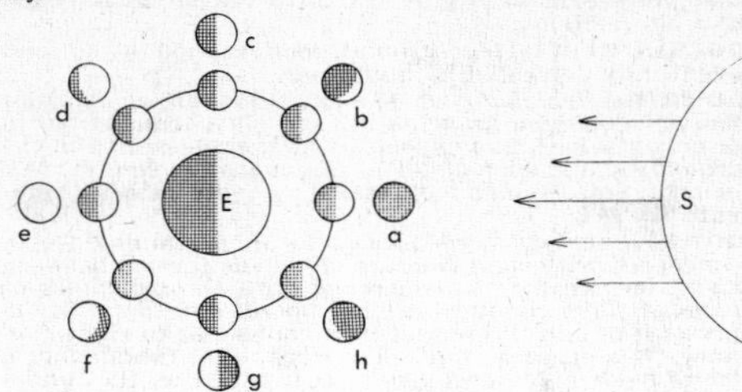

Phases of the moon
Figures on the inner circle show the moon in its orbit; those on the outer circle represent the moon's corresponding phases as seen from the earth; a, New moon (invisible); b, Crescent (waxing moon); c, First quarter (half-moon); d, Gibbous; e, Full moon; f, Gibbous; g, Last quarter (half-moon); h, Crescent (waning moon); S, Sun; E, Earth

Moo·nach·ie (mo͞o nach′ē), *n.* a town in NE New Jersey. 3052 (1960).

Moon′ and Six′pence, The, a novel (1919) by W. Somerset Maugham.

moon·beam (mo͞on′bēm′), *n.* a ray of moonlight. [MOON + BEAM]

moon-blind (mo͞on′blīnd′), *adj.* *Vet. Pathol.* (of horses) afflicted with moon blindness; moon-eyed.

moon′ blind′ness, *Vet. Pathol.* a specific, probably noninfectious disease of horses in which the eyes suffer from recurring attacks of inflammation, and which eventually results in opacity and blindness.

moon·bow (mo͞on′bō′), *n.* a rainbow caused by the refraction and reflection of light from the moon. Also called **lunar rainbow.** [MOON + (RAIN)BOW]

moon·calf (mo͞on′kaf′, -käf′), *n.*, *pl.* **-calves. 1.** a congenital imbecile. **2.** a foolish person. **3.** a person who spends time idly daydreoming. [MOON + CALF¹]

mooned (mo͞ond), *adj.* **1.** ornamented with moons or crescents. **2.** moon- or crescent-shaped. [MOON + -ED³]

moon·eye (mo͞on′ī′), *n.*, *pl.* **-eyes. 1.** *Vet. Pathol.* an eye of a horse affected with moon blindness. **2.** any silvery, herringlike fish of the family *Hiodontidae,* esp. *Hiodon tergisus,* found in fresh waters from Hudson Bay to the lower Mississippi, having large eyes. [MOON + EYE]

moon-faced (mo͞on′fāst′), *adj.* having a very round face, regarded as resembling a full moon.

moon·fish (mo͞on′fish′), *n.*, *pl.* (*esp. collectively*) **-fish,** (*esp. referring to two or more kinds or species*) **-fish·es. 1.** Also called **horsefish, horsehead.** any of several silvery, marine fishes of the genus *Vomer,* having a very compressed body. **2.** the opah. **3.** any of various other rounded, silvery fishes. [MOON + FISH]

moon·flow·er (mo͞on′flou′ər), *n.* a convolvulaceous plant, *Calonyction aculeatum,* having fragrant, white flowers that bloom at night. [MOON + FLOWER]

moon·ish (mo͞o′nish), *adj.* **1.** capricious; inconstant. **2.** fully round or plump and soft. [ME *monish.* See MOON, -ISH¹] —**moon′ish·ly,** *adv.*

moon′ jel′lyfish, a coelenterate, *Aurelia aurita,* found in all seas, having a milky-pink or milky-orange, umbrellalike disk 3–9 inches in diameter. Also called **moon′ jel′ly.**

moon′ knife′, *Tanning.* a crescent-shaped knife used to scrape hides.

moon′ let′ter, *Arabic Gram.* any letter, as *bā* or *mīm,* representing a consonant that does not assimilate the *l* of a prefixed definite article. Cf. **sun letter.** [trans. of Ar *alqamarīyah;* so called from the use of *qamar* (moon) as typical of words with initial consonants that do not assimilate *-l* of *al* (definite article)]

moon·light (mo͞on′līt′), *n.*, *adj.*, *v.*, **-light·ed, -light·ing.** —*n.* **1.** the light of the moon. —*adj.* **2.** pertaining to moonlight. **3.** illuminated by moonlight. **4.** occurring by moonlight, or by night. —*v.i.* **5.** *Informal.* to practice moonlighting. [ME *monelight.*]

moon·light·ing (mo͞on′lī′ting), *n.* *Informal.* working at an additional job after one's regular, full-time employment, as at night. [MOONLIGHT + -ING¹] —**moon′light′er,** *n.*

moon·lit (mo͞on′lit′), *adj.* lighted by the moon. [MOON + LIT¹]

Moon′ of the Car′ib·bees, The (kar′ə bēz′), a play (1918) by Eugene O'Neill. Cf. **Glencairn Cycle.**

moon′ pil′lar, *Astron.* a halo phenomenon in which a vertical streak of light appears above and below the moon, believed to be caused by the reflection of moonlight by ice crystals with vertical axes. Cf. **sun pillar.**

moon·rak·er (mo͞on′rā′kər), *n.* **1.** Also called **moon-sail** (mo͞on′səl, -sāl′). *Naut.* a light square sail set above a skysail. **2.** a simpleton. [MOON + RAKER]

moon·rise (mo͞on′rīz′), *n.* **1.** the rising of the moon above the horizon. **2.** the time at which the moon rises above the horizon. [MOON + RISE]

moon·scape (mo͞on′skāp′), *n.* **1.** the general appearance of the surface of the moon. **2.** an artistic representation of it. [MOON + (LAND)SCAPE]

moon·seed (mo͞on′sēd′), *n.* any climbing herb of the genus *Menispermum,* having greenish-white flowers and crescent-shaped seeds. [MOON + SEED]

moon·set (mo͞on′set′), *n.* **1.** the setting of the moon below the horizon. **2.** the time at which the moon disappears below the horizon. [MOON + SET]

moon·shee (mo͞on′shē), *n.* munshi.

moon′ shell′, **1.** any marine gastropod of the family *Naticidae,* having a rounded, short-spired, smooth shell. **2.** the shell itself.

moon·shine (mo͞on′shīn′), *n.* **1.** *U.S. Informal.* smuggled or illicitly distilled liquor, esp. corn liquor as illicitly distilled in the rural areas of the southern States. **2.** the light of the moon. **3.** empty or foolish talk, ideas, etc.; nonsense. [MOON + SHINE]

moon·shin·er (mo͞on′shī′nər), *n.* *U.S. Informal.* **1.** one who distills or sells liquor illegally, esp. corn liquor in rural areas of the southern states. **2.** one who pursues an illegal trade or activity at night. [MOONSHINE + -ER¹]

moon·shin·y (mo͞on′shī′nē), *adj.* **1.** like moonlight. **2.** moonlit. **3.** fictitious; visionary: *a moonshiny enterprise.* [MOONSHINE + -Y¹]

moon·shot (mo͞on′shot′), *n.* **1.** the act or procedure of launching a missile to the moon. **2.** the missile itself.

moon·sif (mo͞on′sif), *n.* munsif.

moon·stone (mo͞on′stōn′), *n.* **1.** Also called **precious moonstone.** a semitransparent or translucent, opalescent, pearly-blue variety of adularia, used as a gem. **2.** any of several adularescent feldspars, as certain varieties of albite, labradorite, or oligoclase, used as gems. **3.** (not used technically) any milky or girasol stone used as a gem. [MOON + STONE]

Moonstone, The, a mystery novel (1868) by Wilkie Collins.

moon-struck (mo͞on′struk′), *adj.* injuriously affected in mind or body, supposedly by the influence of the moon; dazed; crazed. Also, **moon-strick·en** (mo͞on′strik′ən). [MOON + STRUCK]

moon·wort (mo͞on′wûrt′), *n.* **1.** any fern of the genus *Botrychium,* esp. *B. Lunaria,* having fronds with crescent-shaped pinnae. **2.** honesty (def. 4). [MOON + WORT²]

moon·y (mo͞o′nē), *adj.*, **moon·i·er, moon·i·est. 1.** pertaining to or characteristic of the moon. **2.** resembling the moon in shape. **3.** moonlit. **4.** resembling moonlight. **5.** *Informal.* dreamy, listless, or silly. [MOON + -Y¹] —**moon′i·ly,** *adv.* —**moon′i·ness,** *n.*

moor¹ (mo͝or), *n.* **1.** a tract of open, peaty, waste land, often overgrown with heath, common in high latitudes and altitudes where drainage is poor; a heath. **2.** a tract of land preserved for shooting game. [ME *more,* OE *mōr;* c. D *moer,* G *Moor* marsh] —**moor′y,** *adj.*

moor² (mo͝or), *v.t.* **1.** to secure (a ship, boat, dirigible, etc.) in a particular place, as by cables and anchors or by lines. **2.** to fix firmly; secure. —*v.i.* **3.** to moor a ship, small boat, etc. **4.** to be made secure by cables or the like. —*n.* **5.** the act of mooring. [late ME *more,* akin to OE *mǣrels-* in *mǣrelsrāp* rope for mooring a ship; see MARLINE]

Moor (mo͝or), *n.* **1.** a Muslim of the mixed Berber and Arab people inhabiting NW Africa. **2.** a member of this group that invaded and conquered Spain in the 8th century A.D. [ME *More* < MF, var. of *Maure* < L *Maur(us)* < Gk *Maûros*]

moor·age (mo͝or′ij), *n.* **1.** a place for mooring. **2.** a charge or payment for the use of moorings. **3.** the act or an instance of mooring or the state of being moored. [MOOR² + -AGE]

moor·bird (mo͝or′bûrd′), *n.* moorfowl. [MOOR¹ + BIRD]

moor′ buz′zard, *Brit. Dial.* the marsh harrier.

moor′ cock′, *Brit.* the male red grouse. [ME]

Moore (mo͝or, mōr, môr), *n.* **1. Archibald Lee** (*Archie*), born 1916?, U.S. boxer. **2. Douglas Stuart,** born 1893, U.S. composer. **3. E·li·a·kim Hastings** (i lī′ə kim), 1862–1932, U.S. mathematician. **4. George,** 1852–1933, Irish novelist, critic, and dramatist. **5. G(eorge) E(dward),** 1873–1958, English philosopher. **6. Henry,** born 1898, English sculptor. **7. Sir John,** 1761–1809, British general. **8. John Bas·sett** (bas′it, -et), 1860–1947, U.S. jurist. **9. Marianne (Craig)** (krāg), born 1887, U.S. poet and critic. **10. Thomas,** 1779–1852, Irish poet.

Moore′-Smith′ conver′gence (mo͝or′smith′, mōr′-, môr′-), *Math.* the theory concerned with the convergence of the analogues of sequences in topological spaces. [named after E. H. MOORE and H. L. SMITH]

Moores·ville (mo͝orz′vil), *n.* **1.** a town in central North Carolina. 6918 (1960). **2.** a town in central Indiana. 3856 (1960).

moor·fowl (mo͝or′foul′), *n.*, *pl.* **-fowls,** (*esp. collectively*) **-fowl.** *Brit.* the red grouse. Also called **moorbird.** [MOOR¹ + FOWL]

Moor·head (mōr′hed′, môr′-, mo͝or′-), *n.* a city in W Minnesota. 22,934 (1960).

moor·hen (mo͝or′hen′), *n.* **1.** a common, European gallinule, *Gallinula chloropus.* **2.** *Brit.* the female red grouse. [ME *mor-hen.* See MOOR¹, HEN]

moor·ing (mo͝or′ing), *n.* **1.** the act of one who or that which moors. **2.** Usually, **moorings.** the means by which a vessel is moored. **3. moorings,** a place where a vessel may be moored. [MOOR² + -ING¹]

moor′ing buoy′, *Naut.* a buoy to which vessels can be moored.

moor′ing mast′, the mast or tower to which a dirigible is moored. Also called **moor′ing tow′er.**

moor′ing rack′, *Naut.* a row of piles, connected at the tops, to which vessels can be moored.

moor′ing screw′, *Naut.* a broad, augerlike anchor used for securing buoys in soft-bottomed lakes, rivers, etc. Also called **screw anchor, screw mooring.**

moor′ing tel′egraph, *Naut.* a telegraph for transmitting orders from the bridge of a ship to an officer at the bow in charge of mooring operations; docking telegraph.

Moor·ish (mo͝or′ish), *adj.* **1.** of or pertaining to the Moors. **2.** in the style of the Moors, as architecture, decoration, etc. [late ME *morys.* See MOOR, -ISH¹]

Moor′ish arch′. See **horseshoe arch.**

Moor′ish i′dol, a black, white, and yellow fish, *Zanclus cornutus* (or *canescens*), found in the tropical Indian and Pacific oceans, having a long snout and an elongated dorsal fin.

moor·land (mo͝or′land′), *n.* *Chiefly Brit.* an area of moors, esp. country abounding in heather. [ME *more lond,* OE *morlond.* See MOOR¹, LAND]

moor′ myr′tle. See **sweet gale.**

Moor·park (mo͝or′pärk′, mōr′-, môr′-), *n.* a town in S California. 2902 (1960.

Moor′som sys′tem (mo͝or′səm), *Naut.* a system of measurement of merchant ships in which the unit is a gross ton of 100 cubic feet of permanently enclosed space.

moor·wort (mo͝or′wûrt′), *n.* a low, ericaceous shrub, *Andromeda polifolia,* having pink or white flowers, native to swamplands in the Northern Hemisphere. [MOOR¹ + WORT²]

moose (mo͞os), *n., pl.* **moose. 1.** a large animal, *Alces americanus,* of the deer family, inhabiting Canada and the northern U.S., the male of which has enormous palmate antlers, long legs, and a large head. **2.** a similar species, *A. gigas,* found in Alaska. **3.** the European elk, *A. machlis.* [< Algonquian; kindred forms in Narragansett, Delaware, etc., meaning "he strips or eats off (trees and shrubs)"]

Moose, *Alces americanus* (5½ ft. high at shoulder; length 9 ft.)

Moose′head Lake′ (mo͞os′hed′), a lake in central Maine. 36 mi. long; 120 sq. mi.

Moose′ Jaw′, a city in S Saskatchewan, in SW Canada. 33,206 (1961).

moose·milk (mo͞os′milk′), *n. Canadian Dial.* **1.** homemade or bootleg whiskey. **2.** a cocktail having a base of rum and milk. [MOOSE + MILK]

moose·wood (mo͞os′wo͝od′), *n.* **1.** See **striped maple. 2.** leatherwood. [MOOSE + WOOD[1]]

Moo·sic (mo͞o′sik), *n.* a town in NE Pennsylvania. 4243 (1960).

Moo·sup (mo͞o′səp), *n.* a town in E Connecticut. 2760 (1960).

moot[1] (mo͞ot), *adj.* **1.** subject to argument or discussion; debatable; doubtful: *a moot point.* **2.** of little or no practical value or meaning; purely academic. **3.** not actual; theoretical or hypothetical. **—***v.t.* **4.** to present or introduce (any point, subject, project, etc.) for discussion. **5.** to reduce or remove the practical significance of; make purely theoretical or academic. **6.** *Archaic.* to argue (a case), esp. in a mock court. **—***n.* **7.** an early English assembly of the people, exercising political, administrative, and judicial powers. **8.** an argument or discussion, esp. of a hypothetical legal case. **9.** *Obs.* a debate, argument, or discussion. [ME *mote,* OE (*ge*)*mōt* meeting, assembly; c. Icel *mōt,* D *gemoet* meeting. See MEET[1]] **—moot′er,** *n.* **—moot′ness,** *n.* **—Syn. 1.** disputable, disputed, unsettled. **4.** debate, dispute, discuss. **—Ant. 1.** indisputable. **4.** agree.

moot[2] (mo͞ot), *n.* **1.** a ring gauge for checking the diameters of treenails. **—***v.t.* **2.** to bring (a treenail) to the proper diameter with a moot. [? special use of dial. *moot* tree-stump, block of wood; c. D *moot* piece]

moot′ court′, a mock court for the conduct of hypothetical legal cases, as for students of law.

moot′ hall′, (in certain English villages) a historic building where moots were once held. [ME *Mut-halle*]

mop[1] (mop), *n., v.,* **mopped, mop·ping. —***n.* **1.** a bundle of coarse yarn, a piece of cloth, or the like, fastened at the end of a stick or handle for washing floors, dishes, etc. **2.** *Slang.* a thick mass of hair. **3.** a polishing wheel having several layers of cloth secured by a boss. **—***v.t.* **4.** to rub, wipe, clean, or remove with a mop. **5.** to wipe: *to mop the face with a handkerchief.* **6. mop the floor with.** See **floor** (def. 14). **7. mop up, a.** *Mil.* to clear (ground, trenches, towns, etc.) of scattered or remaining enemy combatants, after attacking forces have gone beyond the place. **b.** *Slang.* to dispose of; complete; finish: *He mopped up the rest of his business and went on a vacation.* [earlier *map,* late ME *mappe,* apocopated var. of *mappel* < ML *mappula* a cloth, equiv. to L *mapp*(*a*) napkin + *-ula* -ULE]

mop[2] (mop), *v.,* **mopped, mop·ping,** *n.* **—***v.i.* **1.** to make a disappointed or unhappy face; grimace: *an unruly child that mops and mows.* **—***n.* **2.** a wry face; grimace. [? akin to D *moppen* to pout]

mop·board (mop′bōrd′, -bôrd′), *n.* baseboard (def. 1). [MOP[1] + BOARD, so called because it adjoins the floor surface, which is cleaned by a mop]

mope (mōp), *v.,* **moped, mop·ing,** *n.* **—***v.i.* **1.** to be sunk in listless apathy or dull dejection. **—***v.t.* **2.** to make listless and dispirited. **—***n.* **3.** a person who mopes or is given to moping. **4. mopes,** low spirits; blues. [? var. of MOP[2]] **—mop′er,** *n.* **—mop′ing·ly,** *adv.*

mo·ped (mō′ped), *n.* a low-powered, heavily built motorized bicycle. [MO(TOR) + PED(AL)] **—mo′ped′er,** *n.*

mop·ey (mō′pē), *adj.,* **-i·er, -i·est.** languishing, listless, droopy, or glum. Also, **mopy.** [MOPE + -Y[1]] **—mop′i·ness,** *n.*

mop·ish (mō′pish), *adj.* given to moping; listless and dejected. [MOPE + -ISH[1]] **—mop′ish·ly,** *adv.* **—mop′ish·ness,** *n.*

mop·per-up (mop′ər up′), *n., pl.* **mop·pers-up.** one who or that which mops up. [n. use of v. phrase *mop up;* see -ER[1]]

mop·pet (mop′it), *n.* a young child. [obs. *mop* rag doll, baby (see MOP[1]) + -ET]

mop·ping-up (mop′ing up′), *adj.* **1.** serving to complete or put the finishing touches to a major phase of a particular action. **2.** serving to complete a military campaign by killing or capturing the few remaining enemy troops: *a mopping-up operation.* [adj. use of v. phrase *mop up;* see -ING[2]]

Mop·po (mop′ō), *n.* Japanese name of **Mokpo.**

Mop·sus (mop′səs), *n. Class. Myth.* **1.** a seer who, with Amphilochus, founded the famous oracle in the city of Mallus in Cilicia. **2.** a son of Ampyeus who joined the Argonauts as a seer.

M.Opt., Master of Optometry.

mop-up (mop′up′), *n.* the act, process, or an instance of mopping up; completion of an operation or action. [n. use of v. phrase *mop up*]

mop·y (mō′pē), *adj.,* **mop·i·er, mop·i·est.** mopey.

mo·quette (mō ket′), *n.* a type of fabric with a thick, velvety pile, used for carpets and in upholstering. [< F, equiv. to *moc*(*ade*) imitation velvet + *-ette* -ETTE]

Mo·qui (mō′kē), *n., pl.* **-quis,** (*esp. collectively*) **-qui.** Moki.

mor., morocco.

mo·ra (mōr′ə, môr′ə), *n., pl.* **mo·rae** (mōr′ē, môr′ē), **mo·ras.** *Pros.* the unit of time equivalent to the ordinary or normal short sound or syllable. [< L: delay, hence, space of time]

mo·ra·ceous (mō rā′shəs, mô-), *adj.* belonging to the *Moraceae,* or mulberry family of plants, comprising the mulberry, breadfruit, fig, hemp, hop, Osage orange, etc. [< NL *Mor*(*us*) the typical genus (L *mōrus* mulberry tree) + -ACEOUS]

Mo·ra·da·bad (mōr′ə də bad′, môr′-, mō′rä dä-bäd′, mô′-), *n.* a city in N Uttar Pradesh, in N India. 180,100 (1961).

morain′al drift′, ground rock carried away and eventually deposited by a glacier.

mo·raine (mə rān′), *n.* **1.** a ridge, mound, or irregular mass of boulders, gravel, sand, and clay, transported in or on a glacier. **2.** a deposit of such material left on the ground by a glacier. [< F < Savoyard *morēna;* cf. ML *morena* embankment of stakes] **—mo·rain′al, mo·rain′ic,** *adj.*

mor·al (môr′əl, mor′-), *adj.* **1.** of, pertaining to, or concerned with right conduct or the distinction between right and wrong. **2.** concerned with the principles or rules of right conduct; ethical: *moral attitudes.* **3.** expressing or conveying truths or counsel as to right conduct, as a speaker, a literary work, etc.; moralizing: *a moral treatise; a moral novel.* **4.** founded on the fundamental principles of right conduct rather than on legalities, enactment, or custom: *moral rights; moral obligations.* **5.** capable of conforming to the rules of right conduct: *Man is a moral being.* **6.** conforming to the rules of right conduct (opposed to *immoral*): *a moral man.* **7.** virtuous in sexual matters; chaste. **8.** of, pertaining to, or acting on the mind, feelings, will, or character: *moral support; a moral victory.* **9.** depending upon what is observed of human nature and actions or of things generally, rather than upon demonstration: *moral evidence.* **10.** resting upon convincing grounds of probability: *a moral certainty.* **—***n.* **11.** the moral teaching or practical lesson contained in a fable, tale, experience, etc. **12.** the embodiment or type of something. **13. morals,** principles or habits with respect to right or wrong conduct. [ME < L *mōrāl*(*is*), equiv. to *mōr-* (s. of *mōs*) usage, custom + *-ālis* -AL[1]] **—mor′al·less,** *adj.*
—Syn. 4. righteous, just. **6.** upright, honest, straightforward, open, virtuous, honorable. **13.** integrity, standards, morality. MORALS, ETHICS refer to rules and standards of conduct and practice. MORALS refers to generally accepted customs of conduct and right living in a society, and to the individual's practice in relation to these: *the morals of our civilization.* ETHICS now implies high standards of honest and honorable dealing, and of methods used, esp. in the professions or in business: *ethics of the medical profession.*

mo·rale (mə ral′), *n.* moral or mental condition with respect to cheerfulness, confidence, zeal, etc.: *the morale of troops; to boost the morale.* [< F, n. use of fem. of *moral* MORAL]

mor′al haz′ard, *Insurance.* an insurance company's risk as to the insured's trustworthiness and honesty.

mor·al·ise (môr′ə līz′, mor′-), *v.i., v.t.,* **-ised, -is·ing.** *Chiefly Brit.* moralize. **—mor′al·i·sa′tion,** *n.* **—mor′al·is′er,** *n.* **—mor′al·is′ing·ly,** *adv.*

mor·al·ism (môr′ə liz′əm, mor′-), *n.* **1.** the habit of moralizing. **2.** a moral maxim. **3.** the practice of morality, as distinct from religion. [MORAL + -ISM]

mor·al·ist (môr′ə list, mor′-), *n.* **1.** a person who teaches or inculcates morality. **2.** a person who practices morality. **3.** a person who believes in regulating the morals of others, as by imposing censorship. [MORAL + -IST] **—mor′al·is′tic,** *adj.* **—mor′al·is′ti·cal·ly,** *adv.*

mo·ral·i·ty (mə ral′i tē, mô-), *n., pl.* **-ties** for 4–6. **1.** conformity to the rules of right conduct; moral or virtuous conduct. **2.** virtue in sexual matters; chastity. **3.** moral quality or character. **4.** a doctrine or system of morals. **5.** moral instruction; a moral lesson or precept; a moralizing discourse or utterance. **6.** See **morality play.** [late ME *moralite* < LL *mōrālitās.* See MORAL, -ITY]
—Syn. 1. See **goodness.**

moral′ity play′, an allegorical form of the drama current from the 14th to 16th centuries and employing personified abstractions, as of virtues and vices. Cf. **miracle play, mystery play.**

mor·al·ize (môr′ə līz′, mor′-), *v.,* **-ized, -iz·ing. —***v.i.* **1.** to make moral reflections. **—***v.t.* **2.** to explain in a moral sense, or draw a moral from. **3.** to improve the morals of. Also, *esp. Brit.,* **moralise.** [late ME *moralise* < ML *mōrāliz*(*āre*). See MORAL, -IZE] **—mor′al·i·za′tion,** *n.* **—mor′al·iz′er,** *n.* **—mor′al·iz′ing·ly,** *adv.*

mor·al·ly (môr′ə lē, mor′-), *adv.* **1.** in a moral manner. **2.** from a moral point of view. **3.** virtuously. **4.** virtually; practically. [late ME; see MORAL, -LY]

Mor′al Major′ity, a political action group formed mainly of Protestant fundamentalists to spread strict conservative morality, as through strong antiabortion laws, school prayer, the teaching of creationism in public schools, the defeat of liberal politicians, and the curbing of books and TV programs considered antireligious or immoral. —**Mo′ral Major′itar′ian.**

Mor′al Re-Ar′ma·ment (rē är′mə mənt), a worldwide ideological movement initiated by Frank Buchman in 1938 as a successor to the Oxford Group, and maintaining that the practice of absolute morality in public and private life is the key to world betterment.

mor′al sense′, the ability to judge the rightness or wrongness of actions.

mor′al tur′pitude, 1. conduct that is regarded as immoral or depraved. **2.** an act or instance of such conduct.

mo·rass (mə ras′), *n.* **1.** a tract of low, soft, wet ground. **2.** a marsh or bog. **3.** marshy ground. [< D *moeras,* alter. (by assoc. with *moer* marsh; see MOOR[1]) of MD *maras* < OF *mareis* < Gmc. See MARSH]

mor·a·to·ri·um (môr′ə tōr′ē əm, -tôr′-, mor′-), *n., pl.* **-to·ri·a** (-tōr′ē ə, -tôr′-), **-to·ri·ums. 1.** a legal authorization to delay payment of money due or of the performance of some other legal obligation, as in an emergency. **2.** the period during which such authorization is in effect. **3.** a temporary cessation of activity, esp. of an activity considered hostile or dangerous: *a moratorium on the testing of atomic bombs.* [< NL, LL, n. use of neut. of *morātōrius* MORATORY]

mor·a·to·ry (môr′ə tōr′ē, -tôr′ē, mor′-), *adj.* authorizing delay of payment: *a moratory law.* [< LL *morātōri*(*us*) dilatory, equiv. to *morāt*(*us*) delayed (ptp. of *morārī;* see MORA) + *-ōrius* -ORY[1]]

Mo·ra·tu·wa (mō rä′to͞o wə), *n.* a city on W Ceylon. 58,160 (1958).

Mo·ra·va (*Czech., Serbo-Croatian.* mô′rä vä), *n.* **1.** German, **March.** a river flowing S from NE Czech Republic, through the SW Slovakia to the Danube. 240 mi. long. **2.** a river in E Yugoslavia, flowing N to the Danube. 134 mi. long. **3.** Czech name of **Moravia.**

Mo·ra·vi·a (mô rā′vē ə, rä′-, mō-; *for 1 also It.* mô rä′vyä), *n.* **1. Al·ber·to** (äl ber′tô), (*Alberto Pincherle*), 1907–90, Italian writer. **2.** Czech, **Morava.** German, **Mähren.** a region in the E Czech Republic: former province of Austria.

Mo·ra·vi·an (mō rā′vē ən, mô-), *adj.* **1.** pertaining to Moravia or its inhabitants. **2.** of or pertaining to the religious denomination of Moravians. **—***n.* **3.** a native or inhabitant of Moravia. **4.** Also called **Herrnhuter.** a member of a Christian denomination descended from the Bohemian Brethren and holding that the Scriptures are the only rule of faith and practice. **5.** a dialect of Czech, spoken in Moravia. [MORAVI(A) + -AN] **—Mo·ra′vi·an·ism,** *n.*

Mora′vian Breth′ren, the Moravian Church.

Mora′vian Gate′, a mountain pass between the Sudeten Mountains and the Tatra range of the Carpathians, leading from S Poland into N Moravia in the NE Czech Republic.

Mo·rav·ská Os·tra·va (mô′räf skä ôs′trä vä), former name of **Ostrava.** German, **Mährisch-Ostrau.**

Mor·ax·el·la (môr′ək sel′ə), *n. Bacteriol.* a genus of rod-shaped, aerobic bacteria, certain species of which, as *M. lacunata,* are parasitic and pathogenic for man and warm-blooded animals. [< NL]

mo·ray (mōr′ā, môr′ā; mō rā′, mô-), *n., pl.* **-rays.** any of numerous chiefly tropical eels of the family *Muraenidae,* having porelike gill openings and no pectoral fins. Also called, **mo′ray eel′.** [< Pg *morēi*(*a*) < L *mūraena* < Gk *mýraina* lamprey]

Mor·ay (mûr′ē), *n.* a county in NE Scotland, on Moray Firth. 49,156 (1961); 476 sq. mi. *Co. seat:* Elgin. Formerly, **Elgin.**

Mor′ay Firth′, an arm of the North Sea projecting into the NE coast of Scotland. Inland portion ab. 30 mi. long.

Mo·ra·zán (mô rä sän′), *n.* **Fran·cis·co** (frän sēs′kô), 1799–1842, Central American statesman and soldier, born in Honduras.

mor·bid (môr′bid), *adj.* **1.** suggesting an unhealthy mental state; unwholesomely gloomy, sensitive, extreme, etc.: *a morbid interest in death.* **2.** affected by, caused by, causing, or characteristic of disease. **3.** pertaining to diseased parts: *morbid anatomy.* **4.** gruesome; grisly. [< L *morbid*(*us*) sickly, equiv. to *morb*(*us*) sickness + *-idus* -ID[4]] **—mor′bid·ly,** *adv.* **—mor′bid·ness,** *n.*
—Syn. 2. unwholesome, diseased, unhealthy, sick, sickly; tainted, corrupted, vitiated. **—Ant. 1.** cheerful. **2.** healthy.

mor·bi·dez·za (môr′bi det′sə; *It.* môr bē det′tsä), *n. Fine Arts.* the effect of extreme softness and delicacy in pictorial and sculptural representations. [< It., equiv. to *morbid*(*o*) delicate (see MORBID) + *-ezza* -ICE]

mor·bid·i·ty (môr bid′i tē), *n.* **1.** a morbid state or quality. **2.** the percentage of deaths resulting from any specific disease as determined by dividing the number of deaths by the total number of people contracting the disease. **3.** the proportion of sickness or of a specific disease in a geographical locality. [MORBID + -ITY]

mor·bif·ic (môr bif′ik), *adj.* causing disease. Also, **mor·bif′i·cal.** [< medical L *morbific*(*us*), equiv. to *morb*(*us*) sickness + *-i-* -I- + *-ficus* -FIC] **—mor·bif′i·cal·ly,** *adv.*

Mor·bi·han (môr bē äN′), *n.* a department in W France. 530,833 (1962); 2738 sq. mi. *Cap.:* Vannes.

mor·bil·li (môr bil′ī), *n.* (*construed as sing.*) *Pathol.* measles (def. 1). [< ML, pl. of *morbillus,* equiv. to L *morb*(*us*) sickness + *-illus* dim. suffix]

mor·ceau (môr sō′), *n., pl.* **-ceaux** (-sō′). *French.* **1.** morsel. **2.** an excerpt or passage of poetry or music.

mord (môrd), *n. Brit. Dial.* mort[3].

mor·da·cious (môr dā′shəs), *adj.* biting or given to biting. [*mordaci*(*ty*) biting power (< L *mordācitās,* equiv. to *mordāci-* (s. of *mordāx* given to biting + *-tās* -TY[2]) + -OUS] **—mor·da′cious·ly,** *adv.* **—mor·dac·i·ty** (môr-das′i tē), *n.*

mor·dan·cy (môr′dᵊn sē), *n.* the quality of being mordant; sharpness; causticity. [MORDAN(T) + -CY]

mor·dant (môr′dᵊnt), *adj.* **1.** caustic or sarcastic, as wit, a speaker, etc. **2.** having the property of fixing colors, as in dyeing. **—***n.* **3.** a substance used in dyeing to fix the coloring matter, esp. a metallic compound, as an oxide or hydroxide, which combines with the organic dye and forms an insoluble colored compound or lake in the fiber. **4.** an adhesive substance for binding gold or silver leaf to a surface. **5.** an acid or other corrosive substance used in etching to eat out the lines, areas, etc. **6.** *Music.* mordent. **—***v.t.* **7.** to impregnate or treat with a mordant. [late ME < MF, prp. of *mordre* to bite < L *mordēre;* see -ANT] **—mor′dant·ly,** *adv.*

mor′dant rouge′, a solution of aluminum acetate in acetic acid, used in dyeing and calico printing. Also called **red liquor.**

Mor·de·cai (môr′də kī′, môr′də kā′ī), *n.* **1.** Also, *Douay Bible,* **Mardochai.** the cousin and guardian of Esther who delivered the Jews from the destruction planned by Haman. Esther 2–8. **2.** a boy's given name.

mor·dent (môr′dᵊnt), *n. Music.* **1.** a melodic embellishment consisting of a rapid alternation of a principal tone with a supplementary tone a half step below it, called *single* or *short* when the supplementary tone occurs but once, and *double* or *long* when this occurs twice or oftener. **2.** See **inverted mordent.** Also, **mordant.** [< G < It *mordente* biting < L *mordentem,* acc. of *mordēns,* prp. of *mordēre* to bite; see -ENT]

Mordents
A, Single; B, Double

mor·di·da (môr thē′thä), *n., pl.* **-das** (-thäs). *Mexican Spanish.* a bribe or kickback. [lit., bite]

Mor·do′vi·an Auton′omous Repub′lic (môr-dō′vē ən), *n.* an autonomous republic in the Russian Federation in Europe. 964,000; 9843 sq. mi. *Cap.:* Saransk. Also, **Mordvinian Autonomous Republic.**

Mor·dred (môr′dred), *n.* Modred.

Mord·vin (môrd′vin), *n.* a Uralic language of the central Volga valley, esp. between Gorki and Saratov. Also, **Mord·vin·i·an** (môrd vin′ē ən).

Mordvin′ian Auton′omous So′viet So′cialist Repub′lic. See **Mordovian Autonomous Soviet Socialist Republic.**

Mor·dy (môr′dē), *n.* a boy's given name, form of **Mordecai.**

more (mōr, môr), *adj., superl.* **most,** *n., adv.* —*adj. compar. of* **much** *or* **many** *with* **most** *as superl.* **1.** in greater quantity, amount, measure, degree, or number: *I need more money.* **2.** additional or further: *Do you need more time? More discussion seems pointless.* —*n.* **3.** an additional quantity, amount, or number: *I would give you more if I had it. He likes her all the more. When I could take no more of such nonsense, I left.* **4.** a greater quantity, amount, or degree: *More is expected of him. The price is more than I thought.* **5.** something of greater importance: *His report is more than a survey.* **6.** (*construed as pl.*) a greater number of a class specified, or the greater number of persons: *More will attend this year than ever before.* —*adv. compar. of* **much** *with* **most** *as superl.* **7.** in or to a greater extent or degree: *more rapid.* **8.** in addition; further; longer; again: *Let's talk more another time. We couldn't stand it any more.* **9.** moreover. **10. more and more,** to an increasing extent or degree; gradually more: *They became involved more and more in stock speculation.* **11. more or less, a.** to some extent; somewhat: *She seemed more or less familiar with the subject.* **b.** in substance; approximately: *We came to more or less the same conclusion.* [ME; OE *māra;* c. OHG *mēro,* Icel *meiri,* Goth *maiza.* See MOST] —**more′ness,** *n.*

More (mōr, môr), *n.* **1. Hannah,** 1745–1833, English writer on religious subjects. **2. Paul Elmer,** 1864–1937, U.S. essayist, critic, and editor. **3. Sir Thomas,** 1478–1535, English humanist, statesman, and author: canonized in 1935.

Mo·re·a (mō rē′ə, mô-), *n.* Peloponnesus.

Mo·reau (mô rō′; *Fr.* mô ʀō′), *n.* **1. Jean Vic·tor** (zhäɴ vēk tôʀ′), 1763–1813, French general. **2. Gus·tave** (gʏs tav′), 1826–98, French painter.

more dict., (in prescriptions) in the manner directed. Also, **mor. dict.** [< L *mōre dictū*]

mo·reen (mə rēn′), *n.* a heavy fabric of wool, or wool and cotton, commonly watered, used for curtains, petticoats, etc. [*mor-* (? var. of MOIRE) + (VELVET)EEN]

More·head (mōr′hed′), *n.* a town in NE Kentucky. 4170 (1960).

More′head Cit′y, a town in E North Carolina. 5583 (1960).

mo·rel[1] (mə rel′), *n.* any edible mushroom of the genus *Morchella,* esp. *M. esculenta.* [< F *morille* < Gmc; cf. OHG *morhila,* equiv. to *morh(a)* carrot (c. OE *more*) + *-ila* dim. suffix]

mo·rel[2] (mə rel′), *n.* any of several nightshades, esp. the black nightshade. Also, **mo·relle′.** [ME *morele* < OF < VL **maurella,* equiv. to L *Maur(us)* Moor + *-ella* dim. suffix; cf. It. *morello* blackish]

Mo·rel (mô rel′; *Fr.* mô ʀel′), *n.* **Jean** (zhäɴ), born 1903, French orchestra conductor.

mo·rel·lo (mə rel′ō), *n., pl.* **-los. 1.** a variety of sour cherry having dark-colored skin and juice. **2.** the tree bearing this fruit. [perh. < It *amarello* AMARELLE, confused (in E) with It *morello* blackish. See MOREL[2]]

Mo·re·los (mô ʀe′lôs), *n.* a state in S central Mexico. 386,264 (1960); 1916 sq. mi. *Cap.:* Cuernavaca.

more·o·ver (mōr ō′vər, môr-, mōr′ō′vər, môr′-), *adv.* beyond what has been said; further; besides. [ME *more over.* See MORE, OVER]

—**Syn.** See **besides.**

Mo·re·ra's the′orem (mô rãr′əz), *Math.* the theorem that a function whose integral about every simple closed curve of finite length in a simply connected domain is zero is an analytic function in the domain. Cf. **Cauchy's integral theorem.**

mo·res (mōr′āz, -ēz, môr′-), *n.pl. Sociol.* folkways of central importance accepted without question and embodying the fundamental moral views of a group. [< L, pl. of *mōs* usage, custom]

more sol., (in prescriptions) in the usual manner. Also, **mor. sol.** [< L *mōre solitō*]

Mo·resque (mə resk′), *adj.* Moorish. [< MF < It *moresco,* equiv. to *Mor(o)* Moor + *-esco* -ESQUE]

More·ton Bay′ pine′ (mōr′tᵊn, môr′-), an evergreen tree, *Araucaria cunninghami,* of Australia, having stiff, sharp leaves, sometimes bluish-green in color, grown as an ornamental. Also called **hoop pine.** [after *Moreton Bay,* Australia]

Mo·re·tus (mô rē′təs), *n.* a walled plain in the third quadrant of the face of the moon: about 75 miles in diameter.

Mor·ga·gni (môʀ gä′nyē), *n.* **Gio·van·ni Bat·tis·ta** (jô vän′nē bät tēs′tä), 1682–1771, Italian anatomist.

Mor·gain le Fay (môr′gān lə fā′, môr′gən). See **Morgan le Fay.**

Mor·gan (môr′gən), *n.* one of a breed of light carriage and saddle horses descended from the stallion *Justin Morgan.* [named after the original sire owned by Justin *Morgan* (1747–98), a New England teacher]

Mor·gan (môr′gən), *n.* **1. Charles Lang·bridge** (lang′brij′), 1894–1958, English novelist and critic. **2. Daniel,** 1736–1802, American Revolutionary general. **3. Sir Henry,** 1635?–88, Welsh buccaneer in the Americas. **4. John Hunt,** 1826–64, Confederate general in the U.S. Civil War. **5. J(ohn) P(ier·pont)** (pēr′pont), 1837–1913, U.S. financier and philanthropist. **6.** his son **John Pierpont,** 1867–1943, U.S. financier. **7. Thomas Hunt,** 1866–1945, U.S. zoologist: Nobel prize for medicine 1933. **8.** a boy's or girl's given name.

Mor·gan·a (môr gan′ə), *n.* a girl's given name.

mor·ga·nat·ic (môr′gə nat′ik), *adj.* designating or pertaining to a form of marriage in which a man of high rank marries a woman of lower station with the stipulation that neither she nor their children, if any, will have any claim to his rank or property. [< NL *morganāticus* (adj.), for ML phrase (*mātrimōnium*) *ad morganāticam* (marriage) to the extent of morning-gift (*morganātica* repr. OHG **morgangeba* (fem.); c. OE *morgengiefu* gift from husband to wife on day after wedding); ML also had *morganāticum* (neut.) < OHG *morgan* MORN + L *-āticum* -AGE] —**mor′ga·nat′i·cal·ly,** *adv.*

Mor·gan·field (môr′gən fēld′), *n.* a town in W Kentucky. 3741 (1960).

Mor′gan Hill′, a town in W California. 3151 (1960).

mor·gan·ic (môr gan′ik), *adj. Rare.* morganatic. [< NL *morganic(us)*]

mor·gan·ite (môr′gə nīt′), *n.* rose-colored beryl. [named after J. P. MORGAN; see -ITE[1]]

Mor·gan le Fay (môr′gən lə fā′), *Celtic and Arthurian Legend.* the fairy sister of King Arthur. Also, **Morgain le Fay.**

Mor·gan·ton (môr′gən tən), *n.* a town in central North Carolina. 9186 (1960).

Mor·gan·town (môr′gən toun′), *n.* a city in N West Virginia. 22,487 (1960).

mor·gen (môr′gən), *n.* **1.** a unit of land measure equal to about two acres, formerly in use in Holland and the Dutch colonies and still used in South Africa. **2.** a unit equal to about two thirds of an acre, formerly used in Prussia, Norway, and Denmark. [< D, G *Morgen* morning (as much land as one plows in a morning)]

Mor·gen·thau (môr′gən thô′), *n.* **Henry, Jr.,** 1891–1967, U.S. statesman: Secretary of the Treasury 1934–45.

morgue (môrg), *n.* **1.** a place in which the bodies of unidentified dead persons, esp. the victims of violence or accidents, are kept pending identification or burial. **2.** *Journalism.* **a.** the reference library of clippings, mats, books, etc., kept by a newspaper, periodical, or other news agency. **b.** the room containing it. **3.** any place, as a room or file, where records, information, or objects are kept for unexpected but possible future use. **4.** such records, information, or objects. [< F; name of building in Paris housing dead bodies not identified]

Mo·ri·ae En·co·mi·um (mōr′ē ē′ en kō′mē əm, môr′-; *Lat.* mō′ʀē ī′ en kō′mē ŏŏm′). See **In Praise of Folly.**

Mo·ri·ah (mō rī′ə, mô-), *n.* **1.** a mountainous region in S Palestine, where Abraham prepared to sacrifice Isaac. Gen. 22:3. **2.** Also, *Douay Bible,* **Mo·ri′a.** a site usually identified with Zion, where Solomon built the Temple. II Chron. 3:1.

mor·i·bund (môr′ə bund′, mor′-), *adj.* **1.** in a dying state; near death. **2.** on the verge of extinction or termination. **3.** not progressing or advancing; stagnant: *a moribund political party.* [< L *moribund(us)* dying, equiv. to *morī* to die + *-bundus* adj. suffix] —**mor′i·bun′di·ty,** *n.* —**mor′i·bund′ly,** *adv.*

Mö·ri·ke (mœ′ʀi kə), *n.* **E·du·ard** (ā′dŏŏ äʀt′), 1804–75, German poet.

Mo·ri·ni (mô rē′nē), *n.* **Erika,** born 1906, U.S. violinist, born in Austria.

mo·ri·on[1] (mōr′ē on′, môr′-), *n.* an open helmet of the 16th and early 17th centuries, worn by common soldiers and usually having a flat or turned-down brim and a crest from front to back. Cf. **cabasset, comb morion.** [< MF < Sp *morrión,* equiv. to *morr(a)* top of head + *-ion* n. suffix]

Morion (16th century)

mo·ri·on[2] (mōr′ē on′, môr′-), *n.* a variety of smoky quartz of a dark-brown or nearly black color. [< L *mōrion* a misreading of *mormorion* a kind of crystal]

Mo·ris·co (mə ris′kō), *adj., n., pl.* **-cos, -coes.** —*adj.* **1.** Moorish. —*n.* **2.** a Moor. **3.** one of the Moors of Spain. [< Sp, equiv. to *Mor(o)* Moor + *-isco* adj. suffix]

Mor·i·son (môr′i sən, mor′-), *n.* **Samuel Eliot,** 1887–1976, U.S. historian.

mo·ri·tu·ri te sa·lu·ta·mus (mō′ʀi tŏŏ′ʀē te sä′lŏŏ tä′mŏŏs; *Eng.* môr′i tyŏŏr′ī tē sal′yŏŏ tā′məs), *Latin.* we who are about to die salute thee: said by Roman gladiators to the emperor as they marched past him.

Mo·ritz (*Ger.* mō′ʀits), *n.* a boy's given name, form of **Maurice.**

Mor·ley (môr′lē), *n.* **1. Christopher Darlington,** 1890–1957, U.S. writer. **2. Edward Williams,** 1838–1923, U.S. chemist and physicist. **3. John, Viscount Morley of Blackburn,** 1838–1923, English statesman, journalist, biographer, and critic. **4. Thomas,** 1557–1603?, English composer, esp. of madrigals.

Mor·mon (môr′mən), *n.* **1.** a member of the Church of Jesus Christ of Latter-day Saints (**Mor′mon Church′**), founded in the U.S. in 1830 by Joseph Smith. **2.** See under **Book of Mormon.** —*adj.* **3.** of or pertaining to the Mormons or their religious system: *the Mormon view of Creation.* —**Mor′mon·dom,** *n.* —**Mor′mon·ism,** *n.*

Mor′mon crick′et, a flightless, long-horned grasshopper, *Anabrus simplex,* of the western U.S., that is very destructive to range grasses and cultivated crops. [so named because found where the Mormons settled]

mor·my·rid (môr mī′rid), *n.* **1.** any of numerous fishes of the family *Mormyridae,* found in the fresh waters of Africa, many species of which have an elongated snout and are capable of producing an electric discharge. —*adj.* **2.** belonging or pertaining to the family *Mormyridae.* [back formation from NL *Mormyridae,* equiv. to *mormyr-* (< Gk *mormýros* a sea-fish) + *-idae* -IDAE]

morn (môrn), *n.* morning. [ME *morn(e),* OE *morne* (dat. of *morgen* morning); c. D, G *Morgen*]

Mor·na (môr′nə), *n.* a girl's given name.

Mor·nay (môʀ nā′), *n.* **Phi·lippe de** (fē lēp′ də), **Sei·gneur du Ples·sis-Mar·ly** (se nyœʀ′ dʏ ple sē′maʀ lē′), ("*Pope of the Huguenots*"), 1549–1623, French statesman and Protestant leader. Also called **Duplessis-Mornay.**

morn·ing (môr′ning), *n.* **1.** the beginning of day; the dawn. **2.** the first part or period of the day, extending from dawn, or from midnight, to noon. **3.** the first or early period of anything: *the morning of life.* —*adj.* **4.** of or pertaining to morning: *the morning hours.* **5.** occurring, appearing, used, etc., in the morning: *the morning sun.* [ME; see MORN, -ING[1], modeled on *evening*]

—**Syn. 1.** morn, daybreak, sunrise. —**Ant.** evening.

morn′ing af′ter, *pl.* **mornings after. 1.** a period, as in the morning, when the aftereffects of excessive self-indulgence are felt, esp. the aftereffects of excessive drinking of alcoholic beverages. **2.** a moment or period of realization in which the consequences of an ill-advised action are recognized or brought home to one: *The morning after of his year of living beyond his means was grim.*

morn′ing coat′, a man's cutaway for wear as part of morning dress.

morn′ing dress′, 1. a simple dress for wear in the home, as for doing housework; housedress. **2.** formal daytime apparel for men, including striped pants, a cutaway, and a silk hat. Cf. **evening dress.**

morn·ing-glo·ry (môr′ning glōr′ē, -glôr′ē), *n., pl.* **-ries.** any of various convolvulaceous plants, esp. of the genera *Ipomoea* and *Convolvolus,* as *I. purpurea,* a twining plant having cordate leaves and funnel-shaped flowers of various colors.

morn′ing gun′, *Mil.* **1.** a gun fired at the first note of reveille. **2.** the firing of this gun.

morn′ing loan′. See **day loan.**

Morn′ing Prayer′, matin (def. 1c).

morn·ings (môr′ningz), *adv.* in or during the morning regularly.

morn′ing sick′ness, nausea occurring in the early part of the day, esp. as a characteristic symptom in the first months of pregnancy.

morn′ing star′, 1. any bright planet seen in the east immediately before sunrise. **2.** an annual plant, *Mentzelia Lindleyi,* of California, having bright-yellow flowers. **3.** Also called **holy water sprinkler, holy water sprinkle.** a medieval shafted weapon having a head in the form of a spiked ball.

morn′ing watch′, *Naut.* the watch from 4 A.M. until 8 A.M.

Mo·ro (mōr′ō, môr′ō), *n., pl.* **-ros,** (*esp. collectively*) **-ro.** a member of any of the various tribes of Muslim Malays in the southern Philippines. [< Sp < L *Maurus* MOOR]

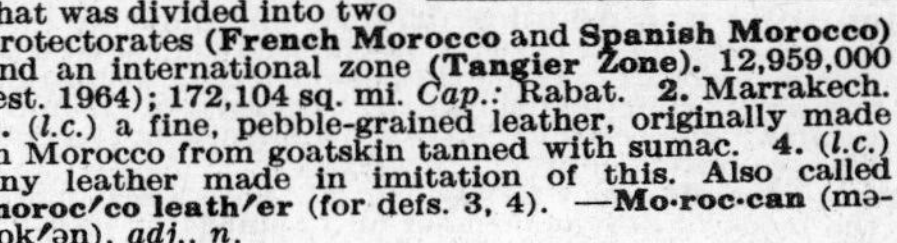

Mo·ro (môr′ō, mor′ō; *It.* mô′ʀô), *n.* **Al·do** (äl′dō; *It.* äl′dô), 1916–78, Italian lawyer, author, and statesman: prime minister 1963–68.

Mo·roc·co (mə rok′ō), *n.* **1.** French, **Maroc.** Spanish, **Marruecos.** a kingdom in NW Africa: formed from a sultanate that was divided into two protectorates (**French Morocco** and **Spanish Morocco**) and an international zone (**Tangier Zone**). 12,959,000 (est. 1964); 172,104 sq. mi. *Cap.:* Rabat. **2.** Marrakech. **3.** (*l.c.*) a fine, pebble-grained leather, originally made in Morocco from goatskin tanned with sumac. **4.** (*l.c.*) any leather made in imitation of this. Also called **moroc′co leath′er** (for defs. 3, 4). —**Mo·roc·can** (mə-rok′ən), *adj., n.*

Mo·ro·go·ro (môr′ə gōr′ō, môr′ə gôr′ō), *n.* a city in E Tanzania. 14,507 (1957).

mo·ron (mōr′on, môr′-), *n.* **1.** a person having an I.Q. of 50–69 and judged incapable of developing beyond a mental age of 8–12. **2.** *Informal.* any stupid person or a person lacking in good judgment. [< Gk, neut. of *mōrós* foolish] —**mo·ron·ic** (mə ron′ik), *adj.* —**mo·ron′i·cal·ly,** *adv.* —**mo′ron·ism, mo·ron·i·ty** (mə-ron′i tē), *n.*

Mo·ron·da·va (mōr′ən dä′və, môr′-), *n.* a seaport on W Madagascar. 9172 (1960).

mo·ror (mô ʀôʀ′), *n. Hebrew.* maror.

Mo·ros (mōr′os, môr′-), *n. Class. Myth.* a child of Nyx, and the personification of fate.

mo·rose (mə rōs′), *adj.* gloomily or sullenly ill-humored, as a person, mood, etc. [< L *mōrōs(us)* fretful, peevish, willful, equiv. to *mōr-* (s. of *mōs*) will, inclination + *-ōsus* -OSE[1]] —**mo·rose′ly,** *adv.* —**mo·rose′ness, mo·ros·i·ty** (mə ros′i tē), *n.*

—**Syn.** moody, sour, sulky, surly. —**Ant.** cheerful.

morph (môrf), *n. Ling.* a sequence of phonemes constituting a minimal unit of grammar or syntax, and, as such, a representation, member, or contextual variant of a morpheme in a specific environment. Cf. **allomorph** (def. 2). [back formation from MORPHEME]

morph-, var. of **morpho-** before a vowel: *morpheme.*

-morph, var. of **morpho-** as final element in compound words: *isomorph.*

mor·pheme (môr′fēm), *n. Ling.* any of the minimal grammatical units of a language, each constituting a word or meaningful part of a word, that cannot be divided into smaller independent grammatical parts, as *the, write,* or the *-ed* of *waited.* Cf. **allomorph** (def. 2), **morph.** [MORPH- + -EME; first formed in F] —**mor·phem′ic,** *adj.* —**mor·phem′i·cal·ly,** *adv.*

Mor·phe·us (môr′fē əs, -fyōōs), *n.* **1.** *Class. Myth.* a son of Hypnos and the god of dreams. **2. in the arms of Morpheus,** asleep; in deep sleep. [ME < L < Gk *morphḗ* form + L *-eus* n. suffix; coined by Ovid, with allusion to the forms seen in dreams] —**Mor′phe·an,** *adj.*

-morphic, an element used as an adjective termination corresponding to **-morph:** *anthropomorphic.* [-MORPH + -IC]

mor·phine (môr′fēn), *n. Pharm.* a white, bitter, crystalline alkaloid, $C_{17}H_{19}NO_3 \cdot H_2O$, the most important narcotic principle of opium, obtained by extraction and crystallization: used chiefly in medicine in the form of its sulfate, hydrochloride, or other salt to dull pain, as a sedative, and to induce sleep. Also, **mor·phi·a** (môr′fē ə). [< G *Morphin.* See MORPHEUS, -INE[2]] —**mor·phin·ic** (môr fin′ik), *adj.*

mor·phin·ism (môr′fə niz′əm), *n. Pathol.* **1.** a morbid condition induced by the habitual use of morphine. **2.** the habitual use of morphine producing this condition. [MORPHINE + -ISM] —**mor′phin·ist,** *n.*

mor·phin·ize (môr′fə nīz′), *v.t.,* **-ized, -iz·ing.** to administer morphine to. [MORPHINE + -IZE]

-morphism, an element forming abstract nouns denoting the state of having a specified form: *monomorphism.* [-MORPH + -ISM]

Mor·pho (môr′fō), *n. Class. Myth.* an epithet of Aphrodite, meaning "shapely."

mor·pho-, a learned borrowing from Greek meaning "form," used in the formation of compound words: *morphology.* Also, *esp. before a vowel,* **morph-.** Cf. **-morph, -morphic, -morphism, -morphous.** [< Gk, comb. form of *morphḗ*]

mor·pho·gen·e·sis (môr′fə jen′i sis), *n. Embryol.* the structural development of an organism or part. [MORPHO- + GENESIS] —**mor·pho·ge·net·ic** (môr′fō jə net′ik), **mor′pho·gen′ic,** *adj.*

morphol., morphology.

mor·pho·line (môr′fə lēn′, -lin), *n. Chem.* a colorless, hygroscopic liquid, $O(CH_2CH_2)_2NH$, used chiefly as a solvent for dyes, resins, and waxes. [*morphol-* (MORPH- + -OL[2]) + -INE[2]]

morpholog′ic construc′tion, *Gram.* a construction that forms a compound or complex word. Cf. **syntactic construction.**

mor·phol·o·gy (môr fol′ə jē), *n.* **1.** the branch of biology dealing with the form and structure of plants and animals. **2.** the form and structure of an organism considered as a whole. **3.** *Gram.* **a.** the patterns of word formation in a particular language, including inflection, derivation, and composition. **b.** the study and description of such patterns. **c.** the study of the behavior and combination of morphemes. **4.** *Phys. Geog.* geomorphology. **5.** the form or structure of anything: *to gain an insight into the morphology of our political system.* **6.** the study of the form or structure of anything. [MORPHO- + -LOGY; first formed in G] —**mor·pho·log·ic** (môr′fə loj′ik), **mor′pho·log′i·cal,** *adj.* —**mor′pho·log′i·cal·ly,** *adv.* —**mor·phol′o·gist,** *n.*

mor·pho·neme (môr fō′nēm), *n. Ling.* morphophoneme. [MOR(PHEME) + PHONEME]

mor·pho·ne·mic (môr′fə nē′mik, -fō-), *adj. Ling.* morphophonemic. [MORPHONEME + -IC]

mor·pho·ne·mics (môr′fə nē′miks, -fō-), *n.* (*construed as sing.*) *Ling.* morphophonemics. [see MORPHONEMIC, -ICS]

mor·pho·pho·neme (môr′fə fō′nēm, -fō-), *n. Ling.* **1.** an abstract phonological unit representing corresponding phonemes in different allomorphs of one morpheme. In English the symbol *F* may be used to represent a morphophoneme occurring in two related allomorphs, as *f* in *leaf,* but *v* in the plural *leaves.* **2.** a phonological entity comprising a bundle of distinctive features used in the representation of a morpheme. **3.** a symbol for a phonological alternation. [MORPH(EME) + -O- + PHONEME]

mor·pho·pho·ne·mic (môr′fō fə nē′mik, -fō nē′-), *adj. Ling.* noting or pertaining to morphophonemics or morphophonemes. [MORPH(EME) + -O- + PHONEMIC]

mor·pho·pho·ne·mics (môr′fō fə nē′miks, -fō nē′-), *n.* (*construed as sing.*) **1.** *Ling.* the study of the relations between morphemes and their phonological realizations, components, or mappings. **2.** the body of data concerning these relations in a given language. [see MORPHOPHONEMIC, -ICS]

mor·pho·sis (môr fō′sis), *n., pl.* **-ses** (-sēz). *Biol.* the mode of development of an organism or part. [< NL < Gk, equiv. to *morph(oûn)* (to) shape + *-ōsis* -OSIS] —**mor·phot·ic** (môr fot′ik), *adj.*

mor·pho·to·ne·mics (môr′fō tə nē′miks, -tō-), *n.* (*construed as sing.*) *Ling.* the morphophonemics of tonal phenomena. [b. MORPHOPHONEMICS and TONE] —**mor′pho·to·ne′mic,** *adj.*

-morphous, an element used as an adjective termination corresponding to **-morph:** *polymorphous.* [< Gk *-morphos,* deriv. of *morphḗ* form; see -OUS]

Mor·rie (môr′ē), *n.* a boy's given name, form of **Maurice.** Also, **Maury.**

Mor′rill Act′ (môr′il, mor′-), *U.S.* **1.** an act of Congress (1862) granting each State 30,000 acres of land for each member it had in Congress, 90 percent of the gross proceeds of which were to be used for the endowment and maintenance of colleges and universities teaching agricultural and mechanical arts and other subjects. **2.** either of two supplementary acts, 1890 and 1907, in which Congress made direct financial grants to assist the land-grant colleges and universities. [named after Justin Smith *Morrill* (1810–98), congressman and senator from Vermont]

Mor·ril·ton (môr′il tən, mor′-), *n.* a town in central Arkansas. 5997 (1960).

Mor·ris (môr′is, mor′-), *n.* **1. Gouv·er·neur** (guv′ər nēr′), 1752–1816, U.S. statesman. **2. Robert,** 1734–1806, U.S. financier and statesman, born in England. **3. William,** 1834–96, English painter, furniture designer, poet, and socialist writer. **4.** a town in NE Illinois. 7935 (1960). **5.** a town in W Minnesota. 4199 (1960). **6.** a boy's given name, form of **Maurice.**

Mor′ris chair′, a large armchair having an adjustable back and loose, removable cushions. [named after William MORRIS]

Morris chair

mor′ris dance′ (môr′is, mor′-), a rural folk dance of north English origin, performed in costume by persons who originally represented characters of the Robin Hood legend, common in England, esp. in May Day festivities. Also called **mor′ris.** [late ME *moreys daunce* Moorish dance; see MOORISH]

Mor·ri·son (môr′i sən, mor′-), *n.* **1. Herbert Stanley,** born 1888, English labor leader and statesman. **2.** a town in NW Illinois. 4159 (1960). **3.** a boy's given name.

Mor′ris Plains′, a town in N New Jersey. 4703 (1960).

Mor′ris Plan′ bank′, a private banking organization, formerly common in the U.S., designed primarily to grant small loans to industrial workers.

Mor·ris·town (môr′is toun′, mor′-), *n.* **1.** a city in N New Jersey: Washington's winter headquarters 1776–77, 1779–80. 17,712 (1960). **2.** a city in E Tennessee. 21,267 (1960).

Mor·ris·ville (môr′is vil′, mor′-), *n.* a town in SE Pennsylvania. 7790 (1960).

mor·ro (môr′ō, mor′ō; *Sp.* mô′rrô), *n., pl.* **-ros** (-rōz; *Sp.* -rôs). a rounded hill, hillock, or promontory. [< Sp: rounded, projecting object. See MORION[1]]

Mor′ro Bay′ (môr′ō, mor′ō), a town in SW California. 3692 (1960).

Mor′ro Cas′tle (môr′ō, mor′ō; *Sp.* mô′rrô), a historic fort at the entrance to the harbor of Havana, Cuba.

mor·row (môr′ō, mor′ō), *n.* **1.** the day next after this or after some other particular day or night. **2.** *Archaic.* morning. [ME *morwe,* var. of *morwen,* OE *morgen* morning. See MORN]

Mor·row (môr′ō, mor′ō), *n.* **Hon·o·ré Will·sie** (on′ə rā′ wil′sē, on′ə rā′), 1880–1940, U.S. novelist.

Mors (môrz), *n.* the ancient Roman personification of death.

morse (môrs), *n. Eccles.* an ornamented metal clasp or brooch for fastening a cope in front. [ME *mors* < OF < L *mors(us)* a catch, lit., bite]

Morse (môrs), *n.* **1. Samuel F(in·ley) B(reese)** (fin′lē brēz), 1791–1872, U.S. artist and inventor: developer of the first successful telegraph in the U.S.; inventor of the most commonly used telegraphic code system. **2.** See **Morse code. 3.** a boy's given name, form of **Maurice.** —*adj.* **4.** noting or pertaining to the Morse code or the system of communications using it. **5.** pertaining to any code resembling the Morse code.

Morse′ code′, a system of dots, dashes, and spaces, or the corresponding sounds or visual signals, used in telegraphy and signaling to represent the letters of the alphabet, numerals, etc. Also called **Morse′ al′phabet.**

mor·sel (môr′səl), *n.* **1.** a bite, mouthful, or small portion of food, candy, etc. **2.** a small piece, quantity, or amount of anything; scrap; bit. —*v.t.* **3.** to distribute in or divide into tiny portions (often fol. by *out*): *She morseled out the last pieces of meat to her family.* [ME < OF, equiv. to *mors* a bite (< L *morsum* something bitten off, n. use of neut. of *morsus,* ptp. of *mordēre* to bite) + *-el* < L *-ellus* dim. suffix]

Morse′ lamp′, a blinker lamp for signaling in Morse code.

mort[1] (môrt), *n.* **1.** *Hunting.* the note played on a hunting horn signifying that the animal hunted has been killed. **2.** *Obs.* death. [ME < MF < L *mort-* (s. of *mors*) death]

mort[2] (môrt), *n.* a three-year-old salmon. [?]

mort[3] (môrt), *n. Brit. Dial.* lard; the fat on ham or bacon. Also, **mord.** [?]

Mort (môrt), *n.* a boy's given name, form of **Mortimer** or **Morton.**

mor·ta·del·la (môr′tə del′ə), *n.* a sausage of pork, beef, and pork fat chopped fine, seasoned with garlic and pepper, cooked, and smoked. [< It, equiv. to L *murtāt(um)* sausage seasoned with myrtle (*murt(um)* myrtle-berry + *-ātum,* neut. of *-ātus* -ATE[1]) + *-ella* dim. suffix]

mor·tal (môr′tᵊl), *adj.* **1.** subject to death; having a transitory life: *all mortal creatures.* **2.** of or pertaining to man as subject to death; human: *this mortal life.* **3.** belonging to this world. **4.** of or pertaining to death: *the mortal hour.* **5.** involving spiritual death (opposed to *venial*): *mortal sin.* **6.** causing or liable to cause death; fatal: *a mortal wound.* **7.** to the death: *mortal combat.* **8.** deadly or implacable: *a mortal enemy.* **9.** severe, dire, grievous, or bitter: *in mortal fear.* **10.** long and wearisome. **11.** extreme; very great: *in a mortal hurry.* —*n.* **12.** a human being. **13.** the condition of being subject to death. [ME < L *mortāl(is),* equiv. to *mort-* (s. of *mors*) death + *-ālis* -AL[1]] —**mor′tal·ly,** *adv.* —**Syn. 6.** See **fatal.**

mor·tal·i·ty (môr tal′i tē), *n., pl.* **-ties. 1.** the state or condition of being subject to death; mortal character, nature, or existence. **2.** mortal beings collectively; humanity. **3.** relative frequency of death, or death rate, as in a district or community. **4.** death or destruction on a large scale, as from war, plague, famine, etc. **5.** *Obs.* death. [ME *mortalite* < MF < L *mortālitās.* See MORTAL, -ITY]

mortal′ity ta′ble, *Insurance.* an actuarial table showing the number of persons who die at any given age, compiled from statistics on selected population groups or on former policyholders. Also called **life table.**

mor′tal mind′, *Christian Science.* the illusion that mind and life arise from matter and are subject to death. Cf. **mind** (def. 17).

mor′tal sin′, *Rom. Cath. Ch.* a willfully committed, serious transgression against the law of God, depriving the soul of divine grace. Cf. **venial sin.**

mor·tar[1] (môr′tər), *n.* **1.** a vessel of hard material, having a bowl-shaped cavity in which substances, as drugs, are reduced to powder with a pestle. **2.** any of various mechanical appliances in which substances are pounded or ground. **3.** a cannon very short in proportion to its bore, for throwing shells at high angles. **4.** some similiar contrivance, as for throwing pyrotechnic bombs or a life line. [ME, OE *mortere* < L *mortār(ium)* vessel to make mortar in (see MORTAR[2]); in defs. 3, 4 trans. of F *mortier*]

A, Mortar
B, Pestle

mor·tar[2] (môr′tər), *n.* **1.** a mixture of lime or cement or a combination of both with sand and water, used as a bonding agent between bricks, stones, etc. **2.** any of various materials or compounds for bonding together bricks, stones, etc.: *Bitumen was used as a mortar.* —*v.t.* **3.** to plaster or fix with mortar. [ME *morter* < OF *mortier* < L *mortār(ium)* contents of vessel. See MORTAR[1]] —**mor′tar·less,** *adj.* —**mor′tar·y,** *adj.*

mor·tar·board (môr′tər bōrd′, -bôrd′), *n.* **1.** a board, usually square, used by masons to hold mortar. **2.** Also called **cap.** a cap with a close-fitting crown surmounted by a stiff, flat, square piece from which a tassel hangs, worn as part of academic costume. [MORTAR[2] + BOARD]

Mortarboard (def. 2)

mor′tar ketch′. See **bomb ketch.**

Morte d'Ar·thur, Le (lə môrt′ där′thər). See **Le Morte d'Arthur.**

mort·gage (môr′gij), *n., v.,* **-gaged, -gag·ing.** —*n.* *Law.* **1.** a conveyance of property to a creditor as security, as for the repayment of money. **2.** the deed by which such a transaction is effected. **3.** the rights conferred by it, or the state of the property conveyed. —*v.t.* **4.** *Law.* to convey or place (property, esp. houses or land) under a mortgage. **5.** to obligate; pledge: *to mortgage one's life to the defense of democracy.* [ME *morgage* < ME, OF, equiv. to *mort* dead (< L *mortuus,* ptp. of *morī* to die) + *gage* pledge, GAGE[1]]

mort′gage bond′, a bond secured by a mortgage on real estate or other property.

mort·ga·gee (môr′gə jē′), *n.* a person to whom property is mortgaged. [MORTGAGE + -EE]

mortgagee′ clause′, *Insurance.* a clause attached to a fire-insurance policy for protecting a mortgagee against loss or damage.

mort·ga·gor (môr′gə jər), *n.* a person who mortgages property. Also, **mort′gag·er.** [MORTGAGE + -OR[2]]

mor·tice (môr′tis), *n., v.t.,* **-ticed, -tic·ing.** mortise.

mor·ti·cian (môr tish′ən), *n.* undertaker (def. 2). [MORT(UARY) + -ICIAN, modeled on *physician*]

Mor·tie (môr′tē), *n.* a boy's given name, form of **Mortimer** or **Morton.** Also, **Morty.**

mor·tif·er·ous (môr tif′ər əs), *adj.* deadly; fatal. [< L *mortiferus* death-bearing, equiv. to *morti-* (s. of *mors*) death + *-ferus* -FEROUS] —**mor·tif′er·ous·ness,** *n.*

mor·ti·fi·ca·tion (môr′tə fə kā′shən), *n.* **1.** humiliation in feeling, as by some wound to pride. **2.** a cause or source of such humiliation. **3.** the practice of asceticism by penitential discipline to overcome desire for sin and to strengthen the will. **4.** *Pathol.* the death of one part of the body while the rest is alive; gangrene. [ME *mortificacion* < eccl. L *mortificātiōn-* (s. of *mortificātiō*), equiv. to *morti-* (see MORTIFY) + *-ficātiōn-* -FICATION]
—**Syn. 1.** See **shame.**

mor·ti·fy (môr′tə fī′), *v.,* **-fied, -fy·ing.** —*v.t.* **1.** to humiliate, as by a blow to the pride or self-respect. **2.** to subjugate (the body, passions, etc.) by abstinence, ascetic discipline, or rigorous austerities. **3.** *Pathol.* to affect with gangrene or necrosis. —*v.i.* **4.** to practice mortification or disciplinary austerities. **5.** *Pathol.* to undergo mortification, or become gangrened or necrosed. [ME *mortifie(n)* < MF *mortifie(r)* < LL *mortificāre* to put to death, equiv. to L *morti-* (s. of *mors*) death + *-ficāre* -FY] —**mor′ti·fied′ly,** *adv.* —**mor′ti·fi′er,** *n.* —**mor′ti·fy′ing·ly,** *adv.*
—**Syn. 1.** humble, abase. **2.** subdue, restrain.

Mor·ti·mer (môr′tə mər), *n.* **1. Roger de** (də), **8th Baron of Wig·more** (wig′mōr′, -môr′) and **1st Earl of March,** 1287–1300, English rebel leader: paramour of Isabella, queen of Edward II of England. **2.** a boy's given name.

Mor·tis (môr′tis), *n.* **Lacus.** See **Lacus Mortis.**

mor·tise (môr′tis), *n., v.,* **-tised, -tis·ing.** —*n.* **1.** a notch, hole, groove, or slot made in a piece of wood or the like to receive a tenon of the same dimensions. **2.** a deep recess cut into wood for any of several other purposes, as for receiving a mortise lock. **3.** *Print.* a space cut out of a plate, esp. for the insertion of type or another plate. —*v.t.* **4.** to secure with a mortise and tenon. **5.** to cut or form a mortise in (a piece of wood or the like). **6.** to join securely. **7.** *Print.* **a.** to cut metal from (a plate). **b.** to cut out metal from a plate and insert (new material) in its place. Also, **mortice.** [ME *mortays* < MF *mortaise,* perh. < Ar *murtazza* made fast] —**mor′tis·er,** *n.*

mor′tise and ten′on joint′. See **mortise joint.** Also, **mor′tise-and-ten′on joint′.**

mor′tise block′, Mach. a block having a shell cut from a single piece of wood.

mor′tise chis′el. See **framing chisel.**

mor′tise joint′, any of various joints between two pieces of timber or the like in which a tenon is housed in or secured to a mortise. Also called **mortise and tenon joint, mortise-and-tenon joint.**

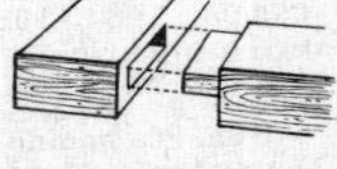

Mortise joint

mor′tise lock′, a lock housed within a mortise in a door or the like, so that the lock mechanism is covered on both sides.

mort·ling (môrt′ling), *n. Brit.* wool obtained from dead sheep. [late ME, deriv. of *mort* fleece of a sheep that died a natural death; see -LING[1]]

mort·main (môrt′mān′), *n. Law.* **1.** the condition of lands or tenements held without right of alienation, as by an ecclesiastical corporation; inalienable ownership. **2.** the perpetual holding of land, esp. by a corporation or charitable trust. [ME *mort(e)mayn(e)* < MF *mortemain,* trans. of ML *mortua manus* dead hand]

Mor·ton (môr′tᵊn), *n.* **1. Jelly Roll** (*Ferdinand Morton*), 1885–1941, U.S. jazz pianist, composer, and band leader. **2. Le·vi Par·sons** (lē′vī pär′sənz), 1824–1920, vice-president of the U.S. 1889–93: governor of New York 1895–96. **3. William Thomas Green,** 1819–68, U.S. dentist: first to employ ether as an anesthetic. **4.** a town in central Illinois. 5325 (1960). **5.** a town in NW Texas. 2731 (1960). **6.** a boy's given name.

Mor′ton Grove′, a city in NE Illinois, near Chicago. 20,533 (1960).

mor·tu·ar·y (môr′cho͞o er′ē), *n., pl.* **-ar·ies,** *adj.* —*n.* **1.** See **funeral home. 2.** a customary gift formerly claimed by and due to the incumbent of a parish in England from the estate of a deceased parishioner. —*adj.* **3.** of or pertaining to the burial of the dead. **4.** pertaining to or connected with death. [ME *mortuarie* < ML *mortuāri(um),* n. use of neut. of L *mortuārius* of the dead, equiv. to *mortu(us)* dead (ptp. of *morī* to die) + *-ārius* -ARY]

Mor·ty (môr′tē), *n.* a boy's given name, form of **Mortimer** or **Morton.** Also, **Mortie.**

mor·u·la (môr′o͝o lə, -yo͞o-), *n., pl.* **-las, -lae** (-lē′). *Embryol.* the mass of cells resulting from the cleavage of the ovum before the formation of a blastula. [< NL, equiv. to L *mōr(um)* mulberry + *-ula* -ULE] —**mor′u·lar,** *adj.*

MOS, military occupational specialty.

mos., months.

mo·sa·ic (mō zā′ik), *n.* **1.** a picture or decoration made of small pieces of inlaid stone, glass, etc. **2.** the process of producing such a picture or decoration. **3.** something resembling such a picture or decoration in composition, esp. in being made up of many fragments or diverse elements: *His essay was just a mosaic of borrowed notions.* **4.** Also called **aerial mosaic.** *Aerial Surveying.* an assembly of aerial photographs taken vertically and matched in such a way as to show a continuous photographic representation of an area (**mosa′ic map′**). **5.** *Archit.* a system of patterns for differentiating the areas of a building or the like, sometimes consisting of purely arbitrary patterns used to separate areas according to function but often consisting of plans of flooring, reflected ceiling plans, overhead views of furnishings and equipment or other items really included in the building or building plan. **6.** Also called **mosa′ic disease′.** *Plant Pathol.* any of several diseases of plants, characterized by mottled green or green and yellow areas on the leaves, caused by certain viruses. **7.** *Biol.* an organism exhibiting mosaicism. **8.** *Television.* a light-sensitive surface in a television camera tube, consisting of a thin mica sheet coated on one side with a large number of small globules of silver and caesium insulated from each other. The image to be televised is focused on this surface and the resulting charges on the globules are scanned by an electron beam. —*adj.* **9.** pertaining to, resembling, or used for making a mosaic or mosaic work: *a mosaic tile.* **10.** composed of a combination of diverse elements. [ME < ML *mosaic(um) (opus),* r. L *mūsīvum (opus)* < Gk *mouseion* mosaic (work), lit., work pertaining to the Muses. See MUSE, -IC] —**mo·sa′i·cal·ly,** *adv.*

Mo·sa·ic (mō zā′ik), *adj.* of or pertaining to Moses or the writings, laws, and principles attributed to him: *the Mosaic view of history.* Also, **Mo·sa′i·cal.** [< NL *Mosaic(us),* equiv. to L *Mōs(ēs)* MOSES + *-aicus,* after *Hebraicus* Hebraic]

mosa′ic glass′, glass having a polychrome pattern made by fusing colors or variously colored canes, rods, strips, or squares together.

mosa′ic gold′, 1. See **stannic sulfide. 2.** ormolu (def. 1). [so called because used in mosaic work]

mo·sa·i·cism (mō zā′i siz′əm), *n. Biol.* a condition in which an organism or part is composed of two or more genetically distinct tissues. [MOSAIC + -ISM]

mo·sa·i·cist (mō zā′i sist), *n.* a person who works in mosaic. [MOSAIC + -IST]

Mosa′ic Law′, 1. the ancient law of the Hebrews, ascribed to Moses. **2.** the part of the Scripture containing this law; the Pentateuch.

mo·sa·saur (mō′sə sôr′), *n.* any of several extinct, carnivorous, marine lizards from the Cretaceous Period, having the limbs modified into broad, webbed paddles. [< NL *Mosasaurus* (1823) genus name, equiv. to L *Mosa* the MEUSE river (where a species was first discovered) + NL *-saurus* -SAUR]

Mos·by (mōz′bē), *n.* **John Sin·gle·ton** (sing′gəl tən), 1833–1916, Confederate cavalry colonel.

mos·chate (mos′kāt, -kit), *adj.* having a musky smell. [< NL *moschāt(us),* equiv. to ML *mosch(us)* musk + L *-ātus* -ATE[1]]

mos·cha·tel (mos′kə tel′, mos′kə tel′), *n.* a small plant, *Adoxa Moschatellina,* having greenish or yellowish flowers with a musky odor. [< F *moscatelle* < It *moscatella,* equiv. to *moscat(o)* musk + *-ella* dim. suffix; *-h-* from botanical name]

Mos·co·viae (mos′kə vē′), *n.* **Mare.** See **Mare Moscoviae.**

Mos·cow (mos′kō *or, for 1, 2,* -kou), *n.* **1.** Russian, **Moskva.** a city in and the capital of the Russian Federation, in the W part: capital of the former Soviet Union. 8,967,000. **2.** Also called **Grand Duchy of Moscow.** Muscovy (def. 1.). **3.** a city in W Idaho. 16,513.

Mos′cow Sea′. See **Mare Moscoviae.**

Mo·sel (mō zel′), *n.* Moselle (def. 1).

Mose·ley (mōz′lē), *n.* **Henry Gwyn Jeffreys** (gwin), 1887–1915, English physicist: pioneer in x-ray spectroscopy.

Mose′ley's law′, *Physics.* the observed law that the square root of the frequencies of lines in atomic x-ray spectra depends linearly on the atomic number of the emitting atom. [named after H.G.J. MOSELEY]

Mo·selle (mō zel′), *n.* **1.** Also, **Mosel.** a river in W central Europe, flowing from the Vosges Mountains in NE France into the Rhine in W West Germany. 320 mi. long. **2.** a department in NE France. 919,412 (1962); 2406 sq. mi. *Cap.:* Metz. **3.** a light, white wine made along the Moselle in West Germany.

Mo·ser (mō′zər), *n.* **Jo·hann Ja·kob** (yō′hän yä′kôp), 1701–85, German jurist and publicist.

Mo·ses (mō′ziz, -zis), *n.* **1.** the Hebrew Patriarch who led the Israelites out of Egypt and was their leader and lawgiver during their years of wandering in the wilderness. **2.** a boy's given name.

Mo·ses (mō′ziz, -zis), *n.* **1. Anna Mary Robertson** ("*Grandma Moses*"), 1860–1961, U.S. painter. **2. Robert,** born 1888, U.S. public official: New York City Commissioner of Parks 1934–60.

Mo′ses bas′ket, *Brit.* a bassinet. [so called from the ark of bulrushes in which the baby Moses was concealed: Exodus 2:3]

Mo′ses boat′, a broad, flat-bottomed rowboat, formerly used for transferring cargo in the West Indies. [? named after a Massachusetts boatwright]

mo·sey (mō′zē), *v.i.,* **-seyed, -sey·ing.** *Informal.* **1.** to leave quickly; decamp. **2.** to shuffle about leisurely, stroll; saunter (often fol. by *along* or *about*). [?]

Mo·shi (mō′shē), *n.* a city in N Tanzania. 13,726 (1956).

Mos·kva (mos kvä′), *n.* Russian name of **Moscow.**

Mosque

Mos·lem (moz′ləm, mos′-), *adj., n., pl.* **-lems, -lem.** Muslim. —**Mos·lem·ic** (moz lem′ik, mos-), *adj.*

Mos·lem·ism (moz′lə miz′əm, mos′-), *n.* the Muslim religion; Islam. [MOSLEM + -ISM]

mosque (mosk, môsk), *n.* a Muslim temple or place of worship. See illus. in preceding column. [? back formation from earlier *mosquee* < MF < It *moschea* << Ar *masjid,* deriv. of *sajada* to worship, lit., prostrate oneself; the *-ee* seems to have been taken as dim. suffix and dropped]

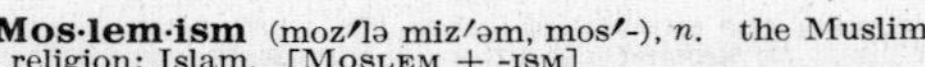

Mosquito, *Culex pipiens* (Length ¼ in.)

mos·qui·to (mə skē′tō), *n., pl.* **-toes.** any of numerous dipterous insects of the family *Culicidae,* the females of which suck the blood of animals and man, some species transmitting certain diseases, as malaria and yellow fever. [< Sp, equiv. to *mosc(a)* fly (< L *musca*) + *-ito* dim. suffix] —**mos·qui′to·ey,** *adj.*

mosqui′to bill′, a perennial herb, *Dodecatheon hendersoni,* of the northwestern coast of the U.S., having purple-spotted, white flowers with yellow anthers. Also called **sailor cap.**

mosqui′to boat′. See **PT boat.**

mos·qui·to·fish (mə skē′tō fish′), *n., pl.* (*esp. collectively*) **-fish,** (*esp. referring to two or more kinds or species*) **-fish·es.** any of several fishes that feed on mosquito larvae, as *Gambusia affinis,* found in the southeastern U.S., now introduced into other parts of the world for mosquito control. [MOSQUITO + FISH]

mosqui′to fleet′, a group or fleet of PT boats or other small, armed boats of high maneuverability.

mosqui′to hawk′, *U.S. Dial.* nighthawk (def. 1). [so called from its nocturnal habits]

mosqui′to net′, a screen, curtain, or canopy of net, gauze, or the like, for keeping out mosquitoes.

mosqui′to net′ting, netting used in the making of mosquito nets.

moss (môs, mos), *n.* **1.** any small, leafy-stemmed, cryptogamic plant of the class *Musci,* growing in tufts, sods, or mats on moist ground, tree trunks, rocks, etc. **2.** a growth of such plants. **3.** any of various similar plants, as Iceland moss or club moss. **4.** *Chiefly Scot. and North Eng.* a swamp or bog. —*v.t.* **5.** to cover with a growth of moss: *to moss a crumbling wall.* [ME *mos(se),* OE *mos* moss, bog; akin to G *Moos,* Icel *mýrr* MIRE] —**moss′like′,** *adj.*

Moss (môs, mos), *n.* a boy's given name, form of **Moses.**

Mos·sa·degh (mō′sä dek′), *n.* **Mohammed,** 1880–1967, Iranian statesman: premier 1951–53.

moss′ ag′ate, a kind of agate or chalcedony containing brown or black mosslike dendritic markings from various impurities.

moss′ an′imal, a bryozoan. [so called because mosslike]

moss·back (môs′bak′, mos′-), *n. Informal.* **1.** a person attached to antiquated notions; an extreme conservative. **2.** a rustic or backwoodsman. **3.** an old turtle. **4.** *Angling.* a large and old fish, as a bass. **5.** a wild bull or cow. [MOSS + BACK[1]]

Möss·bau·er (mûs′bou ər, mos′-; *Ger.* mœs′bou ər), *n.* **Ru·dolf L.** (ro͞o′dôlf), born 1929, German physicist in the U.S. Nobel prize 1961.

Möss′bauer effect′, *Physics.* the phenomenon in which an atom in a crystal undergoes no recoil when emitting a gamma ray, giving all the emitted energy to the gamma ray, resulting in a sharply defined wavelength. [named after Rudolf MÖSSBAUER]

moss·bunk·er (môs′bung′kər, mos′-), *n.* the menhaden. [< D *marsbanker*]

moss′ cam′pion, 1. See **cushion pink. 2.** a related herb, *Silene Schafta,* of the Caucasus, having rose-colored or purple flowers.

Moss′es from an Old′ Manse′, a collection of short stories (1846) by Nathaniel Hawthorne.

moss-grown (môs′grōn′, mos′-), *adj.* **1.** overgrown with moss. **2.** old-fashioned: *moss-grown traditions.*

moss′ hag′, *Scot.* an area, pit, or hole from which peat has been dug.

mos·so (mō′sō; *It.* mōs′sô), *adj. Music.* rapid; fast. [< It, ptp. of *muovere* to MOVE]

Mos·so·ró (mo͞o so͞o RÔ′), *n.* a city in NE Brazil. 41,476 (1960).

moss′ pink′, a phlox, *Phlox subulata,* of the eastern U.S., having showy pink to purple flowers.

Moss′ Point′, a town in SE Mississippi. 6631 (1960).

moss′ rose′, a variety of rose, *Rosa centrifolia muscosa,* having a mosslike growth on the calyx and stem.

moss·troop·er (môs′tro͞o′pər, mos′-), *n.* **1.** one of a class of marauders who infested the mosses, or bogs, of the border between England and Scotland in the 17th century. **2.** any marauder. [MOSS + TROOPER] —**moss′troop′er·y,** *n.* —**moss′troop′ing,** *n., adj.*

moss·y (mô′sē, mos′ē), *adj.,* **moss·i·er, moss·i·est. 1.** overgrown with or abounding in moss: *a mossy stone.* **2.** covered with a mosslike growth. **3.** appearing as if covered with moss. **4.** resembling moss: *a mossy softness.* [MOSS + -Y[1]] —**moss′i·ness,** *n.*

most (mōst), *adj., superl. of* **much** *or* **many** *with* **more** *as compar.* **1.** in the greatest quantity, amount, measure, degree, or number: *to win the most votes.* **2.** in the majority of instances: *Most exercise is beneficial.* **3.** greatest, as in size or extent: *the most talent.* **4. for the most part.** See **part** (def. 18). —*n.* **5.** the greatest quantity, amount, or degree; the utmost: *The most he can hope for is a passing grade.* **6.** the greatest number or the majority of a class specified: *Most of his writing is rubbish. Most of the ornaments were broken.* **7.** the greatest number: *The most this room will seat is 150.* **8.** the majority of persons: *a subject most find to be too difficult; to be more sensitive than most.* **9. at the most,** at the maximum: *It should take, at the most, six more months.* Also, **at most. 10. make the most of,** to use to greatest advantage; utilize fully: *to make the most of an opportunity.* **11. the most,** *U.S. Slang.* the ultimate in something: *He's the most. That movie was the most.* —*adv., superl. of* **much** *with* **more** *as compar.* **12.** in or to the greatest extent or degree (in this sense often used before adjectives and adverbs, and regularly before those of more than two syllables, to form superlative phrases having the same force and effect as the superlative degree formed by the termination *-est*): *most rapid; most wisely.* **13.** *Informal.* almost or nearly. [ME *most(e),* ME *māst* (r. ME *mest(e),* OE *mǣst*); c. G *meist,* Goth *maists.* See MORE]
—**Syn. 13.** See **almost.**

-most, a combining form of **most** occurring in a series of superlatives: *foremost; utmost.* [ME *-most;* r. ME, OE *-mest,* double superl. suffix, equiv. to *-ma* + -EST[1]]

most′-fa′vored-na′tion clause′ (mōst′fā′vərd nā′shən), a clause in a commercial treaty by which each signatory agrees to give the other the same treatment that is accorded any other nation.

Mös·ting (mōs′ting), *n.* a crater in the third quadrant of the face of the moon: about 15 miles in diameter.

most·ly (mōst′lē), *adv.* **1.** for the most part; in the main: *The work is mostly done.* **2.** chiefly. **3.** generally; customarily: *It is at this point that people get mostly involved.* [MOST + -LY]
—**Syn. 2.** especially, particularly. —**Ant. 3.** seldom.

most′ signif′icant dig′it, the digit farthest to the left in a number. *Abbr.:* MSD Cf. **least significant digit.**

Mo·sul (mō so͞ol′), *n.* a city in N Iraq, on the Tigris, opposite the ruins of Nineveh. 215,882 (1963).

Mosz·kow·ski (mōsh kôf′skē), *n.* **Mo·ritz** (mōr′its, mōr′its), 1854–1925, Polish composer and pianist.

mot (mō), *n.* **1.** a pithy or witty remark. **2.** *Archaic.* a note on a horn, bugle, etc. [< F < L *mutt(um)* utterance. See MOTTO]

mote[1] (mōt), *n.* **1.** a particle or speck, esp. of dust. **2.** moit. [ME, OE *mot* speck; c. D *mot* grit, sawdust, Norw *mutt* speck] —**mote′y,** *adj.*

mote[2] (mōt), *v., pt.* **moste** (mōst). *Archaic.* may or might. [ME *mot(e),* OE *mōt* pres. tense (1st sing.); c. G *muss.* See MUST[1]]

mo·tel (mō tel′), *n.* a roadside hotel providing travelers with lodging, typically in bedrooms which are united under one roof but have individual entrances, and with nearby parking space. Also called **tourist court.** [M(OTOR + H)OTEL]

mote′ spoon′, a small spoon with a pierced bowl for removing tea leaves from a cup of tea.

mo·tet (mō tet′), *n. Music.* a vocal composition in polyphonic style, on a Biblical or similar prose text, intended for use in a church service. [ME < MF; see MOT, -ET]

Moth, *Callosamia promethea* (Wingspread 4½ in.)

moth (môth, moth), *n., pl.* **moths** (môthz, mothz, môths, moths). **1.** any of numerous insects of the order *Lepidoptera,* generally distinguished from the butterflies by having antennae of various types, usually not clubbed, and by having nocturnal or crepuscular habits. **2.** See **clothes moth.** [ME *mothe,* OE *moththe;* akin to G *Motte,* Icel *motti*]

moth·ball (môth′bôl′, moth′-), *n.* **1.** a small ball of naphthalene or sometimes of camphor for placing in closets or other storage areas to repel moths from clothing, blankets, etc. **2. in mothballs, a.** in a state or condition of being in disuse or in storage, esp. with reference to out-of-date or obsolete equipment. **b.** in a state or condition of being retired from active participation in something. **c.** (of ideas) in a state of being dismissed as unworthy of further deliberation. —*v.t.* **3.** to put into storage or reserve; inactivate. —*adj.* **4.** inactive; unused; stored away: *a mothball fleet.* [MOTH + BALL[1]]

moth′ bean′. See **mat bean.**

moth-eat·en (môth′ēt′ən, moth′-), *adj.* **1.** eaten or damaged by or as by moths. **2.** decayed. **3.** out of fashion.

moth·er[1] (muth′ər), *n.* **1.** a female parent. **2.** (*often cap.*) one's female parent. **3.** *Informal.* a mother-in-law, stepmother, or adoptive mother. **4.** a term of familiar address for an old or elderly woman. **5.** See **mother superior. 6.** a woman looked upon as a mother, or exercising control or authority like that of a mother: *to be a mother to someone.* **7.** the qualities characteristic of a mother, as maternal affection: *It is the mother in her showing itself.* **8.** something that gives rise to or exercises protecting care over something else. **9.** (in disk recording) a mold electroformed from a master, for molding stampers from which disk records are produced in quantity. —*adj.* **10.** being a mother: *a mother bird.* **11.** of, pertaining to, or characteristic of a mother: *mother love.* **12.** derived from one's mother; native: *He speaks Swahili as if it were his mother tongue.* **13.** bearing a relation like that of a mother, as in giving origin or rise, or in exercising protective care: *the mother company and its affiliates.* —*v.t.* **14.** to be the mother of; give origin or rise to. **15.** to acknowledge oneself the author of; assume as one's own. **16.** to care for or protect as a mother does; act maternally toward. [ME *moder,* OE *mōdor;* c. D *moeder,* G *Mutter,* Icel *mōthir,* L *māter,* Gk *mḗtēr,* Skt *mātar-.* As in *father,* late substitution of *th* for *d,* possibly on pattern of *brother*] —**moth′er·less,** *adj.* —**moth′er·less·ness,** *n.*

moth·er[2] (muth′ər), *n.* a stringy, mucilaginous substance consisting of various bacteria, esp. *Mycoderma aceti,* which forms on the surface of a fermenting liquid and causes fermentation when added to other liquids, as in changing wine or cider to vinegar. Also called **mother of vinegar.** [prob. special use of MOTHER[1], but perh. another word, akin to D *modder* dregs, MLG *moder* swampy land; see MUD]

Moth′er Car′ey's chick′en (kâr′ēz), any of various small petrels, esp. the stormy petrel, *Oceanites oceanicus.* [?]

moth′er church′, 1. a church from which other churches have had their origin or derived their authority. **2.** a cathedral or a metropolitan church. **3.** the particular church attended in one's youth or for the greater part of one's life. [ME *moder chirche*]

moth′er coun′try, 1. the country of one's birth or ancestry. **2.** the country of origin of settlers or colonists in a place: *The Pilgrims' mother country was England.*

Moth′er Goose′, the legendary author of the collection of nursery rhymes first published in English (1760) under the title of *Mother Goose's Melody.*

moth·er·hood (muth′ər ho͝od′), *n.* **1.** the state of being a mother; maternity. **2.** mothers collectively. **3.** the qualities or spirit of a mother. [MOTHER[1] + -HOOD]

Moth′er Hub′bard (hub′ərd), **1.** a full, loose gown, usually fitted at the shoulders, worn by women. **2.** heroine of a nursery rhyme.

moth·er·ing (muth′ər ing), *n.* (in rural England) the custom of visiting one's parents on Laetare Sunday with a present. [MOTHER[1] + -ING[1]]

Moth′ering Sun′day, *Brit.* See **Laetare Sunday.**

moth·er-in-law (muth′ər in lô′), *n., pl.* **moth·ers-in-law.** the mother of one's husband or wife. [late ME *modyr in lawe*]

moth′er-in-law plant′. See **dumb cane.**

moth·er·land (muth′ər land′), *n.* **1.** one's native land. **2.** the land of one's ancestors. [MOTHER[1] + LAND]

moth′er liq′uor, the portion of a solution remaining after crystallization of its important component.

moth′er lode′, *Mining.* a rich or important lode.

moth·er·ly (muth′ər lē), *adj.* **1.** pertaining to, characteristic of, or befitting a mother: *motherly solicitude.* **2.** like a mother: *to take a motherly interest in an orphan.* —*adv.* **3.** in the manner of a mother. [ME *moderly,* OE *mōdorlīc.* See MOTHER[1], -LY] —**moth′er·li·ness,** *n.*

moth·er-na·ked (muth′ər nā′kid), *adj.* stark naked; as naked as when born. [late ME *modur nakyd*]

moth′er of coal′. See **mineral charcoal.**

Moth′er of God′, a title of the Virgin Mary. [late ME *modir of God*]

moth·er-of-pearl (muth′ər əv pûrl′), *n.* **1.** a hard, iridescent substance which forms the inner layer of certain shells, as that of the pearl oyster; nacre. —*adj.* **2.** of or having the qualities of mother-of-pearl, as being iridescent, pearly, etc.: *mother-of-pearl buttons.* [cf. It *madreperla,* obs. F *mère perle*]

moth′er-of-pearl′ cloud′. See **nacreous cloud.**

moth′er-of-pearl′ glass′. See **satin glass.**

moth·er-of-thyme (muth′ər əv tīm′), *n., pl.* **-thymes.** a branched, woody, prostrate herb, *Thymus Serpyllum,* of Eurasia and northern Africa, having wiry stems that root at the joints and small, purplish flowers. Also called **creeping thyme.**

moth′er of vin′egar, mother[2].

moth′er's boy′, a boy or man showing excessive attachment to his mother and lacking normal masculine interests. Also called **mama's boy, mamma's boy.**

Moth′er's Day′, a day, usually the second Sunday in May, devoted to honoring mothers.

moth′er's help′er, a girl or woman who is hired to assist in household chores, esp. caring for children.

moth′er spleen′wort, a fern, *Asplenium bulbiferum,* of tropical Africa and Australasia, the fronds often bearing bulbils which sprout into new plants while still attached, grown as an ornamental.

moth′er supe′rior, *pl.* **mother superiors, mothers superior.** the head of a female religious community.

moth′er tongue′, **1.** the language first learned by a person; native language. **2.** a parent language. [ME *moder tonge*]

Moth·er·well (muth′ər wəl, -wel′), *n.* **Robert,** born 1915, U.S. painter and writer.

Moth·er·well and Wish·aw (muth′ər wel′ ən wish′ō), a burgh in S Scotland. 72,799 (1961).

moth′er wit′, natural or practical intelligence, wit, or sense. [late ME *moderis wytte*]

moth·er·wort (muth′ər wûrt′), *n.* a European, labiate plant, *Leonorus cardica,* an introduced weed in the U.S., having cut leaves with a whorl of flowers in the axils. [ME *moderwort* (see MOTHER[1], WORT[2]), so called because believed helpful for diseases of womb]

moth′er yaw′, *Pathol.* the initial lesion of yaws, occurring at the site of inoculation.

moth′ mul′lein, a weedy, European mullein, *Verbascum Blattaria,* having smooth leaves and white or yellow flowers. [from its mothlike appearance]

moth·proof (môth′proōf′, moth′-), *adj.* **1.** resistant to attack by moths. —*v.t.* **2.** to render (fabric, clothing, etc.) mothproof. [MOTH + -PROOF]

moth·y (mô′thē, moth′ē), *adj.,* **moth·i·er, moth·i·est.** **1.** containing moths. **2.** moth-eaten. [MOTH + -Y[1]]

Mo Ti (mô′ dē′), Mo-tze.

mo·tif (mō tēf′), *n.* **1.** a recurring subject, theme, idea, etc., esp. in an artistic work, as an opera, symphony, or novel. **2.** a distinctive and recurring form, shape, figure, etc., in a design, as in a painting, on a wallpaper, etc. **3.** a dominant idea or feature: *the profit motif of free enterprise.* **4.** a standard, often recurring narrative element in folklore and literature. [< F; see MOTIVE]

mo·tile (mōt′əl, mō′til), *adj.* **1.** *Biol.* moving or capable of moving spontaneously: *motile cells or spores.* —*n.* **2.** *Psychol.* a person in whose mind motor images, rather than visual or auditory images, are predominant or unusually distinct. [< L *mōt(us)* moved, set in motion (ptp. of *movēre*) + -ILE] —**mo·til·i·ty** (mō til′i tē), *n.*

mo·tion (mō′shən), *n.* **1.** the action or process of moving or of changing place or position. **2.** a movement. **3.** power of movement, as of a living body. **4.** the manner of moving the body in walking; gait. **5.** a bodily movement or change of posture; a gesture. **6.** a proposal formally made to a deliberative assembly: *to make a motion to adjourn.* **7.** *Law.* an application made to a court or judge for an order, ruling, or the like. **8.** a suggestion or proposal. **9.** an inward prompting or impulse; inclination: *He will go only of his own motion, and persuasion is useless.* **10.** *Music.* melodic progression, as the change of a voice part from one pitch to another. **11.** *Mach.* **a.** a piece of mechanism with a particular action or function. **b.** the action of such mechanism. **12. in motion,** in active operation; moving: *The ship was now in motion, and the excitement of departure began to diminish.* —*v.t.* **13.** to direct by a significant motion or gesture, as with the hand: *to motion a person to a seat.* —*v.i.* **14.** to make a significant motion, as with the hand; gesture; signal: *to motion to someone to come.* [ME *mocio(u)n* < L *mōtiōn-* (s. of *mōtiō*), equiv. to *mōt(us)* moved (ptp. of *movēre*) + *-iōn-* -ION] —**mo′tion·al,** *adj.* —**mo′tion·er,** *n.*

—**Syn. 1.** MOTION, MOVE, MOVEMENT refer to change of position in space. MOTION denotes change of position, either considered apart from, or as a characteristic of, that which moves; usually the former, in which case it is often a somewhat technical or scientific term: *perpetual motion.* The chief uses of MOVE are founded upon the idea of moving a piece, in chess or a similar game, for winning the game; and hence the word denotes any change of position, condition, or circumstances for the accomplishment of some end: *a shrewd move to win votes.* MOVEMENT is always connected with the person or thing moving, and is usually a definite or particular motion: *the movements of a dance.* **4.** bearing, carriage.

mo·tion·less (mō′shən lis), *adj.* without motion or incapable of motion: *a motionless statue.* [MOTION + -LESS] —**mo′tion·less·ly,** *adv.* —**mo′tion·less·ness,** *n.* —**Syn.** still, stationary, unmoving, inert, stable, fixed, quiescent, quiet. —**Ant.** active.

mo′tion pic′ture, **1.** a sequence of consecutive pictures of objects photographed in motion by a specially designed camera (**mo′tion-pic′ture cam′era**) and thrown on a screen by a projector (**mo′tion-pic′ture projec′tor**) in such rapid succession as to give the illusion of natural movement. **2.** a play, event, or the like, presented in this form. **3. motion pictures,** the art, technique, or business of producing a motion picture. —**mo′tion-pic′ture,** *adj.*

mo′tion sick′ness, *Pathol.* a feeling of nausea and dizziness, sometimes accompanied by vomiting, resulting from stimulation by motion of the semicircular canals of the ear during travel by car, plane, etc.

mo′tion stud′y. See **time and motion study.**

mo′tion work′, clockwork by which the hour hand is driven from the shaft of the minute hand.

mo·ti·vate (mō′tə vāt′), *v.t.,* **-vat·ed, -vat·ing.** to provide with a motive or motives. [MOTIVE + -ATE[1]]

mo·ti·va·tion (mō′tə vā′shən), *n.* **1.** the act or an instance of motivating. **2.** the state or condition of being motivated. **3.** that which motivates; inducement; incentive. [MOTIVE + -ATION] —**mo′ti·va′tion·al,** *adj.* —**mo′ti·va′tive,** *adj.*

motiva′tion research′, the application of the knowledge and techniques of the social sciences, esp. psychology and sociology, to understanding consumer attitudes and behavior: used as a guide in advertising and marketing. Also, **motiva′tional research′.**

mo·tive (mō′tiv), *n., adj., v.,* **-tived, -tiv·ing.** —*n.* **1.** something that prompts a person to act in a certain way or that determines volition; incentive. **2.** the goal or object of one's actions: *His motive was revenge.* **3.** (in art, literature, and music) a motif. —*adj.* **4.** causing, or tending to cause, motion. **5.** pertaining to motion. **6.** prompting to action. **7.** constituting a motive or motives. —*v.t.* **8.** to motivate. **9.** *Obs.* to relate to a motif in a work of art. [ME < ML *mōtīv(um)* that which moves someone to do something, n. use of neut. of *mōtīvus* serving to move, equiv. to L *mōt(us)* moved (ptp. of *movēre*) + *-īvus* -IVE] —**mo′tive·less,** *adj.* —**mo′tive·less·ly,** *adv.* —**mo′tive·less·ness,** *n.*

—**Syn. 1.** motivation, incitement, stimulus, spur; influence, occasion, ground, cause. MOTIVE, INCENTIVE, INDUCEMENT apply to whatever moves one to action. MOTIVE is, literally, that which moves a person; an INDUCEMENT, that which leads him on; an INCENTIVE, that which inspires him. MOTIVE is applied mainly to an inner urge that moves or prompts a person to action, though it may also apply to a contemplated result, the desire for which moves the person: *His motive was a wish to be helpful.* INDUCEMENT is never applied to an inner urge, and seldom to a goal: *The pleasure of wielding authority may be an inducement to get ahead.* It is used mainly of opportunities offered by the acceptance of certain conditions, whether these are offered by a second person or by the factors of the situation: *The salary offered me was a great inducement.* INCENTIVE was once used of anything inspiring or stimulating the emotions or imagination: *incentives to piety;* it has retained of this its emotional connotations, but (rather like INDUCEMENT) is today applied only to something offered as a reward, and offered particularly to stimulate competitive activity: *to create incentives for higher achievement.* **2.** See **reason.**

-motive, a combining form of **motive:** *automotive.*

mo′tive pow′er, **1.** any power used to impart motion. **2.** a source of mechanical energy. **3.** *Railroading.* locomotives or the like which supply tractive power.

mo·tiv·i·ty (mō tiv′i tē), *n.* the power of initiating or producing motion. [MOTIVE + -ITY]

mot juste (mō zhyst′), *pl.* **mots justes** (mō zhyst′). *French.* the exact or appropriate word.

mot·ley (mot′lē), *adj., n., pl.* **-leys.** —*adj.* **1.** exhibiting great diversity of elements; heterogeneous: *a motley crowd.* **2.** being of different colors combined; parti-colored: *a motley flower border.* **3.** wearing a parti-colored garment: *a motley fool.* —*n.* **4.** a combination of different colors. **5.** a parti-colored effect. **6.** the parti-colored garment of a jester: *to wear the motley.* **7.** a heterogeneous assemblage. **8.** a medley. [ME; see MOTE[1], -LY]

Mot·ley (mot′lē), *n.* **John Lo·throp** (lō′thrəp), 1814–77, U.S. historian and diplomat.

mot·mot (mot′mot), *n.* any of several tropical and subtropical American birds of the family *Momotidae,* related to the kingfishers, having a serrate bill and chiefly greenish and bluish plumage. [< AmerSp; repetitive compound, imitating the bird's note]

mo·ton (mōt′ən), *n.* *Armor.* besague. [< F, equiv. to *mot* MOT + *-on* n. suffix]

mo·to·neu·ron (mō′tə nŏŏr′on, -nyŏŏr′-), *n.* *Anat., Physiol.* a motor nerve cell. [*moto-* (comb. form repr. MOTOR) + NEURON]

mo·tor (mō′tər), *n.* **1.** a comparatively small and powerful engine, esp. an internal-combustion engine in an automobile, motorboat, or the like. **2.** any self powered vehicle. **3.** one who or that which imparts motion, esp. a contrivance, as a steam engine, which receives and modifies energy from some natural source in order to utilize it in driving machinery. **4.** *Elect.* a machine that converts electrical energy into mechanical energy. **5. motors,** stocks or bonds in automobile companies. —*adj.* **6.** causing or imparting motion. **7.** pertaining to or operated by a motor. **8.** of, for, by, or pertaining to motor vehicles: *motor freight.* **9.** *Physiol.* conveying an impulse that results or tends to result in motion, as a nerve. **10.** *Psychol., Physiol.* of, pertaining to, or involving muscular movement: *a motor response; motor images.* —*v.i.* **11.** to ride or travel in an automobile: *Bob and Susan plan to motor down for the weekend.* —*v.t.* **12.** *Chiefly Brit.* to drive or transport by car: *He motored his son to school.* [< L: mover, equiv. to *mōt(us)* moved (ptp. of *movēre*) + *-or* -OR[2]]

mo·tor·bike (mō′tər bīk′), *n.* **1.** a bicycle that is propelled by an attached motor. **2.** a motorcycle, esp. one that is small and light. [MOTOR + BIKE[1]]

mo·tor·boat (mō′tər bōt′), *n.* **1.** a boat propelled by its own internal or by an outboard motor. —*v.i.* **2.** to travel in or operate a motorboat: *to motorboat from Hyannis to Martha's Vineyard.* [MOTOR + BOAT]

mo·tor·boat·ing (mō′tər bō′ting), *n.* *Electronics.* oscillation in an electronic circuit or component causing pulses at a very low frequency that produce sounds like that of a motorboat if the circuit is connected to a loudspeaker. [MOTORBOAT + -ING[1]]

mo·tor·bus (mō′tər bus′), *n.* a passenger bus powered by a motor. Also called **motor coach.** [MOTOR + BUS[1]]

mo·tor·cade (mō′tər kād′), *n.* a procession or parade of automobiles. [MOTOR + (CAVAL)CADE]

mo·tor·car (mō′tər kär′), *n.* **1.** an automobile. **2.** *Railroads.* a self-propelled car for freight or passengers. [MOTOR + CAR[1]]

mo′tor coach′, motorbus.

mo′tor court′, motel.

mo·tor·cy·cle (mō′tər sī′kəl), *n., v.,* **-cled, -cling.** —*n.* **1.** a motor vehicle similar to a bicycle, chiefly for one rider and sometimes having an attached sidecar for passengers. —*v.i.* **2.** to ride on or operate a motorcycle. [MOTOR + CYCLE] —**mo·tor·cy·clist** (mō′tər-sī′klist), *n.*

mo′tor drive′, a mechanical system, including an electric motor, used to operate a machine or machines. —**mo·tor-driv·en** (mō′tər driv′ən), *adj.*

mo·tor·drome (mō′tər drōm′), *n.* a rounded course or track for automobile and motorcycle races. [MOTOR + -DROME]

mo·tored (mō′tərd), *adj.* having a motor or motors, esp. of a specified number or type (usually used in combination): *a bimotored airplane.* [MOTOR + -ED[3]]

mo′tor gen′erator, *Elect.* one or more motors mechanically coupled to one or more generators for converting or transforming electric current into mechanical energy. Also called **mo′tor gen′erator set′.**

mo′tor home′, a small bus with a roomlike or apartmentlike area behind the driver's seat, outfitted as living quarters for use in camping, extended motor excursions, etc.

mo·tor·ing (mō′tər ing), *n.* traveling in or driving a car, esp. when considered as a recreation: *a perfect day for motoring in the country.* [MOTOR + -ING[1]]

mo·tor·ise (mō′tə rīz′), *v.t.,* **-ised, -is·ing.** *Chiefly Brit.* motorize. —**mo′tor·i·sa′tion,** *n.*

mo·tor·ist (mō′tər ist), *n.* **1.** a person who drives an automobile. **2.** the user of a privately owned automobile. [MOTOR + -IST]

mo·tor·ize (mō′tə rīz′), *v.t.,* **-ized, -iz·ing.** **1.** to furnish with a motor or motors, as vehicles. **2.** to supply with motor-driven vehicles in the place of horses and horse-drawn vehicles. Also, *esp. Brit.,* **motorise.** [MOTOR + -IZE] —**mo′tor·i·za′tion,** *n.*

mo′tor lodge′, *U.S.* motel. Also called **mo′tor inn′, mo′tor hotel′.**

mo′tor lor′ry, *Brit.* a motor truck, esp. one with open sides.

mo·tor·man (mō′tər mən), *n., pl.* **-men.** **1.** a person who operates or drives an electrically operated vehicle, as a streetcar or subway train. **2.** a person who operates a motor. [MOTOR + MAN[1]]

mo·tor-mind·ed (mō′tər mīn′did), *adj.* disposed to perceive one's environment in terms of mechanical or muscular activity. Cf. **ear-minded, eye-minded.** —**mo′tor-mind′ed·ness,** *n.*

mo′tor sail′er, *Naut.* a yacht having sails and an engine as an alternative means of propulsion.

mo′tor scoot′er, scooter[1] (def. 2).

mo′tor ship′, a ship driven by a diesel or other internal-combustion engine or engines. Also, **mo′tor-ship′.**

mo′tor torpe′do boat′. See **PT boat.**

mo′tor truck′, truck[1] (def. 1).

mo′tor u′nit, *Anat.* a motor nerve cell and the muscle fibers innervated by its axon.

mo′tor van′, *Brit.* a motor truck or van, esp. one with closed sides and a roof to protect the cargo.

mo′tor ve′hicle, an automobile, truck, bus, or similar conveyance equipped with tires and driven on roads.

mo′tor ves′sel, a ship driven by one or more internal-combustion engines.

mo·tor·way (mō′tər wā′), *n.* *Brit.* an expressway. [MOTOR + WAY]

Mo-tse (*Chin.* mô′dzə′), *n.* Mo-tze. Also, **Mo′ Tse′.**

Mott (mot), *n.* **1. John Raleigh,** 1865–1955, U.S. religious leader: Nobel peace prize 1946. **2. Lucretia Coffin,** 1793–1880, U.S. social reformer: advocate of women's rights.

motte (mot), *n.* *Southern and Western U.S.* a grove or clump of trees in prairie land or open country. Also, **mott.** [< MexSp *mata* < L *matta* MAT[1]]

mot·tle (mot′əl), *v.,* **-tled, -tling,** *n.* —*v.t.* **1.** to diversify with spots or blotches of a different color or shade. —*n.* **2.** a diversifying spot or blotch of color. **3.** mottled coloring or pattern. [back formation from MOTLEY] —**mot′tle·ment,** *n.* —**mot′tler,** *n.*

mot·tled (mot′əld), *adj.* spotted or blotched in coloring. [MOTTLE + -ED[2]]

mot′tled enam′el, *Dentistry.* tooth enamel having areas of varying whiteness and abnormally susceptible to staining, caused during the childhood development of teeth by the drinking of water containing excessive levels of fluoride.

mot·to (mot′ō), *n., pl.* **-toes, -tos.** **1.** a maxim adopted as an expression of one's guiding principle. **2.** a sentence, phrase, or word attached to or inscribed on anything as appropriate to it. [< It < L *muttum* utterance. See MOT]

mot·tram·ite (mo′trə mīt′), *n.* *Mineral.* a copper and lead vanadate. [named after *Mottram* St. Andrew's, Cheshire, England, where it was found; see -ITE[1]]

mo·tu pro·pri·o (mō′tōō prō′pri ō′), *Latin.* by one's own volition; of one's own accord: used of certain documents issued by the Pope without counsel from others.

Mo-tze (mô′dzə′), *n.* (*Mo Ti*) fl. 5th century B.C., Chinese philosopher. Also, **Mo′ Tzu′, Mo-tse, Mo Tse.**

mouch (mo͞och), *v.i., v.t., n. Slang.* mooch.

Mou·chez (mo͞o shā′), *n.* a walled plain in the second quadrant of the face of the moon: about 58 miles in diameter.

mou·choir (mo͞o shwar′), *n., pl.* **-choirs** (-shwar′). *French.* a handkerchief.

moue (mo͞o), *n., pl.* **moues** (mo͞o). *French.* a pouting grimace.

mouf·lon (mo͞of′lon), *n.* a wild sheep, *Ovis musimon,* inhabiting the mountainous regions of Sardinia, Corsica, etc., the male of which has large curving horns. Also, **mouf′flon.** [< F < Corsican *mufrone* < LL *mufrōni-* (s. of *mufrō*)]

mouil·lé (mo͞o yā′), *adj. Phonet.* **1.** palatal or palatalized, esp. referring to sounds spelled *ll* and *ñ* in Spanish, *gl* and *gn* in Italian, etc. **2.** (of French sounds) spelled *l* or *ll* and pronounced as a *y* sound. [< F, ptp. of *mouiller* to wet < VL **molliāre* to soften by wetting, deriv. of L *mollis* soft; see MOLLIFY]

mou·jik (mo͞o zhik′, mo͞o′zhik), *n.* muzhik.

Mouk·den (mo͝ok′den′, mo͝ok′-), *n.* Mukden.

mou·lage (mo͞o läzh′), *n.* **1.** the making of a mold, esp. with plaster of Paris, of objects, footprints, tire tracks, etc., as for the purpose of identification. **2.** the mold itself. [< F, equiv. to *moul(er)* (to) mold (deriv. of *moule* MOLD[1]) + *-age* -AGE]

mould (mōld), *n., v.t., v.i. Chiefly Brit.* mold. —**mould′a·bil′i·ty,** *n.* —**mould′a·ble,** *adj.* —**mould′i·ness,** *n.*

mould·board (mōld′bōrd′, -bôrd′), *n. Chiefly Brit.* moldboard.

mould·er[1] (mōl′dər), *v.i., v.t. Chiefly Brit.* molder[1].

mould·er[2] (mōl′dər), *n. Chiefly Brit.* molder[2].

mould·ing (mōl′ding), *n. Chiefly Brit.* molding.

mould·y[1] (mōl′dē), *adj.,* **mould·i·er, mould·i·est.** *Chiefly Brit.* moldy.

mould·y[2] (mōl′dē), *n., pl.* **mould·ies.** *Brit. Mil. Slang.* a torpedo. [prob. orig. Scot and north dial. *moudie* a mole]

mou·lin (mo͞o laN′), *n.* a nearly vertical shaft or cavity worn in a glacier by surface water falling through a crack in the ice. [< F < LL *molīn(um)* MILL[1]]

Mou·lin de la Ga·lette, Le (*Fr.* lə mo͞o laN də la ga let′), a painting (1876) by Auguste Renoir.

Moul·mein (mo͞ol mān′, mōl-), *n.* a seaport in S Burma at the mouth of the Salween River. 108,020 (est. 1958). Also, **Maulmain.**

moult (mōlt), *v.i., v.t., n. Chiefly Brit.* molt. —**moult′er,** *n.*

Moul·trie (mōl′trē, mo͞ol′-), *n.* **1. William,** 1730–1805, U.S. general. **2.** a city in S Georgia. 15,764 (1960). **3. Fort.** See **Fort Moultrie.**

moul·vi (moul′vē), *n.* maulvi.

mound[1] (mound), *n.* **1.** an elevation formed of earth, sand, stones, etc., esp. over a grave or ruins. **2.** a tumulus or other raised work of earth dating from a prehistoric or long-past period. **3.** a natural elevation of earth; a hillock or knoll. **4.** an artificial elevation of earth, as for a defense work, a dam or barrier, or any other purpose; an embankment. **5.** a heap or raised mass: *a mound of papers; a mound of hay.* **6.** *Baseball.* the slightly elevated ground from which the pitcher delivers the ball. Cf. **rubber** (def. 10). —*v.t.* **7.** to furnish with a mound of earth, as for a defense. **8.** to form into a mound; heap up. [OE *mund* hand, hence protection, protector; in 16th century, protective barrier, e.g., fence, earthwork; c. Icel *mund,* MD *mond* protection]

mound[2] (mound), *n.* a golden globe topped with a cross which symbolizes power and constitutes part of the regalia of an English sovereign. [ME < L *mund(us)* world]

Mound (mound), *n.* a town in E Minnesota. 5440 (1960).

Mound′ Build′ers, the various Amerindian tribes who, in prehistoric and early historic times, erected the burial mounds and other earthworks of the Mississippi drainage basin and southeastern U.S.

mound·ing (moun′ding), *n. Pathol.* a localized lumping, due to contraction, of a degenerating muscle upon being firmly struck. [MOUND[1] + -ING[1]]

mounds·man (moundz′mən), *n., pl.* **-men.** *Baseball Slang.* pitcher[2] (def. 2). [MOUND[1] + 's[1] + MAN[1]]

Mounds′ View′, a town in E Minnesota. 6416 (1960).

Mounds·ville (moundz′vil), *n.* a city in NW West Virginia, on the Ohio River. 15,163 (1960).

mount[1] (mount), *v.t.* **1.** to go up; climb; ascend: *He mounted the stairs slowly.* **2.** to get up on (a platform, a horse, etc.). **3.** to set or place at an elevation: *to mount a house on stilts.* **4.** to furnish with a horse or other animal for riding. **5.** to set or place (a person) on horseback. **6.** to raise or put into position for use, as a gun. **7.** (of a fortress or vessel) to have or carry (guns) in position for use. **8.** to go or put on guard, as a sentry or watch. **9.** to fix on or in a support, backing, setting, etc.: *to mount a photograph.* **10.** to provide (a play, musical comedy, etc.) with scenery, costumes, and other equipment for production. **11.** to prepare (an animal body or skeleton) as a specimen. **12.** (of a male animal) to climb upon (a female) for copulation. **13.** *Micros.* **a.** to prepare (a slide) for microscopic investigation. **b.** to prepare (a sample) for examination by a microscope, as by placing it on a slide. —*v.i.* **14.** to rise or go to a higher position, level, degree, etc.; ascend. **15.** to rise in amount (often fol. by *up*): *The cost of small miscellaneous items mounts up.* **16.** to get up on the back of a horse or other animal for riding. **17.** to get up on something, as a platform. —*n.* **18.** the act or a manner of mounting. **19.** a horse, other animal, or sometimes a vehicle, as a bicycle, used, provided, or available for riding. **20.** an act or occasion of riding a horse, esp. in a race. **21.** a support, backing, setting, or the like, on or in which something is, or is to be, mounted or fixed. **22.** an ornamental metal piece applied to a piece of wooden furniture. **23.** *Micros.* a prepared slide. **24.** a distinctive metal feature on a sheath or scabbard, as a locket or chape. **25.** *Philately.* hinge (def. 4). **26.** *Print.* a wooden or metal block to which a plate is secured for printing. [ME *mounte(n)* < OF *munte(r), monte(r)* < VL **montāre* < L *mont-* (s. of *mōns*) MOUNT[2]] —**mount′a·ble,** *adj.* —**mount′less,** *adj.*
—**Syn. 1.** scale. See **climb. 14.** soar. **19.** steed, charger, palfrey. —**Ant. 1, 14.** descend.

mount[2] (mount), *n.* a hill or mountain. [ME, OE *munt* < L *mont-* (s. of *mōns*) mountain, hill]

moun·tain (moun′tən), *n.* **1.** a natural elevation of the earth's surface rising more or less abruptly to a summit, and attaining an altitude greater than that of a hill. **2.** a large mass of something resembling this, as in shape or size. **3.** a huge amount: *A mountain of food covered the table.* **4.** a formidable obstacle: *to make a mountain out of a molehill.* **5.** (*cap.*) a steam locomotive having a four-wheeled front truck, eight driving wheels, and a two-wheeled rear truck. **6. the Mountain,** *Fr. Hist.* (in the revolutionary legislatures) the radical party led by Danton and Robespierre, advocating the ruthless prosecution of the revolution and the Reign of Terror: so called because its members occupied the topmost seats or benches in the legislatures. Cf. **plain** (def. 19). **7.** Also called **moun′tain wine′.** *Brit. Archaic.* a sweet Malaga wine. —*adj.* **8.** of or pertaining to mountains: *mountain air; mountain scenery.* **9.** living, growing, or located in the mountains: *mountain people; mountain flowers.* **10.** resembling or suggesting a mountain, as in size. [ME *mountaine* < OF *montaigne* < VL **montānea,* n. use of fem. of **montāneus,* L *montān(us)* mountainous (*mont-,* s. of *mōns* mountain + *-ānus* -AN) + *-eus* adj. suffix] —**moun′tain·less,** *adj.*

moun′tain ash′, **1.** any of several small, rosaceous trees of the genus *Sorbus,* having small, white, corymbose flowers and bright-red to orange berries. **2.** any of certain other trees, as several Australian species of eucalyptus.

moun′tain av′ens, any evergreen, rosaceous plant of the genus *Dryas,* of northern or alpine regions of the Northern Hemisphere, having showy, solitary, white or yellow flowers.

moun′tain azal′ea, a shrub, *Azalea canescens,* of the southeastern U.S., having nearly odorless, funnel-shaped, pink or white flowers.

moun′tain bea′ver, a small, burrowing rodent, *Aplodontia rufa,* of the Pacific coastal region of North America, considered the most primitive living rodent. Also called **sewellel.**

moun′tain blue′bird, a bluebird, *Siala arctica,* of western North America.

moun′tain blu′et, a European perennial herb, *Centaurea montana,* having raylike blue flowerheads.

Moun′tain Brook′, a city in central Alabama, near Birmingham. 12,680 (1960).

moun′tain camel′lia, a shrub, *Stewartia ovata,* of the mountainous regions from North Carolina and Tennessee to Georgia, having white flowers.

moun′tain cat′, **1.** a cougar. **2.** a bobcat.

moun′tain chain′, **1.** a connected series of mountains. **2.** See **mountain range.**

moun′tain cran′berry, a vacciniaceous shrub, *Vaccinium Vitis-Idaea,* having evergreen leaves, prostrate stems, and tart red berries edible after cooking.

moun′tain creep′er, an evergreen, woody vine, *Thunbergia fragrans,* of India, having white, tubular flowers.

moun′tain cur′rant, an ornamental shrub, *Ribes alpinum,* of Europe, having greenish-yellow flowers and scarlet fruit. Also called **Alpine currant.**

moun′tain dam′son, any of several tropical American trees of the genus *Simaruba,* the bark of the root of which is used as a tonic and astringent.

moun′tain dew′, *Informal.* any whiskey, esp. illegally distilled corn liquor.

moun′tain eb′ony. See **orchid tree.**

moun·tain·eer (moun′tənēr′), *n.* **1.** an inhabitant of a mountainous district. **2.** a climber of mountains. —*v.i.* **3.** to climb mountains. [MOUNTAIN + -EER]

moun·tain·eer·ing (moun′tənēr′ing), *n.* the sport of climbing mountains. [MOUNTAINEER + -ING[1]]

moun′tain fet′terbush, an erect shrub, *Pieris floribunda,* found from Virginia to Georgia, having white flowers in nodding clusters.

moun′tain fleece′, a perennial herb, *Polygonum amplexicaule,* of the Himalayas having white or rose-colored flowers in terminal spikes.

moun′tain fringe′. See **climbing fumitory.**

moun′tain goat′. See **Rocky Mountain goat.**

Moun′tain Grove′, a town in central Missouri. 3176 (1960).

moun′tain heath′, a low, branching, evergreen shrub, *Phyllodoce caerulea,* of northern North America and Eurasia, having bluish-purple flowers.

moun′tain hol′ly fern′, a hardy, evergreen fern, *Polystichum Lonchitis,* of North America, Europe, and Asia, having stiff and leathery fronds.

Moun′tain Home′, a town in SW Idaho. 9344 (1960).

Moun′tain Lakes′, a town in N New Jersey. 4037 (1960).

moun′tain lau′rel, a North American laurel, *Kalmia latifolia,* having terminal clusters of rose to white flowers: the State flower of Connecticut and Pennsylvania.

moun′tain li′on, cougar.

moun′tain magno′lia, a tree, *Magnolia fraseri,* of the southeastern U.S., having fragrant, creamy-white flowers from nine to eleven inches across.

moun′tain ma′ple, a shrub, *Acer spicatum,* of eastern North America, having small, greenish-yellow flowers and winged fruit, the foliage turning from orange to scarlet in autumn.

moun·tain·ous (moun′tənəs), *adj.* **1.** abounding in mountains. **2.** of the nature of a mountain. **3.** resembling a mountain or mountains, as being large and high: *mountainous waves.* [late ME *mounteynous.* See MOUNTAIN, -OUS] —**moun′tain·ous·ly,** *adv.* —**moun′tain·ous·ness,** *n.*

moun′tain oys′ter, the testis of a calf, sheep, pig, etc., used as food. Cf. **prairie oyster.**

moun′tain range′, **1.** a series of more or less connected mountains ranged in a line. **2.** a series of mountains, or of more or less parallel lines of mountains, closely related, as in origin. **3.** an area in which the greater part of the land surface is in considerable degree of slope, upland summits are small or narrow, and there are great differences in elevations within the area (commonly over 2000 feet).

moun′tain rose′. See **coral vine.**

moun′tain rose′bay, a showy, evergreen shrub, *Rhododendron catawbiense,* found in the mountainous regions from Virginia to Georgia, having bell-shaped, purple flowers.

moun′tain sage′, a perennial herb, *Artemisia frigida,* of Asia and the western U.S., having silvery-white foliage and yellow flower heads. Also called **wild sage, wormwood sage.**

moun′tain sand′wort, a sandwort, *Arenaria groenlandica,* of Greenland and North America, having very numerous small leaves, growing in rocky soil. Also called **mountain starwort.**

moun′tain sax′ifrage, a spreading, perennial herb, *Saxifraga oppositifolia,* of Eurasia and northern North America, having purple or rose-colored flowers.

moun′tain sheep′, **1.** the bighorn. **2.** any of various wild sheep inhabiting mountains.

moun′tain sick′ness, *Pathol.* a condition characterized by difficult breathing, headache, nausea, etc., due to the rarefaction of the air at high altitudes.

moun·tain·side (moun′tən sīd′), *n.* the side or slope of a mountain. [ME *mountayne syide.* See MOUNTAIN, SIDE[1]]

Moun·tain·side (moun′tən sīd′), *n.* a town in NE New Jersey. 6325 (1960).

moun′tain star′wort. See **mountain sandwort.**

Moun′tain State′, Montana (used as a nickname).

Moun′tain time′. See under **standard time.**

moun·tain·top (moun′tən top′), *n.* **1.** the top of a mountain. —*adj.* **2.** situated at the top of a mountain: *a mountaintop house.* [MOUNTAIN + TOP[1]]

Moun′tain View′, a city in central California, S of San Francisco. 30,889 (1960).

moun′tain visca′cha, viscacha (def. 2).

moun′tain wave′, the wavelike effect, characterized by severe updrafts and downdrafts, that occurs when rapidly flowing air encounters a sharply rising mountain range. Also called **lee wave.**

moun′tain white′fish, a whitefish, *Prosopium williamsoni,* found in mountain streams and lakes of the western U.S. and Canada. Also called **Rocky Mountain whitefish.**

moun′tain wind′ (wind), a wind descending a mountain valley at night. Cf. **valley wind.**

Mount′ Air′y, a town in NW North Carolina. 7055 (1960).

Mount′ Ar′arat, Ararat.

Mount·bat·ten (mount bat′ən), *n.* **Louis, 1st Earl Mountbatten of Burma,** 1900–79, British admiral: viceroy of India 1947; governor general of India 1947–8.

Mount′ Car′mel, **1.** a borough in E Pennsylvania. 10,760 (1960). **2.** a town in SE Illinois. 8594 (1960).

Mount′ Car′mel man′, an early man of partially Neanderthaloid type, known from skeletal remains from the Würm I period, found in Palestine.

Mount′ Clem′ens (klem′ənz), a city in SE Michigan. 21,016 (1960).

Mount′ Des′ert Is′land (dez′ərt, di zûrt′), an island off the coast of E central Maine: summer resort; forms part of Acadia National Park. 14 mi. long; 8 mi. wide.

Mount′ Do′ra, a town in central Florida. 3756 (1960).

moun·te·bank (moun′tə bangk′), *n.* **1.** a huckster who sells quack medicines from a platform in public places, appealing to his audience by tricks, storytelling, etc. **2.** any charlatan or quack. —*v.i.* **3.** to play the mountebank. [< It *montimbanco* one who climbs on a bench, equiv. to *mont(are)* (to) climb (see MOUNT[1]) + *-im-,* var. of *in* on + *banco* bench (see BANK[2])] —**moun·te·bank·er·y** (moun′tə bangk′ə rē), *n.*
—**Syn. 1.** pitchman. **2.** phony, pretender, fraud.

mount·ed (moun′tid), *adj.* **1.** seated or riding on a horse or other animal. **2.** serving on horseback, or on some special mount, as soldiers, police, etc. **3.** *Mil.* (formerly) permanently equipped with horses or vehicles for transport. Cf. **mobile** (def. 2). **4.** fixed on or in a support, backing, setting, or the like: *mounted gems.* **5.** put into position for use, as guns. [MOUNT[1] + -ED[2]]
—**Ant. 1.** afoot.

Mount′ E′phra·im (ē′frā əm), a town in SW New Jersey. 5447 (1960).

mount·er (moun′tər), *n.* one who or that which mounts. [MOUNT[1] + -ER[1]]

Mount′ Gam′bier (gam′bēr), a city in S Australia. 15,388 (1961).

Mount′ Gay′, a town in SW West Virginia. 3386 (1960).

Mount′ Gil′ead, a town in central Ohio. 2788 (1960).

Mount′ Health′y, a town in SW Ohio. 6553 (1960).

Mount′ Hol′ly, a town in S North Carolina. 4037 (1960).

Moun·tie (moun′tē), *n. Informal.* a member of the Royal Canadian Mounted Police. Also, **Mounty.** [MOUNT(ED) + -IE]

mount·ing (moun′ting), *n.* **1.** the act of one who or that which mounts. **2.** something that serves as a mount, support, setting, or the like: *a new mounting for an heirloom jewel.* [ME; see MOUNT[1], -ING[1]]

Mount′ Joy′, a town in SW Pennsylvania. 3292 (1960).

Mount′ Kis′co (kis′kō), a town in SE New York. 6805 (1960).

Mount′lake Ter′race (mount′lāk′), a town in NW Washington. 9122 (1960).

Mount′ Leb′anon, a town in SW Pennsylvania, SW of Pittsburgh. 35,361 (1960).

Mount′ McKin′ley Na′tional Park′, a national park in central Alaska, including Mounts McKinley and Foraker. 3030 sq. mi.

Mount′ Mor′ris, **1.** a town in central Michigan. 3484 (1960). **2.** a town in central New York. 3250 (1960). **3.** a town in N Illinois. 3075 (1960).

Mount′ Ol′ive, a town in central North Carolina. 4673 (1960).

Mount′ Ol′iver, a town in SW Pennsylvania. 5980 (1960).

Mount′ Penn′, a town in central Pennsylvania. 3574 (1960).

Mount′ Pleas′ant, **1.** a town in NE Texas. 8027 (1960). **2.** a town in SE Iowa. 7339 (1960). **3.** a town in SW Pennsylvania. 6107 (1960). **4.** a town in SE South Carolina. 5116 (1960). **5.** a town in central Tennessee. 2921 (1960).

Mount′ Pros′pect, a city in NE Illinois, near Chicago. 18,906 (1960).

Mount′ Pto′üs, *Class. Myth.* the site in Boeotia of an infallible oracle.

Mount Rai·nier (mount′ rā nēr′ *for 1;* mount′ rā nēr′, rə-, rā′nēr *for 2*), **1.** a town in central Maryland. 9855 (1960). **2.** See **Rainier, Mount.**

Mount′ Rai·nier′ Na′tional Park′ (rā nēr′, rə-, rā′nēr), a national park in W Washington, including Mount Rainier. 378 sq. mi.

Mount′ Rob′son Park′ (rob′sən), a national park in the Rocky Mountains of E British Columbia, Canada.

Mount′ Ster′ling, a town in central Kentucky. 5370 (1960).

Mount′ Un′ion, a town in central Pennsylvania. 4091 (1960).

Mount′ Ver′non, **1.** the home and tomb of George Washington in NE Virginia, on the Potomac, 15 mi. below Washington, D.C. **2.** a city in SE New York, near New York City. 76,010 (1960). **3.** a city in S Illinois. 15,566 (1960). **4.** a town in NW Washington. 7921 (1960). **5.** a town in SW Indiana. 5970 (1960). **6.** a town in E Iowa. 2593 (1960).

Mount·y (moun′tē), *n., pl.* **Mount·ies.** Mountie.

mourn (mōrn, môrn), *v.i.* **1.** to feel or express sorrow or grief. **2.** to grieve or lament for the dead. **3.** to show the conventional or usual signs of sorrow over a person's death. —*v.t.* **4.** to feel or express sorrow or grief over (misfortune, loss, or anything regretted); deplore. **5.** to grieve or lament over (the dead). **6.** to utter in a sorrowful manner. [ME *mo(u)rne(n),* OE *murnan;* c. OHG *mornēn,* Icel *morna,* Goth *maurnan*] —**Syn. 1.** bewail, bemoan. See **grieve.**

mourn·er (mōr′nər, môr′-), *n.* **1.** one who mourns. **2.** one who attends a funeral as a mourning friend or relative of the deceased. **3.** (at religious revival meetings) one who professes penitence for sin, with desire for salvation. [ME; see MOURN, -ER[1]]

mourn′er's bench′, (at religious revival meetings) a bench or seat at the front of the church or room, set apart for mourners or penitent sinners seeking salvation.

Mourn′er's Kad′dish, *Judaism.* Kaddish (def. 2).

mourn·ful (mōrn′fəl, môrn′-), *adj.* **1.** having, expressing, or showing sorrow or grief; sorrowful; sad. **2.** of or pertaining to mourning for the dead. **3.** causing or attended with sorrow or mourning: *a mournful occasion.* **4.** gloomy, somber, or dreary, as in appearance or character: *mournful shadows; a mournful face.* [MOURN + -FUL] —**mourn′ful·ly,** *adv.* —**mourn′ful·ness,** *n.*

mourn·ing (mōr′ning, môr′-), *n.* **1.** the act of one who mourns; sorrowing or lamentation. **2.** the conventional manifestation of sorrow for a person's death, esp. by the wearing of black, the hanging of flags at half-mast, etc. **3.** the outward tokens of such sorrow, as black garments. —*adj.* **4.** of, pertaining to, or used in mourning. [ME (n., adj.); OE *murnung* (n.). See MOURN, -ING[1], -ING[2]] —**mourn′ing·ly,** *adv.* —**Ant. 1.** rejoicing.

mourn′ing band′, a piece of black material which is worn, esp. as a band encircling the upper arm, to indicate mourning.

Mourn′ing Becomes′ Elec′tra, a three-part tragedy (1931) by Eugene O'Neill, including *Homecoming, The Hunted,* and *The Haunted.*

mourn′ing cloak′, an anglewing butterfly, *Nymphalis antiopa,* widely distributed in Europe and North America, having velvety, dark-brown wings with purple spots and pale-yellow edges. Also called **mourn′ing cloak′ but′terfly, Camberwell beauty.**

mourn′ing dove′, a dove *Zenaidura macroura,* of North America, noted for its plaintive cooing.

mourn′ing i′ris, an iris, *Iris susiana,* of Asia Minor and Iran, having solitary, grayish flowers with a black patch and a brownish beard.

mourn′ing war′bler, a North American wood warbler, *Oporornis philadelphia,* olive-green above, yellow below, and with a gray head and throat.

mouse (*n.* mous; *v.* mouz), *n., pl.* **mice** (mīs), *v.,* **moused, mous·ing.** —*n.* **1.** any of numerous small rodents of the family *Muridae,* esp. of the genus *Mus,* introduced into the U.S. from the Old World and of wide distribution. **2.** any similar animal of another family, as *Cricetidae.* **3.** a dance of the early 1960's, derived from the twist. **4.** a small, hand-guided electronic device for positioning the cursor and executing commands in a computer program. **5.** *Slang.* See **black eye. 6.** *Slang.* a girl or woman. **7.** *Boxing Slang.* a swelling under the eye, caused by a blow or blows. —*v.t.* **8.** to hunt out, as a cat hunts out mice. **9.** *Naut.* to secure with mousing. —*v.i.* **10.** to hunt for or catch mice. **11.** to prowl about, as if in search of something: *The burglar moused about for valuables.* **12.** to seek or search stealthily or watchfully, as if for prey. [ME *mous,* OE *mūs* (pl. *mȳs*); c. G *Maus,* Icel *mūs,* L *mūs,* Gk *mŷs*] —**mouse′like′,** *adj.*

House mouse, *Mus musculus* (Total length to 7 in.; tail to 3½ in.)

mouse·bird (mous′bûrd′), *n.* coly. [MOUSE + BIRD]

mouse′ deer′, chevrotain.

mouse-dun (mous′dun′), *n.* a dark brownish-gray color.

mouse-ear (mous′ēr′), *n.* any of various plants having small, hairy leaves, as the hawkweed, *Hieracium Pilosella,* the forget-me-not, *Myosotis palustris,* etc. [ME *mouse-ere.* See MOUSE, EAR[1]]

mouse′-ear chick′weed, any of several weedy, caryophyllaceous herbs of the genus *Cerastium,* as *C. vulgatum,* having small, hairy leaves and white flowers.

mouse·fish (mous′fish′), *n., pl.* (*esp. collectively*) **-fish,** (*esp. referring to two or more kinds or species*) **-fish·es.** sargassumfish. [so called from its size and habitat, which is similar to that of a field mouse]

mouse·hole (mous′hōl′), *n.* **1.** the burrow of a mouse. **2.** the entrance to a mouse's burrow. **3.** a small hole resembling this. [ME; see MOUSE, HOLE]

mouse′ opos′sum. See **murine opossum.**

mouse′ pox′, *Vet. Pathol.* ectromelia (def. 2). Also, **mouse′pox′.**

mous·er (mou′zər), *n.* **1.** an animal that catches mice: *Our cat is a good mouser.* **2.** one who or that which seeks or prowls, as if for prey. [ME; see MOUSE, -ER[1]]

mouse·tail (mous′tāl′), *n.* any ranunculaceous plant of the genus *Myosurus,* esp. *M. minimus,* the flowers of which have a taillike torus. [MOUSE + TAIL[1]]

mouse·trap (mous′trap′), *n., v.,* **-trapped, -trap·ping.** —*n.* **1.** a trap for mice, usually consisting of a rectangular wooden base on which a metal spring is mounted. **2.** Also called **trap, trap play.** *Football.* a play in which a defensive player, usually a guard or tackle, is allowed by the team on offense to cross the line of scrimmage into the backfield and is then blocked out from the side, thereby letting the ball-carrier run through the opening in the line. —*v.t.* **3.** *Football.* to use this play against (a defensive player): *They mousetrapped the left guard and gained 18 yards.* [MOUSE + TRAP[1]]

mous·ey (mou′sē, -zē), *adj.,* **mous·i·er, mous·i·est.** mousy. —**mous′i·ly,** *adv.* —**mous′i·ness,** *n.*

mous·ing (mou′zing), *n.* *Naut.* a wrapping of several turns of small stuff around the shank end of a hook. [MOUSE + -ING[1]]

mous·que·taire (mōōs′kə târ′), *n.* musketeer. [< F]

mousse (mōōs), *n.* *Cookery.* **1.** a sweetened preparation with whipped cream as a base, often stabilized with gelatin and chilled in a mold: *chocolate mousse.* **2.** a similar preparation, unsweetened and containing meat, vegetables, or fish: *salmon mousse.* [< F: moss, froth < Gmc; see MOSS]

mousse·line (mōōs lēn′), *n.* **1.** Also called **chantilly.** hollandaise sauce mixed with whipped cream. **2.** any prepared dish made light and fluffy or airy, as by the mixing in of whipped cream or beaten egg whites. —*adj.* **3.** (of food) prepared or served with whipped cream. [appar. MOUSSE + *-line* taken from F *mousseline* muslin]

mousse·line (mōōs lēn′), *n.* *French.* muslin.

mousse·line de laine (mōōs lēn də len′), *French.* a thin worsted fabric, often having a printed pattern. [lit., muslin of wool]

mousse·line de soie (mōōs lēn də swä′), *French.* a thin, stiff silk or rayon fabric. [lit., muslin of silk]

Mous·sorg·sky (mə zôrg′skē; *Russ.* mōō sôrg′ski), *n.* **Mo·dest Pe·tro·vich** (mo dest′ pe trô′vich), 1839–81, Russian composer. Also, **Mous·sorg′ski, Mussorgski, Mussorgsky.**

mous·tache (mə stash′, mus′tash), *n.* mustache. —**mous·tached′,** *adj.*

mous′tache cup′. See **mustache cup.**

Mous·te·ri·an (mōō stēr′ē ən), *adj.* *Anthropol.* pertaining to Paleolithic human relics having the workmanship, finish, and character of the flint scrapers found in the sands of Moustier, France. Also, **Mous·tie′ri·an.** [< F *moust(i)érien;* see -IAN]

mous·y (mou′sē, -zē), *adj.,* **mous·i·er, mous·i·est. 1.** resembling or suggesting a mouse, as in color, odor, etc. **2.** drab and colorless. **3.** quiet; noiseless: *a mousy tread.* **4.** infested with mice. Also, **mousey.** [MOUSE + -Y[1]] —**mous′i·ly,** *adv.* —**mous′i·ness,** *n.*

mou·tarde (mōō tard′), *n.* *French.* mustard.

mouth (*n.* mouth; *v.* mou*th*), *n., pl.* **mouths** (mou*th*z), *v.* —*n.* **1.** *Anat., Zool.* **a.** the opening through which an animal or man takes in food. **b.** the cavity containing the structures used in mastication. **c.** the structures enclosing or being within this cavity, considered as a whole. **2.** the masticating and tasting apparatus. **3.** a person or animal considered as requiring food or dependent on someone for food or for food and other necessities: *another mouth to feed.* **4.** the oral opening or cavity considered as the source of vocal utterance. **5.** utterance or expression: *to give mouth to one's thoughts.* **6.** talk, esp. loud, empty, or boastful talk, or an inclination to such talk: *That man is all mouth.* **7.** a grimace made with the lips. **8.** an opening leading out of or into any cavity or hollow place or thing: *the mouth of a cave; a bottle's mouth.* **9.** a part of a river or the like where its waters are discharged into some other body of water: *the mouth of the Nile.* **10.** the opening between the jaws of a vise or the like. **11.** the lateral hole of an organ pipe. **12.** the lateral blowhole of a flute. **13. down in the mouth,** *Informal.* having a sad countenance; depressed; disheartened: *Ever since he lost his job, he has been looking very down in the mouth.* **14. word of mouth,** speaking rather than writing; oral transmission: *The information got around by word of mouth.* —*v.t.* **15.** to utter in a sonorous or pompous manner, or with excessive mouth movements: *to mouth a speech.* **16.** to put or take into the mouth, as food. **17.** to press, rub, or chew at with the mouth or lips: *The dog mouthed the child's rubber toys.* **18.** to accustom (a horse) to the use of the bit and bridle. —*v.i.* **19.** to speak sonorously and oratorically, or with excessive mouth movement. **20.** to grimace with the lips. [ME; OE *mūth;* c. Icel *muthr, munnt,* G *Mund*] —**mouth′less,** *adj.*

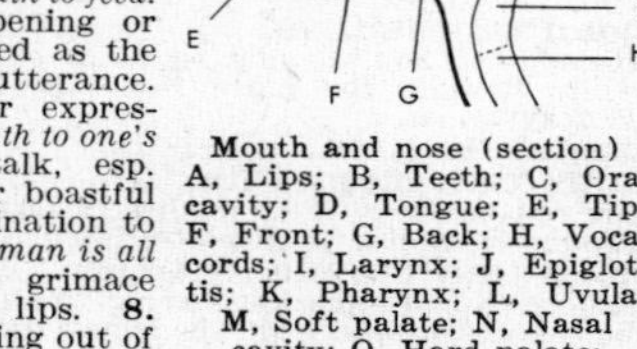

Mouth and nose (section) A, Lips; B, Teeth; C, Oral cavity; D, Tongue; E, Tip; F, Front; G, Back; H, Vocal cords; I, Larynx; J, Epiglottis; K, Pharynx; L, Uvula; M, Soft palate; N, Nasal cavity; O, Hard palate; P, Alveolar ridge

mouth·breed·er (mouth′brē′dər), *n.* any of several fishes of the genera *Tilapia* and *Haplochromis,* which hatch and care for their young in the mouth. [MOUTH + BREEDER]

mouth·ful (mouth′fōōl′), *n., pl.* **-fuls. 1.** as much as a mouth can hold. **2.** as much as is taken into the mouth at one time. **3.** a small quantity. **4.** *Slang.* a spoken remark of special significance or pertinence: *You said a mouthful!* [MOUTH + -FUL]

mouth′ or′gan, harmonica (def. 1).

mouth·part (mouth′pärt′), *n.* Usually, **mouthparts.** the appendages surrounding or associated with the mouth of arthropods. [MOUTH + PART]

mouth·piece (mouth′pēs′), *n.* **1.** a piece placed at or forming the mouth, as of a receptacle, tube, etc. **2.** a piece or part, as of an instrument, to which the mouth is applied or which is held in the mouth: *the mouthpiece of a trumpet.* **3.** the part of a bit or bridle, as for a horse, that passes through the animal's mouth. **4.** a person, newspaper, etc., that conveys the opinions or sentiments of another or others; spokesman. **5.** *Slang.* a lawyer. [MOUTH + PIECE]

mouth′-to-mouth′ meth′od (mouth′tə mouth′), a method of artificial respiration in which a person rhythmically blows air into the patient's lungs, either directly, by placing his mouth over the patient's, or through a tube.

mouth·wash (mouth′wôsh′, -wosh′), *n.* a solution, often containing germicidal, astringent, and breath-sweetening agents, used for cleansing the mouth and teeth, and for gargling. Also called **collutory, collutorium.** [MOUTH + WASH]

mouth-wa·ter·ing (mouth′wô′tər ing, -wot′ər-), *adj.* so appetizing in appearance, aroma, or description as to cause the saliva to flow.

mouth·y (mou′*th*ē, -thē), *adj.,* **mouth·i·er, mouth·i·est.** loud-mouthed; ranting; bombastic. [MOUTH + -Y[1]] —**mouth′i·ly,** *adv.* —**mouth′i·ness,** *n.*

mou·ton (mōō′ton), *n.* sheepskin that has been processed to resemble another fur, esp. seal or beaver. [< F: sheep, sheepskin; see MUTTON]

mou·ton·née (mōōt′ᵊnā′), *adj.* *Phys. Geog.* designating scattered knobs of rock rounded and smoothed by glacial action. Also, **mou′ton·néed′.** [< F: sheep-shaped, equiv. to *mouton* sheep + *-é* -EE]

mov·a·ble (mōō′və bəl), *adj.* **1.** capable of being moved; not fixed in one place, position, or posture. **2.** *Law.* (of property) **a.** not permanent in reference to place; capable of being moved without injury. **b.** personal, as distinguished from real. **3.** changing from one date to another in different years: *a movable feast.* **4.** (of type or matrices) able to be rearranged. —*n.* **5.** an article of furniture which is not fixed in place. **6.** Often, **movables.** *Law.* an article of personal property not attached to land. Also, **moveable.** [ME *mevable.* See MOVE, -ABLE] —**mov′a·ble·ness, mov′a·bil′i·ty,** *n.* —**mov′a·bly,** *adv.*

mov′a·ble-do′ sys′tem (mōō′və bəl dō′), *Music.* a system of solmization in which the syllable "do" can be transposed to the tonic of any key. Cf. **fixed-do system.**

mov′able type′, *Print.* type from which text is printed directly in which each character is on a separate piece of metal.

move (mōōv), *v.,* **moved, mov·ing,** *n.* —*v.i.* **1.** to pass from one place or position to another. **2.** to go from one place of residence to another. **3.** to advance or progress. **4.** to have a regular motion, as an implement or a machine; turn; revolve. **5.** *Com.* to be disposed of by sale, as goods in stock: *That new model is moving well.* **6.** *Informal.* to start off or leave: *It's time to be moving.* **7.** (of the bowels) to discharge or eject the feces; evacuate. **8.** to be active in a particular sphere: *to move in society.* **9.** to take action; proceed. **10.** to make a formal request, application, or proposal: *to move for a new trial.* —*v.t.* **11.** to change from one place or position to another. **12.** to set or keep in motion. **13.** to prompt, actuate, or impel to some action: *What moved you to do this?* **14.** to cause (the bowels) to discharge or eject the feces. **15.** to arouse or excite the feelings or passions of; affect with emotion (usually fol. by *to*): *to move someone to anger.* **16.** to affect with tender or compassionate emotion; touch: *The tale of tragedy moved her to tears.* **17.** *Com.* to dispose of (goods) by sale. **18.** to propose formally, as to a court or judge, or for consideration by a deliberative assembly. **19.** to submit a formal request or proposal to (a sovereign, a court, etc.). —*n.* **20.** the act or an instance of moving; movement. **21.** a change of abode or residence. **22.** an action toward an end; step: *a move in the right direction.* **23.** (in chess, checkers, etc.) a player's right or turn to make a play. **24. get a move on,** *Informal.* to begin; act; hurry: *We'd better get a move on before it rains.* **25. on the move,** *Informal.* **a.** busy; active: *on the move from morning till night.* **b.** going from place to place: *Military personnel are always on the move.* **c.** advancing; progressing: *an industry that is on the move.* [ME *move(n)* < AF *move(r)* < L *movēre*] —**move′less,** *adj.* —**move′less·ly,** *adv.* —**move′less·ness,** *n.* —**mov′er,** *n.*
—**Syn. 1.** stir, budge. See **advance. 2.** remove. **4.** spin, gyrate, rotate, operate. **11.** shift, transfer; propel. **12.** agitate. **13.** influence, induce, incite, instigate, lead. **20.** See **motion.** —**Ant. 11.** fix.

move·a·ble (mōō′və bəl), *adj., n.* movable. —**move′a·bil′i·ty,** —**move′a·ble·ness,** *n.* —**move′a·bly,** *adv.*

move·ment (mōōv′mənt), *n.* **1.** the act, process, or result of moving. **2.** a particular manner of moving. **3.** Usually, **movements.** actions or activities, as of a person or a body of persons. **4.** *Mil., Navy.* a change of position or location of troops or ships. **5.** rapid progress of events, or abundance of events or incidents. **6.** the progress of events, as in a narrative or drama. **7.** *Fine Arts.* the suggestion of motion in a work of art, either by represented gesture in figurative painting or sculpture or by the relationship of structural elements in a design or composition. **8.** a progressive development of ideas toward a particular conclusion: *He could not yet tell where the movement of his thought would take him.* **9.** a series of actions or activities directed or tending toward a particular end: *the movement toward universal suffrage.* **10.** the course, tendency, or trend of affairs in a particular

CONCISE ETYMOLOGY KEY: <, descended or derived from; >, whence; b., blend of, blended; c., cognate with; deriv., derivative; equiv., equivalent; imit., imitative; m., modification of; obl., oblique; r., replacing; s., stem; sp., spelling; trans., translation; ?, origin unknown, perhaps; *, hypothetical. See the full key inside the front cover.

field. 11. a diffusely organized or heterogeneous group of people or organizations tending toward or favoring a generalized common goal: *the antislavery movement; a mixed-bag of political movements; artistic movements.* 12. the price change in the market of some commodity or security: *a steady upward movement in the price of butter.* 13. an evacuation of the bowels. 14. the material evacuated. 15. the working parts or a distinct portion of the working parts of a mechanism, as of a watch. 16. *Music.* **a.** a principal division or section of a sonata, symphony, or the like. **b.** motion; rhythm; time; tempo. 17. *Pros.* rhythmical structure or character. [ME < MF; see MOVE, -MENT] **—Syn. 1.** See **motion. 5.** eventfulness. **—Ant. 1.** inertia, stasis.

mov·ie (mo͞o′vē), *n. Informal.* **1.** See **motion picture. 2.** motion-picture theater (often prec. by *the*): *The movie is next-door to the hardware store.* **3. movies, a.** motion pictures, as an industry (usually prec. by *the*): *The movies have had to meet the challenge of television.* **b.** motion pictures, as a genre of art or entertainment: *cowboy movies; gangster movies; experimental movies.* **c.** the exhibition of a motion picture: *an evening at the movies.* [MOV(ING PICTURE) + -IE]

mov·ie·go·er (mo͞o′vē gō′ər), *n.* a person who goes to see motion pictures often; movie fan. [MOVIE + GOER]

mov·ie·go·ing (mo͞o′vē gō′ing), *n.* **1.** the practice or act of going to see motion pictures. **—adj. 2.** characterized by going to see motion pictures often: *the moviegoing public.* [MOVIE + GOING]

mov′ie house′, *Informal.* a motion-picture theater.

mov·ie·land (mo͞o′vē land′), *n.* **1.** a place where many motion pictures are made, esp. Hollywood, California: *the moguls of movieland.* **2.** the motion-picture industry, esp. considered as including all of the people who work in it, their attitudes, way of life, etc.: *Movieland has yet to produce low-budget films that are consistently good.* [MOVIE + LAND]

mov·ie·mak·er (mo͞o′vē mā′kər), *n.* a person whose profession is producing or directing motion pictures: *the moviemakers of Hollywood.* [MOVIE + MAKER]

Mo·vi·e·o·la (mo͞o′vē ō′lə), *n. Motion Pictures, Trademark.* a projection device for a motion-picture film allowing one person to see the film through a viewer and control its motion and speed, used in film editing, preparing titles, etc.

mov·ing (mo͞o′ving), *adj.* **1.** that moves: *Any moving object attracted the dog's attention.* **2.** causing or producing motion. **3.** actuating, instigating, or impelling: *the moving spirit behind the party.* **4.** exciting the feelings or affecting the emotion, esp. touchingly or pathetically: *a moving scene; a moving story.* [ME *moeving.* See MOVE, -ING[2]] **—mov′ing·ly,** *adv.*

mov′ing pic′ture. See **motion picture.**

mov′ing side′walk, a moving surface, similar to a conveyor belt, for carrying pedestrians.

mov′ing stair′case, escalator (def. 1). Also called **mov′ing stair′way.**

mov′ing tar′get in′dicator, *Electronics.* a Doppler-radar presentation that indicates moving targets only, stationary objects reflecting signals which the system rejects. *Abbr.:* MTI

mow[1] (mō), *v.,* **mowed, mowed** or **mown, mow·ing.** **—v.t. 1.** to cut down (grass, grain, etc.) with a scythe or a machine. **2.** to cut grass, grain, etc., from: *to mow an overgrown lawn.* **3.** to destroy or kill indiscriminately or in great numbers, as men in battle. **—v.i. 4.** to cut down grass, grain, etc. [ME *mowe(n),* OE *māwan;* c. G *mähen*] **—mow′er,** *n.*

mow[2] (mou), *n.* **1.** the place in a barn where hay, sheaves of grain, etc., are stored. **2.** a heap or pile of hay or of sheaves of grain in a barn. [ME *mow(e),* OE *mūwa, mūha, mūga;* c. Icel *mūgi* swath]

mow[3] (mou, mō), *Archaic.* **—n. 1.** a wry or derisive grimace. **—v.i. 2.** to make mows, mouths, or grimaces. Also, **mowe.** [ME *mowe* < MF *moue* lip, pout < Gmc; cf. MD *mouwe* protruded lip]

mowe (mou, mō), *n., v.i.,* **mowed, mow·ing.** *Archaic.* mow[3].

mow·ing (mō′ing), *n.* **1.** the act of leveling or cutting down grass with a mowing machine or scythe. **2.** the quantity of grass cut in a specified period. [MOW[1] + -ING[1]]

mow′ing machine′, a machine for mowing or cutting down standing grass or the like.

mown (mōn), *v.* a pp. of **mow**[1].

mow·rah (mou′rə), *n.* mahua. Also, **mow′ra.**

mow′rah fat′, a yellow, semifluid fat expressed from the seeds of several trees of the genus *Madhuca,* used in making soap and as an adulterant in butter. Also called **mow′rah but′ter, mow′rah oil′.**

mox·a (mok′sə), *n.* **1.** a flammable substance or material obtained from the leaves of certain Chinese and Japanese wormwood plants, esp. *Artemisia moxa.* **2.** this substance or a similar one of cotton, wool, or the like, placed on the skin usually in the form of a cone or cylinder and ignited for use as a counter irritant. [< Jap *mokusa* for *moe kusa* burning herb]

mox·ie (mok′sē), *n. Slang.* **1.** vigor; verve; pep. **2.** courage and aggressiveness; nerve. [after *Moxie,* a trademark (name of a soft drink)]

mox·ie·ber·ry (mok′sē ber′ē), *n., pl.* **-ries.** See **creeping snowberry.** [?]

mo·yen âge (mwa ye näzh′), *French.* See **Middle Ages.**

Mo·yo·bam·ba (mô′yô bäm′bä), *n.* a city in NW Peru. 8850 (1950).

Mozamb., Mozambique.

Mo·zam·bique (mō′zəm bēk′), *n.* **1.** Formerly, **Portuguese East Africa.** a republic in SE Africa; formerly a Portuguese overseas territory. 9,900,000; 297,731 sq. mi. *Cap.:* Maputo. **2.** a seaport on an island just off the NE coast of this colony. 55,000. Portuguese, **Moçambique.**

Mo′zambique′ Chan′nel, a channel in SE Africa, between Mozambique and Madagascar. 950 mi. long; 250–550 mi. wide.

Mo′zambique′ Cur′rent. See **Agulhas Current.**

Moz·ar·ab (mō zar′əb), *n.* a Christian in Spain who, during the Muslim domination, was permitted to practice his own religion. [< Sp *mozárabe* < Ar *musta'rib* a would-be Arab]

Moz·ar·a·bic (mō zar′ə bik), *adj.* **1.** of, pertaining to, or characteristic of the Mozarabs: *Mozarabic culture.* **2.** of or pertaining to church architecture produced, esp. in northern Spain, by the Mozarabs, characterized chiefly by the horseshoe arch. [MOZARAB + -IC]

Mo·zart (mōt′särt), *n.* **Wolf·gang A·ma·de·us** (wo͝olf′gang am′ə dā′əs; *Ger.* vôlf′gäng ä′mä dā′o͝os), 1756–91, Austrian composer. **—Mo·zar′te·an, Mo·zar′ti·an,** *adj.*

moz·za·rel·la (mot′sə rel′ə, mōt′-), *n.* a mild, white, semisoft Italian cheese. [< It, equiv. to *mozza* a kind of cheese (lit., a cut; cf. *mozzare* to cut off) + *-rella* -REL]

moz·zet·ta (mō zet′ə; *It.* môt tset′tä), *n., pl.* **-tas,** *It.* **moz·zet·te** (môt tset′te). *Rom. Cath. Ch.* a short cape which covers the shoulders and can be buttoned over the breast, and to which a hood is attached, worn by the pope and by cardinals, bishops, abbots, and other dignitaries. Also, **mo·zet′ta.** [< It, aph. var. of *almozzetta,* equiv. to *almozz(a)* (cf. ML *almutia* AMICE[1]) + *-etta* -ETTE]

MP, 1. Military Police. **2.** Mounted Police.

mp, *Music.* mezzo piano.

M.P., 1. Member of Parliament. **2.** Metropolitan Police. **3.** Military Police. **4.** Mounted Police.

m.p., 1. melting point. **2.** (in prescriptions) in the manner prescribed; as directed. [< L *mōdō praescriptō*]

M.P.A., 1. Master of Professional Accounting. **2.** Master of Public Administration. **3.** Master of Public Affairs.

M.P.E., Master of Physical Education.

MPers, Middle Persian.

mpg, miles per gallon.

mph, miles per hour. Also, **m.p.h.**

M.Ph., Master of Philosophy.

M.P.H., Master of Public Health.

M.Pharm., Master of Pharmacy.

mphps, miles per hour per second.

M.P.L., Master of Patent Law.

M.P.S., Master of Personnel Service.

MR, 1. motivation research. **2.** Moral Rearmament. Also, **M.R.**

mR, milliroentgen. Also, **mr**

Mr. (mis′tər), *pl.* **Messrs.** (mes′ərz). mister: a title of respect prefixed to a man's name or position: *Mr. Lawson; Mr. President.* Also, *esp. Brit.,* **Mr**

MRA, See **Moral Re-Armament.**

M-ra·di·a·tion (em′rā′dē ā′shən), *n. Physics.* See under **M-line.**

MRBM, *Rocketry.* medium range ballistic missile.

Mr. Bones, the end man in a minstrel troupe who plays the bones. Cf. **Mr. Tambo.**

MRC, Metals Reserve Company.

Mr. Doo·ley (do͞o′lē), a humorous and satirical newspaper character created by Finley Peter Dunne as a vehicle for comment on the Spanish-American War and other events of the early part of the 20th century.

M.R.E., Master of Religious Education.

mrem, millirem; millirems.

Mr. Flood's Party, a poem (1920) by Edwin Arlington Robinson.

M roof, a roof having the form of two parallel gable roofs. Also called **trough roof.**

M.R.P., Master in Regional Planning or Master of Regional Planning.

Mrs. (mis′iz, miz′-), *pl.* **Mrs., Mmes.** (mā däm′, -dam′). a title of respect prefixed to the name of a married woman: *Mrs. Jones.* Also, *esp. Brit.,* **Mrs** [abbr. of MISTRESS]

Mrs. Dal·lo·way (dal′ə wā′), a novel (1925) by Virgina Woolf.

Mrs. Warren's Profession, a comedy (1898) by G. B. Shaw.

Mr. Tam·bo (tam′bō), the end man in a minstrel troupe who plays the tambourine. Cf. **Mr. Bones.**

MS, 1. motor ship. **2.** See **multiple sclerosis.**

Ms. (miz), *n.* a title of respect prefixed to a woman's name or position: unlike Miss or Mrs., it does not depend upon or indicate her marital status. Also, **Ms** [M(ISS + MR)S.]

mS, millisiemens.

MS., *pl.* **MSS.** manuscript.

ms., *pl.* **mss.** manuscript.

M/S, 1. months after sight. **2.** motor ship.

m/s, 1. meters per second. **2.** meters per second per second.

M.S., 1. mail steamer. **2.** Master of Science. **3.** Master in Surgery. **4.** motor ship. **5.** multiple sclerosis.

m.s., modification of the stem of.

M.S.A., Master of Science in Agriculture.

M.S.A.E., Master of Science in Aeronautical Engineering.

M.S.A.M., Master of Science in Applied Mechanics.

M.S.Arch., Master of Science in Architecture.

M.S.B.A., Master of Science in Business Administration.

M.S.B.C., Master of Science in Building Construction.

M.S.Bus., Master of Science in Business.

M.Sc., Master of Science.

M.Sc.D., Doctor of Medical Science.

M.S.C.E., Master of Science in Civil Engineering.

M.S.Ch.E., Master of Science in Chemical Engineering.

M.Sc.Med., Master of Medical Science.

M.S.Cons., Master of Science in Conservation.

M.S.C.P., Master of Science in Community Planning.

MSD, See **most significant digit.**

M.S.D., 1. Doctor of Medical Science. **2.** Master of Science in Dentistry.

M.S.Dent., Master of Science in Dentistry.

M.S.E., 1. Master of Science in Education. **2.** Master of Science in Engineering.

msec, millisecond; milliseconds.

M.S.Ed., Master of Science in Education.

M.S.E.E., Master of Science in Electrical Engineering.

M.S.E.M., 1. Master of Science in Engineering Mechanics. **2.** Master of Science in Engineering of Mines.

M.S.Ent., Master of Science in Entomology.

M-ser·ies (em′sēr′ēz), *n. Physics.* See under **M-line.**

M.S.F., Master of Science in Forestry.

M.S.F.M., Master of Science in Forest Management.

M.S.For., Master of Science in Forestry.

MSG, See **monosodium glutamate.**

M.S.Geol.E., Master of Science in Geological Engineering.

M.S.G.M., Master of Science in Government Management.

M.S.G.Mgt., Master of Science in Game Management.

Msgr., Monsignor.

M.Sgt., master sergeant.

MSH, *Biochem.* a hormone, produced in lower vertebrates by the intermediate lobe of the pituitary gland, that causes dispersal of the black pigment in melanocytes, resulting in generalized blackening of the skin. Also called **melanocyte-stimulating hormone.**

MSH, See **Mohs scale.**

M.S.H.A., Master of Science in Hospital Administration.

M.S.H.E., Master of Science in Home Economics. Also, **M.S.H.Ec.**

M-shell (em′shel′), *n. Physics.* the third shell of electrons surrounding the nucleus of an atom and containing, when filled, eighteen electrons having principal quantum number three. Cf. **K-shell, L-shell, N-shell.**

M.S.Hort., Master of Science in Horticulture.

M.S.Hyg., Master of Science in Hygiene.

M.S.I.E., Master of Science in Industrial Engineering.

M'sieur (mə syœ′), *French.* contraction of *monsieur.*

M.S.J., Master of Science in Journalism.

M.S.L., 1. Master of Science in Linguistics. **2.** mean sea level.

m.s.l., mean sea level.

M.S.M., 1. Master of Sacred Music. **2.** Master of Science in Music.

M.S.M.E., Master of Science in Mechanical Engineering.

M.S.Met.E., Master of Science in Metallurgical Engineering.

M.S.Mgt.E., Master of Science in Management Engineering.

M.S.N., Master of Science in Nursing.

M.S.Orn.Hort., Master of Science in Ornamental Horticulture.

M.S.P.E., Master of Science in Physical Education.

M.S.P.H., Master of Science in Public Health.

M.S.Phar., Master of Science in Pharmacy. Also, **M.S.Pharm.**

M.S.P.H.E., Master of Science in Public Health Engineering.

M.S.P.H.Ed., Master of Science in Public Health Education.

M.S.S., 1. Master of Social Science. **2.** Master of Social Service.

M.S.Sc., Master of Social Science.

M.S.S.E., Master of Science in Sanitary Engineering.

MST, Mountain Standard Time. Also, **m.s.t.**

M.S.T., 1. Master of Science in Teaching. **2.** Mountain Standard Time.

Ms-Th, *Chem.* mesothorium. Also, **MsTh**

M.S.W., 1. Master of Social Welfare. **2.** Master of Social Work or Master in Social Work.

MT, 1. mechanical translation. **2.** megaton; megatons.

Mt., 1. mount: *Mt. Rainier.* **2.** mountain. Also, **mt.**

M.T., 1. metric ton. **2.** Mountain time.

m.t., Mountain time.

m.t.d., (in prescriptions) send such doses. [< L *mitte tālēs dosēs*]

mtg., 1. meeting. **2.** mortgage.

mtge., mortgage.

M.Th., Master of Theology.

MTI, See **moving target indicator.**

mtn, mountain.

MTO, 1. *Mil.* (in World War II) Mediterranean Theater of Operations. **2.** motor transport officer.

Mt. Rev., Most Reverend.

Mts., mountains. Also, **mts.**

M.TV., Master of Television.

M·twa·ra (em twär′ə), *n.* a seaport in SE Tanzania. 10,459 (1957).

mu (myo͞o, mo͞o), *n.* **1.** the 12th letter of the Greek alphabet (M, μ). **2.** the consonant sound represented by this letter. [< Gk]

Mu·ba·rak (mo͞o bär′ək), *n.* **(Mohammed) Hos·ni** (hoz′nē, hos′-), born 1928, Egyptian political leader: president since 1981.

muc-, var. of **muco-** before a vowel: *mucin.*

MU car, *Railroads.* See **multiple-unit car.**

mu·ced·i·nous (myo͞o sed′ənəs), *adj.* of or resembling mold or mildew. [< L *mūcēdin-* mucus (s. of *mūcēdō;* in NL, used in name of family of mold fungi) + -OUS]

much (much), *adj.,* **more, most,** *n., adv.,* **more, most.** **—adj. 1.** being of great quantity, amount, measure, or degree. **—n. 2.** a great quantity or amount; a great deal: *Much of his work has validity.* **3.** a great, important, or notable thing or matter: *The house is not much to look at.* **4. make much of, a.** to treat, represent, or consider as of great importance: *to make much of trivial matters.* **b.** to treat with great consideration; show fondness for; flatter: *She was used to being made much of, and could not adjust to the impartial competition of the business world.* **—adv. 5.** to a great extent or degree; greatly; far: *to talk too much; much pleased.* **6.** nearly, approximately, or about: *This is much like the others.* [ME *muche, moche,* apocopated var. of *muchel, mochel,* OE *mycel;* r. ME *miche(l),* OE *micel* great, much, c. Icel *mikill,* Goth *mikils,* Gk *mégalos* great]

Much′ Ado′ About Noth′ing, a comedy (1598?) by Shakespeare.

much·ness (much′nis), *n. Archaic.* greatness, as in quantity, measure, or degree. [ME *mochenesse.* See MUCH, -NESS]

muci-, var. of **muco-:** *muciferous.*

mu·cic (myo͞o′sik), *adj. Chem.* of or derived from mucic acid. [MUC- + -IC]

mu′cic ac′id, *Chem.* a white, crystalline, water-soluble powder, $HOOC(CHOH)_4COOH$, obtained by the oxidation of certain gums, milk sugar, or galactose, and used chiefly in organic synthesis. Also called **saccharolactic acid, tetrahydroxyadipic acid.**

mu·cid (myo͞o′sid), *adj. Rare.* moldy; musty. [< L *mūcid(us)* musty, moldy, equiv. to *mūc-* (see MUCOR) + *-idus* -ID[4]] —**mu′cid·ness,** *n.*

mu·cif·er·ous (myo͞o sif′ər əs), *adj.* secreting or containing mucus. Also, **mu·cig·en·ous** (myo͞o sij′ə nəs), **muciparous.** [MUC- + -I- + -FEROUS]

mu·ci·gen (myo͞o′si jin, -jen′), *n. Biochem.* any of various substances that can be converted by the body into mucin. [MUC- + -I- + -GEN] —**mu·ci·ge·nous** (myo͞o sij′ə nəs), *adj.*

mu·ci·lage (myo͞o′sə lij), *n.* **1.** any of various preparations of gum, glue, or the like, for causing adhesion. **2.** any of various gummy secretions or gelatinous substances present in plants. [ME *muscilage* < LL *mūcilāgō* a musty juice, akin to *mūcēre* to be musty. See MUCOR]

mu·ci·lag·i·nous (myo͞o′sə laj′ə nəs), *adj.* **1.** of, pertaining to, or secreting mucilage. **2.** of the nature of or resembling mucilage; moist, soft, and viscid. [< LL *mūcilāgin-* (s. of *mūcilāgō*) MUCILAGE + -OUS] —**mu′ci·lag′i·nous·ly,** *adv.*

mu·cin (myo͞o′sin), *n. Biochem.* any of a group of nitrogenous substances found in mucous secretions, varying in composition according to their source. [MUC- + -IN[2]] —**mu′cin·oid′,** *adj.* —**mu·ci·nous** (myo͞o′sə-nəs), *adj.*

mu·cip·a·rous (myo͞o sip′ər əs), *adj.* muciferous. [MUC- + -I- + -PAROUS]

muck (muk), *n.* **1.** farmyard dung, decaying vegetable matter, etc., in a moist state; manure. **2.** a highly organic dark or black soil, less than 50 percent combustible, often used as a manure. **3.** filth; dirt. **4.** *Chiefly Brit. Informal.* something of no value; trash. **5.** (esp. in mining) earth, rock, or other useless matter to be removed in order to get out the mineral or other substances sought. —*v.t.* **6.** to manure. **7.** to make dirty; soil. **8.** to remove muck from. **9.** *Brit. Slang.* **a.** to ruin; bungle. **b.** to put into a state of complete confusion. —*v.i.* **10. muck about,** *Brit. Slang.* to idle; waste time; loiter. [ME *muc, muk* < Scand; cf. Icel *myki* cow dung]

muck′ bar′, *Metall.* a rough bar of wrought iron, rolled from blooms of iron extracted from a puddling furnace.

muck·er (muk′ər), *n.* **1.** *Brit. Slang.* **a.** a vulgar, ill-bred person. **b.** one who often does or says the wrong thing; bungler. **2.** (esp. in mining) one who removes muck. [MUCK + -ER[1]] —**muck′er·ish,** *adj.* —**muck′-er·ism,** *n.*

muck·ing (muk′ing), *adj., adv. Brit. Slang.* damned. [MUCK + -ING[2]]

muck·le[1] (muk′əl), *n. U.S. Dial.* a wooden cudgel used to kill fish. [?]

muck·le[2] (muk′əl), *adj. Brit. Dial.* mickle. [ME, var. of *muchel;* see MUCH]

muck·luck (muk′luk), *n.* mukluk.

muck·rake (muk′rāk′), *v.i.,* **-raked, -rak·ing.** to search for and expose real or alleged corruption, scandal, or the like, esp. in politics. [obs. *muck rake* a rake for use on muck or dung. See MUCK, RAKE[1]] —**muck′-rak′er,** *n.*

muck·worm (muk′wûrm′), *n.* **1.** (not in technical use) the larva of any of several insects, as the dung beetle, which lives in or beneath manure. **2.** a miser. [MUCK + WORM]

muck·y (muk′ē), *adj.,* **muck·i·er, muck·i·est. 1.** of or like muck. **2.** filthy; dirty. **3.** *Brit. Informal.* **a.** obscene: *a mucky story.* **b.** nasty; mean: *a mucky trick.* **c.** (of weather) oppressively humid. [MUCK + -Y[1]]

muc·luc (muk′luk), *n.* mukluk.

muco-, a combining form representing **mucus** or **mucous:** *mucopurulent.* Also, **muc-, muci-.**

mu·coid (myo͞o′koid), *n.* **1.** *Biochem.* any of a group of substances resembling the mucins, occurring in connective tissue, cysts, etc. —*adj.* **2.** Also, **mu·coi·dal** (myo͞o koid′əl). resembling mucus. [MUC(IN) + -OID]

mu·co·pro·tein (myo͞o′kə prō′tēn, -tē in), *n. Biochem.* a protein that yields carbohydrate as well as amino acids on hydrolysis. [MUCO- + PROTEIN]

mu·co·pu·ru·lent (myo͞o′kə pyo͝or′yə lənt, -pyo͝or′-ə-), *adj. Med.* containing or composed of mucus and pus. [MUCO- + PURULENT]

mu·cor (myo͞o′kər), *n.* any phycomycetous fungus of the genus *Mucor,* that forms a furry coating on foodstuffs and dead and decaying vegetable matter. [< NL, L: moldiness, equiv. to *mūc(ēre)* (to) be moldy or musty + *-or* -OR[1]]

mu·co·sa (myo͞o kō′sə), *n., pl.* **-sae** (-sē). *Anat.* See **mucous membrane.** [< NL, n. use of fem. of L *mūcōsus* MUCOUS] —**mu·co′sal,** *adj.*

mu·cous (myo͞o′kəs), *adj.* **1.** pertaining to, consisting of, or resembling mucus. **2.** containing or secreting mucus. [< L *mūcōs(us)* slimy, mucous, equiv. to *mūc(us)* snot + *-ōsus* -OUS] —**mu·cos·i·ty** (myo͞o kos′-i tē), *n.*

mu′cous mem′brane, a lubricating membrane lining an internal surface or an organ, such as the alimentary, respiratory, and genitourinary canals.

mu·co·vis·ci·do·sis (myo͞o′kō vis′i dō′sis), *n. Pathol.* See **cystic fibrosis.** Also, **mu·co·vis·coi·do·sis** (myo͞o′kō vis′koi dō′sis). [< NL; see MUCO-, VISCID, -OSIS]

mu·cro (myo͞o′krō), *n., pl.* **mu·cro·nes** (myo͞o krō′nēz). *Bot., Zool.* a short point projecting abruptly, as at the end of a leaf. [< L: sharp point]

mu·cro·nate (myo͞o′krō nit, -nāt′), *adj. Bot., Zool.* having an abruptly projecting point, as a feather, leaf, etc. Also, **mu′cro·nat′ed.** [< L *mūcrōnāt(us)* pointed, equiv. to *mūcrōn-* (s. of *mūcrō*) point, edge + *-ātus* -ATE[1]] —**mu′cro·na′tion,** *n.*

mu·cus (myo͞o′kəs), *n.* a viscid secretion of the mucous membranes. [< L: snot; akin to Gk *myktḗr* nose, *mŷxa* slime. See MUCID]

mud (mud), *n., v.,* **mud·ded, mud·ding.** —*n.* **1.** wet, soft earth or earthy matter, as on the ground after rain, at the bottom of a pond, or among the discharges from a volcano; mire. —*v.t.* **2.** to cover or smear with mud: *to mud pedestrians with careless driving; to mud the walls of a hut.* **3.** to stir up the mud or sediment in: *waders mudding the clear water; to mud wine by rough handling.* —*v.i.* **4.** to hide in or burrow into mud: *a fish that will mud when attacked.* [ME *mudde, mode* < MLG *mudde.* See MOTHER[2]]

mud′ berth′, *Naut.* a mooring place in which a vessel rests on the bottom at low tide.

mud·cap (mud′kap′), *v.t.,* **-capped, -cap·ping.** to blast (a rock) with an explosive attached to it with a capping of clay. [MUD + CAP]

mud·cat (mud′kat′), *n.* See **flathead catfish.** [MUD + CAT[1]]

mud′ daub′er, any of several wasps of the family *Sphecidae* that build a nest of mud cells and provision it with spiders or insects.

mud·der (mud′ər), *n.* a race horse able to perform well on a track soaked with water or covered with mud. [MUD + -ER[1]]

mud·dle (mud′əl), *v.,* **-dled, -dling,** *n.* —*v.t.* **1.** to mix up in a confused or bungling manner; jumble. **2.** to cause to become mentally confused. **3.** to cause to become confused or stupid with or as if with intoxicating drink. **4.** to mix or stir (a cocktail, chocolate, etc.). **5.** to make muddy or turbid, as water. **6.** *Ceram.* to smooth (clay) by rubbing it on glass. —*v.i.* **7. muddle through,** to come to a successful conclusion without much purposeful effort or planned direction: *to muddle through college.* —*n.* **8.** state or condition of being muddled, esp. a confused mental state. **9.** a confused, disordered, or embarrassing state of affairs; a mess. [MUD + -LE; c. MD *moddelen* to muddy] —**mud′dled·ness, mud′dle·ment,** *n.* —**mud′dling·ly,** *adv.*

mud·dle·head (mud′əl hed′), *n. Informal.* a stupid person; blunderer. [MUDDLE + HEAD]

mud·dle·head·ed (mud′əl hed′id), *adj.* confused in one's thinking; blundering: *a muddleheaded assertion.* [MUDDLE + HEADED]

mud·dler (mud′lər), *n.* **1.** a stick for stirring drinks. **2.** one who muddles or muddles through. **3.** a miller's-thumb. [MUDDLE + -ER[1]]

mud′ drum′, a cylindrical drum for collecting the sediment that settles to the bottom of a boiler.

mud·dy (mud′ē), *adj.,* **-di·er, -di·est,** *v.,* **-died, -dy·ing.** —*adj.* **1.** abounding in or covered with mud. **2.** not clear or pure, as color. **3.** dull, as the complexion. **4.** not clear mentally. **5.** obscure or vague, as thought, expression, literary style, etc. **6.** *Horseracing.* noting the condition of a track after a heavy, continuous rainfall has ceased and been completely absorbed into the surface leaving it the consistency of thick mud. —*v.t.* **7.** to make muddy; soil with mud. **8.** to make turbid. **9.** to render confused or obscure. —*v.i.* **10.** to become muddy. [late ME *moddy.* See MUD, -Y[1]] —**mud′di·ly,** *adv.* —**mud′di·ness,** *n.*

mud·fat (mud′fat′), *adj. Brit., Australian.* (of animals) very fat. [from Australian phrase *as fat as mud*]

Mu·dé·jar (*Sp.* mo͞o the′här), *n., pl.* **-ja·res** (-hä-res′), *adj.* —*n.* **1.** a Christianized Moor living in medieval Spain. **2.** a Muslim living and working in northern or Christian Spain. —*adj.* **3.** of or pertaining to Spanish Christian architecture of the 11th through 16th centuries produced under Moorish influence. [< Sp < Ar *muddajjan* permitted to stay]

mud·fish (mud′fish′), *n., pl.* (*esp. collectively*) **-fish,** (*esp. referring to two or more kinds or species*) **-fish·es.** any of various fishes that live in muddy waters, as the bowfin or mummichog. [MUD + FISH]

mud′ flat′, **1.** a mud-covered, gently sloping tract of land, alternately covered or left bare by tidal waters. **2.** the muddy, nearly level bed of a dry lake.

mud·guard (mud′gärd′), *n.* a guard or shield so placed as to protect riders or passengers from mud thrown by the wheel of a bicycle, automobile, or the like. [MUD + GUARD]

mud′ hen′, any of various marsh-inhabiting birds, esp. the American coot.

mud·hole (mud′hōl′), *n.* a place in which mud collects, as a hole in a road or a low place in a field. [MUD + HOLE]

mud·lark (mud′lärk′), *n.* **1.** *Chiefly Brit.* one who gains a livelihood by searching for iron, coal, old ropes, etc., in mud or low tide. **2.** a gutter urchin; street Arab. **3.** either of two black and white birds, *Grallina cyanoleuca,* of Australia, or *G. bruijni,* of New Guinea, that builds a large, mud nest. —*v.i.* **4.** to grub or play in mud. [MUD + LARK[1]]

mud′ lump′, a small, cone-shaped mound of clay or silt on the bank of a delta.

mud·min·now (mud′min′ō), *n., pl.* (*esp. collectively*) **-now,** (*esp. referring to two or more kinds or species*) **-nows.** any of several small, carnivorous fishes of the genus *Umbra,* found in muddy streams and pools. [MUD + MINNOW]

mud′ pi′lot, *Naut.* **1.** one who navigates by observing the depth of water as shown by its color. **2.** a river pilot.

Mudpuppy, *Necturus maculosus* **(Length 8 in.)**

mud′ pot′, *Geol.* a spring or pit filled with hot mud, usually boiling.

mud·pup·py (mud′pup′ē), *n., pl.* **-pies. 1.** any of several large, aquatic salamanders of the genus *Necturus,* of eastern North America, having bushy, red gills and well-developed limbs. **2.** any of several North American salamanders of the genus *Ambystoma.* [MUD + PUPPY]

mu·dra (mə drä′), *n.* any of a series of subtle hand gestures in India's classical dancing, chiefly to represent certain feelings. [< Skt *mudrā* sign]

mud′ room′, a vestibule in a house, in which wet and muddy clothes or footwear are removed.

mud·sill (mud′sil′), *n.* the lowest sill of a structure, usually placed in or on the ground. Also called **footplate.** [MUD + SILL]

Mudskipper, *Periophthalmus barbarus* **(Length 5½ in.)**

mud·skip·per (mud′skip′ər), *n.* any of several tropical gobies of the genera *Periophthalmus* and *Boleophthalmus,* found from Africa to the East Indies and Japan, noted for the habit of remaining out of water on mud flats for certain periods, and jumping about when disturbed. Also called **mudspringer.** [MUD + SKIPPER[2]]

mud·sling·er (mud′sling′ər), *n.* one who practices mudslinging. [MUD + SLINGER]

mud·sling·ing (mud′sling′ing), *n.* an attempt to discredit one's competitor, opponent, etc., by malicious personal attacks rather than by discussion of legitimate issues, as in political campaigning. [MUD + SLINGING]

mud·spring·er (mud′spring′ər), *n.* mudskipper. [MUD + SPRINGER]

mud·stone (mud′stōn′), *n.* a clayey rock of nearly uniform texture throughout, with little or no lamination. [MUD + STONE]

mud·suck·er (mud′suk′ər), *n.* a goby, *Gillichthys mirabilis,* of California, used as bait. [MUD + SUCKER]

mud′ tur′tle, any of several small, fresh-water turtles of the family *Kinosternidae,* of North, Central, and South America, as the dark-brown *Kinosternum subrubrum,* of the eastern U.S.

mud′ volca′no, a vent in the earth's surface through which escaping gas and vapor issue causing mud to boil and occasionally to overflow, forming a conical mound around the vent.

mud′ wasp′, any of several wasps, as the mud dauber, that construct a nest of mud.

Muel·ler (myo͞o′lər, mul′ər, mil′-), *n.* **Paul,** 1899–1965 Swiss chemist: Nobel prize for medicine 1948.

muen·ster (mo͝on′stər, mun′-, min′-, myn′-), *n.* a white, semisoft, mild cheese made from whole milk. [after *Muenster* in France (Haut Rhin)]

mu·ez·zin (myo͞o ez′in, mo͞o-), *n.* (in Islamic communities) the crier who, from a minaret or other part of a mosque, at stated hours five times daily, intones aloud the call summoning the faithful to prayer. [< Ar *mu'adhdhin*]

muff (muf), *n.* **1.** a thick, tubular case for the hands, covered with fur or other material, used by women and girls for warmth and as a handbag. **2.** a tuft of feathers on the sides of the head of certain fowls. **3.** *Sports.* a failure to catch a ball that may reasonably be expected to be caught. **4.** any failure. —*v.t.* **5.** *Informal.* to bungle; handle clumsily: *He muffed a good opportunity for a big contract.* **6.** *Sports.* to fail to catch (a ball that may reasonably be expected to be caught); fumble. —*v.i.* **7.** *Informal.* to bungle; perform clumsily. [< D *mof,* earlier *moffel* mitten, muff < MF *moufle* mitten] —**muff′y,** *adj.*

muf·fin (muf′in), *n.* **1.** a small, round bread made with wheat flour, corn meal, or the like, and eaten with butter. **2.** See **English muffin.** [?]

muf·fin·eer (muf′ə nēr′), *n.* a caster for sprinkling sugar or other condiments on muffins. [MUFFIN + -EER]

muf′fin stand′, a small stand having several tiers for holding plates and a tea service.

muf·fle (muf′əl), *v.,* **-fled, -fling,** *n.* —*v.t.* **1.** to wrap or envelop in a cloak, shawl, coat, etc., esp. to keep warm or protect the face and neck (often fol. by *up*): *Muffle up the children before they go out.* **2.** to wrap with something to deaden or prevent sound: *to muffle drums.* **3.** to deaden (sound) by wrappings or other means. **4.** to alter temporarily the profile of (a plaster mold) in order to run a base coat of plaster that will later be covered by a finish coat having the true profile. **5.** to wrap (an oar) with soft material in way of the thole or oarlock to silence the rumbling made by ordinary rowing. **6.** to wrap (oneself) in a garment or other covering: *muffled in silk.* —*n.* **7.** something that muffles. **8.** muffled sound. **9.** an oven or arched chamber in a furnace or kiln, used for heating substances without direct contact with the fire. **10.** the thick, bare part of the upper lip and nose of ruminants and rodents. [ME *mufle(n),* prob. < MF; cf. MF *emmoufle* wrapped up]

muf′fle col′or, *Ceram.* a color fired onto an object in a muffle kiln.

muf·fler (muf′lər), *n.* **1.** a heavy neck scarf. **2.** any of various devices for deadening sound, as the sound of escaping gases of an internal-combustion engine. **3.** anything used for muffling. **4.** *Armor.* a mittenlike glove worn with a mail hauberk. [MUFFLE + -ER[1]]

muf·ti (muf′tē), *n., pl.* **-tis. 1.** civilian dress, as opposed to military or other uniform, or as worn by one who usually wears a uniform. **2.** a Muslim legal adviser consulted in applying the religious law. **3.** (in the Ottoman Empire) a deputy of the chief Muslim legal advisor to the Sultan. **4.** (*cap.*) See **Grand Mufti.** [< Ar: lit., one who delivers a judgment, orig. a Muslim legal adviser; def. 1 sense arises from the legal adviser being a civil official]

mug (mug), *n., v.,* **mugged, mug·ging.** —*n.* **1.** a drinking cup, usually cylindrical in shape, having a handle, and often of a heavy substance, as earthenware. **2.** the quantity it holds. **3.** *Slang.* **a.** the face. **b.** the mouth. **c.** an exaggerated facial expression; a grimace, as in acting. **4.** *Slang.* a thug; ruffian. —*v.t.* **5.** *Slang.* to photograph (a person), esp. in compliance with an official or legal requirement. **6.** to assault (a victim), esp. by attacking from the rear and locking the forearm around the neck in a throttling manner, usually with intent to rob. —*v.i.* **7.** *Slang.* to grimace voluntarily; assume an exaggerated facial expression, as in acting. [prob. < Scand; cf. Sw *mugg,* Norw, D *mugge* drinking cup]

mug·ger[1] (mug′ər), *n.* one who mugs, esp. one who assaults a person in order to rob him. [MUG + -ER[1]]

mug·ger[2] (mug′ər), *n.* a broad-snouted crocodile, *Crocodylus palustris,* of southern Asia, that grows to a length of about 12 feet. Also, **mug′gar, mug′gur.** [< Hindi *magar*]

mug·gins (mug′inz), *n.* **1.** a convention in the card game of cribbage in which a player scores points overlooked by an opponent. **2.** a game of dominoes, in which any player, if he can make the sum of two ends of the line equal five or a multiple of five, adds the number so made to his score. **3.** *Brit. Slang.* a fool. [prob. special use of proper name]

mug·gy (mug′ē), *adj.,* **-gi·er, -gi·est.** (of the atmosphere, weather, etc.) humid and oppressive; damp and close. [*mug* to drizzle (n. and v.) (< Scand; cf. Icel *mugga* mist, drizzle) + -Y[1]] —**mug′gi·ly,** *adv.* —**mug′gi·ness,** *n.*
—**Ant.** dry.

mug·wort (mug′wûrt′), *n.* any of several wormwoods, esp. *Artemisia vulgaris.* [ME; OE *mucgwyrt.* See MIDGE, WORT[2]]

mug·wump (mug′wump′), *n. U.S.* **1.** a Republican who refused to support the party nominee, James G. Blaine, in the presidential campaign of 1884. **2.** a person who acts as an independent or affects superiority, esp. in politics. **3.** a person who is unable to make up his mind on an issue, esp. in politics; one who is neutral on a controversial issue. [< Algonquian (Massachusetts): lit., great man] —**mug′wump′er·y, mug′wump′ism,** *n.* —**mug′wump′i·an,** *adj.* —**mug′wump′ish,** *adj.*

Mu·ha·ji·run (mo͝o hä′jə ro͞on′, -hä′jə ro͞on′), *n.pl., sing.* **Mu·ha·jir** (mo͝o hä′jir). those who accompanied Muhammad on the Hegira. [< Ar *muhājirūna*]

Mu·ham·mad (mo͝o ham′əd), *n.* **1.** A.D. 570–632, Arab prophet: founder of Islam. **2.** a boy's given name. Also, **Mohammed, Mahomet.**

Muham′mad Ah′med (äm′ad), ("*the Mahdi*"), 1844–1885, Muslim leader in Anglo-Egyptian Sudan.

Muham′mad Ali′. See **Ali, Muhammad.**

Mu·ham·mad·an (mo͝o ham′i dən), *n., adj.* Muslim. Also, **Mu·ham′med·an.** [MUHAMMAD + -AN]

Mu·ham·mad Gho·ri (mo͝o ham′əd gō rē′, gô-). See **Mohammed of Ghor.**

Muham′mad Ri·za′ Pah·la·vi′ (ri zä′ pä lä vē′, pal′ə vē), 1919–80, shah of Iran 1941–79: in exile after 1979. Also, **Muham′mad Re·za′ Shah′ Pahlavi′, Muham′mad Re·za′ Shah′ Pah·le·vi′** (pä le vē′, pal′ə vē).

Mu·har·ram (mo͞o har′əm), *n.* Moharram.

Mühl·bach (myl′bäkh), *n.* **Lu·i·se** (lo͞o ē′zə), (*Klara Müller Mundt*), 1814–73, German novelist.

Muh·len·berg (myo͞o′lən bûrg′), *n.* **1. Frederick Augustus Conrad,** 1750–1801, U.S. clergyman and statesman: first Speaker of the House 1789–91, 1793–95. **2.** his father, **Henry Mel·chi·or** (mel′kē ôr′), 1711–87, American Lutheran clergyman, born in Germany.

Muir (myo͝or), *n.* **John,** 1838–1914, U.S. naturalist, explorer, and writer.

Muir′ Gla′cier, a glacier in SE Alaska, flowing SE from Mt. Fairweather into Glacier Bay. 350 sq. mi.

mu·jik (mo͞o zhik′, mo͞o′zhik), *n.* muzhik.

muj·ta·hid (mo͞oj tä′hid), *n. Islam.* a person who interprets traditions in his own way. [< Ar: lit., one who exerts himself]

mu·ka·de (mo͞o kä′dä; *Jap.* mo͝o kä′de), *n., pl.* **-de.** the motif of a centipede, often used in the decoration of Japanese arms and armor. [< Jap]

Muk·den (mo͝ok′den′, mo͞ok′-), *n.* a city in S Manchuria, in NE China: former capital of Manchuria; battle 1905. 2,411,000 (est. 1957). Also, **Moukden.** Also called **Fengtien, Shenyang.**

muk·luk (muk′luk), *n.* **1.** a soft boot worn by Eskimos, often lined with fur and usually made of sealskin or reindeer skin. **2.** a similar boot with a soft sole, usually worn for lounging. Also, **mucluc, muckluck.** [< Eskimo *muklok* big seal]

muk·ti (mo͝ok′tē), *n. Hinduism.* moksha. [< Skt]

mu·lat·to (mə lat′ō, myo͞o-), *n., pl.* **-toes,** *adj.* —*n.* **1.** the offspring of one white parent and one Negro parent. **2.** a person whose racial ancestry is mixed Negro and Caucasian, esp. one with light-brown pigmentation of the skin. —*adj.* **3.** of a light-brown color, as resembling the skin of a mulatto. [< Sp *mulato* young mule, equiv. to *mul(o)* MULE[1] + *-ato* < ?]

mul·ber·ry (mul′ber′ē, -bə rē), *n., pl.* **-ries. 1.** the edible, berrylike collective fruit of any tree of the genus *Morus.* **2.** a tree of this genus, as *M. rubra* (**red mulberry** or **American mulberry**), bearing dark-purple fruit, *M. nigra* (**black mulberry**), bearing dark-colored fruit, and *M. alba* (**white mulberry**), bearing nearly white fruit and having leaves used as food for silkworms. [ME *mulberie,* dissimilated var. of *murberie,* OE *mōrberie,* equiv. to *mōr-* (< L *mōrum* mulberry) + *berie* BERRY]

Mul·ber·ry (mul′ber′ē), *n.* **1.** a town in central Florida. 2922 (1960). **2.** a town in central California. 2643 (1960).

mulch (mulch), *Hort.* —*n.* **1.** a covering, as of straw, leaves, manure, etc., spread or left on the ground around plants to prevent excessive evaporation or erosion, enrich the soil, etc. —*v.t.* **2.** to cover with mulch. [n. use of obs. *mulch* (adj.), ME *molsh* soft, OE *myl(i)sc* mellow; c. dial. G *molsch* soft, overripe]

Mul·ci·ber (mul′sə bər), *n.* an ancient Roman epithet of Vulcan, meaning "the Melter."

mulct (mulkt), *n.* **1.** a fine; penalty. —*v.t.* **2.** to punish (a person) by fine or forfeiture. **3.** to obtain (money or the like) by fraud, extortion, etc. **4.** to deprive (someone) of something, as by fraud. [< L *mulct(a)* a fine]

mule[1] (myo͞ol), *n.* **1.** the offspring of a male donkey and a mare, valued as a work animal. **2.** any hybrid between the donkey and the horse. **3.** *Informal.* a stubborn person. **4.** *Biol.* a hybrid, esp. a hybrid between the canary and some other finch. **5.** a machine for spinning cotton or other fibers into yarn and winding the yarn on spindles. **6.** *Naut.* a large triangular staysail set between two masts and having its clew set well aft. **7.** *Numis.* a hybrid coin having the obverse of one issue and the reverse of the succeeding issue, or vice versa. **8.** a dance, deriving from the twist, in which the dancer swings his hips, kicks his feet, and flaps his hands above his head. [ME < OF < L *mūla* she-mule; r. OE *mūl* < L *mūlus*]

Mule,
Equus asinus x caballus
(5 ft. high at shoulder)

mule[2] (myo͞ol), *n.* a slipper that leaves the heel exposed. [< MF < L *mulleus* red shoe]

mule′ chest′, a low chest with drawers, mounted on a low frame.

mule′ deer′, a deer, *Odocoileus hemionus,* of western North America, having large ears.

mule-fat (myo͞ol′fat′), *n.* a shrub, *Baccharis viminea,* of California, having willowlike leaves and clustered flowers, growing in riverbeds. [so called from its being a source of food for mule deer]

Mule·shoe (myo͞ol′sho͞o′), *n.* a town in NW Texas. 3871 (1960).

mule′ skin′ner, *Informal.* a muleteer.

mule′ spin′ning, a process of spinning that produces extremely fine yarn by drawing and twisting the roving, and winding the resultant yarn onto a bobbin or spindle in the form of a cop. Cf. **ring spinning.**

Mule deer
(3½ ft. high at shoulder; total length 6 ft.; tail 7½ in.)

mu·le·ta (mo͞o lā′tə, -let′ə), *n.* a red cloth similar to but smaller than a capa and manipulated by a stick set into one of the three holes in or near the center, for use by a matador in guiding the course of the bull's attack in the stage of the fight preparatory to the kill. [< Sp: prop, support, muleta, dim. of *mula* (fem.) MULE[1]]

mu·le·teer (myo͞o′lə tēr′), *n.* a driver of mules. [< MF *muletier,* equiv. to *mulet* (see MULE[1], -ET) + *-ier* -EER]

mul·ey (myo͞o′lē, mo͝ol′ē), *adj., n., pl.* **-leys.** —*adj.* **1.** (of cattle) hornless; polled. —*n.* **2.** any cow. Also, **mulley.** [var. of dial. *moiley* < Ir *maol* or Welsh *moel* bald, hornless + -EY[2]]

mul′ey saw′, *U.S.* a saw having a long, stiff blade that is not stretched in a gate, but whose motion is directed by clamps at each end mounted on guide rails.

Mul·ha·cén (mo͞ol′ä then′), *n.* a mountain in S Spain: the highest peak in Spain, 11,411 ft.

Mül·hau·sen (myl hou′zən), *n.* German name of **Mulhouse.**

Mül·heim an der Ruhr (myl′hīm än der ro͞or′), a city in W West Germany, near Essen. 189,900 (1963).

Mul·house (my lo͞oz′), *n.* a city in E France, near the Rhine. 110,735 (1962). German, **Mülhausen.**

mu·li·eb·ri·ty (myo͞o′lē eb′ri tē), *n.* **1.** womanly nature or qualities. **2.** womanhood. [< LL *muliēbritās* womanhood, equiv. to *muliēbri(s)* womanly (deriv. of *mulier* woman) + *-tās* -TY[2]] —**mu′li·eb′ral,** *adj.*

mu·li·er[1] (myo͞o′lē ər), *n. Old Eng. Law.* a woman or wife. [ME < AF << L: woman]

mu·li·er[2] (myo͞o′lē ər), *n. Old Eng. Law.* a legitimate child. [ME *mulire, moylere* < AF *muliere* born in wedlock, legitimate < legal L *mulierāt(us).* See MULIER[1], -ATE[1]]

mu′lier puis′ne, *Old Eng. Law.* the legitimate son of parents whose first son was illegitimate. Cf. **bastard eigne.**

mu·li·er·ty (myo͞o′lē ər tē), *n. Old Eng. Law.* state of being of legitimate birth. [< AF *muliertie.* See MULIER[2], -TY[2]]

mul·ish (myo͞o′lish), *adj.* of or like a mule, as being stubborn, obstinate, or intractable. [MULE[1] + -ISH[1]] —**mul′ish·ly,** *adv.* —**mul′ish·ness,** *n.*

Mu·li·us (myo͞o′lē əs), *n.* (in the *Iliad*) the husband of Agamede who was killed by Nestor in the Trojan War where he served as a spearman of King Augeas, his father-in-law.

mull[1] (mul), *v.i.* **1.** to study or ruminate; ponder (often fol. by *over*): *He mulled over the decision for days.* —*v.t.* **2.** to make a mess or failure of. [appar. var. of MUDDLE]

mull[2] (mul), *v.t.* to heat, sweeten, and spice for drinking, as ale, wine, etc.: *mulled cider.* [?]

mull[3] (mul), *n.* a soft, thin muslin. [earlier *mulmul* < Hindi *malmal*]

mull[4] (mul), *v.t. Foundry.* to mix (clay and sand) under a roller for use in preparing a mold. [ME *mulle(n),* deriv. of *mull, mol* powder. See MULLER[1]]

Mull (mul), *n.* an island in the Hebrides, in W Scotland. 2149 (1961); ab. 351 sq. mi.

mul·lah (mul′ə, mo͝ol′ə, mo͞o′lə), *n.* **1.** (in Islamic countries) a title of respect for one who is learned in, teaches, or expounds the sacred law. **2.** (in Turkey) a provincial judge. Also, **mul′la, mollah.** [< Pers or Urdu *mullā* < Ar *mawlā*]

mul·lein (mul′ən), *n.* **1.** Also called **candlewick, flannelleaf, velvet plant.** an Old World weed, *Verbascum Thapsus,* having coarse, woolly leaves and dense spikes of yellow flowers, introduced into North America. **2.** any plant of the same genus, or any of various similar plants. Also, **mul′len.** [ME *moleine* < AF, perh. deriv. of *mol* soft < L *moll(is)*]

mul′lein pink′. See **rose campion** (def. 1).

Mul·lens (mul′ənz), *n.* a town in S West Virginia. 3544 (1960).

mul·ler[1] (mul′ər), *n.* **1.** an implement of stone or other substance with a flat base for grinding paints, powders, etc., on a slab of stone or the like. **2.** any of various mechanical devices for grinding. [perh. formed on ME *mull* powder, OE *myl* dust; see -ER[1]]

mull·er[2] (mul′ər), *n.* **1.** one who or that which mulls. **2.** a vessel for mulling an alcoholic beverage over a fire. [MULL[2] + -ER[1]]

Mul·ler (mul′ər), *n.* **Hermann Joseph,** 1890–1967, U.S. geneticist: Nobel prize for medicine 1946.

Mül·ler (myl′ər; *Ger.* my′lər), *n.* **1. Frie·drich Max** (frē′drik maks; *Ger.* frē′drikh mäks), 1823–1900, English Sanskrit scholar and philologist born in Germany. **2. Jo·hann** (yō′hän), ("*Regiomontanus*"), 1436–76, German mathematician and astronomer. **3. Jo·han·nes Peter** (yō hä′nəs pā′tər), 1801–58, German physiologist and comparative anatomist. **4. Wilhelm** (vil′helm), 1794–1827, German poet.

mul·let[1] (mul′it), *n., pl.* (*esp. collectively*) **-let,** (*esp. referring to two or more kinds or species*) **-lets. 1.** any of several marine or fresh-water, usually gray fishes of the family *Mugilidae,* having a nearly cylindrical body. **2.** a goatfish. **3.** a sucker, esp. of the genus *Moxostoma.* **4.** any of various other fishes. [late ME *mulet* < MF < L *mull(us)* red mullet; see -ET]

mul·let[2] (mul′it), *n. Heraldry.* a starlike charge having five points unless a greater number is specified, used esp. as the cadency mark of a third son. Also, **molet.** Also called **American star, Scottish star.** [ME *molet* < OF *molette* rowel of spur]

mul·ley (mo͝ol′ē), *adj., n., pl.* **-leys.** muley.

mul·li·gan (mul′ə gən), *n.* **1.** *U.S. Slang.* a kind of stew containing meat, vegetables, etc. Also called **mul′ligan stew′. 2.** *Golf.* a shot not counted against the score, permitted in unofficial play to a player whose previous shot was poor. [special use of proper name]

mul·li·ga·taw·ny (mul′ə gə tô′nē), *n.* a curry-flavored soup of East Indian origin, often made with chicken stock. [< Tamil *milakutanni* lit., pepper water]

mul·li·grubs (mul′ə grubz′), *n.* (*construed as sing. or pl.*) *Informal.* ill temper; colic; grumpiness. [earlier *mulligrums,* appar. arbitrary alter. of MEGRIMS]

Mul·lins (mul′ənz), *n.* a town in E South Carolina. 6229 (1960).

mul·lion (mul′yən), *Archit.* —*n.* **1.** a vertical member, as of stone or wood, between the lights of a window, the panels in wainscoting, or the like. **2.** one of the radiating bars of a rose window or the like. —*v.t.* **3.** to furnish with, or to form into divisions by the use of, mullions. [metathetic var. of MONIAL]

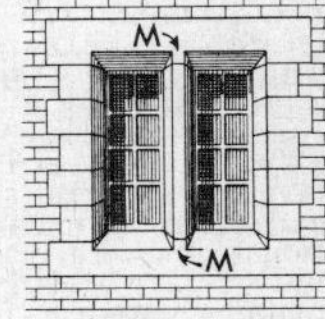

M, Mullion

mull·ite (mul′īt), *n.* a rare clay mineral, aluminum silicate, $Al_6Si_2O_{13}$, produced artificial y during various melting and firing processes. [named after MULL]

mul·lock (mul′ək), *n.* (in Australasia) refuse or rubbish, as rock, earth, or the like, from a mine; muck. [ME *mullok,* equiv. to *mul* dust, mold, rubbish (OE *myl*) + *-ok* -OCK] —**mul′lock·y,** *adj.*

Mu·lock (myo͞o′lok), *n.* **Dinah Maria.** See **Craik, Dinah Maria Mulock.**

Mul·ro·ney (mul rō′nē), *n.* **(Martin) Brian,** born 1939, Canadian political leader: prime minister since 1984.

mult-, var. of **multi-** before a vowel: *multangular.*

Mul·tan (mo͞ol tän′), *n.* a city in W Punjab, in central West Pakistan. 358,000 (est. 1961).

mul·tan·gu·lar (mul tang′gyə lər), *adj.* having many angles; polyangular. [< L *multangul(us)* many-cornered (see MULT-, ANGLE[1]) + -AR[1]]

mul·tan·gu·lum (mul tang′gyə ləm), *n., pl.* **-la** (-lə). *Anat.* either of two bones of the carpus, one (**greater multangular bone**) articulating with the metacarpal bone of the thumb or one (**lesser multangular bone**) articulating with the metacarpal bone of the forefinger. [< NL: polygon. See MULTANGULAR]

multi-, an element of Latin origin meaning "many," "much," "multiple," "many times," "more than one," "more than two," "composed of many like parts," "in many respects," used in the formation of compound words: *multiply; multivitamin.* Also, *esp. before a vowel,* **mult-.** [ME < L, comb. form of *multus* much, many]

mul·ti·an·gu·lar (mul′tē ang′gyə lər, mul′tī-), *adj.* multangular. [MULTI- + ANGULAR]

mul·ti·cel·lu·lar (mul′ti sel′yə lər), *adj.* composed of several or many cells. [MULTI- + CELLULAR]

mul·ti·coil (mul′ti koil′), *adj.* having more than one coil, as an electrical device. [MULTI- + COIL[1]]

mul·ti·col·or (mul′ti kul′ər), *n.* **1.** an arrangement or design of many colors. —*adj.* **2.** (of a printing press) capable of printing more than two colors simultaneously or in a single operation. **3.** of many colors; multicolored. [back formation from MULTICOLORED]

mul·ti·col·ored (mul′ti kul′ərd, mul′tī kul′ərd), *adj.* of many colors. [MULTI- + COLORED]

mul·ti·cyl·in·der (mul′ti sil′in dər), *adj.* having more than one cylinder, as an internal-combustion or steam engine. Also, **mul′ti·cyl′in·dered.** [MULTI- + CYLINDER]

mul·ti·den·tate (mul′ti den′tāt), *adj.* having many teeth or toothlike processes. [MULTI- + DENTATE]

mul·ti·dis·ci·pli·nar·y (mul′tē dis′ə plə ner′ē, mul′tī-), *adj.* composed or made up of several specialized branches of learning, as for achieving a common aim: *a multidisciplinary approach to literature.* [MULTI- + DISCIPLINARY]

mul·ti·fac·et·ed (mul′tē fas′i tid, mul′tī-), *adj.* **1.** having many facets, as a gem. **2.** having many aspects or phases: *a multifaceted problem.* **3.** possessing many talents: *a multifaceted artist.* [MULTI- + FACETED]

mul·ti·far·i·ous (mul′tə fâr′ē əs), *adj.* **1.** having many different parts, elements, forms, etc. **2.** numerous and varied; manifold: *multifarious activities.* [< LL *multifārius* many-sided, manifold, equiv. to L *multi-*

mul′ti·a·re′o·late′, *adj.*
mul′ti·ar·tic′u·lar, *adj.*
mul′ti·ar·tic′u·late, *adj.*
mul′ti·ar·tic′u·lat′ed, *adj.*
mul′ti·ax′i·al, *adj.;* **-ly,** *adv.*
mul′ti·birth′, *n.*
mul′ti·blade′, *n.*
mul′ti·blad′ed, *adj.*
mul′ti·branched′, *adj.*
mul′ti·bran′chi·ate, *adj.*
mul′ti·cap′i·tate′, *adj.*
mul′ti·cap′su·lar, *adj.*
mul′ti·car′i·nate′, *adj.*
mul′ti·car′i·nat′ed, *adj.*
mul′ti·cast′ing, *n.*
mul′ti·cen′tral, *adj.;* **-ly,** *adv.*
mul′ti·cen′tric, *adj.*
mul′ti·chan′nel, *n.*
mul′ti·chan′neled, *adj.*
mul′ti·chan′nelled, *adj.*
mul′ti·charge′, *n.*
mul′ti·chord′, *n.*
mul′ti·chrome′, *n.*
mul′ti·cil′i·ate, *adj.*
mul′ti·cil′i·at′ed, *adj.*
mul′ti·cir′cuit, *n.*
mul′ti·cir′cuit·ed, *adj.*
mul′ti·con·duc′tor, *adj.*
mul′ti·cor′date, *adj., n.*
mul′ti·core′, *n.*
mul′ti·cor′ne·al, *adj.*
mul′ti·cos′tate, *adj.*
mul′ti·course′, *n.*
mul′ti·crys′tal·line′, *adj.*
mul′ti·cus′pid, *n.*
mul′ti·cus′pi·date′, *adj.*
mul′ti·cus′pi·dat′ed, *adj.*
mul′ti·den·tic′u·late, *adj.*
mul′ti·den·tic′u·lat′ed, *adj.*
mul′ti·dig′i·tate′, *adj.*
mul′ti·di·men′sion·al, *adj.*
mul′ti·di·rec′tion·al, *adj.*
mul′ti·dis′ci·pli·nar·y, *adj.*
mul′ti·dis′ci·pline, *n.*
mul′ti·en′gine, *n.*
mul′ti·en′gined, *adj.*
mul′ti·ex·haust′, *n.*
mul′ti·faced′, *adj.*
mul′ti·fac·to′ri·al, *adj.*
mul′ti·fa·mil′ial, *adj.*

fāri(am) on many sides + *-us* -OUS; see MULTI-] —**mul′ti·far′i·ous·ly,** *adv.* —**mul′ti·far′i·ous·ness,** *n.*

mul·ti·fid (mul′tə fid), *adj.* cleft into many parts, divisions, or lobes. [< L *multifid(us)* divided into many parts. See MULTI-, -FID] —**mul′ti·fid′ly,** *adv.*

mul·ti·fil·a·ment (mul′ti fil′ə mənt), *adj.* **1.** having two or more filaments: *multifilament yarn.* —*n.* **2.** yarn constructed of a number of filaments in excess of the standard quantity. Also, **mul·ti·fil** (mul′ti fil′). Cf. **monofilament.** (def. 1) [MULTI- + FILAMENT]

mul′ti·flo′ra rose′ (mul′ti flōr′ə, -flôr′ə, mul′-), a climbing or trailing rose, *Rosa multiflora,* of Japan and Korea, having hooked prickles and fragrant, dense clusters of flowers. [*multiflora* < NL, fem. of ML *multiflōrus* MULTIFLOROUS]

mul·ti·flo·rous (mul′ti flōr′əs, -flôr′-), *adj. Bot.* bearing many flowers, as a peduncle. [< ML *multiflōrus.* See MULTI-, -FLOROUS]

mul·ti·foil (mul′tə foil′), *Archit.* —*n.* **1.** a foil, esp. one having more than five lobes. —*adj.* **2.** (of an arch, window opening, etc.) having the form of a foil with more than five lobes. [MULTI- + FOIL²]

mul·ti·fold (mul′tə fōld′), *adj.* numerous and varied; manifold. [MULTI- + -FOLD]

mul·ti·fo·li·ate (mul′tə fō′lē it, -āt′), *adj. Bot.* having many leaves or leaflets. [MULTI- + FOLIATE]

mul·ti·form (mul′tə fôrm′), *adj.* having many forms; of many different forms or kinds. [< L *multiform(is).* See MULTI-, -FORM] —**mul·ti·for·mi·ty** (mul′tə fôr′mi tē), *n.*

Mul·ti·graph (mul′tə graf′, -gräf′), *n.* **1.** *Trademark.* a rotary typesetting and printing machine, commonly used in making many copies of written matter. —*v.t., v.i.* **2.** (*l.c.*) to print with such a machine.

mul·ti·lat·er·al (mul′ti lat′ər əl), *adj.* **1.** having many sides; many-sided. **2.** *Govt.* participated in by two or more states; multipartite: *multilateral treaty.* [MULTI- + LATERAL] —**mul′ti·lat′er·al·ly,** *adv.*

mul·ti·lay·er (mul′ti lā′ər), *adj.* **1.** having two or more layers, as a color film with different layers of emulsion sensitive to different color ranges. —*n.* **2.** *Physical Chem.* a film consisting of two or more monolayers of different substances. [MULTI- + LAYER]

mul′tilin′ear form′, *Math.* a function or functional of several variables such that when all variables but one are held fixed, the function is linear in the remaining variable. [MULTI- + LINEAR]

mul·ti·lin·gual (mul′ti liŋ′gwəl), *adj.* **1.** able to speak more than two languages with approximately equal facility. **2.** spoken or written in more than two languages: *a multilingual broadcast.* —*n.* **3.** a multilingual person. [MULTI- + LINGUAL]

Mul·ti·lith (mul′ti lith), *n.* **1.** *Trademark.* a small photo-offset printing machine. —*v.t., v.i.* **2.** (*l.c.*) to print on a Multilith.

mul·ti·lob·u·lar (mul′ti lob′yə lər), *adj.* having many lobules. [MULTI- + LOBULAR]

mul·ti·lo·ca·tion (mul′tē lō kā′shən), *n.* the state or power of being in more than two places at the same time. Cf. **bilocation.** [MULTI- + LOCATION]

mul·ti·loc·u·lar (mul′ti lok′yə lər), *adj.* having or consisting of many cells or vesicles. [MULTI- + LOCULAR]

mul·tim·e·ter (mul tim′i tər), *n. Elect.* a device consisting of one or more meters, as an ammeter and voltmeter, used to measure two or more electrical quantities in an electric circuit, as voltage, resistance, and current. Also called **circuit analyzer.** [MULTI- + -METER]

mul·ti·mil·lion·aire (mul′tē mil′yə nâr′, mul′tī-), *n.* one who possesses a fortune that amounts to several million dollars, pounds, francs, etc. [MULTI- + MILLIONAIRE]

mul·ti·na·tion·al (mul′ti nash′ə nəl), *n.* **1.** a giant, usually diversified corporation with operations and subsidiaries in many foreign countries. —*adj.* **2.** of, pertaining to, or composed of many nations or nationalities. **3.** noting or pertaining to a multinational.

mul·ti·nom·i·nal (mul′ti nom′ə nəl), *adj.* having many names. [MULTI- + NOMINAL]

mul·ti·nu·cle·ar (mul′ti nōō′klē ər, -nyōō′-), *adj.* having many or several nuclei, as a cell. [MULTI- + NUCLEAR]

mul·tip·a·ra (mul tip′ər ə), *n., pl.* **-a·rae** (-ə rē′). *Obstet.* a woman who has borne two or more children, or who is parturient for the second time. [n. use of fem. of NL *multiparus* MULTIPAROUS]

mul·tip·a·rous (mul tip′ər əs), *adj.* **1.** producing many, or more than one, at a birth. **2.** *Bot.* (of a cyme) having many lateral axes. [< NL *multipar(us)* bearing many young at a birth. See MULTI-, -PAROUS] —**mul·ti·par·i·ty** (mul′ti par′i tē), *n.*

mul·ti·par·tite (mul′ti pär′tīt), *adj.* **1.** divided into many parts; having many divisions. **2.** *Govt.* multilateral. (def. 2) [< L *multipartīt(us)* divided into many parts. See MULTI-, PARTITE]

mul·ti·ped (mul′tə ped′), *adj.* having many feet. Also, **mul·ti·pede** (mul′tə pēd′). [< L *multiped-* (s. of *multipēs*) many-footed. See MULTI-, -PED]

mul·ti·phase (mul′ti fāz′), *adj. Elect.* having many phases. [MULTI- + PHASE] —**mul′ti·pha′sic,** *adj.*

mul·ti·ple (mul′tə pəl), *adj.* **1.** consisting of, having, or involving many individuals, parts, elements, relations, etc.; manifold. **2.** *Elect.* **a.** (of circuits) arranged in parallel. **b.** (of a circuit or circuits) having a number of points at which connection can be made. **3.** *Bot.* (of a fruit) collective. —*n.* **4.** *Math.* a number which contains another number an integral number of times without a remainder: *12 is a multiple of 3.* **5.** *Elect.* a group of terminals arranged to make a circuit or group of circuits accessible at a number of points at any one of which connection can be made. [< F < LL *multipl(us)* manifold. See MULTIPLEX]

mul′tiple alleles′, *Genetics.* a series of three or more alternative or allelic forms of a gene, only two of which can exist in any normal, diploid individual. —**mul′tiple allel′ism.**

mul′ti·ple-beam′ interferom′eter (mul′tə pəl-bēm′), *Optics.* etalon.

mul·ti·ple-choice (mul′tə pəl chois′), *adj.* consisting of several possible answers from which the correct one must be selected: *a multiple-choice examination.*

mul′tiple crop′ping, *Agric.* the use of the same field for two or more separate crops, whether of the same or of different kinds, successively during a single year.

mul′tiple drill′, a drilling machine having a number of vertical spindles for drilling several holes in a piece simultaneously. Cf. **gang drill.**

mul′tiple fac′tors, *Genetics.* a series of two or more pairs of genes responsible for the development of complex, quantitative characters such as size, yield, etc.

mul′tiple fis′sion, *Biol.* fission into more than two new organisms. Cf. **binary fission.**

mul′tiple in′tegral, *Math.* an integral in which the integrand involves a function of more than one variable and which requires for evaluation repetition of the integration process.

mul′tiple neuri′tis, *Pathol.* inflammation of several nerves at the same time.

mul′tiple personal′ity, *Psychol.* a functionally dissociated personality having distinct, often autonomous personality structures each of a complexity comparable to that of a normal individual. Also called **split personality.**

mul′tiple sclero′sis, *Pathol.* a neurological disease, chiefly of young adults, characterized by speech disturbances, muscular incoordination, weakness, and nystagmus, and caused by sclerotic patches in the brain and spinal cord.

mul′tiple shop′, *Brit.* See **chain store.** Also called **mul′tiple store′.**

mul′tiple star′, *Astron.* three or more stars lying close together in the celestial sphere and usually united in a single gravitational system.

mul·ti·plet (mul′tə plet′, -plit), *n. Physics.* a group of several related spectral lines, usually of nearly the same wavelengths. Also called **mul′tiplet line′.** [MULTI- + (TRI)PLET]

mul′tiple-u′nit car′ (mul′tə pəl yōō′nit), *Railroads.* a self-propelled car, generally used in commuting service, equipped so that a train of such cars can be operated from any one of them. Also called **MU car.**

mul·ti·ple-val·ued (mul′tə pəl val′yōōd), *adj. Math.* many-valued.

mul′tiple vot′ing, the casting of ballots in more than one constituency in one election, as in England before, and to some extent after, the election reform of 1918.

mul·ti·plex (mul′tə pleks′), *adj.* **1.** manifold; multiple: *multiplex aspects of the problem.* **2.** *Telegraphy, Telephony, Radio, Television.* of, pertaining to, or using a telegraph or telephone circuit, or radio or television transmitting and receiving equipment capable of carrying two or more distinct signals simultaneously: *multiplex telegraphy.* —*v.t.* **3.** *Elect.* to arrange a circuit for use by multiplex telegraphy. **4.** to transmit (two or more signals or messages) by a multiplex system, circuit, or the like. —*v.i.* **5.** to send several messages or signals simultaneously, as by multiplex telegraphy. —*n.* **6.** a multiplex electronics system. **7.** (in map making) a device that gives a three-dimensional effect to a combined topographical image when seen through stereoscopic glasses. [< L: manifold, equiv. to *multi-* MULTI- + *-plex* -fold; see PLY²] —**mul′ti·plex′er,** *n.*

mul·ti·pli·a·ble (mul′tə plī′ə bəl), *adj.* capable of being multiplied. Also, **mul·ti·plic·a·ble** (mul′tə plik′ə bəl). [MULTIPLY + -ABLE]

mul·ti·pli·cand (mul′tə pli kand′), *n. Arith.* a number to be multiplied by another. [< L *multiplicand(um),* n. use of neut. of *multiplicandus* to be multiplied, gerundive of *multiplicāre* to MULTIPLY]

mul·ti·pli·cate (mul′tə pli kāt′), *adj.* multiple; manifold. [ME *multiplicat* < L *multiplicāt(us)* multiplied, increased, ptp. of *multiplicāre.* See MULTI-, PLICATE]

mul·ti·pli·ca·tion (mul′tə plə kā′shən), *n.* **1.** the act or process of multiplying or the state of being multiplied. **2.** *Arith.* a mathematical operation, symbolized by $a \times b$, $a \cdot b$, or ab, and signifying, when a and b are positive integers, that a is to be added to itself as many times as there are units in b; the addition of a number to itself as often as is indicated by another number, as in 2×3 or 5×10. **3.** *Math.* any generalization of this operation applicable to numbers other than integers, such as fractions, irrational numbers, etc. [ME *multiplicacio(u)n* < L *multiplicātiōn-* (s. of *multiplicātiō*). See MULTI-, PLICATION] —**mul′ti·pli·ca′tion·al,** *adj.*

multiplica′tion sign′, the symbol (·) or (×) between two mathematical expressions, denoting multiplication of the second expression by the first. In certain algebraic notations the sign is suppressed and multiplication is indicated by immediate juxtaposition or contiguity, as in *ab.*

multiplica′tion ta′ble, a tabular listing of the products of any two numbers of a set, usually of the integers 1 through 10 or 1 through 12.

mul·ti·pli·ca·tive (mul′tə plə kā′tiv, mul′tə plik′ə-), *adj.* **1.** tending to multiply or increase. **2.** having the power of multiplying. [< ML *multiplicātīvus.* See MULTIPLICATE, -IVE] —**mul′ti·pli·ca′tive·ly,** *adv.*

mul′tiplicative ax′iom, *Math. Chiefly Brit.* See **axiom of choice.**

mul′tiplicative group′, *Math.* a group in which the operation of the group is multiplication.

mul·ti·plic·i·ty (mul′tə plis′i tē), *n., pl.* **-ties. 1.** a multitude or great number: *a multiplicity of errors.* **2.** the state of being multiplex or manifold; manifold variety. [< LL *multiplicitās,* equiv. to *multiplic-* (s. of *multiplex*) MULTIPLEX + *-itās* -ITY]

mul·ti·pli·er (mul′tə plī′ər), *n.* **1.** one who or that which multiplies. **2.** *Arith.* a number by which another is multiplied. **3.** *Physics.* a device for intensifying some effect. [ME; see MULTIPLY, -ER¹]

mul·ti·ply¹ (mul′tə plī′), *v.,* **-plied, -ply·ing.** —*v.t.* **1.** to make many or manifold; increase the number, quantity, etc., of. **2.** *Arith.* to find the product of by multiplication. **3.** to breed (animals). **4.** to propagate (plants). **5.** to procreate or increase by procreation. —*v.i.* **6.** to grow in number, quantity, etc.; increase. **7.** *Arith.* to perform the process of multiplication. **8.** to increase in number by procreation or natural generation. [ME *multiplie(n)* < OF *multiplier* < L *multiplicāre.* See MULTI-, PLY²]

mul·ti·ply² (mul′tə plē), *adv.* in a multiple manner; manifoldly. [MULTIPLE + -LY]

mul·ti·ply-con·nect·ed (mul′tə plē kə nek′tid), *adj. Math.* connected but not simply-connected.

mul·ti·po·lar (mul′ti pō′lər), *adj.* **1.** having several or many poles. **2.** *Anat.* (of nerve cells) having more than two dendrites. [MULTI- + POLAR]

mul·ti·pur·pose (mul′ti pûr′pəs), *adj.* able to be used for several purposes: *a multipurpose detergent.* [MULTI- + PURPOSE]

mul′ti·scene control′ board′ (mul′tē sēn′, mul′tī-). See **preset board.**

mul·ti·stage (mul′ti stāj′), *adj.* (of a rocket or guided missile) having more than one stage. [MULTI- + STAGE]

mul′ti·step hy′droplane (mul′ti step′), *Naut.* a motor vessel having a flat bottom built as a series of planes inclined forward, the boat planing on each from stem to stern as its speed increases. [MULTI- + STEP]

mul·ti·sto·ry (mul′ti stōr′ē, -stôr′ē), *adj.* (of a building) having many stories. Also, **mul′ti·sto′ried.** [MULTI- + STORY²]

mul·ti·tude (mul′tə tōōd′, -tyōōd′), *n.* **1.** a great number; host: *a multitude of friends.* **2.** a great number of persons gathered together; a crowd or throng. **3.** the state or character of being many; numerousness. **4.** **the multitude,** the common people; the masses: *the whims of the multitude.* [ME < L *multitūdō.* See MULTI-, -TUDE] —**Syn. 2.** mass. See **crowd.**

mul·ti·tu·di·nous (mul′ti tōōd′ənəs, -tyōōd′-), *adj.* **1.** forming a multitude or great number; existing, occurring, or present in great numbers; very numerous. **2.** comprising many items, parts, or elements. **3.** *Archaic.* crowded or thronged. [< L *multitūdin-* (s. of *multitūdō*) MULTITUDE + -OUS] —**mul′ti·tu′di·nous·ly,** *adv.* —**mul′ti·tu′di·nous·ness,** *n.*

mul·ti·va·lent (mul′tə vā′lənt, mul tiv′ə lənt), *adj. Chem.* having a valence of three or higher. [MULTI- + -VALENT] —**mul′ti·va′lence,** *n.*

mul·ti·val·ued (mul′tə val′yōōd), *adj.* possessing a number of values: *a multivalued book.* [MULTI- + VALUED]

mul·ti·valve (mul′ti valv′), *adj.* **1.** (of a shell) composed of more than two valves or pieces. —*n.* **2.** a multivalve mollusk or its shell. [MULTI- + VALVE]

mul·ti·var·i·ate (mul′tə vâr′ē it), *adj. Statistics.* (of a combined distribution) having more than one variate or variable. [MULTI- + VARIATE]

mul·ti·ver·si·ty (mul′tə vûr′si tē), *n., pl.* **-ties.** a large, decentralized university with several separate campuses [MULTI- + (UNI)VERSITY]

mul·ti·vi·ta·min (mul′tə vī′tə min), *adj.* **1.** containing or consisting of a combination of several vitamins: *multivitamin capsules.* —*n.* **2.** a compound of many vitamins. [MULTI- + VITAMIN]

mul·tiv·o·cal (mul tiv′ə kəl), *adj.* having many or different meanings of equal probability or validity: *a multivocal word.* [MULTI- + VOCAL]

mul·ti·vol·tine (mul′tə vōl′tēn, -tən), *adj. Entomol.* producing several broods in one year, as certain silkworm moths; polyvoltine. [MULTI- + It *volta(a)* turn, time + -INE¹]

mul·ti·vol·ume (mul′tə vol′yōōm), *adj.* consisting of or encompassing many volumes: *a multivolume encyclopedia.* Also, **mul′ti·vol′umed.** [MULTI- + VOLUME]

mul′ti·fe·ta′tion, *n.*
mul′ti·fi′bered, *adj.*
mul′ti·fi′brous, *adj.*
mul′ti·fis′tu·lar, *adj.*
mul′ti·fis′tu·lous, *adj.*
mul′ti·flag′el·late′, *adj.*
mul′ti·flag′el·lat′ed, *adj.*
mul′ti·flo′ra, *n., pl.* **-ras, -rae.**
mul′ti·fo′cal, *adj.*
mul′ti·fur′cate, *adj.*
mul′ti·gan′gli·on′ic, *adj.*
mul′ti·gran′u·lar, *adj.*
mul′ti·gran′u·lat′ed, *adj.*
mul′ti·gy′rate, *adj.*
mul′ti·head′, *n.*
mul′ti·hearth′, *n.*
mul′ti·hued′, *adj.*
mul′ti·jet′, *n.*
mul′ti·ju′gate, *adj.*
mul′ti·la·cin′i·ate′, *adj.*
mul′ti·la·mel′lar, *adj.*
mul′ti·lam′el·late′, *adj.*
mul′ti·lam′i·nar, *adj.*
mul′ti·lam′i·nate′, *adj.*
mul′ti·lam′i·nat′ed, *adj.*
mul′ti·lane′, *n.*
mul′ti·light′ed, *adj.*
mul′ti·lin′e·al, *adj.*
mul′ti·lin′e·ar, *adj.*
mul′ti·lo′bar, *adj.*
mul′ti·lo′bate, *adj.*
mul′ti·lobe′, *n.*
mul′ti·lobed′, *adj.*
mul′ti·mac′u·lar, *adj.*
mul′ti·me′di·al, *adj.*
mul′ti·meg′a·ton′, *n.*
mul′ti·me·tal′lic, *adj.*
mul′ti·mil′lion, *n.*
mul′ti·mod′al, *adj.*
mul′ti·mo·lec′u·lar, *adj.*
mul′ti·mo′tor, *n.*
mul′ti·mo′tored, *adj.*
mul′ti·nerv′ate, *adj.*
mul′ti·nod′al, *adj.*
mul′ti·no′dous, *adj.*
mul′ti·nod′u·lar, *adj.*
mul′ti·nu′cle·ate, *adj.*
mul′ti·nu·cle′o·lar, *adj.*
mul′ti·nu′cle·o·late′, *adj.*
mul′ti·nu′cle·o·lat′ed, *adj.*
mul′ti·o′vu·lar, *adj.*
mul′ti·o′vu·late′, *adj.*
mul′ti·o′vu·lat′ed, *adj.*
mul′ti·par′ti·san, *n.*
mul′ti·path′, *n.*
mul′ti·per′fo·rate, *adj.*
mul′ti·per′fo·rat′ed, *adj.*
mul′ti·per′son·al, *adj.*
mul′ti·pho·tog′ra·phy, *n.*
mul′ti·pin′nate, *adj.*
mul′ti·plat′ed, *adj.*
mul′ti·point′ed, *adj.*
mul′ti·port′ed, *adj.*
mul′ti·ra′cial, *adj.*
mul′ti·ra′cial·ism, *n.*
mul′ti·ra′di·al, *adj.*
mul′ti·ra′di·ate′, *adj.*
mul′ti·ra′di·at′ed, *adj.*
mul′ti·rad′i·cal, *adj.*
mul′ti·ram′i·fied′, *adj.*
mul′ti·ra′mose, *adj.*
mul′ti·ra′mous, *adj.*
mul′ti·re′flex, *n.*
mul′ti·root′ed, *adj.*
mul′ti·sac′cate, *adj.*
mul′ti·sac′cu·late′, *adj.*
mul′ti·sac′cu·lat′ed, *adj.*
mul′ti·seg·men′tal, *adj.*
mul′ti·seg′ment·ed, *adj.*
mul′ti·sep′tate, *adj.*
mul′ti·se′ri·ate, *adj.*
mul′ti·shot′, *n.*
mul′ti·son′ic, *adj.*
mul′ti·so′nor·ous, *adj.;* **-ly,** *adv.;* **-ness,** *n.*
mul′ti·so′nous, *adj.*
mul′ti·speed′, *adj.*
mul′ti·sper′mous, *adj.*
mul′ti·spic′u·lar, *adj.*
mul′ti·spic′u·late, *adj.*
mul′ti·spin′dled, *adj.*
mul′ti·spi′nous, *adj.*
mul′ti·spi′ral, *adj.*
mul′ti·spired′, *adj.*
mul′ti·stam′i·nate, *adj.*
mul′ti·strat′i·fied′, *adj.*
mul′ti·stri′ate, *adj.*
mul′ti·sul′cate, *adj.*
mul′ti·sul′cat·ed, *adj.*
mul′ti·ten′ta·cled, *adj.*
mul′ti·ten·tac′u·late′, *adj.*
mul′ti·test′er, *n.*
mul′ti·thread′ed, *adj.*
mul′ti·tit′u·lar, *adj.*
mul′ti·toed′, *adj.*
mul′ti·toned′, *adj.*
mul′ti·tube′, *adj.*
mul′ti·tu·ber′cu·late, *adj.*
mul′ti·tu′bu·lar, *adj.*
mul′ti·val′vu·lar, *adj.*
mul′ti·vane′, *adj.*
mul′ti·view′, *adj.*
mul′ti·view′ing, *adj.*
mul′ti·voiced′, *adj.*
mul′ti·wall′, *n.*

mul·tum in par·vo (mōōl′tōōm in pär′wō; *Eng.* mul′təm in pär′vō), *Latin.* much in little; a great deal in a small space or in brief.

mul·ture (mul′chər), *n. Scots Law.* a toll or fee given to the proprietor of a mill for the grinding of grain, usually consisting of a fixed proportion of the grain brought or of the flour made. [ME *multir* < OF *molture* < ML *molitūra* a grinding, equiv. to L *molit(us)* ground (ptp. of *molere*) + *-ūra* -URE]

Mul·vane (mul vān′), *n.* a town in S Kansas. 2981 (1960).

mum[1] (mum), *adj.* **1.** silent; not saying a word: *to keep mum.* —*interj.* **2.** say nothing! be silent! **3. mum's the word,** do not reveal what you know (of something); keep silent: *Remember, mum's the word, or the surprise party won't be a surprise.* [ME *momme,* imit.]

mum[2] (mum), *v.i.,* **mummed, mum·ming. 1.** to say "mum"; call for silence. **2.** to act as a mummer. Also, **mumm.** [ME *momme(n),* v. use of MUM[1]; cf. MD *mommen* to act the mummer's part]

mum[3] (mum), *n. Informal.* chrysanthemum. [shortened form]

mum[4] (mum), *n. Chiefly Brit.* mother. [nursery word; see MOM]

mum[5] (mum), *n.* a strong beer or ale first made in Brunswick, Germany. [< G *Mumme,* said to have been named after the brewer who made it]

mum[6] (mum), *n. Chiefly Brit.* madam. [var. of MA'AM]

mum·ble (mum′bəl), *v.,* **-bled, -bling,** *n.* —*v.i.* **1.** to speak indistinctly or unintelligibly, as with partly closed lips; mutter low, indistinct words. **2.** to chew ineffectively, as from loss of teeth: *to mumble on a crust.* —*v.t.* **3.** to utter indistinctly, as with partly closed lips: *He mumbled something about expenses.* **4.** to chew, or try to eat, with difficulty, as from loss of teeth. —*n.* **5.** a low, indistinct utterance or sound. [ME *momele(n),* freq. (with *-el* suffix) based on MUM[1]; cf. D *mommelen,* G *mummeln*] —**mum′bler,** *n.* —**mum′bling·ly,** *adv.*
—**Syn. 3.** See **murmur.** —**Ant. 1.** articulate.

mum·ble·ty·peg (mum′bəl tē peg′), *n.* a children's game played with a pocket knife, the object being to cause the blade to stick in the ground or a wooden surface by flipping the knife in a number of prescribed ways or from a number of prescribed positions. Also, **mum·ble-de-peg,** **mum·ble·dy·peg** (mum′bəl dē-peg′), **mum′ble peg′, mum·ble-the-peg** (mum′bəl-thə peg′), **mum′ble-ty-peg′, mum·bly-peg** (mum′blē-peg′). [from phrase *mumble the peg* (see MUMBLE); so named because the losing player was formerly required to pull a peg from the ground with his teeth]

mum·bo jum·bo (mum′bō jum′bō), *pl.* **mum·bo jum·bos. 1.** meaningless incantation or ritual. **2.** an object of superstitious awe or reverence. **3.** (*caps.*) the guardian of western Sudan Negro villages symbolized by a masked man who combats evil and punishes women for breaches of tribal laws. **4.** senseless or pretentious language, usually designed to obscure an issue, confuse a listener, or the like. [rhyming alter. of Mandingo *Mama Dyumbo* a tribal god]

mu′ me′son, *Physics.* a meson having a mass approximately 207 times that of an electron, with positive or negative charge and spin of 1/2. Also called **muon.**

Mu·met·al (mōō′met′əl, myōō′-), *n.* an alloy containing nickel, iron, and copper, characterized by high magnetic permeability and low hysteresis losses. [short for MUNTZ METAL]

Mum·ford (mum′fərd), *n.* **Lewis,** born 1895, U.S. author and social scientist.

Mu′·min (mōō′min), *n. Islam.* one of the devout. [< Ar: believer]

mumm (mum), *v.i.* mum[2].

mum·mer (mum′ər), *n.* **1.** one who wears a mask or fantastic disguise, esp. as formerly and still in some localities at Christmas, New Year's, and other festive seasons. **2.** an actor. **3.** a pantomimist. [late ME *mommer.* See MUM[2], -ER[1]]

mum·mer·y (mum′ə rē), *n., pl.* **-mer·ies. 1.** performance of mummers. **2.** any performance, ceremony, etc., regarded as absurd, false, or ostentatious. [MUMMER + -Y[3]]

mum·mi·chog (mum′i chog′), *n.* a silver and black killifish, *Fundulus heteroclitus,* found in fresh, brackish, and salt water along the Atlantic coast of the U.S. [< Algonquian (Narragansett) *moamitteaûg,* lit., they swarm]

mum·mi·fy (mum′ə fī′), *v.,* **-fied, -fy·ing.** —*v.t.* **1.** to make (a dead body) into a mummy, as by embalming and drying. **2.** to make (something) resemble a mummy. —*v.i.* **3.** to dry or shrivel up. [MUMMY + -FY] —**mum′-mi·fi·ca′tion,** *n.*

mum·my[1] (mum′ē), *n., pl.* **-mies,** *v.,* **-mied, -my·ing.** —*n.* **1.** the dead body of a human being or animal preserved by the ancient Egyptian process or some similar method of embalming. **2.** a dead body dried and preserved by the agencies of nature. **3.** a withered or shrunken living being. **4.** a dry, shriveled fruit, tuber, or other organ, resulting from any of several fungous diseases. —*v.t.* **5.** to make into or cause to resemble a mummy. [ME *mummie* < ML *mummia* < Ar *mūmiyah* mummy, lit., asphalt]

mum·my[2] (mum′ē), *n., pl.* **-mies.** *Chiefly Brit.* mother. [MUM[4] + -Y[2]]

mump[1] (mump), *Dial.* —*v.t.* **1.** to mumble; mutter. —*v.i.* **2.** *Brit.* to sulk; mope. [imit., equiv. to MUM[1] + intensive *-p*]

mump[2] (mump; *Brit. Dial. also* mōōmp), *Dial.* —*v.t.* **1.** to cheat. —*v.i.* **2.** *Brit.* to beg. [< D *mompe(n)* (obs.)]

mump[3] (mump, mōōmp), *v.i. Brit. Dial.* to grin. [imit.]

mumps (mumps), *n.* (*construed as sing.*) *Pathol.* an infectious disease characterized by inflammatory swelling of the parotid and usually other salivary glands, and sometimes by inflammation of the testes, ovaries, etc. [MUMP[3] + -S[3]]

mun., municipal.

munch (munch), *v.t.* **1.** to chew with steady or vigorous working of the jaws, and often audibly. —*v.i.* **2.** to chew steadily or vigorously, and often audibly. [ME *monche;* imit.] —**munch′er,** *n.*

Munch (mōōngk), *n.* **Ed·vard** (ed′värd), 1863–1944, Norwegian painter and graphic artist.

Münch (mynsh), *n.* **Charles,** 1891–1968, French conductor in the U.S.

Mün·chen (myn′кʜən), *n.* German name of **Munich.**

Mün·chen-Glad·bach (myn′кʜən glät′bäкʜ), *n.* former name of **Mönchen-Gladbach.**

Münch·hau·sen (myngкʜ′hou′zən), *n.* **Karl Frie·drich Hi·e·ro·ny·mus** (kärl frē′drikʜ hē′ā rō′ny-mōōs′), **Baron von** (fən), 1720–97, German soldier, adventurer, and teller of tales. English, **Mun·chau·sen** (mun′chou′zən, munch′hou′-, mun chō′-). —**Mun′-chau′sen·ism,** *n.*

Mun·cie (mun′sē), *n.* a city in E Indiana. 68,603 (1960).

Mun·cy (mun′sē), *n.* a town in central Pennsylvania. 2830 (1960).

Mun·da (mōōn′də), *n.* a group of languages of east-central India that belong to the Austroasiatic family.

mun·dane (mun dān′, mun′dān), *adj.* **1.** of or pertaining to the world, universe, or earth. **2.** of or pertaining to this world or earth as contrasted with heaven; worldly; earthly: *mundane affairs.* **3.** common; ordinary; banal; unimaginative. [< LL *mundān(us),* equiv. to *mund(us)* world + *-ānus* -ANE; r. ME *mondeyne* < MF *mondain*] —**mun·dane′ly,** *adv.*
—**Syn. 2.** secular, temporal. See **earthly.**

mun·di·fy (mun′də fī′), *v.t.,* **-fied, -fy·ing. 1.** to cleanse; deterge: *to mundify a wound before bandaging.* **2.** to purge or purify: *expiation to mundify a person of past sins.* [< LL *mundific(āre),* equiv. to L *mund(us)* clean + *-ificare* -IFY]

Mun·du·gu·mor (mun dōō′gə môr′), *n., pl.* **-mors,** (*esp. collectively*) **-mor.** a member of a Papuan people of New Guinea.

mun·dun·gus (mun dung′gəs), *n. Archaic.* malodorous tobacco. [Latinized var. of Sp *mondongo* tripe]

mung′ bean′ (mung), **1.** the green or yellow, edible seed of an Asian bean, *Phaseolus aureus.* **2.** the plant itself. [*mung* < Tamil *mūngu* < Skt *mudga*]

mun·go (mung′gō), *n., pl.* **-gos.** a low-grade wool from felted rags or waste. Also, **mongo, mongoe.** Cf. **shoddy** (def. 1). [?]

Mun·hall (mun′hôl′), *n.* a city in W Pennsylvania, near Pittsburgh. 17,312 (1960).

Mu·ni (myōō′nē), *n.* **1. Paul** (*Muni Weisenfreund*), 1895–1967, U.S. actor, born in Austria. **2.** a boy's given name.

Mu·nich (myōō′nik), *n.* **1.** German, **München.** a city in and the capital of Bavaria, in SW West Germany. 1,157,300 (1963). **2.** any dishonorable appeasement. Cf. **Munich Pact.**

Mu′nich Pact′, the pact signed by Germany, Great Britain, France, and Italy on September 29, 1938, by which the Sudetenland was ceded to Germany. Also called **Mu′nich Agree′ment.**

mu·nic·i·pal (myōō nis′ə pəl), *adj.* **1.** of or pertaining to the local government of a town or city: *municipal elections.* **2.** *Archaic.* pertaining to the internal affairs of a state or nation rather than to international affairs. [< L *mūnicipāl(is),* equiv. to *mūnicip-* (s. of *mūniceps*) citizen of a free town (*mūni(a)* duties + *-cip-,* var. s. of *capere* to take) + *-ālis* -AL[1]] —**mu·nic′i·pal·ly,** *adv.*

mu·nic·i·pal·ise (myōō nis′ə pə līz′), *v.t.,* **-ised, -is·ing.** *Chiefly Brit.* municipalize. —**mu·nic′i·pal·i·sa′-tion,** *n.*

mu·nic·i·pal·ism (myōō nis′ə pə liz′əm), *n.* **1.** the principle or system of home rule by a municipality. **2.** advocacy of such a principle or system. [MUNICIPAL + -ISM] —**mu·nic′i·pal·ist,** *n.*

mu·nic·i·pal·i·ty (myōō nis′ə pal′i tē), *n., pl.* **-ties. 1.** a city, town, or other district possessing corporate existence. **2.** a community under municipal jurisdiction. **3.** the governing body of such a district or community. [< F *municipalité.* See MUNICIPAL, -ITY]

mu·nic·i·pal·ize (myōō nis′ə pə līz′), *v.t.,* **-ized, -iz·ing. 1.** to make a municipality of. **2.** to bring under municipal ownership or control. Also, *esp. Brit.,* **municipalise.** [MUNICIPAL + -IZE] —**mu·nic′i·pal·i·za′-tion,** *n.*

mu·nif·i·cent (myōō nif′i sənt), *adj.* **1.** extremely liberal in giving or bestowing; very generous. **2.** characterized by great generosity: *a munificent bequest.* [back formation from L *mūnificentia* generosity, equiv. to *mūnific(us)* generous (*mūni-,* comb. form of *mūnus* gift + *-ficus* -FIC) + *-entia* -ENCE] —**mu·nif′i·cence, mu·nif′i·cent·ness,** *n.* —**mu·nif′i·cent·ly,** *adv.*
—**Syn. 1.** bountiful, bounteous. —**Ant. 1.** niggardly.

mu·ni·ment (myōō′nə mənt), *n.* **1. muniments,** *Law.* a document, as a title deed or a charter, by which rights or privileges are defended or maintained. **2.** *Rare.* a defense or protection. [ME < ML *mūniment(um)* document (e.g. title, deed) for use in defense against a claimant, L: defense, protection, orig. fortification, equiv. to *mūnī(re)* (to) fortify + *-mentum* -MENT]

mu′niment room′, *Brit.* a storage or display room in a castle, church, university, or the like, where pertinent historical documents and records are kept.

Mu·nin (mōō′nin), *n. Scand. Myth.* one of the two ravens of Odin that brought him news from the whole world: later regarded as personifying memory. Cf. **Hugin.**

Mu·nip·pus (myōō nip′əs), *n. Class. Myth.* the son of Cilla and Thymoetes who was slain by Priam because of a prophecy that a son of the royal house would cause the fall of Troy.

Mu·ni·sing (myōō′ni sing), *n.* a town in NW Michigan, in the Upper Peninsula. 4228 (1960).

mu·nite (myōō nīt′), *v.t.,* **-nit·ed, -nit·ing.** *Obs.* to fortify. [ME < L *mūnīt(us)* fortified, secured, ptp. of *mūnīre* to wall (a town), fortify; see -ITE[2]]

mu·ni·tion (myōō nish′ən), *n.* **1.** Usually, **munitions.** materials used in war, esp. weapons and ammunition. **2.** material or equipment for carrying on any undertaking. —*v.t.* **3.** to provide with munitions. [< L *mūnītiōn-* (s. of *mūnītiō*) a fortifying, equiv. to *mūnīt(us)* fortified (see MUNITE) + *-iōn-* -ION]

muni′tion ar′mor, armor made in quantity for common soldiers.

Mu·ni·tus (myōō′ni təs), *n. Class. Myth.* an illegitimate son of Laodice and Acamas.

Mun·ká·csy (mōōn′kä chi), *n.* **Mi·há·ly von** (mi′-häl′yᵊ fən), (*Michael Lieb*), 1844–1900, Hungarian painter.

mun·nion (mun′yən), *n.* a mullion or muntin. [assimilated var. of MULLION, MONIAL]

Mu·ñoz Ma·rín (mōō nyôs′ mä rēn′), **Lu·is** (lōō-ēs′), 1898–1980, Puerto Rican political leader: governor 1948–64.

Mun·ro (mən rō′), *n.* **H(ector) H(ugh)** ("*Saki*"), 1870–1916, Scottish novelist and short-story writer, born in Burma.

Mun·roe (mən rō′), *n.* **Charles Edward,** 1849–1938, U.S. chemist.

Munroe′ effect′, *Mil.* the reinforcement of shock waves in the concave, hollow end of a shaped charge, producing a greater resultant wave and concentrating the explosion along the axis of the charge. [named after C. E. MUNROE]

Mun·sey (mun′sē), *n.* **Frank Andrew,** 1854–1925, U.S. publisher.

Mun′sey Park′, a town on NW Long Island, in SE New York. 2847 (1960).

mun·shi (mōōn′shē), *n. Anglo-Indian.* **1.** a native interpreter or language instructor. **2.** a native secretary or assistant. Also, **moonshee.** [< Hindi *munshī* < Ar *munshi′*]

mun·sif (mōōn′sif), *n. Anglo-Indian.* a native law-enforcement officer. Also, **moonsif.** [< Urdu < Ar: lit., honest]

Mun·ster (mun′stər), *n.* **1.** a province in SW Republic of Ireland. 849,203 (1961); 9316 sq. mi. **2.** (*l.c.*) muenster.

mün·ster (mōōn′stər, mun′-, min′-, myn′-), *n.* muenster.

Mün·ster (myn′stər), *n.* a city in NW West Germany: treaty of Westphalia 1648. 189,700 (1963).

Mün·ster·berg (mōōn′stər bûrg′; *Ger.* myn′stər-berкʜ′), *n.* **Hu·go** (hyōō′gō; *Ger.* hōō′gō), 1863–1916, German psychologist and philosopher in the U.S.

mun·tin (mun′tᵊn), *n.* **1.** Also called, *esp. Brit.,* **glazing bar; sash bar.** a bar for holding the edges of windows panes within the sash. See diag. under **double-hung. 2.** (formerly) a vertical bar in a window sash. **3.** a stile within the frame of a door or the like. [var. of *munting* < MF *montant,* n. use of prp. of *monter* to MOUNT[1] with -ING[1] for -ANT]

munt·jac (munt′jak), *n.* **1.** any of various small deer of the genus *Muntiacus,* of southern and eastern Asia and the adjacent islands, esp. *M. muntjac,* of Java, India, etc., having well-developed horns on bony pedicels. **2.** any of the small deer of the related genus *Elaphodus,* of China and Tibet, having minute horns. Also, **munt′jak.** Also called **barking deer.** [< an unrecorded var. of Javanese *mindjangan* deer]

Muntz′ met′al (munts). See **alpha-beta brass.** [named after its inventor, G. F. *Muntz,* 19th-century English metallurgist and manufacturer]

mu·on (myōō′on), *n. Physics.* See **mu meson.** [by shortening]

M.U.P., Master of Urban Planning.

mu·ra (mōōr′ə), *n.* (in Japan) a village; hamlet. [< Jap: village]

mu·rae·nid (myōō rē′nid), *n.* **1.** any fish of the family *Muraenidae,* comprising the morays. —*adj.* **2.** belonging or pertaining to the family *Muraenidae.* [< NL *Muraenid(ae)* name of the family, equiv. to L *muraen(a)* (< Gk *mȳraina* a sea-eel, lamprey) + *-idae* -ID[2]]

mu·rage (myōōr′ij), *n. Eng. Law.* a toll or tax for the repair or construction of the walls or fortifications of a town. [ME < OF, equiv. to *mur(er)* (to) wall about (<< L *mūrus* wall) + *-age* -AGE]

mu·ral (myōōr′əl), *adj.* **1.** of, pertaining to, or resembling a wall. **2.** executed on or affixed to a wall. **3.** pertaining to any of several astronomical instruments that were affixed to a wall aligned on the plane of a meridian, and were formerly used to measure the altitude of celestial bodies: *a mural quadrant; a mural circle.* —*n.* **4.** a mural painting. **5.** a wallpaper pattern representing a landscape or the like, often with very widely spaced repeats so as to produce the effect of a mural painting on a wall of average size; a trompe-l'oeil. [< L *mūrāl(is),* equiv. to *mūr(us)* wall + *-ālis* -AL[1]]

mu′ral crown′, 1. a golden crown formed with indentations to resemble a battlement, bestowed by the ancient Romans on the soldiers who first mounted the wall of a besieged place and there lodged a standard. **2.** Also called **mu′ral cor′onet.** *Heraldry.* a representation of an embattled coronet, often appearing on municipal arms. —**mu′ral·ly,** *adv.*

mu·ral·ist (myōōr′ə list), *n.* an artist who paints murals. [MURAL + -IST]

Mu·ra·no (mōō rä′nō; *It.* mōō rä′nô), *n.* an insular suburb of Venice: cathedral; noted for Venetian glass manufacture. 30,614 (1961).

Mu·ra·sa·ki Shi·ki·bu (mōō′rä sä′kē shē′kē bōō′), **Baroness,** 978?–1031?, Japanese poet and novelist.

Mu·rat (my rä′), *n.* **Jo·a·chim** (zhô ä kēm′), 1767?–1815, French marshal: king of Naples 1808–15.

Mu·rat (mōō rät′), *n.* a river in E Turkey, flowing W to the Euphrates. 425 mi. long. Also called **Mu·rad Su** (mōō räd′ sōō′).

Mur·chi·son (mûr′chi sən), *n.* a walled plain in the northern hemisphere in the first and second quadrants and near the center of the face of the moon: about 35 miles in diameter.

Mur·cia (mōōr′shə; *Sp.* mōōr′thyä), *n.* **1.** a city in SE Spain. 244,683 (est. 1960). **2.** a region in SE Spain: formerly a kingdom.

mur·der (mûr′dər), *n.* **1.** *Law.* the unlawful killing of another human being with malice aforethought. Special statutory definitions and degrees are common in the U.S. **2. get away with murder,** *Slang.* to succeed in a reprehensible activity without harm to oneself: *The new baby-sitter has let the kids get away with murder.* **3. murder will out,** a secret will eventually be exposed. —*v.t.* **4.** *Law.* to kill by an act constituting murder. **5.** to kill or slaughter inhumanly or barbarously. **6.** to spoil or mar by bad execution, representation, pronunciation, etc.: *He murdered that painting when he dulled the background.* —*v.i.* **7.** to commit murder. [ME; var. of MURTHER] —**mur′der·er;** *referring to a woman,* **mur′der·ess,** *n.*
—**Syn. 1.** assassination, homicide. **4, 5.** slay, assassinate, destroy. See **kill**[1]. **6.** ruin.

Mur′der in the Cathe′dral, a verse drama (1935) by T. S. Eliot.

mur·der·ous (mûr′dər əs), *adj.* **1.** of the nature of or involving murder: *a murderous deed.* **2.** guilty of, bent on, or capable of murder. 3. extremely difficult, dangerous, or trying: *a murderous climb; murderous heat.* [MURDER + -OUS] —**mur′der·ous·ly,** *adv.* —**mur′der·ous·ness,** *n.*

Mur·doch (mûr′dok), *n.* a boy's given name.

mur·drum (mûr′drəm), *n. Old Eng. Law.* **1.** the killing of a human being in a secret manner. **2.** the fine payable to the king by the hundred where such a killing occurred, unless the killer was produced or the victim proved to be a Saxon. [< ML < OF *murdre* MURDER]

mure (myŏŏr), *n., v.,* **mured, mur·ing.** —*n.* **1.** *Obs.* a wall. —*v.t.* **2.** to immure. [ME *mure(n)* < MF *mure(r)* < L *mūrāre,* equiv. to *mūr(us)* wall + *-ā-* thematic vowel + *-re* inf. ending]

Mu·res (mŏŏr′esh), *n.* a river in SE central Europe, flowing W from the Carpathian Mountains in central Rumania to the Tirsza River in S Hungary. 400 mi. long. Hungarian, **Maros.** Rumanian, **Mu·reș** (mŏŏ′resh).

mu·rex (myŏŏr′eks), *n., pl.* **mu·ri·ces** (myŏŏr′i sēz′), **mu·rex·es. 1.** any marine gastropod of the genus *Murex,* common in tropical seas, certain species of which yielded the royal purple dye of the ancients. **2.** a shell used as a trumpet, as in representations of Tritons in art. **3.** purplish red. [< NL, L: the shell-fish that yielded Tyrian purple dye]

Murex, *Murex tenuispina* (Shell length 4 to 5 in.)

mu·rex·ide (myŏŏ rek′sīd, -sid), *n. Chem.* a reddish-purple, crystalline, sparingly water-soluble solid, $C_8H_8N_6O_6 \cdot H_2O$, having a green luster: formerly used as a dye. Also called **ammonium purpurate.** [MUREX + -IDE]

murex′ide test′, *Biochem.* a test for detecting uric acid in a substance, usually urine, in which treatment of the specimen with nitric acid and ammonia indicates the presence of uric acid by formation of reddish-purple murexide.

Mur·frees·bor·o (mûr′frēz bûr′ō, -bur′ō), *n.* **1.** a city in central Tennessee: battle of Stone River (or Murfreesboro) 1862. 18,991 (1960). **2.** a town in NE North Carolina. 2643 (1960).

mur·geon (mûr′jən), *n. Scot.* **1.** a grimace; a wry face. **2.** a body contortion, antic, or gesture. [?]

mu·ri·ate (myŏŏr′ē āt′, -it), *n.* (not in scientific use) any chloride, esp. potassium chloride, KCl, used as a fertilizer. [back formation from MURIATIC]

mu·ri·at·ic (myŏŏr′ē at′ik), *adj.* (not in scientific use) of or derived from muriatic acid. [< L *muriātic(us)* pickled, lying in brine, equiv. to *muri(a)* brine + *-āticus;* see -ATE[1], -IC]

mu′riat′ic ac′id, (not in scientific use) See **hydrochloric acid.**

mu·ri·cate (myŏŏr′ə kāt′), *adj. Bot., Zool.* covered with short, sharp points. Also, **mu′ri·cat′ed.** [< L *mūricāt(us)* murexlike, equiv. to *mūric-* (s. of *mūrex*) a purple fish + *-ātus* -ATE[1]]

Mu·ri·el (myŏŏr′ē əl), *n.* a girl's given name.

Mu·ril·lo (myŏŏ ril′ō; *Sp.* mōō rē′lyō), *n.* **Bar·to·lo·mé Es·te·ban** (bär′tô lô me′ es te′vän), 1617–82, Spanish painter.

mu·rine (myŏŏr′in, -in), *adj.* **1.** belonging or pertaining to the *Muridae,* the family of rodents that includes the mice and rats, or to the *Murinae,* the subfamily that includes the domestic species. —*n.* **2.** a murine rodent. [< L *mūrīn(us)* of mice, equiv. to *mūr-* (s. of *mūs*) MOUSE + *-īnus* -INE[1]]

mu′rine opos′sum, any of several grayish, brownish, or russet opossums of the genus *Marmosa,* found in forests of Central and South America, often having a black, masklike marking on the face. Also called **mouse opossum.**

Murj·ite (mûr′jīt), *n. Islam.* a member of a liberal sect asserting that faith is the sole basis upon which a Muslim will be judged after death. [< Ar *murji -ah* body of believers in the doctrines of the sect; see -ITE[1]]

murk (mûrk), *n.* **1.** darkness; gloom: *the oppressing murk of a Victorian parlor.* —*adj.* **2.** dark; with little light; murky. Also, **mirk.** [ME *mirke* < Scand; cf. Icel *myrkr* dark, darkness, c. OE *myrce* dark]

murk·y (mûr′kē), *adj.,* **murk·i·er, murk·i·est. 1.** intensely dark, gloomy, and cheerless. **2.** obscure or thick with mist, haze, etc., as the air. Also, **mirky.** [ME *mirky.* See MURK, -Y[1]] —**murk′i·ly,** *adv.* —**murk′i·ness,** *n.*
—**Syn. 1.** See **dark. 2.** cloudy, dusky, lowering, misty, hazy. —**Ant. 1, 2.** bright, clear.

Mur·man′ Coast′ (mŏŏr män′), an Arctic coastal region in the NW Soviet Union in Europe, on the Kola Peninsula.

Mur·mansk (mŏŏr-mänsk′), *n.* an ice-free seaport and railroad terminus in the NW RSFSR, in the NW Soviet Union, on the Murman Coast. 262,000 (est. 1964).

mur·mur (mûr′mər), *n.* **1.** any low, continuous sound, as of a brook, the wind, trees, etc., or of low, indistinct voices. **2.** a mumbled or private expression of discontent. **3.** Also called **heart murmur.** *Med.* a sound heard on listening to the heart, usually through a stethoscope, produced by the abnormal opening and closing of the valves, the abnormal flow of blood in the chambers of the heart and the great vessels, or esp. the passage of blood through deformed valves. [ME < L] —*v.i.* **4.** to make a low or indistinct sound, esp. continuously. **5.** to speak in a low tone or indistinctly. **6.** to complain in a low tone, or in private. —*v.t.* **7.** to sound by murmurs. **8.** to utter in a low tone. [ME *murmure(n)* < L *murmurāre*] —**mur′mur·er,** *n.* —**mur′mur·less,** *adj.* —**mur′mur·less·ly,** *adv.*
—**Syn. 1.** grumble, susurration, mumble, complaint, mutter. **5.** MURMUR, MUMBLE, MUTTER mean to make sounds which are not fully intelligible. To MURMUR is to utter sounds or words in a low, almost inaudible tone, as in expressing affection, dissatisfaction, etc.: *to murmur disagreement.* To MUMBLE is to utter imperfect or inarticulate sounds with the mouth partly closed, so that the words can be distinguished only with difficulty: *to mumble the answer to a question.* To MUTTER is to utter words in a low, grumbling way, often voicing complaint or discontent, not meant to be fully audible: *to mutter complaints.* **6.** grouse. See **complain.**

mur·mur·a·tion (mûr′mə rā′shən), *n.* **1.** the act or an instance of murmuring: *His words were greeted with a murmuration from the crowd.* **2.** a flock of starlings. [ME < L *murmurātiōn-* (s. of *murmurātiō*). See MURMUR, -ATION]

mur·mur·ous (mûr′mər əs), *adj.* **1.** abounding in or characterized by murmurs. **2.** murmuring: *murmurous waters.* [MURMUR + -OUS] —**mur′mur·ous·ly,** *adv.*

mur·phy (mûr′fē), *n., pl.* **-phies,** *v.,* **-phied, -phy·ing.** *Slang.* —*n.* **1.** an Irish or white potato. **2.** any of various confidence games in which a victim is left with a sealed envelope supposedly containing money, but which contains only newspaper or scrap paper cut to the same size as paper money. —*v.t.* **3.** to victimize or dupe in such a manner. [special uses of *Murphy,* familiar Irish name]

Mur·phy (mûr′fē), *n.* **1. Frank,** 1890–1949, U.S. statesman and jurist: associate justice of the U.S. Supreme Court 1940–49. **2. William Par·ry** (par′ē), born 1892, U.S. physician: Nobel prize for medicine 1934.

Mur′phy bed′, a bed constructed so that it can be folded or swung into a cabinet or closet. [named after William L. *Murphy,* 20th-century American inventor]

Mur·phys·bor·o (mûr′fēz bûr′ō, -bur′ō), *n.* a town in SW Illinois. 8673 (1960).

mur·ra (mûr′ə), *n.* a mineral or stone used in ancient Rome for making fine vases, cups, etc.: believed to have been fluorite. Also, **murrha.** [< L *murra, murrha,* appar. back formation from *murrinus* MURRHINE]

mur·rain (mûr′in), *n.* **1.** *Vet. Pathol.* any of various diseases of cattle, as anthrax, foot-and-mouth disease, and Texas fever. **2.** *Obs.* a plague or pestilence. [ME *moreine, moryne* < MF *morine* a plague, equiv. to *mor(ir)* (to) die (< L *morī*) + *-ine* -INE[1]]

Mur·ray (mûr′ē, mur′ē), *n.* **1. Sir (George) Gilbert (Ai·mé)** (ā mā′), 1866–1957, English classical scholar. **2. Sir James Augustus Henry,** 1837–1915, Scottish lexicographer and philologist. **3. Lind·ley** (lin′lē, lind′-), 1745–1826, English grammarian, born in the U.S. **4. Philip,** 1886–1952, U.S. labor leader: president of the CIO 1940–52. **5.** a river in SE Australia, flowing W along the border between Victoria and New South Wales, through SE South Australia into the Indian Ocean. 1200 mi. long. **6.** a city in N Utah, S of Salt Lake City. 16,806 (1960). **7.** a town in SW Kentucky. 9303 (1960). **8.** a boy's given name.

murre (mûr), *n.* **1.** either of two black and white diving birds of the genus *Uria,* of northern seas, *U. aalge* **(com′mon murre′),** or *U. lomvia* **(thick′-billed′ murre′). 2.** See **razor-billed auk.** [?]

murre·let (mûr′lit), *n.* any of several small, chunky diving birds of the family *Alcidae,* found chiefly about the islands and coasts of the North Pacific. [MURRE + -LET]

mur·rey (mûr′ē), *n.* a dark purplish-red color. [ME *murrey, morrey* < MF *more* < ML *mōrātus,* equiv. to L *mōr(um)* mulberry + *-ātus* -ATE[1]]

mur·rha (mûr′ə), *n.* murra.

mur·rhine (mûr′in, -īn), *adj.* of, pertaining to, or manufactured of murra: *a murrhine vase; a murrhine vessel; a murrhine cup.* Also, **mur′rine.** [< L *murr(h)inus* < Gk *mórrinos,* equiv. to *morr(ía)* murra + *-inos* -INE[1]]

mur′rhine glass′, 1. glassware believed to resemble the murrhine cups of ancient Rome. **2.** a ware composed of glass in which metals, precious stones, or the like are embedded.

Mur·row (mûr′ō, mur′ō), *n.* **Edward R(oscoe),** 1908–65, U.S. news commentator and government official.

Mur·rum·bidg·ee (mûr′əm bij′ē), *n.* a river in SE Australia, flowing W through New South Wales to the Murray River. 1050 mi. long.

Mur·ry (mûr′ē, mur′ē), *n.* a boy's given name, form of **Murray.**

mur·ther (mûr′thər), *n., v.t., v.i. Obs.* murder. [ME *morther,* OE *morthor;* c. Goth *maurthr.* See MORTAL]

mus., 1. museum. **2.** music. **3.** musical. **4.** musician.

mu·sa·ceous (myŏŏ zā′shəs), *adj.* belonging to the *Musaceae,* or banana family of plants. [< NL *Mūsāce(ae)* family name (*Mūs(a)* genus name (< Ar *mawzah* banana) + *-āceae* -ACEAE) + -OUS]

Mu·sae·us (myŏŏ zē′əs), *n. Class. Myth.* an Attic seer and poet sometimes believed to be the son of Orpheus.

mu·saf (mōō′säf), *n. Hebrew.* the religious service celebrated by Jews in addition to and immediately after the morning service on the Sabbath and festivals. [lit., addition]

Mu·sa·ge·tes (myŏŏ saj′i tēz), *n. Class. Myth.* Apollo: so called because he was a patron of the Muses.

Mus.B., Bachelor of Music. Also, **Mus. Bac.** [< L *Musicae Baccalaureus*]

Mus·ca (mus′kə), *n., gen.* **Mus·cae** (mus′ē). *Astron.* the Fly, a small southern constellation between Crux and Chamaeleon. [< NL, L: a fly]

mus·ca·del (mus′kə del′), *n.* muscatel. Also, **mus′ca·delle′.**

mus·ca·dine (mus′kə din, -dīn′), *n.* a grape, *Vitis rotundifolia,* of the southern U.S., having dull purple, thick-skinned musky fruit and being the origin of many grape varieties. [MUSCAD(EL) + -INE[1]]

mus·cae vo·li·tan·tes (mus′ē vol′i tan′tēz), *Ophthalm.* specks that seem to dance in the air before the eyes, due to defects in the vitreous humor of the eye or to other causes. [< NL: lit., flying flies; see MUSCA, VOLITANT]

mus·ca·rine (mus′kər in, -kə rēn′), *n. Chem.* a poisonous compound, $C_8H_{19}NO_3$, found as an alkaloid in certain mushrooms, esp. fly agaric, and as a ptomaine in decaying fish. [< L *muscār(ius)* of flies (*musc(a)* fly + *-ārius* -ARY) + -INE[1]] —**mus·ca·rin·ic** (mus′kə-rin′ik), *adj.*

mus·cat (mus′kət, -kat), *n.* **1.** a variety of grape having a pronounced sweet aroma and flavor, used for making wine. **2.** the vine bearing this fruit. [short for *muscat wine* or *grape* < MF *muscat* musky < OPr, equiv. to *musc* (< L *muscus* MUSK) + *-at* -ATE[1]]

Mus·cat (mus kat′), *n.* a seaport in and the capital of Muscat and Oman, in SE Arabia. 5080 (est. 1960). Arabic, **Masqat.**

Muscat′ and Oman′, a sultanate in SE Arabia. 565,000 (est. 1963); ab. 82,000 sq. mi. *Cap.:* Muscat. Also called **Oman.**

mus·ca·tel (mus′kə tel′, mus′kə tel′), *n.* **1.** a sweet wine made from muscat grapes. **2.** muscat. Also, **muscadel, muscadelle.** [< MF, equiv. to *muscat* MUSCAT + *-el* n. suffix; r. ME *muscadell* < MF, equiv. to *muscad-* (< OPr *muscade,* fem. of *muscat* musky) + *-elle,* fem. of *-el* n. suffix]

Mus·ca·tine (mus′kə tēn′, mus′kə tēn′), *n.* a city in E Iowa, on the Mississippi. 20,997 (1960).

mus·ca·va·do (mus′kə vā′dō, -vä′-), *n.* muscovado.

mus·cic·o·lous (mə sik′ə ləs), *adj. Bot.* growing on or among mosses, as certain lichens. [< NL *Musci* name of class of mosses (L, pl. of *muscus* moss) + -COLOUS]

mus·cid (mus′id), *adj.* **1.** belonging or pertaining to the *Muscidae,* the family of dipterous insects that includes the common housefly. —*n.* **2.** any muscid fly. [< NL *Muscid(ae)* name of the family. See MUSCA, -ID[2]]

mus·cle (mus′əl), *n., v.,* **-cled, -cling.** —*n.* **1.** a tissue composed of cells or fibers, the contraction of which produces movement in the body. **2.** an organ, composed of muscle tissue, that contracts to effect a particular movement. **3.** lean meat. **4.** muscular strength; brawn: *If you want to move this you will need a great deal of muscle.* **5.** power or force, esp. of a coercive nature: *They put muscle into their policy and sent the marines.* **6.** a necessary or fundamental thing, quality, etc.: *He wanted to pare the article down without cutting the muscle from it.* —*v.t.* **7.** *Informal.* to force or compel others to make way for: *He muscled his way into the conversation.* **8.** to make more muscular: *The dancing lessons muscled her legs.* **9.** to strengthen or toughen; put muscle into. —*v.i.* **10.** *Informal.* to make one's way by force or fraud (often fol by *in*). [< medical L *muscul(us)* lit., little mouse (from fancied looks of some muscles), equiv. to *mūs* mouse + *-culus* -CLE] —**mus′cle·less,** *adj.* —**mus′cly,** *adj.*

mus′cle beach′, a beach where scantily clad young men display their muscles, engage in calisthenics, etc.

mus·cle·bound (mus′əl bound′), *adj.* having enlarged and somewhat inelastic muscles, as from excessive exercise: *a muscle-bound weight lifter.* [MUSCLE + -BOUND[1]]

mus′cle fi′ber, one of the structural cells of a muscle.

mus′cle plas′ma, the juice that can be expressed from fresh muscle.

mus′cle sense′, *Psychol., Physiol.* a sense of movement derived from afferent nerves originating in tendons, muscle tissue, skin, and joints.

Mus′cle Shoals′, 1. former rapids of the Tennessee River in SW Alabama, changed into a lake by Wilson Dam: part of the Tennessee Valley Authority. **2.** a town in NW Alabama. 4084 (1960).

mus′cle spin′dle, one of the sensory end organs in skeletal muscle.

mus·cone (mus′kōn), *n. Chem.* an oily, very slightly water-soluble, large cyclic ketone containing a 15-membered ring, $C_{16}H_{30}O$, obtained from musk: used in the perfume industry. Also, **muskone.** [MUSK + -ONE]

Mus·con·gus Bay′ boat′ (məs kong′gəs), a small centerboard sloop used for cod fishing and lobstering off the northern New England coast. Also called **Muscon′gus Bay′ sloop′.**

mus·co·va·do (mus′kə vā′dō, -vä′-), *n.* raw or unrefined sugar, obtained from the juice of the sugar cane by evaporating and draining off the molasses. Also, **muscavado.** [short for *muscovado sugar* < Pg *açucar mascavado* raw sugar, lit., sugar separated (from molasses); *mascavado,* ptp. of *mascavar,* equiv. to *mas-* from (? < L *minus* less) + *-cavar* take (< VL **capāre,* equiv. to L *capere*)]

Mus·co·vite (mus′kə vīt′), *n.* **1.** a native or inhabitant of Moscow, U.S.S.R. **2.** a native or inhabitant of the Grand Duchy of Muscovy. **3.** *Archaic.* a Russian. **4.** (*l.c.*) common light-colored mica, essentially $KAl_3Si_3O_{10}(OH)_2$, used as an electrical insulator. —*adj.* **5.** of, pertaining to, or characteristic of Moscow, Muscovy, or the Muscovites. [MUSCOV(Y) + -ITE[1]]

Mus·co·vit·ic (mus′kə vit′ik), *adj.* of, pertaining to, or characteristic of czarist Russia. [MUSCOVITE + -IC]

Mus·co·vy (mus′kə vē), *n.* **1.** Also called **Grand Duchy of Muscovy.** a principality founded c1271 and centered on the ancient city of Moscow. Its rulers gradually gained control over the neighboring Great Russian principalities and established the Russian Empire under the czars. **2.** *Archaic.* Moscow. **3.** *Archaic.* Russia.

Mus′covy duck′, a large, crested, wild duck, *Cairina moschata,* of tropical America, which has been widely domesticated. Also called **musk duck.**

muscul-, a learned borrowing from Latin meaning "muscle," used in the formation of compound words: *musculamine.* [comb. form repr. L *musculus* a muscle]

mus·cul·a·mine (mus′kyə lə mēn′, -lam′in, mus′kyə-lə mēn′, -lam′in), *n. Biochem.* spermine. [MUSCUL- + AMINE]

mus·cu·lar (mus′kyə lər), *adj.* **1.** of or pertaining to muscle or the muscles. **2.** dependent on or affected by the muscles: *muscular strength.* **3.** having well-developed muscles; brawny. **4.** vigorously and force-

fully expressed, executed, performed, etc., as if by the use of a great deal of muscular power: *muscular painting; muscular poetry.* **5.** broad, energetic, and impactful, esp. with the implication that subtlety and grace are lacking: *a muscular style.* **6.** reflected in physical activity and work: *a muscular religion.* [MUSCUL- + -AR¹] —**mus·cu·lar·i·ty** (mus′kyə lar′i tē), *n.* —**mus′cu·lar·ly,** *adv.*
—**Syn. 3.** sinewy; strong, powerful; stalwart, sturdy.

mus′cular dys′trophy, *Pathol.* a disease of unknown origin that produces a progressive muscular deterioration and wasting.

mus·cu·la·ture (mus′kyə lə chər), *n.* the muscular system of the body or of its parts. [*musculat(ion)* muscular system (see MUSCUL-, -ATION) + -URE]

Mus.D., Doctor of Music. Also, **Mus.Doc., Mus.Dr.** [< L *Musicae Doctor*]

muse (myo͞oz), *v.,* **mused, mus·ing.** —*v.i.* **1.** to reflect or meditate in silence, as on some subject. **2.** to gaze meditatively or wonderingly. —*v.t.* **3.** to meditate on. [ME *muse(n)* (to) mutter, gaze meditatively on, be astonished < MF *muser* < L *mūssāre* to mutter, be at a loss] —**mus′er,** *n.*
—**Syn. 1.** cogitate, ruminate, think; dream. **1, 3.** ponder, contemplate, deliberate.

Muse (myo͞oz), *n.* **1.** *Class. Myth.* **a.** any of a number of sister goddesses, originally given as Aoede (song), Melete (meditation), and Mneme (memory), but latterly and more commonly as the nine daughters of Zeus and Mnemosyne who presided over various arts: Calliope (epic poetry), Clio (history), Erato (lyric poetry), Euterpe (music), Melpomene (tragedy), Polyhymnia (religious music), Terpsichore (dance), Thalia (comedy), and Urania (astronomy); identified by the Romans with the Camenae. **b.** any goddess presiding over a particular art. **2.** (*sometimes l.c.*) the goddess or the power regarded as inspiring a poet. **3.** (*l.c.*) the genius or powers characteristic of a poet. [ME *Muse* < L *Mūsa* < Gk *Moûsa*]

Mu·sée des Beaux Arts (*Fr.* mʏ zā dā bō zar′), a poem (1940) by W. H. Auden.

muse·ful (myo͞oz′fəl), *adj.* *Archaic.* deeply thoughtful; pensive. [MUSE + -FUL] —**muse′ful·ly,** *adv.*

mu·se·ol·o·gy (myo͞o′zē ol′ə jē), *n.* the systematic study of the organization, management, and function of a museum. [MUSE(UM) + -O- + -LOGY] —**mu·se·o·log·i·cal** (myo͞o′zē ə loj′i kəl), *adj.* —**mu′se·ol′o·gist,** *n.*

mu·sette (myo͞o zet′; *Fr.* mʏ zet′), *n., pl.* **-settes** (-zets′; *Fr.* -zet′). **1.** a French bagpipe of the 17th and early 18th centuries, with several chambers and drones, and with the wind supplied by a bellows rather than a blowpipe. **2.** a woodwind instrument similar to but smaller than a shawm. **3.** a short musical piece with a drone bass, often forming the middle section of a gavotte. [ME < MF, equiv. to *muse* bagpipe (deriv. of *muser* to play the bagpipe < L *mūssāre* to hum; see MUSE¹) + *-ette* -ETTE]

musette′ bag′, a small leather or canvas bag for personal belongings of army officers, carried by a shoulder strap. Also called **field bag.**

mu·se·um (myo͞o zē′əm), *n.* a building or place where works of art, scientific specimens, and other objects of permanent value are kept and displayed. [< L < Gk *Mouseîon,* equiv. to *Moûs(a)* MUSE + *-eion* locative suffix]

muse′um piece′, **1.** anything that is very old-fashioned or decrepit, esp. something that has outlived its usefulness: *That car he drives is a museum piece.* **2.** something suitable for keeping and exhibiting in a museum.

mush¹ (mush *or, esp. Dial.,* mo͝osh), *n.* **1.** *U.S.* meal, esp. corn meal, boiled in water or milk until it forms a thick, soft mass, or until it is stiff enough to mold into a loaf for slicing and frying. **2.** any thick, soft mass. **3.** anything unpleasantly lacking in firmness, force, dignity, etc.: *His entire argument was simply mush.* **4.** mawkish sentimentality or amorousness. **5.** *Naut.* brash (def. 5). [obs. *moose* porridge (OE *mōs* food) + (MA)SH]

mush² (mush), *v.i.* **1.** to go or travel, esp. over snow with a dog team and sled. —*interj.* **2.** an order to start or speed up a dog team. —*n.* **3.** a trip or journey, esp. across snow and ice with a dog team. [? < CanF *mouche(r)* (to) make haste, deriv. of F *mouche* fly < L *musca*] —**mush′er,** *n.*

mush·room (mush′ro͞om, -ro͝om), *n.* **1.** any of various fleshy fungi including the toadstools, puffballs, coral fungi, morels, etc. **2.** any of several edible species, esp. of the family *Agaricaceae,* as *Agaricus campestris* (**meadow mushroom** or **field mushroom**), cultivated for food in the U.S. **3.** anything of similar shape or correspondingly rapid growth. **4.** a large, mushroom-shaped cloud of smoke or rubble, which is formed in the atmosphere as a result of an explosion, esp. a nuclear explosion. —*adj.* **5.** of, consisting of, or containing mushrooms: *a mushroom omelet.* **6.** resembling a mushroom in shape or form. **7.** of rapid growth and often brief duration: *mushroom towns of the gold-rush days.* —*v.i.* **8.** to gather mushrooms. **9.** to have or assume the shape of a mushroom. **10.** to spread, grow, or develop quickly. [alter. (by folk etymology) of ME *muscheron, musseroun* < MF *mousseron* << LL *mussiriōn-* (s. of *mussiriō*)] —**mush′room-like′,** *adj.* —**mush′room·y,** *adj.*

A
B
C
D
E

Mushroom
A, Pileus; B, Annulus; C, Stem; D, Volva; E, Gills

mush′room an′chor, *Naut.* a stockless anchor having a bowllike head, used chiefly for semipermanent moorings.

mush′room cloud′, a large, mushroom-shaped cloud, often extending from the ground into the stratosphere, resulting from the explosion of a nuclear bomb above the surface of the earth.

mush′room slab′ construc′tion, beamless reinforced-concrete floor and roof construction employing columns with widely flaring heads having horizontal rings of reinforcement to support the floor or roof slab.

mush′room ven′tilator, a ventilator having at the top of a vertical shaft a broad rounded cap which can be screwed down to close it.

mush·y (mush′ē *or, esp. Dial.,* mo͝osh′ē), *adj.,* **mush·i·er, mush·i·est.** **1.** resembling mush; pulpy. **2.** *Informal.* overly emotional or sentimental, esp. in regard to love, art, humanitarian impulses, etc.: *mushy love letters.* [MUSH¹ + -Y¹] —**mush′i·ly,** *adv.* —**mush′i·ness,** *n.*

Mu·si·al (myo͞o′zē əl, -zhē əl, -zhəl), *n.* **Stanley Frank** ("*Stan the Man*"), born 1920, U.S. baseball player.

mu·sic (myo͞o′zik), *n.* **1.** an art of sound in time which expresses ideas and emotions in significant forms through the elements of rhythm, melody, harmony, and color. **2.** the tones or sounds employed, occurring in single line (melody) or multiple lines (harmony), and sounded or to be sounded by one or more voices or instruments, or both. **3.** musical work or compositions for singing or playing. **4.** the written or printed score of a musical composition. **5.** such scores collectively. **6.** any sweet, pleasing, or harmonious sounds or sound: *the music of the waves.* **7.** appreciation of or responsiveness to musical sounds or harmonies: *Music was in his very soul.* **8.** *Fox Hunting.* the cry of the hounds. **9. face the music,** *Informal.* to meet, take, or accept the consequences of one's mistakes, actions, etc.: *For years he's been selfish and irresponsible, and now he's got to face the music.* [ME *musike* < L *mūsica* < Gk *mousikḗ* (the art) of the Muse, fem. of *mousikós,* equiv. to *Moûs(a)* Muse + *-ikos* -IC] —**mu′sic·less,** *adj.*

mu·si·ca fic·ta (myo͞o′zə kə fik′tə; *Lat.* mo͞o′si kä′ fik′tä), the use of chromatically altered tones in the contrapuntal music of the 10th to the 16th centuries. Also, **mu′sica fal′sa** (myo͞o′zi kə fôl′sə; *Lat.* mo͞o′si-kä′ fäl′sä). [< ML: lit., fashioned music]

mu·si·cal (myo͞o′zi kəl), *adj.* **1.** of, pertaining to, or producing music: *a musical instrument.* **2.** of the nature of or resembling music; melodious; harmonious. **3.** fond of or skilled in music. **4.** set to or accompanied by music: *a musical entertainment.* —*n.* **5.** See **musical comedy.** [ME < ML *mūsicāl(is).* See MUSIC, -AL¹] —**mu′si·cal·ly,** *adv.* —**mu′si·cal′i·ty, mu′si·cal·ness,** *n.*

mu′sical box′, *Brit.* See **music box.**

mu′sical chairs′, a children's game in which any number of players march to music around two rows of chairs placed back to back, there being one chair less than the number of players, the object being to find a seat when the music stops abruptly. The player failing to do so is removed from the game, together with one chair, at each interval. Also called **going to Jerusalem.**

mu′sical com′edy, a play with music, often of a whimsical or satirical nature, based on a slight plot with singing and dancing in solos and groups.

mu·si·cale (myo͞o′zə kal′), *n.* a program of music forming part of a social occasion. [< F, short for *soirée musicale* (fem.) musical evening]

mu′sic box′, a box or case containing an apparatus for producing music mechanically, as by means of a comblike steel plate with tuned teeth sounded by small pegs or pins in the surface of a revolving cylinder or disk. Also, *Brit.,* **musical box.**

mu′sic dra′ma, an opera having more or less continuous musical and dramatic activity without arias, recitatives, or ensembles, using leitmotifs extensively, and having a libretto based on a mythological subject. Cf. **number opera.**

mu′sic hall′, **1.** a hall for musical entertainments. **2.** *Chiefly Brit.* a vaudeville or variety theater.

mu·si·cian (myo͞o zish′ən), *n.* **1.** a person who makes music a profession, esp. as a performer on an instrument. **2.** a person skilled in playing a musical instrument. [ME *musicien* < MF. See MUSIC, -IAN] —**mu·si′cian·ly,** *adj.*

mu·si·cian·ship (myo͞o zish′ən ship′), *n.* knowledge, skill, and artistic sensitivity in performing music. [MUSICIAN + -SHIP]

mu′sic of the spheres′, a music, imperceptible to human ears, formerly supposed to be produced by the movements of the spheres or heavenly bodies.

mu·si·col·o·gy (myo͞o′zə kol′ə jē), *n.* the scholarly or scientific study of music, as in historical research, musical theory, the physical nature of sound, etc. [MUSIC + -O- + -LOGY] —**mu·si·co·log·i·cal** (myo͞o′zə kə loj′i-kəl), *adj.* —**mu′si·co·log′i·cal·ly,** *adv.* —**mu′si·col′o·gist,** *n.*

mu′sic roll′, **1.** a roll of perforated paper for actuating a player piano. **2.** *Informal.* a roll of toilet paper.

mu′sic stand′, a device designed to hold music in position for reading.

Mu·si·do·ra (myo͞o′zi dôr′ ə, -dōr′ə), *n.* a girl's given name.

Mu·si·gny (mo͞o zēn yē′; *Fr.* mʏ zē nyē′), *n.* a dry, red wine of the Burgundy region in France.

Mu·sil (mo͞o′sil, -zil), *n.* **Robert,** 1880–1942, Austrian writer.

mus·ing (myo͞o′zing), *adj.* **1.** absorbed in thought; meditative. —*n.* **2.** contemplation; reflection. [ME; see MUSE, -ING², -ING¹] —**mus′ing·ly,** *adv.*

mu·sique con·crète (mʏ zēk kôɴ kret′), *French.* tape-recorded musical and natural sounds, often electronically distorted, arranged in planned combinations, sequences, and rhythmic patterns to create an artistic work. Cf. **electronic music.**

mus·jid (mus′jid), *n.* *Arabic.* masjid.

musk (musk), *n.* **1.** a substance secreted in a glandular sac under the skin of the abdomen of the male musk deer, having a strong odor, and used in perfumery. **2.** an artificial imitation of the substance. **3.** a similar secretion of other animals, as the civet, muskrat, otter, etc. **4.** the odor of musk, or some similar odor. **5.** *Bot.* any of several plants, as the monkey flower, having a musky fragrance. [ME *muske,* var. of *musco* < LL, abl. sing. of *muscus* < LGk *móschos* < Pers *mushk*]

mus·kal·longe (mus′kə lonj′), *n., pl.* **-longe.** muskellunge.

musk′ bag′, the musk-secreting gland of a male musk deer. Also called **musk′ gland′.**

musk′ deer′, a small, hornless deer, *Moschus moschiferus,* of central Asia, the male of which secretes musk.

musk′ duck′, **1.** See **Muscovy duck.** **2.** an Australian duck, *Biziura lobata,* having a musky odor.

mus·keg (mus′keg), *n.* a bog of northern North America, commonly having sphagnum mosses, sedge, and sometimes stunted black spruce and tamarack trees. [< Algonquian (Ojibwa): grassy bog]

Mus·ke·gon (mus kē′gən), *n.* a port in W Michigan, on Lake Michigan. 46,485 (1960).

Muske′gon Heights′, a city in W Michigan, on Lake Michigan. 19,552 (1960).

mus·kel·lunge (mus′kə lunj′), *n., pl.* **-lunge.** a large game fish, *Esox masquinongy,* of the pike family, found in the lakes and rivers of eastern and middle western North America. Also, **maskalonge, maskanonge, maskinonge, muskallonge.** [dissimilated var. of Ojibwa *mashkinonge* great pike]

mus·ket (mus′kit), *n.* **1.** a heavy, large-caliber hand gun for infantry soldiers, introduced in the 16th century, the predecessor of the modern rifle. **2.** the male sparrow hawk, *Accipiter nisus.* [< MF *mousquet* < It *moschet-t(o)* crossbow arrow, later musket, orig. kind of hawk, equiv. to *mosch(a)* fly (< L *musca*) + *-etto* -ET]

mus·ket·eer (mus′ki tēr′), *n.* a soldier armed with a musket. [MUSKET + -EER; cf. F *mousquetaire,* equiv. to *mousquet* musket + *-aire* -ARY]

mus·ket·ry (mus′ki trē), *n.* **1.** *Mil.* the technique of bringing fire from a group of rifle and automatic weapons to bear on specified targets. **2.** muskets or musketeers collectively. [< F *mousqueterie.* See MUSKET, -RY]

mus·kie (mus′kē), *n.* muskellunge. [MUSK(ELLUNGE) + -IE]

Mus·kie (mus′kē), *n.* **Edmund (Sixtus),** born 1914, U.S. political leader: governor of Maine 1955–59; senator 1959–80; Secretary of State 1980–81.

musk′ mal′low, **1.** Also called **musk rose.** a European mallow, *Malva moschata,* introduced into North America, having musk-scented foliage. **2.** abelmosk.

musk·mel·on (musk′mel′ən), *n.* **1.** a round or oblong melon, occurring in many varieties, having a juicy, often aromatic, sweet, yellow, white, or green, edible flesh. **2.** the plant, *Cucumis Melo,* bearing this fruit. **3.** cantaloupe (def. 1). [MUSK + MELON]

Mus·ko·ge·an (mus kō′gē ən), *n.* a family of American Indian languages of the southeastern U.S., including Choctaw, Creek, and several less well-known languages. Also, **Mus·kho′ge·an.**

Mus·ko·gee (mus kō′gē), *n., pl.* **-gees,** (*esp. collectively*) **-gee** for 2. **1.** a city in E Oklahoma. 38,059 (1960). **2.** a member of an American Indian people formerly constituting part of the Creek Confederacy in Georgia and Alabama and now living in Oklahoma. **3.** Creek (def. 2).

Musk ox
(4 to 5 ft. high at shoulder; length 8 ft.)

mus·kone (mus′kōn), *n.* *Chem.* muscone

musk′ ox′, a bovine ruminant, *Ovibos moschatus,* of arctic regions of North America, that is between an ox and a sheep in size and anatomy. [so called from its odor]

musk·rat (musk′rat′), *n., pl.* **-rats,** (*esp. collectively*) **-rat.** **1.** a large, aquatic, North American rodent, *Ondatra zibethica,* having a musky odor. **2.** its thick, light-brown fur, used for women's coats, as a trimming on women's suits, for hats, etc. [MUSK + RAT, folk-etymological var. of MUSQUASH]

Muskrat
(Total length about 2 ft.; tail to 11 in.)

musk′ rose′, **1.** a rose, *Rosa moschata,* of the Mediterranean region, having white, musk-scented flowers. **2.** See **musk mallow** (def. 1).

musk′ this′tle, a thistle, *Carduus nutans,* having heads of nodding, crimson-purple flowers, introduced into the U.S. from Eurasia.

musk′ tur′tle, any of several aquatic turtles of the genus *Sternothaerus,* of North and Central America, which, when disturbed, emit a musky secretion. [so called from its musky smell]

musk·y¹ (mus′kē), *adj.,* **musk·i·er, musk·i·est.** of or like musk, as an odor: *a musky perfume.* [MUSK + -Y¹] —**musk′i·ness,** *n.*

mus·ky² (mus′kē), *n., pl.* **-kies.** muskellunge. [var. of MUSKIE]

Mus·lem (muz′ləm, mo͝oz′-, mo͝os′-), *adj., n., pl.* **-lems, -lem.** Muslim.

Mus·lim (muz′lim, mo͝oz′-, mo͝os′-), *adj., n., pl.* **-lims, -lim.** —*adj.* **1.** of or pertaining to the religion, law, or civilization of Islam. —*n.* **2.** an adherent of Islam. Also, **Moslem, Muslem.** [< Ar: one who submits. See ISLAM]

mus·lin (muz′lin), *n.* a cotton fabric made in various degrees of fineness, and often printed, woven, or embroidered in patterns, esp. a cotton fabric of plain weave, used for sheets and for a variety of other purposes. [< F *mousseline* < It *mussolina,* equiv. to *Mussol(o)* Mosul, Iraq (where first made) + *-ina* -INE¹]

mus′lin delaine′. See **mousseline de laine.**

mus′lin kail′, *Scot.* barley broth or barley and vegetable soup. [MUSLIN (? in the sense, thin)]

Mus.M., Master of Music. [< L *Musicae Magister*]

mus·nud (mus′nəd), *n.* (in India) a seat or throne of cushions used by native princes. [< Urdu *masnad* < Ar]

Mus·pel·heim (mo͝os′pəl hām′), *n.* *Scand. Myth.* a region of fire, the heat of which turns the ice of Niflheim to mist. Also, **Mus·pels·heim, Mus·pells·heim** (mo͝os′-pəls hām′). Also called **Mus·pell** (mo͝os′pəl).

mus·quash (mus′kwosh), *n.* **1.** muskrat. **2.** *Chiefly Brit.* muskrat fur: *She wore a musquash coat.* [< Algonquian (Virginia): it is red]

mus′quash root′, See **spotted cowbane.**

muss (mus), *n.* **1.** *Informal.* a state of disorder, untidiness, or confusion. —*v.t.* **2.** to put into disorder; make messy; rumple (often fol. by *up*). [appar. M(ESS) + (F)USS]

mus·sel (mus′əl), *n.* any bivalve mollusk, esp. an edible marine bivalve of the family *Mytilidae* and a fresh-water clam of the family *Unionidae*. [ME, OE *muscle* < LL *muscula*, var. of L *musculus* little mouse, sea-mussel. See MUSCLE]

mus′sel crab′, a pea crab, *Pinnotheres maculatus,* the female of which lives as a commensal within the mantle cavity of mussels and other bivalve mollusks.

Mussel, *Mytilus edulis* (Length 4 in.)

Mus·set (my sā′), *n.* **(Louis Charles) Al·fred de** (lwē shärl al fred′ də), 1810–57, French poet, dramatist, and novelist.

mus·si·tate (mus′i tāt′), *v.i.,* **-tat·ed, -tat·ing.** *Obs.* to mutter; mumble. [< L *mussitāt(us)* muttered (ptp. of *mussitāre*), equiv. to *muss(āre)* (to) mutter + *-it-* freq. suffix + *-ātus* -ATE¹]

mus·si·ta·tion (mus′i tā′shən), *n.* **1.** silent movement of the lips in simulation of the movements made in audible speech. **2.** muttering; mumbling; murmuring. [<LL *mussitātiōn-* (s. of *mussitātiō*). See MUSSITATE, -ION]

Mus·so·li·ni (mo͝os′ə lē′nē, mo͞o′sə-; *It.* mo͞os′sô-lē′nē), *n.* **Be·ni·to** (bə nē′tō; *It.* be nē′tô), ("*Il Duce*"), 1883–1945, Italian Fascist leader: premier of Italy 1922–43.

Mus·sorg·sky (mə zôrg′skē; *Russ.* mo͞o′sôrg′ski), *n.* **Mo·dest Pe·tro·vich** (mo dest′ pe trô′vich). See **Moussorgsky, Modest Petrovich.** Also, **Mus·sorg′ski.**

mus·suck (mus′ək), *n.* *Anglo-Indian.* a water bag made of leather, esp. of goatskin. [< Hindi *maśak*]

Mus·sul·man (mus′əl mən), *n., pl.* **-mans.** a Muslim. [< Pers *Musulmān* (pl.) < Ar *Muslimūn*, pl. of *Muslim* MUSLIM]

muss·y (mus′ē), *adj.,* **muss·i·er, muss·i·est.** *Informal.* untidy, messy, or rumpled. [MUSS + -Y¹] —**muss′i·ly,** *adv.* —**muss′i·ness,** *n.*

must¹ (must), *auxiliary verb.* **1.** to be bound or obliged to by an imperative requirement; ought to; should: *I must keep my word.* **2.** to be under the necessity to: *Man must eat to live.* **3.** to be compelled to, as by the use or threat of force: *You must obey the law.* **4.** to be forced to, as by convention, the requirements of honesty, etc.: *I must say, that is a lovely hat.* **5.** to have to: *I must go to the store and buy that book.* **6.** to be reasonably expected to; is bound to: *It must have stopped raining by now. She must be at least 40.* **7.** to be inevitably certain to: *Man must die.* **8.** to be sure to; be certain to: *He must know that!* —*v.i.* **9.** to be obliged; feel compelled: *Do I have to go? I must, I suppose.* **10.** *Archaic.* (sometimes used with ellipsis of *go, get,* or some similar verb readily understood from the context): *We must away.* —*adj.* **11.** necessary; vital: *A raincoat is must clothing in this area.* —*n.* **12.** anything necessary or vital: *This law is a must.* [ME *most(e)*, OE *mōste* past tense; c. G *musste.* See MOTE²]
—**Syn. 1.** MUST, OUGHT, SHOULD express necessity or duty. MUST expresses necessity, or compulsion: *All men must die. I must attend to those patients first. Soldiers must obey orders.* OUGHT (weaker than MUST) expresses obligation, duty, desirability: *You ought to tell your mother.* SHOULD expresses obligation, expectation, or probability: *You are not behaving as you should. Children should be taught to speak the truth. They should arrive at one o'clock.* It also expresses the conditional: *I should be glad to play if I could;* and future intention: *I said I should be home next week.*

must² (must), *n.* new wine; the unfermented juice as pressed from the grape or other fruit. [ME, OE < L *must(um)*, short for *vīnum mustum* new wine]

must³ (must), *n.* mold; moldiness; mustiness: *a castle harboring the must of centuries.* [back formation from MUSTY¹]

must⁴ (must), *n.* musth.

must⁵ (must), *Obs.* —*n.* **1.** musk, esp. a powder made from musk. —*v.t.* **2.** to powder (the hair). [late ME *moist* < MF *must,* var. of *musc* MUSK]

mus·tache (mus′tash, mə stash′), *n.* **1.** the hair growing on the upper lip of men, or either half of such a growth of hair. **2.** such hair when allowed to grow without shaving, and usually trimmed in any of various shapes. **3.** hairs or bristles growing near the mouth of an animal. **4.** a stripe of color, or elongated feathers, suggestive of a mustache on the side of the head of a bird. Also, **mous·tache.** [< MF *moustache* < It *mostaccio;* see MUSTACHIO] —**mus′tached,** *adj.*

mus′tache cup′, a cup having a straight piece inside, just below the rim, for holding back a man's mustache while he is drinking.

mus·ta·chio (mə stä′shō, -shē ō′, -stash′ō, -stash′ē-ō′), *n., pl.* **-chios.** a mustache. [< Sp *mostacho* and its source, It *mostaccio,* var. of *mostacchio* < MGk *moustáki* < DoricGk *mystak-* (s. of *mýstax*) upper lip, mustache] —**mus·ta′chioed,** *adj.*

Mus·ta·fa Ke·mal (mo͝os′tä fä kə mäl′). See **Kemal Atatürk.**

Mus·tagh (mo͞os täkh′), *n.* Karakoram (def. 1).

mus·tang (mus′tang), *n.* **1.** the small, hardy horse of the American plains, descended from Spanish stock. **2.** *U.S. Navy Slang.* a naval officer who received his commission while an enlisted man. [< Sp *mestengo* stray or ownerless beast, n. use of masc. adj.: pertaining to a mixed lot of beasts, equiv. to *mest(a)* such a mixed lot (< L *(animālia) mixta* mixed (beasts), neut. pl. adj., taken as fem. sing. noun; see MIXED) + *-engo* adj. suffix]

mus·tard (mus′tərd), *n.* **1.** a pungent powder or paste prepared from the seed of the mustard plant, much used as a food seasoning or condiment, and medicinally in plasters, poultices, etc. **2.** any of various brassicaceous plants, esp. of the genus *Brassica,* as *B. nigra* **(black mustard),** the chief source of commercial mustard, *B. hirta* **(white mustard),** or *B. juncea* **(leaf mustard),** the leaves of which are used for food. **3. cut the mustard,** *Slang.* to reach or surpass the desired standard of performance: *a pitcher who cuts the mustard with his fast ball.* [ME < OF *moustarde* a relish orig. made of mustard seed and must, equiv. to *moust* MUST² + *-arde* -ARD]

mus′tard gas′, a liquid chemical-warfare agent, $(ClCH_2CH_2)_2S$, producing burns, blindness, and death; introduced by the Germans in World War I. Also called **dichlorodiethyl sulfide.** [so called from its mustard-like effects on eyes and lungs]

mus′tard oil′, oil expressed from the seed of mustard, esp. a carbylamine: used chiefly in making soap.

mus′tard plas′ter, a black, powdered mixture of mustard and rubber in solution, placed on a cloth and used as a counterirritant.

mus·tee (mu stē′, mus′tē), *n.* **1.** the offspring of a white person and a quadroon; octoroon. **2.** a half-breed. [short var. of MESTIZO]

mus·te·lid (mus′tᵊlid), *n.* **1.** any of numerous carnivorous mammals of the family *Mustelidae,* comprising the weasels, martens, skunks, badgers, otters, etc. —*adj.* **2.** belonging or pertaining to the family *Mustelidae.* [< NL *Mustelid(ae),* equiv. to L *mustēl(a)* weasel + *-idae* -ID²]

mus·te·line (mus′tᵊlīn′, -tᵊlin), *adj.* **1.** belonging or pertaining to the family *Mustelidae,* including the martens, skunks, minks, weasels, badgers, otters, etc. **2.** resembling a weasel. **3.** tawny or brown, like a weasel in summer. [< L *mustēlīn(us),* equiv. to *mustēl(a)* weasel (*mūs* mouse + *-ēla,* var. of *-ella* dim. suffix) + *-īnus* -INE¹]

mus·ter (mus′tər), *v.t.* **1.** to assemble (troops, a ship's crew, etc.), as for battle, display, inspection, orders, discharge, etc. **2.** to gather or summon (often fol. by *up*): *He mustered up all his courage and charged into the office.* —*v.i.* **3.** to assemble for inspection, service, etc., as troops or forces. **4.** to come together; collect; gather. **5. muster in** or **out,** to enlist into or discharge from military service: *He will be mustered out of the army in only two more months.* —*n.* **6.** an assembling of troops or men for inspection or other purposes. **7.** an assemblage or collection. **8.** the act of mustering. **9.** Also called **mus′ter roll′.** (formerly) a list of the men enrolled in a military or naval unit. **10. pass muster, a.** to pass a cursory inspection. **b.** to measure up to a certain standard; be adequate: *Your reports better pass muster or you'll be dropped from the committee.* [ME *mostre(n)* < OF *mostre(r)* < L *monstrāre* to show, deriv. of *monstrum* portent; see MONSTER]
—**Syn. 1.** convoke. See **gather. 1, 4.** convene; congregate. **7.** gathering, assembly, convention. —**Ant. 1, 4.** scatter, separate.

musth (must), *n.* a state or condition of violent, destructive frenzy occurring somewhat periodically in male elephants, accompanied by the exudation of an oily substance from glands between the eyes and mouth. Also, **must.** [< Urdu *mast* < Pers: lit., drunk]

must·n't (mus′ənt), contraction of *must not.*

mus·ty¹ (mus′tē), *adj.,* **-ti·er, -ti·est. 1.** having an odor or flavor suggestive of mold, as old buildings, long-closed rooms, food, etc. **2.** made obsolete by time; antiquated: *musty laws.* **3.** dull; apathetic. [? var. of *moisty* (ME; see MOIST, -Y¹) with loss of *i* before *s* as in *master,* etc.] —**mus′ti·ly,** *adv.* —**mus′ti·ness,** *n.*

mus·ty² (mus′tē), *n., pl.* **-ties.** (formerly) a kind of snuff having a musty flavor. [n. use of adj.]

mut¹ (mut), *n.* mutt.

mut² (mut), *n.* *Print.* mutton². [by shortening]

mut., 1. mutilated. **2.** mutual.

mu·ta·ble (myo͞o′tə bəl), *adj.* **1.** liable or subject to change or alteration. **2.** given to changing, or ever changing; fickle or inconstant: *the mutable ways of fortune.* [ME < L *mūtābil(is),* equiv. to *mūtā(re)* (to) change + *-bilis* -BLE] —**mu′ta·bil′i·ty, mu′ta·ble·ness,** *n.* —**mu′ta·bly,** *adv.*
—**Syn. 1.** changeable, variable. **2.** unstable, vacillating, unsettled, wavering, unsteady. —**Ant. 2.** stable.

mu·ta·gen (myo͞o′tə jin, -jen′), *n.* a substance or preparation capable of inducing mutation. [MUTA(TION) + -GEN]

mu·ta·gen·e·sis (myo͞o′tə jen′i sis), *n.* the origin and development of a mutation. [< NL; see MUTATION, GENESIS] —**mu·ta·ge·net·ic** (myo͞o′tə jə-net′ik), *adj.*

mu·ta·gen·ic (myo͞o′tə jen′ik), *adj.* capable of inducing a mutation. [MUTAGEN + -IC] —**mu′ta·gen′i·cal·ly,** *adv.*

mu·tant (myo͞ot′ənt), *adj.* **1.** undergoing mutation; resulting from mutation. —*n.* **2.** a new type of organism produced as the result of mutation. [< L *mūtant-* (s. of *mūtāns*) changing, prp. of *mūtāre;* see -ANT]

mu·ta·ro·ta·tion (myo͞o′tə rō tā′shən), *n.* *Chem.* a gradual change in the optical rotation of freshly prepared solutions of reducing sugars. [< L *mūtā(re)* (to) change + ROTATION]

mu·tase (myo͞o′tās), *n.* *Biochem.* **1.** any of the class of oxido-reductase enzymes that catalyze the simultaneous oxidation and reduction of a single compound, as the conversion of acetaldehyde to acetic acid and ethyl alcohol. **2.** any of various enzymes, as phosphoglucomutase, that catalyze intramolecular rearrangements. [< L *mūt(āre)* (to) change + -ASE]

mu·tate (myo͞o′tāt), *v.,* **-tat·ed, -tat·ing.** —*v.t.* **1.** to change; alter. **2.** *Phonet.* to change by umlaut. —*v.i.* **3.** to change; undergo mutation. [< L *mūtāt(us)* changed, ptp. of *mūtāre;* see -ATE¹] —**mu·ta·tive** (myo͞o′tə tiv), *adj.*

mu·ta·tion (myo͞o tā′shən), *n.* **1.** the act or process of changing. **2.** a change or alteration, as in form, qualities, or nature. **3.** *Biol.* **a.** a sudden departure from the parent type, as when an individual differs from its parents in one or more heritable characteristics, caused by a change in a gene or a chromosome. **b.** an individual, species, or the like, resulting from such a departure. **4.** *Phonet.* umlaut. **5.** *Ling.* (in Celtic languages) syntactically determined morphophonemic phenomena that affect initial sounds of words. [ME *mutacio(u)n* < L *mūtātiōn-* (s. of *mūtātiō*) a changing. See MUTATE, -ION] —**mu·ta′tion·al,** *adj.* —**mu·ta′tion·al·ly,** *adv.*

mu·ta·tis mu·tan·dis (mo͞o tä′tēs mo͞o tän′dēs; *Eng.* myo͞o tā′tis myo͞o tan′dis), *Latin.* the necessary changes having been made.

mu·ta·to no·mi·ne (mo͞o tä′tō nō′mi ne; *Eng.* myo͞o-tā′tō nom′ə nē), *Latin.* the name having been changed.

Mu·ta·zi·la (mo͞o tä′zə lə), *n.* See under **Mutazilite.**

Mu·ta·zi·lite (mo͞o tä′zə līt′), *n.* *Islam.* a member of an extinct theological sect **(Mutazila),** that maintained that nothing but eternity could be predicated of Allah, that the eternal nature of the Koran was questionable, and that man does good or evil of his own free will. [< Ar *mu'tazil(ah)* + -ITE¹] —**Mu·ta′zi·lism,** *n.*

mutch (much), *n.* *Brit. Dial.* a close-fitting linen or muslin cap, as worn by elderly women or babies. [late ME *much* < MD *mutse;* c. G *Mütze* cap. See AMICE²]

mutch·kin (much′kin), *n.* **1.** *Scot.* a unit of liquid measure equal to a little less than a U.S. liquid pint. **2.** a vessel, usually of pewter, holding this quantity. [ME *muchekyn* < MD *mudseken,* equiv. to *mudse-* (dim. of *mudde* << L *modius;* see MODIOLUS) + *-ken* -KIN]

mut′ dash′, *Print.* a dash equal in length to one side of an em quad; em dash.

mute (myo͞ot), *adj., n., v.,* **mut·ed, mut·ing.** —*adj.* **1.** silent; refraining from speech or utterance. **2.** not emitting or having sound of any kind. **3.** incapable of speech; dumb. **4.** (of letters) silent; not pronounced. **5.** *Law.* (of one who has been arraigned) making no plea or giving an irrelevant response when arraigned, or refusing to stand trial (used chiefly in the phrase *to stand mute*). **6.** *Fox Hunting.* (of a hound) hunting a line without giving tongue or cry. —*n.* **7.** a person unable to utter words. **8.** an actor whose part is confined to dumb show. **9.** *Law.* a person who remains mute when arraigned. **10.** *Brit. Obs.* a hired mourner at a funeral; a professional mourner. **11.** Also called **sordino.** a mechanical device of various shapes and materials for muffling the tone of a musical instrument. **12.** *Phonetics.* a stop. —*v.t.* **13.** to deaden or muffle the sound of. **14.** to reduce the intensity of (a color) by the addition of another color. [< L *mūt(us)* dumb; r. ME *muet* < MF < LL **mūtett(us),* equiv. to L *mūt(us)* + *-ettus* dim. suffix] —**mute′ly,** *adv.* —**mute′ness,** *n.*
—**Syn. 3.** still. See **dumb.** —**Ant. 1.** talkative.

mut·ed (myo͞o′tid), *adj.* of low intensity and reduced volume; softened: *She spoke in muted tones.* [MUTE + -ED²] —**mut′ed·ly,** *adv.*

mute′ swan′, a commonly domesticated white swan, *Cygnus olor,* of Europe and Asia.

mu·ti·cous (myo͞o′tə kəs), *adj.* **1.** *Bot.* having no pointed process or awn; awnless. **2.** Also, **mu·tic** (myo͞o′tik). *Zool.* lacking certain defensive structures, as spines, claws, etc. Also, **mu·ti·cate** (myo͞o′tə kāt′, -kit). [< L *muticus* curtailed. See MUTILATE]

mu·ti·late (myo͞ot′ᵊlāt′), *v.t.,* **-lat·ed, -lat·ing. 1.** to deprive (a person or animal) of a limb or other essential part. **2.** to injure, disfigure, or make imperfect by removing or irreparably damaging parts. [< L *mutilāt(us)* cut off, maimed (ptp. of *mutilāre*), equiv. to *mutil(us)* maimed, mutilated + *-ātus* -ATE¹] —**mu′ti·la′tion,** *n.* —**mu′ti·la′tive, mu·ti·la·to·ry** (myo͞ot′ᵊlə tôr′ē, -tōr′ē), *adj.* —**mu′ti·la′tor,** *n.*
—**Syn. 1.** See **maim. 2.** damage, mar, cripple.

mu·ti·neer (myo͞ot′ᵊnēr′), *n.* a person who mutinies. [< MF *mutinier,* equiv. to *mutin* mutiny, mutinous (< VL **movitīn(us);* see MOVE, -ITE², -INE¹) + *-ier* -EER]

mu·ti·nous (myo͞ot′ᵊnəs), *adj.* **1.** disposed to, engaged in, or involving revolt against authority. **2.** characterized by mutiny; rebellious. **3.** difficult to control: *mutinous feelings.* [obs. *mutine* muting (< MF *mutin;* see MUTINEER) + -OUS] —**mu′ti·nous·ly,** *adv.* —**mu′ti·nous·ness,** *n.*
—**Syn. 1.** seditious, insurrectionary, revolutionary, insurgent. **2.** refractory, insubordinate, riotous, disaffected. —**Ant. 1.** patriotic. **2.** obedient.

Mu·ti·nus (myo͞o tī′nəs), *n.* an ancient Italian god of fertility in marriage, identified in Roman mythology with Priapus. Also, **Mu·tu·nus** (myo͞o to͞o′nəs).

mu·ti·ny (myo͞ot′ᵊnē), *n., pl.* **-nies,** *v.,* **-nied, -ny·ing.** —*n.* **1.** revolt or rebellion against constituted authority, esp. by seamen or soldiers against their officers. **2.** rebellion against any authority. —*v.t.* **3.** to commit the offense of mutiny; revolt against authority. [obs. *mutine* to mutiny (< MF *mutine(r),* deriv. of *mutin* mutiny; see MUTINEER) + -Y³]

mut·ism (myo͞o′tiz əm), *n.* *Psychiatry.* a conscious or unconscious refusal to respond verbally to interrogation, present in some mental disorders. [< NL *mūtism(us).* See MUTE, -ISM]

mu·to·scope (myo͞o′tə skōp′), *n.* a machine for giving a peep show in the form of a motion picture, the frames being on a series of cards mounted radially on a rotating drum which are bent down as they come up to the level of the eyepiece, then are released one by one to spring up before the eyepiece. [*muto-* (comb. form repr. L *mūtāre* to change) + -SCOPE]

Mu·tsu·hi·to (mo͞o′tso͞o hē′tō), *n.* 1852–1912, emperor of Japan 1867–1912.

mutt (mut), *n.* *Slang.* **1.** a dog, esp. a mongrel. **2.** a simpleton; a stupid person. Also, **mut.** [short for MUTTONHEAD]

mut·ter (mut′ər), *v.i.* **1.** to utter words indistinctly or in a low tone, often in talking to oneself or in making obscure complaints, threats, etc.; murmur; grumble. **2.** to make a low, rumbling sound. —*v.t.* **3.** to utter indistinctly or in a low tone: *If it's worth saying at all, don't mutter it.* —*n.* **4.** the act or utterance of one who mutters. [ME *motere(n),* perh. freq. of MOOT¹ (OE *mōtian* to speak); see -ER⁶] —**mut′ter·er,** *n.* —**mut′ter·ing·ly,** *adv.*
—**Syn. 1.** See **murmur.**

mut·ton¹ (mut′ən), *n.* **1.** the flesh of sheep, used as food. **2.** the flesh of the full-grown or more mature sheep, as distinguished from lamb. [ME *moton* sheep < OF < Celt; cf. MIr *molt* wether] —**mut′ton·y,** *adj.*

mut·ton² (mut′ən), *n.* *Print.* em (def. 2). Also called **mut.** [code term, coined to differentiate the pronunciation of *em quad* from *en quad*]

mut·ton·chops (mut′ən chops′), *n.pl.* side whiskers that are narrow at the top and broad and trimmed short at the bottom, the chin being shaved both in front and beneath. Also called **mut′tonchop whisk′ers.** [MUTTON + CHOP¹ + -S³; so called from shape]

mut·ton·fish (mut′ən fish′), *n., pl. (esp. collectively)* **-fish,** *(esp. referring to two or more kinds or species)* **-fish·es. 1.** See **ocean pout. 2.** See **mutton snapper.** [MUTTON + FISH, so called for its muttonlike taste]

mut·ton-head (mut′ən hed′), *n.* *Informal.* a slow or stupid person; dolt. [MUTTON + HEAD] —**mut′ton-head′ed,** *adj.*

mut′ton snap′per, *Ichthyol.* a snapper, *Lutjanus analis,* found in the warmer parts of the western Atlantic Ocean, valued as food and game.

mut′ton spank′er, *Naut.* a triangular spanker. Also called **leg-of-mutton spanker.**

Mut·tra (mut′trə), *n.* former name of **Mathura.**

mu·tu·al (myōō′chōō əl), *adj.* **1.** possessed, experienced, performed, etc., by each of two or more with respect to the other or others; reciprocal: *to have mutual respect.* **2.** having the same relation each toward the other or others: *to be mutual enemies.* **3.** of or pertaining to each of two or more, or having in common: *Although they live in different cities, they have many mutual acquaintances.* **4.** pertaining to mutual insurance: *a mutual company.* [ME < LL *mūtuāl(is),* equiv. to L *mūtu(us)* interchanged, reciprocal (akin to *mūtāre;* see MUTATE) + *-ālis* -AL¹] —**mu′tu·al·ly,** *adv.*
—**Syn. 1.** MUTUAL, RECIPROCAL agree in the idea of an exchange or balance between two or more persons or groups. MUTUAL indicates an exchange of a feeling, obligation, etc., between two or more people, or an interchange of some kind between persons or things: *mutual esteem; in mutual agreement.* It is not properly a synonym for COMMON, although often used in that sense (shared by, or pertaining to two or more things), esp. in the phrase *a mutual friend* (a friend of each of two or more other persons), the reason being that COMMON connotes "low," or "ordinary," and people are averse to stigmatizing their friends. RECIPROCAL indicates a relation in which one act, thing, feeling, etc., balances or is given in return for another: *reciprocal promises or favors.*

mu′tual aid′, *Sociol.* the cooperative as opposed to the competitive factors operating in the development of society.

mu′tual fund′. See **open-end investment company.**

mu′tual imped′ance, *Elect.* the ratio of the potential difference between either of two pairs of terminals to the current applied at the other pair of terminals when the circuit is open.

mu′tual induct′ance, *Elect.* the ratio of the electromotive force in one of two circuits to the rate of change of current in the other circuit.

mu′tual induc′tion, *Elect.* the production of an electromotive force in one circuit by a change in current in another circuit.

mu′tual insur′ance, insurance in which those insured become members of a company who reciprocally engage, by payment of certain amounts into a common fund, to indemnify one another against loss.

mu·tu·al·ise (myōō′chōō ə līz′), *v.t., v.i.,* **-ised, -is·ing.** *Chiefly Brit.* mutualize. —**mu′tu·al·i·sa′tion,** *n.*

mu·tu·al·ism (myōō′chōō ə liz′əm), *n.* **1.** a relationship between two species of organisms in which both benefit from the association. **2.** the doctrine that the interdependence of social elements is the primary determinant of individual and social relations, esp. the theory that common ownership of property, or collective effort and control governed by sentiments of brotherhood and mutual aid will be beneficial to both the individual and society. **3.** *Sociol.* the force or principle of mutual aid. [MUTUAL + -ISM] —**mu′tu·al·ist,** *n.* —**mu′tu·al·is′tic,** *adj.*

mu·tu·al·i·ty (myōō′chōō al′i tē), *n.* condition or quality of being mutual; reciprocity; mutual dependence. [MUTUAL + -ITY]

mu·tu·al·ize (myōō′chōō ə līz′), *v.,* **-ized, -iz·ing.** —*v.t.* **1.** to make mutual. **2.** to incorporate with employee or customer ownership of the major or controlling portion of issued shares. —*v.i.* **3.** to become mutual. Also, *esp. Brit.,* **mutualise.** [MUTUAL + -IZE] —**mu′tu·al·i·za′tion,** *n.*

mu′tual sav′ings bank′, a noncapitalized savings bank that distributes its available net earnings to depositors.

mu·tule (myōō′chōōl), *n. Archit.* a projecting flat block under the corona of the Doric cornice, corresponding to the modillion of other orders. [< L *mūtul(us)* a modillion] —**mu·tu·lar** (myōō′chə lər), **mu·tu·la·ry** (myōō′chə ler′ē), *adj.*

Mutule (Grecian Doric)

Mu·tus (myōō′təs), *n.* a crater in the fourth quadrant of the face of the moon: about 50 miles in diameter.

muu·muu (mōō′mōō′), *n.* **1.** a loose dress, often brightly colored or patterned, worn esp. by Hawaiian women. **2.** a similar dress worn as a house dress. [< Hawaiian, name of the dress, lit., cut-off; so called because of its originally lacking a yoke]

Mu·zak (myōō′zak), *n. Trademark.* recorded background music transmitted by radio or telephone to built-in sets in offices, restaurants, waiting rooms, etc.

mu·zhik (mōō zhik′, mōō′zhik), *n.* a Russian peasant. Also, **moujik, mujik, mu·zjik′.** [< Russ: lit., little man, equiv. to *muzh* man + *-ik* dim. suffix]

muzz (muz), *Brit. Slang.* —*v.i.* **1.** to study intensely; grind. —*v.t.* **2.** to confuse (someone); make (someone) muzzy. [back formation from MUZZY]

muz·zle (muz′əl), *n., v.,* **-zled, -zling.** —*n.* **1.** the mouth, or end for discharge, of the barrel of a gun, pistol, etc. **2.** the projecting part of the head of an animal, including jaws, mouth, and nose. **3.** a device, usually an arrangement of straps or wires, placed over an animal's mouth to prevent the animal from biting, eating, etc. —*v.t.* **4.** to put a muzzle on (an animal or its mouth) so as to prevent biting, eating, etc. **5.** to restrain, as from speech or the expression of opinion: *He tried to object to their decision, but they muzzled him.* **6.** *Naut.* to attach the cable to the stock of (an anchor) by means of a light line to permit the anchor to be pulled loose readily. [ME *musel* < MF, equiv. to *muse* snout + *-el* -LE; cf. ML *musellum,* dim. of *musum* snout < ?]

muz·zle·load·er (muz′əl lō′dər), *n.* a firearm that is loaded through the muzzle. Also, **muz′zle-load′er.** [MUZZLE + LOADER] —**muz′zle·load′ing, muz′zle-load′ing,** *adj.*

muz·zler (muz′lər), *n.* **1.** one who or that which muzzles. **2.** Also called **dead muzzler, nose ender.** *Naut.* a strong opposing wind. [MUZZLE + -ER¹]

muz′zle veloc′ity, *Ordn.* the speed of a projectile, usually expressed in feet or meters per second, as it leaves the muzzle of a gun.

muz·zy (muz′ē), *adj.,* **-zi·er, -zi·est.** *Informal.* **1.** confused; muddled. **2.** dull; mentally hazy. [? MU(DDLED + FU)ZZY] —**muz′zi·ly,** *adv.* —**muz′zi·ness,** *n.*

MV, 1. megavolt; megavolts. **2.** motor vessel.

Mv, 1. *Elect.* megavolt. **2.** *Chem.* mendelevium.

mV, millivolt; millivolts. Also, **mv**

m.v., 1. market value. **2.** mean variation. **3.** *Music.* mezza voce.

MVA, megavolt-ampere; megavolt-amperes.

MVD, the secret police of the U.S.S.R. since 1943. Cf. **Cheka, G.P.U., NKVD.** [< Russ *M(inisterstvo) V(nutrennikh) D(el)* Ministry of Home Affairs]

M.V.Ed., Master of Vocational Education.

Mw, *Elect.* megawatt; megawatts.

mW, *Elect.* milliwatt; milliwatts. Also, **mw**

M.W.A., Modern Woodmen of America.

Mwam·bu·tsa IV (mwäm bōō′tsä), born 1912, king of Burundi 1962–66.

Mwan·za (mwän′zä), *n.* a city in N Tanganyika, in Tanzania, on Lake Victoria. 19,877 (1957).

Mwe·ru (mwā′rōō), *n.* a lake in S Africa, between the Republic of the Congo and Zambia. 68 mi. long.

M.W.T., Master of Wood Technology.

mx, maxwell; maxwells.

my (mī), *pron.* **1.** (a form of the possessive case of *I* used as an attributive adjective): *My soup is cold.* —*interj.* **2.** *Informal* (used as an exclamation of surprise): *My, what a big house!* [ME *mī,* var. of *mīn,* OE *mīn;* see MINE¹]
—**Usage.** See **me.**

my-, var. of **myo-** before some vowels: *myalgia.*

my·al·gi·a (mī al′jē ə, -jə), *n. Pathol.* pain in the muscles; muscular rheumatism. Also called **myoneuralgia.** [MY- + -ALGIA] —**my·al′gic,** *adj.*

my·all (mī′ôl), *n.* any of several Australian acacias, esp. *Acacia pendula* **(weeping myall),** having gray foliage and drooping branches. [< native Austral]

My′ An·to·ni′a (an′tə nē′ə, än′tô nyä′), a novel (1918) by Willa Cather.

my·as·the·ni·a (mī′əs thē′nē ə), *n. Pathol.* muscle weakness. [MY- + ASTHENIA] —**my·as·then·ic** (mī′əs then′ik), *adj.*

myasthe′nia gra′vis, *Pathol.* a disease characterized by muscular weakness, affecting esp. the muscles of the face, tongue, and neck, but not involving atrophy. [< NL]

my·a·to·ni·a (mī′ə tō′nē ə), *n. Pathol.* deficient muscle tone. [MY- + ML *atonia* ATONY]

my·at·ro·phy (mī a′trə fē), *n. Pathol.* myoatrophy.

myc-, var. of **myco-** before a vowel: *mycelium.*

my·ce·li·oid (mī sē′lē oid′), *adj.* resembling mycelium. [MYCELI(UM) + -OID]

my·ce·li·um (mī sē′lē əm), *n., pl.* **-li·a** (-lē ə). *Bot.* the vegetative part or thallus of the fungi, being composed of one or more filamentous elements, or hyphae. [MYC- + Gk *(h)ēl(os)* wart, nail + -IUM] —**my·ce′li·al,** *adj.*

My·ce·nae (mī sē′nē), *n.* an ancient city in S Greece, in Argolis: notable ruins.

My·ce·nae·an (mī′si nē′ən), *adj.* **1.** of or pertaining to the ancient city of Mycenae. **2.** denoting or pertaining to the ancient civilization at Mycenae, dating from c1950 to c1100 B.C. [MYCENAE + -AN]

Myc·e·ri·nus (mis′ə rī′nəs), *n.* king of ancient Egypt c2600–2570 B.C.: builder of the third great pyramid at Giza. Also, **Mykerinos.** Also called **Menkure.**

-mycetes, an element meaning "fungi," used esp. in the names of classes: *Myxomycetes.* Also, **-mycete.** [< NL < Gk *mykētes,* pl. of *mýkēs* mushroom, fungus. See MYCETO-]

myceto-, a combining form meaning "fungus": *mycetozoan.* [comb. form repr. Gk *mykēt-,* s. of *mýkēs;* see MYCO-]

my·ce·to·zo·an (mī sē′tə zō′ən), *adj.* **1.** of or pertaining to the order *Mycetozoa,* the classification used by those considering the true slime molds to be animals, or to the class *Myxomycetes,* the classification used by those considering the true slime molds to be plants. —*n.* **2.** a slime mold; myxomycete. [MYCETO + -ZO + -AN]

myco-, a learned borrowing from Greek meaning "fungus," used in the formation of compound words: *mycology.* Also, *esp. before a vowel,* **myc-.** [comb. form repr. Gk *mýkēs* mushroom, fungus]

my·co·bac·te·ri·um (mī′kō bak tēr′ē əm), *n., pl.* **-te·ri·a** (-tēr′ē ə). *Bacteriol.* any of several rod-shaped aerobic bacteria of the genus *Mycobacterium,* certain species of which, as *M. tuberculosis,* are pathogenic for man and animals. [MYCO- + BACTERIUM]

mycobacte′rium paratuberculo′sis (mī′kō bak tēr′ē əm), *Pathol.* See **Johne's disease.**

my·co·ce·cid·i·um (mī′kō si sid′ē əm), *n. Bot.* a gall caused by a parasitic fungus. [< NL, equiv. to *myco-* MYCO- + *cecidium* gall (< Gk *kēkídion* ink-gall, dim. of *kēkid,* s. of *kēkís* oak-gall, a dye made therefrom)]

mycol., mycology.

my·col·o·gy (mī kol′ə jē), *n.* **1.** the branch of botany dealing with fungi. **2.** the fungi found in an area. [MYCO- + -LOGY] —**my·co·log·i·cal** (mī′kə loj′i kəl), **my′co·log′ic,** *adj.* —**my′co·log′i·cal·ly,** *adv.* —**my·col′o·gist,** *n.*

my·cor·rhi·za (mī′kō rī′zə, -kô-), *n., pl.* **-zae** (-zē), **-zas.** *Plant Pathol.* a symbiotic association of the mycelium of a fungus, esp. a basidiomycete, with the roots of certain plants, in which the hyphae form a closely woven mass around the rootlets or penetrate the cells of the root. Also, **my′co·rhi′za.** [MYCO- + -RRHIZA] —**my′cor·rhi′zal, my′co·rhi′zal,** *adj.*

my·co·sis (mī kō′sis), *n. Pathol.* **1.** the presence of parasitic fungi in or on any part of the body. **2.** the condition caused by the presence of such fungi. [MYC- + -OSIS]

my·co·so·zin (mī′kō sō′zin), *n. Biochem.* any sozin that destroys microbes. [MYCO- + SOZIN]

my·co·stat (mī′kō stat′), *n.* a substance or preparation that prevents or inhibits the growth of molds. [MYCO- + -STAT] —**my′co·stat′ic,** *adj.*

My·co·stat·in (mī′kō stat′in), *n. Pharm., Trademark.* nystatin.

my·dri·a·sis (mi drī′ə sis, mī-), *n. Med.* excessive dilatation of the pupil of the eye, as the result of disease, drugs, or the like. Cf. **miosis** (def. 1). [< L < Gk]

myd·ri·at·ic (mid′rē at′ik), *adj.* **1.** pertaining to or producing mydriasis. —*n.* **2.** a mydriatic drug. [MYDRIA(SIS) + -TIC]

myel-, var. of **myelo-** before a vowel: *myelitis.*

my·e·len·ceph·a·lon (mī′ə lən sef′ə lon′), *n., pl.* **-lons, -la** (-lə). *Anat.* the posterior section of the hindbrain comprising the medulla oblongata. [MYEL- + ENCEPHALON] —**my·e·len·ce·phal·ic** (mī′ə lən sə fal′ik), *adj.*

my·e·lin (mī′ə lin), *n. Anat.* a soft, white, fatty substance encasing the axis cylinder of certain nerve fibers. Also, **my·e·line** (mī′ə lēn′). [MYEL- + -IN²] —**my′e·lin′ic,** *adj.*

my·e·li·nat·ed (mī′ə lə nā′tid), *adj. Anat.* (of a nerve) having a myelin sheath; medullated. [MYELIN + -ATE¹ + -ED²]

my·e·li·na·tion (mī′ə lə nā′shən), *n. Anat.* the formation of a myelin sheath. Also, **my·e·lin·i·za·tion** (mī′ə lin i zā′shən). [MYELIN + -ATION]

my′elin sheath′, *Anat.* the sheath of myelin surrounding the axons or fibers of certain nerves. Also called **medullary sheath.** See diag. under **neuron.**

my·e·li·tis (mī′ə lī′tis), *n. Pathol.* **1.** inflammation of the substance of the spinal cord. **2.** inflammation of the bone marrow. [MYEL- + -ITIS]

myelo-, a learned borrowing from Greek used, with the meaning "marrow," "of the spinal cord," in the formation of compound words: *myelocyte.* Also, *esp. before a vowel,* **myel-.** [comb. form repr. Gk *myelós*]

my·e·lo·blast (mī′ə lō blast′), *n. Anat.* an immature myelocyte. [MYELO- + -BLAST] —**my′e·lo·blas′tic,** *adj.*

my·e·lo·cyte (mī′ə lō sīt′), *n. Anat.* a cell of the bone marrow, esp. one developing into a granulocyte. [MYELO- + -CYTE] —**my·e·lo·cyt·ic** (mī′ə lō sit′ik), *adj.*

my·e·lo·gram (mī′ə lō gram′), *n. Med.* an x-ray photograph of the spinal cord, usually following administration of a radiopaque substance into the spinal subarachnoid space. [MYELO- + -GRAM¹]

my·e·log·ra·phy (mī′ə log′rə fē), *n. Med.* the production of myelograms following injection of a radiopaque substance into the spinal subarachnoid space. [MYELO- + -GRAPHY] —**my·e·lo·graph·ic** (mī′ə lō graf′ik), *adj.* —**my′e·lo·graph′i·cal·ly,** *adv.*

my·e·loid (mī′ə loid′), *adj. Anat.* **1.** pertaining to the spinal cord. **2.** marrowlike. **3.** pertaining to marrow. [MYEL- + -OID]

My·ers·town (mī′ərz toun′), *n.* a town in SE Pennsylvania. 3268 (1960).

myg, myriagram; myriagrams.

Myg·don (mig′dən), *n. Class. Myth.* a king of the Bebryces who was killed by Hercules.

my·i·a·sis (mī′ə sis), *n., pl.* **-ses** (-sēz′). *Pathol.* any disease that results from the infestation of tissues or cavities of the body by larvae of flies. [*myi-* (< Gk *myîa* fly) + -ASIS]

Myin·gyan (myin′jän), *n.* a city in central Burma. 36,536 (1953).

Myk·e·ri·nos (mik′ə rī′nəs), *n.* Mycerinus.

myl, myrialiter; myrialiters.

My·les (mī′lēz *for 1;* mīlz *for 2*), *n.* **1.** *Class. Myth.* a Laconian king, believed to have invented the water-powered grain mill. **2.** Also, **Miles.** a boy's given name.

My·lit·ta (mi lit′ə), *n.* Ishtar.

my·lo·hy·oid (mī′lō hī′oid), *Anat.* —*adj.* **1.** Also, **my·lo·hy·oi·de·an** (mī′lō hī oi′dē ən). of, pertaining to, or situated near the lower molar teeth and the hyoid bone. —*n.* **2.** Also, **mylohyoideus.** a flat, triangular mylohyoid muscle that forms the floor of the mouth. [*mylo-* (< Gk *mýlo(s)* molar, lit., mill) + HYOID]

my·lo·hy·oi·de·us (mī′lō hī oi′dē əs), *n., pl.* **-de·i** (-dē ī′). *Anat.* mylohyoid (def. 2). [< NL]

my·lo·nite (mī′lə nīt′, mil′ə-), *n.* a rock that has been crushed and rolled out to such an extent that the original structure has been destroyed. [*mylon-* (< Gk: mill) + -ITE¹]

mym, myriameter; myriameters.

My′ Mor′tal En′emy, a novel (1926) by Willa Cather.

my·na (mī′nə), *n.* any of several Asian birds of the starling family *Sturnidae,* esp. those of the genera *Acridotheres* or *Gracula,* certain species of which have the ability to mimic speech and are kept as pets. Also, **my′nah, mina, minah.** [< Hindi *mainā*]

My·nes (mī′nēz), *n.* (in the *Iliad*) a king of Lyrnessus and husband of Briseis, killed by Achilles in the Trojan War.

Myn·heer (mīn hâr′, -hēr′), *n.* **1.** the Dutch term of address and title of respect corresponding to *sir* and *Mr.* **2.** (*l.c.*) a Dutchman. [sp. var. of D *mijnheer,* equiv. to *mijn* MINE¹ + *heer* lord, sir, Mr.; see HERR]

myo-, a learned borrowing from Greek meaning "muscle," used in the formation of compound words: *myology.* Also, *esp. before a vowel,* **my-.** [comb. form repr. Gk *mŷs* mouse, muscle]

my·o·at·ro·phy (mī′ō a′trə fē), *n. Pathol.* atrophy of muscle. Also, **myatrophy.** [MYO- + ATROPHY]

M.Y.O.B., mind your own business.

myocar′dial infarc′tion, *Pathol.* an infarction, or necrosis caused by blood-deprivation, of the myocardium; coronary thrombosis.

my·o·car·di·o·gram (mī′ə kär′dē ə gram′), *n.* the graphic record produced by a myocardiograph. [MYO- + CARDIOGRAM]

my·o·car·di·o·graph (mī′ə kär′dē ə graf′, -gräf′), *n.* an instrument for recording the movements of the heart. [MYO- + CARDIOGRAPH]

my·o·car·di·tis (mī′ō kär dī′tis), *n. Pathol.* inflammation of the myocardium. [MYO- + CARDITIS]

my·o·car·di·um (mī′ə kär′dē əm), *n., pl.* **-di·a** (-dē ə). *Anat.* the muscular substance of the heart. [< NL < Gk *myo-* MYO- + *-kardion,* dim. of *kardía* heart] —**my′o·car′di·al,** *adj.*

my·o·clo·ni·a (mī′ə klō′nē ə), *n. Pathol.* a disease characterized by myoclonus. [MYOCLON(US) + -IA] —**my·o·clon·ic** (mī′ə klon′ik), *adj.*

my·oc·lo·nus (mī ok′lə nəs), *n. Pathol.* clonic spasm of a muscle. [MYO- + CLONUS]

my·o·coele (mī′ə sēl′), *n. Embryol.* the cavity of a mesodermal somite after the myotome has been established. Also, **my′o·coel′.** [MYO- + -COELE]

my·o·cyte (mī′ə sīt′), *n.* a contractile cell, esp. an elongated cell in sponges that forms a sphincter around body openings. [MYO- + -CYTE]

my·o·e·de·ma (mī′ō i dē′mə), *n. Pathol.* **1.** edema of a muscle. **2.** mounding. [MYO- + EDEMA]

my·o·gen·ic (mī′ə jen′ik), *adj.* originating in muscle, as an impulse, sensation, etc. [MYO- + GENIC] —**my·o·ge·nic·i·ty** (mī′ə jə nis′i tē), *n.*

my·o·glo·bin (mī′ə glō′bin, mī′ə glō′-), *n. Biochem.* hemoglobin of muscle, weighing less and carrying more oxygen and less carbon monoxide than blood hemoglobin. Also, **myohemoglobin.** [MYO- + GLOBIN]

my·o·glo·bi·nu·ri·a (mī′ə glō′bə no͝or′ē ə, -nyo͝or′-), *n. Med.* myohemoglobinuria. [MYOGLOBIN + -URIA]

my·o·gram (mī′ə gram′), *n.* the graphic record produced by a myograph. [MYO- + -GRAM[1]]

my·o·graph (mī′ə graf′, -gräf′), *n.* an instrument for recording the contractions and relaxations of muscles. [MYO- + -GRAPH] —**my·o·graph·ic** (mī′ə graf′ik), *adj.* —**my′o·graph′i·cal·ly,** *adv.* —**my·og·ra·phy** (mī og′rə fē), *n.*

my·o·he·mo·glo·bin (mī′ə hē′mə glō′bin, -hem′ə-, -hē′mə glō′bin, -hem′ə-), *n. Biochem.* myoglobin. [MYO- + HEMOGLOBIN]

my·o·he·mo·glo·bi·nu·ri·a (mī′ə hē′mə glō′bə no͝or′ē ə, -nyo͝or′-), *n. Med.* the presence of myohemoglobin in the urine. Also called **myoglobinuria.** [MYOHEMOGLOBIN + -URIA]

my·o·kym·i·a (mī′ə kim′ē ə), *n. Pathol.* twitching of individual segments of a muscle. [MYO- + *-kymia,* equiv. to Gk *kȳm(a)* something swollen + -IA]

my·ol·o·gy (mī ol′ə jē), *n.* the science or branch of anatomy dealing with muscles. [< NL *myologia.* See MYO-, -LOGY] —**my·o·log·ic** (mī′ə loj′ik), **my′o·log′i·cal,** *adj.* —**my·ol′o·gist,** *n.*

my·o·ma (mī ō′mə), *n., pl.* **-mas, -ma·ta** (-mə tə). *Pathol.* a tumor composed of muscular tissue. [MY- + -OMA] —**my·om·a·tous** (mī om′ə təs, -ō′mə-), *adj.*

my·o·neu·ral (mī′ə no͝or′əl, -nyo͝or′-), *adj.* of or pertaining to both muscle and nerve. [MYO- + NEURAL]

my·o·neu·ral·gia (mī′ō no͝o ral′jə, -nyo͝o-), *n. Pathol.* myalgia. [MYO- + NEURALGIA]

my·o·neu·ras·the·ni·a (mī′ə no͝or′əs thē′nē ə, -nyo͝or′-), *n. Pathol.* muscular weakness associated with neurasthenia. [MYO- + NEURASTHENIA]

my·op·a·thy (mī op′ə thē), *n. Pathol.* any abnormality or disease of muscle tissue. [MYO- + -PATHY] —**my·o·path·ic** (mī′ə path′ik), *adj.*

my·o·pi·a (mī ō′pē ə), *n. Ophthalm.* a condition of the eye in which parallel rays are focused in front of the retina, objects being seen distinctly only when near to the eye; near-sightedness (opposed to *hypermetropia*). [< NL < Gk, equiv. to *myōp-* (s. of *mýōps*) near-sighted, lit., blinking (*mý(ein)* to shut + *ōps* eye) + *-ia* -IA]

my·op·ic (mī op′ik), *adj.* **1.** *Ophthalm.* pertaining to or having myopia; near-sighted. **2.** unable to think clearly or objectively; lacking knowledge, tolerance, or foresight: *a myopic viewpoint.* [MYOP(IA) + -IC] —**my·op′i·cal·ly,** *adv.*

my·o·psy·chop·a·thy (mī′ō sī kop′ə thē), *n. Pathol.* myopathy associated with mental weakness or change. [MYO- + PSYCHOPATHY]

my·o·scope (mī′ə skōp′), *n.* an instrument for observing muscular contraction. [MYO- + -SCOPE]

my·o·sin (mī′ə sin), *n. Biochem.* a globulin occurring in muscle plasma. [MY- + -OSE[2] + -IN[2]]

my·o·sis (mī ō′sis), *n. Med.* miosis (def. 1).

my·o·so·tis (mī′ə sō′tis), *n.* any boraginaceous plant of the genus *Myosotis,* as the forget-me-not. Also, **my·o·sote** (mī′ə sōt′). [< NL, L < Gk: the plant mouse-ear, equiv. to *myòs* (gen. of *mŷs*) MOUSE + *-ōt-* (s. of *oûs*) ear + *-is* n. suffix]

my·ot·ic (mī ot′ik), *adj., n.* miotic.

my·o·tome (mī′ə tōm′), *n.* **1.** *Embryol.* the part of a mesodermal somite contributing to the development of the skeletal muscles. **2.** *Surg.* an instrument for incising muscle. [MYO- + -TOME]

my·ot·o·my (mī ot′ə mē), *n., pl.* **-mies.** *Surg.* incision of a muscle. [< NL *myotomia.* See MYO-, -TOMY]

my·o·to·ni·a (mī′ə tō′nē ə), *n. Pathol.* tonic muscle spasm or muscular rigidity. [*myoton(ic)* (see MYO-, TONIC) + -IA] —**my·o·ton·ic** (mī′ə ton′ik), *adj.*

My·ra (mī′rə), *n.* **1.** an ancient city in SW Asia Minor, in Lycia. **2.** Also, **Mira.** a girl's given name.

myria-, a combining form meaning "10,000," used esp. with units of the metric system: *myriagram.* [comb. form repr. Gk *myriás* ten thousand; see MYRIAD]

myr·i·ad (mir′ē əd), *n.* **1.** an indefinitely great number. **2.** a very great number of persons or things. **3.** ten thousand. —*adj.* **4.** of an indefinitely great number; innumerable: *the myriad stars of a summer night.* **5.** having innumerable phases, aspects, etc.: *the myriad mind of Shakespeare.* **6.** ten thousand. [< Gk *myriad-* (s. of *myriás*) ten thousand; see -AD[1]] —**myr′i·ad·ly,** *adv.*

myr·i·ad-leaf (mir′ē əd lēf′), *n., pl.* **-leaves.** an aquatic plant, *Myriophyllum verticillatum,* of the North Temperate Zone, having hairlike, submerged leaves.

myr·i·a·gram (mir′ē ə gram′), *n. Metric System.* a unit of weight equal to 10,000 grams. *Abbr.:* myg [MYRIA- + -GRAM[2]]

myr·i·a·li·ter (mir′ē ə lē′tər), *n. Metric System.* a unit of capacity equal to 10,000 liters. *Abbr.:* myl [MYRIA- + LITER]

myr·i·a·me·ter (mir′ē ə mē′tər), *n. Metric System.* a unit of distance equal to 10,000 meters. *Abbr.:* mym [MYRIA- + METER[1]]

myr·i·a·pod (mir′ē ə pod′), *n.* **1.** any arthropod of the group *Myriapoda,* having an elongated segmented body with numerous, paired, jointed legs, formerly classified as a class comprising the centipedes and millipedes. —*adj.* **2.** Also, **myr·i·ap·o·dous** (mir′ē ap′ə dəs). belonging or pertaining to the *Myriapoda.* **3.** having very numerous legs. [< NL *Myriapod(a).* See MYRIA-, -POD]

Myr·i·ap·o·da (mir′ē ap′ə də), *n.* (in certain classifications) the class comprising the centipedes and millipedes. [< NL; see MYRIA-, -PODA]

myr·i·are (mir′ē âr′, -är′), *n. Metric System.* a unit of surface measure equivalent to 10,000 ares. [MYRI(A)- + ARE[2]]

my·ri·ca (mi rī′kə), *n.* **1.** the bark of the wax myrtle. **2.** the bark of the bayberry. [< L < Gk *myríkē* a shrub, the tamarisk]

My·ri·na (mi rī′nə), *n.* (in the *Iliad*) the wife of Dardanus.

myr·i·o·pod (mir′ē ə pod′), *n., adj.* myriapod.

myrmeco-, a combining form meaning "ant": *myrmecophile.* [comb. form repr. Gk *myrmēk-* (s. of *mýrmēx*) ant]

myr·me·col·o·gy (mûr′mə kol′ə jē), *n.* the branch of entomology dealing with the ants. [MYRMECO- + -LOGY] —**myr·me·co·log·i·cal** (mûr′mə kə loj′i kəl), *adj.* —**myr′me·col′o·gist,** *n.*

myr·me·coph·a·gous (mûr′mə kof′ə gəs), *adj.* adapted for feeding on ants or termites, as the jaws, teeth, etc., of various anteaters. [MYRMECO- + -PHAGOUS]

myr·me·co·phile (mûr′mə kō fīl′, -fil), *n.* an insect of a foreign species that lives more or less permanently in an ant colony. [MYRMECO- + -PHILE] —**myr·me·coph·i·lism** (mûr′mə kof′ə liz′əm), *n.* —**myr′me·coph′i·ly,** *n.*

myr·me·coph·i·lous (mûr′mə kof′ə ləs), *adj.* **1.** pertaining to a myrmecophile. **2.** of plants frequented by ants. [MYRMECO- + -PHILOUS]

Myr·mi·don (mûr′mi don′, -dən), *n., pl.* **Myr·mi·dons, Myr·mid·o·nes** (mûr mid′ənēz′). **1.** *Class. Myth.* one of the warlike people of ancient Thessaly who accompanied Achilles, their king, to the Trojan War. **2.** (*l.c.*) one who executes without scruple his master's commands. [ME, back formation from L *Myrmidones* (pl.) < Gk *Myrmidónes*]

my·rob·a·lan (mī rob′ə lən, mi-), *n.* the dried plumlike fruit of certain tropical trees of the genus *Terminalia,* used in dyeing, tanning, and making ink. [ME < L *myrobalan(um)* < Gk *myrobálanos* kind of fruit, equiv. to *mýro(n)* balsam + *bálanos* acorn]

my·ron (mē′rôn; *Eng.* mī′ron), *n. Gk. Ch.* chrism. [< Gk: unguent, perfume]

My·ron (mī′rən), *n.* **1.** fl. c450 B.C., Greek sculptor. **2.** a boy's given name.

myrrh (mûr), *n.* an aromatic resinous exudation from certain plants of the genus *Commiphora,* esp. *C. Myrrha,* a spiny shrub: used for incense, perfume, etc. [ME, OE *myrre* < L *myrrha* < Gk *mýrra* << Akkadian *murrū;* akin to Heb *mōr,* Ar *murr*] —**myrrhed,** *adj.* —**myrrh′ic,** *adj.*

Myr·rha (mēr′ə), *n.* **1.** Also called **Smyrna.** *Class. Myth.* a daughter of King Cinyras who had incestuous relations with her father and was changed into a myrrh tree by the gods. Their child, Adonis, was born from the split trunk of the tree. **2.** a girl's given name.

myr·ta·ceous (mûr tā′shəs), *adj.* **1.** belonging to the *Myrtaceae,* or myrtle family of plants, comprising the myrtle, the clove and allspice trees, the guava, the eucalyptus, etc. **2.** of, pertaining to, or resembling the myrtle. [< NL *Myrtace(ae)* family name (L *myrt(us)* MYRTLE + *-āceae* -ACEAE) + -OUS]

Myr·tice (mûr′tis), *n.* a girl's given name.

Myr·ti·lus (mûr′tᵊləs), *n. Class. Myth.* a charioteer of Oenomaus who was bribed to let Pelops win a chariot race against Oenomaus.

myr·tle (mûr′tᵊl), *n.* **1.** any plant of the genus *Myrtus,* esp. *M. communis,* a shrub of southern Europe having evergreen leaves, fragrant white flowers, and aromatic berries. This plant is used as an emblem of love and was anciently held sacred to Venus. **2.** *U.S.* any of certain unrelated plants, as the periwinkle, *Vinca minor,* and California laurel, *Umbellularia californica.* **3.** Also called **myr′tle green′.** dark green with bluish tinge. [ME *mirtile* < ML *myrtill(us),* equiv. to L *myrt(us)* (< Gk *mýrtos*) + *-illus* dim. suffix]

Myr·tle (mûr′tᵊl), *n.* a girl's given name.

Myr′tle Beach′, a town in E South Carolina. 7834 (1960).

Myr′tle Point′, a town in SW Oregon. 2886 (1960).

myr′tle war′bler, a North American wood warbler, *Dendroica coronata,* the male of which is bluish-gray above and white below with a yellow rump.

my·self (mī self′), *pron., pl.* **our·selves** (our selvz′). **1.** (used as an intensive of *me* or *I*): *I myself told her.* **2.** *Nonstandard.* (used as a substitute for *me*): *She wanted John and myself to take charge.* **3.** (used reflexively in place of *me* as the object of a preposition or as the direct or indirect object of a verb): *I gave myself a good rubdown. She asked me for a picture of myself.* **4.** my normal or customary self: *After a few days of rest, I expect to be myself again.* [MY + SELF; r. ME *meself,* OE *mē selfum* (dat.)]

—**Usage. 2.** It is considered nonstandard to use any reflexive pronoun (HIMSELF, HERSELF, ITSELF, YOURSELF, MYSELF, OURSELVES, YOURSELVES, THEMSELVES) in place of the objective form where the latter would normally occur: *He gave it to me* (not *myself*).

My·si·a (mish′ē ə), *n.* **1.** *Class. Myth.* an epithet of Demeter, in reference to Mysius, who entertained Demeter when she was searching for Persephone. **2.** an ancient country in NW Asia Minor. —**My′si·an,** *adj., n.*

my·so·phil·i·a (mī′sə fil′ē ə, -fēl′yə), *n. Psychiatry.* a pathological attraction to filth or dirt. [< NL, equiv. to *myso-* (< Gk *mýsos* filth) + *-philia;* see -PHIL, -IA]

my·so·pho·bi·a (mī′sə fō′bē ə), *n. Psychiatry.* a dread of dirt or filth. [< NL, equiv. to *myso-* (< Gk *mýsos* filth) + *-phobia* -PHOBIA] —**my′so·pho′bic,** *adj.*

My·sore (mī sōr′, -sôr′), *n.* **1.** a state in S India; enlarged in 1956 in conformance with linguistic boundaries. 23,586,772 (1961); 74,326 sq. mi. *Cap.:* Bangalore. **2.** a city in the S part of this state. 253,900 (1961).

mys·ta·gogue (mis′tə gôg′, -gog′), *n.* one who instructs persons before initiation into religious mysteries or before participation in the sacraments. [< L *mystagōg(us)* < Gk *mystagōgós,* equiv. to *mýst(ēs)* (see MYSTIC) + *āgōgos* -AGOGUE] —**mys·ta·go·gy** (mis′tə gō′jē), *n.* —**mys·ta·gog·ic** (mis′tə goj′ik), **mys′ta·gog′i·cal,** *adj.* —**mys′ta·gog′i·cal·ly,** *adv.*

mys·te·ri·ous (mi stēr′ē əs), *adj.* **1.** full of, characterized by, or involving mystery: *a mysterious stranger.* **2.** of obscure nature, meaning, origin, etc.; puzzling; inexplicable. **3.** implying or suggesting a mystery: *a mysterious smile.* [MYSTERY[1] + -OUS] —**mys·te′ri·ous·ly,** *adv.* —**mys·te′ri·ous·ness,** *n.*

—**Syn. 1.** secret, esoteric, occult, cryptic. MYSTERIOUS, INSCRUTABLE, MYSTICAL, OBSCURE refer to that which is not easily comprehended or explained. That which is MYSTERIOUS, by being unknown or puzzling, excites curiosity, amazement, or awe: *a mysterious disease.* INSCRUTABLE applies to that which is impenetrable, so enigmatic that one cannot interpret its significance: *an inscrutable smile.* That which is MYSTICAL has a secret significance, such as that attaching to certain rites, signs, and the like: *mystical symbols.* That which is OBSCURE is discovered or comprehended dimly or with difficulty: *obscure motives.* **2.** unfathomable, unintelligible, incomprehensible, enigmatic, impenetrable.

Myste′rious Stran′ger, The, a short story (1916) by Mark Twain.

mys·ter·y[1] (mis′tə rē, -trē), *n., pl.* **-ter·ies. 1.** anything that is kept secret or remains unexplained or unknown: *the mysteries of nature.* **2.** any affair, thing, or person that presents features or points so obscure as to arouse curiosity or speculation: *a mystery story.* **3.** obscurity, as of something unexplained or puzzling: *The mystery of their disappearance provoked gossip.* **4.** obscure, puzzling, or mysterious quality or character. **5.** any truth unknowable except by divine revelation. **6.** (in the Christian religion) **a.** a sacramental rite. **b.** the Eucharist. **7.** an incident or scene in connection with the life of Christ, regarded as of special significance: *the mysteries of the Passion.* **8.** any of the 15 events in the lives of Christ and the Virgin Mary meditated upon during the recitation of the rosary. **9. mysteries, a.** ancient religions which admitted candidates by secret rites and rituals the meaning of which was known only to initiated worshipers. **b.** any rites or secrets known only to those initiated: *the mysteries of Freemasonry.* **c.** (in the Christian religion) the Eucharistic elements. **10.** See **mystery play.** [ME *mysterie* < L *mystēri(um)* < Gk *mystḗrion,* equiv. to *mýst(ēs)* (see MYSTIC) + *-ērion* n. suffix]

mys·ter·y[2] (mis′tə rē), *n., pl.* **-ter·ies.** *Archaic.* **1.** a craft or trade. **2.** a guild, as of merchants, tradesmen, or the like. [ME *mistery* < ML *mistēri(um),* var. of L *ministerium* MINISTRY]

mys′tery clock′, a clock having no apparent works or place for works.

mys′tery play′, a medieval dramatic form based on a Biblical story, usually dealing with the life, death, and resurrection of Christ. Cf. **miracle play, morality play.**

mys·tic (mis′tik), *adj.* **1.** spiritually significant or symbolic, as the dove used in religious art to symbolize the Holy Ghost. **2.** of the nature of or pertaining to mysteries known only to the initiated: *mystic rites.* **3.** of occult character, power, or significance: *a mystic formula.* **4.** of obscure or mysterious character or significance. **5.** of or pertaining to mystics or mysticism. —*n.* **6.** a person initiated into mysteries. **7.** a person who claims to attain, or believes in the possibility of attaining, insight into mysteries transcending ordinary human knowledge, as by immediate intuition in a state of spiritual ecstasy. [ME *mystik* < L *mystic(us)* < Gk *mystikós,* equiv. to *myst-* (s. of *mýstēs*) an initiate into the mysteries + *-ikos* -IC, akin to *myein* to initiate] —**mys·tic·i·ty** (mi stis′i tē), *n.* —**mys′tic·ly,** *adv.*

Mys·tic (mis′tik), *n.* a town in SE Connecticut. 2536 (1960).

mys·ti·cal (mis′ti kəl), *adj.* **1.** mystic; occult. **2.** of or pertaining to mystics or mysticism: *mystical writings.* **3.** spiritually symbolic. **4.** *Rare.* obscure in meaning; mysterious. [MYSTIC + -AL[1]] —**mys′ti·cal·ly,** *adv.* —**mys′ti·cal′i·ty, mys′ti·cal·ness,** *n.*

—**Syn. 1.** See **mysterious.**

mys′tical theol′ogy, the branch of theology dealing with mysticism and mystical experiences.

mys·ti·cise (mis′ti sīz′), *v.t., v.i.,* **-cised, -cis·ing.** *Chiefly Brit.* mysticize.

mys·ti·cism (mis′ti siz′əm), *n.* **1.** the beliefs, ideas, or mode of thought of mystics. **2.** the doctrine of an immediate spiritual intuition of truths believed to transcend ordinary understanding, or of a direct, intimate union of the soul with God through contemplation and love. **3.** obscure thought or speculation. [MYSTIC + -ISM]

mys·ti·cize (mis′ti sīz′), *v.,* **-cized, -ciz·ing.** —*v.t.* **1.** to make mystical; give mystical meaning to: *to mysticize natural phenomena.* —*v.i.* **2.** to speak or write on mystical subjects: *to mysticize about the Moorish influences on Spanish culture.* Also, *esp. Brit.,* **mysticise.** [MYSTIC + -IZE]

mys·ti·fy (mis′tə fī′), *v.t.,* **-fied, -fy·ing. 1.** to impose upon (a person) by playing upon his credulity; bewilder purposely. **2.** to involve in mystery or obscurity. [< F *mystifie(r),* equiv. to *mysti-* (irreg. deriv. of *mystique* MYSTIC or *mystère* MYSTERY[1]) + *-fier* -FY] —**mys′ti·fi·ca′tion,** *n.* —**mys′ti·fied′ly,** *adv.* —**mys′ti·fi′er,** *n.* —**mys′ti·fy′ing·ly,** *adv.*

mys·tique (mi stēk′), *n.* **1.** a framework of doctrines, ideas, beliefs, or the like, constructed around a person or object, endowing him or it with enhanced value or profound meaning: *the mystique of Poe.* **2.** an aura of mystery or mystical power surrounding a particular occupation or pursuit: *the mystique of science.* [< F (adj.); see MYSTIC]

myth (mith), *n.* **1.** a traditional or legendary story, usually concerning some superhuman being or some alleged person or event, with or without a determinable basis of fact or a natural explanation, esp., a traditional or legendary story that is concerned with deities or demigods and the creation of the world and its inhabitants. **2.** stories or matter of this kind: *in the realm of myth.* **3.** any invented story, idea, or concept: *His rationalizations of his failings are pure myth.* **4.** an imaginary or fictitious thing or person. **5.** an unproved collective belief that is accepted uncritically and is used to justify a social institution, as the belief in the biological inferiority of slaves used in support of slave societies. [< LL *mȳth(us)* < Gk *mŷthos* story, word]

—**Syn. 1.** See **legend.**

myth., **1.** mythological. **2.** mythology.

myth·i·cal (mith′i kəl), *adj.* **1.** pertaining to, of the nature of, or involving a myth or myths. **2.** dealt with in myth, as a period. **3.** dealing with myths, as a writer. **4.** existing only in myth, as a person. **5.** without foundation in fact; imaginary; fictitious: *The story given the public was entirely mythical.* Also, **myth′ic.** [< LL *mȳthic(us)* < Gk *mythikós* of myths (see MYTH, -IC) + -AL¹] —**myth′i·cal·ly,** *adv.* —**myth′i·cal·ness,** *n.*

myth·i·cise (mith′i sīz′), *v.t.*, **-cised, -cis·ing.** *Chiefly Brit.* mythicize. —**myth′i·cis′er,** *n.*

myth·i·cize (mith′i sīz′), *v.t.*, **-cized, -ciz·ing.** to turn into, treat, or explain as a myth. [MYTHIC + -IZE] —**myth′i·ciz′er,** *n.*

myth·i·fy (mith′ə fī′), *v.t.*, **-fied, -fy·ing.** to create a myth about (a person, place, tradition, etc.); cause to become a myth. [MYTH + -IFY] —**myth·i·fi·ca·tion** (mith′ə fə kā′shən), *n.*

myth·mak·er (mith′mā′kər), *n.* a person who creates myths. [MYTH + MAKER] —**myth′mak′ing,** *n.*

mytho-, a combining form of **myth:** *mythogenesis.* [< Gk, comb. form of *mŷthos* MYTH]

myth·o·clast (mith′ə klast′), *n.* a destroyer or debunker of myths. [MYTHO- + -CLAST] —**myth′o·clas′tic,** *adj.*

myth·o·gen·e·sis (mith′ə jen′i sis), *n.*, *pl.* **-ses** (-sēz′). origin, production, or creation of myths. [MYTHO- + GENESIS]

my·thog·ra·pher (mi thog′rə fər), *n.* a person who collects or records myths in writing. Also, **my·thog′ra·phist.** [< Gk *mythográph(os)* mythographer (see MYTHO-, -GRAPH) + -ER¹]

my·thog·ra·phy (mi thog′rə fē), *n.*, *pl.* **-phies.** **1.** a written collection of myths. **2.** expression of myths in artistic, esp. plastic, form. **3.** description of myths. [< Gk *mythographía.* See MYTHO-, -GRAPHY]

mythol., **1.** mythological. **2.** mythology.

myth·o·log·i·cal (mith′ə loj′i kəl), *adj.* of or pertaining to mythology. Also, **myth′o·log′ic.** [< L *mythologic(us)* < Gk *mythologikós* (see MYTHOLOGY, -IC) + -AL¹] —**myth′o·log′i·cal·ly,** *adv.*

my·thol·o·gise (mi thol′ə jīz′), *v.i.*, *v.t.*, **-gised, -gis·ing.** *Chiefly Brit.* mythologize. —**my·thol′o·gi·sa′tion,** *n.* —**my·thol′o·gis′er,** *n.*

my·thol·o·gist (mi thol′ə jist), *n.* **1.** an expert in mythology. **2.** a writer of myths. [< Gk *mythológ(os)* story-teller (see MYTHO-, LOGO-) + -IST]

my·thol·o·gize (mi thol′ə jīz′), *v.*, **-gized, -giz·ing.** —*v.i.* **1.** to classify, explain, or write about myths. **2.** to construct or narrate myths. —*v.t.* **3.** to make into or explain as a myth; make mythical. Also, *esp. Brit.*, **mythologise.** [MYTHOLOG(Y) + -IZE; cf. F *mythologiser*] —**my·thol′o·gi·za′tion,** *n.* —**my·thol′o·giz′er,** *n.*

my·thol·o·gy (mi thol′ə jē), *n.*, *pl.* **-gies.** **1.** a body of myths, as that of a particular people, or that relating to a particular person: *Greek mythology.* **2.** myths collectively. **3.** the science or study of myths. [ME *mythologie* < LL *mythologia* < Gk. See MYTHO-, -LOGY]

myth·o·ma·ni·a (mith′ə mā′nē ə), *n.* *Psychiatry.* lying or exaggerating to an abnormal degree. [MYTHO- + -MANIA] —**myth·o·ma·ni·ac** (mith′ə mā′nē ak′), *n.*, *adj.*

myth·o·poe·ia (mith′ə pē′ə), *n.* a mythopoeic act, circumstance, characteristic, etc. [< LL < Gk *mythopoiía* making of fables, invention, equiv. to *mytho-* MYTHO- + *-poiia* (*poi(eîn)* (to) make + *-ia* n. suffix)]

myth·o·poe·ic (mith′ə pē′ik), *adj.* of or pertaining to the making of myths; causing, producing, or giving rise to a myth or myths. [< Gk *mythopoi(ós)* making tales (*mytho-* MYTHO- + *-poios* making (*poi(eîn)* (to) make + *-os* adj. suffix) + -IC] —**myth′o·poe′ism,** *n.* —**myth′o·poe′ist,** *n.*

myth·o·po·et·ise (mith′ə pō′i tīz′), *v.i.*, **-ised, -is·ing.** *Chiefly Brit.* mythopoetize.

myth·o·po·et·ize (mith′ə pō′i tīz′), *v.i.*, **-ized, -iz·ing.** to produce myths or mythological poetry. [MYTHO- + POETIZE]

Myt·i·le·ne (mit′ᵊlē′nē; *Gk.* mē′tē lē′nē), *n.* **1.** Also called **Lesbos.** a Greek island in the NE Aegean. 140,251 (1961); 836 sq. mi. **2.** Also called **Kastros.** the capital of this island. 27,125 (1951).

My·ti·shchi (mi tyē′shchi), *n.* a city in the W RSFSR, in the central part of the Soviet Union in Europe, NE of Moscow. 107,000 (est. 1962).

myx-, var. of **myxo-** before a vowel: *myxasthenia.*

myx·as·the·ni·a (mik′səs thē′nē ə, mik sas′thə nī′ə), *n.* *Pathol.* defective secretion of mucus. [MYX- + ASTHENIA]

myx·e·de·ma (mik′si dē′mə), *n.* *Pathol.* a disease characterized by thickening of the skin, blunting of the senses and intellect, labored speech, etc., associated with diminished functional activity of the thyroid gland. Also, **myx′oe·de′ma.** [MYX- + EDEMA] —**myx·e·dem·a·tous, myx·oe·dem·a·tous** (mik′si dem′ə təs, -dē′mə-), *adj.* —**myx·e·dem·ic, myx·oe·dem·ic** (mik′si dem′ik), *adj.*

myxo-, a learned borrowing from Greek, where it meant "mucus," "slime," used in the formation of compound words: *myxoneurosis.* Also, *esp. before a vowel,* **myx-.** [comb. form repr. Gk *mýxa*]

myx·oid (mik′soid), *adj.* *Med.* resembling mucus. [MYX- + -OID]

myx·o·ma (mik sō′mə), *n.*, *pl.* **-mas, -ma·ta** (-mə tə). *Pathol.* a soft tumor composed of connective and mucoid tissue. [< NL; see MYX-, -OMA] —**myx·om·a·tous** (mik som′ə təs), *n.*

myx·o·ma·to·sis (mik′sə mə tō′sis), *n.* **1.** *Pathol.* **a.** a condition characterized by the presence of many myxomas. **b.** myxomatous degeneration. **2.** Also called **infectious myxomatosis.** *Vet. Pathol.* a highly infectious viral disease of rabbits: artificially introduced into Great Britain and Australia to reduce the rabbit population. [< NL *myxomat-* (s. of *myxoma;* see MYX-, -OMA) + -OSIS]

myx·o·my·cete (mik′sō mī sēt′), *n.* an organism of the class *Myxomycetes,* the classification used by those considering the true slime molds to be plants. [back formation from NL *myxomycētes.* See MYXO-, -MYCETES]

myx·o·my·ce·tous (mik′sō mī sē′təs), *adj.* of or pertaining to a myxomycete or slime mold. [MYXOMYCET(ES) + -OUS]

myx·o·neu·ro·sis (mik′sō nŏŏ rō′sis, -nyŏŏ-), *n.*, *pl.* **-ses** (-sēz). *Psychiatry.* a neurosis accompanied by excessive secretion from the respiratory or intestinal mucous membranes. [MYXO- + NEUROSIS]

Mzha·va·nadze (mzhä vä näj′), *n.* **Va·si·li Pav·lo·vich** (vä sē′li päv lō′vich), born 1902, Russian government official: alternate member of the Presidium.

N

N, n (en), *n., pl.* **N's** or **Ns, n's** or **ns.** **1.** the 14th letter of the English alphabet, a consonant. **2.** any spoken sound represented by the letter *N* or *n*, as in *now, dinner, son,* etc. **3.** something having the shape of an N. **4.** a written or printed representation of the letter *N* or *n*. **5.** a device, as a printer's type, for reproducing the letter *N* or *n*.

'n (ən), *conj. Informal.* and: *Stop 'n save. Look 'n listen.* Also, **'n'.**

-n, var. of **-an** after a vowel: *Virginian.*

N, **1.** north. **2.** northern.

n, neutron.

N, **1.** the 14th in order or in a series, or, when *I* is omitted, the 13th. **2.** (*sometimes l.c.*) the medieval Roman numeral for 90. Cf. **Roman numerals.** **3.** *Chem.* nitrogen. **4.** *Math.* an indefinite, constant whole number, esp. the degree of a quantic or an equation, or the order of a curve. **5.** *Chess.* knight. **6.** *Print.* en. **7.** See **Avogadro's number.**

n, *Optics.* See **index of refraction.**

N., **1.** National list. **2.** Navy. **3.** New. **4.** Noon. **5.** *Chem.* Normal (strength solution). **6.** Norse. **7.** North. **8.** Northern. **9.** November.

n., **1.** born. [< L *nātus*] **2.** nephew. **3.** neuter. **4.** new. **5.** nominative. **6.** noon. **7.** *Chem.* normal (strength solution). **8.** north. **9.** northern. **10.** noun. **11.** number.

na (nä, nə), *Chiefly Scot.* —*adv.* **1.** no. **2.** not; in no way; by no means. —*conj.* **3.** nor; neither.

Na, *Chem.* sodium. [< NL *natrium*]

n/a, no account.

N.A., **1.** National Army. **2.** North America. **3.** See **numerical aperture.**

NAA, National Aeronautic Association.

NAACP, National Association for the Advancement of Colored People. Also, **N.A.A.C.P.**

nab (nab), *v.t.,* **nabbed, nab·bing.** *Informal.* **1.** to catch or seize, esp. suddenly. **2.** to capture or arrest. [earlier *nap;* perh. < Scand; cf. Dan *nappe,* Sw *nappa* to snatch] —**nab′ber,** *n.*

NAB, National Association of Broadcasters. Also, **N.A.B.**

N.A.B.A.C., National Association of Bank Auditors and Comptrollers. Also, **NABAC**

Na·bal (nā′bəl), *n.* a wealthy Calebite, husband of Abigail, who refused rightful tribute to King David for protecting his flocks. I Sam. 25. —**Na′bal·ism,** *n.* —**Na′bal·ite′,** *n.* —**Na·bal·it·ic** (nā′bə lit′ik), *adj.*

Nab·a·tae·an (nab′ə tē′ən), *n.* **1.** a subject of an ancient Arab kingdom in Palestine that became a Roman province in A.D. 106. **2.** the Aramaic dialect of the Nabataeans. —*adj.* **3.** of or pertaining to the Nabataeans, their kingdom, or their dialect. Also, **Nab′a·te′an.** [< L *Nabatae(a)* name of kingdom + -AN]

na·bi (nä′be), *n. Islam.* a prophet. [< Ar]

Na·bi (nä′bē), *Fine Arts.* —*n.* **1. Nabis,** (*sometimes l.c.*) a group of French artists of the late 19th century whose paintings were characterized chiefly by an emphasis on the organization of flat shapes and the use of high-key colors. Cf. **Synthetism.** —*adj.* **2.** pertaining to or characteristic of the Nabis or their theories. [< F < Heb *nābhi* prophet]

Na·blus (nä blo͞os′), *n.* modern name of **Shechem.**

na·bob (nā′bob), *n.* **1.** Also, **nawab.** a person, esp. a European, who has made a large fortune in India or another country of the East. **2.** any very wealthy or powerful person. **3.** nawab (def. 1). [< Hind *nawwāb.* See NAWAB] —**na·bob·er·y** (nā′bob ə rē, nā bob′ə rē), **na′bob·ism,** *n.* —**na·bob·ish, na·bob′i·cal,** *adj.* —**na′bob·ish·ly, na′bob·i·cal·ly,** *adv.* —**na′bob·ship′,** *n.*

Na·bo·kov (nä bô′kof, nä′bo kôf′), *n.* **Vla·di·mir Vla·di·mi·ro·vich** (vlä dē′mir vlä dē′mi rô′vich), 1899–1977, U.S. novelist, short-story writer, and poet, born in Russia.

Nab·o·nas·sar (nab′ō nas′ər), *n.* died 733? B.C., king of Babylon 747?–733?. Assyrian, **Nab′ū-nas′ir.**

Nab·o·ni·dus (nab′ō nī′dəs), *n.* died 539? B.C., last king of Babylonia 556–539 (father of Belshazzar).

Na·both (nā′both, -bōth), *n.* a man of Jezreel whose vineyard was secured for the covetous Ahab by the scheming of Jezebel. I Kings 21.

Nab·u·cho·don·o·sor (nab′ə kō don′ə sôr′), *n. Douay Bible.* Nebuchadnezzar (def. 1).

NACA, National Advisory Committee for Aeronautics. Also, **N.A.C.A.**

na·celle (nə sel′), *n.* **1.** the enclosed part of an airplane, dirigible, etc., in which the engine is housed or in which cargo or passengers are carried. **2.** the car of a balloon. [< F: a small boat < LL *nāvicella,* r. L *nāvicula,* equiv. to *nāvi(s)* ship (see NAVE[1]) + *-cula* -CULE]

na·cre (nā′kər), *n.* mother-of-pearl. [< ML *nacrum, nacer,* var. of *nacara* kind of drum, nacre < Ar *naqqārah* drum]

na·cred (nā′kərd), *adj.* lined with or resembling nacre. [NACRE + -ED[3]]

na·cre·ous (nā′krē əs), *adj.* **1.** of or pertaining to nacre. **2.** resembling nacre; lustrous; pearly. [NACRE + -OUS]

na′creous cloud′, a rarely seen, luminous, iridescent cloud shaped like a cirrus or altocumulus, approximately 15 miles above the earth, and of unknown composition. Also called **mother-of-pearl cloud.**

N.A.D., National Academy of Design.

Na·dab (nā′dab), *n.* a son of Aaron. Lev. 10. Cf. **Abihu.**

Na-De·ne (nä dā′nē, nä′dā nā′), *n.* **1.** a language stock including Athapaskan, Haida, and Tlingit. Cf. **stock** (def. 13). —*adj.* **2.** of, belonging to, or pertaining to Na-Dene. Also, **Na-de′ne.**

Na·der (nā′dər), *n.* **Ralph,** born 1934, U.S. lawyer, author, and consumer advocate.

na·dir (nā′dər, nā′dēr), *n.* **1.** *Astron.* the point on the celestial sphere directly beneath a given position or observer and diametrically opposite to the zenith. **2.** the lowest point: *the nadir of our hopes.* [ME << Ar *naẓīr* over against, opposite to (the zenith)] —**na′dir·al,** *adj.*

Nad·ja (*Fr.* nad zhä′), *n.* a novel (1928) by André Breton.

nae (nā), *Scot. and North Eng.* —*adv.* **1.** no; not. —*adj.* **2.** no.

nae·thing (nā′thing), *n., adv. Scot.* nothing.

nae·vus (nē′vəs), *n., pl.* **-vi** (-vī). *Med.* nevus. —**nae·void** (nē′void), *adj.*

Na·fl (nä′fl[ə]), *n. Islam.* a prayer other than those prescribed. [< Ar]

Na·fud (na fo͞od′), *n.* See **Nefud Desert.**

nag[1] (nag), *v.,* **nagged, nag·ging,** *n.* —*v.t.* **1.** to torment by persistent faultfinding, complaints, or importunities. —*v.i.* **2.** to find fault or complain in an irritating, wearisome, or relentless manner (often fol. by *at*): *If she starts nagging at her husband, I'm going home.* **3.** to cause pain, discomfort, distress, depression, etc. (often fol. by *at*): *This headache has been nagging at me all day. She had certain misgivings that nagged at her.* —*n.* **4.** the act or an instance of nagging. **5.** Also, **nagger.** a person who nags, esp. habitually. [< Scand; cf. Icel *nagga* to rub, grumble, quarrel; akin to MLG *naggen* to irritate. See GNAW]
—**Syn. 1.** pester, harass, hector; irritate, annoy, vex.

nag[2] (nag), *n.* **1.** an old, inferior, or worthless horse. **2.** *Slang.* any horse, esp. a racehorse. **3.** a small riding horse or pony. [late ME *nagge;* c. obs. D *neg;* akin to NEIGH]

Na·ga (nä′gə), *n. Hindu Myth.* a water spirit, half human and half serpent, supposed to bring safety and prosperity.

Na·ga (nä′gä), *n.* a city on E Cebu, in the E Philippines. 56,238 (1960).

Na·ga·land (nä′gə land′), *n.* a state in E India. 369,200 (1961); 6366 sq. mi. *Cap.:* Kohima.

na·ga′mi kum′quat (nə gä′mē). See **oval kumquat.** [*nagami* < ?]

na·ga·na (nə gä′nə), *n. Vet. Pathol.* **1.** a disease of horses and other animals that occurs only in certain parts of Africa and is caused by the organism *Trypanosoma brucei,* transmitted by a variety of tsetse fly. **2.** certain other African trypanosomal diseases of animals. Also, **n'gana.** [< Zulu *unakane*]

Na·ga·no (nä gä′nô), *n.* a city on central Honshu, in central Japan. 167,470 (1964).

Na·ga·ri (nä′gə rē), *n.* **1.** a group of related scripts, including Devanagari, derived from Brahmi and used for the writing of many of the languages of India. **2.** Devanagari.

Na·ga·sa·ki (nä′gə sä′kē, nag′ə sak′ē; *Jap.* nä′gä-sä′ke), *n.* a seaport on W Kyushu, in SW Japan: second military use of the atomic bomb August 9, 1945. 395,744 (1964).

nag·ger (nag′ər), *n.* nag[1] (def. 5). [NAG[1] + -ER[1]]

nag·ging (nag′ing), *adj.* **1.** tirelessly faultfinding, complaining, or petulant: *a nagging wife.* **2.** persistently recurring; unrelenting: *a nagging backache.* [NAG[1] + -ING[2]] —**nag′ging·ness,** *n.*

nag·gish (nag′ish), *adj.* tending to nag; somewhat nagging. [NAG[1] + -ISH[1]]

nag·gy (nag′ē), *adj.,* **-gi·er, -gi·est.** naggish. [NAG[1] + -Y[1]]

Na·gor′no-Ka·ra·bakh′ Auton′omous Re′gion (nə gôr′nō kär′ə bäk′; *Russ.* nu gôr′nə kə ru bäkh′), an autonomous region in SW Azerbaijan. 199,000; 1700 sq. mi. *Cap.:* Stepanakert.

Na·go·ya (nä′gô yä′), *n.* a city on S Honshu, in central Japan. 1,434,000 (est. 1972).

Nag·pur (nag po͝or′), *n.* a city in NE Maharashtra, in central India: former capital of the Central Provinces and Berar. 713,577 (1965).

na·gual (nä gwäl′, -wäl′), *n.* a guardian spirit among Mexican and Central American Indians, believed to reside in an animal. [< Sp < Nahuatl *nahualli*] —**na·gual′ism,** *n.*

Na·guib (nə gēb′), *n.* **Mohammed,** born 1901, Egyptian general and political leader: premier 1952–54; president 1953–54.

Na·gur·ski (nə gûr′skē), *n.* **Bron·is·law** (bron′i-slof′), ("*Bronko*"), born 1906, U.S. football player.

Na·gy (nod′y[ə], noj), *n.* **Im·re** (im′re), 1896–1958, Hungarian political leader: premier 1953–55, 1956.

Na·gy·vá·rad (nod′yə vä′rod, noj′-), *n.* Hungarian name of **Oradea.**

Nah., Nahum.

Na·hant (nə hant′, -hänt′), *n.* a town in E Massachusetts. 3960 (1960).

Na·hua (nä′wä), *n., pl.* **-huas,** (*esp. collectively*) **-hua,** *adj.* Nahuatl.

Na·hua·tl (nä′wät[ə]l), *n., pl.* **-hua·tls,** (*esp. collectively*) **-hua·tl,** *adj.* —*n.* **1.** a member of any of various peoples of ancient origin ranging from southeastern Mexico to parts of Central America and including the Aztecs. **2.** a Uto-Aztecan language spoken by over half a million people mostly in central Mexico. Cf. **Aztec** (def. 2). —*adj.* **3.** of or pertaining to any of these languages or peoples. [< Nahuatl, equiv. to *Nahua* NAHUA + *-tl* sing. suffix]

Na·hua·tlan (nä′wät lən), *n.* **1.** Nahuatl in all its dialects, often taken as a group of languages, spoken in large areas of central Mexico and El Salvador and in various small, widely dispersed areas throughout southern Mexico and Central America. —*adj.* **2.** of or pertaining to Nahuatl or Nahuatlan. [NAHUATL + -AN]

Na·hum (nā′həm), *n.* **1.** a Minor Prophet of the 7th century B.C. **2.** a book of the Bible bearing his name.

nai·ad (nā′ad, -əd, nī′-), *n., pl.* **-ads, -a·des** (-ə dēz′). **1.** (*sometimes cap.*) *Class. Myth.* any of a class of nymphs presiding over rivers and springs. **2.** a girl swimmer, esp. an expert one. **3.** *Bot.* a plant of the genus *Naias,* or the family *Naiadaceae.* [< L *nāiad-* (s. of *nāias*) < Gk: a water nymph]

na·iant (nā′ənt), *adj. Heraldry.* (of a fish) represented as horizontal, as if swimming: *three pikes naiant.* [< AF **naiant,* equiv. to MF *noiant* swimming < L. See NATANT]

Nai·da (nā′də), *n.* a girl's given name.

na·if (nä ēf′), *adj.* naïve. Also, **na·if′.** [< MF; masc. of NAÏVE]

nail (nāl), *n.* **1.** an extremely slender, typically rod-shaped rigid piece of metal, usually in any of numerous standard lengths from a fraction of an inch to several inches and having one end pointed and the other enlarged and flattened, for hammering into or through wood, other building materials, etc., as used in building, in fastening, to hold separate pieces together, or the like. **2.** *Anat.* a thin, horny plate, consisting of modified epidermis, growing on the upper side of the end of a finger or toe. **3.** a measure of length for cloth, equal to 2¼ inches. **4. hit the nail on the head,** to say or do exactly the right thing; be accurate or correct: *Your analysis really hit the nail on the head.* **5. on the nail,** *Informal.* **a.** of present interest; under discussion. **b.** on the spot; at once: *He was offered a job on the nail.* —*v.t.* **6.** to fasten with a nail or nails: *to nail the cover on a box.* **7.** to enclose or confine (something) by nailing (often fol. by *up*): *to nail up goods in a crate.* **8.** to make fast or keep firmly in one place or position: *Surprise nailed him to the spot.* **9.** *Informal.* **a.** to secure by prompt action; catch or seize: *The police nailed him with the goods.* **b.** to catch (a person) in some difficulty, lie, etc. **c.** to detect and expose (a lie, scandal, etc.). **10.** *Slang.* to hit (a person): *He was nailed on the head with a hard right in the first round.* **11.** *Obs.* to stud with or as if with nails. **12. nail down,** *Informal.* to make final; settle once and for all: *Signing the contract will nail down our agreement.* [ME; OE *nægl*; c. D, G *Nagel*; akin to L *unguis*, Gk *ónyx*] —**nail′er,** *n.* —**nail′less,** *adj.* —**nail′like′,** *adj.*

A B C D E F G

Nails (def. 1)
A, Common nail;
B, Finish nail; C, Brad nail;
D, Cut nail; E, Roofing nail;
F, Screw nail; G, Boat nail

nail-bit·ing (nāl′bī′tiŋ), *n.* **1.** the act or practice of biting one's fingernails, esp. as the result of nervousness. **2.** *Informal.* nervousness: *Washington's announcement that the trade agreement had been signed ended a week of nail-biting on Wall Street.*

nail·brush (nāl′brush′), *n.* a small brush with stiff bristles, used to clean the fingernails. [NAIL + BRUSH[1]]

nail′ enam′el. See **nail polish.**

nail′er joist′, a steel joist having a permanently attached nailing strip, as for nailing down wooden flooring.

nail′ file′, a small file for smoothing or shaping the fingernails.

nail·head (nāl′hed′), *n.* **1.** the enlarged top of a nail, usually flattened but sometimes rounded. **2.** an ornament that suggests or resembles the enlarged top of a nail. [NAIL + HEAD] —**nail′-head′ed,** *adj.*

nail′ing strip′, a strip of wood or other partly yielding material attached to a hard surface, as of steel or concrete, so that objects may be nailed to the surface.

nail′ pol′ish, a polish of quick-drying lacquer, usually colored pink or red, used by women to paint the fingernails.

nail′ set′, a short rod of steel used to drive a nail below, or flush with, a surface.

nail-sick (nāl′sik′), *adj.* *Naut.* iron-sick. —**nail′-sick′ness,** *n.*

nail′ var′nish, *Brit.* See **nail polish.**

nail′ violin′, a musical instrument consisting of a wooden cylinder or half cylinder with a number of nails or U-shaped metal pins inserted into its surface, played with one or two fiddle bows.

nain·sook (nān′so͝ok, nan′-), *n.* a fine, soft-finished cotton fabric, usually white, used for lingerie and infants' wear. [< Urdu (Hindi) *nainsukh*, equiv. to *nain* the eye + *sukh* pleasure]

Nairn (nârn), *n.* a county in N Scotland. 8421 (1960); 163 sq. mi. *Co. seat:* Nairn. Also called **Nairn·shire** (nârn′shēr, -shər).

Nai·ro·bi (nī rō′bē), *n.* a city in and the capital of Kenya, in the SW part. 266,794 (1962).

na·is·kos (nä is′kos), *n., pl.* **-koi** (-koi). a shrine within the cella of a classical temple. [< Gk, dim. of *naós* temple, shrine]

Nai·smith (nā′smith′), *n.* **James,** 1861–1939, U.S. physical-education professor and originator of basketball, born in Canada.

nais·sance (nā′səns), *n.* a birth, an origination, or a growth, as that of a person, an organization, an idea, or a movement: *Public interest brought about the naissance of the State Theater.* [< F, MF, equiv. to *nais-* (s. of *naitre* to be born < L *nascere*; see NATION) + *-ance* -ANCE]

nais·sant (nā′sənt), *adj.* *Heraldry.* (of a beast) represented as issuant from an ordinary. [< MF, prp. of *naitre* to be born. See NASCENT]

na·ive (nä ēv′), *adj.* **1.** having or showing natural simplicity of nature; unsophisticated; ingenuous. **2.** having or showing a lack of experience, judgment, or information; credulous: *She's so naïve she believes anything he tells her. He has a very naïve attitude toward communism.* Also, **na·ive′.** [< F, fem. of *naïf*, OF *naif* natural, instinctive < L *nātīv(us)* NATIVE] —**na·ive′ly, na·ive′ly,** *adv.*
—**Syn. 1.** simple, unaffected; unsuspecting; artless, guileless, candid, open, plain. —**Ant. 1.** sophisticated, artful.

naïve′ re′alism, *Philos.* the theory that the world is perceived exactly as it is. Also called **commonsense realism, natural realism.** —**naïve′ re′alist.**

na·ïve·té (nä ēv tā′), *n.* **1.** Also called **na·ive′ness.** the quality or state of being naïve; artless simplicity. **2.** a naïve action, remark, etc. Also, **na·ïve·té′, na·ïve·te′.** [< F; see NAÏVE, -ITY[2]]

na·ïve·ty (nä ēv′tē), *n., pl.* **-ties.** naïveté.

Na·je·ra′ (nä′jər ə, nä′jə rä′), *n.* a crater in the second quadrant of the face of the moon, in the libration area: about 40 miles in diameter.

na·ked (nā′kid), *adj.* **1.** without clothing or covering; nude: *The children swam naked in the lake.* **2.** without adequate clothing. **3.** bare of any covering, overlying matter, vegetation, foliage, or the like: *naked fields.* **4.** bare, stripped, or destitute (usually fol. by *of*): *The trees were left naked of leaves.* **5.** without the customary covering, container, or protection: *a naked sword; a naked flame.* **6.** without carpets, hangings, or furnishings, as rooms, walls, etc. **7.** (of the eye, sight, etc.) unassisted by a microscope, telescope, or other instrument: *visible to the naked eye.* **8.** defenseless; unprotected; exposed: *naked to invaders.* **9.** simple; unadorned: *the naked realities of the matter.* **10.** not accompanied or supplemented by anything else: *a naked outline of the facts.* **11.** exposed to view or plainly revealed: *the naked evidence in the case; a naked vein of coal.* **12.** plain-spoken; blunt: *the naked truth.* **13.** *Law.* unsupported, as by authority or consideration: *a naked promise.* **14.** *Bot.* **a.** (of seeds) not enclosed in an ovary. **b.** (of flowers) without a calyx or perianth. **c.** (of stalks, branches, etc.) without leaves. **d.** (of stalks, leaves, etc.) without hairs or pubescence. **15.** *Zool.* having no covering of hair, feathers, shell, etc. [ME *naked(e)*, OE *nacod*; c. D *naakt*, G *nackt*, Goth *naqths*; akin to Icel *nakinn*, L *nūdus*, Gk *gymnós*, Skt *nagnás*] —**na′ked·ly,** *adv.* —**na′ked·ness,** *n.*
—**Syn. 1.** uncovered, undressed, unclothed. **4.** desert, denuded. **5.** unsheathed, exposed. **6.** unfurnished. **8.** unarmed, open. **11.** manifest, evident, undisguised. **12.** direct, outspoken. —**Ant. 1.** dressed. **8.** protected.

Na′ked and the Dead′, The, a novel (1948) by Norman Mailer.

na·ked·ize (nā′ki dīz′), *v.,* **-ized, -iz·ing.** —*v.t.* **1.** to make naked. —*v.i.* **2.** to become or go naked; undress. [NAKED + -IZE]

na′ked smut′, *Plant Pathol.* See **loose smut.**

na·ker (nā′kər), *n.* a kettledrum usually played as one of a pair. [ME < OF *naquere*, *naicere* < ML *nacara*, *nacaria* drum, NACRE]

Na·khi·che·van′ Auton′omous Repub′lic (nə-KHē′chə vän′; *Russ.* nə KHyi chyi vän′), an autonomous republic of Azerbaijan, surrounded by Armenia, Iran, and Turkey. 295,000; 2277 sq. mi. *Cap.:* Nakhichevan.

Nal·chik (näl′chik; *Russ.* näl′chyik), *n.* a city in and the capital of Kabardino-Balkar Autonomous Republic in the S Russian Federation. 235,000.

Nal·line (nal′ēn), *n.* *Pharm., Trademark.* nalorphine.

nal·or·phine (nal′ər fēn′, nal ôr′fēn), *n.* *Pharm.* a white, crystalline, water-soluble powder, $C_{19}H_{21}NO_3$, used to nullify respiratory depression due to narcotics and for the diagnosis of addiction to narcotics. [*N-al(lyln)or(mor)phine*]

Nam (näm), *n.* Menam.

NAM, National Association of Manufacturers. Also, **N.A.M.**

Na·ma (nä′mä), *n., pl.* **-mas,** (*esp. collectively*) **-ma. 1.** a member of a Hottentot people of Namaqualand, in SW Africa. **2.** one of the Khoisan languages of the Hottentots.

nam·a·ble (nā′mə bəl), *adj.* **1.** capable of being or liable to being named or revealed. **2.** capable of being said or discussed without shocking a person's sensibilities or sense of decency. Also, **nameable.** [NAME + -ABLE] —**nam′a·bil′i·ty, name′a·bil′i·ty,** *n.*

Na·man·gan (nä′män gän′), *n.* a city in E Uzbekistan, in the SW Soviet Union in Asia. 138,000 (est. 1962).

Na·ma·qua·land (nə mä′kwə land′), *n.* a coastal region in the S part of South-West Africa, extending into the Cape of Good Hope province of the Republic of South Africa: inhabited by Hottentots. Also called **Na·ma·land** (nä′mä land′).

na·ma·ste (num′ə stā′), *n.* a conventional Hindu expression on meeting or parting, used by the speaker usually while holding his palms together vertically in front of the bosom. [?]

nam·ay·cush (nam′i kush′, nam′ā-), *n.* a lake trout. [< Algonquian (Cree) *namekus*, dim. of *namew* fish]

nam·ban (näm bän′), *n., pl.* **-ban.** a motif of dragons and scrolls elaborately worked in iron and used for various Japanese sword mounts. [< Jap, equiv. to *nam* southern + *ban* barbarians]

nam·by-pam·by (nam′bē pam′bē), *adj., n., pl.* **-bies** for 5. —*adj.* **1.** weakly sentimental, pretentious, or affected; insipid. **2.** lacking in character, directness, or moral or emotional strength: *namby-pamby writing.* **3.** without firm methods or policy; weak or indecisive: *namby-pamby handling of juvenile offenders.* —*n.* **4.** namby-pamby verse or prose: *He made a tidy living from namby-pamby.* **5.** a namby-pamby person: *written by and for namby-pambies.* **6.** namby-pamby sentiment: *the harmless namby-pamby of a birthday card.* [special use of nickname *Namby Pamby* for Ambrose Philips; first used 1726 by Henry Carey as title of poem ridiculing Philips' verses] —**nam′by-pam′bi·ness, nam′by-pam′by·ism,** *n.* —**nam′by-pam′by·ish,** *adj.*

name (nām), *n., v.,* **named, nam·ing,** *adj.* —*n.* **1.** a word or a combination of words by which a person, place, or thing, a body or class, or any object of thought is designated or known. **2.** mere designation, as distinguished from fact: *He was a ruler in name only.* **3.** an appellation, title, or epithet, applied descriptively, in honor, abuse, etc. **4.** a reputation of a particular kind given by common report: *to protect one's good name.* **5.** a distinguished, famous, or great reputation; fame: *to make a name for oneself.* **6.** a widely known or famous person: *She's a name in show business.* **7.** an unpleasant or derogatory appellation or expression: *The mother was surprised when her child used those names. Sticks and stones may break my bones but names will never hurt me.* **8.** (*cap.*) a symbol or vehicle of divinity: *to take the Name in vain; the power of the Name.* **9.** a personal or family name as exercising influence or bringing distinction: *She was merely after his name and connections.* **10.** a body of persons grouped under one name, as a family or race. **11.** the verbal or other symbolic representation of a thing, event, property, relation, or concept. **12. by name, a.** personally; individually: *He was always careful to address every employee by name.* **b.** not personally; by repute: *I know him only by name.* **13. call names,** to scold or speak abusively of or to a person: *Better not to call names unless one is larger and considerably stronger than one's adversary.* **14. in the name of, a.** with appeal to: *In the name of mercy, stop that screaming!* **b.** by the authority of: *Open, in the name of the law!* **c.** on behalf of: *to purchase something in the name of another.* **d.** under the name or possession of: *money deposited in the name of a son.* **e.** under the designation of: *murder in the name of justice.* **15. to one's name,** in one's possession: *I haven't a penny to my name.* —*v.t.* **16.** to give a name to: *to name a baby.* **17.** to accuse: *He was named as the thief.* **18.** to call by a specified name: *to name a dog Rufo.* **19.** to identify, specify, or mention by name: *Three persons were named in the report.* **20.** to designate for some duty or office; nominate or appoint: *I have named you for the position.* **21.** to specify; suggest: *Name a price.* **22.** to give the name of: *Can you name the capital of Ohio?* **23.** to speak of. **24.** *Brit.* (in the House of Commons) to cite (a member) for contempt. **25. name names,** to specify people by name, esp. those who have been accomplices in a misdeed: *Several members of the police department requested retirement when the witness in the bribery investigation threatened to name names.* —*adj.* **26.** famous; widely known: *a name actor; a name author; a name brand of tomato juice.* **27.** designed for or carrying a name: *a name tag.* **28.** giving its name or title to a collection or anthology containing it: *the name piece.* [ME; OE *nama*; c. G *Name*, Goth *namō*; akin to Icel *nafn*, L *nōmen*, Gk *ónoma*] —**nam′er,** *n.*
—**Syn. 1.** NAME, TITLE both refer to the label by which a person is known. NAME is the simpler and more general word for appellation: *The name is John.* A TITLE is an official or honorary term bestowed on a person or the specific designation of a book, article, etc.: *He now has the title of Doctor.* Treasure Island *is the title of a book.* **4.** repute, character, credit. **5.** note, distinction, renown, eminence. **6.** celebrity, personality. **18.** title, entitle, dub, denominate. **20.** choose. **21.** mention.

name·a·ble (nā′mə bəl), *adj.* namable.

name·board (nām′bōrd′, -bôrd′), *n.* **1.** a signboard that identifies a place or object. **2.** a name painted, stenciled, etc., on something, as on the side of a ship. [NAME + BOARD]

name-call·er (nām′kô′lər), *n.* a person who constantly resorts to name-calling: *He wasn't so much an arguer as he was a name-caller.*

name-call·ing (nām′kô′liŋ), *n.* the use of abusive epithets to belittle or humiliate another person or to minimize his effectiveness, popularity, vote-getting ability, etc.

name′ day′, 1. the day of the saint after whom a person is named. **2.** the day on which a person is christened.

name-drop (nām′drop′), *v.i.,* **-dropped, -drop·ping.** to indulge in name-dropping.

name-drop·per (nām′drop′ər), *n.* a person who indulges in name-dropping.

name-drop·ping (nām′drop′iŋ), *n.* the introduction into one's conversation, letters, etc., of widely known or famous names as alleged friends or associates, esp. for the purpose of impressing the person addressed

name·less (nām′lis), *adj.* **1.** unknown to fame; obscure: *a nameless poet; nameless defenders of the country.* **2.** having no name. **3.** left unnamed: *a certain person who shall be nameless.* **4.** anonymous: *a nameless source of information.* **5.** having no legitimate paternal name, as a child born out of wedlock. **6.** incapable of being specified or described: *a nameless charm; beset by nameless aches and pains.* **7.** too shocking or vile to be specified: *a nameless crime.* [ME; see NAME, -LESS] —**name′less·ly,** *adv.* —**name′less·ness,** *n.*

name·ly (nām′lē), *adv.* that is to say; explicitly; specifically; to wit: *an item of legislation, namely, the housing bill.* [ME *namely*, *nameliche*. See NAME, -LY]

name·plate (nām′plāt′), *n.* **1.** a flat, usually rectangular piece of metal, wood, or plastic on which the name of a person, company, etc., is printed or engraved. **2.** Also called **masthead.** *Journalism.* a line of type on the front page of a newspaper or the cover of a periodical giving the name of the publication. [NAME + PLATE[1]]

name·sake (nām′sāk′), *n.* **1.** a person named after another. **2.** a person having the same name as another. [alter. of *name's* (NAME + 'S[1]) SAKE[1]]

name′ tape′, a fabric tape on which a person's name is written, woven, or printed: for affixing to garments and other personal belongings for identification.

Nam·hoi (näm′hoi′), *n.* Nanhai.

Na·mib·i·a (nə mib′ē ə), *n.* official (UN) name of **South-West Africa.** —**Na·mib′i·an,** *adj., n.*

nam·ma (nam′ə), *n.* *Australian.* **1.** a pool of water; spring. **2.** a well. [short for *namma hole*, equiv. to native Austral *namma* breast + HOLE]

Nam·mu (nä′mo͞o), *n.* a Sumerian goddess personifying the primeval sea: the mother of the gods and of heaven and earth.

Nam·pa (nam′pə), *n.* a city in W Idaho. 18,013 (1960).

Nam·pu·la (nam po͞o′lə), *n.* a city in E Mozambique. 146,916 (est. 1955).

Nam·tar (näm′tär), *n.* the Sumerian and Akkadian demon personifying death.

Na·mur (nä mo͝or′; *Fr.* NA MYR′), *n.* **1.** a province in S Belgium. 375,634 (est. 1964); 1413 sq. mi. **2.** a city in and capital of this province, on the Sambre and Meuse rivers. 32,467 (est. 1964).

Nan (nan), *n.* **1.** a word formerly used in communications to represent the letter N. **2.** a girl's given name, form of **Ann** or **Anna.**

nan-, var. of **nano-** before a vowel: *nanoid.*

Na·na (*Fr.* NA NA′), *n.* a novel (1880) by Émile Zola.

Na·nak (nä′nək), *n.* ("*Guru*") 1469–1538, Indian religious leader: founder of Sikhism.

na·na·ko (nə nä′kō; *Jap.* nä nä′kō), *n.* a form of Japanese decorative metalwork composed of a pattern of tiny raised dots, used esp. for sword mounts. [< Jap: lit., fish roe]

Na·na·ku·li (nä′nä ko͞o′lē), *n.* a town on SW Oahu, in central Hawaii. 2745 (1960).

Na·nanne (nə nan′; *Fr.* NA NAN′), *n.* a girl's given name.

nance (nans), *n.* *Slang.* **1.** an effeminate male. **2.** a male homosexual, esp. one who assumes the female role. [shortened from given name *Nancy*]

Nan·chang (nän′chäŋ′), *n.* a city in and the capital of Kiangsi, in SE China. 508,000 (est. 1957).

Nan·cy (nan′sē; *Fr.* näN sē′), *n.* **1.** a city in and the capital of Meurthe-et-Moselle, in NE France: battles 1477, 1914, 1944. 695,733 (1962). **2.** Also, **Nan′cee, Nan′cie.** a girl's given name, form of **Ann** or **Anna.**

Nan·da De·vi (nun′də dā′vē), a mountain in N India, in Uttar Pradesh: a peak of the Himalayas. 25,661 ft.

Nan·di (nän′dē), *n.* a town on W Viti Levu, in the Fiji Islands: airport. 1653 (1956).

nan·din (nan′din), *n.* an evergreen shrub, *Nandina domestica,* of China and Japan, bearing red berries, cultivated as an ornamental. Also called **sacred bamboo, heavenly bamboo.** [< Jap]

nane (nān), *pron., adv., adj. Scot.* none.

Na·nette (na net′), *n.* a girl's given name, form of **Ann.**

Nan·ga Par·bat (nuŋ′gə pur′but), a mountain in NW Kashmir, in the Himalayas. 26,660 ft.

Nan·hai (nän′hī′), *n.* a city in W Kwantung, in SE China, near Canton. 96,000 (est. 1950). Also, **Namhoi.** Also called **Fatshan, Foshan.**

na·nism (nā′niz əm, nan′iz-), *n. Med.* the condition of being unusually or abnormally small in size or stature; dwarfism. [NAN- + -ISM; cf. F *nanisme*]

nan·keen (nan kēn′), *n.* **1.** a firm, durable, yellow or buff fabric, formerly made from a natural-colored Chinese cotton. **2.** a twilled material made from other cotton and dyed in imitation of this fabric. **3. nankeens,** garments made of this material. **4.** a yellow or buff color. **5.** Also called **Nan′keen por′celain, Nan′king chi′na, Nanking′ ware′.** a type of Chinese porcelain having blue ornament on a white ground. Also, **nan·kin** (nan′kin). [after *Nankin* NANKING, where first made]

nan′keen lil′y, a bulbous herb, *Lilium testaceum,* having drooping, fragrant, pink-tinged, yellowish or apricot-colored flowers with recurved petals.

Nan·king (nan′kiŋ′; *Chin.* nän′kiŋ′), *n.* a port in and the capital of Kiangsu, in E China, on the Yangtze: a former capital of China. 1,419,000 (est. 1957).

Nan·lee (nan′lē, nan lē′), *n.* a girl's given name.

Nan Ling (nän′ liŋ′), a mountain range in S China. Also called **Nan Shan.**

Nan·na (nän′nä), *n. Scand. Myth.* the wife of Balder.

Nan·na (nä′nä), *n.* the Sumerian god of the moon: the counterpart of the Akkadian god Sin.

Nan·ning (nan′niŋ′; *Chin.* nän′niŋ′), *n.* a city in and the capital of Kwangsi, in S China. 203,000 (est. 1950). Formerly, **Yungning.**

nan·ny (nan′ē), *n., pl.* **-nies.** *Chiefly Brit.* a child's nursemaid. [special use of *Nanny*]

Nan·ny (nan′ē), *n.* a girl's given name, form of **Ann** or **Anna.**

nan·ny·ber·ry (nan′ē ber′ē), *n., pl.* **-ries.** sheepberry (defs. 1, 2). [NANNY (GOAT) + BERRY]

nan′ny goat′, a female goat.

nano-, a learned borrowing from Latin meaning "dwarf"; specialized in certain measurements to mean "one billionth": *nanocurie; nanosecond.* Also, *esp. before a vowel,* **nan-.** [comb. form repr. L *nānus* dwarf < Gk *nânos*]

na·no·cu·rie (nā′nə kyŏŏr′ē, nan′ə-), *n.* one billionth of a curie. *Abbr.:* nC, nc [NANO- + CURIE]

na·no·far·ad (nā′nə far′əd, -ad, nan′ə-), *n.* one billionth of a farad. *Abbr.:* nF, nf [NANO- + FARAD]

na·no·hen·ry (nā′nə hen′rē, nan′ə-), *n., pl.* **-ries, -rys.** one billionth of a henry. *Abbr.:* nH, nh [NANO- + HENRY]

na·noid (nā′noid, nan′oid), *adj. Med.* dwarfish. [NAN- + -OID]

na·no·me·ter (nā′nə mē′tər, nan′ə-), *n. Metric System.* the millionth part of a millimeter. *Abbr.:* nm [NANO- + METER¹]

na·no·sec·ond (nā′nə sek′ənd, nan′ə-), *n.* one billionth of a second. *Abbr.:* ns, nsec [NANO- + SECOND²]

na·no·watt (nā′nə wot′, nan′ə-), *n.* one billionth of a watt. *Abbr.:* nW, nw [NANO- + WATT]

Nan·sen (nan′sən; *Norw.* nän′sən), *n.* **1. Fridt·jof** (frit′yof), 1861–1930, Norwegian arctic explorer, zoologist, and statesman: Nobel peace prize 1922. **2.** a walled plain in the first quadrant of the face of the moon, in the libration area: about 70 miles in diameter.

Nan′sen bot′tle, *Oceanog.* a waterproof container for taking samples of ocean water, several together, usually, being lowered open on a line and each being closed at the desired depth by the action of a falling weight. [named after F. NANSEN]

Nan′sen cast′, *Oceanog.* a series of Nansen bottles lowered on one line and closed by the action of a single weight.

Nan Shan (nän′ shän′), **1.** a mountain range in W China. **2.** See **Nan Ling.**

Nantes (nants; *Fr.* näɴt), *n.* **1.** a seaport in and the capital of Loire-Atlantique, in W France, at the mouth of the Loire River. 246,227 (1962). **2. Edict of,** *Fr. Hist.* a law, promulgated by Henry IV in 1598, granting considerable religious and civil liberty to the Huguenots; revoked by Louis XIV in 1685.

Nan·ti·coke (nan′tə kōk′), *n.* a city in E Pennsylvania. 15,601 (1960).

Nan·tuck·et (nan tuk′it), *n.* **1.** an island off SE Massachusetts: summer resort. 3559 (1960); 15 mi. long. **2.** a town on this island. 2804 (1960).

Nan·ty-Glo (nan′tē glō′), *n.* a town in central Pennsylvania. 4608 (1960).

Naoi·se (nē′sē, nā′-), *n. Irish Legend.* the husband of Deirdre and a nephew of Conchobar, by whom he was treacherously killed.

Na·o·mi (nā ō′mē, -mī, nā′ō mī′, -mē′), *n.* **1.** Also, *Douay Bible,* **Noemi.** the mother-in-law of Ruth. Ruth 1. **2.** a girl's given name.

na·os (nā′os), *n., pl.* **-oi** (-oi). **1.** a temple. **2.** *Archit.* cella. [< Gk *naós* the dwelling of a god, the inner part of a temple, the shrine]

nap¹ (nap), *v.,* **napped, nap·ping,** *n.* —*v.i.* **1.** to sleep for a short time; doze. **2.** to be off one's guard: *The question caught him napping.* —*v.t.* **3.** to sleep or doze through (a period of time, an activity, etc.) (usually fol. by *away*): *I napped the afternoon away. He naps away most of his classes.* —*n.* **4.** a brief period of sleep, often regularly taken, as daily by infants; doze: *Has the baby taken his nap?* [ME *nappe(n),* OE *hnappian;* c. MHG *napfen*]

nap² (nap), *n., v.,* **napped, nap·ping.** —*n.* **1.** the short fuzzy ends of fibers on the surface of cloth, drawn up in napping. **2.** any downy coating, as on plants. —*v.t.* **3.** to raise a nap on. [late ME *noppe,* OE *-hnoppa* (as in *wullcnoppa,* mistake for *wullhnoppa* tuft of wool), c. MD, MLG *noppe;* akin to OE *hnoppian* to pluck] —**nap′less,** *adj.* —**nap′less·ness,** *n.*

nap³ (nap), *n.* napoleon. [shortened form]

Nap (nap), *n.* a boy's given name, form of **Napoleon.**

Nap·a (nap′ə), *n.* a city in W California. 22,170 (1960).

Na·pae·ae (nə pē′ē), *n.pl. Rom. Legend.* the nymphs of a dell.

na·palm (nā′päm), *n. Mil.* a highly incendiary jellylike substance used in fire bombs, flame throwers, etc. [NA(PHTHENE) + PALM(ITATE)]

nape (nāp, nap), *n.* the back of the neck (usually used in the phrase *nape of the neck*). [ME]

na·per·y (nā′pə rē), *n.* **1.** table linen, as tablecloths, napkins, etc. **2.** any linen for household use. [ME *napyre* < MF, equiv. to *nape,* var. of *nappe* tablecloth (see NAPKIN) + *-erie* -ERY]

Naph·ta·li (naf′tə lī′), *n.* **1.** a son of Jacob and Bilhah. Gen. 30:7,8. **2.** one of the 12 tribes of Israel. Also, *Douay Bible,* **Nephtali.**

Naph·ta·lite (naf′tə līt′), *n.* a member of the tribe of Naphtali. [NAPHTAL(I) + -ITE¹]

naphth-, a combining form of **naphtha** or **naphthalene:** *naphthol.*

naph·tha (naf′thə, nap′-), *n.* **1.** a colorless, volatile petroleum distillate, usually an intermediate product between gasoline and benzine, used as a solvent, fuel, etc. **2.** any of various similar liquids distilled from other products. **3.** petroleum. [< L < Gk; akin to Avestan *napta* wet] —**naph′thous,** *adj.*

naph·tha·lene (naf′thə lēn′, nap′-), *n. Chem.* a white, crystalline, water-insoluble hydrocarbon, $C_{10}H_8$, usually obtained from coal tar: used in making dyes, as a moth repellant, etc. Also, **naph′tha·line′, naph·tha·lin** (naf′thə lin, nap′-). [NAPHTH- + -AL³ + -ENE] —**naph·thal·ic** (naf thal′ik, nap-), **naph·tha·len·ic** (naf′thə len′ik, nap′-), *adj.*

naph·tha·lise (naf′thə līz′, nap′-), *v.t.,* **-lised, -lis·ing.** *Chiefly Brit.* naphthalize.

naph·tha·lize (naf′thə līz′, nap′-), *v.t.,* **-lized, -liz·ing.** to mix or saturate with naphtha. [NAPHTHAL(ENE) + -IZE]

naph·thene (naf′thēn, nap′-), *n. Chem.* any of a group of hydrocarbon ring compounds of the general formula, C_nH_{2n}, derivatives of cyclopentane and cyclohexane, found in certain petroleums. [NAPHTH- + -ENE] —**naph·the·nic** (naf thē′nik, -then′ik, nap-), *adj.*

naph·thol (naf′thōl, -thôl, -thol, nap′-), *n. Chem.* **1.** Also called **alpha-naphthol.** one of the two isomeric derivatives of naphthalene, a white or yellow, slightly water-soluble powder or prisms, $C_{10}H_7OH$, darkening on exposure to light: used chiefly in the manufacture of dyes and perfumes; 1-naphthol. **2.** Also called **beta-naphthol.** one of the two isomeric derivatives of naphthalene, a white or yellowish-white, slightly water-soluble, crystalline powder or leafletlike solid, $C_{10}H_7OH$, having a phenollike odor and darkening on exposure to light: used chiefly in the manufacture of dyes, drugs, perfumes, antioxidants for rubber, fats, oils, etc., and as an antiseptic; 2-naphthol. **3.** any of certain hydroxyl derivatives of naphthalene. [NAPHTH- + -OL¹]

naph·thyl (naf′thil, nap′-), *adj. Chem.* containing the naphthyl group. [NAPHTH- + -YL]

naph′thyl group′, *Chem.* **1.** Also called **alpha-naphthyl group, alpha-naphthyl radical.** a univalent group, $C_{10}H_7$–, having a replaceable hydrogen atom in the first, or alpha, position; 1-naphthyl group. **2.** Also called **beta-naphthyl group, beta-naphthyl radical.** a univalent group, $C_{10}H_7$–, having a replaceable hydrogen atom in the second, or beta, position; 2-naphthyl group. Also called **naph′thyl rad′ical.**

na·pier (nā′pēr), *n. Physics.* neper.

Na·pi·er (nā′pē ər *or, for 1–3,* nə pēr′), *n.* **1. Sir Charles James,** 1782–1853, British general. **2.** Also, **Neper. John,** 1550–1617, Scottish mathematician: inventor of logarithms. **3. Robert Cornelis** (*1st Baron Napier of Magdala*), 1810–90, English field marshal. **4.** a seaport on E North Island, in New Zealand. 32,716 (1961).

Na′pier di′agram, *Navig.* a diagram for showing the deviation of a magnetic compass from magnetic north at any heading. [named after John NAPIER]

Na·pier·i·an (nə pēr′ē ən), *adj.* of, pertaining to, or formulated by John Napier. Also, **Na·per′i·an.** [NAPIER + -IAN]

Napier′ian log′arithm, *Math.* See **natural logarithm.**

na·pi·form (nā′pə fôrm′), *adj.* turnip-shaped, as a root. [< L *nāp(us)* a kind of turnip + -I- + -FORM]

nap·kin (nap′kin), *n.* **1.** a rectangular piece of linen, cotton, paper, etc., for use in wiping the lips and fingers and to protect the clothes while eating. **2.** a small towel of linen or cotton cloth. **3.** *Chiefly Brit.* a diaper. **4.** *North Eng. and Scot.* a handkerchief. **5.** *Scot.* a kerchief or neckerchief. [ME < MF *nappe* tablecloth (< L *mappa* napkin); see -KIN]

nap′kin ring′, a ring or band of metal, wood, etc., through which a folded napkin is inserted, often as part of a place setting.

Na·ples (nā′pəlz), *n.* **1.** Italian, **Napoli.** a seaport in SW Italy. 1,179,608 (1961). **2. Bay of,** Italian, **Gol·fo di Na·po·li** (gôl′fô dē nä′pô lē). a bay in SW Italy: Naples located here. 22 mi. long. **3.** a town in S Florida. 4655 (1960).

Na′ples yel′low, *Painting.* a poisonous pigment used in painting and enameling, consisting chiefly of lead antimoniate and characterized by its fugitive yellow color, rapid drying rate, and strong film-forming properties. Also called **antimony yellow.** [so called because originally manufactured in NAPLES, Italy]

na·po·le·on (nə pō′lē ən, -pōl′yən), *n.* **1.** a pastry consisting of thin layers of puff paste interlaid with a cream filling. **2.** a former gold coin of France, equal to 20 francs and bearing a portrait either of Napoleon I or of Napoleon III. **3.** *Cards.* **a.** a game in which the players bid for the privilege of naming the trump, stating the number of tricks they propose to win. **b.** a bid in this game to take all five tricks of a hand. [< F]

Na·po·le·on (nə pō′lē ən), *n.* **1. Louis** (lo͞o′ē; *Fr.* lwē). See **Napoleon III. 2.** a town in NW Ohio. 6739 (1960). **3.** a boy's given name.

Napoleon I, Napoleon Bonaparte (*"the Little Corporal"*) 1769–1821, French general born in Corsica: emperor of France 1804–15.

Napoleon II, Napoleon Bonaparte, *Duke of Reichstadt,* 1811–32, titular king of Rome (son of Napoleon I).

Napoleon III, Louis Napoleon Bonaparte, 1808–73, president of France 1848–52, emperor of France 1852–70.

Na·po·le·on·ic (nə pō′lē on′ik), *adj.* pertaining to, resembling, or suggestive of Napoleon I, or, less often, Napoleon III, or their dynasty: *the Napoleonic era; a Napoleonic attitude toward one's employees.* [NAPOLEON + -IC] —**Na·po′le·on′i·cal·ly,** *adv.*

Napo′leon′ic Wars′, the intermittent wars (1796–1815) waged by France principally against England, Prussia, Austria, and Russia.

Na·po·le·on·ize (nə pō′lē ə nīz′), *v.t.,* **-ized, -iz·ing.** to govern or rule in the manner of Napoleon: *an unwise plan to Napoleonize the new republic.* [NAPOLEON (I) + -IZE]

Na·po·li (nä′pô lē′), *n.* Italian name of **Naples.**

Nap·pa·nee (nap′ə nē′), *n.* a town in N Indiana. 3895 (1960).

nappe (nap), *n.* **1.** *Geol.* a large mass of rock thrust far forward along a nearly horizontal fault plane or in an overturned anticlinal fold. **2.** *Geom.* one of the two equal sections of a cone. [< F: lit., tablecloth, cloth; OF *nappe, nape* < L *mappa;* cf. NAPKIN]

nap·per¹ (nap′ər), *n.* **1.** a textile worker who naps cloth. **2.** a machine for putting a nap on cloth. [NAP² + -ER¹]

nap·per² (nap′ər), *n.* a person who naps or dozes. [NAP¹ + -ER¹]

nap·py¹ (nap′ē), *adj.,* **-pi·er, -pi·est,** *n.* —*adj.* **1.** *Brit. Informal.* (of ale and other malt liquors) heady or strong; foaming and hearty. **2.** *Chiefly Scot. Informal.* mildly drunk; tipsy. —*n.* **3.** *Chiefly Scot.* liquor, esp. ale. [late ME *nopy.* See NAP², -Y¹]

nap·py² (nap′ē), *n., pl.* **-pies.** a small dish, usually round and often of glass, with a flat bottom and sloping sides, for serving food. Also, **nap′pie.** [*nap* (ME; OE *hnæp* bowl) + -Y²]

nap·py³ (nap′ē), *adj.,* **-pi·er, -pi·est.** covered with nap; downy. [NAP² + -Y¹] —**nap′pi·ness,** *n.*

nap·py⁴ (nap′ē), *n., pl.* **-pies.** *Chiefly Brit.* **1.** a baby's napkin or bib. **2.** a diaper. [NAP(KIN) + -Y²]

na·prap·a·thy (nə prap′ə thē), *n.* a system of treatment based on the belief that all diseases are caused by disorders of connective tissue or of ligaments and can be cured by massage. [< Czech *naprá(va)* correction (cf. Russ *napravit′* direct, guide) + -PATHY] —**nap·ra·path** (nap′rə path′), *n.*

Na·ra (nä rä′), *n.* a city on S Honshu, in central Japan: chief Buddhist center of ancient Japan. 152,610 (1964).

Nar·a·ka (nur′ə kə), *n. Hinduism.* a place of torment for the spirits of the wicked.

Nar·ba·da (nər bud′ə), *n.* a river flowing W from central India to the Arabian Sea. 800 mi. long. Also, **Nerbudda.**

Nar·berth (när′bərth), *n.* a town in SE Pennsylvania. 5109 (1960).

Nar·bonne (NAR bôn′), *n.* a city in S France: an important port in Roman times. 35,899 (1962).

Nar·cae·us (när sē′əs), *n. Class. Myth.* a son of Physcoa and Dionysus who initiated the worship of Dionysus in Elis.

narc-, var. of **narco-** before a vowel: *narcoma.*

nar·ce·ine (när′sē ēn′, -in), *n. Pharm.* a white, bitter, crystalline, narcotic alkaloid, $C_{23}H_{27}NO_8$, occurring in opium and acting as a mild relaxant on smooth muscle. [< NL *narcē* (< Gk *nárkē* numbness; see NARCO-) + -INE²]

nar·cis·sism (när′si siz′əm), *n.* **1.** self-love; egocentrism. **2.** *Psychoanal.* erotic gratification derived from admiration of one's own physical or mental attributes, being a normal condition at the infantile level of personality development. Also, **nar·cism** (när′siz əm). [< G *Narzissismus.* See NARCISSUS, -ISM] —**nar′cis·sist, nar′cist,** *n.* —**nar′cis·sis′tic, nar·cis′tic,** *adj.*

nar·cis·sus (när sis′əs), *n., pl.* **-cis·sus, -cis·sus·es, -cis·si** (-sis′ē, -sis′ī) for 1, 2. **1.** any bulbous amaryllidaceous plant of the genus *Narcissus,* having showy flowers with a cup-shaped corona. **2.** the flower of any of these plants. **3.** (*cap.*) *Class. Myth.* a youth who fell in love with his own image reflected in a pool, and who, after eventually wasting away from unsatisfied desire, was transformed into the flower. [< L < Gk *nárkissos* plant name, connected, by virtue of plant's narcotic effects, with *nárkē* numbness, torpor. See NARCOTIC]

narco-, a combining form meaning "stupor," "narcosis": *narcodiagnosis.* Also, *esp. before a vowel,* **narc-.** [< Gk *nárk(ē)* numbness, stiffness + -O-]

nar·co·a·nal·y·sis (när′kō ə nal′i sis), *n.* a method of psychological investigation, conducted by a trained interrogator, in which the conscious or unconscious unwillingness of a subject to confess memories or feelings is diminished by the use of a drug that induces a semisomnolent state. Cf. **truth serum.** [NARCO- + ANALYSIS]

nar·co·di·ag·no·sis (när′kō dī′əg nō′sis), *n. Psychiatry.* the use of drugs to produce narcosis as an aid in diagnosis. [NARCO- + DIAGNOSIS]

nar·co·lep·sy (när′kə lep′sē), *n. Pathol.* a condition characterized by a frequent and uncontrollable need for short periods of deep sleep. [NARCO- + (EPI)LEPSY] —**nar′co·lep′tic,** *adj.*

nar·co·ma (när kō′mə), *n., pl.* **-mas, -ma·ta** (-mə tə). *Med.* stupor produced by narcotics. [NARC- + -OMA] —**nar·com·a·tous** (när kom′ə təs), *adj.*

nar·co·ma·ni·a (när′kə mā′nē ə), *n.* **1.** *Psychiatry.* abnormal craving for a drug to deaden pain. **2.** insanity resulting from addiction to a drug. [NARCO- + -MANIA] —**nar·co·ma·ni·ac** (när′kə mā′nē ak′), *n.* —**nar·co·ma·ni·a·cal** (när′kō mə nī′ə kəl), *adj.*

nar·cose (när′kōs), *adj.* characterized by stupor; stuporous. [NARC- + -OSE¹]

nar·co·sis (när kō′sis), *n.* **1.** a state of sleep or drowsiness. **2.** a state of unconsciousness or drowsiness produced by a drug, or by heat, cold, or electricity. [< NL < Gk *nárkōsis.* See NARC-, -OSIS]

nar·co·syn·the·sis (när′kō sin′thi sis), *n.* a treatment for psychiatric disturbances which uses narcotics. [NARCO- + SYNTHESIS]

nar·co·ther·a·py (när′kō ther′ə pē), *n. Psychiatry.* a method of treating certain mental disorders by injecting barbiturates intravenously. [NARCO- + THERAPY]

nar·cot·ic (när kot′ik), *adj.* **1.** having the power to produce narcosis, as a drug. **2.** pertaining to or of the nature of narcosis. **3.** pertaining to narcotics or their use. **4.** used by, or in the treatment of, narcotic addicts. —*n.* **5.** any of a class of substances that blunt the senses, as opium, morphine, belladonna, and alcohol, that in large quantities produce euphoria, stupor, or coma, that when used constantly can cause habituation or addiction, and that are used in medicine to relieve pain, cause sedation, and induce sleep. **6.** an individual inclined toward the habitual use of such substances. **7.** anything that exercises a soothing or numbing effect or influence: *T.V. is a narcotic for many people.* [ME *narcotik(e)* < ML *narcōticum* < Gk *narkōtikón,* n. use of neut. of *narkōtikós* benumbing, equiv. to *narkō-* (var. s. of *narkoûn* to benumb; see NARCO-) + *-tikos* -TIC] —**nar·cot′i·cal·ly,** *adv.* —**nar·cot′ic·ness, nar·cot′i·cal·ness,** *n.*

nar·co·tise (när′kə tīz′), *v.t., v.i.,* **-tised, -tis·ing.** *Chiefly Brit.* narcotize. —**nar′co·ti·sa′tion,** *n.*

nar·co·tism (när′kə tiz′əm), *n.* **1.** habitual use of narcotics. **2.** the action or influence of narcotics. **3.** narcosis. **4.** an abnormal inclination to sleep. [earlier *narcoticism.* See NARCOTIC, -ISM] —**nar′co·tist,** *n.*

nar·co·tize (när′kə tīz′), *v.,* **-tized, -tiz·ing.** —*v.t.* **1.** to subject to a narcotic; stupefy. **2.** to make dull; deaden the awareness of: *He had used liquor to narcotize his anxieties.* —*v.i.* **3.** to act as a narcotic: *a remedy that does not heal but merely narcotizes.* Also, *esp. Brit.,* **narcotise.** [NARCOT(IC) + -IZE] —**nar′co·ti·za′tion,** *n.*

nard (närd), *n.* **1.** an aromatic, Himalayan plant, believed to be the spikenard, *Nardostachys Jatamansi,* the source of an ointment used by the ancients. **2.** the ointment. [ME *narde* < L *nardus* < Gk *nárdos* < Sem; cf. Heb *nērd*] —**nar·dine** (när′din, -dīn), *adj.*

nar·doo (när′do͞o), *n.* an aquatic herb, *Marsilea drummondi,* of Australia, having wavy-margined, white-hairy leaves. [< native Austral]

nar·es (nâr′ēz), *n.pl., sing.* **nar·is** (nâr′is). *Anat.* the nostrils or the nasal passages. [< L *nārēs,* pl. of *nāris* a nostril]

Na·rew (nä′ʀef), *n.* a river in NE Poland, flowing S and SW into the Bug River: battle 1915. 290 mi. long. Russian, **Na·rev** (nä′ʀef).

nar·ghi·le (när′gə lē, -lā′), *n.* an Oriental tobacco pipe in which the smoke is drawn through water before reaching the lips; hookah. Also, **nar′gi·le, nar′gi·leh.** [< Turk *nargile* < Pers *nārgīleh,* deriv. of *nārgīl* coconut, of which the bowl was formerly made]

nar·i·al (nâr′ē əl), *adj. Anat.* of or pertaining to the nares or nostrils. Also, **nar·ine** (nâr′in, -īn). [< L *nāri(s)* nostril + -AL¹]

nark (närk), *n.* **1.** *Brit. Slang.* See **stool pigeon** (def. 2). **2.** *Chiefly Australian Slang.* an annoying person, esp. a kill-joy. —*v.i.* **3.** *Brit. Slang.* to act as a police informer or stool pigeon. **4.** *Chiefly Australian Slang.* to become annoyed. **5.** **nark it,** *Brit. Slang.* stop it; keep quiet. [< Gypsy *nāk* nose]

Nar·ra·gan·sett (nar′ə gan′sit), *n., pl.* **-setts,** (*esp. collectively*) **-sett.** **1.** a member of a North American Indian tribe of the Algonquian family formerly located in Rhode Island but now extinct. **2.** an Algonquian language, the language of the Narragansett Indians. **3.** a town in S Rhode Island: includes a resort (**Nar′ragan′sett Pier′**). 3444 (1960).

Nar′ragan′sett Bay′, an inlet of the Atlantic in E Rhode Island. 28 mi. long.

nar·rate (nar′āt, na rāt′), *v.,* **-rat·ed, -rat·ing.** —*v.t.* **1.** to give an account or tell the story of (events, experiences, etc.). —*v.i.* **2.** to relate or recount events, experiences, etc., in speech or writing. [< L *narrāt(us)* made known, told (ptp. of *narrāre*), equiv. to *nār(us)* knowing, acquainted with (var. of *gnārus*) + *-ātus* -ATE¹] —**nar′rat·a·ble,** *adj.* —**nar′ra·tor, nar′rat·er,** *n.*
—**Syn. 1.** detail, recite. See **describe.**

nar·ra·tion (na rā′shən), *n.* **1.** that which is narrated; an account or story. **2.** the act or process of narrating. **3.** a recital of events, esp. in chronological order, as the story narrated in a poem or the exposition set forth in a drama. **4.** *Rhet.* (in classical speech) the third part, the exposition of the question. [late ME *narracion* < L *narrātiōn-* (s. of *narrātiō*), equiv. to *narrāt(us)* (see NARRATE) + *-iōn-* -ION] —**nar·ra′tion·al,** *adj.*

nar·ra·tive (nar′ə tiv), *n.* **1.** a story of events, experiences, or the like, whether true or fictitious. **2.** a book, literary work, etc., containing such a story. **3.** the art, technique, or process of narrating: *a master of narrative.* —*adj.* **4.** consisting of or being a narrative: *a narrative poem.* **5.** *Fine Arts.* representing stories or events pictorially or sculpturally: *narrative painting.* Cf. **anecdotal** (def. 2). **6.** of or pertaining to narration: *narrative skill.* [< L *narrātīv(us)* suitable for narration. See NARRATE, -IVE] —**nar′ra·tive·ly,** *adv.*
—**Syn. 1.** chronicle, tale. NARRATIVE, ACCOUNT, RECITAL, HISTORY are terms for a story of an event or events. NARRATIVE is the general term (for a story long or short; of past, present, or future; factual or imagined; told for any purpose; and with or without much detail). The other three terms apply primarily to factual stories of time already past. An ACCOUNT is usually told informally, often for entertainment, with emphasis on details of action, whether about an incident or a series of happenings. A RECITAL is an extended narrative usually with an informative purpose, emphasizing accuracy and exhaustive details of facts and figures. A HISTORY, usually written and at some length, is characterized by a tracing of causes and effects, and by an attempt to estimate, evaluate, and interpret facts.

nar·row (nar′ō), *adj.* **1.** of little breadth or width; not broad or wide: *a narrow path.* **2.** limited in extent or space; affording little room: *narrow quarters.* **3.** limited in range or scope: *a narrow sampling of public opinion.* **4.** lacking breadth of view or sympathy, as persons, the mind, ideas, etc.: *a narrow man, knowing only his professional specialty.* **5.** limited in amount; small; meager: *narrow resources.* **6.** straitened, as circumstances. **7.** with little to spare; barely adequate or successful: *a narrow escape.* **8.** careful or minute, as a scrutiny, search, or inquiry. **9.** *Brit. Dial.* stingy or thrifty; parsimonious. **10.** *Phonet.* **a.** (of a vowel) articulated with the tongue laterally constricted, as the *ee* of *beet,* the *oo* of *boot,* etc.; tense. Cf. **lax** (def. 7). **b.** (of a phonetic transcription) utilizing a unique symbol for each phoneme and whatever supplementary diacritics are needed to indicate its subphonemic varieties. Cf. **broad** (def. 13). **11.** (of livestock feeds) proportionately rich in protein. —*v.i.* **12.** to decrease in width; become narrower: *This is where the road narrows.* —*v.t.* **13.** to make narrower. **14.** to limit or restrict (often fol. by *down*): *to narrow an area of search; to narrow down a contest to three competitors.* **15.** to make narrow-minded: *Living in the provinces has narrowed him.* —*n.* **16.** a narrow part, place, or thing. **17.** a narrow part of a valley, passage, or road. **18.** **narrows,** (*construed as sing. or pl.*) a narrow part of a strait, river, ocean current, etc. **19.** **The Narrows,** a passage from upper to lower New York Bay, between Staten Island and Long Island. 2 mi. long; 1 mi. wide. [ME; OE *nearu;* c. OS *naru* narrow, D *naar* unpleasant; akin to G *Narbe* scar, lit., narrow mark] —**nar′row·ly,** *adv.* —**nar′row·ness,** *n.*

nar·row-fist·ed (nar′ō fis′tid), *adj.* tight-fisted.

nar′row gauge′. See under **gauge** (def. 13). —**nar′row-gauge′;** *esp. in technical use,* **nar′row-gage′,** *adj.* —**nar′row-gauged′;** *esp. in technical use,* **nar′row-gaged′,** *adj.*

nar·row-mind·ed (nar′ō mīn′did), *adj.* **1.** having or showing a prejudiced mind, as persons, opinions, etc. **2.** not receptive to new ideas. **3.** extremely conservative and morally self-righteous. —**nar′row-mind′ed·ly,** *adv.* —**nar′row-mind′ed·ness,** *n.*
—**Syn. 1.** biased, bigoted, partial. **2.** intolerant, illiberal. —**Ant. 2.** tolerant.

nar′row-mouthed toad′ (nar′ō mouthd′), any frog of the family *Microhylidae,* commonly found in the tropics and subtropics, having a narrow, pointed head.

Nar·rows (nar′ōz), *n.* **1.** a town in SW Virginia. 2508 (1960). **2.** **The Narrows,** narrow (def. 19).

nar·thex (när′theks), *n. Archit.* an enclosed passage between the main entrance and the nave of a church. [< LGk, Gk: giant fennel] —**nar·the·cal** (när thē′kəl), *adj.*

Nar·va (när′vä), *n.* a seaport in central Estonia, in the W Soviet Union in Europe: Swedish defeat of Russians 1700. 43,600 (1959).

Nar·vá·ez (när vä′eth, -vä′es), *n.* **Pán·fi·lo de** (päm′fē lô′ the), 1478?–1528, Spanish soldier and adventurer in America.

Nar·vik (när′vik), *n.* a seaport in N Norway. 11,141 (est. 1959).

nar·whal (när′wəl), *n.* an arctic cetacean, *Monodon monoceros,* the male of which has a long, spirally twisted tusk extending forward from the upper jaw. Also, **nar′wal, nar·whale** (när′hwāl′, -wāl′). [< Scand; cf. Norw, Sw, Dan *narhval,* equiv. to *nar-* (of disputed origin) + *hval* WHALE¹] —**nar·whal·i·an** (när wā′lē ən, -wol′ē), *adj.*

Narwhal
(Total length 23 ft.; tusk 9 ft.)

nar·y (nâr′ē), *adj. Dial.* not any; no; never a. [var. of *ne'er a* never a]

N.A.S., National Academy of Sciences. Also, **NAS**

NASA (nas′ə, nä′sə), *n. U.S.* the federal agency that institutes and administers the civilian programs of the government that deal with aeronautical research and the development of space vehicles. [*N(ational) A(eronautics and) S(pace) A(dministration)*]

na·sal¹ (nā′zəl), *adj.* **1.** of or pertaining to the nose: *the nasal cavity.* **2.** *Phonet.* pronounced with the voice issuing through the nose, either partly, as in French nasal vowels, or entirely (as in *m, n,* or the *ng* of *song*). —*n.* **3.** *Phonet.* a nasal speech sound. [< LL *nāsāl(is), equiv. to L *nās(us)* nose + *-ālis* -AL¹] —**na·sal·i·ty** (nā zal′i tē), **na′sal·ism,** *n.* —**na′sal·ly,** *adv.*

na·sal² (nā′zəl), *n. Armor.* a bar or narrow plate used with an open helmet as a defense for the nose. [late ME < ML *nāsāle,* n. use of neut. of LL *nāsālis NASAL¹; r. ME *nasel* < MF < LL *nāsāle]

na′sal con′cha, turbinate (def. 5).

na′sal gleet′, *Vet. Pathol.* gleet (def. 2).

na′sal in′dex, **1.** *Craniom.* (of the skull) the ratio of the distance from nasion to the lower margin of the nasal aperture to that of the maximum breadth of the nasal aperture. **2.** *Cephalom.* (of the head) the ratio of the maximum breadth of the external nose to its height from nasal root to where the septum is confluent with the upper lip.

na·sal·ise (nā′zə līz′), *v.t., v.i.,* **-ised, -is·ing.** *Chiefly Brit.* nasalize. —**na′sal·i·sa′tion,** *n.*

na·sal·ize (nā′zə līz′), *v.,* **-ized, -iz·ing.** *Phonet.* —*v.t.* **1.** to pronounce as a nasal sound. —*v.i.* **2.** to nasalize normally oral sounds. [NASAL¹ + -IZE] —**na′sal·i·za′tion,** *n.*

Nas·by (naz′bē), *n.* **Petroleum V.,** pen name of David Ross Locke.

Nas·ca (näs′kä), *adj.* Nazca.

nas·cent (nas′ənt, nā′sənt), *adj.* **1.** beginning to exist or develop: *the nascent republic.* **2.** *Chem.* (of an element) in the nascent state. [< L *nascent-* (s. of *nascēns,* prp. of *nascī*) being born, arising, equiv. to *nā(tus)* born (var. of *gnātus*) + *-sc-* inceptive suffix + *-ent-* -ENT] —**nas′cence, nas′cen·cy,** *n.*

nas′cent state′, *Chem.* the condition of an element at the instant it is set free from a combination in which it has previously existed. Also called **nas′cent condi′tion.**

NASD, National Association of Securities Dealers. Also, **N.A.S.D.**

nase·ber·ry (nāz′ber′ē, -bə rē), *n., pl.* **-ries.** **1.** the fruit of the sapodilla, *Achras Zapota.* **2.** the sapodilla tree. [< Sp or Pg *néspera* < L *mespila* MEDLAR]

Nase·by (nāz′bē), *n.* a village in W Northamptonshire, in central England: Royalist defeat 1645.

Nash (nash), *n.* **1.** **John,** 1752–1835, English architect and city planner. **2.** **Ogden,** 1902–71, U.S. writer of humorous verse. **3.** Also, **Nashe. Thomas,** ("*Pasquil*"), 1567–1601, English dramatist, novelist, and satirical pamphleteer.

Nash·u·a (nash′o͞o ə), *n.* a city in S New Hampshire, on the Merrimack River. 39,096 (1960).

Nash·ville (nash′vil), *n.* **1.** a city in and the capital of Tennessee, in the central part: battle 1864. 170,874 (1960). **2.** a town in S Georgia. 4070 (1960). **3.** a town in SW Arkansas. 3579 (1960). **4.** a town in SW Illinois. 2606 (1960).

Nash′ville war′bler, a North American wood warbler, *Vermivora ruficapilla,* having a gray head, an olive-green back, and yellow underparts.

Na·si (nä′sē), *n. Jewish Hist.* the head or president of the Sanhedrin. [< Heb: lofty one]

na·si·on (nā′zē on′), *n. Craniom.* the intersection of the internasal suture with the nasofrontal suture in the mid-sagittal plane. [< NL, equiv. to L *nās(us)* NASO- + Gk *-ion,* dim. suffix] —**na′si·al,** *adj.*

Nas·i·red·din (nas′ə red′ən), *n.* a crater in the third quadrant and extending into the fourth quadrant of the face of the moon: about 30 miles in diameter.

Nas·khi (nas′kē), *n.* the cursive variety of Arabic script from which was derived the variety used in modern printed works. [<Ar: copy]

Na·smyth (nā′smith), *n.* a crater in the third quadrant of the face of the moon: about 53 miles in diameter.

naso-, a learned borrowing from Latin meaning "nose," used in the formation of compound words: *nasofrontal.* [comb. form repr. L *nāsus* the nose; see -O-]

na·so·fron·tal (nā′zō frun′tᵊl), *adj.* of or pertaining to the nose and frontal bone. [NASO- + FRONTAL]

na·so·lac·ri·mal (nā′zō lak′rə məl), *adj. Anat.* of or pertaining to the lacrimal structures and the nose. Also, **na′so·lach′ry·mal.** [NASO- + LACRIMAL]

na′solac′rimal duct′, *Anat.* a membranous canal extending from the lacrimal sac to the nasal cavity, through which the tears are discharged into the nose. See diag. under **lacrimal gland.**

na·sol·o·gy (nā zol′ə jē), *n.* the scientific study of noses. [NASO- + -LOGY] —**na·so·log·i·cal** (nā′zə loj′i kəl), *adj.* —**na·sol′o·gist,** *n.*

na·so·pal·a·tine (nā′zō pal′ə tīn′, -tin), *adj. Anat.* of, pertaining to, or involving the nose and palate. Also, **na′so·pal′a·tal.** [NASO- + PALATINE²]

na·so·phar·ynx (nā′zō far′ingks), *n., pl.* **-pha·ryn·ges** (-fə rin′jēz), **-phar·ynx·es.** *Anat.* the part of the pharynx behind and above the soft palate, directly continuous with the nasal passages. Cf. **oropharynx** (def. 2). [NASO- + PHARYNX] —**na·so·pha·ryn·ge·al** (nā′zō fə rin′jē əl, -jəl, -far′ən jē′əl), *adj.*

na·so·scope (nā′zə skōp′), *n. Med.* a rhinoscope. [NASO- + -SCOPE]

Nas·sau (nas′ô; *for 2, 3, also Ger.* nä′sou), *n.* **1.** a seaport on New Providence island: capital of the Bahamas; seaside resort. 50,405 (est. 1958). **2.** a district in central West Germany: formerly a duchy, now a part of Hesse. **3.** a member of a European royal family which ruled chiefly in Germany and the Netherlands until the 19th century. **4.** *Golf.* an eighteen-hole match in which one point each is awarded to the players having the lowest score for the first nine holes, for the second nine holes, and for the entire round.

Nas′sau group′er, a food and game fish, *Epinephelus striatus,* common off the Florida Keys.

Nas′sau Moun′tains, a range in Netherlands New Guinea. Highest peak, Carstensz, 16,404 ft.

Nas·ser (nä′sər, nas′ər), *n.* **1.** **Ga·mal Ab·del** (gə mäl′ ab′del), 1918–70, Egyptian military and political leader: prime minister of Egypt 1954–56; president of Egypt 1956–58; president of the United Arab Republic 1958–1970. **2.** **Lake,** a reservoir in SE United Arab Republic, formed in the Nile River S of Aswan Dam. Projected size: ab. 310 mi. long; 6 mi. wide.

Nast (nast), *n.* **Thomas,** 1840–1902, U.S. cartoonist.

nas·tic (nas′tik), *adj. Plant Physiol.* of or showing sufficiently greater cellular force or growth on one side of an axis to change the form or position of the axis. [< Gk *nast(ós)* pressed close, stamped down, firm (*náss(ein)* (to) press, squeeze + *-tos* ptp. suffix) + -IC]

-nastic, a suffix forming adjectives of nouns with stems in **-nasty:** *hyponastic.* [see NASTIC]

na·stur·tium (na stûr′shəm, nə-), *n.* **1.** any plant of the genus *Tropaeolum,* cultivated for its showy flowers or for its fruit, which is pickled and used like capers. **2.** the flower. [< L *nāsturcium* a kind of cress, lit., something that wrings the nose (referring to its acrid smell). See NOSE, TORT]

nas·ty (nas′tē), *adj.,* **-ti·er, -ti·est.** **1.** physically filthy; disgustingly unclean: *a nasty pigsty of a room.* **2.** offensive to taste or smell; nauseous. **3.** offensive; objectionable: *a nasty habit; their three nasty children.* **4.** morally filthy; obscene: *a nasty joke that wasn't funny.* **5.** vicious, spiteful, or ugly: *a nasty dog; a nasty rumor.* **6.** bad to deal with, encounter, undergo, etc.; dangerous; serious: *a nasty cut; a nasty accident.* **7.** very unpleasant: *nasty weather.* [late ME] —**nas′ti·ly,** *adv.* —**nas′ti·ness,** *n.*
—**Syn. 1.** dirty, foul, loathsome. **2.** nauseating, sickening, repulsive, repellent. **4.** smutty, pornographic. **7.** stormy, inclement. —**Ant. 1.** clean, pure.

-nasty, a combining form indicating irregularity of cellular growth because of some pressure: *hyponasty.* [< Gk *nast(ós)* pressed close (see NASTIC) + -Y³]

na·sute (nā so͞ot′), *n. Entomol.* (of termites) a soldier, characterized by a beaklike snout through which a sticky secretion repellent to other insects is emitted. [< L *nāsūt(us)* big-nosed, equiv. to *nās(ō)-* (comb. form of *nāsus* nose) + *-tus* adj. suffix] —**na·sute′ness,** *n.*

nat (nät), *n.* a nature spirit worshipped in Burma. [< Burmese < Skt *nātha* protection]

Nat (nat), *n.* a boy's given name, form of **Nathan** or **Nathaniel.**

nat., **1.** national. **2.** native. **3.** natural. **4.** naturalist.

na·tal (nāt′ᵊl), *adj.* **1.** of or pertaining to one's birth: *celebrating one's natal day.* **2.** presiding over or affecting one at birth: *natal influences.* **3.** (of places) native: *nostalgia for one's natal town.* [< L *nātāl(is)* of, belonging to one's birth, natal, equiv. to *nāt(us)* born (var. of *gnātus,* ptp. of *nascī*) + *-ālis* -AL¹]

Na·tal (nə tal′, -täl′ *for 1;* nə täl′, -tôl′ *for 2*), *n.* **1.** a province in the E part of the Republic of South Africa. 2,933,447 (1960); 35,284 sq. mi. *Cap.:* Pietermaritzburg. **2.** a seaport in E Brazil. 155,860 (1960). —**Na·tal′i·an,** *adj., n.*

Nat·a·lie (nat′əlē; *Fr.* NA TA LĒ′), *n.* a girl's given name. Also, **Na·tal·ia** (nə tāl′yə, -täl′-), **Nathalie.**

na·tal·i·ty (nā tal′i tē), *n.* See **birth rate.** [NATAL + -ITY]

Natal′ or′ange, a spiny shrub, *Strychnos spinosa*, of central and South Africa, having yellowish-white flowers and edible, berrylike, yellow fruit.

Natal′ plum′, a bushy shrub, *Carissa grandiflora*, of South Africa, having forked spines, white flowers, and egg-shaped, red berries. Also called **amatungula.**

na·tant (nāt′ᵊnt), *adj.* **1.** swimming; floating. **2.** *Bot.* floating on water, as the leaf of an aquatic plant. [< L *natant-* (s. of *natāns*), prp. of *natāre;* see -ANT] **—na′tant·ly,** *adv.*

Na·ta·sha (nə tä′shə), *n.* a girl's given name, Russian form of **Natalie.** Also, **Na·ta′scha.**

na·ta·tion (nā tā′shən, na-), *n.* an act or the art of swimming. [< L *natātiōn-* (s. of *natātiō*), equiv. to *natāt(us)* swum (ptp. of *natāre*) + *-iōn-* -ION] **—na·ta′tion·al,** *adj.*

na·ta·tor (nā′tə tər), *n.* a swimmer. [< L, equiv. to *natāt(us)* (ptp. of *natāre* to swim) + *-or* -OR²]

na·ta·to·ri·al (nā′tə tôr′ē əl, -tōr′-, nat′ə-), *adj.* pertaining to, adapted for, or characterized by swimming: *natatorial birds.* Also, **na′ta·to′ry.** [NATAT(ION) + -ORIAL]

na·ta·to·ri·um (nā′tə tôr′ē əm, -tōr′-, nat′ə-), *n., pl.* **-to·ri·ums, -to·ri·a** (-tôr′ē ə, -tōr′-). a swimming pool, esp. one that is indoors. [< LL: swimming-place, equiv. to L *natāt(us)* (ptp. of *natāre* to swim) + *-ōrium* -ORIUM]

natch (nach), *adv. Slang.* of course; naturally: *He talked about himself, natch.* [by shortening]

Natch·ez (nach′iz), *n., pl.* **-ez** for 2. **1.** a port in SW Mississippi, on the Mississippi River. 23,791 (1960). **2.** a member of an extinct Muskhogean Indian tribe once living on the lower Mississippi River.

na·tes (nā′tēz), *n.pl.* buttocks; rump. [< L *natēs* the rump, buttocks, pl. of *natis;* generally used in the pl.; akin to Gk *nōton* the back]

Nath·a·lie (nat′ᵊlē; *Fr.* NA TA lē′), *n.* a girl's given name. Also, **Natalia, Natalie.**

Na·than (nā′thən), *n.* **1.** a prophet during the reigns of David and Solomon. II Sam. 12; I Kings 1:34. **2. George Jean,** 1882–1958, U.S. drama critic, author, and editor. **3. Robert,** born 1894, U.S. novelist and poet. **4.** a boy's given name.

Na·than·a·el (nə than′ē əl, -than′yəl), *n.* a disciple of Jesus. John 1:45–51.

Na·than·iel (nə than′yəl), *n.* a boy's given name.

nathe·less (nāth′lis, nath′-), *Archaic.* —*adv.* **1.** nevertheless. —*prep.* **2.** notwithstanding. Also, **nath·less** (nath′lis). [ME; OE *nāthēlǣs,* var. of *nāthȳlǣs,* equiv. to *nā* never + *thȳ* for that + *lǣs* less]

Na·tick (nā′tik), *n.* a town in E Massachusetts, W of Boston. 28,831 (1960).

na·tion (nā′shən), *n.* **1.** a body of people, associated with a particular territory, that is sufficiently conscious of its unity to seek or to possess a government peculiarly its own. **2.** the territory or country itself. **3.** a member tribe of an Indian confederation. **4.** an aggregation of persons of the same ethnic family, often speaking the same language or cognate languages. [ME < L *nātiōn-* (s. of *nātiō*) birth, tribe, equiv. to *nāt(us)* born (ptp. of *nāscī*) + *-iōn-* -ION] **—na′tion·hood′,** *n.* **—na′tion·less,** *adj.*
—Syn. 2. state, commonwealth, kingdom, realm. See **race².**

Na·tion (nā′shən), *n.* **Carry** or **Carrie (Amelia Moore),** 1846–1911, U.S. temperance leader.

na·tion·al (nash′ə nᵊl), *adj.* **1.** of, pertaining to, or maintained by a nation as an organized whole or independent political unit: *national affairs.* **2.** peculiar or common to the whole people of a country: *national customs.* **3.** devoted to one's own nation, its interests, etc.; patriotic: *to stir up national pride.* **4.** nationalist. **5.** concerning or encompassing an entire nation: *a national radio network.* **6.** limited to one nation. —*n.* **7.** a citizen or subject of a particular nation who is entitled to its protection: *U.S. nationals living abroad.* [NATION + -AL¹] **—na′tion·al·ly,** *adv.*

Na′tional Aeronau′tics and Space′ Adminis·tra′tion. See **NASA.**

na′tional bank′, **1.** *U.S.* a bank chartered by the national government and formerly authorized to issue notes that served as money. **2.** a bank owned and administered by the government, as in some European countries.

Na′tional Bu′reau of Stand′ards, *U.S.* the federal agency that establishes the standards for units used in measuring the physical properties of substances.

na′tional cem′etery, *U.S.* a cemetery, maintained by the federal government, for persons who have served honorably in the armed forces.

Na′tional Char′ter. See under **Chartism.**

na′tional church′, an independent church within a country, usually representing the prevalent religion. Cf. **established church.**

Na′tional Cit′y, a city in SW California, near San Diego. 32,771 (1960).

Na′tional Conven′tion, **1.** *Fr. Hist.* the legislature of France 1792–95. **2.** *U.S.* a convention held every four years by each of the major political parties to nominate a presidential candidate.

Na′tional Cov′enant, an agreement (1638) among Scottish Presbyterians to uphold their faith in Scotland. Cf. **Solemn League and Covenant.**

na′tional debt′, the financial debt of a national government resulting from deficit spending. Also called **public debt.**

na′tional for′est, *U.S.* a forest maintained and preserved by the federal government.

Na′tional Guard′, *U.S.* State military forces, in part equipped, trained, and quartered by the U.S. government, and paid by the U.S. government, that become an active component of the army when called or ordered into federal service by the President under the authority of the Constitution and implementing laws. Cf. **militia** (def. 2).

Na′tional Guard′ of the Unit′ed States′, one of the reserve components of the Army or Air Force, all members of which belong to the National Guard of the several States.

na′tional hol′iday, **1.** a holiday that is observed throughout a nation. **2.** a holiday that is legally established by a national government rather than by a municipal or state government.

na′tional in′come, the total net earnings from the production of goods and services in a country over a period of time, usually one year, and consisting essentially of wages, salaries, rent, profits, and interest. Cf. **gross national product, net national product.**

Na′tional Indus′trial Recov′ery Act′, an act of Congress (1933, declared unconstitutional in 1936) which enabled the President and the National Recovery Administration to formulate and execute measures for reducing industrial unemployment.

na·tion·al·ise (nash′ə nᵊlīz′), *v.t., v.i.,* **-ised, -is·ing.** *Chiefly Brit.* nationalize. **—na′tion·al·i·sa′tion,** *n.* **—na′tion·al·is′er,** *n.*

na·tion·al·ism (nash′ə nᵊliz′əm), *n.* **1.** national spirit or aspirations. **2.** devotion to the interests of one's own nation. **3.** desire for national advancement or independence. **4.** the policy of asserting the interests of one's own nation, viewed as separate from the interests of other nations or the common interests of all nations. **5.** an idiom or trait peculiar to a nation. [NATIONAL + -ISM]

na·tion·al·ist (nash′ə nᵊlist), *n.* **1.** a person devoted to nationalism. **2.** an advocate of national independence. **3.** (*cap.*) a member of a political group advocating or fighting for national independence, a strong national government, etc. —*adj.* **4.** Also, **na′tion·al·is′tic.** of, pertaining to, or promoting nationalism: *the beginnings of a nationalist movement.* **5.** (*cap.*) of, pertaining to, or noting a group advocating or fighting for national independence, a strong national government, etc. [NATIONAL + -IST] **—na′tion·al·is′ti·cal·ly,** *adv.*

Na′tionalist Chi′na. See **China, Republic of.**

na·tion·al·i·ty (nash′ə nal′i tē), *n., pl.* **-ties** for 1, 2, 5, 6. **1.** the quality of membership in a particular nation, whether original or acquired: *the nationality of an immigrant.* **2.** relationship of property, holdings, etc., to a particular nation, or to one or more of its members: *the nationality of a ship.* **3.** nationalism. **4.** existence as a distinct nation; national independence: *a small protectorate that achieved nationality.* **5.** a nation or people: *the nationalities of the Americas.* **6.** a national quality or character: *Nationalities tend to submerge and disappear in a metropolis.* [NATIONAL + -ITY]

na·tion·al·ize (nash′ə nᵊlīz′), *v.,* **-ized, -iz·ing.** —*v.t.* **1.** to bring under the control or ownership of a nation, as industries, land, etc.: *a movement to nationalize the oil industry.* **2.** to make national in extent or scope: *a magazine article that nationalized a local problem.* **3.** to naturalize. **4.** to make into a nation. —*v.i.* **5.** to become nationalized or naturalized: *Those who remain in the country must nationalize.* Also, *esp. Brit.,* **nationalise.** [NATIONAL + -IZE] **—na′tion·al·i·za′tion,** *n.* **—na′tion·al·iz′er,** *n.*

Na′tional La′bor Rela′tions Act′, an act of Congress (1935) which forbade any interference by employers with the formation and operation of labor unions. Cf. **Taft-Hartley Act.**

Na′tional La′bor Rela′tions Board′, *U.S. Govt.* a board, consisting of five members, originally set up under the National Labor Relations Act but continued under the Labor-Management Relations Act. *Abbr.:* NLRB

Na′tional Libera′tion Front′, a political organization formed by the Vietcong in South Vietnam in 1960 to carry out an insurgent policy. Also called **Na′tional Libera′tion Front′ of South′ Vietnam′.**

na′tional mon′ument, a monument, as a historic site, geographical area, etc., maintained in the public interest by the federal government.

na′tional park′, an area of scenic beauty, historical importance, or the like, maintained by a national government for the use of the people.

Na′tional Park′, a town in SW New Jersey. 3380 (1960).

Na′tional Progres′sive par′ty. See **Progressive party** (def. 1).

Na′tional Recov′ery Administra′tion. See **NRA.**

Na′tional Secur′ity Coun′cil, *U.S. Govt.* the council, composed of the President, Vice-President, Secretaries of State and Defense, and the director of the Office of Civil and Defense Mobilization, that determines means by which domestic, foreign, and military policy can best be integrated for safeguarding the national security. *Abbr.:* NSC

Na′tional So′cialism, the principles and practices of the Nazi party in Germany. **—Na′tional So′cialist.**

Na′tional War′ La′bor Board′, *U.S. Govt.* the board (1942–45) that mediated and arbitrated labor disputes. *Abbr.:* NWLB, WLB Also, **War Labor Board.**

na·tion·hood (nā′shən ho͝od′), *n.* the state or quality of having status as a separate and independent nation: *an African protectorate that achieved nationhood.* [NATION + -HOOD]

na·tion·wide (nā′shən wīd′), *adj.* extending throughout the nation: *The incident aroused nationwide interest.* [NATION + WIDE]

na·tive (nā′tiv), *adj.* **1.** being the place or environment in which a person was born or a thing came into being: *one's native land.* **2.** belonging to a person by birth or to a thing by nature; inherent: *native ability; native grace.* **3.** belonging by birth to a people regarded as natives, esp. outside of the general body of white peoples: *Native guides accompanied the expedition.* **4.** of indigenous origin, growth, or production: *native pottery.* **5.** of, pertaining to, or characteristic of natives: *native customs in Java.* **6.** under the rule of natives: *a native government.* **7.** occupied by natives: *the native quarter of Algiers.* **8.** belonging or pertaining to a person by reason of his birthplace or nationality: *one's native language.* **9.** born in a particular place or country: *native American citizens.* **10.** remaining or growing in a natural state; unadorned or unchanged: *the native beauty of a desert island.* **11.** forming the source or origin of a person or thing: *He returned to his native Kansas.* **12.** originating naturally in a particular country or region, as animals or plants. **13.** found in nature rather than produced artificially, as a mineral substance: *the difference between native and industrial diamonds.* **14.** occurring in nature pure or uncombined, as metals, minerals, etc.: *native copper.* **15.** *Archaic.* belonging to a person as a birthright: *to deprive a person of his native rights.* **16.** *Archaic.* closely related, as by birth. **17. go native,** *Informal.* to affect the manners or imitate the way of life of a country other than one's own, esp. a less civilized country: *The tourists decided to go native and sample the local cuisine.* —*n.* **18.** one of the original inhabitants of a place or country, esp. as distinguished from strangers, foreigners, colonizers, etc.: *the natives of Chile.* **19.** a person born in a particular place or country: *a native of Ohio.* **20.** an animal or plant indigenous to a particular region. **21.** *Brit.* an oyster reared in British waters, esp. in an artificial bed. **22.** *Astrol.* a person born under a particular planet. [< L *nātīv(us)* inborn, natural, equiv. to *nāt(us)* born (ptp. of *nāscī*) + *-īvus* -IVE; r. ME *natif* < MF] **—na′tive·ly,** *adv.* **—na′tive·ness,** *n.*
—Syn. 2. inherited, innate, inbred, congenital. **4.** autochthonous, aboriginal. **10.** real, genuine, original. **18.** aborigine. **—Ant. 2.** acquired. **4.** imported. **10.** decorated. **18.** alien.

na·tive-born (nā′tiv bôrn′), *adj.* born in the place or country indicated: *a native-born Australian.*

na′tive cat′, *Australia.* a dasyure of the genus *Dasyurus,* of Australia and Tasmania.

Na′tive Son′, a novel (1940) by Richard Wright.

Na′tive States′. See **Indian States and Agencies.**

na·tiv·ism (nā′ti viz′əm), *n.* **1.** the policy of protecting the interests of native inhabitants against those of immigrants. **2.** *Philos.* the doctrine that innate ideas exist. [NATIVE + -ISM] **—na′tiv·ist,** *n.* **—na′tiv·is′tic,** *adj.*

na·tiv·i·ty (nə tiv′i tē, nā-), *n., pl.* **-ties.** **1.** birth. **2.** birth with reference to place or attendant circumstances: *of Irish nativity.* **3.** (*cap.*) the birth of Christ. **4.** (*cap.*) the church festival commemorating the birth of Christ; Christmas. **5.** (*cap.*) a representation of the birth of Christ, as in art. **6.** *Astrol.* a horoscope of a person's birth. [ME *nativite(th)* < OF *nativite(d)* < ML *nātīvitāt-* (s. of *nātīvitās*). See NATIVE, -ITY]

natl., national.

NATO (nā′tō), *n.* an organization formed in Washington, D.C. (1949), comprising the 12 nations of the Atlantic Pact together with Greece, Turkey, and the Federal Republic of Germany, for the purpose of collective defense against aggression. [*N(orth) A(tlantic) T(reaty) O(rganization)*]

na·tri·um (nā′trē əm), *n. Obs.* sodium. [< G; see NATRON, -IUM]

nat·ro·lite (na′trə līt′, nā′-), *n.* a zeolite mineral, a hydrous silicate of sodium and aluminum, $Na_2Al_2Si_3O_{10}\cdot 2H_2O$, occurring usually in white or colorless, often acicular crystals. [NATRO(N) + -LITE]

na·tron (nā′tron), *n.* a mineral, hydrated sodium carbonate, $Na_2CO_3\cdot 10H_2O$. [< F < Sp < Ar *naṭrūn,* var. of *niṭrūn* < Gk *nítron* NITER]

Nat·ta (nät′tä), *n.* **Giu·lio** (jo͞o′lyô), born 1903, Italian chemist and engineer: Nobel prize for chemistry 1963.

nat·ter (nat′ər), *v.i.* **1.** *Brit.* to complain; grumble. **2.** *Australian.* to chatter. —*n.* **3.** *Brit.* a chat. **4.** *Canadian.* gossip. [var. of earlier *gnatter* < ?]

nat·ter·jack (nat′ər jak′), *n.* a toad, *Bufo calamita,* of Europe. [?]

nat·ty (nat′ē), *adj.,* **-ti·er, -ti·est.** neatly smart in dress or appearance; spruce; trim: *a natty white uniform.* [? var. of NEAT¹ + -Y¹] **—nat′ti·ly,** *adv.* **—nat′ti·ness,** *n.*

nat·u·ral (nach′ər əl, nach′rəl), *adj.* **1.** existing in or formed by nature (opposed to *artificial*): *a natural bridge.* **2.** based on the state of things in nature; constituted by nature: *Growth is a natural process.* **3.** of or pertaining to nature or the universe: *a natural science.* **4.** of, pertaining to, or occupied with the study of natural science: *conducting natural experiments.* **5.** in a state of nature; uncultivated, as land. **6.** growing spontaneously, without being planted or tended by man, as vegetation. **7.** having a real or physical existence, as opposed to one that is spiritual, intellectual, fictitious, etc. **8.** of, pertaining to, or proper to the nature or essential constitution: *natural ability.* **9.** proper to the circumstances of the case: *a natural result.* **10.** free from affectation or constraint: *a natural manner.* **11.** arising easily or spontaneously: *a natural courtesy to strangers.* **12.** consonant with the nature or character of. **13.** in accordance with the nature of things: *It was natural that he should hit back.* **14.** based upon the innate moral feeling of mankind: *natural justice.* **15.** in conformity with the ordinary course of nature; not unusual or exceptional. **16.** happening in the ordinary course of things, without the intervention of accident, violence, etc. **17.** related only by birth; of no legal relationship; illegitimate: *a natural son.* **18.** based on what is learned from nature, rather than on revelation: *natural religion.* **19.** true to or closely imitating nature: *a natural representation.* **20.** unenlightened or unregenerate: *the natural man.* **21.** being such by nature; born such: *a natural fool.* **22.** *Music.* **a.** neither sharp nor flat; without sharps or flats. **b.** changed in pitch by the sign ♮. **23.** (of a horn or trumpet) having neither side holes nor valves. **24.** *Cards.* **a.** being a card other than a wild card or joker. **b.** (of a set or sequence of cards) containing no wild cards. **25.** *Rare.* having or showing feelings, as affection, gratitude, kindness, etc., considered part of man's basic nature. —*n.* **26.** *Informal.* any person or thing that is or is likely or certain to be extremely suitable to and successful in an endeavor without training or difficulty. **27.** *Music.* **a.** a white key on a piano, organ, or the like. **b.** the sign ♮, placed before a note, canceling the effect of a previous sharp or flat. **c.** a note affected by a ♮, or a tone thus represented. **28.** an idiot. **29.** *Cards.* blackjack (def. 7b). **30.** (in craps) a winning combination of seven or eleven made on the first cast. [ME < L *nātūrāl(is)* (see NATURE, -AL¹); r. ME *naturel* < MF] **—nat′u·ral·ly,** *adv.* **—nat′u·ral·ness,** *n.*

nat′ural aids′, *Manège.* aid (def. 6a).

Nat′ural Bridge′, a natural limestone bridge in western Virginia. 215 ft. high; 90 ft. span.

Nat′ural Bridg′es, a national monument in SE Utah containing three natural bridges. Largest, 222 ft. high; 261 ft. span.

nat′ural child′, *Law.* **1.** an illegitimate child; one born of illicit intercourse. **2.** (in Louisiana) an illegitimate child who has been lawfully acknowledged by its father.

nat′ural child′birth, childbirth, involving little or no use of drugs, for which the mother has been psychologically prepared by an explanation of pertinent facts concerning the birth process and sometimes by special exercises. Cf. **psychoprophylaxis.**

nat′ural death′, death that occurs from natural causes, as disease or old age, rather than from violence or an accident.

nat′ural gas′, *Chem.* combustible gas formed naturally in the earth, as in regions yielding petroleum, consisting usually of over 80 percent of methane together with minor amounts of ethane, propane, butane, nitrogen, and, sometimes, helium: used as a fuel and to make carbon black and acetylene. Cf. **synthesis gas.**

nat′ural gen′der, *Gram.* gender based on the sex (or, for neuter, the lack of sex) of the referent of a noun, as English *girl* (feminine) is referred to by the feminine pronoun *she, boy* (masculine) by the masculine pronoun *he,* and *table* (neuter) by the neuter pronoun *it.* Cf. **grammatical gender.**

nat′ural his′tory, **1.** the sciences, as botany, zoology, etc., dealing with the study of all objects in nature: used esp. in reference to the beginnings of these sciences in former times. **2.** the study of these sciences, esp. of a nontechnical nature. —**nat′ural histo′rian.**

nat·u·ral·ise (nach′ər ə līz′, nach′rə-), *v.t., v.i.,* **-ised, -is·ing.** *Chiefly Brit.* naturalize. —**nat′u·ral·i·sa′tion,** *n.* —**nat′u·ral·is′er,** *n.*

nat·u·ral·ism (nach′ər ə liz′əm, nach′rə-), *n.* **1.** *Literature.* **a.** a manner or technique of treating subject matter that presents, through volume of detail, a deterministic view of man's life and actions. **b.** a deterministic theory of writing in which it is held that a writer should adopt an objective view toward his material, be free of preconceived ideas as to form and content, and represent with clinical accuracy and frankness the details of life. Cf. **realism** (def. 4b). **c.** a representation of natural appearances or natural patterns of speech, manner, etc., in a work of fiction. **d.** the depiction of the physical environment, esp. landscape or the rural environment. **2.** (in a work of art) treatment of forms, colors, space, etc., as they appear or might appear in nature. Cf. **idealism** (def. 4), **realism** (def. 3a). **3.** action arising from or based on natural instincts and desires alone. **4.** *Philos.* **a.** the view of the world which takes account only of natural elements and forces, excluding the supernatural or spiritual. **b.** the belief that all phenomena are covered by laws of science and that all teleological explanations are therefore without value. **5.** *Theol.* **a.** the doctrine that all religious truth is derived from a study of natural processes and not from revelation. **b.** the doctrine that natural religion is sufficient for salvation. **6.** adherence or attachment to what is natural. [NATURAL + -ISM]

nat·u·ral·ist (nach′ər ə list, nach′rə-), *n.* **1.** a person who is versed in or devoted to natural history, esp. a zoologist or botanist. **2.** an adherent of naturalism in literature or art. [NATURAL + -IST]

nat·u·ral·is·tic (nach′ər ə lis′tik, nach′rə-), *adj.* **1.** imitating nature or the usual natural surroundings. **2.** pertaining to naturalists or natural history. **3.** pertaining to naturalism, esp. in literature and art. [NATURAL + -ISTIC] —**nat′u·ral·is′ti·cal·ly,** *adv.*

nat′uralis′tic fal′lacy, *Ethics.* the alleged fallacy of deriving ethical principles from nonethical premises or defining ethical concepts in nonethical terms.

nat·u·ral·ize (nach′ər ə līz′, nach′rə-), *v.,* **-ized, -iz·ing.** —*v.t.* **1.** to invest (an alien) with the rights and privileges of a citizen; confer the rights and privileges of citizenship upon. **2.** to introduce (animals or plants) into a region and cause them to flourish as if native. **3.** to introduce or adopt (foreign practices, words, etc.) into a country or into general use: *to naturalize a French phrase.* **4.** to bring into conformity with nature. **5.** to regard or explain as natural rather than supernatural: *to naturalize miracles.* **6.** to adapt or accustom to a place or to new surroundings. —*v.i.* **7.** to become naturalized. **8.** to adapt as if native to a new environment, set of circumstances, etc. **9.** to study or carry on research in natural history. Also, *esp. Brit.,* **naturalise.** [NATURAL + -IZE] —**nat′u·ral·i·za′tion,** *n.* —**nat′u·ral·iz′er,** *n.*

nat′ural lan′guage, a language used as a native tongue by a group of speakers.

nat′ural law′, a principle or body of laws considered as derived from nature, right reason, or religion and as ethically binding in human society.

na′tural lev′ee, a deposit of sand or mud built up along, and sloping away from, either side of the flood plain of a river or stream. Also called **levee.**

nat′ural log′arithm, *Math.* a logarithm having *e* as a base. *Symbol: ln* Also called **Napierian logarithm.** Cf. **common logarithm.**

nat′ural num′ber, a positive integer.

nat′ural per′son, *Law.* See under **person** (def. 11).

nat′ural philos′ophy, **1.** See **natural science.** **2.** See **physical science.** —**nat′ural philos′opher.**

nat′ural re′alism. See **naïve realism.** —**nat′ural re′alist.**

nat′ural reli′gion, religion based on principles derived solely from reason and the study of nature. Cf. **revealed religion.**

nat′ural re′sources, the natural wealth of a country, consisting of land, forests, mineral deposits, water, etc.

nat′ural right′, any right that exists by virtue of natural law.

nat′ural rub′ber, rubber[1] (def. 1).

nat′ural sci′ence, a science or knowledge of objects or processes observable in nature, as biology, physics, etc., as distinguished from the abstract or theoretical sciences, as mathematics, philosophy, etc.

nat′ural selec′tion, a process in nature resulting in the survival and perpetuation of only those forms of plant and animal life having certain favorable characteristics that best enable them to adapt to a specific environment. Cf. **Darwinism.**

nat′ural theol′ogy, theology based on knowledge of the natural world and on human reason, apart from revelation. Cf. **revealed theology.** —**nat′ural theolo′gian.**

nat′ural var′nish. See under **varnish** (def. 2).

nat′ural vir′tue, (esp. among the scholastics) any moral virtue of which man is capable, esp. the cardinal virtues: justice, temperance, prudence, and fortitude. Cf. **theological virtue.**

na·tu·ra non fa·cit sal·tum (nä to͞o′rä nōn fä′kit säl′to͝om; *Eng.* nə to͝or′ə non fā′sit sal′təm, -tyo͝or′-), *Latin.* nature makes no leap.

na·ture (nā′chər), *n.* **1.** the particular combination of qualities belonging to a person, animal, thing, or class by birth, origin, or constitution; native or inherent character: *the nature of man.* **2.** the instincts or inherent tendencies directing conduct: *a man of good nature.* **3.** character, kind, or sort: *a book of the same nature.* **4.** the characteristic disposition of a person: *a self-willed nature; an evil nature.* **5.** the material world, esp. as surrounding man and existing independently of his activities. **6.** the universe, with all its phenomena. **7.** the natural world as it exists without man or his civilization. **8.** the elements of the natural world, as mountains, trees, animals, rivers, etc. **9.** natural scenery. **10.** the sum total of the forces at work throughout the universe. **11.** reality, as distinguished from any effect of art: *true to nature.* **12.** the physical being. **13.** the original, natural, uncivilized condition of man. **14.** the vital powers: *food sufficient to sustain nature.* **15.** a primitive, wild condition; an uncultivated state. **16.** a simple, uncluttered mode of life without the conveniences or distractions of civilization. **17.** (*cap., italics.*) a prose work (1836), by Ralph Waldo Emerson, expounding transcendentalism. **18.** *Theol.* the moral state as unaffected by grace. **19. by nature,** as a result of inherent qualities; innately: *She is by nature a kind-hearted person.* **20. in a state of nature,** in a nude condition; naked. **21. of** or **in the nature of,** having the character or qualities of: *in the nature of an apology.* [ME *natur(e)* < L *nātūra* blood-kinship, quality, character, natural order, world, equiv. to *nāt(us)* born (ptp. of *nāscī*) + *-ūra* -URE] —**na′ture-like′,** *adj.*

-natured, a combining form of **nature** used in compound adjectives to indicate a specified character, temperament, etc.: *good-natured.* [NATURE + -ED[3]]

na′ture philos′ophy, the philosophy of Haeckel and other 19th-century German thinkers who attempted a philosophical synthesis of the general laws and characteristics of nature. —**na′ture philos′opher.**

na′ture stud′y, the study of the physical world, esp. as a combination of basic botany, zoology, etc., as taught at the primary school level.

na′ture wor′ship, a system of religion based on the deification and worship of natural forces and phenomena. —**na′ture wor′shiper.**

na·tur·o·path (nā′chər ə path′, nach′ər-), *n.* a person who practices naturopathy. [NATURE + -O- + -PATH]

na·tur·op·a·thy (nā′chə rop′ə thē, nach′ə-), *n.* a method of treating disease, using food, exercise, heat, etc., that assists the natural healing processes. [NATURE + -O- + -PATHY] —**na·tur·o·path·ic** (nā′chər ə-path′ik, nach′ər-), *adj.*

Nau·cra·tis (nô′krə tis), *n.* an ancient Greek city in N Egypt, on the Nile delta. Greek, **Nau′kra·tis.**

Naug·a·tuck (nô′gə tuk′), *n.* a city in central Connecticut. 19,511 (1960).

naught (nôt), *n.* **1.** a cipher (0); zero. **2.** nothing. **3.** destruction, ruin, or complete failure: *Her efforts came to naught.* **4. set at naught,** to regard or treat as of no importance; disdain: *He entered a milieu that set his ideals at naught.* —*adj.* **5.** lost; ruined. **6.** *Archaic.* worthless; useless. **7.** *Obs.* morally bad; wicked. —*adv.* **8.** *Obs.* not. Also, **nought.** [ME; OE *nauht, nāwiht* (*nā* NO[1] + *wiht* thing). See NOUGHT, WIGHT[1], WHIT]

naugh·ty (nô′tē), *adj.,* **-ti·er, -ti·est.** **1.** disobedient; mischievous (used esp. in speaking to or about children): *Weren't we naughty not to eat our spinach?* **2.** improper; obscene: *a naughty word.* **3.** *Obs.* wicked; evil. [ME; see NAUGHT, -Y[1]] —**naugh′ti·ly,** *adv.* —**naugh′ti·ness,** *n.*

nau·ma·chi·a (nô mā′kē ə), *n., pl.* **-chi·ae** (-kē ē′), **-chi·as.** **1.** a mock sea fight, given as a spectacle among the ancient Romans. **2.** a place for presenting such spectacles. [< L: mock naval battle < Gk *naumachía* a sea fight, equiv. to *naû(s)* a ship + *mách(ē)* a battle, fight + *-ia* -IA]

nau·ma·chy (nô′mə kē), *n., pl.* **-chies.** naumachia.

Nau·mann (nou′mən), *n.* a crater in the second quadrant of the face of the moon: about 6 miles in diameter.

nau·mann·ite (nô′mə nīt′, nou′-), *n.* a mineral, silver-lead selenide, $(Ag_2Pb)Se$, usually occurring in iron-black cubic crystals. [named after Karl F. *Naumann,* (1797–1873), German mineralogist; see -ITE[1]]

nau·path·i·a (nô path′ē ə), *n.* *Pathol.* seasickness. Cf. **motion sickness.** [< NL < Gk, equiv. to *naû(s)* a ship + *-patheia* -PATHY]

nau·pli·us (nô′plē əs), *n., pl.* **-pli·i** (-plē ī′). (in many crustaceans) a larval form with three pairs of appendages and a single median eye, occurring usually as the first stage of development after leaving the egg. [< L: a kind of shellfish, special use of proper name NAUPLIUS] —**nau′pli·al, nau′pli·form′, nau′pli·oid′,** *adj.*

Nau·pli·us (nô′plē əs), *n.* *Class. Myth.* **1.** a son of Poseidon and a Danaid, credited with discovering a way of navigating by the Great Bear constellation. **2.** a king of Nauplia who was also one of the Argonauts.

Na·u·ru (nä o͞o′ro͞o), *n.* **Republic of,** an island republic in the Pacific, near the equator, W of the Gilbert Islands: administered by Australia before 1968. 4613 (1961); 8¼ sq. mi. Formerly, **Pleasant Island.** —**Na·u′ru·an,** *n.*

nau·se·a (nô′zē ə, -zhə, -sē ə, -shə), *n.* **1.** sickness at the stomach, esp. when accompanied by a loathing for food and an involuntary impulse to vomit. **2.** extreme disgust; loathing; repugnance. **3.** (*cap., italics.*) a novel (1938) by Jean-Paul Sartre. French, **La Nausée.** [< L, var. of *nausia* < Gk: seasickness, deriv. of *naûs* ship; see -IA]

nau·se·ant (nô′zē ənt, -zhē-, -sē-, -shē-), *Med.* —*adj.* **1.** producing nausea. —*n.* **2.** a nauseant agent. [< L *nauseant-* (s. of *nauseāns*) being seasick, prp. of *nauseāre.* See NAUSEA, -ANT]

nau·se·ate (nô′zē āt′, -zhē-, -sē-, -shē-), *v.,* **-at·ed, -at·ing.** —*v.t.* **1.** to affect with nausea; sicken. **2.** to cause to feel extreme disgust: *His behavior nauseates me.* —*v.i.* **3.** to become affected with nausea. [< L *nauseāt(us)* having been seasick (ptp. of *nauseāre*). See NAUSEA, -ATE[1]] —**nau′se·a′tion,** *n.*
—**Syn. 2.** revolt. —**Ant. 2.** attract, delight.

nau·se·at·ing (nô′zē ā′ting, -zhē-, -sē-, -shē-), *adj.* **1.** such as to cause contempt, disgust, loathing, etc.: *I had to listen to the whole nauseating story.* **2.** causing extreme physical revulsion or loathing; sickening. [NAUSEATE + -ING[2]] —**nau′se·at′ing·ly,** *adv.*

Nau·sée, La (*Fr.* lȧ nō zā′), nausea (def. 3).

nau·seous (nô′shəs, -zē əs), *adj.* **1.** causing nausea; sickening. **2.** *Informal.* ill or affected with nausea: *to feel nauseous.* **3.** disgusting; loathsome: *a nauseous sight; a nauseous display of exhibitionism.* [< L *nauseōsus.* See NAUSEA, -OUS] —**nau′seous·ly,** *adv.* —**nau′seous·ness,** *n.*
—**Syn. 3.** revolting, nasty, repellent, abhorrent, detestable, despicable, offensive. —**Ant. 3.** delightful.
—**Usage. 2.** Although it is often used in this sense, NAUSEOUS is frowned upon by teachers and editors as a substitute for NAUSEATED.

Nau·sic·a·ä (nô sik′ē ə, -ā ə, nou-), *n.* *Class. Myth.* a Phaeacian princess who discovered the shipwrecked Odysseus and directed him to the palace of her father, Alcinoüs.

Nau·sith·o·us (nô sith′ō əs), *n.* *Class. Myth.* **1.** a son of Poseidon and Periboea who became a Phaeacian king. **2.** the helmsman of Theseus.

naut., nautical.

nautch (nôch), *n.* **1.** Also called **nautch′ dance′.** a sinuous dance of the Orient, resembling the cooch. **2.** (in India) an exhibition of dancing by professional dancing girls. [< Urdu *nāch* < Prakrit *nachcha* dancing]

Nau·tes (nô′tēz, nō′-), *n.* (in the *Aeneid*) an aged Trojan, taught by Pallas Athena and noted for his wisdom, who advised Aeneas during the journey from Troy.

nau·ti·cal (nô′ti kəl), *adj.* of or pertaining to seamen, ships, or navigation: *nautical terms.* [< L *nautic(us)* pertaining to ships or sailors (< Gk *nautikós,* equiv. to *naû(s)* ship + *-tikos* -TIC) + -AL[1]] —**nau·ti·cal·i·ty** (nô′tə kal′i tē), *n.* —**nau′ti·cal·ly,** *adv.*

nau′tical day′, a period from noon of one day to noon of the next, used in reckoning time aboard ship.

nau′tical mile′, mile (def. 2).

Nautilus, *Nautilus macromphalus* (Shell length 8 in.)

nau·ti·lus (nôt′əl əs), *n., pl.* **nau·ti·lus·es, nau·ti·li** (nôt′əl ī′) for 1, 2. **1.** Also called **chambered nautilus, pearly nautilus.** any cephalopod of the genus *Nautilus,* having a spiral, chambered shell with pearly septa. **2.** See **paper nautilus.** **3.** (*cap.*) the first nuclear-powered submarine launched by the U.S. Navy. [< L: lit., sailor < Gk *nautílos.* See NAUTICAL]

nau·to·phone (nô′tə fōn′), *n.* *Naut.* an electrically operated horn for giving fog warnings. [< Gk *naût(ēs)* sailor + -O- + -PHONE]

nav., **1.** naval. **2.** navigation.

Nav·a·ho (nav′ə hō′, nä′və-), *n., pl.* **-hos, -hoes,** (*esp. collectively*) **-ho** for 1, *adj.* —*n.* **1.** a member of the principal tribe of the southern division of the Athapaskan stock of North American Indians, located in New Mexico and Arizona, and now constituting the largest tribal group in the U.S. **2.** the Athapaskan language of the Navaho Indians. —*adj.* **3.** of, pertaining to, or characteristic of the Navaho Indians, their language, customs, or crafts: *a Navaho blanket.*

Nav·a·jo (nav′ə hō′, nä′və-), *n., pl.* **-jos, -joes,** (*esp. collectively*) **-jo,** *adj.* Navaho.

na·val (nā′vəl), *adj.* **1.** of or pertaining to warships: *a naval battle; naval strength.* **2.** of or pertaining to ships: *naval architecture; naval engineer.* **3.** belonging to, pertaining to, or connected with a navy: *naval affairs.* **4.** possessing a navy: *the great naval powers.* [< L *nāvāl(is),* equiv. to *nāv(is)* ship + *-ālis* -AL[1]] —**na′val·ly,** *adv.*

na′val acad′emy, a collegiate institution for training naval officers.

na′val ar′chitecture, the science of designing ships and other waterborne craft. —**na′val ar′chitect.**

na′val brass′, an alloy of about 60 percent copper and 40 percent zinc, with traces of lead, tin, arsenic, and iron, used in marine and steam-generating equipment.

na′val crown′, *Heraldry.* a representation of a coronet consisting of a circlet adorned with alternate figures of the sterns of ancient ships and figures of square sails upon masts.

na′val mine′, mine[2] (def. 7).

na′val pipe′, *Naut.* spillpipe.

na′val stores′, **1.** supplies for warships. **2.** various products of the pine tree, as resin, pitch, or turpentine, supplied to ships.

Nav. Arch., Naval Architect.

Nav·a·ri·no (nav′ə rē′nō), *n.* a seaport in the SW Peloponnesus, in SW Greece: Turkish and Egyptian fleets defeated near here in a naval battle 1827. Greek, **Pylos, Pilos.**

Na·varre (nə vär′), *n.* a former kingdom in SW France and N Spain. Spanish, **Na·var·ra** (nä-vär′rä). —**Na·varr′i·an,** *adj.*

Nav·a·so·ta (nav′ə sō′tə), *n.* a town in central Texas. 4937 (1960).

nave[1] (nāv), *n.* the principal longitudinal area of a church, extending from the main entrance or narthex to the chancel, usually flanked by aisles of less height and breadth: generally used only by the congregation. See diag. under **basilica.** [< ML *nāvis,* L: ship; so called from the resemblance in shape]

nave[2] (nāv), *n.* **1.** the central part of a wheel; hub. **2.** *Obs.* the navel. [ME; OE *nafu;* c. D *naaf,* Icel *nöf,* G *Nabe;* akin to Skt *nābhi* nave, NAVEL]

Nav. E., Naval Engineer.

na·vel (nā′vəl), *n.* **1.** the mark or depression in the middle of the surface of the abdomen marking the point of attachment of the umbilicus. **2.** the central point or middle of any thing or place. **3.** *Heraldry.* nombril. [ME; OE *nafela;* c. D *navel,* G *Nabel,* Icel *nafli;* akin to Skt *nābhila,* L *umbilīcus,* Gk *omphalós*]

na′vel ill′, *Vet. Pathol.* See **joint ill.**

na′vel or′ange, a variety of orange having at the apex a navellike formation containing a small secondary fruit.

na·vel·wort (nā′vəl wûrt′), *n.* **1.** a European herb, *Cotyledon umbilica*, having fleshy, peltate leaves and yellowish-green flowers. **2.** any of several low, boraginaceous herbs of the genus *Omphalodes*, of Europe and Asia. [ME; see NAVEL, WORT[2]]

na·vette (na vet′; *Fr.* NA vet′), *n., pl.* **-vettes** (-vets′; *Fr.* -vet′). *Jewelry.* a gem, esp. one not a diamond, cut as a marquise. [< F: weaver's shuttle; lit., little ship. See NAVE[1], -ETTE]

nav·i·cert (nav′i sûrt′), *n.* a document, issued by a consular or diplomatic official of a belligerent in a neutral country, certifying that a vessel of that neutral country is carrying noncontraband cargo and may therefore proceed to another specified neutral port without being liable to search or seizure. [NAVI(GATION) + CERT(IFICATE)]

na·vic·u·la (nə vik′yə lə), *n.* *Horol.* a medieval altitude dial in the form of a ship. [< L: a small boat, equiv. to *nāvi(s)* ship + *-cula* -CULE]

na·vic·u·lar (nə vik′yə lər), *Anat.* —*adj.* **1.** boat-shaped, as certain bones. —*n.* Also, **na·vic·u·lar·e** (nə vik′yə lâr′ē, -lär′ē). **2.** the bone at the radial end of the proximal row of the bones of the carpus. **3.** the bone in front of the talus, or anklebone, on the inner side of the foot. [< LL *nāviculār(is)* of, relating to shipping. See NAVICULA, -AR[1]]

navig., navigation.

nav·i·ga·ble (nav′ə gə bəl), *adj.* **1.** deep and wide enough to afford passage to ships: *a navigable channel.* **2.** capable of being steered or guided, as a vessel, aircraft, missile, etc. [< L *nāvigābil(is)*, equiv. to *nāvigā(re)* (to) sail (see NAVIGATE) + *-bilis* -BLE] —**nav′i·ga·bil′i·ty, nav′i·ga·ble·ness,** *n.* —**nav′i·ga·bly,** *adv.*

nav′igable sem′icircle, *Naut.* the less violent half of a cyclone; the half blowing in the direction opposite to that in which the cyclone is moving and in which a vessel can run before the wind.

nav·i·gate (nav′ə gāt′), *v.,* **-gat·ed, -gat·ing.** —*v.t.* **1.** to traverse (the sea, a river, country, etc.) in a vessel or aircraft. **2.** to direct or manage (a ship, aircraft, or guided missile) on its course. **3.** to ascertain or plot and control the course or position of (a ship, aircraft, etc.). **4.** to pass over (the sea or other body of water), as a ship does. **5.** *Informal.* to walk in or across surely and soberly. —*v.i.* **6.** to direct or manage a ship, aircraft, or guided missile on its course. **7.** to pass over the water, as a ship does. **8.** *Informal.* to walk or find one's way surely and soberly. **9.** to travel by ship or boat; sail. [< L *nāvigāt(us)* sailed, equiv. to *nāvigā(re)* (to) sail (*nāv(is)* ship + *-igāre*, comb. form of *agere* to drive) + *-tus* ptp. suffix]

nav′igating bridge′, *Naut.* See **flying bridge.**

nav′igating bridge′ deck′. See **bridge deck** (def. 3).

nav·i·ga·tion (nav′ə gā′shən), *n.* **1.** the act or process of navigating. **2.** the art or science of plotting, ascertaining, or directing the course of a ship or aircraft. [< L *nāvigātiōn-* (s. of *nāvigātiō*) a voyage. See NAVIGATE, -ION] —**nav′i·ga′tion·al,** *adj.*

Naviga′tion Act′, *Eng. Hist.* any of several acts of Parliament between 1651 and 1847 designed primarily to expand British trade and limit trade by British colonies with countries that were rivals of Great Britain.

naviga′tion weir′, stanch[1] (def. 5).

nav·i·ga·tor (nav′ə gā′tər), *n.* **1.** a person who navigates. **2.** a person who practices, or is skilled in, navigation, as of ships, aircraft, etc. **3.** a person who conducts explorations by sea. **4.** *Brit.* a navvy or laborer. [< L *nāvigātor* a sailor, mariner. See NAVIGATE, -OR[2]]

Nav′igator Is′lands, former name of **Samoa.**

Náv·pak·tos (näf′päk tôs), *n.* Greek name of **Lepanto.**

nav·vy (nav′ē), *n., pl.* **-vies.** *Brit. Informal.* a manual laborer employed in excavating for or building railroads, roads, canals, etc. [short for NAVIGATOR]

na·vy (nā′vē), *n., pl.* **-vies. 1.** the whole body of warships and auxiliaries belonging to a country or ruler. **2.** the department of government charged with their management. **3.** (*often cap.*) the complete body of such warships together with their officers and men, equipment, yards, etc., constituting the sea power of a nation. **4.** Also called **na′vy blue′.** a dark blue. **5.** *Archaic.* a fleet of ships. [ME *navie* < MF < VL **navia*, equiv. to L *nāv(is)* ship + *-ia* -Y[3]]

na′vy bean′, a small, white bean, dried for prolonged storage and prepared for eating by soaking and cooking. [so called from wide use in U.S. Navy]

Na′vy Cross′, *U.S. Navy.* a decoration awarded for outstanding heroism in operations against an enemy.

na′vy plug′, a strong, dark tobacco in plug form.

na′vy yard′, a government dockyard where naval vessels are built, repaired, and fitted out, and naval supplies and munitions are laid up.

Na′vy Yard′ Cit′y, a town in W Washington. 3341 (1960).

na·wab (nə wôb′), *n.* **1.** Also, **nabob.** a viceroy or deputy governor under the former Mogul empire in India. **2.** an honorary title conferred upon Muslims of distinction in India and Pakistan. **3.** nabob (def. 1). [< Urdu *nawwāb* < Ar, pl. of *nā'ib* deputy, viceroy] —**na·wab′ship,** *n.*

Nax·os (nak′sos, -sōs; *Gk.* nä′ksôs), *n.* a Greek island in the S Aegean: the largest of the Cyclades group. 18,593 (1951); 169 sq. mi.

nay (nā), *adv.* **1.** no (used in dissent, denial, or refusal). **2.** and not only so, but; indeed: *many good, nay, noble qualities.* —*n.* **3.** a denial or refusal. **4.** a negative vote or voter. **5. say someone nay, a.** to refuse a person's request. **b.** to prohibit or forbid: *She was afraid to say her children nay in anything, and they soon became selfish little monsters.* [ME *nai, nei* < Scand; cf. Icel *nei* no, equiv. to *ne* not + *ei* ever; see AY[1]]

na·ya pai·sa (nə yä′ pī sä′), *pl.* **na·ye pai·se** (nə yā′ pī sā′). **1.** a copper coin of India, the 100th part of a rupee, equivalent to about .002 of a U.S. dollar: first issued in 1950; paisa; pice. **2.** the 100th part of a gulf rupee. **3.** the 100th part of the rupee of Oman. [< Hindi: lit., new pice]

Na·ya·rit (nä′yä RĒT′), *n.* a state in W Mexico. 391,970 (1960); 10,442 sq. mi. *Cap.:* Tepic.

Naz·a·rene (naz′ə rēn′, naz′ə rēn′), *n.* **1.** a native or inhabitant of Nazareth. **2.** one of a sect of early Jewish converts to Christianity who retained the Mosaic ritual. **3. the Nazarene,** Jesus Christ. **4.** *Obs.* (among Jews and Muslims) a Christian. —*adj.* **5.** of or pertaining to Nazareth or the Nazarenes. [< LL *Nazarēnus* < Gk *Nazarēnós*, deriv. of *Nazarét* NAZARETH]

Naz·a·reth (naz′ər əth, -ə rith), *n.* **1.** a town in N Israel: the childhood home of Jesus. 26,400 (est. 1963). **2.** a town in E Pennsylvania. 6209 (1960).

Naz·a·rite (naz′ə rīt′), *n.* **1.** (among the ancient Hebrews) a religious devotee who had taken certain strict vows. **2.** *Rare.* a Nazarene. **3.** *Rare.* Christ. **4.** *Obs.* a Christian. Also, **Nazirite.** [< LL *Nāzar(aeus)* (< Gk *Nāzēraios*, equiv. to *nāzēr* (< Heb *nāzīr* consecrated person) + *-aios* suffix) + -ITE[1]] —**Naz·a·rit·ic** (naz′ə rit′ik), **Naz·a·rit·ish** (naz′ə rī′tish), *adj.*

Naz·ca (näs′kä), *adj.* of or pertaining to a pre-Incan culture of SW Peru, dating from c2000 B.C., characterized by polychrome pottery and the employment of irrigation techniques in agriculture. Also, **Nasca.**

Naze (nāz), *n.* **The,** Lindesnes.

Na·zi (nä′tsē, nat′sē), *n., pl.* **-zis,** *adj.* —*n.* **1.** a member of the National Socialist German Workers' party of Germany, which in 1933, under Adolf Hitler, seized political control of the country, suppressing all opposition and establishing a dictatorship over all cultural, economic, and political activities of the people, and promulgated belief in the supremacy of Hitler as Führer, anti-Semitism, the natural supremacy of the German people, and the establishment of Germany by superior force as a dominant world power. **2.** (*often l.c.*) a person who holds similar views elsewhere. —*adj.* **3.** of or pertaining to the Nazis. [< G *Nazi(onalsozialist)* National Socialist]

na·zi·fy (nä′tsi fī′, nat′si-), *v.t.,* **-fied, -fy·ing.** (*often cap.*) to place under Nazi control or influence. [NAZI + -FY] —**na′zi·fi·ca′tion,** *n.*

Na·zi·mo·va (nə zim′ə və; *Russ.* nä zē′mo vä), *n.* **Al·la** (äl′lä), 1879–1945, Russian actress in the U.S.

na·zir (nä′zir), *n.* **1.** (in Muslim countries) the title of any of various public officials. **2.** (formerly) a title of certain officials serving native rulers in India. [earlier *nasar, naser* < Urdu *nāzir* < Pers < Ar: inspector] —**na′zir·ship′,** *n.*

Naz·i·rite (naz′ə rīt′), *n.* Nazarite.

Na·zism (nä′tsiz əm, nat′siz-, nä′tsē iz′əm, nat′sē-), *n.* the principles or methods of the Nazis. Also, **Na·zi·ism** (nä′tsē iz′əm, nat′sē-). [NAZ(I) + -ISM]

NB, note well; take notice. [< L *notā bene*]

Nb, *Chem.* niobium.

N.B., 1. New Brunswick. **2.** note well; take notice. [< L *notā bene*]

NBA, 1. National Basketball Association. **2.** National Boxing Association.

NbE, See **north by east.**

N-bomb (en′bom′), *n.* See **neutron bomb.**

NBS, National Bureau of Standards. Also, **N.B.S.**

NbW, See **north by west.**

NC, *Mil.* Nurse Corps.

N.C., North Carolina.

NCAA, National Collegiate Athletic Association. Also, **N.C.A.A.**

nCi, nanocurie; nanocuries. Also, **nc**

N.C.O., Noncommissioned Officer.

Nd, *Chem.* neodymium.

n.d., no date.

NDAC, National Defense Advisory Commission.

N.Dak., North Dakota. Also, **N.D.**

Nde·be·le (en′də bē′lē), *n., pl.* **-les,** (*esp. collectively*) **-le.** Matabele.

Ndo·la (ᵊndō′lə), *n.* a city in N Zambia. 96,400 (est. 1964).

NE, 1. northeast. **2.** northeastern. Also, **n.e.**

Ne, *Chem.* neon.

ne-, var. of **neo-** esp. before a vowel: *neencephalon.*

N.E., 1. naval engineer. **2.** New England. **3.** northeast. **4.** northeastern.

N.E.A., 1. National Editorial Association. **2.** National Education Association. **3.** Newspaper Enterprise Association. Also, **NEA**

Ne·ae·ra (nē ēr′ə), *n.* *Class. Myth.* **1.** the mother, by Strymon, of Evadne. **2.** the daughter of Pereus who married her cousin, King Aleus. **3.** (in the *Odyssey*) a nymph, mother of Lampetia and Phaethusa.

Neal (nēl), *n.* a boy's given name. Also, **Neil.**

Ne·an·der (nē an′dər, nā än′-), *n.* a crater in the fourth quadrant of the face of the moon: about 36 miles in diameter.

Ne·an·der·thal (nē an′dər thôl′, -tôl′, -täl′; nā än′dər täl′), *adj.* **1.** *Anthropol.* of or pertaining to Neanderthal man. —*n.* **2.** *Anthropol.* See **Neanderthal man. 3.** a heavily built, crude, and dull-witted person. [after *Neanderthal*, valley in Germany, near Düsseldorf, where evidence of Neanderthal man was first found] —**Ne·an′der·thal′er,** *n.*

Nean′derthal man′, *Anthropol.* a type of powerfully built, Caucasoid man inhabiting Europe and western and central Asia during the Würm I period of the Upper Pleistocene. See illus. under **Pithecanthropus.**

Ne·an·der·thal·oid (nē an′dər thô′loid, -tô′-, -tä′-; nā än′dər tä′loid), *Anthropol.* —*adj.* **1.** resembling or characteristic of the physical type of Neanderthal man. —*n.* **2.** a fossil man having characteristics like those of Neanderthal man. [NEANDERTHAL + -OID]

neap[1] (nēp), *adj.* **1.** designating those tides, midway between spring tides, which attain the least height. —*n.* **2.** neap tide. See diag. under **tide**[1]. [ME *neep*, OE *nēp-*, in *nēpflōd* neap tide]

neap[2] (nēp), *n.* *Dial.* the pole or tongue of a cart, wagon, etc. [?]

neaped (nēpt), *adj.* *Naut.* grounded until the next cycle of spring tides. Also, **beneaped.** [NEAP[1] + -ED[3]]

Ne·a·pol·i·tan (nē′ə pol′i tᵊn), *adj.* **1.** of, pertaining to, or characteristic of Naples: *a Neapolitan love song.* —*n.* **2.** a native or inhabitant of Naples. [< L *Neāpolītānus.* See NAPLES (< Gk *Neápolis*, lit., new town), -ITE[1], -AN]

Ne′apol′itan ice′ cream′, variously flavored and colored ice cream and ice mixtures frozen in layers.

near (nēr), *adv.* **1.** close; to a point or place not far away: *Come near so I won't have to shout.* **2.** at, within, or to a short distance: *to come near.* **3.** close at hand in time: *New Year's draws near.* **4.** close in relation; closely with respect to connection, similarity, etc. (often used in combination): *a near-standing position.* **5.** all but; almost; nearly: *a period of near 30 years.* **6.** *Naut.* close to the wind. —*adj.* **7.** being close by; not distant: *the near meadows.* **8.** being the lesser in distance: *the near side.* **9.** short or direct: *the near road.* **10.** close in time: *the near future.* **11.** closely related or connected: *our nearest relatives.* **12.** close to an original: *a near translation.* **13.** closely affecting one's interests or feelings: *a matter of near consequence to one.* **14.** intimate or familiar: *a near friend.* **15.** narrow or close: *a near escape.* **16.** parsimonious or niggardly: *a near man.* **17.** (of horses or horse-drawn vehicles) on the left side (opposed to *off*): *the near foreleg.* **18. near at hand, a.** in the immediate vicinity: *There is a shopping area near at hand.* **b.** in the near future; soon: *The departure is near at hand.* —*prep.* **19.** at, to, or within a short distance, or no great distance, from or of: *regions near the equator.* **20.** close upon in time: *near the beginning of the year.* **21.** close upon a condition or state: *He is near death.* —*v.t., v.i.* **22.** to come or draw near; approach: *The boat neared the dock. Storm clouds neared.* [ME *nere*, OE *nēar*, comp. of *nēah* NIGH] —**near′ness,** *n.*
—**Syn. 10.** imminent, impending, approaching. **16.** stingy, tight, miserly. —**Ant. 1, 2, 7, 8, 9, 10, 17.** far. **16.** generous.

near′ beer′, any of several malt beverages that are similar to beer but have an alcoholic content of less than ½ percent.

near·by (nēr′bī′), *adj.* **1.** close at hand; not far off; adjacent; neighboring: *a nearby village.* —*adv.* **2.** in the vicinity or neighborhood; close by: *He lives nearby.* [NEAR + BY]

Nearch (nûrch), *n.* a crater in the fourth quadrant of the face of the moon: about 38 miles in diameter.

Ne·arc·tic (nē ärk′tik, -är′-), *adj.* *Zoogeog.* belonging or pertaining to a geographical division comprising temperate and arctic North America and Greenland. [NE- + ARCTIC]

Near′ East′, an indefinite geographical or regional term, usually referring to the Balkan States, United Arab Republic, and the countries of SW Asia. Cf. **Middle East** (def. 1). —**Near′ East′ern.**

Near′er Tibet′, the eastern part of Tibet.

near′ hand′, *Brit. Dial.* **1.** nearly; almost. **2.** close by; close to.

near-hand (nēr′hand′), *Brit. Dial.* —*prep.* **1.** near to; close to. —*adj.* **2.** near. [from phrase *near-(at)-hand*]

near·ly (nēr′lē), *adv.* **1.** all but; almost: *nearly dead with cold.* **2.** with close approximation: *a nearly perfect likeness.* **3.** with close agreement or resemblance: *a plan nearly like our own.* **4.** with close kinship, interest, or connection; intimately: *to be nearly associated in business; two women nearly related.* **5.** *Archaic.* with parsimony; stingily: *He reacted nearly to their plea for aid.* [NEAR + -LY]
—**Syn. 4.** closely.

near′ miss′, 1. a strike by an aerial bomb or other missile that is not a direct hit but is close enough to damage the target. **2.** something that narrowly falls short of its object or of success.

near-point (nēr′point′), *n.* *Ophthalm.* the point nearest the eye at which an object is clearly focused on the retina when accommodation of the eye is at a maximum. Cf. **far-point.**

near′ rhyme. See **slant rhyme.**

near-sight·ed (nēr′sī′tid), *adj.* seeing distinctly for a short distance only; myopic. —**near′-sight′ed·ly,** *adv.* —**near′-sight′ed·ness, near′-sight′,** *n.*

neat[1] (nēt), *adj.* **1.** in a pleasingly orderly condition: *a neat room.* **2.** habitually orderly in appearance or habits: *a neat person.* **3.** of a simple, pleasing appearance, style, design, etc.: *a neat cottage.* **4.** cleverly effective in character or execution: *a neat scheme; a neat solution.* **5.** *Slang.* great; wonderful; fine: *Boy, that's a neat car!* **6.** clever, dexterous, or apt: *She gave a neat characterization of the old woman.* **7.** (of liquor) unadulterated, or undiluted, as with water or soda water; straight: *to prefer one's whiskey neat.* **8.** *Building Trades.* **a.** (of cement) without sand or other aggregate. **b.** (of plaster) without any admixture except hair or fiber. **9.** net: *neat profits.* —*adv.* **10.** neatly. [ME *net* spruce, trim, clean < MF < L *nitidus* shining, polished, handsome, spruce, equiv. to *nit(ēre)* (to) shine + *-idus* -ID[4]] —**neat′ly,** *adv.* —**neat′ness,** *n.*
—**Syn. 1.** spruce, smart. **4.** finished, well-planned. **6.** adroit. **7.** unmixed, pure. —**Ant. 1.** sloppy. **6.** maladroit. **7.** mixed.

neat[2] (nēt), *n., pl.* **neat.** an animal of the genus *Bos*; a bovine. [ME *neet*, OE *nēat*, c. Icel *naut*, MD *noot*; akin to OE *nēotan* to use]

neat·en (nēt′ᵊn), *v.t.* to make (something) neat: *a day spent neatening the kitchen shelves.* [NEAT[1] + -EN[1]]

neath (nēth, nēth), *prep.* *Dial.* beneath. Also, **'neath.** [aph. var. of beneath]

neat·herd (nēt′hûrd′), *n.* *Obs.* cowherd. [ME; see NEAT[2], HERD[1]]

neat′ line′, a line defining a limit or edge of an excavation, cut stone, etc. Also called **net line.**

neat's′-foot oil′ (nēts′fo͝ot′), a pale-yellow fixed oil made by boiling the feet and shinbones of cattle, used chiefly as a dressing for leather.

neb (neb), *n.* **1.** a bill or beak, as of a bird. **2.** *Chiefly Scot.* a person's mouth. **3.** the nose, esp. of an animal. **4.** the tip or pointed end of anything. **5.** the nib of a pen. [ME *nebbe*, OE *nebb*, c. MD, MLG *nebbe*, Icel *nef.* See NIB]

Neb., Nebraska.

neb·bish (neb′ish), *n.* *Slang.* a drab, insignificant person who is generally ignored. [< Yiddish; ? *neb* (var. of obs. *nib* freshman) + -ISH[1]]

NEbE, See **northeast by east.**

Ne·bi·im (nə vē ēm′; *Eng.* neb′ē ēm′), *n.* *Hebrew.* the Prophets, being the second of the three Jewish divisions of the Old Testament. Also, **Neviim.** Cf. **Tanach.**

NEbN, See **northeast by north.**

Ne·bo (nē′bō), *n.* See under **Pisgah.**

Nebr., Nebraska.

Ne·bras·ka (nə bras′kə), *n.* a State in the central United States. 1,411,330 (1960); 77,237 sq. mi. *Cap.:* Lincoln. *Abbr.:* Nebr., Neb.

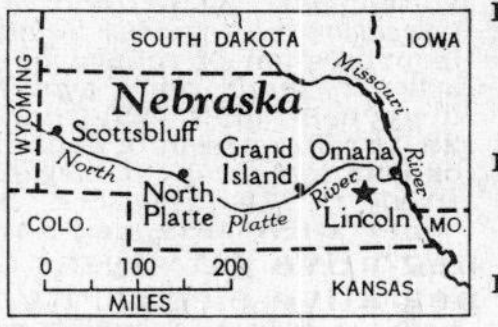

Nebras′ka Cit·y, a town in SE Nebraska. 7252 (1960).

Ne·bras·kan (nə bras′kən), *adj.* **1.** of or pertaining to Nebraska. **2.** *Geol.* of or pertaining to the Nebraskan. —*n.* **3.** a native or inhabitant of Nebraska. **4.** *Geol.* the first stage of the glaciation of North America during the Pleistocene. Cf. **Günz.** [NEBRASK(A) + -AN]

neb·ris (neb′ris), *n.* a fawn skin as worn in Grecian mythology by Dionysus and his followers, and as worn in his honor by his priests and votaries of ancient Greece. [< L < Gk: fawn-skin; akin to *nebrós* fawn]

Ne·broph·o·nus (nə brof′ə nəs), *n.* *Class. Myth.* Thoas (def. 2).

Neb·u·chad·nez·zar (neb′ə kəd nez′ər, neb′yŏŏ-), *n.* **1.** Also, **Neb·u·chad·rez·zar** (neb′ə kəd rez′ər, neb′yŏŏ-); *Douay Bible,* **Nabuchodonosor.** a king of Babylonia, 604?–561? B.C., and conqueror of Jerusalem. II Kings 24, 25. **2.** (*sometimes l. c.*) a bottle for wine holding 20 quarts.

neb·u·la (neb′yə lə), *n., pl.* **-lae** (-lī′), **-las.** **1.** *Astron.* **a.** Also called **diffuse nebula.** a cloudlike, luminous or dark mass composed of gases and small amounts of dust. **b.** Also called **planetary nebula.** a central star surrounded by a gaseous envelope. **c.** Also called **extragalactic nebula.** an exterior galaxy. **2.** *Pathol.* **a.** a faint opacity in the cornea. **b.** cloudiness in the urine. **3.** any liquid medication prepared for use as a spray. [< L: a mist, vapor, cloud; akin to Gk *nephélē* a cloud, G *Nebel* fog, haze] —**neb′u·lar,** *adj.*

neb′ular hypoth′esis, *Astron.* the theory that the solar system evolved from a mass of nebular matter, prominent in the 19th century following its precise formulation by Laplace.

Neb·u·la·rum (neb′yə lâr′əm), *n.* **Palus.** See **Palus Nebularum.**

neb·u·lat·ed (neb′yə lā′tid), *adj.* having dim or indistinct markings, as a bird or other animal. [< LL *nebulāt(us)* (L *nebul(a)* cloud + *-ātus*) + -ED[3]]

neb·u·lé (neb′yə lā′, -lē′), *adj.* **1.** *Heraldry.* **a.** (of a partition line) having deep indentations so as to form a continuous S-curve. **b.** (of a charge, as an ordinary) having the border or borders so indented: *a fess nebulé.* **2.** *Archit.* (of a molding) having an undulating lower edge. Also, **nebuly.** [< MF: lit., clouded. See NEBULATED]

neb·u·lise (neb′yə līz′), *v.t., v.i.,* **-lised, -lis·ing.** *Chiefly Brit.* nebulize. —**neb′u·li·sa′tion,** *n.* —**neb′u·lis′er,** *n.*

neb·u·lize (neb′yə līz′), *v.,* **-lized, -liz·ing.** —*v.t.* **1.** to reduce to fine spray; atomize. —*v.i.* **2.** to become vague, indistinct, or nebulous: *Ideas not developed tend to nebulize.* [NEBUL(A) + -IZE] —**neb′u·li·za′tion,** *n.* —**neb′u·liz′er,** *n.*

neb·u·lose (neb′yə lōs′), *adj.* **1.** cloudlike; nebulous. **2.** hazy or indistinct; nebulous. **3.** having cloudlike markings. [< L *nebulōsus* full of mist, foggy, cloudy. See NEBULA, -OSE]

neb·u·los·i·ty (neb′yə los′i tē), *n., pl.* **-ties.** **1.** nebulous or nebular matter. **2.** a nebulous form, shape, or mass. **3.** the state or condition of being nebulous. [< LL *nebulōsitās.* See NEBULOSE, -ITY]

neb·u·lo·sus (neb′yə lō′səs), *adj.* *Meteorol.* (of a cloud) having indistinct details. [< L: NEBULOUS]

neb·u·lous (neb′yə ləs), *adj.* **1.** hazy, vague, indistinct, or confused: *a nebulous recollection of the meeting; a nebulous distinction between pride and conceit.* **2.** cloudy or cloudlike. **3.** of or resembling a nebula or nebulae; nebular. [< L *nebulōsus* full of mist, foggy, cloudy. See NEBULA, -OUS] —**neb′u·lous·ly,** *adv.* —**neb′u·lous·ness,** *n.*

neb·u·ly (neb′yə lē), *adj.* nebulé.

n.e.c., not elsewhere classified.

nec·es·sar·i·an (nes′i sâr′ē ən), *n., adj.* necessitarian. [NECESSARY + -AN] —**nec′es·sar′i·an·ism,** *n.*

nec·es·sar·i·ly (nes′i sâr′ə lē, nes′i ser′-), *adv.* **1.** by or of necessity: *You don't necessarily have to attend.* **2.** as a necessary result: *That conclusion doesn't follow necessarily from the foregoing.* [late ME; see NECESSARY, -LY]

nec·es·sar·y (nes′i ser′ē), *adj., n., pl.* **-sar·ies.** —*adj.* **1.** being essential, indispensable, or requisite: *a necessary law.* **2.** happening or existing by necessity: *a necessary makeshift.* **3.** acting or proceeding from compulsion or necessity; not free; involuntary: *a necessary agent.* **4.** *Logic.* **a.** (of a proposition) such that a denial of it involves a self-contradiction. **b.** (of an inference or argument) such that it cannot be false if its supporting premises are true. **5.** *Archaic.* (of a servant) rendering indispensable or useful services: *a necessary woman.* —*n.* **6.** something necessary or requisite; necessity. **7.** **necessaries,** *Law.* food, clothing, etc., required by a dependent or incompetent and varying with his social or economic position or that of the person upon whom he is dependent. **8.** *Chiefly New Eng.* a privy or water closet. [ME *necessarie* < L *necessārius* unavoidable, inevitable, needful, equiv. to *necess(e)* (neut. indecl. adj.) unavoidable, necessary + *-ārius* -ARY] —**nec′es·sar′i·ness,** *n.*

—**Syn. 1.** required, needed. NECESSARY, ESSENTIAL, INDISPENSABLE, REQUISITE indicate something vital for the fulfillment of a need. NECESSARY applies to that which is inevitable for the fulfillment of a condition, or that which is inevitable as a consequence of certain causes: *Food is necessary to life. Multiplicity is a necessary result of division.* INDISPENSABLE applies to that which cannot be done without or removed from the rest of a unitary condition: *Food is indispensable to living things. He made himself indispensable as a companion.* That which is ESSENTIAL forms a vital necessary condition of something: *Air is essential to red-blooded animals. It is essential to understand the matter clearly.* REQUISITE applies to what is thought necessary to fill out, complete, or perfect something: *He had all the requisite qualifications for a position.* **6.** requirement, requisite, essential. —**Ant. 1.** dispensable.

nec′essary stool′, close-stool.

ne·ces·si·tar·i·an (nə ses′i târ′ē ən), *n.* **1.** a person who maintains that the action of the will is a necessary effect of antecedent causes (opposed to *libertarian*). —*adj.* **2.** pertaining to necessitarians or necessitarianism. Also, **necessarian.** [NECESSIT(Y) + -ARIAN]

ne·ces·si·tar·i·an·ism (nə ses′ i târ′ē ə niz′əm), *n.* the doctrine of the determination of the will by antecedent causes, as opposed to that of the freedom of the will. [NECESSITARIAN + -ISM]

ne·ces·si·tate (nə ses′i tāt′), *v.t.,* **-tat·ed, -tat·ing.** **1.** to make necessary or unavoidable: *The breakdown of the car necessitated a change in our plans.* **2.** to compel, oblige, or force: *The new wage demand will necessitate a price increase.* [< ML *necessitāt(us)* having been unavoidable, needful, ptp. of *necessitāre.* See NECESSITY, -ATE[1]] —**ne·ces′si·ta′tion,** *n.* —**ne·ces′si·ta′tive,** *adj.*

ne·ces·si·tous (nə ses′i təs), *adj.* **1.** being in or involving necessity; needy; indigent: *to aid a necessitous young mother.* **2.** being essential or unavoidable: *a necessitous discharge of responsibilities.* **3.** requiring immediate attention; urgent: *the necessitous demands of the situation.* [NECESSIT(Y) + -OUS] —**ne·ces′si·tous·ly,** *adv.* —**ne·ces′si·tous·ness,** *n.*

ne·ces·si·tude (nə ses′i tōōd′, -tyōōd′), *n.* *Archaic.* necessity. [< L *necessitūdō,* equiv. to *necess(e)* necessary + *-tūdō* -TUDE]

ne·ces·si·ty (nə ses′i tē), *n., pl.* **-ties.** **1.** something necessary or indispensable: *the necessities of life.* **2.** the fact of being necessary or indispensable; indispensability: *the necessity of adequate housing.* **3.** an imperative requirement or need for something: *the necessity for a quick decision.* **4.** the state or fact of being necessary or inevitable: *to face the necessity of appearing in court.* **5.** an unavoidable need or compulsion to do something: *not by choice but by necessity.* **6.** a state of being in difficulty or need; poverty: *a family in dire necessity.* **7.** *Philos.* **a.** absence of the power to make one's own choices and decisions. Cf. **freedom** (def. 4). **b.** inevitable connection between two happenings. **8.** **of necessity,** as an inevitable result; unavoidably; necessarily: *That discussion must of necessity be postponed for a while.* [ME *necessite* < L *necessitās,* equiv. to *necess(e)* needful + *-itās* -ITY]

—**Syn. 3.** requisite, demand, essential. See **need. 6.** neediness, indigence, need, want.

Ne·cho (nē′kō), *n.* **Prince of Sais** and **Prince of Memphis,** fl. 633? B.C., chief of the Egyptian delta lords (father of Psamtik I). Also called **Necho I.**

neck (nek), *n.* **1.** the part of the body of an animal or man which connects the head and the trunk. **2.** the part of a garment encircling, partly covering, or closest to the neck; neckline. **3.** the length of the neck of a horse or other animal as a measure in racing. **4.** the slender part near the top of a bottle, vase, or similar object. **5.** any narrow, connecting, or projecting part suggesting the neck of an animal. **6.** a narrow strip of land, as an isthmus or a cape. **7.** a strait. **8.** the longer and more slender part of a violin or similar stringed instrument, extending from the body to the head. **9.** *Building Trades, Machinery.* the part on a shank of a bolt next to the head, esp. when it has a special form. **10.** *Anat.* a constricted part of a bone, organ, or the like. **11.** *Dentistry.* the slightly narrowed region of a tooth between the crown and the root. **12.** *Print.* beard (def. 5). **13.** *Archit.* a cylindrical continuation of the shaft of a column above the lower astragal of the capital, as in the Roman Doric and Tuscan orders. **14.** *Geol.* the solidified lava or igneous rock filling a conduit leading either to a vent of an extinct volcano or to a laccolith. **15.** **break one's neck,** *Informal.* to make a great effort: *We broke our necks to get there on time.* **16.** **get it in the neck,** *Slang.* **a.** to suffer punishment or loss: *The trend is to consolidation, and small businesses are getting it in the neck.* **b.** to be rejected or dismissed: *He had worked there for years, but finally got it in the neck when the company moved away.* **17.** **neck and crop,** speedily and completely: *to throw something out, neck and crop.* Also, **neck and heels.** **18.** **neck and neck,** just even or very close; indeterminate as to the outcome: *They were coming toward the finish line neck and neck.* **19.** **neck or nothing,** in a desperate attempt; recklessly: *It was a case of plunging in neck or nothing or letting the opportunity vanish forever.* **20.** **stick one's neck out,** *Slang.* to take a risk; expose oneself to danger; court disaster: *He stuck his neck out by supporting an unpopular candidate.* **21.** **win by a neck, a.** to win by a small amount. **b.** *Racing.* to be first by a head and neck; finish closely. —*v.i.* **22.** *Informal.* (of two persons of opposite sex) to kiss and fondle one another. —*v.t.* **23.** to kiss and fondle, exerting some duress. **24.** to strangle or behead. [ME *nekke,* OE *hnecca,* c. D *nek* nape of neck; akin to G *Nacken,* Icel *hnakki* nape of neck] —**neck′less,** *adj.* —**neck′like′,** *adj.*

Neck·ar (nek′ər; *Ger.* ne′kär), *n.* a river in SW Germany, flowing N and NE from the Black Forest, then W to the Rhine River. 246 mi. long.

neck·band (nek′band′), *n.* **1.** a band of cloth at the neck of a garment. **2.** a band, esp. one of ornamental design, worn around the neck. [late ME *nekband.* See NECK, BAND[2]]

neck·cloth (nek′klôth′, -kloth′), *n., pl.* **-cloths** (-klôthz′, -klothz′, -klôths′, -kloths′). *Obs.* cravat (def. 2). [NECK + CLOTH]

neck′ cord′, lash[1] (def. 7).

Neck·er (nek′ər; *Fr.* ne ker′), *n.* **Jacques** (zhäk), 1732–1804, French statesman, born in Switzerland.

neck·er·chief (nek′ər chif), *n.* a cloth worn round the neck by women or men. [ME; see NECK, KERCHIEF]

neck·ing (nek′ing), *n.* **1.** *Informal.* the act of kissing and fondling. **2.** *Archit.* **a.** a molding or group of moldings between the projecting part of a capital of a column and the shaft. **b.** gorgerin. [NECK + -ING[1]]

neck·lace (nek′lis), *n.* a piece of women's jewelry consisting of a string of stones, beads, jewels, or the like, for wearing around the neck. [NECK + LACE (def. 2)]

neck′lace or′chid, an epiphytic orchid, *Coelogyne dayana,* of Malaya, having reddish-rimmed, white flowers nearly 2½ inches wide in clusters nearly 3 feet long.

neck·let (nek′lit), *n.* something worn around the neck for ornamentation, as a fur piece. [NECK + -LET]

neck·line (nek′līn′), *n.* the opening at the neck of a garment, esp. of a woman's garment, with reference to its shape or its position on the body: *a V-neckline, a high neckline.* [NECK + LINE[1]]

neck·piece (nek′pēs′), *n.* a scarf, esp. one of fur. [NECK + PIECE]

neck′ sweet′bread, sweetbread (def. 2).

neck·tie (nek′tī′), *n.* **1.** a narrow band of decorative fabric worn around the neck, under the collar, by men and tied in front to hang down the front of a shirt. **2.** any band, scarf, or tie fastened at the front of the neck. **3.** *Slang.* a hangman's rope. [NECK + TIE] —**neck′tie′less,** *adj.*

neck′tie par′ty, *Slang.* a lynching by hanging.

neck·wear (nek′wâr′), *n.* articles of dress worn round or at the neck. [NECK + WEAR]

ne·cre·mi·a (nə krē′mē ə, ne-), *n.* *Pathol.* a condition in which a large proportion of the circulating red blood cells are dead. [< NL; see NECR-, -EMIA]

nec·ro (nek′rō), *n.* *Vet. Pathol.* See **necrotic enteritis.** [by shortening]

necro-, a learned borrowing from Greek used, with the meaning "dead," "corpse," "death," in the formation of compound words: *necrology.* Also, *esp. before a vowel,* **necr-.** [< Gk *nekro-,* comb. form of *nekrós* dead body or person]

nec·ro·bac·il·lo·sis (nek′rō bas′ə lō′sis), *n.* *Vet. Pathol.* any disease of cattle, horses, sheep, and swine marked by necrotic areas in which a bacillus, *Sphaerophorus necrophorus,* is found. [NECRO- + BACILLOSIS] —**nec·ro·bac·il·lar·y** (nek′rō bas′ə ler′ē), *adj.*

nec·ro·bi·o·sis (nek′rō bī ō′sis), *n. Med.* the normal, or physiological, death of cells or tissue, as caused by aging or wear. Cf. **necrosis.** [NECRO- + -BIOSIS] —**nec·ro·bi·ot·ic** (nek′rō bī ot′ik), *adj.*

ne·crol·a·try (nə krol′ə trē, ne-), *n.* worship of the dead. [NECRO- + -LATRY]

ne·crol·o·gy (nə krol′ə jē, ne-), *n., pl.* **-gies.** **1.** a notice of death; obituary. **2.** a list of persons who have died within a certain time. [NECRO- + -LOGY] —**nec·ro·log·i·cal** (nek′rə loj′i kəl), **nec′ro·log′ic,** *adj.* —**nec′ro·log′i·cal·ly,** *adv.* —**ne·crol′o·gist,** *n.*

nec·ro·man·cy (nek′rə man′sē), *n.* **1.** magic in general, esp. that practiced by a witch or sorcerer; witchcraft; conjuration. **2.** the alleged art of divination through communication with the dead; the black art. [NECRO- + -MANCY; r. ME *nigromancie* < ML *nigromantīa* for L *necromantīa* < Gk *nekromanteía;* by folk etymology *nigro-* (comb. form of L *niger* black) was substituted in ML for orig. *necro-*] —**nec′ro·man′cer,** *n.* —**nec′ro·man′tic;** *Obs.,* **nec′ro·man′ti·cal,** *adj.* —**nec′ro·man′ti·cal·ly,** *adv.*

—**Syn. 1.** See **magic.**

nec·ro·mi·me·sis (nek′rō mi mē′sis), *n.* *Psychiatry.* a pathological state in which a person believes himself to be dead. [NECRO- + MIMESIS]

ne·croph·a·gous (nə krof′ə gəs, ne-), *adj.* feeding on carrion. [< Gk *nekrophágos.* See NECRO-, -PHAGOUS] —**ne·croph·a·gy** (nə krof′ə jē, ne-), *n.*

nec·ro·phil·i·a (nek′rə fil′ē ə, -fēl′yə), *n.* *Psychiatry.* an erotic attraction to corpses. [< NL; see NECRO-, -PHILIA] —**nec·ro·phile** (nek′rə fīl′), *n.* —**nec·ro·phil·i·ac** (nek′rə fil′ē ak′), **nec′ro·phil′ic,** *adj., n.*

ne·croph·i·lism (nə krof′ə liz′əm, ne-), *n.* *Psychiatry.* necrophilia. [NECRO- + -PHILISM]

nec·ro·pho·bi·a (nek′rə fō′bē ə), *n.* *Psychiatry.* **1.** an abnormal fear of death. **2.** an abnormal fear of dead bodies. [< NL; see NECRO-, -PHOBIA] —**nec′ro·pho′bic,** *adj.*

ne·crop·o·lis (nə krop′ə lis, ne-), *n., pl.* **-lis·es.** **1.** a cemetery, esp. one of large size. **2.** a historic or prehistoric burial ground. [< Gk *nekrópolis* burial place (lit., city of the dead). See NECRO-, -POLIS] —**nec·ro·pol·i·tan** (nek′rə pol′i tᵊn), *adj.*

nec·rop·sy (nek′rop sē), *n., pl.* **-sies.** the examination of a body after death; autopsy. [NECR- + *opsy* (< Gk *ópsis* sight, viewing; see -OPSIS)]

ne·cros·co·py (nə kros′kə pē, ne-), *n., pl.* **-pies.** necropsy. [NECRO- + -SCOPY]

ne·crose (ne krōs′, nek′rōs), *v.t., v.i.,* **-crosed, -cros·ing.** *Pathol.* to affect or be affected with necrosis. [back formation from NECROSIS]

ne·cro·sis (nə krō′sis, ne-), *n.* **1.** death of a circumscribed piece of tissue or of an organ. **2.** *Plant Pathol.* a diseased condition in plants resulting from the death of the tissue. [< NL < Gk *nékrōsis* a making dead, deadness. See NECR-, -OSIS] —**ne·crot·ic** (nə krot′ik, ne-), *adj.*

necrot′ic enteri′tis, *Vet. Pathol.* a disease of swine characterized by extensive ulceration of the intestine. Also called **necro.** [NECRO(SIS) + -TIC]

nec·ro·tise (nek′rə tīz′), *v.i., v.t.,* **-tised, -tis·ing.** *Chiefly Brit.* necrotize.

nec·ro·tize (nek′rə tīz′), *v.,* **-tized, -tiz·ing.** —*v.i.* **1.** to undergo necrosis. —*v.t.* **2.** to cause necrosis in (a tissue, an organ, etc.). [NECROT(IC) + -IZE]

ne·crot·o·my (nə krot′ə mē, ne-), *n., pl.* **-mies.** **1.** *Surg.* the excision of necrosed bone. **2.** the dissection of dead bodies. [NECRO- + -TOMY] —**ne·cro·tom·ic** (nek′rə tom′ik), *adj.* —**ne·crot′o·mist,** *n.*

nec·tar (nek′tər), *n.* **1.** *Bot.* the saccharine secretion of a plant, which attracts the insects or birds that pollinate the flower. **2.** *Class. Myth.* the life-giving drink of the gods. Cf. **ambrosia** (def. 1). **3.** the juice of a fruit, esp. when not diluted, or a blend of fruit juices: *pear nectar; tropical nectar.* **4.** any delicious drink. [< L < Gk *néktar* nectar] —**nec′tar·like′,** *adj.*

Nec·tar (nek′tər), *n.* **1. Sea of.** See **Mare Nectaris.** **2.** a girl's given name.

nec·tar·e·ous (nek târ′ē əs), *adj.* nectarous. Also, **nec·tar′e·an.** [< L *nectare(us)* of, belonging to nectar < Gk *nektáre(os)* like nectar, divine, equiv. to *néktar* NECTAR + *-eos* -EOUS] —**nec·tar′e·ous·ly,** *adv.* —**nec·tar′e·ous·ness,** *n.*

nec·tar·if·er·ous (nek′tə rif′ər əs), *adj.* *Bot.* producing nectar. [NECTAR + -I- + -FEROUS]

nec·tar·ine (nek′tə rēn′, nek′tə rēn′), *n.* **1.** a peach having a smooth, downless skin. **2.** the tree bearing this fruit. [NECTAR + -INE[1]]

Nec·ta·ris (nek târ′is), *n.* **Mare.** See **Mare Nectaris.**

nec·tar·ise (nek′tə rīz′), *v.t.*, **-ised, -is·ing.** *Chiefly Brit.* nectarize.

nec·tar·ize (nek′tə rīz′), *v.t.*, **-ized, -iz·ing.** to mix or saturate with nectar; sweeten. [NECTAR + -IZE]

nec·tar·ous (nek′tər əs), *adj.* **1.** of the nature of or resembling nectar. **2.** delicious; sweet. Also, **nectareous, nectarean.** [NECTAR + -OUS]

nec·ta·ry (nek′tə rē), *n., pl.* **-ries. 1.** *Bot.* an organ or part that secretes nectar. **2.** *Entomol.* a cornicle (formerly thought to secrete honeydew). [< NL *nectarium.* See NECTAR, -Y[3]] **—nec′ta·ried,** *adj.*

nec·to·pod (nek′tə pod′), *n.* (in certain mollusks) an appendage modified for swimming. [< Gk *nēktó(s)* swimming, equiv. to *nēch(ein)* (to) swim + -POD]

Ned (ned), *n.* a boy's given name, form of **Edward.**

N.E.D., New English Dictionary (Oxford English Dictionary). Also, **NED**

Ne·da (nē′də), *n. Class. Myth.* **1.** a river formed on a mountaintop in Arcadia when Rhea prayed to Gaea for water in which to bathe the infant Zeus. **2.** a nymph of this river.

Ned·da (ned′ə), *n.* a girl's given name.

Ne·dra (nē′drə), *n.* a girl's given name.

nee (nā), *adj.* born (placed after the name of a married woman to introduce her maiden name): *Madame de Staël, nee Necker.* Also, **née.** [< F, fem. of *né* (ptp. of *naître* to be born << L *nascī*)]

need (nēd), *n.* **1.** a requirement, necessary duty or obligation, or a lack of something wanted or deemed necessary: *to fulfill the needs of the assignment.* **2.** urgent want, as of something requisite: *He has no need of your charity.* **3.** necessity arising from the circumstances of a case: *There is no need to worry.* **4.** a situation or time of difficulty; exigency: *to help a friend in need; to be a friend in need.* **5.** a condition marked by the lack of something requisite: *the need for leadership.* **6.** destitution; extreme poverty: *The family's need is acute.* **7. if need be,** should the necessity arise. **—*v.t.* 8.** to have need of; require: *to need money.* **—*v.i.* 9.** to be under a necessity (used as an auxiliary, always in an interrogative or in a negative statement, and fol. by infinitive, in certain cases without *to;* in the 3d pers. sing. the form is *need,* not *needs*): *He need not go.* **10.** to be in need or want. **11.** *Archaic.* to be necessary: *There needs no apology.* [ME *nede,* OE *nēd, nīed, nēad,* c. G *Not,* Icel *nauth,* Goth *nauths*] **—need′er,** *n.*

—Syn. 2. urgency. NEED, NECESSITY imply a want, a lack, or a demand, which must be filled. NEED, a word of Old English origin, has connotations which make it strong in emotional appeal: *the need to be appreciated.* NECESSITY, a word of Latin origin, is more formal and impersonal or objective; though much stronger than NEED in expressing urgency or imperative demand, it is less effective in appealing to the emotions: *Water is a necessity for living things.* **4.** emergency. **6.** neediness, indigence, penury, privation. **8.** want, lack. **—Ant. 6.** wealth.

need·fire (nēd′fīᵊr′), *n.* **1.** (formerly, in Europe) a fire kindled by rubbing two pieces of wood together and believed to have supernatural powers, esp. the ability to ward off epidemics among farm animals. **2.** *Scot.* a beacon fire; signal fire. **3.** See **spontaneous combustion. 4.** luminescence, as of rotted or decayed wood. [NEED + FIRE]

need·ful (nēd′fəl), *adj.* **1.** being necessary or required: *needful supplies.* **2.** *Archaic.* needy. **3. the needful,** *Slang.* money, esp. immediately available cash: *They haven't the needful for a car right now.* [ME; see NEED, -FUL] **—need′ful·ly,** *adv.* **—need′ful·ness,** *n.*

Need·ham (nē′dəm), *n.* a town in E Massachusetts, near Boston. 25,793 (1960).

need·i·ness (nē′dē nis), *n.* a state of need; indigence. [ME *nedynes.* See NEEDY, -NESS]

nee·dle (nēd′ᵊl), *n., v.,* **-dled, -dling. —*n.* 1.** a small, slender, rodlike instrument, usually of polished steel, with a sharp point at one end and an eye or hole for thread at the other, for passing thread through cloth to make stitches in sewing. **2.** any of various similar, usually considerably larger, implements for making stitches, as one for use in knitting or one hooked at the end for use in crocheting. **3.** *Med.* **a.** a slender, pointed, steel instrument used in sewing or piercing tissues, as in suturing. **b.** See **hypodermic needle. 4.** *Informal.* an injection of a drug or medicine; shot. **5.** any of various objects resembling or suggesting a needle. **6.** a small, slender, pointed instrument, usually of polished steel or some other material, used to transmit vibrations, as from a phonograph record. **7.** *Elect.* See **magnetic needle. 8.** a pointed instrument, or stylus, used in various recording instruments, engraving, etching, etc. **9.** *Bot.* a needle-shaped leaf, as of a conifer: *a pine needle.* **10.** *Zool.* a slender sharp spicule. **11.** *Chem., Mineral.* a needlelike crystal. **12.** a sharp-pointed mass or pinnacle of rock. **13.** an obelisk, or a tapering, four-sided shaft of stone: *Cleopatra's Needle.* **14.** Also called **nee′dle beam′.** *Building Trades.* a short beam or timber passed though a wall as a temporary support. **15. the needle,** irritating abuse; teasing; heckling (used in the phrases *give someone the needle and get the needle*): *We gave him the needle unmercifully.* **16.** to sew or pierce with or as with a needle: *a skillfully needled patch.* **17.** *Informal.* **a.** to prod or goad (someone) to a specified action: *We needled her into going with us.* **b.** to tease, heckle, or annoy: *We needled him about his big ears.* **—*v.i.* 18.** to form needles in crystallization. **19.** to work with a needle. **20.** *Surg.* to perform a discission. [ME *nedle,* OE *nǣdl,* c. G *Nadel;* akin to L *nēre* to spin] **—nee′dle·like′,** *adj.*

nee′dle-and-ball′ in′dicator (nēd′ᵊl ən bôl′), See **bank-and-turn indicator.**

nee·dle·craft (nēd′ᵊl kraft′, -kräft′), *n.* needlework. [ME *nedle craft.* See NEEDLE, CRAFT]

nee·dle·fish (nēd′ᵊl fish′), *n., pl.* (*esp. collectively*) **-fish,** (*esp. referring to two or more kinds or species*) **-fish·es. 1.** any fish of the family *Belonidae,* found in warm seas and coastal fresh waters, having a sharp beak and needlelike teeth. **2.** a pipefish. [NEEDLE + FISH]

nee·dle·ful (nēd′ᵊl fo͝ol′), *n., pl.* **-fuls.** a suitable length of thread for using at one time with a needle. [NEEDLE + -FUL]

nee′dle hold′er, *Surg.* an instrument for grasping a needle while suturing.

nee·dle·point (nēd′ᵊl point′), *n.* **1.** embroidery upon canvas, usually with uniform spacing of stitches in a pattern. **—*adj.* 2.** noting a lace (**nee′dlepoint lace′**) in which a needle works out the design upon parchment or paper. [NEEDLE + POINT]

Nee·dles (nēd′ᵊlz), *n.* a town in SE California. 4590 (1960).

need·less (nēd′lis), *adj.* unnecessary; not needed or wanted: *a needless waste of food.* [ME *nedles.* See NEED, -LESS] **—need′less·ly,** *adv.* **—need′less·ness,** *n.*

nee′dle valve′, *Mach.* a valve with a needlelike part, a fine adjustment, or a small opening, esp. a valve in which the opening is controlled by a needlelike or conical point which fits into a conical seat.

nee·dle·wom·an (nēd′ᵊl wo͝om′ən), *n., pl.* **-wom·en.** a woman who does needlework. [NEEDLE + WOMAN]

nee·dle·work (nēd′ᵊl wûrk′), *n.* **1.** the art, process, or product of working with a needle, esp. in embroidery, needlepoint, etc. **2.** the occupation or employment of a person skilled in embroidery, needlepoint, etc. Also called **needlecraft.** [ME *nedle werk.* See NEEDLE, WORK]

need·n't (nēd′ᵊnt), contraction of *need not.*

needs (nēdz), *adv.* of necessity; necessarily (often prec. or fol. by *must*): *It must needs be so. It needs must be.* [ME *nedis,* OE *nēdes,* adv. gen. of *nēd* NEED; see -s[1]]

need·y (nē′dē), *adj.,* **need·i·er, need·i·est.** in a state of need or want; without means of subsistence; extremely poor; destitute. [ME *nedi;* see NEED, -Y[1]] **—need′i·ly,** *adv.*

Nee·nah (nē′nə), *n.* a city in E Wisconsin. 18,057 (1960).

ne·en·ceph·a·lon (nē′en sef′ə lon′), *n., pl.* **-lons, -la** (-lə). the more recent part of the brain in the evolutionary development of animals, including the cerebral cortex and its related structures. Also, **neoencephalon.** Cf. **paleencephalon.** [NE- + ENCEPHALON] **—ne·en·ce·phal·ic** (nē′en sə fal′ik), *adj.*

neep (nēp), *n. Brit. Dial.* a turnip. [ME *nepe,* OE *nēp, nǣp* < L *nāpus* turnip]

ne'er (nâr), *adv. Archaic.* never.

ne'er-do-well (nâr′do͞o wel′), *n.* **1.** an idle, worthless person; a person who is ineffectual, unsuccessful, or completely lacking in merit; good-for-nothing. **—*adj.* 2.** worthless; ineffectual; good-for-nothing.

nef (nef), *n.* (in the Middle Ages) a silver or gold table furnishing in the form of a ship, either for holding various utensils or for ornament. [< F: ship < L *nāvis.* See NAVE[1]]

ne·far·i·ous (ni fâr′ē əs), *adj.* extremely wicked; iniquitous: *nefarious deeds.* [< L *nefārius* impious, abominable, wicked, equiv. to *nefās* wickedness (*ne* not + *fās* law, right) + *-ius* -IOUS] **—ne·far′i·ous·ly,** *adv.* **—ne·far′i·ous·ness,** *n.*

—Syn. flagitious, heinous, infamous; vile, atrocious, execrable. **—Ant.** good, honest.

Ne·fer·tem (nā′fer tem′), *n. Egyptian Religion.* Ptah, as the personification of the lotus which keeps Ra alive with its fragrance.

Nef·er·ti·ti (nef′ər tē′tē), *n.* fl. early 14th century B.C., Egyptian queen: wife of Amenhotep IV. Also, **Nef·re·te·te** (nef′ri tē′tē), **Nofretete.**

Ne·fud′ Des′ert (ne fo͞od′), a desert in N Saudi Arabia: areas of reddish sand. Also called **An Nafud, Nafud, Ne·fud′, Nufud, Red Desert.**

neg., 1. negative. **2.** negatively.

ne·gate (ni gāt′, neg′āt, nē′gāt), *v.,* **-gat·ed, -gat·ing. —*v.t.* 1.** to nullify or invalidate (something): *Progress on the study has been negated by the lack of funds.* **2.** to deny the existence, evidence, or truth of (something): *an investigation tending to negate any supernatural influences.* **—*v.i.* 3.** to deny or nullify: *a pessimism which always negates.* [< L *negātus* denied, refused (ptp. of *negāre*), equiv. to *neg-* (var. of *nec* not; see NEGLECT) + *-ā-* v. suffix + *-tus* ptp. suffix] **—ne·gat′ed·ness,** *n.* **—ne·ga′tor, ne·gat′er,** *n.*

ne·ga·tion (ni gā′shən), *n.* **1.** the act of denying: *He shook his head in negation of the charge.* **2.** a denial: *a negation of one's former beliefs.* **3.** that which is without existence; nonentity. **4.** the absence or opposite of that which is actual, positive, or affirmative: *Darkness is the negation of light.* **5.** a negative statement, idea, concept, doctrine, etc.; a contradiction, refutation, or rebuttal: *a shameless lie that demands a negation; answering the party's utopian affirmations with a barrage of negations.* [< L *negātiōn-* (s. of *negātiō*) denial. See NEGATE, -ION] **—ne·ga′tion·al,** *adj.* **—ne·ga′tion·ist,** *n.*

neg·a·tive (neg′ə tiv), *adj., n., v.,* **-tived, -tiv·ing. —*adj.* 1.** expressing or containing negation or denial: *a negative statement.* **2.** expressing refusal to do something: *He maintained a negative attitude about cooperating.* **3.** refusing consent, as to a proposal: *a negative reply to my request.* **4.** prohibitory, as a command or order. **5.** characterized by the absence of distinguishing or marked qualities or features; lacking positive attributes (opposed to *positive*): *a dull, lifeless, negative character.* **6.** lacking in constructiveness, helpfulness, optimism, cooperativeness, or the like: *a man of negative viewpoint.* **7.** being without rewards, results, or effectiveness: *a search of the premises that proved negative.* **8.** *Math., Physics.* **a.** involving or noting subtraction; minus. **b.** measured or proceeding in the direction opposite to that which is considered as positive. **9.** *Bacteriol.* failing to show a positive result in a test for a specific disease caused by either bacteria or viruses. **10.** *Photog.* noting an image in which the brightness values of the subject are reproduced so that the lightest areas are shown as the darkest. **11.** *Physiol.* responding in a direction away from the stimulus. **12.** *Elect.* **a.** of, pertaining to, or characterized by negative electricity. **b.** indicating a point in a circuit that has a lower potential than that of another point, the current flowing from the point of higher potential to the point of lower potential. **13.** of, pertaining to, or noting the south pole of a magnet. **14.** *Chem.* (of an element or group) tending to gain electrons and become negatively charged; acid. **15.** *Logic.* (of a proposition) denying the truth of the predicate with regard to the subject. **—*n.* 16.** a negative statement, answer, word, gesture, etc.: *The ship signaled back a negative.* **17.** a refusal of assent: *to answer a request with a negative.* **18.** the negative form of statement (opposed to *affirmative*). **19.** a person or number of persons arguing against a resolution, statement, etc., esp. a team upholding the negative side in a formal debate. **20.** a negative quality or characteristic. **21.** *Math.* **a.** a minus sign. **b.** a minus sign indicating subtraction. **c.** a negative quantity or symbol. **22.** *Photog.* a negative image, as on a film or the like, used chiefly for making positives. **23.** *Elect.* the negative plate or element in a voltaic cell. **24.** *Archaic.* a veto, or right of veto: *The delegation may exercise its negative.* **25. in the negative,** in expression of refusal or repudiation; no: *The reply, when it finally came, was in the negative.* **—*v.t.* 26.** to deny; contradict. **27.** to refute or disprove (something). **28.** to refuse assent or consent to; veto. **29.** to neutralize or counteract. [< L *negātīv(us)* denying (see NEGATE, -IVE), r. ME *negatif* < MF] **—neg′a·tive·ly,** *adv.* **—neg′a·tive·ness, neg′a·tiv′i·ty,** *n.*

neg′ative cat′alyst, *Chem.* an inhibitor.

neg′ative electric′ity, the electricity present in a body or substance which has an excess of electrons, as the electricity developed on a resin when rubbed with flannel. Cf. **positive electricity.**

neg′ative flag′, the letter "N" in the International Code of Signals, signifying "no" when flown by itself: a square flag having four rows of alternate blue and white squares.

neg′ative glow′, *Physics.* the luminous region between the Crookes dark space and the Faraday dark space in a vacuum tube, occurring when the pressure is low.

neg′ative i′on, *Physics, Chem.* See under **ion** (def. 1).

neg′ative lens′, *Optics.* See **diverging lens.**

neg·a·tiv·ism (neg′ə ti viz′əm), *n.* **1.** *Psychol.* a tendency to resist suggestions or commands, in which the individual responds to what is asked by doing nothing, by doing the opposite, or by doing something wholly unexpected or different. **2.** any system of negative philosophy, as agnosticism, skepticism, etc. [NEGATIVE + -ISM] **—neg′a·tiv·ist,** *n.*

neg·a·tiv·is·tic (neg′ə ti vis′tik), *adj.* of, pertaining to, or characterized by negativism. [NEGATIVIST + -IC]

neg·a·to·ry (neg′ə tōr′ē, -tôr′ē), *adj.* marked by negation; denying; negative. [< LL *negātōrius.* See NEGATE, -ORY[1]]

neg·a·tron (neg′ə tron′), *n.* electron (def. 1). [NEGA(TIVE + ELEC)TRON]

Ne·gau·nee (nə gô′nē), *n.* a town in NW Michigan, in the Upper Peninsula. 6126 (1960).

ne·glect (ni glekt′), *v.t.* **1.** to pay no attention or too little attention to; disregard or slight: *The public neglected his genius for many years.* **2.** to be remiss in care for or treatment of: *to neglect one's family; to neglect one's appearance.* **3.** to omit, through indifference or carelessness: *to neglect to reply to an invitation.* **4.** to fail to carry out or perform (orders, duties, etc.): *to neglect the household chores.* **5.** to fail to take or use: *to neglect no precaution.* **—*n.* 6.** the fault or an instance of neglecting; disregard: *The neglect of the property was shameful.* **7.** the fact or state of being neglected; negligence: *a beauty marred by neglect.* [< L *neglect(us),* var. of *neclectus* slighted (ptp. of *neg- neclegere*), equiv. to *nec* not + *lec-* (var. of *leg-,* base of *legere* to pick up) + *-tus* ptp. suffix] **—ne·glect′ed·ly,** *adv.* **—ne·glect′ed·ness,** *n.* **—ne·glect′er, ne·glec′tor,** *n.* **—ne·glect′·ing·ly,** *adv.*

—Syn. 1. ignore. See **slight. 6, 7.** default, inattention, heedlessness. NEGLECT, DERELICTION, NEGLIGENCE, REMISSNESS imply carelessness, failure, or some important omission in the performance of one's duty, a task, etc. NEGLECT and NEGLIGENCE are occasionally interchangeable, but NEGLECT commonly refers to an instance, NEGLIGENCE to the habit or trait, of failing to attend to or perform what is expected or required: *gross neglect of duty; negligence in handling traffic problems.* DERELICTION implies culpable or reprehensible neglect or failure in the performance of duty: *dereliction in a position of responsibility.* REMISSNESS implies the omission or the careless or indifferent performance of a duty: *Remissness was the cause of tardiness in reporting.* **—Ant. 6.** attention, care.

ne·glect·ful (ni glekt′fəl), *adj.* characterized by neglect; disregardful; careless; negligent (often fol. by *of*): *neglectful of one's health.* [NEGLECT + -FUL] **—ne·glect′ful·ly,** *adv.* **—ne·glect′ful·ness,** *n.*

—Syn. remiss, inattentive, heedless, thoughtless. **—Ant.** careful, thoughtful.

neg·li·gee (neg′li zhā′, neg′li zhā′), *n.* **1.** a dressing gown or robe, usually with soft, flowing lines, worn by women. **2.** easy, informal attire. [< F *négligé* undress, lit., neglected, ptp. of *négliger* < L *neglig(ere)* (to) NEGLECT]

neg·li·gence (neg′li jəns), *n.* **1.** the state or fact of being negligent; neglect: *negligence in discharging one's responsibilities.* **2.** an instance of being negligent: *a downfall brought about by many negligences.* **3.** *Law.* the failure to exercise that degree of care which, under the circumstances, the law requires for the protection of other persons or those interests of other persons which may be injuriously affected by the want of such care. **—*adj.* 4.** pertaining to or involving a civil action for compensation for damages filed by a person who claims to have suffered an injury or loss in an accident caused by another's negligence: *a negligence suit; The injured woman collected a large negligence award.* [ME; var. of *necligence* < L *neg-, necligentia, -legentia.* See NEGLIGENT, -ENCE]

—Syn. 1. See **neglect.**

neg·li·gent (neg′li jənt), *adj.* **1.** guilty of or characterized by neglect, as of duty: *negligent officials.* **2.** indifferent, careless, or offhand: *a negligent, catlike grace that was part of her charm.* [ME; var. of *necligent* < L *neg-, necligent-,* s. of *negligēns,* prp. of *negligere,* var. of *neglegere* to NEGLECT; see -ENT] **—neg′li·gent·ly,** *adv.*

—Syn. 1. neglectful.

neg·li·gi·ble (neg′li jə bəl), *adj.* being so small or trifling that it may safely be neglected or disregarded: *The extra expenses were negligible.* [< F *neglig(ere)* (to) slight, not attend to (see NEGLECT) + -IBLE] **—neg′li·gi·bil′i·ty, neg′li·gi·ble·ness,** *n.* **—neg′li·gi·bly,** *adv.*

ne·go·ti·a·ble (ni gō′shē ə bəl, -shə bəl), *adj.* **1.** (of bills, securities, etc.) transferable by delivery, with or without endorsement, according to the circumstances, the title passing to the transferee. **2.** capable of being negotiated. [NEGOTI(ATE) + -ABLE] **—ne·go′ti·a·bil′i·ty,** *n.*

ne·go·ti·ant (ni gō′shē ənt), *n.* a person who negotiates; negotiator. [< L *negōtiant-* (s. of *negōtiāns*) trading (adj.), trader (n.), prp. of *negōtiārī.* See NEGOTIATE, -ANT]

ne·go·ti·ate (ni gō′shē āt′), *v.,* **-at·ed, -at·ing.** —*v.i.* **1.** to deal or bargain with another or others, as in the preparation of a treaty or in preliminaries to a business deal. —*v.t.* **2.** to arrange for or bring about by discussion and settlement of terms: *to negotiate a loan.* **3.** to manage; transact; conduct: *He negotiated an important business deal.* **4.** to move through, around, or over in a satisfactory manner: *to negotiate a difficult dance step without tripping; to negotiate curves and hills.* **5.** to circulate by endorsement: *to negotiate a bill of exchange.* **6.** to dispose of by sale or transfer: *to negotiate securities.* **7.** to transfer (negotiable paper) by assignment or delivery. [< L *negōtiātus* (ptp. of *negōtiārī*) traded, equiv. to *negōti(um)* business (*neg-* not + *ōtium* leisure) + *-ātus* -ATE[1]] —**ne·go′ti·a′tor,** *n.*

ne·go·ti·a·tion (ni gō′shē ā′shən), *n.* **1.** mutual discussion and arrangement of the terms of a transaction or agreement: *the negotiation of a treaty.* **2.** the act or process of negotiating. **3.** an instance or the result of negotiating. [< L *negōtiātiōn-* (s. of *negōtiātiō*) a doing of business, equiv. to *negōtiāt(us)* (see NEGOTIATE) + *-iōn-* -ION]

Ne·gress (nē′gris), *n.* *Usually Offensive.* a Negro woman or girl. [< F *négresse.* See NEGRO, -ESS]

Ne′gri bod′y (nā′grē), any of the microscopic bodies found in the nerve cells of animals affected with rabies. [named after A. *Negri* (1876–1912), Italian physician]

Ne·gril·lo (ni gril′ō), *n., pl.* **-los,** (*esp. collectively*) **-lo.** a member of any of various dwarfish, Negroid peoples of Africa, as a Pygmy. Cf. **Negrito.** [< Sp *negrillo,* dim. of *negro* black]

Ne·gri Sem·bi·lan (nā′grē sem bē′län, sem′bē län′, nə grē′), a state in Malaysia, on the SW Malay Peninsula. 422,694 (est. 1961); 2580 sq. mi.

Ne·grit·ic (ni grit′ik), *adj.* of or pertaining to Negroes or the Negritos. [NEGRIT(O) + -IC]

Ne·gri·tise (nē′gri tīz′), *v.t.,* **-tised, -tis·ing.** *Chiefly Brit.* Negritize.

Ne·gri·tize (nē′gri tīz′), *v.t.,* **-tized, -tiz·ing.** to give Negro characteristics to; cause to become Negroid. [NEGRIT(IC) + -IZE]

Ne·gri·to (ni grē′tō), *n., pl.* **-tos, -toes.** a member of any of various dwarfish, Negroid peoples of the Philippines, the Malay Peninsula, the Andaman Islands, and southern India. [< Sp *negrito,* equiv. to *negr(o)* black + *-ito* dim. suffix]

Ne·gro (nē′grō), *n., pl.* **-groes,** *adj.* —*n.* **1.** a member of the Negro race, esp. of Africa. **2.** a person having some Negro ancestry, esp. one having dark skin pigmentation. —*adj. Anthropol.* **3.** of, pertaining to, or characteristic of the black race of mankind, esp. the indigenous peoples of Africa, generally characterized by brown to black pigmentation, broad flat nose, prognathism, everted lips, and woolly or crisp hair. **4.** of, pertaining to, or characteristic of a person descended from the African Negro, having dark pigmentation and frequently other Negroid physical characteristics. [< Sp and Pg *negro* black < L *nigrum,* masc. acc. of *niger* black]

Ne·gro (nā′grō; *Sp.* ne′grô), *n.* **Rí·o** (rē′ō; *Sp.* rē′ô), **1.** a river in NW South America, flowing SE from Colombia through N Brazil into the Amazon. 1400 mi. long. **2.** a river in S Argentina, flowing E from the Andes to the Atlantic. 700 mi. long.

Ne·groid (nē′groid), *adj.* **1.** of, pertaining to, or having the characteristics of the Negro race. —*n.* **2.** a Negro. [NEGR(O)- + -OID]

Ne·gro·ise (nē′grō īz′), *v.t.,* **-ised, -is·ing.** *Chiefly Brit.* Negroize.

Ne·gro·ism (nē′grō iz′əm), *n.* **1.** the doctrine or advocacy of equal rights for Negroes. **2.** a quality or manner, as a speech pattern, pronunciation, etc., considered characteristic of the Negro. [NEGRO + -ISM]

Ne·gro·ize (nē′grō īz′), *v.t.,* **-ized, -iz·ing.** **1.** to make or cause to become Negro; give Negro characteristics or qualities to. **2.** to infuse or imbue with Negroism. Also, *esp. Brit.,* **Negroise.** [NEGRO + -IZE]

Ne·gro·phile (nē′grə fīl′, -fil), *n.* (*sometimes l.c.*) a Caucasian or other non-Negro who is esp. sympathetic to Negroes and Negroism. Also, **Ne·gro·phil** (nē′grə fil). [NEGRO + -PHILE] —**Ne·groph·i·lism** (ni grof′ə liz′əm), *n.* —**Ne·groph′i·list,** *n.*

Ne·gro·phobe (nē′grə fōb′), *n.* (*sometimes l.c.*) a person who fears or strongly dislikes Negroes. [NEGRO + -PHOBE]

Ne·gro·pho·bi·a (nē′grə fō′bē ə), *n.* (*sometimes l.c.*) fear or strong dislike of Negroes. [NEGRO + -PHOBIA]

Neg·ro·pont (neg′rō pont′), *n.* Euboea. Italian, **Ne·gro·pon·te** (ne′grô pôn′te).

Ne·gros (nā′grōs; *Sp.* ne′grôs), *n.* an island of the central Philippines. 1,850,410 (est. 1960); 5043 sq. mi.

ne·gus[1] (nē′gəs), *n., pl.* **-gus·es.** **1.** a title of Ethiopian royalty. **2.** (*cap.*) the Emperor of Ethiopia. [< Amharic: king]

ne·gus[2] (nē′gəs), *n.* a beverage made of wine and hot water, with sugar, nutmeg, and lemon. [named after Colonel Francis *Negus* (d. 1732), Englishman who invented it]

Neh., Nehemiah.

Ne·he·mi·ah (nē′ə mī′ə), *n.* **1.** a Hebrew leader of the 5th century B.C. **2.** Also called, *Douay Bible,* **II Esdras.** a book of the Bible bearing his name. **3.** a boy's given name. Also, *Douay Bible,* **Ne·he·mi·as** (nē′ə mī′əs) (for defs. 1, 2).

Neh·ru (nā′ro͞o, ne′ro͞o), *n.* **1.** **Ja·wa·har·lal** (jə wä′hər läl′), 1889–1964, Hindu political leader in India: prime minister of the republic of India 1950–64; father of Indira Gandhi. **2.** his father **Mo·ti·lal** (mō′ti läl), 1861–1931, Indian lawyer and statesman.

neigh (nā), *v.i.* **1.** to utter the cry of a horse; whinny. —*n.* **2.** the cry of a horse; whinny. [ME *nege(n),* OE *hnǣgan,* c. Icel *hneggja.* See NAG[2]]

neigh·bor (nā′bər), *n.* **1.** a person who lives near another. **2.** a person or thing that is near another. **3.** one's fellow human being; a fellow-man: *to be generous toward one's less fortunate neighbors.* **4.** a person who shows kindliness or helpfulness toward his fellow-men: *to be a neighbor to someone in distress.* **5.** (used as a term of address, esp. as a friendly greeting to someone whose name one does not know): *Tell me, neighbor, which way to town?* —*adj.* **6.** living or situated near another: *one of our neighbor nations.* —*v.t.* **7.** to live or be situated near to; adjoin; border on. **8.** to place or bring near. —*v.i.* **9.** to live or be situated nearby. **10.** to associate on the terms of neighbors; be neighborly or friendly (often fol. by *with*). Also, *esp. Brit.,* **neigh′bour.** [ME; OE *neahgebūr, nēahbūr* (*neah* NIGH + *(ge)būr* farmer; see BOER, BOOR); akin to Icel *nābūi,* G *Nachbar,* D *nabuur*] —**neigh′bor·less;** *esp. Brit.,* **neigh′bour·less,** *adj.*

neigh·bor·hood (nā′bər ho͝od′), *n.* **1.** the region surrounding or near some place or thing; vicinity: *the kids of the neighborhood; located in the neighborhood of Jackson and Vine streets.* **2.** a district or locality, often with reference to its character or inhabitants: *a fashionable neighborhood; to move to a nicer neighborhood.* **3.** a number of persons living near one another or in a particular locality: *The whole neighborhood was there.* **4.** neighborly feeling or conduct. **5.** nearness; proximity: *to sense the neighborhood of trouble.* **6.** *Math.* an open set that contains a given point. **7.** **in the neighborhood of,** *Informal.* approximately; nearly; about: *She looks to be in the neighborhood of 40, but stubbornly refuses to admit it.* Also, *esp. Brit.,* **neigh′bour·hood′.** [late ME *neighborehode.* See NEIGHBOR, -HOOD]

neigh′borhood sys′tem, *Math.* the set of all neighborhoods of a given point in a topological space.

neigh·bor·ing (nā′bər ing), *adj.* living or situated near; adjacent: *to visit the neighboring towns.* Also, *esp. Brit.,* **neigh′bour·ing.** [NEIGHBOR + -ING[2]]

neigh·bor·ly (nā′bər lē), *adj.* having or showing qualities befitting a neighbor; friendly. Also, *esp. Brit.,* **neigh′bour·ly.** [NEIGHBOR + -LY] —**neigh′bor·li·ness;** *esp. Brit.,* **neigh′bour·li·ness,** *n.*

Neil (nēl), *n.* a boy's given name. Also, **Neal.**

Nei·la (nē′lə), *n.* a girl's given name.

Ne·i·lah (nə ē lä′), *n.* *Hebrew.* the Jewish religious service marking the conclusion of Yom Kippur.

Neills·ville (nēlz′vil), *n.* a town in central Wisconsin. 2728 (1960).

Neil·son (nēl′sən), *n.* **1.** **William Allan,** 1869–1946, U.S. educator and lexicographer, born in Scotland. **2.** a boy's given name.

Nei·son (nī′sən), *n.* a walled plain in the first quadrant of the face of the moon: about 33 miles in diameter.

Neis·se (nī′sə), *n.* **a river in N Europe, flowing N from the NW Czech Republic along part of the boundary between Germany and Poland to the Oder River. 145 mi. long.**

neis·se·ri·a (nī sēr′ē ə), *n., pl.* **-se·ri·ae** (-sēr′ē ē′). *Bacteriol.* any of several spherical bacteria of the genus *Neisseria,* certain species of which, as *N. gonorrhoeae,* are pathogenic for man. [< NL; named after A.L.S. *Neisser* (1855–1916), German physician; see -IA]

neist (nēst), *adj., adv. Chiefly Scot.* next.

Ne·ith (nē′ith), *n.* an ancient Egyptian personification of femininity and the mother of Ra, the sun god. She was identified by the ancient Greeks with Athena.

nei·ther (nē′thər, nī′-), *conj.* **1.** not either, as of persons or things specified (usually fol. by *nor*): *Neither John nor Betty is at home. Neither color seems right for the room.* **2.** nor; nor yet; no more: *Bob can't go, and neither can I. If she doesn't want it, neither do I.* —*adj.* **3.** not either; not the one or the other: *Neither statement is true.* —*pron.* **4.** not either; not one person or the other; not one thing or the other: *Neither of the suggestions will do. Neither is to be trusted.* [ME, equiv. to *ne* not + EITHER; r. ME *nawther,* OE *nāwther, nāhwæther* (*nā* not + *hwæther* which of two; see WHETHER)]

Nei·va (nā′vä), *n.* a city in W Colombia. 77,410 (est. 1961).

Nejd (nejd, nād), *n.* a region in E central Saudi Arabia: formerly a sultanate of Arabia; inhabited by Wahabis. ab. 3,000,000; ab. 414,000 sq. mi.

Nekh·bet (nek′bet), *n.* *Egyptian Religion.* the guardian goddess of Upper Egypt, often represented as a vulture. Also, **Nekh·e·bet** (nek′ə bet′), **Nekh·e·bit** (nek′ə bit), **Ne·khebt** (ne kebt′).

Ne·koo·sa (nə ko͞o′sə), *n.* a town in central Wisconsin. 2515 (1960).

nek·ton (nek′ton), *n.* the aggregate of actively swimming aquatic organisms in a body of water, able to move independently of water currents. [< G < Gk *nēktón* swimming, neut. of *nēktós* (verbal of *nḗchein* to swim)] —**nek·ton′ic,** *adj.*

Nel·da (nel′də), *n.* a girl's given name.

Ne·le·us (nē′lē əs, -lo͞os), *n.* *Class. Myth.* king of Pylus and father of Nestor by Chloris.

Ne·li·des (nə lī′dēz), *n.* *Class. Myth.* an epithet of Nestor.

Nell (nel), *n.* a girl's given name, form of **Helen.**

Nel·lie (nel′ē), *n.* **1.** a boy's given name, form of **Nelson.** **2.** a girl's given name, form of **Helen.** Also, **Nelly.**

nel·ly (nel′ē), *n.* *Australian Slang.* inferior or cheap wine. [? var. of *nilly* (i.e. *nill he;* see NILL), with pun on NELLY]

Nel·ly (nel′ē), *n.* **1.** a boy's given name, form of **Nelson.** **2.** a girl's given name, form of **Helen.** Also, **Nellie.**

nel·son (nel′sən), *n.* *Wrestling.* a hold in which pressure is applied to the head, back of the neck, and one or both arms of the opponent. Cf. **full nelson, half nelson, quarter nelson, three-quarter nelson.** [special use of name *Nelson*]

Nel·son (nel′sən), *n.* **1.** **Viscount Horatio,** 1758–1805, British admiral. **2.** **(John) Byron,** born 1911, U.S. golf player. **3.** a river in central Canada, flowing NE from Lake Winnipeg to Hudson Bay. 400 mi. long. **4.** a seaport on N South Island, in New Zealand. 25,321 (1961). **5.** a boy's given name.

Nel·son·ville (nel′sən vil′), *n.* a town in SE Ohio. 4834 (1960).

ne·lum·bo (nə lum′bō), *n., pl.* **-bos.** lotus (def. 3). [< NL < Singhalese *nelumbu*] —**ne·lum′bi·an,** *adj.*

Ne·man (nem′ən; *Russ.* ne′män), *n.* Russian name of **Niemen.**

nemat-, var. of **nemato-** before a vowel or *h: nematic.*

nem·a·the·ci·um (nem′ə thē′shē əm, -sē əm), *n., pl.* **-ci·a** (-shē ə, -sē ə). *Bot.* a wartlike protuberance on the thallus of certain red algae, containing tetraspores, antheridia, or cystocarps. [< NL < Gk *nêma* thread + *thēkíon* THECIUM] —**nem·a·the·cial** (nem′ə thē′shəl, -sē əl), *adj.*

nem·a·thel·minth (nem′ə thel′minth), *n.* any worm of the phylum *Nemathelminthes* (now usually broken up into several phyla), including the nematodes, hairworms, etc., having an elongated, unsegmented, cylindrical body. [NEMAT- + HELMINTH]

ne·mat·ic (ni mat′ik), *adj.* *Crystall.* noting a mesomorphic state in which the arrangement of the molecules is linear. Cf. **smectic.** [NEMAT- + -IC]

nemato-, a learned borrowing from Greek, where it meant "thread," used in combination to refer to threadlike things, esp. to *nematodes: nematocyst.* Also, *esp. before a vowel or h,* **nemat-.** [comb. form repr. Gk *nēmat-* (s. of *nêma*) thread, yarn, that which is spun; see -O-]

nem·a·to·blast (nem′ə tə blast′, ni mat′ə-), *n.* *Zool.* the cell from which a nematocyst develops. [NEMATO- + -BLAST] —**nem′a·to·blas′tic,** *adj.*

nem·a·to·cyst (nem′ə tə sist, ni mat′ə-), *n.* *Zool.* an organ in coelenterates consisting of a minute capsule containing a thread capable of being ejected and causing a sting, used for protection and for capturing prey. [NEMATO- + -CYST] —**nem′a·to·cys′tic,** *adj.*

Nem·a·to·da (nem′ə tō′də), *n.* the phylum or class comprising the nematodes. [< NL; see NEMAT-; *-oda,* var. of -OIDEA]

nem·a·tode (nem′ə tōd′), *n.* **1.** any unsegmented worm of the phylum or class *Nematoda,* having an elongated, cylindrical body; a roundworm. —*adj.* **2.** belonging or pertaining to the *Nematoda.* [NEMAT- + -ODE[1]]

nem·a·tol·o·gy (nem′ə tol′ə jē), *n.* the branch of zoology dealing with nematodes. [NEMATO- + -LOGY] —**nem·a·to·log·i·cal** (nem′ə tᵊloj′i kəl), *adj.* —**nem′a·tol′o·gist,** *n.*

Nem·bu·tal (nem′byə tôl′), *n.* *Pharm., Trademark.* pentobarbital.

Nem·bu·tsu (nem bo͞o′tso͞o), *n.* *Japanese.* meditation on the name of Amida.

nem. con., nemine contradicente.

nem. diss., nemine dissentiente.

Ne·me·a (nē′mē ə), *n.* a valley in SE Greece, in ancient Argolis. —**Ne·me·an** (ni mē′ən, nē′mē-), *adj.*

Ne·me·an (ni mē′ən, nē′mē-), *n.* *Class. Myth.* an epithet of Zeus, alluding to his temple at Nemea, in Argolis.

Neme′an Games′, one of the great national festivals of ancient Greece, held at Nemea in the second and fourth year of each Olympiad.

Neme′an li′on, *Class. Myth.* a powerful lion strangled by Hercules as one of his labors.

Ne·mer·te·a (ni mûr′tē ə), *n.* the phylum comprising the nemerteans. Also, **Nem·er·tin·e·a** (nem′ər tin′ē ə), **Nem·er·ti·na** (nem′ər tī′nə, -tē′-). [< NL < Gk *Nēmertḗ(s)* a Nereid + *-a* neut. pl. ending]

ne·mer·te·an (ni mûr′tē ən), *n.* **1.** any unsegmented, marine worm of the phylum *Nemertea* (*Nemertinea* or *Nemertina*), having a protrusible proboscis; a ribbon worm. —*adj.* **2.** belonging or pertaining to any of these worms. Also, **nem·er·tine** (nem′ər tin, -tēn′), **nem·er·toid** (nem′ər toid′, ni mûr′toid). [*Nemerte(a)* + -AN]

Nem·e·sis (nem′i sis), *n., pl.* **-ses** (-sēz′). **1.** Also called **Adrastea.** *Class. Myth.* the goddess of divine retribution. **2.** (*l.c.*) an agent or act of retribution or punishment. **3.** (*l.c.*) that which a person cannot conquer, achieve, etc.: *The performance test proved to be my nemesis.* **4.** (*l.c.*) an opponent or rival whom a person cannot best. [< L < Gk: lit., a dealing out, verbid of *némein* to dispense (justice); see -SIS]

ne·mi·ne con·tra·di·cen·te (ne′mi ne′ kōn′trä diken′te; *Eng.* nem′ə nē′ kon′trə di sen′tē), *Latin.* no one contradicting; unanimously.

ne·mi·ne dis·sen·ti·en·te (ne′mi ne′ di sen′tē en′te; *Eng.* nem′ə nē′ di sen′shē en′tē), *Latin.* no one dissenting; unanimously.

ne·mo (nē′mō), *n., pl.* **-mos.** *Radio and Television.* remote (def. 9). [special use of L *nēmō* nobody, perh. by sound assoc. with REMOTE]

ne·mo me im·pu·ne la·ces·sit (ne′mō me impo͞o′ne lä kes′sit; *Eng.* nē′mō mē im pyo͞o′nē ləses′it), *Latin.* no one attacks me with impunity: motto of Scotland.

ne·mor·i·cole (ni môr′ə kōl′, nem′ər ə-), *adj.* living in a grove. Also, **nem·o·ric·o·line** (nem′ə rik′ə līn′, -lin), **nem·o·ric·o·lous** (nem′ə rik′ə ləs). [< L *nemori-* (s. of *nemus*) grove + *-cola;* see -COLOUS]

Nem·rod (nem′rod), *n.* *Douay Bible.* Nimrod (def. 1).

Ne·mu·nas (nye′mo͝o näs′), *n.* Lithuanian name of **Niemen.**

N. Eng., Northern England.

Nen·ni (nen′nē), *n.* **Pie·tro** (pye′trô), born 1891, Italian socialist leader and author.

neo-, **1.** a learned borrowing from Greek meaning "new," "recent," used freely in the formation of compound words: *Neo-Darwinism; neolithic; neoorthodoxy; neophyte.* **2.** *Chem.* a combining form indicating an isomer having a carbon atom attached to four carbon atoms: *neoarsphenamine.* Also, *esp. before a vowel,* **ne-.** [< Gk *neo-:* new, fresh, recent, young (comb. form of *néos*); akin to NEW]

ne·o·ars·phen·a·mine (nē′ō ärs fen′ə mēn′, -finam′in), *n.* *Pharm.* a yellow-orange medicinal powder, $H_2NC_6H_3(OH)As_2C_6H_3(OH)NHCH_2OSNa$, prepared from, but less toxic than, arsphenamine. [NEO- + ARSPHENAMINE]

Ne·o-Cath·o·lic (nē′ō kath′ə lik, -kath′lik), *adj.* **1.** of or pertaining to those Anglicans who avowedly prefer the doctrines, rituals, etc., of the Roman Catholic Church to those of the Anglican communion. **2.** (in France) of or pertaining to a person who has left the Roman Catholic Church because of his belief in Catholic modernism. —*n.* **3.** a Neo-Catholic person. —**Ne·o-Ca·thol·i·cism** (nē′ō kə thol′i siz′əm), *n.*

Ne·o·cene (nē′ə sēn′), *Geol. Obs.* —*adj.* **1.** noting or pertaining to a division of the Tertiary period including the Pliocene and Miocene epochs. —*n.* **2.** the Neocene division of the Tertiary period or its associated rock series. [NEO- + -CENE]

Ne·o-Chris·ti·an·i·ty (nē′ō kris′chē an′i tē), *n.* any interpretation of Christianity based on the prevalent philosophy of a given period. Also, **ne′o·Chris′ti·an′i·ty.**

ne·o·clas·sic (nē/ō klas/ik), *adj.* **1.** belonging or pertaining to a revival of classic styles or that which is held to resemble classic styles, as in art, literature, music, architecture, etc. **2.** (*sometimes cap.*) *Literature.* of, pertaining to, or designating a style of poetry or prose, developed chiefly in the 17th and 18th centuries, rigidly adhering to canons of form that were derived mainly from classical antiquity, that were exemplified by decorum of style or diction, the three unities, etc., and that emphasized an impersonal expression of universal truths as shown in human actions, representing them principally in satiric and didactic modes. **3.** (*usually cap.*) *Fine Arts.* of, pertaining to, or designating a style of painting and sculpture developed principally from the mid-18th through the mid-19th centuries, characterized chiefly by an iconography derived from classical antiquity, a hierarchical conception of subject matter, severity of composition and, esp. in painting, by an oblique lighting of forms in the early phase and a strict linear quality in the later phase of the style. **4.** *Archit.* of, pertaining to, or designating Neoclassicism. Also, **ne/o·clas/si·cal, ne/o·clas/sic, ne/o·clas/si·cal.** [NEO- + CLASSIC] —**ne/o·clas/si·cist, ne/o·clas/si·cist,** *n.*

Ne·o·clas·si·cism (nē/ō klas/i siz/əm), *n.* **1.** *Archit.* **a.** the trend or movement prevailing in the architecture of Europe, America, and various European colonies at various periods during the late 18th and early 19th centuries, characterized by the introduction and widespread use of Greek orders and decorative motifs, the subordination of detail to simple, strongly geometric overall compositions, the frequent presence of broad, plain wall surfaces, the use of moldings, modillions, recessed panels, etc., to create crisp shadow patterns, the presence of light colors or shades, frequent shallowness of relief in ornamental treatment of façades, and the absence of textural effects. **b.** (*l.c.*) the characteristic of any architecture, esp. of an austere or colorless sort, which utilizes classical forms. **2.** (*often l.c.*) the principles of the neoclassic style in art, literature, etc. **3.** (*sometimes l.c.*) any of various movements based on neoclassic principles in the arts, literature, etc., of the late-17th to mid-19th centuries. Also, **Ne/o·Clas/si·cism, Ne/o·clas/si·cism.** [NEO- + CLASSICISM]

ne·o·co·lo·ni·al·ism (nē/ō kə lō/nē ə liz/əm), *n.* the policy of a strong nation in seeking political and economic hegemony over an independent nation or extended geographical area without necessarily reducing the subordinate nation or area to the legal status of a colony. [NEO- + COLONIALISM] —**ne/o·co·lo/ni·al,** *adj.* —**ne/o·co·lo/ni·al·ist,** *n.*

Ne·o·Con·fu·cian (nē/ō kən fyo͞o/shən), *adj.* **1.** of or pertaining to an eclectic philosophical movement of the 12th to the 16th centuries, incorporating Taoist and Buddhist elements with an adaptation of Confucianism. —*n.* **2.** an advocate or follower of Neo-Confucianism. Also called **Neo-Ju.** —**Ne/o-Con·fu/cian·ism,** *n.*

Ne·o·Con·fu·cian·ist (nē/ō kən fyo͞o/shə nist), *adj.* **1.** of or pertaining to Neo-Confucians or Neo-Confucianism. —*n.* **2.** Neo-Confucian (def. 2).

Ne·o·Dar·win·ism (nē/ō där/wi niz/əm), *n.* *Biol.* the theory of evolution as expounded by later students of Charles Darwin, esp. Weismann, who hold that natural selection accounts for evolution and deny the inheritance of acquired characters. —**Ne/o-Dar·win/i·an,** *adj., n.* —**Ne/o-Dar/win·ist,** *n.*

Ne·o·de·sha (nē/ō də shā/), *n.* a town in SE Kansas. 3594 (1960).

ne·o·dym·i·um (nē/ō dim/ē əm), *n.* *Chem.* a rare-earth, metallic, trivalent element occurring with cerium and other rare-earth metals, and having rose-colored to violet-colored salts. *Symbol:* Nd; *at. wt.:* 144.24; *at. no.:* 60; *sp. gr.:* 6.9 at 20°C. [< NL; see NEO-, DIDYMIUM]

ne·o·en·ceph·a·lon (nē/ō en sef/ə lon/), *n., pl.* **-lons, -la** (-lə). neencephalon.

ne·o·for·ma·tion (nē/ō fôr mā/shən), *n.* *Pathol.* a new and abnormal growth of tissue; tumor; neoplasm. [NEO- + FORMATION] —**ne/o·for/ma·tive,** *adj.*

Ne·o·gae·a (nē/ə jē/ə), *n.* a biogeographical division comprising the Neotropical region. Also, **Ne/o·ge/a.** [< NL; see NEO-, GAEA] —**Ne/o·gae/an, Ne/o·ge/an, Ne/o·gae/al, Ne/o·ge/al, Ne/o·gae/ic, Ne/o·ge/ic,** *adj.*

Ne·o·gene (nē/ə jēn/), *Geol.* —*adj.* **1.** noting or pertaining to the present period, in the system adopted by some geologists, originating 25,000,000 years ago and including the Recent, Pleistocene, Pliocene, and Miocene epochs: corresponds to the Quaternary and the latter half of the Tertiary periods in the system generally used in the U.S. Cf. **Paleogene.** —*n.* **2.** the Neogene period or system. [NEO- + *-gene* (see -GEN)]

Ne·o·Goth·ic (nē/ō goth/ik), *adj.* of, pertaining to, or designating chiefly a style of architecture in which Gothic motifs and forms are imitated.

ne·o·gram·mar·i·an (nē/ō grə mâr/ē ən), *Linguistics.* —*n.* **1.** a member of the *Junggrammatiker.* —*adj.* **2.** of or pertaining to the *Junggrammatiker.* [trans. of G *Junggrammatiker*]

Ne·o·He·ge·li·an·ism (nē/ō hā gā/lē ə niz/əm, -hi jē/-), *n.* *Philos.* Hegelianism as modified by various philosophers of the latter half of the 19th century. —**Ne/o-He·ge/li·an,** *n., adj.*

Ne·o·Im·pres·sion·ism (nē/ō im presh/ə niz/əm), *n.* (*sometimes l.c.*) *Fine Arts.* the theory and practice of a group of Post-Impressionists of about the middle 1880's, characterized chiefly by a systematic juxtaposition of dots or points of pure color according to a concept of the optical mixture of hues. Cf. **Pointillism.** —**Ne/o-Im·pres/sion·ist,** *n., adj.*

Ne·o·Ju (nē/ō zho͞o/), *adj., n.* Neo-Confucian.

Ne·o·Kant·i·an·ism (nē/ō kan/tē ə niz/əm), *n.* *Philos.* Kantianism as modified by various philosophers. —**Ne/o-Kant/i·an,** *n., adj.*

Ne·o·La·marck·ism (nē/ō lə mär/kiz əm), *n.* *Biol.* Lamarckism as expounded by later biologists who hold especially that some acquired characters of organisms may be transmitted to descendants, but that natural selection also is a factor in evolution. —**Ne/o-La·marck/i·an,** *adj., n.* —**Ne/o-La·marck/-ist,** *n.*

Ne·o·Lat·in (nē/ō lat/ən), *n.* the Latin which became current, notably in scientific literature, after the Renaissance, c1500. Also called **New Latin.**

ne·o·lith (nē/ə lith), *n.* a neolithic stone implement. [back formation from NEOLITHIC]

ne·o·lith·ic (nē/ə lith/ik), *adj.* *Anthropol.* (*sometimes l.c.*) of, pertaining to, or characteristic of the last phase of the Stone Age, marked by the domestication of animals, development of agriculture, and the manufacture of pottery and textiles: commonly thought to have begun c8,000–9,000 B.C. in the Middle East. Cf. **Mesolithic, Paleolithic.** [NEO- + -LITHIC]

ne·ol·o·gise (nē ol/ə jīz/), *v.i.*, **-gised, -gis·ing.** *Chiefly Brit.* neologize.

ne·ol·o·gism (nē ol/ə jiz/əm), *n.* **1.** a new word, usage, or phrase. **2.** the introduction or use of new words or new senses of words. **3.** a new doctrine, esp. a new interpretation of sacred writings. [< F *néologisme.* See NEOLOGY, -ISM] —**ne·ol/o·gist,** *n.* —**ne·ol/o·gis/tic, ne·ol/o·gis/ti·cal,** *adj.*

ne·ol·o·gize (nē ol/ə jīz/), *v.i.*, **-gized, -giz·ing.** **1.** to make or use new words or create new meanings for words. **2.** to devise or accept new religious doctrines. Also, *esp. Brit.*, **neologise.** [NEOLOG(Y) + -IZE]

ne·ol·o·gy (nē ol/ə jē), *n., pl.* **-gies.** neologism. [< F *néologie.* See NEO-, -LOGY] —**ne·o·log·i·cal** (nē/ə loj/i kəl), **ne/o·log/ic,** *adj.* —**ne/o·log/i·cal·ly,** *adv.*

Ne·o·Lu·ther·an·ism (nē/ō lo͞o/thər ə niz/əm, -lo͞oth/rə-), *n.* a movement begun in the 19th century in Germany and Scandinavia to revive the orthodox principles, beliefs, and practices of the Lutheran Church. —**Ne/o-Lu/ther·an,** *adj., n.*

Ne·o·Mel·a·ne·sian (nē/ō mel/ə nē/shən, -zhən), *n.* a pidgin language based on English and spoken in Melanesia, New Guinea, and NE Australia. Formerly, **Beach-la-mar.**

ne·o·my·cin (nē/ō mī/sin), *n.* *Pharm.* an antibiotic produced by an actinomycete, *Streptomyces fradiae,* administered orally or locally, used chiefly for skin and eye infections and as an intestinal antiseptic in surgery. [NEO- + MYC- + -IN²]

ne·on (nē/on), *n.* **1.** *Chem.* a chemically inert gaseous element occurring in small amounts in the earth's atmosphere, used chiefly in orange-red tubular electrical discharge lamps. *Symbol:* Ne; *at. wt.:* 20.183; *at. no.:* 10; *weight of one liter of the gas at 0°C and at 760 mm. pressure:* 0.9002 gr. **2.** See **neon lamp.** **3.** a sign or advertising sign formed from neon lamps. —*adj.* **4.** using or containing the gas neon. **5.** made of or formed by a neon lamp or lamps: *a neon sign.* **6.** *Informal.* of, pertaining to, or characteristic of a tawdry urban district or of gaudy nighttime entertainment. [< NL < Gk *néon* new, recent (neut. of *néos*)]

ne·o·na·tal (nē/ō nāt/əl), *adj.* of or pertaining to newborn children. [NEO- + NATAL] —**ne/o·na/tal·ly,** *adv.*

ne·o·nate (nē/ə nāt/), *n.* a newborn child. [NEO- + L *nāt(us)* born; see NATIVE]

ne/on lamp/, a gas-discharge bulb containing two electrodes in neon gas and emitting a glow when a voltage is applied across the electrodes.

ne/on tet/ra, a slender characin fish, *Hyphessobrycon innesi,* having a luminous green and blue stripe running the length of the body, often kept in aquariums.

ne·o·or·tho·dox·y (nē/ō ôr/thə dok/sē), *n.* a movement in Protestant theology, beginning after World War I, stressing the absolute sovereignty of God and chiefly characterized by a reaction against liberal theology and a reaffirmation of certain doctrines of the Reformation. Also, **ne/o-or/tho·dox/y, ne/o·ör/tho·dox/y.** Cf. **crisis theology, dialectical theology.** [NEO- + ORTHODOXY] —**ne/o·or/tho·dox, ne/o-or/tho·dox, ne/o·ör/tho·dox/,** *adj.*

Ne·o·pa·le·o·zo·ic (nē/ō pā/lē ə zō/ik, -pal/ē-), *Geol.* —*n.* **1.** that portion of the Paleozoic comprising the Permian, Pennsylvanian, Mississippian, and Devonian periods. See table under **era.** —*adj.* **2.** of or pertaining to the later part of the Paleozoic Era. [NEO- + PALEOZOIC]

ne·o·phyte (nē/ə fīt/), *n.* **1.** a person newly converted to a belief, as a heathen, heretic, nonbeliever, etc.; proselyte. **2.** *Primitive Church.* a person newly baptized. **3.** *Rom. Cath. Ch.* a novice. **4.** a beginner or tyro: *The neophyte must not despair of mastering the rules and procedures.* [< LL *neophytus* newly planted < Gk *neóphytos.* See NEO-, -PHYTE] —**ne·o·phyt·ic** (nē/ə-fit/ik), **ne·o·phyt·ish** (nē/ə fī/tish), *adj.* —**ne·o·phyt·ism** (nē/ə fī tiz/əm), *n.* —**Syn. 4.** greenhorn, novice.

Ne·o·pi·li·na (nē/ō pi lī/nə, -lē/-), *n.* a genus of primitive mollusks little changed since the Devonian period, exhibiting a serial repetition of internal organs that suggests a close relationship to the annelids. [< NL, equiv. to *neo-* NEO- + *Pilina* genus of mollusks]

ne·o·pla·sia (nē/ō plā/zhə, -zhē ə, -zē ə), *n.* **1.** *Pathol.* tumor growth. **2.** the formation and growth of new tissue. [NEO- + -PLASIA]

ne·o·plasm (nē/ə plaz/əm), *n.* *Pathol.* a new growth of different or abnormal tissue; tumor. [NEO- + PLASM] —**ne·o·plas·tic** (nē/ə plas/tik), *adj.*

Ne·o·Plas·ti·cism (nē/ō plas/ti siz/əm), *n.* (*sometimes l.c.*) *Fine Arts.* the theory and practice of the de Stijl group, chiefly characterized by an emphasis on the formal structure of a work of art, and restriction of spatial or linear relations to vertical and horizontal movements as well as restriction of the artist's palette to black, white, and the primary colors. Also, **ne/o-Plas/ti·cism, Ne/o·plas/ti·cism, ne/o·plas/ti·cism.** —**Ne/o-Plas/tic, ne/o-Plas/tic, Ne/o·plas/tic, ne/o·plas/tic,** *adj.* —**Ne/o-Plas/ti·cist, ne/o-Plas/ti·cist, Ne/o·plas/ti·cist, ne/o·plas/ti·cist,** *n.*

ne·o·plas·ty (nē/ə plas/tē), *n.* the repairing or restoration of a part by plastic surgery. [NEO- + -PLASTY]

Ne·o·pla·to·nism (nē/ō plāt/ᵊniz/əm), *n.* a philosophical system, originated in the 3rd century A.D., founded chiefly on Platonic doctrine and Oriental mysticism, with later influences from Christianity. Also, **Ne/o-Pla/to·nism.** [NEO- + PLATONISM] —**Ne·o·pla·ton·ic, Ne·o-Pla·ton·ic** (nē/ō plə ton/ik), *adj.* —**Ne/o·pla/to·nist, Ne/o-Pla/to·nist,** *n.*

ne·o·prene (nē/ə prēn/), *n.* *Chem.* an oil-resistant synthetic rubber: used chiefly in paints, putties, linings for tanks and chemical apparatus, and in crepe soles for shoes. [NEO- + (CHLORO)PRENE]

Ne·op·tol·e·mus (nē/op tol/ə məs), *n.* *Class. Myth.* the son of Achilles and the killer of Priam. Also called **Pyrrhus.**

Ne·o·Py·thag·o·re·an·ism (nē/ō pi thag/ə rē/ə niz/-əm), *n.* a philosophical system, established in Alexandria and Rome in the second century B.C., consisting mainly of revived Pythagorean doctrines with elements of Platonism and Stoicism. —**Ne/o-Py·thag/o·re/an,** *n., adj.*

Ne·o·Re·al·ism (nē/ō rē/ə liz/əm), *n.* **1.** a philosophy developed chiefly by 20th-century American philosophers, including Montague and Santayana, characterized by a presentationist epistemology and by the assertion of the real status of universals. **2.** any of various movements in literature, motion-picture directing, etc., that are considered as a return to a more realistic style. Also called **New Realism.** —**Ne/o-Re/al·ist,** *n., adj.*

Ne·o·Ro·man·ti·cism (nē/ō rō man/ti siz/əm), *n.* **1.** (*sometimes l.c.*) *Fine Arts.* a style of painting developed in the 20th century, chiefly characterized by forms or images that project a sense of nostalgia and fantasy. **2.** any of various movements or styles in literature, motion picture directing, architecture, etc., considered as a return to a more romantic style. Also, **ne/o-Ro·man/ti·cism, Ne/o·ro·man/ti·cism, ne/o·ro·man/-ti·cism.** —**Ne/o-Ro·man/tic, ne/o-Ro·man/tic, Ne/o-ro·man/tic, ne/o·ro·man/tic,** *adj., n.*

Ne·o·sal·var·san (nē/ō sal/vər san/), *n.* *Pharm., Trademark.* neoarsphenamine.

Ne·o·Scho·las·ti·cism (nē/ō skə las/ti siz/əm), *n.* *Philos., Theol.* a contemporary application of Scholasticism to modern problems and life. —**Ne/o-Scho·las/tic,** *adj., n.*

Ne·o·sho (nē ō/shō, -shə), *n.* a town in SW Missouri. 7452 (1960).

ne·o·stig·mine (nē/ō stig/mēn, -min), *n.* *Pharm.* a synthetic compound, $N(CH_3)_3C_6H_4OC{\cdot}N(CH_3)_2$, used in the form of its bromide or methylsulfate for the treatment of myasthenia gravis, of glaucoma, and for the prevention and treatment of postoperative distention in the urinary bladder. [NEO- + *-stigmine* (as in PROSTIGMIN)]

ne·o·style (nē/ə stīl/), *n., v.,* **-styled, -styl·ing.** —*n.* **1.** a manifolding device similar to the cyclostyle. —*v.t.* **2.** to reproduce (copies, facsimiles, etc.) by means of a neostyle. [NEO- + STYLE]

Ne·o·Syn·eph·rine (nē/ō si nef/rin, -rēn), *n.* *Pharm., Trademark.* phenylephrine.

ne·ot·e·ny (nē ot/ᵊnē), *n.* *Zool.* the capacity or phenomenon of becoming sexually mature in the larval state. [< NL *neotenia* < Gk *neo-* NEO- + *tein(ein)* (to) stretch; see -Y³] —**ne·ot/e·nous,** *adj.*

ne·o·ter·ic (nē/ə ter/ik), *adj.* **1.** modern; new. —*n.* **2.** a modern writer, thinker, etc. [< LL *neōteric(us)* new, modern < Gk *neōterikós* young, youthful, equiv. to *neṓter(os)* younger, newer (comp. degree of *néos*) + *-ikos* -IC] —**ne/o·ter/i·cal·ly,** *adv.*

ne·ot·er·ise (nē ot/ə rīz/), *v.i.*, **-ised, -is·ing.** *Chiefly Brit.* neoterize.

ne·ot·er·ism (nē ot/ə riz/əm), *n.* **1.** an innovation in language, as a new word, term, expression, or the like. **2.** the use of new words, terms, or expressions. [< Gk *neōterismós* an attempt to change, equiv. to *neōter(ízein)* (to) make innovations + *-ismos* -ISM] —**Syn. 1, 2.** neologism.

ne·ot·er·ize (nē ot/ə rīz/), *v.i.*, **-ized, -iz·ing.** to coin new words, terms, or expressions; neologize. Also, *esp. Brit.*, **neoterise.** [< Gk *neōteríz(ein),* equiv. to *neṓter(os)* (see NEOTERIC) + *-izein* -IZE]

Ne·o·trop·i·cal (nē/ō trop/i kəl), *adj.* *Biogeog.* belonging or pertaining to a geographical division comprising that part of the New World extending from the tropic of Cancer southward. [NEO- + TROPICAL]

ne·o·type (nē/ə tīp/), *n.* *Biol.* a specimen selected to replace a holotype that has been lost or destroyed. [NEO- + -TYPE]

ne·o·yt·ter·bi·um (nē/ō i tûr/bē əm), *n.* *Chem. Obs.* ytterbium. [NEO- + YTTERBIUM]

Ne·o·zo·ic (nē/ə zō/ik), *adj., n.* *Obs.* Cenozoic. [NEO- + -ZOIC]

NEP (nep), *n.* See **New Economic Policy.** Also, **Nep, N.E.P.**

Ne·pal (nə pôl/, -päl/, -pal/, nā-), *n.* a constitutional monarchy (since 1959) in the Himalayas between N India and Tibet. 9,700,000 (est. 1963); ab. 54,000 sq. mi. *Cap.:* Katmandu.

Nep·a·lese (nep/ə lēz/, -lēs/), *adj., n., pl.* **-lese** for 2. —*adj.* **1.** of or pertaining to Nepal, its inhabitants, or their language. —*n.* **2.** a native or inhabitant of Nepal. [NEPAL + -ESE]

ne·pen·the (ni pen/thē), *n.* **1.** a drug or drink, or the plant yielding it, mentioned by ancient writers as having the power to bring forgetfulness of sorrow or trouble. **2.** anything inducing a pleasurable sensation of forgetfulness. [< L *nēpenthe(s)* < Gk *nēpenthés* herb for soothing, n. use of neut. of *nēpenthḗs* sorrowless, equiv. to *nē-* not + *pénth(os)* sorrow + *-ēs* adj. suffix] —**ne·pen/the·an,** *adj.*

ne·pen·thes (ni pen/thēz), *n., pl.* **-thes.** nepenthe.

ne·per (nē/pər, nā/-), *n.* *Physics.* **1.** the unit used to express the ratio of two power values, equal to one half the natural logarithm of this ratio; 8.686 decibels. **2.** a unit used to compare two scalar quantities, as currents or voltages, equal to the natural logarithm of the ratio of the two quantities; 8.686 decibels. *Abbr.:* Np Also, **napier.** [named after J. NEPER; see NAPIER]

Ne·per (nā/pər *for 1;* nē/pər, nā/- *for 2*), *n.* **1. John.** See **Napier, John.** **2.** a crater in the first quadrant of the face of the moon, in the libration area: about 70 miles in diameter.

neph-, var. of **nepho-** before a vowel: *nephanalysis.*

neph·a·nal·y·sis (nef/ə nal/i sis), *n., pl.* **-ses** (-sēz/). **1.** a map or chart showing the distribution of types and amounts of clouds and precipitation at a given time. **2.** the preparation of such a map or chart. [NEPH- + ANALYSIS]

Neph·e·le (nef/ə lē), *n.* *Class. Myth.* a woman formed from a cloud by Zeus as a counterfeit of Hera, in order to deceive the lustful Ixion: Mother by Ixion of the centaurs; later the wife of Athamas and the mother by him of Phrixus and Helle.

neph·e·line (nef/ə lin), *n.* a feldspathoid mineral, essentially sodium aluminum silicate, $NaAlSiO_4$, occurring in alkali-rich volcanic rocks. Also, **neph·e·lite** (nef/ə līt/). [< F *néphéline,* equiv. to *néphél-* (< Gk *nephélē* cloud) + *-ine* -INE²]

neph·e·lin·ite (nef/ə lə nīt/), *n.* *Petrog.* a fine-grained, dark rock of volcanic origin, essentially a basalt containing nepheline but no feldspar and little or no olivine. [NEPHELINE + -ITE[1]] —**neph·e·li·nit·ic** (nef′ə lə nit′ik), *adj.*

neph·e·lom·e·ter (nef′ə lom′i tər), *n.* **1.** *Bacteriol.* an apparatus containing a series of barium chloride standards used to determine the number of bacteria in a suspension. **2.** *Physical Chem.* an instrument for studying the density of suspended particles in a liquid by measuring scattered light. [*nephel-* (comb. form repr. Gk *nephélē* cloud; see NEBULA) + -O- + -METER] —**neph·e·lo·met·ric** (nef′ə lə me′trik), **neph′e·lo·met′ri·cal,** *adj.* —**neph′e·lo·met′ri·cal·ly,** *adv.* —**neph′e·lom′e·try,** *n.*

neph·ew (nef′yo͞o *or, esp. Brit.,* nev′yo͞o), *n.* **1.** a son of one's brother or sister. **2.** a son of one's husband's or wife's brother or sister. **3.** a euphemism used in referring to an illegitimate son of a clergyman who has vowed celibacy. **4.** *Obs.* a direct descendant, esp. a grandson. **5.** *Obs.* a remote male descendant, as a grandnephew or cousin. [ME *neveu* < OF < L *nepōtem,* acc. of *nepōs* nephew, grandson; akin to OE *nefa,* Icel *nefi,* D *neef,* G *Neffe*]

Ne·phi (nē′fī), *n.* a town in central Utah. 2566 (1960).

nepho-, a learned borrowing from Greek meaning "cloud," used in the formation of compound words: *nephology.* Also, *esp. before a vowel,* **neph-.** [< Gk *népho(s)* a cloud, mass of clouds; see NEBULA]

neph·o·gram (nef′ə gram′), *n.* a photograph of a cloud or clouds. [NEPHO- + -GRAM]

neph·o·graph (nef′ə graf′, -gräf′), *n.* an instrument for photographing clouds. [NEPHO- + -GRAPH]

ne·phol·o·gy (ne fol′ə jē), *n.* the branch of meteorology that treats of clouds. [NEPHO- + -LOGY] —**neph·o·log·i·cal** (nef′ə loj′i kəl), *adj.* —**ne·phol′o·gist,** *n.*

ne·phom·e·ter (ne fom′i tər), *n.* an instrument for measuring the amount of cloud cover in the sky. [NEPHO- + -METER]

neph·o·scope (nef′ə skōp′), *n.* an instrument for determining the altitude of clouds and the velocity and direction of their motion. [NEPHO- + -SCOPE]

nephr-, var. of **nephro-** before a vowel: *nephralgia.*

ne·phral·gi·a (nə fral′jē ə), *n.* *Pathol.* pain in the kidney or kidneys. [NEPHR- + -ALGIA] —**ne·phral′gic,** *adj.*

ne·phrec·to·mise (nə frek′tə mīz′), *v.t.,* **-mised, -mis·ing.** *Chiefly Brit.* nephrectomize.

ne·phrec·to·mize (nə frek′tə mīz′), *v.t.,* **-mized, -miz·ing.** *Surg.* to perform a nephrectomy upon. [NEPHRECTOM(Y) + -IZE]

ne·phrec·to·my (nə frek′tə mē), *n., pl.* **-mies.** *Surg.* excision of a kidney. [NEPHR- + -ECTOMY]

neph·ric (nef′rik), *adj.* renal. [NEPHR- + -IC]

ne·phrid·i·um (nə frid′ē əm), *n., pl.* **-phrid·i·a** (-frid′ē ə). *Zool.* the excretory organ of many invertebrates, consisting of a tubule with an open or closed motile apparatus at its inner end. [< NL; see NEPHR-, -IDIUM] —**ne·phrid′i·al,** *adj.*

neph·rism (nef′riz əm), *n.* *Pathol.* the unhealthy state produced by a chronic kidney disease. [NEPHR- + -ISM]

neph·rite (nef′rīt), *n.* a mineral, a compact or fibrous variety of actinolite, varying from whitish to dark green: a form of jade. [< G *Nephrit.* See NEPHR-, -ITE[1]]

ne·phrit·ic (nə frit′ik), *adj.* *Pathol.* of, pertaining to, or affected with nephritis. [NEPHRITE + -IC]

ne·phri·tis (nə frī′tis), *n.* *Pathol.* inflammation of the kidneys, esp. in Bright's disease. [< LL *nephrītis* a disease of the kidneys < Gk. See NEPHR-, -ITIS]

nephro-, a learned borrowing from Greek meaning "kidney," used in the formation of compound words: *nephrolith.* Also, *esp. before a vowel,* **nephr-.** [comb. form repr. Gk *nephr(ós)* kidney, kidneys]

neph·ro·cele (nef′rə sēl′), *n.* *Pathol.* hernia of a kidney. [NEPHRO- + -CELE[1]]

ne·phrog·e·nous (nə froj′ə nəs), *adj.* **1.** *Med., Pathol.* originating in the kidney. **2.** *Embryol.* forming or giving rise to kidney tissue. Also, **neph·ro·gen·ic** (nef′rə jen′ik). [NEPHRO- + -GENOUS]

neph·ro·lith (nef′rə lith), *n.* *Pathol.* a renal calculus. [NEPHRO- + -LITH] —**neph′ro·lith′ic,** *adj.*

neph·ro·li·thot·o·my (nef′rō li thot′ə mē), *n., pl.* **-mies.** *Surg.* incision or opening of a kidney pelvis for removal of a calculus or calculi. [NEPHROLITH + -O- + -TOMY]

ne·phrol·o·gy (nə frol′ə jē), *n.* the branch of medical science that deals with the kidney. [NEPHRO- + -LOGY] —**ne·phrol′o·gist,** *n.*

neph·ro·lyt·ic (nef′rə lit′ik), *adj.* *Med.* causing the destruction of renal cells. [NEPHRO- + -LYTIC]

neph·ron (nef′ron), *n.* *Anat., Zool.* a structural and functional unit of a kidney. [< G; alter. of Gk *nephrós* kidney]

ne·phrop·a·thy (nə frop′ə thē), *n.* *Pathol.* any disease of the kidney. [NEPHRO- + -PATHY] —**neph·ro·path·ic** (nef′rə path′ik), *adj.*

ne·phro·sis (nə frō′sis), *n.* *Pathol.* kidney disease, esp. marked by noninflammatory degeneration of the tubular system. [< NL; see NEPHR-, -OSIS] —**ne·phrot·ic** (nə frot′ik), *adj.*

neph·ro·stome (nef′rə stōm′), *n.* **1.** *Zool.* the ciliated opening of a nephridium into the coelom. **2.** *Embryol.* a similar opening from the coelom into a tubule of the embryonic kidney. [NEPHRO- + -STOME] —**ne·phros·to·mous** (nə fros′tə məs), **neph′ro·sto′mi·al,** *adj.*

neph·ro·tome (nef′rə tōm′), *n.* *Embryol.* the part of the mesoderm between the dorsal and lateral zones that develops into the excretory organs of the kidney. [NEPHRO- + -TOME]

ne·phrot·o·mise (nə frot′ə mīz′), *v.t.,* **-mised, -mis·ing.** *Chiefly Brit.* nephrotomize.

ne·phrot·o·mize (nə frot′ə mīz′), *v.t.,* **-mized, -miz·ing.** *Surg.* to perform a nephrotomy upon. [NEPHROTOM(Y) + -IZE]

ne·phrot·o·my (nə frot′ə mē), *n., pl.* **-mies.** *Surg.* incision into the kidney, as for the removal of a calculus. [< NL *nephrotomia.* See NEPHRO-, -TOMY]

neph·ro·tox·ic (nef′rə tok′sik), *adj.* *Med.* toxic to the renal cells; nephrolytic. [NEPHRO- + TOXIC] —**neph·ro·tox·ic·i·ty** (nef′rō tok sis′i tē), *n.*

Neph·ta·li (nef′tᵊlī′), *n.* *Douay Bible.* Naphtali.

ne plus ul·tra (ne plo͝os o͝ol′trä; *Eng.* nē plus ul′trə), *Latin.* **1.** the highest point; acme. **2.** *Archaic.* no more beyond; no further (used in prohibiting an advance or encroachment).

nep·man (nep′mən), *n., pl.* **-men.** (in the Soviet Union) a person who engaged briefly in private enterprise during the New Economic Policy of the 1920's. [NEP + MAN]

Ne·pos (nē′pos, nep′os), *n.* **Cornelius,** 99?–24? B.C., Roman biographer and historian.

nep·o·tism (nep′ə tiz′əm), *n.* patronage bestowed or favoritism shown on the basis of family relationship, as in business and politics. [< It *nepotismo.* See NEPHEW, -ISM] —**ne·pot·ic** (nə pot′ik), **nep′o·tis′tic, nep′o·tis′ti·cal,** *adj.* —**nep′o·tist,** *n.*

Nep·tune (nep′to͞on, -tyo͞on), *n.* **1.** the ancient Roman god of the sea, identified with the Greek god Poseidon. **2.** the sea or ocean: *Neptune's mighty roar.* **3.** *Astron.* the planet eighth in order from the sun, having a diameter of 39,930 miles, a mean distance from the sun of 2,793,500,000 miles, a period of revolution of 164.8 years, and having two satellites. **4.** a town in E New Jersey. 21,487 (1960).

Nep′tune Beach′, a town in NE Florida. 2868 (1960).

Nep′tune Cit′y, a town in E New Jersey. 4013 (1960).

Nep·tu·ni·an (nep to͞o′nē ən, -tyo͞o′-), *adj.* **1.** pertaining to Neptune or the sea. **2.** pertaining to the planet Neptune. **3.** (*often l.c.*) *Geol.* formed by the action of water. [NEPTUNE + -IAN]

nep·tu·ni·um (nep to͞o′nē əm, -tyo͞o′-), *n.* *Chem.* a radioactive transuranic element, not found in nature, produced artificially by the neutron bombardment of U-238. It decays rapidly to plutonium and then to U-235. *Symbol:* Np; *at. no.:* 93; *at. wt.:* 237. [NEPTUNE + -IUM]

ne·ral (nēr′al), *n.* citral b. See under **citral.** [NER(OL) + -AL[3]]

Ner·bud·da (nər bud′ə), *n.* Narbada.

nerd (nûrd), *n.* *Slang.* a boring, dull, or unattractive person. [?]

Ne·re·id (nēr′ē id), *n.* **1.** (*sometimes l.c.*) *Class. Myth.* any of the 50 daughters of Nereus; a sea nymph. **2.** *Astron.* one of the two satellites of Neptune. [< L *Nērēid-* (s. of *Nērēis*) < Gk, s. of *Nērēís.* See NERE(US), -ID[1]]

Ne·re·us (nēr′ē əs, -o͞os), *n.* *Class. Myth.* a sea god, the son of Pontus and Gaea and father of the Nereids.

Ner·gal (nâr′gäl), *n.* (in Akkadian mythology) the god ruling, with Ereshkigal, the world of the dead.

Ne·ri (nâr′ē; *It.* ne′rē), *n.* **Saint Philip** (*Filippo Neri*), 1515–95, Italian priest: founder of Congregation of the Oratory.

ne·rit·ic (nə rit′ik), *adj.* of or pertaining to the region of shallow water along a seacoast. [? NERIT(ES) + -IC]

Ner·i·tes (ner′i tēz′), *n.* *Class. Myth.* a son of Nereus and Doris, changed into a mussel by Aphrodite because he would not go with her when she abandoned the sea.

Nernst (nernst), *n.* **Wal·ther Her·man** (väl′tər her′män), 1864–1941, German physicist and chemist: Nobel prize for chemistry 1920.

Ne·ro (nēr′ō), *n.* **1.** (*Lucius Domitius Ahenobarbus*) ("*Nero Claudius Caesar Drusus Germanicus*") A.D. 37–68, emperor of Rome 54–68. **2.** a boy's given name.

ne·ro an·ti·co (nā′rō an tē′kō, än-), a black marble found in the ruins of buildings dating from the Roman Empire, much used in later times for ornamental purposes. [It: ancient black]

ne·rol (nēr′ōl), *n.* *Chem.* a colorless, liquid, unsaturated alcohol, $C_{10}H_{17}OH$, an isomeric form of geraniol occurring in neroli oil, used in perfumery. [NER(OLI OIL) + -OL[1]]

ner′o·li oil′ (ner′ə lē, nēr′-), a brown essential oil derived from the flowers of the orange tree, *Citrus Bigaradia,* used in the manufacture of perfumes. [< It *Neroli,* title of Anne Marie de la Tremoille, a 17th-century Italian princess of French birth, said to have discovered it]

Ne·ro·nise (nēr′ō nīz′), *v.t.,* **-nised, -nis·ing.** *Chiefly Brit.* Neronize.

Ne·ro·nize (nēr′ō nīz′), *v.t.,* **-nized, -niz·ing. 1.** to characterize (a person) as resembling Nero. **2.** to make depraved in the manner of Nero. **3.** to rule over, tyrannize, or oppress in the manner of Nero. [< L *Nerōn-* (s. of NERO) + -IZE]

Ne·ro's-crown (nēr′ōz kroun′), *n.* See **crape jasmine.**

Ner Ta·mid (nâr′ tä mēd′; *Eng.* nâr′ tä′mid), *Hebrew.* a lamp that is set above and in front of the Holy Ark in a synagogue and is kept burning constantly.

nerts (nûrts), *interj.* *Slang.* nuts (def. 1). Also, **nertz.** [by alter.]

Ne·ru·da (ne ro͞o′thä), *n.* **Pa·blo** (pä′vlô), (*Neftalí Ricardo Reyes Basoalto*), 1904–73, Chilean poet and diplomat.

Ner·va (nûr′və), *n.* **Marcus Coc·ce·ius** (kok sē′yəs), A.D. 32?–98, emperor of Rome 96–98.

nerv·al (nûr′vəl), *adj.* of or pertaining to a nerve or nerves; neural. [< LL *nervāl(is)* of, belonging to nerves, equiv. to L *nerv(us)* NERVE + *-āl(is)* -AL[1]]

Ner·val (ner val′), *n.* **Gé·rard de** (zhā rar′ də), (*Gérard Labrunie*), 1808–55, French writer.

nerv·ate (nûr′vāt), *adj.* *Bot.* (of leaves) having nerves or veins; nerved. [NERVE + -ATE[1]]

ner·va·tion (nûr vā′shən), *n.* venation. Also, **ner·va·ture** (nûr′və cho͝or′, -chər). [NERVE + -ATION]

nerve (nûrv), *n., v.,* **nerved, nerv·ing.** —*n.* **1.** one or more bundles of fibers forming part of a system which conveys impulses of sensation, motion, etc., between the brain or spinal cord and other parts of the body. **2.** *Dentistry.* **a.** the nerve tissue in the pulp of a tooth. **b.** (not in tcehnical use) pulp tissue of a tooth. **3.** a sinew or tendon: *to strain every nerve.* **4.** strength, vigor, or energy: *a test of nerve and stamina.* **5.** firmness or courage under trying circumstances: *an assignment requiring nerve.* **6. nerves,** nervousness: *an attack of nerves.* **7.** *Informal.* impertinence; audacity: *He had the nerve to say that?* **8.** *Bot.* a vein, as in a leaf. **9.** a line, or one of a system of lines, extending across something. **10. get on one's nerves,** to irritate or provoke one: *Women with shrill voices get on his nerves.* —*v.t.* **11.** to give strength, vigor, or courage to: *Encouragement had nerved him for the struggle.* [< L *nervus* sinew, tendon; r. ME *nerf* < MF]
—**Syn. 4.** power, force, might. **5.** steadfastness, intrepidity, fortitude, resolution. **11.** strengthen, fortify, invigorate, steel, brace. —**Ant. 4.** weakness. **11.** weaken.

nerve′ block′, *Med.* a temporary arrest of the passage of impulses through a nerve by means of pressure on the nerve or by injection of an anesthetic into or around the nerve.

nerve′ cell′, *Anat., Physiol.* **1.** any of the cells constituting the cellular element of nerve tissue. **2.** one of the essential cells of a nerve center.

nerve′ cen′ter, a group of nerve cells closely connected with one another and acting together in the performance of some function.

nerve′ deaf′ness, *Pathol.* deafness due to a lesion of the sensory neural mechanism involved in hearing.

nerve′ fi′ber, *Anat., Physiol.* a process, axon, or dendrite of a nerve cell.

nerve′ gas′, *Chem. Warfare.* any of several poison gases, derived chiefly from phosphoric acid, that weaken or paralyze the nervous system, esp. that part of the system controlling respiration.

nerve′ im′pulse, *Physiol.* a progressive wave of electric and chemical activity along a nerve fiber which stimulates or inhibits the action of a muscle, gland, or other nerve cell.

nerve·less (nûrv′lis), *adj.* **1.** without nerves, or nervousness, as in emergencies; cool, calm, and collected. **2.** lacking strength or vigor; feeble; weak. **3.** lacking firmness or courage; spiritless; cowardly. **4.** *Anat., Bot.* having no nerves. [NERVE + -LESS] —**nerve′less·ly,** *adv.* —**nerve′less·ness,** *n.*

nerve-rack·ing (nûrv′rak′ing), *adj.* extremely irritating or trying. Also, **nerve′-wrack′ing.**

nerv·ine (nûr′vēn, -vīn), *adj.* **1.** of or pertaining to the nerves. **2.** acting on or relieving disorders of the nerves; soothing the nerves. —*n.* **3.** a nervine medicine. [< NL *nervīnus,* equiv. to L *nerv(us)* NERVE + *-īnus* -INE[1]]

nerv·ing (nûr′ving), *n.* *Vet. Med.* the excision of part of a nerve trunk. [NERVE + -ING[1]]

ner·vos·i·ty (nûr vos′i tē), *n.* the quality of being nervous; nervousness. [< L *nervōsitas* strength. See NERVOUS, -ITY]

nerv·ous (nûr′vəs), *adj.* **1.** highly excitable; unnaturally or acutely uneasy or apprehensive: *to become nervous under stress.* **2.** of or pertaining to the nerves: *nervous tension.* **3.** having or containing nerves. **4.** affecting the nerves: *nervous diseases.* **5.** suffering from, characterized by, or originating in disordered nerves. **6.** characterized by or attended with acute uneasiness or apprehension: *a nervous moment for us all.* **7.** sinewy or strong. [< L *nervōsus* full of sinews, nervous, equiv. to *nerv(us)* NERVE + *-ōsus* -OUS] —**nerv′ous·ly,** *adv.* —**nerv′ous·ness,** *n.*
—**Syn. 1.** fearful, timid, timorous. —**Ant. 1.** confident, bold.

nerv′ous break′down, nervous debility and exhaustion, as from overwork or prolonged mental strain, characterized by vague complaints of a physical nature in the absence of objectively present causes or lesions; nervous prostration; neurasthenia.

nerv′ous prostra′tion, *Pathol.* nervous breakdown; neurasthenia.

nerv′ous sys′tem, *Anat., Zool.* **1.** the system of nerves and nerve centers in an animal or man, including the brain, spinal cord, nerves, and ganglia. **2.** a particular part of this system. Cf. **autonomic nervous system, central nervous system, cerebrospinal nervous system, peripheral nervous system.**

ner·vule (nûr′vyo͞ol), *n.* *Zool.* a small branch of a nerve in the wing of an insect. [NERVE + -ULE]

ner·vu·ra·tion (nûr′vyə rā′shən), *n.* *Entomol.* the arrangement of the veins in the wing of an insect. Also, **ner·vu·la·tion** (nûr′vyə lā′shən). [NERVURE + -ATION]

ner·vure (nûr′vyo͝or), *n.* **1.** *Bot., Zool.* a vein, as of the wing of an insect. **2.** *Rare.* a rib of a Gothic vault. [< F: rib. See NERVE, -URE]

nerv·y (nûr′vē), *adj.,* **nerv·i·er, nerv·i·est. 1.** *Informal.* brashly presumptuous or insolent; pushy: *a nervy thing to say; a nervy trick to pull.* **2.** having or showing courage: *the nervy feats of the mountaineers.* **3.** strong; sinewy; vigorous: *a hard, nervy physique.* **4.** *Chiefly Brit.* straining one's patience or forbearance; trying. **5.** nervous; excitable; on edge. [NERVE + -Y[1]] —**nerv′i·ly,** *adv.* —**nerv′i·ness,** *n.*

n.e.s., not elsewhere specified. Also, **N.E.S.**

nes·cience (nesh′əns, nesh′ē əns), *n.* **1.** lack of knowledge; ignorance. **2.** agnosticism. [< LL *nescientia* ignorance, equiv. to *ne-* not + *scientia* knowledge; see SCIENCE] —**nes′cient,** *adj.*

ne·so·sil·i·cate (nē′sō sil′ə kit, -kāt′, nes′ō-), *n.* *Mineral.* any silicate having no interlinking of the silicate SiO_4 groups. Cf. **cyclosilicate, inosilicate, sorosilicate, tektosilicate.** [< Gk *nêso(s)* island + SILICATE]

Nes·que·hon·ing (nes′kwə hō′ning, -kə-), *n.* a town in E Pennsylvania. 2714 (1960).

ness (nes), *n.* *Archaic.* a headland; promontory; cape. [< Scand; cf. Icel *nes,* c. OE *næs* headland, akin to nose]

-ness, a native English suffix attached to adjectives and participles, forming abstract nouns denoting quality and state (and often, by extension, something exemplifying a quality or state): *darkness; goodness; kindness; obligingness; preparedness.* [ME, OE *-nes, -nis,* c. G *-nis,* Goth *-(n)assus;* suffix orig. *-assus; -n-* by false division in words like *evenness,* OE *efnes*]

Nes·sel·rode (nes′əl rōd′), *n.* a mixture of preserved fruits, nuts, etc., used as a sauce or in puddings, pies, ice cream, or the like. [said to have been invented by chef of NESSELRODE]

Nes·sel·rode (nes′əl rōd′; *Russ.* nes′sel rô′de), *n.* **Count Karl Rob·ert** (kärl rob′ərt; *Russ.* kärl ro bert′, rô′bert), 1780–1862, Russian diplomat and statesman.

ness·ler·ise (nes′lə rīz′), *v.t., v.i.,* **-ised, -is·ing.** (*sometimes cap.*) *Chiefly Brit.* nesslerize.

ness·ler·ize (nes′lə rīz′), *v.,* **-ized, -iz·ing.** —*v.t.* **1.** (*sometimes cap.*) to test (water, liquid solutions, etc.)

for ammonia by means of Nessler's reagent. —*v.i.* 2. to use Nessler's reagent as a test for ammonia in water or other liquids. [named after Julius *Nessler* (1827–1905), German chemist; see -IZE]

Ness′ler's rea′gent (nes′lərz), an aqueous solution of potassium iodide, mercuric chloride, and potassium hydroxide, used as a test for the presence of ammonia. Also called **Ness′ler's solu′tion.**

Nes·sus (nes′əs), *n. Class. Myth.* a centaur who, on attempting to seduce Deianira, the wife of Hercules, was shot by Hercules with a poisoned arrow. Before Nessus died, he gave to Deianira the poisoned tunic that ultimately caused Hercules' death.

nest (nest), *n.* 1. a pocketlike, usually more or less circular structure of twigs, grass, mud, etc., formed by a bird, often high in a tree, as a place in which to lay and incubate its eggs and rear its young; any protected place used by a bird for these purposes. 2. a place used by insects, fishes, turtles, rabbits, or the like, for depositing their eggs or young. 3. a number of birds or animals inhabiting one such place. 4. a snug retreat or refuge; resting place. 5. an assemblage of things lying or set close together, as a series of boxes, trays, etc., that fit within each other: *a nest of tables.* 6. a place where something bad is fostered or flourishes: *a nest of vice; a robber's nest.* 7. the occupants or frequenters of such a place. —*v.t.* 8. to settle or place (something) in or as if in a nest: *to nest dishes in excelsior.* 9. to fit or place one within another: *to nest boxes for more compact storage.* —*v.i.* 10. to build or have a nest: *The swallows nested under the eaves.* 11. to settle in or as in a nest. 12. to fit together or within another or one another: *bowls that nest easily for storage.* 13. to search for or collect nests: *to go nesting.* [ME, OE, c. D, G *nest;* akin to L *nīdus* nest, Skt *nīda* lair. Basic meaning: sitting-place; see NETHER, SIT] —**nest′a·ble,** *adj.* —**nest′er,** *n.* —**nest′like′,** *adj.* —**nest′y,** *adj.*

n'est-ce pas (nes pä′), *French.* isn't that so?

nest·ed (nes′tid), *adj. Math.* (of an ordered collection of sets or intervals) having the property that each set is contained in the preceding set and the length or diameter of the sets approaches zero as the number of sets tends to infinity. [NEST + -ED[3]]

nest′ egg′, 1. a natural or artificial egg left in a nest to induce a hen to continue laying eggs there. 2. money saved and held in reserve for emergencies, retirement, etc.

nes·tle (nes′əl), *v.,* **-tled, -tling.** —*v.i.* 1. to lie close and snug, like a bird in a nest; snuggle or cuddle. 2. to lie or be located in a sheltered spot; be naturally or pleasantly situated: *a cottage nestling in a pine grove.* 3. *Archaic.* a. to make or have a nest. b. to make one's home; settle in a home. —*v.t.* 4. to provide with or settle in a nest, as a bird. 5. to settle or ensconce snugly: *He nestled himself into the hay for a short nap.* 6. to put or press confidingly or affectionately: *She nestled her head on his shoulder.* [ME *nestle(n),* OE *nestlian,* c. D *nestelen.* See NEST, -LE] —**nes′tler,** *n.*

nest·ling (nest′ling, nes′ling), *n.* 1. a young bird not yet old enough to leave the nest. 2. a young child. [ME; see NEST, -LING[1]]

nest′ of draw′ers, a miniature chest of drawers made in the 18th century.

Nes·tor (nes′tər), *n. Class. Myth.* the wisest and oldest of the Greeks in the Trojan War.

Nes·to·ri·an (ne stôr′ē ən, -stōr′-), *n.* one of a sect of Christians, followers of Nestorius, who denied the hypostatic union and were represented as maintaining the existence of two distinct persons in Christ. [< LL *Nestoriān(us).* See NESTORIUS, -AN] —**Nes·to′ri·an·ism,** *n.*

Nes·to·ri·us (ne stôr′ē əs, -stōr′-), *n.* died A.D. 451?, Syrian ecclesiastic: patriarch of Constantinople 428–431.

net[1] (net), *n., v.,* **net·ted, net·ting.** —*n.* 1. a lacelike fabric with a uniform mesh of cotton, silk, rayon, nylon, etc., often forming the foundation of any of various laces. 2. a piece of meshed fabric designed to serve a specific purpose, as to divide a court in racket games or protect against insects: *a tennis net; a mosquito net.* 3. a bag or other contrivance of strong thread or cord worked into an open, meshed fabric, for catching fish, birds, or other animals: *a butterfly net.* 4. anything serving to catch or ensnare: *a police net to trap the bank robber.* 5. any network or reticulated system of filaments, lines, veins, or the like. 6. (*cap.*) *Astron.* the constellation Reticulum. 7. (in tennis, badminton, etc.) a ball that hits the net. 8. *Math.* the abstraction, in topology, of a sequence; a map from a directed set to a given space. 9. Often, **nets.** the goal in hockey or lacrosse. 10. *Informal.* a radio or television network. —*v.t.* 11. to cover, screen, or enclose with a net or netting: *netting the bed to keep out mosquitoes.* 12. to take with a net: *to net fish.* 13. to set or use nets in (a river, stream, etc.), as for catching fish. 14. to catch or ensnare: *to net a dangerous criminal.* 15. (in tennis, badminton, etc.) to hit (the ball) into the net. [ME *net(te),* OE *net(t),* c. D, Icel *net,* Goth *nati,* G *Netz*] —**net′ta·ble,** *adj.* —**net′like′,** *adj.*

net[2] (net), *adj., n., v.,* **net·ted, net·ting.** —*adj.* 1. remaining after deductions, as for charges, expenses, etc. (opposed to *gross*): *net earnings.* 2. (of weight) after deduction of tare, tret, or both. 3. sold at a stated price with all parts and charges included and with all deductions having been made. 4. final; totally conclusive: *After all that work, what was the net result?* —*n.* 5. net income, profit, or the like. —*v.t.* 6. to gain or produce as clear profit. [var. of NEAT[1]] —**net′ta·ble,** *adj.*

net·ball (net′bôl′), *n. Brit.* a game similar to basketball, played with a soccer ball, usually outdoors. [NET[1] + BALL]

net′ blotch′, *Plant Pathol.* a disease of grasses, characterized by a brown, netlike discoloration of the leaves, caused by fungi of the genus *Helminthosporium.*

Net·cong (net′kông, -kong), *n.* a town in N New Jersey. 2765 (1960).

Ne Te·me·re (nē tem′ə rē′), *Rom. Cath. Ch.* a legislative decree, in effect since 1908, declaring that a marriage of a baptized or lapsed Roman Catholic of the Latin rite is invalid unless celebrated before a priest and at least two witnesses.

Neth., Netherlands.

neth·er (neth′ər), *adj.* 1. lying, or believed to lie, beneath the earth's surface; infernal: *the nether regions.* 2. lower or under: *his nether lip.* [ME *nethere,* OE *neothera, nithera,* deriv. of *nither* down (c. G *nieder*), lit., further down, equiv. to *ni-* down + *-ther* comp. suffix] —**neth′er·ward,** *adj.*

Neth·er·lands (neth′ər ləndz), *n.* **the,** (*construed as sing. or pl.*) a kingdom in W Europe, bordering on the North Sea, West Germany, and Belgium. 11,417,254 (est. 1960); 13,433 sq. mi. *Capitals:* Amsterdam *and* The Hague. Also called **Holland.** —**Neth·er·land·er** (neth′ər lan′dər), *n.* —**Neth′er·land′i·an,** *adj.*

Neth′erlands Antil′les, a Netherlands overseas territory in the Caribbean Sea, N and NE of Venezuela; includes the islands of Aruba, Bonaire, Curaçao, Saba, and St. Eustatius, and the S part of St. Martin: considered an integral part of the Dutch realm. 187,234 (1960); 366 sq. mi. *Cap.:* Willemstad. Also called **Curaçao.** Formerly, **Neth′erlands West′ In′dies, Dutch West Indies.**

Neth′erlands East′ In′dies, a former name of the Republic of Indonesia.

Neth′erlands Gui·an′a, Surinam.

Neth′erlands New′ Guin′ea, a former name of **West Irian.**

Neth′erlands Ti′mor, a former name of **Indonesian Timor.**

neth·er·most (neth′ər mōst′, -məst), *adj.* lowest: *the nethermost depths of the ocean.* [ME *nethermast.* See NETHER, -MOST]

neth′er world′, 1. the infernal regions; hell. 2. the afterworld, or hereafter.

Né·thou (*Fr.* nā to͞o′), *n.* **Pic de** (*Fr.* pēk də), a mountain in NE Spain: highest peak of the Pyrenees. 11,165 ft. Spanish, **Pico de Aneto.**

ne·ti ne·ti (nā′ti nā′ti), *Sanskrit.* neither this nor that (used in Hinduism to describe the undifferentiated and ineffable nature of Brahman).

net′ line′. See **neat line.**

net·man (net′man′, -mən), *n., pl.* **-men** (-men′, -mən). 1. a tennis player. 2. *Tennis.* the partner in a doubles game who stands near the net in the forward part of the court. [NET[1] + MAN[1]]

net′ na′tional prod′uct, the gross national product less allowance for depreciation of capital goods. *Abbr.:* NNP Cf. **national income.**

net′ prof′it, the actual profit made on a business transaction, sale, etc., or during a specific period of business activity, after deducting all costs from gross receipts.

net′ reg′ister ton. See **net ton** (def. 1).

net′ reg′ister ton′nage. See **net tonnage.**

net′ silk′, *Chiefly Brit.* See **thrown silk.**

ne·tsu·ke (net′skē, -skā; *Jap.* ne′tso͞o ke′), *n.* (in Japanese art) a small figure of ivory, wood, metal, or ceramic, originally used as a buttonlike fixture on a man's sash. [< Jap]

net′ted mel′on, a variety of muskmelon, *Cucumis Melo reticulatus,* having reticulate markings on the skin and green to reddish-orange flesh. Also called **nutmeg melon.**

net·ting (net′ing), *n.* any of various kinds of net fabric: *fish netting; mosquito netting.* [NET[1] + -ING[1]]

net′ting knot′. See **sheet bend.**

net·tle (net′əl), *n., v.,* **-tled, -tling.** —*n.* 1. any herb of the genus *Urtica,* covered with stinging hairs. 2. any of various allied or similar plants. —*v.t.* 3. to irritate or provoke. 4. to sting as a nettle does. [ME; OE *netele,* c. D *netel,* Norw *netla,* G *Nessel*] —**net′tle·like′,** *adj.* —**net′tler,** *n.* —**net′tly,** *adj.*

net′tle cell′, *Zool.* a nematocyst.

net·tle·fish (net′əl fish′), *n., pl.* (*esp. collectively*) **-fish,** (*esp. referring to two or more kinds or species*) **-fish·es.** jellyfish. [NETTLE + FISH]

net′tle rash′, *Pathol.* urticaria resulting from contact with various plants causing local irritation.

net·tle·some (net′əl səm), *adj.* 1. causing irritation, vexation, or annoyance: *to cope with a nettlesome situation.* 2. easily provoked or annoyed: *to become nettlesome over trifles.* [NETTLE + -SOME[1]]

net′ ton′, 1. Also called **net register ton.** *Naut.* one gross ton registered as taxable. 2. See **short ton.**

net′ ton′nage, the taxable gross tonnage of a merchant ship. Also called **net register tonnage.**

net·work (net′wûrk′), *n.* 1. any netlike combination of filaments, lines, veins, passages, or the like: *a network of arteries; a network of sewers under the city.* 2. a system of interrelated buildings, offices, stations, etc., esp. over a large area or throughout a country, territory, region, etc.: *a network of supply depots.* 3. a netting or net. 4. *Radio, Television.* a group of transmitting stations linked by wire or microwave relay so that the same program can be broadcast or telecast by all. 5. *Elect.* an arrangement of conducting elements, as resistors, capacitors, inductors, etc., connected by conducting wire. 6. *Telecommunications, Computers.* a system for receiving and transmitting information, based on computers, computer terminals, printers, etc., or interconnected telephone lines. [NET[1] + WORK]

net·work·ing (net′wûr′king), *n.* 1. the act or process of informally sharing information and support, esp. among members of a professional group. 2. the implementation or utilization of a computer network. [NETWORK + -ING[1]]

Neu·châ·tel (*Fr.* nœ shä tel′), *n.* 1. a canton in W Switzerland. 147,633 (1960); 309 sq. mi. 2. the capital of this canton, on the Lake of Neuchâtel. 33,430 (1960). 3. **Lake of,** a lake in W Switzerland. 85 sq. mi. German, **Neu·en·burg** (noi′ən bo͝orkh′).

Neuf·châ·tel (no͞o′shə tel′, no͞o′shə tel′; *Fr.* nœ shä tel′), *n.* a soft, white cheese similar to cream cheese, made from whole or partly skimmed milk in Neufchâtel, a town in N France. Also called **Neuf′châtel cheese′.**

Neuil·ly (nœ yē′), *n.* a suburb of Paris, in N France: treaty of peace (1919) between the Allies and Bulgaria. 73,315 (1962). Also called **Neuil·ly-sur-Seine** (nœ yē syr sen′).

neuk (nyo͞ok), *n. Scot.* nook.

Neu·may·er (no͞o′mā ər, nyo͞o′-), *n.* a walled plain in the fourth quadrant of the face of the moon, in the libration area: about 50 miles in diameter.

Neumes

neume (no͞om, nyo͞om), *n.* any of various symbols representing from one to four notes, used in the musical notation of the Middle Ages, but now employed solely for notating Gregorian chant in the liturgical books of the Roman Catholic Church. [late ME < ML *neuma* < Gk *pneûma* breath] —**neu·mat·ic** (no͞o mat′ik, nyo͞o-), **neu′mic,** *adj.*

Neu·pest (noi′pest′), *n.* German name of **Ujpest.**

Ne·u·quén (ne′o͞o ken′), *n.* a city in central Argentina. 14,000 (est. 1965).

neur-, var. of **neuro-** before a vowel: *neuritis.*

neu·ral (no͝or′əl, nyo͝or′-), *adj.* of or pertaining to a nerve or the nervous system. [NEUR- + -AL[1]] —**neu′ral·ly,** *adv.*

neu·ral·gia (no͝o ral′jə, nyo͝o-), *n. Pathol.* sharp and paroxysmal pain along the course of a nerve. [NEUR- + -ALGIA] —**neu·ral′gic,** *adj.*

neu·ral·gi·form (no͝o ral′jə fôrm′, nyo͝o-), *adj. Pathol.* resembling neuralgia. [NEURALGI(A) + -FORM]

neu′ra·min′ic ac′id (no͝or′ə min′ik, nyo͝or′-, no͝or′-, nyo͝or′-), *Biochem.* an amino compound, $C_9H_{17}NO_8$, that occurs in all animal tissues and is coupled with other compounds as part of the carbohydrate-protein complexes. [NEUR- + AMINE + -IC]

neu·ras·the·ni·a (no͝or′əs thē′nē ə, nyo͝or′-), *n. Pathol.* nervous debility and exhaustion, as from overwork or prolonged mental strain, characterized by vague complaints of a physical nature in the absence of objectively present causes or lesions; nervous prostration; nervous breakdown. [NEUR- + ASTHENIA]

neu·ras·then·ic (no͝or′əs then′ik, nyo͝or′-), *Pathol.* —*adj.* 1. pertaining to or suffering from neurasthenia. —*n.* 2. a person suffering from neurasthenia. [NEURASTHEN(IA) + -IC] —**neu′ras·then′i·cal·ly,** *adv.*

neu·ra·tion (no͝o rā′shən, nyo͝o-), *n.* venation. [NEUR- + -ATION]

neu·rax·i·tis (no͝or′ak sī′tis, nyo͝or′-), *n. Pathol.* 1. inflammation of an axon. 2. encephalitis. [NEUR- + AX(IS)[1] + -ITIS]

neu·rec·to·my (no͝o rek′tə mē, nyo͝o-), *n., pl.* **-mies.** *Surg.* the removal of part or all of a nerve. [NEUR- + -ECTOMY]

neu·ri·dine (no͝or′i dēn′, -din, nyo͝or′-), *n. Biochem.* spermine. [NEUR- + -ID[3] + -INE[2]]

neu·ri·lem·ma (no͝or′ə lem′ə, nyo͝or′-), *n. Anat.* the delicate, membranous sheath of a nerve fiber. [alter. of F *névrilème* (< Gk *neur-* NEUR- + *eílēma* covering), by assoc. with LEMMA[2]] —**neu′ri·lem′mal, neu·ri·lem·mat·ic** (no͝or′ə li mat′ik, nyo͝or′-), **neu·ri·lem·ma·tous** (no͝or′ə lem′ə təs, nyo͝or′-), *adj.*

neu·rite (no͝or′īt, nyo͝or′-), *n. Anat.* axon. [NEUR- + -ITE[1]]

neu·ri·tis (no͝o rī′tis, nyo͝o-), *n. Pathol.* 1. inflammation of a nerve. 2. continuous pain in a nerve, associated with paralysis and sensory disturbances. [NEUR- + -ITIS] —**neu·rit·ic** (no͝o rit′ik, nyo͝o-), *adj.*

neuro-, a learned borrowing from Greek used, with the meaning "nerve," "sinew," "tendon," in the formation of compound words: *neurology.* Also, *esp. before a vowel,* **neur-.** [< Gk *neuro-,* comb. form of *neûron,* akin to L *nervus*]

neu·ro·a·nat·o·mist (no͝or′ō ə nat′ə mist, nyo͝or′-), *n.* a specialist in neuroanatomy. [NEUROANATOM(Y) + -IST]

neu·ro·a·nat·o·my (no͝or′ō ə nat′ə mē, nyo͝or′-), *n., pl.* **-mies.** 1. the branch of anatomy dealing with the nervous system. 2. the nerve structure of man or an animal, or of any of the parts of an organism. [NEURO- + ANATOMY] —**neu·ro·an·a·tom·i·cal** (no͝or′ō an′ə tom′i kəl, nyo͝or′-), **neu′ro·an′a·tom′ic,** *adj.*

neu·ro·blast (no͝or′ə blast′, nyo͝or′-), *n. Embryol.* one of the cells in the embryonic brain and spinal cord of vertebrates, which develop into nerve cells. [NEURO- + -BLAST] —**neu′ro·blas′tic,** *adj.*

neu·ro·cir′cu·la·to·ry asthe′nia (no͝or′ō sûr′kyə lə tôr′ē, -tōr′ē, nyo͝or′-), *Pathol.* See **cardiac neurosis.** [NEURO- + CIRCULATORY]

neu·ro·coele (no͝or′ə sēl′, nyo͝or′-), *n. Embryol.* the system of cavities of the embryonic brain and spinal cord. Also, **neu′ro·coel′, neu′ro·cele′.** [NEURO- + -COELE] —**neu′ro·coel′i·an, neu′ro·cel′i·an,** *adj.*

neu·ro·em·bry·ol·o·gy (no͝or′ō em′brē ol′ə jē, nyo͝or′-), *n.* the branch of embryology dealing with the origin and development of the nervous system. [NEURO- + EMBRYOLOGY] —**neu·ro·em·bry·o·log·i·cal** (no͝or′ō em′brē ə loj′i kəl, nyo͝or′-), **neu′ro·em′bry·o·log′ic,** *adj.* —**neu′ro·em′bry·ol′o·gist,** *n.*

neu·ro·fi·bril (no͝or′ə fī′bril, nyo͝or′-), *n. Anat.* a fibril of a nerve cell. [NEURO- + FIBRIL] —**neu′ro·fi′bri·lar,** *adj.*

neu·ro·fi·bro·ma (no͝or′ō fī brō′mə, nyo͝or′-), *n. Pathol.* a benign neoplasm composed of the fibrous elements of a nerve. [NEURO- + FIBROMA]

neu·ro·gen·ic (no͝or′ə jen′ik, nyo͝or′-), *adj. Med.* originating in a nerve or nerve tissue. Also, **neu·rog·e·nous** (no͝o roj′ə nəs, nyo͝o-). [NEURO- + GENIC]

neu·rog·li·a (no͝o rog′lē ə, nyo͝o-), *n. Anat.* the delicate connective tissue which supports and binds together the essential elements of nerve tissue in the central nervous system. [NEURO- + LGk *glía* glue] —**neu·rog′li·al, neu·rog·li·ac** (no͝o rog′lē ak′, nyo͝o-), **neu·rog′li·ar, neu·rog′lic,** *adj.*

neu·ro·gram (no͝or′ə gram′, nyo͝or′-), *n. Psychiatry.* a hypothesized alteration of the brain produced by and allowing the retention of experience. [NEURO- + -GRAM[1]] —**neu′ro·gram′mic,** *adj.*

neu·rol·o·gist (no͝o rol′ə jist, nyo͝o-), *n.* a physician specializing in neurology. [NEUROLOG(Y) + -IST]

neu·rol·o·gy (no͝o rol′ə jē, nyo͝o-), *n.* the science of the nerves and the nervous system, esp. of the diseases affecting them. [< NL *neurologia.* See NEURO-, -LOGY] —**neu·ro·log·i·cal** (no͝or′ə loj′i kəl, nyo͝or′-), *adj.*

neu·rol·y·sis (no͝o rol′i sis, nyo͝o-), *n. Pathol.* 1. disintegration of nerve tissue. 2. exhaustion of a nerve by excess stimulation. [NEURO- + -LYSIS] —**neu·ro·lyt·ic** (no͝or′ə lit′ik, nyo͝or′-), *adj.*

neu·ro·ma (no͝o rō′mə, nyo͝o-), *n., pl.* **-mas, -ma·ta** (-mə tə). *Pathol.* a tumor formed of nerve tissue. [NEUR- + -OMA] —**neu·rom·a·tous** (no͝o rom′ə təs, nyo͝o-), *adj.*

neu·ro·mast (no͝or′ə mast′, nyo͝or′-), *n.* a rheoreceptor consisting of a group of innervated sensory cells occurring along the lateral line of fishes and aquatic amphibians. [NEURO- + -MAST] —**neu′ro·mas′tic,** *adj.*

neu·ro·mus·cu·lar (no͝or′ə mus′kyə lər, nyo͝or′-), *adj.* pertaining to or affecting both nerves and muscles. [NEURO- + MUSCULAR]

neu·ron (no͝or′on, nyo͝or′-), *n.* *Anat.* a nerve cell with its processes, constituting the structural and functional unit of nerve tissue. Also, **neu·rone** (no͝or′ōn, nyo͝or′-). [< Gk *neûron* sinew, cord, nerve] —**neu·ron·ic** (no͝o ron′ik, nyo͝o-), *adj.*

Neuron
A, Dendrites; B, Cell body; C, Nucleus; D, Axon; E, Myelin sheath

neu·ro·path (no͝or′ə path′, nyo͝or′-), *n.* *Psychiatry.* a person subject to or affected with a functional nervous disease; a neurotic person. [NEURO- + -PATH]

neu·ro·pa·thol·o·gy (no͝or′ō pə thol′ə jē, nyo͝or′-), *n.* the pathology of the nervous system. [NEURO- + PATHOLOGY] —**neu′ro·pa·thol′o·gist,** *n.*

neu·rop·a·thy (no͝o rop′ə thē, nyo͝o-), *n.* any diseased condition of the nervous system. [NEURO- + -PATHY] —**neu·ro·path·ic** (no͝or′ə path′ik, nyo͝or′-), *adj.* —**neu′ro·path′i·cal·ly,** *adv.*

neu·ro·phys·i·ol·o·gy (no͝or′ō fiz′ē ol′ə jē, nyo͝or′-), *n.* the branch of physiology dealing with the nervous system. [NEURO- + PHYSIOLOGY] —**neu·ro·phys·i·o·log·i·cal** (no͝or′ō fiz′ē ə loj′i kəl, nyo͝or′-), **neu′ro·phys′i·o·log′ic,** *adj.* —**neu′ro·phys′i·o·log′i·cal·ly,** *adv.* —**neu′ro·phys′i·ol′o·gist,** *n.*

neu·ro·plasm (no͝or′ə plaz′əm, nyo͝or′-), *n.* *Anat.* the protoplasm of a nerve cell. [NEURO- + -PLASM] —**neu·ro·plas·mat·ic** (no͝or′ō plaz mat′ik, nyo͝or′-), **neu′ro·plas′mic,** *adj.*

neu·ro·psy·chi·a·try (no͝or′ō sī kī′ə trē, nyo͝or′-), *n.* the branch of medicine dealing with diseases involving the mind and nervous system. [NEURO- + PSYCHIATRY] —**neu·ro·psy·chi·at·ric** (no͝or′ō sī′kē a′trik, nyo͝or′-), *adj.* —**neu′ro·psy·chi′a·trist,** *n.*

neu·ro·psy·cho·sis (no͝or′ō sī kō′sis, nyo͝or′-), *n.* *Pathol.* mental derangement in association with nervous disease. [NEURO- + PSYCHOSIS] —**neu·ro·psy·chot·ic** (no͝or′ō sī kot′ik, nyo͝or′-), *adj.*

neu·rop·ter·ous (no͝o rop′tər əs, nyo͝o-), *adj.* *Entomol.* belonging or pertaining to the *Neuroptera,* an order of insects characterized by four membranous wings having netlike venation, comprising the antlions, lacewings, etc. [< NL *Neuropter(a)* + -OUS. See NEURO-, -PTEROUS] —**neu·rop′ter·on,** *n.*

neu·ro·sis (no͝o rō′sis, nyo͝o-), *n., pl.* **-ses** (-sēz). psychoneurosis. [< NL; see NEUR-, -OSIS]

neu·ro·sur·ger·y (no͝or′ō sûr′jə rē, nyo͝or′-), *n.* the branch of medicine dealing with the surgery of nerve tissue. [NEURO- + SURGERY] —**neu·ro·sur·geon** (no͝or′ō sûr′jən, nyo͝or′-), *n.* —**neu′ro·sur′gi·cal,** *adj.*

neu·rot·ic[1] (no͝o rot′ik, nyo͝o-), *adj.* **1.** having a psychoneurosis. —*n.* **2.** a person affected with psychoneurosis. [NEUR(OSIS) + -OTIC] —**neu·rot′i·cal·ly,** *adv.*

neu·rot·ic[2] (no͝o rot′ik, nyo͝o-), *adj.* *Pathol.* pertaining to the nerves or to nerve disease. [NEURO- + -TIC]

neu·rot·o·my (no͝o rot′ə mē, nyo͝o-), *n., pl.* **-mies.** *Surg.* the cutting of a nerve, as to relieve neuralgia. [NEURO- + -TOMY] —**neu·ro·tom·i·cal** (no͝or′ə tom′i kəl, nyo͝or′-), *adj.* —**neu·rot′o·mist,** *n.*

neu·ro·tox·ic (no͝or′ō tok′sik, nyo͝or′-), *adj.* poisonous to nerve tissue, as to the brain or spinal cord. [NEURO- + TOXIC]

neu·ro·tox·in (no͝or′ō tok′sin, nyo͝or′-), *n.* a neurotoxic substance, as rattlesnake venom or the poison of a black widow spider. [NEURO- + TOXIN]

neu·ro·troph·ic (no͝or′ə trof′ik, -trō′fik, nyo͝or′-), *adj.* **1.** of or pertaining to the effect of nerves on the nutritive processes. **2.** neurotropic. [NEURO- + -TROPHIC]

neu·rot·ro·phy (no͝o ro′trə fē, nyo͝o-), *n.* the influence of the nerves on the nutrition and maintenance of body tissue. [NEURO- + -TROPHY]

neu·ro·trop·ic (no͝or′ə trop′ik, -trō′pik, nyo͝or′-), *adj.* *Med.* having an affinity for nerve cells or tissue: *a neurotropic virus; a neurotropic drug.* [NEURO- + -TROPIC]

neu·rot·ro·pism (no͝o ro′trə piz′əm, nyo͝o-), *n.* the quality of being neurotropic. Also, **neu·rot′ro·py.** [NEURO- + -TROPISM]

neu·ro·vas·cu·lar (no͝or′ə vas′kyə lər, nyo͝or′-), *adj.* *Anat.* of, pertaining to, or involving the nerves and blood vessels. [NEURO- + VASCULAR]

neu·ru·la (no͝or′ə lə, nyo͝or′-), *n., pl.* **-las, -lae** (-lē′, -lī′). *Embryol.* an embryo in the stage of development in which part of the ectoderm is differentiated into neural tissue and in which the neural tube, which develops into the brain and spinal cord, is formed. [NEUR- + L *-ula* -ULE] —**neu′ru·lar,** *adj.* —**neu′ru·la′tion,** *n.*

Neu·satz (noi′zäts), *n.* German name of **Novi Sad.**

neus·ton (no͞o′ston, nyo͞o′-), *n.* the aggregate of minute aquatic organisms that float or swim in the surface film of a body of water. [< G; n. use of neut. of Gk *neustós* swimming, verbal of *neîn* to swim] —**neus′tic, neus·ton·ic** (no͞o ston′ik, nyo͞o-), *adj.*

Neus·tri·a (no͞o′strē ə, nyo͞o′-), *n.* the west part of the Frankish kingdom, corresponding roughly to north and northwest France. —**Neus′tri·an,** *adj.*

neut., neuter.

neu·ter (no͞o′tər, nyo͞o′-), *adj.* **1.** *Gram.* **a.** noting or pertaining to a gender in certain languages, as Latin, that refers to things classed as neither masculine nor feminine or to a gender in certain languages, as Swedish, opposed to common, that may be distinguished by formal characteristics, as the nominative *-um* ending in Latin, and by the agreement of modifying adjectives, as in Latin *magnum cor* "big heart." **b.** (of a verb) intransitive. **2.** *Zool.* having imperfectly developed sexual organs, as the worker bees and ants. **3.** *Bot.* having neither stamens nor pistils; asexual. **4.** neutral; siding with no one. —*n.* **5.** *Gram.* **a.** the neuter gender. **b.** a noun of that gender. **c.** another element marking that gender. **d.** an intransitive verb. **6.** an animal made sterile by castration. **7.** *Zool.* a neuter insect. **8.** *Bot.* a plant with neither stamens nor pistils. **9.** one who or that which is neutral. [< L *neuter* neither (of two), equiv. to *ne* not + *uter* either (of two); r. ME *neutre* < MF]

neu·tral (no͞o′trəl, nyo͞o′-), *adj.* **1.** (of a person or government) not taking part or giving assistance in a dispute or war between others. **2.** not aligned with or supporting any side or position in a controversy. **3.** of no particular kind, characteristics, etc.; indefinite: *a neutral personality that made no impression whatever.* **4.** (of a color or shade) **a.** gray; without hue; of zero chroma; achromatic. **b.** matching well with many or most other colors or shades, as white or a pastel: *I'd like a sweater in a neutral shade to match both these skirts.* **5.** *Bot., Zool.* neuter. **6.** *Chem.* exhibiting neither acid nor alkaline qualities: *neutral salts.* **7.** *Elect., Magnetism.* neither positive nor negative; not electrified; not magnetized; electroneutral. —*n.* **8.** a person or a state that remains neutral, as in a controversy or war. **9.** a citizen of a neutral nation during a war. **10.** *Mach.* the position or state of disengaged gears or other interconnecting parts: *in neutral.* [< L *neutrāl(is)* neuter. See NEUTER, -AL[1]] —**neu′tral·ly,** *adv.*

neu′tral acrifla′vine, *Chem.* acriflavine.

neu′tral ax′is, an imaginary line in the cross section of a beam, shaft, or the like, along which no stresses occur.

neu′tral cor′ner, *Boxing.* either of the two corners of the ring not assigned for use between rounds.

neu·tral·ise (no͞o′trə līz′, nyo͞o′-), *v.t., v.i.,* **-ised, -is·ing.** *Chiefly Brit.* neutralize. —**neu′tral·is′er,** *n.*

neu·tral·ism (no͞o′trə liz′əm, nyo͞o′-), *n.* the policy or practice of maintaining strict neutrality in foreign affairs. [NEUTRAL + -ISM]

neu·tral·ist (no͞o′trə list, nyo͞o′-), *n.* a person who advocates or adheres to a policy of strict neutrality in foreign affairs. [NEUTRAL + -IST]

neu·tral·i·ty (no͞o tral′i tē, nyo͞o-), *n.* **1.** the state of being neutral. **2.** the policy or status of a nation which does not participate in a war between other nations: *the continuous neutrality of Switzerland.* **3.** neutral status, as of a seaport during a war. [NEUTRAL + -ITY]

neu·tral·i·za·tion (no͞o′trə li zā′shən, nyo͞o′-), *n.* **1.** the act, process, or an instance of neutralizing. **2.** the quality or condition of being neutralized. **3.** *Ling.* the loss of a distinctive feature of one of a pair of phonemes that are otherwise differentiated solely on the basis of that feature, as the loss of voice as a distinctive feature between the *-t-* and *-d-* of *latter* and *ladder.* Also, *esp. Brit.,* **neu′tral·i·sa′tion.** [NEUTRALIZE + -ATION]

neu·tral·ize (no͞o′trə līz′, nyo͞o′-), *v.,* **-ized, -iz·ing.** —*v.t.* **1.** to make neutral; cause to undergo neutralization. **2.** to make (something) ineffective; counteract; nullify: *carelessness that neutralized our efforts.* **3.** *Mil.* to put out of action or make incapable of action: *to neutralize a bomb; to neutralize an enemy position.* **4.** to declare neutral; invest with neutrality: *to neutralize a city to prevent bombing.* **5.** *Chem.* to add acid to an alkaline solution or an alkali to an acid solution until neutral. **6.** *Elect.* to render electrically or magnetically neutral. —*v.i.* **7.** to become neutral or neutralized; undergo neutralization: *With this additive the solution begins to neutralize.* Also, *esp. Brit.,* **neutralise.** [NEUTRAL + -IZE] —**neu′tral·iz′er,** *n.*

neu′tral mon′ism, *Philos.* the theory that mind and matter consist of different relations between entities which are themselves neither mental nor physical. —**neu′tral mon′ist.**

neu′tral spir′its, nonflavored alcohol of 95 percent, or 190 proof, obtained chiefly from grain or molasses or redistilled from brandy, rum, etc., and used for blending with straight whiskies, and in the making of gin, cordials, liqueurs, and the like.

neu′tral zone′, *Ice Hockey.* the area of a rink between the two blue lines. Cf. **end zone** (def. 2).

neu·tret·to (no͞o tret′ō, nyo͞o-), *n., pl.* **-tos.** *Physics.* a meson with zero charge. [NEUTR(ON) + It *-etto* dim. suffix]

neu·tri·no (no͞o trē′nō, nyo͞o-), *n., pl.* **-nos.** *Physics.* an elementary particle having zero rest mass and charge and spin of ½, emitted with electrons and positrons in certain radioactive-decay processes. [NEUTR(ON) + It *-ino* adj. suffix]

neutro-, a combining form meaning "neutral": *neutrosphere.* [< LL < L *neutr-.* See NEUTER, -O-]

neu·tron (no͞o′tron, nyo͞o′-), *n.* *Physics.* an elementary particle having no charge, mass slightly greater than that of a proton, and spin of ½: a constituent of the nuclei of all atoms except those of hydrogen. *Symbol:* n [NEUTR(O) + -ON[1]]

neu′tron bomb′, a nuclear bomb releasing a shower of neutrons fatal to life with a relatively small amount of blast and small amount of contamination, so that the target area may be occupied and used in a normal manner shortly after the detonation of the bomb. Also called **N-bomb.**

neu′tron num′ber, *Physics.* the number of neutrons in the nucleus of an atom, equal to the mass number minus the atomic number of the atom.

neu′tron star′, a hypothetical nonluminous star so dense that the protons and electrons in its core have coalesced into neutrons.

neu·tro·phil (no͞o′trə fil, nyo͞o′-), *adj.* **1.** (of a cell or cell part) having an affinity for neutral dyes. —*n.* **2.** *Anat.* a phagocytic leukocyte having a lobulate nucleus and neutrophil granules in the cytoplasm. Also, **neu·tro·phile** (no͞o′trə fīl′, nyo͞o′-). [NEUTRO- + -PHIL]

neu·tro·sphere (no͞o′trə sfēr′, nyo͞o′-), *n.* the part of the atmosphere whose constituents are, for the most part, electrically neutral, extending from the earth's surface to the base of the ionosphere. [NEUTRO- + SPHERE]

Nev., Nevada.

Ne·va (nē′və; *for 1 also Russ.* ni vä′), *n.* **1.** a river in the NW Soviet Union in Europe, flowing from Lake Ladoga through Leningrad into the Gulf of Finland: canalized for ships. 40 mi. long. **2.** a girl's given name, form of **Nevada** or **Geneva.**

Ne·vad·a (nə vad′ə, -vä′də *for 1, 4;* nə vä′də *for 2, 3, 4*), *n.* **1.** a State in the W United States. 285,278 (1960); 110,540 sq. mi. *Cap.:* Carson City. *Abbr.:* Nev. **2.** a town in W Missouri. 8416 (1960). **3.** a town in central Iowa. 4227 (1960). **4.** a girl's given name.

OREGON
IDAHO
Winnemucca
Elko
Reno
Nevada
UTAH
Carson City
Ely
SIERRA NEVADA
LAKE TAHOE
Tonopah
Las Vegas
CALIFORNIA
0 50 100 150
MILES
Colorado River
HOOVER DAM
ARIZ.

né·vé (nā vā′), *n.* **1.** granular snow accumulated on high mountains and subsequently compacted into glacial ice. **2.** a field of such snow. Also called **firn.** [< F, alter. of SwissF *nevé* < LL **nivātum,* n. use of neut. of L *nivātus* snow-cooled, equiv. to *niv-* (s. of *nix* snow) + *-ātus* -ATE[1]]

nev·er (nev′ər), *adv.* **1.** not ever; at no time: *Such an idea never occurred to me.* **2.** not at all; absolutely not: *Go back there again? Never!* **3.** to no extent or degree: *He was never the wiser for his experience.* [ME; OE *nǣfre,* equiv. to *ne* not + *ǣfre* EVER]

nev·er·mind (nev′ər mīnd′, nev′ər mīnd′), *n.* *Dial.* **1.** attention; heed; notice (usually used in negative constructions): *Pay him no nevermind.* **2.** business; affair; responsibility (usually used in negative constructions): *It's no nevermind of yours.* [n. use of v. phrase *never mind*]

nev·er·more (nev′ər mōr′, -môr′), *adv.* never again: *And nevermore were the elves seen in that town.* [ME; see NEVER, MORE]

nev·er-nev·er (nev′ər nev′ər), *n.* **1.** any remote, isolated, barren, or sparsely settled region. **2.** an unreal, imaginary, or ideal state, condition, place, etc. **3.** *Brit. Slang.* See **hire-purchase system.** —*adj.* **4.** not real or true; imaginary; illusory: *the never-never world of the cinema.* Also called **nev′er-nev′er land′** (for defs. 1, 2).

Ne·vers (nə ver′), *n.* a city in and the capital of Nièvre, in central France, on the Loire River: Romanesque church. 41,051 (1962).

nev·er·the·less (nev′ər thə les′), *adv.* nonetheless; notwithstanding; however; in spite of that. [ME; see NEVER, THE, LESS] —**Syn.** See **but**[1].

Ne·vi·im (nə vē ēm′), *n.* *Hebrew.* Nebiim.

Nev·il (nev′il), *n.* a boy's given name, form of **Neville.**

Nev·ille (nev′il), *n.* **1. Richard.** See **Warwick, Earl of. 2.** a boy's given name.

Nev·in (nev′in), *n.* **Ethelbert Wood·bridge** (wo͝od′brij), 1862–1901, U.S. composer.

Nev·ins (nev′inz), *n.* **Allan,** born 1890, U.S. historian.

Ne·vis (nē′vis, nev′is), *n.* **1.** one of the Leeward Islands, in the E West Indies: a member of the West Indies Associated States; formerly a British colony. 12,761 (1960); 50 sq. mi. Cf. **St. Kitts-Nevis-Anguilla. 2. Ben.** See **Ben Nevis.**

Nev·ski (nev′skē, nef′-), *n.* **Alexander.** See **Alexander Nevski.**

ne·vus (nē′vəs), *n., pl.* **-vi** (-vī). *Med.* any congenital anomaly of the skin, including various types of birthmarks and all types of moles. Also, **naevus.** [sp. var. of L *naevus:* mole[1]] —**ne·void** (nē′void), *adj.*

new (no͞o, nyo͞o), *adj.* **1.** of recent origin, production, purchase, etc.; having but lately come or been brought into being: *a new book.* **2.** of a kind now existing or appearing for the first time; novel: *a new concept of the universe.* **3.** having but lately or but now come into knowledge: *a new chemical element.* **4.** unfamiliar or strange (often fol. by *to*): *ideas new to us.* **5.** having but lately come to a place, position, status, etc.: *a reception for our new minister.* **6.** unaccustomed (usually fol. by *to*): *men new to such work.* **7.** coming or occurring afresh; further; additional: *new gains.* **8.** fresh or unused: *to start a new sheet of paper.* **9.** (of physical or moral qualities) different and better: *The vacation made a new man of him.* **10.** other than the former or the old: *a new era.* **11.** being the later or latest of two or more things of the same kind: *the New Testament; a new edition.* **12.** (*cap.*) (of a language) in its latest known period, esp. as a living language at the present time: *New High German.* —*adv.* **13.** recently or lately (usually used in combination): *The valley was green with new-planted crops.* **14.** freshly; anew or afresh (often used in combination): *roses new washed with dew; the refreshing smell of new-mown hay.* —*n.* **15.** that which is new; a new object, quality, condition, etc.: *Ring out the old, ring in the new.* [ME *newe,* OE *nēowe,* var. of *nīewe,* c. D *nieuw,* G *neu,* Icel *nýr,* Goth *niujis,* Gk *neîos;* akin to L *novus,* Gk *néos,* Skt *návas*] —**new′ness,** *n.*
—**Syn. 1.** modern; late. NEW, FRESH, NOVEL describe that which is not old. NEW applies to that which has not been long in existence: *a new broom, dress* (one recently made or bought). FRESH suggests a condition of newness, not yet affected by use or the passage of time: *a fresh towel, dress* (newly clean). NOVEL suggests newness which has an unexpected quality, or is strange or striking, but generally pleasing: *a novel experience, dress* (a dress of unusual design, or the like).

New′ Al′bany, 1. a city in S Indiana, on the Ohio River. 37,812 (1960). **2.** a town in N Mississippi. 5151 (1960).

New′ Am′ster·dam (am′stər dam′), a former Dutch town on Manhattan Island: the capital of New Netherland; renamed New York by the British in 1664.

Ne·war (ni wär′), *n., pl.* **-wars,** (*esp. collectively*) **-war.** a member of a Mongoloid people of Nepal.

Ne·wa·ri (ni wär′ē), *n.* a Sino-Tibetan language, the language of the Newars.

New·ark (no͞o′ərk, nyo͞o′-), *n.* **1.** a city in NE New Jersey, on Newark Bay. 405,220 (1960). **2.** a city in central Ohio. 41,790 (1960). **3.** a city in N Delaware. 11,404 (1960). **4.** a town in W California. 9884 (1960).

New′ark Bay′, a bay in NE New Jersey. 6 mi. long; 1 mi. wide.

New′ Atlan′tis, a political allegory by Francis Bacon, published in 1627.

New′ Bal′timore, a town in E Michigan. 3159 (1960).

New′ Bed′ford, a seaport in SE Massachusetts: formerly a chief whaling port. 102,477 (1960).

New·berg (no͞o′bûrg, nyo͞o′-), *n.* a town in NW Oregon. 4204 (1960).

New′ Ber′lin, a city in SE Wisconsin, near Milwaukee. 15,788 (1960).

New′ Bern′, a city in E North Carolina. 15,717 (1960).

New·ber·ry (no͞o′ber′ē, -bə rē, nyo͞o′-), *n.* **1.** a town in NW South Carolina. 8208 (1960). **2.** a town in NW Michigan, in the Upper Peninsula. 2612 (1960).

CONCISE PRONUNCIATION KEY: act, āble, dâre, ärt; ebb, ēqual; if, īce; hot, ōver, ôrder, oil, bo͝ok, o͞oze, out; up, ûrge; chief; sing; shoe; thin, that; zh as in *measure.* ə = *a* as in *alone,* *e* as in *system,* *i* as in *easily,* *o* as in *gallop,* *u* as in *circus;* ᵊ as in *button* (butᵊn), *fire* (fīᵊr), *cradle* (krādᵊl). See the full key inside the front cover.

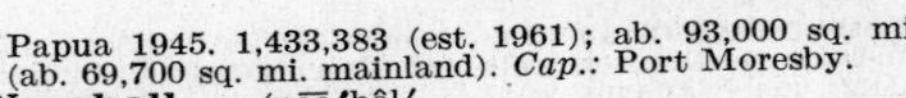

New·ber·y (no͞o′ber/ē, -bə rē, nyo͞o′-), *n.* **John,** 1713–67, English publisher.

New′bery Award′, an annual award for the most distinguished book for juveniles.

New·bold (no͞o′bōld, nyo͞o′-), *n.* a boy's given name.

New·bolt (no͞o′bōlt, nyo͞o′-), *n.* **Sir Henry John,** 1862–1938, English poet, novelist, naval historian, and critic.

new·born (no͞o′bôrn′, nyo͞o′-), *adj., n., pl.* **-born, -borns.** —*adj.* **1.** recently or only just born. **2.** born anew; reborn: *a newborn faith in his fellow-man.* —*n.* **3.** a newborn infant; neonate. [ME; see NEW, BORN]

New′ Bos′ton, 1. a town in S Ohio. 3984 (1960). **2.** a town in NE Texas. 2773 (1960).

New′ Braun′fels (broun′fəlz), a city in S Texas, near San Antonio. 15,631 (1960).

New′ Brigh′ton, 1. a town in W Pennsylvania. 8397 (1960). **2.** a town in E Minnesota. 6448 (1960).

New′ Brit′ain, 1. a city in central Connecticut. 82,201 (1960). **2.** an island in the S Pacific, NE of New Guinea: the largest island in the Bismarck Archipelago. 118,796 including adjacent islands (est. 1961); ab. 14,600 sq. mi. *Cap.:* Rabaul.

New′ Bruns′wick, 1. a province in SE Canada, E of Maine. 597,936 (1961); 27,985 sq. mi. *Cap.:* Fredericton. **2.** a city in central New Jersey. 40,139 (1960).

New·burg (no͞o′bûrg, nyo͞o′-), *adj.* (of sea food) cooked with a sauce of cream, egg yolk, butter, and usually brandy or wine. [? from phrase (*lobster*) *Newburg*]

New·burgh (no͞o′bûrg, nyo͞o′-), *n.* a city in SE New York, on the Hudson. 30,979 (1960).

New′burgh Heights′, a town in N Ohio. 3512 (1960).

New·bur·y·port (no͞o′bə rē pôrt′, -pôrt′, -ber′ē-, nyo͞o′-), a city in NE Massachusetts. 14,004 (1960).

New′ Cal·e·do·ni·a (kal′i dō′nē ə, -dōn′yə), **1.** an island in the S Pacific, ab. 800 mi. E of Australia. 46,643 (1952); 6224 sq. mi. **2.** an overseas territory of France comprising this island and other smaller islands: formerly a penal colony. 78,000 (est. 1960); 7200 sq. mi. *Cap.:* Nouméa.

new′ can′dle, *Optics.* candle (def. 3a).

New′ Carlisle′, a town in central Ohio. 4107 (1960).

New′ Cas·tile′ (ka stēl′), a region in central Spain: formerly a province. 27,933 sq. mi. Spanish, **Castilla la Nueva.**

New′ Cas′tle, 1. a city in W Pennsylvania. 44,790 (1960). **2.** a city in E Indiana. 20,349 (1960). **3.** a town in N Delaware. 4469 (1960).

New·cas·tle (no͞o′kas′əl, -kä′səl, nyo͞o′-), *n.* **1. 1st Duke of.** See **Pelham-Holles, Thomas. 2.** Also called **New·cas·tle-up·on-Tyne** (no͞o′kas′əl ə pon′tīn′, -ə-pôn′-, -kä′səl-, nyo͞o′-), a seaport in SE Northumberland, in NE England, on the Tyne River: shipbuilding. 269,389 (1961). **3.** a seaport in E New South Wales, in SE Australia. 208,630 (1961). **4.** a town in NE Wyoming. 4345 (1960). **5. carry coals to Newcastle, a.** to take something to a place where its kind exists in great quantity, so that it is redundant. **b.** to do something wholly unnecessary.

New′castle disease′, *Vet. Pathol.* a specific virus-induced disease of birds and domestic fowl, as chickens, marked by loss of egg production in old birds and by paralysis in chicks. Also called **avian pneumoencephalitis, avian pseudoplague, Philippine fowl disease, pneumoencephalitis, Rhanikhet disease.** [after *Newcastle-upon-Tyne*]

New′ Church′. See **New Jerusalem Church.**

New·chwang (no͞o′chwäng′, nyo͞o′-), *n.* Yingkow.

New·comb (no͞o′kəm, nyo͞o′-), *n.* **1. Simon,** 1835–1909, U.S. astronomer. **2.** a crater in the first quadrant of the face of the moon: about 32 miles in diameter.

New′ Com′edy, Greek comedy arising toward the end of the 4th century B.C. which employed stock characters and plots, the formulas of which were adopted by later Roman writers for the comic stage. Cf. **Middle Comedy, Old Comedy.**

New·com·en (no͞o kum′ən, nyo͞o-), *n.* **Thomas,** 1663–1729, English inventor.

new·com·er (no͞o′kum′ər, nyo͞o′-), *n.* a person who has recently arrived; new arrival: *a newcomer to our city; a newcomer in the field of advertising.* [NEW + COMER]

New·com·ers·town (no͞o′kum′ərz toun′, nyo͞o′-), *n.* a town in E Ohio. 4273 (1960).

new′ cov′enant, (in Christian exegesis) the promises of salvation made by God to men individually, based on divine grace rather than Mosaic Law.

new′ crit′icism, (*often caps.*) an approach to the critical study of literature which concentrates on textual explication and rejects historical and biographical study as irrelevant to an understanding of the total formal organization of a work (often prec. by *the*). Cf. **explication de texte.** —**new′ crit′ic.**

New′ Cum′berland, a town in central Pennsylvania. 9257 (1960).

New′ Deal′, 1. the principles of the progressive wing of the Democratic party, esp. those advocated under the leadership of President Franklin D. Roosevelt. **2.** the presidential administration of Franklin D. Roosevelt, esp. during the period from 1933 to 1941. Cf. **Fair Deal, Great Society, New Frontier.** —**New′ Deal′er.**

New′ Del′hi, a city in and the capital of India, in the N part, adjacent to Delhi. 261,500 (1961). Cf. **Delhi** (def. 2).

New′ Ea′gle, a town in SW Pennsylvania. 2670 (1960).

New′ Econom′ic Pol′icy, (in the Soviet Union) a program in effect from 1921 to 1928, reviving the wage system and private ownership of some factories and businesses, and abandoning grain requisitions.

new·el (no͞o′əl, nyo͞o′-), *n.* **1.** a central pillar or upright from which the steps of a winding stair radiate. **2.** (on an escalator) the horizontal section of railing at the upper or lower end. **3.** See **newel post.** [earlier *nuel*, ME *nowel* < MF *no(u)el* kernel, newel < LL **nucāle*, n. use of neut. of *nucālis* of a nut, nutlike, equiv. to *nuc-* (s. of *nux*) nut + *-ālis* -AL[1]]

N, Newel

New·ell (no͞o′əl, nyo͞o′-), *n.* a boy's given name.

new′el post′, a post supporting one end of a handrail at the top or bottom of a flight of stairs.

New′ Em′pire. See **New Kingdom.**

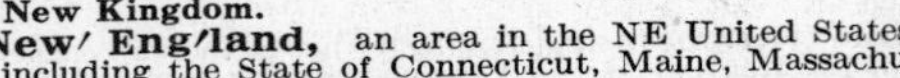

New′ Eng′land, an area in the NE United States, including the State of Connecticut, Maine, Massachusetts, New Hampshire, Rhode Island, and Vermont. —**New′ Eng′lander** —**New′ Eng′landish.**

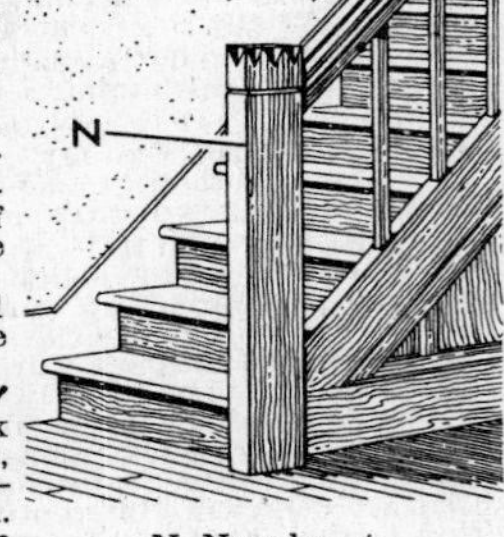

N, Newel post

New′ Eng′land as′ter, a tall aster, *Aster novaeangliae*, of northeastern U.S., the flowers of which have deep-purple rays.

New′ Eng′land boiled′ din′ner. See **boiled dinner.**

New′ Eng′land clam′ chow′der, a thick chowder made from clams, salt pork, onions, potatoes, and milk or cream. Cf. **Manhattan clam chowder.**

New′ Eng′land theol′ogy, Calvinism as modified and interpreted by the descendants of the Puritans in New England, esp. Jonathan Edwards, and which became the dominant theology there from about 1730 to 1880.

New′ Eng′lish. See **Modern English.**

new·fan·gled (no͞o′fang′gəld, nyo͞o′-), *adj.* **1.** of a new kind or fashion: *newfangled ideas.* **2.** fond of or given to novelty: *Only the newfangled teen-agers will go for it.* [ME *newefangel* taken by what is new (*newe* NEW + *-fangel*, OE **-fangol*, equiv. to *fang-* take + *-(o)l* adj. suffix) + -ED[3]] —**new′fan′gled·ly,** *adv.* —**new′fan′gled·ness,** *n.*

new-fash·ioned (no͞o′fash′ənd, nyo͞o′-), *adj.* lately come into fashion; of a new fashion.

New′ For′est, a forest region in S England, in Hampshire: national park. 145 sq. mi.

New·found·land (no͞o′fənd land′, -lənd, -fən-, nyo͞o′-; no͞o-found′lənd, nyo͞o-), *n.* **1.** a large island in E Canada. 444,319 (1961); 42,734 sq. mi. **2.** a province in E Canada, composed of Newfoundland island and Labrador. 457,853 (1961); 155,364 sq. mi. *Cap.:* St. John's. **3.** one of a breed of large, powerful dogs having a dense, oily, usually black coat, raised originally in Newfoundland.

Newfoundland (28 in. high at shoulder)

New·found·land·er (no͞o-found′lən dər, nyo͞o-), *n.* a native or inhabitant of Newfoundland. [NEWFOUNDLAND + -ER[1]]

New′ France′, the French colonies and possessions in North America up to 1763.

New′ Frontier′, the principles of the liberal wing of the Democratic party under the leadership of President John F. Kennedy. Cf. **Fair Deal, Great Society, New Deal.**

New′ Frontiers′man, an advocate or follower of the New Frontier, esp. one in public service. —**New′ Fron·tiers′man·ship′.**

New·gate (no͞o′gāt′, -git, nyo͞o′-), *n.* a prison in London, England: torn down 1902.

New′ Geor′gia, 1. a group of islands in the Solomon Islands: a British protectorate. **2.** the chief island of this group. 50 mi. long; 20 mi. wide.

New′ Glas′gow, a city in N central Nova Scotia, in E Canada. 9782 (1961).

New′ Grana′da, 1. a former Spanish viceroyalty in NW South America, comprising the present republics of Ecuador, Venezuela, Colombia, and Panama. **2.** early name of Colombia (before the secession of Panama).

New′ Greek′. See **Modern Greek.**

new·ground (no͞o′ground′, nyo͞o′-), *n.* *Chiefly Southern U.S.* a tract of land recently cleared for cultivation. [NEW + GROUND[1]]

New′ Guin′ea, 1. Also called **Papua.** a large island N of Australia, divided into the Indonesian province of West Irian and the merged Australian territories of Papua and North East New Guinea. 2,091,373 (est. 1959); ab. 316,000 sq. mi. **2. Territory of,** a territory under the trusteeship of Australia, including North East New Guinea, the Bismarck Archipelago, Bougainville, and other islands: merged with the Territory of Papua 1945. 1,433,383 (est. 1961); ab. 93,000 sq. mi. (ab. 69,700 sq. mi. mainland). *Cap.:* Port Moresby.

New·hall (no͞o′hôl′, nyo͞o′-), *n.* a town in S California. 4705 (1960).

New′ Hamp′shire, 1. a State in the NE United States. 606,921 (1960); 9304 sq. mi. *Cap.:* Concord. *Abbr.:* N.H. **2.** one of an American breed of chestnut-red chickens raised for meat and eggs.

New′ Hamp′ton, a town in NE Iowa. 3456 (1960).

New′ Har′mony, a town in SW Indiana: socialistic community established by Robert Owen 1825. 1121 (1960).

New′ Ha′ven (hā′vən), **1.** a seaport in S Connecticut, on Long Island Sound. 152,048 (1960). **2.** a town in NE Indiana. 3396 (1960).

New′ Ha′ven stem′, *Naut.* a straight stem for flat-bottomed boats in which the ends of the side planking are mitered and covered with a sheet of metal, the stem piece being wholly inside.

New′ Ha′ven theol′ogy, Taylorism.

New′ Heb′rides, an island group in the S Pacific, ab. 1000 mi. NE of Australia: under joint British and French administration. 64,400 (est. 1963); ab. 5700 sq. mi. *Cap.:* Vila.

New′ High′ Ger′man, the High German language since c1500.

New′ Hol′land, a town in SE Pennsylvania. 3425 (1960).

New·house (no͞o′hous′, nyo͞o′-), *n.* **Samuel I(rving),** 1895–1979, U.S. publisher.

New′ Ibe′ria, a city in S Louisiana. 29,062 (1960).

Ne Win (ne′ win′), (*Maung Shu Maung*) born 1911, Burmese general and statesman: prime minister 1958–60 and since 1962.

New′ Ire′land, an island in the S Pacific, in the Bismarck Archipelago, NE of New Guinea. 40,151 with adjacent islands (est. 1961); ab. 3800 sq. mi.

new·ish (no͞o′ish, nyo͞o′-), *adj.* rather new. [NEW + -ISH[1]]

New′ Jer′sey, a State in the E United States, on the Atlantic coast. 6,066,782 (1960); 7836 sq. mi. *Cap.:* Trenton. *Abbr.:* N.J. —**New′ Jer′sey·an, New′ Jer′sey·ite** (jûr′zē īt′).

New′ Jer′sey plan′, *Amer. Hist.* a plan, unsuccessfully proposed at the Constitutional Convention, providing for a single legislative house with equal representation for each State. Cf. **Connecticut Compromise, Virginia plan.**

New′ Jer′sey tea′, a North American shrub, *Ceanothus americanus*, the leaves of which were used as a substitute for tea during the American Revolution. Also called **Indian tea, Walpole tea.**

New′ Jeru′salem, the abode of God and His saints. Rev. 21:2. Also called **Heavenly City, Celestial City.**

New′ Jeru′salem Church′, the church composed of the followers of Swedenborg; the Swedenborgian church. Also called **Church of the New Jerusalem, New Church.**

New′ Ken′sington, a city in W Pennsylvania. 23,485 (1960).

New′ King′dom, the period in the history of ancient Egypt, 1580–1085 B.C., comprising the 18th to 20th dynasties, characterized by the predominance of Thebes. Also called **New Empire.** Cf. **Middle Kingdom, Old Kingdom.**

New·land (no͞o′lənd, nyo͞o′-), *n.* a boy's given name.

New′ Lat′in, Neo-Latin.

New′ Learn′ing, the learning of the 16th century in England, identified mainly with Colet, Erasmus, and More and based on the study of the Bible and the classics.

New′ Left′, *U.S.* a group of liberals, esp. young intellectuals and college students, that (since 1960) has advocated complete racial equality, disarmament, nonintervention in foreign affairs, and radical changes in the political and economic system.

New′ Lex′ington, a town in central Ohio. 4514 (1960).

New·lon (no͞o′lən, nyo͞o′-), *n.* a boy's given name, form of **Newland.**

New′ Lon′don, 1. a seaport in SE Connecticut, on the Thames River: naval base. 34,182 (1960). **2.** a town in central Wisconsin. 5288 (1960).

new′ look′, a new or changed appearance, esp. one characterized by marked departure from the previous or traditional appearance.

new·ly (no͞o′lē, nyo͞o′-), *adv.* **1.** recently; lately: *a newly wedded couple.* **2.** anew or afresh: *a newly repeated slander.* **3.** in a new manner or form: *a room newly decorated.* [ME; OE *nīwlice.* See NEW, -LY]

new·ly·wed (no͞o′lē wed′, nyo͞o′-), *n.* a person who has recently married. [NEWLY + WED]

New′ Madrid′, a town in SE Missouri. 2867 (1960).

New·man (no͞o′mən, nyo͞o′-), *n.* **1. John Henry, Cardinal,** 1801–90, English theologian and author. **2.** a boy's given name.

New·man·ise (no͞o′mə nīz′, nyo͞o′-), *v.i.*, **-ised, -ising.** *Chiefly Brit.* Newmanize.

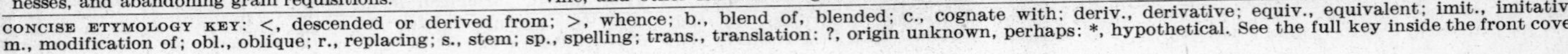

New·man·ism (no͞o′mə niz′əm, nyo͞o′-), *n.* *Theol., Eccles.* the views and theories of John Henry Newman before his conversion to the Roman Catholic Church, in which he held that the Thirty-nine Articles of the Church of England are compatible with Roman Catholicism. [NEWMAN + -ISM]

New·man·ite (no͞o′mə nīt′, nyo͞o′-), *n.* **1.** an adherent of John Henry Newman. **2.** a supporter of Newmanism. [NEWMAN + -ITE[1]]

New·man·ize (no͞o′mə nīz′, nyo͞o′-), *v.i.*, **-ized, -iz·ing.** to adopt or follow Newmanism. Also, *esp. Brit.*, **Newmanise.** [NEWMAN + -IZE]

New·mar·ket (no͞o′mär′kit, nyo͞o′-), *n.* **1.** a town in SE Cambridgeshire, in E England, E of Cambridge: horse races. 20,887 (1961). **2.** a town in SE New Hampshire. 2745 (1960). **3.** (*often l.c.*) Also called **New′market coat′.** a long, close-fitting coat worn in the 19th century as an overcoat by women and as a riding coat by men. **4.** *Brit.* the card game Michigan.

New′ Mar′tinsville, a town in NW West Virginia. 5607 (1960).

new′ math′, a unified, sequential system of teaching arithmetic and mathematics in accord with set theory and to reveal basic concepts: used in some U.S. schools since the 1950's. Also called **new′ mathemat′ics.**

New′ Mex′ico, a State in the SW United States. 951,023 (1960); 121,666 sq. mi. *Cap.:* Santa Fe. *Abbr.:* N. Mex., N.M. —**New′ Mex′i·can.**

New′ Mil′ford, 1. a city in NE New Jersey. 18,810 (1960). **2.** a town in W Connecticut. 3023 (1960).

new-mint (no͞o′mint′, nyo͞o′-), *v.t.* **1.** to mint or coin afresh. **2.** to give a new meaning or sense to (a word, term, or expression). [NEW + MINT[2]]

new-mod·el (no͞o′mod′əl, nyo͞o′-), *adj.* of the latest model: *a new-model automobile.* [NEW + MODEL]

new′ moon′, 1. the moon either when in conjunction with the sun or soon after, being either invisible or visible only as a slender crescent. **2.** the phase of the moon at this time. See diag. under **moon.**

new-mown (no͞o′mōn′, nyo͞o′-), *adj.* recently mown or cut: *the refreshing smell of new-mown hay.*

New′ Neth′erland, a Dutch colony in North America (1613–64), comprising the area along the Hudson River and the lower Delaware River. By 1669 all of the land comprising this colony was taken over by England. *Cap.:* New Amsterdam.

New′ Objectiv′ity. See **Neue Sachlichkeit.**

new′ or′der, 1. a new or revised system of operation, form of government, plan of attack, or the like. **2.** (*caps.*) the system of political and economic control and of social organization that prevailed in Germany and its subject countries during the Nazi era; National Socialism.

New′ Or′le·ans (ôr′lē ənz, ôr lēnz′, ôr′lənz), a seaport in SE Louisiana, on the Mississippi: British defeated (1815) by Americans under Andrew Jackson. 627,525 (1960).

New′ Or′leans lug′ger, a half-decked fishing boat, formerly used on the Gulf of Mexico near New Orleans, having a rather broad hull with centerboard and a single mast with a large dipping lugsail.

New′ Or′leans style′, a style of jazz developed in New Orleans early in the 20th century, influenced by blues, ragtime, marching band music, minstrelsy, etc., and marked by polyphonic group improvisation.

New′ Paltz′ (pôlts), a town in SE New York. 3041 (1960).

New′ Plym′outh, a seaport on W North Island, in New Zealand. 32,387 (1961).

New·port (no͞o′pôrt′, -pōrt′, nyo͞o′-), *n.* **1.** a seaport in S Monmouthshire, in SE Wales, near the Severn estuary. 108,107 (1961). **2.** a seaport and summer resort in SE Rhode Island: naval base. 47,049 (1960). **3.** a city in N Kentucky, on the Ohio River, opposite Cincinnati, Ohio. 30,070 (1960). **4.** a city on the Isle of Wight, in S England. 20,426 (1951). **5.** a town in NE Arkansas. 7007 (1960). **6.** a town in E Tennessee. 6448 (1960). **7.** a town in W Oregon. 5344 (1960). **8.** a town in N Vermont. 5019 (1960). **9.** a town in SW New Hampshire. 3222 (1960).

New′port Beach′, a city in SW California, SE of Los Angeles. 26,564 (1960).

New′port boat′, a catboat, formerly used on Narragansett Bay, having a gaff mainsail and a jib set on a removable bowsprit. Also called **point boat, Providence boat, Providence River boat.**

New′port East′, a town in SE Rhode Island. 2643 (1960).

New′port News′, a seaport in SE Virginia. 113,662 (1960).

New′ Port′ Rich′ey (rich′ē), a town in central Florida. 3520 (1960).

New′ Prague′, a town in S Minnesota. 2533 (1960).

New′ Prov′idence, 1. an island in the W Bahamas. 46,920 (est. 1955); 58 sq. mi. **2.** a town in central Tennessee. 4451 (1960).

New′ Re′alism, *Philos.* Neo-Realism. —**New′ Re′alist.**

new-rich (no͞o′rich′, nyo͞o′-), *adj.* **1.** newly or suddenly wealthy. **2.** characteristic of a newly or suddenly wealthy person: *new-rich vulgarity.* —*n.* **3.** See **nouveau riche.** [NEW + RICH]

New′ Rich′mond, 1. a town in W Wisconsin. 3316 (1960). **2.** a town in SW Ohio. 2834 (1960).

New′ Roads′, a town in central Louisiana. 3965 (1960).

New′ Ro·chelle′ (rō shel′, rə-), a city in SE New York, near New York City. 76,812 (1960).

news (no͞oz, nyo͞oz), *n.* (*construed as sing. or pl.*) **1.** a report of a recent event; intelligence; information: *His family has had no news of his whereabouts for months.* **2.** the presentation of a report on current events in a newspaper or other periodical or on radio or television. **3.** such reports taken collectively: *There's good news tonight.* **4.** a person, thing, or event considered as a choice subject for journalistic treatment: *You may not like her, but she's news.* Cf. **copy** (def. 2). **5.** newspaper. [ME; OE *niwes*, n. use of gen. sing. of *niwe* NEW; see -s[1]] —**news′less,** *adj.* —**news′less·ness,** *n.*

news′ a′gency, 1. a business organization that gathers news for transmittal to its subscribers. Cf. **press association. 2.** a business that sells newspapers at retail.

news·a·gent (no͞oz′ā′jənt, nyo͞oz′-), *n.* *Chiefly Brit.* newsdealer. [NEWS + AGENT]

news′ an′alyst, commentator (def. 2).

news·beat (no͞oz′bēt′, nyo͞oz′-), *n.* beat (def. 50b). [NEWS + BEAT]

news·board (no͞oz′bōrd′, -bôrd′, nyo͞oz′-), *n.* *Brit.* See **bulletin board.** [NEWS + BOARD]

news·boy (no͞oz′boi′, nyo͞oz′-), *n.* a boy who sells or delivers newspapers. [NEWS + BOY]

news·break (no͞oz′brāk′, nyo͞oz′-), *n.* a newsworthy event or incident. [NEWS + BREAK]

news′ case′, *Print.* one of a pair of wooden, metal, or plastic trays, divided into compartments, for the sorting of type. Cf. **case**[2] (def. 8).

news·cast (no͞oz′kast′, -käst′, nyo͞oz′-), *n.* a broadcast of news on radio or television. [NEWS + (BROAD)CAST] —**news′cast′er,** *n.* —**news′cast′ing,** *n.*

news′ con′ference, a press conference, esp. one held by a government official.

New′ Scot′land Yard′. See under **Scotland Yard** (def. 1).

news·deal·er (no͞oz′dē′lər, nyo͞oz′-), *n.* a person who sells newspapers and periodicals. [NEWS + DEALER]

New′ Sea′. See **Mare Novum.**

news′ flash′, *Journalism.* flash (def. 6).

news·girl (no͞oz′gûrl′, nyo͞oz′-), *n.* a girl who sells or delivers newspapers. [NEWS + GIRL]

news·hawk (no͞oz′hôk′, nyo͞oz′-), *n.* *Informal.* a newspaper reporter, esp. one who is energetic and aggressive. Also called **news·hound** (no͞oz′hound′, nyo͞oz′-). [NEWS + HAWK]

news·hen (no͞oz′hen′, nyo͞oz′-), *n.* *Informal.* a female newshawk. [NEWS + HEN]

New′ Shrews′bury, a town in central New Jersey. 7313 (1960).

New′ Sibe′rian Is′lands, a group of islands in the Arctic Ocean, N of the Soviet Union in Asia: part of the Yakutsk Autonomous Republic.

news·let·ter (no͞oz′let′ər, nyo͞oz′-), *n.* **1.** a written report, sometimes illustrated and usually issued periodically, prepared by or for a group or institution, as a business firm, charitable organization, or government agency, to present information to employees, contributors, stockholders, or the like, and often to the press and public. **2.** a written report and analysis of the news, often providing forecasts, typically directed at a special audience, as businessmen, and mailed to subscribers. [NEWS + LETTER]

news·mag·a·zine (no͞oz′mag′ə zēn′, nyo͞oz′-), *n.* a periodical specializing in reports and commentaries on current events, usually issued weekly. [NEWS + MAGAZINE]

news·man (no͞oz′man′, nyo͞oz′-), *n., pl.* **-men. 1.** a person employed to gather or report news, as for a newspaper, a periodical, or a radio or television news bureau; newspaperman. **2.** a person who sells or distributes newspapers, periodicals, etc.; newsdealer. [NEWS + MAN[1]]

news·mon·ger (no͞oz′mung′gər, -mong′-, nyo͞oz′-), *n.* a person who spreads gossip or idle talk; a gossip or gossipmonger. [NEWS + MONGER] —**news′mon′ger·ing, news′mon′ger·y,** *n.*

New′ Smyr′na Beach′, a town in NE Florida. 8781 (1960).

New′ South′ Wales′, a state in SE Australia. 3,917,013 (1961); 309,433 sq. mi. *Cap.:* Sydney.

New′ Spain′, the former Spanish possessions in the Western Hemisphere, at one time including South America (except Brazil), Central America, Mexico, the West Indies, Florida, and most of the land in the U.S. west of the Mississippi River.

news·pa·per (no͞oz′pā′pər, nyo͞oz′-), *n.* **1.** a publication printed on newsprint, issued at regular and usually close intervals, esp. daily or weekly, and commonly containing news, comment, features, and advertising. **2.** a business organization publishing such a publication. **3.** a single issue or copy of such a publication. **4.** newsprint. —*adj.* **5.** of, pertaining to, for, or published in a newspaper. [NEWS + PAPER] —**news′pa′per·dom,** *n.* —**news′pa′per·ish,** *adj.*

news·pa·per·man (no͞oz′pā′pər man′, nyo͞oz′-), *n., pl.* **-men. 1.** a man employed by a newspaper or wire service as a reporter, writer, editor, etc. **2.** the owner or operator of a newspaper or news service. [NEWSPAPER + MAN]

news·pa·per·wom·an (no͞oz′pā′pər wo͝om′ən, nyo͞oz′-), *n., pl.* **-wom·en.** a female newspaperman. [NEWSPAPER + WOMAN]

new·speak (no͞o′spēk′, nyo͞o′-), *n.* an official or semiofficial style of writing or saying one thing in the guise of its opposite, esp. in order to serve a political or ideological cause while pretending to be objective. [NEW + SPEAK, coined by George Orwell in his novel, *1984*]

news′ peg′, 1. a newsworthy event or a news story that forms the basis of or justification for a feature story, editorial, political cartoon, or the like. **2.** the reference in a feature story, editorial, or the like, to the newsworthy event that underlies or justifies it. Also called **peg.**

news·print (no͞oz′print′, nyo͞oz′-), *n.* a low-grade, machine-finished paper made from wood pulp and a small percentage of sulfite pulp, used chiefly for newspapers. [NEWS + PRINT]

new-sprung (no͞o′sprung′, nyo͞o′-), *adj.* newly or suddenly come into existence. [NEW + SPRUNG]

news·read·er (no͞oz′rē′dər, nyo͞oz′-), *n.* *Brit.* a newscaster. [NEWS + READER]

news·reel (no͞oz′rēl′, nyo͞oz′-), *n.* a short motion picture presenting current events. [NEWS + REEL[1]]

news′ release′. See **press release.**

news′ room′, a room in the offices of a newspaper, news service, or broadcasting organization in which the news is processed.

news′ serv′ice, an agency that gathers news stories for its members or subscribers. Cf. **news agency** (def. 1), **press association, wire service.**

news′ stall′, *Brit.* newsstand.

news·stand (no͞oz′stand′, nyo͞oz′-), *n.* a stall or other place at which newspapers and often periodicals are sold, as on a street corner. [NEWS + STAND]

news′ sto′ry, a news report of any length, written in a straightforward style and without editorial comment. Also called **story.** Cf. **editorial, feature story** (def. 1).

New′ Style′, time reckoned according to the Gregorian calendar. Cf. **old style** (def. 2).

news·ven·dor (no͞oz′ven′dər, nyo͞oz′-), *n.* *Chiefly Brit.* a person who sells newspapers and, sometimes, periodicals on a street corner. [NEWS + VENDOR]

news·wom·an (no͞oz′wo͝om′ən, nyo͞oz′-), *n., pl.* **-wom·en. 1.** a newspaperwoman; a woman reporter on a newspaper. **2.** a woman who sells or distributes newspapers, periodicals, etc. [NEWS + WOMAN]

news·wor·thy (no͞oz′wûr′thē, nyo͞oz′-), *adj.* of sufficient potential interest to the public or a special audience to warrant press coverage. [NEWS + WORTHY] —**news′wor′thi·ness,** *n.*

news·y[1] (no͞o′zē, nyo͞o′-), *adj.*, **news·i·er, news·i·est.** *Informal.* **1.** full of news: *a nice long and newsy letter.* **2.** gossipy. [NEWS + -Y[1]] —**news′i·ness,** *n.*

news·y[2] (no͞o′zē, nyo͞o′-), *n., pl.* **news·ies.** *Informal.* a newsboy. [NEWS + -Y[2]]

newt (no͞ot, nyo͞ot), *n.* **1.** any of several brilliantly colored salamanders of the genus *Triturus*, of North America, Europe, and northern Asia, certain of which have a complex aquatic and terrestrial life history. **2.** (loosely) any of various small salamanders. [ME *newte*, *ewte* (*an ewet* being taken as *a newte*), var. of *evet*, OE *efete* EFT]

Newt, *Triturus (Diemictylus) viridescens* (Length 3½ in.)

Newt (no͞ot, nyo͞ot), *n.* a boy's given name, form of **Newton.**

New Test., New Testament.

New′ Tes′tament, 1. the collection of the books of the Bible which were produced by the early Christian church, comprising the Gospels, Acts of the Apostles, the Epistles, and the Revelation of St. John the Divine. **2.** the covenant between God and man in which the dispensation of grace is revealed through Jesus Christ.

new′ theol′ogy, *Prot. Theol.* any departure from strict orthodoxy, used esp. with reference to the liberal movement in American Protestant theology, in the late 19th century.

New′ Thought′, a system of doctrine and practice based on the theory that through the suggestion of favorable and beneficial ideas all physical and mental circumstances of life may be regulated and controlled. —**New′ Thought′er, New′ Thought′ist.**

new·ton (no͞ot′ən, nyo͞ot′-), *n.* *Physics.* the standard meter-kilogram-second unit of force, equal to the force that produces an acceleration of one meter per second per second on a mass of one kilogram. [named after Sir Isaac NEWTON]

New·ton (no͞ot′ən, nyo͞ot′-), *n.* **1. Sir Isaac,** 1642–1727, English philosopher and mathematician: formulator of the law of gravitation. **2.** a city in E Massachusetts, near Boston. 92,384 (1960). **3.** a city in central Iowa, E of Des Moines. 15,381 (1960). **4.** a town in central North Carolina. 6658 (1960). **5.** a town in NW New Jersey. 6563 (1960). **6.** a town in central Mississippi. 3178 (1960). **7.** a town in central Illinois. 2901 (1960). **8.** a walled plain in the third quadrant of the face of the moon: about 70 miles in diameter. **9.** a boy's given name.

New′ton Falls′, a town in NE Ohio. 5038 (1960).

New·to′ni·an flu′id (no͞o tō′nē ən, nyo͞o-), *Hydrodynamics.* any fluid exhibiting a linear relation between the applied shear stress and the rate of deformation. [NEWTON + -IAN]

Newto′nian tel′escope, a reflecting telescope in which a mirror or reflecting prism is mounted on the axis near the eyepiece so that the image may be viewed from outside the telescope tube at right angles to the axis.

new·ton-me·ter (no͞ot′ən mē′tər, nyo͞ot′-), *n.* *Physics.* joule.

New′ton's law′ of gravita′tion, *Physics.* See **law of gravitation.** Also called **New′ton's law′ of univer′sal gravita′tion.**

New′ton's law′ of mo′tion, *Physics.* See **law of motion.**

New′ton's meth′od, *Math.* a process for approximating the roots of an equation by replacing the curve representing the equation by its tangent and finding the intersection of the tangent with the x-axis and iterating this process. [named after Isaac NEWTON]

New′ton's rings′, *Optics.* the pattern of light interference produced by the contact of the convex surface of a lens with a plane glass plate, appearing as a series of concentric, alternately bright and dark rings, which are colored if the light source is white.

New′town Pip′pin (no͞o′toun′, nyo͞o′-). See **Yellow Newtown.**

new′ wave′, (*often caps.*) **1.** a movement, trend, or vogue, as in art, literature, politics, etc., that breaks with traditional concepts, values, techniques, or the like: *the new waves that brought us pop art and the antinovel.* **2.** a group of leaders or representatives of such a movement: *the New Wave among contemporary film makers.* Cf. **nouvelle vague.**

New′ Wind′sor, 1. a town in SE New York. 4041 (1960). 2. Windsor (def. 3).

New′ World′. See **Western Hemisphere.** (def. 1).

New′ World′ mon′key, a platyrrhine monkey.

new′ year′, 1. the year approaching or newly begun. 2. See **New Year's Day.** 3. (*caps.*) the first few days of a year.

New′ Year's′, *Chiefly U.S.* 1. See **New Year's Day.** 2. See **New Year's Eve.**

New′ Year's′ Day′, January 1.

New′ Year's′ Eve′, the night of December 31, usually observed with merrymaking.

New′ York′, 1. Also called **New York State.** a State in the NE United States. 16,782,304 (1960); 49,576 sq. mi. *Cap.:* Albany. *Abbr.:* N.Y. 2. Also called **New′ York′ Cit′y.** a seaport in SE New York at the mouth of the Hudson, comprising the boroughs of Manhattan, Queens, Brooklyn, the Bronx, and Staten Island. 7,071,-639. 3. **Greater,** New York City, the counties of Nassau, Suffolk, Rockland, and Westchester in New York, and the counties of Bergen, Essex, Hudson, Middlesex, Morris, Passaic, Somerset, and Union in New Jersey; the metropolitan area as defined by the U.S. census. 17,412,652. —**New′ York′er.**

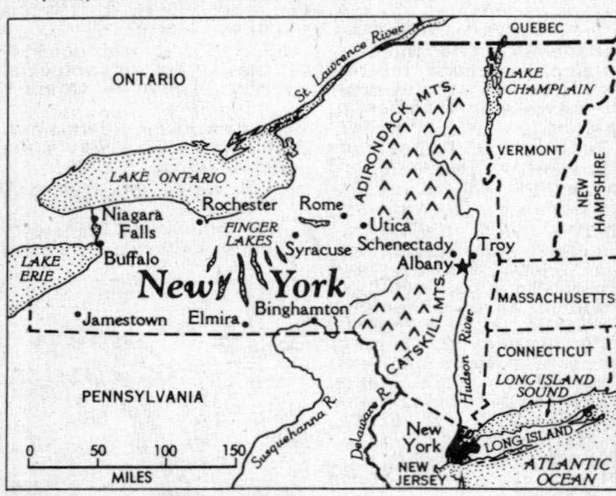

New′ York′ as′ter, a perennial herb, *Aster novi-belgi,* of eastern North America, having numerous bluish-violet flower heads in large, branched clusters.

New′ York′ Bay′, a bay of the Atlantic at the mouth of the Hudson, W of Long Island and E of Staten Island and New Jersey.

New′ York′ Curb′ Exchange′, former name of the **American Stock Exchange.**

New′ York′ cut′, *Chiefly Western and Midwestern U.S.* a porterhouse steak with the fillet and often the bone removed.

New′ York·ese′ (yôr kēz′, -kēs′), the speech thought to be characteristic of a person living in or coming from New York City, as in pronunciation, vocabulary, etc. [NEW YORK + -ESE]

New′ York′ fern′, a shield fern, *Thelypteris noveboracensis,* of eastern North America, having yellowish-green fronds.

New′ York′ Mills′, a town in central New York. 3788 (1960).

New′ York′ sail′ing barge′, a sloop-rigged barge, formerly used in the area of New York harbor, having a boomless gaff mainsail and a jib set on a short bowsprit.

New′ York′ State′. See **New York** (def. 1).

New′ York′ State′ Barge′ Canal′, 1. a New York State waterway system. 575 mi. long. 2. the main canal of this system, between the Hudson River and Lake Erie: consists of the rebuilt Erie Canal. 352 mi. long.

New′ York′ Stock′ Exchange′, the largest stock exchange in the U.S., located in New York City. Cf. **American Stock Exchange.**

New′ Zea′land (zē′lənd), a country in the S Pacific, SE of Australia, consisting of North Island, South Island, and several adjacent small islands: a member of the British Commonwealth of Nations. 3,129,383; 103,416 sq. mi. *Cap.:* Wellington. —**New′ Zea′land·er.**

New′ Zea′land flax′, a large perennial herb, *Phormium tenax,* of New Zealand, having showy, red-margined, leathery leaves and dull red flowers, grown as an ornamental and for the fiber-yielding leaves. Also called **flax lily.**

New′ Zea′land wine′berry, a shrub or small tree, *Aristotelia racemosa,* of New Zealand, having clusters of small, rose-colored flowers and purplish-black fruit.

Nex·ö (nek′sœ), *n.* **Mar·tin An·der·sen** (mär′ten ä′nər sən), 1869–1954, Danish novelist.

next (nekst), *adj.* 1. immediately following in time, order, importance, etc.: *the next day.* 2. nearest in place or position: *the next room.* 3. nearest in relationship or kinship. 4. **next door to, a.** in an adjacent house; neighboring. **b.** in a position of proximity; near to: *They are next door to poverty.* —*adv.* 5. in the nearest place, time, importance, etc.: *Next we're going to the Music Hall. This is my next oldest daughter.* 6. on the first occasion to follow: *when next we meet.* 7. **get next to someone,** *Slang.* to get into the good graces of; become a good friend of; become intimate with: *She concentrates on getting next to the people who can help her career.* —*prep.* 8. adjacent to; nearest: *It's in the closet next the blackboard.* [ME *next(e),* OE *nēxt, nēhst,* superl. of *nēah* NIGH; c. Icel *næstr,* G *nächst*]

next-door (*adv.* neks′dôr′, -dôr′, nekst′-; *adj.* neks′dôr′, -dôr′, nekst′-), *adv., adj.* —*adv.* 1. to, at, or in the next house on the street, esp. if it is very close by, the adjacent apartment, or the like: *Go next-door and get your sister. Your sister is next-door. Her brother lives next-door.* —*adj.* 2. being situated or living next-door (sometimes written as two words, unhyphenated): *next-door neighbors; the girl next-door.*

next′ friend′, *Law.* a person other than a duly appointed guardian who acts on behalf of an infant, married woman, or other person not fully qualified by law to act on his own behalf. Also called **prochain ami.** Cf. **guardian ad litem.**

next′ of kin′, 1. a person's nearest relative or relatives: *The newspaper did not publish the names of casualties until the next of kin had been notified.* 2. *Law.* the nearest relative or relatives who share in the estate, esp. the personal property, of a person who dies intestate.

nex·us (nek′səs), *n., pl.* **nex·us.** 1. a means of connection; tie; link. 2. a connected series or group. [< L *nexus* a binding, joining, fastening (ptp. of *nectere* to bind, fasten, tie)]

Ney (nā), *n.* **Mi·chel** (mē shel′), **Duke of El·ching·en** (el′KHiNG ən), 1769–1815, French revolutionary and Napoleonic military leader: marshal of France 1805–15.

Nez Per·cé (nez′ pûrs′; *Fr.* nā per sā′), *pl.* **Nez Per·cés** (nez′ pûr′siz; *Fr.* nā per sā′), (*esp. collectively*) **Nez Per·cé** for 1. 1. a member of a North American Indian people of the Sahaptin family. 2. the Sahaptin language of the Nez Percé Indians. [< F: lit., pierced nose]

Nez′ Percé′ War′, a war (1877) fought in northwestern U.S. between the U.S. and a band of Nez Percé Indians.

NF, 1. no funds. 2. Norman French.

nF, nanofarad; nanofarads. Also, **nf**

N.F., 1. National Formulary. 2. Newfoundland. 3. no funds. 4. Norman French.

n/f, no funds. Also, **N/F**

NFD., Newfoundland.

NG, *Chem.* nitroglycerin.

N.G., 1. National Guard. 2. New Guinea. 3. no good.

n.g., no good.

n'ga·na (nə gä′nə), *n. Vet. Pathol.* nagana.

Ngan·hwei (*Chin.* ᵊngän′hwā′), *n.* Anhwei.

NGk., New Greek. Also, **N.Gk.**

Ngo Dinh Diem (ᵊngō′ dēn′ dyem′, dzyem′, nō′), 1901–1963, South Vietnamese statesman: president of the Republic of South Vietnam 1956–63.

nH, nanohenry; nanohenries. Also, **nh**

N.H., New Hampshire.

NHA, National Housing Agency. Also, **N.H.A.**

N. Heb., New Hebrides.

NHG, New High German. Also, **NHG., N.H.G.**

N.H.I., *Brit.* National Health Insurance. Also, **NHI**

Ni, *Chem.* nickel.

N.I., Northern Ireland.

NIA, 1. National Intelligence Authority. 2. Newspaper Institute of America.

ni·a·cin (nī′ə sin), *n. Biochem.* See **nicotinic acid.** [NI(COTINIC) AC(ID) + -IN[2]]

ni·a·cin·a·mide (nī′ə sin′ə mīd′), *n. Biochem.* nicotinamide. [NIACIN + AMIDE]

Ni·ag·a·ra (nī ag′rə, -ag′ər ə), *n.* 1. a river on the boundary between W New York and Ontario, Canada, flowing from Lake Erie into Lake Ontario. 34 mi. long. 2. See **Niagara Falls.** 3. **Fort,** a fort in W New York, at the mouth of the Niagara River. 4. (*l.c.*) anything, as utterance, taken as resembling Niagara Falls in force and relentlessness; avalanche; cascade: *She let loose a niagara of billingsgate.* 5. *Hort.* **a.** a variety of white grape, grown for table use. **b.** the vine bearing this fruit.

Niag′ara Falls′, 1. the falls of the Niagara River: in Canada, the Horseshoe Falls, 158 ft. high; 2600 ft. wide; American Falls, 167 ft. high; 1400 ft. wide. 2. a city in W New York, on the U.S. side of the falls. 102,394 (1960). 3. a city in SE Ontario, on the Canadian side of the falls. 22,351 (1961).

Nia·mey (nyä mā′), *n.* a port in and the capital of Niger, in the SW part, on the Niger River. 40,000 (est. 1962).

Ni·an·tic (nī an′tik), *n.* a town in SE Connecticut. 2788 (1960).

Ni·ar·chos (nē är′kōs; *Gk.* nē′är KHôs), *n.* **Stav·ros Spy·ros** (stäv′rôs spē′rôs), born 1909, Greek businessman.

nib (nib), *n., v.,* **nibbed, nib·bing.** —*n.* 1. a bill or beak, as of a bird; neb. 2. *Chiefly Brit.* a penpoint for insertion into a penholder. 3. the point of a pen, or either of its divisions. 4. a point of anything: *a cutting tool with a diamond nib.* 5. any pointed extremity. 6. *Metall.* **a.** a piece of sintered tungsten carbide used as a die for drawing wire or the like. **b.** (in powder metallurgy) a compact at any stage of its manufacture. —*v.t.* 7. *Brit.* to furnish with a nib or point. 8. to mend or trim the nib of. [OE *nybba* (in a place-name), c. Icel *nibba* sharp point, MLG *nibbe* beak. See NIBBLE] —**nib′like′,** *adj.*

nib·ba·na (nib bä′nə), *n. Pali.* nirvana (def. 1).

nib′bing plank′, *Naut.* See **joggling plank.**

nib·ble (nib′əl), *v.,* **-bled, -bling,** *n.* —*v.i.* 1. to bite off small bits. 2. to eat or feed by biting off small pieces: *Give him a graham cracker to nibble on.* 3. to bite slightly or gently (usually fol. by *at*): *She was so upset she could only nibble at her food.* —*v.t.* 4. to bite off small bits of (something). 5. to eat (food) by biting off small pieces. 6. to bite in small bits: *He nibbled each morsel with great deliberation.* —*n.* 7. a small morsel or bit: *Each nibble was eaten with the air of an epicure.* 8. the act or an instance of nibbling. [*nib* to peck, pick (see NIB) + -LE (freq. suffix); akin to MLG *nibbelen* to pick with the beak]

nib·bler (nib′lər), *n.* 1. one who or that which nibbles. 2. any of several fishes of the family *Girellidae,* found in shallow waters on both sides of the Pacific Ocean, having thin, incisorlike teeth. [NIBBLE + -ER[1]]

Ni·be·lung·en·lied (nē′bə lo͝ong′ən lēt′), *n.* a Middle High German epic of c1200, related to the Scandinavian *Volsunga Saga* and telling of the life of Siegfried, his marriage to Kriemhild, his wooing of Brunhild on behalf of Gunther, his murder by Hagen, and the revenge of Kriemhild. [< G; see NIBELUNGS, LIED]

Ni·be·lungs (nē′bə lo͝ongz′), *n.pl., sing.* **Ni·be·lung.** *Teutonic Legend.* 1. a race of dwarfs who possessed a treasure captured by Siegfried. 2. the followers of Siegfried. 3. (in the *Nibelungenlied*) the family of Gunther. Also, **Niblungs.**

nib·lick (nib′lik), *n. Golf.* a club with an iron head the face of which has the greatest slope of all the irons, for hitting the ball with maximum loft. Also called **number nine iron.** [? NIBBLE + -*ick,* var. of -OCK]

Ni·blungs (nē′blo͝ongz), *n.pl., sing.* **Ni·blung.** Nibelungs.

nibs (nibz), *n. Slang.* 1. a person in authority. 2. **his nibs,** *Often Disparaging.* a person who is haughty or tyrannical: *They were careful not to offend his nibs.* [?]

Nic (nik), *n.* a boy's given name, form of **Nicholas.** Also, **Nick.**

Ni·cae·a (nī sē′ə), *n.* an ancient city in NW Asia Minor: Nicene Creed formulated here A.D. 325.

Ni·cae·an (nī sē′ən), *adj.* Nicene.

Nic·a·ra·gua (nik′ə rä′gwə), *n.* 1. a republic in Central America. 1,536,240 (est. 1963); 57,143 sq. mi. *Cap.:* Managua. 2. **Lake,** a lake in SW Nicaragua. 92 mi. long; 34 mi. wide.

nic·co·lite (nik′ə līt′), *n.* a pale copper-red mineral of a metallic luster, nickel arsenide, NiAs, usually occurring massive. [< NL *niccol(um)* nickel + -ITE[1]]

nice (nīs), *adj.,* **nic·er, nic·est.** 1. pleasing; agreeable; delightful: *a nice visit.* 2. amiably pleasant; kind: *They are always nice to strangers.* 3. characterized by or requiring great accuracy, precision, skill, or delicacy: *nice workmanship; a nice shot.* 4. requiring or showing tact or care; delicate: *a nice handling of the situation.* 5. showing minute differences; minutely accurate, as instruments: *a job that requires nice measurements.* 6. minute, fine, or subtle: *a nice distinction.* 7. having or showing delicate, accurate perception: *a nice sense of color.* 8. refined as to manners, language, etc.: *Nice people wouldn't do such things.* 9. virtuous; chaste; respectable; decorous: *a nice girl.* 10. suitable or proper: *That was not a nice remark.* 11. carefully neat as to dress, habits, etc. 12. (esp. of food) dainty or delicious: *That was a nice dinner.* 13. having dainty or fussy tastes: *They're much too nice in their dining habits to enjoy an outdoor barbecue.* 14. *Obs.* coy, shy, or reluctant. 15. *Obs.* unimportant; trivial. [ME: foolish < OF < L *nescius* ignorant, incapable, equiv. to *ne* not + *sci-* (root of *scīre* to know) + *-us* adj. suffix] —**nice′ly,** *adv.* —**nice′ness,** *n.*

—**Syn.** 2. friendly. 3. delicate, exact, exacting, critical, scrupulous. 4. discriminating, discerning, particular. 8. polite. 11, 13. fastidious, finical, finicky. —**Ant.** 1. unpleasant. 2. unkind. 3, 4. careless. 10. improper.

—**Usage.** The semantic history of NICE is quite varied, as the etymology and the obsolete senses attest, and any attempt to insist on only one of its senses as correct will not be in keeping with the facts of the way the word is used. If any criticism is valid, it might be that the word is used too much and has become a cliché to express ideas less dully—and often more precisely—set forth by one or another of the synonyms listed above.

Nice (nēs), *n.* a port in and the capital of Alpes Maritimes, in SE France, on the Mediterranean: resort. 294,976 (1962).

Ni·cene (nī sēn′, nī′sēn), *adj.* of or pertaining to Nicaea. Also, **Nicaean.** [< LL *Nīcēnus,* var. of *Nīcaenus* < Gk *Nīkaîos* (*Nīkai(a)* Nicaea + *-os* adj. suffix), with *-n-* from L adj. suffix *-ānus* -AN]

Ni′cene Coun′cil, either of two church councils which met at Nicaea, the first in A.D. 325 to deal with the Arian heresy, the second in A.D. 787 to consider the question of the veneration of images.

Ni′cene Creed′, 1. a formal statement of the chief tenets of Christian belief, adopted by the first Nicene Council. 2. a later creed of closely similar form (**Niceno-Constantinopolitan Creed** or **Constantinopolitan Creed**) referred, perhaps erroneously, to the Council of Constantinople (A.D. 381), received universally in the Eastern Church and, with an addition introduced in the 6th century A.D., accepted generally throughout western Christendom.

nice′ nel′ly (nel′ē), 1. a girl or woman who professes or exhibits excessive modesty, prudishness, or the like: *too much of a nice nelly to have any fun.* 2. nice-nellyism (def. 2). Also, **nice′ Nel′ly, nice′ nel′lie, nice′ Nel′lie.**

nice-nel·ly (nīs′nel′ē), *adj.* 1. characterized by prudishness or excessive modesty: *The entrance of his nice-nelly wife dammed the flow of risqué stories.* 2. being a euphemism; euphemistic: *She used such nice-nelly expressions that we didn't know what she was talking about.* Also, **nice′-Nel′ly, nice′-nel′lie, nice′-Nel′lie.** [from phrase *nice nelly*]

nice-nel·ly·ism (nīs′nel′ē iz′əm), *n.* 1. excessive modesty; prudishness. 2. a euphemism: *an evasive style of writing, full of circumlocutions and nice-nellyisms.* Also, **nice′-Nel′ly·ism.** [NICE NELLY + -ISM]

Ni·ce′no-Con·stan·ti·no·pol′i·tan Creed′ (nī sē′nō kon stan′tᵊnō pol′i tᵊn). See under **Nicene Creed** (def. 2).

Ni·ce·tas (nī sē′təs), *n.* See **Ignatius, Saint** (def.2).

ni·ce·ty (nī′si tē), *n., pl.* **-ties.** 1. a delicate or fine point; a punctilio: *niceties of protocol.* 2. a fine distinction; subtlety; detail: *the niceties of the filigree work.* 3. Usually, **niceties.** something nice; a refinement or elegance, as of manners or living: *working hard to acquire the niceties of life.* 4. quality of being nice; niceness. 5. delicacy of character, as of something requiring care or tact: *a matter of considerable nicety.* 6. **to a nicety,** to the last detail; precisely: *The schedule was arranged to a nicety.* [ME < OF *niceté.* See NICE, -TY]

Nice·ville (nīs′vil), *n.* a town in NW Florida. 4517 (1960).

niche (nich), *n., v.* **niched, nich·ing.** —*n.* 1. an ornamental recess in a wall or the like, usually semicircular in plan and arched, as for a statue or other decorative object. 2. a place or position suitable or appropriate for a person or thing: *to find one's niche in the business world.* 3. *Ecol.* the position or function of an organism in a community of plants and animals. —*v.t.* 4. to place (something) in a niche. [< F: niche for a statue < It *nicchia,* back formation from *nicchiare* < LL **nīdiculāre* to make a nest. See NEST, -CULE]

Niche (def. 1)

nich·er (niKH′ər), *v.i., n. Scot.* nicker[2].

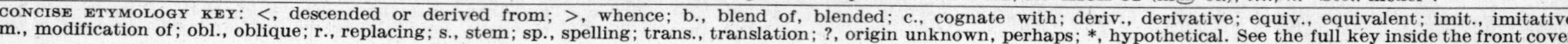
CONCISE ETYMOLOGY KEY: <, descended or derived from; >, whence; b., blend of, blended; c., cognate with; deriv., derivative; equiv., equivalent; imit., imitative; m., modification of; obl., oblique; r., replacing; s., stem; sp., spelling; trans., translation; ?, origin unknown, perhaps; *, hypothetical. See the full key inside the front cover.

Nich·o·las (nik′ə ləs), *n.* **1. of Cu·sa** (kyo͞o′zə), 1401–1464, German cardinal, mathematician, and philosopher. German, **Nikolaus von Cusa. 2. Grand Duke,** 1856–1929, Russian general in World War I. **3. Saint** ("*Santa Claus*"), fl. 4th century A.D., bishop in Asia Minor: patron saint of Russia; protector of children. **4.** a boy's given name.

Nicholas I, 1. Saint ("*Nicholas the Great*"), died A.D. 867, Italian ecclesiastic: pope 858–867. **2.** 1796–1855, emperor of Russia 1825–55.

Nicholas II, 1. (*Gerard*) died 1061, pope 1058–61. **2.** 1868–1918, emperor of Russia 1894–1917: executed 1918.

Nicholas III, (*Giovanni Gaetani Orsini*) died 1280, Italian ecclesiastic: pope 1277–80.

Nicholas IV, (*Girolamo Masci*) died 1292, Italian ecclesiastic: pope 1288–92.

Nicholas V, (*Thomas Parentucelli*) 1397?–1455, Italian ecclesiastic: pope 1447–55.

Nich·o·las·ville (nik′ə ləs vil′), *n.* a town in central Kentucky. 4275 (1960).

Nich′ols Hills′ (nik′əlz), *n.* a town in central Oklahoma. 4897 (1960).

Nich·ol·son (nik′əl sən), *n.* **Sir Francis,** 1655–1728, English colonial administrator in America.

Ni·chrome (nī′krōm′), *n. Trademark.* a nickel-base alloy, containing chromium and iron, having high electrical resistance and stability at high temperatures.

nicht wahr (niKHt vär′), *German.* isn't that so?

Ni·ci·as (nish′ē əs), *n.* died 413 B.C., Athenian statesman and general.

Ni·cip·pe (nī sip′ē), *n. Class. Myth.* the mother, by King Sthenelus, of Eurystheus.

nick (nik), *n.* **1.** a notch, groove, chip, or the like, cut into or existing in a thing. **2.** a hollow place produced in an edge or surface, as of a dish, by breaking, chipping, or the like: *I didn't notice those tiny nicks in the vase when I bought it.* **3.** a small groove on one side of the shank of a printing type, serving as a guide in setting or to distinguish different types. See diag. under **type. 4.** *Brit. Slang.* prison. **5. in the nick of time,** at the propitious or vital moment: *The fire engines arrived in the nick of time.* —*v.t.* **6.** to make a nick or nicks in (something); notch. **7.** to record by means of a notch or notches. **8.** to cut into or through: *I nicked my chin while shaving.* **9.** to incise certain tendons at the root of (a horse's tail) to give it a higher carrying position; make an incision under the tail of (a horse). **10.** to hit, guess, catch, etc., exactly. **11.** to trick, cheat, or defraud: *How much did they nick you for that suit?* **12.** *Brit. Slang.* **a.** to arrest (a criminal or suspect). **b.** to capture. [late ME *nyke;* akin to OE *gehnycned* wrinkled, Icel *hnykla* to wrinkle]

Nick (nik), *n.* **1.** See **Old Nick. 2.** Also, **Nic.** a boy's given name, form of **Nicholas.**

nick·el (nik′əl), *n., v.,* **-eled, -el·ing** or (*esp. Brit.*) **-elled, -el·ling.** —*n.* **1.** *Chem.* a hard, silvery-white, ductile and malleable metallic element, allied to iron and cobalt, not readily oxidized: used chiefly in alloys, in electroplating, and as a catalyst in organic synthesis. *Symbol:* Ni; *at. wt.:* 58.71; *at. no.:* 28; *sp. gr.:* 8.9 at 20°C. **2.** a cupronickel coin of the U.S., the 20th part of a U.S. dollar, equal to five cents. —*v.t.* **3.** to cover or coat with nickel; nickel-plate. [< Sw, abstracted from *kopparnickel* < G *Kupfernickel* niccolite, lit., copper demon (so called because though looking like copper it yielded none); *nickel* demon, special use of *Nickel,* short for *Nikolaus* proper name. See OLD NICK]

nick′el ac′etate, *Chem.* a green, crystalline, water-soluble solid, $(CH_3COO)_2Ni \cdot 4H_2O$, used chiefly in nickel-plating.

nick′el car′bonyl, *Chem.* a colorless or yellow, volatile, water-insoluble, poisonous, flammable liquid, $Ni(CO)_4$, obtained by the reaction of nickel and carbon monoxide, and used for nickel plating. Also called **nickel tetracarbonyl.**

nick·el·ic (ni kel′ik, nik′ə lik), *adj. Chem.* of or containing nickel, esp. in the trivalent state. [NICKEL + -IC]

nickel′ic ox′ide, *Chem.* a gray-black, water-insoluble powder, Ni_2O_3, which, at 600°C, decomposes to nickel oxide: used chiefly in storage batteries as an oxidizing agent. Also called **black nickel oxide, nickel sesquioxide.**

nick·el·if·er·ous (nik′ə lif′ər əs), *adj.* containing or yielding nickel. [NICKEL + -I- + -FEROUS]

nick·el·ise (nik′ə līz′), *v.t.,* **-ised, -is·ing.** *Chiefly Brit.* nickelize.

nick·el·ize (nik′ə līz′), *v.t.,* **-ized, -iz·ing.** to nickel. [NICKEL + -IZE]

nick·el·o·de·on (nik′ə lō′dē ən), *n.* **1.** (formerly) a place of amusement where a film or a variety show could be seen for the admission price of a nickel. **2.** an early jukebox that took nickels. [NICKEL (def. 2) + (MEL)ODEON]

nick·el·ous (nik′ə ləs), *adj. Chem.* containing bivalent nickel. [NICKEL + -OUS]

nick′el ox′ide, *Chem.* a green, water-insoluble powder, NiO, used chiefly in the manufacture of nickel salts and in green pigments for ceramic paints. Also called **nick′el monox′ide, nick′elous ox′ide, nick′el protox′ide.**

nick′el plate′, a thin coating of nickel deposited on the surface of a piece of metal, as by electroplating.

nick·el-plate (nik′əl plāt′), *v.t.,* **-plat·ed, -plat·ing.** to coat with nickel by electroplating or other process.

nick′el sesquiox′ide, *Chem.* See **nickelic oxide.**

nick′el sil′ver. See **German silver.**

nick′el steel′, steel to which up to 5 percent nickel has been added.

nick′el tet·ra·car′bon·yl (te′trə kär′bə nil), *Chem.* See **nickel carbonyl.** [TETRA- + CARBONYL]

nick·el·type (nik′əl tīp′), *n. Print.* an electrotype with a deposit of nickel. [NICKEL + -TYPE]

nick·er¹ (nik′ər), *n.* one who or that which nicks. [NICK + -ER¹]

nick·er² (nik′ər), *v.i., n. Chiefly Dial.* **1.** neigh. **2.** laugh; snicker. [appar. var. of *nicher, neigher,* freq. of NEIGH]

nick·er³ (nik′ər), *n., pl.* **-er, -ers** for 1. **1.** *Brit. Slang.* one pound sterling. **2.** *Australian.* money. [? special use of NICKER¹]

nick·ey (nik′ē), *n., pl.* **-eys.** *Australian.* a mongrel bull. [? NICK (def. 1) + -EY²]

Nick·laus (nik′ləs), *n.* **Jack (William),** born 1940, U.S. golfer.

nick·nack (nik′nak′), *n.* knickknack.

nick·name (nik′nām′), *n., v.,* **-named, -nam·ing.** —*n.* **1.** a name added to or substituted for the proper name of a person, place, etc., as in ridicule or familiarity: *He has always loathed his nickname of "Whizzer."* **2.** a familiar form of a proper name, as *Jim* for *James.* —*v.t.* **3.** to give a nickname to (a person, town, etc.); call by a nickname. **4.** to call by an incorrect or improper name; misname. [late ME *nekename,* for *ekename* (*an ekename* being taken as *a nekename*). See EKE², NAME, NEWT] —**nick′nam′er,** *n.*

Nick·y (nik′ē), *n.* a girl's given name, form of **Nicole.** Also, **Nikky.**

Nic·o·bar·ese (nik′ə bär′ēz, -ēs), *n.* the Austro-asiatic language of the Nicobar Islands.

Nic′o·bar Is′lands (nik′ə bär′). See **Andaman and Nicobar Islands.**

Nic·o·de·mus (nik′ə dē′məs), *n.* a Pharisee and member of the Sanhedrin who became a secret follower of Jesus. John 3:1–21; 7:50–52; 19:39.

Nic·o·la·i (nik′ə lī′; *for 1 also Ger.* nē′kō lä′ē), *n.* **1. (Carl) Ot·to (Eh·ren·fried)** (kärl ôt′ō ā′rən frēt′), 1810–49, German composer. **2.** a crater in the fourth quadrant of the face of the moon: about 27 miles in diameter.

Nic·o·lay (nik′ə lā′), *n.* **John George,** 1832–1901, U.S. biographer.

Ni·cole (ni kōl′; *Fr.* nē kôl′), *n.* a girl's given name.

Ni·co·let (nik′ə lā′; *Fr.* nē kô le′), *n.* **Jean** (zhän), 1598–1642, French explorer in America.

Ni·co·lette (nik′ə let′; *Fr.* nē kô let′), *n.* a girl's given name.

Ni·colle (nē kôl′), *n.* **Charles** (sharl), 1866–1936, French physician: Nobel prize 1928.

Nic·ol·let (nik′ə lit), *n.* a crater in the third quadrant of the face of the moon: about 10 miles in diameter.

Nic′ol prism′ (nik′əl), *Optics.* a prism that produces plane-polarized light by separating a ray of unpolarized light into an ordinary and an extraordinary ray, reflecting the ordinary ray to the side and transmitting the extraordinary ray as plane-polarized light, and that is composed of two pieces of Iceland spar or calcite cemented together at a specified angle by Canada balsam. Also called **Nic′ol.** [named after William *Nicol* (1768–1851), British physicist, its inventor]

Nic·ol·son (nik′əl sən), *n.* **1. Sir Harold George,** 1886–1968, English diplomat, biographer, and journalist (husband of Victoria Mary Sackville-West). **2. Marjorie Hope,** born 1894, U.S. scholar, educator, and author.

Nic·o·si·a (nik′ə sē′ə), *n.* a city on and the capital of Cyprus, in the central part. 47,000 (est. 1963).

Ni·cos·tra·tus (nī kos′trə təs), *n. Class. Myth.* a son of Menelaus and Helen who, with his illegitimate brother Megapenthes, expelled Helen from Sparta when Menelaus died.

ni·co·ti·a·na (ni kō′shē ā′nə, -an′ə, -ä′nə), *n.* any plant of the genus *Nicotiana,* esp. one grown for its ornamental value, as flowering tobacco. [< NL (*herba*) *nicotiana* Nicot's (herb) (named after Jacques *Nicot* (1530–1600), said to have introduced tobacco into France); see -IANA]

nic·o·tin·a·mide (nik′ə tin′ə mīd′, -mid), *n. Biochem.* a colorless, crystalline, water-soluble solid, $C_5H_4NCONH_2$, the amide of nicotinic acid, and a component of the vitamin-B complex, found in meat, liver, fish, whole wheat, and eggs: used in medicine chiefly as an agent for preventing or treating human pellagra or animal black tongue. Also called **niacinamide, nicotin′ic ac′id am′ide.** [NICOTINE + AMIDE]

nic·o·tine (nik′ə tēn′, -tin, nik′ə tēn′), *n. Chem.* a colorless, oily, water-soluble, highly toxic, liquid alkaloid, $C_{10}H_{14}N_2$, obtained from tobacco. [< NL (*herba*) *nicot(iana)* NICOTIANA + F *-ine* -INE²] —**nic′o·tined′,** *adj.* —**nic′o·tine′less,** *adj.* —**nic·o·tin·ic** (nik′ə tin′ik), *adj.*

nic′otin′ic ac′id, *Biochem.* a crystalline acid, $(C_5H_4N)COOH$, that is a component of the vitamin-B complex, found in fresh meat, yeast, etc., produced by the oxidation of nicotine, and used in the prevention and treatment of pellagra. Also called **niacine.** [NICOTINE + -IC]

nic·o·tin·ise (nik′ə tē nīz′, nik′ə tē′nīz), *v.t.,* **-ised, -is·ing.** *Chiefly Brit.* nicotinize.

nic·o·tin·ism (nik′ə tē niz′əm, -ti-, nik′ə tē′niz-), *n.* a pathological condition caused by excessive use of tobacco. [NICOTINE + -ISM]

nic·o·tin·ize (nik′ə tē nīz′, nik′ə tē′nīz), *v.t.,* **-ized, -iz·ing.** to drug or impregnate with nicotine. Also, *esp. Brit.,* **nicotinise.** [NICOTINE + -IZE]

nic·tate (nik′tāt), *v.i.,* **-tat·ed, -tat·ing.** nictitate. —**nic·ta′tion,** *n.*

Nic·the·roy (nik′te roi′), *n.* Niteroi.

nic·ti·tate (nik′ti tāt′), *v.i.,* **-tat·ed, -tat·ing.** to wink. Also, **nictate.** [< ML *nictitāt(us)* (ptp. of *nictitāre*), freq. of L *nictāre* to wink, freq. of *nicere* to beckon; see -ATE¹] —**nic′ti·tant,** *adj.* —**nic′ti·ta′tion,** *n.*

nic′titating mem′brane, a thin membrane, or inner or third eyelid, present in many animals, capable of being drawn across the eyeball, as for protection. [NICTITATE + -ING²]

Ni·da (nid′ə), *n.* a girl's given name, form of **Nydia.**

ni·da·na (ni dä′nə), *n. Buddhism.* any of 12 aspects of Samsara, or the cycle of birth and death, often compared to 12 spokes of a wheel. [< Skt *nidāna* halter, rope]

Ni·da·ros (nē′dä rōs′), *n.* former name of **Trondheim.**

nid·der·ing (nid′ər ing), *n. Archaic.* —*n.* **1.** a cowardly or base person. —*adj.* **2.** cowardly; base. Also, **nid′ering.** [erroneous archaism based on OE *nīthing* < Scand; cf. Icel *nīthingr,* equiv. to *nīth(a)* to act basely (deriv. of *nīth* defamation, c. OE *nīth* spite, G *Neid* envy) + *-ingr* -ING¹]

nide (nīd), *n. Rare.* a nest or brood, esp. of pheasants. [< L *nīdus* nest]

nidge (nij), *v.t.,* **nidged, nidg·ing.** *Masonry.* to dress (a stone) with a pick or kevel. [?]

Nid·hogg (nēd′hôg′), *n. Scand. Myth.* a serpent in Niflheim who gnaws upon the lowermost root of Yggdrasil. Also, **Nid·hug** (nēd′hœg).

ni·dic·o·lous (nī dik′ə ləs), *adj. Ornith.* remaining in the nest for a period after hatching. Cf. **nidifugous.** [< L *nīd-* (s. of *nīdus*) a nest + -I- + -COLOUS]

nid·i·fi·cate (nid′ə fə kāt′), *v.i.,* **-cat·ed, -cat·ing.** to build a nest. [< L *nīdificāt(us)* (ptp. of *nīdificāre*) built a nest; see NIDIFY, -ATE¹] —**nid′i·fi·ca′tion,** *n.* —**nid′i·fi·ca′tion·al,** *adj.*

ni·dif·u·gous (nī dif′yə gəs), *adj. Ornith.* leaving the nest shortly after hatching. Cf. **nidicolous.** [< L *nīd-* (s. of *nīdus*) a nest + *-i-* -I- + *fug(ere)* (to) flee, take flight + -OUS]

nid·i·fy (nid′ə fī′), *v.i.,* **-fied, -fy·ing.** nidificate. [< L *nīdific(āre)* (to) build a nest, equiv. to *nīd-* (s. of *nīdus*) a nest + *-ificāre* -IFY]

ni·dus (nī′dəs), *n., pl.* **-di** (-dī). **1.** a nest, esp. one in which insects, spiders, etc., deposit their eggs. **2.** a place or point in an organism where a germ or other organism can develop or breed. [< L: nest] —**ni′dal,** *adj.*

Nid·wal·den (nēt′väl′dən), *n.* a demicanton of Unterwalden, in central Switzerland. 22,188 (1960); 106 sq. mi. *Cap.:* Stans.

Nie·buhr (nē′bo͝or; *for 1 also Ger.* nē′bo͞or), *n.* **1. Bar·thold Ge·org** (bär′tôlt gā ôrk′), 1776–1831, German historian. **2. Rein·hold** (rīn′hōld), born 1892, U.S. theologian and philosopher.

niece (nēs), *n.* **1.** a daughter of one's brother or sister. **2.** a daughter of one's husband's or wife's brother or sister. **3.** a euphemism used in referring to an illegitimate daughter of a clergyman who has vowed celibacy. [ME *nece* < OF < VL *neptia* for L *neptis* granddaughter; r. ME *nifte* (OE *nift*) niece]

Nie·der·sach·sen (nē′dər zäKH′zən), *n.* German name of **Lower Saxony.**

ni·el·lo (nē el′ō), *n., pl.* **ni·el·li** (nē el′ē), *v.,* **-loed, -lo·ing.** —*n.* **1.** a black metallic substance, consisting of silver, copper, lead, and sulfur, with which an incised design or ground on metal is filled in to produce an ornamental effect. **2.** ornamental work so produced. **3.** a specimen of such work. —*v.t.* **4.** to decorate by means of niello; treat with niello or by the niello process. [< It < L *nigellus* blackish, dim. of *niger* black] —**ni·el′list,** *n.*

Niel·sen (nēl′sən), *n.* **Carl Au·gust** (kärl ou′go͞ost), 1865–1931, Danish composer.

Niel′sen meth′od. See **back pressure-arm lift method.** [named after Holger *Nielsen,* 20th-century Dane who invented it]

Nie·men (nē′mən; *Pol.* nye′men), *n.* a river in the W Soviet Union in Europe, flowing into the Baltic: called Memel in its lower course. 565 mi. long. Lithuanian, **Nemunas.** Russian, **Neman, Nyeman.**

Nie·mey·er (nē′mī ər), *n.* **Oscar,** born 1907, Brazilian architect.

Nie·moel·ler (nē′mœ lər), *n.* **Mar·tin** (mär′tēn), born 1892, German Lutheran clergyman. Also, **Nie′möl·ler.**

Niepce (nyeps), *n.* **Jo·seph Ni·cé·phore** (zhō zef′ nē sā fôr′), 1765–1833, French inventor.

Nier (nēr), *n.* **Alfred Otto Carl,** born 1911, U.S. physicist.

Nier·stein (nēr′stīn; *Ger.* nēr′shtīn′), *n.* a village in central West Germany, SSE of Mainz: noted for its wines.

Nier·stein·er (nēr′stī nər, -shtī-), *n.* a wine from Nierstein in the Rheinhessen wine district of Germany.

Nie·tzsche (nē′chə, -chē), *n.* **Frie·drich Wil·helm** (frē′driKH vil′helm), 1844–1900, German philosopher.

Nie·tzsche·ism (nē′chē iz′əm), *n.* the philosophy of Nietzsche, emphasizing the will to power as the chief motivating force of both the individual and society. Also, **Nie′tzsche·an·ism.** [NIETZSCHE + -ISM] —**Nie′tzsche·an,** *n., adj.*

Nieuw Nick·e·rie (nē′o͞o nik′ə rē), *n.* a seaport in NW Surinam. 4500 (est. 1957).

nieve (nēv), *n. Brit. Dial.* a fist. [ME *neve* < Scand; cf. Icel *hnefr* fist]

Niè·vre (nye′vrə), *n.* a department in central France. 245,921 (1962); 2659 sq. mi. *Cap.:* Nevers.

Ni·fl·heim (niv′əl hām′), *n. Scand. Myth.* a place of eternal cold, darkness, and fog, ruled over by Hel: a place of punishment for the dead. [Icel *Niflheimr,* equiv. to *nifl* mist + *heimr* HOME]

nif·ty (nif′tē), *adj.* **-ti·er, -ti·est,** *n., pl.* **-ties.** *Informal.* —*adj.* **1.** smart, stylish; fine; clever. —*n.* **2.** something nifty, as a clever remark or joke. [orig. theatrical slang]

nig (nig), *v.t.,* **nigged, nig·ging.** *Masonry.* nidge.

Ni·gel (nī′jəl), *n.* a boy's given name, form of **Neil.**

Ni·ger (nī′jər), *n.* **1.** a republic in NW Africa: formerly part of French West Africa. 3,040,673 (est. 1962); 458,976 sq. mi. *Cap.:* Niamey. **2.** a river in W Africa, rising in S Guinea, flowing NE through Mali, and then SE through Nigeria into the Gulf of Guinea. 2600 mi. long.

Ni·ger-Con·go (nī′jər kong′gō), *n.* **1.** a subfamily of Niger-Kordofanian, that comprises a large number of languages of Africa, as Ewe, Ibo, Yoruba, and the Bantu languages, spoken in nearly all of the equatorial forest region and in much of southern Africa. —*adj.* **2.** of, belonging to, or constituting Niger-Congo.

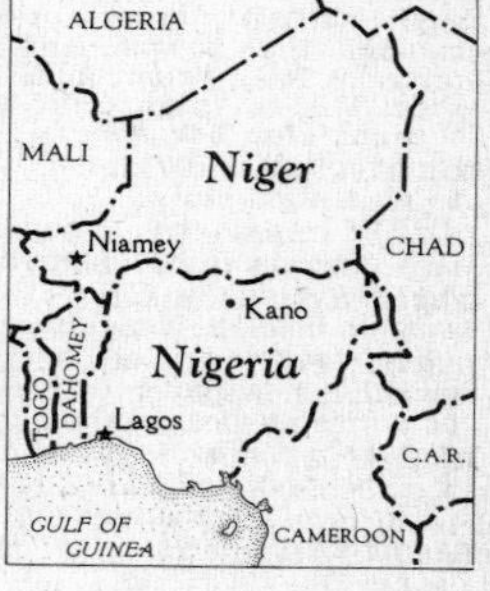

Ni·ge·ri·a (nī jēr′ē ə), *n.* a republic in W Africa: member of the British Commonwealth; formerly a British colony and protectorate. 34,296,000 (est. 1960); 360,000 sq. mi. *Cap.:* Lagos. Official name, **Federation of Nige′ria.** —**Ni·ge′ri·an,** *adj., n.*

Ni·ger-Kor·do·fan·i·an (nī′jər kôr′də fan′ē ən), *n.* a language family comprising Niger-Congo and Kordofanian.

Ni′ger seed′, the black seed of a tropical African, composite plant, *Guizotia abyssinica,* yielding an oil used as food, in the manufacture of soap, etc.

nig·gard (nig′ərd), *n.* **1.** an excessively parsimonious or stingy person. **—***adj.* **2.** niggardly; stingy. [ME *nyggard,* equiv. to *nig* niggard (< Scand; cf. dial. Sw *nygg;* akin to OE *hnēaw* stingy) + -ARD]

nig·gard·ise (nig′ər dīz′), *v.i., v.t.,* **-ised, -is·ing.** *Chiefly Brit.* niggardize.

nig·gard·ize (nig′ər dīz′), *v.,* **-ized, -iz·ing.** *Archaic.* **—***v.i.* **1.** to be niggardly; behave in a niggardly manner. **—***v.t.* **2.** to give (something) in a niggardly manner. [NIGGARD + -IZE]

nig·gard·ly (nig′ərd lē), *adj.* **1.** reluctant to give or spend; stingy. **2.** meanly small or scanty: *a niggardly tip to a waiter.* **—***adv.* **3.** in the manner of a niggard. [NIGGARD + -LY] **—nig′gard·li·ness,** *n.*
—Syn. 1. penurious, miserly, mean, tight, avaricious, mercenary, illiberal, close. **2.** poor. **—Ant. 1.** generous.

nig·ger (nig′ər), *n.* *Offensive and Disparaging.* **1.** a Negro. **2.** a member of any dark-skinned race. **3. nigger in the woodpile,** a dubious or improbable element in a situation, esp. when regarded as possibly harmful or undesirable. **—nig′ger·ish,** *adj.* **—nig′ger·y,** *adj.* [var. of *neger* < F *nègre* < Sp *negro* black, NEGRO]

nig·ger·fish (nig′ər fish′), *n., pl.* (*esp. collectively*) **-fish,** (*esp. referring to two or more kinds or species*) **-fish·es.** coney (def. 1). [NIGGER + FISH]

nig·ger·head (nig′ər hed′), *n.* *Naut.* gypsyhead. [NIGGER + HEAD]

nig′ger heav′en, *Offensive.* the highest balcony in a theater or auditorium.

Nig′ger of the Narcis′sus, The, a novel (1897) by Joseph Conrad.

nig·gle (nig′əl), *v.i.,* **-gled, -gling. 1.** to work ineffectively; trifle: *to niggle with an uninteresting task.* **2.** to spend excessive time and effort on inconsequential details: *It's difficult to be meticulous and not niggle.* **3.** to criticize, esp. constantly or repeatedly, in a peevish manner or over petty details: *to niggle about the fine points of interpretation; preferring to niggle rather than take steps to correct a situation.* [< Scand; cf. Norw *nigla*] **—nig′gler,** *n.*

nig·gling (nig′ling), *adj.* **1.** petty; inconsequential: *to quibble about a niggling difference in terminology.* **2.** demanding excessive care, attention, time, etc.: *niggling chores about the house.* **3.** fussy; overelaborate: *the niggling detail in some naturalistic painting.* **—***n.* **4.** petty, inconsequential, or overelaborate work: *He deplored the amount of niggling in his profession.* [NIGGLE + -ING[2], -ING[1]] **—nig′gling·ly,** *adv.*

nigh (nī), *adv., adj.,* **nigh·er, nigh·est,** *prep., v.* **—***adv.* **1.** near in space, time, or relation (often fol. by *on, onto,* etc.): *The time draws nigh. We've lived here nigh onto 30 years.* **2.** nearly or almost. **—***adj.* **3.** being near; not distant; near in relationship: *The deadline is nigh.* **4.** short or direct: *to take the nighest route.* **5.** (of an animal or vehicle) left or near: *to be astride the nigh horse.* **6.** *Chiefly Dial.* parsimonious; stingy. **—***prep.* **7.** near. **—***v.i., v.t.* **8.** *Archaic.* to approach. [ME *nigh(e), neye,* OE *nēah, nēh,* c. D *na,* Icel *nā-,* Goth *nehw, nehwa,* G *nahe*]

night (nīt), *n.* **1.** the period of darkness between sunset and sunrise. **2.** the beginning of night; nightfall. **3.** the darkness of night; the dark. **4.** a state or time of obscurity, ignorance, misfortune, etc.: *the long night of European history known as the Dark Ages.* **5.** (*sometimes cap.*) an evening used or set aside for a particular event, celebration, or other special purpose: *a night on the town; poker night; New Year's Night.* **6. night and day,** tirelessly; unceasingly; continually: *He worked night and day until the job was done.* **—***adj.* **7.** of or pertaining to night: *the night hours.* **8.** occurring, appearing, or seen at night: *a night raid; a night bloomer.* **9.** used or designed to be used at night: *to take a night coach; the night entrance.* **10.** working at night: *night nurse; the night shift.* **11.** active at night: *the night feeders of the jungle.* [ME; OE *niht, neaht,* c. G *Nacht,* Goth *nahts,* L *nox* (*noctis,* gen.), Gk *nýx*] **—night′less,** *adj.* **—night′less·ly,** *adv.* **—night′like′,** *adj.*

night′ blind′ness, nyctalopia (def. 1). **—night′-blind′,** *adj.*

night′-bloom·ing ce′reus (nīt′blōō′ming), either of two American cactuses, *Selenicereus grandiflorus* or *S. pteranthus,* having large, fragrant flowers that open at night.

night′ bolt′. See **night latch.**

night·cap (nīt′kap′), *n.* **1.** a cap for the head, intended primarily to be worn in bed. **2.** *Informal.* a drink of an alcoholic beverage taken to cap a festive evening or any drink taken at bedtime. **3.** *Sports Informal.* the last event of the program for the day, esp. the second game of a doubleheader in baseball or the last race of the day in horse racing. [ME; see NIGHT, CAP] **—night′capped′,** *adj.*

night′ clothes′, garments for wear in bed.

night′ club′, a restaurant, typically smaller than a cabaret, that is open until early in the morning and provides food, drink, music, a dance floor, and a floor show. Also, **night′club′.** Also called **nightspot. —night′club′ber,** *n.*

night-club (nīt′klub′), *v.i.,* **-clubbed, -club·bing.** to visit night clubs.

night′ crawl′er, *U.S. Dial.* a large earthworm that emerges from its burrow at night.

night·dress (nīt′dres′), *n.* **1.** dress or clothing for wear in bed. **2.** a nightgown. [NIGHT + DRESS]

night′ ed′itor, an editor responsible for getting a morning newspaper to press, for the night operations of a wire service, or the like.

night′ effect′, *Navig.* erratic behavior of radio signals used for taking bearings, observed during the night, esp. after sunset and before sunrise.

night·fall (nīt′fôl′), *n.* the coming of night. [NIGHT + FALL]

night·gown (nīt′goun′), *n.* **1.** a loose gown, worn in bed by women or children. **2.** a man's nightshirt. [ME; see NIGHT, GOWN]

night·hawk (nīt′hôk′), *n.* **1.** any of several long-winged, American goatsuckers of the genus *Chordeiles,* related to the whippoorwill, esp. *C. minor,* having variegated black, white, and buff plumage. **2.** the European goatsucker or nightjar, *Caprimulgus europaeus.* **3.** *Informal.* a person who is habitually up or moving about late at night. [NIGHT + HAWK[1]]

night′ her′on, any of several thick-billed, crepuscular, or nocturnal herons of the genus *Nycticorax* and related genera, as *Nycticorax nycticorax* **(black-crowned night heron),** of the Old and New Worlds, and *Nyctanassa violocea* **(yellow-crowned night heron),** of America.

Nightingale, *Luscinia megarhyncha* (Length 6½ in.)

night·ie (nī′tē), *n.* *Informal.* a nightgown. Also, **nighty.** [NIGHT(GOWN) + -IE]

night·in·gale (nīt′ən gāl′, nī′ting-), *n.* any of several small, Old World, migratory birds of the thrush family, esp. *Luscinia megarhyncha,* of Europe, noted for the melodious song of the male, given chiefly at night during the breeding season. [ME *nightyngale,* nasalized var. of *nightegale,* OE *nihtegale,* c. G *Nachtigall,* lit., night singer; cf. OE *galan* sing, akin to YELL]

Night·in·gale (nīt′ən gāl′, nī′ting-), *n.* **Florence** ("*the Lady with the Lamp*"), 1820–1910, English nurse, reformer of hospital conditions and procedures; reorganizer of nurse's training programs.

night·jar (nīt′jär′), *n.* any Old World goatsucker, esp. the common species, *Caprimulgus europaeus,* of Europe. [NIGHT + JAR[2]]

night′ jas′mine, 1. Also called **hursinghar, sad tree, tree of sadness.** a jasminelike, oleaceous shrub or small tree, *Nyctanthes Arbor-tristis,* of India, having fragrant, white flowers that bloom at night. **2.** a West Indian shrub, *Cestrum nocturnum,* having fragrant, creamy white flowers that bloom at night.

night′ key′, a key for a night latch.

night′ latch′, a door lock operated from the inside by a knob and from the outside by a key. Also called **night bolt.**

night′ let′ter, a telegram, having a minimum charge for 50 words or less that may be sent night or day for delivery the following morning, that is cheaper than a regular telegram.

night′ light′, a usually dim light kept burning at night, as in a child's bedroom or a hallway.

night′ liz′ard, any of several nocturnal, terrestrial lizards of the family *Xantusidae,* of southwestern North America and Cuba.

night·long (nīt′lông′, -long′), *adj.* **1.** lasting all night: *a nightlong snowfall.* **—***adv.* **2.** throughout the night: *They typed nightlong to finish the reports.* [OE *nihtlang.* See NIGHT, LONG]

night·ly (nīt′lē), *adj.* **1.** coming, occurring, appearing, or active at night: *nightly revels.* **2.** coming or occurring each night: *his nightly walk to the newsstand.* **3.** of, pertaining to, or characteristic of night: *the nightly gloom before a storm.* **4.** having the appearance of or resembling night. **—***adv.* **5.** at or by night: *an animal that is seen nightly.* **6.** on every night: *performances given nightly.* [ME; OE *nihtlīc.* See NIGHT, -LY]

night·mare (nīt′mâr′), *n.* **1.** a terrifying dream in which the dreamer experiences feelings of helplessness, extreme anxiety, sorrow, etc. **2.** a condition, thought, or experience suggestive of a nightmare in sleep: *the nightmare of his years in prison.* **3.** (formerly) a monster or evil spirit believed to oppress persons during sleep. [ME; see NIGHT, MARE[2]]
—Syn. 1. phantasmagoria. See **dream.**

night·mar·ish (nīt′mâr′ish), *adj.* resembling a nightmare, esp. in being disquieting, exasperating, or the like: *reappearing with nightmarish regularity.* [NIGHTMARE + -ISH[1]] **—night′mar′ish·ly,** *adv.* **—night′mar′ish·ness,** *n.*

night′ of′fice, *Eccles.* the office for matins.

night′ owl′, *Informal.* a person who often stays up late at night; nighthawk.

night′ pen′nant, *Naut.* a long blue pennant, burgee, or streamer flown at the main truck of a yacht or naval vessel at night in the absence of other flags.

night′ ra′ven, 1. a bird that cries in the night. **2.** *Rare.* the night heron.

night·rid·er (nīt′rī′dər), *n.* **1.** *Southern U.S.* one of a band of mounted men who commit deeds of violence for vengeance or intimidation. **2.** a member of the Ku Klux Klan. [NIGHT + RIDER] **—night′rid′ing,** *n.*

night′ robe′, nightgown. **—night′-robed′,** *adj.*

nights (nīts), *adv.* at or during the night regularly: *He worked during the day and wrote nights.* [ME *nightes,* OE *nihtes* (gen sing.). See NIGHT, -S[1]]

night′ school′, a school held in the evening, esp. for those unable to attend school during the day. Also called **evening school.**

night′ ser′geant, a small damselfish, *Abudefduf taurus,* found in the Atlantic Ocean, related to the sergeant major.

night·shade (nīt′shād′), *n.* **1.** any of various plants of the genus *Solanum,* esp. the black nightshade or the bittersweet. **2.** any of various other solanaceous plants, as the deadly nightshade. [ME; OE *nihtscada.* See NIGHT, SHADE]

night′ shift′, 1. the work force, as of a factory, scheduled to work during the nighttime. **2.** the scheduled period of labor for this work force.

night·shirt (nīt′shûrt′), *n.* a tailored shirt reaching just below the knees, worn in bed originally by men and boys and now also by women. [NIGHT + SHIRT]

night·side (nīt′sīd′), *n.* *Journalism.* the night shift of a newspaper. Cf. **dayside.** [NIGHT + SIDE]

night′ snake′, a nocturnal, mildly venomous New World snake, *Hypsiglena torquata,* having a gray or yellowish body marked with dark brown spots.

night′ soil′, human excrement used as fertilizer.

night·spot (nīt′spot′), *n.* *Informal.* See **night club.** [NIGHT + SPOT]

night·stand (nīt′stand′), *n.* bedstand. [NIGHT + STAND]

night′ stick′, a heavy stick or long club carried by a policeman; billy.

night′ ta′ble, bedstand.

night·tide (nīt′tīd′), *n.* *Poetic.* nighttime. [NIGHT + TIDE[1]]

night·time (nīt′tīm′), *n.* the time between evening and morning. [NIGHT + TIME]

night·walk·er (nīt′wô′kər), *n.* a person who walks or roves about at night, as a thief, prostitute, etc. [NIGHT + WALKER] **—night′walk′ing,** *adj., n.*

night′ watch′, 1. a watch or guard kept during the night. **2.** a person or the persons keeping such a watch. **3.** Usually, **night watches.** the periods or divisions into which the night was divided in ancient times. **—night′ watch′ing.**

Night′ Watch′, The, a painting (1642) by Rembrandt. Also called **The Company of Captain Frans Banning Cog.**

night′ watch′man, a watchman who is on duty at night.

night·wear (nīt′wâr′), *n.* clothes for wearing in bed. [NIGHT + WEAR]

night·y (nī′tē), *n., pl.* **night·ies.** nightie.

night·y-night (nī′tē nīt′), *interj.* *Informal.* See **good night.** [redupl. of (*good*) *night;* see -Y[2]]

ni·gres·cent (nī gres′ənt), *adj.* tending toward black; blackish. [< L *nigrescent-* becoming black, growing dark (s. of *nigrescēns,* prp. of *nigrescere*), equiv. to *nigr-* (s. of *niger*) black *-esc-* -ESC- + *-ent-* -ENT] **—ni·gres′cence,** *n.*

nig·ri·fy (nig′rə fī′), *v.t.,* **-fied, -fy·ing.** to blacken. [< L *nigrific(āre)* (to) make black, blacken, equiv. to *nigr-* (s. of *niger*) black + *-i-* -I- + *-ficāre* -FY] **—nig′ri·fi·ca′tion,** *n.*

nig·ri·tude (nig′ri tōōd′, -tyōōd′, nī′gri-), *n.* **1.** utter or complete darkness; blackness. **2.** *Archaic.* something black or of blackened reputation. [< L *nigritūdō* blackness, black color, equiv. to *nigr-* (s. of *niger*) black + *-i-* -I- + *-tudo* -TUDE] **—nig·ri·tu·di·nous** (nig′ri-tōōd′ənəs, -tyōōd′-), *adj.*

ni·gro·sine (nī′grə sēn′, -sin), *n.* *Chem.* any of the class of deep blue or black dyes obtained by the oxidation of aniline, used as coloring agents in inks and shoe polishes and for dyeing leather, wood, textiles, and furs. Also, **ni·gro·sin** (nī′grə sin). [< L *nigr-* (s. of *niger*) black, dark + -OSE + -INE[1]]

ni·gros′por·a cob′ rot′ (nī gros′pər ə, nī′grə-spôr′ə, -spôr′ə), *Plant Pathol.* a disease of corn, characterized by shredding of the cob, discoloration and disintegration of internal tissues, and bleached, loose kernels, caused by a fungus, *Nigrospora oryzae.* [< NL, equiv. to *nigro-* (comb. form of L *niger* dark) + *-spora* SPORE]

ni·hil (nē′hil; *Eng.* nī′hil), *n.* *Latin.* nothing; a thing of no value.

ni·hil·ism (nī′ə liz′əm, nē′-), *n.* **1.** total rejection of established laws and institutions. **2.** *Philos.* **a.** an extreme form of skepticism: the denial of all real existence or the possibility of an objective basis for truth. **b.** nothingness or nonexistence. **c.** See **ethical nihilism. 3.** (*sometimes cap.*) the principles of a Russian revolutionary group, active in the latter half of the 19th century, holding that existing social and political institutions must be destroyed in order to clear the way for a new state of society and employing extreme measures, including terrorism and assassination. **4.** anarchy, terrorism, or other revolutionary activity. **5.** annihilation of the self, or the individual consciousness, esp. as an aspect of mystical experience. **6.** total and absolute destructiveness, esp. toward the world at large and including oneself: *the power-mad nihilism that so strongly marked Hitler's last years.* [NIHIL + -ISM] **—ni′hil·ist,** *n., adj.* **—ni′hil·is′tic,** *adj.*

ni·hil·i·ty (nī hil′i tē, nē-), *n.* the state of being nothing; nothingness. [NIHIL + -ITY]

ni·hil ob·stat (nē′hil ob′stat), *Rom. Cath. Ch.* permission to publish a book, granted by an official censor who, upon examining it, has certified that it contains nothing contrary to faith or morals. [< L: lit., nothing stands in the way]

Ni·hon (nē′hon), *n.* a Japanese name of **Japan.**

Ni·i·ga·ta (nē′ē gä′tä), *n.* a seaport on NW Honshu, in central Japan. 844,846 (1964).

Ni·i·ha·u (nē′ē hä′ōō), *n.* an island in NW Hawaii, W of Kauai. 254 (1960); 72 sq. mi.

Ni·jin·sky (ni zhin′skē, -jin′-; *Russ.* ni zhēn′ski), *n.* **Was·law** or **Vas·law** (väts läf′), 1890–1950, Russian ballet dancer and choreographer.

Nij·me·gen (nī′mā′gən; *Du.* nī′mā′KHən), *n.* a city in the E Netherlands, on the Waal River: peace treaty 1678. 136,111 (1962). Also, **Nimwegen, Nymwegen.**

Ni·ke (nī′kē), *n.* **1.** the ancient Greek goddess of victory, often identified with Athena; identified by the Romans with Victoria. **2.** one of a series of antiaircraft or antimissile missiles having two or three rocket stages. [< Gk *nīkē* victory, conquest]

Ni′ke of Sam′othrace. See **Winged Victory.**

nik·eth·a·mide (ni keth′ə mīd′, -mid), *n.* *Pharm.* a crystalline solid, or colorless to pale-yellow and slightly viscous liquid, $C_5H_4NCON(C_2H_5)_2$, used chiefly to stimulate circulation and respiration. [*nik-* (comb. form repr. NICOTINIC ACID) + (*di*)*eth*(*yl*) + AMIDE]

Ni·kisch (nē′kish), *n.* **Ar·thur** (ȯR′tōōR), 1855–1922, Hungarian conductor, violinist, and pianist.

Nik·ko (nēk′kō), *n.* a city on NE Honshu, in central Japan: famous for shrines and temples. 32,753 (1964).

nik·kud (nēk kōōd′), *n., pl.* **-ku·dim** (-kōō dēm′). any of the combinations of dots and lines sometimes placed above or below Hebrew consonant symbols to indicate the pronunciation of vowels accompanying and usually following the consonants; vowel point. [< Heb: dot]

Nik·ky (nik′ē), *n.* a girl's given name, form of **Nicole.** Also, **Nicky.**

Ni·ko·la·ev (ni′kô lä′yef), *n.* a city in the S Ukraine, in the SW Soviet Union in Europe. 272,000 (est. 1964). Formerly, **Vernoleninsk.**

Ni·ko·laus von Cu·sa (*Ger.* nē′kō lous fən kōō′zä *or, often,* nē′kō lä′ōōs). Nicholas (def. 1).

Ni·kon (nē′kôn), *n.* 1605–81, patriarch of Russian Orthodox Church 1652–66.

ni·ku-bo·ri (nē kōō′bə rē′; *Jap.* nē kōō′bô RE′), *n.* relief carving in Japanese metalwork, as in the ornamentation of sword mounts. [< Jap]

nil (nil), *n.* **1.** nothing; naught; zero. —*adj.* **2.** having no value or existence: *His credit rating is nil.* [< L: var. (by apocope) of *nīlum*, contr. of *nihilum* nothing, equiv. to *ni* (var. of *ne* not) + *hīlum* trifle. See NIHIL]

nil ad·mi·ra·ri (nēl′ äd′mē rä′rē; *Eng.* nil′ ad′mi râr′ī), *Latin.* to wonder at nothing.

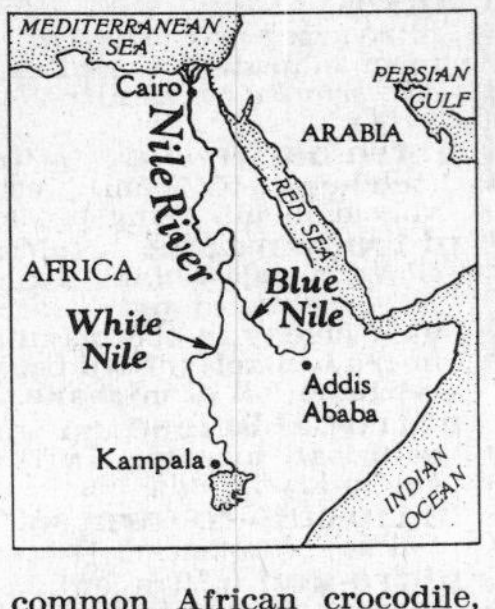

nil de·spe·ran·dum (nēl′ des′pe rän′do͝om; *Eng.* nil′ des′pə ran′dəm), *Latin.* nothing ought be despaired of; never despair.

Nile (nīl), *n.* a river in E Africa, flowing N from Lake Victoria to the Mediterranean. 3473 mi. long; from the headwaters of the Kagera River, 4000 mi. long. Latin, **Nilus.** Cf. **Blue Nile, White Nile.**

Nile′ blue′, pale greenish blue.

Nile′ croc′odile, the common African crocodile, *Crocodylus niloticus*, sometimes growing to a length of 20 feet. Also, **Nilotic crocodile.** See illus. under **crocodile.**

Nile′ green′, pale bluish green.

Niles (nīlz), *n.* **1.** a city in NE Illinois, near Chicago. 20,393 (1960). **2.** a city in NE Ohio. 19,545 (1960). **3.** a boy's given name, form of **Neil.**

nil·gai (nil′gī), *n., pl.* **-gais, -gai.** a large, Indian antelope, *Boselaphus tragocamelus*, the male of which is bluish gray with small horns, the female tawny and hornless. Also, **nylghai, nylghau.** Also called **blue bull.** [< Hindi: lit., blue cow]

Nil′gi·ri Hills′ (nil′gi rē), a group of mountains in S India, in Madras state. Highest peak, Mt. Dodabetta, 8760 ft.

Nilgai (4½ ft. high at shoulder; length 6½ ft.)

nill (nil), *v.t., v.i. Archaic.* to be unwilling: *will he, nill he.* [ME *nille(n)*, OE *nyllan*, equiv. to *ne* not + *willan* WILL¹]

nil ni·si bo·num (nēl nis′ē bō′no͝om; *Eng.* nil nī′sī bō′nəm), *Latin.* See **de mortuis nil nisi bonum.**

Ni·lom·e·ter (nī lom′i tər), *n.* a graduated column or the like used to measure the height of the floods of the Nile. [< Gk *Neilomḗtrion* a device for measuring the flood level of the Nile. See NILUS, -METER] —**Ni·lo·met·ric** (nī′lə me′trik), *adj.*

Ni·lo·te (nī lō′tē), *n., pl.* **-tes,** (*esp. collectively*) **-te.** a member of any of several Negroid peoples of the Sudan and eastern Africa.

Ni·lot·ic (nī lot′ik), *adj.* of or pertaining to the Nile River or the inhabitants of the Nile region. [< L *Nīlōtic(us)* of the Nile < Gk *Neilōtikós*. See NILUS, -OTIC]

Nilot′ic croc′odile. See **Nile crocodile.**

nil·po·tent (nil pōt′ənt), *adj. Math.* equal to zero when raised to a certain power. [NIL + POTENT]

nil si·ne nu·mi·ne (nēl sin′e no͞o′mi ne; *Eng.* nil sī′nī no͞o′mi nē, nyo͞o′-), *Latin.* nothing without the divine will: motto of Colorado.

Nils·son (nil′sən), *n.* **(Mär·ta) Bir·git** (mär′tä bir′git; *Eng.* mär′tə bûr′git), born 1918, Swedish soprano.

Ni·lus (nē′lo͞os; *Eng.* nī′ləs), *n.* Latin name of the **Nile.**

nim¹ (nim), *v.,* **nam** (näm, nam) or **nimmed, no·men** (nō′mən) or **nome** (nōm), **nim·ming.** *Archaic.* —*v.t.* **1.** to take or steal. —*v.i.* **2.** to steal; pilfer. [ME *nimen*, OE *niman*, c. Goth *niman*, Icel *nema*, G *nehmen* to take]

nim² (nim), *n.* a game in which two players alternate in drawing counters, pennies, or the like, from a set of 12 arranged in three rows of 3, 4, and 5 counters, respectively, the object being to draw the last counter, or, sometimes, to avoid drawing it. [special use of NIM¹]

nim·ble (nim′bəl), *adj.,* **-bler, -blest. 1.** quick and light in movement; moving with ease; agile; active; rapid: *nimble feet.* **2.** quick in apprehending, devising, etc.: *a nimble mind.* **3.** cleverly contrived: *a story with a nimble plot.* [late ME *nymel*, ME *nemel*, OE *nǣmel* capable, equiv. to *nǣm-* (var. s. of *niman* to take; see NUMB) + *-el* adj. suffix] —**nim′ble·ness,** *n.* —**nim′bly,** *adv.*
—**Syn. 1.** lively, brisk, swift. **2.** alert. —**Ant. 1.** clumsy.

nimbo-, a combining form of **nimbus:** *nimbostratus.*

nim·bo·stra·tus (nim′bō strā′təs, -strat′əs), *n., pl.* **-tus.** a cloud of a class characterized by a formless layer that is almost uniformly dark gray; a rain cloud of the layer type, of low altitude, usually below 8000 feet. [NIMBO- + STRATUS]

nim·bus (nim′bəs), *n., pl.* **-bi** (-bī), **-bus·es. 1.** *Class. Myth.* a shining cloud sometimes surrounding a deity when on earth. **2.** a cloud, aura, atmosphere, etc., surrounding a person or thing: *The candidate was encompassed with a nimbus of fame.* **3.** halo (def. 1). **4.** *Obs.* the type of clouds or mass of clouds, dense, with ragged edges, that yields rain or snow; a rain cloud. [< L: a rain-storm, rain-cloud, thunder-cloud, cloud; akin to *nebula* and Gk *nephélē, néphos* cloud] —**nim′bused,** *adj.*

Nîmes (nēm), *n.* a city in and the capital of Gard, in S France: Roman ruins. 105,199 (1962).

ni·mi·e·ty (ni mī′i tē), *n., pl.* **-ties. 1.** excess; overabundance: *nimiety of mere niceties in conversation.* **2.** an instance of this: *nimieties that are to be found in so many of his writings.* [< LL *nimietās*, equiv. to *nimi(us)* too much + *-etās*, var. (after *i-*) of *-itās* -ITY]

nim·i·ny-pim·i·ny (nim′ə nē pim′ə nē), *adj.* affectedly nice or refined; mincing; effeminate: *A niminy-piminy shyness makes frankness impossible.* [rhyming compound; cf. NAMBY-PAMBY] —**nim′i·ny-pim′i·ni·ness,** *n.* —**nim′i·ny-pim′i·ny·ism,** *n.*

Nim·itz (nim′its), *n.* **Chester William,** 1885–1966, U.S. admiral.

n'im·porte (naN pôrt′), *French.* it does not matter.

Nim·rod (nim′rod), *n.* **1.** Also, *Douay Bible,* **Nemrod.** the great-grandson of Noah: noted as a great hunter. Gen. 10:8–10. **2.** a person expert in or devoted to hunting. —**Nim·rod′i·an, Nim·rod′ic, Nim·rod′i·cal,** *adj.*

Nim·rud (nim ro͞od′), *n.* modern name of the site of the ancient city of Kalakh.

Nim·we·gen (*Ger.* nim′vā′ɢən), *n.* Nijmegen.

Ni·na (nē′nə, nī′-), *n.* a girl's given name, Russian form of **Anna.**

Ni·ña (nēn′yə, nē′nə; *Sp.* nē′nyä), *n.* one of the three ships under the command of Columbus when he made his first voyage of discovery to America in 1492.

nin·com·poop (nin′kəm po͞op′, ning′-), *n.* a fool or simpleton. [?] —**nin′com·poop′er·y,** *n.* —**nin′com·poop′ish,** *adj.*

nine (nīn), *n.* **1.** a cardinal number, eight plus one. **2.** a symbol for this number, as 9 or IX. **3.** a set of this many persons or things. **4.** a baseball team. **5.** a playing card with nine pips. **6. dressed to the nines,** *Informal.* looking one's best; dressed smartly, splendidly, etc.: *All the girls were dressed to the nines for their graduation.* Also, **dressed up to the nines. 7. the Nine,** the nine Muses. —*adj.* **8.** amounting to nine in number. [ME; OE *nigan, nigon,* c. D *negen,* akin to Icel *nīu,* Goth *niun,* G *neun,* L *novem,* Gk *ennéa,* Skt *nava*]

nine′-band·ed armadil′lo (nīn′ban′did), an armadillo, *Dasypus novemcinctus,* of the southern U.S. to Argentina, having nine hinged bands of bony plates, the female of which usually gives birth to quadruplets that are always of the same sex. Also called **peba, Texas armadillo.**

nine·bark (nīn′bärk′), *n.* any of several rosaceous shrubs of the genus *Physocarpus,* having bark which separates into thin layers. [NINE + BARK²]

nine′ days′ won′der, an event that arouses considerable but short-lived interest or excitement.

Nine′ Drag′on Scroll′, a Chinese scroll (1244?) painted in ink on paper.

nine·fold (nīn′fōld′), *adj.* **1.** having nine elements or parts. **2.** nine times as great or as much. —*adv.* **3.** in a ninefold manner or measure; to or by nine times as much: *to increase one's income ninefold.* [NINE + -FOLD]

nine·pence (nīn′pens′, -pəns), *n.* **1.** (*construed as pl.*) *Brit.* nine pennies. **2.** a former shilling of Great Britain, issued under Elizabeth I for use in Ireland, debased so that it was used in England as a ninepenny piece. [NINE + PENCE]

nine·pen·ny (nīn′pen′ē), *adj.* **1.** noting a nail 2¾ inches long. *Abbr.:* 9d **2.** of the value of ninepence. [NINE + -PENNY]

nine·pins (nīn′pinz′), *n.* **1.** (*construed as sing.*) tenpins played without the head pin. **2. ninepin,** a pin used in this game. [NINE + PINS]

nine-spot (nīn′spot′), *n. Slang.* a playing card the face of which bears nine pips.

nine·teen (nīn′tēn′), *n.* **1.** a cardinal number, ten plus nine. **2.** a symbol for this number, as 19 or XIX. **3.** a set of this many persons or things. **4. talk nineteen to the dozen,** to talk very rapidly or vehemently: *Whenever she is excited she talks nineteen to the dozen.* —*adj.* **5.** amounting to nineteen in number. [ME *nintene,* OE *nigontȳne.* See NINE, -TEEN]

1984, an anti-utopian novel (1949) by George Orwell.

1919, a novel (1932) by John Dos Passos. Cf. **U.S.A.** (def. 4).

nine·teenth (nīn′tēnth′), *adj.* **1.** next after the eighteenth; being the ordinal number for 19. **2.** being one of 19 equal parts. —*n.* **3.** a nineteenth part, esp. of one (1/19). **4.** the nineteenth member of a series. [ME *nyntenthe* (see NINETEEN, -TH²), r. *nientethe,* OE *nigontēotha;* see NINE, TITHE]

nine′teenth hole′, the clubhouse or any other place where golfers gather to relax, talk, or have a drink after play.

nine·ti·eth (nīn′tē ith), *adj.* **1.** next after the eighty-ninth; being the ordinal number for 90. **2.** being one of 90 equal parts. —*n.* **3.** a ninetieth part, esp. of one (1/90). **4.** the ninetieth member of a series. [ME *nyntithe,* OE *nigenteotha.* See NINETY, -ETH²]

Ni·nette (ni net′), *n.* a girl's given name, form of **Ann.**

nine·ty (nīn′tē), *n., pl.* **-ties,** *adj.* —*n.* **1.** a cardinal number, ten times nine. **2.** a symbol for this number, as 90 or XC. **3.** a set of this many persons or things. **4. nineties,** the numbers 90 through 99, esp. as in computation of age, time, temperature, etc.: *His grandmother is in her nineties.* —*adj.* **5.** amounting to 90 in number. [ME *nineti,* OE *nigontig.* See NINE, -TY¹]

nine′ty-day won′der (nīn′tē dā′), an officer commissioned in a branch of the armed forces after an unusually short training period, esp. after a three-months officers' training course during World War II.

nine·ty-eight (nīn′tē āt′), *n.* **1.** a cardinal number, 90 plus 8. **2.** a symbol for this number, as 98 or XCVIII. **3.** a set of this many persons or things. —*adj.* **4.** amounting to 98 in number.

nine·ty-eighth (nīn′tē ātth′), *adj.* **1.** next after the ninety-seventh; being the ordinal number for 98. **2.** being one of 98 equal parts. —*n.* **3.** a ninety-eighth part, esp. of one (1/98). **4.** the ninety-eighth member of a series.

nine·ty-fifth (nīn′tē fifth′), *adj.* **1.** next after the ninety-fourth; being the ordinal number for 95. **2.** being one of 95 equal parts. —*n.* **3.** a ninety-fifth part, esp. of one (1/95). **4.** the ninety-fifth member of a series.

nine·ty-first (nīn′tē fûrst′), *adj.* **1.** next after the ninetieth; being the ordinal number for 91. **2.** being one of 91 equal parts. —*n.* **3.** a ninety-first part, esp. of one (1/91). **4.** the ninety-first member of a series.

nine·ty-five (nīn′tē fīv′), *n.* **1.** a cardinal number, 90 plus 5. **2.** a symbol for this number, as 95 or XCV. **3.** a set of this many persons or things. —*adj.* **4.** amounting to 95 in number.

Nine′ty-Five The′ses, the theses of Luther against the sale of indulgences in the Roman Catholic Church, posted by him on the door of a church in Wittenberg, October 31, 1517.

nine·ty-four (nīn′tē fôr′, -fōr′), *n.* **1.** a cardinal number, 90 plus 4. **2.** a symbol for this number, as 94 or XCIV. **3.** a set of this many persons or things. —*adj.* **4.** amounting to 94 in number.

nine·ty-fourth (nīn′tē fôrth′, -fōrth′), *adj.* **1.** next after the ninety-third; being the ordinal number for 94. **2.** being one of 94 equal parts. —*n.* **3.** a ninety-fourth part, esp. of one (1/94). **4.** the ninety-fourth member of a series.

nine·ty-nine (nīn′tē nīn′), *n.* **1.** a cardinal number, 90 plus 9. **2.** a symbol for this number, as 99 or XCIX. **3.** a set of this many persons or things. —*adj.* **4.** amounting to 99 in number.

nine·ty-ninth (nīn′tē nīnth′), *adj.* **1.** next after the ninety-eighth; being the ordinal number for 99. **2.** being one of 99 equal parts. —*n.* **3.** a ninety-ninth part, esp. of one (1/99). **4.** the ninety-ninth member of a series.

nine·ty-one (nīn′tē wun′), *n.* **1.** a cardinal number, 90 plus 1. **2.** a symbol for this number, as 91 or XCI. **3.** a set of this many persons or things. —*adj.* **4.** amounting to 91 in number.

nine·ty-sec·ond (nīn′tē sek′ənd), *adj.* **1.** next after the ninety-first; being the ordinal number for 92. **2.** being one of 92 equal parts. —*n.* **3.** a ninety-second part, esp. of one (1/92). **4.** the ninety-second member of a series.

nine·ty-sev·en (nīn′tē sev′ən), *n.* **1.** a cardinal number, 90 plus 7. **2.** a symbol for this number, as 97 or XCVII. **3.** a set of this many persons or things. —*adj.* **4.** amounting to 97 in number.

nine·ty-sev·enth (nīn′tē sev′ənth), *adj.* **1.** next after the ninety-sixth; being the ordinal number for 97. **2.** being one of 97 equal parts. —*n.* **3.** a ninety-seventh part, esp. of one (1/97). **4.** the ninety-seventh member of a series.

nine·ty-six (nīn′tē siks′), *n.* **1.** a cardinal number, 90 plus 6. **2.** a symbol for this number, as 96 or XCVI. **3.** a set of this many persons or things. —*adj.* **4.** amounting to 96 in number.

nine·ty-sixth (nīn′tē siksth′), *adj.* **1.** next after the ninety-fifth; being the ordinal number for 96. **2.** being one of 96 equal parts. —*n.* **3.** a ninety-sixth part, esp. of one (1/96). **4.** the ninety-sixth member of a series.

nine·ty-third (nīn′tē thûrd′), *adj.* **1.** next after the ninety-second; being the ordinal number for 93. **2.** being one of 93 equal parts. —*n.* **3.** a ninety-third part, esp. of one (1/93). **4.** the ninety-third member of a series.

nine·ty-three (nīn′tē thrē′), *n.* **1.** a cardinal number, 90 plus 3. **2.** a symbol for this number, as 93 or XCIII. **3.** a set of this many persons or things. —*adj.* **4.** amounting to 93 in number.

nine·ty-two (nīn′tē to͞o′), *n.* **1.** a cardinal number, 90 plus 2. **2.** a symbol for this number, as 92 or XCII. **3.** a set of this many persons or 'things. —*adj.* **4.** amounting to 92 in number.

Nin·e·veh (nin′ə və), *n.* the ancient capital of Assyria: its ruins are opposite Mosul, on the Tigris River, in N Iraq. See map under **Babylon.** —**Nin·e·vite** (nin′ə vīt′), *n.* —**Nin·e·vit·i·cal** (nin′ə vit′i kəl), *adj.* —**Nin·e·vit·ish** (nin′ə vī′tish), *adj.*

Nine′ Worth′ies, three pagan, three Jewish, and three Christian heroes mentioned together in medieval romances, usually including Hector, Alexander the Great, Julius Caesar, Joshua, David, Judas Maccabaeus, Arthur, Charlemagne, and Godefroy de Bouillon.

Nin·gal (nin′gal), *n.* a Sumerian goddess, the consort of Nanna and mother of Utu.

Ning·po (ning′pō′), *n.* a seaport in E Chekiang, in E China. 240,000 (est. 1951).

Ning·sia (ning′shyä′), *n.* former province in NW China; now part of Inner Mongolia.

Ni·nib (nē′nib), *n. Obs.* Ninurta.

Ni·ni·gi (nē nē′gē), *n. Japanese Legend.* the grandson of Amaterasu and first ruler of Japan.

Nin·lil (nin′lil), *n.* a Sumerian goddess of the air.

nin·ny (nin′ē), *n., pl.* **-nies.** a fool; simpleton. [? *(a)n inn(ocent)* + -Y²] —**nin′ny·ish,** *adj.*

nin·ny·ham·mer (nin′ē ham′ər), *n.* a fool; simpleton; dolt; ninny. [NINNY + HAMMER]

ni·non (nē nôN′), *n.* a sturdy chiffon or voile constructed in either plain or novelty weaves and generally used in the manufacture of women's garments, curtains, and drapery. [< F: special use of nickname for Anne]

ninth (nīnth), *adj.* **1.** next after the eighth; being the ordinal number for nine. **2.** being one of nine equal parts. —*n.* **3.** a ninth part, esp. of one (1/9). **4.** the ninth member of a series. **5.** *Music.* **a.** a tone distant from another tone by an interval of an octave and a second. **b.** the interval between such tones. **c.** harmonic combination of such tones. [ME *ninthe* (see NINE, -TH²), r. ME *niend* (OE *nigend*), *neogethe, nigethe* (OE *nigotha*), etc.; akin to OS *nigutho,* Icel *nīundi,* Goth *niunda*] —**ninth′ly,** *adv.*

ninth′ chord′, *Music.* a chord formed by the superposition of four thirds.

Ninth′ of Ab′, *Judaism.* See **Tishah b'Ab.**

Ni·nur·ta (ni no͝or′tä), *n.* a Sumerian and Babylonian hero god, the personification of the stormy south wind and the son and avenger of Enlil.

Ni·nus (nī′nəs), *n.* the legendary husband of Semiramis and founder of Nineveh.

ni·o·bate (nī′ə bāt′), *n. Chem.* any salt of niobic acid; columbate. [NIOB(IUM) + -ATE²]

Ni·o·be (nī′ō bē′), *n. Class. Myth.* the daughter of Tantalus and wife of Amphion of Thebes. She provoked Apollo and Artemis to vengeance by taunting their mother, Leto, with the number and beauty of her own children; Niobe's children were slain and Zeus turned her into stone, in which state she continued to weep over her loss. —**Ni′o·be′an,** *adj.*

ni·o·bic (nī ō′bik, -ob′ik), *adj. Chem.* **1.** of or pertaining to niobium; columbic. **2.** of or derived from niobic acid. [NIOB(IUM) + -IC]

nio′bic ac′id, *Chem.* a white, water-insoluble solid, $Nb_2O_5 \cdot nH_2O$.

Ni·o·bid (nī′ō bid), *n. Class. Myth.* any of the children of Niobe.

ni·o·bi·um (nī ō′bē əm), *n. Chem.* a steel-gray metallic element resembling tantalum in its chemical properties; used chiefly in alloy steels. *Symbol:* Nb; *at. no.:* 41; *at. wt.:* 92.906; *sp. gr.:* 8.4 at 20°C. [< NL; see NIOBE, -IUM]

ni·o·bous (nī ō′bəs), *adj.* **1.** *Chem.* containing trivalent niobium, as niobous chloride, $NbCl_3$. **2.** of or pertaining to niobium. [NIOB(IUM) + -OUS]

Ni·o·brar·a (nī′ə brâr′ə), *n.* a river flowing E from E Wyoming through Nebraska to the Missouri. 431 mi. long.

Niord (nyôrd), *n. Scand. Myth.* the god of winds, navigation, and prosperity, and the father of Frey and Freya; king of the Vanir. Also, **Njord, Njorth.**

Niort (nyôʀ), *n.* a city in and the capital of Deux-Sèvres, in W France. 39,165 (1962).

nip[1] (nip), *v.*, **nipped, nip·ping,** *n.* —*v.t.* **1.** to compress tightly between two surfaces or points; pinch; bite. **2.** to take off by pinching, biting, or snipping (usually fol. by *off*): *He nipped off a piece of steak and gave it to the dog.* **3.** to check in growth or development. **4.** to affect sharply and painfully or injuriously, as cold does: *a cold wind that nips the fingers.* **5.** *Informal.* to snatch away suddenly. **6.** *Informal.* to steal. **7.** *Naut.* **a.** (of ice) to press (a vessel) from opposite sides. **b.** to seize (a taut rope) to another rope, as an anchor cable to a messenger from a capstan. **c.** to hold (an anchor cable) after partial heaving in while a messenger from a capstan is attached to heave it in farther. —*v.i.* **8.** *Chiefly Brit. Slang.* to leave stealthily; sneak away; flee (often fol. by *away*). **9. nip in the bud.** See **bud** (def. 6). —*n.* **10.** act of nipping; a pinch: *The dog took several nips at his heels.* **11.** a sharp or biting remark. **12.** a biting quality, as in cold or frosty air: *There's a nip in the air this morning.* **13.** sharp cold; a sharp touch of frost: *The trees had felt the first nip of winter.* **14.** the biting taste or tang in cheese. **15.** a small bit or quantity of anything: *a nip of bread to stave off hunger.* **16.** *Naut.* **a.** an abrupt turn or twist in a rope. **b.** a part of a rope or chain bound by a seizing or nipper. **17.** Usually, **nips.** nipper (def. 2). **18. nip and tuck,** *U.S. Informal.* (in a race or other contest) with one competitor equaling the speed or efforts of the other; very close: *It was nip and tuck as to which sailboat would reach port first.* [ME *nyppe* to pinch < Scand; cf. Icel *hnippa* to poke (someone) in the ribs]

nip[2] (nip), *n.*, *v.*, **nipped, nip·ping.** —*n.* **1.** a small drink of liquor; sip: *a person who relishes an occasional nip.* **2.** *Brit.* a small tankard of ale, about a half pint. **3.** *Chiefly Brit.* split (def. 28). —*v.t.*, *v.i.* **4.** to drink (liquor) in small sips, esp. repeatedly. [short for *nipperkin* vessel holding half-pint or less, small amount, ? < D; cf. *nippertje* nip and tuck; see -KIN]

Nip (nip), *n.*, *adj. Offensive and Disparaging.* Japanese. [short for NIPPON]

ni·pa (nē′pə, nī′-), *n.* a palm, *Nipa fruticans,* of the East Indies, Philippines, etc., whose foliage is used for thatching, basketry, etc. [< NL < Malay *nīpah*]

niph·a·blep·si·a (nif′ə blep′sē ə), *n.* See **snow blindness.** [< NL, equiv. to Gk *niph(a)* snow + *a-* A-[6] + *blepsia* sight]

Nip·is·sing (nip′i sing), *n.* a lake in SE Canada, in Ontario, N of Georgian Bay. 330 sq. mi.

Nip·muck (nip′muk), *n.*, *pl.* **-mucks,** (*esp. collectively*) **-muck.** a member of an Algonquian Indian people living in the vicinity of Worcester, Massachusetts.

nip·per (nip′ər), *n.* **1.** one who or that which nips. **2.** Usually, **nippers.** a device for nipping, as pincers or forceps. **3.** one of the large claws of a crustacean. **4.** *Metalworking.* dog (def. 14). **5. nippers,** *Slang.* handcuffs. **6.** *Chiefly Brit. Informal.* **a.** a small boy. **b.** a costermonger's helper or assistant. **7.** *Naut.* **a.** a short rope for seizing an anchor cable to a messenger from a capstan. **b.** a short iron clamp for seizing an anchor chain to a chain messenger from a capstan or for securing it in place; devil's claw. **8. nipper off,** *Naut.* to hold (an anchor cable) in place after partial heaving in while a messenger from a capstan is attached to heave it in further; nip. [NIP[1] + -ER[1]]

nip·ping (nip′ing), *adj.* **1.** characterized by nips; being one who or that which nips. **2.** sharp or biting, as cold. **3.** (of a person, remark, tone, etc.) sarcastic; caustic; bitter. [NIP[1] + -ING[2]] —**nip′ping·ly,** *adv.*

nip·ple (nip′əl), *n.* **1.** a protuberance of the mamma or breast where, in the female, the milk ducts discharge; teat. **2.** something resembling it, as the mouthpiece of a nursing bottle, a sugar-tit, pacifier, etc. **3.** a short piece of pipe with threads on each end, used for joining valves. [OE *nypel* proboscis, orig., projecting part; akin to Dan *nip* point] —**nip′ple·less,** *adj.*

Nip·pon (nē pôn′; *Eng.* ni pon′, nip′on), *n.* a Japanese name of **Japan.**

Nippon′ chrysan′themum, a perennial garden plant, *Chrysanthemum nipponicum,* of Japan, having thickish, blunt leaves and solitary, white flowers. Also called **Nippon′ dai′sy.**

Nip·pon·ese (nip′ə nēz′, -nēs′), *n.*, *pl.* **-ese,** *adj.* Japanese. [NIPPON + -ESE] —**Nip·pon·ism** (nip′ə-niz′əm), *n.*

Nip·pur (nip po͝or′), *n.* an ancient Sumerian and Babylonian city in SE Iraq: partially excavated.

nip·py (nip′ē), *adj.*, **-pi·er, -pi·est.** **1.** tending to nip; sharp; biting: *morning air that feels a bit nippy; a nippy taste.* **2.** *Chiefly Brit. Informal.* nimble; agile. [NIP[1] + -Y[1]]

NIRA, National Industrial Recovery Act. Also, **N.I.R.A.**

Ni·re·us (nī′rē əs, -ro͞os), *n.* (in the *Iliad*) a son of Aglaia and Charopus who, after Achilles, was the handsomest Greek warrior at Troy.

Nir·ma·lin (nir mä′lin), *n.* one of a group of Sikh ascetics devoted to the study of sacred writings.

nir·va·na (nir vä′nə, -van′ə, nər-), *n.* **1.** (*often cap.*) Pali, **nibbana.** *Buddhism.* freedom from the endless cycle of personal reincarnations, with their consequent suffering, as a result of the extinction of individual passion, hatred, and delusion: attained by the Arhat as his goal, but postponed by the Bodhisattva. **2.** (*often cap.*) *Hinduism.* salvation through the union of Atman with Brahma; Moksha. **3.** a place or state characterized by freedom from or oblivion to pain, worry, and the external world. [< Skt *nirvāṇa* a blowing out] —**nir·va′nic,** *adj.*

Niš (nēsh), *n.* a city in SE Serbia, in E Yugoslavia: a former capital of Serbia. 74,500 (est. 1959). Also, **Nish.**

Ni·san (nis′ən; *Heb.* nē sän′), *n.* a month of the Jewish calendar. Also, **Nissan.** Cf. **Jewish calendar.**

Ni·sei (nē′sā′), *n.*, *pl.* **-sei.** a person of Japanese descent, born and educated in the U.S. (distinguished from *Kibei*). Also, **ni′sei′.** Cf. **Issei, Sansei.** [< Jap, equiv. to *ni* second + *sei* generation]

Ni·sha·pur (nē′shä po͝or′), *n.* a town in NE Iran: the birthplace of Omar Khayyám. 24,270 (est. 1949).

Ni·shi·no·mi·ya (nē′shē nô′mē yä′), *n.* a city on S Honshu, in central Japan. 262,608 (1964).

ni·si (nī′sī), *conj.* unless (used, esp. in law, to indicate that a judgment or decree will become final on a particular date unless set aside or invalidated by certain specified contingencies): *to grant a decree nisi.* [< L *nisi* if not, unless]

ni·si pri·us (nī′sī prī′əs), *Law.* **1.** Also called **ni′si pri′us court′.** a trial court for the hearing of civil cases before a judge and jury. **2.** *Brit. Law.* **a.** a writ commanding a sheriff of a county to summon a jury and bring it to the court in Westminster on a certain day, unless the judges of assizes previously came to that county. **b.** the clause with the words "nisi prius" introducing this writ. **c.** the system of judicial circuits to which judges are assigned for local trials of civil and criminal cases. [< L: lit., unless previously, unless before] —**ni′si-pri′us,** *adj.*

Nis·san (nis′ən; *Heb.* nē sän′), *n.* Nisan.

Nis′sen hut′ (nis′ən), a prefabricated shelter with the shape of a long, slightly flattened cylinder, insulated, esp. for military troops in arctic regions; Quonset hut. [named after P.N. *Nissen* (1871–1930), British military engineer who invented it]

Nis·tru (nē′stro͞o), *n.* Rumanian name of **Dniester.**

ni·sus (nī′səs), *n.*, *pl.* **-sus.** a striving toward a particular goal or attainment; effort; impulse. [< L: effort, equiv. to *nīs-*, ptp. s. of *nītī* to exert oneself + *-us* n. suffix (4th decl.)]

Ni·sus (nī′səs), *n.* **1.** *Class. Myth.* a son of Pandion whose life and fate of his kingdom depended upon a lock of hair on his head. **2.** *Rom. Legend.* the son of Hyrtacus and the nymph Ida: a companion of Aeneas on the flight from Troy.

nit[1] (nit), *n.* **1.** the egg of a parasitic insect, esp. of a louse, often attached to a hair or a fiber of clothing. **2.** the young of such an insect. [ME *nite,* OE *hnitu,* c. D *neet,* Norw *nit,* G *Niss*]

nit[2] (nit), *n.* a unit of luminous intensity equal to one candela per square meter. *Abbr.:* nt [< L *nit(or)* brightness]

Ni·ta (nē′tə; *Sp.* nē′tä), *n.* a girl's given name, form of **Juanita.**

nitch·ie (nich′ē, nē′chē), *n. Chiefly Canadian Dial. Disparaging.* an Indian. [?]

ni·ter (nī′tər), *n.* **1.** potassium nitrate, a white salt, KNO_3, used in the manufacture of gunpowder, fireworks, etc.; saltpeter. **2.** sodium nitrate, a white salt, $NaNO_3$, used as a fertilizer, in dynamite, etc.; Chile saltpeter. Also, *esp. Brit.,* **nitre.** [late ME *nitre* < L *nitrum* < Gk *nítron* natron]

Ni·te·roi (nē′te roi′), *n.* a seaport in and the capital of Rio de Janeiro state, in SE Brazil. 229,025 (1960). Also, **Nictheroy.**

nit·id (nit′id), *adj.* bright; lustrous. [< L *nitid(us)* shining, bright, equiv. to *nit(ēre)* (to) glisten + *-idus* -ID[4]] —**ni·tid·i·ty** (ni tid′i tē), *n.*

nit-lamp (nit′lamp′), *n. Canadian.* See **jack light.**

ni·ton (nī′ton), *n.* (formerly) radon. *Symbol:* Nt [< L *nit(ēre)* (to) shine + Gk *-on* neut. suffix]

nit-pick (nit′pik′), *v.i. Informal.* to be excessively concerned with inconsequential details. [NIT[1] + PICK[1]]

nitr-, var. of **nitro-** before a vowel: *nitramine.*

Ni·tral·loy (nī′trə loi′), *n. Trademark.* a type of nitriding steel.

ni·tra·mine (nī′trə mēn′, nī tram′in), *n. Chem.* **1.** any of a class of compounds containing the nitramino group. **2.** tetryl. [NITR- + AMINE]

ni·tra·mi·no (nī′trə mē′nō, nī tram′ə nō′), *adj. Chem.* containing the nitramino group. [NITR- + AMINO]

nitrami′no group′, *Chem.* the univalent group, $-NHNO_2$. Also called **nitram′ino rad′ical.**

ni·trate (nī′trāt), *n.*, *v.*, **-trat·ed, -trat·ing.** —*n.* **1.** *Chem.* a salt or ester of nitric acid, or any compound containing the univalent group $-ONO_2$ or $-NO_3$. **2.** fertilizer consisting of potassium nitrate or sodium nitrate. —*v.t.* **3.** to treat with nitric acid or a nitrate. **4.** to convert into a nitrate. [NITR- + -ATE[2]] —**ni·tra′tion,** *n.*

ni·tre (nī′tər), *n. Chiefly Brit.* niter.

ni·tric (nī′trik), *adj.* **1.** *Chem.* containing nitrogen, usually in the pentavalent state. **2.** of or pertaining to niter. [NITR- + -IC, modeled on F *nitrique*]

ni′tric ac′id, *Chem.* a colorless or yellowish, fuming, suffocating, caustic, corrosive, water-soluble liquid, HNO_3, having powerful oxidizing properties, usually obtained from ammonia or from Chile saltpeter: used chiefly in the manufacture of explosives, fertilizers, and in organic synthesis. Also called **aqua fortis.**

ni′tric bacte′ria, nitrobacteria.

ni′tric e′ther, *Chem.* See **ethyl nitrate.**

ni′tric ox′ide, *Chem.* a colorless, slightly water-soluble gas, NO, formed by the action of dilute nitric acid on copper: used chiefly as an intermediate in the manufacture of nitric acid from ammonia.

ni·tride (nī′trīd, -trid), *n. Chem.* a compound, containing two elements only, of which the more electronegative one is nitrogen. [NIT(E)R + -IDE]

ni·trid·ing (nī′trī ding), *n. Metall.* a process of casehardening in which nitrogen is introduced into the metal by keeping it at a suitable temperature in the presence of a nitrogen source. [NITRIDE + -ING[1]]

ni′triding steel′, any steel suitable for casehardening by nitriding.

ni·tri·fi·ca·tion (nī′trə fə kā′shən), *n.* **1.** the act of nitrifying. **2.** the introduction of a nitro group into an organic compound, usually by means of mixed nitric and sulfuric acids. [NITR- + -I- + -FICATION]

ni·tri·fi·er (nī′trə fī′ər), *n.* one who or that which nitrifies. [NITRIFY + -ER[1]]

ni·tri·fy (nī′trə fī′), *v.t.*, **-fied, -fy·ing.** **1.** to oxidize (ammonia, ammonium compounds, or atmospheric nitrogen) to nitrites, nitrates, or their respective acids, esp. by bacterial action. **2.** to impregnate with nitrogen or nitrogen compounds. **3.** to treat or combine with nitrogen or its compounds. **4.** *Obs.* to convert into niter. [< F *nitrifier.* See NITRE, -FY] —**ni′tri·fi′a·ble,** *adj.*

ni·trile (nī′tril, -trīl), *n. Chem.* any of a class of organic compounds with the general formula $RC{\equiv}N$. [NITR- + -ILE]

ni·trite (nī′trit), *n. Chem.* a salt or ester of nitrous acid. [NITR- + -ITE[1]]

ni·tro (nī′trō), *adj. Chem.* containing the nitro group. [see NITRO-]

Ni·tro (nī′trō), *n.* a town in W West Virginia. 6894 (1960).

nitro-, *Chem.* **1.** a combining form indicating the nitro group: *nitroglycerin.* **2.** (erroneously) a combining form indicating the nitrate group: *nitrocellulose.* Also, *esp. before a vowel,* **nitr-.** [comb. form of Gk *nítron.* See NITER]

ni·tro·bac·te·ri·a (nī′trō bak tēr′ē ə), *n.pl.*, *sing.* **-te·ri·um** (-tēr′ē əm). certain bacteria in the soil involved in nitrifying processes. [NITRO- + BACTERIA]

ni·tro·ben·zene (nī′trō ben′zēn, -ben zēn′), *n. Chem.* a pale-yellow, toxic, water-soluble liquid, $C_6H_5NO_2$, produced by nitrating benzene with nitric acid: used chiefly in the manufacture of aniline. Also called **ni·tro·ben·zol** (nī′trō ben′zōl, -zōl, -zol), **essence of mirbane, oil of mirbane.** [NITRO- + BENZENE]

ni·tro·cel·lu·lose (nī′trə sel′yə lōs′), *n. Chem.* See **cellulose nitrate.** [NITRO- + CELLULOSE] —**ni′tro·cel′lu·los′ic,** *adj.*

ni·tro·chlo·ro·form (nī′trə klôr′ə fôrm′, -klōr′-), *n. Chem.* chloropicrin. [NITRO- + CHLOROFORM]

ni·tro·gen (nī′trə jən), *n. Chem.* a colorless, odorless, gaseous element that constitutes about four fifths of the volume of the atmosphere and is present in combined form in animal and vegetable tissues, esp. in proteins: used chiefly in the manufacture of ammonia, nitric acid, cyanide, explosives, fertilizer, dyes, as a cooling agent, etc. *Symbol:* N; *at. wt.:* 14.0067; *at. no.:* 7. [< F *nitrogène.* See NITRO-, -GEN]

ni′trogen cy′cle, the continuous sequence of changes by which atmospheric nitrogen and nitrogenous compounds in the soil are converted, as by nitrification and nitrogen fixation, into substances that can be utilized by green plants, the substances returning to their previous state after the plants decay, and by denitrification into substances that cannot be utilized by the plants.

ni′trogen diox′ide, *Chem.* a reddish-brown, highly poisonous gas, NO_2, used as an intermediate in the manufacture of nitric and sulfuric acids, and as a nitrating and oxidizing agent.

ni′trogen fixa′tion, **1.** any process of combining atmospheric nitrogen with other elements, either by chemical means or by bacterial action: used chiefly in the preparation of fertilizers, industrial products, etc. **2.** this process as performed by certain bacteria found in the nodules of leguminous plants, which make the resulting nitrogenous compounds available to their host plants.

ni′trogen fix′er, any of various microorganisms in the soil involved in the process of nitrogen fixation.

ni·tro·gen-fix·ing (nī′trə jən fik′sing), *adj.* involved in or aiding the process of nitrogen fixation.

ni·trog·en·ise (nī troj′ə nīz′), *v.t.*, **-ised, -is·ing.** *Chiefly Brit.* nitrogenize. —**ni·trog′en·i·sa′tion,** *n.*

ni·tro·gen·ize (nī′trə jə nīz′, nī troj′ə-), *v.t.*, **-ized, -iz·ing.** to combine with nitrogen or add nitrogenous material to. [NITROGEN + -IZE] —**ni′tro·gen·i·za′tion, ni′tro·ge·na′tion,** *n.*

ni′trogen mus′tard, *Chem.* any of the class of poisonous, blistering compounds, as $(ClCH_2CH_2)_2NCH_3$, analogous in composition to mustard gas but containing nitrogen instead of sulfur: used in the treatment of cancer and similar diseases.

ni′trogen narco′sis. See **caisson disease.**

ni·trog·e·nous (nī troj′ə nəs), *adj.* containing nitrogen. [NITROGEN + -OUS]

ni′trogen tetrox′ide, *Chem.* a poisonous compound, N_2O_4, occurring as a colorless, water-soluble solid, as a yellow liquid, or as a red-brown gas: used chiefly as an oxidizer, esp. in rocket fuels, as a nitrating agent, and as an intermediate in the manufacture of nitric acid.

ni·tro·glyc·er·in (nī′trə glis′ər in), *n. Chem., Pharm.* a colorless, thick, oily, flammable, highly explosive, slightly water-soluble liquid, $CH_2NO_3CHNO_3CH_2NO_3$, prepared from glycerol with nitric and sulfuric acids: used chiefly as a constituent of dynamite and other explosives, in rocket propellants, and in medicine as a vasodilator in the treatment of angina pectoris. Also, **ni·tro·glyc·er·ine** (nī′trə glis′ər in, -ə rēn′). Also called **glonoin, glyceryl trinitrate, trinitroglycerin.** [NITRO- + GLYCERIN]

ni′tro group′ (nī′trō), *Chem.* the univalent group, $-NO_2$. Also called **nitro radical.**

ni′tro·hy·dro·chlo′ric ac′id (nī′trə hī′drə klôr′ik, -klōr′-, nī′-), *Chem.* See **aqua regia.** [NITRO- + HYDROCHLORIC ACID]

ni·trol·ic (nī trol′ik), *adj. Chem.* of or noting a series of acids of the type, $RC(=NOH)NO_2$, whose salts form deep-red solutions. [NITR- + -OL[1] + -IC]

ni·tro·man·ni·tol (nī′trə man′i tōl′, -tôl′, -tol′), *n. Chem.* See **mannitol hexanitrate.** Also, **ni·tro·man·nite** (nī′trə man′īt). [NITRO- + MANNITOL]

ni·tro·mer·sol (nī′trə mûr′sōl, -sôl, -sol), *n. Chem.* a brownish-yellow or yellow, granular, water-insoluble powder, $C_6H_2(CH_3)(NO_2)(OHg)$: used in alkaline solution chiefly as an antiseptic. [NITRO- + MER(CURIC) + (CREO)SOL]

ni·trom·e·ter (nī trom′i tər), *n.* an apparatus for determining the amount of nitrogen or nitrogen compounds in a substance or mixture. [NITRO- + -METER] —**ni·tro·met·ric** (nī′trō me′trik), *adj.*

ni·tro·meth·ane (nī′trə meth′ān), *n. Chem.* a colorless, oily, slightly water-soluble, poisonous liquid, CH_3NO_2, used chiefly as a solvent and in organic synthesis. [NITRO- + METHANE]

ni·tro·par·af·fin (nī′trə par′ə fin), *n. Chem.* any of a class of compounds derived from the methane series replacing a hydrogen atom by the nitro group. [NITRO- + PARAFFIN]

ni·tro·phe·nol (nī′trə fē′nōl, -nôl, -nol), *n. Chem.* **1.** any compound derived from phenol by the replacement of one or more of its ring hydrogen atoms by the nitro group. **2.** any of three water-soluble, crystalline isomers of such a derivative, having the formula $O_2NC_6H_4OH$, occurring in yellow **(ortho-nitrophenol),** pale-yellow **(meta-nitrophenol),** and yellowish **(para-nitrophenol)** solids, used chiefly as intermediates in organic synthesis and as indicators. [NITRO- + PHENOL]

ni′tro rad′ical. See **nitro group.**

ni·tros·a·mine (nī′trōs ə mēn′, -am′in), *n. Chem.*

any of a series of compounds with the type formula R_2NNO. [NITROS- + AMINE]

ni·tro·so (nī trō′sō), *adj. Chem.* (esp. of organic compounds) containing the nitroso group; nitrosyl. [special use of NITROSO-]

nitroso-, a combining form of the nitroso group: *nitrosobenzene.* Also, *esp. before a vowel,* **nitros-.** [< L *nitrōs(us)* full of natron, equiv. to *nitr(um)* native soda, natron (< Gk *nítron* soda) + *-ōsus* -OSE[1]]

ni·tro·so·ben·zene (nī trō′sō ben′zēn, -ben zēn′), *n. Chem.* a blue, crystalline, water-insoluble solid, C_6H_5NO, that is green as a molten solid or in solution. [NITROSO- + BENZENE]

nitro′so group′, *Chem.* the univalent group, O=N–. Also called **nitro′so rad′ical.**

ni·tro·syl (nī′trə sil, nī′trə sēl′, nī trō′sil), *adj. Chem.* nitroso. [NITROS- + -YL]

ni·tro·syl·sul·fu·ric (nī′trə sil sul fyŏŏr′ik), *adj. Chem.* of or derived from nitrosylsulfuric acid. Also, **ni′tro·syl·sul·phu′ric.** [NITROSYL + SULFURIC]

ni′trosylsulfu′ric ac′id, *Chem.* a clear, straw-colored, oily, corrosive liquid, $NOHSO_4$, used chiefly in the manufacture of dyes. [NITROSYL + SULFURIC ACID]

ni·tro·tri·chlo·ro·meth·ane (nī′trō trī klôr′ə-meth′ān, -klōr′-), *n. Chem.* chloropicrin. [NITRO- + TRICHLOROMETHANE]

ni·trous (nī′trəs), *adj. Chem.* **1.** pertaining to compounds obtained from niter, usually containing less oxygen than the corresponding nitric compounds. **2.** containing nitrogen, usually in the trivalent state. [< L *nitrōsus* full of natron. See NITROSO-]

ni′trous ac′id, *Chem.* an acid, HNO_2, known only in solution.

ni′trous bacte′ria, nitrobacteria that convert ammonia derivatives into nitrites by oxidation.

ni′trous e′ther, *Chem.* See **ethyl nitrite.**

ni′trous ox′ide, *Chem., Pharm.* a colorless, sweet-smelling, sweet-tasting, nonflammable, slightly water-soluble gas, N_2O, that sometimes produces a feeling of exhilaration when inhaled: used chiefly as an anesthetic in dentistry and surgery, in the manufacture of chemicals, and as an aerosol. Also called **laughing gas.**

ni′tro·xan′thic ac′id (nī′trō zan′thik, nī′-), *Chem.* See **picric acid.** [NITRO- + XANTHIC ACID]

Nit·ti (nēt′tē), *n.* **Fran·ces·co Sa·ve·rio** (fʀän ches′kô sä ve′ʀyô), 1868–1953, Italian lawyer, statesman, and economist.

nit·ty (nit′ē), *adj.,* **-ti·er, -ti·est.** full of nits. [NIT[1] + -Y[1]]

nit·ty-grit·ty (nit′ē grit′ē), *n. Slang.* the essential, sometimes burdensome details of a matter or problem; brass tacks. [perh. < NIT[1] (as in NIT-PICK) + GRITTY]

nit·wit (nit′wit′), *n.* a slow-witted or foolish person. [nit (< G; dial. var. of *nicht* not) + WIT]

Ni·u·e (nē ōō′ā), *n.* an island in the S Pacific between Tonga and Cook Islands: possession of New Zealand. 4781 (est. 1960); ab. 100 sq. mi. Also called **Savage Island.** —**Ni·u·an** (nē ōō′ən), *adj., n.*

ni·val (nī′vəl), *adj.* of or growing in snow: *nival flora.* [< L *nivāl(is)* of, belonging to snow, snowy, equiv. to *niv-* (s. of *nix*) snow + *-ālis* -AL[1]]

ni·va·tion (nī vā′shən), *n.* erosion resulting from the action of névé beneath or at the edges of a snowdrift. [< L *niv-* (s. of *nix*) snow + -ATION]

niv·e·ous (niv′ē əs), *adj.* resembling snow, esp. in whiteness; snowy. [< L *niveus* snowy, snow-white, of, from snow, equiv. to *niv-* (s. of *nix*) snow + *-eus* -EOUS]

Ni·ver·nais (nē veʀ ne′), *n.* a former province in central France. *Cap.:* Nevers.

Ni·vôse (nē vōz′), *n.* (in the French Revolutionary calendar) the fourth month of the year, extending from December 21 to January 19. [< F < L *nivōsus* snowy, equiv. to *niv-* (s. of *nix*) snow + *-ōsus* -OSE[1]]

nix[1] (niks), *Slang.* —*n.* **1.** nothing. —*adv.* **2.** no. —*interj.* **3.** (used as an exclamation, esp. of warning): *Nix, the cops!* —*v.t.* **4.** to veto; refuse to agree to; prohibit: *to nix the project.* [< G: var. of *nichts* nothing]

nix[2] (niks), *n., pl.* **nix·es.** *Germanic Folklore.* a water spirit, usually small, and either good or bad. Also, *referring to a female,* **nix·ie** (nik′sē). [< G *Nix,* OHG *nihhus,* c. OE *nicor* sea monster]

Nix·on (nik′sən), *n.* **Richard M(il·hous)** (mil′hous), born 1913, 37th president of the U.S., 1969–74 (resigned).

ni·ya·ma (ni′yə mə), *n. Yoga.* one of five observances, composing one of the eight practices, or angas, which are cleanliness of mind and body, equanimity, temperance or tapas, self-appraisal, and attentiveness to God, who is conceived of as a completely free spirit. [< Skt]

Ni·zam (ni zäm′, -zam′), *n.* **1.** the title of the ruler of Hyderabad from the beginning of the 18th century to 1950. **2.** (*l.c.*) a soldier of the Turkish regular army. [(def. 1) < Urdu *Nizām-al-mulk* governor of the realm; (def. 2) < Turk *nizāmiye* regular army; both < Ar *nizām* order, arrangement, etc.]

ni·zam·ate (ni zä′māt, -zam′āt), *n.* the position held or territory governed by a Nizam. [NIZAM + -ATE[3]]

Nizh·ni Nov·go·rod (*Russ.* nēzh′ni nôv′go ʀot), former name of the city of **Gorki.**

Nizh′ni Ta·gil′ (tä gēl′), a city in the RSFSR, in the W Soviet Union in Asia, on the E slope of the Ural Mountains. 359,000 (est. 1962).

N.J., New Jersey.

Njord (nyōrd), *n.* Niord. Also, **Njorth** (nyôrth, nyôrth).

Nkru·mah (ənkrōō′mə, əngkrōō′-), *n.* **Kwa·me** (kwä′mē), 1909–72, president of Ghana 1960–66.

NKVD, the secret police of the Soviet Union (1935–43). Also, **N.K.V.D.** Cf. **Cheka, G.P.U., MVD.**

NL, New Latin; Neo-Latin. Also, **NL., N.L.**

N.L., *Baseball.* National League.

n.l., **1.** *Print.* new line. **2.** it is not permitted. [< L *non licet*] **3.** it is not clear or evident. [< L *non liquet*]

N. Lat., north latitude. Also, **N. lat.**

N. L. F., See **National Liberation Front.**

NLRB, National Labor Relations Board. Also, **N.L.R.B.**

nm, **1.** nanometer. **2.** nautical mile. **3.** nonmetallic.

N.M., New Mexico. Also, **N. Mex.**

N.M.U., National Maritime Union. Also, **NMU**

NNE, north-northeast. Also, **N.N.E.**

NNP, See **net national product.**

NNW, north-northwest. Also, **N.N.W.**

no[1] (nō), *adv., n., pl.* **noes, nos.** —*adv.* **1.** (a negative used to express dissent, denial, or refusal, as in response to a question, request, etc.) **2.** (used to emphasize or introduce a negative statement): *No one came to the party, no, not a one.* **3.** not in any degree; not at all (used with a comparative): *He is no better.* **4.** not: *whether or no.* —*n.* **5.** an utterance of the word "no." **6.** a denial or refusal: *He responded with a definite no.* **7.** a negative vote or voter: *The noes have it.* [ME; OE *nā,* equiv. to *ne* not + *ā* ever; see AY[1]]

no[2] (nō), *adj.* **1.** not any: *no money.* **2.** not at all; far from being: *He is no genius.* [var. of NONE[1]]

Nō (nō), *n.* classic drama of Japan, developed chiefly in the 14th century, employing verse, prose, choral song, and dance in highly conventionalized formal and thematic patterns derived from religious sources and folk myths. Also, **No, Noh.** Also called **Nogaku.** Cf. **kabuki.** [< Jap: lit., ability, capacity]

No, *Chem.* nobelium.

no., **1.** north. **2.** northern. **3.** number. Also, **No.**

no-ac·count (nō′ə kount′), *Informal.* —*adj.* **1.** worthless; trifling. —*n.* **2.** a worthless person; good-for-nothing. Also, **no-count.**

No·a·chi·an (nō ā′kē ən), *adj.* of or pertaining to the patriarch Noah or his time. Also, **No·ach·ic** (nō-ak′ik, -ā′kik), **No·ach′i·cal, No·a·hic** (nō ā′ik). [*Noach* (var. of NOAH) + -IAN]

No·ah (nō′ə), *n.* **1.** Also, *Douay Bible,* **Noe.** the Hebrew patriarch who built a vessel **(Noah's Ark)** in which he, his family, and animals of every species survived the Flood. Gen. 5–9. **2.** a boy's given name.

No′ah's Ark′, **1.** See under **Noah** (def. 1). **2.** an ark shell, *Arca noae.*

No′ah's Dove′, *Astron.* the constellation Columba.

No′ank boat′ (nō′angk), a centerboard lobstering vessel, formerly built in the area of Noank and New London, Connecticut, sloop-rigged with a gaff mainsail and a jib and having a sharp bow and transom stern with a well amidships for the lobsters. Also called **No′ank sloop′.**

nob[1] (nob), *n.* **1.** *Slang.* the head. **2.** *Cribbage.* the jack of the same suit as the card turned up, counting one to the holder. [? var. of KNOB]

nob[2] (nob), *n. Chiefly Brit. Slang.* a person of wealth or social distinction. [? special use of NOB[1]]

no′ ball′, *Cricket.* an unfairly bowled ball.

nob·ble (nob′əl), *v.t.,* **-bled, -bling.** *Brit. Slang.* **1.** to drug or disable (a race horse) to prevent its winning a race. **2.** to convince (a person) by fraudulent methods; misrepresent or lie to. **3.** to swindle; defraud. **4.** to seize (a person); hold for arrest. [back formation from *nobbler,* var. of HOBBLER (*an 'obbler* being taken as *a nobbler*)] —**nob′bler,** *n.*

nob·by (nob′ē), *adj.,* **-bi·er, -bi·est.** *Brit. Slang.* **1.** fashionable or elegant. **2.** excellent; first-rate. [NOB[2] + -Y[1]] —**nob′bi·ly,** *adv.*

No·bel (nō bel′), *n.* **1. Al·fred Bern·hard** (äl′fʀed beʀ′närd), 1833–96, Swedish engineer, manufacturer, and philanthropist. **2.** a boy's given name.

No·bel·ist (nō bel′ist), *n.* a person who is awarded a Nobel prize. [NOBEL (PRIZE) + -IST]

no·be·li·um (nō bē′lē əm), *n. Chem.* a synthetic, radioactive element. *Symbol:* No; *at. no.:* 102. [< NL; named after NOBEL Institute where first discovered; see -IUM]

No′bel prize′, one of a group of prizes awarded annually from the bequest of Alfred B. Nobel for achievement during the preceding year in physics, chemistry, medicine or physiology, literature, and the promotion of peace; an annual award in economics was instituted in 1969 from private funds.

No·bi·le (nô′bē le), *n.* **Um·ber·to** (ōōm beʀ′tô), 1885–1978, Italian aeronautical engineer and arctic explorer.

no·bil·i·ar·y (nō bil′ē er′ē), *adj.* of or pertaining to the nobility. [< F *nobiliaire* < L **nōbiliārius.* See NOBLE, -ARY]

no·bil·i·ty (nō bil′i tē), *n., pl.* **-ties.** **1.** the noble class or the body of nobles in a country. **2.** (in Britain) the peerage. **3.** the state or quality of being noble. **4.** noble birth or rank. **5.** nobleness of mind or spirit; exalted moral excellence. **6.** grandeur or magnificence. [late ME *nobilite* < L *nōbilitās.* See NOBLE, -ITY]

no·ble (nō′bəl), *adj.,* **-bler, -blest,** *n.* —*adj.* **1.** distinguished by rank or title. **2.** pertaining to persons so distinguished. **3.** of, belonging to, or constituting a hereditary class possessing special social or political status in a country or state; of or pertaining to the aristocracy. **4.** of an exalted moral character or excellence: *a noble thought.* **5.** admirable in dignity of conception, manner of expression, execution, or composition: *a noble poem.* **6.** imposing in appearance; stately; magnificent: *a noble monument.* **7.** of an admirably high quality; notably superior. **8.** *Chem.* inert; chemically inactive. **9.** *Falconry.* noting a hawk with long wings that stoops to its quarry at a single swoop. —*n.* **10.** a person of noble birth or rank; nobleman. **11.** a former gold coin of England, first issued in 1346 by Edward III, equal to half a mark or 6s. 8d., replaced in 1464 under Edward IV by the rose noble. **12.** (in Britain) a peer. [ME < OF < L *(g)nōbilis* notable, of high rank, equiv. to *(g)nō-* KNOW + *-bilis* -BLE] —**no′ble·ness,** *n.*

—**Syn. 3.** highborn, aristocratic. **4.** lofty, honorable. NOBLE, HIGH-MINDED, MAGNANIMOUS agree in referring to lofty principles and loftiness of mind or spirit. NOBLE implies a loftiness of character or spirit that scorns the petty, mean, base, or dishonorable: *a noble deed.* HIGH-MINDED implies having elevated principles and consistently adhering to them: *a high-minded pursuit of legal reforms.* MAGNANIMOUS suggests greatness of mind or soul, esp. as manifested in generosity or in overlooking injuries: *magnanimous toward his former enemies.* **6.** impressive, grand, lordly, splendid. **10.** peer, aristocrat. —**Ant. 3.** lowborn, base.

no′ble fir′, a fir, *Abies procera,* of the northwestern U.S., which may grow to a height of 250 feet, or its soft, light wood, used for pulpwood and plywood.

no·ble·man (nō′bəl mən), *n., pl.* **-men.** a man of noble birth or rank; noble. [NOBLE + MAN[1]] —**no′ble-man·ly,** *adv.*

no′ble met′al, any of a number of metals, as gold, silver, mercury, platinum, etc., that resist oxidation when heated in air, and solution by inorganic acids.

no·ble-mind·ed (nō′bəl mīn′did), *adj.* characterized by noble, upright thought; righteous; worthy. —**no′ble-mind′ed·ly,** *adv.* —**no′ble-mind′ed·ness,** *n.*

no′ble o′pal. See **precious opal.**

no·blesse o·blige (nō bles′ ō blēzh′; *Fr.* nô bles′ ô blēzh′), the moral obligation of the rich or highborn to display honorable or charitable conduct. [< F: lit., nobility obliges]

No·bles·ville (nō′bəlz vil′), *n.* a town in central Indiana. 7664 (1960).

no·ble·wom·an (nō′bəl wŏŏm′ən), *n., pl.* **-wom·en.** a woman of noble birth or rank. [NOBLE + WOMAN]

no·bly (nō′blē), *adv.* **1.** in a noble manner. **2.** courageously; bravely; gallantly. **3.** splendidly; superbly; magnificently. **4.** of noble ancestry: *nobly born.* [ME *nobliche.* See NOBLE, -LY]

no·bod·y (nō′bod′ē, -bə dē), *pron., n., pl.* **-bod·ies.** —*pron.* **1.** no person; not anyone; no one: *Nobody answered, so I hung up.* —*n.* **2.** *Informal.* a person of no importance, esp. socially. [ME; see NO[2], BODY]

no′-bot·tom sound′ing (nō′bot′əm), *Naut.* a sounding with a lead at a depth greater than the length of the lead line.

no·car·di·a (nō kär′dē ə), *n. Bacteriol.* any of several filamentous or rod-shaped, aerobic bacteria of the genus *Nocardia,* certain species of which are pathogenic for man and animals. [< NL; named after Edmond I.E. *Nocard* (1850–1903), French biologist; see -IA]

no·cent (nō′sənt), *adj.* **1.** harmful; injurious. **2.** *Archaic.* guilty. [< L *nocent-,* s. of *nocēns* doing harm, prp. of *nocēre;* see -ENT]

nock (nok), *n.* **1.** a metal or plastic piece at the end of an arrow, having a notch for the bowstring. **2.** a notch or groove at the end of an arrow into which the bowstring fits. **3.** a notch or groove at each end of the bow, to hold the bowstring in place. **4.** *Naut.* throat (def. 6a). —*v.t.* **5.** to furnish with a nock. **6.** to adjust (the arrow) to the bowstring, in readiness to shoot. [ME *nocke;* akin to D *nok,* LG *nok(ke)* tip]

No·co·na (nə kō′nə), *n.* a town in N Texas. 3127 (1960).

no-count (nō′kount′), *adj., n.* no-account.

noct-, var. of **nocti-** before a vowel.

noc·tam·bu·lism (nok tam′byə liz′əm), *n.* somnambulism. Also, **noc·tam′bu·la′tion.** [NOCT- + L *ambul(āre)* (to) walk + -ISM] —**noc·tam′bu·list, noc·tam·bule** (nok tam′byōōl), *n.*

noc·tam·bu·lous (nok tam′byə ləs), *adj.* of, pertaining to, or given to sleepwalking. Also, **noc·tam′bu·lant, noc·tam′bu·lis′tic.** [NOCTAMBUL(ISM) + -OUS]

nocti-, a learned borrowing from Latin meaning "night," used in the formation of compound words: *noctilucent.* Also, *esp. before a vowel,* **noct-.** [< L *nocti-,* comb. form of *nox* night]

noc·ti·lu·ca (nok′tə lōō′kə), *n., pl.* **-cae** (-sē). a dinoflagellate of the genus *Noctiluca,* capable of producing light and responsible for much of the luminous appearance of the sea. [< L *noctilūca* shiner by night, equiv. to *nocti-* NOCTI- + *-lūca* shiner, akin to *lūcēre* to shine] —**noc′ti·lu′can,** *adj.*

noc·ti·lu·cent (nok′tə lōō′sənt), *adj. Meteorol.* (of clouds) very high and cirruslike, visible during the short night of summer and believed to be of meteor dust shining with reflected sunlight. [NOCTI- + LUCENT] —**noc′ti·lu′cence,** *n.*

noc·tis (nok′tis), *adj.* (in prescriptions) of the night. [< L, gen. sing. of *nox* night]

noc·to·graph (nok′tə graf′, -gräf′), *n.* a frame used to aid the blind in writing. [NOCT- + -O- + -GRAPH]

noc·tu·id (nok′chōō id), *n.* **1.** Also called **owlet moth.** any of numerous moths of the family *Noctuidae,* comprising dull-colored moths, the larvae of which include the armyworms and cutworms. —*adj.* **2.** belonging or pertaining to the family *Noctuidae.* [< NL *Noctuid(ae)* name of family of moths, equiv. to *noctu-* (s. of L *noctua* night-owl; see NOCTI-) + *-idae* -ID[2]]

noc·tule (nok′chōōl), *n.* a large reddish insectivorous bat, *Nyctalus noctula,* common to Europe and Asia. [< F < It *nottola* a bat, owl, alter. of L *noctua* night owl. See NOCT-, -ULE]

noc·turn (nok′tûrn), *n. Rom. Cath. Ch.* the office of matins, consisting of nine psalms and either three or nine lessons. [ME *nocturne* < ML *nocturna,* n. use of fem. of L *nocturnus* by night; r. OE *noctern*]

noc·tur·nal (nok tûr′nəl), *adj.* **1.** of or pertaining to the night (opposed to *diurnal*). **2.** done, occurring, or coming by night. **3.** active by night, as animals (opposed to *diurnal*). **4.** opening by night and closing by day, as certain flowers (opposed to *diurnal*). —*n.* **5.** *Archaic.* an astrolabe for telling time or for determining latitude by the position of certain stars in reference to Polaris. [< LL *nocturnāl(is).* See NOCTURN, -AL[1]] —**noc·tur·nal·i·ty** (nok′tər nal′i tē), *n.* —**noc·tur′nal·ly,** *adv.*

noctur′nal arc′, *Astron.* the portion of the diurnal circle that is below the horizon of a given point. Cf. **diurnal arc.**

noc·turne (nok′tûrn), *n. Music.* **1.** a piece appropriate to the night or evening. **2.** an instrumental composition of a dreamy or pensive character. [< F *nocturne.* See NOCTURN]

noc·u·ous (nok′yōō əs), *adj.* likely to cause damage or injury; noxious. [< L *nocuus* harmful, injurious, equiv. to *nocu-* (perf. s. of *nocēre* to harm) + *-us* -OUS] —**noc′u·ous·ly,** *adv.* —**noc′u·ous·ness,** *n.*

nod (nod), *v.,* **nod·ded, nod·ding,** *n.* —*v.i.* **1.** to make a slight, quick inclination of the head, as in assent, greeting, command, etc. **2.** to let the head fall forward with a sudden, involuntary movement when sleepy. **3.** to become careless, inattentive, or listless; make an error or mistake through lack of attention. **4.** (of trees, flowers, plumes, etc.) to droop, bend, or incline with a swaying motion. —*v.t.* **5.** to incline (the head) in a short, quick movement, as of assent, greeting, etc. **6.** to express or signify by such a movement of the head: *to nod approval; to nod agreement.* **7.** to summon, bring, or send by a nod of the head. **8.** to cause (something) to lean or sway; incline. —*n.* **9.** a short, quick inclination of the head, as in assent, greeting, command, or drowsiness. **10.** a brief period of sleep; nap. **11.** a bending or swaying movement. **12. on the nod,** *Brit.* on credit. [ME *nodde* < ?] —**nod′ding·ly,** *adv.*

Nod (nod), *n.* **1.** the land east of Eden where Cain went to dwell. Gen. 4:16. **2.** See **land of Nod.**

nod·al (nōd′əl), *adj.* pertaining to or of the nature of a node. [NODE + -AL[1]] —**no·dal·i·ty** (nō dal′i tē), *n.*

nod′al plane′, *Optics.* a plane through a nodal point, normal to the axis of a lens or other optical system.

nod′al point′, *Optics.* either of two points on the axis of a lens or other optical system, determined by extending an incident oblique ray and the corresponding refracted ray to the axis for the pair of rays which are parallel outside the optical system. Also called **node.**

nod′ding acquain′tance, 1. an incomplete or superficial knowledge (of something): *He had only a nodding acquaintance with Italian and didn't trust it to get him through the tour.* 2. someone with whom one is only slightly acquainted: *I don't really know what he's like, he's only a nodding acquaintance.*

nod′ding li′lac, a showy lilac, *Syringa reflexa,* of China, having nodding clusters of deep-pink flowers.

nod′ding tril′lium, a hardy, perennial herb, *Trillium cernuum,* of the eastern coast of North America, having wavy-petalled, white or pinkish flowers on short, recurved stalks. Also called **ground lily, jew's-harp.**

nod·dle[1] (nod′əl), *n.* *Informal.* the head. [late ME *nodel*]

nod·dle[2] (nod′əl), *v.t., v.i.,* **-dled, -dling.** to nod slightly or frequently. [NOD + -LE (freq. suffix)]

nod·dy (nod′ē), *n., pl.* **-dies.** 1. any of several dark-bodied terns found about the coasts and islands in warm seas of both the New and Old Worlds, often so tame as to seem stupid. 2. a fool or simpleton; noodle. [? n. use of *noddy* (adj.) silly. See NOD, -Y[1]]

node (nōd), *n.* 1. a knot, protuberance, or knob. 2. a centering point of component parts. 3. *Bot.* **a.** a joint in a stem. **b.** a part of a stem that normally bears a leaf. 4. *Geom.* a point on a curve or surface at which there can be more than one tangent line or tangent plane. 5. *Physics.* a point, line, or region in a standing wave at which there is relatively little or no vibration. 6. *Astron.* either of the two points at which the orbit of a heavenly body intersects a given plane, esp. the plane of the ecliptic or of the celestial equator. Cf. **ascending node, descending node.** 7. *Optics.* See **nodal point.** 8. *Pathol.* circumscribed swelling. 9. *Engineering.* See **panel point.** 10. nodus. [< L *nōdus* a knot]

N
N

N, Node on stem of polygonum

nod·i·cal (nod′i kəl, nō′di-), *adj.* *Astron.* of or pertaining to a node or the nodes. [NODE + -ICAL]

nod′ical month′. See under **month** (def. 5).

no·dose (nō′dōs, nō dōs′), *adj.* having nodes. [< L *nōdōsus* full of knots, knotty, equiv. to *nōd(us)* NODE + *-ōsus* -OSE[1]] —**no·dos·i·ty** (nō dos′i tē), *n.*

no·dous (nō′dəs), *adj.* full of knots. [< L *nōdōsus.* See NODOSE]

nod·u·lar (noj′ə lər), *adj.* 1. of, pertaining to, or characterized by nodules. 2. shaped like or occurring in nodules: *limestone of nodular structure.* [NODULE + -AR[1]]

nod·ule (noj′o͞ol), *n.* 1. a small node, knot, or knob. 2. a small, rounded mass or lump. 3. *Bot.* a tubercle. [< L *nōdulus* a little knot, equiv. to *nōd(us)* NODE + *-ulus* -ULE]

nod·u·lous (noj′ə ləs), *adj.* having nodules. Also, **nod·u·lose** (noj′ə lōs′, noj′ə lōs′). [NODULE + -OUS]

nod·u·lus (noj′ə ləs), *n., pl.* **-li** (-lī′). *Anat.* a small node, esp. on the vermis of the cerebellum. [< L: little knot; see NODULE]

no·dus (nō′dəs), *n., pl.* **-di** (-dī). a difficult or intricate point, situation, plot, etc. [< L *nōdus* a knot]

No·e (nō′ə), *n.* *Douay Bible.* Noah (def. 1).

no·e·gen·e·sis (nō′ē jen′i sis), *n.* the production of new knowledge from sensory or intellectual experience. [< NL < Gk *noē-* (comb. form repr. *nóēsis* intelligence, or *nóēma* perception, thought) + GENESIS] —**no·e·ge·net·ic** (nō′ē jə net′ik), *adj.*

No·el (nō el′), *n.* 1. the Christmas season; yuletide. 2. (*l.c.*) a Christmas song or carol. [< F << L *nātālis* birthday, n. use of *nātālis* NATAL]

No·el-Ba·ker (nō′əl bā′kər), *n.* **Philip John,** born 1889, British statesman and author: Nobel peace prize 1959.

No·e·mi (nō′ə mī′), *n.* *Douay Bible.* Naomi (def. 1).

No·e·mon (nō ē′mən), *n.* (in the *Odyssey*) an Ithacan inspired by Athena to supply Telemachus with a ship to search for Odysseus.

no·e·sis (nō ē′sis), *n.* 1. (in Greek philosophy) the exercise of reason. 2. *Psychol.* cognition; the functioning of the intellect. [< Gk *nóēsis* thought, intelligence, equiv. to *noē-* (verbid s. of *noein* to think) + *-sis* -SIS]

no·et·ic (nō et′ik), *adj.* 1. of or pertaining to the mind. 2. originating in and apprehended by the reason. [< Gk *noētikós* intelligent, equiv. to *nóē(sis)* NOESIS + *-tikos* -TIC]

no·et·ics (nō et′iks), *n.* (*construed as sing.*) *Logic.* the science of the intellect. [see NOETIC, -ICS]

Noeud de Vi·pères, Le (*Fr.* lə nœ də vē per′). See **Viper's Tangle, The.**

No′ Ex′it, a play (1945) by Jean-Paul Sartre. French, **Huis Clos.**

no-fault (nō′fôlt′), *n.* 1. Also called **no′-fault′ in·sur′ance.** a form of automobile insurance designed to enable the policyholder in case of an accident to collect a certain basic compensation promptly for his economic loss from his own insurance company without determination of liability. —*adj.* 2. of, pertaining to, or requiring the use of such insurance: *a no-fault law; no-fault coverage.*

Nof·re·te·te (nof′ri tē′tē), *n.* Nefertiti.

no-frills (nō′frilz′), *adj.* not providing or including normally expected or available features or comfort; reduced to essentials: *a no-frills air fare.*

nog[1] (nog), *n.* 1. *U.S.* any beverage made with beaten eggs, usually with alcoholic liquor; eggnog. 2. a kind of strong ale. Also, **nogg.** [?]

nog[2] (nog), *n., v.,* **nogged, nog·ging.** —*n.* 1. a block of wood, as one inserted into brickwork to provide a hold for nails. 2. any wooden peg, pin, or block. 3. Also, **nogging.** one of a number of wooden pieces fitted between the principal timbers of a half-timbered wall. —*v.t.* 4. to fill (a framed wall or partition) with small masonry, as bricks or stones. [? var. of *knag,* ME *knagge* spur, peg]

No·ga·ku (nō′gä ko͞o′), *n.* (*often l.c.*) *Japanese.* Nō.

No·gal·es (nə gal′is), *n.* a town in S Arizona. 7286 (1960).

nogg[1] (nog), *n.* nog[1].

nogg[2] (nog), *n.* *Carpentry.* a shave for shaping dowels and handles. [special use of NOG[2]]

Nög·ge·rath (nō′gə rath′), *n.* a crater in the third quadrant of the face of the moon: about 22 miles in diameter.

nog·gin (nog′ən), *n.* 1. a small cup or mug. 2. a small amount of liquor, usually a gill. 3. *Informal.* the head. [?]

nog·ging (nog′ing), *n.* 1. (in frame construction) the act of filling the spaces between studs or nogs with small masonry, as bricks. 2. masonry employed in nogging. 3. nog[2] (def. 3). [NOG[2] + -ING[1]]

No·gu·chi (nō go͞o′chē), *n.* 1. **Hi·de·yo** (hē′de yô′), 1876–1928, Japanese physician and bacteriologist in the U.S. 2. **I·sa·mu** (ē′sä mo͞o′), born 1904, U.S. sculptor and designer.

Noh (nō), *n.* Nō.

no-hit (nō′hit′), *adj.* *Baseball.* of, pertaining to, or noting a game in which the same pitcher pitches throughout the full game without allowing a base hit to the opposing team: *a no-hit pitcher; a no-hit game.*

no-hit·ter (nō′hit′ər), *n.* *Baseball.* a no-hit game. Cf. **perfect game.**

no·how (nō′hou′), *adv.* *Chiefly Dial.* in no manner; not at all: *I can't learn this nohow.* [NO[2] + HOW]

-noia, an element appearing in loan words from Greek, where it meant "thought": *paranoia.* [< Gk *-noia,* equiv. to *nó(os)* mind + *-ia* -Y[3]]

n.o.i.b.n., not otherwise indexed by name.

noil (noil), *n.* a short fiber of cotton, wool, worsted, etc., separated from the long fibers in combing. [?] —**noil′y,** *adj.*

noir (NWAR), *adj.* noting the black numbers in roulette. [< F: lit., black]

noise (noiz), *n., v.,* **noised, nois·ing.** —*n.* 1. sound, esp. of a loud, harsh, or confused kind: *deafening noises.* 2. a nonharmonious or discordant group of sounds. 3. a sound of any kind: *to hear a noise at the door.* 4. loud shouting, outcry, or clamor. 5. an electric disturbance in a communications system that interferes with or prevents reception of a signal or of information, as the buzz on a telephone, or snow on a television screen. 6. *Obs.* rumor or common talk, esp. slander. —*v.t.* 7. to spread as a report or rumor: *A new scandal is being noised about.* —*v.i.* 8. to talk much or publicly. 9. to make a noise, outcry, or clamor. [ME < OF < L *nausea* seasickness. See NAUSEA]
—**Syn.** 1. clatter, blare, uproar, tumult. NOISE, CLAMOR, DIN, HUBBUB, RACKET refer to unmusical or confused sounds. NOISE is the general word and is applied equally to soft or loud, confused or inharmonious sounds: *street noises.* CLAMOR and HUBBUB are alike in referring to loud noises resulting from shouting, cries, animated or excited tones, and the like; but in CLAMOR the emphasis is on the meaning of the shouting, and in HUBBUB the emphasis is on the confused mingling of sounds: *the clamor of an angry crowd; His voice could be heard above the hubbub.* DIN suggests a loud, resonant noise, painful if long continued: *the din of a boiler works.* RACKET suggests a loud, confused noise of the kind produced by clatter or percussion: *She always makes a racket when she cleans up the dishes.* 3. See **sound**[1].

noise′ fac′tor, *Radio, Electronics.* (in an amplifier or transducer) the ratio of the noise power per unit bandwidth in the output to the noise power per unit bandwidth which would occur in the output if the device were to operate with a noise corresponding only to the thermal noise inherent in the input termination at a standard temperature. Also called **noise′ fig′ure.**

noise·less (noiz′lis), *adj.* accompanied by or making no noise; silent; quiet: *a noiseless step.* [NOISE + -LESS] —**noise′less·ly,** *adv.* —**noise′less·ness,** *n.*
—**Syn.** inaudible, soundless. See **still**[1].

noise′ lim′iter, *Electronics.* an electronic circuit that cuts off all noise peaks that are stronger than some specific maximum for the desired input signal, thus limiting atmospheric and other interference. Also called **noise suppressor.**

noise·mak·er (noiz′mā′kər), *n.* one who or that which makes noise, as a reveler on New Year's Eve, Halloween, etc., or a rattle, horn, or similar device used on such an occasion. [NOISE + MAKER] —**noise′mak′ing,** *n., adj.*

noise·proof (noiz′pro͞of′), *adj.* soundproof. [NOISE + -PROOF]

noise′ suppres′sor, *Electronics.* 1. squelch (def. 8). 2. See **noise limiter.**

noi·some (noi′səm), *adj.* 1. offensive or disgusting, as an odor. 2. harmful, injurious, or noxious. [ME *noy* (aph. var. of ANNOY) + -SOME[1]] —**noi′some·ly,** *adv.* —**noi′some·ness,** *n.*
—**Syn.** 1. fetid, putrid, rotten, stinking, mephitic.

nois·y (noi′zē), *adj.,* **nois·i·er, nois·i·est.** 1. making much noise: *noisy children.* 2. abounding in or full of noise: *a noisy assembly hall.* [NOISE + -Y[1]] —**nois′i·ly,** *adv.* —**nois′i·ness,** *n.*
—**Syn.** 1. clamorous, tumultuous, uproarious; vociferous. See **loud.** —**Ant.** 1. quiet.

no·lens vo·lens (nō′lens vō′lens), *Latin.* whether willing or not; willy-nilly.

no·li me tan·ge·re (nō′lī mē tan′jə rē; *Lat.* nō′lē me täng′ge re′), 1. one who or that which must not be touched or interfered with. 2. a picture representing Jesus appearing to Mary Magdalene after his resurrection. 3. Also, **no′li-me-tan′ge·re.** the touch-me-not. [< L: touch me not]

nol·le pros·e·qui (nol′ē pros′ə kwī′), *Law.* an entry made upon the records of a court when the plaintiff or prosecutor will proceed no further in a suit or action. *Abbr.:* nol. pros. [< L: be unwilling to pursue, do not prosecute]

no·lo con·ten·de·re (nō′lō kən ten′də rē), *Law.* (in a criminal case) a defendant's pleading which does not admit guilt but subjects him to punishment as though he had pleaded guilty, the determination of guilt remaining open in other proceedings. [< L: I am unwilling to contend]

nol-pros (nol′pros′), *v.t.,* **-prossed, -pros·sing.** *Law.* to determine by a nolle prosequi.

nol. pros., *Law.* See **nolle prosequi.**

Nol·u·dar (nol′yə där′), *n.* *Pharm., Trademark.* methyprylon.

nom., nominative.

no·ma (nō′mə), *n., pl.* **-mas.** *Pathol.* a gangrenous ulceration of the mouth and cheeks and sometimes other parts, occurring mainly in debilitated children. [< NL, equiv. to L *nom(ē)* a sore, ulcer < Gk *nomḗ* a feeding, grazing (akin to *némein* to feed, graze, consume) + L *-a* n. suffix]

no·mad (nō′mad, nom′ad), *n.* 1. a member of a race or tribe which has no fixed abode, but moves about from place to place according to the state of the pasturage or food supply. 2. any wanderer. —*adj.* 3. nomadic. [< L *nomad-* < Gk, s. of *nomás* pasturing flocks, akin to *némein* to pasture] —**no′mad·ism,** *n.*

no·mad·ic (nō mad′ik), *adj.* of, pertaining to, or characteristic of nomads. [NOMAD + -IC] —**no·mad′i·cal·ly,** *adv.*

no·mad·ise (nō′ma dīz′), *v.i., v.t.,* **-ised, -is·ing.** *Chiefly Brit.* nomadize.

no·mad·ize (nō′ma dīz′), *v.,* **-ized, -iz·ing.** —*v.i.* 1. to live in the manner of a nomad. —*v.t.* 2. to cause (a person, tribe, etc.) to become nomadic: *The invaders had succeeded in nomadizing the country's people.* [NOMAD + -IZE]

no′ man's′ land′, 1. a tract of land between opposing armies, over which no control has been established. 2. an unowned or unclaimed tract of usually barren land. 3. *Informal.* (in tennis, handball, etc.) the area of a court in which a player is at a tactical disadvantage, as the area of a tennis court about midway between the net and the base line.

nom·arch (nom′ärk), *n.* the governor of a nome or a nomarchy. [< Gk *nomárch(ēs)* the chief of a province, equiv. to *nom(ós)* a province, district + *árch(ein)* (to) rule + *-ēs* n. suffix]

nom·ar·chy (nom′är kē), *n., pl.* **-chies.** one of the provinces into which modern Greece is divided. [< Gk *nomarchía* rule of a province. See NOMARCH, -Y[3]]

nom·bles (num′bəlz), *n.pl.* numbles.

nom·bril (nom′bril), *n.* *Heraldry.* the point in an escutcheon between the middle of the base and the fess point. Also called **navel.** [< F: lit., navel]

Nom. Cap., nominal capital.

nom de guerre (nôN də geR′; *Eng.* nom′ də gâr′), *pl.* **noms de guerre** (nôN də geR′; *Eng.* nomz′ də gâr′). *French.* an assumed name, as one under which a person fights, paints, writes, etc.; pseudonym. [lit., war name]

nom de plume (nom′ də plo͞om′; *Fr.* nôN də plym′), *pl.* **noms de plume** (nomz′ də plo͞om′; *Fr.* nôN də plym′). See **pen name.** [coined in E < F words: lit., pen name]

nome (nōm), *n.* 1. one of the provinces of ancient Egypt. 2. nomarchy. [< Gk *nom(ós)* a pasture, district, akin to *némein* to pasture]

Nome (nōm), *n.* 1. a seaport in W Alaska. 2316 (1960). 2. **Cape,** a cape in W Alaska, on Seward Peninsula, W of Nome.

no·men (nō′men), *n., pl.* **nom·i·na** (nom′ə nə). (in ancient Rome) the second name of a citizen, indicating his gens, as "Gaius *Julius* Caesar." [< L: A NAME]

no·men·cla·tor (nō′mən klā′tər), *n.* *Archaic.* 1. a person who calls or announces things or persons by their names. 2. a person who assigns names, as in scientific classification; classifier. [< L: var. of *nōmenculātor* a name-caller, equiv. to *nōmen* NAME + *-culātor,* var. of *calātor* a crier (*calā(re)* (to) call + *-tor* agent suffix)]

no·men·cla·ture (nō′mən klā′chər, nō men′klə-), *n.* 1. a set or system of names or terms, as those used in a particular science or art, by an individual or community, etc. 2. the names or terms comprising a set or system. [< L *nōmenclātūra* a calling by name, list of names. See NOMENCLATOR, -URE] —**no′men·cla′tur·al, no·men·cla·to·ri·al** (nō′mən klə tôr′ē əl, -tōr′-), **no·men·cla·tive** (nō′mən klā′tiv), *adj.*

No·mi·a (nō′mē ə), *n.* *Class. Myth.* a nymph who blinded Daphnis because he was unfaithful to her.

nom·i·nal (nom′ə nəl), *adj.* 1. being such in name only; so-called: *a nominal treaty; a nominal committee.* 2. (of a price, consideration, etc.) named as a mere matter of form, being trifling in comparison with the actual value. 3. of, pertaining to, or constituting a name or names. 4. *Gram.* **a.** of, pertaining to, or producing a noun or nouns: *a nominal suffix.* **b.** functioning as or like a noun. 5. assigned to a person by name: *nominal shares of stock.* 6. containing, bearing, or giving a name or names. [< L *nōmināl(is)* of, belonging to a name, nominal, equiv. to *nōmin-* (s. of *nōmen*) a name + *-ālis* -AL[1]]
—**Syn.** 1. titular, formal.

nom′inal dam′ages, *Law.* damages of a small amount awarded to a plaintiff in cases where the loss sustained was not proved or does not entitle him to substantial compensation.

nom·i·nal·ism (nom′ə nəliz′əm), *n.* (in medieval philosophy) the doctrine that general or abstract words do not stand for objectively existing entities, and that universals are no more than names assigned to them. Cf. **conceptualism, realism** (def. 5a). [< F *nominalisme.* See NOMINAL, -ISM] —**nom′i·nal·ist,** *n.* —**nom′i·nal·is′tic,** *adj.* —**nom′i·nal·is′ti·cal·ly,** *adv.*

nom·i·nal·ize (nom′ə nəlīz′), *v.t.,* **-ized, -iz·ing.** to convert (another part of speech) into a noun: *Usage has nominalized the adjective "lowly" into "the lowly."* [NOMINAL + -IZE]

nom·i·nal·ly (nom′ə nəlē), *adv.* by or as regards name; in name; ostensibly: *He was, nominally, the leader, but others actually wielded the power.* [NOMINAL + -LY]

nom′inal par′, *Finance.* See under **par** (def. 3).

nom′inal sen′tence, *Gram.* a sentence consisting of a subject and complement without a linking verb, as *Very interesting, those books.*

nom′inal val′ue, book or par value, as of securities; face value.

nom′inal wag′es, *Econ.* wages measured in terms of money and not by their ability to command goods and services. Cf. **real wages.**

nom·i·nate (*v.* nom′ə nāt′; *adj.* nom′ə nit), *v.,* **-nat·ed, -nat·ing,** *adj.* —*v.t.* 1. to propose (someone) as a proper person for appointment or election to an office. 2. to appoint to a duty or office. 3. *Horse Racing.* to register (a horse) as an entry in a race. 4. *Archaic.* to entitle; name; designate. 5. *Obs.* to specify. —*adj.* 6. having a particular name. [< L *nōmināt(us)* called by name, named (ptp. of *nōmināre*), equiv. to *nōmin-* (s. of *nōmen*) a name + *-ātus* -ATE[1]] —**nom′i·na′tor,** *n.*

nom·i·na·tion (nom′ə nā′shən), *n.* **1.** the act or an instance of nominating, esp. to office: *The floor is open for nomination of candidates for the chairmanship.* **2.** the state of being nominated. [< L *nōminātiōn-* (s. of *nōminātiō*) a naming, nomination. See NOMINATE, -ION]

nom·i·na·tive (nom′ə nə tiv, -nā′tiv, nom′nə-), *adj.* **1.** *Gram.* **a.** (in certain inflected languages, as Sanskrit, Latin, and Russian) noting a case having as its function the indication of the subject of a finite verb, as in Latin *Nauta bonus est* "The sailor is good," with *nauta* "sailor" in the nominative case. **b.** similar to such a case in function or meaning. **2.** nominated; appointed by nomination. **3.** made out in a person's name, as a certificate, security, etc. —*n.* *Gram.* **4.** the nominative case. **5.** a word in the nominative case. **6.** a form or construction of similar function or meaning. [< L *nōminātīv(us)* (see NOMINATE, -IVE), r. ME *nominatif* < MF] —**nom′i·na·tive·ly,** *adv.*

nom′inative ab′solute, *Gram.* an absolute in the nominative case.

nom′inative of address′, *Gram.* a noun naming the person to whom one is speaking.

nom·i·nee (nom′ə nē′), *n.* a person nominated, as to run for elective office, fill a particular post, etc. [NOMIN(ATE) + -EE]

no·mism (nō′miz əm), *n.* conduct in a religion, based on a law or laws. [NOM(O)- + -ISM] —**no·mis′tic,** *adj.*

nomo-, a learned borrowing from Greek meaning "custom," "law," used in the formation of compound words: *nomology.* [< Gk *nomo-*, comb. form of *nómos* law, custom; akin to *némein* (to) manage, control]

no·mo·can·on (nō′mə kan′ən), *n.* a compendium of Greek Orthodox ecclesiastical laws and Byzantine imperial laws that related to ecclesiastical matters. [< MGk *nomokanōn.* See NOMO-, CANON]

nom·o·gram (nom′ə gram′, nō′mə-), *n.* **1.** a graph, usually containing three parallel scales graduated for different variables so that when a straight line connects values of any two, the related value may be read directly from the third at the point intersected by the line. **2.** any similar graph used to show the relation between quantities, values, numbers, and so on. Also called **nom·o·graph** (nom′ə graf′, -gräf′, nō′mə-), **alignment chart.** [NOMO- + -GRAM¹]

no·mog·ra·phy (nō mog′rə fē), *n., pl.* **-phies** for 1. **1.** the art of or a treatise on drawing up laws. **2.** the art of making and using a nomogram for solving a succession of nearly identical problems. [< Gk *nomographía* the writing of laws. See NOMO-, -GRAPHY] —**no·mog′ra·pher,** *n.* —**nom·o·graph·ic** (nom′ə graf′ik), **nom′o·graph′i·cal,** *adj.* —**nom′o·graph′i·cal·ly,** *adv.*

no·mol·o·gy (nō mol′ə jē), *n.* **1.** the science of law. **2.** the science of the laws of the mind. [NOMO- + -LOGY] —**nom·o·log·i·cal** (nom′ə loj′i kəl), *adj.* —**no·mol′o·gist,** *n.*

nom·o·thet·ic (nom′ə thet′ik), *adj.* **1.** lawgiving; legislative. **2.** founded upon or derived from law. **3.** *Psychol.* pertaining to or involving the study of cases or events as universals, with a view to formulating general laws (opposed to *idiographic*). [< Gk *nomothetik(ós).* See NOMO-, THETIC]

No·mu·ra (nō′mōō rä′), *n.* **Ki·chi·sa·bu·ro** (kē′chē-sä′bōō rō′), 1877–1964, Japanese diplomat.

-nomy, a combining form of Greek origin meaning "distribution," "arrangement," "management," or having reference to laws or government: *astronomy; economy; taxonomy.* [< Gk *-nomia* law. See NOMO-, -Y³]

non-, a combining form meaning "not," freely used as an English formative, usually with a simple negative force as implying mere negation or absence of something (rather than the opposite or reverse of it, as often expressed by **un-**¹): *nonadherence; noninterference; nonpayment; nonprofessional.* [comb. form repr. L adv. *nōn* not]

no·na (nō′nə), *n.* *Pathol.* See **sleeping sickness** (def. 2). [< L *nōna (hōra)* ninth (hour); i.e., late stage in life of patient]

No·na (nō′nə), *n.* a girl's given name.

non·age (non′ij, nō′nij), *n.* **1.** the period of legal minority. **2.** any period of immaturity. [late ME < MF (see NON-, AGE), r. ME *nounage* < AF *nounage*]

non·a·ge·nar·i·an (non′ə jə nâr′ē ən, nō′nə jə-), *adj.* **1.** of the age of 90 years, or between 90 and 100 years old. —*n.* **2.** a nonagenarian person. [< L *nōnāgēnāri(us)* that contains ninety, that consists of ninety (*nōnāgēn(i)* ninety each + *-ārius* -ARY) + -AN]

non·ag·gres·sion (non′ə gresh′ən) *n.* **1.** abstention from aggression, esp. by a nation. —*adj.* **2.** of or pertaining to abstention from aggression: *a nonaggression pact.* [NON- + AGGRESSION] —**non′ag·gres′sive,** *adj.* —**non′ag·gres′sive·ly,** *adv.* —**non′ag·gres′sive·ness,** *n.*

non·a·gon (non′ə gon′), *n.* a polygon having nine angles and nine sides. Also called **enneagon.** [< L *nōn(a)-*, comb. form of *nōn(us)* ninth + -GON] —**non·ag·o·nal** (non ag′ə nᵊl), *adj.*

140°

Nonagon

non·ag·ri·cul·tur·al (non′ag rə kul′chər əl), *adj.* not applied to or practicing agriculture: *a nonagricultural nation.* [NON- + AGRICULTURAL]

non·al·co·hol·ic (non′al kə hô′lik, -hol′ik), *adj.* not being or containing alcohol: *nonalcoholic beverages.* [NON- + ALCOHOLIC]

non·a·lign·ment (non′ə līn′mənt), *n.* **1.** the state or condition of not being aligned. **2.** a national policy repudiating alliance with either the U.S. or the Soviet Union. [NON- + ALIGNMENT]

non·al·ler·gen·ic (non′al ər jen′ik), *adj.* not causing an allergic reaction: *nonallergenic cosmetics.* [NON- + ALLERGENIC]

non′a·no′ic ac′id (non′ə nō′ik, non′-), *Chem.* See **pelargonic acid.** [*nonane* < L *nōnus* ninth + -ANE + -OIC (-O- + -IC)]

non·ap·pear·ance (non′ə pēr′əns), *n.* failure or neglect to appear, as in a court. [NON- + APPEARANCE]

no·na·ry (nō′nə rē), *adj., n., pl.* **-ries.** —*adj.* **1.** consisting of nine. **2.** of, pertaining to, or noting a numerical system based on the number 9. —*n.* **3.** a number in

non′a·ban′don·ment, *n.*
non′ab·di·ca′tion, *n.*
non·ab′di·ca′tive, *adj.*
non′a·bid′ing, *adj.;* **-ly,** *adv.;* **-ness,** *n.*
non′ab·ju·ra′tion, *n.*
non′ab·jur′a·to′ry, *adj.*
non′ab·o·li′tion, *n.*
non′a·bor′tive, *adj.;* **-ly,** *adv.;* **-ness,** *n.*
non′a·bra′sive, *adj.;* **-ly,** *adv.;* **-ness,** *n.*
non′a·bridg′a·ble, *adj.*
non′a·bridg′ment, *n.*
non·ab′ro·ga·ble, *adj.*
non′ab·sen·ta′tion, *n.*
non·ab′so·lute′, *adj., n.;* **-ly,** *adv.;* **-ness,** *n.*
non′ab·so·lu′tion, *n.*
non·ab′so·lut′ist, *n.*
non′ab·so·lu·tis′tic, *adj.*
non′ab·so·lu·tis′ti·cal·ly, *adv.*
non′ab·sorb′a·bil′i·ty, *n.*
non′ab·sorb′a·ble, *adj.*
non′ab·sorb′en·cy, *n.*
non′ab·sorb′ent, *adj., n.*
non′ab·sorb′ing, *adj.*
non′ab·sorp′tion, *n.*
non′ab·sorp′tive, *adj.*
non′ab·stain′er, *n.*
non′ab·stain′ing, *adj.*
non′ab·ste′mi·ous, *adj.;* **-ly,** *adv.;* **-ness,** *n.*
non′ab·sten′tion, *n.*
non·ab′stract, *adj., n.;* **-ly,** *adv.;* **-ness,** *n.*
non′ab·stract′ed, *adj.;* **-ly,** *adv.;* **-ness,** *n.*
non′a·bu′sive, *adj.;* **-ly,** *adv.;* **-ness,** *n.*
non′ac·a·dem′ic, *adj., n.*
non′ac·a·dem′i·cal, *adj.;* **-ly,** *adv.;* **-ness,** *n.*
non′ac·ced′ence, *n.*
non′ac·ced′ing, *adj.*
non′ac·cel′er·a′tion, *n.*
non′ac·cel′er·a′tive, *adj.*
non′ac·cel′er·a·to′ry, *adj.*
non·ac′cent, *n.*
non·ac′cent·ed, *adj.*
non′ac·cent′ing, *adj.*
non′ac·cen′tu·al, *adj.;* **-ly,** *adv.*
non′ac·cept′ance, *n.*
non′ac·cept′ant, *adj.*
non′ac·cep·ta′tion, *n.*
non′ac·ces′sion, *n.*
non′ac·ces′so·ry, *adj., n., pl.* **-ries.**
non′ac·ci·den′tal, *adj., n.;* **-ly,** *adv.;* **-ness,** *n.*
non′ac·com′mo·da·ble, *adj.;* **-bly,** *adv.*
non′ac·com′mo·dat′ing, *adj.;* **-ly,** *adv.;* **-ness,** *n.*
non′ac·com′pa·ni·ment, *n.*
non′ac·com′pa·ny·ing, *adj.*
non′ac·cord′, *n.*
non′ac·cord′ant, *adj.;* **-ly,** *adv.*
non′ac·cred′it·ed, *adj.*
non′ac·cre′tion, *n.*
non′ac·cre′tive, *adj.*
non′ac·crued′, *adj.*
non′ac·cru′ing, *adj.*
non′ac·cul′tur·at′ed, *adj.*
non′ac·cu′mu·lat′ing, *adj.*
non′ac·cu·mu·la′tion, *n.*
non′ac·cu′mu·la′tive, *adj.;* **-ly,** *adv.;* **-ness,** *n.*
non′ac·cus′ing, *adj.*
non·ac′id, *n., adj.*
non′a·cid′ic, *adj.*
non′a·cid′i·ty, *n.*
non′a·cous′tic, *adj., n.*
non′a·cous′ti·cal, *adj.;* **-ly,** *adv.*
non′ac·quaint′ance, *n.*
non′ac·quaint′ance·ship′, *n.*
non′ac·qui·es′cence, *n.*
non′ac·qui·es′cent, *adj.;* **-ly,** *adv.*
non′ac·qui·esc′ing, *adj.*
non′ac·quis′i·tive, *adj.;* **-ly,** *adv.;* **-ness,** *n.*
non′ac·quit′tal, *n.*
non′ac·tin′ic, *adj.*
non′ac·tin′i·cal·ly, *adv.*
non·ac′tion, *n.*
non·ac′tion·a·ble, *adj.;* **-bly,** *adv.*
non′ac·ti·va′tion, *n.*
non·ac′ti·va′tor, *n.*
non·ac′tive, *adj., n.*
non′ac·tiv′i·ty, *n., pl.* **-ties.**
non·ac′tu·al, *adj.;* **-ness,** *n.*
non′ac·tu·al′i·ty, *n., pl.* **-ties.**
non′a·cu′i·ty, *n.*
non′a·cu′le·ate, *adj.*
non′a·cu′le·at′ed, *adj.*
non′a·cute′, *adj.;* **-ly,** *adv.;* **-ness,** *n.*
non′a·dapt′a·bil′i·ty, *n.*
non′a·dapt′a·ble, *adj.;* **-ness,** *n.*
non′a·dapt′ing, *adj.*
non′ad·ap·ta′tion, *n.*
non′ad·ap·ta′tion·al, *adj.*
non′a·dap′tive, *adj.*
non′a·dapt′er, *n.*
non′a·dap′tor, *n.*
non·ad′dict, *n.*
non′ad·dict′ed, *adj.*
non′ad·dict′ing, *adj.*
non′ad·dic′tive, *adj.*
non′a·dept′, *adj.;* **-ly,** *adv.;* **-ness,** *n.*
non′ad·her′ence, *n.*
non′ad·her′ent, *adj., n.*
non′ad·her′ing, *adj.*
non′ad·he′sion, *n.*
non′ad·he′sive, *adj.;* **-ly,** *adv.;* **-ness,** *n.*
non′ad·ja′cen·cy, *n., pl.* **-cies.**
non′ad·ja′cent, *adj.;* **-ly,** *adv.*
non′ad·jec·ti′val, *adj.;* **-ly,** *adv.*
non·ad′jec·tive·ly, *adv.*
non′ad·join′ing, *adj.*
non′ad·journ′ment, *n.*
non′ad·ju′di·cat′ed, *adj.*
non′ad·ju′di·ca′tion, *n.*
non′ad·ju′di·ca′tive, *adj.;* **-ly,** *adv.*
non′ad·junc′tive, *adj.;* **-ly,** *adv.*
non′ad·just′a·bil′i·ty, *n.*
non′ad·just′a·ble, *adj.;* **-bly,** *adv.*
non′ad·just′er, *n.*
non′ad·just′ment, *n.*
non′ad·jus′tor, *n.*
non′ad·min′is·tra·ble, *adj.*
non′ad·min′is·trant, *adj.*
non′ad·min′is·tra′tive, *adj.;* **-ly,** *adv.*
non′ad·mis′si·bil′i·ty, *n.*
non′ad·mis′si·ble, *adj.;* **-ble·ness,** *n.;* **-bly,** *adv.*
non′ad·mis′sion, *n.*
non′ad·mis′sive, *adj.*
non′ad·mit′ted, *adj., n.;* **-ly,** *adv.*
non′a·dopt′a·ble, *adj.*
non′a·dopt′er, *n.*
non′a·dop′tion, *n.*
non′a·dorn′er, *n.*
non′a·dorn′ing, *adj.*
non′a·dorn′ment, *n.*
non′a·dult′, *adj., n.*
non′ad·vance′ment, *n.*
non′ad·van·ta′geous, *adj.;* **-ly,** *adv.;* **-ness,** *n.*
non′ad·ven·ti′tious, *adj.;* **-ly,** *adv.;* **-ness,** *n.*
non′ad·ven′tur·ous, *adj.;* **-ly,** *adv.;* **-ness,** *n.*
non′ad·ver′bi·al, *adj.;* **-ly,** *adv.*
non′ad·vert′ence, *n.*
non′ad·vert′en·cy, *n.*
non·ad′vo·ca·cy, *n.*
non·ad′vo·cate, *n.*
non·aer′at·ed, *adj.*
non·aer′at·ing, *adj.*
non′aes·thet′ic, *adj.*
non′aes·thet′i·cal, *adj.;* **-ly,** *adv.*
non′af·fec·ta′tion, *n.*
non′af·fect′ing, *adj.;* **-ly,** *adv.*
non′af·fec′tive, *adj.*
non′af·fil′i·at′ed, *adj.*
non′af·fil′i·at′ing, *adj.*
non′af·fil′i·a′tion, *n.*
non′af·fin′i·tive, *adj.*
non′af·fin′i·ty, *n., pl.* **-ties.**
non′af·firm′ance, *n.*
non′af·fir·ma′tion, *n.*
non-Af′ri·can, *adj., n.*
non′ag·glom′er·a′tive, *adj.*
non′ag·glu′ti·nant, *adj., n.*
non′ag·glu′ti·nat′ing, *adj.*
non′ag·glu′ti·na′tive, *adj.*
non′a·grar′i·an, *adj., n.*
non′a·gree′ment, *n.*
non′-Al·ex·an′dri·an, *adj.*
non′al·ge·bra′ic, *adj.*
non′al·ge·bra′i·cal, *adj.;* **-ly,** *adv.*
non·al′ien, *n., adj.*
non·al′ien·at′ing, *adj.*
non′al·ien·a′tion, *n.*
non′a·lign′a·ble, *adj.*
non′a·ligned′, *adj.*
non′a·lined′, *adj.*
non′a·line′ment, *n.*
non·al′ka·loid′, *n., adj.*
non′al·ka·loi′dal, *adj.*
non′al·le·ga′tion, *n.*
non′al·le′giance, *adj.*
non′al·le·gor′ic, *adj.*
non′al·le·gor′i·cal, *adj.;* **-ly,** *adv.*
non′al·lel′ic, *adj.*
non′al·lit′er·at′ed, *adj.*
non′al·lit′er·a′tive, *adj.;* **-ly,** *adv.;* **-ness,** *n.*
non′al·lot′ment, *n.*
non′al·lu′vi·al, *adj., n.*
non′al·pha·bet′ic, *adj.*
non′al·pha·bet′i·cal, *adj.;* **-ly,** *adv.*
non·al′ter·nat′ing, *adj.*
non′al·tru·is′tic, *adj.*
non′al·tru·is′ti·cal·ly, *adv.*
non′am·bi·gu′i·ty, *n., pl.* **-ties.**
non′am·bi′tious, *adj.;* **-ly,** *adv.;* **-ness,** *n.*
non·am′bu·la·to′ry, *adj., n., pl.* **-ties.**
non′a·me′na·bil′i·ty, *n.*
non′a·me′na·ble, *adj.;* **-ble·ness,** *n.;* **-bly,** *adv.*
non′a·mend′a·ble, *adj.*
non′a·mend′ment, *n.*
non′-A·mer′i·can, *adj., n.*
non·am′o·rous, *adj.;* **-ly,** *adv.;* **-ness,** *n.*
non′am·phib′i·an, *adj.*
non′am·phib′i·ous, *adj.;* **-ly,** *adv.;* **-ness,** *n.*
non′am·pu·ta′tion, *n.*
non′a·nach′ro·nis′tic, *adj.*
non′a·nach′ro·nis′ti·cal·ly, *adv.*
non′a·nach′ro·nous, *adj.;* **-ly,** *adv.*
non′a·nae′mic, *adj.*
non′an·a·log′ic, *adj.*
non′an·a·log′i·cal, *adj.;* **-ly,** *adv.;* **-ness,** *n.*
non′a·nal′o·gous, *adj.;* **-ly,** *adv.;* **-ness,** *n.*
non′an·a·lyt′ic, *adj.*
non′an·a·lyt′i·cal, *adj.;* **-ly,** *adv.*
non·an′a·lyz′a·ble, *adj.*
non·an′a·lyzed′, *adj.*
non′an·ar′chic, *adj.*
non′an·ar′chi·cal, *adj.;* **-ly,** *adv.*
non′an·ar·chis′tic, *adj.*
non′an·a·tom′ic, *adj.*
non′an·a·tom′i·cal, *adj.;* **-ly,** *adv.*
non′an·ces′tral, *adj.;* **-ly,** *adv.*
non′a·ne′mic, *adj.*
non′an·es·thet′ic, *adj., n.*
non′an·es′the·tized′, *adj.*
non′an·gel′ic, *adj.*
non-An′gli·can, *adj., n.*
non·an′gling, *adj.*
non·an′guished, *adj.*
non·an′i·mal, *n., adj.*
non′an·i·mal′i·ty, *n.*
non·an′i·mate, *adj.*
non·an′i·mat′ed, *adj.*
non·an′i·mat′ing, *adj.;* **-ly,** *adv.*
non′an·i·ma′tion, *n.*
non′an·nex′a·ble, *adj.*
non′an·nex·a′tion, *n.*
non′an·ni′hi·la·bil′i·ty, *n.*
non′an·ni′hi·la·ble, *adj.*
non′an·nul′ment, *n.*
non′an·o·nym′i·ty, *n.*
non′a·non′y·mous·ness, *n.*
non′an·tag′o·nis′tic, *adj.*
non′an·tag′o·nis′ti·cal·ly, *adv.*
non′an·tic′i·pa′tion, *n.*
non′an·tic′i·pa′tive, *adj.;* **-ly,** *adv.*
non′an·tic′i·pa·to′ri·ly, *adv.*
non′an·tic′i·pa·to′ry, *adj.*
non′a·pha′si·ac′, *n.*
non′a·pha′sic, *adj., n.*
non′a·phet′ic, *adj.*
non′aph·o·ris′tic, *adj.*
non′aph·o·ris′ti·cal·ly, *adv.*
non′a·pol′o·get′ic, *adj.*
non′a·pol′o·get′i·cal, *adj.;* **-ly,** *adv.*
non′ap·os·tol′ic, *adj.*
non′ap·o·stol′i·cal, *adj.;* **-ly,** *adv.*
non′ap·par′ent, *adj.;* **-ly,** *adv.;* **-ness,** *n.*
non′ap·pa·ri′tion·al, *adj.*
non′ap·peal′a·bil′i·ty, *n.*
non′ap·peal′a·ble, *adj.*
non′ap·peal′ing, *adj.;* **-ly,** *adv.;* **-ness,** *n.*
non′ap·peas′a·bil′i·ty, *n.*
non′ap·peas′a·ble, *adj.*
non′ap·peas′ing, *adj.*
non′ap·pel′late, *adj.*
non′ap·pend′ance, *n.*
non′ap·pend′ant, *adj.*
non′ap·pend′ence, *n.*
non′ap·pend′ent, *adj.*
non′ap·pen·dic′u·lar, *adj.*
non′ap·pli·ca·bil′i·ty, *n.*
non·ap′pli·ca·ble, *adj.;* **-ness,** *n.*
non′ap·pli·ca′tion, *n.*
non·ap′pli·ca′tive, *adj.*
non·ap′pli·ca·to′ry, *adj.*
non′ap·poin′tive, *adj.*
non′ap·por′tion·a·ble, *adj.*
non′ap·por′tion·ment, *n.*
non′ap·pos′a·ble, *adj.*
non′ap·pre′ci·a′tion, *n.*
non′ap·pre′ci·a′tive, *adj.;* **-ly,** *adv.;* **-ness,** *n.*
non′ap·pre·hen′si·bil′i·ty, *n.*
non′ap·pre·hen′si·ble, *adj.*
non′ap·pre·hen′sion, *n.*
non′ap·pre·hen′sive, *adj.*
non′ap·proach′a·ble, *adj.;* **-ness,** *n.*
non′ap·proach′a·bil′i·ty, *n.*
non′ap·pro′pri·a·ble, *adj.*
non′ap·pro′pri·a′tive, *adj.*
non′a·quat′ic, *adj.*
non·a′que·ous, *adj.*
non-Ar′ab, *n., adj.*
non-Ar′a·bic, *adj.*
non·ar′bi·tra·ble, *adj.*
non·ar′bi·trar′i·ly, *adv.*
non·ar′bi·trar′i·ness, *n.*
non·ar′bi·trar′y, *adj.*
non′ar·chi·tec·ton′ic, *adj.*
non′ar·chi·tec′tur·al, *adj.;* **-ly,** *adv.*
non′ar·gen·tif′er·ous, *adj.*
non·ar′gu·a·ble, *adj.*
non′ar·gu·men′ta·tive, *adj.;* **-ly,** *adv.;* **-ness,** *n.*
non′a·ris′to·crat′ic, *adj.*
non′a·ris′to·crat′i·cal, *adj.;* **-ly,** *adv.*
non′ar·ith·met′ic, *adj.*
non′ar·ith·met′i·cal, *adj.;* **-ly,** *adv.*
non·ar′ma·ment, *n.*
non′ar·mig′er·ous, *adj.*
non′ar·o·mat′ic, *adj.*
non′ar·o·mat′i·cal·ly, *adv.*
non′ar·raign′ment, *n.*
non′ar·rest′ing, *adj.*
non′ar·riv′al, *n.*
non·ar′ro·gance, *n.*
non·ar′ro·gan·cy, *n.*
non′ar·sen′ic, *adj.*
non′ar·sen′i·cal, *adj.*
non′ar·te′ri·al, *adj.*
non′ar·tic′u·late, *adj.;* **-ly,** *adv.;* **-ness,** *n.*
non′ar·tic′u·la′tive, *adj.*
non′ar·tis′tic, *adj.*
non′ar·tis′ti·cal, *adj.;* **-ly,** *adv.*
non-Ar′y·an, *n., adj.*
non′as·bes′tine, *adj.*
non′as·cend′ance, *n.*
non′as·cend′an·cy, *n.*
non′as·cend′ant, *adj.;* **-ly,** *adv.*
non′as·cend′ence, *n.*
non′as·cend′en·cy, *n.*
non′as·cend′ent, *adj.;* **-ly,** *adv.*
non′as·cer·tain′a·ble, *adj.;* **-ble·ness,** *n.;* **-bly,** *adv.*
non′as·cer·tain′ment, *n.*
non′as·cet′ic, *n., adj.*
non′as·cet′i·cal, *adj.;* **-ly,** *adv.*
non′as·cet′i·cism, *n.*
non′a·sep′tic, *adj.*
non′a·sep′ti·cal·ly, *adv.*
non-A′sian, *adj., n.*
non′-A·si·at′ic, *adj., n.*
non′as·per′sion, *n.*
non·as′pi·rate, *n., adj.*
non·as′pi·rat′ed, *adj.*
non·as′pi·rat′ing, *adj.*
non′as·pi′ra·to′ry, *adj.*
non′as·pir′ing, *adj.*
non′as·sault′, *n.*
non′as·sent′ing, *adj.*
non′as·ser′tion, *n.*
non′as·ser′tive, *adj.;* **-ly,** *adv.;* **-ness,** *n.*

a nonary system. [< L *nōnāri(us)* of, belonging to the ninth (hour), equiv. to *nōn(us)* ninth + *-ārius* -ARY]

non·as·sess·a·ble (non/ə ses/ə bəl), *adj.* (of stock) exempting the investor from any expense or liability beyond the amount of his investment. [NON- + ASSESSABLE] —**non/as·ses/sa·bil/i·ty,** *n.*

non·at·tend·ance (non/ə ten/dəns), *n.* failure to attend: *Members of the society were reminded of their records of nonattendance.* [NON- + ATTENDANCE]

non·be·liev·er (non/bi lē/vər), *n.* a person who lacks faith, esp. in God. [NON- + BELIEVER]

non·bel·lig·er·en·cy (non/bə lij/ər ən sē), *n.* **1.** the state or status of not participating in a war. **2.** the status or policy of a nation which does not participate openly in a war but supports, often with direct aid, the cause of one of the participants. [NON- + BELLIGERENCY]

non·bel·lig·er·ent (non/bə lij/ər ənt), *adj.* **1.** of or pertaining to a country whose status or policy is one of nonbelligerency. —*n.* **2.** a nation that does not engage officially in a war, but gives aid to one of the active participants. [NON- + BELLIGERENT]

non·can·cel·a·ble (non kan/sə lə bəl), *adj.* not subject to cancellation, as certain insurance policies. Also, **non·can/cel·la·ble.** [NON- + CANCELABLE] —**non·can/cel·a·bil/i·ty, non·can/cel·la·bil/i·ty,** *n.*

non·ca·non·i·cal (non/kə non/i kəl), *adj.* **1.** not included within a canon or group of rules. **2.** not belonging to the canon of Scripture. [NON- + CANONICAL]

non cau·sa pro cau·sa (non kô/zə prō kô/zə; *Lat.* nōn kou/sä prō kou/sä), *Logic.* the fallacy of giving as a reason for a conclusion a proposition not actually relevant to that conclusion. [< L: lit., no cause for cause]

nonce (nons), *n.* the present, or immediate, occasion or purpose (usually used in the phrase *for the nonce*). [ME *nones,* in phrase *for the nones,* where *the nones* was earlier *then ones* THE ONCE (ME *then* dat. sing. of THE), by wrong division into syllables]

non·cel·lu·lar (non sel/yə lər), *adj.* not composed of or containing cells: *Protoplasm is noncellular.* [NON- + CELLULAR]

nonce/ word/, a word coined and used only for the particular occasion.

non·cha·lance (non/shə läns/, non/shə ləns), *n.* the state or quality of being nonchalant; cool indifference or lack of concern; casualness. [< F; see NONCHALANT, -ANCE]

non·cha·lant (non/shə länt/, non/shə lənt), *adj.* coolly unconcerned, indifferent, or unexcited; casual. [< F *nonchalant,* prp. of obs. *nonchaloir* to lack warmth (of heart), be indifferent, equiv. to *non-* NON- + *chaloir* < L *calēre* to be warm. See -ANT]
—**Syn.** cool, calm, collected, composed. —**Ant.** excitable.

non·col·le·giate (non/kə lē/jit, -jē it), *adj.* **1.** *Brit.* belonging to the body of students in a university not attached to any particular college or hall. **2.** below the level usually associated with college or university study. **3.** (of a university) not composed of colleges. [NON- + COLLEGIATE]

non·com (non/kom/), *n.* *Informal.* a noncommissioned officer. [short for NONCOMMISSIONED]

noncom., noncommissioned.

non·com·bat (non kom/bat), *adj.* not including or requiring combat: *noncombat duty.* [NON- + COMBAT]

non·com·bat·ant (non kom/bə tənt, non/kəm bat/ənt), *n.* **1.** a person who is not a combatant; a civilian in time of war. **2.** a person connected with a military force in some capacity other than that of a fighter, as a surgeon, a chaplain, etc. [NON- + COMBATANT]

non·com·bus·ti·ble (non/kəm bus/tə bəl), *adj.* **1.** not flammable. —*n.* **2.** a noncombustible substance. [NON- + COMBUSTIBLE] —**non/com·bus/ti·bil/i·ty,** *n.*

non·com·mis·sioned (non/kə mish/ənd), *adj.* not commissioned, applied esp. to military officers, as

non/as·sign/a·bil/i·ty, *n.*
non/as·sign/a·ble, *adj.;* -bly, *adv.*
non/as·signed/, *adj.*
non/as·sign/ment, *n.*
non/as·sim/i·la·bil/i·ty, *n.*
non/as·sim/i·la·ble, *adj.*
non/as·sim/i·lat/ing, *adj.*
non/as·sim/i·la/tion, *n.*
non/as·sim/i·la/tive, *adj.*
non/as·sim/i·la·to/ry, *adj.*
non/as·sist/ant, *n.*
non/as·sist/er, *n.*
non/as·so/ci·a·bil/i·ty, *n.*
non/as·so/ci·a·ble, *adj.*
non/as·so/ci·a/tion, *n.*
non/as·so/ci·a/tion·al, *adj.*
non/as·so/ci·a/tive, *adj.;* -ly, *adv.*
non·as/so·nance, *n.*
non·as/so·nant, *adj., n.*
non/as·sumed/, *adj.*
non/as·sump/tion, *n.*
non/as·sump/tive, *adj.*
non/asth·mat/ic, *adj., n.*
non/asth·mat/i·cal·ly, *adv.*
non·as/tral, *adj.*
non/as·trin/gen·cy, *n.*
non/as·trin/gent, *adj.;* -ly, *adv.*
non/as·tro·nom/ic, *adj.*
non/as·tro·nom/i·cal, *adj.;* -ly, *adv.*
non/a·the·is/tic, *adj.*
non/a·the·is/ti·cal, *adj.;* -ly, *adv.*
non·ath/lete, *n.*
non/ath·let/ic, *adj.*
non/ath·let/i·cal·ly, *adv.*
non/at·mos·pher/ic, *adj.*
non/at·mos·pher/i·cal, *adj.;* -ly, *adv.*
non/a·tom/ic, *adj.*
non/a·tom/i·cal, *adj.;* -ly, *adv.*
non/a·troph/ic, *adj.*
non·at/ro·phied, *adj.*
non/at·tach/ment, *n.*
non/at·tack/ing, *adj.*
non/at·tain/a·bil/i·ty, *n.*
non/at·tain/a·ble, *adj.*
non/at·tain/ment, *n.*
non/at·tes·ta/tion, *n.*
non-At/tic, *adj., n.*
non/at·trib/u·tive, *adj.;* -ly, *adv.;* -ness, *n.*
non/au·di·bil/i·ty, *n.*
non·au/di·ble, *adj.;* -ble·ness, *n.;* -bly, *adv.*
non/aug·ment/a·tive, *adj., n.*
non/au·ric/u·lar, *adj.*
non/au·rif/er·ous, *adj.*
non/au·then/tic, *adj.*
non/au·then/ti·cal, *adj.*
non/au·then/ti·cat/ed, *adj.*
non/au·then/ti·ca/tion, *n.*
non/au·then·tic/i·ty, *n.*
non/au·thor/i·ta/tive, *adj.;* -ly, *adv.;* -ness, *n.*
non/au·to·bi/o·graph/i·cal, *adj.;* -ly, *adv.*
non·au/to·mat/ed, *adj.*
non/au·to·mat/ic, *adj.*
non/au·to·mat/i·cal·ly, *adv.*
non/au·to·mo/tive, *adj.*
non/au·ton/o·mous, *adj.;* -ly, *adv.;* -ness, *n.*
non/a·vail/a·bil/i·ty, *n.*
non/a·void/a·ble, *adj.;* -ble·ness, *n.;* -bly, *adv.*
non/a·void/ance, *n.*
non/ax·i·o·mat/ic, *adj.*
non/ax·i·o·mat/i·cal, *adj.;* -ly, *adv.*
non·bach/e·lor, *n.*
non/bac·te/ri·al, *adj.;* -ly, *adv.*
non·bail/a·ble, *adj.*
non·bal/lot·ing, *n.*
non·ban/ish·ment, *n.*
non·bank/a·ble, *adj.*
non-Ban/tu, *n., adj.*
non-Bap/tist, *n.*
non/bar·bar/i·an, *adj., n.*
non/bar·bar/ic, *adj.*
non·bar/ba·rous, *adj.;* -ly, *adv.;* -ness, *n.*
non/ba·ro/ni·al, *adj.*
non·base/, *n., adj.*
non·ba/sic, *adj.*
non·bath/ing, *adj.*
non·beard/ed, *adj.*
non·bear/ing, *adj.*
non/be·a·tif/ic, *adj.*
non/be·a·tif/i·cal·ly, *adv.*
non·beau/ty, *n., pl.* -ties.
non·be/ing, *n., adj.*
non/be·liev/ing, *adj.;* -ly, *adv.*
non·bend/ing, *adj.*
non·ben/e·ficed, *adj.*
non/be·nef/i·cence, *n.*
non/be·nef/i·cent, *adj.;* -ly, *adv.*
non/ben·e·fi/cial, *adj.;* -ly, *adv.;* -ness, *n.*
non/be·nev/o·lence, *n.*
non/be·nev/o·lent, *adj.;* -ly, *adv.*
non·bi/ased, *adj.*
non-Bib/li·cal, *adj.;* -ly, *adv.*
non·bib/u·lous, *adj.;* -ly, *adv.;* -ness, *n.*
non·big/ot·ed, *adj.;* -ly, *adv.*
non/bi·la/bi·ate/, *adj.*
non·bil/ious, *adj.;* -ly, *adv.;* -ness, *n.*
non·bill/a·ble, *adj.*
non·bind/ing, *adj.;* -ly, *adv.;* -ness, *n.*
non/bi·o·graph/i·cal, *adj.;* -ly, *adv.*
non/bi·o·log/i·cal, *adj.;* -ly, *adv.*
non·bit/ing, *adj.*
non·bit/ter, *adj.*
non/bi·tu/mi·nous, *adj.*
non·black/, *adj., n.*
non·blam/a·ble, *adj.;* -ble·ness, *n.;* -bly, *adv.*
non·blame/ful, *adj.;* -ly, *adv.;* -ness, *n.*
non·blas/phe·mous, *adj.;* -ly, *adv.;* -ness, *n.*
non·blas/phe·my, *n., pl.* -mies.
non·bleach/, *n.*
non·bleed/ing, *adj., n.*
non·blend/ed, *adj.*
non·blend/ing, *adj., n.*
non·blind/ing, *adj.;* -ly, *adv.*
non·block/ad/ed, *adj.*
non·block/ing, *adj., n.*
non·bloom/ing, *adj., n.*
non·blun/der·ing, *adj., n.;* -ly, *adv.*
non·boast/er, *n.*
non·boast/ing, *adj., n.;* -ly, *adv.*
non·bod/i·ly, *adj.*
non·bod/ing, *adj.;* -ly, *adv.*
non·boil/ing, *adj.*
non-Bol/she·vik, *n.*
non-Bol/she·vism, *n.*
non-Bol/she·vist, *n.*
non/-Bol·she·vis/tic, *adj.*
non·book/ish, *adj.;* -ly, *adv.;* -ness, *n.*
non·bor/row·er, *n.*
non·bor/row·ing, *adj.*
non/bo·tan/ic, *adj.*
non/bo·tan/i·cal, *adj.;* -ly, *adv.*
non/bour·geois/, *n., pl.* -geois, *adj.*
non/-Brah·man/ic, *adj.*
non/-Brah·man/i·cal, *adj.*
non/-Brah·min/ic, *adj.*
non/-Brah·min/i·cal, *adj.*
non·brand/ed, *adj.*
non·breach/, *n.*
non·breach/ing, *adj.*
non·break/a·ble, *adj.*
non·breed/er, *n.*
non·breed/ing, *adj., n.*
non·bris/tled, *adj.*
non-Brit/ish, *adj.*
non/bro·mid/ic, *adj.*
non·brood/ing, *adj., n.*
non·brows/er, *n.*
non·brows/ing, *adj., n.*
non·bru/tal, *adj.;* -ly, *adv.*
non-Bud/dhist, *n., adj.*
non/-Bud·dhis/tic, *adj.*
non·bud/ding, *adj., n.*
non/bul·ba/ceous, *adj.*
non·bul/bar, *adj.*
non/bul·bif/er·ous, *adj.*
non·bul/bous, *adj.*
non·buoy/an·cy, *n.*
non·buoy/ant, *adj.;* -ly, *adv.*
non·bur/den·some, *adj.;* -ly, *adv.;* -ness, *n.*
non/bu·reau·crat/ic, *adj.*
non/bu·reau·crat/i·cal·ly, *adv.*
non·burg/age, *n.*
non·burn/a·ble, *adj.*
non·burn/ing, *adj., n.*
non·burst/ing, *adj., n.*
non·bus/i·ly, *adv.*
non·busi/ness, *adj.*
non·bus/y, *adj.*
non·bus/y·ness, *n.*
non·but/tressed, *adj.*
non·buy/ing, *adj., n.*
non·ca/denced, *adj.*
non·ca/dent, *adj.*
non·caf·feine/, *n.*
non/caf·fein/ic, *adj.*
non·cak/ing, *adj., n.*
non/cal·car/e·ous, *adj.*
non·cal/ci·fied/, *adj.*
non·cal/cu·la·ble, *adj.;* -bly, *adv.*
non·cal/cu·lat/ing, *adj.*
non·cal/cu·la/tive, *adj.*
non/ca·lor/ic, *adj.*
non/ca·lum/ni·at/ing, *adj.*
non/ca·lum/ni·ous, *adj.*
non-Cal/vin·ist, *n., adj.*
non/-Cal·vin·is/tic, *adj.*
non/-Cal·vin·is/ti·cal, *adj.*
non·can/cer·ous, *adj.*
non/can·des/cence, *n.*
non/can·des/cent, *adj.;* -ly, *adv.*
non/can·ni·bal·is/tic, *adj.*
non/can·ni·bal·is/ti·cal·ly, *adv.*
non/cap·il·lar/i·ty, *n.*
non·cap/il·lar/y, *adj., n., pl.* -lar·ies.
non·cap/i·tal, *adj., n.*
non·cap/i·tal·ist, *n.*
non/cap·i·tal·is/tic, *adj.*
non/cap·i·tal·is/ti·cal·ly, *adv.*
non·cap/i·tal·ized/, *adj.*
non/ca·pit/u·la/tion, *n.*
non/ca·pri/cious, *adj.;* -ly, *adv.;* -ness, *n.*
non/cap·siz/a·ble, *adj.*
non·cap/tious, *adj.;* -ly, *adv.;* -ness, *n.*
non/car·bo·hy/drate, *n.*
non/car·bol/ic, *adj.*
non·car/bon, *n.*
non·car/bo·nate/, *n.*
non·car/bo·nat/ed, *adj.*
non/car·niv/o·rous, *adj.;* -ly, *adv.;* -ness, *n.*
non·car/ri·er, *n.*
non·car/tel·ized/, *adj.*
non·cash/, *adj.*
non·cas/ti·gat/ing, *adj.*
non/cas·ti·ga/tion, *n.*
non/cas·u·is/tic, *adj.*
non/cas·u·is/ti·cal, *adj.;* -ly, *adv.*
non/cat·a·clys/mal, *adj.*
non/cat·a·clys/mic, *adj.*
non/cat·a·lyt/ic, *adj.*
non/cat·a·lyt/i·cal·ly, *adv.*
non/ca·tar/rhal, *adj.*
non/cat·a·stroph/ic, *adj.*
non/cat·e·chis/tic, *adj.*
non/cat·e·chis/ti·cal, *adj.*
non/cat·e·gor/i·cal, *adj.;* -ly, *adv.;* -ness, *n.*
non/ca·thar/tic, *adj., n.*
non/ca·thar/ti·cal, *adj.*
non-Cath/o·lic, *adj., n.*
non/cath·o·lic/i·ty, *n.*
non/-Cau·ca/sian, *adj., n.*
non/-Cau·cas/ic, *adj.*
non-Cau/ca·soid, *adj., n.*
non·caus/a·ble, *adj.*
non·caus/al, *adj.;* -ly, *adv.*
non/cau·sal/i·ty, *n.*
non/cau·sa/tion, *n.*
non·caus/a·tive, *adj.;* -ly, *adv.;* -ness, *n.*
non·caus/tic, *adj.*
non·caus/ti·cal·ly, *adv.*
non/cel·e·bra/tion, *n.*
non/ce·les/tial, *adj.;* -ly, *adv.*
non·cel/lu·lous, *adj.*
non-Celt/ic, *adj.*
non·cen/sored, *adj.*
non/cen·so/ri·ous, *adj.;* -ly, *adv.;* -ness, *n.*
non·cen/sur·a·ble, *adj.;* -ble·ness, *n.,* -bly, *adv.*
non·cen/tral, *adj.;* -ly, *adv.*
non·ce/re·al, *adj.*
non·cer/e·bral, *adj.*
non/cer·e·mo/ni·al, *adj.;* -ly, *adv.*
non/cer·e·mo/ni·ous, *adj.;* -ly, *adv.;* -ness, *n.*
non·cer/tain·ty, *n., pl.* -ties.
non/cer·ti·fi·ca/tion, *n.*
non·cer/ti·fied/, *adj.*
non·cer/ti·tude/, *n.*
non·chaf/ing, *adj.*
non·chalk/y, *adj.*
non·chal/leng·er, *n.*
non·chal/leng·ing, *adj.*
non·cham/pi·on, *n.*
non·change/a·ble, *adj.;* -ble·ness, *n.;* -bly, *adv.*
non·chan/neled, *adj.*
non·chan/nel·ized/, *adj.*
non/cha·ot/ic, *adj.*
non/cha·ot/i·cal·ly, *adv.*
non/char·ac·ter·is/tic, *adj.*
non/char·ac·ter·is/ti·cal·ly, *adv.*
non·char/ac·ter·ized/, *adj.*
non·charge/a·ble, *adj.*
non/char·is·mat/ic, *adj.*
non·char/i·ta·ble, *adj.;* -ble·ness, *n.;* -bly, *adv.*
non·chas/tise·ment, *n.*
non·chas/ti·ty, *n.*
non/-Chau·ce/ri·an, *adj., n.*
non·chem/i·cal, *adj., n.*
non·chem/ist, *n.*
non/chi·mer/ic, *adj.*
non/chi·mer/i·cal, *adj.;* -ly, *adv.*
non/-Chi·nese/, *n., pl.* -nese, *adj.*
non·chiv/al·ric, *adj.*
non·chiv/al·rous, *adj.;* -ly, *adv.;* -ness, *n.*
non·chol/er·ic, *adj.*
non-Chris/tian, *adj., n.*
non/chro·mat/ic, *adj.*
non/chro·mat/i·cal·ly, *adv.*
non/chro·mo·so/mal, *adj.*
non·chron/ic, *adj.*
non·chron/i·cal, *adj.;* -ly, *adv.*
non·church/, *n.*
non·churched/, *adj.*
non·church/go/er, *n.*
non·church/go/ing, *adj.*
non·cil/i·ate, *adj.*
non·cil/i·at/ed, *adj.*
non·cir/cuit·ed, *adj.*
non/cir·cu/i·tous, *adj.;* -ly, *adv.;* -ness, *n.*
non·cir/cu·lar, *adj.;* -ly, *adv.*
non·cir/cu·lat/ing, *adj.*
non/cir·cu·la/tion, *n.*
non·cir/cu·la·to/ry, *adj.*
non·cir/cum·scribed/, *adj.*
non/cir·cum·scrip/tive, *adj.*
non·cir/cum·spect/, *adj.;* -ly, *adv.;* -ness, *n.*
non/cir·cum·stan/tial, *adj.;* -ly, *adv.*
non/cir·cum·val/lat·ed, *adj.*
non·cit/a·ble, *adj.*
non/ci·ta/tion, *n.*
non·cite/a·ble, *adj.*
non·cit/i·zen, *n.*
non/ci·vil/ian, *n.*
non·civ/i·li/za·ble, *adj.*
non·civ/i·lized/, *adj.*
non·claim/a·ble, *adj.*
non·clam/or·ous, *adj.;* -ly, *adv.*
non/clar·i·fi/a·ble, *adj.*
non/clar·i·fi·ca/tion, *n.*
non·clar/i·fied, *adj.*
non·clas/sic, *adj.*
non·clas/si·cal, *adj.;* -ly, *adv.*
non/clas·si·cal/i·ty, *n.*
non·clas/si·fi/a·ble, *adj.*
non/clas·si·fi·ca/tion, *n.*
non·clas/si·fied/, *adj.*
non·clas/tic, *adj.*
non·clear/ance, *n.*
non/cleis·to·gam/ic, *adj.*
non/cleis·tog/a·mous, *adj.*
non·cler/i·cal, *adj.;* -ly, *adv.*
non/cli·mac/tic, *adj.*
non/cli·mac/ti·cal, *adj.*
non·climb/a·ble, *adj.*
non·climb/ing, *adj.*
non·cling/ing, *adj.*
non·clin/i·cal, *adj.;* -ly, *adv.*
non·clois/tered, *adj.*
non·close/, *adj.*
non·close/ly, *adv.*
non·clo/sure, *n.*
non·clot/ting, *adj.*
non/co·ag/u·la·bil/i·ty, *n.*
non/co·ag/u·la·ble, *adj.*
non/co·ag/u·lat/ing, *adj.*
non/co·ag/u·la/tion, *n.*
non/co·ag/u·la/tive, *adj.*
non/co·a·les/cence, *n.*
non/co·a·les/cent, *adj.*
non/co·a·les/cing, *adj.*
non·cod/i·fied/, *adj.*
non/co·er/ci·ble, *adj.*
non/co·er/cion, *n.*
non/co·er/cive, *adj.;* -ly, *adv.;* -ness, *n.*
non·co/gen·cy, *n.*
non·co/gent, *adj.;* -ly, *adv.*
non·cog/nate, *adj., n.*
non/cog·ni/tion, *n.*
non·cog/ni·tive, *adj.*
non/cog·ni/za·ble, *adj.;* -bly, *adv.*
non·cog/ni·zance, *n.*
non·cog/ni·zant, *adj.;* -ly, *adv.*
non/co·hab/i·ta/tion, *n.*
non/co·her/ence, *n.*
non/co·her/en·cy, *n.*
non/co·her/ent, *adj.;* -ly, *adv.*
non/co·he/sion, *n.*
non/co·he/sive, *adj.;* -ly, *adv.;* -ness, *n.*
non·coin/age, *n.*
non/co·in/ci·dence, *n.*
non/co·in/ci·dent, *adj.*
non/co·in/ci·den/tal, *adj.;* -ly, *adv.*
non/col·lab/o·ra/tion, *n.*
non/col·laps/a·ble, *adj.*
non/col·laps/i·bil/i·ty, *n.*
non/col·laps/i·ble, *adj.*
non/col·lect/a·ble, *adj.*
non/col·lect/i·ble, *adj.*
non/col·lec/tion, *n.*
non/col·lec/tive, *adj.;* -ly, *adv.*
non/col·lec/tiv·is/tic, *adj.*
non/col·lin/e·ar, *adj.*
non·col/loid, *n.*
non/col·loi/dal, *adj.*
non/col·lu/sion, *n.*
non/col·lu/sive, *adj.;* -ly, *adv.;* -ness, *n.*
non/co·lo/ni·al, *adj., n.;* -ly, *adv.*
non/col·or·a·bil/i·ty, *n.*
non·col/or·a·ble, *adj.;* -ble·ness, *n.;* -bly, *adv.*
non·col/or·ing, *adj., n.*
non/com·bi·na/tion, *n.*
non/com·bi/na·tive, *adj.*
non/com·bin/ing, *adj.*
non/com·bus/tion, *n.*
non/com·bus/tive, *adj.*
non·com/ic, *adj., n.*
non·com/i·cal, *adj.;* -ly, *adv.;* -ness, *n.*
non/com·i·cal/i·ty, *n.*
non/com·mem/o·ra/tion, *n.*
non/com·mem/o·ra/tion·al, *adj.*
non/com·mem/o·ra/tive, *adj.;* -ly, *adv.*
non/com·mem/o·ra·to/ry, *adj.*
non/com·mence/ment, *n.*
non/com·mend/a·ble, *adj.;* -ble·ness, *n.;* -bly, *adv.*
non/com·men/da·to/ry, *adj.*
non/com·mer/cial, *adj., n.;* -ly, *adv.*
non/com·mer/ci·al/i·ty, *n.*
non/com·mis/er·a/tion, *n.*
non/com·mis/er·a/tive, *adj.;* -ly, *adv.*

CONCISE ETYMOLOGY KEY: <, descended or derived from; >, whence; b., blend of, blended; c., cognate with; deriv., derivative; equiv., equivalent; imit., imitative; m., modification of; obl., oblique; r., replacing; s., stem; sp., spelling; trans., translation; ?, origin unknown, perhaps; *, hypothetical. See the full key inside the front cover.

sergeants and corporals, ranking below warrant officer. [NON- + COMMISSIONED]

non′commis′sioned of′ficer, *Mil.* an enlisted person holding any of various ranks below commissioned or warrant officers.

non·com·mit·tal (non′kə mit′ᵊl), *adj.* not committing oneself, or not involving committal, to a particular view, course, or the like: *a noncommittal answer.* [NON- + COMMITTAL] —**non′com·mit′tal·ly,** *adv.*

non·com·mu·ni·ca·ble (non′kə myo͞o′nə kə bəl), *adj.* not communicable, esp. with reference to a disease that is not transmitted through contact with an infected or afflicted person. [NON- + COMMUNICABLE]

non·com·mu·ni·cant (non′kə myo͞o′nə kənt), *n.* **1.** a person who is not a communicant. **2.** a person who does not communicate. [NON- + COMMUNICANT]

non·com·pli·ance (non′kəm plī′əns), *n.* failure or refusal to comply. [NON- + COMPLIANCE] —**non′com·pli′ant,** *n.*

non com·pos men·tis (nōn kōm′pōs men′tis; *Eng.* non kom′pəs men′tis), *Latin.* not of sound mind; mentally incapable.

non·con·cur·rence (non′kən kûr′əns, -kur′-), *n.* refusal or failure to concur. [NON- + CONCURRENCE]

non′condens′ing en′gine, a steam engine releasing exhaust steam to the atmosphere rather than condensing it to hot feedwater. [NON- + CONDENSING]

non·con·duc·tor (non′kən duk′tər), *n.* a substance that does not readily conduct heat, sound, or electricity. [NON- + CONDUCTOR] —**non′con·duc′ting,** *adj.*

non·con·form·ance (non′kən fôr′məns), *n.* lack of conformity. [NON- + CONFORMANCE]

non·con·form·ist (non′kən fôr′mist), *n.* **1.** a person who refuses to conform, as to established customs. **2.** (*often cap.*) a Protestant in England who is not a member of the Church of England; dissenter. [NON- + CONFORMIST]

non·con·form·i·ty (non′kən fôr′mi tē), *n.* **1.** lack of conformity or agreement. **2.** failure or refusal to conform, as with established customs. **3.** (*often cap.*) refusal to conform to the Church of England. [NON- + CONFORMITY]

non·con·tra·dic·tion (non′kon trə dik′shən), *n.* absence or lack of contradiction. [NON- + CONTRADICTION]

non·con·tras·tive (non′kən tras′tiv), *adj.* **1.** not contrastive. **2.** *Ling.* in complementary distribution; in free variation. [NON- + CONTRASTIVE]

non·co·op·er·a·tion (non′kō op′ə rā′shən), *n.* **1.** failure or refusal to cooperate. **2.** a method or practice, established in India by Gandhi, of showing opposition to acts or policies of the government by refusing to participate in civic and political life or to obey governmental regulations. Cf. **civil disobedience** (def. 1), **passive resistance.** Also, **non′co-op′er·a′tion, non′-co·öp′er·a′tion.** [NON- + COOPERATION] —**non′co-op′er·a′tive, non′co-op′er·a′tive, non′co·öp′er·a′-tive,** *adj.* —**non′co·op′er·a′tor, non′co-op′er·a′tor, non′co·öp′er·a′tor,** *n.* —**non′co-op′er·a′tion·ist, non′co·op′er·a′tion·ist, non′co·öp′er·a′tion·ist,** *n.*

non·cum·u·la·tive (non kyo͞o′myə lā′tiv, -lə tiv), *adj.* of or pertaining to preferred stock the dividends of which are skipped and not accrued. [NON- + CUMULATIVE]

non·de·creas·ing (non′di krē′sing), *adj.* **1.** not decreasing. **2.** *Math.* increasing (def. 2). [NON- + DECREASING]

non′com·mit′ment, *n.*
non′com·mo′di·ous, *adj.;* **-ly,** *adv.;* **-ness,** *n.*
non′com·mu′nal, *adj.;* **-ly,** *adv.*
non′com·mu′ni·cat′ing, *adj.*
non′com·mu′ni·ca′tion, *n.*
non′com·mu′ni·ca′tive, *adj.;* **-ly,** *adv.;* **-ness,** *n.*
non·com′mu·nist, *n., adj.*
non′com·mu·nis′tic, *adj.*
non′com·mu·nis′ti·cal, *adj.;* **-ly,** *adv.*
non·com′mu·ta′tive, *adj.*
non·com′pen·sa′ting, *adj.*
non′com·pen·sa′tion, *n.*
non·com′pen·sa′tive, *adj.*
non′com·pen′sa·to′ry, *adj.*
non·com′pe·ten·cy, *n.*
non·com′pe·tent, *adj.;* **-ly,** *adv.*
non′com·pet′ing, *adj.*
non′com·pet′i·tive, *adj.;* **-ly,** *adv.;* **-ness,** *n.*
non′com·pla′cence, *n.*
non′com·pla′cen·cy, *n., pl.* **-cies.**
non′com·pla′cent, *adj.;* **-ly,** *adv.*
non′com·plai′sance, *n.*
non′com·plai′sant, *adj.;* **-ly,** *adv.*
non′com·ple′tion, *n.*
non′com·plic′i·ty, *n., pl.* **-ties.**
non′com·ply′ing, *adj., n.*
non·com·pos′ite, *adj., n.;* **-ly,** *adv.;* **-ness,** *n.*
non′com·po′sure, *n.*
non′com·pound′a·ble, *adj.*
non′com·pre·hend′i·ble, *adj.*
non′com·pre·hend′ing, *adj.;* **-ly,** *adv.*
non′com·pre·hens′i·ble, *adj.;* **-ly,** *adv.*
non′com·pre·hen′sion, *n.*
non′com·pre·hen′sive, *adj.;* **-ly,** *adv.;* **-ness,** *n.*
non′com·pres′si·bil′i·ty, *n.*
non′com·pres′si·ble, *adj.*
non′com·pres′sion, *n.*
non′com·pres′sive, *adj.;* **-ly,** *adv.*
non·com′pro·mised′, *adj.*
non·com′pro·mis′ing, *adj.*
non′com·pul′sion, *n.*
non′com·pul′sive, *adj.;* **-ly,** *adv.*
non′com·pul′so·ri·ly, *adv.*
non′com·pul′so·ri·ness, *n.*
non′com·pul′so·ry, *adj.*
non·com′pu·ta′tion, *n.*
non′con·ceal′ment, *n.*
non′con·ceiv′ing, *n., adj.*
non·con′cen·trat′ed, *adj.*
non·con′cen·tra′tion, *n.*
non·con′cen·tra′tive, *adj.;* **-ness,** *n.*
non′con·cen′tric, *adj.*
non′con·cen′tri·cal, *adj.;* **-ly,** *adv.*
non′con·cen·tric′i·ty, *n.*
non′con·cep′tu·al, *adj.;* **-ly,** *adv.*
non′con·ces′sion, *n.*
non′con·ces′sive, *adj.*
non′con·cil′i·at′ing, *adj.*
non′con·cil′i·a·to′ry, *adj.*
non′con·ci′sion, *n.*
non′con·clud′ing, *adj.*
non′con·clu′sion, *n.*
non′con·clu′sive, *adj.;* **-ly,** *adv.;* **-ness,** *n.*
non′con·cord′ant, *adv.;* **-ly,** *adv.*
non′con·cur′rent, *adj., n.;* **-ly,** *adv.*
non′con·dem·na′tion, *n.*
non′con·den′sa·ble, *adj.*
non′con·den·sa′tion, *n.*
non′con·densed′, *adj.*
non′con·den′si·bil′i·ty, *n.*
non′con·den′si·ble, *adj.*
non′con·dens′ing, *adj.*
non′con·de·scend′ing, *adj.;* **-ly,** *adv.;* **-ness,** *n.*
non′con·de·scen′sion, *n.*
non·con′di·ment, *n.*
non′con·di·men′tal, *adj.*
non′con·di′tion·al, *adj.*
non′con·di′tioned, *adj.*
non′con·do·na′tion, *n.*
non′con·du′cive, *adj.;* **-ness,** *n.*
non′con·duc′ti·bil′i·ty, *n.*
non′con·duc′ti·ble, *adj.*
non′con·duc′tive, *adj.*
non′con·fed′er·ate, *adj., n.*
non′con·fed′er·a′tion, *n.*
non′con·fer′ra·ble, *adj.*
non·con′fi·dence, *n.*
non·con′fi·dent, *adj.;* **-ly,** *adv.*
non′con·fi·den′tial, *adj.;* **-ly,** *adv.;* **-ness,** *n.*
non′con·fi·den′ti·al′i·ty, *n.*
non′con·fid′ing, *adj.*
non′con·fined′, *adj.*
non′con·fine′ment, *n.*
non′con·fin′ing, *adj.*
non′con·fir·ma′tion, *n.*
non′con·firm′a·tive, *adj.*
non′con·firm′a·to′ry, *adj.*
non′con·firm′ing, *adj.*
non′con·fis′ca·ble, *adj.*
non′con·fis·ca′tion, *n.*
non′con·flict′ing, *adj.*
non′con·flic′tive, *adj.*
non′con·fron·ta′tion, *n.*
non′con·geal′ing, *adj., n.*
non′con·gen′i·tal, *adj.*
non′con·ges′tion, *n.*
non′con·ges′tive, *adj.*
non′con·grat′u·la·to′ry, *adj.*
non′-Con·gre·ga′tion·al, *adj.*
non·con′gre·ga′tive, *adj.*
non′-Con·gres′sion·al, *adj.*
non·con′gru·ence, *n.*
non·con′gru·en·cy, *n.*
non·con′gru·ent, *adj.;* **-ly,** *adv.*
non′con·gru′i·ty, *n., pl.* **-ties.**
non·con′gru·ous, *adj.;* **-ly,** *adv.;* **-ness,** *n.*
non′con·jec′tur·a·ble, *adj.;* **-bly,** *adv.*
non·con′ju·gal, *adj.;* **-ly,** *adv.*
non′con·ju·gal′i·ty, *n.*
non·con′ju·gate, *adj., n.*
non′con·ju·ga′tion, *n.*
non′con·junc′tion, *n.*
non′con·junc′tive, *adj.;* **-ly,** *adv.*
non′con·nec′tive, *adj., n.;* **-ly,** *adv.*
non′con·nec·tiv′i·ty, *n.*
non′con·niv′ance, *n.*
non′con·niv′ence, *n.*
non·con′no·ta′tive, *adj.;* **-ly,** *adv.*
non′con·nu′bi·al, *adj.;* **-ly,** *adv.*
non′con·nu′bi·al′i·ty, *n.*
non′con·sci·en′tious, *adj.;* **-ly,** *adv.;* **-ness,** *n.*
non·con′scious, *adj.;* **-ly,** *adv.;* **-ness,** *n.*
non′con·script′a·ble, *adj.*
non′con·scrip′tion, *n.*
non′con·se·cra′tion, *n.*
non′con·sec′u·tive, *adj.;* **-ly,** *adv.;* **-ness,** *n.*
non′con·sent′, *n.*
non′con·sent′ing, *adj., n.*
non·con′se·quence, *n.*
non·con′se·quent, *adj.*
non′con·se·quen′tial, *adj.;* **-ly,** *adv.;* **-ness,** *n.*
non′con·se·quen′ti·al′i·ty, *n.*
non′con·ser·va′tion, *n.*
non′con·ser·va′tion·al, *adj.*
non′con·ser′va·tive, *adj., n.*
non′con·serv′ing, *adj., n.*
non′con·sid′er·a′tion, *n.*
non′con·sign′ment, *n.*
non′con·sis·to′ri·al, *adj.*
non′con·sol′a·ble, *adj.*
non′con·sol′i·da′tion, *n.*
non′con·sol′ing, *adj.;* **-ly,** *adv.*
non·con′so·nance, *n.*
non′con·sort′ing, *adj.*
non′con·spir′a·tor, *n.*
non′con·spir′a·to′ri·al, *adj.*
non′con·spir′ing, *adj.*
non·con′stant, *n., adj.*
non′con·stit′u·ent, *adj., n.*
non·con′sti·tut′ed, *adj.*
non′con·sti·tu′tion·al, *adj.*
non′con·strain′ing, *adj.*
non′con·straint′, *n.*
non′con·strict′ed, *adj.*
non′con·strict′ing, *adj.*
non′con·stric′tive, *adj.*
non′con·stru′a·bil′i·ty, *n.*
non′con·stru′a·ble, *adj.*
non′con·struc′tive, *adj.;* **-ly,** *adv.;* **-ness,** *n.*
non·con′su·lar, *adj.*
non′con·sult′a·tive, *adj.*
non′con·sul′ta·to′ry, *adj.*
non′con·sum′a·ble, *adj.*
non′con·sum′ing, *adj.*
non′con·sum·ma′tion, *n.*
non′con·sump′tion, *n.*
non′con·sump′tive, *adj.;* **-ly,** *adv.;* **-ness,** *n.*
non·con′tact, *n.*
non′con·ta′gion, *n.*
non′con·ta′gious, *adj.;* **-ly,** *adv.;* **-ness,** *n.*
non′con·tam′i·na·ble, *adj.*
non′con·tam′i·na′tion, *n.*
non′con·tam′i·na′tive, *adj.*
non·con′tem·pla′tive, *adj.;* **-ly,** *adv.;* **-ness,** *n.*
non′con·tem′po·ra′ne·ous, *adj.;* **-ly,** *adv.;* **-ness,** *n.*
non′con·tem′po·rar′y, *adj., n., pl.* **-rar·ies.**
non′con·tempt′i·bil′i·ty, *n.*
non′con·tempt′i·ble, *adj.;* **-ble·ness,** *n.;* **-bly,** *adv.*
non′con·temp′tu·ous, *adj.;* **-ly,** *adv.;* **-ness,** *n.*
non′con·tend′ing, *adj.*
non′con·ten′tion, *n.*
non′con·ten′tious, *adj.;* **-ly,** *adv.*
non′con·ter′mi·nal, *adj.*
non′con·ter′mi·nous, *adj.;* **-ly,** *adv.*
non′con·tes·ta′tion, *n.*
non′con·tex′tual, *adj.;* **-ly,** *adv.*
non′con·ti·gu′i·ty, *n., pl.* **-ties.**
non′con·tig′u·ous, *adj.;* **-ly,** *adv.;* **-ness,** *n.*
non·con′ti·nence, *n.*
non·con′ti·nen·cy, *n.*
non′con·ti·nen′tal, *adj., n.*
non′con·tin′gent, *adj.;* **-ly,** *adv.*
non′con·tin′u·a·ble, *adj.;* **-bly,** *adv.*
non′con·tin′u·ance, *n.*
non′con·tin′u·a′tion, *n.*
non′con·tin·u′i·ty, *n.*
non′con·tin′u·ous, *adj.;* **-ly,** *adv.;* **-ness,** *n.*
non·con′tra·band′, *n., adj.*
non′con·trac′tion, *n.*
non′con·tra·dic′to·ry, *adj., n., pl.* **-ries.**
non′con·tra·ri′e·ty, *n., pl.* **-ties.**
non′con·trib′u·ta·ble, *adj.*
non′con·trib′u·ting, *adj.*
non′con·tri·bu′tion, *n.*
non′con·trib′u·tive, *adj.;* **-ly,** *adv.;* **-ness,** *n.*
non′con·trib′u·tor, *n.*
non′con·trib′u·to′ry, *adj., n., pl.* **-ries.**
non′con·triv′ance, *n.*
non′con·troll′a·ble, *adj.;* **-ly,** *adv.*
non′con·trolled′, *adj.*
non′con·trol′ling, *adj.*
non′con·tro·ver′sial, *adj.;* **-ly,** *adv.*
non′con·tu·ma′cious, *adj.;* **-ly,** *adv.;* **-ness,** *n.*
non′con·vec′tive, *adj.;* **-ly,** *adv.*
non′con·ven′tion·al, *adj.;* **-ly,** *adv.*
non′con·ver′gence, *n.*
non′con·ver′gen·cy, *n.*
non′con·ver′gent, *adj.*
non′con·verg′ing, *adj.*
non′con·ver′sa·ble, *adj.;* **-ble·ness,** *n.;* **-bly,** *adv.*
non′con·ver′sance, *n.*
non′con·ver′san·cy, *n.*
non′con·ver′sant, *adj.;* **-ly,** *adv.*
non′con·ver·sa′tion·al, *adj.;* **-ly,** *adv.*
non′con·ver′sion, *n.*
non′con·vert′i·bil′i·ty, *n.*
non′con·vert′i·ble, *adj.;* **-ble·ness,** *n.;* **-bly,** *adv.*
non′con·vey′ance, *n.*
non′con·vic′tion, *n.*
non′con·viv′i·al, *adj.;* **-ly,** *adv.*
non′con·viv′i·al′i·ty, *n.*
non′co·or′di·nat′ing, *adj.*
non′co·or′di·na′tion, *n.*
non′co·pla′nar, *adj.*
non·cor′po·rate, *adj.;* **-ly,** *adv.*
non′cor·po·ra′tion, *n.*
non·cor′po·ra′tive, *adj.*
non′cor·po′re·al, *adj.*
non′cor·po′re·al′i·ty, *n.*
non′cor·pus′cu·lar, *adj.*
non′cor·rec′tion, *n.*
non′cor·rec′tion·al, *adj.*
non′cor·rec′tive, *adj., n.;* **-ly,** *adv.*
non·cor′re·lat′ing, *adj.*
non′cor·re·la′tion, *n.*
non′cor·rel′a·tive, *adj.;* **-ly,** *adv.;* **-ness,** *n.*
non′cor·res·pond′ence, *n.*
non′cor·res·pond′ent, *adj., n.*
non′cor·res·pond′ing, *adj., n.;* **-ly,** *adv.*
non′cor·rob′o·rat′ing, *adj.*
non′cor·rob′o·ra′tion, *n.*
non′cor·rob′o·ra′tive, *adj.;* **-ly,** *adv.*
non′cor·rob′o·ra·to′ry, *adj.*
non′cor·rod′i·ble, *adj.*
non′cor·rod′ing, *adj., n.*
non′cor·ro′sive, *adj.;* **-ly,** *adv.;* **-ness,** *n.*
non′cor·rupt′, *adj.;* **-ly,** *adv.;* **-ness,** *n.*
non′cor·rupt′er, *n.*
non′cor·rupt′i·bil′i·ty, *n.*
non′cor·rupt′i·ble, *adj.;* **-ble·ness,** *n.;* **-bly,** *adv.*
non′cor·rup′tive, *adj.*
non·cor′ti·cal, *adj.;* **-ly,** *adv.*
non·cos′mic, *adj.*
non·cos′mi·cal·ly, *adv.*
non′cos·mo·pol′i·tan, *adj., n.*
non′cos·mo·pol′i·tan·ism, *n.*
non′cos·mop′o·lite′, *n.*
non′cos·mop′o·lit′ism, *n.*
non·cot′tag·er, *n.*
non′cot·y·le′don·al, *adj.*
non′cot·y·le′don·ar′y, *adj.*
non′cot·y·le′don·ous, *adj.*
non′coun·ter·ac′tive, *adj.*
non·coun′ter·feit, *adj.*
non·cov′et·ous, *adj.;* **-ly,** *adv.;* **-ness,** *n.*
non·crank′ing, *adj.*
non′cre·a′tive, *adj.;* **-ly,** *adv.;* **-ness,** *n.*
non′cre·a·tiv′i·ty, *n.*
non·cre′dence, *n.*
non·cre′dent, *adj.*
non′cred·i·bil′i·ty, *n.*
non·cred′i·ble, *adj.;* **-ble·ness,** *n.;* **-bly,** *adv.*
non·cred′it·a·ble, *adj.;* **-ble·ness,** *n.;* **-bly,** *adv.*
non·cred′i·tor, *n.*
non·cred′u·lous, *adj.;* **-ly,** *adv.;* **-ness,** *n.*
non·creep′ing, *adj.*
non·cre′nate, *adj.*
non·cre′nat·ed, *adj.*
non′cre·ta′ceous, *adj.*
non·crim′i·nal, *adj., n.;* **-ly,** *adv.*
non′crim·i·nal′i·ty, *n.*
non·cri′noid, *adj.*
non·crit′i·cal, *adj.;* **-ly,** *adv.;* **-ness,** *n.*
non·crit′i·ciz′ing, *adj., n.*
non·cru′cial, *adj.;* **-ly,** *adv.*
non·cru′ci·form′, *adj.;* **-ly,** *adv.*
non′cru·sad′ing, *adj.*
non′crus·ta′ceous, *adj.*
non·cryp′tic, *adj.*
non·cryp′ti·cal, *adj.;* **-ly,** *adv.*
non·crys′tal·line, *adj.*
non·crys′tal·liz′a·ble, *adj.*
non·crys′tal·lized′, *adj.*
non·crys′tal·liz′ing, *adj.*
non·cul′mi·nat′ing, *adj.*
non′cul·mi·na′tion, *n.*
non′cul·pa·bil′i·ty, *n.*
non·cul′pa·ble, *adj.;* **-ble·ness,** *n.;* **-bly,** *adv.*
non·cul′ti·va·bil′i·ty, *n.*
non·cul′ti·va·ble, *adj.*
non·cul′ti·vat′a·ble, *adj.*
non·cul′ti·vat′ed, *adj.*
non′cul·ti·va′tion, *n.*
non·cul′tur·al, *adj.;* **-ly,** *adv.*
non·cul′ture, *n.*
non·cul′tured, *adj.*
non·cum′brous, *adj.;* **-ly,** *adv.;* **-ness,** *n.*
non·cur′a·tive, *adj.;* **-ly,** *adv.;* **-ness,** *n.*
non·cur′dling, *adj., n.*
non′cu·ri·os′i·ty, *n.*
non·cu′ri·ous, *adj.;* **-ly,** *adv.;* **-ness,** *n.*
non·cur′rent, *adj.;* **-ly,** *adv.*
non·cur′sive, *adj.;* **-ly,** *adv.*
non′cur·tail′ing, *adj.*
non′cur·tail′ment, *n.*
non·cus′pi·date′, *adj.*
non·cus′pi·dat′ed, *adj.*
non′cus·to′di·al, *adj.*
non′cus′tom·ar′i·ly, *adv.*
non·cus′tom·ar′y, *adj.*
non·cut′ting, *adj., n.*
non·cy′clic, *adj.*
non·cy′cli·cal, *adj.;* **-ly,** *adv.*
non-Cym′ric, *adj.*
non-Czech′, *adj., n.*
non′-Czech·o·slo·vak′i·an, *adj., n.*
non·dam′age·a·ble, *adj.*
non·dam′ag·ing, *adj.;* **-ly,** *adv.*
non′dam·na′tion, *n.*
non·danc′er, *n.*
non·dan′ger·ous, *adj.;* **-ly,** *adv.;* **-ness,** *n.*
non-Dan′ish, *adj.*
non·dark′, *adj.*
non′-Dar·win′i·an, *adj., n.*
non′da·ti′val, *adj.*
non·dead′ly, *adj.*
non·deaf′, *adj.;* **-ly,** *adv.;* **-ness,** *n.*
non·deaf′ened, *adj.*
non·deaf′en·ing, *adj.;* **-ly,** *adv.*
non′de·bat′a·ble, *adj.*
non′de·bat′er, *n.*
non′de·bat′ing, *adj.*
non′de·bil′i·tat′ing, *adj.*
non′de·bil′i·ta′tion, *n.*
non′de·bil′i·ta′tive, *adj.*
non·debt′or, *n.*
non·dec′a·dence, *n.*
non·dec′a·den·cy, *n.*
non·dec′a·dent, *adj., n.*
non′de·cal′ci·fi·ca′tion, *n.*
non′de·cal′ci·fied′, *adj.*
non′dec·a·syl·lab′ic, *adj.*
non·dec′a·syl′la·ble, *n.*
non′de·cayed′, *adj.*
non′de·cay′ing, *adj.*
non′de·ceit′, *n.*
non′de·ceiv′a·ble, *adj.*
non′de·ceiv′ing, *adj.*
non′de·cel′er·a′tion, *n.*
non′de·cep′tion, *n.*
non′de·cep′tive, *adj.;* **-ly,** *adv.;* **-ness,** *n.*
non′de·cid′u·ous, *adj.;* **-ly,** *adv.;* **-ness,** *n.*
non′de·ci′sion, *n.*
non′de·ci′sive, *adj.;* **-ly,** *adv.;* **-ness,** *n.*
non′de·clam′a·to′ry, *adj.*
non′dec·la·ra′tion, *n.*
non′de·clar′a·tive, *adj.;* **-ly,** *adv.*
non′de·clar′a·to′ry, *adj.*
non′de·clar′er, *n.*
non′de·cliv′i·tous, *adj.*
non·dec′o·rat′ed, *adj.*
non′dec·o·ra′tion, *n.*
non·dec′o·ra′tive, *adj.*
non·dec′o·rous, *adj.;* **-ly,** *adv.;* **-ness,** *n.*
non′ded·i·ca′tion, *n.*
non·ded′i·ca′tive, *adj.*
non·ded′i·ca·to′ry, *adj.*
non′de·duc′i·ble, *adj.*
non′de·duct′i·ble, *adj., n.*
non′de·duc′tion, *n.*
non′de·duc′tive, *adj.;* **-ly,** *adv.*
non·deep′, *adj.*
non′de·fal·ca′tion, *n.*
non′de·fam′a·to′ry, *adj.*
non′de·fault′ing, *adj., n.*
non′de·fea′sance, *n.*
non′de·fea′si·bil′i·ty, *n.*
non′de·fea′si·ble, *adj.;* **-ness,** *n.*
non′de·feat′, *n.*
non′de·fect′ing, *adj.*
non′de·fec′tion, *n.*
non′de·fec′tive, *adj.;* **-ly,** *adv.;* **-ness,** *n.*
non′de·fec′tor, *n.*
non′de·fend′ant, *n.*

non·dense (non dens′), *adj.* *Math.* nowhere-dense. [NON- + DENSE]

non·de·script (non′di skript′), *adj.* **1.** of no recognized, definite, or particular type or kind: *a nondescript color.* —*n.* **2.** a person or a thing of no particular type or kind. [NON- + L *dēscrīpt(us)* described, defined, represented (ptp. of *dēscrībere;* see DESCRIBE)]
—**Syn. 1.** odd, peculiar, amorphous, indescribable, unclassifiable.

non·di·rec·tion·al (non′di rek′shə nəl, -dī-), *adj.* **1.** without direction; not directional. **2.** functioning equally well in all directions; omnidirectional. [NON- + DIRECTIONAL]

non′di·rec′tive ther′apy, (non′di rek′tiv). See **client-centered therapy.** [NON- + DIRECTIVE]

non·dis·junc·tion (non′dis jungk′shən), *n.* *Biol.* the failure of chromosomes to follow normal separation into daughter cells at division. [NON- + DISJUNCTION]

non·dis·tinc·tive (non′di stingk′tiv), *adj.* *Ling.* not serving to distinguish meanings: *a nondistinctive difference in sound.* [NON- + DISTINCTIVE] —**non′dis·tinc′tive·ly,** *adv.*

none[1] (nun), *pron.* **1.** no one; not one: *None of the members is going.* **2.** not any, as of something indicated: *That is none of your business.* **3.** no part; nothing. **4.** (*construed as pl.*) no or not any persons or things: *None were left when I came.* —*adv.* **5.** to no extent; in no way; not at all: *The supply is none too great.* —*adj.* **6.** *Archaic.* not any; no (usually used only before a vowel or *h*): *Thou shalt have none other gods but me.* [ME *non,* OE *nān,* equiv. to *ne* not + *ān* one]
—**Usage.** Since many construe NONE in its etymological sense of "not one," they insist that precision demands its being treated as a singular, followed by a singular verb, as in def. 1, above. However, the word is very often felt to have the sense of def. 4, and there is ample evidence for such use dating back to the earliest English writings.

none[2] (nōn), *n.* sing. of **nones**[1]. Also, **None.** [ME; OE *nōn* < L *nōna* (*hōra*) ninth (hour). See NOON]

non·ef·fec·tive (non′i fek′tiv), *adj.* **1.** not effective. **2.** not fit for duty or active service, as a soldier or sailor. —*n.* **3.** a noneffective person. [NON- + EFFECTIVE]

non·e·go (non ē′gō, -eg′ō), *n.* *Metaphys.* all that is not the ego or conscious self; object as opposed to subject. [< L *nōn* not + *ego* I]

non′de·fense′, *n.*
non′de·fen′si·bil′i·ty, *n.*
non′de·fen′si·ble, *adj.;* **-ble·ness,** *n.;* **-bly,** *adv.*
non′de·fen′sive, *adj.;* **-ly,** *adv.;* **-ness,** *n.*
non′de·fer′a·ble, *adj.*
non·def′er·ence, *n.*
non·def′er·ent, *adj.*
non′def·er·en′tial, *adj.;* **-ly,** *adv.*
non′de·fer′ra·ble, *adj.*
non′de·fi′ance, *n.*
non′de·fi′ant, *adj.;* **-ly,** *adv.;* **-ness,** *n.*
non′de·fi′cien·cy, *n., pl.* **-cies.**
non′de·fi′cient, *adj.;* **-ly,** *adv.*
non′de·file′ment, *n.*
non′de·fil′ing, *adj.*
non′de·fin′a·bil′i·ty, *n.*
non′de·fin′a·ble, *adj.;* **-bly,** *adv.*
non′de·fined′, *adj.*
non′de·fin′er, *n.*
non′de·fin′ing, *adj.*
non·def′i·nite, *adj.;* **-ly,** *adv.;* **-ness,** *n.*
non′de·fin′i·tive, *adj.;* **-ly,** *adv.;* **-ness,** *n.*
non′de·fla′tion, *n.*
non′de·fla′tion·ar′y, *adj.*
non′de·flect′ed, *adj.*
non′de·flec′tion, *n.*
non′de·flec′tive, *adj.*
non′de·for·ma′tion, *n.*
non′de·formed′, *adj.*
non′de·for′mi·ty, *n., pl.* **-ties.**
non′de·funct′, *adj.*
non′de·gen′er·a·cy, *n., pl.* **-cies.**
non′de·gen′er·ate, *adj., n.;* **-ly,** *adv.;* **-ness,** *n.*
non′de·gen′er·a′tion, *n.*
non′de·gen′er·a′tive, *adj.*
non′deg·ra·da′tion, *n.*
non′de·grad′ing, *adj.*
non′de·his′cent, *adj.*
non·de′ist, *n.*
non′de·is′tic, *adj.*
non′de·is′ti·cal, *adj.;* **-ly,** *adv.*
non·del′e·gate, *n.*
non′del·e·ga′tion, *n.*
non′del·e·te′ri·ous, *adj.;* **-ly,** *adv.;* **-ness,** *n.*
non′de·lib′er·ate, *adj.;* **-ly,** *adv.;* **-ness,** *n.*
non′de·lib′er·a′tion, *n.*
non·del′i·cate, *adj.;* **-ly,** *adv.;* **-ness,** *n.*
non′de·lin′e·a′tion, *n.*
non′de·lin′e·a′tive, *adj.*
non′de·lin′quent, *adj.*
non′del·i·ques′cence, *n.*
non′del·i·ques′cent, *adj.*
non′de·lir′i·ous, *adj.;* **-ly,** *adv.;* **-ness,** *n.*
non′de·liv′er·ance, *n.*
non′de·liv′er·y, *n., pl.* **-er·ies.**
non′de·lud′ed, *adj.*
non′de·lud′ing, *adj.*
non′de·lu′sive, *adj.*
non′de·mand′ing, *adj.*
non′de·mise′, *n.*
non′de·mo′bi·li·za′tion, *n.*
non′de·moc′ra·cy, *n., pl.* **-cies.**
non′dem·o·crat′ic, *adj.*
non′dem·o·crat′i·cal, *adj.;* **-ly,** *adv.*
non′dem·o·li′tion, *n.*
non′de·mon′stra·bil′i·ty, *n.*
non′de·mon′stra·ble, *adj.;* **-ble·ness,** *n.;* **-bly,** *adv.*
non′de·mon′stra·tive, *adj.;* **-ly,** *adv.;* **-ness,** *n.*
non·den′droid, *adj.*
non′den·droi′dal, *adj.*
non′de·ni′al, *n.*
non′de·nom′i·na′tion·al, *adj.;* **-ly,** *adv.*
non′de·no′ta·tive, *adj.;* **-ly,** *adv.*
non·dense′ness, *n.*
non·den′si·ty, *n.*
non′de·nun′ci·at′ing, *adj.*
non′de·nun′ci·a′tion, *n.*
non′de·nun′ci·a′tive, *adj.*
non′de·nun′ci·a·to′ry, *adj.*
non′de·o′dor·ant, *n., adj.*
non′de·o′dor·iz′ing, *adj.*
non′de·part·men′tal, *adj.;* **-ly,** *adv.*
non′de·par′ture, *n.*
non′de·pend′a·bil′i·ty, *n.*
non′de·pend′a·ble, *adj.;* **-ble·ness,** *n.;* **-bly,** *adv.*
non′de·pend′ance, *n.*
non′de·pend′an·cy, *n., pl.* **-cies.**
non′de·pend′ence, *n.*
non′de·pend′en·cy, *n., pl.* **-cies.**
non′de·ple′tion, *n.*
non′de·ple′tive, *adj.*
non′de·ple′to·ry, *adj.*
non′de·por·ta′tion, *n.*
non′de·port′ed, *adj., n.*
non′de·pos′i·tor, *n.*
non′dep·ra·va′tion, *n.*
non′de·praved′, *adj.*
non′de·prav′i·ty, *n., pl.* **-ties.**
non·dep′re·cat′ing, *adj.;* **-ly,** *adv.*
non·dep′re·ca′tive, *adj.;* **-ly,** *adv.*
non·dep′re·ca·to′ri·ly, *adv.*
non·dep′re·ca·to′ry, *adj.*
non′de·pre′ci·at′ing, *adj.*
non′de·pre′ci·a′tion, *n.*
non′de·pre′ci·a′tive, *adj.;* **-ly,** *adv.*
non′de·pre′ci·a·to′ry, *adj.*
non′de·pressed′, *adj.*
non′de·press′ing, *adj.;* **-ly,** *adv.*
non′de·pres′sion, *n.*
non′de·pres′sive, *adj.;* **-ly,** *adv.*
non′de·priv′a·ble, *adj.*
non′dep·ri·va′tion, *n.*
non′der·e·lict, *adj., n.*
non′de·ris′i·ble, *adj.*
non′de·ri′sive, *adj.*
non′de·riv′a·bil′i·ty, *n.*
non′de·riv′a·ble, *adj.*
non′de·riv′a·tive, *adj., n.;* **-ly,** *adv.*
non′der·o·ga′tion, *n.*
non′de·rog′a·tive, *adj.;* **-ly,** *adv.*
non′de·rog′a·to′ri·ly, *adv.*
non′de·rog′a·to′ri·ness, *n.*
non′de·rog′a·to′ry, *adj.*
non′de·scrib′a·ble, *adj.*
non′de·scrip′tive, *adj.;* **-ly,** *adv.;* **-ness,** *n.*
non′des·e·cra′tion, *n.*
non·des′ig·nate, *adj.*
non·des′ig·na′tive, *adj.*
non′de·signed′, *adj.*
non′de·sir′ous, *adj.*
non′de·sist′ance, *n.*
non′de·sist′ence, *n.*
non′de·sist′ing, *adj., n.*
non′des·pot′ic, *adj.*
non′des·pot′i·cal·ly, *adv.*
non′de·struc′tion, *n.*
non′de·struc′tive, *adj.;* **-ly,** *adv.;* **-ness,** *n.*
non′de·sul′fu·ri·za′tion, *n.*
non′de·sul′fu·rized′, *adj.*
non′de·tach′a·bil′i·ty, *n.*
non′de·tach′a·ble, *adj.*
non′de·tach′ment, *n.*
non′de·tailed′, *adj.*
non′de·ten′tion, *n.*
non′de·te′ri·o·ra′tion, *n.*
non′de·ter′mi·na·ble, *adj.*
non′de·ter′mi·nant, *n.*
non′de·ter′mi·na′tion, *n.*
non′de·ter′mi·na′tive, *adj., n.;* **-ly,** *adv.;* **-ness,** *n.*
non′de·ter′min·ist, *n., adj.*
non′de·ter′min·is′tic, *adj.*
non′de·ter′rent, *adj.*
non·det′o·nat′ing, *adj.*
non′de·trac′tive, *adj.;* **-ly,** *adv.*
non′de·trac′to·ry, *adj.*
non′det·ri·men′tal, *adj.;* **-ly,** *adv.*
non′de·vel′op·a·ble, *adj.*
non′de·vel′op·ing, *adj.*
non′de·vel′op·ment, *n.*
non′de·vel′op·men′tal, *adj.;* **-ly,** *adv.*
non·de′vi·ant, *adj., n.*
non·de′vi·at′ing, *adj.*
non′de·vi·a′tion, *n.*
non·de′vi·ous, *adj.;* **-ly,** *adv.;* **-ness,** *n.*
non′de·vo′tion·al, *adj.;* **-ly,** *adv.*
non′de·vout′, *adj.;* **-ly,** *adv.;* **-ness,** *n.*
non′dex·ter′i·ty, *n.*
non·dex′ter·ous, *adj.;* **-ly,** *adv.;* **-ness,** *n.*
non·dex′trous, *adj.*
non′di·a·bet′ic, *adj.*
non′di·a·bol′ic, *adj.*
non′di·a·bol′i·cal, *adj.;* **-ly,** *adv.;* **-ness,** *n.*
non′di·ag′o·nal, *adj., n.;* **-ly,** *adv.*
non′di·a·gram·mat′ic, *adj.*
non′di·a·gram·mat′i·cal, *adj.;* **-ly,** *adv.*
non′di·a·lec′tal, *adj.;* **-ly,** *adv.*
non′di·a·lec′tic, *adj., n.*
non′di·a·lec′ti·cal, *adj.;* **-ly,** *adv.*
non·di′a·lyz′ing, *adj.*
non′di·am′e·tral, *adj.;* **-ly,** *adv.*
non′di·aph′a·nous, *adj.;* **-ly,** *adv.;* **-ness,** *n.*
non′di·a·sta′sic, *adj.*
non′di·a·stat′ic, *adj.*
non′di·a·ther′ma·nous, *adj.*
non′di·cho·gam′ic, *adj.*
non′di·chog′a·mous, *adj.*
non′di·chog′a·my, *n.*
non′di·chot′o·mous, *adj.;* **-ly,** *adv.*
non′dic·ta′tion, *n.*
non′dic·ta·to′ri·al, *adj.;* **-ly,** *adv.;* **-ness,** *n.*
non′di·dac′tic, *adj.*
non′di·dac′ti·cal·ly, *adv.*
non′di·e·tet′ic, *adj.*
non′di·e·tet′i·cal·ly, *adv.*
non·di′et·ing, *adj., n.*
non′dif·fer·en′ti·a·ble, *adj.*
non′dif·fer·en′ti·a′tion, *n.*
non·dif′fi·cult′, *adj.*
non·dif′fi·dence, *n.*
non·dif′fi·dent, *adj.;* **-ly,** *adv.*
non′dif·frac′tive, *adj.;* **-ly,** *adv.;* **-ness,** *n.*
non′dif·fuse′, *adj.*
non′dif·fused′, *adj.*
non′dif·fus′i·ble, *adj.;* **-ble·ness,** *n.;* **-bly,** *adv.*
non′dif·fus′ing, *adj.*
non′dif·fu′sion, *n.*
non′di·gest′i·bil′i·ty, *n.*
non′di·gest′i·ble, *adj.;* **-ble·ness,** *n.;* **-bly,** *adv.*
non′di·gest′ing, *adj.*
non′di·ges′tion, *n.*
non′di·ges′tive, *adj.*
non′di·lap′i·dat′ed, *adj.*
non′di·lat′a·bil′i·ty, *n.*
non′di·lat′a·ble, *adj.*
non′di·la′tion, *n.*
non·dil′i·gence, *n.*
non·dil′i·gent, *adj.;* **-ly,** *adv.*
non′di·lu′tion, *n.*
non′di·men′sioned, *adj.*
non′di·min′ish·ing, *adj.*
non′di·oc′e·san, *adj.*
non′diph·the′ri·al, *adj.*
non′diph·ther′ic, *adj.*
non′diph·the·rit′ic, *adj.*
non′diph·thon′gal, *adj.*
non′di·plo′ma·cy, *n.*
non′dip·lo·mat′ic, *adj.*
non′dip·lo·mat′i·cal·ly, *adv.*
non·dip′ter·ous, *adj.*
non′di·rec′tive, *adj.*
non′dir·i·gi·bil′i·ty, *n.*
non·dir′i·gi·ble, *adj., n.*
non′dis·a·gree′ment, *n.*
non′dis·ap·pear′ing, *adj.*
non′dis·ar′ma·ment, *n.*
non′dis·as′trous, *adj.;* **-ly,** *adv.;* **-ness,** *n.*
non′dis·burs′a·ble, *adj.*
non′dis·bursed′, *adj.*
non′dis·burse′ment, *n.*
non′dis·cern′ing, *adj.*
non′dis·cern′ment, *n.*
non′dis·charg′ing, *adj., n.*
non·dis′ci·plin′a·ble, *adj.*
non·dis′ci·pli·nar′y, *adj.*
non·dis′ci·plined, *adj.*
non·dis′ci·plin·ing, *adj.*
non′dis·clo′sure, *n.*
non′dis·con·tin′u·ance, *n.*
non′dis·cord′ant, *adj.*
non′dis·count′a·ble, *adj.*
non′dis·cov′er·a·ble, *adj.*
non′dis·cov′er·y, *n., pl.* **-er·ies.**
non′dis·cre′tion·ar′y, *adj.*
non′dis·crim′i·nat′ing, *adj.;* **-ly,** *adv.*
non′dis·crim′i·na′tion, *n.*
non′dis·crim′i·na′tive, *adj.;* **-ly,** *adv.*
non′dis·crim′i·na·to′ry, *adj.*
non′dis·cur′sive, *adj.;* **-ly,** *adv.;* **-ness,** *n.*
non′dis·eased′, *adj.*
non′dis·fig′ure·ment, *n.*
non′dis·fran′chised, *adj.*
non′dis·guised′, *adj.*
non′dis·in·gen′u·ous, *adj.;* **-ly,** *adv.;* **-ness,** *n.*
non′dis·in′te·grat′ing, *adj.*
non′dis·in·te·gra′tion, *n.*
non′dis·in′ter·est·ed, *adj.*
non′dis·junc′tive, *adj.;* **-ly,** *adv.*
non′dis·mem′ber·ment, *n.*
non′dis·mis′sal, *n.*
non′dis·par′ag·ing, *adj.*
non·dis′pa·rate, *adj.;* **-ly,** *adv.;* **-ness,** *n.*
non′dis·par′i·ty, *n., pl.* **-ties.**
non′dis·pens′a·ble, *adj.*
non′dis·pen·sa′tion, *n.*
non′dis·pen·sa′tion·al, *adj.*
non′dis·pens′i·ble, *adj.*
non′dis·per′sal, *n.*
non′dis·per′sion, *n.*
non′dis·per′sive, *adj.*
non′dis·pos′a·ble, *adj.*
non′dis·pos′al, *n.*
non′dis·posed′, *adj.*
non′dis·pu·ta′tious, *adj.;* **-ly,** *adv.;* **-ness,** *n.*
non′dis·qual′i·fy′ing, *adj.*
non′dis·rupt′ing, *adj.;* **-ly,** *adv.*
non′dis·rup′tive, *adj.*
non′dis·sent′ing, *adj., n.*
non·dis′si·dence, *n.*
non·dis′si·dent, *adj., n.*
non·dis′si·pat′ed, *adj.;* **-ly,** *adv.;* **-ness,** *n.*
non·dis′si·pa′tive, *adj.*
non′dis·so·lu′tion, *n.*
non′dis·solv′ing, *adj.*
non′dis·till′a·ble, *adj.*
non′dis·til·la′tion, *n.*
non′dis·tin′guish·a·ble, *adj.;* **-ble·ness,** *n.;* **-bly,** *adv.*
non′dis·tin′guished, *adj.*
non′dis·tin′guish·ing, *adj.*
non′dis·tort′ed, *adj.;* **-ly,** *adv.;* **-ness,** *n.*
non′dis·tort′ing, *adj.;* **-ly,** *adv.*
non′dis·tor′tion, *n.*
non′dis·tor′tive, *adj.*
non′dis·tract′ed, *adj.;* **-ly,** *adv.*
non′dis·tract′ing, *adj.;* **-ly,** *adv.*
non′dis·trac′tive, *adj.*
non′dis·tri·bu′tion, *n.*
non′dis·tri·bu′tion·al, *adj.*
non′dis·trib′u·tive, *adj.;* **-ly,** *adv.;* **-ness,** *n.*
non′dis·turb′ance, *n.*
non′dis·turb′ing, *adj.*
non′di·ver′gence, *n.*
non′di·ver′gen·cy, *n., pl.* **-cies.**
non′di·ver′gent, *adj.;* **-ly,** *adv.*
non′di·verg′ing, *adj.*
non′di·ver′si·fi·ca′tion, *n.*
non′di·vin′i·ty, *n., pl.* **-ties.**
non′di·vis′i·bil′i·ty, *n.*
non′di·vis′i·ble, *adj.*
non′di·vi′sion, *n.*
non′di·vi′sion·al, *adj.*
non′di·vi′sive, *adj.;* **-ly,** *adv.;* **-ness,** *n.*
non′di·vorce′, *n.*
non′di·vorced′, *adj.*
non′di·vul′gence, *n.*
non′di·vulg′ing, *adj.*
non′doc·tri·naire′, *adj.*
non·doc′tri·nal, *adj.;* **-ly,** *adv.*
non′doc·u·men′tal, *adj.*
non′doc·u·men′ta·ry, *adj., n., pl.* **-ries.**
non′dog·mat′ic, *adj.*
non′dog·mat′i·cal, *adj.;* **-ly,** *adv.*
non′do·mes′tic, *adj., n.*
non′do·mes′ti·cal·ly, *adv.*
non′do·mes′ti·cat′ed, *adj.*
non′do·mes′ti·cat′ing, *adj.*
non·dom′i·nance, *n.*
non·dom′i·nant, *adj., n.*
non·dom′i·nat′ing, *adj.*
non′dom·i·na′tion, *n.*
non′dom·i·neer′ing, *adj.*
non·dor′mant, *adj.*
non·doubt′a·ble, *adj.*
non·doubt′er, *n.*
non·doubt′ing, *adj.;* **-ly,** *adv.*
non′dra·mat′ic, *adj.*
non′dra·mat′i·cal·ly, *adv.*
non·drink′a·ble, *adj.*
non·drink′er, *n.*
non·drink′ing, *adj., n.*
non·driv′er, *n.*
non·drop′si·cal, *adj.*
non·drop′si·cal·ly, *adv.*
non-Dru′id, *n.*
non′dru·id′ic, *adj.*
non′dru·id′i·cal, *adj.*
non·dry′ing, *adj.*
non·du′al·ism, *n.*
non′du·al·is′tic, *adj.*
non′du·al·is′ti·cal·ly, *adv.*
non′du·al′i·ty, *n.*
non·duc′tile, *adj.*
non′duc·til′i·ty, *n.*
non·du′pli·cat′ing, *adj.*
non′du·pli·ca′tion, *n.*
non·du′pli·ca′tive, *adj.*
non′du·plic′i·ty, *n.*
non′du·ra·bil′i·ty, *n.*
non·du′ra·ble, *adj.;* **-ble·ness,** *n.;* **-bly,** *adv.*
non·du′ti·a·ble, *adj.*
non′dy·nam′ic, *adj.*
non′dy·nam′i·cal, *adj.;* **-ly,** *adv.*
non′dy·nas′tic, *adj.*
non′dy·nas′ti·cal, *adj.;* **-ly,** *adv.*
non′dys·pep′tic, *adj.*
non′dys·pep′ti·cal, *adj.;* **-ly,** *adv.*
non·ea′ger, *adj.;* **-ly,** *adv.;* **-ness,** *n.*
non·earn′ing, *adj., n.*
non·east′ern, *adj.*
non·eat′a·ble, *adj.*
non′e·bul′lience, *n.*
non′e·bul′lien·cy, *n.*
non′e·bul′lient, *adj.;* **-ly,** *adv.*
non′ec·cen′tric, *adj.*
non′ec·cen′tri·cal·ly, *adv.*
non′ec·cle′si·as′tic, *adj., n.*
non′ec·cle′si·as′ti·cal, *adj.;* **-ly,** *adv.*
non′e·cho′ic, *adj.*
non′ec·lec′tic, *adj., n.*
non′ec·lec′ti·cal·ly, *adv.*
non′e·clipsed′, *adj.*
non′e·clips′ing, *adj.*
non′e·clip′tic, *adj.*
non′e·clip′ti·cal, *adj.;* **-ly,** *adv.*
non′e·co·nom′ic, *adj.*
non′e·co·nom′i·cal, *adj.;* **-ly,** *adv.*
non′e·con′o·my, *n., pl.* **-mies.**
non′ec·stat′ic, *adj.*
non′ec·stat′i·cal·ly, *adv.*
non′ec·u·men′ic, *adj.*
non′ec·u·men′i·cal, *adj.*
non′ed·i·bil′i·ty, *n.*
non·ed′i·ble, *adj., n.;* **-ness,** *n.*
non·ed′i·fied′, *adj.*
non′ed·i·to′ri·al, *adj.;* **-ly,** *adv.*
non·ed′u·ca·ble, *adj.*
non·ed′u·cat′ed, *adj.*
non′ed·u·ca′tion, *n.*
non′ed·u·ca′tion·al, *adj.;* **-ly,** *adv.*
non·ed′u·ca′tive, *adj.*
non·ed′u·ca·to′ry, *adj.*
non′ef·fer·ves′cent, *adj.;* **-ly,** *adv.*
non′ef·fete′, *adj.;* **-ly,** *adv.;* **-ness,** *n.*
non′ef·fi·ca′cious, *adj.;* **-ly,** *adv.*
non·ef′fi·ca·cy, *n.*
non′ef·fi′cien·cy, *n.*
non′ef·fi′cient, *adj.;* **-ly,** *adv.*
non′ef·fu′sion, *n.*
non′ef·fu′sive, *adj.;* **-ly,** *adv.;* **-ness,** *n.*
non′e·go·cen′tric, *adj.*
non′e·go·is′tic, *adj.*
non′e·go·is′ti·cal, *adj.;* **-ly,** *adv.*
non′e·go·tis′tic, *adj.*
non′e·go·tis′ti·cal, *adj.;* **-ly,** *adv.*
non′e·gre′gious, *adj.;* **-ly,** *adv.;* **-ness,** *n.*
non′-E·gyp′tian, *adj., n.*
non′ei·det′ic, *adj.*
non′e·jac′u·la·to′ry, *adj.*
non′e·ject′ing, *adj.*
non′e·jec′tion, *n.*
non′e·jec′tive, *adj.*
non′e·lab′o·rate, *adj.;* **-ly,** *adv.;* **-ness,** *n.*
non′e·lab′o·rat′ing, *adj.*
non′e·lab′o·ra′tive, *adj.*
non′e·las′tic, *adj.*
non′e·las′ti·cal·ly, *adv.*
non′e·las·tic′i·ty, *n.*
non′e·lect′, *n.*
non′e·lec′tion, *n.*
non′e·lec′tive, *adj., n.;* **-ly,** *adv.;* **-ness,** *n.*
non′e·lec′tor, *n.*
non′e·lec′tric, *adj., n.*
non′e·lec′tri·cal, *adj.;* **-ly,** *adv.*
non′e·lec′tri·fi·ca′tion, *n.*
non′e·lec′tri·fied′, *adj.*
non′e·lec′trized, *adj.*
non′e·lec′tro·lyte′, *n.*

non·emp·ty (non emp′tē), *adj. Math.* (of a set, group, collection, etc.) containing at least one element. [NON- + EMPTY]

non·en·ti·ty (non en′ti tē), *n., pl.* **-ties. 1.** a person or thing of no importance. **2.** something which does not exist, or exists only in imagination. **3.** nonexistence. [NON- + ENTITY]

nones[1] (nōnz), *n. Eccles.* the fifth of the seven canonical hours, or the service for it, originally fixed for the ninth hour of the day (or 3 P.M.). [pl. of NONE[2]]

nones[2] (nōnz), *n.pl., sing.* **none.** (in the ancient Roman calendar) the ninth day before the ides, both days included: the seventh of March, May, July, and October, and the fifth of the other months. [ME < L *nōnae*, orig. fem. pl. of *nōnus* ninth]

none-so-pret·ty (nun′sō prit′ē, -prit′ē), *n., pl.* **-ties.** See **sweet william catchfly.**

non·es·sen·tial (non′i sen′shəl), *adj.* **1.** not essential; not necessary: *Nonessential use of gasoline must be eliminated.* —*n.* **2.** a nonessential thing or person. [NON- + ESSENTIAL]

non est (non′ est′), *Law.* the returning of a sheriff's writ when the person to be arrested or served with it cannot be found in the sheriff's jurisdiction. [< L: short for *non est inventus* he was not found]

none·such (nun′such′), *n.* **1.** a person or thing without equal; paragon. **2.** See **black medic.** Also, **nonsuch.** [NONE[1] + SUCH]
—Syn. 1. ideal, model, pattern, nonpareil.

no·net (nō net′), *n. Music.* **1.** a group of nine performers or instruments. **2.** a composition for a nonet. [< It *nonetto*, deriv. of *nono* ninth < L *nōnus.* See -ET]

none·the·less (nun′thə les′), *adv.* however; nevertheless. [from the phrase *none the less*]

non′-Eu·clid′e·an geom′etry (non′yōō klid′ē ən), geometry based upon one or more postulates that differ from those of Euclid, esp. from the postulate that only one line may be drawn through a given point parallel to a given line. [NON- + EUCLIDEAN]

non·ex·ist·ence (non′ig zis′təns), *n.* **1.** absence of existence. **2.** a thing that has no existence. [NON- + EXISTENCE]

non·ex·por·ta·tion (non′eks pōr tā′shən, -pôr-), *n.* failure or refusal to export. [NON- + EXPORTATION]

non·fat (non′fat′), *adj.* without fat or fat solids; having the fat solids removed, as skim milk: *nonfat dry milk.* [NON- + FAT]

non·fea·sance (non fē′zəns), *n. Law.* the omission of some act which ought to have been performed. Cf. **malfeasance, misfeasance** (def. 2). [NON- + obs. *feasance;* see MALFEASANCE]

non·fer·rous (non fer′əs), *adj.* **1.** (of a metal) containing no iron or very little. **2.** noting or pertaining to metals other than iron or steel. [NON- + FERROUS]

non·fic·tion (non fik′shən), *n.* **1.** the branch of literature comprising works of narrative prose dealing with or offering opinions or conjectures upon facts and reality, including biography, history, and the essay (opposed to *fiction* and distinguished from *poetry* and

non′e·lec′tro·lyt′ic, *adj.*
non′el·ee·mos′y·nar′y, *adj.*
non′el·e·men′tal, *adj.;* **-ly,** *adv.*
non′el·e·men′ta·ry, *adj.*
non·el′e·vat′ing, *adj.*
non′el·e·va′tion, *n.*
non′e·lic′it·ed, *adj.*
non′el·i·gi·bil′i·ty, *n.*
non·el′i·gi·ble, *adj.;* **-bly,** *adv.*
non′e·lim′i·na′tion, *n.*
non′e·lim′i·na′tive, *adj.*
non′e·lim′i·na·to′ry, *adj.*
non′e·lite′, *n.*
non′el·lip′tic, *adj.*
non′el·lip′ti·cal, *adj.;* **-ly,** *adv.*
non′e·lon·ga′tion, *n.*
non′e·lope′ment, *n.*
non·el′o·quence, *n.*
non·el′o·quent, *adj.;* **-ly,** *adv.*
non′e·lu′ci·dat′ing, *adj.*
non′e·lu′ci·da′tion, *n.*
non′e·lu′ci·da′tive, *adj.*
non′e·lu′sive, *adj.;* **-ly,** *adv.;* **-ness,** *n.*
non·em′a·nant, *adj.*
non·em′a·nat′ing, *adj.*
non′e·man′ci·pa′tion, *n.*
non′e·man′ci·pa′tive, *adj.*
non′em·bar·ka′tion, *n.*
non′em·bel′lished, *adj.*
non′em·bel′lish·ing, *adj.*
non′em·bel′lish·ment, *n.*
non′em·bez′zle·ment, *n.*
non′em·bry·o′nal, *adj.*
non′em·bry·on′ic, *adj.*
non′em·bry·on′i·cal·ly, *adv.*
non′e·mend′a·ble, *adj.*
non′e·men·da′tion, *n.*
non′e·mer′gence, *n.*
non′e·mer′gent, *adj.*
non·em′i·grant, *n., adj.*
non′em·i·gra′tion, *n.*
non′e·mis′sion, *n.*
non′e·mo′tion·al, *adj.;* **-ly,** *adv.*
non′e·mo′tion·al·ism, *n.*
non′e·mo′tive, *adj.;* **-ly,** *adv.;* **-ness,** *n.*
non′em·path′ic, *adj.*
non′em·path′i·cal·ly, *adv.*
non′em·pir′ic, *n., adj.*
non′em·pir′i·cal, *adj.;* **-ly,** *adv.*
non′em·pir′i·cism, *n.*
non′em·ploy′ing, *adj.*
non′em·ploy′ment, *n.*
non′em·u·la′tion, *n.*
non·em′u·la′tive, *adj.*
non·em′u·lous, *adj.;* **-ly,** *adv.;* **-ness,** *n.*
non′en·act′ment, *n.*
non′en·clo′sure, *n.*
non′en·croach′ment, *n.*
non′en·cy′clo·pae′dic, *adj.*
non′en·cy′clo·pe′dic, *adj.*
non′en·cy′clo·pe′di·cal, *adj.*
non′en·dem′ic, *adj.*
non′en·dorse′ment, *n.*
non′en·dow′ment, *n.*
non′en·dur′a·ble, *adj.*
non′en·dur′ing, *adj.*
non·en′e·my, *n., pl.* **-mies.**
non′en·er·get′ic, *adj.*
non′en·er·get′i·cal·ly, *adv.*
non·en′er·vat′ing, *adj.*
non′en·force′a·ble, *adj.*
non′en·forced′, *adj.;* **-ly,** *adv.*
non′en·force′ment, *n.*
non′en·forc′ing, *adj.*
non′en·gage′ment, *n.*
non′en·gi·neer′ing, *n., adj.*
non-Eng′lish, *adj., n.*
non′en·gross′ing, *adj.;* **-ly,** *adv.*
non′en·ig·mat′ic, *adj.*
non′en·ig·mat′i·cal, *adj.;* **-ly,** *adv.*
non′en·light′ened, *adj.*
non′en·light′en·ing, *adj.*
non′en·rolled′, *adj.*
non′en·tailed′, *adj.*
non′en·ter′ic, *adj.*
non·en′ter·pris′ing, *adj.*
non′en·ter·tain′ing, *adj.*
non′en·ter·tain′ment, *n.*
non′en·thu′si·as′tic, *adj.*
non′en·thu′si·as′ti·cal·ly, *adv.*
non′en·tic′ing, *adj.;* **-ly,** *adv.*
non′en·to·mo·log′ic, *adj.*
non′en·to·mo·log′i·cal, *adj.*
non·en′trant, *n.*
non·en′treat′ing, *adj.;* **-ly,** *adv.*
non·en′try, *n., pl.* **-tries.**
non′e·nu′mer·at′ed, *adj.*
non′e·nu′mer·a·tive, *adj.*
non′e·nun′ci·a′tion, *n.*
non′e·nun′ci·a′tive, *adj.*
non′e·nun′ci·a·to′ry, *adj.*
non·en′vi·a·ble, *adj.;* **-ble·ness,** *n.;* **-bly,** *adv.*
non·en′vi·ous, *adj.;* **-ly,** *adv.;* **-ness,** *n.*
non′en·vi′ron·men′tal, *adj.;* **-ly,** *adv.*
non′e·phem′er·al, *adj.;* **-ly,** *adv.*
non·ep′ic, *adj., n.*
non·ep′i·cal, *adj.;* **-ly,** *adv.*
non′ep·i·cu·re′an, *adj., n.*
non′ep·i·gram·mat′ic, *adj.*
non′ep·i·gram·mat′i·cal·ly, *adv.*
non′ep·i·lep′tic, *adj., n.*
non′e·pis′co·pal, *adj.;* **-ly,** *adv.*
non′e·pis′co·pa′lian, *adj.*
non′-E·pis′co·pa′lian, *n.*
non′ep·i·sod′ic, *adj.*
non′ep·i·sod′i·cal, *adj.;* **-ly,** *adv.*
non′ep·i·the′li·al, *adj.*
non·ep′och·al, *adj.*
non′eq·ua·bil′i·ty, *n.*
non·eq′ua·ble, *adj.;* **-ble·ness,** *n.;* **-bly,** *adv.*
non·e′qual, *adj., n.*
non′e·qual·i·za′tion, *n.*
non·e′qual·ized′, *adj.*
non·e′qual·iz′ing, *adj.*
non′e·qua′tion, *n.*
non′e·qua·to′ri·al, *adj.;* **-ly,** *adv.*
non′e·ques′tri·an, *adj., n.*
non′e·qui·lat′er·al, *adj.;* **-ly,** *adv.*
non′e·qui·lib′ri·um, *n.*
non·eq′ui·ta·ble, *adj.;* **-bly,** *adv.*
non′e·quiv′a·lence, *n.*
non′e·quiv′a·len·cy, *n.*
non′e·quiv′a·lent, *adj., n.;* **-ly,** *adv.*
non′e·quiv′o·cal, *adj.;* **-ly,** *adv.*
non′e·quiv′o·cat′ing, *adj.*
non′e·rad′i·ca·ble, *adj.*
non′e·rad′i·ca′tive, *adj.*
non′e·ra′sure, *n.*
non′e·rect′ing, *adj.*
non′e·rec′tion, *n.*
non′e·rod′ed, *adj.*
non′e·rod′ent, *adj.*
non′e·rod′ing, *adj.*
non′e·ro′sive, *adj.*
non′e·rot′ic, *adj.*
non′e·rot′i·cal·ly, *adv.*
non·er′rant, *adj.;* **-ly,** *adv.*
non′er·rat′ic, *adj., n.*
non′er·rat′i·cal·ly, *adv.*
non′er·ro′ne·ous, *adj.;* **-ly,** *adv.,* **-ness,** *n.*
non·er′u·dite′, *adj.;* **-ly,** *adv.;* **-ness,** *n.*
non′er·u·di′tion, *n.*
non′e·rup′tion, *n.*
non′e·rup′tive, *adj.*
non′es·o·ter′ic, *adj.*
non′es·o·ter′i·cal·ly, *adv.*
non·es′pi·o·nage′, *n.*
non′es·pous′al, *n.*
non′es·tab′lish·ment, *n.*
non′es·thet′ic, *adj.*
non′es·thet′i·cal, *adj.;* **-ly,** *adv.*
non·es′ti·ma·ble, *adj.;* **-ble·ness,** *n.;* **-bly,** *adv.*
non′e·su′ri·ent, *adj.;* **-ly,** *adv.*
non′e·ter′nal, *adj.;* **-ly,** *adv.;* **-ness,** *n.*
non′e·ter′ni·ty, *n.*
non′e·the′re·al, *adj.;* **-ly,** *adv.;* **-ness,** *n.*
non′e·the′re·al′i·ty, *n.*
non·eth′ic, *adj.*
non·eth′i·cal, *adj.;* **-ly,** *adv.;* **-ness,** *n.*
non·eth′nic, *adj.*
non·eth′ni·cal, *adj.;* **-ly,** *adv.*
non′eth·no·log′ic, *adj.*
non′eth·no·log′i·cal, *adj.;* **-ly,** *adv.*
non·eth′yl, *n.*
non′-Eu·clid′e·an, *adj.*
non′eu·gen′ic, *adj.*
non′eu·gen′i·cal, *adj.;* **-ly,** *adv.*
non′eu·pho′ni·ous, *adj.;* **-ly,** *adv.;* **-ness,** *n.*
non′-Eu·ro·pe′an, *adj., n.*
non′e·vac′u·a′tion, *n.*
non′e·vad′a·ble, *adj.*
non′e·vad′i·ble, *adj.*
non′e·vad′ing, *adj.;* **-ly,** *adv.*
non′e·val′u·a′tion, *n.*
non′ev·a·nes′cent, *adj.;* **-ly,** *adv.*
non′e·van·gel′ic, *adj.*
non′e·van·gel′i·cal, *adj.;* **-ly,** *adv.*
non′e·vap′o·ra·ble, *adj.*
non′e·vap′o·rat′ing, *adj.*
non′e·vap′o·ra′tion, *n.*
non′e·vap′o·ra′tive, *adj.*
non′e·va′sion, *n.*
non′e·va′sive, *adj.;* **-ly,** *adv.;* **-ness,** *n.*
non′e·vic′tion, *n.*
non·ev′i·dent, *adj.*
non′ev·i·den′tial, *adj.*
non·e′vil, *adj.;* **-ly,** *adv.;* **-ness,** *n.*
non′e·vin′ci·ble, *adj.*
non′e·vin′cive, *adj.*
non′e·voc′a·tive, *adj.*
non′ev·o·lu′tion·al, *adj.;* **-ly,** *adv.*
non′ev·o·lu′tion·ar′y, *adj.*
non′ev·o·lu′tion·ist, *n.*
non′e·volv′ing, *adj.*
non′ex·act′a·ble, *adj.*
non′ex·act′ing, *adj.;* **-ly,** *adv.;* **-ness,** *n.*
non′ex·ac′tion, *n.*
non′ex·ag′ger·at′ed, *adj.;* **-ly,** *adv.*
non′ex·ag′ger·at′ing, *adj.*
non′ex·ag′ger·a′tion, *n.*
non′ex·ag′ger·a′tive, *adj.*
non′ex·ag′ger·a·to′ry, *adj.*
non′ex·ca·va′tion, *n.*
non′ex·cept′ed, *adj.*
non′ex·cept′ing, *adj.*
non′ex·cep′tion·al, *adj.;* **-ly,** *adv.*
non′ex·ces′sive, *adj.;* **-ly,** *adv.;* **-ness,** *n.*
non′ex·change′a·bil′i·ty, *n.*
non′ex·change′a·ble, *adj.*
non′ex·cit′a·ble, *adj.;* **-ble·ness,** *n.;* **-bly,** *adv.*
non′ex·cit′a·tive, *adj.*
non′ex·cit′a·to′ry, *adj.*
non′ex·cit′ing, *adj.*
non′ex·clam′a·to′ry, *adj.*
non′ex·clu′sion, *n.*
non′ex·clu′sive, *adj.*
non′ex·cul′pa·ble, *adv.*
non′ex·cul·pa′tion, *n.*
non′ex·cul′pa·to′ry, *adj.*
non′ex·cus′a·ble, *adj.;* **-ble·ness,** *n.;* **-bly,** *adv.*
non·ex′e·cut′a·ble, *adj.*
non′ex·e·cu′tion, *n.*
non′ex·ec′u·tive, *adj., n.*
non′ex·em′pla·ry, *adj.*
non′ex·em′pli·fi·ca′tion, *n.*
non′ex·empt′, *adj., n.*
non′ex·emp′tion, *n.*
non·ex′er·cis′a·ble, *adj.*
non·ex′er·cise′, *n.*
non·ex′er·cis′er, *n.*
non′ex·er′tion, *n.*
non′ex·er′tive, *adj.*
non′ex·haust′ed, *adj.*
non′ex·haust′i·ble, *adj.*
non′ex·haus′tive, *adj.;* **-ly,** *adv.;* **-ness,** *n.*
non′ex·hi·bi′tion, *n.*
non′ex·hi·bi′tion·ism, *n.*
non′ex·hi·bi′tion·is′tic, *adj.*
non′ex·hib′i·tive, *adj.*
non′ex·hor·ta′tion, *n.*
non′ex·hor′ta·tive, *adj.*
non′ex·hor′ta·to′ry, *adj.*
non·ex′i·gent, *adj.;* **-ly,** *adv.*
non′ex·is·ten′tial, *adj.;* **-ly,** *adv.*
non′ex·is·ten′tial·ism, *n.*
non′ex·ist′ing, *adj.*
non′ex·ot′ic, *adj.*
non′ex·ot′i·cal·ly, *adv.*
non′ex·pand′ed, *adj.*
non′ex·pand′ing, *adj.*
non′ex·pan′si·bil′i·ty, *n.*
non′ex·pan′si·ble, *adj.*
non′ex·pan′sile, *adj.*
non′ex·pan′sion, *n.*
non′ex·pan′sive, *adj.;* **-ly,** *adv.;* **-ness,** *n.*
non′ex·pect′ant, *adj.;* **-ly,** *adv.*
non′ex·pe′di·ence, *n.*
non′ex·pe′di·en·cy, *n.*
non′ex·pe′di·ent, *adj.;* **-ly,** *adv.*
non′ex·pe·di·en′tial, *adj.*
non′ex·pe·di′tious, *adj.;* **-ly,** *adv.;* **-ness,** *n.*
non′ex·pend′a·ble, *adj.*
non′ex·pe′ri·enced, *adj.*
non′ex·pe′ri·en′tial, *adj.;* **-ly,** *adv.*
non′ex·per′i·men′tal, *adj.;* **-ly,** *adv.*
non′ex·pert′, *adj.*
non·ex′pert, *n.*
non·ex′pi·a·ble, *adj.*
non′ex·pi·a′tion, *n.*
non·ex′pi·a·to′ry, *adj.*
non′ex·pi·ra′tion, *n.*
non′ex·pir′ing, *adj.*
non′ex·pi′ry, *n., pl.* **-ries.**
non′ex·plain′a·ble, *adj.*
non′ex·plan′a·tive, *adj.*
non′ex·plan′a·to′ry, *adj.*
non·ex′pli·ca·ble, *adj.*
non·ex′pli·ca′tive, *adj.*
non′ex·ploi·ta′tion, *n.*
non′ex·plor′a·tive, *adj.*
non′ex·plor′a·to′ry, *adj.*
non′ex·plo′sive, *adj., n.;* **-ly,** *adv.;* **-ness,** *n.*
non′ex·po·nen′tial, *adj.;* **-ly,** *adv.*
non′ex·po′ni·ble, *adj.*
non′ex·port′a·ble, *adj.*
non′ex·po′sure, *n.*
non′ex·pres′sion·is′tic, *adj.*
non′ex·pres′sive, *adj.;* **-ly,** *adv.;* **-ness,** *n.*
non′ex·pul′sion, *n.*
non′ex·pul′sive, *adj.*
non·ex′tant, *adj.*
non′ex·tem′po·re, *adv., adj.*
non′ex·tend′ed, *adj.*
non′ex·tend′i·ble, *adj.;* **-ble·ness,** *n.*
non′ex·ten′si·bil′i·ty, *n.*
non′ex·ten′si·ble, *adj.;* **-ness,** *n.*
non′ex·ten′sile, *adj.*
non′ex·ten′sion, *n.*
non′ex·ten′sion·al, *adj.*
non′ex·ten′sive, *adj.;* **-ly,** *adv.,* **-ness,** *n.*
non′ex·ten′u·at′ing, *adj.;* **-ly,** *adv.*
non′ex·ten′u·a′tive, *adj.*
non′ex·ter′mi·na′tion, *n.*
non′ex·ter′mi·na′tive, *adj.*
non′ex·ter′mi·na·to′ry, *adj.*
non′ex·ter′nal, *adj., n.;* **-ly,** *adv.*
non′ex·ter·nal′i·ty, *n.*
non′ex·ter′nal·ized′, *adj.*
non′ex·tinct′, *adj.*
non′ex·tinc′tion, *n.*
non′ex·tin′guish·a·ble, *adj.*
non′ex·tin′guished, *adj.*
non′ex·tor′tion, *n.*
non′ex·tor′tive, *adj.*
non′ex·tract′a·ble, *adj.*
non′ex·tract′ed, *adj.*
non′ex·tract′i·ble, *adj.*
non′ex·trac′tion, *n.*
non′ex·trac′tive, *adj.*
non·ex′tra·dit′a·ble, *adj.*
non′ex·tra·di′tion, *n.*
non′ex·tra′ne·ous, *adj.;* **-ly,** *adv.;* **-ness,** *n.*
non·ex′tri·ca·ble, *adj.;* **-bly,** *adv.*
non′ex·tri·ca′tion, *n.*
non′ex·trin′sic, *adj.*
non′ex·trin′si·cal, *adj.;* **-ly,** *adv.*
non′ex·tru′sive, *adj.*
non′ex·u′ber·ance, *n.*
non′ex·u′ber·an·cy, *n.*
non′ex·ud′ing, *adj.*
non′ex·ult′ant, *adj.;* **-ly,** *adv.*
non′ex·ul·ta′tion, *n.*
non′fa·ce′tious, *adj.;* **-ly,** *adv.;* **-ness,** *n.*
non′fa·cil′i·ty, *n.*
non′fac′tious, *adj.;* **-ly,** *adv.;* **-ness,** *n.*
non′fac·ti′tious, *adj.;* **-ly,** *adv.;* **-ness,** *n.*
non·fac′tu·al, *adj.;* **-ly,** *adv.*
non·fac′ul·ta′tive, *adj.*
non·fad′dist, *n.*
non·fail′ure, *n.*
non′fal·la′cious, *adj.;* **-ly,** *adv.;* **-ness,** *n.*
non·fal′ter·ing, *adj.;* **-ly,** *adv.*
non′fa·mil′ial, *adj.*
non′fa·mil′iar, *adj.;* **-ly,** *adv.*
non·fam′i·ly, *n., pl.* **-lies.**
non′fa·nat′ic, *n., adj.*
non′fa·nat′i·cal, *adj.;* **-ly,** *adv.*
non·fan′ta·sy, *n., pl.* **-sies.**
non·far′ci·cal, *adj.;* **-ly,** *adv.;* **-ness,** *n.*
non′far·ci·cal′i·ty, *n.*
non·farm′, *adj.*
non·fas′cist, *n., adj.*
non·fash′ion·a·ble, *adj.;* **-ble·ness,** *n.;* **-bly,** *adv.*
non′fas·tid′i·ous, *adj.;* **-ly,** *adv.;* **-ness,** *n.*
non·fa′tal, *adj.;* **-ly,** *adv.;* **-ness,** *n.*
non′fa·tal·is′tic, *adj.*
non′fa·tal′i·ty, *n., pl.* **-ties.**
non·fat′i·ga·ble, *adj.*
non·fault′y, *adj.*
non·fa′vor·a·ble, *adj.;* **-ble·ness,** *n.;* **-bly,** *adv.*
non·fa′vored, *adj.*
non·fa′vor·ite, *n.*
non·fe′al·ty, *n., pl.* **-ties.**
non′fea·si·bil′i·ty, *n.*
non·fea′si·ble, *adj.;* **-ble·ness,** *n.;* **-bly,** *adv.*
non·fea′tured, *adj.*
non′fe·brile, *adj.*
non·fe′cund, *adj.*
non′fe·cun′di·ty, *n.*
non·fed′er·al, *adj.*
non·fed′er·at′ed, *adj.*
non·fee′ble, *adj.;* **-ble·ness,** *n.;* **-bly,** *adv.*
non·feed′ing, *adj.*
non·feel′ing, *adj.;* **-ly,** *adv.*
non′feld·spath′ic, *adj.*
non′fe·lic′i·tous, *adj.;* **-ly,** *adv.;* **-ness,** *n.*
non′fe·lic′i·ty, *n.*
non′fe·lo′ni·ous, *adj.;* **-ly,** *adv.;* **-ness,** *n.*
non′fe·nes′trat·ed, *adj.*
non′fer·ment′a·bil′i·ty, *n.*
non′fer·ment′a·ble, *adj.*
non′fer·men·ta′tion, *n.*
non′fer·men′ta·tive, *adj.*
non′fer·ment′ed, *adj.*
non′fer·ment′ing, *adj.*
non′fe·ro′cious, *adj.;* **-ly,** *adv.;* **-ness,** *n.*
non′fe·roc′i·ty, *n.*
non·fer′tile, *adj.*
non′fer·til′i·ty, *n.*
non·fer′vent, *adj.;* **-ly,** *adv.;* **-ness,** *n.*
non·fer′vid, *adj.;* **-ly,** *adv.;* **-ness,** *n.*
non·fes′tive, *adj.;* **-ly,** *adv.;* **-ness,** *n.*
non·feu′dal, *adj.;* **-ly,** *adv.*
non·fe′ver·ish, *adj.;* **-ly,** *adv.;* **-ness,** *n.*
non·fe′ver·ous, *adj.;* **-ly,** *adv.*
non·fi′brous, *adj.*
non′fic·ti′tious, *adj.;* **-ly,** *adv.;* **-ness,** *n.*
non·fic′tive, *adj.;* **-ly,** *adv.*
non′fi·del′i·ty, *n.*
non′fi·du′ci·ar′y, *adj., n., pl.* **-ar·ies.**
non·fight′er, *n.*
non·fig′ur·a·tive, *adj.;* **-ly,** *adv.;* **-ness,** *n.*
non′fil·a·men′tous, *adj.*
non·fil′i·al, *adj.*
non·fil′ter, *n.*
non·fil′ter·a·ble, *adj.*
non·fim′bri·ate, *adj.*
non·fim′bri·at′ed, *adj.*
non′fi·nan′cial, *adj.;* **-ly,** *adv.*
non·find′ing, *n.*
non·fin′ish·ing, *adj., n.*
non·fi′nite, *adj., n.;* **-ly,** *adv.;* **-ness,** *n.*
non·fire′proof′, *adj.*
non·fis′cal, *adj.;* **-ly,** *adv.*
non·fish′er·man, *n., pl.* **-men.**
non·fis′sile, *adj.*
non′fis·sil′i·ty, *n.*
non·fis′sion·a·ble, *adj.*
non′fix·a′tion, *n.*
non·flag′el·late, *adj.*
non·flag′el·lat′ed, *adj.*
non′fla·gi′tious, *adj.;* **-ly,** *adv.;* **-ness,** *n.*

drama). **2.** works of this class: *She admired Hersey's nonfiction.* **3.** (esp. in cataloguing books, as in a library or bookstore) all writing or books not fiction, poetry, or drama, including nonfictive narrative prose and reference works; the broadest category of written works. [NON- + FICTION] —**non·fic′tion·al,** *adj.* —**non·fic′tion·al·ly,** *adv.*

non·flam·ma·ble (non flam′ə bəl), *adj.* not flammable; not combustible or easily set on fire. [NON- + FLAMMABLE]

non/for/fei·ture val/ue (non fôr′fi chər), *Insurance.* any benefit, as cash or other form of insurance, available to a life-insurance policyholder who discontinues premium payments on his policy. Also called **nonfor′feiture ben′efit.** [NON- + FORFEITURE]

non·freez·ing (non frē′ziŋ), *adj.* not given or subject to freezing. [NON- + FREEZING]

non·ful·fill·ment (non′fo͝ol fil′mənt), *n.* neglect or failure to fulfill. [NON- + FULFILLMENT]

non·gram·mat·i·cal (non′grə mat′i kəl), *adj.* (of a sentence or expression) not conforming to the grammatical rules of a given language. [NON- + GRAMMATICAL]

non′har·mon′ic tone′ (non′här mon′ik), *Music.* a tone sounding with a chord of which it is not a chord tone. [NON- + HARMONIC]

non·i·de·al (non′ī dē′əl, -dēl′), *adj. Physics.* (of a gas or solution) differing in behavior from that of an ideal gas or solution. [NON- + IDEAL]

no·nil·lion (nō nil′yən), *n., pl.* **-lions,** (*as after a numeral*) **-lion,** *adj.* —*n.* **1.** a cardinal number represented in the U.S. and France by one followed by 30 zeros, and in Great Britain and Germany, by one followed by 54 zeros. —*adj.* **2.** amounting to one nonillion in number. [< F, equiv. to *non-* (< L *nōnus* ninth) + (*m*)*illion*] —**no·nil′lionth,** *n., adj.*

non·im·por·ta·tion (non′im pōr tā′shən, -pôr-), *n.* failure or refusal to import. [NON- + IMPORTATION]

non·in·creas·ing (non′in krē′siŋ), *adj.* **1.** not increasing. **2.** *Math.* decreasing (def. 2). [NON- + INCREASING]

non·in·duc·tive (non′in duk′tiv), *adj. Elect.* not inductive: *a noninductive resistance.* [NON- + INDUCTIVE] —**non′in·duc′tive·ly,** *adv.* —**non′in·duc·tiv′i·ty,** *n.*

non·fla′grance, n.
non·fla′gran·cy, n.
non·fla′grant, adj.; -ly, adv.
non·flak′i·ly, adv.
non·flak′i·ness, n.
non·flak′y, adj.
non·flat′u·lence, n.
non·flat′u·len·cy, n.
non·flat′u·lent, adj.; -ly, adv.
non·flawed′, adj.
non-Flem′ish, adj., n.
non′flex·i·bil′i·ty, n.
non·flex′i·ble, adj.; -ble·ness, n.; -bly, adv.
non′flir·ta′tious, adj.; -ly, adv.; -ness, n.
non·float′ing, adj.; -ly, adv.
non′flo·rif′er·ous, adj.
non·flow′er·ing, adj.
non·fluc′tu·at′ing, adj.
non′fluc·tu·a′tion, n.
non·flu′en·cy, n.
non·flu′ent, adj.; -ly, adv.; -ness, n.
non·flu′id, n.; -ly, adv.
non′flu·id′ic, adj.
non′flu·id′i·ty, n.
non′flu·o·res′cence, n.
non′flu·o·res′cent, adj.
non·flux′, n.
non·fly′a·ble, adj.
non·fly′ing, adj.
non·fol′low·ing, adj.
non·food′, n.
non′for·bear′ance, n.
non′for·bear′ing, adj.; -ly, adv.
non′fore·clos′ing, adj.
non′fore·clo′sure, n.
non·for′eign, adj.; -ness, n.
non′fo·ren′sic, adj.
non′fo·ren′si·cal·ly, adv.
non·for′est, n.
non·for′est·ed, adj.
non·for′feit·a·ble, adj.
non·for′feit·ing, adj.
non·for′fei·ture, n.
non′for·giv′ing, adj.
non·form′, n.
non·for′mal, adj.; -ly, adv.; -ness, n.
non·for′mal·ism, n.
non′for·mal·is′tic, adj.
non′for·ma′tion, n.
non·form′a·tive, adj.; -ly, adv.
non′for·mi·da·bil′i·ty, n.
non·for′mi·da·ble, adj.; -ble·ness, n.; -bly, adv.
non·form′ing, adj.
non′for·mu·la′tion, n.
non·for′ti·fi′a·ble, adj.
non′for·ti·fi·ca′tion, n.
non·for′ti·fy′ing, adj.
non′for·tu′i·tous, adj.; -ly, adv.; -ness, n.
non′fos·sil·if′er·ous, adj.
non·foul′ing, adj.
non·frag′ile, adj.; -ly, adv.; -ness, n.
non′fra·gil′i·ty, n.
non·frag′ment·ed, adj.
non·fra′grant, adj.
non′fran·gi·bil′i·ty, n.
non·fran′gi·ble, adj.
non′fra·ter′nal, adj.; -ly, adv.
non′fra·ter′ni·ty, n.
non·fraud′u·lence, n.
non·fraud′u·len·cy, n.
non·fraud′u·lent, adj.; -ly, adv.
non·free′dom, n.
non·free′man, n., pl. -men.
non·freez′a·ble, adj.
non-French′, adj., n.
non′fre·net′ic, adj.
non′fre·net′i·cal·ly, adv.
non·fre′quence, n.
non·fre′quen·cy, n.
non·fre′quent, adj.; -ly, adv.
non·fric′a·tive, adj., n.
non·fric′tion, n.
non·frig′id, adj.; -ly, adv.; -ness, n.
non′fri·gid′i·ty, n.
non·frost′ed, adj.
non·frost′ing, adj.
non·fru′gal, adj.; -ly, adv.; -ness, n.
non′fru·gal′i·ty, n.
non′fru·i′tion, n.
non′frus·tra′tion, n.
non·fu′gi·tive, adj., n.; -ly, adv.; -ness, n.
non·ful′mi·nat′ing, adj.
non·func′tion·al, adj.; -ly, adv.
non·func′tion·ing, adj.
non′fun·da·men′tal, adj., n.; -ly, adv.
non′fun·da·men′tal·ist, n.
non·fund′ed, adj.
non·fun′gi·ble, adj.
non·fused′, adj.
non′fu·si·bil′i·ty, n.
non·fu′si·ble, adj.
non·fu′sion, n.
non·fu′tile, adj.
non′fu·tur·is′tic, adj.
non-Gael′ic, adj.
non′ga·lac′tic, adj.
non·gal′va·nized′, adj.
non′gan·gli·on′ic, adj.
non·gan′gre·nous, adj.
non′gar·ru′li·ty, n.
non·gar′ru·lous, adj.; -ly, adv.; -ness, n.
non·gas′, n., pl. -gas·es.
non·gas′e·ous, adj.; -ness, n.
non·gas′sy, adj.
non′ge·lat′i·niz′ing, adj.
non′ge·lat′i·nous, adj.; -ly, adv.; -ness, n.
non·gel′ling, adj.
non′ge·ne·a·log′ic, adj.
non′ge·ne·a·log′i·cal, adj.; -ly, adv.
non·gen′er·al·ized′, adj.
non·gen′er·at′ing, adj.
non·gen′er·a′tive, adj.
non′ge·ner′ic, adj.
non′ge·ner′i·cal, adj.; -ly, adv.
non′ge·net′ic, adj.
non′ge·net′i·cal, adj.; -ly, adv.
non·gen′tile, adj.
non·gen′u·ine, adj.; -ly, adv.; -ness, n.
non′ge·o·graph′ic, adj.
non′ge·o·graph′i·cal, adj.; -ly, adv.
non′ge·o·log′ic, adj.
non′ge·o·log′i·cal, adj.; -ly, adv.
non′ge·o·met′ric, adj.
non′ge·o·met′ri·cal, adj.; -ly, adv.
non-Ger′man, adj., n.
non′ger·mane′, adj.
non′-Ger·man′ic, adj.
non·ger′mi·nal, adj.
non·ger′mi·nat′ing, adj.
non′ger·mi·na′tion, n.
non·ger′mi·na′tive, adj.
non′ge·run′di·al, adj.
non′ge·run′dive, adj.; -ly, adv.
non·ges′tic, adj.
non·ges′ti·cal, adj.
non·gild′ed, adj.
non·gilled′, adj.
non·gla′cial, adj.; -ly, adv.
non·glan′dered, adj.
non·glan′du·lar, adj.
non·glan′du·lous, adj.
non·glare′, n.
non·glazed′, adj.
non·glob′u·lar, adj.; -ly, adv.
non·glu′cose, n.
non·glu′te·nous, adj.
non·god′, n.
non·gold′, n., adj.
non·golf′er, n.
non·gos′pel, adj.
non-Goth′ic, adj.
non-Goth′i·cal·ly, adv.
non·gov′ern·ance, n.
non·gov′ern·ment, n.
non′gov·ern·men′tal, adj.
non·grace′ful, adj.; -ly, adv.; -ness, n.
non′gra·ci·os′i·ty, n.
non·gra′cious, adj.; -ly, adv.; -ness, n.
non·grad′u·ate, n.
non·grad′u·at′ed, adj.
non′grad·u·a′tion, n.
non·grain′, n.
non·grained′, adj.
non·gran′u·lar, adj.
non·gran′u·lat′ed, adj.
non·graph′ic, adj.
non·graph′i·cal, adj.; -ly, adv.; -ness, n.
non′gra·phit′ic, adj.
non′grat·i·fi·ca′tion, n.
non·grat′i·fy′ing, adj.; -ly, adv.
non′gra·tu′i·tous, adj.; -ly, adv.; -ness, n.
non·grav′en, adj.
non′grav·i·ta′tion, n.
non′grav·i·ta′tion·al, adj.; -ly, adv.
non·grav′i·ta′tive, adj.
non·grav′i·ty, n., pl. -ties.
non·greas′y, adj.
non-Greek′, adj., n.
non·green′, adj.
non′gre·gar′i·ous, adj.; -ly, adv.; -ness, n.
non·gre′mi·al, adj.
non·grieved′, adj.
non·griev′ing, adj.
non·griev′ous, adj.; -ly, adv.; -ness, n.
non·groom′ing, adj.
non·ground′ed, adj.
non·ground′ing, adj.
non′guar·an·tee′, n.
non·guar′an·ty, n., pl. -ties.
non·guid′a·ble, adj.
non·guid′ance, n.
non·guilt′, n.
non·gut′tur·al, adj.; -ly, adv.; -ness, n.
non·gym′nast, n.
non-Gyp′sy, n., pl. -sies.
non′hab·it·a·bil′i·ty, n.
non·hab′it·a·ble, adj.; -ble·ness, n.; -bly, adv.
non′hab·i·ta′tion, n.
non′ha·bit′u·al, adj.; -ly, adv.; -ness, n.
non·hack′neyed, adj.
non′hal·lu′ci·na′tion, n.
non′hal·lu′ci·nat′ed, adj.
non′hal·lu′ci·na·to′ry, adj.
non′-Ha·mit′ic, adj.
non·hand′i·cap′, n.
non′har·mon′ic, adj.
non′har·mo′ni·ous, adj.; -ly, adv.; -ness, n.
non·har′mo·ny, n., pl. -nies.
non·haz′ard·ous, adj.; -ly, adv.; -ness, n.
non·head′ing, n.
non·hea′then, n., pl. -thens; -then, adj.
non′-He·bra′ic, adj.
non′-He·bra′i·cal·ly, adv.
non-He′brew, n., adj.
non·hec′tic, adj.
non·hec′ti·cal·ly, adv.
non′he·don′ic, adj.
non′he·don′i·cal·ly, adv.
non′he·do·nis′tic, adj.
non′he·do·nis′ti·cal·ly, adv.
non·hei′nous, adj.; -ly, adv.; -ness, n.
non′-Hel·len′ic, adj.
non′he·mat′ic, adj., n.
non′he·mo·phil′ic, adj.
non′he·pat′ic, adj., n.
non′he·red′i·ta·bil′i·ty, n.
non′he·red′i·ta·ble, adj.; -bly, adv.
non′he·red′i·tar′i·ly, adv.
non′he·red′i·tar′i·ness, n.
non′he·red′i·tar′y, adj.
non′he·ret′i·cal, adj.; -ly, adv.
non′her·it·a·bil′i·ty, n.
non·her′it·a·ble, adj.; -bly, adv.
non·her′i·tor, n.
non·he′ro, n., pl. -roes.
non′he·ro′ic, adj.
non′he·ro′i·cal, adj.; -ly, adv.; -ness, n.
non′he·ro′ic·ness, n.
non·hes′i·tant, adj.; -ly, adv.
non′heu·ris′tic, adj.
non′-Hi·ber′ni·an, adj., n.
non′hi·er·ar′chic, adj.
non′hi·er·ar′chi·cal, adj.; -ly, adv.
non′hi·er·at′ic, adj.
non′hi·er·at′i·cal, adj.; -ly, adv.
non-Hin′du, n., adj.
non′his·tor′ic, adj.
non′his·tor′i·cal, adj.; -ly, adv.; -ness, n.
non′his·tri·on′ic, adj.
non′his·tri·on′i·cal, adj.; -ly, adv.; -ness, n.
non′-Ho·mer′ic, adj.
non′ho·mi·let′ic, adj.
non′ho·mo·ge·ne′i·ty, n.
non′ho·mo·ge′ne·ous, adj.; -ly, adv.; -ness, n.
non′ho·mog′e·nous, adj.
non′ho·mol′o·gous, adj.
non·hos′tile, adj.; -ly, adv.
non′hos·til′i·ty, n.
non·house′hold′er, n.
non′hu·bris′tic, adj.
non·hu′man, adj.; -ness, n.
non·hu′ma·nist, n.
non′hu·man·is′tic, adj.
non·hu′man·ized′, adj.
non·hu′mor·ous, adj.; -ly, adv.; -ness, n.
non·hu′mus, n.
non·hunt′ing, adj.
non·hy′drat·ed, adj.
non′hy·drau′lic, adj.
non′hy·drog′e·nous, adj.
non′hy·dro·pho′bic, adj.
non′hy·gro·met′ric, adj.
non′hy·gro·scop′ic, adj.
non′hy·gro·scop′i·cal·ly, adv.
non′hy·per·bol′ic, adj.
non′hy·per·bol′i·cal, adj.; -ly, adv.
non′hyp·not′ic, adj., n.
non′hyp·not′i·cal·ly, adv.
non′hy·po·stat′ic, adj.
non′hy·po·stat′i·cal, adj.; -ly, adv.
non′i·con′o·clas′tic, adj.
non′i·con′o·clas′ti·cal·ly, adv.
non′i·de′al·is′tic, adj.
non′i·de′al·is′ti·cal·ly, adv.
non′i·de·a′tion·al, adj.; -ly, adv.
non′i·den′ti·cal, adj.
non′i·den′ti·fi·ca′tion, n.
non′i·den′ti·ty, n.
non′i·de·o·log′ic, adj.
non′i·de·o·log′i·cal, adj.; -ly, adv.
non′id·i·o·mat′ic, adj.
non′id·i·o·mat′i·cal, adj.; -ly, adv.; -ness, n.
non′i·dol′a·trous, adj.; -ly, adv.; -ness, n.
non′i·dyl′lic, adj.
non′i·dyl′li·cal·ly, adv.
non·ig′ne·ous, adj.
non′ig·nit′a·bil′i·ty, n.
non′ig·nit′a·ble, adj.
non′ig·nit′i·bil′i·ty, n.
non′ig·nit′i·ble, adj.
non′ig·no·min′i·ous, adj.; -ly, adv.; -ness, n.
non·ig′no·rant, adj.; -ly, adv.
non·il′la·tive, adj.; -ly, adv.
non′il·lu′mi·nant, n.
non′il·lu′mi·nat′ing, adj.; -ly, adv.
non′il·lu′mi·na′tion, n.
non′il·lu′mi·na′tive, adj.
non′il·lu′sion·al, adj.
non′il·lu′sive, adj.; -ly, adv.; -ness, n.
non′il·lus·tra′tion, n.
non′il·lus′tra·tive, adj.; -ly, adv.
non′im·ag′i·nar′i·ly, adv.
non′im·ag′i·nar′i·ness, n.
non′im·ag′i·nar′y, adj.
non′im·ag′i·na′tion·al, adj.
non·im′bri·cate′, adj.; -ly, adv.
non·im′bri·cat′ed, adj.
non·im′bri·cat′ing, adj.
non·im′bri·ca′tive, adj.
non′im·i·ta·bil′i·ty, n.
non·im′i·ta·ble, adj.
non·im′i·tat′ing, adj.
non′im·i·ta′tion·al, adj.
non·im′i·ta′tive, adj.; -ly, adv.; -ness, n.
non·im′ma·nence, n.
non·im′ma·nen·cy, n.
non·im′ma·nent, adj.; -ly, adv.
non′im·mer′sion, n.
non·im′mi·grant, n., adj.
non′im·mi·gra′tion, n.
non′im·mune′, adj.
non′im·mu′ni·ty, n., pl. -ties.
non′im·mu·ni·za′tion, n.
non·im′mu·nized′, adj.
non·im′pact, n.
non′im·pact′ed, adj.
non′im·pair′ment, n.
non′im·par·ta′tion, n.
non′im·part′ment, n.
non′im·peach′a·bil′i·ty, n.
non′im·peach′a·ble, adj.
non′im·peach′ment, n.
non′im·ped′i·men′tal, adj.
non′im·ped′i·men′ta·ry, adj.
non′im·per′a·tive, adj.; -ly, adv.; -ness, n.
non′im·pe′ri·al, adj.; -ly, adv.; -ness, n.
non′im·pe′ri·al·is′tic, adj.
non′im·pe′ri·al·is′ti·cal·ly, adv.
non′im·pe′ri·ous, adj.; -ly, adv.; -ness, n.
non·im′ple·ment, n.
non′im·ple·men′tal, adj.
non′im·pli·ca′tion, n.
non·im′pli·ca′tive, adj.; -ly, adv.
non′im·po·si′tion, n.
non′im·preg′nat·ed, adj.
non′im·pres′sion·a·bil′i·ty, n.
non′im·pres′sion·a·ble, adj.; -ness, n.
non′im·pres′sion·is′tic, adj.
non′im·prove′ment, n.
non′im·pul′sive, adj.; -ly, adv.; -ness, n.
non′im·put′a·bil′i·ty, n.
non′im·put′a·ble, adj.; -ble·ness, n.; -bly, adv.
non′im·put′a·tive, adj.; -ly, adv.; -ness, n.
non′in·can·des′cence, n.
non′in·can·des′cent, adj.; -ly, adv.
non′in·car′nate, adj.
non′in·car′nat·ed, adj.
non′in·ces′tu·ous, adj.; -ly, adv.; -ness, n.
non·in′ci·dent, n., adj.
non′in·ci·den′tal, adj.; -ly, adv.
non′in·cite′ment, n.
non′in·clin′a·ble, adj.
non′in·cli·na′tion, n.
non′in·cli·na′tion·al, adj.
non′in·cli′na·to′ry, adj.
non′in·clu′sion, n.
non′in·clu′sive, adj.; -ly, adv.; -ness, n.
non′in·cor′po·rat′ed, adj.
non′in·cor′po·ra′tive, adj.
non′in·creas′a·ble, adj.
non·in′crease, n.
non′in·crim′i·nat′ing, adj.
non′in·crim′i·na′tion, n.
non′in·crim′i·na·to′ry, adj.
non′in·crust′ing, adj., n.
non′in·de·pend′ent, adj.; -ly, adv.
non·in′dexed, adj.
non-In′di·an, adj., n.
non′in·dict′a·ble, adj.
non′in·dict′ment, n.
non′in·dig′e·nous, adj.
non′in·di·vid′u·al, adj.
non′in·di·vid′u·al·is′tic, adj.
non′in·di·vid′u·al′i·ty, n., pl. -ties.
non-In′do-Eu·ro·pe′an, adj., n.
non′in·duced′, adj.
non′in·duc′i·ble, adj.
non′in·dul′gence, n.
non′in·dul′gent, adj.; -ly, adv.
non′in·du′rat·ed, adj.
non′in·du′ra·tive, adj.
non′in·dus′tri·al, adj., n.; -ly, adv.
non′in·dus′tri·al·i·za′tion, n.
non′in·dus′tri·ous, adj.; -ly, adv.; -ness, n.
non′in·ert′, adj.; -ly, adv.; -ness, n.
non′i·ner′tial, adj.
non′in·fal′li·bil′i·ty, n.
non′in·fal′li·ble, adj.; -ble·ness, n.; -bly, adv.
non·in′fan·try, n.
non′in·fect′ed, adj.
non′in·fect′ing, adj.
non′in·fec′tion, n.
non′in·fec′tious, adj.; -ly, adv.; -ness, n.
non′in·fer′a·ble, adj.; -bly, adv.
non′in·fer·en′tial, adj.; -ly, adv.
non·in′fi·nite, adj., n.; -ly, adv.; -ness, n.
non′in·flam′ma·bil′i·ty, n.
non′in·flam′ma·ble, adj.; -ble·ness, n.; -bly, adv.
non′in·flam′ma·to′ry, adj.
non′in·fla′tion, n.
non′in·fla′tion·ar′y, adj.
non′in·flect′ed, adj.
non′in·flec′tion·al, adj.; -ly, adv.
non·in′flu·ence, n.
non′in·flu·en′tial, adj.; -ly, adv.
non′in·for·ma′tion·al, adj.
non′in·for′ma·tive, adj.; -ly, adv.; -ness, n.
non′in·frac′tion, n.
non′in·fu′si·bil′i·ty, n.
non′in·fu′si·ble, adj.; -ness, n.
non′in·hab′it·a·bil′i·ty, n.
non′in·hab′it·a·ble, adj.
non′in·hab′it·ance, n.
non′in·hab′it·an·cy, n., pl. -cies.
non′in·her′ence, n.
non′in·her′ent, adj.; -ly, adv.

non·i·ni·tial (non′i nish′əl), *adj.* **1.** not occurring as the first letter of a word. **2.** not occurring at the beginning of anything. [NON- + INITIAL] —**non′in·i′tial·ly,** *adv.*

non·in·ter·course (non in′tər kōrs′, -kôrs′), *n.* suspension of interchange in relations, esp. commercial or political relations. [NON- + INTERCOURSE]

Nonin′tercourse Act′, *U.S. Hist.* the act of Congress (1809) prohibiting French and British ships from entering American ports.

non·in·ter·fer·ence (non′in tər fēr′əns), *n.* the policy or practice of refraining from interference, esp. in political affairs. [NON- + INTERFERENCE]

non·in·ter·ven·tion (non′in tər ven′shən), *n.* **1.** abstention by a state from interference in the affairs of other states or in those of its own political subdivisions. **2.** failure or refusal to intervene. [NON- + INTERVENTION] —**non′in·ter·ven′tion·al,** *adj.* —**non′in·ter·ven′tion·al·ist, non′in·ter·ven′tion·ist,** *n.*

non·i·ron (non ī′ərn), *adj. Brit.* drip-dry.

Non·i·us (non′ē əs), *n.* a walled plain in the fourth quadrant of the face of the moon: about 20 miles in diameter.

non·join·der (non join′dər), *n. Law.* failure to join, as of a person who should have been a party to an action. [NON- + JOINDER]

non·ju·ror (non jŏŏr′ər), *n.* **1.** a person who refuses to take a required oath, as of allegiance. **2.** (*often cap.*) *Eng. Hist.* any of the clergymen of the Church of England who in 1689 refused to swear allegiance to William and Mary. [NON- + JUROR]

non·le·gal (non lē′gəl), *adj.* not related to, qualified for, or phrased in the manner of the practice of law (distinguished from *illegal*): *a nonlegal explanation; the commission's nonlegal employees.* [NON- + LEGAL]

non·life (non līf′), *n.* lack or absence of life.

non·lin·e·ar·i·ty (non′lin ē ar′i tē), *n.* **1.** *Math.* the quality of a function that expresses a relationship which is not one of direct proportion. **2.** *Elect.* deviation of an input-output relationship from one of direct proportionality. [NON- + LINEARITY]

non·lit·er·ate (non lit′ər it), *adj. Anthropol.* lacking a written language: *a nonliterate people.* [NON- + LITERATE]

non·ma·te·ri·al (non′mə tēr′ē əl), *adj.* **1.** not material or composed of matter. **2.** of or pertaining to the spirit or soul; spiritual: *to minister to man's nonmaterial needs.* **3.** cultural, aesthetic, or the like: *the nonmaterial benefits of one's community.* [NON- + MATERIAL]

non′mate′rial cul′ture, *Sociol.* the aggregate of values, mores, norms, etc., of a society; the ideational structure of a culture that provides the values and meanings by which it functions. Cf. **material culture.**

non·mem·ber (non mem′bər), *n.* a person who is not a member: *a club-sponsored lecture open to nonmembers.* [NON- + MEMBER] —**non·mem′ber·ship′,** *n.*

non·met·al (non met′əl), *n. Chem.* **1.** an element not having the character of a metal, as carbon, nitrogen, etc. **2.** an element incapable of forming simple positive ions in solution. [NON- + METAL]

non·me·tal·lic (non′mə tal′ik), *adj. Chem.* **1.** of or relating to a nonmetal. **2.** not of a metallic quality: *a nonmetallic appearance.* [NON- + METALLIC]

non·mis·ci·ble (non mis′ə bəl), *adj.* not miscible. [NON- + MISCIBLE] —**non·mis·ci·bil·i·ty** (non′mis ə bil′i tē), *n.*

non·mor·al (non môr′əl, -mor′-), *adj.* having no relation to morality; neither moral nor immoral: *It was a completely nonmoral problem and involved only judg-*

non′in·her′it·a·bil′i·ty, *n.*
non′in·her′it·a·ble, *adj.;* **-ness,** *n.*
non′in·her′it·ed, *adj.*
non′in·hib′i·tive, *adj.*
non′in·hib′i·to′ry, *adj.*
non′in·ju′ri·ous, *adj.;* **-ly,** *adv.;* **-ness,** *n.*
non·in′ju·ry, *n., pl.* **-ries.**
non′in·oc′u·la′tion, *n.*
non′in·oc′u·la′tive, *adj.*
non′in·quir′ing, *adj.;* **-ly,** *adv.*
non·in′sect, *n.*
non′in·ser′tion, *n.*
non′in·sist′ence, *n.*
non′in·sist′en·cy, *n., pl.* **-cies.**
non′in·sist′ent, *adj.*
non′in·spis′sat·ing, *adj.*
non′in·stinc′tive, *adj.;* **-ly,** *adv.*
non′in·stinc′tu·al, *adj.;* **-ly,** *adv.*
non′in·sti·tu′tion, *n.*
non′in·sti·tu′tion·al, *adj.;* **-ly,** *adv.*
non′in·struc′tion·al, *adj.;* **-ly,** *adv.*
non′in·struc′tive, *adj.;* **-ly,** *adv.;* **-ness,** *n.*
non′in·stru·men′tal, *adj.;* **-ly,** *adv.*
non′in·stru·men′tal·is′tic, *adj.*
non′in·sur′ance, *n.*
non·in′te·gra·ble, *adj.*
non′in·te·gra′tion, *n.*
non′in·tel·lec′tu·al, *adj., n.;* **-ly,** *adv.;* **-ness,** *n.*
non′in·tel′li·gence, *n.*
non′in·tel′li·gent, *adj.;* **-ly,** *adv.*
non′in·ter·ac′tive, *adj.*
non′in·ter·cept′ing, *adj.*
non′in·ter·cep′tive, *adj.*
non′in·ter·change′a·bil′i·ty, *n.*
non′in·ter·change′a·ble, *adj.;* **-ble·ness,** *n.;* **-bly,** *adv.*
non′in·ter·de·pend′ence, *n.*
non′in·ter·de·pend′en·cy, *n.*
non′in·ter·de·pend′ent, *adj.;* **-ly,** *adv.*
non′in·ter·fer′ing, *adj.;* **-ly,** *adv.*
non′in·ter·mit′tence, *n.*
non′in·ter·mit′tent, *adj.;* **-ly,** *adv.;* **-ness,** *n.*
non′in·ter·na′tion·al, *adj.;* **-ly,** *adv.*
non′in·ter′po·lat′ing, *adj.*
non′in·ter′po·la′tion, *n.*
non′in·ter′po·la′tive, *adj.*
non′in·ter·po·si′tion, *n.*
non′in·ter′pret·a·bil′i·ty, *n.*
non′in·ter′pret·a·ble, *adj.*
non′in·ter′pre·ta′tion·al, *adj.*
non′in·ter′pre·ta′tive, *adj.;* **-ly,** *adv.*
non′in·ter′pre·tive, *adj.;* **-ly,** *adv.;* **-ness,** *n.*
non′in·ter·rupt′ed, *adj.;* **-ly,** *adv.;* **-ness,** *n.*
non′in·ter·rup′tive, *adj.*
non′in·ter·sect′ing, *adj.*
non′in·ter·sec′tion·al, *adj.*
non′in·tox′i·cant, *adj.*
non′in·tox′i·cat′ing, *adj.;* **-ly,** *adv.*
non′in·tox′i·ca′tive, *adj.*
non′in·tro·spec′tive, *adj.;* **-ly,** *adv.;* **-ness,** *n.*
non′in·tro·ver′sive, *adj.;* **-ly,** *adv.;* **-ness,** *n.*
non·in′tro·vert′ed, *adj.;* **-ly,** *adv.;* **-ness,** *n.*
non′in·tu′i·tive, *adj.,* **-ly,** *adv.,* **-ness,** *n.*
non′in·vert′ed, *adj.*
non′in·vid′i·ous, *adj.;* **-ly,** *adv.;* **-ness,** *n.*
non′in·vin′ci·bil′i·ty, *n.*
non′in·vin′ci·ble, *adj.;* **-ble·ness,** *n.;* **-bly,** *adv.*
non·i′o·dized′, *adj.*
non′i·on′ic, *adj.*
non′-I·on′ic, *adj., n.*
non·i′on·ized′, *adj.*
non·i′on·iz′ing, *adj.*
non·i′rate, *adj.;* **-ly,** *adv.*
non′i·ren′ic, *adj.*
non′i·ren′i·cal, *adj.*
non′ir·i·des′cence, *n.*
non′ir·i·des′cent, *adj.;* **-ly,** *adv.*
non-I′rish, *adj., n., pl.* **-I·rish.**
non′i·ron′ic, *adj.*
non′i·ron′i·cal, *adj.;* **-ly,** *adv.;* **-ness,** *n.*
non′ir·ra′di·at′ed, *adj.*
non′ir·ra′tion·al, *adj., n.;* **-ly,** *adv.;* **-ness,** *n.*
non′ir·rev′o·ca·bil′i·ty, *n.*
non′ir·rev′o·ca·ble, *adj.;* **-ble·ness,** *n.;* **-bly,** *adv.*
non·ir′ri·ga·ble, *adj.*
non·ir′ri·gat′ed, *adj.*
non·ir′ri·gat′ing, *adj.*
non′ir·ri·ga′tion, *n.*
non′ir·ri·ta·bil′i·ty, *n.*
non·ir′ri·ta·ble, *adj.;* **-ble·ness,** *n.;* **-bly,** *adv.*
non·ir′ri·tan·cy, *n.*
non·ir′ri·tant, *adj.*
non·ir′ri·tat′ing, *adj.*
non′-Is·lam′ic, *adj.*
non′-Is·lam·it′ic, *adj.*
non′i·so·e·las′tic, *adj.*
non·i′so·la·ble, *adj.*
non′i·so·trop′ic, *adj.*
non′i·sot′ro·pous, *adj.*
non-Is′ra·el·ite′, *n.*
non′-Is·ra·el·it′ic, *adj.*
non-Is′ra·el·it′ish, *adj.*
non·is′su·a·ble, *adj.;* **-bly,** *adv.*
non′-I·tal′ian, *adj., n.*
non′-I·tal′ic, *adj., n.*
non′-Jap·an·ese′, *adj., n., pl.* **-ese.**
non-Jew′, *n.*
non-Jew′ish, *adj.*
non′jour·nal·is′tic, *adj.*
non′jour·nal·is′ti·cal·ly, *adv.*
non·ju′di·ca·ble, *adj.*
non·ju′di·ca′tive, *adj.*
non·ju′di·ca·to′ry, *adj., n., pl.* **-ries.**
non′ju·di′ci·a·ble, *adj.*
non′ju·di′cial, *adj.;* **-ly,** *adv.*
non′ju·rid′ic, *adj.*
non′ju·rid′i·cal, *adj.;* **-ly,** *adv.*
non′ju·ris′tic, *adj.*
non′ju·ris′ti·cal, *adj.;* **-ly,** *adv.*
non·ju′ry, *n., pl.* **-ries.**
non-Kaf′fir, *n.*
non′ki·net′ic, *adj.*
non·knowl′edge·a·ble, *adj.*
non·ko′sher, *adj., n.*
non·la′bel·ing, *adj., n.*
non·la′bel·ling, *adj., n.*
non·lac′te·al, *adj.;* **-ly,** *adv.*
non·lac′te·ous, *adj.*
non′lac·tes′cent, *adj.*
non·lac′tic, *adj.*
non·lam′i·na·ble, *adj.*
non·lam′i·nat′ed, *adj.*
non·lam′i·na′ting, *adj., n.*
non·lam′i·na′tive, *adj.*
non·lar′ce·nous, *adj.*
non-Lat′in, *adj., n.*
non·lay′ered, *adj.*
non·lay′ing, *adj.*
non·lead′ed, *adj.*
non·leak′ing, *adj.*
non′le·ga′to, *adj.*
non·leg′is·la′tive, *adj.;* **-ly,** *adv.*
non′le·git′i·ma·cy, *n.*
non′le·git′i·mate, *adj.*
non·leg′ume, *n.*
non′le·gu′mi·nous, *adj.*
non′lep·i·dop′ter·al, *adj.*
non′lep·i·dop′ter·an, *adj., n.*
non′lep·i·dop′ter·ous, *adj.*
non·lep′rous, *adj.;* **-ly,** *adv.*
non·le′thal, *adj.;* **-ly,** *adv.*
non′le·thar′gic, *adj.*
non′le·thar′gi·cal, *adj.;* **-ly,** *adv.*
non·lev′el, *adj.*
non·lev′u·lose′, *adj.*
non′li·a·bil′i·ty, *n., pl.* **-ties.**
non·li′a·ble, *adj.*
non·li′bel·ous, *adj.;* **-ly,** *adv.*
non·lib′er·al, *adj.*
non·lib′er·al·ism, *n.*
non′lib·er·a′tion, *n.*
non′li·bid′i·nous, *adj.;* **-ly,** *adv.;* **-ness,** *n.*
non·li′cens·a·ble, *adj.*
non·li′censed, *adj.*
non′li·cen′ti·ate, *n.*
non′li·cen′tious, *adj.;* **-ly,** *adv.;* **-ness,** *n.*
non·lick′ing, *adj.*
non·lim′i·ta′tion, *n.*
non·lim′i·ta′tive, *adj.*
non·lim′it·ing, *adj.*
non·lin′e·al, *adj.*
non·lin′e·ar, *adj.*
non·lin·guis′tic, *adj.*
non·link′age, *adj.*
non·liq′ue·fi′a·ble, *adj.*
non·liq′ue·fy′ing, *adj.*
non·liq′uid, *adj., n.;* **-ly,** *adv.*
non·liq′ui·dat′ing, *adj.*
non′liq·ui·da′tion, *n.*
non·list′ing, *adj.*
non·lit′er·a·cy, *n.*
non·lit′er·al, *adj.;* **-ly,** *adv.;* **-ness,** *n.*
non·lit′er·ar′i·ly, *adv.*
non·lit′er·ar′i·ness, *n.*
non·lit′er·ar′y, *adj.*
non′lit·i·ga′tion, *n.*
non′li·ti′gious, *adj.;* **-ly,** *adv.;* **-ness,** *n.*
non′li·tur′gic, *adj.*
non′li·tur′gi·cal, *adj.;* **-ly,** *adv.*
non·live′, *adj.*
non·liv′ing, *adj., n.*
non′lix·iv′i·at′ed, *adj.*
non′lix·iv′i·a′tion, *n.*
non·lo′cal, *adj., n.;* **-ly,** *adv.*
non·lo′cal·iz′a·ble, *adj.*
non·lo′cal·ized′, *adj.*
non′lo·ca′tion, *n.*
non·log′ic, *n.*
non·log′i·cal, *adj.;* **-ly,** *adv.;* **-ness,** *n.*
non′log·i·cal′i·ty, *n.*
non′lo·gis′tic, *adj.*
non′lo·gis′ti·cal, *adj.*
non·los′a·ble, *adj.*
non·los′er, *n.*
non·lov′er, *n.*
non·lov′ing, *adj.*
non′lox·o·drom′ic, *adj.*
non′lox·o·drom′i·cal, *adj.*
non·loy′al, *adj.;* **-ly,** *adv.*
non·loy′al·ty, *n., pl.* **-ties.**
non·lu′bri·cant, *n.*
non·lu′bri·cat′ing, *adj.*
non′lu·bri′cious, *adj.;* **-ly,** *adv.;* **-ness,** *n.*
non·lu′cid, *adj.;* **-ly,** *adv.;* **-ness,** *n.*
non′lu·cid′i·ty, *n.*
non·lu′cra·tive, *adj.;* **-ly,** *adv.;* **-ness,** *n.*
non′lu·gu′bri·ous, *adj.;* **-ly,** *adv.;* **-ness,** *n.*
non′lu·mi·nes′cence, *n.*
non′lu·mi·nes′cent, *adj.*
non′lu·mi·nos′i·ty, *n.*
non·lu′mi·nous, *adj.;* **-ly,** *adv.;* **-ness,** *n.*
non·lus′ter, *n.*
non·lus′trous, *adj.;* **-ly,** *adv.;* **-ness,** *n.*
non-Lu′ther·an, *adj., n.*
non′lym·phat′ic, *adj.*
non·lyr′ic, *adj.*
non·lyr′i·cal, *adj.;* **-ly,** *adv.;* **-ness,** *n.*
non·lyr′i·cism, *n.*
non′mag·net′ic, *adj.*
non′mag·net′i·cal, *adj.;* **-ly,** *adv.*
non·mag′net·ized′, *adj.*
non-Mag′yar, *n., adj.*
non·main′te·nance, *n.*
non′ma·jor′i·ty, *n., pl.* **-ties.**
non·make′up′, *adj.*
non′ma·lar′i·al, *adj.*
non′ma·lar′i·an, *adj.*
non′ma·lar′i·ous, *adj.*
non′-Ma·lay, *adj., n.*
non′-Ma·lay′an, *adj., n.*
non′ma·li′cious, *adj.;* **-ly,** *adv.;* **-ness,** *n.*
non′ma·lig′nance, *n.*
non′ma·lig′nan·cy, *n.*
non′ma·lig′nant, *adj.;* **-ly,** *adv.*
non′ma·lig′ni·ty, *n.*
non′mal·le·a·bil′i·ty, *n.*
non·mal′le·a·ble, *adj.;* **-ness,** *n.*
non′-Mal·thu′si·an, *adj., n.*
non′mam·ma′li·an, *n., adj.*
non·man′age·ment, *n.*
non·man′da·to′ry, *adj., n., pl.* **-ries.**
non·man′i·fest′, *adj.;* **-ly,** *adv.;* **-ness,** *n.*
non′man·i·fes·ta′tion, *n.*
non′ma·nip′u·la′tive, *adj.*
non′ma·nip′u·la·to′ry, *adj.*
non·man′nered, *adj.*
non′man·ner·is′tic, *adj.*
non·man′u·al, *adj.;* **-ly,** *adv.*
non′man·u·fac′ture, *n.*
non′man·u·fac′tured, *adj.*
non′man·u·fac′tur·ing, *n.*
non′ma·rine′, *adj., n.*
non·mar′i·tal, *adj.;* **-ly,** *adv.*
non·mar′i·time′, *adj.*
non·mar′ket, *n.*
non′mar·ket·a·bil′i·ty, *n.*
non·mar′ket·a·ble, *adj.*
non·mar′riage, *n.*
non′mar·riage·a·bil′i·ty, *n.*
non·mar′riage·a·ble, *adj.;* **-ness,** *n.*
non·mar′ry·ing, *adj.*
non·mar′tial, *adj.;* **-ly,** *adv.;* **-ness,** *n.*
non·mas′cu·line, *adj.;* **-ly,** *adv.;* **-ness,** *n.*
non′mas·cu·lin′i·ty, *n.*
non·ma′son, *n.*
non·mas′ter·y, *n., pl.* **-ter·ies.**
non′ma·te′ri·al·is′tic, *adj.*
non′ma·te′ri·al·is′ti·cal·ly, *adv.*
non′ma·ter′nal, *adj.;* **-ly,** *adv.*
non′math·e·mat′ic, *adj.*
non′math·e·mat′i·cal, *adj.;* **-ly,** *adv.*
non′math·e·ma·ti′cian, *n.*
non′mat·ri·mo′ni·al, *adj.;* **-ly,** *adv.*
non·mat′ter, *n.*
non′mat·u·ra′tion, *n.*
non·mat′u·ra′tive, *adj.*
non′ma·ture′, *adj.;* **-ly,** *adv.;* **-ness,** *n.*
non′ma·tu′ri·ty, *n.*
non′meas·ur·a·bil′i·ty, *n.*
non·meas′ur·a·ble, *adj.;* **-ble·ness,** *n.;* **-bly,** *adv.*
non′me·chan′i·cal, *adj.;* **-ly,** *adv.;* **-ness,** *n.*
non′mech·a·nis′tic, *adj.*
non′me·di·a′tion, *n.*
non·me′di·a′tive, *adj.*
non·med′i·ca·ble, *adj.*
non·med′i·cal, *adj.;* **-ly,** *adv.*
non·med′i·ca′tive, *adj.*
non′me·dic′i·nal, *adj.;* **-ly,** *adv.*
non·med′i·ta′tive, *adj.;* **-ly,** *adv.;* **-ness,** *n.*
non′-Med·i·ter·ra′ne·an, *n., adj.*
non·med′ul·lat′ed, *adj.*
non′me·lod′ic, *adj.*
non′me·lod′i·cal·ly, *adv.*
non′me·lo′di·ous, *adj.;* **-ly,** *adv.;* **-ness,** *n.*
non′mel·o·dra·mat′ic, *adj.*
non′mel·o·dra·mat′i·cal·ly, *adv.*
non·melt′ing, *adj.*
non·men′ac·ing, *adj.*
non′-Men·de′li·an, *adj.*
non·men′di·can·cy, *n.*
non·men′di·cant, *adj.*
non·me′ni·al, *adj.;* **-ly,** *adv.*
non·men′tal, *adj.;* **-ly,** *adv.*
non·mer′can·tile, *adj.*
non·mer′cen·ar′y, *adj., n., pl.* **-ar·ies.**
non′met·al·lif′er·ous, *adj.*
non′met·al·lur′gic, *adj.*
non′met·al·lur′gi·cal, *adj.;* **-ly,** *adv.*
non′met·a·mor′phic, *adj.*
non′met·a·mor′pho·sis, *n., pl.* **-ses.**
non′met·a·mor′phous, *adj.*
non′met·a·phor′ic, *adj.*
non′met·a·phor′i·cal, *adj.;* **-ly,** *adv.*
non′met·a·phys′i·cal, *adj.;* **-ly,** *adv.*
non′me·te·or′ic, *adj.*
non′me·te·or′i·cal·ly, *adv.*
non′me·te·or·o·log′ic, *adj.*
non′me·te·or·o·log′i·cal, *adj.;* **-ly,** *adv.*
non′me·thod′ic, *adj.*
non′me·thod′i·cal, *adj.;* **-ly,** *adv.;* **-ness,** *n.*
non-Meth′od·ist, *n., adj.*
non′-Meth·od·is′tic, *adj.*
non·met′ric, *adj.*
non·met′ri·cal, *adj.;* **-ly,** *adv.*
non′met·ro·pol′i·tan, *adj., n.*
non′mi·cro′bic, *adj.*
non′mi·cro·scop′ic, *adj.*
non′mi·cro·scop′i·cal, *adj.;* **-ly,** *adv.*
non·mi′grant, *adj., n.*
non·mi′grat·ing, *adj., n.*
non′mi·gra′tion, *n.*
non·mi′gra·to′ry, *adj.*
non·mil′i·tan·cy, *n.*
non·mil′i·tant, *adj., n.;* **-ly,** *adv.*
non′mil·lion·aire′, *n.*
non′mi·met′ic, *adj.*
non′mi·met′i·cal·ly, *adv.*
non·min′er·al, *n., adj.*
non′min·er·al·og′i·cal, *adj.;* **-ly,** *adv.*
non·min′i·mal, *adj.*
non′min·is·te′ri·al, *adj.;* **-ly,** *adv.*
non′min·is·tra′tion, *n.*
non′mi·rac′u·lous, *adj.;* **-ly,** *adv.;* **-ness,** *n.*
non·mis′chie·vous, *adj.;* **-ly,** *adv.;* **-ness,** *n.*
non·mis′sion·ar′y, *adj., n., pl.* **-ar·ies.**
non′mit·i·ga′tion, *n.*
non·mit′i·ga′tive, *adj.*
non·mit′i·ga·to′ry, *adj.*
non·mo′bile, *adj.*
non′mo·bil′i·ty, *n.*
non·mod′al, *adj.;* **-ly,** *adv.*
non·mod′er·ate, *adj., n.;* **-ly,** *adv.;* **-ness,** *n.*
non·mod′ern, *adj., n.;* **-ly,** *adv.;* **-ness,** *n.*
non′mod·ern·is′tic, *adj.*
non·mod′i·fi·ca′tive, *adj.*
non·mod′i·fi·ca·to′ry, *adj.*
non·mod′i·fy′ing, *adj.*
non′-Mo·ham′med·an, *adj., n.*
non·mo′lar, *adj., n.*
non′mo·lec′u·lar, *adj.*
non·mo′men·tar′i·ness, *n.*
non·mo′men·tar′y, *adj.*
non′mo·nar′chal, *adj.;* **-ly,** *adv.*
non′mo·nar′chi·al, *adj.*
non′mo·nar′chic, *adj.*
non′mo·nar′chi·cal·ly, *adv.*
non·mon′ar·chist, *n.*
non′mon·ar·chis′tic, *adj.*
non′mo·nas′tic, *adj.*
non′mo·nas′ti·cal·ly, *adv.*
non-Mon′gol, *n., adj.*
non′-Mon·go′li·an, *adj., n.*
non·mon′ist, *n.*
non′mo·nis′tic, *adj.*
non′mo·nis′ti·cal·ly, *adv.*
non′mo·nog′a·mous, *adj.;* **-ly,** *adv.*
non′mo·nop′o·lis′tic, *adj.*
non-Mor′mon, *n., adj.*
non·mor′tal, *adj., n.;* **-ly,** *adv.*
non-Mos′lem, *adj., n., pl.* **-lems, -lem.**
non·mo′tile, *adj.*
non′mo·til′i·ty, *n.*
non·mo′tion, *n.*
non·mo′ti·vat′ed, *adj.*
non′mo·ti·va′tion, *n.*
non′mo·ti·va′tion·al, *adj.*
non·mo′tor·ing, *adj.*
non·mo′tor·ist, *n.*
non·moun′tain·ous, *adj.;* **-ly,** *adv.*
non′move·a·bil′i·ty, *n.*
non·move′a·ble, *adj.;* **-ble·ness,** *n.;* **-bly,** *adv.*
non′mu·ci·lag′i·nous, *adj.*
non·mu′cous, *adj.*
non′-Mu·ham′mad·an, *adj., n.*

ments as to efficacy. [NON- + MORAL] —**non′mo·ral′i·ty,** *n.* —**non·mor′al·ly,** *adv.*
—**Syn.** See **immoral.**

non·na·sal (non nā′zəl), *adj.* 1. not nasal. 2. *Phonet.* oral (def. 6). [NON- + NASAL] —**non·na·sal·i·ty** (non′nā zal′i tē), *n.* —**non·na′sal·ly,** *adv.*

non·neg·a·tive (non neg′ə tiv), *adj.* *Math.* (of a real number) greater than or equal to zero. [NON- + NEGATIVE]

non·ni·trog·e·nous (non′nī troj′ə nəs), *adj.* containing no nitrogen. [NON- + NITROGENOUS]

non·o·be·di·ence (non′ō bē′dē əns), *n.* absence or lack of obedience. [NON- + OBEDIENCE]

non·ob·jec·tive (non′əb jek′tiv), *adj.* *Fine Arts.* not representing objects known in physical nature; nonrepresentational. [NON- + OBJECTIVE]

non·ob·serv·ance (non′əb zûr′vəns), *n.* absence or lack of observance. [NON- + OBSERVANCE]

non obst., non obstante.

non ob·stan·te (nōn ōb stän′te; *Eng.* non ob stan′tē), *Latin.* notwithstanding. [late ME < AL: short for *nōn obstante aliquō statūtō in contrārium* any statute to the contrary notwithstanding]

non·oc·cur·rence (non′ə kûr′əns, -kur′-), *n.* absence or lack of occurrence. [NON- + OCCURRENCE]

non·par·a·met·ric (non′par ə me′trik), *adj.* *Statistics.* (of a test or method) not requiring assertions about parameters or about the form of the underlying distribution. [NON- + PARAMETRIC]

non·pa·reil (non′pə rel′), *adj.* 1. having no equal; peerless. —*n.* 2. a person or thing having no equal. 3. a small pellet of multicolored sugar for decorating candy, cake, and cookies. 4. a flat, round, bite-sized piece of chocolate covered with this sugar. 5. See **painted bunting.** 6. *Print.* a. a 6-point type. b. a slug occupying 6 points of space between lines. [late ME *nonparaille* < MF *nonpareil,* equiv. to *non-* NON- + *pareil* equal < VL **pariculum* (L *pari-* (s. of *pār*) equal + *-culum* -CULE)]
—**Syn.** 1. unparalleled. 2. nonesuch. —**Ant.** 1. ordinary.

non·par·ous (non par′əs), *adj.* *Physiol.* having borne no children. [NON- + -PAROUS]

non·par·tic·i·pant (non′pär tis′ə pənt), *n.* a person who does not participate. [NON- + PARTICIPANT]

non·par·tic·i·pat·ing (non′pär tis′ə pā′ting), *adj.* *Insurance.* having or imparting no right to dividends or to a distribution of surplus. [NON- + PARTICIPATING]

non·par·tic·i·pa·tion (non′pär tis′ə pā′shən), *n.* absence of participation: *Nonparticipation of citizens in political matters hampers efforts toward better government.* [NON- + PARTICIPATION]

non·par·ti·san (non pär′ti zən), *adj.* 1. not partisan; objective. 2. not supporting any of the established or regular parties. —*n.* 3. a person who is nonpartisan. Also, **non·par′ti·zan.** [NON- + PARTISAN] —**non·par′ti·san·ship′, non·par′ti·zan·ship′,** *n.*

Nonpar′tisan League′, a political organization of farmers, founded in North Dakota, in 1915 and extending to many States west of the Mississippi, with the aim of influencing agricultural legislation in State legislatures.

non·pay·ment (non pā′mənt), *n.* failure or neglect to pay: *His property was confiscated for nonpayment of taxes.* [late ME; see NON-, PAYMENT]

non·per·form·ance (non′pər fôr′məns), *n.* failure or neglect to perform. [NON- + PERFORMANCE] —**non′per·form′er,** *n.* —**non′per·form′ing,** *adj.*

non·per·ish·a·ble (non per′i shə bəl), *adj.* 1. not subject to rapid deterioration or decay: *A supply of nonperishable food was kept for emergencies.* —*n.* 2. Usually, **nonperishables.** articles or items, esp. of food, not subject to rapid spoilage. [NON- + PERISHABLE]

non pla·cet (nōn plä′ket; *Eng.* non plā′sit), *Latin.* it is not pleasing.

---

non′-Mu·ham′med·an, *adj., n.*
non·mulched′, *adj.*
non·mul′ti·ple, *adj., n.*
non′mul·ti·pli·ca′tion, *n.*
non′mul·ti·pli·ca′tion·al, *adj.*
non·mul′ti·pli·ca′tive, *adj.;* **-ly,** *adv.*
non′mu·nic′i·pal, *adj.;* **-ly,** *adv.*
non·mus′cu·lar, *adj.;* **-ly,** *adv.*
non·mu′si·cal, *adj.;* **-ly,** *adv.;* **-ness,** *n.*
non-Mus′lem, *adj., n., pl.* **-lems, -lem.**
non-Mus′lim, *adj., n., pl.* **-lims, -lim.**
non′mu·ta·bil′i·ty, *n.*
non·mut′a·ble, *adj.;* **-ble·ness,** *n.;* **-bly,** *adv.*
non′mu·ta′tion·al, *adj.;* **-ly,** *adv.*
non·mu′ta·tive, *adj.*
non·mu′ti·nous, *adj.;* **-ly,** *adv.;* **-ness,** *n.*
non·mu′tu·al, *adj.;* **-ly,** *adv.*
non′mu·tu·al′i·ty, *n.*
non′my·op′ic, *adj.*
non′my·op′i·cal·ly, *adv.*
non·mys′tic, *adj., n.*
non·mys′ti·cal, *adj.;* **-ly,** *adv.;* **-ness,** *n.*
non·mys′ti·cism, *n.*
non·myth′i·cal, *adj.;* **-ly,** *adv.*
non′myth·o·log′ic, *adj.*
non′myth·o·log′i·cal, *adj.;* **-ly,** *adv.*
non·nar′cism, *n.*
non′nar·cis′sism, *n.*
non′nar·cis·sis′tic, *adj.*
non′nar·cot′ic, *adj., n.*
non′nar·ra′tion, *n.*
non·nar′ra·tive, *adj., n.*
non·na′tion·al, *adj., n.;* **-ly,** *adv.*
non·na′tion·al·ism, *n.*
non′na·tion·al·is′tic, *adj.*
non′na·tion·al·is′ti·cal·ly, *adv.*
non′na·tion·al·i·za′tion, *n.*
non·na′tive, *adj., n.;* **-ly,** *adv.;* **-ness,** *n.*
non·nat′ti·ly, *adv.*
non·nat′ti·ness, *n.*
non·nat′ty, *adj.*
non·nat′u·ral, *adj.;* **-ly,** *adv.;* **-ness,** *n.*
non·nat′u·ral·ism, *n.*
non·nat′u·ral·ist, *n.*
non·nat·u·ral·is′tic, *adj.*
non·nau′ti·cal, *adj.;* **-ly,** *adv.*
non·na′val, *adj.*
non′nav·i·ga·bil′i·ty, *n.*
non·nav′i·ga·ble, *adj.;* **-ble·ness,** *n.;* **-bly,** *adv.*
non′nav·i·ga′tion, *n.*
non·neb′u·lar, *adj.*
non·neb′u·lous, *adj.;* **-ly,** *adv.;* **-ness,** *n.*
non′ne·ces′si·tous, *adj.;* **-ly,** *adv.;* **-ness,** *n.*
non′ne·ces′si·ty, *n., pl.* **-ties.**
non′ne·ga′tion, *n.*
non·neg′a·tiv·ism, *n.*
non′neg·a·tiv·is′tic, *adj.*
non′neg·a·tiv′i·ty, *n.*
non·neg′li·gence, *n.*
non·neg′li·gent, *adj.;* **-ly,** *adv.*
non′neg·li·gi·bil′i·ty, *n.*
non·neg′li·gi·ble, *adj.;* **-ble·ness,** *n.;* **-bly,** *adv.*
non′ne·go′ti·a·bil′i·ty, *n.*
non′ne·go′ti·a·ble, *adj.*
non′ne·go′ti·a′tion, *n.*
non′-Ne·grit′ic, *adj.*
non-Ne′gro, *n., pl.* **-groes,** *adj.*
non′ne·phrit′ic, *adj.*
non·ner′vous, *adj.;* **-ly,** *adv.;* **-ness,** *n.*
non·nes′cience, *n.*
non·nes′cient, *adj.*
non·neu′ral, *adj.*
non·neu·rot′ic, *adj., n.*
non·neu′tral, *adj., n.;* **-ly,** *adv.*
non′neu·tral′i·ty, *n.*
non′-New·to′ni·an, *adj., n.*
non′-Ni·cene′, *adj.*
non′nic·o·tin′ic, *adj.*
non·ni′hil·ism, *n.*
non·ni′hil·ist, *n.*
non′ni·hil·is′tic, *adj.*
non·ni′tric, *adj.*
non·ni′tro·gen·ized′, *adj.*
non·ni′trous, *adj.*
non′no·bil′i·ty, *n.*
non′noc·tur′nal, *adj.;* **-ly,** *adv.*
non·no′mad, *n., adj.*
non′no·mad′ic, *adj.*
non′no·mad′i·cal·ly, *adv.*
non′nom·i·nal·is′tic, *adj.*
non′nom·i·na′tion, *n.*
non-Nor′dic, *adj., n.*
non·nor′mal, *adj.;* **-ly,** *adv.;* **-ness,** *n.*
non′nor·mal′i·ty, *n.*
non-Nor′man, *n., adj.*
non-Norse′, *adj., n.*
non·not′a·ble, *adj.;* **-ble·ness,** *n.;* **-bly,** *adv.*
non′no·ta′tion·al, *adj.*
non′no·ti·fi·ca′tion, *n.*
non·no′tion·al, *adj.*
non·nou′me·nal, *adj.;* **-ly,** *adv.*
non·nour′ish·ing, *adj.*
non·nour′ish·ment, *n.*
non′nul·li·fi·ca′tion, *n.*
non·nu′mer·al, *n., adj.*
non·nu′tri·ent, *adj., n.*
non·nu′tri·ment, *n.*
non′nu·tri′tious, *adj.;* **-ly,** *adv.;* **-ness,** *n.*
non·nu′tri·tive, *adj.;* **-ly,** *adv.;* **-ness,** *n.*
non′o·be′di·ent, *adj.;* **-ly,** *adv.*
non′ob·jec′ti·fi·ca′tion, *n.*
non′ob·jec′tion, *n.*
non′ob·jec′ti·vis′tic, *adj.*
non·ob′li·gat′ed, *adj.*
non′ob·lig′a·to′ri·ly, *adv.*
non′ob·lig′a·to′ry, *adj.*
non′ob·scu′ri·ty, *n., pl.* **-ties.**
non′ob·serv′a·ble, *adj.;* **-bly,** *adv.*
non′ob·ser′vant, *adj.;* **-ly,** *adv.*
non′ob·ser·va′tion, *n.*
non′ob·ser·va′tion·al, *adj.*
non′ob·serv′ing, *adj.;* **-ly,** *adv.*
non′ob·ses′sion, *n.*
non′ob·ses′sion·al, *adj.*
non′ob·ses′sive, *adj.;* **-ly,** *adv.;* **-ness,** *n.*
non′ob·stet′ric, *adj.*
non′ob·stet′ri·cal, *adj.;* **-ly,** *adv.*
non′ob·struc′tive, *adj.;* **-ly,** *adv.;* **-ness,** *n.*
non·ob′vi·ous, *adj.;* **-ly,** *adv.;* **-ness,** *n.*
non′oc·ci·den′tal, *adj.;* **-ly,** *adv.*
non′oc·clu′sion, *n.*
non′oc·clu′sive, *adj.*
non′oc·cult′, *adj.*
non′oc·cult′ing, *adj.*
non·oc′cu·pant, *n.*
non′oc·cu·pa′tion, *n.*
non′oc·cu·pa′tion·al, *adj.*
non′o·dor·if′er·ous, *adj.;* **-ly,** *adv.;* **-ness,** *n.*
non·o′dor·ous, *adj.;* **-ly,** *adv.;* **-ness,** *n.*
non′oec·u·men′ic, *adj.*
non′oec·u·men′i·cal, *adj.*
non′of·fend′er, *n.*
non′of·fen′sive, *adj.;* **-ly,** *adv.;* **-ness,** *n.*
non·of′fice·hold′er, *n.*
non′of·fi′cial, *adj.;* **-ly,** *adv.*
non′of·fic′i·nal, *adj.*
non·oil′y, *adj.*
non′ol·fac′to·ry, *adj., n., pl.* **-ries.**
non·ol′i·gar′chic, *adj.*
non·ol′i·gar′chi·cal, *adj.*
non′o·mis′si·ble, *adj.*
non′o·mis′sion, *n.*
non·on′er·ous, *adj.;* **-ly,** *adv.;* **-ness,** *n.*
non′o·pac′i·ty, *n., pl.* **-ties.**
non·op′er·a·ble, *adj.*
non′op·er·at′ic, *adj.*
non′op·er·at′i·cal·ly, *adv.*
non·op′er·at′ing, *adj.*
non′op·er·a′tion·al, *adj.*
non·op′er·a′tive, *adj.*
non′o·pin′ion·at′ed, *adj.;* **-ness,** *n.*
non′o·pin′ion·a′tive, *adj.;* **-ly,** *adv.;* **-ness,** *n.*
non′op·pos′a·ble, *adj.*
non′op·pos′ing, *adj.*
non′op·po·si′tion, *n.*
non′op·pres′sion, *n.*
non′op·pres′sive, *adj.;* **-ly,** *adv.;* **-ness,** *n.*
non′op·pro′bri·ous, *adj.;* **-ly,** *adv.;* **-ness,** *n.*
non·op′tic, *adj.*
non·op′ti·cal, *adj.;* **-ly,** *adv.*
non′op·ti·mis′tic, *adj.*
non′op·ti·mis′ti·cal, *adj.;* **-ly,** *adv.*
non·op′tion·al, *adj.;* **-ly,** *adv.*
non·o′ral, *adj.;* **-ly,** *adv.*
non′or·ches′tral, *adj.;* **-ly,** *adv.*
non·or′dered, *adj.*
non′or·di·na′tion, *n.*
non′or·gan′ic, *adj.*
non′or·gan′i·cal·ly, *adv.*
non′or·gan·i·za′tion, *n.*
non′o·ri·en′ta·ble, *adj.*
non′o·ri·en′tal, *adj., n.*
non′o·ri·en·ta′tion, *n.*
non′o·rig′i·nal, *adj., n.;* **-ly,** *adv.*
non′or·na·men′tal, *adj.;* **-ly,** *adv.*
non′or·na·men·tal′i·ty, *n.*
non·or′tho·dox′, *adj.;* **-ly,** *adv.*
non′or·tho·graph′ic, *adj.*
non′or·tho·graph′i·cal, *adj.;* **-ly,** *adv.*
non-Os′can, *adj., n.*
non·os′cine, *adj.*
non′os·mot′ic, *adj.*
non′os·mot′i·cal·ly, *adv.*
non′os·ten′si·ble, *adj.;* **-bly,** *adv.*
non′os·ten′sive, *adj.;* **-ly,** *adv.*
non′os·ten·ta′tion, *n.*
non·out′law′ry, *n., pl.* **-ries.**
non·o′ver·head′, *n., adj.*
non·o′ver·lap′ping, *adj., n.*
non·own′er, *n.*
non·own′ing, *adj.*
non·ox′i·dat′ing, *adj.*
non′ox·i·da′tion, *n.*
non·ox′i·da′tive, *adj.*
non·ox′i·diz′a·ble, *adj.*
non′ox·i·di·za′tion, *n.*
non·ox′i·diz′ing, *adj.*
non·ox′y·gen·at′ed, *adj.*
non′pac·i·fi′a·ble, *adj.*
non′pa·cif′ic, *adj.*
non′pa·cif′i·cal, *adj.;* **-ly,** *adv.*
non′pac·i·fi·ca′tion, *n.*
non′pa·cif′i·ca·to′ry, *adj.*
non·pac′i·fist, *n.*
non′pac·i·fis′tic, *adj.*
non·pa′gan, *n., adj.*
non·pa′gan·ish, *adj.*
non·paid′, *adj.*
non·paint′er, *n.*
non′pal·at·a·bil′i·ty, *n.*
non·pal′at·a·ble, *adj.;* **-ble·ness,** *n.;* **-bly,** *adv.*
non·pal′a·tal, *adj., n.*
non′pal·a·tal·i·za′tion, *n.*
non′pal·li·a′tion, *n.*
non·pal′li·a′tive, *adj.;* **-ly,** *adv.*
non′pal·pa·bil′i·ty, *n.*
non·pal′pa·ble, *adj.;* **-bly,** *adv.*
non′pan·the·is′tic, *adj.*
non′pan·the·is′ti·cal, *adj.;* **-ly,** *adv.*
non·pa′pal, *adj.*
non·pap′ist, *n.*
non′pa·pis′tic, *adj.*
non′pa·pis′ti·cal, *adj.*
non·par′, *n., adj.*
non′par·a·bol′ic, *adj.*
non′par·a·bol′i·cal, *adj.;* **-ly,** *adv.*
non′par·a·dox′i·cal, *adj.;* **-ly,** *adv.;* **-ness,** *n.*
non·par′al·lel′, *adj., n.*
non·par′al·lel′ism, *n.*
non′pa·ral′y·sis, *n., pl.* **-ses.**
non′par·a·lyt′ic, *adj., n.*
non′par·a·sit′ic, *adj.*
non′par·a·sit′i·cal, *adj.;* **-ly,** *adv.*
non·par′a·sit′ism, *n.*
non·par′don·ing, *adj.*
non·par′ent, *n.*
non′pa·ren′tal, *adj.;* **-ly,** *adv.*
non′pa·rish′ion·er, *n.*
non′-Pa·ri′sian, *adj., n.*
non·par′i·ty, *n.*
non·par′lia·men′ta·ry, *adj.*
non′pa·ro′chi·al, *adj.;* **-ly,** *adv.*
non·par′tial, *adj.;* **-ly,** *adv.*
non′par·ti·al′i·ty, *n., pl.* **-ties.**
non·par′ti·ble, *adj.*
non·part′ner, *n.*
non·par′ty, *adj.*
non·pas′sen·ger, *n.*
non·pas′ser·ine, *adj., n.*
non·pas′si·ble, *adj.*
non·pas′sion·ate, *adj.;* **-ly,** *adv.;* **-ness,** *n.*
non·pas′to·ral, *adj., n.;* **-ly,** *adv.*
non′pat·ent·a·bil′i·ty, *n.*
non·pat′ent·a·ble, *adj.*
non·pat′ent·ed, *adj.*
non·pat′ent·ly, *adv.*
non′pa·ter′nal, *adj.;* **-ly,** *adv.*
non′path·o·gen′ic, *adj.*
non′path·o·log′ic, *adj.*
non′path·o·log′i·cal, *adj.;* **-ly,** *adv.*
non′pa·tri·ot′ic, *adj.*
non′pa·tri·ot′i·cal·ly, *adv.*
non·pat′terned, *adj.*
non·pause′, *n.*
non·pay′ing, *adj.*
non·peaked′, *adj.*
non′pe·cu′ni·ar′y, *adj.*
non′ped·a·gog′ic, *adj.*
non′ped·a·gog′i·cal, *adj.;* **-ly,** *adv.*
non′pe·des′tri·an, *n., adj.*
non·ped′i·greed′, *adj.*
non′pe·jo′ra·tive, *adj.;* **-ly,** *adv.*
non′pe·lag′ic, *adj.*
non·pel′tast, *n.*
non·pe′nal, *adj.*
non·pe′nal·ized′, *adj.*
non·pend′ant, *adj.*
non·pend′en·cy, *n.*
non·pend′ent, *adj.;* **-ly,** *adv.*
non·pend′ing, *adj.*
non′pen·e·tra·bil′i·ty, *n.*
non·pen′e·tra·ble, *adj.;* **-bly,** *adv.*
non·pen′e·trat′ing, *adj.*
non′pen·e·tra′tion, *n.*
non·pen′i·tent, *adj., n.*
non·pen′sion·a·ble, *adj.*
non·pen′sion·er, *n.*
non′per·ceiv′a·ble, *adj.;* **-bly,** *adv.*
non′per·ceiv′ing, *adj.*
non′per·cep′ti·bil′i·ty, *n.*
non′per·cep′ti·ble, *adj.;* **-ble·ness,** *n.;* **-bly,** *adv.*
non′per·cep′tion, *n.*
non′per·cep′tion·al, *adj.*
non′per·cep′tive, *adj.;* **-ly,** *adv.;* **-ness,** *n.*
non′per·cep·tiv′i·ty, *n.*
non′per·cep′tu·al, *adj.;* **-ly,** *adv.*
non′per·cip′i·ence, *n.*
non′per·cip′i·en·cy, *n.*
non′per·cip′i·ent, *adj.*
non′per·cus′sive, *adj.*
non′per·fect′ed, *adj.*
non′per·fect·i·bil′i·ty, *n.*
non′per·fect′i·ble, *adj.*
non′per·fec′tion, *n.*
non·per′fo·ra′ted, *adj.*
non·per′fo·rat′ing, *adj.*
non·per′il·ous, *adj.;* **-ly,** *adv.*
non′pe·ri·od′ic, *adj.*
non′pe·ri·od′i·cal, *adj., n.;* **-ly,** *adv.*
non·per′ish·ing, *adj.*
non·per′jured, *adj.*
non·per′ju·ry, *n., pl.* **-ries.**
non·per′ma·nence, *n.*
non·per′ma·nen·cy, *n.*
non·per′ma·nent, *adj.;* **-ly,** *adv.*
non·per′me·a·bil′i·ty, *n.*
non·per′me·a·ble, *adj.*
non′per·me·a′tion, *n.*
non·per′me·a′tive, *adj.*
non′per·mis′si·bil′i·ty, *n.*
non′per·mis′si·ble, *adj.;* **-bly,** *adv.*
non′per·mis′sion, *n.*
non′per·mis′sive, *adj.;* **-ly,** *adv.;* **-ness,** *n.*
non′per·mit′ted, *adj.*
non′per·pen·dic′u·lar, *adj., n.;* **-ly,** *adv.*
non′per·pen·dic′u·lar′i·ty, *n.*
non′per·pe·tra′tion, *n.*
non′per·pet′u·al, *adj.;* **-ly,** *adv.*
non′per·pet′u·ance, *n.*
non′per·pet′u·a′tion, *n.*
non′per·pe·tu′i·ty, *n., pl.* **-ties.**
non·per′se·cut′ing, *adj.*
non′per·se·cu′tion, *n.*
non·per′se·cu′tive, *adj.*
non·per′se·cu·to′ry, *adj.*
non′per·se·ver′ance, *n.*
non′per·se·ver′ant, *adj.*
non′per·se·ver′ing, *adj.*
non′per·sist′ence, *n.*
non′per·sist′en·cy, *n.*
non′per·sist′ent, *adj.;* **-ly,** *adv.*
non′per·sist′ing, *adj.*
non·per′son·al, *adj.;* **-ly,** *adv.*
non′per·son′i·fi·ca′tion, *n.*
non′per·spec′tive, *n., adj.*
non′per·suad′a·ble, *adj.*
non′per·sua′si·ble, *adj.*
non′per·sua′sive, *adj.;* **-ly,** *adv.;* **-ness,** *n.*
non·per′ti·nence, *n.*
non·per′ti·nen·cy, *n.*
non·per′ti·nent, *adj.;* **-ly,** *adv.*
non′per·turb′a·ble, *adj.*
non′per·turb′ing, *adj.*
non′-Pe·ru′vi·an, *adj., n.*
non′per·verse′, *adj.;* **-ly,** *adv.;* **-ness,** *n.*
non′per·ver′sion, *n.*
non′per·ver′si·ty, *n., pl.* **-ties.**
non′per·ver′sive, *adj.*
non′per·vert′ed, *adj.;* **-ly,** *adv.*
non′per·vert′i·ble, *adj.*
non′pes·si·mis′tic, *adj.*
non′pes·si·mis′ti·cal·ly, *adv.*
non·pes′ti·lent, *adj.;* **-ly,** *adv.*
non′pes·ti·len′tial, *adj.*
non′phag·o·cyt′ic, *adj.*
non′phar·ma·ceu′tic, *adj.*
non′phar·ma·ceu′ti·cal, *adj.;* **-ly,** *adv.*
non′phe·no′lic, *adj.*
non′phe·nom′e·nal, *adj.;* **-ly,** *adv.*
non′phil·an·throp′ic, *adj.*
non′phil·an·throp′i·cal, *adj.*
non′phil·o·log′ic, *adj.*
non′phil·o·log′i·cal, *adj.*
non′phil·o·soph′ic, *adj.*
non′phil·o·soph′i·cal, *adj.;* **-ly,** *adv.*
non′phi·los′o·phy, *n., pl.* **-phies.**
non·pho′bic, *adj.*
non′pho·ne′mic, *adj.*
non′pho·ne′mi·cal·ly, *adv.*
non′pho·net′ic, *adj.*
non′pho·net′i·cal, *adj.;* **-ly,** *adv.*
non′phos·phat′ic, *adj.*
non·phos′pho·rous, *adj.*
non′pho·to·graph′ic, *adj.*
non′pho·to·graph′i·cal, *adj.;* **-ly,** *adv.*
non′phre·net′ic, *adj.*
non′phre·net′i·cal·ly, *adv.*
non·phys′i·cal, *adj.;* **-ly,** *adv.*
non′phys·i·o·log′ic, *adj.*
non′phys·i·o·log′i·cal, *adj.;* **-ly,** *adv.*
non′pic·to′ri·al, *adj.;* **-ly,** *adv.*
non·pig′ment·ed, *adj.*
non′pi·na′ceous, *adj.*
non′pla·cen′tal, *adj.*

---

non·plus (non plus′, non′plus), *v.*, **-plused, -plus·ing** or (*esp. Brit.*) **-plussed, -plus·sing,** *n.* —*v.t.* **1.** to make utterly perplexed; puzzle completely. —*n.* **2.** a state of utter perplexity: *Her question put me in a nonplus.* [< L *nōn plūs*: lit., not more, no further] —**Syn. 1.** perplex, confuse, confound, disconcert.

non·po·lar (non pō′lər), *adj.* *Physical Chem.* containing no permanently dipolar molecules; lacking a dipole. [NON- + POLAR]

non·pos·i·tive (non poz′i tiv), *adj.* *Math.* (of a real number) less than or equal to zero. [NON- + POSITIVE]

non pos·su·mus (nōn pō′so͞o mo͞os′; *Eng.* non pos′ə məs), *Latin.* we cannot.

non·pro·duc·tive (non′prə duk′tiv), *adj.* **1.** not producing goods directly, as employees in charge of personnel, inspectors, etc. **2.** unproductive. [NON- + PRODUCTIVE] —**non′pro·duc′tive·ly,** *adv.* —**non′pro·duc′tive·ness, non·pro·duc·tiv·i·ty** (non′prō duk tiv′i tē), *n.*

non·pro·fes·sion·al (non′prə fesh′ə nəl), *adj.* **1.** not a member of or trained in a specific profession. **2.** *Sports.* not engaged in as a means of livelihood or for any financial gain; amateur. —*n.* **3.** a person who is not a professional. **4.** an amateur athlete. [NON- + PROFESSIONAL]

non·pro·fi·cien·cy (non′prə fish′ən sē), *n.* absence or lack of proficiency. [NON- + PROFICIENCY] —**non′pro·fi′cient,** *adj.*

non·prof·it (non prof′it), *adj.* not yielding a return; not entered into for profit: *a nonprofit association.* [NON- + PROFIT]

non·pro·lif·er·a·tion (non′prō lif′ə rā′shən), *n.* **1.** failure or refusal to proliferate, as in budding or cell division. **2.** the action or practice of curbing or controlling an excessive, rapid spread: *nonproliferation of nuclear weapons.* [NON- + PROLIFERATION]

non-pros (non′pros′), *v.t.*, **-prossed, -pros·sing.** *Law.* to adjudge (a plaintiff) in default. [shortened form of NON PROSEQUITUR]

non pros., non prosequitur.

non pro·se·qui·tur (non prō sek′wi tər), *Law.* a judgment entered against the plaintiff in a suit when he does not appear in court to prosecute it. [< L: lit., he does not pursue (prosecute)]

non·rec·og·ni·tion (non′rek əg nish′ən), *n.* absence or lack of recognition. [NON- + RECOGNITION]

non·re·gent (non rē′jənt), *n.* (at English universities) a Master of Arts whose regency has terminated. [NON- + REGENT]

non′rel·a·tiv·is′tic quan′tum mechan′ics

non·plan′e·tar′y, *adj.*
non·plas′tic, *adj., n.*
non′plas·tic′i·ty, *n.*
non·plat′ed, *adj.*
non′plat·i·tu′di·nous, *adj.*; **-ly,** *adv.*
non·plau·si·bil′i·ty, *n.*
non·plau′si·ble, *adj.*; **-ble·ness,** *n.*; **-bly,** *adv.*
non·plead′a·ble, *adj.*
non·plead′ing, *adj.*
non·plead′ing·ly, *adv.*
non′pli·a·bil′i·ty, *n.*
non·pli′a·ble, *adj.*; **-ble·ness,** *n.*; **-bly,** *adv.*
non·pli′an·cy, *n.*
non·pli′ant, *adj.*; **-ly,** *adv.*; **-ness,** *n.*
non′plu·ral·is′tic, *adj.*
non′plu·ral′i·ty, *n.*, *pl.* **-ties.**
non′plu·to·crat′ic, *adj.*
non′plu·to·crat′i·cal, *adj.*
non′pneu·mat′ic, *adj.*
non′pneu·mat′i·cal·ly, *adv.*
non·po′et, *n.*
non′po·et′ic, *adj.*
non·poi′son·ous, *adj.*; **-ly,** *adv.*; **-ness,** *n.*
non′po·lar′i·ty, *n.*
non·po′lar·iz′a·ble, *adj.*
non·po′lar·iz′ing, *adj.*
non′po·lem′ic, *n., adj.*
non′po·lem′i·cal, *adj.*; **-ly,** *adv.*
non-Pol′ish, *adj., n.*
non′po·lit′i·cal, *adj.*; **-ly,** *adv.*
non′pon·der·a·bil′i·ty, *n.*
non·pon′der·a·ble, *adj.*
non′pon·der·os′i·ty, *n.*
non·pon′der·ous, *adj.*; **-ly,** *adv.*; **-ness,** *n.*
non·pop′u·lar, *adj.*
non′pop·u·lar′i·ty, *n.*
non·pop′u·lar·ly, *adv.*
non·pop′u·lous, *adj.*; **-ly,** *adv.*; **-ness,** *n.*
non·por′no·graph′ic, *adj.*
non·po′rous, *adj.*; **-ness,** *n.*
non′por·phy·rit′ic, *adj.*
non′port·a·bil′i·ty, *n.*
non·port′a·ble, *adj.*
non′por·ten′tous, *adj.*; **-ly,** *adv.*; **-ness,** *n.*
non′por·tray′a·ble, *adj.*
non′por·tray′al, *n.*
non′-Por·tu·guese′, *adj., n., pl.* **-guese.**
non′pos·i·tiv·is′tic, *adj.*
non′pos·sessed′, *adj.*
non′pos·ses′sion, *n.*
non′pos·ses′sive, *adj.*; **-ly,** *adv.*; **-ness,** *n.*
non·pos′si·ble, *adj.*
non·pos′si·bly, *adv.*
non·post′hu·mous, *adj.*
non′post·pone′ment, *n.*
non·po′ta·ble, *adj., n.*
non′po·ten′tial, *adj., n.*
non′prac·ti·ca·bil′i·ty, *n.*
non·prac′ti·ca·ble, *adj.*; **-ble·ness,** *n.*; **-bly,** *adv.*
non·prac′ti·cal, *adj.*; **-ly,** *adv.*; **-ness,** *n.*
non′prac·ti·cal′i·ty, *n.*
non·prac′tice, *n.*
non·prac′ticed, *adj.*
non′prag·mat′ic, *adj., n.*
non′prag·mat′i·cal, *adj.*; **-ly,** *adv.*
non·preach′ing, *adj., n.*
non·prec′e·dent, *n.*
non′pre·ced′ent, *adj.*
non·prec′e·den′tial, *adj.*
non·pre′cious, *adj.*; **-ly,** *adv.*; **-ness,** *n.*
non′pre·cip′i·ta′tion, *n.*
non′pre·cip′i·ta′tive, *adj.*
non·pred′a·to·ri·ly, *adv.*
non·pred′a·to′ri·ness, *n.*
non·pred′a·to′ry, *adj.*
non·pred′i·ca′tive, *adj.*; **-ly,** *adv.*
non′pre·dict′a·ble, *adj.*
non′pre·dic′tive, *adj.*
non′pref·er·a·bil′i·ty, *n.*
non·pref′er·a·ble, *adj.*; **-ble·ness,** *n.*; **-bly,** *adv.*
non·pref′er·ence, *n.*
non′pref·er·en′tial, *adj.*; **-ly,** *adv.*
non′pref·er·en′tial·ism, *n.*
non′pre·formed′, *adj.*
non·preg′nant, *adj.*
non′pre·hen′sile, *adj.*
non·prej′u·diced, *adj.*
non′prej·u·di′cial, *adj.*; **-ly,** *adv.*
non′pre·lat′ic, *adj.*
non·pre′mi·um, *n.*
non′prep·a·ra′tion, *n.*
non′pre·par′a·tive, *adj.*
non′pre·par′a·to′ry, *adj.*
non′prep·o·si′tion·al, *adj.*; **-ly,** *adv.*
non·pres′by·ter, *n.*
non′-Pres·by·te′ri·an, *adj., n.*
non·pre′sci·ent, *adj.*; **-ly,** *adv.*
non′pre·scribed′, *adj.*
non′pre·scrib′er, *n.*
non′pre·scrip′tive, *adj.*
non·pres′ence, *n.*
non′pre·sent′a·bil′i·ty, *n.*
non′pre·sent′a·ble, *adj.*; **-ble·ness,** *n.*; **-bly,** *adv.*
non·pres′en·ta′tion, *n.*
non′pres·en·ta′tion·al, *adj.*
non′pre·serv′a·ble, *adj.*
non′pres·er·va′tion, *n.*
non′pre·serv′a·tive, *adj.*
non′pres·i·den′tial, *adj.*
non·press′ing, *adj.*
non·pres′sure, *n., adv.*
non′pre·sump′tive, *adj.*; **-ly,** *adv.*
non·prev′a·lence, *n.*
non·prev′a·lent, *adj.*; **-ly,** *adv.*
non′pre·vent′a·ble, *adj.*
non′pre·vent′i·ble, *adj.*
non′pre·ven′tion, *n.*
non′pre·ven′tive, *adj.*; **-ly,** *adv.*; **-ness,** *n.*
non·priest′ly, *adj.*
non·prim′i·tive, *adj., n.*; **-ly,** *adv.*; **-ness,** *n.*
non·prin′ci·pled, *adj.*
non·print′a·ble, *adj.*
non·print′ing, *adj.*
non·priv′i·leged, *adj.*
non·priv′i·ty, *n.*, *pl.* **-ties.**
non′prob·a·bil′i·ty, *n.*, *pl.* **-ties.**
non·prob′a·ble, *adj.*; **-bly,** *adv.*
non′pro·ba′tion, *n.*
non·pro′ba·tive, *adj.*
non·pro′ba·to′ry, *adj.*
non′prob·lem·at′ic, *adj.*
non′prob·lem·at′i·cal, *adj.*; **-ly,** *adv.*
non′pro·ces′sion·al, *adj.*
non′pro·cre·a′tion, *n.*
non′pro·cre′a·tive, *adj.*
non′pro·cur′a·ble, *adj.*
non′proc·u·ra′tion, *n.*
non′pro·cure′ment, *n.*
non′pro·duc′er, *n.*
non′pro·duc′i·ble, *adj.*
non′pro·duc′ing, *adj.*
non′pro·duc′tion, *n.*
non′pro·fane′, *adj.*; **-ly,** *adv.*; **-ness,** *n.*
non′pro·fan′i·ty, *n.*, *pl.* **-ties**
non′pro·fessed′, *adj.*
non′pro·fes′sion, *n.*
non′pro·fes′sion·al·ism, *n.*
non′pro·fes·so′ri·al, *adj.*; **-ly,** *adv.*
non′prof·it·a·bil′i·ty, *n.*
non·prof′it·a·ble, *adj.*; **-ly,** *adv.*; **-ness,** *n.*
non′prof·it·eer′ing, *n.*
non′prog·nos′ti·ca′tive, *adj.*
non′pro·gres′sive, *adj., n.*; **-ly,** *adv.*; **-ness,** *n.*
non′pro·hi·bi′tion, *n.*
non′pro·hib′i·tive, *adj.*; **-ly,** *adv.*
non′pro·hib′i·to′ri·ly, *adv.*
non′pro·hib′i·to′ry, *adj.*
non′pro·ject′ing, *adj.*
non′pro·jec′tion, *n.*
non′pro·jec′tive, *adj.*
non′pro·le·tar′i·an, *adj., n.*
non′pro·le·tar′i·at, *n.*
non′pro·lif′er·ous, *adj.*
non′pro·lif′ic, *adj.*; **-ness,** *n.*
non′pro·lif′i·ca·cy, *n.*
non′pro·lif′i·cal·ly, *adv.*
non′pro·lix′, *adj.*; **-ly,** *adv.*; **-ness,** *n.*
non′pro·lix′i·ty, *n.*
non′pro·lon·ga′tion, *n.*
non·prom′i·nence, *n.*
non·prom′i·nent, *adj.*; **-ly,** *adv.*
non′pro·mis′cu·ous, *adj.*; **-ly,** *adv.*; **-ness,** *n.*
non·prom′is·so′ry, *adj.*
non′pro·mo′tion, *n.*
non′pro·mo′tive, *adj.*
non′pro·mul·ga′tion, *n.*
non′pro·nun′ci·a′tion, *n.*
non·prop′a·ga·ble, *adj.*
non′prop·a·gan′dist, *n., adj.*
non′prop·a·ga′tion, *n.*
non·prop′a·ga′tive, *adj.*
non′pro·pel′lent, *adj., n.*
non′pro·phet′ic, *adj.*
non′pro·phet′i·cal, *adj.*; **-ly,** *adv.*
non′pro·pi′ti·a·ble, *adj.*
non′pro·pi′ti·a′tion, *n.*
non′pro·pi′ti·a′tive, *adj.*
non′pro·por′tion·a·ble, *adj.*
non′pro·por′tion·al, *adj.*; **-ly,** *adv.*
non′pro·por′tion·ate, *adj.*; **-ly,** *adv.*; **-ness,** *n.*
non′pro·por′tioned, *adj.*
non′pro·pri′e·tar′y, *adj., n.*, *pl.* **-tar·ies.**
non′pro·pri′e·tor, *n.*
non′pro·pri′e·ty, *n.*
non′pro·ro·ga′tion, *n.*
non′pro·sa′ic, *adj.*; **-ness,** *n.*
non′pro·sa′i·cal·ly, *adv.*
non′pro·scrip′tion, *n.*
non′pro·scrip′tive, *adj.*; **-ly,** *adv.*
non′pros·e·cu′tion, *n.*
non·pros′pect, *n.*
non′pros·per′i·ty, *n.*
non·pros′per·ous, *adj.*; **-ly,** *adv.*; **-ness,** *n.*
non′pro·tect′ing, *adj.*
non′pro·tec′tion, *n.*
non′pro·tec′tive, *adj.*; **-ly,** *adv.*
non·pro′te·in, *n.*
non-Prot′es·tant, *n., adj.*
non′prot·es·ta′tion, *n.*
non′pro·test′ing, *adj.*
non′pro·trac′tile, *adj.*
non′pro·trac′tion, *n.*
non′pro·tru′sion, *n.*
non′pro·tru′sive, *adj.*; **-ly,** *adv.*; **-ness,** *n.*
non′pro·tu′ber·ance, *n.*
non′pro·tu′ber·an·cy, *n.*, *pl.* **-cies.**
non′pro·tu′ber·ant, *adj.*; **-ly,** *adv.*
non·prov′a·ble, *adj.*
non′pro·vid′ed, *adj.*
non·prov′i·dent, *adj.*; **-ly,** *adv.*
non′prov·i·den′tial, *adj.*; **-ly,** *adv.*
non′pro·vid′er, *n.*
non′pro·vin′cial, *adj.*; **-ly,** *adv.*
non′pro·vi′sion·al, *adj.*; **-ly,** *adv.*
non′pro·vi′sion·ar′y, *adj.*
non′prov·o·ca′tion, *n.*
non′pro·voc′a·tive, *adj.*; **-ly,** *adv.*; **-ness,** *n.*
non′prox·im′i·ty, *n.*
non·pru′dence, *n.*
non·pru′dent, *adj.*; **-ly,** *adv.*
non′pru·den′tial, *adj.*; **-ly,** *adv.*
non-Prus′sian, *n., adj.*
non′psy·chi·at′ric, *adj.*
non′psy′chic, *adj., n.*
non′psy′chi·cal, *adj.*; **-ly,** *adv.*
non′psy·cho·an′a·lyt′ic, *adj.*
non′psy·cho·an′a·lyt′i·cal, *adj.*; **-ly,** *adv.*
non′psy·cho·log′ic, *adj.*
non′psy·cho·log′i·cal, *adj.*; **-ly,** *adv.*
non′psy·cho·path′ic, *adj.*
non′psy·cho·path′i·cal·ly, *adv.*
non′psy·chot′ic, *adj.*
non·pub′lic, *adj.*
non′pub·li·ca′tion, *n.*
non′pub·lic′i·ty, *n.*
non·pub′lish·a·ble, *adj.*
non·pu′er·ile, *adj.*; **-ly,** *adv.*
non′pu·er·il′i·ty, *n.*, *pl.* **-ties.**
non·pul′mo·nar′y, *adj.*
non·pul′sat·ing, *adj.*
non′pul·sa′tion, *n.*
non·pul′sa·tive, *adj.*
non·punc′tu·al, *adj.*; **-ly,** *adv.*; **-ness,** *n.*
non·punc′tu·at′ing, *adj.*
non′punc·tu·a′tion, *n.*
non·punc′tur·a·ble, *adj.*
non·pun′gen·cy, *n.*
non·pun′gent, *adj.*; **-ly,** *adv.*
non·pun′ish·a·ble, *adj.*
non·pun′ish·ing, *adj.*
non·pun′ish·ment, *n.*
non·pu′ni·tive, *adj.*
non′pu′ni·to′ry, *adj.*
non·pur′chas·a·bil′i·ty, *n.*
non·pur′chas·a·ble, *adj.*
non·pur′chase, *n.*
non·pur′chas·er, *n.*
non′pur·ga′tion, *n.*
non·pur′ga·tive, *adj.*; **-ly,** *adv.*
non·pur′ga·to′ri·al, *adj.*
non′pu·ri·fi·ca′tion, *n.*
non·pu′ri·fy′ing, *adj.*
non′pu·ris′tic, *adj.*
non·pur′pos·ive, *adj.*; **-ly,** *adv.*; **-ness,** *n.*
non′pur·su′ance, *n.*
non′pur·su′ant, *adj.*; **-ly,** *adv.*
non·pu′ru·lence, *n.*
non·pu′ru·lent, *adj.*; **-ly,** *adv.*
non′pur·vey′ance, *n.*
non′pu·tres′cence, *n.*
non′pu·tres′cent, *adj.*
non′pu·tres′ci·ble, *adj.*
non′py·o·gen′ic, *adj.*
non-Quak′er, *n., adj.*
non-Quak′er·ish, *adj.*
non′qual·i·fi·ca′tion, *n.*
non·qual′i·fy′ing, *adj.*
non·qual′i·ta′tive, *adj.*; **-ly,** *adv.*
non·qual′i·ty, *n.*, *pl.* **-ties.**
non·quan′ti·ta′tive, *adj.*; **-ly,** *adv.*; **-ness,** *n.*
non′rab·bin′i·cal, *adj.*
non·ra′cial, *adj.*; **-ly,** *adv.*
non·ra′di·ance, *n.*
non·ra′di·an·cy, *n.*
non·ra′di·ant, *adj.*; **-ly,** *adv.*
non·ra′di·at′ing, *adj.*
non′ra·di·a′tion, *n.*
non·ra′di·a′tive, *adj.*
non·rad′i·cal, *adj., n.*; **-ness,** *n.*
non·rad′i·cal·ly, *adv.*
non′ra·di·o·ac′tive, *adj.*
non·rais′a·ble, *adj.*
non·raise′a·ble, *adj.*
non·raised′, *adj.*
non·ran′dom, *adj.*; **-ly,** *adv.*; **-ness,** *n.*
non·rang′ing, *adj.*
non′rap·port′, *n.*
non′rat·a·bil′i·ty, *n.*
non·rat′a·ble, *adj.*; **-ble·ness,** *n.*; **-bly,** *adv.*
non′rate·a·bil′i·ty, *n.*
non·rate′a·ble, *adj.*; **-ble·ness,** *n.*; **-bly,** *adv.*
non·rat′ed, *adj.*
non′rat·i·fi·ca′tion, *n.*
non·rat′i·fy′ing, *adj.*
non·ra′tion·al, *adj.*; **-ly,** *adv.*
non·ra′tion·al·ism, *n.*
non·ra′tion·al·ist, *n.*
non·ra′tion·al·is′tic, *adj.*
non·ra′tion·al·is′ti·cal, *adj.*; **-ly,** *adv.*
non·ra′tion·al′i·ty, *n.*
non·ra′tion·al·i·za′tion, *n.*
non·ra′tion·al·ized′, *adj.*
non′re·ac′tion, *n.*
non′re·ac′tion·ar′y, *adj., n., pl.* **-ar·ies.**
non′re·ac′tive, *adj.*
non′re·ac′tor, *n.*
non′read·a·bil′i·ty, *n.*
non·read′a·ble, *adj.*; **-ble·ness,** *n.*; **-bly,** *adv.*
non·read′er, *n.*
non·read′ing, *n.*
non·re′al·ism, *n.*
non·re′al·ist, *n.*
non′re·al·is′tic, *adj.*
non′re·al·is′ti·cal·ly, *adv.*
non′re·al′i·ty, *n.*, *pl.* **-ties.**
non′re·al·iz′a·ble, *adj.*
non′re·al·i·za′tion, *n.*
non·re′al·iz′ing, *adj.*
non′rea·son·a·bil′i·ty, *n.*
non·rea′son·a·ble, *adj.*; **-ble·ness,** *n.*; **-bly,** *adv.*
non·rea′son·er, *n.*
non·rea′son·ing, *adj.*
non·reb′el, *n., adj.*
non′re·bel′lion, *n.*
non′re·bel′lious, *adj.*; **-ly,** *adv.*; **-ness,** *n.*
non′re·cal′ci·trance, *n.*
non′re·cal′ci·tran·cy, *n.*
non′re·cal′ci·trant, *adj.*
non′re·ceipt′, *n.*
non′re·ceiv′a·ble, *adj.*
non′re·ceiv′ing, *adj.*
non′re·cep′tion, *n.*
non′re·cep′tive, *adj.*; **-ly,** *adv.*; **-ness,** *n.*
non′re·cep·tiv′i·ty, *n.*
non′re·cess′, *n.*
non′re·ces′sion, *n.*
non′re·ces′sive, *adj.*
non′re·cip′i·ence, *n.*
non′re·cip′i·en·cy, *n.*
non′re·cip′i·ent, *adj., n.*
non′re·cip′ro·cal, *adj., n.*; **-ly,** *adv.*
non′re·cip′ro·cat′ing, *adj.*
non′rec·i·proc′i·ty, *n.*
non′re·ci′sion, *n.*
non′re·cit′al, *n., adj.*
non′rec·i·ta′tion, *n.*
non·rec′i·ta′tive, *adj.*
non′re·claim′a·ble, *adj.*
non′rec·la·ma′tion, *n.*
non′re·clu′sive, *adj.*
non·rec′og·nized′, *adj.*
non′re·coil′, *n.*
non′re·coil′ing, *adj.*
non′rec·ol·lec′tion, *n.*
non′rec·ol·lec′tive, *adj.*
non′re·con·cil′a·bil′i·ty, *n.*
non′re·con·cil′a·ble, *adj.*; **-ble·ness,** *n.*; **-bly,** *adv.*
non′re·con·cil′i·a′tion, *n.*
non·re′course, *n.*
non′re·cov′er·a·ble, *adj.*
non′rec·tan′gu·lar, *adj.*; **-ly,** *adv.*
non′rec·tan′gu·lar′i·ty, *n.*
non′rec·ti·fi′a·ble, *adj.*
non·rec′ti·fied′, *adj.*
non′re·cu′per·a′tion, *n.*
non′re·cu′per·a′tive, *adj.*; **-ness,** *n.*
non′re·cu′per·a·to′ry, *adj.*
non′re·cur′rent, *adj.*; **-ly,** *adv.*
non′re·cur′ring, *adj.*
non′re·deem′a·ble, *adj.*
non′re·demp′ti·ble, *adj.*
non′re·demp′tion, *n.*
non′re·demp′tive, *adj.*
non′re·dress′ing, *adj., n.*
non′re·duced′, *adj.*
non′re·duc′i·bil′i·ty, *n.*
non′re·duc′i·ble, *adj.*; **-bly,** *adv.*
non′re·duc′ing, *adj.*
non′re·duc′tion, *n.*
non′re·duc′tion·al, *adj.*
non′re·duc′tive, *adj.*
non·ref′er·ence, *n.*
non′re·fill′a·ble, *adj.*
non′re·fined′, *adj.*
non′re·fine′ment, *n.*
non′re·flect′ed, *adj.*
non′re·flect′ing, *adj.*
non′re·flec′tion, *n.*
non′re·flec′tive, *adj.*; **-ly,** *adv.*; **-ness,** *n.*
non′re·flec′tor, *n.*
non′ref·or·ma′tion, *n.*
non′ref·or·ma′tion·al, *adj.*
non′re·fract′ing, *adj.*
non′re·frac′tion, *n.*
non′re·frac′tion·al, *adj.*
non′re·frac′tive, *adj.*; **-ly,** *adv.*; **-ness,** *n.*
non′re·frig′er·ant, *adj., n.*
non′re·fu′el·ing, *adj.*
non′re·fu′el·ling, *adj.*
non′re·fut′al, *n.*
non′ref·u·ta′tion, *n.*
non′re·gen′er·ate, *adj.*
non′re·gen′er·at′ing, *adj.*
non′re·gen′er·a′tion, *n.*
non′re·gen′er·a′tive, *adj.*; **-ly,** *adv.*
non′reg·i·men′tal, *adj.*
non·reg′i·ment′ed, *adj.*
non·reg′is·tered, *adj.*
non·reg′is·tra·ble, *adj.*
non′reg·is·tra′tion, *n.*
non′re·gres′sion, *n.*
non′re·gres′sive, *adj.*; **-ly,** *adv.*
non′reg·u·la′tion, *n.*
non·reg′u·la′tive, *adj.*
non·reg′u·la·to′ry, *adj.*
non′re·ha·bil′i·ta′tion, *n.*
non·reign′ing, *adj.*
non′re·im·burse′ment, *n.*
non′re·in·force′ment, *n.*
non′re·in·state′ment, *n.*
non′re·jec′tion, *n.*
non′re·join′der, *n.*
non′re·lat′ed, *adj.*
non′re·la′tion, *n.*
non′re·la′tion·al, *adj.*
non·rel′a·tive, *n., adj.*; **-ness,** *n.*
non·rel′a·tive·ly, *adv.*
non′rel·a·tiv′i·ty, *n.*

(non′rel ə ti vis′tik, non′-), *Physics.* See under **quantum mechanics** (def. 1). [NON- + RELATIVISTIC]

non rep., non repetatur.

non re·pe·ta·tur (non rep′i tā′tər), (in prescriptions) do not repeat. [< L]

non·rep·re·sen·ta·tion·al (non′rep ri zen tā′shə nəl), *adj.* not resembling any object in physical nature: *a nonrepresentational painting.* [NON- + REPRESENTATIONAL] —**non′rep·re·sen·ta′tion·al·ism,** *n.*

non·res·i·dent (non rez′i dənt), *adj.* **1.** not resident in a particular place. **2.** not residing where official duties require a person to reside. —*n.* **3.** a person who is nonresident. [NON- + RESIDENT] —**non·res′i·dence, non·res′i·den·cy,** *n.*

non·re·sis·tance (non′ri zis′təns), *n.* the policy or practice of not resisting violence or tyrannical authority by force. [NON- + RESISTANCE]

non·re·sis·tant (non′ri zis′tənt), *adj.* **1.** not resistant; passively obedient. —*n.* **2.** a person who does not resist force. **3.** a person who maintains that violence should not be resisted by force. [NON- + RESISTANT]

non·re·straint (non′ri strānt′), *n.* **1.** *Psychiatry.* the treatment of the mentally ill without mechanical means of restraint. **2.** absence of restraint. [NON- + RESTRAINT]

non·re·stric·tive (non′ri strik′tiv), *adj. Gram.* descriptive of a modified element rather than limiting its meaning: *a nonrestrictive word.* Cf. **restrictive** (def. 4). [NON- + RESTRICTIVE]

non′restric′tive clause′, *Gram.* See **descriptive clause.**

non·rig·id (non rij′id), *adj.* **1.** not rigid. **2.** designating a type of airship having a flexible gas container without a supporting structure and held in shape only by the pressure of the gas within. [NON- + RIGID]

non·sched·uled (non skej′o͞old; *Brit.,* non shed′yo͞old), *adj.* **1.** not scheduled; not entered on or having a schedule; unscheduled: *nonscheduled delays.* **2.** of, pertaining to, or characteristic of a nonscheduled airline. [NON- + SCHEDULED]

non′scheduled air′line, an airline authorized to carry passengers or freight between specified points as demand warrants, rather than on a regular schedule.

non·sec·tar·i·an (non′sek târ′ē ən), *adj.* not affiliated with any specific religious denomination. [NON- + SECTARIAN]

non·sense (non′sens), *n.* **1.** that which makes no sense or is lacking in sense. **2.** words without sense or conveying absurd ideas. **3.** senseless or absurd action; foolish conduct, notions, etc.: *to have tolerated enough nonsense.* **4.** something absurd; an absurdity: *the utter nonsense of such a suggestion.* **5.** anything of trifling importance or of little or no use. [NON- + SENSE] —**non·sen·si·cal** (non sen′si kəl), *adj.* —**non·sen′si·cal·ly,** *adv.* —**non·sen′si·cal·ness, non·sen·si·cal·i·ty** (non′sen si kal′i tē), *n.*
—**Syn. 1.** twaddle, balderdash, moonshine, absurdity.

non seq., non sequitur.

non se·qui·tur (nōn se′kwi to͝or′; *Eng.* non sek′wi tər), *Latin.* an inference or a conclusion which does not follow from the premises. [lit., it does not follow]

non·sin·gu·lar (non sing′gyə lər), *adj. Math.* **1.** not singular. **2.** of or pertaining to a one-to-one linear transformation from a vector space to itself. **3.** of or

non′rel·a·tiv′i·ty, *n.*
non′re·lax·a′tion, *n.*
non′re·lease′, *n.*
non′re·lent′ing, *adj.*
non′re·li′a·bil′i·ty, *n.*
non′re·li′a·ble, *adj.;* **-ble·ness,** *n.;* **-bly,** *adv.*
non′re·li′ance, *n.*
non′re·liev′ing, *adj.*
non′re·li′gion, *n.*
non′re·li′gious, *adj.;* **-ly,** *adv.;* **-ness,** *n.*
non′re·lin′quish·ment, *n.*
non′re·me′di·a·bil′i·ty, *n.*
non′re·me′di·a·ble, *adj.;* **-bly,** *adv.*
non′re·me′di·al, *adj.;* **-ly,** *adv.*
non·rem′e·dy, *n., pl.* **-dies.**
non′re·mem′brance, *n.*
non′re·mis′si·ble, *adj.*
non′re·mis′sion, *n.*
non′re·mit′ta·ble, *adj.;* **-bly,** *adv.*
non′re·mon′strance, *n.*
non′re·mon′strant, *adj.*
non′re·mov′a·ble, *adj.*
non′re·mu′ner·a′tion, *n.*
non′re·mu′ner·a′tive, *adj.;* **-ly,** *adv.*
non′ren·di′tion, *n.*
non′re·new′a·ble, *adj.*
non′re·new′al, *n.*
non′re·nounc′ing, *adj.*
non′re·nun′ci·a′tion, *n.*
non′re·pair′, *n.*
non′re·pair′a·ble, *adj.*
non·rep′a·ra·ble, *adj.*
non′rep·a·ra′tion, *n.*
non′re·pa′tri·a·ble, *adj.*
non′re·pa′tri·a′tion, *n.*
non′re·pay′a·ble, *adj.*
non′re·pay′ing, *adj.*
non′re·peal′a·ble, *adj.*
non′re·peat′, *n.*
non′re·peat′ed, *adj.*
non′re·peat′er, *n.*
non′re·pel′lence, *n.*
non′re·pel′len·cy, *n.*
non′re·pel′lent, *adj.*
non′re·pel′ler, *n.*
non′re·pent′ance, *n.*
non′re·pent′ant, *adj.;* **-ly,** *adv.*
non′rep·e·ti′tion, *n.*
non′rep·e·ti′tious, *adj.;* **-ly,** *adv.;* **-ness,** *n.*
non′re·pet′i·tive, *adj.;* **-ly,** *adv.*
non′re·place′a·ble, *adj.*
non′re·place′ment, *n.*
non·rep′li·cate, *adj.*
non·rep′li·cat′ed, *adj.*
non′rep·li·ca′tion, *n.*
non′re·port′a·ble, *adj.*
non′rep·re·hen′si·bil′i·ty, *n.*
non′rep·re·hen′si·ble, *adj.;* **-ble·ness,** *n.;* **-bly,** *adv.*
non′rep·re·sent′a·ble, *adj.*
non′rep·re·sen·ta′tion, *n.*
non′rep·re·sent′a·tive, *n., adj.;* **-ly,** *adv.;* **-ness,** *n.*
non′re·pressed′, *adj.*
non′re·press′i·ble, *adj.;* **-ble·ness,** *n.;* **-bly,** *adv.*
non′re·pres′sion, *n.*
non′re·pres′sive, *adj.*
non′re·pris′al, *n.*
non′re·pro·duc′i·ble, *adj.*
non′re·pro·duc′tion, *n.*
non′re·pro·duc′tive, *adj.;* **-ly,** *adv.;* **-ness,** *n.*
non′re·pub′li·can, *adj., n.*
non′re·pu′di·a·ble, *adj.*
non′re·pu′di·a′tion, *n.*
non′re·pu′di·a′tive, *adj.*
non·rep′ut·a·ble, *adj.;* **-bly,** *adv.*
non′re·quir′a·ble, *adj.*
non′re·quire′ment, *n.*
non·req′ui·site, *adj., n.;* **-ly,** *adv.;* **-ness,** *n.*
non′req·ui·si′tion, *n.*
non′re·quit′al, *n.*
non′re·scis′si·ble, *adj.*
non′re·scis′sion, *n.*
non′re·scis′so·ry, *adj.*
non·res′cue, *n.*
non′re·sem′blance, *n.*
non′re·serv′a·ble, *adj.*
non′res·er·va′tion, *n.*
non′re·serve′, *n., adj.*
non′res·i·den′tial, *adj.*
non′re·sid′u·al, *adj.*
non′res·ig·na′tion, *n.*
non′re·sil′i·ence, *n.*
non′re·sil′i·en·cy, *n.*
non′re·sil′i·ent, *adj.;* **-ly,** *adv.*
non′re·sist′i·bil′i·ty, *n.*
non′re·sist′i·ble, *adj.*
non′re·sist′ing, *adj.*
non′re·sis′tive, *adj.*
non′res·o·lu′tion, *n.*
non′re·solv′a·bil′i·ty, *n.*
non′re·solv′a·ble, *adj.;* **-ness,** *n.;* **-bly,** *adv.*
non·res′o·nant, *adj.;* **-ly,** *adv.*
non′re·spect′a·bil′i·ty, *n., pl.* **-ties.**
non′re·spect′a·ble, *adj.;* **-ble·ness,** *n.;* **-bly,** *adv.*
non′re·spir′a·ble, *adj.*
non′re·spon′si·bil′i·ty, *n., pl.* **-ties.**
non′re·spon′si·ble, *adj.;* **-ble·ness,** *n.;* **-bly,** *adv.*
non′re·spon′sive, *adj.;* **-ly,** *adv.*
non′res·ti·tu′tion, *n.*
non′res·to·ra′tion, *n.*
non′re·stor′a·tive, *adj., n.*
non′re·strained′, *adj.*
non′re·strict′ed, *adj.;* **-ly,** *adv.*
non′re·strict′ing, *adj.*
non′re·stric′tion, *n.*
non′re·sump′tion, *n.*
non′res·ur·rec′tion, *n.*
non′res·ur·rec′tion·al, *adj.*
non′re·sus′ci·ta·ble, *adj.*
non′re·sus′ci·ta′tion, *n.*
non′re·sus′ci·ta′tive, *adj.*
non·re′tail, *adj.*
non′re·tain′a·ble, *adj.*
non′re·tain′ment, *n.*
non′re·tal′i·a′tion, *n.*
non′re·tar·da′tion, *n.*
non′re·tard′a·tive, *adj.*
non′re·tard′a·to′ry, *adj.*
non′re·tard′ed, *adj.*
non′re·tard′ment, *n.*
non′re·ten′tion, *n.*
non′re·ten′tive, *adj.;* **-ly,** *adv.;* **-ness,** *n.*
non·ret′i·cence, *n.*
non·ret′i·cent, *adj.;* **-ly,** *adv.*
non·ret′i·nal, *adj.*
non′re·tired′, *adj.*
non′re·tire′ment, *n.*
non′re·tir′ing, *adj.*
non′re·trace′a·ble, *adj.*
non′re·trac′tile, *adj.*
non′re·trac·til′i·ty, *n.*
non′re·trac′tion, *n.*
non′re·trench′ment, *n.*
non′ret·ro·ac′tive, *adj.;* **-ly,** *adv.*
non′ret·ro·ac·tiv′i·ty, *n.*
non′re·turn′, *n.*
non′re·turn′a·ble, *adj.*
non′re·val′u·a′tion, *n.*
non′re·veal′ing, *adj.*
non′rev·e·la′tion, *n.*
non′re·venge′, *n.*
non′re·veng′er, *n.*
non·rev′e·nue′, *adj.*
non·rev′er·ence, *n.*
non·rev′er·ent, *adj.;* **-ly,** *adv.*
non′rev·er·en′tial, *adj.;* **-ly,** *adv.*
non′re·verse′, *adj., n.*
non′re·versed′, *adj.*
non′re·vers′i·bil′i·ty, *n.*
non′re·vers′i·ble, *adj.;* **-ble·ness,** *n.;* **-bly,** *adv.*
non′re·vers′ing, *adj.*
non′re·ver′sion, *n.*
non′re·vert′i·ble, *adj.*
non′re·ver′tive, *adj.*
non′re·view′a·ble, *adj.*
non′re·vi′sion, *n.*
non′re·viv′al, *n.*
non′re·viv′al·ist, *n.*
non′rev·o·ca·bil′i·ty, *n.*
non·rev′o·ca·ble, *adj.;* **-bly,** *adv.*
non′rev·o·ca′tion, *n.*
non′re·vok′a·ble, *adj.*
non′re·volt′ing, *adj.;* **-ly,** *adv.*
non′rev·o·lu′tion, *n.*
non′rev·o·lu′tion·ar′y, *adj., n., pl.* **-ar·ies.**
non′re·volv′ing, *adj.*
non′rhe·tor′i·cal, *adj.;* **-ly,** *adv.*
non′rheu·mat′ic, *adj., n.*
non·rhyme′, *n.*
non·rhymed′, *adj.*
non·rhym′ing, *adj.*
non·rhythm′, *n.*
non·rhyth′mic, *adj.*
non·rhyth′mi·cal, *adj.;* **-ly,** *adv.*
non·rid′ing, *adj., n.*
non·ri′ot·er, *n.*
non·ri′ot·ing, *adj.*
non′ri·par′i·an, *adj., n.*
non′rit·u·al·is′tic, *adj.*
non′rit·u·al·is′ti·cal·ly, *adv.*
non·ri′val, *n., adj.*
non-Ro′man, *adj., n.*
non′ro·man′tic, *adj., n.*
non′ro·man′ti·cal·ly, *adv.*
non′ro·man′ti·cism, *n.*
non·ro′tat·a·ble, *adj.*
non·ro′tat·ing, *adj.*
non′ro·ta′tion, *n.*
non′ro·ta′tion·al, *adj.*
non·ro′ta·tive, *adj.*
non·round′, *adj.*
non·rous′ing, *adj.*
non′rou·tine′, *adj., n.*
non·roy′al, *adj.;* **-ly,** *adv.*
non·roy′al·ist, *n.*
non·roy′al·ty, *n.*
non·rub′ber, *n.*
non′ru·di·men′tal, *adj.*
non′ru·di·men′ta·ri·ly, *adv.*
non′ru·di·men′ta·ri·ness, *n.*
non′ru·di·men′ta·ry, *adj.*
non·ru′in·a·ble, *adj.*
non·ru′in·ous, *adj.;* **-ly,** *adv.;* **-ness,** *n.*
non·rul′ing, *n., adj.*
non·ru′mi·nant, *n., adj.*
non·ru′mi·nat′ing, *adj.;* **-ly,** *adv.*
non′ru·mi·na′tion, *n.*
non′ru·mi·na′tive, *adj.*
non·run′, *adj.*
non·rup′tur·a·ble, *adj.*
non·rup′ture, *n.*
non·ru′ral, *adj.;* **-ly,** *adv.*
non-Rus′sian, *adj., n.*
non·rust′a·ble, *adj.*
non·rus′tic, *adj.*
non·rus′ti·cal·ly, *adv.*
non′-Sab·bat′ic, *adj., n.*
non′-Sab·bat′i·cal, *adj., n.;* **-ly,** *adv.*
non·sac′cha·rin, *adj., n.*
non·sac′cha·rine, *adj., n.*
non′sac·cha·rin′i·ty, *n.*
non′sac·er·do′tal, *adj.;* **-ly,** *adv.*
non′sac·ra·men′tal, *adj.*
non·sa′cred, *adj.;* **-ly,** *adv.;* **-ness,** *n.*
non·sac′ri·fice′, *n.*
non′sac·ri·fi′cial, *adj.*
non′sac·ri·fic′ing, *adj.*
non′sac·ri·le′gious, *adj.;* **-ly,** *adv.;* **-ness,** *n.*
non·sail′or, *n.*
non′sal·a·bil′i·ty, *n.*
non·sal′a·ble, *adj.;* **-bly,** *adv.*
non·sal′a·ried, *adj.*
non·sale′, *n.*
non′sale·a·bil′i·ty, *n.*
non·sale′a·ble, *adj.;* **-bly,** *adv.*
non·sa′line, *adj.*
non′sa·lin′i·ty, *n.*
non′sa·lu′bri·ous, *adj.;* **-ly,** *adv.;* **-ness,** *n.*
non·sal′u·tar′i·ly, *adv.*
non·sal′u·tar′i·ness, *n.*
non·sal′u·tar′y, *adj.*
non′sal·u·ta′tion, *n.*
non·sal′vage·a·ble, *adj.*
non′sal·va′tion, *n.*
non·san′a·tive, *adj.*
non′sanc·ti·fi·ca′tion, *n.*
non′sanc·ti·mo′ni·ous, *adj.;* **-ly,** *adv.;* **-ness,** *n.*
non·sanc′ti·mo′ny, *n.*
non·sanc′tion, *n.*
non·sanc′ti·ty, *n., pl.* **-ties.**
non·sane′, *adj.;* **-ly,** *adv.;* **-ness,** *n.*
non·san′guine, *adj.;* **-ly,** *adv.;* **-ness,** *n.*
non·san′i·ty, *n.*
non′-San·skrit′ic, *adj.*
non′sa·pon′i·fi′a·ble, *adj.*
non′sa·pon′i·fi·ca′tion, *n.*
non′sap·o·rif′ic, *adj.*
non′sa·ti·a·bil′i·ty, *n.*
non·sa′ti·a·ble, *adj.*
non′sa·ti·a′tion, *n.*
non·sat′ire, *n.*
non′sa·tir′ic, *adj.*
non′sa·tir′i·cal, *adj.;* **-ly,** *adv.;* **-ness,** *n.*
non·sat′i·riz′ing, *adj.*
non′sat·is·fac′tion, *n.*
non·sat′is·fy′ing, *adj.*
non·sat′u·rat′ed, *adj.*
non′sat·u·ra′tion, *n.*
non·sav′ing, *adj.*
non·saw′ing, *adj.*
non-Sax′on, *n., adj.*
non·scald′ing, *adj.*
non·scal′ing, *adj.*
non·scan′dal·ous, *adj.;* **-ly,** *adv.*
non′-Scan·di·na′vi·an, *adj., n.*
non·scar′ci·ty, *n., pl.* **-ties.**
non·scent′ed, *adj.*
non′sche·mat′ic, *adj.*
non′sche·mat′i·cal·ly, *adv.*
non·sche′ma·tized′, *adj.*
non′schis·mat′ic, *adj.*
non′schis·mat′i·cal, *adj.*
non′schiz·o·phren′ic, *adj.*
non·schol′ar, *n.;* **-ly,** *adj.*
non′scho·las′tic, *adj.*
non′scho·las′ti·cal, *adj.;* **-ly,** *adv.*
non·school′ing, *n.*
non′sci·at′ic, *adj.*
non·sci′ence, *n.*
non′sci·en·tif′ic, *adj.*
non′sci·en·tif′i·cal·ly, *adv.*
non·sci′en·tist, *n.*
non·scor′ing, *adj.*
non·scrap′ing, *adj.*
non·scrip′tur·al, *adj.*
non·scru′ti·ny, *n., pl.* **-nies.**
non·sculp′tur·al, *adj.;* **-ly,** *adv.*
non·sculp′tured, *adj.*
non·sea′son·a·ble, *adj.;* **-ble·ness,** *n.;* **-bly,** *adv.*
non·sea′son·al, *adj.;* **-ly,** *adv.*
non·sea′soned, *adj.*
non′se·ces′sion, *n.*
non′se·ces′sion·al, *adj.*
non′se·clud′ed, *adj.;* **-ly,** *adv.;* **-ness,** *n.*
non′se·clu′sion, *n.*
non′se·clu′sive, *adj.;* **-ly,** *adv.;* **-ness,** *n.*
non·se′cre·cy, *n., pl.* **-cies.**
non·se′cret, *adj., n.;* **-ly,** *adv.*
non′sec·re·tar′i·al, *adj.*
non′se·cre′tion, *n.*
non′se·cre′tion·ar′y, *adj.*
non′se·cre′tive, *adj.;* **-ly,** *adv.*
non′se·cre′to·ry, *adj., n., pl.* **-ries.**
non·sec′tion·al, *adj.;* **-ly,** *adv.*
non′sec·to′ri·al, *adj.*
non·sec′u·lar, *adj.*
non′se·cu′ri·ty, *n., pl.* **-ties.**
non·sed′en·tar′i·ly, *adv.*
non·sed′en·tar′i·ness, *n.*
non·sed′en·tar′y, *adj.*
non′se·di′tious, *adj.;* **-ly,** *adv.;* **-ness,** *n.*
non′seg·men′tal, *adj.;* **-ly,** *adv.*
non·seg′men·tar′y, *adj.*
non′seg·men·ta′tion, *n.*
non·seg′ment·ed, *adj.*
non·seg′re·ga·ble, *adj.*
non·seg′re·gat′ed, *adj.*
non′seg·re·ga′tion, *n.*
non·seg′re·ga′tive, *adj.*
non·seis′mic, *adj.*
non·sei′zure, *n.*
non′se·lect′ed, *adj.*
non′se·lec′tion, *n.*
non′se·lec′tive, *adj.*
non′self-gov′ern·ing, *adj.*
non·sell′ing, *adj.*
non′se·man′tic, *adj.*
non′se·man′ti·cal·ly, *adv.*
non·Sem′ite, *n.*
non′-Se·mit′ic, *adj.*
non′sen·a·to′ri·al, *adj.*
non·sen′sate, *adj.*
non′sen·sa′tion, *n.*
non′sen·sa′tion·al·is′tic, *adj.*
non′sen·si·bil′i·ty, *n.*
non·sen′si·ble, *adj.;* **-ble·ness,** *n.;* **-bly,** *adv.*
non·sen′si·tive, *adj.;* **-ly,** *adv.;* **-ness,** *n.*
non′sen·si·tiv′i·ty, *n., pl.* **-ties.**
non′sen·si·ti·za′tion, *n.*
non·sen′si·tized′, *adj.*
non·sen′si·tiz′ing, *adj.*
non′sen·so′ri·al, *adj.*
non·sen′so·ry, *adj.*
non·sen′su·al, *adj.;* **-ly,** *adv.*
non′sen·su·al·is′tic, *adj.*
non′sen·su·al′i·ty, *n.*
non·sen′su·ous, *adj.;* **-ly,** *adv.;* **-ness,** *n.*
non′sen·ten′tious, *adj.;* **-ly,** *adv.;* **-ness,** *n.*
non·sen′tience, *n.*
non·sen′tien·cy, *n.*
non·sen′tient, *adj.;* **-ly,** *adv.*
non′sep·a·ra·bil′i·ty, *n.*
non·sep′a·ra·ble, *adj.;* **-ble·ness,** *n.;* **-bly,** *adv.*
non·sep′a·rat′ing, *adj.*
non′sep·a·ra′tion, *n.*
non·sep′a·ra′tive, *adj.*
non·sep′tate, *adj.*
non·sep′tic, *adj.*
non′se·qua′cious, *adj.;* **-ly,** *adv.;* **-ness,** *n.*
non′se·quac′i·ty, *n.*
non·se′quent, *adj.*
non′se·quen′tial, *adj.;* **-ly,** *adv.*
non′se·ques′tered, *adj.*
non′se·ques·tra′tion, *n.*
non′se·raph′ic, *adj.*
non′se·raph′i·cal, *adj.;* **-ly,** *adv.*
non·se′ri·al, *n., adj.;* **-ly,** *adv.*
non·se′ri·ate, *adj.;* **-ly,** *adv.*
non·se′ri·ous, *adj.;* **-ly,** *adv.;* **-ness,** *n.*
non·se′rous, *adj.*
non′serv·ice·a·bil′i·ty, *n.*
non·serv′ice·a·ble, *adj.;* **-ble·ness,** *n.;* **-bly,** *adv.*
non·ser′vile, *adj.;* **-ly,** *adv.;* **-ness,** *n.*
non·set′ting, *adj.*
non·set′tle·ment, *n.*
non·sev′er·a·ble, *adj.*
non·sev′er·ance, *n.*
non′se·ver′i·ty, *n., pl.* **-ties.**
non·sex′linked′, *adj.*
non·sex′u·al, *adj.;* **-ly,** *adv.*
non′-Shake·spear′e·an, *adj.*
non′-Shake·spear′i·an, *adj.*
non·shar′ing, *adj., n.*
non·shat′ter, *n.*
non·shat′ter·ing, *adj.*
non·shed′ding, *adj.*
non·ship′per, *n.*
non·ship′ping, *adj.*
non·shred′ding, *adj.*
non·shrink′a·ble, *adj.*
non·shrink′ing, *adj.;* **-ly,** *adv.*
non·sib′i·lance, *n.*
non·sib′i·lan·cy, *n.*
non·sib′i·lant, *adj., n.;* **-ly,** *adv.*
non·sic′ca·tive, *adj., n.*
non′si·de′re·al, *adj.*
non·sign′a·ble, *adj.*
non·sig′na·to′ry, *adj., n., pl.* **-ries.**
non′sig·nif′i·cance, *n.*
non′sig·nif′i·can·cy, *n.*
non′sig·nif′i·cant, *adj.;* **-ly,** *adv.*
non′sig·ni·fi·ca′tion, *n.*
non′sig·nif′i·ca′tive, *adj.*
non·sil′i·cate, *n.*
non′si·li′ceous, *adj.*
non′si·li′cious, *adj.*
non·sil′ver, *n., adj.*
non·sim′i·lar, *adj.;* **-ly,** *adv.*
non′sim·i·lar′i·ty, *n.*
non′si·mil′i·tude′, *n.*
non′sim·plic′i·ty, *n.*
non′sim·pli·fi·ca′tion, *n.*
non·sim′u·lar, *n., adj.*
non·sim′u·late, *adj.*
non′sim·u·la′tion, *n.*
non·sim′u·la′tive, *adj.*
non′sin·gu·lar′i·ty, *n., pl.* **-ties.**

pertaining to a matrix having a determinant not equal to zero. [NON- + SINGULAR]

non·sked (non sked′), *n. Informal.* a nonscheduled airline: *He got his training with the nonskeds.* [NON- + *sked* (short for SCHEDULE)]

non·skid (non′skid′), *adj.* having the wheel rim or tire with a ridged or otherwise skid-resistant surface. [NON- + SKID]

non·smok·er (non smō′kər), *n.* a person who does not smoke. [NON- + SMOKER] —**non·smok′ing,** *adj.*

non·sol·vent (non sol′vənt), *n. Chem.* a substance incapable of dissolving a given component of a solution or mixture. [NON- + SOLVENT] —**non·sol′ven·cy,** *n.*

non·stand·ard (non′stan′dərd), *adj.* differing in usage from the speech or writing of those whose language is generally considered to be correct or preferred: *nonstandard pronunciation; nonstandard English.* [NON- + STANDARD]

non·stop (non′stop′), *adj., adv.* without a single stop en route: *a nonstop bus; to fly nonstop from New York to Paris.* [NON- + STOP]

non·stri·at·ed (non strī′ā tid), *adj.* not striated; unstriped, as certain muscular tissue. [NON- + STRIATED]

non·such (non′such′), *n.* nonesuch.

non·suit (non′sōōt′), *Law.* —*n.* **1.** a judgment given against a plaintiff who neglects to prosecute, or who fails to show a legal cause of action or to bring sufficient evidence. —*v.t.* **2.** to subject to a nonsuit. [NON- + SUIT; r. ME *nounsuyt* < AF *nounsute*]

non·sul·fide (non sul′fīd), *adj.* (of minerals) not containing a sulfide. Also, **non·sul′phide.** [NON- + SULFIDE]

non·sup·port (non′sə pôrt′, -pōrt′), *n. Law.* failure to support a wife, child, or other dependent as required by law. [NON- + SUPPORT]

---

non·sink′a·ble, *adj.*
non·sis′ter, *n., adj.*
non·skel′e·tal, *adj.;* **-ly,** *adv.*
non·skep′tic, *adj., n.*
non·skep′ti·cal, *adj.*
non·skilled′, *adj.*
non·skip′ping, *adj., n.*
non·slan′der·ous, *adj.*
non·slave′hold′ing, *adj., n.*
non-Slav′ic, *adj.*
non·slip′, *adj.*
non·slip′per·y, *adj.*
non·slip′ping, *adj., n.*
non·so′ber, *adj.;* **-ly,** *adv.;* **-ness,** *n.*
non·so′ber·ing, *adj.*
non′so·bri′e·ty, *n.*
non′so·cia·bil′i·ty, *n.*
non·so′cia·ble, *adj.;* **-ble·ness,** *n.;* **-bly,** *adv.*
non·so′cial, *adj.;* **-ly,** *adv.;* **-ness,** *n.*
non·so′cial·ist, *n., adj.*
non′so·cial·is′tic, *adj.*
non′so·ci·al′i·ty, *n.*
non′so·ci′e·tal, *adj.*
non′so·ci′e·ty, *n.*
non′so·ci·o·log′i·cal, *adj.*
non·so′lar, *adj.*
non·sol′dier, *n.*
non′so·lic′i·ta′tion, *n.*
non′so·lic′i·tous, *adj.;* **-ly,** *adv.;* **-ness,** *n.*
non·sol′id, *adj., n.;* **-ly,** *adv.*
non′sol·i·dar′i·ty, *n.*
non′so·lid′i·fi·ca′tion, *n.*
non′so·lid′i·fied′, *adj.*
non′so·lid′i·fy′ing, *adj.*
non·sol′u·ble, *adj.;* **-ble·ness,** *n.;* **-bly,** *adv.*
non′so·lu′tion, *n.*
non′solv·a·bil′i·ty, *n.*
non·solv′a·ble, *adj.;* **-ble·ness,** *n.*
non·so′nant, *adj., n.*
non′so·phis′tic, *adj.*
non′so·phis′ti·cal, *adj.;* **-ly,** *adv.;* **-ness,** *n.*
non′sop·or·if′ic, *adj., n.*
non·sov′er·eign, *n., adj.;* **-ly,** *adv.*
non·spa′cious, *adj.;* **-ly,** *adv.;* **-ness,** *n.*
non·spall′ing, *adj.*
non-Span′ish, *adj., n.*
non·spar′ing, *adj.*
non·spark′ing, *adj.*
non·spar′kling, *adj.*
non-Spar′tan, *adj., n.*
non·spa′tial, *adj.;* **-ly,** *adv.*
non·spa·ti·al′i·ty, *n.*
non·speak′er, *n.*
non·speak′ing, *adj.*
non·spe′cial, *adj., n.;* **-ly,** *adv.*
non·spe′cial·ist, *n.*
non·spe′cial·ized′, *adj.*
non·spe′cial·iz′ing, *adj.*
non·spec′i·fi′a·ble, *adj.*
non′spe·cif′ic, *adj.*
non′spe·cif′i·cal·ly, *adv.*
non′spec·i·fi·ca′tion, *n.*
non′spec·i·fic′i·ty, *n.*
non·spec′i·fied′, *adj.*
non·spe′cious, *adj.;* **-ly,** *adv.;* **-ness,** *n.*
non′spec·tac′u·lar, *adj.;* **-ly,** *adv.*
non·spec′tral, *adj.;* **-ly,** *adv.*
non′spec·tral′i·ty, *n.*
non′spec·u·la′tion, *n.*
non·spec′u·la′tive, *adj.;* **-ly,** *adv.;* **-ness,** *n.*
non·spec′u·la·to′ry, *adj.*
non·spher′al, *adj.*
non·spher′ic, *adj.*
non·spher′i·cal, *adj.;* **-ly,** *adv.*
non′spher·i·cal′i·ty, *n.*
non·spill′, *adj.*
non·spill′a·ble, *adj.*
non·spi′nal, *adj.*
non·spin′ning, *n., adj.*
non·spi′nose, *adj.;* **-ly,** *adv.*
non′spi·nos′i·ty, *n.*
non·spin′y, *adj.*
non·spi′ral, *adj., n.*
non·spir′it, *n.*
non·spir′it·ed, *adj.;* **-ly,** *adv.;* **-ness,** *n.*
non·spir′it·ous, *adj.*
non·spir′it·u·al, *adj., n.;* **-ly,** *adv.;* **-ness,** *n.*
non·spir·it·u·al′i·ty, *n.*
non·spir′it·u·ous, *adj.;* **-ness,** *n.*
non′spon·ta′ne·ous, *adj.;* **-ly,** *adv.;* **-ness,** *n.*
non·spore′-form′ing, *adj.*
non·sport′ing, *adj.;* **-ly,** *adv.*
non·spot′ta·ble, *adj.*
non·sprout′ing, *adj.*
non·spu′ri·ous, *adj.;* **-ly,** *adv.;* **-ness,** *n.*
non·sta′bile, *adj.*
non′sta·bil′i·ty, *n.*
non·sta′ble, *adj.;* **-ble·ness,** *n.;* **-bly,** *adv.*
non·stain′a·ble, *adj.*
non·stain′er, *n.*
non·stain′ing, *adj.*
non·stamp′a·ble, *adj.*
non·stand′ard·ized′, *adj.*
non′stan·za′ic, *adj.*
non·sta′ple, *n.*
non·start′er, *n.*
non·start′ing, *adj.*
non·state′ment, *n.*
non·stat′ic, *adj.*
non·sta′tion·ar′y, *adj., n., pl.* **-ar·ies.**
non′sta·tis′tic, *adj.*
non′sta·tis′ti·cal, *adj.;* **-ly,** *adv.*
non·stat′u·ta·ble, *adj.*
non·stat′u·to′ry, *adj.*
non·stel′lar, *adj.*
non·ster′e·o·typed′, *adj.*
non′ster·e·o·typ′ic, *adj.*
non′ster·e·o·typ′i·cal, *adj.*
non·ster′ile, *adj.;* **-ly,** *adv.*
non′ste·ril′i·ty, *n.*
non′ster·i·li·za′tion, *n.*
non·stick′y, *adj.*
non·stim′u·la·ble, *adj.*
non·stim′u·lant, *n., adj.*
non·stim′u·lat′ing, *adj.*
non′stim·u·la′tion, *n.*
non·stim′u·la′tive, *adj.*
non′stip·u·la′tion, *n.*
non·stock′, *n., adj.*
non-Sto′ic, *adj., n.*
non·sto′i·cal, *adj.;* **-ly,** *adv.;* **-ness,** *n.*
non·stoop′ing, *adj.*
non·stor′a·ble, *adj.*
non·stor′age, *n.*
non′stra·te′gic, *adj.*
non′stra·te′gi·cal, *adj.;* **-ly,** *adv.*
non·strat′i·fied′, *adj.*
non·stress′, *n.*
non·stretch′a·ble, *adj.*
non·stric′tured, *adj.*
non·strik′er, *n.*
non·strik′ing, *adj.*
non·strin′gent, *adj.*
non·striped′, *adj.*
non·stroph′ic, *adj.*
non·struc′tur·al, *adj.;* **-ly,** *adv.*
non·struc′ture, *n.*
non·struc′tured, *adj.*
non·stu′dent, *n.*
non·stud′ied, *adj.*
non·stu′di·ous, *adj.;* **-ly,** *adv.;* **-ness,** *n.*
non·stud′y, *n.*
non′stul·ti·fi·ca′tion, *n.*
non′sty·li·za′tion, *n.*
non·styl′ized, *adj.*
non·styp′tic, *adj.*
non·styp′ti·cal, *adj.*
non′stip·tic′i·ty, *n.*
non′sub·con′scious, *adj.;* **-ly,** *adv.;* **-ness,** *n.*
non·sub′ject, *n., adj.*
non′sub·ject′ed, *adj.*
non′sub·jec′ti·fi·ca′tion, *n.*
non′sub·jec′tion, *n.*
non′sub·jec′tive, *adj.;* **-ly,** *adv.;* **-ness,** *n.*
non′sub·jec·tiv′i·ty, *n.*
non·sub′ju·ga·ble, *adj.*
non′sub·ju·ga′tion, *n.*
non′sub·li·ma′tion, *n.*
non′sub·lim′i·nal, *adj.;* **-ly,** *adv.*
non′sub·merged′, *adj.*
non′sub·mer′gence, *n.*
non′sub·mer′gi·bil′i·ty, *n.*
non′sub·mer′gi·ble, *adj.*
non′sub·mers′i·ble, *adj.*
non′sub·mis′si·ble, *adj.*
non′sub·mis′sion, *n.*
non′sub·mis′sive, *adj.;* **-ly,** *adv.;* **-ness,** *n.*
non′sub·or′di·nate, *adj.*
non′sub·or′di·nat′ing, *adj.*
non′sub·or′di·na′tion, *n.*
non′sub·scrib′er, *n.*
non′sub·scrib′ing, *adj.*
non′sub·scrip′tion, *n.*
non·sub·sid′i·ar′y, *adj., n., pl.* **-ar·ies.**
non·sub′sid·ing, *adj.*
non·sub′si·dy, *n., pl.* **-dies.**
non′sub·sist′ence, *n.*
non′sub·sist′ent, *adj.*
non′sub·stan′tial, *adj.;* **-ly,** *adv.;* **-ness,** *n.*
non′sub·stan′ti·al′i·ty, *n.*
non′sub·stan′ti·a′tion, *n.*
non′sub·stan·ti′val, *adj.;* **-ly,** *adv.*
non·sub′stan·tive, *adj.;* **-ly,** *adv.;* **-ness,** *n.*
non·sub′sti·tut′ed, *adj.*
non′sub·sti·tu′tion, *n.*
non′sub·sti·tu′tion·al, *adj.;* **-ly,** *adv.*
non′sub·sti·tu′tion·ar′y, *adj.*
non·sub′sti·tu′tive, *adj.*
non·sub′tile, *adj.;* **-ly,** *adv.;* **-ness,** *n.*
non′sub·til′i·ty, *n.*
non·sub′tle, *adj.;* **-tle·ness,** *n.;* **-tly,** *adv.*
non·sub′tle·ty, *n., pl.* **-ties.**
non′sub·trac′tion, *n.*
non′sub·trac′tive, *adj.;* **-ly,** *adv.*
non′sub·ur′ban, *adj., n.*
non′sub·ver′sion, *n.*
non′sub·ver′sive, *adj.;* **-ly,** *adv.;* **-ness,** *n.*
non′suc·cess′, *n.*
non′suc·cess′ful, *adj.;* **-ly,** *adv.*
non′suc·ces′sion, *n.*
non′suc·ces′sion·al, *adj.;* **-ly,** *adv.*
non′suc·ces′sive, *adj.;* **-ly,** *adv.;* **-ness,** *n.*
non·suc′cor, *n.*
non·suc′tion, *n.*
non′suc·to′ri·al, *adj.*
non·suds′ing, *adj.*
non·suf′fer·a·ble, *adj.;* **-ble·ness,** *n.;* **-bly,** *adv.*
non·suf′fer·ance, *n.*
non·suf′frage, *n.*
non·sug′ar, *n.*
non′sug·gest′i·ble, *adj.*
non′sug·ges′tion, *n.*
non′sug·ges′tive, *adj.;* **-ly,** *adv.;* **-ness,** *n.*
non·sul′fur·ous, *adj.*
non·sul′phur·ous, *adj.*
non·sum′mons, *n.*
non′su·per·vi′sion, *n.*
non′sup·ple·men′tal, *adj.;* **-ly,** *adv.*
non′sup·ple·men′ta·ry, *adj.*
non·sup′pli·cat′ing, *adj.*
non′sup·pli·ca′tion, *n.*
non′sup·port′a·bil′i·ty, *n.*
non′sup·port′a·ble, *adj.;* **-ble·ness,** *n.;* **-bly,** *adv.*
non′sup·port′er, *n.*
non′sup·port′ing, *adj.*
non′sup·posed′, *adj.*
non′sup·pos′ing, *adj.*
non′sup·po·si′tion·al, *adj.;* **-ly,** *adv.*
non′sup·pos′i·tive, *adj., n.;* **-ly,** *adv.*
non′sup·pressed′, *adj.*
non′sup·pres′sion, *n.*
non′sup·pres′sive, *adj.;* **-ly,** *adv.;* **-ness,** *n.*
non·sup′pu·ra′tive, *adj.*
non·sur′face, *n., adj.*
non·sur′gi·cal, *adj.;* **-ly,** *adv.*
non′sur·re′al·is′tic, *adj.*
non′sur·re′al·is′ti·cal·ly, *adv.*
non′sur·ren′der, *n.*
non′sur·viv′al, *n.*
non′sur·vi′vor, *n.*
non′sus·cep′ti·bil′i·ty, *n.*
non′sus·cep′ti·ble, *adj.;* **-ble·ness,** *n.;* **-bly,** *adv.*
non′sus·cep′tive, *adj.;* **-ness,** *n.*
non′sus·cep·tiv′i·ty, *n.*
non·sus′pect, *n., adj.*
non′sus·pend′ed, *adj.*
non′sus·pen′sion, *n.*
non′sus·pen′sive, *adj.;* **-ly,** *adv.;* **-ness,** *n.*
non′sus·tain′a·ble, *adj.*
non′sus·tained′, *adj.*
non′sus·tain′ing, *adj.*
non·sus′te·nance, *n.*
non·sweat′ing, *adj.*
non-Swed′ish, *adj., n.*
non·swim′mer, *n.*
non·swim′ming, *adj.*
non-Swiss′, *adj., n.*
non′syl·lo·gis′tic, *n., adj.*
non′syl·lo·gis′ti·cal, *adj.;* **-ly,** *adv.*
non·syl′lo·giz′ing, *adj.*
non′sym·bi·ot′ic, *adj.*
non′sym·bi·ot′i·cal, *adj.;* **-ly,** *adv.*
non′sym·bol′ic, *adj.*
non′sym·bol′i·cal, *adj.;* **-ly,** *adv.;* **-ness,** *n.*
non·sym′me·try, *n., pl.* **-tries.**
non′sym·pa·thet′ic, *adj.*
non′sym·pa·thet′i·cal·ly, *adv.*
non·sym′pa·thiz′er, *n.*
non·sym′pa·thiz′ing, *adj.;* **-ly,** *adv.*
non·sym′pa·thy, *n., pl.* **-thies.**
non′sym·phon′ic, *adj.*
non′sym·phon′i·cal·ly, *adv.*
non′sym·pho′ni·ous, *adj.;* **-ly,** *adv.;* **-ness,** *n.*
non′symp·to·mat′ic, *adj.*
non′syn·chro′nal, *adj.*
non′syn·chron′ic, *adj.*
non′syn·chron′i·cal, *adj.;* **-ly,** *adv.*
non·syn′chro·nous, *adj.;* **-ly,** *adv.;* **-ness,** *n.*
non′syn·co·pa′tion, *n.*
non·syn′di·cat′ed, *adj.*
non′syn·di·ca′tion, *n.*
non′syn·es·thet′ic, *adj.*
non′syn·od′ic, *adj.*
non′syn·od′i·cal, *adj.;* **-ly,** *adv.*
non′syn·on′y·mous, *adj.;* **-ly,** *adv.*
non′syn·op′tic, *adj., n.*
non′syn·op′ti·cal, *adj.;* **-ly,** *adv.*
non′syn·tac′tic, *adj.*
non′syn·tac′ti·cal, *adj.;* **-ly,** *adv.*
non·syn′the·sis, *n., pl.* **-ses.**
non·syn′the·sized′, *adj.*
non′syn·thet′ic, *adj.*
non′syn·thet′i·cal, *adj.:* **-ly,** *adv.*
non′syn·ton′ic, *adj.*
non′syn·ton′i·cal, *adj.;* **-ly,** *adv.*
non-Syr′i·an, *adj., n.*
non′sys·tem·at′ic, *adj.*
non′sys·tem·at′i·cal, *adj.;* **-ly,** *adv.*
non·tab′u·lar, *adj.;* **-ly,** *adv.*
non·tab′u·lat′ed, *adj.*
non·tac′tic, *n., adj.*
non·tac′ti·cal, *adj.;* **-ly,** *adv.*
non·tac′tile, *adj.*
non′tac·til′i·ty, *n.*
non·tal′ent·ed, *adj.*
non·talk′a·tive, *adj.;* **-ly,** *adv.;* **-ness,** *n.*
non·tan′, *adj.*
non′tan·gen′tal, *adj.*
non′tan·gen′tial, *adj.;* **-ly,** *adv.*
non·tan′gi·ble, *adj.;* **-ble·ness,** *n.;* **-bly,** *adv.*
non·tan′nic, *adj.*
non·tan′nin, *n.*
non·tan′ning, *adj.*
non·tar′nish·a·ble, *adj.*
non·tar′nished, *adj.*
non·tar′nish·ing, *adj.*
non·tarred′, *adj.*
non-Tar′tar, *n., adj.*
non′tau·to·log′i·cal, *adj.;* **-ly,** *adv.*
non′tau·to·mer′ic, *adj.*
non′tau·tom′er·iz′a·ble, *adj.*
non·tax′, *n.*
non′tax·a·bil′i·ty, *n.*
non·tax′a·ble, *adj., n.;* **-ble·ness,** *n.;* **-bly,** *adv.*
non′tax·a′tion, *n.*
non·tax′er, *n.*
non′tax·o·nom′ic, *adj.*
non′tax·o·nom′i·cal, *adj.;* **-ly,** *adv.*
non·teach′a·bil′i·ty, *n.*
non·teach′a·ble, *adj.;* **-ble·ness,** *n.;* **-bly,** *adv.*
non·teach′er, *n.*
non·teach′ing, *adj.*
non·tech′ni·cal, *adj.;* **-ly,** *adv.;* **-ness,** *n.*
non′tech·no·log′ic, *adj.*
non′tech·no·log′i·cal, *adj.;* **-ly,** *adv.*
non·tee′to·tal·er, *n.*
non·tee′to·tal·ist, *n.*
non′tel·e·graph′ic, *adj.*
non′tel·e·graph′i·cal, *adj.;* **-ly,** *adv.*
non′tel·e·o·log′i·cal, *adj.;* **-ly,** *adv.*
non′tel·e·path′ic, *adj.*
non′tel·e·path′i·cal·ly, *adv.*
non′tel·e·phon′ic, *adj.*
non′tel·e·phon′i·cal·ly, *adv.*
non′tel·e·scop′ic, *adj.*
non·tel′e·scop′ing, *adj.*
non·tel′ic, *adj.*
non·tem′per·a·ble, *adj.*
non′tem·per·a·ment′al, *adj.;* **-ly,** *adv.*
non·tem′per·ate, *adj.;* **-ly,** *adv.;* **-ness,** *n.*
non·tem′pered, *adj.*
non·tem′po·ral, *adj., n.;* **-ly,** *adv.*
non·tem′po·rar′i·ly, *adv.*
non·tem′po·rar′i·ness, *n.*
non·tem′po·rar′y, *adj.*
non·tem′po·riz′ing, *adj.;* **-ly,** *adv.*
non′temp·ta′tion, *n.*
non′ten·a·bil′i·ty, *n.*
non·ten′a·ble, *adj.;* **-ble·ness,** *n.;* **-bly,** *adv.*
non·ten′ant, *n.*
non·ten′ant·a·ble, *adj.*
non·ten′sile, *adj.*
non′ten·sil′i·ty, *n.*
non·ten′ta·tive, *adj.;* **-ly,** *adv.;* **-ness,** *n.*
non′ten·u′ri·al, *adj.;* **-ly,** *adv.*
non·ter′mi·na·bil′i·ty, *n.*
non·ter′mi·na·ble, *adj.;* **-ble·ness,** *n.;* **-bly,** *adv.*
non·ter′mi·nal, *adj.;* **-ly,** *adv.*
non·ter′mi·na′tion, *n.*
non·ter′mi·na′tive, *adj.;* **-ly,** *adv.*
non′ter·res′tri·al, *adj., n.*
non′ter·ri·to′ri·al, *adj.;* **-ly,** *adv.*
non·ter·ri·to′ri·al′i·ty, *n.*
non·test′a·ble, *adj.*
non′tes·ta·men′ta·ry, *adj.*
non·test′ing, *adj.*
non-Teu′ton, *n., adj.*
non′-Teu·ton′ic, *adj.*
non·tex′tu·al, *adj.;* **-ly,** *adv.*
non·tex′tur·al, *adj.;* **-ly,** *adv.*
non′the·at′ric, *adj.*
non′the·at′ri·cal, *adj.;* **-ly,** *adv.*
non′the·is′tic, *adj.*
non′the·is′ti·cal, *adj.;* **-ly,** *adv.*
non′the·mat′ic, *adj.*
non′the·mat′i·cal·ly, *adv.*
non′the·o·crat′ic, *adj.*
non′the·o·crat′i·cal, *adj.;* **-ly,** *adv.*
non′the·o·log′ic, *adj.*
non′the·o·log′i·cal, *adj.;* **-ly,** *adv.*
non′the·o·ret′ic, *adj.*
non′the·o·ret′i·cal, *adj.;* **-ly,** *adv.*
non′the·o·soph′ic, *adj.*
non′the·o·soph′i·cal, *adj.;* **-ly,** *adv.*
non′ther·a·peu′tic, *adj.*
non′ther·a·peu′ti·cal, *adj.;* **-ly,** *adv.*
non·ther′mal, *adj.;* **-ly,** *adv.*
non′ther·mo·plas′tic, *adj., n.*
non·think′er, *n.*
non·think′ing, *adj.*
non′tho·rac′ic, *adj.*
non·thread′ed, *adj.*
non·threat′en·ing, *adj.;* **-ly,** *adv.*
non·tid′al, *adj.*
non·till′a·ble, *adj.*
non·tim′bered, *adj.*
non·tint′ed, *adj.*
non′ti·tan·if′er·ous, *adj.*
non·ti′tled, *adj.*
non·tit′u·lar, *adj.;* **-ly,** *adv.*
non·tol′er·a·ble, *adj.;* **-ble·ness,** *n.;* **-bly,** *adv.*
non·tol′er·ance, *n.*
non·tol′er·ant, *adj.;* **-ly,** *adv.*
non·tol′er·at′ed, *adj.*
non′tol·er·a′tion, *n.*
non·tol′er·a′tive, *adj.*
non′to·nal′i·ty, *n.*
non·toned′, *adj.*
non·ton′ic, *adj.*
non′top·o·graph′i·cal, *adj.*
non·tor′tuous, *adj.;* **-ly,** *adv.*
non′to·tal′i·tar′i·an, *adj.*
non·tour′ist, *n.*
non·tox′ic, *adj.*
non·tox′i·cal·ly, *adv.*
non′trace·a·bil′i·ty, *n.*
non·trace′a·ble, *adj.;* **-ble·ness,** *n.;* **-bly,** *adv.*
non′trac·ta·bil′i·ty, *n.*
non·trac′ta·ble, *adj.;* **-ble·ness,** *n.;* **-bly,** *adv.*
non·trac′tion, *n.*
non·trade′, *n.*
non·trad′er, *n.*
non·trad′ing, *adj.*
non′tra·di′tion, *n.*
non′tra·di′tion·al, *adj.;* **-ly,** *adv.*
non′tra·di′tion·ar′y, *adj.*
non′tra·di′tion·al·ist, *n., adj.*
non′tra·di′tion·al·is′tic, *adj.*
non·trag′e·dy, *n., pl.* **-dies.**
non·trag′ic, *adj.*
non·trag′i·cal, *adj.;* **-ly,** *adv.;* **-ness,** *n.*
non·trail′ing, *adj.*
non·trained′, *adj.*
non·train′ing, *adj., n.*
non·trai′tor·ous, *adj.;* **-ly,** *adv.;* **-ness,** *n.*

---

non·triv·i·al (non triv′ē əl), *adj.* **1.** not trivial. **2.** *Math.* noting a solution of a linear equation in which the value of at least one variable of the equation is not equal to zero. [NON- + TRIVIAL]

non trop·po (non trop′ō; *It.* nôn trôp′pô), *Music.* not too much: *non troppo allegro.* [< It]

non-U (non yōō′), *adj.* *Informal.* not characteristic of or appropriate to the upper class, esp. of Britain: *certain figures of speech that are considered absolutely non-U.* [NON- + U (initial of *upper*)]

non·un·ion (non yōōn′yən), *adj.* **1.** not belonging to, or not in accordance with the rules of, a trade union. **2.** antiunion. —*n.* **3.** *Med.* failure of a broken bone to heal. [NON- + UNION]

non·un·ion·ism (non yōōn′yə niz′əm), *n.* disregard of or opposition to trade unions. [NON- + UNIONISM] —**non·un′ion·ist,** *n.*

non′union shop′, a shop or business in which the employer fixes terms and conditions of employment unilaterally without recognizing or dealing with a union. Cf. **union shop.**

non·vi·o·lence (non vī′ə ləns), *n.* the policy or practice of refraining from the use of violence, as in reaction to oppressive authority. [NON- + VIOLENCE] —**non·vi′o·lent,** *adj.* —**non·vi′o·lent·ly,** *adv.*

non·vot·er (non vō′tər), *n.* **1.** a person who does not vote. **2.** a person who is not eligible to vote. [NON- + VOTER]

non·white (non hwīt′, -wīt′), *n.* **1.** a person who is not Caucasian. —*adj.* **2.** not Caucasian: *self-governing programs for the nonwhite peoples of Africa.* **3.** of or pertaining to nonwhite persons or peoples: *the growth of nonwhite communities.* [NON- + WHITE]

non·wo·ven (non wō′vən), *adj.* (of a fabric) made of fibers autogenously bonded through the action of a chemical agent or heating device, or adhering by means of resinous substances. [NON- + WOVEN]

non′yl al′cohol (non′il, -ēl, nō′nil, -nēl), *Chem.* any of several colorless or light-yellow, liquid, water-soluble isomers of the formula $C_9H_{19}OH$, esp. $CH_3(CH_2)_7CH_2OH$, having a roselike odor: used chiefly in perfumery and flavoring. [*non*(*ane*) (see NONANOIC) + -YL]

non·ze·ro (non zēr′ō), *adj.* not equal to zero. [NON- + ZERO]

noo·dle[1] (nōōd′əl), *n.* a narrow strip of unleavened egg dough that has been rolled thin and dried, usually boiled and served in soups, casseroles, etc.; a ribbon-shaped pasta. [< G *Nudel*]

noo·dle[2] (nōōd′əl), *n.* **1.** *Slang.* the head. **2.** a fool or simpleton. [? var. of NOODLE[1] (with *oo* from FOOL)]

noo·dle[3] (nōōd′əl), *v.i.*, **-dled, -dling.** *Music.* to practice or play idly on a musical instrument, as in warming up for a performance. [v. use of NOODLE[2] (def. 2); cf. FOOL (def. 9)]

noo·dle·head (nōōd′əl hed′), *n.* fool; simpleton; dolt; blockhead. [NOODLE[2] + HEAD]

nook (nŏŏk), *n.* **1.** a corner, as in a room. **2.** any retired or obscure corner. **3.** any small recess: *a breakfast nook.* **4.** a remote spot: *a shady nook that was ideal for a picnic.* [ME *nok*] —**nook′like′,** *adj.*

nook·er·y (nŏŏk′ə rē), *n., pl.* **-er·ies.** a snug, secure, or cozy nook. [NOOK + -ERY]

nook·ie (nŏŏk′ē), *n.* **1.** full of or abounding in nooks or like a nook. **2.** *Slang* (*vulgar*). coitus. Also, **nook′y.** [NOOK + -IE]

nook′ shaft′, *Archit.* a freestanding column or colonette set into a reentering angle, as in the splay of some medieval doorways.

noon (nōōn), *n.* **1.** midday. **2.** twelve o'clock in the daytime. **3.** the highest, brightest, or finest point or part: *the noon of one's career.* **4.** *Chiefly Literary.* midnight. [ME *none,* OE *nōn* < L *nōna* ninth hour. See NONE[2]]

noon·day (nōōn′dā′), *adj.* **1.** of or at noonday: *the noonday meal.* —*n.* **2.** midday; noon. [NOON + DAY]

no′ one′, no person; not anyone; nobody: *No one is home.* Also, **no′-one′.**

noon·ing (nōō′ning), *n.* *Chiefly Dial.* **1.** noontime. **2.** an interval at noon for rest or food. **3.** a rest or meal at noon. [NOON + -ING[1]]

noon·tide (nōōn′tīd′), *n.* **1.** the time of noon; midday. **2.** the highest or best point or part: *the noontide of one's prosperity.* **3.** *Chiefly Literary.* midnight. [ME *nonetyde,* OE *nōntīd.* See NOON, TIDE]

noon·time (nōōn′tīm′), *n.* noon; noontide; noonday: *Will he be home at noontime?* [ME *none tyme.* See NOON, TIME]

noose (nōōs), *n., v.,* **noosed, noos·ing.** —*n.* **1.** a loop with a running knot, as in a snare, lasso, hangman's halter, etc., which tightens as the rope is pulled. **2.** a tie or bond; snare. —*v.t.* **3.** to secure by or as by a noose. **4.** to make a noose with or in (a rope or the like). [late ME *nose* < ?] —**noos′er,** *n.*

Noot·ka (nōōt′kə, nŏŏt′-), *n., pl.* **-kas,** (*esp. collectively*) **-ka.** **1.** a Wakashan language spoken in SW Canada on the western coast of Vancouver Island. **2.** a member of an Indian people of Washington and Vancouver Island speaking this language.

Noot′ka cy′press. See **Alaska cedar.**

Noot′ka fir′, (in the Pacific Northwest) See **Douglas fir.**

NOP, not our publication. Also, **N.O.P.**

no·pal (nō′pəl), *n.* **1.** any cactus or fruit of the genera *Opuntia* and *Nopalea.* **2.** See **prickly pear.** [< Sp < Nahuatl *nopalli*]

no-par (nō′pär′), *adj.* without par or face value: *no-par stock.* [special use of phrase *no par* (*value*)]

nope (nōp), *adv.* *Informal.* no.

nor (nôr; *unstressed* nər), *conj.* **1.** (used in negative phrases, esp. after *neither,* to introduce the second member in a series, or any subsequent member): *Neither he nor I will be there. They won't wait for you, nor for me, nor for anybody.* **2.** (used to continue the force of a negative, as *not, no, never,* etc., occurring in a preceding clause): *He left and I never saw him again, nor did I regret it.* **3.** (used after an affirmative clause, or as a continuative, in the sense of *and not*): *They are happy, nor need we worry.* **4.** *Dial.* than. **5.** *Archaic.* (used without a preceding *neither,* the negative force of which is understood): *He nor I was there.* **6.** *Archaic.* (used instead of *neither* as correlative to a following *nor*): *Nor he nor I was there.* [ME; contr. of *nother,* OE *nōther,* equiv. to *ne* not + *ōther* (contr. of *ōhwæther*) either]

nor-, *Chem.* a combining form of a normal or parent compound: *l-norepinephrine.* [short for NORMAL]

Nor., **1.** Norman. **2.** North. **3.** Northern. **4.** Norway. **5.** Norwegian.

nor., **1.** north. **2.** northern.

No·ra (nôr′ə, nōr′ə), *n.* a girl's given name, form of **Honora.**

Nor·bert (nôr′bərt), *n.* a boy's given name.

Nor·ber·ta (nôr bûr′tə), *n.* a girl's given name.

Nor·co (nôr′kō), *n.* **1.** a town in S California. 4964 (1960). **2.** a town in SE Louisiana. 4682 (1960).

Nord (nôʀ), *n.* a department in N France. 2,293,112 (1962); 2229 sq. mi. *Cap.:* Lille.

Nor·dau (nôr′dou), *n.* **Max Si·mon** (mäks zē′môn), 1849–1923, Jewish-Hungarian author, physician, and leader in the Zionist movement.

Nor·den·skjöld (nōōʀ′dən shœld′), *n.* **1. Baron Nils A·dolf E·rik** (nils ä′dôlf ā′ʀik), 1832–1901, Swedish arctic explorer, geographer, and geologist;

---

non′tran·scrib′ing, *adj.*
non′tran·scrip′tion, *n.*
non′tran·scrip′tive, *adj.*
non′trans·fer·a·bil′i·ty, *n.*
non′trans·fer′a·ble, *adj.*
non·trans′fer·ence, *n.*
non′trans·fer·en′tial, *adj.*
non′trans·for·ma′tion, *n.*
non′trans·form′ing, *adj.*
non′trans·gres′sion, *n.*
non′trans·gres′sive, *adj.*; -ly, *adv.*
non·tran′sience, *n.*
non·tran′sien·cy, *n.*
non·tran′sient, *adj.*; -ly, *adv.*; -ness, *n.*
non′tran·si′tion·al, *adj.*; -ly, *adv.*
non·tran′si·tive, *adj., n.*; -ly, *adv.*; -ness, *n.*
non′trans·lo·ca′tion, *n.*
non′trans·mis′sion, *n.*
non′trans·mit′tal, *adj.*
non′trans·mit′tance, *n.*
non′trans·mit′ti·ble, *adj.*
non′trans·par′ence, *n.*
non′trans·par′en·cy, *n.*
non′trans·par′ent, *adj.*; -ly, *adv.*; -ness, *n.*
non′trans·port′a·bil′i·ty, *n.*
non′trans·port′a·ble, *adj.*
non′trans·por·ta′tion, *n.*
non′trans·pos′a·ble, *adj.*
non′trans·pos′ing, *adj.*
non′trans·po·si′tion, *n.*
non·trav′el·er, *n.*
non·trav′el·ing, *adj.*
non·trav′el·ler, *n.*
non·trav′el·ling, *adj.*
non·trav′ers·a·ble, *adj.*
non·trea′son·a·ble, *adj.*; -ble·ness, *n.*; -bly, *adv.*
non·treat′a·ble, *adj.*
non·treat′ed, *adj.*
non·treat′ment, *n.*
non·trea′ty, *n., pl.* -ties.
non·tres′pass, *n.*
non·tri′al, *n.*
non·trib′al, *adj.*; -ly, *adv.*
non·tribes′man, *n., pl.* -men.
non·trib′u·tar′y, *adj.*
non·tri′er, *n.*
non′trig·o·no·met′ric, *adj.*
non′trig·o·no·met′ri·cal, *adj.*; -ly, *adv.*
non′-Trin·i·tar′i·an, *adj., n.*
non·triv′i·al′i·ty, *n.*
non·trop′ic, *adj.*
non·trop′i·cal, *adj.*; -ly, *adv.*
non·trou′bling, *adj.*
non·tru′an·cy, *n.*
non·tru′ant, *n., adj.*
non·trunked′, *adj.*
non·trust′, *n.*
non·trust′ing, *adj.*
non·truth′, *n.*
non′tu·ber′cu·lar, *adj.*; -ly, *adv.*
non′tu·ber′cu·lous, *adj.*
non·tu′bu·lar, *adj.*
non·tu′mor·ous, *adj.*
non′tu·mul′tu·ous, *adj.*; -ly, *adv.*; -ness, *n.*
non·tuned′, *adj.*
non·tur′bi·nate, *adj.*
non·tur′bi·nat′ed, *adj.*
non-Turk′, *n.*
non-Tur′kic, *adj.*
non-Turk′ish, *adj., n.*
non-Tus′can, *adj., n.*
non′tu·to′ri·al, *adj.*; -ly, *adv.*
non′ty·phoi′dal, *adj.*
non·typ′i·cal, *adj.*; -ly, *adv.*; -ness, *n.*
non′ty·po·graph′ic, *adj.*
non′ty·po·graph′i·cal, *adj.*; -ly, *adv.*
non′ty·ran′nic, *adj.*
non′ty·ran′ni·cal, *adj.*; -ly, *adv.*; -ness, *n.*
non·tyr′an·nous, *adj.*; -ly, *adv.*; -ness, *n.*
non′u·biq′ui·tar′y, *adj.*
non′u·biq′ui·tous, *adj.*; -ly, *adv.*; -ness, *n.*
non′-U·krain′i·an, *adj., n.*
non·ul′cer·ous, *adj.*; -ly, *adv.*; -ness, *n.*
non′um·bil′i·cal, *adj.*
non-Um′bri·an, *adj., n.*
non′u·nan′i·mous, *adj.*; -ly, *adv.*; -ness, *n.*
non′un·der·grad′u·ate, *n., adj.*
non′un·der·stand′a·ble, *adj.*
non′un·der·stand′ing, *adj., n.*; -ly, *adv.*
non′un·der·stood′, *adj.*
non·un′du·lant, *adj.*
non·un′du·late, *adj.*
non·un′du·lat′ing, *adj.*
non·un′du·la·to′ry, *adj.*
non′u·ni·fi·ca′tion, *n.*
non·u′ni·fied′, *adj.*
non·u′ni·form′, *adj.*
non′u·ni·for′mi·ty, *n., pl.* -ties.
non′u·nique′, *adj.*; -ly, *adv.*; -ness, *n.*
non·u′ni·son, *n.*
non′u·nit′a·ble, *adj.*
non′u·ni·tar′i·an, *n.*
non′-U·ni·tar′i·an, *adj., n.*
non′u·nite′a·ble, *adj.*
non′u·nit′ed, *adj.*
non′u·nit′ing, *adj.*
non·u′ni·ty, *n.*
non′u·ni·ver′sal, *adj., n.*; -ly, *adv.*
non′u·ni·ver′sal·ist, *n., adj.*
non′u·ni·ver·sal′i·ty, *n.*
non′u·ni·ver′si·ty, *n., pl.* -ties; *adj.*
non·up′right, *adj., n.*; -ly, *adv.*; -ness, *n.*
non′-U·ra′li·an, *n.*
non·ur′ban, *adj.*
non·ur′ban·ite′, *n.*
non·ur′gent, *adj.*; -ly, *adv.*
non·us′a·ble, *adj.*
non·us′age, *n.*
non·use′, *n.*
non·use′a·ble, *adj.*
non·us′er, *n.*
non·us′ing, *adj.*
non′u·su′ri·ous, *adj.*; -ly, *adv.*; -ness, *n.*
non′u·surp′ing, *adj.*; -ly, *adv.*
non·u′ter·ine, *adj.*
non′u·til′i·tar′i·an, *adj., n.*
non′u·til′i·ty, *n., pl.* -ties.
non·u′til·i·za′tion, *n.*
non·u′til·ized′, *adj.*
non·ut′ter·ance, *n.*
non·va′can·cy, *n., pl.* -cies.
non·va′cant, *adj.*; -ly, *adv.*
non′vac·ci·na′tion, *n.*
non·vac′il·lat′ing, *adj.*
non′vac·il·la′tion, *n.*
non·vac′u·ous, *adj.*; -ly, *adv.*; -ness, *n.*
non·vac′u·um, *n., pl.* -vac·u·ums, -vac·u·a; *adj.*
non·vag′i·nal, *adj.*
non·va′gran·cy, *n., pl.* -cies.
non·va′grant, *adj.*; -ly, *adv.*; -ness, *n.*
non·val′id, *adj.*; -ly, *adv.*; -ness, *n.*
non′val·i·da′tion, *n.*
non′va·lid′i·ty, *n., pl.* -ties.
non·val′or·ous, *adj.*; -ly, *adv.*; -ness, *n.*
non·val′u·a·ble, *adj.*
non·val′ue, *n.*
non·val′ued, *adj.*
non·van′ish·ing, *adj.*
non′vap·o·ros′i·ty, *n.*
non·vap′or·ous, *adj.*; -ly, *adv.*; -ness, *n.*
non·var′i·a·bil′i·ty, *n.*
non·var′i·a·ble, *adj.*; -ble·ness, *n.*; -bly, *adv.*
non·var′i·ance, *n.*
non·var′i·ant, *adj., n.*
non·var′i·a′tion, *n.*
non·var′ied, *adj.*
non′va·ri′e·ty, *n., pl.* -ties.
non·var′i·ous, *adj.*; -ly, *adv.*; -ness, *n.*
non·vas′cu·lar, *adj.*; -ly, *adv.*
non·vas′cu·lose′, *adj.*
non·vas′cu·lous, *adj.*
non·vas′sal, *n.*
non-Ve′dic, *adj.*
non·veg′e·ta·ble, *n., adj.*
non′veg·e·ta′tion, *n.*
non·veg′e·ta′tive, *adj.*; -ly, *adv.*; -ness, *n.*
non·veg′e·tive, *adj.*
non·ve′he·ment, *adj.*; -ly, *adv.*
non·ve′nal, *adj.*; -ly, *adv.*
non′vend·i·bil′i·ty, *n.*
non·vend′i·ble, *adj.*; -ble·ness, *n.*; -bly, *adv.*
non′ve·ne′re·al, *adj.*
non′-Ve·ne′tian, *adj., n.*
non·ven′om·ous, *adj.*; -ly, *adv.*; -ness, *n.*
non·ve′nous, *adj.*; -ly, *adv.*; -ness, *n.*
non·ven′ti·la′tion, *n.*
non·ven′ti·la′tive, *adj.*
non′ve·ra′cious, *adj.*; -ly, *adv.*; -ness, *n.*
non′ve·rac′i·ty, *n.*
non·ver′bal, *adj.*; -ly, *adv.*
non·ver′bal·ized′, *adj.*
non′ver·bos′i·ty, *n.*
non·ver′i·fi′a·ble, *adj.*
non·ver′i·fi·ca′tion, *n.*
non·ver′i·ta·ble, *adj.*; -ble·ness, *n.*; -bly, *adv.*
non·ver′min·ous, *adj.*; -ly, *adv.*; -ness, *n.*
non′ver·nac′u·lar, *adj.*
non′ver·sa·til′i·ty, *n.*
non·ver′te·bral, *adj.*
non·ver′te·brate′, *adj., n.*
non·ver′ti·cal, *adj.*; -ly, *adv.*; -ness, *n.*
non′ver·ti·cal′i·ty, *n.*
non′ve·sic′u·lar, *adj.*; -ly, *adv.*
non·vest′ing, *adj., n.*
non·ves′ture, *n.*
non·vet′er·an, *n.*
non·vet′er·i·nar′y, *n., pl.* -nar·ies, *adj.*
non′vex·a′tious, *adj.*; -ly, *adv.*; -ness, *n.*
non′vi·a·bil′i·ty, *n.*
non·vi′a·ble, *adj.*
non·vi′bra·tile, *adj.*
non·vi′brat·ing, *adj.*
non′vi·bra′tion, *n.*
non·vi′bra·tor, *n.*
non·vi′bra·to′ry, *adj.*
non′vi·car′i·ous, *adj.*; -ly, *adv.*; -ness, *n.*
non·vic′to·ry, *n., pl.* -ries.
non·vig′i·lance, *n.*
non·vig′i·lant, *adj.*; -ly, *adv.*; -ness, *n.*
non·vil′lag·er, *n.*
non·vil′lain·ous, *adj.*; -ly, *adv.*; -ness, *n.*
non·vin′di·ca·ble, *adj.*
non′vin·di·ca′tion, *n.*
non′vi·nos′i·ty, *n.*
non·vi′nous, *adj.*
non·vin′tage, *adj., n.*
non′vi·o·la·bil′i·ty, *n.*
non·vi′o·la·ble, *adj.*; -ble·ness, *n.*; -bly, *adv.*
non′vi·o·la′tion, *n.*
non·vi′o·la′tive, *adj.*
non·vir′gin·al, *adj.*; -ly, *adv.*
non′-Vir·gin′ian, *adj., n.*
non·vir′ile, *adj.*
non′vi·ril′i·ty, *n.*
non·vir′tue, *n.*
non·vir′tu·ous, *adj.*; -ly, *adv.*; -ness, *n.*
non·vir′u·lent, *adj.*; -ly, *adv.*
non·vis′cer·al, *adj.*
non·vis′cid, *adj.*; -ly, *adv.*; -ness, *n.*
non′vis·cid′i·ty, *n.*
non·vis′cous, *adj.*; -ly, *adv.*; -ness, *n.*
non′vis·i·bil′i·ty, *n., pl.* -ties.
non·vis′i·ble, *adj.*; -bly, *adv.*
non·vi′sion·al, *adj.*
non·vi′sion·ar′y, *adj., n.*
non·vis′it·ing, *adj.*
non·vis′u·al, *adj.*
non·vis′u·al·ized′, *adj.*
non·vi′tal, *adj.*; -ly, *adv.*; -ness, *n.*
non′vi·tal′i·ty, *n.*
non·vi′tal·ized′, *adj.*
non′vi·ti·a′tion, *n.*
non·vit′ri·fied′, *adj.*
non′vit·ri·ol′ic, *adj.*
non′vi·tu′per·a′tive, *adj.*; -ly, *adv.*
non′viv·i·par′i·ty, *n.*
non′vi·vip′a·rous, *adj.*; -ly, *adv.*; -ness, *n.*
non·vo′ca·ble, *adj.*
non·vo′cal, *adj., n.*; -ly, *adv.*; -ness, *n.*
non′vo·cal′ic, *adj.*
non′vo·cal′i·ty, *n.*
non′vo·cal·i·za′tion, *n.*
non′vo·ca′tion·al, *adj.*; -ly, *adv.*
non·void′, *adj., n.*
non·void′a·ble, *adj.*
non·vo′lant, *adj.*
non·vol′a·tile, *adj.*; -ness, *n.*
non′vol·a·til′i·ty, *n.*
non·vol′a·til·iz′a·ble, *adj.*
non·vol′a·til·ized′, *adj.*
non′vol·can′ic, *adj.*
non′vo·li′tion, *n.*
non′vo·li′tion·al, *adj.*
non′vol·u·bil′i·ty, *n.*
non·vol′u·ble, *adj.*; -ble·ness, *n.*; -bly, *adv.*
non·vol′un·tar′y, *adj.*
non·vot′ing, *adj.*
non·vul′can·ized′, *adj.*
non′vul·gar′i·ty, *n., pl.* -ties.
non·vul′val, *adj.*
non·vul′var, *adj.*
non·walk′ing, *adj., n.*
non·war′, *n.*
non·war′rant·a·ble, *adj.*; -bly, *adv.*
non·war′rant·ed, *adj.*
non·wash′a·ble, *adj.*
non·wast′ing, *adj., n.*
non·wa′ter·tight′, *adj.*
non·wav′er·ing, *adj.*
non·wax′ing, *adj.*
non·weak′ness, *n.*
non-Welsh′, *adj., n.*
non·west′ern, *adj., n.*
non·wet′ted, *adj.*
non·winged′, *adj.*
non·with′er·ing, *adj.*
non·wood′y, *adj.*
non·work′er, *n.*
non·work′ing, *adj.*
non·yield′ing, *adj.*
non·zeal′ous, *adj.*; -ly, *adv.*; -ness, *n.*
non-Zi′on·ist, *n., adj.*
non·zo′di·a·cal, *adj.*
non·zon′al, *adj.*; -ly, *adv.*
non·zon′ate, *adj.*
non·zon′at·ed, *adj.*
non′zo·o·log′ic, *adj.*
non′zo·o·log′i·cal, *adj.*; -ly, *adv.*

born in Finland. **2.** his nephew **Nils Ot·to Gus·taf** (nils ôt′tōō gōōs′täv), 1869–1928, Swedish arctic and antarctic explorer.

Nor′denskjöld Sea′. See **Laptev Sea.**

Nord·hau·sen (nôrt′hou′zən), *n.* a city in SW East Germany: site of a former Nazi concentration camp. 39,200 (est. 1959).

Nor·dic (nôr′dik), *adj.* **1.** *Anthropol.* of, pertaining to, or characteristic of a Caucasoid racial subtype marked by tall stature, blond hair, blue eyes, and elongated head, exemplified chiefly by Scandinavians, Britons, and their descendants. —*n.* **2.** a member of the Nordic race. [< F *nordique*, equiv. to *nord* north + *-ique* -IC] —**Nor·dic·i·ty** (nôr dis′i tē), *n.*

Nor·di·ca (nôr′də kə), *n.* **Lillian** (*Lillian Norton*), 1859–1914, U.S. soprano.

Nord′kyn Cape′ (nôr′kyn), a cape in N Norway: the northernmost point of the European mainland.

Nord·land (nōr′län, nōōr′-), *n.* a county in N Norway. 237,322 (est. 1959); 14,797 sq. mi. *Co. seat:* Bodö.

Nord·ma·ling (nōōrd′mä′ling), *n.* a city in E Sweden, on the Gulf of Bothnia. 8972 (1964).

Nor·doff (nôr′dof, -dôf), *n.* **1. Charles Bernard,** 1887–1947, U.S. novelist. **2. Paul,** born 1909, U.S. composer and teacher.

Nord·rhein-West·fa·len (nôrt′rīn vest′fä′lən), *n.* German name of **North Rhine-Westphalia.**

nor′east·er (nôr′ē′stər), *n.* northeaster.

No·reen (nô rēn′, nôr′ēn), *n.* a girl's given name, Irish form of **Nora.** Also, **No·rene′.**

Nor·folk (nôr′fək), *n.* **1.** a county in E England. 561,980 (1961); 2054 sq. mi. *Co. seat:* Norwich. **2.** a seaport in SE Virginia: naval base. 305,872 (1960). **3.** a city in NE Nebraska. 13,111 (1960).

Nor′folk Is′land, an island in the S Pacific between New Caledonia and New Zealand: a territory of Australia. 844 (est. 1961); 13 sq. mi.

Nor′folk Is′land Pine′, an evergreen tree, *Araucaria excelsa*, of Norfolk Island, having sharp-pointed leaves that curve at the tip: grown for timber and as an ornamental.

Nor′folk jack′et, a loosely belted single-breasted jacket, with box pleats in front and back. Also called **Nor′folk coat′.** [named after NORFOLK county in England]

Nor·ge (nôr′gə), *n.* Norwegian name of **Norway.**

no·ri·a (nōr′ē ə, nôr′-), *n.* a device consisting of a series of buckets on a wheel, used in Spain and the Orient for raising water. [< Sp < Ar *nā′ūra*]

Nor·i·cum (nôr′i kəm, nor′-), *n.* an ancient Roman province in central Europe, roughly corresponding to the part of Austria south of the Danube.

No·rilsk (no rēlsk′), *n.* a city in the N RSFSR, in the NW Soviet Union in Asia, near the mouth of the Yenisei River. 117,000 (est. 1962).

nor·ite (nôr′īt), *n.* a granular rock, the lighter minerals of which are calcic plagioclase feldspars, and the darker minerals of which are orthorhombic pyroxenes. [< Norw *norit*. See NORWAY, -ITE[1]] —**nor·it·ic** (nô rit′ik), *adj.*

nor·land (nôr′lənd), *n.* *Chiefly Dial.* northland. [NOR(TH) + LAND]

Nor·lene (nôr lēn′), *n.* a girl's given name, form of **Nora.**

norm (nôrm), *n.* **1.** standard, model, or pattern. **2.** general level or average: *Two cars per family is the norm in most suburban communities.* **3.** *Educ.* **a.** a designated standard of average performance of people of a given age, background, etc. **b.** a standard based on the past average performance of a given individual. **4.** *Math.* **a.** a real-valued, nonnegative function whose domain is a vector space and which has the properties that the function of a vector is zero only when the vector is zero, the function of a scalar times a vector is equal to the absolute value of the scalar times the function of the vector, and the function of the sum of two vectors is less than or equal to the sum of the functional values of each vector. The norm of a real number is its absolute value. **b.** the greatest difference between two successive points of a given partition. [< L *norm(a)* a carpenter's square, a rule, pattern] —**norm′less,** *adj.*

Norm., Norman.

Nor·ma (nôr′mə), *n., gen.* **-mae** (-mē). *Astron.* the Rule, a small southern constellation between Lupus and Ara. [< L; see NORM]

Nor·ma (nôr′mə), *n.* a girl's given name.

nor·mal (nôr′məl), *adj.* **1.** conforming to the standard or the common type; usual; not abnormal; regular; natural. **2.** serving to fix a standard. **3.** *Psychol.* **a.** approximately average in any psychological trait, as intelligence, personality, or emotional adjustment. **b.** free from any mental disorder; sane. **4.** *Math.* **a.** being at right angles, as a line; perpendicular. **b.** of the nature of or pertaining to a mathematical normal. **c.** (of an orthogonal system of real functions) defined so that the integral of the square of the absolute value of any function is 1. **d.** (of a topological space) having the property that corresponding to every pair of disjoint closed sets are two disjoint open sets, each containing one of the closed sets. **e.** (of a subgroup) having the property that the same set of elements results when all the elements of the subgroup are operated on consistently on the left and consistently on the right by any element of the group; invariant. **5.** *Chem.* **a.** (of a solution) containing one equivalent weight of the constituent in question in one liter of solution. **b.** pertaining to an aliphatic hydrocarbon having a straight unbranched carbon chain, each carbon atom of which is joined to no more than two other carbon atoms. **c.** of or pertaining to a neutral salt in which any replaceable hydroxyl groups or hydrogen atoms have been replaced by other groups or atoms, as sodium sulfate, Na_2SO_4. **6.** *Biol., Med.* **a.** free from any infection or other form of disease or malformation, or from experimental therapy or manipulation. **b.** of natural occurrence. —*n.* **7.** the standard or type. **8.** the normal form or state; the average or mean: *Production may fall below normal.* **9.** *Math.* **a.** a perpendicular line or plane, esp. one perpendicular to a tangent line of a curve, or a tangent plane of a surface, at the point of contact. **b.** the portion of this perpendicular line included between its point of contact with the curve and the *x*-axis. [< L *normāl(is)* made according to a carpenter's square, a rule, pattern, equiv. to *norm(a)* (see NORM) + *-ālis* -AL[1]] —**nor·mal·i·ty** (nôr mal′i tē), **nor′mal·ness,** *n.*

nor′mal curve′, *Statistics.* a bell-shaped curve showing a distribution of probability associated with different values of a variate. Also called **Gaussian curve.**

nor·mal·cy (nôr′məl sē), *n.* the character or state of being normal, as the general economic, political, and social conditions of a nation; normality: *After months of living in a state of tension, all yearned for a return to normalcy.* [NORMAL + -CY]

nor′mal distribu′tion, *Statistics.* a theoretical frequency distribution represented by a normal curve. Also called **Gaussian distribution.**

nor′mal divi′sor, *Math.* a normal subgroup.

nor′mal equiv′alent de′viate, *Statistics.* a value *x* such that the integral of a normal curve over all those values of the independent variable less than *x* is equal to the given probability.

nor·mal·ise (nôr′mə līz′), *v.t., v.i.,* **-ised, -is·ing.** *Chiefly Brit.* normalize. —**nor′mal·i·sa′tion,** *n.*

nor·mal·ize (nôr′mə līz′), *v.,* **-ized, -iz·ing.** —*v.t.* **1.** to make normal. **2.** *Metall.* to heat (a steel alloy) to a suitable temperature above the transformation range and then to cool it in still air at the environmental temperature. —*v.i.* **3.** to become normal; resume a normal state: *Prices soon normalized after the war.* [NORMAL + -IZE] —**nor′mal·i·za′tion,** *n.*

nor·mal·iz·er (nôr′mə lī′zər), *n.* **1.** one who or that which normalizes. **2.** *Math.* **a.** the subgroup consisting of elements that commute with a given element. **b.** the set of elements of a group which commute with every element of a given subgroup. [NORMALIZE + -ER[1]]

nor·mal·ly (nôr′mə lē), *adv.* according to rule, general custom, etc.; as a rule. [NORMAL + -LY]

nor′mal magnifica′tion, *Optics.* the magnification produced by a telescope or microscope such that the diameter of the exit pupil of the instrument is equal to the diameter of the pupil of the eye.

nor′mal orthog′onal, *Math.* orthonormal.

nor′mal pen′tane, *Chem.* pentane (def. 2).

nor′mal pitch′, *Mach.* See under **pitch**[1] (def. 45a).

nor′mal sa′line solu′tion, *Pharm.* See **isotonic sodium chloride solution.**

nor′mal school′, a school giving a two-year course to high-school graduates preparing to be teachers.

nor′mal se′ries, *Math.* a collection of subgroups of a given group so arranged that the first subgroup is the identity, the last subgroup is the group itself, and each subgroup is a normal subgroup of the succeeding subgroup.

nor′mal tax′, the initial tax levied on incomes at a fixed rate irrespective of the base amount. Cf. **surtax** (def. 2).

nor′mal Zee′man effect′, *Physics, Optics.* See under **Zeeman effect.**

nor·man (nôr′mən), *n., pl.* **-mans.** *Naut.* **1.** a bar passed through a hole in a bollard to prevent lines from slipping up. **2.** a pin passed through a hole in a rudder head to prevent its loss. [?]

Nor·man (nôr′mən), *n.* **1.** a member of that branch of the Northmen or Scandinavians who in the 10th century conquered Normandy. **2.** Also called **Norman French.** one of the mixed Scandinavian and French people who inhabited Normandy and conquered England in 1066. **3.** a native or inhabitant of Normandy. **4.** See **Norman French** (def. 1). **5.** a city in central Oklahoma. 33,412 (1960). **6.** a boy's given name. —*adj.* **7.** of or pertaining to the Normans. **8.** noting or pertaining to a variety of Romanesque architecture built by the Normans, esp. in England after 1066.

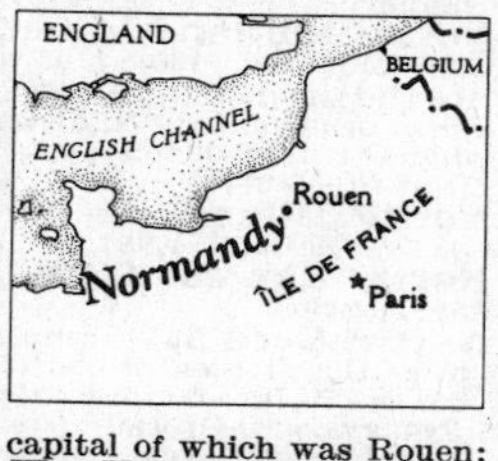

Nor′man Con′quest, the conquest of England by the Normans, under William the Conqueror, in 1066.

Nor·man·dy (nôr′mən dē), *n.* **1.** a region in N France along the English Channel: invaded and settled by Scandinavians in the 10th century, becoming a duchy in A.D. 911; later a province, the capital of which was Rouen; Allied invasion in World War II began here June 6, 1944. **2.** a town in E Missouri. 4452 (1960).

Nor·man·esque (nôr′mə nesk′), *adj.* in the style of Norman architecture. [NORMAN + -ESQUE]

Nor′man French′ **1.** Also called **Norman.** the French of the Normans or of Normandy. **2.** Norman (def. 2). —**Nor′man-French′,** *adj.*

Nor·man·ise (nôr′mə nīz′), *v.t., v.i.,* **-ised, -is·ing.** *Chiefly Brit.* Normanize. —**Nor′man·i·sa′tion,** *n.* —**Nor′man·is′er,** *n.*

Nor·man·ize (nôr′mə nīz′), *v.t., v.i.,* **-ized, -iz·ing.** to make or become Norman in customs, language, etc. [NORMAN + -IZE] —**Nor′man·i·za′tion,** *n.* —**Nor′man·iz′er,** *n.*

Nor′man Wells′, a settlement in the W Northwest Territories, in NW Canada, on the Mackenzie River: oil wells. 600 (1956).

nor·ma·tive (nôr′mə tiv), *adj.* **1.** of or pertaining to a norm, esp. an assumed norm regarded as the standard of correctness in behavior, speech, writing, etc. **2.** tending or attempting to establish such a norm, esp. by the prescription of rules: *normative grammar.* **3.** reflecting the assumption of such a norm, or favoring its establishment: *a normative attitude.* [< L **normātivus.* See NORM, -ATIVE] —**nor′ma·tive·ly,** *adv.* —**nor′ma·tive·ness,** *n.*

normed′ con′jugate (nôrmd), *Math.* See **dual space** (def. 3).

normed′ space′, *Math.* any vector space on which a norm is defined.

nor·mo·cyte (nôr′mə sīt′), *n.* *Anat.* an erythrocyte of normal size. [NORM + -O- + -CYTE] —**nor·mo·cyt·ic** (nôr′mə sit′ik), *adj.*

nor·mo·ten·sive (nôr′mō ten′siv), *Pathol.* —*adj.* **1.** characterized by normal arterial tension or blood pressure. —*n.* **2.** a normotensive person. [NORM + -O- + TENSIVE]

Norn (nôrn), *n.* *Scand. Myth.* a personification of fate, usually in the form of a virgin goddess. Cf. **Skuld, Urd, Urdar, Verdandi.**

No·ro·dom Si·ha·nouk (nôr′ə dom′ sē′ä nōōk′), **Prince,** born 1922, Cambodian statesman: premier 1952–60; chief of state since 1960.

Nor·ris (nôr′is, nor′-), *n.* **1. Charles Gilman,** 1881–1945, U.S. novelist and editor. **2. Frank,** 1870–1902, U.S. novelist (brother of Charles Gilman). **3. George William,** 1861–1947, U.S. senator 1913–43. **4. Kathleen (Thompson),** 1880–1966, U.S. novelist and short-story writer (wife of Charles Gilman). **5.** a boy's given name.

Nor′ris-La Guar′di·a Act′ (nôr′is lə gwär′dē ə, nor′-), an act of Congress in 1932 limiting the use of court injunctions against striking, picketing, and boycotting, with a clause outlawing yellow-dog contracts.

Nor·ris·town (nôr′is toun′, nor′-), *n.* a borough in SE Pennsylvania, near Philadelphia. 38,925 (1960).

Norr·kö·ping (nôr′chœ′ping), *n.* a seaport in SE Sweden. 93,161 (1965).

Norse (nôrs), *adj.* **1.** belonging or pertaining to Norway, esp. ancient Norway with its colonies, or to ancient Scandinavia generally. —*n.* **2.** (*construed as pl.*) the Norwegians. **3.** (*construed as pl.*) the ancient Norwegians. **4.** (*construed as pl.*) the Northmen or ancient Scandinavians generally. **5.** the Norwegian language, esp. in its older forms. Cf. **Old Norse.** [perh. < D *noorsch*, obs. var. of *noordsch* (now *noords*), equiv. to *noord* NORTH + *-sch* -ISH[1]. Cf. Norw, Sw, Dan *Norsk* Norwegian, Norse]

Norse·man (nôrs′mən), *n., pl.* **-men.** Northman. [NORSE + MAN[1]]

Nor·stad (nôr′stad, -städ), *n.* **Lau·ris** (lôr′is, lōr′-), born 1907, U.S. Air Force general: Supreme Allied Commander of NATO 1956–63.

nor·te·a·me·ri·ca·no (nôr′te ä me′rē kä′nô), *n., pl.* **-nos** (-nôs), *adj.* *Spanish.* —*n.* **1.** a North American. **2.** a citizen or inhabitant of the U.S., esp. as distinguished from the peoples of Spanish-speaking America. —*adj.* **3.** of, pertaining to, or characteristic of the *norteamericano.*

north (nôrth), *n.* **1.** a cardinal point of the compass, lying in the plane of the meridian and to the left of a person facing the rising sun. **2.** the direction in which this point lies. **3.** (*usually cap.*) a region or territory situated in this direction. **4.** (*cap.*) the northern area of the United States, esp. the States that fought with the Union in the Civil War, lying to the north of the Ohio River, and usually including Missouri and Maryland. **5.** (*cap.*) See **North Country. 6.** the north wind. —*adj.* **7.** situated in the north: *north woods.* **8.** directed or proceeding toward the north: *a north course.* **9.** coming from the north: *a north wind.* **10.** (*usually cap.*) designating the northern part of a region, nation, country, etc.: *North Atlantic.* —*adv.* **11.** from the north: *a wind blowing north.* **12.** toward the north: *sailing north.* [ME, OE, c. D *noord*, Icel *northr*, G *nord*]

North (nôrth), *n.* **1. Christopher,** pen name of John Wilson. **2. Frederick, 2nd Earl of Guil·ford** (gil′fərd) (*"Lord North"*), 1732–92, British statesman: prime minister 1770–82. **3. Sir Thomas,** 1535?–1601?, English translator.

North′ Ad′ams, a city in NW Massachusetts. 19,905 (1960).

North′ Af′rica, the northern part of Africa, esp. the region north of the tropical rain forest and comprised of Morocco, Algeria, Tunisia, Libya, and that part of the United Arab Republic west of the Gulf of Suez. —**North′ Af′rican.**

Nor·tham (nôr′thəm), *n.* a boy's given name.

North′ Amer′ica, the northernmost continent of the Western Hemisphere, extending from Central America to the Arctic Ocean. Highest point, Mt. McKinley, 20,300 ft.; lowest, Death Valley, 276 ft. below sea level. (including Central America) 261,348,038 (est. 1960); ab. 8,440,000 sq. mi. —**North′ Amer′ican.**

North·amp·ton (nôr thamp′tən, north hamp′-), *n.* **1.** a city in and the county seat of Northamptonshire, in central England. 105,361 (1961). **2.** a city in central Massachusetts. 30,058 (1960). **3.** a town in E Pennsylvania. 8866 (1960).

North·amp·ton·shire (nôr thamp′tən shēr′, -shər), *n.* a county in central England. 398,132 (1961); 914 sq. mi. *Co. seat:* Northampton. Also called **Northampton.**

North′an·ger Ab′bey (nôrth′ān jər, -ang′gər), a novel (1818) by Jane Austen.

North′ Ar′lington, a city in NE New Jersey. 17,477 (1960).

North′ Atlan′tic Cur′rent, an ocean current formed from the northern terminus of the Gulf Stream SE of Newfoundland, flowing NE toward the British Isles. Also called **North′ Atlan′tic Drift′.**

North′ Atlan′tic Trea′ty, the treaty (1949) signed by 12 countries, providing for the establishment of NATO.

North′ Atlan′tic Trea′ty Organiza′tion. See **NATO.**

North′ Austral′ia, a former division of Australia; now part of the Northern Territory. —**North′ Austral′ian.**

North′ Bal′timore, a town in NW Ohio. 3011 (1960).

North′ Bat′tle·ford (bat′əl fərd), a city in W central Saskatchewan, in central Canada. 11,230 (1961).

North′ Bay′, a city in SE Ontario, in S Canada. 23,781 (1961).

North′ Belle·ver·non (bel vûr′nən), a town in SW Pennsylvania. 3148 (1960).

North′ Bell′more, a town on W Long Island, in SE New York. 19,639 (1960).

North′ Bel′mont, a town in S North Carolina. 8328 (1960).

North′ Bend′, a town in SW Oregon. 7512 (1960).

North′ Ber′gen, a town in NE New Jersey. 42,387 (1960).

North′ Bor′neo, a former name of **Sabah.**

North·bor·ough (nôrth′bûr′ō, -bur′ō), *n.* a town in central Massachusetts. 2516 (1960).

north·bound (nôrth′bound′), *adj.* going toward the north: *northbound traffic.* [NORTH + -BOUND[2]]

North′ Brabant′, a province in the S Netherlands. 1,484,671 (est. 1960); 1965 sq. mi. *Cap.:* 's Hertogenbosch.

North′ Brook′field, a town in central Massachusetts. 2615 (1960).

north′ by east′, *Navig., Survey.* a point on the compass 11°15′ east of north. *Abbr.:* NbE

north′ by west′, *Navig., Survey.* a point on the compass 11°15′ west of north. *Abbr.:* NbW

North′ Cald′well, a town in NE New Jersey. 4163 (1960).

North′ Can′ton (kan′tən), a town in central Ohio. 7727 (1960).

North′ Cape′, 1. a point of land on an island at the N tip of Norway: the northernmost point of Europe. 2. the northern end of North Island, New Zealand.

North′ Caroli′na, a State in the SE United States, on the Atlantic coast. 4,556,155 (1960); 52,712 sq. mi. *Cap.:* Raleigh. *Abbr.:* N.C. **—North′ Carolin′ian.**

North′ Cat·a·sau′qua (kat′ə sô′kwə), a town in E Pennsylvania. 2805 (1960).

North′ Cauca′sian, 1. a language family including all the Caucasian languages north of the Caucasian divide, as Kabardian and the Circassian language proper, and a few between the divide and the Black Sea, as Abkhazian. 2. of or pertaining to this language family.

North′ Cau′casus, a region in the S Soviet Union in Europe, E of the Black Sea.

North′ Chan′nel, a strait between SW Scotland and NE Ireland. 14 mi. wide at the narrowest point.

North′ Chica′go, a city in NE Illinois, on Lake Michigan. 20,517 (1960).

North·cliffe (nôrth′klif), *n.* **Viscount.** See **Harmsworth, Alfred Charles William.**

North′ Coun′try, 1. the part of England north of the Humber estuary. 2. Alaska and the Yukon territory of Canada (as a geographical and economic unit).

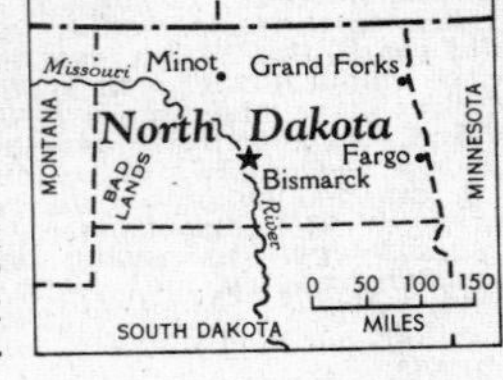

North′ Dako′ta, a State in the N central United States. 632,446 (1960); 70,665 sq. mi. *Cap.:* Bismarck. *Abbr.:* N. Dak. **—North′ Dako′tan.**

North′ East′, a town in NW Pennsylvania. 4217 (1960).

north·east (nôrth′ēst′; *Naut.* nôr′ēst′), *n.* 1. a point on the compass midway between north and east. 2. a region in this direction. 3. **the Northeast,** the northeastern part of the United States, esp. the New England States. —*adv.* 4. from this point: *a wind blowing northeast.* 5. toward this point: *sailing northeast.* —*adj.* 6. coming from this point: *a northeast wind.* 7. directed toward this point: *a northeast course.* [OE; see NORTH, EAST] **—north′east′ern,** *adj.*

northeast′ by east′, *Navig., Survey.* a point on the compass 11°15′ east of northeast. *Abbr.:* NEbE

northeast′ by north′, *Navig., Survey.* a point on the compass 11°15′ north of northeast. *Abbr.:* NEbN

north·east·er (nôrth′ē′stər; *Naut.* nôr′ē′stər), *n.* 1. a wind or gale from the northeast. 2. *Meteorol.* See **northeast storm.** Also, **nor′easter.** [NORTHEAST + -ER[1]]

north·east·er·ly (nôrth′ē′stər lē; *Naut.* nôr′ē′stər lē), *adj.* 1. of or located in the northeast. 2. toward or from the northeast. —*adv.* 3. toward or from the northeast. [NORTHEASTER + -LY]

north·east·ern·er (nôrth′ē′stər nər), *n.* 1. a native or inhabitant of the northeast. 2. (*cap.*) a native or inhabitant of the northeastern U.S. [NORTHEASTERN + -ER[1]]

North′ East′ New′ Guin′ea, the NE part of the Australian Territory of New Guinea. ab. 70,000 sq. mi.

North′east Pas′sage, a ship route along the N coast of Europe and Asia, between the North Sea and the Pacific.

north′east storm′, a cyclonic storm that moves northeastward within several hundred miles of the eastern coast of the U.S. and Canada, particularly in fall and winter, its often strong northeast winds causing high seas and coastal damage and bearing rain or snow. Also called **northeaster, nor′easter.**

north·east·ward (nôrth′ēst′wərd; *Naut.* nôr′ēst′wərd), *adv., adj.* 1. Also, **north′east′ward·ly.** toward the northeast. —*n.* 2. the northeast. [NORTHEAST + -WARD]

north·east·wards (nôrth′ēst′wərdz; *Naut.* nôr′ēst′wərdz), *adv.* northeastward.

north·er (nôr′thər), *n.* 1. (in the U.S. Gulf Coast region) a cold gale from the north, formed during the winter by a vigorous outbreak of continental polar air behind a cold front. 2. a wind or storm from the north. [NORTH + -ER[1]]

nor·ther·ly (nôr′thər lē), *adj., adv., n., pl.* **-lies.** —*adj.* 1. moving, directed, or situated toward the north. 2. (esp. of a wind) coming from the north: *a northerly gale.* —*adv.* 3. toward the north. 4. from the north. —*n.* 5. a wind that blows from the north. [NORTHER + -LY] **—nor′ther·li·ness,** *n.*

north·ern (nôr′thərn), *adj.* 1. lying toward or situated in the north. 2. directed or proceeding northward. 3. coming from the north, as a wind. 4. (*often cap.*) of or pertaining to the North, esp. the northern U.S. 5. *Astron.* north of the celestial equator or of the zodiac: *a northern constellation.* —*n.* 6. a person living in a northern region or country. [ME, OE; see NORTH, -ERN] **—north′ern·ness,** *n.*

North′ern Bucovi′na, Bucovina.

North′ern Cameroons′. See under **Cameroons** (def. 2).

north′ern canoe′, *Canadian.* a large, heavy canoe used to transport supplies. Cf. **York boat.**

North′ern Coal′sack, *Astron.* See under **Coalsack.**

North′ern Cross′, *Astron.* six stars in the constellation Cygnus, arranged in the form of a cross.

North′ern Crown′, *Astron.* the constellation Corona Borealis.

North·ern·er (nôr′thər nər), *n.* (*sometimes l.c.*) a native or inhabitant of the North, esp. of the northern U.S. [NORTHERN + -ER[1]]

north′ern har′vestfish. See under **harvestfish** (def. 1).

North′ern Hem′isphere, the half of the earth between the North Pole and the equator.

North′ern Ire′land, a political division of the United Kingdom, in the NE part of the island of Ireland. 1,425,462 (1961); 5238 sq. mi. *Cap.:* Belfast.

North·ern·ise (nôr′thər nīz′), *v.t.,* **-ised, -is·ing.** (*sometimes l.c.*) *Chiefly Brit.* Northernize.

North·ern·ize (nôr′thər nīz′), *v.t.,* **-ized, -iz·ing.** (*sometimes l.c.*) to make northern; impart qualities considered typical of the North, esp. of the Northern U.S. [NORTHERN + -IZE]

north′ern king′fish, *Ichthyol.* a drum, *Menticirrhus saxatilis,* found along the Atlantic coast of the U.S. Also called **king-whiting, northern whiting.**

north′ern lights′. See **aurora borealis.**

North′ern Mich′igan. See **Upper Peninsula.**

north·ern·most (nôr′thərn mōst′ *or, esp. Brit.,* -məst), *adj.* farthest north. [NORTHERN + -MOST]

North′ern Paiute′, 1. a member of an American Indian people of Nevada, Oregon, and California, allied to the Paiute. 2. See under **paiute** (def. 2).

north′ern pike′, a pike, *Esox lucius,* found in North America and Eurasia, valued as a game fish.

north′ern red′ cur′rant, an unarmed shrub, *Ribes rubrum,* of Eurasia, having drooping clusters of greenish-brown flowers and red, edible fruit.

North′ern Rhode′sia, former name of **Zambia.** **—North′ern Rhode′sian.**

north′ern sen′net. See under **sennet[1].**

North′ern Spor′ades. See under **Sporades.**

North′ern Spy′, 1. an American variety of red-striped apple that ripens in autumn or early winter. 2. the tree bearing this fruit.

north′ern stud′fish. See under **studfish.**

North′ern Ter′ritories, a former British protectorate in W Africa; now a part of N Ghana.

North′ern Ter′ritory, a territory in N Australia. 27,095 (1961); 523,620 sq. mi. *Cap.:* Darwin.

north′ern whit′ing. See **northern kingfish.**

North·field (nôrth′fēld′), *n.* 1. a town in SE Minnesota. 8707 (1960). 2. a town in SE New Jersey. 5849 (1960). 3. a town in NE Illinois. 4005 (1960).

North′ Fond′ du Lac′, a town in E Wisconsin. 2549 (1960).

North′ Frig′id Zone′, the part of the earth's surface between the Arctic Circle and the North Pole.

North′ German′ic, the subbranch of Germanic that includes the languages of Scandinavia and Iceland. Also called **Scandinavian.**

North′ Hale′don (hāl′dən), a town in NE New Jersey. 6026 (1960).

North′ High′lands, a town in central California, near Sacramento. 21,271 (1960). **—North′ High′lander.**

North′ Hol′land, a province in the W Netherlands. 2,054,509 (est. 1960); 1163 sq. mi. *Cap.:* Haarlem.

north·ing (nôr′thing, -thing), *n.* 1. northward movement or deviation. 2. distance due north. 3. distance due north made on any course tending northward. [NORTH + -ING[1]]

North′ Is′land, the northernmost principal island of New Zealand. 1,684,139 (est. 1961); 44,281 sq. mi.

North′ Kan′sas Cit′y, a town in W Missouri. 5657 (1960).

North′ Kore′a, a country in E Asia: formed 1948 after the division of the former country of Korea at 38° N. 10,700,000 (est. 1963); 50,000 sq. mi. *Cap.:* Pyongyang. Official name, **Democratic People's Republic of Korea.** Cf. **Korea.**

north·land (nôrth′lənd), *n.* 1. the land or region in the north. 2. the northern part of a country. 3. (*cap.*) the peninsula containing Norway and Sweden. [ME, OE: see NORTH, LAND] **—north′land·er,** *n.*

North′ Las′ Ve′gas, a city in S Nevada. 18,422 (1960).

North′ Lit′tle Rock′, a city in central Arkansas, on the Arkansas River. 58,032 (1960).

North·man (nôrth′mən), *n., pl.* **-men.** a member of the Scandinavian group which from about the 8th to the 11th century made many raids and established settlements in Great Britain, Ireland, many parts of continental Europe, and probably in parts of North America. [OE *northman;* see NORTH, MAN[1]]

North′ Man′chester, a town in N Indiana. 4377 (1960).

North′ Manka′to, a town in S Minnesota. 5927 (1960).

North′ Miam′i, a city in SE Florida. 28,708 (1960).

North′ Miam′i Beach′, a city in SE Florida. 21,405 (1960).

north·most (nôrth′mōst′ *or, esp. Brit.,* -məst), *adj.* northernmost. [NORTH + -MOST]

North′ Muske′gon, a town in SW Michigan. 3855 (1960).

North′ New′ Hyde′ Park′, a town on W Long Island, in SE New York. 17,929 (1960).

north-north·east (nôrth′nôrth′ēst′; *Naut.* nôr′nôr′ēst′), *n.* 1. the point on the compass midway between north and northeast. —*adj.* 2. coming from this point: *a north-northeast wind.* 3. directed toward this point: *a north-northeast course.* —*adv.* 4. from this point: *The wind is blowing north-northeast.* 5. toward this point: *sailing north-northeast.* *Abbr.:* NNE [late ME *north north est;* see NORTH, NORTHEAST]

north-north·east·ward (nôrth′nôrth′ēst′wərd; *Naut.* nôr′nôr′ēst′wərd), *adv., adj.* toward the north-northeast. Also, **north′-north′east′ward·ly.** [NORTH-NORTH-EAST + -WARD]

north-north·west (nôrth′nôrth′west′; *Naut.* nôr′nôr′west′), *n.* 1. the point on the compass midway between north and northwest. —*adj.* 2. coming from this point: *a north-northwest wind.* 3. directed toward this point: *a north-northwest course.* —*adv.* 4. from this point: *The wind is blowing north-northwest.* 5. toward this point: *sailing north-northwest.* *Abbr.:* NNW [ME; see NORTH, NORTHWEST]

north-north·west·ward (nôrth′nôrth′west′wərd, *Naut.* nôr′nôr′west′wərd), *adv., adj.* toward the north-northwest. Also, **north′-north′west′ward·ly.**

North′ Og′den, a town in N Utah. 2621 (1960).

North′ Olm′sted, a city in NE Ohio, near Cleveland. 16,290 (1960).

North′ Osse′tian Auton′omous Repub′lic, an autonomous republic in the Russian Federation in SE Europe. 634,000; 3088 sq. mi. *Cap.:* Vladikavkaz.

North′ Pacif′ic cur′rent, a warm ocean current moving eastward: the southern branch of the Kuroshio extension.

North′ Palm′ Beach′, a town in E Florida. 2684 (1960).

North′ Pel′ham, a town in SE New York. 5326 (1960).

North′ Plain′field, a city in NE New Jersey. 16,993 (1960).

North′ Platte′, 1. a river flowing from N Colorado through SE Wyoming and W Nebraska into the Platte. 618 mi. long. 2. a city in central Nebraska. 17,184 (1960).

North′ Plym′outh, a town in SE Massachusetts. 3467 (1960).

North′ Pole′, 1. *Geog.* the end of the earth's axis of rotation marking the northernmost point on the earth. 2. *Astron.* the point at which the extended axis of the earth cuts the northern half of the celestial sphere, about 1° from the North Star; the north celestial pole. 3. (*l.c.*) the pole of a magnet that seeks the earth's north magnetic pole. 4. (*l.c.*) See under **magnetic pole** (def. 1).

North·port (nôrth′pōrt′, -pôrt′), *n.* 1. a town on N Long Island, in SE New York. 5972 (1960). 2. a town in central Alabama. 5245 (1960).

North′ Prince′ton, a town in W New Jersey. 4506 (1960).

North′ Rhine′-West·pha′li·a (rīn′west fā′lē ə, -fāl′yə), a state in W West Germany; formerly a part of Rhine province. 16,280,000 (1963); 13,111 sq. mi. *Cap.:* Dusseldorf. German, **Nordrhein-Westfalen.**

North′ Rich′land Hills′, a town in N Texas. 8662 (1960).

North′ Rid′ing (rī′ding), an administrative division of Yorkshire, in N England. 354,382 (1961); 2127 sq. mi. *Co. seat:* Northallerton.

North′ Riv′er, a part of the Hudson River between NE New Jersey and SE New York.

North′ Riv′erside, a town in NE Illinois. 7989 (1960).

Nor·throp (nôr′thrəp), *n.* **John Howard,** born 1891, U.S. biochemist: Nobel prize 1946.

North′ Roy′al·ton (roi′əl tən), a town in N Ohio. 9290 (1960).

Nor·thrup (nôr′thrəp), *n.* a boy's given name.

North′ Scit′uate, a town in E Massachusetts. 3421 (1960).

North′ Sea′, an arm of the Atlantic between Great Britain and the European mainland. ab. 201,000 sq. mi.; greatest depth, 1998 ft. Formerly, **German Ocean.**

North′ Shreve′port, a town in NW Louisiana. 7701 (1960).

North′ Star′, *Astron.* Polaris.

North St. Paul, a town in E Minnesota. 8520 (1960).

North′ Syr′acuse, a town in central New York. 7412 (1960).

North′ Tar′rytown, a town in SE New York. 8818 (1960).

North′ Tem′perate Zone′, the part of the earth's surface between the tropic of Cancer and the Arctic Circle.

North′ Ton·a·wan′da (ton′ə won′də), a city in W New York. 34,757 (1960).

North′ Tur′lock, a town in central California. 2535 (1960).

North·um·ber·land (nôr thum′bər lənd), *n.* 1. a county in NE England. 818,988 (1961); 2019 sq. mi. *Co. seat:* Newcastle. 2. a town in central Pennsylvania. 4156 (1960).

North·um·bri·a (nôr thum′brē ə), *n.* an early English kingdom extending N from the Humber to the Firth of Forth. See map under **Mercia.**

North·um·bri·an (nôr thum′brē ən), *adj.* 1. of or pertaining to Northumbria, Northumberland, or the inhabitants or dialect of either. —*n.* 2. a native or inhabitant of Northumbria or Northumberland. 3. the English dialect of Northumbria or Northumberland. [NORTHUMBRI(A) + -AN]

North·vale (nôrth′vāl′), *n.* a town in NE New Jersey. 2892 (1960).

North′ Val′ley Stream′, a town on W Long Island, in SE New York. 17,239 (1960).

North′ Ver′non, a town in SE Indiana. 4062 (1960).

North′ Vietnam′, a former country in SE Asia that comprised Vietnam N of about 17° N latitude: now part of reunified Vietnam. Cf. **Vietnam, South Vietnam.**

North·ville (nôrth′vil), *n.* a town in SE Michigan. 3967 (1960).

North′ Virgin′ia Beach′, a town in SE Virginia. 2587 (1960).

North′ Wales′, a town in SE Pennsylvania. 3673 (1960).

north·ward (nôrth′wərd; *Naut.* nôr′thərd), *adv.* **1.** Also, **north′wards.** toward the north. —*adj.* **2.** moving, bearing, facing, or situated toward the north. —*n.* **3.** the northward part, direction, or point. Also, **north′wardly.** [ME; OE *northweard.* See NORTH, -WARD]

north·west (nôrth′west′; *Naut.* nôr′west′), *n.* **1.** a point on the compass midway between north and west. **2.** a region in this direction. **3. the Northwest, a.** the northwestern part of the United States, esp. Washington, Oregon, and Idaho. **b.** the northwestern part of the United States when its western boundary was the Mississippi River. **c.** the northwestern part of Canada. —*adj.* **4.** Also, **north′west′ern.** coming from this point: *a northwest wind.* **5.** directed toward this point: *a northwest course.* —*adv.* **6.** from this point: *a wind blowing northwest.* **7.** toward this point: *sailing northwest.* [ME, OE; see NORTH, WEST]

northwest′ by north′, *Navig., Survey.* a point on the compass, 11°15′ north of northwest. *Abbr.:* NWbN

northwest′ by west′, *Navig., Survey.* a point on the compass, 11°15′ west of northwest. *Abbr.:* NWbW

north·west·er (nôrth′wes′tər; *Naut.* nôr′wes′tər), *n.* a wind or gale from the northwest. Also, **nor′-wester.** [NORTHWEST + -ER[1]]

north·west·er·ly (nôrth′wes′tər lē; *Naut.* nôr′-wes′tər lē), *adj., adv.* toward or from the northwest. [NORTHWESTER + -LY]

north·west·ern·er (nôrth′wes′tər nər), *n.* **1.** a native or inhabitant of the northwest. **2.** (*cap.*) a native or inhabitant of the northwestern U.S. [NORTHWESTERN + -ER[1]]

North′-West Frontier′ Prov′ince (nôrth′west′, -west′), **1.** a former province in Pakistan, bordering Punjab and Kashmir on the west: included in West Pakistan province October 1955; a former province of British India. 13,560 sq. mi. *Cap.:* Peshawar. **2.** the former agencies and tribal areas between this province and the Afghanistan border. 25,699 sq. mi.

North′west Or′dinance, the act of Congress in 1787 providing for the government of the Northwest Territory and setting forth the steps by which its subdivisions might become States.

North′west Pas′sage, a ship route along the Arctic coast of Canada and Alaska, joining the Atlantic and Pacific oceans.

North′west Pas′sage, a historical novel (1937) by Kenneth Roberts.

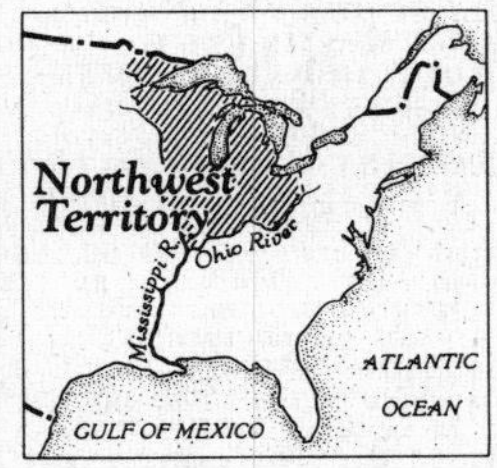

North′west Ter′ritories, a territory of Canada lying N of the provinces and extending E from Yukon territory to Davis Strait. 22,998 (1961); 1,304,903 sq. mi. Also called **Old Northwest.**

North′west Ter′ritory, the region north of the Ohio River, organized by Congress in 1787, comprising Ohio, Indiana, Illinois, Michigan, Wisconsin, and the eastern part of Minnesota.

north·west·ward (nôrth′west′wərd; *Naut.* nôr′-west′wərd), *adv., adj.* **1.** Also, **north′west′ward·ly.** toward the northwest. —*n.* **2.** the northwest. [ME; see NORTHWEST, -WARD]

north·west·wards (nôrth′west′wərdz; *Naut.* nôr′-west′wərdz), *adv.* northwestward.

North′ Wild′wood, a town in S New Jersey. 3598 (1960).

North′ Wilkes′bor·o (wilks′bûr ō, -bur ō), a town in NW North Carolina. 4197 (1960).

North·woods (nôrth′wo͝odz′), *n.* a town in E Missouri. 4701 (1960).

Nor·ton (nôr′tən), *n.* **1. Charles Eliot,** 1827–1908, U.S. scholar. **2. Thomas,** 1532–84, English author. **3.** a town in SW Virginia. 4996 (1960). **4.** a town in NW Kansas. 3345 (1960). **5.** a boy's given name.

Nor·vin (nôr′vin), *n.* a boy's given name.

Norw., **1.** Norway. **2.** Norwegian.

Nor·walk (nôr′wôk), *n.* **1.** a city in SW California. 88,739 (1960). **2.** a city in SW Connecticut. 67,775 (1960).

Nor·way (nôr′wā), *n.* **1.** a kingdom in N Europe, in the W part of the Scandinavian Peninsula. 3,667,000 (est. 1963); 124,555 sq. mi. *Cap.:* Oslo. Norwegian, **Norge. 2.** a town in NW Michigan, in the Upper Peninsula. 3171 (1960). **3.** a town in W Maine. 2654 (1960).

Nor′way ma′ple, a European maple, *Acer platanoides*, having bright green leaves, grown as a shade tree in the U.S.

Nor′way rat′, an Old World rat, *Rattus norvegicus*, having a grayish-brown body with whitish underparts and a long, scaly tail, now common in the U.S. in or near homes, barns, wharves, etc. Also called **brown rat.**

Nor′way salt′peter, *Chem.* See **ammonium nitrate.**

Nor′way spruce′, a European spruce, *Picea abies*, grown as an ornamental.

Nor·we·gian (nôr wē′jən), *adj.* **1.** of or pertaining to Norway, its inhabitants, or their language. —*n.* **2.** a native or inhabitant of Norway. **3.** the speech of Norway in any of its forms, whether Dano-Norwegian, the local dialects, or the standard language based on these, all being closely related to one another and to the other Scandinavian languages. [earlier *Norvegian* < ML *Norvegi(a)* NORWAY + -AN]

Norwe′gian Cur′rent, an ocean current formed from the terminus of the North Atlantic Current, flowing N along the Norwegian coast into the Barents Sea. Also called **Norwe′gian Coast′al Cur′rent.**

Norwe′gian elk′hound, one of a breed of dogs having a short, compact body, short, pointed ears, and a thick, gray coat, raised originally in Norway for hunting elk and other game.

Norwe′gian salt′peter, *Chem.* See **calcium nitrate.**

Norwe′gian Sea′, part of the Arctic Ocean, N and E of Iceland and between Greenland and Norway.

nor′west·er (nôr wes′tər), *n.* **1.** southwester (def. 3). **2.** northwester. [NOR(TH)WESTER]

Nor·wich (nôr′ich, -ij, nor′- *for 1;* nôr′wich *for 2,3*), *n.* **1.** a city in E Norfolk, in E England: cathedral. 119,904 (1960). **2.** a city in SE Connecticut, on the Thames River. 38,506 (1960). **3.** a town in central New York. 9175 (1960).

Nor′wich ter′rier, one of an English breed of small, short-legged terriers having a straight, wiry, red, gray, or black-and-tan coat.

Nor·wood (nôr′wo͝od′), *n.* **1.** a city in SW Ohio, near Cincinnati. 34,580 (1960). **2.** a town in E Massachusetts. 24,898 (1960). **3.** a town in SE Pennsylvania. 6729 (1960). **4.** a town in NE New Jersey. 2852 (1960).

nos-, var. of **noso-** before a vowel.

nos., numbers. Also, **Nos.**

n.o.s., not otherwise specified.

nos·ce te ip·sum (nōs′ke tā ip′so͝om; *Eng.* nō′sē te ip′səm), *Latin.* know thyself.

nose (nōz), *n., v.,* **nosed, nos·ing.** —*n.* **1.** the part of the face or facial region in man and certain animals which contains the nostrils and the organs of smell and functions as the usual passageway for air in respiration: in man it is a prominence in the center of the face formed of bone and cartilage, and serves also to modify or modulate the voice. **2.** this part as the organ of smell. **3.** the sense of smell: *fragrances appealing to the nose.* **4.** a faculty of perceiving or detecting: *to have a nose for secretive dealings.* **5.** something regarded as resembling the nose of a person or animal, as a spout or nozzle. **6.** the prow of a ship. **7.** the forward end of an aircraft: *Keep the nose up in landing.* **8.** the forward edge of the head of a golf club. **9.** a projecting part of anything: *the nose of a pair of pliers.* **10.** the human nose regarded as a symbol of meddling or prying: *Why can't he keep his nose out of my business?* **11.** the length of a nose, as of a horse. **12.** the bouquet of an alcoholic drink. **13. by a nose,** *Slang.* by a very narrow margin: *He passed the examination by a nose.* **14. count noses,** to count the number of people in attendance: *Each time the troop left an exhibit the leader counted noses.* **15. cut off one's nose to spite one's face,** to create a disadvantage to oneself through one's own spiteful action. **16. follow one's nose, a.** to go forward in a straight course. **b.** to guide oneself by instinct: *It had been many years since my last visit, but I found the house by following my nose.* **17. lead by the nose,** to exercise complete control over; reduce to submission: *He lets his wife lead him by the nose.* **18. look down one's nose at,** *Informal.* to regard with disdain or condescension: *He had always looked down his nose at foreigners.* **19. on the nose,** *Slang.* **a.** precisely; correctly. **b.** exactly on time: *We made it at 10 o'clock on the nose.* **20. pay through the nose,** to pay an excessive price: *They patronize small and exclusive shops where they cheerfully pay through the nose.* **21. put someone's nose out of joint, a.** to supersede a person in another's regard, devotion, etc. **b.** to thwart someone; spoil one's plans. **22. turn up one's nose at,** to regard with contempt; scorn: *Our cat turns up her nose at fish. My friend turns up his nose at anyone who hasn't had a college education.* **23. under one's nose,** plainly visible; in full view: *The theft took place right under the detective's nose.* Also, **under one's very nose.** —*v.t.* **24.** to perceive by or as by the nose or the sense of smell: *a cheese that could be nosed at some distance; a man who could always nose a crime.* **25.** to approach the nose to, as in smelling or examining; sniff. **26.** to move or push forward with or as with the nose: *The dog nosed its pup back into the yard. The boat nosed its way toward shore.* **27.** to defeat (an opponent), esp. by a narrow margin (often fol. by *out*): *The other candidate had been nosed out in the final returns.* **28.** to touch or rub with the nose; nuzzle. —*v.i.* **29.** to smell or sniff. **30.** to seek as if by smelling or scent: *The dogs nosed after their quarry.* **31.** to move or push forward: *to nose into the wind.* **32.** to meddle or pry (often fol. by *about, into,* etc.): *She lives vicariously, always nosing about in other people's lives.* **33.** (of a locomotive or self-propelled rail car) to swing horizontally from side to side at high speed. [ME; OE *nosu*, akin to D *neus*, G *Nase*, L *nāsus*, Skt *nāsā*] —**nose′less,** *adj.* —**nose′like′,** *adj.*

nose′ bag′. See **feed bag** (def. 1).

nose·band (nōz′band′), *n.* that part of a bridle or halter that passes over the animal's nose. [NOSE + BAND[2]] —**nose′band′ed,** *adj.*

nose·bleed (nōz′blēd′), *n.* **1.** bleeding from the nose. **2.** See **red trillium.** [NOSE + BLEED]

nose′ cone′, *Rocketry.* the cone-shaped forward section of a rocket or guided missile, including a heat shield and containing the payload.

nose′ dive′, **1.** a plunge of an aircraft with the forward part pointing downward. **2.** any sudden drop or rapid decline: *a time when market values were in a nose dive.*

nose-dive (nōz′dīv′), *v.i.,* **-dived** or **-dove, -dived, -div·ing.** to go into a nose dive: *a warning that prices might nose-dive.*

nose′ drops′, medicine for use in the nose and applied with a dropper.

nose′ end′er, *Naut.* muzzler (def. 2).

nose·gay (nōz′gā′), *n.* a small bunch of flowers; bouquet; posy. [late ME; a *gay* (obs., something pretty) for the NOSE (i.e., to smell)]

nose′ glass′es, eyeglasses held in place by a spring which clamps them to the bridge of the nose; pince-nez.

nose′ leaf′, a leaflike outgrowth of skin on the nose of various bats, thought to be sensitive to vibrations of the air.

nose·piece (nōz′pēs′), *n.* **1.** a protective cover for the nose. **2.** the part of a microscope where the object slide is attached. See diag. under **microscope. 3.** a noseband. **4.** the part of a frame for eyeglasses that rests on the bridge of the nose. [NOSE + PIECE]

nose′ ring′, **1.** a ring inserted in the nose of an animal, as to facilitate leading it. **2.** a ring worn as an ornament in the nose.

nose·wheel (nōz′hwēl′, -wēl′), *n.* the landing wheel under the nose of an aircraft. [NOSE + WHEEL]

nose·wing (nōz′wing′), *n.* the flared portion of each side of the nose; a nasal ala. [NOSE + WING]

nos·ey (nō′zē), *adj.,* **nos·i·er, nos·i·est.** nosy. —**nos′i·ly,** *adv.* —**nos′i·ness,** *n.*

Nos·ey Par·ker (nō′zē pär′kər), *Informal.* See **Nosy Parker.** Also, **nos′ey Par′ker.**

nosh (nosh), *v.i.* **1.** to eat between meals, esp. to nibble at tidbits. —*n.* **2.** a tidbit or snack eaten between meals. [< Yiddish; cf. G *naschen* to nibble, eat on the sly; c. Dan *naske*, Sw *snaska*]

nosh·er (nosh′ər), *n.* a person who eats tidbits, esp. often or continuously. [< Yiddish; see NOSH, -ER[1]]

no-show (nō′shō′), *n. Informal.* a person who makes a reservation on a plane, ship, or train and doesn't use it. [NO[2] + SHOW]

nos·ing (nō′zing), *n. Archit.* a projecting edge, as the part of the tread of a step extending beyond the riser, or a projecting part of a buttress. [NOSE + -ING[1]]

noso-, a learned borrowing from Greek meaning "disease," used in the formation of compound words: *nosology.* Also, *esp. before a vowel,* **nos-.** [comb. form repr. Gk *nóso(s)* disease, sickness, malady]

nos·o·gen·e·sis (nos′ə jen′i sis), *n.* pathogenesis. Also, **no·sog·e·ny** (nō soj′ə nē). [NOSO- + GENESIS] —**nos·o·ge·net·ic** (nos′ə jə net′ik), *adj.*

nos·o·ge·og·ra·phy (nos′ō jē og′rə fē), *n.* the study of the geographical causes and distribution of diseases. Also called **nos·och·tho·nog·ra·phy** (nos′ok thə nog′-rə fē). [NOSO- + GEOGRAPHY] —**nos·o·ge·o·graph·ic** (nos′ō jē′ə graf′ik), **nos′o·ge′o·graph′i·cal,** *adj.*

no·sog·ra·phy (nō sog′rə fē), *n.* the systematic description of diseases. [NOSO- + -GRAPHY] —**no·sog′ra·pher,** *n.* —**no·so·graph·ic** (nō′sə graf′ik), **no′so·graph′i·cal,** *adj.* —**no′so·graph′i·cal·ly,** *adv.*

no·sol·o·gy (nō sol′ə jē), *n.* **1.** the systematic classification of diseases. **2.** the knowledge of a disease. [< NL *nosologia.* See NOSO-, -LOGY] —**nos·o·log·i·cal** (nos′ə loj′i kəl), *adj.* —**nos′o·log′i·cal·ly,** *adv.* —**no·sol′o·gist,** *n.*

nos·o·pho·bi·a (nos′ə fō′bē ə), *n. Psychiatry.* an abnormal fear of disease. [NOSO- + -PHOBIA]

nos·tal·gia (no stal′jə, -jē ə, nə-), *n.* a desire to return in thought or in fact to a former time in one's life, to one's home, or to one's family and friends. [< NL < Gk *nóst(os)* a return home + *-algia* -ALGIA] —**nos·tal′gic,** *adj.* —**nos·tal′gi·cal·ly,** *adv.*

nos·tal·gy (no stal′jē, nə-), *n., pl.* **-gies.** *Archaic.* nostalgia.

nos·toc (nos′tok), *n.* any fresh-water, blue-green alga of the genus *Nostoc*, often found in jellylike colonies in moist places. [< NL, coined by Paracelsus]

nos·tol·o·gy (no stol′ə jē), *n.* geriatrics. [< Gk *nósto(s)* a return home + -LOGY] —**nos·to·log·ic** (nos′tə loj′ik), *adj.*

nos·to·ma·ni·a (nos′tə mā′nē ə, -mān′yə), *n.* intense homesickness; an irresistible compulsion to return home. [< Gk *nósto(s)* a return home + -MANIA]

Nos·tra·da·mus (nos′trə dā′məs, -dä′-), *n.* 1503–66, French astrologer. —**Nos·tra·dam·ic** (nos′trə dam′ik), *adj.*

nos·tril (nos′trəl), *n.* one of the external openings of the nose. [ME *nostrill*, OE *nosterl*, var. of *nosthyrl*, equiv. to *nosu* nose + *thyrel* hole; see THIRL]

Nos·tro·mo (no strō′mō), *n.* a novel (1904) by Joseph Conrad.

nos·trum (nos′trəm), *n.* **1.** a patent medicine. **2.** a quack medicine. **3.** a medicine made by the person who recommends it. **4.** a pet scheme, theory, device, etc., esp. one to remedy social or political ills; panacea. [< L *nostrum* our, ours (neut. sing. of *noster*); referring to the seller's calling the drug "our" drug]

nos·y (nō′zē), *adj.,* **nos·i·er, nos·i·est.** *Informal.* prying; inquisitive. Also, **nosey.** [NOSE + -Y[1]]

Nos·y Par·ker (nō′zē pär′kər), *Informal.* a nosy, prying person; busybody. Also, **Nosey Parker.**

not (not), *adv.* (used to express negation, denial, refusal, or prohibition): *You must not do that. It's not far from here.* [ME; weak var. of NOUGHT]

not-, var. of **noto-** before a vowel.

no·ta be·ne (nō′tä be′ne; *Eng.* nō′tə bē′nē), *Latin.* note well; take notice.

no·ta·bil·i·ty (nō′tə bil′i tē), *n., pl.* **-ties. 1.** the state or quality of being notable; distinction; prominence. **2.** *Chiefly Brit.* a notable person. [ME *notabilite.* See NOTABLE, -ITY]

no·ta·ble (nō′tə bəl), *adj.* **1.** worthy of note or notice; noteworthy: *a play which is a notable success; a notable theory.* **2.** prominent, important, or distinguished, as persons. **3.** *Archaic.* capable, thrifty, and industrious: *a notable housekeeper.* —*n.* **4.** a notable person; a prominent or important person. **5.** (*usually cap.*) *Fr. Hist.* **a.** one of a number of prominent men, usually of the aristocracy, called by the king on extraordinary occasions. **b. Notables,** Also called **Assembly of the Notables.** an assembly of high-ranking nobles, ecclesiastics, and state functionaries having deliberative but not legislative or administrative powers, convoked by the king principally in 1554, 1786, and 1788, in the lattermost year to establish the manner for selecting the States-General. **6.** *Obs.* a notable fact or thing. [ME *notab(i)le* < L *notābilis.* See NOTE, -ABLE] —**no′ta·ble·ness,** *n.* —**no′ta·bly,** *adv.*
—**Syn. 1, 2.** conspicuous, memorable, great, remarkable, noticeable, noted, outstanding, unusual, uncommon, eminent. **2.** celebrated, famous. —**Ant. 1.** ordinary. **2.** unknown.

no·tar·i·al (nō târ′ē əl), *adj.* **1.** of, pertaining to, or characteristic of a notary. **2.** drawn up or executed by a notary. [NOTARY + -AL[1]] —**no·tar′i·al·ly,** *adv.*

no·ta·rize (nō′tə rīz′), *v.t.,* **-rized, -riz·ing.** to certify (a document, contract, etc.) or cause to become certified through a notary public. [NOTAR(Y) + -IZE]

no·ta·ry (nō′tə rē), *n., pl.* **-ries.** See **notary public.** [ME < L *notārius* clerk, equiv. to *not(āre)* (to) note, mark + *-ārius* -ARY] —**no′ta·ry·ship′,** *n.*

no′tary pub′lic, *pl.* **notaries public.** a public officer or other person authorized to authenticate contracts, acknowledge deeds, take affidavits, protest bills of exchange, take depositions, etc.

no·ta·tion (nō tā′shən), *n.* **1.** a system of graphic symbols for a specialized use, other than ordinary writing: *musical notation; dance notation.* **2.** the process of noting or setting down by means of a special system of signs or symbols. **3.** the act of noting, marking, or setting down in writing. **4.** a note, jotting, or record: *notations in the margin.* [< L *notātiōn-* (s. of *notātiō*) a marking, equiv. to *notāt(us)* noted (ptp. of *notāre*) + *-iōn-* -ION] —**no·ta′tion·al,** *adj.*

notch (noch), *n.* **1.** an angular cut, indentation, or hollow in an object, surface, or edge. **2.** a cut or nick made in a stick or other object for record, as in keeping a score: *The marshal's revolver had six notches on the handle.* **3.** a deep, narrow opening or pass between mountains; defile. **4.** *Metall.* a taphole in a blast furnace: *iron notch; cinder notch.* **5.** *Informal.* a step, degree, or grade: *This one is a notch better than the other.* —*v.t.* **6.** to cut or make a notch or notches in. **7.** to make notches in by way of record: *He notched a stick each time he shot a hawk.* **8.** to record by a notch or notches: *He notched each hawk he killed on the stick.* **9.** to score, as in a game: *He notched another win in his record.* [a notch (by false division) for *an* *otch < OF *oche* notch] —**notch′y,** *adj.*

note (nōt), *n., v.,* **not·ed, not·ing.** —*n.* **1.** a brief record of something written down to assist the memory, or for reference, development, etc. **2. notes,** a record or outline of a speech, statement, testimony, etc., or of one's impressions of something. **3.** an explanatory or critical comment, or a reference to authority quoted, appended to a passage in a book or the like: *a note on the purpose of this book.* **4.** a brief written or printed statement giving particulars or information. **5.** *Library Science.* additional information about a book, such as its special series or some other significant identification, entered on the library catalog card. **6.** a short, informal letter: *to write a thank-you note.* **7.** a formal diplomatic or official communication in writing: *a note delivered by the ambassador.* **8.** a paper acknowledging a debt and promising payment; promissory note. **9.** a certificate, as of a government or a bank, current as money. **10.** eminence or distinction: *a man of note.* **11.** importance or consequence: *few events of particular note.* **12.** notice, observation, or heed: *Please take note of those warning signs. There are few plays worthy of note this season.* **13.** a characteristic or distinguishing feature: *There was a note of whimsy in the design of the house.* **14.** a mark, quality, or indication of something, esp. as a submerged but ubiquitous element: *There was just a note of sadism in his films.* **15.** a signal, announcement, or intimation: *a note of warning in her voice.* **16.** a musical sound or tone. **17.** *Music.* **a.** a sign or character used to represent a tone, its position and form indicating the pitch and duration of the tone. **b.** a key, as of a piano. **18.** a sound of musical quality uttered by a bird: *attentive to the thrush's note.* **19.** any call, cry, or sound of a bird, fowl, etc. **20.** a tone sounded on a musical instrument.

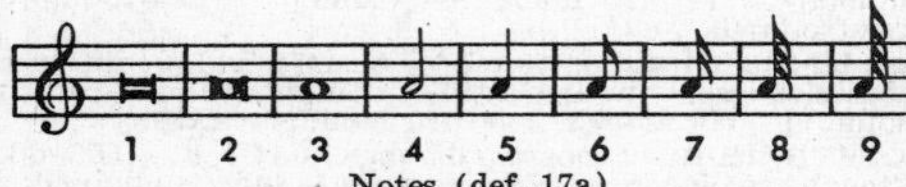

Notes (def. 17a)
1, 2, Breve; 3, Whole note or semibreve; 4, Half note or minim; 5, Quarter note or crotchet; 6, Eighth note or quaver; 7, Sixteenth note or semiquaver; 8, Thirty-second note or demisemiquaver; 9, Sixty-fourth note or hemidemisemiquaver

21. *Informal.* a new or unexpected element in a situation. **22.** a way of speaking or thinking: *His critics had begun to change their note.* **23.** a mark or sign, as of punctuation, used in writing or printing. **24.** *Archaic.* a melody, tune, or song. **25. compare notes,** to exchange views, ideas, or impressions: *The returning tourists were sitting on the sun deck comparing notes.* —*v.t.* **26.** to mark down, as in writing; make a memorandum of: *to note the places of interest in a travel diary.* **27.** to make particular mention of in a writing: *Please note that in your letter.* **28.** to annotate. **29.** to observe carefully; give attention or heed to: *Note the fine brushwork in this painting.* **30.** to take notice of; perceive: *We noted his concern at the announcement.* **31.** to set down in or furnish with musical notes. **32.** to indicate or designate; signify; denote. [ME < ML *nota* sign for musical tone, L, mark] —**not′er,** *n.*
—**Syn. 1.** memorandum, minute. **3.** commentary, annotation. See **remark. 9.** bill. **10.** repute, celebrity, fame, renown, reputation, name. **26.** register, record. **30.** see, spot, remark. **32.** mention.

note·book (nōt′bŏŏk′), *n.* **1.** a book of or for notes. **2.** a book in which promissory notes are entered, registered, recorded, etc. [NOTE + BOOK]

note′ bro′ker, *Finance.* a broker who buys and sells commercial paper.

note·case (nōt′kās′), *n.* *Chiefly Brit.* billfold. [NOTE + CASE[2]]

not·ed (nō′tid), *adj.* **1.** celebrated; famous. **2.** provided with musical notation, a musical score, etc.: *The text is illustrated with noted examples from the symphonies.* [NOTE + -ED[2]] —**not′ed·ly,** *adv.* —**not′ed·ness,** *n.*
—**Syn. 1.** distinguished, renowned, eminent. —**Ant. 1.** obscure, unknown.

note·less (nōt′lis), *adj.* **1.** of no note; undistinguished; unnoticed. **2.** unmusical or voiceless. [NOTE + -LESS] —**note′less·ly,** *adv.* —**note′less·ness,** *n.*

note′ of hand′. See **promissory note.**

note·pap·er (nōt′pā′pər), *n.* writing paper, esp. that used in personal correspondence. [NOTE + PAPER]

note′ row′ (rō), *Music Chiefly Brit.* See **tone row.**

Notes′ from the Un′derground, a novel (1864) by Dostoevsky.

note ver·bale (nôt ver bȧl′), *pl.* **notes ver·bales** (nôt ver bȧl′). *French.* a diplomatic communication prepared in the third person and unsigned: less formal than a note but more formal than an aide-mémoire.

note·wor·thy (nōt′wûr′thē), *adj.* worthy of notice or attention; notable; remarkable: *a noteworthy addition to our collection of rare books.* [NOTE + WORTHY] —**note′wor′thi·ly,** *adv.* —**note′wor′thi·ness,** *n.*

noth·ing (nuth′ing), *n.* **1.** no thing; not anything; naught: *to say nothing.* **2.** no part, share, or trace (usually fol. by *of*): *The house showed nothing of its former magnificence.* **3.** that which is nonexistent: *The sound faded to nothing.* **4.** something of no importance or significance: *Money is nothing when you're without health.* **5.** a trivial action, matter, circumstance, thing, or remark: *to exchange a few nothings when being introduced.* **6.** a person of no importance; a nobody: *He says he's happy being a nothing.* **7.** that which is without quantity or magnitude. **8.** a cipher or naught: *Nothing from nine leaves nine.* **9. for nothing, a.** free of charge. **b.** for no apparent reason or motive. **c.** futilely; to no avail: *They had gone to a great deal of expense for nothing.* **10. make nothing of, a.** to treat lightly; regard as easy. **b.** to be unsuccessful in comprehending: *He could make nothing of the complicated directions.* **11. nothing doing,** *Informal.* **a.** emphatically no; certainly not. **b.** no inducement, activity, advantage, etc., present to the eye: *We drove through the town but there seemed to be nothing doing.* **12. nothing less than** or **short of,** absolutely; completely: *She was used to nothing less than the best.* **13. think nothing of,** to treat casually; regard as insignificant: *He thinks nothing of lying to conceal his incompetence.* —*adv.* **14.** in no respect or degree; not at all: *It was nothing like that. Nothing dismayed, he repeated his question.* **15. nothing but,** nothing other than; only: *We could see nothing but fog.* [orig. two words.]

noth·ing·ness (nuth′ing nis), *n.* **1.** the state of being nothing. **2.** that which is nonexistent: *a view of man as suspended between infinity and nothingness.* **3.** lack of being; nonexistence: *The sound faded into nothingness.* **4.** unconsciousness or death: *She remembered a dizzy feeling, then nothingness.* **5.** utter insignificance, emptiness, or worthlessness; triviality: *She had never been dismayed by the nothingness of her life.* **6.** something insignificant or without value. [NOTHING + -NESS]

no·thus (nō′thəs, noth′əs), *adj.* *Meteorol.* (not in technical use) spissatus. [< L < Gk *nóthos* spurious, mongrel, hybrid]

no·tice (nō′tis), *n., v.,* **-ticed, -tic·ing.** —*n.* **1.** information or intelligence: *to give notice of one's departure.* **2.** an intimation; warning: *to serve notice that smoking is not allowed.* **3.** a note, placard, or the like conveying information or a warning: *to post a notice about the fire laws.* **4.** a notification of the termination, at a specified time, of an agreement, as for renting or employment, given by one of the parties to the agreement: *George had been with the firm 12 years when he suddenly gave notice and headed for Acapulco.* **5.** observation, perception, attention, or heed: *a book worthy of notice.* **6.** interested or favorable attention: *to take notice of an unusual feature in the construction of a building.* **7.** critical attention, appraisal, or evaluation: *Only a few of the entries were singled out for notice.* **8.** a brief written mention or critique, as of a newly published book; review: *The notices of the play were mostly favorable.* —*v.t.* **9.** to pay attention to or take notice of: *Did you notice her hat?* **10.** to perceive; become aware of: *Did you notice the fear in her voice?* **11.** to treat with attention, politeness, or favor: *The hostess barely noticed him.* **12.** to acknowledge acquaintance with: *She noticed him merely with a nod.* **13.** to mention or refer to; point out, as to a person: *a circumstance that was noticed in an earlier chapter.* **14.** to give notice to; serve with a notice: *to notice a householder that taxes are overdue.* [late ME < MF < L *nōtitia* a knowing, a being known] —**no′tic·er,** *n.*
—**Syn. 1.** advice, news, notification, announcement. **3.** sign, poster. **5.** note, cognizance. **7.** comment, mention. **9.** see, regard, heed, observe. **10.** note, mark, remark; descry, distinguish, discriminate, recognize, understand. NOTICE, DISCERN, PERCEIVE imply becoming aware of, and paying attention to, something. All are "point-action" verbs. To NOTICE is to become aware of something which has caught one's attention: *to notice a newspaper headline; to notice a road sign.* DISCERN suggests distinguishing (sometimes with difficulty) and recognizing a thing for what it is, discriminating it from its surroundings: *In spite of the fog, we finally discerned the outline of the harbor.* PERCEIVE, often used as a formal substitute for see or notice, may convey also the idea of understanding meanings and implications: *After examining the evidence he perceived its significance.*

no·tice·a·ble (nō′ti sə bəl), *adj.* **1.** such as to attract notice or attention; capable of being noticed: *a noticeable lack of restraint.* **2.** worthy or deserving of notice or attention; noteworthy: *a book that is noticeable for its vivid historical background.* [NOTICE + -ABLE] —**no′tice·a·bil′i·ty,** *n.* —**no′tice·a·bly,** *adv.*
—**Syn. 1, 2.** conspicuous, prominent, notable. —**Ant. 1, 2.** inconspicuous.

no·ti·fi·ca·tion (nō′tə fə kā′shən), *n.* **1.** the act of notifying, making known, or giving notice. **2.** a formal notifying or informing. **3.** an instance of notifying; notice. [ME *notificacioun* < ML *notificātiōn-* (s. of *notificātiō*). See NOTIFY, -ATION]

no·ti·fy (nō′tə fī′), *v.t.,* **-fied, -fy·ing. 1.** to inform or give notice of (something): *to notify the police of a crime.* **2.** *Chiefly Brit.* to make known; give information of: *The sale was notified in the newspapers.* [ME *notifien* < MF *notifier* < L *nōtificāre,* equiv. to *(g)nōt(us)* known (ptp. of *(g)nōscere* to come to know) + *-ificāre* -IFY] —**no′ti·fi′a·ble,** *adj.* —**no′ti·fi′er,** *n.*

no·tion (nō′shən), *n.* **1.** a general, vague, or imperfect conception or idea of something: *a notion of how something should be done.* **2.** an opinion, view, or belief: *That's his notion, not mine.* **3.** conception or idea. **4.** a fanciful or foolish idea; whim: *It was her mother's notion to have the party.* **5.** an ingenious article; device; contrivance; knickknack. **6. notions,** small articles, as buttons, thread, ribbon, and other personal items, esp. such items displayed together for sale, as in a five-and-ten. [< L *nōtiōn-* (s. of *nōtiō*) examination, idea, equiv. to *nōt(us)* examined, known (ptp. of *nōscere*) + *-iōn-* -ION] —**no′tion·less,** *adj.*
—**Syn. 1, 3.** See **idea.**

no·tion·al (nō′shə nəl), *adj.* **1.** pertaining to or expressing a notion or idea. **2.** of the nature of a notion or idea: *a notional response to the question.* **3.** abstract, theoretical, or speculative, as reflective thought. **4.** not real or actual; ideal or imaginary: *to create a notional world for oneself.* **5.** given to or full of foolish or fanciful ideas or moods. **6.** *Gram.* **a.** relating to the meaning expressed by a linguistic form. **b.** having full lexical meaning, in contrast to relational. **7.** *Semantics.* belonging to a class of words that express clear concepts rather than relations between concepts; presentive. Cf. **relational** (def. 3), **symbolic** (def. 4). [NOTION + -AL[1]] —**no·tion·al·i·ty** (nō′shə nal′i tē), *n.* —**no′tion·al·ly,** *adv.*

no·tion·ate (nō′shə nit), *adj.* *U.S. Informal.* **1.** strong-willed; headstrong; stubborn. **2.** having foolish and fanciful notions. [NOTION + -ATE[1]]

noto-, a learned borrowing from Greek meaning "the back," used in the formation of compound words: *notochord.* Also, *esp. before a vowel,* **not-.** [comb. form repr. Gk *nôton* the back]

no·to·chord (nō′tə kôrd′), *n.* *Biol., Embryol.* a rodlike cord of cells that forms the chief axial supporting structure of the body of the lower chordates, as amphioxus and the cyclostomes, and of the embryos of the higher vertebrates. [NOTO- + CHORD] —**no′to·chord′al,** *adj.*

No·to·gae·a (nō′tə jē′ə), *n.* a biogeographical division comprising the Australian region. Also, **No′to·ge′a.** [< NL < Gk *nóto(s)* the south + *gaîa* earth, soil, land] —**No′to·gae′an, No′to·ge′an,** *n., adj.* —**No′to·gae′al, No′to·ge′al, No′to·gae′ic, No′to·ge′ic,** *adj.*

no·to·ri·e·ty (nō′tə rī′i tē), *n., pl.* **-ties. 1.** the state or character of being notorious or widely known: *a craze for notoriety.* **2.** *Chiefly Brit.* a notorious or celebrated person. [< ML *nōtōrietās,* equiv. to *nōtōri(us)* NOTORIOUS + *-etās* -ety, var. of -ITY]

no·to·ri·ous (nō tôr′ē əs, -tōr′-), *adj.* **1.** widely but unfavorably known: *a notorious gambler.* **2.** publicly or generally known: *a metal that is notorious for its resistance to rust.* [< ML *nōtōrius* evident, equiv. to *nōt(us)* known, recognized (ptp. of *nōscere*) + *-ōrius* -ORY[1]] —**no·to′ri·ous·ly,** *adv.* —**no·to′ri·ous·ness,** *n.*

no·tor·nis (nō tôr′nis), *n.* any of several rare, flightless, gallinulelike birds of the genus *Notornis,* of New Zealand. [< NL: name of the genus < Gk *nót(os)* the south + *órnis* a bird]

no·to·un·gu·late (nō′tō ung′gyə lit, -lāt′), *n.* **1.** one of the herbivorous, hoofed mammals of the extinct order *Notoungulata,* best known from the Paleocene to the Pleistocene epochs of South America. —*adj.* **2.** belonging or pertaining to the *Notoungulata.* Also, **notungulate.** [< NL *Notoungulata.* See NOTUNGULATE]

No·tre Dame (nō′trə dām′, dăm′, nō′tər), a famous early Gothic cathedral in Paris (started 1163). Also called **Notre Dame de Paris.**

No·tre Dame de Pa·ris (*Fr.* nô trᵊ dȧm də pȧ rē′), **1.** (*italics*) See **Hunchback of Notre Dame, The. 2.** See **Notre Dame.**

no-trump (nō′trump′), *Bridge.* —*adj.* **1.** (of a hand, bid, or contract) without a trump suit; noting a bid or contract to be played without naming a trump suit. —*n.* **2.** the declaration to play a no-trump contract.

no-trump·er (nō′trum′pər), *n.* *Bridge.* the player who bids or plays a no-trump contract. [NO-TRUMP + -ER[1]]

Not·ting·ham (not′ing əm), *n.* **1.** a city in SW Nottinghamshire, in central England. 311,645 (1961). **2.** Nottinghamshire.

Not·ting·ham·shire (not′ing əm shēr′, -shər), *n.* a county in central England. 902,966 (1961); 844 sq. mi. *Co. seat:* Nottingham. Also **Nottingham, Notts** (nots).

not·tur·no (nə tŏŏr′nō, nō-; *It.* nôt tŏŏr′nô), *n., pl.* **-ni** (-nē). *Music.* **1.** an 18th-century composition for chamber orchestra, similar to a serenade or a divertimento. **2.** nocturne. [< It: of the night. See NOCTURN]

no·tum (nō′təm), *n., pl.* **-ta** (-tə). a dorsal plate or sclerite of the thorax of an insect. [< NL < Gk *nôton* the back] —**no′tal,** *adj.*

not′ un′der command′, *Naut.* (of a vessel) not under control because of breakage or failure of equipment.

not′-un·der-com·mand′ lights′ (not′un′dər kə mand′), *Naut.* two red lights, one six feet directly above the other and visible at least two miles away, displayed to show that a vessel is not under command. Also called **breakdown lights, not′-un·der-con·trol′ lights′** (not′un′dər kən trōl′).

no·tun·gu·late (nō tung′gyə lit, -lāt′), *n., adj.* notoungulate. [< NL *Notungulata* name of order, equiv. to *not(o)-* (< Gk *nôtos* the south) + *ungulata* UNGULATE]

No·tus (nō′təs), *n.* the ancient Greek personification of the south wind. Cf. **Auster.** [< L < Gk *Nótos* the south wind, the south]

not·with·stand·ing (not′with stan′ding, -with-), *prep.* **1.** without being opposed or prevented by; in spite of: *Notwithstanding a brilliant defense, he was found guilty. He went to the game anyway, doctor's orders notwithstanding.* —*conj.* **2.** in spite of the fact that; although: *It was the same material, notwithstanding the texture seemed different.* —*adv.* **3.** nevertheless; anyway; yet: *We were invited notwithstanding.* [ME; see NOT, WITHSTAND, -ING[2]]
—**Syn. 1.** NOTWITHSTANDING, DESPITE, IN SPITE OF imply that something is true even though there are obstacles or opposing conditions. The three expressions may be used practically interchangeably. NOTWITHSTANDING suggests, however, a hindrance of some kind: *Notwithstanding the long delay, I shall still go.* DESPITE, now literary and somewhat archaic, indicates that there is an active opposition: *Despite procrastination and disorganization, they finished the project.* IN SPITE OF, the modern equivalent on an informal level, implies meeting strong opposing forces or circumstances which must be taken into account: *He succeeded in spite of many discouragements.* —**Ant. 1.** because of, on account of.

Nouak·chott (nwäk shot′), *n.* a city in and the capital of Mauritania, on the W coast. 10,000 (est. 1961).

nou·gat (nōō′gət, nōō′gä), *n.* a chewy or brittle confection containing almonds or other nuts and sometimes fruit. [< F < Pr << L **nucātum,* n. use of neut. of **nucātus,* equiv. to *nuc-* (s. of *nux*) nut + *-ātus* -ATE[1]]

nou·ga·tine (nōō′gə tēn′), *n.* a chocolate-coated nougat. [NOUGAT + -INE[1]]

nought (nôt), *n., adj., adv.* naught. [ME; OE *nōht,* contr. of *nōwiht,* equiv. to *ne* not + *ōwiht* OUGHT[3]]

noughts-and-cross·es (nôts′ən krô′siz, -kros′iz), *n.* *Brit.* tick-tack-toe (def. 1).

Nou·mé·a (nōō mā′ ə), *n.* a city in and the capital of New Caledonia, on the SW coast. 30,000 (est. 1960).

nou·me·non (nōō′mə non′, nou′-), *n., pl.* **-na** (-nə). **1.** the object, itself inaccessible to experience, to which a phenomenon is referred for the basis or cause of its sense content. **2.** a thing in itself, as distinguished from a phenomenon or thing as it appears. **3.** *Kantianism.* that which can be the object only of a purely intellectual, nonsensuous intuition. [< Gk *nooúmenon* a thing being perceived, n. use of neut. of prp. passive of *noeîn* to perceive; akin to NOUS] —**nou′me·nal,** *adj.* —**nou′-**

me·nal·ism, *n.* —**nou′me·nal·ist,** *n.* —**nou′me·nal′i·ty,** *n.* —**nou′me·nal·ly,** *adv.*

noun (noun), *n.* **1.** *Gram.* any member of a class of words that are formally distinguished in many languages, as in English, typically by the plural and possessive endings and that function as the main or only elements of subjects, as *deed, belief, writing, man, Ohio, whiteness.* Nouns are often thought of as referring to persons, places, things, states, or qualities. —*adj.* **2.** Also, **noun′al.** of or resembling a noun. [ME *nowne* < AF *noun* < L *nōmen* NAME] —**noun′al·ly,** *adv.*

nour·ish (nûr′ish, nur′-), *v.t.* **1.** to sustain with food or nutriment; supply with what is necessary for maintaining life. **2.** to cherish, foster, keep alive, etc.: *He had long nourished the dream of living abroad.* **3.** to strengthen, build up, or promote: *to nourish discontent among the have-nots; to nourish the arts in one's community.* [ME *norisshe* < OF *noriss-,* long s. of *norir* < L *nūtrīre* to feed; see -ISH²] —**nour′ish·a·ble,** *adj.* —**nour′ish·er,** *n.* —**nour′ish·ing·ly,** *adv.*
—**Syn. 1.** See **nurse. 3.** encourage, help, aid, back, advance. —**Ant. 3.** discourage.

nour·ish·ment (nûr′ish mənt, nur′-), *n.* **1.** that which nourishes; food, nutriment, or sustenance. **2.** the act of nourishing. **3.** the state of being nourished. **4.** a process, system, method, etc., of providing or administering nourishment: *a treatise on the nourishment of international trade.* [late ME *norysshement* < MF *norissement.* See NOURISH, -MENT]

nous (nōōs, nous), *n.* **1.** *Gk. Philos.* mind or intellect. **2.** *Neoplatonism.* the first and purest emanation of the One, regarded as the self-contemplating order of the universe. [< Gk *noûs,* contracted var. of *nóos* mind]

nou·veau riche (nōō vō rēsh′; *Eng.* nōō′vō rēsh′), *pl.* ***nou·veaux riches*** (nōō vō rēsh′; *Eng.* nōō′vō rēsh′). *French. Usually Disparaging.* a person who is newly rich: *the ostentation of the* nouveaux riches *of the 1920's.*

nou·veau·té (nōō vō tā′), *n., pl.* **-tés** (-tā′). *French.* newness; novelty.

nou·velle cui·sine (nōō vel kwē zēn′), (*sometimes caps.*) *French.* a modern style of French cooking that emphasizes the use of the finest and freshest ingredients simply and imaginatively prepared, often with fresh herbs, the artful arrangement and presentation of food, and the use of reduced stocks in place of flour-thickened sauces. [lit., new cooking]

Nou·velle Hé·lo·ïse, La (*Fr.* LA nōō vel ā lô ēz′). See **La Nouvelle Héloïse.**

nou·velles (nōō vel′), *n.pl. French.* news.

nou·velle vague (nōō vel VAG′), *pl.* **nou·velles vagues** (nōō vel VAG′). *French.* a new wave, trend, movement, phase, etc., esp. in an art form, as that manifested in French and Italian motion-picture making of the early 1960's. [lit., new wave]

Nov., November.

nov., novelist.

no·va (nō′və), *n., pl.* **-vae** (-vē), **-vas.** *Astron.* a star that suddenly becomes thousands of times brighter and then gradually fades to its original intensity. Cf. **supernova.** [< NL: n. use of fem. of L *novus* NEW]

no·vac·u·lite (nō vak′yə līt′), *n. Petrog.* a very hard rock, probably sedimentary, composed essentially of microcrystalline quartz. [< L *novācul(a)* a sharp knife, razor + -ITE¹]

No·va·lis (nō vä′lis), *n.* pen name of Friedrich von Hardenberg.

No·va Lis·bo·a (*Port.* nô′və lēzh bô′ə), a city in central Angola. 37,381 (est. 1955). Formerly, **Huambo.**

No·va·ra (nō vär′ə; *It.* nô vä′rä), *n.* a city in NE Piedmont, in NW Italy. 86,190 (1961).

No·va Sco·tia (nō′və skō′shə), a peninsula and province in SE Canada: once a part of the French province of Acadia. 737,007 (1961); 21,068 sq. mi. *Cap.:* Halifax. —**No′va Sco′tian.**

no·va·tion (nō vā′shən), *n.* **1.** *Law.* the substitution of a new obligation for an old one, usually by the substitution of a new debtor or of a new creditor. **2.** *Rare.* the introduction of something new; innovation. [< L *novātiōn-* (s. of *novātiō*) a renewing, equiv. to *novāt(us)* renewed (ptp. of *novāre;* see NOVA) + *-iōn-* -ION]

No·va·to (nō vä′tō, nə-), *n.* a city in W California, N of San Francisco. 17,881 (1960).

No·va·ya Zem·lya (nô′vä yä zem lyä′), two large islands in the Arctic Ocean, N of the Soviet Union in Europe, belonging to the Soviet Union: test center for nuclear warheads. 35,000 sq. mi. Also, **No·va Zem·bla** (nō′və zem blä′).

nov·el¹ (nov′əl), *n.* **1.** a fictitious prose narrative of considerable length and complexity, portraying characters and presenting a sequential organization of action and scenes. **2.** (formerly) novella (def. 1). [< It *novella* < L: short for *novella narrātiō* new kind of story. See NOVEL²] —**nov′el·like′,** *adj.*

nov·el² (nov′əl), *adj.* of a new kind, or different from anything seen or known before: *a novel idea.* [late ME < L *novellus* fresh, young, novel, dim. of *novus* NEW]
—**Syn.** See **new.**

nov·el³ (nov′əl), *n.* **1.** *Roman Law.* **a.** imperial enactments subsequent and supplementary to an imperial compilation and codification of authoritative legal materials. **b.** Usually, **Novels.** imperial enactments subsequent to the promulgation of Justinian's Code and supplementary to it: one of the four divisions of the Corpus Juris Civilis. **2.** *Civil Law.* an amendment to a statute. [<LL *novella* (*constitūtiō*) a new (regulation, order). See NOVEL²]

nov·el·ette (nov′ə let′), *n.* a short novel. [NOVEL¹ + -ETTE]

nov·el·ist (nov′ə list), *n.* a person who writes novels. [NOVEL¹ + -IST]

nov·el·is·tic (nov′ə lis′tik), *adj.* of, pertaining to, or characteristic of novels. [NOVEL¹ + -ISTIC] —**nov′el·is′ti·cal·ly,** *adv.*

nov·el·ize (nov′ə līz′), *v.t.,* **-ized, -iz·ing. 1.** to put into the form of a novel. **2.** to make fictional; fictionalize: *He was called in to novelize the history of the past 10 years.* Also, *esp. Brit.,* **nov′el·ise′.** [NOVEL¹ + -IZE] —**nov′el·i·za′tion,** *n.*

no·vel·la (nō vel′ə; *It.* nô vel′lä), *n., pl.* **-vel·las, -vel·le** (-vel′ā; *It.* -vel′le). **1.** a tale or short story of the type contained in the *Decameron* of Boccaccio. **2.** a fictional prose narrative that is longer and more complex than a short story; a short novel. [< It; see NOVEL¹]

nov·el·ty (nov′əl tē), *n., pl.* **-ties,** *adj.;* —*n.* **1.** state or quality of being novel; novel character; newness: *the novelty of the Space Age.* **2.** a novel occurrence, experience, or proceeding: *His sarcastic witticisms had ceased being an entertaining novelty.* **3.** an article of trade whose value is chiefly decorative, comic, or the like and whose appeal is often transitory: *a wild emporium for every novelty from a pocket-size icecube maker to a life-size plastic python on a leash.* —*adj.* **4.** *Textiles.* **a.** (of a weave) consisting of a combination of basic weaves. **b.** (of a fabric or garment) having a pattern or design produced by a novelty weave. **c.** (of yarn) having irregularities within the fibrous structure. **5.** of or pertaining to novelties as articles of trade: *novelty goods; novelty items.* **6.** having or displaying novelties: *novelty shop.* [ME *novelte* < MF *novelete* < LL *novellitās* newness. See NOVEL², -ITY]

nov′elty sid′ing. See **drop siding.**

No·vem·ber (nō vem′bər), *n.* **1.** the eleventh month of the year, containing 30 days. **2.** a word used in communications to represent the letter N. [ME, OE < L *novembris* the ninth month of the early Roman calendar]

no·vem·de·cil·lion (nō′vəm di sil′yən), *n., pl.* **-lions** (*as after a numeral*) **-lion,** *adj.* —*n.* **1.** a cardinal number represented in the United States and France by one followed by 60 zeros, and in Great Britain and Germany, by one followed by 114 zeros. —*adj.* **2.** amounting to one novemdecillion in number. [< L *novemdec(im)* nineteen (*novem* nine + *decem* ten) + (M)ILLION] —**no′vem·de·cil′lionth,** *adj., n.*

no·ve·na (nō vē′nə, nə-), *n., pl.* **-nae** (-nē). *Rom. Cath. Ch.* a devotion consisting of prayers or services on nine consecutive days. [< ML, n. use of fem. sing. of L *novēnus* nine each]

no·ver·cal (nō vûr′kəl), *adj.* of, like, or befitting a stepmother. [< L *novercāl(is),* equiv. to *noverc(a)* stepmother + *-ālis* -AL¹]

Nov·go·rod (nôv′go rot), *n.* a city in the W RSFSR, in the NW Soviet Union in Europe, SE of Leningrad: a former capital of Russia. 61,000 (1959).

No·vi (nō′vī), *n.* a town in SE Michigan. 6390 (1960).

nov·ice (nov′is), *n.* **1.** a person who is new to the circumstances, work, etc., in which he is placed; beginner; tyro: *a novice in politics.* **2.** a person who has been received into a religious order or congregation for a period of probation before taking vows. **3.** a person newly become a church member. **4.** a recent convert to Christianity. [ME *novyce* < MF *novice* < ML *novitius* convent novice, var. of L *novīcius* newly come into a particular status, deriv. of *novus* new. See -ITIOUS] —**nov′ice·hood′,** *n.* —**nov′ice·like′,** *adj.*
—**Syn. 1.** newcomer. **1, 2.** neophyte.

Nov·ice (nov′is), *n.* a boy's given name.

No·vi Sad (nô′vē säd′), a city in NE Yugoslavia, on the Danube. 123,000 (1961). German, **Neusatz.**

no·vi·ti·ate (nō vish′ē it, -āt′), *n.* **1.** state or period of being a novice of a religious order or congregation. **2.** the quarters occupied by religious novices during probation. **3.** the state or period of being a beginner in anything. **4.** a novice. Also, **no·vi′ci·ate.** [< ML, equiv. to *novīti(us)* NOVICE + *-ātus* -ATE³]

no·vo·bi·o·cin (nō′vō bī′ə sin), *n. Pharm.* a paleyellow, crystalline, antibiotic powder, $C_{31}H_{36}N_2O_{11}$, produced by the fermentation of *Streptomyces niveus* and *S. spheroides,* used in the treatment of gram-positive bacterial infections, esp. of *Staphylococcus aureus.* [*novo-* (comb. form repr. L *novus* new) + (*anti*)*bio*(*tic*) + (*streptomy*)*cin*]

No·vo·caine (nō′və kān′), *n. Pharm., Trademark.* procaine.

No·vo·cher·kassk (nô′vo chər käsk′), *n.* a city in the SW RSFSR, in the S Soviet Union in Europe, in the Donets Basin. 104,000 (est. 1962).

No·vo·kuz·netsk (nô′vo ko͝oz netsk′), *n.* a city in the S RSFSR, in the E Soviet Union in Asia: a planned industrial center is located here because of coal deposits of the Kuznetsk Basin. 410,000 (est. 1962). Formerly, **Stalinsk.**

No·vo·mos·kovsk (nô′vo mos kôfsk′), *n.* a city in the west RSFSR, in the central Soviet Union in Europe, S of Moscow. 114,000 (est. 1962).

No·vo·ros·siysk (nô′vo ro sēsk′), *n.* a seaport in the SW RSFSR, in the S Soviet Union in Europe, on the Black Sea. 104,000 (est. 1962). Also, **No′vo·ros·siisk′.**

No·vo·shakh·tinsk (nô′vo shäkh′tinsk), *n.* a city in the S RSFSR, in the SW Soviet Union in Europe, NE of the Sea of Azov. 108,000 (est. 1962).

No·vo·si·birsk (nô′vo si bērsk′), *n.* a city in the SW RSFSR, in the W Soviet Union in Asia, on the Ob. 1,013,000 (est. 1964). Formerly, **No·vo·ni·ko·la·evsk** (nô′vo ni ko lä′yefsk).

No·vot·ný (nô′vôt nē′), *n.* **An·to·nín** (än′tô nyēn′), 1904–75, Czech political leader: president 1957–68.

No·vum (nō′vəm), *n.* **Mare.** See **Mare Novum.**

No·vum Or·ga·num (nō′vəm ôr′gə nəm, ôr gä′nəm, -gan′əm; *Lat.* nō′wo͝om ôr′gä no͝om′), a philosophical work in Latin (1620), by Francis Bacon, presenting an inductive method for scientific and philosophical inquiry.

no·vus or·do se·clo·rum (nō′wo͝os ōr′dō se klō′ro͝om; *Eng.* nō′vəs ôr′dō se klôr′əm, -klōr′-), *Latin.* a new order of the ages (is born): motto on the reverse of the great seal of the United States (adapted from Vergil's *Eclogues* IV:5).

now (nou), *adv.* **1.** at the present time or moment: *He is here now.* **2.** without further delay; immediately; at once: *Either do it now or not at all.* **3.** at this time or juncture in some period under consideration or in some course of proceedings described: *The case was now ready for the jury.* **4.** at the time or moment only just past: *I saw him just now on the street.* **5.** in these present times; nowadays: *Now you rarely see the word.* **6.** under the present or existing circumstances; as matters stand: *I see now what you meant.* **7.** (used to introduce a statement or question): *Now, you don't really mean that.* **8.** (used to strengthen a command, entreaty, or the like): *Now stop that!* **9. now and again,** occasionally. Also, **now and then. 10. now that,** inasmuch as; since: *Now that he is rich and famous, he is constantly being besieged by appeals for aid.* —*conj.* **11.** inasmuch as; since: *Now you're here, why not stay?* —*n.* **12.** the present time or moment: *Up to now there's been only one.* [ME; OE *nū,* c. Icel, Goth *nū;* akin to G *nun,* L *num,* Skt *nu,* Gk *nŷ, nŷn*] —**now′ness,** *n.*

now·a·days (nou′ə dāz′), *adv.* **1.** at the present day; in these times: *One rarely sees that nowadays.* —*n.* **2.** the present: *The houses of nowadays are much more efficient.* [ME *nou adaies,* OE *nū on dæge;* see -S¹]

No·wa·ta (nə wä′tə), *n.* a town in NE Oklahoma. 4163 (1960).

no·way (nō′wā′), *adv.* in no way, respect, or degree; not at all: *He was noway responsible for the accident.* Also, **no′ways′.** [ME; see NO², WAY]

nowed (noud, nōō′id), *adj. Heraldry.* represented as tied into a loose knot: *a serpent nowed.* [< MF *nou(e)* knotted (see NOWY) + -ED³]

now·el (nō el′), *n. Archaic.* Noel (def. 2). [ME < MF *no(u)el* NOEL]

No·well (nō′əl), *n.* a boy's given name, form of **Noel.**

no·where (nō′hwâr′, -wâr′), *adv.* **1.** in, at, or to no place; not anywhere: *The missing pen was nowhere to be found. We went nowhere last weekend.* —*n.* **2.** the state of nonexistence or seeming nonexistence: *A gang of thieves appeared from nowhere.* **3.** anonymity or obscurity: *She came from nowhere to win the championship.* [ME; OE *nāhwær, nōhwær.* See NO¹, WHERE]

no·where-dense (nō′hwâr dens′, -wâr-), *adj. Math.* (of a set in a topological space) having a closure that contains no open set with any points in it; nondense.

no·wheres (nō′hwârz, -wârz), *adv. U.S.* nowhere.

no·whith·er (nō′hwith′ər, -with′-), *adv.* to no place; nowhere: *paths leading nowhither.* [ME *nohwider,* OE *nāhwider.* See NO¹, WHITHER]

no·wise (nō′wīz′), *adv.* in no wise; noway; not at all: *a plan nowise agreeable to the committee.* [NO¹ + -WISE]

nowt¹ (nout), *n., pl.* **nowt.** *Scot. and North Eng.* **1.** an ox. **2.** a herd of cattle. [ME < Scand; cf. Icel *naut,* NEAT²]

nowt² (nōt), *n. Brit. Dial.* naught; nothing.

now·y (nou′ē, nō′ē), *adj. Heraldry.* noting a partition line or charge in which one or more curves interrupt a normally straight line or lines, usually halfway along their length: *per fess nowy; a cross nowy.* [< MF *noue* knotted < L *nōdātus.* See NODE, -ATE¹]

Nox (noks), *n.* the ancient Roman goddess personifying night.

nox·ious (nok′shəs), *adj.* **1.** harmful or injurious to health or physical well-being: *noxious fumes; a noxious swamp.* **2.** morally harmful; pernicious: *a noxious plan to spread dissension.* [< L *noxius* harmful, hurtful, injurious, equiv. to *nox(a)* harm, hurt, injury (akin to *noc(ēre)* (to) do harm, inflict injury) + *-ius* -IOUS] —**nox′ious·ly,** *adv.* —**nox′ious·ness,** *n.*
—**Syn. 1.** hurtful, unwholesome, unhealthy, nocuous, detrimental, deleterious. **2.** corruptive. —**Ant. 1, 2.** harmless.

no·yade (nwä yäd′; *Fr.* NWA YAD′), *n.* destruction or execution by drowning, esp. as practiced at Nantes, France, in 1793–94, during the Reign of Terror. [< F: drowning, equiv. to *noy(er)* (to) drown (< L *necāre*) + *-ade* -ADE¹]

Noyes (noiz), *n.* **1. Alfred,** 1880–1958, English poet. **2. John Humphrey,** 1811–86, U.S. social reformer: founder of the Oneida Community.

Noz·ze di Fi·ga·ro, Le (*It.* le nôt′tse dē fē′gä RÔ). See **Marriage of Figaro, The.**

noz·zle (noz′əl), *n.* **1.** a projecting spout, terminal discharging pipe, or the like, as of a bellows or a hose. **2.** the socket of a candlestick. **3.** the spout of a teapot. **4.** *Slang.* the nose. [NOSE + -LE (dim. suffix)]

NP, neuropsychiatric.

Np, **1.** *Physics.* neper. **2.** *Chem.* neptunium.

N.P., **1.** new paragraph. **2.** nisi prius. **3.** no protest. **4.** Notary Public.

n.p., **1.** net proceeds. **2.** new paragraph. **3.** nisi prius. **4.** no pagination. **5.** no place of publication. **6.** no protest. **7.** notary public.

n.p. or d., no place or date.

n.p.t., normal pressure and temperature. Also, **npt**

nr., near.

NRA, *U.S. Govt.* National Recovery Administration: the former federal agency (1933–36) charged with administering the provisions of the National Industrial Recovery Act. Also, **N.R.A.**

NRAB, National Railroad Adjustment Board.

NRPB, National Resources Planning Board.

NS, **1.** not sufficient (funds). **2.** nuclear ship.

Ns, nimbo-stratus.

ns, nanosecond; nanoseconds. Also, **nsec**

N.S., **1.** New Style. **2.** Nova Scotia.

n.s., not specified.

NSA, **1.** National Shipping Authority. **2.** National Standards Association. **3.** National Student Association. Also, **N.S.A.**

NSC, See **National Security Council.**

NSF, **1.** National Science Foundation. **2.** not sufficient funds. Also, **N.S.F.**

N/S/F, not sufficient funds.

N-shell (en′shel′), *n. Physics.* the fourth shell of electrons surrounding the nucleus of an atom and containing, when filled, thirty-two electrons having principal quantum number four. Cf. **K-shell, L-shell, M-shell.**

N.S.P.C.A., National Society for the Prevention of Cruelty to Animals.

N.S.P.C.C., National Society for the Prevention of Cruelty to Children.

n.s.p.f., not specifically provided for.

NSRB, National Security Resources Board.

N.S.W., New South Wales.

-n't, an adverbial combining form of **not:** *didn't; won't; mustn't.* [by contr.]

NT, New Testament. Also, **NT.**

nt, nit; nits.

Nt, *Chem.* niton.

N.T., **1.** New Testament. **2.** Northern Territory.

nth (enth), *adj.* **1.** being the last in a series of infinitely decreasing or increasing values, amounts, etc. **2.** *Informal.* (of an item in a series of occurrences, planned events, things used, etc., that is thought of as being infinitely large) being the latest, or most recent: *This* *is the nth time I've told you to eat slowly.* **3. the nth degree or power, a.** a high degree or power. **b.** the utmost degree or extent: *The jewel sparkled to the nth degree.* [n (the letter) + -TH²]

n-tu·ple (en to͞o′pəl, -tyo͞o′-, -tup′əl; en′to͝o pəl, -tyo͞o-), *n. Math.* a set of *n* objects or quantities, where *n* is an integer, esp. such a set arranged in a specified order (**ordered n-tuple**). [N + *-tuple* (abstracted from words such as *quintuple, octuple*)]

nt. wt., net weight.

nu¹ (no͞o, nyo͞o), *n.* **1.** the 13th letter of the Greek alphabet (N, ν). **2.** the consonant sound represented by this letter. [< Gk < Sem; cf. Heb *nun*]

nu² (no͞o), *interj.* well? so? so what? [< Yiddish; c. OHG, MHG *nū* (adv. and conj.), G *nu* (dial. and colloquial) well! well now! See NOW]

Nu (no͞o), *n.* **U** (o͞o), born 1907, Burmese statesman.

nu·ance (no͞o′äns, nyo͞o′-, no͞o äns′, nyo͞o-; *Fr.* NY-äns′), *n., pl.* **-anc·es** (-än siz, -än′siz; *Fr.* NY äns′). a subtle shade of color, expression, or variation. [< F: shade, hue, equiv. to *nu(er)* (to) shade (lit., to cloud < VL **nūba*, r. L *nūbēs* cloud) + *-ance* -ANCE]

nub (nub), *n.* **1.** a knob or protuberance. **2.** a lump or small piece: *a nub of coal; a nub of pencil.* **3.** *Informal.* the point, gist, or heart of something. **4.** a small mass of fibers produced on a card, dyed brilliant colors, and introduced into yarn during the spinning process. [var. of *knub* < MLG *knubbe* KNOB]

nub·bin (nub′in), *n.* **1.** a small lump or stunted piece; stub. **2.** a small or imperfect ear of corn. **3.** an undeveloped fruit. [? NUB + *-in*, var. of -ING¹]

nub·ble (nub′əl), *n.* **1.** a small lump or piece. **2.** a small knob or protuberance. [NUB + -LE (dim. suffix)]

nub·bly (nub′lē), *adj.,* **-bli·er, -bli·est. 1.** full of small protuberances. **2.** in the form of small lumps. [NUBBLE + -Y¹]

nub·by (nub′ē), *adj.* **-bi·er, -bi·est.** having nubs. [NUB + -Y¹]

nu·bi·a (no͞o′bē ə, nyo͞o′-), *n.* a light, knitted woolen head scarf for women. [< L *nūb(ēs)* a cloud + -IA]

Nu·bi·a (no͞o′bē ə, nyo͞o′-), *n.* a region in the S United Arab Republic and the Sudan, N of Khartoum, extending from the Nile to the Red Sea.

Nu·bi·an (no͞o′bē ən, nyo͞o′-), *n.* **1.** one of a Negroid people of mixed descent inhabiting Nubia. **2.** a language of the Nile valley below Khartoum. **3.** a Nubian or Negro slave. **4.** a Nubian horse. **—*adj.* 5.** of, pertaining to, or characteristic of Nubia, its people, or their language. [NUBI(A) + -AN]

Nu′bian Des′ert, an arid region in the NE Sudan.

nu·bile (no͞o′bil, nyo͞o′-), *adj.* (of a girl or young woman) suitable for marriage, esp. in regard to age or physical development. [< L *nūbilis*, equiv. to *nūb(ere)* (to) marry + *-ilis* -ILE] **—nu·bil′i·ty,** *n.*

nu·bi·lous (no͞o′bə ləs, nyo͞o′-), *adj.* **1.** cloudy or foggy. **2.** obscure; vague; indefinite. [< L *nūbilus*, equiv. to *nūb(ēs)* cloud + *-ilus* adj. suffix. See -OUS]

Nu·bi·um (no͞o′bē əm, nyo͞o′-), *n.* **Mare.** See **Mare Nubium.**

nu·cel·lus (no͞o sel′əs, nyo͞o-), *n., pl.* **-cel·li** (-sel′ī). *Bot.* the central cellular mass of the body of the ovule, containing the embryo sac. [< NL: alter. of L *nucella* little nut, equiv. to *nuc-* (s. of *nux*) nut + *-ella* dim. suffix] **—nu·cel′lar,** *adj.*

nu·cha (no͞o′kə, nyo͞o′-), *n., pl.* **-chae** (-kē). nape. [< ML: nape of neck < Ar *nukhā* spinal marrow]

nuci-, a learned borrowing from Latin meaning "nut," used in the formation of compound words: *nuciform.* [comb. form repr. L *nuci-* (s. of *nux*) nut]

nu·ci·form (no͞o′sə fôrm′, nyo͞o′-), *adj.* nut-shaped. [NUCI- + -FORM]

nucle-, var. of **nucleo-** before a vowel: *nuclear.*

nu·cle·ar (no͞o′klē ər, nyo͞o′-), *adj.* **1.** of, pertaining to, or forming a nucleus. **2.** pertaining to or involving atomic weapons: *nuclear war.* **3.** operated or powered by atomic energy: *a nuclear submarine.* **4.** (of a nation or group of nations) having atomic bombs. [NUCLE- + -AR¹; cf. F *nucléaire*]

nu′clear cross′ sec′tion, *Physics.* See **cross section** (def. 8).

nu′clear en′ergy. See **atomic energy.**

nu′clear fam′ily, *Anthropol.* a social unit composed of father, mother, and children. Cf. **extended family.**

nu′clear fis′sion, fission (def. 3).

nu′clear fu′sion, fusion (def. 4).

nu′clear i′somer, *Physics.* isomer (def. 2).

nu′clear isom′erism, *Physics.* isomerism (def. 2).

nu′clear mag′neton, *Physics.* a unit of magnetic moment, used to measure proton spin and approximately equal to $^1/_{1836}$ Bohr magneton.

nu′clear phys′ics, the branch of physics that deals with the behavior, structure, and component parts of atomic nuclei. **—nu′clear phys′icist.**

nu′clear reac′tion, reaction (def. 8).

nu′clear reac′tor, *Physics.* reactor (def. 4).

nu′clear war′head. See **atomic warhead.**

nu·cle·ase (no͞o′klē ās′, nyo͞o′-), *n. Biochem.* any of the class of enzymes comprising the nucleinases, nucleotidases, and nucleosidases, and that serve to break down nucleic acids, found in plant and animal tissue. [NUCLE- + -ASE]

nu·cle·ate (no͞o′klē it, -āt′, nyo͞o′-), *adj., v.,* **-at·ed, -at·ing. —*adj.* 1.** having a nucleus. **—*v.t.* 2.** to form (something) into a nucleus. **—*v.i.* 3.** to form a nucleus. [< L *nucleātus* having a kernel or stone. See NUCLE-, -ATE¹] **—nu·cle·a·tion** (no͞o′klē ā′shən, nyo͞o′-), *n.* **—nu′cle·a′tor,** *n.*

nu·cle·i (no͞o′klē ī′, nyo͞o′-), *n.* pl. of **nucleus.** [< L *nuclei* small nuts, kernels (nom. pl. of *nucleus*)]

nu·cle′ic ac′id (no͞o klē′ik, nyo͞o-), *Biochem.* any of a group of complex acids occurring in all living cells, esp. as a component of cell-nucleus proteins, and composed of a phosphoric acid group, a carbohydrate, two purines, and two pyrimidines. Cf. **DNA, RNA.** [NUCLE- + -IC]

nu·cle·in (no͞o′klē in, nyo͞o′-), *n. Biochem.* any of a class of phosphorus-containing protein substances occurring in cell nuclei. [NUCLE- + -IN²]

nu·cle·in·ase (no͞o′klē ə nās′, nyo͞o′-), *n. Biochem.* any of a class of enzymes that split nucleic acids into nucleotides. [NUCLEIN + -ASE]

nucleo-, a combining form of **nucleus, nuclear,** or **nucleic acid:** *nucleoprotein.* Also, *esp. before a vowel,* **nucle-.**

nucleol-, a combining form of **nucleolus:** *nucleolated.*

nu·cle·o·lar (no͞o klē′ə lər, nyo͞o-), *adj.* of, pertaining to, or forming a nucleolus. [NUCLEOL- + -AR¹]

nu·cle·o·lat·ed (no͞o′klē ə lā′tid, nyo͞o′-), *adj.* containing a nucleolus or nucleoli. Also, **nu′cle·o·late′.** [NUCLEOL- + -ATE¹ + -ED³]

nu·cle·o·lus (no͞o klē′ə ləs, nyo͞o-), *n., pl.* **-li** (-lī′). *Biol.* a conspicuous, often rounded body within the nucleus of a cell. Also, **nu·cle·ole** (no͞o′klē ōl′, nyo͞o′-). [< L: dim. of *nucleus* kernel. See NUCLEUS] **—nu·cle′o·loid′,** *adj.*

nu·cle·on (no͞o′klē on′, nyo͞o′-), *n. Physics.* a proton or neutron, esp. when considered as a component of a nucleus. [NUCLE- + -ON¹]

nu·cle·on·ics (no͞o′klē on′iks, nyo͞o′-), *n.* (*construed as sing.*) the branch of science that deals with atomic nuclei, esp. practical applications, as in industrial engineering. [NUCLEON + -ICS]

nu·cle·o·phil·ic (no͞o′klē ə fil′ik, nyo͞o′-), *adj. Chem.* of or pertaining to electron contribution in covalent bonding (opposed to *electrophilic*). [NUCLEO- + -PHILIC]

nu·cle·o·plasm (no͞o′klē ə plaz′əm, nyo͞o′-), *n. Biol.* karyoplasm. [NUCLEO- + -PLASM] **—nu′cle·o·plas′mic, nu·cle·o·plas·mat·ic** (no͞o′klē ō plaz mat′ik, nyo͞o′-), *adj.*

nu·cle·o·pro·tein (no͞o′klē ə prō′tēn, -tē in, nyo͞o′-), *n. Biochem.* any of the class of conjugated proteins found in plant and animal cells and consisting of a protein combined with a nucleic acid, essential for cell division and reproduction. [NUCLEO- + PROTEIN]

nu·cle·o·sid·ase (no͞o′klē ə sī′dās, nyo͞o′-), *n. Biochem.* any of the class of enzymes that catalyze the hydrolysis of nucleosides. [NUCLEOSIDE + -ASE]

nu·cle·o·side (no͞o′klē ə sīd′, nyo͞o′-), *n. Biochem.* any of the class of compounds derived by the hydrolysis of nucleic acids or nucleotides, consisting typically of desoxyribose or ribose combined with adenine, or guanine and cytosine, uracil, or thymine. [NUCLE- + -OSE² + -IDE]

nu·cle·o·tid·ase (no͞o′klē ə tī′dās, nyo͞o′-), *n. Biochem.* any of the class of enzymes that catalyze the hydrolysis of nucleotides into nucleosides and phosphoric acid. Also called **nu·cle·o·phos·pha·tase** (no͞o′klē ō-fos′fə tās′, nyo͞o′-), **phosphonuclease.** [NUCLEOTIDE + -ASE]

nu·cle·o·tide (no͞o′klē ə tīd′, nyo͞o′-), *n. Biochem.* any of the class of esters formed by the interaction of phosphoric acid and a nucleoside or by the partial hydrolysis of nucleic acids. [alter. of NUCLEOSIDE]

nu·cle·us (no͞o′klē əs, nyo͞o′-), *n., pl.* **-cle·i** (-klē ī′), **-cle·us·es. 1.** a central part about which other parts are grouped; core: *A few faithful friends formed the nucleus of the club.* **2.** *Biol.* a specialized, usually spherical mass of protoplasm encased in a membrane, and found in most living cells, forming an essential element in their growth, metabolism, and reproduction, and in the transmission of genic characters. See illus. under **amoeba. 3.** *Anat.* a mass of gray matter in the brain and spinal cord in which incoming nerve fibers form connections with outgoing fibers. **4.** *Chem.* a fundamental arrangement of atoms, as the benzene ring, that may occur in many compounds by substitution of atoms without a change in structure. **5.** *Physics.* the positively charged mass within an atom, composed of neutrons and protons, and possessing most of the mass but occupying only a small fraction of the volume of the atom. **6.** *Astron.* the condensed portion of the head of a comet. **7.** *Meteorol.* a particle upon which condensation of water vapor occurs to form water drops or ice crystals. **8.** *Phonet.* the vocalic or vowellike element in a syllable, as the *a*-sound in *cat.* [< L: kernel, syncopated var. of *nuculeus*, equiv. to *nucul(a)* little nut (*nuc-*, s. of *nux* nut, + *-ula* -ULE) + *-eus* adj. suffix]
—Syn. 1. center, kernel, heart.

nu′cleus count′er. See **dust counter.**

nu·clide (no͞o′klīd, nyo͞o′-), *n. Physics.* **1.** an atomic species in which all atoms have the same atomic number and mass number. **2.** an individual atom in such a species. [NUCL- + *-ide* < Gk *eidos* shape]

Nudd (nyth), *n.* Llud.

nude (no͞od, nyo͞od), *adj.* **1.** naked or unclothed, as a person or the body. **2.** without the usual coverings, furnishings, etc.; bare: *a nude stretch of land laid waste by brush fires.* **3.** *Law.* unsupported; made without a consideration: *a nude pact.* **4.** having the color nude. **—*n.* 5.** a nude figure in art. **6.** an unclothed human figure. **7. the nude,** the condition of being unclothed. **8.** a light grayish-yellow brown to brownish-pink color. [< L *nūdus* NAKED] **—nude′ly,** *adv.* **—nude′ness,** *n.*
—Syn. 1. uncovered, undressed, undraped, exposed. **—Ant. 1.** covered.

nudge (nuj), *v.,* **nudged, nudg·ing,** *n.* **—*v.t.* 1.** to push slightly or jog, esp. with the elbow. **—*v.i.* 2.** to give a nudge. **—*n.* 3.** a slight push or jog. [var. of dial. *(k)nidge*, akin to OE *cnucian, cnocian* to KNOCK] **—nudg′er,** *n.*

nudi-, a learned borrowing from Latin meaning "naked," "bare," used in the formation of compound words: *nudicaul.* [comb. form repr. L *nūd(us)* naked]

nu·di·branch (no͞o′də brangk′, nyo͞o′-), *n.* a shell-less, marine snail of the suborder *Nudibranchia*, having external, often branched respiratory appendages on the back and sides. [< F *nudibranche*, equiv. to *nudi* NUDI- + *branche* gills (< L *branchia* BRANCHIA)]

nu·di·bran·chi·ate (no͞o′də brang′kē it, -āt′, nyo͞o′-), *n.* **1.** nudibranch. **—*adj.* 2.** belonging or pertaining to the *Nudibranchia.* Also, **nu·di·bran·chi·an** (no͞o′də brang′kē ən, nyo͞o′-). [< NL *Nudibranchiata* name of suborder of mollusks. See NUDI-, BRANCHIATE]

nu·di·caul (no͞o′də kôl′, nyo͞o′-), *adj. Bot.* having leafless stems. Also, **nu′di·cau′lous.** [NUDI- + CAUL]

nud·ie (no͞o′dē, nyo͞o′-), *n. Slang.* **1.** a show or motion picture in which a nude or nearly nude female or females perform. **2.** a nude female performer or model. [NUD(E) + -IE]

nud·ism (no͞o′diz əm, nyo͞o′-), *n.* the practice of going nude in the belief that such practice benefits health. [NUDE + -ISM] **—nud′ist,** *n., adj.*

nu·di·ty (no͞o′di tē, nyo͞o′-), *n., pl.* **-ties** for 2. **1.** the state or fact of being nude; nakedness. **2.** something nude or naked. [< L *nūditās.* See NUDE, -ITY]

nud·nik (no͝od′nik), *n. Slang.* a stupid person; dope; jerk. [< Yiddish < Russ]

nu·dum pac·tum (nyo͞o′dəm pak′təm), *Law.* a simple contract or promise involving no legal considerations. [< L: lit., a nude pact]

Nu·e·ces (no͞o ā′səs), *n.* a river in S Texas, flowing SE to Corpus Christi Bay, on the Gulf of Mexico. 338 mi. long.

nu·ée ar·dente (*Fr.* NY ā′ AR dänt′), *pl.* **nu·ées ar·dentes** (*Fr.* NY ā′ ZAR dänt′). *Geol.* (in a volcanic eruption) a swiftly expanding cloud of hot gases, ashes, and lava fragments. [F: lit., burning cloud]

Nue·va Ge·ro·na (nwe′vä he rô′nä), a town on the Isle of Pines, S of Cuba. 2935 (1953).

Nue·va O·co·te·pe·que (nwe′vä ô kô′te pe′ke), a city in W Honduras. 4120 (1961).

Nue·vo La·re·do (nwe′vô lä re′thô), a city in NE Mexico, on the Rio Grande. 117,728 (est. 1965).

Nue·vo Le·ón (nwā′vō lā ōn′, no͞o ā′-; *Sp.* nwe′vô le ôn′), a state in NE Mexico. 1,078,848 (1960); 25,136 sq. mi. *Cap.:* Monterrey.

Nu·fud (ne fo͞od′), *n.* See **Nefud Desert.**

nu·gae (no͞o′gī; *Eng.* nyo͞o′jē), *n.pl. Latin.* trifles.

nu·ga·to·ry (no͞o′gə tōr′ē, -tôr′ē, nyo͞o′-), *adj.* **1.** trifling; of no real value; worthless. **2.** of no force or effect; futile; vain. [< L *nūgātōrius* worthless, useless, trifling, equiv. to *nūgāt(us)* (ptp. of *nūgārī* to trifle) + *-ōrius* -ORY¹]
—Syn. 1. trivial, insignificant, frivolous. **2.** useless, ineffective.

nug·get (nug′it), *n.* **1.** a lump of something, as of precious metal. **2.** a lump of native gold. **3.** *Welding.* (in a spot-weld) the metal fused. **4.** *Australian.* **a.** a powerful, heavy animal. **b.** a strong, thickset man. [? dim. of obs. *nug* small piece, var. of NOG²; see -ET] **—nug′get·y,** *adj.*

nui·sance (no͞o′səns, nyo͞o′-), *n.* **1.** an obnoxious or annoying person, thing, practice, etc.: *a monthly meeting that was more nuisance than pleasure.* **2.** *Law.* something offensive or annoying to individuals or to the community, esp. in violation of their legal rights. [late ME *nu(i)sa(u)nce* < AF, equiv. to *nuis(er)* (to) harm (< L *nocēre*) + *-ance* -ANCE]

nui′sance ground′, *Canadian Dial.* a garbage dump.

nui′sance tax′, a tax paid in small amounts, usually by consumers.

nuke ((no͞ok, nyo͞ok), *n., adj., v.,* **nuked, nuk·ing.** *Slang.* **—*n.* 1.** a nuclear weapon. **2.** a thermonuclear weapon. **—*adj.* 3.** of or pertaining to a nuclear or thermonuclear weapon. **—*v.t.* 4.** to attack or destroy with or as with nuclear weapons. [by shortening]

Nü-kua (NY′kwä′), *n.* a Chinese goddess who repaired and restored order to heaven and earth when they were damaged, and who created the human race.

NUL, National Urban League. Also **N.U.L.**

null (nul), *adj.* **1.** without value, effect, consequence, or significance. **2.** being or amounting to nothing; lacking; nonexistent. **3.** *Math.* (of a set) containing no elements; empty; void. **4.** being or amounting to zero. **5. null and void,** without legal force or effect; not valid: *This check is null and void.* [< L *nullus*, equiv. to *n(e)* not + *ullus* any]

nul·lah (nul′ə), *n.* (in the East Indies) **1.** an intermittent watercourse. **2.** a gully or ravine. [< Hindi *nālā* brook, ravine]

nul·la-nul·la (nul′ə nul′ə), *n. Australian.* an aboriginal club or cudgel for use in hunting and war. [< native Austral name]

nulli-, a combining form meaning "none," "null": *nullify.* [< L *nulli-* not any, none, no (comb. form of *null(us)* NULL)]

nul·li·fi·ca·tion (nul′ə fə kā′shən), *n.* **1.** the act or an instance of nullifying. **2.** the state of being nullified. **3.** (*often cap.*) *U.S.* failure of a State to aid in enforcement of federal laws within its limits. [< LL *nullificātiōn-* (s. of *nullificātiō*) contempt, equiv. to *nullificāt(us)* despised (ptp. of *nullificāre*) + *-iōn-* -ION. See NULLIFY] **—nul′li·fi·ca′tion·ist, nul′li·fi·ca′tor,** *n.*

nul·li·fid·i·an (nul′ə fid′ē ən), *n.* a person who has no faith or religion; skeptic. [NULLI- + L *fid-* (s. of *fidēs*) faith + -IAN]

nul·li·fy (nul′ə fī′), *v.t.,* **-fied, -fy·ing. 1.** to deprive (something) of value or effectiveness; make futile or of no consequence. **2.** to render or declare legally void or inoperative: *to nullify a contract.* [< LL *nullificāre* to despise. See NULLI-, -FY] **—nul′li·fi′er,** *n.*
—Syn. 1, 2. invalidate, annul, void.

nul·ling (nul′ing), *n.* knulling.

nul·lip·a·ra (nu lip′ər ə), *n., pl.* **-a·rae** (-ə rē′). *Obstet.* a woman who has never borne a child. [< NL: *nulli-* NULLI- + *-para*, fem. of *-parus* -PAROUS] **—nul·li·par·i·ty** (nul′ə par′i tē), *n.* **—nul·lip′a·rous,** *adj.*

nul·li·pore (nul′ə pōr′, -pôr′), *n. Bot.* any of the coralline algae with a crustlike plant body. [NULLI- + PORE²] **—nul·lip·o·rous** (nu lip′ər əs, nul′ə pōr′əs, -pôr′-), *adj.*

nul·li·ty (nul′i tē), *n., pl.* **-ties** for 2, 3. **1.** the state or quality of being null; nothingness; invalidity. **2.** something null. **3.** something of no legal force or validity. [< ML *nullitas.* See NULL, -ITY]

nul·li·us fi·li·us (no͞ol′lē o͝os′ fē′lē o͝os′; *Eng.* nul′ē əs fē′lē əs), *Latin.* (esp. in law) son of nobody; bastard.

nul·li·us ju·ris (no͞ol′lē o͝os′ yo͞o′ris; *Eng.* nul′ē əs jo͝or′is), *Latin.* (esp. in old English law) of no legal force.

null-man·i·fold (nul′man′ə fōld′), *n. Math.* null-space.

nul·lo (nul′ō), *n., pl.* **-los.** (in certain card games) a bid to take no tricks. [< It: none < L *nullus* NULL]

null′ se′quence, *Math.* a sequence that has zero as its limit.

null-space (nul′spās′), *n. Math.* the set of elements of a vector space that a given linear transformation maps to zero. Also called **null-manifold.**

Num., Numbers.

num., 1. number. 2. numeral; numerals.

Nu·man·ti·a (no͞o man′shē ə, -shə, nyo͞o-), *n.* an ancient city in N Spain: besieged and taken 134–133 B.C. by Scipio the Younger.

Nu·ma·nus (no͞o mā′nəs, nyo͞o-), *n. Rom. Legend.* the brother-in-law of Turnus, killed in the war between Turnus and Aeneas.

Nu·ma Pom·pil·i·us (no͞o′mə pom pil′ē əs, nyo͞o′-mə), died 673? B.C., 2nd legendary Sabine king of Rome 715–673?.

numb (num), *adj.* **1.** deprived of or deficient in the physical or mental power of sensation and movement: *fingers numb with cold; a person numb with grief.* **2.** of the nature of numbness: *a numb sensation.* —*v.t.* **3.** to make numb. [ME *nome,* lit., taken, seized, var. of *nomen, numen,* OE *numen,* ptp. of *niman* to take] —**numb′ly,** *adv.* —**numb′ness,** *n.*

num·bat (num′bat), *n.* See **banded anteater.** [< native Austral name]

num·ber (num′bər), *n.* **1.** the sum, total, count, or aggregate of a collection of units, or any generalization of this concept. **2.** a numeral. **3.** the particular numeral assigned to an object so as to designate its place in a series: *house number; license number.* **4.** a word or symbol, or a combination of words or symbols, used in counting or in noting a total. **5.** one of a series of things distinguished by numerals. **6.** a single part of a book published in parts. **7.** a single issue of a periodical: *several numbers of a popular magazine.* **8.** any of a collection of poems or songs: *to sing several numbers.* **9.** a single part of a program made up of a number of similar parts: *For her third number she played a nocturne.* **10.** *Theat.* a single or distinct performance within a show, as a song, dance, etc.: *The comic routine followed the dance number.* **11.** a tune or arrangement for singing or dancing. **12.** the full count of a collection or company. **13.** a collection or company. **14.** a quantity of individuals: *Their number was above 20,000.* **15.** a certain collection, company, or quantity not precisely reckoned, but usually considerable or large: *I've gone there a number of times.* **16. numbers, a.** a considerable amount or quantity; many: *Numbers flocked to the city to see the parade.* **b.** metrical feet; verse. **c.** musical periods, measures, or groups of notes. **d.** See **numbers pool** (def. 1). **e.** *Obs.* arithmetic. **17.** numerical strength or superiority; complement: *The garrison is not up to its full number.* **18.** quantity as composed of units: *to increase the number of eligible voters.* **19.** *Gram.* a category of substantival and verbal inflection found in many languages, as English, Latin, Arabic, used to indicate whether a word has one or more than one referent. There may be a two-way distinction in number, as between singular and plural, three-way, as between singular, dual, and plural, or more. **20.** a distinct part of an extended musical work, or one in a sequence of compositions. **21.** conformity in music or verse to regular beat or measure; rhythm. **22.** *Informal.* a girl or young woman: *a cute little blonde number.* **23.** an article of merchandise, esp. of wearing apparel, offered for sale: *Put those numbers in the display window.* **24.** mathematics regarded as a science, a basic concept, and a mode of thought: *Number is the basis of science.* **25. get** or **have someone's number,** *Slang.* to become informed about someone's real motives, character, intentions, etc.: *He was only interested in her fortune, but she got his number fast.* **26. have one's number on it,** *Slang.* to be thought of as the instrument of fate in the death of a person: *That bullet had his number on it.* **27. one's number is (was, will be) up,** *Slang.* **a.** one is (was, will be) in serious trouble. **b.** one is (was, will be) on the point of death: *Convinced that her number was up anyway, she refused to see doctors.* **28. the numbers.** See **numbers pool** (def. 1). **29. without number,** of unknown or countless number; vast: *stars without number.* —*v.t.* **30.** to ascertain the number of. **31.** to mark with or distinguish by a number or numbers. **32.** to count over one by one; tell: *to number one's beads in prayer.* **33.** to mention one by one; enumerate: *They numbered the highlights of their trip at length.* **34.** to fix the number of; limit in number; make few in number: *to number the hours until the attack should begin.* **35.** to consider or include in a number: *I number myself among his friends.* **36.** to live or have lived (a number of years). **37.** to amount to or comprise in number; total: *The town numbers 12,000 inhabitants. The crew numbers 50 men.* **38.** to apportion or divide: *The players were numbered into two teams.* **39.** to apportion; divide. —*v.i.* **40.** to count. **41.** to be numbered or included (usually fol. by *among* or *with*): *Several eminent scientists number among his friends.* **42.** to make a total; reach an amount: *Casualties numbered in the thousands.* [ME; var. of *nombre* < OF < L *numerus*] —**num′ber·a·ble,** *adj.* —**num′ber·er,** *n.*

—**Syn. 1.** NUMBER, SUM both imply the total of two or more units. NUMBER applies to the result of a count or estimate in which the units are considered as individuals; it is used of groups of persons or things: *to have a number of items on the agenda.* SUM applies to the result of addition, in which only the total is considered: *a large sum of money.* **2.** digit, figure. **7.** copy, edition. **30.** calculate, compute, reckon. **33.** numerate.

num′ber eight′ i′ron, *Golf.* See **pitching niblick.**

num′ber five′ i′ron, *Golf.* mashie.

num′ber four′ i′ron, *Golf.* See **mashie iron.**

num′ber four′ wood′, *Golf.* baffy.

num·ber·less (num′bər lis), *adj.* **1.** innumerable; countless; myriad. **2.** without a number or numbers. [NUMBER + -LESS]

—**Syn. 1.** uncounted, untold; numerous.

num′ber nine′ i′ron, *Golf.* niblick.

num′ber one′, *Informal.* **1.** one's own well-being; oneself: *to look out for number one.* **2.** of the best quality; first-rate: *a number one performance.* **3.** *Informal.* urination.

num′ber one′ i′ron, *Golf.* See **driving iron.**

num′ber one′ wood′, *Golf.* driver (def. 7).

num′ber op′era, an opera in which the arias, ensembles, recitatives, and other sections are clearly separated from one another. Cf. **music drama.**

Num·bers (num′bərz), *n.* (*construed as sing.*) the fourth book of the Old Testament, containing the census of the Israelites after the Exodus from Egypt.

num′ber sev′en i′ron, *Golf.* pitcher² (def. 3).

num′ber six′ i′ron, *Golf.* See **mashie niblick.**

num′bers pool′, 1. Also called **numbers, num′bers game′, num′bers rack′et.** an illegal daily lottery in which money is wagered on the appearance of certain numbers in some statistical listing or tabulation published in a daily newspaper, racing form, etc. **2.** policy² (def. 2a).

num′ber the′ory, *Math.* the study of integers and their relation to one another.

num′ber three′ i′ron, *Golf.* mid-mashie.

num′ber three′ wood′, *Golf.* spoon (def. 4).

num′ber two′, *Informal.* defecation.

num′ber two′ i′ron, *Golf.* midiron.

num′ber two′ wood′, *Golf.* brassie.

numb·fish (num′fish′), *n., pl.* (*esp. collectively*) **-fish,** (*esp. referring to two or more kinds or species*) **-fish·es.** an electric ray: so called from its power of numbing its prey by means of electric shocks. [NUMB + FISH]

numb·ing (num′ing), *adj.* causing numbness or insensibility; paralyzing; stupefying: *the numbing effects of grief; a story she told with numbing regularity.* [NUMB + -ING²] —**numb′ing·ly,** *adv.*

num·bles (num′bəlz), *n.pl. Archaic.* certain of the inward parts of an animal, esp. of a deer, used as food. Also, **nombles.** [ME < MF *nombles* fillet of venison, pl. of *nomble,* dissimilated var. of **lomble* < L *lumbulus,* dim. of *lumbus* loin. See -ULE]

numb·skull (num′skul′), *n.* numskull.

nu·men (no͞o′min, nyo͞o′-), *n., pl.* **-mi·na** (-mə nə). divine power or spirit; a deity, esp. one presiding locally or believed to inhabit a particular object. [< L: a nod, command; divine will, power or being; akin to *nūtāre* to nod again and again]

nu·mer·a·ble (no͞o′mər ə bəl, nyo͞o′-), *adj.* capable of being numbered or counted. [< L *numerābilis* that can be counted, equiv. to *numer(āre)* (to) number + *-ābilis* -ABLE] —**nu′mer·a·ble·ness,** *n.* —**nu′mer·a·bly,** *adv.*

nu·mer·al (no͞o′mər əl, nyo͞o′-), *n.* **1.** a word or words expressing a number: *cardinal numerals.* **2.** a letter or figure, or a group of letters or figures, expressing a number: *the Roman numerals.* —*adj.* **3.** of, pertaining to, or consisting of numbers or numerals. **4.** expressing or noting a number or numbers. [< LL *numerālis* of, belonging to number, equiv. to L *numer(us)* number + *-ālis* -AL¹]

nu·mer·ar·y (no͞o′mə rer′ē, nyo͞o′-), *adj.* of or pertaining to a number or numbers. [< ML *numerārius* of, relating to number, equiv. to L *numer(us)* number + *-ārius* -ARY]

nu·mer·ate (no͞o′mə rāt′, nyo͞o′-), *v.t.,* **-at·ed, -at·ing. 1.** to number; count; enumerate. **2.** to read (a numerical expression) in words. [< L *numerātus* numbered, counted, reckoned (ptp. of *numerāre*), equiv. to *numer-* number + *-ātus* -ATE¹]

nu·mer·a·tion (no͞o′mə rā′shən, nyo͞o′-), *n.* **1.** the act, process, or result of numbering or counting. **2.** the process or a method of reckoning or calculating. **3.** the act, art, or method of expressing or reading off numbers set down in numerals, esp. those written decimally. [< L *numerātiōn-* (s. of *numerātiō*) a counting out, paying, equiv. to *numerāt(us)* NUMERATE + *-iōn-* -ION] —**nu′mer·a′tive,** *adj.*

nu·mer·a·tor (no͞o′mə rā′tər, nyo͞o′-), *n.* **1.** *Arith.* the term of a fraction, usually above the line, that indicates the number of equal parts which are to be added together; the dividend placed over a divisor: *The numerator of the fraction ⅔ is 2.* **2.** one who or that which numbers. [< LL *numerātor* a counter, numberer, equiv. to L *numerāt(us)* NUMERATE + *-or* -OR²]

nu·mer·i·cal (no͞o mer′i kəl, nyo͞o-), *adj.* **1.** of or pertaining to numbers; of the nature of a number. **2.** indicating a number: *numerical symbols.* **3.** bearing or designated by a number. **4.** expressed by numbers instead of letters: *numerical cryptography; numerical equations.* **5.** of or pertaining to one's skill at working with numbers, solving mathematical problems, etc.: *tests for rating numerical aptitude.* **6.** *Math.* absolute (def. 12). Also, **nu·mer′ic.** [< L *numer(us)* number + -ICAL] —**nu·mer′i·cal·ly,** *adv.* —**nu·mer′i·cal·ness,** *n.*

numer′ical ap′erture, *Optics.* a measure of the resolving power of a microscope, equal to the index of refraction of the medium in which the object is placed multiplied by the sine of the angle made with the axis by the most oblique ray entering the instrument, the resolving power increasing as the product increases. *Abbr.:* N.A.

numer′ical weath′er predic′tion, a method of predicting weather through the use of high-speed computers, specifically by the time integration of the fundamental equations of hydrodynamics in a mathematically modeled atmosphere. Also called **numer′ical fore′casting.**

nu·mer·ol·o·gy (no͞o′mə rol′ə jē, nyo͞o′-), *n.* the study of numbers, as the figures designating the year of one's birth, to determine their supposed influence on one's life, future, etc. [< L *numer(us)* a number + -O- + -LOGY] —**nu·mer·o·log·i·cal** (no͞o′mər ə loj′i kəl, nyo͞o′-), *adj.*

nu·mer·ous (no͞o′mər əs, nyo͞o′-), *adj.* **1.** very many; being or existing in great quantity: *numerous visits to the doctor; numerous fish in the lake.* **2.** consisting of or comprising a great number of units or individuals: *Recent audiences have been more numerous.* [< L *numerōsus* consisting of a great number, numerous, equiv. to *numer(us)* a number + *-ōsus* -OUS] —**nu′mer·ous·ly,** *adv.* —**nu′mer·ous·ness, nu·me·ros·i·ty** (no͞o′mə ros′i tē, nyo͞o′-), *n.*

—**Syn. 1.** See **many.**

Nu·mid·i·a (no͞o mid′ē ə, nyo͞o-), *n.* an ancient country in N Africa, corresponding roughly to modern Algeria. —**Nu·mid′i·an,** *adj., n.*

Numid′ian crane′. See **demoiselle crane.** [NUMIDI(A) + -AN]

nu·mi·na (no͞o′mə nə, nyo͞o′-), *n.* pl. of **numen.**

nu·mi·nous (no͞o′mə nəs, nyo͞o′-), *adj.* **1.** of, pertaining to, or like a numen; spiritual or supernatural. **2.** surpassing comprehension or understanding; mysterious: *that element in artistic expression which remains numinous.* **3.** arousing one's elevated feelings of duty, honor, loyalty, etc.: *a benevolent and numinous paternity.* [< L *numin-* (s. of *nūmen*) NUMEN + -OUS]

numis., 1. numismatic. **2.** numismatics. Also, **numism.**

nu·mis·mat·ic (no͞o′miz mat′ik, -mis-, nyo͞o′-), *adj.* **1.** of, pertaining to, or consisting of coins, medals, or the like. **2.** pertaining to numismatics. Also, **nu′mis·mat′i·cal.** [< NL *numismatic(us)* < Gk *nomismatikós* of coins, equiv. to *nomismat-* (s. of *nómisma*) currency + *-ikos* -IC, akin to *nómos* usage, law] —**nu′mis·mat′i·cal·ly,** *adv.*

nu·mis·mat·ics (no͞o′miz mat′iks, -mis-, nyo͞o′-), *n.* (*construed as sing.*) the study or collecting of coins, medals, and the like. Also, **numismatology.** [see NUMISMATIC, -ICS]

nu·mis·ma·tist (no͞o miz′mə tist, -mis′-, nyo͞o-), *n.* **1.** a specialist in numismatics. **2.** a person who collects numismatic items, esp. coins. [< L *numismat-* (s. of *numisma*) coin + -IST]

nu·mis·ma·tol·o·gy (no͞o miz′mə tol′ə jē, -mis′-, nyo͞o-), *n.* numismatics. [NUMISMAT(ICS) + -O- + -LOGY] —**nu·mis′ma·tol′o·gist,** *n.*

Nu·mi·tor (no͞o′mi tôr′, nyo͞o′-), *n. Rom. Legend.* a king of Alba Longa, the father of Rhea Silvia and the grandfather of Romulus and Remus.

num·ma·ry (num′ə rē), *adj.* **1.** of or pertaining to coins or money. **2.** dealing in coins or money. [< L *nummārius* of, belonging to money, equiv. to *numm(us)* coin + *-ārius* -ARY]

num·mu·lar (num′yə lər), *adj.* **1.** pertaining to coins or money; nummary. **2.** having the shape of a coin; coin-shaped. [< L *nummul(ī)* petty cash, small change (*numm(us)* money + *-ulī,* pl. of *-ulus* -ULE) + -AR¹]

num·mu·lite (num′yə līt′), *n.* a fossil foraminifer of the genus *Camerina* (*Nummulites*), having a calcareous, usually disklike shell. [NUMMUL(AR) + -ITE¹] —**num·mu·lit·ic** (num′yə lit′ik), *adj.*

num·skull (num′skul′), *n. Informal.* a dull-witted person; dunce; dolt. Also, **numbskull.** [NUM(B) + SKULL]

nun¹ (nun), *n.* **1.** a woman bound by solemn vows to a religious order. **2.** a woman living in a convent under solemn vows of poverty, chastity, and obedience. [ME, OE *nunne* < eccl. L *nonna,* fem. of *nonnus* monk] —**nun′like′,** *adj.*

nun² (no͝on, no͞on), *n.* **1.** the 14th letter of the Hebrew alphabet. **2.** the consonant sound represented by this letter. [< Heb; see NU¹]

nūn (no͝on, no͞on), *n.* the 25th letter of the Arabic alphabet. [< Ar; see NUN², NU¹]

Nun (no͞on), *n.* the major channel of the Niger River, in W Africa.

Nun (no͞on), *n. Egyptian Religion.* Nunu.

nun·a·tak (nun′ə tak′), *n.* a hill or mountain that has been completely encircled by a glacier. [< Eskimo]

nun·a·tion (nun nā′shən), *n. Arabic Gram.* the doubling, in writing, of the final vowel symbol to indicate the addition, in speech, of the indefinite suffix *n* to certain nouns. Also, **nunnation.** [< NL *nunnātiōn-* (s. of *nunnātiō*), equiv. to *nūn* (< Ar; see NŪN) + *-ātiōn-* -ATION] —**nun′a·ted,** *adj.*

nun′ buoy′ (nun), an unlighted buoy having a conical form above water, used in various ways as a channel marker, esp. one placed on the starboard side of a channel entering from seaward, in which case it is painted red and given an even number. Cf. **can buoy.** [*nun* spinning top + BUOY]

nunc (no͝ongk; *Eng.* nungk), *adv. Latin.* now.

Nunc Di·mit·tis (nungk′ di mit′is, no͝ongk′), **1.** (*italics*) the canticle beginning with the words of Simeon, in Luke 2:29–32, "Lord, now lettest thou thy servant depart in peace." **2.** (*l.c.*) permission to depart; dismissal; departure. [< L]

Nun·ci·a·ta (nun′shē ā′tə), *n.* a girl's given name, form of **Annunciata.**

nun·ci·a·ture (nun′shē ə chər), *n.* the office or the term of service of a nuncio. [< It *nunziatura.* See NUNCIO, -ATE¹, -URE]

nun·ci·o (nun′shē ō′), *n., pl.* **-ci·os.** a permanent diplomatic representative of the pope at a foreign court or capital. Cf. **apostolic delegate.** [< It *nuncio, nunzio* < L *nuncius, nuntius* messenger]

nun·cle (nung′kəl), *n. Chiefly Brit. Dial.* uncle. [*mine uncle,* taken as *my nuncle;* cf. NEWT]

nun·cu·pa·tive (nung′kyə pā′tiv, nung kyo͞o′pə tiv), *adj.* (esp. of a will) oral; not written. [< LL *nuncupātīv(us)* so-called, specified name, equiv. to *nuncupāt(us)* named (ptp. of *nuncupāre* for *nōmen capere* to take a name, i.e., utter it publicly) + *-īvus* -IVE]

nun′cupative will′, *Law.* a will made by the oral declaration of the testator, valid only under special circumstances. Cf. **holographic will.**

nun·hood (nun′ho͝od), *n.* status, vocation, or responsibilities of a nun. Also called **nun′ship.** [NUN¹ + -HOOD]

Nun·kiang (no͞on′kyäng′), *n.* a former province in Manchuria, in NE China. 25,856 sq. mi. *Cap.:* Tsitsihar.

nun·na·tion (nu nā′shən), *n.* nunation. —**nun′-nat·ed,** *adj.*

nun·ner·y (nun′ə rē), *n., pl.* **-ner·ies.** a religious house for nuns; convent. [ME *nonnerie.* See NUN¹, -ERY]

nun's′ fid′dle. See **trumpet marine.**

nun's′ veil′ing, a thin, plain-woven, worsted fabric, originally for nuns' veils but now also for dresses, coats, etc.

Nu·nu (no͞o′no͞o), *n. Egyptian Religion.* a god personifying the ocean, the primeval chaos from which the world was formed. Also, **Nun.**

Nu·per·caine (no͞o′pər kān′, nyo͞o′-), *n. Pharm., Trademark.* dibucaine.

nup·tial (nup′shəl), *adj.* **1.** of or pertaining to marriage or the marriage ceremony: *the nuptial day.* —*n.* **2.** Usually, **nuptials.** a wedding or marriage. [< L *nuptiāl(is)* of, belonging to a marriage, deriv. of *nuptiae* a marriage, wedding, equiv. to *nūpt(a)* married, lit., veiled (fem. ptp. of *nūbere* to cover) + *-iae* pl. of *-ia* -IA. See -AL¹] —**nup′tial·ly,** *adv.*

—**Syn. 2.** See **marriage.**

nup′tial plum′age, *Ornith.* the plumage assumed by a bird during the courtship period, applied chiefly to those species that are particularly more colorful at this period. Also called **breeding plumage.**

nuque (no͞ok, nyo͞ok), *n.* the back of the neck. [< F; see NUCHA]

nu·ra·ghe (no͞o rä′gā), *n., pl.* **-ghi** (-gē), **-ghes.** any of the large, tower-shaped, prehistoric stone structures found in Sardinia. [< It, c. *nurage* (Sardinian dial.), akin to *mura* in same sense < L *mūrus* wall]

Nu·rem·berg (no͝or′əm-bûrg′, nyo͝or′-), *n.* a city in central Bavaria, in SE West Germany: site of trials (1945–46) of Nazis accused of war crimes. 466,100 (1963). German, **Nürnberg.**

Nu′remberg egg′, *Horol.* an egg-shaped watch of the 16th century: one of the earliest watches.

Nu′remberg vi′olet. See **manganese violet.**

Nu·re·yev (no͞o rā′ef, -ev; *Russ.* no͞o re′yef), *n.* **Rudolf (Ha·me·to·vich)** (hä me′to vich), born 1938, Russian ballet dancer.

Nu·ri·stan (no͝or′i stan′), *n.* a mountainous region in NE Afghanistan. 5000 sq. mi. Formerly, **Kafiristan.**

nurl (nûrl), *n., v.t.* knurl.

Nur·mi (nûr′mē; *Fin.* no͞or′mē), *n.* **Paa·vo Jo·han·nes** (pä′vô yô hän′nes), born 1897, Finnish athlete.

Nürn·berg (nyrn′berkh), *n.* German name of **Nuremberg.**

nurse (nûrs), *n., v.,* **nursed, nurs·ing.** —*n.* **1.** a person, esp. a woman, who takes care of the sick or infirm. **2.** a woman who has the general care of a child or children; dry nurse. **3.** a woman employed to suckle an infant; wet nurse. **4.** any fostering agency or influence. **5.** *Entomol.* a worker that attends the young in a colony of social insects. **6.** *Billiards.* the act of maintaining the position of billiard balls in preparation for a carom. —*v.t.* **7.** to tend, or minister to, in sickness or infirmity. **8.** to seek to cure (an ailment) by taking care of oneself: *to nurse a cold.* **9.** to look after carefully so as to promote growth, development, etc.; foster; cherish: *to nurse one's meager talents.* **10.** to treat or handle with adroit care in order to further one's own interests: *to nurse one's nest egg.* **11.** to bring up, train, or nurture. **12.** to clasp or handle carefully or fondly: *to nurse a plate of food on one's lap; to nurse a memento.* **13.** to suckle (an infant). **14.** to feed and tend in infancy. **15.** *Billiards.* to maintain the position of for a series of caroms. —*v.i.* **16.** to act as nurse; tend the sick or infirm: *a teacher who nurses in her spare time.* **17.** to suckle a child, esp. one's own: *The young mother learned she would be unable to nurse.* **18.** (of a child) to suckle: *The child did not nurse after he was three months old.* [ME, var. of *nurice* < OF < LL *nūtrīcia,* n. use of fem. of L *nūtrīcius* NUTRITIOUS]

—**Syn. 9.** encourage, abet, help, aid, back. **14.** rear, raise. NURSE, NOURISH, NURTURE may be used almost interchangeably to refer to bringing up the young. NURSE, however, suggests attendance and service; NOURISH emphasizes providing whatever is needful for development; and NURTURE suggests tenderness and solicitude in training mind and manners. —**Ant. 7, 9.** neglect.

nurse′ crop′, a crop planted in the same field with another crop, esp. to minimize the growth of weeds.

nurse·ling (nûrs′ling), *n.* nursling.

nurse·maid (nûrs′mād′), *n.* a maidservant employed to take care of children. Also called **nurs′er·y·maid′.** [NURSE + MAID]

nurs·er (nûr′sər), *n.* **1.** one who or that which nurses. **2.** See **nursing bottle.** [ME; see NURSE, -ER[1]]

nurs·er·y (nûr′sə rē), *n., pl.* **-er·ies.** **1.** a room or place set apart for young children. **2.** a nursery school or day nursery. **3.** any place in which something is bred, nourished, or fostered: *The institute has been the nursery of the region's arts.* **4.** any situation, condition, circumstance, practice, etc., serving to foster something: *Slums are nurseries for young criminals.* **5.** a place where young trees or other plants are raised for transplanting or for sale. [ME *norcery.* See NURSE, -ERY]

nurs·er·y·man (nûr′sə rē mən), *n., pl.* **-men.** a person who owns or conducts a nursery for plants. [NURSERY + MAN[1]]

nurs′ery rhyme′, a short, simple poem or song for very young children.

nurs′ery school′, a prekindergarten school.

nurse′'s aide′, a person who assists professional nurses, as in a hospital, by performing such routine tasks as making beds, serving meals, and the like.

nurse′ shark′, any of several sharks of the family *Orectolobidae,* esp. *Ginglymostoma cirratum,* found in shallow waters from the Florida Keys to Brazil.

nurs′ing bot′tle, a bottle with a rubber nipple, from which an infant sucks milk, water, etc.

nurs′ing home′, **1.** a private residence or the like equipped to care for persons unable to look after themselves, as the aged or infirm. **2.** *Chiefly Brit.* a private hospital; a hospital owned by one person or a group of individuals and supported solely by the fees of patients.

nurs·ling (nûrs′ling), *n.* **1.** an infant, child, or young animal being nursed or being cared for by a nurse. **2.** any person or thing under fostering care, influences, or conditions. Also, **nurseling.** [NURSE + -LING[1]]

nur·ture (nûr′chər), *v.,* **-tured, -tur·ing,** *n.* —*v.t.* **1.** to promote the development of by providing nourishment, support, encouragement, etc., during the stages of growth, as children or young; rear: *to nurture promising musicians; to nurture a young business.* **2.** to bring up; train; educate. —*n.* **3.** upbringing; training; breeding. **4.** education; tutelage: *The nurture of young artists is a difficult and long process.* **5.** that which nourishes; nourishment; food. [ME < MF, var. of *nourriture* < LL *nūtrītūra* a nourishing, equiv. to L *nūtrīt(us)* nourished (ptp. of *nūtrīre*) + *-ūra* -URE] —**nur′tur·a·ble,** *adj.* —**nur′ture·less,** *adj.* —**nur′tur·er,** *n.*

—**Syn. 1.** See **nurse.**

Nus·ku (no͞os′ko͞o), *n.* a Sumerian and Babylonian deity originally the vizier of Enlil.

nut (nut), *n., adj., v.,* **nut·ted, nut·ting.** —*n.* **1.** a dry fruit consisting of an edible kernel or meat enclosed in a woody or leathery shell. **2.** the kernel itself. **3.** *Bot.* a hard, indehiscent, one-seeded fruit, as the chestnut or the acorn. **4.** any of various devices or ornaments resembling a nut. **5.** *Slang.* the head. **6.** *Slang.* a person who is very enthusiastic about something; buff. **7.** *Slang.* a foolish, silly, or eccentric person. **8.** *Slang.* an insane person; psychotic. **9.** a block, usually of metal, perforated with a threaded hole so that it can be screwed down on a bolt to hold together objects through which the bolt passes. **10.** *Music.* (in instruments of the violin family) **a.** the ledge, as of ebony, at the upper end of the finger board, over which the strings pass. **b.** the movable piece at the lower end of the bow, by means of which the hairs may be slackened or tightened. **11.** *Slang.* total operating expenses, esp. of a theatrical or television production. **12.** *Slang* (vulgar). a testis. **13.** *Print.* en (def. 2). **14. hard nut to crack, a.** a problem difficult to solve; a formidable undertaking. **b.** a person difficult to know, understand, or convince. Also **tough nut to crack. 15. off one's nut,** *Slang.* **a.** insane; mad. **b.** confused; unreasonable. **c.** erroneous; wrong: *You're off your nut if you think such a plan can succeed.* —*adj.* **15.** *Coal Mining.* **a.** noting a size of anthracite of less than 1⁵/₈ inches and more than ¹⁵/₁₆ of an inch in the longest dimension. **b.** noting a size of bituminous coal of less than 2 inches and more than ³/₄ of an inch in the longest dimension. —*v.i.* **17.** to seek for or gather nuts: *to go nutting in late autumn.* [ME *nute,* OE *hnutu;* c. D *noot,* Icel *hnot,* G *Nuss;* akin to L *nux*] —**nut′like′,** *adj.*

Nut (no͞ot), *n.* *Egyptian Religion.* the goddess of the sky, sometimes shown as a cow bearing Ra on her back and the stars on her underside.

N.U.T., *Brit.* National Union of Teachers.

nu·tant (no͞ot′ənt, nyo͞ot′-), *adj.* *Bot.* drooping; nodding. [< L *nūtant-* (s. of *nūtāns*) nodding often, prp. of *nūtāre.* See NUMEN, -ANT]

nu·ta·tion (no͞o tā′shən, nyo͞o-), *n.* **1.** the act or an instance of nodding one's head, esp. involuntarily or spasmodically. **2.** *Bot.* spontaneous movements of plant parts during growth. **3.** *Astron.* the periodic oscillation observed in the precession of the earth's axis and the precession of the equinoxes. **4.** the variation of the inclination of the axis of a gyroscope to the vertical. [< L *nūtātiōn-* (s. of *nūtātiō*), equiv. to *nūtāt(us)* (ptp. of *nūtāre* to nod repeatedly; *nū-* nod + *-tā-* freq. suffix + *-re* inf. ending) + *-iōn-* -ION] —**nu·ta′tion·al,** *adj.*

nut·brown (nut′broun′), *adj.* brown, as many nuts when ripe. [ME *nute brun.* See NUT, BROWN]

nut·crack·er (nut′krak′ər), *n.* **1.** an instrument for cracking nuts. **2.** any of several corvine birds of the genus *Nucifaga* which feed on nuts, as the common nutcracker, *N. caryocatactes,* of Europe. [NUT + CRACKER]

Nut′cracker Suite′, a ballet and concert suite (1892) by Peter Ilych Tschaikovsky.

nut′ dash′, *Print.* a dash equal in length to the width of an en quad; en dash.

nut·gall (nut′gôl′), *n.* a nutlike gall or excrescence, esp. one formed on an oak. [NUT + GALL[3]]

nut′ grass′, any of various sedges of the genus *Cyperus,* esp. *C. rotundus,* bearing small, nutlike tubers.

nut·hatch (nut′hach′), *n.* any of numerous small, short-tailed, sharp-beaked birds of the family *Sittidae* that creep on trees and feed on small nuts and insects. [ME *notehache, nuthagge, nuthak,* lit., nut hacker. See NUT, HACK[1]]

Nuthatch,
Sitta carolinensis
(Length 6 in.)

nut′ house′, *Slang.* an insane asylum.

nut·let (nut′lit), *n.* **1.** a small nut; a small nutlike fruit or seed. **2.** the stone of a drupe. [NUT + -LET]

Nut·ley (nut′lē), *n.* a city in NE New Jersey. 29,513 (1960).

nut·meat (nut′mēt′), *n.* the edible kernel of a nut. [NUT + MEAT]

nut·meg (nut′meg), *n.* **1.** the hard, aromatic seed of the fruit of an East Indian tree, *Myristica fragrans,* used as a spice. **2.** the similar product of certain other trees of the same genus or other genera. **3.** a tree bearing such seeds. [ME *notemug(g)e,* perh. back formation from *notemugede (-ede being taken as -ED[3]), equiv. to *note* NUT + *mugede* < OF < LL *muscāta* musky; see MUSK, -ATE[1]] —**nut′megged,** *adj.*

nut′meg gera′nium, a perennial herb, *Pelargonium odoratissimum,* of South Africa, having hairy leaves with scalloped margins and nutmeg-scented clusters of white flowers, of which the two upper petals are veined deep pink.

nut′meg mel′on. See **netted melon.**

Nut′meg State′, Connecticut (used as a nickname).

nut·pick (nut′pik′), *n.* a sharp-pointed table device for removing the meat from nuts. [NUT + PICK]

nut′ pine′, any of various trees of the southwestern U.S. and Rocky Mountains, as *Pinus monophylla, P. edulis,* etc., bearing edible nuts.

nut′ quad′, *Print.* a quad one en wide; en quad.

nu·tri·a (no͞o′trē ə, nyo͞o′-), *n.* **1.** the coypu. **2.** the fur of the coypu, resembling beaver, used for making women's coats, hats, suit trimmings, etc. [< Sp: otter, var. of *lutria* < ML, r. L *lutra*]

nu·tri·ent (no͞o′trē ənt, nyo͞o′-), *adj.* **1.** containing or conveying nutriment, as solutions or vessels of the body. **2.** nourishing; providing nourishment or nutriment. —*n.* **3.** a nutrient substance. [< L *nūtrient-* (s. of *nūtriēns*) feeding, prp. of *nūtrīre;* see -ENT]

nu·tri·lite (no͞o′trə lit′, nyo͞o′-), *n.* *Biochem.* any of several substances that, in minute quantities, serve as nutrients for microorganisms. [NUTRI(MENT + METABO)-LITE]

nu·tri·ment (no͞o′trə mənt, nyo͞o′-), *n.* **1.** any matter that, taken into a living organism, serves to sustain it in its existence, promoting growth, replacing loss, and providing energy. **2.** that which nourishes; nourishment; food. [< L *nūtrīment(um)* nourishment, equiv. to *nūtrī(re)* (to) nourish, feed + *-mentum* -MENT] —**nu·tri·men·tal** (no͞o′trə men′tᵊl, nyo͞o′-), *adj.*

nu·tri·tion (no͞o trish′ən, nyo͞o-), *n.* **1.** the act or process of nourishing or of being nourished. **2.** the process by which plants and animals take in and utilize food material. **3.** food; nutriment. **4.** the science or study of or a course of study in nutrition, esp. of humans, or the pursuit of this science as an occupation. [< LL *nūtrītiōn-* (s. of *nūtrītiō*) a feeding, equiv. to L *nūtrīt(us)* fed (ptp. of *nūtrīre* + *-iōn-* -ION] —**nu·tri′tion·al, nu·tri′tion·ar′y,** *adj.* —**nu·tri′tion·al·ly,** *adv.*

nu·tri·tion·ist (no͞o trish′ə nist, nyo͞o-), *n.* a person whose occupation is nutrition. [NUTRITION + -IST]

nu·tri·tious (no͞o trish′əs, nyo͞o-), *adj.* providing nourishment, esp. to a high degree; nourishing. [< L *nūtrīti(us)* that suckles, nourishes, var. of *nūtrīcius,* equiv. to *nūtrīci-* (s. of *nūtrix*) NURSE + *-us* -OUS] —**nu·tri′tious·ly,** *adv.* —**nu·tri′tious·ness,** *n.*

nu·tri·tive (no͞o′tri tiv, nyo͞o′-), *adj.* **1.** serving to nourish; providing nutriment; nutritious. **2.** of, pertaining to, or concerned with nutrition: *foods with high nutritive value.* —*n.* **3.** an item of nourishing food: *a breakfast of cereals, fruits, and other nutritives.* [< LL *nūtrītīv(us),* equiv. to *nūtrīt-* (see NUTRITION) + *-īvus* -IVE; r. late ME *nutritif* < MF] —**nu′tri·tive·ly,** *adv.* —**nu′tri·tive·ness,** *n.*

nuts (nuts), *Slang.* —*interj.* **1.** Also, **nerts, nertz.** (used to express defiance, disgust, disapproval, despair, etc., often fol. by *to*). —*adj.* **2.** crazy; insane. **3. be nuts about** or **on,** to be wildly enthusiastic about; be fervent in one's admiration of: *Both of them are nuts about chamber music.* [pl. of NUT]

nut·shell (nut′shel′), *n.* **1.** the shell of a nut. **2. in a nutshell,** in very brief form; in a few words: *Just tell me the story in a nutshell.* [ME *nuteschell;* see NUT, SHELL]

nut·ter (nut′ər), *n.* a person who gathers nuts. [NUT + -ER[1]]

nut·ting (nut′ing), *n.* the act of seeking or gathering nuts. [NUT + -ING[1]]

Nut·ting (nut′ing), *n.* **Wallace,** 1861–1941, U.S. antiquary, author, and illustrator.

nut·ty (nut′ē), *adj.,* **-ti·er, -ti·est.** **1.** abounding in or producing nuts. **2.** nutlike, esp. in taste. **3.** full of flavor or zest; lively; stimulating; meaty: *He offered several rich, nutty ideas on the subject.* **4.** *Informal.* silly or ridiculous: *That's a nutty suggestion.* **5.** *Slang.* insane. [NUT + -Y[1]] —**nut′ti·ly,** *adv.* —**nut′ti·ness,** *n.*

nut′ wee′vil, any of several snout beetles of the genus *Balaninus,* the larvae of which live in and feed on nuts and acorns.

nut·wood (nut′wo͝od′), *n.* **1.** any of various nut-bearing trees, as the hickory, walnut, etc. **2.** the wood of such a tree. [NUT + WOOD[1]]

nu·val·ue (no͞o′val′yo͞o, nyo͞o′-), *n.* *Optics.* See **Abbe number.**

N.U.W.W., *Brit.* National Union of Women Workers.

nux vom·i·ca (nuks vom′ə kə), **1.** the seed of the orangelike fruit of an East Indian, loganiaceous tree, *Strychnos Nux-vomica,* containing strychnine, used in medicine. **2.** the tree itself. [< NL: lit., vomiting nut]

nuz·zle (nuz′əl), *v.,* **-zled, -zling,** *n.* —*v.i.* **1.** to burrow or root with the nose, as an animal does: *a rabbit nuzzling into the snow.* **2.** to thrust the nose: *The dog nuzzled up to his master.* **3.** to lie close to or cuddle or snuggle up with someone or something. —*v.t.* **4.** to root up with the nose or snout: *training pigs to nuzzle truffles from the ground.* **5.** to touch or rub with the nose. **6.** to thrust the nose against or into: *The horse was nuzzling my pocket for sugar.* **7.** to thrust (the nose or head), as into something. **8.** to lie close to or snuggle or cuddle up to. —*n.* **9.** an affectionate embrace or cuddle. [ME *nosele.* See NOSE, -LE]

NW, **1.** northwest. **2.** northwestern. Also, **N.W., n.w.**

nW, nanowatt; nanowatts. Also, **nw**

NWbN, See **northwest by north.**

NWbW, See **northwest by west.**

NWC, *Mil.* National War College.

NWLB, National War Labor Board.

n. wt., net weight.

N.W.T., Northwest Territories (Canada).

N.Y., New York.

NYA, National Youth Administration. Also, **N.Y.A.**

Ny·ack (nī′ak), *n.* a town in SE New York. 6062 (1960).

nya·la (nyä′lə), *n.* an antelope, *Tragelaphus angasii,* of southeastern Africa, the male of which has a grayish body marked with white stripes. [<Bantu (SE Africa)]

Nya·la (nyä′lä), *n.* a city in the W Sudan. 12,278 (1956).

Nyan·ja (nyan′jə), *n.* a Bantu language spoken south of Lake Nyasa.

ny·an·za (nē an′zə, nī-), *n.* (in central and East Africa) a large body of water, esp. a lake.

Nya·sa (nyä′sä, nī as′ə), *n.* a lake in SE Africa, between Malawi, Tanzania, and Mozambique. 11,000 sq. mi. Also, **Nyas′sa.**

Nya·sa·land (nyä′sä land′, nī as′ə-), *n.* former name of **Malawi.**

Nya·ya (nyä′yə), *n.* (in ancient India) a philosophical school emphasizing logical analysis of knowledge, which is considered as deriving from perception, inference, analogy, and reliable testimony. [< Skt: lit., a going back (to prototype)]

N.Y.C., **1.** New York Central. **2.** New York City.

nyck·el·har·pa (nik′əl här′pə), *n.* an old-time Swedish stringed musical instrument, similar to the hurdy-gurdy but sounded with a bow instead of a wheel. [< Sw, equiv. to *nyckel* fret + *harpa* HARP]

nyct-, a combining form meaning "night": *nyctalgia.* Also, **nycti-, nycto-.** [< Gk *nykt-,* s. of *nýx* night]

nyc·ta·gi·na·ceous (nik′tə jə nā′shəs), *adj.* belonging to the *Nyctaginaceae,* or four-o'clock family of plants. [< NL *Nyctāgin-* (s. of *Nyctāgō* old name of genus; see NYCT-, LUMBAGO, -ACEOUS]

nyc·tal·gia (nik tal′jə, -jē ə), *n.* *Pathol.* night pain that occurs in the sleep. [NYCT- + -ALGIA]

nyc·ta·lo·pi·a (nik′tᵊlō′pē ə), *n.* *Ophthalm.* **1.** Also called **night blindness.** a condition of the eyes in which sight is normal in the day or in a strong light, but is abnormally poor or wholly gone at night or in a dim light. **2.** hemeralopia (def. 1). [< LL < Gk *nyktálōps*) blind + *-ōpia* -OPIA] —**nyc·ta·lop·ic** (nik′tᵊlop′ik), *adj.*

Nyc·te·us (nik′tē əs, -to͞os, -tyo͞os), *n.* *Class. Myth.* the brother of Lycus and the father of Antiope.

nycti-, var. of **nyct-.**

Nyc·tim·e·ne (nik tim′ə nē′), *n.* *Class. Myth.* a princess of Lesbos who was changed into an owl after being raped by her father, Epopeus.

Nyc·ti·mus (nik′tə məs), *n.* *Class. Myth.* the youngest son of Lycaon of Arcadia.

nyc·ti·trop·ic (nik′ti trop′ik), *adj. Bot.* tending to assume at or just before nightfall positions unlike those maintained during the day, as the leaves of certain plants. [NYCTI- + -TROPIC] —**nyc·tit·ro·pism** (nik-ti′trə piz′əm), *n.*

nycto-, var. of **nyct-**.

nyc·to·pho·bi·a (nik′tə fō′bē ə), *n. Psychiatry.* an abnormal fear of night or darkness. [NYCTO- + -PHOBIA]

Nyd·i·a (nid′ē ə), *n.* a girl's given name.

Nye (nī), *n.* **1. Edgar Wilson** ("*Bill Nye*"), 1850–96, U.S. humorist. **2.** a boy's given name, form of **Aneurin.**

Nye·man (nye′män), *n.* Russian name of **Niemen.**

Nye·re·re (*Swahili.* nye re′re; *Eng.* ni rãr′ē), *n.* **Julius Kam·ba·ra·ge** (*Swahili.* käm bä′rä gə), born 1921, African statesman: president of Tanzania since 1964.

Nyí·regy·há·za (nyi′redyᵊ hä′zo), *n.* a city in NE Hungary. 53,000 (1956).

nyl·ghai (nil′gī), *n., pl.* **-ghais,** (*esp. collectively*) **-ghai.** nilgai.

nyl·ghau (nil′gô), *n., pl.* **-ghaus,** (*esp. collectively*) **-ghau.** nilgai.

ny·lon (nī′lon), *n.* **1.** any of a class of thermoplastic polyamides capable of extrusion when molten into fibers, sheets, etc., of extreme toughness, strength, and elasticity, synthesized by the interaction of a dicarboxylic acid with a diamine: used for yarn, as for hosiery, for bristles, as for brushes, etc. **2. nylons,** stockings made of nylon, esp. sheer, full-length ones for women. [formerly a trademark]

nymph (nimf), *n.* **1.** one of a numerous class of lesser deities of mythology, conceived of as beautiful maidens inhabiting the sea, rivers, woods, trees, mountains, meadows, etc., and frequently mentioned as attending a superior deity. **2.** a beautiful or graceful young woman. **3.** a maiden. **4.** the young of an insect that undergoes incomplete metamorphosis. [ME *nimphe* < L *nympha* < Gk *nýmphē* bride, nymph] —**nym′phal, nym·phe·an** (nim′fē ən), *adj.*
—**Syn. 1.** naiad, nereid, oread, dryad, hamadryad. See **sylph.**

nym·pha (nim′fə), *n., pl.* **-phae** (-fē). **1.** *Anat.* one of the inner labia of the vulva. **2.** nymph (def. 4). [< L *nympha* a bride, young woman, NYMPH]

Nym·phae·a (nim fē′ə), *n. Class. Myth.* an epithet of Aphrodite, meaning "bridal."

nym·phae·a·ceous (nim′fē ā′shəs), *adj.* belonging to the *Nymphaeaceae,* or water-lily family of plants. [< L *nymphae(a)* the water-lily (< Gk *nymphaia,* n. use of fem. of *nymphaîos,* sacred to the nymphs; see NYMPHAEUM) + -ACEOUS]

nym·phae·um (nim fē′əm), *n., pl.* **-phae·a** (-fē′ə). **1.** a room or area having a fountain, statues, flowers, etc. **2.** an architecturally treated outlet of a reservoir or aqueduct. [< L < Gk *nymphaîon* place sacred to nymphs, n. use of neut. of *nymphaîos,* equiv. to *nýmph(ē)* nymph + *-aios* adj. suffix]

nym·pha·lid (nim′fə lid), *n.* **1.** a butterfly of the family *Nymphalidae,* comprising the brush-footed butterflies. —*adj.* **2.** belonging or pertaining to the family *Nymphalidae.* [< NL *Nymphalid(ae)* name of family, equiv. to *Nymphāl(is)* name of genus (L, equiv. to *nymph(a)* NYMPH + *-ālis* -AL[1]) + *-idae* -ID[2]]

nymph·et (nim fet′, nim′fit), *n.* **1.** a young and particularly beautiful nymph. **2.** a sexually attractive young girl. **3.** a girl or young woman of loose morals. [< MF *nymphette.* See NYMPH, -ET]

nym·pho (nim′fō), *n., pl.* **-phos.** *adj. Slang.* nymphomaniac. [by shortening]

nym·pho·lep·sy (nim′fə lep′sē), *n., pl.* **-sies. 1.** an ecstasy supposed by the ancients to be inspired by nymphs. **2.** a frenzy of emotion, as for something unattainable. [b. NYMPHOLEPT and EPILEPSY] —**nym·pho·lep·tic** (nim′fə lep′tik), *adj.*

nym·pho·lept (nim′fə lept′), *n.* a person seized with nympholepsy. [< Gk *nymphólēpt(os)* caught by nymphs, equiv. to *nýmph(ē)* NYMPH + *-o-* -O- + *lēptos,* verbid of *lambánein* to seize]

nym·pho·ma·ni·a (nim′fə mā′nē ə), *n. Pathol.* abnormal and uncontrollable sexual desire in women. [< Gk *nympho-* (see NYMPH, -O-) + -MANIA] —**nym·pho·ma·ni·ac** (nim′fə mā′nē ak′), *adj., n.* —**nym·pho·ma·ni·a·cal** (nim′fō mə nī′ə kəl), *adj.*

Nym·we·gen (nim′vā gən), *n.* Nijmegen.

Ny·norsk (ny′nôshk′; *Eng.* nē′nôrsk, -nōrsk), *n. Norwegian.* a literary language based on western Norwegian dialects and Old Norse and in 1885 adopted as one of the two official languages of Norway. Also called **Landsmål.** Cf. **Bokmål.** [lit., new Norse]

NYP, not yet published. Also, **N.Y.P.**

Ny·sa (nī′sə), *n. Class. Myth.* **1.** the mountain where Zeus sent the infant Dionysus to protect him from the vindictive wrath of Hera. **2.** one of the Nysaean Nymphs.

Ny·sae′an Nymphs′ (nī sē′ən), *Class. Myth.* the nymphs who cared for the infant Dionysus on Nysa. Also called **Ny·se·i·des** (nī sē′i dēz′).

Nys·sa (nis′ə), *n.* a town in E Oregon. 2611 (1960).

nys·tag·mus (ni stag′məs), *n. Pathol.* an involuntary oscillation of the eyeball, usually lateral but sometimes rotatory or vertical. [< NL < Gk *nystagm(ós)* nodding, akin to *nystázein* to nod] —**nys·tag′mic,** *adj.*

nys·ta·tin (nis′tə tin), *n. Pharm.* a light-yellow, water-insoluble antibiotic powder, $C_{46}H_{77}NO_{19}$, produced by the fermentation of *Streptomyces noursei* and *S. aureus,* used chiefly in the treatment of fungal infections. [*N(ew) Y(ork) Stat(e),* where originated + -IN[2]]

ny·tril (nī′tril), *n.* a synthetic fiber which produces a soft, elastic fabric, polymerized chiefly with the vinylidine dinitrile group, $-CH_2C(CN)_2-$. [(VI)NY(LIDINE) (DINI)TRILE]

Nyx (niks), *n.* an ancient Greek goddess personifying night.

N.Z., New Zealand. Also, **N. Zeal.**

O

O, o (ō), *n., pl.* **O's** or **Os; o's** or **os** or **oes. 1.** the fifteenth letter of the English alphabet, a vowel. **2.** any spoken sound represented by the letter *O* or *o*, as in *box, note, do,* etc. **3.** something having the shape of an O. **4.** a written or printed representation of the letter *O* or *o*. **5.** a device, as a printer's type, for reproducing the letter *O* or *o*.

O (ō), *interj., n., pl.* **O's.** —*interj.* **1.** (used before a name in direct address, esp. in solemn or poetic language, to lend earnestness to an appeal): *Hear me, O Israel!* **2.** (used as an expression of surprise, pain, annoyance, longing, gladness, etc.) —*n.* **3.** the exclamation "O."

O, 1. *Elect.* ohm. **2.** Old.

O, 1. the fifteenth in order or in a series. **2.** the Arabic cipher; zero. **3.** (*sometimes l.c.*) the medieval Roman numeral for 11. Cf. **Roman numerals. 4.** a major blood group or type usually enabling a person whose blood is of this group to donate blood to persons of group O, A, B, or AB and to receive blood from persons of group O. **5.** *Chem.* oxygen. **6.** *Logic.* See **particular negative.**

o' (ə, ō), *prep.* **1.** an abbreviated form of *of*, now chiefly dialectal or informal except in *o'clock, will-o'-the-wisp,* etc. **2.** an abbreviated form of *on.* [ME; by alter.]

O', a prefix meaning "descendant," in Irish family names: *O'Brien; O'Connor.* [repr. Ir ō descendant, OIr *au*]

o-[1], *Chem.* an abridgment of **ortho-.**

o-[2], var. of **ob-** before *m: omission.*

o-[3], var. of **oo-**: *oidium.*

-o-, the typical ending of the first element of compounds of Greek origin (as **-i-** is, in compounds of Latin origin), used regularly in forming new compounds with elements of Greek origin and often used in English as a connective irrespective of etymology: *Franco-Italian; geography; seriocomic; speedometer.* Cf. **-i-.** [ME (< OF) < L < Gk]

O., 1. Ocean. **2.** (in prescriptions) a pint. [< L *octārius*] **3.** octavo. **4.** October. **5.** Ohio. **6.** Old. **7.** Ontario. **8.** Oregon.

o., 1. pint. [< L *octārius*] **2.** octavo. **3.** off. **4.** old. **5.** only. **6.** order. **7.** *Baseball.* out; outs.

oaf (ōf), *n.* **1.** a simpleton; dunce; blockhead. **2.** a clumsy, stupid person; lout. **3.** a deformed or mentally deficient child. **4.** a changeling. [var. of *auf*, ME *alfe*, OE *ælf* ELF; c. G *Alp* nightmare] —**oaf′ish,** *adj.* —**oaf′ish·ly,** *adv.* —**oaf′ish·ness,** *n.*
—**Syn. 1.** dolt, ninny. **2.** churl, boor.

O·a·hu (ō ä′ho͞o), *n.* an island in central Hawaii: third largest and most important island of the State; location of Honolulu. 500,409 (1960); 589 sq. mi.

oak (ōk), *n.* **1.** any fagaceous tree or shrub of the genus *Quercus*, bearing the acorn as fruit. **2.** the hard, durable wood of such a tree, used in making furniture and in construction. **3.** the leaves of this tree, esp. as worn in a chaplet. **4.** anything made of the wood of this tree, as an item of furniture, a door, etc. **5. sport one's oak,** *Brit.* (of a university student) to indicate that one is not at home to visitors by closing the outer door of one's lodgings. [ME *ook*, OE *āc*; c. D *eik*, G *Eiche*] —**oak′like′,** *adj.*

oak′ ap′ple, any of various roundish galls produced on oaks. Also called **oak′ gall′.** [ME]

Oak′ Creek′, a town in SE Wisconsin. 9372 (1960).

Oak·dale (ōk′dāl′), *n.* **1.** a town in central Louisiana. 6618 (1960). **2.** a town in central California. 4980 (1960).

oak·en (ō′kən), *adj.* **1.** made of oak: *the old oaken bucket.* **2.** of or pertaining to the oak tree. [ME; see OAK, -EN[2]]

Oak′ For′est, a town in NE Illinois. 3724 (1960).

Oak′ Har′bor, 1. a town in NW Washington. 3942 (1960). **2.** a town in N Ohio. 2903 (1960).

Oak′ Hill′, a town in central West Virginia. 4711 (1960).

Oak·hurst (ōk′hûrst), *n.* a town in E New Jersey. 4374 (1960).

Oak·land (ōk′lənd), *n.* **1.** a seaport in W California, on San Francisco Bay. 367,548 (1960). **2.** a town in NE New Jersey. 9446 (1960).

Oak′land Cit′y, a town in SW Indiana. 3016 (1960).

Oak′land Park′, a town in S Florida. 5331 (1960).

Oak′ Lawn′, a city in NE Illinois, near Chicago. 27,471 (1960).

oak′ leaf′ clus′ter, a U.S. military decoration in the form of a small bronze twig bearing four oak leaves and three acorns, worn on the ribbon of another decoration for valor, wounds, or distinguished service to signify a second award of the same medal.

oak′ leath′er, *Bot.* a thick sheet of mycelium occurring in decayed oak wood.

oak′-leaved gera′nium (ōk′lēvd′), a perennial herb, *Pelargonium guercifolium*, of South Africa, having oaklike leaves and sparse clusters of purple flowers with darker markings.

Oak·ley (ōk′lē), *n.* **1. Annie** (*Phoebe Anne Oakley Mozee*), 1860–1926, U.S. markswoman. **2.** *Slang.* See **Annie Oakley.**

Oak·lyn (ōk′lin), *n.* a town in SW New Jersey. 4778 (1960).

Oak·mont (ōk′mont), *n.* a town in SW Pennsylvania. 7504 (1960).

oak·moss (ōk′môs′, -mos′), *n.* a lichen, *Evernia pranastri*, growing on oak and other trees, yielding a resin used in the manufacture of perfumes. [OAK + MOSS]

Oak′ Park′, a city in NE Illinois, near Chicago. 61,093 (1960).

Oak′ Ridge′, a city in E Tennessee, near Knoxville: atomic research center. 27,169 (1960).

oa·kum (ō′kəm), *n.* loose fiber obtained by untwisting and picking apart old ropes, used for calking the seams of ships. [ME *okome*, OE *ācum(a)*, var. of *ācumba*, lit., offcombings; see COMB[1]]

oak′ wilt′, *Plant Pathol.* a disease of oaks, characterized by wilting and discoloration of the leaves and defoliation, usually starting at and spreading from the top of the tree and the ends of the branches, caused by a fungus, *Ceratocystis fagacearum.*

Oak·wood (ōk′wo͝od′), *n.* a town in W Pennsylvania. 3303 (1960).

OAO, Orbiting Astronomical Observatory.

OAPC, Office of Alien Property Custodian.

oar (ōr, ôr), *n.* **1.** a long shaft with a broad blade at one end, used as a lever for rowing or otherwise propelling or steering a boat. **2.** something resembling this or having a similar purpose. **3.** an oarsman. **4.** to meddle in; interfere with: *If she tries to put in her oar just once more, I'll tell her to keep her advice to herself.* **5. rest on one's oars, a.** to depend on one's reputation for past achievements rather than on one's present efforts for recognition. **b.** to relax after exertion; stop working after success or completing a task: *After making sure of a decent income, he was content to rest on his oars.* —*v.t.* **6.** to propel with or as if with oars; row. **7.** to traverse or make (one's way) by, or as if by, rowing. —*v.i.* **8.** to row. **9.** to move or advance as if by rowing. [ME *ore*, OE *ār*; c. Icel *ār*] —**oar′less,** *adj.* —**oar′like′,** *adj.*

oared (ōrd, ôrd), *adj.* furnished with oars. [OAR + -ED[3]]

oar·fish (ōr′fish′, ôr′-), *n., pl.* (*esp. collectively*) **-fish,** (*esp. referring to two or more kinds or species*) **-fish·es.** any pelagic fish of the genus *Regalecus*, having a compressed, tapelike body from 12 to over 20 feet long. Also called **king-of-the-herrings.** [OAR + FISH]

oar·lock (ōr′lok′, ôr′-), *n.* any of various devices providing a pivot for an oar in rowing, esp. a swiveling, crutchlike or ringlike metal device projecting above a gunwale. Also called **rowlock.** [ME *orlok*, OE *ārloc*. See OAR, LOCK[1]]

O, Oarlock

oars (ōrz, ôrz), *interj.* *Naut.* (used as a command to the crew of a scull or other similar boat to cease rowing and hold the oars horizontal with blades feathered.)

oars·man (ōrz′mən, ôrz′-), *n., pl.* **-men.** a person who rows a boat or other vessel; rower. [OAR + 'S[1] + MAN[1]] —**oars′man·ship′,** *n.*

oar·y (ōr′ē, ôr′ē), *adj.* *Archaic.* oarlike. [OAR + -Y[1]]

OAS, See **Organization of American States.**

o·a·sis (ō ā′sis, ō′ə sis), *n., pl.* **-ses** (-sēz, -sēz′). **1.** a small fertile or green area in a desert region, usually having a spring or well. **2.** something serving as a pleasant relief, refuge, or change from the usual, the annoying, or the difficult: *He worked hard six days a week and looked forward to his day off as an oasis of rest and relaxation.* [< LL < Gk; ? < Egypt *wāh*] —**o·a·sit·ic** (ō′ə sit′ik), **o·a′sal, o·a·se·an** (ō ā′sē ən), *adj.*

oast (ōst), *n.* *Chiefly Brit.* a kiln for drying hops or malt. [ME *ost*, OE *āst*; c. D *eest*]

oast-house (ōst′hous′), *n., pl.* **-hous·es** (-hou′ziz). *Chiefly Brit.* **1.** oast. **2.** a building housing several oasts.

oat (ōt), *n.* **1.** a cereal grass, *Avena sativa*, cultivated for its edible seed. **2.** Usually, **oats.** the seed of this plant, used as a food for man and animals. **3.** any of several plants of the same genus, as the wild oat. **4.** *Archaic.* a musical pipe made of an oat straw. **5. feel one's oats,** *Informal.* **a.** to feel gay or lively. **b.** to become aware of and use one's importance or power. **6. sow one's wild oats.** See **wild oat** (def. 3). [ME *ote*, OE *āte*] —**oat′like′,** *adj.*

oat·cake (ōt′kāk′), *n.* a cake, usually thin and brittle, made of oatmeal. [OAT + CAKE]

-oate, *Chem.* a combining form indicating the presence of the ester or >C=O group: *benzoate.* [-*o(ic)* (as in *benzoic*) + -ATE[2]]

oat·en (ōt′ᵊn), *adj.* **1.** of, pertaining to, or made of oats. **2.** of or made of oatmeal. **3.** made of an oat straw. [ME; see OAT, -EN[2]]

oat·er (ō′tər), *n.* *Slang.* a western movie, television play, etc.; horse opera. [OAT + -ER[1]]

Oates (ōts), *n.* **Titus,** 1649–1705, English imposter; instigator of the Popish Plot scare.

oat′ grass′, 1. any of certain oatlike grasses. **2.** any wild species of oat.

oath (ōth), *n., pl.* **oaths** (ōthz). **1.** a solemn appeal to God, or to some revered person or thing, to witness one's determination to speak the truth or to keep a promise: *to testify upon oath.* **2.** a statement or promise strengthened by such an appeal. **3.** a formally affirmed statement or promise accepted as an equivalent of an appeal to God or a revered person or thing; affirmation. **4.** the form of words in which such a statement or promise is made. **5.** an irreverent or blasphemous use of the name of God or anything sacred. **6.** any profane expression; curse; swearword: *He slammed the door with a muttered oath.* **7. take oath,** to swear solemnly; vow: *He took oath that he had seen the defendant leaving the scene of the crime.* [ME *ooth*, OE *āth*; c. G *Eid*]
—**Syn. 2.** vow, pledge. **5.** profanity.

oat·meal (ōt′mēl′, -mēl′), *n.* **1.** meal made from oats. **2.** a cooked breakfast food made from this. —*adj.* **3.** made with or containing oatmeal: *oatmeal cookies.* [ME; see OAT, MEAL[2]]

OAWR, Office for Agricultural War Relations.

Oa·xa·ca (wä hä′kä, wə hä′kə), *n.* **1.** a state in S Mexico. 1,727,266 (1960); 36,375 sq. mi. **2.** a city in and the capital of this state, in the central part. 74,370 (1960).

ob (ob), *n. Meteorol. Slang.* weather observation. [short for OBSERVATION]

Ob (ôp), *n.* **1.** a river in the W Soviet Union in Asia, flowing NW to the Gulf of Ob. 2500 mi. long. **2. Gulf of,** an inlet of the Arctic Ocean. ab. 500 mi. long.

ob-, a prefix meaning "toward," "to," "on," "over," "against," orig. occurring in loan words from Latin, but now used also, with the sense of "reversely," "inversely," to form Neo-Latin and English scientific terms: *object; obligate; oblanceolate.* Also, **o-, oc-, of-, op-.** [ME (< OF) < L, repr. *ob* (prep.); in some scientific terms, < NL, L *ob-*]

ob., **1.** obiit. **2.** incidentally. [< L *obiter*] **3.** oboe.

O.B., **1.** opening of books. **2.** ordered back. Also, **OB, O/B**

Obad., Obadiah.

O·ba·di·ah (ō′bə dī′ə), *n.* **1.** a Minor Prophet. **2.** a book of the Bible bearing his name. **3.** a boy's given name. Also, *Douay Bible,* **Abdias** (for defs. 1, 2).

obb., obbligato.

ob·bli·ga·to (ob′lə gä′tō; *It.* ôb′blē gä′tô), *adj., n., pl.* **-tos,** *It.* **-ti** (-tē). *Music.* —*adj.* **1.** (used as a musical direction) obligatory or indispensable; so important that it cannot be omitted (opposed to *ad libitum*). —*n.* **2.** an obbligato part or accompaniment. **3.** a continuing or persistent subordinate or background motif. **4.** a subordinate part of a solo. Also, **obligato.** [< It: bound, obliged < L *obligāt(us)*; see OBLIGATE]

ob·cla·vate (ob klā′vāt), *adj.* inversely clavate. [< NL; see OB-, CLAVATE]

ob·con·i·cal (ob kon′i kəl), *adj. Bot.* conical, with the attachment at the pointed end. Also, **ob·con′ic.** [OB- + CONICAL]

ob·cor·date (ob kôr′dāt), *adj. Bot.* heart-shaped, with the attachment at the pointed end, as a leaf. [OB- + CORDATE]

ob·cu·ne·ate (ob kyōō′nē āt′, -it), *adj.* inversely cuneate. [OB- + CUNEATE]

obdt., obedient.

ob·du·ce (ob dōō′sē, -dyōō′-), *v. imp.* (in prescriptions) cover; conceal; coat. [< L]

ob·du·rate (ob′dŏŏ rit, -dyŏŏ-), *adj.* **1.** unmoved by persuasion, pity, or tender feelings; unyielding. **2.** stubbornly resistant to moral influence; persistently impenitent: *an obdurate sinner.* [ME *obdurat* < L *obdūrāt(us)* hardened (ptp. of *obdūrāre*), equiv. to *ob-* OB- + *dūr(us)* hard + *-ātus* -ATE¹] —**ob′du·rate·ly,** *adv.* —**ob′du·rate·ness,** *n.*
—**Syn. 1.** hard, obstinate, callous, stubborn, unbending, inflexible. **2.** unregenerate, reprobate, shameless. —**Ant. 1.** soft, tractable. **2.** humble, repentant.

O.B.E., **1.** Officer (of the Order) of the British Empire. **2.** Order of the British Empire.

o·be·ah (ō′bē ə), *n.* obi². —**o′be·ah·ism,** *n.*

o·be·che (ō bē′chē), *n.* **1.** a tropical African tree *Triplochiton scleroxylon.* **2.** the hard, white to pale-yellow wood of this tree, used for making furniture. [< native Nigerian name]

o·be·di·ence (ō bē′dē əns), *n.* **1.** the state or quality of being obedient. **2.** the act or practice of obeying; dutiful or submissive compliance: *Military service demands obedience from its members.* **3.** a sphere of authority or jurisdiction, esp. ecclesiastical. **4.** *Chiefly Eccles.* **a.** conformity to a monastic rule or the authority of a religious superior, esp. on the part of one who has vowed such conformance. **b.** the rule or authority that exacts such conformance. [ME < OF < L *oboedient-* OBEDIENT + *-ia;* see -ENCE]

o·be·di·ent (ō bē′dē ənt), *adj.* obeying, or willing to obey; complying with or submissive to one in authority: *an obedient son.* [ME < OF < L *oboedient-* (s. of *oboediēns*), prp. of *oboedīre* to OBEY; see -ENT]
—**Syn.** compliant, docile, tractable, yielding, deferential, respectful. —**Ant.** recalcitrant.

O·beid (ō bād′), *n.* See **El Obeid.**

o·bei·sance (ō bā′səns, ō bē′-), *n.* **1.** a movement of the body expressing deep respect or deferential courtesy, as before a superior; a bow, curtsy, or other similar gesture. **2.** deference or homage: *The nobles gave obeisance to the new king.* [ME *obeisaunce* < MF *obeissance,* deriv. of OF *obeissant,* prp. of *obeir* to OBEY; see -ANCE] —**o·bei′sant,** *adj.* —**o·bei′sant·ly,** *adv.*

O·bel·ia (ō bēl′yə, ō bē′lē ə), *n.* a girl's given name.

O·be·lia (ō bēl′yə, ō bē′lē ə), *n.* a genus of colonial hydroids common in temperate seas and appearing as a delicate, mosslike growth on rocks, pilings, etc. [< NL < Gk *obelía(s)* a loaf toasted on a spit, equiv. to *obel(ós)* a spit (see OBELISK) + *-ias* derivative suffix]

ob·e·lise (ob′ə līz′), *v.t.,* **-lised, -lis·ing.** *Chiefly Brit.* obelize.

ob·e·lisk (ob′ə lisk), *n.* **1.** a tapering, four-sided shaft of stone, usually monolithic and having a pyramidal apex. **2.** something resembling such a shaft. **3.** an obelus. **4.** *Print.* dagger (def. 2). [< L *obelisc(us)* < Gk *obelískos* small spit, equiv. to *obel(ós)* spit, pointed pillar + *-iskos* dim. suffix] —**ob′e·lis′cal,** *adj.* —**ob′e·lis′koid,** *adj.*

Obelisk

ob·e·lize (ob′ə līz′), *v.t.,* **-lized, -liz·ing.** to mark (a word or passage) with an obelus. Also, *esp. Brit.,* **obelise.** [< Gk *obelíz(ein),* equiv. to *obel(ós)* OBELUS + *-izein* -IZE] —**ob′e·lism,** *n.*

O·be·lon (ō′bə lən, -lon′), *n.* a boy's given name.

ob·e·lus (ob′ə ləs), *n., pl.* **-li** (-lī′). **1.** a mark (— or ÷) used in ancient manuscripts to point out spurious, corrupt, doubtful, or superfluous words or passages. **2.** *Print.* dagger (def. 2). [< LL < Gk *obelós* spit, pointed pillar]

O·ber·am·mer·gau (ō′bər äm′ər gou′), *n.* a village in S West Germany, SW of Munich: famous for the passion play performed every ten years. 5325 (1950).

O·ber·hau·sen (ō′bər hou′zən), *n.* a city in W West Germany, in the lower Ruhr valley. 259,800 (1963).

O·ber·land (ō′bər land′; *Ger.* ō′bər länt′), *n.* a mountain region in central Switzerland, mostly in S Bern canton.

O·ber·lin (*Fr.* ô ber laN′ *for 1;* ō′bər lin *for 2*), *n.* **1. Jean Fré·dé·ric** (*Fr.* zhäN frā dā rēk′), 1740–1826, Alsatian clergyman. **2.** a village in N Ohio. 8198 (1960).

O·ber·on (ō′bə ron′), *n.* **1.** (in medieval folklore and in Shakespeare's *A Midsummer Night's Dream*) the king of the fairies and husband of their queen, Titania. **2.** *Astron.* one of the five satellites of Uranus.

o·bese (ō bēs′), *adj.* excessively fat; corpulent; overweight: *a diet program for obese people.* [< L *obēs(us),* ptp. of *obēdere* to eat away, equiv. to *ob-* OB- + *ēdere* to EAT] —**o·bese′ly,** *adv.* —**o·bese′ness, o·bes·i·ty** (ō bē′si tē), *n.*
—**Syn.** gross.

o·bey (ō bā′), *v.t.* **1.** to comply with or follow the commands, restrictions, wishes, or instructions of: *to obey one's parents.* **2.** to comply with or follow (a command, restriction, wish, instruction, etc.): *to obey orders.* **3.** (of things) to respond conformably in action to: *The car obeyed the slightest touch of the wheel.* **4.** to submit or conform in action to (some guiding principle, impulse, etc.): *Obey your conscience.* —*v.i.* **5.** to be obedient: *to love, honor, and obey.* [ME *obeie(n)* < OF *obei(r)* < L *oboedīre,* equiv. to *ob-* OB- + *audīre* to hear] —**o·bey′a·ble,** *adj.* —**o·bey′er,** *n.* —**o·bey′ing·ly,** *adv.*

ob·fus·cate (ob fus′kāt, ob′fə skāt′), *v.t.,* **-cat·ed, -cat·ing.** **1.** to confuse, bewilder, or stupefy. **2.** to make obscure: *to obfuscate a problem with extraneous information.* **3.** to darken. [< LL *obfuscāt(us)* darkened (ptp. of *obfuscāre*), equiv. to L *ob-* OB- + *fusc-* dark + *-ātus* -ATE¹] —**ob′fus·ca′tion,** *n.*
—**Syn. 1.** muddle, perplex. **2.** cloud. —**Ant. 1.** clarify.

o·bi¹ (ō′bē; *Jap.* ô′bē), *n., pl.* **o·bis,** *Jap.* **o·bi.** a long, broad sash tied about the waist over a Japanese kimono. [< Jap: belt, sash, equiv. to ? ō thong + *bi* beautiful]

o·bi² (ō′bē), *n., pl.* **o·bis** for 2. **1.** a kind of sorcery practiced by the Negroes of Africa, the West Indies, etc. **2.** a fetish or charm used in it. Also called **obeah.** [< WAfr, perh. Bini (spoken in Nigeria)] —**o′bi·ism,** *n.*

O·bie (ō′bē), *n.* a boy's given name, form of **Obadiah.**

o·bi·it (ō′bi it; *Eng.* ō′bē it, ob′ē-), *Latin.* he died; she died.

o·bit (ō′bit, ob′it), *n.* **1.** the date of a person's death. **2.** an obituary. **3.** *Obs.* a Requiem Mass. [ME *obite* < L *obit(us)* dead, equiv. to *ob-* OB- + *-i-* go + *-tus* ptp. suffix]

ob·i·ter dic·tum (ob′i tər dik′təm), *pl.* **ob·i·ter dic·ta** (ob′i tər dik′tə). **1.** an incidental or passing remark, opinion, etc. **2.** *Law.* an incidental or supplementary opinion by a judge in deciding a case, upon a matter not essential to the decision, and therefore not binding. [< L: (a) saying by the way]

o·bit·u·ar·y (ō bich′ōō er′ē), *n., pl.* **-ar·ies,** *adj.* —*n.* **1.** a notice of the death of a person, often with a brief biographical sketch, as in a newspaper. —*adj.* **2.** of, pertaining to, or recording a death or deaths: *an obituary notice; the obituary page of a newspaper.* [< ML *obituārī(us),* equiv. to L *obitu(s)* death (see OBIT) + *-ārius* -ARY]

obj., **1.** object. **2.** objection. **3.** objective.

ob·ject (*n.* ob′jikt, -jekt; *v.* əb jekt′), *n.* **1.** anything that is visible or tangible and is stable in form. **2.** anything that may be apprehended intellectually: *objects of thought.* **3.** a person or thing with reference to the impression made on the mind or the feeling or emotion elicited in an observer: *an object of curiosity and pity.* **4.** a thing, person, or matter to which thought or action is directed: *an object of medical investigation.* **5.** the end toward which effort is directed; goal; purpose: *Investigation of business prospects is the object of his trip to London.* **6.** *Gram.* (in many languages, as English) a noun, noun phrase, or noun substitute representing by its syntactical position either the goal of the action of a verb with which it combines to form a verb phrase or the goal of a preposition in a prepositional phrase, as *ball* in *John hit the ball, Venice* in *He came to Venice, coin* and *her* in *He gave her a coin.* Cf. **direct object, indirect object. 7.** *Metaphys.* something toward which a cognitive act is directed. —*v.i.* **8.** to offer a reason or argument in opposition. **9.** to express or feel disapproval, dislike, or distaste; be averse. **10.** to refuse or attempt to refuse to permit some action, speech, etc. —*v.t.* **11.** to state, claim, or cite in opposition; put forward in objection: *Some persons objected that the proposed law would harm world trade.* **12.** to refuse to permit. **13.** *Archaic.* to bring forward or adduce in opposition. [ME < LL *object(us)* act of placing before or opposite, n. use of L *objectus* (ptp. of *objicere*), equiv. to *ob-* OB- + *jec-* (comb. form of *jac-* throw; see JET¹) + *-tus* ptp. suffix] —**ob·jec′tor,** *n.*
—**Syn. 5.** objective, target, destination, intent, intention, motive. See **aim.**

object., **1.** objection. **2.** objective.

ob′ject ball′, *Billiards, Pool.* **1.** the first ball struck by the cue ball in making a carom. Cf. **carom ball. 2.** a ball to be struck by the cue ball; any ball except the cue ball.

ob′ject glass′, *Optics.* objective (def. 3).

ob·jec·ti·fy (əb jek′tə fī′), *v.t.,* **-fied, -fy·ing.** to present as an object, esp. of sight, touch, or other physical sense; make objective; externalize. [< ML *object(um)* OBJECT + -IFY] —**ob·jec′ti·fi·ca′tion,** *n.*

ob·jec·tion (əb jek′shən), *n.* **1.** something said or offered in disagreement, opposition, refusal, or disapproval; an adverse reason or argument. **2.** the act of objecting. **3.** a ground or cause for objecting. **4.** a feeling of disapproval, dislike, or disagreement. [ME *objeccioun* < LL *objectiōn-* (s. of *objectiō*), equiv. to L *object(us)* OBJECT + *-iōn-* -ION]

ob·jec·tion·a·ble (əb jek′shə nə bəl), *adj.* **1.** causing or tending to cause an objection, disapproval, or protest. **2.** offensive to good taste, manners, etiquette, propriety, etc.: *an objectionable paragraph in a book.* **3.** offensive or insulting to a person or group, esp. a racial, religious, or ethnic group. [OBJECTION + -ABLE] —**ob·jec′tion·a·bil′i·ty, ob·jec′tion·a·ble·ness,** *n.* —**ob·jec′tion·a·bly,** *adv.*

ob·jec·tive (əb jek′tiv), *n.* **1.** something that one's efforts are intended to attain or accomplish; purpose; goal; target: *the objective of a military mission; the objective of a fund-raising drive.* **2.** *Gram.* **a.** Also called **objec′tive case′.** (in English and some other languages) a case specialized for the use of a form as the object of a transitive verb or of a preposition, as *him* in *The boy hit him,* or *me* in *He comes to me with his troubles.* **b.** a word in that case. **3.** Also called **object glass, object lens.** *Optics.* (in a telescope, microscope, camera, or other optical system) the lens or combination of lenses which first receives the rays from the object and forms the image in the focal plane of the eyepiece, as in a microscope, or on a plate or screen, as in a camera. See diag. under **microscope.** —*adj.* **4.** being the object of perception or thought; belonging to the object of thought rather than to the thinking subject (opposed to *subjective*). **5.** free from personal feelings or prejudice; based on facts; unbiased: *an objective analysis of the role of religion in politics.* **6.** being the object or goal of one's endeavors or actions. **7.** intent upon or dealing with things external to the mind rather than with thoughts or feelings, as a person, a book, etc. **8.** of or pertaining to that which can be known, or to that which is an object or a part of an object; existing independent of thought or an observer as part of reality. **9.** being part of or pertaining to an object to be drawn: *an objective plane.* **10.** *Med.* (of a symptom) discernible to others as well as the patient. **11.** *Gram.* **a.** pertaining to the use of a form as the object of a transitive verb or of a preposition. **b.** (in English and some other languages) noting the objective case. **c.** similar to such a case in meaning. [< ML *objectīv(us),* equiv. to L *object(us)* (see OBJECT) + *-īvus* -IVE] —**ob·jec′tive·ly,** *adv.* —**ob·jec′tive·ness,** *n.*
—**Syn. 1.** object, destination, aim. **5.** impartial, fair, impersonal, disinterested. —**Ant. 5.** subjective, personal.

objec′tive com′plement, *Gram.* a word or a group of words used in the predicate following a factitive verb to modify or qualify its direct object, as *chairman* in *We appointed him chairman, white* in *He painted his house white,* or *a nice chap* in *They thought him a nice chap.* Also called **objec′tive pred′icate.**

objec′tive correl′ative, *Literature.* a situation or chain of events which objectifies a particular emotion and may be used in a work of literature to produce or evoke that emotion in the reader.

objec′tive ide′alism, *Philos.* a form of idealism asserting that the act of experiencing has a reality combining and transcending the natures of the object experienced and of the mind of the observer. Cf. **subjective idealism.** —**objec′tive ide′alist.**

objec′tive lens′, *Optics.* the lens of an optical instrument closest to the object being viewed.

objec′tive rel′ativism, *Epistemology.* the doctrine that knowledge of real objects is relative to the individual. —**objec′tive rel′ativist.**

objec′tive spir′it, *Hegelianism.* the human spirit, insofar as it has become capable of a rational identification of its individual self with the community of other spirits but is not yet capable of the identification with the absolute idea that characterizes the absolute spirit.

ob·jec·tiv·ism (əb jek′tə viz′əm), *n.* **1.** a tendency to lay stress on the objective or external elements of cognition. **2.** the tendency, as of a writer, to deal with things external to the mind rather than with thoughts or feelings. **3.** a doctrine characterized by this tendency. [OBJECTIVE + -ISM] —**ob·jec′tiv·ist,** *n., adj.* —**ob·jec′ti·vis′tic,** *adj.*

ob·jec·tiv·i·ty (ob′jek tiv′i tē), *n.* **1.** the state or quality of being objective: *He tries to maintain objectivity in his opinions.* **2.** intentness on objects external to the mind. **3.** external reality. [OBJECTIVE + -ITY]

ob·jec·tiv·ize (əb jek′tə vīz′), *v.t.,* **-ized, -iz·ing.** to cause to become concrete or objective; objectify: *to objectivize a plan.* [OBJECTIVE + -IZE] —**ob·jec′ti·vi·za′tion,** *n.*

ob′ject lan′guage, the language to which a meta-language refers.

ob′ject lens′, *Optics.* objective (def. 3).

ob·ject·less (ob′jikt lis), *adj.* **1.** not directed toward any end or goal; purposeless; aimless. **2.** having no object: *an objectless preposition.* [OBJECT + -LESS] —**ob′ject·less·ly,** *adv.* —**ob′ject·less·ness,** *n.*

ob′ject les′son, **1.** a practical or concrete illustration of a principle. **2.** a lesson in which instruction is conveyed by means of a material object.

ob·jet d'art (ôb zhe dar′), *pl.* **ob·jets d'art** (ôb zhe dar′). *French.* an object of artistic worth or curiosity, esp. a small object.

ob·jet trou·vé (ôb zhe trōō vā′). *French.* See **found object.**

ob·jur·gate (ob′jər gāt′, əb jûr′gāt), *v.t.,* **-gat·ed, -gat·ing.** to reproach or denounce vehemently; upbraid harshly; berate sharply. [< L *objurgāt(us)* rebuked, ptp. of *objurgāre,* equiv. to *ob-* OB- + *jurgāre* to rebuke, equiv. to *jur-* (s. of *jus*) law + *(a)g-* do, drive + *-ātus* -ATE¹] —**ob′jur·ga′tion,** *n.* —**ob′jur·ga′tor,** *n.* —**ob·jur′ga·to·ri·ly** (əb jûr′gə tôr′ə lē, -tōr′-), **ob·jur·ga·tive·ly** (əb jûr′gə tiv lē), *adv.* —**ob·jur′ga·to′ry, ob·jur′ga·tive,** *adj.*

obl., **1.** oblique. **2.** oblong.

ob·lan·ce·o·late (ob lan′sē ə lit, -lāt′), *adj. Bot.* inversely lanceolate, as a leaf. [OB- + LANCEOLATE]

ob·last (ob′last, -läst; *Russ.* ôb′läst), *n., pl.* **-lasts,** *Russ.* **-las·ti** (-läs tē). **1.** (in the Soviet Union) an administrative division corresponding to an autonomous province. **2.** region; province. [< Russ *oblast′* < OSlav, equiv. to *ob-* against, on + *vlast′* administration]

ob·late¹ (ob′lāt, o blāt′), *adj.* flattened at the poles, as a spheroid generated by the revolution of an ellipse about its shorter axis (opposed to *prolate*). See diag. under **prolate.** [< NL *oblāt(us)* lengthened, equiv. to L *ob-* OB- + *lātus* carried] —**ob′late·ly,** *adv.*

ob·late² (ob′lāt, o blāt′), *n.* **1.** a person offered to the service of and living in a monastery, but not under monastic vows or full monastic rule. **2.** a layman of any of various Roman Catholic societies devoted to special religious work. [< ML *oblāt(us)* offered, ptp. of *offerre* to OFFER]

ob·la·tion (o blā′shən), *n.* **1.** the offering to God of the elements of bread and wine in the Eucharist. **2.** the whole office of the Eucharist. **3.** the act of making an offering, now esp. to God or a deity. **4.** any offering for religious or charitable uses. [ME *oblacion* < LL *oblātiōn-* (s. of *oblātiō*), equiv. to *oblāt(us)* offered (see OBLATE²) + *-iōn-* -ION] —**ob·la·to·ry** (ob′lə tôr′ē, -tōr′ē), **ob·la′tion·al,** *adj.*

ob·li·gate (*v.* ob′lə gāt′; *adj.* ob′lə git, -gāt′), *v.*, **-gat·ed, -gat·ing,** *adj.* —*v.t.* **1.** to oblige or bind morally or legally: *to obligate oneself by contract to purchase a building.* **2.** to pledge, commit, or bind (funds, property, etc.) to meet an obligation. —*adj.* **3.** morally or legally bound; constrained. **4.** necessary; essential. **5.** *Biol.* restricted to a particular condition of life, as certain parasites which must live in close association with their usual hosts in order to survive (opposed to *facultative*). [ME *obligat* < L *obligāt(us)* bound (ptp. of *obligāre*), equiv. to *ob-* OB- + *ligātus;* see LIGATE] —**ob·li·ga·ble** (ob′lə gə bəl), *adj.* —**ob′li·ga′tor,** *n.*

ob·li·ga·tion (ob′lə gā′shən), *n.* **1.** something by which a person is bound to do certain things, and which arises out of a sense of duty or results from custom, law, etc. **2.** something that is done or is to be done for such reasons: *to fulfill one's obligations.* **3.** a binding promise, contract, sense of duty, etc. **4.** the act of binding oneself by a promise, contract, etc. **5.** *Law.* **a.** an agreement enforceable by law, originally applied to promises under seal. **b.** a document containing such an agreement. **c.** a bond containing a penalty, with a condition annexed for payment of money, performance of covenants, etc. **d.** any bond, note, bill, certificate, or the like, as of a government or a corporation, serving as evidence of indebtedness. **6.** an indebtedness or amount of indebtedness. **7.** a favor, service, or benefit for which gratitude is due. **8.** a debt of gratitude: *He felt an obligation to his benefactor.* **9.** the state of being under a debt, as of gratitude, for a favor, service, or benefit. [ME *obligacioun* < OF *obligation* < L *obligātiōn-* (s. of *obligātiō*) a binding, equiv. to *obligāt(us)* bound (see OBLIGATE) + *-iōn-* -ION]
—**Syn. 1.** responsibility. See **duty. 5.** contract, covenant.

ob·li·ga·tive (ob′lə gā′tiv), *adj.* implying or involving obligation: *an obligative commitment.* [< L *obligāt(us)* (see OBLIGATE) + -IVE]

ob·li·ga·to (ob′lə gä′tō), *adj., n., pl.* **-tos, -ti** (-tē). obbligato.

ob·lig·a·to·ry (ə blig′ə tôr′ē, -tōr′ē, ob′lə gə-), *adj.* **1.** imposing moral or legal obligation; binding: *an obligatory promise.* **2.** required as a matter of obligation; mandatory: *A reply is desirable but not obligatory.* **3.** incumbent or compulsory (usually fol. by *on* or *upon*): *duties obligatory on all.* **4.** creating or recording an obligation, as a document. [ME < LL *obligātōri(us)* binding, equiv. to L *obligāt(us)* bound (see OBLIGATE) + *-ōrius* -ORY[1]] —**ob·lig·a·to·ri·ly** (ə blig′ə tôr′ə lē, -tôr′-, ob′lə gə-; ə blig′ə tôr′ə lē, -tôr′-, ob′lə gə-), *adv.* —**ob·lig′a·to′ri·ness,** *n.*

o·blige (ə blīj′), *v.,* **o·bliged, o·blig·ing.** —*v.t.* **1.** to require or constrain, as by law, command, conscience, or force of necessity. **2.** to bind morally or legally, as by a promise, contract, or the like. **3.** to make (an action, policy, etc.) necessary or obligatory: *Your recalcitrance obliges firmness on my part.* **4.** to place under a debt of gratitude for some benefit, favor, or service: *I'm much obliged for the ride.* **5.** to put (one) in a debt of gratitude, as by a favor or accommodation: *Mr. Weems will oblige us with a song.* —*v.i.* **6.** to be kindly accommodating: *I'll do anything within reason to oblige.* [ME *oblige(n)* < OF *obligie(r)* < L *obligāre* to bind. See OBLIGATE] —**o·blig·ed·ly** (ə blī′jid lē), *adv.* —**o·blig′ed·ness,** *n.* —**o·blig′er,** *n.*
—**Syn. 1.** compel, force. **2.** obligate. **5.** OBLIGE, ACCOMMODATE imply making a gracious and welcome gesture of some kind. OBLIGE emphasizes the idea of conferring a favor or benefit (and often of taking some trouble to do it): *to oblige someone with a loan.* ACCOMMODATE emphasizes doing a service or furnishing a convenience: *to accommodate someone with lodgings and meals.*

ob·li·gee (ob′lə jē′), *n.* **1.** *Law.* **a.** a person to whom another is bound. **b.** a person to whom a bond is given. **2.** a person who is under obligation for a favor, service, or benefit. [OBLIGE + -EE]

o·blig·ing (ə blī′jing), *adj.* **1.** willing or eager to do favors, offer one's services, etc.; accommodating: *The clerk was most obliging.* **2.** obligating. [OBLIGE + -ING[2]] —**o·blig′ing·ly,** *adv.* —**o·blig′ing·ness,** *n.*
—**Syn. 1.** helpful, kind, friendly.

ob·li·gor (ob′lə gôr′, ob′lə gôr′), *n.* *Law.* **1.** a person who is bound to another. **2.** a person who gives a bond. [OBLIGE + -OR[2]]

ob·lique (ə blēk′; *Mil.* ə blīk′), *adj., adv., v.,* **-liqued, -liqu·ing,** *n.* —*adj.* **1.** neither perpendicular nor parallel to a given line or surface; slanting; sloping. **2.** *Geom.* (of a solid) not having the axis perpendicular to the plane of the base. **3.** diverging from a given straight line or course. **4.** not straight or direct, as a course. **5.** indirectly stated or expressed; not straightforward: *some oblique remarks about his honesty.* **6.** indirectly aimed at or reached, as ends, results, etc.; deviously achieved. **7.** morally, ethically, or mentally wrong; underhand; perverse. **8.** *Rhet.* indirect (applied to discourse in which the original words of a speaker or writer are assimilated to the language of the reporter). **9.** *Gram.* noting or pertaining to any case of noun inflection except nominative and vocative, or except these two and accusative: *Latin genitive, dative, and ablative cases are said to be oblique.* **10.** *Anat.* pertaining to muscles running obliquely in the body as opposed to those running transversely or longitudinally. **11.** *Bot.* having unequal sides, as a leaf. **12.** *Typography.* (of a letter) slanting toward the right, as a form of sans-serif, gothic, or square-serif type. **13.** *Drafting.* designating a method of projection **(oblique′ projec′tion)** in which a three-dimensional object is represented by a drawing **(oblique′ draw′ing)** in which the face, usually parallel to the picture plane, is represented in accurate or exact proportion, and all other faces are shown at any convenient angle other than 90°. Cf. **axonometric, cabinet** (def. 17), **isometric** (def. 4). —*adv.* **14.** *Mil.* at an angle of 45°. —*v.i.* **15.** to have or take an oblique direction; slant: *The wall obliques from the gate at a sharp angle.* **16.** *Mil.* to change direction obliquely. —*n.* **17.** *Gram.* the oblique case. **18.** something that is oblique. **19.** any of several oblique muscles, esp. in the walls of the abdomen. [ME *oblike* < L *oblīquus* slanter, equiv. to *ob-* OB- + OL *līquus* < ?] —**ob·lique′ness,** *n.*

oblique′ an′gle, an angle that is not a right angle; an acute or obtuse angle. —**ob·lique′-an′gled,** *adj.*

oblique′ cir′cular cone′, *Geom.* a cone whose surface is generated by lines joining a fixed point to the points of a circle, the fixed point lying on a line that is not perpendicular to the circle at its center. Cf. **right circular cone.**

oblique′ cir′cular cyl′inder, *Geom.* a cylinder generated by the revolution of a parallelogram other than a rectangle about one of its sides. Cf. **right circular cylinder.**

oblique′ coor′dinates, *Math.* a coordinate system in which the axes do not meet at right angles.

ob·lique·ly (ə blēk′lē; *Mil.* ə blīk′-), *adv.* in an oblique manner or direction. [OBLIQUE + -LY]

oblique′ mo′tion, *Music.* the relative motion of two melodic parts in which one remains in place or moves relatively little while the other moves more actively.

oblique′ sail′ing, the navigation of a vessel on a point of the compass other than one of the cardinal points.

oblique′ sec′tion, a representation of an object as it would appear if cut by a plane that is other than parallel or perpendicular to its longest axis.

ob·liq·ui·ty (ə blik′wi tē), *n., pl.* **-ties. 1.** the state of being oblique. **2.** divergence from moral conduct, rectitude, etc.; immorality, dishonesty, or the like. **3.** a moral delinquency. **4.** mental perversity. **5.** an instance of mental perversity. **6.** an inclination or a degree of inclination. **7.** a confusing or obscure statement or passage of writing, esp. one deliberately made obscure. **8.** Also called **obliq′uity of the eclip′tic.** *Astron.* the angle between the plane of the earth's orbit and that of the earth's equator, equal to 23°27′; the inclination of the earth's equator. [ME *obliquitee* < MF *obliquite* < L *oblīquitāt-* (s. of *oblīquitās*), equiv. to *obliqu(us)* OBLIQUE + *-itāt-* -ITY] —**ob·liq′ui·tous,** *adj.*

ob·lit·er·ate (ə blit′ə rāt′), *v.t.,* **-at·ed, -at·ing. 1.** to remove all traces of; do away with; destroy completely. **2.** to blot out or render undecipherable (writing, marks, etc.); cancel; efface. [< L *oblitterāt(us)* blotted out (ptp. of *oblitterāre*), equiv. to *ob-* OB- + *litter(a)* letter + *-ātus* -ATE[1]] —**ob·lit·er·a·ble** (ə blit′ər ə bəl), *adj.*
—**Syn. 2.** expunge. See **cancel.**

ob·lit·er·a·tion (ə blit′ə rā′shən), *n.* **1.** the act of obliterating or the state of being obliterated. **2.** *Pathol., Surg.* closure of an orifice or lumen or the removal of a part as a result of disease or surgery. [< L *oblitterātiōn-* (s. of *oblitterātiō*), equiv. to *oblitterāt(us)* (see OBLITERATE) + *-iōn-* -ION] —**ob·lit·er·a·tive** (ə blit′ə rā′tiv, -ər ə tiv), *adj.*

ob·li·ves·cence (ob′lə ves′əns), *n.* the process of forgetting. [< L *oblīvīsc(ī)* (to) forget + -ENCE]

ob·liv·i·on (ə bliv′ē ən), *n.* **1.** the state of being forgotten, as by the public: *a former star of the theater now in oblivion.* **2.** the state of forgetting or of being mentally withdrawn: *The nap gave him 30 minutes of oblivion.* **3.** official disregard or overlooking of offenses; pardon; amnesty. [ME < MF < L *oblīviōn-* (s. of *oblīviō*), equiv. to *oblīv(īscī)* (to) forget (*ob-* OB- + *līv-*, s. of *līvēre* to darken, forget) + *-iōn-* -ION]

ob·liv·i·ous (ə bliv′ē əs), *adj.* **1.** forgetful; without remembrance or memory: *oblivious of my former failure.* **2.** unmindful; unconscious; unaware (usually fol. by *of* or *to*): *She was oblivious of his admiration.* **3.** inducing forgetfulness. [ME < L *oblīviōs(us)* forgetful, equiv. to *oblīvī(scī)* (to) forget (see OBLIVION) + *-ōsus* -OUS] —**ob·liv′i·ous·ly,** *adv.* —**ob·liv′i·ous·ness,** *n.*
—**Syn. 1.** See **absent-minded.**

Oblong leaf

ob·long (ob′lông′, -long′), *adj.* **1.** elongated, usually from the square or circular form. **2.** in the form of a rectangle one of whose dimensions is greater than the other. —*n.* **3.** an oblong figure. [ME *oblonge* < L *oblong(us)* rather long, equiv. to *ob-* OB- + *long-* LONG[1]] —**ob′long·ish,** *adj.* —**ob′long·ly,** *adv.* —**ob′long·ness,** *n.*

ob·long·a·ta (ob′lông gä′tə, -long-), *n., pl.* **-tas, -tae** (-tē). See **medulla oblongata.** [< NL: lit., OBLONG; see -ATE[1]]

ob·lo·quy (ob′lə kwē), *n., pl.* **-quies. 1.** discredit, disgrace, or bad repute resulting from public blame, abuse, or denunciation. **2.** censure, blame, or abusive language aimed at a person or thing, esp. by numerous persons or by the general public. [< L *obloqui(um)* contradiction, equiv. to *obloqu(ī)* (to) contradict (*ob-* OB- + *loquī* to speak) + *-ium* -Y[3]] —**ob·lo·qui·al** (o blō′kwē əl), *adj.*
—**Syn. 2.** reproach, calumny; aspersion, revilement, disgrace. —**Ant. 1.** credit. **2.** praise.

ob·nounce (ob nouns′), *v.i.,* **-nounced, -nounc·ing.** (in ancient Rome) to announce an unfavorable omen with reference to a proposed public action. [< L *obnunti(āre)*, equiv. to *ob-* OB- + *nuntiāre* to tell (*nunti(us)* messenger + *-āre* inf. suffix)]

ob·nox·ious (əb nok′shəs), *adj.* **1.** objectionable; offensive; odious: *obnoxious behavior that led to his being ostracized by society.* **2.** annoying or objectionable due to being a showoff or attracting undue attention to oneself, as by talking loudly or being boisterous: *an obnoxious little brat.* **3.** exposed or liable to harm, evil, or anything objectionable. **4.** *Obs.* liable to punishment or censure; reprehensible. [< L *obnoxiōs(us)* harmful, equiv. to *ob-* OB- + *noxiōsus* NOXIOUS] —**ob·nox′ious·ly,** *adv.* —**ob·nox′ious·ness,** *n.*
—**Syn. 1.** See **hateful. 2.** subject, answerable. —**Ant. 1.** delightful.

o·boe (ō′bō), *n.* **1.** a woodwind instrument having a slender conical, tubular body and a double-reed mouthpiece. **2.** (in an organ) a reed stop with a sound like that of an oboe. **3.** a word formerly used in communication to represent the letter *O.* [< It < F *hautbois,* equiv. to *haut* high + *bois* wood]

Oboe

O·boe (ō′bō), *n.* *Electronics.* a navigation system utilizing two ground stations that use radar to measure the distance to an aircraft and then radio the information to the aircraft. [special use of OBOE]

o·bo·ist (ō′bō ist), *n.* a player of the oboe. [OBOE + -IST]

ob·ol (ob′əl), *n.* **1.** a silver coin of ancient Greece, the sixth part of a drachma. **2.** obole. [see OBOLUS]

ob·ole (ob′ōl), *n.* a silver-alloy coin of France issued during the Middle Ages, the 24th part of a sol, or one-half denier. Also, **obol, obolus.** [< F < L *obol(us)* OBOLUS]

ob·o·lus (ob′ə ləs), *n., pl.* **-li** (-lī′). **1.** a modern Greek unit of weight equal to 0.1 gram. **2.** obole. [< L < Gk *obolós* small coin, weight]

ob·o·vate (ob ō′vāt), *adj.* inversely ovate; ovate with the narrow end at the base. [OB- + OVATE]

ob·o·void (ob ō′void), *adj.* inversely ovoid; ovoid with the narrow end at the base, as certain fruits. [OB- + OVOID]

Obovate leaf

O'Boyle (ō boil′), *n.* **Patrick Aloysius,** born 1896, U.S. Roman Catholic clergyman: archbishop of Washington, D.C., since 1947.

ob·pyr·i·form (ob pir′ə fôrm′), *adj.* inversely pear-shaped; pear-shaped with the narrow end at the base. [OB- + PYRIFORM]

O·brecht (ō′brekht), *n.* **Ja·cob** (yä′kôp), 1430–1505, Dutch composer and conductor. Also, **Hobrecht.**

O·bre·gón (ô′vre gôn′), *n.* **Al·va·ro** (äl′vä rô), 1880–1928, Mexican general and statesman: president 1920–24.

O·bre·no·vić (*Serbo-Croatian.* ô bre′no vich), *n.* **A·lek·san·dar** (*Serbo-Croatian.* ä′le ksän′där). See **Alexander I.**

O·bren·o·vich (ō bren′ə vich′), *n.* **Alexander.** See **Alexander I.**

ob·rep·tion (o brep′shən), *n.* **1.** *Canon Law.* fraud in obtaining or attempting to obtain something from an official. Cf. **subreption** (def. 1). **2.** *Scots Law.* the act of obtaining something, as an escheat, by falsehood. Cf. **subreption** (def. 2). [< L *obreptiōn-* (s. of *obreptiō*) a surprise, equiv. to *ob-* OB- + *rept(us)* crept (see REPTILE) + *-iōn-* -ION] —**ob·rep·ti·tious** (ob′rep tish′əs), *adj.* —**ob′rep·ti′tious·ly,** *adv.*

ob·ro·ga·tion (ob′rə gā′shən), *n.* *Civil Law.* the annulment or alteration of a law by the enactment of a new one. [< L *obrogātiōn-* (s. of *obrogātiō*), equiv. to *ob-* OB- + *rogātiōn-* ROGATION]

obs., 1. observation. **2.** observatory. **3.** obsolete. Also, **Obs.**

ob·scene (əb sēn′), *adj.* **1.** offensive to modesty or decency; indecent; lewd: *obscene pictures.* **2.** causing, or intended to cause, sexual excitement or lust. **3.** abominable; disgusting; repulsive: *an obscene exhibition of public discourtesy.* [< L *obscēn(us), obscaen(us),* prob. akin to *caenum, cēnum* dirt, filth] —**ob·scene′ly,** *adv.* —**ob·scene′ness,** *n.*
—**Syn. 1.** pornographic, smutty, filthy, lubricious.

ob·scen·i·ty (əb sen′i tē, -sē′ni-), *n., pl.* **-ties** for 2, 3. **1.** the character or quality of being obscene; indecency. **2.** something obscene, as a picture or story. **3.** an obscene word or expression, esp. when used as an invective. [< F *obscenité* < L *obscēnitāt-* (s. of *obscēnitās*), equiv. to *obscēn(us)* OBSCENE + *-itāt-* -ITY]

ob·scu·rant (əb skyŏŏr′ənt), *n.* **1.** a person who strives to prevent the increase and spread of knowledge. **2.** a person who obscures. —*adj.* **3.** pertaining to or characteristic of obscurants. [< L *obscūrant-* (s. of *obscūrāns*, prp. of *obscūrāre*), equiv. to *obscūr(us)* dark + *-ant-* -ANT]

ob·scu·rant·ism (əb skyŏŏr′ən tiz′əm, ob′skyŏŏ ran′tiz əm), *n.* **1.** opposition to the increase and spread of knowledge. **2.** deliberate obscurity or evasion of clarity. [< F; see OBSCURANT, -ISM] —**ob·scu′rant·ist,** *n., adj.*

ob·scu·ra·tion (ob′skyŏŏ rā′shən), *n.* **1.** the act of obscuring. **2.** the state of being obscured. [< L *obscūrātiōn-* (s. of *obscūrātiō*) a darkening, equiv. to *obscūrāt(us)*, ptp. of *obscūrāre*, (*obscūr(us)* dark + *-ātus* -ATE[1]) + *-iōn-*; see -ATION]

ob·scure (əb skyŏŏr′), *adj.,* **-scur·er, -scur·est,** *v.,* **-scured, -scur·ing,** *n.* —*adj.* **1.** (of meaning) not clear or plain; uncertain. **2.** (of language, style, a speaker, etc.) not expressing the meaning clearly or plainly. **3.** inconspicuous or unnoticeable: *the obscure beginnings of a great movement.* **4.** of little or no prominence, note, or distinction: *an obscure French artist.* **5.** far from public notice, worldly affairs, or important activities; remote; retired: *an obscure little town.* **6.** indistinct to the sight or any other sense; not readily seen, heard, etc.; faint. **7.** (of a vowel) having the reduced or neutral sound usually represented by the schwa (ə). **8.** lacking in light or illumination; dark; dim; murky: *an obscure back room.* **9.** enveloped in, concealed by, or frequenting darkness. **10.** not bright or lustrous; dull or darkish, as color or appearance. **11.** not clear to the understanding; ambiguous: *obscure motivations.* —*v.t.* **12.** to conceal or conceal by confusing (the meaning of a statement, poem, etc.). **13.** to make dark, dim, indistinct, etc. **14.** to reduce or neutralize (a vowel) to the sound usually represented by a schwa (ə). —*n.* **15.** obscurity. [ME < OF *oscur, obscur* < L *obscūr(us)* dark] —**ob·scur·ed·ly** (əb skyŏŏr′id lē), **ob·scure′ly,** *adv.* —**ob·scure′ness,** *n.*
—**Syn. 1.** doubtful, dubious, vague, ambiguous. See **mysterious. 4.** undistinguished, unnoted, unknown. **5.** secluded, inconspicuous, unnoticeable, unnoticed. **6.** blurred, veiled. **8.** cloudy, dusky, somber. See **dark.** —**Ant. 1.** certain. **4.** noted. **5.** conspicuous. **6.** clear. **8.** bright.

ob·scu·ri·ty (əb skyŏŏr′i tē), *n., pl.* **-ties. 1.** the state or quality of being obscure. **2.** uncertainty of meaning or expression; ambiguity. **3.** the condition of being unknown. **4.** an unknown or unimportant person or thing. **5.** darkness; dimness; indistinctness. [< MF *obscurite* < L *obscūritāt-* (s. of *obscūritās*), equiv. to *obscūr(us)* OBSCURE + *-itāt-* -ITY]

ob·se·crate (ob′sə krāt′), *v.t.,* **-crat·ed, -crat·ing.** to entreat solemnly; beseech; supplicate. [< L *obsecrāt(us)* supplicated (ptp. of *obsecrāre*), equiv. to *ob-* OB- + *secr-* sacred (var. of *sacr-*, s. of *sacer*) + *-ātus* -ATE[1]] —**ob′se·cra′tion,** *n.*

ob·se·quence (ob′sə kwəns), *n.* willingness or eagerness to serve, comply, please, etc.; the state of being obsequious. Also, **ob·se·que·ence** (ob sē′kwē əns). [< L *obsequentia*. See OBSEQUENT, -ENCE]

ob·se·quent (ob′sə kwənt), *adj. Obs.* obsequious; compliant; obedient. [< L *obsequent-* (s. of *obsequēns*), prp. of *obsequī* to comply with (*ob-* OB- + *sequī* to follow); see -ENT]

ob′sequent stream′, *Geol.* a stream flowing in a direction opposite to that of the dip of the local strata. Cf. **consequent stream.**

ob·se·qui·ous (əb sē′kwē əs), *adj.* **1.** servilely compliant or deferential: *obsequious servants.* **2.** characterized by or showing servile complaisance or deference: *an obsequious bow.* **3.** *Archaic.* obedient; dutiful. [< L *obsequiōs(us)*, equiv. to *obsequi(um)* compliance (deriv. of *obsequī*; see OBSEQUENT) + *-ōsus* -OUS] —**ob·se′qui·ous·ly,** *adv.* —**ob·se′qui·ous·ness,** *n.*
—**Syn. 1.** cringing, submissive. See **servile. 2.** fawning, sycophantic, flattering.

ob·se·quy (ob′sə kwē), *n., pl.* **-quies.** Usually, **obsequies.** a funeral rite or ceremony. [ME *obseque* < MF < LL *obsequi(ae)* (confused with *exsequiae* funeral), pl. of L *obsequium*; see OBSEQUIOUS]

ob·serv·a·ble (əb zûr′və bəl), *adj.* **1.** capable of being or liable to be observed; noticeable; visible; discernible. **2.** worthy or important enough to be celebrated, followed, or observed: *an observable holiday.* **3.** worthy or deserving of attention, notice, or celebration; noteworthy. [< L *observābil(is)* remarkable, equiv. to *observā(re)* (to) OBSERVE + *-bilis* -BLE] —**ob·serv′a·bil′i·ty, ob·serv′a·ble·ness,** *n.* —**ob·serv′a·bly,** *adv.*

ob·serv·ance (əb zûr′vəns), *n.* **1.** the act or an instance of following, obeying, or conforming to: *the observance of traffic laws.* **2.** a keeping or celebration by appropriate procedure, ceremonies, etc. **3.** a procedure, ceremony, or rite, as for a particular occasion: *patriotic observances.* **4.** a rule or custom to be followed or obeyed; a customary practice. **5.** *Rom. Cath. Ch.* **a.** a rule or discipline for a religious house or order. **b.** a house or order observing a rule or discipline. **6.** the act or an instance of watching, noting, or perceiving; observation. **7.** respectful attention or service. **8.** *Archaic.* respectful or courteous attention as to a person; dutiful service. [ME *observaunce* < OF < LL *observantia*, L: esteem, attention, deriv. of *observant-* (s. of *observāns*), prp. of *observāre.* See OBSERVE, -ANCE]

ob·serv·ant (əb zûr′vənt), *adj.* **1.** observing or regarding attentively; watchful. **2.** quick to notice or perceive; alert. **3.** careful in the observing of a law, custom, religious ritual, or the like. —*n.* **4.** an observer of law or rule. **5.** (*cap.*) Also, **Ob·ser·van·tine** (ob zûr′vən tin, -tēn′). a member of a Franciscan order that observes the strict rule of St. Francis. [< F, prp. of *observer.* See OBSERVE, -ANT] —**ob·serv′ant·ly,** *adv.*
—**Syn. 1.** attentive, heedful, mindful, aware. **2.** perceptive. **3.** obedient. —**Ant. 1.** heedless. **2.** dull, slow.

ob·ser·va·tion (ob′zûr vā′shən), *n.* **1.** the act or an instance of noticing or perceiving. **2.** the act or an instance of regarding attentively or watching. **3.** the faculty or habit of observing or noticing. **4.** notice: *to escape a person's observation.* **5.** the act or an instance of viewing or noting a fact or occurrence for some scientific or other special purpose. **6.** the information or record secured by such an act. **7.** something that is learned in the course of observing things: *My observation is that such clouds mean a storm.* **8.** a remark, comment, or statement based on what one has observed. **9.** the condition of being observed. **10.** *Navig.* **a.** the measurement of the altitude or azimuth of a heavenly body for navigational purposes. **b.** the information obtained by such a measurement. **11.** *Obs.* observance, as of the law. [< L *observātiōn-* (s. of *observātiō*), equiv. to *observāt(us)* (ptp. of *observāre* OBSERVE) + *-iōn-* -ION]
—**Syn. 3.** attention. **8.** pronouncement, opinion. See **remark.**

ob·ser·va·tion·al (ob′zûr vā′shə nəl), *adj.* of, pertaining to, or founded on observation, esp. founded on observation rather than experiment. [OBSERVATION + -AL[1]] —**ob′ser·va′tion·al·ly,** *adv.*

observa′tion car′, a railroad passenger car, usually at the end of a train, having a platform or lounge from which the scenery may be observed.

observa′tion post′, *Mil.* a forward position, usually on high ground, from which enemy activity can be observed and, particularly, from which artillery or mortar fire can be directed.

observa′tion train′, a train run along a river, or the like, to allow the passengers to watch a boat race.

ob·serv·a·to·ry (əb zûr′və tōr′ē, -tôr′ē), *n., pl.* **-ries. 1.** a place or building equipped and used for making observations of astronomical, meteorological, or other natural phenomena, esp. a place equipped with a powerful telescope for observing the planets and stars. **2.** an institution which controls or carries on the work of such a place. **3.** a place or structure for affording an extensive view; lookout. [< L *observāt(us)* (see OBSERVATION) + -ORY[2]]

ob·serve (əb zûrv′), *v.,* **-served, -serv·ing.** —*v.t.* **1.** to see, watch, perceive, or notice: *He idly observed the passersby in the street.* **2.** to regard with attention, so as to see or learn something: *to observe a surgical operation; I want you to observe his reaction to the question and judge whether he is telling the truth or not.* **3.** to watch, view, or note for a scientific, official, or other special purpose: *to observe an eclipse.* **4.** to state by way of comment; remark: *He observed frequently that goods in the stores are not as well made as they used to be.* **5.** to keep or maintain in one's action, conduct, etc.: *You must observe quiet.* **6.** to obey, comply with, or conform to: *to observe all laws.* **7.** to show regard for by some appropriate procedure, ceremonies, etc.: *to observe a holiday.* **8.** to perform duly or solemnize (ceremonies, rites, etc.). **9.** to note or inspect closely for an omen or sign of future events. —*v.i.* **10.** to notice. **11.** to act as an observer. **12.** to remark or comment (usually fol. by *on* or *upon*). [ME *observe(n)* < MF *observe(r)* < L *observāre* to watch, regard, attend to, equiv. to *ob-* OB- + *servāre* to keep, save, pay heed to] —**ob·serv·ed·ly** (əb zûr′vid lē), *adv.* —**ob·serv′ing·ly,** *adv.*
—**Syn. 1.** discover, detect. **2.** note. OBSERVE, WITNESS imply paying strict attention to what one sees or perceives. Both are "continuative" in action. TO OBSERVE is to mark or be attentive to something seen, heard, etc.; to consider carefully; to watch steadily: *to observe the behavior of birds, a person's pronunciation.* To WITNESS, formerly to be present when something was happening, has added the idea of having observed with sufficient care to be able to give an account as evidence: *to witness an accident.* **4.** mention, say. **6.** follow, fulfill. **7.** celebrate, keep. —**Ant. 1-3, 6-8.** ignore.

ob·serv·er (əb zûr′vər), *n.* **1.** one who or that which observes. **2.** *Air Force.* **a.** a member of an aircrew, other than the pilot, holding an aeronautical rating. **b.** a person who maintains observation in an aircraft during flight. **3.** Also called **air observer, aircraft observer.** *U.S. Army.* a person who serves in an aircraft as a reconnoiterer and directs artillery fire. **4.** a delegate to an assembly or gathering, who is sent to observe and report but not to take part officially in its activities. [OBSERVE + -ER[1]] —**ob·serv′er·ship′,** *n.*

ob·sess (əb ses′), *v.t.* to dominate or preoccupy the thoughts, feelings, or desires of (a person); beset, trouble, or haunt persistently or abnormally: *Suspicion obsessed him.* [< L *obsess(us)*, ptp. of *obsidēre* to besiege] —**ob·sess′ing·ly,** *adv.* —**ob·ses′sor,** *n.*

ob·ses·sion (əb sesh′ən), *n.* **1.** the domination of one's thoughts or feelings by a persistent idea, image, desire, etc. **2.** the idea, image, desire, feeling, etc., itself. **3.** the state of being obsessed. **4.** the act of obsessing. [< L *obsessiōn-* (s. of *obsessiō*) blockade, siege, equiv. to *obsess(us)* (see OBSESS) + *-iōn-* -ION] —**ob·ses′sion·al,** *adj.*

ob·ses·sive (əb ses′iv), *adj.* **1.** being, pertaining to, or resembling an obsession: *obsessive fears.* **2.** causing an obsession. **3.** excessive, esp. extremely so. [OBSESS(ION) + -IVE]

ob·sid·i·an (əb sid′ē ən), *n.* a volcanic glass similar in composition to granite, usually dark but transparent in thin pieces, and having a good conchoidal fracture. [< L *Obsidiān(us)*, prop. *Obsiānus* pertaining to *Obsius*, the discoverer (according to Pliny) of a similar mineral in Ethiopa; see -AN]

ob·sid′i·o·nal coin′ (əb sid′ē ə nəl). See **siege piece.** [< L *obsidiōnālis* of a siege, equiv. to *obsid(ēre)* to besiege + *-iōn-* -ION + *-ālis* -AL[1]]

obsolesc., obsolescent.

ob·so·lesce (ob′sə les′), *v.i.,* **-lesced, -lesc·ing.** to be or become obsolete or obsolescent. [< L *obsolesc(ere)*; see OBSOLETE]

ob·so·les·cence (ob′sə les′əns), *n.* the state, process, or condition of being or becoming obsolete. [OBSOLESC(ENT) + -ENCE]

ob·so·les·cent (ob′sə les′ənt), *adj.* **1.** becoming obsolete; passing out of use, as a word. **2.** becoming outdated or outmoded, as machinery, weapons, etc. **3.** *Biol.* gradually disappearing or imperfectly developed, as vestigial organs, marks, etc. [< L *obsolescent-* (s. of *obsolescēns*, prp. of *obsolescere* to grow old). See OBSOLETE, -ESCENT] —**ob′so·les′cent·ly,** *adv.*

ob·so·lete (ob′sə lēt′, ob′sə lēt′), *adj., v.,* **-let·ed, -let·ing.** —*adj.* **1.** no longer in general use; fallen into disuse: *an obsolete expression.* **2.** of a discarded or outmoded type; out of date: *an obsolete battleship.* **3.** (of a word or other linguistic unit) no longer in use, esp., out of use for at least a century. Cf. **archaic. 4.** effaced by wearing down or away. **5.** *Biol.* imperfectly developed or rudimentary in comparison with the corresponding character in other individuals, as of the opposite sex or of a related species. —*v.t.* **6.** to make obsolete by replacing with something newer or better; antiquate: *Automation has obsoleted many unskilled workers.* [< L *obsolēt(us)* worn out, ptp. of *obsolescere* (*obs-* toward + *ol-* age, c. OLD + *-esc(ere)* -ESCE)] —**ob′so·lete′ly,** *adv.* —**ob′so·lete′ness,** *n.*
—**Syn. 2.** antiquated, ancient, old. —**Ant. 1, 2.** new, modern.

ob·sta·cle (ob′stə kəl), *n.* something that stands in the way or obstructs progress. [ME < OF < L *obstācul(um)*, equiv. to *ob-* OB- + *stā-* stand + *-culum* -CLE]
—**Syn.** OBSTACLE, OBSTRUCTION, HINDRANCE, IMPEDIMENT refer to that which interferes with or prevents action or progress. An OBSTACLE is something, material or nonmaterial, which stands in the way of literal or figurative progress: *Lack of imagination is an obstacle to one's advancement.* An OBSTRUCTION is something which more or less completely blocks a passage: *A blood clot is an obstruction to the circulation.* A HINDRANCE keeps back by interfering and delaying: *Interruptions are a hindrance to one's work.* An IMPEDIMENT interferes with proper functioning: *an impediment in one's speech.* —**Ant.** help.

ob′stacle course′, a military training area having obstacles that must be surmounted or crossed in succession, as hurdles, ditches, walls, etc.

ob′stacle race′, a foot race in which the contestants are prevented in a specific way from running the full course at top speed, as by having hurdles to jump, sacks enclosing the legs, potatoes to pick up, etc. —**ob′stacle rac′er.**

obstet., 1. obstetric. 2. obstetrics.

ob·stet·ric (əb ste′trik), *adj.* **1.** of or pertaining to the care and treatment of women in childbirth and during the period before and after delivery. **2.** of or pertaining to childbirth or obstetrics. Also, **ob·stet′ri·cal.** [< NL *obstetric(us)* pertaining to a midwife, alter. of L *obstetrīcius*, deriv. of *obstetrix*, equiv. to *ob-* OB- + *ste-* (var. s. of *stāre*) stand + *-trix* -TRIX] —**ob·stet′ri·cal·ly,** *adv.*

ob·ste·tri·cian (ob′sti trish′ən), *n.* a physician who specializes in obstetrics. [< L *obstetrīci(a)* midwifery (n. use of fem. of *obstetrīcius*; see OBSTETRIC) + -AN]

ob·stet·rics (əb ste′triks), *n.* (*construed as sing.*) the branch of medical science concerned with childbirth and caring for and treating women in or in connection with childbirth. [see OBSTETRIC, -ICS]

ob·sti·na·cy (ob′stə nə sē), *n., pl.* **-cies** for 5. **1.** the quality or state of being obstinate. **2.** unyielding or stubborn adherence to one's purpose, opinion, etc. **3.** stubborn persistence: *The garrison fought on with incredible obstinacy.* **4.** resistance to cure, relief, or treatment, as a disease. **5.** an instance of being obstinate; an obstinate act, viewpoint, etc. [ME < ML *obstinātia*, deriv. of L *obstinātus* OBSTINATE; see -CY]

ob·sti·nate (ob′stə nit), *adj.* **1.** firmly or perversely adhering to one's purpose, opinion, etc.; not yielding to argument, persuasion, or entreaty. **2.** characterized by inflexible persistence or an unyielding attitude; inflexibly persisted in or carried out: *obstinate advocacy of high tariffs.* **3.** not easily controlled or overcome: *the obstinate growth of weeds.* **4.** not yielding readily to treatment, as a disease. [< L *obstināt(us)* determined (ptp. of *obstināre*), equiv. to *ob-* OB- + *stin-* (var. s. of *stāre*) stand + *-ātus* -ATE[1]] —**ob′sti·nate·ly,** *adv.* —**ob′sti·nate·ness,** *n.*
—**Syn. 1.** mulish, obdurate, unyielding, unbending, intractable, perverse, inflexible, refractory, pertinacious. See **stubborn.** —**Ant. 1.** submissive, tractable.

ob·sti·pant (ob′stə pənt), *n.* a substance that produces obstipation. [OBSTIP(ATION) + -ANT]

ob·sti·pa·tion (ob′stə pā′shən), *n.* obstinate constipation. [< LL *obstipātiōn-* (s. of *obstipātiō*) close pressure, equiv. to *ob-* OB- + *stīpāt(us)* (ptp. of *stīpāre* to press) + *-iōn-* -ION]

ob·strep·er·ous (əb strep′ər əs), *adj.* **1.** resisting control in a noisy and difficult manner; unruly. **2.** noisy, clamorous, or boisterous. [< L *obstreperus* clamorous, akin to *obstrepere* to make a noise at (*ob-* OB- + *strepere* to rattle); see -OUS] —**ob·strep′er·ous·ly,** *adv.* —**ob·strep′er·ous·ness, ob·strep·e·ros·i·ty** (əb strep′ə ros′i tē), *n.*
—**Syn. 1.** uncontrolled. —**Ant. 1.** obedient. **2.** calm.

ob·struct (əb strukt′), *v.t.* **1.** to block or close up with an obstacle or obstacles, as a road, channel, etc.; make difficult to pass. **2.** to interrupt, hinder, or oppose the passage, progress, course, etc., of. **3.** to block from sight; to be or come in the way of (a view, passage, etc.). [< L *obstruct(us)* built against (ptp. of *obstruere*). See OB-, CONSTRUCT] —**ob·struct′ed·ly,** *adv.* —**ob·struct′er, ob·struc′tor,** *n.* —**ob·struct′ing·ly,** *adv.* —**ob·struc′tive,** *adj.* —**ob·struc′tive·ly,** *adv.* —**ob·struc′tive·ness, ob·struc·tiv·i·ty** (ob′struk tiv′i tē), *n.*
—**Syn. 1.** stop, choke, clog, hinder, impede, prevent; check, slow, retard, arrest. —**Ant. 1.** encourage, further.

ob·struc·tion (əb struk′shən), *n.* **1.** something that obstructs, blocks, or closes up with an obstacle or obstacles; obstacle or hindrance: *obstructions to navigation.* **2.** the act or an instance of obstructing. **3.** the delaying or preventing of business before a deliberative body, esp. a legislative group, by parliamentary contrivances. **4.** the state of being obstructed. [< L *obstructiōn-* (s. of *obstructiō*) barrier. See OBSTRUCT, -ION]
—**Syn. 1.** barrier, bar, impediment. See **obstacle. 4.** stoppage. —**Ant. 1, 4.** encouragement.

ob·struc·tion·ist (əb struk′shə nist), *n.* a person who deliberately delays or prevents progress, esp. of business before a legislative body, by parliamentary contrivances or legalistic maneuvers: *The obstructionists in Congress kept the bill from coming to a vote.* [OBSTRUCTION + -IST] —**ob·struc′tion·ism,** *n.* —**ob·struc′tion·is′tic,** *adj.*

obstruc′tion to vi′sion, *Meterol.* any of a class of atmospheric phenomena, other than precipitation, that reduce surface visibility, as fog, haze, blowing dust, and smoke.

ob·stru·ent (ob′stro͞o ənt), *adj.* **1.** *Med.* (of a substance) producing an obstruction. **2.** *Phonet.* occlusive. Cf. **sonorant.** —*n.* **3.** *Med.* a medicine that closes the natural passages of the body. **4.** *Phonet.* an obstruent speech sound. Cf. **sonorant.** [< L *obstruent-* (s. of *obstruēns*, prp. of *obstruere*), equiv. to *ob-* OB- + *stru-* build + *-ent-* -ENT]

ob·tain (əb tān′), *v.t.* **1.** to come into possession of; get or acquire; procure, as through an effort or by a request: *to obtain some information.* **2.** *Archaic.* to attain or reach. —*v.i.* **3.** to be prevalent, customary, or in vogue: *the morals that obtained in Rome.* **4.** *Archaic.* to succeed. [ME *obtein(en)* < MF *obten(ir)* < L *obtinēre* to take hold of, equiv. to *ob-* OB- + *-tinēre* (comb. form of *tenēre* to hold)] —**ob·tain′a·ble,** *adj.* —**ob·tain′er,** *n.* —**ob·tain′ment,** *n.*
—**Syn. 1.** gain, achieve, earn, win, attain. See **get.** —**Ant. 1.** lose, forgo.

ob·tect (ob tekt′), *adj.* (of a pupa) having the antennae, legs, and wings glued to the surface of the body by a hardened secretion. Also, **ob·tect′ed.** Cf. **exarate.** [< L *obtect(us)* covered over (ptp. of *obtegere*, var. of *obtigere*), equiv. to *ob-* OB- + *teg-* cover (see THATCH, TOGA) + *-t-* ptp. suffix]

Obtect pupa of swallowtail, Genus *Papilio*

ob·test (ob test′), *v.t.* **1.** to invoke as witness. **2.** to supplicate earnestly; beseech. —*v.i.* **3.** to protest. [< L *obtest(ārī)*, equiv. to *ob-* OB- + *test-* bear witness + *-ārī* inf. suffix] —**ob′tes·ta′tion,** *n.*

ob·trude (əb tro͞od′), *v.,* **-trud·ed, -trud·ing.** —*v.t.* **1.** to thrust (something) forward or upon a person, esp. without warrant or invitation: *to obtrude one's opinions upon others.* **2.** to thrust forth; push out. —*v.i.* **3.** to thrust oneself or itself forward, esp. unduly; intrude. [< L *obtrūde(re)* (to) thrust against, equiv. to *ob-* OB- + *trūd-* THRUST + *-ere* inf. suffix] —**ob·trud′er,** *n.*
—**Syn. 1.** impose, force. **3.** shove, push.

ob·tru·sion (əb tro͞o′zhən), *n.* **1.** the act of obtruding. **2.** something obtruded. [< LL *obtrūsiōn-* (s. of *obtrūsiō*), equiv. to L *obtrūs(us)* (*ob-* OB- + *trū-* THRUST + *-s-* ptp. suffix) + *-iōn-* -ION] —**ob·tru′sion·ist,** *n.*

ob·tru·sive (əb tro͞o′siv), *adj.* **1.** having or showing a disposition to obtrude. **2.** (of a thing) obtruding itself: *an obtrusive error.* **3.** protruding. [< L *obtrūs(us)* thrust against (ptp. of *obtrūdere*; see OBTRUDE) + -IVE] —**ob·tru′sive·ly,** *adv.* —**ob·tru′sive·ness,** *n.*
—**Syn. 2.** blatant.

ob·tund (ob tund′), *v.t.* to blunt; dull; deaden. [< L *obtund(ere)* to beat at, equiv. to *ob-* OB- + *tundere* to strike (c. THUNDER)] —**ob·tund′ent,** *adj.* —**ob·tun′di·ty,** *n.*

ob·tu·rate (ob′tə rāt′, -tyə-), *v.t.,* **-rat·ed, -rat·ing. 1.** to stop up; close. **2.** *Ordn.* to close (a hole or cavity) so as to prevent a flow of gas through it, esp. the escape of explosive gas from a gun tube during firing. [< L *obtūrāt(us)* stopped at (ptp. of *obtūrāre*), equiv. to *ob-* OB- + *tūr-* stop + *-ātus* -ATE[1]] —**ob′tu·ra′tion,** *n.* —**ob′tu·ra′tor,** *n.*

ob·tuse (əb to͞os′, -tyo͞os′), *adj.* **1.** not sharp, acute, or pointed; blunt in form. **2.** (of a leaf, petal, etc.) rounded at the extremity. **3.** not quick or alert in perception, feeling, or intellect; not sensitive or observant; dull; stupid. **4.** indistinctly felt or perceived,

as pain, sound, etc. [< L *obtūs(us)* dulled (ptp. of *obtundere*), equiv. to *ob-* OB- + *tū(d)-* beat + *-s-* ptp. suffix] —**ob·tuse′ly,** *adv.* —**ob·tuse′ness,** *n.*
—**Syn. 3.** unfeeling, tactless, insensitive; blind, imperceptive, unobservant; gauche, boorish; slow, dim.

obtuse′ an′gle, an angle greater than 90° but less than 180°. See diag. under **angle.** —**ob·tuse′-an′gled, ob·tuse′-an′gu·lar,** *adj.*

obtuse′ bisec′trix, *Crystall.* See under **bisectrix** (def. 1).

obtuse′ tri′angle, *Geom.* a triangle with one obtuse angle. See diag. under **triangle.**

O·bu·da (ō′bŏŏ do), *n.* a former city in Hungary, in the N part: incorporated into Budapest 1873.

OBulg., Old Bulgarian. Also, **OBulg**

ob·um·brant (ob um′brənt), *adj. Zool.* overhanging; projecting over another part. [< L *obumbrant-* (s. of *obumbrāns*) overshadowing (prp. of *obumbrāre*), equiv. to *ob-* OB- + *umbr-* shadow + *-ant-* -ANT]

ob·um·brate (ob um′brāt), *v.*, **-brat·ed, -brat·ing,** *adj.* —*v.t.* **1.** to darken, overshadow, or cloud. —*adj.* **2.** *Obs.* overshadowed, darkened. [< L *obumbrāt(us),* ptp. of *obumbrāre,* equiv. to *ob-* OB- + *umbrāre* to shadow, deriv. of *umbr(a)* shadow; see -ATE[1]] —**ob′um·bra′tion,** *n.*

ob·verse (*n.* ob′vûrs; *adj.* ob vûrs′, ob′vûrs), *n.* **1.** the side of a coin, medal, etc., that bears the principal design (opposed to *reverse*). **2.** the front or principal surface of anything. **3.** a counterpart. **4.** *Logic.* a proposition obtained from another by obversion. —*adj.* **5.** turned toward or facing the observer. **6.** corresponding to something else as a counterpart. **7.** having the base narrower than the top, as a leaf. [< L *obvers(us)* turned towards, against (ptp. of *obvertere*), equiv. to *ob-* OB- + *ver(t)-* turn + *-s-* ptp. suffix]

ob·ver·sion (ob vûr′zhən, -shən), *n.* **1.** the act or an instance of obverting. **2.** something that is obverted. **3.** *Logic.* a form of inference in which a negative proposition is obtained from an affirmative, or vice versa, as "No men are immortal" is obtained by obversion from "All men are mortal." [< L *obversiōn-* (s. of *obversiō*) a turning towards, equiv. to *obvers(us)* (see OBVERSE) + *-iōn-* -ION]

ob·vert (ob vûrt′), *v.t.* **1.** to turn (something) so as to show a different surface. **2.** *Logic.* to change (a proposition) by obversion. [< L *obvert(ere)* (to) turn towards, equiv. to *ob-* OB- + *vertere* to turn]

ob·vi·ate (ob′vē āt′), *v.t.*, **-at·ed, -at·ing.** to prevent or eliminate (difficulties, disadvantages, etc.) by effective measures; render unnecessary: *This pump obviates the necessity of priming before use.* [< L *obviāt(us)* prevented, opposed (ptp. of *obviāre*), equiv. to *ob-* OB- + *vi(am)* the way + *-ātus* -ATE[1]] —**ob·vi·a·ble** (ob′vē ə bəl), *adj.* —**ob′vi·a′tion,** *n.* —**ob′vi·a′tor,** *n.*
—**Syn.** preclude, avert, anticipate.

ob·vi·ous (ob′vē əs), *adj.* **1.** easily seen, recognized, or understood; open to view or knowledge: *an obvious advantage.* **2.** *Obs.* being or standing in the way. [< L *obvius* in the way, meeting, equiv. to *ob-* OB- + *vi(a)* way + *-us* -OUS] —**ob′vi·ous·ly,** *adv.* —**ob′vi·ous·ness,** *n.*
—**Syn. 1.** plain, manifest, evident, clear, palpable, unmistakable. See **apparent.** —**Ant. 1.** hidden.

ob·vo·lute (ob′və lōōt′), *adj.* **1.** rolled or turned in. **2.** *Bot.* noting or pertaining to a vernation in which two leaves are folded together in the bud so that one half of each is exterior and the other interior. [< L *obvolūt(us)* wrapped up (ptp. of *obvolvere*), equiv. to *ob-* OB- + *vol-* roll + *-ū-* v. suffix + *-t-* ptp. suffix; see VOLUTE] —**ob′vo·lu′tion,** *n.* —**ob′vo·lu′tive,** *adj.*

Ob·wal·den (*Ger.* ôp′väl′dᵊn), *n.* one of the two divisions of the canton of Unterwalden, in central Switzerland. 23,135 (1960); 189 sq. mi. *Cap.:* Sarnen.

oc-, var. of **ob-** (by assimilation) before *c: occident.*

OC., ocean. Also, **oc.**

o/c, overcharge.

O.C., *Philately.* original cover.

o.c., **1.** *Archit.* on center. See **center** (def. 17). **2.** in the work cited. [< L *opere citāto*]

O·cal·a (ō kal′ə), *n.* a city in central Florida. 13,598 (1960).

oc·a·ri·na (ok′ə rē′nə), *n.* a simple musical wind instrument shaped somewhat like an elongated egg with a mouthpiece and finger holes. Also called **sweet potato.** [< It, dim. of *oca* goose < LL **avica,* equiv. to *auc(a)* (L *avis* bird) + *-ica* dim. suffix]

Ocarina

O′Ca·sey (ō kā′sē), *n.* **Sean** (shôn, shän), 1880–1964, Irish playwright.

Oc·cam (ok′əm), *n.* **William of,** died 1349?, English scholastic philosopher. Also, **Ockham.** —**Oc′cam·ism,** *n.* —**Oc′cam·ist, Oc′cam·ite′,** *n.* —**Oc′cam·is′tic,** *adj.*

Oc′cam's ra′zor, the maxim that assumptions introduced to explain a thing must not be multiplied beyond necessity. Also, **Ockham's razor.** [after William of OCCAM]

occas., **1.** occasional. **2.** occasionally.

oc·ca·sion (ə kā′zhən), *n.* **1.** a particular time, esp. as marked by certain circumstances or occurrences: *They met on three occasions.* **2.** a special or important time, event, ceremony, celebration, etc.: *His birthday will be quite an occasion.* **3.** a convenient or favorable time, opportunity, or juncture: *This slack period would be a good occasion to take inventory.* **4.** (in the philosophy of Whitehead) the coincidence of the eternal objects forming a specific point-event. **5.** the ground, reason, or incidental cause of some action or result: *What is the occasion for this uproar? Last spring I had occasion to be in Baghdad.* **6. occasions,** *Obs.* **a.** needs or necessities. **b.** necessary business matters: *to go about one's lawful occasions.* **7. on occasion,** now and then; occasionally: *He visits New York on occasion to see the new plays.* —*v.t.* **8.** to give occasion or cause for; bring about. [ME *occasioun* < OF *occasion* < L *occāsiōn-* (s. of *occāsiō*), equiv. to *oc-* OC- + *cās(us)* (ptp. of *cadere* to fall) + *-iōn-* -ION]
—**Syn. 3.** chance, opening. **5.** motive, inducement, influence. See **cause. 8.** motivate, originate, produce, create.

oc·ca·sion·al (ə kā′zhə nᵊl), *adj.* **1.** occurring or appearing at irregular or infrequent intervals; occurring now and then: *an occasional visitor; an occasional publication.* **2.** intended for supplementary use when necessary: *an occasional chair.* **3.** pertaining to, arising out of, or intended for the occasion: *occasional verses; occasional decrees.* **4.** acting or serving for the occasion or on particular occasions. **5.** serving as the occasion or incidental cause. [OCCASION + -AL[1]] —**oc·ca′sion·al·ness, oc·ca′sion·al′i·ty,** *n.*

oc·ca·sion·al·ism (ə kā′zhə nᵊliz′əm), *n. Philos.* the doctrine that the apparent interaction of mind and matter is to be explained by the supposition that God takes an act of the will as the occasion of producing a corresponding movement of the body and a state of the body as the occasion of producing a corresponding mental state. [OCCASIONAL + -ISM] —**oc·ca′sion·al·is′tic,** *adj.*

oc·ca·sion·al·ly (ə kā′zhə nᵊlē), *adv.* at times; now and then: *He takes a cocktail occasionally.* [OCCASIONAL + -LY]

occa′sional ta′ble, a small table having no specific purpose.

Oc·ci·dent (ok′si dənt), *n.* **1. the Occident, a.** the West; the countries of Europe and America. **b.** See **Western Hemisphere. 2.** (*l.c.*) the west; the western regions. [ME < MF < L *occident-* (s. of *occidēns,* prp. of *occidere* to set), equiv. to *oc-* OC- + *cid-* fall (comb. form of *cadere*) + *-ent-* -ENT]

oc·ci·den·tal (ok′si den′tᵊl), *adj.* **1.** (*usually cap.*) of, pertaining to, or characteristic of the Occident or its natives and inhabitants. **2.** western. —*n.* **3.** (*usually cap.*) a native or inhabitant of the Occident. [ME < L *occidentāl(is)* western, equiv. to *occident-* OCCIDENT + *-ālis* -AL[1]] —**oc·ci·den·tal·i·ty** (ok′si den tal′i tē), *n.* —**oc′ci·den′tal·ly,** *adv.*

Oc·ci·den·tal·ise (ok′si den′tᵊlīz′), *v.t.*, **-ised, -is·ing.** *Chiefly Brit.* Occidentalize. —**Oc′ci·den′tal·i·sa′tion,** *n.*

Oc·ci·den·tal·ism (ok′si den′tᵊliz′əm), *n.* Occidental character or characteristics. [OCCIDENTAL + -ISM] —**Oc′ci·den′tal·ist,** *n., adj.*

Oc·ci·den·tal·ize (ok′si den′tᵊlīz′), *v.t.*, **-ized, -iz·ing.** to make Occidental. Also, *esp. Brit.,* **Occidentalise.** [OCCIDENTAL + -IZE] —**Oc′ci·den′tal·i·za′tion,** *n.*

oc·cip·i·tal (ok sip′i tᵊl), *Anat.* —*adj.* **1.** of, pertaining to, or situated near the occiput or the occipital bone. —*n.* **2.** any of several parts of the occiput, esp. the occipital bone. [< ML *occipitāl(is),* equiv. to L *occipit-* (s. of *occiput*) OCCIPUT + *-ālis* -AL[1]] —**oc·cip′i·tal·ly,** *adv.*

occip′ital bone′, *Anat.* a curved, compound bone forming the back and part of the base of the skull. See diag. under **skull.**

occip′ital lobe′, *Anat.* the most posterior lobe of each cerebral hemisphere, behind the parietal and temporal lobes.

occipito-, a combining form of "occiput." [< NL, comb. form of L *occipit-* (s. of *occiput*) + *-o-* -o-]

oc·ci·put (ok′sə put′, -pət), *n., pl.* **oc·ci·puts, oc·cip·i·ta** (ok sip′i tə). *Anat.* the back part of the head or skull. [< L, equiv. to *oc-* OC- + *-ciput,* comb. form of *caput* head]

Oc·cleve (ok′lēv), *n.* Hoccleve.

oc·clude (ə klōōd′), *v.*, **-clud·ed, -clud·ing.** —*v.t.* **1.** to close, shut, or stop up (a passage, opening, etc.). **2.** to shut in, out, or off. **3.** *Physical Chem.* (of certain metals and other solids) to incorporate (gases and other foreign substances), as by absorption or adsorption. —*v.i.* **4.** *Dentistry.* to shut or close, with the cusps of the opposing teeth of the upper and lower jaws fitting together. **5.** *Meteorol.* to form an occluded front. [< L *occlūd(ere)* (to) shut up, close up, equiv. to *oc-* OC- + *clūd-* shut (var. of *claud-*)] —**oc·clud′ent,** *adj.*

occlud′ed front′, *Meteorol.* a composite front formed when a cold front overtakes a warm front and forces it aloft. Also called **occlusion.**

oc·clu·sion (ə klōō′zhən), *n.* **1.** the act or state of occluding or the state of being occluded. **2.** *Dentistry.* the fitting together of the teeth of the lower jaw with the corresponding teeth of the upper jaw when the jaws are closed. **3.** *Phonet.* momentary complete closure at some area in the vocal tract, causing stoppage of the breathstream and accumulation of pressure. **4.** *Meteorol.* **a.** the formation of an occluded front. **b.** See **occluded front.** [prob. < NL **occlūsiōn-* (s. of **occlūsiō*), equiv. to *occlūs(us)* (ptp. of *occlūdere* to OCCLUDE) + *-iōn-* -ION] —**oc·clu·sal** (ə klōō′səl), *adj.*

oc·clu·sive (ə klōō′siv), *adj.* **1.** occluding or tending to occlude. **2.** *Phonet.* characterized by or having occlusion. —*n. Phonet.* **3.** a stop that is unreleased, as the *p*-sound in *stop,* or deviously released, as the *k*-sound in *acme, acne,* or *action,* the *t*-sound of *catnip,* the *g*-sound of *pygmy, ugly,* etc. **4.** (not in technical use) any stop sound. [< L *occlus(us)* (see OCCLUSION) + -IVE] —**oc·clu′sive·ness,** *n.*

oc·cult (ə kult′, ok′ult), *adj.* **1.** beyond the range of ordinary knowledge; mysterious. **2.** secret; disclosed or communicated only to the initiated. **3.** (in early science) **a.** not apparent on mere inspection but discoverable by experimentation. **b.** of a nature not understood, as physical qualities. **c.** dealing with such qualities; experimental: *occult science.* **4.** of or pertaining to magic, astrology, and other alleged sciences claiming use or knowledge of secret, mysterious, or supernatural agencies. **5.** hidden from view. —*n.* **6.** occult studies or sciences (usually prec. by *the*). **7.** the supernatural or supernatural agencies and affairs. **8.** anything occult. —*v.t.* **9.** to block or shut off (an object) from view; hide. **10.** *Astron.* to hide (a body) by occultation. —*v.i.* **11.** to become hidden or shut off from view. [< L *occult(us)* covered over, concealed (ptp. of *occulere*), equiv. to *oc-* OC- + LL *cul-* hide (var. of L *cel-*) + *-t-* ptp. suffix] —**oc·cult′er,** *n.* —**oc·cult′ly,** *adv.* —**oc·cult′ness,** *n.*
—**Syn. 1.** metaphysical, supernatural. **2.** concealed, unrevealed; veiled, shrouded; mystical, cabalistic.

oc·cul·ta·tion (ok′ul tā′shən), *n.* **1.** *Astron.* the passage of one celestial body in front of a second, thus hiding the second from view: applied esp. to the moon's coming between an observer and a star or planet. **2.** disappearance from view or notice. **3.** the act of blocking or hiding from view. **4.** the resulting hidden or concealed state. [ME < L *occultātiōn-* (s. of *occultātiō*) a hiding, equiv. to *occultāt(us)* hidden, ptp. of *occultāre* (*oc-* OC- + *cult-* hide + *-ātus* -ATE[1]) + *-iōn-* -ION]

occult′ bal′ance, asymmetrical balance of visual elements in an artistic composition.

occult′ing light′, *Navig.* a beacon having a light covered briefly at regular intervals.

oc·cult·ism (ə kul′tiz əm), *n.* belief in the existence of certain secret, mysterious, or supernatural agencies that can be known and communicated with by human beings. [OCCULT + -ISM] —**oc·cult′ist,** *n., adj.*

oc·cu·pan·cy (ok′yə pən sē), *n., pl.* **-cies. 1.** the act, state, or condition of being or becoming a tenant or of living in or taking up quarters or space in or on something: *Our firm's occupancy of the office depends on a rent reduction.* **2.** the possession or tenancy of a property: *You can have occupancy on June 1st.* **3.** the act of taking possession, as of a property. **4.** the term during which one is an occupant. **5.** the use to which property is put. **6.** exercise of dominion over property which has no owner so as to become the legal owner. [OCCUPAN(T) + -CY]

oc·cu·pant (ok′yə pənt), *n.* **1.** a person who or family, group, or organization that lives in, occupies, or has quarters or space in or on something: *the occupants of a taxicab.* **2.** a tenant of a house, estate, office, etc. **3.** *Law.* **a.** an owner through occupancy. **b.** one who is in actual possession. [< MF *occupant,* prp. of *occuper.* See OCCUPY, -ANT]

oc·cu·pa·tion (ok′yə pā′shən), *n.* **1.** one's usual or principal work or business, esp. as a means of earning a living: *His occupation was dentistry.* **2.** any activity in which one is engaged. **3.** possession, settlement, or use of land or property. **4.** the act of occupying. **5.** the state of being occupied. **6.** tenure or the holding of an office or official function: *during his occupation of the presidency.* **7.** the seizure and control of an area by military forces, esp. foreign territory. **8.** the term of control of a territory by foreign military forces: *a history of Danish resistance organizations during the German occupation.* [ME *occupacioun* < MF *occupation* < L *occupātiōn-* (s. of *occupātiō*), equiv. to *occupāt(us)* occupied (ptp. of *occupāre;* see OCCUPY) + *-iōn-* -ION] —**oc′cu·pa′tion·less,** *adj.* —**oc′cu·pa′tive,** *adj.*
—**Syn. 1.** vocation, employment, pursuit, craft, metier. OCCUPATION, BUSINESS, PROFESSION, TRADE refer to the activity to which one regularly devotes himself, esp. his regular work, or means of getting a living. OCCUPATION is the general word: *a pleasant or congenial occupation.* BUSINESS esp. suggests a commercial or mercantile occupation: *the printing business.* PROFESSION implies an occupation requiring special knowledge and training in some field of science or learning: *the profession of teaching.* TRADE suggests an occupation involving manual training and skill: *one of the building trades.* **3.** occupancy.

oc·cu·pa·tion·al (ok′yə pā′shə nᵊl), *adj.* **1.** of or pertaining to occupation: *occupational risks; occupational troops.* **2.** of or pertaining to an occupation, trade, or calling: *occupational guidance.* [OCCUPATION + -AL[1]] —**oc′cu·pa′tion·al·ly,** *adv.*

occupa′tional disease′, **1.** Also called **industrial disease.** a disease caused by the conditions or hazards of a particular occupation. **2.** a trait or tendency that develops among members of a particular profession: *Cynicism was thought to be an occupational disease of reporters.*

oc′cupa′tional haz′ard, a danger or hazard to workers that is inherent in a particular occupation: *The chance of severe burns forms an occupational hazard for bakers. Silicosis is an occupational hazard of miners.*

oc′cupa′tional ther′apy, *Med.* therapy consisting of light work, such as basketry, carpentry, etc., that provides mental diversion for the patient and frequently serves to exercise an affected part of the body or to give vocational training.

Occupa′tion Day′, July 25, a holiday celebrated in Puerto Rico to mark the anniversary of the landing of United States troops in 1898.

occupa′tion lay′er, (on an archaeological site) a layer of remains left by a single culture, from which the culture can be dated or identified. Also called **occupa′tion lev′el.**

oc·cu·py (ok′yə pī′), *v.*, **-pied, -py·ing.** —*v.t.* **1.** to take or fill up (space, time, etc.). **2.** to engage or employ (the mind, one's attention, etc.). **3.** to take possession and control of (a place), as by military invasion. **4.** to hold (a position, office, etc.). **5.** to be a resident or tenant of; dwell in. —*v.i.* **6.** *Obs.* to take or hold possession. [ME *occupie(n)* < MF *occup(er)* < L *occupāre* to seize, take hold, equiv. to *oc-* OC- + *cup-* seize (var. of *cap-*) + *-āre* inf. suffix] —**oc′cu·pi′a·ble,** *adj.* —**oc′cu·pi′er,** *n.*
—**Syn. 1–4.** See **have. 2.** use, busy. **3.** capture, seize.

oc·cur (ə kûr′), *v.i.*, **-curred, -cur·ring. 1.** to happen; take place; come to pass. **2.** to be met with or found; present itself; appear. **3.** to suggest itself in thought (usually fol. by *to*): *An idea occurred to me.* [< L *occurr(ere)* (to) run, equiv. to *oc-* OC- + *currere* to run]
—**Syn. 1.** befall. See **happen. 2.** arise, offer.

oc·cur·rence (ə kûr′əns, ə kur′-), *n.* **1.** the action or fact of occurring. **2.** something that happens; event; incident: *We were delayed by several unexpected occurrences.* [prob. OCCURR(ENT) + -ENCE] —**oc·cur′rent,** *adj.*
—**Syn. 2.** circumstance. See **event.**

OCD, Office of Civilian Defense.

OCDM, See **Office of Civil and Defense Mobilization.**

o·cean (ō′shən), *n.* **1.** the vast body of salt water which covers almost three fourths of the earth's surface. **2.** any of the geographical divisions of this body, commonly given as the Atlantic, Pacific, Indian, Arctic, and Antarctic oceans. **3.** a vast expanse or quantity: *an ocean of grass.* [ME < L *ōcean(us)* ocean < Gk *Ōkeanós* OCEANUS] —**o′cean·like′,** *adj.*

O′cean Cit′y, a town in SE New Jersey. 7618 (1960).

o·cean·front (ō′shən frunt′), *n.* the land along the shore of an ocean. [OCEAN + FRONT]

o·cean-go·ing (ō′shən gō′ing), *adj.* noting any vessel designed and equipped to go on the open sea.

O·ce·an·i·a (ō′shē an′ē ə, -ä′nē ə), *n.* the islands of the central and S Pacific, including Micronesia, Melanesia, Polynesia, and sometimes Australasia and the Malay Archipelago. Also, **O·ce·an·i·ca** (ō′shē an′ə kə). —**O′ce·an′i·an,** *adj., n.*

o·ce·an·ic (ō′shē an′ik), *adj.* **1.** of, living in, belonging to, or produced by the ocean; pelagic: *oceanic currents; oceanic mammals.* **2.** immensely large; vast. [< ML *ōceanic(us),* equiv. to L *ōcean(us)* OCEAN + *-icus* -IC]

o·ce·a·nic·i·ty (ō′shē ə nis′i tē, ō′shə nis′-), *n.* the degree to which the climate of a place is influenced by the sea. Cf. **continentality.** Also called **o·ce·an·i·ty** (ō′shē an′i tē). [OCEANIC + -ITY]

O·ce·a·nid (ō sē′ə nid), *n., pl.* **O·ce·an·i·des** (ō′sē an′i dēz′). *Class. Myth.* any of the daughters of Oceanus and Tethys; a sea nymph. [< Gk *Okeanid(es)* daughter(s) of Ocean (nom. pl. of *Okeanís,* deriv. of *Okean(ós)* OCEANUS + *-ides* -ID[1]]

o′cean lin′er, a vessel carrying a large number of passengers and a small amount of freight on ocean voyages, operating either as one unit of a regular scheduled service or as a cruise ship.

o′cean marine′ insur′ance, insurance covering risks involving the transporting of persons or goods on the high seas. Cf. **inland marine insurance.**

O′cean of Storms′. See **Oceanus Procellarum.**

oceanog., oceanography.

o·ce·a·nog·ra·phy (ō′shē ə nog′rə fē, ō′shə nog′-), *n.* the branch of physical geography dealing with the ocean. [OCEAN + -O- + -GRAPHY] —**o′ce·a·nog′ra·pher,** *n.* —**o·ce·a·no·graph·ic** (ō′shē ə nə graf′ik, ō′shə nə-), **o′ce·a·no·graph′i·cal,** *adj.* —**o′ce·a·no·graph′i·cal·ly,** *adv.*

o′cean perch′, redfish (def. 1).

O·cean·port (ō′shən pōrt′, -pôrt′), *n.* a town in E New Jersey. 4937 (1960).

o′cean pout′, an eelpout, *Macrozoarces americanus,* found along the northeastern coast of North America.

O·cean·side (ō′shən sīd′), *n.* **1.** a town on SW Long Island, in SE New York. 30,448 (1960). **2.** a city in SW California. 24,971 (1960).

O′cean Springs′, a town in SE Mississippi. 5025 (1960).

o′cean sun′fish, a brown and gray mola, *Mola mola,* found in tropical and temperate seas, having the posterior half of the body sharply truncated behind the elongated dorsal and anal fins. Also called **headfish.**

O·ce·a·nus (ō sē′ə nəs), *n. Class. Myth.* **1.** a Titan who was the son of Uranus and Gaea, the consort of Tethys, and the father of the river gods and Oceanids. **2.** a great stream of water encircling the earth and believed to be the source of all rivers, lakes, etc.

O·ce·a·nus Pro·cel·la·rum (ō′shē ā′nəs prō′se lär′əm, -an′əs), the largest dark plain on the face of the moon, in the second and third quadrants, extending from Sinus Roris in the north to Mare Humorum in the south: about 2,000,000 square miles. Also called **Ocean of Storms.**

Ocellated marking on peacock feather

o·cel·lar (ō sel′ər), *adj.* pertaining to an ocellus. [OCELL(US) + -AR[1]]

oc·el·lat·ed (os′ə lā′tid, ō sel′ā tid), *adj.* **1.** (of a spot or marking) eyelike. **2.** having ocelli, or eyelike spots. Also, **oc·el·late** (os′ə lāt′, ō sel′it, -āt). [< L *ocellāt(us)* (*ocell(us)* OCELLUS + *-ātus* -ATE[1]) + -ED[3]]

oc′ellated tur′key, a wild turkey, *Agriocharis ocellata,* of Yucatán, British Honduras, and Guatemala, typically having green, blue, reddish-brown, and yellowish-brown plumage of a metallic luster and eyelike spots on the tail.

oc·el·la·tion (os′ə lā′shən), *n.* an eyelike spot or marking. [OCELLATE + -ION]

o·cel·lus (ō sel′əs), *n., pl.* **o·cel·li** (ō sel′ī). **1.** a type of eye common to invertebrates, consisting of retinal cells, pigments, and nerve fibers. **2.** an eyelike spot, as on a peacock feather. [< L: little eye, equiv. to *oc-* (s. of *oculus*) EYE + *-ellus* dim. suffix]

Ocelot (Total length about 4 ft.; tail 14 in.)

o·ce·lot (ō′sə lot′, os′ə-), *n.* a spotted leopardlike cat, *Felis pardalis,* ranging from Texas through South America. [< F < Nahuatl *ocelotl* jaguar] —**o′ce·loid′,** *adj.*

och (OKH), *interj. Scot., Irish Eng.* (used as an expression of surprise, disapproval, regret, etc.) [Scot, IrGael]

o·cher (ō′kər), *n., adj., v.,* **o·chered, o·cher·ing.** —*n.* **1.** any of a class of natural earths, mixtures of hydrated oxide of iron with various earthy materials, ranging in color from pale yellow to orange and red, and used as pigments. **2.** the color of this, ranging from pale yellow to an orangish or reddish yellow. **3.** *Slang.* money, esp. gold coin. —*adj.* **4.** of the color of ocher. —*v.t.* **5.** to color or mark with ocher. Also, **ochre.** [ME *oker* < OF *ocre* < L *ōchra* < Gk: yellow ocher] —**o′cher·ous, o′cher·y,** *adj.*

Och·i·mus (ok′ə məs), *n. Class. Myth.* a king of Rhodes who was one of the seven sons of Helius, the husband of the nymph Hegetoria and the father of Cydippe.

och·le·sis (ok lē′sis), *n. Pathol.* any disease caused by overcrowding. [< Gk *óchlēsis* disturbance, distress, equiv. to *óchl(os)* mob, crowd + *-ēsis* result of] —**och·le·sit·ic** (ok′li sit′ik), **och·let·ic** (ok let′ik), *adj.*

och·loc·ra·cy (ok lok′rə sē), *n.* government by the mob; mobocracy; mob rule. [< Gk *ochlokratía,* equiv. to *óchl(os)* mob + *-kratia* -CRACY] —**och·lo·crat** (ok′lə krat′), *n.* —**och′lo·crat′ic, och′lo·crat′i·cal,** *adj.* —**och′lo·crat′i·cal·ly,** *adv.*

och·lo·pho·bi·a (ok′lə fō′bē ə), *n. Psychiatry.* an abnormal fear of crowds. [< Gk *ochlophobía,* equiv. to *óchlo(s)* mob + *-phobia* -PHOBIA] —**och′lo·pho′bist,** *n.*

O·cho·a (ō chō′ə; *Sp.* ô chô′ä), *n.* **Se·ve·ro** (sə vâr′ō; *Sp.* se ve′rô), born 1905, U.S. biochemist, born in Spain: Nobel prize for medicine 1959.

o·chone (ə KHōn′), *interj. Scot. and Irish Eng.* ohone.

Och·o·zath (ok′ə zath′), *n. Douay Bible.* Ahuzzath.

Och·o·zi·as (ok′ə zī′əs), *n. Douay Bible.* Ahaziah.

o·chre (ō′kər), *n., adj., v.t.,* **o·chred, o·chring.** ocher. —**o·chre·ous** (ō′kər əs, ō′krē əs), **o·chrous** (ō′krəs), **o·chry** (ō′krē), *adj.*

och·re·a (ok′rē ə), *n., pl.* **-re·ae** (-rē ē′). ocrea.

o·chroid (ō′kroid), *adj.* yellow as ocher. [< Gk *ōchroeid(ēs)* pallid, equiv. to *ōchr-* OCHER + *-oeidēs* -OID]

Ochs (oks), *n.* **Adolph Simon,** 1858–1935, U.S. newspaper publisher.

OCIAA, Office of Coordinator of Inter-American Affairs.

O·cie (ō′sē), *n.* a girl's given name.

O·cil·la (ō sil′ə), *n.* a town in central Georgia. 3217 (1960).

-ock, a native English suffix of nouns, used to form descriptive names (*ruddock,* lit., the red one), diminutives (*hillock*), etc. [ME *-ok,* OE *-oc, -uc*]

Ock·e·ghem (ok′ə gem′), *n.* **Jo·han·nes** (yō hä′nəs). See **Okeghem, Jean d′** or **Jan van.** Also, **Ock·en·heim** (ok′ən hīm′, ō′kən-).

Ock·ham (ok′əm), *n.* **William of.** See **Occam.**

Ock′ham's ra′zor. See **Occam's razor.**

o'clock (ə klok′), *adv.* **1.** of, by, or according to the clock (used in specifying the hour of the day): *It is now 1 o'clock.* **2.** according to a method for indicating relative position whereby a plane in space is considered to be numbered as a clock's face, with 12 o'clock considered as directly ahead in horizontal position or straight up in vertical position: *Enemy aircraft were approaching at 6 o'clock. The arrow struck the target at 9 o'clock.*

Oc·nus (ok′nəs), *n.* **1.** *Class. Myth.* the personification of unavailing effort, often depicted endlessly plaiting a straw rope which his donkey eats as fast as he makes it. **2.** *Rom. Legend.* the son of the Tuscan river god and the seeress Manto who founded the town of Mantua.

O·co·ee (ō kō′ē), *n.* a town in central Florida. 2628 (1960).

O'Con·nell (ō kon′əl), *n.* **Daniel,** 1775–1847, Irish political agitator and orator.

O'Con·nor (ō kon′ər), *n.* **1. Frank** (*Michael Donovan*), 1903–66, Irish writer. **2. (Mary) Flannery,** 1925–64, U.S. novelist and short-story writer. **3. Sandra Day,** born 1930, U.S. jurist: associate justice of the U.S. Supreme Court since 1981; first woman appointed to that position. **4. Thomas Power,** 1848–1929, Irish journalist, author, and political leader.

O·con·o·mo·woc (ə kon′ə mə wok′), *n.* a town in SE Wisconsin. 6682 (1960).

O·con·to (ō kon′tō), *n.* a town in NE Wisconsin. 4805 (1960).

o·co·til·lo (ō′kə tēl′yō; *Sp.* ô′kô tē′yô), *n., pl.* **-til·los** (-tēl′yōz; *Sp.* -tē′yôs). a spiny, woody shrub, *Fouquieria splendens,* of arid regions of Mexico and the southwestern U.S. [< MexSp, dim. of *ocote* kind of pine < Aztec *ocotl*]

O, Ocrea

oc·re·a (ok′rē ə, ō′krē ə), *n., pl.* **oc·re·ae** (ok′rē ē′, ō′krē ē′). *Bot., Zool.* a sheathing part, as a pair of stipules united about a stem. Also, **ochrea.** [< L: greave, legging < Gk *ókris* prominence, crag, c. *ákris* peak]

oc·re·ate (ok′rē it, -āt′, ō′krē-), *adj.* having an ocrea or ocreae; sheathed. [< L *ocreāt(us)* greaved, equiv. to *ocre(a)* greave (see OCREA) + *-ātus* -ATE[1]]

OCS, 1. Office of Contract Settlement. **2.** *Mil.* officer candidate school.

oct-, var. of **octa-** or **octo-** before a vowel: *octal.*

Oct., October.

oct., octavo.

octa-, an element occurring in loan words from Greek and Latin, where it meant "eight" (*octagon; octastyle*), on this model, used in the formation of compound words, and in chemical terms specialized to mean "having eight atoms" (*octavalent*). Also, **oct-, octo-.** [< Gk *okta-,* comb. form of *oktṓ* EIGHT]

oc·ta·chord (ok′tə kôrd′), *n.* **1.** any musical instrument with eight strings. **2.** a diatonic series of eight tones. [< Gk *oktáchord(os)* having eight strings. See OCTA-, CHORD[1]] —**oc′ta·chor′dal,** *adj.*

oc·tad (ok′tad), *n.* **1.** a group or series of eight. **2.** *Chem.* an element, atom, or group having a valence of eight. [< Gk *oktad-* (s. of *oktás*) group of eight, equiv. to *okt-* OCT- + *-ad* -AD] —**oc·tad′ic,** *adj.*

oc′ta·dec·a·no′ic ac′id (ok′tə dek′ə nō′ik, ok′-), *Chem.* See **stearic acid.** [OCTA- + DECANE + -O- + -IC]

Octagon

oc·ta·gon (ok′tə gon′, -gən), *n.* a polygon having eight angles and eight sides. Also called **octangle.** [< L *octagōn(os)* eight-cornered (sp. var. of *octōgōnos*) < Gk *oktágōnos* octangular, equiv. to *okta-* OCTA- + *gōn(ía)* angle; see -GON]

oc·tag·o·nal (ok tag′ə nəl), *adj.* having eight angles and eight sides. [< NL *octōgōnāl(is),* equiv. to L *octōgōn-* OCTAGON + *-ālis* -AL[1]] —**oc·tag′o·nal·ly,** *adv.*

oc′tagon scale′, *Carpentry.* a scale used in laying out octagonal figures of various sizes.

oc·ta·he·dral (ok′tə hē′drəl), *adj.* having the form of an octahedron. [OCTAHEDR(ON) + -AL[1]]

oc·ta·he·drite (ok′tə hē′drīt), *n.* anatase. [< LL *octahedr(os)* eight-sided < Gk *oktáedr(on)* (see OCTAHEDRON) + -ITE[1]]

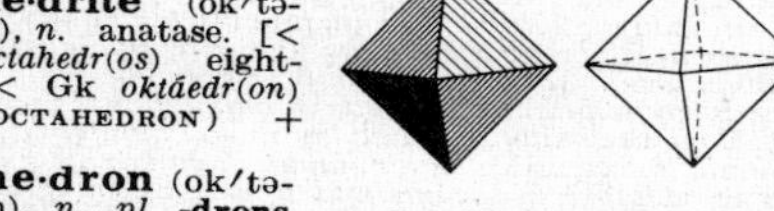
Octahedrons (Regular)

oc·ta·he·dron (ok′tə hē′drən), *n., pl.* **-drons, -dra** (-drə). a solid figure having eight faces. [< Gk *oktáedron* eight-sided (neut. of *oktáedros*), equiv. to *okta-* OCTA- + *-hedron* -HEDRON]

oc·tal (ok′təl), *adj.* **1.** octonary. **2.** (of a vacuum tube) having eight pins in its base for electrical connections. —*n.* **3.** octonary (def. 6). [OCT- + -AL[1]]

oc·tam·er·ous (ok tam′ər əs), *adj.* **1.** consisting of or divided into eight parts. **2.** *Bot.* (of flowers) having eight members in each whorl. [< Gk *oktamer(ḗs)* having eight parts, equiv. to *okta-* OCTA- + *mér(os)* -MEROUS] —**oc·tam·er·ism** (ok tam′ə riz′əm), *n.*

oc·tam·e·ter (ok tam′i tər), *Pros.* —*adj.* **1.** consisting of eight measures or feet. —*n.* **2.** an octameter verse. [< LL < Gk *oktámetr(os),* equiv. to *okta-* OCTA- + *métro(n)* -METER]

oc·tan (ok′tən), *adj.* **1.** (of a fever) occurring every eighth day. —*n.* **2.** an octan fever. [< F *octane, octaine* < L *octān(us)* (applied to a soldier in the 8th legion), equiv. to *oct-* OCT- + *-ānus* -AN]

oc·tane (ok′tān), *n. Chem.* any of 18 isomeric saturated hydrocarbons having the formula C_8H_{18}, some of which are obtained in the distillation and cracking of petroleum. [OCT- + -ANE]

oc′tane num′ber, (of gasoline) a designation of antiknock quality, numerically equal to the percentage of isooctane, or 2, 2, 4 trimethylpentane, by volume in a mixture of isooctane and normal heptane that matches the given gasoline in antiknock characteristics. Also called **oc′tane rat′ing.**

oc·tan·gle (ok′tang gəl), *adj.* **1.** octangular. —*n.* **2.** octagon. [< LL *octangul(us)* eight-angled, equiv. to L *oct-* OCT- + *angulus* ANGLE]

oc·tan·gu·lar (ok tang′gyə lər), *adj.* having eight angles. [< LL *octangul(us)* (see OCTANGLE) + -AR[1]] —**oc·tan′gu·lar·ness,** *n.*

Oc·tans (ok′tanz), *n., gen.* **Oc·tan·tis** (ok tan′tis). *Astron.* the Octant, a southern constellation that contains the south celestial pole. [< LL: eighth part of a circle, equiv. to *oct-* OCT- + *-āns* (see -ANT)]

oc·tant (ok′tənt), *n.* **1.** the eighth part of a circle. **2.** *Math.* any of the eight parts into which three mutually perpendicular planes divide space. **3.** an instrument having an arc of 24°, used by navigators for measuring angles up to 90°. **4.** the position of one heavenly body when 45° distant from another. **5.** (*cap.*) *Astron.* the constellation Octans. [< LL *octant-* (s. of *octāns*); see OCTANS] —**oc·tan·tal** (ok tan′təl), *adj.*

oc·tar·chy (ok′tär kē), *n., pl.* **-chies. 1.** a government by eight persons. **2.** a group of eight states or kingdoms. [OCT- + -ARCHY]

oc·ta·style (ok′tə stīl′), *adj. Archit.* **1.** having eight columns. **2.** (of a classical temple or building in the style of one) having eight columns on one or either front. [< L *octastȳl(os)* < Gk *oktástȳlos,* equiv. to *okta-* OCTA- + *stŷlos* pillar]

oc·ta·sty·los (ok′tə stī′los), *n.* an octastyle building, as a classical temple. Also, **oktastylos.** [< L (adj.); see OCTASTYLE]

oc·ta·teuch (ok′tə to͞ok′, -tyo͞ok′), *n.* the first eight books of the Old Testament or a volume containing them. [< LL *octateuch(us)* < Gk *oktáteuchos,* equiv. to *okta-* OCTA- + *teûchos* container for scrolls]

oc·ta·va·lent (ok′tə vā′lənt), *adj. Chem.* having a valence of eight. [OCTA- + -VALENT]

oc·tave (ok′tiv, -tāv), *n.* **1.** *Music.* **a.** a tone on the eighth degree from a given tone. **b.** the interval encompassed by such tones. **c.** the harmonic combination of such tones. **d.** a series of tones, or of keys of an instrument, extending through this interval. **2.** a pipe-organ stop whose pipes give tones an octave above the normal pitch of the keys used. **3.** a series or group of eight. **4.** Also called **octet.** *Pros.* **a.** a group of eight lines of verse, esp. the first eight lines of a sonnet in the Italian form. Cf. **sestet** (def. 1). **b.** a stanza of eight lines. **5.** the eighth of a series. **6.** *Eccles.* **a.** the eighth day from a feast day, counting the feast day as the first. **b.** the period of eight days beginning with a feast day. **7.** one eighth of a pipe of wine. **8.** *Fencing.* the eighth of eight defensive positions. —*adj.* **9.** pitched an octave higher. [ME < L *octāva* eighth, fem. of *octāvus,* equiv. to *oct-* OCT- + *-āvus* adj. suffix] —**oc·ta·val** (ok tā′vəl, ok′tə-), *adj.*

Oc·ta·vi·a (ok tā′vē ə), *n.* **1.** died 11 B.C., sister of Roman emperor Augustus and wife of Marc Anthony. **2.** A.D. c42–62 Roman empress, wife of Nero. **3.** a girl's given name.

Oc·ta·vi·an (ok tā′vē ən), *n.* Augustus.

Oc·ta·vi·us (ok tā′vē əs), *n.* a boy's given name.

oc·ta·vo (ok tā′vō, -tä′-), *n., pl.* **-vos,** *adj.* —*n.* **1.** a book size of about 6 × 9 inches, determined by printing on sheets folded to form 8 leaves or 16 pages. *Abbr.:* 8vo, 8° **2.** a book of this size. —*adj.* **3.** in octavo. [short for NL *in octāvō* in an eighth (of a sheet)]

oc·ta·vus (ōk tä′wo͝os; *Eng.* ok tā′vəs), *adj. Latin.* eighth.

oc·ten·ni·al (ok ten′ē əl), *adj.* **1.** occurring every eight years. **2.** of or for eight years. [< LL *octenn(ium)* eight-year period, equiv. to *oct-* OCT- + *-enn* (comb. form of *annus* year) + -IAL] —**oc·ten′ni·al·ly,** *adv.*

oc·tet (ok tet′), *n.* **1.** a company of eight singers or musicians. **2.** a musical composition for eight voices or instruments. **3.** *Pros.* octave (def. 4). **4.** any group of eight. Also, **oc·tette′.** [OCT- + *-et,* as in *duet*]

oc·til·lion (ok til′yən), *n., pl.* **-lions,** (*as after a numeral*) **-lion,** *adj.* —*n.* **1.** a cardinal number represented in the U.S. and France by a one followed by 27 zeros, and in Great Britain and Germany by a one followed by 48 zeros. —*adj.* **2.** amounting to one octillion in number. [< F, equiv. to *oct-* OCT- + *-illion,* as in *million*] —**oc·til′lionth,** *n., adj.*

octo-, var. of **octa-:** *octosyllabic.*

Oc·to·ber (ok tō′bər), *n.* **1.** the tenth month of the year, containing 31 days. **2.** *Brit.* ale brewed in this month. [ME, OE < L: the eighth month of the early Roman year, equiv. to *octō-* OCTO- + *-ber* adj. suffix]

Octo′ber Revolu′tion. See **Russian Revolution** (def. 2).

Oc·to·brist (ok tō′brist), *n.* **1.** a member of a Russian political party that advocated constitutional monarchism: so called because it was organized after the Czar's manifesto in October, 1905. **2.** a member of a communist organization in the Soviet Union for children ranging in age from eight to ten. Cf. **Komsomol, Pioneer.** [trans. of Russ *oktyabrist*]

oc·tode (ok′tōd), *n. Electronics.* a vacuum tube containing eight electrodes, usually a cathode, an anode, a control electrode, and five grids. [OCT- + -ODE[2]]

oc·to·de·cil·lion (ok′tō di sil′yən), *n., pl.* **-lions,** (*as after a numeral*) **-lion,** *adj.* —*n.* **1.** a cardinal number represented in the U.S. and France by a one followed by 57 zeros, and in Great Britain and Germany by a one followed by 108 zeros. —*adj.* **2.** amounting to one octodecillion in number. [< L *octodec(im)* eighteen + *-illion,* as in *million*] —**oc′to·de·cil′lionth,** *adj., n.*

oc·to·dec·i·mo (ok′tə des′ə mō′), *n., pl.* **-mos** for 2. *adj.* —*n.* **1.** a book size of about 4 × 6¼ inches, determined by printing on sheets folded to form 18 leaves or 36 pages. *Abbr.:* 18mo, 18° **2.** a book of this size. —*adj.* **3.** in octodecimo. Also called **eighteenmo.** [short for NL *in octōdecimō* in an eighteenth (of a sheet)]

oc·to·foil (ok′tə foil′), *n. Heraldry.* See **double quatrefoil.** [OCTO- + FOIL[2]]

oc·to·ge·nar·i·an (ok′tə jə nâr′ē ən), *adj.* Also, **oc·tog·e·nar·y** (ok toj′ə ner′ē). **1.** of the age of 80 years. **2.** between 80 and 90 years old. —*n.* **3.** an octogenarian person. [< L *octōgēnāri(us)* belonging to eighty, equiv. to *octōgēn(ī)* eighty each + *-ārius* -ARY + -AN] —**oc′to·ge·nar′i·an·ism,** *n.*

oc·to·nar·y (ok′tə ner′ē), *adj., n., pl.* **-nar·ies.** —*adj.* **1.** pertaining to the number 8. **2.** consisting of eight. **3.** proceeding by eight. **4.** of, pertaining to, or noting a numerical system based on the number 8. —*n.* **5.** a group of eight; an ogdoad. **6.** *Pros.* a stanza of eight lines. **7.** a number in an octonary system. Also, **octal** (for defs. 1–4, 6). [< L *octōnāri(us)* consisting of eight each, equiv. to *octō-* OCTO- + *-n-* connective + *-ārius* -ARY]

oc·to·pod (ok′tə pod′), *n.* any eight-armed cephalopod of the order or suborder *Octopoda,* including the octopuses and paper nautiluses. [< NL *Octopod(a)* name of the order < Gk *oktṓpoda* neut. pl. of *oktṓpous* eight-footed. See OCTO-, -POD]

Octopus, *Octopus vulgaris* (Radial span about 10 ft.)

oc·to·pus (ok′tə pəs), *n., pl.* **-pus·es, -pi** (-pī′). **1.** any animal of the genus *Octopus,* having a soft, oval body and eight sucker-bearing arms, living mostly at the bottom of the sea. **2.** any octopod. **3.** something likened to an octopus, as an organization or a person of far-reaching influence or control. [< NL < Gk *oktṓpous* eight-footed]

Octopus, The, a novel (1901) by Frank Norris.

oc·to·roon (ok′tə ro͞on′), *n.* a person having one-eighth Negro ancestry; the offspring of a quadroon and a white. [OCTO- + *-roon,* modeled on *quadroon*]

oc·to·syl·lab·ic (ok′tō si lab′ik), *adj.* **1.** consisting of or pertaining to eight syllables. —*n.* **2.** an octosyllable. [< LL *octosyllab(us)* (< Gk *oktasýllabos,* equiv. to *okta-* OCTO- + *-syllabos* syllabic) + -IC]

oc·to·syl·la·ble (ok′tə sil′ə bəl), *n.* a word or line of verse of eight syllables. [part trans. of L *octōsyllabus;* see OCTOSYLLABIC, -LE]

oc·troi (ok′troi; *Fr.* ôk TRWA′), *n., pl.* **-trois** (-troiz; *Fr.* -TRWA′). **1.** (formerly esp. in France and Italy) a local tax levied on certain articles, such as foodstuffs, on their entry into a city. **2.** the place at which such a tax is collected. **3.** the officials collecting it. **4.** the act of a sovereign in granting a constitution or other charter to his subjects. [< F, back formation from *octroyer* to grant, OF *otreier* < ML *auctorizāre;* see AUTHORIZE]

oc·tu·ple (ok′to͝o pəl, -tyo͝o-; ok to͞o′pəl, -tyo͞o′-), *adj., v.,* **-pled, -pling,** *n.* —*adj.* **1.** eightfold; eight times as great. **2.** having eight effective units or elements. —*v.t.* **3.** to make eight times as great. —*n.* **4.** *Rowing.* a shell rowed by eight oarsmen each using a pair of oars. [< L *octupl(us),* equiv. to *octō-* OCTO- + *-plus* -FOLD]

oc·tup·let (ok tup′lit, -to͞o′plit, -tyo͞o′-; ok′to͝o plit, -tyo͝o-), *n.* **1.** a group, series, or combination of eight related items. **2.** *Music.* a group of eight notes which are to be played or sung in the same time as six notes of equal value. [OCTUPLE + -ET]

oc·tu·pli·cate (ok to͞o′plə kit, -kāt′, -tyo͞o′-), *adj.* **1.** having or consisting of eight identical parts; eightfold. —*n.* **2.** a group, series, or set of eight identical copies (usually prec. by *in*): *issuing orders in octuplicate.* [< L *octuplicāt(us),* equiv. to *octupl(us)* OCTUPLE + *-ātus* -ATE[1], modeled after *quadruplus, quadruplicātus*]

oc′tyl al′cohol (ok′təl), *Chem.* any of a group of isomers having the formula $C_8H_{17}OH$, esp. $CH_3(CH_2)_6CH_2OH$ and $CH_3(CH_2)_5CHOHCH_3$, used in making perfumes, and $CH_3(CH_2)_3CH(C_2H_5)CH_2OH$, used as a solvent. [OCT(ANE) + -YL]

oc′tyl phe′nol, *Chem.* a white to pink, water-insoluble, flakey substance composed of $C_8H_{17}C_6H_4OH$, used chiefly in the manufacture of commercial surface active agents.

ocul-, var. of **oculo-** before a vowel: *oculist.*

oc·u·lar (ok′yə lər), *adj.* **1.** of, pertaining to, or for the eye or eyes: *ocular movements.* **2.** of the nature of an eye: *an ocular organ.* **3.** performed or perceived by the eye or eyesight. —*n.* **4.** *Optics.* eyepiece. [< L *oculār(is),* equiv. to *ocul(us)* eye + *-āris* -AR[1]] —**oc′u·lar·ly,** *adv.*

oc·u·list (ok′yə list), *n.* a doctor of medicine skilled in the examination and treatment of the eye; ophthalmologist. [< F *oculiste.* See OCUL-, -IST] —**oc′u·lis′tic,** *adj.*

oculo-, a learned borrowing from Latin used, with the meaning "eye," "ocular," in the formation of compound words: *oculomotor.* Also, *esp. before a vowel,* **ocul-.** [comb. form of L *oculus* eye; see -o-]

oc·u·lo·mo·tor (ok′yə lō mō′tər), *adj.* moving the eyeball. [OCULO- + MOTOR]

oculomo′tor nerve′, *Anat.* either one of the third pair of cranial nerves, consisting chiefly of motor fibers that innervate most of the muscles of the eyeball. See diag. under **brain.**

oc·u·lus (ok′yə ləs), *n., pl.* **-li** (-lī′). **1.** an eye. **2.** *Archit.* a circular opening, esp. one at the apex of a dome. [< L: eye]

O·cyp·e·te (ō sip′i tē′), *n. Class. Myth.* one of the Harpies.

O·cyr·rho·ë (ō sir′ō ē′), *n. Class. Myth.* a daughter of Chiron and the nymph Chariclo who predicted the circumstances of her father's death and foresaw the divine anger that her prophetic gift would excite.

od (od, ōd), *n.* a hypothetical force formerly held to pervade all nature and to manifest itself in magnetism, mesmerism, chemical action, etc. Also, **odyl, odyle.** [arbitrary name coined by Baron Karl von Reichenbach (1788–1869), German scientist]

Od (od), *interj. Archaic.* a shortened form of "God" (used interjectionally and in minced oaths). Also, **'Od, Odd.**

OD, 1. See **officer of the day. 2.** Ordnance Department. **3.** outside diameter.

od, 1. on demand. **2.** outside diameter. **3.** outside dimensions. **4.** overdraft. **5.** overdrawn.

OD., Old Dutch.

O.D., 1. Doctor of Optometry. **2.** (in prescriptions) the right eye. [< L *oculus dexter*] **3.** Officer of the Day. **4.** Old Dutch. **5.** (of a military uniform) olive drab. **6.** ordinary seaman. **7.** outside diameter. **8.** overdraft. **9.** overdrawn.

o.d., 1. (in prescriptions) the right eye. [< L *oculus dexter*] **2.** olive drab. **3.** on demand. **4.** outside diameter.

o·da·lisque (ōd′ᵊlisk), *n.* **1.** a female slave or concubine in a harem, esp. in that of the Sultan of Turkey. **2.** (*cap.*) any of a number of representations of such a woman or of a similar subject, as by Ingres or Matisse. Also, **o′da·lisk.** [< F, misspelling (with orig. mute *s*) of Turk *odalik* concubine, equiv. to *oda* room + *-lik* n. suffix]

odd (od), *adj.* **1.** differing in nature from what is ordinary, usual, or expected: *an odd choice.* **2.** singular or peculiar in a freakish or eccentric way: *an odd person; odd manners.* **3.** fantastic; bizarre: *Her taste in clothing was rather odd.* **4.** out-of-the-way; secluded: *a tour to the odd parts of the Far East.* **5.** more or less, esp. a little more (used in combination with a round number): *I owe three hundred-odd dollars.* **6.** being a small amount in addition to what is counted or specified: *I have five gross and a few odd dozens. Five dollars and some odd cents were all he had.* **7.** being part of a pair, set, or series of which the rest is lacking: *an odd glove.* **8.** remaining after all others are paired, grouped, or divided into equal numbers or parts: *Everybody gets two hamburgers and I get the odd one.* **9.** left over after all others are used, consumed, etc. **10.** (of a pair) not matching: *Do you know you're wearing an odd pair of socks?* **11.** leaving a remainder of 1 when divided by 2, as a number (opposed to *even*): *Numbers like 3, 15, and 181 are odd numbers.* **12.** *Math.* (of a function) having a sign that changes when the sign of each independent variable is changed at the same time. **13.** not regular or full-time; occasional; casual: *to do odd jobs.* **14.** not forming part of any particular group, set, or class: *to pick up odd bits of information.* —*n.* **15.** that which is odd. **16.** *Golf.* **a.** a stroke more than the opponent has played. **b.** *Brit.* a stroke taken from a player's total score for a hole in order to give him odds. [ME *odde* < Scand; cf. Icel *odda-tala* odd number] —**odd′ly,** *adv.* —**odd′ness,** *n.*
—**Syn. 1.** extraordinary, unusual, rare, uncommon. See **strange.** —**Ant. 1.** ordinary, usual, common.

odd′ and e′ven. See **odd or even.**

odd·ball (od′bôl′), *Slang.* —*n.* **1.** one who or that which is atypical, bizarre, eccentric, or nonconforming, esp. a person having beliefs that are unusual and unattractive but harmless. —*adj.* **2.** whimsically free-spirited; eccentric; atypical: *an oddball scheme.* [ODD + BALL[1]]

odd′-e′ven check′ (od′ē′vən). See **parity check.**

Odd·fel·low (od′fel′ō), *n.* a member of a secret social and benevolent society "Independent Order of Odd-fellows," originated in England in the 18th century. —**Odd′fel′low·ship′,** *n.*

odd·ish (od′ish), *adj.* rather odd; queer. [ODD + -ISH[1]]

odd·i·ty (od′i tē), *n., pl.* **-ties** for 1, 3. **1.** an odd or remarkably unusual person, thing, or event. **2.** the quality of being odd; singularity, strangeness, or eccentricity. **3.** an odd characteristic; peculiarity. [ODD + -ITY]

odd′ lot′, 1. a quantity or amount less than the conventional unit of trading. **2.** *Stock Exchange.* (in a transaction) a quantity of stock less than the established 100-share unit for active issues or the 10-share unit for designated inactive issues. Also called **broken lot.** Cf. **round lot.** —**odd′-lot′,** *adj.*

odd′ man′ out′, 1. a method of selecting or isolating a person from a group, as by matching coins, esp. in preparation for playing a game. **2.** the person so selected or isolated. **3.** a game consisting of this method. **4.** outsider (def. 2).

odd·ment (od′mənt), *n.* **1.** an odd article, bit, remnant, or the like. **2.** an article belonging to a broken or incomplete set. **3.** *Print.* any individual portion of a book excluding the text, as the frontispiece, index, etc. [ODD + MENT]

odd′ or e′ven, any of various games of chance in which one bets on an odd or even number, as one in which two players alternately draw from a pile of an odd number of counters any desired number up to a prearranged limit, the object being to have drawn an odd number of counters at the end of the game. Also, **odd and even, odds or evens.**

odd′ permuta′tion, *Math.* a permutation of a set of n elements, $x_1, x_2, \ldots, x_n$, which permutes the product of all differences of the form $(x_i - x_j)$ where i is less than j, into the negative of the product. Cf. **even permutation.**

odd-pin·nate (od′pin′āt, -it), *adj. Bot.* pinnate with an odd terminal leaflet.

odds (odz), *n.* (*usually construed as pl.*) **1.** the probability that something is so, will occur, or is more likely to occur than something else: *The odds are that it will rain today.* **2.** the ratio of probability that something is so, will occur, or is more likely to occur than something else. **3.** this ratio used as the basis of a bet; the ratio by which the bet of one party to a wager exceeds that of the other, granted by one of two betting opponents to equalize the chances favoring one of them: *The odds are two-to-one that it won't rain today. Track odds on the seven horse are nine-to-five.* **4.** an equalizing allowance, as that given the weaker person or team in a contest; handicap. **5.** an advantage or degree of superiority on the side of two contending parties; a difference favoring one of two contestants. **6.** an amount or degree by which one thing is better or worse than another. **7. at odds,** at variance; in disagreement: *They were usually at odds over political issues.* **8. by all odds,** in every respect; by far; undoubtedly: *She is by all odds the prettiest girl in the family.* Also, **by long odds, by odds.** [special use of ODD]

odds′ and ends′, fragments; remnants; scraps; bits: *She made a meal of the odds and ends that were left in the refrigerator.*

odd·side (od′sīd′), *n. Foundry.* a temporary support for a pattern below the joint of a mold, used while the mold is being made. [ODD + SIDE[1]]

odds-on (odz′on′, -ôn′), *adj.* being the one more or most likely to win, succeed, attain or achieve something, etc.: *Native Dancer was the odds-on favorite for the race.*

odds′ or e′vens. See **odd or even.**

odd′ trick′, 1. *Bridge.* each trick exceeding six that is taken by the declarer. **2.** *Whist.* the seventh trick taken by a partnership.

ode (ōd), *n.* **1.** a lyric poem typically of elaborate or irregular metrical form and expressive of exalted or enthusiastic emotion. **2.** (originally) a poem intended to be sung. Cf. **Horatian ode, Pindaric ode.** [< MF < LL *ōd(a)* < Gk *ōidḗ,* contr. of *aoidḗ* song, deriv. of *aeíd(ein)*]

-ode[1], a suffix of nouns, appearing in loan words from Greek, where it meant "like"; used in the formation of compound words: *phyllode.* Cf. **-oid.** [< Gk *-ōdēs,* contr. of *-oeidēs* -OID]

-ode[2], a learned borrowing from Greek meaning "way," "road," used in the formation of compound words: *anode; electrode.* [< Gk *-odos,* comb. form of *hodós*]

O·dell (ō del′), *n.* a boy's given name.

O·dels·ting (ōd′ᵊls ting′), *n.* Storting. Also, **O′dels·thing′.** [< ON, equiv. to *odel* noble (c. OE *æthele* noble) + *-s* 's[1] + *ting* THING[2]]

O·den·se (ō′thən sə), *n.* a seaport on Fyn island, in S Denmark. 129,833 (1960).

Ode′ on a Gre′cian Urn′, a poem (1819) by Keats.

Ode′ on In′dolence, a poem (1819) by Keats.

Ode′ on Mel′ancholy, a poem (1819) by Keats.

O·der (ō′dər), *n.* a river in central Europe, flowing from the NE Czech Republic, N through SW Poland and along the border between Germany and Poland into the Baltic. 562 mi. long.

O′der-Neis′se Line′ (ō′dər nī′sə), the provisional boundary between Poland and East Germany.

O·des·sa (ō des′ə; *Russ.* o de′sä), *n.* **1.** a seaport in the S Ukraine, in the SW Soviet Union in Europe, on the Black Sea: the principal export center of Ukrainian grain. 735,000 (1965). **2.** a city in W Texas. 80,338 (1960).

Ode′ to a Night′ingale, a poem (1819) by Keats.

Ode′ to Au′tumn, a poem (1819) by Keats.

Ode′ to Du′ty, a poem (1807) by Wordsworth.

Ode′ to Psy′che, a poem (1819) by Keats.

Ode′ to the West′ Wind′, a poem (1820) by Shelley.

O·dets (ō dets′), *n.* **Clifford,** 1906–63, U.S. dramatist and director.

O·det·ta (ō det′ə), *n.* **1.** (*Odetta Holmes*), born 1930, U.S. folk singer. **2.** a girl's given name.

O·dette (ō det′), *n.* a girl's given name, form of **Odille.**

o·de·um (ō dē′əm), *n., pl.* **o·de·a** (ō dē′ə). **1.** a hall or structure for musical or dramatic performances. **2.** (in ancient Greece and Rome) a roofed building for musical performances. [< LL: music hall < Gk *ōideion,* equiv. to *ōid(ḗ)* song, ODE + *-eion* place]

od·ic[1] (ō′dik), *adj.* of an ode. [ODE + -IC] —**od′i·cal·ly,** *adv.*

od·ic[2] (od′ik, ō′dik), *adj.* of or pertaining to the hypothetical force od. [OD + -IC]

O·dille (ō dil′), *n.* a girl's given name. Also, **O·dil·la** (ō dil′ə).

O·din (ō′din), *n. Scand. Myth.* the ruler of the Aesir and god of war, poetry, knowledge, and wisdom; Wotan. Also, **Othin.** —**O·din′i·an, O·din′ic, O′din·it′ic,** *adj.* —**O′din·ism,** *n.* —**O′din·ist,** *n.*

o·di·ous (ō′dē əs), *adj.* **1.** deserving or causing hatred; hateful; repugnant; detestable. **2.** highly offensive; disgusting. [ME < L *odiōs(us),* equiv. to *od(ium)* hate, ODIUM + *-ōsus* -OUS] —**o′di·ous·ly,** *adv.* —**o′di·ous·ness,** *n.*
—**Syn. 1.** abominable, objectionable, despicable, execrable. See **hateful. 2.** loathsome, repellent, repulsive. —**Ant. 1.** attractive, lovable.

o·di·um (ō′dē əm), *n.* **1.** intense hatred or dislike, esp. toward someone or something regarded as contemptible, despicable, or repugnant. **2.** the reproach, discredit, or opprobrium attaching to something hated or repugnant. **3.** the state or quality of being hated. [< L: hate, cf. *ōdī* I hate]
—**Syn. 1.** detestation, abhorrence, antipathy. **2.** obloquy. —**Ant. 1, 2.** love.

O·do·a·cer (ō′dō ā′sər), *n.* A.D. 434?–493, first barbarian ruler of Italy 476–493. Also, **Odovacar.**

o·do·graph (ō′də graf′, -gräf′), *n.* **1.** a recording odometer. **2.** a pedometer. **3.** *Naut.* an instrument for recording courses steered by a vessel with the distances or lengths of time run on each. [var. of *hodograph* < Gk *hodó(s)* way + -GRAPH]

o·dom·e·ter (ō dom′i tər), *n.* an instrument for measuring distance passed over, as by an automobile. Also, **hodometer.** [var. of *hodometer* < Gk *hodó(s)* way + -METER] —**o·do·met·ri·cal** (ō′də me′tri kəl), *adj.* —**o·dom′e·try,** *n.*

odont-, var. of **odonto-** before a vowel: *odontiasis.*

-odont, var. of **odonto-** as final element of compounds.

o·don·tal·gia (ō′don tal′jə, -jē ə), *n. Dentistry.* pain in a tooth; toothache. [ODONT- + -ALGIA] —**o′don·tal′gic,** *adj.*

o·don·ti·a·sis (ō′don tī′ə sis), *n. Dentistry.* dentition (def. 2). [< Gk *odontiā(n)* (to) cut teeth + -SIS]

odonto-, a learned borrowing from Greek meaning "tooth," used in the formation of compound words: *odontology.* Also, **odont-, -odont.** Cf. **denti-, -odus.** [< Gk *odónt-,* s. of *odoús* or *odṓn* tooth]

o·don·to·blast (ō don′tə blast′), *n. Anat.* one of a layer of cells lining the pulp cavity of a tooth, from which dentin is formed. [ODONTO- + -BLAST] —**o·don′to·blas′tic,** *adj.*

o·don·tog·e·ny (ō′don toj′ə nē), *n. Dentistry.* the development of teeth. Also, **o·don·to·gen·e·sis** (ō don′tə jen′i sis). [ODONTO- + -GENY] —**o·don·to·gen·ic** (ō don′tə jen′ik), *adj.*

o·don·to·glos·sum (ō don′tə glos′əm), *n.* any epiphytic orchid of the genus *Odontoglossum*, of the mountainous regions from Bolivia to Mexico. [< NL < Gk *odonto-* ODONTO- + *glôss(a)* tongue + NL *-um* neut. n. suffix]

o·don·to·graph (ō don′tə graf′, -gräf′), *n.* an instrument for laying out the forms of gear teeth or ratchets. [ODONTO- + -GRAPH] —**o·don′to·graph′ic,** *adj.* —**o·don·tog·ra·phy** (ō′don tog′rə fē), *n.*

o·don·toid (ō don′toid), *adj.* **1.** of or resembling a tooth; toothlike. **2.** *Anat.* of or pertaining to the odontoid process. —*n.* **3.** See **odontoid process.** [< Gk *odontoeid(ēs)* toothlike. See ODONT-, -OID]

odon′toid proc′ess, *Anat.* a toothlike process of the axis or second cervical vertebra upon which the atlas rotates.

o·don·to·lite (ō don′tᵊlīt′), *n.* See **bone turquoise.** [< F; see ODONTO-, -LITE]

o·don·tol·o·gy (ō′don tol′ə jē, od′on-), *n.* **1.** the science dealing with the study of the teeth and their surrounding tissues and with the prevention and cure of their diseases. **2.** dentistry. [ODONTO- + -LOGY] —**o·don·to·log·i·cal** (ō don′tᵊloj′i kəl), *adj.* —**o′don·tol′o·gist,** *n.*

o·don·to·phore (ō don′tə fōr′, -fôr′), *n.* *Zool.* a structure in the mouth of most mollusks over which the radula is drawn backward and forward in the process of breaking up food. [< Gk *odontophór(os)* bearing teeth. See ODONTO-, -PHORE] —**o·don·toph·o·ral** (ō′don tof′ər əl), **o·don·toph·o·rine** (ō′don tof′ə rīn′, -ər in), **o′don·toph′or·ous,** *adj.*

o·dor (ō′dər), *n.* **1.** that property of a substance which affects the sense of smell: *rank odors.* **2.** a sensation perceived by the sense of smell; scent. **3.** an agreeable scent; fragrance. **4.** a disagreeable smell. **5.** a quality or property characteristic or suggestive of something: *An odor of suspicion surrounded his testimony.* **6.** repute or estimation: *in bad odor with the whole community.* Also, *esp. Brit.,* **o′dour.** [ME < OF < L] —**o′dor·ful, o′dour·ful,** *adj.* —**o′dor·less, o′dour·less,** *adj.* —**Syn. 3.** aroma, redolence, perfume.

o·dor·if·er·ous (ō′də rif′ər əs), *adj.* yielding or diffusing an odor, esp. a fragrant one. [ME < L *odōrifer* bringing odors, equiv. to *odōr-* ODOR + *-i-* -I- + *-fer* -FER + -OUS] —**o′dor·if′er·ous·ly,** *adv.* —**o′dor·if′er·ous·ness, o·dor·if·er·os·i·ty** (ō′də rif′ə ros′i tē), *n.* —**Syn.** odorous, fragrant, aromatic, perfumed, redolent.

o·dor·ous (ō′dər əs), *adj.* odoriferous. [< L *odōrus* fragrant. See ODOR, -OUS] —**o′dor·ous·ly,** *adv.* —**o′dor·ous·ness, o·dor·os·i·ty** (ō′də ros′i tē), *n.*

O·do·va·car (ō′dō vā′kər), *n.* Odoacer.

Ods·bod·i·kins (odz bod′ə kinz), *interj.* Gadsbodikins. Also, **Ods·bod·kins** (odz bod′kinz).

ODT, Office of Defense Transportation.

O·dus (ō′dəs), *n.* a boy's given name, form of **Otis.**

-odus, *Zool.* a suffix occurring in names of genera, used to mean "having a (certain kind of) tooth": *ceratodus.* [< NL, comb. form repr. Gk *odoús* tooth. See ODONTO-]

od·yl (od′il, ō′dil), *n.* od. Also, **od′yle.** [OD + -YL] —**o·dyl·ic** (ō dil′ik), *adj.* —**od′yl·ism,** *n.* —**od′yl·ist,** *n.*

-odynia, a learned borrowing from Greek meaning "pain," used in the formation of compound words: *pododynia.* Cf. **-algia.** [< NL < Gk, equiv. to *odýn(ē)* pain + *-ia* -Y³]

O·dys·se·us (ō dis′ē əs, ō dis′yōōs), *n.* *Class. Myth.* king of Ithaca; son of Laertes; one of the heroes of the *Iliad* and protagonist of the *Odyssey:* wisest and shrewdest of the Greek leaders in the Trojan War.

Od·ys·sey (od′i sē), *n.* **1.** (*italics*) an epic poem attributed to Homer, describing Odysseus' adventures in his ten-year attempt to return home to Ithaca after the Trojan War. **2.** (*often l.c.*) a long series of wanderings, esp. when filled with notable experiences, hardships, etc. —**Od′ys·se′an,** *adj.*

Od·zooks (od zōōks′, -zōōks′), *interj.* Gadzooks. Also, **Od·zook·ers** (od zōōk′ərz, -zōō′kərz).

oe¹ (ō), *n.* a whirlwind that occurs in the vicinity of the Faeroe Islands. [< Faeroese *ōthi,* deriv. of *ōthur* wild, demented < ON *ōthr;* see WOOD²]

oe² (oi), *n.* *Scot.* oy.

oe-, var. spelling of *e-,* appearing in some words of Latin and Greek origin: *oecology; oenology; oesophagus.* [< L, repr. Gk *oi-,* as in *oikos* house (see ECONOMY), *oînos* wine (see OENOLOGY)]

OE, Old English. Also, **OE., O.E.**

Oe, oersted; oersteds.

O.E., omissions excepted. Also, **o.e.**

o.e., omissions excepted. Also, **oe**

Oe·a·grus (ē′ə grəs), *n.* *Class. Myth.* a Thracian king, the father, by the muse Calliope, of Orpheus and probably of Linus the musician.

Oe·ax (ē′aks), *n.* *Class. Myth.* a son of Nauplius and Clymene who, in seeking revenge for the slaying of his brother, Palamedes, provoked Clytemnestra to murder Agamemnon.

Oe·ba·lus (ē′bə ləs), *n.* *Class. Myth.* a Spartan king, the father of Hippocoön, Tyndareus, and Icarius.

OECD, Organization for Economic Cooperation and Development.

oe·col·o·gy (i kol′ə jē), *n.* ecology. —**oec·o·log·i·cal** (ek′ə loj′i kəl, ē′kə-), **oec′o·log′ic,** *adj.* —**oec′o·log′i·cal·ly,** *adv.* —**oe·col′o·gist,** *n.*

oec·u·men·i·cal (ek′yōō men′i kəl *or, esp. Brit.,* ē′kyōō-), *adj.* ecumenical. Also, **oec′u·men′ic.**

oe·cus (ē′kəs), *n., pl.* **oe·ci** (ē′sī). (in an ancient Roman house) an apartment, esp. a dining room, decorated with columns. [< L < Gk *oikos* house]

O.E.D., Oxford English Dictionary. Also, **OED**

oe·de·ma (i dē′mə), *n., pl.* **-ma·ta** (-mə tə). *Pathol.* edema.

oed·i·pal (ed′ə pəl, ē′də-), *adj.* (*often cap.*) of, characterized by, or resulting from the Oedipus complex. [OEDIP(US COMPLEX) + -AL¹]

Oed·i·pe·an (ed′ə pē′ən), *adj.* of, pertaining to, or characteristic of Oedipus or the Oedipus complex. [OEDIP(US) + *-ean,* var. of -IAN]

Oed·i·pus (ed′ə pəs, ē′də-), *n.* *Gk. Legend.* a king of Thebes, the son of Laius and Jocasta, and the father by Jocasta of Eteocles, Polynices, and Antigone: as was prophesied at his birth, he unwittingly killed his father and married his mother and was blinded and exiled for having done so.

Oed′ipus at Co·lo′nus (kə lō′nəs), a tragedy by Sophocles, written toward the end of his life and produced posthumously in 401? B.C.

Oed′ipus com′plex, *Psychoanal.* **1.** the unresolved desire of a child for sexual gratification through the parent of the opposite sex. This involves, first, identification with and, later, hatred for the parent of the same sex, who is considered by the child as a rival. **2.** sexual desire of a son for his mother.

Oed′ipus Rex′, a tragedy (c430 B.C.) by Sophocles. Also called **Oed′ipus Ty·ran′nus** (ti ran′əs).

OEEC, Organization for European Economic Cooperation.

oeil-de-boeuf (œ′yᵊ də bœf′), *n., pl.* **oeils-de-boeuf** (œ′yᵊ də bœf′). *French.* a comparatively small round or oval window, as in a frieze. Also called **oxeye.** [lit., bull's eye]

oeil·lade (œ yad′), *n., pl.* **oeil·lades** (œ yad′). *French.* an amorous glance; ogle.

Oel·wein (ōl′wīn), *n.* a town in NE Iowa. 8282 (1960).

OEM, Office for Emergency Management.

oe·nan′thic es′ter (ē nan′thik), *Chem.* See **ethyl oenanthate.** Also called **oenan′thic e′ther.** [< L *oenanth(ē)* (< Gk *oinánthē,* equiv. to *oínē* vine + *ánthē* blossom) + -IC]

Oe·ne·us (ē′nē əs, -nōōs, -nyōōs), *n.* *Class. Myth.* a king of Calydon believed to have been the first man to cultivate grapes: when he once forgot to honor Artemis in a sacrifice, she sent the Calydonian boar to ravage his land.

Oe·no (ē′nō), *n.* *Class. Myth.* a daughter of Anius who was empowered by Dionysus to change anything into wine.

oe·noch·o·e (ē nok′ō ē′), *n., pl.* **oe·noch·o·es, oe·noch·o·ai** (ē nok′ō ī′). oinochoe.

oe·nol·o·gy (ē nol′ə jē), *n.* the science of viniculture. Also, **enology.** [< Gk *oin-* (s. of *oînos*) wine + -LOGY] —**oe·no·log·i·cal** (ēn′ᵊloj′i kəl), *adj.* —**oe·nol′o·gist,** *n.*

Oe·no·ma·us (ē′nə mā′əs), *n.* *Class. Myth.* a Pisan king, the father of Hippodamia.

oe·no·mel (ē′nə mel′, en′ə-), *n.* **1.** a drink made of wine mixed with honey. **2.** something combining strength with sweetness. [< LL *oenomel(um)* (sp. var. of *oenomeli*) < Gk *oinómel(i),* equiv. to *oino(s)* wine + *méli* honey]

Oe·no·ne (ē nō′nē), *n.* *Class. Myth.* a nymph of Mount Ida who was the wife of Paris, but was deserted by him for Helen.

Oe·nop·i·des (ē nop′i dēz′), *n.* a walled plain in the second quadrant of the face of the moon: about 42 miles in diameter.

Oe·no·pi·on (ē nō′pē on′), *n.* *Class. Myth.* a king of Chios who kept postponing the marriage of his daughter Merope to Orion: when Orion, in a drunken stupor, assaulted Merope, Oenopion blinded him.

OEO, See **Office of Economic Opportunity.**

Oe·o·nus (ē ō′nəs), *n.* *Class. Myth.* a relative of Hercules who was beaten to death by the owners of a dog he had killed in self-defense.

o'er (ōr, ôr), *prep., adv.* over.

oer·sted (ûr′sted), *n.* **1.** *Elect.* a centimeter-gram-second unit of magnetic intensity, equal to the magnetic pole of unit strength when undergoing a force of one dyne in a vacuum. **2.** *Obs.* the unit of magnetic reluctance equal to the reluctance of a centimeter cube of vacuum between parallel surfaces. *Abbr:* Oe [named after H. C. OERSTED]

Oer·sted (ûr′sted; *for 1 also Dan.* œʀ′stiṫh), *n.* **1.** **Hans Christian** (häns kʀis′tyän), 1777–1851, Danish physicist. **2.** (*cap.*) a walled plain in the first quadrant of the face of the moon: about 25 miles in diameter.

Oe·sel (œ′zəl), *n.* German name of **Saaremaa.**

oesophag-, var. of **esophag-.**

oe·soph·a·ge·al (i sof′ə jē′əl, ē′sə faj′ē əl), *adj.* esophageal.

oe·soph·a·gus (i sof′ə gəs), *n., pl.* **-gi** (-jī′). esophagus.

oes·tra·di·ol (es′trə dī′ōl, -ôl, -ol, ē′strə-), *n.* *Biochem.* estradiol.

oes·trin (es′trin, ē′strin), *n.* *Biochem.* estrone.

oes·tri·ol (es′trē ōl′, -ôl′, -ol′, ē′strē-), *n.* *Biochem.* estriol.

oes·tro·gen (es′trə jən, ē′strə-), *n.* *Biochem.* estrogen.

oes·trone (es′trōn, ē′strōn), *n.* *Biochem.* estrone.

oes·trous (es′trəs, ē′strəs), *adj.* estrous.

oes·trus (es′trəs, ē′strəs), *n.* **1.** Also, **oes·trum** (es′trəm, ē′strəm). estrus. **2.** passion or passionate impulse. **3.** a stimulus. [< L < Gk *oîstros* gadfly, sting, frenzy] —**oes·tru·al** (es′trōō əl, ē′strōō-), *adj.*

oeuvre (œ′vʀᵊ), *n., pl.* **oeuvres** (œ′vʀᵊ). *French.* **1.** the works of a writer, painter, or the like, taken as a whole. **2.** any one of the works of a writer, painter, or the like.

of¹ (uv, ov, *unstressed* əv), *prep.* **1.** (used to indicate distance or direction from, separation, deprivation, etc.): *within a mile of the church; south of Tahiti; to be robbed of one's money.* **2.** (used to indicate derivation, origin, or source): *a man of good family; the plays of O'Neill; a piece of cake.* **3.** (used to indicate cause, motive, occasion, or reason): *to die of hunger.* **4.** (used to indicate material, component parts, substance, or contents): *a dress of silk; an apartment of three rooms; a package of cheese.* **5.** (used to indicate apposition or identity): *Is that idiot of a salesman calling again?* **6.** (used to indicate specific identity or a particular item within a category): *the city of Chicago; thoughts of love.* **7.** (used to indicate possession, connection, or association): *the king of France; the property of the church.* **8.** (used to indicate inclusion in a number, class, or whole): *one of us.* **9.** (used to indicate the objective relation, the object of the action noted by the preceding noun or the application of a verb or adjective): *the ringing of bells; He writes her of home; I'm tired of working.* **10.** (used to indicate reference or respect): *talk of peace.* **11.** (used to indicate qualities or attributes): *a man of tact.* **12.** (used to indicate time): *They arrived of an evening.* **13.** (used to indicate time to or before a designated hour of the clock): *twenty minutes of five.* **14.** on the part of: *It was very mean of you to insult her.* **15.** in respect to: *fleet of foot.* **16.** *Archaic.* (used to indicate the agent by whom or by which an action is carried through): *consumed of worms.* [ME, OE; c. G, L *ab,* Gk *apó.* See OFF]

of² (əv), *auxiliary v.* *Nonstandard.* have: *He should of asked me first.*

of-, var. of **ob-** (by assimilation) before *f: offend.*

OF, Old French. Also, **OF., O.F.**

O'Fal·lon (ō fal′ən), *n.* **1.** a town in SW Illinois. 4018 (1960). **2.** a town in E Missouri. 3770 (1960).

O'Fao·láin (ō fā′lən, ō fal′ən), *n.* **Seán** (shôn), born 1900, Irish writer and teacher.

o·fay (ō′fā), *n.* *Disparaging.* a white person. Also, **fay.** [?]

off (ôf, of), *adv.* **1.** so as to be no longer supported or attached: *This drawer pull is about to come off.* **2.** so as to be no longer covering or enclosing: *Take your hat off. Can you get the wrapping off?* **3.** away from a place: *to run off; to look off toward the west.* **4.** away from a path, course, etc.; aside: *This road branches off to Grove City.* **5.** away from or out of association or relation: *to cast off.* **6.** away from what is considered normal, regular, standard, or the like: *to go off on a tangent.* **7.** from a charge or price: *He took 10 percent off for all cash purchases.* **8.** at a distance in space or future time: *Back off a few feet. Summer is only a week off.* **9.** out of operation or effective existence: *Turn the lights off.* **10.** so as to interrupt continuity or cause discontinuance: *Negotiations have been broken off.* **11.** in absence from work, service, a job, etc.: *We get two days off at Christmas. We have Friday off.* **12.** completely; utterly: *to kill off.* **13.** with prompt or ready performance: *to dash a letter off.* **14.** to fulfillment, or into execution or effect: *The contest came off on the day fixed.* **15.** into nothingness: *My headache passed off soon.* **16.** so as to be delineated, divided, or apportioned: *Mark it off into three equal parts.* **17.** away from a state of consciousness: *I must have dozed off.* **18.** *Naut.* away from the land, a ship, the wind, etc. **19. be off,** to depart; leave: *I must be off now.* **20. off and on, a.** Also, **on and off.** with intervals between; intermittently: *to work off and on.* **b.** *Naut.* on alternate tacks. **21. off with,** take away! remove!: *Off with him! Off with his head!* —*prep.* **22.** so as to no longer to be supported by, attached to, on, resting on, or unified with: *Take your feet off the table! Break off a piece of bread.* **23.** deviating from: *off balance; You are off course.* **24.** below or less than the usual or expected level or standard: *25 percent off the marked price; I was off my golf game and finished in the 90's.* **25.** away, disengaged, or resting from: *to be off duty on Tuesdays.* **26.** *Informal.* refraining or abstaining from; denying oneself the pleasure, company, practice, etc., of: *He's off women since she jilted him. I'm off gambling.* **27.** away from; apart or distant from: *a village off the main road.* **28.** leading into or away from: *an alley off 12th Street.* **29.** not fixed on or directed toward, as the gaze, eyes, etc.: *His eyes weren't off the king for a moment.* **30.** *Informal.* from (a specified source): *I bought it off him.* **31.** from or of, indicating material or component parts: *to make a meal off fish.* **32.** so as to no longer covering or enclosing: *Take the lid off the box.* **33.** *Naut.* at some distance to seaward of: *off Cape Hatteras.* —*adj.* **34.** in error; wrong: *You are off on that point.* **35.** slightly abnormal or not quite sane: *He is a little off, but he's really harmless.* **36.** not up to standard; not so good or satisfactory as usual; inferior or subnormal: *The accompanist's playing was slightly off during the second song.* **37.** no longer in effect, in operation, or in process: *The agreement is off. The electricity is off because of the storm.* **38.** noting a state of being, condition, circumstances, etc.: *He's well off now. You're better off this way.* **39.** (of time) free from work or duty; nonworking: *a pastime for one's off hours.* **40.** of less than the ordinary activity, liveliness, or lively interest: *an off season in the woolen trade.* **41.** more distant; farther: *the off side of a wall.* **42.** (in riding or driving) on the right (opposed to *near*). **43.** starting; beginning: *I'm off to Europe on Monday. They're off and running in the third race at Aqueduct.* **44.** not working at one's usual occupation: *We're off Wednesdays during the summer.* **45.** *Naut.* noting one of two like things that is the farther from the shore; seaward: *the off side of the ship.* **46.** *Cricket.* noting or pertaining to that side of the wicket or of the field opposite that on which the batsman stands. —*n.* **47.** the state or fact of being off. **48.** *Cricket.* the off side. —*interj.* **49.** be off! stand off! off with you! [ME, OE *of,* var. of OF¹ when stressed]

—**Usage.** Despite the frequency with which it is heard, OFF OF in a construction like, *I asked him to keep off of the freshly varnished floor,* is considered nonstandard, largely because it is redundant and poor style. OFF, without OF, is sufficient to express the same notion.

off., **1.** offered. **2.** office. **3.** officer. **4.** official.

of·fal (ô′fəl, of′əl), *n.* **1.** the parts of a butchered animal that are considered inedible by human beings; carrion. **2.** refuse in general; rubbish; garbage. [ME, equiv. to *of* OFF + *fal* FALL]

Of·fa·ly (ô′fə lē, of′ə-), *n.* a county in Leinster, in the central Republic of Ireland. 51,533 (1961); 760 sq. mi. *Co. seat:* Tullamore.

off·beat (*adj.* ôf′bēt′, of′-; *n.* ôf′bēt′, of′-), *adj.* **1.** differing from the usual or expected; unconventional: *an offbeat theatrical presentation with the performers dressed in rehearsal clothes.* —*n.* **2.** *Music.* an unaccented beat of a measure. [OFF + BEAT]

off′ Broad′way, professional drama produced in New York City away from the Broadway area and characterized chiefly by experimental and low-budget productions. —**off′-Broad′way,** *adj.*

off·cast (ôf′kast′, -käst′, of′-), *adj.* **1.** discarded or rejected; castoff: *his offcast suits.* —*n.* **2.** a castoff person or thing. [adj., n. use of v. phrase *cast off*]

off-cen·ter (ôf′sen′tər, of′-), *adj.* Also, **off′-cen′tered.** 1. missing or diverging from the exact center. 2. out of balance or alignment: *Isn't that painting off-center?* 3. out of proportion, or reason: *an off-center argument.* —*adv.* 4. so as to be out of balance or alignment: *to hang a painting off-center.*

off′ chance′, a very slight possibility or likelihood; remote chance.

off-col·or (ôf′kul′ər, of′-), *adj.* 1. not having the usual or standard color: *an off-color gem.* 2. of doubtful propriety or taste; risqué: *an off-color joke.* 3. not in one's usual health: *to feel off-color.* Also, *esp. Brit.,* **off′-col′our.**

Of·fen·bach (ô′fən bäk′, of′ən-; *for 1 also Fr.* ô fen-bak′; *for 2 also Ger.* ôf′ən bäᴋʜ′), *n.* 1. **Jacques** (zhäk), 1819–80, French composer. 2. a city in S Hesse, in central West Germany, on the Main River, near Frankfurt. 118,000 (1963).

of·fence (ə fens′, ô′fens, of′ens), *n.* offense.

of·fend (ə fend′), *v.t.* 1. to irritate or vex the mind or feelings of; cause resentful displeasure in: *Even the mildest criticism offends her.* 2. to affect (the sense, taste, etc.) disagreeably. 3. to violate or transgress a religious or moral law. 4. to hurt or cause pain to. 5. (in Biblical use) to cause to fall into sinful ways. —*v.i.* 6. to cause resentful displeasure; give offense: *a commercial so blatant it can only offend.* 7. to err in conduct; commit a sin, crime, or fault. [ME *offend(en)* < MF *offend(re)* < L *offendere* to strike against, displease, equiv. to *of-* OF- + *fendare* to strike] —**of·fend′a·ble, of·fend′i·ble,** *adj.* —**of·fend′ed·ly,** *adv.* —**of·fend′ed·ness,** *n.* —**of·fend′er,** *n.*
—**Syn.** 1. provoke, annoy, chafe, nettle, affront, insult. 7. transgress. —**Ant.** 1. please.

of·fense (ə fens′, ô′fens, of′ens), *n.* 1. a violation or breaking of a law or rule; transgression; sin. 2. a transgression of the criminal law, esp. one which is not a felony. 3. a cause of transgression or wrong. 4. something that offends or displeases. 5. the act of offending or displeasing. 6. the feeling of resentful displeasure caused: *to give offense.* 7. the act of attacking; attack or assault: *weapons of offense.* 8. a person, side, team, army, etc., attacking. 9. *Obs.* injury, harm, or hurt. Also, **offence.** [ME *offence, offense* < MF *offense* << L *offēns(a),* fem. ptp. of *offendere* to strike against (see OFFEND)]
—**Syn.** 1. trespass, misdemeanor, felony, fault. See **crime.** 6. umbrage, resentment, wrath, indignation. 7. aggression. 8. besiegers, attackers, enemy, foe. —**Ant.** 6. pleasure. 7. defense.

of·fense·less (ə fens′lis), *adj.* 1. without offense. 2. incapable of offense or attack. 3. not offensive. Also, **of·fence′less.** [OFFENSE + -LESS] —**of·fense′less·ly,** *adv.*

of·fen·sive (ə fen′siv, ô′fen-, of′en-), *adj.* 1. causing resentful displeasure; highly irritating or annoying: *offensive television commercials.* 2. unpleasant or disagreeable to the sense: *an offensive smell.* 3. repugnant to the moral sense, good taste, or the like; insulting: *an offensive remark; an offensive joke.* 4. pertaining to offense or attack: *offensive movements.* 5. characterized by attack; aggressive: *offensive warfare.* —*n.* 6. the position or attitude of aggression or attack: *to take the offensive.* 7. an aggressive movement or attack: *the Vietcong summer offensive.* [< ML *offensīv(us),* equiv. to L *offens(us)* (see OFFENSE) + *-īvus* -IVE] —**of·fen′sive·ly,** *adv.* —**of·fen′sive·ness,** *n.*
—**Syn.** 1. displeasing, vexatious, vexing, unpleasant. See **hateful.** 2, 3. distasteful, disgusting, revolting, repellent. 3. repulsive, shocking. 4. invading, attacking. —**Ant.** 1, 2. pleasing. 4. defensive.

of·fer (ô′fər, of′ər), *v.t.* 1. to present for acceptance or rejection; proffer: *He offered me a cigarette.* 2. to propose or put forward for consideration: *to offer a suggestion.* 3. to make a show of intention (to do something): *We did not offer to go first.* 4. to propose or volunteer (to do something): *She offered to accompany me.* 5. to present or volunteer (oneself) to someone as a spouse. 6. to present solemnly as an act of worship or devotion, as to God, a deity, a saint, etc.; sacrifice. 7. to give, make, or promise: *She offered no response. The doctor offered no hope.* 8. to attempt to inflict, do, or make: *to offer battle.* 9. to do, make, or threaten (violence, resistance, etc.): *to offer someone a blow.* 10. to present to sight or notice; introduce or present for exhibition or performance. 11. to present for sale: *He offered the painting to me at a reduced price.* 12. to tender or bid as a price: *to offer ten dollars for a radio.* 13. to render (homage, thanks, etc.). —*v.i.* 14. to make a proposal or suggestion. 15. to suggest oneself to someone for marriage; propose. 16. to present itself; occur: *Whenever an occasion offered, he slipped off to town.* 17. to present something as an act of worship or devotion; sacrifice. 18. *Archaic.* to make an attempt (fol. by *at*). —*n.* 19. the act or an instance of offering: *an offer of help.* 20. a proposal of marriage. 21. a proposal or bid to give or pay something as the price of something else; bid: *an offer of $30,000 for a house.* 22. the condition of being offered: *an offer for sale.* 23. something offered. 24. *Law.* a proposal which requires only acceptance in order to create a contract. 25. an attempt or endeavor. 26. a show of intention. [ME *offre(n),* OE *offrian* < L *offerre,* equiv. to *ob-* OB- + *ferre* to BEAR[1]] —**of′fer·a·ble,** *adj.* —**of′fer·er, of′fer·or,** *n.*
—**Syn.** 1. OFFER, PROFFER, TENDER mean to present for acceptance or refusal. OFFER is a common word in general use for presenting something to be accepted or rejected: *to offer assistance.* PROFFER, with the same meaning, is now chiefly a literary word: *to proffer one's services.* TENDER (no longer used in reference to concrete objects) is a ceremonious term for a more or less formal or conventional act: *to tender one's resignation.* 2. give, move, propose. —**Ant.** 1. withdraw, withhold. 19. refusal, denial.

Of·fer (ô′fər, of′ər), *n.* a boy's given name.

of·fer·ing (ô′fər ing, of′ər-), *n.* 1. something offered in worship or devotion, as to God, a deity, etc.; an oblation or sacrifice. 2. a contribution given to or through the church for a particular purpose, as at a service. 3. anything offered as a gift. 4. something presented for inspection or sale. 5. a sale: *our spring offering of furniture.* 6. the act of one who offers. [ME; OE *offrun.* See OFFER, -ING[1]]

of·fer·to·ry (ô′fər tôr′ē, -tōr′ē, of′ər-), *n., pl.* **-ries.** 1. (*sometimes cap.*) the offering of the unconsecrated elements that is made to God by the celebrant in a Eucharistic service. 2. *Eccles.* **a.** the verses, anthem, or music said, sung, or played while the offerings of the people are received at a religious service. **b.** that part of a service at which offerings are made. **c.** the offerings themselves. [ME *offertorie* < ML *offetōri(um)* place to which offerings were brought, offering, oblation, equiv. to L *offert(us)* (ptp. of *offerre* to OFFER) + *-ōrium* -ORY[2]] —**of′fer·to′ri·al,** *adj.*

off·hand (ôf′hand′, of′-), *adv.* 1. without previous thought or preparation; extempore: *to decide offhand to take a trip.* 2. cavalierly, curtly, or brusquely: *to reply offhand.* —*adj.* 3. Also, **off′hand′ed.** done or made offhand. 4. informal or casual: *an offhand manner.* 5. *Glassmaking.* working manually and without the use of molds: *offhand blowing; offhand glass fabrication.* [OFF + HAND] —**off′hand′ed·ly,** *adv.* —**off′hand′ed·ness,** *n.*
—**Syn.** 2. short, abrupt. 4. impromptu, extempore. —**Ant.** 4. considered.

off-hour (*n.* ôf′our′, -ou′ər, -our′, -ou′ər, of′-; *adj.* ôf′our′, -ou′ər, of′-), *n.* 1. an hour or other period when one is off duty: *I spent my off-hour reading.* 2. a period outside of rush hours or greatest activity: *Travel by subway during the off-hours. Go to the fish market in the off-hours.* —*adj.* 3. of, pertaining to, or during an off-hour: *hoping the off-hour traffic would be lighter.*

of·fice (ô′fis, of′is), *n.* 1. a room, set of rooms, or building where the business of a commercial or industrial organization or of a professional person is transacted: *the home office of an insurance company; a doctor's office.* 2. a room assigned to a specific person or a group of persons in a commercial or industrial organization: *All employees come to my office in five minutes.* 3. a business or professional organization: *He went to work in an architect's office.* 4. a building or a set of rooms devoted to the business of a branch of a governmental organization: *a post office.* 5. the staff or designated part of a staff at a commercial or industrial organization: *The whole office was at her wedding. The accounting office starts work at nine thirty.* 6. a position of duty, trust, or authority, esp. in the government, a corporation, a society, or the like: *He was elected twice to the office of president.* 7. employment or position as an official: *to seek office.* 8. the duty, function, or part of a particular person or agency: *to act in the office of adviser.* 9. a service or task to be performed; assignment; chore: *little domestic offices.* 10. *Slang.* hint, signal, or warning (prec. by *the*). 11. Often, **offices.** something, whether good or bad, done or said for or to another: *He obtained a position through the good offices of a friend.* 12. *Eccles.* **a.** the prescribed order or form for a service of the church or for devotional use. **b.** the services so prescribed. **c.** Also called **divine office.** the prayers, readings from Scripture, and psalms that must be recited every day by all who are in major orders. **d.** a ceremony or rite, esp. for the dead. 13. (*cap.*) *Chiefly Brit.* a major administrative unit of the national government; a govermental department: *the Foreign Office.* 14. **offices,** *Chiefly Brit.* **a.** the parts of a house, as the kitchen, pantry, laundry, etc., devoted to household work. **b.** the stables, barns, cowhouses, etc., of a farm. [ME < OF < L *offic(ium)* service, duty, ceremony, equiv. to *op(us)* work + *-fic* -FIC + *-ium* n. suffix] —**of′fice·less,** *adj.*
—**Syn.** 6. post, station, berth, situation. See **appointment.** 8. responsibility, charge, trust. 9. work, duty.

of′fice block′, *Brit.* a large office building.

of′fice-block bal′lot (ô′fis blok′, of′is-), a ballot on which the candidates are listed alphabetically, with or without their party designations, in columns under the office for which they were nominated. Cf. **Indiana ballot, Massachusetts ballot.**

of′fice boy′, a boy employed in an office to run errands, do odd jobs, etc.

of·fice·hold·er (ô′fis hōl′dər, of′is-), *n.* a person filling a governmental position. [OFFICE + HOLDER]

of′fice hours′, 1. the hours a person spends working in an office. 2. the hours during which a professional man or an office conducts regular business.

Of′fice of Civ′il and Defense′ Mobiliza′tion, *U.S.* the division of the Executive Office of the President that institutes and administers all federal programs dealing with the defense by civilians of their homes, families, communities, etc., in the event of enemy attack. *Abbr.:* OCDM

Of′fice of Defense′ Transporta′tion, *U.S.* the former federal agency (1941–1945) that regulated the transport over public routes of goods considered vital to the war effort. *Abbr.:* ODT

Of′fice of Econom′ic Opportun′ity, (in the U.S.) a division of the Executive Office of the President that administers and coordinates federal programs of basic education and job training to eliminate poverty. *Abbr.:* OEO

Of′fice of Price′ Administra′tion. See **OPA.**

Of′fice of War′ Informa′tion. See **OWI.**

of·fi·cer (ô′fi sər, of′i-), *n.* 1. one who holds a position of rank or authority in the army, navy, or any similar organization, esp. one who holds a commission in the army or navy. 2. a policeman or constable. 3. a person licensed to take full or partial responsibility for the operation of a merchant vessel or other large civilian vessel; a master or mate. 4. a person appointed or elected to some position of responsibility or authority in the government, a corporation, a society, etc. 5. (in some honorary orders) a member of any rank except the lowest. 6. *Obs.* an agent. —*v.t.* 7. to furnish with officers. 8. to command or direct as an officer does. 9. to direct, conduct, or manage. [ME < MF *officier* < ML *officiār(ius),* equiv. to L *offici(um)* OFFICE + *-ārius* -ER[1]] —**of·fi·ce·ri·al** (ô′fi sēr′ē əl, of′i-), *adj.* —**of′fi·cer·less,** *adj.* —**of′fi·cer·ship′, of′fi·cer·hood′,** *n.*

of′ficer of the day′, *Mil.* an officer who has charge of the guard and prisoners on an assigned day at a military installation. *Abbr.:* O.D.

of′ficer of the guard′, *Mil.* an officer, acting under the officer of the day, who is responsible for the instruction, discipline, and performance of duty of the guard in a post, camp, or station.

of′ficer of the watch′, *Naut.* the officer primarily responsible for the navigation of a ship, in the absence of the captain, during a certain watch.

of′fice seek′er, a person who seeks public office.

of·fi·cial (ə fish′əl), *n.* 1. a person appointed or elected to an office or charged with certain duties, esp. in the government. —*adj.* 2. of or pertaining to an office or position of duty, trust, or authority: *official powers.* 3. authorized or issued authoritatively: *an official report.* 4. holding office. 5. appointed or authorized to act in a designated capacity: *an official representative.* 6. (of an activity or event) intended for the notice of the public and performed or held on behalf of officials or of an organization; formal: *the official opening of a store; the official laying of a cornerstone.* 7. *Pharm.* noting drugs or drug preparations which are recognized by and which conform to the standards of the *United States Pharmacopeia* or the *National Formulary.* [< LL *officiāl(is)* of duty, equiv. to L *offici(um)* OFFICE + *-ālis* -AL[1]] —**of·fi′cial·ly,** *adv.*

of·fi·cial·dom (ə fish′əl dəm), *n.* 1. the position or domain of officials. 2. the class or entire body of officials; officials as a whole. [OFFICIAL + -DOM]

of·fi·cial·ese (ə fish′ə lēz′, -lēs′), *n.* a style of language used in official pronouncements, often criticized for its use of polysyllabic jargon and obscure, pretentiously wordy phrasing. [OFFICIAL + -ESE]

of·fi·cial·ise (ə fish′ə līz′), *v.t.,* **-ised, -is·ing.** *Chiefly Brit.* officialize. —**of·fi′cial·i·sa′tion,** *n.*

of·fi·cial·ism (ə fish′ə liz′əm), *n.* 1. official methods or systems. 2. excessive attention to official regulations and routines. 3. officials collectively. [OFFICIAL + -ISM]

of·fi·cial·ize (ə fish′ə līz′), *v.t.,* **-ized, -iz·ing.** to make official; place under official authority or control. Also, *esp. Brit.,* **officialise.** [OFFICIAL + -IZE] —**of·fi′cial·i·za′tion,** *n.*

of·fi·ci·ant (ə fish′ē ənt), *n.* a person who officiates at a religious service or ceremony. [< ML *officiant-* (s. of *officiāns,* prp. of *officiāre*) officiating, equiv. to L *offici(um)* OFFICE + *-ant-* -ANT]

of·fi·ci·ar·y (ə fish′ē er′ē), *adj.* 1. pertaining to or derived from an office, as a title. 2. having a title or rank derived from an office, as a dignitary. [< L *offici(um)* OFFICE + -ARY]

of·fi·ci·ate (ə fish′ē āt′), *v.,* **-at·ed, -at·ing.** —*v.i.* 1. to perform the duties or function of some office or position. 2. to perform the office of a priest or minister, as at divine service. —*v.t.* 3. to perform, carry out, or fulfill (an official duty or function). 4. to serve as the priest or minister of (a divine service, religious ceremony, etc.): *Father O'Toole officiated the wedding.* 5. to act as a referee, umpire, timekeeper, or other official for (a sports contest or game). [< ML *officiāt(us)* officiated (ptp. of *officiāre*), equiv. to L *offici(um)* + *-ātus* -ATE[1]] —**of·fi′ci·a′tion,** *n.* —**of·fi′ci·a′tor,** *n.*

of·fic·i·nal (ə fis′ə nəl), *adj.* 1. kept in stock by apothecaries, as a drug. Cf. **magistral** (def. 1). 2. recognized by a pharmacopoeia. —*n.* 3. an officinal medicine. [< ML *officināl(is)* of a storeroom, equiv. to L *officīn(a)* workshop, sp. var. of *opificīna* (*opific-,* s. of *opifex* artisan, equiv. to *opi-,* var. of *opus* work + *-fic* -FIC, + *-in(a)* -INE[1]) + *-ālis* -AL[1]] —**of·fic′i·nal·ly,** *adv.*

of·fi·cious (ə fish′əs), *adj.* 1. objectionably forward in offering one's unrequested and unwanted services, help, or advice; meddlesome: *an officious person.* 2. marked by or proceeding from such forwardness: *officious interference.* 3. *Obs.* ready to serve; obliging. [< L *officiōs(us)* obliging, dutiful, equiv. to *offici(um)* OFFICE + *-ōsus* -OUS] —**of·fi′cious·ly,** *adv.* —**of·fi′cious·ness,** *n.*
—**Syn.** 1. interfering, meddling. —**Ant.** 1. retiring.

offi′cious will′, *Law.* a will by which the testator gives his property to the natural objects of his bounty, as his family. Also called **offi′cious tes′tament.** Cf. **inofficious will.**

off·ing (ô′fing, of′ing), *n.* 1. the more distant part of the sea seen from the shore, beyond the anchoring ground. 2. a position at a distance from shore. 3. **in the offing, a.** at a distance but within sight. **b.** in the projected future; likely to happen: *I saw them together yesterday, and I would venture to say that a wedding is in the offing.* [OFF + -ING[1]]

off·ish (ô′fish, of′ish), *adj.* *Informal.* aloof; unapproachable. [OFF + -ISH[1]] —**off′ish·ly,** *adv.* —**off′ish·ness,** *n.*

off·lap (ôf′lap′, of′-), *n.* *Geol.* 1. the retreat of a sea from its shore. 2. the layer or layers or rock formed on a sea floor such a retreat. Cf. **onlap.** [OFF + LAP[3]]

off-li·cense (ôf′lī′səns, of′-), *Brit.* —*n.* 1. a license permitting a store to sell sealed bottles of liquor but not allowing drinking on the premises or the sale of individual drinks. 2. a store having such a license; package store. —*adj.* 3. possessing such a license.

off-lim·its (ôf′lim′its, of′-), *adj.* forbidden to be patronized or frequented, as by certain persons: *a bar off-limits to soldiers.*

off-line (ôf′līn′, of′-), *adj.* (in data processing) operating independently of the main computer.

off-mike (ôf′mīk′, of′-), *adj.* located at a distance from or not projected directly into a microphone: *off-mike sound effects.*

off-peak (ôf′pēk′, of′-), *adj.* lower than the maximum: *off-peak operation.*

off·print (ôf′print′, of′-), *n.* 1. Also called **separate.** a reprint in separate form of an article which originally appeared as part of a larger publication. —*v.t.* 2. to reprint separately, as an article from a larger publication. [trans. of G *Abdruck*]

off·scour·ing (ôf′skour′ing, -skou′ər-, of′-), *n.* Often, **offscourings.** that which is scoured off; filth; refuse. [OFF + SCOURING, after v. phrase *scour off*]

off·screen (ôf′skrēn′, of′-), *adj.* 1. occurring, existing, or done away from the motion-picture screen, or in actual life: *The star's offscreen personality was at variance with her movie image.* —*adv.* 2. outside the range of the motion-picture camera, or in actual life. [OFF + SCREEN]

off-sea·son (ôf′sē′zən, of′-), *adj.* 1. being a time of year other than the regular or most popular season for a specific activity; out of season: *an off-season jaunt to the beach; an off-season job for a baseball player in the winter.* —*adv.* 2. in or during the off-season: *Traveling off-season is the easiest way to save vacation money.* —*n.* 3. a time of year other than the regular or most popular one for a specific activity: *Fares* *are lower when one travels in the off-season.* **4.** a time of year when business, manufacturing activity, etc., is less than normal or at an unusually low point.

off·set (*n., adj.* ôf′set′, of′-; *v.* ôf′set′, of′-), *n. adj., v.,* **-set, -set·ting.** —*n.* **1.** something that juxtaposes or counterbalances; a compensating equivalent. **2.** the start, beginning, or outset. **3.** a short lateral shoot by which certain plants are propagated. **4.** an offshoot or branch of a family or race. **5.** any offshoot; branch. **6.** a spur of a mountain range. **7.** Also called **offset lithography.** *Lithog.* **a.** a process in which a lithographic stone or metal or paper plate is used to make an inked impression on a rubber blanket which transfers it to the paper being printed, instead of being made directly on the paper. **b.** the impression itself. **8.** Also called **setoff.** *Print.* an unintentional transfer of excess or undried ink from one printed sheet to another. **9.** *Mach.* a jog or short displacement in an otherwise straight and continuous line, as in a pipe, lever, rod, etc., made to avoid objects or to connect with other parts. **10.** *Archit.* setoff (def. 3). **11.** *Survey.* **a.** a short distance measured perpendicularly from a main survey line. **b.** Also called **off′set line′.** a line a short distance from and parallel to a main survey line. **12.** *Naval Archit.* any of the coordinates by which any point on a hull being planned is located. —*adj.* **13.** of, noting, or pertaining to an offset. **14.** *Lithog.* pertaining to, printed by, or suitable for printing by, offset. **15.** placed off a center line; off-center. **16.** placed at an angle to something, as to the axis of a form, shape, object, etc.; not parallel. —*v.t.* **17.** to juxtapose with something else, as for purposes of comparison: *to offset debits against credits.* **18.** to counterbalance as an equivalent does; compensate for: *The gains offset the losses.* **19.** *Print.* **a.** to make an offset of. **b.** to print by the process of offset lithography. **20.** *Archit.* to build with a setoff, as a wall. **21.** *Survey.* to establish (a line) parallel to a main survey line at an offset. —*v.i.* **22.** to project as an offset or branch. **23.** *Print.* to make an offset. [OFF + SET, after v. phrase *set off*]
—**Syn. 2.** onset. **18.** match, parallel; counterweight, counterpoise; counteract.

off′set lithog′raphy, *Lithog.* offset (def. 7).

off·shoot (ôf′sho͞ot′, of′-), *n.* **1.** a branch or lateral shoot from a main stem, as of a plant. **2.** a branch, or a descendant or scion, of a family or race. **3.** anything conceived of as springing or proceeding from a main stock: *an offshoot of a discussion.* [OFF + SHOOT]

off·shore (ôf′shôr′, -shōr′, of′-), *adv.* **1.** off or away from the shore: *They pushed the boat offshore.* **2.** at a distance from the shore. —*adj.* **3.** moving or tending away from the shore: *an offshore wind.* **4.** located or operating at some distance from the shore: *offshore fisheries; offshore oil.* [OFF + SHORE[1]]

off′shore dock′, *Naut.* a floating dock moored to pilings, dolphins, etc., used for cleaning and repairing medium-sized vessels.

off·side (ôf′sīd′, of′-), *adj., adv.* **1.** *Sports.* illegally beyond a prescribed line or area or in advance of the ball or puck at the beginning of or during play or a play: *The touchdown was nullified because the left tackle was offside. The guard ran offside.* **2.** with or in doubtful propriety or taste; risqué: *an offside joke; He spoke offside.* [OFF + SIDE[1]]

off·sid·er (ôf′sī′dər, of′-), *n.* *Australian.* **1.** an assistant or helper. **2.** a follower or supporter of a person or cause. [OFFSIDE + -ER[1]]

off·spring (ôf′spring′, of′-), *n., pl.* **-spring, -springs.** **1.** children or young of a particular parent or progenitor. **2.** a child or animal in relation to its parent or parents. **3.** a descendant. **4.** descendants collectively. **5.** the product, result, or effect of something: *the offspring of an inventive mind.* [ME, OE; see OFF, SPRING (v.)]

off·stage (ôf′stāj′, of′-), *adv.* **1.** off the stage or in the wings; away from the view of the audience (opposed to *onstage*). —*adj.* **2.** not in view of the audience; backstage, in the wings, etc.: *a terrible offstage crash.* [OFF + STAGE]

off′ stump′, *Cricket.* the outside stump opposite the one at which the batsman takes his position. Cf. **leg stump, middle stump.**

off·take (ôf′tāk′, of′-), *n.* a pipe or passage for conducting smoke, a current of air, or the like, to an uptake or downtake. [n. use of v. phrase *take off*]

off-the-cuff (ôf′thə kuf′, of′-), *adj.* *Informal.* with little or no preparation; impromptu: *a speaker with a good off-the-cuff delivery.*

off-the-face (ôf′thə fās′, of′-), *adj.* **1.** (of the style of a woman's hairdo or hat) not covering, framing, or shading the face: *replacing her picture hat with an off-the-face model.* —*adv.* **2.** so as not to cover, frame, or shade the face: *She wears her hair off-the-face. Although it was designed to dip in front, she wore the hat off-the-face.*

off-the-peg (ôf′thə peg′, of′-), *adj.* *Brit.* ready-to-wear.

off-the-wall (ôf′thə wôl′, of′-), *adj.* *Slang.* **1.** surprisingly unusual or unconventional: *an off-the-wall remark.* **2.** bizarre; freakish: *off-the-wall behavior.* **3.** impromptu; unexpected.

off-white (ôf′hwīt′, -wīt′, of′-), *adj.* **1.** white mixed with a small amount of gray, yellow, or other light color. —*n.* **2.** an off-white color.

off′ year′, **1.** a year marked by reduced or inferior production or activity in a particular field, as farming, business, sports, etc.: *With its wet, cold summer, this was an off year for grapes.* **2.** a year without a major election. —**off′-year′,** *adj.*

Of Hu′man Bond′age, a novel (1915) by W. Somerset Maugham.

O'Fla·her·ty (ō fla′hər tē), *n.* **Li·am** (lē′əm), born 1896, Irish novelist.

OFlem, Old Flemish.

O.F.M., Order of Friars Minor (Franciscan). [< L *Ordo Fratrum Minorum*]

Of Mice′ and Men′, a novel (1937) and play (1938) by John Steinbeck.

OFr., Old French.

OFris., Old Frisian.

oft (ôft, oft), *adv.* *Literary.* often. [ME *oft(e),* OE *oft;* c. G *oft*]

of·ten (ô′fən, of′ən *or, sometimes,* ôf′tən, of′-), *adv.* **1.** many times; frequently. **2.** in many cases. —*adj.* **3.** *Archaic.* frequent. [ME *oftin,* var. before vowels of *ofte* OFT] —**of′ten·ness,** *n.*
—**Syn. 1, 2.** repeatedly, customarily. OFTEN, FREQUENTLY, GENERALLY, USUALLY refer to experiences which are customary. OFTEN and FREQUENTLY may be used interchangeably in most cases, but OFTEN implies numerous repetitions and, sometimes, regularity of recurrence: *We often go there;* FREQUENTLY suggests esp. repetition at comparatively short intervals: *It happens frequently.* GENERALLY refers to place and means universally: *It is generally understood. He is generally liked;* but it is often used as a colloquial substitute for USUALLY. In this sense, GENERALLY, like USUALLY, refers to time, and means in numerous instances. GENERALLY, however, extends in range from the merely numerous to a majority of possible instances; whereas USUALLY means practically always: *The train is generally on time. We usually have hot summers.* —**Ant. 1, 2.** seldom.

of·ten·times (ô′fən tīmz′, of′ən- *or, sometimes,* ôf′tən, of′-), *adv.* often. Also, **oft·times** (ôft′tīmz′, oft′-, ôf′-, of′-). [ME; see OFTEN, TIME, -S[1]]

Of Time′ and the Riv′er, a novel (1935) by Thomas Wolfe.

O.G., **1.** Officer of the Guard. **2.** *Archit.* ogee (def. 2). **3.** *Philately.* See **o.g.** (def. 1).

o.g., **1.** *Philately.* original gum: the gum on the back of a stamp when it is issued to the public. **2.** *Archit.* ogee (def. 2).

O·gal·lal·a (ō′gə lal′ə), *n.* a town in central Nebraska. 4250 (1960).

og·am (og′əm, ō′gəm), *n.* ogham.

O·ga·sa·wa·ra Ji·ma (ō′gä sä wä′rä jē′mä), Japanese name of **Bonin Islands.**

O gauge, **1.** a model railroad gauge of 1¼ inches, used either with a scale of ¼ inch or 17/64 inch to the foot. **2.** Also called **Q gauge.** a model railroad gauge of 13/16 inches with a scale of ¼ inch to the foot.

Og·bo·mo·sho (og′bə mō′shō), *n.* a city in SW Nigeria. 319,881 (1963).

Og·burn (og′bûrn), *n.* **William Fielding,** 1886–1959, U.S. sociologist and educator.

Og·den (ôg′den, og′-), *n.* **1. Charles Kay,** 1889–1957, British psychologist and linguist, inventor of Basic English. **2.** a city in N Utah. 70,197 (1960). **3.** a boy's given name.

Og·dens·burg (ôg′dənz bûrg′, og′-), *n.* a city in NE New York, on the St. Lawrence River. 16,122 (1960).

og·do·ad (og′dō ad′), *n.* **1.** the number eight. **2.** a group of eight. **3.** (*cap.*) *Egyptian Religion.* See under **heh deity.** [< LL *ogdoad-* (s. of *ogdoas*) < Gk *ogdoad(a),* equiv. to *oktō* OCTO- + *-ad* -AD[1]]

o·gee (ō jē′, ō′jē), *n.* **1.** a double curve, resembling the letter S, formed by the union of a concave and a convex line. **2.** Also called **gula.** *Archit.* a molding with such a curve for a profile; cyma. *Abbr.:* O.G., o.g. [var. of OGIVE]

o′gee arch′, *Archit.* an arch each haunch of which is an ogee with the concave side uppermost. See illus. under **arch.**

og·ham (og′əm, ō′gəm), *n.* **1.** an alphabetical script used originally for inscriptions in an archaic form of Irish, from about the 5th to the 10th centuries. **2.** any of the 20 characters of this script, each consisting of one or more straight lines drawn or carved perpendicularly or at an angle to a single long line or to the edge of a stone or piece of wood. **3.** an inscription employing this script. Also, **ogam.** [< Ir; MIr, OIr *ogam, ogum*]

O·gil·vie (ō′gəl vē), *n.* **John,** 1797–1867, Scottish lexicographer.

o·give (ō′jīv, ō jīv′), *n.* **1.** *Archit.* **a.** a diagonal vaulting rib. **b.** a pointed arch. **2.** *Statistics.* the distribution curve of a frequency distribution. **3.** *Rocketry.* the curved nose of a missile or rocket. [ME < MF *ogive, augive* < ?]

o·gle (ō′gəl), *v.,* **o·gled, o·gling,** *n.* —*v.t.* **1.** to look at amorously, flirtatiously, or impertinently. **2.** to eye; look or stare at. —*v.i.* **3.** to look amorously, flirtatiously, or impertinently. **4.** to look or stare. —*n.* **5.** an amorous, flirtatious, or impertinent glance. [appar. < freq. (cf. LG *oegeln,* G *äugeln*) of D *oogen* to eye, deriv. of *oog* eye]

O·gles·by (ō′gəlz bē), *n.* a town in N Illinois. 4215 (1960).

O·gle·thorpe (ō′gəl thôrp′), *n.* **James Edward,** 1696–1785, British general: founder of the colony of Georgia.

Og·ma (og′mə), *n.* *Irish Myth.* a god of poetry and eloquence and the inventor of the Ogham letters: one of the Tuatha De Danann.

Og·mi·os (og′mē ōs′), *n.* the ancient Gallic god of eloquence, identified by the Romans with Mercury.

OGO, Orbiting Geophysical Observatory.

Og·pu (og′po͞o), *n.* See **G.P.U.**

o·gre (ō′gər), *n.* **1.** a monster in fairy tales and popular legend, usually represented as a hideous giant who feeds on human flesh. **2.** a monstrously ugly, cruel, or barbarous person. [< F, ? < L *Orcus* ORCUS] —**o·gre·ish** (ō′gər ish), **o·grish** (ō′grish), *adj.* —**o′gre·ish·ly, o′grish·ly,** *adv.* —**o′gre·ism, o′grism,** *n.*

o·gress[1] (ō′gris), *n.* a female ogre. [< F *ogresse.* See OGRE, -ESS]

o·gress[2] (ō′gris), *n.* *Heraldry.* a roundel sable. Also called **pellet.** [?]

O·gyg·i·a (ō jij′ē ə), *n.* *Gk. Legend.* the island of Calypso.

Og·y·gus (oj′ə gəs), *n.* *Class. Myth.* a Boeotian king, the son of either Poseidon or the soil.

oh (ō), *interj., n., pl.* **oh's, ohs,** *v.* —*interj.* **1.** (used as an expression of surprise, pain, disapprobation, etc.) **2.** (used in direct address to attract the attention of the person spoken to): *Oh, John, will you take these books, please.* —*n.* **3.** the exclamation "oh." —*v.i.* **4.** to utter or exclaim "oh." [ME *o*]

O'Har·a (ō hâr′ə, ō har′ə), *n.* **John (Henry),** 1905–70, U.S. journalist, novelist, short-story writer, and scenarist.

O'Hare (ō hâr′), *n.* an airport in Chicago.

O. Hen·ry (ō hen′rē), pen name of William S. Porter.

OHG, Old High German. Also, **OHG., O.H.G.**

O'Hig·gins (ō hig′inz; *Sp.* ō ē′gēns), *n.* **1. Am·bro·sio** (äm brō′syō), (*Marqués de Osorno*), 1720?–1801, Irish soldier and administrator in South America. **2.** his son, **Ber·nar·do** (ber när′thō), (*Liberator of Chile*), 1778–1842, Chilean general and statesman.

O·hi·o (ō hī′ō), *n.* **1.** a State in the NE central United States: a part of the Midwest. 9,706,397 (1960); 41,222 sq. mi. *Cap.:* Columbus. *Abbr.:* O. **2.** a river formed by the confluence of the Allegheny and Monongahela rivers, flowing SW from Pittsburgh, Pennsylvania to the Mississippi in S Illinois. 981 mi. long.

Ohi′o buck′eye. See under **buckeye** (def. 1).

ohm (ōm), *n.* *Elect.* the meter-kilogram-second unit of resistance, equal to the resistance in a conductor in which one volt of potential difference produces a current of one ampere. *Symbol:* Ω [named after G. S. OHM] —**ohmic** (ō′mik), *adj.*

Ohm (ōm), *n.* **Georg Simon,** 1787–1854, German physicist.

ohm·age (ō′mij), *n.* *Elect.* electric resistance expressed in ohms. [OHM + -AGE]

ohm′ic resist′ance, *Elect.* resistance (def. 4a).

ohm·me·ter (ōm′mē′tər), *n.* *Elect.* an instrument for measuring electric resistance in ohms. [OHM + -METER]

O.H.M.S., On His Majesty's Service; On Her Majesty's Service.

Ohm's′ law′, *Elect.* the law that for any circuit the electric current is directly proportional to the voltage and is inversely proportional to the resistance. [named after G. S. OHM]

o·ho (ō hō′), *interj.* (used as an exclamation to express surprise, taunting, exultation, etc.) [ME]

o·hone (ə khōn′), *interj.* *Scot. and Irish Eng.* alas! Also, **ochone.** [< Scot, IrGael *ohōn*]

O·hře (ôr′zhə), *n.* a river in central Europe, flowing NE from Germany through the W Czech Republic to the Elbe. 193 mi. long. German, **Eger.**

Ohr·mazd (ôr′məzd), *n.* *Zoroastrianism.* See **Ahura Mazda.**

oi (oi), *interj.* oy[1].

OIcel, Old Icelandic.

-oid, a learned borrowing from Greek, meaning "resembling," "like," used in the formation of adjectives and nouns (and often implying an incomplete or imperfect resemblance to what is indicated by the preceding element): *alkaloid; anthropoid; cardioid; cuboid; lithoid; ovoid; planetoid.* Cf. **-ode**[1]. [< Gk *-oeidēs,* equiv. to *-ō-* -o- + *-eidēs* having the form of, deriv. of *eîdos* form]

-oidea, a suffix used in naming zoological classes or entomological superfamilies. [< NL, deriv. of *-oidēs* -OID; see -A]

o·id·i·um (ō id′ē əm), *n., pl.* **o·id·i·a** (ō id′ē ə). *Bot.* **1.** one of the conidia that are borne in chains by certain fungi. **2.** (in certain fungi) a thin-walled spore derived from the fragmentation of a hypha into its component cells. [< NL < Gk *ōi(ón)* egg (c. L *ovum;* see o-[3]) + *-idium* -IDIUM] —**o·id′i·oid′,** *adj.*

oik (oik), *n., pl.* **oicks, oiks.** *Brit. Slang.* a member of the lower classes, as one who tends to pronounce an (ī) sound as (oi).

oil (oil), *n.* **1.** any of a large class of substances typically unctuous, viscous, combustible, liquid at ordinary temperatures, and soluble in ether or alcohol but not in water; used for anointing, perfuming, lubricating, illuminating, heating, smoothing waves at sea in a storm, etc. **2.** a substance of this or similar consistency. **3.** petroleum. **4.** *Painting.* **a.** See **oil color. b.** See **oil painting. 5.** *Slang.* unctuous insincerity; flattery. **6.** an oilskin garment. **7. pour oil on troubled waters,** to attempt to calm a quarrel or a disturbance; pacify; calm. **8. strike oil, a.** to discover oil, esp. to bring in a well. **b.** to have good luck, esp. financially; make an important discovery: *They struck oil only after years of market research.* —*v.t.* **9.** to smear, lubricate, or supply with oil. **10.** to bribe. **11.** to make unctuous or smooth: *She oiled her words in order to sound persuasive.* **12.** to convert into oil by melting, as butter. —*adj.* **13.** pertaining to or resembling oil. **14.** concerned with the production or use of oil. **15.** made with oil. **16.** using oil, esp. as a fuel. **17.** obtained from oil. [ME *olie, oile* < OF < L *oleum* (olive) oil, deriv. of *olea* olive tree < Gk *elaía* OLIVE] —**oil′-less,** *adj.* —**oil′less·ness,** *n.* —**oil′like′,** *adj.*

oil′ bee′tle, any of several blister beetles of the genus *Meloe* that exude an oily fluid from the joints of their legs.

oil·bird (oil′bûrd′), *n.* guacharo. [OIL + BIRD]

oil′ cake′, a cake or mass of linseed, cottonseed, soybean, or the like, from which the oil has been extracted or expressed, used as food for livestock.

oil·can (oil′kan′), *n.* a can having a long spout through which oil is poured or squirted to lubricate machinery or the like. [OIL + CAN[2]]

Oil′ Cit′y, a city in NW Pennsylvania, on the Allegheny River. 17,692 (1960).

oil·cloth (oil′klôth′, -kloth′), *n., pl.* **-cloths** (-klôthz′, -klothz′, -klôths′, -kloths′) for 2. —*n.* **1.** a cotton fabric made waterproof by being treated with oil and pigment, for use as tablecloths, shelf coverings, and the like. **2.** a piece of this fabric. [OIL + CLOTH]

oil′ col′or, a paint made by grinding a pigment in oil, usually linseed oil.

oil·cup (oil′kup′), *n.* a closed cup or can supplying lubricant to a bearing or bearings. Also called **grease cup.** [OIL + CUP]

O·il′e·an A′jax (ō il′ē ən), *Class. Myth.* Ajax (def. 2).

oil·er (oi′lər), *n.* **1.** one who or that which oils. **2.** a workman employed to oil machinery. **3.** any of several devices, other than pressure devices, for feeding lubricating oil to a bearing. **4.** a can with a long spout, used for oiling machinery. **5.** Often, **oilers.** an oilskin garment, esp. a coat. **6.** a ship using oil as fuel. **7.** a cargo ship designed to transport oil; tanker. [OIL + -ER[1]]

O·i·le·us (ō il′ē əs, -ē o͞os′), *n.* *Class. Myth.* a king in Locris who was one of the Argonauts and the father of Ajax the Less and of Medon.

oil′ field′, an area in which there are large deposits of oil.

oil·fish (oil′fish′), *n., pl.* **-fish·es,** (*esp. collectively*) **-fish.** a snake mackerel, *Ruvettus pretiosus,* commonly found in deep, marine waters. [OIL + FISH]

oil′ gild′ing, gilding of glass or ceramic ware by using a size of japan or lacquer. Also, **oil′-gild′ing.**

oil′ gland′. See **uropygial gland.**

oil·let (oi′lit), *n.* eyelet (def. 4). [ME *oilet*]

oil·man (oil′man′, -mən), *n., pl.* **-men** (-men′, -mən). **1.** a person who owns or operates oil wells. **2.** a person who retails or delivers oil: *The oilman can't bring our order before Monday.* [OIL + MAN[1]]

oil′ meal′, oil cake ground into small particles for livestock feed.

oil′ of ben′. See under **ben**[2] (def. 1).

oil′ of cade′. See under **cade**[1].

oil′ of catechu′mens, holy oil used in baptism, the ordination of a cleric, the coronation of a sovereign, or in the consecration of a church.

oil′ of mir′bane (mûr′bān), nitrobenzene. Also, **oil′ of myr′bane.** [?]

oil′ of the sick′, holy oil used in the sacrament of extreme unction.

oil′ of tur′pentine, a colorless, flammable, volatile essential oil having a penetrating odor and a pungent, bitter taste, obtained from turpentine oleoresin by distillation: used in paints and varnishes, and in medicine as a carminative, vermifuge, expectorant, rubefacient, and, formerly, as a diuretic. Also called **spirits of turpentine, turpentine.**

oil′ of vit′riol, *Chem.* See **sulfuric acid.**

oil′ of win′tergreen. See **methyl salicylate.**

oil′ paint′, **1.** See **oil color.** **2.** a commercial paint in which a drying oil is the vehicle.

oil′ paint′ing, **1.** the art or technique of painting with oil colors. **2.** a painting executed in oil colors. **—oil′ paint′er.**

oil′ palm′, an African feather palm, *Elaeis guineensis,* the fruits of which yield palm oil.

oil·pa·per (oil′pā′pər), *n.* a paper made waterproof and translucent by treatment with oil. [OIL + PAPER]

oil-plant (oil′plant′), *n.* any of several plants, as the castor-oil plant or sesame, the seeds of which yield an oil.

Oil′ Riv′ers, a region in W Africa, comprising the vast Niger River delta: formerly a British protectorate; now a part of Nigeria.

oil·seed (oil′sēd′), *n.* any of several seeds, as the castor bean or cottonseed, from which an oil is expressed. [OIL + SEED]

oil′ shale′, *Geol.* a black or dark brown shale or siltstone rich in bitumens, from which shale oil is obtained by destructive distillation.

oil·skin (oil′skin′), *n.* **1.** a cotton fabric made waterproof by treatment with oil and used for rain gear and fishermen's clothing. **2.** a piece of this. **3.** Often, **oilskins.** a garment made of this, esp. a long, full-cut raincoat or a loose-fitting suit of pants and jacket as worn by sailors for protection against rain. [OIL + SKIN]

oil′ slick′, a smooth area on the surface of water caused by the presence of oil.

oil′spot glaze′ (oil′spot′), a brown or black ceramic glaze dotted with silvery spots caused by impurities. [OIL + SPOT]

oil·stone (oil′stōn′), *n.* a block of fine-grained stone, usually oiled, for putting the final edge on certain cutting tools by abrasion. [OIL + STONE]

oil·tight (oil′tīt′), *adj.* proof against the passage of oil: *an oiltight bulkhead.* [OIL + TIGHT]

oil′ var′nish. See under **varnish** (def. 1).

oil′ well′, a well that yields or has yielded oil.

oil·y (oi′lē), *adj.,* **oil·i·er, oil·i·est,** *adv.* —*adj.* **1.** of or pertaining to oil. **2.** full of or containing oil. **3.** smeared or covered with oil; greasy: *an oily road surface.* **4.** of the nature of, consisting of, or resembling oil. **5.** smooth or unctuous, as in manner or speech: *an oily hypocrite.* —*adv.* **6.** in an oily manner. [OIL + -Y[1]] **—oil′i·ness,** *n.*

Oinochoe

oi·noch·o·e (oi nok′ō ē′), *n., pl.* **-noch·o·es, -noch·o·ai** (-nok′ō ī′). *Gk. and Rom. Antiq.* a wine pitcher or jug, characterized by a curved handle extending from the lip to the shoulder, and a round or trefoil mouth. Also, **oenochoe.** [< Gk *oinochóē* wine jug, equiv. to *oíno(s)* wine + *choē-* pouring (s. of *chéai* to pour)]

oint·ment (oint′mənt), *n.* *Pharm.* a soft, unctuous preparation, often medicated, for application to the skin; an unguent. [obs. *oint* (aph. var. of ANOINT) + -MENT; r. ME *oignement* < OF < VL **unguimentum* for L *unguentum;* see UNGUENT] **—Syn.** salve, balm; nar[illegible].

OIr., Old Irish. Also, **OIr**

Oir·each·tas (er′əkh thəs), *n.* **1.** the parliament of the Republic of Ireland, consisting of the Dail Eireann and the Seanad Eireann. **2.** an annual assembly, usually in Dublin, held by Gaelic-speaking people to celebrate, exhibit, and encourage the use of the Gaelic language, traditions, and arts. [< Ir: assembly, conference]

Oise (wäz), *n.* **1.** a river in W Europe, flowing SW from S Belgium through N France to the Seine, near Paris. 186 mi. long. **2.** a department in N France. 495,227 (1962); 2273 sq. mi. *Cap.:* Beauvais.

Oi·sin (u shēn′), *n.* Ossian.

Oi·strakh (oi′sträk), *n.* **Da·vid** (dä′vid), born 1908, Russian violinist.

OIt, Old Italian.

oi·ti·ci·ca (oi′ti sē′kə), *n.* a rosaceous tree, *Licania rigida,* of Brazil, the seeds of which yield oiticica oil. [< Pg < Tupi]

oitici′ca oil′, a light yellow drying oil expressed from the seeds of the oiticica tree, used as a vehicle for paints, varnishes, etc.

O·ïz·ys (ō′i zis, ō iz′is), *n.* *Class. Myth.* a child of Nyx, the personification of pain.

O·jai (ō′hī), *n.* a town in S California. 4495 (1960).

O·jib·wa (ō jib′wā, -wə), *n., pl.* **-was,** (*esp. collectively*) **-wa.** **1.** a member of a large tribe of North American Indians divided geographically between the U.S. and Canada in the Lake Superior region. **2.** an Algonquian language used by the Ojibwa, Algonquian, and Ottawa Indians. Also, **Ojibway.** Also called **Chippewa.** [< AmerInd (Algonquian) *ojibway* to roast until puckered up, equiv. to *ojib* to pucker up + *ub-way* to roast, deriv. of *way* heat, with reference to the puckered seams on their moccasins]

O·jib·way (ō jib′wā), *n., pl.* **-ways,** (*esp. collectively*) **-way.** Ojibwa.

o·jo (ō′hō), *n.* *Southwestern U.S.* a spring of water. [< Sp: eye, opening, well]

o·jo ca·lien·te (ō′hō käl yen′tā), *Southwestern U.S.* a hot spring. [< Sp]

O.K., (*adj., adv.* ō′kā′; *v., n.* ō′kā′), *adj., adv., v.,* **O.K.'d, O.K.'ing,** *n., pl.* **O.K.'s.** *Informal.* —*adj., adv.* **1.** all right; correct: *O.K., I'll get it for you. Everything is O.K.* —*v.t.* **2.** to put "O.K." on (a bill, check, etc.); endorse; sanction; approve. —*n.* **3.** an approval, agreement, or endorsement. Also, **OK, okay, okeh, okey.** [prob. after the *O.K. Club,* formed in 1840 by partisans of Martin Van Buren, who allegedly named their organization in allusion to "Old Kinderhook," his birthplace being Kinderhook, New York; but cf. also the Bostonian phrase *all correct*]

o·ka (ō′kə), *n.* **1.** a unit of weight in Turkey and neighboring countries, equal to about 2¾ pounds. **2.** a unit of liquid measure, equal to about 1⅓ U.S. liquid quarts. Also, **oke.** [< It *occa* < Turk *ōqa* < Ar (cf. *ūqiyya*) < Gk *ounkía;* c. L *uncia;* see OUNCE[1]]

O·ka (ō kä′), *n.* a river in the central Soviet Union in Europe, flowing NE to the Volga at Gorki. 950 mi. long.

o·ka·pi (ō kä′pē), *n., pl.* **-pis,** (*esp. collectively*) **-pi.** an African mammal, *Okapia johnstoni,* closely related to and resembling the giraffe, but smaller and with a much shorter neck. [< a Central Afr language]

Okapi, (5 ft. high at shoulder; total length 7½ ft; tail 16 in.)

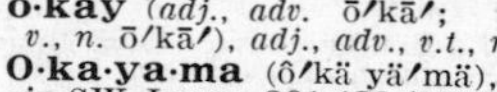

O·ka·van·go (ō′kä vāŋ′gō), *n.* Okovanggo.

o·kay (*adj., adv.* ō′kā′; *v., n.* ō′kā′), *adj., adv., v.t., n.* O.K.

O·ka·ya·ma (ō′kä yä′mä), *n.* a city on SW Honshu, in SW Japan. 301,438 (1964).

O·ka·za·ki (ō′kä zä′kē), *n.* a city on S central Honshu, in central Japan. 188,603 (1964).

oke[1] (ōk), *n.* oka.

oke[2] (ōk), *adj.* *Informal.* all right; O.K.

O·kee·cho·bee (ō′kē chō′bē), *n.* **1. Lake.** Also called **O′kee·cho′bee.** a lake in S Florida, in the N part of the Everglades. 35 mi. long; 30 mi. wide. **2.** a town in central Florida. 2947 (1960).

O'Keeffe (ō kēf′), *n.* **Georgia,** 1887–1986, U.S. painter.

O·ke·fe·no′kee Swamp′ (ō′kə fə nō′kē, -fə nok′ē), a large wooded swamp area in SE Georgia.

O·ke·ghem (ō′kə gem′), *n.* **Jean** (zhän) **d'** or **Jan van** (yän vän), c1430–c95, Flemish composer. Also, **Ockeghem, Ockenheim.**

O'Kel·ley (ō kel′ē), *n.* **Seán Thomas** (shôn, shän), 1882–1966, Irish statesman: president 1945–59.

O·ke·mah (ō kē′mə), *n.* a town in central Oklahoma. 2836 (1960).

O·ken (ō′kən), *n.* a crater in the fourth quadrant of the face of the moon: about 50 miles in diameter. Also, **Ö′ken.**

o·key (*adj., adv.* ō′kā′; *v., n.* ō′kā′), *adj., adv., v.t., n.* O.K. Also, **o′keh′.**

o·key-doke (ō′kē dōk′), *adj.* *Informal.* perfectly all right; O.K. Also, **o·key-do·key** (ō′kē dō′kē), **okle-dokle.** [rhyming redupl. of OKE[2]]

O·khotsk (ō kotsk′; *Russ.* o khôtsk′), *n.* **Sea of,** an arm of the N Pacific enclosed by the Kamchatka Peninsula, the Kurile Islands, Sakhalin, and the Soviet Union in Asia. 582,000 sq. mi.; greatest depth, 10,554 ft.

Okhotsk′ Cur′rent. See **Oyashio Current.**

O·kie (ō′kē), *n.* **1.** *Informal.* a migrant worker from Oklahoma. **2.** *Disparaging.* a native or inhabitant of Oklahoma. [OK(LAHOMA) + -IE]

O·kie (ō′kē), *Disparaging.* —*n.* **1.** a native of Okinawa. —*adj.* **2.** belonging to the Okinawan people. [OK(INAWA) + -IE]

O·ki·na·wa (ō′kə nou′wə, -nä′wə; *Jap.* ō′kē-nä′wä), *n.* the largest of the Ryukyu Islands, in the N Pacific, SW of Japan: taken by U.S. forces April–June 1945 in the last major amphibious campaign of World War II. 718,500 (est. 1959); 544 sq. mi. **—O′ki·na′wan,** *adj., n.*

Okla., Oklahoma.

O·kla·ho·ma (ō′klə hō′mə), *n.* a State in the S central United States. 2,328,284 (1960): 69,919 sq. mi. *Cap.:* Oklahoma City. *Abbr.:* Okla. **—O′kla·ho′man,** *adj., n.*

O′klaho′ma Cit′y, a city in and the capital of Oklahoma, in the central part. 324,253 (1960).

o·kle-do·kle (ō′kəl dō′kəl), *adj.* okey-doke. [by alter.]

Ok·mul·gee (ōk mul′gē), *n.* a city in E Oklahoma. 15,951 (1960).

O·ko·lo·na (ō′kə lō′nə), *n.* a town in central Mississippi. 2622 (1960).

o·kou·me (ō′kə mā′), *n.* gaboon. [< F *okoumé,* of Afr orig.]

O·ko·vang·go (ō′kə vaŋ′gō), *n.* a river in central Africa, flowing SE from Angola to Botswana. ab. 1000 mi. long. Also, **Okavango.** Also called **Kubango.**

o·kra (ō′krə), *n.* **1.** a malvaceous shrub, *Hibiscus esculentus,* bearing beaked, mucilaginous pods. **2.** the pods, used in soups, stews, etc. **3.** a dish made with the pods; gumbo. [< a WAfr language]

ok·ta·sty·los (ok′tə stī′los), *n.* octastylos.

O·ku·ni·nu·shi (ō ko͞o′nē no͞o′shē), *n.* *Japanese Legend.* a son of Susanowo and, in some legends, creator of the world.

-ol[1], a suffix used in the names of chemical derivatives, representing "alcohol" (*glycerol; naphthol; phenol*), or sometimes "phenol" or less definitely assignable phenol derivatives (*resorcinol*). [short for ALCOHOL or PHENOL]

-ol[2], var. of **-ole.**

OL, Old Latin. Also, **OL., O.L.**

O.L., (in prescriptions) the left eye. Also, **o.l.** [< L *oculus laevus*]

ol., (in prescriptions) oil. [< L *oleum*]

O·la (ō′lə), *n.* a girl's given name, form of **Olga.**

O·laf (ō′ləf; *Dan., Nor.* ō′läf; *Swed.* o͞o′läf, -läv), *n.* a boy's given name. Also, **O·lav** (ō′läv).

O·laf I (ō′läf; *Eng.* ō′ləf), (*Olaf Tryggressön*) A.D. 969–1000, king of Norway 995–1000. Also, **Olav I.**

Olaf II, Saint (*Olaf Haraldssön*), A.D. 995–1030, king of Norway 1016–29; patron saint of Norway. Also, **Olav II.**

Olaf V, born 1903, king of Norway since 1957. Also, **Olav V.**

Ö·land (œ′länd′), *n.* an island in SE Sweden, separated from the mainland by Kalmar Sound. 25,534 (1964); 519 sq. mi.

Ol·bers (ōl′bərz), *n.* a crater in the second quadrant of the face of the moon: about 40 miles in diameter.

Ol·cott (ol′kət), *n.* **Chauncey** (*Chancellor John Olcott*), 1860–1932, U.S. tenor, actor, and song writer.

old (ōld), *adj.,* **old·er, old·est** or **eld·er, eld·est,** *n.* —*adj.* **1.** far advanced in the years of one's or its life: *an old man; an old horse.* **2.** of or pertaining to the latter part of the life or term of existence of a person or thing: *old age.* **3.** as if or appearing to be far advanced in years: *Worry had made him old.* **4.** having lived or existed for a specified time: *a man thirty years old; a century-old organization.* **5.** having lived or existed as specified with relation to younger or newer persons or things: *Jim is our oldest boy. There is no learned society in the world as old as this one.* **6.** having been aged for a specified time: *This whisky is eight years old.* **7.** having been aged for a comparatively long time: *old brandy.* **8.** long known or in use: *the same old excuse.* **9.** belonging to the past: *the good old days.* **10.** having been in existence since the distant past: *a fine old family.* **11.** no longer in general use: *This typewriter is an old model.* **12.** acquired, made, or in use by one prior to the acquisition, making, or use of something more recent: *When the new house was erected, the old one was made into servants' quarters.* **13.** of, pertaining to, or originating in an earlier period or date: *old maps showing America to be in the Orient.* **14.** prehistoric; ancient: *There may have been an old land bridge between Asia and Alaska.* **15.** of, originating in, or belonging to an early period or stage in the growth of a language, literature, or culture: *Old French; an old illuminated manuscript.* **16.** experienced: *He's an old hand at welding.* **17.** of long standing; having been such for a comparatively long time: *an old and trusted employee; an old trouper.* **18.** (of colors) dull, faded, or subdued: *old rose.* **19.** deteriorated through age or long use; worn, decayed, or dilapidated: *old clothes.* **20.** *Phys. Geog.* (of topographical features) far advanced in reduction by erosion or the like. **21.** sedate, sensible, or wise, as if from mature years: *an old head on young shoulders.* **22.** (used to indicate affection, familiarity, disparagement, or a personalization): *good old Bob; that old dear; the old brain cells; that dirty old thing.* **23.** *Informal.* (used as an intensive) great; uncommon: *a high old time.* **24.** former; having been so formerly: *a dinner for old Etonians.* —*n.* **25.** (*construed as pl.*) old persons collectively (usually prec. by *the*): *appropriations to care for the old.* **26.** a person or animal of a specified age or age group (used in combination): *a class for six-year-olds.* **27.** old or former time, often time long past: *days of old.* [ME; OE *eald, ald;* c. D *old,* G *alt,* Goth *altheis;* akin to OIcel *ala* to nourish, L *-ul-* of *adultus* ADULT] **—old′ness,** *n.* **—Syn. 1.** OLD, AGED, ELDERLY all mean well along in years. An OLD person has lived long, nearly to the end of the usual period of life. An AGED person is very far advanced in years, and is usually afflicted with the infirmities of age. An ELDERLY person is somewhat old, but usually has the mellowness, satisfactions, and joys of age before him. **9.** olden, early. **—Ant. 1.** young.

old′ Ad′am, (in theology) man in his unredeemed state; human nature lacking in grace. Also called **old man.**

old′ age′, the last period of human life, generally considered to be the years after 65. [ME]

Old′ Bai′ley (bā′lē), the main criminal court of London, England

Old′ Believ′er, Raskolnik.

old boy (ōld′ boi′ *for 1;* ōld′ boi′ *for 2;* ōld′ boi′ *for 3*), **1.** a vivacious, elderly man. **2.** *Brit.* an alumnus, esp. of a preparatory or public school. **3.** *Chiefly Brit.* See **old chap.**

Old′ Brit′ish, Brythonic as used before A.D. 800. *Abbr.:* OBrit

Old′ Bulgar′ian, the Bulgarian language of the Middle Ages. Cf. **Old Church Slavonic.**

Old′ Cai′ro, al-Fustat.

Old′ Cas·tile′ (ka stēl′), a region in N Spain: formerly a province. Spanish, **Castilla la Vieja.**

Old·cas·tle (ōld′kas′əl, -kä′səl), *n.* **Sir John.** See **Cobham, John Oldcastle, Lord.**

Old′ Cath′olic, **1.** a member of any of several European churches professing to be truly Catholic but rejecting certain modern Roman Catholic doctrines, dogmas, and practices, esp. the dogma of papal infallibility. **2.** a member of any of several minor churches, esp. in the U.S., differing from the Roman Catholic Church chiefly in their rejection of the ecclesiastical authority of the Roman Catholic hierarchy.

old′ chap′, *Chiefly Brit.* (used in direct address to a close friend.) Also called **old boy, old fellow.**

Old′ Church′ Slavon′ic, the oldest attested Slavic language, an ecclesiastical language written first by Cyril and Methodius in a Bible translation of the 9th century and continued in use for about two centuries. It represents the South Slavic, Bulgarian dialect of 9th-century Salonika with considerable addition of other South and West Slavic elements. Also called **Old′ Church′ Slavic′, Old Slavic, Old Slavonic.** Cf. **Church Slavic.**

Old′ Com′edy, Greek comedy of the 5th century B.C. which derived from fertility rites in honor of Dionysus and combined robust humor with biting personal and political satire. Cf. **Middle Comedy, New Comedy.**

old′ coun′try, *U.S.* the original home country of an immigrant or a person's ancestors, esp. a European country: *a visit to relatives back in the old country.* **—old′-coun′try,** *adj.*

old′ cov′enant, (in Christian exegesis) **1.** the covenant between God and the ancient Israelites, based on the Mosaic Law. **2.** (*cap.*) the Old Testament.

Old′ Curios′ity Shop′, The, a novel (1840–41) by Dickens.

Old′ Del′hi, Delhi (def. 2).

Old′ Domin′ion, the State of Virginia (used as a nickname).

old·en (ōl′dən), *adj. Archaic.* **1.** old. **2.** of or pertaining to the distant past; ancient. **3.** of or pertaining to former days. [ME; see OLD, -EN²]

Ol·den·burg (ōl′dən bûrg′; *Ger.* ōl′dən bŏŏrkh′), *n.* **1.** a former state in Germany, including the three scattered provinces of Oldenburg in NW Germany, Birkenfeld in SW Germany, and Lübeck on the Baltic; now a part of Lower Saxony. **2.** a city in NW West Germany: former capital of Oldenburg. 126,200 (1963).

Old′ Eng′lish, 1. Also called **Anglo-Saxon.** the English language of A.D. c450–c1150. **2.** *Print.* a style of black letter.

Old′ Eng′lish cut′, *Jewelry.* See **single cut.**

Old′ Eng′lish pat′tern, a spoon pattern having a stem curving backward at the end.

Old′ Eng′lish sheep′dog, one of an English breed of medium-sized dogs having a long, shaggy, gray or blue-merle and white coat that hangs over the eyes.

old·er (ōl′dər), *adj.* a comparative of **old.**
—Syn. OLDER, ELDER imply having greater age than something or someone else. OLDER is the usual form of the comparative of old: *This building is older than that one.* ELDER, now greatly restricted in application, is used chiefly to indicate seniority in age as between any two people but especially priority of birth as between children born of the same parents: *The elder brother became king.* **—Ant.** newer, younger.

old·est (ōl′dist), *adj.* a superlative of **old.**

old·fan·gled (ōld′fang′gəld), *adj.* old-fashioned; of an older or former kind. [formed after *newfangled*] **—old′fan′gled·ness,** *n.*

Old′ Fash′ioned, 1. a cocktail made with whiskey, bitters, water, and sugar, garnished with citrus fruit slices and a cherry, and served in an Old Fashioned glass. **2.** Also called **Old′ Fash′ioned glass′.** a short, broad cocktail glass holding usually six ounces.

old-fash·ioned (ōld′fash′ənd), *adj.* **1.** of a style or kind that is no longer in vogue: *an old-fashioned suit.* **2.** favored or prevalent in former times: *old-fashioned ideas.* **3.** having the conservative behavior, ways, ideas, or tastes of earlier times: *an old-fashioned girl.* **—old′-fash′ioned·ly,** *adv.* **—old′-fash′ioned·ness,** *n.*
—Syn. 1. outmoded, obsolete. See **ancient.**

old′ fel′low, *Chiefly Brit.* See **old chap.**

old′ field′, land no longer under cultivation because the fertility of the soil has been exhausted.

Old Flemish, The Flemish language before C1300.

old′ fo′gy, a person who is excessively conservative or old-fashioned in ideas, manners, etc. Also, **old′ fo′gey.** **—old′-fo′gy·ish, old′-fo′gey·ish,** *adj.*

Old′ Forge′, a town in NE Pennsylvania. 8928 (1960).

Old′ Franco′nian, the Franconian language before 1100; Frankish.

Old′ French′, the French language of the 9th through the 13th century.

Old′ Fri′sian, the Frisian language before c1500.

old′ fus′tic, fustic (defs. 1–3).

Old′ Glo′ry. See **Stars and Stripes.**

old′ goat′, *Slang.* **1.** an elderly man who is disliked, esp. for being mean to or disapproving of younger people. **2.** a lecherous but no longer youthful man.

old′ gold′, a color ranging in hue from medium yellow to light olive brown.

Old′ Guard′, 1. the imperial guard created in 1804 by Napoleon: it made the last French charge at Waterloo. **2.** *U.S.* the conservative element of any political party, esp. the Republican party. **3.** (*usually l.c.*) the influential, established, more conservative members of any body, group, movement, etc.: *the old guard of New York society.* [trans. of F *Vieille Garde*]

Old′ Guard′ism (gär′dĭz əm), political conservatism. [OLD GUARD + -ISM] **—Old′ Guard′ist.**

Old·ham (ōl′dəm; *locally* ou′dəm), *n.* a city in SE Lancashire, in NW England, near Manchester. 115,426 (1961).

old′ hand′, a person who is experienced in or familiar with a subject, area, procedure, etc.: *He is an old hand at leading safaris.*

Old′ Har′ry, Satan.

old′ hat′, *Informal.* old-fashioned; dated.

Old′ High′ Ger′man, High German before 1100.

Old′ Icelan′dic, Old Norse as used in Iceland.

old·ie (ōl′dē), *n. Informal.* a popular song, joke, movie, etc., that was in vogue at a time considerably in the past. [OLD + -IE]

Old′ Ion′ic, epic (def. 9).

Old′ I′rish, the Irish language before the 11th century.

Old′ I′ronsides, the U.S. frigate *Constitution* (used as a nickname).

old·ish (ōl′dish), *adj.* somewhat old: *an oldish man.* [OLD + -ISH¹]

Old′ Ital′ian, the Italian language of the 10th to the 14th centuries.

Old′ King′, The, a painting (1916–36) by Georges Rouault.

Old′ King′dom, the period in the history of ancient Egypt, 2780–2280 B.C., comprising the 3rd to 6th dynasties, characterized by the predominance of Memphis. Cf. **Middle Kingdom, New Kingdom.**

old′ la′dy, *Informal.* **1.** a mother, usually one's own. **2.** a wife, usually one's own.

Old′ La′dy of Thread′nee·dle Street′ (thred′nēd′əl), the Bank of England (used as a nickname).

Old′ Lat′in, the Latin language represented in written records of the 7th to the 1st centuries B.C.

old-line (ōld′līn′), *adj.* **1.** following or supporting conservative or traditional ideas, beliefs, customs, etc. **2.** long established; traditional: *old-line society.*

Old′ Low′ Fran·co′ni·an (frang kō′nē ən), a Low German dialect of the Franks of the lower Rhine valley before c1100. Also called **Old′ Low′ Frank′ish.**

Old′ Low′ Ger′man, the language of the German lowlands before c1100.

old′ maid′, 1. an elderly or confirmed spinster. **2.** a person having the characteristics considered typical of an old maid, as fussiness, prudishness, etc. **3.** *Cards.* **a.** a simple game in which the players draw from one another to match pairs and the one holding an odd queen at the end loses. **b.** the loser of such a game. **4.** *Facetious.* the person who takes or receives the last item of a group, esp. the person who takes the last piece or portion of food from a serving platter: *I'm going to be the old maid and eat this last piece of cake.*

old-maid·ish (ōld′mā′dish), *adj.* characteristic of or resembling an old maid, esp. in being prudish, fussy, prone to gossip, etc.

old′ man′, *Informal.* **1.** a father, usually one's own: *His old man's letting him have the car for the prom.* **2.** a husband, usually one's own: *My old man is finally retiring on our golden anniversary.* **3.** (*sometimes cap.*) a person in a position of authority, esp. an employer or a commanding officer: *The Old Man has ordered an inspection for Saturday morning.* **4.** (used affectionately in direct address to an old friend): *What courses are you taking next semester, old man?* **5.** a person who has had long experience in an occupation, business, or the like. **6.** southernwood.

Old′ Man′ and the Sea′, The, a novel (1952) by Ernest Hemingway.

old′-man cac′tus (ōld′man′), a Mexican cactus, *Cephalocereus senilis,* having a columnar body from 30 to 40 feet high with thatchlike, long, white hairs on the top, and red flowers with white centers.

Old′ Man′ of the Sea′, 1. (in *The Arabian Nights' Entertainments*) an old man who clung to the shoulders of Sindbad the Sailor for many days and nights. **2.** a burden, annoyance, care, or the like, from which it is extremely difficult to free oneself.

old-man's-beard (ōld′manz′bērd′), *n.* **1.** See **fringe tree. 2.** traveler's-joy.

old′ mas′ter, 1. an eminent artist of an earlier period, esp. from the 15th–18th centuries. **2.** a painting by such an artist.

old′ mine′ cut′, *Jewelry.* a brilliant cut, common in the 19th century, retaining a relatively high proportion of the original stone and having a large culet and small table compared to modern brilliants.

old′ moon′. See **waning moon.**

Old′ Nick′, the devil; Satan.

Old′ Norse′, the Germanic language of medieval Scandinavia.

Old′ North′ French′, the dialect of Old French spoken in northern France.

Old′ Northwest′. See **Northwest Territories.**

Old′ Or′chard Beach′, a resort town in S Maine. 4431 (1960).

Old′ Per′sian, an ancient West Iranian language attested by cuneiform inscriptions.

Old′ Pretend′er. See **Stuart, James Francis Edward.**

Old′ Prus′sian, a Baltic language extinct since the 17th century.

Old′ Rit′ualist, Raskolnik.

old′ riv′er, a river bed left dry because the river has changed its course.

old′ rose′, rose color with a purplish or grayish cast. **—old′-rose′,** *adj.*

Old′ Rus′sian, Russian as used in documents c1300–c1600.

Old′ Sax′on, the Saxon dialect of Low German as spoken before c1100.

old′ school′, advocates or supporters of established custom or of conservatism: *a military man of the old school.* **—old′-school′,** *adj.*

old′ school′ tie′, 1. a necktie striped in the colors that represent a specific English public school, esp. as worn by a graduate to indicate his educational background. **2.** an alumnus of an English public school. **3.** the conservative manners, accent, dress, and attitudes associated with students and graduates of the English public schools. **4.** snobbishness, clannishness, or extreme conservatism.

Old′ Scratch′, Satan.

Old′ Slav′ic. See **Old Church Slavonic.** Also called **Old′ Slavon′ic.**

old′ sledge′. See **all fours** (def. 2).

Old′ South′, the U.S. South before the Civil War.

Old′ Span′ish, the Spanish language of the 12th to the 16th centuries.

old′ squaw′, a sea duck, *Clangula hyemalis,* of arctic and subarctic regions.

old′ stag′er, stager (def. 1).

old·ster (ōld′stər), *n.* **1.** *Informal.* an old or elderly person. **2.** (in the British navy) a midshipman of four years' standing. [OLD + -STER, modeled on *youngster*]

Old′ Sto′a (stō′ə), the earliest phase of Stoicism, lasting from the latter part of the 4th century to the early part of the 3rd century B.C.

old′ style′, 1. Also, **old-style** (ōld′stīl′). *Print.* a type style differentiated from modern by the more or less uniform thickness of all strokes and by slanted serifs. **2.** (*caps.*) time reckoned according to the Julian calendar. Cf. **New Style.** **—***adj.* **3.** *Typography.* noting or descriptive of a font of numerals of which some part extends below the baseline. **—old′-style′,** *adj.*

Old Test., Old Testament.

Old′ Tes′tament, 1. the first of the two main divisions of the Christian Bible, comprising the Law, the Prophets, and the Hagiographia. In the Vulgate translation all but two books of the Apocrypha are included in the Old Testament. **2.** this testament considered as the complete bible of the Jews. **3.** the covenant between God and Israel on Mount Sinai, constituting the basis of the Hebrew religion. Ex. 19–24; Jer. 31:31–34; II Cor. 3:6, 14. [ME, trans. of LL *Vetus Testament(um),* trans. of Gk *Palaiá Diathḗkē*]

old-time (ōld′tīm′), *adj.* **1.** belonging to or characteristic of old or former times, methods, ideas, etc.: *old-time sailing ships; an old-time piano player.* **2.** being long established: *efforts to be accepted by the old-time residents.*

old-tim·er (ōld′tī′mər), *n. Informal.* **1.** a person whose residence, membership, or experience began long ago and has been continuing for a considerable length of time; veteran. **2.** an old person. **3.** (used as a form of familiar direct address to an elderly man.) [OLD-TIME + -ER¹]

Old′ Town′, a town in central Maine. 8626 (1960).

Ol′du·vai Gorge′ (ôl′dŏŏ vī′), a gorge in Tanzania in which is located a site containing Australopithecine and human skeletal and cultural remains.

Old′ Vic′ (vik), a repertory theater in London, England, famous for its productions of Shakespearean plays.

old·wife (ōld′wīf′), *n., pl.* **-wives. 1.** any of various fishes, as the alewife, the menhaden, or a West Indian fish of the family *Balistidae.* **2.** See **old squaw.** [OLD + WIFE]

Old′ Wives′ sum′mer, a period of fine, summerlike weather occurring in Europe in autumn. Cf. **Indian summer.**

old′ wives′ tale′, a belief, story, or idea that is often of a superstitious nature, as those traditionally passed on by old women: *Modern medicine has dispelled many old wives' tales about childbearing.*

Old′ Wives′ Tale′, The, a novel (1908) by Arnold Bennett.

old-wom·an·ish (ōld′wŏŏm′ə nish), *adj.* characteristic of an old woman, as excessive fussiness. **—old′-wom′an·ish·ness,** *n.*

Old′ World′, 1. Europe, Asia, and Africa. **2.** See **Eastern Hemisphere.**

old-world (ōld′wûrld′), *adj.* **1.** of or pertaining to the ancient world or to a former period of history. **2.** of or pertaining to the Old World. **—old′-world′ly,** *adj.* **—old′-world′li·ness,** *n.*

Old′ World′ mon′key, a catarrhine monkey.

-ole, var. of **oleo-** as final element of compounds: *thiazole.* Also, **-ol².**

O·le·a (ō′lē ə), *n.* the genus comprising the olive trees and shrubs. [< NL, L: olive tree; see OIL]

o·le·a·ceous (ō′lē ā′shəs), *adj.* belonging to the *Oleaceae,* or olive family of plants, comprising the ash, jasmine, etc. [OLE(A) + -ACEOUS]

o·le·ag·i·nous (ō′lē aj′ə nəs), *adj.* **1.** having the nature or qualities of oil. **2.** containing oil. **3.** producing oil. **4.** oily or unctuous. [< L *oleāginus* of the olive, deriv. of *olea* olive tree; see OIL] **—o′le·ag′i·nous·ness,** *n.*

O·le·an (ō′lē an′), *n.* a city in SW New York. 21,868 (1960).

o·le·an·der (ō′lē an′dər, ō′lē an′-), *n.* any apocynaceous plant of the genus *Nerium,* esp. the poisonous evergreen *N. Oleander,* having showy rose-colored or white flowers or *N. odorum,* of India, having fragrant flowers. [< ML < ? cf. LL *lorandrum,* var. of L *rhododendron* RHODODENDRON]

o·le·an·do·my·cin (ō′lē an′dō mī′sin), *n. Pharm.* an antibiotic compound, $C_{35}H_{61}NO_{12}$, produced by the fermentation of *Streptomyces antibioticus:* used chiefly in the form of its hydrochloride in the treatment of infections of Gram-positive bacteria which have become resistant to the more commonly used antibiotics. [OLEAND(ER) + -O- + MYC- + -IN²]

o·le·as·ter (ō′lē as′tər), *n.* an ornamental shrub or small tree, *Elaeagnus angustifolia,* of southern Europe and western Asia, having fragrant yellow flowers and an olivelike fruit. Also called **Russian olive, Trebizond date.** [ME < L: wild olive tree, deriv. of *olea* olive tree; see OIL]

o·le·ate (ō′lē āt′), *n.* **1.** *Chem.* an ester or a salt of oleic acid. **2.** *Pharm.* a preparation, as an ointment, composed of medicated oleic acid. [OLE(IC) + -ATE²]

o·lec·ra·non (ō lek′rə non′, ō′lə krā′non), *n. Anat.* the part of the ulna beyond the elbow joint. [< NL < Gk *ōlékranon* point of the elbow, short for *ōlenókranon,* equiv. to *ōlénē* elbow + *kraníon* head; see CRANIUM] **—o·lec·ra·nal** (ō lek′rə nəl, ō′lə krān′əl), **o′le·cra′ni·al, o′le·cra′ni·an, o′le·cra′ni·oid′,** *adj.*

o·le·fi′ant gas′ (ō′lə fī′ənt, ō lē′fē-, ō lef′ē-), ethylene (def. 2). [part trans. of F *gaz oléfiant,* equiv. to *olé-* -OLE + *fiant,* prp. of *-fier* -FY; see -ANT]

o·le·fin (ō′lə fin), *n. Chem.* any member of the alkene series. Also, **o·le·fine** (ō′lə fin, -fēn′). [< F *oléf(iant)* (see OLEFIANT GAS) + -IN²] **—o′le·fin′ic,** *adj.*

o′lefin se′ries, *Chem.* See **alkene series.**

o·le·ic (ō lē′ik, ō′lē ik), *adj. Chem.* pertaining to or derived from oleic acid. [< L *ole(um)* OIL + -IC]

ole′ic ac′id, *Chem.* a colorless, odorless, liquid, water-insoluble, unsaturated acid, $CH_3(CH_2)_7CH{=}CH(CH_2)_7COOH$, obtained from animal tallow and natural vegetable oils, in which it occurs as the glycerol ester: used chiefly in the manufacture of soap, commercial oleates, and cosmetics.

o·le·in (ō′lē in), *n. Chem.* **1.** Also called **glyceryl trioleate, triolein.** a colorless to yellowish, oily, water-insoluble liquid, $(C_{17}H_{33}COO)_3C_3H_5$, the triglyceride of oleic acid, present in many vegetable oils. **2.** the oily or lower-melting fractions of a fat as distinguished from the solid or higher-melting constituents. [< F *oléine,* equiv. to *olé-* (< L *ole(um)* OIL) + *-ine* -IN²]

O·len (ō′lən), *n. Class. Myth.* a Lycian poet believed to have originated the singing of hymns in the worship of Apollo at Delphi.

O·lene (ō lēn′), *n.* a girl's given name.

o·le·o (ō′lē ō), *n.* oleomargarine. [by shortening]

oleo-, 1. a learned borrowing from Latin meaning "oil," used in the formation of compound words: *oleograph.* 2. *Chem.* a combining form representing the oleoyl group. Also, **-ol, -ole.** [< L, comb. form repr. *oleum* OIL]

o·le·o·graph (ō′lē ə graf′, -gräf′), *n.* a chromolithograph printed in oil colors on canvas or cloth. [OLEO- + -GRAPH] —**o·le·o·graph·ic** (ō′lē ə graf′ik), *adj.* —**o·le·og·ra·phy** (ō′lē og′rə fē), *n.*

o·le·o·mar·ga·rine (ō′lē ō mär′jə rin, -rēn′, -märj′rin, -rēn), *n.* butter substitute used as a cooking and table fat, made by combining animal oils such as oleo oil and refined lard, and sometimes cottonseed oil, with milk. Also, **o′le·o·mar′ga·rin.** Also called **margarine.** [< F *oléomargarine.* See OLEO-, MARGARINE] —**o·le·o·mar·gar·ic** (ō′lē ō mär gär′ik), *adj.*

o′leo oil′, a product obtained from beef fat and consisting chiefly of a mixture of olein and palmitin, used for making butterlike foods.

o·le·o·res·in (ō′lē ō rez′ən), *n.* 1. a mixture of an essential oil and a resin, found in nature. 2. *Pharm.* an oil holding resin in solution, extracted from a substance, as ginger, by means of alcohol, ether, or acetone. [OLEO- + RESIN]

o·le·o·res·in·ous (ō′lē ō rez′ə nəs), *adj.* 1. pertaining to, characteristic of, or containing oleoresin. 2. (of a varnish or paint vehicle) consisting of drying oils and resins that usually have been cooked. [OLEORESIN + -OUS]

o′leo strut′, a hydraulic device used as a shock absorber in the landing gear of aircraft, consisting of an oil-filled cylinder fitted with a hollow, perforated piston into which oil is slowly forced when a compressive force is applied to the landing gear, as in a landing.

o·le·o·yl (ō lē′ō il), *adj.* *Chem.* containing the oleoyl group. [OLEO- + -YL]

ole′oyl group′, *Chem.* the univalent group, $C_{17}H_{33}CO$—, derived from oleic acid. Also called **ole′oyl rad′ical.**

ol·er·i·cul·ture (ol′ər ə kul′chər), *n.* the cultivation of vegetables for the home or market. [< L *oler-* (s. of *olus* or *holus*) vegetable, kitchen herb + CULTURE] —**ol′er·i·cul′tur·al,** *adj.* —**ol′er·i·cul′tur·al·ly,** *adv.* —**ol′er·i·cul′tur·ist,** *n.*

O·le·ta (ō lē′tə), *n.* a girl's given name.

o·le·threu·tid (ō′lə thrōō′tid), *n.* 1. any of numerous brown or gray moths of the family *Olethreutidae* having mottled or banded wings and forewings each with a truncated tip, including many crop pests, as the codling moth, oriental fruit moth, etc. —*adj.* 2. belonging or pertaining to the family *Olethreutidae.* [< NL *Olethreutid(ae)* name of the family, equiv. to *Olethreut(es)* name of the genus (< Gk *olethreú(ein)* (to) destroy, deriv. of *ólethros* destruction) + *-idae* -ID²]

o·le·um (ō′lē əm), *n., pl.* **o·le·a** (ō′lē ə) for 1, **o·le·ums** for 2. 1. *Pharm.* oil. 2. *Chem.* See **pyrosulfuric acid.** [< L: OIL]

o·le′yl al′cohol (ō lē′il), *Chem.* an unsaturated, fatty alcohol, derived from oleic acid, $CH_3(CH_2)_7CH{=}CH(CH_2)_7CH_2OH$, used chiefly in organic synthesis. [OLE(UM) + -YL]

ol·fac·tion (ol fak′shən), *n.* 1. the act of smelling. 2. the sense of smell. [< L *olfact(us)* smelled (see OLFACTORY) + -ION]

ol·fac·to·re·cep·tor (ol fak′tō ri sep′tər), *n.* *Physiol., Biol.* a receptor stimulated by odor. [< L *olfact(us)* (see OLFACTORY) + -O- + RECEPTOR]

ol·fac·to·ry (ol fak′tə rē, -trē), *adj., n., pl.* **-ries.** —*adj.* 1. of or pertaining to the sense of smell: *olfactory organs.* —*n.* 2. Usually, **olfactories.** an olfactory organ. 3. See **olfactory nerve.** [< L *olfactōri(us),* deriv. of *olfactor* one who smells (*olfact(us)* smelled, ptp. of *olfactāre* to smell (freq. of *olfacere,* equiv. to *ol(ere)* (to) smell + *facere* to make, do) + *-or* -OR²); see -ORY¹] —**ol·fac′to·ri·ly,** *adv.*

olfac′tory bulb′, *Anat.* the enlarged terminal part of each olfactory lobe from which the olfactory nerve originates.

olfac′tory cell′, *Anat.* one of the sensory nerve cells in the mucous membranes of the nose receptive to odor stimuli.

olfac′tory lobe′, *Anat.* the anterior part of each cerebral hemisphere, involved with olfactory functions.

olfac′tory nerve′, *Anat.* either one of the first pair of cranial nerves, consisting of sensory fibers that conduct to the brain the impulses from the mucous membranes of the nose.

O.L.G., Old Low German. Also, **OLG**

Ol·ga (ol′gə; *Russ.* ôl′gä), *n.* 1. **Saint,** died A.D. 968?, regent of Kiev until 955: saint of the Russian Orthodox Church. 2. a girl's given name.

o·lib·a·num (ō lib′ə nəm), *n.* frankincense. [ME < ML, var. of LL *liban(us)* < Gk *líbanos,* of Sem orig.; cf. Heb *lebhonāh*]

olig-, var. of **oligo-** before a vowel: *oligarchy.*

ol·i·garch (ol′ə gärk′), *n.* one of the rulers in an oligarchy. [< Gk *oligárch(ēs),* equiv. to *olig(os)* OLIG- + *-archēs* -ARCH]

ol·i·gar·chic (ol′ə gär′kik), *adj.* of, pertaining to, or having the form of an oligarchy. Also, **ol′i·gar′chi·cal.** [< Gk *oligarchik(ós),* equiv. to *oligarch(ía)* OLIGARCHY + *-ikos* -IC] —**ol′i·gar′chi·cal·ly,** *adv.*

ol·i·gar·chy (ol′ə gär′kē), *n., pl.* **-chies.** 1. a form of government in which the power is vested in a few persons or in a dominant class or clique; government by the few. 2. a state or organization so ruled. 3. the persons or class so ruling. [< LL *oligarchia* < Gk *oligarchía.* See OLIG-, -ARCHY]

oligo-, a learned borrowing from Greek meaning "few," "little," used in the formation of compound words: *oligopoly.* Also, *esp. before a vowel,* **olig-.** [< Gk, comb. form of *olígos* little, few (in pl.)]

ol·i·go·car·pous (ol′ə gō kär′pəs), *adj.* *Bot.* bearing few fruits. [OLIGO- + -CARPOUS]

Ol·i·go·cene (ol′ə gō sēn′), *Geol.* —*adj.* 1. noting or pertaining to an epoch either of the Tertiary or Paleogene period, occurring from 25,000,000 to 40,000,000 years ago and characterized by the presence of saber-toothed cats. See table under **era.** —*n.* 2. the Oligocene epoch or series. [OLIGO- + -CENE]

Ol·i·go·chae·ta (ol′ə gō kē′tə, ə lig′ə-), *n.* the class comprising the oligochaetes. [< NL; see OLIGOCHAETE]

ol·i·go·chaete (ol′ə gō kēt′), *n.* any of a group of annelids, including earthworms and certain small, freshwater species, having locomotory setae sunk directly in the body wall. [< NL *Oligochaet(a).* See OLIGO-, CHAETA] —**ol′i·go·chae′tous,** *adj.*

ol·i·go·clase (ol′ə gō klās′), *n.* *Mineral.* a kind of plagioclase feldspar occurring commonly in crystals of white color, sometimes shaded with gray, green, or red. [OLIGO- + Gk *klás(is)* a breaking]

ol·i·go·cy·the·mia (ol′ə gō sī thē′mē ə), *n.* *Pathol.* a form of anemia in which there is a reduction in the number of corpuscles in the blood. Also, **ol′i·go·cy·thae′mi·a.** [OLIGO- + CYT- + -HEMIA] —**ol′i·go·cy·the′mic, ol′i·go·cy·thae′mic,** *adj.*

ol·i·go·don·tia (ol′ə gō don′shə, -shē ə), *n.* *Dentistry.* an abnormal condition in which fewer than the normal number of teeth develop. [< NL; see OLIG-, -ODONT, -IA]

ol·i·goph·a·gous (ol′ə gof′ə gəs), *adj.* (esp. of insects) feeding on a limited variety of foods. Cf. **monophagous.** [OLIGO- + -PHAGOUS]

ol·i·go·phre·ni·a (ol′i gō frē′nē ə, ə lig′ə-), *n.* *Pathol.* less than normal mental development; feeblemindedness. [< NL; see OLIGO-, PHREN-, -IA] —**ol·i·go·phren·ic** (ol′i gō fren′ik, ə lig′ə-), *adj.*

ol·i·gop·o·ly (ol′ə gop′ə lē), *n.* the market condition that exists when there are few sellers. Cf. **duopoly, monopoly** (def. 1). [OLIGO- + (MONO)POLY] —**ol·i·gop·o·lis·tic** (ol′ə gop′ə lis′tik), *adj.*

ol·i·gop·so·ny (ol′ə gop′sə nē), *n.* the market condition that exists when there are few buyers. Cf. **duopsony, monopsony.** [OLIG- + Gk *opsōnía* purchase of victuals] —**ol′i·gop′so·nis′tic,** *adj.*

ol·i·go·sac·cha·ride (ol′ə gō sak′ə rīd′, -ər id), *n.* *Chem.* any carbohydrate yielding few monosaccharides on hydrolysis, as two, three, or four. [OLIGO- + SACCHARIDE]

ol·i·go·troph·ic (ol′ə gō trof′ik), *adj.* *Ecol.* (of a lake) characterized by a low accumulation of dissolved nutrient salts, supporting but a sparse plant and animal life, and having a high oxygen content owing to the low organic content. [OLIGO- + -TROPHIC]

ol·i·got·ro·phy (ol′ə go′trə fē), *n.* *Ecol.* the state of being oligotrophic. [OLIGO- + -TROPHY]

ol·i·gu·ri·a (ol′ə gyŏŏr′ē ə), *n.* *Pathol.* scantiness of urine due to diminished secretion. Also, **ol·i·gu·re·sis** (ol′ə gyŏŏ rē′sis). [OLIG- + -URIA] —**ol·i·gu·ret·ic** (ol′ə gyŏŏ ret′ik), *adj.*

O·lin (ō′lin), *n.* a boy's given name.

o·li·o (ō′lē ō′), *n., pl.* **o·li·os.** 1. a dish of many ingredients. 2. a mixture of heterogeneous elements. 3. a medley or potpourri, as of musical or literary selections; miscellany. 4. *Theat.* **a.** a specialty act performed downstage while the upstage set is changed. **b.** a performance, as a musical number, presented between scenes or acts. **c.** See **drop scene** (def. 1). [< Sp *olla* pot, stew < LL: pot, jar]

Ol·i·phant (ol′ə fənt), *n.* **Margaret Wilson,** 1828–97, Scottish novelist.

ol·i·va·ceous (ol′ə vā′shəs), *adj.* of a deep shade of green; olive. [< NL *olivāceus,* equiv. to L *olīv(a)* OLIVE + *-āceus* -ACEOUS]

ol·i·va·ry (ol′ə ver′ē), *adj.* 1. shaped like an olive. 2. of or pertaining to an olivary body. [< L *olīvāri(us)* belonging to olives. See OLIVE, -ARY]

ol′ivary bod′y, *Anat.* one of two oval bodies or prominences composed of nerve tissue, one on each side of the anterior surface of the medulla oblongata.

ol·ive (ol′iv), *n.* 1. an evergreen tree, *Olea europaea,* of Mediterranean and other warm regions, cultivated chiefly for its fruit, but also yielding a wood valued for ornamental work. 2. the fruit of this tree, a small oval drupe, used as a relish and as a source of oil. 3. any of various related or similar trees. 4. the foliage of this tree. 5. See **olive branch.** 6. a wreath of it. 7. an ochre green or dull yellow green. —*adj.* 8. of, pertaining to, or made of olives, their foliage, or their fruit. 9. of the color olive. 10. tinged with this color: *an olive complexion.* [ME < OF < L *olīv(a);* akin to Gk *elaía* olive tree. See OIL]

Ol·ive (ol′iv), *n.* a girl's given name.

ol′ive-backed thrush′ (ol′iv bakt′), a North American thrush, *Hylocichla ustulata,* wintering south to Argentina, having olive upper parts. Also called **Swainson's thrush.**

ol′ive branch′, 1. a branch of the olive tree as an emblem of peace. 2. something offered as a token of peace.

ol′ive drab′, *pl.* **olive drabs** for 3. 1. a deep olive color. 2. woolen cloth of this color used for U.S. Army uniforms. 3. a uniform made from this cloth.

ol·ive-green (ol′iv grēn′), *n., adj.* green with a yellowish or brownish tinge.

Ol·ive·hurst (ol′iv hûrst′), *n.* a town in central California. 4835 (1960).

o·liv·en·ite (ō liv′ə nīt′, ol′ə və-), *n.* a mineral, basic copper arsenate, $Cu_4As_2O_8(OH)_2$, occurring in crystals and in masses, usually olive-green in color. [< G *Oliven(erz)* (obl. of *Olive*) olive (ore) + -ITE¹]

ol′ive oil′, an oil expressed from the olive fruit, used with food, in medicine, etc.

Ol·i·ver (ol′ə vər), *n.* 1. one of the 12 paladins of Charlemagne. Cf. **Roland.** 2. a town in SW Pennsylvania. 3015 (1960). 3. a boy's given name.

Ol′iver Twist′, a novel (1838) by Dickens.

Ol·ives (ol′ivz), *n.* **Mount of,** a small ridge E of Jerusalem, in what is now Jordan. Highest point, 2737 ft. Also, **Ol·i·vet** (ol′ə vet′, -vit).

ol′ive shell′, 1. any marine gastropod of the family *Olividae,* having a polished, highly colored, elongated shell and a large mantle that, when extended, surrounds the shell. 2. the shell itself.

ol·i·vette (ol′ə vet′), *n.* *Theat.* a large floodlight having a single bulb. Also, **ol·i·vet** (ol′ə vet′, ol′ə vet′). [< F; see OLIVE, -ETTE]

Ol·i·vette (ol′ə vet′), *n.* a town in E Missouri. 8257 (1960).

O·liv·i·a (ō liv′ē ə), *n.* a girl's given name, form of **Olive.**

O·liv·i·er (ō liv′ē ā′), *n.* **Sir Laurence (Kerr)** (kûr; *Brit.* kär, kär), born 1907, English actor and director.

ol·i·vine (ol′ə vēn′, ol′ə vēn′), *n.* 1. a common mineral, magnesium iron silicate, $(Mg,Fe)_2SiO_4$, occurring commonly in olive-green to gray-green masses as an important constituent of basic igneous rocks. 2. a rare, transparent variety of this, used as a gem; peridot. Also called **chrysolite.** [< G *Olivin,* equiv. to *Olive* OLIVE + *-in* -INE²] —**ol·i·vin·ic** (ol′ə vin′ik), **ol·i·vin·it·ic** (ol′ə vi nit′ik), *adj.*

o·lla (ô′lyä, ô′yä; *Eng.* ol′ə), *n.* *Spanish.* 1. an earthen pot or jar for holding water, for cooking, etc. 2. a dish of meat and vegetables cooked in such a pot.

OLLA, Office of Lend Lease Administration.

ol·la-po·dri·da (ol′ə pə drē′də; *Sp.* ô′lyä pô drē′dä, ô′yä-), *n.* 1. a Spanish stew of meat and vegetables. 2. an incongruous mixture or collection; miscellany. [< Sp: lit., rotten pot]

Ol·len (ol′ən), *n.* a boy's given name, form of **Olin.**

Ol·lie (ol′ē), *n.* 1. a boy's given name, form of **Oliver.** 2. a girl's given name, form of **Olive.**

Olm·sted (ōm′stid, -sted), *n.* **Frederick Law,** 1822–1903, U.S. landscape architect.

Ol·ney (ol′nē), *n.* 1. a town in SE Illinois. 8780 (1960). 2. a town in N Texas. 3872 (1960). 3. a boy's given name.

ol·o·gy (ol′ə jē), *n., pl.* **-gies.** *Informal.* any science or branch of knowledge. [abstracted from words like BIOLOGY, GEOLOGY where the element -LOGY is preceded by *-o-;* see -O-]

O·lo·mouc (ô′lô mōts), *n.* a city in central Moravia, in the E Czech Republic. 107,000. German, **Olmütz** (ôl′myts).

O·lo·nos (*Gk.* ô′lô nôs′), *n.* Erymanthus.

o·lo·ro·so (ō′lə rō′sō), *n.* a sweet, dark dessert sherry. [< Sp: lit., sweet-smelling, equiv. to *olor* smell (< L *olēre* to smell) + *-oso* -OUS]

ol·pe (ol′pē), *n., pl.* **-pes, -pae** (-pē). a form of the oinochoe. [< Gk *ólpē* oil-flask]

Olpe

-olus, a Latin diminutive suffix used to form derivative nouns in scientific terminology: *nucleolus.* [< NL, L]

Ol·wen (ol′wen), *n.* *Welsh Legend.* a princess, the daughter of Yspadaden Penkawr.

O·lym·pi·a (ō lim′pē ə), *n.* 1. a plain in ancient Elis, Greece, where the Olympic Games were held. 2. a city in and the capital of Washington, in the W part, on Puget Sound. 18,273 (1960). 3. a girl's given name.

O·lym·pi·ad (ō lim′pē ad′), *n.* (*often cap.*) 1. a period of four years reckoned from one celebration of the Olympic Games to the next, by which the Greeks computed time from 776 B.C. 2. a celebration of the modern Olympic Games. [ME < L *Olympiad-* (s. of *Olympias*) < Gk. See OLYMPIA, -AD] —**O·lym′pi·ad′ic,** *adj.*

O·lym·pi·an (ō lim′pē ən), *adj.* 1. pertaining to Mount Olympus or dwelling thereon, as the gods of classical Greece. 2. pertaining to Olympia in Elis. 3. of, resembling, characteristic of, or suitable to the gods of Olympus; majestic; aloof; incomparably superior: *a landscape of Olympian beauty; an Olympian disregard for everyday matters.* —*n.* 4. an Olympian deity. 5. a contender in the Olympic Games. 6. a native or inhabitant of Olympia. [< LL *Olympiān(us),* equiv. to L *Olympi(us)* (< Gk *Olýmpios,* deriv. of *Ólymp(os)* OLYMPUS) + *-iānus* -IAN] —**O·lym′pi·an·ly,** *adv.*

O·lym·pic (ō lim′pik), *adj.* 1. of or pertaining to the Olympic Games: *Olympic event; Olympic year.* 2. of or pertaining to Olympia, in Greece. 3. pertaining to Mount Olympus, in Greece. 4. Olympian (def. 3). —*n.* 5. an Olympian deity. 6. **Olympics.** See **Olympic Games.** [< L *Olympic(us)* of Olympia < Gk *Olympikós.* See OLYMPUS, -IC]

Olym′pic Games′, 1. Also called **Olym′pian Games′.** the greatest of the games or festivals of ancient Greece, held every four years in the plain of Olympia in Elis, in honor of Zeus. 2. a modern revival of these games, held once every four years, consisting of athletic contests involving participants from many countries.

Olym′pic Moun′tains, a mountain system in NW Washington, part of the Coast Range. Highest peak, Mt. Olympus, 7954 ft.

Olym′pic Na′tional Park′, a national park in NW Washington. 1323 sq. mi.

ALBANIA
Salonika
Mt. Olympus
AEGEAN SEA
GREECE
Athens
PELOPONNESUS

O·lym·pi·o (ə lim′pē ō′), *n.* **Sylvanus,** 1902–63, African statesman: first president of the Republic of Togo 1961–63.

O·lym·pus (ō lim′pəs), *n.* **Mount,** 1. a mountain in NE Greece, on the boundary between Thessaly and Macedonia: mythical abode of the greater Grecian gods. 9730 ft. 2. a mountain in NW Washington: highest peak of the Olympic Mountains. 7954 ft.

O·lyn·thus (ō lin′thəs), *n.* an ancient city in NE Greece, on Chalcidice Peninsula. —**O·lyn·thi·ac** (ō lin′thē ak′), **O·lyn′thi·an,** *adj., n.*

Ol·y·phant (ol′ə fənt), *n.* a town in NE Pennsylvania. 5864 (1960).

Om (ōm), *n.* *Hinduism.* a mantric word thought to be a complete expression of Brahman and interpreted as having three sounds representing Brahma or creation, Vishnu or preservation, and Siva or destruction, or as consisting of the same three sounds, representing waking, dreams, and deep sleep, along with the following silence, which is fulfillment. Also, **Aum.** [< Skt]

Om., Ostmark.

O. M., *Brit.* Order of Merit.

-oma, *pl.* **-omas, -omata.** a noun suffix appearing in loan words from Greek, specialized in terms from pathology to indicate a tumor: *carcinoma; glaucoma; sarcoma.* [< Gk *-ōma*]

O·ma·ha (ō′mə hô′, -hä′), *n., pl.* **-has,** (*esp. collectively*) **-ha** for 2. 1. a city in E Nebraska, on the Missouri River. 301,598 (1960). 2. a member of a Siouan people formerly living in northeastern Nebraska.

O·mak (ō′mak), *n.* a town in N Washington. 4068 (1960).

O·man (ō män′), *n.* **1.** See **Muscat and Oman. 2. Gulf of,** a NW arm of the Arabian Sea, at the entrance to the Persian Gulf.

O·mar (ō′mär), *n.* a boy's given name.

O·mar Khay·yám (ō′mär kī yäm′, -yam′, ō′mər), died 1123?, Persian poet and mathematician.

o·ma·sum (ō mā′səm), *n., pl.* **-sa** (-sə). the third stomach of a ruminant, between the reticulum and the abomasum; the manyplies. See diag. under **ruminant.** [< NL, L *omāsum* bullock's tripe]

O·may·yad (ō mī′ad), *n., pl.* **-yads, -ya·des** (-ə dēz′). **1.** a member of the dynasty that ruled at Damascus A.D. 661–750, claiming descent from Omayya, cousin of the grandfather of Muhammad the Prophet. **2.** a member of the dynasty of caliphs that ruled in southern Spain, A.D. 756–1031: related to the Damascus dynasty. Also, **Ommiad, Umayyad.**

om·ber (om′bər), *n.* **1.** a card game popular in the 17th and 18th centuries and played, usually by three persons, with forty cards. **2.** the player undertaking to win the pool in this game. Also, **hombre;** *esp. Brit.,* **om′bre.** [< F *(h)ombre* < Sp *hombre,* lit., man < L *hom-in-* (s. of *homō*) man. See HOMAGE]

om·brel·li·no (om′brə lē′nō), *n., pl.* **-nos.** *Western Ch.* the white silk canopy held over the Eucharist while transferring it from one place to another, esp. from the main altar to a side altar. [< It: lit., parasol, sunshade]

om·buds·man (ôm′bŏŏdz man′; *Sw.* ôm′bʏds män′), *n., pl.* **-men;** *Sw.* **-man** (-men′). a commissioner appointed by a legislature, as in some Scandinavian countries, New Zealand, and elsewhere, to hear and investigate complaints by private citizens against government officials or agencies. [< Sw: commissioner]

Om·dur·man (om′dŏŏr män′), *n.* a city in the central Sudan, on the White Nile opposite Khartoum: British victory 1898. 171,000 (est. 1964).

o·me·ga (ō mē′gə, -mā′-, ō meg′ə, ō′meg ə), *n.* **1.** the 24th letter of the Greek alphabet (Ω, ω). **2.** the vowel sound represented by this letter. **3.** the last of any series; the end. [< Gk *ō méga,* lit., great *o.* Cf. OMICRON]

o·me′ga-3 fat′ty ac′id (ō mē′gə thrē′, ō mā′-, ō meg′ə-), a polyunsaturated fatty acid, essential for proper retinal function, that lowers cholesterol and triglyceride levels, and reduces inflammatory and immune reactions. [so named because its 1st double bond occurs after the 3d carbon atom counting from the methyl or *omega* end of the molecule]

ome′ga mi′nus, *Physics.* a subatomic particle that decays into a cascade particle on collision with a pi meson.

om·e·let (om′ə lit, om′lit), *n.* eggs beaten until frothy, often combined with other ingredients, as chopped ham, cheese, or jelly, and cooked until set. Also, **om′e·lette.** [< F *omelette,* earlier *amelette,* metathetic form of *alemette,* var. of *alemelle,* lit., thin plate, var. of OF *lemelle* < L *lamella.* See LAMELLA, -ET]

o·men (ō′mən), *n.* **1.** anything perceived or happening that is believed to portend a good or evil event or circumstance in the future; portent. **2.** a prognostic. **3.** prophetic significance; presage: *a bird of ill omen.* —*v.t.* **4.** to be an omen of; portend. **5.** to divine, as if from omens. [< L; OL *osmen,* equiv. to *os-* (deriv. of **augs-,* akin to *augur* AUGURY) + *-men* n. suffix]
—Syn. 1. augury, foreboding. See **sign.**

o·men·tum (ō men′təm), *n., pl.* **-ta** (-tə). *Anat.* a fold or duplication of the peritoneum passing between certain of the viscera. Cf. **greater omentum, lesser omentum.** [< L: fat-skin] **—o·men′tal,** *adj.*

o·mer (ō′mər), *n.* **1.** a Hebrew unit of dry measure, the tenth part of an ephah. **2.** *(usually cap.) Judaism.* the period of 49 days extending from the second day of Passover to the first day of Shabuoth. [< Heb *'ōmer*]

O·mer (ō′mər), *n.* a boy's or girl's given name.

om·i·cron (om′ə kron′, ō′mə-), *n.* **1.** the 15th letter of the Greek alphabet (O, o). **2.** the vowel sound represented by this letter. [< Gk *ō mikrón,* lit., small *o.* Cf. OMEGA]

om·i·nous (om′ə nəs), *adj.* **1.** portending evil or harm; foreboding; threatening; inauspicious: *an ominous bank of dark clouds; an ominous scowl.* **2.** having the significance of an omen. [< L *ōminōs(us)* portentous, equiv. to *ōmin-* (s. of *ōmen*) OMEN + *-ōsus* -OUS] **—om′i·nous·ly,** *adv.* **—om′i·nous·ness,** *n.* **—Syn. 1.** portentous.

o·mis·si·ble (ō mis′ə bəl), *adj.* capable of being or allowed to be omitted. [< L *omiss(us)* let go (see OMISSION) + -IBLE]

o·mis·sion (ō mish′ən), *n.* **1.** the act of omitting. **2.** the state of being omitted. **3.** something left out, not done, or neglected: *an omission in a report.* [ME < LL *omissiōn-* (s. of *omissiō*), equiv. to L *omiss(us)* let go (ptp. of *omittere;* see OMIT) + *-iōn-* -ION; see MISSION]

o·mis·sive (ō mis′iv), *adj.* neglecting; leaving out. [< L *omiss(us)* let go (see OMISSION) + -IVE] **—o·mis′sive·ly,** *adv.*

o·mit (ō mit′), *v.t.,* **o·mit·ted, o·mit·ting. 1.** to leave out; fail to include or mention: *to omit a passage from a text. Why did you omit my name in your list of students?* **2.** to forbear or fail to do, make, use, send, etc.: *to omit a greeting.* [ME *omitt(en)* < L *omitt(ere)* (to) let go, equiv. to *o-* o-[2] + *mitt-* send] **—o·mit′ter,** *n.*

om·ma·te·um (om′ə tē′əm), *n., pl.* **-te·a** (-tē′ə). *Zool.* See **compound eye.** [< NL < Gk *ommat-* (s. of *ómma*) eye + NL *-eum* n. suffix] **—om′ma·te′al,** *adj.*

om·ma·tid·i·um (om′ə tid′ē əm), *n., pl.* **-tid·i·a** (-tid′ē ə). *Zool.* one of the radial elements composing a compound eye. [< NL < Gk *ommatídion* little eye. See OMMATEUM, -IDION] **—om′ma·tid′i·al,** *adj.*

om·mat·o·phore (ə mat′ə fōr′, -fôr′), *n. Zool.* a tentacle or movable stalk bearing an eye, as in certain snails. [< Gk *ommat-* eye (see OMMATEUM) + -o- + -PHORE] **—om·ma·toph·or·ous** (om′ə tof′ər əs), *adj.*

Om·mi·ad (ō mī′ad), *n., pl.* **-ads, -a·des** (-ə dēz′). Omayyad.

omn. bih., (in prescriptions) every two hours. [< L *omnī bihoriō*]

omn. hor., (in prescriptions) every hour. [< L *omnī horā*]

omni-, an element of Latin origin meaning "all," used in combination with various words: *omnifarious; omnipotence; omniscient.* [< L, comb. form of *omnis*]

om·ni·a vin·cit a·mor (om′nē ä′ wĕng′kit ä′mōr; *Eng.* om′nē ə vin′sit ā′mōr), *Latin.* love conquers all.

om·ni·bear·ing (om′nə bâr′ing), *n.* the magnetic bearing of an omnirange station. [OMNI- + BEARING]

om·ni·bus (om′nə bus′, -bəs), *n., pl.* **-bus·es,** *adj.* —*n.* **1.** a bus (def. 1). **2.** a volume of reprinted works of a single author or of works related in interest or theme. —*adj.* **3.** pertaining to or dealing with numerous objects or items at once: *an omnibus bill submitted to a legislature.* [< F < L: for all (dat. pl. of *omnis*)]

om′nibus clause′, *Insurance.* a clause, esp. in an automobile liability policy, extending coverage to persons other than the insured named in the policy.

om·ni·di·rec·tion·al (om′nē di rek′shə nəl), *adj. Electronics.* sending or receiving signals in all directions: *an omnidirectional microphone.* [OMNI- + DIRECTIONAL]

om·ni·dis·tance (om′ni dis′təns), *n.* the distance between an omnirange station and a receiver. [OMNI- + DISTANCE]

om·ni·far·i·ous (om′nə fâr′ē əs), *adj.* of all forms, varieties, or kinds. [< LL *omnifārius* (deriv. of L *omnifāriam* on all sides), equiv. to L *omni-* OMNI- + *-fārius* -fold] **—om′ni·far′i·ous·ly,** *adv.* **—om′ni·far′i·ous·ness,** *n.*

om·nif·ic (om nif′ik), *adj.* creating all things. [< NL *omnific(us).* See OMNI-, -FIC]

om·nif·i·cent (om nif′i sənt), *adj.* creating all things; having all powers of creation. [OMNI- + *-ficent,* as in *beneficent*] **—om·nif′i·cence,** *n.*

om·ni·graph (om′nə graf′, -gräf′), *n.* a device for converting Morse Code signals that are punched on a tape into audio signals, used in the training of telegraph operators. [OMNI- + -GRAPH]

om·ni ma·ne (om′nī mā′nē), (in prescriptions) every morning.

om·nip·o·tence (om nip′ə təns), *n.* **1.** the quality or state of being omnipotent. **2.** *(cap.)* God. [< LL *omnipotentia,* equiv. to L *omnipotent-* OMNIPOTENT + *-ia;* see -ENCE]

om·nip·o·tent (om nip′ə tənt), *adj.* **1.** almighty, or infinite in power, as God or a deity. **2.** having very great or unlimited authority or power. —*n.* **3.** an omnipotent being. **4. the Omnipotent,** God. [ME < L *omnipotent-* (s. of *omnipotēns*), equiv. to *omni-* OMNI- + *potent-* (see POTENT[1])] **—om·nip′o·tent·ly,** *adv.*

om·ni·pres·ent (om′nə prez′ənt), *adj.* present everywhere at the same time: *the omnipresent God.* [< ML *omnipraesent-* (s. of *omnipraesēns*), equiv. to L *omni-* OMNI- + *praesent-* PRESENT[1]] **—om′ni·pres′ence,** *n.*
—Syn. OMNIPRESENT, UBIQUITOUS refer to the quality of being everywhere. OMNIPRESENT emphasizes in a lofty or dignified way the power, usually divine, of being present everywhere at the same time, as though all-enveloping: *Divine law is omnipresent.* UBIQUITOUS is applied to that which seems to appear in many and all sorts of places, or in an undignified or humorous way is "all over the place," often when unwanted: *A bore seems to be ubiquitous.* **—Ant.** nowhere.

om·ni·range (om′nə rānj′), *n.* a radio navigational aid in which stations emit distinctive signals on each of 360°, giving the bearing of each degree with reference to magnetic north. Also called **omni, VOR** [OMNI- + RANGE]

om·nis·cience (om nish′əns), *n.* **1.** the quality or state of being omniscient. **2.** infinite knowledge. **3.** *(cap.)* God. [< ML *omniscientia,* equiv. to L *omni-* OMNI- + *scientia* knowledge; see SCIENCE]

om·nis·cient (om nish′ənt), *adj.* **1.** having complete or infinite knowledge, awareness, or understanding; perceiving all things. —*n.* **2.** an omniscient being. **3. the Omniscient,** God. [< NL *omniscient-* (s. of *omnisciēns*), equiv. to L *omni-* OMNI- + *scient-* (s. of *sciēns*) knowing; see SCIENCE] **—om·nis′cient·ly,** *adv.*

om·ni·um-gath·er·um (om′nē əm gath′ər əm), *n., pl.* **-ums.** a miscellaneous collection. [< L *omnium* of all (gen. pl. of *omnis*) + *gatherum* a gathering, pseudo-L deriv. of GATHER]

om·ni·vore (om′nə vōr′, -vôr′), *n.* **1.** one who or that which is omnivorous. **2.** an omnivorous animal. [< NL *Omnivor(a)* name of the group, equiv. to L *omnivor(us)* OMNIVOROUS + *-a* neut. pl. n. suffix]

om·niv·or·ous (om niv′ər əs), *adj.* **1.** eating all kinds of foods indiscriminately. **2.** eating both animal and plant foods. **3.** taking in everything, as with the mind: *an omnivorous reader.* [< L *omnivorus,* equiv. to *omni-* OMNI- + *-vorus* -VOROUS] **—om·niv′o·rous·ly,** *adv.* **—om·niv′o·rous·ness,** *n.*

omn. man., (in prescriptions) every morning. [< L *omnī mane*]

omn. noct., (in prescriptions) every night. [< L *omnī nocte*]

omn. quadr. hor., (in prescriptions) every quarter of an hour. [< L *omnī quādrante hōrae*]

O·moo (ō mōō′), *n.* (A Narrative of Adventures in the South Seas) a novel (1847) by Herman Melville.

o·mo·pha·gia (ō′mə fā′jə, -jē ə), *n.* the eating of raw flesh or raw food. [< NL < Gk *ōmophagía,* equiv. to *ōmó(s)* raw + *-phagia* -PHAGY] **—o·mo·phag·ic** (ō′mə faj′ik), **o·moph·a·gous** (ō mof′ə gəs), *adj.* **—o·moph·a·gist** (ō mof′ə jist), *n.*

o·mo·pho·ri·on (ō′mə fōr′ē ən, -fôr′-, om′ə-), *n., pl.* **-pho·ri·a** (-fōr′ē ə, -fôr′-). *Eastern Ch.* a liturgical stole, resembling a pallium, worn by bishops. [< LGk *ōmophórion,* equiv. to Gk *ōmo-* (deriv. of *ōmos* shoulder) + LGk *-phorion,* deriv. of Gk *phérein* to bear]

om·pha·cite (om′fə sīt′), *n. Mineral.* a pale green variety of pyroxene similar to olivine, found in eclogite rocks. [< G *Omphazit* < Gk *omphakít(ēs)* green stone, equiv. to *omphak-* (s. of *ómphax*) unripe grape + *-ītēs* -ITE[1]]

Om·pha·le (om′fə lē′), *n. Class. Myth.* a Lydian queen whom Hercules served in bondage for three years.

omphalo-, a learned borrowing from Greek used, with the meaning "navel," "umbilical," in the formation of compound words: *omphaloskepsis.* [< Gk *omphalós* navel]

om·phal·o·cele (om′fə lō sēl′), *n. Pathol.* See **umbilical hernia.** [OMPHALO- + -CELE[1]]

om·pha·los (om′fə ləs), *n.* **1.** the navel. **2.** the central point. **3.** *Gk. Antiq.* a rounded or conical stone in the temple of Apollo at Delphi, thought to mark the center of the earth. [< Gk: lit., navel]

om·pha·lo·skep·sis (om′fə lō skep′sis), *n.* contemplation of one's navel as part of a mystical exercise. [OMPHALO- + Gk *sképsis* act of looking]

Om·ri (om′rī), *n.* a king of Israel and the father of Ahab. I Kings 16:16–28. Also, *Douay Bible,* **Amri.**

Omsk (ômsk), *n.* a city in the S RSFSR, in the W Soviet Union in Asia on the Irtish River. 722,000 (1965).

O·mu·ta (ō′mōō tä′), *n.* a seaport on W Kyushu, in SW Japan. 158,431 (1964). Also, **O·mu·da** (ō′mōō dä′).

on (on, ôn), *prep.* **1.** so as to be or remain supported by or suspended from: *Put your package down on the table. Hang your hat on the hook.* **2.** so as to be attached to or unified with: *a picture on the wall; Glue on the broken part.* **3.** so as to be a covering or wrapping for: *Put the blanket on the baby. Put the wax paper on the cake.* **4.** in connection, association, or cooperation with; as a part or element of: *to serve on a jury.* **5.** so as to be a supporting part, base, backing, etc., of: *a painting on canvas; mounted on cardboard; legs on a chair.* **6.** (used to indicate place, location, situation, etc.): *a scar on the face; the book on the table; a house on 19th street.* **7.** (used to indicate immediate proximity): *a house on the lake; to border on absurdity.* **8.** in the direction of: *on the left; to sail on a southerly course.* **9.** (used to indicate a means of conveyance or a means of supporting or supplying movement): *on the wing; The car runs on gas. Can you walk on your hands? I'll be there on the noon plane.* **10.** by the agency or means of: *drunk on wine; talking on the phone; I saw it on television.* **11.** with respect or regard to (used to indicate the object of an action directed against or toward): *Let's play a joke on him. Write a term paper on Shakespeare.* **12.** in a state, condition, or process of: *on strike; The house is on fire!* **13.** (used to indicate a source or one who or that which serves as a source or agent): *a duty on imported goods; She depends on her father for money.* **14.** (used to indicate a basis or ground): *on my word of honor; The movie is based on the book.* **15.** (used to indicate risk or liability): *on pain of death.* **16.** (used to indicate time or occasion): *on Sunday; We demand cash on delivery.* **17.** (used to indicate the object or end of motion): *to march on the capital.* **18.** (used to indicate the object or end of action, thought, desire, etc.): *to gaze on a scene.* **19.** (used to indicate subject, reference, or respect): *views on public matters.* **20.** (used to indicate an encounter): *to happen on a person.* **21. on the bow,** *Naut.* within 45° to the heading of the vessel. **22. on the quarter,** *Naut.* abaft the beam, esp. at an angle of 45° with the beam or the fore-and-aft line. —*adv.* **23.** in, into, or onto a position of being supported or attached: *Put the coffee on.* **24.** in, into, or onto a position of covering or wrapping: *Put your clothes on.* **25.** fast to a thing, as for support: *Hold on!* **26.** toward a place, point, activity, or object: *to look on while others work.* **27.** forward, onward, or along, as in any course or process: *further on.* **28.** with continuous activity: *to work on.* **29.** into or in active operation or performance: *Turn the gas on.* **30. on and off,** off (def. 20). **31. on and on,** at great length, so as to become tiresome: *They rambled on and on about their grandchildren.* —*adj.* **32.** operating or in use: *The television set was on. Is your brake on?* **33.** taking place; occurring: *Don't you know there's a war on?* **34.** performing or broadcasting: *The radio announcer told us we were on.* **35.** scheduled or planned: *Anything on after supper?* **36.** *Baseball.* on a base or bases: *They had two men on when he hit the home run.* **37.** *Cricket.* noting that side of the wicket, or of the field, on which the batsman stands. **38. on to,** *Informal.* aware of the true nature, motive, or meaning of: *I'm on to your little game.* —*n.* **39.** the state of being on. **40.** *Cricket.* the on side. [ME *on, an,* OE: on, in, to; c. D *aan,* G *an,* OIcel *ā,* Goth *ana;* akin to Gk *ana* on, upon. See ANA-]

On (on), *n. Bible.* Heliopolis.

-on[1], a formal element used in the naming of elementary particles: *neutron; proton.* [abstracted from such words as ION, ELECTRON]

-on[2], a formal element used in the naming of inert gaseous elements: *neon.* [<< Gk *-on,* neut. of *-os,* masc. sing. adj. ending]

ON, Old Norse. Also, **ON., O.N.**

O·na (ō′nə), *n., pl.* **O·nas,** *(esp. collectively)* **O·na. 1.** a member of a people of Tierra del Fuego. **2.** Also, **Oona, Oonagh, Una.** a girl's given name.

on·a·ger (on′ə jər), *n., pl.* **-gri** (-grī′), **-gers. 1.** a wild ass, *Equus hemionus,* of southwestern Asia. **2.** an ancient and medieval engine of war for throwing stones. [ME (in LL: scorpion (colloquial), hence machine for throwing projectiles) < L, var. of *onagrus* wild ass < Gk *ónagr(os),* equiv. to *ón(os)* ass + *-agros* field]

Onager (4½ ft. high at shoulder)

on·a·gra·ceous (on′ə grā′shəs), *adj.* belonging to the *Onagraceae,* or evening-primrose family of plants. [< NL *Onagrāce(ae)* name of the family (L *onagr(a),* fem. of *onagrus* wild ass (see ONAGER) + *-āceae* -ACEAE) + -OUS]

On·a·las·ka (on′ə las′kə), *n.* a town in W Wisconsin. 3161 (1960).

o·nan·ism (ō′nə niz′əm), *n.* **1.** withdrawal in sexual intercourse so that ejaculation takes place outside the vagina. **2.** masturbation. [after *Onan,* son of Judah (Gen. 38:9); see -ISM] **—o′nan·ist,** *n.* **—o′nan·is′tic,** *adj.*

O·nas·sis (ō nas′is, -näs′is), *n.* **Aristotle Socrates,** born 1906?, Greek-Argentine businessman, born in Turkey.

O·ña·te (ô nyä′te), *n.* **Juan de** (hwän de), 1550?–1624, Spanish explorer who colonized New Mexico.

On·a·wa (on′ə wə, -wä′), *n.* a town in W Iowa. 3176 (1960).

once (wuns), *adv.* **1.** at one time in the past; formerly: *a once powerful nation.* **2.** a single time: *We go to a movie once a week.* **3.** even a single time; at any time; ever: *If the facts once become known, it will be just too bad.* **4.** by a single step, degree, or grade: *a cousin once removed.* **5. once and again,** repeatedly: *He has been told once and again not to slam the door.* **6. once and for all,** decisively; finally. Also, **once for all. 7. once in a while,** at intervals; occasionally: *She stops in to see us once in a while.* **8. once or twice,** a very few times; infrequently: *I've seen her in the elevator once or twice.* **9. once upon a time,** at some unspecified past time, esp. a long time ago: *Once upon a time the kingdom was divided into many duchies.* —*adj.* **10.** former; having at one time been. —*conj.* **11.** if or when at any time; if ever. **12.** whenever. —*n.* **13.** a single occasion; one time only: *Once is enough.* **14. all at once, a.** simultaneously: *He is a planner, supervisor, and public-relations man all at once.* **b.** suddenly: *All at once the wind came up.* **15. at once, a.** at the same time; simultaneously: *Don't all speak at once.* **b.** immediately; promptly: *Tell him to come at once!* [ME *ones,* OE *ānes* (adv.), orig. gen. of *ān* ONE; r. ME *enes,* OE *ǣnes* once, equiv. to *ǣne* once + *-es* adv. suffix]

once-o·ver (wuns′ō′vər), *n. Informal.* **1.** a quick look, examination, or appraisal. **2.** a quick, superficial job: *He gave the car just a once-over with a rag.*

once-o·ver-light·ly (wuns′ō′vər līt′lē), *n.* a hasty or superficial treatment, look, examination, etc.; once-over: *The maid gave the room the once-over-lightly.*

on·col·o·gy (oŋ kol′ə jē), *n.* the branch of medical science dealing with tumors. [< Gk *ónko(s)* mass, bulk + -LOGY] —**on·co·log·ic** (oŋ′kə loj′ik), **on′co·log′i·cal,** *adj.*

on·com·ing (on′kum′iŋ, ôn′-), *adj.* **1.** approaching; nearing: *the oncoming train.* —*n.* **2.** the approach; onset: *the oncoming of winter.* [adj., n. use of v. phrase *come on*]

on·co·sis (oŋ kō′sis), *n., pl.* **-ses** (-sēz). *Pathol.* **1.** any condition characterized by the development of tumors. **2.** any swelling or tumor. [< Gk *ónkōsis,* deriv. of *ónkos* mass] —**on·cot·ic** (oŋ kot′ik), *adj.*

on·dine (on dēn′, ôn-; *for 1 also Fr.* ôɴ dēn′), *n.* **1.** (*cap., italics.*) a play (1939) by Jean Giraudoux. **2.** undine.

on·ding (on′diŋ), *n. Scot.* the act of continued outpouring or falling; a continuing torrent, as of rain. [ON + DING[2]]

on dit (ôɴ dē′), *French.* one says; they say; it is said.

on·do·gram (on′də gram′), *n.* an autographic record made on an ondograph. [prob. < F *onde* wave (< L *unda*) + -o- + -GRAM[1]]

on·do·graph (on′də graf′, -gräf′), *n.* an instrument for graphically recording oscillatory variations, as in alternating currents. [< F *ondographe,* equiv. to *onde* wave (< L *unda*) + *-o-* + *-graphe* -GRAPH]

on·dom·e·ter (on dom′i tər), *n.* an instrument for measuring the wavelengths of radio waves. [< F *onde* wave (< L *unda*) + -o- + -METER]

on·do·scope (on′də skōp′), *n. Electronics.* a gas-filled tube that gives off a visible glow discharge in the presence of high-frequency radio waves due to ionization of the gas: used to detect high-frequency radiation. [< F *onde* wave (< L *unda*) + -o- + -SCOPE]

one (wun), *adj.* **1.** being or amounting to a single unit or individual or entire thing, item, or object rather than two or more; a single: *one apple.* **2.** being a person, thing, or individual instance or member of a number, kind, group, or category indicated: *one member of the party.* **3.** noting some indefinite day or time in the future: *You will see him one day.* **4.** existing, acting, or considered as a single unit, entity, or individual. **5.** of the same or a single kind, nature, or condition: *All our pomp of yesterday is one with Nineveh and Tyre! We both belong to one team.* **6.** a certain (often used in naming a person otherwise unknown or undescribed): *One John Smith was chosen.* **7.** being a particular, unique, or only individual, item, or unit: *He's the one man I trust.* **8.** noting some indefinite day or time in the past: *We all had dinner together one evening last week.* **9.** of no consequence as to the character, outcome, etc.; the same: *It's all one to me whether they go or not.* —*n.* **10.** the first and lowest whole number, being a cardinal number; unity. **11.** a symbol of this number, as 1 or I. **12.** a single person or thing: *If only problems would come one at a time!* **13.** a die face or a domino face having one pip. **14.** (*cap.*) *Neoplatonism.* the ultimate reality, seen as a central source of being by whose emanations all entities, spiritual and corporeal, have their existence, the corporeal ones containing the fewest of the emanations. **15. at one, a.** in a state of agreement; of one opinion. **b.** united in thought or feeling; attuned: *Alone on the plains in the starry night, he felt at one with his Creator.* **16. one and all,** everyone: *They came, one and all, to welcome him home.* **17. one by one,** singly and successively: *One by one the children married and moved away.* **18. one for the road.** See **road** (def. 8). —*pron.* **19.** a person or thing of number or kind indicated or understood: *one of the poets.* **20.** (in certain pronominal combinations) a person unless definitely specified otherwise: *every one.* **21.** (with a defining clause or other qualifying words) a person or a personified being or agency: *the evil one.* **22.** any person indefinitely; anyone: *as good as one would desire.* **23.** a person of the speaker's kind; such as the speaker himself: *to press one's own claims.* **24.** something of the kind just mentioned: *The portraits are fine ones. These qualities are good ones to have.* [ME *oon,* OE *ān;* c. D *een,* G *ein,* Goth *ains,* L *ūnus* (OL *oinos*); akin to Gk *oínē* ace on a die]

-one, a noun suffix of Greek origin, specialized in chemical terminology to indicate chemical derivatives, esp. ketones. [< Gk, abstracted from fem. patronymics in *-ōnē*]

one-a-cat (wun′ə kat′), *n.* See **one old cat.**

one-act·er (wun′ak′tər), *n. Theat.* a play consisting of one act, esp. a short play.

one′ anoth′er, one of two or more; each other. —**Usage.** See usage note at EACH OTHER.

one-bag·ger (wun′bag′gər), *n. Baseball Slang.* See **one-base hit.**

one′-base hit′ (wun′bās′), *Baseball.* a base hit that enables a batter to reach first base safely; single. Also called **one-bagger, single.**

one′-com·part·ment ves′sel (wun′kəm pärt′mənt), *Naut.* a vessel having a floodable length equal to any one watertight compartment.

one-eyed (wun′īd′), *adj.* **1.** having but one eye. **2.** *Cards Slang.* being, of, pertaining to, or using a face card or cards on which the figure is shown in profile, such cards being the jack of spades, the jack of hearts, and the king of diamonds in standard packs of cards: *One-eyed jacks are wild.*

O·ne·ga (ō nē′gə; *Russ.* o ne′gä), *n.* **1. Lake,** a lake in the NW Soviet Union in Europe: second largest lake in Europe. 3764 sq. mi. **2.** a river in the NW Soviet Union in Europe, flowing N to Onega Bay. 250 mi. long.

One′ga Bay′, a bay in the NW Soviet Union in Europe, at the SW end of the White Sea. 100 mi. long.

O·neg Shab·bat (ō neg′ shä bät′), *Hebrew.* a Jewish celebration in honor of the Sabbath that takes place on Friday evening or Saturday afternoon and usually includes a program of songs, a lecture, and refreshments.

one-hand·ed (wun′han′did), *adj.* **1.** having or using only one hand: *a one-handed catcher; a one-handed catch.* —*adv.* **2.** with one hand: *to catch a ball one-handed.*

one-horse (wun′hôrs′, -hôrs′), *adj.* **1.** using or having only a single horse: *a one-horse shay.* **2.** *Informal.* small and unimportant; limited: *a one-horse town.*

O·nei·da (ō nī′də), *n., pl.* **-das,** (*esp. collectively*) **-da** for 1. **1.** a member of an Iroquois people formerly inhabiting the region east of Oneida Lake. **2.** the Iroquoian language of the Oneida Indians, noted for its complex system of verbs. [< Iroquois *tiionenyote* a rock which someone set up and which is still standing (with reference to a boulder near an ancient village)]

Onei′da Commu′nity, a society of religious perfectionists established by John Humphrey Noyes, in 1848 at Oneida, N.Y., on the theory that sin can be eliminated through social reform: dissolved and reorganized in 1881 as a joint-stock company.

Onei′da Lake′, a lake in central New York. 20 mi. long; 5 mi. wide.

one-i·de·aed (wun′ī dē′əd), *adj.* characterized by or having only one idea.

O'Neill (ō nēl′), *n.* **1. Eugene (Gladstone),** 1888–1953, U.S. playwright: Nobel prize 1936. **2. Thomas P(hilip)** ("Tip"), born 1912, U.S. politician: congressman 1953–87; speaker of the House 1977–87.

o·nei·ric (ō nī′rik), *adj.* of or pertaining to dreams. [< Gk *óneir(os)* dream + -IC]

o·nei·ro·crit·ic (ō nī′rə krit′ik), *n.* **1.** an interpreter of dreams. **2.** oneirocriticism. [< Gk *oneirokritik(ós)* pertaining to the interpretation of dreams, equiv. to *óneir(os)* dream + *kritikós* skilled in judgment; see CRITIC] —**o·nei′ro·crit′i·cal,** *adj.* —**o·nei′ro·crit′i·cal·ly,** *adv.*

o·nei·ro·crit·i·cism (ō nī′rə krit′i siz′əm), *n.* the art of interpreting dreams. [ONEIROCRITIC + -ISM]

o·nei·ro·man·cy (ō nī′rə man′sē), *n.* divination through dreams. [< Gk *óneiro(s)* dream + -MANCY] —**o·nei′ro·man′cer,** *n.*

O·nei·ros (ō nī′ros), *n.* an ancient Greek god of dreams. Also, **Oniros.**

one-legged (wun′legd′, -leg′id), *adj.* **1.** having one leg. **2.** one-sided, as an argument, point of view, etc. **3.** ineffectual because certain basic elements, measures, etc., are lacking: *one-legged legislation.*

one-lung (wun′luŋ′), *adj.* **1.** having or equipped with only one lung. **2.** *Slang.* (of an engine, automobile, etc.) equipped with only one cylinder: *The boys had built a one-lung car.* Also, **one′-lunged′.** —**one′-lung′er,** *n.*

one-man (wun′man′), *adj.* of or operated, performed, or used by one person: *a one-man office; a one-man show.*

one-man·y (wun′men′ē; *usually read as* wun′tə men′ē), *adj. Logic, Math.* (of a relation) having the property that an element may be assigned to several elements but that given an element, only one may be assigned to it.

one·ness (wun′nis), *n.* **1.** the quality of being one; singleness; unity; sameness. **2.** agreement; concord; unity of thought, feeling, belief, aim, etc. [ONE + -NESS]

one-night·er (wun′nī′tər), *n.* See **one-night stand.**

one′-night stand′ (wun′nīt′), **1.** a single performance in one locale, as by a touring theatrical company, before moving on to the next engagement. **2.** a place, as a town or theater, where such a performance is given.

one old cat (wun′ə kat′), *Games.* a greatly modified form of baseball in which there is a home plate and one other base, and in which a player remains at bat and scores runs by hitting the ball and running to the base and back without being put out. Also, **one′ o' cat′, one-a-cat.**

one-one (wun′wun′; *usually read as* wun′tə wun′), *adj.* one-to-one (def. 1).

O·ne·on·ta (ō′nē on′tə), *n.* a city in E central New York. 13,412.

one-piece (wun′pēs′), *adj.* **1.** complete in one piece, as a garment: *a one-piece snowsuit.* —*n.* **2.** Also called **one′-piec′er.** a one-piece garment.

one′-point perspec′tive (wun′point′). See under **linear perspective.**

on·er·ous (on′ər əs, ō′nər-), *adj.* **1.** burdensome, oppressive, or troublesome; causing hardship: *onerous duties.* **2.** having or involving obligations or responsibilities, esp. legal ones, that outweigh the advantages. [ME < L *onerōs(us),* equiv. to *oner-* (s. of *onus*) burden + *-ōsus* -OUS] —**on′er·ous·ly,** *adv.* —**on′er·ous·ness, o·ne·ros·i·ty** (ō′nə ros′i tē), *n.*
—**Syn. 1.** heavy, crushing, grievous; irksome, galling, harassing; laborious, arduous, difficult, hard.

one·self (wun self′, wunz-), *pron.* **1.** a person's self (often used for emphasis or reflexively): *One hurts oneself by such methods.* **2. be oneself, a.** to be in one's normal state of mind or physical condition. **b.** to be unaffected and sincere: *One makes more friends by being oneself than by putting on airs.* **3. by oneself, a.** without a companion; alone. **b.** through one's own efforts; unaided: *It's hard to become a millionaire by oneself.* **4. come to oneself, a.** Also, **come to.** to regain consciousness. **b.** to regain one's self-possession; come to one's senses. Also, **one's self′.** [orig. *one's self*]

one′ shot′, **1.** a magazine that is published but one time, with no subsequent issues intended, usually containing articles and photographs devoted to one topical subject, the life of a celebrity, etc. **2.** a single appearance by a performer, as in a play, motion picture, radio or television program, etc. **3.** a close-up camera shot of one person.

one-sid·ed (wun′sī′did), *adj.* **1.** considering but one side of a matter or question; partial, unjust, or unfair: *a one-sided judgment.* **2.** *Law.* involving the action of one person only. **3.** with one party, contestant, side, etc., vastly superior; unbalanced; unequal: *a one-sided fight.* **4.** existing or occurring on one side only. **5.** having but one side, or but one developed or finished side. **6.** having one side larger or more developed than the other. **7.** having the parts all on one side, as an inflorescence. —**one′-sid′ed·ly,** *adv.* —**one′-sid′ed·ness,** *n.*

one-spot (wun′spot′), *n.* the upward face of a die bearing one pip or a domino one half of which bears one pip.

one-step (wun′step′), *n.* **1.** a round dance performed by couples to ragtime. **2.** a piece of music for this dance.

one-time (wun′tīm′), *adj.* having been as specified at one time; former: *his one-time partner.*

one-to-one (wun′tə wun′), *adj.* **1.** Also, **one-one.** (of the relationship between two or more groups of things) corresponding element by element. **2.** *Math.* associating with each element in one set a unique element in a second set: *a one-to-one function.*

one-track (wun′trak′), *adj.* **1.** having only one track. **2.** *Informal.* **a.** incapable of coping with more than one idea, action, etc., at a time; limited. **b.** absorbed in or attentive to just one thing; narrow; obsessed: *a one-track mind.*

one-two (wun′to͞o′), *n.* **1.** Also called **one′-two′ punch′.** *Boxing.* a left-hand jab immediately followed by a right cross. **2.** *Informal.* any strong or effective combination of two people or things: *The old one-two of a good passer and a good receiver is the best way to win football games.* **3.** *Fencing.* a type of attack made up of two movements. —*adj.* **4.** employing or suggesting a one-two; with one major or powerful thing or person combined with or following another.

one′ up′, **1.** *Print.* with only one reproduction of a form per sheet or on a given sheet: *We must print this job one up.* **2.** *Journ.* using one more column of space than of type. **3.** having gained an advantage in some way that betokens success, esp. over rivals. **4.** leading an opponent by one point or one scoring unit: *The home team was one up on the visitors.* **5.** one each: *The score was one up in the ninth inning.*

one-up·man·ship (wun′up′mən ship′), *n.* the art or practice of achieving, demonstrating, or assuming superiority in society or business or in one's rivalry with a friend or opponent by obtaining privilege, status, or status symbols, or by proving one's worth in either serious or facetious ways: *the one-upmanship of owning a yacht.* [from the phrase to be *one up* + *-manship,* as in *horsemanship*]

one-way (wun′wā′), *adj.* **1.** moving, or allowing movement in one direction only: *a one-way street.* **2.** without a reciprocal feeling, responsibility, relationship, etc.: *It's a one-way friendship.*

ONF, Old North French.

On First′ Look′ing into Chap′man's Ho′mer, a sonnet (1815) by John Keats.

ONFr., Old North French.

on·go·ing (on′gō′iŋ, ôn′-), *adj.* continuing without termination or interruption: *three ongoing research projects next year.* [adj. use of v. phrase *go on*]

ONI, Office of Naval Intelligence.

o·ni·o·ma·ni·a (ō′nē ə mā′nē ə, -mān′yə), *n.* an uncontrollable desire to buy things. [< NL < Gk *ōni(os)* for sale (deriv. of *ōnos* price) + *-o-* + LL *mania* -MANIA] —**o·ni·o·ma·ni·ac** (ō′nē ə mā′nē ak′), *n.*

on·ion (un′yən), *n.* **1.** a liliaceous plant, *Allium cepa,* having an edible, succulent, pungent bulb. **2.** any of certain similar plants. **3.** the bulb of the onion plant. **4.** the flavor or odor of this bulb. **5.** *Slang.* a person: *He's a tough onion.* **6. know one's onions,** *Slang.* to know one's subject or business thoroughly; be capable or proficient. —*adj.* **7.** containing or cooked with onions: *onion omelet.* **8.** of, pertaining to, or resembling an onion. [ME *onyon* < OF *oignon* < L *ūniōn-* (s. of *ūniō*) large pearl, onion; see UNION] —**on′ion·like′,** *adj.* —**on′ion·y,** *adj.*

on′ion dome′, *Archit.* a bulbous, domelike roof ending in a sharp point, characteristically used in Russian Orthodox church architecture to cover cupolas or towers.

On·ions (un′yənz), *n.* **Charles Tal·but** (tôl′bət, tal′-), 1873–1965, English lexicographer and philologist.

on·ion·skin (un′yən skin′), *n.* a translucent, glazed paper. [ONION + SKIN]

O·ni·ros (ō nī′ros), *n. Class. Myth.* Oneiros.

On·ke·los (oŋ′kə los′), *n.* fl. 2nd century A.D., author of an Aramaic Targum of the Pentateuch known as the Targum of Onkelos.

on·ker (oŋ′kər), *n. Naut. Slang.* (formerly) a sailing vessel engaged in the timber trade between Great Britain and ports on the Baltic Sea. [so called from the sound of the bilge pumps which worked constantly in these ships]

on·lap (on′lap′, ôn′-), *n. Geol.* **1.** the advance of a sea beyond its former shore. **2.** the layer or layers of rock formed on a sea floor during this advance. Cf. **offlap.** [ON + LAP[3]]

on·lay (*n.* on′lā′, ôn′-; *v.* on lā′, ôn-), *n., v.,* **-laid, -lay·ing.** —*n.* **1.** an overlay, esp. one in relief. —*v.t.* **2.** to place or mount (an onlay) on a surface, esp. for decorative purposes. [ON + LAY[1], after v. phrase *lay on*]

On Lib′erty, a treatise (1859) by John Stuart Mill on the rights of the individual within the state.

on-lim·its (on′lim′its, ôn′-), *adj.* open or not prohibited to certain persons, as military personnel: *an on-limits area.*

on-line (on′līn′, ôn′-), *adj.* (in data processing) operating as part of or directly connected with the main computer.

on·look·er (on′lo͝ok′ər, ôn′-), *n.* spectator. [n. use of v. phrase *look on*]

on·look·ing (on′lo͝ok′iŋ, ôn′-), *adj.* **1.** looking on; observing; perceiving. **2.** looking onward or foreboding. [adj. use of v. phrase *look on*]

on·ly (ōn′lē), *adv.* **1.** without others or anything further; alone; solely; exclusively: *This information is for your eyes only. Only he remained.* **2.** no more than; merely; just: *If it were only true! I cook only on week-*

ends. **3.** as recently as: *I saw him only yesterday.* **4.** in the final outcome or decision: *You will only regret your harsh words to him.* **5.** singly; as the only one: *the only begotten Son of God.* **6. only too, a.** as a matter of fact, extremely: *I am only too glad to go.* **b.** unfortunately, very: *It is only too likely to happen.* **—*adj.*** **7.** being the single one or the relatively few of the kind: *He was the only child in the room.* **8.** having no sibling or no sibling of the same sex: *an only child; an only son.* **9.** single in superiority or distinction; unique; the best: *the one and only Joe Louis.* **—*conj.*** **10.** but (introducing a single restriction, restraining circumstance, or the like): *I would have gone, only you objected.* **11.** *Chiefly Dial.* except; but: *Only for him you would not be here.* [ME *oonlich*, OE *ānlich*, *ǣnlich*. See ONE, -LY]
—Syn. 5. uniquely. **7.** solitary, lone. **9.** exclusive. **—Ant. 7.** plentiful, common.
—Usage. The placement of ONLY can change the entire meaning of even the simplest sentence. For example, *Only he sees the book* means "He, and no other person, sees the book." *He only sees the book* means "He sees the book (but does not or cannot touch it, feel it, smell it, read it, etc.)." *He sees only the book* means "He sees the book and nothing else." *He sees the only book* means "He sees the single, solitary book that can be seen." *He sees the book only* means "He sees or is capable of seeing the book and nothing but the book." Although some people insist that ONLY be placed as close as possible to the word it modifies, the most careful writers feel that ONLY may be varied in position as long as the meaning of the context remains clear.

on-mike (on′mīk′, ôn′-), *adj.* located close to or projected directly into the microphone.

on·o·mas·tic (on′ə mas′tik), *adj.* **1.** of or pertaining to onomastics. **2.** of or pertaining to proper names. **3.** *Law.* (of a signature) written in the handwriting other than that of the document, instrument, etc., to which it is appended. [< Gk *onomastik(ós)*, equiv. to *onomast(ós)* named (ptp. of *onomázein*, deriv. of *ónoma* NAME) + *-ikos* -IC]

on·o·mas·tics (on′ə mas′tiks), *n.* (*construed as sing.*) the study of the origin and history of proper names. [< F *onomastique*, n. use of *onomastique* (adj.) ONOMASTIC; see -ICS]

on·o·ma·tol·o·gy (on′ō mə tol′ə jē), *n.* onomastics. [< MGk *onomatología*, equiv. to Gk *onomatológ(os)* word-gathering (*onomato-*, comb. form of *ónoma* NAME + *-logos*) + *-ia*; see -LOGY] **—on·o·mat·o·log·ic** (on′ə-mat′əloj′ik), **on′o·mat′o·log′i·cal,** *adj.* **—on′o·mat′o·log′i·cal·ly,** *adv.* **—on′o·ma·tol′o·gist,** *n.*

on·o·mat·o·poe·ia (on′ə mat′ə pē′ə), *n.* **1.** the formation of a word, as *cuckoo* or *boom*, by imitation of a sound made by or associated with its referent. **2.** a word so formed. **3.** *Rhet.* the use of imitative and naturally suggestive words for rhetorical effect. [< LL < Gk *onomatopoiía* making of words, equiv. to *onomato-* (comb. form of *ónoma* NAME) + *poi-* make (s. of *poiein* to make) + *-ia* -IA] **—on′o·mat′o·poe′ic, on·o·mat·o·po·et·ic** (on′ə mat′ə pō et′ik), **on·o·mat·o·poi·et·ic** (on′ə mat′ə poi et′ik), **on′o·mat′o·poe′ial,** *adj.* **—on′o·mat′o·poe′i·cal·ly, on′o·mat′o·po·et′i·cal·ly,** *adv.*

On·on·da·ga (on′ən dô′gə, -dä′-), *n., pl.* **-gas,** (*esp. collectively*) **-ga** for 1. **1.** a member of a tribe of Iroquoian Indians formerly inhabiting the region of Onondaga Lake. **2.** the dialect of the Seneca language spoken by these Indians. **3. Lake,** a salt lake in central New York. 5 mi. long; 1 mi. wide. [< Iroquois *ononytá′geh* on top of hill] **—On′on·da′gan,** *adj.*

on·rush (on′rush′, ôn′-), *n.* a strong forward rush, flow, etc. [n. use of v. phrase *rush on*] **—on′rush′ing,** *adj.*

on·set (on′set′, ôn′-), *n.* **1.** a beginning or start: *the onset of winter.* **2.** an assault or attack: *a violent onset.* [n. use of v. phrase *set on*]

on·shore (on′shôr′, -shōr′, ôn′-), *adv.* **1.** onto or in the direction of the shore: *a breeze blowing onshore.* **2.** close to or parallel with the shore: *to sail a boat onshore.* **3.** on land, esp. within the area adjoining a port; ashore: *to land and shop onshore.* **—*adj.*** **4.** moving or proceeding toward shore or onto land: *an onshore breeze.* **5.** located on or close to the shore: *an onshore lighthouse; an onshore buoy.* **6.** done or taking place on land: *onshore liberty for the crew.* [ON + SHORE[1]]

on·side (on′sīd′, ôn′-), *adj., adv. Sports.* not offside; being within the prescribed line or area at the beginning of or during play or a play: *The field captain argued that his penalized teammate was indeed onside when the ball was snapped.* [ON + SIDE[1]]

on·slaught (on′slôt′, ôn′-), *n.* an onset, assault, or attack, esp. a vigorous or furious one. [< D *aanslag* plot, attack; c. G *Anschlag* (*-t* possibly by influence of *slaughter*)]

Ons·low (onz′lō), *n.* a boy's given name.

on·stage (on′stāj′, ôn′-), *adv.* **1.** on or onto the stage (opposed to *offstage*): *The director shouted, "Onstage, everybody!"* **—*adj.*** **2.** of, pertaining to, or used in the acting area, or that part of the stage that is in view of the audience. [ON + STAGE]

Ont., Ontario.

On·tar·i·o (on târ′ē ō′), *n.* **1.** a province in S Canada, bordering on the Great Lakes. 6,236,092 (1961); 412,582 sq. mi. *Cap.:* Toronto. **2. Lake,** a lake between the NE United States and S Canada, between New York and Ontario province: the smallest of the Great Lakes. 193 mi. long; 7540 sq. mi. **3.** a city in SW California, E of Los Angeles. 46,617 (1960). **4.** a town in E Oregon. 5101 (1960). **—On·tar′i·an, On·tar′ic** (on tar′ik), *adj., n.*

On the Knock′ing at the Gate′ in Macbeth′, a critical essay (1823) by Thomas De Quincey.

On the Morn′ing of Christ's′ Nativ′ity, a poem (1629) by John Milton.

on·to (on′tōō, ôn′-; *unstressed* on′tə, ôn′-), *prep.* **1.** to a place or position on; upon; on: *to get onto a horse.* **2.** *Informal.* in or into a state of awareness about: *I'm onto your little tricks.* **—*adj.*** **3.** *Math.* pertaining to a function or map from one set to another set, the range of which is the entire second set. [ON + TO]

onto-, a learned borrowing from Greek meaning "being," used in the formation of compound words: *ontogeny.* [< NL < Gk *ont-* (s. of *ṓn*, prp. of *einai* to be) + *-o-* -O-]

on·tog·e·ny (on toj′ə nē), *n. Biol.* the development or course of development of an individual organism. Also, **on·to·gen·e·sis** (on′tə jen′i sis). Cf. **phylogeny.** [ONTO- + -GENY] **—on·to·ge·net·ic** (on′tō jə net′ik), **on′to·ge·net′i·cal, on′to·gen′ic,** *adj.* **—on′to·ge·net′i·cal·ly, on′to·gen′i·cal·ly,** *adv.* **—on·tog′e·nist,** *n.*

on′tolog′ical ar′gument, *Philos.* an a priori argument for the existence of God, asserting that as existence is a perfection, and as God is described as the most perfect being, it follows that God must exist; originated by Anselm, later used by Duns Scotus, Descartes, and Leibniz. Also called **on′tolog′ical proof′.**

on·tol·o·gise (on tol′ə jīz′), *v.t.,* **-gised, -gis·ing.** *Chiefly Brit.* ontologize.

on·tol·o·gism (on tol′ə jiz′əm), *n. Theol.* the doctrine that the human intellect has an immediate cognition of God as its proper object and the principle of all its cognitions. [ONTOLOG(Y) + -ISM]

on·tol·o·gize (on tol′ə jīz′), *v.t.,* **-gized, -giz·ing.** to express in ontological terms; regard from an ontological viewpoint. Also, *esp. Brit.,* **ontologise.** [ONTOLOG(Y) + -IZE]

on·tol·o·gy (on tol′ə jē), *n.* **1.** the branch of metaphysics that studies the nature of existence or being as such, as distinct from material existence, spiritual existence, etc. **2.** metaphysics. [< NL *ontologia.* See ONTO-, -LOGY] **—on·to·log·i·cal** (on′tᵊloj′i kəl), **on′to·log′ic, on·to·lo·gis·tic** (on tol′ə jis′tik), *adj.* **—on·tol′o·gist,** *n.*

o·nus (ō′nəs), *n., pl.* **o·nus·es.** a burden; a responsibility. [< L: load, burden]

o·nus pro·ban·di (ō′nōōs prō bän′dē; *Eng.* ō′nəs-prō ban′dī, -dē), *Latin.* the burden of proof.

on·ward (on′wərd, ôn′-), *adv.* Also, **on′wards. 1.** toward a point ahead or in front; forward, as in space or time. **2.** at a position or point in advance. **—*adj.*** **3.** directed or moving onward or forward; forward. [ME; see ON, -WARD]
—Syn. 1. See **forward. —Ant. 1, 3.** backward.

o·nych·i·a (ō nik′ē ə), *n. Pathol.* inflammation of the matrix of the nail. [< NL, pl. of *onychium* < Gk *onýchion* little claw, nail, equiv. to *onych-* nail (see ONYX) + *-ion* dim. suffix]

on·y·cho·pha·gia (on′ə kō fā′jə, -jē ə), *n. Psychiatry.* the practice of biting one's nails, esp. when done habitually and as a symptom of emotional disturbance. [< Gk *onycho-* (comb. form of *ónyx* nail, claw; see ONYX) + -PHAGIA] **—on·y·choph·a·gist** (on′ə-kof′ə jist), *n.*

on·y·choph·o·ran (on′ə kof′ər ən), *n.* any terrestrial, caterpillarlike animal of the phylum *Onychophora*, having characteristics of both the annelids and the arthropods. [< NL *Onychophor(a)* name of the class (< Gk *onycho-*, comb. form of *ónyx* nail, claw; see ONYX) + NL *-phora* -PHORE + -AN]

-onym, a combining form of Greek origin, meaning "word," "name": *pseudonym.* [< Gk *-onym(os)*, comb. form of *ónoma* name]

on·yx (on′iks, ō′niks), *n.* **1.** a variety of chalcedony having straight parallel bands of alternating colors. Cf. **Mexican onyx. 2.** (not used technically) an unbanded chalcedony dyed for ornamental purposes. **3.** black, esp. a pure or jet black. **4.** *Med.* a nail of a finger or toe. **5.** *Pathol.* the presence of pus between layers of the cornea. **—*adj.*** **6.** black, esp. jet black. [ME *onix* < L *onyx* < Gk: nail, claw, veined gem]

o·nyx·is (ō nik′sis), *n. Pathol.* an ingrowing of a fingernail or toenail. [< NL, irreg. < Gk *onych-* (s. of *ónyx*) nail; see -SIS]

on′yx mar′ble, 1. See **Mexican onyx. 2.** any compact, banded calcareous tufa that can be given a high polish.

o-o (ō′ō), *n., pl.* **o-os.** a large, extinct honey eater, *Moho nobilis*, of the Hawaiian Islands, that had black plumage and two tufts of yellow plumes, formerly used to make ceremonial robes for the Hawaiian kings. [< Hawaiian *'ō'ō*]

oo-, a learned borrowing from Greek meaning "egg," used in the formation of compound words: *oogamous.* Also, **oö-.** [< Gk *ōio-*, comb. form of *ōión* EGG[1]]

OOC, Office of Censorship.

o·o·cyte (ō′ə sīt′), *n. Biol.* a female germ cell **(primary oocyte)** that gives rise by meiosis to a polar body and a haploid cell **(secondary oocyte)**, which in turn gives rise to a second polar body and an ootid. Also, **o′ö·cyte′.** [OO- + -CYTE]

oo·dles (ōōd′ᵊlz), *n.* (*sometimes construed as sing.*) *Informal.* a large quantity: *oodles of books; oodles of money.* [?]

o·og·a·mous (ō og′ə məs), *adj. Biol.* **1.** having structurally dissimilar gametes, the female gamete being large and nonmotile and the male gamete being small and motile. **2.** reproducing by the union of such gametes. Also, **o·ög′a·mous.** [OO- + -GAMOUS] **—o·og′a·my, o·ög′a·my,** *n.*

OO gauge, a model railroad gauge of 19 millimeters.

o·o·gen·e·sis (ō′ə jen′i sis), *n. Biol.* the origin and development of the ovum. Also, **o′ö·gen′e·sis.** [OO- + GENESIS] **—o·o·ge·net·ic, o·ö·ge·net·ic** (ō′ə jə net′ik), *adj.*

o·o·go·ni·um (ō′ə gō′nē əm), *n., pl.* **-ni·a** (-nē ə), **-ni·ums. 1.** *Biol.* one of the undifferentiated germ cells giving rise to oocytes. **2.** *Bot.* the one-celled female reproductive organ in certain thallophytic plants, usually a more or less spherical sac containing one or more eggs. Also, **o′ö·go′ni·um.** [< NL; see OO-, -GONIUM] **—o′o·go′ni·al, o′ö·go′ni·al,** *adj.*

o·o·kin·e·sis (ō′ə ki nē′sis, -kī-), *n. Biol.* the series of nuclear changes occurring in the ovum during maturation and fertilization. Also, **o′ö·ki·ne′sis.** [OO- + Gk *kínēsis* movement, action, verbid of *kinein* to move; see -SIS] **—o·o·ki·net·ic, o·ö·ki·net·ic** (ō′ə ki net′ik, -kī-), *adj.*

oo·la·chan (ōō′lə kän′), *n., pl.* **-chans,** (*esp. collectively*) **-chan.** *Chiefly Canadian.* eulachon.

o·o·lite (ō′ə līt′), *n. Geol.* **1.** Also called **egg stone.** a limestone composed of minute rounded concretions resembling fish roe, in some places altered to ironstone by replacement with iron oxide. **2.** (*cap.*) an upper division of the European Jurassic, largely composed of oolitic limestone. Also, **o′ö·lite′.** [earlier *oolites* < NL. See OO-, -LITE] **—o·o·lit·ic, o·ö·lit·ic** (ō′ə lit′ik), *adj.*

o·o·lith (ō′ə lith), *n. Geol.* any of the component concretions of a piece of oolite. Also, **o′ö·lith.** [OO- + -LITH]

o·ol·o·gy (ō ol′ə jē), *n.* the branch of ornithology dealing with the study of birds' eggs. Also, **o·öl′o·gy.** [OO- + -LOGY] **—o·o·log·i·cal, o·ö·log·i·cal** (ō′ə loj′i-kəl), *adj.* **—o·ol′o·gist, o·öl′o·gist,** *n.*

oo·long (ōō′lông′, -long′), *n.* a brown or amber tea grown in China and Taiwan and partially fermented before being dried. [< Chin *wu-lung*, lit., black dragon]

oo·mi·ak (ōō′mē ak′), *n.* umiak. Also, **oo′mi·ac′.**

Oom Pa·ul (ōōm pō′ōōl), *n.* See **Kruger, Stephanus Johannes Paulus.**

oomph (ŏŏmf), *n. Slang.* **1.** energy; vitality; enthusiasm. **2.** sex appeal. [? orig. attempt to represent in writing a nasal exclamation of approval; cf. *yum-yum*]

Oo·nagh (ōō′nə), *n.* a girl's given name. Also, **Ona, Oo′na, Una.**

oophor-, a learned borrowing from Greek used, with meaning "ovary," in the formation of compound words: *oophoritis.* Also, **oöphor-.** [< NL < Gk *ōophór(os)* bearing eggs. See OO-, -PHORE]

o·o·phore (ō′ə fôr′, -fōr′), *n. Bot.* an oophyte. Also, **o′ö·phore′.** [OO- + -PHORE] **—o·o·phor·ic, o·ö·phor·ic** (ō′ə fôr′ik, -for′-), *adj.*

o·o·pho·rec·to·mize (ō′ə fə rek′tə mīz′), *v.t.,* **-mized, -miz·ing.** *Surg.* to perform an oophorectomy on; ovariectomize. Also, **o′ö·pho·rec′to·mize.** [OOPHOREC-TOM(Y) + -IZE]

o·o·pho·rec·to·my (ō′ə fə rek′tə mē), *n., pl.* **-mies.** *Surg.* the operation of removing one or both ovaries; ovariectomy. Also, **o′ö·pho·rec′to·my.** [< NL; see OOPHOR, -ECTOMY]

o·o·pho·ri·tis (ō′ə fə rī′tis), *n. Pathol.* inflammation of an ovary, usually combined with an inflammation of the Fallopian tubes; ovaritis. Also, **o′ö·pho·ri′tis.** [< NL; see OOPHOR-, -ITIS]

o·o·phyte (ō′ə fīt′), *n. Bot.* the gametophyte of a moss, fern, or liverwort, resulting from the development of a fertilized egg. Also, **o′ö·phyte′.** [OO- + -PHYTE] **—o·o·phyt·ic, o·ö·phyt·ic** (ō′ə fit′ik), *adj.*

oops (ŏŏps, ōōps), *interj.* (used to express mild dismay, chagrin, surprise, etc., as at one's own mistake, a clumsy act or social blunder, etc.) [?]

oo·ry (ōō′rē), *adj. Scot.* ourie.

o·o·sperm (ō′ə spûrm′), *n. Biol.* a fertilized egg; zygote. Also, **o′ö·sperm′.** [OO- + -SPERM]

o·o·sphere (ō′ə sfēr′), *n. Bot.* an unfertilized egg within an oogonium. Also, **o′ö·sphere′.** [OO- + -SPHERE]

o·o·spore (ō′ə spōr′, -spôr′), *n. Bot.* a fertilized egg within an oogonium. Also, **o′ö·spore′.** [OO- + -SPORE] **—o·o·spor·ic, o·ö·spor·ic** (ō′ə spôr′ik, -spor′-), **o·os·por·ous, o·ös·por·ous** (ō os′pər əs, ō′ə spôr′əs, -spōr′-), *adj.*

Oost (ōst), *n.* **Ja·cob van** (yä′kôp vän), 1600?–71, and his son, **Jacob van,** 1639?–1713, Flemish painters.

o·o·the·ca (ō′ə thē′kə), *n., pl.* **-cae** (-sē). a case or capsule containing eggs, as that of certain gastropods and insects. Also, **o′ö·the′ca.** [< NL; see OO-, THECA] **—o′o·the′cal, o′ö·the′cal,** *adj.*

o·o·tid (ō′ə tid), *n. Biol.* the cell that results from the meiotic divisions of an oocyte and matures into an ovum. Also, **o′ö·tid.** [OO- + (SPERMA)TID]

ooze[1] (ōōz), *v.,* **oozed, ooz·ing,** *n.* **—*v.i.*** **1.** (of moisture, liquid, etc.) to flow, percolate, or exude slowly, as through holes or small openings. **2.** (of air, sound, etc.) to pass slowly or gradually as if through pores or small openings. **3.** (of a substance) to exude moisture. **4.** (of something abstract, as information or courage) to appear or become publicly known, or to disappear, slowly or imperceptibly (often fol. by *out* or *away*). **—*v.t.*** **5.** to make by oozing. **6.** to exude (moisture, air, etc.) slowly. **—*n.*** **7.** the act of oozing. **8.** that which oozes. **9.** an infusion of oak bark, sumac, etc., used in tanning. [ME *wose(n)*, deriv. of *wos* (n.), OE *wōs* juice, moisture]

ooze[2] (ōōz), *n.* **1.** a calcareous mud composed chiefly of the shells of small organisms, covering parts of the ocean bottom. **2.** soft mud, or slime. **3.** a marsh or bog. [ME *wose*, OE *wāse* mud]

ooze′ leath′er, leather prepared from calfskin or other skin and having a soft, velvety finish on the flesh side.

ooz·y[1] (ōō′zē), *adj.,* **ooz·i·er, ooz·i·est. 1.** exuding moisture. **2.** damp with moisture. [OOZE[1] + -Y[1]]

ooz·y[2] (ōō′zē), *adj.,* **ooz·i·er, ooz·i·est.** of or like ooze, soft mud, or slime. [ME *wosi.* See OOZE[2], -Y[1]] **—ooz′i·ly,** *adv.* **—ooz′i·ness,** *n.*

op-, var. of **ob-** (by assimilation) before *p*: *oppose.*

OP, observation post. Also, **O.P.**

Op., opus.

op., **1.** opera. **2.** operation. **3.** opposite. **4.** opus.

O.P., 1. *Theat.* opposite prompt. **2.** Order of Preachers (Dominican). [< L *Ordo Praedicatōrum*] **3.** out of print. **4.** overproof.

o.p., out of print.

o·pa (ō′pə), *n., pl.* **o·pai** (ō′pī). (in a classical temple) a socket for a roof beam. [< Gk *opá*, var. of *opḗ* hole, in technical senses]

OPA, *U.S. Govt.* Office of Price Administration: the former federal agency (1941–46) charged with regulating rents and the distribution and prices of goods.

o·pac·i·fy (ō pas′ə fī′), *v.,* **-fied, -fy·ing. —*v.t.*** **1.** to cause to become opaque. **—*v.i.*** **2.** to become opaque. [< L *opāc(us)* shaded + -IFY] **—o·pac′i·fi·ca′tion,** *n.* **—o·pac′i·fi′er,** *n.*

o·pa·cim·e·ter (ō′pə sim′i tər), *n.* an instrument for measuring the opacity of a substance, often used to determine the turbidity of a liquid. [< L *opāc(us)* shaded + -I- + -METER]

o·pac·i·ty (ō pas′i tē), *n., pl.* **-ties. 1.** the state or quality of being opaque. **2.** something opaque. **3.** the degree to which a substance is opaque; capacity for being opaque. **4.** *Photog.* the proportion of the light that is absorbed by the emulsion on any given area of a film or plate. **5.** obscurity of meaning. **6.** mental dullness. [< L *opācitās* shade. See OPAQUE, -ITY]

o·pa·cus (ō pā′kəs), *adj. Meteorol.* (of a cloud) dense enough to obscure the sun or moon. [< NL, L; see OPAQUE]

o·pah (ō′pə), *n.* a large, deep-bodied, brilliantly colored, oceanic food fish, *Lampris regius.* [< WAfr (Niger-Congo coast)]

o·pai·on (ō pī′on), *n.* **1.** (in ancient Greek and Roman architecture) a vent for the escape of smoke. **2.** (in ancient Greek architecture) a lacunar. [< Gk: an opening, neut. of *opaios* holed]

o·pal (ō′pəl), *n.* **1.** a mineral, an amorphous form of silica, SiO_2 with some water of hydration, found in many varieties and colors, including a form that is milky white. **2.** an iridescent variety of this that is used as a gem. **3.** a gem of this. [< L *opal(us)* < Gk *opállios* opal, gem < Skt *úpala* stone]

O·pal (ō′pəl), *n.* a girl's given name.

o·pal·esce (ō′pə les′), *v.i.*, **-esced, -esc·ing.** to exhibit a play of colors like that of the opal. [back formation from OPALESCENT]

o·pal·es·cent (ō′pə les′ənt), *adj.* **1.** exhibiting a play of colors like that of the opal. **2.** having a milky iridescence. [OPAL + -ESCENT] **—o′pal·es′cence,** *n.*

o·pal·eye (ō′pəl ī′), *n., pl.* **-eyes,** (*esp. collectively*) **-eye.** a green game fish, *Girella nigricans*, found off rocky shores from California southward, having opalescent blue eyes. Also called **greenfish.** [OPAL + EYE]

o′pal glass′, a translucent or opaque glass, usually of a milky white hue.

o·pal·ine (ō′pə lin, -līn′), *adj.* of or like opal; opalescent. [OPAL + -INE[1]]

O·pa-Lock·a (ō′pə lok′ə), *n.* a town in S Florida. 9810 (1960).

o·paque (ō pāk′), *adj., n., v.*, **o·paqued, o·paqu·ing.** **—*adj.*** **1.** not transparent or translucent; impenetrable to light; not allowing light to pass through. **2.** not transmitting radiation, sound, heat, etc. **3.** not shining or bright; dark; dull. **4.** hard to understand; not clear or lucid; obscure: *The problem remains opaque despite explanations.* **5.** dull, stupid, or unintelligent: *an opaque stare.* **—*n.*** **6.** something that is opaque. **7.** *Photog.* a coloring matter, usually black or red, used to render part of a negative opaque. **—*v.t.*** **8.** *Photog.* to remove blemishes from (a negative), esp. for making a printing plate. **9.** to cause to become opaque. [late ME *opake* < L *opāc(us)* shaded] **—o·paque′ly,** *adv.* **—o·paque′ness,** *n.*

opaque′ projec′tor, a machine for projecting opaque objects as books, on a screen, by means of reflected light. **—opaque′ project′ing.**

op′ art′ (op), a style of abstract art in which forms and space are organized in such a way as to provide optical illusions of an ambiguous nature, as alternately advancing and receding squares on a flat surface. [OP(TICAL)]

op. cit. (op′ sit′), in the work cited. [< L *opere citātō*]

OPCW, Office of Petroleum Coordinator for War.

ope (ōp), *adj., v.t., v.i.*, **oped, op·ing.** *Archaic.* open.

OPEC (ō′pek), Organization of Petroleum Exporting Countries.

Op-Ed (op′ed′), *n.* *U.S.* a newspaper page devoted to signed articles by commentators, essayists, humorists, etc., of varying viewpoints: *the Op-Ed page of today's* New York Times. Also called **Op′Ed′ page.** [*op(posite)-ed(itorial page)*]

O·pe·li·ka (ō′pə lī′kə), *n.* a city in E Alabama. 15,678 (1960).

Op·e·lou·sas (op′ə lo͞o′səs), *n.* a city in S Louisiana. 17,417 (1960).

O·pelt (ō′pəlt), *n.* a walled plain in the third quadrant of the face of the moon: about 33 miles in diameter.

o·pen (ō′pən), *adj.* **1.** not closed or barred at the time, as a doorway or passageway by a door, a window by a sash, or a gateway by a gate: *to leave the windows open at night.* **2.** (of a door, gate, window sash, or the like) set so as to permit passage through the opening it is intended to close. **3.** having no means of closing or barring: *an open field; an open portico.* **4.** having the interior immediately accessible, as a box with the lid raised or a drawer that is pulled out. **5.** relatively free of obstructions to sight, movement, or internal arrangement: *an open floor plan.* **6.** constructed so as to be without cover or enclosure on the top or on some or all sides: *an open boat; an open shelter.* **7.** having relatively large or numerous voids or intervals: *an open architectural screen; open ranks of soldiers.* **8.** perforated or porous: *an open texture.* **9.** relatively unoccupied by buildings, fences, trees, etc.: *open country.* **10.** extended or unfolded: *an open newspaper.* **11.** without restrictions as to who may participate: *an open competition; an open session.* **12.** accessible or available: *the only course still open to one.* **13.** not taken or filled; not preempted: *Is the job still open?* **14.** not engaged or committed: *Have you any open time on Monday?* **15.** not restricted as to the kind of game that may be legally hunted, nor as to where or when it may be taken: *open season.* **16.** free from frost; mild or moderate: *an open winter.* **17.** *Informal.* without effective or enforced legal, commercial, or moral regulations: *an open town.* **18.** undecided; unsettled: *several open questions.* **19.** liable or subject: *open to question; open to retaliation.* **20.** accessible, as to appeals, ideas, offers, etc.: *to be open to suggestion.* **21.** exposed to general view or knowledge; existing, carried on, etc., without concealment: *open disregard of rules.* **22.** acting publicly or without concealment, as a person. **23.** unreserved, candid, or frank, as persons or their speech, aspect, etc.: *an open manner.* **24.** generous, liberal, or bounteous: *to give with an open hand.* **25.** free of ice, as a body of water or a seaport. **26.** (of a seaport) available for foreign trade; not closed by government regulations or by considerations of health. **27.** free of navigational hazards: *an open coast.* **28.** noting the part of the sea beyond headlands or enclosing areas of land. **29.** *Stockbreeding.* (of a female animal) not pregnant. **30.** *Print.* **a.** (of type) in outline form. **b.** widely spaced or leaded, as printed matter. **31.** not yet balanced or adjusted, as an account. **32.** *Music.* **a.** (of an organ pipe) not closed at the far end. **b.** (of a string) not stopped by a finger. **c.** (of a note) produced by such a pipe or string or, on a wind instrument, without the aid of a slide, key, etc. **33.** not constipated, as the bowels. **34.** *Phonet.* **a.** (of a vowel) articulated with a relatively large opening above the tongue or with a relatively large oral aperture, as the vowel sound of *cot* compared with that in *caught.* **b.** (of a syllable) ending with its vowel. **c.** (of a consonant) continuant (opposed to *stopped*). **35.** *Math.* **a.** (of an interval) containing neither endpoint. **b.** (of a set) consisting of points having neighborhoods wholly contained in the set, as the set of points within a circle. **c.** (of a map from one topological space to another) having the property that the image of an open set is an open set. **—*v.t.*** **36.** to move (a door, window sash, etc.) from a shut or closed position so as to admit of passage. **37.** to render (a doorway, gateway, window, etc.) unobstructed by moving a door, window sash, etc., away from it. **38.** to render the interior of (a box, drawer, etc.) readily accessible. **39.** to give access to; make accessible or available, as for use: *to open a port for trade.* **40.** to recall or revoke (a judgment, decree, etc.) for the purpose of allowing further contest or delay. **41.** to clear (a passage, channel, etc.) of obstructions. **42.** to clear (bodily passages). **43.** to uncover, lay bare, or expose to view. **44.** to disclose, reveal, or divulge: *to open one's mind.* **45.** to render accessible to knowledge, enlightenment, sympathy, etc. **46.** to expand, unfold, or spread out: *to open a map.* **47.** to make less compact, less closely spaced, or the like: *to open ranks.* **48.** to establish for business purposes or for public use: *to open an office.* **49.** to set in action, begin, start, or commence (sometimes fol. by *up*): *to open a campaign.* **50.** to cut, blast, or break into: *to open a safe with nitro.* **51.** to make an incision or opening in: *to open a boil.* **52.** to make or produce (an opening) by cutting or breaking, or by pushing aside or removing obstructions: *to open a way through a crowd.* **53.** *Naut.* to sail (a course) so that the apparent location of a distant fixed object changes with relation to a nearer fixed object (sometimes fol. by *out*). **54.** *Law.* to make the first statement of (a case) to the court or jury. **55.** *Cards.* to begin a hand by making (the first bid), placing (the first bet), or playing (a given card or suit) as the lead. **—*v.i.*** **56.** to become open, as a door, building, box, enclosure, etc. **57.** to afford access (into, to, etc.): *a door that opens into a garden.* **58.** (of a building, theater, etc.) to open its doors to the public: *The museum opens at one o'clock.* **59.** to begin a session or term, as a school. **60.** to begin a season, series of performances, or tour as a theatrical company: *The play will open in Boston.* **61.** to have an opening, passage, or outlet (into, upon, etc.): *The room opens into a corridor.* **62.** to part, or seem to part, so as to allow or reveal a passage: *At last the cliffs opened to show us that we were heading for the sea.* **63.** to unfold or expand, as a blossom, so as to reveal the interior. **64.** to become disclosed or revealed. **65.** to come into view, or become more visible or plain. **66.** to become receptive to knowledge, sympathy, etc., as the mind. **67.** to disclose or reveal one's knowledge, thoughts, feelings, etc. **68.** to spread out or expand, as the hand or a fan. **69.** to open a book, newspaper, etc.: *Open to page 32.* **70.** to become less compact, less closely spaced, or the like: *The ranks began to open.* **71.** to begin, start, or commence an activity: *The session opened with a prayer.* **72.** *Hunting.* (of hounds) to begin to bark, as on the scent of game. **73.** *Cards.* to make the first bet, bid, or lead in beginning a hand. **74. open up,** *Slang.* **a.** to go into action, esp. to begin firing. **b.** to become familiar. **c.** to disclose confidential information: *After hours of grilling, the prisoner opened up.* **d.** to increase speed or the speed of (a vehicle). **—*n.*** **75.** an open or clear space. **76.** the open air. **77.** the open water, as of the sea. **78.** the situation of one who does not use or seek concealment: *All of his dealings are in the open.* **79.** an opening or aperture. **80.** an opening or opportunity. **81.** a contest or tournament in which both amateurs and professionals may compete, esp. in golf. **82. the open, a.** the unenclosed or unobstructed country. **b.** the outdoors: *Vacations in the open are fine for the entire family.* **c.** the condition of being publicly known or recognized: *The scandal is now out in the open.* [ME, OE; c. D *open*, G *offen*, OIcel *opinn*; based on root of UP] **—o′pen·ly,** *adv.* **—o′pen·ness,** *n.*

o′pen account′. See **current account** (def. 1).

o′pen air′, the unconfined atmosphere; outdoor air.

o·pen-air (ō′pən âr′), *adj.* existing in, taking place in, or characteristic of the open air; outdoor: *He conducted three open-air concerts last summer.* **—o′pen-air′ish,** *adj.* **—o′pen-air′ish·ness,** *n.* **—o′pen-air′ness,** *n.*

o·pen-and-shut (ō′pən ən shut′), *adj.* immediately obvious upon consideration; easily decided: *an open-and-shut case of murder.*

O′pen Boat′, The, a short story (1897) by Stephen Crane.

o′pen book′, a person, thing, or situation easily known or understood; something obvious or easy to know or interpret: *Her face is an open book.*

o′pen chain′, *Chem.* a series of atoms linked in a chain not joined together at its ends, and so represented in its structural formula. Cf. **closed chain.** **—o′pen-chain′,** *adj.*

o′pen cir′cuit, *Elect.* a discontinuous circuit through which no current can flow. Cf. **closed circuit.** **—o′pen-cir′cuit,** *adj.*

o′pen cit′y, *Mil.* a city that is officially declared to be of no military value and not to be defended or subjected to bombing or military attack by an enemy.

o′pen commun′ion, *Eccles.* a communion service in which members of all denominations can participate. Cf. **close communion, intercommunion.**

o′pen cou′plet, a couplet that concludes with a run-on line. Cf. **closed couplet.**

o′pen cov′er, *Math.* a cover of a set consisting entirely of open sets.

o′pen diapa′son. See under **diapason** (def. 4).

o′pen door′, **1.** the policy of admitting all nations or people of all nationalities to a country upon equal terms, as for trade or immigration. **2.** admission or access; unrestricted opportunity: *His experience had given him an open door to success in his field.* **—o′pen-door′,** *adj.*

o·pen-end (ō′pən end′), *adj.* not having fixed limits; permitting a broad interpretation: *open-end agreements; an open-end conception of man's potential.* Also, **o′pen-end′ed.**

o′pen-end invest′ment com′pany, an investment company that issues its shares continuously and without limit and is obliged to redeem or repurchase them from owners on demand. Also called **mutual fund.** Cf. **closed-end investment company.**

o·pen·er (ō′pə nər), *n.* **1.** one who or that which opens. **2.** a device for opening sealed containers: *can opener.* **3.** the first of several theatrical numbers, variety acts, sports events, etc.: *a humorous monologue as an opener; The home team won the opener.* **4. openers,** *Poker.* cards in a hand, as a pair of jacks or better, that according to a given standard are worth enough to enable the holder to make the first bet of a deal. [OPEN + -ER[1]]

o·pen-eyed (ō′pən īd′), *adj.* **1.** having the eyes open. **2.** having the eyes wide open, as in wonder. **3.** watchful; alert. **4.** done or experienced with full awareness: *an open-eyed commission of a crime.* **—o·pen-ey·ed·ly** (ō′pən ī′id lē, -īd′-), *adv.*

o·pen-faced (ō′pən fāst′), *adj.* **1.** having a frank or ingenuous face. **2.** (of a watch) having the dial covered only by the crystal. **3.** (of a pie, sandwich, etc.) without a layer of dough, crust, bread, etc., on top; having an uncovered filling.

o′pen frac′ture. See **compound fracture.**

o′pen frame′, *Bowling.* a frame in which a bowler fails to make a strike or a spare.

o′pen-frame′ gird′er (ō′pən frām′), a girder made on the principle of a Vierendeel truss.

Op·en·glop·ish (op′ən glop′ish), *n.* a secret language, often used by children, that is derived from ordinary language by inserting the letters *op* before each vowel sound of a word, as *Dopon't foporgopet hopim* (Don't forget him).

o·pen-hand·ed (ō′pən han′did), *adj.* generous; liberal: *open-handed hospitality.* Also, **o′pen-hand′ed.** **—o′pen-hand′ed·ly, o′pen-hand′ed·ly,** *adv.* **—o′pen-hand′ed·ness, o′pen-hand′ed·ness,** *n.*

o′pen hand′ knot′. See **loop knot.**

o·pen-heart·ed (ō′pən-här′tid), *adj.* **1.** unreserved, candid, or frank: *open-hearted advice.* **2.** kindly; benevolent: *an open-hearted gift to charity.* **—o′pen-heart′ed·ly,** *adv.* **—o′pen-heart′ed·ness,** *n.*

o·pen-hearth (ō′pən-härth′), *adj.* noting, pertaining to, or produced by the open-hearth process.

Open-hearth furnace (Cross section)
A, Charging door; **B,** Hearth; **C,** Checkers; **D,** Air; **E,** Gas

o′pen-hearth′ proc′ess, a process of steelmaking in which the charge is laid in a furnace (**o′pen-hearth′ fur′nace**) on a shallow hearth over which play flames of burning gas and hot air.

o′pen-heart′ sur′gery (ō′pən härt′), surgery performed on the exposed heart while a heart-lung machine pumps and oxygenates the blood and diverts it from the heart.

o′pen house′, **1.** a party or a time during which one's home is open to all friends and relatives who may wish to visit, often to share in a celebration, meet a special guest, etc.: *We have open house on the first Sunday of each month. He's giving an open house from three until seven today so we can all meet his friend from Italy.* **2.** a time during which a school, institution, etc., is open to the public for exhibition or for some specific occasion. **3.** a house hospitably open to all friends who may wish to visit it or enjoy its entertainment. **4. keep open house,** to be prepared to entertain visitors at any time: *They keep open house for artists and writers.*

o′pen hous′ing, *U.S.* the elimination of racial discrimination in the sales and rentals of private housing. Also called **fair housing.** **—o′pen-hous′ing,** *adj.*

o·pen·ing (ō′pə ning), *n.* **1.** the act or an instance of making or becoming open. **2.** the act of one who or that which opens. **3.** an unobstructed or unoccupied space or place. **4.** a void in solid matter; a gap, hole, or aperture. **5.** a tract of land thinly wooded as compared with adjoining forest tracts. **6.** the act of beginning; start; commencement: *the opening of a new session of Congress.* **7.** the first part or initial stage of anything. **8.** an employment vacancy; an unfilled position or job: *There are no openings for clerks today.* **9.** an opportunity. **10.** a formal or official beginning, as of a sport season or a season's sale of goods: *the opening of the deer-hunting season; Swimsuits sold well at the summer opening.* **11.** the first performance of a theatrical production. **12.** the first public showing or use of something: *the opening of an art exhibition.* **13.** a celebration of the first public showing or performance or of the first use or start of something: *The new supermarket is going to give away prizes at its opening.* **14.** *Law.* the statement of the case made by counsel to the court or jury preliminary to adducing evidence. **15.** a mode of beginning a game: *a manual of chess openings.* [ME; see OPEN, -ING[1]] **—Syn. 4.** orifice; slit, breach, rift, chasm, cleft, fissure, rent. **—Ant. 1.** closing.

o′pen let′ter, a letter, usually of protest or criticism, addressed to a specific person, but meant to be published in a newspaper, broadcast by radio, or otherwise brought to widespread public attention. **—o′pen-let′ter,** *adj.*

o·pen-mind·ed (ō′pən mīn′did), *adj.* **1.** having or showing a mind receptive to new ideas or arguments. **2.** unprejudiced. **—o′pen-mind′ed·ly,** *adv.* **—o′pen-mind′ed·ness,** *n.*

o·pen-mouthed (ō′pən mouthd′, -moutht′), *adj.* **1.** having the mouth open. **2.** gaping, as with surprise or astonishment. **3.** greedy, ravenous, or rapacious. **4.** clamoring at the sight of game or prey, as hounds. **5.** vociferous or clamorous. **6.** having a wide mouth, as a pitcher or jar. **—o·pen-mouth·ed·ly** (ō′pən mou′thid lē, -moutht′lē), *adv.* **—o′pen-mouth′ed·ness,** *n.*

o′pen or′der, *Mil.* a troop formation for drill or basic combat training, the intervals between the individuals being greater than those in close order. Also called **extended order.**

o′pen pol′icy, *Insurance.* a continuous policy covering goods of a class subject to changes in volume, usually requiring periodic reports of values.

o′pen posi′tion, *Music.* the arrangement of a chord with wide intervals between the parts.

o′pen pri′mary, a direct primary election in which voters need not meet a test of party membership.

o′pen quote′, **1.** the quotation mark used to begin a quotation (" or '). **2.** (used by a speaker to signify that he is beginning a quotation.) Also, **o′pen quotes′.**

o′pen sand′wich, a sandwich served on one slice of bread, without a covering slice.

o′pen sea′, the main body of a sea or ocean, esp. that part which is outside territorial waters and not enclosed, or partially enclosed, by land.

o/pen se/cret, something supposedly secret but actually known quite generally.

o/pen ses/ame, any marvelously effective means for bringing about a desired result: *He seems to think that wealth is the open sesame to happiness.* [from the use of these words by Ali Baba to open the door of the robbers' den]

o·pen-shelf (ō/pən shelf/), *adj.* of or pertaining to a system of library management in which patrons have direct access to bookshelves for browsing and for selecting books.

o/pen-shel/ter-deck ves/sel (ō/pən shel/tər-dek/), *Naut.* a cargo vessel not considered sufficiently watertight in all cargo spaces to have the legal maximum draft. Also called **shelter-deck vessel.**

o/pen shop/, 1. a shop in which a union, chosen by a majority of the employees, acts as representative of all the employees in making agreements with the employer, but in which union membership is not a condition of employment. **2.** *Rare.* a nonunion shop which may or may not employ union members together with nonmembers, but which does not recognize or deal with a union as the representative of the employees. Cf. **nonunion shop. 3.** *Rare.* an antiunion shop in which union members are not knowingly employed. **—o/pen-shop/,** *adj.*

o·pen-sid·ed (ō/pən sī/did), *adj.* having a side or sides open.

o/pen sight/, (on a firearm) a rear sight consisting of a notch across which the gunner aligns the front sight on the target. Cf. **peep sight.**

o/pen space/, *Naut.* (in tonnage computation) any covered space above an upper deck that has only temporary means of closing it, theoretically regarded as nonwatertight or as insufficient to exclude the weather. It is exempt from taxation. Cf. **open-shelter deck vessel, tonnage opening.**

o/pen sphere/, *Math.* the set of points whose distance from a given point is less than some specified number. Cf. **closed sphere.**

o/pen stock/, *Com.* merchandise, esp. china, silverware, and glassware, sold in sets with individual pieces available from stock for future purchases, as for replacement.

o/pen string/, a staircase string whose top follows the profile of the steps in such a way that the treads project beyond its outer face.

o/pen sys/tem, *Physics, Chem.* a region separated from its surroundings by a boundary that admits a transfer of matter across it. Cf. **closed system.**

o·pen-tim·bered (ō/pən tim/bərd), *adj.* (of a roof, ceiling, etc.) constructed so that the timbers are exposed.

o/pen trail/er, any dog which barks or bays on the trail of its quarry. Cf. **still trailer.**

o/pen un/ion, a labor union that does not impose rigid restrictions on the admission of new members. Cf. **closed union.**

o·pen-web (ō/pən web/), *adj.* (of a metal joist or girder) having a web of zigzag or crisscross lacing.

o·pen·work (ō/pən wûrk/), *n.* any kind of work, esp. ornamental, as of metal, stone, wood, embroidery, lace, etc., showing openings through its substance. [OPEN + WORK]

OPer., Old Persian.

op·er·a[1] (op/ər ə, op/rə), *n.* **1.** an extended dramatic composition in which all parts are sung to instrumental accompaniment, that usually includes arias, choruses, and recitatives, and that sometimes includes ballet. Cf. **comic opera, grand opera. 2.** the form or branch of musical and dramatic art represented by such compositions. **3.** the score or the words of such a composition. **4.** a performance of one: *to go to the opera.* **5.** an opera house: *the Paris Opera.* [< It: work, opera < L: service, work, a work, pl. of *opus*]

o·per·a[2] (ō/pər ə, op/ər ə), *n.* *Chiefly Music.* a pl. of **opus.**

op·er·a·ble (op/ər ə bəl), *adj.* **1.** capable of being put into use, operation, or practice. **2.** admitting of a surgical operation without undue risk. Cf. **inoperable** (def. 2). [< LL *operābil(is)*, equiv. to *operā(rī)* (to) work + *-bilis* -BLE] **—op/er·a·bil/i·ty,** *n.* **—op/er·a·bly,** *adv.*

o·pé·ra bouffe (op/ər ə bo͞of/, op/rə; *Fr.* ô pā RA bo͞of/), *pl.* **o·pé·ra bouffes, o·pé·ras bouffe,** *Fr.* **o·pé·ras bouffes** (ô pā RA bo͞of/). a comic opera, esp. of farcical character. [< F]

o·pe·ra buf·fa (op/ər ə bo͞o/fə, op/rə; *It.* ô/pe RÄ bo͞of/fä), *pl.* **o·pe·ra buf·fas, o·pe·ras buf·fa,** *It.* **o·pe·re buf·fe** (ô/pe RE bo͞of/fe). **1.** an Italian farcical comic opera originating in the 18th century and containing recitativo secco, patter songs, and ensemble finales. **2.** the operatic genre comprising such works. [< It]

o·pé·ra co·mique (op/ər ə ko mēk/, op/rə; *Fr.* ô pā RA kô mēk/), *pl.* **o·pé·ra co·miques, o·pé·ras co·mique,** *Fr.* **o·pé·ras co·miques** (ô pā RA kô mēk/). See **comic opera.** [< F]

op/era glass/es, a small, low-power pair of binoculars for use at plays, concerts, and the like. Also, **op/era glass/.**

op/era hat/, a man's tall, collapsible top hat, held open or in shape by springs and usually covered with a black, silky fabric. Also called **gibus.** Cf. **beaver**[1] (def. 4), **silk hat, top hat.**

op/era house/, 1. a theater devoted chiefly to operas. **2.** *U.S. Dial.* a theater or exhibition hall.

op·er·and (op/ə rand/), *n.* *Math.* a quantity upon which a mathematical operation is performed. [< L *operand(um)*, neut. of ger. of *operārī* to OPERATE]

op·er·ant (op/ər ənt), *adj.* **1.** operating; producing effects. **2.** *Psychol.* (of a response) emitted by or elicited from an organism without a specific or identifiable stimulus: *operant conditioning; operant learning.* **—*n.* 3.** one who or that which operates. [< L *operant-* (s. of *operāns*, prp. of *operārī*), equiv. to *oper(ā)-* OPERATE + *-ant-* -ANT]

o·pe·ra se·ria (op/ər ə sēr/ē ə, op/rə; *It.* ô/pe RÄ se/ryä), *pl.* **o·pe·ra se·rias, o·pe·ras se·ria,** *It.* **o·pe·re se·rie** (ô/pe RE se/RYE). Italian dramatic opera of the 18th century based typically on a classical subject and characterized by extensive use of the aria da capo and recitative. [< It: lit., serious opera]

op·er·ate (op/ə rāt/), *v.,* **-at·ed, -at·ing.** **—*v.i.* 1.** to work, perform, or function, as a machine does. **2.** to work or use a machine, apparatus, or the like. **3.** to act effectively; produce an effect; exert force or influence (often fol. by *on* or *upon*): *Their propaganda is beginning to operate on the minds of the people.* **4.** to perform some process of work or treatment. **5.** *Surg.* to perform some manual act or series of acts with instruments upon the body of a patient to remedy or remove deformity, injury, or disease. **6.** (of a drug) to produce the effect intended. **7.** *Mil.* **a.** to carry on operations in war. **b.** to give orders and accomplish military acts, as distinguished from doing staff work. **8.** to carry on transactions in securities, or some commodity, esp. speculatively or on a large scale. **—*v.t.* 9.** to manage or use (a machine, device, etc.): *to operate a switchboard.* **10.** to put or keep (a factory, industrial system, ranch, etc.) working or in operation: *to operate a coal mine.* **11.** to bring about, effect, or produce, as by action or the exertion of force or influence. [< L *operāt(us)* having done work (ptp. of *operārī*), equiv. to *oper-* (s. of *opus*) work + *-ātus* -ATE[1]] **—op/er·at/a·ble,** *adj.*

op·er·at·ic (op/ə rat/ik), *adj.* **1.** of, pertaining to, or resembling opera: *operatic music.* **2.** resembling or suitable for opera: *a voice of operatic caliber.* **—*n.* 3.** Usually, **operatics.** (*construed as sing. or pl.*) **a.** technique or method of producing or staging operas. **b.** wildly exaggerated or melodramatic behavior, often thought to be characteristic of operatic acting: *She went into her usual operatics when she didn't get her way.* [OPERA[1] + -TIC, after *drama, dramatic*] **—op/er·at/i·cal·ly,** *adv.*

op·er·a·tion (op/ə rā/shən), *n.* **1.** the act or an instance, process, or manner of functioning or operating. **2.** the state of being operative (usually prec. by *in* or *into*): *a rule no longer in operation.* **3.** the power to act; efficacy, influence, or force. **4.** the exertion of force or influence; agency: *the operation of alcohol on the mind.* **5.** a process of a practical or mechanical nature in some form of work or production: *a delicate operation in watchmaking.* **6.** a course or procedure of productive or industrial activity: *building operations.* **7.** a particular process or course: *mental operations.* **8.** a business transaction, esp. one of a speculative nature or on a large scale: *operations in oil.* **9.** *Surg.* a process or method of operating on the body of a patient, with instruments, to remedy injury, malformation, etc. **10.** *Math.* **a.** a mathematical process, as addition, multiplication, differentiation, etc. **b.** the action of applying a mathematical process to a quantity or quantities. **11.** *Mil.* **a.** a campaign, mission, maneuver, or action. **b.** Usually, **operations.** the conduct of a campaign, mission, etc. **c. operations,** a headquarters, office, or place from which a military campaign, air traffic to and from an airfield, or any of various other activities, is planned, conducted, and controlled. **d. operations,** the people who work at such a headquarters. [ME *operacioun* < L *operātiōn-* (s. of *operātiō*), equiv. to *operāt(us)* (see OPERATE) + *-iōn-* -ION]

op·er·a·tion·al (op/ə rā/shə nəl), *adj.* **1.** able to function or be used; functional: *How soon will the truck be operational?* **2.** *Mil.* **a.** of, pertaining to, or involved in military operations. **b.** on active service or combat duty: *All units of the command are operational.* **3.** of or pertaining to operations or an operation. [OPERATION + -AL[1]] **—op/er·a/tion·al·ly,** *adv.*

op·er·a·tion·al·ism (op/ə rā/shə nəliz/əm), *n.* *Philos.* the doctrine that the meaning of a proposition consists of the operation or operations performed in proving it or in applying it to specific situations. Also, **op/er·a/tion·ism.** [OPERATIONAL + -ISM]

opera/tions research/, the analysis, usually involving mathematical treatment, of a process, problem, or operation to determine its purpose and effectiveness and to gain maximum efficiency.

op·er·a·tive (op/ə rā/tiv, -ər ə tiv, op/rə tiv), *n.* **1.** a worker; a person engaged, employed, or skilled in some branch of work, esp. productive or industrial work; a workman, artisan, or factory hand. **2.** a detective. **3.** a secret agent; spy. **—*adj.* 4.** operating, or exerting force or influence. **5.** having force; being in effect or operation: *laws operative in this city.* **6.** effective or efficacious. **7.** engaged in, concerned with, or pertaining to work or productive activity. **8.** *Med.* concerned with, involving, or pertaining to remedial operations: *operative surgery.* [< MF *operatif* < L *operāt(us)* having done work (see OPERATE) + MF *-if* -IVE] **—op/er·a/tive·ly,** *adv.* **—op/er·a/tive·ness, op·er·a·tiv·i·ty** (op/ər ə tiv/i tē), *n.* **—Syn. 2.** investigator, agent. **6.** effectual, serviceable.

op·er·a·tor (op/ə rā/tər), *n.* **1.** a person who operates a machine, apparatus, or the like: *a telegraph operator.* **2.** a woman who operates a telephone switchboard, esp. for a telephone company. **3.** a person who conducts some working or industrial establishment, enterprise, or system: *the operators of a mine.* **4.** a person who trades in securities, esp. speculatively or on a large scale. **5.** a person who performs a surgical operation. **6.** *Math.* **a.** a symbol for expressing a mathematical operation. **b.** a function, esp. one transforming a function, set, etc., into another: *a differential operator.* **7.** *Slang.* **a.** a person who accomplishes his purposes by cleverness of method, persuasiveness, etc. **b.** a person who is adroit at overcoming, avoiding, or evading difficulties, regulations, or restrictions. **c.** a person who is successful in a large-scale financial activity. **d.** a person who is extremely successful with or charmingly persuasive to members of the opposite sex. **e.** a person who can talk convincingly and persuasively about many things. [< LL, equiv. to L *operāt(us)* having done work (see OPERATE) + *-or* -OR[2]]

o·per·cle (ō/pər kəl), *n.* an operculum, esp. the posterior bone of the operculum of a fish. [< L *opercul(um)* cover. See OPERCULUM]

o·per·cu·late (ō pûr/kyə lit, -lāt/), *adj.* having an operculum. Also, **o·per/cu·lat/ed.** [< L *opercul(um)* cover (see OPERCULUM) + -ATE[1]]

o·per·cu·lum (ō pûr/kyə ləm), *n., pl.* **-la** (-lə), **-lums. 1.** *Bot., Zool.* a part or organ serving as a lid or cover, as a covering flap on a seed vessel. **2.** *Zool.* **a.** the gill cover of fishes and amphibians. See diag. under **fish. b.** (in many gastropods) a horny plate which closes the opening of the shell when the animal is retracted. [< NL, L: lid, cover, equiv. to *oper(īre)* (to) cover + *-cul-* -CULE + *-um* n. suffix] **—o·per/cu·lar,** *adj.*

o·pe·re ci·ta·to (ô/pe RE/ ki tä/tō; *Eng.* op/ə rē/ sī-tā/tō), *Latin.* See **op. cit.**

op·er·et·ta (op/ə ret/ə), *n.* a short opera, commonly of a light, amusing character. [< It, dim. of *opera* OPERA[1]] **—op/er·et/tist,** *n.*

op·er·ose (op/ə rōs/), *adj.* **1.** industrious, as a person. **2.** done with or involving much labor. [< L *operōs(us)* busy, active, equiv. to *oper-* (s. of *opus*) work + *-ōsus* -OSE[1]] **—op/er·ose/ly,** *adv.* **—op/er·ose/ness,** *n.*

OPers, Old Persian.

O·phel·ia (ō fēl/yə), *n.* a girl's given name.

O·phel·tes (ə fel/tēz), *n.* *Class. Myth.* the son of King Lycurgus of Nemea who was killed in infancy by a serpent and in whose memory the Nemean games were held. Also called **Archemorus.**

O·phi·a (ō fē/ə), *n.* a girl's given name, form of **Ophelia.**

oph·i·cleide (of/ə klīd/), *n.* a musical wind instrument, a development of the old wooden serpent, consisting of a conical metal tube bent double. [< F *ophicléide* < Gk *óphi(s)* serpent + *kleid-* (s. of *kleís*) key] **—oph/i·clei/de·an,** *adj.*

o·phid·i·an (ō fid/ē ən), *adj.* **1.** belonging or pertaining to the suborder *Ophidia*, comprising the snakes. **—*n.* 2.** a snake. [< NL *Ophidi(a)* (pl.) name of the suborder (< Gk *ophídion*, equiv. to *óph(is)* serpent + *-idion* dim. suffix) + -AN]

o·phid·i·id (ō fid/ē id, of/i dī/id, ō/fi-), *n.* **1.** any fish of the family *Ophidiidae*, comprising the cusk-eels. **—*adj.* 2.** belonging or pertaining to the family *Ophidiidae.* [< NL *Ophidiid(ae)* name of the family, equiv. to *Ophidi(on)* name of the genus (< L *ophidion* snakelike fish < Gk; see OPHIDIAN) + *-idae* -ID[2]]

oph·i·ol·a·try (of/ē ol/ə trē, ō/fē-), *n.* the worship of snakes. [< Gk *óphi(s)* snake + (ID)OLATRY] **—oph/i·ol/a·ter,** *n.* **—oph/i·ol/a·trous,** *adj.*

oph·i·ol·o·gy (of/ē ol/ə jē, ō/fē-), *n.* the branch of herpetology dealing with snakes. [< Gk *óphi(s)* snake + -o- + -LOGY] **—oph·i·o·log·i·cal** (of/ē ə loj/i kəl), **oph/i·o·log/ic,** *adj.* **—oph/i·ol/o·gist,** *n.*

O·phi·on (ə fī/ən), *n.* *Class. Myth.* a serpent created from the north wind by Eurynome as a mate.

O·phir (ō/fər), *n.* a country of uncertain location, possibly southern Arabia or the eastern coast of Africa, from which gold and precious stones and trees were brought for Solomon. I Kings 10:11.

oph·ite (of/īt, ō/fīt), *n.* *Mineral.* an ophitic diabase. [< L *ophīt(ēs)* serpentine stone < Gk *ophī́tēs (líthos)* serpentine (stone), equiv. to *óph(is)* serpent + *-ītēs* -ITE[1]]

o·phit·ic (ō fit/ik), *adj.* noting or pertaining to a rock texture exhibited by certain ophites, in which elongate feldspar crystals are embedded in a matrix. [OPHITE + -IC]

Oph·i·u·chus (of/ē yo͞o/kəs, ō/fē-), *n., gen.* **-chi** (-kī). *Astron.* the Serpent Bearer, a constellation on the celestial equator between Libra and Aquila.

ophthalm-, var. of **ophthalmo-** before a vowel: *ophthalmitis.*

ophthalm., opthalmology. Also, **ophthalmol.**

oph·thal·mi·a (of thal/mē ə, op-), *n.* *Ophthalm.* inflammation of the eye, esp. of its membranes or external structures. [< LL < Gk *ophthalmía*, equiv. to *ophthalm(ós)* OPHTHALM- + *-ia* -IA] **—oph·thal·mi·ac** (of thal/mē ak/), *n.*

ophthal/mia ne·o·na·to/rum (nē/ə nə tōr/əm, -tôr/-), *Pathol.* inflammation of the eyes of a newborn child due to a gonorrheal infection contracted during birth from the infected mother. [< NL: ophthalmia of the newborn (pl.)]

oph·thal·mic (of thal/mik, op-), *adj.* of or pertaining to the eye; ocular. [< L *ophthalmic(us)* < Gk *ophthalmikós*, equiv. to *ophthalm(ós)* OPHTHALM- + *-ikos* -IC]

oph·thal·mi·tis (of/thal mī/tis, op/-), *n.* *Ophthalm.* ophthalmia. [< NL; see OPHTHALM-, -ITIS] **—oph·thal·mit·ic** (of/thal mit/ik), *adj.*

Oph·thal·mi·tis (of/thal mī/tis), *n.* *Class. Myth.* an epithet of Athena meaning "of the eye."

ophthalmo-, a learned borrowing from Greek meaning "eye," used in the formation of compound words: *ophthalmology.* Also, *esp. before a vowel,* **ophthalm-.** [< Gk, comb. form of *ophthalmós*]

oph·thal·mo·dy·na·mom·e·ter (of thal/mō dī/nə-mom/i tər, -din/ə-, op-), *n.* **1.** a device for measuring the blood pressure of the retinal blood vessels. **2.** a device for determining the nearest point of ocular convergence. [OPHTHALMO- + DYNAMOMETER]

oph·thal·mol·o·gist (of/thal mol/ə jist, -thəl-, -thə-, op/-), *n.* a doctor of medicine specializing in ophthalmology. [OPHTHALMOLOG(Y) + -IST]

oph·thal·mol·o·gy (of/thal mol/ə jē, -thəl-, -thə-, op/-), *n.* the branch of medical science dealing with the anatomy, functions, and diseases of the eye. [OPHTHALMO- + -LOGY] **—oph·thal·mo·log·i·cal** (of thal/mə-loj/i kəl, op-), **oph·thal/mo·log/ic,** *adj.*

oph·thal·mom·e·ter (of/thal mom/i tər, -thəl-, -thə-, op/-), *n.* *Ophthalm.* an instrument for measuring the reflection of an image on the surface of the cornea and other capacities of the eye, used chiefly for determining the presence and degree of astigmatism. [OPHTHALMO- + -METER] **—oph·thal·mo·met·ric** (of thal/mə me/trik, op-), **oph·thal/mo·met/ri·cal,** *adj.* **—oph/thal·mom/e·try,** *n.*

oph·thal·mo·ple·gi·a (of thal/mə plē/jə, -jē ə, op-), *n.* *Ophthalm.* paralysis of one or more motor nerves of the eye. [< NL; see OPHTHALMO-, -PLEGIA] **—oph·thal·mo·ple·gic** (of thal/mə plē/jik, -plej/ik, op-), *adj.*

oph·thal·mo·scope (of thal/mə skōp/, op-), *n.* an instrument for viewing the interior of the eye or examining the retina. [OPHTHALMO- + -SCOPE] **—oph·thal·mo·scop·ic** (of thal/mə skop/ik, op-), **oph·thal/mo·scop/i·cal,** *adj.*

oph·thal·mos·co·py (of/thal mos/kə pē, op/-), *n., pl.* **-pies.** the use of or technique of using an ophthalmoscope. [OPHTHALMO- + -SCOPY] **—oph/thal·mos/co·pist,** *n.*

-opia, a learned borrowing from Greek, added to nouns indicating a condition of sight or of the visual organs: *diplopia; hemeralopia; myopia.* [< Gk *-ōpia*, deriv. of *ṓps* eye]

o·pi·ate (*n., adj.* ō/pē it, -āt/; *v.* ō/pē āt/), *n., adj., v.,* **-at·ed, -at·ing.** **—*n.* 1.** a medicine containing opium, used for inducing sleep and relieving pain. **2.** *Informal.* any sedative, soporific, or narcotic. **3.** anything that causes dullness or inaction, or that soothes the feelings. **—*adj.* 4.** mixed or prepared with opium. **5.** inducing sleep; soporific; narcotic. **6.** causing dullness or inaction. **—*v.t.* 7.** to subject to an opiate; stupefy. **8.** to dull or deaden. [< ML *opiāt(us)* bringing sleep, equiv. to L *opi(um)* OPIUM + *-ātus* -ATE[1]] **—Syn. 2.** drug. **3.** anodyne. **5.** sedative. **—Ant. 2.** stimulant.

o·pi·at·ic (ō′pē at′ik), *adj.* of, pertaining to, or resembling opiates. [OPIATE + -IC]

o·pine (ō pīn′), *v.t., v.i.,* **o·pined, o·pin·ing.** to hold or express an opinion. [< L *opīn(ārī)* (to) think, deem]

o·pin·i·cus (ō pin′ə kəs), *n., pl.* **-cus·es.** a heraldic monster having the head, neck, and wings of an eagle, the body of a lion, and the tail of a bear. [?]

o·pin·ion (ə pin′yən), *n.* **1.** a belief or judgment that rests on grounds insufficient to produce certainty. **2.** a personal view, attitude, or appraisal: *public opinion.* **3.** the expression of a personal view, attitude; appraisal, or judgment: *to give an opinion on tariffs.* **4.** the expression of a formal or professional judgment: *to ask a doctor for his opinion.* **5.** *Law.* the formal statement by a judge or court of the reasoning and the principles of law used in reaching a decision of a case. **6.** a judgment or estimate of a person or thing with respect to character, merit, etc.: *to forfeit someone's good opinion.* **7.** a favorable estimate; esteem: *I haven't much of an opinion of him.* [ME < OF < L *opīniōn-* (s. of *opīniō*), akin to *opīnārī* to OPINE]

—Syn. 1. persuasion, notion, idea, impression. OPINION, SENTIMENT, VIEW are terms for one's conclusion about something. An OPINION is a belief or judgment that falls short of absolute conviction, certainty, or positive knowledge; it is a conclusion that certain facts, ideas, etc., are probably true or likely to prove so: *political opinions; an opinion about art; In my opinion this is true.* SENTIMENT (usually *pl.*) refers to an opinion or judgment arrived at as the result of deliberation and representing a rather fixed conviction; it usually has a tinge of emotion about it: *These are my sentiments.* VIEW is an estimate of something, an intellectual judgment, a critical survey based on a mental examination, particularly of a public matter: *views on governmental planning.*

o·pin·ion·at·ed (ə pin′yə nā′tid), *adj.* obstinate or conceited with regard to one's opinions; conceitedly dogmatic. [OPINION + -ATE[1] + -ED[3]] **—o·pin′ion·at′ed·ly,** *adv.* **—o·pin′ion·at′ed·ness,** *n.*
—Syn. prejudiced, biased; bigoted; stubborn.

o·pin·ion·a·tive (ə pin′yə nā′tiv), *adj.* **1.** of, pertaining to, or of the nature of opinion. **2.** opinionated. [OPINION + -ATIVE] **—o·pin′ion·at′ive·ly,** *adv.* **—o·pin′ion·at′ive·ness,** *n.*

O·pis (ō′pis), *n. Class. Myth.* a companion of Artemis.

o·pis·the·nar (ə pis′thə när′), *n. Anat.* the back of the hand. [< NL < Gk *ópis(then)* behind + *thénar* THENAR]

op·is·thod·o·mos (op′is thod′ə məs, -mos′), *n., pl.* **-mos·es. 1.** Also called **posticum.** a small room in the cella of a classical temple, as for a treasury. **2.** epinaos. [< Gk, equiv. to *opistho-* (comb. form of *ópisthen* behind) + *dómos* house]

op·is·thog·na·thous (op′is thog′nə thəs), *adj. Zool.* having receding jaws. [< Gk *ópisth(en)* behind + -o- + -GNATHOUS] **—op′is·thog′na·thism,** *n.*

o·pis·tho·graph (ə pis′thə graf′, -gräf′), *n.* a manuscript, parchment, or book having writing on both sides of the leaves. Cf. **anopisthograph.** [< L *opisthograph(us)* having writing on the back < Gk *opisthógraphos,* equiv. to *opistho-* (comb. form of *ópisthen* behind) + *-graphos* -GRAPH]

o·pi·um (ō′pē əm), *n.* **1.** the inspissated juice of a poppy, *Papaver somniferum,* that has a narcotic, soporific, analgesic, and astringent effect and contains morphine, codeine, papaverine, and other alkaloids now used in medicine in their isolated or derived forms: a narcotic substance, poisonous in large doses. **2.** anything that causes dullness or inaction or soothes the mind or emotions. [ME < L < Gk *ópion* poppy juice, equiv. to *op(ós)* sap, juice + *-ion* dim. suffix]

o·pi·um·ism (ō′pē ə miz′əm), *n.* **1.** the habitual smoking of opium as a stimulant or intoxicant. **2.** a pathological condition caused by the habitual use of opium. [OPIUM + -ISM]

o′pium pop′py, a Eurasian poppy, *Papaver somniferum,* having white, pink, red, or purple flowers, cultivated as the source of opium, for its oily seeds, and as an ornamental.

op·o·del·doc (op′ə del′dok), *n. Pharm. Obs.* any of various liniments containing soap, camphor, alcohol, etc. [prob. coined by Paracelsus]

O·por·to (ō pōr′tō, ō pôr′-), *n.* a port in NW Portugal, near the mouth of the Douro River. 303,424 (1960). Portuguese, **Porto.**

o·pos·sum (ə pos′əm, pos′-əm), *n., pl.* **-sums,** (*esp. collectively*) **-sum. 1.** a prehensile-tailed marsupial, *Didelphis virginiana,* of the eastern U.S., the female having an abdominal pouch in which its young are carried: noted for the habit of feigning death when in danger. **2.** any of various animals of related genera. [< Algonquian; cf. Renape (Virginia) *apässum* white beast, Ojibwa *wabäsim* white dog]

Opossum, *Didelphis virginiana* (Total length about 3 ft.; tail 13 in.)

opos′sum shrimp′, any small, shrimplike crustacean of the order *Mysidacea,* the females of which carry their eggs in a pouch between the legs.

Opp (op), *n.* a town in S Alabama. 5535 (1960).

Opp., opuses; opera.

opp., 1. opposed. **2.** opposite.

Op·pen·heim (op′ən hīm′), *n.* **E(dward) Phillips,** 1866–1946, English novelist.

Op·pen·heim·er (op′ən hī′mər), *n.* **J(ulius) Robert,** 1904–67, U.S. nuclear physicist: Fermi prize in nuclear physics 1963.

op·pi·dan (op′i dən), *adj.* **1.** of a town; urban. **—***n.* **2.** a townsman. [< L *oppidān(us),* equiv. to *oppid(um)* town (OL *oppedum,* prob. equiv. to L *op-* OP- + *pedum* field < Gk *pédon*) + *-ānus* -AN]

op·pi·late (op′ə lāt′), *v.t.,* **-lat·ed, -lat·ing.** to stop up; fill with obstructing matter; obstruct. [< L *oppīlā-t(us)* stopped up (ptp. of *oppīlāre*), equiv. to *op-* OP- + *pīl-* ram + *-ātus* -ATE[1]] **—op′pi·la′tion,** *n.*

op·po·nen·cy (ə pō′nən sē), *n.* **1.** the act or an instance of opposing. **2.** the state of being an opponent. [OPPONEN(T) + -CY]

op·po·nens (ə pō′nenz), *n., pl.* **op·po·nen·tes** (op′ə-nen′tēz). *Anat.* any of several muscles of the hand or foot, the action of which tends to bring one of the lateral digits toward the other digits, making a hollow of the palm or sole. [< NL, L *oppōnēns,* nom. of *oppōnent-;* see OPPONENT]

op·po·nent (ə pō′nənt), *n.* **1.** a person who is on an opposing side in a contest, controversy, or the like; adversary. **—***adj.* **2.** being opposite, as in position. **3.** opposing; adverse; antagonistic. **4.** *Anat.* bringing parts together or into opposition, as a muscle. [< L *oppōnent-* (s. of *oppōnēns,* prp. of *oppōnere*), equiv. to *op-* OP- + *pōn-* place + *-ent-* -ENT]

—Syn. 1. antagonist; contestant. OPPONENT, COMPETITOR, RIVAL refer to persons engaged in a contest. OPPONENT is the most impersonal, meaning merely one who opposes; perhaps one who continually blocks and frustrates or one who happens to be on the opposite side in a temporary contest: *an opponent in a debate.* COMPETITOR emphasizes the action in striving against another, or others, for a definite, common goal: *competitors in business.* RIVAL has both personal and emotional connotations; it emphasizes the idea that (usually) two persons are struggling to attain the same object: *rivals for an office.* **—Ant. 1.** ally, friend.

op·por·tune (op′ər tōōn′, -tyōōn′), *adj.* **1.** appropriate, favorable, or suitable: *an opportune phrase for the occasion.* **2.** occurring or coming at an appropriate time; timely: *an opportune warning.* [ME < L *opportūn(us)* convenient, equiv. to *op-* OP- + *portus* access, PORT[1] + *-ūnus* adj. suffix] **—op′por·tune′ly,** *adv.* **—op′por·tune′ness,** *n.*

—Syn. 1. apt; fortunate, propitious. **2.** convenient. OPPORTUNE, SEASONABLE, TIMELY refer to that which is particularly fitting or suitable for a certain time. OPPORTUNE refers to that which is well-timed and meets exactly the demands of the time or occasion: *an opportune remark.* That which is SEASONABLE is right or proper for the time or season or occasion: *seasonable weather.* That which is TIMELY occurs or is done at an appropriate time, esp. in time to meet some need: *timely intervention.*

op·por·tun·ism (op′ər tōō′niz əm, -tyōō′-), *n.* **1.** the policy or practice, as in politics or business, of adapting actions, decisions, etc., to expediency, regardless of the sacrifice of principle. **2.** action or judgment in accordance with this policy. [< It *opportunismo,* equiv. to *opportun(o)* (< L *opportūnus;* see OPPORTUNE) + *-ismo* -ISM] **—op′por·tun′ist,** *n.* **—op′por·tun·is′tic,** *adj.* **—op′por·tun·is′ti·cal·ly,** *adv.*

op·por·tu·ni·ty (op′ər tōō′ni tē, -tyōō′-), *n., pl.* **-ties. 1.** an appropriate or favorable time or occasion. **2.** a situation or condition favorable for attainment of a goal. **3.** a good position, chance, or prospect for advancement. [ME *opportunite* < MF < L *opportūnitāt-* (s. of *opportūnitās*) fitness, equiv. to *opportūn(us)* (see OPPORTUNE) + *-itāt-* -ITY]

op·pos·a·ble (ə pō′zə bəl), *adj.* **1.** capable of being placed opposite to something else. **2.** capable of being resisted, fought, or opposed. [OPPOSE + -ABLE] **—op·pos′a·bil′i·ty,** *n.*

op·pose (ə pōz′), *v.,* **-posed, -pos·ing.** **—***v.t.* **1.** to act against or provide forceful resistance to; combat. **2.** to stand in the way of; hinder or obstruct. **3.** to set as an opponent or adversary. **4.** to be hostile or adverse to, as in opinion: *to oppose a resolution in a debate.* **5.** to set as an obstacle or hindrance. **6.** to set against in some relation, as of offsetting, comparison, or contrast: *to oppose advantages to disadvantages.* **7.** to use or take as being opposite or contrary. **8.** to set (something) over against something else in place, or to set (two things) so as to face or be opposite to one another. **—***v.i.* **9.** to be or act in opposition. [ME < OF *oppose(r),* b. L *oppōnere* to set against and OF *poser* to POSE[1]] **—op·pos′er,** *n.* **—op·pos′ing·ly,** *adv.*

—Syn. 1. confront, contravene. OPPOSE, RESIST, WITHSTAND imply setting up a force against something. The difference between OPPOSE and RESIST is somewhat that between offensive and defensive action: to OPPOSE is mainly to fight against, in order to thwart, certain tendencies, procedures, of which one does not approve: *He opposed the passage of the bill.* RESIST suggests that the subject is already threatened by the forces, or by the imminent possibility, against which he struggles: *to resist temptation.* Again, whereas OPPOSE always suggests an attitude of great disapproval, RESIST may imply an inner struggle in which the will is divided: *She tried unsuccessfully to resist his charm.* WITHSTAND generally implies successful resistance; it may refer to endurance that allows one to emerge unharmed (*to withstand a shock*), as well as to active resistance: *to withstand an attack.* **2.** prevent. **4.** contradict. **—Ant. 1.** support, help.

op·posed′-pis′ton en′gine (ə pōzd′pis′tən), a reciprocating engine, as a diesel engine, in which each cylinder has two pistons which move simultaneously away from or toward the center, connection of all pistons with a common crankshaft being made by a system of rods and yokes.

op·po·site (op′ə zit, -sit), *adj.* **1.** situated, placed, or lying face to face with something else or each other, or in corresponding positions with relation to an intervening line, space, or thing: *opposite ends of a room.* **2.** contrary or radically different in some respect common to both, as in nature, qualities, direction, result, or significance; opposed: *opposite purposes; opposite sides in a controversy; We left in opposite directions.* **3.** *Bot.* **a.** situated on diametrically opposed sides of an axis, as leaves when there are two on one node. **b.** having one organ vertically above another; superimposed. **4.** *Obs.* adverse or inimical. **—***n.* **5.** one who or that which is opposite or contrary. **6.** an antonym. **7.** *Archaic.* an opponent; antagonist. **—***prep.* **8.** across from; facing: *The guest of honor sat opposite me at the banquet.* **9.** in a role parallel or complementary to: *He has played opposite many leading ladies.* **—***adv.* **10.** on opposite sides. [ME < MF < L *opposit(us)* set against, ptp. of *oppōnere.* See OPPOSE, -ITE[2]] **—op′po·site·ly,** *adv.* **—op′po·site·ness,** *n.*

Opposite leaves (def. 3a)

—Syn. 1. facing. **2.** incompatible, irreconcilable, unlike, differing. OPPOSITE, CONTRARY, REVERSE imply that two things differ from each other in such a way as to indicate a definite kind of relationship. OPPOSITE suggests symmetrical antithesis in position, action, or character: *opposite ends of a pole, sides of a road, views.* CONTRARY sometimes adds to OPPOSITE the idea of conflict or antagonism: *contrary statements, beliefs.* REVERSE suggests that which faces or moves in the opposite direction: *the reverse side of a coin; a reverse gear.* **—Ant. 2.** same, like.

op′posite num′ber, *Chiefly Brit.* a counterpart; an equal or comparable title, person, job, idea, object, or word in a different country, system, class, situation, or language: *The American Secretary of the Treasury, inheritance tax, and the New York City subway are opposite numbers of the British Chancellor of the Exchequer, death duty, and the London underground.*

op′posite prompt′, *Theat. Chiefly Brit.* the offstage area to the right as one faces the audience. *Abbr.:* O.P. Also, **op′posite prompt′ side′.**

op·po·si·tion (op′ə zish′ən), *n.* **1.** the action of opposing, resisting, or combating. **2.** antagonism or hostility. **3.** a person or group of people opposing, criticising, or protesting something, someone, or another group. **4.** the major political party opposed to the party in power: *His Majesty's loyal opposition.* **5.** the act of placing opposite, or the state or position of being placed opposite. **6.** the act of opposing, or the state of being opposed by way of offset, comparison, or contrast. **7.** *Logic.* **a.** the relation between two propositions which have the same subject and predicate, but which differ in quantity or quality, or in both. **b.** the relation between two propositions in virtue of which the truth or falsity of one of them determines the truth or falsity of the other. **8.** *Astron.* the situation of two heavenly bodies when their longitudes or right ascensions differ by 180°: *The moon is in opposition to the sun when the earth is directly between them.* **9.** *Elect.* the condition that exists when two waves of the same frequency are out of phase by one-half of a period. [< L *oppositiōn-* (s. of *oppositiō*), equiv. to *opposit(us)* set against (see OPPOSITE) + *-iōn-* -ION; r. ME *opposicioun* < OF *opposicion*] **—op′po·si′tion·al, op′po·si′tion·ar′y,** *adj.* **—op′po·si′tion·less,** *adj.*

op·press (ə pres′), *v.t.* **1.** to lie heavily upon (the mind, a person, etc.): *Care and sorrow oppressed them.* **2.** to burden with cruel or unjust impositions or restraints; subject to a burdensome or harsh exercise of authority or power: *a people oppressed by totalitarianism.* **3.** to weigh down, as sleep or weariness does. **4.** *Archaic.* to put down, subdue or suppress. **5.** *Obs.* to press upon or against; crush. [ME *oppress(en)* < MF *oppress(er)* < ML *oppressāre* (freq.), deriv. of L *oppress(us)* crushed, ptp. of *opprimere,* equiv. to *op-* OP- + *-primere* (comb. form of *premere*) to PRESS[1]] **—op·pres′si·ble,** *adj.* **—op·pres′sor,** *n.*

—Syn. 1, 2. OPPRESS, DEPRESS, both having the literal meaning to press down upon, to cause to sink, are today mainly limited to figurative applications. To OPPRESS is usually to subject (a people) to burdens, to undue exercise of authority, and the like; its chief application, therefore, is to a social or political situation: *The tyrant oppressed his subjects.* DEPRESS suggests mainly the psychological effect, upon the individual, of unpleasant conditions, situations, etc., which sadden and discourage: *depressed by the news.* When OPPRESS is sometimes used in this sense, it suggests a psychological attitude of more complete hopelessness: *oppressed by a sense of failure.* **2.** maltreat, persecute. **—Ant. 1.** uphold, encourage.

op·pres·sion (ə presh′ən), *n.* **1.** the exercise of authority or power in a burdensome, cruel, or unjust manner. **2.** the act or an instance of oppressing. **3.** the state of being oppressed. **4.** the feeling of being oppressed by something weighing down the bodily powers or depressing the mind. [< MF < L *oppressiōn-* (s. of *oppressiō*) a pressing down, equiv. to *oppress(us)* crushed (see OPPRESS) + *-iōn-* -ION]

—Syn. 1. tyranny, despotism, persecution. **3.** hardship, misery, suffering. **—Ant. 1.** kindness, justice.

op·pres·sive (ə pres′iv), *adj.* **1.** burdensome, unjustly harsh, or tyrannical, as a king, taxes, measures, etc. **2.** causing discomfort by being excessive, intense, elaborate, etc.: *oppressive heat; oppressive decoration.* **3.** distressing or grievous: *oppressive sorrows.* [< ML *oppressīv(us),* equiv. to *oppress(us)* crushed (see OPPRESS) + *-īvus* -IVE] **—op·pres′sive·ly,** *adv.* **—op·pres′sive·ness,** *n.*

op·pro·bri·ous (ə prō′brē əs), *adj.* **1.** conveying or expressing opprobrium, as language, a speaker, etc.: *opprobrious invectives.* **2.** disgraceful or shameful: *opprobrious conduct.* [ME < LL *opprobriōs(us),* equiv. to L *opprobri(um)* OPPROBRIUM + *-ōsus* -OUS] **—op·pro′bri·ous·ly,** *adv.* **—op·pro′bri·ous·ness,** *n.*

—Syn. 1. reproachful, abusive, vituperative, contemptuous. **2.** dishonorable, ignominious. **—Ant. 1.** laudatory. **2.** reputable.

op·pro·bri·um (ə prō′brē əm), *n.* **1.** the disgrace or the reproach incurred by conduct considered outrageously shameful; infamy. **2.** a cause or object of such disgrace or reproach. [< L: reproach, equiv. to *op-* OP- + *probrium* infamy, disgrace]

op·pugn (ə pyōōn′), *v.t.* **1.** to assail by criticism, argument, or action. **2.** to call in question; dispute. [ME < L *oppugn(āre)* (to) oppose, attack, equiv. to *op-* OP- + *pugn-* fight, deriv. of *pugnus* fist; see PUGILISM] **—op·pugn′er,** *n.*

op·pug·nant (ə pug′nənt), *adj.* opposing; antagonistic; contrary. [< L *oppugnant-* (s. of *oppugnāns*) opposing, prp. of *oppugnāre.* See OPPUGN, -ANT] **—op·pug′nan·cy,** *n.*

OPr., Old Provençal.

OPruss, Old Prussian.

O·prille (ō′pril), *n.* a girl's given name.

OPruss, Old Prussian.

Ops (ops), *n.* the ancient Roman goddess of plenty, and the wife of Saturn and mother of Jupiter: identified with the Greek goddess Rhea.

OPS, Office of Price Stabilization. Also, **O.P.S.**

op·sin (op′sin), *n. Biochem.* any of several compounds that form the protein component of the light-sensitive retina pigment, rhodopsin. [prob. back formation from RHODOPSIN]

-opsis, a learned borrowing from Greek indicating apparent likeness: *coreopsis.* [< Gk *ópsis* appearance, sight]

op·son·ic (op son′ik), *adj. Bacteriol.* of, pertaining to, or influenced by opsonin. [OPSON(IN) + -IC]

opson′ic in′dex, the ratio of the number of bacteria taken up by phagocytes in the blood serum of a patient or test animal to the number taken up in normal blood serum.

op·so·nin (op′sə nin), *n. Bacteriol.* a constituent of normal or immune blood serum that makes invading bacteria more susceptible to the destructive action of the phagocytes. [< L *opsōn(ium)* victuals, hors d'oeuvre < Gk *opsṓnion*, deriv. of *opsōn(eîn)* (to) buy provisions] —**op′so·noid′,** *adj.*

op·so·nize (op′sə nīz′), *v.t.*, **-nized, -niz·ing.** *Immunol.* to increase the susceptibility of (bacteria) to ingestion by phagocytes. [OPSON(IN) + -IZE] —**op′so·ni·za′tion,** *n.*

opt (opt), *v.i.* to make a choice; choose (usually fol. by *for* or by an infinitive clause). [< F *opt(er)* (to) choose, divide < L *optāre* to select]

opt., 1. optative. 2. optical. 3. optician. 4. optics.

op·ta·tive (op′tə tiv), *Gram.* —*adj.* 1. designating or pertaining to a verb mood, as in Greek, that has among its functions the expression of a wish, as Greek *ídoimen* "may we go, we wish we might go." —*n.* 2. the optative mood. 3. a verb in it. [< LL *optātīv(us)*, equiv. to L *optāt(us)* (ptp. of *optāre*; see OPT) + *-īvus* -IVE] —**op′ta·tive·ly,** *adv.*

op·tic (op′tik), *adj.* 1. of or pertaining to the eye or sight. 2. optical. [< ML *optic(us)* < Gk *optikós* (cf. *optḗr* spy), equiv. to *opt(ós)* seen (verbid of *ópesthai*) + *-ikos* -IC]

op·ti·cal (op′ti kəl), *adj.* 1. of, pertaining to, or applying optics or the principles of optics. 2. constructed to assist sight or to correct defects in vision. 3. of or pertaining to sight or vision; visual: *optical illusions.* 4. of or pertaining to the eye. 5. dealing with or skilled in optics. [OPTIC + -AL[1]]

op′tical activ′ity, *Physical Chem.* the ability of a substance to rotate the plane of polarization of plane-polarized light.

op′tical air′ mass′, *Astron.* See **air mass** (def. 2).

op′tical bench′, an apparatus, as a special table, rigid beam, etc., for the precise positioning of light sources, screens, and optical instruments used for optical and photometric studies, having a ruled bar to which these devices can be attached and along which they can be readily adjusted.

op′tical cen′ter, *Print.* a point about 10 percent above the exact center of a printed page or layout.

op′tical disk′, a computer disk for holding digitized data that is stored on it and read from it by a laser beam.

op′tical dou′ble star′. See under **double star.**

op′tical glass′, *Optics.* any of several types of high-quality, homogeneous, color-free glass, as flint or crown glass, having specified refractive properties, used in lenses and other components of optical systems.

op′tical i′somer, *Chem.* any of two or more isomers exhibiting optical isomerism.

op′tical isom′erism, *Chem.* stereoisomerism in which the isomers are identical in molecular weight and most chemical and physical properties but differ in their effect on the rotation of polarized light. Cf. **dextrorotatory, levorotatory, racemism.**

op′tical ma′ser, a maser that amplifies radiation of frequencies within or near the range of visible light. Also called **laser.**

op′tical path′, the path of light through a medium, having a magnitude equal to the geometric distance through the system times the index of refraction of the medium.

op′tical rota′tion, *Physical Chem.* the angle at which the plane of polarized light is rotated when passed through an optically active substance.

op′tical scan′ning, *Computer Technol.* a process for recording impulses on magnetic tape by using a photoelectric device capable of distinguishing written or printed letters, numerals, and special characters and converting the information to electric impulses.

op′tical tool′ing, the technique of establishing precise reference lines and planes by means of telescopic sights, esp. for the purpose of aligning machinery, machine-shop work, etc.

op′tic ax′is, *Crystall.* (in a crystal exhibiting double refraction) the direction or directions, uniaxial or biaxial respectively, along which this phenomenon does not occur.

op′tic cen′ter. See **optical center.**

op·ti·cian (op tish′ən), *n.* 1. a person who makes or sells glasses for remedying defects of vision in accordance with the prescriptions of oculists. 2. a maker or seller of optical glasses and instruments. [< F *opticien* < ML *optic(a)* (see OPTICS) + F *-ien* -IAN]

op′tic nerve′, *Anat.* either one of the second pair of cranial nerves, consisting of sensory fibers that conduct impulses from the retina to the brain. See diag. under **eye.**

op·tics (op′tiks), *n.* (*construed as sing.*) the branch of physical science that deals with the properties and phenomena of both visible and invisible light and with vision. [< ML *optic(a)* (pl.) < Gk *optiká*, neut. pl. of *optikós*; see OPTIC] —**op′tic·ly,** *adv.*

op′tic thal′amus, thalamus (def. 1).

op·ti·mal (op′tə məl), *adj.* best; most desirable: *the optimal degree of economic recovery.* [OPTIM(UM) + -AL[1]]

op·ti·me (op′tə mē′), *n.* (formerly at Cambridge University, England) a student taking second or third honors in the mathematical tripos. Cf. **wrangler** (def. 2). [abstracted from L phrase *optimē* (*disputasti*) (you have argued) very well]

op·ti·mise (op′tə mīz′), *v.i., v.t.*, **-mised, -mis·ing.** *Chiefly Brit.* optimize. —**op′ti·mi·sa′tion,** *n.*

op·ti·mism (op′tə miz′əm), *n.* 1. a disposition or tendency to look on the more favorable side of happenings and to anticipate the most favorable result. 2. the belief that good ultimately predominates over evil in the world. 3. the doctrine that the existing world is the best of all possible worlds. 4. the belief that goodness pervades reality. [< F *optimisme* < L *optim(um)* what is best (see OPTIMUM) + F *-isme* -ISM]

op·ti·mist (op′tə mist), *n.* 1. an optimistic person. 2. a person who holds the belief or the doctrine of optimism. [< F *optimiste* < L *optim(um)* what is best (see OPTIMUM) + F *-iste* -IST]

op·ti·mis·tic (op′tə mis′tik), *adj.* 1. disposed to take a favorable view of things and to anticipate favorable results. 2. reflecting optimism: *an optimistic plan.* 3. of or pertaining to optimism. Also, **op′ti·mis′ti·cal.** [OPTIMIST + -IC] —**op′ti·mis′ti·cal·ly,** *adv.*

op·ti·mize (op′tə mīz′), *v.*, **-mized, -miz·ing.** —*v.i.* 1. to be optimistic. —*v.t.* 2. to make as effective, perfect, or useful as possible. 3. to make the best of. 4. *Computer Technol.* **a.** to prepare (a program) that automatically adjusts itself to operate a computer at maximum efficiency. **b.** to rewrite (a program) to obtain maximum efficiency. Also, *esp. Brit.,* **optimise.** [OPTIM(UM) + -IZE] —**op′ti·mi·za′tion,** *n.*

op·ti·mum (op′tə məm), *n., pl.* **-ma** (-mə), **-mums,** *adj.* —*n.* 1. the best or most favorable point, degree, amount, etc., as of temperature, light, and moisture for the growth or reproduction of an organism. 2. the greatest degree or best result obtained or obtainable under specific conditions. —*adj.* 3. best or most favorable: *optimum conditions.* [< L: best, neut. of *optimus*, superl. of *bonus* good]

op′timum pro′gramming, *Computer Technol.* See **minimum access programming.**

op·tion (op′shən), *n.* 1. the power or right of choosing. 2. something that may be or is chosen; choice. 3. the act of choosing. 4. See **stock option.** 5. a privilege acquired, as by the payment of a premium or consideration, of demanding, within a specified time, the carrying out of a transaction upon stipulated terms; the right, as granted in a contract or by an initial payment, of acquiring something in the future: *We bought one lot and took a 90-day option on an adjoining one. MGM has an option on his next script.* [< L *optiōn-* (s. of *optiō*) choice, equiv. to *opt(āre)* (to) select (see OPT) + *-iōn-* -ION] —**Syn.** 2. See **choice.** 2, 3. selection, election.

op·tion·al (op′shə nəl), *adj.* 1. left to one's choice; not mandatory: *Formal dress is optional.* 2. leaving something to choice. [OPTION + -AL[1]] —**op·tion·al·i·ty** (op′shə nal′i tē), *n.* —**op′tion·al·ly,** *adv.*

op·tion·ee (op′shə nē′), *n.* a person who acquires or holds a legal option. [OPTION + -EE]

opto-, a learned borrowing from Greek used, with the meaning "optic," "vision," in the formation of compound words: *optometry.* [< Gk *optó(s)*, verbal of *ópsesthai* to be about to see]

op·tom·e·ter (op tom′i tər), *n.* any of various instruments for measuring the refractive error of an eye. [OPTO- + -METER]

op·tom·e·trist (op tom′i trist), *n.* a person skilled in optometry. [OPTOMETR(Y) + -IST]

op·tom·e·try (op tom′i trē), *n.* the practice or profession of testing the eyes, by means of suitable instruments or appliances, for defects of vision in order to prescribe corrective glasses. [OPTO- + -METRY] —**op′to·met·ri·cal** (op′tə me′tri kəl), *adj.*

op·to·type (op′tə tīp′), *n. Ophthalm.* type used on an eye chart. [OPTO- + -TYPE]

op·u·lence (op′yə ləns), *n.* 1. wealth, riches, or affluence. 2. abundance, as of resources, goods, etc.; plenty. 3. the state of being opulent. Also, **op′u·len·cy.** [< L *opulentia* wealth. See OPULENT, -ENCE]

op·u·lent (op′yə lənt), *adj.* 1. wealthy, rich, or affluent, as persons or places. 2. richly supplied; abundant or plentiful: *opulent sunshine.* [< L *opulent(us)* wealthy, equiv. to *op-* (s. of *opēs* wealth, pl. of *ops* power) + *-ulentus* -ULENT] —**op′u·lent·ly,** *adv.* —**Syn.** 1. sumptuous, luxurious. See **rich.** —**Ant.** 1. poor; squalid.

o·pun·ti·a (ō pun′shē ə, -shə), *n.* 1. any cactaceous fleshy herb, shrubby plant, or tree of the genus *Opuntia*, having branches usually composed of flattened or globose joints, and having usually yellow flowers and pear-shaped or ovoid, often edible fruit. 2. See **prickly pear.** [< NL, L, after *Opuntius* pertaining to *Opūs* a town in Locris, Greece; see -IA]

o·pus (ō′pəs), *n., pl.* **o·pus·es** or, esp. for 2, 3, **o·pe·ra** (op′ər ə). 1. a literary work or composition, as a book. 2. a musical composition. 3. one of the compositions of a composer, usually numbered according to the order of publication. 4. *Informal.* a radio or television play or a motion picture. *Abbr.:* op. [< L: work, labor, a work]

o·pus·cule (ō pus′kyōōl), *n.* 1. a small or minor work. 2. a literary or musical work of small size. [< F < L *opuscul(um)*, equiv. to *opus* work + *-culum* -CULE] —**o·pus′cu·lar,** *adj.*

o′pus in·cer′tum (in sûr′təm), ancient Roman masonry faced with irregular stonework or brickwork. [< L: lit., uncertain work]

o′pus i·sod′o·mum (ī sod′ə məm), (in Roman masonry) coursed ashlar having courses of equal height. Also called **isodomum.** Cf. **opus pseudoisodomum.** [< L: lit., evenly built work]

o′pus pseu·do·i·sod′o·mum (sōō′dō ī sod′ə məm), (in Roman masonry) coursed ashlar having courses of unequal height. Cf. **opus isodomum.** [< L: lit., disproportionate work]

o′pus re·tic·u·la′tum (ri tik′yə lā′təm), Roman masonry faced with small, squared stones set obliquely. [< L: lit., reticulated work]

o′pus spi·ca′tum (spī kā′təm), Roman masonry faced with stones or tiles laid edge outward in a herringbone pattern. [< L: lit., work shaped like ears of corn]

o′pus tes·ta′ce·um (te stā′shē əm, -sē əm), Roman masonry faced with flat, triangular tiles, set so that one angle points inward toward the core of rubble or concrete. [< L: lit., work of tile]

-opy, var. of **-opia.**

o·quas·sa (ō kwas′ə, ō kwä′sə), *n., pl.* **-sas,** (*esp. collectively*) **-sa.** a small, dark blue trout, *Salvelinus oquassa*, found in Maine lakes. [said to be after one of the Rangeley lakes]

or[1] (ôr; *unstressed* ər), *conj.* 1. (used to connect words, phrases, or clauses representing alternatives): *to be or not to be.* 2. (used to connect alternative terms for the same thing): *the Hawaiian or Sandwich Islands.* 3. (used in correlation): *either . . . or; or . . . or; whether . . . or.* 4. (used to correct or rephrase what was previously said): *His autobiography, or rather memoirs, is ready for publication.* [ME, orig. unstressed member of correlative *other . . . or*, earlier *other . . . other*, OE *āther*, *ā-hwæther* (*oththe*) . . . *oththe* either . . . or]

or[2] (ôr), *prep., conj. Archaic.* before; ere. [ME, OE *ār* soon, early; c. OIcel *ār*, Goth *air* early; cf. OE *ǣr* soon, before, ERE]

or[3] (ôr), *Heraldry.* —*n.* 1. the tincture, or metal, gold: represented either by gold or by yellow. —*adj.* 2. of the tincture, or metal, gold: *a lion or.* [ME < MF < L *aur(um)* gold]

-or[1], a formal element appearing in nouns (of various origins) denoting action, state or condition, result, a quality or property, etc.: *ardor; color; error; honor; labor; odor; tremor; valor; vigor.* [< L; in some cases r. ME *-our* < AF (equiv. to F *-eur*) << L]

-or[2], a suffix of nouns denoting who or that which does something, or has some particular function or office (*actor; confessor; creditor; distributor; elevator; emperor; governor; juror; refractor; tailor; traitor*). It occurs chiefly in nouns originally Latin or formed from Latin stems. In some cases it is used as an alternative or substitute for the homonymous native English suffix **-er**[1], esp. in legal terms (often correlative with forms in **-ee**) or with some other differentiation of use (*assignor; grantor; lessor; sailor; survivor; vendor*). [< L; in some cases r. ME *-our* < AF *-(e)our* (equiv. to F *-eur*) << L *-or, -ātor,* etc.]

O.R., owner's risk. Also, **O.R.**

o·ra[1] (ôr′ə, ōr′ə), *n.* pl. of **os**[2].

o·ra[2] (ôr′ə, ōr′ə), *n., pl.* **o·ras, o·rae** (ôr′ē, ōr′ē). a money of account of Anglo-Saxon England, introduced by the Danes and equal to about two shillings. [OE *ōra* < Scand]

O·ra (ôr′ə, ōr′ə), *n.* a girl's given name.

O·ra·belle (ôr′ə bel′, ōr′-), *n.* a girl's given name. Also, **Or′a·bel′.**

or·ach (ôr′əch, or′-), *n.* any plant of the genus *Atriplex*, esp. *A. hortensis*, cultivated for use like spinach. Also, **or′ache.** [ME *orage, arage* < OF *arache* < VL *atripica*, var. of L *atriplic-* (s. of *atriplex*) < Gk *atrá-phaxis*]

or·a·cle (ôr′ə kəl, or′-), *n.* 1. (esp. in ancient Greece) an utterance, often ambiguous or obscure, given by a priest or priestess at a shrine as the response of a god to an inquiry. 2. the agency or medium giving such responses, or a shrine or place at which they were given: *the oracle of Apollo at Delphi.* 3. a divine communication or revelation. 4. **oracles,** the Scriptures. 5. the holy of holies of the Temple built by Solomon in Jerusalem. I Kings 6:16, 19–23. 6. any person or thing serving as an agency of divine communication. 7. any utterance made or received as authoritative, extremely wise, or infallible. 8. a person who delivers authoritative, wise, or highly regarded and influential pronouncements. [ME < OF < L *ōrācul(um)*, equiv. to *ōrā(re)* (to) plead (see ORATION) + *-culum* -CLE]

O·ra·con (ôr′ə kon′, ōr′-), *n. Pharm., Trademark.* two types of pills, containing estrogenic and progestational compounds, for administering in a certain series to women during the menstrual cycle for preventing conception.

o·rac·u·lar (ō rak′yə lər, ō rak′-), *adj.* 1. of the nature of, resembling, or suggesting an oracle: *an oracular response.* 2. giving forth utterances or decisions as if by special inspiration or authority. 3. uttered or delivered as if divinely inspired or infallible; sententious. 4. ambiguous or obscure. 5. portentous; ominous. [< L *ōrācul(um)* ORACLE + -AR[1]] —**o·rac′u·lar·ly,** *adv.* —**o·rac·u·lar·i·ty** (ō rak′yə lar′i tē), **o·rac′u·lar·ness,** *n.* —**Syn.** 1. prophetic. 2. authoritative, dogmatic. 4. equivocal.

o·rad (ôr′ad, ōr′-), *adv. Anat., Zool.* toward the mouth or the oral region. [< L *ōr-* (s. of *ōs*) mouth + *ad* toward]

O·ra·dea (ô rä′dyä), *n.* a city in NW Rumania. 110,719 (est. 1964). Also called **Ora′dea Ma′re** (mä′re). German, **Grosswardein.** Hungarian, **Nagyvárad.**

O·ra·dell (ôr′ə del′, ōr′-), *n.* a town in NE New Jersey. 7487 (1960).

o·ral (ôr′əl, ōr′-), *adj.* 1. uttered by the mouth; spoken: *oral testimony.* 2. of or using speech: *oral training in French; oral methods of teaching.* 3. of or pertaining to the mouth: *the oral cavity.* 4. done, taken, or administered through the mouth: *an oral dose of medicine.* 5. *Zool.* pertaining to that surface of polyps and marine animals that contains the mouth and tentacles. 6. *Phonet.* articulated with none of the voice issuing through the nose, as the normal English vowels and the consonants *b* and *v.* 7. *Psychoanal.* **a.** of or pertaining to the first stage of libidinal development in which sexual desire is undifferentiated from the desire for food, and gratification is derived from sucking, biting, etc. **b.** of or pertaining to the sublimation of feelings experienced during the oral stage of childhood: *oral anxiety.* **c.** of or pertaining to gratification by stimulation of the lips or membranes of the mouth, as in sucking, eating, talking, etc. —*n.* 8. an oral examination in a school, college, or university, given esp. to a candidate for an advanced degree. [< L *ōr-* (s. of *ōs*) mouth (c. Skt *āsya*) + -AL[1]] —**o′ral·ly,** *adv.* —**Syn.** 1. vocal. ORAL, VERBAL are not properly synonyms. ORAL is properly applied to that which is uttered by word of mouth, as opposed to what is conveyed in writing: *oral message.* VERBAL is often used for oral: *a verbal agreement.* Literally, however, VERBAL applies to the words, spoken or written, in which thought or feeling is conveyed: *a verbal picture.* —**Ant.** 6. nasal.

O·ral (ôr′əl), *n.* a boy's or girl's given name.

o·ra·le (ō rā′lē, ō rā′-), *n. Eccles.* fanon (def. 2). [< ML, equiv. to L *ōr-* (s. of *ōs*) mouth + *-āle*, neut. of *-ālis* -AL[1]]

o′ral groove′, a groovelike depression that forms the walls of the mouth of paramecia and other ciliate protozoans.

o′ral interpreta′tion, the study and practice of vocally expressing the meaning of written compositions, esp. of literature.

O·ran (ō ran′, ô ran′; *Fr.* ô räN′), *n.* 1. a seaport in NW Algeria. 392,637 with suburbs (1960). 2. a boy's given name, form of **Oren.**

o·rang (ō rang′), *n.* orang-utan.

or·ange (ôr′inj, or′-), *n.* 1. a globose, reddish-yellow, bitter or sweet, edible citrus fruit. 2. any white-flowered, evergreen rutaceous trees of the genus *Citrus*, bearing this fruit, as *C. aurantium* (**bitter orange, Seville orange,** or **sour orange**) and *C. sinensis* (**sweet orange**), cultivated in warm countries. 3. any of several other citrus trees, as the trifoliate orange. 4. any of several trees or fruits resembling an orange. 5. a color between yellow and red in the spectrum; reddish yellow. —*adj.* 6. of or pertaining to the orange. 7. made or prepared with oranges or orangelike flavoring: *orange sherbet.* 8. of the color orange; reddish-yellow. [ME < OF (b. with *or* gold), c. Sp *naranja* < Ar *nāranj* < Pers *nārang* < Skt *nāranja*]

Or·ange (ôr′inj, or′-; *Fr.* ô RÄNZH′ *for* 3, 7), *n.* **1.** a member of a European princely family ruling in the United Kingdom from 1688 to 1694 and in the Netherlands since 1815. **2.** a river in the Republic of South Africa, flowing W from Lesotho to the Atlantic. 1300 mi. long. **3.** a former small principality of W Europe: now in the SE part of France. **4.** a city in NE New Jersey, near Newark. 35,789 (1960). **5.** a city in SW California, near Los Angeles. 26,444 (1960). **6.** a city in SE Texas. 25,605 (1960). **7.** a town in SE France, near Avignon: Roman ruins. 21,450 (1962). **8.** a town in N Massachusetts. 3689 (1960). **9.** a town in central Virginia. 2955 (1960). **10. Fort.** See **Fort Orange.**

orange III, *Chem.* See **methyl orange.**

or·ange·ade (ôr′inj ād′, -in jād′, or′-), *n.* a beverage consisting of orange juice, sweetener, and water, sometimes carbonated. [< F; see ORANGE, -ADE[2]]

or′ange blos′som, 1. the white flower of an orange tree, esp. of the genus *Citrus*, much used in wreaths, bridal bouquets, etc.: the State flower of Florida. **2.** a cocktail made of gin, orange juice, and sugar, shaken together with ice.

Or·ange·burg (ôr′inj bûrg′, or′-), *n.* a city in central South Carolina. 13,852 (1960).

Or′ange Cit′y, a town in NW Iowa. 2707 (1960).

or′ange cone′flower, a perennial herb, *Rudbeckia fulgida*, found from New Jersey to Virginia and Indiana, having hairy leaves and orange-based, golden-yellow flowers with purplish-black disks.

Or′ange Cove′, a town in central California. 2885 (1960).

or′ange-eye but′terfly bush′ (ôr′inj ī′, or′-), a shrub, *Buddleia davidi*, of China, having fragrant, orange-throated, lilac-colored flowers.

Or′ange Free′ State′, a province in the central Republic of South Africa: a Boer republic 1854–1900; a British colony (**Or′ange Riv′er Col′ony**) 1900–10. 1,373,790 (1960); 49,647 sq. mi. *Cap.:* Bloemfontein.

or′ange gum′, gum-myrtle.

or′ange hawk′weed, a European hawkweed, *Hieracium aurantiacum*, having orange flowers, growing as a weed, esp. in eastern North America. Also called **devil's paintbrush.**

Or·ange·ism (ôr′in jiz′əm, or′-), *n.* the principles and practices of the Orangemen. [ORANGE + -ISM] —**Or′ange·ist,** *n.*

or′ange lil′y, a bulbous herb, *Lilium croceum*, of the mountainous regions of southern Europe, having erect, crimson-spotted, orange flowers.

Or·ange·man (ôr′inj mən, or′-), *n., pl.* **-men. 1.** a member of a secret society formed in the north of Ireland in 1795, having as its object the maintenance and political ascendancy of Protestantism. **2.** a Protestant of Northern Ireland. [ORANGE + MAN[1]]

Or′angemen's Day′, July 12, an annual celebration in Northern Ireland and certain cities having a large Irish section, esp. Liverpool, to mark both the victory of William III over James II at the Battle of the Boyne, July 1, 1690, and the Battle of Augbrim, July 12, 1690.

or′ange milk′weed. See **butterfly weed** (def. 1).

or′ange milk′wort, a milkwort, *Polygala lutea*, having racemes of orange-yellow flowers.

Or′ange Moun′tains, a range in E central Netherlands New Guinea. Highest peak, Wilhelmina, 15,584 ft.

Or′ange Park′, a town in NE Florida. 2624 (1960).

or′ange pe′koe, 1. a black tea composed of only the smallest top leaves and grown in India and Ceylon. **2.** any India or Ceylon tea of good quality.

or′ange puccoon′, a perennial herb, *Lithospermum canescens*, found mainly in eastern North America, having hairy stems and orange-yellow flowers.

or′ange rust′, *Plant Pathol.* a disease of blackberries and raspberries, characterized by an orange, powdery mass of spores on the undersides of the leaves and stunted, misshapen foliage, caused by a rust fungus, *gymnoconia interstitialis*.

or·ange·ry (ôr′inj rē, or′-), *n., pl.* **-ries.** a place, as a greenhouse, in which orange trees are cultivated. [< F *orangerie*, equiv. to *orang(er)* orange tree (deriv. of *orange* ORANGE) + *-erie* -ERY]

or′ange sul′phur. See **alfalfa butterfly.**

or′ange sun′flower, a perennial herb, *Heliopsis scabra*, of the eastern U.S., having rough leaves and orange-yellow flowers.

or·ange·wood (ôr′inj wo͝od′, or′-), *n.* the hard, fine-grained, yellowish wood of the orange tree, used in inlaid work and fine turnery. [ORANGE + WOOD[1]]

Orang-utan (4½ ft. high; arm spread 7½ ft.)

o·rang-u·tan (ō rang′o͞o tan′, ō rang′-), *n.* a large, long-armed anthropoid ape, *Pongo pygmaeus*, of arboreal habits, found in Borneo and Sumatra. Also, **o·rang′u·tan′, o·rang′u·tang′, o·rang-ou·tang** (ō rang′o͞o tang′, ō rang′-, ə rang′-). Also called **orang.** [< Malay: man of the woods]

or·ang·y (ôr′in jē, or′-), *adj.* resembling or suggesting an orange, as in taste, appearance, color, etc.: *decorated with orangy-pink flowers.* Also, **or′ang·ey.** [ORANGE + -Y[1]]

o·rans (ôr′anz, ôr′-), *n., pl.* **o·ran·tes** (ō ran′tēz, ô ran′-). orant.

o·rant (ôr′ənt, ôr′-), *n. Fine Arts.* a representation of a female figure, with outstretched arms and palms up in a gesture of prayer, in ancient and early Christian art. Also, **o·ran·te** (ō ran′tē, ô ran′-), **orans.** [< ML *ōrant-* (s. of *ōrāns*) praying, prp. of *ōrāre* to plead. See ORATION, -ANT]

o·ra pro no·bis (ôr′ä prō nō′bis, ôr′ä), *Latin.* pray for us.

o·rar·i·on (ə rár′ē ən), *n., pl.* **o·rar·i·a** (ə rár′ē ə). *Eastern Ch.* a stole worn by deacons. Also, **orarium.** [< MGk < LL *ōrārium*, L: napkin, equiv. to *ōr-* (s. of *ōs*) mouth + *-ārium* -ARY]

o·rar·i·um (ə rár′ē əm), *n., pl.* **o·rar·i·a** (ə rár′ē ə). orarion.

o·rate (ō rāt′, ô rāt′, ôr′āt, ōr′āt), *v.i., v.t.,* **-rat·ed, -rat·ing.** to deliver an oration; speak pompously or pretentiously; declaim. [back formation from ORATION]

o·ra·te fra·tres (ō rä′tā frä′tres, -trāz), *Rom. Cath. Ch.* the call to prayer, addressed by the celebrant to the people just before the Secret. [< L: pray, brothers]

o·ra·tion (ō rā′shən, ô rā′-), *n.* **1.** a formal speech, esp. one delivered on a special occasion, as on an anniversary, at a funeral, or at academic exercises. **2.** a speech characterized by a studied or elevated style, diction, or delivery. [ME *oracion* < L *ōrātiōn-* (s. of *ōrātiō*) speech, prayer, equiv. to *ōrāt(us)* pleaded (ptp. of *ōrāre* deriv. of *ōr-*, s. of *ōs*, mouth) + *-iōn-* -ION] —**Syn. 1.** See **speech. 2.** discourse, declamation.

or·a·tor (ôr′ə tər, or′-), *n.* **1.** a person who delivers an oration; a public speaker, esp. one of great eloquence: *Demosthenes was one of the great orators of ancient Greece.* **2.** *Law. Obs.* a plaintiff in a case in a court of equity. [< L: speaker, suppliant, equiv. to *ōrāt(us)* pleaded (see ORATION) + *-or* -OR[2]; r. ME *oratour* < AF] —**or′a·tor·like′,** *adj.* —**or′a·tor·ship′,** *n.*

Or·a·to·ri·an (ôr′ə tôr′ē ən, -tōr′-, or′-), *Rom. Cath. Ch.* —*n.* **1.** a member of an Oratory. —*adj.* **2.** of or pertaining to the Oratorians. [ORATORY[2] + -AN]

or·a·tor·i·cal (ôr′ə tôr′i kəl, or′ə tor′-), *adj.* **1.** of, pertaining to, or characteristic of an orator or oratory: *His oratorical prowess has been a major factor in gaining him political success.* **2.** given to oratory: *Even in private conversation, he is an oratorical speaker.* [ORATOR, ORATOR(Y)[1] + -ICAL] —**or′a·tor′i·cal·ly,** *adv.*

or·a·to·ri·o (ôr′ə tôr′ē ō′, -tōr′-, or′-), *n., pl.* **-ri·os.** an extended musical composition with a text more or less dramatic in character and usually based upon a religious theme, for solo voices, chorus, and orchestra, and performed without action, costume, or scenery. [< It: small chapel < LL *ōrātōri(um)* ORATORY[2]; so named from the musical services in the church of the Oratory of St. Philip Neri in Rome]

or·a·to·ry[1] (ôr′ə tôr′ē, -tōr′ē, or′-), *n.* **1.** the exercise of eloquence; eloquent speaking: *As an evangelist, he has moved thousands to repentance with his oratory.* **2.** the art of an orator; art of public speaking. [< L *ōrātōri(a)*, n. use of fem. of *ōrātōrius* of an orator. See ORATOR, -Y[3]]

or·a·to·ry[2] (ôr′ə tôr′ē, -tôr′ē, or′-), *n., pl.* **-ries. 1.** a place of prayer, as a small chapel or a room for private devotions. **2.** (*cap.*) *Rom. Cath. Ch.* any of the religious societies of secular priests who live in religious communities but do not take vows. [ME < LL *ōrātōri(um)* place of prayer, n. use of neut. of L *ōrātōrius* oratorical. See ORATOR, -ORY[2]]

or·a·trix (ôr′ə triks, or′-), *n., pl.* **or·a·tri·ces** (ôr′ə trī′sēz, or′-). a female orator. Also called **or·a·tress** (ôr′ə tris, or′-). [< L, fem. of *ōrātor*. See ORATOR, -TRIX]

orb (ôrb), *n.* **1.** one of the heavenly bodies: *He lay on the greensward, warmed by that orb of day, the sun.* **2.** a sphere or globe: *the Christmas tree all hung with crystal orbs.* **3.** the eyeball or eye: *He looks with blind orbs on a blind world.* **4.** a globe bearing a cross; the mound or emblem of sovereignty, esp. as part of the regalia of England. **5.** *Archaic.* a circle or something circular. **6.** *Astron. Obs.* the orbit of a heavenly body. **7.** *Astrol.* the space within which the influence of a planet, star, etc., is supposed to act. **8.** *Obs.* the earth. —*v.t.* **9.** to form into a circle or sphere. **10.** *Archaic.* to encircle; enclose. —*v.i.* **11.** to move in an orbit. **12.** to form into an orb or globe; round out. [< L *orb-* (s. of *orbis*) circle, disk, orb] —**orb′less,** *adj.* —**orb′like′,** *adj.* —**Syn. 2.** See **ball**[1].

or·bic·u·lar (ôr bik′yə lər), *adj.* like an orb; circular; ringlike; spherical; rounded. [ME < LL *orbiculār(is)* circular, equiv. to L *orbicul(us)* small disk (*orbi(s)* ORB + *-culus* -CULE) + *-āris* -AR[1]] —**or·bic′u·lar′i·ty,** *n.* **or·bic′u·lar·ness,** *n.* —**or·bic′u·lar·ly,** *adv.*

or·bi·cu·lar·is (ôr bik′yə lâr′is, -lär′-), *n., pl.* **-la·res** (-lâr′ēz, -lär′-). *Anat.* a muscle encircling an orifice of the body, as the mouth or eye. [< NL, LL: circular, ORBICULAR]

or·bic·u·late (ôr bik′yə lit, -lāt′), *adj.* orbicular; rounded. Also, **or·bic′u·lat′ed.** [< L *orbiculāt(us)* gone round in a circle (ptp. of *orbiculāri*), equiv. to *orbicul(us)* small disk (see ORBICULAR) + *-ātus* -ATE[1]] —**or·bic′u·late·ly,** *adv.* —**or·bic′u·la′tion,** *n.*

or·bit (ôr′bit), *n.* **1.** the curved path, usually elliptical, described by a planet, satellite, etc., about a celestial body, as the sun. **2.** the usual course of one's life or range of one's activities. **3.** *Anat.* **a.** the bony cavity of the skull which contains the eye; eye socket. **b.** the eye. **4.** *Zool.* the part surrounding the eye of a bird or insect. **5.** an orb or sphere. **6.** *Physical Chem.* the path traced by an electron revolving around the nucleus of an atom. —*v.t.* **7.** to move or travel around in an orbital or elliptical path: *The earth orbits the sun once every 365.25 days.* **8.** to send into orbit, as a satellite. —*v.i.* **9.** to go or travel in an orbit. [< L *orbit(a)* wheel track, course, circuit] —**or′bit·al, or′bit·ar′y,** *adj.*

or′bital an′gular momen′tum, *Physics.* the component of angular momentum of an electron in an atom or a nucleon in a nucleus, arising from its orbital motion rather than from its spin.

or·bi·ta·le (ôr′bi tā′lē), *n.* **1.** *Craniom.* the lowermost point on the lower margin of the left orbit, located instrumentally on the skull. **2.** *Cephalom.* the lowermost point on the lower margin of the left orbit, located by palpation on the head. [< NL, L: of an orbit, equiv. to *orbit(a)* ORBIT + *-āle*, neut. of *-ālis* -AL[1]]

or′bital in′dex, *Craniom.* the ratio of the maximum breadth to the maximum height of the orbital cavity.

or′bital quan′tum num′ber, *Physics.* See **azimuthal quantum number.**

or′bital veloc′ity, the minimum velocity at which a body must move to maintain a given orbit. Cf. **circular velocity.**

orb·y (ôr′bē), *adj.,* **or·bi·er, or·bi·est.** *Archaic.* like or pertaining to an orb. [ORB + -Y[1]]

orc (ôrk), *n.* **1.** (loosely) any of several cetaceans, as a grampus. **2.** a mythical monster, as an ogre. [< L *orc(a)* whale]

O.R.C., Officers' Reserve Corps.

or·ca (ôr′kə), *n.* the killer whale, *Grampus orca.* [< NL, L: whale]

or·ce·in (ôr′sē in), *n. Chem.* a red dye, the principal coloring matter of cudbear and orchil, obtained by oxidizing an ammoniacal solution of orcinol. [arbitrary alter. of *orcin;* see ORCINOL]

orch., orchestra.

or·chard (ôr′chərd), *n.* **1.** an area, often enclosed, devoted to the cultivation of fruit trees. **2.** a group or collection of such trees. [ME *orch(i)ard*, OE *orceard;* r. *ortyard*, ME *ortyerd*, OE *ortigeard* (cf. Goth *aurtigards* garden), equiv. to *ort-* (cf. L *hortus* garden) + *geard* YARD[2]]

or′chard grass′, a weedy grass, *Dactylis glomerata*, often grown for pastures.

or·chard·ist (ôr′chər dist), *n.* a person who cultivates an orchard. [ORCHARD + -IST]

or′chard o′riole, a North American oriole, *Icterus spurius*, the male of which is chestnut and black.

Or′chard Park′, a town in W New York. 3278 (1960).

or′chard valve′, an alfalfa valve of lesser diameter than the pipe it closes.

or·chec·to·my (ôr kek′tə mē), *n., pl.* **-mies.** *Surg.* orchiectomy.

or·ches·tra (ôr′ki strə), *n.* **1.** a company of performers on various musical instruments, including esp. stringed instruments of the viol class, clarinets and flutes, cornets and trombones, drums, cymbals, etc., for playing concert music, as symphonies, operas, and other compositions. **2.** (in a modern theater) **a.** the space reserved for the musicians, usually the front part of the main floor (**or′chestra pit′**). **b.** the entire main-floor space for spectators. **c.** the parquet. **3.** (in the ancient Greek theater) the circular space in front of the stage, allotted to the chorus. **4.** (in the Roman theater) a similar space reserved for persons of distinction. [< L < Gk: the space on which the chorus danced] —**or′ches·tra·less,** *adj.*

or·ches·tral (ôr kes′trəl), *adj.* **1.** of, pertaining to, or resembling an orchestra. **2.** composed for or performed by an orchestra: *orchestral works.* [ORCHESTR(A) + -AL[1]] —**or·ches′tral·ly,** *adv.*

or·ches·trate (ôr′ki strāt′), *v.t., v.i.,* **-trat·ed, -trat·ing.** to compose or arrange (music) for performance by an orchestra. [< F *orchestr(er)* (deriv. of *orchestre* ORCHESTRA) + -ATE[1]] —**or′ches·tra′tion,** *n.* —**or′ches·tra′tor, or′ches·trat′er,** *n.*

or·ches·tri·on (ôr kes′trē ən), *n.* a mechanical musical instrument, resembling a barrel organ but more elaborate, for producing the effect of an orchestra. [ORCHESTR(A) + *-ion*, as in *accordion*]

orchi-, var. of **orchido-.**

or·chid (ôr′kid), *n.* **1.** any terrestrial or epiphytic, perennial herb of the family *Orchidaceae*, of temperate and tropical regions, having usually showy flowers. **2.** a bluish to reddish purple. [< NL *Orchid(eae)* (later *Orchidaceae*), equiv. to L *orch(is)* a plant (see ORCHIS) + *-ideae* -ID[2]]

Orchid, Genus *Cattleya*

orchid-, var. of **orchido-** before a vowel: *orchidology.*

or·chi·da·ceous (ôr′ki dā′shəs), *adj.* belonging to the *Orchidaceae*, or orchid family of plants. [< NL *Orchidace(ae).* See ORCHID-, -ACEOUS]

or·chi·dec·to·my (ôr′ki dek′tə mē), *n., pl.* **-mies.** *Surg.* orchiectomy.

orchido-, a combining form used, with the meaning "orchid," "testicle," in the formation of compound words: *orchidology; orchidotomy.* Also, **orchi-, orchid-.** [*orchid-* (erroneously supposed s. of Gk *órchis* ORCHIS) + -O-]

or·chid·ol·o·gy (ôr′ki dol′ə jē), *n.* the branch of botany or horticulture dealing with orchids. [ORCHIDO- + -LOGY] —**or′chid·ol′o·gist,** *n.*

or·chi·dot·o·my (ôr′ki dot′ə mē), *n., pl.* **-mies.** *Surg.* incision of a testis. Also, **orchotomy.** [ORCHIDO- + -TOMY]

or′chid tree′, a tree, *Bauhinia variegata*, of southeastern Asia, having lavender or purple flowers clustered in the leaf axils. Also called **mountain ebony.**

or·chi·ec·to·my (ôr′kē ek′tə mē), *n., pl.* **-mies.** *Surg.* castration; excision of one or both testes. Also, **orchectomy, orchidectomy.** [ORCHI- + -ECTOMY]

or·chil (ôr′kil, -chil), *n.* **1.** a violet coloring matter obtained from certain lichens, chiefly species of *Roccella.* **2.** any lichen yielding this dye. Also, **archil, orseille.** [late ME < OF]

or·chis (ôr′kis), *n.* **1.** any orchid. **2.** any of various terrestrial orchids, esp. of the genus *Orchis*, of temperate regions, having spicate flowers. **3.** See **fringed orchis.** [< L < Gk *órchis* testicle, plant with roots like testicles]

or·chi·tis (ôr kī′tis), *n. Pathol.* inflammation of the testis. Also, **or·chi·di·tis** (ôr′ki dī′tis). [< NL; see ORCHI-, -ITIS] —**or·chit·ic** (ôr kit′ik), *adj.*

or·chot·o·my (ôr kot′ə mē), *n., pl.* **-mies.** *Surg.* orchidotomy.

or·ci·nol (ôr′sə nōl′, -nôl′, -nol′), *n. Chem.* a white, crystalline, water-soluble solid, $CH_3C_6H_3(OH)_2 \cdot H_2O$, sweet but unpleasant in taste, which reddens on exposure to air: obtained from many lichens or produced synthetically and used chiefly as a reagent for certain carbohydrates. Also, **or·cin** (ôr′sin). [< NL *orcin(a)* (< It *orcello* ORCHIL, by alter.) + -OL[2]]

or′ cir′cuit, a circuit in an electronic computer that is energized when any of its inputs is energized.

Or·cus (ôr′kəs), *n.* **1.** the ancient Roman god of the underworld, identified with the Greek Pluto, or Hades. **2.** the ancient Roman underworld; Hades; Dis.

ord., **1.** order. **2.** ordinal. **3.** ordinance. **4.** ordinary. **5.** ordnance.

or·dain (ôr dān′), *v.t.* **1.** *Eccles.* to invest with ministerial or sacerdotal functions; confer holy orders upon: *Twenty seminary students were ordained last week.* **2.** to enact or establish by law, edict, etc.: *to ordain a new type of government.* **3.** to decree; give orders for: *He ordained that the restrictions were to be lifted.* **4.** (of God, fate, etc.) to destine or predestine: *It seemed that fate had ordained the meeting.* —*v.i.* **5.** to order or

CONCISE ETYMOLOGY KEY: <, descended or derived from; >, whence; b., blend of, blended; c., cognate with; deriv., derivative; equiv., equivalent; imit., imitative; m., modification of; obl., oblique; r., replacing; s., stem; sp., spelling; trans., translation; ?, origin unknown, perhaps; *, hypothetical. See the full key inside the front cover.

command: *Thus do the gods ordain.* **6.** *Obs.* to select for or appoint to an office. [ME *ordein(en)* < OF *ordene(r)* < L *ordināre* to order, arrange, appoint. See ORDINATION] —**or·dain′a·ble,** *adj.* —**or·dain′er,** *n.* —**or·dain′ment,** *n.*
—**Syn. 4.** order, prescribe, determine. **5.** predetermine.

or·deal (ôr dēl′, -dē′əl, ôr′dēl), *n.* **1.** any extremely severe or trying test, experience, or trial. **2.** a primitive form of trial to determine guilt or innocence by subjecting the accused person to fire, poison, or other serious danger, the result being regarded as a divine or preternatural judgment. [ME *ordal,* OE *ordāl;* c. D *oordeel,* G *Urteil.* See DOLE[1]]

Ordeal′ of Rich′ard Fev′er·el, The (fev′ər əl), a novel (1859) by George Meredith concerning the education of a young man.

or·der (ôr′dər), *n.* **1.** an authoritative direction or instruction; command; mandate. **2.** a command of a court or judge. **3.** a command or notice issued by the Army, Navy, or Air Force or by a military commander to troops under him. **4.** the disposition of things following one after another, as in space, time, etc.; succession or sequence: *The cards were filed in alphabetical order.* **5.** a condition in which each thing is properly disposed with reference to other things and to its purpose; methodical or harmonious arrangement: *You must try to give order to your life.* **6.** formal disposition or array: *Put the chessmen in order.* **7.** proper or satisfactory condition: *My watch is out of order.* **8.** state or condition generally: *His affairs were in good order.* **9.** *Gram.* **a.** the arrangement of the elements of a construction in a particular sequence, as the placing of *John* before the verb and of *George* after it in *John saw George. John saw George* and *George was seen by John* differ only in order. **b.** the hierarchy of grammatical rules applying to a construction; the rank of immediate constituents. **10.** any class, kind, or sort, as of persons or things, distinguished from others by nature or character: *talents of a high order.* **11.** *Biol.* the usual major subdivision of a class or subclass in the classification of plants and animals, consisting of several families. **12.** a rank, grade, or class of persons in a community. **13.** a group or body of persons of the same profession, occupation, or pursuits: *the clerical order.* **14.** a body or society of persons living by common consent under the same religious, moral, or social regulations. **15.** *Eccles.* any of the degrees or grades of clerical office. Cf. **major order, minor order. 16.** any of the nine grades of angels in medieval angelology. Cf. **angel** (def. 1). **17.** a monastic society or fraternity: *the Franciscan order.* **18. orders,** the rank or status of an ordained Christian minister. **19.** Usually, **orders.** the rite or sacrament of ordination. **20.** a prescribed form of divine service, or of administration of a rite or ceremony. **21.** the service itself. **22.** the visible structures essential or desirable to the nature of the church, involving esp. ministry, polity, and sacraments. **23.** *Hist.* a society or fraternity of knights, of combined military and monastic character, as, in the Middle Ages, the Knights Templars. **24.** a modern organization or society more or less resembling the knightly orders: *fraternal orders.* **25.** conformity or obedience to law or established authority; absence of disturbance, riot, revolt, unruliness, etc.: *A police officer was there to maintain order.* **26.** customary mode of procedure; established practice or usage. **27.** the customary or prescribed mode of proceeding in debates or the like, or in the conduct of deliberative or legislative bodies, public meetings, etc.: *We follow* Robert's Rules of Order. **28.** conformity to this. **29.** prevailing course of things, or an established system or regime: *The old order is changing.* **30.** a direction or commission to make, provide, or furnish something: *shoes made to order.* **31.** a quantity of goods purchased or sold: *The druggist is sending the order right over.* **32.** a written direction to pay money or deliver goods, given by a person legally entitled to dispose of it: *delivery order; exchange order.* **33.** *Chiefly Brit.* a pass for admission to a theater, museum, or the like. **34.** *Archit.* **a.** any arrangement of columns with an entablature. **b.** any of five such arrangements typical of classical architecture, including the Doric, Ionic, and Corinthian orders invented by the Greeks and adapted by the Romans, the Tuscan order, invented by the Romans, and the Composite order, first named during the Renaissance. **c.** any of several concentric rings composing an arch, especially when each projects beyond the one below.

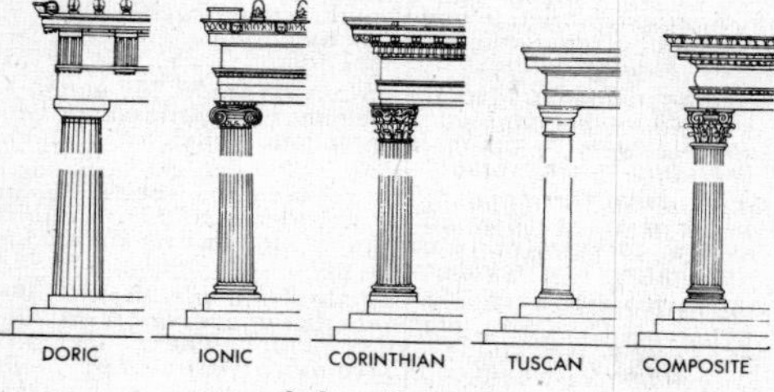

Orders (def. 34b)

35. *Math.* **a.** degree, as in algebra. **b.** the number of rows or columns of a square matrix or determinant. **c.** the number of times a function has been differentiated to produce a given derivative: *a second order derivative.* **d.** the order of the highest derivative appearing in a given differential equation: $\frac{d^2y}{dx^2} + 3y\frac{dy}{dx} - 6 = 0$ is a differential equation of order two. **e.** the number of elements of a given group. **f.** the smallest positive integer such that a given element in a group raised to that integer equals the identity. **g.** the least positive integer *n* such that permuting a given set *n* times under a given permutation results in the set in its original form. **36. a tall order,** a formidable task, requirement, or demand: *Getting the crop harvested with so few hands to help was a tall order, but we did it.* Also, **a large order. 37. call to order,** to begin (a meeting): *The meeting was called to order at 3 o'clock.* **38. in order, a.** fitting; appropriate: *It appears that a toast is in order.* **b.** in a state of proper arrangement, preparation, or readiness: *Everything is in order for the departure.* **c.** correct according to the rules of parliamentary procedure: *Questions from the floor are now in order.* **39. in order that,** to the end that: *We ought to leave early in order that we may not miss the train.* **40. in order to,** as a means to; with the purpose of: *She worked summers in order to save money for college.* **41. in short order,** with promptness or speed; rapidly: *The merchandise arrived in short order.* **42. on order,** ordered but not yet received: *We're out of stock in that item, but it's on order.* **43. on the order of,** resembling to some extent; like: *I would like a dress on the order of the one I saw in the display window.* **44. out of order, a.** inappropriate; unsuitable: *His remark was certainly out of order.* **b.** not operating properly; in disrepair: *The air conditioner is out of order again.* **c.** incorrect according to the rules of parliamentary procedure: *The chairman told him that he was out of order.*
—*v.t.* **45.** to give an order, direction, or command to: *The infantry divisions were ordered to advance.* **46.** to direct or command to go or come (as specified): *to order a person out of one's house.* **47.** to give an order for: *I forgot to order a taxi to take us to the airport.* **48.** to prescribe: *The doctor ordered rest for his patient.* **49.** to direct to be made, supplied, or furnished: *to order a copy of a book.* **50.** to regulate, conduct, or manage: *to order one's life for greater leisure.* **51.** to arrange methodically or suitably: *to order chessmen for a game.* **52.** *Math.* to arrange (the elements of a set) so that if one element precedes another, it cannot be preceded by the other or by elements which the other precedes. **53.** to ordain, as God or fate does. **54.** to invest with clerical rank or authority.
—*v.i.* **55.** to give an order or issue orders: *I would like to order, but the waitress is busy.* [ME *ordre* < OF < L *ōrdin-* (s. of *ordō*) row, rank, regular arrangement] —**or′der·a·ble,** *adj.* —**or′dered·ness,** *n.* —**or′der·er,** *n.* —**or′der·less,** *adj.*
—**Syn. 1.** ukase; ordinance, prescription, instruction. **5.** regularity. **12.** degree. **14.** fraternity, community. **45.** instruct, bid, require; ordain. See **direct. 50.** run, operate, adjust, arrange, systematize.

or′der arms′, 1. a position, in the manual of arms in close order drill, in which the rifle is held at the right side, with its butt on the ground. **2.** (as an interjection) the command to move the rifle to this position.

or′der bill′ of lad′ing, a bill of lading that is issued to the order of a shipper or consignee for delivery of the goods and that can be transferred by endorsement to third parties. Cf. **straight bill of lading.**

or′dered field′, *Math.* a field containing a subset of elements closed under addition and multiplication and having the property that every element in the field is either zero, in the subset, or has its additive inverse in the subset.

or′dered pair′, *Math.* two quantities written in such a way as to indicate that one quantity precedes or is to be considered before the other, as (3, 4) indicates the Cartesian coordinates of a point in the plane.

or·der·ly (ôr′dər lē), *adj., adv., n., pl.* **-lies.** —*adj.* **1.** arranged or disposed in a neat, tidy manner or in a regular sequence: *an orderly desk.* **2.** observant of or governed by system or method, as persons, the mind, etc.: *One must approach scientific study with an orderly mind.* **3.** characterized by or observant of law, rule, or discipline; law-abiding: *an orderly assemblage of citizens.* **4.** pertaining to or charged with the communication or execution of orders. —*adv.* **5.** according to established order or rule. **6.** methodically; regularly. —*n.* **7.** *Mil.* a soldier selected to perform various menial chores for a commanding officer. **8.** a hospital attendant, usually male, having general, non-medical duties. [ME (adv.); see ORDER, -LY] —**or′der·li·ness,** *n.*
—**Syn. 1, 2.** ORDERLY, METHODICAL, SYSTEMATIC characterize that which is neat, in order, and planned. These three words are sometimes used interchangeably. However, ORDERLY emphasizes neatness of arrangement: *an orderly array of books.* METHODICAL suggests a logical plan, a definite order of actions or method from beginning to end: *a methodical examination.* SYSTEMATIC suggests thoroughness, an extensive and detailed plan, together with regularity of action: *a systematic review.* —**Ant. 1.** chaotic, haphazard.

or′derly of′ficer, *Mil.* officer of the day, as in the British army, or, formerly, in the U.S. Army.

Or′der of the Gar′ter, the highest order of British knighthood, instituted by Edward III about 1348.

or′der port′, a port at which a merchant vessel calls for orders regarding the loading or discharge of cargo.

or·di·naire (ôʀ dē neʀ′), *adj.* *French.* ordinary; common.

or·di·nal[1] (ôr′dᵊnᵊl), *adj.* **1.** of or pertaining to an order, as of animals or plants. —*n.* **2.** an ordinal number or numeral. [< LL *ordināl(is)* in order, equiv. to L *ordin-* (s. of *ordō*) ORDER + *-ālis* -AL[1]] —**or′di·nal·ly,** *adv.*

or·di·nal[2] (ôr′dᵊnᵊl), *n.* **1.** a directory of ecclesiastical services. **2.** a book containing the forms for the ordination of priests, consecration of bishops, etc. [ME < ML, m. LL *ordināle* in order (neut. of *ordinālis*). See ORDINAL[1]]

or′dinal num′ber, 1. Also called **or′dinal nu′meral.** any of the numbers that express degree, quality, or position in a series, as *first, second,* and *third* (distinguished from *cardinal number*). **2.** *Math.* a symbol denoting both the cardinal number and the ordering of a given set, being identical for two ordered sets that have elements which can be placed into one-to-one correspondence, the correspondence preserving the order of the elements.

or·di·nance (ôr′dᵊnəns), *n.* **1.** an authoritative rule or law; a decree or command. **2.** a public injunction or regulation: *a city ordinance against excessive horn blowing.* **3.** *Eccles.* **a.** an established rite or ceremony. **b.** a sacrament. **c.** the communion. [ME *ordinaunce* < OF *ordenance,* ML *ordinantia,* deriv. of L *ordinant-* (s. of *ordināns*) arranging, prp. of *ordināre.* See ORDINATION, -ANCE]
—**Syn. 1.** order.

or·di·nand (ôr′dᵊnand′), *n.* *Eccles.* a candidate for ordination. [< LL *ordinand(us),* ger. of *ordināre* to ORDAIN]

or·di·nar·i·ate (ôr′dᵊnâr′ē it, -āt′), *n.* *Rom. Cath. Ch.* (formerly) a province in which the faithful of an Eastern rite were under the rule of a prelate of their rite who had no territorial jurisdiction. [ORDINARY (n.) + -ATE[1]]

or·di·nar·i·ly (ôr′dᵊnâr′ə lē, ôr′dᵊner′ə lē), *adv.* **1.** in ordinary cases; usually: *Ordinarily he sleeps until the last possible minute.* **2.** in an unexceptional manner or fashion; modestly: *a plain girl who was dressed quite ordinarily.* **3.** to the usual extent; reasonably: *to expect someone to be ordinarily honest.* [ORDINARY + -LY]

or·di·nar·y (ôr′dᵊner′ē), *adj., n., pl.* **-nar·ies.** —*adj.* **1.** of the usual kind; not exceptional; commonplace: *an ordinary day at work; a simple, ordinary man.* **2.** somewhat inferior or below average; plain or undistinguished: *a pretty face but ordinary clothes.* **3.** customary; normal: *for all ordinary purposes.* **4.** (of jurisdiction) immediate, as contrasted with that which is delegated. **5.** (of officials) belonging to the regular staff or the fully recognized class. —*n.* **6.** the commonplace or average condition, degree, etc.: *ability far above the ordinary.* **7.** something regular, customary, or usual. **8.** *Eccles.* **a.** an order or form for divine service, esp. that for saying Mass. **b.** the service of the Mass exclusive of the canon. **9.** *Hist.* a clergyman appointed to prepare condemned prisoners for death. **10.** *Eng. Eccles. Law.* a bishop, archbishop, or other ecclesiastic or his deputy, in his capacity as an *ex officio* ecclesiastical authority. **11.** *U.S.* (in some States) a judge of a court of probate. **12.** *Brit.* **a.** (in a restaurant or inn) a complete meal in which all courses are included at one fixed price, as opposed to à la carte service. **b.** *Obs.* a restaurant or inn, or its dining room. **13.** a high bicycle of an early type, with one large wheel in front and one small wheel behind. **14.** *Heraldry.* **a.** any of the simplest and commonest charges, usually having straight or broadly curved edges. **b.** See **honorable ordinary.** Cf. **subordinary. 15. in ordinary,** in regular service: *a physician in ordinary to the king.* **16. out of the ordinary,** exceptional; unusual: *The food was something truly out of the ordinary.* [ME *ordinarie* < L *ordinār(ius)* regular, of the usual order, equiv. to *ordin-* ORDER + *-ārius* -ARY] —**or′di·nar′i·ness,** *n.*
—**Syn. 1.** plain. See **common. 2.** mediocre, indifferent. **3.** regular, accustomed. —**Ant. 1.** extraordinary, unusual.

or′dinary differen′tial equa′tion, *Math.* an equation containing derivatives but not partial derivatives. Cf. **partial differential equation.**

or′dinary ju′bilee. See under **jubilee** (def. 3a).

or′di·nar·y-lan′guage philos′ophy (ôr′dᵊner′ē lang′gwij), the practice of those modern philosophers who use existing language, esp. nontechnical language, to analyze concepts.

or′dinary life′ insur′ance, life insurance with premiums paid throughout the lifetime of the insured.

or′dinary point′, *Math.* a point in a domain in which a given function of a complex variable is analytic. Cf. **singular point.**

or′dinary ray′, *Optics, Crystall.* the part of a doubly refracted ray that has unvarying velocity with direction in the crystal and has vibrations perpendicular to the plane containing the ray and the optic axis of the crystal.

or′dinary sea′man, a seaman insufficiently skilled to be classified as an able-bodied seaman. *Abbr.:* O.D., O.S., o.s.

or′dinary share′, *Brit.* a share of common stock.

or′dinary stock′, *Brit.* See **common stock.**

or′dinary wave′, *Radio.* (of the two waves into which a radio wave is divided in the ionosphere under the influence of the earth's magnetic field) the wave with characteristics less different from those that the undivided wave would have exhibited in the absence of the magnetic field. Also called **O-wave.** Cf. **extraordinary wave.**

or·di·nate (ôr′dᵊnāt′, -dᵊnit), *n.* *Math.* (in plane Cartesian coordinates) the y-coordinate of a point: its distance from the x-axis measured parallel to the y-axis. Cf. **abscissa.** [abstracted from NL (*linea*) *ordināte* (*applicāta*) line applied in order; NL *ordināte* (adv.), deriv. of L *ordinātus* arranged. See ORDINATION]

Ordinate
P, Any point; AO and PB, Ordinate of P; YY, Axis of ordinate; OB and AP, Abscissa of P; XX, Axis of abscissa

or·di·na·tion (ôr′dᵊnā′shən), *n.* **1.** *Eccles.* the act or ceremony of ordaining. **2.** the fact of being ordained. **3.** a decreeing. **4.** the act of arranging. **5.** the resulting state; disposition; arrangement: *the ordination of animal species.* [ME *ordinacioun* < LL *ordinātiōn-* (s. of *ordinātiō*) ordainment, an ordering, equiv. to *ordināt(us)* ordered (ptp. of *ordināre* to order, arrange, deriv. of *ordin-,* s. of *ordō* order) + *-iōn* -ION]

ordn., ordnance.

ord·nance (ôrd′nəns), *n.* **1.** cannon or artillery. **2.** military weapons of all kinds with their equipment, ammunition, etc. **3.** the branch of an army that procures, stores, and issues weapons, munitions, and combat vehicles and maintains arsenals for their development and testing. [syncopated var. of ORDINANCE]

or·do (ôr′dō), *n., pl.* **or·di·nes** (ôr′dᵊnēz′). *Rom. Cath. Ch.* a booklet containing short and abbreviated directions for the contents of the office and Mass of each day in the year. [< ML, L: series, row, order]

or·don·nance (ôr′dᵊnəns; *Fr.* ôʀ dô näɴs′), *n., pl.* **-don·nanc·es** (-dᵊnən siz; *Fr.* -dô näɴs′). **1.** arrangement or disposition of parts, as of a building, a picture, or a literary composition. **2.** an ordinance, decree, or law. [< F, alter. of MF *ordenance* ORDINANCE, by influence of *donner* to give] —**or′don·nant,** *adj.*

Or·do·vi·cian (ôr′də vish′ən), *Geol.* —*adj.* **1.** noting or pertaining to a period of the Paleozoic era, occurring 440,000,000 to 500,000,000 years ago, and characterized by the advent of conodonts and ostracods and the presence of algae and seaweeds. See table under **era.** —*n.* **2.** the Ordovician period or system. [named after the *Ordovic(es)* (pl.) (< L) an ancient British tribe in northern Wales; see -IAN]

or·dure (ôr′jər, -dyŏŏr), *n.* dung; manure; excrement. [ME < OF, equiv. to *ord* filthy (< L *horrid(us)* HORRID) + *-ure* -URE] —**or′dur·ous,** *adj.*

Or·dzho·ni·kid·ze (ôʀ jo ni kēd′ze), *n.* a city in the RSFSR, in the S Soviet Union in Europe, in Caucasia. 202,000 (est. 1964). Also, **Orjonikidze.** Formerly, **Vladikavkaz.**

ore (ōr, ôr), *n.* **1.** a metal-bearing mineral or rock, or a native metal, esp. when valuable enough to be mined. **2.** a mineral or natural product serving as a source of some nonmetallic substance, as sulfur. [ME *oor* metal, ore, OE *ār* brass]

ö·re (œ′ʀə), *n., pl.* **ö·re. 1.** a bronze coin of Norway, the 100th part of a krone, equivalent to about .0014 of a U.S. dollar. **2.** a zinc coin of Denmark, the 100th part of a krone, equivalent to about .0015 of a U.S. dollar. **3.** a bronze coin of Sweden, the 100th part of a krona, equivalent to about .002 of a U.S. dollar. **4.** a fractional currency of the Faeroe Islands, the 100th part of a krona, equivalent to about .0015 of a U.S. dollar. Also, **øre** (for defs. 1, 2). [all << L *aureus* a gold coin]

Ore., Oregon.

o·re·ad (ōr′ē ad′, ôr′-), *n. Class. Myth.* any of a group of mountain nymphs who were the companions of Artemis. [< L *Oread-* (s. of *Oreas*) < Gk *oreiad-* (s. of *oreiás*), equiv. to *ór(os)* mountain + *-ad* -AD[1]]

ore·bod·y (ōr′bod′ē, ôr′-), *n., pl.* **-bod·ies.** a quantity of ore as it exists before mining. [ORE + BODY]

Ö·re·bro (œ′ʀə bʀōō′), *n.* a city in S Sweden. 79,727 (1965).

o·rec·tic (ō rek′tik, ô rek′-), *adj. Philos.* of or pertaining to desire; appetitive. [< Gk *orektik(ós)* appetitive, equiv. to *orekt(ós)* stretched out (deriv. of *orégein* to grasp for, desire) + *-ikos* -IC]

ore′ dress′ing, *Metall.* the art of separating the valuable minerals from an ore without chemical changes.

Oreg., Oregon.

o·reg·a·no (ə reg′ə nō′, ô reg′-), *n.* any menthaceous plant of the genus *Origanum*, related to but spicier than marjoram, used in cookery. [< AmerSp *orégano*, Sp: wild marjoram < L *origan(um)*. See ORIGAN]

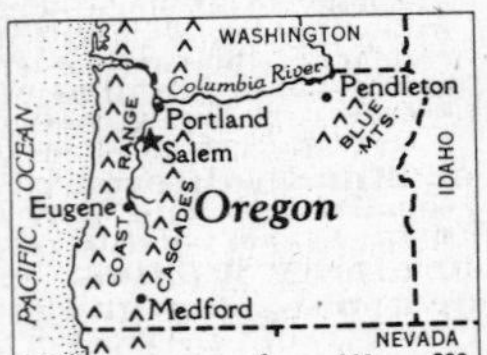

Or·e·gon (ôr′ə gən, -gon′, or′-), *n.* **1.** a State in the NW United States, on the Pacific coast. 1,768,687 (1960). 96,981 sq. mi. *Cap.:* Salem. *Abbr.:* Oreg., Ore. **2.** a town in N Illinois. 3732 (1960). —**Or·e·go·ni·an** (ôr′ə gō′nē ən, or′-), *adj., n.*

Or′egon ce′dar. See **white cedar.**

Or′egon Cit′y, a town in NW Oregon. 7996 (1960).

Or′egon crab′ ap′ple, a shrub or small tree, *Malus fusca*, of the northwestern coast of North America, having hairy leaves, white flowers, and yellow or green fruit with a red flush.

Or′egon fir′. See **Douglas fir.**

Or′egon grape′, 1. an evergreen shrub, *Mahonia Aquifolium*, of the western coast of the U.S., having yellow flowers and small, blue, edible berries: the State flower of Oregon. **2.** the berry itself. **3.** Also called **water holly.** a related shrub, *M. nervosa*, found from British Columbia to California, having bright-yellow flowers and dark-blue, edible fruit.

Or′egon myr′tle. See **California laurel** (def. 1).

Or′egon pine′. See **Douglas fir.**

Or′egon Trail′, a former route used during the westward migrations, esp. in the period from 1840 to 1860, starting in Missouri and ending in Oregon. ab. 2000 miles long.

ore′ hearth′, a small blast furnace for smelting lead. Also called **Scotch furnace, Scotch hearth.**

O·re·kho·vo-Zu·ye·vo (o ʀe′ᴋʜo vo zōō′ye vo), *n.* a city in the W RSFSR, in the central Soviet Union in Europe, E of Moscow. 113,000 (est. 1962).

O·rel (ō rel′, ô rel′; *Russ.* o ʀyôl′), *n.* a city in the W RSFSR, in the central Soviet Union in Europe, SSW of Moscow. 190,000 (est. 1964).

O·rem (ōr′əm, ôr′-), *n.* a city in N Utah. 18,394 (1960).

O·ren (ōr′ən, ôr′-), *n.* a boy's given name.

O·ren·burg (ōr′ən bûrg′, ôr′-; *Russ.* o ʀen bŏŏʀᴋ′), *n.* Chkalov.

o·ren·da (ō ren′də, ô ren′-), *n.* a supernatural force believed by the Iroquois Indians to be present, in varying degrees, in all objects or persons, and to be the spiritual force by which human accomplishment is attained or accounted for. [< Wyandot]

O·ren·se (ô ʀen′se), *n.* a city in N Spain. 66,403 (est. 1963).

O·re·o·pi·the·cus (ōr′ē ō pi thē′kəs, -pith′ə kəs, ôr′-), *n.* a genus of fossil hominids from the late Miocene or early Pliocene period in Italy. [< NL < Gk *ore-* (s. of *óros*) hill, mountain + *-o-* -O- + *píthekos* ape]

o·re ro·tun·do (ō′ʀe ʀō tōōn′dō; *Eng.* ôr′ē rō tun′dō, ôr′ē), *Latin.* with full, round voice.

ore·shoot (ōr′shōōt′, ôr′-), *n.* a rich mineral concentration in an orebody. [ORE + SHOOT]

O·res·te·ia (ôr′e stē′ə, ôr′-), *n.* a trilogy of tragic dramas (458 B.C.) by Aeschylus, consisting of the *Agamemnon*, the *Choëphori*, and the *Eumenides*.

O·res·tes (ō res′tēz, ô res′-), *n.* **1.** *Class. Myth.* the son of Agamemnon and Clytemnestra, and the brother of Electra and Iphigenia: he avenged the murder of Agamemnon by killing Clytemnestra and her lover, Aegisthus. **2.** (*italics*) a tragedy (408 B.C.) by Euripides.

Ores′tes com′plex, *Psychoanal.* an unconscious desire of a son to kill his mother.

Ö·re·sund (œ′ʀə sŏŏnd′), *n.* Swedish and Danish name of **The Sound.**

ore′ tank′er, *Naut.* a ship built to carry ore or some liquid, as petroleum.

O·re·tha (ə rē′thə), *n.* a girl's given name.

O·ret·ic (ô ret′ik), *n. Pharm., Trademark.* hydrochlorothiazide.

-orexia, an element occurring in loan words from Greek and used with the meaning "desire," "appetite," in the formation of compound words: *anorexia*. [< Gk *-orexia*. See OREXIS, -Y[3]]

o·rex·is (ō rek′sis, ô rek′-), *n. Psychol.* the affective and conative character of mental activity as contrasted with its cognitive aspect; the appetitive aspect of an act. [< L: longing, appetite < Gk *órexis* desire, equiv. to *orég(ein)* (to) desire + *-sis* -SIS] —**o·rec·tic** (ō rek′tik, ô rek′-), *adj.*

Or·fe·o (*It.* ôʀ fe′ô), *n.* See **Favola d'Orfeo, La.**

Or·fe·o ed E·u·ri·di·ce (*It.* ôʀ fe′ô ed e ōō ʀē dē′che), an opera (1762) by Christopher Willibald von Gluck.

Orff (ôrf), *n.* **Carl,** born 1895, German composer and conductor.

org., 1. organic. **2.** organized.

or·gan (ôr′gən), *n.* **1.** Also called **pipe organ.** a musical instrument consisting of one or more sets of pipes sounded by means of compressed air, played by means of one or more keyboards, and capable of producing a wide range of musical effects. **2.** any of various similar instruments, as a reed organ or an electronic organ. **3.** a barrel organ or hand organ. **4.** a differentiated part or member having a specific function in a plant or animal. **5.** an instrument or means, as of action, performance, etc.: *This committee will be the chief organ of administration.* **6.** a newspaper, magazine, or other means of communicating thoughts, opinions, etc., esp. in behalf of some organization, political group, or the like. **7.** *Obs.* any of various musical instruments, esp. wind instruments. [ME < L *organ(um)* < Gk *órganon* implement, tool, bodily organ, musical instrument, akin to *érgon* work]

or·ga·na[1] (ôr′gə nə), *n.* a pl. of **organon.**

or·ga·na[2] (ôr′gə nə), *n.* a pl. of **organum.**

or·gan·dy (ôr′gən dē), *n.* a fine, thin, cotton fabric usually having a durable crisp finish, white, dyed, or printed: used for blouses, dresses, curtains, trimmings, etc. Also, **or′gan·die.** [< F *organdi* <?]

or·gan·elle (ôr′gə nel′, ôr′gə nel′), *n. Biol.* a specialized part of a cell having some specific function; a cell organ. [< NL *organella*, dim. of L *organum* ORGAN]

or′gan grind′er, a street musician who earns his living by playing a hand organ or hurdy-gurdy.

or·gan·ic (ôr gan′ik), *adj.* **1.** noting or pertaining to a class of compounds that formerly comprised only those existing in or derived from plants or animals, but that now includes all other compounds of carbon. Cf. **inorganic** (def. 3). **2.** characteristic of, pertaining to, or derived from living organisms: *organic remains found in rocks.* **3.** of or pertaining to an organ or the organs of an animal or a plant. **4.** of, pertaining to, or affecting living tissue: *organic pathology.* **5.** *Psychol.* caused by structural impairment or change: *organic disorder.* Cf. **functional** (def. 6). **6.** *Philos.* having an organization similar in its complexity to that of living things. **7.** characterized by the systematic arrangement of parts; organized; systematic: *elements fitting together into a unified, organic whole.* **8.** of or pertaining to the constitution or structure of a thing; constitutional; structural: *The flaws in his writing are too organic to be easily remedied.* **9.** developing in a manner analogous to the natural growth and evolution characteristic of living organisms; arising as a natural outgrowth. **10.** viewing organisms; or explaining something as having a growth and development analogous to that of living organisms: *an organic theory of history.* **11.** of, pertaining to, involving, or grown with the use of fertilizers or pesticides of animal or vegetable origin, as distinguished from manufactured chemicals: *organic farming.* **12.** *Law.* of or pertaining to the constitutional or essential law or laws organizing the government of a state. **13.** *Archit.* noting or pertaining to any work of architecture regarded as analogous to plant or animal forms in having a structure and a plan that fulfill perfectly the functional requirements for the building and that form in themselves an intellectually lucid, integrated whole. **14.** *Fine Arts.* of or pertaining to the shapes or forms in a work of art that are of irregular contour and seem to resemble or suggest forms found in nature. —*n.* **15.** a substance, as a fertilizer or pesticide, of animal or vegetable origin. [< LL *organic(us)* instrumental < Gk *organikós*, equiv. to *órgan(on)* ORGAN + *-ikos* -IC] —**or·gan′i·cal·ness, or·ga·nic·i·ty** (ôr′gə nis′i tē), *n.*
—**Syn. 8.** inherent, fundamental, essential. —**Ant. 1.** inorganic.

or·gan·i·cal·ly (ôr gan′ik lē), *adv.* **1.** in an organic manner; by or with organs. **2.** with reference to organic structure. **3.** by or through organization: *Both ideas are organically connected to the central theme.* [ORGANIC + -AL[1] + -LY]

organ′ic chem′istry, the branch of chemistry dealing with the compounds of carbon, originally limited to substances found only in living organisms.

organ′ic disease′, *Pathol.* a disease in which there is a structural alteration (opposed to *functional disease*).

or·gan·i·cism (ôr gan′i siz′əm), *n.* **1.** *Biol., Philos.* the theory that vital activities arise not from any one part of an organism but from its autonomous composition. **2.** *Pathol.* the doctrine that all symptoms arise from organic disease. **3.** a view of society as an autonomous entity analogous to and following the same developmental pattern as a biological organism. [ORGANIC + -ISM] —**or·gan′i·cis′mal, or·gan′i·cis′tic,** *adj.* —**or·gan′i·cist,** *n.*

or·gan·ise (ôr′gə nīz′), *v.t., v.i.,* **-ised, -is·ing.** *Chiefly Brit.* organize. —**or′gan·is′a·bil′i·ty,** *n.* —**or′gan·is′a·ble,** *adj.*

or·gan·ism (ôr′gə niz′əm), *n.* **1.** a form of life composed of mutually dependent parts that maintain various vital processes. **2.** any form of animal or plant life: *microscopic organisms.* **3.** any organized body or system conceived of as analogous to a living being: *the governmental organism.* **4.** *Philos.* any complex thing or system having properties and functions determined not only by the properties and relations of its individual parts, but by the character of the whole which they compose and by the relations of the parts to the whole. [ORGAN + -ISM] —**or′gan·is′mic, or′gan·is′mal,** *adj.* —**or′gan·is′mi·cal·ly,** *adv.*

or·gan·ist (ôr′gə nist), *n.* a person who plays an organ. [< ML *organist(a)*, equiv. to L *organ(um)* ORGAN + *-ista* -IST]

or·gan·i·za·tion (ôr′gə ni zā′shən), *n.* **1.** the act or process of organizing. **2.** the state or manner of being organized. **3.** that which is organized. **4.** organic structure; composition: *The organization of this painting is quite remarkable.* **5.** a body of persons organized for some end or work: *a nonprofit organization.* **6.** the administrative personnel or apparatus of a business. **7.** the functionaries of a political party along with the offices, committees, etc., that they fill. **8.** an organism. Also, *esp. Brit.,* **or′gan·i·sa′tion.** [late ME *organizacion* < ML *organizātiōn-* (s. of *organizātiō*), equiv. to *organizāt(us)* organized (ptp. of *organizāre*; see ORGANIZE) + *-iōn-* -ION] —**or′gan·i·za′tion·al;** *esp. Brit.,* **or′gan·i·sa′tion·al,** *adj.* —**or′gan·i·za′tion·al·ly;** *esp. Brit.,* **or′gan·i·sa′tion·al·ly,** *adv.*

Organiza′tion of Amer′ican States′, an organization formed in Bogotá, Colombia (1948), comprising the U.S., Mexico, Dominican Republic, Haiti, and the sixteen republics of Central and South America, for the purpose of cooperative, coordinated action in economic, political, and military matters. *Abbr.:* OAS

or·gan·ize (ôr′gə nīz′), *v.,* **-ized, -iz·ing.** —*v.t.* **1.** to form as or into a whole consisting of interdependent or coordinated parts, esp. for harmonious or united action: *to organize a committee.* **2.** to systematize: *to organize the files of an office.* **3.** to give organic structure or character to: *to organize the elements of a composition.* **4.** to build a labor union among: *to organize workers.* **5.** to enlist the employees of into a labor union: *to organize a factory.* —*v.i.* **6.** to combine in an organized company, party or the like. **7.** *Informal.* to put (oneself) in a state of mental competence to perform a task: *We can't have any slipups, so you'd better get organized.* **8.** to assume organic structure: *Only in the last movement does the music begin to organize.* Also, *esp. Brit.,* **organise.** [ME *organyse(n)* < ML *organiz(āre)*, equiv. to L *organ(um)* ORGAN + *-izāre* -IZE] —**or′gan·iz′a·bil′i·ty,** *n.* —**or′gan·iz′a·ble,** *adj.*
—**Syn. 1.** dispose, frame. **2.** order. —**Ant. 1.** destroy.

or′ganized fer′ment, ferment (def. 1).

or′ganized la′bor, all workers who are organized in labor unions.

or′ganized mili′tia, a former military organization functioning under both state and federal authority.

or·gan·iz·er (ôr′gə nī′zər), *n.* **1.** a person who organizes, esp. one who enlists employees into membership in a union. **2.** a multiple folder in which correspondence, papers, etc., are sorted by subject, date, or otherwise, for systematic handling. **3.** *Embryol.* any part of an embryo that stimulates the development and differentiation of another part. Also, *esp. Brit.,* **or′gan·is′er.** [ORGANIZE + -ER[1]]

organo-, an element of Greek origin used, with the meaning "organ (of the body)," or "organic," in the formation of compound words: *organology; organosilicon.* [< Gk, comb. form of *órganon* ORGAN]

or′gan of Cor′ti (kôr′tē), *Anat., Zool.* a structure in the cochlea of a mammal, consisting of hair cells that serve as receptors for auditory stimuli. [named after Alfonso CORTI]

or·ga·no·gen·e·sis (ôr′gə nō jen′i sis, ôr gan′ə-), *n. Biol.* the origin and development of an organ. Also, **or·ga·nog·e·ny** (ôr′gə noj′ə nē). [ORGANO- + -GENESIS] —**or·ga·no·ge·net·ic** (ôr′gə nō jə net′ik, ôr gan′ō-), *adj.* —**or·ga·no·ge·net′i·cal·ly,** *adv.*

or·ga·nog·ra·phy (ôr′gə nog′rə fē), *n., pl.* **-phies.** the description of the organs of animals or plants. [ORGANO- + -GRAPHY] —**or·ga·no·graph·ic** (ôr′gə nə graf′ik), **or′ga·no·graph′i·cal,** *adj.* —**or′ga·nog′ra·phist,** *n.*

or·ga·nol·o·gy (ôr′gə nol′ə jē), *n.* **1.** the branch of biology that deals with the structure and functions of the organs of animals or plants. **2.** phrenology. [ORGANO- + -LOGY] —**or·ga·no·log·ic** (ôr′gə nəloj′ik), **or′ga·no·log′i·cal,** *adj.* —**or′ga·nol′o·gist,** *n.*

or·ga·no·mag·ne·si·um (ôr′gə nō mag nē′zē əm, -zhəm, -shē əm, ôr gan′ō-), *adj. Chem.* pertaining to or noting an organic compound, esp. an organic halide, containing magnesium linked to carbon. [ORGANO- + MAGNESIUM]

or·ga·no·me·tal·lic (ôr′gə nō mə tal′ik, ôr gan′ō-), *adj. Chem.* pertaining to or noting an organic compound containing a metal or a metalloid linked to carbon. [ORGANO- + METALLIC]

or·ga·non (ôr′gə non′), *n., pl.* **-na** (-nə), **-nons. 1.** an instrument of thought or knowledge. **2.** *Philos.* a system of rules or principles of demonstration or investigation. [< Gk; see ORGAN]

or·ga·no·sil·i·con (ôr′gə nō sil′ə kən, -kon′, ôr gan′ə-), *adj. Chem.* pertaining to or noting an organic compound containing silicon, esp. where attached directly to a carbon atom. [ORGANO- + SILICON]

or·ga·no·si·lox·ane (ôr′gə nō si lok′sān, ôr gan′ō-), *adj. Chem.* a siloxane containing an organic group. [ORGANO- + SILOXANE]

or·ga·no·ther·a·peu·tics (ôr′gə nō ther′ə pyōō′tiks ôr gan′ō), *n.* (*construed as sing.*) organotherapy. [ORGANO- + THERAPEUTICS]

or·ga·no·ther·a·py (ôr′gə nō ther′ə pē, ôr gan′ō-), *n.* the branch of therapeutics which deals with the use of remedies prepared from the organs of animals, as from the thyroid gland, the pancreas, the suprarenal bodies, etc. [ORGANO- + THERAPY]

or′gan pipe′, 1. one of the pipes of a pipe organ. **2.** something resembling such a pipe.

or′gan-pipe cac′tus (ôr′gən pīp′), a treelike or columnar cactus, *Pachycereus Marginatus*, of Mexico, having a central, erect spine surrounded by spreading spines in clusters of five to eight, and funnel-shaped, brownish-purple flowers.

or′gan-pipe cor′al, an alcyonarian coral of the genus *Tubipora*, occurring in tropical waters, and forming a complex colony of brick-red, vertical tubules joined at intervals by transverse plates.

or′gan screen′, 1. an ornamental screen closing off an organ chamber in a church. 2. a rood screen or the like supporting an organ.

or·ga·num (ôr′gə nəm), *n., pl.* **-na** (-nə), **-nums.** 1. an organon. 2. *Music.* **a.** the doubling, or simultaneous singing, of a melody at an interval of either a fourth, a fifth, or an octave. **b.** the second part in such singing. [< L; see ORGAN]

or′gan whis′tle, a steam or air whistle in which the jet is forced up against the thin edge of a pipe closed at the top.

or·gan·za (ôr gan′zə), *n.* a sheer rayon, nylon, or silk fabric constructed in plain weave, used in the manufacture of evening dresses, trimmings, etc. [?]

or·gan·zine (ôr′gən zēn′), *n.* silk that has been additionally twisted in opposite directions, used warpwise in weaving silk fabrics. Cf. **tram.** [< F *organsin* < It *organzin(o)*]

or·gasm (ôr′gaz əm), *n.* 1. the physical and emotional sensation experienced at the culmination of a sexual act, as intercourse or masturbation, being a result of stimulation of the sexual organs, and typically followed in the male by ejaculation. 2. an instance of experiencing this. 3. intense or unrestrained excitement. 4. an instance or occurrence of such excitement. [< NL *orgasm(us)* < Gk *orgasmós* excitement, deriv. of *orgâein* to swell, be excited] —**or·gas′mic, or·gas′tic,** *adj.*

or·geat (ôr′zhat; *Fr.* ôR zhA′), *n.* a syrup or drink made originally from barley but later from almonds, prepared with sugar and a solution of orange flowers. [< F < Pr *orjat*, deriv. of *orge* barley < L *horde(um)*]

Or·get·o·rix (ôr jet′ə riks), *n.* fl. c60 B.C., Helvetian chieftain.

or·gi·as·tic (ôr′jē as′tik), *adj.* 1. of, pertaining to, or having the nature of an orgy. 2. tending to arouse or excite unrestrained emotion: *orgiastic rhythms.* 3. *Sociol.* (of an expressive crowd) reaching a peak of emotional intensity, often of an ecstatic nature and frequently expressed by uninhibited behavior: *People celebrating the armistice behaved like an orgiastic mob.* [< Gk *orgiastik(ós)*, equiv. to *orgiáz(ein)* (to) celebrate orgies (deriv. of *órgia* secret rites; see ORGY) + *-tikos* -TIC]

or′gone box (ôr′gōn), a cabinetlike device constructed of layers of wood and other materials, as tin, claimed by its inventor, Wilhelm Reich, to restore orgone energy to persons sitting in it, thereby aiding in the cure of impotence, cancer, the common cold, etc. Also called **or′gone-en′er·gy accu′mulator** (ôr′gōn en′ər jē). [prob. ORG(ASM) + -ONE]

or′gone en′ergy, (in Reichian theory) a vital, primal, nonmaterial element believed to permeate the universe.

or·gy (ôr′jē), *n., pl.* **-gies.** 1. wild, drunken, or licentious festivity or revelry. 2. any proceedings marked by unbridled indulgence of passions: *an orgy of killing.* 3. **orgies,** (in ancient Greece) esoteric religious rituals, used esp. in the worship of Demeter and Dionysus, characterized in later times by wild dancing, singing, and drinking. [< MF *orgie* < L *orgia* (neut. pl.) < Gk *órgia*, akin to *érgon* work]

-orial, a suffix used to form adjectives from nouns with stems in **-or** or **-ory:** *professorial; purgatorial.* [ME *-oriale.* See -OR², -ORY², -AL¹]

O·ri·an·a (ôr′ē an′ə, ōr′-), *n.* a girl's given name.

or·i·bi (ôr′ə bē, or′-), *n., pl.* **-bis.** a small tan-colored antelope, *Ourebia ourebi*, of South and East Africa, with spikelike horns. [< SAfrD < Hottentot *arab*]

or·i·chal·cum (ôr′ə kal′kəm), *n.* a brass rich in zinc, prepared by the ancients. [< L < Gk *oreíchalk(on)*, lit., mountain-copper, equiv. to *ór(os)* mountain + *chalkós* copper]

o·ri·el (ôr′ē əl, ōr′-), *n.* 1. a bay window, esp. one cantilevered or corbeled out from a wall. 2. (in medieval architecture) a large bay window of a hall or chamber. [ME < OF *oriol* porch, passage, gallery << L *aureol(us)* gilded]

Oriel

o·ri·ent (*n., adj.* ôr′ē ənt, ōr′ē ent′, ôr′-; *v.* ôr′ē ent′, ōr′-), *n.* 1. **the Orient, a.** the East; the countries to the E and SE of the Mediterranean. **b.** See **Eastern Hemisphere.** 2. *Jewelry.* **a.** an orient pearl. **b.** the iridescence of a pearl. 3. *Archaic.* the east; the eastern region of the heavens or the world. —*adj.* 4. (of a gem or pearl) exceptionally fine and lustrous; oriental. 5. *Archaic.* eastern or oriental. 6. *Archaic.* rising or appearing, esp. as from beneath the horizon: *the orient sun.* —*v.t.* 7. to adjust with relation to, or bring into due relation to, surroundings, circumstances, facts, etc.: *to orient one's ideas to new conditions.* 8. to familiarize (a person) with new surroundings, circumstances, or the like: *lectures designed to orient the new draftees.* 9. to place in any definite position with reference to the points of the compass or other locations: *to orient a building north and south.* 10. to direct or position toward a particular object: *Orient it toward that house.* 11. to determine the position of in relation to the points of the compass; get the bearings of. 12. to place so as to face the east, esp. to build (a church) with the chief altar to the east and the chief entrance to the west. 13. *Survey.* **a.** to turn (a map or plane-table sheet) so that its north direction is toward the north. **b.** to set (the horizontal circle of a surveying instrument) so that readings of the circle give correct azimuths. 14. *Math.* to assign (to a surface) a constant, outward direction at each point. —*v.i.* 15. to turn toward the east or in any specified direction. [ME < MF < L *orient-* (s. of *oriēns*) the east, sunrise, n. use of prp. of *orīrī* to rise; see -ENT]

o·ri·en·tal (ôr′ē en′tᵊl, ōr′-), *adj.* 1. (*usually cap.*) of, pertaining to, or characteristic of the Orient, or East. 2. (*cap.*) *Zoogeog.* belonging to a geographical division comprising southern Asia and the Malay Archipelago as far as and including the Philippines, Borneo, and Java. 3. of the orient or east; eastern. 4. *Jewelry.* **a.** (*usually cap.*) designating various gems which are varieties of corundum: *Oriental aquamarine; Oriental ruby.* **b.** fine or precious; orient: *oriental agate; oriental garnet.* **c.** designating certain natural salt-water pearls found esp. in the Orient. —*n.* 5. (*usually cap.*) a native or inhabitant of the Orient, esp. one belonging to a native race. [ME < MF < L *orientāl(is)*, equiv. to *orient-* the east (see ORIENT) + *-ālis* -AL¹] —**o′ri·en′tal·ly,** *adv.*

O′rien′tal al′abaster, alabaster (def. 2).

O′rien′tal bee′tle, a scarabaeid beetle, *Anomala orientalis*, introduced into the U.S. from the Orient, the larvae of which feed on the roots of sugarcane and other grasses. Also called **Asiatic beetle.**

O′rien′tal car′pet. See **Oriental rug.**

O′rien′tal cat′s′-eye, *Jewelry.* a chatoyant variety of chrysoberyl, used as a gem.

o′rien′tal cock′roach, a dark-brown cockroach, *Blatta orientalis*, thought to have originated in the Orient but now nearly cosmopolitan in distribution. Also called **o′rien′tal roach′, blackbeetle.**

O′rien′tal fruit′ moth′, an olethreutid moth, *Grapholitha molesta*, introduced into the U.S. from the Orient, the larvae of which infest and feed on the twigs and fruits of peach, plum, and related trees.

O·ri·en·ta·li·a (ôr′ē ən tā′lē ə, -tāl′yə, ōr′-), *n.pl.* objects pertaining to the Orient and Oriental art culture, history, folklore, or the like. [< NL, n. use of neut. pl. of L *orientālis* ORIENTAL]

O·ri·en·ta·lis (ôr′ē ən tā′lis, ōr′-), *n.* **Mare.** See **Mare Orientalis.**

O·ri·en·tal·ise (ôr′ē en′tᵊlīz′, ōr′-), *v.t., v.i.,* **-ised, -is·ing.** (*often l.c.*) *Chiefly Brit.* Orientalize. —**O′ri·en′tal·i·sa′tion,** *n.*

O·ri·en·tal·ism (ôr′ē en′tᵊliz′əm, ōr′-), *n.* (*often l.c.*) 1. a peculiarity or idiosyncrasy of the Oriental peoples. 2. the character or characteristics of the Oriental peoples. 3. the knowledge and study of Oriental languages, literature, etc. [ORIENTAL + -ISM] —**O′ri·en′tal·ist,** *n.*

O·ri·en·tal·ize (ôr′ē en′tᵊlīz′, ōr′-), *v.t., v.i.,* **-ized, -iz·ing.** (*often l.c.*) to make or become Oriental. Also, *esp. Brit.,* **Orientalise.** [ORIENTAL + -IZE] —**O′ri·en′tal·i·za′tion,** *n.*

O′rien′tal pop′py, a poppy, *Papaver orientale*, of Asia, having hispid stems and leaves and showy scarlet, pink, or white flowers, cultivated as an ornamental.

O′rien′tal rug′, a rug or carpet woven usually in Asia and characterized by hand-knotted pile, used in the Orient for various purposes, in the U.S. chiefly as a floor covering. Also called **Oriental carpet.** Cf. **Persian carpet, Turkish rug, Turkoman rug.**

o·ri·en·tate (ôr′ē en tāt′, ōr′-, ôr′ē en′tāt, ōr′-), *v.t., v.i.,* **-tat·ed, -tat·ing.** to orient. [< F *orient(er)* (to) ORIENT + -ATE¹]

o·ri·en·ta·tion (ôr′ē en tā′shən, ōr′-), *n.* 1. the act or process of orienting. 2. the state of being oriented. 3. *Psychol., Psychiatry.* the ability to locate oneself in one's environment with reference to time, place, and people. 4. the ascertainment of one's true position, as in a novel situation, with respect to attitudes, judgments, etc. 5. an introduction, as to guide one in adjusting to new surroundings, employment, activity, or the like: *All new employees must receive two days of orientation.* 6. *Chem.* **a.** the relative positions of certain atoms or groups, especially in aromatic compounds. **b.** the determination of the position of substituted atoms or groups in a compound. [ORIENTATE + -ION] —**o′ri·en·ta′tive,** *adj.*

O·ri·en·te (ô′rē en′te), *n.* 1. a region in Ecuador, E of the Andes: the border long disputed by Peru. 2. a province in E Cuba. 1,797,606 (1953); 14,132 sq. mi. *Cap.:* Santiago de Cuba.

o·ri·en·teer·ing (ôr′ē en tēr′ing, ōr′-), *n.* a competitive sport in which participants must find their way through unknown terrain using only a compass and topographical map. [alter. of Sw *orientering*]

or·i·fice (ôr′ə fis, or′-), *n.* a mouth or aperture, as of a tube or pipe; a mouthlike opening or hole; vent. [< MF < LL *ōrific(ium)*, equiv. to L *ōr-* (s. of *ōs*) mouth + *-fic* -FIC + *-ium* n. suffix] —**or·i·fi·cial** (ôr′ə fish′əl, or′-), *adj.*

or·i·flamme (ôr′ə flam′, or′-), *n.* 1. the red banner of St. Denis, near Paris, carried before the early kings of France as a military ensign. 2. any ensign, banner, or standard, esp. one that serves as a rallying point or symbol. [late ME *oriflam* < MF *oriflamme*, OF, equiv. to *orie* golden (< L *aurea*, fem. of *aureus*, deriv. of *aurum* gold) + *flamme* FLAME]

orig., 1. origin. 2. original. 3. originally.

o·ri·ga·mi (ôr′ə gä′mē), *n., pl.* **-mis** for 2. 1. a technique of folding paper into a variety of decorative or representational forms. 2. an object made by origami. [< Jap]

Or·i·gen (ôr′i jen′, -jən, or′-), *n.* (*Origenes Admantius*) A.D. 185?–254?, Alexandrian writer, Christian theologian, and teacher. —**Or′i·gen′i·an,** *adj., n.* —**Or′i·gen·ism,** *n.* —**Or′i·gen′ist,** *n.* —**Or′i·gen·is′tic,** *adj.*

or·i·gin (ôr′i jin, or′-), *n.* 1. the source; that from which anything arises or is derived; fountainhead: *to follow a stream to its origin.* 2. rise or derivation from a particular source: *the origin of a word.* 3. the first stage of existence; beginning: *the origin of Quakerism in America.* 4. birth; parentage; extraction: *Scottish origin.* 5. *Anat.* **a.** the point of derivation. **b.** the more fixed portion of a muscle. 6. *Math.* **a.** the point in a Cartesian coordinate system where the axes intersect. **b.** Also called **pole.** the point from which rays designating specific angles originate in a polar coordinate system with no axes. [ME < L *origin-* (s. of *origo*) beginning, source, rise, deriv. of *orīrī* to rise] —**Syn.** 1. root, foundation. 4. ancestry, lineage.

o·rig·i·nal (ə rij′ə nᵊl), *adj.* 1. belonging or pertaining to the origin or beginning of something, or to a thing at its beginning: *The book still has its original binding.* 2. new; fresh; novel: *an original way of advertising.* 3. arising or proceeding independently of anything else: *an original view of history.* 4. capable of or given to thinking or acting in an independent, creative, or individual manner: *an original thinker.* 5. created, undertaken, or presented for the first time: *to give the original performance of a string quartet; to do original research.* 6. being that from which a copy, a translation, or the like is made: *The original document is in Washington.* —*n.* 7. a primary form or type from which varieties are derived. 8. an original work, writing, or the like, as opposed to any copy or imitation: *The original of this is in the British Museum.* 9. the person or thing represented by a picture, description, etc.: *The original is said to have been the painter's mistress.* 10. a person who is original in his ways of thinking or acting: *In a field of brilliant technicians he looms as a true original.* 11. *Archaic.* an eccentric person. 12. *Archaic.* a source of being; an author or originator. [ME < L *orīgināl(is)* (ML *orīgināle*, n. use of neut. adj.), equiv. to *origin-* ORIGIN + *-ālis* -AL¹]
—**Syn.** 1. primary, primordial, primeval, primitive, aboriginal. 7. archetype, pattern, prototype, model. —**Ant.** 1. secondary. 7. copy.

orig′inal gum′, *Philately.* See **o.g.**

o·rig·i·nal·i·ty (ə rij′ə nal′i tē), *n., pl.* **-ties.** 1. the quality or state of being original. 2. ability to think or express oneself in an independent and individual manner; creative ability. 3. freshness or novelty, as of an idea, method, or performance: *to admire the originality of another's work.* [< F *originalité.* See ORIGINAL, -ITY]

o·rig·i·nal·ly (ə rij′ə nᵊlē), *adv.* 1. with respect to origin; by origin: *Originally he was from California.* 2. at the origin; at first: *Originally this was to be in three volumes.* 3. in the first place; primarily: *Originally nomads, they first learned agriculture from the missionaries.* 4. in an original, novel, or distinctively individual manner: *Originally planned houses are much in demand.* 5. *Archaic.* from the beginning; from the first; inherently: *the latent brutality originally in each man.* [ORIGINAL + -LY]

orig′inal sin′, 1. *Theol.* **a.** a depravity, or tendency to evil, held to be innate in mankind and transmitted from Adam to the race in consequence of his sin. **b.** inclination to evil, inherent in human nature. 2. *Rom. Cath. Theol.* the privation of sanctifying grace in consequence of the sin of Adam. [ME; trans. of ML *peccātum orīgināle*]

o·rig·i·nate (ə rij′ə nāt′), *v.,* **-nat·ed, -nat·ing.** —*v.i.* 1. to take its origin or rise; arise; spring: *The practice originated during the middle ages.* 2. (of a train, bus, or other public conveyance) to begin its scheduled run at a specified place: *This train originates at Philadelphia.* —*v.t.* 3. to give origin or rise to; initiate; invent: *to originate a new filing system.* [prob. back formation from *origination*] —**o·rig·i·na·ble** (ə rij′ə nə bəl), *adj.* —**o·rig′i·na′tion,** *n.* —**o·rig′i·na′tor,** *n.* —**Syn.** 3. See **discover.**

o·rig·i·na·tive (ə rij′ə nā′tiv), *adj.* having or characterized by the power of originating; creative. [ORIGINATE + -IVE] —**o·rig′i·na′tive·ly,** *adv.*

Or′igin of Spe′cies, The, (*On the Origin of Species by Means of Natural Selection, or the Preservation of Favoured Races in the Struggle for Life*) a treatise (1859) by Charles Darwin setting forth his theory of evolution.

o·ri·hon (ôr′ē hon′, ōr′-), *n.* 1. a manuscript scroll having columns running across the width, folded in accordion fashion along the separating margins. 2. a book consisting of leaves, printed on one side only, that remain uncut at the fore edge. [< Jap, prob. equiv. to *ori* fold + *hon* book]

o·ri·na·sal (ôr′ē nā′zəl, ōr′-), *Phonet.* —*adj.* 1. pronounced with the voice issuing through the mouth and the nose simultaneously, as in the nasalized vowels of French. —*n.* 2. an orinasal sound. Also, **oronasal.** [< L *ōr-* (s. of *ōs*) mouth + -I- + NASAL¹] —**o′ri·na′sal·ly,** *adv.*

O·rin·da (ō rin′də, ô rin′-), *n.* a town in W California. 4712 (1960).

Orin′da Vil′lage, a town in W California. 5568 (1960).

O·ri·no·co (ôr′ə nō′kō, ōr′-; *Sp.* ô′Rē nô′kô), *n.* a river in N South America, flowing N from the border of Brazil, along the E border of Colombia, and NE through Venezuela to the Atlantic. 1600 mi. long.

o·ri·ole (ôr′ē ōl′, ōr′-), *n.* 1. any of several usually brightly colored, passerine birds of the family *Oriolidae*, of the Old World. Cf. **golden oriole.** 2. any of several brightly colored, passerine birds of the family *Icteridae*, of America. Cf. **Baltimore oriole, orchard oriole.** [< F *oriol*, OF < ML *oriol(us)*, var. of L *aureolus* golden, equiv. to *aure(us)* golden (deriv. of *aurum* gold) + *-olus* dim. suffix]

O·ri·on (ō rī′ən, ô rī′-), *n., gen.* **Or·i·o·nis** (ôr′ē ō′nis, or′-, ə rī′ə nis) for 2. 1. *Class. Myth.* a giant-sized hunter who pursued the Pleiades, was eventually slain by Artemis, and was then placed in the sky as a constellation. 2. *Astron.* the Hunter, a constellation lying on the celestial equator between Canis Major and Taurus, containing the bright stars Betelgeuse and Rigel.

O·ris·ka·ny (ō ris′kə nē, ô ris′-), *n.* a village in central New York, near Utica: battle 1777. 1580 (1960). —**Or·is·ka·ni·an** (ôr′is kā′nē ən, or′-), *adj., n.*

or·i·son (ôr′i zən, or′-), *n.* a prayer. [ME < OF < LL *ōrātiōn-* (s. of *ōrātiō*) plea, prayer, ORATION]

O·ris·sa (ō ris′, ô ris′ə), *n.* a state in E India. 17,548,846 (1961); 60,136 sq. mi. *Cap.:* Cuttack.

Or·i·thy·ia (ôr′ə thī′ə), *n.* *Class. Myth.* a daughter of King Erechtheus who was abducted by Boreas and taken to Thrace. Also, **Or·i·the·a** (ôr′ə thē′ə).

-orium, a suffix occurring in loan words from Latin, denoting a place or an instrument: *emporium; moratorium.* See **-ory².** Cf. **-arium.** [< L]

O·ri·ya (ô rē′yə), *n.* an Indic language, the language of Orissa.

O·ri·za·ba (ôr′ə zä′bə, ōr′-; *Sp.* ô′Rē sä′vä), *n.* 1. Also called **Citlaltepetl.** an inactive volcano in SE Mexico, in Veracruz state. 18,546 ft. 2. a city near this peak. 55,531 (1960).

Or·jo·ni·kid·ze (*Russ.* ôʀ jo ni kēd′ze), *n.* Ordzhonikidze.

Or·khon (ôr′kon), *n.* a river in E central Asia, flowing E, N, and then NE from the N central Mongolian People's Republic to the Selenga River. ab. 400 mi. long.

Ork′ney Is′lands (ôrk′nē), an island group off the NE tip of Scotland, constituting a county in Scotland. 18,743 (1961); 376 sq. mi. *Co. seat:* Kirkwall.

Or·land (ôr′lənd, ôr′-), *n.* a town in central California. 2534 (1960).

Or·lan·do (ôr lan′dō; *also, for 1, 2, It.* ôʀ län′dô), *n.* **1. Vit·to·rio E·ma·nu·e·le** (vēt tô′ʀyô e′mä nōō e′le), 1860–1952, Italian statesman. **2.** the Italian name for Roland, as in Ariosto's *Orlando Furioso,* Boiardo's *Orlando Innamorato,* etc. **3.** (*italics*) a novel (1928) by Virginia Woolf. **4.** a city in central Florida: resort. 88,135 (1960). **5.** a boy's given name.

Or·lan·do Fu·rio·so (*It.* ôʀ län′dô fōō ʀyô′zô), an epic poem (1532) by Ariosto.

Orlan′do In·na·mo·ra′to (*It.* ēn nä′mô ʀä′tô), an epic poem (1487?) by Matteo Maria Boiardo.

Or′land Park′, a town in NE Illinois. 2592 (1960).

orle (ôrl), *n.* **1.** *Heraldry.* **a.** a charge in the form of a narrow band following the form of the escutcheon within the edge, so that the extreme outer edge of the escutcheon is of the field tincture. **b.** an arrangement in orle of small charges: *azure, an orle of bezants.* **2.** *Armor.* a thick roll of cloth or leather on a helmet forming a base for an ornamental crest. **3.** Also called **or·let** (ôr lā′), **orlo.** *Archit.* **a.** a border, as one formed by a fillet. **b.** a fillet at the upper end of the shaft of a column. Cf. **cincture** (def. 3). **c.** a fillet between two flutes of a column. **4. in orle,** *Heraldry.* (of small charges) arranged within the edge of an escutcheon in the manner of an orle. [< MF: border, edge < VL **ōrul(us),* dim. of L *ōra* border]

Or·lé·a·nais (ôʀ lā ᴀ ne′), *n.* a former province in N France. *Cap.:* Orléans.

Or·le·an·ist (ôr′lē ə nist), *n.* a supporter of the Orleans branch of the former French royal family and of its claim to the throne of France through descent from the younger brother of Louis XIV. [< F *Orléaniste,* after ORLÉANS + *-iste* -IST] **—Or′le·an·ism,** *n.*

Or·lé·ans (ôr′lē ənz; *Fr.* ôʀ lā äɴ′), *n.* a city in and the capital of Loiret, in central France, SSW of Paris: English siege of the city raised by Joan of Arc 1428. 88,105 (1962).

Or·lé·ans, d′ (dôʀ lā äɴ′), *n.* **Louis Phi·lippe Jo·seph** (lwē fē lēp′ zhô zef′), **Duc** (*Philippe Égalité*), 1747–93, French political leader.

orl′ fly′ (ôrl), *Brit.* an alderfly, *Sialis lutaria.* [*orl,* dial. var. of ALDER]

Or·lich (ôr′lich; *Sp.* ôʀ′lēch), *n.* **Fran·cis·co J.** (frän sēs′kô), born 1906, Costa Rican engineer and statesman: president since 1962.

Or·lin (ôr′lin), *n.* a boy's given name.

or·lo (ôr′lō), *n., pl.* **-los.** *Archit.* **1.** a plinth supporting the base of a column. **2.** orle (def. 3). [< It: border, deriv. of *orlare* to hem < VL; see ORLE]

Or·lon (ôr′lon), *n. Trademark.* a synthetic, acrylic textile fiber of light weight, good wrinkle resistance, and high resistance to weathering and many chemicals.

or·lop (ôr′lop), *n. Naut.* **1.** the lowermost of four or more decks above the space at the bottom of a hull. **2.** *Obs.* a single weather deck on a small vessel. Also called **or′lop deck′.** [late ME < MLG *overlōp* covering, lit., an over-leap equiv. to *over-* OVER + *-loop(en)* (to) run, extend; see LEAP]

Or·ly (ôr′lē; *Fr.* ôʀ lē′), *n.* a suburb SE of Paris, France: international airport. 18,469 (1962).

Or·man·dy (ôr′mən dē), *n.* **Eugene,** born 1899, U.S. conductor and violinist, born in Hungary.

Or·mazd (ôr′məzd), *n.* See **Ahura Mazda.** Also, **Or′muzd.**

Orme (ôrm), *n.* a boy's given name.

or·mer (ôr′mər), *n.* **1.** an abalone, *Haliotis tuberculata,* found in the Channel Islands. **2.** any abalone. [< F *ormier* (< L *auris maris* ear of the sea) + *mier* (< L *mer(us)* pure)]

or·mo·lu (ôr′mə lōō′), *n.* **1.** an alloy of copper and zinc used to imitate gold. **2.** gilded metal, esp. brass or bronze. **3.** gold or gold powder prepared for use in gilding. [< F *or moulu* ground gold, equiv. to *or* (< L *aur(um)* + *moulu,* ptp. of *moudre* to grind < L *molere*]

Or·mond (ôr′mənd), *n.* a boy's given name.

Or′mond Beach′, a town in NE Florida. 8658 (1960).

Or·muz (ôr′muz), *n.* **Strait of.** See **Hormuz, Strait of.**

or·na·ment (*n.* ôr′nə mənt; *v.* ôr′nə ment′), *n.* **1.** an accessory, article, or detail used to beautify the appearance or general effect: *architectural ornaments.* **2.** any adornment, or means of adornment. **3.** a person who adds luster, as to his surroundings, to society, etc.: *The theologian was an ornament of the university.* **4.** the act of adorning. **5.** the state of being adorned. **6.** mere outward display: *a speech more of ornament than of ideas.* **7.** *Chiefly Eccles.* any accessory, adjunct, or equipment. **8.** *Music.* a tone or group of tones applied as decoration to a principal melodic tone. —*v.t.* **9.** to furnish with ornaments: *to ornament a musical composition.* **10.** to be an ornament to: *Several learned men were acquired to ornament the society.* [< L *ornāment(um)* equipment, ornament, equiv. to *ornā(re)* (to) equip + *-mentum* -MENT; r. ME *ornement* < OF < L] **—or′na·ment′er,** *n.*
—Syn. 1. embellishment. **2.** decoration. **9.** beautify, embellish, trim. **9, 10.** decorate, adorn, grace.

or·na·men·tal (ôr′nə men′tᵊl), *adj.* **1.** used or grown for ornament: *ornamental plants.* **2.** such as to ornament; decorative. **3.** of or pertaining to ornament. —*n.* **4.** something ornamental. **5.** a plant cultivated for decorative purposes. [ORNAMENT + -AL¹] **—or′na·men·tal′i·ty,** *n.* **—or′na·men′tal·ly,** *adv.*

or·na·men·ta·tion (ôr′nə men tā′shən), *n.* **1.** the act of ornamenting. **2.** the state of being ornamented. **3.** something with which a thing is ornamented; embellishment. [ORNAMENT + -ATION]

or·na·ment·ed (ôr′nə men′tid), *adj. Typography.* (of a character) highly embellished or ornate; altered by embellishment. [ORNAMENT + -ED²]

or·nate (ôr nāt′), *adj.* **1.** elaborately or sumptuously adorned, often excessively or showily so: *She bought a highly ornate Louis XIV sofa.* **2.** embellished with rhetoric; florid or high-flown: *an ornate style of writing.* [ME < L *ornāt(us)* adorned, ptp. of *ornāre* to equip; see -ATE¹] **—or·nate′ly,** *adv.* **—or·nate′ness,** *n.*
—Syn. 1. showy, ostentatious; rich, lavish.

Orne (ôʀn), *n.* a department in NW France. 280,549 (1962); 2372 sq. mi. *Cap.:* Alençon.

or·ner·y (ôr′nə rē), *adj. Informal.* **1.** ugly in disposition or temper: *That old man is just plain ornery and mean.* **2.** stubborn: *I can't do a thing with that ornery mule.* **3.** low or vile. **4.** *Chiefly Dial.* inferior or common; ordinary. [contr. of ORDINARY] **—or′ner·i·ness,** *n.*

Or·ne·us (ôr′nē əs), *n. Class. Myth.* a son of King Erechtheus who, with his brother Metion, drove another brother, Cecrops, heir apparent to the throne, out of Athens.

or·nis (ôr′nis), *n., pl.* **or·ni·thes** (ôr nī′thēz). an avifauna. [< G < Gk *órnis* bird; akin to OE *earn* eagle, G *Aar*]

ornith-, var. of **ornitho-** before a vowel: *ornithoid.*

ornith., **1.** ornithological. **2.** ornithology.

or·nith·ic (ôr nith′ik), *adj.* of or pertaining to birds. [< Gk *ornīthik(ós)* birdlike, equiv. to *ornīth-* ORNITH- + *-ikos* -IC]

or·ni·thine (ôr′nə thēn′), *n. Biochem.* an amino acid, $H_2N(CH_2)_3CH(NH)_2COOH$, obtained by the hydrolysis of arginine. [*ornith(uric acid),* secreted by birds + -INE²]

or·nith·is·chi·an (ôr′nə this′kē ən), *n.* **1.** any herbivorous dinosaur of the order *Ornithischia,* having a pelvis resembling that of a bird. Cf. **saurischian.** —*adj.* **2.** belonging or pertaining to the *Ornithischia.* [< NL *Ornithischi(a)* (*ornith-* ORNITH- + *-ischia* < Gk *ischíon* ISCHIUM) + -AN]

ornitho-, a learned borrowing from Greek meaning "bird," used in the formation of compound words: *ornithology.* Also, *esp. before a vowel,* **ornith-.** [comb. form repr. Gk *ornīth-* (s. of *órnis*) bird]

or·ni·thoid (ôr′nə thoid′), *adj.* resembling a bird. [ORNITH- + -OID]

ornithol., **1.** ornithological. **2.** ornithology.

or·ni·thol·o·gy (ôr′nə thol′ə jē), *n.* the branch of zoology that deals with birds. [< NL *ornithologia.* See ORNITHO-, -LOGY] **—or·ni·tho·log·i·cal** (ôr′nə thə loj′i kəl), **or′ni·tho·log′ic,** *adj.* **—or′ni·tho·log′i·cal·ly,** *adv.* **—or′ni·thol′o·gist,** *n.*

or·ni·tho·pod (ôr′nə thə pod′, ôr nī′thə-), *n.* any herbivorous dinosaur of the suborder *Ornithopoda* whose members usually walked erect on their hind legs. [< NL *Ornithopod(a)* (pl.). See ORNITHO-, -POD]

or·ni·thop·ter (ôr′nə thop′tər), *n.* a heavier-than-air craft sustained in and propelled through the air by flapping wings. Also, **orthopter.** [ORNITHO- + Gk *pter(ón)* wing]

or·ni·tho·rhyn·chus (ôr′nə thə ring′kəs), *n.* the duck-bill. [ORNITHO- + Gk *rhýnchos* bill]

or·ni·tho·sis (ôr′nə thō′sis), *n. Vet. Pathol.* psittacosis, esp. of birds other than those of the parrot family, easily transmissible to man. [< NL; see ORNITH-, -OSIS]

Or·ny·tus (ôr′ni təs), *n. Class. Myth.* Teuthis.

oro-¹, a learned borrowing from Greek meaning "mountain," used in the formation of compound words: *orography.* [< Gk, comb. form of *óros*]

oro-², a learned borrowing from Latin meaning "mouth," used in the formation of compound words: *oropharynx.* [< L, comb. form of *ōs*]

or·o·ban·cha·ceous (ôr′ō bang kā′shəs, or′ō-), *adj.* belonging to the *Orobanchaceae,* the broomrape family of parasitic herbs. [< L *orobanch(ē)* broomrape (< Gk *orobánchē*) + -ACEOUS]

o·rog·e·ny (ō roj′ə nē, ô roj′-), *n. Geol.* the process of mountain making or upheaval. [ORO-¹ + -GENY] **—or·o·gen·ic** (ôr′ə jen′ik, or′ə-), **or′o·ge·net′ic,** *adj.*

or′ograph′ic cloud′, any cloud whose existence and form are largely controlled by the disturbed flow of air over and around mountains, as the banner cloud and crest cloud.

orograph′ic precipita′tion, precipitation caused by the lifting of moist air over a mountain barrier.

o·rog·ra·phy (ō rog′rə fē, ô rog′-), *n.* the branch of physical geography dealing with mountains. [ORO-¹ + -GRAPHY] **—or·o·graph·ic** (ôr′ə graf′ik, or′ə-), **or′o·graph′i·cal,** *adj.* **—or′o·graph′i·cal·ly,** *adv.*

or·o·ide (ôr′ō īd′, ôr′-), *n.* an alloy containing copper, tin, etc., used to imitate gold. [< F, equiv. to *or* gold (<< L *aur(um)*) + *-oide* -OID]

o·rol·o·gy (ō rol′ə jē, ô rol′-), *n.* the science of mountains. [ORO-¹ + -LOGY] **—or·o·log·i·cal** (ôr′ə loj′i kəl, or′ə-), *adj.* **—o·rol′o·gist,** *n.*

o·rom·e·ter (ō rom′i tər, ô rom′-), *n.* an aneroid barometer with a scale giving elevations above sea level, used to determine altitudes of mountains, volcanoes, etc. [ORO-¹ + -METER]

or·o·met·ric (ôr′ə me′trik, ôr′-), *adj.* **1.** of or pertaining to orometry. **2.** of or pertaining to an orometer. [ORO-¹ + METRIC²]

o·rom·e·try (ō rom′i trē, ô rom′-), *n.* the measurement of mountains. [ORO-¹ + -METRY]

or·o·na·sal (ôr′ō nā′zəl, ôr′ō-), *adj., n.* orinasal. **—o′ro·na′sal·ly,** *adv.*

O·ro·no (ôr′ə nō′, ôr′-), *n.* **1.** a town in central Minnesota. 5643 (1960). **2.** a town in S Maine. 3234 (1960).

O·ron·tes (ō ron′tēz, ô ron′-), *n.* a river in W Asia, flowing N from Lebanon through NW Syria and then SW past Antioch, Turkey, to the Mediterranean. 250 mi. long.

O·ron·ti·us (ō ron′tē əs), *n.* a walled plain in the third quadrant of the face of the moon: about 77 miles in diameter.

or·o·pen·do·la (ôr′ō pen′dᵊ lə, ôr′ō-), *n.* any of several arboreal, tropical American birds of the family *Icteridae,* noted for their colonies of long, pensile nests.

o·ro·phar·ynx (ôr′ō far′ingks, ôr′-), *n., pl.* **-pha·ryn·ges** (-fə rin′jēz), **-phar·ynx·es.** *Anat.* **1.** the part of the pharynx between the soft palate and the upper edge of the epiglottis. **2.** the pharynx as distinguished from the nasopharynx and laryngeal pharynx. [ORO-² + PHARYNX] **—o·ro·pha·ryn·ge·al** (ôr′ō fə rin′jē əl, -far′in-jē′əl, ôr′-), *adj.*

O·ro·si·us (ō rō′zhē əs), *n.* **Pau·lus** (pô′ləs), fl. 5th century A.D., Spanish theologian and historian.

o·ro·tund (ôr′ə tund′, ôr′-), *adj.* **1.** (of the voice or speech) characterized by strength, fullness, richness, and clearness. **2.** (of a style of speaking) pompous or bombastic. [< L *ōre rotundō,* lit., with round mouth] **—o·ro·tun·di·ty** (ôr′ə tun′di tē, ôr′-), *n.*

o·ro y pla·ta (ôʀ′ô ē plä′tä; *Eng.* ôr′ō ē plä′tə), *Spanish.* gold and silver: motto of Montana.

O·roz·co (ô rôs′kô), *n.* **Jo·sé Cle·men·te** (hô se′ kle-men′te), 1883–1949, Mexican painter.

Or·pen (ôr′pən), *n.* **Sir William New·en·ham Montague** (nōō′ə nəm, nyōō′-), 1878–1931, Irish painter.

or·phan (ôr′fən), *n.* **1.** a child who has lost both parents through death, or, less commonly, one parent. **2.** a young animal that has been deserted by or has lost its mother. **3.** one who or that which is without protection, sponsorship, etc.: *The committee is an orphan of the previous administration.* —*adj.* **4.** bereft of parents. **5.** of or for orphans: *an orphan home.* —*v.t.* **6.** to deprive of parents or a parent through death: *He was orphaned at the age of twelve.* [late ME < LL *orphan(us)* destitute, without parents (akin to L *orbus* bereaved) < Gk *orphanós* bereaved] **—or′phan·hood′,** *n.*

or·phan·age (ôr′fə nij), *n.* **1.** an institution for the housing and care of orphans. **2.** the state of being an orphan; orphanhood. **3.** *Archaic.* orphans collectively. [ORPHAN + -AGE]

or′phans′ court′, a probate court in certain U.S. States.

Or·phe·us (ôr′fē əs, -fyōōs), *n.* **1.** *Gk. Legend.* a poet and musician, a son of Calliope, who followed his dead wife, Eurydice, to the underworld. By charming Hades, he obtained permission to lead her away, provided he did not look back at her until they had returned to earth. But at the last moment he looked, and she was lost to him forever. Later, Orpheus was torn to pieces by maenads. **2.** (*italics*) a ballet (1947) by Stravinsky. **—Orphe·an** (or fē′ ən, ôr′fē ən), *adj.*

Or·phic (ôr′fik), *adj.* **1.** of or pertaining to Orpheus. **2.** resembling the music attributed to Orpheus; entrancing. **3.** pertaining to a religious or philosophical school maintaining a form of the cult of Dionysus, or Bacchus, ascribed to Orpheus as founder: *Orphic mysteries.* **4.** (*often l.c.*) mystic; oracular. [< Gk *Orphik(ós)* (c. L *Orphicus*), equiv. to *Orph(eús)* + *-ikos* -IC] **—Or′phi·cal·ly,** *adv.*

Or·phism (ôr′fiz əm), *n.* **1.** the religious or philosophical system of the Orphic school. **2.** (*sometimes l.c.*) *Fine Arts.* a style of painting developed in the early 20th century, chiefly characterized by the use of vivid color and a generally nonrepresentational development of the forms and space characteristic of Cubism. [ORPH(EUS) + -ISM]

Or·phist (ôr′fist), *n.* **1.** (*sometimes l.c.*) a person who paints in the style of Orphism. —*adj.* **2.** (*sometimes l.c.*) pertaining to Orphism. [ORPH(ISM) + -IST]

or·phrey (ôr′frē), *n., pl.* **-phreys.** **1.** an ornamental band or border, esp. on an ecclesiastical vestment. **2.** gold embroidery. **3.** rich embroidery of any sort. **4.** a piece of richly embroidered material. [ME *orfreis* < OF < LL *aurifris(ium),* var. of L *aurumphrygium* gold embroidery, lit., Phrygian gold] **—or′phreyed,** *adj.*

or·pi·ment (ôr′pə mənt), *n.* a mineral, arsenic trisulfide, As_2S_3, found usually in soft yellow foliated masses, used as a pigment. [ME < OF < L *auripigment(um)* pigment of gold; see PIGMENT]

or·pine (ôr′pin), *n.* a perennial, crassulaceous herb, *Sedum Telephium,* having purplish flowers. Also, **or′pin.** [ME < MF, back formation from *orpiment* ORPIMENT]

Or·ping·ton (ôr′ping tən), *n.* one of a breed of large, white-skinned chickens. [after *Orpington,* town in Kent, England]

or·ra (ôʀ′ə, oʀ′ə), *adj. Scot.* not regular or scheduled; occasional; miscellaneous; odd: *orra work.* Also, **orrow.** [?]

or·rer·y (ôr′ə rē, or′-), *n., pl.* **-rer·ies.** **1.** an apparatus for representing the motions and phases of the planets, satellites, etc., in the solar system. **2.** any of certain similar machines, as a planetarium. [named after Charles Boyle, Earl of *Orrery* (1676–1731), for whom it was first made]

Or·rin (ôr′in, or′-), *n.* a boy's given name.

or·ris¹ (ôr′is, or′-), *n.* an iris, esp. *Iris florentina,* having a fragrant rootstock. Also, **or′rice.** [unexplained alter. of IRIS]

or·ris² (ôr′is, or′-), *n.* **1.** a lace or braid made of gold or silver, much used in the 18th century. **2.** a galloon used in upholstering. [perh. alter. (by influence of *arras*) of earlier *orfrays* ORPHREY]

or·ris·root (ôr′is rōōt′, -ro͝ot′, or′-), *n.* the rootstock of the orris, used in perfumery, medicine, etc. [ORRIS¹ + ROOT¹]

or·row (ô′ʀə, o′ʀə), *adj. Scot.* orra.

Orr·ville (ôr′vil), *n.* a town in central Ohio. 6511 (1960).

or·seille (ôr sāl′, -sā′, -sel′), *n. Chem.* orchil. [< F]

Orsk (ôʀsk), *n.* a city in the S RSFSR, in the E Soviet Union in Europe, on the Ural River. 199,000 (est. 1962).

Or·son (ôr′sən), *n.* a boy's given name.

ort (ôrt), *n.* Usually, **orts.** a fragment of food left at a meal. [ME; c. LG *ort,* early D *oorete,* equiv. to *oor-* rejected (lit., out, from) + *etes;* cf. OE *or-, ǣt*]

Or·te·gal (ôʀ te gäl′), *n.* **Cape,** a cape in NW Spain, on the Bay of Biscay.

Or·te·ga Sa·a·ve·dra (ôʀ te′gä sä′ä ve′thʀä), **(Jo·sé) Da·niel** (hô se′ dä nyel′), born 1945, Nicaraguan political leader: president since 1985.

Or·te·ga y Gas·set (ôr tā′gə ē gä set′; *Sp.* ôʀ te′gä ē gäs set′), **Jo·sé** (hô se′), 1883–1955, Spanish philosopher, journalist, and critic.

orth-, var. of **ortho-** before a vowel: *orthicon.*

Orth., Orthodox.

Or·thae·a (ôr thē′ə), *n. Class. Myth.* a daughter of Hyacinthus.

Or·thi·a (ôr′thē ə), *n. Class. Myth.* an epithet of Artemis, meaning "upright," in reference to an image of the goddess held upright by willow tendrils.

or·thi·con (ôr′thə kon′), *n. Television.* a camera tube, more sensitive than the Iconoscope, in which a beam of low-velocity electrons scans a photoemissive mosaic. Also, **or·thi·con·o·scope** (ôr′thə kon′ə skōp′). [ORTH- + ICON(OSCOPE)]

or·tho (ôr′thō), *adj.* *Chem.* pertaining to or occupying two adjacent positions in the benzene ring. Cf. **meta²**, **para²**. [independent use of ORTHO-]

ortho-, **1.** an element occurring in loan words from Greek, where it meant "straight," "upright," "right," "correct" (*orthodox*) and on this model used in the formation of compound words (*orthopedic*). **2.** *Chem.* **a.** a prefix indicating that acid of a series that contains most water (*orthoboric acid*). Cf. **meta-**, **pyro-**. **b.** a prefix applied to a salt of one of these acids: if the acid ends in *-ic*, the corresponding salt ends in *-ate* (*orthoboric acid* (H_3BO_3) and *potassium orthoborate* (K_3BO_3)); if the acid ends in *-ous*, the corresponding salt ends in *-ite* (*orthoantimonous acid* (H_3SbO_3) and *potassium orthoantimonite* (K_3SbO_3)). **c.** a prefix designating the 1, 2 position in the benzene ring. Also, *esp. before a vowel*, **orth-**. [< Gk, comb. form of *orthós* straight, upright, correct]

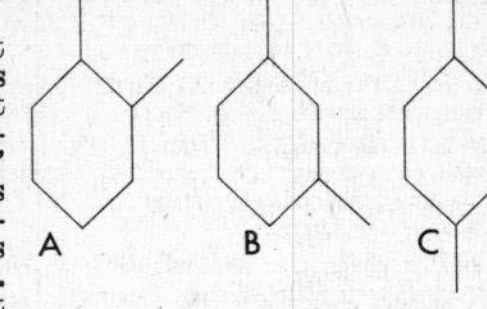

A, Ortho; B, Meta; C, Para

or/tho·bo/ric ac/id (ôr′thə bôr′ik, -bôr′-, ôr′thə-), *Chem.* See **boric acid** (def. 1). Cf. **ortho-** (def. 2). [ORTHO- + BORIC ACID]

or·tho·cen·ter (ôr′thə sen′tər), *n.* *Geom.* the point of intersection of the three altitudes of a triangle. [ORTHO- + CENTER]

or·tho·ce·phal·ic (ôr′thō sə fal′ik), *adj.* having the relation between the height of the skull and the breadth or the length medium or intermediate. Also, **or·tho·ceph·a·lous** (ôr′thə sef′ə ləs). [< NL *orthocephal(us)* (see ORTHO-, CEPHAL-) + -IC] —**or′tho·ceph′a·ly**, *n.*

or·tho·chro·mat·ic (ôr′thə krō mat′ik, -thō krə-), *adj.* *Photog.* **1.** representing correctly the relations of colors as found in a subject; isochromatic. **2.** (of an emulsion) sensitive to all visible colors except red; isochromatic. [ORTHO- + CHROMATIC]

or·tho·clase (ôr′thə klās′, -klāz′), *n.* a common white or pink mineral of the feldspar group, $KAlSi_3O_8$, having two good cleavages at right angles, and found in high-silicon igneous rocks: used in the manufacture of porcelain. [ORTHO- + Gk *klás(is)* cleavage, breaking]

or·tho·clas·tic (ôr′thə klas′tik), *adj.* *Crystall.* (of a crystal) having cleavages at right angles to each other. [< G *orthoklastisch*, equiv. to *ortho-* ORTHO- + *-klastisch* CLASTIC]

or·tho·cous·in (ôr′thə kuz′in, ôr′thə kuz′-), *n.* See **parallel cousin.**

or·tho·don·tics (ôr′thə don′tiks), *n.* (*construed as sing.*) the branch of dentistry dealing with the prevention and correction of irregular teeth. Also, **or·tho·don·tia** (ôr′thə don′shə, -shē ə). [ORTH- + -ODONT + -ICS] —**or′tho·don′tic**, *adj.*

or·tho·don·tist (ôr′thə don′tist), *n.* a specialist in orthodontics. [ORTH- + -ODONT + -IST]

or·tho·dox (ôr′thə doks′), *adj.* **1.** sound or correct in opinion or doctrine, esp. theological or religious doctrine. **2.** conforming to the Christian faith as represented in the creeds of the early church. **3.** (*cap.*) of, pertaining to, or designating the Eastern Church, esp. the Greek Orthodox Church. **4.** (*cap.*) of, pertaining to, or characteristic of Orthodox Jews or Orthodox Judaism. **5.** of, pertaining to, or conforming to the approved form of any doctrine, philosophy, ideology, etc. **6.** approved; conventional. [< LL *orthodox(us)* < Gk *orthódoxos* right in opinion, deriv. of *orthodoxein* to have the right opinion, equiv. to *ortho-* ORTHO- + *dóx(a)* belief, opinion] —**or′tho·dox′ness**, *n.*

Or′thodox Church′, **1.** the Christian church comprising the local and national Eastern churches that are in communion with the ecumenical patriarch of Constantinople; Byzantine Church. **2.** (originally) the Christian church of those countries formerly comprising the Eastern Roman Empire and of countries evangelized from it; Greek Orthodox Church.

Or′thodox Jew′, a Jew who adheres faithfully to the principles and practices of traditional Judaism as evidenced chiefly by a devotion to and study of the Torah, daily synagogue attendance if possible, and strict observance of the Sabbath, religious festivals, holy days, and the dietary laws. Cf. **Conservative Jew, Reform Jew.**

Or′thodox Ju′daism, Judaism as observed by Orthodox Jews.

or·tho·dox·y (ôr′thə dok′sē), *n., pl.* **-dox·ies. 1.** orthodox belief or practice. **2.** orthodox character. [< LL *orthodoxia* < Gk *orthodoxía*, equiv. to *orthódox(os)* (see ORTHODOX) + *-ia* -Y³]

Or′thodoxy Sun′day. See under **Feast of Orthodoxy.**

or·tho·e·py (ôr thō′ə pē, ôr′thō ep′ē), *n.* the study of correct pronunciation. Also, **or·tho′ë·py.** [< Gk *orthoépeia* correctness of diction, equiv. to *ortho-* ORTHO- + *epe-* (s. of *épos*) word + *-ia* -Y³] —**or·tho·ep·ic, or·tho·ëp·ic** (ôr′thō ep′ik), **or′tho·ep′i·cal, or′tho·ëp′i·cal**, *adj.* —**or′tho·ep′i·cal·ly, or′tho·ëp′i·cal·ly**, *adv.* —**or·tho′e·pist, or·tho′ë·pist**, *n.* —**or′tho·e·pis′tic, or′tho·ë·pis′tic**, *adj.*

or·tho·for·mate (ôr′thə fôr′māt), *n.* *Chem.* an ester of orthoformic acid. [ORTHO- + FORMATE]

or′tho·for′mic ac′id (ôr′thə fôr′mik, ôr′thə-), *Chem.* a hypothetical acid, $HC(OH)_3$, known only in the form of its esters. [ORTHO- + FORMIC ACID]

or·tho·gen·e·sis (ôr′thə jen′i sis), *n.* **1.** *Biol.* the evolution of species in definite lines which are predetermined by the constitution of the germ plasm. **2.** *Sociol.* a hypothetical parallelism between the stages through which every culture necessarily passes, in spite of secondary conditioning factors. [< NL; see ORTHO-, GENESIS]

or·tho·ge·net·ic (ôr′thō jə net′ik), *adj.* pertaining to or exhibiting orthogenesis. [< NL *orthogenet-* (s. of *orthogenesis*) ORTHOGENESIS + -IC]

or·tho·gen·ic (ôr′thə jen′ik), *adj.* **1.** *Psychol.* of, concerned with, or providing corrective treatment for mentally retarded or seriously disturbed children: *orthogenic class.* **2.** orthogenetic. [ORTHO- + -GENIC]

or·thog·na·thous (ôr thog′nə thəs), *adj.* *Craniom.* straight-jawed; having the profile of the face vertical or nearly so; having a gnathic index below 98. Also, **or·thog·nath·ic** (ôr′thog nath′ik, -thog-). See diag. under **facial angle.** [ORTHO- + -GNATHOUS] —**or·thog·na·thism** (ôr thog′nə thiz′əm), **or·thog′na·thy**, *n.*

or·thog·o·nal (ôr thog′ə nəl), *adj.* **1.** *Math.* **a.** pertaining to or involving right angles or perpendiculars: *an orthogonal projection.* **b.** (of a system of real functions) defined so that the integral of the product of any two different functions is zero. **c.** (of a system of complex functions) defined so that the product of a function times the complex conjugate of any other function equals one. **d.** (of two vectors) having an inner product equal to 0. **e.** (of a linear transformation) defined so that the length of a vector under the transformation equals the length of the original vector. **f.** (of a square matrix) defined so that its product with its transpose results in the identity matrix. **2.** *Crystall.* referable to a rectangular set of axes. [obs. *orthogon(ium)* (< LL < Gk *orthogṓnion* (neut.) right-angled, equiv. to *ortho-* ORTHO- + *-gōnion* -GON) + -AL¹] —**or·thog·o·nal·i·ty** (ôr thog′ə nal′i tē), *n.* —**or·thog′o·nal·ly**, *adv.*

or·thog·o·nal·ize (ôr thog′ə nəlīz′), *v.t.*, **-ized, -iz·ing.** *Math.* to make (vectors, functions, etc.) orthogonal. [ORTHOGONAL + -IZE] —**or·thog′o·nal·i·za′tion**, *n.*

orthog′onal trajec′tory, *Math.* the locus of a point whose path cuts each curve of a family of curves at right angles.

or·thog·ra·pher (ôr thog′rə fər), *n.* **1.** a person versed in orthography or spelling. **2.** a person who spells correctly. Also, **or·thog′ra·phist.** [< LL *orthograph(us)* (L *ortho-* ORTHO- + *-graphus* -GRAPH) + -ER¹]

or·tho·graph·ic (ôr′thə graf′ik), *adj.* **1.** of or pertaining to orthography. **2.** orthogonal (def. 1a). Also, **or′tho·graph′i·cal.** [ORTHOGRAPH(Y) + -IC] —**or′tho·graph′i·cal·ly**, *adv.*

or·thog·ra·phise (ôr thog′rə fīz′), *v.t., v.i.*, **-phised, -phis·ing.** *Chiefly Brit.* orthographize.

or·thog·ra·phize (ôr thog′rə fīz′), *v.*, **-phized, -phiz·ing.** —*v.t.* **1.** to spell correctly or according to the rules of orthography. —*v.i.* **2.** to apply the rules of correct spelling. [ORTHOGRAPH(Y) + -IZE]

or·thog·ra·phy (ôr thog′rə fē), *n., pl.* **-phies. 1.** the art of writing words with the proper letters, according to accepted usage; correct spelling (opposed to *cacography*). **2.** that part of grammar which treats of letters and spelling. **3.** a method of spelling, as by the use of an alphabet or other system of symbols. **4.** a system of such symbols: *Missionaries provided the first orthography for the language.* **5.** an orthogonal projection, or an elevation drawn by means of it. [ME *ortografye* < L *orthographia* correct writing, orthogonal projection < Gk. See ORTHO-, -GRAPHY]

or·tho·hy·dro·gen (ôr′thə hī′drə jən), *n.* *Physics, Chem.* the form of molecular hydrogen in which the nuclei of the two hydrogen atoms contained in the molecule have spins in the same direction. Cf. **parahydrogen.** [ORTHO- + HYDROGEN]

or′tho·mor′phic projec′tion (ôr′thə môr′fik, ôr′-), *Cartog.* See **conformal projection.** [ORTHO- + -MORPHIC]

or·tho·ni·tro·phe·nol (ôr′thō nī′trō fē′nōl, -nôl, -nol), *n.* See under **nitrophenol** (def. 2).

or·tho·nor·mal (ôr′thə nôr′məl), *adj.* *Math.* **1.** (of a system of functions) normal; normalized. **2.** (of a set of vectors) having the properties that any two vectors are perpendicular and that each vector has length of one unit. [ORTHO- + NORMAL]

or·tho·pe·dic (ôr′thə pē′dik), *adj.* of or pertaining to orthopedics. Also, **or′tho·pae′dic.** [ORTHO- + Gk *paid-* (s. of *pais*) child + -IC] —**or′tho·pe′di·cal·ly, or′tho·pae′di·cal·ly**, *adv.*

or·tho·pe·dics (ôr′thə pē′diks), *n.* (*construed as sing.*) (esp. of children) the correction or cure of deformities and diseases of the spine, bones, joints, muscles, or other parts of the skeletal system. Also, **or′tho·pae′dics, or′tho·pe′dy, or′tho·pae′dy.** [see ORTHOPEDIC, -ICS]

or·tho·pe·dist (ôr′thə pē′dist), *n.* a person skilled in orthopedics. Also, **or′tho·pae′dist.** [ORTHOPED(Y) + -IST]

or·tho·phos·phor·ic (ôr′thō fos fôr′ik, -for′-), *adj.* *Chem.* of or derived from orthophosphoric acid. [ORTHO- + PHOSPHORIC]

or′thophosphor′ic ac′id, *Chem.* a colorless, crystalline solid, H_3PO_4, the tribasic acid of pentavalent phosphorus: used chiefly in fertilizers, as a source of phosphorus salts, and in soft drinks as an acidulant and flavoring agent.

or·tho·phos·pho·rous (ôr′thə fos′fər əs, -thō fos-fôr′əs, -fōr′-), *adj.* *Chem.* of or derived from orthophosphorous acid. [ORTHO- + PHOSPOROUS]

or′thophos′phorous ac′id, *Chem.* a white to yellowish, crystalline, hygroscopic, water-soluble solid, H_3PO_3, used chiefly in the synthesis of phosphites.

or·tho·phy·ric (ôr′thə fī′rik), *adj.* *Petrog.* of or pertaining to a texture of groundmass including closely packed, short, quadrilateral crystals of feldspar larger than those in a trachytic groundmass. [ORTHO- + -PHYRE + -IC]

or·thop·ne·a (ôr thop′nē ə, ôr′thop nē′ə), *n.* *Med.* difficult or painful breathing except in an erect sitting or standing position. Also, **or·thop′noe·a.** [< Gk *orthópnoia*, deriv. of *orthópno(os)* breathing upright, equiv. to *ortho-* ORTHO- + *pnoḗ* breath] —**or′thop·ne′ic, or′thop·noe′ic**, *adj.*

or·tho·prax·i·a (ôr′thə prak′sē ə), *n.* *Med.* the correction of deformities; orthopedics. Also, **orthopraxy.** [ORTHO- + Gk *prâx(is)* PRAXIS + -IA]

or·tho·prax·y (ôr′thə prak′sē), *n.* **1.** correctness or orthodoxy of action or practice. **2.** *Med.* orthopraxia. [ORTHO- + PRAX(IS) + -Y³]

or·tho·psy·chi·a·try (ôr′thō si kī′ə trē, -sī-), *n.* the science that concerns itself with the study and treatment of behavior disorders, esp. of young people. [ORTHO- + PSYCHIATRY] —**or·tho·psy·chi·at·ric** (ôr′thō sī′kē a′trik), **or′tho·psy′chi·at′ri·cal**, *adj.* —**or′tho·psy·chi′a·trist**, *n.*

or·thop·ter (ôr thop′tər), *n.* ornithopter. [< F *orthoptère*, equiv. to *ortho-* ORTHO- + *-ptère*, as in *helicopter*]

or·thop·ter·an (ôr thop′tər ən), *adj.* **1.** orthopterous. —*n.* **2.** an orthopterous insect. [< NL *Orthopter(a)* (see ORTHOPTERON) + -AN]

or·thop·ter·on (ôr thop′tə ron′, -tər ən), *n., pl.* **-ter·a** (-tər ə). an orthopterous insect. [< NL, sing. of *Orthopter(a)* name of the order. See ORTHOPTEROUS]

or·thop·ter·ous (ôr thop′tər əs), *adj.* belonging or pertaining to the *Orthoptera*, an order of insects comprising the crickets, grasshoppers, cockroaches, etc., characterized by leathery forewings and membranous hind wings. [< NL *orthopterus* straight-winged. See ORTHO-, -PTEROUS]

or·thop·tic (ôr thop′tik), *adj.* *Ophthalm.* pertaining to or producing normal binocular vision. [ORTH- + OPTIC]

orthop′tic ex′ercises, a method of exercising the eye and its muscles in order to cure strabismus or improve vision.

or·tho·rhom·bic (ôr′thə rom′bik), *adj.* *Crystall.* noting or pertaining to a system of crystallization characterized by three unequal axes intersecting at right angles; rhombic; trimetric. [ORTHO- + RHOMBIC]

or·tho·scope (ôr′thə skōp′), *n.* *Ophthalm.* an instrument for examining the internal structures of the eye through a layer of water which neutralizes the refraction of the cornea. [ORTHO- + -SCOPE]

or·tho·scop·ic (ôr′thə skop′ik), *adj.* *Ophthalm.* pertaining to, characterized by, or produced by normal vision; presenting objects correctly to the eye. [ORTHO- + -SCOPE + -IC]

or·tho·se·lec·tion (ôr′thō si lek′shən), *n.* *Biol.* a type of natural evolution that promotes adaptive evolution, which in turn affects orthogenesis. [ORTHO- + SELECTION]

or·tho·stat (ôr′thə stat′), *n.* (in a classical temple) any of a number of large stone slabs revetting the lower part of the cella. [< Gk *orthostát(ēs)*, equiv. to *ortho-* ORTHO- + *státēs* that stands; see -STAT]

or·thos·ta·tes (ôr thos′tə tēz′), *n., pl.* **-tai** (-tī′). orthostat.

or·thos·ti·chy (ôr thos′tə kē), *n., pl.* **-chies.** *Bot.* **1.** a vertical rank or row. **2.** an arrangement of members, as leaves, at different heights on an axis so that their median planes coincide. [ORTHO- + Gk *-stichia* alignment, equiv. to *stích(os)* row (see STICH) + *-ia* -Y³] —**or·thos′ti·chous**, *adj.*

or·tho·style (ôr′thə stīl′), *adj.* *Archit.* **1.** (of columns) erected in a straight row. **2.** having columns in a straight row or in straight rows. [ORTHO- + Gk *stŷl(os)* column]

or·tho·to·lu·i·dine (ôr′thō tə lōō′i dēn′, -din), *n.* *Chem.* a light-yellow, very slightly water-soluble liquid, $CH_3C_6H_4NH_2$, the ortho isomer of toluidine: used in the manufacture of dyes, saccharin, and other organic compounds, and in textile printing processes.

or·tho·trop·ic (ôr′thə trop′ik), *adj.* *Bot.* noting, pertaining to, or exhibiting a mode of growth which is more or less vertical. [ORTHO- + -TROPIC]

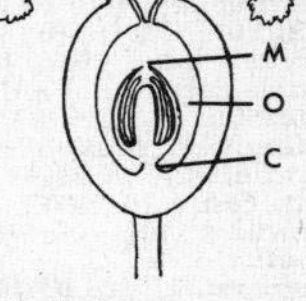

Orthotropous ovule
M, Micropyle;
C, Chalaza; O, Ovule

or·thot·ro·pism (ôr thot′rə piz′əm), *n.* *Bot.* orthotropic tendency or growth. [ORTHO- + -TROPISM]

or·thot·ro·pous (ôr thot′rə pəs), *adj.* *Bot.* (of an ovule) straight and symmetrical, with the chalaza at the evident base and the micropyle at the opposite extremity. [< NL *orthotropus* < Gk *orthótropos*. See ORTHO-, -TROPOUS]

or·tho·xy·lene (ôr′thō zī′lēn), *n.* *Chem.* a clear, colorless, poisonous, flammable liquid, $C_6H_4(CH_3)_2$, the ortho isomer of xylene: used chiefly in the synthesis of phthalic anhydride.

or·thros (ôʀ′thʀôs; *Eng.* ôr′thros), *n.* *Gk. Orth. Ch.* the morning office, corresponding to matins. [< LGk, Gk *órthros* dawn]

Or·thrus (ôr′thrəs), *n.* *Class. Myth.* a two-headed monster guarding the cattle of Geryon, killed by Hercules.

Or·ting (ôr′ting), *n.* a town in central Washington. 2697 (1960).

Ort·ler (ôrt′lər), *n.* **1.** a range of the Alps in N Italy. **2.** the highest peak of this range. 12,802 ft.

or·to·lan (ôr′tᵊlən), *n.* **1.** an Old World bunting, *Emberiza hortulana*, esteemed as a table delicacy. **2.** the bobolink. **3.** the sora. [< F < Pr: lit., gardener (i.e., frequenting gardens) < L *hortulān(us)*, equiv. to *hortul(us)* little garden (*hort(us)* garden + *-ulus* -ULE) + *-ānus* -AN]

Or·ton·ville (ôr′tᵊn vil), *n.* a town in W Minnesota. 2674 (1960).

O·ru·ro (ô rōō′rô), *n.* a city in W Bolivia: a former capital. 77,874 (est. 1959); over 12,000 ft. high.

ORuss, Old Russian.

Or·vi·e·to (ôr′vē ā′tō; *It.* ôʀ vye′tô), *n.* a white wine, from dry to sweet, from Umbria, Italy.

Or·ville (ôr′vil), *n.* a boy's given name.

Or·well (ôr′wel, -wəl), *n.* **George** (*Eric Arthur Blair*), 1903–50, English novelist and essayist.

-ory¹, a suffix of adjectives borrowed from Latin, meaning "having the function or effect of": *compulsory; contributory; declaratory; illusory.* [< L *-ōrius*, suffix of adjectives associated esp. with agent nouns in *-or*. See -OR²]

-ory², a suffix of nouns borrowed from Latin, denoting esp. a place or an instrument: *directory; dormitory; purgatory.* [< L *-ōrium*, neut. of *-ōrius* -ORY¹]

o·ryx (ôr′iks, ōr′-), *n., pl.* **o·ryx·es**, (*esp. collectively*) **o·ryx.** a large African antelope, *Oryx beisa*, grayish with black markings and having long, nearly straight horns. [ME < L < Gk: pickax, oryx]

os¹ (os), *n., pl.* **os·sa** (os′ə). *Anat., Zool.* a bone. [< L]

os² (os), *n., pl.* **o·ra** (ôr′ə, ōr′ə). *Anat.* a mouth, opening, or entrance. [< L: mouth]

os³ (ōs), *n., pl.* **o·sar** (ō′sär). *Geol.* an esker, esp. when of great length. [< Sw *as* (pl. *asar*) ridge]

OS, Old Saxon. Also, **OS.**

Os, *Chem.* osmium.

O/S, (of the calendar) Old Style.

o/s, **1.** (of the calendar) Old Style. **2.** out of stock. **3.** (in banking) outstanding.

O.S., **1.** (in prescriptions) the left eye. [< L *oculus sinister*] **2.** Old Saxon. **3.** Old School. **4.** Old Series. **5.** (of the calendar) Old Style. **6.** See **ordinary seaman.**

o.s., **1.** (in prescriptions) the left eye. [< L *oculus sinister*] **2.** See **ordinary seaman.**

O.S.A., Order of St. Augustine (Augustinian).

O·sage (ō′sāj, ō sāj′), *n., pl.* **O·sag·es,** (*esp. collectively*) **O·sage.** 1. a dialect mutually intelligible with Ponca and belonging to the Siouan language family. 2. a member of an American Indian people speaking this dialect. 3. a river flowing E from E Kansas to the Missouri River in central Missouri. 500 mi. long. 4. a town in N Iowa. 3753 (1960).

O′sage or′ange, 1. an ornamental, moraceous tree, *Maclura pomifera*, native to Arkansas and adjacent regions, used for hedges. 2. its fruit, which resembles a warty orange.

O·sa·ka (ō sä′kə; *Jap.* ô′sä kä′), *n.* a city on S Honshu, in S Japan. 3,214,330 (1964).

o·sar (ō′sär), *n.* pl. of **os**[3].

O·sa·wat·o·mie (ō′sə wot′ə mē, os′ə-), *n.* a town in E Kansas. 4622 (1960).

O.S.B., Order of St. Benedict (Benedictine).

Os·bert (oz′bərt), *n.* a boy's given name.

Os·born (oz′bərn), *n.* 1. **Henry Fair·field** (fâr′fēld′), 1857–1935, U.S. paleontologist and author. 2. a boy's given name.

Os·borne (oz′bərn), *n.* 1. **John (James),** born 1929, English playwright. 2. **Thomas Mott,** 1859–1926, U.S. prison reformer.

Os·can (os′kən), *n.* 1. one of an ancient people of south-central Italy. 2. the Indo-European, Italic language of the Oscans, replaced by Latin. —*adj.* 3. of or pertaining to the Oscans or their language.

Os·car (os′kər), *n.* one of a group of statuettes awarded annually by the Academy of Motion Picture Arts and Sciences for professional achievements in motion-picture production and performance. [said to have been named in 1931 by an employee of the Academy of Motion Picture Arts and Sciences, after her uncle]

Os·car (os′kər), *n.* 1. a word used in communications to represent the letter O. 2. a boy's given name.

Oscar II, 1829–1907, king of Sweden 1872–1907; king of Norway 1872–1905.

Os·ce·o·la (os′ē ō′lə), *n.* 1. 1804–38, U.S. Indian leader: chief of the Seminole tribe. 2. a town in NE Arkansas. 6189 (1960). 3. a town in S Iowa. 3350 (1960).

Os·cho·pho·ri·a (os′kə fōr′ē ə, -fôr′-), *n.* (*sometimes construed as pl.*) one of the festivals in ancient Athens composing the Dionysia, an autumn festival celebrating the ripening of grapes. [< NL < Gk *oschophória*, equiv. to *oschophór(os)* bearing vine branches (*óscho(s)* (vine) branch + *-phoros* -PHORE) + *-ia* -Y[3]]

os·cil·late (os′ə lāt′), *v.,* **-lat·ed, -lat·ing.** —*v.i.* 1. to swing or move to and fro, as a pendulum does; vibrate. 2. to fluctuate between differing beliefs, opinions, conditions, etc.: *He oscillates regularly between elation and despair.* 3. *Physics.* to have, produce, or generate oscillations: *A vacuum tube oscillates.* 4. *Math.* (of a function, sequence, etc.) to tend to no limit, including infinity: *The sequence 0, 1, 0, 1, . . . oscillates.* —*v.t.* 5. to cause to move to and fro; vibrate. [< L *oscillāt(us)* swung (ptp. of *oscillāre*), equiv. to *oscill(um)* swing + *-ātus* -ATE[1]]
—**Syn.** 1. See **swing**[1]. 2. vacillate, vary.

os′cillating en′gine, a steam engine having piston rods connected directly to the crankshaft and cylinders oscillating on trunnions.

os·cil·la·tion (os′ə lā′shən), *n.* 1. the act or fact of oscillating. 2. a single swing or movement in one direction of an oscillating body. 3. fluctuation between beliefs, opinions, conditions, etc. 4. *Physics.* a. an effect expressible as a quantity that repeatedly and regularly fluctuates above and below some mean value, as the pressure of a sound wave or the voltage of an alternating current. b. a single fluctuation between maximum and minimum values in such an effect. 5. *Math.* a. the difference between the least upper bound and the greatest lower bound of the functional values of a function in a given interval. b. Also called **saltus.** the limit of the oscillation in an interval containing a given point, as the length of the interval approaches zero. [< L *oscillātiōn-* (s. of *oscillātiō*) a swinging, equiv. to *oscillāt(us)* swung (see OSCILLATE) + *-iōn-* -ION]

os·cil·la·tor (os′ə lā′tər), *n.* 1. a device or machine producing oscillations. 2. an electronic circuit that produces an alternating output current of a certain frequency determined by the characteristics of the circuit components. 3. one who or that which oscillates. [< NL, equiv. to L *oscillāt(us)* swung (see OSCILLATE) + *-or* -OR[2]]

os·cil·la·to·ry (os′ə lə tōr′ē, -tôr′ē), *adj.* characterized by or involving oscillation. [< NL *oscillātōri(us)*, equiv. to L *oscillāt(us)* swung (see OSCILLATE) + *-ōrius* -ORY[1]]

os·cil·lo·gram (ə sil′ə gram′), *n.* the record produced by the action of an oscillograph or oscilloscope. [< L *oscill(āre)* (to) swing (see OSCILLATE) + -O- + -GRAM[1]]

os·cil·lo·graph (ə sil′ə graf′, -gräf′), *n.* *Elect.* a device for recording the wave-forms of changing currents, voltages, or any other quantity which can be translated into electric energy, as sound waves. [< L *oscill(āre)* (to) swing (see OSCILLATE) + -O- + -GRAPH] —**os·cil·lo·graph·ic,** (ə sil′ə graf′ik, -gräf′-), *adj.* —**os·cil·log·ra·phy** (os′ə log′rə fē), *n.*

os·cil·lom·e·ter (os′ə lom′i tər), *n.* *Med.* an instrument for measuring the fluctuations of the arterial pulse. [< L *oscill(āre)* (to) swing (see OSCILLATE) + -O- + -METER] —**os·cil·lo·met·ric** (os′ə lō me′trik, ə sil′ə-), *adj.* —**os′cil·lom′e·try,** *n.*

os·cil·lo·scope (ə sil′ə skōp′), *n.* *Elect.* a device that depicts on a screen periodic changes in an electric quantity, as voltage or current, using a cathode-ray tube or similar instrument. [< L *oscill(āre)* (to) swing (see OSCILLATE) + -O- + -SCOPE]

os·cine (os′in, -īn), *adj.* 1. of, belonging to, or pertaining to the suborder *Oscines*, of the order *Passeriformes*, comprising the songbirds that have highly developed vocal organs. —*n.* 2. an oscine bird. [back formation from NL *Oscines* name of the suborder, equiv. to L *oscin-* (s. of *oscen*) songbird (*os-*, var. of *ob-* OB- + *cin-*, var. of *can-* sing) + *-es* nom. pl. n. suffix]

os·ci·tant (os′i tənt), *adj.* 1. yawning, as with drowsiness; gaping. 2. drowsy; inattentive. 3. dull; lazy; negligent. [< L *ōscitant-* (s. of *ōscitāns*) yawning, (prp. of *ōscitāre*), equiv. to *ōscit-* open the mouth wide (*ōs* mouth + *cit-* put in motion) + *-ant-* -ANT] —**os′ci·tance, os′ci·tan·cy,** *n.*

Os·coe (os′kō), *n.* a boy's given name.

Os·co-Um·bri·an (os′kō um′brē ən), *n.* a major division of Italic languages that contains Oscan and Umbrian.

os·cu·lant (os′kyə lənt), *adj.* 1. united by certain common characteristics. 2. *Zool.* adhering closely; embracing. [< L *ōsculant-* (s. of *ōsculāns*) kissing (prp. of *ōsculārī*; see OSCULATE) + *-ant-* -ANT]

os·cu·lar (os′kyə lər), *adj.* 1. pertaining to an osculum. 2. pertaining to the mouth or kissing: *oscular stimulation.* —**os·cu·lar·i·ty** (os′kyə lar′i tē), *n.*

os·cu·late (os′kyə lāt′), *v.,* **-lat·ed, -lat·ing.** —*v.i.* 1. to kiss. 2. to come into close contact or union. 3. *Geom.* (of a curve) to touch another curve or another part of the same curve so as to have the same tangent and curvature at the point of contact. —*v.t.* 4. to bring into close contact or union. 5. *Geom.* (of a curve) to touch (another curve or another part of the same curve) in osculation. 6. *Archaic.* to kiss (someone or something). [< L *ōsculāt(us)* kissed (ptp. of *ōsculārī*), equiv. to *ōscul(um)* kiss, a little mouth (see OSCULUM) + *-ātus* -ATE[1]] —**os·cu·la·to·ry** (os′kyə lə tōr′ē, -tôr′ē), *adj.*

os′culating cir′cle, *Math.* See **circle of curvature.**

os′culating plane′, *Math.* the plane containing the circle of curvature of a point on a given curve.

os·cu·la·tion (os′kyə lā′shən), *n.* 1. the act of kissing. 2. a kiss. 3. close contact. 4. *Geom.* the contact between two osculating curves or the like. [< L *ōsculātiōn-* (s. of *ōsculātiō*) a kissing, equiv. to *ōsculāt(us)* kissed (see OSCULATE) + *-iōn-* -ION]

os·cu·lum (os′kyə ləm), *n., pl.* **-la** (-lə). a small mouthlike aperture, as of a sponge. [< NL, L, equiv. to *ōs* mouth + *-culum* -CULE]

OSD, Office of the Secretary of Defense.

O.S.D., Order of St. Dominic (Dominican).

-ose[1], a suffix occurring in adjectives borrowed from Latin, meaning "full of," "abounding in," "given to," "like": *frondose; globose; jocose; otiose; verbose.* [< L *-ōsus*. Cf. -OUS]

-ose[2], a suffix used in chemical terminology to form the names of sugars and other carbohydrates (*amylose; fructose; hexose; lactose*), and of other protein derivatives (*proteose*). [abstracted from GLUCOSE]

O·see (ō′zē, ō′sē), *n.* *Douay Bible.* Hosea.

Ö·sel (œ′zəl), *n.* German name of **Saaremaa.**

O·se·tian (o sē′shən), *adj., n.* Ossetian.

O·set·ic (o set′ik), *adj., n.* Ossetic.

O.S.F., Order of St. Francis (Franciscan).

OSFCW, Office of Solid Fuels Coordinator for War.

Os·good (oz′go͝od′), *n.* a boy's given name.

Osh·kosh (osh′kosh), *n.* a city in E Wisconsin, on Lake Winnebago. 45,110 (1960).

O·shog·bo (ō shog′bō), *n.* a city in SW Nigeria. 210,384 (1963).

o·sier (ō′zhər), *Chiefly Brit.* —*n.* 1. any of various willows, as the red osier, having tough, flexible twigs or branches which are used for wickerwork. 2. a twig from such a willow. [ME < MF; akin to ML *ausaria* willow bed] —**o′siered,** *adj.* —**o′sier-like′,** *adj.*

O·si·ris (ō sī′ris), *n.* *Egyptian Religion.* the king and judge of the dead, the husband and brother of Isis and father (or brother) of Horus, killed by Set but later resurrected (after Horus killed Set): usually depicted as a man, partly wrapped as a mummy, having a beard and wearing the atef-crown. —**O·si·ri·an** (ō sī′rē ən), *adj.*

Osiris

-osis, a suffix occurring in loan words from Greek, where it denoted action, process, state, condition (*metamorphosis*); used in the formation of many pathological terms (*tuberculosis*). [< Gk, suffix forming nouns from verbs with infinitives in *-oein, -oun*]

-osity, a combination of **-ose** (or **-ous**) and **-ity,** used to form nouns from stems in **-ose** (or **-ous**): *verbosity; generosity.* [OSE[1] + -ITY, repr. L *-ōsitas* and F *-osité*]

OSlav, Old Slavic.

Os·ler (ōs′lər, ōz′-), *n.* **Sir William,** 1849–1919, Canadian physician and professor of medicine.

Os·lo (oz′lō, os′-, ōs′-; *Norw.* o͝os′lo͝o), *n.* a seaport in and the capital of Norway, in the SE part, at the head of Oslo Fiord. 484,747 (est. 1964). Formerly, **Christiania.**

Os′lo Fiord′, an inlet of the Skagerrak, in SE Norway. 75 mi. long.

osm-, a learned borrowing from Greek meaning "smell," used in the formation of compound words: *osmics.* [< Gk, comb. form of *osmḗ*]

Os·man (oz′mən, os′-; *Turk.* os män′), *n.* 1259–1326, Turkish emir 1299–1326: founder of the Ottoman dynasty. Also, **Othman.**

Os·man·li (oz man′lē, os-), *n., pl.* **-lis,** *adj.* —*n.* 1. an Ottoman. 2. the language of the Ottoman Turks. —*adj.* 3. Ottoman. (defs. 3, 4).

os·ma·te·ri·um (oz′mə tēr′ē əm), *n., pl.* **-te·ri·a** (-tēr′ē ə). osmeterium.

os·me·te·ri·um (oz′mi tēr′ē əm), *n., pl.* **-te·ri·a** (-tēr′ē ə). a forked, eversible process of the first thoracic segment of certain caterpillars, from which a sometimes disagreeable odor is emitted. Also, **osmaterium.** [< NL, irreg. < Gk *osmḗ* smell]

os·mic (oz′mik), *adj.* *Chem.* of or containing osmium in its higher valences, esp. the tetravalent state. [OSM(IUM) + -IC]

os·mics (oz′miks), *n.* (*construed as sing.*) the science dealing with the sense of smell. [OSM- + -ICS]

os·mi·dro·sis (oz′mi drō′sis), *n.* *Med.* bromhidrosis. [< NL, equiv. to *osm-* OSM- + *hidrōsis*; see HIDROSIS]

os·mi·ous (oz′mē əs), *adj.* *Chem.* of or containing osmium in its lower valences. [OSMI(UM) + -OUS]

os·mi·rid·i·um (oz′mə rid′ē əm), *n.* iridosmine. [< G; see OSMIUM, IRIDIUM]

os·mi·um (oz′mē əm), *n.* *Chem.* a hard, heavy, metallic element having the greatest density of the known elements and forming octavalent compounds, as OsO_4 and OsF_8: used chiefly as a catalyst, in alloys, and in the manufacture of electric-light filaments. [< NL, equiv. to *osm-* OSM- + *-ium* -IUM; named from the penetrating odor of one of its oxides]

os·mom·e·ter (oz mom′i tər), *n.* an instrument used in osmometry. [OSMO- + -METER]

os·mom·e·try (oz mom′i trē), *n.* *Physical Chem.* measurement of osmotic pressure. [OSMO- + -METRY] —**os·mo·met·ric** (oz′mə me′trik), *adj.* —**os′mo·met′ri·cal·ly,** *adv.*

Os·mond (oz′mənd), *n.* a boy's given name.

os·mose (oz′mōs, os′-), *v.,* **-mosed, -mos·ing,** *n.* —*v.i.* 1. to undergo osmosis. —*v.t.* 2. to subject to osmosis. —*n.* 3. osmosis. [abstracted from *endosmose* and *exosmose* as representing the common element; cf. Gk *ōsmós* a push, thrust]

os·mo·sis (oz mō′sis, os-), *n.* 1. *Physical Chem.* a. the tendency of a fluid to pass through a semipermeable membrane into a solution where its concentration is lower, thus equalizing the conditions on either side of the membrane. b. the diffusion of fluids through membranes or porous partitions. Cf. **endosmosis, exosmosis.** 2. a subtle or gradual absorption or mingling: *We can teach you some of the things you'll have to know, but the rest you'll have to pick up by osmosis.* [< NL < Gk *ōsmó(s)* a push, thrust + *-sis* -SIS] —**os·mot·ic** (oz mot′ik, os-), *adj.* —**os·mot′i·cal·ly,** *adv.*

osmot′ic pres′sure, *Physical Chem.* the force that a dissolved substance exerts on a semipermeable membrane, through which it cannot penetrate, when separated by it from pure solvent.

os·mund[1] (oz′mənd, os′-), *n.* any fern of the genus *Osmunda*, esp. the royal fern. [ME *osmunde* < ?]

os·mund[2] (oz′mənd, os′-), *n.* a superior quality of iron, formerly used for fishhooks, arrowheads, etc. [ME *osmond* < MLG *osemunt* < OSw *osmund(er)*]

Os·na·brück (oz′nə bro͝ok′; *Ger.* ôs′nä brʏk′), *n.* a city in N West Germany, in Hanover. 141,000 (1963).

Os·na·burg (oz′nə bûrg′), *n.* a heavy, coarse cotton in a plain weave, for grain sacks and sportswear and also finished into cretonne. [irreg. after OSNABRÜCK, known for its linen]

O·sor·no (ô sôr′nô), *n.* a city in S Chile. 50,909 (est. 1959).

os·o·phone (os′ə fōn′), *n.* a telephone receiver that applies audio vibrations directly to the bones of the head, for use by partly deaf persons. [OS[1] + -O- + (TELE)PHONE]

OSP, he died without issue. [< L *obiit sine prole*]

OSp, Old Spanish.

os·prey (os′prē), *n., pl.* **-preys.** 1. Also called **fish hawk.** a large hawk, *Pandion haliaetus*, which feeds on fish. 2. a plume for trimming hats. [ME *ospray(e)* < MF *orfraie, offraie* < L *ossifraga*, lit., bone-breaker. See OSSIFRAGE]

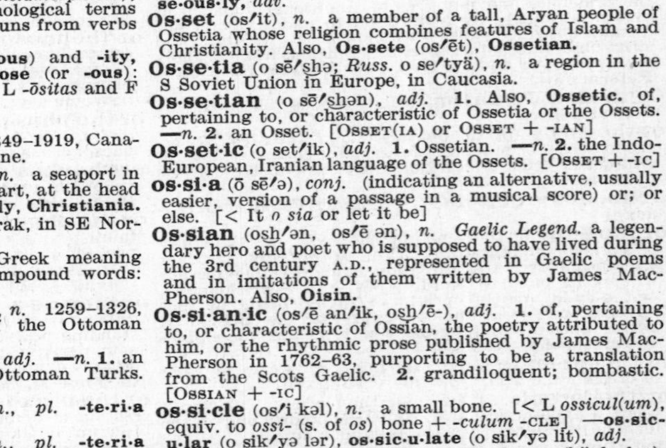

Osprey (Length 2 ft.; wingspread 4½ ft.)

OSRD, Office of Scientific Research and Development.

OSS, Office of Strategic Services. Also, **O.S.S.**

os·sa (os′ə), *n.* pl. of **os**[1].

Os·sa (os′ə), *n.* a mountain in E Greece, in Thessaly. 6490 ft.

os·se·in (os′ē in), *n.* *Biochem.* the organic basis of bone, remaining after the mineral matter has been removed by treatment with dilute acid. [< L *osse(us)* OSSEOUS + -IN[2]]

os·se·let (os′ə lit), *n.* *Vet. Pathol.* a hard nodule on the leg of a horse, esp. one on the inner side of the knee or the outer side of the fetlock. [< F: lit., little bone, OF, equiv. to *ossel* bone (<< L *os* bone) + *-et* -ET]

os·se·ous (os′ē əs), *adj.* 1. composed of, containing, or resembling bone; bony. 2. ossiferous. [< L *osseus* bony, equiv. to *oss-* (s. of *os*) bone + *-eus* -EOUS] —**os′se·ous·ly,** *adv.*

Os·set (os′it), *n.* a member of a tall, Aryan people of Ossetia whose religion combines features of Islam and Christianity. Also, **Os·sete** (os′ēt), **Ossetian.**

Os·se·tia (o sē′shə; *Russ.* o se′tyä), *n.* a region in the S Soviet Union in Europe, in Caucasia.

Os·se·tian (o sē′shən), *adj.* 1. Also, **Ossetic.** of, pertaining to, or characteristic of Ossetia or the Ossets. —*n.* 2. an Osset. [OSSET(IA) or OSSET + -IAN]

Os·set·ic (o set′ik), *adj.* 1. Ossetian. —*n.* 2. the Indo-European, Iranian language of the Ossets. [OSSET + -IC]

os·si·a (ō sē′ə), *conj.* (indicating an alternative, usually easier, version of a passage in a musical score) or; or else. [< It *o sia* or let it be]

Os·sian (osh′ən, os′ē ən), *n.* *Gaelic Legend.* a legendary hero and poet who is supposed to have lived during the 3rd century A.D., represented in Gaelic poems and in imitations of them written by James MacPherson. Also, **Oisin.**

Os·si·an·ic (os′ē an′ik, osh′ē-), *adj.* 1. of, pertaining to, or characteristic of Ossian, the poetry attributed to him, or the rhythmic prose published by James MacPherson in 1762–63, purporting to be a translation from the Scots Gaelic. 2. grandiloquent; bombastic. [OSSIAN + -IC]

os·si·cle (os′i kəl), *n.* a small bone. [< L *ossicul(um)*, equiv. to *ossi-* (s. of *os*) bone + *-culum* -CLE] —**os·sic·u·lar** (o sik′yə lər), **os·sic·u·late** (o sik′yə lit), *adj.*

Os·si·etz·ky (ô′sē ets′kē), *n.* **Carl von** (kärl fən), 1889–1938, German pacifist leader: Nobel peace prize 1935.

os·si·fer (os′ə fər), *n.* *Facetious.* officer.

os·sif·er·ous (o sif′ər əs), *adj.* containing bones, esp. fossil bones: *ossiferous caves and rock beds.* [< L *ossi-* (s. of *os*) bone + -FEROUS]

os·si·fi·ca·tion (os′ə fə kā′shən), *n.* 1. the act or process of ossifying. 2. the state of being ossified. 3. something that ossified; a bony formation. [< NL *ossificātiōn- (s. of *ossificātiō), equiv. to *ossificāt(us)* ossified (ptp. of *ossificāre*, deriv. of *ossi-*, s. of *os*) bone + *-ficātiōn-* -FICATION]

os·si·fied (os′ə fīd′), *adj.* 1. hardened like or into bone. 2. *Slang.* drunk. [OSSIFY + -ED[2]]

os·si·frage (os′ə frij), *n.* 1. the lammergeier. 2. *Rare.* the osprey. [< L *ossifraga* sea eagle, lit., bone-breaker (fem. of *ossifragus*), equiv. to *ossi-* (s. of *os*) bone + *frag-* break + *-a* fem. n. suffix]

os·si·fy (os′ə fī′), *v.*, **-fied, -fy·ing.** —*v.t.* **1.** to convert into or cause to harden like bone. —*v.i.* **2.** to become bone or harden like bone. **3.** to become rigid or inflexible in habits, attitudes, opinions, etc.: *a young man who began to ossify right after college.* [< L *ossi-* (s. of *os*) bone + -FY] —**os′si·fi′er,** *n.*

Os·si·ning (os′ə ning), *n.* a town in SE New York, on the Hudson: the site of Sing Sing, a state prison. 18,662 (1960). Formerly, **Sing Sing.**

os·su·ar·i·um (osh′o͞o âr′ē əm, os′-), *n.*, *pl.* **-ar·i·a** (-âr′ē ə). ossuary.

os·su·ar·y (osh′o͞o er′ē, os′-), *n.*, *pl.* **-ar·ies.** a place or receptacle for the bones of the dead. Also, **ossuarium.** [< LL *ossuāri(um)*, var. of *ossārium*, equiv. to *oss-* (s. of *os*) bone + *-ārium* -ARY]

oste-, var. of **osteo-** before a vowel: *osteitis.*

os·te·al (os′tē əl), *adj.* osseous. [OSTE- + -AL[1]]

os·tec·to·my (o stek′tə mē), *n.*, *pl.* **-mies.** *Surg.* excision of part or all of a bone. Also, **osteectomy.** [OST(E)- + -ECTOMY]

os·te·ec·to·my (os′tē ek′tə mē), *n.*, *pl.* **-mies.** *Surg.* ostectomy.

Os·teen (os′tēn), *n.* a boy's given name.

Os·te·ich·thy·es (os′tē ik′thē ēz′), *n.* the class comprising the bony fishes. [< NL < Gk *ostéo(on)* OSTE- + *ichthŷes* fish (pl. of *ichthŷs*)]

os·te·i·tis (os′tē ī′tis), *n.* *Pathol.* inflammation of the substance of bone. [OSTE- + -ITIS] —**os·te·it·ic** (os′tē it′ik), *adj.*

Ost·end (os tend′), *n.* a seaport in NW Belgium. 57,063 (est. 1964). French, **Os·tende** (ôs tãnd′).

Ostend′ Manifes′to, a declaration (1854) issued from Ostend, Belgium, by the U.S. ministers to England, France, and Spain, stating that the U.S. would be justified in seizing Cuba if Spain did not sell it to the U.S.

os·ten·si·ble (o sten′sə bəl), *adj.* **1.** given out or outwardly appearing as such; professed; pretended: *an ostensible heartiness that ill concealed his true malevolence.* **2.** apparent; conspicuous: *the ostensible truth of his theories.* [< F < L *ostens(us)* displayed (see OSTENTATION) + F *-ible* -IBLE] —**os·ten′si·bly,** *adv.*

os·ten·sive (o sten′siv), *adj.* **1.** clearly or manifestly demonstrative. **2.** ostensible. [< LL *ostensīv(us)*, equiv. to L *ostens(us)* displayed (see OSTENTATION) + *-īvus* -IVE] —**os·ten′sive·ly,** *adv.*

os·ten·so·ri·um (os′tən sôr′ē əm, -sōr′-), *n.*, *pl.* **-so·ri·a** (-sôr′ē ə, -sōr′ē ə). *Rom. Cath. Ch.* ostensory.

os·ten·so·ry (o sten′sə rē), *n.*, *pl.* **-ries.** *Rom. Cath. Ch.* monstrance. Also, **ostensorium.** [< ML *ostensōri(um)*, equiv. to L *ostens(us)* displayed (see OSTENTATION) + *-ōrium* -ORY[2]]

os·ten·ta·tion (os′ten tā′shən), *n.* **1.** pretentious show; display intended to impress others. **2.** *Archaic.* the act of showing or exhibiting; display. [ME *ostentacioun* < MF *ostentation* < L *ostentātiōn-* (s. of *ostentātiō*), equiv. to *ostentāt(us)* displayed, ptp. of *ostentāre* (*ostent(us)*, ptp. of *ostendere*, equiv. to *os-*, var of *ob-* OB- + *tendere* to stretch + *-ātus* -ATE[1]) + *-iōn-* -ION]
—**Syn. 1.** pretension, semblance. See **show.**

os·ten·ta·tious (os′ten tā′shəs), *adj.* **1.** characterized by or given to ostentation or pretentious show: *evidences of wealth too ostentatious to be ignored.* **2.** (of actions, manner, qualities exhibited, etc.) intended to attract notice: *Lady Bountiful's ostentatious charity.* [OSTENTAT(ION) + -IOUS] —**os′ten·ta′tious·ly,** *adv.* —**os′ten·ta′tious·ness,** *n.*

osteo-, a learned borrowing from Greek meaning "bone," used in the formation of compound words: *osteometry.* Also, *esp. before a vowel,* **oste-.** [< Gk, comb. form of *ostéon*]

os·te·o·ar·thri·tis (os′tē ō är thrī′tis), *n.* *Pathol.* a degenerative disease of the joints, esp. those that bear weight, occurring in elderly people. Also called **degenerative joint disease.** [OSTEO- + ARTHRITIS]

os·te·o·blast (os′tē ə blast′), *n.* *Anat.* a bone-forming cell. [OSTEO- + -BLAST] —**os′te·o·blas′tic,** *adj.*

os·te·oc·la·sis (os′tē ok′lə sis), *n.* **1.** *Anat.* the breaking down or absorption of osseous tissue. **2.** *Surg.* the fracturing of a bone to correct deformity. [OSTEO- + Gk *klásis* fracture]

os·te·o·clast (os′tē ə klast′), *n.* **1.** *Anat.* one of the large multinuclear cells in growing bone concerned with the absorption of osseous tissue, as in the formation of canals. **2.** *Surg.* an instrument for effecting osteoclasis. [OSTEO- + Gk *klast(ós)* broken] —**os′te·o·clas′tic,** *adj.*

os·te·o·cope (os′tē ə kōp′), *n.* *Med.* severe pain in the bones, esp. that occurring at night in syphilitic persons. [< Gk *osteokóp(os)*, equiv. to *osteo-* OSTEO- + *kópos* beat, toil, fatigue]

os·te·o·gen·e·sis (os′tē ə jen′i sis), *n.* the formation of bone. [OSTEO- + GENESIS] —**os·te·o·ge·net·ic** (os′tē ō jə net′ik), **os·te·o·gen′ic, os·te·og·e·nous** (os′tē oj′ə nəs), *adj.*

os·te·oid (os′tē oid′), *adj.* resembling bone; bonelike. [OSTE- + -OID]

os·te·ol·o·gy (os′tē ol′ə jē), *n.* the branch of anatomy dealing with the skeleton. [< NL *osteologia.* See OSTEO-, -LOGY] —**os·te·o·log·i·cal** (os′tē ə loj′i kəl), **os′te·o·log′ic,** *adj.* —**os′te·o·log′i·cal·ly,** *adv.* —**os′te·ol′o·gist, os′te·ol′o·ger,** *n.*

os·te·o·ma (os′tē ō′mə), *n.*, *pl.* **-mas, -ma·ta** (-mə tə). *Pathol.* a tumor composed of osseous tissue. [OSTE- + -OMA]

os·te·o·ma·la·cia (os′tē ō mə lā′shə, -shē ə, -sē ə), *n.* *Pathol.* a condition, esp. of women during pregnancy, characterized by a softening of the bones with subsequent flexibility, deformity, weakness, and pain, caused by a deficiency of calcium, phosphorus, and vitamin D. [< NL; see OSTEO-, MALACIA] —**os′te·o·ma·la′cial, os·te·o·ma·lac·ic** (os′tē ō mə las′ik), *adj.*

os·te·om·e·try (os′tē om′i trē), *n.* the anthropometric measurement of bones. [OSTEO- + -METRY] —**os·te·o·met·ric** (os′tē ə me′trik), **os′te·o·met′ri·cal,** *adj.*

os·te·o·my·e·li·tis (os′tē ō mī′ə lī′tis), *n.* *Pathol.* a purulent inflammation of the bone. [OSTEO- + MYELITIS]

os·te·o·path (os′tē ə path′), *n.* a person who practices osteopathy. Also, **os·te·op·a·thist** (os′tē op′ə thist). [back formation from OSTEOPATHY]

os·te·op·a·thy (os′tē op′ə thē), *n.* a therapeutic system based upon the premise that restoring or preserving health can best be accomplished by manipulation of the skeleton and of the muscles. [OSTEO- + -PATHY] —**os·te·o·path·ic** (os′tē ə path′ik), *adj.* —**os′te·o·path′i·cal·ly,** *adv.*

os·te·o·phyte (os′tē ə fīt′), *n.* *Pathol.* a small osseous excrescence or outgrowth on bone. [OSTEO- + -PHYTE] —**os·te·o·phyt·ic** (os′tē ə fit′ik), *adj.*

os·te·o·plas·tic (os′tē ə plas′tik), *adj.* **1.** *Surg.* pertaining to osteoplasty. **2.** *Physiol.* pertaining to bone formation. [OSTEO- + -PLASTIC]

os·te·o·plas·ty (os′tē ə plas′tē), *n.* *Surg.* the transplanting or inserting of bone, or surgical reconstruction of bone, to repair a defect or loss. [OSTEO- + -PLASTY]

os·te·o·po·ro·sis (os′tē ō pə rō′sis), *n.* Pathol. a disorder in which the bones become increasingly porous, brittle, and subject to fracture, owing to loss of calcium and other mineral components, sometimes resulting in pain, decreased height, and skeletal deformities: common in older persons, primarily postmenopausal women, but also associated with long-term steroid therapy and certain endocrine disorders. [OSTEO- + Gk *pōr(os)* passage, PORE[2] + -OSIS]

os·te·o·tome (os′tē ə tōm′), *n.* *Surg.* a double-beveled chisellike instrument for cutting or dividing bone. [< NL *osteotom(us).* See OSTEO, -TOME]

os·te·ot·o·my (os′tē ot′ə mē), *n.*, *pl.* **-mies.** *Surg.* the dividing of a bone, or the excision of part of it. [OSTEO- + -TOMY] —**os′te·ot′o·mist,** *n.*

Ös·ter·reich (œ′stər rīkh′), *n.* German name of **Austria.**

Os·ti·a (os′tē ə; *It.* ô′styä), *n.* a town in central Italy, SW of Rome: ruins from 4th century B.C.; site of ancient port of Rome. 2364 (1951).

Os·ti·ak (os′tē ak′), *n.* Ostyak.

os·ti·ar·y (os′tē er′ē), *n.*, *pl.* **-ar·ies. 1.** Also called **doorkeeper, porter.** *Rom. Cath. Ch.* **a.** a member of the lowest-ranking of the four minor orders. **b.** the order itself. Cf. **acolyte** (def. 2), **exorcist** (def. 2), **lector** (def. 2). **2.** a doorkeeper, as of a church. [< L *ostiāri(us)* doorkeeper, equiv. to *osti(um)* door, entrance + *-ārius* -ARY]

os·ti·na·to (os′ti nä′tō; *It.* ôs′tē nä′tô), *n.*, *pl.* **-tos.** *Music.* a constantly recurring melodic fragment. [< It: lit., obstinate < L *obstinātus* OBSTINATE]

os·ti·ole (os′tē ōl′), *n.* a small opening or orifice. [< L *ostiol(um)* little door, equiv. to *osti(um)* door + *-olum* dim. suffix] —**os·ti·o·lar** (os′tē ə lər, o stī′-), *adj.*

ost·ler (os′lər), *n.* hostler.

ost·mark (ôst′märk′, ost′-), *n.* (formerly) a cupro-nickel coin and monetary unit of East Germany: replaced by the Deutsche mark in 1990. [< G: east mark]

os·to·sis (o stō′sis), *n.* *Physiol.* the formation of bone; ossification. [< NL; see OSTE-, -OSIS]

Ost·preus·sen (ôst′proi′sən), *n.* German name of **East Prussia.**

os·tra·cise (os′trə sīz′), *v.t.*, **-cised, -cis·ing.** *Chiefly Brit.* ostracize.

os·tra·cism (os′trə siz′əm), *n.* **1.** the act of ostracizing. **2.** the fact or state of being ostracized. **3.** (in ancient Greece) temporary banishment of a citizen, decided upon by popular vote, as recorded on potsherds or earthenware tablets. [< NL *ostracism(us)* < Gk *ostrakismós* banishment, equiv. to *ostrakíz(ein)* (to) OSTRACIZE + *-ismos* -ISM]

os·tra·cize (os′trə sīz′), *v.t.*, **-cized, -ciz·ing. 1.** to exclude, by general consent, from society, privileges, etc.: *Her friends ostracized her after her husband's arrest.* **2.** to banish (a person) from his native country; expatriate. **3.** (in ancient Greece) to banish (a citizen) temporarily by popular vote. Also, *esp. Brit.*, **ostracise.** [< Gk *ostrakíz(ein)*, equiv. to *óstrak(on)* potsherd, tile, ballot (akin to *óstreion* OYSTER, shell) + *-izein* -IZE] —**os′tra·ciz′a·ble,** *adj.* —**os′tra·ci·za′tion,** *n.* —**os′tra·ciz′er,** *n.*
—**Syn. 1.** exile. **2.** disenfranchise, excommunicate.

os·tra·cod (os′trə kod′), *n.* any of numerous minute, marine and fresh-water crustaceans of the subclass *Ostracoda*, having the body enclosed in a hinged, bivalve shell. [< NL *Ostracod(a)* name of the subclass < Gk *ostrakṓdēs*, equiv. to *óstrak(on)* shell, tile + *-ōdēs* -ODE[1]] —**os·tra·co·dan** (os′trə kōd′ən), **os′tra·co′dous,** *adj.*

os·tra·co·derm (os′trə kō dûrm′), *n.* any of several extinct jawless fish of the Ordovician, Silurian, and Devonian periods, having the body enclosed in an armor of bony plates. Cf. **anaspid, heterostracan, osteostracan.** [< NL *Ostracoderm(i)* < Gk *ostrakóderm(os)* with a shell, equiv. to *óstrako(n)* shell, tile + *dérm(a)* -DERM]

os·tra·con (os′trə kon′), *n.*, *pl.* **-ca** (-kə). (in ancient Greece) a potsherd, esp. one used as a ballot on which the name of a person voted to be ostracized was inscribed. Also, **ostrakon.** [< Gk *óstrakon*; see OSTRACIZE]

os·tra·kon (os′trə kon′), *n.*, *pl.* **-ka** (-kə). ostracon.

Os·tra·va (*Czech.* ô′strä vä), *n.* a city in N Moravia, in the NE Czech Republic. 328,000. Formerly, **Moravská Ostrava.**

Ostrich, *Struthio camelus* (Height 8 ft.; length 6 ft.)

os·trich (ô′strich, os′trich), *n.* **1.** a large, two-toed, swift-footed, flightless bird, *Struthio camelus*, indigenous to Africa and Arabia, domesticated for its plumage: the largest of living birds. **2.** Also called **American ostrich.** (not used scientifically) a rhea. [ME *ostrice* < OF *ostruce* < LL *avi(s) strūthio* ostrich < Gk *strouthíōn*] —**os′trich·like′,** *adj.*

os′trich fern′, a tall, North American fern, *Pteretis pensylvanica.*

os·trin·ger (ô′strin jər), *n.* astringer.

Os·tro·goth (os′trə goth′), *n.* a member of the easterly division of the Goths, maintaining a monarchy in Italy, A.D. 493–555. Cf. **Visigoth.** [< LL *Ostrogoth(ī)* (pl.) < L *Austrogotī* < Goth] —**Os′tro·goth′ic, Os′tro·goth′i·an,** *adj.*

Ost·wald (ôst′vält), *n.* **Wil·helm** (vil′helm), 1853–1932, German chemist: Nobel prize 1909.

Os·ty·ak (os′tē ak′), *n.* **1.** an Ugric language of the Uralic family of languages, spoken in NW Siberia in the Ob River basin. **2.** a member of a Finnic people dwelling in western Siberia and the Ural Mountains. Also, **Ostiak.**

Os·wald (oz′wôld), *n.* a boy's given name.

Os·we·go (o swē′gō), *n.* **1.** a port in W New York, on Lake Ontario. 22,155 (1960). **2.** a town in NW Oregon. 8906 (1960). —**Os·we·gan** (o swē′gən), *adj.*, *n.*

Oswe′go tea′, a North American, labiate herb, *Monarda didyma*, having showy, bright-red flowers.

Oś·wię·cim (ôsh vyan′chim), *n.* Polish name of **Auschwitz.**

ot-, var. of **oto-** before a vowel: *otalgia.*

OT, Old Testament. Also, **OT., O.T.**

O·tage, L' (*Fr.* lō tȧzh′). See **Hostage, The** (def. 2).

O·ta·hei·te (ō′tə hē′tē, -hā′-), *n.* former name of **Tahiti.**

Otahei′te ap′ple, 1. a tree, *Spondias cytherea*, of the Society Islands, having whitish flowers and yellow, edible, plumlike fruit. **2.** the fruit itself. Also called **ambarella, vi apple.**

o·tal·gi·a (ō tal′jē ə, -jə), *n.* *Pathol.* earache. [< NL < Gk *ōtalgía*, equiv. to *ōt-* OT- + *-algia* -ALGIA] —**o·tal′gic,** *adj.*

O·ta·ru (ô′tä ro͞o′), *n.* a city in W Hokkaido, in N Japan. 206,620 (1964).

O.T.C., 1. Officers' Training Camp. **2.** Officers' Training Corps.

O·tel·ia (ō tēl′yə, ə tēl′-), *n.* a girl's given name.

O·tel·lo (ō tel′lô), *n.* an opera (1887) by Giuseppe Verdi, with a libretto by Arrigo Boito based on Shakespeare's *Othello.*

O tem·po·ra! O mo·res! (ō tem′pō rä′ ō mō′rās; *Eng.* ō tem′pər ə ō mōr′ēz, môr′-), *Latin.* O times! O customs!

O·thel (ō thel′, ə thel′), *n.* a boy's given name, form of **Othello.**

O·thel·lo (ō thel′ō, ə thel′ō), *n.* **1.** (*italics*) a tragedy (1604) by Shakespeare. **2.** a town in SE Washington. 2669 (1960). **3.** a boy's given name.

oth·er (uth′ər), *adj.* **1.** additional or further: *he and one other person.* **2.** different or distinct from the one or ones mentioned or implied: *in some other city.* **3.** different in nature or kind: *I would not have him other than he is.* **4.** being the remaining one of two or more: *the other hand.* **5.** (used with plural nouns) being the remaining ones of a number: *the other men.* **6.** former: *sailing ships of other days.* **7. every other,** every alternate: *a meeting every other week.* **8. the other day (night, evening,** etc.), a day (night, evening, etc.) or two ago; lately: *That thunderstorm the other night frightened the baby half to death.* —*n.* **9.** the other one: *Each praises the other.* —*pron.* **10.** Usually, **others.** other persons or things: *others in the medical profession; others who follow his example.* **11.** some person or thing else: *Surely some friend or other will help me.* —*adv.* **12.** otherwise; differently (usually fol. by *than*): *We can't collect the rent other than by suing the tenant.* [ME; OE *ōther*; c. G *ander*, Goth *anthar*; akin to Skt *antara-*] —**oth′er·ness,** *n.*

oth·er-di·rect·ed (uth′ər di rek′tid), *adj.* guided by a set of values that is derived from current trends or outward influences rather than from within oneself. Cf. **inner-directed.** —**oth′er-di·rect′ed·ness,** *n.* —**oth′er-di·rec′tion,** *n.*

oth·er·guess (uth′ər ges′), *adj.* *Archaic.* of another kind; different. [var. of *othergets*, var. of ME *othergates.* See OTHER, GATE[2], -S[1]]

oth′er half′, a group or class of people at the opposite extreme from one's own or from that to which reference is being made, esp. with respect to economic or social standing: *Her experience as a social worker gave her insight into the problems of the other half.*

oth·er·where (uth′ər hwâr′, -wâr′), *adv.* *Archaic.* elsewhere. [OTHER + WHERE]

oth·er·while (uth′ər hwīl′, -wīl′), *adv.* *Archaic.* **1.** at another time or other times. **2.** sometimes. Also, **oth′er·whiles′.** [ME *otherwhil, otherwhiles.* See OTHER, WHILE]

oth·er·wise (uth′ər wīz′), *adv.* **1.** under other circumstances: *Otherwise they may get broken.* **2.** in another manner; differently: *Under the circumstances, I can't believe otherwise.* **3.** in other respects: *an otherwise happy life.* —*adj.* **4.** other or different; of another nature or kind: *We hoped his behavior would be otherwise.* **5.** in other or different circumstances: *An otherwise pleasure had become a grinding chore.* [ME; OE (*on*) *ōthre wīsan* (in) other manner. See OTHER, -WISE]

oth′er world′, the world after death; the future world: *He fell to wondering what it would be like in the other world.*

oth·er·world·ly (uth′ər wûrld′lē), *adj.* of, pertaining to, or devoted to another world, as the world of imagination or the world to come. [OTHER WORLD + -LY] —**oth′er·world′li·ness,** *n.*

O·thin (ō′thin), *n.* Odin.

Oth·man (oth′mən; *for 1 also Arab.* ōōth män′), *n.*, *pl.* **-mans. 1.** Osman. **2.** Ottoman (defs. 3, 4).

Oth·ni·el (oth′nē əl), *n.* a judge of Israel. Judges 3:9. Also, *Douay Bible,* **Othoniel.**

O·tho (ō′thō), *n.* a boy's given name, form of **Otto.**

Otho I. See **Otto I.**

O·tho·ni·el (ə thō′nē əl), *n.* *Douay Bible.* Othniel.

o·tic (ō′tik, ot′ik), *adj.* *Anat.* of or pertaining to the ear; auricular. [< Gk *ōtik(ós).* See OT-, -IC]

-otic, an adjective suffix of Greek origin, often corresponding to nouns with stems in *-osis*, denoting a relationship to an action, process, state, or condition indicated by the preceding element: *hypnotic; neurotic.* See **-tic.** Cf. **-osis.** [< Gk *-ōtikos*]

o′tic ves′icle. See **auditory vesicle.**

O·ti·o·ni·a (ō′shē ō′nē ə), *n.* *Class. Myth.* a daughter of King Erechtheus who willingly offered herself as a sacrifice when an oracle told her father that her death would secure an Athenian victory against the Eleusinians.

o·ti·ose (ō′shē ōs′, ō′tē-), *adj.* **1.** leisured; idle; indolent. **2.** ineffective or futile. **3.** superfluous or useless. [< L *ōtiōs(us)* at leisure, equiv. to *ōti(um)* leisure + *-ōsus* -OSE¹] —**o′ti·ose′ly,** *adv.* —**o·ti·os·i·ty** (ō′shē os′i tē, ō′tē-), **o′ti·ose′ness,** *n.*
—**Syn. 1.** lazy, slothful. **2.** idle, vain, profitless. **3.** redundant, worthless, pointless.

O·tis (ō′tis), *n.* **1. Elisha Graves,** 1811–61, U.S. inventor. **2. James,** 1725–83, American patriot. **3.** a boy's given name.

o·ti·tis (ō tī′tis), *n.* *Pathol.* inflammation of the ear. [OT- + -ITIS]

oti′tis ex·ter′na (ik stûr′nə), *Pathol.* inflammation of the external ear. [< NL: external otitis]

oti′tis in·ter′na (in tûr′nə), *Pathol.* labyrinthitis. [< NL: internal otitis]

oti′tis me′di·a (mē′dē ə), *Pathol.* inflammation of the middle ear. [< NL: middle otitis]

o·ti·um cum dig·ni·ta·te (ō′ti ōōm′ kōōm dig′ni tä′te; *Eng.* ō′shē əm kum dig′ni tā′tē), *Latin.* leisure with dignity.

oto-, a learned borrowing from Greek meaning "ear," used in the formation of compound words: *otology.* Also, *esp. before a vowel,* **ot-.** [< Gk, comb. form of *oûs*]

o·to·cyst (ō′tə sist), *n.* **1.** a statocyst. **2.** See **auditory vesicle.** [OTO- + -CYST] —**o·to·cys·tic** (ō′tə sis′tik), *adj.*

o·to·hem·i·neur·as·the·ni·a (ō′tō hem′ē nōōr′əs thē′nē ə, -nyōōr′-), *n.* *Pathol.* a condition in which a person hears with only one ear due to a nerve defect in the other. [< NL; see OTO-, HEMI-, NEURASTHENIA]

o·to·lar·yn·gol·o·gy (ō′tō lar′ing gol′ə jē), *n.* otorhinolaryngology. [OTO- + LARYNGOLOGY] —**o′to·lar′yn·gol′o·gist,** *n.* —**o·to·la·ryn·go·log·i·cal** (ō′tō lə ring′gə loj′i kəl), *adj.*

o·to·lith (ōt′əlith), *n.* **1.** *Anat., Zool.* a calcareous concretion in the internal ear of vertebrates. **2.** statolith (def. 1). [OTO- + -LITH]

o·tol·o·gy (ō tol′ə jē), *n.* the science of the ear and its diseases. [OTO- + -LOGY] —**o·to·log·i·cal** (ōt′əloj′i kəl), *adj.* —**o·tol′o·gist,** *n.*

o·to·neur·as·the·ni·a (ō′tō nōōr′əs thē′nē ə, -nyōōr′-), *n.* *Pathol.* a functional disorder of the nervous system, caused by ear disease. Cf. **neurasthenia.** [< NL; see OTO-, NEURASTHENIA]

o·to·plas·ty (ō′tə plas′tē), *n.* plastic surgery of the external ear. [OTO- + -PLASTY] —**o′to·plas′tic,** *adj.*

o·to·rhi·no·lar·yn·gol·o·gy (ō′tō rī′nō lar′ing gol′ə jē), *n.* the branch of medicine that deals with the anatomy, function, and diseases of the ear, nose, and throat. Also, **otolaryngology.** [OTO- + RHINO- + LARYNGOLOGY] —**o·to·rhi·no·la·ryn·go·log·i·cal** (ō′tō rī′nō lə ring′gə loj′i kəl), **o′to·rhi′no·la·ryn′go·log′ic,** *adj.* —**o′to·rhi′no·lar′yn·gol′o·gist,** *n.*

o·tor·rhe·a (ō′tə rē′ə), *n.* *Pathol.* a mucopurulent discharge from the ear. [< NL; see OTO-, -RRHEA]

o·to·scle·ro·sis (ō′tə skli rō′sis), *n.* *Pathol.* formation of new bone about the stapes, resulting in deafness. [< NL; see OTO-, SCLEROSIS]

o·to·scope (ō′tə skōp′), *n.* *Med.* **1.** an instrument for examining the external canal and tympanic membrane of the ear. **2.** an instrument for auscultation in the ear. [OTO- + -SCOPE] —**o·to·scop·ic** (ō′tə skop′ik), *adj.* —**o·tos·co·py** (ō tos′kə pē), *n.*

O·tran·to (ō trän′tō; *It.* ô′trän tô), *n.* **Strait of,** a strait between SE Italy and Albania, connecting the Adriatic and the Mediterranean. 44 mi. wide.

Ot·se·go (ot sē′gō), *n.* a town in N Michigan. 4142 (1960).

ot·tar (ot′ər), *n.* attar.

ot·ta·va (ō tä′və; *It.* ôt tä′vä), *adv.* *Music.* (of notes in a score) at an octave higher than written (when placed above the staff) or lower than written (when placed below the staff). *Abbr.:* 8 va. [< It: OCTAVE]

ot·ta·va ri·ma (ō tä′və rē′mə), *pl.* **ot·ta·va ri·mas.** an Italian stanza of eight lines, each of eleven syllables (or, in the English adaptation, of ten or eleven syllables), the first six lines rhyming alternately and the last two forming a couplet with a different rhyme: used in Keats' *Isabella* and Byron's *Don Juan.* [< It: octave rhyme]

Ot·ta·wa (ot′ə wə), *n., pl.* **-was,** (*esp. collectively*) **-wa** for 5. **1.** a city in and the capital of Canada, in SE Ontario. 304,462 (1981). **2.** a river in SE Canada, flowing SE along the boundary between Ontario and Quebec into the St. Lawrence at Montreal. 685 mi. long. **3.** a city in NE Illinois, SW of Chicago. 19,408 (1960). **4.** a town in N Ohio. 3245 (1960). **5.** a member of a tribe of Algonquian Indians of Canada, forced into the Lake Superior and Lake Michigan regions by the Iroquois confederacy. **6.** the Ojibwa language as used by the Ottawa Indians.

Ot′tawa Hills′, a town in NW Ohio. 3870 (1960).

ot·ter (ot′ər), *n., pl.* **-ters,** (*esp. collectively*) **-ter.** any of several aquatic, fur-bearing, carnivorous, musteline mammals of the genus *Lutra* and related genera, having webbed feet and a long, slightly flattened tail. [ME *otter, oter,* OE *otor, ottor;* c. D, G *otter;* akin to Gk *hýdra,* Skt *udrá-* water-snake. See HYDRA]

Otter, *Lutra canadensis*
(Total length about 4 ft.; tail to 1½ ft.)

Ot·ter (ot′ər), *n.* (in the Volsunga Saga) a son of Hreidmar, who assumed the form of an otter when fishing, and who was killed by Loki while in that form.

Ot·ter·bein (ot′ər bīn′), *n.* **Philip William,** 1726–1813, American clergyman, originator of the United Brethren, born in Germany.

Ot·ter·burn (ot′ər bûrn′), *n.* a village in central Northumberland, in NE England: battle of Chevy Chase 1388.

ot′ter gear′, *Naut.* the gear by which a paravane is handled.

ot·ter·hound (ot′ər hound′), *n.* one of an English breed of water dogs having a thick, shaggy, oily coat, trained to hunt otter. [OTTER + HOUND¹]

ot′ter shrew′, a chiefly aquatic insectivore, *Potamogale velox,* of W Africa, that resembles an otter, having sleek, brown fur and a flattened tail. Also called **potamogale.**

ot·to (ot′ō), *n.* attar.

Ot·to (ot′ō; *Ger.* ôt′ō), *n.* a boy's given name.

Otto I, ("*the Great*") A.D. 912–973, king of the Germans 936–973; emperor of the Holy Roman Empire 962–973. Also, **Otho I.**

Ot·to·man (ot′ə mən), *adj., n., pl.* **-mans.** —*adj.* **1.** of or pertaining to the Ottoman Empire. **2.** of or pertaining to the lands, peoples, and possessions of the Ottoman Empire. —*n.* **3.** a Turk. **4.** a Turk of the family or tribe of Osman. **5.** (*l.c.*) a kind of divan or sofa, with or without a back. **6.** (*l.c.*) a low cushioned seat without back or arms. **7.** (*l.c.*) a cushioned footstool. **8.** (*l.c.*) a corded silk or rayon fabric with large cotton cord for filling. Also, **Othman** (for defs. 3, 4). [< F < It *ottoman(o),* after the founder of the empire (Ar *'othmān*)] —**Ot′to·man·like′,** *adj.*

Ot′toman Em′pire, a former Turkish empire that was founded about 1300 by Osman and reached its greatest territorial extent under Suleiman in the 16th century, collapsed after World War I, and was replaced by the republic of Turkey. *Cap.:* Constantinople. Also called **Turkish Empire.**

Ot·to·ni·an (o tō′nē ən), *adj.* **1.** of or pertaining to the German dynasty (Otto I, II, III) that ruled as emperors of the Holy Roman Empire from 962 to 1002. **2.** pertaining to or designating the arts or culture of the Ottonian period, characterized chiefly by the development of forms derived from both Carolingian and Byzantine concepts: *an Ottonian revival.* [< G *Otton(en),* pl. of *Otto* + -IAN]

ot′to of ros′es. See **rose oil.**

Ot′to Stru′ve. See **Struve, O.**

ot·tre·lite (o′trə līt′), *n.* *Mineral.* a gray or black member of the chlorite group containing manganese. [< F *ottrélite,* named after *Ottrez,* Belgium, where it is found; see -LITE]

Ot·tum·wa (ə tum′wə), *n.* a city in SE Iowa, on the Des Moines River. 33,871 (1960).

O·tus (ō′təs), *n.* *Class. Myth.* a son of Poseidon and the brother of Ephialtes.

Ot·way (ot′wā), *n.* **Thomas,** 1652–85, English dramatist.

oua·ba·in (wä bä′in), *n.* *Pharm.* a glycoside occurring as a white, crystalline powder, $C_{29}H_{44}O_{12}$, obtained from the seeds of a shrub, *Strophanthus gratus,* or from the wood of a tree, *Acokanthera schimperi:* used in medicine chiefly as a cardiac stimulant. Also called **G-strophanthin.** [< F *ouabaï(o)* (< Somali *waba yo* the name of a tree) + -IN²]

Ouach·i·ta (wosh′i tô′, wô′shi-), *n., pl.* **-tas,** (*esp. collectively*) **-ta.** **1.** a river flowing SE from W Arkansas through NE Louisiana to the Red River. 605 mi. long. **2.** a member of a former North American Indian tribe, apparently of the Caddoan stock, of NE Louisiana. Also, **Washita.**

Ouach′ita Moun′tains, a range extending from SE Oklahoma to W Arkansas.

Oua·ga·dou·gou (wä′gə dōō′gōō), *n.* a city in and the capital of Upper Volta, in the central part. 59,126 (1961).

oua·na·niche (wä′nə nēsh′; *Fr.* WA NA nēsh′), *n., pl.* **-niche.** a landlocked salmon found in Quebec province and adjacent regions. [< CanF < Montagnais *awanas* salmon + *-iš* little]

Ou·ban·gi (ōō bäN gē′), *n.* French name of **Ubangi.**

Ou·ban·gi-Cha·ri (ōō bäN gē′shA rē′), *n.* French name of **Ubangi-Shari.**

ou·bli·ette (ōō′blē et′), *n.* a secret dungeon with an opening only at the top, as in certain old castles. [< F, MF, equiv. to *oubli(er)* (to) forget, OF *oblider* < VL **oblītāre,* deriv. of L *oblīt(us)* forgotten (ptp. of *oblīvīscī*) + MF *-ette* -ETTE]

ouch¹ (ouch), *interj.* (an exclamation expressing sudden pain.) [< G *autsch*]

ouch² (ouch), *Archaic.* —*n.* **1.** a clasp, buckle, or brooch, esp. one worn for ornament. **2.** the setting of a precious stone. —*v.t.* **3.** to adorn with or as with ouches. [ME *ouche,* for *nouche* (*a nouche* taken as *an ouche;* cf. APRON) < OF < LL *nusca* brooch, perh. << Celt]

oud (ōōd), *n.* an Arabian lute. [< Ar *'ūd,* lit., wood]

Oudh (oud), *n.* a former part of the United Provinces of Agra and Oudh in N India: now part of Uttar Pradesh.

O·udts·hoorn (ō′ōōts hōōrn′), *n.* a city in the S Republic of South Africa. 18,729 (1951).

Oues·sant (we säN′), *n.* French name of **Ushant.**

Oue·ta (wē′tə), *n.* a girl's given name.

ought¹ (ôt), *auxiliary verb.* **1.** (used to express duty or moral obligation): *Every citizen ought to help.* **2.** (used to express justice, moral rightness, or the like): *He ought to be punished. You ought to be ashamed.* **3.** (used to express propriety, appropriateness, etc.): *You ought to be home early. We ought to bring her some flowers.* **4.** (used to express probability or natural consequence): *That ought to be the postman.* —*n.* **5.** duty or obligation. [ME *ought, aught,* OE *āhte,* pret. of *āgan* to OWE]
—**Syn. 1.** See **must**¹.

ought² (ôt), *n., adv.* aught¹. [var. of *nought, a nought* being taken as *an ought;* cf. OUCH²]

ought³ (ôt), *n.* aught².

ought·lins (ôKHT′linz), *adv.* *Scot.* in the least; to the least degree. Also, **aughtlins.** [OUGHT³ + *-lins,* var. of -LING² + -S¹]

oughtn't (ôt′ənt), contraction of *ought not.*

oui (wē), *adv., n.* *French.* yes.

Oui·da (wē′də), *n.* **1.** pen name of Louise de la Ramée. **2.** a girl's given name.

Oui·ja (wē′jə), *n.* *Trademark.* a device consisting of a small board on legs, which rests on a larger board marked with words, letters of the alphabet, etc., and which, by moving over the larger board and touching the words, letters, etc., while the fingers of spiritualists, mediums, or others rest lightly upon it, is employed to answer questions, give messages, etc. Also, **oui′ja.** Also called **oui′ja board′.**

Ouj·da (ōōj dä′), *n.* a city in NE Morocco. 128,645 (1960).

Ou·lu (ou′lōō), *n.* a city in W Finland, on the Gulf of Bothnia. 78,545 (est. 1965).

ounce¹ (ouns), *n.* **1.** a unit of weight equal to 437.5 grains or 1/16 pound avoirdupois. **2.** a unit of 480 grains, 1/12 pound troy or apothecaries' weight. **3.** a fluid ounce. **4.** a small quantity or portion. [ME *unce* < MF < L *uncia* twelfth part, inch, ounce, deriv. of *unus* ONE]

ounce² (ouns), *n.* a long-haired, leopardlike feline, *Panthera uncia,* of mountain ranges of central Asia. Also called **snow leopard.** [ME < OF, var. of *lonce* (taken as *l'once* the ounce) < VL **luncea,* deriv. of L *lync-* (s. of *lynx*) LYNX]

Ounce²
(Total length 7 ft.; tail 3 ft.)

ouphe (ouf, ōōf), *n.* an elf or goblin. [scribal var. of OAF]

our (our, ou′ər; *unstressed* är), *pron.* (a form of the possessive case of *we* used as an attributive adjective): *Our team is going to win. Do you mind our going on ahead?* Cf. **ours.** [ME *oure,* OE *ūre,* gen. pl. See US]
—**Usage.** See **me.**

ou·ra·ri (ōō rär′ē), *n.* curare.

Our′ Fa′ther. See **Lord's Prayer.**

ou·rie (ōō′rē), *adj.* *Scot.* **1.** shabby; dingy. **2.** melancholy; languid. Also, **oory.** [ME (north) *ouri,* perh. < Scand]

Ou·ri·nhos (ō rē′nyōōs), *n.* a city in E Brazil. 25,717 (1960).

Our′ La′dy, a title of the Virgin Mary. [ME]

our'n (ourn, ou′ərn, ärn), *pron.* *Dial.* ours. Also, **ourn.** [ME *ouren, ourn,* equiv. to *oure* OUR + *-n* (by analogy with *my, mine; thy, thine*)]

ours (ourz, ou′ərz *or, often,* ärz), *pron.* **1.** (a form of the possessive case of *we* used as a predicate adjective): *Which house is ours?* **2.** that or those belonging to us: *Ours was given second prize. Ours are in the car.* [ME *ures, oures.* See OUR, 's¹]

our·self (är self′, our-, ou′ər-), *pron.* **1.** (a form corresponding to *ourselves,* used of a single person, esp. in the regal or formal style, as *we* for *I*): *We have taken unto ourself such powers as may be necessary.* **2.** one's own person, individuality, etc., considered as private and apart from others: *It is for ourself that we should strive for greater knowledge.* [ME *oure self;* modeled on OURSELVES]
—**Usage.** See **myself.**

our·selves (är selvz′, our-, ou′ər-), *pron.pl.* **1.** (used reflexively as the direct or indirect object of a verb or as the object of a preposition): *We are deceiving ourselves. Give us a moment to ourselves.* **2.** (used as an intensive with *we*): *We ourselves would never say such a thing.* **3.** (used as an intensive in place of *us*): *When it satisfies ourselves it will be ready to market. Nobody likes it but ourselves.* **4.** (used for emphasis in place of *we* or *we ourselves*): *The ones who really want it are ourselves. No one loves it more than ourselves.* **5.** our healthy, normal selves: *After a good rest, we're almost ourselves again.* [ME *oure selven.* See OUR, SELVES]
—**Usage.** See **myself.**

Our′ Town′, a play (1938) by Thornton Wilder.

-ous, **1.** an adjective suffix, occurring with stems of any origin, meaning "full of," "abounding in," "given to," "characterized by," "having," "like," etc. (*glorious; joyous; mucous; nervous; sonorous; wondrous*). **2.** a suffix in chemical terms, specialized in opposition to corresponding terms in *-ic* to mean the lower of two possible valences (*stannous chloride,* $SnCl_2$, and *stannic chloride,* $SnCl_4$). Also, **-eous, -ious.** [ME < OF < L *-ōsus;* often repr. L *-us* (adj.), Gk *-os* (adj.); in some words (e.g., *wondrous*), attached to native stems]

Ouse (ōōz), *n.* **1.** a river in NE England, in Yorkshire, flowing SE to the Humber. 57 mi. long. **2.** Also called **Great Ouse.** a river in E England, flowing NE to the Wash. 160 mi. long. **3.** a river in SE England, flowing S to the English Channel. 30 mi. long.

ou·sel (ōō′zəl), *n.* ouzel.

Ou·spen·sky (ōō spen′skē; *Russ.* ōō spen′ski), *n.* **Pe·ter De·mia·no·vich** (pyô′tər de myä′no vich), 1878–1947, Russian philosopher and author.

oust (oust), *v.t.* **1.** to expel from a place or position occupied: *The union ousted several troublemakers.* **2.** *Law.* to eject; dispossess. [< AF *oust(er)* (to) remove, equiv. to OF *oster* < L *obstare* to stand in the way, oppose (*ob-* OB- + *stare* to stand)]

oust·er (ou′stər), *n.* **1.** expulsion from a place or position occupied: *The opposition called for the ouster of the cabinet minister.* **2.** *Law.* **a.** an ejection; dispossession. **b.** a wrongful exclusion from real property. [< AF, n. use of inf. See OUST]

out (out), *adv.* **1.** away from, or not in, the normal or usual place, position, state, etc.: *out of alphabetical order; to go out to dinner.* **2.** away from one's home, country, work, etc., as specified: *to go out of town.* **3.** in or into the outdoors: *to go out for a walk.* **4.** to exhaustion, extinction, or depletion: *to pump a well out.* **5.** to the end or conclusion; to a final decision or resolution: *to fight it out; to see a crisis out.* **6.** to a point or into a state of extinction, nonexistence, etc.: *The lamp went out.* **7.** in or into a state of neglect, disuse, etc.; not in vogue or fashion: *That style has gone out.* **8.** in or into public notice or knowledge: *The truth is out at last.* **9.** seeking openly and energetically to do or have: *to be out for a good time.* **10.** in or into society, as a result of one's debut: *a debutante who will be coming out this season.* **11.** not in present or personal possession or use, as on loan: *The librarian said that the book was still out.* **12.** on strike: *The miners are going out.* **13.** so as to project or extend: *to stretch out.* **14.** in or into activity, existence, or outward manifestation: *A rash broke out on her arm.* **15.** from a source or material, as specified: *made out of scraps.* **16.** from a state of composure, satisfaction, or harmony: *to be put out over trifles.* **17.** in or into a state of confusion, vexation, dispute, variance, or unfriendliness: *to fall out about trifles.* **18.** so as to deprive or be deprived: *to cheat out of money.* **19.** so as to use the last of: *to run out of coal.* **20.** from a number, stock, or store: *to pick out.* **21.** aloud or loudly:

to call out. **22.** with completeness or effectiveness: *to fill out.* **23.** thoroughly; completely; entirely: *The children tired me out.* **24.** so as to obliterate or make undecipherable: *to paint out; to ink out.* **25.** (used as a radio communications term to signify that the sender has finished his message and is not expecting or prepared to receive a reply.) Cf. **over** (def. 28). **26.** *Sports.* in a manner resulting in an out: *He struck out and the side was retired.* **27. all out,** *Informal.* with maximum effort; thoroughly: *They went all out to finish within the specified time.* **28. out and away,** to a surpassing degree; by far: *It was out and away the best apple pie she had ever eaten.* **29. out from under,** *Informal.* out of a difficult situation: *They tried brainstorming to find a way of getting out from under.*
—*adj.* **30.** exposed; made bare, as by holes in one's clothing: *out at the knees.* **31.** beyond fixed or regular limits: *The ball was declared out.* **32.** beyond the usual range, size, weight, etc. (often in combination): *an outsize bed.* **33.** incorrect or inaccurate: *His calculations are out.* **34.** not in practice; unskillful from lack of practice: *Your bow hand is out.* **35.** having a pecuniary loss to an indicated extent: *I'm out ten dollars.* **36.** wanting; lacking; without (often fol. by *of*): *We are out of butter. We had some, but now we're out.* **37.** removed from or not in effective operation, play, a turn at bat, or the like, as in a game: *He's out for the season because of an injury.* **38.** unconscious; senseless: *She was out for 10 minutes after the box fell on her. Two drinks and he's usually out.* **39.** *Baseball.* **a.** (of a batter) not succeeding in getting on base: *He was out at first on an attempted bunt.* **b.** (of a base runner) not successful in an attempt to advance a base or bases: *He was out in attempting to steal second base.* **40.** *Cricket.* not having its innings: *the out side.* **41.** no longer having or holding (a public office, a job, etc.); unemployed; disengaged (usually fol. by *of*): *to be out of work.* **42.** at variance; at odds; unfriendly: *They are out with each other over the most trivial matter.* **43.** finished; ended: *before the week is out.* **44.** inoperative; extinguished: *The engine is out. Are the lights out?* **45.** not in power, authority, or the like: *a member of the out party.* **46.** moving or directed outward; outgoing: *an out box for mail; the out train.* **47.** of or pertaining to the playing of the first nine holes of an eighteen-hole golf course (opposed to *in*): *His out score on the second round was 33.* **48.** not stylish or fashionable: *Fitted waistlines are out this season.* **49.** not available, plentiful, etc.: *Mums are out till next fall.* **50.** *Obs.* external; exterior; outer. **51.** *Obs.* located at a distance; outlying. **52. out of, a.** foaled by (a dam): *Grey Dancer out of Lady Grey.* **b.** as a result of; from: *She did it out of pity.* **53. out of trim,** *Naut.* (of a vessel) drawing excessively at the bow or stern.
—*prep.* **54.** (used to indicate movement or direction from the inside to the outside of something): *He looked out the window. He ran out the door.* **55.** (used to indicate location: *He lives out back.* **56.** (used to indicate movement away from a central point): *Let's drive out the old mill-road.*
—*interj.* **57.** begone! away! **58.** *Archaic.* (an exclamation of abhorrence, indignation, reproach, or grief (usually fol. by *upon*): *Out upon you!*
—*n.* **59.** something that is out, as a projecting corner. **60.** a means of escape, as from a place, punishment, retribution, responsibility, etc.: *He always left himself an out.* **61.** a person who lacks status or authority, esp. in relation to a particular group or situation: *He joined a fraternity because he was afraid of becoming an out.* **62.** *Baseball.* a put-out. **63.** (in tennis, squash, handball, etc.) a return or service that does not land within the in-bounds limits of a court or section of a court (opposed to *in*). **64.** Usually, **outs.** persons not in office or political power (distinguished from *ins*). **65.** *Print.* **a.** the omission of a word or words. **b.** the word or words omitted. **66.** *Dial.* an outing. **67. be on the** or **at outs with,** *Informal.* to be estranged from (another person); be on bad terms with: *He is on the outs with his brother.*
—*v.i.* **68.** to go or come out. **69.** to become public, evident, etc.: *The truth will out.* **70.** to make known; tell; utter (fol. by *with*): *Out with the truth!*
—*v.t.* **71.** *Archaic.* to put out; expel; discharge; oust. [ME; OE *ūt*; c. D *uit*, G *aus*, Icel, Goth *ūt*; akin to Skt *ud-*]

out-, a prefixal use of **out,** adv., occurring in various senses in compounds (*outcast, outcome, outside*), and serving also to form many transitive verbs denoting a going beyond, surpassing, or outdoing in the particular action indicated (*outbid, outdo, outgeneral, outlast, outstay, outrate*). [ME; OE *ūt*]

out·act (out/akt/), *v.t.* to outdo in acting. [OUT- + ACT]

out·age (ou/tij), *n.* **1.** a stoppage in the functioning of a machine or mechanism due to a failure in the supply of power or electricity. **2.** a period during which such a failure in the supply of electrical power occurs. **3.** the quantity of goods lost or lacking from a shipment. Cf. **innage** (def. 1). **4.** *Aeron.* the amount of fuel used from the fuel tanks of an aircraft during a flight. Cf. **innage** (def. 2). [OUT + -AGE]

out-and-out (out/ᵊnout/, -ᵊnd out/), *adj.* thoroughgoing; thorough; complete; unqualified: *That is an out-and-out lie.* [ME]

out·ar·gue (out/är/gyo͞o), *v.t.*, **-gued, -gu·ing.** to outdo or defeat in arguing: *Given the chance, that man could outargue the Devil himself.* [OUT- + ARGUE]

out·back (*n.* out/bak/; *adj., adv.* out/bak/), *Australian.* —*n.* **1.** (*often cap.*) the back country or remote settlements; the bush (usually prec. by *the*): *We lived in the Outback for several years.* —*adj.* **2.** (*sometimes cap.*) of, pertaining to, or located in the back country: *outback settlements.* —*adv.* **3.** (*sometimes cap.*) in or to the back country: *They moved outback many years ago.* [OUT + BACK²]

out·bal·ance (out/bal/əns), *v.t.*, **-anced, -anc·ing.** to outweigh: *The bad in his character is outbalanced by the good.* [OUT- + BALANCE]

out·bid (out/bid/), *v.t.*, **-bid, -bid·den** or **-bid, -bid·ding.** to outdo in bidding: *The big corporations can usually outbid the small companies for a contract.* [OUT- + BID] —**out/bid/der,** *n.*

out·bluff (out/bluf/), *v.t.* to surpass in bluffing: *to outbluff one's opponents at cards.* [OUT- + BLUFF²]

out·board (out/bōrd/, -bôrd/), *adj.* **1.** located on the exterior of a hull or aircraft. **2.** located farther from the center, as of an aircraft: *the outboard end of a wing.* **3.** (of a motorboat) having an outboard motor. —*adv.* **4.** outside or away from the center of a hull or aircraft. Cf. **inboard.** —*n.* **5.** an outboard motor. **6.** a boat equipped with an outboard motor. [OUT- + BOARD]

out/board mo/tor, a portable gasoline engine with propeller and tiller, clamped on the stern of a boat.

out/board pro/file, *Naval Archit.* an exterior side elevation of a vessel, showing all deck structures, rigging, fittings, etc.

out·bond (out/bond/), *adj.* *Masonry.* composed mainly or entirely of stretchers (opposed to *inbond*). [OUT- + BOND]

out·bound (out/bound/), *adj.* outward bound: *an outbound freighter.* [OUT- + -BOUND²]

out·box (out/boks/), *v.t.* to outdo in boxing: *I've seen the champ outbox better fighters than this one.* [OUT- + BOX²]

out·brave (out/brāv/), *v.t.*, **-braved, -brav·ing.** **1.** to stand up to; face defiantly: *to outbrave charges of misconduct.* **2.** to surpass in bravery or daring: *None can outbrave the great heroes of the past.* **3.** *Archaic.* to surpass in beauty, splendor, etc. [OUT- + BRAVE]

out·break (out/brāk/), *n.* **1.** a breaking out; an outburst: *an outbreak of temper.* **2.** a sudden and active manifestation: *an outbreak of hives.* **3.** a public disturbance; insurrection; riot. [OUT- + BREAK]

out·breed (out/brēd/), *v.t.*, **-bred, -breed·ing.** to breed outside the limits of the family, within a breed or variety. [OUT- + BREED]

out·build (out/bild/), *v.t.*, **-built, -build·ing.** to exceed in building, or in durability of building: *The two construction crews engaged in a contest to see which could outbuild the other.* [OUT- + BUILD]

out·build·ing (out/bil/ding), *n.* a detached building subordinate to a main building. [OUT- + BUILDING]

out·burst (out/bûrst/), *n.* **1.** a bursting forth; eruption. **2.** a sudden and violent outpouring: *an outburst of tears.* **3.** a sudden spell of activity, energy, etc. [OUT- + BURST]

out·by (*adv.* out/bī/; *adj.* out/bī/), *Scot. and North Eng.* —*adv.* **1.** outside; outdoors. **2.** toward the exterior or outside; closer to the outside. **3.** (of a mine) toward or near the shaft or surface. **4.** a short distance away. —*adj.* **5.** outside; exterior. Also, **out/bye/.** [ME (Scot); see OUT, BY (adv.)]

out·cast¹ (out/kast/, -käst/), *n.* **1.** a person who is rejected or cast out, as from home or society: *In the beginning, the area was settled by outcasts, adventurers, and felons.* **2.** a homeless wanderer; vagabond. **3.** *Archaic.* rejected matter; refuse. —*adj.* **4.** cast out, as from one's home or society: *He enjoyed his role as the outcast son.* **5.** pertaining to or characteristic of an outcast: *outcast misery.* **6.** rejected or discarded: *outcast opinions.* [ME; see OUT-, CAST]

out·cast² (out/kast/, -käst/), *n.* *Scot.* a falling out; quarrel. [n. use of v. phrase (Scot) *cast out*]

out·caste (out/kast/, -käst/), *n.* **1.** a person of no caste. **2.** (in India) a person who has forfeited membership in his caste. [OUT- + CASTE]

Out/cast of the Is/lands, An, a novel (1896) by Joseph Conrad.

out·class (out/klas/, -kläs/), *v.t.* to surpass in class or quality; be superior: *He far outclasses the other runners in the race.* [OUT- + CLASS]

out-clear·ing (out/klēr/ing), *n.* *Brit.* **1.** a check, bill of exchange, etc., presented to a clearing house by one member bank for collection from another member bank. **2.** the total amount of such items collectible by one member bank. Cf. **in-clearing.**

out·climb (out/klīm/), *v.t.*, **-climbed** or (*Archaic*) **-clomb; -climbed** or (*Archaic*) **-clomb; -climb·ing.** to outdo in climbing: *As a child, I could outclimb any kid on the block.* [OUT- + CLIMB]

out·come (out/kum/), *n.* **1.** that which results from something; the consequence or issue. **2.** a conclusion reached through a process of logical thinking. [ME *utcume.* See OUT-, COME]
—**Syn. 1, 2.** See **end¹.**

out·coun·try (out/kun/trē), *n.* a remote area or region; hinterland.

out·crop (*n.* out/krop/; *v.* out/krop/), *n., v.*, **-cropped, -crop·ping.** —*n.* **1.** a cropping out, as of a stratum or vein at the surface of the earth. **2.** the emerging part. **3.** something that emerges suddenly or violently in the manner of an outcrop; outbreak: *an outcrop of student demonstrations.* —*v.i.* **4.** to crop out, as strata. [OUT- + CROP, n. use of v. phrase *crop out*]

out·cross (*v.* out/krôs/, -kros/; *n.* out/krôs/, -kros/), *v.t.* **1.** to produce (a hybrid) by outcrossing. —*n.* **2.** a hybrid animal or plant so produced. **3.** an act of outcrossing. [OUT- + CROSS]

out·cross·ing (out/krô/sing, -kros/ing), *n.* the crossing of animals or plants that are of different strains but usually, esp. of livestock, within the same breed. [OUTCROSS + -ING¹]

out·cry (*n.* out/krī/; *v.* out/krī/), *n., pl.* **-cries,** *v.* **-cried, -cry·ing.** —*n.* **1.** a crying out. **2.** a cry of distress, indignation, or the like: *The neighbors heard her outcries and called the police.* **3.** loud clamor: *the outcry of police sirens and blaring automobile horns.* **4.** an auction. —*v.t.* **5.** to outdo in crying; cry louder than. [ME; see OUT-, CRY]

out·curve (out/kûrv/), *n.* *Baseball.* a pitch that breaks outward from the batter. Also called **outshoot.** Cf. **incurve** (def. 2). [OUT- + CURVE]

out·dare (out/dâr/), *v.t.*, **-dared, -dar·ing.** **1.** to surpass in daring. **2.** to defy; brave. [OUT- + DARE]

out·date (out/dāt/), *v.t.*, **-dat·ed, -dat·ing.** to put out of date; make antiquated or obsolete: *The advent of the steamship outdated sailing vessels as commercial carriers.* [OUT- + DATE¹]

out·dis·tance (out/dis/təns), *v.t.*, **-tanced, -tanc·ing.** to leave behind, as in running; outstrip: *The winning horse outdistanced the second-place winner by five lengths.* [OUT- + DISTANCE]

out·do (out/do͞o/), *v.t.*, **-did, -done, -do·ing.** to surpass in execution or performance: *The cook outdid herself last night.* [ME; see OUT-, DO¹]
—**Syn.** See **excel.**

out·door (out/dōr/, -dôr/), *adj.* **1.** Also, **outdoors.** characteristic of, located, or belonging outdoors: *an outdoor barbecue; outdoor sports.* **2.** *Chiefly Brit.* **a.** (of aid) given or administered outside of a poorhouse, hospital, etc.: **b.** (of people) aided while living outside of an institution. [earlier *out (of) door*]

out·doors (out/dōrz/, -dôrz/), *adv.* **1.** out of doors; in the open air: *He's happiest when he's outdoors.* —*n.* **2.** (*construed as sing.*) the world outside of houses; open air: *Our whole family likes the outdoors.* —*adj.* **3.** outdoor: *an outdoors man.* [earlier *out (of) doors*]

out·doors·y (out/dōr/zē, -dôr/-), *adj.* **1.** characteristic of or suitable to the outdoors: *a rugged, outdoorsy life; heavy, outdoorsy clothes.* **2.** unusually fond of outdoor life: *an outdoorsy type who always swam before breakfast.* [OUTDOORS + -Y¹]

out·draw (out/drô/), *v.t.*, **-drew, -drawn, -draw·ing.** **1.** to draw a gun, revolver, etc., faster than (one's opponent or competitor): *She could outdraw any member of the club.* **2.** to excel in drawing power; prove a greater attraction than: *She outdraws all male stars at the box office.* [OUT- + DRAW]

out·dwel·ler (out/dwel/ər), *n.* a person who dwells away from or is remote from (a particular place). [OUT- + DWELLER]

out·er (ou/tər), *adj.* of, pertaining to, or situated on or toward the outside; farther out; external; exterior: *an outer corridor; outer garments.* [ME; see OUT, -ER⁴] —**out/er·ness,** *n.*

out/er automor/phism, *Math.* an automorphism which is not an inner automorphism. Cf. **inner automorphism.**

out/er bar/, *Eng. Law.* a body of the junior counsel who sit and plead outside the dividing bar in the court, ranking below the King's Counsel or Queen's Counsel. Also, **utter bar.** Cf. **inner bar.**

out/er bar/rister, *Eng. Law.* a barrister belonging to the outer bar. Also, **utter barrister.** Cf. **inner barrister.**

out/er ear/. See **external ear.**

Out/er Heb/rides. See under **Hebrides.**

out/er jib/, *Naut.* a headsail next forward from an inner jib and aft of a flying jib.

Out/er Mongo/lia, former name of **Mongolian People's Republic.**

out·am/bush, *v.t.*
out·awe/, *v.t.*, **-awed, -aw·ing.**
out·bab/ble, *v.t.*, **-bled, -bling.**
out·bake/, *v.t.*, **-baked, -bak·ing.**
out·ban/, *v.t.*, **-banned, -ban·ning.**
out·ban/ter, *v.t.*
out·bar/, *v.t.*, **-barred, -bar·ring.**
out·bar/gain, *v.t.*
out·bark/, *v.t.*
out·bar/ter, *v.t.*
out·bat/, *v.t.*, **-bat·ted, -bat·ting.**
out·bat/ter, *v.t.*
out·bawl/, *v.t.*
out·beam/, *v.t.*
out·beg/, *v.t.*, **-begged, -beg·ging.**
out·belch/, *v.t.*
out·bel/low, *v.t.*
out·bend/, *v.t.*, **-bent, -bend·ing.**
out·bet/ter, *v.t.*
out·blaze/, *v.t.*, **-blazed, -blaz·ing.**
out·bleat/, *v.t.*
out·bleed/, *v.t.*, **-bled, -bleed·ing.**
out·bless/, *v.t.*
out·bloom/, *v.t.*
out·blos/som, *v.t.*
out·blot/, *v.t.*, **-blot·ted, -blot·ting.**
out·blow/, *v.t.*, **-blew, -blown, -blow·ing.**
out·blun/der, *v.t.*
out·blush/, *v.t.*
out·blus/ter, *v.t.*
out·boast/, *v.t.*
out·bow/, *v.t.*
out·bowl/, *v.t.*
out·brag/, *v.t.*, **-bragged, -brag·ging.**
out·branch/, *v.t.*
out·bray/, *v.t.*
out·bra/zen, *v.t.*
out·breathe/, *v.t.*, **-breathed, -breath·ing.**
out·bribe/, *v.t.*, **-bribed, -brib·ing.**
out·bridge/, *v.t.*, **-bridged, -bridg·ing.**
out·bring/, *v.t.*, **-brought, -bring·ing.**
out·bud/, *v.t.*, **-bud·ded, -bud·ding.**
out·bulge/, *v.*, **-bulged, -bulg·ing**
out·bulk/, *v.t.*
out·bul/ly, *v.t.*, **-lied, -ly·ing.**
out·burn/, *v.t.*, **-burned** or **-burnt, -burn·ing.**
out·bus/tle, *v.t.*, **-tled, -tling.**
out·buzz/, *v.t.*
out·cant/, *v.t.*
out·ca/per, *v.t.*
out·car/ol, *v.t.*, **-oled, -ol·ing** or (*esp. Brit.*) **-olled, -ol·ling.**
out·cav/il, *v.t.*, **-iled, -il·ing** or (*esp. Brit.*) **-illed, -il·ling.**
out·charm/, *v.t.*
out·chase/, *v.t.*, **-chased, -chas·ing.**
out·chat/ter, *v.t.*
out·cheat/, *v.t.*
out·chide/, *v.t.*, **-chid·ed** or **-chid; -chid·ed, chid** or **-chid·den; -chid·ing.**
out/cit/y, *n., pl.* **-cit·ies.**
out·clam/or, *v.t.*
out/clerk/, *n.*
out·com/pass, *v.t.*
out·com/pli·ment/, *v.t.*
out·court/, *v.t.*
out·crawl/, *v.t.*
out·creep/, *v.t.*, **-crept, -creep·ing.**
out·crick/et, *v.t.*
out·crow/, *v.t.*
out·crowd/, *v.t.*
out·cull/, *v.t.*
out·cure/, *v.t.*, **-cured, -cur·ing.**
out·curse/, *v.t.*, **-cursed, -curs·ing.**
out·cut/, *v.t.*, **-cut, -cut·ting.**
out·dance/, *v.t.*, **-danced, -danc·ing.**
out·daz/zle, *v.t.*, **-zled, -zling.**
out/des·patch/, *v.t.*
out·de/vil, *v.t.*, **-iled, -il·ing** or (*esp. Brit.*) **-illed, -ill·ing.**
out/dis·patch/, *v.t.*
out/dis/trict, *n.*
out·dodge/, *v.t.*, **-dodged, -dodg·ing.**
out·dress/, *v.t.*
out·drink/, *v.t.*, **-drank** or (*Nonstandard*) **-drunk; -drunk** or, often, **-drank; -drink·ing.**
out·drive/, *v.t.*, **-drove, -driv·en, -driv·ing.**
out·dwell/, *v.t.*, **-dwelt** or **-dwelled, -dwell·ing.**
out/dwell/ing, *n.*
out·eat/, *v.t.*, **-ate, -eat·en, -eat·ing.**
out·ech/o, *v.t.*, **-ech·oed, -ech·o·ing.**
out·edge/, *v.t.*, **-edged, -edg·ing.**
out·e·quiv/o·cate/, *v.t.*, **-cat·ed, -cat·ing.**

out·er·most (ou′tər mōst′ *or, esp. Brit.,* -məst), *adj.* farthest out; remotest from the interior or center: *the outermost reaches of space.* [OUTER + -MOST]

out′er prod′uct, *Math.* See **cross product.**

out′er space′, space beyond the atmosphere of the earth. Cf. **deep space.**

out·er·wear (ou′tər wâr′), *n.* **1.** outer garments; clothing, as dresses, sweaters, suits, etc., worn over undergarments. **2.** garments, as raincoats, overcoats, etc., worn over other clothing for warmth or protection outdoors; overclothes. [OUTER + WEAR]

out·face (out/fās′), *v.t.*, **-faced, -fac·ing.** **1.** to face or stare down. **2.** to face or confront boldly; defy. [OUT- + FACE]

out·fall (out′fôl′), *n.* the outlet or place of discharge of a river, drain, sewer, etc. [OUT- + FALL]

out·field (out′fēld′), *n.* **1.** *Baseball.* **a.** the part of the field beyond the diamond. **b.** the positions played by the right, center, and left fielders. **c.** the outfielders considered as a group (contrasted with *infield*). **2.** *Cricket.* the part of the field farthest from the batsman. **3.** *Agric.* **a.** the outlying land of a farm. **b.** land not regularly tilled but normally used for pasture. Cf. **infield** (def. 3). **4.** an outlying region. [OUT- + FIELD]

out·field·er (out′fēl′dər), *n.* *Sports.* one of the players stationed in the outfield. [OUT- + FIELDER]

out·fit (out′fit′), *n., v.,* **-fit·ted, -fit·ting.** —*n.* **1.** an assemblage of articles for fitting out or equipping: *an explorer's outfit.* **2.** (esp. for a woman) a complete costume, usually including shoes, coat, hat, dress, and other matching or harmonious accessories; ensemble: *a new spring outfit.* **3.** a set of articles for any purpose: *a cooking outfit.* **4.** *Informal.* **a.** a group associated in an undertaking requiring close cooperation, as a military unit. **b.** a business firm engaged in a particular form of commercial enterprise: *a construction outfit.* **c.** any company, party, or set. **5.** the act of fitting out or equipping for any purpose, as for a voyage, journey, or expedition. **6.** mental, physical, or moral equipment. —*v.t.* **7.** to furnish with an outfit; fit out; equip: *to outfit an expeditionary party to the South Pole.* **8.** *Naut.* to finish equipping (a vessel) at a dock. —*v.i.* **9.** to furnish oneself with an outfit. [OUT- + FIT¹] —**out′fit′ter,** *n.*
—**Syn. 1, 3.** kit. **7.** appoint, supply, rig.

out′fit car′, a railroad car used as a dormitory for construction and maintenance workers. Also called **camp car.**

out·flank (out′flangk′), *v.t.* **1.** to go or extend beyond the flank of (an opposing military unit); turn the flank of. **2.** to get around (an opposing force); outmaneuver; bypass: *If the senator appeals to his constituents, he may be able to outflank the opposition.* [OUT- + FLANK] —**out′flank′er,** *n.*

out·flow (out′flō′), *n.* **1.** the act of flowing out: *We need flood control to stem the river's outflow.* **2.** that which flows out: *to measure the outflow in gallons per minute.* **3.** any outward movement: *the outflow of gold; the annual outflow of tourists.* [OUT- + FLOW]

out·flux (out′fluks′), *n.* **1.** the act of flowing out; outflow (opposed to *influx*). **2.** a place of flowing out; outlet. [OUT- + FLUX]

out·fly (out′flī′), *v.t.*, **-flew, -flown, -fly·ing.** **1.** to surpass in flying, esp. in speed or distance: *to outfly the speed of sound.* **2.** *Archaic.* to fly out or forth. [OUT- + FLY¹]

out·foot (out′fo͝ot′), *v.t.* **1.** to outsail; excel (another boat) in speed. **2.** to surpass (another person) in running, walking, etc. [OUT- + FOOT]

out·fox (out′foks′), *v.t.* to outwit; outsmart: *Politics is often the art of knowing how to outfox the opposition.* [OUT- + FOX]

out·frown (out′froun′), *v.t.* *Archaic.* to outdo in frowning; silence or put down by frowning. [OUT- + FROWN]

out·gen·er·al (out′jen′ər əl), *v.t.*, **-aled, -al·ing** or (*esp. Brit.*) **-alled, -al·ling.** to outdo in generalship. [OUT- + GENERAL]

out·go¹ (out′gō′), *n., pl.* **-goes.** **1.** the act or process of going out: *Her illness occasioned a tremendous outgo of affectionate concern.* **2.** money paid out; expenditure: *a record of income and outgo.* **3.** that which goes out; outflow: *The outgo of electrical energy had to be increased.* [n. use of OUTGO²]

out·go² (out gō′), *v.t.*, **-went, -gone, -go·ing.** **1.** to go beyond; outdistance: *to outgo the minimum requirements.* **2.** to surpass, excel, or outdo: *Each man was encouraged to outgo his colleagues.* **3.** *Archaic.* to go faster than; excel in speed. [OUT- + GO¹]

out·go³ (out′gō′), *v.i.*, **-went, -gone, -go·ing.** *Obs.* to go out. [ME *outgon,* OE *ūtgān.* See OUT-, GO¹]

out·go·ing (out′gō′ing), *adj.* **1.** going out; departing: *outgoing trains.* **2.** interested in and responsive to others: *an outgoing personality.* —*n.* **3.** Usually, **outgoings.** *Chiefly Brit.* expenses; money expended. **4.** the act of going out: *The ship's outgoing proved more difficult than its incoming.* **5.** that which goes out; an effluence: *an outgoing measured in kilowatt hours.* [ME (n.); see OUT-, GOING]

out·group (out′gro͞op′), *n.* *Sociol.* people outside one's own group, esp. as considered to be inferior or alien; a group perceived as other than one's own. Cf. **ingroup.** [OUT- + GROUP]

out·grow (out′grō′), *v.*, **-grew, -grown, -grow·ing.** —*v.t.* **1.** to grow too large for: *to outgrow one's clothes.* **2.** to leave behind or lose in the changes incident to development or the passage of time: *to outgrow one's early prejudices; to outgrow childish toys.* **3.** to surpass in growing: *watching one child outgrow another.* —*v.i.* **4.** *Archaic.* to grow out; burst forth; protrude: *First one leaf outgrows and then another.* [OUT- + GROW]

out·growth (out′grōth′), *n.* **1.** a natural development, product, or result: *Juvenile delinquency among the wealthy is most often an outgrowth of parental neglect of the child.* **2.** an additional, supplementary result. **3.** a growing out or forth: *pruning to retard the outgrowth.* **4.** that which grows out; offshoot; excrescence. [OUT- + GROWTH]

out·guard (out′gärd′), *n.* *Mil.* a guard attached to an outpost and posted as near as possible to the enemy. [OUT- + GUARD]

out·guess (out′ges′), *v.t.* to outwit. [OUT- + GUESS]

out·haul (out′hôl′), *n.* *Naut.* a rope used for hauling out a sail on a boom, yard, etc. [OUT- + HAUL]

out-Her·od (out′her′əd), *v.t.* to outdo in extravagance or excess: *His cruelty out-Herods Herod; She out-Herods Queen Victoria in prudery.* [OUT- + HEROD (ANTIPAS)]

out·house (out′hous′), *n., pl.* **-hous·es** (-hou′ziz). **1.** an outbuilding. **2.** an outside privy. [OUT- + HOUSE]

out·ing (ou′ting), *n.* **1.** a pleasure trip, excursion, picnic, or the like: *the annual outing for the senior class.* **2.** the part of the sea out from the shore. [ME; see OUT, -ING¹]

out′ing flan′nel, a light cotton flannel with a short, dense nap.

out·jock·ey (out′jok′ē), *v.t.*, **-eyed, -ey·ing.** to outmaneuver: *His racer is faster than mine, but I can try to outjockey him on the turns.* [OUT- + JOCKEY]

out·laid (out′lād′), *v.* pt. and pp. of **outlay.**

out·land (*n.* out′land′; *adj.* out′land′, -lənd), *n.* **1.** Usually, **outlands.** the outlying districts or remote regions of a country; provinces: *a name unknown in the outlands.* **2.** (formerly) the outlying land of a feudal estate, usually granted to tenants. **3.** *Archaic.* a foreign land. —*adj.* **4.** outlying, as districts. **5.** *Archaic.* foreign. [ME; OE *ūtland.* See OUT-, LAND]

out·land·er (out′lan′dər), *n.* **1.** a foreigner; alien. **2.** *Informal.* an outsider. [OUTLAND + -ER¹]

out·land·ish (out lan′dish), *adj.* **1.** freakishly or grotesquely strange or odd, as appearance, dress, objects, ideas, practices, etc.; bizarre: *outlandish clothes; outlandish questions.* **2.** having a foreign appearance. **3.** out-of the-way, as places. **4.** *Archaic.* foreign. [ME; OE *ūtlendisc.* See OUTLAND, -ISH¹] —**out·land′ish·ly,** *adv.* —**out·land′ish·ness,** *n.*
—**Syn. 1.** peculiar, queer, eccentric, curious. **3.** remote.

out·last (out′last′, -läst′), *v.t.* to last longer than: *The pyramids have outlasted the civilization that built them.* [OUT- + LAST²]
—**Syn.** outlive, survive.

out·law (out′lô′), *n.* **1.** a person, group, or thing excluded from the benefits and protection of the law. **2.** a person under sentence of outlawry. **3.** a habitual criminal. **4.** a horse that cannot be broken; a mean, intractable horse. **5.** any rogue animal. —*v.t.* **6.** to deprive of the benefits and protection of the law: *After the Civil War, members of Confederate guerrilla bands who refused to surrender were outlawed.* **7.** to make unlawful: *The Eighteenth Amendment outlawed the manufacture, sale, or transportation of intoxicating beverages in the U.S.* **8.** to remove from legal jurisdiction; deprive of legal force. **9.** to prohibit: *to outlaw smoking in a theater.* [ME *outlawe,* OE *ūtlage* < Scand; cf. Icel *ūtlagi.* See OUT, LAW¹]
—**Syn. 3.** robber, thief; bandit, brigand. **9.** proscribe.

out·law·ry (out′lô′rē), *n., pl.* **-ries.** **1.** the act or process of outlawing. **2.** the state of being outlawed. **3.** disregard or defiance of the law: *a man whose outlawry had made him a folk hero.* [ME *outlagerie, outlagarie* < AF *utlagerie,* ML *utlagāria* < ME *outlage* OUTLAW + AF *-erie* -RY, ML *-āria* -ARY]

out′law strike′. See **wildcat strike.**

out·lay (*n.* out′lā′; *v.* out′lā′), *n., v.,* **-laid, -lay·ing.** —*n.* **1.** an expending or expenditure, as of money. **2.** an amount expended. —*v.t.* **3.** to expend, as money. [OUT- + LAY¹]

out·leap (out′lēp′), *v.*, **-leaped** or **-leapt, -leap·ing.** —*v.t.* **1.** to leap ahead of or over. **2.** to surpass in leaping. —*v.i.* **3.** to leap forth. [OUT- + LEAP]

out·let (out′let, -lit), *n.* **1.** an opening or passage by which anything is let out; a vent or exit. **2.** *Elect.* **a.** a point on a wiring system at which current is taken to supply electric devices. **b.** Also called **outlet box.** the metal box or receptacle designed to facilitate connections to a wiring system. **3.** *Com.* **a.** a market for goods. **b.** (of a wholesaler or manufacturer) a store, merchant, or agency selling one's goods: *He has 50 good outlets.* **4.** a means of expression or satisfaction: *an outlet for one's artistic inclinations.* **5.** a local radio or television station that broadcasts the programs of a large network. **6.** a river or stream flowing from a body of water, as a lake or pond. **7.** the channel such a river or stream follows. **8.** the lower end or mouth of a river where it meets a large body of water, as a lake or the sea. [early ME *utlete.* See OUT, LET¹]

out′let box′, *Elect.* outlet (def. 2b).

out·li·er (out′lī′ər), *n.* **1.** one who or that which lies outside. **2.** a person residing outside the place of his business, duty, etc. **3.** *Geol.* a part of a formation left detached through the removal of surrounding parts by denudation. [OUT- + LIER]

out·line (out′līn′), *n., v.,* **-lined, -lin·ing.** —*n.* **1.** the line by which a figure or object is defined or bounded; contour. **2.** a drawing or sketch restricted to line without shading or modeling of form. **3.** a general sketch, account, or report, indicating only the main features, as of a book, subject, project, etc.: *an outline of medieval history; an outline of freshman English.* **4.** **outlines,** the essential features or main aspects of something under discussion: *At the first meeting, we gave him only the outlines of the project.* **5.** an ornamented type in which the outside contours of each character appear in black with the inside left white. —*v.t.* **6.** to draw the outline of, or draw in outline, as a figure or object. **7.** to give an outline of; sketch the main features of: *On the first day, the professor just outlined the course for us.* [OUT- + LINE¹]
—**Syn. 1.** silhouette. See **form. 3.** plan, draft, rough. **6, 7.** delineate, draft.

out·live (out′liv′), *v.t.*, **-lived, -liv·ing.** **1.** to live longer than; survive (a person, period, etc.): *She outlived her husband by many years. Spiritually, he was an Edwardian who had outlived his time.* **2.** to outlast; live or last through: *The ship outlived the storm.* [ME *outleve(n).* See OUT-, LIVE¹] —**out′liv′er,** *n.*
—**Syn. 1.** See **survive.**

out·look (out′lo͝ok′), *n.* **1.** the view or prospect from a place. **2.** mental view: *one's outlook on life.* **3.** prospect of the future: *the political outlook.* **4.** the place from which an observer looks out; lookout. **5.** the act or state of looking out. **6.** a watch kept; vigilance; lookout: *a careful outlook to prevent forest fires.* [OUT- + LOOK]
—**Syn. 1, 3.** scene. **2.** attitude, picture, interpretation, approach.

out·ly·ing (out′lī′ing), *adj.* **1.** lying at a distance from the center or the main body; remote; out-of-the-way: *outlying military posts.* **2.** lying outside the boundary or limit. [OUT- + LYING²]

out·man (out′man′), *v.t.*, **-manned, -man·ning.** **1.** to surpass in manpower. **2.** *Archaic.* to surpass in manliness. [OUT- + MAN¹]

out·ma·neu·ver (out′mə no͞o′vər), *v.t.* to outdo in or get the better of by maneuvering. [OUT- + MANEUVER]

out·ma·noeu·vre (out′mə no͞o′vər), *v.t.*, **-vred, -vring.** outmaneuver.

out·march (out′märch′), *v.t.* to outdo in marching; march faster or farther than. [OUT- + MARCH¹]

out·match (out′mach′), *v.t.* to surpass; outdo: *The home team seems to have been completely outmatched by the visitors.* [OUT- + MATCH²]

out·mode (out′mōd′), *v.*, **-mod·ed, -mod·ing.** —*v.t.* **1.** to cause (something) to go out of style or become obsolete: *The feather bob quickly outmoded the pageboy hairdo.* —*v.i.* **2.** to go out of style or become obsolete: *I predict it will outmode overnight.* [out (of) mode]

out·mod·ed (out′mō′did), *adj.* **1.** gone out of style; no longer fashionable: *the quickly outmoded fripperies of the postwar years.* **2.** not acceptable by present standards; no longer usable; obsolete: *outmoded dwellings; outmoded teaching methods.* [out (of) mode + -ED²]

out·most (out′mōst′ *or, esp. Brit.,* -məst), *adj.* farthest out; outermost. [ME; see OUT-, -MOST]

out·num·ber (out′num′bər), *v.t.* to exceed in number: *The enemy outnumbered us by three to one.* [OUT- + NUMBER]

out′ of bounds′, beyond the established limits.

out-of-bounds (out′əv boundz′), *adj.* **1.** *Sports.* being beyond or passing the limits of a field, course, etc., marking the area within which the ball, puck, or the like is legally in play. **2.** further than or beyond established limits, as of behavior, thought, etc.

out′ of date′, no longer in style or fashion: *His ideas are out of date.*

out-of-date (out′əv dāt′), *adj.* gone out of style; outmoded; obsolete: *All her clothing is of the most out-of-date fashion.* —**out′-of-date′ness,** *n.*

out′ of doors′, in the open air; not within a house or building; outdoors: *We often hold class out of doors in the spring.*

out-of-doors (out′əv dōrz′, -dôrz′), *adj.* **1.** Also, **out′-of-door′.** outdoor. —*n.* **2.** (*construed as sing.*) outdoors.

out′ of pock′et, **1.** lacking money. **2.** not making a profit and suffering a loss.

out-of-pock·et (out′əv pok′it), *adj.* **1.** paid out or owed in cash: *The out-of-pocket expenses of maintaining the estate were prohibitive.* **2.** without funds or assets: *an out-of-pocket student who stayed with us.*

out′ of print′, no longer published.

out-of-print (out′əv print′), *adj.* **1.** being no longer published: *He runs a shop specializing in out-of-print books.* —*n.* **2.** a book, pamphlet, etc., that is no longer published.

---

out·eyed′, *adj.*
out·fa′ble, *v.t.*, **-bled, -bling.**
out·fame′, *v.t.*, **-famed, -fam·ing.**
out·fast′, *v.t.*
out·fawn′, *v.t.*
out·feast′, *v.t.*
out·feed′, *v.t.*, **-fed, -feed·ing.**
out·fence′, *v.t.*, **-fenced, -fenc·ing.**
out·fer′ret, *v.t.*
out·fight′, *v.t.*, **-fought, -fight·ing.**
out·fig′ure, *v.t.*, **-ured, -ur·ing.**
out·fish′, *v.t.*
out·flame′, *v.t.*, **-flamed, -flam·ing.**
out·flare′, *v.t.*, **-flared, -flar·ing.**
out·flash′, *v.t.*
out·flat′ter, *v.t.*
out·flee′, *v.t.*, **-fled, fleeing.**
out·fling′, *v.t.*, **-flung, -fling·ing.**
out·float′, *v.t.*
out·flour′ish, *v.t.*
out·fool′, *v.t.*
out·froth′, *v.t.*
out·gab′ble, *v.t.*, **-bled, -bling.**
out·gain′, *v.t.*
out·gal′lop, *v.t.*
out·gam′ble, *v.t.*, **-bled, -bling.**
out·game′, *v.t.*, **-gamed, -gam·ing.**
out·gaze′, *v.t.*, **-gazed, -gaz·ing.**
out·glare′, *v.t.*, **-glared, -glar·ing.**
out·gleam′, *v.t.*
out·glit′ter, *v.t.*
out·gloom′, *v.t.*
out·glow′, *v.t.*
out·gnaw′, *v.t.*, **-gnawed, -gnawed** or **-gnawn, -gnaw·ing.**
out·green′, *v.t.*
out·grin′, *v.t.*, **-grinned, -grin·ning.**
out·gun′, *v.t.*, **-gunned, -gun·ning.**
out·gush′, *v.t.*
out·ham′mer, *v.t.*
out·has′ten, *v.t.*
out·hear′, *v.t.*, **-heard, -hear·ing.**
out·hire′, *v.t.*, **-hired, -hir·ing.**
out·hiss′, *v.t.*
out·hit′, *v.t.*, **-hit, -hit·ting.**
out·hor′ror, *v.t.*
out·howl′, *v.t.*
out·hu′mor, *v.t.*
out·hunt′, *v.t.*
out·hurl′, *v.t.*
out′hy·per′bo·lize′, *v.t.*, **-lized, -liz·ing.**
out′in·vent′, *v.t.*
out·is′sue, *v.t.*, **-sued, -su·ing.**
out·jest′, *v.t.*
out·jet′, *v.t.*, **-jet·ted, -jet·ting.**
out·jinx′, *v.t.*
out·jour′ney, *v.t.*, **-neyed, -ney·ing.**
out·jug′gle, *v.t.*, **-gled, -gling.**
out·jump′, *v.t.*
out·jut′, *v.t.*, **-jut·ted, -jut·ting.**
out·kick′, *v.t.*
out·kill′, *v.t.*
out·king′, *v.t.*
out·kiss′, *v.t.*
out′kitch′en, *n.*
out·la′bor, *v.t.*
out·lance′, *v.t.*, **-lanced, -lanc·ing.**
out·lash′, *v.t.*
out·laugh′, *v.t.*
out·launch′, *v.t.*
out·lead′, *v.t.*, **-led, -lead·ing.**
out·learn′, *v.t.*
out·length′en, *v.t.*
out·light′en, *v.t.*
out·limn′, *v.t.*
out·lin′ger, *v.t.*
out·lip′, *v.t.*, **-lipped, -lip·ping.**
out·love′, *v.t.*, **-loved, -lov·ing.**
out·lus′ter, *v.t.*
out·mal′a·prop′, *v.t.*, **-propped, -prop·ping.**
out·mar′ry, *v.t.*, **-ried, -ry·ing.**
out·mas′ter, *v.t.*
out·mate′, *v.t.*, **-mat·ed, -mat·ing.**
out·meas′ure, *v.t.*, **-ured, -ur·ing.**
out′mer′chant, *n.*
out·mount′, *v.t.*
out·mouth′, *v.t.*
out·move′, *v.t.*, **-moved, -mov·ing.**
out′of′fice, *n.*

out′ of the way′, **1.** remote from a populous or much-traveled region. **2.** rarely seen or encountered; unusual. **3.** offensive or improper.

out-of-the-way (out′əv thə wā′), *adj.* **1.** remote from much-traveled, frequented, or populous regions; secluded: *They bought an out-of-the-way place up in the hills.* **2.** seldom ecountered; unusual: *an out-of-the-way style of writing.* **3.** giving offense; improper: *an out-of-the-way remark.*

out-of-town·er (out′əv tou′nər), *n. Informal.* a stranger or visitor from another town: *The World's Fair brought many out-of-towners to New York.*

out·par·ish (out′par′ish), *n.* a parish located outside the boundaries of or at a distance from a town or city; an outlying parish. [OUT- + PARISH]

out·pa·tient (out′pā′shənt), *n.* a patient receiving treatment at a hospital but not being an inmate. [OUT- + PATIENT]

out·play (out′plā′), *v.t.* to play better than; defeat. [OUT- + PLAY]

out·point (out′point′), *v.t.* **1.** to excel in number of points, as in a competition or contest. **2.** *Naut.* to sail closer to the wind than (another vessel). [OUT- + POINT]

out·port (out′pōrt′, -pôrt′), *n.* a secondary seaport close to a larger one but beyond its corporate limits or jurisdiction. [OUT- + PORT[1]]

out·post (out′pōst′), *n.* **1.** a station established at a distance from the main body of an army to protect it from surprise attack: *We keep only a small garrison of men at our desert outposts.* **2.** the body of troops stationed there. [OUT- + POST[2]]

out·pour (*n.* out′pōr′, -pôr′; *v.* out′pōr′, -pôr′), *n.* **1.** outpouring. —*v.t.* **2.** to pour out. [OUT- + POUR] —**out′pour′er,** *n.*

out·pour·ing (out′pōr′ing, -pôr′-), *n.* that which pours out or is poured out; an outflow, overflow, or effusion: *an outpouring of sympathy from her friends.* [OUT- + POURING]

out·preach (out′prēch′), *v.t.* to surpass in preaching. [OUT- + PREACH]

out·put (out′po͝ot′), *n.* **1.** the act of turning out; production: *The output begins as soon as the machine is activated.* **2.** the quantity or amount produced, as in a given time: *to increase one's daily output.* **3.** the product or yield, as of a mine: *The output is of high quality and should fetch a good price.* **4.** the current, voltage, power, or signal produced by an electrical or electronic circuit or device. Cf. **input.** (def. 3). **5.** *Computer Technol.* **a.** information in a form suitable for transmission from internal to external units of a computer, or to an outside apparatus. **b.** the process of transferring data from internal storage to an external device. **6.** the power or force produced by a machine. [OUT- + PUT]

out·rage (out′rāj), *n., v.,* **-raged, -rag·ing.** —*n.* **1.** an act of wanton violence; any gross violation of law or decency. **2.** anything that outrages the feelings. **3.** *Obs.* passionate or violent behavior or language; fury or insolence. —*v.t.* **4.** to subject to grievous violence or indignity. **5.** to anger or offend; make resentful; shock: *I am outraged by his whole attitude.* **6.** to offend against (right, decency, feelings, etc.) grossly or shamelessly: *Such conduct outrages our normal sense of decency.* **7.** to rape (a woman). [ME < OF *outrage, ultrage,* equiv. to *outr(er)* (to) push beyond bounds (deriv. of *outre* beyond < L *ultrā*) + *-age* -AGE] —**Syn. 2.** affront, insult, offense, abuse, indignity. **7.** violate.

out·ra·geous (out rā′jəs), *adj.* **1.** of the nature of or involving gross injury or wrong: *an outrageous slander.* **2.** grossly offensive to the sense of right or decency: *outrageous behavior; an outrageous remark.* **3.** passing reasonable bounds; intolerable or shocking: *an outrageous price.* **4.** violent in action or temper. **5.** highly unusual or unconventional; extravagant: *a child of the most outrageous precocity; a fancy dive performed with outrageous ease.* [ME < MF *outrageus.* See OUTRAGE, -OUS] —**out·ra′geous·ly,** *adv.* —**out·ra′geous·ness,** *n.* —**Syn. 2.** repugnant, insulting, shocking, revolting. **3.** unthinkable, appalling.

out·ran (out′ran′), *v.* pt. of **outrun.**

ou·trance (o͞o träns′), *n. French.* the utmost extremity, as in combat.

out·rang (out′rang′), *v.* pt. of **outring.**

out·range (out′rānj′), *v.t.,* **-ranged, -rang·ing.** **1.** to have a longer or greater range than. **2.** to sail out of the range of (a gun or guns). [OUT- + RANGE]

out·rank (out′rangk′), *v.t.* to rank above: *A major outranks a captain in the army.* [OUT- + RANK[1]]

ou·tré (o͞o trā′), *adj. French.* passing the bounds of what is usual or considered proper.

out·reach (*v.* out′rēch′; *n.* out′rēch′), *v.t.* **1.** to reach beyond; exceed: *The demand has outreached our supply.* **2.** *Archaic.* to reach out; extend: *to outreach one's hand as a token of friendship.* —*v.i.* **3.** to reach out. —*n.* **4.** the act or an instance of reaching out. **5.** length of reach. [OUT- + REACH]

out-re·lief (out′ri lēf′), *n. Brit.* public relief administered to people who do not reside in a poorhouse or similar institution.

ou·tre·mer (o͞o trə mer′), *French.* —*adj.* **1.** ultramarine (def. 2). —*n.* **2.** ultramarine.

out·ride (*v.* out′rīd′; *n.* out′rīd′), *v.,* **-rode, -rid·den, -rid·ing,** *n.* —*v.t.* **1.** to outdo or outstrip in riding. **2.** (of a vessel) to come safely through (a storm) by lying to. —*v.i.* **3.** to act as an outrider. —*n.* **4.** *Pros.* an unaccented syllable or syllables added to a metrical foot, esp. in sprung rhythm. [OUT- + RIDE]

out·rid·er (out′rī′dər), *n.* **1.** a mounted attendant riding before or beside a carriage. **2.** someone who goes in advance of an automobile or person to clear a passage. **3.** a person who leads the way or is a member of a vanguard. **4.** a man who rides out or forth, esp. a scout, cowboy, ranch hand, or the like. [ME: official in a monastery; see OUT-, RIDER]

out·rig·ger (out′rig′ər), *n.* **1.** a framework extended outboard from the side of a boat, esp., as in South Pacific canoes, supporting a float which gives stability. **2.** a bracket extending outward from the side of a racing shell, to support an oarlock. **3.** the shell itself. **4.** a spar rigged out from a ship's rail or the like, as for extending a sail. **5.** a long, flexible rod, attached to a fishing boat near the stern, along which a fishing line may be threaded to keep it clear of the boat's wake when trolling. **6.** any of various propelling frames or parts on an airplane, as for supporting a rudder. **7.** a projecting beam, as for supporting a hoisting tackle. **8.** a horizontal steel beam extending the base of a crane. [OUT- + RIGGER]

Outrigger (def. 2)

out·right (*adj.* out′rīt′; *adv.* out′rīt′, -rīt′), *adj.* **1.** complete or total: *an outright loss.* **2.** downright or unqualified: *an outright refusal.* **3.** *Archaic.* directed straight out or on. —*adv.* **4.** completely; entirely. **5.** without restraint, reserve, or concealment; openly: *Tell me outright what's bothering you.* **6.** at once; instantly: *to be killed outright.* **7.** *Archaic.* straight out or ahead; directly onward. [ME; see OUT, RIGHT] —**out′right′ness,** *n.*

out·ring (out′ring′), *v.,* **-rang, -rung, -ring·ing.** —*v.t.* **1.** to outdo in ringing; ring louder than. —*v.i.* **2.** to ring out: *church bells outringing over the countryside.* [ME (v.i.); see OUT-, RING[2]]

out·roar (out′rōr′, -rôr′), *v.t.* to surpass in roaring; roar louder than. [OUT- + ROAR]

out·root (out′ro͞ot′, -ro͝ot′), *v.t.* to root out; eradicate. [OUT- + ROOT[1]]

out·row (out′rō′), *v.t.* to surpass in rowing; row faster than. [OUT- + ROW[2]]

out·run (out′run′), *v.t.,* **-ran, -run, -run·ning.** **1.** to run faster or farther than. **2.** to escape by or as by running: *He managed to outrun the police net.* **3.** to exceed; excel; surpass. [OUT- + RUN]

out·run·ner (out′run′ər), *n.* **1.** one who or that which runs out or outside. **2.** an attendant who runs before or beside a carriage. **3.** the leader of a team of dogs. **4.** a forerunner. [OUT- + RUNNER]

out·rush (out′rush′), *n.* a rapid or intense outflow: *an outrush of water from a bursting pipe.* [OUT- + RUSH[1]]

out·sail (out′sāl′), *v.t.* to outdo in sailing; sail farther or faster than; outstrip: *He won the race not only on speed but on his ability to outsail the other boats.* [OUT- + SAIL]

out·sang (out′sang′), *v.* pt. of **outsing.**

out·sat (out′sat′), *v.* pt. and pp. of **outsit.**

out·sell (out′sel′), *v.t.,* **-sold, -sell·ing.** **1.** to outdo in selling; sell more than: *He outsells all our other salesmen.* **2.** to be sold more than: *a soap that outsells all other brands.* **3.** to exceed in value. [OUT- + SELL[1]]

out·sen·try (out′sen′trē), *n., pl.* **-tries.** *Archaic.* a sentry posted in advance of a position, or one stationed at an outpost. [OUT- + SENTRY]

out·sert (out′sûrt′), *n. Bookbinding.* an additional folded signature or sheet into which another is bound. Also called **outset, wrap-around.** [OUT- + (IN)SERT]

out·set (out′set′), *n.* **1.** the beginning or start: *He wanted to explain the situation at the outset.* **2.** outsert. [OUT- + SET]

out·set·tle·ment (out′set′əl mənt), *n.* a distant or remote settlement. [OUT- + SETTLEMENT]

out·set·tler (out′set′lər), *n.* a person who inhabits a remote settlement or area. [OUT- + SETTLER]

out·shine (out′shīn′), *v.,* **-shone, -shin·ing.** —*v.t.* **1.** to surpass in shining. **2.** to surpass in splendor, excellence, etc.: *a product that outshone all competitors; to outshine one's classmates.* —*v.i.* **3.** *Archaic.* to shine out or forth: *a small light outshining in the darkness.* [OUT- + SHINE]

out·shoot (*v.* out′sho͞ot′; *n.* out′sho͞ot′), *v.,* **-shot, -shoot·ing,** *n.* —*v.t.* **1.** to surpass in shooting. **2.** to shoot beyond. **3.** to shoot (something) out; send forth: *a tree outshooting its roots.* —*v.i.* **4.** to shoot forth; project: *sparks outshooting from the fire.* —*n.* **5.** the act or an instance of shooting out: *an outshoot of his fist that staggered his opponent.* **6.** something that shoots out: *a row of outshoots from the soil.* **7.** *Baseball.* outcurve. [OUT- + SHOOT]

out·shot (out′shot′), *n.* an annex to a building, adjoining it but structurally independent. Also called **out·shut** (out′shut′). [OUT- + SHOT[1]]

out·shout (out′shout′), *v.t.* **1.** to surpass (someone) in shouting; shout louder than. **2.** to outdo in advocacy, as of one's position or point of view: *He outshouted all critics of his scheme.* [OUT- + SHOUT]

out·side (*n.* out′sīd′, -sīd′; *adj.* out′sīd′, out′-; *adv.* out′sīd′; *prep.* out′sīd′, out′sīd′), *n.* **1.** the outer side, surface, or part; the exterior: *the outside of the house; the outside of the road.* **2.** the external aspect or appearance. **3.** something merely external: *a pretense of learning that was only an outside.* **4.** the space without or beyond an enclosure, boundary, etc.: *a prisoner about to resume life on the outside.* **5.** *Chiefly Brit. Informal.* an outside passenger or place on a coach or other vehicle. **6. at the outside,** at the utmost limit; at the maximum: *There weren't more than ten at the outside.* —*adj.* **7.** being, acting, done, or originating beyond an enclosure, boundary, etc.: *outside noises.* **8.** situated on or pertaining to the outside; exterior; external: *an outside television antenna.* **9.** not belonging to or connected with a specified institution, society, etc.: *outside influences.* **10.** extremely unlikely or remote: *an outside chance for recovery.* **11.** *Baseball.* (of a pitched ball) passing, but not going over, home plate on the side opposite the batter: *The fast ball was high and outside.* —*adv.* **12.** on or to the outside, exterior, or space without: *Take the dog outside.* —*prep.* **13.** on or toward the outside of: *There was a noise outside the door.* **14.** *Informal.* with the exception of; aside from: *Outside her cooking, what does she have?* **15. outside of,** *Informal.* other than; exclusive of; excepting: *Outside of her, no one else came to the party.* [OUT- + SIDE[1]]

out′side loop′, *Aeron.* a loop during which the back of the airplane is on the outer side of the curve described by the course of flight. Cf. **inside loop.**

out′side port′, **1.** a seaport or area of a seaport where absence of docking facilities forces transfer of goods by lighters or other vessels. **2.** a port not usually visited by the ships of a certain line.

out·sid·er (out′sī′dər), *n.* **1.** a person or thing not within an enclosure, boundary, etc. **2.** a person not belonging to a particular group, set, party, etc.: *Society often regards the artist as an outsider.* **3.** a person unconnected or unacquainted with the matter in question: *Not being a parent, I was regarded as an outsider.* **4.** a race horse, sports team, etc., not classified among the best or among those expected to win. [OUTSIDE + -ER[1]]

out·sing (out′sing′), *v.,* **-sang, -sung, -sing·ing.** —*v.t.* **1.** to sing better than. **2.** to sing louder than. —*v.i.* **3.** to sing out; break out in song: *A bird outsings from the topmost branch.* [OUT- + SING]

out′ sis′ter, a nun, esp. in a cenobite order, who handles the outside affairs of the convent to which she belongs.

out·sit (out′sit′), *v.t.,* **-sat, -sit·ting.** **1.** to sit longer than; outwait: *He was determined to outsit his rival.* **2.** to sit beyond the time of: *We realized we were outsitting our welcome.* [OUT- + SIT]

out·size (out′sīz′), *n.* **1.** an uncommon or irregular size. **2.** a garment of such a size, esp. if larger than average. —*adj.* **3.** Also, **out′sized′.** being unusually or abnormally large, heavy, extensive, etc.: *a rack of outsize dresses; an outsize woman; pampering an outsize ego.* [OUT- + SIZE[1]]

out·skirt (out′skûrt′), *n.* **1.** Often, **outskirts.** the outlying district or region, as of a city, metropolitan area, or the like: *to live on the outskirts of town; a sparsely populated outskirt.* **2.** Usually, **outskirts.** the border or fringes of a specified quality, condition, or the like: *the outskirts of respectability.* [OUT- + SKIRT]

out·sleep (out′slēp′), *v.t.,* **-slept, -sleep·ing.** **1.** to sleep through or later than (a specified time). **2.** to sleep until the end of: *to outsleep a thunderstorm.* [OUT- + SLEEP]

out·smart (out′smärt′), *v.t.* **1.** to get the better of (someone); outwit. **2. outsmart oneself,** to defeat oneself unintentionally by intrigue, elaborate scheming, or the like: *This time, he may have outsmarted himself.* [OUT- + SMART (adj.)]

out·soar (out′sōr′, -sôr′), *v.t.* to soar beyond. [OUT- + SOAR]

out·sold (out′sōld′), *v.* pt. and pp. of **outsell.**

out·sole (out′sōl′), *n.* the outer sole of a shoe. [OUT- + SOLE[2]]

---

out·pace′, *v.t.,* **-paced, -pac·ing.**
out·paint′, *v.t.*
out·pass′, *v.t.*
out·path′, *n.*
out·peep′, *v.t.*
out·peo′ple, *v.t.,* **-pled, -pling.**
out′per·form′, *v.t.*
out·pick′, *v.t.*
out·pipe′, *v.t.,* **-piped, -pip·ing.**
out·pitch′, *v.t.*
out·pit′y, *v.t.,* **-pit·ied, -pit·y·ing.**
out·plan′, *v.t.,* **-planned, -plan·ning.**
out·please′, *v.t.,* **-pleased, -pleas·ing.**
out·plod′, *v.t.,* **-plod·ded, -plod·ding.**
out·plot′, *v.t.,* **-plot·ted, -plot·ting.**
out·poi′son, *v.t.*
out·poll′, *v.t.*
out·pop′, *v.t.,* **-popped, -pop·ping.**
out·pop′u·late′, *v.t.,* **-lat·ed, -lat·ing.**
out·prac′tice, *v.t.,* **-ticed, -tic·ing.**
out·praise′, *v.t.,* **-praised, -prais·ing.**
out·pray′, *v.t.,* **-prayed, -pray·ing.**
out·preen′, *v.t.*
out·price′, *v.t.,* **-priced, -pric·ing.**
out′pro·duce′, *v.t.,* **-duced, -duc·ing.**
out·prom′ise, *v.t.,* **-ised, -is·ing.**
out·pry′, *v.t.,* **-pried, -pry·ing.**
out·pull′, *v.t.*
out·pu′pil, *n.*
out·purl′, *v.t.*
out′pur·sue′, *v.t.,* **-sued, -su·ing.**
out·push′, *v.t.*
out·quaff′, *v.t.*
out′quar′ters, *n.*
out·que′ry, *v.t.,* **-ried, -ry·ing.**
out·ques′tion, *v.t.*
out·quib′ble, *v.t.,* **-bled, -bling.**
out·quote′, *v.t.,* **-quot·ed, -quot·ing.**
out·race′, *v.t.,* **-raced, -rac·ing.**
out·rail′, *v.t.*
out·rant′, *v.t.*
out·rap′, *v.t.,* **-rapped, -rap·ping.**
out·rate′, *v.t.,* **-rat·ed, -rat·ing.**
out·rave′, *v.t.,* **-raved, -rav·ing.**
out·read′, *v.t.,* **-read, -read·ing.**
out·rea′son, *v.t.*
out·reck′on, *v.t.*
out·red′den, *v.t.*
out·reign′, *v.t.*
out·rhyme′, *v.t.,* **-rhymed, -rhym·ing.**
out·rib′, *v.t.,* **-ribbed, -rib·bing.**
out·rick′, *v.t.*
out·rig′, *v.t.,* **-rigged, -rig·ging.**
out·ri′val, *v.t.,* **-valed, -val·ing** or (*esp. Brit.*) **-valled, -val·ling.**
out·rogue′, *v.t.,* **-rogued, -ro·guing.**
out′ro·mance′, *v.t.,* **-manced, -manc·ing.**
out·rove′, *v.t.,* **-roved, -rov·ing.**
out·saint′, *v.t.*
out·sal′ly, *v.t.,* **-lied, -ly·ing.**
out·sat′is·fy′, *v.t.,* **-fied, -fy·ing.**
out·sa′vor, *v.t.*
out·say′, *v.t.,* **-said, -say·ing.**
out·scent′, *v.t.*
out·scold′, *v.t.*
out·score′, *v.t.,* **-scored, -scor·ing.**
out·scorn′, *v.t.*
out·scream′, *v.t.*
out·search′, *v.t.*
out·see′, *v.t.* **-saw, -seen, -see·ing.**
out·seek′, *v.t.,* **-sought, -seek·ing.**
out·shame′, *v.t.,* **-shamed, -sham·ing.**
out·shape′, *v.t.,* **-shaped, -shap·ing.**
out·shoul′der, *v.t.*
out·shove′, *v.t.,* **-shoved, -shov·ing.**
out·show′, *v.t.,* **-showed, -shown** or **-showed, -show·ing.**
out·show′er, *v.t.*
out·shriek′, *v.t.*
out·shrill′, *v.t.*
out·sift′, *v.t.*
out·sigh′, *v.t.*
out·sin′, *v.t.,* **-sinned, -sin·ning.**
out·skill′, *v.t.*
out·skip′, *v.t.,* **-skipped, -skip·ping.**
out·skir′mish, *v.t.*
out·slan′der, *v.t.*
out·slang′, *v.t.*
out·slide′, *v.t.,* **-slid, -slid** or **-slid·den, -slid·ing.**
out·slink′, *v.t.*
out·smell′, *v.t.*
out·smile′, *v.t.,* **-smiled, -smil·ing.**
out·snatch′, *v.t.*
out·snore′, *v.t.,* **-snored, -snor·ing.**

out·span (*v.* out′span′; *n.* out′span′), *v.*, **-spanned, -span·ning,** *n. South African Eng.* —*v.t.* **1.** to unyoke or unhitch, as oxen from a wagon. —*v.i.* **2.** to remove the yoke, harness, etc., from animals. —*n.* **3.** the act or a place of outspanning. [trans of SAfrD *uitspan*]

out·speak (out′spēk′), *v.*, **-spoke, -spo·ken, -speak·ing.** —*v.t.* **1.** to outdo or excel in speaking. **2.** to utter frankly or boldly: *to outspeak one's grievances.* —*v.i.* **3.** to speak out: *to outspeak in defense of one's beliefs.* [OUT- + SPEAK]

out·spent (out′spent′), *adj.* worn-out; exhausted. [OUT- + SPENT]

out·spo·ken (out′spō′kən), *adj.* **1.** uttered or expressed with frankness or lack of reserve: *outspoken criticism.* **2.** free or unreserved in speech: *outspoken people.* —*v.* **3.** pp. of **outspeak.** —**out′spo′ken·ly,** *adv.* —**out′spo′ken·ness,** *n.*
—**Syn. 1.** See **frank.** —**Ant. 1.** taciturn.

out·spread (*v.* out′spred′; *adj.* out′spred′; *n.* out′spred′), *v.*, **-spread, -spread·ing,** *adj., n.* —*v.t., v.i.* **1.** to spread out; extend: *an eagle outspreading its wings; a storm outspreading across the countryside.* —*adj.* **2.** spread out; stretched out: *outspread papers on a desk; outspread arms.* **3.** diffused abroad; widely disseminated: *The outspread news had traveled quickly.* —*n.* **4.** the act of spreading out; expansion: *the rapid outspread of the early American colonists.* **5.** that which is spread out; an expanse: *a vast outspread of rich farmland.* [ME *outspredd(en)* (v.). See OUT-, SPREAD]

out·stand (out′stand′), *v.*, **-stood, -stand·ing.** —*v.i.* **1.** (of a ship) to sail out to sea. **2.** *Archaic.* to be prominent. —*v.t. Archaic.* **3.** to stay or remain beyond: *to outstand the visit.* **4.** to withstand. [OUT- + STAND]

out·stand·ing (out′stan′ding), *adj.* **1.** prominent; conspicuous; striking: *an outstanding example.* **2.** continuing in existence; remaining unsettled, unpaid, etc.: *outstanding debts.* **3.** standing out; projecting; detached: *a stiff, outstanding fabric.* **4.** *Archaic.* that resists or opposes. [OUTSTAND + -ING[2]] —**out′stand′ing·ly,** *adv.* —**out′stand′ing·ness,** *n.*
—**Syn. 1.** eminent. **2.** owing, due.

out·stare (out′stâr′), *v.t.*, **-stared, -star·ing. 1.** to outdo in staring; stare down. **2.** to cause (someone) discomfort or embarrassment: *a small company that fearlessly outstared a great corporation.* [OUT- + STARE]

out·sta·tion (out′stā′shən), *n.* an auxiliary station, esp. on the outskirts of a district. [OUT- + STATION]

out·stay (out′stā′), *v.t.* **1.** to stay longer than. **2.** to stay beyond the time or duration of: *to outstay one's welcome.* [OUT- + STAY[1]]

out·stretch (out′strech′), *v.t.* **1.** to stretch forth; extend: *to outstretch one's hand in welcome.* **2.** to stretch beyond: *His behavior outstretches my patience.* **3.** to stretch out; expand: *The rising population has outstretched the city.* **4.** *Obs.* to strain. [OUT- + STRETCH] —**out′stretch′er,** *n.*

out·strip (out′strip′), *v.t.*, **-stripped, -strip·ping. 1.** to outdo; surpass; excel: *a supply that far outstrips demand.* **2.** to outdo or pass in running or swift travel: *a car that can outstrip the fastest train.* **3.** to get ahead of or leave behind in a race or in any course of competition: *to outstrip the previous attendance record.* [OUT- + STRIP[1]]

out·stroke (out′strōk′), *n.* **1.** a stroke in an outward direction. **2.** (in an engine) the stroke during which the piston rod moves outward from the cylinder. [OUT- + STROKE[1]]

out·sung (out′sung′), *v.* pp. of **outsing.**

out·swear (out′swâr′), *v.t.*, **-swore** or (*Archaic*) **-sware; -sworn; -swear·ing.** to outdo in swearing: *She's one woman who can outswear any man I know.* [OUT- + SWEAR]

out·swing·er (out′swing′ər), *n.* **1.** *Cricket.* a ball that when bowled veers from leg side to off side. Cf. **inswinger.** [OUT- + SWINGER]

out·talk (out′tôk′), *v.t.* to outdo or overcome in talking. [OUT- + TALK]

out·tell (out′tel′), *v.t.*, **-told, -tell·ing. 1.** to outdo in telling; surpass in effect: *so ridiculous as to outtell any comment.* **2.** to tell to the end; say completely: *He outtold the tale to his amazed listeners.* **3.** to speak out; tell openly; declare: *The guilty heart outtells its inmost thoughts.* [OUT- + TELL[1]]

out·think (out′thingk′), *v.t.*, **-thought, -think·ing. 1.** to excel in thinking; think faster, more accurately, or more perceptively than: *outthinking most of his contemporaries in the field of human relations.* **2.** to get the advantage of (someone) by quick or clever thinking; outwit: *only a split second to outthink his opponent.* [OUT- + THINK[1]]

out·throw (out′thrō′), *v.t.*, **-threw, -thrown, -throw·ing. 1.** to throw out; extend: *outthrowing his arms.* **2.** to surpass in throwing; throw farther and more accurately than: *He can outthrow all his teammates.* [ME: to throw out. See OUT-, THROW]

out·thrown (out′thrōn′), *adj.* thrown or extended outward: *arms outthrown in greeting.* [OUT- + THROWN]

out·thrust (*v., adj.* out′thrust′; *n.* out′thrust′), *v.*, **-thrust, -thrust·ing,** *adj., n.* —*v.t., v.i.* **1.** to thrust out or extend: *outthrusting his hand when we met; branches outthrusting in the treetops.* —*adj.* **2.** thrust or extended outward: *a friendly, outthrust hand.* —*n.* **3.** something that thrusts or extends outward: *an outthrust of the tall building.* [OUT- + THRUST]

out·turn (out′tûrn′), *n.* **1.** a quantity produced; output. **2.** the quality or condition of something produced or manufactured. [n. use of v. phrase *turn out*]

out·vote (out′vōt′), *v.t.*, **-vot·ed, -vot·ing.** to outdo or defeat in voting: *The rural districts outvoted the urban districts. The measure was outvoted by the farmers.* [OUT- + VOTE]

out·wait (out′wāt′), *v.t.* **1.** to surpass in waiting or expecting. **2.** *Archaic.* to lie in ambush longer than. [OUT- + WAIT]

out·walk (out′wôk′), *v.t.* **1.** to outdo in walking. **2.** to walk beyond: *to outwalk the lights of the city.* [OUT- + WALK]

out·ward (out′wərd), *adj.* **1.** pertaining to or being what is seen or apparent, as distinguished from the underlying nature, facts, etc.; pertaining to surface qualities only; superficial: *outward appearances.* **2.** pertaining to the outside of the body; external. **3.** pertaining to the body, as opposed to the mind or spirit. **4.** belonging or pertaining to external actions or appearances, as opposed to inner feelings, mental states, etc.: *an outward show of grief.* **5.** belonging or pertaining to what is external to oneself: *outward influences.* **6.** proceeding or directed toward the outside or exterior, or away from a central point: *the outward flow of gold; the outward part of a voyage.* **7.** that lies toward the outside; that is on the outer side: *an outward court.* **8.** of or pertaining to the outside, outer surface, or exterior: *to make repairs on the outward walls of a house.* **9.** *Archaic.* not directly concerned or interested. —*n.* **10.** *Archaic.* that which is without; the external or material world. **11.** *Archaic.* outward appearance. —*adv.* Also, **out′wards. 12.** toward the outside; out. **13.** visibly expressing one's inner feelings, mental state, etc. **14.** away from port: *a ship bound outward.* **15.** *Obs.* on the outside; without. [ME; OE *ūtweard.* See OUT, -WARD] —**out′ward·ness,** *n.*

out·ward-bound (out′wərd bound′), *adj.* (of a ship) headed out to sea; bound for foreign ports: *We passed an outward-bound ship as we came into the harbor.*

Out′ward Bound′, a play (1923) by Sutton Vane.

out·ward·ly (out′wərd lē), *adv.* **1.** as regards appearance or outward manifestation: *She is outwardly charming.* **2.** toward the outside: *The pier stretched outwardly from the shore.* **3.** on the outside or outer surface; externally: *Outwardly, the fruit was rough to the touch.* [ME; see OUTWARD, -LY]

out·wash (out′wosh′, -wôsh′), *n. Geol.* the material, chiefly sand or gravel, washed from a glacier by the action of meltwater. [OUT- + WASH]

out·watch (out′woch′, -wôch′), *v.t.* **1.** to outdo in watching. **2.** to watch, or maintain a vigil, until the end of: *The mourners had outwatched the night.* [OUT- + WATCH]

out·wear (out′wâr′), *v.t.*, **-wore, -worn, -wear·ing. 1.** to wear or last longer than; outlast: *a well-made product that outwears its competition.* **2.** to outlive or outgrow: *Perhaps he will outwear those eccentricities.* **3.** to wear out; destroy by wearing: *A child outwears his clothes so quickly.* **4.** to exhaust in strength or endurance: *The daily toil had soon outworn him.* **5.** to pass (time): *trying to outwear the hours by reading.* [OUT- + WEAR]

out·weep (out′wēp′), *v.t.*, **-wept, -weep·ing.** to surpass or outdo in weeping. [OUT- + WEEP[1]]

out·weigh (out′wā′), *v.t.* **1.** to exceed in value, importance, influence, etc.: *The advantages of the plan outweighed its defects.* **2.** to be too heavy or burdensome for: *Collapse may follow if the load outweighs its supports.* **3.** to exceed in weight: *The champion will probably outweigh his opponent.* [OUT- + WEIGH]

out·went (out′went′), *v.* pt. of **outgo.**

out·wind (out′wind′), *v.t.* to cause to be out of breath: *A fierce race had outwinded the runners.* [OUT- + WIND[1]]

out·wit (out′wit′), *v.t.*, **-wit·ted, -wit·ting. 1.** to get the better of by superior ingenuity or cleverness: *to outwit an obstreperous child.* **2.** *Archaic.* to surpass in wisdom or knowledge. [OUT- + WIT[1]]
—**Syn. 1.** outdo, outmaneuver, outthink, finesse.

out·work (*v.* out′wûrk′; *n.* out′wûrk′), *v.t.*, **-worked** or **-wrought, -work·ing,** *n.* —*v.t.* **1.** to surpass in working; work harder or faster than. **2.** to work out or carry on to a conclusion; finish: *a problem to be outworked in after generations.* **3.** *Archaic.* to outdo in workmanship. —*n.* **4.** a minor defense lying outside the principal fortification limits. [ME: to complete; see OUT-, WORK] —**out′work′er,** *n.*

out·worn (out′wōrn′, -wôrn′), *adj.* **1.** out-of-date; obsolete, as opinions, ideas, etc. **2.** worn out, as clothes. **3.** exhausted in strength or endurance, as persons. —*v.* **4.** pp. of **outwear.**

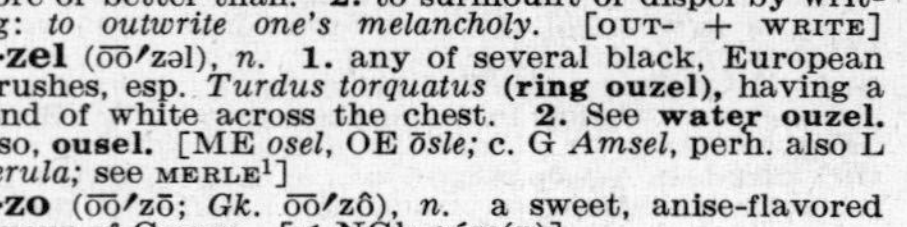

out·write (out′rīt′), *v.t.*, **-wrote** or (*Archaic*) **-writ; -writ·ten** or (*Archaic*) **-writ; -writ·ing. 1.** to write more or better than. **2.** to surmount or dispel by writing: *to outwrite one's melancholy.* [OUT- + WRITE]

ou·zel (o͞o′zəl), *n.* **1.** any of several black, European thrushes, esp. *Turdus torquatus* **(ring ouzel),** having a band of white across the chest. **2.** See **water ouzel.** Also, **ousel.** [ME *osel,* OE *ōsle;* c. G *Amsel,* perh. also L *merula;* see MERLE[1]]

ou·zo (o͞o′zō; *Gk.* o͞o′zô), *n.* a sweet, anise-flavored liqueur of Greece. [< NGk *oúzo(n)*]

o·va (ō′və), *n.* pl. of **ovum.**

o·val (ō′vəl), *adj.* **1.** having the general form, shape, or outline of an egg; egg-shaped. **2.** ellipsoidal or elliptical. —*n.* **3.** any of various objects of oval shape. **4.** a body or plane figure that is oval in shape or outline. **5.** an elliptical field or a field on which an elliptical track is laid out, as for athletic contests. **6.** *Informal.* a football. [< NL *ōvāl(is),* equiv. to L *ōv(um)* egg + *-ālis* -AL[1]] —**o′val·ly,** *adv.* —**o′val·ness,** *n.*

o·val-faced (ō′vəl fāst′), *adj.* having an oval face.

o·val·i·ty (ō val′i tē), *n.* **1.** the quality or state of being oval. **2.** *Metalworking.* distortion in section of drawn wire or the like. [OVAL + -ITY]

o′val kum′quat, a spineless shrub or small tree, *Fortunella margarita,* of Japan, having ovalish-oblong fruit with sweet and acid flesh. Also called **nagami kumquat.**

O·va·lle (ō vä′yə), *n.* a city in central Chile. 17,573 (1951).

o′vals of Cassi′ni, *Geom.* the locus of a point such that the product of the distances from the point to two fixed points is constant. Equation: $(x^2+y^2)^2-2a^2(x^2-y^2)+a^4-k^4=0$, where k is the constant and a is one half the length of the fixed side.

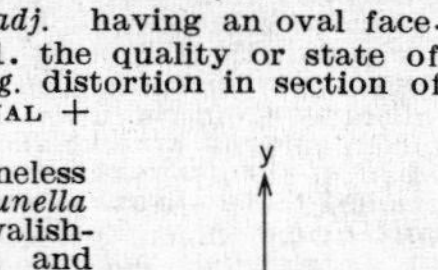

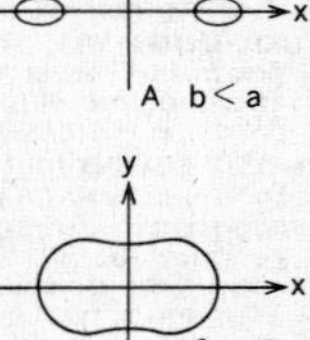

Ovals of Cassini

o·var·i·an (ō vâr′ē ən), *adj.* of or pertaining to an ovary. [OVARY + -AN]

o·var·i·ec·to·mize (ō vâr′ē ek′tə mīz′), *v.t.*, **-mized, -miz·ing.** *Surg.* to perform an ovariectomy on; oophorectomize. [OVARIECTOM(Y) + -IZE]

o·var·i·ec·to·my (ō vâr′ē ek′tə mē), *n., pl.* **-mies.** *Surg.* the operation of removing one or both ovaries; oophorectomy. [OVARI(UM) + -ECTOMY]

o·var·i·o·tome (ō vâr′ē ə tōm′), *n. Surg.* a cutting instrument for performing an ovariotomy. [back formation from OVARIOTOMY]

o·var·i·ot·o·my (ō vâr′ē ot′ə mē), *n., pl.* **-mies.** *Surg.* incision into or removal of an ovary. [< NL *ōvāriotomia,* equiv. to *ōvāri(um)* OVARY + *-o-* -O- + *-tomia* -TOMY] —**o·var′i·ot′o·mist,** *n.*

o·va·ri·tis (ō′və rī′tis), *n. Pathol.* oophoritis. [< NL, equiv. to *ōvār(ium)* OVARY + *-itis* -ITIS]

o·var·i·um (ō vâr′ē əm), *n., pl.* **o·var·i·a** (ō vâr′ē ə). *Archaic.* ovary. [< NL; see OVARY]

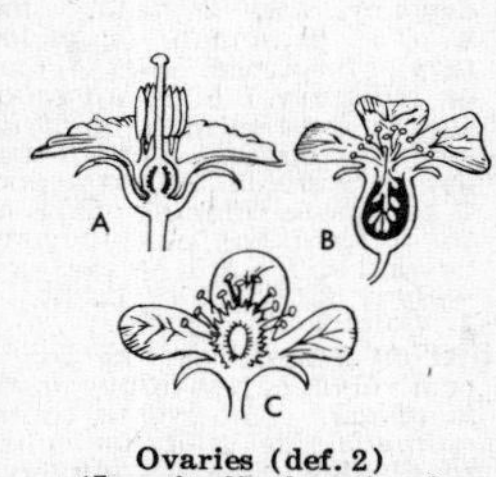

Ovaries (def. 2)
(Longitudinal sections)
A, Potato flower; B, Rose;
C, Strawberry flower

o·va·ry (ō′və rē), *n., pl.* **-ries. 1.** *Anat., Zool.* the female gonad or reproductive gland, in which the ova and the hormones that regulate female secondary sex characteristics develop. **2.** *Bot.* the enlarged lower part of the pistil in angiospermous plants, enclosing the ovules or young seeds. [< NL *ōvāri(um).* See OVUM, -ARY]

o·vate (ō′vāt), *adj.* **1.** egg-shaped. **2.** *Bot.* **a.** having a plane figure like the longitudinal section of an egg. **b.** having such a figure with the broader end at the base, as a leaf. [< L *ōvāt(us),* equiv. to *ōv(um)* egg + *-ātus* -ATE[1]] —**o′vate·ly,** *adv.*

Ovate leaf

o·va·tion (ō vā′shən), *n.* **1.** an enthusiastic public reception of a person; enthusiastic applause. **2.** *Rom. Hist.* the ceremonial entrance into Rome of a commander whose victories were of a lesser degree of im-

out·son′net, *v.t.*
out′so·phis′ti·cate′, *v.t.,* **-cat·ed, -cat·ing.**
out·sound′, *v.t.*
out·spar′kle, *v.t.,* **-kled, -kling.**
out·speed′, *v.t.,* **-sped** or **-speed·ed, -speed·ing.**
out·spell′, *v.t.*
out·spill′, *v.t.*
out·spin′, *v.t.,* **-spinned, -spin·ning.**
out·spir′it, *v.t.*
out·spit′, *v.t.,* **-spat** or **-spit, -spit·ting.**
out·splen′dor, *v.t.*
out·sport′, *v.t.*
out·spring′, *v.t.,* **-sprang** or **-sprung, -sprung, -spring·ing.**
out·sprint′, *v.t.*
out·sprue′, *v.t.,* **-sprued, -spru·ing.**
out·spurn′, *v.t.*
out·spurt′, *v.t.*
out·spy′, *v.t.,* **-spied, -spy·ing.**
out·stag′ger, *v.t.*
out·star′tle, *v.t.,* **-tled, -tling.**
out·state′, *v.t.,* **-stat·ed, -stat·ing.**
out·stat′ure, *v.t.,* **-ured, -ur·ing.**
out·steal′, *v.t.,* **-stole, -sto·len, -steal·ing.**
out·steam′, *v.t.*
out·step′, *v.t.,* **-stepped, -step·ping.**
out·sting′, *v.t.,* **-stung, -sting·ing.**
out·stink′, *v.t.,* **-stank** or **-stunk, -stunk, -stink·ing.**
out·storm′, *v.t.*
out·strain′, *v.t.*
out·stream′, *v.t.*
out·stride′, *v.t.,* **-strode, -strid·den, -strid·ing.**
out·strike′, *v.t.,* **-struck, -struck** or **-strick·en, -strik·ing.**
out·strive′, *v.t.,* **-strove, -striv·en, -striv·ing.**
out·strut′, *v.t.,* **-strut·ted, -strut·ting.**
out·stud′y, *v.t.,* **-stud·ied, -stud·y·ing.**
out·stunt′, *v.t.*
out·suck′, *v.t.*
out·suf′fer, *v.t.*
out·sulk′, *v.t.*
out·sum′, *v.t.,* **-summed, -sum·ming.**
out·swag′ger, *v.t.*
out·swarm′, *v.t.*
out·sweep′, *v.t.*
out·sweet′en, *v.t.*
out·swim′, *v.,* **-swam, -swum, -swim·ming.**
out·swin′dle, *v.t.,* **-dled, -dling.**
out·swing′, *v.t.,* **-swung, -swing·ing.**
out·swirl′, *v.t.*
out·tear′, *v.t.,* **-tore, -torn, -tear·ing.**
out·tease′, *v.t.,* **-teased, -teas·ing.**
out·thieve′, *v.t.,* **-thieved, -thiev·ing.**
out·threat′en, *v.t.*
out·throb′, *v.t.,* **-throbbed, -throb·bing.**
out·thun′der, *v.t.*
out·thwack′, *v.t.*
out·tin′kle, *v.t.,* **-kled, -kling.**
out·tire′, *v.t.,* **-tired, -tir·ing.**
out·toil′, *v.t.*
out·tongue′, *v.t.,* **-tongued, -tongu·ing.**
out·tow′er, *v.t.*
out·trade′, *v.,* **-trad·ed, -trad·ing.**
out·trav′el, *v.t.,* **-eled, -el·ing,** or (*esp. Brit.*) **-elled, -el·ling.**
out·trick′, *v.t.*
out·trot′, *v.t.,* **-trot·ted, -trot·ting.**
out·trump′, *v.t.*
out·tyr′an·nize′, *v.t.,* **-nized, -niz·ing.**
out·val′ue, *v.t.,* **-ued, -u·ing.**
out·van′ish, *v.t.*
out·vaunt′, *v.t.*
out·vel′vet, *v.t.*
out·ven′om, *v.t.*
out·vic′tor, *v.t.*
out·vie′, *v.t.,* **-vied, -vy·ing.**
out·vig′il, *v.t.*
out′vo·cif′er·ate′, *v.t.,* **-at·ed, -at·ing.**
out·voice′, *v.t.,* **-voiced, -voic·ing.**
out·voy′age, *v.t.,* **-aged, -ag·ing.**
out·wal′lop, *v.t.*
out·wan′der, *v.t.*
out·war′, *v.t.,* **-warred, -war·ring.**
out·war′ble, *v.t.,* **-bled, -bling.**
out·waste′, *v.t.,* **-wast·ed, -wast·ing.**
out·wa′ter, *v.t.*
out·wave′, *v.t.,* **-waved, -wav·ing.**
out·weap′oned, *adj.*
out·wea′ry, *v.t.,* **-ried, -ry·ing.**
out·weave′, *v.t.,* **-wove, -wo·ven, -weav·ing.**
out·weed′, *v.t.*
out·well′, *v.t.*
out·whirl′, *v.t.*
out·wig′gle, *v.t.,* **-gled, -gling.**
out·wile′, *v.t.,* **-wiled, -wil·ing.**
out·will′, *v.t.*
out·wing′, *v.t.*
out·wish′, *v.t.*
out·word′, *v.t.*
out·wran′gle, *v.t.,* **-gled, -gling.**
out·wrench′, *v.t.*
out·wres′tle, *v.t.,* **-tled, -tling.**
out·wrig′gle, *v.t.,* **-gled, -gling.**
out·wring′, *v.t.,* **-wrung, -wring·ing.**
out·yell′, *v.t.*
out·yelp′, *v.t.*
out·yield′, *v.t.*

CONCISE ETYMOLOGY KEY: <, descended or derived from; >, whence; b., blend of, blended; c., cognate with; deriv., derivative; equiv., equivalent; imit., imitative; m., modification of; obl., oblique; r., replacing; s., stem; sp., spelling; trans., translation; ?, origin unknown, perhaps; *, hypothetical. See the full key inside the front cover.

portance than that for which a triumph was accorded. Cf. **triumph** (def. 3). [< L *ovātiōn-* (s. of *ovātiō*) a rejoicing, shouting, equiv. to *ovāt(us)* rejoiced (ptp. of *ovāre*) + *-iōn-* -ION] —**o·va′tion·al,** *adj.*

ov·en (uv′ən), *n.* a heated chamber or compartment, as in a stove, for baking, roasting, heating, drying, etc. [ME; OE *ofen;* c. G *Ofen,* Icel *ofn*] —**ov′en·like′,** *adj.*

ov·en·bird (uv′ən bûrd′), *n.* **1.** an American warbler, *Seiurus aurocapillus,* which builds an oven-shaped nest of leaves, twigs, etc., on the forest floor. **2.** any of several South American passerine birds of the genus *Furnarius* or of the family *Furnariidae,* certain species of which build an oven-shaped nest. [OVEN + BIRD]

ov·en·ware (uv′ən wâr′), *n.* heat-resistant dishes of glass, pottery, etc., for baking and serving food. [OVEN + WARE¹]

ov·en·wood (uv′ən wo͝od′), *n.* brushwood; dead wood fit only for burning. [OVEN + WOOD¹]

o·ver (ō′vər), *prep.* **1.** above in place or position: *the roof over one's head.* **2.** above and to the other side of: *to leap over a wall.* **3.** above in authority, rank, power, etc., so as to govern, control, or conquer: *She is over the department now. He will be over the occupied zone.* **4.** so as to rest on or cover; on or upon: *Throw a sheet over the bed.* **5.** on or upon, so as to cause an apparent change in one's mood, attitude, etc.: *I can't imagine what has come over her.* **6.** on or on top of: *to hit someone over the head.* **7.** here and there on or in: *at various places over the country.* **8.** through all parts of; all through: *to roam over the estate; to show someone over the house.* **9.** to and fro on or in: *to travel over Europe.* **10.** from side to side of; to the other side of; across: *to go over a bridge.* **11.** on the other side of; across: *lands over the sea.* **12.** reaching higher than, so as to submerge: *The water is over his shoulders.* **13.** in excess of; more than: *over a mile; not over five dollars.* **14.** above in degree, quantity, etc.: *a big improvement over last year's turnout.* **15.** in preference to: *chosen over another applicant.* **16.** throughout the length of: *The message was sent over a great distance.* **17.** until after the end of: *to adjourn over the holidays.* **18.** throughout the duration of: *over a long period of years.* **19.** in reference to, concerning, or about: *to quarrel over a matter.* **20.** while engaged in or occupied with: *to fall asleep over one's work.* **21.** across; to the other side of: *to sell drugs over the counter.* **22.** (used to indicate a means of communication): *He told me over the phone. I heard it over the radio.* **23. over and above,** in addition to; besides: *a great deal of work, over and above what they had anticipated.* —*adv.* **24.** beyond the top or upper surface or edge of something: *a roof that hangs over.* **25.** so as to cover the surface, or affect the whole surface: *to paint a thing over.* **26.** through a region, area, etc.: *He traveled the country over.* **27.** at some distance, as in a direction indicated: *He lives over by the hill.* **28.** from side to side; across; to the other side: *to sail over.* **29.** across an intervening space: *Toss the ball over, will you?* **30.** from beginning to end; throughout: *to read a thing over.* **31.** from one person, party, etc., to another: *Hand the money over. He made the property over to his brother.* **32.** on the other side, as of a sea, a river, or any space: *over in Europe.* **33.** so as to bring the upper end or side down or under: *to knock something over.* **34.** once more; again: *to do a thing over.* **35.** in repetition or succession: *twenty times over.* **36.** in excess or addition: *to pay the full sum and something over.* **37.** in excess of or beyond a certain amount: *Five goes into seven once, with two over.* **38.** throughout or beyond a period of time: *to stay over till Monday.* **39.** to one's residence, office, or the like: *Why don't you come over tonight? Come over and we'll close the deal.* **40. all over, a.** over the entire surface of; everywhere: *material printed all over with a floral design.* **b.** thoroughly; entirely. **c.** finished: *The war was all over, and the soldiers came home.* **41. all over with,** ended; finished: *It seemed impossible that the business was all over with.* **42. over again,** in repetition; once more: *The director had the choir sing one passage over again.* **43. over against,** against (def. 10). **44. over and over,** several times; repeatedly: *They played the same record over and over.* **45. over there,** *U.S. Informal.* (during and after World War I) in or to Europe: *Many of the boys who went over there never came back.* —*adj.* **46.** upper; higher up. **47.** higher in authority, station, etc. **48.** serving, or intended to serve, as an outer covering; outer. **49.** remaining or additional, surplus; extra: *After paying the rent, this much is over.* **50.** too great; excessive (usually used in combination): *Insufficient tact and over-aggressiveness are two of his problems.* **51.** ended; done; past: *when the war was over.* —*n.* **52.** an amount in excess or addition; extra. **53.** *Mil.* a shot that strikes or bursts beyond the target. **54.** *Cricket.* **a.** the number of balls, usually six, delivered between successive changes of bowlers. **b.** the part of the game played between such changes. —*v.t.* **55.** to go or get over; leap over. **56.** *Dial.* to recover from. [ME; OE *ofer;* c. D *over,* G *ober;* akin to L *super,* Gk *hypér,* Skt *upari.* See UP, HYPER-]

over-, a prefixal use of **over,** *prep., adv.,* or *adj.,* occurring in various senses in compounds (*overboard; overcoat; overhang; overlap; overlord; overrun; overthrow*), and especially employed, with the sense of "over the limit," "to excess," "too much," "too," to form verbs, adjectives, adverbs, and nouns (*overact; overcapitalize; overcrowd; overfull; overmuch; oversupply; overweight*), and many others, mostly self-explanatory: a hyphen, which is commonly absent from old or well-established formations, is often used in new coinages, or in any words whose component parts it may be desirable to set off distinctly. [ME; OE *ofer-.* See OVER]

o·ver·a·bound (ō′vər ə bound′), *v.i.* to be too abundant or plentiful: *The land overabounds in vegetation.* [ME; see OVER-, ABOUND]

o·ver·a·bun·dance (ō′vər ə bun′dəns), *n.* an excessive amount or abundance; surfeit: *an overabundance of wheat in Canada.* [ME; see OVER-, ABUNDANCE] —**o′ver·a·bun′dant,** *adj.* —**o′ver·a·bun′dant·ly,** *adv.*

o·ver·act (ō′vər akt′), *v.t., v.i.* to act in an exaggerated manner: *He overacted the part of the king. One of the most difficult things for a performer to learn is how not to overact.* [OVER- + ACT] —**o′ver·ac′tion,** *n.*

o·ver·ac·tive (ō′vər ak′tiv), *adj.* active to excess; too active. [OVER- + ACTIVE] —**o′ver·ac·tiv′i·ty, o′ver·ac′tive·ness,** *n.*

o·ver·age¹ (ō′vər āj′), *adj.* beyond the required or desired age: *overage for the draft.* [OVER- + AGE]

o·ver·age² (ō′vər ij), *n.* *Com.* **1.** an excess supply of merchandise. **2.** the value of goods in excess of the amount called for by stock records; money in excess of the amount called for by sales records. [OVER- + -AGE]

o·ver·all (*adv.* ō′vər ôl′; *adj., n.* ō′vər ôl′), *adv., adj.* **1.** from one extreme limit of a thing to the other: *the overall length of a bridge.* **2.** covering or including everything: *an overall survey; to view something overall.* —*n.* **3. overalls, a.** loose, stout trousers, usually with a part extending up over the breast, often worn over other trousers to protect them, as by workmen, farmers, etc. **b.** long waterproof leggings. **4.** *Brit.* a smock or loose housedress. [ME *overal* (adv.), OE *ofer eall* OVER ALL]

o·ver·anx·ious (ō′vər angk′shəs, -ang′-), *adj.* excessively anxious. [OVER- + ANXIOUS] —**o·ver·anx·i·e·ty** (ō′vər ang zī′i tē), **o′ver·anx′ious·ness,** *n.* —**o′ver·anx′ious·ly,** *adv.*

o·ver·arch (ō′vər ärch′), *v.t.* **1.** to span with or like an arch: *A new bridge overarches the river.* —*v.i.* **2.** to form an arch over something: *a cerulean sky overarching in the early twilight.* [OVER- + ARCH¹]

o·ver·arm (ō′vər ärm′), *adj.* thrown or performed with the arm above the shoulder: *an overarm pitch; an overarm swimming stroke.* [OVER- + ARM¹]

o·ver·as·sess·ment (ō′vər ə ses′mənt), *n.* **1.** the act or an instance of assessing to an excessive degree or amount. **2.** the state or condition of being assessed to excess. [OVER- + ASSESSMENT]

o·ver·ate (ō′vər āt′), *v.* pt. of **overeat.**

o·ver·awe (ō′vər ô′), *v.t.,* **-awed, -aw·ing.** to restrain or subdue by inspiring awe; intimidate: *He often used that scowl to overawe his subordinates.* [OVER- + AWE]

o·ver·bal·ance (*v.* ō′vər bal′əns; *n.* ō′vər bal′əns), *v.,* **-anced, -anc·ing,** *n.* —*v.t.* **1.** to outweigh: *The opportunity overbalances the disadvantages of leaving town.* **2.** to cause to lose balance or to fall or turn over: *He accidently overbalanced a vase.* —*n.* **3.** an excessive weight or amount. **4.** something that more than balances or more than equals: *An overbalance of imports depleted the country's treasury.* [OVER- + BALANCE]

o·ver·bank (ō′vər bangk′), *v.i.* *Horol.* (of a lever escapement) to have the balance staff oscillate so greatly that the fork of the lever fails to engage with the ruby pin, which then returns and forces the end of the lever against one of the banking pins, thereby stopping the timepiece. [OVER- + BANK¹]

o·ver·bear (ō′vər bâr′), *v.,* **-bore, -borne, -bear·ing.** —*v.t.* **1.** to bear over or down by weight or force: *With his superior strength he easily overbore his opponent in the fight.* **2.** to overcome or overwhelm: *A spirited defense had overborne the enemy attack.* **3.** to prevail over or overrule (wishes, objections, etc.): *He quickly overbore all objections to his plan.* **4.** to treat in a domineering way; dominate: *to overbear one's children with threats of violence.* **5.** *Naut.* (of a sailing vessel) to have the advantage of (another sailing vessel) because of an ability to carry more canvas safely. —*v.i.* **6.** to produce fruit or progeny so abundantly as to impair the health. [OVER- + BEAR¹] —**o′ver·bear′er,** *n.*

o·ver·bear·ing (ō′vər bâr′ing), *adj.* domineering; dictatorial; haughtily or rudely arrogant. [OVERBEAR + -ING²] —**o′ver·bear′ing·ly,** *adv.* —**o′ver·bear′ing·ness,** *n.*

o·ver·bid (*v.* ō′vər bid′; *n.* ō′vər bid′), *v.,* **-bid, -bid·ding,** *n.* —*v.t.* **1.** to bid more than the value of (a thing): *to overbid one's cards.* **2.** to outbid: *She overbid him for the painting.* —*v.i.* **3.** to bid more than the actual value or worth: *a tendency to overbid at auctions; to overbid at bridge.* —*n.* **4.** a higher bid. [OVER- + BID¹]

o·ver·bite (ō′vər bīt′), *n.* *Dentistry.* occlusion in which the upper incisor teeth overlap the lower. [OVER- + BITE]

o·ver·blouse (ō′vər blous′, -blouz′), *n.* a blouse designed to be worn outside the waistband of a skirt or a pair of slacks. [OVER- + BLOUSE]

o·ver·blow (ō′vər blō′), *v.,* **-blew, -blown, -blow·ing.** —*v.t.* **1.** to give excessive importance or value to: *to overblow one's writing and reduce its credibility.* **2.** to overinflate. **3.** to blow over the surface of, as the wind, sand, or the like does: *dead leaves overblowing the yard.* **4.** to blow (a wind instrument or an organ pipe) in such a way as to produce overtones. **5.** *Archaic.* to blow (clouds, fog, etc.) over or away. —*v.i.* **6.** *Music.* to blow a wind instrument with extra pressure in order to produce specific overtones instead of the fundamental tones. **7.** *Archaic.* to pass away or blow over, as a storm. [ME; see OVER-, BLOW²]

o·ver·blown¹ (ō′vər blōn′), *adj.* **1.** overdone or excessive: *overblown praise.* **2.** of unusually large size or proportions: *a majestic, overblown figure.* **3.** overinflated; turgid; bombastic; pretentious: *a specialist in windy, overblown prose.* —*v.* **4.** pp. of **overblow.** [OVER- + BLOWN¹]

o·ver·blown² (ō′vər blōn′), *adj.* (of a flower) more than full-blown: *an overblown rose.* [OVER- + BLOWN²]

o·ver·board (ō′vər bōrd′, -bôrd′), *adv.* **1.** over the side of a ship or boat, esp. into or in the water: *to fall overboard.* **2. go overboard,** to go to extremes, esp. in regard to approval or disapproval of a person or thing: *I think the critics went overboard in panning that new show.* [ME *over bord,* OE *ofer bord.* See OVER, BOARD]

o·ver·bold (ō′vər bōld′), *adj.* excessively bold; presumptuous; rash. [OVER- + BOLD] —**o′ver·bold′ly,** *adv.* —**o′ver·bold′ness,** *n.*

o·ver·bore (ō′vər bōr′, -bôr′), *v.* pt. of **overbear.**

o·ver·borne (ō′vər bōrn′, -bôrn′), *adj.* **1.** overcome; crushed; oppressed. —*v.* **2.** pp. of **overbear.**

o·ver·bought (ō′vər bôt′), *adj.* marked by prices considered to be unjustifiably high because of extensive buying: *overbought market.* Cf. **oversold.** [OVER- + BOUGHT]

o·ver·break (ō′vər brāk′), *n.* earth excavated outside of neat lines. Also, **o′ver·break′age.** [OVER- + BREAK]

o·ver·build (ō′vər bild′), *v.t.,* **-built, -build·ing.** **1.** to cover or surmount with a building or structure. **2.** to erect too many buildings on (an area). **3.** to build (a structure) on too great or elaborate a scale. [OVER- + BUILD]

o·ver·bur·den (*v.* ō′vər bûr′dᵊn; *n.* ō′vər bûr′dᵊn), *v.t.* **1.** to load with too great a burden; overload: *She was overburdened with cares.* —*n.* **2.** an excessive burden. **3.** Also called **capping.** waste earth and rock covering a mineral deposit. [OVER- + BURDEN¹]

o·ver·bur·den·some (ō′vər bûr′dᵊn səm), *adj.* excessively burdensome. [OVER- + BURDENSOME]

o·ver·buy (ō′vər bī′), *v.,* **-bought, -buy·ing.** —*v.t.* **1.** to purchase in excessive quantities. **2.** *Finance.* to buy on margin in excess of one's ability to provide added security in an emergency, as in a falling market. —*v.i.* **3.** to buy regardless of one's financial ability. [ME *overbiggen.* See OVER-, BUY]

o′ver·a′ble, *adj.;* **-bly,** *adv.*
o′ver·ab·sorb′, *v.t.*
o′ver·ab·sorp′tion, *n.*
o′ver·ab·stain′, *v.i.*
o′ver·ab·ste′mi·ous, *adj.;* **-ly,** *adv.;* **-ness,** *n.*
o′ver·a·buse′, *v.t.,* **-bused, -bus·ing,** *n.*
o′ver·a·bu′sive, *adj.;* **-ly,** *adv.;* **-ness,** *n.*
o′ver·ac·cel′er·ate′, *v.,* **-at·ed, -at·ing.**
o′ver·ac·cel′er·a′tion, *n.*
o′ver·ac·cen′tu·ate′, *v.t.,* **-at·ed, -at·ing.**
o′ver·ac·cen′tu·a′tion, *n.*
o′ver·ac·cu′mu·late′, *v.,* **-lat·ed, -lat·ing.**
o′ver·ac·cu′mu·la′tion, *n.*
o′ver·a·cid′i·ty, *n.*
o′ver·ac′ti·vate′, *v.t.,* **-vat·ed, -vat·ing.**
o′ver·a·cute′, *adj.;* **-ly,** *adv.;* **-ness,** *n.*
o′ver·ad·dic′tion, *n.*
o′ver·a·dorn′, *v.t.*
o′ver·a·dorned′, *adj.*
o′ver·ad·vance′, *v.,* **-vanced, -vanc·ing,** *n.*
o′ver·af·fect′, *v.t.*
o′ver·af·fect′, *n.*
o′ver·af·fect′ed, *adj.*
o′ver·af·firm′, *v.*
o′ver·af′fir·ma′tion, *n.*
o′ver·af·firm′a·tive, *adj.;* **-ly,** *adv.;* **-ness,** *n.*
o′ver·af·flict′, *v.t.*
o′ver·af·flic′tion, *n.*
o′ver·ag′gra·vate′, *v.t.,* **-vat·ed, -vat·ing.**
o′ver·ag′gra·va′tion, *n.*
o′ver·ag·gres′sive, *adj.;* **-ly,** *adv.;* **-ness,** *n.*
o′ver·ag′i·tate′, *v.t.,* **-tat·ed, -tat·ing.**
o′ver·ag′i·ta′tion, *n.*
o′ver·al′co·hol·ize′, *v.t.,* **-ized, -iz·ing.**
o′ver·al·le′giance, *n.*
o′ver·al′le·go·rize′, *v.t.,* **-rized, -riz·ing.**
o′ver·am·bi′tioned, *adj.*
o′ver·am·bi′tious, *adj.;* **-ly,** *adv.;* **-ness,** *n.*
o′ver·a·nal′y·sis, *n.*
o′ver·an′a·lyt′i·cal, *adj.;* **-ly,** *adv.*
o′ver·an′a·lyze′, *v.,* **-lyzed, -lyz·ing.**
o′ver·an′gry, *adj.*
o′ver·an′i·mat′ed, *adj.;* **-ly,** *adv.*
o′ver·an′i·ma′tion, *n.*
o′ver·an′no·tate′, *v.,* **-tat·ed, -tat·ing.**
o′ver·ap·par′eled, *adj.*
o′ver·ap·plaud′, *v.*
o′ver·ap·prais′al, *n.*
o′ver·ap·praise′, *v.t.,* **-praised, -prais·ing.**
o′ver·ap·pre′ci·a′tion, *n.*
o′ver·ap·pre′ci·a′tive, *adj.;* **-ly,** *adv.;* **-ness,** *n.*
o′ver·ap′pre·hen′sion, *n.*
o′ver·ap′pre·hen′sive, *adj.;* **-ly,** *adv.;* **-ness,** *n.*
o′ver·apt′, *adj.;* **-ly,** *adv.;* **-ness,** *n.*
o′ver·ar′gue, *v.,* **-gued, -gu·ing.**
o′ver·ar′gu·men′ta·tive, *adj.;* **-ly,** *adv.;* **-ness,** *n.*
o′ver·ar′ti·fi′cial, *adj.;* **-ly,** *adv.*
o′ver·ar′ti·fi′ci·al′i·ty, *n.*
o′ver·as·sert′, *v.t.*
o′ver·as·ser′tion, *n.*
o′ver·as·ser′tive, *adj.;* **-ly,** *adv.;* **-ness,** *n.*
o′ver·as·sess′, *v.t.*
o′ver·as·sume′, *v.t.,* **-sumed, -sum·ing.**
o′ver·as·sump′tion, *n.*
o′ver·as·sump′tive, *adj.;* **-ly,** *adv.*
o′ver·as·sured′, *adj.;* **-ly,** *adv.;* **-ness,** *n.*
o′ver·at·tached′, *adj.*
o′ver·at·tach′ment, *n.*
o′ver·at·ten′tion, *n.*
o′ver·at·ten′tive, *adj.;* **-ly,** *adv.;* **-ness,** *n.*
o′ver·at·ten′u·ate′, *v.t.,* **-at·ed, -at·ing.**
o′ver·bait′, *v.t.*
o′ver·bake′, *v.,* **-baked, -bak·ing.**
o′ver·bal′last, *v.t.*
o′ver·bash′ful, *adj.;* **-ly,** *adv.;* **-ness,** *n.*
o′ver·bet′, *v.,* **-bet** or **-bet·ted, -bet·ting.**
o′ver·bet′, *n.*
o′ver·big′, *adj.;* **-ness,** *n.*
o′ver·bill′, *v.t.*
o′ver·bit′ter, *adj.;* **-ly,** *adv.;* **-ness,** *n.*
o′ver·blame′, *v.t.,* **-blamed, -blam·ing.**
o′ver·blanch′, *v.t.*
o′ver·bleach′, *v.t.*
o′ver·blind′ly, *adv.*
o′ver·blithe′, *adj.*
o′ver·boast′, *n., v.i.*
o′ver·boast′ful, *adj.;* **-ly,** *adv.;* **-ness,** *n.*
o′ver·book′, *v.t.*
o′ver·book′ish, *adj.;* **-ly,** *adv.;* **-ness,** *n.*
o′ver·boom′ing, *adj.*
o′ver·bor′row, *v.*
o′ver·boun′te·ous, *adj.;* **-ly,** *adv.;* **-ness,** *n.*
o′ver·brace′, *v.t.,* **-braced, -brac·ing.**
o′ver·brag′, *v.,* **-bragged, -brag·ging.**
o′ver·brake′, *v.t.,* **-braked, -brak·ing.**
o′ver·bra·va′do, *n.*
o′ver·brave′, *adj.;* **-ly,** *adv.;* **-ness,** *n.*
o′ver·brav′er·y, *n.*
o′ver·breed′, *v.t.,* **-bred, -breed·ing.**
o′ver·bright′, *adj.;* **-ly,** *adv.;* **-ness,** *n.*
o′ver·bril′liance, *n.*
o′ver·bril′lian·cy, *n.*
o′ver·bril′liant, *adj.;* **-ly,** *adv.*
o′ver·broad′en, *v.*
o′ver·broil′, *v.*
o′ver·brown′, *v.*
o′ver·browse′, *v.t.,* **-browsed, -brows·ing.**
o′ver·brush′, *v.t.*
o′ver·bru′tal, *adj.;* **-ly,** *adv.*
o′ver·bru·tal′i·ty, *n., pl.* **-ties.**
o′ver·bru′tal·i·za′tion, *n.*
o′ver·bru′tal·ize′, *v.t.,* **-ized, -iz·ing.**
o′ver·bulk′i·ly, *adv.*
o′ver·bulk′i·ness, *n.*
o′ver·bul′ky, *adj.*
o′ver·bump′tious, *adj.;* **-ly,** *adv.;* **-ness,** *n.*
o′ver·bus′i·ly, *adv.*
o′ver·bus′y, *adj.;* **-ness,** *n.*

o·ver·call (*v.* ō′vər kôl′, ō′vər kôl′; *n.* ō′vər kôl′), *Cards.* —*v.t., v.i.* **1.** to make an overcall. —*n.* **2.** a bid higher than the previous bid. **3.** *Bridge.* a bid on a higher level than, or in a higher ranking suit than, the previous bid of an opponent that was not followed by a bid or double by one's partner. [OVER- + CALL]

o·ver·came (ō′vər kām′), *v.* pt. of **overcome.**

o·ver·cap·i·tal·ise (ō′vər kap′i tᵊlīz′), *v.t.,* **-ised, -is·ing.** *Chiefly Brit.* overcapitalize. —**o′ver·cap′i·tal·i·sa′tion,** *n.*

o·ver·cap·i·tal·ize (ō′vər kap′i tᵊlīz′), *v.t.,* **-ized, -iz·ing. 1.** to fix the total amount of securities of a company in excess of the limits set by law or by sound financial policy. **2.** to overestimate the capital value of (a business property or enterprise). **3.** to provide an excessive amount of capital (for a business enterprise). [OVER- + CAPITALIZE] —**o′ver·cap′i·tal·i·za′tion,** *n.*

o·ver·care·ful (ō′vər kâr′fəl), *adj.* excessively or unduly careful. [OVER- + CAREFUL] —**o′ver·care′ful·ly,** *adv.* —**o′ver·care′ful·ness,** *n.*

o·ver·cast (*adj.* ō′vər kast′, -käst′, ō′vər kast′, -käst′; *v.* ō′vər kast′, -käst′, ō′vər kast′, -käst′; *n.* ō′vər kast′, -käst′), *adj., v.,* **-cast, -cast·ing,** *n.* —*adj.* **1.** overspread or covered with clouds; cloudy: *an overcast sky.* **2.** *Meteorol.* (of the sky) more than 95 percent covered by clouds. **3.** dark; gloomy. **4.** *Sewing.* sewn by overcasting. —*v.t.* **5.** to overcloud, darken, or make gloomy: *Ominous clouds began to overcast the sky.* **6.** to sew with stitches passing successively over an edge, esp. long stitches set at intervals to prevent raveling. —*v.i.* **7.** to become cloudy or dark: *By noon it had begun to overcast.* —*n.* **8.** *Meteorol.* the condition of the sky when more than 95 percent covered by clouds. **9.** *Mining.* a crossing of two passages, as airways, dug at the same level, in which one rises to pass over the other without opening into it. Cf. **undercast** (def. 1). [ME (v.); see OVER-, CAST[1]]

o·ver·cast·ing (ō′vər kas′ting, -kä′sting), *n. Sewing.* **1.** the act of sewing along the edges of material with long, spaced stitches to prevent raveling. **2.** the stitch used to overcast. [OVERCAST + -ING[1]]

o·ver·cau·tious (ō′vər kô′shəs), *adj.* excessively or unnecessarily cautious: *He is overcautious in business.* [OVER- + CAUTIOUS] —**o′ver·cau′tious·ly,** *adv.* —**o′ver·cau′tious·ness,** *n.*

o·ver·cer·ti·fy (ō′vər sûr′tə fī′), *v.t.,* **-fied, -fy·ing.** *Banking.* to certify (a bank check) for an amount greater than the drawer's balance in his account. [OVER- + CERTIFY] —**o′ver·cer′ti·fi·ca′tion,** *n.*

o·ver·charge (*v.* ō′vər chärj′; *n.* ō′vər chärj′), *v.,* **-charged, -charg·ing,** *n.* —*v.t.* **1.** to charge (someone) too high a price: *We stopped using his services, because he continually overcharged us.* **2.** to fill too full; overload: *He had overcharged his writing with too much colorless hyperbole.* **3.** to exaggerate: *to overcharge the importance of a matter.* —*v.i.* **4.** to make an excessive charge; charge too much for something: *If you're going to overcharge, I'll go somewhere else.* —*n.* **5.** a charge in excess of a just price. **6.** an act of charging excessively. **7.** an excessive load. [ME; see OVER-, CHARGE] —**o′ver·charg′er,** *n.*

o·ver·check (ō′vər chek′), *n.* **1.** a checkrein passing from the bit, over a horse's head, to the saddle of a harness. **2.** a textile pattern having one checked design superimposed on another so that both are visible. **3.** a fabric having this pattern. [OVER- + CHECK]

o·ver·clothes (ō′vər klōz′, -klōthz′), *n.* (*construed as pl.*) clothing worn outside other garments. [OVER- + CLOTHES]

o·ver·cloud (ō′vər kloud′), *v.t.* **1.** to overspread with or as if with clouds: *a summer storm that briefly overclouds the sun; to overcloud one's pleasure with solemn thoughts.* **2.** to darken; obscure; make gloomy: *a childhood that was overclouded by the loss of her parents.* —*v.i.* **3.** to become clouded over or overcast: *Toward evening the sky began to overcloud.* [OVER- + CLOUD]

o·ver·coat (*n.* ō′vər kōt′; *v.* ō′vər kōt′, ō′vər kōt′), *n.* **1.** a coat worn over the ordinary clothing, as in cold weather; a greatcoat. **2.** Also called **overcoating.** an added coating, as of paint, applied for protection. —*v.t.* **3.** to apply an additional coat of paint to (a surface). [OVER- + COAT]

Overcoat, The, a short story (1842) by Gogol.

o·ver·coat·ing (ō′vər kō′ting), *n.* **1.** material for overcoats. **2.** overcoat (def. 2). [OVERCOAT + -ING[1]]

o·ver·coil (ō′vər koil′), *n. Horol.* **1.** a fixed end of a spiral hairspring consisting of an upwardly and inwardly bent continuation of the outermost coil of the spring: used to offset the asymmetry of the common spiral spring when tight, which impairs isochronism. **2.** a hairspring having such a fixed end. [OVER- + COIL[1]]

o·ver·come (ō′vər kum′), *v.,* **-came, -come, -com·ing.** —*v.t.* **1.** to get the better of in a struggle or conflict; conquer; defeat: *to overcome the enemy.* **2.** to prevail over (opposition, objections, temptations, etc.); surmount: *to overcome one's weaknesses.* **3.** to overpower or overwhelm in body or mind, as does liquor, a drug, exertion, emotion, etc.: *She was overcome with grief.* **4.** *Archaic.* to overspread or overrun. —*v.i.* **5.** to gain the victory; win; conquer: *a plan to overcome by any means possible.* [ME; OE *ofercuman.* See OVER-, COME] —**o′ver·com′er,** *n.*
—**Syn. 1.** vanquish. See **defeat.**

o·ver·com·pen·sa·tion (ō′vər kom′pən sā′shən), *n. Psychoanal.* an exaggerated striving to neutralize and conceal a strong but unacceptable character trait by substituting for it an opposite trait. [OVER- + COMPENSATION] —**o·ver·com·pen·sa·to·ry** (ō′vər kəm pen′sə tôr′ē, -tōr′ē), *adj.*

o·ver·con·fi·dent (ō′vər kon′fi dənt), *adj.* too confident. [OVER- + CONFIDENT] —**o′ver·con′fi·dence,** *n.* —**o′ver·con′fi·dent·ly,** *adv.*

o·ver·crit·i·cal (ō′vər krit′i kəl), *adj.* excessively critical; hypercritical. [OVER- + CRITICAL] —**o′ver·crit′i·cal·ly,** *adv.* —**o′ver·crit′i·cal·ness,** *n.*

o·ver·crop (*v.* ō′vər krop′; *n.* ō′vər krop′), *v.,* **-cropped, -crop·ping,** *n.* —*v.t.* **1.** *Agric.* to crop (land) to excess; exhaust the fertility of by continuous cropping. —*n.* **2.** a mark of identification for cattle, which is made by cutting a piece from the upper margin of the ear. [OVER- + CROP]

o·ver·crowd (ō′vər kroud′), *v.t., v.i.* to crowd to excess: *Enthusiastic listeners overcrowded the dance floor. The store overcrowded as the early shoppers poured in.* [OVER- + CROWD[1]]

o·ver·cu·ri·ous (ō′vər kyŏŏr′ē əs), *adj.* excessively inquisitive: *Young children tend to be so overcurious.* [OVER- + CURIOUS] —**o′ver·cu′ri·ous·ly,** *adv.* —**o·ver·cu·ri·os·i·ty** (ō′vər kyŏŏr′ē os′i tē), **o′ver·cu′ri·ous·ness,** *n.*

o·ver·cur·rent (ō′vər kûr′ənt, -kur′-), *n. Elect.* a current of a magnitude that is greater than a limiting value, as the value at which a fuse melts. [OVER- + CURRENT]

o·ver·date (ō′vər dāt′), *n. Numis.* a coin stamped from a die altered to show a year subsequent to that for which it was cut. [OVER- + DATE[1]]

o·ver·dear (ō′vər dēr′), *adj.* excessively dear, esp. too expensive: *The articles in that antique shop are overdear for my budget.* [ME *over dere.* See OVER-, DEAR[1]] —**o′ver·dear′ly,** *adv.* —**o′ver·dear′ness,** *n.*

o·ver·del·i·cate (ō′vər del′ə kit), *adj.* extremely or excessively delicate: *an overdelicate constitution.* [OVER- + DELICATE] —**o·ver·del·i·ca·cy** (ō′vər del′ə kə sē), **o′ver·del′i·cate·ness,** *n.* —**o′ver·del′i·cate·ly,** *adv.*

o·ver·de·vel·op (ō′vər di vel′əp), *v.t., v.i.* to develop to excess: *to overdevelop a photograph; active muscles that overdeveloped and inactive muscles that atrophied.* [OVER- + DEVELOP] —**o′ver·de·vel′op·ment,** *n.*

o·ver·do (ō′vər dōō′), *v.,* **-did, -done, -do·ing.** —*v.t.* **1.** to do to excess: *to overdo exercise.* **2.** to carry to excess or beyond the proper limit: *She puts on so much charm that she overdoes it.* **3.** to overact (a part); exaggerate. **4.** to overtax the strength of; fatigue; exhaust: *He's worked too hard and overdone himself.* **5.** to cook too much or too long; overcook: *Don't overdo the hamburgers.* —*v.i.* **6.** to do too much; go to an extreme: *Exercise is good, but one mustn't overdo.* [ME *overdo(n),* OE *oferdōn.* See OVER-, DO[1]] —**o′ver·do′er,** *n.*

o·ver·done (ō′vər dun′), *v.* **1.** pp. of **overdo.** —*adj.* **2.** (of food) cooked too much: *The roast was overdone. She gave us overdone steak.* **3.** excessive; exaggerated: *Don't you think his politeness is overdone? Such overdone piety really puts me off.* **4.** overtaxed; exhausted: *You're looking a bit overdone from that hike.*

o·ver·door (ō′vər dōr′, -dôr′), *adj.* **1.** situated above a doorway: *an overdoor panel.* —*n.* **2.** an ornamented carving, painting, or section of decorated woodwork over a doorway. [OVER- + DOOR]

o·ver·dose (*n.* ō′vər dōs′; *v.* ō′vər dōs′), *n., v.,* **-dosed, -dos·ing.** —*n.* Also, **o′ver·dos′age. 1.** an excessive dose: *an overdose of pills.* —*v.t.* **2.** to give an overdose to; dose to excess: *She overdosed herself with barbiturates.* [OVER- + DOSE]

o·ver·draft (ō′vər draft′, -dräft′), *n.* **1.** a draft in excess of one's credit balance, or the amount of the excess. **2.** an excess draft or demand made on anything. **3.** the action of overdrawing an account, as at a bank. **4.** a draft made to pass over a fire, as in a furnace. **5.** a draft passing downward through a kiln. **6.** *Metalworking.* a tendency of a rolled piece to curve upwards after passing through a stand occurring when the lower roll is faster than the upper. Cf. **underdraft.** [OVER- + DRAFT]

o·ver·draw (ō′vər drô′), *v.,* **-drew, -drawn, -draw·ing.** —*v.t.* **1.** to draw upon (an account, allowance, etc.) in excess of the balance standing to one's credit or at one's disposal: *It was the first time he had ever overdrawn his account.* **2.** to strain, as a bow, by drawing too far. **3.** to exaggerate in drawing, depicting, or describing: *The author has overdrawn the villain to the point of absurdity.* —*v.i.* **4.** to overdraw an account or the like: *It ruins one's credit to overdraw at a bank.* **5.** (of a stove, fireplace, etc.) to draw excessively; have too strong an updraft: *When the flue overdraws, all the heat goes right up the chimney.* [ME; see OVER-, DRAW]

o·ver·draw·er (ō′vər drô′ər), *n.* a person who overdraws something, esp. his bank account. [OVERDRAW + -ER[1]]

---

o′ver·can′ny, *adj.*
o′ver·ca′pa·bil′i·ty, *n.*
o′ver·ca′pa·ble, *adj.*
o′ver·ca·pac′i·ty, *n., pl.* **-ties.**
o′ver·cap′tious, *adj.;* **-ly,** *adv.;* **-ness,** *n.*
o′ver·care′, *n.*
o′ver·care′less, *adj.;* **-ly,** *adv.;* **-ness,** *n.*
o′ver·cas′u·al, *adj.;* **-ly,** *adv.;* **-ness,** *n.*
o′ver·cas·u·is′ti·cal, *adj.*
o′ver·caus′tic, *adj.*
o′ver·caus′ti·cal·ly, *adv.*
o′ver·caus·tic′i·ty, *n.*
o′ver·cau′tion, *n., v.t.*
o′ver·cen′sor, *v.t.*
o′ver·cen·so′ri·ous, *adj.;* **-ly,** *adv.;* **-ness,** *n.*
o′ver·cen′tral·i·za′tion, *n.*
o′ver·cen′tral·ize′, *v.,* **-ized, -iz·ing.**
o′ver·ce·re′bral, *adj.*
o′ver·chafe′, *v.,* **-chafed, -chaf·ing.**
o′ver·char′i·ta·ble, *adj.;* **-ble·ness,** *n.;* **-bly,** *adv.*
o′ver·char′i·ty, *n.*
o′ver·chase′, *v.,* **-chased, -chas·ing.**
o′ver·cheap′, *adj.;* **-ly,** *adv.;* **-ness,** *n.*
o′ver·cher′ish, *v.t.*
o′ver·cher′ished, *adj.*
o′ver·child′ish, *adj.;* **-ly,** *adv.;* **-ness,** *n.*
o′ver·chill′, *adj.*
o′ver·chill′, *v.*
o′ver·cir′cum·spect′, *adj.*
o′ver·cir′cum·spec′tion, *n.*
o′ver·civ′il, *adj.;* **-ly,** *adv.*
o′ver·ci·vil′i·ty, *n.*
o′ver·civ′i·li·za′tion, *n.*
o′ver·civ′i·lize′, *v.,* **-lized, -liz·ing.**
o′ver·claim′, *v.t.*
o′ver·clean′, *adj.;* **-ly,** *adv.;* **-ness,** *n.*
o′ver·clem′en·cy, *n.*
o′ver·clem′ent, *adj.*
o′ver·clev′er, *adj.;* **-ly,** *adv.;* **-ness,** *n.*
o′ver·clin′i·cal, *adj.;* **-ly,** *adv.;* **-ness,** *n.*
o′ver·clog′, *v.t.,* **-clogged, -clog·ging.**
o′ver·close′, *adj.;* **-ly,** *adv.;* **-ness,** *n.*
o′ver·cloy′, *v.t.*
o′ver·clut′ter, *v.t.*
o′ver·cold′, *adj.;* **-ly,** *adv.*
o′ver·col′or, *v.t.*
o′ver·col′or·a′tion, *n.*
o′ver·com·mend′, *v.t.*
o′ver·com·mer′cial·i·za′tion, *n.*
o′ver·com·mer′cial·ize′, *v.t.,* **-ized, -iz·ing.**
o′ver·com′mon, *adj.;* **-ly,** *adv.;* **-ness,** *n.*
o′ver·com·mu′ni·ca′tive, *adj.*
o′ver·com·pet′i·tive, *adj.;* **-ly,** *adv.;* **-ness,** *n.*
o′ver·com·pla′cence, *n.*
o′ver·com·pla′cen·cy, *n.*
o′ver·com·pla′cent, *adj.;* **-ly,** *adv.*
o′ver·com·plex′, *adj.*
o′ver·com·plex′i·ty, *n.*
o′ver·com·pli′ant, *adj.*
o′ver·com′pli·cate′, *v.t.,* **-cat·ed, -cat·ing.**
o′ver·con′cen·trate′, *v.,* **-trat·ed, -trat·ing.**
o′ver·con′cen·tra′tion, *n.*
o′ver·con·cern′, *n., v.t.*
o′ver·con′den·sa′tion, *n.*
o′ver·con·dense′, *v.,* **-densed, -dens·ing.**
o′ver·con′sci·en′tious, *adj.;* **-ly,** *adv.;* **-ness,** *n.*
o′ver·con′scious, *adj.;* **-ly,** *adv.;* **-ness,** *n.*
o′ver·con·serv′a·tism, *n.*
o′ver·con·serv′a·tive, *adj.;* **-ly,** *adv.;* **-ness,** *n.*
o′ver·con·sid′er·ate, *adj.;* **-ly,** *adv.;* **-ness,** *n.*
o′ver·con·sid′er·a′tion, *n.*
o′ver·con′stant, *adj.;* **-ly,** *adv.;* **-ness,** *n.*
o′ver·con·sume′, *v.,* **-sumed, -sum·ing.**
o′ver·con·sump′tion, *n.*
o′ver·con·tent′ed, *adj.;* **-ly,** *adv.;* **-ness,** *n.*
o′ver·con·ten′tious, *adj.;* **-ly,** *adv.;* **-ness,** *n.*
o′ver·con·tent′ment, *n.*
o′ver·con·tract′, *v.t.*
o′ver·con·trac′tion, *n.*
o′ver·con·trib′ute, *v.,* **-ut·ed, -ut·ing.**
o′ver·con′tri·bu′tion, *n.*
o′ver·con·trite′, *adj.;* **-ly,** *adv.;* **-ness,** *n.*
o′ver·con·trol′, *v.t.,* **-trolled, -trol·ling.**
o′ver·con·trol′, *n.*
o′ver·cook′, *v.t.*
o′ver·cool′, *adj.;* **-ly,** *adv.;* **-ness,** *n.*
o′ver·co′pi·ous, *adj.;* **-ly,** *adv.;* **-ness,** *n.*
o′ver·cor·rect′, *adj., v.*
o′ver·cor·rupt′, *v., adj.;* **-ly,** *adv.*
o′ver·cor·rup′tion, *n.*
o′ver·cost′li·ness, *n.*
o′ver·cost′ly, *adj.*
o′ver·cour′te·ous, *adj.;* **-ly,** *adv.;* **-ness,** *n.*
o′ver·cour′te·sy, *n.*
o′ver·cov′et·ous, *adj.;* **-ly,** *adv.;* **-ness,** *n.*
o′ver·coy′, *adj.;* **-ly,** *adv.;* **-ness,** *n.*
o′ver·cred′it, *v.*
o′ver·cre·du′li·ty, *n.*
o′ver·cred′u·lous, *adj.;* **-ly,** *adv.;* **-ness,** *n.*
o′ver·crit′i·cism, *n.*
o′ver·crit′i·cize′, *v.,* **-cized, -ciz·ing.**
o′ver·crowd′ed·ly, *adv.*
o′ver·crowd′ed·ness, *n.*
o′ver·cull′, *v.t.*
o′ver·cul′ti·vate′, *v.t.,* **-vat·ed, -vat·ing.**
o′ver·cul′ti·va′tion, *n.*
o′ver·cul′tured, *adj.*
o′ver·cum′ber, *v.*
o′ver·cun′ning, *adj.;* **-ly,** *adv.;* **-ness,** *n.*
o′ver·cured′, *adj.*
o′ver·daint′i·ly, *adv.*
o′ver·daint′i·ness, *n.*
o′ver·dain′ty, *adj.*
o′ver·daz′zle, *v.,* **-zled, -zling.**
o′ver·deal′, *v.*
o′ver·de·bate′, *v.,* **-bat·ed, -bat·ing.**
o′ver·de·bil′i·tate′, *v.t.,* **-tat·ed, -tat·ing.**
o′ver·dec′a·dence, *n.*
o′ver·dec′a·dent, *adj.;* **-ly,** *adv.*
o′ver·dec′o·rate′, *v.,* **-rat·ed, -rat·ing.**
o′ver·dec′o·ra′tion, *n.*
o′ver·dec′o·ra′tive, *adj.;* **-ly,** *adv.;* **-ness,** *n.*
o′ver·ded′i·cate′, *v.t.,* **-cat·ed, -cat·ing.**
o′ver·ded′i·ca′tion, *n.*
o′ver·deep′, *adj.*
o′ver·deep′en, *v.t.*
o′ver·de·fen′sive, *adj.;* **-ly,** *adv.;* **-ness,** *n.*
o′ver·def′er·en′tial, *adj.;* **-ly,** *adv.*
o′ver·de·fi′ant, *adj.;* **-ly,** *adv.;* **-ness,** *n.*
o′ver·de·lib′er·ate′, *v.,* **-at·ed, -at·ing.**
o′ver·de·lib′er·ate, *adj.;* **-ly,** *adv.;* **-ness,** *n.*
o′ver·de·lib′er·a′tion, *n.*
o′ver·de·li′cious, *adj.;* **-ly,** *adv.;* **-ness,** *n.*
o′ver·de·mand′, *v., n.*
o′ver·de·mand′ing·ly, *adv.;* **-ness,** *n.*
o′ver·de·nun′ci·a′tion, *n.*
o′ver·de·pend′ence, *n.*
o′ver·de·pend′ent, *adj.*
o′ver·de·press′, *v.t.*
o′ver·de·pres′sive, *adj.;* **-ly,** *adv.;* **-ness,** *n.*
o′ver·de·ride′, *v.t.,* **-rid·ed, -rid·ing.**
o′ver·de·ri′sive, *adj.;* **-ly,** *adv.;* **-ness,** *n.*
o′ver·de·scribe′, *v.t.,* **-scribed, -scrib·ing.**
o′ver·de·scrip′tive, *adj.;* **-ly,** *adv.;* **-ness,** *n.*
o′ver·de·sire′, *n.*
o′ver·de·sir′ous, *adj.;* **-ly,** *adv.;* **-ness,** *n.*
o′ver·de·struc′tive, *adj.;* **-ly,** *adv.;* **-ness,** *n.*
o′ver·de·tailed′, *adj.*
o′ver·de·vot′ed, *adj.;* **-ly,** *adv.;* **-ness,** *n.*
o′ver·dif·fuse′, *v.,* **-fused, -fus·ing,** *adj.;* **-ly,** *adv.;* **-ness,** *n.*
o′ver·dif·fu′sion, *n.*
o′ver·di·gest′, *v.*
o′ver·dig′ni·fy′, *v.t.,* **-fied, -fy·ing.**
o′ver·di′late, *v.,* **-lat·ed, -lat·ing.**
o′ver·di·la′tion, *n.*
o′ver·dil′i·gence, *n.*
o′ver·dil′i·gent, *adj.;* **-ly,** *adv.;* **-ness,** *n.*
o′ver·di·lute′, *v.,* **-lut·ed, -lut·ing,** *adj.*
o′ver·di·lu′tion, *n.*
o′ver·dis′ci·pline, *v.,* **-plined, -plin·ing.**
o′ver·dis′count, *v.t.*
o′ver·dis·cour′age, *v.t.,* **-aged, -ag·ing.**
o′ver·dis·cour′age·ment, *n.*
o′ver·dis·creet′, *adj.;* **-ly,** *adv.;* **-ness,** *n.*
o′ver·dis·crim′i·nat′ing, *adj.;* **-ly,** *adv.*
o′ver·dis·cuss′, *v.t.*
o′ver·dis′tant, *adj.;* **-ly,** *adv.*
o′ver·dis·tend′, *v.*
o′ver·dis·ten′tion, *n.*
o′ver·dis·tort′, *v.t.*
o′ver·dis·tor′tion, *n.*
o′ver·dis·trait′, *adj.*
o′ver·dis·traught′, *adj.*
o′ver·di·verse′, *adj.;* **-ly,** *adv.;* **-ness,** *n.*
o′ver·di·ver′si·fi·ca′tion, *n.*
o′ver·di·ver′si·fy′, *v.,* **-fied, -fy·ing.**
o′ver·di·ver′si·ty, *n.*
o′ver·doc′tri·naire′, *adj.*
o′ver·dog·mat′ic, *adj.*
o′ver·dog·mat′i·cal, *adj.;* **-ly,** *adv.;* **-ness,** *n.*
o′ver·dog′ma·tism, *n.*
o′ver·do·mes′ti·cate′, *v.t.,* **-cat·ed, -cat·ing.**
o′ver·dom′i·nate′, *v.t.,* **-nat·ed, -nat·ing.**
o′ver·doubt′, *v.t.*
o′ver·doze′, *v.i.,* **-dozed, -doz·ing.**
o′ver·drain′, *v.*
o′ver·drain′age, *n.*
o′ver·dra·mat′ic, *adj.*
o′ver·dra·mat′i·cal·ly, *adv.*
o′ver·dram′a·tize′, *v.,* **-tized, -tiz·ing.**

o·ver·dress (*v.* ō′vər dres′; *n.* ō′vər dres′), *v.*, **-dressed, -dress·ing,** *n.* —*v.t., v.i.* **1.** to dress too warmly or with too much display: *She tends to overdress her children. He can't abide these women who overdress.* —*n.* **2.** a dress worn over another which it covers either partially or completely. [OVER- + DRESS]

o·ver·drive (*v.* ō′vər drīv′; *n.* ō′vər drīv′), *v.*, **-drove, -driv·en, -driv·ing,** *n.* —*v.t.* **1.** to push or carry to excess; overwork. **2.** to drive too hard. —*n.* **3.** *Mach.* a device containing a gear set at such ratio and arrangement as to provide, when engaged, a drive shaft speed greater than the engine crankshaft speed. [ME *overdrive(n)* (v.). See OVER-, DRIVE]

o·ver·due (ō′vər do͞o′, -dyo͞o′), *adj.* **1.** past due, as a belated train or a bill not paid by the assigned date; late. **2.** too long awaited; needed or expected for an undue length of time: *Improvements in our highway system have been long overdue.* **3.** more than sufficiently advanced, mature, or ready: *That country is overdue for revolution.* [OVER- + DUE]

o·ver·dye (ō′vər dī′, ō′vər dī′), *v.t.*, **-dyed, -dy·ing. 1.** to dye too long or too much. **2.** to dye over another color. [OVER- + DYE] —**o′ver·dy′er,** *n.*

o·ver·ea·ger (ō′vər ē′gər), *adj.* excessively or unduly eager: *overeager for riches.* [OVER- + EAGER[1]] —**o′ver·ea′ger·ly,** *adv.* —**o′ver·ea′ger·ness,** *n.*

o·ver·eat (ō′vər ēt′), *v.*, **-ate, -eat·en, -eat·ing.** —*v.i.* **1.** to eat too much: *If you overeat, you're bound to get fat.* —*v.t.* **2.** to eat more than is good for (oneself): *It was such a feast we overate ourselves.* [OVER- + EAT] —**o′ver·eat′er,** *n.*

o·ver·e·lab·o·rate (*adj.* ō′vər i lab′ər it; *v.* ō′vər i lab′ə rāt′), *adj., v.*, **-rat·ed, -rat·ing.** —*adj.* **1.** excessively or fussily elaborate, ornate, detailed, etc. —*v.t.* **2.** to fill or supply with excessive or fussy detail: *He so overelaborates his jokes that they lose their humor.* —*v.i.* **3.** to add excessive details, as in writing or speaking: *He overelaborates to an extent that his novels must be cut radically before being published.* [OVER- + ELABORATE] —**o′ver·e·lab′o·rate·ly,** *adv.* —**o′ver·e·lab′o·ra′tion, o′ver·e·lab′o·rate·ness,** *n.*

o·ver·es·ti·mate (*v.* ō′vər es′tə māt′; *n.* ō′vər es′tə mit), *v.*, **-mat·ed, -mat·ing,** *n.* —*v.t.* **1.** to estimate at too high a value, amount, rate, or the like: *Don't overestimate the car's trade-in value.* —*n.* **2.** an estimate that is too high. [OVER- + ESTIMATE] —**o′ver·es′ti·ma′tion,** *n.*

o·ver·ex·cite (ō′vər ik sīt′), *v.t.*, **-cit·ed, -cit·ing.** to excite too much. [OVER- + EXCITE] —**o′ver·ex·cit′a·bil′i·ty,** *n.* —**o′ver·ex·cit′a·bly,** *adv.* —**o′ver·ex·cit′a·ble,** *adj.* —**o′ver·ex·cite′ment,** *n.*

o·ver·ex·ert (ō′vər ig zûrt′), *v.t.* to exert too much. [OVER- + EXERT] —**o′ver·ex·ert′ed·ly,** *adv.* —**o′ver·ex·er′tion,** *n.*

o·ver·ex·pose (ō′vər ik spōz′), *v.t.*, **-posed, -pos·ing. 1.** to expose too much, as to the sun, cold, light rays, etc. (often used reflexively): *Be careful of overexposing yourself to the sun.* **2.** *Photog.* to expose (a film or the like) for too long a time. [OVER- + EXPOSE]

o·ver·ex·po·sure (ō′vər ik spō′zhər), *n.* excessive exposure, esp. of photographic film or a sensitized plate to light rays. [OVER- + EXPOSURE]

o·ver·falls (ō′vər fôlz′), *n.* **1.** water made rough by a strong current moving over ridges, by an opposing current, or by winds blowing against the current. **2.** *Obs.* a cataract or waterfall. [OVER- + FALL + -S[3]]

o·ver·feed (ō′vər fēd′), *v.t., v.i.*, **-fed, -feed·ing.** to feed or eat to excess: *Be careful of overfeeding the goldfish. When she's nervous, she overfeeds.* [OVER- + FEED]

o·ver·fill (ō′vər fil′), *v.t.* **1.** to fill too full, so as to cause overflowing. —*v.i.* **2.** to become too full. [ME *overfill(en)*, OE *oferfyllan.* See OVER-, FILL]

o·ver·fish (ō′vər fish′), *v.t.* **1.** to fish (an area) excessively; to exhaust the supply of usable fish in (certain waters): *Scientists are concerned that thoughtless competitors may overfish our coastal waters.* —*v.i.* **2.** to fish so as to deplete the supply of fish in certain waters: *If the trawlers are going to overfish here, we'll need legislation to restrict their hauls.* [OVER- + FISH]

o·ver·flap (ō′vər flap′), *n.* a protective paper cover for artwork, usually of kraft paper. [OVER- + FLAP]

o·ver·flight (ō′vər flīt′), *n.* an air flight that passes over a specific area or territory: *Overflights by planes from Western countries were sharply curtailed.* [OVER- + FLIGHT[1]]

o·ver·flow (*v.* ō′vər flō′; *n.* ō′vər flō′), *v.*, **-flowed, -flown, -flow·ing,** *n.* —*v.i.* **1.** to flow or run over, as rivers, water, etc.: *After the thaw, the river overflows, causing great damage.* **2.** to have the contents flowing over, as an overfull vessel: *Stop pouring or your glass is going to overflow.* **3.** to pass from one place or part to another as if flowing from an overfull space: *The population overflowed into the adjoining territory.* **4.** to be filled or supplied with in great measure: *a heart overflowing with gratitude; a region overflowing with orchards and vineyards.* —*v.t.* **5.** to flow over; flood; inundate: *The river overflowed several farms.* **6.** to flow over or beyond (the brim, banks, borders, etc.). **7.** to cause to overflow. **8.** to flow over the edge or brim of (a vessel, container, etc.). **9.** to fill to the point of running over. —*n.* **10.** an overflowing: *the annual overflow of the Nile.* **11.** that which flows or runs over: *to carry off the overflow from a fountain.* **12.** an excess or superabundance: *an overflow of applicants for the job.* **13.** a portion crowded out of an overfilled place: *to house the overflow of the museum's collection in another building.* **14.** an outlet for excess liquid: *The tank is equipped with an overflow.* [ME *overflowe(n)*, OE *oferflōwan.* See OVER-, FLOW] —**o′ver·flow′a·ble,** *adj.* —**o′ver·flow′ing·ly,** *adv.*

o·ver·fly (ō′vər flī′), *v.*, **-flew, -flown, -fly·ing.** —*v.t.* **1.** to fly over (a specified area, territory, country, etc.): *The plane had got lost and overflown Russian territory.* **2.** to fly farther than or beyond; overshoot: *The plane overflew Shannon and landed in the ocean.* —*v.i.* **3.** to fly over a particular territory, country, etc.: *The plane approached the border but never overflew.* [OVER- + FLY[1]]

o·ver·full (ō′vər fo͝ol′), *adj.* excessively full: *The auditorium was overfull.* [ME; OE *oferfull.* See OVER-, FULL[1]] —**o′ver·full′ness,** *n.*

o·ver·gar·ment (ō′vər gär′mənt), *n.* an outer garment. [ME; see OVER-, GARMENT]

o·ver·gild (ō′vər gild′), *v.t.*, **-gild·ed** or **-gilt, -gild·ing. 1.** to cover with gilding. **2.** to tint with a golden color: *morning sunlight that overgilds the rooftops.* [ME *overgild(en)*, OE *ofergyldan.* See OVER-, GILD[1]]

o·ver·glance (ō′vər glans′, -gläns′), *v.t.*, **-glanced, -glanc·ing.** *Archaic.* to glance over. [OVER- + GLANCE[1]]

o·ver·glaze (*n., adj.* ō′vər glāz′; *v.* ō′vər glāz′, ō′vər-glāz′), *n., v.*, **-glazed, -glaz·ing,** *adj. Ceram.* —*n.* **1.** a color or glaze applied to an existing glaze. —*v.t.* **2.** to cover or decorate (a ceramic object) with an overglaze. —*adj.* **3.** used as an overglaze. [OVER- + GLAZE]

o·ver·graze (ō′vər grāz′, ō′vər grāz′), *v.t.*, **-grazed, -graz·ing.** to graze (land) to excess. [OVER- + GRAZE[1]]

o·ver·grow (ō′vər grō′, ō′vər grō′), *v.*, **-grew, -grown, -grow·ing.** —*v.t.* **1.** to grow over; cover with a growth of something. **2.** to outdo in growing; choke or supplant by a more exuberant growth. **3.** to grow beyond, grow too large for, or outgrow. —*v.i.* **4.** to grow to excess; grow too large: *When the vegetable overgrows, it tends to be woody.* **5.** to grow over, as with weeds; become grown over: *An untended garden will quickly overgrow.* [ME *overgrow(en).* See OVER-, GROW]

o·ver·growth (ō′vər grōth′), *n.* **1.** a growth overspreading or covering something. **2.** excessive or too exuberant growth: *to prune a young tree so as to prevent overgrowth.* **3.** *Crystall.* a crystal which continues to grow when placed in a saturated solution of another substance. [OVER- + GROWTH]

o·ver·hand (ō′vər hand′), *adj.* **1.** thrown or performed overhand: *overhand stroke.* **2.** overarm. —*adv.* Also, **o′ver·hand′ed. 3.** with the hand over the object: *to grasp one's fork overhand.* **4.** with the hand and part or all of the arm raised above the shoulder: *to pitch overhand.* **5.** (in sewing and embroidery) with close, shallow stitches over two edges. —*n.* **6.** an overhand stroke or delivery. —*v.t.* **7.** to sew overhand. [OVER- + HAND]

o′verhand knot′, a simple knot of various uses which slips easily. See illus. under **knot.**

o·ver·hang (*v.* ō′vər hang′; *n.* ō′vər hang′), *v.*, **-hung, -hang·ing,** *n.* —*v.t.* **1.** to hang or be suspended over: *A great chandelier overhung the ballroom.* **2.** to extend, project, or jut over: *A wide balcony overhangs the garden. A dark canopy overhangs the path.* **3.** to impend over, or threaten, as danger or evil: *the threat of war which overhung Europe.* **4.** to spread throughout; permeate; pervade: *the melancholy which overhung the proceedings.* —*v.i.* **5.** to hang over; project or jut out over something below: *A balcony that juts out is said to overhang.* —*n.* **6.** something that extends or juts out over; projection. **7.** the extent of projection, as of the bow of a vessel. **8.** *Archit.* a projecting upper part of a building, as a roof or balcony. **9.** *Aeron.* the amount by which an upper wing of a biplane projects laterally beyond the corresponding lower wing. [OVER- + HANG]

o·ver·hap·py (ō′vər hap′ē), *adj.* excessively or unusually happy. [OVER- + HAPPY] —**o′ver·hap′pi·ly,** *adj.* —**o′ver·hap′pi·ness,** *n.*

o·ver·hast·y (ō′vər hā′stē), *adj.* excessively hasty; rash: *overhasty judgment.* [ME; see OVER-, HASTY] —**o′ver·hast′i·ly,** *adv.* —**o′ver·hast′i·ness,** *n.*

o·ver·hat·ted (ō′vər hat′id), *adj. Naut.* equipped with excessive sail on one or more masts. [OVER- + HATTED]

o·ver·haul (*v.* ō′vər hôl′, ō′vər hôl′; *n.* ō′vər hôl′), *v.t.* **1.** to investigate or examine thoroughly, as for repair, revision, etc.: *It's time to overhaul the car again. Next year we're going to overhaul the curriculum.* **2.** to make necessary repairs on; restore to serviceable condition: *My car was overhauled by an expert mechanic.* **3.** to haul or turn over for examination. **4.** to gain upon or overtake, as in a race. **5.** *Naut.* **a.** to slacken (a rope) by hauling in the opposite direction to that in which it was drawn taut. **b.** to release the blocks of (a tackle). —*n.* **6.** Also, **o′ver·haul′ing.** a general examination and repair: *The state roads were badly in need of a major overhaul.* [OVER- + HAUL] —**o′ver·haul′er,** *n.*

o·ver·head (*adv.* ō′vər hed′; *adj., n.* ō′vər hed′), *adv.* **1.** over one's head; aloft; up in the air or sky, esp. near the zenith: *There was a cloud overhead.* **2.** so as to be completely submerged or deeply involved: *to plunge overhead in water; to sink overhead in debt.* —*adj.* **3.** situated, operating, or passing above, aloft, or over the head: *an overhead sprinkler system.* **4.** general; average; not specific or particular: *overhead expenses; an overhead charge.* —*n.* **5.** the general cost of running a business. **6.** *Accounting.* that part of manufacturing costs for which cost per unit produced is not readily assignable. **7.** (in a hoistway) the distance between the last floor level served and the beam supporting the hoisting sheaves or machinery. **8.** *Tennis, Badminton.* a stroke in which the ball or shuttlecock is hit with a downward motion from above the head; smash. [OVER- + HEAD]

o′verhead rail′way, *Brit.* See **elevated railroad.**

---

o′ver·dredge′, *v.t.*, **-dredged, -dredg·ing.**
o′ver·dri′ly, *adv.*; **-ness,** *n.*
o′ver·drink′, *v.t.*
o′ver·dry′, *adj.*
o′ver·ear′nest, *adj.*; **-ly,** *adv.*; **-ness,** *n.*
o′ver·eas′i·ly, *adv.*
o′ver·eas′i·ness, *n.*
o′ver·eas′y, *adj.*
o′ver·ed′it, *v.*
o′ver·ed′i·to′ri·al·ize′, *v.i.*, **-ized, -iz·ing.**
o′ver·ed′u·cate′, *v.t.*, **-cat·ed, -cat·ing.**
o′ver·ed′u·ca′tion, *n.*
o′ver·ed′u·ca′tive, *adj.*; **-ly,** *adv.*
o′ver·ef′fort, *n.*
o′ver·ef·fu′sive, *adj.*; **-ly,** *adv.*; **-ness,** *n.*
o′ver·e·late′, *v.t.*, **-lat·ed, -lat·ing,** *adj.*
o′ver·el′e·gance, *n.*
o′ver·el′e·gant, *adj.*; **-ly,** *adv.*; **-ness,** *n.*
o′ver·el·lip′ti·cal, *adj.*; **-ly,** *adv.*
o′ver·em·bel′lish, *v.t.*
o′ver·em·bel′lish·ment, *n.*
o′ver·em·broi′der, *v.t.*
o′ver·e·mo′tion·al, *adj.*; **-ly,** *adv.*; **-ness,** *n.*
o′ver·e·mo′tion·al·ize′, *v.t.*, **-ized, -iz·ing.**
o′ver·em′pha·sis, *n.*
o′ver·em′pha·size′, *v.t.*, **-sized, -siz·ing.**
o′ver·em·phat′ic, *adj.*
o′ver·em·phat′i·cal, *adj.*; **-ly,** *adv.*; **-ness,** *n.*
o′ver·em·pir′i·cal, *adj.*; **-ly,** *adv.*
o′ver·em·ploy′, *v.t.*
o′ver·em·ploy′ment, *n.*
o′ver·emp′ty, *adj.*
o′ver·em′u·late′, *v.t.*, **-lat·ed, -lat·ing.**
o′ver·em′u·la′tion, *n.*
o′ver·en·thu′si·asm, *n.*
o′ver·en·thu′si·as′tic, *adj.*
o′ver·en·thu′si·as′ti·cal·ly, *adv.*
o′ver·en′vi·ous, *adj.*; **-ly,** *adv.*; **-ness,** *n.*
o′ver·ex·act′ing, *adj.*
o′ver·ex·ag′ger·ate′, *v.*, **-at·ed, -at·ing.**
o′ver·ex′er·cise′, *v.t.*, **-cised, -cis·ing,** *n.*
o′ver·ex·pand′, *v.*
o′ver·ex·pan′sion, *n.*
o′ver·ex·pan′sive, *adj.*; **-ly,** *adv.*; **-ness,** *n.*
o′ver·ex·pect′, *v.*
o′ver·ex·pect′ant, *adj.*; **-ly,** *adv.*; **-ness,** *n.*
o′ver·ex·pend′, *v.*
o′ver·ex·pen′di·ture, *n.*
o′ver·ex·plain′, *v.*
o′ver·ex′pla·na′tion, *n.*
o′ver·ex·plic′it, *adj.*
o′ver·ex·press′, *v.t.*
o′ver·ex·pres′sive, *adj.*; **-ly,** *adv.*; **-ness,** *n.*
o′ver·ex′qui·site, *adj.*
o′ver·ex·tend′, *v.*
o′ver·ex·treme′, *adj.*
o′ver·ex·u′ber·ance, *n.*
o′ver·ex·u′ber·ant, *adj.*; **-ly,** *adv.*; **-ness,** *n.*
o′ver·eye′, *v.t.*, **-eyed, -ey·ing.**
o′ver·fac′ile, *adj.*; **-ly,** *adv.*
o′ver·fa·cil′i·ty, *n.*
o′ver·fac′tious, *adj.*; **-ly,** *adv.*; **-ness,** *n.*
o′ver·fac·ti′tious, *adj.*
o′ver·fag′, *v.*, **-fagged, -fag·ging.**
o′ver·faint′, *adj.*; **-ly,** *adv.*; **-ness,** *n.*
o′ver·faith′ful, *adj.*; **-ly,** *adv.*; **-ness,** *n.*
o′ver·famed′, *adj.*
o′ver·fa·mil′iar, *adj.*; **-ly,** *adv.*
o′ver·fa·mil′i·ar′i·ty, *n.*
o′ver·fa′mous, *adj.*
o′ver·fan′ci·ful, *adj.*; **-ly,** *adv.*; **-ness,** *n.*
o′ver·far′, *adv., adj.*
o′ver·fast′, *adj.*
o′ver·fas·tid′i·ous, *adj.*; **-ly,** *adv.*; **-ness,** *n.*
o′ver·fat′, *adj.*
o′ver·fa·tigue′, *v.*, **-tigued, -ti·guing.**
o′ver·fat′ten, *v.t.*
o′ver·fa′vor, *v.t.*
o′ver·fa′vor·a·ble, *adj.*; **-ble·ness,** *n.*; **-bly,** *adv.*
o′ver·fear′ful, *adj.*; **-ly,** *adv.*; **-ness,** *n.*
o′ver·feast′, *v.*
o′ver·fee′, *n.*
o′ver·feel′, *v.*
o′ver·fem′i·nine, *adj.*; **-ly,** *adv.*
o′ver·fem′i·nin′i·ty, *n.*
o′ver·fem′i·nize′, *v.*, **-nized, -niz·ing.**
o′ver·fer′tile, *adj.*
o′ver·fer·til′i·ty, *n.*
o′ver·fer′vent, *adj.*; **-ly,** *adv.*; **-ness,** *n.*
o′ver·few′, *adj.*
o′ver·fierce′, *adj.*; **-ly,** *adv.*; **-ness,** *n.*
o′ver·fil′ter, *v.t.*
o′ver·fit′, *adj.*
o′ver·fix′, *v.*
o′ver·flat′, *adj.*; **-ly,** *adv.*; **-ness,** *n.*
o′ver·flat′ten, *v.t.*
o′ver·fla′vor, *v.*
o′ver·fleshed′, *adj.*
o′ver·flex′ion, *n.*
o′ver·flog′, *v.t.*, **-flogged, -flog·ging.**
o′ver·flood′, *v.*
o′ver·flor′id, *adj.*; **-ly,** *adv.*; **-ness,** *n.*
o′ver·flour′, *v.*
o′ver·flu′en·cy, *n.*
o′ver·flu′ent, *adj.*; **-ly,** *adv.*; **-ness,** *n.*
o′ver·fond′, *adj.*; **-ly,** *adv.*; **-ness,** *n.*
o′ver·fon′dle, *v.*, **-dled, -dling.**
o′ver·fool′ish, *adj.*; **-ly,** *adv.*; **-ness,** *n.*
o′ver·force′, *n.*
o′ver·force′, *v.*, **-forced, -forc·ing.**
o′ver·forged′, *adj.*
o′ver·for′mal·ize′, *v.*, **-ized, -iz·ing.**
o′ver·formed′, *adj.*
o′ver·for′ward, *adj.*; **-ly,** *adv.*; **-ness,** *n.*
o′ver·foul′, *adj.*; **-ly,** *adv.*; **-ness,** *n.*
o′ver·frag′ile, *adj.*
o′ver·frag′ment·ed, *adj.*
o′ver·frail′, *adj.*; **-ly,** *adv.*; **-ness,** *n.*
o′ver·frail′ty, *n.*
o′ver·fran′chised, *adj.*
o′ver·frank′, *adj.*; **-ly,** *adv.*; **-ness,** *n.*
o′ver·fraught′, *adj.*
o′ver·free′, *adj.*; **-ly,** *adv.*
o′ver·free′dom, *n.*
o′ver·freight′, *v.t.*
o′ver·fre′quen·cy, *n.*
o′ver·fre′quent, *adj.*; **-ly,** *adv.*
o′ver·fright′en, *v.*
o′ver·fru′gal, *adj.*; **-ly,** *adv.*
o′ver·fru·gal′i·ty, *n.*
o′ver·fruit′ful, *adj.*; **-ly,** *adv.*; **-ness,** *n.*
o′ver·frus·tra′tion, *n.*
o′ver·func′tion·ing, *adj.*
o′ver·fur′nish, *v.t.*
o′ver·gam′ble, *v.t.*, **-bled, -bling.**
o′ver·gar′nish, *v.t.*
o′ver·gar′ri·son, *v.t.*
o′ver·gen′er·al·i·za′tion, *n.*
o′ver·gen′er·al·ize′, *v.t.*, **-ized, -iz·ing.**
o′ver·gen′er·os′i·ty, *n.*
o′ver·gen′er·ous, *adj.*; **-ly,** *adv.*
o′ver·gen′ial, *adj.*; **-ly,** *adv.*; **-ness,** *n.*
o′ver·ge′ni·al′i·ty, *n.*
o′ver·gen′tle, *adj.*
o′ver·gen′tly, *adv.*
o′ver·ges·tic′u·late′, *v.*, **-lat·ed, -lat·ing.**
o′ver·ges·tic′u·la′tion, *n.*
o′ver·ges·tic′u·la′tive, *adj.*; **-ly,** *adv.*; **-ness,** *n.*
o′ver·gift′ed, *adj.*
o′ver·gird′, *v.t.*, **-gird·ed** or **-girt, -gird·ing.**
o′ver·glad′, *adj.*; **-ly,** *adv.*
o′ver·gloom′i·ly, *adv.*
o′ver·gloom′i·ness, *n.*
o′ver·gloom′y, *adj.*
o′ver·glut′, *v.t.*
o′ver·goad′, *v.t.*
o′ver·gov′ern, *v.t.*
o′ver·gra′cious, *adj.*; **-ly,** *adv.*; **-ness,** *n.*
o′ver·grade′, *v.t.*, **-grad·ed, -grad·ing.**
o′ver·grad′u·at′ed, *adj.*
o′ver·grasp′ing, *adj.*
o′ver·grate′ful, *adj.*; **-ly,** *adv.*; **-ness,** *n.*
o′ver·grat′i·fi·ca′tion, *n.*
o′ver·grat′i·fy′, *v.t.*, **-fied, -fy·ing.**
o′ver·grat′i·tude′, *n.*
o′ver·greas′i·ness, *n.*
o′ver·greas′y, *adj.*
o′ver·great′, *adj.*; **-ly,** *adv.*; **-ness,** *n.*
o′ver·greed′i·ly, *adv.*
o′ver·greed′i·ness, *n.*
o′ver·greed′y, *adj.*
o′ver·grieve′, *v.t.*, **-grieved, -griev·ing.**
o′ver·griev′ous, *adj.*; **-ly,** *adv.*; **-ness** *n.*
o′ver·gross′, *adj.*; **-ly,** *adv.*; **-ness,** *n.*
o′ver·guilt′y, *adj.*
o′ver·hand′i·cap′, *v.t.*, **-capped, -cap·ping.**
o′ver·han′dle, *v.t.*, **-dled, -dling.**
o′ver·har′ass, *v.t.*
o′ver·har′ass·ment, *n.*
o′ver·hard′, *adj.*; **-ness,** *n.*
o′ver·hard′en, *v.t.*
o′ver·har′dy, *adj.*
o′ver·harsh′, *adj.*; **-ly,** *adv.*; **-ness,** *n.*
o′ver·has′ten, *v.*
o′ver·haugh′ti·ly, *adv.*; **-ness,** *n.*
o′ver·haugh′ty, *adj.*
o′ver·head′i·ness, *n.*

o·ver·hear (ō′vər hēr′), *v.t.*, **-heard, -hear·ing.** to hear (speech or a speaker) without the speaker's intention or knowledge: *I accidentally overheard what they were saying.* [OVER- + HEAR] —**o′ver·hear′er,** *n.*

o·ver·heat (ō′vər hēt′), *v.t.* **1.** to heat to excess. **2.** to excite or agitate; make vehement: *a crowd overheated by rabble-rousers.* —*v.i.* **3.** to become overheated: *a stove that overheats alarmingly; a temper that overheats with little provocation.* —*n.* **4.** the state or condition of being overheated; excessive heat, agitation, or vehemence. [ME *overhet(en).* See OVER-, HEAT]

o·ver·hung (*v.* ō′vər hung′; *adj.* ō′vər hung′), *v.* **1.** pt. and pp. of **overhang.** —*adj.* **2.** hung or suspended from above: *an overhung door.*

O·ver·ijs·sel (ō′vər ī′səl), *n.* a province in the E Netherlands. 835,494 (1962); 1254 sq. mi. *Cap.:* Zwolle.

o·ver·in·dulge (ō′vər in dulj′), *v.t., v.i.,* **-dulged, -dulg·ing.** to indulge to excess: *to overindulge one's fondness for candy.* [OVER- + INDULGE] —**o′ver·in·dul′gence,** *n.* —**o′ver·in·dul′gent,** *adj.* —**o′ver·in·dul′gent·ly,** *adv.*

o·ver·is·sue (ō′vər ish′o͞o *or, esp. Brit.,* -is′yo͞o), *n.* an excessive issue of stocks or bonds, as in excess of the needs of the business or in excess of charter authorization. [OVER- + ISSUE]

o·ver·joy (ō′vər joi′), *v.t.* to cause to feel great joy or delight: *It overjoys me to hear of your good fortune. I was overjoyed at her safe arrival.* [OVER- + JOY]

o·ver·kill (ō′vər kil′), *n.* **1.** the capacity of a nation to destroy, by nuclear weapons, more of an enemy than would be necessary for a military victory. **2.** an instance of such destruction. [OVER- + KILL[1]]

o·ver·kind (ō′vər kīnd′), *adj.* too kind: *She means well but is overkind to the point of annoyance.* [ME *overkinde.* See OVER-, KIND[1]] —**o′ver·kind′ly,** *adv.* —**o′ver·kind′ness,** *n.*

o·ver·la·bor (ō′vər lā′bər), *v.t.* to labor too much, esp. to elaborate excessively: *to overlabor an argument.* [OVER- + LABOR]

o·ver·lade (ō′vər lād′), *v.t.,* **-lad·ed, -lad·en** or **-lad·ed, -lad·ing.** to overload (usually used in pp. *overladen*): *a table overladen with rich food.* [ME *overlade(n),* equiv. to *over* OVER- + *laden* to load; see LADE]

o·ver·land (ō′vər land′, -lənd), *adv.* **1.** by land: *to travel overland rather than by sea.* **2.** over or across the land: *a road that winds overland.* —*adj.* **3.** proceeding, performed, or carried on overland: *the overland route.* [ME *overlond.* See OVER-, LAND]

O·ver·land (ō′vər lənd), *n.* a city in E Missouri, near St. Louis. 22,763 (1960).

O′verland Park′, a town in E Kansas, near Kansas City. 21,110 (1960).

o′verland stage′, a stagecoach used in the Western U.S. during the middle of the 19th century.

o·ver·lap (*v.* ō′vər lap′; *n.* ō′vər lap′), *v.,* **-lapped, -lap·ping,** *n.* —*v.t.* **1.** to lap over (something else or each other); extend over and cover a part of. **2.** to cover and extend beyond (something else): *The ends of cloth overlap the table.* **3.** to coincide in part with; have in common with: *two lives that overlapped each other.* —*v.i.* **4.** to lap over: *two territories that overlap; fields of knowledge that overlap.* —*n.* **5.** the act or an instance of overlapping. **6.** the extent or amount of overlapping: *The second story of the building has an overlap of ten feet.* **7.** an overlapping part. **8.** the place of overlapping. **9.** (in yacht racing) the position of two yachts side by side so that the overtaking boat, to pass the other on the opposite side, must fall back or so that neither can turn toward the other without danger of collision. [OVER- + LAP[2]]

o·ver·large (ō′vər lärj′), *adj.* excessively large: *an overlarge size.* [OVER- + LARGE]

o·ver·lay[1] (*v.* ō′vər lā′; *n.* ō′vər lā′), *v.,* **-laid, -lay·ing,** *n.* —*v.t.* **1.** to lay or place (one thing) over or upon another. **2.** to cover, overspread, or surmount with something. **3.** to finish with a layer or applied decoration of something: *wood richly overlaid with gold.* **4.** *Print.* to put an overlay upon. —*n.* **5.** something laid over something else; covering. **6.** a layer or decoration of something applied: *an overlay of gold.* **7.** *Print.* **a.** a shaped piece of paper, or a sheet of paper reinforced at the proper places by shaped pieces, put on the tympan of a press to increase or equalize the impression. **b.** a method of preparing copy for multicolor printing, in which matter for each color is prepared on a transparent sheet which is placed over a key plate, usually the one to be printed in black. **c.** the sheet or sheets so prepared. **8.** a sheet of transparent paper placed over a photograph, a dummy, or other artwork for noting corrections, instructions, mechanical separations, etc. **9.** a transparent sheet giving special military information not ordinarily shown on maps, used by being placed over the map on which it is based. **10.** *Scot.* a cravat. [ME; see OVER-, LAY[1]]

o·ver·lay[2] (ō′vər lā′), *v.* pt. of **overlie.**

o′verlay glass′. See **case glass.**

o·ver·leaf (ō′vər lēf′), *adv.* on the other side of the page or sheet: *continued overleaf.* [OVER- + LEAF]

o·ver·leap (ō′vər lēp′), *v.t.* **-leaped** or **-leapt, -leap·ing.** **1.** to leap over or across: *to overleap a fence.* **2.** to overreach (oneself) by leaping too far: *to overleap oneself with ambition.* **3.** to pass over or omit: *to overleap important steps and proceed to erroneous conclusions.* **4.** *Archaic.* to leap farther than; outleap. [ME *overlep(en),* OE *oferhlēapan.* See OVER-, LEAP]

o·ver·lib·er·al (ō′vər lib′ər əl, -lib′rəl), *adj.* excessively liberal. [OVER- + LIBERAL] —**o′ver·lib′er·al′i·ty,** *n.* —**o′ver·lib′er·al·ly,** *adv.*

o·ver·lie (ō′vər lī′), *v.t.,* **-lay, -lain, -ly·ing.** **1.** to lie over or upon, as a covering, stratum, etc. **2.** to smother (an infant) by lying upon it, as in sleep. [ME *overlie(n), overligg(en).* See OVER-, LIE[2]]

o·ver·line (ō′vər līn′), *n.* **1.** *Journalism.* a cutline, usually of one line, appearing over a cut. **2.** kicker (def. 7). [OVER- + LINE[1]]

o·ver·live (ō′vər liv′), *v.,* **-lived, -liv·ing.** *Archaic.* —*v.t.* **1.** to live or last longer than (another person, an era, etc.); outlast. —*v.i.* **2.** to survive or continue to live; live too long. [ME *overlive(n),* OE *oferlibben.* See OVER-, LIVE[1]] —**o′ver·liv′er,** *n.*

o·ver·load (*v.* ō′vər lōd′; *n.* ō′vər lōd′), *v.t.* **1.** to load to excess; overburden: *Don't overload the raft or it will sink.* —*n.* **2.** an excessive load. [OVER- + LOAD]

o·ver·long (ō′vər lông′, -long′), *adj., adv.* too long: *a book that was overlong; to stay overlong.* [ME; see OVER-, LONG[1]]

o·ver·look (*v.* ō′vər lo͝ok′; *n.* ō′vər lo͝ok′), *v.t.* **1.** to fail to notice, perceive, or consider: *to overlook a misspelled word.* **2.** to disregard or ignore indulgently, as faults, misconduct, etc.: *Only a mother could overlook that kind of behavior.* **3.** to look over, as from a higher position: *a balcony that overlooks the ballroom.* **4.** to afford a view down over: *a hill overlooking the sea.* **5.** to rise above: *The Washington Monument overlooks the Tidal Basin.* **6.** to excuse; pardon: *a minor infraction we can overlook this time.* **7.** to look over in inspection, examination, or perusal: *He allowed us to overlook the proposed contract.* **8.** to look after, oversee, or supervise: *She has to overlook a large number of employees.* **9.** to look upon with the evil eye; bewitch. —*n.* **10.** terrain, as on a cliff, that affords a view: *Miles of landscape could be seen from the overlook.* [ME; see OVER-, LOOK]
—**Syn. 1.** miss. See **slight. 2.** excuse, forgive, pardon.

o·ver·look·er (ō′vər lo͝ok′ər), *n.* *Brit.* overseer. [ME; see OVERLOOK, -ER[1]]

o·ver·lord (ō′vər lôrd′), *n.* **1.** a person who is lord over another or over other lords: *to obey the will of one's sovereign and overlord.* **2.** a person of great influence, authority, power, or the like: *the overlords of industry.* —*v.t.* **3.** to rule or govern arbitrarily or tyrannically; domineer. [ME; see OVER-, LORD] —**o′ver·lord′ship,** *n.*

o·ver·lust·y (ō′vər lus′tē), *adj.* excessively lusty; too robust or powerful: *an overlusty appetite.* [OVER- + LUSTY] —**o′ver·lust′i·ness,** *n.*

o·ver·ly (ō′vər lē), *adv.* overmuch; excessively; too: *a voyage not overly dangerous.* [ME; OE *oferlīce.* See OVER, -LY]

o·ver·ly·ing (ō′vər lī′ing), *v.* ppr. of **overlie.**

o·ver·man (*n.* ō′vər mən *for 1, 2,* ō′vər man′ *for 3; v.* ō′vər man′), *n., pl.* **-men** (-mən *for 1, 2;* -men′ *for 3*), *v.,* **-manned, -man·ning.** —*n.* **1.** a foreman or overseer. **2.** *Chiefly Scot.* a person who arbitrates a dispute; an arbiter or umpire. **3.** *Archaic.* a superman. —*v.t.* **4.** to oversupply with men, esp. for service: *Indiscriminate hiring had overmanned the factory.* [ME; see OVER-, MAN[1]]

o·ver·man·tel (ō′vər man′tᵊl), *adj.* **1.** situated above a mantelpiece. —*n.* **2.** an ornament or panel situated above a mantelpiece. [OVER- + MANTEL]

o·ver·mast (ō′vər mast′, -mäst′), *v.t.* *Naut.* to fit (a vessel) with excessively high or heavy masts. [OVER- + MAST[1]]

o·ver·mas·ter (ō′vər mas′tər, -mä′stər), *v.t.* to gain mastery over; overpower: *The sudden impulse had quite overmastered me.* [ME *overmaistre(n).* See OVER-, MASTER] —**o′ver·mas′ter·ing·ly,** *adv.*

o·ver·match (ō′vər mach′), *v.t.* **1.** to outmatch; surpass; defeat: *an assignment that clearly overmatched his abilities; an able task force that overmatched the enemy fleet.* **2.** to match (a competitor) against another of superior strength, ability, or the like: *His managers must have known that they were overmatching him.* [ME *overmacche(n).* See OVER-, MATCH[2]]

o·ver·mat·ter (ō′vər mat′ər), *n.* *Print.* overset (def. 6). [OVER- + MATTER]

o·ver·meas·ure (ō′vər mezh′ər), *n.* an excessive or surplus measure or amount: *an overmeasure of exuberance.* [OVER- + MEASURE]

o·ver·mod·est (ō′vər mod′ist), *adj.* too modest: *overmodest about one's achievements.* [OVER- + MODEST] —**o′ver·mod′est·ly,** *adv.* —**o′ver·mod′est·y,** *n.*

o·ver·much (ō′vər much′), *adj., n., adv.* too much: *He didn't show overmuch concern. We tried not to regret it overmuch.* [ME; see OVER-, MUCH]

---

o′ver·head′y, *adj.*
o′ver·heap′, *v.t.*
o′ver·heart′i·ly, *adv.*
o′ver·heart′i·ness, *n.*
o′ver·heart′y, *adj.*
o′ver·heav′i·ly, *adv.*
o′ver·heav′i·ness, *n.*
o′ver·heav′y, *adj.*
o′ver·help′ful, *adj.;* **-ly,** *adv.;* **-ness,** *n.*
o′ver·high′, *adj.;* **-ly,** *adv.*
o′ver·home′li·ness, *n.*
o′ver·home′ly, *adj.*
o′ver·hon′est, *adj.;* **-ly,** *adv.;* **-ness,** *n.*
o′ver·hon′es·ty, *n.*
o′ver·hon′or, *v.t.*
o′ver·hos′tile, *adj.;* **-ly,** *adv.*
o′ver·hos·til′i·ty, *n.*
o′ver·hot′, *adj.;* **-ly,** *adv.*
o′ver·huge′, *adj.;* **-ly,** *adv.;* **-ness,** *n.*
o′ver·hu′man, *adj.*
o′ver·hu·mane′, *adj.*
o′ver·hu·man′i·ty, *n.*
o′ver·hu′man·ize′, *v.,* **-ized, -iz·ing.**
o′ver·hum′ble, *adj.;* **-ble·ness,** *n.;* **-bly,** *adv.*
o′ver·hunt′, *v.t.*
o′ver·hur′ried, *adj.;* **-ly,** *adv.*
o′ver·hur′ry, *v.,* **-ried, -ry·ing.**
o′ver·hys·ter′i·cal, *adj.*
o′ver·i·de′al·ism, *n.*
o′ver·i·de′al·is′tic, *adj.*
o′ver·i·de′al·ize′, *v.,* **-ized, -iz·ing.**
o′ver·i·den′ti·fy′, *v.,* **-fied, -fy·ing.**
o′ver·i′dle, *adj.;* **-ness,** *n.*
o′ver·i′dly, *adv.*
o′ver·i·dol′a·trous, *adj.;* **-ly,** *adv.;* **-ness,** *n.*
o′ver·il′lus·trate′, *v.t.,* **-trat·ed, -trat·ing.**
o′ver·il′lus·tra′tion, *n.*
o′ver·il·lus′tra·tive, *adj.;* **-ly,** *adv.*
o′ver·im·ag′i·na′tive, *adj.;* **-ly,** *adv.;* **-ness,** *n.*
o′ver·im′i·tate′, *v.t.,* **-tat·ed, -tat·ing.**
o′ver·im′i·ta′tion, *n.*
o′ver·im′i·ta′tive, *adj.;* **-ly,** *adv.;* **-ness,** *n.*
o′ver·im′mu·nize′, *v.t.,* **-nized, -niz·ing.**
o′ver·im·port′, *v.t.*
o′ver·im′por·ta′tion, *n.*
o′ver·im·pose′, *v.t.,* **-posed, -pos·ing.**
o′ver·im·press′, *v.t.*
o′ver·im·press′i·ble, *adj.;* **-bly,** *adv.*
o′ver·im·press′i·bil′i·ty, *n.*
o′ver·im·pres′sion·a·bil′i·ty, *n.*
o′ver·im·pres′sion·a·ble, *adj.;* **-ble·ness,** *n.;* **-bly,** *adv.*
o′ver·in·clin′a·ble, *adj.*
o′ver·in′cli·na′tion, *n.*
o′ver·in·cline′, *v.,* **-clined, -clin·ing.**
o′ver·in′di·vid′u·al·ism, *n.*
o′ver·in′di·vid′u·al·is′tic, *adj.*
o′ver·in′di·vid′u·al·is′ti·cal·ly, *adv.*
o′ver·in′di·vid′u·a·li·za′tion, *n.*
o′ver·in·dus′tri·al·ism, *n.*
o′ver·in·dus′tri·al·i·za′tion, *n.*
o′ver·in·dus′tri·al·ize′, *v.,* **-ized, -iz·ing.**
o′ver·in·flate′, *v.t.,* **-flat·ed, -flat·ing.**
o′ver·in·fla′tion, *n.*
o′ver·in·fla′tion·ar′y, *adj.*
o′ver·in′flu·ence, *v.t.,* **-enced, -enc·ing.**
o′ver·in′flu·en′tial, *adj.*
o′ver·in·hib′it, *v.t.*
o′ver·in·hib′it·ed, *adj.*
o′ver·in·sist′, *v.i.*
o′ver·in·sist′ence, *n.*
o′ver·in·sist′en·cy, *n., pl.* **-cies.**
o′ver·in·sist′ent, *adj.;* **-ly,** *adv.*
o′ver·in′so·lence, *n.*
o′ver·in′so·lent, *adj.;* **-ly,** *adv.*
o′ver·in·struct′, *v.t.*
o′ver·in·struc′tion, *n.*
o′ver·in·struc′tive, *adj.;* **-ly,** *adv.;* **-ness,** *n.*
o′ver·in·sure′, *v.t.,* **-sured, -sur·ing.**
o′ver·in′tel·lec′tu·al, *adj.;* **-ly,** *adv.;* **-ness,** *n.*
o′ver·in′tel·lec′tu·al·ism, *n.*
o′ver·in′tel·lec′tu·al·i·za′tion, *n.*
o′ver·in′tel·lec′tu·al·ize′, *v.,* **-ized, -iz·ing.**
o′ver·in·tense′, *adj.;* **-ly,** *adv.;* **-ness,** *n.*
o′ver·in·ten′si·fi·ca′tion, *n.*
o′ver·in·ten′si·fy′, *v.,* **-fied, -fy·ing.**
o′ver·in·ten′si·ty, *n.*
o′ver·in′ter·est, *n.*
o′ver·in′ter·est·ed, *adj.;* **-ly,** *adv.;* **-ness,** *n.*
o′ver·in′ter·fer′ence, *n.*
o′ver·in′ven·to′ried, *adj.*
o′ver·in·vest′, *v.*
o′ver·in·vest′ment, *n.*
o′ver·in·volve′, *v.t.,* **-volved, -volv·ing.**
o′ver·i′o·dize′, *v.t.,* **-dized, -diz·ing.**
o′ver·ir′ri·gate′, *v.t.,* **-gat·ed, -gat·ing.**
o′ver·ir′ri·ga′tion, *n.*
o′ver·jade′, *v.t.,* **-jad·ed, -jad·ing**
o′ver·jeal′ous, *adj.;* **-ly,** *adv.;* **-ness,** *n.*
o′ver·joc′u·lar, *adj.;* **-ly,** *adv.*
o′ver·joc′u·lar′i·ty, *n.*
o′ver·joy′ful, *adj.;* **-ly,** *adv.;* **-ness,** *n.*
o′ver·joy′ous, *adj.;* **-ly,** *adv.;* **-ness,** *n.*
o′ver·ju·di′cious, *adj.;* **-ly,** *adv.;* **-ness,** *n.*
o′ver·keen′, *adj.;* **-ly,** *adv.;* **-ness,** *n.*
o′ver·kick′, *v.t.*
o′ver·lac′tate, *v.i.,* **-tat·ed, -tat·ing.**
o′ver·lac·ta′tion, *n.*
o′ver·lard′, *v.t.*
o′ver·las·civ′i·ous, *adj.;* **-ly,** *adv.;* **-ness,** *n.*
o′ver·late′, *adj.;* **-ness,** *n.*
o′ver·lath′er, *v.t.*
o′ver·laud′, *v.t.*
o′ver·lau·da′tion, *n.*
o′ver·laud′a·to′ry, *adj.*
o′ver·lav′ish, *adj.;* **-ly,** *adv.;* **-ness,** *n.*
o′ver·lax′, *adj.;* **-ly,** *adv.;* **-ness,** *n.*
o′ver·learn′, *v.t.*
o′ver·learn′ed, *adj.;* **-ly,** *adv.;* **-ness,** *n.*
o′ver·leg′is·late′, *v.,* **-lat·ed, -lat·ing.**
o′ver·lewd′, *adj.;* **-ly,** *adv.;* **-ness,** *n.*
o′ver·lib′er·al·i·za′tion, *n.*
o′ver·lib′er·al·ize′, *v.,* **-ized, -iz·ing.**
o′ver·li·cen′tious, *adj.;* **-ly,** *adv.;* **-ness,** *n.*
o′ver·light′, *adj.;* **-ly,** *adv.;* **-ness,** *n.*
o′ver·light′, *n.*
o′ver·lik′ing, *n.*
o′ver·lim′it, *v.t.*
o′ver·lin′ger, *v.i.*
o′ver·lit′er·ar′i·ly, *adv.*
o′ver·lit′er·ar′i·ness, *n.*
o′ver·lit′er·ar′y, *adj.*
o′ver·live′li·ness, *n.*
o′ver·live′ly, *adj.*
o′ver·loan′, *v.t.*
o′ver·loath′, *adj.*
o′ver·loft′i·ly, *adv.*
o′ver·loft′i·ness, *n.*
o′ver·loft′y, *adj.*
o′ver·log′i·cal, *adj.;* **-ly,** *adv.;* **-ness,** *n.*
o′ver·log′i·cal′i·ty, *n.*
o′ver·loose′, *adj.;* **-ly,** *adv.;* **-ness,** *n.*
o′ver·loud′, *adj.;* **-ly,** *adv.;* **-ness,** *n.*
o′ver·love′, *v.,* **-loved, -lov·ing.**
o′ver·low′ness, *n.*
o′ver·loy′al, *adj.;* **-ly,** *adv.*
o′ver·loy′al·ty, *n., pl.* **-ties.**
o′ver·lu′bri·cate′, *v.t.,* **-cat·ed, -cat·ing.**
o′ver·lu′bri·ca′tion, *n.*
o′ver·lus′cious, *adj.;* **-ly,** *adv.;* **-ness,** *n.*
o′ver·lush′, *adj.;* **-ly,** *adv.;* **-ness,** *n.*
o′ver·lux·u′ri·ance, *n.*
o′ver·lux·u′ri·an·cy, *n.*
o′ver·lux·u′ri·ant, *adj.;* **-ly,** *adv.*
o′ver·lux·u′ri·ous, *adj.;* **-ly,** *adv.;* **-ness,** *n.*
o′ver·mag·net′ic, *adj.*
o′ver·mag·net′i·cal·ly, *adv.*
o′ver·mag′ni·fi·ca′tion, *n.*
o′ver·mag′ni·fy′, *v.t.,* **-fied, -fy·ing.**
o′ver·mag′ni·tude′, *n.*
o′ver·man′age, *v.t.,* **-aged, -ag·ing.**
o′ver·man′y, *adj.*
o′ver·march′, *v.*
o′ver·mas′ter·ful, *adj.;* **-ly,** *adv.;* **-ness,** *n.*
o′ver·ma·ture′, *adj.;* **-ly,** *adv.;* **-ness,** *n.*
o′ver·mean′, *adj.;* **-ly,** *adv.;* **-ness,** *n.*
o′ver·med′dle, *v.i.,* **-dled, -dling.**
o′ver·meek′, *adj.;* **-ly,** *adv.;* **-ness,** *n.*
o′ver·mel′low, *adj.;* **-ly,** *adv.;* **-ness,** *n.*
o′ver·me·lo′di·ous, *adj.;* **-ly,** *adv.;* **-ness,** *n.*
o′ver·melt′, *v.*
o′ver·mer′ci·ful, *adj.;* **-ly,** *adv.;* **-ness,** *n.*
o′ver·mer′it, *v.*
o′ver·mer′ri·ly, *adv.*
o′ver·mer′ri·ment, *n.*
o′ver·mer′ri·ness, *n.*
o′ver·mer′ry, *adj.*
o′ver·met′tled, *adj.*
o′ver·might′y, *adj.*
o′ver·mild′, *adj.*
o′ver·mil′i·ta·ris′tic, *adj.*
o′ver·mil′i·ta·ris′ti·cal·ly, *adv.*
o′ver·mill′, *v.t.*
o′ver·mi·nute′, *adj.;* **-ly,** *adv.;* **-ness,** *n.*
o′ver·mit′i·gate′, *v.,* **-gat·ed, -gat·ing.**
o′ver·mix′, *v.*
o′ver·mo′bi·lize′, *v.,* **-lized, -liz·ing.**
o′ver·mod′ern·i·za′tion, *n.*
o′ver·mod′ern·ize′, *v.,* **-ized, -iz·ing.**
o′ver·mod′i·fi·ca′tion, *n.*
o′ver·mod′i·fy′, *v.,* **-fied, -fy·ing.**
o′ver·moist′, *adj.*
o′ver·mois′ten, *v.*
o′ver·mo·nop′o·lize′, *v.t.,* **-lized, -liz·ing.**
o′ver·mor′al, *adj.;* **-ly,** *adv.*
o′ver·mor′al·is′tic, *adj.*
o′ver·mor′al·ize′, *v.,* **-ized, -iz·ing.**
o′ver·mor′al·iz′ing·ly, *adv.*
o′ver·mort′gage, *v.,* **-gaged, -gag·ing.**
o′ver·mourn′, *v.*
o′ver·mourn′ful, *adj.;* **-ly,** *adv.;* **-ness,** *n.*

o·ver·nice (ō′vər nīs′), *adj.* excessively nice; too fastidious: *overnice tastes; unhampered by overnice manners.* [ME; see OVER-, NICE] —**o′ver·nice′ly,** *adv.* —**o′ver·nice′ness,** *n.*

o·ver·night (*adv.* ō′vər nīt′; *adj., n.* ō′vər nīt′), *adv.* **1.** for or during the night: *to stay overnight.* **2.** on the previous evening: *Preparations were made overnight.* **3.** very quickly; suddenly: *new suburbs sprang up overnight.* —*adj.* **4.** done, occurring, or continuing during the night: *an overnight stop.* **5.** staying for one night: *a group of overnight guests.* **6.** designed to be used on a trip or for a journey lasting one night or a very few nights: *an overnight bag containing an extra shirt and sundries.* **7.** valid for one night: *The corporal got an overnight pass.* **8.** of or pertaining to the previous evening: *an overnight decision.* **9.** occurring suddenly or within a very short time: *a comedian who became an overnight sensation.* —*n.* **10.** *Informal.* a permit for overnight absence, as from a college dormitory: *She had an overnight the night of the prom.* **11.** *Archaic.* the previous evening. [ME; see OVER-, NIGHT]

o·ver·op·ti·mism (ō′vər op′tə miz′əm), *n.* excessive or unfounded optimism. [OVER- + OPTIMISM] —**o′ver·op′ti·mist,** *n.* —**o′ver·op′ti·mis′tic,** *adj.* —**o′ver·op′ti·mis′ti·cal·ly,** *adv.*

o·ver·or·gan·i·za·tion (ō′vər ôr′gə ni zā′shən), *n.* emphasis on status, rules, and details in an organization at the expense of purpose or function. [OVER- + ORGANIZATION]

o·ver·or·gan·ize (ō′vər ôr′gə nīz′), *v.t.,* **-ized, -iz·ing.** —*v.t.* **1.** to stress status, rules, and details excessively. —*v.i.* **2.** to become overorganized. [OVER- + ORGANIZE] —**o′ver·or′gan·iz′er,** *n.*

o·ver·pass (*n.* ō′vər pas′, -päs′; *v.* ō′vər pas′, -päs′), *n., v.,* **-passed** or **-past, -pass·ing.** —*n.* **1.** a highway or railway bridge crossing some barrier, as another highway or railroad tracks. —*v.t.* **2.** to pass over or traverse (a region, space, etc.): *We had overpassed the frontier during the night.* **3.** to pass beyond (specified limits, bounds, etc.); exceed; overstep; transgress: *to overpass the bounds of good judgment.* **4.** to get over (obstacles, difficulties, etc.); surmount: *to overpass the early days of privation and uncertainty.* **5.** to go beyond, exceed, or surpass: *Greed had somehow overpassed humanitarianism.* **6.** to pass through (time, experiences, etc.): *to overpass one's apprenticeship.* **7.** to overlook; disregard; omit: *We could hardly overpass such grievous faults. The board overpassed him when promotions were awarded.* —*v.i.* **8.** to pass over; pass by: *Under the bridge there was the din of cars overpassing.* [ME; see OVER-, PASS]

o·ver·pay (ō′vər pā′), *v.t.,* **-paid, -pay·ing.** **1.** to pay more than (an amount due): *I received a credit after overpaying the bill.* **2.** to pay (a person) in excess: *We were certain we had overpaid him for helping us.* [OVER- + PAY¹] —**o·ver·pay·ment** (ō′vər pā′mənt, ō′vər-pā′mənt), *n.*

o·ver·peo·ple (ō′vər pē′pəl), *v.t.,* **-pled, -pling.** to overpopulate: *The town has been overpeopled by those leaving the farms.* [OVER- + PEOPLE]

o·ver·per·suade (ō′vər pər swād′), *v.t.,* **-suad·ed, -suad·ing.** **1.** to persuade (a person) against his inclination or intention: *By threats and taunts they had overpersuaded him to steal the car.* **2.** to bring over by persuasion: *She had overpersuaded him to renounce his bachelorhood.* [OVER- + PERSUADE] —**o′ver·per·sua′sion,** *n.*

o·ver·play (ō′vər plā′), *v.t.* **1.** to exaggerate or overemphasize (one's performance in a play, an emotion, an effect, etc.): *The young actor overplayed his role shamelessly. The director of the movie had overplayed the pathos.* **2.** to overstress the value or importance of: *A charitable biographer had overplayed the man's piety and benevolence.* **3.** *Archaic.* outplay. —*v.i.* **4.** to exaggerate one's part, an effect, etc.; overact: *Without a firm director she invariably overplays.* **5.** *Golf.* to hit (the ball) past the putting green. [OVER- + PLAY]

o·ver·plus (ō′vər plus′), *n.* an excess over a particular amount; surplus: *After the harvest the overplus was distributed among the tenantry. We have an overplus of chiefs but no Indians.* [ME; partial trans. of OF *surplus* SURPLUS]

o·ver·pop·u·late (ō′vər pop′yə lāt′), *v.t.,* **-lat·ed, -lat·ing.** to fill with an excessive number of people: *Expanding industry has overpopulated the western suburbs.* [OVER- + POPULATE] —**o′ver·pop′u·la′tion,** *n.*

o·ver·po·ten·tial (ō′vər pə ten′shəl), *n. Elect.* overvoltage. [OVER- + POTENTIAL]

o·ver·pow·er (ō′vər pou′ər), *v.t.* **1.** to overcome or overwhelm in feeling; affect or impress excessively: *We were overpowered with joy at her good fortune.* **2.** to overcome, master, or subdue by superior force: *to overpower a maniac.* **3.** to overmaster the bodily powers or mental faculties of: *a strong drink that had quickly overpowered him.* **4.** to furnish or equip with excessive power: *a giant motor that had overpowered the machine.* [OVER- + POWER]
—**Syn. 2.** vanish, subjugate, conquer, defeat, beat.

o·ver·pow·er·ing (ō′vər pou′ər ing), *adj.* that overpowers; overwhelming: *an overpowering conviction of the truth.* [OVERPOWER + -ING²] —**o′ver·pow′er·ing·ly,** *adv.* —**o′ver·pow′er·ing·ness,** *n.*

o·ver·praise (ō′vər prāz′), *v.,* **-praised, -prais·ing,** *n.* —*v.t.* **1.** to praise excessively or unduly. —*n.* **2.** excessive or undeserved praise. [ME; see OVER-, PRAISE]

o·ver·print (*v.* ō′vər print′; *n.* ō′vər print′), *v.t.* **1.** *Print.* to print additional material or another color on a form or sheet previously printed. —*n.* **2.** *Print.* a quantity of printing in excess of that desired; overrun. **3.** *Philately.* **a.** any word, inscription, or device written or printed on the face of a stamp which alters, limits, or describes its use, place of issue, or character. **b.** a stamp so marked. [OVER- + PRINT]

o·ver·prize (ō′vər prīz′), *v.t.,* **-prized, -priz·ing.** to prize too highly; overvalue: *One cannot overprize honor.* [OVER- + PRIZE²] —**o′ver·priz′er,** *n.*

o·ver·pro·duce (ō′vər prə do͞os′, -dyo͞os′), *v.t., v.i.,* **-duced, -duc·ing.** to produce in excess of demand or of a stipulated amount. [OVER- + PRODUCE]

o·ver·pro·duc·tion (ō′vər prə duk′shən), *n.* excessive production; production in excess of the demand. [OVER- + PRODUCTION]

o·ver·pro·nounce (ō′vər prə nouns′), *v.,* **-nounced, -nounc·ing.** —*v.t.* **1.** to pronounce (a word, syllable, etc.) in an exaggerated, affected, or overcareful manner: *In overpronouncing individual words, one loses the important stress in the sentence.* —*v.i.* **2.** to pronounce or speak overcarefully, affectedly, exaggeratedly, etc.: *When he overpronounces that way, he seems to be patronizing his audience.* [OVER- + PRONOUNCE] —**o·ver·pro·nun·ci·a·tion** (ō′vər prə nun′sē ā′shən), *n.*

o·ver·proof (ō′vər pro͞of′), *adj.* containing a greater proportion of alcohol than proof spirit does. [OVER- + PROOF]

o·ver·pro·por·tion (*v.* ō′vər prə pôr′shən, -pōr′-; *n.* ō′vər prə pôr′shən, -pōr′-), *v.t.* **1.** to make or measure in excess of the true or desired proportion. —*n.* **2.** the excessiveness of something in relation to another or to what is considered correct, desirable, or normal: *the overproportion of expenditure to savings.* [OVER- + PROPORTION] —**o′ver·pro·por′tion·ate,** *adj.* —**o′ver·pro·por′tion·ate·ly,** *adv.* —**o′ver·pro·por′tioned,** *adj.*

o·ver·proud (ō′vər proud′), *adj.* excessively proud: *He is a man overproud of his success.* [ME *over prowde,* OE *ofer-prūt.* See OVER-, PROUD] —**o′ver·proud′ly,** *adv.*

o·ver·quick (ō′vər kwik′), *adj.* excessively quick: *She is overquick to criticize.* [OVER- + QUICK] —**o′ver·quick′ly,** *adv.*

o·ver·rake (ō′vər rāk′), *v.t.,* **-raked, -rak·ing.** *Naut.* (of water) to break over the bow of (a vessel) in a solid mass. [OVER- + RAKE¹]

o·ver·ran (ō′vər ran′), *v.* pt. of **overrun.**

o·ver·rate (ō′vər rāt′), *v.t.,* **-rat·ed, -rat·ing.** to rate too highly; overestimate: *I think you overrate his political influence.* [OVER- + RATE¹]

o·ver·reach (ō′vər rēch′), *v.t.* **1.** to reach or extend over or beyond: *The shelf overreached the nook and had to be planed down.* **2.** to reach for or aim at but go beyond, as a thing sought, a mark, etc.: *an arrow that had overreached the target.* **3.** to stretch to excess, as by a straining effort: *to overreach one's arm and strain a muscle.* **4.** to defeat (oneself) by overdoing matters, often by excessive eagerness or cunning: *In trying to promote disunity he had overreached himself.* **5.** to strain or exert (oneself or itself) to the point of exceeding the purpose. **6.** to get the better of, esp. by deceit or trickery; outwit: *Every time you deal with them you wonder if they're overreaching you.* **7.** *Obs.* to overtake; overpower. —*v.i.* **8.** to reach or extend over something. **9.** to reach too far: *In grabbing for the rope he overreached and fell.* **10.** to cheat others. **11.** (of a horse) to strike, or strike and injure, the forefoot with the hind foot. **12.** *Naut.* to sail on a tack longer than is desirable or was intended; overstand. [ME; see OVER-, REACH]

o·ver·re·fine (ō′vər ri fīn′), *v.t.,* **-fined, -fin·ing.** to refine excessively, as with oversubtle distinctions. [OVER- + REFINE]

o·ver·re·fine·ment (ō′vər ri fīn′mənt), *n.* excessive or unnecessary refinement. [OVER- + REFINEMENT]

o·ver·ride (*v.* ō′vər rīd′; *n.* ō′vər rīd′), *v.* **-rode, -rid·den, -rid·ing,** *n.* —*v.t.* **1.** to trample or crush by riding over: *to override an enemy position.* **2.** to assert one's will, authority, etc., in disregard of: *to override one's advisers.* **3.** to prevail over: *a decision that overrides all previous decisions.* **4.** to ride (a horse) too much: exhaust by excessive riding. **5.** *Fox Hunting.* to ride too closely behind (the hounds). **6.** to pass or extend over: *the glacier that once overrode the plain.* **7.** *Surg.* to overlap, as one piece of a fractured bone over another. —*n.* **8.** a commission, as that paid on sales or profits: *His yearly override exceeds his salary.* **9.** a manually applied, auxiliary device for supplementing or correcting the operation of an automatic device. [ME *override(n),* OE *oferrīdan.* See OVER-, RIDE]

o·ver·rid·ing (ō′vər rī′ding), *adj.* taking precedence over all other considerations. [OVERRIDE + -ING²]

o·ver·ripe (ō′vər rīp′), *adj.* too ripe; more than ripe: *overripe tomatoes.* [OVER- + RIPE¹] —**o′ver·ripe′ly,** *adv.* —**o′ver·ripe′ness,** *n.*

o′ver·mul′ti·pli·ca′tion, *n.*
o′ver·mul′ti·ply′, *v.,* **-plied, -ply·ing.**
o′ver·mys′ti·fi·ca′tion, *n.*
o′ver·mys′ti·fy′, *v.t.,* **-fied, -fy·ing.**
o′ver·nar′row, *adj.;* **-ly,** *adv.;* **-ness,** *n.*
o′ver·na′tion·al·i·za′tion, *n.*
o′ver·na′tion·al·ize′, *v.t.,* **-ized, -iz·ing.**
o′ver·near′, *adj., adv.;* **-ness,** *n.*
o′ver·neat′, *adj.;* **-ly,** *adv.;* **-ness,** *n.*
o′ver·neg·lect′, *v.t.*
o′ver·neg·lect′ful, *adj.;* **-ly,** *adv.;* **-ness,** *n.*
o′ver·neg′li·gence, *n.*
o′ver·neg′li·gent, *adj.;* **-ly,** *adv.;* **-ness,** *n.*
o′ver·ner′vous, *adj.;* **-ly,** *adv.;* **-ness,** *n.*
o′ver·neu′tral·i·za′tion, *n.*
o′ver·neu′tral·ize′, *v.t.,* **-ized, -iz·ing.**
o′ver·neu′tral·iz′er, *n.*
o′ver·ni′ce·ty, *n., pl.* **-ties.**
o′ver·no′ble, *adj.;* **-ble·ness,** *n.;* **-bly,** *adv.*
o′ver·nor′mal, *adj.;* **-ly,** *adv.*
o′ver·nor·mal′i·ty, *n.*
o′ver·nor′mal·i·za′tion, *n.*
o′ver·nor′mal·ize′, *v.t.,* **-ized, -iz·ing.**
o′ver·nour′ish, *v.t.*
o′ver·nour′ish·ing·ly, *adv.*
o′ver·nour′ish·ment, *n.*
o′ver·nu′mer·ous, *adj.;* **-ly,** *adv.;* **-ness,** *n.*
o′ver·nurse′, *v.t.,* **-nursed, -nurs·ing.**
o′ver·o·be′di·ence, *n.*
o′ver·o·be′di·ent, *adj.;* **-ly,** *adv.*
o′ver·o·bese′, *adj.;* **-ly,** *adv.;* **-ness,** *n.*
o′ver·o·bes′i·ty, *n.*
o′ver·ob·ject′, *v.*
o′ver·ob·jec′ti·fi·ca′tion, *n.*
o′ver·ob·jec′ti·fy′, *v.t.,* **-fied, -fy·ing.**
o′ver·ob·se′qui·ous, *adj.;* **-ly,** *adv.;* **-ness,** *n.*
o′ver·of·fend′, *v.t.*
o′ver·of·fen′sive, *adj.;* **-ly,** *adv.;* **-ness,** *n.*
o′ver·of·fi′cious, *adj.;* **-ly,** *adv.;* **-ness,** *n.*
o′ver·or′na·ment′, *v.t.*
o′ver·or′na·men′tal, *adj.;* **-ly,** *adv.*
o′ver·or′na·men·tal′i·ty, *n.*
o′ver·ox′i·di·za′tion, *n.*
o′ver·ox′i·dize′, *v.,* **-dized, -diz·ing.**
o′ver·pack′, *v.*
o′ver·pained′, *adj.*
o′ver·pain′ful, *adj.;* **-ly,** *adv.;* **-ness,** *n.*
o′ver·pam′per, *v.t.*
o′ver·park′, *v.*
o′ver·par′tial, *adj.;* **-ly,** *adv.;* **-ness,** *n.*
o′ver·par′ti·al′i·ty, *n.*
o′ver·par·tic′u·lar, *adj.;* **-ly,** *adv.;* **-ness,** *n.*
o′ver·pas′sion·ate, *adj.;* **-ly,** *adv.;* **-ness,** *n.*
o′ver·pa′tient, *adj.*
o′ver·pa′tri·ot′ic, *adj.*
o′ver·pa′tri·ot′i·cal·ly, *adv.*
o′ver·pa′tri·ot·ism, *n.*
o′ver·pe′nal·i·za′tion, *n.*
o′ver·pe′nal·ize′, *v.t.,* **-ized, -iz·ing.**
o′ver·pen′sive, *adj.;* **-ly,** *adv.;* **-ness,** *n.*
o′ver·per·emp′to·ri·ly, *adv.*
o′ver·per·emp′to·ri·ness, *n.*
o′ver·per·emp′to·ry, *adj.*
o′ver·per′se·cute′, *v.t.,* **-cut·ed, -cut·ing.**
o′ver·pes′si·mism, *n.*
o′ver·pes′si·mis′tic, *adj.*
o′ver·pes′si·mis′ti·cal·ly, *adv.*
o′ver·pet′, *v.t.*
o′ver·phi·los′o·phize′, *v.i.,* **-phized, -phiz·ing.**
o′ver·pic·to′ri·al·ize′, *v.,* **-ized, -iz·ing.**
o′ver·pit′e·ous, *adj.;* **-ly,** *adv.;* **-ness,** *n.*
o′ver·plain′, *adj.;* **-ly,** *adv.;* **-ness,** *n.*
o′ver·plant′, *v.t.*
o′ver·plau′si·ble, *adj.;* **-ble·ness,** *n.;* **-bly,** *adv.*
o′ver·please′, *v.,* **-pleased, -pleas·ing.**
o′ver·plen′i·tude′, *n.*
o′ver·plen′te·ous, *adj.;* **-ly,** *adv.;* **-ness,** *n.*
o′ver·plen′ti·ful, *adj.;* **-ly,** *adv.;* **-ness,** *n.*
o′ver·plen′ty, *n.*
o′ver·plow′, *v.*
o′ver·plump′, *adj.;* **-ness,** *n.*
o′ver·ply′, *v.,* **-plied, -ply·ing.**
o′ver·po·et′i·cize′, *v.,* **-cized, -ciz·ing.**
o′ver·po·lem′i·cal, *adj.;* **-ly,** *adv.;* **-ness,** *n.*
o′ver·po·lice′, *v.t.,* **-liced, -lic·ing.**
o′ver·pol′ish, *v.t.*
o′ver·pol′i·tic′, *adj.*
o′ver·po·lit′i·cal, *adj.;* **-ly,** *adv.*
o′ver·pol′li·nate′, *v.t.,* **-nat·ed, -nat·ing.**
o′ver·pon′der·ous, *adj.;* **-ly,** *adv.;* **-ness,** *n.*
o′ver·pop′u·lar, *adj.;* **-ly,** *adv.*
o′ver·pop′u·lar′i·ty, *n.*
o′ver·pop′u·lous, *adj.;* **-ly,** *adv.;* **-ness,** *n.*
o′ver·pos′i·tive, *adj.;* **-ly,** *adv.;* **-ness,** *n.*
o′ver·po′ten·cy, *n.*
o′ver·po′tent, *adj.;* **-ly,** *adv.;* **-ness,** *n.*
o′ver·pow′er·ful, *adj.;* **-ly,** *adv.;* **-ness,** *n.*
o′ver·prac′tice, *v.t.,* **-ticed, -tic·ing.**
o′ver·pre·cise′, *adj.;* **-ly,** *adv.;* **-ness,** *n.*
o′ver·pre·ci′sion, *n.*
o′ver·pre·oc′cu·pa′tion, *n.*
o′ver·pre·oc′cu·py′, *v.t.,* **-pied, -py·ing.**
o′ver·press′, *v.t.*
o′ver·pre·sump′tion, *n.*
o′ver·pre·sump′tive, *adj.;* **-ly,** *adv.;* **-ness,** *n.*
o′ver·pre·sump′tu·ous, *adj.;* **-ly,** *adv.;* **-ness,** *n.*
o′ver·price′, *v.t.,* **-priced, -pric·ing.**
o′ver·pro·cras′ti·na′tion, *n.*
o′ver·pro·fi′cien·cy, *n.*
o′ver·pro·fi′cient, *adj.;* **-ly,** *adv.*
o′ver·pro·lif′ic, *adj.;* **-ness,** *n.*
o′ver·pro·lif′i·cal·ly, *adv.*
o′ver·pro·lix′, *adj.;* **-ly,** *adv.;* **-ness,** *n.*
o′ver·pro·lix′i·ty, *n.*
o′ver·prom′i·nence, *n.*
o′ver·prom′i·nent, *adj.;* **-ly,** *adv.;* **-ness,** *n.*
o′ver·prom′ise, *v.t.,* **-ised, -is·ing.**
o′ver·prompt′, *adj.;* **-ly,** *adv.;* **-ness,** *n.*
o′ver·prone′, *adj.;* **-ness,** *n.*
o′ver·pros′per·ous, *adj.;* **-ly,** *adv.;* **-ness,** *n.*
o′ver·pro·tect′, *v.t.*
o′ver·pro·tec′tion, *n.*
o′ver·pro·tract′, *v.t.*
o′ver·pro·trac′tion, *n.*
o′ver·prove′, *v.t.,* **-proved, -prov·ing.**
o′ver·pro·vide′, *v.t.,* **-vid·ed, -vid·ing.**
o′ver·prov′i·dent, *adj.;* **-ly,** *adv.;* **-ness,** *n.*
o′ver·pro·vi′sion, *n.*
o′ver·prov′o·ca′tion, *n.*
o′ver·pro·voke′, *v.,* **-voked, -vok·ing.**
o′ver·prune′, *v.t.,* **-pruned, -prun·ing.**
o′ver·psy·chol′o·gize′, *v.,* **-gized, -giz·ing.**
o′ver·pub·lic′i·ty, *n.*
o′ver·pub′li·cize′, *v.t.,* **-cized, -ciz·ing.**
o′ver·pu′is·sant, *adj.;* **-ly,** *adv.*
o′ver·pun′ish, *v.t.*
o′ver·pun′ish·ment, *n.*
o′ver·pur′chase, *v.t.,* **-chased, -chas·ing.**
o′ver·qual′i·fi·ca′tion, *n.*
o′ver·qual′i·fy′, *v.t.,* **-fied, -fy·ing.**
o′ver·qui′et, *adj.;* **-ly,** *adv.;* **-ness,** *n.*
o′ver·rank′, *v.t., adj.;* **-ness,** *n.*
o′ver·rash′, *adj.;* **-ly,** *adv.;* **-ness,** *n.*
o′ver·ra′tion·al, *adj.;* **-ly,** *adv.*
o′ver·ra′tion·al·i·za′tion, *n.*
o′ver·ra′tion·al·ize′, *v.,* **-ized, -iz·ing.**
o′ver·re·act′, *v.*
o′ver·re·ac′tion, *n.*
o′ver·re·ac′tive, *adj.*
o′ver·read′i·ly, *adv.*
o′ver·read′i·ness, *n.*
o′ver·read′y, *adj.*
o′ver·re′al·ism, *n.*
o′ver·re′al·is′tic, *adj.*
o′ver·re′al·is′ti·cal·ly, *adv.*
o′ver·re·duce′, *v.,* **-duced, -duc·ing.**
o′ver·re·duc′tion, *n.*
o′ver·re·flec′tion, *n.*
o′ver·re·flec′tive, *adj.;* **-ly,** *adv.;* **-ness,** *n.*
o′ver·reg′i·ment′, *v.t.*
o′ver·reg′i·men·ta′tion, *n.*
o′ver·reg′u·late′, *v.,* **-lat·ed, -lat·ing.**
o′ver·reg′u·la′tion, *n.*
o′ver·re·lax′, *v.*
o′ver·re·li′ance, *n.*
o′ver·re·li′ant, *adj.*
o′ver·re·li′gi·os′i·ty, *n.*
o′ver·re·li′gious, *adj.;* **-ly,** *adv.;* **-ness,** *n.*
o′ver·re·miss′, *adj.;* **-ly,** *adv.;* **-ness,** *n.*
o′ver·rep′re·sent′, *v.t.*
o′ver·rep′re·sen·ta′tion, *n.*
o′ver·rep′re·sent′a·tive, *adj.;* **-ly,** *adv.;* **-ness,** *n.*
o′ver·re·press′, *v.t.*
o′ver·rep′ri·mand′, *v.t.*
o′ver·re·served′, *adj.*
o′ver·re·serv′ed·ly, *adv.*
o′ver·re·serv′ed·ness, *n.*
o′ver·re·sist′, *v.*
o′ver·res′o·lute′, *adj.;* **-ly,** *adv.;* **-ness,** *n.*
o′ver·re·strain′, *v.t.*
o′ver·re·straint′, *adj.*
o′ver·re·strict′, *v.t.*
o′ver·re·stric′tion, *n.*
o′ver·re·ten′tion, *n.*
o′ver·re·ward′, *v.*
o′ver·rich′, *adj.;* **-ly,** *adv.;* **-ness,** *n.*
o′ver·rife′, *adj.*
o′ver·rigged′, *adj.*
o′ver·right′eous, *adj.;* **-ly,** *adv.;* **-ness,** *n.*
o′ver·rig′id, *adj.;* **-ly,** *adv.;* **-ness,** *n.*
o′ver·ri·gid′i·ty, *n.*
o′ver·rig′or·ous, *adj.;* **-ly,** *adv.;* **-ness,** *n.*

o·ver·ruff (*v.* ō′vər ruf′; *n.* ō′vər ruf′), *Cards.* —*v.t., v.i.* **1.** to overtrump. —*n.* **2.** the act of overtrumping. [OVER- + RUFF²]

o·ver·rule (ō′vər ro͞ol′), *v.t.*, **-ruled, -rul·ing. 1.** to rule against or disallow the arguments of (a person): *The senator was overruled by the committee chairman.* **2.** to rule or decide against (a plea, argument, etc.); disallow: *to overrule an objection.* **3.** to prevail over so as to change the purpose or action: *a delay that overruled our plans.* **4.** to exercise rule or influence over: *belief in a beneficent deity that overrules the universe.* [OVER- + RULE] —**o′ver·rul′er,** *n.* —**o′ver·rul′ing·ly,** *adv.*

o·ver·run (*v.* ō′vər run′; *n.* ō′vər run′), *v.*, **-ran, -run, -run·ning,** *n.* —*v.t.* **1.** to rove over (a country, region, etc.); invade; ravage: *a time when looting hordes had overrun the province.* **2.** to swarm over in great numbers, as animals, esp. vermin: *The house had been overrun by rats.* **3.** to spread or grow rapidly over, as plants, esp. vines, weeds, etc.: *a garden overrun with weeds.* **4.** to attack and defeat decisively; overwhelm; crush: *Wellington overran Napoleon's army at Waterloo.* **5.** to spread rapidly throughout, as a new idea, spirit, etc.: *a rekindling of scholarship that had overrun Europe.* **6.** to run beyond: *The new jet had overrun the landing field.* **7.** to exceed: *to overrun one's allotted time.* **8.** to run over; overflow: *During the flood season, the river overruns its banks for several miles.* **9.** *Print.* to print copies of (a book, brochure, etc.) in excess of those ordered. **10.** *Print.* to print additional copies of (a magazine, special article, etc.) so as to meet an abnormally heavy demand: *We overran a million copies of the memorial issue.* **11.** *Naut.* **a.** to sail past (an intended stopping or turning point) by accident. **b.** (of a vessel) to complete (a schedule of calls) more rapidly than anticipated. **12.** *Archaic.* to outrun; overtake in running. —*v.i.* **13.** to run over; overflow: *a stream that always overruns at springtime.* **14.** to exceed the proper, desired, or normal limit: *If he overran, he knew he would be cut off the air. Do you want to overrun on this next issue?* —*n.* **15.** the act or an instance of overrunning. **16.** an amount in excess; surplus: *an overrun of 10,000 copies of a new book.* [ME *overrin(en),* OE *oferyrnan.* See OVER-, RUN]

o·ver·score (ō′vər skōr′, -skôr′), *v.t.*, **-scored, -scor·ing.** to score over, as with strokes or lines. [OVER- + SCORE]

o·ver·scru·pu·lous (ō′vər skro͞o′pyə ləs), *adj.* excessively scrupulous: *overscrupulous about details.* [OVER- + SCRUPULOUS] —**o′ver·scru′pu·lous·ly,** *adv.* —**o′ver·scru′pu·lous·ness,** *n.*

o·ver·seas (*adv., n.* ō′vər sēz′; *adj.* ō′vər sēz′), *adv.* **1.** over, across, or beyond the sea; abroad: *to be sent overseas.* —*adj.* **2.** of or pertaining to passage over the sea: *overseas travel.* **3.** situated beyond the sea: *overseas territories.* **4.** pertaining to countries beyond the sea: *overseas military service; overseas commitments.* —*n.* **5.** (*construed as sing.*) countries or territories across the sea; foreign lands: *He just got back from overseas.* Also, *esp. Brit.,* **o·ver·sea** (*adv.* ō′vər sē′; *adj.* ō′vər sē′) (for defs. 1-4). [late ME *over see,* OE *ofersǣwisc* (see OVER-, SEA) + -S³]

overseas′ cap′, *U.S. Mil.* a wedge-shaped cap of cotton or woolen fabric, worn as part of the service uniform. Also called **garrison cap.**

o·ver·see (ō′vər sē′), *v.t.*, **-saw, -seen, -see·ing. 1.** to direct (work or workers); supervise; manage: *He was hired to oversee the construction crews.* **2.** to see or observe secretly or unintentionally: *He happened to oversee the burglar leaving the premises. He was overseen stealing the letters.* **3.** *Archaic.* to survey or watch, as from a higher position. **4.** *Archaic.* to look over; inspect. [ME *oversee(n),* OE *ofersēon.* See OVER-, SEE¹]

o·ver·se·er (ō′vər sē′ər, -sēr′), *n.* **1.** a person who oversees; supervisor: *the overseer of a plantation.* **2.** (in Britain) a minor parish official, appointed annually, who performs various administrative details and is in charge of relief to the poor. [ME; see OVERSEE, -ER¹]

o·ver·sell (ō′vər sel′), *v.*, **-sold, -sell·ing.** —*v.t.* **1.** to sell more of (a stock, product, etc.) than can be delivered. **2.** to sell aggressively, as by using high-pressure merchandising techniques. **3.** to emphasize the good points of excessively: *She so oversold the picnic that I became convinced I'd have a better time at the movies.* —*v.i.* **4.** to sell something aggressively. **5.** to make extreme claims for something or someone. [OVER- + SELL¹]

o·ver·sen·si·tive (ō′vər sen′si tiv), *adj.* excessively or unduly sensitive: *oversensitive to noise.* [OVER- + SENSITIVE] —**o′ver·sen′si·tiv′i·ty, o′ver·sen′si·tive·ness,** *n.*

o·ver·set (*v.* ō′vər set′; *n.* ō′vər set′), *v.*, **-set, -set·ting,** *n.* —*v.t.* **1.** to upset or overturn; overthrow. **2.** to throw into confusion; disorder physically or mentally. —*v.i.* **3.** to become upset, overturned, or overthrown. **4.** *Print.* **a.** (of type or copy) to set in or to excess. **b.** (of space) to set too much type for. —*n.* **5.** the act or fact of oversetting; an upset or overturn. **6.** Also called **overmatter.** *Print.* matter set up in excess of space. [ME; see OVER-, SET] —**o′ver·set′ter,** *n.*

o·ver·sew (ō′vər sō′, ō′vər sō′), *v.t.*, **-sewed, -sewn** or **-sewed, -sew·ing.** to sew with stitches passing successively over an edge, esp. closely, so as to cover the edge or make a firm seam. [OVER- + SEW¹]

o·ver·shade (ō′vər shād′), *v.t.*, **-shad·ed, -shad·ing. 1.** to cast shade over. **2.** to make dark or gloomy. [OE *ofer sceadth* (ptp.). See OVER-, SHADE]

o·ver·shad·ow (ō′vər shad′ō), *v.t.* **1.** to diminish the importance of, or render insignificant in comparison: *For years he was overshadowed by his illustrious father.* **2.** to cast a shadow over; cover with shadows, clouds, darkness, etc.: *clouds overshadowing the moon.* **3.** to make dark or gloomy: *a disappointment that overshadowed his last years.* **4.** *Archaic.* to shelter or protect. [ME *overschadew(en),* OE *ofersceadwian.* See OVER-, SHADOW] —**o′ver·shad′ow·er,** *n.* —**o′ver·shad′ow·ing·ly,** *adv.*

o·ver·sharp (ō′vər shärp′), *adj.* excessively sharp: *an oversharp wit.* [late ME; see OVER-, SHARP]

o·ver·shine (ō′vər shīn′), *v.t.*, **-shone** or **-shined, -shin·ing. 1.** to outshine: *One star seemed to overshine all others.* **2.** to surpass in splendor, excellence, etc.: *Her singing overshone that of the opera company's more widely known contraltos.* **3.** *Archaic.* to shine over or upon. [OE *oferscīn(an).* See OVER-, SHINE]

o·ver·shirt (ō′vər shûrt′), *n.* a pull-over sport shirt, worn outside the waistband of a skirt or pair of slacks. [OVER- + SHIRT]

o·ver·shoe (ō′vər sho͞o′), *n.* a shoe or boot usually worn over another and intended for protection against wet or cold weather, esp. a waterproof outer shoe of rubber. [OVER- + SHOE]

o·ver·shoot (ō′vər sho͞ot′), *v.*, **-shot, -shoot·ing.** —*v.t.* **1.** to shoot or go over, beyond, or above; miss: *The missile overshot its target; to overshoot the enemy's defenses.* **2.** to pass or go by or beyond (a point, limit, etc.): *to overshoot a stop sign.* **3.** to shoot or pour down over: *turbulent water overshooting the falls; power provided when the stream overshoots a water wheel.* **4.** to overreach (oneself or itself); go further than is intended or proper; go too far: *It looked as though his self-confidence had overshot itself.* **5.** *Aeron.* (of an aircraft or pilot) to fly too far along a landing strip in attempting to land. —*v.i.* **6.** to fly or go beyond. **7.** to shoot over or above a mark. [ME; see OVER-, SHOOT]

o·ver·shot (ō′vər shot′), *adj.* **1.** driven over the top of, as by water passing over from above. **2.** having the upper jaw projecting beyond the lower, as a dog. —*v.* **3.** pt. and pp. of **overshoot.**

o′vershot wheel′, a water wheel in which the water enters the buckets tangentially near the top of the wheel.

Overshot wheel

o·ver·side (ō′vər sīd′), *adv.* **1.** over the side, as of a ship. **2.** on the opposite side (of a phonograph record): *Overside we are given an example of early Ellington.* —*adj.* **3.** effected over the side of a vessel: *overside delivery of cargo.* **4.** placed or located on the opposite side (of a phonograph record): *The overside selections are more agreeably sung.* —*n.* **5.** the opposite side (of a phonograph record): *On the overside we have a potpourri of Strauss waltzes.* [short for *over the side*]

o·ver·sight (ō′vər sīt′), *n.* **1.** failure to notice or consider: *Owing to my oversight, the letter was sent unsigned.* **2.** an omission or error due to carelessness: *My bank statement is full of oversights.* **3.** supervision; watchful care: *a man responsible for the oversight of the organization.* [ME; see OVER-, SIGHT]
—**Syn. 1.** lapse, neglect, inattention. **1, 2.** mistake, blunder, slip. **2.** erratum. **3.** management, direction, control; surveillance.

o·ver·size (*adj.* ō′vər sīz′; *n.* ō′vər sīz′), *adj.* Also, **o′ver·sized′. 1.** of excessive size; unusually large: *a man smoking an oversize cigar.* **2.** of a size larger than is necessary or required. —*n.* **3.** something that is oversize; an oversize article or object. **4.** a size larger than the proper or usual size. [OVER- + SIZE¹]

o·ver·skirt (ō′vər skûrt′), *n.* **1.** an outer skirt. **2.** a skirt worn over the skirt of a dress and caught up or draped to reveal it. [OVER- + SKIRT]

o·ver·slaugh (ō′vər slô′), *v.t.* to pass over or disregard (a person) by giving a promotion, position, etc., due him to another. [< D *overslag,* akin to *overslaan* to pass over, omit]

o·ver·sleep (ō′vər slēp′), *v.*, **-slept, -sleep·ing.** —*v.i.* **1.** to sleep beyond the proper time of waking: *He overslept and missed his train.* —*v.t.* **2.** to sleep beyond (a certain hour): *She had overslept her usual time of arising.* **3.** to let (oneself) sleep past the hour of arising: *Of all mornings to oversleep herself!* [ME; see OVER-, SLEEP]

o·ver·slip (ō′vər slip′), *v.t.*, **-slipped** or **-slipt, -slip·ping.** *Obs.* **1.** to leave out; miss. **2.** to elude; evade. [late ME; see OVER-, SLIP¹]

o·ver·sold (ō′vər sōld′), *v.* **1.** pt. and pp. of **oversell.** —*adj.* **2.** marked by prices considered to be unjustifiably low because of extensive selling: *oversold market.* Cf. **overbought.**

o·ver·so·lic·i·tous (ō′vər sə lis′i təs), *adj.* too solicitous: *oversolicitous concerning one's health.* [OVER- + SOLICITOUS]

o·ver·soul (ō′vər sōl′), *n.* *Philos.* (esp. in transcendentalism) a supreme reality or mind; the spiritual unity of all being. [OVER- + SOUL]

o·ver·sparred (ō′vər spärd′), *adj.* *Naut.* **1.** (of a sailing vessel) having spars of excessive length or weight; overhatted. **2.** *Slang.* tipsy; drunk. [OVER- + SPAR¹ + -ED³]

o·ver·spend (ō′vər spend′), *v.*, **-spent, -spend·ing.** —*v.i.* **1.** to spend more than one can afford: *Receiving a small inheritance, she began to overspend alarmingly.* —*v.t.* **2.** to spend in excess of: *He was overspending his yearly salary by several thousand dollars.* **3.** to spend beyond one's means (used reflexively): *When the bills arrived, he realized he had foolishly overspent himself.* **4.** *Archaic.* to wear out; exhaust. [OVER- + SPEND]

o·ver·spill (*v.* ō′vər spil′; *n.* ō′vər spil′), *v.*, **-spilled** or **-spilt, -spill·ing,** *n.* —*v.i.* **1.** to spill over. —*n.* **2.** the act of spilling over. **3.** that which spills over. **4.** *Brit.* overflow. [OVER- + SPILL¹]

o·ver·spin (ō′vər spin′), *n.* See **top spin.** [OVER- + SPIN]

o·ver·spread (ō′vər spred′), *v.t.*, **-spread, -spread·ing.** to spread or diffuse over: *A blush of embarrassment overspread his face.* [ME; OE *ofersprǣdan.* See OVER-, SPREAD]

o·ver·stand (ō′vər stand′), *v.i.*, **-stood, -stand·ing.** *Naut.* overreach (def. 12). [ME; see OVER-, STAND]

o·ver·state (ō′vər stāt′), *v.t.*, **-stat·ed, -stat·ing.** to state too strongly; exaggerate: *to overstate one's position in a controversy.* [OVER- + STATE] —**o′ver·state′ment,** *n.*

o·ver·stay (ō′vər stā′), *v.t.* **1.** to stay beyond the time or duration of; outstay: *to overstay one's welcome.* **2.** *Finance Informal.* to remain in (the market) beyond the point where a sale would have yielded the greatest profit. [OVER- + STAY¹]

o·ver·stayed (ō′vər stād′), *adj.* *Naut.* **1.** (of a mast) pulled too far forward by its stays. **2.** (of a vessel) having excessively taut or heavy stays. [OVER- + STAY³ + -ED³]

o·ver·step (ō′vər step′), *v.t.*, **-stepped, -step·ping.** to step or pass over or beyond: *to overstep one's authority.* [ME *overstepp(en),* OE *ofersteppan.* See OVER-, STEP]

o·ver·stitch (*n.* ō′vər stich′; *v.* ō′vər stich′), *Sewing.* —*n.* **1.** a stitch made with a sewing machine, for binding or finishing a raw edge or hem. —*v.t., v.i.* **2.** to sew with overstitches. [OVER- + STITCH¹]

o·ver·stock (*v.* ō′vər stok′; *n.* ō′vər stok′), *v.t.* **1.** to stock to excess: *We are overstocked on this item.* —*n.* **2.** a stock in excess of need or demand. [OVER- + STOCK]

o·ver·stood (ō′vər sto͝od′), *v.* pt. and pp. of **overstand.**

o·ver·stow·age (ō′vər stō′ij), *n.* *Naut.* improper stowage of cargo so that some of the cargo is buried inaccessibly beneath other cargo that is scheduled to be discharged at a later time. [OVER- + STOWAGE]

o·ver·stowed (ō′vər stōd′), *adj.* *Naut.* (of cargo) inaccessible because of overstowage. [OVER- + STOWED]

o·ver·strain (ō′vər strān′), *v.t., v.i.* to strain to excess. [OVER- + STRAIN¹]

o·ver·stretch (ō′vər strech′), *v.t.* **1.** to stretch excessively: *to overstretch a bow.* **2.** to stretch or extend over: *We came to an old bridge overstretching the river.* [ME; see OVER-, STRETCH]

o·ver·strict (ō′vər strikt′), *adj.* excessively or unduly strict: *an overstrict schoolmaster.* [OVER- + STRICT]

o·ver·stride (ō′vər strīd′), *v.t.*, **-strode, -strid·den, -strid·ing. 1.** to surpass: *to overstride one's competitors.* **2.** to stand or sit astride of; bestride: *a great statue overstriding the entrance; to overstride a horse.* **3.** to tower

---

o′ver·rip′en, *v.*
o′ver·roast′, *v.*
o′ver·ro·man′ti·cize′, *v.*, **-cized, -ciz·ing.**
o′ver·rough′, *adj.*; **-ly,** *adv.*; **-ness,** *n.*
o′ver·rude′, *adj.*; **-ly,** *adv.*; **-ness,** *n.*
o′ver·sac′ri·fi′cial, *adj.*; **-ly,** *adv.*; **-ness,** *n.*
o′ver·sad′, *adj.*; **-ly,** *adv.*; **-ness,** *n.*
o′ver·salt′, *v.t.*
o′ver·salt′y, *adj.*
o′ver·san′guine, *adj.*; **-ly,** *adv.*; **-ness,** *n.*
o′ver·sate′, *v.t.*, **-sat·ed, -sat·ing.**
o′ver·sa·ti′e·ty, *n.*
o′ver·sat′u·rate′, *v.t.*, **-rat·ed, -rat·ing.**
o′ver·sat′u·ra′tion, *n.*
o′ver·sau′cy, *adj.*
o′ver·scent′ed, *adj.*
o′ver·scep′ti·cal, *adj.*; **-ly,** *adv.*; **-ness,** *n.*
o′ver·scep′ti·cism, *n.*
o′ver·scrub′, *v.*, **-scrubbed, -scrub·bing.**
o′ver·scru′ple, *v.*, **-pled, -pling.**
o′ver·sea′son, *v.t.*
o′ver·se·crete′, *v.t.*, **-cret·ed, -cret·ing.**
o′ver·se·cre′tion, *n.*
o′ver·se·cure′, *adj.*, *v.t.*, **-cured, -cur·ing; -ly,** *adv.*
o′ver·se·cu′ri·ty, *n.*
o′ver·se·da′tion, *n.*
o′ver·seed′, *v.*
o′ver·sen′si·ble, *adj.*; **-ble·ness,** *n.*; **-bly,** *adv.*
o′ver·sen′si·tize′, *v.*, **-tized, -tiz·ing.**
o′ver·sen′ti·men′tal, *adj.*; **-ly,** *adv.*
o′ver·sen′ti·men′tal·ism, *n.*
o′ver·sen′ti·men·tal′i·ty, *n.*
o′ver·sen′ti·men′tal·ize′, *v.*, **-ized, -iz·ing.**
o′ver·se·rene′, *adj.*; **-ly,** *adv.*
o′ver·se·ren′i·ty, *n.*
o′ver·se′ri·ous, *adj.*; **-ly,** *adv.*; **-ness,** *n.*
o′ver·ser′vile, *adj.*; **-ly,** *adv.*; **-ness,** *n.*
o′ver·ser·vil′i·ty, *n.*
o′ver·set′tle, *v.*, **-tled, -tling.**
o′ver·set′tle·ment, *n.*
o′ver·se·vere′, *adj.*; **-ly,** *adv.*; **-ness,** *n.*
o′ver·se·ver′i·ty, *n.*
o′ver·short′, *adj.*; **-ness,** *n.*
o′ver·short′en, *v.*
o′ver·shrink′, *v.*
o′ver·si′lence, *n.*
o′ver·si′lent, *adj.*; **-ly,** *adv.*; **-ness,** *n.*
o′ver·sim′ple, *adj.*; **-ple·ness,** *n.*; **-ply,** *adv.*
o′ver·sim·plic′i·ty, *n.*
o′ver·sim′pli·fi·ca′tion, *n.*
o′ver·sim′pli·fy′, *v.t.*, **-fied, -fy·ing.**
o′ver·skep′ti·cal, *adj.*; **-ly,** *adv.*; **-ness,** *n.*
o′ver·skep′ti·cism, *n.*
o′ver·slack′, *adj.*
o′ver·slav′ish, *adj.*; **-ly,** *adv.*; **-ness,** *n.*
o′ver·slight′, *adj.*
o′ver·slow′, *adj.*; **-ly,** *adv.*; **-ness,** *n.*
o′ver·smooth′, *adj.*; **-ly,** *adv.*; **-ness,** *n.*
o′ver·soak′, *v.*
o′ver·soap′, *v.t.*
o′ver·so′cial, *adj.*; **-ly,** *adv.*
o′ver·so′cial·ize′, *v.t.*, **-ized, -iz·ing.**
o′ver·soft′, *adj.*; **-ly,** *adv.*; **-ness,** *n.*
o′ver·soft′en, *v.*
o′ver·sol′emn, *adj.*; **-ly,** *adv.*; **-ness,** *n.*
o′ver·so·lem′ni·ty, *n.*
o′ver·so·lid′i·fi·ca′tion, *n.*
o′ver·so·lid′i·fy′, *v.t.*, **-fied, -fy·ing.**
o′ver·sooth′ing, *adj.*; **-ly,** *adv.*
o′ver·so·phis′ti·cat′ed, *adj.*
o′ver·so·phis′ti·ca′tion, *n.*
o′ver·sor′row·ful, *adj.*; **-ly,** *adv.*; **-ness,** *n.*
o′ver·sour′, *adj.*; **-ly,** *adv.*; **-ness,** *n.*
o′ver·spa′cious, *adj.*; **-ly,** *adv.*; **-ness,** *n.*
o′ver·spar′ing, *adj.*; **-ly,** *adv.*; **-ness,** *n.*
o′ver·spe′cial·i·za′tion, *n.*
o′ver·spe′cial·ize′, *v.*, **-ized, -iz·ing.**
o′ver·spec′u·late′, *v.i.*, **-lat·ed, -lat·ing.**
o′ver·spec′u·la′tion, *n.*
o′ver·spec′u·la′tive, *adj.*; **-ly,** *adv.*; **-ness,** *n.*
o′ver·speed′, *v.*
o′ver·speed′i·ly, *adv.*
o′ver·speed′i·ness, *n.*
o′ver·speed′y, *adj.*
o′ver·spice′, *v.*, **-spiced, -spic·ing.**
o′ver·squeam′ish, *adj.*; **-ly,** *adv.*; **-ness,** *n.*
o′ver·stale′, *adj.*; **-ly,** *adv.*; **-ness,** *n.*
o′ver·starch′, *v.*
o′ver·stead′fast, *adj.*; **-ly,** *adv.*; **-ness,** *n.*
o′ver·stead′i·ly, *adv.*
o′ver·stead′i·ness, *n.*
o′ver·stead′y, *adj.*
o′ver·steer′, *v.*
o′ver·stiff′, *adj.*; **-ly,** *adv.*; **-ness,** *n.*
o′ver·stiff′en, *v.*
o′ver·stim′u·late′, *v.*, **-lat·ed, -lat·ing.**
o′ver·stim′u·la′tion, *n.*
o′ver·stim′u·la′tive, *adj.*; **-ly,** *adv.*; **-ness,** *n.*
o′ver·stir′, *v.*, **-stirred, -stir·ring.**
o′ver·stock′ing, *n.*
o′ver·store′, *v.*, **-stored, -stor·ing.**
o′ver·stout′, *adj.*; **-ly,** *adv.*; **-ness,** *n.*
o′ver·straight′, *adj.*; **-ly,** *adv.*; **-ness,** *n.*
o′ver·straight′en, *v.*
o′ver·strength′en, *v.*
o′ver·stress′, *v.t.*

over; dominate: *He overstrides the committee with loud aggressiveness.* **4.** to stride or step over or across: *At its narrowest point, one can easily overstride the stream.* **5.** to stride more rapidly than or beyond: *a downward path where he easily overstrode his companion.* [ME; see OVER-, STRIDE]

o·ver·strike (*v.* ō′vər strīk′; *n.* ō′vər strīk′), *v.*, **-struck, -struck, -strik·ing,** *n. Numis.* —*v.t.* **1.** to stamp a new device, value, or inscription on (a coin). —*n.* **2.** a coin that has been overstruck without complete obliteration of the original design. [OVER- + STRIKE]

o·ver·string (ō′vər string′), *v.t.*, **-strung; -strung** or (*Rare*) **-stringed; -string·ing.** **1.** *Music.* to arrange the strings of (a piano) so that the bass strings cross over the treble. **2.** *Archery.* to string (a bow) too tightly. [OVER- + STRING]

o·ver·strung (ō′vər strung′), *adj.* **1.** too highly strung: *Their nerves were badly overstrung.* **2.** *Archery.* (of a bow) strung too tightly. [OVER- + STRUNG]

o·ver·stud·y (*v.* ō′vər stud′ē; *n.* ō′vər stud′ē), *v.*, **-stud·ied, -stud·y·ing,** *n.* —*v.t., v.i.* **1.** to study too much or too hard (sometimes used reflexively): *to overstudy a letter for hidden meanings; to overstudy to the point of exhaustion; He overstudied himself and forgot half of what he had read.* —*n.* **2.** excessive study. [OVER- + STUDY[1]]

o·ver·stuff (ō′vər stuf′), *v.t.* **1.** to force too much into: *If you overstuff your valise, the fastenings may not hold.* **2.** *Furniture.* to envelop completely with deep upholstery. [OVER- + STUFF]

o·ver·stuffed (ō′vər stuft′), *adj.* **1.** *Furniture.* having the entire frame covered by stuffing and upholstery, so that only decorative woodwork or the like is exposed: *an overstuffed sofa.* **2.** overlong; filled with tedious or extraneous material: *an overstuffed biography that should have been cut by half.* **3.** obese; corpulent: *an overstuffed man who was a compulsive eater.* [OVERSTUFF + -ED[2]]

o·ver·sub·scribe (ō′vər səb skrīb′), *v.t.*, **-scribed, -scrib·ing.** to subscribe for in excess of what is available or required: *The charity drive was oversubscribed by several thousand dollars.* [OVER- + SUBSCRIBE] —**o′ver·sub·scrib′er,** *n.* —**o·ver·sub·scrip·tion** (ō′vər-səb skrip′shən), *n.*

o·ver·sub·tle (ō′vər sut′əl), *adj.* excessively subtle: *an oversubtle distinction.* [OVER- + SUBTLE] —**o′ver-sub′tly,** *adv.*

o·ver·sub·tle·ty (ō′vər sut′əl tē), *n., pl.* **-ties.** **1.** excessive or unnecessary subtlety. **2.** something that is excessively subtle. **3.** an instance of oversubtlety. [OVER- + SUBTLETY]

o·ver·sup·ply (*n.* ō′vər sə plī′; *v.* ō′vər sə plī′), *n., pl.* **-plies,** *v.*, **-plied, -ply·ing.** —*n.* **1.** an excessive supply. —*v.t.* **2.** to supply in excess. [OVER- + SUPPLY[1]]

o·ver·sweet (ō′vər swēt′), *adj.* excessively sweet: *an oversweet cake.* [OVER- + SWEET] —**o′ver·sweet′ly,** *adv.* —**o′ver·sweet′ness,** *n.*

o·vert (ō vûrt′, ō′vûrt), *adj.* **1.** open to view or knowledge; not concealed or secret: *overt hostility.* **2.** *Heraldry.* (of a device, as a purse) represented as open: *a purse overt.* [ME < OF, ptp. of *ouvrir* to open < VL *ōperīre, var. of L aperīre] —**Syn. 1.** plain, manifest, apparent, public. —**Ant. 1.** private, concealed.

o·ver·take (ō′vər tāk′), *v.*, **-took, -tak·en, -tak·ing,** —*v.t.* **1.** to catch up with in traveling or in pursuit: *By taking a cab to the next town, we managed to overtake and board the train.* **2.** to catch up with or pass in any course of action: *to overtake one's backlog of work; to overtake all other countries in steel production.* **3.** to happen to or befall suddenly or unexpectedly, as death, night, a storm, etc.: *The rain overtook them near the edge of the city.* **4.** *Chiefly Brit.* to pass (another vehicle). —*v.i.* **5.** *Chiefly Brit.* to pass another vehicle: *Never overtake on a curve.* [ME; see OVER-, TAKE]

o·ver·task (ō′vər task′, -täsk′), *v.t.* to impose too heavy a task upon: *work that would overtask the hardiest constitution.* [OVER- + TASK]

o·ver·tax (ō′vər taks′), *v.t.* **1.** to tax too heavily. **2.** to make too great demands on: *I had overtaxed my strength.* [OVER- + TAX] —**o′ver·tax·a′tion,** *n.*

o′ver the coun′ter, **1.** other than on an organized securities exchange; directly to the buyer or from the seller: *He sold his stocks over the counter.* **2.** *Pharm.* without a doctor's prescription but within the law.

o·ver-the-coun·ter (ō′vər thə koun′tər), *adj.* **1.** (of stocks and securities) sold or purchased other than on an organized securities exchange; unlisted: *over-the-counter stocks; over-the-counter market.* **2.** *Pharm.* noting drugs which may be sold legally without a doctor's prescription.

o·ver·throw (*v.* ō′vər thrō′; *n.* ō′vər thrō′), *v.*, **-threw, -thrown, -throw·ing,** *n.* —*v.t.* **1.** to depose, as from a position of power; overcome, defeat, or vanquish: *to overthrow a tyrant.* **2.** to put an end to by force, as governments or institutions. **3.** to throw over; upset; overturn: *The heavy winds overthrew numerous telephone poles and trees.* **4.** to knock down and demolish. **5.** to throw (something) too far: *He overthrew the ball and they lost the game.* **6.** *Archaic.* to destroy the sound condition of (the mind). —*v.i.* **7.** to throw too far: *If he hadn't overthrown, it would have been a sure touchdown.* —*n.* **8.** the act of overthrowing; state or condition of being overthrown. **9.** deposition from power. **10.** defeat; destruction; ruin. [ME; see OVER-, THROW] —**o′ver·throw′er,** *n.* —**Syn. 1.** conquer, overpower. **4.** destroy, raze, level. **10.** fall.

o·ver·thrust (ō′vər thrust′), *n. Geol.* **1.** a thrust fault with a deep dip and a large slip. **2.** a thrust fault in which the hanging wall was the one that moved (opposed to *underthrust*). [OVER- + THRUST]

o·ver·time (*n., adv., adj.* ō′vər tīm′; *v.* ō′vər tīm′), *n., adv., adj., v.*, **-timed, -tim·ing.** —*n.* **1.** time during which one works before or after regularly scheduled working hours; extra working time. **2.** pay for such time (distinguished from *straight time*). **3.** time in excess of a prescribed period. **4.** *Sports.* an additional unit of play for deciding the winner of a game in which the contestants are tied at the end of the regular playing period. —*adv.* **5.** during extra time: *to work overtime.* —*adj.* **6.** of or pertaining to overtime: *overtime pay.* —*v.t.* **7.** to give too much time to (a photographic exposure). [OVER- + TIME]

o·ver·tire (ō′vər tīər′), *v.i., v.t.*, **-tired, -tir·ing.** to tire to the point of exhaustion; tire out: *He overtires very easily. He has overtired himself by working such long hours.* [OVER- + TIRE[1]]

o·vert·ly (ō vûrt′lē, ō′vûrt lē), *adv.* openly; publicly. [ME; see OVERT, -LY]

O·ver·ton (ō′vər tən), *n.* a boy's given name.

o·ver·tone (ō′vər tōn′), *n.* **1.** *Music.* An acoustical frequency that is higher in frequency than the fundamental. **2.** an additional, usually subsidiary and implicit, meaning or quality: *an aesthetic theory with definite political overtones.* [trans. of G *Oberton.* See OVER-, TONE]

o·ver·took (ō′vər to͝ok′), *v.* pt. of **overtake.**

o·ver·top (ō′vər top′), *v.t.*, **-topped, -top·ping.** **1.** to rise over or above the top of: *scalded by hot coffee overtopping the cup.* **2.** to rise above in authority; take precedence over; override: *No individual shall overtop the law.* **3.** to surpass or excel: *a rise in sales that overtopped everyone in the industry.* [OVER- + TOP[1]]

o·ver·trade (ō′vər trād′), *v.i.*, **-trad·ed, -trad·ing.** to trade in excess of one's capital or the requirements of the market. [OVER- + TRADE]

o·ver·train (ō′vər trān′), *v.t., v.i.* to train to excess. [OVER- + TRAIN]

o·ver·trick (ō′vər trik′), *n. Bridge.* a trick won by declarer in excess of the number of tricks necessary to make his contract. Cf. **undertrick.** [OVER- + TRICK]

o·ver·trump (ō′vər trump′, ō′vər trump′), *v.t., v.i. Cards.* to play a higher trump than has already been played. [OVER- + TRUMP[1]]

o·ver·ture (ō′vər chər, -cho͝or′), *n., v.*, **-tured, -tur·ing.** —*n.* **1.** an opening or initiating move toward negotiations, establishment of a relationship, etc.; a formal or informal proposal or offer: *overtures of peace; a shy man who rarely made overtures of friendship.* **2.** *Music.* **a.** an orchestral composition forming the prelude or introduction to an opera, oratorio, etc. **b.** an independent piece of similar character. **3.** an introductory part, as of a poem. **4.** (in Presbyterian churches) **a.** the action of an ecclesiastical court in submitting a question or proposal to presbyteries. **b.** the proposal or question so submitted. **5.** Also called **o′verture and begin′ners.** *Theat.* an act call summoning performers for the beginning of a performance. —*v.t.* **6.** to submit as an overture or proposal; make an overture or proposal to: *to overture conditions for a cease-fire; to overture one's adversary through a neutral party.* [ME < OF; see OVERT, -URE] —**Syn. 1.** See **proposal.**

o·ver·turn (*v.* ō′vər tûrn′; *n.* ō′vər tûrn′), *v.t.* **1.** to destroy the power of; overthrow; defeat; vanquish. **2.** to turn over on its side, face, or back; upset: *to overturn a vase.* —*v.i.* **3.** to turn on its side, face, or back; upset; capsize: *The boat overturned during the storm.* —*n.* **4.** the act of overturning; state of being overturned. [ME; see OVER-, TURN] —**o′ver·turn′a·ble,** *adj.* —**Syn. 1.** conquer. **2.** See **upset.**

o·ver-un·der (ō′vər un′dər), *adj.* **1.** (of double-barreled firearms) with one barrel mounted over the other. —*n.* **2.** such a firearm.

o·ver·use (*v.* ō′vər yo͞oz′; *n.* ō′vər yo͞os′), *v.*, **-used, -us·ing,** *n.* —*v.t.* **1.** to use too much or too often: *to overuse an expression.* —*n.* **2.** excessive use: *to strain one's voice through overuse.* [OVER- + USE]

o·ver·val·ue (ō′vər val′yo͞o), *v.t.*, **-ued, -u·ing.** to value too highly; put too high a value on: *He should be careful not to overvalue himself.* [OVER- + VALUE] —**o′ver·val′u·a′tion,** *n.*

o·ver·view (ō′vər vyo͞o′), *n.* a general idea or outline of a subject; an over-all impression, as of a field of activity or study; survey. [OVER- + VIEW]

o·ver·volt·age (ō′vər vōl′tij), *n.* **1.** *Elect.* excess voltage. **2.** *Physics.* the amount by which the voltage applied to an ionization chamber exceeds the Geiger-Müller threshold. [OVER- + VOLTAGE]

o·ver·watch (ō′vər woch′, -wôch′), *v.t.* **1.** to watch over. **2.** *Archaic.* to weary by keeping awake. [OVER- + WATCH] —**o′ver·watch′er,** *n.*

o·ver·wear (ō′vər wâr′), *v.t.*, **-wore, -worn, -wear·ing.** to use or wear excessively; wear out; exhaust: *a laborer overworn by toil; clothing overworn by active children; phrases overworn by repetition.* [OVER- + WEAR]

o·ver·wea·ry (*adj.* ō′vər wēr′ē; *v.* ō′vər wēr′ē), *adj., v.*, **-ried, -ry·ing.** —*adj.* **1.** excessively weary; tired out. —*v.t.* **2.** to weary to excess; overcome with weariness. [OVER- + WEARY]

o·ver·ween (ō′vər wēn′), *v.i. Archaic.* to be conceited or arrogant. [ME; see OVER-, WEEN] —**o′ver·ween′er,** *n.*

o·ver·ween·ing (ō′vər wē′ning), *adj.* **1.** (of a person) conceited, overconfident, or presumptuous: *a brash, insolent, overweening fellow.* **2.** (of opinions, pretensions, characteristics, etc.) exaggerated, excessive, or arrogant: *overweening prejudice; overweening pride.* [ME; see OVERWEEN, -ING[2]] —**o′ver·ween′ing·ly,** *adv.* —**o′ver·ween′ing·ness,** *n.*

o·ver·weigh (ō′vər wā′), *v.t.* **1.** to exceed in weight; overbalance or outweigh: *a respected opinion that overweighs the others.* **2.** to weigh down; oppress: *gloom that overweighs one's spirits.* [ME; see OVER-, WEIGH]

o·ver·weight (*n.* ō′vər wāt′; *adj.* ō′vər wāt′), *n.* **1.** extra or excess weight above what law or regulation allows, as of baggage, freight, etc.: *The overweight will cost us $12.* **2.** weight in excess of that considered normal, proper, healthful, etc.: *Her overweight has become quite a problem.* **3.** greater effect or importance; preponderance. —*adj.* **4.** weighing too much or more than is considered normal, proper, etc.: *overweight luggage; an overweight woman; two letters that may be overweight.* [OVER- + WEIGHT]

o·ver·whelm (ō′vər hwelm′, -welm′), *v.t.* **1.** to overpower, esp. with superior forces; destroy; crush: *Roman troops were overwhelmed by barbarians.* **2.** to overcome completely in mind or feeling: *overwhelmed by remorse.* **3.** to load, heap, treat, or address with an overpowering or excessive amount of anything: *a child overwhelmed with presents; to overwhelm someone with questions.* **4.** to cover or bury beneath a mass of something, as flood waters, debris, an avalanche, etc.: *Lava from erupting Vesuvius overwhelmed the city of Pompeii.* **5.** *Archaic.* to overthrow. [ME; see OVER-, WHELM]

o·ver·whelm·ing (ō′vər hwel′ming, -wel′-), *adj.* **1.** that overwhelms: *The temptation to give up may become overwhelming.* **2.** so great as to render opposition useless: *an overwhelming majority.* [OVERWHELM + -ING[2]] —**o′ver·whelm′ing·ly,** *adv.* —**o′ver·whelm′ing·ness,** *n.*

o·ver·wind (ō′vər wīnd′), *v.t.*, **-wound, -wind·ing.** to wind beyond the proper limit; wind too far: *He has a tendency to overwind his watch.* [OVER- + WIND[2]]

o·ver·win·ter (ō′vər win′tər), *v.i.* to pass the winter: *to overwinter on the Riviera.* [OVER- + WINTER; prob. trans. of Norw *overvintre*]

o·ver·wire (ō′vər wīər′), *n.* a spiral-bound book in which the spiral is covered by the spine. [OVER- + WIRE]

o·ver·wise (ō′vər wīz′), *adj.* excessively wise: *overwise for a child of his age.* [OVER- + WISE[1]]

o·ver·word (ō′vər wûrd′), *n.* a word that is repeated, as a refrain in a song. [OVER- + WORD]

o·ver·wore (ō′vər wōr′, -wôr′), *v.* pt. of **overwear.**

o·ver·work (*v.* ō′vər wûrk′; *n.* ō′vər wûrk′), *v.*, **-worked** or **-wrought, -work·ing,** *n.* —*v.t.* **1.** to cause to work too hard or too long; weary or exhaust with work (often used reflexively): *Don't overwork yourself on that new job.* **2.** to work up, stir up, or excite excessively: *to overwork a mob to the verge of frenzy.* **3.** to employ or elaborate to excess: *an appeal*

o′ver·stri′dence, *n.*
o′ver·stri′den·cy, *n.*
o′ver·stri′dent, *adj.;* **-ly,** *adv.;* **-ness,** *n.*
o′ver·strive′, *v.i.,* **-strove, -striv·en, -striv·ing.**
o′ver·strong′, *adj.;* **-ly,** *adv.;* **-ness,** *n.*
o′ver·stu′di·ous, *adj.;* **-ly,** *adv.;* **-ness,** *n.*
o′ver·suf·fi′cien·cy, *n.*
o′ver·suf·fi′cient, *adj.;* **-ly,** *adv.*
o′ver·sup′, *v.,* **-supped, -sup·ping.**
o′ver·su′per·sti′tious, *adj.;* **-ly,** *adv.;* **-ness,** *n.*
o′ver·sure′, *adj.;* **-ly,** *adv.;* **-ness,** *n.*
o′ver·sure′ty, *n.*
o′ver·sus·cep′ti·bil′i·ty, *n.*
o′ver·sus·cep′ti·ble, *adj.;* **-ble·ness,** *n.;* **-bly,** *adv.*
o′ver·sus·pi′cious, *adj.;* **-ly,** *adv.;* **-ness,** *n.*
o′ver·sys′tem·at′ic, *adj.*
o′ver·sys′tem·at′i·cal·ly, *adv.*
o′ver·sys′tem·at′i·cal·ness, *n.*
o′ver·sys′tem·a·tize′, *v.t.,* **-tized, -tiz·ing.**
o′ver·talk′a·tive, *adj.;* **-ly,** *adv.;* **-ness,** *n.*
o′ver·talk′er, *n.*
o′ver·tame′, *adj.;* **-ly,** *adv.;* **-ness,** *n.*
o′ver·tart′, *adj.;* **-ly,** *adv.;* **-ness,** *n.*
o′ver·teach′, *v.,* **-taught, -teach·ing.**
o′ver·tech′ni·cal, *adj.;* **-ly,** *adv.*
o′ver·tech′ni·cal′i·ty, *n.*
o′ver·te′di·ous, *adj.;* **-ly,** *adv.;* **-ness,** *n.*
o′ver·te·na′cious, *adj.;* **-ly,** *adv.;* **-ness,** *n.*
o′ver·te·nac′i·ty, *n.*
o′ver·ten′der, *adj.;* **-ly,** *adv.;* **-ness,** *n.*
o′ver·tense′, *adj.;* **-ly,** *adv.;* **-ness,** *n.*
o′ver·ten′sion, *n.*
o′ver·the·at′ri·cal, *adj.*
o′ver·the·at′ri·cal·ly, *adv.*
o′ver·the·at′ri·cal·ness, *n.*
o′ver·the′o·ri·za′tion, *n.*
o′ver·the′o·rize′, *v.i.,* **-rized, -riz·ing.**
o′ver·thick′, *adj.;* **-ly,** *adv.;* **-ness,** *n.*
o′ver·thin′, *adj.;* **-ly,** *adv.;* **-ness,** *n.*
o′ver·thought′ful, *adj.;* **-ly,** *adv.;* **-ness,** *n.*
o′ver·thrift′i·ly, *adv.*
o′ver·thrift′i·ness, *n.*
o′ver·thrift′y, *adj.*
o′ver·throng′, *v.*
o′ver·tight′, *adj.;* **-ly,** *adv.;* **-ness,** *n.*
o′ver·tim′bered, *adj.*
o′ver·tim′id, *adj.;* **-ly,** *adv.;* **-ness,** *n.*
o′ver·ti·mid′i·ty, *n.*
o′ver·tim′or·ous, *adj.;* **-ly,** *adv.;* **-ness,** *n.*
o′ver·tin′sel, *v.t.,* **-seled, -sel·ing** or (*esp. Brit.*) **-selled, -sel·ling.**
o′ver·tint′, *v.*
o′ver·tint′, *n.*
o′ver·tip′ple, *v.i.,* **-pled, -pling.**
o′ver·toil′, *v.*
o′ver·tol′er·ance, *n.*
o′ver·tol′er·ant, *adj.;* **-ly,** *adv.*
o′ver·tor′ture, *v.t.,* **-tured, -tur·ing.**
o′ver·tread′, *n.*
o′ver·treat′ment, *n.*
o′ver·trim′, *v.,* **-trimmed, -trim·ming.**
o′ver·trou′ble, *v.,* **-bled, -bling.**
o′ver·true′, *adj.*
o′ver·tru′ly, *adv.*
o′ver·trust′, *v.*
o′ver·trust′ful, *adj.;* **-ly,** *adv.;* **-ness,** *n.*
o′ver·truth′ful, *adj.;* **-ly,** *adv.;* **-ness,** *n.*
o′ver·twist′, *v.*
o′ver·un′ion·ize′, *v.,* **-ized, -iz·ing.**
o′ver·ur′ban·i·za′tion, *n.*
o′ver·ur′ban·ize′, *v.,* **-ized, -iz·ing.**
o′ver·urge′, *v.,* **-urged, -urg·ing.**
o′ver·val′iant, *adj.;* **-ly,** *adv.;* **-ness,** *n.*
o′ver·val′u·a·ble, *adj.;* **-ble·ness,** *n.;* **-bly,** *adv.*
o′ver·var′i·a′tion, *n.*
o′ver·va·ri′e·ty, *n.*
o′ver·var′y, *v.,* **-var·ied, -var·y·ing.**
o′ver·ve′he·mence, *n.*
o′ver·ve′he·ment, *adj.;* **-ly,** *adv.;* **-ness,** *n.*
o′ver·ven′ti·late′, *v.t.,* **-lat·ed, -lat·ing.**
o′ver·ven′ti·la′tion, *n.*
o′ver·ven′ture·some, *adj.*
o′ver·ven′tur·ous, *adj.;* **-ly,** *adv.;* **-ness,** *n.*
o′ver·vig′or·ous, *adj.;* **-ly,** *adv.;* **-ness,** *n.*
o′ver·vi′o·lent, *adj.;* **-ly,** *adv.;* **-ness,** *n.*
o′ver·war′i·ly, *adv.*
o′ver·war′i·ness, *n.*
o′ver·warmed′, *adj.*
o′ver·war′y, *adj.*
o′ver·weak′, *adj.;* **-ly,** *adv.;* **-ness,** *n.*
o′ver·wealth′, *n.*
o′ver·wealth′y, *adj.*
o′ver·wet′, *adj.; v.t.,* **-wet** or **-wet·ted, -wet·ting; -ly,** *adv.;* **-ness,** *n.*
o′ver·whip′, *v.t.,* **-whipped, -whip·ping.**
o′ver·wide′, *adj.;* **-ly,** *adv.;* **-ness,** *n.*
o′ver·wild′, *adj.;* **-ly,** *adv.;* **-ness,** *n.*
o′ver·will′ing, *adj.;* **-ly,** *adv.;* **-ness,** *n.*
o′ver·wil′y, *adj.*
o′ver·with′ered, *adj.*

for sympathy that has been overworked by many speakers. **4.** to work or decorate all over; decorate the surface of: *white limestone overworked with inscriptions.* —*v.i.* **5.** to work too hard; work to excess: *You look as though you've been overworking.* —*n.* **6.** work beyond one's strength or capacity. **7.** extra or excessive work. [OE *oferwyrc(an).* See OVER-, WORK]

o·ver·worn (ō′vər wōrn′, -wôrn′), *v.* pp. of **overwear.**

o·ver·write (ō′vər rīt′), *v.*, **-wrote, -writ·ten, -writ·ing.** —*v.t.* **1.** to write in too elaborate, burdensome, diffuse, or prolix a style: *He overwrites his essays to the point of absurdity.* **2.** to write in excess of the requirements, esp. so as to defeat the original intention: *The young playwright tends to overwrite his big scenes.* **3.** to write on or over; cover with writing: *a flyleaf overwritten with a dedication.* —*v.i.* **4.** to write too elaborately: *The problem with so many young authors is that they tend to overwrite.* [OVER- + WRITE]

o·ver·wrought (ō′vər rôt′, ō′vər-), *adj.* **1.** worked up or excited excessively: *to become overwrought on hearing bad news; an overwrought personality.* **2.** elaborated to excess; overworked: *written in a florid, overwrought style.* **3.** *Archaic.* wearied or exhausted by overwork. —*v.* **4.** a pt. and pp. of **overwork.**

o·ver·zeal·ous (ō′vər zel′əs), *adj.* too zealous: *overzealous for reform.* [OVER- + ZEALOUS] —**o′ver·zeal′ous·ly,** *adv.* —**o′ver·zeal′ous·ness,** *n.*

O·ve·ta (ō vē′tə), *n.* a girl's given name.

ovi-, a learned borrowing from Latin meaning "egg," used in the formation of compound words: *oviferous.* [< L, comb. form of *ōvum*]

Ov·id (ov′id), *n.* (*Publius Ovidius Naso*) 43 B.C.–A.D. 17?, Roman poet. —**O·vid·i·an** (ō vid′ē ən), *adj.*

o·vi·duct (ō′vi dukt′), *n.* *Anat., Zool.* either of a pair of tubes that transport the ova from the ovary to the exterior, the distal ends of which are fused to form the uterus and vagina in higher mammals. [< NL *ōviduct(us).* See OVI-, DUCT] —**o·vi·du·cal** (ō′vi do͞o′kəl, -dyo͞o′-), **o′vi·duc′tal,** *adj.*

O·vie·do (ō vye′dō), *n.* a city in NW Spain. 134,424 (est. 1960).

o·vif·er·ous (ō vif′ər əs), *adj.* *Anat., Zool.* bearing eggs. [OVI- + -FEROUS]

o·vi·form (ō′və fôrm′), *adj.* having a shape resembling that of an egg; egg-shaped. [OVI- + -FORM]

o·vine (ō′vīn, ō′vin), *adj.* pertaining to, of the nature of, or like sheep. [< LL *ovīn(us),* equiv. to L *ov(is)* sheep + *-īnus* -INE¹]

o·vip·a·ra (ō vip′ər ə), *n.pl.* egg-laying animals. [< NL, L, neut. pl. of *ōviparus* OVIPAROUS]

o·vip·a·rous (ō vip′ər əs), *adj.* *Zool.* producing eggs that mature and hatch after being expelled from the body, as birds, most reptiles and fishes, certain mammals, etc. [< L *ōviparus.* See OVI-, -PAROUS] —**o·vi·par·i·ty** (ō′vi par′i tē), **o·vip′ar·ous·ness,** *n.* —**o·vip′ar·ous·ly,** *adv.*

o·vi·pos·it (ō′vi poz′it, ō′vi poz′-), *v.i.* to deposit or lay eggs, esp. by means of an ovipositor. [OVI- + L *posit(us)* placed; see POSIT] —**o·vi·po·si·tion** (ō′vi pə zish′ən), *n.*

O, Ovipositor (of field cricket)

o·vi·pos·i·tor (ō′vi poz′i tər), *n.* **1.** (in certain female insects) an organ at the end of the abdomen, by which eggs are deposited. **2.** a similar organ in other animals, as certain fishes. [OVIPOSIT + -OR²]

o·vi·sac (ō′vi sak′), *n.* *Zool.* a sac or capsule containing an ovum or ova. [OVI- + SAC] —**o′vi·sac′like′,** *adj.*

o·void (ō′void), *adj.* **1.** egg-shaped; having the solid form of an egg. **2.** ovate (def. 2). —*n.* **3.** an ovoid body. [< NL *ōvoid(es).* See OVI-, -OID]

o·vo·lo (ō′və lō′), *n., pl.* **-li** (-lī′). *Archit.* a convex molding forming or approximating in section a quarter of a circle or ellipse. See illus. under molding. [< It, var. (now obs.) of *uovolo,* dim. of *uovo* egg < L *ōvum*]

o·vo·vi·tel·lin (ō′vō vi tel′in), *n.* *Biochem.* vitellin. [OV(I)- + -O- + VITELLIN]

o·vo·vi·vip·a·rous (ō′vō vī vip′ər əs), *adj.* *Zool.* producing eggs which are hatched within the body, so that the young are born alive but without placental attachment, as certain reptiles, fishes, etc. [OV(I)- + -O- + VIVIPAROUS] —**o′vo·vi·vip′ar·ism, o·vo·vi·vi·par·i·ty** (ō′vo vī′və par′i tē), **o′vo·vi·vip′ar·ous·ness,** *n.* —**o′vo·vi·vip′ar·ous·ly,** *adv.*

o·vu·lar (ō′vyə lər), *adj.* pertaining to or of the nature of an ovule. [< NL *ōvulār(is).* See OVULE, -AR¹]

o·vu·late (ō′vyə lāt′), *v.i.,* **-lat·ed, -lat·ing.** *Biol.* to shed eggs from an ovary or ovarian follicle. [OVULE + -ATE¹] —**o′vu·la′tion,** *n.*

o·vule (ō′vyo͞ol), *n.* **1.** *Bot.* **a.** a rudimentary seed. **b.** the body that contains the embryo sac and hence the female germ cell, which after fertilization develops into a seed. **2.** *Biol.* a small egg. [< L *ōvul(um)* little egg. See OVUM, -ULE]

o·vum (ō′vəm), *n., pl.* **o·va** (ō′və). **1.** *Biol.* **a.** the female reproductive cell or gamete of animals, which is capable of developing, usually only after fertilization, into a new individual. **b.** the female reproductive cell or gamete of plants. **2.** *Archit.* an oval ornament, as in an egg-and-dart molding. [< L: egg; c. Gk *ōión*]

ow (ou), *interj.* (used esp. as an expression of intense or sudden pain.)

o-wave (ō′wāv′), *n.* *Radio Rare.* See **ordinary wave.**

owe (ō), *v.,* **owed, ow·ing.** —*v.t.* **1.** to be indebted or beholden for (usually fol. by *to*): *to owe one's fame to good fortune.* **2.** to be under obligation to for payment or repayment (often fol. by an indirect object): *to owe money to the bank; to owe the bank interest on a mortgage.* **3.** to be in debt to: *He says he doesn't owe anybody.* **4.** to have or cherish (a certain feeling) toward a person: *to owe someone a debt of gratitude.* **5.** *Obs.* to possess; own. —*v.i.* **6.** to be in debt: *That's a lot to owe. Who owes for the antipasto?* [ME *owe(n),* OE *āgan;* c. OHG *eigan,* OIcel *eiga.* See OWN, OUGHT¹]

O·we·go (ō wē′gō), *n.* a town in S New York. 5417 (1960).

Ow·en (ō′in), *n.* **1. Robert,** 1771–1858, Welsh social reformer. **2. Wilfred,** 1893–1918, English poet. **3.** a boy's given name.

Ow·en·ism (ō′ə niz′əm), *n.* the socialistic philosophy of Robert Owen. [OWEN + -ISM] —**Ow′en·ist, Ow′en·ite′,** *n.*

Ow·ens (ō′ənz), *n.* **1. Jesse** (*John Cleveland*), 1913–80, U.S. athlete. **2.** a town in central North Carolina. 5207 (1960).

Ow·ens·bor·o (ō′inz bûrō, -burō), *n.* a city in NW Kentucky, on the Ohio River. 42,471 (1960).

O′wen Stan′ley, a mountain range in SE New Guinea. Highest peak, Mt. Victoria, 13,240 ft.

OWI, *U.S. Govt.* Office of War Information: the former federal agency (1942–45) charged with disseminating information about World War II, as changes in Allied military policy, casualty statistics, etc.

ow·ing (ō′ing), *adj.* **1.** owed or due: *to pay what is owing.* **2.** *Archaic.* that owes or is under obligation. **3.** *Archaic.* indebted. **4. owing to,** attributable to; because of: *Owing to a mistake in the payroll department, some of us were issued incorrect checks.* [ME; see OWE, -ING²]

Great horned owl, *Bubo virginianus* (Length 2 ft.)

Ow′ings-Mills′ (ō′ingz milz′), *n.* a town in central Maryland. 3810 (1960).

owl (oul), *n.* **1.** any of numerous, chiefly nocturnal birds of prey, of the order *Strigiformes,* having a broad head with large eyes that are usually surrounded by disks of modified feathers and directed forward. They feed on mice, small birds and reptiles, etc. **2.** one of a breed of domestic pigeons having an owllike appearance. **3.** a person who habitually stays up late at night. **4.** a person of owllike solemnity or appearance. —*adj.* **5.** operating late at night or all night: *an owl train.* [ME *oule,* OE *ūle;* c. LG *ūle,* D *uil;* akin to Icel *ugla,* G *Eule*] —**owl′like′,** *adj.*

owl′ but′terfly, any of several South American nymphalid butterflies of the genus *Caligo,* esp. *C. eurylochus,* having a spot like an owl's eye on each hind wing.

owl·et (ou′lit), *n.* **1.** a young owl. **2.** See **little owl.** [OWL + -ET]

owl′et moth′, noctuid (def. 1).

owl′et night′jar, any of several birds of the family *Aegothelidae,* of Australia and New Guinea, related to the nightjars but resembling small owls.

owl·ish (ou′lish), *adj.* resembling an owl: *His thick glasses give him an owlish appearance.* [OWL + -ISH¹] —**owl′ish·ly,** *adv.* —**owl′ish·ness,** *n.*

owl's-crown (oulz′kroun′), *n.* See **wood cudweed.**

own (ōn), *adj.* **1.** of, pertaining to, or belonging to oneself or itself (usually used after a possessive to emphasize the idea of ownership, interest, or relation conveyed by the possessive): *He spent only his own money. This example is my own.* **2.** (used as an intensifier to indicate oneself as the sole agent of some activity or action, prec. by a possessive): *He insists on being his own doctor. She does her own housework.* **3. come into one's own, a.** to take possession of that which is due one. **b.** to receive the recognition which one's abilities merit: *In his latest exhibition, he comes into his own as a sculptor of the first magnitude.* **4. hold one's own, a.** to maintain one's position or condition: *The stock market seems to be holding its own these days.* **b.** to be equal to the opposition; be a match for: *He can hold his own in any fight.* **5. of one's own,** belonging to oneself: *She had never had a room of her own.* **6. on one's own,** *Informal.* **a.** on one's own responsibility or resources; independently: *Because she spoke the language, she got around the country very well on her own.* **b.** being on one's own responsibility or resources; independent: *My son's been on his own for several years.* [ME *owen,* OE *āgen* (c. G *eigen,* Icel *eigenn*), orig. ptp. of *āgan* to have, possess. See OWE]
—*v.t.* **7.** to have or hold as one's own; possess: *They own several homes.* **8.** to acknowledge or admit: *to own a fault.* **9.** to acknowledge as one's own; recognize as having full claim, authority, power, dominion, etc.: *He owned his child before the entire assembly. They owned the king as their lord.* —*v.i.* **10.** to confess (often fol. by *to* or *up*): *I own to being uncertain about that. The one who did it had better own up.* [ME *own(en),* OE *āgnian, āhnian,* deriv. of *āgen* own (adj.)]
—**Syn. 7.** See **have.** —**Ant. 7.** lack, need.

own·er (ō′nər), *n.* a person who owns; proprietor. [ME; see OWN, -ER¹]

own·er·ship (ō′nər ship′), *n.* **1.** the state or fact of being an owner. **2.** legal right of possession; proprietorship. [OWNER + -SHIP]

O·wos·so (ō wos′ō), *n.* a city in central Michigan. 17,006 (1960).

owse (ous), *n., pl.* **ows·en** (ou′sən, -zən). *Scot. and North Eng.* ox.

ox (oks), *n., pl.* **ox·en** for 1, 2, **ox·es** for 3. **1.** the adult castrated male of the genus *Bos,* used as a draft animal and for food. **2.** any member of the bovine family. **3.** a clumsy, stupid fellow. [ME *oxe,* OE *oxa;* c. G *Ochse*] —**ox′like′,** *adj.*

ox-, *Chem.* a combining form meaning "containing oxygen": *oxazine.* [short for OXYGEN]

Ox., Oxford. [< L *Oxonia*]

oxa-, *Chem.* a combining form denoting oxygen when it replaces carbon. [var. of OX- or OXY-¹]

ox·a·late (ok′sə lāt′), *n.* *Chem.* a salt or ester of oxalic acid. [OXAL(IC) + -ATE²]

ox·al·ic (ok sal′ik), *adj.* *Chem.* of or derived from oxalic acid. [< F *oxalique.* See OXALIS, -IC]

oxal′ic ac′id, *Chem.* a white, crystalline, water-soluble, poisonous acid, $HOOCCOOH \cdot 2H_2O$, first discovered in the juice of the wood sorrel species of oxalis and obtained by reacting carbon monoxide with sodium hydroxide or certain carbohydrates with acids or alkalis: used chiefly for bleaching, as a cleanser, and as a laboratory reagent. Also called **ethanedioic acid.**

ox·a·lis (ok′sə lis, ok sal′is), *n.* any plant of the genus *Oxalis,* comprising the wood sorrels. [< L: garden sorrel, sour wine < Gk, deriv. of *oxýs* sharp]

ox·a·zine (ok′sə zēn′, -zin), *n.* *Chem.* any of a group of 13 compounds having the formula C_4H_5NO, containing four carbon atoms, one oxygen atom, and one nitrogen atom, arranged in a six-membered ring. [OX- + AZINE]

ox′ ball′, *U.S.* an ornamental ball forming the top of a flagstaff or the track of a mast.

ox·blood (oks′blud′), *n.* Also, **ox′blood red′.** a deep dull red color. [OX + BLOOD]

ox·bow (oks′bō′), *n.* **1.** a U-shaped piece of wood placed under and around the neck of an ox with its upper ends in the bar of the yoke. **2.** *Phys. Geog. U.S.* **a.** a bow-shaped bend in a river, or the land embraced by it. **b.** a bow-shaped lake formed in an abandoned channel of a river. [ME; see OX, BOW²]

ox′bow chest′, a chest of drawers having a front convex at the sides and concave in the center without vertical divisions.

ox′bow front′, *Furniture.* a front, as of a chest of drawers, having a horizontal compound curve with a concave section between two convex ones. Also called **yoke front.** Cf. **serpentine front.**

Oxbow front (England, 1720)

Ox′-Bow In′cident, The (oks′-bō′), a novel (1940) by Walter Van Tilburg Clark.

Ox·bridge (oks′brij′), *Brit.* —*n.* **1.** Oxford or Cambridge University, or both: *He is eager to have his son educated at Oxbridge.* **2.** upper-class intellectual life in England, as felt to be under the influence of Oxford and Cambridge universities: *a bitter attack on Oxbridge by the younger writers.* —*adj.* **3.** of, pertaining to, or characteristic of Oxford and Cambridge: *a career formerly open only to Oxbridge graduates; to voice the proper Oxbridge sentiments.*

ox·cart (oks′kärt′), *n.* an ox-drawn cart. [OX + CART]

ox·en (ok′sən), *n.* a pl. of **ox.**

Ox·en·stier·na (o͝ok′sən shēr′nä), *n.* **Count Ax·el** (äk′səl), 1583–1654, Swedish statesman. Also, **Ox′en·stjer′na.**

ox·eye (oks′ī′), *n., pl.* **-eyes. 1.** any of various plants having flowers composed of a disk with marginal rays, as the mayweed and the oxeye daisy. **2.** *Dial.* any of several shore birds, as the least sandpiper. **3.** *Archit.* oeil-de-boeuf. [late ME; see OX, EYE]

ox′eye cam′omile. See **golden marguerite.**

ox-eyed (oks′īd′), *adj.* having large, round eyes similar to those of an ox. [OXEYE + -ED³]

ox′eye dai′sy, a composite plant, *Chrysanthemum leucanthemum,* having flowers with white rays and a yellow disk.

ox·ford (oks′fərd), *n.* **1.** Also called **Oxford shoe, Oxford tie.** a low shoe laced or buttoned over the instep. **2.** Also called **ox′ford cloth′.** a rayon or cotton fabric, in plain, twill, or basket weave, constructed on a pattern of two fine yarns woven as one warpwise and one loosely twisted yarn weftwise, for shirts, skirts, and summer sportswear. [after OXFORD (def. 2)]

Ox·ford (oks′fərd), *n.* **1. 1st Earl of.** See **Harley, Robert. 2.** a city in S Oxfordshire, in S England, NW of London: university, founded in 12th century. 106,124 (1961). **3.** Oxfordshire. **4.** a town in SW Ohio. 7828 (1960). **5.** a town in S Massachusetts. 6985 (1960). **6.** a town in N North Carolina. 6978 (1960). **7.** a town in N Mississippi. 5283 (1960). **8.** a town in E Alabama. 3603 (1960). **9.** a town in SE Pennsylvania. 3376 (1960). **10.** Also called **Ox′ford Down′.** one of an English breed of large, hornless sheep, noted for its market lambs and heavy fleece of medium length.

Ox′ford cor′ners, *Print.* ruled border lines about the text of a page that cross and project slightly at the corners. —**ox′ford cor′nered.**

Ox′ford gray′, medium to dark gray.

Ox′ford Group′, an organization founded at Oxford University in 1921 by Frank Buchman, advocating absolute morality in public and private life. Cf. **Moral Re-Armament.**

Ox′ford move′ment, the movement toward High Church principles within the Church of England, originating at Oxford University in 1833 in opposition to liberalizing, rationalizing, and evangelical tendencies and emphasizing the principles of primitive and patristic Christianity as well as the historic and catholic character of the church. Cf. **Tractarianism.**

Ox′ford rule′, *Typography.* a type that prints a thick line together with and parallel to a thin one.

Ox·ford·shire (oks′fərd shēr′, -shər), *n.* a county in S England. 309,458 (1961); 749 mi. *Co. seat:* Oxford. Also called **Oxford, Oxon.**

Ox′ford shoe′, oxford (def. 1). Also called **Ox′ford tie′.**

Ox′ford the′ory, the theory attributing the authorship of Shakespeare's plays to Edward de Vere, Earl of Oxford, 1550–1604. Cf. **Baconian theory.**

ox·gang (oks′gang′), *n.* bovate. [ME; OE *oxan gang,* lit., ox's going. See OX, GANG¹]

ox·heart (oks′härt′), *n.* any large, heart-shaped variety of sweet cherry. [OX + HEART]

ox·i·dase (ok′si dās′, -dāz′), *n.* *Biochem.* any of a class of oxidoreductase enzymes that catalyze the oxidation of molecular oxygen. [OXIDE + -ASE] —**ox·i·da·sic** (ok′si dā′sik, -zik), *adj.*

ox·i·date (ok′si dāt′), *v.,* **-dat·ed, -dat·ing,** *n.* *Chem.* —*v.t., v.i.* **1.** to oxidize. —*n.* **2.** *Geochem.* any of the class of sediments consisting chiefly of oxides of iron or manganese. [OXIDE + -ATE²] —**ox′i·da′tion,** *n.* —**ox′i·da′tion·al, ox′i·da′tive,** *adj.*

oxida′tion num′ber. *Chem.* See **oxidation state.**

oxida′tion poten′tial, *Physical Chem.* (in a galvanic cell) the potential of the electrode at which oxidation occurs. Cf. **reduction potential.**

oxida′tion state′, *Chem.* the state of an element or ion in a compound with regard to the electrons gained or lost by the element or ion in the reaction that formed the compound, expressed as a positive or negative number indicating the ionic charge of the element or ion. Also called **oxidation number.**

ox·ide (ok′sīd, -sid), *n.* *Chem.* **1.** a compound containing oxygen and one or more elements, as mercuric oxide, HgO. **2.** a compound containing oxygen and one or more groups, as ethyl oxide, $(C_2H_5)_2O$. Also, **ox·id** (ok′sid). [< F, b. *oxygène* and *acide.* See OXYGEN, ACID] —**ox·id·ic** (ok sid′ik), *adj.*

ox·i·dim·e·try (ok′si dim′i trē), *n.* a technique of analytical chemistry that utilizes oxidizing agents for titrations. [OXIDE + -I- + -METRY] —**ox·i·di·met·ric** (ok′si di me′trik), *adj.*

ox·i·dise (ok′si dīz′), *v.t., v.i.,* **-dised, -dis·ing.** *Chiefly Brit.* oxidize. —**ox′i·dis′a·bil′i·ty,** *n.* —**ox′i·dis′a·ble,** *adj.* —**ox′i·di·sa′tion,** *n.* —**ox′i·dis′er,** *n.*

ox·i·dize (ok′si dīz′), *v.,* **-dized, -diz·ing.** *Chem.* —*v.t.* **1.** to convert (an element) into its oxide; combine with oxygen. **2.** to cover with a coating of oxide, or rust. **3.** to take away hydrogen, as by the action of oxygen; add oxygen or any nonmetal. **4.** to increase the valence of (an element). **5.** to remove electrons from. —*v.i.* **6.** to become oxidized. [OXIDE + -IZE] —**ox′i·diz′a·bil′i·ty,** *n.* —**ox′i·diz′a·ble, ox·i·da·ble** (ok′si də bəl), *adj.* —**ox′i·di·za′tion,** *n.* —**ox′i·diz′er,** *n.*

ox·i·do·re·duc·tase (ok′si dō ri duk′tās), *n. Biochem.* any of a class of enzymes that act as a catalyst, some of them conjointly, causing the oxidation and reduction of compounds. Also, **ox′i·do-re·duc′tase.** [OXIDE + -O- + REDUCTASE]

ox·ime (ok′sēm, -sim), *n. Chem.* any of a group of compounds containing the group >C=NOH produced by the condensation of ketones or aldehydes with hydroxylamine. [OX(YGEN) + IM(ID)E]

ox·im·e·ter (ok sim′i tər), *n. Med.* an instrument for measuring the oxygen saturation of the hemoglobin in a sample of blood. [OX- + -I- + -METER] —**ox·i·met·ric** (ok′si me′trik), *adj.*

ox·im·e·try (ok sim′i trē), *n. Med.* the measuring of oxygen saturation of the blood by means of an oximeter. [OX- + -I- + -METRY]

ox·lip (oks′lip′), *n.* a primrose, *Primula elatior,* having pale-yellow flowers. [ME; OE *oxan slyppe,* lit., ox's slime. See SLIP² and cf. COWSLIP]

Ox·nard (oks′närd), *n.* a city in SW California, NW of Los Angeles. 40,265 (1960).

Ox·on (ok′son), *n.* Oxfordshire.

Oxon., 1. Oxford. [< L *Oxonia*] **2.** of Oxford. [< L *Oxoniensis*]

Ox·o·ni·an (ok sō′nē ən), *adj.* **1.** of or pertaining to Oxford, England, or to Oxford University. —*n.* **2.** a member or graduate of Oxford University. **3.** a native or inhabitant of Oxford. [< ML *Oxoni(a)* Oxford + -AN]

ox·o·ni·um com′pound (ok sō′nē əm), *Chem.* a salt formed by the reaction of an acid with an organic compound containing a basic oxygen atom. [OX- + NL *-onium* (abstracted from *ammonium*)]

ox/o proc′ess (ok′sō), *Chem.* a process for producing carbonyl compounds, esp. alcohols and aldehydes, by adding, under high pressure, carbon monoxide and hydrogen to an olefin in the presence of a cobalt catalyst. Also called **ox′o reac′tion.** [OX- + -O-]

ox·peck·er (oks′pek′ər), *n.* either of two African starlings of the genus *Buphagus,* characterized by their habit of riding on large, wild animals and domestic cattle to feed on ticks. [OX + PECKER]

ox·tail (oks′tāl′), *n.* the skinned tail of an ox or steer, used as an ingredient in soup, stew, etc. [ME; see OX, TAIL¹]

ox·ter (ok′stər), *n. Scot. and North Eng.* the armpit. [akin to OE *ōcusta* armpit, Icel *ōst(r)* throat]

ox·tongue (oks′tung′), *n.* any of various plants having rough, tongue-shaped leaves, as the bugloss, *Anchusa officinalis.* [ME; see OX, TONGUE]

ox′-tongue par′tisan (oks′tung′), a shafted weapon having a long, wide, tapering blade. Also called **langue de boeuf.**

Ox·us (ok′səs), *n.* See **Amu Darya.**

oxy-¹, a learned borrowing from Greek used, with the meaning "sharp," "acute," "keen," "pointed," "acid," in the formation of compound words: *oxycephalic; oxygen; oxymoron.* [< Gk, comb. form of *oxýs* sharp, keen, acid]

oxy-², a combining form of **oxygen,** sometimes used as an equivalent of *hydroxy-*: *oxychloride.*

ox·y·a·cet·y·lene (ok′sē ə set′ᵊlēn′, -ᵊlin), *adj.* noting or pertaining to a mixture of oxygen and acetylene used in a blowpipe for cutting steel plates or the like. [OXY-² + ACETYLENE]

ox·y·ac·id (ok′sē as′id), *n. Chem.* an inorganic acid containing oxygen. Also, **oxygen acid.** [OXY-² + ACID]

ox·y·al·de·hyde (ok′sē al′də hīd′), *n. Chem.* an aldehyde containing the hydroxyl group. [OXY-² + ALDEHYDE]

ox·y·ben·zene (ok′si ben′zēn, -ben zēn′), *n. Chem.* phenol (def. 1). [OXY-² + BENZENE]

ox·y·cal·ci·um (ok′si kal′sē əm), *adj.* pertaining to or produced by oxygen and calcium. [OXY-² + CALCIUM]

oxycal′cium light′. See **calcium light.**

ox·y·cel·lu·lose (ok′si sel′yə lōs′), *n. Chem.* any substance formed naturally or synthetically by the oxidation of cellulose. [OXY-² + CELLULOSE]

ox·y·ce·phal·ic (ok′sē sə fal′ik), *adj.* of, pertaining to, or marked by oxycephaly. Also, **ox·y·ceph·a·lous** (ok′si sef′ə ləs). [OXY¹ + -CEPHALIC]

ox·y·ceph·a·ly (ok′si sef′ə lē), *n. Pathol.* acrocephaly. [< G *Oxycephalie,* prob. < Gk *oxyképhal(os)* sharp-headed (*oxy-* OXY-¹ + *kephalē* -CEPHALY)]

ox·y·chlo·ride (ok′si klōr′īd, -id, -klôr′-), *n. Chem.* a compound having oxygen and chlorine atoms bonded to another element, as bismuth oxychloride, BiOCl. [OXY-² + CHLORIDE] —**ox′y·chlo′ric,** *adj.*

ox·y·dase (ok′si dās′), *n.* oxidase. —**ox·y·da·sic** (ok′si dā′sik, -zik), *adj.*

ox·y·da·tion (ok′si dā′shən), *n.* oxidation.

Ox·y·der·ces (ok′si dûr′sēz), *n. Class. Myth.* an epithet of Athena, meaning "bright-eyed."

ox′y·di·a·ce′tic ac′id (ok′si dī′ə sē′tik, -set′ik, ok′-), *Chem.* See **diglycolic acid.** [OXY-² + DI-¹ + ACETIC]

ox·y·gen (ok′si jən), *n. Chem.* a colorless, odorless, gaseous element constituting about one fifth of the volume of the atmosphere and present in a combined state in nature. It is the supporter of combustion in air and was the standard of atomic, combining, and molecular weights until 1961, when carbon 12 became the new standard. *Weight of 1 liter at 0°C and 760 mm. pressure:* 1.4290 grams. *Symbol:* O; *at. wt.:* 15.9994; *at. no.:* 8. [< F *oxygène,* equiv. to *oxy-* OXY-¹ + *-gène* -GEN] —**ox·y·gen·ic** (ok′si jen′ik), **ox·yg·e·nous** (ok sij′ə nəs), *adj.* —**ox′y·gen·ic′i·ty,** *n.*

ox′ygen ac′id, oxyacid.

ox·y·gen·ate (ok′si jə nāt′), *v.t.,* **-at·ed, -at·ing.** to treat, combine, or enrich with oxygen: *to oxygenate the blood.* [OXYGEN + -ATE¹] —**ox′y·gen·a′tion,** *n.* —**ox′y·gen·a′tor,** *n.*

ox′y·gen-hy′dro·gen weld′ing (ok′si jən hī′drə-jən), welding done by means of a blowpipe using a mixture of oxygen and hydrogen.

ox·y·gen·ize (ok′si jə nīz′), *v.t.,* **-ized, -iz·ing.** oxygenate. [OXYGEN + -IZE] —**ox′y·gen·iz′a·ble,** *adj.* —**ox′y·ge·niz′er,** *n.*

ox′ygen lance′, a tube for conveying oxygen, used in various thermal cutting or steelmaking operations.

ox′ygen mask′, a masklike device placed or worn over the nose and mouth when inhaling supplementary oxygen from an attached tank.

ox′ygen tent′, a small tentlike canopy for placing over a sick person for delivering and maintaining a flow of oxygen at critical periods.

ox·y·he·mo·glo·bin (ok′si hē′mə glō′bin, -hem′ə-, -hē′mə glō′-, -hem′ə-), *n. Biochem.* See under **hemoglobin.** *Symbol:* HbO_2 [OXY-² + HEMOGLOBIN]

ox·y·hy·dro·gen (ok′si hī′drə jən), *adj.* **1.** pertaining to or involving a mixture of oxygen and hydrogen. —*n.* **2.** a mixture of oxygen and hydrogen, used in a blowpipe for cutting steel plates or the like. [OXY-² + HYDROGEN]

Ox·y·lus (ok′si ləs), *n. Class. Myth.* an exiled Aetolian who, upon returning home on a one-eyed mule, was chosen by the Heraclidae to lead their invasion of the Peloponnesus. They believed him to be the three-eyed man who, according to an oracle, would lead them.

ox·y·mo·ron (ok′si mōr′on, -môr′-), *n., pl.* **-mo·ra** (-mōr′ə, môr′ə). *Rhet.* a figure of speech by which a locution produces an effect by a seeming self-contradiction, as in "cruel kindness" or "to make haste slowly." [< NL < Gk *oxýmōron* pointedly foolish, neut. of *oxýmōros,* equiv. to *oxý(s)* OXY-¹ + *mōrós* foolish]

ox·y·neu·rine (ok′si nŏŏr′ēn, -in, -nyŏŏr′-), *n. Chem.* betaine. [OXY-² + NEUR- + -INE²]

ox·y·salt (ok′si sôlt′), *n. Chem.* **1.** any salt of an oxyacid. **2.** a salt containing oxygen as well as a given anion, as FeOCl or $BiONO_3$. [OXY-² + SALT¹]

ox·y·sul·fide (ok′si sul′fīd, -fid), *n. Chem.* a sulfide in which part of the sulfur is replaced by oxygen. [OXY-² + SULFIDE]

ox·y·te·tra·cy·cline (ok′si te′trə sī′klīn, -klin), *n. Pharm.* a dull yellow, slightly water-soluble, crystalline antibiotic powder, $C_{22}H_{24}N_2O_9$, isolated from the metabolic products produced by *Streptomyces rimosus,* used chiefly in treating infections caused by streptococci, staphylococci, Gram-negative bacilli, rickettsiae, and by certain protozoans and viruses. [OXY-² + TETRACYCLINE]

ox·y·to·ci·a (ok′si tō′shē ə, -shə), *n. Med.* rapid childbirth. [< NL, equiv. to *oxy-* OXY-¹ + *toc-* (< Gk *tók(os)* childbirth) + *-ia* -IA]

ox·y·to·cic (ok′si tō′sik, -tos′ik), *Med.* —*adj.* **1.** of or causing the stimulation of the involuntary muscle of the uterus. **2.** promoting or accelerating childbirth. —*n.* **3.** an oxytocic substance or drug. [OXYTOC(IA) + -IC]

ox·y·to·cin (ok′si tō′sən), *n.* **1.** *Biochem.* a polypeptide hormone, produced by the posterior lobe of the pituitary gland, that stimulates contraction of the smooth muscle of the uterus. **2.** *Pharm.* a commercial form of this substance, obtained from beef and hog pituitary glands or esp. by synthesis, and used chiefly in obstetrics to induce labor and to control postnatal hemorrhage. Also called **alpha-hypophamine.** [OXYTOC(IC) + -IN²]

ox·y·tone (ok′si tōn′), *Classical Gk. Gram.* —*adj.* **1.** having an acute accent on the last syllable. —*n.* **2.** an oxytone word. [< Gk *oxýton(os)* shrill-toned. See OXY-¹, TONE]

oy¹ (oi), *interj.* (used to express dismay, pain, annoyance, grief, etc.) Also, **oi.**

oy² (oi), *n. Scot.* **1.** a grandchild. **2.** *Obs.* a nephew or niece. Also, **oe.** [ME (north) *o* < Celt]

O·ya·ma (ô′yä mä′), *n.* **I·wa·o** (ē′wä ô′), 1842–1916, Japanese field marshal.

O′ya·shi′o Cur′rent (oi′ə shē′ō; *Jap.* ô′yä shē′ô), *n.* a cold ocean current flowing SW from the Bering Sea, E of the Kurile Islands, along the E coast of Japan where it meets the Japan Current. Also, **Okhotsk Current.**

oye·let (oi′lit), *n.* eyelet (def. 4).

o·yer (ō′yər, oi′ər), *n. Law.* **1.** *Obs.* a hearing in open court involving the production of some document pleaded by one party and demanded by the other, the party pleading the document being said to *make profert.* **2.** See **oyer and terminer.** [ME < AF, c. OF *oïr* to hear < L *audīre*]

o′yer and ter′mi·ner (tûr′mə nər), *Law.* **1.** *U.S.* (in some States) any of various higher criminal courts. **2.** *Brit.* **a.** a commission or writ directing the holding of a court to try offenses. **b.** the court itself. [ME < AF: lit., to hear and determine]

o·yez (ō′yes, ō′yez), *interj.* **1.** hear! attend! (a cry uttered usually three times by a public or court crier to command silence and attention before making a proclamation). —*n.* **2.** a cry of "oyez." Also, **o′yes.** [< AF, 2nd pers. pl. impv. of *oyer;* see OYER]

oy·let (oi′lit), *n.* eyelet (def. 4).

oys·ter (oi′stər), *n.* **1.** any of several edible, marine bivalve mollusks of the family *Ostreidae,* having an irregularly shaped shell, found on the bottom or adhering to rocks or other objects in shallow water. **2.** the oyster-shaped bit of dark meat in the front hollow of the side bone of a fowl. **3.** *Slang.* a close-mouthed or uncommunicative person, esp. one who keeps secrets well. **4.** something from which one may extract or derive advantage: *The world was his oyster.* **5.** See **oyster white.** —*v.i.* **6.** to dredge for or otherwise take oysters. [ME *oistre* < MF < L *ostrea* < Gk *óstreon*]

Oyster,
Ostrea virginica
(Length 2 to 6 in.)

oys′ter bed′, a place where oysters breed or are cultivated.

oys′ter canoe′, *Naut.* a canoe used for oystering in the Chesapeake Bay area, having slabs of hollowed logs for a keel and gar boards with washboards above, and rigged with leg-of-mutton sails on two masts.

oys·ter·catch·er (oi′stər kach′ər), *n.* any of several long-billed wading birds of the genus *Haematopus* that have chiefly black and white plumage and that feed on oysters, clams, mussels, etc. Also, **oys′ter catch′er.** [OYSTER + CATCHER]

oys′ter crab′, a pea crab, *Pinnotheres ostreum,* the female of which lives as a commensal within the mantle cavity of oysters.

oys′ter crack′er, a small, round, usually salted cracker, served with oysters, soup, etc.

oys·tered (oi′stərd), *adj. Furniture.* veneered with matched flitches having a figure of concentric rings. [OYSTER + -ED³]

oys′ter farm′, a place where oyster beds are kept.

oys·ter·fish (oi′stər fish′), *n., pl.* **-fish·es,** (*esp. collectively*) **-fish.** the oyster toadfish. See under **toadfish** (def. 1). [OYSTER + FISH]

oys′ter fork′, a small, three-pronged fork, used esp. in eating raw oysters or clams, lobster, shrimp cocktails, etc.

oys·ter·ing (oi′stər ing), *n.* **1.** veneering of furniture with matched flitches having a figure of concentric rings. **2.** flitches used on an oystered piece. [OYSTER + -ING¹]

oys·ter·man (oi′stər mən), *n., pl.* **-men. 1.** a man who gathers, cultivates, or sells oysters. **2.** a boat specially equipped for gathering oysters. Also called **oys′ter·er.** [OYSTER + MAN¹]

oys′ter plant′, 1. salsify. **2.** See **sea lungwort.**

oys′ter rake′, a rake with a long handle and with iron, usually hooked teeth, for taking oysters from a bed too deep in the water to be reached by tongs.

oys′ter scale′. See **oystershell scale.**

oys′ter schoon′er, any of various small schooners used for oystering along the east and southeast coasts of the U.S.

oys′ter scow′, a scow used for oystering along the Pacific Coast of the U.S.

oy′stershell scale′ (oi′stər shel′), a scale insect, *Lepidosaphes ulmi,* having a scale shaped like the shell of an oyster, which infests various deciduous trees and shrubs. Also called **oyster scale.** [OYSTER + SHELL]

oys′ter sloop′, *Naut.* plunger (def. 5).

oys′ter thief′, a balloon-shaped brown alga, *Colpomenia sinuosa,* having a sucking disk by which it adheres to seaweed, rocks, oysters, etc.

oys′ter toad′fish. See under **toadfish** (def. 1).

oys′ter white′, a slightly greyish white; off-white.

oys·ter·wom·an (oi′stər wŏŏm′ən), *n., pl.* **-wom·en.** a woman who gathers, cultivates, or sells oysters. [OYSTER + WOMAN]

oz., ounce; ounces.

Oz·a·lid (oz′ə lid), *n.* **1.** *Trademark.* a process for reproducing line drawings, manuscripts, and the like on a sensitized paper developed by ammonia vapor. **2.** (*sometimes l.c.*) a reproduction made by this process. —*adj.* **3.** (*sometimes l.c.*) of or pertaining to the Ozalid process.

oz. ap., *Pharm.* ounce apothecary's.

O·zark (ō′zärk), *n.* a town in SE Alabama. 9534 (1960).

O′zark Moun′tains, a group of low mountains in S Missouri, N Arkansas, and NE Oklahoma. Also called **O′zarks.**

oz. av., ounce avoirdupois.

O·zen·fant (ō zän fän′), *n.* **A·mé·dée** (a mā dā′), 1886–1966, French painter and writer, in the U.S. after 1938.

ozo-, an element of Greek origin meaning "smell," used in the formation of compound words: *ozocerite; ozostomia.* [< Gk, comb. form of *ózō* a smell (whether good or bad), ODOR]

o·zo·ce·rite (ō zō′kə rīt′, -sə rīt′, ō′zō sēr′īt), *n.* wax-like mineral resin; mineral wax. Also, **o·zo·ke·rite** (ō zō′kə rīt′, ō′zō kēr′īt). [< G *Ozokerit* < Gk *ózō* ozo- + *kēr(ós)* wax + G *-it* -ITE¹]

ozon-, var. of **ozono-** before a vowel: *ozonide.*

O·zo·na (ō zō′nə), *n.* a town in W Texas. 3361 (1960).

o·zone (ō′zōn, ō zōn′), *n.* **1.** a form of oxygen, O_3, having three atoms to the molecule, with a peculiar odor suggesting that of weak chlorine, produced when an electric spark is passed through air or oxygen. It is found in the atmosphere in minute quantities, esp. after a thunderstorm, and is a powerful oxidizing agent: used for bleaching, sterilizing water, etc. **2.** clear, fresh, invigorating air: *I'm going outside to fill my lungs full of ozone.* [< F; see OZO-, -ONE] —**o·zon·ic** (ō zon′ik, ō zō′nik), *adj.*

o′zone lay′er, ozonosphere.

ozon′ic e′ther, *Chem.* a solution of hydrogen peroxide in ethyl ether.

o·zo·nide (ō′zə nīd′, ō′zō-), *n. Chem.* any compound, usually explosive, formed by the addition of ozone to the double or triple bond of an organic compound. [OZON- + -IDE]

o·zo·nif·er·ous (ō′zə nif′ər əs, ō′zō-), *adj.* containing ozone. [OZON- + -I- + -FEROUS]

o·zo·nise (ō′zə nīz′, ō′zō-), *v.t., v.i.,* **-ised, -is·ing.** *Chiefly Brit.* ozonize.

o·zo·ni·za·tion (ō′zə ni zā′shən, ō′zō-), *n.* **1.** the treatment of a compound with ozone. **2.** the conversion of oxygen into ozone. Also, *esp. Brit.,* **o′zo·ni·sa′tion.** [OZONIZE + -ATION]

o·zon·ize (ō′zə nīz′, ō′zō-), *v.,* **-ized, -iz·ing.** —*v.t.* **1.** to impregnate or treat with ozone. **2.** to convert (oxygen) into ozone. —*v.i.* **3.** (of oxygen) to be converted into ozone. Also, *esp. Brit.,* **ozonise.** [OZON- + -IZE]

o·zon·iz·er (ō′zə nī′zər, ō′zō-), *n. Chem.* an apparatus for converting oxygen into ozone. Also, *esp. Brit.,* **o′zon·is′er.** [OZONIZE + -ER¹]

ozono-, a combining form of **ozone:** *ozonosphere.* Also, *esp. before a vowel,* **ozon-.**

o·zo·nol·y·sis (ō′zə nol′i sis, ō′zō-), *n. Chem.* the reaction of ozone with hydrocarbons. [OZONO- + -LYSIS]

o·zo·no·sphere (ō zō′nə sfēr′), *n.* the region in the upper atmosphere where most atmospheric ozone is concentrated, from about 8 to about 30 miles above the earth, maximum ozone occurring at an altitude of about 12 miles. Also called **ozone layer.** [OZONO- + -SPHERE]

o·zo·nous (ō′zə nəs, ō′zō-), *adj.* of or containing ozone. [OZON- + -OUS]

o·zos·to·mi·a (ō′zə stō′mē ə), *n. Med.* bad breath; halitosis. [< NL < Gk *ozóstom(os)* (*ozo-* OZO- + *-stomos* -STOMOUS) + *-ia* -IA]

ozs., ounces.

oz. t., ounce troy.

Oz·zie (oz′ē), *n.* a boy's given name, form of **Oswald.**

P

P, p (pē), *n., pl.* **P's** or **Ps, p's** or **ps. 1.** the sixteenth letter of the English alphabet, a consonant. **2.** any spoken sound represented by the letter *P* or *p*, as in *pet, supper, top*, etc. **3.** something having the shape of a P. **4.** a written or printed representation of the letter *P* or *p*. **5.** a device, as a printer's type, for reproducing the letter *P* or *p*. **6. mind one's p's and q's,** to be careful of one's behavior; be circumspect or wary: *The children were told to mind their p's and q's.*

p. 1. passing. **2.** *Chess.* pawn. **3.** poise². **4.** poor.

P, 1. the 16th in order or in a series, or, when *I* is omitted, the 15th. **2.** (*sometimes l.c.*) the medieval Roman numeral for 400. Cf. **Roman numerals. 3.** *Chem.* phosphorous. **4.** *Physics.* **a.** power. **b.** pressure. **c.** P-state. **5.** *Genetics.* parental.

p, *Music.* softly [< It *piano*]

P-, *U.S. Mil.* (in designations of fighter aircraft): pursuit: *P-38.*

p-, *Chem.* para-¹.

P., 1. pastor. **2.** father. [< L *Pater*] **3.** peseta. **4.** peso. **5.** post. **6.** president. **7.** pressure. **8.** priest. **9.** prince. **10.** progressive.

p., 1. page. **2.** part. **3.** participle. **4.** past. **5.** father. [< L *pater*] **6.** *Chess.* pawn. **7.** penny. **8.** per. **9.** peseta. **10.** peso. **11.** *Music.* softly. [< It *piano*] **12.** pint. **13.** pipe. **14.** *Baseball.* pitcher. **15.** pole. **16.** population. **17.** after. [< L *post*]

pa (pä), *n. Informal.* father. [short for PAPA]

PA, 1. press agent. **2.** public-address system.

Pa, *Chem.* protactinium.

Pa., Pennsylvania.

P.A., 1. passenger agent. **2.** post adjutant. **3.** power of attorney. **4.** press agent. **5.** publicity agent. **6.** purchasing agent.

p.a., 1. participial adjective. **2.** per annum. **3.** press agent.

Paa·si·ki·vi (pä′si ki vi), *n.* **Ju·ho Kus·ti** (yo͞o′hō ko͝os′tē), 1870–1956, Finnish statesman: president 1946–56.

PABA, para-aminobenzoic acid.

Pa·blo (pä′blō; *Sp.* pä′vlō), *n.* a boy's given name, Spanish form of **Paul**.

Pab·lum (pab′ləm), *n.* **1.** *Trademark.* a form of cereal for infants. **2.** (*l.c.*) banal or simple-minded ideas or writings; intellectual pap.

pab·u·lum (pab′yə ləm), *n.* **1.** something that nourishes an animal or vegetable organism; food. **2.** material for intellectual nourishment. [< L: food, nourishment, equiv. to *pā(scere)* to feed + *-bulum* n. suffix of means, instrument. See FOOD]

PAC (pak), *n.* Political Action Committee.

Pac., Pacific.

P.A.C., Political Action Committee.

pa·ca (pä′kə, pak′ə), *n.* a large, white-spotted, almost tailless rodent, *Cuniculus paca*, of Central and South America. Also called **spotted cavy.** [< Sp or Pg < Tupi]

Paca
(Length 2½ ft.)

Pac·ce·ka (pät chā′kə), *n. Pali.* pratyeka.

pac·cha (pät′chä), *n.* an Incan wooden vessel for holding liquids. [< Quechua]

pace¹ (pās), *n., v.,* **paced, pac·ing.** —*n.* **1.** a rate of movement, esp. in stepping, walking, etc.: *to hike at a pace of three miles an hour.* **2.** a rate of activity, progress, growth, performance, etc.; tempo. **3.** any of various standard lineal measures, representing the space naturally measured by the movement of the feet in walking. Cf. **geometrical pace, military pace, Roman pace. 4.** a single step: *She took three paces in the direction of the door.* **5.** the distance covered in a step: *Stand six paces inside the gates.* **6.** a manner of stepping; gait. **7.** a gait of a horse or other animal in which the feet on the same side are lifted and put down together. **8.** any of the gaits of a horse. **9.** a raised step or platform. **10. put one through one's paces,** to cause to prove ability or show skill: *The French teacher put her pupils through their paces for the visitors.* **11. set the pace,** to act as an example for others to rival; be the most progressive or successful: *an agency that sets the pace in advertising.* **12.** *Obs.* a herd of asses. —*v.t.* **13.** to set the pace for, as in racing. **14.** to traverse or go over with steps: *He paced the floor nervously.* **15.** to measure by paces. **16.** to train to a certain pace; exercise in pacing: *to pace a horse.* **17.** (of a horse) to run (a distance) at a pace: *Hanover II paced a mile.* —*v.i.* **18.** to take slow, regular steps. **19.** to walk up and down nervously, as to expend nervous energy. **20.** (of a horse) to go at a pace; amble. [ME *pas* < OF < L *pass(us)* step, pace, n. use of ptp. of *pandere* to spread (the legs, in walking)]
—**Syn. 8.** step, amble, rack, trot, jog, canter, gallop, walk, run, singlefoot. **18, 19.** PACE, PLOD, TRUDGE refer to a steady and monotonous kind of walking. PACE suggests steady, measured steps as of one completely lost in thought or impelled by some distraction: *to pace up and down.* PLOD implies a slow, heavy, laborious, weary walk: *The mailman plods his weary way.* TRUDGE implies a spiritless but usually steady and doggedly persistent walk: *The farmer trudged to his village to buy his supplies.* —**Ant. 18.** scurry, scamper, skip.

pa·ce² (pā′sē; *Lat.* pä′ke), *prep.* with the permission of (a courteous form used to mention one who disagrees): *I do not, pace my rival, hold with the ideas of the reactionists.* [< L *pāce* in peace, by favor (abl. sing. of *pax* peace, favor, pardon, grace)]

paced (pāst), *adj.* **1.** having a specified or indicated pace (usually used in combination): *slow-paced.* **2.** counted out or measured by paces. **3.** run at a pace set by a pacemaker. [PACE¹ + -ED³]

pace′ egg′ (pās), *Brit.* See **Easter egg.** [ME (Scot and north) *paas, pase, pask* Easter. See PASCH]

pace·mak·er (pās′mā′kər), *n.* **1.** one who sets the pace, as in racing. **2.** a person, group, or organization that is the most progressive or successful and serves as a model to be imitated, followed, etc. **3.** *Med.* an instrument implanted beneath the skin for providing a normal heartbeat by electrical stimulation of the heart muscle, used in certain heart conditions. Also called **pacesetter** (for defs. 1, 2). [PACE¹ + MAKER] —**pace′mak′ing,** *n.*

Pa·cem in Ter·ris (pä′chem in ter′is), *Latin.* Peace on Earth (opening words and the title of an encyclical of Pope John XXIII issued in 1963 on world political unity).

pac·er (pā′sər), *n.* **1.** one who paces. **2.** a pacemaker. **3.** a standard-bred horse that is used for pacing in harness racing. [PACE¹ + -ER¹]

pace·set·ter (pās′set′ər), *n.* pacemaker (defs. 1, 2). [PACE¹ + SETTER]

pa·cha (pə shä′, pash′ə), *n.* pasha. —**pa·cha′dom,** *n.*

pa·cha·lic (pə shä′lik), *n.* pashalik.

Pach·el·bel (päкн′əl bel′), *n.* **Jo·hann** (yō′hän), 1653–1706, German organist and composer.

pa·chin·ko (pə ching′kō), *n.* a Japanese pinball game played on a vertical machine in which slots struck by the player's ball release other balls that in turn are exchanged for noncash prizes. [< Jap]

pa·chi·si (pə chē′zē, pä-), *n.* parcheesi.

Pach·mann (päкн′män′), *n.* **Vla·di·mir de** (vlä dē′mir də), 1848–1933, Russian pianist.

Pa·cho·mi·us (pə kō′mē əs), *n.* **Saint,** A.D. 292?–348?, Egyptian ascetic: founder of the cenobitical form of monasticism. —**Pa·cho′mi·an,** *adj., n.*

pach·ou·li (pach′o͝o lē, pə cho͞o′lē), *n.* patchouli.

Pa·chu·ca (pä cho͞o′kä), *n.* a city in and the capital of Hidalgo, in central Mexico: silver mines. 69,432 (1960).

pach·y·derm (pak′i dûrm′), *n.* **1.** any of the thick-skinned nonruminant ungulates, as the elephant, hippopotamus, and rhinoceros. **2.** an elephant. **3.** a person who is not sensitive to criticism, ridicule, etc.; a thick-skinned person. [back formation from NL *pachydermata* < Gk *pachý(s)* thick + *dérmata*, pl. of *dérma* skin] —**pach′y·der′mal, pach′y·der′mous, pach′y·der′mic, pach′y·der′moid,** *adj.*

pach·y·der·ma·tous (pak′i dûr′mə təs), *adj.* **1.** of, pertaining to, or characteristic of pachyderms. **2.** thick-skinned; insensitive: *a pachydermatous indifference to insults.* [< NL *Pachydermat(a)* a classification of mammals (see PACHYDERM) + -OUS] —**pach′y·der′ma·tous·ly,** *adv.*

pach·y·lo·sis (pak′ə lō′sis), *n. Med.* scaling and thickening of the skin, esp. of the legs. [< NL, equiv. to Gk *pachyl(ós)* thickish + *-ōsis* -OSIS]

pach·y·san·dra (pak′i san′drə), *n.* any plant of the genus *Pachysandra*, as the Allegheny spurge or Japanese spurge, often used as a ground cover in the U.S. [< NL, equiv. to Gk *pachýs* thick + NL *-andra*, fem. of *-andrus* -ANDROUS]

pa·cif·ic (pə sif′ik), *adj.* **1.** tending to make peace; conciliatory: *pacific overtures.* **2.** not warlike; peaceable; mild: *a pacific disposition.* **3.** at peace; peaceful: *a pacific era in history.* **4.** calm; tranquil: *The Wabash is a pacific river.* **5.** (*cap.*) of or pertaining to the Pacific Ocean. **6.** (*cap.*) of or pertaining to the region bordering on the Pacific Ocean: *the Pacific States.* —*n.* (*cap.*) **7.** See **Pacific Ocean. 8.** a steam locomotive having a four-wheeled front truck, six driving wheels, and a two-wheeled rear truck. [< L *pācific(us)*, lit., peacemaking, equiv. to *pāci-* (s. of *pāx*) peace + *-ficus* -FIC]
—**Syn. 1.** appeasing. PACIFIC, PEACEABLE, PEACEFUL describe that which is in a state of peace. That which is PACIFIC tends toward the making, promoting, or preserving of peace: *pacific intentions.* That which is PEACEABLE desires to be at peace or is free from the disposition to quarrel: *peaceable citizens.* That which is PEACEFUL is in a calm state, characteristic of, or characterized by, peace: *a peaceful death.* **2.** quiet, gentle, still. —**Ant. 1.** hostile. **2.** agitated.

Pa·cif·ic (pə sif′ik), *n.* a town in E Missouri. 2795 (1960).

Pa·cif·i·ca (pə sif′i kə), *n.* a city in W California, S of San Francisco. 20,995 (1960).

pa·cif·i·cal (pə sif′i kəl), *n. Archaic.* pacific (defs. 1–4). [< L *pācific(us)* PACIFIC + -AL¹]

pa·cif·i·cal·ly (pə sif′ik lē), *adv.* peaceably, mildly, calmly, or quietly. [PACIFICAL + -LY]

pa·cif·i·cate (pə sif′ə kāt′), *v.t.,* **-cat·ed, -cat·ing.** to pacify. [< L *pācificāt(us)* made peace (ptp. of *pācificāre*). See PACIFY, -ATE¹] —**pac·i·fi·ca·tion** (pas′ə fə kā′shən), *n.* —**pa·cif′i·ca′tor,** *n.* —**pa·cif·i·ca·to·ry** (pə sif′ə kə tôr′ē, -tōr′ē), *adj.*

Pacif′ic barracu′da, a small, slender barracuda, *Sphyraena argentea*, found from Alaska to Lower California, used for food. Also called **California barracuda, scooter.**

Pacif′ic dog′wood, a dogwood, *Cornus nuttalli*, of western central North America, having red or orange fruit and petallike, white or pinkish bracts.

Pacif′ic high′, a semipermanent, atmospheric, high-pressure system of the Pacific Ocean, centered, in the mean, about 1000 miles northeast of Hawaii: one of the subtropical highs.

pa·cif·i·cism (pə sif′i siz′əm), *n. Brit.* pacifism. [PACIFIC + -ISM] —**pa·cif′i·cist,** *n.*

Pacif′ic madro′ne, madroño.

pa·ci·fi·co (pä thē′fē kô′, -sē′-), *n., pl.* **-cos** (-kôs′). *Spanish.* **1.** a peaceful person. **2.** a native of Cuba or the Philippine Islands who did not resist Spanish occupation of his country.

Pacif′ic O′cean, an ocean bordered by the American continents, Asia, and Australia: largest ocean in the world; divided by the equator into the North Pacific and the South Pacific. 70,000,000 sq. mi.; greatest known depth, 35,433 ft.

Pacif′ic stur′geon. See **white sturgeon.**

Pacif′ic time′. See under **standard time.**

Pacif′ic tree′ frog′, a terrestrial frog, *Hyla regilla*, of western North America, having a dark stripe along each side of the head.

pac·i·fi·er (pas′ə fī′ər), *n.* **1.** one who or that which pacifies. **2.** any rubber or plastic device, often shaped into a nipple, for a baby to suck on. **3.** See **teething ring.** [PACIFY + -ER¹]

pac·i·fism (pas′ə fiz′əm), *n.* **1.** opposition to war or violence of any kind. **2.** the principle or policy of establishing and maintaining universal peace or such relations among all nations that all differences may be adjusted without recourse to war. **3.** nonresistance to aggression. [< F *pacifisme.* See PACIFIC, -ISM]

pac·i·fist (pas′ə fist), *n.* **1.** a person who believes in pacifism or is opposed to war or to violence of any kind. **2.** a man whose personal belief in pacifism causes him to refuse being drafted into military service. Cf. **conscientious objector. 3.** a person who refuses to resist violence or aggression. **—***adj.* **4.** pacifistic. [< F *pacifiste.* See PACIFIC, -IST]

pac·i·fis·tic (pas′ə fis′tik), *adj.* of or pertaining to pacifism or pacifists. [PACIF(IC) + -ISTIC] **—pac′-i·fis′ti·cal·ly,** *adv.*

pac·i·fy (pas′ə fī′), *v.t.,* **-fied, -fy·ing. 1.** to bring or restore to a state of peace or tranquillity; quiet; calm: *to pacify an angry man.* **2.** to appease: *to pacify one's appetite.* **3.** to reduce to a submissive state; subdue. [late ME < L *pācific(āre)* (to) make peace. See PACIFIC, -FY] **—pac′i·fi′a·ble,** *adj.* **—pac′i·fy′ing·ly,** *adv.*

pack[1] (pak), *n.* **1.** a group of things wrapped or tied up for easy handling or carrying; a bundle, esp. one to be carried on the back of an animal or a person: *a mule pack; a hiker's pack.* **2.** a definite quantity or standard measure of something wrapped up for merchandising: *a pack of cigarettes.* **3.** the quantity of something that is packaged, canned, or the like, at one time, in one season, etc.: *last year's salmon pack.* **4.** a group of people or things: *a pack of fools.* **5.** a group of certain animals of the same kind, esp. predatory ones: *a pack of wolves.* **6.** *Hunting.* a number of hounds, esp. foxhounds and beagles, regularly used together in a hunt. **7.** a complete set of playing cards, usually 52 in number; deck. **8.** a considerable area of pieces of floating ice driven or packed together. **9.** *Metalworking.* a pile of metal sheets for hot-rolling together. **10.** *Med.* **a.** a wrapping of the body in wet or dry cloths for therapeutic purposes. **b.** the cloths so used. **c.** *Obs.* the state of being so wrapped. **11.** *Mining.* **a.** Also called **pack wall.** a rubble wall for supporting a roof. **b.** any of various other roof supports of timber, timber and rubble, or rubble and wire mesh. **12.** a cosmetic material, usually of a pastelike consistency, applied either to the face or to the hair and scalp: *a mud pack; a beauty pack; a henna pack.* **13.** *Obs.* a plot; conspiracy. **14.** *Obs.* a low or worthless person.
—*v.t.* **15.** to make into a pack or bundle. **16.** to form into a group or compact mass. **17.** to fill with anything compactly arranged: *to pack a trunk.* **18.** to press or crowd together within; cram: *The crowd packed the gallery.* **19.** to prepare for marketing by putting into containers or packages: *to pack fruit for shipping.* **20.** to make airtight, vaportight, or watertight by stuffing: *to pack the piston of a steam engine.* **21.** to cover or envelop with something pressed closely around. **22.** to load, as with a pack or packs: *We packed the mules and then set off for the lake.* **23.** to carry or wear, esp. as part of one's usual equipment: *to pack a gun.* **24.** to send off summarily (sometimes fol. by *off, away,* etc.): *We packed her off to her mother because she wouldn't follow the rules here.* **25.** *Slang.* to be able to deliver (a powerful blow): *He packs a better punch than any heavyweight in years.* **26.** to treat with a therapeutic pack.
—*v.i.* **27.** to pack goods in compact form, as for transportation or storage (often fol. by *up*). **28.** to place clothes and personal items in a suitcase, trunk, etc., preparatory to traveling. **29.** to be capable of or suitable for compact storage or packing for transportation: *articles that pack well.* **30.** to crowd together, as persons: *The audience packed into the auditorium.* **31.** to become compacted: *Wet snow packs readily.* **32.** to collect into a group: *The grouse began to pack.* **33.** to leave hastily (usually fol. by *off, away,* etc.). **34. pack in** or **up,** *Brit.* to relinquish or give up; quit: *to pack in football; to pack up smoking.*
—*adj.* **35.** transporting, or used in transporting, a pack: *pack animals.* **36.** *Chiefly Scot.* (of animals) tame. **37.** compressed into a pack; packed. **38.** used in or adapted for packing: *pack equipment.* [ME *pak, packe* < MFlem *pac*] **—pack′a·ble,** *adj.*
—Syn. 1. knapsack. See **package. 4.** band, company, crew. **5.** See **flock**[1].

pack[2] (pak), *v.t.* to choose, collect, arrange, or manipulate (cards, persons, facts, etc.) so as to serve one's own purposes: *to pack a jury.* [? var. of PACT]

pack[3] (pak), *adj. Scot.* on terms of close friendship; intimate. [? special use of PACK[1]]

pack·age (pak′ij), *n., v.,* **-aged, -ag·ing. —***n.* **1.** a bundle of something, usually of small or medium size, that is packed and wrapped or boxed; parcel. **2.** a container, as a box, case, etc., in which something may be packed. **3.** *Informal.* something conceived of as a compact unit having particular characteristics: *That girl is a neat little package.* **4.** the packing of goods, freight, etc. **5.** a finished product contained in a unit that is suitable for immediate installation and operation, as a power or heating unit. **6.** a group, combination, or series of related parts or elements to be accepted or rejected as a single unit. **7.** a completed program or series of programs, as for radio or television, sold to an advertiser or network, usually for a lump sum. **—***v.t.* **8.** to put into wrappings or a container. **9.** to design and manufacture a package for (a product or series of related products): *They package their soaps in eye-catching wrappers.* **10.** to group or combine (a series of related parts) into a single unit. [< D *pakkage.* See PACK[1], -AGE]
—Syn. 1. PACKAGE, PACK, PACKET, PARCEL refer to a bundle or to something fastened together. A PACKAGE is a bundle of things packed and wrapped: *a package from the drug store.* A PACK is a large bundle or bale of things put or fastened together, usually wrapped up or in a bag, case, etc., to be carried by a person or a beast of burden: *a peddler's pack.* A PACKET, originally a package of letters or dispatches, is a small package or bundle: *a packet of gems.* A PARCEL is an object or objects wrapped up to form a single, small bundle: *a parcel containing two dresses.* **2.** carton.

pack′age deal′, 1. an agreement in which one pays a stipulated price for a group of related products or services: *a package deal from a book club.* **2.** the products or services included in such an agreement: *We got a package deal of maid, cook, gardener, and chauffeur with the rent.* **3.** an agreement or plan in which the approval of one proposal is contingent upon the approval of another: *The union wanted management to approve a package deal increasing wages, retirement benefits, and the number of paid holidays.*

pack′age mill′, *Metalworking.* a mill having its own individual foundation.

pack′age store′, a store selling sealed bottles of alcoholic beverages that may only be consumed off the premises.

pack′age tour′, a planned tour in which one fee is charged for all expenses: *offering package tours of the chateau country.* Also, **pack′aged tour′.**

pack·er (pak′ər), *n.* **1.** one who or that which packs. **2.** a person who engages in packing as an occupation or business, esp. a person who packs food for market: *a meat packer.* [PACK[1] + -ER[1]]

pack·et (pak′it), *n.* **1.** a small pack or package of anything: *a packet of letters.* **2.** a boat that carries mail, passengers, and goods regularly on a fixed route. **3.** any ship. **4.** *Cards.* a part of a pack of cards after being cut. **5.** *Chiefly Brit.* **a.** *Informal.* a sizeable amount of money, esp. unearned money. **b.** *Slang.* a painful blow or beating. **c.** *Slang.* misfortune or failure. **—***v.t.* **6.** to bind up in a package or parcel. [< MF *pacquet,* equiv. to *pacq(uer)* (to) PACK[1] + *-et* -ET]
—Syn. 1. See **package.**

pack·horse (pak′hôrs′), *n.* **1.** a horse used for carrying goods, freight, supplies, etc. **2.** *Archaic.* a drudge. [PACK[1] + HORSE]

pack′ ice′, a large area of floating ice formed over a period of many years and consisting of pieces of ice driven together by wind, current, etc. Also called **ice pack.**

pack·ing (pak′ing), *n.* **1.** the act or work of one who or that which packs. **2.** the preparation and packaging of foodstuffs, esp. to be sold at wholesale. **3.** the way in which something is packed. **4.** the act or an instance of transporting supplies, goods, etc., on the backs of horses, mules, or men. **5.** material used to cushion or protect goods packed in a container. **6.** material, often in the form of a grease-impregnated fibrous ring, compressed inside a stuffing box or the like to prevent leakage around the moving shaft of an engine, pump, or valve. **7.** *Print.* rubber, paper, or other material fastened to the tympan or cylinder of a press to provide pressure to produce a printed impression. [ME *pakking.* See PACK[1], -ING[1]]

pack′ing box′, a box or crate in which goods are packed for transport or storage. Also called **pack′ing case′.**

pack′ing frac′tion, *Physics.* a measure of the stability of an atomic nucleus, equal to the quotient of the difference of the mass number and the mass of the atom divided by the mass number.

pack′ing house′, an establishment for processing and packing foods, to be sold at wholesale, esp. meat.

pack′ing nut′. See **stuffing nut.**

pack′ing ring′. See **piston ring.**

pack·man (pak′mən), *n., pl.* **-men.** a peddler. [PACK[1] + MAN[1]]

pack·plane (pak′plān′), *n.* an airplane having a detachable main cargo compartment. [PACK[1] + PLANE[1]]

pack′ rat′, 1. a large, bushy-tailed rodent, *Neotoma cinerea,* of North America, noted for carrying away small articles which it then keeps in its nest. **2.** *Informal.* **a.** an old prospector or guide. **b.** a person who collects, saves, or hoards useless small items.

pack′ roll′ing, *Metalworking.* the hot rolling of metal sheets in two or more thicknesses to produce composite sheets. Also called **ply rolling.**

pack·sack (pak′sak′), *n.* a leather or canvas carrying bag, usually one that can be strapped over the shoulder and used to carry food and personal items when a person is traveling. [PACK[1] + SACK[1]]

pack·sad·dle (pak′sad′əl), *n.* a saddle specifically designed for supporting the load on a pack animal. [ME *pakke saddil.* See PACK[1], SADDLE]

pack·thread (pak′thred′), *n.* a strong thread or twine for sewing or tying up packages. [ME *pakthrede.* See PACK[1], THREAD] **—pack′thread′ed,** *adj.*

pack·train (pak′trān′), *n.* a line or succession of animals, as mules, burros, etc., used to transport food and supplies, over terrain unsuitable for wagons or other vehicles. [PACK[1] + TRAIN]

pack′ wall′, pack (def. 11a).

pact (pakt), *n.* **1.** an agreement, covenant, or compact: *We made a pact not to argue any more.* **2.** an agreement or treaty between two or more nations: *a pact between Germany and Italy.* [late ME *pact(e)* < MF < L *pact(um),* n. use of neut. of ptp. of *paciscī* to make a bargain, contract]
—Syn. 1. contract, bond, bargain, deal. **2.** league, union, alliance.

pac·tion (pak′shən), *n.* an agreement. [late ME *pactyon* < L *pactiōn-* (s. of *pactiō*) bargain, agreement. See PACT, -ION] **—pac′tion·al,** *adj.* **—pac′tion·al·ly,** *adv.*

Pac·to·lus (pak tō′ləs), *n.* a small river in Asia Minor, in ancient Lydia: famous for the gold washed from its sands.

Pa·cy (pā′sē), *n.* a boy's given name.

pad[1] (pad), *n., v.,* **pad·ded, pad·ding. —***n.* **1.** a cushionlike mass of soft material used for comfort, protection, or stuffing. **2.** a soft, stuffed cushion used as a saddle; a padded leather saddle without a tree. **3.** a number of sheets of paper held together at one edge to form a tablet. **4.** a soft, ink-soaked block of absorbent material for inking a rubber stamp. **5.** one of the cushionlike protuberances on the underside of the feet of dogs, foxes, and some other animals. See diag. under **dog. 6.** the foot, as of a fox, hare, or wolf. **7.** a piece or fold of gauze or other absorbent material for use as a surgical dressing or a protective covering. **8.** *Zool.* a pulvillus as on the tarsus or foot of an insect. **9.** the large floating leaf of the water lily. **10.** *Rocketry.* See **launch pad. 11.** *Slang.* **a.** one's apartment or home. **b.** one's room. **c.** one's bed. **d.** a room where people gather to take narcotics; an addicts' den. **12.** *Elect.* a nonadjustable attenuator consisting of a network of fixed resistors. **13.** *Shipbuilding.* **a.** a metal plate riveted or welded to a surface as a base or attachment for bolts, hooks, eyes, etc. **b.** a piece of wood laid on the back of a deck beam to give the deck surface a desired amount of camber. **14.** *Carpentry.* **a.** a handle for holding various small, interchangeable saw blades. **b.** Also, **pod.** a socket in a brace for a bit. **15.** *Foundry.* a raised surface on a casting. **16.** a small deposit of weld metal, as for building up a worn surface. **—***v.t.* **17.** to furnish, protect, fill out, or stuff with a pad or padding. **18.** to expand (writing or speech) deliberately with unnecessary material or language. **19.** *Foundry.* to add metal to (a casting) above its required dimensions, to insure the flow of enough metal to all parts. **—***v.i.* **20.** to insure the proper forging of a piece. [special uses of obs. *pad* bundle to lie on, ? b. PACK[1] and BED]

pad[2] (pad), *n., v.,* **pad·ded, pad·ding. —***n.* **1.** a dull sound, as of footsteps on the ground. **2.** a road horse, as distinguished from a hunter or workhorse. **3.** a highwayman. **4.** *Brit. Dial.* a path, lane, or road. [< D; c. PATH]
—*v.t.* **5.** to travel along on foot. **6.** to beat down by treading. **—***v.i.* **7.** to travel on foot; walk. **8.** to walk so that one's footsteps make a dull sound. [< MD *pad(en)* (to) make or follow a path: c. OE *pæththan* to traverse. See FOOTPAD]

PaD, Pennsylvania Dutch.

Pa·dang (pä däng′), *n.* a seaport in W central Sumatra, in W Indonesia. 143,699 (1961).

pa·dauk (pe douk′), *n.* See **padouk wood.**

pad′ded cell′, a room, as in a mental hospital, with heavily padded walls for the confinement of violent inmates.

pad·ding (pad′ing), *n.* **1.** material, as cotton or straw, used to pad something. **2.** unnecessary verbal material used deliberately to lengthen a speech, essay, etc. **3.** the act of one who or that which pads. [PAD[1] + -ING[1]]

Pad·ding·ton (pad′ing tən), *n.* a residential borough of W London, England. 115,322 (1961).

pad·dle[1] (pad′əl), *n., v.,* **-dled, -dling. —***n.* **1.** a short, flat bladed oar for propelling and steering a canoe, usually held in both hands and moved more or less through a vertical arc. **2.** any of various similar implements used for mixing, stirring, or beating. **3.** any of various similar but smaller implements with a short handle for holding in one hand and a wide or rounded blade, used for a racket in paddle tennis, ping-pong, etc. **4.** such an implement, or a similarly shaped makeshift one, used to spank a child or in hazing freshmen, initiates to a fraternity, etc. **5.** an implement used for beating garments while washing them in running water, as in a stream. **6.** Also called **float.** a blade of a paddle wheel. **7.** See **paddle wheel. 8.** Also called **float.** any of the blades by which a water wheel is turned. **9.** a flipper or limb of a penguin, turtle, whale, etc. **10.** an act of paddling. **11.** Also, **pattle.** *Brit. Dial.* a small spade with a long handle, used to dig up thistles. **12.** (in a gate of a lock or sluice) a panel that slides to permit the passage of water. **—***v.i.* **13.** to propel or travel in a canoe or the like by using a paddle. **14.** to row lightly or gently with oars. **15.** to move by means of paddle wheels, as a steamer. **—***v.t.* **16.** to propel with a paddle: *to paddle a canoe.* **17.** to spank with or as with a paddle. **18.** to stir, mix, or beat with or as with a paddle. **19.** to convey by paddling, as in a canoe. **20.** to hit (a ping-pong ball or the like) with a paddle. [late ME *padell*] **—pad′dler,** *n.*

pad·dle[2] (pad′əl), *v.i.,* **-dled, -dling. 1.** to move the feet or hands playfully in shallow water; dabble. **2.** to toy with the fingers. **3.** to toddle. [?] **—pad′-dler,** *n.*

pad·dle·board (pad′əl bōrd′, -bôrd′), *n.* a type of surfboard with one end rounded and the other tapered to a point, used chiefly in surfing and often in lifesaving. [PADDLE[1] + BOARD]

pad′dle box′, a structure enclosing a paddle wheel.

pad·dle·fish (pad′əl fish′), *n., pl.* **-fish·es,** (*esp. collectively*) **-fish.** a large ganoid fish, *Polyodon spathula,* found in the Mississippi River and its larger tributaries, having a long, flat, paddlelike snout. [PADDLE[1] + FISH]

pad′dle ten′nis, a variety of tennis played with wooden paddles and a ball of sponge rubber on a court about half the size of and having a lower net than a tennis court.

pad′dle wheel′, an engine-driven wheel for propelling a vessel, having a number of paddles entering the water more or less perpendicularly. **—pad′dle-wheel′,** *adj.*

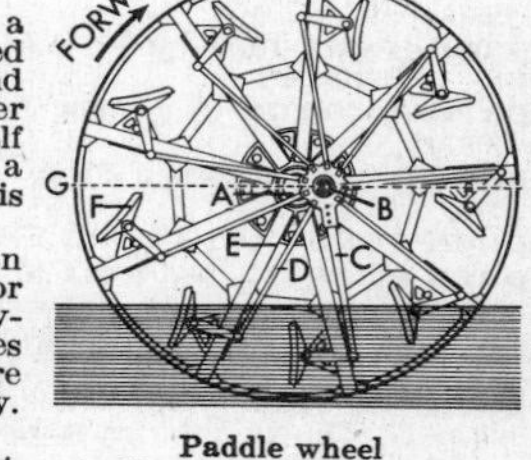

Paddle wheel
A, Shaft; B, Hub of radius rods; C, Principal radius rod; D, Radius rod; E, Arm; F, Paddle; G, Level of main deck

pad′dle wing′, *Naut.* sponson (def. 3).

pad·dock[1] (pad′ək), *n.* **1.** a small, usually enclosed field near a stable or barn for pasturing or exercising animals. **2.** *Horse Racing.* the enclosure in which the horses are saddled and mounted. **3.** *Australian.* any enclosed field or pasture. **—***v.t.* **4.** to confine or enclose in or as in a paddock. [var. of ME *parrok,* OE *pearroc* enclosure, orig. fence. See PARK]

pad·dock[2] (pad′ək), *n. Scot. and North Eng.* a frog or toad. Also, **poddock, puddock.** [ME *paddok(e),* deriv. of early ME *pad* toad; akin to D, LG *pad,* Icel *padda;* see -OCK]

pad·dy (pad′ē), *n., pl.* **-dies. 1.** a rice field. **2.** rice. **3.** rice in the husk, uncut or gathered. [< Malay *pādī*]

Pad·dy (pad′ē), *n., pl.* **-dies. 1.** *Slang.* an Irishman or one of Irish descent. **2.** a boy's given name. [familiar var. of Ir *Padraig* Patrick]

pad·dy·mel·on (pad′ē mel′ən), *n.* pademelon.

pad′dy wag′on, *Slang.* See **patrol wagon.** [prob. PADDY (policeman)]

pad·dy·whack (pad′ē hwak′, -wak′), *n.* **1.** *Brit. Informal.* a fit of temper; rage. **2.** *Informal.* a spanking. —v.t. 3. Informal. to spank or beat. Also, **pad·dy-wack** (pad′ē wak′). [PADDY + WHACK]

pad·e·mel·on (pad′ē mel′ən), n. any of several small, Australian wallabies, esp. of the genus *Thylogale*, growing to a length of about three feet, excluding the tail. Also, **paddymelon.** [alter. (by assoc. with *melon*) of an Australian native name]

Pa′den Cit′y (pād′ən), a town in NW West Virginia. 3137 (1960).

Pa·de·rew·ski (pä′de ref′ski; Eng. pad′ə ref′skē, -rev′-), n. **I·gnace** (Fr. ē nyas′) or **Ig·na·cy Jan** (Pol. ig nä′tse yän), 1860–1941, Polish pianist, composer, patriot, and statesman.

pad·eye (pad′ī′), n., pl. **-eyes.** a ring fixed to the structure of a vessel as a hold for small lines, tackles, etc. Also called **lug pad.** [PAD[1] + EYE]

pad′ foot′, *Furniture.* any of various kinds of feet to a cabriole leg, as club, slipper, trifid, or web, having the form of a flattened extension of its lines.

Pad foot

Pa·di·shah (pä′di shä′), n. great king; emperor (a title applied formerly to the Shah of Iran, the Sultan of Turkey, and to the British sovereign as emperor in India). Also, **pa′di·shah′.** [< Pers (poetical form), equiv. to *pādi-* (earlier *pati*) lord + *shāh* SHAH]

pa·dle (pād′əl), n. *Scot.* a hoe. Also, **paidle.** [var. of PADDLE[1]]

pad·lock (pad′lok′), n. 1. a portable or detachable lock with a pivoted or sliding shackle that can be passed through a staple, link, ring, or the like. —v.t. 2. to fasten with or as with a padlock. [ME *padlok.* See POD[3], LOCK[1]]

pad·nag (pad′nag′), n. a slow-moving, old or run-down horse; ambling nag. [PAD[2] + NAG[2]]

pa·douk′ wood′ (pə do͞ok′), an ornamental wood mottled in shades of yellowish red from a Malaysian tree, *Pterocarpus indicus*, used in inlaying and for making small articles. Also called **pa·douk′, padauk.** [*padouk* < Burmese native name]

Pa·do·va (pä′dô vä), n. Italian name of **Padua.**

pad·pa·rad′schah sap′phire (päd′pə rä′zhə), an orange, synthetic sapphire. [?]

pa·dre (pä′drā, -drē; Sp. pä′ᵺre; It. pä′dre), n., pl. **-dres** (-drāz, -drēz; Sp. -ᵺres), It. **-dri** (-drē). 1. father (used esp. in addressing or referring to a priest or clergyman). 2. a chaplain in military or naval service. [< Sp, Pg, It: father < L *pater*]

pa·dro·ne (pə drō′nē, -nā; It. pä drô′ne), n., pl. **-nes** (-nēz, -nāz), It. **-ni** (-nē). 1. a master; head. 2. an employer who almost entirely controls the lives of his employees for exploitative purposes by providing communal housing and eating arrangements, rigidly controlling occupational activities, etc. 3. the master or captain of a ship. 4. an innkeeper. [< It; see PATRON] —**pa·dro·nism** (pə drō′niz əm), n.

pad′ saw′, a small compass saw with a pad.

pad′ stone′, *Building Trades.* a stone templet.

Pad·u·a (paj′o͞o ə, pad′yo͞o ə), n. a city in NE Italy. 198,403 (1961). Italian, **Padova.** —**Pad′u·an,** adj.

pad·u·a·soy (paj′o͞o ə soi′), n., pl. **-soys.** 1. a smooth, strong, rich, silk fabric. 2. a garment made of this. [alter. of F *pou de soie* (var. of *poult de soie*, lit., pelt of silk) by assoc. with PADUA]

Pa·du·cah (pə do͞o′kə, -dyo͞o′-), n. a city in W Kentucky, at the junction of the Tennessee and Ohio rivers. 34,479 (1960).

Pa·dus (pā′dəs), n. ancient name of **Po.**

p. ae., (in prescriptions) equal parts. [< L *partes aequāles*]

pae·an (pē′ən), n. 1. any song of praise, joy, or triumph. 2. a hymn of invocation or thanksgiving to Apollo or some other ancient Greek deity. 3. (cap.) Also, **Paeon.** *Class. Myth.* a god serving as a physician to the Olympian gods, later identified with Apollo. Also, **pean** (for defs. 1, 2). [< L: religious or festive hymn, special use of *Paean* appellation of Apollo < Gk *Paiān* physician of the gods] —**pae′an·ism,** n.

paed-, var. of **ped-**[1]. Also, **paedo-.**

paed·a·gog·ic (ped′ə goj′ik, -gō′jik, pē′də-), adj. pedagogic.

paed·a·gog·ism (ped′ə gog′iz əm, -gô′giz-, pē′də-), n. pedagogism.

paed·a·gogue (ped′ə gog′, -gôg′, pē′də-), n. pedagogue.

paed·a·go·gy (ped′ə gō′jē, -goj′ē, pē′də-), n. pedagogy.

paed·er·ast (ped′ə rast′, pē′də-), n. pederast.

paed·er·as·ty (ped′ə ras′tē, pē′də-), n. pederasty. —**paed′er·as′tic,** adj. —**paed′er·as′ti·cal·ly,** adv.

pae·di·a·tri·cian (pē′dē ə trish′ən, ped′ē-), n. *Chiefly Brit.* pediatrician.

pae·di·at·rics (pē′dē a′triks, ped′ē-), n. (construed as sing.) *Chiefly Brit.* pediatrics. —**pae′di·at′ric,** adj.

paedo-, var. of **pedo-**[1]. Also, esp. before a vowel, **paed-.**

pae·do·bap·tism (pē′dō bap′tiz əm), n. pedobaptism.

pae·do·bap·tist (pē′dō bap′tist), n. pedobaptist.

pae·do·gen·e·sis (pē′də jen′i sis), n. reproduction by animals in the larval state, often by parthenogenesis. [< NL; see PAEDO-, -GENESIS] —**pae·do·ge·net·ic** (pē′dō jə net′ik), **pae′do·gen′ic,** adj.

pa·el·la (pä ā′lə, -el′ə, pə-; Sp. pä e′lyä, -e′yä), n. a Spanish dish prepared by simmering together chicken, rice, vegetables, saffron and other seasonings, and often meat and shellfish. [< Sp < Catalan: lit., frying pan, pot < MF *paelle* < L *patella* pan. See PATELLA]

pae·nu·la (pēn′yə lə), n., pl. **-lae** (-lē′), **-las.** a long, circular cloak, sleeveless and often hooded, worn by the poorer classes in ancient Rome. [< L]

pae·on (pē′ən), n. 1. *Class. Pros.* a foot of one long and three short syllables in any order. 2. (cap.) *Class. Myth.* paean (def. 3). [< L < Gk *paiōn*, Attic var. of *paiān* PAEAN]

Pae·o·ni·a (pē ō′nē ə), n. *Class. Myth.* an epithet of Athena, meaning "healer."

Pa·e·siel·lo (It. pä′e zyel′lô), n. **Gio·van·ni** (It. jô vän′nē). See **Paisiello, Giovanni.**

Paes·tum (pes′təm), n. an ancient coastal city of Lucania, in S Italy: the extant ruins include three Greek temples and a Roman amphitheater.

PaG, Pennsylvania German.

pa·gan (pā′gən), n. 1. one of a people or community professing a polytheistic religion, as the ancient Romans, Greeks, etc. 2. a person who is not a Christian, Jew, or Muslim. 3. an irreligious or hedonistic person. —adj. 4. pertaining to the worship or worshipers of any religion that is neither Christian, Jewish, nor Muslim. 5. of, pertaining to, or characteristic of pagans. 6. irreligious and hedonistic. [ME < ML, LL (eccl.) *pāgānus* worshiper of false gods, civilian (i.e., not a soldier of Christ), L: peasant, n. use of *pāgānus* (adj.), deriv. of *pāgus* village, rural district (akin to *pangere* to fix, make fast); see -AN] —**pa′gan·ish,** adj. —**pa′gan·ish·ly,** adv.
—**Syn. 2.** heathen, idolater, gentile. **5.** See **heathen. 6.** idolatrous.

pa·gan·dom (pā′gən dəm), n. 1. the part of the world inhabited by pagans. 2. pagans collectively. [PAGAN + -DOM]

Pa·ga·ni·ni (pag′ə nē′nē; It. pä′gä nē′nē), n. **Nic·co·lò** (nēk′kô lô′), 1784–1840, Italian composer and violinist.

pa·gan·ise (pā′gə nīz′), v.t., v.i., **-ised, -is·ing.** *Chiefly Brit.* paganize. —**pa′ga·ni·sa′tion,** n. —**pa′ga·nis′er,** n.

pa·gan·ism (pā′gə niz′əm), n. 1. pagan spirit or attitude in religious or moral questions. 2. the beliefs or practices of pagans. 3. the state of being a pagan. [ME *pāganysme* < LL *pāgānism(us)*, equiv. to L *pāgān(us)* PAGAN + *-ismus* -ISM] —**pa′gan·ist,** adj., n. —**pa′gan·ist′ic,** adj.

pa·gan·ize (pā′gə nīz′), v., **-ized, -iz·ing.** —v.t. 1. to make pagan. —v.i. 2. to become pagan. Also, esp. Brit., **paganise.** [PAGAN + -IZE] —**pa′gan·i·za′tion,** n. —**pa′gan·iz′er,** n.

page[1] (pāj), n., v., **paged, pag·ing.** —n. 1. one side of a leaf of something printed or written, as a book, manuscript, or letter. 2. the entire leaf of such a printed or written thing: *He tore out one of the pages.* 3. a single sheet of paper for writing. 4. any noteworthy or distinctive event or period: *a reign that formed a gloomy page in English history.* 5. *Print.* the type set and arranged for a page. —v.t. 6. to paginate. [< MF < L *pāgina*, akin to *pangere* to fix, make fast]

page[2] (pāj), n., v., **paged, pag·ing.** —n. 1. a boy servant or attendant. 2. a youth in attendance on a person of rank or, in medieval times, a youth being trained for knighthood. 3. a young male attendant or employee, usually in uniform, who carries messages, ushers guests, runs errands, etc. 4. a boy or man employed by a legislature to carry messages and run errands for the members, as in the U.S. Congress. —v.t. 5. to summon formally by calling out the name of repeatedly: *He had his father paged in the hotel lobby.* 6. to attend as a page. [ME < OF < It *paggio* < ?]

Page (pāj), n. 1. **Thomas Nelson,** 1853–1922, U.S. novelist and diplomat. 2. **Walter Hines** (hīnz), 1855–1918, U.S. journalist, editor, and diplomat. 3. a town in N Arizona. 2960 (1960). 4. a boy's given name.

pag·eant (paj′ənt), n. 1. an elaborate public spectacle illustrative of the history of a place, institution, or the like, often given in dramatic form or as a procession of colorful floats. 2. a costumed procession, masque, allegorical tableau, or the like forming part of public or social festivities. 3. something comparable to such a spectacle or procession in its colorful variety, splendor, or grandeur: *the pageant of Renaissance history.* 4. a pretentious display or show that conceals a lack of real importance or meaning. 5. a platform or stage, usually moving on wheels, on which scenes from the medieval mystery plays were presented. 6. a stage bearing any kind of spectacle. [ME *pagyn* < AL *pāgina* a stage for plays, scene, platform, special use of L *pāgina* PAGE[1]] —**pag′eant·eer′,** n. —**pa·gean·tic** (pə jan′tik), adj.

pag·eant·ry (paj′ən trē), n., pl. **-ries.** 1. spectacular display; pomp: *the pageantry of a coronation.* 2. mere show; empty display. 3. pageants collectively; pageants and the performance of pageants. [PAGEANT + -RY]

page·boy (pāj′boi′), n. 1. a woman's hair style in which the hair is rolled under at shoulder-length. 2. a youth or man who works as a page, as at a hotel. Also, **page′ boy′.** [PAGE[2] + BOY]

page′ chair′. See **porter chair.**

Page·dale (pāj′dāl′), n. a town in E Missouri. 5106 (1960).

Pag·et (paj′it), n. **Sir James,** 1814–99, English surgeon and pathologist.

pag·i·nal (paj′ə nəl), adj. 1. of or pertaining to pages. 2. consisting of pages. 3. page for page: *a paginal reprint.* [< LL *pāgināl(is)* of, belonging to a page. See PAGE[1], -AL[1]]

pag·i·nate (paj′ə nāt′), v.t., **-nat·ed, -nat·ing.** to indicate the sequence of (pages) by numbers or other characters on each leaf of a book; to number the pages of. [< L *pāgin(a)* PAGE[1] + -ATE[1]]

pag·i·na·tion (paj′ə nā′shən), n. *Bibliog.* 1. the number of pages or leaves of a book, identified in bibliographical description or in cataloging the book. 2. the figures by which pages are numbered. 3. the act of paginating. [< L *pāgin(a)* PAGE[1] + -ATION]

Pa·gliac·ci, I (It. ē pä lyät′chē), an opera (1892) by Ruggiero Leoncavallo.

pagne (Fr. pan′yᵊ), n., pl. **pagnes** (Fr. pan′yᵊ). a garment, worn by the natives in some parts of Africa, consisting of a rectangular strip of cloth worn as a loincloth or wrapped around the torso to form a short skirt. [< F < Sp *paño* cloth << L *pann(um)*]

Pa·gnol (pa nyôl′), n. **Mar·cel** (mar sel′), 1895–1974, French playwright.

pa·go·da (pə gō′də), n. 1. (in India, Burma, China, etc.) a temple or sacred building, usually more or less pyramidal or forming a tower with upward-curving roofs over the individual stories. 2. any of several gold or silver coins of southern India, usually bearing a figure of such a temple, first issued by natives in the late 16th century and later also by British, French, and Dutch traders. [< Pg *pagode* temple << Pers *butkadah* (*but* idol + *kadah* temple, dwelling)] —**pa·go′da·like′,** adj.

pago′da tree′, a spreading, round-headed tree, *Sophora japonica*, of China and Korea, having yellowish white flowers in loose, showy clusters. Also called **Chinese scholar tree, Japanese pagoda tree.**

pag·o·dite (pag′ə dīt′, pə gō′dīt), n. a soft stone similar to pinite but containing more silica, and yellowish, greenish, or grayish in color: used in China to make small carvings. Also called **agalmatolite.** [< F (see PAGODA, -ITE[1]); so called because carved into pagodalike objects]

Pa·go Pa·go (päng′ō päng′ō), the chief harbor and town of American Samoa, on Tutuila island: naval station. 1251 (1960). Also, **Pa′go·pa′go, Pango Pango.**

Pagoda (Chinese), 11th century

pa·gu·ri·an (pə gyo͝or′ē ən), n. 1. a hermit crab, esp. of the genus *Pagurus.* —adj. 2. pertaining to or characteristic of a hermit crab. [< NL *Pagūr(us)* the typical genus (L: crab < Gk *págouros*; see PAGURID) + -IAN]

pa·gu·rid (pə gyo͝or′id, pag′yə rid), n. a pagurian. [back formation from NL *Pagūridae* the Pagurus family < Gk *Pagouridai* crab family, equiv. to *págour(os)* crab (see -PAGUS, URO-[2]) + *-idai* -ID[2]]

-pagus, a learned borrowing from Greek, used in pathological terminology to denote a fetal monster having a fixation specified by the preceding element of the compound: *thoracopagus.* [< NL < Gk *pagós* fixation, something fixed, solid]

pah (pä, pa), interj. (used as an exclamation of disgust or disbelief.)

Pa·hang (pä häng′), n. a state in Malaysia, on the SE Malay Peninsula. 354,316 (est. 1961); 13,820 sq. mi. *Cap.:* Kuala Lipis.

Pa·ha·ri (pä hä′rē), n., pl. **-ri, -ris.** 1. one of several hill peoples inhabiting the area in India SW of the Ganges river. 2. a member of these peoples. 3. a group of Indic languages or dialects spoken by the Pahari.

Pah·la·vi (pä′lə vē′), n., pl. **-vis** for 3, 4. 1. See **Riza Shah Pahlavi.** 2. See **Muhammad Riza Pahlavi.** 3. a member of the dynasty ruling in Iran from 1925 to 1979, founded by Riza Shah Pahlavi. 4. (l.c.) a former gold coin of Iran, equal to 20 rials. Also, **Pah′le·vi′.**

Pah·la·vi (pä′lə vē′), n. 1. the Indo-European, Iranian language of the Zoroastrian literature of the 3rd to the 10th centuries. 2. the script used in writing this language, derived from the Aramaic alphabet. [< Pers: Parthian]

pa·ho[1] (pä′hō, pä hō′), n., pl. **-hos.** a Philippine tree, *Mangifera altissima*, bearing an edible, mangolike fruit. Also called **pahutan.** [< Tagalog]

pa·ho[2] (pä′hō, -hōō), n., pl. **-hos.** a prayer stick of the Hopi Indians. [< Hopi *pāaho*]

pa·ho·e·ho·e (pə hō′ē hō′ē), n. basaltic lava having a smooth or billowy surface. Cf. **aa.** [< Hawaiian]

Pa·ho·kee (pə hō′kē), n. a town in Florida. 4709 (1960).

pa·hu·tan (pə ho͞o′tän), n. paho[1]. [< Tagalog *pahūtan*]

Pah′vant Val′ley plague′ (pä′vənt), *Pathol., Vet. Pathol.* tularemia.

paid (pād), v. a pt. and pp. of **pay**[1].

paid-in (pād′in′), adj. having paid the dues, initiation fees, etc., required by any organization or association: *The union has a paid-in membership of 60,000.* [adj. use of v. phrase *pay in*]

paid′-in sur′plus, *Accounting.* surplus paid in by purchasers of stock certificates sold at a premium.

pai·dle (pād′əl), n. *Scot.* padle.

paido-, var. of **pedo-**[1].

pai·dol·o·gy (pā dol′ə jē, pī-), n. *Rare.* pedology[2].

paik (pāk), *Scot. and North Eng.* —n. 1. a firm blow or hit. —v.t. 2. to hit or strike solidly. [?] —**paik′er,** n.

pail (pāl), n. 1. a cylindrical or nearly cylindrical container made of metal, wood, plastic, etc., with a semicircular handle, used for holding liquids or solids; bucket. 2. the amount filling a pail. [ME *payle* wooden vessel, OE *pægel* wine vessel, liquid measure < ML *pagella* liquid measure >> G *Pegel* water gauge]

pail·ful (pāl′fo͝ol′), n., pl. **-fuls.** a quantity sufficient to fill a pail. [PAIL + -FUL]

pail·lasse (pal yas′, pal′yas), n. *Chiefly Brit.* a mattress of straw; pallet. Also, **palliasse.** [< F < It *pagliaccio* straw pallet, equiv. to *pagli(a)* straw (< L *palea* chaff) + *-accio* pejorative n. suffix]

pail·lette (pal yet′, pə let′; Fr. pä yet′), n., pl. **pail·lettes** (pal yets′, pə lets′; Fr. pä yet′). 1. a spangle for ornamenting a costume. 2. (in enameling) a decorative piece of gold, silver, or colored foil. [< F; see PALLET[1]] —**pail·let′ted,** adj.

pail·lon (Fr. pä yôN′), n., pl. **pail·lons** (Fr. pä yôN′). a sheet of thin metallic foil used decoratively in enameling and gilding. [< F, special use of *paille* straw (see PALLET[1]) + *-on* n. suffix]

pai-loo (pī′lo͞o′), n., pl. **-loo, -loos.** (in Chinese architecture) a decorative or monumental gateway having a trabeated form with three compartments, the central one higher than the others. [< Chin, equiv. to *p'ai* tablet + *lou* tower]

pain (pān), n. 1. bodily suffering or distress, as due to injury, illness, etc. 2. a distressing sensation in a particular part of the body: *a back pain.* 3. mental or emotional suffering or torment: *I am sorry my news causes you such pain.* 4. **pains, a.** laborious or careful efforts; assiduous care: *Great pains have been taken to finish the project.* **b.** the suffering of childbirth. 5. **on** or **upon pain of,** liable to the penalty of: *on pain of death.* Also, **under pain of.** —v.t. 6. to cause physical pain to; hurt. 7. to cause (someone) mental or emotional pain;

distress: *Her sarcasm pained him.* —*v.i.* **8.** to have or give pain. [ME *peine* < OF < L *poena* penalty, pain < Gk *poinē* penalty]

—**Syn. 1, 2, 3.** torture, misery, torment. PAIN, ACHE, AGONY, ANGUISH are terms for sensations causing suffering or torment. PAIN and ACHE refer usually to physical sensations (except *heartache*); AGONY and ANGUISH may be physical or mental. PAIN suggests a sudden sharp twinge: *a pain in one's ankle.* ACHE applies to a continuous pain, whether acute or dull: *headache; muscular aches.* AGONY implies a continuous, excruciating, scarcely endurable pain: *in agony from a wound.* ANGUISH suggests not only extreme and long-continued pain, but also a feeling of despair. **2.** pang, twinge, stitch. **4.** See **care. 7.** afflict, torment; trouble, grieve. —**Ant. 3.** joy, delight. **7.** please.

painch (pānch), *n. Brit. Dial.* paunch.

Paine (pān), *n.* **1. Albert Big·e·low** (big′ə lō′), 1861–1937, U.S. author and editor. **2. Robert Treat,** 1731–1814, U.S. jurist and statesman. **3. Thomas,** 1737–1809, U.S. patriot and writer on government and religion, born in England.

pained (pānd), *adj.* **1.** hurt; injured. **2.** giving the appearance of distress, anguish, or resentment: *a pained look in reply to a sarcastic remark.* [ME; see PAIN, -ED[2]]

Paines·ville (pānz′vil), *n.* a city in NE Ohio, on Lake Erie. 16,116 (1960).

pain·ful (pān′fəl), *adj.* **1.** affected with, causing, or characterized by pain: *a painful wound; a painful night; a painful memory.* **2.** laborious; exacting; difficult: *a painful life.* **3.** *Archaic.* painstaking; careful. [ME; see PAIN, -FUL] —**pain′ful·ly,** *adv.* —**pain′ful·ness,** *n.*

—**Syn. 1.** distressing, torturing, agonizing, tormenting, excruciating. **2.** arduous. —**Ant. 1.** pleasant. **2.** easy.

pain·kil·ler (pān′kil′ər), *n. Informal.* something that relieves pain, esp. an analgesic. [PAIN + KILLER]

pain·less (pān′lis), *adj.* **1.** without pain; causing no pain: *painless dentistry; a painless cure.* **2.** *Informal.* not difficult; requiring little or no hard work or exertion. [PAIN + -LESS] —**pain′less·ly,** *adv.* —**pain′less·ness,** *n.*

pains·tak·ing (pānz′tā′king, pān′stā′-), *adj.* **1.** taking or characterized by taking pains or trouble; expending or showing diligent care and effort; careful: *a painstaking craftsman; painstaking research.* —*n.* **2.** careful and diligent effort. [PAIN + -S[3] + TAKING] —**pains′-tak′ing·ly,** *adv.* —**pains′tak′ing·ness,** *n.*

paint (pānt), *n.* **1.** a substance composed of solid coloring matter suspended in a liquid medium and applied as a protective or decorative coating to various surfaces, or to canvas or other materials in producing a work of art. **2.** an application of this. **3.** the dried surface pigment: *Don't scuff the paint.* **4.** the solid coloring matter alone; pigment. **5.** facial cosmetics, esp. lipstick, rouge, etc., designed to heighten natural color. **6.** *Chiefly Western U.S.* a pied, calico, or spotted horse or pony; pinto. —*v.t.* **7.** to produce (a picture, design, etc.) in paint: *to paint a portrait.* **8.** to represent in paint, as in oils, tempera, or water color: *to paint an actress as the Muse of tragedy.* **9.** to depict as if by painting; describe vividly in words: *The ads painted the resort as a winter wonderland.* **10.** to coat, cover, or decorate (something) with paint: *to paint a fence.* **11.** to color by or as if by painting: *Sunset painted the clouds pink.* **12.** to apply like paint, as a liquid medicine, cosmetic, etc.: *to paint a cut with iodine.* —*v.i.* **13.** to coat or cover anything with paint. **14.** to engage in painting as an art: *She has begun to paint in her spare time.* **15.** to put on or use facial cosmetics: *She's upstairs, primping and painting before her mirror.* **16. paint the town red,** *Slang.* to celebrate boisterously, esp. by making a round of stops at bars and night clubs. Also, **paint the town.** —*adj.* **17.** *Western U.S.* (of a horse) pinto. [ME *peinte(n)* < OF *peint,* ptp. of *peindre* < L *pingere* to paint] —**paint′less,** *adj.*

paint′ bridge′. See under **bridge**[1] (def. 18a).

paint·brush (pānt′brush′), *n.* **1.** any brush for applying paint, as one used in painting houses or one used in painting pictures. **2.** any plant of the figwort family. [PAINT + BRUSH[1]]

paint·ed (pān′tid), *adj.* **1.** reproduced or represented in paint: *a painted image.* **2.** covered with a coating of paint: *a painted chair.* **3.** unreal; artificial; feigned: *a painted life.* **4.** exaggerated or misrepresented: *a luridly painted version of what really happened.* **5.** covered with make-up, esp. to excess: *a painted showgirl.* **6.** brightly colored or multicolored (used in combinations). [ME; see PAINT, -ED[2]]

paint′ed beau′ty, a butterfly, *Vanessa virginiensis,* having brownish-black and orange wings and hind wings each with two eyespots, the larvae of which feed on the everlasting plant.

paint′ed bunt′ing, a brilliantly colored bunting, *Passerina ciris,* of the southern U.S.

paint′ed cup′, any of several plants of the genus *Castilleja,* having highly colored dilated bracts about the flowers.

Paint′ed Des′ert, a region in N central Arizona, E of the Colorado River: many-colored rock surfaces.

paint′ed green′ling, a greenling, *Oxylebius pictus,* found along the Pacific coast of North America, having a whitish body marked with black bands. Also called **convictfish.**

paint′ed horse′, paint (def. 6). Also called **paint′ed po′ny.**

paint′ed la′dy, a butterfly, *Vanessa cardui,* having brownish-black and orange wings and hind wings each with four eyespots, the larvae of which feed on thistles.

paint′ed port′, *Naut.* one of a series of imitation gun ports used as camouflage or decoration on some British, American, and French merchant vessels from the middle 19th century to the early 20th century, usually painted on a black hull with a broad white band and having typically the form of a black square extending from the very top of the white band to a point near its bottom.

Paint′ed Post′, a town in S New York. 2570 (1960).

paint′ed snipe′, either of two snipelike birds of the family *Rostratulidae,* of South America and the Old World tropics, the female of which is larger and more brightly colored than the male.

paint′ed tongue′, an annual herb, *Salpiglossis sinuata,* of Chile, having large, funnel-shaped, variously colored flowers.

paint′ed tril′lium, a North American trillium, *Trillium undulatum,* having white flowers streaked with red or purple. Also called **smiling wakerobin.**

paint′ed tur′tle, a fresh-water turtle, *Chrysemys picta,* common in the U.S., having bright yellow markings on the head and neck and red markings on the margin of the carapace.

paint′ed wom′an, 1. a prostitute. **2.** a promiscuous and cynical woman.

paint·er[1] (pān′tər), *n.* **1.** an artist who paints pictures. **2.** a person who coats walls or other surfaces with paint, esp. one who does so as an occupation. **3.** (*cap.*) *Astron.* the constellation Pictor. [PAINT + -ER[1]; r. ME *peyntour* < AF *peintour*]

paint·er[2] (pān′tər), *n.* a rope, usually at the bow, for fastening a boat to a ship, stake, etc. [ME *paynter,* prob. < MF *pentoir,* var. of *pendoir* rope, cord for hanging things on. See PEND, -ER[2]]

paint·er[3] (pān′tər), *n.* cougar. [var. of PANTHER]

paint·er·ly (pān′tər lē), *adj.* **1.** of, pertaining to, or characteristic of a painter. **2.** *Fine Arts.* characterized by qualities of color, stroke, or texture perceived as distinctive to the art of painting, esp. the rendering of forms and images in terms of color or tonal relations rather than of contour or line. [PAINTER[1] + -LY]

paint′er's col′ic, *Pathol.* lead poisoning causing intense intestinal pain.

paint′ horse′, paint (def. 6). Also called **paint′ po′ny.**

paint·ing (pān′ting), *n.* **1.** a picture or design executed in paints. **2.** the act, art, or work of one who paints. **3.** the works of art painted in or at a particular place or period: *a book on Flemish painting.* **4.** an instance of covering a surface with paint. [ME; see PAINT, -ING[1]]

paint′ pot′, 1. Also, **paint′pot′.** a container, as a jar, pail, bucket, etc., for holding paint while it is being applied. **2.** *Geol.* a spring or pit filled with boiling colored mud.

paint′ roll′er, a roller of absorbent material, mounted on a handle, that is rolled in a trough of paint and then rolled over a flat surface to be painted.

Paints·ville (pānts′vil), *n.* a town in E Kentucky. 4025 (1960).

paint·y (pān′tē), *adj.,* **paint·i·er, paint·i·est. 1.** of, coated with, or soiled with paint: *a painty finish; painty overalls.* **2.** having a crudely or clumsily painted surface: *The stage set consisted chiefly of painty scenery.* [PAINT + -Y[1]] —**paint′i·ness,** *n.*

pair (pâr), *n., pl.* **pairs, pair,** *v.* —*n.* **1.** two identical, similar, or corresponding things that are matched for use together: *a pair of gloves; a pair of earrings.* **2.** something consisting of or regarded as having two parts or pieces joined together: *a pair of scissors; a pair of slacks.* **3.** two people or animals who are similar or in some way associated: *a pair of liars; a very handsome pair of poodles.* **4.** a married, engaged, or dating couple. **5.** two mated animals. **6.** a span or team: *a pair of horses.* **7.** the part of a staircase within one story. **8.** *Govt.* **a.** two members on opposite sides in a deliberative body who for convenience, as to permit absence, arrange together to forgo voting on a given occasion. **b.** the arrangement thus made. **9.** *Cards.* **a.** two cards of the same denomination without regard to suit or color. **b. pairs,** two players who are matched together against different contestants. **10.** Also called **kinematic pair.** *Mech.* two parts or pieces so connected that they mutually constrain relative motion. **11.** *Philately.* two postage stamps joined together either vertically or horizontally. **12.** *Chiefly Dial.* a set or combination of more than two objects forming a collective whole: *a pair of arrows; a pair of beads.* —*v.t.* **13.** to arrange or designate in pairs or groups of two: *She paired dancers for the gavotte.* **14.** to form into a pair, as by matching, joining, etc.; match; couple: *to pair freshly washed socks.* **15.** (of animals) to cause to mate. —*v.i.* **16.** to separate into pairs or groups of two (usually fol. by *off*): *to pair off for a procession.* **17.** to form a pair or pairs. **18.** to be a member of a pair. **19.** to match with or resemble another. **20.** to unite in close association with another, as in a business partnership, friendship, marriage, etc. **21.** (of animals) to mate. **22.** (in a deliberative body) to form or arrange a pair. [ME *paire* < OF < L *pāria,* pl. (taken as fem. sing.) of *pār* a pair. See PAR] —**pair′-wise′,** *adv.*

—**Syn. 1.** PAIR, BRACE, COUPLE, SPAN, YOKE are terms for groups of two. PAIR is used of two things naturally or habitually associated in use, or necessary to each other to make a complete set (*a pair of horses*). It is used also of one thing composed of two similar and complementary parts: *a pair of trousers.* BRACE is a hunter's term, used of a pair of dogs, ducks, etc., or a pair of pistols or slugs: *a brace of partridges.* In COUPLE the idea of combination or interdependence has become greatly weakened; it may be used loosely for two of anything (*a couple of apples*), and even for more than two (= several): *I have to see a couple of people.* SPAN is used of a matched pair of horses harnessed together side by side. YOKE applies to the two animals hitched together under a yoke for drawing and pulling: *a yoke of oxen.*

pair (per), *adj. French.* noting any even number, esp. in roulette.

pair′ annihila′tion, *Physics.* annihilation (def. 3a).

pair′ case′, 1. a multiple casing for a watch, usually consisting of a plain case for the movement with an outer decorative case, sometimes also with an outermost protective case. **2.** an outer decorative case covering a plainer case for the movement.

pairle (pârl, perl), *n. Heraldry.* a device representing the front of an ecclesiastical pallium, consisting of a broad Y-shaped form covered with crosses. Also called **pall.** [< F, prob. alter. of OF *paile* PALL[1]]

pair′ masts′, *Naut.* See under **goal-post mast.**

pair-oar (pâr′ōr′, -ôr′), *n.* **1.** a pair-oared shell. —*adj.* **2.** pair-oared.

pair-oared (pâr′ōrd′, -ôrd′), *adj.* (of a racing shell) having two oarsmen with one oar each.

pair′ produc′tion, *Physics.* the simultaneous creation of a particle and its antiparticle by a nucleus or particle in an excited state, as when a photon is absorbed.

pair′ roy′al, *Cribbage.* a set of three cards of the same denomination. Cf. **double pair royal.**

pai·sa (pī′sä), *n., pl.* **-se** (-sä). **1.** See **naya paisa. 2.** Also, **pice.** a copper coin of Pakistan, the 100th part of a rupee, equivalent to about .0021 of a U.S. dollar. [< Hindi *paisā*]

pai·sa·no (pī sä′nō; *Sp.* pī sä′nô), *n., pl.* **-nos** (-nōz; *Sp.* -nôs). **1.** *Slang.* **a.** pal; buddy; comrade. **b.** compatriot. **2.** *Southwestern U.S.* **a.** a rustic or peasant. **b.** a roadrunner. [< Sp < F *paysan.* See PEASANT]

Pai·siel·lo (pī zyel′lô), *n.* **Gio·van·ni** (jô vän′nē), 1741–1816, Italian composer. Also, **Paesiello.**

pais·ley (pāz′lē), *n., pl.* **-leys,** *adj.* —*n.* **1.** a soft woolen fabric woven with a pattern of colorful and minutely detailed figures. **2.** a shawl, scarf, or other article made of this fabric. **3.** a silk print simulating this fabric and weave. **4.** Also called **pais′ley print′.** a pattern resembling the design or figure on this fabric or material. —*adj.* **5.** made of paisley: *a paisley shawl.* **6.** having the pattern of a paisley. [after PAISLEY]

Pais·ley (pāz′lē), *n.* a city in central Renfrew, SW Scotland, W of Glasgow: thread factories. 95,753 (1961).

Pai·ute (pī o͞ot′), *n., pl.* **-utes,** (*esp. collectively*) **-ute. 1.** a member of a group of North American Indians of Uto-Aztecan family dwelling in California, Nevada, Utah, and Arizona. **2.** either of two mutually unintelligible Shoshonean dialects (**North′ern Paiute′** and **South′ern Paiute′**). Also, **Piute.**

pajam′a par′ty, a party at which teen-age girls dress in night clothes and stay overnight at a friend's home.

pa·jam·as (pə jä′məz, -jam′əz), *n.* (*construed as pl.*) **1.** night clothes consisting of loose-fitting trousers and jacket. **2.** loose trousers, usually of silk or cotton, worn by both sexes in the Orient. Also, *esp. Brit.,* **pyjamas.** [pl. of *pajama* < Hindi, var. of *pāejāma* < Pers *pāe* leg + *jāma* garment] —**pa·ja′maed,** *adj.*

Pa·kan·ba·ru (pä′kän bär′o͞o), *n.* a city on central Sumatra, in W Indonesia. 69,147 (1961).

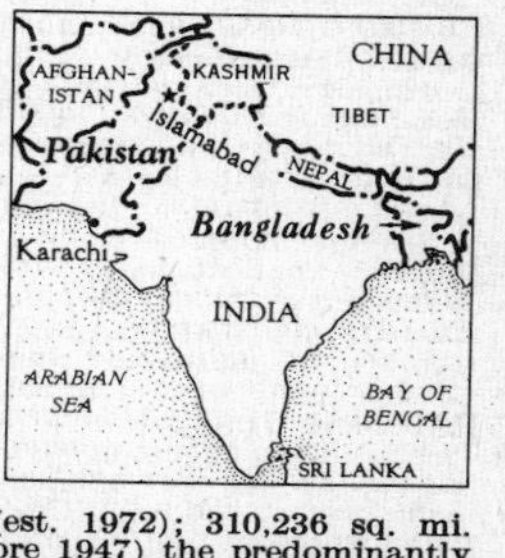

pak-choi (bäk′choi′), *n., pl.* **-choi, -chois.** a cabbagelike plant, *Brassica chinensis,* of China, having a loose head of dark-green leaves. [< Chin *paak ts'oi,* lit., white plant]

Pa·ki·stan (pak′i stan′, pä′ki stän′), *n.* **1. Is·lam′ic Repub′lic of,** a republic in S Asia, W of India: formerly part of India; from 1947–71 divided into West Pakistan and East Pakistan (now Bangladesh). 64,900,000 (est. 1972); 310,236 sq. mi. *Cap.:* Islamabad. **2.** (before 1947) the predominantly Muslim areas of the peninsula of India as distinguished from Hindustan, the predominantly Hindu areas.

Pa·ki·sta·ni (pä′ki stä′nē), *n., pl.* **-nis, -ni,** *adj.* —*n.* **1.** a native or inhabitant of Pakistan. —*adj.* **2.** of, pertaining to, or characteristic of Pakistan or its inhabitants.

Pa·kok·ku (pə kôk′ko͞o), *n.* a city in central Burma. 30,943 (1953).

Pak·se (päk sā′), *n.* a city in S Laos, on the Mekong River. 9000 (est. 1957).

pal (pal), *n., v.,* **palled, pal·ling.** *Informal.* —*n.* **1.** a comrade; chum. **2.** an accomplice. —*v.i.* **3.** to associate as comrades or chums: *to pal around with the kid next door.* [< E Gypsy: brother, mate, dissimilated var. of continental Gypsy *pral, plal* << Skt *bhrātr* brother]

Pal., Palestine.

pal., **1.** paleography. **2.** paleontology.

pa·la·bra (pä lä′vrä), *n., pl.* **-bras** (-vräs). *Spanish.* **1.** a word. **2.** speech; talk.

pal·ace (pal′is), *n.* **1.** the official residence of a sovereign, bishop, or other exalted personage. **2.** a large and stately mansion or building. **3.** a large and usually pretentiously ornate place for entertainment, exhibitions, etc. [late ME < ML *palāc(ium),* sp. var. of *palātium,* sing. of L *palātia* palace (L *Palātium* was name of a hill on which the emperor's palace was situated; hence pl. meaning); r. ME *paleis* < OF << L *Palāt(ium)*] —**pal′aced,** *adj.* —**pal′ace·like′,** *adj.* —**pal′ace·ward,** *adv.*

Pa·la·cios (pə lash′əz), *n.* a town in S Texas. 3676 (1960).

Pa·la·cio Val·dés (pä lä′thyô väl dēs′), **Ar·man·do** (är män′dô), 1853–1938, Spanish novelist and critic.

pal·a·din (pal′ə din), *n.* **1.** one of the 12 legendary peers or knightly champions in attendance on Charlemagne. **2.** any knightly or heroic champion. **3.** any determined advocate or defender of a noble cause. [< F < It *paladin(o)* < LL *palātinus* imperial functionary, n. use of adj.; see PALATINE[1]]

palae-, var. of **pale-.** Also, *esp. before a consonant,* **palaeo-.**

Pa·lae·arc·tic (pā′lē ärk′tik, pal′ē-), *n.* Palearctic.

Pa·lae·mon (pə lē′mən), *n. Class. Myth.* Melicertes, after being changed into a sea god.

palaeo-, var. of **paleo-.** Also, *before some vowels,* **palae-.**

pa·lae·o·bi·ol·o·gy (pā′lē ō bī ol′ə jē, pal′ē-), *n.* paleobiology. —**pa·lae·o·bi·o·log·i·cal** (pā′lē ō bī′ə loj′i kəl), **pa′lae·o·bi′o·log′ic,** *adj.* —**pa′lae·o·bi·ol′o·gist,** *n.*

pa·lae·o·bot·a·ny (pā′lē ō bot′ənē, pal′ē-), *n.* paleobotany. —**pa·lae·o·bo·tan·ic** (pā′lē ō bə tan′ik, pal′ē-), **pa′lae·o·bo·tan′i·cal,** *adj.* —**pa′lae·o·bo·tan′i·cal·ly,** *adv.* —**pa′lae·o·bot′a·nist,** *n.*

Pa·lae·o·cene (pā′lē ə sēn′, pal′ē-), *n., adj.* Paleocene.

pa·lae·o·cli·ma·tol·o·gy (pā′lē ō klī′mə tol′ə jē, pal′ē-), *n.* paleoclimatology. —**pa·lae·o·cli·ma·to·log·i·cal** (pā′lē ō klī′mə tᵊloj′i kəl, pal′ē-), **pa′lae·o·cli′ma·to·log′ic,** *adj.* —**pa′lae·o·cli′ma·tol′o·gist,** *n.*

pa·lae·o·e·col·o·gy (pā′lē ō i kol′ə jē, pal′ē-), *n.* paleoecology. —**pa·lae·o·ec·o·log·i·cal** (pā′lē ō ek′ə loj′i kəl, pal′ē-), **pa′lae·o·ec′o·log′ic,** *adj.* —**pa′lae·o·e·col′o·gist,** *n.*

pa·lae·o·en·ceph·a·lon (pā′lē ō en sef′ə lon′, pal′ē-), *n., pl.* **-la** (-lə). paleoencephalon.

pa·lae·o·en·to·mol·o·gy (pā′lē ō en′tə mol′ə jē, pal′ē-), *n.* paleoentomology. —**pa·lae·o·en·to·mo·log·i·cal** (pā′lē ō en′tə mə loj′i kəl, pal′ē-), **pa′lae·o·en′to·mo·log′ic,** *adj.* —**pa′lae·o·en′to·mol′o·gist,** *n.*

Pa·lae·o·gene (pā′lē ə jēn′, pal′ē-), *adj., n.* Paleogene.

pa·lae·o·gen·e·sis (pā′lē ō jen′i sis, pal′ē-), *n. Biol.* paleogenesis. —**pa·lae·o·ge·net·ic** (pā′lē ō jə net′ik, pal′ē-), *adj.*

pa·lae·o·ge·og·ra·phy (pā′lē ō jē og′rə fē), *n.* paleogeography. —**pa′lae·o·ge·og′ra·pher,** *n.* —**pa·lae·o·ge·o·graph·ic** (pā′lē ō jē′ə graf′ik, pal′ē-), **pa′lae·o·ge′o·graph′i·cal,** *adj.* —**pa′lae·o·ge′o·graph′i·cal·ly,** *adv.*

Pa·lae·o·lith·ic (pā′lē ə lith′ik, pal′ē-), *adj.* paleolithic.

Pa·lae·ol·o·gus (pā′lē ol′ə gəs, pal′ē-), *n.* family name of Byzantine rulers 1259–1453.

pa·lae·ol·o·gy (pā′lē ol′ə jē, pal′ē-), *n.* paleology. —**pa·lae·o·log·i·cal** (pā′lē ə loj′i kəl, pal′ē-), *adj.* —**pa′lae·ol′o·gist,** *n.*

pa·lae·on·tog·ra·phy (pā′lē ən tog′rə fē, pal′ē-), *n.* paleontography. —**pa·lae·on·to·graph·ic** (pā′lē on′tə graf′ik, pal′ē-), **pa′le·on′to·graph′i·cal,** *adj.*

palaeontol., palaeontology.

pa·lae·on·tol·o·gy (pā′lē ən tol′ə jē, pal′ē-), *n., pl.* **-gies.** paleontology. —**pa·lae·on·to·log·ic** (pā′lē on′tᵊloj′ik, pal′ē-), **pa′lae·on′to·log′i·cal,** *adj.* —**pa′lae·on′to·log′i·cal·ly,** *adv.* —**pa′lae·on·tol′o·gist,** *n.*

pa·lae·o·pa·thol·o·gy (pā′lē ō pə thol′ə jē, pal′ē-), *n.* paleopathology. —**pa·lae·o·path·o·log·i·cal** (pā′lē ō path′ə loj′i kəl, pal′ē-), **pa′lae·o·path′o·log′ic,** *adj.* —**pa′lae·o·pa·thol′o·gist,** *n.*

pa·lae·o·pe·dol·o·gy (pā′lē ō pi dol′ə jē, pal′ē-), *n.* paleopedology.

pa·lae·o·trop·i·cal (pā′lē ō trop′i kəl, pal′ē-), *adj.* paleotropical.

Pa·lae·o·zo·ic (pā′lē ə zō′ik, pal′ē-), *n., adj.* Paleozoic.

pa·lae·o·zo·ol·o·gy (pā′lē ō zō ol′ə jē, pal′ē-), *n.* paleozoology. Also, **pa′lae·o·zo·öl′o·gy.** —**pa·lae·o·zo·o·log·i·cal** (pā′lē ō zō′ə loj′i kəl, pal′ē-), **pa′lae·o·zo′o·log′ic,** *adj.* —**pa′lae·o·zo·ol′o·gist,** *n.*

pa·laes·tra (pə les′trə), *n., pl.* **-tras, -trae** (-trē), *Gk. Antiq.* palestra. —**pa·laes′tral, pa·laes′tric,** *adj.* —**pa·laes′tri·an,** *adj.*

pa·lais (pᴀ le′), *n., pl.* **-lais.** *French.* a palace, esp. a French government or municipal building.

pa·lais de danse (pa lā′ də däns′; *Fr.* pᴀ le də däns′), *pl.* **pa·lais de danse.** a dance hall, esp. one that is highly ornate or pretentiously elegant. [< F]

Pal·a·me·des (pal′ə mē′dēz), *n. Class. Myth.* a lieutenant of Agamemnon who tricked Odysseus into going to the Trojan War against his will and who was later killed through the plotting of Odysseus.

pal·am·pore (pal′əm pōr′, -pôr′), *n.* a cotton print woven in India and used for clothing, canopies, etc. Also, **pal·am·poor** (pal′əm po͝or′). [prob. named after *Palanpur,* city in Rajputana, India]

pal·an·quin (pal′ən kēn′), *n.* (in India and other Eastern countries) a passenger carriage, usually for one person, consisting of a covered or boxlike litter carried by means of poles resting on the shoulders of several men. Also, **pal′an·keen′.** [< MF < D *pallankin* < Pg *palanquim* << Pali *palanki* palanquin < Prakrit *pallanka* couch, bed] —**pal′an·quin′er, pal′an·keen′er,** *n.* —**pal′an·quin′ing·ly, pal′an·keen′ing·ly,** *adv.*

pal·at·a·ble (pal′ə tə bəl), *adj.* **1.** pleasing to the palate or taste; agreeable; savory: *palatable food.* **2.** pleasing or agreeable to the mind or feelings; acceptable: *palatable ideas.* [PALATE + -ABLE] —**pal′at·a·bil′i·ty, pal′at·a·ble·ness,** *n.* —**pal′at·a·bly,** *adv.*
—**Syn. 1.** tasty, delicious, delectable. **2.** pleasing, satisfactory. —**Ant. 1.** distasteful.

pal·a·tal (pal′ə tᵊl), *adj.* **1.** *Anat.* of or pertaining to the palate. **2.** *Phonet.* articulated with the blade of the tongue held close to or touching the hard palate. —*n.* **3.** *Phonet.* a palatal consonant. [< F; see PALATE, -AL[1]] —**pal′a·tal·ism, pal·a·tal·i·ty** (pal′ə tal′i tē), *n.* —**pal′a·tal·ly,** *adv.*

pal·a·tal·ize (pal′ətᵊlīz′), *v.,* **-ized, -iz·ing.** *Phonet.* —*v.t.* **1.** to articulate (a consonant other than a normal palatal) as a palatal or with relatively more contact between the blade of the tongue and the hard palate, as in certain pronunciations of the *l*-sound in *million.* —*v.i.* **2.** to palatalize a consonant. [PALATAL + -IZE] —**pal′a·tal·i·za′tion,** *n.*

pal·a·tal·ized (pal′ə tᵊlīzd′), *adj. Phonet.* pronounced with secondary palatal articulation. [PALATALIZE + -ED[2]]

pal·ate (pal′it), *n.* **1.** *Anat.* the roof of the mouth, consisting of an anterior bony portion **(hard palate)** and a posterior muscular portion **(soft palate)** that separate the oral cavity from the nasal cavity. See diag. under **mouth. 2.** the sense of taste: *a dinner to delight the palate.* **3.** intellectual or aesthetic taste; mental appreciation. [ME *palat* < L *palāt(um)* roof of the mouth] —**pal′ate·less,** *adj.* —**pal′ate·like′,** *adj.*

pa·la·tial (pə lā′shəl), *adj.* **1.** of, pertaining to, or resembling a palace: *a palatial home.* **2.** befitting or suitable for a palace; stately; magnificent: *a palatial tapestry.* [< L *palāti(um)* PALACE + -AL[1]] —**pa·la′tial·ly,** *adv.* —**pa·la′tial·ness,** *n.*

Pa·lat·i·nate (pə lat′ᵊnāt′, -ᵊnit), *n.* **1. The.** Also called **Lower Palatinate, Rhine Palatinate.** German, **Pfalz.** a district in SW Germany, W of the Rhine: belonged to Bavaria until 1945; formerly, with portions of the neighboring territory **(Upper Palatinate),** constituted an electorate of the Holy Roman Empire; now part of Rhineland-Palatinate state. **2.** a native or inhabitant of the Palatinate. **3.** (*l.c.*) the territory under the jurisdiction of a palatine. [PALATINE[1] + -ATE[1]] —**pa·lat′i·nal,** *adj.*

pal·a·tine[1] (pal′ə tīn′, -tin), *adj.* **1.** having royal privileges: *a count palatine.* **2.** of or pertaining to a count palatine, earl palatine, or county palatine. **3.** of or pertaining to a palace; palatial: *a palatine chapel.* **4.** (*cap.*) of or pertaining to the Palatinate. —*n.* **5.** a vassal exercising royal privileges in a province; a count or earl palatine. **6.** an important officer of an imperial palace. **7.** a high official of an empire. **8.** (*cap.*) a native or inhabitant of the Palatinate. **9.** (*cap.*) one of the seven hills on which ancient Rome was built. **10.** a shoulder cape, usually of fur or lace, formerly worn by women. [late ME < ML, L *palātīn(us)* of the imperial house, imperial; orig., of the hill *Palātium* in Rome, where the emperor's palace was situated. See PALADIN, -INE[1]]

pal·a·tine[2] (pal′ə tīn′, -tin), *adj.* of, near, or in the palate; palatal: *the palatine bones.* [< F *palatin, -ine.* See PALATE, -INE[1]]

Pal′atine Anthol′ogy, The. See **Greek Anthology, The.**

pa·la·ti·um (pə lā′shē əm, -shəm; *Lat.* pä lä′tē o͝om′), *n., pl.* **-ti·a** (-shē ə, -shə; *Lat.* -tē ä′). a palace, esp. the palace of an ancient Roman emperor. [< L]

Pa·lau′ Is′lands (pä lou′), a group of Pacific islands in the W part of the Caroline group: taken by U.S. forces after severe fighting 1944; formerly a Japanese mandate, now under U.S. trusteeship. 9320 (1960); 171 sq. mi. Also, **Pelew Islands.**

pa·lav·er (pə lav′ər, -lä′vər), *n.* **1.** a long parley, esp. one with primitive natives. **2.** a conference or long discussion. **3.** profuse and idle talk; chatter. **4.** persuasive talk; flattery; cajolery. —*v.i.* **5.** to talk profusely and idly. **6.** to parley or confer. —*v.t.* **7.** to cajole or persuade. [< Pg *palavra* word, speech, talk < LL *parabola* PARABLE] —**pa·lav′er·er, pa·lav′er·ist,** *n.* —**pa·lav′er·ment,** *n.* —**pa·lav′er·ous,** *adj.*

Pa·la·wan (pä lä′wän), *n.* an island in the SW Philippines. 132,670 (est. 1960); 5697 sq. mi. *Cap.:* Puerto Princesa.

pa·laz·zo (pä lät′sô), *n., pl.* **-laz·zi** (-lät′sē). *Italian.* an impressive public building or private residence; palace.

pale[1] (pāl), *adj.,* **pal·er, pal·est,** *v.,* **paled, pal·ing.** —*adj.* **1.** lacking intensity of color; colorless or whitish: *a pale complexion.* **2.** of a low degree of chroma, saturation, or purity; approaching white or gray: *pale yellow.* **3.** not bright or brilliant; dim: *the pale moon.* **4.** faint; feeble; lacking vigor: *a pale protest.* —*v.i., v.t.* **5.** to make or become pale: *to pale at the sight of blood.* [ME < MF < L *pallid(us)* PALLID] —**pale′ly,** *adv.* —**pale′ness,** *n.*
—**Syn. 1.** ashy, ashen. PALE, PALLID, WAN imply an absence of color, esp. from the human countenance. PALE implies a faintness or absence of color, which may be natural when applied to things: *the pale blue of a violet,* but when used to refer to the human face usually means an unnatural and often temporary absence of color, as arising from sickness or sudden emotion: *pale cheeks.* PALLID, limited mainly to the human countenance, implies an excessive paleness induced by intense emotion, disease, or death: *the pallid lips of the dying man.* WAN implies a sickly paleness, as after a long illness: *wan and thin;* the suggestion of weakness may be more prominent than that of lack of color: *a wan smile.* **5.** blanch, whiten. —**Ant. 1.** ruddy. **5.** darken.

pale[2] (pāl), *n., v.,* **paled, pal·ing.** —*n.* **1.** a stake or picket, as of a fence. **2.** an enclosing or confining barrier; enclosure. **3.** an enclosed area. **4.** limits; bounds: *outside the pale of his jurisdiction.* **5.** a district or region within fixed bounds. **6.** (*cap.*) Also called **English Pale, Irish Pale.** a district in E Ireland included in the Angevin Empire of King Henry II and his successors. **7.** *Heraldry.* an ordinary in the form of a broad vertical stripe at the center of an escutcheon. **8.** *Shipbuilding.* a shore used inside to support the deck beams of a hull under construction. **9. beyond the pale,** beyond the limits of propriety, courtesy, protection, safety, etc.: *Their conduct is certainly beyond the pale.* **10. in pale,** *Heraldry.* **a.** (of two charges) with one directly over the other. **b.** (of a single charge) placed upright at the center of the escutcheon. **11. per pale,** *Heraldry.* from top to bottom at the center: *party per pale.* —*v.t.* **12.** to enclose with pales; fence. **13.** to encircle or encompass. [ME (north), OE *pāl* < L *pāl(us)* stake. See PEEL[3], POLE]

pale-, var. of **paleo-** before most vowels: *paleethnology.* Also, **palae-.**

pa·le·a (pā′lē ə), *n., pl.* **-le·ae** (-lē ē′). *Bot.* **1.** a chafflike scale or bract. **2.** the scalelike, membranous organ in the flowers of grasses that is situated upon a secondary axis in the axil of the flowering glume and envelops the stamens and pistil. [< NL, special use of L *palea* chaff] —**pa·le·a·ceous** (pā′lē ā′shəs), **pa·le·ate** (pā′lē it, -āt′), *adj.*

Pa·le·arc·tic (pā′lē ärk′tik, -är′tik), *adj. Zoogeog.* belonging or pertaining to a geographical division comprising Europe, Africa north of the tropic of Cancer, the northern part of the Arabian Peninsula, and Asia north of the Himalayas. Also, **Palaearctic.** [PALE- + ARCTIC]

pale′ coryd′alis. See **pink corydalis.**

pa·le·en·ceph·a·lon (pā′lē en sef′ə lon′, pal′ē-), *n., pl.* **-lons, -la** (-lə). the more primitive part of the brain in the evolutionary development of animals, including all parts except the cerebral cortex and its related structures. Also, **palaeoencephalon.** Cf. **neencephalon.** [< NL; see PALE-, ENCEPHALON]

pa·le·eth·nol·o·gy (pā′lē eth nol′ə jē, pal′ē-), *n.* the branch of ethnology concerned with the earliest or most primitive races of mankind. [PALE- + ETHNOLOGY] —**pa·le·eth·no·log·ic** (pā′lē eth′nəloj′ik, pal′ē-), **pa′le·eth′no·log′i·cal,** *adj.* —**pa′le·eth·nol′o·gist,** *n.*

pale·face (pāl′fās′), *n. Sometimes Disparaging.* a white person as distinguished from a North American Indian. [PALE[1] + FACE, expression attributed to North American Indians]

Pale′ Horse′, a representation of Death, as in literature, the Bible, etc. [after the Biblical *pale horse* on which Death rides, Rev. 6:8]

Pale′ Horse′, Pale′ Rid′er, a trilogy of short novels (1939) by Katherine Anne Porter.

pale′ lau′rel. See **swamp laurel** (def. 1).

Pa·lem·bang (pä′lem bäng′), *n.* a city in SE Sumatra, in W Indonesia. 458,661 (est. 1961).

Pa·len·que (pä leng′ke), *n.* a village in SE Mexico, in Chiapas state: ruins of ancient Mayan city.

paleo-, a learned borrowing from Greek meaning "old," used in the formation of compound words: *paleobotany.* Also, **pale-, palae-, palaeo-.** [< Gk *palaio-,* comb. form of *palaiós*]

Pa·le·o-A·si·at·ic (pā′lē ō ā′zhē at′ik, -shē-, pal′ē-), *n.* **1.** a member of any of various Mongoloid peoples of northeastern Asia. —*adj.* **2.** Paleosiberian.

pa·le·o·bi·ol·o·gy (pā′lē ō bī ol′ə jē, pal′ē-), *n.* the branch of paleontology dealing with fossil plants and animals, esp. with reference to their origin, growth, structure, etc. Also, **palaeobiology.** [PALEO- + BIOLOGY] —**pa·le·o·bi·o·log·i·cal** (pā′lē ō bī′ə loj′i kəl, pal′ē-), **pa′le·o·bi′o·log′ic,** *adj.* —**pa′le·o·bi·ol′o·gist,** *n.*

pa·le·o·bot·a·ny (pā′lē ō bot′ᵊnē, pal′ē-), *n.* the branch of paleontology dealing with fossil plants. Also, **palaeobotany.** [PALEO- + BOTANY] —**pa·le·o·bo·tan·i·cal** (pā′lē ō bə tan′i kəl, pal′ē-), **pa′le·o·bo·tan′ic,** *adj.* —**pa′le·o·bot′a·nist,** *n.*

Pa·le·o·cene (pā′lē ə sēn′, pal′ē-), *Geol.* —*adj.* **1.** noting or pertaining to an epoch either of the Tertiary or Paleogene period, occurring from 60,000,000 to 70,000,000 years ago, and characterized by the advent of birds, mammals, and placental mammals. See table under **era.** —*n.* **2.** the Paleocene epoch or series. Also, **Palaeocene.** [PALEO- + -CENE]

pa·le·o·cli·ma·tol·o·gy (pā′lē ō klī′mə tol′ə jē, pal′ē-), *n.* the branch of paleogeography dealing with the study of climates of past geologic ages. Also, **palaeoclimatology.** [PALEO- + CLIMATOLOGY] —**pa·le·o·cli·ma·to·log·i·cal** (pā′lē ō klī′mə tᵊloj′i kəl, pal′ē-), **pa′le·o·cli′ma·to·log′ic,** *adj.* —**pa′le·o·cli′ma·tol′o·gist,** *n.*

pa·le·o·e·col·o·gy (pā′lē ō i kol′ə jē, pal′ē-), *n.* the study of the ecological relationships prevailing in past geologic ages. Also, **palaeoecology.** [PALEO- + ECOLOGY] —**pa·le·o·ec·o·log·i·cal** (pā′lē ō ek′ə loj′i kəl, pal′ē-), **pa′le·o·ec′o·log′ic,** *adj.* —**pa′le·o·e·col′o·gist,** *n.*

pa·le·o·en·ceph·a·lon (pā′lē ō en sef′ə lon′, pal′ē-), *n., pl.* **-lons, -la** (-lə). paleencephalon. Also, **palaeoencephalon.**

pa·le·o·en·to·mol·o·gy (pā′lē ō en′tə mol′ə jē, pal′ē-), *n.* the branch of paleontology dealing with fossil insects. Also, **palaeoentomology.** [PALEO- + ENTOMOLOGY] —**pa·le·o·en·to·mo·log·i·cal** (pā′lē ō en′tə mə loj′i kəl, pal′ē-), **pa′le·o·en′to·mo·log′ic,** *adj.* —**pa′le·o·en′to·mol′o·gist,** *n.*

paleog., paleography.

Pa·le·o·gene (pā′lē ə jēn′, pal′ē-), *Geol.* —*adj.* **1.** noting or pertaining to the earlier part of the Cenozoic era, in the system adopted by some geologists, occurring from 25,000,000 to 70,000,000 years ago and including the Oligocene, Eocene, and Paleocene epochs: corresponds to the earlier part of the Tertiary period in the system generally used in the U.S. Cf. **Neogene.** —*n.* **2.** the Paleogene period or system. Also, **Palaeogene.** [< G *Paläogen,* equiv. to *paläo-* PALEO- + *-gen* (< Gk *genésthai* be born); cf. -GEN]

pa·le·o·gen·e·sis (pā′lē ō jen′i sis, pal′ē-), *n. Biol.* palingenesis (def. 2a). Also, **palaeogenesis.** [PALEO- + -GENESIS] —**pa·le·o·ge·net·ic** (pā′lē ō jə net′ik, pal′ē-), *adj.*

pa·le·o·ge·og·ra·phy (pā′lē ō jē og′rə fē, pal′ē-), *n.* the science of representing the earth's geographic features belonging to any part of the geologic past. Also, **palaeogeography.** [PALEO- + GEOGRAPHY] —**pa′le·o·ge·og′ra·pher,** *n.* —**pa·le·o·ge·o·graph·ic** (pā′lē ō jē′ə graf′ik, pal′ē-), **pa′le·o·ge′o·graph′i·cal,** *adj.* —**pa′le·o·ge′o·graph′i·cal·ly,** *adv.*

pa·le·o·ge·ol·o·gy (pā′lē ō jē ol′ə jē, pal′ē-), *n.* the science of representing geologic conditions of some given time in past earth history. [PALEO- + GEOLOGY] —**pa·le·o·ge·o·log·ic** (pā′lē ō jē′ə loj′ik, pal′ē-), *adj.*

pa·le·og·ra·phy (pā′lē og′rə fē, pal′ē-), *n.* **1.** ancient forms of writing, as in documents and inscriptions. **2.** the study of ancient writing, including determination of origin and date, decipherment, etc. [PALEO- + -GRAPHY] —**pa′le·og′ra·pher,** *n.* —**pa·le·o·graph·ic** (pā′lē ə graf′ik, pal′ē-), **pa′le·o·graph′i·cal,** *adj.* —**pa′le·o·graph′i·cal·ly,** *adv.*

pa·le·o·lith (pā′lē ə lith, pal′ē-), *n.* a paleolithic stone implement. [PALEO- + -LITH]

Pa·le·o·lith·ic (pā′lē ə lith′ik, pal′ē-), *adj. Anthropol.* (*sometimes l.c.*) of, pertaining to, or characteristic of the cultures of the Pleistocene epoch or early phase of the Stone Age, marked by the development of bone or flint tools and, during its later stage, by cave paintings and sculptured figurines: usually divided into three periods **(Low′er Paleolith′ic,** c500,000 B.C.–c250,000 B.C., **Mid′dle Paleolith′ic,** c250,000 B.C.–c60,000 B.C., **Up′per Paleolith′ic,** c60,000 B.C.–c10,000 B.C.). Also, **Palaeolithic.** [PALEO- + -LITHIC]

pa′leolith′ic man′, any of the primitive species of man, as Neanderthal man, living in the Pleistocene epoch.

pa·le·ol·o·gy (pā′lē ol′ə jē, pal′e-), *n.* the study of antiquities. Also, **palaeology.** [PALEO- + -LOGY] —**pa·le·o·log·i·cal** (pā′lē ə loj′i kəl, pal′ē-), *adj.* —**pa′le·ol′o·gist,** *n.*

pa·le·o·mag·net·ism (pā′lē ō mag′ni tiz′əm), *n.* the magnetism acquired by a rock at the time of its formation. [PALEO- + MAGNETISM] —**pa·le·o·mag·net·ic** (pā′lē ō mag net′ik), *adj.*

paleon., paleontology.

pa·le·on·tog·ra·phy (pā′lē ən tog′rə fē, pal′ē-), *n.* descriptive paleontology. Also, **palaeontography.** [< F *paléontographie.* See PALE-, ONTO-, -GRAPHY] —**pa·le·on·to·graph·ic** (pā′lē on′tə graf′ik, pal′ē-), **pa′le·on′to·graph′i·cal,** *adj.*

paleontol., paleontology.

pa·le·on·tol·o·gy (pā′lē ən tol′ə jē, pal′ē-), *n., pl.* **-gies. 1.** the science of the forms of life existing in former geologic periods, as represented by fossil animals and plants. **2.** a treatise on paleontology. Also, **palaeontology.** [< F *paléontologie.* See PALE-, ONTOLOGY] —**pa·le·on·to·log·ic** (pā′lē on′tᵊloj′ik, pal′ē-), **pa′le·on′to·log′i·cal,** *adj.* —**pa′le·on′to·log′i·cal·ly,** *adv.* —**pa′le·on·tol′o·gist,** *n.*

pa·le·o·pa·thol·o·gy (pā′lē ō pə thol′ə jē, pal′ē-), *n.* the study of pathological conditions in fossil organisms. Also, **palaeopathology.** [PALEO- + PATHOLOGY] —**pa·le·o·path·o·log·i·cal** (pā′lē ō path′ə loj′i kəl, pal′ē-), **pa′le·o·path′o·log′ic,** *adj.* —**pa′le·o·pa·thol′o·gist,** *n.*

pa·le·o·pe·dol·o·gy (pā′lē ō pi dol′ə jē, pal′ē-), *n.* the branch of pedology dealing with the soils of past geologic ages. Also, **palaeopedology.** [PALEO- + PEDOLOGY]

pa·le·o·psy·chic (pā′lē ō sī′kik, pal′ē-), *adj.* of or pertaining to paleopsychology. [PALEO- + PSYCHIC]

pa·le·o·psy·chol·o·gy (pā′lē ō sī kol′ə jē, pal′ē-), *n.* the study of psychological processes considered to be vestigial remains of an earlier evolutionary stage. [PALEO- + PSYCHOLOGY] —**pa·le·o·psy·cho·log·i·cal** (pā′lē ō sī′kə loj′i kəl, pal′ē-), *adj.*

Pa·le·o·si·be·ri·an (pā′lē ō sī bēr′ē ən, pal′ē-), *adj.* of or pertaining to those languages of Siberia that do not belong to the Indo-European, Altaic, Uralic, or Eskimo-Aleut language families; Hyperborean; Paleo-Asiatic. [PALEO- + SIBERIAN]

pa·le·o·trop·i·cal (pā′lē ō trop′i kəl), *adj. Biogeog.* belonging or pertaining to a geographical division comprising the Ethiopian and Oriental regions. Also, **palaeotropical.** [PALEO- + TROPICAL]

Pa·le·o·zo·ic (pā′lē ə zō′ik, pal′ē-), *Geol.* —*adj.* **1.** noting or pertaining to an era occurring between 220,000,000 and 600,000,000 years ago, characterized by the appearance of fish, insects, and reptiles. See table under **era.** —*n.* **2.** the Paleozoic era or group of systems. Also, **Palaeozoic.** [PALEO- + Gk *zōik(ós)*; see ZO-, -IC]

pa·le·o·zo·ol·o·gy (pā′lē ō zō ol′ə jē, pal′ē-), *n.* the branch of paleontology dealing with fossil animals. Also, **palaeozoology, pa′le·o·zo·öl′o·gy.** [PALEO- + ZOOLOGY] —**pa·le·o·zo·o·log·i·cal, pa·le·o·zo·ö·log·i·cal** (pā′lē ō zō′ə loj′i kəl, pal′ē-), **pa′le·o·zo′o·log′ic, pa′le·o·zo′ö·log′ic,** *adj.* —**pa′le·o·zo·ol′o·gist, pa′le·o·zo·öl′o·gist,** *n.*

Pa·ler·mo (pə lûr′mō, -lâr′-; *It.* pä leR′mô), *n.* a seaport in and the capital of Sicily, in the NW part. 587,063 (1961). —**Pa·ler·mi·tan** (pə lûr′mi tᵊn, -lâr′-), *adj., n.*

Pa·les (pā′lēz), *n.* an ancient Roman deity, a protector of flocks and shepherds, whose festival was celebrated on April 21, the legendary anniversary day of the founding of Rome.

Pal·es·tine (pal′i stīn′), *n.* **1.** Also called **Holy Land.** Biblical name, **Canaan.** an ancient country in SW Asia, on the E coast of the Mediterranean. **2.** a former British mandate comprising part of this country, divided in 1948 between Israel, Jordan, and Egypt: the Jordanian and Egyptian parts were occupied by Israel in 1967.

Pal·es·tin·i·an (pal′i stin′ē ən), *n.* **1.** a native or inhabitant of Palestine. **2.** Also called **Palestin′ian Ar′ab.** an Arab formerly living in Palestine who advocates the establishment of an Arab homeland there. —*adj.* **3.** of or pertaining to Palestine or Palestinians. **4.** of or pertaining to Palestinian Arabs: *Palestinian guerrillas.*

pa·les·tra (pə les′trə), *n., pl.* **-tras, -trae** (-trē). *Gk. Antiq.* a public place for training or exercise in wrestling or athletics. Also, **palaestra.** [late ME *palestre* < L *palaestra* a wrestling school, place of exercise < Gk *palaístra,* equiv. to *palaí(ein)* (to) wrestle + *-stra* n. suffix of place]

Pa·le·stri·na (pal′i strē′nə; *It.* pä′le stRē′nä), *n.* **1. Gio·van·ni Pier·lu·i·gi da** (jō vän′nē pyeR′lo͞o ē′jē dä), 1526?–94 Italian composer. **2.** Ancient, **Praeneste.** a town in central Italy, ESE of Rome.

pal·et (pal′it), *n. Heraldry.* pallet³.

pal·e·tot (pal′i tō′, pal′tō), *n.* **1.** a loose overcoat. **2.** a close-fitting jacket differing in material from the rest of a costume, worn by women esp. in the 19th century. [< F, MF, var. of *paletoc* < ME *paltok* a jacket, peasant's coat]

pal·ette (pal′it), *n.* **1.** a thin and usually oval or oblong board or tablet with a thumb hole at one end, used by painters for holding and mixing colors. **2.** any other flat surface used by a painter for this purpose. **3.** the set of colors on such a board or surface. **4.** the range of colors used by a particular artist. **5.** (in Egyptian art) a slate object having a recessed circular area on one side that in the smaller, often circular or rectangular pieces are believed to have been used for eye make-up and in the larger, scutiform pieces are believed to have been used as commemorative objects. **6.** Also, **pallette.** *Armor.* a small plate defending the front of the armpit when the arm is lifted; gusset. [< F, MF < It *paletta,* dim. of *pala* shovel < L; see -ETTE] —**pal′ette-like′,** *adj.*

pal′ette knife′, *Painting.* a thin blade of varying flexibility set in a handle and used for mixing colors or applying them to a canvas.

Pal′ette of Nar′mer (när′mər), an Egyptian slate tablet bearing a relief sculpture, c3000 B.C.

pale·wise (pāl′wīz′), *adv. Heraldry.* in the manner or direction of a pale; vertically. Also, **pale·ways** (pāl′wāz′). [PALE² + -WISE]

Pa·ley (pā′lē), *n.* **William,** 1743–1805, English theologian, philosopher, and clergyman.

pal·frey (pôl′frē), *n., pl.* **-freys.** **1.** a riding horse, as distinguished from a war horse. **2.** a saddle horse particularly suitable for a woman. [ME *palefrei* < OF, earlier *palefreid* < LL *paraverēd(us)* post-horse < Gk *pará* near, beside (see PARA-) + L *verēdus* swift hunting-horse < Celt; cf. Welsh *gorwydd* horse, akin to RIDE] —**pal′freyed,** *adj.*

Pal·grave (pôl′grāv, pal′-), *n.* **Francis Turner,** 1824–97, English critic, poet, and anthologist.

pa·li (pä′lē), *n.* (in Hawaii) a steep slope or cliff. [< Hawaiian]

Pa·li (pä′lē), *n.* the Prakrit language of the Buddhist scriptures. [short for Skt *pāli-bhāṣa* language of the canonical texts, equiv. to *pāli* line, row, canon + *bhāṣa* language]

Pa′li Can′on, *Buddhism.* a collection of scriptures, originally recorded from oral traditions in the 1st century B.C., divided into three parts **(Pitakas),** comprising sermons **(Sutta Pitaka),** the rules of the Buddhist order **(Vinaya Pitaka),** and a treatise on philosophy and psychology **(Abhidhamma Pitaka).** Also called **Tripitaka.**

pal·i·kar (pal′i kär′), *n.* a Greek militiaman in the Greek war for independence against the Turks 1821–28. Also, **pellekar.** [< NGk *palikári* lad, youth, var. of LGk *pallēkárion* camp boy (Gk *pallēk-,* s. of *pállēx* a youth + *-arion* dim. suffix)]

Pal·i·li·ci·um (pal′ə lish′ē əm), *n.pl. Rom. Legend.* the Hyades.

pal·i·mo·ny (pal′ə mō′nē), *n. Informal.* a form of alimony awarded, usually to a woman, after the breakup of a relationship in which two unmarried people have lived together as husband and wife for a considerable length of time. [PAL + (AL)IMONY]

pal·imp·sest (pal′imp sest′), *n.* a parchment or the like from which writing has been partially or completely erased to make room for another text. [< L *palimpsēst(us)* < Gk *palímpsēstos* rubbed again (*pálin* again + *psēstós* scraped, rubbed, verbid of *psēn* to rub smooth)] —**pal′imp·ses′tic,** *adj.*

pal·im·scope (pal′im skōp′), *n.* a hand instrument that produces concentrated ultraviolet light for reading palimpsests and other research materials. [PALIM(PSEST) + -SCOPE]

pal·in·drome (pal′in drōm′), *n.* a word, line, verse, etc., reading the same backward as forward, as *Madam, I'm Adam* or *Poor Dan is in a droop.* [< Gk *palíndrom(os)* recurring, equiv. to *pálin* again, back + *drómos* -DROME] —**pa·lin·dro·mist** (pə lin′drō mist), *n.* —**pal·in·drom·ic** (pal′in drom′ik, -drō′mik), **pal′in·drom′i·cal,** *adj.* —**pal′in·drom′i·cal·ly,** *adv.*

pal·ing (pā′ling), *n.* **1.** a fence of pales. **2.** a pale or picket for a fence. **3.** pales collectively. **4.** the act of one who builds a fence with pales. [ME; see PALE², -ING¹]

pal·in·gen·e·sis (pal′in jen′i sis), *n.* **1.** rebirth; regeneration. **2.** *Biol.* **a.** the development of an individual that reproduces the ancestral features (opposed to *cenogenesis*). **b.** *Obs.* the supposed generation of organisms from others preformed in the germ cells. **3.** baptism in the Christian faith. **4.** the doctrine of transmigration of souls. [< NL < Gk *pálin* again + *génesis* GENESIS] —**pal·in·ge·ne·si·an** (pal′in jə nē′zhē ən), **pal·in·ge·net·ic** (pal′in jə net′ik), *adj.* —**pal′in·ge·net′i·cal·ly,** *adv.*

pal·in·gen·e·sist (pal′in jen′i sist), *n.* a person who believes in a doctrine of rebirth or transmigration of souls. Also, **pal·in·gen·ist** (pal′in jen′ist). [PALINGENES(IS) + -IST]

pal·i·node (pal′ə nōd′), *n.* **1.** a poem in which the poet retracts something said in an earlier poem. **2.** a recantation. [< LL *palinōd(ia)* < Gk *palinōidía* a singing again, especially a recanting, equiv. to *pálin* again, back + *ōid(ḗ)* ODE + *-ia* -IA] —**pal′i·nod′ist,** *n.*

Pal·i·nur·us (pal′ə no͝or′əs, -nyo͝or′-), *n. Class. Myth.* a steersman of Aeneas, murdered by Italian natives and buried at the intervention of Aeneas.

pal·i·sade (pal′i sād′), *n., v.,* **-sad·ed, -sad·ing.** —*n.* **1.** a fence of pales or stakes set firmly in the ground, as for enclosure or defense. **2.** any of a number of pales or stakes pointed at the top and set firmly in the ground in a close row with others to form a defense. **3. palisades,** a line of cliffs. —*v.t.* **4.** to furnish or fortify with a palisade. [< F *palissade* < OPr *palissad(a),* equiv. to *paliss(a)* paling (deriv. of *pal* stake < L *pālus*) + *-ada* -ADE¹]

Pal·i·sades (pal′i sādz′), *n.* the line of cliffs in NE New Jersey and SE New York extending along the W bank of the lower Hudson River. ab. 40 mi. long.

pal·i·sa·do (pal′i sā′dō), *n., pl.* **-does,** *v.t.,* **-doed, -do·ing.** palisade. [< Sp *palizada*]

palisa′do crown′, *Heraldry.* **1.** a representation of a crown having flat rays that are pointed at the top and attached to the circlet by rivets. **2.** (loosely) a crown vallary.

pal·i·san·der (pal′i san′dər, pal′i san′dər), *n.* See **Brazilian rosewood.** [< F *palissandre* < ?]

pal·ish (pā′lish), *adj.* somewhat pale. [ME; see PALE¹, -ISH¹]

Pa·lis·sy (pA lē sē′), *n.* **Ber·nard** (beR naR′), c1510–89, French potter, enameler, and author.

Pa·litzsch (pä′lich), *n.* an elliptical, walled plain in the fourth quadrant of the face of the moon: about 60 miles long and 20 miles wide.

pal·ki (päl′kē), *n. Anglo-Indian.* a palanquin; sedan chair. Also, **pal′kee.** [< Hindi *pālkī*]

pall¹ (pôl), *n.* **1.** a cloth, often of velvet, for spreading over a coffin, bier, or tomb. **2.** a coffin. **3.** something that covers, shrouds, or overspreads, esp. with darkness or gloom. **4.** *Eccles.* **a.** pallium (def. 2a). **b.** a linen cloth or a square cloth-covered piece of cardboard used to cover a chalice. **5.** *Heraldry.* pairle. **6.** *Archaic.* a cloth spread upon an altar; corporal. **7.** *Archaic.* a garment, esp. a robe, cloak, or the like. —*v.t.* **8.** to cover with or as with a pall. [ME; OE *pæll* < L *pall(ium)* cloak] —**pall′-like′,** *adj.*

pall² (pôl), *v.i.* **1.** to have a wearying effect (usually fol. by *on* or *upon*). **2.** to become distasteful or unpleasant. **3.** to become satiated or cloyed with something. —*v.t.* **4.** to satiate or cloy. **5.** to make dull, distasteful, or unpleasant. [ME *palle(n)*; aph. var. of APPALL]
—**Syn. 4.** glut, sate, surfeit. **5.** weary.

pal·la (pal′ə), *n., pl.* **pal·lae** (pal′ē). a voluminous square of cloth draped around the body as a mantle or wrap, worn by women of ancient Rome. [< L]

Pal·la·di·an (pə lā′dē ən), *adj.* **1.** pertaining to, introduced by, or in the style of Andrea Palladio. —*n.* **2.** a disciple of Andrea Palladio, specifically one of the circle of Lord Burlington in 18th-century England. [PALLADI(O) + -AN]

Palladian window

Pal·la·di·an (pə lā′dē ən), *adj.* **1.** of or pertaining to the goddess Pallas. **2.** pertaining to wisdom, knowledge, or study. [< L *Palladi(us)* of Pallas (< Gk *Pallādios;* see PALLADIUM) + -AN]

Palla′dian win′dow, a window in the form of a round-headed archway with a narrower compartment on either side, the side compartments usually being capped with entablatures on which the arch of the central compartment rests. Also called **Diocletian window, Venetian window.**

pal·lad·ic (pə lad′ik, -lā′dik), *adj. Chem.* of or containing palladium, esp. in the tetravalent state. [PALLAD(IUM) + -IC]

pal·la·di·nize (pal′ə dᵊnīz′), *v.t.,* **-ized, iz·ing.** palladiumize. [irreg. < NL *pallad(ium)*; see -IZE]

Pal·la·dio (päl lä′dyô), *n.* **An·dre·a** (än dRe′ä), 1508–80, Italian architect.

pal·la·di·um (pə lā′dē əm), *n. Chem.* a rare metallic element of the platinum group, silver-white, ductile and malleable, harder and fusing more readily than platinum: used chiefly as a catalyst and in dental and other alloys. *Symbol:* Pd; *at. wt.:* 106.4; *at. no.:* 46; *sp. gr.:* 12 at 20°C. [special use of PALLADIUM; named (1803) after the asteroid PALLAS, then newly discovered; see -IUM]

Pal·la·di·um (pə lā′dē əm), *n., pl.* **-di·a** (-dē ə). **1.** a statue of Pallas Athene, esp. one on the citadel of Troy on which the safety of the city was supposed to depend. **2.** (*usually l.c.*) anything believed to provide protection or safety; safeguard. [< L *Palladium* < Gk *Pallādion,* n. use of neut. of *Pallādios* of Pallas, equiv. to *Pallad-* (s. of *Pallás*) PALLAS + *-ios* adj. suffix]

pal·la·di·um·ize (pə lā′dē ə mīz′), *v.t.,* **-ized, -iz·ing.** to treat or cover a surface with palladium. Also, **palladinize, palladize.** [PALLADIUM + -IZE]

pal·la·dize (pal′ə dīz′), *v.t.,* **-dized, -diz·ing.** palladiumize. [PALLAD(IUM) + -IZE]

pal·la·dous (pə lā′dəs, pal′ə dəs), *adj. Chem.* containing bivalent palladium. [PALLAD(IUM) + -OUS]

Pal·las (pal′əs), *n.* **1.** *Class. Myth.* **a.** a name given to or used with the name of Athena. **b.** a daughter of Triton who was killed while playing with the youthful Athena. The goddess adopted her name and made an effigy of her. **2.** *Astron.* the second largest and one of the four brightest asteroids. **3.** a walled plain in the second quadrant of the face of the moon: about 30 miles in diameter.

pal·las·ite (pal′ə sīt′), *n. Mineral.* a type of meteorite containing crystals of olivine embedded in nickel iron. [named after Peter S. *Pallas* (d. 1811), German naturalist; see -ITE¹]

pall·bear·er (pôl′bâr′ər), *n.* one of several persons who carry or attend the coffin at a funeral. [PALL¹ + BEARER]

pal·let¹ (pal′it), *n.* **1.** a bed or mattress of straw. **2.** a small or makeshift bed. [ME *pailet* < AF *paillete,* equiv. to OF *paille* straw (< L *palea* chaff) + *-ete* -ETTE]

pal·let² (pal′it), *n.* **1.** a shaping tool used by potters and consisting of a flat blade or plate with a handle at one end. **2.** a flat board or metal plate used to support ceramic articles during drying. **3.** *Horol.* **a.** a lever with three projections, two of which intermittently lock and receive impulses from the escape wheel and one which transmits these impulses to the balance. **b.** either of the two projections of this lever that engage and release the escape wheel. **4.** (on a pawl) a lip or projection that engages with the teeth of a ratchet wheel. **5.** (in gilding) an instrument used to take up the gold leaves from the pillow and to apply and extend them. **6.** *Print.* typeholder. **7.** a platform on which goods are placed for storage or transportation. **8.** a painter's palette. **9.** *Bookbinding.* **a.** a tool for decorating the spine of a book. **b.** the stamping of the name of the binder on the inside covers of a book. [< MF *palette* small shovel. See PALETTE]

pal·let³ (pal′it), *n. Heraldry.* a diminutive of the pale, about one half the usual width and often used in pairs. Also, **palet.** [PALE² + -ET]

pal·let·ed (pal′i tid), *adj.* (of the binding of a book) stamped with the name of the binder. [PALLET² + -ED³]

pal·let·ize (pal′i tīz′), *v.t.,* **-ized, -iz·ing.** **1.** to place (materials) upon pallets for handling or transportation. **2.** to perform (a materials handling operation) with the aid of pallets. [PALLET² + -IZE] —**pal′let·i·za′tion,** *n.*

pal′let knife′, *Cookery.* a small flat utensil for picking up and handling pastry paste.

pal·lette (pal′it), *n. Armor.* palette (def. 6).

pal·li·al (pal′ē əl), *adj.* **1.** of or pertaining to the mantle of a mollusk. **2.** of or pertaining to the cerebral cortex. [PALLI(UM) + -AL¹]

pal·liasse (pal yas′, pal′yas), *n. Chiefly Brit.* paillasse.

pal·li·ate (pal′ē āt′), *v.t.,* **-at·ed, -at·ing.** **1.** to attempt to mitigate or conceal the gravity of (an offense) by excuses, apologies, etc.; extenuate. **2.** to relieve without curing; mitigate; alleviate. [< LL *palliāt(us)* cloaked, covered. See PALLIUM, -ATE¹] —**pal′li·a′tion,** *n.* —**pal′li·a′tor,** *n.*

pal·li·a·tive (pal′ē ā′tiv, -ē ə tiv), *adj.* **1.** serving to palliate. —*n.* **2.** something that palliates. [< F *palliatif.* See PALLIATE, -IVE] —**pal′li·a′tive·ly,** *adv.*

pal·lid (pal′id), *adj.* **1.** pale; wan; faint or deficient in color: *a pallid countenance.* **2.** lacking in vitality or interest: *a pallid musical performance.* [< L *pallid(us)* sallow, equiv. to *pall(ēre)* (to) be pale + *-idus* -ID⁴] —**pal′lid·ly,** *adv.* —**pal′lid·ness,** *n.*
—**Syn. 1.** See **pale¹.**

pal·li·um (pal′ē əm), *n., pl.* **pal·li·a** (pal′ē ə), **pal·li·ums.** **1.** a large, rectangular mantle worn by men in ancient Greece and Rome. **2.** *Eccles.* **a.** a woolen vestment worn by the pope and conferred by him on archbishops, consisting, in its present form, of a narrow ringlike band that rests on the shoulders, with two dependent bands or lappets, one in front and one behind. **b.** an altar cloth; a pall. **3.** *Anat.* the entire cortex of the cerebrum. **4.** *Zool.* a mantle. [ME, OE < L; see PALL¹]

Pall Mall (pel′ mel′, pal′ mal′, pôl′ môl′), a street in London, England, famed for its clubs.

pall-mall (pel′mel′), *n.* **1.** a game, popular in the 17th century, in which a ball of boxwood was struck with a mallet in an attempt to drive it through a raised iron ring at the end of a playing alley. **2.** a playing alley on which this game was played. [< MF *pallemaille* < It *pallamaglio,* equiv. to *palla* ball (< Langobardish) + *maglio* mallet (< L *malleus*). See BALL¹, MALL]

pal·lor (pal′ər), *n.* unnatural paleness, as from fear, ill health, or death; wanness. [< L: paleness, equiv. to *pall(ēre)* (to) be pale + *-or* -OR¹]

palm¹ (päm), *n.* **1.** the part of the inner surface of the hand which extends from the wrist to the bases of the fingers. **2.** the corresponding part of the forefoot of an animal. **3.** the part of a glove covering this part of the hand. **4.** Also called **sailmaker's palm.** a stiff rawhide or metal shield worn over this part of the hand by sailmakers to serve as a thimble. **5.** a linear measure of from three to four inches, based on the breadth of the hand. **6.** a linear measure of from seven to ten inches, based on the length of the hand. **7.** the flat, expanded part of the horn or antler of a deer. **8.** a flat, widened part at the end of an armlike projection. **9.** *Naut.* **a.** the blade of an oar. **b.** the inner face of an anchor fluke. **c.** (loosely) an anchor fluke. **10.** a flat-topped bearing member at the head of a stanchion. **11. cross** or **grease someone's palm,** to give money to, esp. as a bribe: *Before any work could begin it was necessary to grease the superintendent's palm.* —*v.t.* **12.** to conceal in the palm, as in cheating at cards or dice or in juggling. **13.** to pick up stealthily. **14.** to hold in the hand. **15.** to impose (something) fraudulently (usually fol. by *on* or *upon*): *to palm stolen jewels on someone.* **16.** to touch or stroke with the palm or hand. **17.** to shake hands with. **18.** *Basketball.* to grip (the ball) momentarily with the hand in the act of dribbling. **19.** **palm off,** to dispose of by fraud; substitute (something) with intent to deceive: *Someone had palmed off a forgery on the museum officials.* [< L *palm(a)* (c. OE *folm* hand); r. ME *paume* < MF < L *palma*]

palm[2] (päm), *n.* **1.** any of numerous plants of the family *Palmaceae,* most species being tall, unbranched trees surmounted by a crown of large pinnate or palmately cleft leaves. **2.** any of various other trees or shrubs that resemble this. **3.** a leaf or branch of such a tree, esp. as formerly borne to signify victory or as used on festive occasions. **4.** a representation of such a leaf or branch, as on a military or other decoration of honor. **5.** the reward of honor due to a victor. **6.** victory; triumph; success: *He carried off the palm by sheer perseverance.* [ME, OE < L *palma* palm tree, special use of *palma* PALM[1]] **—palm′like′,** *adj.*

Royal palm, *Roystonea regia*

Pal·ma (päl′mä), *n.* **1.** Also called **Palma de Mallorca.** a seaport in and the capital of the Balearic Islands, on W Majorca. 162,155 (est. 1960). **2.** one of the Canary Islands, off the NW coast of Africa. 164,963 (est. 1963); 281 sq. mi. *Cap.:* Santa Cruz de la Palma.

pal·ma·ceous (pal mā′shəs, päl-, pä mā′-), *adj.* belonging to the *Palmaceae,* or palm family of plants. [PALM[2] + -ACEOUS]

Pal·ma de Ma·llor·ca (*Sp.* päl′mä the mä lyôr′kä), Palma (def. 1).

pal·mar (pal′mər, päl′-, pä′mər), *adj.* of, pertaining to, or located in or on the palm of the hand or to the corresponding part of the forefoot of an animal. [< L *palmār(is)* a hand's breadth. See PALM[1], -AR[1]]

pal·ma·ry (pal′mə rē, pal′-, pä′mə-), *adj.* having or deserving to have the palm of victory or success; praiseworthy: *a palmary achievement.* [< L *palmāri(us)* of, belonging to palms. See PALM[2], -ARY]

Pal·mas (päl′mäs), *n.* **Las.** See **Las Palmas.**

pal′ma sa·man·do′ca (pal′mə sä′mən dō′kə), a treelike plant, *Samuela carnerosana,* of Mexico, having showy, white flowers nearly four inches wide. [< MexSp]

pal·mate (pal′māt, -mit, päl′-, pä′māt), *adj.* **1.** shaped like an open palm or like a hand with the fingers extended, as a leaf or an antler. **2.** *Bot.* lobed or divided so that the sinuses point to or reach the apex of the petiole irrespective of the number of lobes. **3.** *Zool.* web-footed. **4.** *Furniture.* **a.** decorated with palmettes. **b.** (in furniture of the 17th century) having bands of semicircles enclosing a radiating leaf form. Also, **pal′mat·ed.** [< LL *palmāt(us)* marked with the palm of a hand, shaped like a palm. See PALM[1], -ATE[1]] **—pal′mate·ly,** *adv.*

Palmate leaf

pal·ma·tion (pal mā′shən, päl-, pä mā′-), *n.* **1.** a palmate state or formation. **2.** a palmate structure. [PALMATE + -ION]

Palm′ Beach′, a town in SE Florida: seaside winter resort. 6055 (1960).

palm′ cab′bage, **1.** See **cabbage palm. 2.** the edible bud of a cabbage palm.

palm′ cat′, any of various viverrine animals of southeastern Asia, the East Indies, etc., chiefly arboreal in habit, about the size of the domestic cat, and having a spotted or striped fur and a long curled tail. Also called **palm′ civ′et.**

palm′ chat′, a passerine bird, *Dulus dominicus,* of Hispaniola and Gonave, noted for its huge, communal nest, occupied by several pairs of birds.

palm′ crab′. See **coconut crab.**

palm·er[1] (pä′mər, pal′mər), *n.* **1.** a pilgrim, esp. of the Middle Ages, who had returned from the Holy Land, in token of which he bore a palm branch. **2.** any pilgrim. **3.** palmerworm. **—*v.i.* 4.** *Scot. and North Eng.* to wander; go idly from place to place. [ME *palmer(e)* < AF *palmer,* equiv. to OF *palmier* < ML *palmār(ius),* special use of L *palmārius* PALMARY]

palm·er[2] (pä′mər), *n.* one who palms a card, die, or other object, as in cheating at cards or performing a magic trick. [PALM[1] + -ER[1]]

Pal·mer (pä′mər), *n.* **1. Alice Elvira,** 1855–1902, U.S. educator. **2. Arnold,** born 1929, U.S. golfer. **3. Daniel David,** 1845–1913, Canadian originator of chiropractic medicine. **4. George Herbert,** 1842–1933, U.S. educator, philosopher, and author. **5.** a town in S Massachusetts. 3888 (1960).

Palm′er Land′, the southern part of the Antarctic Peninsula.

Palm′er Penin′sula, former name of **Antarctic Peninsula.**

Palm·er·ston (pä′mər stən), *n.* **Henry John Temple, 3rd Viscount,** 1784–1865, British statesman: prime minister 1855–58; 1859–65.

Palm·er·ton (pä′mər tən), *n.* a town in E Pennsylvania. 5942 (1960).

palm·er·worm (pä′mər wûrm′), *n.* the larva of a tineid moth, *Dichomeris ligulella,* of the eastern U.S., that feeds on the leaves of apple and other fruit trees. [PALMER[1] + WORM]

pal·mette (pal met′), *n.* a conventionalized shape in the form of palmately spread leaves or sections, used as ornamentation. Cf. **anthemion, lotus** (def. 5). See diag. under **volute.** [< F; see PALM[2], -ETTE]

pal·met·to (pal met′ō), *n., pl.* **-tos, -toes.** any of various palms having fan-shaped leaves, as of the genera *Sabal, Serenoa, Thrinax,* etc. [earlier *palmito* < Sp, dim. of *palma* PALM[2], *-etto* by assoc. with -ETTE]

Pal·met·to (pal met′ō), *n.* a town in SW Florida. 5556 (1960).

Palmet′to State′, the State of South Carolina (used as a nickname).

palm′ grass′, a perennial grass, *Setaria palmifolia,* of the East Indies, having showy foliage, grown as an ornamental.

Palm·gren (päm′grən; *Fin.* pälm′grən), *n.* **Se·lim** (sel′im, sā′lim; *Fin.* se′lim), 1878–1951, Finnish pianist and composer.

Pal·mi·ra′ (päl mē rä′), *n.* a city in W Colombia. 148,510 (est. 1964).

pal·miste (pal mēst′, pal′mēst), *n.* See **Barbados royal palm.** [< F < Creole < Sp *palmito* PALMETTO]

palm·is·try (pä′mi strē), *n.* the art or practice of telling fortunes and interpreting character by the lines and configurations of the palm of the hand. [late ME *pawmestry,* equiv. to *pawm* PALM[1] + *-estr-* (var. of *-istr-* < MF *-istre*) + *-y* -Y[3]] **—palm′ist,** *n.*

pal·mi·tate (pal′mi tāt′, päl′-, pä′mi-), *n.* *Chem.* a salt or ester of palmitic acid. [PALMIT(IN) + -ATE[2]]

pal·mit·ic (pal mit′ik, päl-, pä mit′-), *adj.* *Chem.* of or derived from palmitic acid. [< F *palmitique.* See PALM[2], -ITE[1], -IC]

palmit′ic ac′id, *Chem.* a white, crystalline, water-insoluble solid, $CH_3(CH_2)_{14}COOH$, obtained by hydrolysis from palm oil and natural fats, in which it occurs as the gylceride, and from spermaceti: used in the manufacture of soap. Also called **cetylic acid, hexadecanoic acid.**

pal·mi·tin (pal′mi tin, päl′-, pä′mi-), *n.* *Chem.* a white, crystalline, water-insoluble powder, $(C_{15}H_{31}COO)_3C_3H_5$, prepared from glycerol and palmitic acid: used in the manufacture of soap. Also called **glyceryl tripalmitate, tripalmitin.** [< F *palmitine.* See PALM[2], -ITE[1], -IN[2]]

palm′ leaf′, the leaf or frond of a palm tree, esp. that of a fan palm, used in making fans, hats, thatch, mats, etc.

palm′ oil′, **1.** a yellow butterlike oil derived from the fruit of the oil palm and used as an edible fat and for making soap, candles, etc. **2.** oil obtained from various species of palm.

Palm′ Springs′, a city in S California: resort. 13,468 (1960).

palm′ sug′ar, sugar from the sap of certain palm trees.

Palm′ Sun′day, the Sunday before Easter, celebrated in commemoration of Christ's triumphal entry into Jerusalem. [ME *palmesonday,* OE *palmsunnandæg*]

palm′ war′bler, a North American wood warbler, *Dendroica palmarum,* brown above and whitish or yellowish below.

palm′ wine′, wine made from distilled palm-tree sap.

palm·y (pä′mē), *adj.,* **palm·i·er, palm·i·est. 1.** glorious, prosperous, or flourishing: *the palmy days of yesteryear.* **2.** abounding in or shaded with palms: *palmy islands.* **3.** palmlike. [PALM[2] + -Y[1]]

pal·my·ra (pal mī′rə), *n.* a tropical Asian fan palm, *Borassus flabellifer.* Also called **palmy′ra palm′.** [alter. of Pg *palmeira* PALM[2]]

Pal·my·ra (pal mī′rə), *n.* **1.** Biblical name, **Tadmor.** an ancient city in central Syria, NE of Damascus: reputedly built by Solomon. **2.** a town in SW New Jersey. 7036 (1960). **3.** a town in central Pennsylvania. 6999 (1960). **4.** a town in W New York. 3476 (1960). **5.** a town in NE Missouri. 2933 (1960).

Pal·o Al·to (pal′ō al′tō *for 1;* pä′lō äl′tō *for 2*), **1.** a city in W California, SE of San Francisco. 52,287 (1960). **2.** a battlefield in S Texas, near Brownsville: first battle of Mexican War fought here in 1846.

pa·lo·lo (pə lō′lō), *n., pl.* **-los.** See **palolo worm.** [< Samoan or Tongan]

palo′lo worm′, a polychaete worm, *Eunice viridis,* that lives in burrows among the coral reefs of several South Pacific islands, producing sperm or eggs in posterior segments that are cast off periodically in enormous numbers.

Pa·lo·ma (pə lō′mə), *n.* a girl's given name.

pal·o·met·a (pal′ə met′ə), *n.* **1.** a pompano, *Trachinotus glaucus,* found in the tropical and temperate areas of the Atlantic Ocean, having long, tapering fins. **2.** any of several stromateid butterfishes. [< Sp, dim. of *paloma* dove < L *palumbēs;* see -ET]

pal·o·mi·no (pal′ə mē′nō), *n., pl.* **-nos.** one of a breed of horses developed chiefly in the southwestern U.S. and characterized by a golden color and a flaxen mane and tail. [< AmerSp, special use of Sp *palomino* of, resembling a dove < L *palumbīnus,* equiv. to *palumb(ēs)* dove + *-īnus* -INE[1]]

pa·loo·ka (pə lo͞o′kə), *n.* *Slang.* **1.** an athlete, esp. a boxer, lacking in ability, experience, or competitive spirit. **2.** a stupid, clumsy person [?]

Pa·los (pä′lôs), *n.* a seaport in SW Spain: starting point of Columbus' first voyage westward. 2280 (1950).

Pal′os Ver′des Estates′ (pal′əs vûr′dis), a town in S California. 9564 (1960).

pal·o·ver·de (pal′ō vûr′dē, -vûrd′), *n.* a spiny, desert shrub, *Cercidium torreyanum,* of the southwestern U.S. and Mexico, having green bark. Also called **green-barked acacia.** [< AmerSp: lit., green tree]

palp (palp), *n.* a palpus.

pal·pa·ble (pal′pə bəl), *adj.* **1.** readily or plainly seen, heard, perceived, etc.; obvious; evident: *a palpable lie; palpable absurdity.* **2.** capable of being touched or felt; tangible. **3.** *Med.* perceptible by palpation. [ME < LL *palpābil(is)* that can be touched, equiv. to *palpā(re)* (to) touch + *-bilis* -BLE] **—pal′pa·bil′i·ty, pal′pa·ble·ness,** *n.* **—pal′pa·bly,** *adv.*
—Syn. 1. manifest, plain. **2.** material, corporeal.
—Ant. 1. obscure.

pal·pate[1] (pal′pāt), *v.t.,* **-pat·ed, -pat·ing.** to examine by touch, esp. for the purpose of diagnosing disease or illness. [< L *palpāt(us)* ptp. of *palpāre* to feel, touch; see -ATE[1]] **—pal·pa′tion,** *n.* **—pal·pa·to·ry** (pal′pə tôr′ē, -tōr′ē), *adj.*

pal·pate[2] (pal′pāt), *adj.* *Zool.* having a palpus or palpi. [PALP(US) + -ATE[1]]

pal·pe·bral (pal′pə brəl), *adj.* of or pertaining to the eyelids. [< LL *palpebrāl(is)* of, on the eyelids, equiv. to L *palpebr(a)* eyelid (sp. var. of *palpebrum*) + *-ālis* -AL[1]]

pal·pe·brate (pal′pə brāt′, pal pē′brit), *adj.* having eyelids. [< NL *palpebrāt(us),* equiv. to L *palpebr(a)* eyelid + *-ātus* -ATE[1]]

pal·pi (pal′pī), *n.* pl. of **palpus.**

pal·pi·tant (pal′pi tənt), *adj.* palpitating. [< L *palpitant-* (s. of *palpitāns*) throbbing, prp. of *palpitāre.* See PALPITATE, -ANT]

pal·pi·tate (pal′pi tāt′), *v.i.,* **-tat·ed, -tat·ing. 1.** to pulsate with unnatural rapidity from exertion, emotion, disease, etc.; flutter: *His heart palpitated wildly.* **2.** to pulsate; quiver; throb; tremble. [< L *palpitāt(us)* throbbed, ptp. of *palpitāre,* freq. of *palpāre* to stroke. See PALPUS, -ATE[1]] **—pal′pi·tat′ing·ly,** *adv.*
—Syn. 1. See **pulsate.**

pal·pi·ta·tion (pal′pi tā′shən), *n.* **1.** the act of palpitating. **2.** an abnormally rapid or violent beating of the heart. [< L *palpitātiōn-* (s. of *palpitātiō*) a throbbing. See PALPITATE, -ION]

pal·pus (pal′pəs), *n., pl.* **-pi** (-pī). an appendage attached to an oral part and serving as an organ of sense in insects, crustaceans, etc. See diag. under **insect.** [< NL, special use of L *palpus* soft palm of the hand, akin to *palma* PALM[1]]

Pal·se·ar (pal′sē är′), *n.* a boy's given name.

pal·sen (päl′sən), *n.pl.* *Geol.* mounds of earth pushed up by or formed near the edge of a glacier, found in alpine and arctic areas. [< Sw, equiv. to *palo* (< Lappish *palsa*) + *-en* the]

pals·grave (pôlz′grāv, palz′-), *n.* a German count palatine. [< D *paltsgrave* (now *paltsgraaf*); c. G *Pfalzgraf* imperial count. See MARGRAVE, PALATINE[1]]

pals·gra·vine (pôlz′grə vēn′, palz′-), *n.* the wife or widow of a palsgrave. [< D *paltsgravin.* See PALSGRAVE, -INE[2]]

pal·stave (pôl′stāv′, pal′-), *n.* *Archaeol.* a bronze celt fitted into a split wooden handle. Also, **pal·staff** (pôl′staf′, -stäf′, pal′-). [< Dan *pålstav,* special use of Icel *pālstafr* javelin < OE *palster* spike, taken (by folk etymology) as **pālstæf;* see POLE, STAFF[1]]

pal·sy[1] (pôl′zē), *n., pl.* **-sies,** *v.,* **-sied, -sy·ing. —*n.* 1.** paralysis. **2.** any of a variety of atonal muscular conditions characterized by tremors of the body parts, as of the hands, arms, or legs, or of the entire body. **—*v.t.* 3.** to paralyze. [ME, var. of *parlesie* < MF *paralisie* < L *paralysis* PARALYSIS] **—pal′sy·like′,** *adj.*

pal·sy[2] (pal′zē), *adj.* *Slang.* palsy-walsy. [PAL + -S[3] + -Y[1]]

pal·sy-wal·sy (pal′zē wal′zē), *adj.* *Slang.* friendly or appearing to be friendly in an intimate or hearty way: *The police kept their eye on him because he was trying to get palsy-walsy with the night watchman.* [rhyming compound, based on PALSY[2]]

pal·ter (pôl′tər), *v.i.* **1.** to talk or act insincerely; lie or use trickery. **2.** to bargain with; haggle. **3.** to act carelessly; trifle. [earliest sense: to speak indistinctly; perh. alter. of FALTER in same sense, with *p-* from PALSY[1]] **—pal′ter·er,** *n.*

pal·try (pôl′trē), *adj.,* **-tri·er, -tri·est. 1.** trifling; petty: *a paltry sum.* **2.** trashy or worthless: *paltry rags.* **3.** mean or contemptible: *a paltry coward.* [< LG *paltrig* ragged, equiv. to **palter* rag (dial. G *Palter*) + *-ig* -Y[1]] **—pal′tri·ly,** *adv.* **—pal′tri·ness,** *n.*
—Syn. 1. minor, inconsiderable, slight, insignificant. See **petty. —Ant. 1.** important, major.

pa·lu·dal (pə lo͞od′əl, pal′yə dəl), *adj.* **1.** of or pertaining to marshes. **2.** produced by marshes, as miasma or disease. [< L *palūd-* (s. of *palūs*) swamp, marsh + -AL[1]]

pa·lu·da·men·tum (pə lo͞o′də men′təm), *n., pl.* **-ta** (-tə). a cloak worn by officials and military officers of ancient Rome, esp. during wartime. Also, **pa·lu·da·ment** (pə lo͞o′də mənt). [< L; cf. PALLA]

pal·u·dism (pal′yə diz′əm), *n.* *Pathol.* malaria. [< L *palūd-* (s. of *palūs*) swamp, marsh + -ISM]

Pal·u·drine (pal′yə drēn′, -drin, pə lo͞o′drin), *n.* *Pharm., Trademark.* chloroguanide.

Pa·lus Ep·i·dem·i·a·rum (pä′ləs ep′i dem′ē är′əm), a dark plain in the third quadrant of the face of the moon at the southern edges of Mare Nubium and Mare Humorum: about 6,700 square miles. Also called **Marsh of Epidemics.**

Pa′lus Neb·u·la′rum (neb′yə lär′əm), a hilly area in the first quadrant of the face of the moon at the edge of Mare Imbrium. Also called **Marsh of Mists.**

Pa′lus Pu·tre′di·nis (po͞o trăd′ənis), a hilly area in the northern hemisphere of the face of the moon in the first and second quadrants, at the edge of Mare Imbrium: about 3,600 square miles. Also called **Marsh of Decay.**

Pa′lus Som′ni (som′nē), a hilly area in the first quadrant of the face of the moon at the edge of Mare Tranquillitatis: about 11,000 square miles. Also, **Pa′lus Som′ni·i** (som′nē ē′). Also called **Marsh of Sleep.**

pal·y[1] (pā′lē), *adj.* *Archaic.* pale. [PALE[1] + -Y[1]]

pal·y[2] (pā′lē), *adj.* *Heraldry.* dividend palewise, or vertically, into equal parts of alternating tinctures. [ME < MF *palé.* See PALE[2], -EE]

pal·y-bend·y (pā′lē ben′dē), *adj.* *Heraldry.* (of an escutcheon) divided palewise and bendwise to form a lozengy pattern, usually of two alternating tinctures: *paly-bendy argent and gules.*

pal·y·nol·o·gy (pal′ə nol′ə jē), *n.* the science dealing with the study of live and fossil spores and with pollen grains and other microscopic plant structures. [< Gk *palŷn(ein)* (to) sprinkle, scatter (akin to *pálē* dust) + -o- + -LOGY] **—pal·y·no·log·i·cal** (pal′ə nᵊloj′i kəl), *adj.* **—pal′y·no·log′i·cal·ly,** *adv.*

pam (pam), *n.* *Cards.* **1.** the jack of clubs, esp. in a form of loo in which it is the best trump. **2.** a game in which this card is trump. [short for F *pamphile,* special use of *Pamphile* man's name, Gk *Pámphilos.* See PAN-, -PHILE]

Pam (pam), *n.* a girl's given name, form of **Pamela.**

pam., pamphlet.

pam·a·quine (pam′ə kwīn′, -kwēn′, -kwin), *n.* a compound, $C_{19}H_{29}N_3O$, prepared in the form of its yellow to yellow-orange, water-insoluble naphthoate, $C_{42}H_{45}N_3O_7$: used in medicine chiefly in the treatment of malaria. Also, **pam·a·quin** (pam′ə kwin). Also called **aminoquin, plasmoquin, plasmoquine.** [P(ENTYL) + AM(INO) + *-a-* connective + QUIN(OLINE)]

Pam·e·la (pam′ə lə), *n.* a girl's given name.

Pam·e·la (pam′ə lə), *n.* (or *Virtue Rewarded*) an epistolary novel (1740) by Samuel Richardson.

pam′ head′. See **pan head.**

Pa·mir·i (pä mēr′ī), *n., pl.* **-mir·is,** (*esp. collectively*) **-mir·i.** a member of a Caucasoid people inhabiting the Pamirs.

Pa·mirs, the (pä mērz′), a plateau in central Asia, where the Hindu Kush, Tien Shan, and Himalaya mountain ranges converge: highest peaks, ab. 25,000 ft. Also called **Pa·mir′.**

Pam′li·co Sound′ (pam′lə kō′), a sound between the North Carolina mainland and coastal islands.

Pam·pa (pam′pə), *n.* a city in N Texas. 24,664 (1960).

pam·pas (pam′pəz; *attributively* pam′pəs; *Sp.* päm′päs), *n.pl., sing.* **-pa** (-pə; *Sp.* -pä). the vast grassy plains of S South America, esp. in Argentina. [< AmerSp, pl. of *pampa* < Quechua *bamba* plain] —**pam·pe·an** (pam pē′ən, pam′pē ən), *adj.*

pam′pas grass′, a tall, ornamental grass, *Cortaderia Sellona,* native to South America, having large, thick, feathery, silvery-white panicles.

Pam·pe·lu·na (päm′pe lo͞o′nä), *n.* Pamplona.

pam·per (pam′pər), *v.t.* to treat or gratify with extreme or excessive indulgence, kindness, or care: *to pamper a child; to pamper one's stomach.* [ME *pamper(en),* prob. < MFlem; cf. Flem *pamperen*] —**pam′pered·ly,** *adv.* —**pam′pered·ness,** *n.* —**pam′per·er,** *n.*
—**Syn.** humor, coddle, baby, spoil. —**Ant.** discipline.

pam·pe·ro (päm pâr′ō; *Sp.* päm pe′rô), *n., pl.* **-ros** (-rōz; *Sp.* -rôs). a cold and dry southwesterly wind that sweeps over the pampas of Argentina and northeastward to the Brazilian coast, following barometric depression. [< AmerSp: lit., of the pampas]

pamph., pamphlet.

pam·phlet (pam′flit), *n.* **1.** a short treatise or essay, generally a controversial tract, on some subject of contemporary interest: *a political pamphlet.* **2.** a complete, unbound publication of generally less than 80 pages stitched or stapled together. [ME *pamflet* < AL *panflet(us),* syncopated var. of *Pamphiletus,* dim. of ML *Pamphilus,* title of a 12th-century Latin comedy. See PAM, -ET] —**pam′phlet·ar′y,** *adj.*

pam·phlet·eer (pam′fli tēr′), *n.* **1.** a writer of pamphlets. —*v.i.* **2.** to write and issue pamphlets. [PAMPHLET + -EER]

pam·phlet·ize (pam′fli tīz′), *v.,* **-ized, -iz·ing.** —*v.i.* **1.** to write a pamphlet. —*v.t.* **2.** to write a pamphlet on (a specific subject). [PAMPHLET + -IZE]

Pam·phyl·i·a (pam fil′ē ə), *n.* an ancient country in S Asia Minor: later a Roman province.

pam·ple·gia (pam plē′jə, -jē ə), *n. Pathol.* panplegia.

Pam·plo·na (pam plō′nə; *Sp.* päm plô′nä), *n.* a city in N Spain. 105,397 (est. 1963). Also, **Pampeluna.**

pam·pre (pam′pər), *n.* a running undercut ornament for filling continuous hollows, as a cavetto molding, usually having the form of a grapevine. [< F < L *pampinus* shoot of a vine, foliage of a vine]

pam·pro·dac·ty·lous (pam′prō dak′tᵊləs), *adj. Ornith.* having all four toes directed forward, as in swifts and colies. Also, **pam′pro·dac′tyl.** [*pam-* (var. of PAN-) + PRO- + -DACTYL + -OUS] —**pam′pro·dac′tyl·ism,** *n.*

pan[1] (pan), *n., v.,* **panned, pan·ning.** —*n.* **1.** a broad, shallow container of metal, usually having sides flaring outward toward the top, used in various forms for frying, baking, washing, etc. **2.** any dishlike receptacle or part, as the scales of a balance. **3.** any of various open or closed vessels used in industrial or mechanical processes. **4.** a vessel in which silver ores are ground and amalgamated. **5.** a container in which gold or other heavy, valuable metals are separated from gravel or other substances by agitation with water. **6.** *Slang.* the face. **7.** a drifting piece of flat, thin ice, as formed on a shore or bay. **8.** a natural depression in the ground, as one containing water, mud, or mineral salts. **9.** a similar depression made artificially, as for evaporating salt water to make salt. **10.** hardpan. **11.** (in old guns) the depressed part of the lock, holding the priming. —*v.t.* **12.** to wash (gravel, sand, etc.) in a pan to separate gold or other heavy valuable metal. **13.** to separate (gold or other heavy valuable metal) by such washing. **14.** to cook (oysters, clams, etc.) in a pan. **15.** *Informal.* to criticize severely, as in a review of a play. —*v.i.* **16.** to wash gravel, sand etc., in a pan in seeking gold or the like. **17.** to yield gold or the like, as gravel washed in a pan. **18. pan out,** *Informal.* to turn out, esp. successfully: *The peace talks did not pan out and fighting was resumed.* [ME, OE *panne;* c. D *pan,* G *Pfanne,* Icel *panna*]

pan[2] (pän), *n.* **1.** the leaf of the betel. **2.** a substance, esp. betel nut or a betel-nut mixture, used for chewing. [< Hindi < Skt *parna* feather, leaf]

pan[3] (pan), *v.,* **panned, pan·ning.** —*v.i.* **1.** to photograph or televise while rotating a camera on its vertical or horizontal axis in order to keep a moving person or object in view or allow the film to record a panorama: *to pan leisurely from one end of the playing field to the other during the opening of the football game.* **2.** (of a camera) to be moved or manipulated in such a manner: *The cameras panned occasionally during the scene.* —*v.t.* **3.** to move (a camera) in such a manner: *to pan the camera across the scene.* **4.** to photograph or televise (a scene, moving character, etc.) by panning the camera. [shortening of PANORAMA]

Pan

pan[4] (pan), *n.* **1.** a major vertical division of a wall. **2.** a nogged panel of half-timber construction. [< F, MF: PANE]

Pan (pan), *n.* the ancient Greek god of forests, pastures, flocks, and shepherds, represented with the head, chest, and arms of a man and the legs and sometimes the horns and ears of a goat.

pan-, a learned borrowing from Greek meaning "all," occurring originally in loan words from Greek (*panacea; panoply*), but now used freely as a general formative (*panleukopenia; panorama; pantelegraph; pantheism; pantonality*), and esp. in terms, formed at will, implying the union of all branches of a group (*Pan-Christian; Panhellenic; Pan-Slavism*). The hyphen and the second capital tend with longer use to be lost, unless they are retained in order to set off clearly the component parts. Also, **pant-, panto-.** [< Gk *pan-* comb. form of Gk *pân* all]

Pan., Panama.

Pa·na (pā′nə), *n.* a town in central Illinois. 6432 (1960).

pan·a·ce·a (pan′ə sē′ə), *n.* **1.** a remedy for all disease or ills; cure-all. **2.** an answer for all problems or solution to all difficulties: *His philosophy is a good one, but he tries to use it as a panacea.* [< L < Gk *panákeia,* equiv. to *panakē(s)* all-healing (*pan-* PAN- + *akēs* a cure) + *-ia* -IA] —**pan′a·ce′an,** *adj.*

Pan·a·ce·a (pan′ə sē′ə), *n.* an ancient Greek goddess of healing.

pa·nache (pə nash′, -näsh′), *n.* **1.** an ornamental plume of feathers, tassels, or the like, esp. one worn on a helmet or cap. **2.** *Archit.* the surface of a pendentive. **3.** *Rare.* web (def. 7). **4.** a grand or flamboyant manner; verve; style; flair: *The actor who would play Cyrano must have panache.* [var. (after F) of *pennache* < MF < early It *pennachio* < LL *pinnāculum,* dim. of *pinna* wing; identical in form with *pinnāculum* PINNACLE]

pa·na·da (pə nä′də, -nā′-), *n.* a thick sauce or paste made with bread crumbs, milk, and seasonings, often served with roast wild fowl or meat. [< Sp, equiv. to *pan-* bread (< L *pānis*) + *-ada* -ADE[1]]

Pan-Af·ri·can·ism (pan′af′rə kə niz′əm), *n.* the idea or advocacy of a political alliance or union of all the African nations. —**Pan′-Af′ri·can,** *adj., n.* —**Pan′-Af′ri·can·ist,** *n.*

Pa·na·gi·a (pä′nä yē′ä), *n., pl.* **-gi·as** for 1. *Eastern Ch.* **1.** a ceremony in a monastery, commemorating the assumption of the Virgin Mary, in which a loaf of bread on a plate is elevated before being distributed to the monks. **2.** (*l.c.*) encolpion. [< LGk *Panágia* the Virgin, fem. of Gk, *panágios* all-holy, equiv. to *pan-* PAN- + *hágios* holy]

Pan·a·ma (pan′ə mä′) *n.* **1.** a republic in S Central America, enclosing but not including the Panama Canal. 1,287,000 (est. 1966); 28,575 sq. mi. **2.** Also called **Panama City.** a city in and the capital of Panama, at the Pacific end of the Panama Canal, though not in the Canal Zone. 331,474 (est. 1965). **3. Isthmus of.** Formerly, **Isthmus of Darien.** an isthmus between North and South America. **4. Gulf of,** the portion of the Pacific in the bend of the Isthmus of Panama. **5.** (*sometimes l.c.*) See **Panama hat.** Also, **Pa·na·má** (pä′nä mä′) (for 1, 2). —**Pan·a·ma·ni·an** (pan′ə mā′nē ən, -mä′-), *adj., n.* —**Pan·am·ic** (pə nam′ik), *adj.*

Pan′ama Canal′, a canal extending SE from the Atlantic to the Pacific across the Isthmus of Panama. 40 mi. long.

Pan′ama Canal′ Zone′. See **Canal Zone.**

Pan′ama Cit′y, **1.** Panama (def. 2). **2.** a city in NW Florida. 33,275 (1960).

Pan′ama hat′, a hat made of finely plaited young leaves of a palmlike plant, *Carludovica palmata,* of Central and South America. Also called **Panama.**

Pan-A·mer·i·can (pan′ə mer′i kən), *adj.* of, pertaining to, or representing all the countries or people of North, Central, and South America.

Pan-A·mer·i·can·ism (pan′ə mer′i kə niz′əm), *n.* **1.** the idea or advocacy of a political alliance or union of all the countries of North, Central, and South America. **2.** a movement for or the idea or advocacy of close economic, cultural, and military cooperation among the Pan-American countries. [PAN-AMERICAN + -ISM]

Pan′ Amer′ican Un′ion, an organization of the 21 American republics dedicated to furthering understanding and peace.

pan·a·mi·ga (pan′ə mē′gə), *n.* a low, foliage plant, *Pilea pubescens,* of America, having toothed, velvety, brownish-green leaves and small, green flowers in clusters. [< AmerSp: lit., all-friend]

Pan′a·mint Moun′tains (pan′ə mint), a mountain range in E California. Highest peak, Telescope Peak, 11,045 ft.

Pan-Ar·a·bism (pan′ar′ə biz′əm), *n.* the idea or advocacy of a political alliance or union of all the Arab nations. —**Pan′-Ar′ab, Pan′-Ar′ab·ic,** *adj., n.*

pan·a·tel·la (pan′ə tel′ə), *n.* panetella. Also, **pan′a·tel′a.**

Pan·ath·e·nae·a (pan′ath ə nē′ə), *n.* a festival in honor of the goddess Athene, celebrated yearly in ancient Athens, with each fourth year reserved for greater pomp, marked by contests, as in athletics and music, and highlighted by a solemn procession of women to the Acropolis bearing a peplos embroidered for the goddess.

Pan·ath·e·na·ic (pan′ath ə nā′ik), *adj.* (*sometimes l.c.*) of or pertaining to a Panathenaea. Also, **Pan·ath·e·nae·an** (pan′ath ə nē′ən). [PANATHENA(EA) + -IC]

pan·at·ro·phy (pan a′trə fē), *n. Pathol.* atrophy of all parts of a structure or of the whole body. [PAN- + ATROPHY] —**pan·a·troph·ic** (pan′ə trof′ik), *adj.*

Pa·nay (pä nī′), *n.* an island in the Central Philippines. 1,813,000 (est. 1965); 4446 sq. mi. *Cap.:* Iloilo.

pan·cake (pan′kāk′), *n., v.,* **-caked, -cak·ing.** —*n.* **1.** a flat cake of batter cooked in a pan or on a griddle; griddlecake or flapjack. **2.** an airplane landing made by pancaking. **3.** Also called **pan′cake make′-up, cake make-up.** a make-up in cake form, used alone or with powder, applied with a damp sponge. —*v.i.* **4.** (of an airplane or the like) to drop flat to the ground after leveling off a few feet above it. —*v.t.* **5.** to cause (an airplane) to pancake. [late ME; see PAN[1], CAKE]

pan′cake ice′, newly formed ice in flat pieces too small and thin to obstruct navigation.

pan·car·di·tis (pan′kär dī′tis), *n. Pathol.* inflammation of the entire heart: the pericardium, myocardium, and endocardium. [PAN- + CARDITIS]

Pan·chai·a (pän che′ə), *n.* an area in the northern hemisphere of Mars, appearing as a dark region when viewed telescopically from the earth.

Pan·cha Si·la (pun′chə sē′lə), *Buddhism.* a standard recitation of Hinayanists, including repetitions of formulas and of vows to abstain from anger, lust, cowardice, malevolence, and to abstain from the desire for possessions and unwholesome pleasures. [< Pali: five utterances]

Pan·cha·tan·tra (pun′chə tun′trə). *n.* a collection of fables of the 3rd or 4th century A.D., written in Sanskrit.

Pan′chen La′ma (pän′chen). See **Tashi Lama.** Also called **Pan′chen Rim·po′che** (rim pō′chā). [*panchen* < Chin *pan ch'an,* lit., treasure of great value]

pan·chet·to (pan chet′ō; *It.* pän ket′tô), *n., pl.* **-tos,** *It.* **-ti** (-tē). *Ital. Furniture.* a Renaissance chair having three splayed legs and a shaped back joined into a solid wooden seat. [< It: stool]

panch′ mat′ (panch), *Naut.* See **paunch mat.**

pan·chro·mat·ic (pan′krō mat′ik, -krə-), *adj.* sensitive to all visible colors, as a photographic film. [PAN- + CHROMATIC] —**pan·chro·ma·tism** (pan krō′mə tiz′əm), *n.*

Pan·cra·tis (pan′krə tis), *n. Class. Myth.* a daughter of Aloeus and Iphimedia.

pan·cra·ti·um (pan krā′shē əm), *n., pl.* **-ti·a** (-shē ə). (in ancient Greece) an athletic contest combining wrestling and boxing. [< L < Gk *pankrátion* all-power exercise, equiv. to *pan-* PAN- + *krát(os)* strength, mastery + *-ion,* neut. of *-ios* adj. suffix] —**pan·crat·ic** (pan krat′ik), *adj.*

pan·cre·as (pan′krē əs, pang′-), *n. Anat., Zool.* a gland, situated near the stomach, which secretes a digestive fluid into the intestine through one or more ducts and also secretes the hormone insulin. Cf. **islet of Langerhans, pancreatic juice.** [< NL < Gk *pánkreas* sweetbread, equiv. to *pan-* PAN- + *kréas* flesh, meat] —**pan·cre·at·ic** (pan′krē at′ik, pang′-), *adj.*

pancreat-, var. of **pancreato-** before a vowel: *pancreatin.*

pan·cre·a·tec·to·mize (pan′krē ə tek′tə mīz′, pang′-), *v.t.,* **-mized, -miz·ing.** *Surg.* to excise the pancreas. [PANCREATECTOM(Y) + -IZE]

pan·cre·a·tec·to·my (pan′krē ə tek′tə mē, pang′-), *n., pl.* **-mies.** *Surg.* excision of part or all of the pancreas. [PANCREAT- + -ECTOMY]

pancreat′ic fibro′sis, *Pathol.* See **cystic fibrosis.**

pancreat′ic juice′, *Biochem.* a thick, colorless, very alkaline fluid secreted by the pancreas, containing enzymes that break down protein, fat, and starch.

pan·cre·a·tin (pan′krē ə tin, pang′-), *n.* **1.** *Biochem.* a substance containing the pancreatic enzymes, trypsin, amylase, and lipase. **2.** a commercial preparation of this substance, obtained from the pancreas of the hog or ox, and used chiefly as a digestive. [PANCREAT- + -IN[2]]

pan·cre·a·ti·tis (pan′krē ə tī′tis, pang′-), *n. Pathol.* inflammation of the pancreas. [< NL; see PANCREAT-, -ITIS]

pancreato-, a combining form of **pancreas:** *pancreatotomy.* Also, *esp. before a vowel,* **pancreat-.** [< NL < Gk *pankreat-* (s. of *pánkreas*); see -o-]

Giant panda, *Ailuropoda melanoleuca* (2 ft. high at shoulder; length 5 ft.)

pan·cre·a·tot·o·my (pan′krē ə tot′ə mē, pang′-), *n., pl.* **-mies.** *Surg.* incision of the pancreas. [PANCREATO- + -TOMY]

pan·da (pan′də), *n.* **1.** Also called **lesser panda.** a reddish-brown carnivore, *Ailurus fulgens,* of the Himalayas, having the face marked with white and a long, bushy tail marked with pale rings. **2.** Also called **giant panda.** a large, bearlike carnivore, *Ailuropoda melanoleuca,* of Tibet and southern China, white with black limbs, shoulders, and ears, and with a black ring around each eye. [after a Nepalese name for the animal]

pan·dal (pan′dᵊl), *n.* (in India) a temporary shed, esp. one used for public meetings. [< Tamil *pantal*]

pan·da·na·ceous (pan′də nā′shəs), *adj.* belonging to the *Pandanacea,* or pandanus family of trees and shrubs. [PANDAN(US) + -ACEOUS]

pan·da·nus (pan dā′nəs), *n., pl.* **-nus·es.** any plant of the genus *Pandanus,* comprising the screw pines. [< NL < Malay *pandan*]

Pan·dar·e·us (pan dâr′ē əs), *n. Class. Myth.* a son of Merops who was turned to stone for stealing the golden dog created by Hephaestus to guard the temple of Zeus.

Pan·da·rus (pan′dər əs), *n. Class. Myth.* **1.** a Trojan who, at the instigation of Athena, attempted to assassinate Menelaus, thereby violating a truce between the Greeks and the Trojans and prolonging the Trojan War: in Chaucerian and other medieval accounts, he is the procurer of Cressida for Troilus. **2.** a son of Alcanor and a companion of Aeneas.

Pan·da·vas (pun′də vəz), *n.* (*construed as pl.*) (in the Mahabharata) the family of Arjuna, at war with their cousins, the Kauravas.

Pan·de·an (pan dē′ən), *adj.* of or pertaining to the god Pan. [irreg. PAN + *-e-* (< L *-aeus*) + -AN]

Pande′an pipes′, panpipe.

pan·dect (pan′dekt), *n.* **1. pandects,** a complete body or code of laws. **2.** a comprehensive digest. **3. Pandects,** *Roman Law.* digest (def. 12b). [< LL

Pandect(ēs) < Gk *pandéktēs* all-receiver (*pan-* PAN- + *déktēs* receiver, container), encyclopedia (pl.)]

pan·dem·ic (pan dem′ik), *adj.* **1.** (of a disease) prevalent throughout an entire country, continent, or the whole world. **2.** general; universal: *pandemic fear of atomic war.* —*n.* **3.** a pandemic disease. [< LL *pandēm(us)* < Gk *pándēmos* common, public (*pan-* PAN- + *dêm(os)* the people + *-os* adj. suffix) + -IC] —**pan·de·mi·a** (pan dē′mē ə), *n.* —**pan·de·mic·i·ty** (pan′də mis′i tē), *n.*

pan·de·mo·ni·um (pan′də mō′nē əm), *n.* **1.** wild lawlessness or uproar; tumult or chaos. **2.** a place or scene of riotous uproar or utter chaos. **3.** (*often cap.*) the abode of all the demons. **4.** hell. [after *Pandaemonium*, Milton's name for the capital of hell; see PAN-, DEMON] —**pan′de·mo′ni·ac′, pan·de·mo·ni·a·cal** (pan′də mə nī′i kəl), **pan·de·mon·ic** (pan′də mon′ik), *adj.* —**pan′de·mo′ni·an,** *adj., n.*

Pan·de·mos (pan dē′mos), *n. Class. Myth.* an epithet of Aphrodite as goddess of earthly love.

pan·der (pan′dər), *n.* Also, **pan′der·er. 1.** a go-between in amorous intrigues. **2.** a person who furnishes clients for a prostitute or supplies women for illicit sexual intercourse; procurer; pimp. **3.** a person who caters to or profits from the weaknesses or vices of others. —*v.t.* **4.** to act as a pander for. —*v.i.* **5.** to act as a pander; cater basely: *to pander to the tastes of vulgar persons.* [earlier *pandar(e)*, generalized use of ME name *Pandare* PANDARUS] —**pan′der·age,** *n.* —**pan′der·ing·ly,** *adv.* —**pan′der·ism,** *n.* —**pan′der·ly,** *adj.*

pan·dic·u·la·tion (pan dik′yə lā′shən), *n. Med.* the act of stretching. [< L *pandiculāt(us)*, ptp. of *pandiculārī* to stretch oneself, deriv. of *pandere* to stretch; see -ATE[1]]

Pan·di·on (pan′dē on′), *n. Class. Myth.* **1.** a son of Phineus and Cleopatra who, with his brother Plexippus, was blinded by his father when Idaea, his stepmother, made false accusations against him. **2.** a king of Athens and the father of Erechtheus, Butes, Procne, and Philomela. **3.** a companion of the skilled archer Teucer.

Pan′dion the Young′er, *Class. Myth.* an Athenian king who was driven out of Athens with his sons and who later reigned in Megara.

pan·dit (pun′dit; *spelling pron.* pan′dit), *n.* (in India) a man held in high respect for his great wisdom or learning; scholar. [< Hindi < Skt *paṇḍita*]

Pan·dit (pun′dit), *n.* **Vi·ja·ya Lak·shmi** (vi jī′ə läk′shmē), born 1900, Indian statesman: president of the General Assembly of the United Nations 1953–54 (sister of Jawaharlal Nehru).

P. and L., profit and loss. Also, **P. & L., p. and l.**

pan·do·ra (pan dōr′ə, -dôr′ə), *n.* bandore. Also, **pan·dore** (pan dōr′, -dôr′, pan′dōr, -dôr).

Pan·do·ra (pan dōr′ə, -dôr′ə), *n.* **1.** *Class. Myth.* the first woman, created by Hephaestus, endowed by the gods with all the graces and treacherously presented to Epimetheus along with a box in which Prometheus had confined all the evils that could trouble mankind. As the gods had anticipated, Pandora opened the box, allowing the evils to escape, thereby frustrating the efforts of Prometheus. In some versions, the box contained blessings, all of which escaped but hope. **2.** a girl's given name. [< L < Gk: lit., all-gifted, equiv. to *pan-* PAN- + *dôron* gift]

Pan·do·rae Fre·tum (pan dōr′ē frē′təm, -dôr′ē), an area in the southern hemisphere of Mars.

Pando′ra's box′, a source of extensive but unforseen troubles or problems: *The senate investigation turned out to be a Pandora's box for the administration.*

pando′ra shell′, 1. any marine bivalve of the genus *Pandora*, having a scimitar-shaped shell with a pronounced ridge along the hinge. **2.** the shell itself.

pan·dour (pan′dŏŏr), *n.* **1.** *Hist.* a member of a local militia in Croatia, formed as a regiment in the Austrian army in the 18th century and noted for its ruthlessness and cruelty. **2.** a brutal, marauding soldier. [< F < Hung *pandur* guard, prob. < ML *bandora* band of soldiers. See BANNER]

pan·dow·dy (pan dou′dē), *n., pl.* **-dies.** *U.S.* a pudding or deep pie made with apples, and usually sweetened with molasses. Also called **apple pandowdy.** [? var. of obs. dial. (Somerset) *pan-doulde* custard; see PAN[1]]

Pan·dro·sos (pan′drə səs), *n. Class. Myth.* a daughter of Cecrops and Agraulos who was first priestess of Athena.

pan·du·rate (pan′dyə rāt′), *adj.* shaped like a fiddle, as a leaf. Also, **pan·du·ri·form** (pan dŏŏr′ə fôrm′, -dyŏŏr′-). [< L *pandūr(a)* musical instrument (see BANDORE) + -ATE[1]]

Pandurate leaf

pan·dy (pan′dē), *n., pl.* **-dies,** *v.,* **-died, -dy·ing.** *Chiefly Scot.* —*n.* **1.** a stroke on the palm of the hand with a cane or strap given as a punishment in school. —*v.t.* **2.** to hit on the palm of the hand. [< L *pande* stretch out! (impv. of *pandere*), i.e., open your hand to take the blow]

pane (pān), *n.* **1.** one of the divisions of a window or the like, consisting of a single plate of glass in a frame. **2.** a plate of glass for such a division. **3.** a panel, as of a wainscot, ceiling, door, etc. **4.** a flat section, side, or surface, as one of the sides of a bolthead. **5.** *Philately.* a sheet of stamps or any large portion of one, as a half or a quarter, as issued by the post office. [ME *pane, pan* strip of cloth, section < MF *pan* < L *pann(us)* cloth; akin to OE *fana* flag; see VANE] —**pane′less,** *adj.*

pa·né (*Fr.* PA NĀ′), *adj.* (of food) prepared with bread crumbs; breaded. [< F]

paned (pānd), *adj.* having panes (usually used in combination): *a diamond-paned window.* [PANE + -ED[3]]

pan·e·gyr·ic (pan′i jir′ik, -jī′rik), *n.* **1.** an oration, discourse, or writing in praise of a person or thing; eulogy. **2.** formal or elaborate commendation. [< L, n. use of *panegyric(us)* of, belonging to a public assembly < Gk *panēgyrikós* (deriv. of *panḗgyris* solemn assembly, equiv. to *pan-* PAN- + *ágyris* gathering) + *-ikos* -IC] —**pan′e·gyr′i·cal,** *adj.* —**pan′e·gyr′i·cal·ly,** *adv.*

pan·e·gy·rise (pan′i jə rīz′), *v.t., v.i.,* **-rised, -ris·ing.** *Chiefly Brit.* panegyrize.

pan·e·gyr·ist (pan′i jir′ist, -jī′rist, pan′i jir′ist, -jī′rist), *n.* a person who panegyrizes; eulogist. [< LL *panēgyrist(a)* < Gk *panēgyristḗs* one who takes part in a public festival or assembly, equiv. to *panēgyr(ízein)* (to) celebrate a public festival + *-istēs* -IST]

pan·e·gy·rize (pan′i jə rīz′), *v.,* **-rized, -riz·ing.** —*v.t.* **1.** to pronounce or write a panegyric upon; eulogize. —*v.i.* **2.** to indulge in panegyric; bestow praises. Also, *esp. Brit.,* **panegyrise.** [< Gk *panēgyríz(ein)* (to) celebrate a public festival, equiv. to *panḗgyr(is)* (see PANEGYRIC) + *-izein* -IZE]

pan·el (pan′əl), *n., v.,* **-eled, -el·ing** or (*esp. Brit.*) **-elled, -el·ling.** —*n.* **1.** a distinct portion, section, or division of a wall, wainscot, ceiling, door, shutter, fence, etc., esp. of any surface sunk below or raised above the general level or enclosed by a frame or border. **2.** a pane, as in a window. **3.** a comparatively thin, flat piece of wood or the like, as a large piece of plywood. **4.** *Painting.* **a.** a flat piece of wood of varying kinds on which a picture is painted. **b.** a picture painted on such a piece of wood. **5.** a photograph much longer in one dimension than the other. **6.** a broad strip of material set vertically, in or on a dress, skirt, etc. **7.** *Law.* **a.** a list of persons summoned for service as jurors. **b.** the body of persons composing a jury. **c.** (in Scotland) the person or persons arraigned for trial. **8.** a group of persons gathered to conduct a public discussion, judge a contest, serve as advisers, be players on a radio or television quiz game, or the like: *a panel of political scientists meeting to discuss French foreign policy.* **9.** a public discussion by such a group. **10.** a mount for or surface or section of a machine containing the controls and dials. **11.** (in Britain) a list of approved or cooperating doctors available to patients under a health insurance program. **12.** the section between the two bands on the backbone of a bound book. **13.** *Elect.* a switchboard or control board, or a division of a switchboard or control board containing a set of related cords, jacks, relays, etc. **14.** *Engineering, Building Trades.* **a.** the space on the chord of a truss between any two adjacent joints made by principal web members with the chord. **b.** the space within the web of a truss between any two such joints and a corresponding pair of joints or a single joint on an opposite chord: usually quadrangular, bounded by web members perpendicular to one or both chords, and crossed by one or more diagonals, the triangular panels of the Warren truss being the principal exception. **15.** *Aeron.* **a.** a lateral subdivision of an airfoil with internal girder construction. **b.** a section of the hull of a rigid airship marked off by a set of transverse and lateral girders. **16.** *Mining.* an area of a coal seam separated for mining purposes from adjacent areas by extra thick masses or ribs of coal. **17.** a pad placed under a saddle. **18.** a pad, cloth, or the like, serving as a saddle. **19.** a slip of parchment. —*v.t.* **20.** to arrange in or furnish with a panel or panels. **21.** to ornament with a panel or panels. **22.** to set in a frame as a panel. **23.** to select (a jury). **24.** *Scots Law.* to bring to trial. [ME < OF *panel* a piece (of anything), dim. of *pan* piece of cloth or the like. See PANE]

pan·el·board (pan′əl bōrd′, -bôrd′), *n.* **1.** panel (def. 3). **2.** a compact pressboard for use in constructing sides of cabinets, paneling for walls, and in other nonstructural applications. [PANEL + BOARD]

pan′el discus′sion, an organized discussion before an audience for which the topic, speakers, etc., have been selected in advance.

pan′el heat′ing, heating of a room or building by means of wall, ceiling, floor, or basebord panels containing heating pipes or electric conductors.

pan′el house′, a brothel having rooms with secret entrances, as sliding panels, for admitting panel thieves.

pan·el·ing (pan′əling), *n.* **1.** wood or other material made into panels. **2.** a surface of panels, esp. of decorative wood or woodlike panels. **3.** panels collectively. Also, *esp. Brit.,* **pan′el·ling.** [PANEL + -ING[1]]

pan·el·ist (pan′əlist), *n.* a member of a small group of persons gathered for public discussion, judging, playing a radio or television quiz or guessing game, etc. [PANEL + -IST]

pan′el light′ing, lighting of a room or building by means of flat sheets of material that glow brightly when a coating of a phosphor is excited by an electrical charge.

pan′el patch′, a patch made to one of the outer veneers of a sheet of plywood after manufacture.

pan′el point′, *Engineering.* a joint between two or more members of a truss. Also called **node.**

pan′el saw′, a small ripsaw or crosscut saw.

pan′el strip′, one of a number of strips of wood or metal laid upon the surface of a wall, ceiling, etc., so as to divide it into a number of broad areas, usually in order to conceal joints between sheets of composition material forming the surface.

pan′el thief′, a thief who secretly robs the customers in a panel house.

pan′el truck′, a small truck having a fully enclosed body, used mainly to deliver light or small objects.

pan·e·tel·la (pan′i tel′ə), *n.* a long, slender cigar, usually with straight sides and tapering to a point at the closed end. Also, **pan′e·tel′a, panatella, panatela.** [< AmerSp *panatela* a kind of bread, long, slender biscuit < It, dim. of *panata* PANADA]

pan·e·tière (pan′i tyâr′; *Fr.* PAN° TYER′), *n., pl.* **-tières** (-tyârz′; *Fr.* -TYER′). *Fr. Furniture.* a small, decorative livery cupboard, made esp. in Provence in the 18th century. [< F, OF, equiv. to *panet(erie)* bread room (see PANTRY) + *-iere*, fem. of *-ier* -ER[2]]

pan·et·to·ne (pan′i tō′nē; *It.* pä′net tô′ne), *n., pl.* **-nes** (-nēz), *It.* **-ni** (-nē). an Italian yeast-leavened bread, traditionally eaten on holidays, usually made with raisins, candied fruit peels, almonds, and brandy. [< It, deriv. of *panetto* little loaf, equiv. to *pan(e)* bread (< L *panis*) + *-etto* dim. suffix]

Pan-Eu·ro·pe·an (pan′yŏŏr ə pē′ən), *adj.* of or pertaining to all or most of the countries of Europe.

pan·fish (pan′fish′), *n., pl.* **-fish·es,** (*esp. collectively*) **-fish.** any small, fresh-water nongame food fish, as a perch or sunfish, usually eaten panfried. [PAN[1] + FISH]

pan-fry (pan′frī′), *v.t.,* **-fried, -fry·ing.** to fry in a small amount of fat, as in a skillet or shallow pan; sauté. [PAN[1] + FRY[1]]

pang (pang), *n.* **1.** a sudden feeling of mental or emotional distress or longing: *a pang of remorse; a pang of desire.* **2.** a sudden, brief, sharp pain or physical sensation; spasm: *a hunger pang.* [?]

pan·ga (päng′gə), *n.* a large, broad-bladed African knife used as a weapon or as an implement for cutting heavy jungle growth, sugar cane, etc.; machete. [< native African name]

pan·gen·e·sis (pan jen′i sis), *n. Biol.* the theory that a reproductive cell or body contains gemmules or invisible germs which were derived from the individual cells from every part of the organism and which are the bearers of hereditary attributes. [PAN- + GENESIS] —**pan·ge·net·ic** (pan′jə net′ik), *adj.* —**pan′ge·net′i·cal·ly,** *adv.*

Pan-Ger·man·ism (pan′jûr′mə niz′əm), *n.* the idea or advocacy of a union of all the German peoples in one political organization or state. [PAN- + GERMANISM] —**Pan′-Ger′man,** *adj., n.* —**Pan-Ger·man·ic** (pan′jər man′ik), *adj.*

pan·go·lin (pang gō′lin), *n.* any mammal of the order *Pholidota*, of Africa and tropical Asia, having a covering of broad, overlapping, horny scales and feeding on ants and termites. Also called **scaly anteater.** [< Malay *penggōling* roller]

Pangolin, Genus *Manis* (Total length 4 ft.; tail 2 ft.)

Pang·o Pang·o (päng′ō päng′ō). See **Pago Pago.**

pan′ gra′vy, meat juices, as from a roast, seasoned but not thickened. Cf. **dish gravy.**

pan·guin·gue (päng gēng′gē), *n.* a card game of the rummy family that is played with from five to eight regular 52-card packs from which the eights, nines, and tens have been removed, the object being to win bonuses by melding certain groups of cards during the play and extra bonuses by melding all the cards in the hand. [< Tagalog]

pan·han·dle[1] (pan′han′dəl), *n.* **1.** the handle of a pan. **2.** (*sometimes cap.*) a long, narrow, projecting strip of territory that is not a peninsula, esp. such a part of a specified state: *the panhandle of Alaska; the West Virginia Panhandle.* [PAN[1] + HANDLE]

pan·han·dle[2] (pan′han′dəl), *v.,* **-dled, -dling.** *Informal.* —*v.i.* **1.** to accost passers-by on the street and beg from them. —*v.t.* **2.** to accost and beg from. **3.** to obtain by accosting and begging from someone. [back formation from PANHANDLER; so called from the resemblance of the extended arm to a PANHANDLE[1]] —**pan′han′dler,** *n.*

Pan′handle State′, the State of West Virginia (used as a nickname).

pan′ head′, *Photog.* a tripod head permitting vertical or horizontal rotation of a camera to any position. Also called **pam head.**

pan·head (pan′hed′), *n.* a rivet or screw head having the form of a truncated cone. [PAN[1] + HEAD] —**pan′-head′ed,** *adj.*

Pan·hel·len·ic (pan′hə len′ik), *adj.* **1.** of or pertaining to all Greeks or to Panhellenism. **2.** of, pertaining to, or noting collegiate fraternities and sororities. Also, **pan′hel·len′ic.** [PAN- + HELLENIC]

Pan·hel·len·ism (pan hel′ə niz′əm), *n.* the idea or advocacy of a union of all Greeks in one political body. [PAN- + HELLENISM] —**Pan·hel′len·ist,** *n.*

Pan·hel·le·ni·us (pan′hə lē′nē əs), *n. Class. Myth.* an epithet of Zeus, meaning "god of all Greeks."

pan·ic[1] (pan′ik), *n., adj., v.,* **-icked, -ick·ing.** —*n.* **1.** a sudden overwhelming fear, with or without cause, that produces hysterical or irrational behavior, and that often spreads quickly through a group of persons or animals. **2.** an instance, outbreak, or period of such fear. **3.** *Finance.* a sudden widespread fear concerning financial affairs leading to credit contraction and widespread sale of securities at depressed prices in an effort to acquire cash. **4.** *Slang.* someone who or something that is considered hilariously funny. —*adj.* **5.** (of fear, terror, etc.) suddenly destroying the self-control and impelling to some frantic action. **6.** of the nature of, caused by, or evidencing panic: *panic haste.* **7.** (*cap.*) of or pertaining to the god Pan. —*v.t.* **8.** to affect with panic; terrify and cause to flee or lose self-control. **9.** *Slang.* to keep (an audience or the like) highly amused. —*v.i.* **10.** to be stricken with panic; become frantic with fear: *The herd panicked and stampeded.* [earlier *panique* < F < Gk *Panik(ós)* of PAN; see -IC] —**pan′ick·y,** *adj.*
—**Syn. 1.** alarm. See **terror.**

pan·ic[2] (pan′ik), *n.* **1.** Also called **pan′ic grass′.** any grass of the genus *Panicum*, many species of which bear edible grain. **2.** the grain. [late ME < L *pānic(um)* a kind of millet, appar. back formation from *pānicula*, dim. of *pānus* ear of millet. See PANICLE]

pan′ic bolt′, (on an exit door) a latch operated by pressure on a bar that spans the door on its interior side. Also called **pan′ic bar′.**

pan′ic but′ton, *Facetious.* a button that is supposed to actuate a device or system that will set everything to rights and is pushed only as a last resort when everything seems to go wrong. Cf. **chicken switch, egads button.**

pan·i·cle (pan′i kəl), *n. Bot.* **1.** a compound raceme. **2.** any loose, diversely branching flower cluster. [< L *pānicul(a)* tuft (on plants), dim. of *pānus* thread wound on a bobbin, a swelling, ear of millet < Doric Gk *pânos*, var. of Attic *pênos* a web; see -I-, -CLE] —**pan′i·cled,** *adj.*

pan·ic-strick·en (pan′ik strik′ən), *adj.* overcome with, characterized by, or resulting from fear, panic, or the like: *a panic-stricken mother looking for her child; a panic-stricken phone call.* Also **pan·ic-struck** (pan′ik-struk′).

pa·nic·u·late (pə nik′yə lāt′, -lit), *adj. Bot.* arranged in panicles. Also, **pa·nic′u·lat′ed.** [< NL *pāniculāt(us)* panicled. See PANICLE, -ATE[1]] —**pa·nic′u·late′ly,** *adv.*

pan·ier (pan′yər), *n.* pannier.

Pa·ni·ni (pä′nē nē *for 1;* pä nē′nē *for 2*), *n.* **1.** fl. c400 B.C., Indian grammarian of Sanskrit. **2.** See **Pannini, Giovanni Paolo.**

Pan·Is·lam·ism (pan/is/lə miz/əm, -iz/-), *n.* the idea or advocacy of a political union of all Muslim nations. [PAN- + ISLAMISM] —**Pan-Is·lam·ic** (pan/-is lam/ik, -läm/ik, -iz-), *adj.*

pa·niv·o·rous (pa niv/ər əs), *adj.* subsisting on bread; bread-eating. [< L *pān(is)* bread + -I- + -VOROUS]

Pan·ja·bi (pun jä/bē), *n., pl.* **-bis.** **1.** Punjabi (def. 1). **2.** Also, **Punjabi.** an Indic language of the Punjab.

pan·jan·drum (pan jan/drəm), *n.* a self-important or pretentious official. [pseudo-Latin word (based on PAN-) made up by Samuel Foote (1720–77), English dramatist and actor, for a nonsensical context]

Pank·hurst (pangk/hûrst), *n.* **Emmeline (Goul·den)** (go͝ol/dən), 1858–1928, English suffragist leader.

P'an-ku (pän/ko͞o/), *n.* *Chinese Myth.* a being personifying the primeval stuff from which heaven and earth were formed.

pan·leu·ko·pe·ni·a (pan/lo͞o kə pē/nē ə), *n.* *Vet. Pathol.* distemper[1] (def. 1c). Also, **pan/leu·co·pe/ni·a.** [PAN- + LEUKOPENIA]

pan·lo·gism (pan/lə jiz/əm), *n.* *Philos.* the doctrine that the universe is a realization or act of the logos. [< G *Panlogism(us).* See PAN-, LOGOS, -ISM] —**pan·log·i·cal** (pan loj/i kəl), **pan/lo·gis/tic, pan/lo·gis/ti·cal,** *adj.* —**pan/lo·gist,** *adj., n.* —**pan/lo·gis/ti·cal·ly,** *adv.*

Pan·mun·jon (pän/mo͞on/jon/), *n.* a small community along the boundary between North Korea and South Korea: site of the truce talks at the close of the Korean War.

panne (pan), *n.* a soft, lustrous, lightweight velvet with flattened pile. [< F, OF, var. of *pen(n)e,* equiv. to ML *panna, penna* skin, fur, appar. special use of L *penna* feather; cf. MHG *federe* kind of fur]

pan·nic·u·lus (pə nik/yə ləs), *n., pl.* **-li** (-lī/). *Anat.* a layer of tissue, esp. a subcutaneous layer of fat. [< L: small piece of cloth, rag, equiv. to *pann(us)* cloth, rag + *-i-* -I- + *-culus* (dim. suffix). See PANICLE] —**pan·nic/u·lar,** *adj.*

pan·nier (pan/yər, -ē ər), *n.* **1.** a basket, esp. a large one, for carrying goods, provisions, etc. **2.** a basket for carrying on a person's back, or one of a pair to be slung across the back of a beast of burden. **3.** (on a dress, skirt, etc.) a puffed arrangement of drapery at the hips. **4.** an oval framework formerly used for distending the skirt of a woman's dress at the hips. Also, **panier.** [ME *panier* < MF < L *pānār(ium)* breadbasket, equiv. to *pān(is)* bread + *-ārium* -ER[2]] —**pan/niered,** *adj.*

pan·ni·kin (pan/ə kin), *n.* *Chiefly Brit.* a small pan or metal cup. [PAN[1] + -I- + -KIN]

Pan·ni·ni (pän nē/nē), *n.* **Gio·van·ni (Pa·o·lo)** (jô vän/nē pä ô/lô), 1692?–1765, Italian painter. Also, **Panini.**

Pan·no·ni·a (pə nō/nē ə), *n.* an ancient country and Roman province in central Europe, S and W of the Danube: now mostly in Hungary and Yugoslavia. —**Pan·no/ni·an,** *adj., n.* —**Pan·non·ic** (pə non/ik), *adj.*

pan·nose (pan/ōs), *adj.* *Bot.* having the texture of felt or woolen cloth. [< L *pannōs(us)* full of rags, tattered, equiv. to *pann(us)* cloth, rag + *-ōsus* -OSE[1]] —**pan/nose·ly,** *adv.*

pan·nus (pan/əs), *n.* **1.** *Pathol.* an abnormal thickening of the cornea. **2.** *Meteorol.* a group of ragged cloud fragments hanging below a cloud. [< NL, L: piece of cloth, rag]

pa·no·cha (pə nō/chə), *n.* **1.** Also, **penuche.** a coarse grade of sugar made in Mexico. **2.** penuche (def. 1). Also, **pa·no·che** (pə nō/chē). [< MexSp, dim. of Sp *pan* bread]

Pa·nof·sky (pa nof/skē), *n.* **Erwin,** born 1892, U.S. art historian, born in Germany.

Pan·om·phae·us (pan/om fē/əs), *n.* *Class. Myth.* Zeus: so called because of his inauspicious and prophetic utterances. [< Gk *panomphaios,* equiv. to *pan-* PAN- + *omphaios* prophetic]

Pan·o·peus (pan/ə pyo͞os/), *n.* *Class. Myth.* a son of Phocus and Asteria who was a lifelong enemy of his twin brother, Crisus.

pan·o·ply (pan/ə plē), *n., pl.* **-plies.** **1.** a complete suit of armor. **2.** a complete covering or array of something. [< Gk *panoplía*]

Pan·op·tes (pan op/tēz), *n.* *Class. Myth.* an epithet of Argus, meaning "all eyes."

pan·op·tic (pan op/tik), *adj.* **1.** permitting the viewing of all parts or elements: *a panoptic stain used in microscopy; a panoptic aerial photograph of an enemy missile base.* **2.** considering all parts or elements; all inclusive: *a panoptic criticism of modern poetry.* Also, **pan·op/ti·cal.** [< Gk *panóptēs* all-seeing. See PAN-, OPTIC] —**pan·op/ti·cal·ly,** *adv.*

pan·op·ti·con (pan op/tə kon/), *n.* a prison or workhouse so arranged that all parts of the interior are visible from a single point. [PAN- + Gk *optikón* sight, seeing (neut. of *optikós*); see OPTIC]

pan·o·ram·a (pan/ə ram/ə, -rä/mə), *n.* **1.** an unobstructed and wide view of an extensive area in all directions. **2.** an extended pictorial representation or a cyclorama of a landscape or other scene, often exhibited a part at a time and made to pass continuously before the spectators. **3.** a building for exhibiting such a pictorial representation. **4.** a continuously passing or changing scene or an unfolding of events: *the panorama of recent history.* **5.** a comprehensive survey, as of a subject. [PAN- + Gk *hórama* view, sight, deriv. of *horân* to see, look] —**pan/o·ram/ic,** *adj.* —**pan/o·ram/i·cal·ly,** *adv.*

pan/oram/ic sight/, an artillery sight that can be rotated horizontally in a full circle.

pan·pipe (pan/pīp/), *n.* a primitive wind instrument consisting of a series of hollow pipes of graduated length, the tones being produced by blowing across the upper ends. Also, **Pan's/ pipes/, pan/pipes/.** [PAN + PIPE[1]]

Panpipe

pan·ple·gi·a (pan plē/jē ə, -jə), *n.* *Pathol.* paralysis of all four extremities. Also, **pamplegia.** [PAN- + -PLEGIA]

pan·pneu·ma·tism (pan no͞o/mə tiz/əm, -nyo͞o/-), *n.* the philosophy of von Hartmann, combining elements of pantheism and panlogism. [PAN- + PNEUMAT- + -ISM]

pan·psy·chism (pan sī/kiz əm), *n.* *Philos.* the doctrine that each object in the universe has either a mind or an unconscious psyche. [PAN- + PSYCH- + -ISM] —**pan·psy/chic,** *adj.*

pan·psy·chist (pan sī/kist), *n.* a person who believes in or advocates panpsychism. [PANPSYCH(ISM) + -IST] —**pan/psy·chis/tic,** *adj.*

Pan·sil (pun/sēl), *n.* *Buddhism.* See **Pancha Sila.** [< Singhalese << Skt]

Pan-Slav·ism (pan/slä/viz əm, -slav/iz-), *n.* the idea or advocacy of a political union of all the Slavic races. [PAN- + SLAVISM] —**Pan/-Slav/, Pan/-Slav/ic,** *adj.*

pan·soph·ism (pan/sə fiz/əm), *n.* a claim or pretension to pansophy. [< Gk *pánsoph(os)* all-wise + -ISM. See PAN-, SOPHISM] —**pan/so·phist,** *n.*

pan·so·phy (pan/sə fē), *n.* universal wisdom or knowledge. [PAN- + -SOPHY] —**pan·soph·ic** (pan-sof/ik), **pan·soph/i·cal,** *adj.* —**pan·soph/i·cal·ly,** *adv.*

pan·sper·mi·a (pan spûr/mē ə), *n.* *Biol.* the theory that life exists and is distributed throughout the universe in the form of germs or spores that develop in the right environment. Also, **pan·sper·ma·tism** (pan spûr/mə tiz/əm), **pan·sper·my** (pan/spûr/mē). [< NL < Gk *panspermía* mixture of all seeds. See PAN-, -SPERM, -IA] —**pan·sper/mic,** *adj.*

pan·sy (pan/zē), *n., pl.* **-sies.** **1.** a violet, *Viola tricolor hortensis,* cultivated in many varieties, having richly and variously colored flowers. **2.** the flower of this plant. **3.** *Slang.* **a.** a male homosexual. **b.** an effeminate man. [< MF *pensée* pansy, lit., thought, n. use of fem. of ptp. of *penser* to think < L *pensāre* to weigh, consider. See PENSIVE]

Pan·sy (pan/zē), *n.* a girl's given name.

pant[1] (pant), *v.i.* **1.** to breathe hard and quickly, as after exertion. **2.** to emit steam or the like in loud puffs. **3.** to gasp, as for air. **4.** to long with breathless or intense eagerness; yearn: *to pant for revenge.* **5.** to throb or heave violently or rapidly; palpitate. **6.** *Naut.* (of the bow or stern of a vessel) to work with the shock of contact with a succession of waves. —*v.t.* **7.** to breathe or utter gaspingly. —*n.* **8.** the act of panting. **9.** a short, quick, labored effort at breathing; gasp. **10.** a puff, as of an engine. **11.** a throb or heave, as of the breast. [late ME *pant(en)* < MF *pant(a)is(i)er* < LL **phantasiāre* to have visions < Gk *phantasioûn* to have or form images. See FANTASY] —**pant/ing·ly,** *adv.*

—**Syn. 1.** puff, blow. PANT, GASP suggest breathing with more effort than usual. PANT suggests rapid, convulsive breathing, as from violent exertion or excitement: *to pant after a run for the train.* GASP suggests catching one's breath in a single quick intake, as from amazement, terror, and the like, or a series of such quick intakes of breath as in painful breathing: *to gasp with horror; to gasp for breath.* **4.** thirst, hunger.

pant[2] (pant), *adj.* **1.** of or pertaining to pants: *pant legs.* —*n.* **2.** a leg of a pair of pants. [back formation from PANTS]

pant-, var. of **panto-** before a vowel.

pan·ta·graph (pan/tə graf/, -gräf/), *n.* pantograph (def. 1).

Pan·tag·ru·el (pan tag/ro͞o el/; *Fr.* pän tA grY el/), *n.* **1.** (in Rabelais' *Gargantua* and *Pantagruel*) the huge son of Gargantua, represented as dealing with serious matters in a spirit of broad and somewhat cynical good humor. **2.** (*italics.*) a satirical novel (1532) by Rabelais. Cf. **Gargantua.** —**Pan·ta·gru·el·i·an** (pan/tə gro͞o-el/ē ən), *adj.* —**Pan/ta·gru·el/i·cal·ly,** *adv.* —**Pan·ta·gru·el·ism** (pan/tə gro͞o/ə liz/əm, pan tag/ro͞o ə-liz/əm), *n.* —**Pan/ta·gru/el·ist,** *n.*

pan·ta·lets (pan/tᵊlets/), *n.pl.* **1.** long drawers extending below the dress, with a frill or other finish at the bottom of the leg, commonly worn by women and girls in the 19th century. **2.** a pair of separate frilled or trimmed pieces for attaching to the legs of women's drawers. Also, **pan/ta·lettes/.** Also called **trousers.** [PANTAL(OON) + -ET + -S[3]] —**pan/ta·let/ted,** *adj.*

pan·ta·loon (pan/tᵊlo͞on/), *n.* **1.** **pantaloons,** a man's close-fitting garment for the hips and legs, worn esp. in the 19th century, but varying in form from period to period; trousers. **2.** (in the modern pantomime) a foolish, vicious old man, the butt and accomplice of the clown. **3.** (*usually cap.*) Also, **Pan·ta·lo·ne** (pan/tᵊlō/nā, pän/-; *It.* pän/tä lô/ne). (in commedia dell'arte) a foolish old Venetian merchant, usually the head of a household, generally lascivious, and frequently deceived in the course of lovers' intrigues. [< MF *Pantalon* < It *Pantalone* (Venetian dial.) nickname for a Venetian, var. of *Pantaleone,* name of a 4th-century saint once a favorite with the Venetians]

pan·tech·ni·con (pan tek/nə kon/, -kən), *n.* *Brit.* **1.** a warehouse, esp. a furniture warehouse. **2.** Also called **pantech/nicon van/,** a furniture van; moving van. **3.** *Obs.* a bazaar or exhibition of art objects, crafts, etc. [PAN- + Gk *technikón* artistic, skillful (neut. of *technikós*); see TECHNIC]

pan·tel·e·graph (pan tel/ə graf/, -gräf/), *n.* an early type of facsimile telegraph. [orig. It *pantelegrafo.* See PAN-, TELEGRAPH] —**pan·te·leg·ra·phy** (pan/tə-leg/rə fē), *n.*

Pan·tel·le·ri·a (pän tel/le RĒ/ä), *n.* an Italian island in the Mediterranean between Sicily and Tunisia. 10,306 (1951); 32 sq. mi. Ancient name, **Cosyra.**

pan·ter (pan/tər), *n.* *Archaic.* pantler. [ME *paneter* < AF < ML *pānetār(ius);* cf. L *pān-* (s. of *panis*) bread; see -ER[2]]

Pan-Teu·ton·ism (pan/to͞ot/ᵊniz/əm, -tyo͞ot/-), *n.* Pan-Germanism.

pan·the·ism (pan/thē iz/əm), *n.* **1.** the doctrine that God is the transcendent reality of which the material universe and man are only manifestations: it involves a denial of God's personality and expresses a tendency to identify God and nature. **2.** any religious belief or philosophical doctrine which identifies the universe with God. [< F *panthéisme.* See PAN-, THEISM] —**pan/the·ist,** *n.* —**pan/the·is/tic, pan/the·is/ti·cal,** *adj.* —**pan/the·is/ti·cal·ly,** *adv.*

Pan·the·on (pan/thē on/, -ən, pan thē/ən), *n.* **1.** a domed circular temple at Rome, erected A.D. 120–124 by Hadrian using an older porch built by Agrippa 27 B.C., used as a church since A.D. 609. **2.** (*l.c.*) a public building containing tombs or memorials of the illustrious dead of a nation. **3.** (*l.c.*) a temple dedicated to all the gods. **4.** (*l.c.*) the gods of a particular mythology considered collectively. **5.** (*l.c.*) the place of the heroes or idols of any group, individual, movement, party, etc., or the heroes or idols themselves: *to earn a place in the pantheon of American literature.* [ME *panteon* < L *Panthēon* < Gk *Pántheion,* n. use of neut. of *pántheios* of all gods, equiv. to *pan-* PAN- + *the(ós)* god + *-ios* adj. suffix] —**pan/the·on/ic,** *adj.*

Pan·thé·on (pän tā ôN/), *n.* a national monument in Paris, France, used as a sepulchre for famous Frenchmen, begun in 1764 by Soufflot as the church of Ste. Geneviève, and secularized in 1885. Also called **Panthéon/ Fran·çais/** (fRäN se/).

pan·ther (pan/thər), *n., pl.* **-thers,** (*esp. collectively*) **-ther,** *adj.* —*n.* **1.** the cougar or puma, *Felis concolor.* **2.** the leopard, *Panthera pardus.* **3.** any leopard in the black color phase. **4.** *Informal.* anyone who is very fierce. —*adj.* **5.** fierce; strong and violent. Also, *referring to a female,* **pan·ther·ess** (pan/thər is). [< L *panther(a)* < Gk *pánthēr;* r. ME *pantere* (< OF) and OE *pandher* (< L)]

Pan·tho·us (pan/thō əs), *n.* *Class. Myth.* a priest of Apollo and a trusted counselor of Priam.

pant·ie (pan/tē), *n.* panties. [back formation from PANTIES]

pant·ies (pan/tēz), *n.pl.* underpants or undershorts for women and children. Also, **pantie, panty.** [pl. of PANTY]

pan·tile (pan/tīl/), *n.* **1.** a roofing tile straight in its length but curved in its width to overlap the next tile. **2.** a tapered, semicylindrical roofing tile laid either convex side up to overlap flanking similar tiles laid concave side up or vice versa. [PAN[1] + TILE]

Pantiles

pant·ler (pant/lər), *n.* *Archaic.* the servant or household officer in charge of the pantry, esp. in acquiring and dispensing bread. Also, **panter.** [ME; alter. (cf. BUTLER) of PANTER]

pan·to (pan/tō), *n., pl.* **-tos.** *Brit.* pantomime (def. 2). [by shortening]

panto-, a combining form synonymous with **pan-:** *pantology.* Also, *esp. before a vowel,* **pant-.** [comb. form repr. Gk *pant-* all (s. of *pân,* neut. of *pâs*)]

Pan·toc·ra·tor (pan tok/rə tər), *n.* *Fine Arts.* a representation of Christ as ruler of the universe. Also, **Pan·tok/ra·tor.** [< Gk *pantokrátōr* almighty, equiv. to *panto-* PANTO- + *krátōr* ruler; cf. -CRAT]

pan·to·fle (pan/tə fəl, pan tof/əl, -to͞o/fəl), *n.* **1.** a slipper. **2.** a cork-soled patten covering the forepart of the foot, worn in the 16th century. Also, **pan/tof·fle.** [late ME *pantufle* < MF *pantoufle* < OIt *pantofola* < MGk *pantóphellos* cork shoe, lit., all-cork. See PANTO-, PHELLOGEN]

pan·to·graph (pan/tə graf/, -gräf/), *n.* **1.** an instrument for the mechanical copying of plans, diagrams, etc., on any desired scale. **2.** *Elect.* a current collector for transferring current from an overhead wire to a vehicle, as a trolley car, usually consisting of two parallel, hinged, double-diamond frames. [PANTO- + -GRAPH] —**pan·tog·ra·pher** (pan tog/rə fər), *n.* —**pan·to·graph·ic** (pan/tə graf/ik), **pan/to·graph/i·cal,** *adj.* —**pan/to·graph/i·cal·ly,** *adv.* —**pan·tog·ra·phy** (pan tog/rə fē), *n.*

pan·tol·o·gy (pan tol/ə jē), *n.* a systematic view of all human knowledge. [PANTO- + -LOGY] —**pan·to·log·ic** (pan/tᵊloj/ik), **pan/to·log/i·cal,** *adv.* —**pan·tol/o·gist,** *n.*

pan·to·mime (pan/tə mīm/), *n., v.,* **-mimed, -miming.** —*n.* **1.** a play or entertainment in which the performers express themselves by mute gestures, often to the accompaniment of music. **2.** Also called **Christmas pantomime.** a form of theatrical spectacle common in England during the Christmas season, generally adapted from a fairy tale and including stock character types who perform songs and dances, tell jokes, etc. **3.** an actor in dumb show, as in ancient Rome. **4.** significant gesture without speech. **5.** the art or technique of conveying emotions, actions, feelings, etc. by mute gestures. —*v.t.* **6.** to represent or express in pantomime. —*v.i.* **7.** to express oneself in pantomime. [earlier *pantomimus* < L < Gk *pantómīmos.* See PANTO-, MIME] —**pan·to·mim·ic** (pan/tə mim/ik), **pan/to·mim/i·cal,** *adj.* —**pan/to·mim/i·cal·ly,** *adv.* —**pan/to·mim/ic·ry,** *n.*

pan·to·mim·ist (pan/tə mī/mist), *n.* **1.** a person who acts in pantomime. **2.** the author of a pantomime. [PANTOMIME + -IST]

pan·ton·al (pan tōn/ᵊl), *adj.* *Music.* marked by or using pantonality. [PAN- + TONAL]

pan·to·nal·i·ty (pan/tō nal/i tē), *n.* *Music.* See **twelve-tone technique.** [PANTONAL + -ITY]

pan/to·then/ic ac/id (pan/tə then/ik, pan/-), *Biochem.* an oily, hydroxy acid, $HOCH_2C(CH_3)_2CHOHCONHCH_2CH_2COOH$, found in plant and animal tissues, rice, bran, etc., and essential for cell growth. [< Gk *pántothen* from all quarters (*panto-* PANTO- + *-then* suffix of motion from) + -IC]

pan·to·there (pan/tə thēr/), *n.* any animal of the extinct group *Pantotheria,* believed to be the ancestor of the marsupial and placental mammals. [< NL *Pantothēr(ia)* name of group, equiv. to *panto-* PANTO- + *-thēria* < Gk *thēría,* pl. of *thēríon* wild animal, beast]

pan·toum (pan to͞om/), *n.* a Malay verse form consisting of an indefinite number of quatrains with the second and fourth lines of each quatrain repeated as the first and third lines of the following one. Also, **pantun.** [< Malay]

pan·trop·ic (pan trop/ik, -trō/pik), *adj.* (esp. of viruses) attracted toward or affecting many types of body tissues. [PAN- + -TROPIC] —**pan·trop/i·cal·ly,** *adv.*

pan·trop·i·cal (pan trop/i kəl), *adj.* living or growing throughout the tropics. [PAN- + TROPICAL]

pan·try (pan/trē), *n., pl.* **-tries.** **1.** a room or closet in which bread and other provisions, or silverware, dishes, etc., are kept. **2.** a room between the kitchen and dining room in which food is arranged for serving, glassware and dishes are stored, etc. [ME *panetrie* < AF, equiv. to OF *paneterie* bread room, equiv. to *panet(er)* (to) bake bread (deriv. of *pan* bread < L *pānis*) + *-erie* -ERY]

pan·try·man (pan′trē mən), *n., pl.* **-men.** a man who works in or has charge of a pantry, as aboard ship, in a hospital, etc. [PANTRY + MAN[1]]

pants (pants), *n.pl.* **1.** trousers (def. 1). **2.** underpants, esp. for women and children; panties. **3.** *Brit.* men's underpants, esp. long drawers. **4. wear the pants,** to assume the dominant role: *Anyone can tell that she wears the pants in that family.* [short for PANTALOONS]

pants′ suit′. See **slack suit** (def. 2). Also, **pant′ suit′.**

pan·tun (pan to͞on′), *n.* pantoum.

pant·y (pan′tē), *n., pl.* **pant·ies.** panties. [PANT(S) + -Y[2]]

pant′y gir′dle, a girdle with a crotch.

pant′y hose′, a one-piece, skintight garment worn by women, combining panties and stockings.

pant·y·waist (pan′tē wāst′), *n.* **1.** a child's undergarment consisting of short pants and a shirt that button together at the waist. Cf. **underwaist. 2.** *Informal.* a cowardly or effeminate man; sissy. —*adj. Informal.* **3.** childish. **4.** cowardly or effeminate. [PANTY + WAIST]

Pan·urge (pan ûrj′; *Fr.* pA nyrzh′), *n.* (in Rabelais' *Gargantua and Pantagruel*) a rascal, the companion of Pantagruel. —**pan·urg′ic,** *adj.*

pa·nus (pā′nəs), *n. Pathol. Obs.* an inflamed, nonsuppurating lymph gland. [< L: swelling, tumor]

Pan·za (pan′zə; *Sp.* pän′thä), *n.* **Sancho.** See **Sancho Panza.**

pan·zer (pan′zər; *Ger.* pän′tsər), *adj.* **1.** armored: *a panzer unit.* **2.** of or pertaining to a panzer division: *a panzer attack.* —*n.* **3.** a vehicle, esp. a tank, forming part of a German panzer division. [< G; MHG *panzier* < OF *panciere* coat of mail, lit., belly piece. See PAUNCH, -ER[2]]

pan′zer divi′sion, an armored division of the German army, esp. in World War II, consisting chiefly of tanks and organized for making rapid attacks.

Pão de A·çú·car (poun′ də ä so͞o′kər), Portuguese name of **Sugarloaf Mountain.**

Pa·o·la (pā ō′lə, pī-), *n.* a town in E Kansas. 4784 (1960).

Pa·o·li (pā ō′lē, pī-), *n.* a town in S Indiana. 2754 (1960).

Pao·shan (bou′shän′), *n.* a town in W Yunnan, in SW China, on the Burma Road.

Pao·ting (bou′ding′), *n.* former name of **Tsingyuan.**

pap[1] (pap), *n.* **1.** soft food for infants or invalids, as bread soaked in water or milk. **2.** an idea, talk, book, or the like, lacking substance or real value. **3.** *Slang.* profits, favors, or privileges secured through political patronage. [late ME; imit. of a baby's call for food; corresponds to D *pap,* G *Pappe,* It *pappa,* L *pappa,* etc.] —**pap′like′,** *adj.*

pap[2] (pap), *n. Chiefly Dial.* **1.** a teat; nipple. **2.** something resembling a teat or nipple. [ME *pap(pe);* a nursery word identical in origin with PAP[1]; cf. dial. Norw, Sw *pappe,* L *papilla* nipple]

pa·pa[1] (pä′pə, pə pä′), *n.* **1.** father. **2.** (*cap.*) a word used in communications to represent the letter P. [< F; MF *pappa* (nursery word); cf. L *pāpa* father (see POPE), Icel *pāpi, pabbi* father. See PAPAS, PAP[1]]

pa·pa[2] (pä′pä), *n. Rare.* the Roman Catholic pontiff; pope. [< It: pope]

pa·pa·ble (pā′pə bəl), *adj.* suitable or not unlikely to become pope. [< MF; see PAPA[2], -BLE] —**pa′pa·bil′i·ty,** *n.*

pa·pa·cy (pā′pə sē), *n., pl.* **-cies.** *Rom. Cath. Ch.* **1.** the office, dignity, or jurisdiction of the pope. **2.** the system of ecclesiastical government in which the pope is recognized as the supreme head. **3.** the period during which a certain pope is in office. **4.** the succession or line of the popes. [ME *papacie* < ML *pāpātia.* See POPE, -ACY]

Pa·pa·ga·yo (pä′pə gī′ō; *Sp.* pä′pä gä′yô), *n.* **1. Gulf of,** an inlet of the Pacific, on the NW coast of Costa Rica. 15 mi. long; 25 mi. wide. **2.** a violent northerly wind occurring along the W coast of Central America, esp. on the Gulf of Papagayo.

pa·pa·in (pə pā′in, -pī′in, pā′pə-), *n.* **1.** *Chem.* a proteolytic enzyme found in the fruit of the papaya tree, *Carica Papaya.* **2.** *Pharm.* a commercial preparation of this used as a meat tenderizer and in medicine as a digestant. [PAPA(YA) + -IN[2]]

pa·pal (pā′pəl), *adj.* **1.** of or pertaining to the pope or the papacy. **2.** of or pertaining to the Roman Catholic Church. [ME < ML *pāpāl(is).* See POPE, -AL[1]] —**pa′pal·ly,** *adv.*

pa′pal cross′, a cross with three horizontal crosspieces. See illus. under **cross.**

pa′pal infallibil′ity, *Rom. Cath. Ch.* the dogma that the pope cannot err in a solemn teaching addressed to the whole church on a matter of faith or morals.

pa·pal·ise (pā′pə līz′), *v.i., v.t.,* **-ised, -is·ing.** *Chiefly Brit.* papalize. —**pa′pal·i·sa′tion,** *n.*

pa·pal·ism (pā′pə liz′əm), *n.* the papal system. [PAPAL + -ISM] —**pa′pal·ist,** *adj., n.* —**pa′pal·is′tic,** *adj.*

pa·pal·ize (pā′pə līz′), *v.i., v.t.,* **-ized, -iz·ing.** to become or render papal. Also, *esp. Brit.,* **papalise.** [PAPAL + -IZE] —**pa′pal·i·za′tion,** *n.*

Pa′pal States′, the areas comprising a large district in central Italy ruled as a temporal domain by the popes from A.D. 755 until the greater part of it was annexed in 1860, by Victor Emmanuel II: the remaining part, Rome and its environs, was absorbed into the kingdom of Italy in 1870. Also called **States of the Church.** Cf. **Vatican City.**

Pa·pan·dre·ou (pä′pən drā′o͞o), *n.* **George,** 1888–1968, Greek statesman: premier 1944, 1963–65.

pa·pa·raz·zo (pä′pä rät′tsō; *Eng.* pä′pə rät′sō), *n., pl.* **-raz·zi** (-rät′tsē; *Eng.* -rät′sē). *Italian.* a free-lance photographer.

pa·pav·er·a·ceous (pə pav′ə rā′shəs), *adj.* belonging to the *Papaveraceae,* or poppy family of plants. [< NL, L *papāver* poppy + -ACEOUS]

pa·pav·er·ine (pə pav′ə rēn′, -ər in, pə pā′və rēn′, -vər in), *n. Pharm.* a white, crystalline, water-insoluble, non-narcotic, alkaloidal powder, $C_{20}H_{21}NO_4$, obtained from opium, but not a morphine derivative and not habit-forming or addicting: used usually in the form of its hydrochloride in the treatment of spasms of involuntary muscle, esp. of the stomach, bronchi, and arteries. [< L *papāver* poppy + -INE[2]]

pa·paw (pô′pô, pə pô′), *n.* **1.** the small fleshy fruit of a temperate North American bush or small tree, *Asimina triloba.* **2.** the tree itself. Also, **pawpaw.** [unexplained var. of PAPAYA]

pa·pa·ya (pə pä′yə), *n.* **1.** the large, yellow, melonlike fruit of a tropical American shrub or small tree, *Carica Papaya.* **2.** the tree itself. [< Sp < Carib (Hispaniola)] —**pa·pa′yan,** *adj.*

Pa·pe·e·te (pä′pē ā′tā), *n.* a city on NW Tahiti, in the Society Islands: capital of the Society Islands and of French Polynesia. 20,302 (1962).

pa·pe·le·ra (pä′pe le′rä), *n., pl.* **-ras** (-räs). *Sp. Furniture.* a small Renaissance cabinet for papers and writing materials, mounted on a small stand. [< Sp, equiv. to *papel* paper + *-era* (fem.); see -ER[2]]

pap·é·lon·né (pap′ə lə nā′), *adj. Heraldry.* divided into a fish-scale pattern. [< F; lit., butterflied. See PAVILION, -EE]

Pa·pen (pä′pən), *n.* **Franz von** (fränts fən), 1879–1969, German diplomat, statesman, and soldier.

pa·per (pā′pər), *n.* **1.** a substance made from rags, straw, wood, or other fibrous material, usually in thin sheets, used to bear writing or printing or for wrapping things, decorating walls, etc. **2.** something resembling this substance, as papyrus. **3.** a piece, sheet, or leaf of this. **4.** a written or printed document or the like. **5.** negotiable notes, bills, etc.: *Only silver, please, no paper.* **6.** Often, **papers.** a document establishing or verifying identity, status, or the like: *citizenship papers.* **7. papers,** *Naut.* See **ship's papers. 8.** a set of questions for an examination, an individual set of written answers to them, or any written piece of schoolwork. **9.** an essay, article, or dissertation on a particular topic: *a paper on early Armenian artifacts.* **10.** a newspaper or journal. **11.** a sheet or card of paper with pins or needles stuck through it in rows. **12.** wallpaper. **13.** stationery. **14.** *Slang.* a free pass to a place of entertainment. **15. on paper, a.** in written or printed form. **b.** in theory rather than in practice. **c.** existing only in a preliminary state; in a plan or design: *The university building program is still on paper.* —*v.t.* **16.** to cover with wallpaper or apply wallpaper to: *They papered the bedroom last summer.* **17.** to line or cover with paper. **18.** to write or set down on paper. **19.** to describe in writing. **20.** to fold, enclose, or wrap in paper. **21.** to supply with paper. **22.** *Slang.* to fill (a theater or the like) with spectators by giving away free tickets or passes. —*v.i.* **23.** to apply wallpaper to walls. —*adj.* **24.** made of paper or paperlike material: *a paper bag.* **25.** paperlike; thin; flimsy; frail. **26.** of, pertaining to, or noting routine clerical duties. **27.** pertaining to or carried on by means of letters, articles, books, etc.: *a paper war.* **28.** written or printed on paper. **29.** existing on paper only and not in reality: *paper profits.* **30.** indicating the first event of a series, as a wedding anniversary. **31.** *Slang.* containing many patrons admitted on free passes, as an audience for a theatrical performance: *It's a paper house tonight.* [ME, OE < L *papȳr(us)* PAPYRUS] —**pa′per·like′,** *adj.*

pa·per·back (pā′pər bak′), *n.* **1.** a book bound in a flexible paper cover, often a low-priced edition of a hard-cover book: *a successful series of paperbacks on foreign policy.* —*adj.* **2.** (of a book) bound in a flexible paper cover: *a paperback edition of Chaucer.* **3.** of, for, or pertaining to paperbacks: *the paperback market; a paperback bookstore.* Cf. **hardcover.** [PAPER + BACK[1]]

pa′per·bark ma′ple (pā′pər bärk′), a tree, *Acer macrophyllum,* of China, having winged, hanging fruit, hairy clusters of flowers, and papery, gray, flaking bark. [PAPER + BARK[2]]

pa′per birch′, a North American birch, *Betula papyrifera,* having a tough bark and yielding a valuable wood: the State tree of New Hampshire. Also called **canoe birch.**

pa·per·board (pā′pər bōrd′, -bôrd′), *n.* **1.** a thick, stiff cardboard composed of layers of paper or paper pulp compressed together; pasteboard. —*adj.* **2.** of, pertaining to, or made of paperboard. [PAPER + BOARD]

pa·per·bound (pā′pər bound′), *n., adj.* paperback. [PAPER + BOUND[1]]

pa·per·boy (pā′pər boi′), *n.* a youth or man whose job consists of hawking newspapers on the street or delivering them to homes; newsboy. [PAPER + BOY]

pa′per bush′, cajuput.

pa′per chase′. See **hare and hounds.** —**pa′per chas′er.** —**pa′per-chas′ing,** *adj., n.*

pa′per chromatog′raphy, *Chem.* See under **chromatography.**

pa′per clip′, a flat wire clip bent so that it can clasp sheets of paper between two of its projecting parts.

pa′per cut′ter, **1.** any device for cutting or trimming many sheets of paper at once, typically a weighted, powered, or spring-hinged blade mounted on or over a ruled board or table on which stacks of paper may be aligned for cutting. **2.** See **paper knife.** —**pa′per-cut′ting,** *adj.*

pa′per doll′, **1.** a paper or cardboard, usually two-dimensional, representation of the human figure, used as a child's toy. **2.** Usually, **paper dolls.** a connected series of doll-like figures cut from folded paper.

pa·per·er (pā′pər ər), *n.* **1.** a paperhanger. **2.** one who papers. [PAPER + -ER[1]]

pa·per·hang·er (pā′pər hang′ər), *n.* **1.** a person whose job is covering walls with wallpaper. **2.** *Slang.* a person who forges and passes worthless checks. Also, **pa′per hang′er.** [PAPER + HANGER]

pa·per·hang·ing (pā′pər hang′ing), *n.* **1.** the activity or business of a paperhanger. **2. paper-hangings,** *Rare.* wallpaper. [PAPER + HANGING]

pa′per knife′, **1.** a small, often decorative, knife-like instrument with a blade of metal, ivory, wood, or the like, for slitting open envelopes, the leaves of books, folded papers, etc. **2.** the blade of a paper cutter.

pa·per-mâ·ché (pā′pər mə shā′, -ma-), *n., adj.* papier-mâché.

pa·per·mak·er (pā′pər mā′kər), *n.* one who or that which makes paper. [PAPER + MAKER] —**pa′per·mak′ing,** *n.*

pa′per match′. See **book match.**

pa′per mon′ey, currency in paper form, as government and bank notes.

pa′per mul′berry, a moraceous tree, *Broussonetia papyrifera,* of eastern Asia, grown as a shade tree. [so called because its bark is used to make paper]

pa′per nau′tilus, any dibranchiate cephalopod of the genus *Argonauta,* the female of which has a delicate, white shell.

pa·per-shelled (pā′pər sheld′), *adj.* having a thin, easily broken shell: *paper-shelled nuts.*

pa′per ti′ger, one who or that which has the appearance of strength or power but is actually weak or ineffectual: *The Chinese communists claim that the U.S. is a paper tiger.*

pa′per wasp′, any of several social wasps, as the yellowjacket or hornet, that constructs a nest of a paperlike substance consisting of chewed plant material.

Paper wasp, *Polistes annularis* (Length 1⅛ in.)

pa·per·weight (pā′pər wāt′), *n.* a small, heavy object of glass, metal, etc., laid on papers to keep them from scattering. [PAPER + WEIGHT]

pa′per work′, written or clerical work, as records, reports, etc., forming a necessary but incidental part of some work or job.

pa·per·y (pā′pə rē), *adj.* like paper; thin or flimsy: *the papery petals of the narcissus.* [PAPER + -Y[1]] —**pa′per·i·ness,** *n.*

pap·e·terie (pap′i trē; *Fr.* pApᵊ trē′), *n., pl.* **-teries** (-trēz; *Fr.* -trē′). a case or box of paper and other materials for writing. [< F, equiv. to *papet(ier)* paper maker or dealer (irreg. deriv. of *papier* PAPER; see -ER[2]) + *-erie* -ERY]

Pa·phi·an (pā′fē ən), *adj.* **1.** of or pertaining to Paphos, an ancient city of Cyprus sacred to Aphrodite. **2.** of or pertaining to love, esp. illicit sexual love. **3.** noting or pertaining to Aphrodite or to her worship or service. —*n.* **4. the Paphian,** Aphrodite: so called from her cult center at Paphos. [< L *Paphi(us)* (< Gk *Páphios* of Paphos, of Aphrodite) + -AN]

Pa′phian God′dess, *Class. Myth.* Aphrodite, worshiped in Cyprus as the goddess of sexual love.

Paph·la·go·ni·a (paf′lə gō′nē ə), *n.* an ancient country and Roman province in N Asia Minor, on the S coast of the Black Sea.

Pa·phos (pā′fos), *n.* **1.** an ancient city in SW Cyprus. **2.** Also, **Pa·phus** (pā′fəs). *Class. Myth.* the son of Pygmalion and Galatea who inherited the throne of Cyprus from his father.

Pa·pia·men·to (pä′pyä men′tô), *n.* a creolized language based on Spanish and spoken on Curaçao. [? < Pg *papea(r)* to chatter (back formation from *papagaio* parrot) + *-mento* -MENT]

pa·pier col·lé (pA pyā′ kô lā′), *pl.* ***pa·piers col·lés*** (pA pyā′ kô lā′). *French.* an arrangement of various objects and materials pasted on a flat surface to achieve a formal design, used especially in Cubism about 1912–14. Cf. **collage.** [lit., glued paper]

pa·pier-mâ·ché (pā′pər mə shā′; *Fr.* pA pyā′mA-shā′), *n.* **1.** a substance made of pulped paper or paper pulp mixed with glue and other materials or of layers of paper glued and pressed together, molded when moist to form various articles, and becoming hard and strong when dry. —*adj.* **2.** made of papier-mâché. **3.** easily destroyed or discredited; false; pretentious; illusory: *a papier-mâché façade of friendship.* Also, **paper-mâché.** [< F: lit., chewed paper]

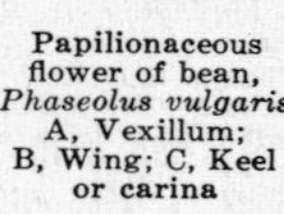

Papilionaceous flower of bean, *Phaseolus vulgaris* A, Vexillum; B, Wing; C, Keel or carina

pa·pil·i·o·na·ceous (pə pil′ē ə nā′shəs), *adj. Bot.* **1.** having an irregular corolla shaped somewhat like a butterfly, as the pea and other leguminous plants. **2.** belonging to the family *Papilionaceae* (*Fabaceae*), which is often included as part of the *Leguminosae.* [< L *pāpiliōn-* (s. of *pāpiliō*) butterfly + -ACEOUS]

pa·pil·la (pə pil′ə), *n., pl.* **-pil·lae** (-pil′ē). **1.** any small, nipplelike process or projection. **2.** one of certain small protuberances concerned with the senses of touch, taste, and smell: *the papillae of the tongue.* **3.** a small vascular process at the root of a hair. **4.** a papule or pimple. [< L: nipple, teat, akin to *papula* pimple. See PAP[2]] —**pap·il·lar** (pap′ə lər, pə pil′ər), *adj.*

pap·il·lar·y (pap′ə ler′ē, pə pil′ə rē), *adj.* **1.** of, pertaining to, or of the nature of a papilla or papillae. **2.** having or covered with papillae. [< L *papill(a)* nipple + -ARY]

pap′illary mus′cle, *Anat.* one of the small bundles of muscles attached to the ventricle walls and to the chordae tendineae that tighten these tendons during ventricular contraction.

pa·pil·li·form (pə pil′ə fôrm′), *adj.* resembling a papilla. [PAPILL(A) + -I- + -FORM]

pap·il·lo·ma (pap′ə lō′mə), *n., pl.* **-ma·ta** (-mə tə), **-mas.** *Pathol.* a tumor of skin or mucous membrane consisting of a hypertrophied papilla or group of papillae, as a wart or a corn. [< NL; see PAPILLA, -OMA] —**pap·il·lo′ma·to′sis,** *n.* —**pap·il·lo·ma·tous** (pap′ə lō′mə təs, -lom′ə-), *adj.*

pap·il·lon (pap′ə lon′), *n.* one of a breed of toy spaniels having a long, silky coat and large, erect ears held so that they resemble the wings of a butterfly. [< F: butterfly < L *pāpiliōn-* (s. of *pāpiliō*)]

pap·il·lose (pap′ə lōs′), *adj.* full of papillae. [PAPILL(A) + -OSE[1]] —**pap·il·los·i·ty** (pap′ə los′i tē), *n.*

pap·il·lote (pap′ə lōt′), *n.* **1.** a decorative curled paper placed over the end of the bone of a cutlet or chop. **2.** See **en papillote.** [< F, irreg. deriv. of *papillon* butterfly. See PAPILLON]

Pa·pin·i·an (pə pin′ē ən), *n.* (*Aemilius Papinianus*) died A.D. 212, Roman jurist and writer.

pap·ism (pā′piz əm), *n. Usually Disparaging.* the papal system, popery, or Roman Catholicism. [< MF *papisme.* See POPE, -ISM]

pa·pist (pā′pist), *Usually Disparaging.* —*n.* **1.** a Roman Catholic, esp. one regarded as being a strong advocate of the papacy. —*adj.* **2.** papistical. [earlier *papista* < NL. See POPE, -IST] —**pa′pist·like′,** *adj.* —**pa′pist·ly,** *adv.*

pa·pis·ti·cal (pā pis′ti kəl, pə-), *adj. Usually Disparaging.* of or pertaining to the Roman Catholic Church. [prob. < MF *papistique* (see PAPIST, -IC) + -AL[1]]

pa·pist·ry (pā′pi strē), *n. Usually Disparaging.* the system, doctrines, or practices of the Roman Catholic Church. [PAPIST + -RY]

pa·poose (pa po͞os′, pə-), *n.* a North American Indian baby or young child. Also, **pap·poose′.** [< Algonquian (New England) *papeisses*, deriv. of *peisses* child]

pa·poose-root (pa po͞os′ro͞ot′, -ro͝ot′), *n.* the blue cohosh. See under **cohosh.**

pap·pen·hei·mer (pap′ən hī′mər), *n.* a heavy rapier of the 17th century, having a swept guard with two perforated plates. Also called **Walloon sword.** [named after Gottfried Heinrich Graf zu *Pappenheim* (1594–1632), German leader in 30 Years' War]

pap·pose (pap′ōs), *adj. Bot.* **1.** having or forming a pappus. **2.** downy. Also, **pap·pous** (pap′əs). [PAPP(US) + -OSE[1]]

pap·pus (pap′əs), *n., pl.* **pap·pi** (pap′ī). *Bot.* a downy, bristly, or other tuftlike appendage of the achene of certain plants, as the dandelion and the thistle. [< NL < Gk *páppos* down, lit., grandfather (taken as greybeard, white hairs, down)]

pap·py[1] (pap′ē), *adj.,* **-pi·er, -pi·est.** like pap, mushy. [PAP[1] + -Y[1]]

pap·py[2] (pap′ē), *n., pl.* **-pies.** *Chiefly Midland and Southern U.S.* father. [PAP(A)[1] + -Y[2]]

pap·ri·ka (pa prē′kə, pə-, pap′rə kə), *n.* **1.** a red, powdery condiment derived from dried, ripe sweet peppers. —*adj.* **2.** cooked or seasoned with paprika. [< G < Hung < Croatian, deriv. of *papar* PEPPER]

Pap′ test′ (pap), a test for cancer of the uterus, consisting of the staining of a vaginal smear (**Pap′ smear′**) for examination of exfoliated cells. [named after George *Papanicolaou* (1883–1962), American scientist who developed the staining method]

Pap·u·a (pap′yo͞o ə, pä′po͞o ä′), *n.* **1.** See **New Guinea** (def. 1). **2. Territory of,** a former Australian territory in SE New Guinea: now part of Papua New Guinea. **3. Gulf of,** a gulf of the Coral Sea, off the SE coast of New Guinea.

Pap·u·an (pap′yo͞o ən), *adj.* **1.** of or pertaining to Papua. **2.** noting or pertaining to the native Negroid race of New Guinea, characterized by a black or sooty-brown complexion and crisp, frizzled hair. **3.** of or pertaining to any of the unaffiliated languages indigenous to New Guinea and other islands nearby, esp. Timor, the Bismarck Archipelago, the Moluccas, and the Solomons. —*n.* **4.** a native or inhabitant of New Guinea. [PAPU(A) + -AN]

Pap′ua New′ Guin′ea, a republic in the W Pacific Ocean, comprising the E part of New Guinea and numerous nearby islands: former territory of Australia; independent since 1975. 3,000,000; 178,260 sq. mi. *Cap.:* Port Moresby. —**Pap′ua New′ Guin′ean.**

pap·u·la (pap′yə lə), *n., pl.* **-lae** (-lē′). one of the small, ciliated projections of the body wall of an echinoderm, serving for respiration and excretion. [< NL, L: pimple, pustule. See PAPULE]

pap·ule (pap′yo͞ol), *n. Pathol.* a small, somewhat pointed elevation of the skin, usually inflammatory but nonsuppurative. [< L *papul(a)* pimple, pustule, akin to *papilla* nipple. See PAP[2], -ULE] —**pap′u·lar,** *adj.* —**pap·u·lose** (pap′yə lōs′), *adj.*

pap·y·ra·ceous (pap′ə rā′shəs), *adj.* papery. [< L *papȳr(us)* PAPYRUS + -ACEOUS]

pap·y·rol·o·gy (pap′ə rol′ə jē), *n.* the study of papyrus manuscripts. [PAPYR(US) + -O- + -LOGY] —**pa·py·ro·log·i·cal** (pə pī′rə loj′i kəl, pa per′ə-), *adj.* —**pap′y·rol′o·gist,** *n.*

pa·py·rus (pə pī′rəs), *n., pl.* **-py·ri** (-pī′rī). **1.** a tall, aquatic, cyperaceous plant, *Cyperus Papyrus*, of the Nile valley. **2.** a material on which to write, prepared from thin strips of the pith of this plant laid together, soaked, pressed, and dried, used by the ancient Egyptians, Greeks, and Romans. **3.** an ancient document, manuscript, or scroll written on this material. [< L < Gk *pápyros*] —**pa·py′ral, pa·pyr·i·an** (pə pir′ē ən), —**pa·py·rine** (pə pī′rin), *adj.* —**pap·y·ri·tious** (pap′ə rish′əs), *adj.*

Papyrus, ***Cyperus Papyrus*** **(Height 3 to 10 ft.)**

par (pär), *n., adj., v.,* **parred, par·ring.** —*n.* **1.** an equality in value or standing; a level of equality: *The gains and the losses are on a par.* **2.** an average or normal amount, degree, quality, condition, standard, or the like: *above par; below par.* **3.** *Finance.* **a.** the legally established value of the monetary unit of one country in terms of that of another using the same metal as a standard of value. **b.** the state of the shares of any business, undertaking, loan, etc., when they may be purchased at the original price (**issue par**) or at their face value (**nominal par**). **4.** *Golf.* the number of strokes set as a standard for a hole or a complete course. **5. at par,** *Finance.* (of a share) purchasable at issue par or nominal par. —*adj.* **6.** average or normal. **7.** *Finance.* at or pertaining to par: *the par value of a bond.* —*v.t.* **8.** *Golf.* to equal par on (a hole or course). [< L: equal]

par., 1. paragraph. **2.** parallel. **3.** parenthesis. **4.** parish.

pa·ra[1] (pä rä′, pä′rä), *n., pl.* **-ras, -ra.** a former copper coin of Turkey, the 40th part of a piaster. [< Turk < Pers *pārah*, lit., piece]

pa·ra[2] (pä rä′, pä′rä), *n., pl.* **-ras, -ra.** a money of account of Yugoslavia, the 100th part of a dinar, equal to about .000013 of a U.S. dollar. [< Serbo-Croatian < Turk; see PARA[1]]

par·a[3] (par′ə), *adj. Chem.* pertaining to or occupying two positions in the benzene ring that are separated by two carbon atoms. Cf. **ortho, meta.** [independent form of PARA-[1]]

Pa·rá (pä rä′), *n.* **1.** Belém. **2.** an estuary in N Brazil: an arm of the Amazon. 200 mi. long; 40 mi. wide. **3.** See **Pará rubber.**

para-[1], **1.** an element appearing in loan words from Greek, where it meant "beside" (*paradigm; paragraph*); on this model, used also with the meanings "near," "beyond," "aside," "amiss," and sometimes implying alteration or modification (*parablast; paragenesis; parapsychology*). **2.** *Chem.* a combining form designating the para position in the benzene ring. *Abbr.:* p-. Cf. **meta-** (def. 2b), **ortho-** (def. 2b). Also, *esp. before a vowel,* **par-.** [< Gk *para-*, comb. form repr. *pará* (prep.) beside, alongside of, by, beyond]

para-[2], a combining form meaning "guard against," used in a few words: *parachute; parasol.* [< F < It *para*, impv. of *parare* to prepare against, ward off < L *parāre* to prepare]

Para., Paraguay.

par′a-am·i·no·ben·zo′ic ac′id (par′ə ə mē′nō-ben zō′ik, -am′ə nō-), *Chem.* a white or yellowish, crystalline, slightly water-soluble solid, $H_2NC_6H_4COOH$, the para isomer of aminobenzoic acid: used chiefly in the manufacture of dyes and pharmaceuticals. [PARA-[1] + AMINO- + BENZOIC ACID]

pa·rab·a·sis (pə rab′ə sis), *n., pl.* **-ses** (-sēz′). *Greek.* (in ancient Greek drama) a choral ode addressed to the audience, esp. of comedy, and independent of the action of the play: usually following the *agon* and, in the earliest forms of comedy, serving often to end the play.

par·a·bi·o·sis (par′ə bī ō′sis), *n. Biol.* experimental or natural union of two individuals with exchange of blood. [PARA-[1] + -BIOSIS] —**par·a·bi·ot·ic** (par′ə bī-ot′ik), *adj.*

par·a·blast (par′ə blast′), *n. Biol.* the nutritive yolk of a meroblastic ovum or egg. [PARA-[1] + -BLAST] —**par′a·blas′tic,** *adj.*

par·a·ble (par′ə bəl), *n.* **1.** a short allegorical story designed to convey some truth, religious principle, or moral lesson. **2.** a statement or comment that conveys a meaning indirectly by the use of comparison, analogy, or the like. [ME *parabil* < LL *parabol(a)* comparison, parable, word < Gk *parabolḗ* comparison, equiv. to *para-* PARA-[1] + *bolḗ* a putting] —**pa·rab·o·list** (pə rab′ə list), *n.*

pa·rab·o·la (pə rab′ə lə), *n. Geom.* a plane curve formed by the intersection of a right circular cone with a plane parallel to a generator of the cone; the set of points in a plane that are equidistant from a fixed line and a fixed point in the same plane or in a parallel plane. Equation: $y^2 = 2px$ or $x^2 = 2py$. See diag. under **conic section.** [< NL < Gk *parabolḗ* a putting aside. See PARABLE]

Parabola (common)
AB, Directrix;
F, Focus; P, Point on parabola;
PQ, Always equal to PF; XX, Axis

pa·rab·o·le (pə rab′ə lē), *n. Rhet.* a comparison, esp. a simile using an existing or imagined event or object. [< Gk *parabolḗ* comparison. See PARABLE]

par·a·bol·ic[1] (par′ə bol′ik), *adj.* **1.** having the form or outline of a parabola. **2.** having a longitudinal section in the form of a paraboloid or parabola: *a parabolic reflector.* **3.** of, pertaining to, or resembling a parabola. [PARABOL(A) + -IC]

par·a·bol·ic[2] (par′ə bol′ik), *adj.* of, pertaining to, or involving a parable. Also, **par′a·bol′i·cal.** [< LL *parabolic(us)* metaphoric < LGk *parabolikós* figurative, equiv. to Gk *parabol(ḗ)* PARABLE + *-ikos* -IC] —**par′a·bol′i·cal·ism,** *n.* —**par′a·bol′i·cal·ly,** *adv.*

pa·rab·o·lise (pə rab′ə līz′), *v.t.,* **-lised, -lis·ing.** *Chiefly Brit.* parabolize.

pa·rab·o·lize[1] (pə rab′ə līz′), *v.t.,* **-lized, -liz·ing.** to tell or explain in a parable or parables. [< LL *parabol(a)* PARABLE + -IZE] —**pa·rab′o·li·za′tion,** *n.* —**pa·rab′o·liz′er,** *n.*

pa·rab·o·lize[2] (pə rab′ə līz′), *v.t.,* **-lized, -liz·ing.** to form as a parabola or paraboloid. [PARABO-L(A) + -IZE] —**pa·rab′o·li·za′tion,** *n.* —**pa·rab′o·liz′er,** *n.*

Paraboloids
A, Hyperbolic
B, Elliptic

pa·rab·o·loid (pə rab′ə loid′), *n. Geom.* a solid or surface generated by the revolution of a parabola about its axis, or a surface of the second degree some of whose plane sections are parabolas. Equation: $x^2/a^2 + y^2/b^2 = 2cz$. [PARABOL(A) + -OID] —**pa·rab·o·loi·dal** (pə rab′ə-loid′ᵊl, par′ə bə-), *adj.*

par·a·bomb (par′ə bom′), *n.* a bomb that has typically a delayed-action fuze and is dropped by parachute from an aircraft. [PARA-[2] + BOMB]

par·a·brake (par′ə brāk′), *n.* See **parachute brake.**

par·a·ca·sein (par′ə kā′sēn, -sē in, -kā sēn′), *n. Biochem.* casein. [PARA-[1] + CASEIN]

Par·a·cel·sus (par′ə sel′səs), *n.* **1. Phil·ip·pus Au·re·o·lus** (fi lip′əs ô rē′ō ləs), (*Theophrastus Bombastus von Hohenheim*), 1493?–1541, Swiss physician and alchemist. **2.** (*italics.*) a dramatic poem (1835) by Robert Browning, based on the life of Paracelsus. —**Par′a·cel′si·an,** *adj., n.* —**Par′a·cel′si·an·ism,** *n.* —**Par′a·cel′sic, Par′a·cel·sis′tic,** *adj.* —**Par′a·cel′sist,** *n.*

par·a·cen·te·sis (par′ə sen tē′sis), *n., pl.* **-ses** (-sēz). *Surg.* puncture of the wall of a cavity to drain off fluid. Also called **tapping.** [< L *paracentēsis* perforation, tapping < Gk *parakéntēsis*, equiv. to *parakent(eîn)* (to) prick beside (*para-* PARA-[1] + *kentein* to prick, pierce) + *-ē-* (v. suffix) + *-sis* -SIS]

par·ac·et·al·de·hyde (par′as i tal′də hīd′), *n. Chem.* paraldehyde. [PARA-[1] + ACETALDEHYDE]

par·a·chor (par′ə kōr′, -kôr′), *n. Physics, Chem.* a ratio that is essentially constant for a given liquid and that equals the product of the molecular weight and the fourth root of the surface tension of the liquid divided by the difference between its density and the density of its vapor, both densities being measured at the same temperature. [PARA-[1] + Gk *chṓr(a)* place, spot, space]

pa·rach·ro·nism (pə rak′rə niz′əm), *n.* a chronological error in which a person, event, etc., is assigned a date later than the actual one. Cf. **anachronism, prochronism.** [PARA-[1] + CHRON- + -ISM] —**pa·rach′ro·nis′tic,** *adj.*

par·a·chute (par′ə sho͞ot′), *n., v.,* **-chut·ed, -chut·ing.** —*n.* **1.** a folding, umbrellalike, fabric device with cords supporting a harness or straps for allowing a man, object, package, etc., to descend safely through the air from a great height, esp. from an aircraft, rendered effective by the resistance of the air which expands it during the descent and then reduces the velocity of its motion. **2.** See **parachute brake. 3.** *Horol.* a shock-proofing device for the balance staff of a watch, consisting of a yielding, springlike support for the bearing at either end. —*v.t.* **4.** to drop or land (troops, equipment, supplies, etc.) by parachute. —*v.i.* **5.** to descend by parachute. [< F, equiv. to *para-* PARA-[2] + *chute* fall] —**par′a·chut′ic,** *adj.* —**par′a·chut′ism,** *n.* —**par′a·chut′ist, par′a·chut′er,** *n.*

par′achute brake′, a parachute opened horizontally from the tail of an airplane upon landing, used as an aid in braking. Also called **parabrake.**

par′achute rig′ger, a person who inspects, repairs, and packs or folds, parachutes.

par′achute spin′naker, *Naut.* a spinnaker having its head well below the masthead and its foot well above the deck and having such an expanse of cloth as to assume a nearly hemispherical form when filled. Also called **double spinnaker.**

par·a·clete (par′ə klēt′), *n.* **1.** one called in to aid; an advocate or intercessor. **2.** (*cap.*) the Holy Spirit; the Comforter. [< eccl. L *Paraclēt(us)* < LGk *Paráklētos* comforter, lit., (person) called in (to help), verbal of *parakalein*, equiv. to *para-* PARA-[1] + *kalein* to call; r. late ME *paraclit* < eccl. L *Paraclīt(us)*, repr. MGk *Paráklētos*]

par·a·cu·sis (par′ə kyo͞o′sis), *n. Med.* defective hearing. Also, **par·a·cu·sia** (par′ə kyo͞o′zhə, -zhē ə, -zē ə). [PAR- + Gk *ákousis* hearing; see ACOUSTIC, -SIS] —**par′a·cu′sic,** *adj.*

par·a·cy·e·sis (par′ə sī ē′sis), *n., pl.* **-ses** (-sēz). *Med.* See **extrauterine pregnancy.** [PARA-[1] + CYESIS]

par·a·cy·mene (par′ə sī′mēn), *n. Chem.* a colorless liquid, $CH_3C_6H_4CH(CH_3)_2$, derived from benzene, found in various essential oils, and obtained as a by-product of paper making. Cf. **cymene.** [PARA-[1] + CYMENE]

par·a·cys·ti·tis (par′ə si stī′tis), *n. Med.* inflammation of the connective tissue around the urinary bladder. [PARA-[1] + CYSTITIS]

pa·rade (pə rād′), *n., v.,* **-rad·ed, -rad·ing.** —*n.* **1.** a large public procession, usually including a marching band and of a festive nature, held in honor of an anniversary, a person, an event, etc., and accompanied by band music. **2.** a military ceremony involving the formation and marching of troop units, often combined with saluting the lowering of the flag at the end of the day. **3.** the orderly assembly of troops for inspection or display. **4.** a place where troops regularly assemble for this. **5.** an ostentatious display: *to make a parade of one's beliefs.* **6.** *Chiefly Brit.* **a.** a group or procession of promenaders. **b.** a promenade. **7.** *Fort.* the level space forming the interior or enclosed area of a fortification. **8.** *Fencing.* a parry. —*v.t.* **9.** to walk up and down on or in. **10.** to make parade of; display ostentatiously. **11.** to cause to march or proceed for display. —*v.i.* **12.** to march in a procession. **13.** to promenade in a public place, esp. for the purpose of showing off. **14.** to assemble in military order for display. [< F, MF < Sp *parada* a stop, stopping place, n. use of fem. of *parado*, ptp. of *parar* to stop, end < L *parāre* to set. See COMPARE, PARRY, -ADE[1]] —**pa·rade′ful,** *adj.* —**pa·rade′less,** *adj.* —**pa·rade′like′,** *adj.* —**pa·rad′er,** *n.* —**pa·rad′ing·ly,** *adv.*
—**Syn. 10.** show, flaunt, flourish. —**Ant. 10.** conceal.

parade′ ar′mor, ornamented armor worn only for ceremonial purposes.

parade′ bed′, *Hist.* a royal bed from which levees were held.

parade′ rest′, *Mil., Navy.* **1.** a position assumed by a soldier or sailor in which the feet are 12 inches apart, the hands are clasped behind the back, and the head is held motionless and facing forward. **2.** a command to assume this position.

par·a·di·chlor·o·ben·zene (par′ə dī klôr′ō ben′zēn, -ben zēn′, -klōr′-), *n. Chem.* a white, crystalline, volatile, water-insoluble solid, $C_6H_4Cl_2$, of the benzene series, having a penetrating odor: used chiefly as a moth repellent. Also, **par′a·di·chlo′ro·ben′zene.** Also called **PDB** [PARA-[1] + DI-[1] + CHLORO-[2] + BENZENE]

par·a·did·dle (par′ə did′ᵊl, par′ə did′ᵊl), *n.* a drum roll, esp. on the snare drum, in which the beat is struck by the left and right drumstick in succession. [partly imit.; cf. DIDDLE[2]]

par·a·digm (par′ə dim, -dīm′), *n.* **1.** *Gram.* **a.** a set of forms all of which contain a particular element, esp. the set of all inflected forms based on a single stem or theme. **b.** a display in fixed arrangement of such a set, as *boy, boy's, boys, boys'.* **2.** an example; pattern. [late ME < LL *paradīgm(a)* < Gk *parádeigma* pattern, akin to *paradeiknýnai* to show side by side, equiv. to *para-* PARA-[1] + *deiknýnai* to show; see DEICTIC] —**par·a·dig·mat·ic** (par′ə dig mat′ik), **par′a·dig·mat′i·cal,** *adj.* —**par′a·dig·mat′i·cal·ly,** *adv.*
—**Syn. 2.** model, mold, ideal, standard, paragon, touchstone.

par′adigm case′, *Logic, Philos.* a perfectly clear and uncontroversial use of a word or expression the meaning of which is being investigated.

par·a·di·sa·i·cal (par′ə di sā′i kəl, -zā′-), *adj.* paradisiacal. Also, **par′a·di·sa′ic.** [PARADISE + *-aic* (suffix abstracted from words like *prosaic, algebraic,* etc.) + -AL[1]] —**par′a·di·sa′i·cal·ly,** *adv.*

par·a·dise (par′ə dīs′, -dīz′), *n.* **1.** heaven, as the final abode of the righteous. **2.** an intermediate place for the departed souls of the righteous awaiting resurrection. **3.** See **Garden of Eden. 4.** a place of extreme beauty, delight, or happiness. **5.** supreme happiness or a state of supreme happiness. **6.** *Archit.* **a.** parvis. **b.** an enclosure beside a church, as an atrium or cloister. **7.** (*cap., italics.*) Italian, **Pa·ra·di·so** (pä′rä dē′zō). the third and concluding part of Dante's *Divine Comedy*, depicting heaven, through which he is guided by Beatrice. Cf. **inferno** (def. 3), **purgatory** (def. 2). [ME, OE *paradīs* < LL *paradīs(us)* < Gk *parádeisos* park, pleasure-grounds < Iranian; cf. Avestan *pairidaēza-* enclosure, equiv. to *pairi-* PERI- + *daēza-* wall]

Par·a·dise (par′ə dīs′, -dīz′), *n.* **1.** a town in N California. 8268 (1960). **2.** a town in W California. 5616 (1960).

par′adise fish′, any small fresh-water fish of the genus *Macropodus*, found in southeastern Asia, often kept in aquariums.

par′adise flow′er. See **Costa Rica nightshade.**

Par′adise Lost′, an epic poem (1667) by John Milton.

Par′adise Regained′, an epic poem (1671) by John Milton.

par·a·di·si·a·cal (par′ə di sī′ə kəl, -zī′-), *adj.* of, like, or befitting paradise. Also, **par·a·dis·i·ac** (par′ə dis′ē ak′). [< L *paradīsiac(us)* < Gk *paradeisiakós* (see PARADISE, -IAC) + -AL[1]] —**par′a·di·si′a·cal·ly,** *adv.*

par·a·doc·tor (par′ə dok′tər), *n.* a doctor who parachutes to patients in remote areas. [PARA(CHUTE) + DOCTOR]

par·a·dos (par′ə dos′), *n.* *Fort.* the bank behind a trench for protecting men from enemy fire and from being seen against the skyline. [< F; see PARA-[2], REREDOS]

par·a·dox (par′ə doks′), *n.* **1.** a statement or proposition seemingly self-contradictory or absurd but in reality expressing a possible truth. **2.** a self-contradictory and false proposition. **3.** any person, thing, or situation exhibiting an apparently contradictory nature. **4.** an opinion or statement contrary to commonly accepted opinion. [< L *paradox(um)* < Gk *parádoxon,* n. use of neut. of *parádoxos* unbelievable, lit., beyond what is thought. See PARA-[1], ORTHODOX] —**par′a·dox′i·cal, par′a·dox′al,** *adj.* —**par′a·dox′i·cal·ly,** *adv.* —**par′a·dox′i·cal·ness, par′a·dox′i·cal′i·ty,** *n.* —**par′a·dox·ol′o·gy,** *n.*

par·a·drop (par′ə drop′), *n., v.t.,* **-dropped, -drop·ping.** airdrop. [PARA(CHUTE) + DROP]

Pa·rae·bi·us (pə rē′bē əs), *n.* *Class. Myth.* a youth who was cursed because his father had cut down a hamadryad's tree.

par·aes·the·sia (par′is thē′zhə, -zhē ə, -zē ə), *n.* *Pathol.* paresthesia. —**par·aes·thet·ic** (par′is thet′ik), *adj.*

par. aff., (in prescriptions) to the part affected. [< L *pars affecta*]

par·af·fin (par′ə fin), *n.* **1.** a white or colorless, tasteless, odorless, water-insoluble, solid substance not easily acted upon by reagents, consisting of a mixture of hydrocarbons chiefly of the alkane series, obtained from crude petroleum: used in candles, for forming preservative coatings and seals, for waterproofing paper, etc. **2.** *Chem.* **a.** any member of the alkane series. **b.** one of the higher members of the alkane series, solid at ordinary temperatures, having a boiling point above 300°C, which largely constitutes the commercial form of this substance. **3.** Also called **par′affin oil′.** *Brit.* kerosene. —*v.t.* **4.** to cover or impregnate with paraffin. [< G < L *par(um)* barely + *affin(is)* connected; so called from its slight affinity for other substances; see AFFINITY]

par·af·fine (par′ə fin, -fēn′), *n., v.t.,* **-fined, -fin·ing.** paraffin.

par·af·fin·ic (par′ə fin′ik), *adj.* of, noting, or characteristic of paraffin wax or a paraffin hydrocarbon. [PARAFFIN + -IC]

par·af·fin·ize (par′ə fi nīz′), *v.t.,* **-ized, -iz·ing.** paraffin (def. 4). [PARAFFIN + -IZE]

par·af·fin·oid (par′ə fi noid′). *adj.* resembling a paraffin. [PARAFFIN + -OID]

par′affin se′ries, *Chem.* See **alkane series.**

par′affin wax′, paraffin in its solid state.

par·a·form·al·de·hyde (par′ə fôr mal′də hīd′), *n.* *Chem.* a white, crystalline solid, $(HCOH)_n$, having the odor of formaldehyde, obtained from formaldehyde by evaporation of its aqueous solution: used chiefly as an antiseptic. Also called **par·a·form** (par′ə fôrm′). [PARA-[1] + FORMALDEHYDE]

par·a·gen·e·sis (par′ə jen′i sis), *n.* *Geol.* the origin of minerals or mineral deposits in contact so as to affect one another's formation. Also, **par·a·ge·ne·sia** (par′ə jə nē′zhə, -zhē ə, -zē ə). [< NL; see PARA-[1], GENESIS] —**par·a·ge·net·ic** (par′ə jə net′ik), *adj.*

par·a·geu·sia (par′ə gyōō′zhə, -zhē ə, -zē ə), *n.* *Psychiatry.* an abnormal or hallucinatory sense of taste. [< NL, equiv. to *para-* PARA-[1] + Gk *geûs(is)* taste + L *-ia* -IA] —**par·a·geu·sic** (par′ə gyōō′sik), *adj.*

par·a·glid·er (par′ə glī′dər), *n.* a steerable glider with inflatable wings proposed for use as an emergency vehicle for travel between a space station and the earth or for the recovery of rocket boosters. [PARA(CHUTE) + GLIDER]

par·a·glos·sa (par′ə glos′ə, glô′sə), *n., pl.* **-glos·sae** (-glos′ē, -glô′sē). one of a pair of lateral lobes in the labium of an insect. [< NL, equiv. to *para-* PARA-[1] + Gk *glôssa* tongue; see GLOSS[2]]

par·a·glos·sate (par′ə glos′āt, -glô′sāt), *adj.* having paraglossae. [< NL; see PARAGLOSSA, -ATE[1]]

par′a·glyph print′ing (par′ə glif), the printing of the positive and negative of a radiograph superimposed in slight misalignment to give the effect of a relief. [cf. Gk *paraglyph(ein)* (to) counterfeit. See PARA-[1], GLYPH]

par·a·go·ge (par′ə gō′jē), *n.* the addition of a sound or group of sounds at the end of a word, as in the nonstandard pronunciation of *height* as *height-th.* [< L *paragōgē* addition to a word, lengthening of a word < Gk *paragōgḗ* a leading by, alteration, change, deriv. of *parágein* to lead by, past. See PARA-[1], -AGOGUE] —**par·a·gog·ic** (par′ə goj′ik), **par′a·gog′i·cal,** *adj.* —**par′a·gog′i·cal·ly,** *adv.*

par·a·gon (par′ə gon′, -gən), *n.* **1.** a model or pattern of excellence or of a particular excellence. **2.** *Print.* a 20-point type. **3.** an unusually large, round pearl. —*v.t.* **4.** *Archaic.* to compare; parallel. **5.** *Archaic.* to be a match for; rival. **6.** *Obs.* to surpass. **7.** *Obs.* to regard as a paragon. [< MF < OIt *paragone* comparison, ? < Gk *parágōn,* prp. of *parágein* to bring side by side] —**par′a·gon′less,** *adj.*
—**Syn. 1.** ideal, standard; nonesuch, nonpareil.

pa·rag·o·nite (pə rag′ə nīt′), *n.* *Mineral.* a mica, similar in composition and appearance to muscovite but containing sodium instead of potassium. [< Gk *parágōn* misleading, leading aside (prp. of *parágein;* see PARAGOGE) + -ITE[1]] —**pa·rag·o·nit·ic** (pə rag′ə nit′ik), *adj.*

Par·a·gould (par′ə gōōld′), *n.* a town in NE Arkansas. 9947 (1960).

par·a·graph[1] (par′ə graf′, -gräf′), *n.* **1.** a distinct portion of written or printed matter dealing with a particular idea, usually beginning with an indentation on a new line. **2.** a note, item, or brief article, as in a newspaper. —*v.t.* **3.** to divide into paragraphs. **4.** to write or publish paragraphs about, as in a newspaper. **5.** to express in a paragraph. [earlier *paragraphe* < Gk *paragraphḗ* marked passage] —**par′a·graph·ism,** *n.* —**par·a·gra·phis·ti·cal** (par′ə grə fis′ti kəl), *adj.*

par·a·graph[2] (par′ə graf′, -gräf′), *n.* a character, usually ¶, used to indicate the beginning of a distinct or separate portion of a text, or as a mark of reference. [earlier *paragraf(f)e* < ML *paragraph(us)* < Gk *parágraphos* mark made beside (usually below) to set off part of a text. See PARA-[1], -GRAPH]

par·a·graph·er (par′ə graf′ər, -grä′fər), *n.* a person who writes short pieces or fillers for a newspaper. Also, *esp. Brit.,* **par′a·graph′ist.** [PARAGRAPH[1] + -ER[1]]

par·a·graph·i·a (par′ə graf′ē ə), *n.* *Psychiatry.* a mental disorder marked by the writing of words or letters other than those intended, or the loss of the ability to express ideas in writing. [< NL; see PARA-[1], -GRAPH, -IA]

par·a·graph·ic (par′ə graf′ik), *adj.* **1.** of, pertaining to, or forming a paragraph. **2.** divided into paragraphs. Also, **par′a·graph′i·cal.** [PARAGRAPH[1] + -IC] —**par′a·graph′i·cal·ly,** *adv.*

Par·a·guay (par′ə gwā′, -gwī′; *Sp.* pä′rä gwī′), *n.* **1.** a republic in central South America between Bolivia, Brazil, and Argentina. 1,816,890 (1962); 157,047 sq. mi. *Cap.:* Asunción. **2.** a river in central South America, flowing S from W Brazil through Paraguay to the Paraná. 1500 mi. long. —**Par′a·guay′an,** *adj., n.*

Par′aguay tea′, maté.

par·a·hy·dro·gen (par′ə hī′drə jən), *n.* *Physics Chem.* the form of molecular hydrogen in which the nuclei of the two hydrogen atoms contained in the molecule have spins in opposite directions. Cf. **orthohydrogen.** [PARA-[1] + HYDROGEN]

Pa·ra·í·ba (pä′rə ē′bə), *n.* a state in E Brazil. 2,018,023 (1960); 21,760 sq. mi. *Cap.:* João Pessoa.

par·ai·son (par′ə zon′), *n.* parison.

par·a·keet (par′ə kēt′), *n.* any of numerous small, slender parrots, usually having a long, pointed, graduated tail, often kept as pets and noted for the ability to mimic speech. Also, **paraquet, paroquet, parrakeet, parroket, parroquet.** [earlier *parrachito* < It *parochito* (Florio), var. of *parrochetto,* dim. of *parroco* parson. See PAROCHIAL, -ET]

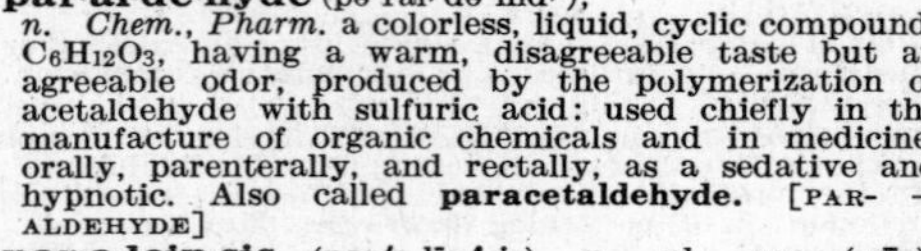

Parakeet (Budgerigar), *Melopsittacus undulatus* (Length 7 in.)

par·al·de·hyde (pə ral′də hīd′), *n.* *Chem., Pharm.* a colorless, liquid, cyclic compound, $C_6H_{12}O_3$, having a warm, disagreeable taste but an agreeable odor, produced by the polymerization of acetaldehyde with sulfuric acid: used chiefly in the manufacture of organic chemicals and in medicine, orally, parenterally, and rectally, as a sedative and hypnotic. Also called **paracetaldehyde.** [PAR- + ALDEHYDE]

par·a·leip·sis (par′ə līp′sis), *n., pl.* **-ses** (-sēz). paralipsis.

par·a·lep·sis (par′ə lep′sis), *n., pl.* **-ses** (-sēz). paralipsis.

par·a·lex·i·a (par′ə lek′sē ə), *n.* an impairment of reading ability characterized by the transposition of letters or words. [< NL, equiv. to *para-* PARA-[1] + Gk *léx(is)* speaking, speech; see -IA] —**par′a·lex′ic,** *adj.*

par·a·li·pom·e·na (par′ə li pom′ə nə, -lī-), *n.pl.* things omitted or neglected that are added as a supplement. [< Gk *(tà) paraleipómena* (things) omitted, not told (prp. of *paraleípein*), equiv. to *para-* PARA-[1] + *leíp(ein)* (to) leave behind + *-omena* neut. pl. prp. suffix]

Par·a·li·pom·e·non (par′ə li pom′ə non′, -lī-), *n., pl.* **-na** (-nə). *Douay Bible.* Chronicles. [< LL; sing. of PARALIPOMENA]

par·a·lip·sis (par′ə lip′sis), *n., pl.* **-ses** (-sēz). *Rhet.* the suggestion, by deliberately concise treatment of a topic, that much of significance is being omitted, as in "not to mention other faults." Also, **paraleipsis, paralepsis.** Also called **preterition.** [< LL *paralīpsis* < Gk *paráleipsis* an omitting, equiv. to *paraleíp(ein)* (to) leave on one side (*para-* PARA-[1] + *leípein* to leave) + *-sis* -SIS]

par·al·lax (par′ə laks′), *n.* **1.** the apparent displacement of an observed object due to a change in the position of the observer. **2.** *Astron.* the apparent displacement of a celestial body due to its being observed from the surface instead of from the center of the earth (**diurnal parallax** or **geocentric parallax**) or due to its being observed from the earth instead of from the sun (**annual parallax** or **heliocentric parallax**). **3.** apparent change in the position of cross hairs as viewed through a telescope, when the focusing is imperfect. **4.** the difference between the view of an object as seen through the picture-taking lens of a camera and the view as seen through a separate viewfinder. [< Gk *parállax(is)* change, equiv. to *parallak-* (verbid s. of *parallássein,* equiv. to *para-* PARA-[1] + *allássein* to vary, akin to *állos* other; see ELSE, ALIEN) + *-sis* -SIS] —**par·al·lac·tic** (par′ə lak′tik), *adj.* —**par′al·lac′ti·cal·ly,** *adv.*

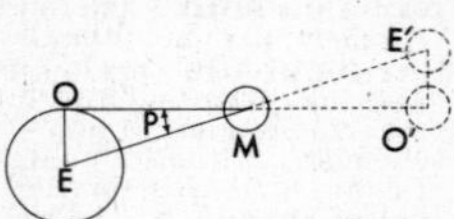

Parallax (geocentric) of the moon
P, Parallax; O, Observer; E, Center of earth; M, Moon; E′, Image of E; O′, Image of O

par·al·lel (par′ə lel′), *adj., n., v.,* **-leled, -lel·ing** or (*esp. Brit.*) **-lelled, -lel·ling.** —*adj.* **1.** extending in the same direction, equidistant at all points, and never converging or diverging: *parallel rows of trees.* **2.** having the same direction, course, nature, or tendency; corresponding; similar; analogous: *Canada and the U.S. have many parallel interests.* **3.** *Geom.* **a.** (of straight lines) lying in the same plane but never meeting no matter how far extended. **b.** (of planes) having common perpendiculars. **c.** (of a single line, plane, etc.) equidistant from another or others at all corresponding points (usually fol. by *to* or *with*). **4.** *Music.* **a.** (of two voice parts) progressing so that the interval between them remains the same. **b.** (of a tonality or key) having the same tonic but differing in mode. **5.** *Elect.* consisting of or having component parts connected in parallel: *a parallel circuit; a parallel generator.* —*n.* **6.** anything parallel or comparable in direction, course, nature, or tendency to something else. **7.** a parallel line or plane. **8.** Also called **parallel of latitude.** *Geog.* **a.** an imaginary circle on the earth's surface formed by the intersection of a plane parallel to the plane of the equator, bearing east and west and designated in degrees of latitude north or south of the equator along the arc of any meridian. **b.** the line representing this circle on a chart or map. **9.** a match or counterpart: *a case history without a known parallel.* **10.** correspondence or analogy: *These two cases have some parallel with each other.* **11.** a comparison of things as if regarded side by side. **12.** *Print.* a pair of vertical parallel lines (||) used as a mark for reference. **13.** *Elect.* an arrangement of the components, as resistances, of a circuit in such a way that all positive terminals are connected to one point and all negative terminals are connected to a second point, the same voltage flowing through each component. Cf. **series** (def. 8). **14.** *Fort.* a trench cut in the ground before a fortress, parallel to its defenses, for the purpose of covering a besieging force. **15.** *Theat.* a trestle for supporting a platform (**parallel top**). —*v.t.* **16.** to make parallel. **17.** to provide or show a parallel for; match. **18.** to form a parallel to; be equivalent to; equal. **19.** to go or be in a parallel course, direction, etc., to: *The road parallels the river.* **20.** to show the similarity of; compare. [< L *parallēl(us)* < Gk *parállēlos* side by side, equiv. to *para-* PARA-[1] + *allḗlos* one another; see ELSE] —**par′al·lel′a·ble,** *adj.* —**par′al·lel′less,** *adj.* —**par′al·lel′ly,** *adv.*
—**Syn. 2.** like, alike. **9.** similarity, likeness, resemblance. —**Ant. 2.** divergent; unlike; unique. **9.** dissimilarity.

par′allel ax′iom, *Geom.* See **parallel postulate.**

par′allel bars′, a gymnasium apparatus consisting of two wooden bars on uprights, adjustable in height, and used for swinging, vaulting, balancing exercises, etc.

Parallel bars

par′allel cous′in, a cousin who is the child either of one's mother's sister or of one's father's brother. Also called **ortho-cousin.** Cf. **cross-cousin.**

par′allel cous′in mar′riage, marriage between the children of two brothers or two sisters. Cf. **cross-cousin marriage.**

Parallelepiped

par·al·lel·e·pi·ped (par′ə lel′ə pī′pid, -pip′id), *n.* a prism with six faces, all parallelograms. Also, **par·al·lel·e·pip·e·don** (par′ə lel′ə pip′i don′, -dən), **par′al·lel′o·pi′ped.** [< Gk *parallēlepíped(on)* body with parallel surfaces, equiv. to *parállēl(os)* PARALLEL + *epípedon* plane, n. use of neut. of *epípedos* flat, equiv. to *epi-* EPI- + *pédon* ground] —**par·al·lel·e·pip·e·dic** (par′ə lel′ə pip′i dik), **par′al·lel′e·pip′e·don·al, par′al·lel′e·pip′e·dous,** *adj.*

par′allel forc′es, *Mech.* forces acting in parallel lines of action.

par·al·lel·ise (par′ə lel īz′, -lə līz′), *v.t.,* **-ised, -is·ing.** *Chiefly Brit.* parallelize. —**par′al·lel′i·sa′tion,** *n.*

par·al·lel·ism (par′ə lel′iz əm), *n.* **1.** the position or relation of parallels. **2.** agreement in direction, tendency, or character; the state or condition of being parallel. **3.** a parallel or comparison. **4.** *Metaphys.* the doctrine that mental and bodily processes are concomitant, each varying with variation of the other, but that there is no causal relation of interaction between the two. [PARALLEL + -ISM]

par·al·lel·ist (par′ə lel′ist), *n.* **1.** one who seeks or makes a comparison. **2.** an adherent of the metaphysical doctrine of parallelism. [PARALLEL + -IST]

par·al·lel·is·tic (par′ə lel is′tik, -lə lis′-), *adj.* **1.** of, pertaining to, or of the nature of a parallelism. **2.** of or pertaining to the metaphysical doctrine of parallelism or to its adherents. **3.** resembling, approaching, or characterized by parallelism. [PARALLELIST + -IC]

par·al·lel·ize (par′ə lel īz′, -lə līz′), *v.t.,* **-ized, -iz·ing.** **1.** to make parallel; place so as to be parallel. **2.** to draw a parallelism or analogy between. Also, *esp. Brit.,* **parallelise.** [< Gk *parallēlíz(ein).* See PARALLEL, -IZE] —**par′al·lel′i·za′tion,** *n.*

par′allel mid′dle bod′y, *Naut.* a middle body of a hull, or part of one, that is absolutely parallel to the fore-and-aft centerline at all levels.

par′allel mo′tion, an arrangement of links and levers permitting rectilinear motion of a rod moving with a lever oscillating through an arc.

par′allel of al′titude, *Astron.* almucantar.

par′allel of lat′itude, parallel (def. 8).

Parallelograms

par·al·lel·o·gram (par′ə lel′ə gram′), *n.* a quadrilateral having both pairs of opposite sides parallel to each other. [< LL *parallēlogramm(um)* < Gk *parallēlógrammon.* See PARALLEL, -GRAM[1]] —**par′al·lel′o·gram·mat′ic, par′al·lel′o·gram·mat′i·cal, par′al·lel′o·gram′mic, par′al·lel′o·gram′mi·cal,** *adj.*

parallel′ogram law′, **1.** *Math.* a rule for adding two vectors by placing the point of application of one at the point of origin of the other and obtaining their sum by constructing the line connecting the two remaining end points. **2.** *Math., Physics.* the law that the sum of two vectors is equal to the diagonal of the parallelogram whose sides are the two given vectors, when all three vectors originate at the same point.

parallel′ogram of forc′es, *Physics.* a parallelogram in which two sides and a diagonal represent two forces acting on a body and their resultant force: an application of the parallelogram law.

par′allel opera′tion, *Computer Technol.* **1.** the simultaneous use of two or more data channels for the transfer of information in a computer. **2.** the simultaneous performance of two or more programs or operations by a computer. Cf. **serial operation.**

par′allel pos′tulate, *Geom.* the axiom in Euclidean geometry that only one line can be drawn through a given point so that the line is parallel to a given line that does not contain the point. Also called **parallel axiom.**

par′allel projec′tion, *Geom.* a projection from one plane to a second plane in which the lines joining points on the first plane and corresponding images are parallel.

par′allel rul′ers, a pair of straightedges connected by two pivoted crosspieces of equal length so as to be parallel at all times, used for various navigational purposes, esp. for transferring the bearing of a plotted course to a compass rose.

par′allel sail′ing, sailing along a parallel of latitude.

par′allel top′. See under **parallel** (def. 15).

par·a·lo·gism (pə ral′ə jiz′əm), *n. Logic.* **1.** argument violating principles of valid reasoning. **2.** a conclusion reached through such argument. [< LL *paralogism(us)* < Gk *paralogismós.* See PARA-[1], LOGO-, -ISM] —**pa·ral′o·gist,** *n.* —**pa·ral′o·gis′tic,** *adj.*

pa·ral·o·gize (pə ral′ə jīz′), *v.i.,* **-gized, -giz·ing.** to draw conclusions that do not follow logically from a given set of assumptions. [< ML *paralogiz(āre)* < Gk *paralogízesthai* to reason falsely, equiv. to *parálog(os)* (see PARA-[1], LOGOS) + *-izesthai* -IZE]

par·a·lyse (par′ə līz′). *v.t.,* **-lysed, -lys·ing.** *Chiefly Brit.* paralyze. —**par′a·ly·sa′tion,** *n.* —**par′a·lys′er,** *n.*

pa·ral·y·sis (pə ral′i sis), *n., pl.* **-ses** (-sēz′). **1.** *Pathol.* **a.** a loss or impairment of sensation or esp. of muscle function, caused by injury or disease of the nerves, brain, or spinal cord. **b.** a disease characterized by this, esp. palsy. **2.** a crippling or stoppage, as of powers or activities: *a paralysis of trade.* [< L < Gk, equiv. to *paralý(ein)* (to) loosen (i.e., disable) on one side (*para-* PARA-[1] + *lýein* to loosen) + *-sis* -SIS]

paral′ysis ag′i·tans (aj′i tanz′), *Pathol.* See **Parkinson's disease.** [< NL: lit., shaking paralysis]

par·a·lyt·ic (par′ə lit′ik), *n.* **1.** a person affected with paralysis. —*adj.* **2.** affected with or subject to paralysis. **3.** pertaining to or of the nature of paralysis. [ME *paralitik* < L *paralytic(us)* < Gk *paralytikós,* equiv. to *paralý(ein)* (to) disable on one side (see PARALYSIS) + *-tikos* -TIC] —**par′a·lyt′i·cal·ly,** *adv.*

par·a·lyze (par′ə līz′), *v.t.,* **-lyzed, -lyz·ing. 1.** to affect with paralysis. **2.** to bring to a condition of helpless inactivity: *the strike paralyzed communications.* Also, *esp. Brit.,* **paralyse.** [back formation from PARALYSIS, modeled on *analyze*] —**par′a·lyz′ant,** *adj., n.* —**par′a·ly·za′tion,** *n.* —**par′a·lyz′er,** *n.* —**par′a·lyz′ing·ly,** *adv.* —**Syn. 2.** See **shock**[1].

par·a·mag·net (par′ə mag′nit), *n. Physics.* a body or substance having paramagnetic properties. [back formation from PARAMAGNETIC] —**par′a·mag′net·ism,** *n.*

par·a·mag·net·ic (par′ə mag net′ik), *adj. Physics.* noting or pertaining to a substance that, placed in a magnetic field, possesses magnetization in direct proportion to the field strength; noting or pertaining to a substance in which the magnetic moments of the atoms have random directions. Cf. **antiferromagnetic, diamagnetic, ferromagnetic.** [PARA-[1] + MAGNETIC]

Par·a·mar·i·bo (par′ə mar′ə bō′), *n.* a seaport in and the capital of Surinam, in NE South America. 135,000 (est. 1971).

Par·am·at·man (pur′ə mät′mən), *n. Hinduism.* absolute Atman. [< Skt: lit., beyond Atman]

par·a·mat·ta (par′ə mat′ə), *n.* a light, twilled dress fabric, having a silk or cotton warp and a woolen weft. Also, **parramatta.** [named after *Parramatta,* town in New South Wales]

par·a·me·ci·um (par′ə mē′shē əm, -sē əm), *n., pl.* **-ci·a** (-shē ə, -sē ə). any ciliated fresh-water protozoan of the genus *Paramecium,* having an oval body and a long, deep oral groove. [< NL < Gk *paramḗk(ēs)* oblong, oval; see -IUM]

par·a·med·ic (*n.* par′ə med′ik; *adj.* par′ə med′ik), *n.* **1.** *Mil.* a medic in the paratroops. **2.** a doctor who parachutes into remote areas to give medical care. —*adj.* **3.** of or pertaining to a paramedic or to paramedics. [PARA(CHUTE) + MEDIC[1]]

par·a·med·i·cal (par′ə med′i kəl), *adj.* related to the medical profession in a secondary or supplementary capacity. [PARA-[1] + MEDICAL]

par·a·ment (par′ə mənt), *n., pl.* **par·a·ments, par·a·men·ta** (par′ə men′tə). **1.** a decoration for a room, as a tapestry. **2.** an ecclesiastical vestment. [ME < LL *parāment(um)* an ornament, equiv. to *parā(re)* (to) adorn (L: prepare) + *-mentum* -MENT]

pa·ram·e·ter (pə ram′i tər), *n.* **1.** *Math.* **a.** a constant or variable term in a function that determines the specific form of the function but not its general nature, as *a* in $f(x) = ax$, where *a* determines only the slope of the line described by $f(x)$. **b.** one of the independent variables in a set of parametric equations. **2.** *Statistics.* a variable entering into the mathematical form of any distribution such that the possible values of the variable correspond to different distributions. [< NL *parametrum.* See PARA-[1], -METER] —**par·a·met·ric** (par′ə me′trik), **par′a·met′ri·cal,** *adj.*

par′amet′ric equa′tion, *Math.* one of two or more equations expressing the location of a point on a curve by determining each coordinate separately.

par·a·mil·i·tar·y (par′ə mil′i ter′ē), *adj.* noting or pertaining to an organization operating in substitution for or as a supplement to a regular military force: *a paramilitary police unit.* [PARA-[1] + MILITARY]

pa·ra·mi·ta (pä rum′i tə), *n. Buddhism.* any of the practices prescribed for one aspiring to nirvana. [< Skt *pāramitā* (adj.) transcendent, equiv. to *pāras* goal + *mitās* fixed]

par·am·ne·sia (par′am nē′zhə, -zhē ə, -zē ə), *n. Psychiatry.* a distortion of memory in which fact and fantasy are confused. Also called **pseudomemory.** [< NL; see PAR-, AMNESIA]

par·a·mo (par′ə mō′), *n., pl.* **-mos.** a high plateau region in the tropical areas of South America. [< Sp *páramo* barren plain]

par·a·morph (par′ə môrf′), *n. Mineral.* a pseudomorph formed by a change in crystal structure but not in chemical composition. [PARA-[1] + -MORPH] —**par′a·mor′phic, par′a·mor′phous,** *adj.*

par·a·mor·phism (par′ə môr′fiz əm), *n.* **1.** the process by which a paramorph is formed. **2.** the state of being a paramorph. [PARA-[1] + -MORPHISM]

par·a·mount (par′ə mount′), *adj.* **1.** chief in importance; supreme; preeminent: *a point of paramount significance.* **2.** above others in rank or authority; superior in power or jurisdiction. —*n.* **3.** an overlord; supreme ruler. [< AF *paramont* above, equiv. to *par* PER- + *a mont* < L *ad montem* to the mountain, hence, in OF: upward, above; see AD-, MOUNT[2]] —**par′a·mount′cy,** *n.* —**par′a·mount′ly,** *adv.*
—**Syn. 1.** See **dominant.** —**Ant. 1.** unimportant.

Par·a·mount (par′ə mount′), *n.* a city in SW California, near Los Angeles. 27,249 (1960).

par·a·mour (par′ə mo͝or′), *n.* **1.** an illicit lover, esp. of a married person, as a man's mistress. **2.** any lover. **3.** a beloved one. [ME, from the phrase *par amour* with love < OF]

Pa·ram·us (pə ram′əs), *n.* a city in NE New Jersey. 23,238 (1960).

Pa·ra·ná (par′ə nä′; *Port.* pä′rə nä′), *n.* **1.** a river in central South America, flowing from S Brazil along the SE boundary of Paraguay and through E Argentina into the Río de la Plata. 2050 mi. long. **2.** a city in E Argentina, on the Paraná River: the capital of Argentina 1852–61. 184,000 (est. 1965).

Pa·ra·na·guá (pä′rə nə gwä′), *n.* a seaport in S Brazil. 28,755 (1960).

par·a·na·sal (par′ə nā′zəl), *adj. Anat.* situated near the nasal cavities. [PARA-[1] + NASAL[1]]

par·a·neph·ros (par′ə nef′ros), *n., pl.* **-roi** (-roi). *Anat. Obs.* adrenal gland. [< NL < Gk *para-* PARA-[1] + *nephrós* kidney] —**par·a·neph·ric** (par′ə nef′rik), *adj.*

pa·rang (pä′räng), *n.* a large, heavy knife used as a tool or a weapon by the Malays. [< Malay]

par·a·ni·tro·phe·nol (par′ə nī′trō fē′nōl, -nôl, -nol), *n.* See under **nitrophenol** (def. 2).

par·a·noi·a (par′ə noi′ə), *n. Psychiatry.* mental disorder characterized by systematized delusions and the projection of personal conflicts, which are ascribed to the supposed hostility of others: the disorder often exists for years without any disturbance of consciousness. Also, **par·a·noe·a** (par′ə nē′ə). [< NL < Gk: madness. See PARA-, NOUS, -IA]

par·a·noi·ac (par′ə noi′ak), *adj.* **1.** of, like, or suffering from paranoia. —*n.* **2.** a person suffering from paranoia. Also, **par′a·noid′, par·a·noe·ac** (par′ə nē′ak). [PARANOI(A) + -AC]

par·a·nymph (par′ə nimf′), *n.* **1.** a groomsman or a bridesmaid. **2.** (in ancient Greece) **a.** a friend who accompanied the bridegroom when he went to bring home the bride. **b.** the bridesmaid who escorted the bride to the bridegroom. [< LL *paranymph(us)* < Gk *pará-nymphos* (common gender) groomsman, bridesmaid, lit., person beside the bride. See PARA-[1], NYMPH]

par·a·pa·re·sis (par′ə pə rē′sis, -par′i sis), *n. Pathol.* partial paralysis, esp. of the lower limbs. [< NL; see PARA-[1], PARESIS]

par·a·pet (par′ə pit, -pet′), *n.* **1.** *Fort.* **a.** a defensive wall or elevation, as of earth or stone, in a fortification. See diag. under **bastion. b.** an elevation raised above the main wall or rampart of a permanent fortification. **2.** any low protective wall or barrier at the edge of a balcony, roof, bridge, or the like. [< It *parapett(o).* See PARA-[2], PETTO] —**par′a·pet·ed,** *adj.* —**par′a·pet·less,** *adj.*

par·aph (par′əf), *n.* a flourish made after a signature, as in a document, originally as a precaution against forgery. [ME *paraf* < It *paraf(o)* or MF *paraphe* PARAGRAPH[2] (by syncope)]

par′a·phase am′plifier (par′ə fāz′), *Electronics.* an amplifier that produces a push-pull output from a single input. [PARA-[1] + PHASE]

par·a·phe·net·i·dine (par′ə fə net′i dēn′, -din), *n. Chem.* See under **phenetidine.**

par·a·pher·nal·ia (par′ə fər nāl′yə, -fə nāl′-), *n.* **1.** (*construed as pl.*) personal belongings. **2.** (*construed as pl.*) *Law.* the personal articles, apart from dower, reserved by law to a married woman. **3.** (*sometimes construed as sing.*) equipment, apparatus, or furnishing: *a golfer's paraphernalia.* [< ML *paraphernālia* (*bona*) a bride's goods, beyond her dowry, equiv. to LL *parapherna*) a bride's property (< Gk *parápherna,* equiv. to *para-* PARA-[1] + *phern(ḗ)* dowry, deriv. of *phérein* to carry) + L *-ālia,* neut. pl. (n.) of *-ālis* -AL[1]] —**par′a·pher·na′li·an, par·a·pher·nal** (par′ə fûr′nᵊl), *adj.*
—**Syn. 1.** effects. **3.** appointments, appurtenances, accouterments, trappings.

par·a·phrase (par′ə frāz′), *n., v.,* **-phrased, -phras·ing.** —*n.* **1.** a restatement of a text or passage giving the meaning in another form, as for clearness; rewording. **2.** the act or process of restating or rewording —*v.t.* **3.** to render the meaning of in a paraphrase: *to paraphrase a technical paper for lay readers.* —*v.i.* **4.** to make a paraphrase or paraphrases. [< MF < L *paraphrasis* < Gk. See PARA-[1], PHRASE] —**par′a·phras′a·ble,** *adj.* —**par′a·phras′er,** *n.*
—**Syn. 1.** See **translation. 3.** summarize; explain.

pa·raph·ra·sis (pə raf′rə sis), *n., pl.* **-ses** (-sēz′). paraphrase. [< L]

par·a·phrast (par′ə frast′), *n.* a person who paraphrases. [< LL *paraphrast(ēs)* < Gk, deriv. of *paraphrázein* to retell in other words, equiv. to *para-* PARA-[1] + *phrázein* to tell, declare]

par·a·phras·tic (par′ə fras′tik), *adj.* having the nature of a paraphrase. [< ML *paraphrastic(us)* < Gk *paraphrastikós.* See PARAPHRAST, -IC] —**par′a·phras′ti·cal·ly,** *adv.*

par·a·phyl·li·um (par′ə fil′ē əm), *n., pl.* **-phyl·li·a** (-fil′ē ə). *Bot.* one of the branched, filamentous or stipuliform outgrowths of the stem, between the leaves of certain mosses. [< NL; see PARA-[1], PHYLL-, -IUM]

pa·raph·y·sis (pə raf′i sis), *n., pl.* **-ses** (-sēz′). *Bot.* one of the sterile, usually filamentous, outgrowths often occurring among the reproductive organs in many cryptogamous plants. [< NL < Gk: lit., a growing beside, by-growth, equiv. to *para-* PARA-[1] + *phýsis* growth, nature; see PHYSIC] —**pa·raph′y·sate,** *adj.*

par·a·ple·gi·a (par′ə plē′jē ə, -jə), *n. Pathol.* paralysis of both lower limbs due to spinal disease or injury. [< NL < Gk *paraplēgía.* See PARA-[1], -PLEGIA] —**par·a·ple·gic** (par′ə plē′jik, -plej′ik), *adj., n.*

par·a·po·di·um (par′ə pō′dē əm), *n., pl.* **-di·a** (-dē ə). *Zool.* one of the unjointed lateral locomotor processes or series of rudimentary limbs of many worms, as annelids. [PARA-[1] + -PODIUM] —**par′a·po′di·al,** *adj.*

par·a·pro·fes·sion·al (par′ə prə fesh′ə nᵊl), *n.* **1.** a person trained to assist a professional, as a doctor's assistant or a part-time teaching assistant. —*adj.* **2.** of or pertaining to paraprofessionals.

par·a·psy·chol·o·gy (par′ə sī kol′ə jē), *n.* the branch of psychology that deals with the investigation of psychic phenomena, as clairvoyance, extrasensory perception, telepathy, and the like. [PARA-[1] + PSYCHOLOGY] —**par′a·psy′cho·log′i·cal,** *adj.*

par·a·quet (par′ə ket′), *n.* parakeet.

par·a·res·cue (par′ə res′kyo͞o), *n.* a rescue, as of persons caught in a disaster, accomplished by parachutists. [PARA(CHUTE) + RESCUE]

Pará′ rhat′any. See under **rhatany** (def. 1).

Pará′ rub′ber, India rubber obtained from the euphorbiaceous tree *Hevea brasiliensis* and other species of the same genus of tropical South America.

par·a·sail (par′ə sāl′), *n.* **1.** a kind of parachute kept open to provide lift, used in parasailing. —*v.i.* **2.** to engage in parasailing. [PARA(CHUTE) + SAIL]

par·a·sail·ing (par′ə sā′ling), *n.* the sport of soaring while attached to a parasail that is towed by a fast-moving vehicle, as a motorboat or car, from which one may release oneself to float freely. [PARASAIL + -ING[1]]

par·a·sang (par′ə sang′), *n.* a Persian unit of distance, of varying length, anciently about 3⅖ miles. [< L *parasang(a)* < Gk *parasángēs* < OPers; akin to Pers *farsang*]

par·a·scen·i·um (par′ə sē′nē əm), *n., pl.* **-ni·a** (-nē ə). either of two wings flanking and extending forward from the skene of an ancient Greek theater. [< NL < Gk *paraskḗnion* space at sides of stage. See PARA-[1], SCENE]

par·a·se·le·ne (par′ə si lē′nē), *n., pl.* **-nae** (-nē). *Meteorol.* a bright moonlike spot on a lunar halo; a mock moon. Cf. **parhelion.** [< NL, equiv. to *para-* PARA-[1] + Gk *selḗnē* the moon] —**par·a·se·le·nic** (par′ə si lē′nik, -len′ik), *adj.*

Par·a·shah (pär′ə shä′), *n., pl.* **Par·a·shoth** (pär ä shōt′), **Par·a·shi·oth** (pär ä shē ōt′). *Judaism.* **1.** a portion of the Torah chanted or read each week in the synagogue on the Sabbath. **2.** a selection from such a portion, chanted or read in the synagogue on Mondays, Thursdays, and holy days. [< Heb: division]

Par·a·shu·ra·ma (par′ə sho͝o rä′mə), *n. Hindu Myth.* a Rama and avatar of Vishnu who rid the earth of Kshatriyas.

par·a·site (par′ə sīt′), *n.* **1.** an animal or plant that lives on or in an organism of another species, known as the host, from the body of which it obtains nutriment. **2.** a person who receives support, advantage, or the like, from another or others without giving any useful or proper return, esp. one who lives on the hospitality of others. **3.** (in ancient Greece) a person who received free meals in return for his amusing or impudent conversation. [< L *parasīt(us)* < Gk *parásītos* one who eats at another's table, orig. adj.: feeding beside, equiv. to *para-* PARA-[1] + *sīt(os)* grain, food + *-os* adj. suffix]
—**Syn. 2.** sycophant, toady, leech, flatterer, hanger-on, freeloader.

par′asite drag′, *Aeron.* the component of drag caused by skin friction and the shape of the surfaces not contributing to lift.

par·a·sit·ic (par′ə sit′ik), *adj.* **1.** of, pertaining to, or characteristic of parasites. **2.** (of diseases) due to parasites. Also, **par′a·sit′i·cal.** [< L *parasīitic(us)* < Gk *parasitikós.* See PARASITE, -IC] —**par′a·sit′i·cal·ly,** *adv.* —**par′a·sit′i·cal·ness,** *n.*

par·a·sit·i·cide (par′ə sit′i sīd′), *adj.* **1.** destructive to plant or animal parasites. —*n.* **2.** an agent or preparation that destroys parasites. [PARASITE + -I- + -CIDE] —**par′a·sit′i·cid′al,** *adj.*

par·a·sit·ism (par′ə sī′tiz əm), *n.* **1.** a parasitic mode of life or existence. **2.** *Zool., Bot.* a relation between organisms in which one lives as a parasite on another. **3.** *Pathol.* a diseased condition due to parasites. [PARASITE + -ISM]

par·a·si·tize (par′ə si tīz′, -sī-), *v.t.,* **-tized, -tiz·ing.** to live on (a host) as a parasite. Also, *esp. Brit.,* **par′a·si·tise′.** [PARASITE + -IZE]

par·a·sit·ol·o·gy (par′ə sī tol′ə jē, -si-), *n.* the branch of biology dealing with parasites and the effects of parasitism. [PARASITE + -O- + -LOGY] —**par·a·si·to·log·i·cal** (par′ə sīt′ᵊloj′i kəl), *adj.* —**par′a·si·tol′o·gist,** *n.*

par·a·si·to·sis (par′ə sī tō′sis, -si-), *n. Pathol.* any disease or condition caused by parasites. [PARASITE + -OSIS]

par·a·sol (par′ə sôl′, -sol′), *n.* a woman's small or light sun umbrella; sunshade. [< F, MF < It *parasole.* See PARA-[2], SOL] —**par′a·soled′,** *adj.*

par′asol ant′. See **leaf-cutting ant.**

pa·ras·ti·chy (pə ras′tə kē), *n., pl.* **-chies.** *Bot.* one of a number of secondary spirals or oblique ranks seen to wind around the stem or axis to the right and left in a spiral arrangement of leaves, scales, etc., where the internodes are short and the members closely crowded, as in the houseleek and the pine cone. [PARA-[1] + STICH + -Y[3]]

par·a·sym·pa·thet·ic (par′ə sim′pə thet′ik), *Anat., Physiol.* —*adj.* **1.** pertaining to that part of the autonomic system consisting of nerves and ganglia that arise from the cranial and sacral regions and function in opposition to the sympathetic system, as in inhibiting heart beat, contracting the pupil of the eye, etc. —*n.* **2.** a nerve of the parasympathetic system. [PARA-[1] + SYMPATHETIC]

par·a·syn·ap·sis (par′ə si nap′sis), *n. Biol.* the conjugation of chromosomes side by side; synapsis. [PARA-[1] + SYNAPSIS] —**par′a·syn·ap′tic,** *adj.* —**par′a·syn·ap′tist,** *n.*

par·a·syn·the·sis (par′ə sin′thi sis), *n. Gram.* the formation of a word by the addition of an affix to a phrase or compound, as of *great-hearted,* which is *great heart* plus *-ed.* [PARA-[1] + SYNTHESIS] —**par·a·syn·thet·ic** (par′ə sin thet′ik), *adj.*

par·a·tax·ic (par′ə tak′sik), *adj. Psychol.* **1.** of or characterized by emotional maladjustment. **2.** of or related to a lack of harmony between attitudes, ideas, etc., and other aspects of an individual's personality. [PARATAX(IS) + -IC]

par·a·tax·is (par′ə tak′sis), *n.* the placing together of sentences, clauses, or phrases without a conjunctive word, as *Hurry up, it is getting late! I came—I saw—I conquered.* [< NL < Gk *paràtaxis* an arranging in order for battle. See PARA-[1], -TAXIS] —**par′a·tac·tic** (par′ə tak′tik), **par′a·tac′ti·cal,** *adj.* —**par′a·tac′ti·cal·ly,** *adv.*

par·a·thi·on (par′ə thī′on), *n. Chem.* a deep-brown to yellow, poisonous liquid, $(C_2H_5O)_2P(S)OC_6H_4NO_2$, used as an insecticide. [PARA-[1] + THI- + ON(E)]

Par·a·thor·mone (par′ə thôr′mōn), *n. Pharm., Trademark.* See **parathyroid extract.**

par·a·thy·roid (par′ə thī′roid), *Anat.* —*adj.* **1.** situated near the thyroid gland. —*n.* **2.** See **parathyroid gland.** [PARA-[1] + THYROID]

par·a·thy·roid·ec·to·mize (par′ə thī′roi dek′tə mīz′), *v.t.*, **-mized, -miz·ing.** *Surg.* to excise the parathyroid glands. [PARATHYROIDECTOM(Y) + -IZE]

par·a·thy·roid·ec·to·my (par′ə thī′roi dek′tə mē), *n., pl.* **-mies.** *Surg.* the excision of a parathyroid gland. [PARATHYROID + -ECTOMY]

par′athy′roid ex′tract, *Pharm.* an aqueous preparation obtained from the parathyroid gland of cattle, used in medicine chiefly in cases of parathyroid deficiency and in veterinary medicine in the treatment of tetanic convulsions.

parathy′roid gland′, *Anat.* any of several small glands or oval masses of epitheloid cells usually lying near or embedded in the thyroid gland, the internal secretions of which control the calcium content of the blood.

par·a·to·lu·i·dine (par′ə tə lo͞o′i dēn′, -din), *n. Chem.* a white, flaky, lustrous, very slightly water-soluble solid, $CH_3C_6H_4NH_2$, the para isomer of toluidine, used in the manufacture of dyes, in organic synthesis, and as a reagent in tests for nitrite, lignin, and phloroglucinol.

par·a·troop (par′ə tro͞op′), *adj.* **1.** of or pertaining to a paratrooper or a parachute unit: *paratroop boots.* —*n.* **2.** paratrooper. [back formation from PARATROOPER]

par·a·troop·er (par′ə tro͞o′pər), *n. Mil.* a member of an army infantry unit trained to attack or land in combat areas by parachuting from airplanes. [PARA(CHUTE) + TROOPER]

par·a·troph·ic (par′ə trof′ik), *adj.* obtaining nourishment from living organic matter; parasitic. [PARA-[1] + -TROPHIC]

par·a·tu·ber·cu·lin (par′ə to͞o bûr′kyə lin, -tyo͞o-), *n. Vet. Med.* johnin. [PARA-[1] + TUBERCULIN]

par·a·tu·ber·cu·lo·sis (par′ə to͞o bûr′kyə lō′sis, -tyo͞o-), *n. Vet. Pathol.* See **Johne's disease.** [< NL; see PARA-[1], TUBERCULOSIS] —**par·a·tu·ber·cu·lous** (par′ə to͞o bûr′kyə ləs, -tyo͞o-), *adj.*

par·a·ty·phoid (par′ə tī′foid), *Pathol.* —*n.* **1.** Also called **paraty′phoid fe′ver.** an infectious disease, similar in some of its symptoms to typhoid but usually milder, caused by the paratyphoid bacillus. —*adj.* **2.** of or pertaining to paratyphoid. **3.** resembling typhoid. [PARA-[1] + TYPHOID]

paraty′phoid bacil′lus, any of several bacteria of the genus *Salmonella,* as *S. paratyphi* and *S. schottmuelleri,* causing paratyphoid.

par·a·vail (par′ə vāl′, par′ə vāl′), *adj. Old Eng. Law.* being below or inferior to all others; specifically, being a tenant of one who holds land of another who himself is a tenant: *a tenant paravail.* [< OF *par aval* down (of direction, position), equiv. to *par* through, by + *aval, a val* down < L *ad vallem,* lit., to the valley]

par a·vance (PA RA väns′), *French.* in advance; in expectation.

par·a·vane (par′ə vān′), *n.* a device consisting of a pair of torpedo-shaped vanes towed at the bow of a vessel, usually of a minesweeper, at the ends of cables that cut the cable of a moored mine, causing the mine to rise to the surface where it can be destroyed by gunfire. [PARA-[1] + VANE]

par·a·vent (par′ə vent′), *n.* a screen against a draft or the wind. [< F: lit., against wind, equiv. to *para-* PARA-[2] + *vent* WIND[1]]

pa·ra·vid·ya (pär′ə vid′yä), *n. Hinduism.* transcendental knowledge. Cf. **aparavidya.** [< Skt *pāravidyā,* equiv. to *pāra* bringing across + *vidyā* knowledge]

par a·vion (PA RA vyôN′), *French.* by plane (used esp. as a designation on matter to be sent by air mail).

par·ax·i·al (par ak′sē əl), *adj. Optics.* making a small angle with and lying close to the axis of an optical system: *paraxial ray.* [PAR-[1] + AXIAL]

par·boil (pär′boil′), *v.t.* to boil partially, or for a short time; precook. [late ME *parboyle(n)* (to) boil partly, earlier, boil fully < MF *parboill(ir)* < LL *perbullīre* to boil through and through (see PER-, BOIL); change of meaning by confusion of *par-* with *part*]

par·buck·le (pär′buk′əl), *n., v.,* **-led, -ling.** —*n.* **1.** a kind of tackle for raising or lowering a cask or similar object along an inclined plane or a vertical surface, consisting of a rope looped over a post or the like, with its two ends passing around the object to be moved. **2.** a kind of double sling made with a rope, as around a cask to be raised or lowered. —*v.t.* **3.** to raise, lower, or move with a parbuckle. [earlier *parbunkel* < ?]

Par·ca (pär′kə), *n.* **1.** an ancient Roman goddess of childbirth and destiny. Cf. **Parcae. 2.** any one of the Parcae.

Par·cae (pär′sē), *n. pl., sing.* **-ca** (-kə). the three Fates of ancient Rome, developed out of the goddess Parca by identification with the Moerae of Greek mythology.

par·cel (pär′səl), *n., v.,* **-celed, -cel·ing** or (*esp. Brit.*) **-celled, -cel·ling,** *adv.* —*n.* **1.** an object, article, container or quantity of something wrapped or packed up; package; bundle: *a parcel improperly tied for mailing.* **2.** a quantity or unit of something, as of a commodity for sale; a lot. **3.** any group or assemblage of persons or things. **4.** something that is or is treated as being distinct or separate from other such things: *a parcel of land for sale.* **5.** a part, portion, or fragment. —*v.t.* **6.** to divide into or distribute in parcels or portions (usually fol. by *out*). **7.** to make into a parcel or wrap as a parcel. **8.** *Naut.* to cover or wrap (a rope) with strips of canvas. —*adv.* **9.** in part; partially. [ME < MF *parcelle* < LL **particella* for L *particula;* see PARTICLE] —**Syn. 1.** See **package. 3.** batch, collection. **6.** mete, apportion, deal, allot.

par′cel gild′ing, *Furniture.* the gilding of isolated areas or ornaments of a piece. —**par′cel-gild′er,** *n.* —**par′cel-gilt′,** *adj.*

par·cel·ing (pär′sə liṅg), *n.* **1.** the act of separating or dividing into parts and distributing; allotting or apportioning. **2.** *Naut.* odd strips of canvas for wrapping around a rope. [PARCEL + -ING[1]]

par′cel post′, 1. a branch of a postal service charged with conveying parcels. **2.** the service this branch renders. **3.** parcels handled by this branch.

par·ce·nar·y (pär′sə ner′ē), *n. Law.* coheirship; the undivided holding of land by two or more coheirs. [< AF *parcenarie,* OF *parconerie* coheirship, equiv. to *parçon* (see PARCENER) + *-erie* -ERY]

par·ce·ner (pär′sə nər), *n. Law.* a joint heir; coheir. [ME < AF: coheir, equiv. to *parcen* (OF *parçon* < VL **partiōn-* for L *partitiōn-* PARTITION) + *-er* -ER[2]]

parch (pärch), *v.t.* **1.** to make excessively or completely dry, as heat, sun, and wind do. **2.** to make dry, hot, or thirsty: *Walking in the sun parched his throat.* **3.** to dry (peas, beans, grain, etc.) by exposure to heat without burning; to toast or roast slightly: *A staple of the Indian diet was parched corn.* **4.** to dry or shrivel from cold. —*v.i.* **5.** to suffer from heat or thirst, esp. to be thirsty or in need of water. **6.** to become parched; undergo drying by heat. **7.** to dry (usually fol. by *up*). [ME *perche(n)* < ?] —**parch′a·ble,** *adj.* —**parch′ed·ly,** *adv.* —**parch′ed·ness,** *n.* —**parch′ing·ly,** *adv.*

par·chee·si (pär chē′zē), *n.* **1.** a game similar to backgammon, played in India, in which cones and cowrie shells are used instead of counters and dice. **2.** a simplified form of this game played elsewhere in which each player attempts to be the first to advance all his pieces around a board, making moves in accordance with the throw of dice. Also, **pachisi, parche′si, par·chi′si.** [< Hindi, alter. of *pachisi,* deriv. of *pachis* twenty-five (the highest throw in the game)]

parch·ment (pärch′mənt), *n.* **1.** the skin of sheep, goats, etc., prepared for use as a material on which to write. **2.** a manuscript or document on such material. **3.** a paper resembling this material. **4.** a diploma. [late ME *parchment* < MF, OF *parche* (< L *Parthica* (*pellis*) Parthian leather); see -MENT (cf. ML *percamentum,* D *perkament*); r. ME *parchemin* < OF (-*min* < ML (*perga*)*mīnum,* var. of *pergamēnum* for LL *Pergamēna charta* paper of PERGAMUM)] —**parch′ment-like′, parch′ment·y,** *adj.*

parch·ment·ise (pärch′mən tīz′), *v.t.,* **-ised, -is·ing.** *Chiefly Brit.* parchmentize.

parch·ment·ize (pärch′mən tīz′), *v.t.,* **-ized, -iz·ing.** to change (paper or the like) into a parchmentlike substance. [PARCHMENT + -IZE]

parch′ment pa′per, a waterproof and grease-resistant paper produced by treating a paper with concentrated sulfuric acid.

parch′ment worm′, any of several polychaete worms of the genus *Chaetopterus* that secrete and live in a U-shaped, parchmentlike tube.

par·close (pär′klōz′), *n.* (in a church) a screen dividing one area from another, as a chapel from an aisle. Also, **perclose.** [ME < MF, n. use of fem. of *parclos,* ptp. of *parclore* to enclose fully. See PER-, CLOSE]

pard[1] (pärd), *n. Archaic.* a leopard or panther. [ME *parde,* OE *pardus* < L < Gk *párdos* (masc.), deriv. of *párdalis* (fem.)] —**pard·ine** (pär′dīn, -din), *adj.*

pard[2] (pärd), *n. Slang.* partner; companion. [by alter. and shortening of PARTNER]

par·dah (pûr′də), *n.* purdah.

par·di (pär dē′), *adv., interj. Archaic.* verily; indeed. Also, **par·die′, pardy, perdie.** [late ME *pardie,* ME *parde* < OF *par De* < L *per Deum* by God]

pard·ner (pärd′nər), *n. U.S. Dial.* **1.** (in direct address) friend. **2.** partner. [alter. of PARTNER]

par·don (pär′dᵊn), *n.* **1.** kind indulgence, as in forgiveness of an offense or discourtesy, or in tolerance of a distraction or inconvenience: *I beg your pardon, but which way is Spruce Street?* **2.** *Law.* **a.** a release from the penalty of an offense; a remission of penalty, as by an executive. **b.** the deed or warrant by which such remission is declared. **3.** forgiveness of an offense or offender. **4.** *Obs.* a papal indulgence. —*v.t.* **5.** to remit the penalty of (an offense): *The governor will not pardon your crime.* **6.** to release (a person) from liability for an offense. **7.** to make courteous allowance for or to excuse: *Pardon me, madam.* [ME < OF: remission, indulgence, back formation from *pardoner* < ML *perdōnāre* to remit, overlook, equiv. to L *per-* FOR- + *dōnāre* to give; see DONATE. ML v. perh. a trans. of Gmc] —**par′don·a·ble,** *adj.* —**par′don·a·ble·ness,** *n.* —**par′don·a·bly,** *adv.* —**par′don·less,** *adj.*
—**Syn. 3.** absolution, remission, amnesty. **5.** forgive, absolve, condone, overlook. **6.** acquit, clear. See **excuse.** —**Ant. 7.** censure, blame.

par·don·er (pär′dᵊnər), *n.* **1.** a person who pardons. **2.** *Obs.* an ecclesiastical official charged with the granting of indulgences. [ME; see PARDON, -ER[1]]

par·dy (pär dē′), *adv., interj. Archaic.* pardi.

pare (pâr), *v.t.,* **pared, par·ing. 1.** to cut off the outer coating, layer, or part of: *to pare potatoes.* **2.** to remove (an outer coating, layer, or part) by cutting (often fol. by *off* or *away*). **3.** to reduce or remove by or as by cutting; diminish or decrease gradually: *to pare down one's expenses.* [ME *pare(n)* < MF *par(er)* (to) make ready, trim < L *parāre* to prepare] —**pare′a·ble,** *adj.*
—**Syn. 1.** See **peel**[1]. **3.** clip, shave, lessen. —**Ant. 3.** increase.

Pa·ré (PA RĀ′), *n.* **Am·broise** (äN BRWAZ′), 1510–90, French surgeon.

pa·re·cious (pə rē′shəs), *adj. Bot.* paroicous. —**pa·re′cious·ly,** *adv.* —**pa·re′cious·ness, pa·re′cism, pa·re′cy,** *n.*

pa·reg·me·non (pə reg′mə non′), *n. Rhet.* the juxtaposition of words that have a common derivation, as in "sense and sensibility." [< Gk *parēgménon* derived, neut. of perf. pass. ptp. of *parágein* to bring side by side, derive. See PAR-, PARAGON]

par·e·gor·ic (par′ə gôr′ik, -gor′-), *Pharm.* —*n.* **1.** a soothing medicine; anodyne. **2.** a camphorated tincture of opium, used chiefly to check diarrhea in children. —*adj.* **3.** assuaging pain; soothing. [< LL *parēgoric(us)* < Gk *parēgorikós* soothing, equiv. to *parēgor(os)* pertaining to consolatory speech (see PARA-[1], AGORA) + *-ikos* -IC]

pa·rei·ra (pə râr′ə), *n.* the root of a South American vine, *Chondodendron tomentosum,* used as a source of curare, a diuretic, etc. [short for PAREIRA BRAVA]

parei′ra bra′va (brä′və, brā′-), pareira. [< Pg *parreira brava,* lit., wild vine]

paren., parenthesis.

pa·ren·chy·ma (pə reṅg′kə mə), *n.* **1.** *Bot.* the fundamental tissue of plants, composed of thin-walled cells. **2.** *Anat., Zool.* the specific tissue of an animal organ as distinguished from its connective or supporting tissue. **3.** *Zool.* a type of connective tissue in certain lower animals, consisting of a spongy mass of cells. **4.** *Pathol.* the functional tissue of a morbid growth. [< NL < Gk: lit., something poured in beside, equiv. to *par-* PAR- + *énchyma* infusion; see EN-[2], CHYME] —**par·en·chym·a·tous** (par′eṅg kim′ə təs), *adj.*

parens., parentheses.

par·ent (pâr′ənt, par′-), *n.* **1.** a father or a mother. **2.** an ancestor, precursor, or progenitor. **3.** a source, origin, or cause. **4.** a protector or guardian. **5.** *Biol.* any organism that produces or generates another. [late ME < L *parent-* (s. of *parēns*), n. use of prp. of *parere* to bring forth, breed; in obs. sense, kinsman < MF] —**par′ent·less,** *adj.* —**par′ent·like′,** *adj.*

par·ent·age (pâr′ən tij, par′-), *n.* **1.** derivation or descent from parents or ancestors; birth, origin, or lineage: *a man of distinguished parentage.* **2.** the state or relation of a parent. [< MF; see PARENT, -AGE]
—**Syn. 1.** descent, ancestry, extraction, stock.

pa·ren·tal (pə ren′tᵊl), *adj.* **1.** of or pertaining to a parent: *the parental relation.* **2.** proper to or characteristic of a parent: *parental feelings.* **3.** having the relation of a parent. **4.** *Genetics.* pertaining to the sequence of generations preceding the filial generation, each generation being designated by a P followed by a subscript number indicating its place in the sequence. [< L *parentāl(is)* of, belonging to parents, equiv. to *parent-* PARENT + *-ālis* -AL[1]] —**pa·ren′tal·ly,** *adv.*

paren′tal home′, a school for problem children. Also called **paren′tal school′.**

Par·en·ta·li·a (pâr′ən tā′lē ə, -tāl′yə), *n.* (*sometimes construed as pl.*) (in ancient Rome) an annual festival in honor of the Manes.

par′ent com′pany, a corporation or other business enterprise that owns controlling interests in one or more subsidiary companies (distinguished from *holding company*).

par′ent com′pound, *Chem.* a compound from which derivatives may be obtained.

par·en·ter·al (pa ren′tər əl), *adj. Anat., Med., Physiol.* **1.** taken into the body in a manner other than through the digestive canal. **2.** not within the intestine; not intestinal. [PAR- + ENTER- + -AL[1]] —**par·en′ter·al·ly,** *adv.*

pa·ren·the·sis (pə ren′thi sis), *n., pl.* **-ses** (-sēz′). **1.** either or both of a pair of signs () used in writing to mark off an interjected explanatory or qualifying remark, to indicate separate groupings of symbols in mathematics and symbolic logic, etc. **2.** *Gram.* a qualifying, explanatory, or appositive word, phrase, clause, sentence, or other sequence which interrupts a syntactic construction without otherwise affecting it, having often a characteristic intonation and indicated in writing by commas, parentheses, or dashes, as in *William Smith—you must know him—is coming tonight.* **3.** an interval. [< LL < Gk. See PAR-, EN-[2], THESIS]

pa·ren·the·sise (pə ren′thi sīz′), *v.t.,* **-sised, -sis·ing.** *Chiefly Brit.* parenthesize.

pa·ren·the·size (pə ren′thi sīz′), *v.t.,* **-sized, -siz·ing. 1.** to insert (a word, phrase, etc.) as a parenthesis. **2.** to put between marks of parenthesis: *to parenthesize the pronunciation of a word.* **3.** to interlard with parenthetic remarks, as a speech. [PARENTHES(IS) + -IZE]

par·en·thet·ic (par′ən thet′ik), *adj.* **1.** of, pertaining to, noting, or of the nature of a parenthesis: *several unnecessary parenthetic remarks.* **2.** characterized by the use of parentheses. Also, **par′en·thet′i·cal.** [back formation from *parenthetical* < Gk *parénthet(os)* putting in beside (verbid of *parentithénai,* equiv. to *par-* PAR- + *-en* -EN[2] + *tithénai* to put) + -IC + -AL[1]] —**par·en·thet·i·cal·i·ty** (par′ən thet′i kal′i tē), **par′en·thet′i·cal·ness,** *n.* —**par′en·thet′i·cal·ly,** *adv.*

par·ent·hood (pâr′ənt ho͝od′, par′-), *n.* the state, position, or relation of a parent. [PARENT + -HOOD]

pa·ren·ti·cide (pə ren′ti sīd′), *n.* **1.** a person who kills one or both of his or her parents. **2.** the act of killing one's parent or parents. [PARENT + -I- + -CIDE]

par·ent-in-law (pâr′ənt in lô′, par′-), *n., pl.* **par·ents-in-law.** the father or mother of one's wife or husband.

Par′ent-Teach′er Asso′ciation (pâr′ənt tē′chər, par′-), an organization of teachers and the parents of their students, as within a public school, to promote mutual understanding and to increase the effectiveness of the educational program. *Abbr.:* P.T.A.

pa·re·sis (pə rē′sis, par′i sis), *n. Pathol.* **1.** partial motor paralysis. **2.** See **general paralysis.** [< NL < Gk *páresis* paralysis, a letting go, equiv. to *pare-* (var. s. of *pariénai* to let go; see PAR-) + *-sis* -SIS]

par·es·the·sia (par′is thē′zhə, -zhē ə, -zē ə), *n. Pathol.* an abnormal sensation, as prickling, itching, etc. Also, **paraesthesia.** [< NL; see PAR-, ESTHESIA] —**par·es·thet·ic** (par′is thet′ik), *adj.*

pa·ret·ic (pə ret′ik, pə rē′tik), *Pathol.* —*n.* **1.** a person who has general paresis. —*adj.* **2.** pertaining to or affected with paresis. [< NL *paretic(us)* < Gk *páret(os)* relaxed, palsied (verbid of *pariénai*) + *-ikos* -IC] —**pa·ret′i·cal·ly,** *adv.*

Pa·re·to (pä RE′tô), *n.* **Vil·fre·do** (vēl fRe′dô), 1848–1923, Italian sociologist and economist in Switzerland.

pa·ret·ta (pə ret′ə), *n. Masonry.* roughcast having a pebbly surface. [?]

pa·re·u (pä′rä o͞o′), *n.* lava-lava. [< Tahitian]

pa·re·ve (pär′ə və), *adj. Judaism.* having no meat or milk in any form as an ingredient and being permissible for use with both meat and dairy meals as stated in the dietary laws: *a pareve bread; pareve soup.* Also, **parve.** [< Yiddish *parev*]

par ex·cel·lence (PA REK sə läNs′; *Eng.* pär ek′sə läns′), *French.* being an example of excellence; superior; preeminent: *a chef* par excellence.

par ex·em·ple (PAR eg zäN′plə), *French.* **1.** for example. **2.** (used as an expression of indignation or surprise): well! indeed!

par·fait (pär fā′), *n.* **1.** a dessert of ice cream and fruit or ice cream and syrup in alternate layers, often topped with whipped cream and served in a tall dessert glass. **2.** a rich frozen dessert of whipped cream and egg, variously flavored. [< F: lit., perfect < L *perfect(us).* See PERFECT]

par·fleche (pär′flesh, pär flesh′), *n.* **1.** a rawhide which has been dried after having been soaked in a solution of lye and water to remove the hair. **2.** an article or object, as a case, pouch, etc., made of such rawhide. [< CanF *parflèche,* equiv. to F *par(er)* (to) parry (see PARA-[2]) + *flèche* arrow]

par·gas·ite (pär′gə sīt′), *n. Mineral.* a green or blue-green variety of hornblende. [named after *Pargas,* town in Finland; see -ITE[1]]

par·get (pär′jit), *n., v.,* **-get·ed, -get·ing** or (*esp. Brit.*) **-get·ted, -get·ting.** —*n.* **1.** any of various plasters or roughcasts for covering walls or other surfaces, esp. a mortar of lime, hair, and cow dung for lining chimney flues. **2.** gypsum. **3.** pargeting (defs. 2, 3). —*v.t.* **4.** to cover or decorate with parget or pargeting. [ME < MF *pargeter,* equiv. to *par-* PER- + *geter,* sp. var. of *jeter* JET[1]]

par·get·ing (pär′ji ting), *n.* **1.** the act of one who pargets. **2.** ornamental or fine plasterwork, esp. exterior plasterwork bearing designs in low relief. **3.** a lining of mortar or plaster for a chimney flue or the like. Also, *esp. Brit.,* **par′get·ting; parget** (for defs. 2, 3). [ME; see PARGET, -ING[1]]

parg·ing (pär′jing), *n.* a thin coat of plaster or mortar for giving a relatively smooth surface to rough masonry or for sealing it against moisture. [*parge* (by shortening from PARGET) + -ING[1]]

par·he·li·a·cal (pär′hi lī′ə kəl), *adj.* of, pertaining to, or constituting a parhelion or parhelia. Also, **par·he·lic** (pär hē′lik, -hel′ik). [PARHELI(ON) + -AC + -AL[1]]

parhe′lic cir′cle, *Meteorol.* a white, horizontal band passing through the sun, either incomplete or extending around the horizon, produced by the reflection of the sun's rays from the vertical faces of ice prisms in the atmosphere. Also called **par′heli′acal ring′.**

par·he·li·on (pär hē′lē ən), *n., pl.* **-li·a** (-lē ə). *Meteorol.* a bright circular spot on a solar halo; a mock sun: usually one of two or more such spots seen on opposite sides of the sun, and often accompanied by additional luminous arcs and bands. Also called **sundog.** [etym. alter. of L *parēlion* < Gk, n. use of neut. of *parēlios* beside the sun. See PAR-, HELIO-]

pari-, a learned borrowing from Latin meaning "equal," used in the formation of compound words: *paripinnate.* [comb. form repr. L *pari-* (s. of *pār*). See PAR]

Par·i·a (pâr′ē ə), *n. Class. Myth.* a nymph, the beloved of Minos, who was the mother of Eurymedon, Nephalion, Chryses, and Philolaus.

pa·ri·ah (pə rī′ə, par′ē ə, pär′-), *n.* **1.** an outcast. **2.** any person or animal generally despised. **3.** (*cap.*) a member of a low caste in southern India. [< Tamil *paraiyar,* pl. of *paraiyan,* lit., drummer (from a hereditary duty of the caste), deriv. of *parai* a festival drum] —**pa·ri′ah·dom,** *n.* —**pa·ri′ah·ism,** *n.*

Par·i·an (pâr′ē ən, par′-), *adj.* **1.** of or pertaining to Paros, noted for its white marble. **2.** noting or pertaining to a fine, unglazed porcelain resembling this marble. **3.** of, pertaining to, or resembling a native or inhabitant of Paros. —*n.* **4.** a native or inhabitant of Paros. **5.** See **Parian ware.** [< L *Pari(us)* of PAROS + -AN]

Par′ian ware′, an English and American hard-paste porcelain ware introduced c1850, having a white, hard surface and used mainly for biscuit figures.

Pa·ri·cu·tín (pä rē ko͞o tēn′), *n.* a volcano in W central Mexico: the most recently formed volcano on earth; first eruption 1943; now dormant. 8200 ft.

par·i·es (pâr′ē ēz′), *n., pl.* **pa·ri·e·tes** (pə rī′i tēz′). Usually, **parietes.** *Biol.* a wall, as of a hollow organ; an investing part. [< NL, special use of L *pariēs* a wall, partition]

pa·ri·e·tal (pə rī′i təl), *adj.* **1.** *Anat.* of, pertaining to, or situated near the side and top of the skull or the parietal bone. **2.** *Biol.* of or pertaining to parietes or structural walls. **3.** *Bot.* pertaining to or arising from a wall: usually applied to ovules when they proceed from or are borne on the walls or sides of the ovary. **4.** pertaining to or having authority over residence within the walls or buildings of a college or university: *a listing of the parietal regulations for the law students' dormitory.* —*n.* **5.** *Anat.* any of several parts in the parietal region of the skull, esp. the parietal bone. [< LL *parietāl(is)* of, belonging to walls, equiv. to L *pariet-* (s. of *pariēs*) wall + *-ālis* -AL[1]]

pari′etal bone′, *Anat.* either of a pair of membrane bones forming, by their union at the sagittal suture, part of the sides and top of the skull. See diag. under **skull.**

pari′etal cell′, *Anat.* any of the cells in the mucous membranes of the stomach that secrete hydrochloric acid. Also called **acid cell.**

pari′etal eye′, a median outgrowth of the diencephalon anterior to the pineal apparatus, having visual structual adaptations in cyclostomes and certain reptiles.

pari′etal lobe′, *Anat.* the middle part of each cerebral hemisphere, behind the central sulcus.

par·i·mu·tu·el (par′i myo͞o′cho͞o əl), *n.* **1.** a form of betting and of handling the betting on horse races at race tracks, in which those holding winning tickets divide the total amount bet in proportion to their wagers, less a percentage for the management, taxes, etc. **2.** Also called **parimu′tuel machine′.** an electronic machine that registers bets in parimutuel betting as they are made and calculates and posts the changing odds and final payoffs. [< F: lit., mutual bet]

par·ing (pâr′ing), *n.* **1.** the act of one who or that which pares. **2.** a piece or part pared off: *apple parings.* [ME; see PARE, -ING[1]]

par′ing chis′el, a woodworking chisel moved by steady hand pressure to make long, light cuts.

par′ing gouge′, a woodworker's gouge having the bezel on the concave face.

pa·ri pas·su (pä′rē päs′so͞o; *Eng.* pâr′ī pas′o͞o, par′ē), *Latin.* **1.** with equal pace or progress; side by side. **2.** without partiality; equably; fairly.

par·i·pin·nate (par′i pin′āt), *adj. Bot.* **1.** evenly pinnate. **2.** pinnate without an odd terminal leaflet. [PARI- + PINNATE]

Par·is (par′is; *for 2 also Fr.* PA RĒ′), *n.* **1. Matthew.** See **Matthew of Paris. 2.** Ancient, **Lutetia Parisiorum, Pa·ris·i·i** (pə riz′ē ī′). a city in and the capital of France, in the N part, on the Seine. 2,317,227. **3.** a city in NE Texas. 20,977 (1960). **4.** a town in E Illinois. 9823 (1960). **5.** a town in NW Tennessee. 9325 (1960). **6.** a town in central Kentucky. 7791 (1960). **7.** a town in W Arkansas. 3007 (1960).

Par·is (par′is), *n. Class. Myth.* a Trojan prince, son of Priam and Hecuba and brother of Cassandra, who awarded the apple of discord to Aphrodite and was by her help enabled to abduct Helen.

Par′is Com′mune, commune[3] (def. 6).

Par′is dai′sy, marguerite (def. 2).

Par′is green′, **1.** Also called **copper acetoarsenite, Schweinfurth green.** *Chem.* an emerald-green, poisonous, water-insoluble powder having the approximate formula, $3Cu(AsO_2)_2 \cdot Cu(C_2H_3O_2)_2$, produced from arsenic trioxide and copper acetate: used chiefly as a pigment, insecticide, and wood preservative. **2.** (*sometimes l.c.*) a variable hue ranging from light to vivid yellow-green in color.

par·ish (par′ish), *n.* **1.** an ecclesiastical district having its own church and clergyman. **2.** a local church with its field of activity. **3.** *Chiefly Brit.* a civil district or administrative division. **4.** (in Louisiana) a county. **5.** the people of an ecclesiastical or civil parish. **6.** *Curling.* house (def. 16). **7. on the parish,** *Brit.* **a.** receiving charity from local authorities. **b.** *Informal.* meagerly or inadequately supplied. [ME, var. of *parosshe* < MF *paroisse* < LL *parochia,* alter. of *paroecia* < LGk, deriv. of Gk *pároikos* neighbor (see PAROICOUS), in Christian usage, sojourner; see -IA]

par′ish house′, **1.** a building used by a church chiefly for administrative and social purposes. **2.** (esp. in the Roman Catholic Church) the residence of a cleric; parsonage.

pa·rish·ion·er (pə rish′ə nər), *n.* one of the community or inhabitants of a parish. [earlier *parishion,* ME *paroschian, -ien, -en* < OF *paroissien.* See PARISH, -IAN, -ER[1]] —**pa·rish′ion·er·ship′,** *n.*

par′ish reg′ister, *Eccles.* the register of the christenings, marriages, and burials in a parish.

par·ish-rigged (par′ish rigd′), *adj. Naut. Slang.* (of a sailing vessel) meagerly or inadequately outfitted.

Pa·ri·sian (pə rizh′ən, -rē′zhən, -riz′ē ən), *n.* **1.** a native or inhabitant of Paris, France. —*adj.* **2.** of, pertaining to, or characteristic of Paris, France. [< F *parisien.* See PARIS, -IAN] —**Pa·ri′sian·ly,** *adv.*

par·i·son (par′i sən), *n.* a partially shaped mass of molten glass. Also, **paraison.** [< F *paraison,* deriv. of *parer* to prepare < L *parāre*] —**par·i·son·ic** (par′i-son′ik), *adj.*

par·i·ty[1] (par′i tē), *n.* **1.** equality, as in amount, status, or character. **2.** equivalence; correspondence; similarity; analogy. **3.** *Finance.* **a.** equivalence in value in the currency of another country. **b.** equivalence in value at a fixed ratio between moneys of different metals. **4.** *Physics.* a property of a wave function, expressed as +1 or −1 and noting the relation of the given function to the function formed when each variable is replaced by its negative, +1 indicating that the functions are identical and −1 that the second function is the negative of the first. **5.** a system of regulating prices of farm commodities, usually by government price supports, to provide farmers with the same purchasing power they had in a selected base period. **6.** *Computer Technol.* the condition of the number of items in a set, as bits in a word, words in a column, etc., being either even or odd: used as a means for detecting certain errors. [< L *páritās.* See PAR, -ITY]

par·i·ty[2] (par′i tē), *n. Obstet.* the condition or fact of having borne offspring. [< L *par(ere)* (to) bring forth + -ITY]

par′ity check′, *Computer Technol.* a system for finding errors in a computer operation, as by counting a digit (**par′ity dig′it**) to determine whether a block of coded data results in an odd or even figure, represented in the former instance by one and in the latter by zero. Also called **odd-even check, redundant check.**

park (pärk), *n.* **1.** an area of land, usually in a natural state, for the enjoyment of the public, having facilities for rest and recreation, usually owned, set apart, and managed by a city, state, or nation. **2.** an enclosed area or a stadium used for sports: *a baseball park.* **3.** a considerable extent of land forming the grounds of a country house. **4.** *Brit.* a tract of land reserved for wild animals; game preserve. **5.** *U.S.* a broad valley in a mountainous region. **6.** a space where vehicles, esp. automobiles, may be assembled or stationed. **7.** *Mil.* **a.** the space occupied by the assembled guns, tanks, or vehicles of a military unit. **b.** the assemblage so formed. **c.** (formerly) the ammunition trains and reserve artillery of an army. —*v.t.* **8.** to halt (one's vehicle) with the intention of not using it again immediately. **9.** *Informal.* to put or leave: *He decided to park his package at her office. She parked the child at Grandmother's house.* **10.** to assemble (equipment or supplies) in a military park. **11.** to enclose in or as in a park. —*v.i.* **12.** to park a car, bicycle, etc. **13.** *Informal.* to engage in love-making in a parked car: *They used to park for hours on the drive near the water tower.* [ME < OF *parc* enclosure < LL **parric(us)* < Gmc. See PADDOCK[1]] —**park′like′,** *adj.*

Park (pärk), *n.* **1. Mun·go** (mung′gō), 1771–1806?, Scottish explorer in Africa. **2. Robert E.,** 1864–1944, U.S. sociologist. **3.** a boy's given name.

par·ka (pär′kə), *n.* **1.** a fur coat, shirtlike and hooded, for wear in the arctic and other regions of extreme cold. **2.** a hip-length jacket or overshirt with an attached hood, often of wool or of a windproof, water-repellent material lined or trimmed with wool, used by skiers, hunters, the military, etc. **3.** any coat or jacket with a hood, as a hooded raincoat or windbreaker. [< Aleut < Russ: pelt < Samoyed]

Park′ Av′enue, a street in New York City which, because of its large, expensive apartment houses, has come to represent luxury and fashion.

Par·ker (pär′kər), *n.* **1. Charles Christopher, Jr.** ("*Bird*"), 1920–55, U.S. jazz saxophonist and composer. **2. Dorothy (Rothschild),** born 1893, U.S. author. **3. Sir Gilbert,** 1862–1932, Canadian novelist and politician in England. **4. Horatio William,** 1863–1919, U.S. composer, organist, and teacher. **5. John,** 1729–75, American Revolutionary patriot. **6. Matthew,** 1504–75, English theologian. **7. Theodore,** 1810–60, U.S. preacher, theologian, and reformer. **8** a boy's given name.

Par′ker House′ roll′, a bread roll made by folding a flat disk of dough in half. [after the *Parker House* hotel in Boston, which originally served the rolls]

Par·kers·burg (pär′kərz bûrg′), *n.* a city in NW West Virginia, on the Ohio River. 44,797 (1960).

Parkes·burg (pärks′bûrg), *n.* a town in SE Pennsylvania. 2759 (1960).

Park′ Falls′, a town in N Wisconsin. 2919 (1960).

Park′ For′est, a city in NE Illinois. 29,993 (1960).

Park′ Hills′, a town in N Kentucky. 4076 (1960).

par·kin (pär′kin), *n. Brit. Dial.* gingerbread made with oatmeal flour. [?]

park·ing (pär′king), *n.* **1.** the act of one who or that which parks, esp. a vehicle. **2.** space in which to park vehicles, as at a place of business or a public event: *There's plenty of free parking at the Fair.* **3.** permission to park vehicles: *Is there parking on this side of the street?* **4.** the activity or occupation of one who operates or works in a parking lot, garage, or the like. **5.** *Informal.* the act of making love in a parked car. —*adj.* **6.** of, pertaining to, used for, or engaged in parking, esp. of vehicles: *a parking problem; parking regulations; parking ticket; parking lot; parking space; parking attendant.* [PARK + -ING[1], -ING[2]]

park′ing me′ter, a mechanical device for registering and collecting payment for the length of time that a vehicle occupies a parking space, consisting typically of a timer, actuated by a coin which a driver deposits upon parking, set in a headpiece mounted on a pole.

park′ing ramp′, apron (def. 6).

Par·kin·son (pär′kin sən), *n.* **C(yril) North·cote** (nôrth′kət), born 1909, English author and historian.

par·kin·so·ni·an (pär′kin sō′nē ən), *adj. Pathol.* of, related to, or resembling Parkinson's disease. [see PARKINSON'S DISEASE, -IAN]

Par′kin·son's disease′ (pär′kin sənz), *Pathol.* a nerve disease, characterized by tremors, esp. of fingers and hands, rigidity of muscles, slowness of movements and speech, and a masklike, expressionless face. Also called **Par′kin·son·ism, paralysis agitans, shaking palsy.** [named after James *Parkinson* (1755–1854), English physician who first described it]

Par′kin·son's law′, the idea, stated facetiously as a law of physics, that work expands to fill the time allotted to it, as by a worker's slowing his pace or embellishing a task so that he does not finish it ahead of schedule.

park·land (pärk′land′), *n.* a grassland region with isolated or grouped trees, usually in temperate regions.

Park·man (pärk′mən), *n.* **Francis,** 1823–93, U.S. historian.

Park′ Range′, a range of the Rocky Mountains in central Colorado. Highest peak, Mt. Lincoln, 14,287 ft.

Park′ Rap′ids, a town in central Minnesota. 3047 (1960).

Park′ Ridge′, **1.** a city in NE Illinois. 32,659 (1960). **2.** a town in NE New Jersey. 6389 (1960).

Park·ville (pärk′vil), *n.* a town in S Pennsylvania. 4516 (1960).

park·way (pärk′wā′), *n.* **1.** a broad thoroughfare with a dividing strip or side strips planted with grass, trees, etc. **2.** a walk and planted border beside the roadway of a street. [PARK + WAY]

Parl., **1.** Parliament. **2.** Parliamentary. Also, **parl.**

par·lance (pär′ləns), *n.* **1.** a way or manner of speaking; vernacular; idiom: *legal parlance.* **2.** speech, esp. a formal discussion or debate. **3.** *Archaic.* talk; parley. [< AF; see PARLE, -ANCE]

par·lan·do (pär län′dō), *adj. Music.* sung or played as though speaking or reciting (a musical direction). [< It, prp. of *parlare* to speak; see PARLE]

par·lay (pär′lē, pär lā′), *U.S.* —*v.t.* **1.** to bet (an original amount and its winnings) on a subsequent race, contest, etc. **2.** *Informal.* to use (one's money, talent, or other assets) to obtain spectacular wealth or success: *He parlayed a modest inheritance into a fortune.* —*n.* **3.** a bet of an original sum and the subsequent winnings. [alter. of earlier *paroli* < F < Neapolitan It, pl. of *parolo,* ? deriv. of *paro* equal < L *pār;* see PAIR]

parle (pärl), *n., v.i., v.t.,* **parled, parl·ing.** *Archaic.* talk; parley. [ME *parle(n)* < MF *parle(r)* (to) speak < LL *parabolāre;* see PARABLE]

par·le·ment (pär′lə mənt), *n. Obs.* parliament.

Par′lement of Fowl′es, The (fo͞o′lis), a poem (1381–82?) by Geoffrey Chaucer.

par·ley (pär′lē), *n., pl.* **-leys,** *v.,* **-leyed, -ley·ing.** —*n.* **1.** a discussion or conference. **2.** an informal conference between enemies under truce, to discuss terms, conditions of surrender, etc. —*v.i.* **3.** to hold an informal conference with an enemy, under a truce, as between active hostilities. **4.** to speak, talk, or confer. [earlier *parlee* < MF, n. use of fem. of *parle,* ptp. of *parler* to PARLE] —**par′ley·er,** *n.* —**Syn. 1.** talk, conversation. **4.** discuss, converse.

Par·ley (pär′lē), *n.* **Peter,** pen name of Samuel Griswold Goodrich.

par·lia·ment (pär′lə mənt), *n.* **1.** (*usually cap.*) the legislature of Great Britain, historically the assembly of the three estates, now composed of Lords Spiritual and Lords Temporal, forming together the House of Lords, and representatives of the counties, cities, boroughs, and universities, forming the House of Commons. **2.** (*usually cap.*) the legislature of certain British colonies and possessions. **3.** any legislative body in other countries. **4.** *Fr. Hist.* any of several high courts of justice in France before 1789. **5.** a meeting or assembly for conference on public or national affairs. **6.** *Cards.* fan-tan (def. 1). [late ME < AL *parliament(um),* alter. of ML *parlāmentum* < OF *parlement* a speaking, conference (see PARLE, -MENT); r. ME *parlement* < OF]

par·lia·men·tar·i·an (pär′lə men târ′ē ən), *n.* **1.** a person who is expert in the formal rules and procedures of deliberative assemblies and other formal organizations. 2. (*sometimes cap.*) *Brit.* a member of Parliament. 3. (*cap.*) a partisan of the British Parliament in opposition to Charles I. [PARLIAMENT + -ARIAN]

par·lia·men·tar·i·an·ism (pär′lə men târ′ē ə niz′əm), *n.* advocacy of a parliamentary system of government. [PARLIAMENTARIAN + -ISM]

par·lia·men·ta·ry (pär′lə men′tə rē, -trē), *adj.* 1. of or pertaining to a parliament or any of its members. 2. enacted or established by a parliament. 3. having a parliament. 4. of the nature of a parliament. 5. in accordance with the formal rules governing the methods of procedure, discussion, and debate in deliberative bodies and organized assemblies: *parliamentary order.* [PARLIAMENT + -ARY] —**par′lia·men′ta·ri·ly,** *adv.*

Par′liament hinge′, a butt hinge the knuckle of which protrudes from the door so that the door when fully opened stands away from the wall.

par·lor (pär′lər), *n.* 1. a room for the reception and entertainment of visitors; living room. 2. a semi-private room in a hotel, club, or the like, for relaxation, conversation, etc.; lounge. 3. Also called **locutorium.** a room in a monastery or the like where the inhabitants may converse with visitors or with each other. 4. a room, apartment, or building forming a business place for certain businesses or professions: *funeral parlor; ice-cream parlor; shoe-shine parlor; beauty parlor.* Also, *esp. Brit.,* **parlour.** [ME *parlur* < AF, equiv. to OF *parleor* < LL **parabolātōrium.* See PARABLE, -ATE[1], -ORY[2]] —**par′lor·ish,** *adj.*

par′lor car′, a railroad passenger car having individual reserved seats and more comfortable than a day coach.

par′lor game′, any game usually played indoors, esp. in the living room or parlor, as a word game or a quiz, requiring little or no physical activity.

par′lor house′, *Slang.* a brothel.

par·lor·maid (pär′lər mād′), *n.* a maid who takes care of a parlor, answers the door, waits on guests, etc. [PARLOR + MAID]

par·lour (pär′lər), *n.* *Chiefly Brit.* parlor. —**par′lour·ish,** *adj.*

par·lous (pär′ləs), *Archaic.* —*adj.* 1. perilous; dangerous. 2. clever; shrewd. —*adv.* 3. to a large extent; greatly. [ME, var. of *perlous;* syncopated var. of PERILOUS] —**par′lous·ly,** *adv.* —**par′lous·ness,** *n.*

parl. proc., parliamentary procedure.

Par·ma (pär′mə; *for 1 also It.* pär′mä), *n.* 1. a city in N Italy, SE of Milan. 140,844 (1961). 2. a city in NE Ohio. 82,845 (1960).

Par′ma Heights′ (pär′mə), a city in NE Ohio, near Cleveland. 18,100 (1960).

Par·men·i·des (pär men′i dēz′), *n.* fl. c450 B.C., Greek Eleatic philosopher. —**Par·me·nid·e·an** (pär′mə nid′ē ən), *adj.*

Par·men·tier (pär′men tyā′; *Fr.* PAR män tyā′), *adj.* (*sometimes l.c.*) (of food) prepared or served with potatoes: *potage Parmentier.* Also, **Par·men·tière** (pär′men tyâr′; *Fr.* PAR män tyer′). [named after A. A. *Parmentier* (1737–1813), French promoter of economic botany]

Par·me·san (pär′mi zan′, -zän′, -zən, pär′mi zan′, -zän′), *adj.* 1. of or from Parma, in northern Italy. —*n.* 2. Also called **Par′mesan cheese′.** a hard, dry variety of Italian cheese made from skim milk, usually grated and sprinkled over pasta dishes and soups. [< MF < It *parmigiano* pertaining to Parma]

par·mi·gia·na (pär′mə zhä′nə; *It.* pär′mē jä′nä), *adj.* *Italian Cookery.* cooked with Parmesan cheese: *veal parmigiana; eggplant parmigiana.* Also, **par·mi·gia·no** (pär′mə zhä′nō; *It.* pär′mē jä′nō). [< It, fem. of *parmigiano* Parmesan]

Par·na·í·ba (pär′nə ē′bə), *n.* 1. a seaport in NE Brazil. 39,951 (1960). 2. a river in NE Brazil, flowing NE to the Atlantic. 900 mi. long. Also, **Par′na·hi′ba, Par′na·hy′ba.**

Par·nas·si·an (pär nas′ē ən), *adj.* 1. pertaining to Mount Parnassus. 2. pertaining to poetry. 3. of, pertaining to, or noting a school of French poets of the latter half of the 19th century, characterized chiefly by a belief in art for art's sake, by an emphasis on metrical form, and by the repression of emotive elements: so called from *Le Parnasse Contemporain,* the title of their first collection of poems, published in 1866. —*n.* 4. a member of the Parnassian school of French poets. [< L *Parnāsi(us)* of PARNASSUS + -AN] —**Par·nas′si·an·ism, Par·nas′sism,** *n.*

Par·nas·sus (pär nas′əs), *n.* 1. **Mount.** Modern, **Liakoura.** a mountain in central Greece, N of the Gulf of Corinth. ab. 8000 ft. 2. a collection of poems or of elegant literature. 3. the world of poetry or poets collectively: *a rhymester striving to enter and be recognized by Parnassus.* 4. any center of poetry or artistic activity: *Greenwich Village was once the Parnassus of the U.S.*

Par·nell (pär′nəl, pär nel′), *n.* **Charles Stewart,** 1846–91, Irish political leader. —**Par′nell·ism,** *n.* —**Par′nell·ite′,** *n.*

Par·no·pi·us (pär nō′pē əs), *n.* *Class. Myth.* an epithet of Apollo, meaning "locust-god," having reference to his once having ended a plague of locusts.

pa·ro·chi·al (pə rō′kē əl), *adj.* 1. of or pertaining to a parish or parishes. 2. of or pertaining to parochial schools or the education they provide. 3. of very limited or narrow scope or outlook; provincial: *parochial views; a parochial mentality.* [late ME *parochialle* < LL *parochiāl(is)* (see PARISH, -AL[1]); r. ME *parochiele* < AF *parochiel*] —**pa·ro′chi·al·ly,** *adv.* —**pa·ro′chi·al·ness,** *n.*

Paro′chial Church′ Coun′cil, *Ch. of Eng.* the ruling body of a parish, composed of the vicar, the churchwardens, and elected laymen.

pa·ro·chi·al·ise (pə rō′kē ə līz′), *v.t., v.i.,* **-ised, -is·ing.** *Chiefly Brit.* parochialize.

pa·ro·chi·al·ism (pə rō′kē ə liz′əm), *n.* a parochial character, spirit, or tendency; excessive narrowness of interests or view; provincialism. [PAROCHIAL + -ISM] —**pa·ro′chi·al·ist,** *n.* —**pa·ro′chi·al·i·za′tion,** *n.*

pa·ro·chi·al·ize (pə rō′kē ə līz′), *v.,* **-ized, -iz·ing.** —*v.t.* 1. to make parochial. —*v.i.* 2. to work in or for a parish. Also, *esp. Brit.,* **parochialise.** [PAROCHIAL + -IZE]

paro′chial school′, *U.S.* an elementary or high school maintained and operated by a religious organization.

pa·rod·ic (pə rod′ik), *adj.* having or of the nature of a parody or burlesque. Also, **pa·rod′i·cal.** [PAROD(Y) + -IC]

par·o·dist (par′ə dist), *n.* a person who composes parodies, esp. the author of a literary parody. [< F *parodiste.* See PARODY, -IST]

par·o·dis·tic (par′ə dis′tik), *adj.* parodic. [PARODIST + -IC]

par·o·don·ti·um (par′ə don′shē əm), *n., pl.* **-ti·a** (-shē ə). *Dentistry.* periodontium.

par·o·dos (pär′ə dos′), *n., pl.* **-doi** (-doi′). *Greek.* (in ancient Greek drama) an ode sung by the chorus at their entrance, usually beginning the play and preceding the *proagōn* in comedy or the alteration of *epeisodia* and *stasima* in tragedy.

par·o·dy (par′ə dē), *n., pl.* **-dies,** *v.,* **-died, -dy·ing.** —*n.* 1. a humorous or satirical imitation of a serious piece of literature or writing. 2. the genre of literary composition represented by such imitations. 3. a burlesque imitation of a musical composition. 4. any humorous, satirical, or burlesque imitation, as of a person, event, etc. 5. the use in the 16th century of borrowed material in a musical setting of the Mass. (**par′ody Mass′**). 6. a poor or feeble imitation; travesty: *His acting is a parody of his past greatness.* —*v.t.* 7. to imitate (a composition, author, etc.) for purposes of ridicule or satire. 8. to imitate poorly or feebly; travesty. [< L *parōdia* a parody < Gk *parōidía* a burlesque song or poem. See PAR-, ODE, -Y[3]] —**par′o·di·a·ble,** *adj.* —**pa·rod·ic** (pə rod′ik), **pa·rod′i·cal, pa·ro·di·al** (pə rō′dē əl), *adj.* —**par′o·dis′tic,** *adj.* —**par′o·dis′ti·cal·ly,** *adv.*
—**Syn. 1, 2.** See **burlesque.**

pa·roi·cous (pə roi′kəs), *adj.* *Bot.* (of certain mosses) having the male and female reproductive organs beside or near each other. Also, **parecious, pa·roe·cious** (pə rē′shəs). [< Gk *pároikos* dwelling beside (adj.), neighbor (n.), equiv. to *par-* PAR- + *oîk(os)* house + *-os* -OUS]

pa·rol (pə rōl′, par′əl), *n.* 1. **by parol,** by word of mouth; orally. —*adj.* 2. given by word of mouth; oral; not contained in documents: *parol evidence.* [late ME *parole* < AF, OF < VL **paraula,* syncopated var. of **paravola,* for L *parabola* PARABLE]

pa·role (pə rōl′), *n., v.,* **-roled, -rol·ing,** *adj.* —*n.* 1. *Penol.* a. the conditional release of a person from prison prior to the end of the maximum sentence imposed. b. such release or its duration. c. an official document authorizing such a release. 2. *Mil.* a. the promise, usually written, of a prisoner of war, that if he is released he either will return to custody at a specified time or will not again take up arms against his captors. b. (formerly) a password given by authorized personnel in passing by a guard. 3. word of honor given or pledged. 4. (in U.S. immigration laws) the temporary admission of aliens into the U.S. for emergency reasons or on grounds considered in the public interest, as authorized by the Attorney General at his discretion. 5. *Law.* parol. —*v.t.* 6. to put on parole. 7. *U.S.* to admit (an alien) under the parole provision: *An increased number of Hungarian refugees were paroled into the United States.* —*adj.* 8. of or pertaining to parole or parolees: *a parole record.* [< MF, short for *parole d'honneur* word of honor. See PAROL] —**pa·rol′a·ble,** *adj.*

pa·rol·ee (pə rō lē′), *n.* one who is released from prison on parole. [PAROLE + -EE]

par·o·no·ma·sia (par′ə nō mā′zhə, -zhē ə, -zē ə), *n.* *Rhet.* 1. the use of a word in different senses or the use of words similar in sound to achieve a specific effect, as humor or a dual meaning; punning. 2. a pun. [< L < Gk: a slight name-change, deriv. of *paronomázein* to make such a change (*par-* PAR- + *onomázein* to name, deriv. of *ónoma* a name); see -IA] —**par·o·no·mas·tic** (par′ə nə mas′tik), *adj.* —**par′o·no·mas′ti·cal·ly,** *adv.*

par·o·nych·i·a (par′ə nik′ē ə), *n.* *Pathol.* inflammation of the folds of skin bordering a nail of a finger or toe, usually characterized by infection and pus formation; felon. [< L *parōnychia* < Gk *parōnychía* whitlow, equiv. to *par-* PARA-[1] + *onych-* (s. of *ónyx*) claw, nail + *-ia* -IA] —**par′o·nych′i·al,** *adj.*

par·o·nym (par′ə nim), *n.* *Gram.* a paronymous word. [< Gk *parṓnym(on),* neut. of *parṓnymos,* equiv. to *par-* PAR- + *ónyma* name] —**par′o·nym′ic,** *adj.*

pa·ron·y·mous (pə ron′ə məs), *adj.* *Gram.* containing the same root or stem: *"Wise" and "wisdom" are paronymous words.* [< Gk *parṓnym(os).* See PARONYM, -OUS]

par·o·quet (par′ə ket′), *n.* parakeet.

Par·os (pâr′os; *Gk.* pä′rôs), *n.* a Greek island of the Cyclades, in the S Aegean: noted for its white marble. 9022 (1951); 77 sq. mi.

pa·ro·tic (pə rō′tik, -rot′ik), *adj.* *Anat., Zool.* situated about or near the ear. [< NL *parōtic(us)* < Gk *par-* PAR- + *ōtikós* of the ear; see OTO-, IC]

pa·rot·id (pə rot′id), *Anat.* —*n.* 1. a salivary gland situated at the base of each ear. —*adj.* 2. of, pertaining to, or situated near either parotid. [< NL *parōtid-* (s. of *parōtis*) parotid gland; L, Gk: tumor near the ear. See PAR- OTO-, -ID[1]] —**pa·rot′i·de′an,** *adj.*

par·o·tit·ic (par′ə tit′ik), *adj.* of or pertaining to parotitis. [PAROTIT(IS) + -IC]

par·o·ti·tis (par′ə tī′tis), *n.* *Pathol.* 1. inflammation of a parotid. 2. mumps. Also, **pa·rot·i·di·tis** (pə-rot′i dī′tis). [PAROT(ID) + -ITIS]

pa·ro·toid (pə rō′toid), *Zool.* —*adj.* 1. resembling a parotid. 2. denoting certain cutaneous glands forming warty masses or excrescences near the ear in certain salientians, as toads. —*n.* 3. a parotoid. [PAROT(ID) + -OID]

-parous, a learned borrowing from Latin meaning "bearing," "producing," used in the formation of compound words: *oviparous; viviparous.* [< L *-parus* bearing, equiv. to *par(ere)* (to) bear, bring forth + *-us* -OUS]

Par·ou·si·a (pa rōō′zē ə, -sē ə, pə-), *n.* 1. advent (def. 4). 2. (*l.c.*) *Platonism.* the presence in any thing of the idea after which it was formed. [< Gk *parousía* a being present, presence, equiv. to *par-* PAR- + *ous-* (s. of *ṓn,* prp. of *eînai* to be) + *-ia* -IA]

par·ox·ysm (par′ək siz′əm), *n.* 1. any sudden, violent outburst; a fit of violent action or emotion: *paroxysms of rage.* 2. *Pathol.* a severe attack or an increase in violence of a disease, usually recurring periodically. [earlier *paroxismos* < Gk *paroxysmós* irritation, deriv. of *paroxýnein* to irritate. See PAR-, OXY-[1], -ISM] —**par′ox·ys′mal, par′ox·ys′mic,** *adj.* —**par′ox·ys′mal·ly,** *adv.*

paroxys′mal tachycar′dia, *Med.* tachycardia that begins and subsides suddenly.

par·ox·y·tone (pa rok′si tōn′), *Classical Gk. Gram.* —*adj.* 1. having an acute accent on the next to the last syllable. —*n.* 2. a paroxytone word. [< NL *paroxytōn(us)* < Gk *paroxýtonos.* See PAR-, OXYTONE] —**par·ox·y·ton·ic** (par′ok si ton′ik), *adj.*

par·pen (pär′pən), *n.* perpend[1].

par·quet (pär kā′, -ket′), *n., v.,* **-queted, -quet·ing,** —*n.* 1. a floor composed of short strips of wood forming a pattern, sometimes with inlays of other woods or other materials. 2. the part of the main floor of a theater, opera house, etc., that is between the musicians' area and the parterre or rear division or, esp. in the U.S., the entire floor space for spectators. —*v.t.* 3. to construct (a floor) of parquetry. [< F, dim. of *parc* PARK; see -ET]

Parquetry

par′quet cir′cle, the part of the main floor of a theater, opera house, etc., behind the parquet, often including the area under the galleries. Also called **orchestra circle, parterre.**

par·quet·ry (pär′ki trē), *n.* mosaic work of wood used for floors, wainscoting, etc.; marquetry. [< F *parqueterie.* See PARQUET, -ERY]

parr (pär), *n., pl.* **parrs,** (*esp. collectively*) **parr.** 1. a young salmon, having dark crossbars on its sides. 2. the young of certain other fishes, as the codfish. [?]

Parr (pär), *n.* **Catherine,** 1512–48, 6th wife of Henry VIII: queen of England 1543–47.

par·ra·keet (par′ə kēt′), *n.* parakeet.

par·ra·mat·ta (par′ə mat′ə), *n.* paramatta.

Par·ran (par′ən), *n.* **Thomas,** born 1892, U.S. physician: surgeon general of U.S. Public Health Service 1936–48.

par·rel (par′əl), *n.* 1. Also, **par′ral.** *Naut.* a sliding ring or collar of rope, wood, or metal, that confines a yard or the jaws of a gaff to the mast but allows vertical movement. 2. *Rare.* a chimney breast. [late ME *perell,* var. of ME *parail,* aph. var. of *aparail* APPAREL]

par·ri·cide (par′i sīd′), *n.* 1. the act of killing one's father. 2. a person who kills his mother or someone else to whom he owes reverence. [< L *parricīd(um)* act of kin-murder, *parricīd(a)* kin-killer, var. of OL *pāricīdum, -a,* equiv. to *pāri-* (akin to Gk *pāós,* Attic *pēós* kinsman) + *-cīdum, -a* -CIDE] —**par′ri·cid′al,** *adj.*

Par·ring·ton (par′ing tən), *n.* **Vernon Louis,** 1871–1929, U.S. literary historian and critic.

Par·rish (par′ish), *n.* 1. **Anne,** 1888–1957, U.S. novelist and author of books for children. 2. **Max·field** (maks′fēld), 1870–1966, U.S. painter and illustrator.

par·ro·ket (par′ə ket′), *n.* parakeet. Also, **par′ro·quet′.**

par·rot (par′ət), *n.* 1. any of numerous hook-billed, often brilliantly colored birds of the order *Psittaciformes,* as the cockatoo, lory, macaw, parakeet, etc., having the ability to mimic speech and often kept as pets. 2. a person who, without thought or understanding, merely repeats the words or imitates the actions of another. —*v.t.* 3. to repeat or imitate without thought or understanding. 4. to teach to repeat or imitate in such a fashion. [unexplained var. of PARAKEET] —**par′rot·like′,** *adj.* —**par′rot·y,** *adj.*

Par·rot (par′ət), *n.* a walled plain in the fourth quadrant of the face of the moon: about 40 miles in diameter.

par·rot-beak (par′ət bēk′), *n.* parrot's-bill.

par′rot fe′ver, *Pathol.* psittacosis. Also called **par′rot disease′.**

par·rot·fish (par′ət fish′), *n., pl.* (*esp. collectively*) **-fish,** (*esp. referring to two or more kinds or species*) **-fish·es.** any of various chiefly tropical marine fishes, esp. of the families *Scaridae* and *Labridae:* so called because of their coloring or the shape of their jaws. Also called **pollyfish.** [PARROT + FISH]

par·rot's-bill (par′əts bil′), *n.* a showy, vinelike plant, *Clianthus puniceus,* of New Zealand, having clusters of eight white-streaked, crimson flowers. Also called **parrot-beak, red kowhai.**

par·rot's-feath·er (par′əts feth′ər), *n.* either of two South American water milfoils, *Myriophyllum brasiliense,* or *M. proserpinacoides,* commonly cultivated as aquarium plants.

par·ry (par′ē), *v.,* **-ried, -ry·ing,** *n., pl.* **-ries.** —*v.t.* 1. to ward off (a thrust, stroke, weapon, etc.), as in fencing; avert. 2. to turn aside; evade; avoid; dodge: *to parry an embarrassing question.* —*v.i.* 3. to parry a thrust, blow, etc. —*n.* 4. the act or an instance of parrying, as in fencing. 5. a defensive movement in fencing. [< F *parez,* impv. of *parer* to ward off, set off < L *parāre* to set. See PARADE] —**par′ri·a·ble,** *adj.* —**par′ri·er,** *n.*
—**Syn. 2.** avert; elude; prevent, obviate, preclude.

Par·ry (par′ē), *n.* 1. **William Edward,** 1790–1855, English arctic explorer. 2. a walled plain in the third quadrant of the face of the moon: about 28 miles in diameter. 3. a boy's given name.

pars (pärz), *n., pl.* **par·tes** (pär′tēz). (in prescriptions) a part. [< L]

parse (pärs, pärz), *v.t.,* **parsed, pars·ing.** *Gram.* to describe (a word or series of words) grammatically, telling the part of speech, inflectional form, syntactic relations, etc. [< L *pars* part, as in *pars ōrātiōnis* part of speech] —**pars′a·ble,** *adj.* —**pars′er,** *n.*

par·sec (pär′sek′), *n.* *Astron.* a unit of distance equal to that required to cause a heliocentric parallax of one second of an arc, equivalent to 206,265 times the distance from the earth to the sun or 3.26 light years. [PAR(ALLAX) + SEC(OND)[2]]

Par·see (pär′sē, pär sē′), *n.* 1. an Indian Zoroastrian descended from Persian Zoroastrians who came to India in the 7th and 8th centuries to escape Muslim persecution. 2. the Middle Persian dialect of the Parsee scriptures. Also, **Par′si.** [< Pers *Pārsī* Persian, equiv. to *Pārs* Persia + *-ī* suffix of appurtenance]

Par·see·ism (pär′sē iz′əm, pär sē′iz əm), *n.* the religion and customs of the Parsees. Also, **Par′si·ism.** [PARSEE + -ISM]

Par·si·fal (pär′sə fəl, -fäl′), *n.* **1.** (*italics.*) a music drama by Richard Wagner: composed 1877–82; première 1882. **2.** *German Legend.* Parzival.

par·si·mo·ni·ous (pär′sə mō′nē əs), *adj.* characterized by or showing parsimony; sparing or frugal, esp. to excess. [PARSIMON(Y) + -IOUS] **—par′si·mo′ni·ous·ly,** *adv.* **—par′si·mo′ni·ous·ness,** *n.*
—Syn. stingy, tight, close, niggardly, miserly, illiberal, mean, penurious; avaricious, covetous. **—Ant.** generous.

par·si·mo·ny (pär′sə mō′nē), *n.* extreme or excessive economy or frugality; stinginess, or niggardliness. [late ME *parcimony* < L *parcimōnia*, var. of *parsimōnia* frugality, thrift, equiv. to *parsi-* (comb. form of *parsus*, ptp. of *parcere* to economize) or *parci-* (comb. form of *parcus* sparing) + *-mōnia* -MONY]

pars·ley (pärs′lē), *n.* **1.** a garden herb, *Petroselinum crispum*, having aromatic leaves. **2.** the leaves of this plant, used to garnish or season food. **3.** any of certain allied or similar plants. **—***adj.* **4.** cooked or garnished with parsley: *parsley potatoes.* [ME *persely*, b. OE *petersilie* + OF *persil*, both < LL **petrosilium*, alter. of L *petroselīnum* < Gk *petrosélīnon* rock-parsley. See PETRO-, CELERY] **—pars′ley·like′,** *adj.*

pars·nip (pär′snip), *n.* **1.** a plant, *Pastinaca sativa*, cultivated varieties of which have a large, whitish, edible root. **2.** the root of this plant. [ME *pas(t)nep(e)* < L *past(ināca)* parsnip (deriv. of *pastinum* forked dibble); see NEEP]

par·son (pär′sən), *n.* **1.** a clergyman; minister; preacher. **2.** the holder or incumbent of a parochial benefice. [ME *persone* < ML *persōna* parish priest, L: personage. See PERSON] **—par·son·ic** (pär son′ik), **par·son′i·cal,** *adj.* **—par·son′i·cal·ly,** *adv.* **—par′son·ish, par′son·like′,** *adj.*

par·son·age (pär′sə nij), *n.* **1.** the residence of a parson or clergyman, as provided by the parish or church. **2.** *Eng. Eccles. Law.* the benefice of a parson. [ME *personage* < AF, equiv. to ML *persōnāticum* benefice. See PARSON, -AGE]

par′son bird′, tui.

Par·sons (pär′sənz), *n.* **Tal·cott** (tôl′kot, tal′-), born 1902, U.S. sociologist and author.

par′son's nose′, *Slang.* See **pope's nose.**

Pars·va (pärsh′və, pärs′-), *n.* *Jainism.* a semi-legendary Tirthankara of the 8th century B.C., said to have been born after a series of pious incarnations in each of which he was killed by an antagonist who had originally been his elder brother: the twenty-third Tirthankara.

part (pärt), *n.* **1.** a portion or division of a whole that is separate either in reality or in thought only; a piece, fragment, fraction, or section; constituent: *the rear part of the house.* **2.** an essential or integral attribute or quality: *a sense of humor is part of a healthy personality.* **3.** a section or division of a literary work. **4.** a portion, member, or organ of an animal body. **5.** any of a number of more or less equal quantities that compose a whole or into which a whole is divided: *A third part of the world is hungry. Use two parts sugar to one part cocoa.* **6.** an allotted portion; share. **7.** Usually, **parts. a.** a region, quarter, or district: *an ocean journey to foreign parts.* **b.** a quality or attribute establishing the possessor as a person of importance or superior worth: *Being both a diplomat and a successful businessman, he is widely regarded as a man of parts.* **8.** one of the opposing sides in a contest, question, agreement, etc. **9.** the dividing line formed in separating the hair of the head and combing it in different directions. **10.** a constituent piece of a machine or tool either included at the time of manufacture or set in place as a replacement for the original piece. **11.** *Music.* **a.** a voice, either vocal or instrumental. **b.** the written or printed matter extracted from the score which a single performer or section uses in the performance of concerted music: *a horn part.* **c.** a section or division of a composition: *the allegro part of the first movement.* **12.** participation, interest, or concern in something: *The Commies have some part in this!* **13.** one's share in some action; a duty, function, or office: *Everyone has to do his part if we're to finish by tonight.* **14.** a character or role acted in a play or sustained in real life. **15. for one's part,** as far as concerns one: *For my part, you can do whatever you please.* **16. for the most part,** with respect to the greatest part; usually; mostly: *They are good students, for the most part.* **17. in good part, a.** without offense; amiably: *She was able to take teasing in good part.* **b.** to a great extent; largely: *His success is in good part ascribable to dogged determination.* **18. in part,** in some measure or degree; to some extent: *The crop failure was due in part to unusual weather conditions.* **19. on the part of, a.** so far as pertains to or concerns one: *He expressed appreciation on the part of himself and his colleagues.* **b.** as done or manifested by: *attention on the part of the audience.* Also, **on one's part. 20. part and parcel,** an essential or integral part: *Her love for her child was part and parcel of her life.* **21. take someone's part,** to align oneself with; support; defend: *His mother took his part, even though he was obviously in the wrong.* **22. take part,** to participate; partake: *They refused to take part in any of the activities of the community.*
—*v.t.* **23.** to divide (a thing) into parts; break; cleave; divide. **24.** to comb (the hair) away from a dividing line. **25.** to dissolve (a connection, relationship, etc.) by separation of the parts, persons, or things involved: *She parted company with her sisters.* **26.** to divide into shares; distribute in parts; apportion. **27.** to put or keep apart; separate: *They parted the calves from the herd.* **28.** *Metall.* **a.** to separate (silver) from gold in refining. **b.** to cut (one part) away from a piece, as an end from a billet. **c.** to keep the surface of (a casting) separate from the sand of the mold. **29.** *Obs.* to leave. **—***v.i.* **30.** to be or become divided into parts; break or cleave: *The frigate parted amidships.* **31.** to go or come apart; separate, as two or more things. **32.** to go apart from each other or one another, as persons: *We'll part no more.* **33.** to be or become separated from something else (usually fol. by *from*). **34.** *Naut.* to break or become torn apart, as a cable. **35.** to depart. **36.** to die. **37. part with,** to give up; relinquish: *to part with one's possessions.* [ME, OE < L *part-* (s. of *pars*) piece, portion]
—Syn. 1. component, ingredient, division, sector. PART, PIECE, PORTION, SEGMENT, SECTION, FRACTION, FRAGMENT refer to that which is less than the whole. PART is the general word: *part of a house.* A PIECE suggests a part which is itself a complete unit, often of standardized form: *a piece of pie.* A PORTION is a part allotted or assigned to a person, purpose, etc.: *a portion of food.* A SEGMENT is often a part into which something separates naturally: *a segment of an orange.* SECTION suggests a relatively substantial, clearly separate part that fits closely with other parts to form a whole: *a section of a fishing rod, a book.* FRACTION suggests a less substantial but still clearly delimited part, often separate from other parts: *a fraction of his former income.* FRAGMENT suggests a broken, inconsequential, incomplete part, with irregular or imprecise outlines or boundaries: *a fragment of broken pottery, of a manuscript leaf, of information.* **6.** apportionment, lot. **13.** responsibility. **27.** sever, sunder, dissociate, disconnect, disjoin, detach. **—Ant. 1.** whole. **23.** join.

part., **1.** participle. **2.** particular.

part. adj., participial adjective.

Par·tage de Mi·di (*Fr.* PAR TAZH də mē dē′), a play (1906) by Paul Claudel.

par·take (pär tāk′), *v.*, **-took, -tak·en, -tak·ing. —***v.i.* **1.** to take or have a part or share in common with others: participate (usually fol. by *in*): *He wouldn't partake in the festivities.* **2.** to receive, take, or have a share (usually fol. by *of*): *to partake of a meal.* **3.** to have something of the nature or character (usually fol. by *of*): *Feelings partaking of both joy and regret.* **—***v.t.* **4.** to take or have a part in; share. [back formation from *partaking*, ME *part taking*, trans. of L *participātiō* participation] **—par·tak′a·ble,** *adj.* **—par·tak′er,** *n.*
—Syn. 1. See **share**[1].

par·tan (pär′tᵊn), *n.* *Scot.* a crab. [late ME (Scot) < Gael: crab]

part·ed (pär′tid), *adj.* **1.** divided into parts; cleft. **2.** set or kept apart; separated. **3.** *Bot.* (of a leaf) separated into rather distinct portions by incisions that extend nearly to the midrib or the base. **4.** *Heraldry.* party (def. 14). **5.** *Archaic.* deceased. [ME; see PART, -ED[2]] **—part′ed·ness,** *n.*

part′ed and fret′ty, *Heraldry.* (of a cross) having the vertical arms divided into two endorses, and the horizontal arms into two barrulets, which pass alternately over and under each other from edge to edge; double-parted and fretty: *a cross parted and fretty.*

part′ed per tierce′, *Heraldry.* tierced.

par·terre (pär târ′), *n.* **1.** See **parquet circle. 2.** an ornamental arrangement of flower beds of different shapes and sizes. [< F, n. use of phrase *par terre* on the ground. See PER, TERRA] **—par·terred′,** *adj.*

Par·the·ni·a (pär thē′nē ə), *n.* *Class. Myth.* an epithet of Athena, meaning "virgin."

Par·then·i·us (pär then′ē əs), *n.* *Class. Myth.* Plexippus (def. 2).

partheno-, a learned borrowing from Greek meaning "virgin," used in the formation of compound words: *parthenogenesis.* [< Gk, comb. form repr. *parthénos* maiden]

par·the·no·car·pic (pär′thə nō kär′pik), *adj.* exhibiting parthenocarpy. Also, **par′the·no·car′pi·cal, par′the·no·car′pous.** [PARTHENOCARP(Y) + -IC] **—par′the·no·car′pi·cal·ly,** *adv.*

par·the·no·car·py (pär′thə nō kär′pē), *n.* *Bot.* the production of fruit without fertilization of an egg in the ovary. [PARTHENO- + *-carpy*; see -CARP, -Y[3]]

par·the·no·gen·e·sis (pär′thə nō jen′i sis), *n.* *Biol.* development of an egg without fertilization. [PARTHENO- + GENESIS] **—par·the·no·ge·net·ic** (pär′thə nō jə net′ik), *adj.* **—par′the·no·ge·net′i·cal·ly,** *adv.*

par·the·no·gone (pär′thə nə gōn′), *n.* *Rare.* an organism produced by parthenogenesis. [PARTHENO- + *-gone* (appar. back formation from -GONY)]

Par·the·non (pär′thə non′, -nən), *n.* the temple of Athena Parthenos on the Acropolis at Athens, completed c438 B.C. by Ictinus and Callicrates and decorated by Phidias: regarded as the first and finest peripteral Doric temple.

Par·the·no·pae·us (pär′thə nō pē′əs), *n.* *Class. Myth.* a son of Hippomenes and Atalanta, and one of the Seven against Thebes.

Par·then·o·pe (pär then′ə pē′), *n.* *Class. Myth.* a siren who drowned herself when Odysseus escaped from the influence of the sirens' singing. **—Par·then·o·pe·an** (pär′thə nə pē′ən), *adj.*

Par·the·nos (pär′thə nos′, -nōs′), *n.* an epithet of certain ancient Greek deities, esp. Athena, meaning "virgin."

par·the·no·spore (pär′thə nō spōr′, -spôr′), *n.* *Bot.* a spore developed without fertilization. [PARTHENO- + -SPORE]

Par·thi·a (pär′thē ə), *n.* an ancient country in W Asia, SE of the Caspian Sea: conquered by the Iranians A.D. 226; now a part of NE Iran.

Par·thi·an (pär′thē ən), *n.* **1.** a native or inhabitant of Parthia. **2.** an Iranian language of ancient and medieval Parthia. **—***adj.* **3.** of, pertaining to, or characteristic of Parthia, its inhabitants, or their language. [PARTHI(A) + -AN]

Par′thian shot′, **1.** a rearward shot by a fleeing mounted archer. **2.** a sharp, telling remark made in departing. [so called from the custom of the ancient Parthian cavalry of shooting arrows while in real or feigned flight]

par-three (pär′thrē′), *adj.* of, pertaining to, or noting a small-scale golf course, usually having 18 holes of 150 yards in length from tee to cup on 7 to 40 acres of land. Cf. **pitch-and-putt.**

par·ti (pär tē′, pär′tē), *n.* *Archit.* the basic scheme or concept of an architectural design. [< F: task assigned, treatment, n. use of ptp. of *partir* to PART]

par·tial (pär′shəl), *adj.* **1.** pertaining to or affecting a part. **2.** being such in part only; not total or general; incomplete: *partial blindness; a partial payment of a debt.* **3.** *Bot.* secondary or subordinate: *a partial umbel.* **4.** being a part; component; constituent. **5.** biased or prejudiced in favor of a person, group, side, etc., as in a controversy: *a partial witness.* **6. partial to,** having a liking for; particularly fond of: *I'm partial to chocolate cake.* **—***n.* **7.** *Bridge:* part-score. **8.** *Chiefly Music.* See **partial tone.** [late ME *parcial* biased, particular < MF < LL *partiāl(is)* pertaining to a part, equiv. to L *parti-* (s. of *pars*) PART + *-ālis* -AL[1]] **—par′tial·ly,** *adv.* **—par′tial·ness,** *n.*
—Syn. 2. unfinished, imperfect, limited. **5.** one-sided, unfair, unjust. **—Ant. 1, 2.** complete. **5.** unbiased, fair.

par′tial-awn′ing-deck ves′sel (pär′shəl ô′ning-dek′), *Naut.* a merchant vessel having a long poop connected with the bridge house and having an awning deck running forward between the bridge house and the forecastle.

par′tial den′ture. See under **denture.**

par′tial deriv′ative, *Math.* the derivative of a function with respect to one of its variables with all other variables held constant.

par′tial differen′tial, *Math.* an expression obtained from a given function of several variables by taking the partial derivative with respect to one of the variables and multiplying by the increment in that variable.

par′tial differen′tial equa′tion, *Math.* a differential equation containing partial derivatives. Cf. **ordinary differential equation.**

par′tial frac′tions, *Algebra.* one of the fractions into which a given fraction can be resolved, the sum of such simpler fractions being equal to the given fraction: *Partial fractions of* $\frac{5}{(x^2-x)}$ *are* $\frac{5}{x-1}$ *and* $\frac{-5}{x}$.

par·tial·ise (pär′shə līz′), *v.t.*, **-ised, -is·ing.** *Chiefly Brit.* partialize.

par·ti·al·i·ty (pär shal′i tē, pär′shē al′-), *n., pl.* **-ties. 1.** the state or character of being partial. **2.** a favorable bias or prejudice: *the partiality of parents for their own children.* **3.** a special fondness or liking (usually fol. by *to* or *for*): *a partiality for country living.* [late ME *parcialite* < ML *partiālitās.* See PARTIAL, -ITY]
—Syn. 2. favoritism. **3.** leaning, inclination, bent, predilection. **—Ant. 2.** justice. **3.** dislike.

par·tial·ize (pär′shə līz′), *v.t.*, **-ized, -iz·ing.** to make partial; bias. Also, *esp. Brit.,* **partialise.** [< F *partialis(er).* See PARTIAL, -IZE]

par′tially or′dered set′, *Math.* a set in which a relation as "less than or equal to" holds for some pairs of elements of the set, but not for all. Cf. **totally ordered set, well-ordered set.**

par′tial or′dering, *Math.* a relation defined on a set, having the properties that each element is in relation to itself, the relation is transitive, and if two elements are in relation to each other, the two elements are equal.

par′tial pres′sure, *Physics, Chem.* the pressure that a gas in a mixture of gases would exert if it occupied the same volume as the mixture at the same temperature. Cf. **Dalton's law.**

par′tial score′, *Bridge.* part-score.

par′tial sum′, *Math.* one of a series of sums of elements of a given sequence, the first sum being the first element, the second sum being the first element added to the second element, the third sum being equal to the sum of the first three elements, and so on.

par′tial tone′, *Chiefly Music.* one of the pure tones forming a part of a complex tone; the fundamental tone or a harmonic. Also called **partial.**

par′tial vac′uum, an enclosed space from which part of the air or another gas has been removed.

par·ti·ble (pär′tə bəl), *adj.* capable of being divided or separated; divisible. [< LL *partibil(is)* divisible, equiv. to L *part(īrī)* (to) divide, PART + *-ibilis* -IBLE] **—par′ti·bil′i·ty,** *n.*

par·ti·ceps cri·mi·nis (pär′ti seps′ krim′ə nis), *Law.* an accomplice in a crime. [< L]

par·tic·i·pa·ble (pär tis′ə pə bəl), *adj.* capable of being shared. [late ME *partycypable* < LL *participābil(is)* which can be shared, equiv. to L *particip(āre)* (to) PARTICIPATE + *-ābilis* -ABLE]

par·tic·i·pance (pär tis′ə pəns), *n.* participation. Also, **par·tic′i·pan·cy.** [PARTICIP(ANT) + -ANCE]

par·tic·i·pant (pär tis′ə pənt), *n.* **1.** a person who participates; partaker. **—***adj.* **2.** participating; sharing. [< L *participant-* (s. of *participāns*), prp. of *participāre.* See PARTICIPATE, -ANT] **—par·tic′i·pant·ly,** *adv.*

partic′ipant observa′tion, a technique of field research, used in anthropology and sociology, by which an investigator studies the life of a group by sharing in its activities.

partic′ipant observ′er, a field researcher using the methods of participant observation.

par·tic·i·pate (pär tis′ə pāt′), *v.*, **-pat·ed, -pat·ing. —***v.i.* **1.** to take or have a part or share, as with others; partake; share (usually fol. by *in*): *to participate in profits; to participate in a play.* **—***v.t.* **2.** to take or have a part or share in; partake in; share. [< L *participāt(us)* shared (ptp. of *participāre*), equiv. to *particip-* (s. of *particeps*) taking part, partner (see PARTICIPLE) + *-ātus* -ATE[1]] **—par·tic′i·pat′ing·ly,** *adv.* **—par·tic′i·pa′tive,** *adj.* **—par·tic′i·pa′tive·ly,** *adv.* **—par·tic′i·pa′tor,** *n.* **—par·tic·i·pa·to·ry** (pär tis′ə pə tōr′ē, -tôr′ē), *adj.*
—Syn. 1. See **share**[1].

partic′ipating insur′ance, insurance in which the policyholders receive dividends and share in the surplus earnings of the company.

partic′ipating preferred′, *Stock Exchange.* a preferred stock entitled to its fixed dividend and to additional ones on a specified basis after payment of dividends on common stock.

par·tic·i·pa·tion (pär tis′ə pā′shən), *n.* **1.** the act or an instance of participating. **2.** a taking part, as in some action or attempt: *participation in a burglary.* **3.** a sharing, as in benefits or profits: *participation in a distribution of increased earnings.* [< LL *participātiōn-*, s. of *participātiō* (see PARTICIPATE, -ION); r. ME *participacioun* < AF]

par·ti·cip·i·al (pär′ti sip′ē əl), *Gram.* —*adj.* **1.** of or pertaining to a participle. **2.** similar to or formed from a participle. —*n.* **3.** a participle. [< L *participiāl(is)*, equiv. to *participi(um)* PARTICIPLE + *-ālis* -AL[1]] —**par·ti·cip·i·al·i·ty** (pär′ti sip′ē al′i tē), *n.* —**par′ti·cip′i·al·ly**, *adv.*

par·ti·cip·i·al·ise (pär′ti sip′ē ə līz′), *v.t.*, **-ised, -is·ing.** *Chiefly Brit.* participialize. —**par′ti·cip′i·al·i·sa′tion**, *n.*

par·ti·cip·i·al·ize (pär′ti sip′ē ə līz′), *v.t.*, **-ized, -iz·ing.** to form (a word) into a participle; make participial. [PARTICIPIAL + -IZE] —**par′ti·cip′i·al·i·za′tion**, *n.*

par·ti·ci·ple (pär′ti sip′əl, -sə pəl), *n.* *Gram.* an adjective or complement to certain auxiliaries that is regularly derived from the verb in many languages and refers to participation in the action or state of the verb; a verbal form used as an adjective. It does not specify person or number in English, but may have a subject or object, show tense, etc., as *burning*, in *a burning candle*, or *devoted* in *his devoted friend.* [ME < MF, var. of *participe* < L *participium*, deriv. of *particeps* taking part, equiv. to *parti-* (s. of *pars*) PART + *-cep-* (var. s. of *capere* to take) + *-s* nom. sing. ending]

par·ti·cle (pär′ti kəl), *n.* **1.** a minute portion, piece, or amount; a very small bit: *a particle of dust; not a particle of supporting evidence.* **2.** *Physics.* **a.** one of the extremely small constituents of matter, as an atom or nucleus. **b.** See **elementary particle. c.** a body considered as possessing finite mass but infinitesimal dimensions. **d.** a body in which the internal motion is negligible. **3.** a clause or article, as of a document. **4.** *Rom. Cath. Ch.* a small piece of the Host given to each lay communicant in a Eucharistic service. **5.** *Gram.* **a.** (in some languages) one of the major form classes, or parts of speech, consisting of words that are neither nouns nor verbs, or of all uninflected words, or the like. **b.** such a word. **c.** a small word of functional or relational use, such as an article, preposition, or conjunction, whether of a separate form class or not. [ME < L *particula.* See PART, -I-, -CLE] —**par′ti·cled**, *adj.*
—**Syn. 1.** mite, whit, iota, jot, tittle, grain, speck.

par′ticle accel′erator, accelerator (def. 7).

par′ticle board′, any of various composition boards formed from small particles of wood, as flakes or shavings, bonded together with a resin.

par′ticle veloc′ity, *Physics.* the velocity of a point in a medium that is undergoing wave motion. Cf. **group velocity, phase velocity.**

par·ti-col·ored (pär′tē kul′ərd), *adj.* having different colors in different parts; variegated: *a parti-colored dress.* Also, **party-colored;** *esp. Brit.*, **par′ti-col′oured, party-coloured.** [ME *parti* variegated < MF << L *partīt(us)* divided, ptp. of *partīre.* See PARTY]

par·tic·u·lar (pər tik′yə lər), *adj.* **1.** of or pertaining to a single or specific person, thing, group, class, occasion, etc., rather than to others or all; special rather than general: *one's particular interests.* **2.** immediately present or under consideration: *Look at this particular item in the contract.* **3.** distinguished or different from others or from the ordinary; noteworthy; marked; unusual: *She sang with particular warmth at last evening's concert.* **4.** exceptional or especial: *Take particular pains with this job.* **5.** being such in an exceptional degree: *a particular friend of mine.* **6.** dealing with or giving details, as an account, description, etc., of a person; detailed; minute; circumstantial. **7.** exceptionally selective, attentive, or exacting; fussy; fastidious: *to be particular about one's food.* **8.** *Logic.* **a.** not general; referring to an indefinite part of a whole class. **b.** (of a proposition) containing only existential quantifiers. **c.** partaking of the nature of an individual as opposed to a class. **9.** *Law.* **a.** noting an estate which precedes a future or ultimate ownership, as lands devised to a widow during her lifetime and after that to her children. **b.** noting the tenant of such an estate. —*n.* **10.** an individual or distinct part, as an item of a list or enumeration. **11.** Usually, **particulars.** specific points, details, or circumstances: *to give an investigator the particulars of a case.* **12.** *Logic.* an individual or a specific group within a general class. **13. in particular,** particularly; especially: *There is one book in particular that may help you.* [ME *particuler* < MF < LL *particulār(is)*, equiv. to L *particul(a)* PARTICLE + *-āris* -AR[1]]
—**Syn. 1.** See **special. 1, 2.** specific. **2.** distinct; discrete. **3.** notable. **6.** scrupulous, careful, exact, precise. **7.** discriminating; finical, finicky. PARTICULAR, DAINTY, FASTIDIOUS imply great care, discrimination, and taste in choices, in details about one's person, etc. PARTICULAR implies esp. care and attention to details: *particular about one's clothes.* DAINTY implies delicate taste and exquisite cleanliness: *a dainty dress.* FASTIDIOUS implies being difficult to please and critical of small or minor points: *a fastidious taste in styles.* **10.** item, feature, particularity. —**Ant. 3.** ordinary. **6.** inexact. **7.** undiscriminating.

partic′ular affirm′ative, *Logic.* a proposition of the form "Some S is P." *Symbol:* I,i

par·tic·u·lar·ise (pər tik′yə lə rīz′), *v.t., v.i.*, **-ised, -is·ing.** *Chiefly Brit.* particularize. —**par·tic′u·lar·i·sa′tion**, *n.* —**par·tic′u·lar·is′er**, *n.*

par·tic·u·lar·ism (pər tik′yə lə riz′əm), *n.* **1.** exclusive attention or devotion to one's own particular interests, party, etc. **2.** the principle of leaving each state of a federation free to retain its laws and promote its interests. **3.** *Theol.* the doctrine that divine grace is provided only for the elect. [< F *particularisme.* See PARTICULAR, -ISM] —**par·tic′u·lar·ist**, *n.* —**par·tic′u·lar·is′tic**, *adj.* —**par·tic′u·lar·is′ti·cal·ly**, *adv.*

par·tic·u·lar·i·ty (pər tik′yə lar′i tē), *n., pl.* **-ties. 1.** the quality or state of being particular. **2.** a special, peculiar, or individual character. **3.** detailed, minute, or circumstantial character, as of description or statement. **4.** attention to details; special care. **5.** fastidiousness. **6.** something that is particular; a particular or characteristic feature or trait. [< MF *particularite* < LL *particulāritāt-* (s. of *particulāritās*) state of being apart. See PARTICULAR, -ITY]

par·tic·u·lar·ize (pər tik′yə lə rīz′), *v.*, **-ized, -iz·ing.** —*v.t.* **1.** to make particular. **2.** to mention or indicate specifically; specify. **3.** to state or treat in detail. —*v.i.* **4.** to speak or treat particularly or specifically. Also, *esp. Brit.*, **particularise.** [< MF *particularis(er).* See PARTICULAR, -IZE] —**par·tic′u·lar·i·za′tion**, *n.* —**par·tic′u·lar·iz′er**, *n.*

par·tic·u·lar·ly (pər tik′yə lər lē), *adv.* **1.** in a particular or to an exceptional degree; especially: *He read it with particularly great interest.* **2.** in a particular manner; specifically; individually. **3.** in detail; minutely. [ME *particulerly.* See PARTICULAR, -LY]
—**Syn. 1.** exceptionally, specially. See **especially. 3.** scrupulously. —**Ant. 1.** generally; commonly.

partic′ular neg′ative, *Logic.* a proposition of the form "Some S is not P." *Symbol:* O,o

partic′ular quan′tifier, *Logic.* See **existential quantifier.**

partic′ular solu′tion, *Math.* a solution of a differential equation containing no arbitrary constants. Cf. **general solution.**

par·tic·u·late (pər tik′yə lit, -lāt′), *adj.* of, pertaining to, or composed of distinct particles. [< NL *particulāt(us)*, equiv. to L *particul(a)* PARTICLE + *-ātus* -ATE[1]]

part·ing (pär′ting), *n.* **1.** the act of one who or that which parts. **2.** a division or separation. **3.** a departure; leave-taking. **4.** death. **5.** a place of division or separation. **6.** something that serves to part or separate things. **7.** *Crystall.* a fracture of a crystal along a plane determined by twinning or pressure rather than along a cleavage plane. **8.** *Foundry.* the line on which the cope and drag of a mold meet. —*adj.* **9.** given, taken, done, etc., at parting: *a parting remark.* **10.** of or pertaining to parting, leave-taking, departure, or death: *parting words.* **11.** departing: *the parting day.* **12.** dying. **13.** dividing; separating. [ME *partyng* (n.). See PART, -ING[1], -ING[2]]

part′ing gate′, *Foundry.* a gate designed to separate and retain slag and scum.

part′ing shard′, a potsherd separating two ceramic pieces being fired.

part′ing slip′, a parting strip for separating two sash weights. Also called **wagtail.**

part′ing strap′, *Naut.* a strap used as part of a line otherwise composed of rope or wire of higher strength so that excessive tension on the line will cause the strap to yield before the rope or wire is harmed.

part′ing strip′, a strip, as of wood, used to keep two parts separated, as one in each side of the frame of a window to keep the sashes apart when lowered or raised. Also called **part′ing bead′, part′ing stop′.** See diag. under **double-hung.**

par·ti pris (PAR tē′ PRē′), *French.* a position or attitude resolved upon or taken in advance.

par·tis (pär′tis), *adj.* (in prescriptions) of a part. [< L]

par·ti·san[1] (pär′ti zən), *n.* **1.** an adherent or supporter of a person, party, or cause. **2.** *Mil.* a member of a party of light or irregular troops engaged in harassing an enemy, esp. a native engaged in fighting or sabotage against an occupying army. —*adj.* **3.** of, pertaining to, or characteristic of partisans; partial to a specific party, person, etc.: *partisan politics.* **4.** of, pertaining to, or carried on by military partisans or guerrillas. Also, **partizan.** [< MF < It *partigiano.* See PARTY, -IAN] —**par′ti·san·ship′, par′ti·san·ry**, *n.*
—**Syn. 1.** See **follower. 3.** biased, partial. —**Ant. 1.** opponent.

Partisan[2] (Head)

par·ti·san[2] (pär′ti zən), *n.* a shafted weapon having as a head a long spear blade with a pair of curved lobes at the base. Also, **partizan.** [< MF *partisane* < It *partigiana* halberd < OHG *part(a)* halberd + It suffix; see PARTISAN[1]]

par·ti·san·ism (pär′ti zə niz′əm), *n.* partisan action or spirit. [PARTISAN[1] + -ISM]

par·ti·ta (pär tē′tə; *It.* pär tē′tä), *n., pl.* **-tas,** *It.* **-te** (-te). *Music.* **1.** an instrumental suite common chiefly in the 18th century. **2.** a set of variations. [< It, fem. of *partito* divided. See PARTY]

par·tite (pär′tīt), *adj.* **1.** divided into parts, usually into a specified number of parts (usually used in combination): *a tri-partite agreement.* **2.** *Bot.* parted. [< L *partīt(us)* divided (ptp. of *partīrī*). See PART-, -ITE[2]]

par·ti·tion (pär tish′ən), *n.* **1.** a division into or distribution in portions or shares. **2.** a separation, as of two or more things. **3.** something that separates or divides. **4.** a part, division, or section. **5.** an interior wall or barrier dividing a room, area of a building, enclosure, etc., into separate areas. **6.** a septum or dissepiment, as in a plant or animal structure. **7.** *Law.* a division of property among joint owners or tenants in common or a sale of such property followed by a division of the proceeds. **8.** *Logic.* the separation of a whole into its integrant parts. **9.** *Math.* **a.** a mode of separating a positive whole number into a sum of positive whole numbers. **b.** the decomposition of a set into disjoint subsets whose union is the original set: *A partition of the set (1, 2, 3, 4, 5) is the collection of subsets (1), (2,3), (4), and (5).* **10.** *Rhet.* (in a speech organized on classical principles) the second, usually brief section or part in which a speaker announces the chief lines of thought he proposes to discuss in support of his theme. —*v.t.* **11.** to divide into parts or portions. **12.** to divide or separate by interior walls, barriers, or the like: *to partition a room into cubicles.* **13.** *Law.* to divide property among several owners, either in specie or by sale and division of the proceeds. [< L *partītiōn-* (s. of *partītiō*) division, equiv. to *partīt(us)* divided (see PARTY) + *-iōn-* -ION] —**par·ti′tion·ar′y**, *adj.* —**par·ti′tion·er, par·ti′tion·ist**, *n.* —**par·ti′tion·ment**, *n.*
—**Syn. 1.** See **division. 11.** portion, apportion. —**Ant. 2.** unity. **11.** unite.

parti′tion bulk′head, *Shipbuilding.* a nonstructural, nonwatertight bulkhead used as a partition between two successive decks. Also called **joiner bulkhead.**

parti′tion line′, *Heraldry.* a plain or figured edge between two adjacent areas of an escutcheon, between an ordinary and the field of an escutcheon, or between two adjacent ordinaries. Also called **boundary line.**

par·ti·tive (pär′ti tiv), *adj.* **1.** serving to divide into parts. **2.** *Gram.* noting part of a whole: *the Latin partitive genitive.* —*n.* **3.** *Gram.* a partitive word or formation, as *of the men* in *half of the men.* [< ML *partītīv(us)* divisive, equiv. to L *partīt(us)* divided (see PARTY) + *-īvus* -IVE] —**par′ti·tive·ly**, *adv.*

par·ti·zan[1] (pär′ti zən), *n., adj.* partisan[1]. —**par′ti·zan·ship′**, *n.*

par·ti·zan[2] (pär′ti zən), *n.* partisan[2].

part·let (pärt′lit), *n.* a garment for the neck and shoulders, usually ruffled and having a collar, worn in the 16th century. [unexplained var. of late ME *patelet* < MF *patelette* strip of cloth, band, lit., little paw, equiv. to OF *pate* paw + *-lete* -LET]

part·ly (pärt′lē), *adv.* in part; to some extent or degree; not wholly: *His statement is partly true.* [PART + -LY]

part′ mu′sic, music, esp. vocal music, with parts for two or more independent performers.

part·ner (pärt′nər), *n.* **1.** one who shares or is associated with another in some action or endeavor; sharer; associate. **2.** *Law.* **a.** one associated with another or others as a principal or a contributor of capital in a business or a joint venture, usually sharing its risks and profits. **b.** See **special partner. 3.** See **silent partner. 4.** a husband or a wife; spouse. **5.** one's companion in a dance. **6.** a player on the same side or team as another: *My tennis partner was an excellent player.* **7. partners,** *Naut.* a framework of timber round a hole in a ship's deck, to support a mast, capstan, pump, etc. —*v.t.* **8.** to associate as a partner or partners with. **9.** to serve as the partner of. [ME *partener;* alter. of PARCENER by assoc. with PART] —**part′ner·less**, *adj.*
—**Syn. 1.** colleague, accessory, accomplice.

part′ner plate′, *Shipbuilding.* a heavy metal deck plate having a hole for a mast.

part′ners' desk′, a desk having a kneehole and drawers on two fronts.

part·ner·ship (pärt′nər ship′), *n.* **1.** the state or condition of being a partner; participation; association; joint interest. **2.** *Law.* **a.** the relation subsisting between partners. **b.** the contract creating this relation. **c.** an association of persons joined as partners in business. [PARTNER + -SHIP]

part′ of speech′, *Gram.* any of the classes into which words in some languages, as Latin and English, have traditionally been divided on the basis of their meaning, form, or syntactic function. The usual parts of speech in English are noun, pronoun, verb, adverb, adjective, preposition, conjunction, and interjection.

par·took (pär to͝ok′), *v.* pt. of **partake.**

Gray partridge, *Perdix perdix* (Length 1 to 1½ ft.)

par·tridge (pär′trij), *n., pl.* **-tridg·es,** (*esp. collectively*) **-tridge. 1.** any of several Old World, gallinaceous game birds of the subfamily *Perdicinae*, esp. *Perdix perdix* **(gray partridge),** of Europe. **2.** *Chiefly New England.* the ruffed grouse. **3.** *Southern U.S.* bobwhite. **4.** any of several other North American, gallinaceous game birds. **5.** any of various South and Central American tinamous. [ME *partrich*, var. of *pertrich* < MF *pertris*, var. of *perdris*, OF *perd(r)iz* < L *perdix* < Gk] —**par′tridge·like′**, *adj.*

par·tridge·ber·ry (pär′trij ber′ē), *n., pl.* **-ries.** a North American, trailing, rubiaceous plant, *Mitchella repens*, having roundish evergreen leaves, fragrant white flowers, and scarlet berries. [PARTRIDGE + BERRY]

part-score (pärt′skōr′, -skôr′), *n.* *Bridge.* **1.** a contract to make less than the number of tricks required for game: *to bid a part-score of three diamonds.* **2.** the number of points gained by making such a contract: *a part-score of 60 points.* Also called **partial, partial score.**

part′ song′, a song with parts for several voices, esp. one meant to be sung without accompaniment. —**part′ sing′ing.**

part′ time′, a period of time that is less than the usual or full time. Cf. **full time.**

part-time (pärt′tīm′), *adj.* **1.** employed to work, expected to function, used, etc., less than the usual or full time: *a part-time clerk.* **2.** of, pertaining to, or noting such work, function, or use: *part-time employment.* —*adv.* **3.** on a part-time basis: *to work part-time.* Cf. **full-time.** [adj., adv. use of PART TIME]

part-tim·er (pärt′tī′mər), *n.* one who is employed to work part-time.

par·tu·ri·ent (pär to͝or′ē ənt, -tyo͝or′-), *adj.* **1.** bringing forth or about to bring forth young; travailing. **2.** pertaining to parturition. **3.** bringing forth or about to produce something, as an idea. [< L *parturient-* (s. of *parturiēns*) being in labor, lit., desiring to bring forth (prp. of *parturīre*), equiv. to *part(us)* brought forth, born (ptp. of *parere*) + *-uri-* desiderative suffix + *-ent-* -ENT] —**par·tu′ri·en·cy**, *n.*

par·tu·ri·fa·cient (pär to͝or′ə fā′shənt, -tyo͝or′-), *Med.* —*adj.* **1.** inducing or accelerating labor, or childbirth; oxytocic. —*n.* **2.** a parturifacient agent. [< L *parturi-* (s. of *parturīre* to be in labor; see PARTURIENT) + -FACIENT]

par·tu·ri·tion (pär′to͞o rish′ən, -tyo͞o-, -cho͞o-), *n.* the act of bringing forth young; childbirth. [< LL *parturītiōn-* (s. of *parturītiō*) travail, equiv. to L *parturīt(us)* (ptp. of *parturīre;* see PARTURIENT) + *-iōn* -ION]

part. vic., (in prescriptions) in divided doses. [< L *partibus vicibus*]

part·way (pärt′wā′, -wā′), *adv.* **1.** at or to a part of the way or distance: *Shall I walk you partway? I'm already partway home.* **2.** in some degree or part; partly; partially: *intentions that were only partway realized.* [PART + WAY]

par·ty (pär′tē), *n., pl.* **-ties,** *adj., v.,* **-tied, -ty·ing.** —*n.* **1.** a social gathering, as of invited guests at a private home, for conversation, refreshments, entertainment, etc.: *a cocktail party.* **2.** a group gathered for some special purpose or task: *a fishing party; a search party.* **3.** a detachment or detail of troops assigned to perform some particular service. **4.** a group of persons with common purposes or opinions who support one side of a dispute, question, debate, etc. **5.** a group of persons with common political opinions

and purposes organized for gaining political influence and governmental control and for directing government policy: *the Republican party; the Democratic party.* **6.** the system of taking sides on public or political questions or the like. **7.** attachment or devotion to one side or faction; partisanship: *to put considerations of party first.* **8.** *Law.* **a.** one of the litigants in a legal proceeding; a plaintiff or defendant in a suit. **b.** a signatory to a legal instrument. **c.** one participating in or otherwise privy to a crime. **9.** a person who or group that participates in some action, affair, plan, etc.; participant: *He was a party to the deal.* **10.** the person under consideration; a specific individual: *Look at the party in the green necktie. Your party doesn't answer.* **11.** a person or, usually, two or more persons together patronizing a restaurant, attending a social or cultural function, etc.: *The headwaiter asked how many were in our party; a party of 12 French physicists touring the labs; a party of one at the small table.* **12.** any occasion or activity likened to a social party, as specified; session: *The couple in the next apartment are having their usual dish-throwing party.* **13.** an advantageous or pleasurable situation or combination of circumstances of some duration and often of questionable character: *The police broke in and suddenly the party was over for the nation's most notorious gunman.* **—adj. 14.** of or pertaining to a party or faction; partisan: *party politics.* **15.** of or for a social gathering: *her new party dress.* **16.** *Heraldry.* (of an escutcheon) having the field divided into a number of parts, usually two; parted. **—v.i. 17.** *Informal.* to go to parties, esp. a series of parties. **18.** *Slang.* to enjoy oneself thoroughly and without restraint. [ME *partie* < OF, n. use of fem. of *parti* (ptp. of *partir*) < L *partītus*, *-a-*, *-um* divided, ptp. of *partīre.* See PART] **—par′ty·less,** *adj.*
—Syn. 1. gathering, assemblage. See **company. 4.** faction, circle, coterie, ring.
—Usage. When used in ordinary speech or writing in place of "person," "man," etc., as in def. 10, PARTY is considered rather poor style, and is avoided by those who are careful about their forms of expression.

par·ty-col·ored (pär′tē kul′ərd), *adj.* parti-colored. Also, *esp. Brit.*, **par′ty-col′oured.**

par′ty-col·umn bal′lot (pär′tē kol′əm). See **Indiana ballot.**

par′ty girl′, 1. a physically attractive young woman hired to attend parties and entertain men. **2.** *Slang.* a girl or woman who is interested in little else besides attending parties.

par·ty·ism (pär′tē iz′əm), *n.* **1.** adherence to a political party or organization. **2.** the organization of political affairs into parties; the political system of a state, region, etc. (often used in combination): *Two-partyism was never significant in continental politics.* [PARTY + -ISM] **—par′ty·ist,** *n.*

par·ty line (pär′tē līn′ *for 1, 2;* pär′tē līn′ *for 3, 4*), **1.** a telephone line connecting the telephones of a number of subscribers by one circuit to a central office. **2.** the boundary line separating adjoining properties. **3.** the authoritatively announced policies and practices of a group, esp. of the Communist party, usually followed by the members without deviation. **4.** the guiding policy, tenets, or practices of a political party: *The judge was chosen on party lines.*

par′ty lin′er, a person who follows a party line, esp. the Communist party line. [PARTY LINE + -ER[1]]

par′ty man′, a man belonging to a political party, esp. one who adheres strictly to the principles and policy of his party.

par′ty per tierce′, *Heraldry.* tierced.

par′ty pol′itics, politics based on strict adherence to the policies and principles of a political party regardless of the public interest.

par′ty poop′er (po͞o′pər), *Slang.* one who hasn't the interest or vitality to participate actively in a social party and thereby lessens others' enjoyment; killjoy. [POOP + -ER[1]]

par′ty wall′, *Law.* a wall used, or usable, as a part of contiguous structures. **—par′ty-walled′,** *adj.*

par′ty whip′, *Politics.* whip (def. 23).

par′u·la war′bler (par′yə lə, -ə lə), a North American wood warbler, *Parula americana*, having bluish plumage with a yellow throat and breast. [< NL, dim. (fem.) of L *pārus* titmouse; see -ULE]

pa·ru·lis (pə ro͞o′lis), *n. Pathol.* gumboil. [< NL < Gk *paroulís*, equiv. to *par-* PAR- + *-oulis*, cf. *oûlon* gum]

pa·rure (pə ro͝or′; *Fr.* PA RYR′), *n., pl.* **-rures** (-ro͝orz′; *Fr.* -RYR′). a matching set of jewels or ornaments. [< F: lit., adornment; OF *pareure* peeling < L *parātūra* (*parāt-*, ptp. s. of *parāre* to prepare + *-ūra* -URE)]

par′ val′ue. See **face value** (def. 1).

Par·va·ti (pär′və tē), *n. Hinduism.* Devi (def. 2).

par·ve (pär′və), *adj. Judaism.* pareve.

par·ve·nu (pär′və no͞o′, -nyo͞o′), *n.* **1.** a person who has recently or suddenly acquired wealth, importance, position, or the like, but has not yet developed the appropriate manners, dress, surroundings, etc. **—adj. 2.** being or resembling a parvenu. **3.** characteristic of a parvenu. [< F: upstart, n. use of ptp. of *parvenir* to arrive, reach < L *pervenīre*, equiv. to *per-* PER- + *venīre* to come] **—par′ve·nu′dom,** *n.* **—par′ve·nu′·ism,** *n.*

par·vis (pär′vis), *n.* **1.** a vacant enclosed area in front of a church. **2.** a colonnade or portico in front of a church. Also called **paradise.** [ME < MF; OF *pare(v)is* < LL *paradīs(us)* a church courtyard, orig. the one before St. Peter's, Rome. See PARADISE]

par·vu·lus (pär′vyo͝o ləs), *n., pl.* **-li** (-lī′). (in prescriptions) an infant. [< L]

Par·vum (pär′vəm), *n.* **Mare.** See **Mare Parvum.**

par·vus (pär′vəs), *adj.* (in prescriptions) little. [< L]

Par·zi·val (pär′tsi fäl′), *n.* the German counterpart of Percival.

pas (pä), *n., pl.* **pas. 1.** a step or series of steps in ballet. **2.** right of precedence. [< F < L *pass(us)*. See PACE[1]]

Pas·a·de·na (pas′ə dē′nə), *n.* **1.** a city in SW California, near Los Angeles. 116,407 (1960). **2.** a city in SE Texas, near Houston. 58,737 (1960).

Pa·sar·ga·dae (pə sär′gə dē′), *n.* an ancient ruined city in S Iran, NE of Persepolis: an early capital of ancient Persia; tomb of Cyrus the Great.

Pas·ca·gou·la (pas′kə go͞o′lə), *n.* a city in SE Mississippi, on the Gulf of Mexico. 17,139 (1960).

Pas·cal (pas kal′, pas′kəl; *Fr.* PA SKAL′), *n.* **1. Blaise** (blez), 1623–62, French philosopher and mathematician. **2.** a boy's given name.

Pascal's′ law′, *Physics.* the law that an external pressure applied to a fluid in a closed vessel is uniformly transmitted throughout the fluid. [named after PASCAL]

Pascal's′ the′orem, *Geom.* the theorem that the lines joining adjacent vertices of a hexagon intersect the same straight line if alternate vertices lie on two intersecting straight lines. [named after PASCAL]

Pascal's′ tri′angle, *Math.* a triangular arrangement of the binomial coefficients of the expansion $(x + y)^n$ for positive integral values of *n*. [named after PASCAL]

Pasch (pask), *n. Archaic.* **1.** the Jewish festival of Passover. **2.** Easter. [early ME < eccl. L *Pascha* < Gk *Páscha* < Aram: Passover, var. of Heb *Pesakh* PESACH]

pas·chal (pas′kəl), *adj.* **1.** of or pertaining to the Passover. **2.** of or pertaining to Easter. **—n. 3.** a paschal candle or candlestick. [ME *paschall* < LL *paschāl(is)*. See PASCH, -AL[1]]

Paschal I (pas′kəl), died A.D. 824, pope 817–824.

Paschal II, (*Ranieri*) died 1118, Italian ecclesiastic: pope 1099–1118.

pas′chal can′dle, *Rom. Cath. Ch.* a tall candle, symbolizing Christ, that is blessed and placed on the gospel side of the altar on Holy Saturday and kept burning until Ascension Day. Also called **Easter candle.**

pas′chal flow′er, pasqueflower.

pas′chal lamb′, 1. *Jewish Hist.* a lamb slaughtered and eaten on the eve of the first day of Passover. Ex. 12:3–11. **2.** (*caps.*) Christ. **3.** (*caps.*) any of several symbolic representations of Christ, as the Agnus Dei. **4.** (*caps.*) Also called **Holy Lamb.** *Heraldry.* a representation of a lamb passant having around its head a nimbus and supporting on the dexter shoulder a cross-like staff bearing a flag argent charged with a cross gules.

pas′chal let′ter, (in the early Christian church) a letter, written by a patriarch, archbishop, or bishop to a cleric under his authority, announcing the date of the next Easter festival.

Pa′schen-Back′ effect′ (pä′shən bäk′), *Physics.* a splitting of spectral lines observed when a strong magnetic field is introduced at the source of a radiation, caused when the vectors associated with the spin and orbital angular momentum exhibit individual rather than common precession. Cf. **total angular momentum quantum number, Zeeman effect.** [named after Friedrich *Paschen* (1865–1947) and Ernst *Back* (b. 1881), German physicists]

Pa′schen se′ries (pä′shən), *Physics.* a series of lines in the infrared spectrum of hydrogen. [named after Friedrich *Paschen*]

Pas·cin (pä skan′), *n.* **Jules** (zhyl), (*Julius Pincas*), 1885–1930, French painter, born in Bulgaria.

Pas·co (pas′kō), *n.* a city in S Washington, on the Columbia River. 14,522 (1960).

Pas·coag (pas′kōg), *n.* a town in NW Rhode Island. 2983 (1960).

Pas′co West′, a town in S Washington. 2894 (1960).

pas d'ac·tion (*Fr.* pä dak syôn′), *pl.* **pas d'action.** a dramatic, pantomimic dance sequence serving to advance the plot in the classic ballet. [< F: step of action]

pas d'âne (pä dän′), *pl.* **pas d'âne.** a pair of rings set below and at right angles to the quillons of a sword as a guard for the forefinger. [< F: a guard on a hilt, lit., ass's step]

pas de basque (*Fr.* pä də bäsk′), *pl.* **pas de basque.** *Ballet.* a step in which the dancer swings one foot to the side, springs onto it, and swings the other foot against it. [< F: Basque step]

pas de bour·rée (*Fr.* pä də bo͞o rā′), *pl.* **pas de bourrée.** *Ballet.* a short running step. [< F: bourrée step]

Pas-de-Ca·lais (päd[ə] ka le′), *n.* a department in N France. 1,366,282 (1962); 2607 sq. mi. *Cap.:* Arras.

Pas de Ca·lais (päd[ə] ka le′). French name of the **Strait of Dover.**

pas de chat (*Fr.* pä də sha′), *pl.* **pas de chat.** *Ballet.* a jump of one foot over the other. [< F: cat step]

pas de che·val (*Fr.* pä də shə val′), *pl.* **pas de cheval.** *Ballet.* a step in which the dancer hops on one foot and paws the ground with the other. [< F: horse step]

pas de cô·té (*Fr.* päd[ə] kō tā′), *Dressage.* a two-track. [< F: (a) step sideways]

pas de deux (*Fr.* pä də dœ′), *pl.* **pas de deux.** *Ballet.* **1.** a dance by two persons. **2.** (in classical ballet) a set dance for a ballerina and a danseur noble, consisting typically of an entrée, an adagio, a variation for each dancer, and a coda. [< F: lit., step for two]

pas de trois (*Fr.* pä də trwä′), *pl.* **pas de trois.** *Ballet.* a dance for three dancers. [< F: lit., step for three]

pas du tout (pä dy to͞o′), *French.* not at all.

pa·se (pä′sā), *n.* a maneuver by a bullfighter with the capa or muleta to gain the attention of the bull and to guide the course of its attack. [< Sp: lit., a pass, n. use of *pase* let him pass, 3rd person sing. pres. subj. of *pasar* to pass]

pa·se·o (pä sā′ō), *n., pl.* **-se·os. 1.** a slow, idle, or leisurely walk or stroll. **2.** a public place or path designed for walking; promenade. [< Sp]

pash[1] (pash), *Chiefly Brit. Dial.* **—v.t. 1.** to hurl or dash. **2.** to smash or shatter. **—v.i. 3.** to dash or strike violently. [ME *pas(s)he(n)*; appar. imit.]

pash[2] (pash), *n. Chiefly Scot.* the head. [?]

pa·sha (pə shä′, pash′ə, pä′shə), *n.* a title, placed after the name, formerly borne by civil and military officials of high rank in Turkish dominions. Also, **pacha.** [< Turk; see BASHAW] **—pa·sha′dom,** *n.*

pa·sha·lik (pə shä′lik), *n.* the territory governed by a pasha. Also, **pachalic, pa·sha′lic.** [< Turk, equiv. to *pāshā* PASHA + *-lik* suffix of quality or condition]

pashm (push′əm), *n.* the fine woolly underhair of goats raised in northern India. Also, **pash·im** (push′ēm), **pash·mi·na** (push mē′nə), **pushmina.** [< Pers: wool]

Pash·to (push′tō), *n.* an Indo-European, Iranian language that is the official language of Afghanistan and the chief vernacular of the eastern part of the nation. Also, **Pushtu.** Also called **Afghan.**

Pa·siph·a·ë (pə sif′ə ē′), *n. Class. Myth.* the wife of Minos, mother of Ariadne, and mother of the Minotaur by the Cretan bull.

Pa·sith·e·a (pə sith′ē ə), *n. Class. Myth.* one of the Graces.

pa·so do·ble (pä′sō dō′blā; *Sp.* pä′sô dô′vle), *pl.* **pa·so do·bles,** *Sp.* **pa·sos do·bles** (pä′sôs dô′vles). **1.** a quick, light march often played at bullfights. **2.** a two-step, esp. one done to Latin-American rhythms. [< Sp: lit., double step]

Pas·o Ro·bles (pä′sō rō′blās). See **El Paso de Robles.**

Pas·qua·le (pə skwä′lē; *It.* pä skwä′le), *n.* a boy's given name.

Pas·qua·li·na (pas′kwə lē′nə; *It.* pä′skwä lē′nä), *n.* a girl's given name.

pasque·flow·er (pask′flou′ər), *n.* **1.** an Old World, ranunculaceous plant, *Anemone Pulsatilla*, having purple flowers blooming about Easter. **2.** a related plant, *A. ludoviciana*, having similar flowers: the State flower of South Dakota. [*Pasque* (var. sp. of PASCH) + FLOWER (so named by the herbalist Gerarde in 1597); r. *passe-flower* < MF *passefleur.* See PASS (v.), FLOWER]

pas·quil (pas′kwil), *n.* a pasquinade. [< NL *pasquill(us)* < It *Pasquillo*, dim. of *Pasquino;* see PASQUINADE] **—pas·quil′ic, pas·quil′lic,** *adj.*

pas·quin·ade (pas′kwə nād′), *n., v.,* **-ad·ed, -ad·ing.** **—n. 1.** a satire or lampoon, esp. one posted in a public place. **—v.t. 2.** to assail in a pasquinade or pasquinades. [*Pasquin* (< It *Pasquino*, name given an antique Roman statue (unearthed in 1501) which was annually decorated and posted with verses) + -ADE[1]; r. *pasquinata* < It] **—pas′quin·ad′er,** *n.* **—pas·quin′i·an,** *adj.*

pass (pas, päs), *v.t.* **1.** to move past; go by: *to pass someone on the road.* **2.** to let go without notice, action, remark, etc.; leave unconsidered; disregard; overlook: *Pass the preface and go on to the text.* **3.** to omit the usual or regular payment of: *to pass a dividend in a certain year.* **4.** to cause or allow to go through or over a barrier, obstacle, etc.: *The guard checked the identification papers, then passed the visitor.* **5.** to go across or over (a stream, threshold, etc.); cross. **6.** to undergo: *They passed the worst night of their lives.* **7.** to undergo or complete successfully: *to pass an examination.* **8.** to cause or permit to complete successfully (an investigation, examination, course of study, etc.): *I am passing the whole class this term.* **9.** to go beyond (a point, degree, stage, etc.); transcend; exceed; surpass. **10.** to cause to go or move onward: *to pass a rope through a hole.* **11.** to cause to go, move, or march by: *to pass troops in review.* **12.** to live during (a portion of time); spend: *He decided to pass a year abroad, improving his German.* **13.** to live through without tedium: *How to pass the time?* **14.** to cause to circulate or spread: *to pass rumors all over a naval base.* **15.** to cause to be accepted or received: *to pass a worthless check.* **16.** to convey, transfer, or transmit; deliver: *Pass this on after reading.* **17.** to convey from one person, hand, etc., to another: *Please pass the mustard.* **18.** to pledge: *to pass one's word of honor to remain loyal.* **19.** to utter, pronounce, or speak: *She passed a remark about every passer-by.* **20.** to cause to go through something, as a process or agency: *to pass returning travelers through customs.* **21.** to discharge or void from the body, as excrement. **22.** to sanction or approve, esp. by vote: *Congress passed the bill.* **23.** to obtain the approval or sanction of (a legislative body, committee, etc.), esp. by a vote: *The bill passed Congress on the second vote.* **24.** to express or pronounce, as an opinion: *to pass judgment without knowing the facts.* **25.** *Law.* to place legal title or interest in (another) by a conveyance, a will, or other transfer. **26.** (in feats of magic) to perform a pass on. **27.** *Baseball.* (of a pitcher) to give a base on balls to (a batter). **28.** *Tennis.* to make a passing shot against (an opponent). **29.** *Sports.* to transfer (the ball or puck) to a teammate. **—v.i. 30.** to go or move onward; proceed: *Your papers are in order, and you may pass.* **31.** to come to or toward, then go beyond: *to pass by a shop; to pass through town.* **32.** to go away; depart: *The lightheaded feeling will pass in a minute.* **33.** to elapse or slip by; be spent: *The day passed very quickly for him.* **34.** to come to an end: *The crisis soon passed.* **35.** to die. **36.** to take place; happen; occur: *What passed while I was on vacation?* **37.** to go by or move past: *The funeral procession passed slowly.* **38.** to go about or circulate; be current. **39.** to serve as a marginally acceptable substitute: *The facsimile isn't very good but it will pass.* **40.** to live or be known as a member of a racial, religious, or ethnic group other than one's own, esp. to live and be known as a white person although having some Negro ancestry. **41.** to be transferred or conveyed: *The crown passed to the king's nephew.* **42.** to be interchanged, as between two persons: *Sharp words passed between them.* **43.** to undergo transition or conversion: *to pass from a solid to a liquid state.* **44.** to go or get through a barrier, test, course of study, etc., successfully: *Of the twenty who took the exam, only twelve passed.* **45.** to go unheeded, uncensured, or unchallenged: *He decided to let the insult pass.* **46.** to express or pronounce an opinion, judgment, verdict, etc. (usually fol. by *on* or *upon*): *Will you pass on the authenticity of this drawing?* **47.** to be voided, as excrement. **48.** to obtain the vote of approval or sanction of a legislative body, official committee, or the like: *The new tax bill finally passed.* **49.** *Law.* **a.** (of a member of an inquest or other deliberative body) to sit (usually fol. by *on* or *upon*): *to pass on a case of manslaughter.* **b.** to adjudicate. **c.** to vest title or other legal interest in real or personal property in a new owner. **50.** to throw a ball from one person to another, as in a game of catch. **51.** *Sports.* to make a pass, as in football or ice hockey. **52.** *Cards.* **a.** to forgo one's opportunity to bid, play, etc. **b.** to throw in one's hand. **53.**

Fencing Obs. to thrust or lunge. **54. bring to pass,** to cause to happen; bring about: *His wife's death brought a change to pass in his attitude toward religion.* **55. come to pass,** to occur; happen: *Strange things came to pass.* **56. pass away, a.** to cease; end: *All this trouble will pass away.* **b.** to die: *He passed away during the night.* **57. pass current,** to be received or believed; circulate openly: *There is a scandalous story about them that is passing current in town.* **58. pass for,** to be accepted as; be considered: *material that passed for silk.* **59. pass off, a.** to present or offer (something) under false pretenses; dispose of deceptively: *to pass off a spurious Rembrandt on someone.* **b.** to cause to be accepted or received under a false identity: *He passed himself off as a doctor.* **c.** to cease gradually; end: *The headache passed off in the late afternoon.* **d.** to disregard; ignore. **e.** to continue to completion; occur: *The meeting passed off without incident.* **60. pass on,** to die: *Her childhood friends had all passed on.* **61. pass out,** *Informal.* **a.** to lose consciousness; faint. **b.** to die: *The accident victim passed out in the ambulance on the way to the hospital.* **62. pass over, a.** to disregard; ignore: *Just pass over the first part of his letter.* **b.** to omit purposely to notice: *Boys passed her over in favor of her prettier sister.* **63. pass up,** *Informal.* to refuse or neglect to take advantage of; reject: *The opportunity may not come again, so you had better not pass it up.* —*n.* **64.** a narrow route across a relatively low notch or depression in a mountain barrier. **65.** a road, channel, or other way providing a means of passage, as through an obstructed region or other barrier. **66.** a navigable channel, as at the mouth or in the delta of a river. **67.** a permission or license to pass, go, come, or enter. **68.** *Mil.* **a.** a military document granting the right to cross lines or to enter or leave a military or naval base or building. **b.** written authority given a soldier to leave a station or duty for a specified period of time. **69.** a free ticket or permit: *two passes to a concert; a railroad pass.* **70.** *Chiefly Brit.* the act of passing a university or school examination or course without honors or distinction. **71.** *Sports.* the transfer of a ball or puck from one teammate to another. **72.** *Baseball.* See **base on balls. 73.** *Fencing.* a thrust or lunge. **74.** a single movement, effort, maneuver, etc.: *He made a pass at the control tower of the enemy airfield.* **75.** *Informal.* **a.** a gesture or action that is intended to be sexually inviting. **b.** a jab or poke with the arm, esp. one that misses its mark. **76.** *Cards.* the act or statement of not bidding or raising another bid: *There have been two passes and now it's your bid.* **77.** (in feats of magic) **a.** a passing of the hand over, along, or before anything. **b.** the transference or changing of objects by or as by sleight of hand; a manipulation, as of a juggler. **78.** a particular stage or state of affairs: *The economic situation had come to a dreadful pass.* **79.** *Bullfighting.* a pase. **80.** an act of passing. **81.** one passage of a tool over work, or of work through a machine. **82.** *Archaic.* a sally of wit; a witty thrust. [ME *pass(en)* < OF *pass(er)* < LL **passāre*, deriv. of L *passus* step. See PACE¹] —**pass′less,** *adj.*

—**Syn. 2.** ignore. **9.** excel. **23.** enact. **32.** leave. **34.** expire, cease, terminate, vanish, fade, disappear. See **die**¹. **64.** saddle, col. **78.** juncture, situation, condition.

pass., **1.** passenger. **2.** passim. **3.** passive.

pass·a·ble (pas′ə bəl, pä′sə-), *adj.* **1.** capable of being passed through or over; fit to be traversed, penetrated, crossed, etc., as a road, forest, or stream. **2.** adequate; acceptable: *a passable knowledge of French.* **3.** capable of being circulated legally or having a valid currency, as a coin. **4.** capable of being or liable to be ratified or enacted: *passable legislation.* [late ME < MF; see PASS, -ABLE] —**pass′a·ble·ness,** *n.*

pass·a·bly (pas′ə blē, pä′sə-), *adv.* fairly; moderately: *a passably good novel.* [PASSABLE + -LY]

pas·sa·ca·glia (pä′sə käl′yə, pas′ə-), *n.* **1.** a slow, dignified dance of Spanish origin. **2.** the music for this dance, based on an ostinato figure. [earlier *passacalle* < Sp *pasacalle*, lit., step (i.e., dance) in the street (*pasa-*, comb. form of *paso* step, PACE¹, + *calle* street < L *callem*, acc. of *callis* path); *-aglia* is a sp. change made to give word an Italian look]

pas·sade (pə sād′), *n.* *Manège.* a turn or course of a horse backward or forward on the same ground. [< F < It *passata.* See PASS (V.), -ADE¹]

pas·sa·do (pə sä′dō), *n., pl.* **-dos, -does.** *Fencing.* a forward thrust with the weapon while advancing with one foot. [alter. of Sp *pasada* or It *passata.* See PASSADE, PASS]

pas·sage¹ (pas′ij), *n., v.,* **-saged, -sag·ing.** —*n.* **1.** a portion or section of a written work; a paragraph, verse, etc.: *a passage of Scripture.* **2.** a phrase or other division of a musical work. **3.** *Fine Arts.* an area, section, or detail of a work, esp. with respect to its qualities of execution: *passages of sensitive brushwork.* **4.** the act or an instance of passing from one place, condition, etc., to another. **5.** the permission, right, or freedom to pass: *to refuse passage through a territory.* **6.** the route or course by which a person or thing passes or travels. **7.** *Chiefly Brit.* a hall or corridor; passageway. **8.** an opening or entrance into, through, or out of something: *the nasal passages.* **9.** a voyage by water or air from one point to another: *a rough passage across the English Channel.* **10.** the privilege of conveyance as a passenger: *to book passage on an ocean liner.* **11.** a lapse or passing, as of time. **12.** a progress or course, as of events. **13.** the enactment into law of a legislative measure. **14.** an interchange of communications, confidences, etc., between persons. **15.** an exchange of blows; altercation or dispute: *a passage at arms.* **16.** the act of causing something to pass; transference; transmission. **17.** an evacuation of the bowels. **18.** *Archaic.* an occurrence, incident, or event. **19. on passage,** *Naut.* (of a merchant vessel) loaded with all its cargo and on the way to its destination. —*v.i.* **20.** to make a passage; cross; pass; voyage. [ME < OF, equiv. to *pass(er)* (to) PASS + *-age* -AGE]

pas·sage² (pas′ij, pə säzh′), *n., v.,* **-saged, -sag·ing.** *Dressage.* —*n.* **1.** a slow, cadenced trot executed with great elevation of the feet and characterized by a moment of suspension before the feet strike the ground. —*v.i.* **2.** (of a horse) to execute such a movement. **3.** (of a rider) to cause a horse to execute such a movement. —*v.t.* **4.** to cause (a horse) to passage. [< F *passag(er)*, var. of *passéger* < It *passegiare* to walk; see PACE¹]

pas′sage hawk′, **1.** a young hawk during its first migration. **2.** *Falconry.* a hawk captured during its migration.

pas′sage sail′, *Naut.* a sail used in a trade wind rig.

Pas′sage to In′dia, A, a novel (1924) by E. M. Forster.

pas·sage·way (pas′ij wā′), *n.* a way for passing into, through, or out of something, as within a building or between buildings; a hall, alley, catwalk, or the like. [PASSAGE¹ + WAY]

pas·sage-work (pas′ij wûrk′), *n.* *Music.* **1.** writing that is often extraneous to the thematic material of a work and is typically of a virtuosic or decorative character: *passage-work consisting of scales, arpeggios, trills, and double octaves.* **2.** the performance of such writing: *The pianist's passage-work is brilliantly clear and smooth.*

Pas·sa·ic (pə sā′ik), *n.* a city in NE New Jersey. 53,963 (1960).

Pas′sa·ma·quod′dy Bay′ (pas′ə mə kwod′ē), an inlet of the Bay of Fundy, between Maine and New Brunswick, at the mouth of the St. Croix River.

pas·sa·ment (pas′ə mənt), *n.* passement.

pas·sant (pas′ənt), *adj.* *Heraldry.* (of a beast) represented as in the act of walking, with one forepaw raised, and as looking forward to the dexter side of the escutcheon unless specified as guardant: *a lion passant; a lion passant guardant.* [< MF, prp. of *passer* to PASS; see -ANT]

passaree′ boom′ (pas′ə rē′), *Naut.* See **placery boom.**

pass·book (pas′bŏŏk′, päs′-), *n.* **1.** a bankbook. **2.** *Archaic.* a customer's book in which a merchant or trader makes entries of goods sold on credit. [PASS + BOOK]

Pass Chris·ti·an (pas kris′chē an′, päs), a town in SE Mississippi. 3881 (1960).

pass′ degree′, (in English universities) an ordinary bachelor's degree conferred without honors.

passe (pɑs), *n.* *French.* the numbers 19 through 36 in roulette. [lit., passing, pass]

pas·sé (pa sā′, pas′ā; *Fr.* pɑ sā′), *adj., n., pl.* **pas·sés** (pa sāz′, pas′āz; *Fr.* pɑ sā′). —*adj.* **1.** out-of-date; antiquated; outmoded: *passé fashions.* **2.** past: *time passé.* **3.** past one's prime; aged. —*n.* **4.** *Ballet.* a movement in which one leg passes behind or in front of the other. [< F, ptp. of *passer* to PASS; see -EE]

passed (past, päst), *adj.* **1.** having completed the act of passing. **2.** having received a passing grade on an examination or test or successfully completed a school course, year, or program of study. **3.** *Navy.* having successfully completed an examination for promotion, and awaiting a vacancy in the next grade: *a passed chief engineer.* **4.** *Finance.* noting a dividend not paid at the usual dividend date. [late ME; see PASS, -ED²]

passed′ ball′, *Baseball.* a pitched ball that the catcher can reasonably be expected to catch but misses, resulting in a base runner's or runners' advancing one or more bases or in the batter's reaching first base safely. Cf. **wild pitch.**

pas·sel (pas′əl), *n.* a group or lot of indeterminate number: *a passel of dignitaries.* [alter. of PARCEL]

passe·ment (pas′mənt), *n.* a garment trimming of gold, silver, linen, or silk thread. Also, **passament.** [< F, for *passeman* < Sp *pasamano* railing (so called because one passes one's hand along it in going up and down stairs), hence edging for clothes. See PASS, MANUAL]

passe·men·terie (pas men′trē; *Fr.* päs män trē′), *n.* trimming of braid, cord, bead, etc., in any of various forms. [< F; see PASSEMENT, -ERY]

pas·sen·ger (pas′ən jər), *n.* **1.** a person who is carried or conveyed in an automobile, bus, train, airplane, or other conveyance. **2.** a wayfarer; traveler. [ME *passager* < MF, n. use of *passag(i)er* (adj.) passing, temporary; see PASSAGE, -AR¹. For *-n-* cf. MESSENGER, HARBINGER, SCAVENGER, POPINJAY]

pas′senger mile′, a unit of measurement, consisting of one mile traveled by a passenger, that airlines, railroads, and other public transportation facilities use in recording volume of traffic. —**pas′senger mile′age.**

pas′senger pi′geon, an extinct pigeon, *Ectopistes migratorius*, once found in great numbers in North America, noted for its sustained migratory flights.

passe-par·tout (pas′pär to͞o′; *Fr.* päs pär to͞o′), *n., pl.* **-touts** (-to͞oz′; *Fr.* -to͞o′). **1.** an ornamental mat for a picture. **2.** a method of framing in which a piece of glass is placed over a picture and is affixed to a backing by means of adhesive strips of paper or other material pasted over the edges. **3.** paper prepared for this purpose. **4.** something that passes everywhere or provides a universal means of passage. **5.** a master key; skeleton key. [< F: lit., pass everywhere]

passe·pied (päs pyā′), *n., pl.* **-pieds** (-pyā′). **1.** a lively dance in triple meter popular in France in the 17th and 18th centuries. **2.** a dance form in moderately fast 3/8 or 6/8 meter, occasionally constituting part of the 17th- and 18th-century instrumental suite. [< F *passe-pied*, lit., pass (the) foot, i.e. move it, dance. See PASS, -PED]

pass·er (pas′ər, pä′sər), *n.* **1.** one who or that which passes or causes something to pass. **2.** a passer-by. [ME; see PASS, -ER¹]

pass·er-by (pas′ər bī′, -bī′, pä′sər-), *n., pl.* **pass·ers-by** (pas′ərz bī′, pä′sərz-). a person passing by: *A passer-by noticed the fire and turned in the alarm.* Also, **pass′er·by′.**

pas·ser·i·form (pas′ər ə fôrm′, pə ser′ə-), *adj.* of or pertaining to the order *Passeriformes*; passerine. [< NL *Passeriform(es)*, equiv. to L *passer* sparrow + NL *-iformes*; see -I-, *-form*]

pas·ser·ine (pas′ər in, -ə rīn′, -ə rēn′), *adj.* **1.** of, belonging, or pertaining to the order *Passeriformes*, comprising more than half of all birds and typically having the feet adapted for perching. **2.** oscine (def. 1). —*n.* **3.** any bird of the order *Passeriformes*. [< L *passerin(us)* of a sparrow, equiv. to *passer-* (s. of *passer*) sparrow + *-inus* -INE¹]

pas seul (*Fr.* pä sœl′), *pl.* **pas seuls** (*Fr.* pä sœl′). *Ballet.* a dance performed by one person; dance solo. [< F: lit., solo step]

pas·si·ble (pas′ə bəl), *adj.* capable of feeling; susceptible of sensation or emotion; impressionable. [ME < ML *passibil(is).* See PASSION, -IBLE] —**pas′si·bil′i·ty** *n.*

pas·si·flo·ra·ceous (pas′ə flō rā′shəs, -flō-), *adj.* belonging to the *Passifloraceae*, or passionflower family of plants. [< NL *Passiflor(a)* the typical genus (see PASSION, FLORA) + -ACEOUS]

pas·sim (pas′im), *adv.* *Latin.* here and there: used to indicate the repetition of an idea, phrase, etc., throughout an author's writings or a single work.

pass·ing (pas′ing, pä′sing), *adj.* **1.** going by or past; elapsing: *He was feeling better with each passing day.* **2.** fleeting; transitory; not lasting: *to take a passing fancy to something.* **3.** done, given, etc., in passing; cursory: *a passing mention.* **4.** surpassing, preeminent, or extreme. **5.** indicating that one has passed: *a passing grade on a test.* —*adv.* **6.** *Archaic.* surpassingly; exceedingly; very. —*n.* **7.** the act of one who or that which passes or causes something to pass. **8.** a means or place of passage. **9. in passing,** by the way; incidentally: *The speaker mentioned his latest book in passing.* [ME; see PASS, -ING², -ING¹] —**pass′ing·ly,** *adv.* —**pass′ing·ness,** *n.*

pass′ing bell′, **1.** a bell tolled to announce a death or funeral. **2.** a portent or sign of the passing away of anything.

pass′ing modula′tion, *Music.* See **transient modulation.**

pass′ing note′, *Music.* a note that is foreign to a harmony and is introduced between two successive chord tones in order to produce a melodic transition. Also called **pass′ing tone′.**

pass′ing shot′, *Tennis.* a shot played to one side of and beyond the reach of an opponent coming to or stationed at the net.

pass′ing spring′, *Horol.* (in a chronometer escapement) a flat gold spring projecting from the free end of the spring detent in such a way as to engage the pallet on the balance when it travels in one direction, thereby depressing the detent and unlocking the escape wheel but allowing the pallet to travel freely in the other direction.

pas·sion (pash′ən), *n.* **1.** any emotion or feeling, as love, desire, anger, hate, fear, grief, joy, hope, etc., esp. when of a powerful or compelling nature. **2.** strong amorous feeling or desire; love. **3.** strong sexual desire; lust. **4.** an instance or experience of strong love or sexual desire. **5.** a person toward whom one feels strong love or sexual desire. **6.** a strong or extravagant fondness, enthusiasm, or desire for anything: *a passion for music.* **7.** the object of such a fondness or desire: *Accuracy became a passion with him.* **8.** an outburst of strong emotion or feeling: *She suddenly broke into a passion of tears.* **9.** violent anger. **10.** the state of being acted upon or affected by something external, esp. something alien to one's nature or one's customary behavior (contrasted with *action*). **11.** (*often cap.*) *Theol.* **a.** the sufferings of Christ on the cross or His sufferings subsequent to the Last Supper. **b.** the narrative of Christ's sufferings as recorded in the Gospels. **12.** *Archaic.* the sufferings of a martyr. [ME, OE < eccl. L *passiōn-* (s. of *passiō*) Christ's sufferings on the cross, any of the biblical accounts of these, special use of LL *passiō* suffering, submission, deriv. of L *passus* suffered, submitted, ptp. of *pati*; see -ION] —**pas′sion·ful,** *adj.* —**pas′sion·ful·ly,** *adv.* —**pas′sion·ful·ness,** *n.* —**pas′sion·like′,** *adj.*

—**Syn. 1.** See **feeling. 6.** fervor, zeal, ardor. **9.** ire, fury, wrath, rage. —**Ant. 1.** apathy.

pas·sion·al (pash′ə nəl), *adj.* **1.** of, pertaining to, or marked by passion. **2.** caused by or attended with passion: *a passional crime.* —*n.* **3.** a book containing descriptions of the sufferings of saints and martyrs, for reading on their festivals. [< ML *passiōnāl(is)*, equiv. to LL *passiōn-* PASSION + L *-ālis* -AL¹; in n. use, + *-āle* (neut.- of *-ālis*) -AL¹]

pas·sion·ar·y (pash′ə ner′ē), *n., pl.* **-ar·ies.** passional (def. 3). [< ML *passiōnāri(um)*, equiv. to LL *passiōn-* PASSION + L *-ārium* -ARY]

pas·sion·ate (pash′ə nit), *adj.* **1.** influenced or dominated by intense emotion or strong feeling: *a passionate advocate of socialism.* **2.** expressing, showing, or marked by intense emotion or strong feeling: *passionate language.* **3.** intense or vehement, as emotions or feelings: *passionate grief.* **4.** easily affected with or influenced by sexual desire; ardently sensual. **5.** easily moved to anger; quick-tempered; irascible. [< ML *passiōnāt(us)*, equiv. to LL *passiōn-* PASSION + L *-ātus* -ATE¹] —**pas′sion·ate·ly,** *adv.* —**pas′sion·ate·ness,** *n.*

—**Syn. 1.** excitable, emotional, impulsive, zealous. **1-3.** ardent, impassioned, excited, fervent, fervid, warm, enthusiastic, earnest, glowing, burning, fiery; animated, impetuous, violent. **5.** testy, choleric, hasty, short-tempered, fiery, hot-headed. —**Ant. 1-3,** **5.** cool, calm.

Pas′sion cross′, *Heraldry.* See **Latin cross.**

pas·sion·flow·er (pash′ən flou′ər), *n.* any chiefly American climbing vine or shrub of the genus *Passiflora*, having showy flowers and a pulpy berry or fruit that in some species is edible. [trans. of NL *flōs passiōnis*, lit., flower of the Passion; so named because likened to Christ's wounds, crown of thorns and other marks of suffering]

Passionflower, *Passiflora incarnata*

pas·sion·fruit (pash′ən fro͞ot′), *n.* any edible fruit of a passionflower, as the maypop. [PASSION + FRUIT]

Pas·sion·ist (pash′ə nist), *n.* *Rom. Cath. Ch.* a member of the "Congregation of Barefooted Clerks of the Most Holy Cross and Passion of Our Lord Jesus Christ," founded in 1720, engaged chiefly in missionary work. [< It *passionist(a).* See PASSION, -IST]

pas·sion·less (pash′ən lis), *adj.* not feeling or moved by passion; cold or unemotional; calm or detached. [PASSION + -LESS] —**pas′sion·less·ly,** *adv.* —**pas′sion·less·ness,** *n.*

pas′sion nail′, *Heraldry.* a very narrow pile, usually one of a number, used as a symbol of the Passion.

pas′sion play′, a dramatic representation of the passion of Christ, such as that given every 10 years at the Bavarian village of Oberammergau. Also, **Pas′sion Play′.**

Pas′sion Sun′day, the fifth Sunday in Lent, being the second week before Easter. [ME *Passioun Sonday*]

Pas·sion·tide (pash′ən tīd′), *n.* the two-week period from Passion Sunday to Holy Saturday. [PASSION + TIDE[1]]

Pas′sion Week′, **1.** the week preceding Easter; Holy Week. **2.** the week before Holy Week, beginning with Passion Sunday. [ME *passion-woke*]

pas·si·vate (pas′ə vāt′), *v.t.,* **-vat·ed, -vat·ing.** *Metall.* to treat (a metal) to render its surface less reactive chemically. [PASSIVE + -ATE[1]]

pas·sive (pas′iv), *adj.* **1.** not reacting visibly to something that might be expected to produce manifestations of an emotion or feeling. **2.** not participating readily or actively: *a passive member of a committee.* **3.** not involving visible reaction or active participation: *to play a passive role.* **4.** inactive; inert; quiescent. **5.** influenced, acted upon, or affected by some external force, cause, or agency; being the object of action rather than causing action (opposed to *active*). **6.** receiving or characterized by the reception of impressions or influences from external sources. **7.** produced or caused by an external agency. **8.** receiving, enduring, or submitting without resistance: *a passive hypnotic subject.* **9.** *Gram.* **a.** noting a voice in the inflection of the verb in some languages which is used to indicate that the subject undergoes the action of the verb. Latin *portātur,* "he, she, or it is carried," is in the passive voice. **b.** noting or pertaining to a construction similar to this in meaning, as English *He is carried.* **10.** *Chem.* inactive, esp. under conditions in which chemical activity is to be expected. **11.** *Med.* of or pertaining to certain unhealthy but dormant conditions; inactive, as opposed to active or spontaneous. **12.** *Electronics.* designed to relay signals without electronic devices: *a passive communications satellite.* **13.** *Metall.* (of a metal) treated so as to be abnormally unresponsive to certain environments. **—***n.* *Gram.* **14.** the passive voice. **15.** a passive form or construction. [ME < L *passīv(us),* lit., submissive, equiv. to *pass(us)* submitted (ptp. of *patī* to experience, undergo) + *-īvus* -IVE] **—pas′sive·ly,** *adv.* **—pas′sive·ness, pas·siv′i·ty,** *n.*
—Syn. 8. submissive, unresisting. **—Ant. 1–3.** active. **8.** recalcitrant.

pas′sive immu′nity, *Immunol.* immunity resulting from the injection of antibodies from another organism or, in infants, from the transfer of antibodies through the placenta or from colostrum.

pas′sive noun′, *Gram.* a noun whose referent is the recipient of an action, as *trainee, multiplicand.*

pas′sive rea′son, *Aristotelianism.* the reasoning faculty existing only within an individual mind, limited in scope and perishing with the body. Cf. **active reason.**

pas′sive resist′ance, (esp. of a minority or of a subject people) the action or expression of disapproval of a government or of specific governmental laws by the use of noncooperative and nonviolent methods, as economic boycotts and protest marches. Cf. **civil disobedience, noncooperation** (def. 2). **—pas′sive resist′er.**

pas·siv·ism (pas′ə viz′əm), *n.* **1.** the quality of being passive. **2.** the principle or practice of passive behavior. [PASSIVE + -ISM] **—pas′siv·ist,** *n.*

pass·key (pas′kē′, päs′-), *n., pl.* **-keys. 1.** See **master key. 2.** See **skeleton key. 3.** a private key. **4.** a latchkey. [PASS + KEY[1]]

Pas·so Fun·do (päs′sŏŏ fōōnn′dŏŏ), a city in S Brazil. 50,559 (1960).

Pass·o·ver (pas′ō′vər, päs′-), *n.* **1.** Also called **Pesach.** a Jewish festival that commemorates the exodus of the Jews from Egypt and is marked chiefly by the Seder ritual and the eating of matzoth. It begins on the eve of the 14th day of the month of Nisan and is celebrated for eight days by Orthodox and Conservative Jews outside of Israel and for seven days by Reform Jews and Jews in Israel. **2.** (*l.c.*) See **paschal lamb.** [n. use of v. phrase *pass over*]

pass′ point′, *Survey.* a point located photogrammetrically and used as a reference point for other photographs.

pass·port (pas′pōrt, -pôrt, päs′-), *n.* **1.** an official document issued by the government of a country to one of its citizens and, varying from country to country, authorizing him to travel to foreign countries and authenticating his identity, citizenship, right to protection while abroad, and right to re-enter his native country. **2.** any authorization to pass or go somewhere. **3.** a document issued to a ship, esp. to neutral merchant vessels in time of war, granting or requesting permission to proceed without molestation in certain waters. **4.** a certificate intended to secure admission. **5.** anything that ensures admission or acceptance. [earlier *passeport* < MF, equiv. to *passe* (impv. of *passer* to PASS) + *port* PORT[1]] **—pass′port·less,** *adj.*

pas·sus (pas′əs), *n., pl.* **-sus, -sus·es.** a section or division of a story, poem, etc.; canto. [< ML, L: step. See PACE[1]]

pass·word (pas′wûrd′, päs′-), *n.* a secret word or expression known only to authorized persons for their use and identification in being allowed to pass guards; watchword. Cf. **countersign.** [PASS + WORD]

Pas·sy (pa sē′), *n.* **1. Fré·dé·rick** (frā dā rek′), 1822–1912, French economist and statesman: Nobel peace prize 1901. **2.** his son, **Paul É·douard** (pôl ā dwar′), 1859–1940, French phonetician.

past (past, päst), *adj.* **1.** gone by or elapsed in time: *It was a bad time, but it's all past now.* **2.** of, having existed in, or having occurred in a time previous to the present; bygone: *the past glories of Greece.* **3.** gone by just before the present time; just passed: *during the past year.* **4.** ago: *six days past.* **5.** having formerly been or served as; previous; earlier: *three past presidents of the club.* **6.** *Gram.* designating a tense, or other verb formation or construction, which refers to events or states in time gone by. **—***n.* **7.** the time gone by: *He could remember events far back in the past.* **8.** the history of a person, nation, etc.: *Our country's glorious past.* **9.** what has existed or has happened at some earlier time: *Try to forget the past, now that your troubles are over.* **10.** the events, phenomena, conditions, etc., that characterize an earlier historical period: *That hat is something out of the past.* **11.** an earlier period of one's life, career, etc., that is thought to be of a shameful or embarrassing nature: *A woman with a past couldn't be accepted socially.* **12.** *Gram.* **a.** the past tense, as *he ate, he smoked.* **b.** another verb formation or construction with past meaning. **c.** a form in the past tense. **—***adv.* **13.** so as to pass by or beyond; by: *The troops marched past.* **—***prep.* **14.** beyond in time; after: *past noon; half past six.* **15.** beyond in space or position; farther on than: *the house just past the church.* **16.** in a direction so as to pass by or go beyond: *We went past the house by mistake.* **17.** beyond in amount, number, etc.: *past the maximum age for enlisting in the army.* **18.** beyond the reach, scope, influence, or power of: *He is past hope of recovery.* [ME; var. sp. of *passed,* ptp. of PASS]

pas·ta (pä′stə), *n.* any of various flour-and-egg food preparations of Italian origin, made of thin, unleavened dough and produced in a variety of forms, usually served with a sauce and sometimes stuffed. [< It < LL. See PASTE]

paste (pāst), *n., v.,* **past·ed, past·ing.** **—***n.* **1.** a mixture of flour and water, often with starch or the like, used for causing paper or other material to adhere to something. **2.** any material or preparation in a soft or plastic mass. **3.** dough, esp. when prepared with shortening, as for making pie crust and other pastry: *puff paste.* **4.** pasta. **5.** any of various semisoft fruit confections of pliable consistency: *almond paste; guava paste.* **6.** a preparation of fish, tomatoes, or other food reduced to a smooth, soft mass, as for a relish or for seasoning. **7.** a mixture of clay, water, etc., for making earthenware or porcelain. **8.** *Jewelry.* **a.** a brilliant, heavy glass, as strass, used for making imitation gems. **b.** an imitation gem of this material. **9.** *Slang.* a hard smack, blow, or punch, esp. on the face. **—***v.t.* **10.** to fasten or stick with paste or the like. **11.** to cover with something applied by means of paste. **12.** *Slang.* to strike hard at; beat or punch, as on the face or body. [ME < MF < LL *pasta* dough < Gk: barley porridge, n. use of neut. pl. of *pastós,* verbid of *pássein* to strew, sprinkle; a *pasta* was orig. a kind of gruel sprinkled with salt]

paste·board (pāst′bōrd′, -bôrd′), *n.* **1.** a stiff, firm board made of sheets of paper pasted or layers of paper pulp pressed together. **2.** *Slang.* a card, as a visiting card or a playing card. **3.** *Slang.* a ticket, as for an entertainment. **—***adj.* **4.** made of pasteboard. **5.** unsubstantial, flimsy, or sham. [PASTE + BOARD] **—paste′board′y,** *adj.*

pas·tel[1] (pa stel′, pas′tel), *n.* **1.** a color having a soft, subdued shade. **2.** a kind of dried paste made of pigments ground with chalk and compounded with gum water. **3.** a chalklike stick made from such paste. **4.** the art of drawing with such crayons. **5.** a drawing so made. **6.** a short, slight prose study or sketch. **—***adj.* **7.** having a soft, subdued shade. **8.** drawn with pastels: *a pastel portrait.* [< F < It *pastell(o)* < LL *pastellus,* dim. of *pasta* PASTE]

pas·tel[2] (pas′tel), *n.* **1.** the woad plant. **2.** the dye made from it. [< MF < Pr < ML *pastell(um)* woad (orig. woad-paste), var. of LL *pastellus,* dim. of *pasta* PASTE; change of gender by influence of L *glastum* woad]

pas·tel·ist (pa stel′ist, pas′tel ist), *n.* an artist who draws with pastels. Also, *esp. Brit.,* **pas′tel·list.** [PASTEL[1] + -IST]

pastel′ or′ange. See **sun tan** (def. 3).

paste′ mold′, *Glassmaking.* a mold lined with a moist carbonized paste, for shaping glass as it is blown.

past·er (pā′stər), *n.* **1.** a slip of paper gummed on the back, to be pasted on or over something, as over a name on a ballot. **2.** one who or that which pastes. [PASTE + -ER[1]]

pas·tern (pas′tərn), *n.* **1.** the part of the foot of a horse, cow, etc., between the fetlock and the hoof. See diag. under **horse. 2.** either of the two bones of this part, the upper or first phalanx **(great pastern bone)** and the lower or second phalanx **(small pastern bone),** between which is a joint **(pas′tern joint′).** [ME *pastron* shackle, prob. same word as MF *pasturon, pastern* < VL **pastōr(ia)* herding (see PASTOR, -IA) + ME, MF *-on* n. suffix]

Pas·ter·nak (pas′tər nak′), *n.* **Bo·ris Le·o·ni·do·vich** (bō rēs′ le o nē′do vich), 1890–1960, Russian poet, novelist, and translator: declined 1958 Nobel prize.

paste-up (pāst′up′), *n.* *Print.* a mechanical. [n. use of v. phrase *paste up*]

Pas·teur (pa stûr′; *Fr.* pä stœr′), *n.* **Louis** (lo͞o′ē; *Fr.* lwē), 1822–95, French chemist and bacteriologist. **—Pas·teur′i·an,** *adj.*

Pasteur′ effect′, the inhibiting of fermentation by oxygen. [named after Louis PASTEUR]

pas·teu·rel·la (pas′tə rel′ə), *n., pl.* **-rel·lae** (-rel′ē), **-rel·las.** *Bacteriol.* any of several rod-shaped bacteria of the genus *Pasturella,* certain species of which, as *P. pestis,* are parasitic and pathogenic for men and animals. [< NL; named after Louis PASTEUR + *-ella* dim. n. suffix]

pas·teu·rel·lo·sis (pas′tər ə lō′sis), *n.* *Vet. Pathol.* See **hemorrhagic septicemia.** [< NL; see PASTEURELLA, -OSIS]

pas·teur·ise (pas′chə rīz′, pas′tə-), *v.t.,* **-ised, -is·ing.** *Chiefly Brit.* pasteurize. **—pas′teur·i·sa′tion,** *n.*

pas·teur·ism (pas′chə riz′əm, pas′tə-), *n.* **1.** a treatment devised by Pasteur for preventing certain diseases, esp. hydrophobia, by inoculation with virus of gradually increasing strength. **2.** the act or process of pasteurizing milk, cheese, etc. [PASTEUR + -ISM]

pas·teur·ize (pas′chə rīz′, pas′tə-), *v.t.,* **-ized, -iz·ing. 1.** to expose (milk, cheese, etc.) to a high temperature for a given period of time to destroy certain microorganisms and prevent or arrest fermentation. **2.** to subject to pasteurism in order to prevent certain diseases, esp. hydrophobia. Also, *esp. Brit.,* **pasteurise.** [PASTEUR + -IZE] **—pas′teur·i·za′tion,** *n.*

pas·teur·iz·er (pas′chə rī′zər, pas′tə-), *n.* an apparatus for pasteurizing milk and other liquids. [PASTEURIZE + -ER[1]]

pas·tic·cio (pa stē′chō; *It.* päs tēt′chô), *n., pl.* **-ci** (-chē). a pastiche. [< It < ML *pasticius* pasty, pie. See PASTE, -ICE]

pas·tiche (pa stēsh′, pä-), *n.* **1.** a literary, musical, or artistic piece consisting wholly or chiefly of motifs or techniques borrowed from one or more sources. **2.** an incongruous combination of materials, forms, motifs, etc., taken from different sources; hodgepodge. [< F < It *pasticcio* PASTICCIO]

pas·ti·cheur (pas tē shœr′), *n., pl.* **-cheurs** (-shœr′). *French.* **1.** a person who makes, composes, or concocts a pastiche. **2.** a person who imitates the work of others.

pas·ti·cheuse (pas tē shœz′), *n., pl.* **-cheuses** (-shœz′). *French.* a female pasticheur.

pas·ti·glia (pä stēl′yə; *It.* päs tē′lyä), *n.* a plaster used during the Italian Renaissance for bas-relief ornament of furniture, being applied in layers, molded, carved, and gilded. [< It < Sp *pastilla.* See PASTILLE]

pas·tille (pa stēl′, -stil′), *n.* **1.** a flavored lozenge, usually containing some medicine; troche. **2.** a roll or cone of paste containing aromatic substances, burned as a disinfectant or deodorant. **3.** pastel for crayons. **4.** a crayon made of pastel. Also, **pas·til** (pas′til). [< F < Sp *pastilla;* akin to L *pastilus* lump of meal, lozenge, pill]

pas·time (pas′tīm′, päs′-), *n.* something that serves to make time pass agreeably; amusement; recreation; sport: *to play cards as a pastime.* [late ME *pas(s)e tyme,* trans. of MF *passe-temps*]
—Syn. entertainment.

past·i·ness (pā′stē nis), *n.* the quality of being pasty. [PASTY[1] + -NESS]

past′ mas′ter, 1. a person who has held the office of master in a guild, lodge, etc. **2.** a person who is thoroughly experienced in a profession, art, etc.: *a past master at chess.*

past′ mis′tress, a woman who is thoroughly expert in a profession, field, etc.: *She is a past mistress of the art of singing popular ballads.*

Pas·to (päs′tô), *n.* **1.** a city in SW Colombia. 119,600 (est. 1961); ab. 8350 ft. high. **2.** a volcanic peak near this city. 13,990 ft.

pas·tor (pas′tər), *n.* **1.** a minister or priest in charge of a church. **2.** one having spiritual care of a number of persons. **3.** *Ornith.* any of various starlings, esp. *Sturnus roseus* **(rosy pastor)** of Europe and Asia. [< L: shepherd, lit., feeder, equiv. to *pāst(us)* pastured, (ptp. of *pāscere* to put to pasture) + *-or* -OR[2]; r. ME *pastour* < AF] **—pas′tor·less,** *adj.* **—pas′tor·like′, pas′tor·ly,** *adj.*

pas·tor·age (pas′tər ij, pä′stər-), *n.* pastorate. [PASTOR + -AGE]

pas·to·ral (pas′tər əl, pä′stər-), *adj.* **1.** of, pertaining to, or consisting of shepherds. **2.** used for pasture, as land. **3.** having the simplicity, charm, serenity, or other characteristics generally attributed to rural areas: *pastoral scenery; the pastoral life.* **4.** pertaining to the country or to life in the country; rural; rustic. **5.** portraying or suggesting idyllically the life of shepherds or of the country, as a work of literature, art, or music: *pastoral poetry; a pastoral symphony.* **6.** of or pertaining to a minister or clergyman or to his duties: *pastoral visits to a hospital.* **—***n.* **7.** a poem, play, or the like, dealing with the life of shepherds, commonly in a conventional or artificial manner, or with simple rural life generally; a bucolic. **8.** a picture or work of art representing the shepherds' life. **9.** *Music.* pastorale. **10.** a treatise on the duties of a minister or clergyman. **11.** a letter from a spiritual pastor to his people. **12.** a letter from a bishop to his clergy or people. **13.** Also called **pas′toral staff′.** crosier (def. 1). [ME < L *pastōrāl(is),* equiv. to *pāstōr-* (see PASTOR) + *-ālis* -AL[1]] **—pas′to·ral·ly,** *adv.*
—Syn. 3. rustic, rural, simple. **5.** bucolic, idyllic. **7.** eclogue, idyl; georgic.

pas·to·rale (pas′tə räl′, -ral′, -rä′lē; *It.* päs′tô rä′le), *n., pl.* **-rales,** *It.* **-ra·li** (-rä′lē). *Music.* **1.** an opera, cantata, or the like, with a pastoral subject. **2.** a piece of music suggestive of pastoral life. [< It, n. use of *pastorale* PASTORAL]

pas·to·ral·ise (pas′tər ə līz′), *v.t.,* **-ised, -is·ing.** *Chiefly Brit.* pastoralize. **—pas′to·ral·i·sa′tion,** *n.*

pas·to·ral·ism (pas′tər ə liz′əm, pä′stər-), *n.* the practice of herding as the primary economic activity of a society. [PASTORAL + -ISM]

pas·to·ral·ize (pas′tər ə līz′), *v.t.,* **-ized, -iz·ing. 1.** to make pastoral or rural. **2.** to celebrate in a pastoral or set in a pastoral form. Also, *esp. Brit.,* **pastoralise.** [PASTORAL + -IZE] **—pas′to·ral·i·za′tion,** *n.*

pas′toral prayer′, the main prayer in a church service.

pas′toral staff′, crosier (def. 1).

Pas′toral Sym′phony, The, **1.** French, **La Symphonie Pastorale.** a novel (1919) by André Gide. **2.** the Symphony No. 6 in F major (1807–8) by Ludwig van Beethoven.

pas′toral theol′ogy, the branch of theology dealing with the responsibilities of a clergyman to the people under his care. Also called **poimenics.**

pas·tor·ate (pas′tər it, pä′stər-), *n.* **1.** the office or term of office of a pastor. **2.** a body of pastors. **3.** parsonage (def. 1). [< ML *pāstōrāt(us),* equiv. to L *pāstor* (see PASTOR) + *-ātus* -ATE[1]]

pas·to·ri·um (pa stōr′ē əm, -stôr′-, pä-), *n.* *Southern U.S.* a parsonage. [< NL, n. use of L *pastōrius,* equiv. to *pastōr-* (see PASTOR) + *-ōrium* -ORY[2]]

pas·tor·ship (pas′tər ship′, pä′stər-), *n.* the dignity or office of a pastor. [PASTOR + -SHIP]

pas·tose (pa stōs′), *adj.* having a heavy impasto. [< It *pastoso* doughy. See PASTE, -OSE[1]] **—pas·tos·i·ty** (pa stos′i tē), *n.*

past′ par′ticiple, *Gram.* a participle with past or perfect meaning; perfect participle, as *fallen, sung, defeated.*

past′ per′fect, *Gram.* pluperfect.

pas·tra·mi (pə strä′mē), *n.* **1.** a highly seasoned cut of smoked or pickled beef, usually from the shoulder section. **2.** a slice of this. [< Yiddish < Pol << Turk]

pas·try (pā′strē), *n., pl.* **-tries. 1.** a sweet baked food made of paste, esp. the shortened paste used for pie crust and the like. **2.** any item of food of which such paste forms an essential part, as a pie, tart, napoleon, etc. [PASTE + -RY]

pas′try tube′, a conical tube of light metal with a patterned hole at one end, fitted over the opening of a cloth funnel (**pas′try bag′**), for shaping icings, food pastes, etc., as they are forced through by squeezing the bag.

pas·tur·a·ble (pas′chər ə bəl, päs′-), *adj.* capable of affording pasture, as land. [PASTURE + -ABLE] —**pas′-tur·a·bil′i·ty,** *n.*

pas·tur·age (pas′chər ij, päs′-), *n.* **1.** grass or herbage grown for grazing livestock. **2.** grazing ground. **3.** the activity or business of pasturing livestock. [PASTURE + -AGE]

pas·ture (pas′chər, päs′-), *n., v.,* **-tured, -tur·ing.** —*n.* **1.** ground covered with grass or herbage used or suitable for the grazing of livestock; grassland. **2.** a specific area or piece of such ground. **3.** grass or herbage for feeding livestock. —*v.t.* **4.** to feed (livestock) by putting them to graze on pasture. **5.** (of land) to furnish pasturage for. **6.** (of livestock) to graze upon. [ME < MF < LL *pāstūra,* equiv. to L *pāst(us)* (see PASTOR) + *-ūra* -URE] —**pas′tur·al,** *adj.* —**pas′ture·less,** *adj.* —**pas′tur·er,** *n.*

Pas·ture (*Fr.* pä styr′), *n.* **Ro·gier** (*Fr.* rô zhē ā′) or **Ro·ger** (*Fr.* rô zhā′) **de la** (*Fr.* də la). See **Weyden, Rogier van der.**

pas′ture rose′, a bristly-stemmed rose, *Rosa carolina,* of the eastern U.S., having slender, straight prickles and solitary, rose-pink flowers nearly two inches wide.

past·y[1] (pā′stē), *adj.,* **past·i·er, past·i·est,** *n., pl.* **past·ies.** —*adj.* **1.** of or like paste in consistency, appearance, etc. —*n.* **2. pasties,** a pair of small, cuplike coverings for the nipples of a striptease dancer. [PASTE + -Y[1]]

past·y[2] (pas′tē, pä′stē), *n., pl.* **past·ies.** *Chiefly Brit.* a pie filled with game, fish, or the like. [ME *pastee* < MF. See PASTE, -EE]

past·y-faced (pā′stē fāst′), *adj.* having a pale, unhealthy, pastelike complexion: *an awkward, pasty-faced youth.*

PA system. See **public-address system.** Also, **P.A. system, p.a. system.**

pat[1] (pat), *v.,* **pat·ted, pat·ting,** *n.* —*v.t.* **1.** to strike lightly or gently with something flat, as with a paddle or the palm of the hand, usually in order to flatten, smooth, or shape: *to pat dough into pastry forms.* **2.** to stroke or tap gently with the palm or fingers as an expression of affection, approbation, etc. **3.** to strike (the floor, ground, etc.) with light footsteps. —*v.i.* **4.** to strike lightly or gently. **5.** to walk or run with light footsteps. **6. pat on the back,** *Informal.* to encourage, congratulate, or praise: *He has been patting himself on the back for the deal he made yesterday.* —*n.* **7.** a light stroke, tap, or blow with the palm, fingers, or a flat object. **8.** the sound of a light stroke or of light footsteps. **9.** a small piece or mass, usually flat and square, formed by patting, cutting, etc.: *a pat of butter.* **10. a pat on the back,** *Informal.* a word of encouragement or praise: *Everyone needs a pat on the back now and then.* [ME; perh. var. of PUTT]

pat[2] (pat), *adj.* **1.** exactly to the point or purpose; apt; opportune; ready: *a pat answer; a pat solution to a problem.* **2.** excessively glib; unconvincingly facile: *His answers were too pat to suit the examining board.* **3.** learned, known, or mastered perfectly or exactly: *to have something pat.* —*adv.* **4.** exactly or perfectly. **5.** aptly; opportunely. **6. stand pat, a.** to cling or hold firm to one's decision, policy, or beliefs: *The government must stand pat in its policy.* **b.** (in poker) to play a hand as dealt, without drawing other cards. [? special use of PAT[1]] —**pat′ness,** *n.* —**pat′ter,** *n.*

Pat (pat), *n.* **1.** a boy's given name, form of **Patrick. 2.** a girl's given name, form of **Patricia.**

PAT, *Football.* point after touchdown; points after touchdown.

pat., **1.** patent. **2.** patented.

pa·ta·ca (pə tä′kə), *n.* a silver coin and monetary unit of Macao, equal to 100 avos and equivalent to about .18 of a U.S. dollar. [< Pg << Ar *abu taqa* a kind of coin]

pat-a-cake (pat′ə kāk′), *n.* a form of amusement among very young children, in which a child claps his hands, usually in a regular pattern, to the words of a nursery rhyme. Also, **patty-cake.** [named after opening words of rhyme that accompanies the game]

pa·ta·gi·um (pə tā′jē əm), *n., pl.* **-gi·a** (-jē ə). **1.** a wing membrane, as of a bat. **2.** the extensible fold of skin of a gliding mammal or reptile, as a flying squirrel. [< NL, special use of L *patagium* gold edging on a Roman tunic < Gk *patageion* a gold tunic border]

Pat·a·go·ni·a (pat′ə gō′nē ə, -gōn′yə), *n.* **1.** the tableland region constituting the southern tip of Argentina. **2.** a region in S South America, in S Argentina and S Chile, extending from the Andes to the Atlantic. —**Pat′-a·go′ni·an,** *adj., n.*

pa·ta·gua (pə tô′gwə), *n.* a tree, *Crinodendron patagua,* of Chile, having prominently veined leaves and fragrant, cup-shaped, white flowers. [< Sp < AmerInd (? Araucanian)]

Pa·tan·ja·li (pə tun′jə lē), *n.* fl. late 2nd century B.C., Indian scholar and philosopher: sometimes regarded as the founder of Yoga.

patch[1] (pach), *n.* **1.** a piece of material used to mend a tear or break, to cover a hole, or to strengthen a weak place: *patches at the elbows of a jacket.* **2.** a piece of material used to cover or protect a wound, an injured part, etc.: *a patch over the eye.* **3.** any of the pieces of cloth sewed together to form patchwork. **4.** a small piece, scrap, or area of anything: *a patch of ice on the road.* **5.** a piece or tract of land; plot. **6.** a small field, plot, or garden, esp. one in which a specific type of plant grows or is cultivated: *a cabbage patch; a bean patch.* **7.** See **beauty spot** (def. 1). **8.** *Mil.* a cloth emblem worn on the upper uniform sleeve to identify the military unit of the wearer. —*v.t.* **9.** to mend, cover, or strengthen with or as with a patch or patches. **10.** to repair or restore, esp. in a hasty or makeshift way (usually fol. by *up*). **11.** to make by joining patches or pieces together: *to patch a quilt.* **12.** to settle or smooth over (a quarrel, difference, etc.) (often fol. by *up*): *They patched up their quarrel before the company arrived.* [ME *pacche;* ? akin to OPr *pedas* piece to cover a hole < VL **pedaceum,* lit., something measured; cf. ML *pedāre* to measure in feet; see PED-] —**patch′a·ble,** *adj.* —**patch′er,** *n.* —**patch′less,** *adj.*
—**Syn. 9.** See **mend. 12.** fix. —**Ant. 9.** break.

patch[2] (pach), *n.* a clown, fool, or booby. [? < It *pazzo* fool]

Patch (pach), *n.* **Alexander McCar·rell** (mə kar′əl), 1889–1945, U.S. World War II general.

Patch·en (pach′ən), *n.* **Kenneth,** born 1911, U.S. poet and novelist.

Pat·chogue (pat′chôg, -chog), *n.* a town on S Long Island, in SE New York. 8838 (1960).

patch·ou·li (pach′o͝o lē, pə cho͞o′lē), *n.* **1.** either of two East Indian, menthaceous plants, *Pogostemon Heyneanus* or *P. Cablin,* which yield a fragrant oil. **2.** a penetrating perfume derived from it. Also, **pachouli, patch′ou·ly.** [< Tamil *pacculi*]

patch′ pock′et, a pocket formed by sewing a piece of shaped material to the outside of a garment.

patch·stand (pach′stand′), *n.* a small tazza. [PATCH[1] + STAND]

patch′ test′, a test for allergy in which an allergic condition is indicated by an inflammatory reaction to a patch of material impregnated with an allergen applied to the skin.

patch·work (pach′wûrk′), *n.* **1.** work made of pieces of cloth or leather of various colors or shapes sewed together, used esp. for covering quilts, cushions, etc. **2.** something made up of an incongruous variety of pieces or parts: *a patchwork of verse forms.* [PATCH[1] + WORK] —**patch′work′y,** *adj.*

patch·y (pach′ē), *adj.,* **patch·i·er, patch·i·est. 1.** characterized by or made up of patches. **2.** occurring in, forming, or like patches. **3.** of inconsistent or irregular quality, texture, etc.; not uniform: *patchy acting; patchy areas of fog.* [PATCH[1] + -Y[1]] —**patch′i·ly,** *adv.* —**patch′i·ness,** *n.*

patd., patented.

pate (pāt), *n.* **1.** the head. **2.** the crown or top of the head. **3.** the brain. [ME]

pâte (pät), *n.* porcelain paste used in ceramic work. [< F; see PASTE]

pâ·té (pä tā′), *n., pl.* **-tés** (-tāz′; *Fr.* -tā′). **1.** *French Cookery.* a paste or spread made of liver, meat, fish, game, etc., often baked in a pastry and served as an hors d'oeuvre. **2.** See under **foie gras.** [< F; see PASTY[2]]

pâte à chou (pä ta sho͞o′), *French Cookery.* See **cream puff paste.** [< F: lit., cabbage paste]

-pated, a combining form of **pate:** *addlepated.* [PATE + -ED[3]]

pâ·té de foie gras (pä tā′ də fwä′ grä′; *Fr.* pä-tā′ də fwa grä′), *pl.* **pâ·tés de foie gras** (pä tāz′ də fwä′ grä′; *Fr.* pä tā′ də fwa grä′). See under **foie gras.** [< F: goose-liver pâté]

pâte de verre (pät də ver′), *French.* a decorative glass made in a mold in which powdered glass of various hues is mixed, blended, and fused. [lit., glass paste]

pâte dure (*Fr.* pät dyr′). See **hard paste.** [< F: lit., hard paste]

pa·tel·la (pə tel′ə), *n., pl.* **-tel·lae** (-tel′ē). **1.** *Anat.* the flat, movable bone at the front of the knee; kneecap. See diag. under **skeleton. 2.** *Biol.* a panlike or cuplike formation. **3.** *Archaeol.* a small pan or shallow vessel. [< L, dim. of *patina, patena* pan, lit., something wide open. See PATENT] —**pa·tel′lar,** *adj.*

patel′lar re′flex. See **knee jerk.**

pa·tel·late (pə tel′it, -āt), *adj.* **1.** having a patella. **2.** patelliform. [PATELL(A) + -ATE[1]]

pa·tel·li·form (pə tel′ə fôrm′), *adj.* having the form of a patella; shaped like a saucer, kneecap, or limpet shell. [PATELL(A) + -I- + -FORM]

pat·en (pat′ən), *n.* a metal plate on which the bread is placed in the celebration of the Eucharist. Also, **patin, patine.** [ME *pateyn(e)* < OF *patene* < ML *patena, patina* Eucharistic plate (L: pan); akin to Gk *patánē*]

pa·ten·cy (pāt′ən sē), *n.* **1.** the state of being patent. **2.** *Med.* the condition of not being blocked or obstructed. **3.** *Phonet.* openness of articulation, found more or less in all phonemes except stops. [PATEN(T) + -CY]

pat·ent (pat′ənt *or, esp. Brit.,* pāt′ənt), *n.* **1.** a government grant to an inventor, his heirs, or assigns, for a stated period of time, conferring the exclusive right to make, use, licence, or vend an invention, process, etc. **2.** an invention, process, etc., that has been patented. **3.** an official document conferring some right, privilege, or the like. **4.** the instrument by which the United States conveys the legal fee-simple title to public land. —*adj.* **5.** protected by a patent; patented: *a patent cooling device.* **6.** pertaining to or dealing with patents, as upon inventions: *a patent attorney; a patent law.* **7.** conferred by a patent, as a right or privilege. **8.** appointed by a patent, as a person. **9.** open to notice or observation; evident; obvious: *a patent breach of good manners.* **10.** lying open; not enclosed or shut in: *a patent field.* **11.** *Chiefly Bot.* expanded or spreading. **12.** open, as a doorway or a passage. **13.** *Phonet.* open, in various degrees, to the passage of the breath stream. —*v.t.* **14.** to take out a patent on; obtain the exclusive rights to (an invention, process, etc.) by a patent. **15.** to originate and establish as one's own. **16.** *Metall.* to heat and quench (wire) so as to prepare its molecular structure for cold-drawing. **17.** to grant (public land) by a patent. [ME < L *patent-* (s. of *patēns*) open, orig. prp. of *patēre* to stand wide open; as n., short for *letters patent,* trans. of ML *litterae patentēs* open letters] —**pat′ent·a·bil′i·ty,** *n.* —**pat′ent·a·ble,** *adj.* —**pat′ent·a·bly,** *adv.* —**pat′-ent·ly,** *adv.*
—**Syn. 9.** clear, apparent, palpable, conspicuous, unconcealed. See **apparent.** —**Ant. 9.** dim, obscure, hidden.

pat′ent an′chor, *Naut.* **1.** (loosely) any of various stockless anchors housed in hawseholes. **2.** any anchor whose design is patented.

pat′ent-cut jib′ (pat′ənt kut′), *Naut.* See **mitered jib.**

pat·ent·ee (pat′ən tē′), *n.* a person to whom or a group or company to which a patent is granted. [late ME; see PATENT, -EE]

pat′ent eye′. See **rope socket.**

pat′ent flour′, a fine grade of flour, consisting chiefly of the inner part of the endosperm.

pat′ent fora′men ova′le, *Pathol.* a congenital heart defect resulting from failure of the foramen ovale to close shortly after birth.

pat′ent ham′mer, a hammer for dressing stone, having a head with two faces formed of a number of broad, thin chisels bolted side by side.

pat′ent leath′er (pat′ənt, pat′ən *or, esp. Brit.,* pāt′ənt), a hard, glossy, smooth leather, used esp. in shoes and accessories.

pat′ent log′, *Naut.* any of various devices for determining the speed of a vessel by means of a vaned rotor streamed at the end of a log line upon which it exerts a torsion transmitted to a registering device on board.

pat′ent med′icine, 1. a medicine sold in drugstores or by salesmen without the buyer's needing a doctor's prescription. **2.** a medicine distributed by a company having a patent on its manufacture.

pat′ent of′fice, a governmental agency that administers and regulates patents and trademarks, in the U.S. forming a division of the Department of Commerce.

pat·en·tor (pat′ən tər), *n.* a person who grants patents. [PATENT + -OR[2]]

pat′ent right′, the exclusive right granted by a patent, as on an invention.

pat′ent slip′, *Brit.* See **marine railway.**

pa·ter (pā′tər; *also for 2, 3* pat′ər), *n.* **1.** *Brit. Informal.* father. **2.** (*often cap.*) the paternoster; Lord's Prayer. **3.** a recitation of it. [< L: father]

Pa·ter (pā′tər), *n.* **Walter Horatio,** 1839–94, English critic, essayist, and novelist.

pat·er·a (pat′ər ə), *n., pl.* **-er·ae** (-ə rē′). **1.** *Rom. Antiq.* a cup similar in shape and use to the phiale. **2.** an embossed ornament in the shape of a circle or ovoid. [< L, akin to *patēre* to be wide open]

pa·ter·fa·mil·i·as (pā′tər fə mil′ē əs, pä′-, pat′ər-), *n., pl.* **pa·ter·fa·mil·i·as·es** for 1, **pa·tres·fa·mil·i·as** (pā′trēz fə mil′ē əs, pä′-, pa′-) for 2. **1.** the male head of a household or family, usually the father. **2.** *Roman Law.* **a.** the head of the Roman family; a juridical entity who holds the patria potestas. **b.** a person who is not under the patria potestas of another. [< L: lit., father (i.e., master) of the household; see FAMILY] —**pa′ter·fa·mil′iar,** *adj.* —**pa′ter·fa·mil′iar·ly,** *adv.*

pa·ter·nal (pə tûr′nəl), *adj.* **1.** characteristic of or befitting a father; fatherly: *a kind and paternal reprimand.* **2.** of or pertaining to a father. **3.** related on the father's side: *one's paternal grandfather.* **4.** derived or inherited from a father: *paternal traits.* [< LL *paternāl(is),* equiv. to L *patern(us)* paternal (*pater* father + *-nus* adj. suffix) + *-ālis* -AL[1]] —**pa·ter′nal·ly,** *adv.*

pa·ter·nal·ism (pə tûr′nəlˌiz′əm), *n.* the system, principle, or practice of managing or governing individuals, businesses, nations, etc., in the manner of a father dealing with his children: *The employees objected to the paternalism of the old president.* [PATERNAL + -ISM] —**pa·ter′nal·ist,** *n., adj.* —**pa·ter′nal·is′tic,** *adj.* —**pa·ter′nal·is′ti·cal·ly,** *adv.*

pa·ter·ni·ty (pə tûr′ni tē), *n.* **1.** the state of being a father; fatherhood. **2.** derivation or acquirement from a father. **3.** origin or authorship. —*adj.* **4.** noting or pertaining to a legal dispute in which an unwed mother accuses a man of fathering her child: *a paternity suit.* [late ME *paternite* < eccl. L *paternitās* quality of fatherhood in God (said of or to a monk or priest). See PATERN(AL), -ITY]

pa·ter·nos·ter (pā′tər nos′tər, pat′ər-), *n.* **1.** (*often cap.*) Also, **Pa′ter Nos′ter.** the Lord's Prayer, esp. in the Latin form. **2.** a recitation of this prayer as an act of worship. **3.** one of certain beads in a rosary, regularly every 11th bead, differing in size or material from the rest and indicating that the Lord's Prayer is to be said. **4.** any statement or recital of words used as a prayer or magical charm. **5.** an elevator for persons or goods, having platforms or shelves rising and falling on an endless moving chain, used esp. in Europe. **6.** (*cap.*) *Archit.* See **pearl molding.** [ME, OE: Lord's prayer, named from L *pater noster* our father, its first two words in Vulgate version (Matthew VI. 9)]

Pa·ter Pa·tri·ae (pä′ter pä′trē ī′; *Eng.* pā′tər pā′-trē ē′), *Latin.* father of his country.

Pat·er·son (pat′ər sən), *n.* a city in NE New Jersey. 143,663 (1960).

pâte sur pâte (pät′ sər pät′), *Ceram.* a technique of decoration employing layers of slip, often of different colors or shades. [< F: lit., paste on paste]

pâte ten·dre (*Fr.* pät tän′drə). See **soft paste.** [< F]

path (path, päth), *n., pl.* **paths** (pathz, päthz, paths, päths). **1.** a way beaten or trodden by the feet of men or animals. **2.** a narrow walk or way: *a path through a garden; a bicycle path.* **3.** a route, course, or track along which something moves: *the path of a hurricane.* **4.** a course of action, conduct, or procedure: *the path of righteousness.* **5. cross one's path,** to encounter or meet unexpectedly: *Tragedy crossed our path again.* [ME; OE *pæth;* c. G *Pfad*]
—**Syn. 1.** footpath, pathway. PATH, LANE, TRAIL are passages or routes not as wide as a way or road. A PATH is a way for passing on foot; a track, beaten by feet, not specially constructed, often along the side of a road: *a path through a field.* A LANE is a narrow road or track, generally between fields, often enclosed with fences or trees; sometimes an alley or narrow road between buildings in towns: *a lane leading to a farmhouse; Drury Lane.* A TRAIL is a rough way made or worn through woods, or across mountains, prairies, or other untraveled regions: *an Indian trail.*

path-, var. of **patho-** before a vowel: *pathosis.*

-path, 1. an element occurring in agent nouns corresponding to nouns with stems ending in **-pathy** (*homeopath*). **2.** var. of **patho-** as final element of compounds (*psychopath*). Cf. **-pathia, -pathic, -pathy.**

path., **1.** pathological. **2.** pathology.

Pa·than (pə tän′, pət hän′), *n.* **1.** an Afghan. **2.** an Afghan dwelling in India.

Pa·than·kot (pə tän′kōt), *n.* a city in N Punjab, in N India. 46,300 (1961).

pa·thet·ic (pə thet′ik), *adj.* **1.** causing or evoking pity, sympathetic sadness, sorrow, etc.; pitiable: *a pathetic letter; a pathetic sight.* **2.** affecting or moving the feelings. **3.** pertaining to or caused by the feelings. **4.** miserably inadequate: *In return for our investment we get a pathetic three percent interest.* Also, **pa·thet′i·cal.** [< LL *pathēticus* < Gk *pathētikós* sensitive, equiv. to *pathēt(ós)* made or liable to suffer (verbid of *páschein* to suffer) + *-ikos* -IC] —**pa·thet′i·cal·ly,** *adv.* —**pa·thet′i·cal·ness,** *n.*
—**Syn. 1.** plaintive. **2.** touching, tender. **3.** emotional.

pathet′ic fal′lacy, the endowment of nature, inanimate objects, etc., with human traits and feelings, as in *the smiling skies; the undaunted cliffs of Dover.* [coined by John Ruskin in *Modern Painters*, Vol. III, Part IV (1856)]

path·find·er (path′fīn′dər, päth′-), *n.* **1.** a person who finds or makes a path, way, route, etc., esp. through a wilderness. **2.** an airplane, or a person dropped from a plane, sent into a target area to illuminate the area for succeeding aircraft. **3.** a radar beacon beamed into a target area to provide guidance for missiles seeking the target. [PATH + FINDER] —**path′find′ing,** *n.*

Pathfinder, The, a historical novel (1840) by James Fenimore Cooper. Cf. **Leather-Stocking Tales.**

-pathia, an obsolete var. of **-pathy:** *psychopathia.* [< NL; see -PATH, -IA]

-pathic, an element used to form adjectives from nouns with stems in **-pathy:** *psychopathic.* [< NL; see -PATH(Y), -IC]

path·less (path′lis, päth′-), *adj.* without paths; trackless; untrodden: *a pathless forest.* [PATH + -LESS] —**path′less·ness,** *n.*

patho-, a learned borrowing from the Greek meaning "suffering," "disease," "feeling," used in the formation of compound words: *pathology.* Also, *esp. before a vowel,* **path-.** Cf. **-path, -pathia, -pathic, -pathy.** [comb. form repr. Gk *páthos;* see PATHOS]

path·o·bi·ol·o·gy (path′ō bī ol′ə jē), *n.* pathology. [PATHO- + BIOLOGY] —**path·o·bi·o·log·i·cal** (path′ə-bī′ə loj′i kəl), *adj.* —**path′o·bi·ol′o·gist,** *n.*

path·o·cure (path′ə kyŏŏr′), *n.* *Psychiatry.* cessation of a neurosis with the appearance of an organic disease. [PATHO- + CURE]

path·o·for·mic (path′ə fôr′mik), *adj.* *Pathol.* pertaining to the beginning of a disease, esp. to symptoms that occur in the preliminary stages of mental disease. [PATHO- + -FORM + -IC]

path·o·gen (path′ə jən), *n.* any disease-producing organism. Also, **path·o·gene** (path′ə jēn′). [PATHO- + -GEN]

path·o·gen·e·sis (path′ə jen′i sis), *n.* the production and development of disease. Also, **pa·thog·e·ny** (pə thoj′ə nē). [< NL; see PATHO-, -GENESIS] —**path·o·ge·net·ic** (path′ō jə net′ik), *adj.*

path·o·gen·ic (path′ə jen′ik), *adj.* disease-producing. [PATHO- + GENIC]

path·o·ge·nic·i·ty (path′ō jə nis′i tē), *n.* the disease-producing capacity of a microorganism. [PATHOGENIC + -ITY]

pa·thog·no·mon·ic (pə thog′nə mon′ik), *adj.* *Med.* characteristic or diagnostic of a specific disease: *a pathognomonic sign of pneumonia.* [< Gk *pathognōmonik(ós)* skilled in judging disease. See PATHO-, GNOMON, -IC] —**pa·thog′no·mon′i·cal·ly,** *adv.*

pa·thog·no·my (pə thog′nə mē), *n.* *Med.* the study of the symptoms or characteristics of a disease; diagnosis. [PATHOGNOM(IC) + -Y³]

pa·thog·ra·phy (pə thog′rə fē), *n.* *Pathol.* a treatise on or a description of a disease. [PATHO- + -GRAPHY] —**path·o·graph·ic** (path′ə graf′ik), *adj.*

pathol., **1.** pathological. **2.** pathology.

path·o·log·i·cal (path′ə loj′i kəl), *adj.* **1.** of or pertaining to pathology. **2.** caused by or involving disease; morbid. **3.** dealing with diseases: *a pathological casebook.* Also, **path′o·log′ic.** [*pathologic* pertaining to disease (< Gk *pathologik(ós);* see PATHOLOG(Y), -IC) + -AL¹] —**path′o·log′i·cal·ly,** *adv.*

patholog′ic anat′omy, the branch of pathology dealing with the morphologic changes in tissues as observed through a microscope. —**path·o·log·i·co-an·a·tom·ic** (path′ə loj′i kō an′ə tom′ik), *adj.*

pa·thol·o·gy (pə thol′ə jē), *n., pl.* **-gies. 1.** the science or the study of the origin, nature, and course of diseases. **2.** the conditions and processes of a disease. **3.** any deviation from a healthy, normal, or efficient condition. [earlier *pathologia* < L < Gk. See PATHO-, -LOGY] —**pa·thol′o·gist,** *n.*

path·o·morph·ism (path′ə môr′fiz əm), *n.* abnormal morphology. [PATHO- + -MORPH + -ISM]

path·o·neu·ro·sis (path′ə nŏŏ rō′sis, -nyŏŏ-), *n.* *Psychiatry.* a neurotic concentration upon an actual illness or a part of the body affected by it. [PATHO- + NEUROSIS]

pa·thos (pā′thos), *n.* **1.** the quality or power, in literature, music, speech, or other expressive forms, of evoking a feeling of pity or compassion. **2.** pity. **3.** *Obs.* suffering. [< Gk: suffering, sensation, verbal n. of *páschein* to suffer]

pa·tho·sis (pə thō′sis), *n.* a diseased condition. [< NL; see PATH-, -OSIS]

path·way (path′wā′, päth′-), *n.* a path, course, route, or way. [PATH + WAY] —**path′wayed′,** *adj.*

-pathy, a noun element occurring in loan words from Greek, where it meant "suffering," "feeling" (*antipathy; sympathy*); in compound words of modern formation, often used with the meaning "morbid affection," "disease" (*arthropathy; deuteropathy; neuropathy; psychopathy*), and hence used also in names of systems or methods of treating disease (*allopathy; homeopathy; hydropathy; osteopathy*). Cf. **-path, -pathia.** [comb. form repr. Gk *pátheia* suffering, feeling, equiv. to *páth(os)* PATHOS + *-eia* -Y³]

Pa·ti·a·la (put′ē ä′lə), *n.* **1.** an important state of the former Punjab States: now part of Punjab in NW India. **2.** a city in E Punjab, in N India. 125,200 (1961).

pa·tience (pā′shəns), *n.* **1.** the bearing of provocation, annoyance, misfortune, pain, etc., without complaint, loss of temper, irritation, or the like. **2.** an ability or willingness to suppress restlessness or annoyance in waiting: *to have patience with a slow learner.* **3.** quiet perseverance; even-tempered care; diligence: *to work with patience.* **4.** *Cards.* solitaire. **5.** *Obs.* sufferance; leave; permission. **6.** Also called **pa′tience dock′.** a European dock, *Rumex Patientia,* having leaves used as a vegetable. [ME *pacience* < OF < L *patientia.* See PATIENT, -ENCE]
—**Syn. 1.** composure, stability, self-possession; submissiveness, sufferance. PATIENCE, ENDURANCE, FORTITUDE, STOICISM imply qualities of calmness, stability, and persistent courage in trying circumstances. PATIENCE may denote calm, self-possessed, and unrepining bearing of pain, misfortune, annoyance, or delay; or painstaking and untiring industry or (less often) application in the doing of something: *to bear afflictions with patience.* ENDURANCE denotes the ability to bear exertion, hardship, or suffering (without implication of moral qualities required or shown): *Running in a marathon requires great endurance.* FORTITUDE implies not only patience but courage and strength of character in the midst of pain, affliction, or hardship: *to show fortitude in adversity.* STOICISM is calm fortitude, with such repression of emotion as to seem almost like indifference to pleasure or pain: *The American Indians were noted for stoicism under torture.* **3.** indefatigability, persistence, assiduity.

Pa·tience (pā′shəns), *n.* a girl's given name.

pa·tient (pā′shənt), *n.* **1.** a person who is under medical or surgical treatment. **2.** *Rare.* a person or thing that undergoes some action. **3.** *Archaic.* a sufferer or victim. —*adj.* **4.** bearing misfortune, provocation, annoyance, delay, hardship, pain, etc., with fortitude and calm and without complaint, anger, or the like. **5.** characterized by or expressing such a quality: *a patient smile.* **6.** quietly persevering or diligent, esp. in detail or exactness: *a patient worker.* **7.** *Rare.* undergoing the action of another (opposed to *agent*). **8. patient of, a.** having or showing the capacity for endurance: *a man patient of distractions.* **b.** susceptible of: *This statement is patient of criticism.* [ME *pacient* < MF < L *patient-* (s. of *patiēns*), prp. of *pati* to undergo, suffer, bear; see -ENT] —**pa′tient·less,** *adj.* —**pa′tient·ly,** *adv.* —**pa′tient·ness,** *n.*
—**Syn. 1.** invalid. **4.** uncomplaining, long-suffering, forbearing, resigned, passive, calm. **5.** quiet, serene, unruffled, unexcited, self-possessed, composed. **6.** sedulous, assiduous, untiring. —**Ant. 4.** hostile. **5.** impatient, agitated.

pat·in (pat′ᵊn), *n.* paten. Also, **pat′ine.**

pat·i·na¹ (pat′ᵊnə), *n.* **1.** a film or incrustation, usually green, produced by oxidation on the surface of old bronze and esteemed as being of ornamental value. **2.** a similar film or coloring on some other substance. **3.** a surface calcification of implements, usually indicating great age. [< It: coating < L: pan. See PATEN]

pat·i·na² (pat′ᵊnə), *n., pl.* **-nae** (-nē′). a broad, shallow dish of the ancient Romans. [< L; see PATEN]

pat·i·nat·ed (pat′ᵊnā′tid), *adj.* covered with or having a patina. [PATIN(A)¹ + -ATE¹ + -ED²]

pat·i·na·tion (pat′ᵊnā′shən), *n.* **1.** the state of having or being covered with a patina. **2.** the process of forming or encrusting with a patina. [PATIN(A)¹ + -ATE¹ + -ION]

pat·i·nous (pat′ᵊnəs), *adj.* patinated. [PATIN(A)¹ + -OUS]

pa·ti·o (pat′ē ō′, pä′tē ō′), *n., pl.* **-ti·os. 1.** a courtyard, esp. of a house, surrounded by low buildings or walls. **2.** an area, usually paved, adjoining a house and serving as an area for outdoor living. [< Sp, OSp: courtyard, perh. orig. open area; cf. ML *patium* meadow, pasturage, ? deriv. of L **patius,* ptp. of *patēre* to lie open. See PATENT]

pa·tis·se·rie (pə tis′ə rē; *Fr.* pä tēsᵊ ʀē′), *n., pl.* **-ries** (-rēz; *Fr.* -ʀē′). **1.** an establishment where pastry, esp. French pastry, is made and sold. **2.** See **French pastry.** [< F *pâtisserie,* OF *pastiserie.* See PASTE¹, -ERY]

Pat·more (pat′mōr, -môr), *n.* **Co·ven·try (Ker·sey Digh·ton)** (kov′ən trē kûr′zē dīt′ᵊn, kuv′ən-), 1823–96, English poet and essayist.

Pat·mos (pat′mos, -mōs, pät′mōs), *n.* one of the Dodecanese Islands, off the SW coast of Asia Minor: St. John is supposed to have been exiled here. (Rev. 1:9). 2613 (1951); 13 sq. mi. Italian, **Pat·mo** (pät′mō). —**Pat′mi·an,** *adj.*

Pat·na (pat′nə, put′nä′), *n.* a city in and the capital of Bihar, in NE India, on the Ganges. 363,700 (1961).

Pat. Off., Patent Office.

pat·ois (pat′wä; *Fr.* pa twa′), *n., pl.* **pat·ois** (pat′wäz; *Fr.* pa twa′). **1.** a rural or provincial form of speech, esp. of French. **2.** an ungrammatical mixture of two or more languages. **3.** jargon; cant; argot. [< F: lit., clumsy speech; akin to OF *patoier* to handle clumsily, deriv. of *pate* paw; see -ESE]

Pa·ton (pāt′ᵊn), *n.* **Alan (Stewart),** born 1903, South African novelist.

pa·tonce (pə tons′), *adj.* *Heraldry.* (of a cross) split into three points at the end of each arm: *a cross patonce.* [alter. of late ME (*crosse*) *patife,* adj. of uncertain orig. and meaning]

pat. pend., patent pending.

Pa·tras (pə tras′, pa′trəs), *n.* **1.** Greek, **Pa·trai** (pä′-trē). a seaport in the Peloponnesus, in W Greece, on the Gulf of Patras. 95,364 (1961). **2. Gulf of,** an inlet of the Ionian Sea in the NW Peloponnesus. 10 mi. long; 25 mi. wide.

Pa·tre·cia (pə trē′shə), *n.* a girl's given name. Also, **Patricia.**

pa·tres con·scrip·ti (pä′tres kōn skrip′tē; *Eng.* pā′-trēz kən skrip′tī), *Latin.* See **conscript fathers.**

pa·tres·fa·mil·i·as (pā′trēz fə mil′ē əs, pä′-, pa′-), *n.* a pl. of **paterfamilias.**

Pa·tri (pä′trē), *n.* **An·ge·lo** (an′jə lō′), born 1877, U.S. educator and writer, born in Italy.

patri-, an element meaning "father," occurring originally in loan words from Greek and Latin (*patriarch; patrician*), and used in the formation of new compounds (*patrilineal*). [comb. form repr. L *pater,* Gk *patēr* FATHER]

pa·tri·a po·tes·tas (pä′trē ə pō tes′tas; *Lat.* pä′-trē ä′ pō tes′täs), *Roman Law.* the power vested in the paterfamilias or head of the Roman family with respect to his wife, natural or adopted children, and agnatic descendants: title to family property is vested exclusively in the paterfamilias. Property acquired by a family member becomes family property, and no family member can enter into a transaction in his own right. [< L: lit., paternal power]

pa·tri·arch (pā′trē ärk′), *n.* **1.** any of the earlier Biblical personages regarded as the fathers of the human race, comprising those from Adam to Noah (**antediluvian patriarchs**) and those between the Deluge and the birth of Abraham. **2.** any of the three great progenitors of the Israelites: Abraham, Isaac, or Jacob. **3.** any of the sons of Jacob (the **twelve patriarchs**), from whom the tribes of Israel were descended. **4.** (in the early Christian church) any of the bishops of any of the ancient sees of Alexandria, Antioch, Constantinople, Jerusalem, or Rome having authority over other bishops. **5.** *Gk. Orth. Ch.* the head of any of the ancient sees of Alexandria, Antioch, Constantinople, or Jerusalem, and sometimes including other sees of chief cities. Cf. **ecumenical patriarch. 6.** the head of certain other churches in the East, as the Coptic, Nestorian, and Armenian churches, that are not in full communication with the ecumenical patriarch of Constantinople. **7.** *Rom. Cath. Ch.* **a.** the pope as patriarch of the West. **b.** a bishop ranking next after the pope with either titular or active jurisdiction. **c.** the head of a Uniat church. **8.** *Mormon Ch.* any of the high dignitaries who pronounce the blessing of the church; Evangelist. **9.** one of the elders or leading older members of a community. **10.** a venerable old man. **11.** the male head of a family or tribal line. **12.** a person regarded as the father or founder of an order, class, etc. [ME; OE *patriarcha* < LL < Gk *patriárchēs* high-ranking bishop (eccl.), family head, equiv. to *patri(á)* family (deriv. of *patēr* father) + *-archēs* for *archós* ruler] —**pa′tri·ar′chal, pa′tri·ar′chic, pa′tri·ar′chi·cal,** *adj.* —**pa′tri·ar′chal·ly, pa′tri·ar′chi·cal·ly,** *adv.* —**pa′tri·arch′dom, pa′tri·arch·ship′,** *n.*

pa′triar′chal cross′, a Latin cross having a shorter crosspiece above the customary one. Also called **archiepiscopal cross.** See illus. under **cross.**

pa·tri·ar·chate (pā′trē är′kit), *n.* **1.** the office, dignity, jurisdiction, province, or residence of an ecclesiastical patriarch. **2.** a patriarchy. [< ML *patriarchātus,* equiv. to LL *patriarch(a)* (see PATRIARCH) + L *-ātus* -ATE¹]

pa·tri·ar·chy (pā′trē är′kē), *n., pl.* **-chies. 1.** a form of social organization in which the father is the supreme authority in the family, clan, or tribe and descent is reckoned in the male line, with the children belonging to the father's clan or tribe. **2.** a society, community, or country based on this social organization. [< Gk *patriarchía.* See PATRIARCH, -Y³]

Pa·tri·cia (pə trish′ə, -trē′shə), *n.* a girl's given name. Also, **Patrecia.**

pa·tri·cian (pə trish′ən), *n.* **1.** a member of the original senatorial aristocracy in ancient Rome. **2.** (under the later Roman and Byzantine Empires) a title or dignity conferred by the emperor. **3.** a member of an influential and hereditary ruling class in certain medieval German, Swiss, and Italian free cities. **4.** any person of noble or high rank; aristocrat. —*adj.* **5.** of or belonging to the patrician families of ancient Rome. **6.** of high social rank or noble family. **7.** befitting or characteristic of aristocrats: *patrician tastes.* [< L *patrici(us)* patrician (*pat(e)r* father + *-ic-* -IC + *-ius* adj. suffix) + -AN; r. late ME *patricion* (-ION for -IAN)] —**pa·tri′cian·hood′, pa·tri′cian·ship′,** *n.* —**pa·tri′cian·ism,** *n.* —**pa·tri′cian·ly,** *adv.*

pa·tri·ci·ate (pə trish′ē it, -āt′), *n.* **1.** the patrician class. **2.** patrician rank. [< ML *patriciāt(us),* equiv. to L *patrici(us)* (see PATRICIAN) + *-ātus* -ATE¹]

pat·ri·cide (pa′tri sīd′, pā′-), *n.* **1.** the act of killing one's father. **2.** a person who kills his father. [PATRI- + -CIDE] —**pat′ri·cid′al,** *adj.*

Pat·rick (pa′trik), *n.* **1. Saint,** A.D. 389?–461?, English missionary and bishop in Ireland: patron saint of Ireland. **2.** a boy's given name.

pat·ri·lat·er·al (pa′trə lat′ər əl, pā′-), *adj.* related through the father. Cf. **matrilateral.** [PATRI- + LATERAL]

pat·ri·lin·e·age (pa′trə lin′ē ij, pā′-), *n.* lineal descent traced through the male line. [PATRI- + LINEAGE¹]

pat·ri·lin·e·al (pa′trə lin′ē əl, pā′-), *adj.* inheriting or determining descent through the male line. Cf. **matrilineal.** [PATRI- + LINEAL] —**pat′ri·lin′e·al·ly,** *adv.*

pat·ri·lin·e·ar (pa′trə lin′ē ər, pā′-), *adj.* patrilineal. [PATRI- + LINEAR] —**pat′ri·lin′e·ar·ly,** *adv.*

pat·ri·li·ny (pa′trə lī′nē, pā′-), *n., pl.* **-nies.** the tracing of descent through the father's line of a family. [PATRILIN(EAL) + -Y³]

pat·ri·lo·cal (pa′trə lō′kəl, pā′-), *adj.* **1.** *Anthropol.* living with or located near the husband's relatives; virilocal. **2.** of or pertaining to residence with the family or tribe of one's husband. Cf. **matrilocal.** [PATRI- + LOCAL] —**pat·ri·lo·cal·i·ty** (pa′trə lō kal′i-tē), *n.*

pat·ri·mo·ny (pa′trə mō′nē), *n., pl.* **-nies. 1.** an estate inherited from one's father or ancestors. **2.** any quality, characteristic, etc., that is inherited; heritage. **3.** the aggregate of one's property. **4.** the estate or endowment of a church, religious house, etc. [ME *patrimonie* < MF < L *patrimoni(um).* See PATRI-, -MONY] —**pat′ri·mo′ni·al,** *adj.* —**pat′ri·mo′ni·al·ly,** *adv.*
—**Syn. 1.** inheritance.

pa·tri·ot (pā′trē ət, -ot′ *or, esp. Brit.,* pa′trē ət), *n.* a person who loves, supports, and defends his country and its interests with devotion. [< MF *patriote* < LL *patriōta* fellow-countryman < Gk *patriṓtēs,* deriv. of *pátrio(s)* of one's fathers, deriv. of *patrís* one's fatherland]

pa·tri·ot·ic (pā′trē ot′ik *or, esp. Brit.,* pa′-), *adj.* **1.** of, like, suitable for, or characteristic of a patriot. **2.** expressing or inspired by patriotism: *a patriotic ode.* [< LL *patriōtic(us)* < Gk *patriōtikós.* See PATRIOT, -IC] —**pa′tri·ot′i·cal·ly,** *adv.*

pa·tri·ot·ism (pā′trē ə tiz′əm *or, esp. Brit.,* pa′-), *n.* devoted love, support, and defense of one's country; national loyalty. [PATRIOT + -ISM]

Pa′triots' Day′, April 19th, the anniversary of the battle of Lexington in 1775, observed as a legal holiday in Massachusetts and Maine.

Pat·ri·pas·si·an (pa/trə pas/ē ən, pā/-), *n.* a person who advocates Patripassianism. Also, **Pat/ri·pas/si·an·ist.** [< LL *patripassiān(us).* See PATRI-, PASSION, -IAN] —**Pat/ri·pas/si·an·ly,** *adv.*

Pat·ri·pas·si·an·ism (pa/trə pas/ē ə niz/əm, pā/-), *n.* the doctrine that God the Father suffered in the sufferings of Jesus Christ. [PATRIPASSIAN + -ISM]

pat·ri·po·tes·tal (pa/trə pō tes/tᵊl, pā/-), *adj. Anthropol.* of or pertaining to the authority exercised by a father or a father's blood relatives. [PATRI- + POTESTAL]

pa·tris·tic (pə tris/tik), *adj.* of or pertaining to the fathers of the Christian church or their writings. Also, **pa·tris/ti·cal.** [PATR(I)- + -ISTIC] —**pa·tris/ti·cal·ly,** *adv.* —**pa·tris/ti·cal·ness,** *n.*

pa·tris·tics (pə tris/tiks), *n.* (*construed as sing.*) patrology (def. 1). [see PATRISTIC, -ICS]

pa·trix (pā/triks), *n., pl.* **-tri·ces** (-tri sēz/), **-trix·es.** *Print.* a mold of a Linotype for casting right-reading type for use in dry offset. [< NL; see PATRI-, MATRIX]

Pa·tro·clus (pə trō/kləs), *n. Class. Myth.* a friend of Achilles who was slain by Hector and whose death led Achilles to return to battle.

pa·trol (pə trōl/), *v.,* **-trolled, -trol·ling,** *n.* —*v.i.* **1.** (of a policeman, soldier, etc.) to pass along a road, beat, etc., or around or through a specified area in order to maintain order and security. —*v.t.* **2.** to maintain the order and security of (a road, beat, area, etc.) by passing along or through it. —*n.* **3.** a person or group of persons assigned to patrol an area, road, etc. **4.** an automobile, ship, plane, squadron, fleet, etc., assigned to patrol an area. **5.** *Mil.* a detachment of two or more men, often a squad or platoon, detailed for reconnaissance or combat. **6.** the act of patrolling. **7.** See **patrol wagon. 8.** (in the Boy Scouts and Girl Scouts) a subdivision of a troop, usually consisting of about eight members. [< F *patrouille* (n.), *patrouiller* (v.) patrol, orig. a pawing (n.), to paw (v.) in mud; deriv. (with suffixal *-ouille*) of *patte* paw; *-r-* unexplained] —**pa·trol/ler,** *n.*

pa·trol·man (pə trōl/mən), *n., pl.* **-men. 1.** a policeman who is assigned to patrol a specific district, route, etc. **2.** a man who patrols. [PATROL + MAN[1]]

pa·trol·o·gist (pə trol/ə jist), *n.* a student of patrology. [PATROLOG(Y) + -IST]

pa·trol·o·gy (pə trol/ə jē), *n., pl.* **-gies. 1.** Also called **patristics.** the branch of theology dealing with the teachings of the church fathers. **2.** a collection of the writings of the early church fathers. [< NL *patrologia.* See PATRI-, -O-, -LOGY] —**pat·ro·log·ic** (pa/trə loj/ik), **pat/ro·log/i·cal,** *adj.*

patrol/ wag/on, an enclosed truck or van used by the police to transport prisoners. Also called **police wagon.**

pa·tron (pā/trən), *n.* **1.** a person who is a customer, client, or paying guest, esp. a regular one, of a store, hotel, or the like. **2.** a person who supports with money, gifts, efforts, or endorsement an artist, writer, museum, charity, institution, or the like: *a patron of scholars; art patrons.* **3.** one whose support or protection is solicited or acknowledged by the dedication of a book or other work. **4.** See **patron saint. 5.** *Rom. Hist.* the protector of a dependent or client, often the former master of a freedman still retaining certain rights over him. **6.** *Eccles.* a person who has the right of presenting a clergyman to a benefice. Also, *referring to a woman,* **pa·tron·ess** (pā/trə nis, pa/-). [ME < ML, L *patrōn(us)* legal protector, advocate (ML: lord, master) deriv. of *pater* father. See PATTERN] —**pa/tron·al, pa/tron·ly,** *adj.* —**pa/tron·dom, pa/tron·ship/,** *n.* —**pa/tron·less,** *adj.*

pa·tron·age (pā/trə nij, pa/-), *n.* **1.** the financial support or business afforded a store, hotel, or the like, by customers, clients, or paying guests. **2.** the position, encouragement, influence, or support of a patron, as toward an artist, institution, etc. **3.** the control of or power to make appointments to government jobs or the power to grant other political favors. **4.** offices, jobs, or other favors so controlled. **5.** the distribution of jobs and favors on a political basis, as to those who have supported one's party or political campaign. **6.** a condescending manner or attitude in granting favor; condescension: *an air of patronage toward his social inferiors.* **7.** the right of presentation to an ecclesiastical benefice; advowson. [ME < MF; see PATRON, -AGE]

pa·tron·ise (pā/trə nīz/), *v.t.,* **-ised, -is·ing.** *Chiefly Brit.* patronize. —**pa/tron·is/a·ble,** *adj.* —**pa/tron·is/er,** *n.*

pa·tron·is·ing (pa/trə nī/ziŋ), *adj. Chiefly Brit.* patronizing. —**pa/tron·is/ing·ly,** *adv.*

pa·tron·ize (pā/trə nīz/, pa/-), *v.t.,* **-ized, -iz·ing. 1.** to give (a store, restaurant, hotel, etc.) one's regular patronage; trade with. **2.** to behave in an offensively condescending manner toward: *a professor who patronizes his students.* **3.** to act as a patron toward (an artist, institution, etc.); support. Also, *esp. Brit.,* **patronise.** [PATRON + -IZE] —**pa/tron·iz/a·ble,** *adj.* —**pa/tron·iz/er,** *n.*

pa·tron·iz·ing (pā/trə nī/ziŋ, pa/-), *adj.* displaying or indicative of an unpleasantly condescending manner: *a patronizing greeting, accompanied by a smirk.* [PATRONIZE + -ING[2]] —**pa/tron·iz/ing·ly,** *adv.*

pa/tron saint/, a saint regarded as the special guardian of a person, group, trade, place, country, etc.

pat·ro·nym·ic (pa/trə nim/ik), *adj.* **1.** (of names) derived from the name of a father or ancestor, esp. by the addition of a suffix or prefix indicating descent. **2.** (of a suffix or prefix) indicating such descent. —*n.* **3.** a patronymic name, as *Williamson* (son of William) or *Macdonald* (son of Donald). **4.** a family name; surname. [< LL *patrōnymic(us)* < Gk *patrōnymikós,* equiv. to *patrōnym(os)* (see PATRI-, -ONYM) + *-ikos* -IC] —**pat/ro·nym/i·cal·ly,** *adv.*

pa·troon (pə trōōn/), *n.* one who held an estate in land with certain manorial privileges granted under the old Dutch governments of New York and New Jersey. [< D < L *patrōn(us).* See PATRON] —**pa·troon/ship,** *n.*

pat·sy (pat/sē), *n., pl.* **-sies.** *Slang.* **1.** a person upon whom the blame for something falls; scapegoat; fall guy. **2.** a person who is easily swindled, deceived, coerced, persuaded, etc. **3.** a person who is the object of a joke, ridicule, or the like. [?]

Pat·sy (pat/sē), *n.* **1.** a boy's given name, form of **Patrick. 2.** a girl's given name, form of **Patricia.**

pat·tée (pa tā/, pat/ē), *adj.* paty.

pat·ten (pat/ᵊn), *n.* **1.** any of various kinds of footwear, as a wooden shoe, a shoe with a wooden sole, a chopine, etc., to protect the feet from mud or wetness. **2.** a separate sole attached to a shoe or boot for this purpose. **3.** *Building Trades.* any stand or support, esp. one of a number resting on unbroken ground as a substitute for a foundation. [ME *paten* < MF *patin* wooden shoe, perh. deriv. of *pate* paw] —**pat/tened,** *adj.*

pat·ter[1] (pat/ər), *v.i.* **1.** to make a succession of light, tapping sounds: *Raindrops patter on the windowpane.* **2.** to move or walk lightly or quickly: *The child pattered across the room.* —*v.t.* **3.** to cause to patter. **4.** to spatter with something. —*n.* **5.** a rapid succession of light tapping sounds: *the steady patter of rain.* **6.** the act of pattering. [PAT[1] + -ER[6]]

pat·ter[2] (pat/ər), *n.* **1.** the usually glib and rapid speech or talk used by a magician while performing, a barker at a circus or sideshow, a comedian or other entertainer, a salesman of questionable wares, or the like; stylized or rehearsed talk used to attract attention, entertain, etc. **2.** meaningless, rapid talk; mere chatter; gabble. **3.** the jargon or cant of any class, group, etc. **4.** amusing lines delivered rapidly by an entertainer or performer, as in a comedian's routine or a song. —*v.i.* **5.** to talk glibly or rapidly, esp. with little regard to meaning; chatter. **6.** to repeat a paternoster or other prayer in a rapid, mechanical way. —*v.t.* **7.** to recite or repeat (prayers, verses, etc.) in a rapid, mechanical way. **8.** to repeat or say rapidly or glibly. [var. of PATER] —**pat/ter·er, pat/ter·ist,** *n.*

pat·ter[3] (pat/ər), *n.* one who or that which pats. [PAT[1] + -ER[1]]

pat·tern (pat/ərn), *n.* **1.** a decorative design, as for china, wallpaper, textile fabrics, etc. **2.** decoration or ornament having such a design. **3.** a natural or chance marking, configuration, or design: *patterns of frost on the window.* **4.** a distinctive style, model, or form: *a new pattern of army rifle.* **5.** a combination of qualities, acts, tendencies, etc., forming a consistent or characteristic arrangement: *the behavior patterns of teenagers.* **6.** an original or model considered for or deserving of imitation: *Our constitution has been a pattern for those of many new republics.* **7.** anything fashioned or designed to serve as a model or guide for something to be made: *a paper pattern for a dress.* **8.** a sufficient quantity of material for making a garment. **9.** a diagram of lines transmitted occasionally by a television station to aid in adjusting receiving sets; test pattern. **10.** *Foundry.* a model or form, usually of wood or metal, used for giving the shape of the interior of a mold. **11.** *Numis.* a coin, either the redesign of an existing piece or the model for a new one, submitted for authorization as a regular issue. **12.** the path of flight established for an aircraft approaching an airport at which it is to land. **13.** an example, instance, sample, or specimen. **14.** *Gunnery, Aerial Bombing.* **a.** the distribution of strikes around a target at which a shotgun or a number of rifle or artillery rounds has been fired or on which bombs have been dropped. **b.** a diagram showing such distribution. —*v.t.* **15.** to make or fashion after or according to a pattern. **16.** to cover or mark with a pattern. **17.** *Chiefly Brit. Dial.* **a.** to imitate. **b.** to attempt to match or duplicate. [ME *patron* < ML *patrōn(us)* model, special use of L *patrōnus* PATRON] —**pat/tern·a·ble,** *adj.* —**pat/tern·er,** *n.* —**pat/tern·less,** *adj.* —**pat/tern·like/,** *adj.* —**pat/tern·y,** *adj.*
—**Syn. 1.** figure. **4.** kind, sort. **6.** example, exemplar. **15.** copy, follow, imitate.

pat/tern bomb/ing, aerial bombing in which bombs are dropped on a target in a predetermined pattern. Also called **carpet bombing, saturation bombing.** Cf. **area bombing, precision bombing.**

pat·tern·ize (pat/ər nīz/), *v.t.,* **-ized, -iz·ing.** to conform to or arrange in a pattern. [PATTERN + -IZE]

pat·tern·mak·er (pat/ərn mā/kər), *n.* one who makes patterns, as for clothing, embroidery, etc. Also, **pat/tern mak/er.** [PATTERN + MAKER] —**pat/tern·mak/ing,** *n.*

Pat·ter·son (pat/ər sən), *n.* **1. Floyd,** born 1935, U.S. boxer: world heavyweight champion 1956–59, 1960–62. **2.** a town in S Louisiana. 2923 (1960).

pat/ter song/, a comic song depending for its humorous effect on rapid enunciation of the words, occurring most commonly in comic opera and operetta.

Pat·ti (pat/ē; *It., Sp.* pät/tē), *n.* **1. A·de·li·na** (ä/də lē/nä), (*Adela Juana Maria Patti*), 1843–1919, Italian operatic soprano, born in Spain. **2.** a girl's given name.

pat·tle (pat/ᵊl, pät/ᵊl), *n. Brit. Dial.* paddle[1] (def. 9).

Pat·ton (pat/ᵊn), *n.* **1. George Smith,** 1885–1945, U.S. general. **2.** a town in central Pennsylvania. 2880 (1960).

pat·ty (pat/ē), *n., pl.* **-ties. 1.** a little pie; pâté. **2.** any item of food covered with dough, batter, etc., and fried or baked: *oyster patties.* **3.** a thin, round piece of finely divided food, as of meat or the like: *hamburger patty.* **4.** a thin, round piece, as of candy: *peppermint patties.* [alter. of PÂTÉ]

Pat·ty (pat/ē), *n.* a girl's given name, form of **Patience, Patrecia,** or **Patricia.** Also, **Patti.**

pat·ty-cake (pat/i kāk/), *n.* pat-a-cake.

pat/ty pan/, 1. a small pan for baking patties. **2.** a variety of summer squash having a fluted rind.

pat/ty shell/, a cup-shaped shell of light, flaky pastry, for serving vegetable, fish, or meat mixtures, usually with a sauce.

pat·u·lous (pach/ə ləs), *adj.* **1.** open; gaping; expanded. **2.** *Bot.* **a.** spreading, as a tree or its boughs. **b.** spreading slightly, as a calyx. **c.** bearing the flowers loose or dispersed, as a peduncle. [< L *patulus* standing wide-open. See PATENT, -ULOUS] —**pat/u·lous·ly,** *adv.* —**pat/u·lous·ness,** *n.*

pat·y (pat/ē), *adj. Heraldry.* (of a cross) having arms of equal length, each expanding outward from the center; formée: *a cross paty.* Also, **pattée.** [late ME *pattee* < MF, equiv. to *patte* paw + *-ee,* fem. of *-é;* see -EE, -ATE[1]]

Pau (pō), *n.* a city in and the capital of Basses-Pyrénées, in SW France: winter resort. 61,468 (1962).

P.A.U., Pan American Union.

pau·cis ver·bis (pou/kis wer/bis; *Eng.* pô/sis vûr/bis), *Latin.* in few words; with or by few words.

pau·ci·ty (pô/si tē), *n.* smallness or insufficiency of number or amount; scarcity; scantiness: *a country marked by a paucity of resources.* [late ME *paucite* < L *paucitās* fewness, deriv. of *pauc(us)* few; see -ITY]

paugh·ty (pô/tē, päᴋʜ/-), *adj. Scot. and North Eng.* **1.** haughty; proud. **2.** insolent; impertinent. Also, **pauch/ty.** [?]

Paul (pôl *for 1, 2, 4;* poul *for 3*), *n.* **1.** died A.D. c67, the apostle to the gentiles: author of several of the Epistles. **2. Elliot (Harold),** 1891–1958, U.S. novelist. **3. Jean** (zhäN), pen name of Jean Paul Friedrich Richter. **4.** a boy's given name.

Paul I, 1. died A.D. 767, pope 757–767. **2.** Russian, **Pavel Petrovich** 1754–1801, emperor of Russia 1796–1801 (son of Peter III). **3.** 1901–64, king of Greece 1947–64.

Paul II, (*Pietro Barbo*) 1417–71, Italian ecclesiastic: pope 1464–71.

Paul III, (*Alessandro Farnese*) 1468–1549, Italian ecclesiastic: pope 1534–49.

Paul IV, (*Gian Pietro Caraffa*) 1476–1559, Italian ecclesiastic: pope 1555–59.

Paul V, (*Camillo Borghese*) 1552–1621, Italian ecclesiastic: pope 1605–21.

Paul VI, (*Giovanni Batista Montini*) 1897–1978, Italian ecclesiastic: pope 1963–78.

Pau·la (pô/lə), *n.* a girl's given name.

Paul-Bon·cour (pôl bôN kōōr/), *n.* **Jo·seph** (zhô zef/), 1873–1972, French lawyer and statesman: premier 1932–33.

Paul/ Bun/yan, a giant lumberjack, an American folk hero.

Paul·ding (pôl/diŋ), *n.* a town in NW Ohio. 2936 (1960).

paul·dron (pôl/drən), *n. Armor.* a piece of plate armor for the shoulder and the uppermost part of the arm, often overlapping the adjacent parts of the chest and back. Also called **epaulière.** Cf. **spaulder.** See diag. under **armor.** [earlier *paleron, poleron* (late ME *polronds,* pl.) < MF *(es)palleron* shoulder. See EPAULET]

Pau·lette (pô let/), *n.* a girl's given name.

Pau·li (pô/lē; *Ger.* pou/lē), *n.* **Wolf·gang** (wo͝olf/gaŋ; *Ger.* vôlf/gäŋ), 1900–1958, Austrian physicist in the U.S.: Nobel prize 1945.

Pau/li exclu/sion prin/ciple, *Physics.* See **exclusion principle.** [named after W. PAULI]

Paul·ine (pô/līn), *adj.* of or pertaining to the apostle Paul or to his doctrines or writings. [< ML *Paulīn(us).* See PAUL, -INE[1]]

Pau·line (pô lēn/), *n.* a girl's given name.

Paul/ine priv/ilege, *Rom. Cath. Ch.* (in canon law) the privilege given to converts to dissolve a marriage with an unbaptized spouse if either obstructs the religious practices of the other.

Paul·ing (pô/liŋ), *n.* **Li·nus Carl** (lī/nəs), born 1901, U.S. chemist: Nobel prize in chemistry 1954, Nobel prize for peace 1962.

Paul·in·ism (pô/lə niz/əm), *n.* the body of theologica doctrine taught by or attributed to the apostle Paul [PAULINE + -ISM] —**Paul/in·ist,** *n.* —**Paul/in·is/tic,** *adj.* —**Paul/in·is/ti·cal·ly,** *adv.*

Paul·in·ize (pô/lə nīz/), *v.,* **-ized, -iz·ing.** —*v.i.* **1.** to follow the doctrines of St. Paul the apostle. —*v.t.* **2.** to imbue with Paulinism. [PAULINE + -IZE]

Pau·li·nus (pô lī/nəs), *n.* **Saint,** died A.D. 644, Roman missionary in England with Augustine: 1st archbishop of York 633–644.

Paul·ist (pô/list), *n. Rom. Cath. Ch.* a member of the "Missionary Society of St. Paul the Apostle," a community of priests founded in New York in 1858. [PAUL + -IST]

Paull (pôl), *n.* a boy's given name, form of **Paul.**

pau·low·ni·a (pô lō/nē ə), *n.* **1.** a tree, *Paulownia tomentosa,* of Japan, having showy, pale-violet or blue flowers blossoming in early spring. **2.** any other tree of the genus *Paulownia.* [< NL; named after Anna *Paulovna,* daughter of Paul I of Russia; see -IA]

Paul/ Pry/, an inquisitive, meddlesome person. [from name of title-character of *Paul Pry* (1853) by John Poole (1786–1872), English playwright]

Pauls·bor·o (pôlz/bûr ō, -bur ō), *n.* a town in SW New Jersey. 8121 (1960).

Pauls/ Val/ley, a town in central Oklahoma. 6856 (1960).

Paum·gart·ner (poum/gärt/nər), *n.* **Bern·hard** (bern/härt), born 1887, Austrian composer, conductor, and musicologist.

Pa·u·mo·tu Archipel/ago (pä/ōō mō/tōō). See **Tuamotu Archipelago.**

paunch (pônch, pänch), *n.* **1.** the belly or abdomen. **2.** a large and protruding belly; potbelly. **3.** the rumen. [ME *paunche* < AF, equiv. to MF *pance,* deriv. of *pantices* (pl.) bowels] —**paunched,** *adj.*

paunch/ mat/, *Naut.* a mat woven from strands and used in sliding heavy objects or as a pad to prevent chafing. Also, **panch mat, punch mat.**

paunch·y (pôn/chē, pän/-), *adj.,* **paunch·i·er, paunch·i·est.** having a large and protruding belly: *a paunchy middle-aged man.* [PAUNCH + -Y[1]] —**paunch/i·ness,** *n.*

pau·per (pô/pər), *n.* **1.** a very poor person. **2.** a person without any means of support, esp. a destitute person who depends on aid from tax-based welfare funds. [< L: poor] —**pau/per·age, pau/per·dom,** *n.*

pau·per·ise (pô/pə rīz/), *v.t.,* **-ised, -is·ing.** *Chiefly Brit.* pauperize. —**pau/per·i·sa/tion,** *n.* —**pau/per·is/er,** *n.*

pau·per·ism (pô/pə riz/əm), *n.* the state or condition of utter poverty. [PAUPER + -ISM]

pau·per·ize (pô/pə rīz/), *v.t.,* **-ized, -iz·ing.** to make a pauper of: *His extravagance pauperized him.* Also, *esp. Brit.,* **pauperise.** [PAUPER + -IZE] —**pau/per·i·za/tion,** *n.* —**pau/per·iz/er,** *n.*

Paur (pour, pou/ər; *Ger.* pouʀ), *n.* **E·mil** (ā/mēl), 1855–1932, Austrian violinist and conductor.

pau·ra·que (pou rä/kā; *Sp.* pou ʀä/ke), *n., pl.* **-ques** (-kāz; *Sp.* -kes). a large, tropical American goatsucker, *Nyctidromus albicollis.* [< MexSp]

Pau·rice (pô rēs/), *n.* a boy's given name, form of **Paul** and **Maurice.**

Pau·sa·ni·as (pô sā/nē əs), *n.* fl. A.D. c175, Greek traveler, geographer, and author.

pause (pôz), *n.*, *v.*, **paused, paus·ing.** —*n.* **1.** a temporary stop or rest, esp. in speech or action: *a short pause after each stroke of the oar.* **2.** a cessation of activity because of doubt or uncertainty; hesitation. **3.** any comparatively brief stop, delay, wait, etc.: *I would like to make a pause in my talk, and continue after lunch.* **4.** a break or rest in speaking or reading to emphasize meaning, grammatical relation, metrical division, etc., or in writing or printing, depending on punctuation. **5.** *Pros.* a break or suspension, as a caesura, in a line of verse. **6.** *Music.* a fermata. **7. give pause,** to cause to hesitate, as from surprise, doubt, etc.: *These frightening statistics give us pause.* —*v.i.* **8.** to make a brief stop or delay; wait; hesitate: *He paused at the edge of the pool for a moment. I'll pause in my lecture so we can adjourn for lunch.* **9.** to dwell or linger (usually fol. by *upon*): *to pause upon a particular point.* [ME < L *pausa* < Gk *paûsis* a halt, equiv. to *paú(ein)* (to) stop + *-sis* -SIS] —**paus′al,** *adj.* —**pause′ful,** *adj.* —**pause′ful·ly,** *adv.* —**pause′less,** *adj.* —**pause′less·ly,** *adv.* —**paus′er,** *n.* —**paus′ing·ly,** *adv.*
—**Syn. 1, 2, 3.** suspension, interruption, break, halt; hiatus, lacuna. **8.** rest, waver. **9.** tarry, delay.

pav·age (pā′vij), *n.* *Eng. Law.* a tax for the paving of streets or highways. [< AF, OF. See PAVE, -AGE]

pa·vane (pə vän′, -van′; *Fr.* PA VAN′), *n.*, *pl.* **pa·vanes** (pə vänz′, -vanz′; *Fr.* PA VAN′). **1.** a stately dance dating from the 16th century. **2.** the music for this dance. Also, **pav·an** (pav′ən), **pavin.** [< MF < Sp *pavana,* deriv. of *pavo* peacock; see -AN]

pave (pāv), *v.t.*, **paved, pav·ing. 1.** to cover or lay (a road, walk, etc.) with stones, bricks, tiles, wood, concrete, or the like, so as to make a firm, level surface. **2. pave the way to** or **for,** to prepare for and facilitate the entrance of; lead up to: *Such a line of reasoning paves the way for a complete loss of faith.* [ME *pave(n)* < MF *pav(er)* < VL **pavare* for L *pavīre* to beat, ram, or tread down]

pa·vé (pə vā′, pav′ā; *Fr.* PA VĀ′), *n.*, *pl.* **pa·vés** (pə vāz′, pav′āz; *Fr.* PA VĀ′), *adv.* —*n.* **1.** a pavement. **2.** *Jewelry.* a setting of stones placed close together so as to show no metal between them. —*adv.* **3.** *Jewelry.* in the manner of a pavé; as a pavé: *diamonds set pavé.* [< F, ptp. of *paver.* See PAVE]

Pa·vel Pe·tro·vich (*Russ.* pä′vəl pə trô′vich). See **Paul I.**

pave·ment (pāv′mənt), *n.* **1.** a paved road, highway, etc. **2.** a surface, ground covering, or floor made by paving. **3.** a material used for paving. **4.** *Chiefly Brit.* sidewalk. [ME < OF < L *pavīment(um).* See PAVE, -MENT] —**pave·men·tal** (pāv men′tᵊl), *adj.*

pave′ment art′ist, *Chiefly Brit.* See **sidewalk artist.**

pave′ment light′. See **vault light.**

pav·er (pā′vər), *n.* **1.** one who or that which paves. **2.** an unglazed paving tile, esp. one larger than six inches square. [ME; see PAVE, -ER¹]

Pa·vi·a (pə vē′ə), *n.* a city in N Italy, S of Milan. 73,503 (1961).

pav·id (pav′id), *adj.* timid; afraid; fearful; frightened. [< L *pavid(us)* trembling, timid, deriv. of *pavēre* to quake; see -ID⁴]

pa·vil·ion (pə vil′yən), *n.* **1.** a light, usually open building used for shelter, concerts, exhibits, etc., as in a park or fair. **2.** *Archit.* a projecting element of a façade, used esp. at the center or at each end and usually treated so as to suggest a tower. **3.** any of a number of separate or attached buildings forming a hospital or the like. **4.** a tent, esp. a large and elaborate one. **5.** a small, ornamental building in a garden. **6.** Also called **base.** *Jewelry.* the part of a cut gem below the girdle. **7.** *Anat. Rare.* the auricle of the ear. —*v.t.* **8.** to shelter in or as in a pavilion. **9.** to furnish with pavilions. [ME *pavilon* < OF *paveillon* < L *pāpiliōn-* (s. of *pāpiliō*) butterfly]

pavil′ion roof′, a pyramidal hip roof.

pa·vil·lon (*Fr.* PA VĒ YÔN′), *n.*, *pl.* **-vil·lons** (*Fr.* -VĒ-YÔN′). *Music.* the bell of a wind instrument. [< F: lit., pavilion]

pa·vil·lon Chi·nois (*Fr.* PA VĒ YÔN′ SHĒ NWA′), *pl.* **pa·vil·lons Chi·nois** (*Fr.* PA VĒ YÔN′ SHĒ NWA′). crescent (def. 7). [< F: lit., Chinese pavilion]

pav·in (pav′ən), *n.* pavane.

pav·ing (pā′ving), *n.* **1.** a pavement. **2.** material for paving. [late ME; see PAVE, -ING¹]

pav·ior (pāv′yər), *n.* a paver. Also, *esp. Brit.,* **pav′·iour.** [alter. of late ME *pavier,* itself alter. of PAVER]

Pa·vi·o·tso (pä′vē ōt′sō), *n.*, *pl.* **-tsos,** (*esp. collectively*) **-tso.** See **Northern Paiute** (def. 1).

pav·is (pav′is), *n.* a large oblong shield of the late 14th through the early 16th centuries, often covering the entire body and used esp. by archers and infantrymen. Also, **pav′ise.** [ME *paveys* < MF *pavais* < OIt *pavese,* lit., of PAVIA; see -ESE]

pav·is·er (pav′i sər), *n.* a person armed with or bearing a pavis. [ME < OF *paves(s)ier.* See PAVIS, -ER²]

Pav·lo·dar (päv lo där′), *n.* a city in NE Kazakstan in the S Soviet Union in Asia. 130,000 (est. 1964).

Pav·lov (pav′lov; *Russ.* päv′lof), *n.* **I·van Pe·tro·vich** (i vän′ pe trô′vich), 1849–1936, Russian physiologist: Nobel prize for medicine 1904.

Pav·lo·va (päv lō′və; *Russ.* päv′lo vä), *n.* **An·na** (än′nä), 1885–1931, Russian ballet dancer.

Pa·vo (pā′vō), *n.*, *gen.* **Pa·vo·nis** (pə vō′nis). *Astron.* the Peacock, a southern constellation between Triangulum Australe and Indus. [< L: peacock]

pav·o·nine (pav′ə nīn′, -nin), *adj.* **1.** of or like the peacock. **2.** resembling the feathers of a peacock, as in coloring. [< L *pāvōnīn(us),* deriv. of *pāvō* (s. *pāvōn-*) peacock; see -INE¹]

paw¹ (pô), *n.* **1.** the foot of an animal having claws. **2.** the foot of any animal. **3.** *Informal.* the human hand: *Keep your paws off my property.* —*v.t.* **4.** to strike or scrape with the paws or feet: *a dog pawing the door.* **5.** *Informal.* to handle clumsily, rudely, or with unwelcome familiarity. —*v.i.* **6.** to beat or scrape the floor, ground, etc., with the paws or feet. **7.** *Informal.* to handle someone or something in a clumsy or rude manner or with unwelcome familiarity. [ME *pawe,* var. of *powe* < MF *poue* (c. Pr *pauta*) < Gmc; cf. D *poot,* G *Pfote*] —**paw′er,** *n.*

paw² (pô), *n.* *Informal.* father; pa. [by alter.]

Paw·ca·tuck (pô′kə tuk′), *n.* a town in SE Connecticut. 4389 (1960).

Paw·hus·ka (pô hus′kə), *n.* a town in N Oklahoma. 5414 (1960).

pawk·y (pô′kē), *adj.*, **pawk·i·er, pawk·i·est.** *Scot. and North Eng.* cunning; sly. [*pawk* trick (Scot) + -Y¹] —**pawk′i·ly,** *adv.* —**pawk′i·ness,** *n.*

pawl (pôl), *n.* **1.** a pivoted bar adapted to engage with the teeth of a ratchet wheel or the like so as to prevent movement or to impart motion. —*v.t.* **2.** to check or hold with a pawl. [? < D *pal;* see PALE²]

pawn¹ (pôn), *v.t.* **1.** to deposit as a security, as for money borrowed, esp. with a pawnbroker: *to pawn a watch.* **2.** to pledge; stake; risk: *to pawn one's life.* —*n.* **3.** the state of being deposited or held as security, esp. with or by a pawnbroker: *jewels in pawn.* **4.** something given or deposited as security, as for money borrowed. **5.** a person serving as security; hostage. **6.** the act of pawning. [late ME (Scot) *paun* pledge (r. 12th-century *pand,* found in Latinized form) < MFlem *paen;* akin to D *pand,* G *Pfand* pledge; cf. OF *pan(d)* < Gmc] —**pawn′a·ble,** *adj.* —**pawn·er** (pô′nər), **pawn·or** (pô′nər, -nôr), *n.*
—**Syn. 4.** pledge.

pawn² (pôn), *n.* **1.** *Chess.* one of eight men of one color and of the lowest value, usually moved one square at a time vertically and capturing diagonally. **2.** one who is used or manipulated to further another person's ends. [ME *poun* < AF, equiv. to MF *poon,* var. of *paon,* earlier *pe(h)on,* lit., walker; see PEON]

pawn·age (pô′nij), *n.* the act of pawning. [PAWN¹ + -AGE]

pawn·bro·ker (pôn′brō′kər), *n.* a person whose business is lending money at interest on personal, movable property deposited with him until redeemed. [PAWN¹ + BROKER] —**pawn′bro′king, pawn′bro′·ker·age, pawn′bro′ker·y,** *n.*

Paw·nee (pô nē′), *n.*, *pl.* **-nees,** (*esp. collectively*) **-nee. 1.** a member of a confederacy of North American Plains Indians of Caddoan stock formerly located along the Platte River valley, Nebraska, and now living in northern Oklahoma. **2.** the Caddoan language of the Pawnee Indians.

pawn·shop (pôn′shop′), *n.* the shop of a pawnbroker, esp. one where unredeemed items are displayed and sold. [PAWN¹ + SHOP]

pawn′ tick′et, a receipt given for goods left with a pawnbroker.

Paw Paw (pô′ pô′), a town in SW Michigan. 2970 (1960).

paw·paw (pô′pô′), *n.* papaw.

Paw′ Paw′ Lake′, a town in SW Michigan. 3518 (1960).

Paw·tuck·et (pô tuk′it), *n.* a city in NE Rhode Island. 81,001 (1960).

pax (paks), *n.* **1.** *Rom. Cath. Ch.* an embrace exchanged in turn by the celebrants during the Agnus Dei in a High Mass. **2.** (*cap.*) a period in history marked by the absence of major wars, usually imposed by a predominant nation. **3.** See **kiss of peace.** [< L: peace]

Pax (paks), *n.* the ancient Roman goddess of peace, identified with the Greek goddess Irene.

PAX, private automatic exchange.

Pax′ Bri·tan′ni·ca (bri tan′ə kə), a peace imposed by Great Britain upon hostile nations, esp. in the 19th century. [< L: British peace]

pax in bel·lo (päks′ in bel′ō; *Eng.* paks′ in bel′ō), *Latin.* peace in war.

Pax·os (pak′sos, -sōs), *n.* one of the Ionian Islands, off the NW coast of Greece. 7 sq. mi. Greek, **Pa·xoi** (pä ksē′).

Pax Ro·ma·na (paks′ rō mä′nə; *Lat.* päks′ RŌ-mä′nä), **1.** the terms of peace imposed by ancient Rome on its dominions. **2.** peace imposed by a strong nation on weaker nations that cannot afford to go against its wishes. **3.** an uneasy or hostile peace. [< L: Roman peace]

Pax·ton (paks′tən), *n.* **1. Sir Joseph,** 1801–65, English horticulturist and architect. **2.** a town in E Illinois. 4370 (1960). **3.** a boy's given name.

pax vo·bis·cum (päks′ wō bis′ko͝om; *Eng.* paks′ vō bis′kəm), *Latin.* peace be with you.

pax·wax (paks′waks′), *n.* *Brit. Dial.* the neck ligament; nuchal ligament. [late ME, alter. of ME *fax wax,* lit., hair growth (OE *feax* hair, *weaxan* to grow; see WAX²); cf. G *Haarwachs* sinew, lit., hair growth]

pay¹ (pā), *v.*, **paid** or (*Obs. except for def. 12*) **payed; pay·ing;** *n.*; *adj.* —*v.t.* **1.** to discharge (a debt, obligation, etc.), as by transferring money, goods, or doing something: *Please pay your bill.* **2.** to give (money, goods, etc.) in exchange for goods or in discharge of a debt or obligation: *He paid six dollars for the shirt.* **3.** to transfer money as compensation or recompense for work done or services rendered; to satisfy the claims of (a person, organization, etc.), as by giving money due: *He paid me for my work.* **4.** to defray (cost or expense). **5.** to give compensation for. **6.** to yield a recompense or return to; be profitable to: *Your training will pay you well in the future.* **7.** to yield as a return: *The stock pays four percent.* **8.** to requite, as for good, harm, offense, etc. (usually fol. by *back*). **9.** to retaliate upon or punish (usually fol. by *back, off,* or *out*): *He paid me back by refusing to talk to me.* **10.** to give or render (attention, regard, court, compliments, etc.) as if due or fitting. **11.** to make (a call, visit, etc.). **12.** *Naut.* to let (a vessel) fall off to leeward. —*v.i.* **13.** to transfer money, goods, etc., as in making a purchase or settling a debt. **14.** to discharge a debt or obligation. **15.** to yield a return, profit, or advantage; be worthwhile: *It pays to be honest.* **16.** to give compensation, as for damage or loss sustained. **17.** to suffer or be punished for something: *The murderer paid with his life.* **18. pay as you go, a.** to pay for (goods, services, etc.) at the time of purchase, as opposed to buying on credit. **b.** to spend no more than income permits; keep out of debt. **c.** to pay income tax by regular deductions from salary or wages. **19. pay down,** to give partial payment at the time of purchase, with the stipulation that the balance be paid in installments: *On this plan you pay only ten percent down.* **20. pay off, a.** to pay someone everything that is due him, esp. to do so and discharge from one's employ. **b.** to pay a debt in full. **c.** *Slang.* to bribe. **d.** to retaliate upon or punish. **e.** *Naut.* to fall off to leeward. **f.** to result in success or failure: *The risk payed off handsomely.* **21. pay one's** or **its way, a.** to pay one's portion of shared expenses. **b.** to yield a return on one's investment sufficient to repay one's expenses: *It will take time for the restaurant to begin paying its way.* **22. pay out, a.** to distribute (money, wages, etc.); disburse. **b.** to get revenge upon for an injury; punish. **c.** to let out (a rope) by slackening. **23. pay up, a.** to pay fully. **b.** to pay upon demand: *The gangsters used threats of violence to force the shopkeepers to pay up.*
—*n.* **24.** the act of paying or being paid; payment. **25.** wages, salary, or stipend. **26.** a person with reference to his solvency or reputation for meeting obligations: *The bank regards him as good pay.* **27.** paid employ: *in the pay of the enemy.* **28.** reward or punishment; requital. **29.** a rock stratum from which petroleum is obtained.
—*adj.* **30.** (of earth) containing a sufficient quantity of metal or other value to be profitably worked by the miner. **31.** having a mechanism with a slot into which coins are placed in payment for use: *a pay telephone; a pay toilet.* [ME *pay(en)* < OF *pai(er)* < L *pācāre* to pacify (by force of arms), ML: to satisfy, settle (a debt). See PEACE]
—**Syn. 1.** settle, liquidate. **3.** reward, reimburse, indemnify. **25.** remuneration, emolument, fee, honorarium, income, allowance. PAY, WAGE or WAGES, SALARY, STIPEND, EARNINGS are terms for amounts of money or equivalent benefits, usually given at a regular rate or at regular intervals, in return for services. PAY is the general term: *His pay went up every year.* WAGE usually designates the pay given at an hourly, daily, or weekly rate, often for manual or semiskilled work; WAGES usually means the cumulative amount paid at regular intervals for such work: *an hourly wage; weekly wages.* SALARY designates a fixed, periodic payment for regular work or services, usually computed on a monthly or yearly basis: *an annual salary paid in twelve equal monthly installments.* STIPEND designates a periodic payment, either as a professional salary or, more commonly, as a salary for a limited term of months or years in return for special services or as a grant in support of creative or scholarly work: *an annual stipend for work as a consultant; a stipend to cover living expenses.*

pay² (pā), *v.t.*, **payed, pay·ing.** *Naut.* to coat or cover (seams, a ship's bottom, etc.) with pitch, tar, or the like. [< MF, OF *pei(er)* < L *picāre* to smear with pitch, deriv. of *pix* (s. *pic-*) PITCH²]

pay·a·ble (pā′ə bəl), *adj.* **1.** owed; to be paid; due: *a loan payable in 30 days.* **2.** capable of being or liable to be paid. **3.** profitable. **4.** *Law.* imposing an obligation on the debtor. [late ME; see PAY¹, -ABLE] —**pay′a·bil′i·ty, pay′a·ble·ness,** *n.* —**pay′a·bly,** *adv.*

pay·box (pā′boks′), *n.* *Brit.* See **box office** (def. 1). [PAY¹ + BOX¹]

pay·day (pā′dā′), *n.* **1.** the day on which wages are given, payment is made, etc. **2.** *Slang.* a day or period during which a great deal of money, success, fame, etc., is won or obtained: *Payday came when she was given a screen test by a big Hollywood studio.* [PAY¹ + DAY]

pay′ dirt′, 1. dirt, gravel, or ore that can be mined profitably. **2.** *Informal.* any source of success or wealth; a fortunate discovery or profitable venture: *After months of experimentation, the scientists finally hit pay dirt.* **3.** *Football Slang.* See **end zone.**

pay·ee (pā ē′), *n.* a person to whom money is paid or is to be paid. [PAY¹ + -EE]

pay·er (pā′ər), *n.* **1.** a person who pays. **2.** the person named in a bill or note who has to pay the holder. [ME; see PAY¹, -ER¹]

Pay·ette (pā et′), *n.* a town in W Idaho. 4451 (1960).

pay·load (pā′lōd′), *n.* **1.** *Com.* **a.** the part of a cargo producing revenue or income, usually expressed in weight. **b.** the number of paying passengers, as on an airplane. **2.** *Rocketry, Aeron.* **a.** the bomb load, warhead, cargo, or passengers of an aircraft, a rocket, missile, etc., for delivery at a target or destination. **b.** the explosive energy of the warhead of a missile or of the bomb load of an aircraft: *a payload of 50 megatons.* [PAY¹ + LOAD]

pay·mas·ter (pā′mas′tər, -mä′stər), *n.* a person authorized by a company, government, etc., to pay out wages or salaries. [PAY¹ + MASTER] —**pay′mas′ter·ship′,** *n.*

pay·ment (pā′mənt), *n.* **1.** the act of paying. **2.** something that is paid; an amount paid; compensation; recompense. **3.** reward or punishment; requital. [ME, var. of *paiement* < MF. See PAY¹, -MENT]

Payne (pān), *n.* **John Howard,** 1791–1852, U.S. actor and dramatist.

pay·nim (pā′nim), *n.* *Archaic.* **1.** a pagan or heathen. **2.** a Muslim. [ME, var. of *painime* < OF < LL *paganism(us)* PAGANISM] —**pay′nim·hood′,** *n.*

pay·off (pā′ôf′, -of′), *n.* **1.** the payment of a salary, debt, wager, etc. **2.** the time at which such payment is made. **3.** a settlement or reckoning, as in retribution or reward. **4.** *Informal.* the consequence, outcome, or final sequence in a series of events, actions or circumstances: *The payoff was when they fired him.* **5.** *Informal.* the climax of something, esp. a story or joke. —*adj.* **6.** yielding results, esp. rewarding or decisive results: *a payoff play giving a team its chance.* [n. use of v. phrase *pay off*]

pay·o·la (pā ō′lə), *n.* *Informal.* a secret or private payment in return for the promotion of a product, service, etc., through the abuse of one's position, influence, or facilities. [humorous coinage: PAY¹ + *-ola,* as in *Victrola*]

pay·roll (pā′rōl′), *n.* **1.** a list of persons to be paid, with the amount due to each. **2.** the sum total of these amounts. **3.** the actual money to be paid out: *The bandits got away with the payroll.* **4.** the total number of people employed by a business firm or organization. Also, **pay′ roll′.** [PAY¹ + ROLL]

pay′roll deduc′tion insur′ance. See **salary savings insurance.**

Pay·san·dú (pī′sän do͞o′), *n.* a city in W Uruguay, on the Uruguay River. 44,000 (est. 1954).

Pay·son (pā′sən), *n.* a town in central Utah. 4237 (1960).

pay′ sta′tion, a public telephone, esp. one operated by a coin device.

payt., payment.

Pay·ton (pāt′ᵊn), *n.* a boy's given name.

pay-TV (pā′tē′vē′), *n.* See **subscription television.**

Paz Es·tens·so·ro (päs′ es′tens sô′rô), *n.* **Vic·tor** (bēk′tôr), born 1907, Bolivian economist and statesman: president 1952–56 and 1960–64.

Pb, *Chem.* lead. [< L *plumbum*]

P.B., 1. British Pharmacopoeia. [< L *Pharmacopoeia Britannica*] 2. Prayer Book.

p.b., *Baseball.* passed ball; passed balls.

P.B.A., Patrolmen's Benevolent Association.

PBI, *Med.* the protein-bound iodine in the blood.

PBX, a telephone system for private use, as for routing interoffice calls, usually having outside lines. [*P*(*rivate*) *B*(*ranch*) *Ex*(*change*)]

PC, personal computer: a microcomputer designed for individual use.

pc., 1. *pl.* **pcs.** piece. 2. prices.

P/C, 1. petty cash. 2. price current. Also, **p/c**

P.C., 1. Past Commander. 2. *Brit.* Police Constable. 3. Post Commander. 4. *Brit.* Prince Consort. 5. *Brit.* Privy Council.

p.c., 1. percent. 2. petty cash. 3. postal card. 4. (in prescriptions) after eating; after meals. [< L *post cibōs*] 5. price current.

PCB, *Chem.* polychlorinated biphenyl: any of a family of highly toxic compounds, now banned in the U.S., formerly used in industry and manufacturing and frequently discharged into rivers in chemical wastes: known to cause skin diseases in humans and suspected of causing birth defects and cancer in animals.

P-Celt·ic (pē′sel′tik, -kel′-), *n.* 1. the subbranch of Celtic in which the Proto-Indo-European *kw*-sound became a *p*-sound. Welsh, Breton, Cornish, and Gaulish belong to P-Celtic. —*adj.* 2. of or belonging to P-Celtic.

pcf, pounds per cubic foot.

pci, pounds per cubic inch.

PCP, *Slang.* a powerful illicit hallucinogenic drug made from phencyclidine. [*p*(*hen*)*c*(*yclidine*) + perh. (*peace*) *p*(*ill*), earlier designation]

pct., percent.

Pd, *Chem.* palladium.

pd., paid.

P.D., 1. per diem. 2. Police Department.

p.d., 1. per diem. 2. potential difference.

PDB, paradichlorobenzene.

Pd.B., Bachelor of Pedagogy.

Pd.D., Doctor of Pedagogy.

pdl, poundal.

Pd.M., Master of Pedagogy.

P.D.Q., *Slang.* immediately; at once: *You'd better get started P.D.Q.* [*p*(*retty*) *d*(*amn*) *q*(*uick*)]

pe (pā), *n.* 1. the 17th letter of the Hebrew alphabet. 2. either of the consonant sounds represented by this letter. Also, **peh.** [< Heb]

P.E., 1. Petroleum Engineer. 2. Presiding Elder. 3. See **printer's error.** 4. *Statistics.* probable error. 5. Professional Engineer. 6. Protestant Episcopal.

p.e., See **printer's error.**

pea[1] (pē), *n., pl.* **peas,** (*Archaic or Brit. Dial.*) **pease,** *adj.* —*n.* 1. the round, highly nutritious seed of a leguminous plant, *Pisum sativum.* 2. the plant itself. 3. any of various related or similar plants or their seed, as the chickpea. 4. something resembling a pea, esp. in being small and round. —*adj.* 5. pertaining to, growing, containing, or cooked with peas: *We cultivated some tomato vines and a pea patch.* 6. small or small and round (usually in combination). 7. *Coal Mining.* **a.** noting a size of anthracite of less than $^{13}/_{16}$ of an inch and more than $^3/_8$ of an inch in the longest dimension. **b.** noting a size of bituminous coal of less than $^3/_4$ of an inch and more than $^3/_8$ of an inch in the longest dimension. [back formation from PEASE, wrongly taken as pl.] —**pea′like′,** *adj.*

pea[2] (pē), *n. Naut.* bill[3] (def. 4). [? short for peak[1]]

pea′ bean′, a variety of kidney bean having a small, white seed, used dried for food.

Pea·bod·y (pē′bod′ē, -bə dē), *n.* 1. **Endicott,** 1857–1944, U.S. educator. 2. **George,** 1795–1869, U.S. merchant, banker, and philanthropist in England. 3. a city in NE Massachusetts. 32,202 (1960).

pea′body bird′, *Chiefly New England.* the white-throated sparrow. [prob. imit.]

peace (pēs), *n., v.,* **peaced, peac·ing,** *interj.* —*n.* 1. the normal, nonwarring condition of a nation, group of nations, or the world. 2. an agreement or treaty between warring or antagonistic nations, groups, etc., to end hostilities and abstain from further fighting or antagonism: *the Peace of Ryswick.* 3. a state of mutual harmony between people or groups, esp. in personal relations: *Try to live in peace with your neighbors.* 4. the normal freedom from civil commotion and violence of a community; public order and security: *He was arrested for being drunk and breaking the peace.* 5. cessation of or freedom from any strife or dissension. 6. freedom of the mind from annoyance, distraction, anxiety, an obsession, etc.; tranquility; serenity. 7. a state of tranquility or serenity: *May he rest in peace.* 8. a state or condition conducive to, proceeding from, or characterized by tranquility: *the peace of a mountain resort.* 9. silence; stillness: *The cawing of a crow broke the afternoon's peace.* 10. (*cap., italics*) a comedy (421 B.C.) by Aristophanes. 11. **hold one's peace,** to refrain from or cease speaking; keep silent: *He told her to hold her peace until he had finished.* 12. **keep the peace,** to maintain order; cause to refrain from creating a disturbance: *Several officers of the law were on hand to keep the peace.* 13. **make one's peace,** to become reconciled; acquiesce: *He repaired the fence he had broken and made his peace with the neighbor on whose property it stood.* 14. **make peace,** to ask for or arrange a cessation of hostilities or antagonism. —*v.i.* 15. *Obs.* to be or become silent. —*interj.* 16. keep still! silence! [ME *pes* < OF, var. of *pais* < L *pāc*(*em*), acc. of *pax* peace; akin to PACT] —**peace′less,** *adj.* —**peace′less·ness,** *n.* —**peace′like′,** *adj.*
—**Syn. 2.** armistice, truce, pact, accord. **3.** rapport.

peace·a·ble (pē′sə bəl), *adj.* 1. inclined to avoid strife or dissension; disposed to peace; quiet: *a peaceable person; to have a peaceable disposition.* 2. peaceful; tranquil: *in peaceable periods; a peaceable adjustment of a dispute.* [ME *pesible* < MF *paisible.* See PEACE, -ABLE] —**peace′a·ble·ness,** *n.* —**peace′a·bly,** *adv.*
—**Syn. 1.** amicable, friendly, amiable. See **pacific.** —**Ant. 1.** quarrelsome, hostile.

Peace′ Corps′, a civilian organization sponsored by the U.S. government to help natives of developing countries carry out practical technological, agricultural, educational, and public-health projects.

peace·ful (pēs′fəl), *adj.* 1. characterized by peace; free from war, strife, commotion, violence, or disorder: *a peaceful reign; a peaceful demonstration.* 2. of, pertaining to, or characteristic of a state or time of peace: *peaceful uses of atomic energy.* 3. peaceable; not argumentative or quarrelsome: *a peaceful disposition.* [ME *pesful.* See PEACE, -FUL] —**peace′ful·ly,** *adv.* —**peace′ful·ness,** *n.*
—**Syn. 1.** PEACEFUL, PLACID, SERENE, TRANQUIL refer to what is characterized by lack of strife or agitation. PEACEFUL today is rarely applied to persons; it refers to situations, scenes and activities free of disturbances, or, occasionally, of warfare: *a peaceful life.* PLACID, SERENE, TRANQUIL are used mainly of persons; when used of things (usually elements of nature) there is a touch of personification. PLACID suggests an unruffled calm that verges on complacency: *a placid disposition; a placid stream.* SERENE is a somewhat nobler word; when used of persons it suggests dignity, composure, and graciousness: *a serene old age;* when applied to nature there is a suggestion of mellowness: *the serene landscapes of autumn.* TRANQUIL implies a command of emotions, often because of strong faith, which keeps one unagitated even in the midst of excitement or danger. See **pacific.**

peace·mak·er (pēs′mā′kər), *n.* a person who or group or nation that tries to make peace, esp. by reconciling parties who disagree, quarrel, or fight. [ME; see PEACE, MAKER] —**peace′mak′ing,** *n., adj.*

peace′ offen′sive, an active program, policy, propaganda campaign, etc., by a national government for the purpose of terminating a war or period of hostility, lessening international tensions, or promoting peaceful cooperation with other nations.

peace′ of′fering, 1. a sacrificial offering made in order to assure communion with God. Ex. 20:24; Lev. 7:11–18. 2. any offering made to procure peace.

peace′ of′ficer, a civil officer appointed to preserve the public peace, as a sheriff or constable.

peace′ pipe′, calumet.

Peace′ Riv′er, a river in W Canada, flowing NE from the Rocky Mountains in E British Columbia through Alberta to the Slave River. 1050 mi. long.

peace·time (pēs′tīm′), *n.* 1. a time or period of peace. —*adj.* 2. of or for such a period: *peacetime uses of atomic energy.* [PEACE + TIME]

peach[1] (pēch), *n.* 1. the subacid, juicy, drupaceous fruit of a tree, *Prunus Persica.* 2. the tree itself, cultivated in temperate climates. 3. a light pinkish yellow, as of a peach. 4. *Informal.* a person or thing that is especially admired or enjoyed. —*adj.* 5. of the color peach. 6. made or cooked with peaches or a flavor like that of a peach: *peach pie.* [ME *peche* < MF < LL *persica,* fem. sing., L, neut. pl. of *Persicus* Persian; r. OE *persic* (masc.) < L *Persic*(*us*)] —**peach′like′,** *adj.*

peach[2] (pēch), *Slang.* —*v.i.* 1. to inform against an accomplice or associate. —*v.t.* 2. to inform against; betray. [late ME *peche,* aph. var. of ME *apeche* < AF *apech*(*er*) < LL *impedicāre* to hold up. See IMPEACH] —**peach′er,** *n.*

peach′ bark′ bee′tle, a bark beetle, *Phloeotribus liminaris,* that feeds on and nests in peach and other drupaceous trees.

peach′ bell′, a perennial herb, *Campanula persicifolia,* of Europe, having showy blue or white flowers.

peach′ blos′som, the flower of the peach tree: the State flower of Delaware.

peach·blow (pēch′blō′), *n.* a delicate purplish pink. [PEACH[1] + BLOW[2]]

peach′blow glass′, an American art glass made in various pale colors and sometimes having an under layer of milk glass.

peach′ bran′dy, brandy distilled from the fermented juice of peaches.

peach′ Mel′ba, a dessert consisting of half a cooked peach served with vanilla ice cream and Melba sauce. Also, **peach′ mel′ba, pêche Melba.**

peach′ tree′ bor′er, the larva of any of several clearwing moths, as *Sanninoidea exitiosa,* that bore into the wood of the peach and other drupaceous trees.

peach′ twig′ bor′er. See under **twig borer.**

peach·y (pē′chē), *adj.,* **peach·i·er, peach·i·est.** 1. resembling a peach, as in color or appearance. 2. *Informal.* (often used ironically) excellent, wonderful. [PEACH[1] + -Y[1]] —**peach′i·ness,** *n.*

pea·coat (pē′kōt′), *n.* See **pea jacket.** [*pea* (see PEA JACKET) + COAT]

Peacock (Peafowl), *Pavo cristatus* (Length 6½ to 7½ ft.)

pea·cock (pē′kok′), *n., pl.* **-cocks,** (*esp. collectively*) **-cock.** *v.* —*n.* 1. the male of the peafowl distinguished by its long, erectile, greenish, iridescent tail coverts that are brilliantly marked with ocellated spots. 2. any peafowl. 3. a vain, self-conscious person. 4. (*cap.*) *Astron.* the constellation Pavo. —*v.i.* 5. to make a vainglorious display; strut like a peacock. [ME *pecok,* equiv. to *pe-* (OE *pēa* peafowl < L *pāvōn*- PAVO) + *cok* (OE *coc* COCK[1])] —**pea′cock′er·y, pea′cock′ism,** *n.* —**pea′cock′ish, pea′cock′y,** *adj.* —**pea′cock′ish·ly,** *adv.* —**pea′cock′ish·ness,** *n.*

Pea·cock (pē′kok′), *n.* **Thomas Love,** 1785–1866, English poet and novelist.

pea′cock blue′, a lustrous greenish blue, as of certain peacock feathers.

pea·cock-flow·er (pē′kok′flou′ər), *n.* 1. See **Barbados pride** (def. 1). 2. See **royal poinciana.**

pea′cock i′ris, an herb, *Moraea Pavonia,* of South Africa, having hairy leaves and dark-spotted, orange-red flowers.

pea′cock ore′, bornite.

pea′cock worm′. See **feather-duster worm.**

pea′ crab′, any of several tiny crabs of the family *Pinnotheridae,* the female of which lives as a commensal in the shells of bivalve mollusks.

pea·fowl (pē′foul′), *n., pl.* **-fowls,** (*esp. collectively*) **-fowl.** any of several gallinaceous birds of the genera *Pavo,* of India, Ceylon, southeastern Asia, and the East Indies, and *Afropavo,* of Africa. Cf. **peacock, peahen.** [*pea* + FOWL; see PEACOCK]

peag (pēg), *n.* wampum (def. 1). [< AmerInd; see WAMPUM]

pea′ green′, a medium or yellowish green.

pea·hen (pē′hen′), *n.* the female peafowl. [late ME *pehenne.* See PEACOCK, HEN]

pea′ jack′et, a short coat of thick wool, usually double-breasted and navy in color, worn esp. by seamen. [*pea,* var. sp. of *pay, pee, pie* coat of coarse woolen cloth (late ME *pee, pey, pie;* akin to D *pij,* EFris *pey,* dial. Sw *paje*) + JACKET; ? modeled on NFris *pijekkat*]

peak[1] (pēk), *n.* 1. the pointed top of a mountain or ridge. 2. a mountain with a pointed summit. 3. the pointed top of anything. 4. the highest or most important point or level: *the peak of his career.* 5. the maximum point, degree, or volume of anything: *Traffic reaches its peak on this road about five o'clock.* 6. *Physics.* **a.** the maximum value of a quantity during a specified time interval: *a voltage peak.* **b.** the maximum power consumed or produced by a unit or group of units in a stated period of time. 7. a projecting point: *the peak of a man's beard.* 8. See **widow's peak.** 9. a projecting front piece, or vizor, of a cap. 10. *Naut.* **a.** the contracted part of a ship's hull at the bow or the stern. **b.** the upper after corner of a sail that is extended by a gaff. **c.** the outer extremity of a gaff. —*v.t.* 11. *Naut.* to raise the after end of (a yard, gaff, etc.) to or toward an angle above the horizontal. —*v.i.* 12. to project in a peak. [? < MLG *pēk* pick, pike] —**peak′less,** *adj.* —**peak′like′,** *adj.*
—**Syn. 2, 4.** pinnacle. **4.** acme, zenith. —**Ant. 4.** abyss, nadir.

peak[2] (pēk), *v.i.* to become weak, thin, and sickly. [?] —**peak′i·ly,** *adv.* —**peak′i·ness,** *n.* —**peak′ish,** *adj.* —**peak′ish·ly,** *adv.* —**peak′ish·ness,** *n.* —**peak′y,** *adj.*

peaked[1] (pēkt, pē′kid), *adj.* having a peak: *a peaked cap.* [late ME *pekyd.* See PEAK[1], -ED[3]]

peak·ed[2] (pē′kid), *adj.* pale; sickly; emaciated: *to have a peaked look about the face.* [PEAK[2] + -ED[2]] —**peak′ed·ly,** *adv.* —**peak′ed·ness,** *n.*

peal (pēl), *n.* 1. a loud, prolonged ringing of bells. 2. a set of bells tuned to one another. 3. a series of changes rung on a set of bells. 4. any loud, sustained sound or series of sounds, as of cannon, thunder, applause, laughter, etc. —*v.t.* 5. to sound loudly and sonorously: *to peal the bells of a tower.* 6. *Obs.* to assail with loud sounds. —*v.i.* 7. to sound forth in a peal; resound. [ME *pele,* akin to *peal* to beat, strike (now dial.)]

Peale (pēl), *n.* 1. **Charles Will·son** (wil′sən), 1741–1827, and his brother **James,** 1749–1831, U.S. painters. 2. **Raph·a·elle** (raf′ā el′, -ē el′, rä′fä-, -fē-), 1774–1825, and his brother **Rem·brandt** (rem′brant), 1778–1860, U.S. painters (sons of Charles Willson Peale).

pea·mouth (pē′mouth′), *n., pl.* **-mouths** (-mouŧħz′). a minnow, *Mylocheilus caurinus,* found in the northwestern U.S. and British Columbia. [PEA[1] + MOUTH]

pe·an[1] (pē′ən), *n.* paean (defs. 1, 2).

pean[2] (pēn), *n. Heraldry.* ermine or a fur similar to ermine in having gold spots on a black field. [< MF *pene,* lit., feather < L *penna*]

Pe·a·no (pe ä′nō; *It.* pe ä′nô), *n.* **Giu·sep·pe** (jo͞o zep′pe), 1858–1932, Italian mathematician.

Pea′no curve′, *Math.* a curve that passes through every point of a two-dimensional region. [named after G. PEANO]

Pea′no's pos′tulates, *Math.* a collection of axioms concerning the properties of the set of all positive integers, including the principle of mathematical induction. Also called **Pea′no's ax′ioms.** Cf. **principle of mathematical induction.** [named after G. PEANO]

pea·nut (pē′nut′), *n.* 1. the pod or fruit or the enclosed edible seed of a leguminous plant, *Arachis hypogaea.* The pod is forced underground in growing, where it ripens. 2. the plant itself. 3. **peanuts,** *Slang.* any small or insignificant person or thing, esp. a very small amount of money: *working for peanuts.* —*adj.* 4. of or pertaining to the peanut or peanuts. 5. made with or from peanuts. 6. *Slang.* small, insignificant, or petty. [PEA[1] + NUT]

Peanut, *Arachis hypogaea*

pea′nut but′ter, a smooth paste made from finely ground roasted peanuts, used as a spread or in cookery.

pea′nut gal′lery, 1. *Informal.* the rearmost section of seats in the balcony of a theater. 2. *Slang.* a source of insignificant criticism: *No remarks from the peanut gallery.*

pea′nut oil′, a yellow to greenish oil expressed or extracted from peanuts, used chiefly as a salad oil, as a vehicle for medicines, and in the manufacture of margarine and soap. Also called **arachis oil.**

pea′nut worm′, any small, unsegmented, marine worm of the phylum *Sipunculoidea,* which when disturbed retracts its anterior portion into the body, giving the appearance of a peanut seed.

pea·pod (pē′pod′), *n.* a small, double-ended boat used for lobstering along the coast of Maine and either rowed or rigged with a single gaff sail or spritsail. [PEA[1] + POD[1]]

pear (pâr), *n.* 1. the edible fruit, typically rounded but elongated and growing smaller toward the stem, of a rosaceous tree, *Pyrus communis.* 2. the tree itself. [ME *pe*(*e*)*re,* OE *peru* < LL *pira,* fem. sing., L pl. of *pirum* pear] —**pear′like′,** *adj.*

pear′ haw′, a shrub or small tree, *Crataegus uniflora,* of the eastern and southern coastal areas of the U.S., having pear-shaped, orange-red fruit. Also called **blackthorn.**

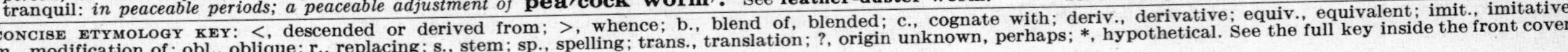
CONCISE ETYMOLOGY KEY: <, descended or derived from; >, whence; b., blend of, blended; c., cognate with; deriv., derivative; equiv., equivalent; imit., imitative; m., modification of; obl., oblique; r., replacing; s., stem; sp., spelling; trans., translation; ?, origin unknown, perhaps; *, hypothetical. See the full key inside the front cover.

pearl[1] (pûrl), *n.* **1.** a smooth, rounded concretion of aragonite or calcite with conchiolin, formed within the shells of certain mollusks to enclose irritating foreign objects, and valued as a gem when lustrous and finely colored. **2.** something resembling this, as various man-made substances for use in costume jewelry. **3.** something similar in form, luster, etc., as a dewdrop or a capsule of medicine. **4.** something precious or choice; the finest example of anything: *pearls of wisdom; a pearl among women.* **5.** a very pale gray approaching white but commonly with a bluish tinge. **6.** mother-of-pearl: *a pearl-handled revolver.* **7.** *Print.* a 5-point type. **8.** Also called **epithelial pearl.** *Pathol.* a rounded mass of keratin occurring in certain carcinomas of the skin. **9. cast pearls before swine,** to offer or give something of value to those incapable of appreciating it: *She read them Shakespeare, but it was casting pearls before swine.* —*v.t.* **10.** to adorn or stud with or as with pearls. **11.** to make like pearls, as in form or color. —*v.i.* **12.** to dive, fish, or search for pearls. **13.** to assume a pearllike form or appearance. —*adj.* **14.** of the color or luster of pearl; nacreous. **15.** of or pertaining to pearls. **16.** set with a pearl or pearls or covered or inlaid with pearls or mother-of-pearl. **17.** having or reduced to small, rounded grains. [ME *perle* < MF < It *perla* < VL **pernula,* dim. of L *perna* sea mussel] —**pearl′er,** *n.* —**pearl′ish,** *adj.* —**pearl′like′,** *adj.*

pearl[2] (pûrl), *v.t., n.* purl[2].

Pearl (pûrl), *n.* a girl's given name. Also, **Perle.**

pearl·ash (pûrl′ash′), *n.* commercial potassium carbonate. [PEARL[1] + ASH[1]]

pearl′ bar′ley, barley milled into small, round grains, used in cooking, esp. in soups.

pearl′ blue′, a light bluish gray. —**pearl′ blu′ish.**

pearl′ cot′ton, a two-ply mercerized cotton thread used chiefly in handweaving and needlework. Also, **perle cotton.**

pearl′ es′sence, a lustrous, silvery-white substance obtained from the scales of certain fishes or derived synthetically, as from mercuric chloride: used chiefly in the manufacture of simulated pearls and as a pigment in lacquers (**pearl′ lac′quers**).

pearl·eye (pûrl′ī′), *n., pl.* **-eyes,** (*esp. collectively*) **-eye.** any of several deep-sea fishes of the family *Scopelarchidae,* having large, hooked teeth on the tongue and a luminous organ on each eye. [PEARL[1] + EYE] —**pearl′-eyed′,** *adj.*

pearl·fish (pûrl′fish′), *n., pl.* **-fish·es,** (*esp. collectively*) **-fish.** any of several small fishes of the family *Carapidae,* living within pearl oysters, sea cucumbers, starfishes, etc. [PEARL[1] + FISH]

pearl′ gray′, a very pale bluish gray.

Pearl′ Har′bor, a harbor near Honolulu, on S Oahu, in Hawaii: surprise attack by Japan on the U.S. naval base December 7, 1941.

pearl·ite (pûr′līt), *n.* **1.** *Metall.* a microscopic lamellar structure found in iron or steel, composed of alternating layers of ferrite and cementite. **2.** *Petrog.* perlite. [PEARL[1] + -ITE[1]] —**pearl·it·ic** (pûr lit′ik), *adj.*

pearl·ized (pûr′līzd), *adj.* resembling or made to resemble mother-of-pearl; iridescent: *pearlized buttons; pearlized lipstick.* [PEARL[1] + -IZE + -ED[2]]

pearl′ mil′let, a tall grass, *Pennisetum glaucum,* cultivated in Africa, the Orient, and the southern U.S. for its edible seeds and as a forage plant. Also called **African millet, Indian millet.**

pearl′ mold′ing, *Archit.* a molding having the form of a row of pearls. Also called **bead molding, Paternoster.**

pearl′ oys′ter, any of several marine bivalve mollusks of the family *Pteriidae,* some of which form pearls of great value. Found in eastern Asia and off the coasts of Panama and Lower California.

Pearl′ Riv′er, **1.** a river flowing from central Mississippi into the Gulf of Mexico. 485 mi. long. **2.** Chu-Kiang.

pearl′ tapio′ca. See under **tapioca.**

pearl·y (pûr′lē), *adj.,* **pearl·i·er, pearl·i·est. 1.** like a pearl, esp. in being white or lustrous; nacreous. **2.** adorned with or abounding in pearls, pearl, or mother-of-pearl. [late ME *peerly.* See PEARL[1], -Y[1]] —**pearl′i·ness,** *n.*

pearl′y everlast′ing, an everlasting, *Anaphalis margaritacea,* of the North Temperate Zone, having white flowers.

Pearl′y Gates′, *Informal.* the entrance to heaven.

pearl′y nau′tilus, nautilus (def. 1).

pearl′y ra′zorfish. See under **razorfish.**

pear·main (pâr′mān), *n.* any of several varieties of apple. [late ME *parmayn* a kind of cooking pear, warden < MF *parmain,* lit., of PARMA; see -AN]

Pear′ Ridge′, a town in SE Texas. 3470 (1960).

Pear·sall (pēr′sôl), *n.* a town in SW Texas. 4957 (1960).

pear-shaped (pâr′shāpt′), *adj.* **1.** having the shape of a pear; tapering near the top and bulging toward the base or bottom: *a pear-shaped vase; a woman with a pear-shaped figure.* **2.** (of a vocal tone) clear, resonant, and without harshness; full-bodied.

Pear·son (pēr′sən), *n.* **1. Karl,** 1857–1936, English statistician. **2. Lester Bowles** (bōlz), born 1897, Canadian diplomat and politician: Nobel peace prize 1957; prime minister 1963–68.

peart (pērt, pyert), *adj. Dial.* lively; brisk; cheerful. [var. of PERT] —**peart′ly,** *adv.* —**peart′ness,** *n.*

Pea·ry (pēr′ē), *n.* **Robert Edwin,** 1856–1920, U.S. admiral and arctic explorer.

peas·ant (pez′ənt), *n.* **1.** one of a class of persons, as in European countries, of inferior social rank, usually engaged in agricultural labor. **2.** a rude, unsophisticated, usually uneducated person of little financial means, esp. one from the country; rustic. —*adj.* **3.** of, pertaining to, or characteristic of peasants or their traditions, way of life, crafts, etc. [late ME *paissaunt* < AF, MF *paisant,* OF *paisenc,* equiv. to *pais* country (< L *pāgus* country district + *-ēnsis* -ESE) + *-enc* < Gmc; see -ING[1]] —**peas′ant-like′,** *adj.*

peas′ant propri′etor, a peasant who owns land, esp. the land he tills. —**peas′ant propri′etorship.**

peas·ant·ry (pez′ən trē), *n.* **1.** peasants collectively. **2.** the status or character of a peasant. [PEASANT + -RY]

pease (pēz), *n., pl.* **pease.** *Archaic.* **1.** a pea. **2.** pl. of **pea.** [ME *pese,* OE *peose, pise* < LL *pisa* fem. sing., L pl. of *pisum* < Gk *píson* pea, pulse] —**pease′like′,** *adj.*

pease·cod (pēz′kod′), *n.* **1.** the pod of the pea. **2.** the front of a 16th-century doublet, quilted or stuffed to form a pointed bulge over the stomach and abdomen. Also, **peas′cod′.** [ME *pesecodde.* See PEASE, COD[2]]

pease′cod breast′plate, *Armor.* a breastplate having a long central ridge terminating in a raised area overhanging the waistline.

pease′ pud′ding, *Chiefly Brit.* a pudding of strained split peas mixed with egg.

pea·shoot·er (pē′sho͞o′tər), *n.* a tube through which dried peas, beans, etc., are blown, used as a toy. [PEA[1] + SHOOTER]

pea′ shrub′. See **pea tree** (def. 2).

pea′ soup′, **1.** a thick soup made from split peas. **2.** *Informal.* dense, yellow fog.

pea′ soup′er, **1.** *Chiefly Brit. Informal.* a thick fog. **2.** *Canadian Slang.* a French Canadian. [PEA SOUP + -ER[1]]

peat[1] (pēt), *n.* **1.** a highly organic soil, more than 50 percent combustible, composed of partially decayed vegetable matter found in marshy or damp regions, which is cut and then dried for use as fuel. **2.** such vegetable matter as a substance for fuel. [ME *pete* (AL *peta*) < ?]

peat[2] (pēt), *n. Obs.* a merry young girl; darling (used as a term of endearment). [?]

peat′ moss′, **1.** any moss, esp. of the genus *Sphagnum,* from which peat may form. **2.** such moss after it has been dried, used chiefly as a mulch or seed bed, for acidification.

pea′ tree′, **1.** a tree, *Agati grandiflora,* of tropical Asia, having very showy, red or white flowers. **2.** Also called **pea shrub.** a shrub, *Caragana arborescens,* of Siberia, having showy, yellow, pealike flowers, grown as an ornamental.

peat·y (pē′tē), *adj.,* **peat·i·er, peat·i·est.** of, pertaining to, resembling, or containing the substance peat. [PEAT[1] + -Y[1]]

peau de soie (pō′ də swä′, pō′ də swä′), a soft, satiny cloth of silk or rayon, grainy and having a dull luster, for dresses, coats, trimmings, etc. [< F: lit., pelt of silk]

pea·vey (pē′vē), *n., pl.* **-veys.** a cant hook having a sharply pointed end. [named after Joseph *Peavey,* the inventor]

pea·vy (pē′vē), *n., pl.* **-vies.** peavey.

pea′ wee′vil, a seed beetle, *Bruchus pisorum,* the larvae of which live in and feed on the seeds of the pea plant.

peb·a (peb′ə), *n.* See **nine-banded armadillo.** [short for Tupi *tatu-peba,* equiv. to *tatu* armadillo + *peba* low]

peb·ble (peb′əl), *n., v.,* **-bled, -bling.** —*n.* **1.** a small, rounded stone, esp. one worn by the action of water. **2.** Also called **peb′ble leath′er.** leather that has been given a granulated surface. **3.** a transparent colorless rock crystal used for the lenses of eyeglasses. **4.** a lens made from this crystal. —*v.t.* **5.** to prepare (leather) so as to have a granulated surface. **6.** to pelt with or as with pebbles. [ME *pibbil, puble,* etc., OE *pæbbel* (in place names)]

peb′ble dash′, an exterior wall finish composed of mortar against which, while still wet, small pebbles have been thrown and pressed in. Cf. **depeter, roughcast.** —**peb′ble-dashed′,** *adj.*

peb′ble heat′er, a heat exchanger utilizing refractory pellets to store and give off heat.

peb·bly (peb′lē), *adj.* **1.** having or covered with pebbles: *the pebbly beach at Nice.* **2.** (of a texture, design, etc.) having a granular or pebbled surface: *shoes with a pebbly finish.* [PEBBLE + -Y[1]]

pe·brine (pā brēn′), *n.* an infectious disease of silkworms, characterized by a black spotting of the integument and by stunted growth, caused by the protozoan *Nosema bomycis.* [< F < Pr *pebrino,* lit., peppery, with reference to the black spots. See PEPPER, -INE[1]]

pe·can (pi kän′, pi kan′, pē′kan), *n.* **1.** a hickory tree, *Carya illinoensis* (*C. Pecan*), indigenous to the lower Mississippi valley and grown in the southern U.S. for its oval, smooth-shelled nut having a sweet, oily, edible kernel: the State tree of Texas. **2.** the nut. [< Cree *pakan*]

pec·ca·ble (pek′ə bəl), *adj.* liable to sin or error. [< ML *peccābil(is).* See PECCAVI, -BLE] —**pec′ca·bil′i·ty,** *n.*

pec·ca·dil·lo (pek′ə dil′ō), *n., pl.* **-loes, -los.** a petty sin or offense; a trifling fault. [< Sp, dim. of *peccado* sin < L *peccātum* transgression, n. use of neut. of ptp. of *peccāre* to err, offend]

pec·cant (pek′ənt), *adj.* **1.** sinning; guilty of moral offense. **2.** violating a rule; faulty; wrong. [< L *peccant-* (s. of *peccāns,* prp. of *peccāre*), equiv. to *pecc-* sin + *-ant-* -ANT] —**pec′can·cy, pec′cant·ness,** *n.* —**pec′cant·ly,** *adv.*

Collared peccary, *Tayassu angulatus* (About 2 ft. high at shoulder; length 3 ft.)

pec·ca·ry (pek′ə rē), *n., pl.* **-ries,** (*esp. collectively*) **-ry.** any of several piglike, artiodactylous, hoofed mammals of the genus *Tayassu,* of North and South America, as *T. angulatus* (**collared peccary**), having a dark gray coat with a white collar. [< Carib; akin to Apalai dial. *pakira*]

pec·ca·to·pho·bi·a (pə kā′tə fō′bē ə, -kä′-), *n. Psychiatry.* an abnormal fear of sinning. [< L *peccāt(um)* sin + -o- + -PHOBIA]

pec·ca·vi (pe kä′vē, -kā′vē), *n., pl.* **-vis.** any confession of guilt or sin. [< L, perf. 1st. pers. sing. of *peccāre* to go wrong]

pech (pekʜ), *Scot. and North Eng. Dial.* —*n.* **1.** a short breath or gasp, as after exertion. —*v.i.* **2.** to breathe heavily from exertion; pant. Also, **pegh.** [late ME; imit.]

pech·an (pekʜ′ən), *n. Scot.* the stomach. [?]

pêche′ Mel′ba (pech, pesh), *pl.* **pêch·es Mel·ba** (pe′chiz, pesh). See **peach Melba.**

Pe·chen·ga (pe cheng′gä), *n.* Russian name of **Petsamo.**

Pe·cho·ra (pe chô′rä), *n.* a river in the NE Soviet Union in Europe, flowing from the Ural Mountains to the Arctic Ocean. 1110 mi. long.

peck[1] (pek), *n.* **1.** a dry measure of 8 quarts; the fourth part of a bushel, equal to 537.6 cubic inches. **2.** a container for measuring this quantity. *Abbr.:* pk, pk. **3.** a considerable quantity: *a peck of trouble.* [ME *pek* < OF < ?]

peck[2] (pek), *v.t.* **1.** to strike or indent with the beak, as a bird does, or with some pointed instrument, esp. with quick, repeated movements. **2.** to make (a hole, puncture, etc.) by such strokes. **3.** to take (food) bit by bit, with or as with the beak. —*v.i.* **4.** to make strokes with the beak or a pointed instrument. **5.** to pick or nibble at food (usually fol. by *at*). **6.** to carp or nag (usually fol. by *at*). —*n.* **7.** a quick stroke, as in pecking. **8.** a hole or mark made by or as by pecking. **9.** (in timber) incipient decay from fungi, occurring in isolated spots. [ME *pekk(en)* < MFlem; akin to PICK[1]]

peck·er (pek′ər), *n.* **1.** one who or that which pecks. **2.** a bird's bill. **3.** a woodpecker. **4.** *Slang* (*vulgar*). penis. **5.** *Brit. Slang.* one's spirits or courage: *Keep your pecker up!* [PECK[2] + -ER[1]]

peck·er·wood (pek′ər wo͝od′), *n.* **1.** *Southern and Midland U.S.* woodpecker. **2.** See **poor white.** [PECKER + WOOD[1]; inversion of WOODPECKER]

peck′ or′der, **1.** *Ornith.* a social relationship, esp. among domestic birds of the same species, in which a member of a flock that has asserted its dominance over one or more other members can peck the dominated without retaliation. **2.** *Informal.* a sequence or hierarchy of authority in an organization or social group. Also, **peck′ing or′der.**

Peck·sniff·i·an (pek snif′ē ən), *adj.* hypocritically affecting benevolence or high moral principles. [after Seth *Pecksniff,* character in *Martin Chuzzlewit* by Dickens; see -IAN] —**Peck′sniff′er·y, Peck·sniff′i·an·ism, Peck′sniff·ism,** *n.*

peck·y (pek′ē), *adj.,* **peck·i·er, peck·i·est.** (of timber) spotted with fungi. [PECK[2] + -Y[1]]

Pe·cos (pā′kəs, -kōs), *n.* a river flowing SE from N New Mexico through W Texas to the Rio Grande. 735 mi. long.

Pe′cos Bill′, the legendary cowboy of the American frontier who performed such fabulous feats as digging the Rio Grande River.

Pecs (pāch), *n.* a city in SW Hungary. 114,713 (1960). German, **Fünfkirchen.**

pec·tase (pek′tās), *n. Biochem.* an enzyme found in various fruits and involved in the formation of pectic acid from pectin. [PECT(IN) + -ASE]

pec·tate (pek′tāt), *n. Chem.* a salt or ester of pectic acid. [PECT(IC) + -ATE[2]]

pec·ten (pek′tən), *n., pl.* **-tens, -ti·nes** (-tə nēz′). **1.** *Zool., Anat.* **a.** a comblike part or process. **b.** a pigmented vascular membrane with parallel folds suggesting the teeth of a comb, projecting into the vitreous humor of the eye in birds and reptiles. **2.** any bivalve mollusk of the genus *Pecten;* scallop. [< L *pecten* comb, akin to *pectere,* Gk *pékein* to comb, card]

pec·tic (pek′tik), *adj.* pertaining to pectin. [< Gk *pēktik(ós)* congealing, equiv. to *pēkt(ós)* congealed (verbid of *pēgnýein* to make solid) + *-ikos* -IC]

pec′tic ac′id, *Chem.* any of several water-insoluble products of the hydrolysis of pectin esters.

pec·tin (pek′tin), *n. Biochem.* a white, amorphous, colloidal carbohydrate of high molecular weight occurring in ripe fruits, esp. in apples, currants, etc., and used as a base for fruit jellies and in pharmaceuticals and cosmetics because of its thickening and emulsifying properties and its ability to solidify to a gel. [< Gk *pēkt(ós)* fixed (see PECTIC) + -IN[2]] —**pec·ti·na·ceous** (pek′tə nā′shəs), *adj.*

pec·ti·nate (pek′tə nāt′), *adj.* formed into or having closely parallel, toothlike projections; comblike. Also, **pec′ti·nat′ed.** [< L *pectināt(us),* ptp. of *pectināre.* See PECTEN, -ATE[1]] —**pec′ti·nate′ly,** *adv.* —**pec′ti·na′tion,** *n.*

pec·ti·na·tel·la (pek′tə nā tel′ə, -nə-), *n.* a genus of fresh-water bryozoans, characterized by a gelatinous matrix in which the individuals forming the colony are embedded, growing as a jellylike mass on submerged stones, twigs, etc. [< NL, equiv. to L *pectināt(us)* PECTINATE + *-ella* dim. suffix]

pec·tin·o·gen (pek tin′ə jin, -jen′), *n. Biochem.* protopectin. [PECTIN + -O- + -GEN]

pec·tin·ose (pek′tə nōs′), *n. Chem.* arabinose. Also called **pec′tin sug′ar.** [PECTIN + -OSE[2]]

pec·tise (pek′tīz), *v.t., v.i.,* **-tised, -tis·ing.** *Chiefly Brit.* pectize. —**pec′tis·a·ble,** *adj.* —**pec′ti·sa′tion,** *n.*

pec·tize (pek′tīz), *v.t., v.i.,* **-tized, -tiz·ing.** to change into a jelly; jellify; gel; gelatinize; gelatinate. [< Gk *pēkt(ós)* fixed (see PECTIC) + -IZE] —**pec′tiz·a·ble,** *adj.* —**pec′ti·za′tion,** *n.*

pec·to·lite (pek′tə līt′), *n.* a mineral, hydrous calcium-sodium silicate, usually occurring in radiating groups of crystals in rock cavities. [< Gk *pēktó(s)* made solid (see PECTIC) + -LITE]

pec·to·ral (pek′tər əl), *adj.* **1.** of, in, on, or pertaining to the chest or breast; thoracic. **2.** worn on the breast or chest. **3.** proceeding from the heart or inner consciousness. **4.** *Speech.* (of a vocal quality) appearing to come from resonance in the chest; full or deep. **5.** of or for diseases of the lungs. —*n.* **6.** something worn on the breast for ornament, protection, etc., as a breastplate. **7.** See **pectoral fin.** **8.** *Anat.* a pectoral part or organ, as a muscle. [late ME < L *pectorāl(is)* of the breast (*pector-,* s. of *pectus* breast, + *-ālis* -AL[1]); *pectorāle* breastplate (n. use of neut. of adj.)] —**pec′to·ral·ly,** *adv.*

pec′toral cross′, *Eccles.* a cross worn on the breast by various prelates, as a designation of office.

pec′toral fin′, (in fishes) either of a pair of fins usually situated behind the head, one on each side, and corresponding to the forelimbs of higher vertebrates. See diag. under **fish.**

pec′toral gir′dle, **1.** (in vertebrates) a bony or cartilaginous arch supporting the forelimbs. **2.** (in man) the bony arch, formed by the clavicle or collarbone and scapula or shoulder blade, which attaches the upper limb to the axial skeleton. Also called **pec/toral arch/.**

pec·to·ra·lis (pek/tə ral/is, -rā/lis, -rä/-), *n., pl.* **-ra·les** (-ral/ēz, -rā/lēz, -rä/-). *Anat.* either of two muscles on each side of the upper and anterior part of the thorax, the action of the larger (**pec/toral/is ma/jor**) assisting in drawing the shoulder forward and rotating the arm inward, and the action of the smaller (**pec/toral/is mi/nor**) assisting in drawing the shoulder downward and forward. [< L; see PECTORAL]

pec/toral sand/piper, an American sandpiper, *Erolia melanotos,* the male of which, when courting, inflates its chest conspicuously.

pec·tose (pek/tōs), *n. Biochem.* protopectin. [PECT(IC) + -OSE[2]]

pec·tous (pek/təs), *adj. Biochem.* of, pertaining to, or consisting of pectin or protopectin. [*pect-* (repr. PECTIC, PECTIN, PECTOSE) + -OUS]

pec·u·late (pek/yə lāt/), *v.i., v.t.,* **-lat·ed, -lat·ing.** to steal or take dishonestly (money, esp. public funds, or property entrusted to one's care); embezzle. [v. use of *peculate* embezzlement (now obs.) < L *pecūlāt(us)* (4th decl. n.), deriv. of ptp. s. of *pecūlārī* to embezzle, lit., to make public property private. See PECULIAR, -ATE[1]] —**pec/u·la/tion,** *n.* —**pec/u·la/tor,** *n.*

pe·cul·iar (pi kyōōl/yər), *adj.* **1.** strange; queer; odd: *peculiar happenings.* **2.** uncommon; unusual: *the peculiar hobby of stuffing and mounting bats.* **3.** distinguished in nature or character from others. **4.** belonging characteristically (usually fol. by *to*): *an expression peculiar to Canadians.* **5.** belonging exclusively to some person, group, or thing: *the peculiar properties of a drug.* —*n.* **6.** a property or privilege belonging exclusively or characteristically to a person. **7.** *Brit.* a particular parish or church that is exempted from the jurisdiction of the ordinary or bishop in whose diocese it lies and is governed by another. **8. peculiars.** Also called **arbitraries.** *Print. Brit.* special characters not generally included in standard type fonts, as phonetic symbols, mathematical symbols, etc. [< L *pecūliār(is)* as one's own. See PECULIUM, -AR[1]] —**pe·cu/liar·ly,** *adv.*
—**Syn. 1.** eccentric, bizarre. See **strange. 2.** extraordinary, singular, exceptional. **3.** distinctive. **5.** individual, personal, particular, special, unique. —**Ant. 2, 5.** common.

pecu/liar institu/tion, *U.S. Archaic.* Negro slavery in the southern U.S. before the Civil War.

pe·cu·liar·ise (pi kyōōl/yə rīz/), *v.t.,* **-ised, -is·ing.** *Chiefly Brit.* peculiarize.

pe·cu·li·ar·i·ty (pi kyōō/lē ar/i tē, -kyōōl yar/-), *n., pl.* **-ties. 1.** a trait, manner, characteristic, or habit that is odd or unusual. **2.** oddity; singularity; eccentricity. **3.** the quality or condition of being peculiar. **4.** a distinguishing quality or characteristic. [< LL *pecūliāritās.* See PECULIAR, -ITY]
—**Syn. 1.** idiosyncrasy, eccentricity. **2.** irregularity. **4.** See **feature.**

pe·cu·liar·ize (pi kyōōl/yə rīz/), *v.t.,* **-ized, -iz·ing.** to make peculiar, unusual, distinguished, etc.: *to peculiarize a room with period furnishings.* Also, *esp. Brit.,* **peculiarise.** [PECULIAR + -IZE]

pecu/liar peo/ple, 1. the Jews as being God's chosen people. Deut. 14:2. **2.** a name adopted by certain fundamentalist Christians, signifying their refusal to conform to any rule of conduct which is contrary to the letter or spirit of the Bible.

pe·cu·li·um (pi kyōō/lē əm), *n.* **1.** private property. **2.** *Roman Law.* property given by a paterfamilias to those subject to him, or by a master to his slave, to be treated as though the property of the recipient. [< L, dim. of *pecū* money, orig. flock of sheep, akin to *pecus* cattle. See FEE]

pe·cu·ni·ar·y (pi kyōō/nē er/ē), *adj.* **1.** consisting of or given or exacted in money: *pecuniary tributes.* **2.** of or pertaining to money: *pecuniary difficulties.* **3.** (of a crime, violation, etc.) involving a money penalty or fine. [< L *pecūniāri(us),* deriv. of *pecūnia* property, money (*pecū* flock of sheep + unexplained *-n-* + *-ia* -IA); see -ARY] —**pe·cu·ni·ar·i·ly** (pi kyōō/nē âr/ə lē), *adv.*
—**Syn. 1.** See **financial.**

ped-[1], var. of **pedo-**[1] before a vowel: *pedagogic.* Also, **paed-, paedo-.**

ped-[2], var. of **pedi-**[1] before a vowel.

ped-[3], var. of **pedo-**[2] before a vowel: *pedalfer.*

-ped, var. of **pedi-**[1], as final element of compound words: *pinnatiped.* Also, **-pede.** Cf. **-pod.**

ped., **1.** pedal. **2.** pedestal.

ped·a·gog·ic (ped/ə goj/ik, -gō/jik), *adj.* of or pertaining to a pedagogue or pedagogy. Also, **ped/a·gog/i·cal, paedagogic.** [< Gk *paidagōgik(ós)* of a boy's tutor. See PEDAGOGUE, -IC] —**ped/a·gog/i·cal·ly,** *adv.*

ped·a·gog·ics (ped/ə goj/iks, -gō/jiks), *n.* (*construed as sing.*) the science or art of teaching or education; pedagogy. [PEDAGOG(Y) + -ICS]

ped·a·gog·ism (ped/ə gog/iz əm, -gô/giz-), *n.* the principles, manner, method, or characteristics of pedagogues. Also, **ped·a·gogu·ism** (ped/ə gog/iz əm, -gô/giz-). [PEDAGOG(Y) + -ISM]

ped·a·gogue (ped/ə gog/, -gôg/), *n.* **1.** a teacher; schoolteacher. **2.** a person who is pedantic, dogmatic, and formal. Also, **ped/a·gog/, paedagogue.** [ME *pedagoge* < L *paedagōg(us)* < Gk *paidagōgós* a boy's tutor. See PED-[1], -AGOGUE] —**ped/a·gogu/er·y, ped/a·gog/er·y,** *n.* —**ped/a·gogu/ish, ped/a·gog/ish,** *adj.*

ped·a·go·gy (ped/ə gō/jē, -goj/ē), *n., pl.* **-gies. 1.** the function or work of a teacher; teaching. **2.** the art or science of teaching; instructional methods. Also, **paedagogy.** [< Gk *paidagōgía* office of a boy's tutor. See PEDAGOGUE, -Y[3]]

ped·al (ped/əl *for 1–5;* pēd/əl *for 6–8*), *n., v.,* **-aled, -al·ing** or (*esp. Brit.*) **-alled, -al·ling,** *adj.* —*n.* **1.** a foot-operated lever used to control certain mechanisms, as powered vehicles, or to play or modify the sounds of certain musical instruments, as pianos, organs, or harps. **2.** *Music.* **a.** a foot-operated keyboard, as on an organ or harpsichord. **b.** any of the keys of such a keyboard. **c.** See **pedal point. 3.** a leverlike part worked by the foot to supply power in various mechanisms, as the sewing machine, bicycle, etc.; treadle. —*v.i.* **4.** to work or use the pedals, as in playing an organ, propelling a bicycle, etc. —*v.t.* **5.** to work the pedals of (an organ, bicycle, etc.). —*adj.* **6.** of or pertaining to a foot or the feet. **7.** of or pertaining to a pedal or pedals. **8.** using pedals: *a pedal mechanism.* [< L *pedāl(is)* of the feet. See PED-[2], -AL[1]]

pe·dal·fer (pi dal/fər), *n.* a soil rich in alumina and iron, with few or no carbonates. Cf. **pedocal.** [< Gk *pé̄d(on)* the ground + L *al(ūmen)* ALUM + *fer(rum)* iron]

ped/al key/board, pedal (def. 2a).

ped/al point/, *Music.* **1.** a tone sustained by one part, usually the bass, while other parts progress without reference to it. **2.** a passage containing it.

ped/al push/ers, slacks that extend to about the midpoint of the calf, originally worn for cycling.

ped·ant (ped/ənt), *n.* **1.** a person who makes an excessive or inappropriate show of learning. **2.** a person who overemphasizes rules or minor details. **3.** a person who adheres rigidly to book knowledge without regard to common sense. **4.** *Obs.* a schoolmaster. [< It *pedante* teacher, pedant, equiv. to *ped-,* *piede* foot (in meaning of servile follower); see -ANT] —**ped/ant·esque/,** *adj.* —**ped/ant·hood/,** *n.* —**pe·dan·tic** (pə dan/tik), **pe·dan/ti·cal,** *adj.* —**pe·dan/ti·cal·ly,** *adv.* —**pe·dan/ti·cal·ness,** *n.*

pe·dan·ti·cism (pə dan/ti siz/əm), *n.* pedantry. Also, **ped·ant·ism** (ped/ən tiz/əm). [PEDANTIC + -ISM]

ped·ant·ry (ped/ən trē), *n., pl.* **-ries. 1.** the character, qualities, practices, etc., of a pedant, esp. undue display of learning. **2.** slavish attention to rules, details, etc. **3.** an instance of being pedantic: *the pedantries of modern criticism.* [earlier *pedanteria* < It. See PEDANT, -RY]

Pedate leaves
A, Bird's-foot violet, *Viola pedata;* B, Arum, Genus *Arum*

Pe·da·sus (pē/də səs), *n.* (in the *Iliad*) the twin brother of Aesepus, killed in the Trojan War by Euryalus.

ped·ate (ped/āt), *adj.* **1.** having a foot or feet. **2.** resembling a foot. **3.** having divisions like toes. **4.** *Bot.* (of a leaf) palmately parted or divided with the lateral lobes or divisions cleft or divided. [< L *pedāt(us).* See PED-[2], -ATE[1]] —**ped/ate·ly,** *adv.*

pedati-, a combining form meaning "pedate," used in the formation of compound words: *pedatifid.* [comb. form repr. L *pedāt(us)* PEDATE + -I-]

pe·dat·i·fid (pə dat/ə fid, -dā/tə-), *adj. Bot.* pedately cleft. [PEDATI- + -FID]

pe·dat·i·lob·ate (pə dat/ə lō/bāt, -dā/tə-), *adj.* (of a leaf) pedately lobed. Also, **pe·dat/i·lobed/.** [PEDATI- + LOBATE]

Ped.D., Doctor of Pedagogy.

ped·dle (ped/əl), *v.,* **-dled, -dling.** —*v.t.* **1.** to carry (goods, wares, etc.) from place to place for sale at retail; hawk. **2.** to deal out, distribute, or dispense, esp. in small quantities: *to peddle radical ideas.* —*v.i.* **3.** to travel from place to place with goods, wares, etc., for sale at retail. **4.** to occupy oneself with trifles; trifle. [appar. back formation from PEDDLER and confused with PIDDLE]

ped·dler (ped/lər), *n.* a person who peddles. Also, **pedlar, pedler.** [ME *pedlere,* unexplained var. of *peder* (ME *peoddare*), deriv. of *ped* basket (ME *pedde*); the peder carried his wares in a ped]

ped·dler·y (ped/lə rē), *n., pl.* **-dler·ies. 1.** the business of a peddler. **2.** peddlers' wares. **3.** trumpery. Also, **pedlary, pedlery.** [PEDDLER + -Y[3]]

ped·dling (ped/ling), *adj.* trifling; paltry; piddling. [PEDDLE + -ING[2]] —**ped/dling·ly,** *adv.*

-pede, var. of **-ped:** *centipede.*

ped·er·ast (ped/ə rast/, pē/də-), *n.* a person who engages in pederasty. Also, **paederast.** [< Gk *paiderast(ḗs)* lover of boys, equiv. to *paid-* (s. of *paîs*) boy, child + *erastḗs* lover, deriv. of *erân* to love]

ped·er·as·ty (ped/ə ras/tē, pē/də-), *n.* unnatural sexual relations between two males, esp. when one is a young boy. Also, **paederasty.** [< NL *pederastia* < Gk *paiderastía* love of boys. See PEDERAST, -Y[3]] —**ped/er·as/tic,** *adj.* —**ped/er·as/ti·cal·ly,** *adv.*

pe·de·sis (pi dē/sis), *n., pl.* **-ses** (-sēz). See **Brownian movement.** [< Gk, equiv. to *pēd(ân)* (to) leap + *-ēsis* state of]

ped·es·tal (ped/i stəl), *n., v.,* **-taled, -tal·ing** or (*esp. Brit.*) **-talled, -tal·ling.** —*n.* **1.** an architectural support for a column, statue, vase, or the like. **2.** a supporting structure or piece; base. **3.** *Furniture.* **a.** a support for a desk, consisting of a boxlike frame containing drawers one above the other. **b.** a columnar support for a table top. **4.** *Building Trades.* a bulge cast at the bottom of a concrete pile. **5. set** or **put on a pedestal,** to glorify; idealize: *She married a man who set her on a pedestal.* —*v.t.* **6.** to put on or supply with a pedestal. [alter. of MF *piedestal* < It *piedestallo,* var. of *piedistallo,* lit., foot of stall. See PED-[2], DE-, STALL[1]]

ped/estal ta/ble, a table supported upon a central shaft, or upon several shafts along its center line, each resting upon a spreading foot or feet.

pe·des·tri·an (pə des/trē ən), *n.* **1.** one who goes or travels on foot; walker. —*adj.* **2.** going or performed on foot; walking. **3.** of or pertaining to walking. **4.** lacking in vitality, imagination, distinction, etc.; commonplace; prosaic; dull: *a pedestrian commencement speech.* [< L *pedestri-* (s. of *pedester* on foot, deriv. of *pedes* on foot; see PEDI-) + -AN]

pe·des·tri·an·ise (pə des/trē ə nīz/), *v.i., v.t.,* **-ised, -is·ing.** *Chiefly Brit.* pedestrianize.

pe·des·tri·an·ism (pə des/trē ə niz/əm), *n.* **1.** the exercise or practice of walking. **2.** commonplace or prosaic manner, quality, etc. [PEDESTRIAN + -ISM]

pe·des·tri·an·ize (pə des/trē ə nīz/), *v.i., v.t.,* **-ized, -iz·ing.** to go on foot; walk. Also, *esp. Brit.,* **pedestrianise.** [PEDESTRIAN + -IZE]

pede/ win/dow (pēd), (in a church) a window supposed, from its relative size and position, to symbolize the feet of Christ. [*pede* < L *ped-* (s. of *pēs*) foot]

pedi-[1], a learned borrowing from Latin meaning "foot," used in the formation of compound words: *pediform.* Also, **ped-**[2], **-ped.** [comb. form of L *ped-* (s. of *pēs*)]

pedi-[2], var. of **pedo-**[1].

pe·di·a·tri·cian (pē/dē ə trish/ən, ped/ē-), *n.* a physician who specializes in pediatrics. Also called **pe·di·at·rist** (pē/dē a/trist, ped/ē-). [PEDIATRIC(S) + -AN]

pe·di·at·rics (pē/dē a/triks, ped/ē-), *n.* (*construed as sing.*) the science dealing with the medical and hygienic care of children or with the diseases of children. Also, **paediatrics.** [PEDI-[1] + -IATRIC; see -ICS] —**pe/di·at/ric,** *adj.*

ped·i·cab (ped/ə kab/), *n.* (esp. in Southeast Asia) a three-wheeled public conveyance operated by pedals, typically one having a hooded cab for two passengers mounted behind the driver. [PEDI-[1] + CAB[1]]

ped·i·cel (ped/i səl, -sel/), *n.* **1.** *Bot.* **a.** a small stalk. **b.** an ultimate division of a common peduncle. **c.** one of the subordinate stalks in a branched inflorescence, bearing a single flower. **2.** *Zool., Anat.* a peduncle, as that supporting an organ or other structure. [< NL *pedīcell(us),* dim. of L *pediculus* a little foot. See PEDICLE] —**ped·i·cel·lar** (ped/i sel/ər), *adj.*

A, Pedicel
B, Peduncle

ped·i·cel·late (ped/i sel/it, -āt, ped/i sə lit, -lāt/), *adj.* having a pedicel or pedicels. [PEDICEL + -ATE[1]] —**ped/i·cel·la/tion,** *n.*

ped·i·cle (ped/i kəl), *n. Biol.* a small stalk or stalklike support; a pedicel or peduncle. [< L *pedicul(us),* dim. of *pēs* foot. See PEDI-[1], -CLE]

pe·dic·u·lar (pə dik/yə lər), *adj.* of or pertaining to lice. [< L *pediculār(is),* deriv. of *pediculus,* dim. of *pedis* louse; see -CULE, -AR[1]]

pe·dic·u·late (pə dik/yə lit, -lāt/), *adj.* **1.** of or related to the *Pediculati,* a group of teleost fishes, characterized by the elongated base of their pectoral fins, simulating an arm or peduncle. —*n.* **2.** a pediculate fish. [< L *pedicul(us)* little foot (see PEDICLE) + -ATE[1]]

pe·dic·u·li·cide (pə dik/yə li sīd/), *adj.* **1.** Also, **pe·dic/u·li·ci/dal.** destructive to lice. —*n.* **2.** a pediculicide agent. [< L *pedicul(us)* louse (see PEDICULAR) + -I- + -CIDE]

pe·dic·u·lo·sis (pə dik/yə lō/sis), *n. Pathol.* the state of being infested with lice. [< L *pedicul(us)* louse (see PEDICULAR) + -OSIS] —**pe·dic·u·lous** (pə dik/yə ləs), *adj.*

ped·i·cure (ped/ə kyŏŏr/), *n.* **1.** professional care or treatment of the feet. **2.** one who makes a business of caring for the feet; chiropodist. [< F *pédicure* foot-care. See PEDI-[1], CURE] —**ped/i·cur/ist,** *n.*

ped·i·form (ped/ə fôrm/), *adj.* in the form of a foot; footlike. [PEDI-[1] + -FORM]

ped·i·gree (ped/ə grē/), *n.* **1.** an ancestral line; line of descent; lineage; ancestry. **2.** a genealogical table, chart, list, or record: *a family pedigree.* **3.** distinguished, excellent, or pure ancestry. **4.** derivation, origin, or history: *the pedigree of a word.* [late ME *pedegru* < AF, equiv. to MF *pie de grue,* lit., foot of crane, a fanciful way of describing the appearance of the lines of a genealogical chart] —**ped/i·gree/less,** *adj.*
—**Syn. 2.** PEDIGREE, GENEALOGY refer to an account of ancestry. A PEDIGREE is a table or chart recording a line of ancestors, either of persons or (more especially) of animals, as horses, cattle, and dogs; in the case of animals, such a table is used as proof of superior qualities: *a detailed pedigree.* A GENEALOGY is an account of the descent of a person or family traced through a series of generations, usually from the first known ancestor: *a genealogy that includes a king.*

ped·i·greed (ped/ə grēd/), *adj.* having established purebred ancestry: *a pedigreed collie.* [PEDIGREE + -ED[3]]

ped·i·ment (ped/ə mənt), *n.* **1.** (in classical architecture) a low gable, typically triangular with a horizontal cornice and raking cornices, surmounting a colonnade, an end wall, or a major division of a façade. **2.** any imitation of this, often fancifully treated, used to crown an opening, a monument, etc., or to form part of a decorative scheme. **3.** *Geol.* a gently sloping rock surface at the foot of a steep slope, as of a mountain, usually thinly covered with alluvial products. [earlier *peremint,* illiterate mishearing and misapplication of PYRAMID; the current form goes back to Evelyn's guess that L *pedāmentum* vine-stake was the word the illiterates were trying to use] —**ped·i·men·tal** (ped/ə men/təl), *adj.* —**ped·i·ment·ed** (ped/ə men/tid, -mən-), *adj.*

Pediments
A, Pointed; B, Curved; C, Broken

ped·i·o·coc·cus (ped/ē ə kok/əs), *n., pl.* **-coc·ci** (-kok/sī). *Bacteriol.* any of several spherical, facultatively anaerobic bacteria of the genus *Pediococcus,* producing acid and clouding in beer and wort. [< NL; see PEDI-[1], COCCUS] —**ped·i·o·coc·cal** (ped/ē ə kok/əl), **ped·i·o·coc·cic** (ped/ē ə kok/sik), *adj.*

ped·i·palp (ped/ə palp/), *n.* (in arachnids) one member of the usually longer pair of appendages immediately behind the chelicerae. [< NL *Pedipalp(us).* See PEDI-[1], PALP] —**ped/i·pal/pal,** *adj.* —**ped·i·pal·pate** (ped/ə pal/pāt), *adj.*

P.E.Dir., Director of Physical Education.

ped·lar (ped/lər), *n.* peddler. Also, **ped/ler.**

ped·lar·y (ped/lə rē), *n., pl.* **-lar·ies.** peddlary.

ped·ler·y (ped/lə rē), *n., pl.* **-ler·ies.** peddlery.

pedo-[1], a learned borrowing from Greek meaning "child," used in the formation of compound words: *pedophilia.* Also, **paed-, paedo-, ped-**[1], **pedi-**[2]. [var. sp. of *paedo-,* Gk *paido-,* comb. form of *paid-* (s. of *paîs*) child]

pedo-[2], a learned borrowing from Greek meaning "soil," used in the formation of compound words: *pedocal.* Also, *esp. before a vowel,* **ped-**[3]. [< Gk, comb. form of *pédon*]

pe·do·bap·tism (pē/dō bap/tiz əm), *n.* the baptism of infants. Also, **paedobaptism.** [earlier *paedobaptism.* See PEDO-[1], BAPTISM]

pe·do·bap·tist (pē/dō bap/tist), *n.* one who advocates or practices pedobaptism. Also, **paedobaptist.** [PEDOBAPT(ISM) + -IST]

ped·o·cal (ped/ə kal/), *n.* a soil rich in carbonates, esp. those of lime. Cf. **pedalfer.** [PEDO-[2] + *-cal* < L *calc-* (s. of *calx*) lime]

pe·do·don·tics (pē/də don/tiks), *n.* (*construed as sing.*) the branch of dentistry dealing with the care and treatment of children's teeth. Also, **pe·do·don·tia** (pē/də don/shə, -shē ə). [PED-[1] + -ODONT + -ICS] —**pe/do·don/tic,** *adj.*

pe·do·don·tist (pē/də don/tist), *n.* a specialist in pedodontics. [PEDODONT(ICS) + -IST]

ped·o·graph (ped/ə graf/, -gräf/), *n.* an imprint on paper of the foot. [PED-[2] + -O- + -GRAPH]

pe·dol·o·gy[1] (pi dol/ə jē), *n.* the science that deals with the study of soils. Also called **soil science.** [PEDO-[2] + -LOGY] —**pe·do·log·i·cal** (pēd/ᵊloj/i kəl), *adj.* —**pe·dol/o·gist,** *n.*

pe·dol·o·gy[2] (pi dol/ə jē), *n.* **1.** the scientific study of the nature and development of children. **2.** pediatrics. [earlier *paidology, paedology.* See PEDO-[1], -LOGY] —**pe·do·log·i·cal** (pēd/ᵊloj/i kəl), *adj.* —**pe·dol/o·gist,** *n.*

pe·dom·e·ter (pə dom/i tər), *n.* an instrument for recording the number of steps taken in walking, thereby showing approximately the distance traveled. [< F *pédomètre.* See PED-[2], -O-, -METER] —**pe·do·met·ri·cal** (ped/ə me/tri kəl), *adj.* —**ped/o·met/ri·cal·ly,** *adv.* —**pe·dom/e·trist,** *n.*

pe·do·phil·i·a (pē/də fil/ē ə, -fēl/yə, ped/ə-), *n.* *Psychiatry.* sexual desire in an adult for a child. [< NL; see PEDO-[1], -PHILIA] —**pe/do·phil/ic,** *adj.*

Pe·drell (pā drel/; *Sp.* pe tʜrel/), *n.* **Fe·li·pe** (fe lē/pe), 1841–1922, Spanish musicologist and composer.

pe·dro (pē/drō, pā/-), *n., pl.* **-dros.** *Cards.* **1.** any of several varieties of all fours in which the five of trumps counts at its face value. **2.** the five of trumps. [< Sp: lit., Peter]

Pe·dro Xi·me·nez (pā/drō hē mā/nās, -men/is; *Sp.* pe/tʜrō he me/neth), a rich, sweet sherry of Spain, sometimes blended with other wines or with brandy, and sometimes used in blending whiskey. [< Sp; after proper name]

pe·dun·cle (pi dung/kəl), *n.* **1.** *Bot.* **a.** a flower stalk, supporting either a cluster or a solitary flower. **b.** the stalk bearing the fructification in fungi. **2.** *Zool.* a stalk or stem; a stalklike part or structure. **3.** *Anat.* a stalklike structure composed of white matter connecting various regions of the brain. [< NL *pedunculus*, alter. of L *pediculus* little foot. See PED-[2], CARBUNCLE, -CLE] —**pe·dun/cled, pe·dun·cu·lar** (pi dung/kyə lər), *adj.*

P, Peduncle

pe·dun·cu·late (pi dung/kyə lit, -lāt/), *adj.* **1.** having a peduncle. **2.** growing on a peduncle. Also, **pe·dun/cu·lat/ed.** [< NL *pedunculāt(us).* See PEDUNCLE, -ATE[1]] —**pe·dun/cu·la/tion,** *n.*

pee (pē), *v.,* **peed, pee·ing,** *n. Slang.* —*v.i.* **1.** to urinate. —*n.* **2.** urine. **3.** the act of urinating. [euphemism for *piss*]

Pee·bles (pē/bəlz), *n.* a county in S Scotland. 14,117 (1961); 347 sq. mi. *Co. seat:* Peebles. Also called **Pee·bles·shire** (pē/bəlz shēr/, -shər), **Tweeddale.**

Pee Dee (pē/ dē/), a river flowing through central North Carolina and NE South Carolina into the Atlantic. 435 mi. long. Cf. **Yadkin.**

peek (pēk), *v.i.* **1.** to look or glance briefly or furtively, esp. through a small opening or from a concealed location; peep; peer. —*n.* **2.** a brief or furtive look or glance; peep. [ME *pike(n),* ? dissimilated var. of *kike* to peep < MD *kiken, kieken*]
—**Syn. 1.** See **peep**[1].

peek·a·boo (pēk/ə bōō/), *n.* **1.** Also called **bopeep.** a game played by very young children, typically in which one covers his face or hides himself and then suddenly uncovers his face or reappears, calling "Peekaboo!" —*adj. Clothing.* **2.** decorated with openwork. **3.** made of a revealing material, as some blouses for women. [PEEK + *-a-* connective + BOO]

Peeks·kill (pēk/skil), *n.* a city in SE New York, on the Hudson. 18,737 (1960).

peel[1] (pēl), *v.t.* **1.** to strip (something) of its skin, rind, bark, etc.: *to peel an orange.* **2.** to strip (the skin, rind, bark, etc.) from something. **3.** *Croquet.* to cause (another player's ball) to go through a wicket. —*v.i.* **4.** (of skin, bark, etc.) to come off; become separated. **5.** to lose the skin, rind, bark, etc. **6.** *Informal.* to undress. **7.** *Foundry.* (of a malleable iron casting) to lose, or tend to lose, the outer layer. **8. keep one's eyes peeled,** *Slang.* to watch closely or carefully; be alert: *Keep your eyes peeled for an exit sign.* **9. peel off,** *Aeron.* to leave a flying formation of aircraft with a banking turn, usually from one end of an echelon. —*n.* **10.** the skin or rind of a fruit, vegetable, etc. **11.** Also called **peeling disease.** *Foundry.* the presence of a brittle outer layer on a malleable iron casting. [ME *pel(en),* OE *pilian* to strip, skin < L *pilāre* to remove hair, deriv. of *pilus* hair. See PILL[2]] —**peel/a·ble,** *adj.*
—**Syn. 1.** PEEL, PARE agree in meaning to remove the skin or rind from something. PEEL means to pull or strip off the natural external covering or protection of something: *to peel an orange, a potato.* PARE is used of trimming off chips, flakes, or superficial parts from something, as well as of cutting off the skin or rind: *to pare the nails; to pare a potato.* **2.** flay.

peel[2] (pēl), *n.* **1.** a shovellike implement for putting bread, pies, etc., into the oven or taking them out. **2.** *Metall.* **a.** a long, shovellike iron tool for charging an open-hearth furnace. **b.** an arm having a similar function on a machine for charging an open-hearth furnace. [ME *pele* < MF < L *pāla* spade. See PALETTE]

peel[3] (pēl), *n.* a fortified tower for residence or use in emergencies, common in the border counties of England and Scotland in the 16th century. Also, **pele.** [ME *pele* fortress < AF *pel* stockade, MF *pel* stake < L *pal(us)* stake. See PALE[2]]

Peel (pēl), *n.* **1. Sir Robert,** 1788–1850, British statesman: prime minister 1834–35; 1841–46. **2.** a seaport on W Isle of Man: castle; resort. 2582 (1951).

Peele (pēl), *n.* **George,** 1558?–97?, English dramatist.

peel·er[1] (pē/lər), *n.* **1.** one who or that which peels. **2.** a long-staple cotton raised originally in the regions along the Yazoo River and the Mississippi River delta. **3.** a yarn made from this cotton. **4.** *Slang.* stripper (def. 3). [ME *peler.* See PEEL[1], -ER[1]]

peel·er[2] (pē/lər), *n. Brit. Slang. Obs.* a policeman. [named after Sir Robert PEEL, who founded the Irish constabulary]

peel·ing (pē/ling), *n.* **1.** the act of one who or that which peels. **2.** that which is peeled from something, as a piece of the skin or rind of a fruit. [PEEL[1] + -ING[1]]

peel/ing disease/, peel[1] (def. 11).

peen (pēn), *n.* **1.** a wedgelike, spherical, or other striking end of a hammer head opposite the face. —*v.t.* **2.** to enlarge, straighten, or smooth with a peen. **3.** to strengthen (a metal surface) by light hammering or by bombardment with steel balls or shot. Also, **pein.** [earlier *pen* < Scand; cf. Sw, Norw *pen* (n.) in same sense; akin to G *Pinne* peen. See PIN]

Pee·ne (pā/nə), *n.* a river in N East Germany, flowing E to the Baltic Sea. ab. 97 mi. long.

Pee·ne·mün·de (pā/nə mʏn/də), *n.* a village in NE East Germany: German missile and rocket center in World War II.

peenge (pēnj), *v.i.,* **peenged, peeng·ing.** *Scot. and North Eng.* to complain; whine. Also, **pinge.** [earlier *pinge,* ME *pinsen* to torture, OE *pinsian* to examine, judge. Changes in meaning by assoc. with PINE[2] torture and *whinge* to whine]

peep[1] (pēp), *v.i.* **1.** to look through a small opening or from a concealed location. **2.** to look slyly, pryingly, or furtively. **3.** to look curiously or playfully. **4.** to come partially into view; begin to appear: *the first crocuses peeping through the ground.* —*v.t.* **5.** to show or protrude slightly. —*n.* **6.** a quick or furtive look or glance. **7.** the first appearance, as of dawn. **8.** an aperture for looking through. [late ME *pepe;* assimilated var. of PEEK]
—**Syn. 1, 2.** PEEP, PEEK, PEER mean to look through, over, or around something. To PEEP or PEEK is usually to give a quick look through a narrow aperture or small opening, often furtively, slyly, or pryingly; or to look over or around something curiously or playfully: *to peep over a wall; to peek into a room.* PEEK is often associated with children's games. To PEER is to look continuously and narrowly for some time, esp. in order to penetrate obscurity or to overcome some obstacle in the way of vision: *The fireman peered through the smoke.*

peep[2] (pēp), *n.* **1.** a short, shrill little cry or sound, as of a young bird; cheep; squeak. **2.** any of various small sandpipers. —*v.i.* **3.** to utter the short, shrill little cry of a young bird, a mouse, etc.; cheep; squeak. **4.** to speak in a thin, weak voice. [ME *pepe(n), pipen;* cf. D, G *piepen,* OF *piper,* L *pipāre,* all imit.]

peep[3] (pēp), *n.* jeep. [appar. alter. of JEEP]

pee·pee (pē/pē/), *v.i.,* **-peed, -pee·ing,** *n. Baby Talk.* pee.

peep·er[1] (pē/pər), *n.* **1.** one who or that which emits or utters a peeping sound. **2.** any of several frogs having a peeping call, esp. the spring peeper. [PEEP[2] + -ER[1]]

peep·er[2] (pē/pər), *n.* **1.** a person who peeps, esp. in an abnormal prying manner. **2.** a person, esp. a man, who indulges in voyeurism. **3.** Usually, **peepers.** *Slang.* an eye. [PEEP[1] + -ER[1]]

peep·hole (pēp/hōl/), *n.* a hole or opening through which to peer or look, as in a door. [PEEP[1] + HOLE]

Peep/ing Tom/, a person who obtains sexual gratification by observing others from hiding; voyeur: *A Peeping Tom has been reported in that area.* [allusion to the man who peeped at Lady Godiva as she rode through Coventry]

peep/ show/, an exhibited display of objects or pictures viewed through a small opening that is usually fitted with a magnifying lens.

peep/ sight/, a plate containing a small hole through which a gunner peeps in sighting.

pee·pul (pē/pəl), *n.* pipal.

peer[1] (pēr), *n.* **1.** a person of the same rank or standing; a legal equal: *a jury of one's peers.* **2.** a person who is equal to another in abilities, qualifications, etc. **3.** a nobleman. **4.** a member of any of the five degrees of the nobility in Great Britain and Ireland, namely, duke, marquis, earl, viscount, and baron. **5.** *Archaic.* a companion. [ME *per* < OF *pere* < L *par* equal]

peer[2] (pēr), *v.i.* **1.** to look narrowly or searchingly, as in the effort to discern clearly. **2.** to peep out or appear slightly. **3.** to come into view. [< Flem *pier(en)* (to) look narrowly] —**peer/ing·ly,** *adv.*
—**Syn. 1.** See **peep**[1].

peer·age (pēr/ij), *n.* **1.** the rank or dignity of a peer. **2.** the body of peers of a country or state. **3.** a book listing the peers and giving their genealogies. [late ME *perage.* See PEER[1], -AGE]

Peerce (pērs), *n.* **Jan** (*Jacob Pincus Perelmuth*), born 1904, U.S. singer.

peer·ess (pēr/is), *n.* **1.** the wife or widow of a peer. **2.** a woman having in her own right the rank of a peer. [PEER[1] + -ESS]

Peer Gynt (pēr/ gint/; *Norw.* pâr/ gʏnt/), a play (1867) by Henrik Ibsen.

peer·ie (pēr/ē), *n. Chiefly Scot.* peery.

peer·less (pēr/lis), *adj.* having no equal; matchless; unrivaled. [ME *pereles.* See PEER[1], -LESS] —**peer/less·ly,** *adv.* —**peer/less·ness,** *n.*
—**Syn.** unmatched, unequaled; unique, unsurpassed.

peer/ of the realm/, *pl.* **peers of the realm.** any of a class of peers in Great Britain and Ireland entitled to sit in the House of Lords.

peer·y (pēr/ē), *n., pl.* **peer·ies.** *Chiefly Scot.* a child's peg top. Also, **peerie.** [? dim. of ME *pere* pear]

peet·weet (pēt/wēt), *n. U.S. Dial.* the spotted sandpiper. [imit. rhyming compound; cf. PEWEE, PEWIT]

peeve (pēv), *v.,* **peeved, peev·ing,** *n.* —*v.t.* **1.** to render peevish; annoy. —*n.* **2.** a source of annoyance or irritation: *a pet peeve.* [back formation from PEEVISH]
—**Syn. 2.** gripe.

peeved (pēvd), *adj.* annoyed; irritated; vexed. [PEEVE + -ED[2]] —**peev·ed·ly** (pē/vid lē, pēvd/-), *adv.* —**peev/ed·ness,** *n.*

peev·ish (pē/vish), *adj.* **1.** cross, querulous, or fretful, as from vexation or discontent: *a peevish retort.* **2.** *Obs.* perverse. [ME *pevysh* < ?] —**pee/vish·ly,** *adv.* —**pee/vish·ness,** *n.*
—**Syn. 1.** petulant, irritable, snappish. See **cross.** —**Ant. 1.** equable, amiable.

pee·wee (pē/wē/), *Informal.* —*adj.* **1.** very small; tiny. —*n.* **2.** a person who is unusually small. **3.** an animal that is small for its kind; runt. **4.** *Marbles.* a small, cheap playing marble, as one made of clay rather than glass. **5.** a very small playing marble. [rhyming compound based on WEE]

pee·wit (pē/wit, pyōō/it), *n.* pewit.

peg (peg), *n., v.,* **pegged, peg·ging,** *adj.* —*n.* **1.** a pin of wood or other material driven or fitted into something, as to fasten parts together, to hang things on, to make fast a rope or string on, to stop a hole, or to mark some point. **2.** *Informal.* a leg, either real or wooden: *still on his pegs at 99.* **3.** an occasion; reason: *a peg to hang a grievance on.* **4.** *Informal.* a degree: *to come down a peg.* **5.** Also called **pin.** *Music.* a pin of wood or metal in the neck of a stringed instrument, one end of a string being fastened to the pin, which may be turned in its socket to adjust the string's tension. **6.** *Chiefly Baseball Slang.* a throw: *The peg to the plate was late.* **7.** See **news peg. 8.** *Brit., Anglo-Indian.* a highball, esp. whiskey and soda or brandy and soda. **9.** *Brit.* clothespin. **10. take down a peg,** *Informal.* to humble: *I guess that'll take him down a peg!* —*v.t.* **11.** to drive or insert a peg into. **12.** to fasten with or as with pegs. **13.** to mark with pegs. **14.** to strike or pierce with or as with a peg. **15.** to keep the commodity price, exchange rate, etc., at a set level, as by manipulation, law, etc. **16.** *Chiefly Baseball Slang.* to throw (a ball). **17.** *Journalism.* to base (an article, feature story, etc.) upon; justify by (usually fol. by *on*): *The feature on the Chief of Police was pegged on the riots.* **18.** *Slang.* to identify: *to peg someone as a good prospect.* —*v.i.* **19.** to work or continue persistently or energetically: *to peg away at a homework assignment.* **20.** *Chiefly Baseball Slang.* to throw a ball. **21.** *Croquet.* to strike a peg, as in completing a game. —*adj.* **22.** tapered toward the bottom of the leg: *peg trousers.* [ME *pegge* < MD *pegge* (n.), *peggen* (v.)] —**peg/less,** *adj.* —**peg/like/,** *adj.*

Peg (peg), *n.* a girl's given name, form of **Peggy.**

Pe·gae (pē/jē), *n. Class. Myth.* Dryope's spring, in Mysia.

Peg·a·sus (peg/ə səs), *n., gen.* **-si** (-sī/) for 2. **1.** *Class. Myth.* a winged horse, created from the blood of Medusa, which opened the spring of Hippocrene with a stroke of its hoof, and which carried Bellerophon in his attack on the Chimera. **2.** *Astron.* the Winged Horse, a northern constellation between Cygnus and Aquarius. —**Pe·ga·si·an** (pə gā/sē ən), *adj.*

Pegasus

peg·board (peg/bōrd/, -bôrd/), *n.* **1.** a board having holes into which pegs are placed in specific patterns, used for playing or scoring certain games. **2.** composition board with regular perforations for the insertion of pegs or hooks. [PEG + BOARD]

peg·box (peg/boks/), *n.* the widened end of the neck of a stringed instrument, to which the tuning pegs are fixed. [PEG + BOX[1]]

Peg·gy (peg/ē), *n.* a girl's given name.

pegh (pекн), *n., v.i. Scot. and North Eng.* pech.

peg/ leg/, **1.** a wooden leg. **2.** a person with a wooden leg. —**peg/legged/,** *adj.*

peg·ma·tite (peg/mə tīt/), *n.* **1.** a graphic intergrowth of quartz and feldspar; graphic granite. **2.** a coarsely crystalline granite or other high-silica rock occurring in veins or dikes. [< Gk *pēgmat-* (s. of *pēgma*) anything fastened together, a bond (cf. *pēgnyein* to stick) + -ITE[1]] —**peg·ma·tit·ic** (peg/mə tit/ik), *adj.*

peg/ tank/ard, a tankard of c1700, having pegs inside marking some unit of measure.

peg/ top/, **1.** a child's wooden top that spins on a metal peg. **2. peg tops,** peg-top trousers. **3.** a peg-top skirt.

peg-top (peg/top/), *adj.* wide at the hips and narrowing to the ankle: *peg-top trousers; peg-top skirts.* [adj. use of PEG TOP]

Pe·gu (pe gōō/), *n.* a city in central Burma: pagodas. 47,378 (1953). —**Pe·gu/an,** *adj., n.*

peg·wood (peg/wŏŏd/), *n.* a rod of boxwood of about ⅛ inch diameter, cut in various ways at the end and used by watchmakers for cleaning jewels. [PEG + WOOD[1]]

peh (pā), *n.* pe.

Peh·le·vi (pā/lə vē/), *n.* the Pahlavi language.

P.E.I., Prince Edward Island.

Pei-ching (*Chin.* bā/jing/), *n.* Peking.

peign·oir (pān wär/, pen-, pān/wär, pen/-), *n.* **1.** a woman's dressing gown. **2.** a cloak or gown of terry cloth for wear after swimming or, esp. in France, after the bath. [< F: lit., comber, i.e., something worn while one's hair is being combed, equiv. to *peign(er)* (to) comb (< LL *pectināre;* see PECTEN) + *-oir* n. suffix]

pein (pēn), *n., v.t.* peen.

Pei·ping (bā/ping/), *n.* former name of **Peking.**

Pei·pus (pī/pəs), *n.* a lake in the W Soviet Union in Europe, on the E boundary of Estonia. 93 mi. long; 356 sq. mi. Russian, **Chudskoye Ozero.** Estonian, **Peip·si** (pāp/sē).

Pei·rae·us (pī rē/əs), *n.* Piraeus.

Pei·rai·evs (pē/re efs/), *n.* Greek name of **Piraeus.**

Peirce (pûrs *for 1, 2, 4;* pērs *for 3, 4*), *n.* **1. Benjamin,** 1809–80, U.S. mathematician. **2. Charles San·ders** (san/dərz), 1839–1914, U.S. philosopher, mathematician, and physicist. **3.** a crater in the first quadrant of the face of the moon: about 12 miles in diameter. **4.** a boy's given name.

peise (pāz, pēz), *v.,* **peised, peis·ing.** *Brit. Dial.* —*v.t.* **1.** to weigh, as in a balance. **2.** to weigh down;

burden. —*v.i.* **3.** to have weight; weigh. **4.** to press down by weight or force. [ME *peys, peis* < OF, ONF, AF (F *poids*) < L *pens(um)* weight, deriv. of *pendere.* See POISE]

Pei·se·nor (pī sē′nôr), *n.* (in the *Odyssey*) an Ithacan herald famous for his wise counsel.

Pei·sis·tra·tus (pē sis′trə təs), *n.* Pisistratus.

Pei·tho (pī′thō), *n. Class. Myth.* **1.** the personification of persuasion, usually a companion of Aphrodite. **2.** Aphrodite.

pej·o·ra·tion (pej′ə rā′shən, pē′jə-), *n.* **1.** depreciation; a lessening in worth, quality, etc. **2.** *Historical Ling.* semantic change in a word to a lower, less approved, or less respectable meaning. Cf. **melioration** (def. 1). [< ML *pējōrātiōn-* (s. of *pējōrātiō*) a making worse, equiv. to *pējōrāt(us)* (ptp. of *pējōrāre,* deriv. of *pējor* worse) + *-iōn-* -ION]

pe·jo·ra·tive (pi jôr′ə tiv, -jor′-, pej′ə rā′-, pē′jə-), *adj.* **1.** having a disparaging effect or force: *the pejorative affix -ling in princeling.* —*n.* **2.** a pejorative form or word, as *poetaster.* [< L *pējōrāt(us)* made worse (see PEJORATION) + -IVE] —**pe·jo′ra·tive·ly,** *adv.*
—**Syn. 1.** deprecatory.

pek·an (pek′ən), *n.* the fisher, *Martes pennanti.* [< CanF < Algonquian (Abnaki) *pēkanē*]

pe·kin (pē′kin′), *n.* (*often cap.*) a silk fabric in which broad stripes of equal width and in various colors or weaves are alternated. [< F *pékin;* after PEKING]

Pe·kin (pē′kin′), *n.* one of a hardy breed of yellowish-white domestic ducks, raised originally in China. [after PEKING]

Pe·kin (pē′kin), *n.* a city in central Illinois. 28,146 (1960).

Pe·kin·ese (pē′kə nēz′, -nēs′), *n., pl.* **-ese.** Pekingese.

Pe·king (pē′king′; *Chin.* bā′ging′), *n.* a city in and the capital of the People's Republic of China, in the NE part, in central Hopeh province: traditional capital of China. 7,570,000. Also, **Peiching.** Formerly (1928–49), **Peiping.** Pinyin spelling, **Beijing.**

Pe·king·ese (pē′king ēz′, -ēs′, -kə nēz′, -nēs′), *n., pl.* **-ese** for 1, 4, *adj.* —*n.* **1.** one of a Chinese breed of small dogs having a long, silky coat. **2.** the standard Chinese language. **3.** the dialect of Peking. **4.** a native or inhabitant of Peking. —*adj.* **5.** of, pertaining to, or characteristic of Peking. Also, **Pekinese.** [PEKING + -ESE]

Pekingese (11 in. high at shoulder)

Pe′king man′, a fossil man known from skeletal remains found in a Middle Pleistocene cave near Peking, China, and regarded as being generically related to but more advanced than Java man.

pe·koe (pē′kō *or, esp. Brit.,* pek′ō), *n.* a superior kind of black tea from Ceylon, India, and Java, made from leaves smaller than those used for orange pekoe. [< Chin (Amoy dial.) *pek-ho* white down]

pel·age (pel′ij), *n.* the hair, fur, wool, or other soft covering of a mammal. [< F, deriv. of *poil* (OF *peil;* see POILU); see -AGE] —**pe·la·gi·al** (pə lā′jē əl), *adj.*

Pe·la·gi·an (pə lā′jē ən), *n.* **1.** a follower of Pelagius, a British monk who lived in Rome in the early part of the 5th century A.D. and who denied original sin and maintained the freedom of the will and its power to attain righteousness. —*adj.* **2.** of or pertaining to Pelagius or Pelagianism. [< LL *Pelagiān(us);* see -AN] —**Pe·la′gi·an·ism,** *n.*

Pe·la·gi·an·ize (pə lā′jē ə nīz′), *v.i., v.t.,* **-ized, -iz·ing.** to become or make Pelagian. [PELAGIAN + -IZE] —**Pe·la′gi·an·iz′er,** *n.*

pe·lag·ic (pə laj′ik), *adj.* **1.** of or pertaining to the seas or oceans. **2.** living or growing at or near the surface of the ocean, far from land, as certain animals or plants. [< L *pelagic(us)* < Gk *pelagikós,* equiv. to *pélag(os)* the sea (c. L *pelagus*) + *-ikos* -IC]

Pe·la·gi·us (pə lā′jē əs), *n.* 360?–420?, English monk and theologian.

Pelagius I, died A.D. 561, pope 556–561.

Pelagius II, died A.D. 590, pope 579–590.

Pel·a·gon (pel′ə gon′), *n.* (in the *Iliad*) a Lycian ally of Sarpedon in the Trojan War.

pel·ar·gon·ic (pel′är gon′ik, -gō′nik), *adj. Chem.* of or derived from a pelargonium or pelargonic acid. [PELARGON(IUM) + -IC]

pel′argon′ic ac′id, *Chem.* a colorless, oily, water-immiscible liquid, $CH_3(CH_2)_7COOH$, occurring as an ester in a volatile oil in species of pelargonium: used chiefly in organic synthesis and in the manufacture of lacquers and plastics. Also called **nonanoic acid.**

pel·ar·go·ni·um (pel′är gō′nē əm), *n.* any plant of the genus *Pelargonium,* the cultivated species of which are usually called geranium. Cf. **geranium** (def. 2). [< NL < Gk *pelargó(s)* the stork + *(gerá)nion* GERANIUM]

Pe·las·gi (pə laz′jē), *n.pl.* the Pelasgians. [< L < Gk *Pelasgoí*]

Pe·las·gi·an (pə laz′jē ən), *adj.* **1.** of or pertaining to the Pelasgians. —*n.* **2.** a member of a prehistoric people inhabiting Greece, Asia Minor, and the islands of the eastern Mediterranean. [<< Gk *Pelásgi(os)* Pelasgian (< *Pelasg(oí)* PELASGI + *-ios* adj. suffix) + -AN]

Pe·las·gic (pə laz′jik), *adj.* Pelasgian. [<< Gk *Pelasgik(ós).* See PELASGI, -IC]

Pe·las·gis (pə laz′jis), *n. Class. Myth.* Demeter: named for Pelasgus, the founder of her sanctuary at Argos.

Pe·las·gus (pə laz′gəs), *n. Class. Myth.* the first man, father of Lycaon and founder of the Pelasgians. Also called **Corynetes.**

pele (pēl), *n.* peel[3].

pe·lec·y·pod (pə les′ə pod′), *n.* **1.** any mollusk of the class *Pelecypoda* (*Lamellibranchiata*), characterized by a bivalve shell enclosing the headless body and lamellate gills, comprising the oysters, clams, mussels, scallops, etc. —*adj.* **2.** Also, **pel·e·cyp·o·dous** (pel′i sip′ə dəs). belonging or pertaining to the *Pelecypoda* (*Lamellibranchiata*). [< NL *Pelecypod(a)* < Gk *péleky(s)* hatchet; see -POD]

Pe·lée (pə lā′), *n.* **Mount,** a volcano in the West Indies, on the island of Martinique: eruption 1902. 4428 ft.

Pe·le·gon (pē′lə gon′), *n.* (in the *Iliad*) a river god and the father of Asteropaeus.

pel·er·ine (pel′ə rēn′), *n.* a woman's cape of fur or cloth, usually waist-length in back and with long descending ends in front. [< F *pèlerine,* fem. of *pèlerin* pilgrim]

Pe′le's hair′ (pā′lāz, pē′lēz), volcanic glass thread, usually basaltic, caused by the solidification of exploding or ejected lava in the open air. [trans. of Hawaiian *ranoho o Pele* hair of Pele (goddess of the volcano Kilauea)]

Pe′le's tears′, drops of volcanic glass, often with pendent threads, thrown out during a volcanic eruption. [named after *Pele;* see PELE'S HAIR]

Pe·le·us (pē′lē əs, pēl′yo͞os), *n. Class. Myth.* a king of the Myrmidons, the son of Aeacus and father of Achilles.

Pe·lew′ Is′lands (pē lo͞o′). See **Palau Islands.**

pelf (pelf), *n. Disparaging.* money or riches. [ME, OF *pelfre* booty]

Pel·ham (pel′əm), *n.* a bit that is used with two pairs of reins, designed to serve the purpose of a full bridle. [after the proper name *Pelham*]

Pel·ham (pel′əm), *n.* **1. Henry,** 1696–1754, British statesman: prime minister 1743–54 (brother of Thomas Pelham-Holles). **2.** a town in SW Georgia. 4609 (1960).

Pel·ham-Hol·les (pel′əm hol′is), *n.* **Thomas, 1st Duke of Newcastle,** 1693–1768, British statesman: prime minister 1754–56, 1757–62 (brother of Henry Pelham).

Pel′ham Man′or, a town in SE New York. 6114 (1960).

Pe·li·as (pē′lē əs, pel′ē-), *n. Class. Myth.* a son of Poseidon and uncle of Jason, whom he sent to recover the Golden Fleece.

pel·i·can (pel′ə kən), *n.* **1.** any of several large, totipalmate, fish-eating birds of the family *Pelecanidae,* having a large bill with a distensible pouch. **2.** *Alchemy.* a still with two tubes that leave the body from the neck, curve in opposite directions, and reenter the body through the belly. [ME, OE *pellican* < LL *pelicān(us),* var. of *pelecānus* < Gk *pelekân*]

Pelican, *Pelecanus erythrorhynchos* (Length 5 ft.)

pel·i·can-flow·er (pel′ə kən flou′ər), *n.* a woody vine, *Aristolochia grandiflora,* of the West Indies, having heart-shaped leaves and purple-spotted, purple-veined flowers from 18 to 24 inches wide with a long, taillike structure at the tip of the corolla.

pel′ican hook′, a hooklike device for holding the link of a chain or the like, consisting of a long shackle with a hinged rod closed against the end of the shackle by a sliding ring. Also called **slip hook.**

Pel′ican State′, Louisiana (used as a nickname).

Pelican hook

Pe·li·des (pə lī′dēz), *n. Class. Myth.* **1.** a descendant of Peleus. **2.** a patronymic of Achilles or Neoptolemus.

pel·i·ke (pel′ə kē′), *n., pl.* **-kai** (-kī′). *Gk. and Rom. Antiq.* a two-handled storage jar with the handles extending from the lip to the shoulder, characterized by an oval body that is wider at the base than at the neck and rests on a foot. Cf. **amphora, stamnos.** [< Gk: pitcher]

Pe·li·on (pē′lē ən; *Gk.* pē′lē ôn′), *n.* **Mount,** a mountain near the E coast of Greece, in Thessaly. 5252 ft.

pe·lisse (pə lēs′), *n.* **1.** an outer garment lined or trimmed with fur. **2.** a woman's long cloak with slits for the arms. [< F < LL *pellicia* mantle, n. use of fem. of *pellicius* of skin, deriv. of *pellis* skin]

pe·lite (pē′līt), *n. Geol.* any clay rock. [< Gk *pēl(ós)* clay, earth + -ITE[1]] —**pe·lit·ic** (pi lit′ik), *adj.*

Pel·la (pel′ə), *n.* **1.** a ruined city in N Greece, NW of Salonika: the capital of ancient Macedonia; birthplace of Alexander the Great. **2.** a town in central Iowa. 5198 (1960).

pel·la·gra (pə lā′grə, -lag′rə, -lä′grə), *n. Pathol.* a disease caused by a deficiency of niacin in the diet, characterized by skin changes, severe nerve dysfunction, and diarrhea. [< It < medical L: skin disease, equiv. to *pell(is)* skin + *-agra* < Gk *ágra* seizure] —**pel·la·grose** (pə lā′grōs, -lag′rōs, -lä′grōs), **pel·la·grous** (pə lā′grəs, -lag′rəs, -lä′grəs), *adj.*

pel·la′gra-pre·ven′tive fac′tor (pə lā′grə pri ven′tiv, -lag′rə-, -lä′grə-), *Biochem.* nicotinic acid or its amide, nicotinamide, being the vitamin-B-complex members that serve to prevent pellagra. Also called **P.P. factor.**

pel·la·grin (pə lā′grin, -lag′rin, -lä′grin), *n. Pathol.* a person affected with pellagra. [PELLAGR(A) + -IN[1]]

Pel·lan (*Fr.* pe län′), *n.* **Al·fred** (*Fr.* al fred′), born 1906, Canadian painter.

Pell′ Cit′y, a town in central Alabama. 4165 (1960).

Pel·le·as (pel′ē as′), *n.* **Sir,** *Arthurian Romance.* a knight of King Arthur's court who loved Ettarre.

Pel·lé·as et Mé·li·sande (*Fr.* pe lā as′ ā mā lē zänd′), **1.** a play (1892) by Maurice Maeterlinck. **2.** an opera (1902) by Claude Debussy, based on this play.

pel·le·kar (pel′ə kär′), *n.* palikar.

Pel·les (pel′ēz), *n.* **King,** *Arthurian Romance.* a character in the story of Lancelot's quest for the Holy Grail: father of Elaine.

pel·let (pel′it), *n.* **1.** a small, rounded or spherical body, as of food or medicine. **2.** a ball, usually of stone, formerly used as a missile. **3.** one of a charge of small shot, as for a shotgun. **4.** a bullet. **5.** a small wad or ball of wax, paper, etc., for throwing, shooting, or the like. **6.** Also called **cast.** *Ornith.* a small, roundish mass of matter regurgitated by certain predatory birds, consisting of the indigestible remains, as the fur, feathers, and bones, of the prey. **7.** (in Romanesque architecture) a hemispherical or disklike carved ornament. **8.** *Heraldry.* ogress[2]. —*v.t.* **9.** to form into pellets. **10.** to hit with pellets. [ME *pelet* < MF *pelote* < Pr *pelota,* deriv. of L *pila* ball. See PILL[1], -ET] —**pel′let·like′,** *adj.*

Pel·le·tier (pel′i tēr′; *Fr.* pelə tyā′), *n.* **Wilfrid,** 1896–1982, Canadian orchestra conductor.

pel·let·y (pel′i tē), *adj. Heraldry.* semé of pellets or ogresses. [PELLET + -Y[1]]

pel·li·cle (pel′i kəl), *n.* a thin skin or membrane; film; scum. [< L *pellicul(a),* deriv. of *pellis* skin; see -CLE] —**pel·lic·u·lar** (pə lik′yə lər), **pel·lic·u·late** (pə lik′yə lit, -lāt′), *adj.*

pel·li·to·ry (pel′i tōr′ē, -tôr′ē), *n., pl.* **-ries.** an asteraceous plant, *Anacyclus Pyrethrum,* of Southern Europe, whose root is used as a local irritant. [alter. of ME *peletre* < AF, MF *piretre* < L *pyrethrum* < Gk *pýrethron*]

pell-mell (pel′mel′), *adv.* **1.** in a confused or jumbled mass, crowd, manner, etc. **2.** in disorderly, headlong haste; in a recklessly hurried manner. —*adj.* **3.** indiscriminate; disorderly; confused: *a pell-mell dash after someone.* —*n.* **4.** a confused or jumbled mass, crowd, etc. **5.** disorderly, headlong haste. Also, **pell′mell′.** [< MF *pelemele,* OF *pesle mesle,* rhyming compound based on *mesler* to mix. See MEDDLE]

pel·lu·cid (pə lo͞o′sid), *adj.* **1.** allowing the maximum passage of light; translucent. **2.** clear or limpid: *pellucid waters.* **3.** clear in meaning, expression, or style: *a pellucid phrase.* [< L *pellūcid(us),* var. of *perlūcidus.* See PER-, LUCID] —**pel·lu·cid·i·ty** (pel′o͝o sid′i tē), **pel·lu′cid·ness,** *n.* —**pel·lu′cid·ly,** *adv.*
—**Syn. 2.** transparent. —**Ant. 1, 2.** opaque. **3.** obscure.

pel·oid (pel′oid), *n. Med.* mud used therapeutically. [< Gk *pēl(ós)* mud, clay + -OID]

Pe·lo·pi·a (pə lō pī′ə), *n. Class. Myth.* the mother of Aegisthus. Pelopia was raped by her father, Thyestes, and killed herself on learning that he was her attacker. Also, **Pe·lo·pe·a** (pə lō pē′ə).

Pe·lop·i·dae (pə lop′i dē′), *n.pl. Class. Myth.* the descendants of Pelops.

Pe·lop·i·das (pə lop′i dəs), *n.* died 364 B.C., Greek general and statesman of Thebes.

Pel′oponne′sian War′, a war between Athens and Sparta, 431–404 B.C., which resulted in the transfer of hegemony in Greece from Athens to Sparta.

AEGEAN SEA
GREECE
Athens
Peloponnesus
IONIAN SEA
MEDITERRANEAN SEA

Pel·o·pon·ne·sus (pel′ə pə nē′səs), *n.* a peninsula forming the S part of Greece: seat of the early Mycenaean civilization and the powerful city-states of Argos, Sparta, etc. 1,096,654 (1961); 8356 sq. mi. Also, **Pel·o·pon·nese** (pel′ə pə nēz′, -nēs′), **Pel·o·pon·ne·sos** (pel′ə pə nē′sos, -sôs, -sōs). Also called **Morea.** [< L < Gk *Pelopónnēsos,* lit., island of PELOPS. See INDONESIA] —**Pel·o·pon·ne·sian** (pel′ə pə nē′zhən, -shən), *adj., n.*

Pe·lops (pē′lops), *n. Class. Myth.* a son of Tantalus and brother of Niobe, served by Tantalus to the gods as food, but restored to life by Hermes.

pe·lo·ri·a (pə lōr′ē ə, -lôr′-), *n. Bot.* regularity of structure occurring abnormally in flowers normally irregular. [< NL < Gk *pélōr(os)* monstrous (*pélōr* monster + *-os* adj. suffix) + *-ia* -IA] —**pe·lor·ic** (pə lōr′ik, -lor′-), **pe·lo′ri·an, pe·lo·ri·ate** (pə lōr′ē it, -āt′, -lôr′-), *adj.*

pel·o·rize (pel′ə rīz′), *v.t.,* **-rized, -riz·ing.** *Bot.* to affect with peloria. [PELOR(IA) + -IZE] —**pel′o·ri·za′tion,** *n.*

pe·lo·rus (pə lōr′əs, -lôr′-), *n., pl.* **-rus·es.** *Navig.* a device for measuring in degrees the relative bearings of observed objects. Also called **dumb compass.** [? < L *Pelōrus,* now Faro in Sicily, a cape the rounding of which requires skill in navigation]

Pe·lo·rus (pə lōr′əs, -lôr′-), *n. Class. Myth.* one of the Sparti.

pelo′rus card′, *Navig.* a disk calibrated in degrees, mounted on or serving as a pelorus.

pe·lo·ta (pə lō′tə; *Sp.* pe lô′tä), *n., pl.* **-tas** (-təz; *Sp.* -täs). **1.** a Basque and Spanish game from which jai alai was developed. **2.** the game of jai alai. **3.** the ball used in pelota and jai alai. [< Sp < Pr; see PELLET]

Pe·lo·tas (pə lô′təs), *n.* a city in S Brazil. 78,014 (1950).

pelt[1] (pelt), *v.t.* **1.** to attack or assail with repeated blows or with missiles. **2.** to throw (missiles). **3.** to drive by blows or missiles: *The child pelted the cows home from the fields.* **4.** to assail with abuse. **5.** to beat or rush against with repeated forceful blows: *The wind and rain pelted the roofs and walls of the houses for four days.* —*v.i.* **6.** to strike blows; beat with force or violence. **7.** to throw missiles. **8.** to hurry. **9.** to beat or pound unrelentingly: *The wind, rain, and snow pelted against the castle walls.* **10.** *Rare.* to cast abuse. —*n.* **11.** the act of pelting. **12.** a vigorous stroke; whack. **13.** a blow with something thrown. **14.** speed. **15.** an unrelenting or repeated beating, as of rain, wind, etc. [?]

pelt[2] (pelt), *n.* **1.** the hide or skin of an animal. **2.** *Facetious.* the human skin. **3. in one's pelt,** *Facetious.* naked. [late ME; ? back formation from PELTRY] —**pelt′ish,** *adj.* —**pelt′less,** *adj.*
—**Syn. 1.** See **skin.**

pel·ta (pel′tə), *n., pl.* **-tae** (-tē). a small, light shield used by foot soldiers in ancient Greece. [< L < Gk *péltē* kind of shield]

pel·tast (pel′tast), *n.* an ancient Greek foot soldier armed with a pelta. [< L *peltast(a)* < Gk *peltastḗs.* See PELTA, -IST]

pel·tate (pel′tāt), *adj. Bot.* having the stalk or support attached to the lower surface at a distance from the margin, as a leaf; shield-shaped. [< L *peltāt(us)* having a PELTA; see -ATE[1]] —**pel′tate·ly,** *adv.* —**pel·ta′tion,** *n.*

Peltate leaf

pelt·er (pel′tər), *n.* **1.** one who or that which pelts. **2.** *Poker.* skeet[2]. [PELT[1] + -ER[1]]

Pel′tier effect′ (pel′tyā), the change in temperature of either junction of a thermocouple when a current is maintained in the thermocouple and after allowance is made for a temperature change due to resistance. [named after Jean C. A. *Peltier* (1785–1845), French physicist who discovered it]

A, Pelton wheel; B, Thrust and reaction of water impinging on bucket

Pel′tier heat′, *Physics.* the heat gained or lost at a junction of a thermocouple due to the Peltier effect.

pelt·ing (pel′ting), *adj. Archaic.* paltry; petty; mean. [? dial. *pelt* rags, rubbish (akin to Dan *pjalt* rag) + -ING². See PALTRY] —**pelt′ing·ly,** *adv.*

Pel′ton wheel′ (pel′tᵊn), a high-pressure impulse water turbine in which one or more free jets of water are directed against the buckets of the rotor. [named after L. A. *Pelton* (d. 1908), American engineer, its inventor]

pelt·ry (pel′trē), *n., pl.* **-ries. 1.** fur skins; pelts collectively. **2.** a pelt. [late ME < AF *pelterie,* OF *peleterie* furrier's wares, equiv. to *peleter* furrier (deriv. of L *pilus* hair; see -ER²) + *-ie* -Y³]

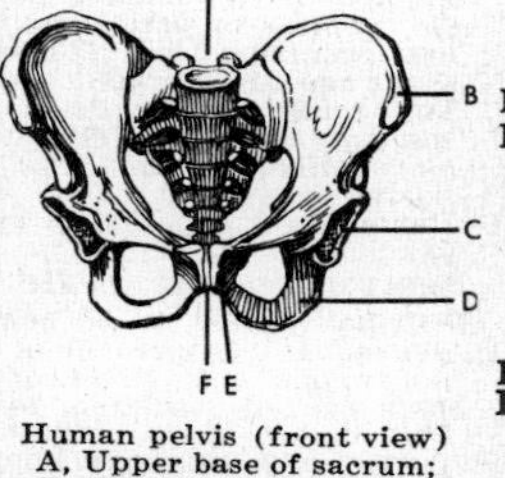

P, Pelvic fin

pel·vic (pel′vik), *adj.* of or pertaining to the pelvis. [PELV(IS) + -IC]

pel′vic fin′, (in fishes) either of a pair of fins on the lower surface of the body, corresponding to the hind limbs of a land vertebrate; ventral fin.

pel′vic gir′dle, 1. (in vertebrates) a bony or cartilaginous arch supporting the hind limbs or analogous parts. **2.** (in man) the arch, formed by the innominate bones, which attaches the lower limb to the axial skeleton. Also called **pel′vic arch′.**

pel·vis (pel′vis), *n., pl.* **-vis·es, -ves** (-vēz). *Anat., Zool.* **1.** the basinlike cavity in the lower part of the trunk of many vertebrates, formed in man by the innominate bones, sacrum, etc. **2.** the bones forming this cavity. **3.** the cavity of the kidney which receives the urine before it is passed into the ureter. See diag. under **kidney.** [< L: basin; akin to Gk *pellis* bowl]

Human pelvis (front view) A, Upper base of sacrum; B, Ilium; C, Acetabulum; D, Ischium; E, Pubis; F, Pubic symphysis

Pem·ba (pem′bə), *n.* an island near the E coast of equatorial Africa: formerly part of Zanzibar protectorate; now a part of Tanzania. 133,858 (1958); 380 sq. mi.

Pem·broke (pem′bro͝ok, -brōk), *n.* **1.** a municipal borough in and the county seat of Pembrokeshire, in SW Wales. 12,737 (1961). **2.** Pembrokeshire. **3.** one of a variety of Welsh corgi having a short or docked tail. Cf. **Cardigan** (def. 2).

Pem·broke·shire (pem′bro͝ok shēr′, -shər, -brōk-), *n.* a county in SW Wales. 93,980 (1961); 614 sq. mi. *Co. seat:* Pembroke. Also called **Pembroke.**

Pembroke table

Pem′broke ta′ble, a drop-leaf table with fly rails and with a drawer at one end or each end of the skirt. Also, **pem′broke ta′ble.** [? after *Pembroke* English aristocratic family]

pem·mi·can (pem′ə kən), *n.* dried meat pounded into a powder and mixed with hot fat and dried fruits or berries, pressed into a loaf or into small cakes, originally prepared by North American Indians. Also, **pem′i·can.** [< Cree *pimikān,* akin to *pimii* grease, fat]

pem·phi·gus (pem′fə gəs, pem fī′-), *n. Pathol.* a serious disease, commonly fatal, characterized by vesicles and bullae on the skin and mucous membranes. [< NL < Gk *pemphig-* (s. of *pémphix*) bubble + L *-us* n. suffix] —**pem·phi·goid** (pem′fə goid′), *n.* —**pem′phi·gous,** *adj.*

pen¹ (pen), *n., v.,* **penned, pen·ning.** —*n.* **1.** any of various instruments for writing or drawing with ink. **2.** a detachable metal penpoint, filled by dipping or with a quill; nib. **3.** such a penpoint with its penholder. **4.** the pen as the instrument of writing or authorship: *The pen is mightier than the sword.* **5.** one's style or quality of writing: *He writes with a witty, incisive pen.* **6.** a writer or author: *I leave this theme to abler pens.* **7.** the profession of writing: *a master of the pen.* **8.** *Ornith.* **a.** a quill. **b.** a pinfeather. **9.** something resembling or suggesting a feather or quill. **10.** *Zool.* an internal, corneous or chitinous, feather-shaped structure in certain cephalopods, as the squid. —*v.t.* **11.** to write with or as with a pen; put down in writing; write: *to pen an essay.* [ME *penne,* OE *pinn* < LL *penna* pen, feather, L: feather, ML *pinnicula* pen, dim. of *pinna* feather. See PENNON] —**pen′like′,** *adj.* —**pen′ner,** *n.*

pen² (pen), *n., v.,* **penned** or **pent, pen·ning.** —*n.* **1.** a small enclosure for domestic animals. **2.** animals so enclosed: *We have a pen of twenty sheep.* **3.** an enclosure used for confinement or safekeeping: *We have built several pens to hold our harvest of corn.* **4.** playpen. **5.** See **bull pen. 6.** a dock having a protective, concrete structure overhead, used to service and repair submarines. —*v.t.* **7.** to confine in or as in a pen. [ME *penne,* OE *penn* < ?]

pen³ (pen), *n. Slang.* penitentiary. [shortened form]

pen⁴ (pen), *n.* a female mute swan. [?]

Pen (pen), *n.* a girl's given name, form of **Penelope.**

pen-, var. of **pene-** before a vowel: *penannular.*

Pen., peninsula. Also, **pen.**

P.E.N., International Association of Poets, Playwrights, Editors, Essayists, and Novelists.

pe·nal (pēn′ᵊl), *adj.* **1.** of, pertaining to, or involving punishment, as for crimes or offenses. **2.** prescribing punishment: *penal laws.* **3.** constituting punishment: *He survived the years of penal hardship.* **4.** used as a place of punishment: *a penal colony.* **5.** subject to or incurring punishment: *a penal offense.* **6.** payable or forfeitable as a penalty: *a penal sum.* [ME < L *poenāl(is),* equiv. to *poen(a)* penalty (< Gk *poinḗ* fine) + *-ālis* -AL¹] —**pe·nal·i·ty** (pi nal′i tē), *n.* —**pe′nal·ly,** *adv.*

pe′nal code′, *Law.* the aggregate of statutory enactments dealing with crimes and their punishment.

pe·nal·ise (pēn′ᵊlīz′, pen′-), *v.t.,* **-ised, -is·ing.** *Chiefly Brit.* penalize. —**pe′nal·is′a·ble,** *adj.* —**pe′nal·i·sa′tion,** *n.*

pe·nal·ize (pēn′ᵊlīz′, pen′-), *v.t.,* **-ized, -iz·ing. 1.** to subject to a penalty, as a person. **2.** to declare (an action, deed, etc.) punishable by law or rule. **3.** to put under a disadvantage or handicap. [PENAL + -IZE] —**pe′nal·iz′a·ble,** *adj.* —**pe′nal·i·za′tion,** *n.*

pe′nal ser′vitude, *Eng. Crim. Law.* imprisonment together with hard labor.

pen·al·ty (pen′ᵊl tē), *n., pl.* **-ties. 1.** a punishment imposed or incurred for a violation of law or rule. **2.** a loss, forfeiture, suffering, or the like, to which a person subjects himself by nonfulfillment of some obligation. **3.** something that is forfeited, as a sum of money. **4.** consequence or disadvantage attached to any action, condition, etc. **5.** *Sports.* a disadvantage imposed upon one of the competitors or upon one side for infraction of the rules. [<< ML *poenālitās.* See PENAL, -TY²]

pen′alty box′, *Ice Hockey.* an enclosed space immediately adjacent to the rink and usually on the side opposite the benches of the teams, for penalized players, the penalty timekeeper, and the official scorer.

pen′alty dou′ble, *Bridge.* See **business double.**

pen·ance (pen′əns), *n.* **1.** a punishment undergone in token of penitence for sin. **2.** a penitential discipline imposed by church authority. **3.** a sacrament, as in the Roman Catholic Church, consisting in a confession of sin, made with sorrow and with the intention of amendment, followed by the forgiveness of the sin. [ME *penaunce* < AF; OF *peneance* < L *paenitentia* PENITENCE] —**pen′ance·less,** *adj.*

pe·nang (pə nang′), *n.* a heavyweight percale. [?]

Pe·nang (pē nang′, -näng′, pi-), *n.* **1.** an island in SE Asia, off the W coast of the Malay Peninsula. 338,866 (1957); 110 sq. mi. **2.** a state including this island and parts of the adjacent mainland: now part of the federation of Malaysia; formerly one of the Straits Settlements and part of the former Federation of Malaya. 680,865 (est. 1963); 400 sq. mi. *Cap.:* George Town. **3.** See **George Town.**

pen·an·nu·lar (pen an′yə lər), *adj.* having the shape or design of an incomplete circle. [PEN- + ANNULAR]

Pen Ar·gyl (pen′ är′jil), a town in E Pennsylvania. 3693 (1960).

pe·nar·i·a (pə nâr′ē ə), *n.* (in an ancient Roman house) a minor room, as a storeroom or sleeping room. [< L: storehouse, akin to *penus* victuals, provision of food]

pe·na·tes (pə nā′tēz), *n.pl. Rom. Religion.* gods who watched over the home or community to which they belonged: originally, two deities of the storeroom. Also, **Pe·na′tes.** Cf. **lares.** [< L, akin to *penitus* inner, *penes* within]

Pen·brook (pen′bro͝ok′), *n.* a town in central Pennsylvania. 3671 (1960).

pen·ca·tite (pen kä′tīt), *n.* a crystalline limestone rock composed of brucite and calcite. [named after Count J. Marzari-*Pencati;* see -ITE¹]

pence (pens), *n. Brit.* a pl. of **penny:** used when the number of pennies is indicated (usually used in combination): *He gave two pennies for tuppence worth. Twelve pence equals one shilling.* —**pence′less,** *adj.*

pen·cel (pen′səl), *n.* a small pennon, as at the head of a lance. Also, **pensil.** [ME < AF, syncopated var. of *penoncel* PENNONCEL]

pen·chant (pen′chənt; *Fr.* päN shäN′), *n.* a strong inclination, taste, or liking for something: *a penchant for outdoor sports.* [< F, n. use of prp. of *pencher* to incline, lean, deriv. of L *pendēre* to hang]

pen·cil (pen′səl), *n., v.,* **-ciled, -cil·ing** or (*esp. Brit.*) **-cilled, -cil·ling.** —*n.* **1.** a slender tube of wood, metal, plastic, etc., containing a core or strip of graphite, a solid coloring material, or the like, used for writing or drawing. **2.** style or skill in drawing or delineation: *He favored the late products of the artist's pencil.* **3.** a slender, pointed piece of a substance used for marking. **4.** a stick of cosmetic coloring material for use on the eyebrows, eyelids, etc. **5.** anything shaped or used like a pencil, as a stick of medicated material: *a styptic pencil.* **6.** a narrow set of lines, light rays, or the like, diverging from or converging to a point. **7.** *Math.* the collection of lines, planes, or surfaces passing through a given point or set of points and satisfying a given equation or condition. Cf. **axial pencil. 8.** *Archaic.* an artist's paintbrush, esp. for fine work. —*v.t.* **9.** to use a pencil on. **10.** to write, draw, mark, or color with, or as with, a pencil. [ME *pencel* < MF *pincel* << L *pēnicill(us)* painter's brush or pencil, dim. of *pēniculus* little tail. See PENIS, -CULE] —**pen′cil·er;** *esp. Brit.,* **pen′cil·ler,** *n.* —**pen′cil·like′,** *adj.*

pen′cil beam′, a cone-shaped radar beam.

pen′cil flow′er, any of several leguminous plants of the genus *Stylosanthes,* of the warmer regions of the world, having spikes of small, tubular flowers.

pen′cil gate′, *Foundry.* any of a large number of narrow gates used for rapid distribution of metal in large castings.

pen′cil gat′ing, *Foundry.* the use of pencil gates.

pen·cil·i·form (pen sil′ə fôrm′, pen′sə lə-), *adj.* **1.** having a pencillike shape. **2.** (of a set of lines, rays, or the like) parallel or nearly parallel. [PENCIL + -I- + -FORM]

pen·cil·ing (pen′sə ling), *n. Obs.* fine or delicate work done with a pencil or brush on a painting or drawing. [PENCIL + -ING¹]

pen′cil push′er, *Informal.* someone, as a bookkeeper, whose work involves a considerable amount of writing.

pen′cil sharp′ener, a rotary device for sharpening pencils or the like. —**pen′cil sharp′ening.**

pend (pend), *v.i.* **1.** to remain undecided or unsettled. **2.** to hang. **3.** *Obs.* to depend. [< L *pend(ēre)* (to) hang, depend]

pend·ant (pen′dənt), *n.* **1.** a hanging ornament, as an earring or the main piece in a necklace. **2.** an ornament suspended from roof, vault, or ceiling. **3.** a hanging electrical lighting fixture; chandelier. **4.** that by which something is suspended, as the ringed stem of a watch. **5.** a match, parallel, companion, or counterpart. **6.** Also, **pennant.** *Naut.* a length of rope attached to a masthead, the end of a yardarm, etc., and having a block or thimble secured to its free end. —*adj.* **7.** pendent. [ME *pendaunt* < MF *pendant,* n. use of prp. of *pendre* to hang < VL **pendere,* r. L *pendēre.* See PEND, -ANT] —**pend′ant·ed,** *adj.* —**pend′ant-like′,** *adj.*

pen′dant cloud′, tuba (def. 4).

pen′dant tack′le, *Naut.* a tackle suspended from a pendant, esp. one from a lower masthead.

pen·da·tive (pen dā′tiv), *n.* one segment of a dome having a polygonal plan. [PEND + -ATIVE]

pend·ent (pen′dənt), *adj.* **1.** hanging or suspended: *a pendent lamp.* **2.** overhanging; jutting; projecting: *a pendent rock formation.* **3.** impending. **4.** undecided; undetermined; pending: *a lawsuit that is still pendent.* —*n.* **5.** pendant. [< L *pendent-* (s. of *pendēns*), prp. of *pendēre* to hang; r. *pendant* (adj.) < MF; see PENDANT] —**pend′en·cy,** *n.* —**pend′ent·ly,** *adv.*

pen·den·te li·te (pen den′tē lī′tē), *Law.* during litigation; while a suit is in progress. [< L: lit., with a lawsuit pending]

pen·den·tive (pen den′tiv), *n. Archit.* **1.** any of several spandrels, in the form of spherical triangles, forming a transition between the circular plan of a dome and the polygonal plan of the supporting masonry. **2.** any of several masonry devices, as squinches or trompes, for forming a transition between a circular or polygonal construction, as a dome or lantern, and supporting masonry of a different plan. —*adj.* **3.** functioning as, or substituting for, a pendentive: *pendentive corbeling.* **4. in pendentive,** *Print.* (of type) set in the form of a triangle resting on its apex. [PENDENT + -IVE, modeled on F *pendentif*]

P, Pendentive

pend′ent post′, (in a timber roof) a short post placed against the wall to receive the lower end of a brace, strut, or beam forming part of the roof framework.

pend·ing (pen′ding), *prep.* **1.** while awaiting; until: *pending his return.* **2.** in the period before the decision or conclusion of; during: *pending the negotiations.* —*adj.* **3.** remaining undecided; awaiting decision or settlement; unfinished: *pending business; pending questions; pending litigation.* **4.** about to take place; impending. [PEND(ENT) + -ING²]

Pen·dle·ton (pen′dᵊl tən), *n.* **1.** a city in N Oregon. 14,434 (1960). **2.** a boy's given name.

pen·drag·on (pen drag′ən), *n.* the supreme leader: the title of certain ancient British chiefs. [< Welsh: lit., head dragon] —**pen·drag′on·ish,** *adj.* —**pen·drag′on·ship′,** *n.*

Pen·drag·on (pen drag′ən), *n.* either of two kings of ancient Britain. Cf., **Arthur** (def. 2), **Uther.**

pen·du·lous (pen′jə ləs, pen′də-, -dyə-), *adj.* **1.** hanging down loosely: *pendulous blossoms.* **2.** swinging freely; oscillating. **3.** vacillating; fluctuating: *pendulous enthusiasm.* [< L *pendul(us)* hanging, swinging. See PEND, -ULOUS] —**pen′du·lous·ly,** *adv.* —**pen′du·lous·ness,** *n.*

pen·du·lum (pen′jə ləm, pen′də-, -dyə-), *n.* **1.** a body so suspended from a fixed point as to move to and fro by the action of gravity and acquired momentum. **2.** *Horol.* a swinging lever, weighted at the lower end, for regulating the speed of a clock mechanism. [< NL, n. use of neut. of L *pendulus* PENDULOUS] —**pen′du·lum·like′,** *adj.*

pen′dulum watch′, (formerly) a watch having a balance wheel, esp. a balance wheel bearing a fake pendulum bob oscillating behind a window in the dial.

pene-, a prefix borrowed from Latin meaning "almost," used in the formation of compound words: *penecontemporaneous.* Also, *esp. before a vowel,* **pen-.** [< L *paene-,* comb. form of *paene*]

pe·ne·con·tem·po·ra·ne·ous (pē′nē kən tem′pə rā′nē əs), *adj. Geol.* formed during or shortly after the formation of the containing rock stratum: *penecontemporaneous minerals.* [PENE- + CONTEMPORANEOUS]

Pe·nei·os (pē′nē ôs′), *n.* Modern Greek name of **Salambria.**

Pe·nel·o·pe (pə nel′ə pē), *n.* **1.** *Class. Myth.* the wife of Odysseus, who remained faithful to him during his absence at Troy in spite of having numerous suitors. **2.** a faithful wife. **3.** a girl's given name.

pe·ne·plain (pē′nə plān′, pē′nə plān′), *n. Geol.* an area reduced almost to a plain by erosion. Also, **pe′ne·plane′.** [PENE- + PLAIN¹] —**pe·ne·pla·na·tion** (pē′nə plə nā′shən), *n.*

pen·e·tra·ble (pen′i trə bəl), *adj.* capable of being penetrated. [< L *penetrābil(is),* equiv. to *penetrā(re)* (to) PENETRATE + *-bilis* -BLE] —**pen′e·tra·bil′i·ty, pen′e·tra·ble·ness,** *n.* —**pen′e·tra·bly,** *adv.*

pen·e·tra·li·a (pen′i trā′lē ə), *n.pl.* the innermost parts or recesses of a place or thing. [< L, n. use of neut. pl. of *penetrālis* inner, equiv. to *penetr(āre)* penetrate + *-ālis* -AL¹] —**pen′e·tra′li·an,** *adj.*

pen·e·tram·e·ter (pen′i tram′i tər), *n.* penetrometer (def. 1).

pen·e·trance (pen′i trəns), *n. Genetics.* the frequency, expressed as a percentage, with which a particular gene produces its effect in a group of organisms. Cf. **expressivity.** [PENETR(ANT) + -ANCE]

pen·e·trant (pen′i trənt), *n.* **1.** one who or that which penetrates. **2.** *Zool.* a large nematocyst discharging a barbed thread that penetrates the body of the prey and injects a toxic fluid. **3.** a substance that lowers the surface tension of water; wetting agent. **4.** a compound that penetrates the skin, as a cosmetic, lotion, cream, or the like. —*adj.* **5.** penetrating. [< L *penetrant-* (s. of *penetrāns*) penetrating, prp. of *penetrāre.* See PENETRATE, -ANT]

pen·e·trate (pen′i trāt′), *v.,* **-trat·ed, -trat·ing.** —*v.t.* **1.** to pierce or pass into or through: *The bullet penetrated the wall. The foglights penetrated the mist.* **2.** to enter the interior of: *to penetrate a forest.* **3.** to enter and diffuse itself through; permeate. **4.** to extend influence, usually peacefully, into the life of (another country). **5.** to obtain a share of (a market): *to penetrate the Canadian coffee market.* **6.** to affect or impress (the mind or feelings) deeply. **7.** to arrive at the truth or meaning of; understand; comprehend: *to penetrate a mystery.* —*v.i.* **8.** to enter, reach, or pass through something, as by piercing: *We penetrated to the interior of the Casbah.* **9.** to diffuse itself through something. **10.** to understand or read the meaning of something. **11.** to have a deep effect or impact on someone. [< L *penetrāt(us)* penetrated (ptp. of *penetrāre*), equiv. to *pene(s)* inside + *-trā(re)* to go (see ENTER) + *-tus* ptp. suffix; see -ATE¹] —**pen′e·tra′tor,** *n.*
—**Syn. 1.** See **pierce. 6.** touch. **7.** fathom, discern.

pen·e·trat·ing (pen′i trā′ting), *adj.* **1.** that penetrates; piercing; sharp: *a penetrating shriek; a penetrating glance.* **2.** acute; discerning: *a penetrating observation.* **3.** *Surg.* noting a wound produced by an agent or missile such that depth is its salient feature, as a wound entering a member. Also, **penetrant.** [PENETRATE + -ING²] —**pen′e·trat′ing·ly,** *adv.* —**pen′e·trat′ing·ness,** *n.*
—**Syn. 2.** keen, sharp. See **acute.** —**Ant. 1.** blunt. **2.** obtuse.

pen·e·tra·tion (pen′i trā′shən), *n.* **1.** the act or power of penetrating. **2.** the extension, usually peaceful, of the influence of one culture in the life of another. **3.** the obtaining of a share of a market for some commodity or service. **4.** mental acuteness, discernment, or insight: *a scholar of rare penetration.* **5.** *Gunnery.* the depth to which a projectile goes into the target. **6.** *Microscopy.* See **depth of field. 7.** the measure of relative depth of field of a telescope or microscope, esp. a binocular microscope. [< LL *penetrātiōn-* (s. of *penetrātiō*). See PENETRATE, -ION]
—**Syn. 4.** understanding, perception, discrimination, depth, profundity.

pen·e·tra·tive (pen′i trā′tiv), *adj.* **1.** tending to penetrate; piercing. **2.** acute; keen. [late ME < ML *penetrātīv(us).* See PENETRATE, -IVE] —**pen′e·tra′tive·ly,** *adv.* —**pen′e·tra′tive·ness, pen·e·tra·tiv·i·ty** (pen′i trə tiv′i tē), *n.*

pen·e·trom·e·ter (pen′i trom′i tər), *n.* **1.** Also, **penetrameter.** Also called **qualimeter.** a device for measuring the penetrating power of x-ray or other radiations. **2.** a device for measuring the penetrability of a solid. [PENETR(ATE) + -O- + -METER]

Pe·ne·us (pə nē′əs), *n.* **1.** ancient name of **Salambria. 2.** *Class. Myth.* the god of the river Peneus and the father of Hypseus and Daphne.

Peng·hu (*Chin.* pung′hōō′), *n.* Pescadores. Also, **Peng·hu·tao** (*Chin.* pung′hōō′dou′).

pen·gő (peng′gœ′), *n., pl.* **-gő, -gős** (-gœz′). a silver coin and monetary unit of Hungary, replaced by the forint in 1946, equal to 100 fillér. [< Hung: lit., sounding; prp. of *pengeni* to sound, jingle]

Emperor penguin, *Aptenodytes forsteri* (Length 4 ft.)

pen·guin (pen′gwin, peng′-), *n. Ornith.* **1.** any of several flightless, aquatic birds of the family *Spheniscidae,* of the Southern Hemisphere, having webbed feet and wings reduced to flippers. **2.** *Obs.* See **great auk.** [? named after *Penguin Island* (near Newfoundland), lit., white head island (i.e. one with a snow-capped height of land < Welsh *pen* head, peak + *gwyn* white), where many auks were found]

Pen′guin Is′land, a novel (1908) by Anatole France. French, **L'Île de Pingouins.**

pen·hold·er (pen′hōl′dər), *n.* **1.** a holder in which a penpoint is placed. **2.** a rack for a pen or pens. [PEN¹ + HOLDER]

-penia, a combining form indicating deficiency: *leucopenia.* [< NL, comb. form repr. Gk *penía* poverty, need]

pen·i·cil (pen′i sil), *n.* a small, brushlike tuft of hairs, as on a caterpillar. [< L *pēnicill(us)* painter's brush or pencil. See PENCIL]

pen·i·cil·late (pen′i sil′it, -āt), *adj.* having a penicil or penicils. [< L *pēnicill(us)* (see PENCIL) + -ATE¹] —**pen′i·cil′late·ly,** *adv.* —**pen′i·cil·la′tion,** *n.*

pen·i·cil·lin (pen′i sil′in), *n. Pharm.* an antibiotic, produced by molds of the genus *Penicillium,* having primarily a bacteriostatic rather than a bactericidal effect, used in medicine chiefly for infections caused by gonococci, meningococci, pneumococci, staphylococci, streptococci, and treponemata. [PENICILL(IUM) + -IN²]

pen·i·cil·li·um (pen′i sil′ē əm), *n., pl.* **-cil·li·ums, -cil·li·a** (-sil′ē ə). any fungus of the genus *Penicillium,* certain species of which are used in cheesemaking and as the source of penicillin. [< NL < L *pēnicill(us)* brush (see PENCIL) + *-ium* -IUM]

pen·in·su·la (pə nin′sə lə, -nins′yə lə), *n.* **1.** an area of land almost completely surrounded by water except for an isthmus connecting it with the mainland. **2. the Peninsula, a.** Spain and Portugal together; Iberian Peninsula; Iberia. **b.** a district in SE Virginia between the York and James rivers: Civil War battles. [< L *paenīnsula,* contr. of *paene īnsula* almost island] —**pen·in′su·lar,** *adj.* —**pen·in′su·lar·ism, pen·in·su·lar·i·ty** (pə nin′sə lar′i tē, -nins′yə-), *n.*

Penin′sular State′, Florida (used as a nickname).

Penin′sula War′, a war (1808–14) in Spain and Portugal, with British, Spanish, and Portuguese troops opposing the French.

pe·nis (pē′nis), *n., pl.* **-nes** (-nēz), **-nis·es.** the male organ of urination and copulation. [< L *pēnis* a tail, the penis] —**pe·nile** (pēn′əl, pē′nil), **pe·ni·al** (pē′nē əl), *adj.*

pe′nis en′vy, *Psychoanal.* the repressed wish of a female to possess a penis.

pen·i·tence (pen′i təns), *n.* the state of being penitent; regret for one's wrongdoing or sinning; contrition; repentance. [< eccl. L *pēnitentia,* var. sp. of L *paenitentia* a regretting. See PENITENT, -ENCE, PENANCE]
—**Syn.** See **regret.**

pen·i·tent (pen′i tənt), *adj.* **1.** feeling or expressing sorrow for sin or wrongdoing and disposed to atonement and amendment; repentant; contrite. —*n.* **2.** a penitent person. **3.** *Rom. Cath. Ch.* one who confesses sin and submits to a penance. [ME < eccl. L *pēnitent-,* var. sp. of L *paenitent-* (s. of *paenitēns*) regretting, prp. of *paenitēre;* r. ME *penaunt* < AF] —**pen′i·tent·ly,** *adv.*

Pen·i·ten·te (pen′i ten′tā, -tē), *n.* a member of a fanatical religious order (**Los Hermanos Penitentes**), prevalent chiefly in Spanish-American communities in New Mexico, known for their practice of self-flagellation, esp. in Holy Week. [< Sp, sing. of *Penitentes,* short for *Los Hermanos Penitentes* the penitent brothers]

pen·i·ten·tial (pen′i ten′shəl), *adj.* **1.** of, pertaining to, proceeding from, or expressive of penitence or repentance. —*n.* **2.** a penitent. **3.** a book or code of canons relating to penance, its imposition, etc. [< ML *poenitentiāl(is).* See PENITENT, -IAL] —**pen′i·ten′tial·ly,** *adv.*

pen′iten′tial Psalm′, any of the Psalms (the 6th, 32nd, 38th, 51st, 102nd, 130th, and 143rd) that give expression to feelings of penitence and that are used in various Christian liturgical services.

pen·i·ten·tia·ry (pen′i ten′shə rē), *n., pl.* **-ries,** *adj.* —*n.* **1.** a place for imprisonment, reformatory discipline, or punishment. **2.** a prison, esp. one maintained in the U.S. by a State or the federal government. **3.** *Rom. Cath. Ch.* a tribunal in the Curia Romana, presided over by a cardinal (**grand penitentiary**), having jurisdiction over certain matters, as penance, confession, dispensation, absolution, and impediments, and dealing with questions of conscience reserved for the Holy See. —*adj.* **4.** (of an offense) punishable by imprisonment in a penitentiary. **5.** of, pertaining to, or intended for imprisonment, reformatory discipline, or punishment. **6.** penitential. [ME < ML *poenitentiāri(us).* See PENITENCE, -ARY]

pen·knife (pen′nīf′), *n., pl.* **-knives.** a small pocketknife, formerly one used for making and repairing quill pens. [late ME *pen(ne)knif.* See PEN¹, KNIFE]

pen·light (pen′līt′), *n.* a flashlight similar in size and shape to a fountain pen. Also, **pen′lite′.** [PEN¹ + LIGHT¹]

pen·man (pen′mən), *n., pl.* **-men. 1.** a person who writes or copies; scribe; copyist. **2.** an expert in penmanship. **3.** a writer or author. [PEN¹ + MAN¹]

pen·man·ship (pen′mən ship′), *n.* **1.** the art of handwriting; the use of the pen in writing. **2.** one's style or manner of handwriting: *clear penmanship; poor penmanship.* [PENMAN + -SHIP]

Penn (pen), *n.* **1. Sir William,** 1621–70, British admiral. **2.** his son, **William,** 1644–1718, English Quaker: founder of Pennsylvania 1682.

Penn., Pennsylvania. Also, **Pa., Penna.**

pen·na (pen′ə), *n., pl.* **pen·nae** (pen′ē). *Ornith.* a contour feather, as distinguished from a down feather, plume, etc. [< L: feather. See PEN¹]

pen·na·ceous (pə nā′shəs), *adj.* having the texture of a penna; not downy. [< NL *pennaceus.* See PENNA, -ACEOUS]

pen′ name′, a name used by an author instead of his real name; pseudonym; nom de plume.

pen·nant (pen′ənt), *n.* **1.** a long, tapering flag or burgee of distinctive form and special significance, borne on naval or other vessels and used in signaling or for identification. **2.** any relatively long, tapering flag. **3.** a flag serving as an emblem of victory or championship: *He says the Mets may win the pennant next year.* **4.** *Music.* hook (def. 11). **5.** *Naut.* pendant (def. 6). [b. PENNON + PENDANT]

pen·nate (pen′āt), *adj.* winged; feathered. Also, **pen′nat·ed.** [< L *pennāt(us).* See PENNA, -ATE¹]

Pen·nell (pen′əl), *n.* **Joseph;** 1860–1926, U.S. etcher, illustrator, and writer.

Penn′ Hills′, a town in W Pennsylvania. 51,512 (1960).

pen·ni (pen′ē), *n., pl.* **pen·ni·a** (pen′ē ə), **pen·nis.** a copper coin of Finland, the 100th part of a markka, equivalent to about .0031 of a U.S. dollar. [< Finnish < LG *pennig* PENNY]

Pen·nie (pen′ē), *n.* a girl's given name, form of **Penelope.** Also, **Penny.**

pen·ni·less (pen′ē lis), *adj.* without any money whatsoever; totally impoverished. [ME *peniles.* See PENNY, -LESS] —**pen′ni·less·ly,** *adv.* —**pen′ni·less·ness,** *n.*
—**Syn.** indigent. See **poor.** —**Ant.** rich.

Pen′nine Alps′ (pen′īn), a mountain range on the border between Switzerland and Italy: part of the Alps. Highest peak, Monte Rosa, 15,217 ft.

Pen′nine Chain′, a range of hills in N England, extending from the S Midlands to the Cheviot Hills.

pen·ning (pen′ing), *n.* pitching. [PEN² + -ING¹]

pen′ning gate′, a sluice gate that opens by lifting upward.

pen·ni·nite (pen′ə nīt′), *n. Mineral.* a member of the chlorite group, rhombohedral in habit. Also called **pen·nine** (pen′in, -īn). [< G *Pennin* (after PENNINE ALPS) + -ITE¹]

pen·non (pen′ən), *n.* **1.** a distinctive flag in any of various forms, as tapering, triangular, swallow-tailed, etc., formerly one borne on the lance of a knight. **2.** a pennant. **3.** any flag or banner. **4.** a wing or pinion. [ME *penon* < MF, aug. of OF *pene* < L *penna* or *pinna* feather. See PEN¹] —**pen′noned,** *adj.*

pen·non·cel (pen′ən sel′), *n.* pencel. Also, **penoncel.** [ME *penonceal* < MF *penoncel,* dim. of *penon* PENNON]

Penn·sau·ken (pen sô′kin), *n.* a town in W New Jersey, on the Delaware River. 33,771 (1960).

Penns′ Grove′, a town in SW New Jersey. 6176 (1960).

Penn·syl·va·ni·a (pen′səl vā′nē ə, -vān′yə), *n.* a State in the E United States. 11,319,366 (1960); 45,333 sq. mi. *Cap.:* Harrisburg. *Abbr.:* Pa., Penn., Penna.

Penn′sylva′nia Dutch′, **1.** the descendants of 18th-century settlers in Pennsylvania from SW Germany. **2.** Also called **Pennsylvania German.** a German dialect spoken mainly in eastern Pennsylvania, developed from the language of these settlers. **3.** the folk style of applied and decorative art developed by the Pennsylvania Dutch. —**Penn′syl·va′ni·a-Dutch′,** *adj.*

Penn′sylva′nia Ger′man, the German dialect of eastern Pennsylvania; Pennsylvania Dutch.

Penn·syl·va·ni·an (pen′səl vā′nē ən, -vān′yən), *adj.* **1.** of or pertaining to the State of Pennsylvania. **2.** *Geol.* noting or pertaining to a period of the Paleozoic era, occurring from 270,000,000 to about 300,000,000 years ago and characterized by warm climates, swampy land areas, and the development of large reptiles and insects: sometimes considered as an epoch of the Carboniferous period. See table under **era.** —*n.* **3.** a native or inhabitant of Pennsylvania. **4.** *Geol.* the Pennsylvanian period or system. [PENNSYLVANI(A) + -AN]

Penn′sylva′nia ri′fle. See **Kentucky rifle.**

pen·ny (pen′ē), *n., pl.* **pen·nies,** (*esp. collectively for 2*) **pence. 1.** a bronze coin of the U.S., the 100th part of a dollar; one cent. **2.** a bronze coin of Great Britain, the 12th part of a shilling, equivalent to about .012 of a U.S. dollar. **3.** a bronze coin of Canada, the 100th part of a dollar, equivalent to about .00925 of a U.S. dollar. **4.** the 12th part of the shillings of various nations and territories, as Australia, Ghana, Ireland, Jamaica, New Guinea, New Zealand, and Nigeria. **5.** a sum of money: *to spend every penny of one's income.* **6.** the length of a nail in terms of certain standard designations from twopenny to sixtypenny. **7. a bad penny,** someone or something undesirable: *At every party I went to that year he'd keep turning up like a bad penny.* **8. a pretty penny,** *Informal.* a considerable sum of money: *Their car must have cost them a pretty penny.* **9. turn an honest penny,** to earn one's living honestly; make money by fair means: *He's never turned an honest penny in his life.* [ME *peni,* OE *penig, pening, pending,* lit., something connected with *Penda,* 8th-century English (Mercian) king who coined the piece of money so named (see -ING¹) where D *penning,* G *Pfennig,* Icel *pen(n)ingr,* etc.] —**pen′nied,** *adj.*

Pen·ny (pen′ē), *n.* a girl's given name, form of **Penelope.** Also, **Pennie.**

-penny, a suffix forming adjectives that denote price or value (as used in *fourpenny nails, fivepenny nails,* etc., formerly meaning "nails costing fourpence, fivepence, etc., a hundred," but now nails of certain arbitrary sizes).

pen·ny-a-line (pen′ē ə līn′), *adj. Chiefly Brit. Archaic.* **1.** (of writing) paid for at the rate of one cent for each line written. **2.** (of books, newspaper articles, etc.) containing cheap or inferior writing.

pen·ny-a-lin·er (pen′ē ə lī′nər), *n. Chiefly Brit. Archaic.* a hack writer. [PENNY-A-LINE + -ER¹]

Penn′ Yan′ (yan), a town in central New York. 5770 (1960).

pen′ny an′te, **1.** *Cards.* a game of poker in which the ante or limit is one cent. **2.** *Informal.* any business arrangement or transaction involving a trifling or paltry sum of money: *That deal of his is just penny ante compared to the one I'm offering you.*

pen′ny arcade′, a hall or walk, as in an amusement park or carnival, that contains entertainment devices that can be operated for a penny or other small sum.

pen·ny-cress (pen′ē kres′), *n.* any of several cruciferous herbs of the genus *Thalaspi,* esp. *T. alpestre,* of Europe, bearing somewhat round, flat pods.

pen′ny dread′ful, a cheap, sensational novel of adventure, crime, or violence; dime novel.

pen′ny fee′, *Scot. Archaic.* small pay; a low wage.

pen′ny pinch′er, a miserly, niggardly, or stingy person. —**pen′ny-pinch′ing,** *n., adj.*

pen·ny-plain (pen′ē plān′), *adj. Brit.* plain or simple; without frills or decoration.

pen′ny post′, (formerly) any of various postal systems delivering mail for a penny a letter.

pen·ny·roy·al (pen′ē roi′əl), *n.* any herbaceous, labiate plant, as *Mentha Pulegium,* of the Old World, or *Hedeoma pulegioides,* of America, used medicinally and yielding a pungent aromatic oil. [PENNY + ROYAL; r. late ME *puliol real* < AF; MF *poliol* (< L **pulegiōl-(um),* dim. of *pulegium* pennyroyal) + *real,* earlier form of *royal*]

pen′ny stocks′, *Stock Exchange.* common stocks, usually highly speculative, selling for less than a dollar a share.

pen·ny-stone (pen′ē stōn′), *n. Scot. and North Eng.* **1.** a round stone used as a quoit. **2.** the game of quoits. [ME *penystan.* See PENNY, STONE]

pen·ny·weight (pen′ē wāt′), *n.* (in troy weight) a unit of 24 grains or 1/20 of an ounce. *Abbr.:* dwt [ME *penyweight,* OE *penega gewihte.* See PENNY, WEIGHT]

pen′ny wheep′ (hwēp, wēp), *n. Chiefly Scot.* a small glass of beer; a short beer. [PENNY + *wheep,* Scot var. of WHIP (to drink fast)]

pen·ny-wise (pen′ē wīz′), *adj.* prudent or saving, esp. short-sightedly, in regard to small sums: *penny-wise and pound-foolish.* —**pen′ny wis′dom.**

pen·ny·wort (pen′ē wûrt′), *n.* any of several plants having round or roundish leaves, as the navelwort. [late ME *penywort.* See PENNY, WORT[2]]

pen·ny·worth (pen′ē wûrth′), *n.* **1.** as much as may be bought for a penny. **2.** a small quantity. **3.** a bargain. [ME *penyworth,* OE *penigweorth.* See PENNY, WORTH[1]]

Pe·nob·scot (pə nob′skot, -skət), *n., pl.* **-scots,** (*esp. collectively*) **-scot** for 2. **1.** a river flowing S from N Maine into Penobscot Bay. 350 mi. long. **2.** a member of an Algonquian Indian tribe of the Abnaki confederacy, which occupied territory on both sides of the Penobscot Bay and River. **3.** the dialect of the Abnaki language used by the Penobscot Indians.

Penob′scot Bay′, an inlet of the Atlantic in S Maine. 30 mi. long.

pe·nol·o·gy (pē nol′ə jē), *n.* **1.** the science of the punishment of crime, in both its deterrent and its reformatory aspects. **2.** the science of the management of prisons. Also, **poenology.** [*peno-* (comb. form repr. Gk *poinḗ* penalty) + -LOGY] —**pe·no·log·i·cal** (pēn′əloj′i kəl), *adj.* —**pe·nol′o·gist,** *n.*

pen·on·cel (pen′ən sel′), *n.* pennoncel.

pen′ pal′, a person who keeps up an exchange of letters, usually with someone who is so far away that a personal meeting is unlikely.

pen·point (pen′point′), *n.* **1.** the point or writing end of a pen, esp. a small, tapering, metallic device having a split tip for drawing up ink and for writing; nib. **2.** the tip or point of a ball-point pen. [PEN[1] + POINT]

Pen·rod (pen′rod), *n.* a novel (1914) by Booth Tarkington.

Pen·sa·co·la (pen′sə kō′lə), *n.* a seaport in NW Florida, on Pensacola Bay. 56,752 (1960).

Pen′saco′la Bay′, an inlet of the Gulf of Mexico, in NW Florida. ab. 30 mi. long.

Pen′saco′la pi′lot boat′, a fishing boat, used in the area of Pensacola, Florida, having a centerboard hull and spritsails on three masts: originally used as a pilot boat.

pen·sée (päN sā′), *n., pl.* **-sées** (-sā′). *French.* a reflection or thought.

Pen·sées (päN sāz′, päN-; *Fr.* päN sā′), *n.* a collection of notes, essays, etc., dealing with religious and philosophical matters by Blaise Pascal, published posthumously in 1670.

Pen·se·ro·so, Il (il pen′sə rō′sō; *It.* ēl pen′se rô′sô). See **Il Penseroso.**

pen·sil (pen′səl), *n.* pencil.

pen·sile (pen′sil), *adj.* **1.** hanging, as the nests of certain birds. **2.** building a hanging nest. [< L *pensil(is)* hanging down, equiv. to *pens-* (a ptp. s. akin to *pendēre* to hang) + *-ilis* -ILE] —**pen′sile·ness, pen·sil′i·ty,** *n.*

pen·sion (pen′shən; *for 3, 4 Fr.* päN syôN′), *n., pl.* **-sions** (-shənz; *for 3, 4 Fr.* -syôN′), *v.* —*n.* **1.** a fixed amount, other than wages, paid at regular intervals to a person or his surviving dependents in consideration of his past services, age, merit, poverty, injury or loss sustained, etc.: *a retirement pension.* **2.** an allowance, annuity, or subsidy. **3.** (in France and elsewhere on the Continent) a boarding house or school. **4.** (on the continent of Europe) room and board. —*v.t.* **5.** to grant a pension to. **6.** to cause to retire on a pension (usually fol. by *off*). [late ME < L *pensiōn-* (s. of *pensiō*) a weighing out, hence, a paying out, installment paying, equiv. to *pens(us)* (ptp. of *pendere* to weigh out, pay by weight) + *-iōn-* -ION; r. ME *pensioun* < AF] —**pen′sion·a·ble,** *adj.* —**pen′sion·a·bly,** *adv.* —**pen′sion·less,** *adj.*

pen·sion·ar·y (pen′shə ner′ē), *n., pl.* **-ar·ies,** *adj.* —*n.* **1.** a pensioner. **2.** a hireling. —*adj.* **3.** of the nature of a pension. **4.** receiving a pension. [< ML *pensiōnāri(us).* See PENSION, -ARY]

pen·sion·er (pen′shə nər), *n.* **1.** a person who receives a pension. **2.** a hireling. **3.** a student at Cambridge University who pays for his commons and other expenses, and is not supported by any foundation. **4.** *Obs.* a gentleman-at-arms. [late ME < AF; see PENSION, -ER[2]] —**pen′sion·er·ship′,** *n.*

pen·sive (pen′siv), *adj.* **1.** dreamily or wistfully thoughtful: *a pensive mood.* **2.** expressing thoughtfulness or sadness: *a pensive adagio.* [< F (fem.); r. ME *pensif* < MF (masc.), deriv. of *penser* to think < L *pensāre* to weigh, consider. See PENSION, -IVE] —**pen′sive·ly,** *adv.* —**pen′sive·ness,** *n.*

—**Syn. 1.** PENSIVE, MEDITATIVE, REFLECTIVE suggest quiet modes of apparent or real thought. PENSIVE, the weakest of the three, suggests dreaminess or wistfulness, and may involve little or no thought to any purpose: *a pensive, faraway look.* MEDITATIVE involves thinking of certain facts or phenomena, perhaps in the religious sense of "contemplation", without necessarily having a goal of complete understanding or of action: *meditative but unjudicial.* REFLECTIVE has a strong implication of orderly, perhaps analytic, processes of thought, usually with a definite goal of understanding: *a careful and reflective critic.* —**Ant. 1.** thoughtless.

pen·ste·mon (pen stē′mən, pen′stə mən), *n.* pentstemon.

pen·stock (pen′stok′), *n.* **1.** a pipe conducting water from the head gates to a water wheel. **2.** a conduit for conveying water to a power plant. See diag. under **dam**[1]. **3.** a sluicelike contrivance used to control the flow of water. [PEN[2] + STOCK]

pent[1] (pent), *v.* **1.** a pt. and pp. of **pen**[2]. —*adj.* **2.** shut in; confined. [ptp. of late ME *pend* (now obs.), var. of PEN[2] (v.); cf. LEND]

pent[2] (pent), *n.* penthouse (def. 3). [by shortening]

Pent., Pentecost.

penta-, an element occurring in loan words from Greek, meaning "five" (*Pentateuch*); on this model, used in the formation of compound words (*pentavalent*). Also, *esp. before a vowel,* **pent-.** [< Gk *pent-, penta-,* comb. forms repr. *pénte* five]

pen·ta·bo·rane (pen′tə bôr′ān, -bôr′-), *n. Chem.* a liquid, B_5H_9, that ignites spontaneously in air: used as a rocket propellant. [PENTA- + BOR(ON) + -ANE]

pen·ta·chlo·ro·phe·nol (pen′tə klôr′ō fē′nōl, -nôl, -nol, -klōr′-), *n. Chem.* a white, crystalline, water-insoluble powder, C_6Cl_5OH used chiefly in fungicides, disinfectants, and wood preservatives. [PENTA- + CHLORO-[2] + PHENOL]

pen·ta·cle (pen′tə kəl), *n.* **1.** pentagram. **2.** a similar figure, as a hexagram. [< It *pentacolo* five-cornered object. See PENTA-, -CLE]

pen·tad (pen′tad), *n.* **1.** a period of five years. **2.** *Chem.* a pentavalent element or group. **3.** a group of five. **4.** the number five. [< Gk *pentad-* (s. of *pentás*) group of five. See PENT-, -AD[1]]

pen·ta·dac·tyl (pen′tə dak′təl, -til), *adj.* **1.** having five digits on each hand or foot. **2.** having five fingerlike projections or parts. [< L *pentadactyl(us)* < Gk *pentadáktylos.* See PENTA-, DACTYL] —**pen′ta·dac′tyl·ism,** *n.*

pen·ta·dec·a·gon (pen′tə dek′ə gon′), *n. Geom.* a polygon having fifteen angles and fifteen sides. [PENTA- + DECAGON]

pen·ta·e·ryth·ri·tol (pen′tə i rith′ri tōl′, -tôl′, -tol′), *n. Chem.* a white, crystalline, water-soluble powder, $C(CH_2OH)_4$, used chiefly in the manufacture of alkyd resins, varnishes, plasticizers, and explosives. [PENTA- + ERYTHRITOL]

pen′taeryth′ritol tetrani′trate, *Chem., Pharm.* a white, crystalline, water-insoluble, explosive solid, $C(CH_2ONO_2)_4$, used chiefly as a high explosive and as a vasodilator in treating angina pectoris. Also called **PETN**

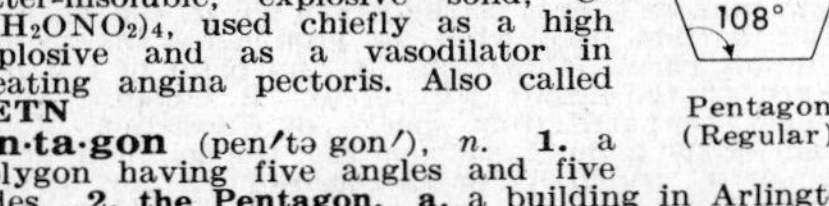

Pentagon (Regular)

pen·ta·gon (pen′tə gon′), *n.* **1.** a polygon having five angles and five sides. **2. the Pentagon, a.** a building in Arlington, Virginia, containing most U.S. Defense Department offices. **b.** *Informal.* the U.S. Department of Defense. [< LL *pentagōn(um)* < Gk *pentágōnon,* n. use of neut. of *pentágōnos* five-angled. See PENTA-, -GON] —**pen·tag·o·nal** (pen tag′ə nəl), *adj.* —**pen·tag′o·nal·ly,** *adv.*

pentag′onal dodecahe′dron, *Crystall.* pyritohedron.

pen·tag·o·noid (pen tag′ə noid′), *adj.* like a pentagon in shape.

Pentagram

pen·ta·gram (pen′tə gram′), *n.* a five-pointed, star-shaped figure made by extending the sides of a regular pentagon until they meet, used as a symbolic figure by the Pythagoreans and later philosophers, by magicians, etc. Also called **pentacle, pentangle, pentalpha.** [< Gk *pentágramm(on).* See PENTA-, -GRAM[1]] —**pen·ta·gram·mat·ic** (pen′tə grə mat′ik), *adj.*

pen·ta·grid (pen′tə grid′), *adj. Electronics.* (of a vacuum tube) having five grids. [PENTA- + GRID]

pen·ta·he·dron (pen′tə hē′drən), *n., pl.* **-drons, -dra** (-drə). a solid figure having five faces. [PENTA- + -HEDRON] —**pen′ta·he′dral, pen′ta·he′dri·cal, pen′ta·he′drous,** *adj.*

pen·ta·hy·drate (pen′tə hī′drāt), *n. Chem.* a hydrate that contains five molecules of water, as potassium molybdate, $KMoO_4 \cdot 5H_2O$. [PENTA- + HYDRATE] —**pen′ta·hy′drat·ed,** *adj.*

pen·ta·hy·dric (pen′tə hī′drik), *adj. Chem.* (esp. of alcohols and phenols) pentahydroxy. [PENTA- + -HYDRIC]

pen·ta·hy·drox·y (pen′tə hī drok′sē), *adj. Chem.* (of a molecule) containing five hydroxyl groups. [PENTA- + HYDROXY]

pen·tal·pha (pen tal′fə), *n.* pentagram. [< Gk *péntalpha* (see PENT-, ALPHA); so called from the *A* represented at each point]

pen·tam·er·ous (pen tam′ər əs), *adj.* **1.** consisting of or divided into five parts. **2.** *Bot.* (of flowers) having five members in each whorl. [< NL *pentamerus.* See PENTA-, -MEROUS] —**pen·tam′er·ism, pen·tam′er·y,** *n.*

pen·tam·e·ter (pen tam′i tər), *Pros.* —*n.* **1.** a verse of five feet. **2.** Also called **elegiac pentameter.** *Class. Pros.* a verse consisting of two dactyls, one long syllable, two more dactyls, and another long syllable. **3.** unrhymed verse of five iambic feet; heroic verse. —*adj.* **4.** consisting of five metrical feet. [< L *pentameter* < Gk *pentámetros.* See PENTA-, -METER] —**pen·tam′e·trist,** *n.*

pen·ta·meth·yl·ene (pen′tə meth′ə lēn′), *n. Chem.* cyclopentane. [PENTA- + METHYLENE]

pen·ta·meth·yl·ene·di·a·mine (pen′tə meth′ə lēn-dī′ə mēn′, -min, -dī′ə mēn′), *n. Biochem.* cadaverine. [PENTA- + METHYLENE + DIAMINE]

pen·tane (pen′tān), *n. Chem., Pharm.* **1.** a hydrocarbon, C_5H_{12}, of the methane series, existing in three liquid isomeric forms. **2.** Also called **normal pentane.** the most important isomer of pentane, a colorless, flammable, water-insoluble, very volatile liquid, $CH_3(CH_2)_3CH_3$, obtained from petroleum by distillation: used chiefly as a solvent and in medicine as an anesthetic. [PENT- + -ANE]

pen·tan·gle (pen′taŋ gəl), *n.* pentagram. [PENT- + ANGLE]

pen·tan·gu·lar (pen taŋ′gyə lər), *adj.* having five angles and five sides; pentagonal. [PENT- + ANGULAR]

pen·tap·o·dy (pen tap′ə dē), *n., pl.* **-dies.** *Pros.* a measure consisting of five feet. [PENTA- + -POD + -Y[3]] —**pen·ta·pod·ic** (pen′tə pod′ik), *adj.*

pen·ta·prism (pen′tə priz′əm), *n.* a prism that has five faces with four angles of 112.5° and one of 90° on each face and that has the property that all rays parallel to the major face are deviated 90°: used as a reflector in rangefinders. [PENTA- + PRISM]

pen·tap·tych (pen′tap tik), *n.* a work of art consisting of five panels or sections. [PENTA- + Gk *ptych(ḗ)* a fold]

pen·tar·chy (pen′tär kē), *n., pl.* **-chies. 1.** a government by five persons. **2.** a governing body of five persons. **3.** a union of five states or kingdoms, each under its own ruler. [< Gk *pentarchía.* See PENT-, -ARCHY] —**pen′tarch,** *n.* —**pen·tar′chi·cal,** *adj.*

pen·ta·stich (pen′tə stik′), *n. Pros.* a strophe, stanza, or poem consisting of five lines or verses. [< NL *pentastich(us)* < Gk *pentástichos.* See PENTA-, STICH]

pen·ta·style (pen′tə stīl′), *adj. Archit.* **1.** having five columns. **2.** (of a classical temple or a building in the style of one) having five columns on one or each front. [PENTA- + Gk *stŷl(os)* pillar]

pen·ta·sty·los (pen′tə stī′los), *n.* a pentastyle building, as a classical temple. [< NL; see PENTASTYLE]

pen·ta·syl·la·ble (pen′tə sil′ə bəl), *n.* a word or line of verse of five syllables. [PENTA- + SYLLABLE] —**pen·ta·syl·lab·ic** (pen′tə si lab′ik), *adj.* —**pen′ta·syl′la·bism,** *n.*

Pen·ta·teuch (pen′tə to͞ok′, -tyo͞ok′), *n.* the first five books of the Old Testament. [< LL *Pentateuch(os)* < LGk *pentáteuchos* (*biblos*), equiv. to Gk *penta-* PENTA- + *teûch(os)* tool, implement > LGk: book] —**Pen′ta·teuch′al,** *adj.*

pen·tath·lon (pen tath′lən), *n.* an athletic contest comprising five different track and field events and won by the contestant gaining the highest total score. [< Gk *pénthathlon,* equiv. to *pent-* PENT- + *âthlon* contest]

pen′taton′ic scale′ (pen′tə ton′ik, pen′-), *Music.* a scale having five tones to an octave, as the five black keys of a piano octave. [PENTA- + TONIC]

pen·ta·tron (pen′tə tron′), *n. Electronics.* a duotriode having one cathode, which functions for both triodes. [PENTA- + -TRON]

pen·ta·va·lent (pen′tə vā′lənt, pen tav′ə-), *adj. Chem.* **1.** having a valence of 5: *pentavalent arsenic.* **2.** quinquevalent (def. 2). [PENTA- + -VALENT]

Pen·te·cost (pen′tə kôst′, -kost′), *n.* **1.** a Christian festival celebrated on the seventh Sunday after Easter, commemorating the descent of the Holy Ghost upon the apostles; Whitsunday. **2.** Shabuoth. [ME *pentecoste,* OE *pentecosten* < LL *pentēcostē* < Gk *pentēkostḗ* fiftieth (day)]

Pen·te·cos·tal (pen′tə kô′stəl, -stəl, -kos′təl, -təl), *adj.* **1.** of or pertaining to Pentecost. **2.** noting or pertaining to any of the Christian groups, often fundamentalist, that emphasize the activity of the Holy Spirit, stress holiness of living, and express their religious feelings uninhibitedly, as by speaking in tongues. —*n.* **3.** a member of any Pentecostal denomination. [< LL *pentēcostāl(is).* See PENTECOST, -AL[1]]

pen·te·cos·ta·ri·on (pen′dē kôs tä′rē ôn; *Eng.* pen′tə ko stâr′ē on′), *n., pl.* **-cos·ta·ri·a** (-kôs tä′rē ä; *Eng.* -ko stâr′ē ə). *Gk. Orth. Ch.* a service book of offices for the period from Easter to the Sunday after Pentecost. [< LGk *pentēkostárion,* equiv. to Gk *pentēkost(ḗ)* PENTECOST + *-arion* n. suffix]

Pen·tel·i·cus (pen tel′ə kəs), *n.* a mountain in SE Greece, near Athens: noted for its fine marble. 3640 ft. Also, **Pen·tel·i·kon** (pen tel′ə kon′). —**Pen·tel′ic, Pen·tel′i·can,** *adj.*

Pen·the·si·le·a (pen′thə sə lē′ə), *n.* **1.** *Class. Myth.* an Amazon queen killed by Achilles at Troy. **2.** (*italics.*) a tragedy (1808) by Heinrich von Kleist.

Pen·the·us (pen′thē əs, -tho͞os), *n. Class. Myth.* a Theban king who was torn to pieces by his mother, Agave, and other frenzied followers of Dionysus, whose divinity the king had denied.

pent·house (pent′hous′), *n., pl.* **-hous·es** (-hou′ziz). **1.** a separate apartment or dwelling on a roof. **2.** a structure on a roof for housing elevator machinery, a water tank, etc. **3.** Also called **appentice, pent, pentice.** a shed with a sloping roof, or a sloping roof, projecting from a wall or the side of a building, as to shelter a door. **4.** any rooflike shelter or overhanging part. **5.** See **shed roof. 6.** *Court Tennis.* a corridor having a slanted roof and projecting from three walls of the court. [alter. (by folk etymology) of ME *pentis* < OF *apentis* annex; akin to APPENDIX] —**pent′house′like′,** *adj.*

pen·tice (pen′tis), *n.* penthouse (def. 3).

Pen·tic·ton (pen tik′tən), *n.* a city in S British Columbia, in SW Canada. 13,859 (1961).

pen·ti·men·to (pen′tə men′tō), *n., pl.* **-ti** (-tē). *Painting.* the presence or emergence of earlier images, forms, or strokes that have been changed and painted over. [< It, equiv. to *penti(re)* (to) repent (< L *paenitēre* to regret) + *-mento* -MENT]

Pent·land (pent′lənd), *n.* a walled plain in the fourth quadrant of the face of the moon: about 45 miles in diameter.

pent·land·ite (pent′lən dīt′), *n.* a mineral, sulfide of nickel, occurring in the form of bronze-colored granular aggregates, found with pyrrhotite: the principal source of nickel. [< F; named after Joseph B. *Pentland* (d. 1873), Irish scientist; see -ITE[1]]

pen·to·bar·bi·tal (pen′tə bär′bi tal′, -tôl′), *n. Pharm.* a barbiturate, $C_{11}H_{18}N_2O_3$, used chiefly in the form of its sodium or calcium salt as a hypnotic and as a sedative. [PENT- + -O- + BARBITAL]

pen·tode (pen′tōd), *n. Electronics.* a vacuum tube having five electrodes, usually a plate, three grids, and a cathode, within the same envelope. [PENT- + -ODE[2]]

pen·to·lite (pen′tə līt′), *n.* a high explosive consisting of pentaerythritol tetranitrate and TNT. [PENT- + -OL[1] + -ITE[1]]

pen·tom·ic (pen tom′ik), *adj. Mil.* pertaining to or characterizing the organization of an army division into five groups, each with supporting units, geared to maneuver in keeping with the requirements of atomic warfare. [PENT- + (AT)OMIC]

pen·to·san (pen′tə san′), *n. Biochem.* any of a class of polysaccharides that occur in plants, humus, etc., and form pentoses upon hydrolysis. [PENTOSE + -AN]

pen·tose (pen′tōs), *n. Chem.* a monosaccharide containing five atoms of carbon, as xylose, $C_5H_{10}O_5$, or produced from pentosans by hydrolysis. [PENT- + -OSE[2]]

pen′tose nucle′ic ac′id, *Biochem.* **1.** a nucleic acid containing a pentose. **2.** See **RNA.**

Pen·to·thal (pen′tə thôl′), *n. Pharm., Trademark.* thiopental.

pent·ste·mon (pent stē′mən), *n.* any of several North American plants of the genus *Pentstemon*, certain species of which are cultivated for their showy flowers. Also, **penstemon.** [< NL, equiv. to *pent-* PENT- + Gk *stēmon* warp, thread]

pent-up (pent′up′), *adj.* confined; restrained; curbed: *pent-up emotions; pent-up rage.*

pen·tyl (pen′til), *adj.* *Chem.* containing a pentyl group; amyl. [PENT- + -YL]

pen·tyl·ene·tet·ra·zol (pen′tᵊlēn te′trə zôl′, -zōl′), *n.* *Pharm.* a white, crystalline, bitter-tasting, water-soluble powder, $C_6H_{10}N_4$, used as a respiratory and circulatory stimulant, esp. in the treatment of barbiturate poisoning, and to induce a convulsive state in the treatment of certain mental diseases. [PENT- + (METH)YLENE + TETRA- + AZ- + -OL²]

pen′tyl group′, *Chem.* any of the univalent, isomeric groups having the formula C_5H_{11}–.

pe·nu·che (pə nōō′chē), *n.* **1.** Also, **panocha.** a candy made of brown sugar, butter, and milk, usually with nuts. **2.** panocha (def. 1). [var. of PANOCHA]

pe·nuch·le (pē′nuk əl), *n.* pinochle. Also, **pen′-nuck·le.**

pe·nult (pē′nult, pi nult′), *n.* the last syllable but one in a word. Also, **pe·nul·ti·ma** (pi nul′tə mə). [< L *paenult(ima)* (*syllaba*), contr. of *paene ultima* almost the last; see ULTIMA]

pe·nul·ti·mate (pi nul′tə mit), *adj.* **1.** next to the last: *the penultimate scene of the play.* **2.** of or pertaining to a penult or penults. —*n.* **3.** a penult. [see PENULT, ULTIMATE]

pe·num·bra (pi num′brə), *n., pl.* **-brae** (-brē), **-bras.** *Astron.* **1.** the partial or imperfect shadow outside the complete shadow of an opaque body, as a planet, where the light from the source of illumination is only partly cut off. **2.** the grayish marginal portion of a sunspot. Cf. **umbra** (def. 3). [< NL contr. of L *paene* almost + *umbra* shade] —**pe·num′bral, pe·num′brous,** *adj.*

pe·nu·ri·ous (pə nŏŏr′ē əs, -nyŏŏr′-), *adj.* **1.** extremely stingy; parsimonious; miserly. **2.** extremely poor; destitute; indigent. **3.** poorly or inadequately supplied; lacking in means or resources. [< ML *pēnūriōs(us).* See PENURY, -OUS] —**pe·nu′ri·ous·ly,** *adv.* —**pe·nu′ri·ous·ness,** *n.*
—**Syn. 1.** tight, close, niggardly. —**Ant. 1.** generous.

pen·u·ry (pen′yə rē), *n.* **1.** extreme poverty; destitution. **2.** scarcity; dearth; inadequacy; insufficiency. [late ME < L *pēnūria;* akin to Gk *peîna* hunger, *penía* poverty]
—**Syn. 1.** indigence, need, want. —**Ant. 1.** wealth.

Pe·nu·ti·an (pə nōō′tē ən, -shən), *n.* **1.** a tentatively established North American Indian linguistic stock that includes several linguistic families formerly regarded as unrelated, distributed from California northward through Oregon and British Columbia. —*adj.* **2.** of or pertaining to Penutian. [*Penuti* (learned coinage, combining *pen* two and *uti* two, taken from different languages of the stock) + -AN]

Pen·za (pen′zä), *n.* a city in the W RSFSR, in the central Soviet Union, in Europe. 305,000 (1964).

Pen·zance (pen zans′), *n.* a seaport in SW Cornwall, in the SW extremity of England: resort. 19,433 (1961).

pe·on¹ (pē′ən, pē′on), *n.* **1.** (in Spanish America and southwestern U.S.) **a.** one who tends a horse or mule. **b.** See **day laborer. 2.** (esp. in Mexico) one held in servitude to work off debts or other obligations. [< Sp *peón* peasant, day laborer < LL **pedōn-* (s. of **pedō*) walker (whence ML *pedōnes* infantry, OF *peon* pawn), deriv. of L *ped-* (s. of *pēs*) foot]

pe·on² (pē′ən, pē′on), *n.* (in India and Ceylon) **1.** a messenger or attendant. **2.** a native soldier. **3.** See **foot soldier.** [< Pg *peão,* F *pion* foot soldier, pedestrian, day laborer. See PEON¹]

pe·on·age (pē′ə nij), *n.* **1.** the condition or service of a peon. **2.** the practice of holding persons in servitude or partial slavery, as to work off a debt or to serve a penal sentence. [PEON¹ + -AGE]

pe·on·ism (pē′ə niz′əm), *n.* *Archaic.* peonage. [PEON¹ + -ISM]

pe·o·ny (pē′ə nē), *n., pl.* **-nies. 1.** any ranunculaceous herb or shrub of the genus *Paeonia,* having large, showy flowers. **2.** the flower. [ME *pione* (< AF), OE *peonie* < LL *peōnia,* L *paeōnia* < Gk *paiōnía* peony, akin to *paiṓnios* healing]

Pe·o·ny (pē′ə nē), *n.* a girl's given name.

peo·ple (pē′pəl), *n., pl.* **-ple, -ples** for 1, *v.,* **-pled, -pling.** —*n.* **1.** the whole body of persons constituting a community, tribe, race, or nation because of a common culture, history, religion, or the like: *the people of Australia; the Jewish people.* **2.** the persons of any particular group, company, or number: *the people of a parish.* **3.** persons in relation to a ruler, leader, employer, etc.: *the king and his people.* **4.** a person's family or relatives: *He took me to meet his people.* **5.** the members of any group or number to which one belongs. **6.** the body of enfranchised citizens of a state: *representatives chosen by the people.* **7.** the ordinary persons, as distinguished from those who have wealth, rank, etc.: *a man of the people.* **8.** persons indefinitely, whether men or women: *People may say what they please.* **9.** human beings, as distinguished from animals. **10.** animals of a specific kind: *the monkey people of the forest.* —*v.t.* **11.** to furnish with people; populate. **12.** to supply or stock as if with people: *a meadow peopled with wild flowers.* [ME *peple* < AF *poeple,* OF *pueple* < L *popul(us).* See POPULAR] —**peo′ple·less,** *adj.* —**peo′pler,** *n.*
—**Syn. 1.** See **race².**

Peo′ple's Char′ter. See under **Chartism.**

Peo′ple's Com′missar, commissar.

peo′ple's front′. See **popular front.**

Peo′ple's par′ty, *U.S. Politics.* a political party (1891–1904), advocating expansion of currency, state control of railroads, the placing of restrictions upon ownership of land, etc.

Peo′ple's Repub′lic of Chi′na, official name of **Communist China.**

Pe·o·ri·a (pē ōr′ē ə, -ôr′-), *n.* **1.** a city in central Illinois, on the Illinois River. 103,162 (1960). **2.** a town in central Arizona. 2593 (1960). —**Pe·o′ri·an,** *adj., n.*

Peo′ria Heights′, a town in central Illinois. 7064 (1960).

pep (pep), *n., v.,* **pepped, pep·ping.** *Informal.* —*n.* **1.** spirit or animation; vigor; energy. —*v.t.* **2. pep up,** to make spirited, vigorous, or lively; animate: *We need something to pep up this party.* [short for PEPPER] —**pep′ful,** *adj.*

pep·er·i·no (pep′ə rē′nō), *n.* *Geol.* a volcanic rock composed of cinders and scoriae cemented together. [< It < LL *piperīn(us),* equiv. to *piper* PEPPER + *-īnus* -INE¹] —**pep·er·ine** (pep′ər in, -ə rin′), *adj.*

pep·er·o·ni (pep′ə rō′nē), *n.* a highly seasoned, hard sausage of beef and pork. Also, **pepperoni.** [< It, pl. of *peperone* Cayenne pepper plant, aug. of *pepe* PEPPER]

Pep·in (pep′in), *n.* ("*Pepin the Short*") died A.D. 768, king of the Franks 751–768 (father of Charlemagne).

pe·pi·no (pə pē′nō), *n., pl.* **-nos. 1.** a rounded, cone-shaped hill in a karstic area. **2.** Also called **melon pear, melon shrub.** a perennial herb, *Solanum muricatum,* of Peru, having spiny foliage, bright blue flowers, and purple-marked, yellow, egg-shaped fruit. [< Sp: cucumber < L *pepō* a species of melon; see -INE¹]

Pe·pi·ta (pə pē′tə; *Sp.* pe pē′tä), *n.* a girl's given name.

pep·los (pep′ləs), *n., pl.* **-los·es.** a voluminous outer garment worn, draped in folds, by women in ancient Greece. Also, **peplus.** [< Gk] —**pep·losed** (pep′ləst), *adj.*

pep·lum (pep′ləm), *n., pl.* **-lums, -la** (-lə). **1.** a short full flounce or an extension of a garment below the waist, covering the hips. **2.** a short skirt attached to a bodice or jacket. **3.** *Obs.* a peplos. [< L < Gk **péplon* (only pl. *pépla* occurs). See PEPLOS]

pep·lus (pep′ləs), *n., pl.* **-lus·es.** peplos.

pe·po (pē′pō), *n., pl.* **-pos.** the characteristic fruit of cucurbitaceous plants, having a fleshy, many-seeded interior and a hard or firm rind, as the gourd, melon, cucumber, etc. [< L *pepō* large melon, pumpkin < Gk *pépōn,* short for *pépōn* (*síkyos*) a ripe (gourd)]

Pep·per (pep′ər), *n.* **1.** a pungent condiment obtained from various plants of the genus *Piper,* esp. from the dried berries, used whole or ground, of the tropical, climbing shrub *P. nigrum.* **2.** any plant of the genus *Piper,* or the family *Piperaceae.* **3.** cayenne, or red pepper, prepared from species of Capsicum. **4.** any plant of the genus *Capsicum,* esp. the common, garden pepper, *C. frutescens,* or its green or red, hot or sweet fruit. **5.** *Baseball.* See **pepper game.** —*v.t.* **6.** to season with or as with pepper. **7.** to sprinkle, as with pepper; dot; stud. **8.** to sprinkle like pepper. **9.** to pelt with shot or missiles. **10.** to discharge (shot or missiles) at something. [ME *peper, piper,* OE *piper* < L < Gk *péperi.* Cf. D *peper,* G *Pfeffer,* Icel *piparr*] —**pep′per·er,** *n.* —**pep′per·ish,** *adj.* —**pep′per·ish·ly,** *adv.*

Pep·per (pep′ər), *n.* a boy's given name.

pep·per-and-salt (pep′ər ən sôlt′), *adj.* **1.** composed of a fine mixture of black with white, as cloth. —*n.* **2.** an apparel fabric having a pepper-and-salt effect. **3.** the harbinger-of-spring.

pep·per·box (pep′ər boks′), *n.* a small box with perforations in the top, for sprinkling pepper. Also called **pepper pot.** [PEPPER + BOX¹]

pep′per bush′, a bushy shrub, *Leucothoë racemosa,* of the eastern coast of the U.S., having numerous white flowers in clusters. Also called **sweetbells, white osier.**

pep·per·corn (pep′ər kôrn′), *n.* **1.** the berry of the pepper plant, *Piper nigrum,* dried and used in pickling. **2.** anything very small, insignificant, or trifling. —*adj.* **3.** (of hair) growing in tightly spiraled clumps. [ME *pepercorn* < OE *piporcorn.* PEPPER, CORN] —**pep′per·corn′ish, pep′per·corn′y,** *adj.*

pep′per game′, *Baseball.* a pregame warm-up performed at a brisk rate, in which one batter bunts back balls tossed to him by fielders stationed a short distance away.

pep·per·grass (pep′ər gras′, -gräs′), *n.* any pungent plant of the genus *Lepidium,* used as a potherb or salad vegetable. Cf. **garden cress.** [PEPPER + GRASS]

pep·per·idge (pep′ər ij), *n.* the tupelo. [?]

pep·per·mint (pep′ər mint′), *n.* **1.** a labiate herb, *Mentha piperita,* cultivated for its aromatic, pungent oil. **2.** Also called **pep′permint oil′.** this oil, or some preparation of it. **3.** a lozenge or confection flavored with it. [PEPPER + MINT¹]

pep′permint cam′phor, menthol.

pep′permint gera′nium, a shrubby plant, *Pelargonium tomentosum,* of South Africa, having velvety leaves and clusters of white flowers.

pep′permint gum′, a tree, *Eucalyptus amygdalina,* of Australia, having peppermint-scented foliage and growing to as much as 300 feet in height.

pep′permint spir′it, a green or colorless alcoholic solution of the volatile oil produced by the peppermint leaf, used as a carminative and flavoring agent.

pep·per·o·ni (pep′ə rō′nē), *n.* peperoni.

Pep′per Pike′, a town in N Ohio. 3217 (1960).

pep′per pot′, 1. a West Indian stew, the principal flavoring of which is cassareep, with meat or fish and vegetables. **2.** Also called **Philadelphia pepper pot.** a highly seasoned soup made of tripe and sometimes containing small balls of dough. **3.** See **pepperbox.**

pep·per·shrike (pep′ər shrīk′), *n.* either of two New World, oscine birds ef the family *Cyclarhidae,* resembling a vireo but having a large shrikelike bill. [PEPPER + SHRIKE]

pep′per spot′, *Plant Pathol.* a disease of clover and alfalfa, characterized by numerous black specks on the leaves, premature yellowing, and defoliation, caused by a fungus, *Pseudoplea trifolii.*

pep′per tree′, any of several chiefly South American, evergreen trees of the genus *Schinus,* cultivated in subtropical regions as an ornamental.

pep·per·wood (pep′ər wŏŏd′), *n.* See **California laurel** (def. 1). [PEPPER + WOOD¹]

pep·per·y (pep′ə rē), *adj.* **1.** full of or tasting like pepper; hot; pungent. **2.** of, pertaining to, or resembling pepper. **3.** sharp or stinging: *a peppery speech.* **4.** easily angered; irritable; irascible: *the peppery leader of a political faction.* [PEPPER + -Y¹] —**pep′per·i·ly,** *adv.* —**pep′per·i·ness,** *n.*
—**Syn. 1.** spicy. **3.** biting. **4.** hot-tempered, hot-headed, testy, choleric. —**Ant. 1.** mild, bland. **4.** placid.

pep′ pill′, a pill, tablet, or capsule that consists typically of a form of the stimulant drug amphetamine.

pep·py (pep′ē), *adj.,* **-pi·er, -pi·est.** *Informal.* energetic; vigorous; lively. [PEP + -Y¹] —**pep′pi·ly,** *adv.* —**pep′pi·ness,** *n.*

pep′ ral′ly, a meeting, esp. of students before an interscholastic contest, to stimulate group enthusiasm by songs, cheers, talks, etc.

pep·sin (pep′sin), *n.* *Biochem.* **1.** an enzyme, produced in the stomach, that in the presence of hydrochloric acid splits proteins into proteoses and peptones. **2.** a commercial form of this substance, obtained from the stomachs of hogs, used as a digestive, as a ferment in the manufacture of cheese, etc. Also, **pep′sine.** [< Gk *péps(is)* digestion (*pép(tein)* (to) digest + *-sis* -SIS) + -IN²]

pep·sin·ate (pep′sə nāt′), *v.t.,* **-at·ed, -at·ing.** to treat, prepare, or mix with pepsin. [PEPSIN + -ATE¹]

pep·sin·o·gen (pep sin′ə jən), *n.* *Biochem.* a zymogen, occurring in the gastric glands, that during digestion is converted into pepsin. [PEPSIN + -O- + -GEN] —**pep·si·no·gen·ic** (pep′sə nō jen′ik), **pep·si·nog·e·nous** (pep′sə noj′ə nəs), *adj.*

pep′ talk′, a vigorous talk, as to a person or group, calculated to arouse support for a cause, increase the determination to succeed, etc.

pep·talk (pep′tôk′), *v.t.* **1.** to give a pep talk to (a person, group, etc.): *He peptalked the players just before a football game.* —*v.i.* **2.** to deliver a pep talk. [v. use of PEP TALK]

pep·tic (pep′tik), *adj.* **1.** pertaining to or associated with digestion; digestive. **2.** promoting digestion. **3.** of or pertaining to pepsin. —*n.* **4.** a substance promoting digestion. [< Gk *peptik(ós)* conducive to digestion, equiv. to *pept(ós)* digested (verbid of *péptein*) + *-ikos* -IC]

pep′tic ul′cer, an erosion of the mucous membrane of the stomach or duodenum, caused in part by the corrosive action of the gastric juice. Cf. **gastric ulcer.**

pep·ti·dase (pep′ti dās′), *n.* *Biochem.* any of the class of enzymes that catalyze the hydrolysis of peptides or peptones to amino acids. [PEPTIDE + -ASE]

pep·tide (pep′tīd, -tid), *n.* *Biochem.* a compound containing two or more amino acids in which the carboxyl group of one acid is linked to the amino group of the other, as $H_2NCH_2CONHCH_2COOH$. [PEPT(IC) + -IDE]

pep·ti·do·lyt·ic (pep′ti dō lit′ik), *adj.* *Biochem.* causing the hydrolysis of peptides. [PEPTIDE + -O- + -LYTIC]

pep·tize (pep′tīz), *v.t.,* **-tized, -tiz·ing.** to disperse (a substance) into colloidal form, usually in a liquid. [? < Gk *pépt(ein)* (to) digest + -IZE] —**pep·tiz′a·ble,** *adj.* —**pep′ti·za′tion,** *n.* —**pep′tiz·er,** *n.*

pep·to·lyt·ic (pep′tə lit′ik), *adj.* *Biochem.* causing the hydrolysis of peptones. [PEPTO(NE) + -LYTIC] —**pep·tol·y·sis** (pep tol′i sis), *n.*

pep·tone (pep′tōn), *n.* *Biochem.* any of a class of diffusible, soluble substances into which proteins are converted by partial hydrolysis. [< G *Pepton* < Gk *peptón,* neut. of *peptós* cooked, digested, verbid of *péptein*] —**pep′tone·like′,** *adj.* —**pep·ton·ic** (pep-ton′ik), *adj.* —**pep·to·noid** (pep′tə noid′), *n.*

pep·to·nise (pep′tə nīz′), *v.t.,* **-nised, -nis·ing.** *Chiefly Brit.* peptonize. —**pep′to·ni·sa′tion,** *n.* —**pep′to·nis′er,** *n.*

pep·to·nize (pep′tə nīz′), *v.t.,* **-nized, -niz·ing. 1.** to subject (food) to an artificial, partial digestion by pepsin or pancreatic extract in order to aid digestion. **2.** to hydrolyze or dissolve by a proteolytic enzyme, as pepsin. [PEPTONE + -IZE] —**pep′to·ni·za′tion,** *n.* —**pep′to·niz′er,** *n.*

Pe·pusch (pā′pŏŏsh), *n.* **Jo·hann Chris·toph** (yō′hän kris′tôf), or **John Christopher,** 1667–1752, German composer and music theorist in England.

Pepys (pēps, peps, pē′pis, pep′is), *n.* **Samuel,** 1633–1703, English diarist and naval official. —**Pepys·i·an** (pēp′sē ən, pep′-), *adj.*

Pepys′ Di′ary, a diary kept by Samuel Pepys from January 1, 1660, to May 31, 1669, in which are recorded his impressions of contemporary London life, the life of the court, and the administration of the navy.

Pe·quot (pē′kwot), *n., pl.* **-quots,** (*esp. collectively*) **-quot.** a member of a former tribe of Algonquin Indians, in southern New England in the early 17th century. [? shortened var. of Narragansett *paquatanog* destroyers]

per (pûr; *unstressed* pər), *prep.* through; by; for each: *Membership costs ten dollars per year. This cloth is two dollars per yard.* [< L, ML, OF: through, by, for, for each. See FOR]
—**Usage.** PER is generally restricted to commercial use, and A is the word most stylists prefer in formal contexts: *Admission to the movie was $2.50 a person.*

per-, 1. a prefix meaning "through," "thoroughly," "utterly," "very": *pervert; pervade; perfect.* **2.** *Chem.* a prefix applied to inorganic acids and their salts to indicate that they possess an access of the designated element: *percarbonic* ($H_2C_2O_5$), *permanganic* ($HMnO_4$), *persulfuric* ($H_2S_2O_5$), *acids; potassium permanganate* ($KMnO_4$); *potassium persulfate* ($K_2S_2O_5$). [< L, comb. form of *per* PER, and used as an intensive]

Per., 1. Persia. **2.** Persian.

per., 1. period. **2.** person.

Pe·ra (pe′rä), *n.* a modern section of Istanbul, Turkey, N of the Golden Horn: populated chiefly by Europeans. 218,433 (1965). Also called **Beyoglu.**

per·ac·id (pər as′id), *n.* *Chem.* an oxyacid, the primary element of which is in its highest possible oxidation state, as perchloric acid, $HClO_4$, and permanganic acid, $HMnO_4$. [PER- + ACID]

per·ad·ven·ture (pûr′əd ven′chər, per′-), *n.* **1.** chance or uncertainty. **2.** surmise. —*adv.* **3.** *Archaic.* it may be; maybe; possibly; perhaps. [ME *per aventure* < OF. See PER, ADVENTURE]

Pe·rae·a (pə rē′ə), *n.* a region in ancient Palestine, E of the Jordan and the Dead Sea.

Pe·rak (pā′rak, -räk, per′ə, pēr′ə), *n.* a state in Malaysia, on the SW Malay Peninsula. 1,384,321 (est. 1961); 7980 sq. mi. *Cap.:* Taiping.

Pe·ral·ta (pe räl′tä), *n.* **En·ri·que** (en rē′ke), (*Enrique Peralta Azurdia*), born 1908, Guatemalan military leader: president since 1963.

per·am·bu·late (pər am′byə lāt′), *v.,* **-lat·ed, -lat·ing.** —*v.t.* **1.** to walk through, about, or over; travel through; traverse. **2.** to traverse in order to examine or inspect. **—*v.i.*** **3.** to walk or travel about; stroll. [< L *perambulāt(us)* walked through, ptp. *perambulāre*. See PER-, AMBULATE] **—per·am/bu·la/tion,** *n.* **—per·am·bu·la·to·ry** (pər am/byə lə tōr/ē, -tôr/ē), *adj.*

per·am·bu·la·tor (pər am/byə lā/tər), *n.* **1.** See **baby carriage. 2.** Also called **ambulator.** an odometer pushed by a person walking. **3.** one who makes a tour of inspection on foot. [< ML; see PERAMBULATE, -OR[2]]

per an., per annum.

per an·num (pər an/əm), by the year; yearly. [< L]

per·bo·rate (pər bōr/āt, -bôr/-), *n.* *Chem.* a salt of perboric acid, as sodium perborate, $NaBO_2 \cdot H_2O_2 \cdot 3H_2O$, used for bleaching, disinfecting, etc. Also, **peroxyborate.** [PER- + BORATE]

per·bo·rax (pər bōr/aks, -aks, -bôr/-), *n.* *Chem.* See **sodium perborate.** [PER- + BORAX]

per·bo/ric ac/id (pər bōr/ik, -bôr/-), *Chem.* a hypothetical acid, HBO_3, known only in the form of its salts. [PER- + BORIC ACID]

Per·bu·nan (pûr byōō/nən), *n.* *Trademark.* a synthetic rubber made by copolymerizing acrylonitrile with butadiene.

per·cale (pər kāl/), *n.* a closely woven, smooth-finished, plain or printed cambric. [< F < Pers *pargālah* rag; r. *percalla* < Pers]

per·ca·line (pûr/kə lēn/), *n.* a fine, lightweight cotton fabric, usually finished with a gloss and dyed in one color, used esp. for linings. [< F; see PERCALE, -INE[2]]

per cap·i·ta (pər kap/i tə), **1.** by or for the individual person: *income per capita.* **2.** *Law.* noting or pertaining to a method of dividing an estate by which all those equally related to the decedent take equal shares individually without regard to the number of lines of descent. Cf. **per stirpes.** [< L: lit., by heads]

per·ceiv·a·ble (pər sē/və bəl), *adj.* capable of being perceived; perceptible. [ME *perceyvable.* See PERCEIVE, -ABLE] **—per·ceiv/a·bil/i·ty, per·ceiv/a·ble·ness,** *n.* **—per·ceiv/a·bly,** *adv.*

per·ceive (pər sēv/), *v.t.*, **-ceived, -ceiv·ing. 1.** to become aware of, know, or identify by means of the senses: *I perceived an object looming through the mist. I perceived that it was a gasworks.* **2.** to apprehend, envision, or understand: *I perceive a note of sarcasm in your voice. This is a nice idea, but I perceive difficulties in putting it into practice.* [ME *perceive(n)* < OF **perceivre, perçoivre* < L *percipere* to lay hold of, grasp, equiv. to *per-* PER- + *-cipere,* comb. form of *capere* to take] **—per·ceiv·ed·ly** (pər sē/vid lē, -sēvd/-), *adv.* **—per·ceiv/ed·ness,** *n.* **—per·ceiv/er,** *n.* **—per·ceiv/ing·ness,** *n.*
—Syn. 1. note, discover, observe, descry, distinguish. See **notice.**

per·cent (pər sent/), *n.* **1.** Also called **per centum.** one one-hundredth part; $^1/_{100}$. **2.** percentage (def. 1). **3.** *Brit.* stocks, bonds, etc., that bear an indicated rate of interest. **—*adj.*** **4.** reckoned on the basis of a rate or proportion per hundred (used in combination with a number in expressing rates of interest, proportions, etc.): *to get three percent interest. Symbol:* % Also, **per cent.** [short for ML *per centum* for each hundred. See PER, CENT] **—per·cent/al,** *adj.*
—Usage. PERCENT is now found more often spelled as one word than as two, and the practice of considering CENT as an abbreviation for *centum,* hence written with a period after it, is becoming an archaism.

per·cent·age (pər sen/tij), *n.* **1.** Also called **percent.** a rate or proportion per hundred. **2.** an allowance, duty, commission, or rate of interest on a hundred items. **3.** a proportion in general: *Only a small percentage of the class will graduate with honors.* **4.** *Informal.* gain; personal advantage. [PERCENT + -AGE] **—per·cent/aged,** *adj.*

per·cen·tile (pər sen/tīl, -til), *Statistics.* **—*n.*** **1.** one of the values of a variable which divides the distribution of the variable into 100 groups having equal frequencies. Thus, there are 100 percentiles, numbered from 0 to 99, inclusively: *the first percentile; the second percentile.* **—*adj.*** **2.** of or pertaining to a percentile or a division of a distribution by percentiles. [PERCENT + -ILE]

per cen·tum (pər sen/təm), percent (def. 1). [< L: lit., by the hundred]

per·cept (pûr/sept), *n.* **1.** the mental result or product of perceiving, as distinguished from the act of perceiving. **2.** that which is perceived; the object of perception. [< L *percept(um)* something perceived, n. use of neut. of *perceptus,* ptp. of *percipere* to PERCEIVE]

per·cep·ti·ble (pər sep/tə bəl), *adj.* capable of being perceived; recognizable; appreciable: *a perceptible difference.* [< LL *perceptibil(is).* See PERCEPT, -IBLE] **—per·cep/ti·bil/i·ty, per·cep/ti·ble·ness,** *n.* **—per·cep/ti·bly,** *adv.*
—Syn. discernible, apparent.

per·cep·tion (pər sep/shən), *n.* **1.** the act or faculty of apprehending by means of the senses or of the mind; cognition; understanding. **2.** immediate or intuitive recognition, as of moral or aesthetic qualities: *an artist of rare perception.* **3.** the result or product of perceiving, as distinguished from the act of perceiving; percept. **4.** *Psychol.* a single unified awareness derived from sensory processes while a stimulus is present. **5.** *Law.* the taking into possession of rents, crops, profits, etc. [late ME < L *perceptiōn-* (s. of *perceptiō*) comprehension, lit., a taking in. See PERCEPT, -ION] **—per·cep/tion·al,** *adj.*

percep/tion deaf/ness, *Pathol.* deafness or hearing impairment that results from disease of or injury to the inner ear or to the central mechanism involved in hearing.

per·cep·tive (pər sep/tiv), *adj.* **1.** having the power or faculty of perceiving. **2.** of, pertaining to, or showing perception. **3.** having or showing keenness of insight, understanding, or intuition: *a perceptive analysis of the problems involved.* [< L *percept(us)* (see PERCEPT) + -IVE] **—per·cep/tive·ly,** *adv.* **—per/cep·tiv/i·ty, per·cep/tive·ness,** *n.*

per·cep·tu·al (pər sep/chōō əl), *adj.* of or pertaining to perception. [PERCEPT + (CONCEPT)UAL] **—per·cep/tu·al·ly,** *adv.*

Per·ce·val (pûr/sə vəl), *n.* **1. Spencer,** 1762–1812, British statesman: prime minister 1809–12. **2.** *Arthurian Romance.* Percival.

perch[1] (pûrch), *n.* **1.** a pole or rod, usually fixed horizontally, serving as a roost for birds. **2.** any place or object, as a sill, fence, branch, twig, or the like, for a bird, animal, or person to alight or rest upon. **3.** a high or elevated position, resting place, or the like. **4.** a small, elevated seat for the driver of any of certain vehicles. **5.** a pole connecting the fore and hind running parts of a spring carriage or other vehicle. **6.** a post set up as a navigational aid on a navigational hazard or on a buoy. **7.** a linear or square rod. **8.** a solid measure for stone, commonly 16½ feet by 1½ feet by 1 foot. **9.** *Textiles.* an apparatus consisting of two vertical posts and a horizontal roller, used for inspecting cloth after it leaves the loom. **10.** *Obs.* any pole, rod, or the like. **—*v.i.*** **11.** to alight or rest upon a perch, as a bird. **12.** to settle or rest in some elevated position, as if on a perch. **—*v.t.*** **13.** to set or place on, or as if on a perch. **14.** to inspect (cloth) for defects and blemishes after it has been taken from the loom and placed upon a perch. [ME *perche* < OF < L *pertica* pole, staff, measuring rod] **—perch/a·ble,** *adj.*

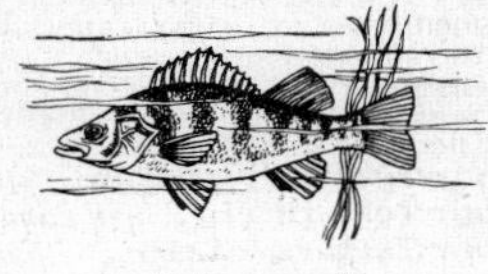

Yellow perch,
Perca flavescens
(Length 1 ft.)

perch[2] (pûrch), *n., pl.* (*esp. collectively*) **perch,** (*esp. referring to two or more kinds or species*) **perch·es. 1.** any spiny-finned, fresh-water food fish of the genus *Perca,* as *P. flavescens* **(yellow perch),** found in the U.S., or *P. fluviatilis,* found in Europe. **2.** any of various other spiny-finned, related fishes. **3.** any of several embiotocid fishes, as *Hysterocarpus traski* **(tule perch)** of California. [ME *perche* < MF < L *perca* < Gk *pérkē*]

per·chance (pər chans/, -chäns/), *adv.* *Literary.* **1.** maybe; possibly. **2.** by chance. [ME, var. of *par chance* by chance < AF. See PER, CHANCE]

Perche (pârsh; *Fr.* persh), *n.* a former division of N France.

perch·er (pûr/chər), *n.* **1.** one who or that which perches. **2.** a bird whose feet are adapted for perching. [PERCH[1] + -ER[1]]

Per·che·ron (pûr/chə ron/, -shə-), *n.* one of a French breed of draft horses, having a gray or black coat. [< F; named after *Perche,* French district where first bred]

perchlor-, var. of **perchloro-:** *perchlorperazine.*

per·chlo·rate (pər klōr/āt, -klôr/-), *n.* *Chem.* a salt or ester of perchloric acid, as potassium perchlorate, $KClO_4$. [PER- + CHLORATE]

per·chlo·ric (pər klōr/ik, -klôr/-), *adj.* *Chem.* of or derived from perchloric acid. [PER- + CHLORIC]

perchlo/ric ac/id, *Chem.* a colorless, syrupy hygroscopic liquid, $HClO_4$, an acid of chlorine containing one more oxygen atom than chloric acid: used chiefly as a reagent in analytical chemistry.

per·chlo·ride (pər klōr/īd, -id, -klôr/-), *n.* *Chem.* the chloride of any particular element or group with the maximum proportion of chlorine. [PER- + CHLORIDE]

per·chlo·ri·nate (pər klōr/ə nāt/, -klôr/-), *v.t.*, **-nat·ed, -nat·ing.** *Chem.* to combine with the maximum proportion of chlorine. [PER- + CHLORINATE] **—per·chlo/ri·na/tion,** *n.*

perchloro-, a combination of **per-** and **chloro-**[2]: *perchloromethane.*

per·chlo·ro·eth·yl·ene (pər klōr/ō eth/ə lēn/, -klôr/-), *n.* *Chem.* tetrachlorethylene. [PERCHLORO- + ETHYLENE]

per·chlo·ro·meth·ane (pər klōr/ō meth/ān, -klôr/-), *n.* *Chem.* See **carbon tetrachloride.** [PERCHLORO- + METHANE]

per·chlor·per·a·zine (pûr/klōr per/ə zēn/, -klôr-), *n.* *Pharm.* a compound, $C_{20}H_{24}ClN_3S$, used in the form of its maleate or ethanedisulfonate as a tranquillizer and in the treatment of nausea. [PERCHLOR- + (PI)PERAZINE]

per·chro·mate (pər krō/māt), *n.* *Chem.* a salt of perchromic acid. [PER- + CHROMATE]

per·chro·mic (pər krō/mik), *adj.* *Chem.* of or derived from perchromic acid. [PER- + CHROMIC]

perchro/mic ac/id, *Chem.* an unstable acid, $(HO)_4$-$Cr(OOH)_3$ or $H_3CrO_8 \cdot 2H_2O$, known chiefly in the form of its salts.

Perch·ta (perkн/tä), *n.* *Germanic Myth.* the goddess of death and of fertility: sometimes identified with Holle. Also, **Berchta.**

per·cip·i·ent (pər sip/ē ənt), *adj.* **1.** perceiving. **2.** having perception; discerning; discriminating: *a percipient selection of wines.* **—*n.*** **3.** one who or that which perceives. [< L *percipient-* (s. of *percipiēns*) taking in, prp. of *percipere.* See PERCEIVE, -ENT] **—per·cip/i·ence, per·cip/i·en·cy,** *n.*

Per·ci·val (pûr/sə vəl), *n.* **1.** Also, **Perceval, Per/ci·vale.** *Arthurian Romance.* a knight of King Arthur's court who sought the Holy Grail. **2.** a boy's given name.

per·close (pûr/klōz), *n.* parclose.

per·coid (pûr/koid), *adj.* **1.** belonging to the *Percoidea,* a group of acanthopterygian fishes comprising the true perches and related families, and constituting one of the largest natural groups of fishes. **2.** resembling a perch. Also, **per·coi·de·an** (pər koi/dē ən). [< L *perc(a)* PERCH[2] + -OID]

per·co·late (*v.* pûr/kə lāt/; *n.* pûr/kə lit, -lāt/), *v.*, **-lat·ed, -lat·ing,** *n.* **—*v.t.*** **1.** to cause (a liquid) to pass through a porous body; filter. **2.** (of a liquid) to filter through; permeate. **3.** to brew (coffee) in a percolator. **—*v.i.*** **4.** to pass through a porous substance; filter; ooze. **5.** to become percolated: *The coffee is starting to percolate.* **6.** to become active, lively, or spirited. **—*n.*** **7.** a percolated liquid. [< L *percolāt(us)* filtered, ptp. of *percolāre.* See PER-, COLANDER, -ATE[1]] **—per/co·la·ble,** *adj.* **—per/co·la/tive,** *adj.*

per·co·la·tion (pûr/kə lā/shən), *n.* **1.** the act or state of percolating or of being percolated. **2.** *Pharm.* the extraction of the soluble principles of a crude drug by the passage of a suitable liquid through it. [< L *percolātiōn-* (s. of *percolātiō*). See PERCOLATE, -ION]

per·co·la·tor (pûr/kə lā/tər), *n.* **1.** a kind of coffee pot in which boiling water is forced up a hollow stem, filters through ground coffee, and returns to the pot below. **2.** that which percolates. [PERCOLATE + -OR[2]]

per con·tra (pər kon/trə; *Lat.* per kōn/trä), on the other hand; on the contrary. [< L]

per cu·ri·am (pər kyōōr/ē am/), *Law.* noting an anonymous opinion of a court as a whole, as contrasted with an opinion delivered in the name and upon the responsibility of a particular judge. [< ML: lit., through the court]

per·cur·rent (pər kûr/ənt, -kur/-), *adj.* *Bot.* extending through the entire length, as a midrib through a leaf. [< L *percurrent-* (s. of *percurrēns*) running through, prp. of *percurrere.* See PER-, CURRENT]

per·cuss (pər kus/), *v.t.* **1.** to strike (something) so as to shake or cause a shock to. **2.** *Med.* to strike or tap for diagnostic or therapeutic purposes. [< L *percuss(us)* struck hard, beaten, ptp. of *percutere,* equiv. to *per-* PER- + *-cutere,* comb. form of *quatere* to shake. See QUASH[1]]

per·cus·sion (pər kush/ən), *n.* **1.** the striking of one body against another with some sharpness; impact. **2.** *Med.* the striking or tapping of a part of the body for diagnostic or therapeutic purposes. **3.** the striking of musical instruments to produce tones. **4.** a sharp blow for detonating a percussion cap or the fuze of an artillery shell. **5.** the act of percussing. [< L *percussiōn-* (s. of *percussiō*) a beating. See PERCUSS, -ION] **—per·cus/sion·al,** *adj.*

percus/sion cap/, a small metallic cap or cup containing fulminating powder, formerly exploded by percussion to fire the charge of small arms.

percus/sion in/strument, a musical instrument, as the drum, cymbal, piano, etc., which is struck to produce a sound, as distinguished from string or wind instruments.

per·cus·sion·ist (pər kush/ə nist), *n.* a musician who plays percussion instruments. [PERCUSSION + -IST]

percus/sion lock/, a gunlock on a firearm that fires by striking a percussion cap. Cf. **flintlock.**

per·cus·sive (pər kus/iv), *adj.* of, pertaining to, or characterized by percussion. [PERCUSS(ION) + -IVE] **—per·cus/sive·ly,** *adv.* **—per·cus/sive·ness,** *n.*

per·cus·sor (pər kus/ər), *n.* plexor. [< NL, L: one that beats. See PERCUSSION, -OR[2]]

Per·cy (pûr/sē), *n.* **1. Sir Henry** (*"Hotspur"*), 1364–1403, English military and rebel leader. **2. Thomas,** 1729–1811, English poet and antiquary: bishop of Dromore 1782–1811. **3.** a boy's given name.

Per·di·do (*Sp.* per ᵺē/ᵺō), *n.* **Mon·te** (*Sp.* môn/te), a mountain in NE Spain, a peak of the Pyrenees. 10,994 ft. French, **Mont Perdu.**

per·die (pər dē/), *adv., interj.* *Archaic.* pardi.

per di·em (pər dē/əm, dī/əm), **1.** by the day. **2.** a daily allowance, usually for living expenses while traveling in connection with one's work. [< L]

per·di·fume (pûr/də fyōōm/, per/-), *n.* *Obs.* a cap for catching soot from a gaslight.

Per·di·ta (pûr dē/tə), *n.* a girl's given name.

per·di·tion (pər dish/ən), *n.* **1.** a state of final spiritual ruin; loss of the soul; damnation. **2.** the future state of the wicked. **3.** hell. **4.** utter destruction or ruin. [< L *perditiōn-* (s. of *perditiō*) destruction, equiv. to *perdit(us)* ruined (ptp. of *perdere* to do for (*per-* PER- + *-dere,* comb. form of *dāre* to give)) + *-iōn* -ION; r. ME *perdiciun* < OF]

Per·dix (pûr/diks), *n.* *Class. Myth.* the sister of Daedalus who committed suicide and was changed into a partridge when her son was jealously killed by her brother. Also called **Polycaste.** Cf. **Talos** (def. 1).

per·du (pər dōō/, -dyōō/, per-), *adj.* **1.** hidden; concealed; obscured. **—*n.*** **2.** *Obs.* a soldier placed in a dangerous position. Also, **per·due/.** [< F: lost, ptp. of *perdre* < L *perdere* to lose]

Per·du (per dʏ/), *n.* **Mont** (môɴ), French name of **Monte Perdido.**

per·dur·a·ble (pər dōōr/ə bəl, -dyōōr/-), *adj.* permanent; everlasting; imperishable. [ME < LL *perdūrābil(is).* See PER-, DURE[2], -ABLE] **—per·dur/a·bil/i·ty, per·dur/a·ble·ness,** *n.* **—per·dur/a·bly,** *adv.*

per·dure (pər dōōr/, -dyōōr/), *v.i.*, **-dured, -dur·ing.** to continue or last permanently; endure. [ME *perdure(n)* < L *perdūr(āre).* See PER-, DURE[2]]

père (per; *Eng.* pâr), *n., pl.* **pères** (per; *Eng.* pârz). *French.* **1.** father. **2.** senior: *Dumas père.*

per·e·gri·nate (per/ə grə nāt/), *v.*, **-nat·ed, -nat·ing. —*v.i.*** **1.** to travel or journey, esp. on foot. **—*v.t.*** **2.** to travel over; traverse. [< L *peregrīnāt(us)* traveled abroad (ptp.). See PEREGRINE, -ATE[1]] **—per/e·gri·na/tor,** *n.*

per·e·gri·na·tion (per/ə grə nā/shən), *n.* **1.** travel from one place to another, esp. on foot. **2.** a course of travel; journey. [< L *peregrīnātiōn-* (s. of *peregrīnātiō*) a traveling abroad. See PEREGRINATE, -ION]

per·e·grine (per/ə grin, -grēn/, -grīn/), *adj.* **1.** foreign; alien; coming from abroad. **—*n.*** **2.** See **peregrine falcon.** [< L *peregrīn(us)* foreign, deriv. of *peregrē* abroad, lit., through (i.e., beyond the borders of) the (home) field, equiv. to *per-* PER- + *-egr-,* comb. form of *ager* field + *-ē* adv. suffix; see -INE[1]] **—per·e·grin·i·ty** (per/ə grin/i tē), *n.*

per/egrine fal/con, a cosmopolitan falcon, *Falco peregrinus,* much used in falconry because of its swift flight. See illus. under **falcon.**

pe·rei·on (pə rī/on, -rā/-, -rē/-), *n., pl.* **-rei·a** (-rī/ə, -rā/ə, -rē/ə). (in a crustacean) the thorax. [< NL, repr. Gk *peraíon* transporting, carrying about (prp. of *peraioûn*); so called from the location of limbs on the thorax]

pe·rei·o·pod (pə rī/ə pod/, -rā/-, -rē/-), *n.* (in a crustacean) an appendage of the thorax. [< NL; see PEREI(ON), -POD]

Pe·rei·ra (pe rā/rä), *n.* a city in W Colombia. 223,500 (est. 1964).

pe·rei/ra bark/ (pə râr/ə), the bark of any of several South American, apocynaceous trees of the genus *Geissospermum,* esp. *G. vellosii,* from which pereirine is derived. [*pereira* < NL, named after J. *Pereira* (1804–53) English professor of medicine]

pe·rei·rine (pə râr/ēn, -in), *n.* *Chem.* a brown, amorphous, water-insoluble powder, $C_{19}H_{24}ON_2$, obtained from pereira bark: used chiefly as a quinine substitute for reducing or preventing fever. [PEREIR(A BARK) + -INE[1]]

Perel·man (pûrl/mən), *n.* **S(idney) J(oseph),** born 1904, U.S. author.

per·emp·to·ry (pə remp/tə rē, per/əmp tōr/ē, -tôr/ē), *adj.* **1.** leaving no opportunity for denial or refusal; imperative: *a peremptory command.* **2.** imperious or dic-

tatorial. 3. *Law.* **a.** that precludes or does not admit of debate, question, etc.: *a peremptory edict.* **b.** decisive or final. **c.** in which a command is absolute and unconditional: *a peremptory writ.* 4. positive or assertive in speech, tone, manner, etc. [< legal L *peremptōri(us)* final, decisive, lit., deadly, destructive, equiv. to *perempt(us)* (ptp. of *perimere* to take away fully, destroy, slay (*per-* PER- + *-imere,* comb. form of *emere* to buy, orig. to take)) + *-ōrius* -ORY[1]] —**per·emp/to·ri·ly,** *adv.* —**per·emp/to·ri·ness,** *n.*
—**Syn. 2.** arbitrary, dogmatic.

peremp/tory chal/lenge, *Law.* a formal objection to the service of a juror that requires no showing of cause.

peremp/tory excep/tion, *Law.* a plea in bar of an action. Also, **peremp/tory plea/.**

per·en·ni·al (pə ren/ē əl), *adj.* 1. lasting for an indefinitely long time; enduring. 2. *Bot.* having a life cycle lasting more than two years. 3. lasting or continuing throughout the year, as a stream. 4. perpetual; everlasting; continuing; recurrent. —*n.* 5. a perennial plant. 6. something that is continuing or recurrent. [< L *perenni(s)* lasting the whole year through (*per-* PER- + *-enn-,* comb. form of *annus* year + *-is* adj. suffix) + -AL[1]] —**per·en·ni·al·i·ty** (pə ren/ē al/i tē), *n.* —**per·en/ni·al·ly,** *adv.*
—**Syn. 1.** perdurable; constant, incessant, continual. 4. imperishable, undying, eternal, immortal.

peren/nial pea/. See **everlasting pea** (def. 2).

peren/nial phlox/. See **garden phlox.**

peren/nial rye/grass. See under **ryegrass.**

Per·etz (per/its; *Yiddish.* pe/rets), *n.* **I(saac) L(eob)** or **Yitz·chok Lei·bush** (yits/khôk lā/bŏŏsh), 1852–1915, Polish author: writer of plays, poems, and short stories in Yiddish. Also, **Per/ez.**

Pé·rez de Cué·llar (per/ez də kwā/yär; *Sp.* pe/res the kwe/yär), **Ja·vier** (hä vyer/), born 1920, Peruvian diplomat: secretary-general of the United Nations since 1982.

perf., 1. perfect. 2. perforated.

per·fect (*adj., n.* pûr/fikt; *v.* pər fekt/, pûr/fikt), *adj.* 1. conforming absolutely to the description or definition of the type: *a perfect sphere; a perfect gentleman.* 2. excellent or complete beyond practical or theoretical improvement: *There is no perfect legal code. The proportions of this temple are almost perfect.* 3. exactly fitting the need in a certain situation or for a certain purpose: *a perfect actor to play Mr. Micawber; a perfect saw for cutting out keyholes.* 4. without any of the flaws or shortcomings that might be present: *a perfect apple.* 5. correct in every detail: *a perfect copy.* 6. thorough; complete; utter: *perfect strangers.* 7. pure or unmixed: *perfect yellow.* 8. unqualified; absolute: *He has perfect control over his servants.* 9. unmitigated; out-and-out: *He made a perfect fool of himself.* 10. *Bot.* **a.** having all parts or members present. **b.** monoclinous. 11. *Gram.* **a.** noting an action or state brought to a close prior to some temporal point of reference, in contrast to imperfect or incomplete action. **b.** designating a tense or other verb formation or construction with such meaning. 12. *Music.* **a.** applied to the consonances of unison, octave, fifth, and fourth, as distinguished from those of a third and sixth, which are called imperfect. **b.** applied to the intervals, harmonic or melodic, of an octave, fifth, and fourth in their normal form, as opposed to augmented and diminished. 13. *Math.* (of a set) equal to its set of accumulation points. 14. *Obs.* assured or certain. —*n.* *Gram.* 15. the perfect tense. 16. any verb formation or construction in the perfect tense. 17. a perfect form, as English *He had cooked the meal before six o'clock,* or Latin *ōrāculum audīvī* "I heard the oracle." —*v.t.* 18. to bring to completion; finish. 19. to bring to perfection; make faultless. 20. to bring nearer to perfection; improve. 21. to make fully skilled. 22. *Print.* to print the reverse of (a printed sheet). [< L *perfect(us)* done, finished, ptp. of *perficere* (*per-* PER- + *-ficere,* comb. form of *facere* to do); r. ME *parfit* < OF] —**per·fect/ed·ly,** *adv.* —**per·fect/er,** *n.* —**per/fect·ness,** *n.*
—**Syn. 1, 2.** See **complete.** 4. unblemished. —**Ant. 1.** incomplete. 2. imperfect.

per/fect bind/ing, a technique for binding books by machine that cuts off the backs of the sections and glues the leaves to a cloth or paper backing.

per/fect ca/dence, *Music.* a cadence in which the tonic chord has its root in both bass and soprano.

per/fect contri/tion. See under **contrition** (def. 2).

per/fect game/, *Baseball.* a game in which the same player pitches throughout the full game without allowing any player of the opposing team to reach first base by a base hit, error, base on balls, or any other means. Cf. **no-hitter.**

per/fect gas/, *Physics.* See **ideal gas.**

per·fect·i·ble (pər fek/tə bəl), *adj.* capable of becoming or of being made perfect. [< F < ML *perfectibil(is).* See PERFECT, -IBLE] —**per·fect/i·bil·ist,** *n.* —**per·fect/i·bil/i·ty,** *n.*

perfect/ing press/, *Print.* a rotary press for printing both sides of a sheet or web in one operation.

per·fec·tion (pər fek/shən), *n.* 1. the state or quality of being or becoming perfect. 2. the highest degree of proficiency, skill, or excellence, as in some art. 3. a perfect embodiment of something. 4. a quality, trait, or feature of the highest degree of excellence. 5. the highest or most nearly perfect degree of a quality or trait. 6. the act or fact of perfecting. [< L *perfectiōn-* (s. of *perfectiō*) a finishing (see PERFECT, -ION); r. ME *perfectiun, perfeccioun* < AF]

per·fec·tion·ism (pər fek/shə niz/əm), *n.* 1. any of various doctrines holding that religious, moral, social, or political perfection is attainable. 2. a personal standard, attitude, or philosophy that demands perfection and rejects anything less. [PERFECTION + -ISM]

per·fec·tion·ist (pər fek/shə nist), *n.* 1. one who adheres to or believes in perfectionism. 2. one who demands perfection of himself and his work. —*adj.* 3. of, pertaining to, or distinguished by perfection or perfectionism. [PERFECTION + -IST] —**per·fec/tion·is/tic,** *adj.*

per·fec·tive (pər fek/tiv), *adj.* 1. tending to make perfect; conducive to perfection. 2. *Gram.* noting an aspect of verbal inflection, as in Russian, which indicates completion of the action or state denoted by the verb. —*n.* *Gram.* 3. the perfective aspect. 4. a form in the perfective. [< ML *perfectīv(us).* See PERFECT, -IVE] —**per·fec/tive·ly,** *adv.* —**per·fec/tive·ness, per·fec·tiv·i·ty** (pûr/fek tiv/i tē), *n.*

per·fec·tiv·ise (pər fek/tə vīz/), *v.t.,* **-ised, -is·ing.** *Chiefly Brit.* perfectivize.

per·fec·tiv·ize (pər fek/tə vīz/), *v.t.,* **-ized, -iz·ing.** to make perfective. [PERFECTIVE + -IZE]

per·fect·ly (pûr/fikt lē), *adj.* 1. in a perfect manner or to a perfect degree: *to sing an aria perfectly.* 2. completely; adequately: *This will suit my purpose perfectly.* [PERFECT + -LY; r. ME *parfitly*]

per/fect num/ber, *Math.* a positive number that is equal to the sum of all positive integers which are submultiples of it, as 6, which is equal to the sum of 1, 2, and 3. Cf. **abundant number, deficient number.**

per·fec·to (pər fek/tō), *n., pl.* **-tos.** a rather thick, medium-sized cigar tapering toward both ends. [< Sp: lit., perfect]

per·fec/tor press/ (pər fek/tər), *Print.* a flatbed press for printing both sides of a sheet in one operation. [*perfector* < L. See PERFECT, -OR[2]]

per/fect par/ticiple. See **past participle.**

per/fect pitch/. See **absolute pitch** (def. 2).

per/fect ra/diator, *Physics.* See **black body.**

per/fect ream/. See under **ream**[1] (def. 1).

per/fect rhyme/, 1. rhyme of two words spelled or pronounced identically but differing in meaning, as *rain, reign;* rich rhyme. 2. See **full rhyme.**

Per·fec·tus (pər fek/təs), *n., pl.* **-ti** (-tī). a member of the elite body of Cathari that practiced an extreme form of asceticism. [< L; see PERFECT]

per/fect year/. See under **Jewish calendar.**

per·fer·vid (pər fûr/vid), *adj.* very fervid: *perfervid patriotism.* [< NL *perfervid(us).* See PER-, FERVID] —**per/fer·vid/i·ty, per·fer/vid·ness,** *n.* —**per·fer/vid·ly,** *adv.* —**per·fer/vor;** *esp. Brit.,* **per·fer/vour,** *n.*

per·fide Al·bion (per fēd/ al byôn/), *French.* perfidious Albion: an epithet applied to England by Napoleon I.

per·fid·i·ous (pər fid/ē əs), *adj.* deliberately faithless; treacherous; deceitful: *a perfidious lover.* [< L *perfidiōs(us)* faithless, dishonest. See PERFIDY, -OUS] —**per·fid/i·ous·ly,** *adv.* —**per·fid/i·ous·ness,** *n.*
—**Syn.** false, disloyal; unfaithful, traitorous. —**Ant.** faithful.

per·fi·dy (pûr/fi dē), *n., pl.* **-dies.** 1. deliberate breach of faith or trust; faithlessness; treachery: *perfidy that goes unpunished.* 2. an act or instance of faithlessness or treachery. [< L *perfidia* faithlessness, equiv. to *perfid(us)* faithless, lit., through (i.e., beyond the limits of) faith (*per-* PER- + *fid(ēs)* faith + *-us* adj. suffix) + *-ia* -Y[3]]
—**Syn.** See **disloyalty.**

Perfoliate leaves

per·fo·li·ate (pər fō/lē it, -āt/), *adj.* *Bot.* having the stem apparently passing through the leaf, owing to congenital union of the basal edges of the leaf round the stem: *a perfoliate leaf.* [< NL *perfoliāt(us)* (see PER-, FOLIATE), the fem. of which, *perfoliāta,* was formerly used as the name of a plant with a stalk that seemed to grow through (pierce) its leafage] —**per·fo/li·a/tion,** *n.*

per·fo·rate (*v.* pûr/fə rāt/; *adj.* pûr/fə rit, -rāt/), *v.,* **-rat·ed, -rat·ing,** *adj.* —*v.t.* 1. to make a hole or holes through by boring, punching, piercing, or the like. 2. to pierce through or to the interior of; penetrate. —*v.i.* 3. to make a way through or into; penetrate. —*adj.* 4. perforated. [< L *perforāt(us)* bored through, ptp. of *perforāre* to BORE through; see PER-] —**per/for·a·ble,** *adj.* —**per/fo·ra/tive,** *adj.* —**per/fo·ra/tor,** *n.*

per·fo·rat·ed (pûr/fə rā/tid), *adj.* 1. pierced with a hole or holes. 2. *Philately.* (of a number of stamps joined together) having rows of closely spaced perforations dividing each stamp from the others. Also, **perforate.** [PERFORATE + -ED[2]]

per/forated trac/ery. See **plate tracery.**

per·fo·ra·tion (pûr/fə rā/shən), *n.* 1. a hole, or one of a number of holes, bored or punched through something, as those between individual postage stamps of a sheet to facilitate separation. 2. a hole made or passing through a thing. 3. the act of perforating, or the state of being perforated. [late ME < LL *perforātiōn-* (s. of *perforātiō*) a boring through. See PERFORATE, -ION]

per·force (pər fōrs/, -fôrs/), *adv.* of necessity; by force of circumstance: *The story must perforce be true.* [PER + FORCE; r. ME *par force* < MF]

per·form (pər fôrm/), *v.t.* 1. to carry out; execute; do: *to perform miracles.* 2. to go through or execute in the proper or established manner: *to perform the marriage ceremony.* 3. to carry into effect; fulfill: *Perform what you promise.* 4. to act (a play, part, etc.), as on the stage. 5. to render (music), as by playing or singing. 6. to accomplish (any action involving skill or ability), as before an audience: *to perform a juggling act.* 7. *Obs.* to complete. —*v.i.* 8. to fulfill a command, promise, or undertaking. 9. to execute or do something. 10. to act in a play: *to perform in the role of Romeo.* 11. to perform music. 12. to go through any performance. [ME *parform(en)* < AF *parformer,* alter. (by assoc. with *forme* FORM) of OF, MF *parfournir* to accomplish. See PER-, FURNISH] —**per·form/a·ble,** *adj.* —**per·form/er,** *n.*
—**Syn. 1.** PERFORM, DISCHARGE, EXECUTE, TRANSACT mean to carry to completion a prescribed course of action. PERFORM is the general word, often applied to ordinary activity as a more formal expression than DO, but usually implying regular, methodical, or prolonged application or work: *to perform an exacting task.* DISCHARGE implies carrying out an obligation, often a formal or legal one: *to discharge one's duties as a citizen.* EXECUTE means either to carry out an order, or to carry through a plan or program: *to execute a maneuver.* TRANSACT, meaning to conduct or manage, has commercial connotations: *to transact business.* 3. accomplish, achieve, effect.

per·for·mance (pər fôr/məns), *n.* 1. a musical, dramatic, or other entertainment. 2. the act of performing a ceremony, play, piece of music, etc. 3. the execution or accomplishments of work, acts, feats, etc. 4. a particular action, deed, or proceeding. 5. an action or proceeding of an unusual or spectacular kind: *His temper tantrum was quite a performance.* 6. the act of performing. 7. the manner in which or the efficiency with which something reacts or fulfills its intended purpose. [PERFORM + -ANCE]

perfor/mance test/, *Psychol.* a test requiring little or no use of language, the test materials being designed to elicit manual or behavioral responses rather than verbal ones.

per·form·a·tive (pər fôr/mə tiv), *adj.* *Logic, Philos.* (of an expression or statement) performing an act by the very fact of being uttered, as with the expression "I promise," which performs the act of promising. [PERFORM + -ATIVE]

perform/ing arts/, arts or skills which require public performance, as acting, singing, dancing, etc.

perf. part., perfect participle.

per·fume (*n.* pûr/fyōōm, pər fyōōm/; *v.* pər fyōōm/), *n., v.,* **-fumed, -fum·ing.** —*n.* 1. a substance, extract, or preparation for diffusing or imparting an agreeable or attractive smell. 2. the scent, odor, or volatile particles emitted by substances that smell agreeably. —*v.t.* 3. (of substances, flowers, etc.) to impart a pleasant fragrance to. 4. to impregnate with a sweet odor; scent. [earlier *parfume* (n.) < MF *parfum,* back formation from *parfumer* (v.). See PER-, FUME] —**per/fume·less,** *adj.* —**per/fum·y,** *adj.*
—**Syn. 1.** essence, attar, scent; incense. 2. PERFUME, AROMA, FRAGRANCE all refer to agreeable odors. PERFUME often indicates a strong, rich smell, natural or manufactured: *the perfume of flowers.* FRAGRANCE is best used of fresh, delicate, and delicious odors, esp. from growing things: *fragrance of new-mown hay.* AROMA is restricted to a somewhat spicy smell: *the aroma of coffee.* —**Ant. 2.** stench.

per·fum·er (pər fyōō/mər), *n.* 1. one who or that which perfumes. 2. a maker or seller of perfumes. [PERFUME + -ER[1]]

per·fum·er·y (pər fyōō/mə rē), *n., pl.* **-er·ies.** 1. perfumes collectively. 2. a perfume. 3. the art or business of a perfumer. 4. the place of business of a perfumer. 5. the preparation of perfumes. [PERFUMER + -Y[3]]

per·func·to·ry (pər fungk/tə rē), *adj.* 1. performed merely as an uninteresting or routine duty; hasty and superficial: *perfunctory courtesy.* 2. without interest, care, or enthusiasm; indifferent: *In his lectures he reveals himself to be merely a perfunctory speaker.* [< LL *perfunctōr(ius)* negligent, lit., behaving like a *perfunctor,* one who is satisfied to get through, equiv. to *perfunct(us)* experienced, undergone (ptp. of *perfungī*) + *-ōr-* -OR[2] + *-ius* adj. suffix. See PER-, FUNCTION] —**per·func/to·ri·ly,** *adv.* —**per·func/to·ri·ness,** *n.*
—**Syn. 1, 2.** negligent, heedless, thoughtless, uninterested. —**Ant. 1, 2.** careful, diligent.

per·fuse (pər fyōōz/), *v.t.,* **-fused, -fus·ing.** 1. to overspread with moisture, color, etc. 2. to diffuse (a liquid, color, etc.) through or over something. [< L *perfūs(us)* drenched, ptp. of *perfundere.* See PER-, FUSE[2]] —**per·fu·sive** (pər fyōō/siv), *adj.*

per·fu·sion (pər fyōō/zhən), *n.* 1. the act of perfusing. 2. *Surg.* the pumping of a fluid through an organ or a tissue. [< L *perfūsiōn-* (s. of *perfūsiō*) a drenching. See PERFUSE, -ION]

Per·ga·mum (pûr/gə məm), *n.* 1. an ancient Greek kingdom on the coast of Asia Minor: later a Roman province. 2. the ancient capital of this kingdom; now the site of Bergama, in W Turkey. 3. ancient name of **Bergama.** Also, **Per·ga·mon** (pûr/gə mon), **Pergamus, Pergamos.** —**Per·ga·mene** (pûr/gə mēn/), **Per·gam·ic** (pər gam/ik), *adj.* —**Per/ga·me/ni·an,** *adj., n.*

Per·ga·mus (pûr/gə məs), *n.* 1. *Class. Myth.* a son of Neoptolemus and Andromache. 2. Also, **Per/ga·mos.** Pergamum.

per·gel·i·sol (pər jel/i sôl/, -sol/), *n.* permafrost. [PER(MANENT) + L *gel(āre)* (to) freeze + -I- + *sol(um)* ground, land]

pergel/isol ta/ble. See **permafrost table.**

Pergola

per·go·la (pûr/gə lə), *n.* 1. an arbor formed of horizontal trelliswork supported on columns or posts, over which vines or other plants are trained. 2. a colonnade having the form of such an arbor. [< It < L *pergula* projecting roof, arbor]

Per·go·le·si (per/gô le/zē), *n.* **Gio·van·ni Bat·tis·ta** (jô vän/nē bät tēs/tä), 1710–36, Italian composer.

perh., perhaps.

per·haps (pər haps/), *adv.* maybe; possibly: *Perhaps the package will arrive today.* [earlier *perhappes* by haps. See PER, HAP]

per·hy·dro·gen·ate (pər hī/drə jə nāt/, pûr/hī droj/ə-), *v.t.,* **-at·ed, -at·ing.** to hydrogenate as completely as possible. [PER- + HYDROGENATE] —**per·hy/dro·gen·a/tion,** *n.*

per·hy·dro·gen·ize (pər hī/drə jə nīz/, pûr/hī droj/ə-), *v.t.,* **-ized, -iz·ing.** perhydrogenate. [PER- + HYDROGENIZE]

per·hy·drol (pər hī/drôl, -drol), *n.* a 30 percent solution of hydrogen peroxide in water. [PER- + HYDR-[2] + -OL[1]]

pe·ri (pēr/ē), *n., pl.* **-ris.** 1. one of a race of beautiful, fairylike beings of Persian mythology, represented as descended from fallen angels and excluded from paradise till their penance is accomplished. 2. any lovely, graceful person. [< Pers *perī,* var. of *parī* fairy, MPers *parīk* < Avestan *pairikā* witch]

Pe·ri (pe/re), *n.* **Ja·co·po** (yä/kô pô), (*Il Zazzerino*), 1561–1633, Italian composer.

peri-, a prefix meaning "about," "around," "beyond," appearing in loan words from Greek (*peripeteia*); on this model, used in the formation of compound words (*perimorph*). [< Gk, comb. form of *perí* (adv. and prep.)]

Per·i·al·la (per/ē al/ə), *n.* *Class. Myth.* a priestess of Delphi who was discredited for taking a bribe.

Per·i·an·der (per′ē an′dər), *n.* died 585 B.C., tyrant of Corinth.

per·i·anth (per′ē anth′), *n.* *Bot.* the envelope of a flower, whether calyx or corolla or both. [earlier *perianthium* < NL. See PERI-, ANTH-, -IUM] —**per′i·an′thi·al,** *adj.*

Per·i·a·pis (per′ē ā′pis), *n.* *Class. Myth.* a woman believed to be the mother of Patroclus. Also, **Periopis.**

per·i·apt (per′ē apt′), *n.* an amulet. [< Gk *periapt(on)* amulet, n. use of neut. of *periaptos* hung around, equiv. to *peri-* PERI- + *haptós*, verbid of *háptein* to fasten]

per·i·ar·ter·i·tis (per′ē är′tə rī′tis), *n.* *Pathol.* inflammation of the outer coat and tissues surrounding an artery. [< NL; see PERI-, ARTERITIS]

periarteri′tis nodo′sa, *Pathol.* polyarteritis. [*nōdōsa* < L, fem. of *nōdōsus* NODOSE]

per·i·as·tron (per′ē as′trən, -tron), *n., pl.* **-tra** (-trə). *Astron.* the point at which the stars of a binary system are closest (opposed to *apastron*). [< Gk *peri* PERI- + *ástron* a star; modeled on *perihelion*] —**per′i·as′tral,** *adj.*

per·i·au·ger (per′ē ô′gər), *n.* a flat-bottomed, leeboard sailing barge formerly used in the U.S. on the east coast and on the Mississippi and tributary rivers. Also, **piragua, pirogue.** [alter. of Sp *piragua* PIRAGUA]

per·i·blast (per′ə blast′), *n.* *Embryol.* the peripheral, nucleate area of an expanding blastodisk. [PERI- + -BLAST] —**per′i·blas′tic,** *adj.*

per·i·blem (per′ə blem′), *n.* *Bot.* the histogen in plants which gives rise to the cortex. [< Gk *períblēm(a)* a cloak, covering, akin to *peribállein* to throw about, put on. See PERI-, BALLISTA]

Per·i·boe·a (per′ə bē′ə), *n.* *Class. Myth.* **1.** the mother of the Telamonian Ajax. **2.** a daughter of Hipponous of Olenus, sent to Oeneus of Calydon to be murdered. Instead, she married him and became the mother of Tydeus. **3.** the wife of Polybus, king of Corinth, and the foster mother of Oedipus. **4.** (in the *Iliad*) the mother of Pelegon.

pe·rib·o·los (pə rib′ə ləs, -los′), *n., pl.* **-loi** (-loi′). a wall enclosing a sacred precinct or sanctuary. Also, **peribolus.** [< Gk: an enclosure, circuit, akin to *peribállein;* see PERIBLEM]

pe·rib·o·lus (pə rib′ə ləs), *n., pl.* **-li** (-lī′). peribolos.

per·i·car·di·al (per′ə kär′dē əl), *adj.* of or pertaining to the pericardium. Also, **per′i·car′di·ac′.** [PERICARDI(UM) + -AL[1]]

per·i·car·di·tis (per′ə kär dī′tis), *n.* *Pathol.* inflammation of the pericardium. [PERICARD(IUM) + -ITIS] —**per·i·car·dit·ic** (per′ə kär dit′ik), *adj.*

per·i·car·di·um (per′ə kär′dē əm), *n., pl.* **-di·a** (-dē ə). *Anat.* the membranous sac enclosing the heart. [< NL < Gk *perikárdion*, n. use of neut. of *perikárdios* heart-surrounding. See PERI-, CARDI-, -OUS]

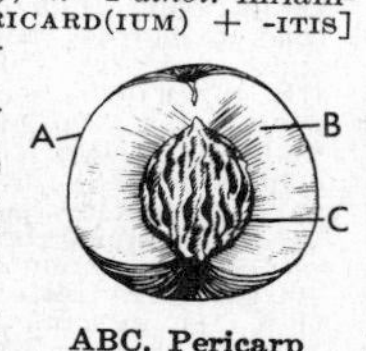

per·i·carp (per′ə kärp′), *n.* **1.** *Bot.* the walls of a ripened ovary or fruit, sometimes consisting of three layers, the epicarp, mesocarp, and endocarp. **2.** a membranous envelope around the cystocarp of red algae. **3.** a seed vessel. [< NL *pericarp(ium)* < Gk *perikárpion* pod. See PERI-, -CARP] —**per·i·car′pi·al, per′i·car′pic,** *adj.* —**per′i·car·poi′dal,** *adj.*

ABC, Pericarp of fruit of peach
A, Epicarp
B, Mesocarp
C, Endocarp

per·i·ce·men·tum (per′ē si men′təm), *n.* *Dentistry.* See **periodontal membrane.** [< NL; see PERI-, CEMENTUM] —**per′i·ce·men′tal,** *adj.*

per·i·cen·ter (per′i sen′tər), *n.* *Astron.* the point at which a heavenly body orbiting around a primary other than the earth or sun is closest to the primary. Cf. **apocenter.** [PERI- + CENTER] —**per′i·cen′tral, per′i·cen′tric,** *adj.*

per·i·chae·ti·um (per′ə kē′tē əm), *n., pl.* **-ti·a** (-tē ə). *Bot.* the envelope of modified leaves surrounding the archegonia in mosses. Cf. **perigonium.** [< NL, equiv. to *peri-* PERI- + Gk *chaít(ē)* flowing hair, mane, foliage (of trees); see -IUM] —**per′i·chae′ti·al,** *adj.*

per·i·chon·dri·um (per′ə kon′drē əm), *n., pl.* **-dri·a** (-drē ə). *Anat.* the membrane of fibrous connective tissue covering the surface of cartilages except at the joints. [< NL < Gk *peri-* PERI- + *khondríon*, dim. of *khóndros* cartilage] —**per′i·chon′dral, per′i·chon′dri·al,** *adj.*

per·i·clase (per′ə klās′, -klāz′), *n.* a cubic mineral, native magnesia, MgO, occurring usually in metamorphosed dolomite. [< G *Periklas*, short for NL *periclasia* < Gk *períklas(is)* a breaking round (*peri-* PERI- + *kla-*, root of *kláein* to break + *-sis* -SIS) + *-ia* -IA]

Per·i·cle·an (per′ə klē′ən), *adj.* of or pertaining to Pericles or to the age (**Per′icle′an Age′**) when Athens was intellectually and materially preeminent. [PERICLE(S) + -AN]

Per·i·cles (per′ə klēz′), *n.* c490–429 B.C., Athenian statesman.

Per′icles, Prince′ of Tyre′, a drama (1608–09?) by Shakespeare.

per·i·cline (per′ə klīn′), *n.* a mineral, a variety of albite, occurring in large white opaque crystals. [< Gk *periklinē(s)* sloping on all sides]

Per·i·cly·me·nus (per′ə klī′mə nəs), *n.* *Class. Myth.* **1.** a son of Neleus who assumed whatever shape he wished, killed by Hercules while defending Neleus's kingdom against the latter. **2.** a Theban son of Poseidon who defended his city in the war of the Seven against Thebes.

pe·ric·o·pe (pə rik′ə pē′), *n., pl.* **-pes, -pae** (-pē′). **1.** a selection or extract from a book. **2.** lection (def. 2). [< L: section < Gk *perikopḗ* a cutting, equiv. to *peri-* PERI- + *kopḗ* a cutting] —**pe·ric′o·pal, per·i·cop·ic** (per′ə kop′ik), *adj.*

per·i·cra·ni·um (per′ə krā′nē əm), *n., pl.* **-ni·a** (-nē ə). **1.** *Anat.* the external periosteum of the cranium. **2.** *Archaic.* the skull or brain. [< NL < Gk *perikránion*, n. use of neut. of *perikránios* skull-surrounding, equiv. to *peri-* PERI- + *kraní(on)* CRANIUM + *-os* -OUS] —**per′i·cra′ni·al,** *adj.*

per·i·cy·cle (per′i sī′kəl), *n.* *Bot.* the outmost cell layer of the stele, frequently becoming a multilayered zone. [< Gk *perikykl(os)*. See PERI-, CYCLE]

per·i·den·tal (per′i den′tᵊl), *adj.* *Dentistry.* periodontal. [PERI- + DENTAL]

per′iden′tal mem′brane, *Dentistry.* See **periodontal membrane.**

per·i·derm (per′i dûrm′), *n.* *Bot.* the cork-producing tissue of stems together with the cork layers and other tissues derived from it. [short for NL *peridermis*. See PERI-, DERMIS] —**per′i·der′mal, per′i·der′mic,** *adj.*

pe·rid·i·ole (pə rid′ē ōl′), *n.* *Bot.* any of several lenticular structures containing the basidiospores in the peridium of the bird's-nest fungi. [PERIDI(UM) + -OLE]

pe·rid·i·o·lum (pə rid′ē ō′ləm), *n., pl.* **-la** (-lə). *Bot.* peridiole. [< NL]

pe·rid·i·um (pə rid′ē əm), *n., pl.* **-rid·e·a** (-rid′ē ə). *Bot.* the outer enveloping coat of the fruit body in many fungi, sometimes itself differentiated into outer and inner layers, exoperidium and endoperidium respectively. [< NL < G *perídion*, dim. of *péra* wallet] —**pe·rid′i·al,** *adj.* —**pe·rid·i·i·form** (pə rid′ē ə fôrm′), *adj.*

per·i·dot (per′i dot′), *n.* a transparent, usually green variety of olivine, used as a gem. [< F *péridot;* r. ME *peritot* < MF] —**per′i·dot′ic,** *adj.*

per·i·do·tite (per′i dō′tīt, pə rid′ə tīt′), *n.* any of a group of igneous rocks of granite texture, composed chiefly of olivine with an admixture of various other minerals, but nearly or wholly free of feldspar. [< F; see PERIDOT, -ITE[1]] —**per·i·do·tit·ic** (per′i dō tit′ik, pə rid′ə-), *adj.*

per′idot of Ceylon′, *Jewelry.* a honey-colored tourmaline, used as a gem: not a true peridot.

per·i·drome (per′i drōm′), *n.* (in a classical temple) the space between the peristyle and the cella. Also, **peridromos.** [< Gk *perídrom(os)*. See PERI-, DROME]

pe·rid·ro·mos (per′i drō′məs, -mos), *n., pl.* **-moi** (-moi). peridrome.

Per·i·e·res (per′ē ēr′ēz), *n.* *Class. Myth.* a Messenian king, the father, by Gorgophone, of Aphareus and Leucippus.

per′ige′an tide′, an ocean tide that occurs in the spring, when the moon is at its perigee.

per·i·gee (per′i jē′), *n.* *Astron.* the point in the orbit of a heavenly body, esp. the moon, or of an artificial satellite at which it is nearest to the earth. See diag. under **apogee.** [< NL *perigē(um)*, var. of *perigaeum* < Gk *perígeion*, n. use of neut. of *perígeios* close to the earth, equiv. to *peri-* PERI- + *gé(a)* earth + *-ios* -IOUS] —**per′i·ge′al, per′i·ge′an,** *adj.*

per·i·gon (per′ə gon′), *n.* an angle of 360°. Also called **round angle.** [PERI- + -GON]

per·i·gone (per′ə gōn′), *n.* *Bot.* perigonium.

per·i·go·ni·um (per′ə gō′nē əm), *n., pl.* **-ni·a** (-nē ə). *Bot.* the envelope of modified leaves surrounding the antheridia in mosses. Also, **perigone.** Cf. **perichaetium.** [< NL; see PERI-, -GONIUM] —**per′i·go′ni·al, per′i·go′nal,** *adj.*

Pé·ri·gord (pā rē gôr′), *n.* a division of the former province of Guienne, in SW France.

Per·i·gor·di·an (per′ə gôr′dē ən), *adj.* of, pertaining to, or characteristic of an Upper Paleolithic cultural epoch in southern France, esp. of the Périgord region. [PÉRIGORD + -IAN]

Per·i·gu·ne (per′ə gyōō′nē), *n.* *Class. Myth.* the mother, by Theseus, of Melanippus.

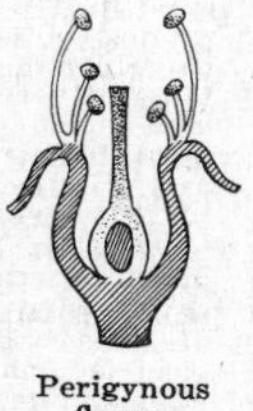

pe·rig·y·nous (pə rij′ə nəs), *adj.* *Bot.* **1.** situated around the pistil on the edge of a cuplike receptacle, as stamens, petals, etc. **2.** having stamens, petals, etc., so arranged. [< NL *perigynus*. See PERI-, -GYNOUS]

Perigynous flower (section)

pe·rig·y·ny (pə rij′ə nē), *n.* perigynous condition. [PERIGYN(OUS) + -Y[3]]

per·i·he·li·on (per′ə hē′lē ən, -hēl′yən), *n., pl.* **-he·li·a** (-hē′lē ə, -hēl′yə). *Astron.* the point in the orbit of a planet or comet at which it is nearest to the sun. Cf. **aphelion.** See diag. under **aphelion.** [< NL *perihēli(um)* < Gk *peri-* PERI- + *hḗli(os)* sun + *-on* neut. n. suffix] —**per′i·he′li·al, per′i·he′li·an,** *adj.*

Per·i·kei·rom·e·ne (per′ə kī rom′ə nē), *n.* a comedy (313? B.C.) by Menander, extant only as a fragment. Also, **Per′i·ki·rom′e·ne.** Also called **The Rape of the Ringlets.**

per·il (per′əl), *n., v.,* **-iled, -il·ing** or (*esp. Brit.*) **-illed, -il·ling.** —*n.* **1.** exposure to injury, loss, or destruction; risk; jeopardy; danger: *They faced the peril of falling rocks.* —*v.t.* **2.** to expose to danger; imperil; risk. [ME < OF < L *perīcul(um)* trial, test, danger] —**per′il·less,** *adj.* —**Syn. 1.** See **danger.**

Per·i·la·us (per′ə lā′əs), *n.* *Class. Myth.* a son of Icarius who demanded vengeance for the murder of his cousin, Clytemnestra.

pe·ril′la oil′ (pə ril′ə), a light yellow oil, obtained from the seeds of mints of the genus *Perilla*, used in the Orient as a cooking oil and elsewhere in the manufacture of varnish, printing ink, and artificial leather. [*perilla* < NL < ?]

per·il·ous (per′ə ləs), *adj.* involving or full of risk or peril; hazardous; dangerous: *a perilous undertaking.* [ME < AF *perillous* < L *perīculōs(us)*. See PERIL, -OUS] —**per′il·ous·ly,** *adv.* —**per′il·ous·ness,** *n.* —**Syn.** risky. —**Ant.** safe.

per′il point′, *U.S.* the lower limit of a tariff on a commodity at which import of that commodity would have a seriously adverse effect on the local producers.

per·i·lune (per′i lōōn′), *n.* the point in a lunar orbit that is nearest to the moon. Cf. **apolune.** [PERI- + *lune* < L *lūna* moon]

per·i·lymph (per′ə limf′), *n.* *Anat.* the fluid between the bony and membranous labyrinths of the ear. [PERI- + LYMPH] —**per′i·lym·phat′ic,** *adj.*

Per·i·me·des (per′ə mē′dēz), *n.* *Class. Myth.* **1.** a son of Eurystheus. **2.** (in the *Odyssey*) one of the companions of Odysseus on his trip to the underworld.

Per·i·me·le (per′ə mē′lē), *n.* *Class. Myth.* a daughter of Hippodamas who was ravished by Achelous and later was changed into an island.

pe·rim·e·ter (pə rim′i tər), *n.* **1.** the circumference, border, or outer boundary of a two-dimensional figure. **2.** the length of such a boundary. **3.** *Ophthalm.* an instrument for determining the extent and defects of the visual field. [< F *périmètre* < L *perimetr(os)*. See PERI-, -METER] —**pe·rim′e·ter·less,** *adj.* —**pe·rim′e·tral, per·i·met·ric** (per′ə me′trik), **per′i·met′ri·cal,** *adj.* —**per′i·met′ri·cal·ly,** *adv.* —**pe·rim′e·try,** *n.* —**Syn. 1.** periphery.

per·i·morph (per′ə môrf′), *n.* a mineral enclosing another mineral. Cf. **endomorph** (def. 1). [PERI- + -MORPH] —**per′i·mor′phic, per′i·mor′phous,** *adj.* —**per′i·mor′phism,** *n.*

per·in·de (pər in′dē), *adv.* (in prescriptions) in the same manner as before. [< L]

per·i·neph·ri·um (per′ə nef′rē əm), *n., pl.* **-neph·ri·a** (-nef′rē ə). *Anat.* the capsule of connective tissue which envelops the kidney. [< NL; see PERI-, NEPHR-, -IUM] —**per′i·neph′ral, per′i·neph′ri·al, per′i·neph′ric,** *adj.*

per·i·ne·um (per′ə nē′əm), *n., pl.* **-ne·a** (-nē′ə). *Anat.* **1.** the area in front of the anus extending to the fourchette of the vulva in the female and to the scrotum in the male. **2.** the diamond-shaped area corresponding to the outlet of the pelvis, containing the anus and vulva or the roots of the penis. [< NL, var. of *perinaeum* < Gk *perínaion* (neut.), *perínaios* (masc.), var. of *perineos*, equiv. to *peri-* PERI- + *iné(ein)* (to) discharge, evacuate + *-os* adj. suffix] —**per′i·ne′al,** *adj.*

per·i·neu·ri·tis (per′ə nŏŏ rī′tis, -nyŏŏ-), *n.* *Pathol.* inflammation of the perineurium. [PERI- + NEURITIS]

per·i·neu·ri·um (per′ə nŏŏr′ē əm, -nyŏŏr′-), *n., pl.* **-neu·ri·a** (-nŏŏr′ē ə, -nyŏŏr′-). *Anat.* the sheath of connective tissue that encloses a bundle of nerve fibers. [< NL; see PERI- NEUR-, -IUM] —**per′i·neu′ri·al,** *adj.*

pe·ri·od (pēr′ē əd), *n.* **1.** a rather large interval of time that is meaningful in the life of a person, in history, etc., because of its particular characteristics: *a period of illness; a period of expansion for a company; a period of social unrest in Germany.* **2.** any specified division or portion of time: *architecture of the period 1530–1800.* **3.** *Educ.* a specific length of time during school hours that a student spends in a classroom, laboratory, etc., or has free. **4.** a definite, timed part of a game: *a rest between periods.* **5.** *Music.* a division of a composition, usually a passage of eight or sixteen measures, complete or satisfactory in itself, commonly consisting of two or more contrasted or complementary phrases ending with a conclusive cadence. **6.** *Geol.* the basic unit of geological time, during which a standard rock system is formed: comprising several epochs and included with other periods in an era. **7.** *Physics.* the duration of one complete cycle of a wave or oscillation; the reciprocal of the frequency. **8.** *Astron.* **a.** Also called **period of rotation.** the time in which a body rotates once on its axis. **b.** Also called **period of revolution.** the time in which a planet or satellite revolves once about its primary. **9.** a round of time or series of years by which time is measured. **10.** a round of time marked by the recurrence of some phenomenon or occupied by some recurring process of action. **11.** the point of completion of a round of time or of the time during which something lasts or happens. **12.** *Physiol.* a time of the month during which menstruation occurs. **13.** the time during which anything runs its course. **14.** the present time. **15.** the point or character (.) used to mark the end of a declarative sentence, indicate an abbreviation, etc. **16.** a full pause, as is made at the end of a complete sentence. **17.** a sentence, esp. a well-balanced, impressive sentence; a periodic sentence: *stately periods.* **18.** *Class. Pros.* a group of two or more cola. —*adj.* **19.** noting, pertaining to, evocative of, imitating, or representing a historical period or the styles current during a specific period of history: *period piece; period costumes; period play.* [late ME *peryod* < ML, L *period(us)* < Gk *períodos* circuit, period of time, period in rhetoric, lit., way around. See PERI-, -ODE[2]] —**Syn. 1.** interval. See **age. 2.** term.

per·i·o·date (pə rī′ə dāt′), *n.* *Chem.* a salt of a periodic acid, as sodium periodate, $Na_2H_3IO_6$. [PERIOD(IC ACID) + -ATE[2]]

pe·ri·od·ic[1] (pēr′ē od′ik), *adj.* **1.** recurring at intervals of time: *periodic revivals of the arts-and-crafts ideas.* **2.** occurring or appearing at regular intervals: *periodic visits of a mail steamer to an island.* **3.** repeated at irregular intervals; intermittent: *periodic outbreaks of violence in the summer of 1964.* **4.** *Physics.* recurring at equal intervals of time. **5.** *Astron.* **a.** characterized by a series of successive circuits or revolutions, as the motion of a planet or satellite. **b.** of or pertaining to a period, as of the revolution of a heavenly body. **6.** pertaining to or characterized by rhetorical periods, or periodic sentences. [< L *periodic(us)* < Gk *periodikós*. See PERIOD, -IC] —**pe′ri·od′i·cal·ly,** *adv.*

per·i·od·ic[2] (pûr′ī od′ik), *adj.* *Chem.* of or derived from a periodic acid. [PER- + IODIC]

per′i·od′ic ac′id (pûr′ī od′ik, pûr′-), *Chem.* any of a series of acids derived from I_2O_7 by the addition of water molecules, as HIO_4 or H_5IO_6.

pe·ri·od·i·cal (pēr′ē od′i kəl), *n.* **1.** a magazine or other journal that is issued at regularly recurring intervals. —*adj.* **2.** published at regularly recurring intervals. **3.** of or pertaining to such publications. **4.** periodic[1]. [PERIODIC[1] + -AL[1]] —**pe′ri·od′i·cal·ism,** *n.* —**pe′ri·od′i·cal·ist,** *n.* —**pe′ri·od′i·cal·ly,** *adv.* —**pe′ri·od′i·cal·ness,** *n.*

period′ical cica′da, a cicada, *Magicicada septendecim*, of the eastern U.S. having nymphs that live in the soil, usually emerging in great numbers after 17 years in the North or 13 years in the South. Also called **seventeen-year locust.**

pe·ri·o·dic·i·ty (pēr′ē ə dis′i tē), *n.* the character of being periodic; the tendency to recur at regular intervals. [< F *périodicité*. See PERIODIC[1], -ITY]

pe′ri·od′ic law′ (pēr′ē od′ik, pēr′-), *Chem.* **1.** the law that the properties of the elements are periodic functions of their atomic numbers. **2.** Also called **Mendeleev's law.** (originally) the statement that the chemical and physical properties of the chemical elements recur periodically when the elements are arranged in the order of their atomic weights.

pe′ri·od′ic mo′tion (pēr′ē od′ik, pēr′-), *Physics.* any motion that recurs in identical forms at equal intervals of time.

pe′ri·od′ic sen′tence (pēr′ē od′ik, pēr′-), a sentence that, by leaving the completion of its main clause to the end, produces an effect of suspense. Cf. **loose sentence.**

pe′ri·od′ic sys′tem (pēr′ē od′ik, pēr′-), *Chem.* a system of classification of the elements based on the periodic law.

pe′ri·od′ic ta′ble (pēr′ē od′ik, pēr′-), *Chem.* a table illustrating the periodic system, in which the chemical elements, formerly arranged in the order of their atomic weights and now according to their atomic numbers, are shown in related groups. See table on page 462.

per·i·o·dide (pə rī′ə dīd′, -did), *n.* *Chem.* an iodide with the maximum proportion of iodine. [PERIOD(IC ACID) + -IDE]

pe′riod of revolu′tion, *Astron.* period (def. 8b).

pe′riod of rota′tion, *Astron.* period (def. 8a).

per·i·o·don·tal (per′ē ə don′təl), *adj.* *Dentistry.* **1.** of or pertaining to the periodontium. **2.** of or pertaining to periodontics. **3.** of or pertaining to the periodontal membrane. Also, **peridental.** [PERI- + -ODONT + -AL[1]]

per′iodon′tal mem′brane, *Dentistry.* the collagenous, fibrous connective tissue between the cementum of the tooth and the alveolus. Also, **pericementum.**

per·i·o·don·tics (per′ē ə don′tiks), *n.* (*construed as sing.*) the branch of dentistry dealing with the study and treatment of diseases of the periodontium. Also, **per·i·o·don·tia** (per′ē ə don′shə, -shē ə). [< NL; see PERIODONTIUM, -ICS] **—per′i·o·don′tic,** *adj.*

per·i·o·don·tist (per′ē ə don′tist), *n.* a specialist in periodontics. [PERIODONT(ICS) + -IST]

per·i·o·don·tium (per′ē ə don′shəm, -shē əm), *n., pl.* **-tia** (-shə, -shē ə). *Dentistry.* the bone, connective tissue, and gum surrounding and supporting a tooth. Also called **parodontium.** [< NL; see PERI-, -ODONT, -IUM]

pe′riod piece′, something, as a novel, painting, building, etc., of little interest or value aside from the fact that it evokes or epitomizes a particular period of history.

Per·i·oe·ci (per′ē ē′sī), *n.pl., sing.* **-cus** (-kəs). the inhabitants of ancient Laconia, constituting a dependent people of Sparta, who governed themselves and had a monopoly on trade and manufacture. Cf. **Helot** (def. 1), **Spartiate.** [< ML *perioecī* < Gk *períoikoi* countryside dwellers, n. use of pl. of *períoikos* dwelling round, equiv. to *peri-* PERI- + *oik(os)* house + *-os* adj. suffix] **—per′i·oe′cic, per′i·oe′cid,** *adj.*

per·i·o·nych·i·a[1] (per′ē ō nik′ē ə), *n.* *Pathol.* inflammation of the perionychium. [< NL < Gk *perí* PERI- + *onych-* (s. of *ónyx*) nail (see ONYX) + *-ia* -IA]

per·i·o·nych·i·a[2] (per′ē ō nik′ē ə), *n.* pl. of **perionychium.**

per·i·o·nych·i·um (per′ē ō nik′ē əm), *n., pl.* **-nych·i·a** (-nik′ē ə). *Anat.* the epidermis surrounding the base and sides of a fingernail or toenail. [< NL; see PERIONYCHIA[1], -IUM]

Per·i·o·pis (per′ē ō′pis), *n.* *Class. Myth.* Periapis.

per·i·os·te·um (per′ē os′tē əm), *n., pl.* **-te·a** (-tē ə). *Anat.* the normal investment of bone, consisting of a dense, fibrous outer layer and a more delicate, inner layer capable of forming bone. [< NL, var. of LL *periosteon* < Gk. See PERI-, OSTEO-] **—per′i·os′te·al, per′i·os′te·ous,** *adj.* **—per′i·os′te·al·ly,** *adv.*

per·i·os·ti·tis (per′ē o stī′tis), *n.* *Pathol.* inflammation of the periosteum. [PERIOST(EUM) + -ITIS] **—per·i·os·tit·ic** (per′ē o stit′ik), *adj.*

per·i·os·tra·cum (per′ē os′trə kəm), *n., pl.* **-ca** (-kə). the external, chitinlike covering of the shell of certain mollusks, which protects the limy portion from acids. [PERI- + *ostracum* < Gk *óstrakon* a shell. See OYSTER] **—per′i·os′tra·cal,** *adj.*

per·i·o·tic (per′ē ō′tik, -ot′ik), *adj.* *Anat.* **1.** surrounding the ear. **2.** noting or pertaining to certain bones or bony elements which form or help to form a protective capsule for the internal ear, being usually confluent or fused, and in man constituting part of the temporal bone. [PERI- + -OTIC]

Per·i·pa·tet·ic (per′ə pə tet′ik), *adj.* **1.** of or pertaining to Aristotle, who taught philosophy while walking in the Lyceum of ancient Athens. **2.** of or pertaining to the Aristotelian school of philosophy. **3.** (*l.c.*) walking or traveling about; itinerant. **—*n.* 4.** a member of the Aristotelian school. **5.** (*l.c.*) one who walks or travels about. [late ME *perypatetik* < L *peripatēticus* < Gk *peripatētikós* of Aristotle and his school, lit., walking about, equiv. to *peripatē-* (verbid s. of *peripatein* to walk about) + *-tikos* -TIC] **—per′i·pa·tet′i·cal·ly,** *adv.* **—per′i·pa·tet′i·cism,** *n.*
—Syn. 3. wandering, roving; vagrant.

per·i·pe·tei·a (per′ə pi tī′ə), *n.* *Literature.* a sudden turn of events or reversal in the action, esp. of a dramatic work. Also, **per′i·pe·ti′a, pe·rip·e·ty** (pə rip′i tē). [< Gk: sudden change, equiv. to *peripet(ḗs)*, lit., falling round (*peri-* PERI- + *pet-* fall, s. of *píptein* to fall) + *-eia* -Y[3]]

Per·i·phas (per′ə fəs), *n.* **1.** (in the *Iliad*) **a.** a son of Epytus who served as a Trojan herald. **b.** the most valiant Aetolian warrior in the Trojan War. **2.** *Class. Myth.* an Attic king whom Zeus changed into an eagle.

pe·riph·er·al (pə rif′ər əl), *adj.* **1.** pertaining to, situated in, or constituting the periphery. **2.** concerned with the comparatively superficial or not really essential aspects of the subject in question: *These peripheral criticisms of the quality of the printing and illustrations should not, however, deter anyone from buying the book.* **3.** *Anat.* outside of; external. **4.** *Computer Technol.* pertaining to hardware separate or separable from a computer. Also, **peripheric.** [< Gk *peripher(ḗs)* (see PERIPHERY) + -AL[1]] **—pe·riph′er·al·ly,** *adv.*

periph′eral nerv′ous sys′tem, the part of the nervous system comprising the autonomic nervous system and the cranial and spinal nerves.

per·i·pher·ic (per′ə fer′ik), *adj.* peripheral. **—per′i·pher′i·cal·ly,** *adv.*

pe·riph·er·y (pə rif′ə rē), *n., pl.* **-er·ies.** **1.** the external boundary of any surface or area. **2.** the external surface of a body. **3.** the relatively superficial or external aspects of the subject in question: *The preliminary researches did not, of course, take me beyond the periphery of my problem.* **4.** *Anat.* the area in which nerves end. [ME *periferie* < ML *periferia*, var. sp. of *peripheria* < Gk *periphéreia* circumference, lit., a bearing round, equiv. to *peri-* PERI- + *phér(ein)* to bear + *-eia* -Y[3]]
—Syn. 1. circumference, perimeter. **—Ant. 1, 2.** center.

Per·i·phe·tes (per′ə fē′tēz), *n.* *Class. Myth.* **1.** a lame giant killed with his own club by Theseus. Cf. **Corynetes. 2.** the son of Copreus of Mycenae. **3.** a Mysian ally of the Trojans in the Trojan War.

pe·riph·ra·sis (pə rif′rə sis), *n., pl.* **-ses** (-sēz′). **1.** a roundabout way of speaking; circumlocution. **2.** an expression phrased in such fashion. Also, **per·i·phrase** (per′ə frāz′). [< L < Gk *periphrasis.* See PERI-, PHRASE, -SIS]

per·i·phras·tic (per′ə fras′tik), *adj.* **1.** circumlocutory; roundabout. **2.** *Gram.* noting a construction of two or more words having the same syntactic function as an inflected word, as *of Mr. Smith* in *the son of Mr. Smith*, which is equivalent to *Mr. Smith's* in *Mr. Smith's son.* [< Gk *periphrastik(ós)*, deriv. of *periphrázein.* See PERI-, PHRASE, -TIC] **—per′i·phras′ti·cal·ly,** *adv.*

per·i·proct (per′ə prokt′), *n.* (in certain echinoids) that part of the body surface bordering the anus. [PERI- + *proct* < Gk *prōkt(ós)* anus] **—per′i·proc′tal, per′i·proc′tic, per′i·proc′tous,** *adj.*

pe·rip·ter·al (pə rip′tər əl), *adj.* (of a classical temple) surrounded by a single row of columns. [< L *peripter(on)* < Gk, n. use of neut. of *perípteros* encompassed round with columns; see PERI-, -PTEROUS) + -AL[1]]

pe·rip·ter·os (pə rip′tə ros′), *n., pl.* **-ter·oi** (-tə roi′). a peripteral building. Also, **periptery.** [< L < Gk *perípteros*. See PERIPTERAL]

pe·rip·ter·y (pə rip′tə rē), *n., pl.* **-ter·ies.** peripteros. [< Gk *perípter(os)* (see PERIPTERAL) + -Y[3]]

pe·rique (pə rēk′), *n.* a rich-flavored tobacco produced in Louisiana. [said to have its name from *Périque*, nickname of Pierre Chenet, Louisiana grower who first developed it]

per·i·sarc (per′i särk′), *n.* *Zool.* the horny or chitinous outer case or covering with which the soft parts of hydrozoans are often protected. [PERI- + SARC-] **—per′i·sar′cal, per′i·sar′cous,** *adj.*

per·i·scope (per′i skōp′), *n.* an optical instrument for viewing objects that are above the level of direct sight or in an otherwise obstructed field of vision, consisting essentially of a tube with an arrangement of prisms or mirrors and, usually, lenses. [back formation from PERISCOPIC. See PERISCOPIC]

per·i·scop·ic (per′i skop′ik), *adj.* **1.** *Optics.* (of certain lenses in special microscopes, cameras, etc.) giving distinct vision obliquely, or all around, as well as, or instead of, in a direct line. **2.** pertaining to periscopes or their use. Also, **per′i·scop′i·cal.** [< Gk *periskop(eîn)* (to) look about (see PERI-, -SCOPE) + -IC]

per·ish (per′ish), *v.i.* **1.** to die unseasonably through violence, privation, etc.: *to perish in an earthquake.* **2.** to pass away; decay; disappear: *an age of elegance that has forever perished.* **3.** to suffer destruction: *His valuable paintings perished in the fire.* **4.** to suffer spiritual death: *Save us, lest we perish.* [ME *periss(en)* < OF *periss-*, long s. of *perir* < L *perīre* to perish, lit., go through, spend fully, equiv. to *per-* PER- + *īre* to go] **—per′ish·less,** *adj.* **—per′ish·ment,** *n.*
—Syn. 1. expire. See **die**[1]. **2.** wither, shrivel, rot, molder, vanish. **—Ant. 2.** appear.

per·ish·a·ble (per′i shə bəl), *adj.* **1.** subject to decay or destruction. **—*n.* 2.** Usually, **perishables.** something perishable, esp. food. [PERISH + -ABLE] **—per′ish·a·bil′i·ty, per′ish·a·ble·ness,** *n.* **—per′ish·a·bly,** *adv.*

per·ish·ing (per′i shing), *adj.* causing destruction, extreme discomfort, or death: *lost in the perishing cold.* [ME; see PERISH, -ING[2]] **—per′ish·ing·ly,** *adv.*

Per′ish in Their Pride′, a novel (1934) by Henry de Montherlant. French, **Les Célibataires.**

per·i·sphere (per′i sfēr′), *n.* *Physics.* the region about a body in which its gravitation, magnetic, or electric fields are capable of producing significant effects. [PERI- + SPHERE] **—per·i·spher·ic** (per′i sfer′ik), **per′i·spher′i·cal,** *adj.*

per·i·spore (per′i spōr′, -spôr′), *n.* *Bot.* a membrane surrounding a spore. [PERI- + -SPORE]

pe·ris·so·dac·tyl (pə ris′ō dak′təl, -til), *adj.* **1.** having an uneven number of toes or digits on each foot. **—*n.* 2.** any mammal of the order *Perissodactyla*, comprising the odd-toed hoofed quadrupeds and including the tapirs, rhinoceroses, and horses. Also, **pe·ris·so·dac·tyle** (pə ris′ō dak′təl, -til, -tīl). [< NL *perissodactyl(us)* < Gk *perissó(s)* uneven (deriv. of *perí* over; see PERI-) + *-daktylos* fingered, toed; see DACTYL, -OUS] **—pe·ris′so·dac′ty·lous,** *adj.*

Pe·ris·so·dac·ty·la (pə ris′ō dak′tələ), *n.* the order comprising the perissodactyls. [< NL, neut. pl. of *perissodactylus* PERISSODACTYL]

pe·ris·ta·lith (pə ris′tə lith), *n.* a group of stones encircling a mound, dolmen, or the like. [< Gk *perísta-(tos)* surrounded (verbid of *periistanai* to stand round, equiv. to *peri-* PERI- + *histanai* to stand) + -LITH]

per·i·stal·sis (per′i stôl′sis, -stal′-), *n., pl.* **-ses** (-sēz). *Physiol.* the progressive wave of contraction and relaxation of a tubular muscular system, esp. the alimentary canal, by which the contents are forced through the system. [< NL < Gk *peri-* PERI- + *stálsis* contraction, equiv. to *stal-* (var. s. of *stéllein* to set, bring together, compress) + *-sis* -SIS]

per·i·stal·tic (per′i stôl′tik, -stal′-), *adj.* *Physiol.* of, pertaining to, or resembling peristalsis. [< Gk *peristaltik(ós)* compressing, equiv. to *peri-* PERI- + *stal-* (see PERISTALSIS) + *-tikos* -TIC] **—per′i·stal′ti·cal·ly,** *adv.*

pe·ris·te·rite (pə ris′tə rīt′), *n.* a whitish, iridescent variety of albite, used as a gem. [< Gk *peristér(ā)* pigeon, dove + -ITE[1]]

per·i·stome (per′i stōm′), *n.* **1.** *Bot.* the one or two circles of small, pointed, toothlike appendages around the orifice of a capsule or urn of mosses, appearing when the lid is removed. **2.** *Zool.* any of various structures or sets of parts which surround or form the walls of a mouth or mouthlike opening. [< NL *peristom(a).* See PERI-, -STOME] **—per′i·sto′mal, per·i·sto·mat·ic** (per′i stə mat′ik), **per′i·sto′mi·al,** *adj.*

per·i·style (per′i stīl′), *n.* *Archit.* **1.** a colonnade surrounding a building or an open space. **2.** an open space, as a courtyard, surrounded by a colonnade. [< L *peristȳl(um)* < Gk *peristȳlon*, n. use of neut. of *peristȳlos* columned round, equiv. to *peri-* PERI- + *stȳl(os)* column + *-os* -OUS] **—per′i·sty′lar,** *adj.*

per·i·sty·li·um (per′i stī′lē əm, -stil′ē-), *n., pl.* **-sty·li·a** (-stī′lē ə, -stil′ē ə). a peristyle. [< L; see PERISTYLE]

per·i·tec·tic (per′i tek′tik), *adj.* *Physical Chem.* of or noting the phase intermediate between a solid and the liquid that results from the melting of the solid. [PERI- + Gk *tēktik(ós)* able to dissolve, akin to *tḗkein* to melt]

per·i·the·ci·um (per′ə thē′shē əm, -sē əm), *n., pl.* **-ci·a** (-shē ə, -sē ə). *Bot.* the fructification of certain fungi, typically a minute, more or less completely closed, globose or flask-shaped body enclosing the asci. [< NL; see PERI-, THECA, -IUM] **—per′i·the′ci·al,** *adj.*

per·i·the·li·um (per′ə thē′lē əm), *n., pl.* **-li·a** (-lē ə). *Anat.* the connective tissue surrounding certain small vessels, as capillaries. [< NL < Gk *perí* + *thēl(ḗ)* nipple + L *-ium* -IUM] **—per′i·the′li·al,** *adj.*

per·i·to·ne·al·ize (per′i tə nē′ə līz′), *v.t.,* **-ized, -iz·ing.** *Surg.* to cover with peritoneum. [PERITONEAL + -IZE]

per·i·to·ne·um (per′i tənē′əm), *n., pl.* **-to·ne·ums, -to·ne·a** (-tənē′ə). *Anat.* the serous membrane lining the abdominal cavity and investing its viscera. [< LL, var. sp. of *peritonaeum* < Gk *peritónaion*, n. use of neut. of *peritónaios*, synonymous deriv. of *perítonos* stretched round. See PERI-, TONE, -EOUS] **—per′i·to·ne′al, per′i·to·nae′al,** *adj.* **—per′i·to·ne′al·ly, per′i·to·nae′al·ly,** *adv.*

per·i·to·ni·tis (per′i tənī′tis), *n.* *Pathol.* inflammation of the peritoneum. [PERITON(EUM) + -ITIS] **—per·i·to·nit·ic** (per′i tənit′ik), **per′i·to·nit′al,** *adj.*

Per·i·trate (per′i trāt′), *n.* *Pharm., Trademark.* See **pentaerythritol tetranitrate.**

pe·rit·ri·chate (pə ri′trə kit, -kāt′), *adj.* (of bacteria) having flagella on the entire surface. Also, **per·i·trich·ic** (per′i trik′ik). [PERI- + TRICH- + -ATE[1]] **—per′i·trich, pe·rit·ri·chan** (pə ri′trə kən), *n.*

per·i·vis·cer·al (per′ə vis′ər əl), *adj.* *Anat.* surrounding or situated about the viscera. [PERI- + VISCERAL]

per·i·wig (per′i wig′), *n.* a peruke or wig. [earlier *perwyke*, alter. of MF *perruque* PERUKE]

per′iwig chair′, a chair of c1700 having a high, caned back with an elaborately carved cresting.

Periwinkle[1], ***Littorina littorea*** **(Length to 1 in.)**

per·i·win·kle[1] (per′i wing′kəl), *n.* **1.** any of various marine gastropods or sea snails, esp. *Littorina littorea*, used for food in Europe. **2.** the shell of any of these animals. [dissimilated var. of OE *pinewincle*, equiv. to *pine* (< L *pīna* < Gk *pína*, var. of *pínna* kind of mollusk) + *wincle*, c. dial. Dan *vinkel* snail shell]

per·i·win·kle[2] (per′i wing′kəl), *n.* any trailing, evergreen, apocynaceous plant of the genus *Vinca*, as *V. minor*, having blue, white, or purple flowers, or *V. major* **(large periwinkle),** having blue or variegated flowers. [late ME *perwinke*, earlier *pervinke*, OE *pervincae* < L *pervinca*] **—per′i·win′kled,** *adj.*

per·jure (pûr′jər), *v.t.,* **-jured, -jur·ing.** to render (oneself) guilty of swearing falsely, or of willfully making a false statement under oath or solemn affirmation. [late ME < L *pejūr(āre)* (to) swear falsely, equiv. to *per-* through, i.e., beyond the limits, + *jūrāre* to swear, lit., to be at law, deriv. of *jūs* JUS; r. *parjure* < AF] **—per′jure·ment,** *n.* **—per′jur·er,** *n.*

per·jured (pûr′jərd), *adj.* **1.** guilty of perjury. **2.** characterized by or involving perjury: *perjured testimony.* [late ME; see PERJURE, -ED[2]] **—per′jured·ly,** *adv.* **—per′jured·ness,** *n.*

per·ju·ry (pûr′jə rē), *n., pl.* **-ries.** *Law.* the willful utterance of a false statement under oath or affirmation, before a competent tribunal, upon a point material to a legal inquiry. [ME < L *perjūri(um)*, equiv. to *perjūr(us)* swearing falsely (see PERJURE) + *-ium* -Y[3]; r. *parjury* < AF] **—per·ju·ri·ous** (pər jo͝or′ē əs), *adj.* **—per·ju′ri·ous·ly,** *adv.* **—per·ju′ri·ous·ness,** *n.*

perk[1] (pûrk), *v.i.* **1.** to act, or carry oneself, in a jaunty manner. **2.** to become lively or vigorous, as after depression or sickness (usually fol. by *up*). **3.** to put oneself forward briskly or presumptuously. **—*v.t.* 4.** to raise smartly or briskly (often fol. by *up* or *out*): *to perk one's head up.* **5.** to dress smartly; make trim or jaunty (sometimes fol. by *up* or *out*): *to perk up a suit with a new white blouse.* **—*adj.* 6.** perky; jaunty: *a perk manner.* [ME *perke(n)*; ? akin to PEER[2]] **—perk′ing·ly,** *adv.* **—perk′ish,** *adj.*

perk[2] (pûrk), *v.i., v.t.* *Informal.* to percolate: *Is the coffee perking yet?* [by shortening]

perk[3] (pûrk), *n.* *Brit. Informal.* perquisite (def. 2). [by shortening]

Per·ka·sie (pûr′kə sē), *n.* a town in SE Pennsylvania. 4650 (1960).

Per·kin (pûr′kin), *n.* **Sir William Henry,** 1838–1907, English chemist.

Per·kins (pûr′kinz), *n.* **Frances,** 1882–1965, U.S. sociologist: Secretary of Labor 1933–45.

perk·nite (pûrk′nīt), *n.* any of the group of coarse-grained, dark-colored igneous rocks consisting of pyroxenites and amphibolites and having no feldspar.

perk·y (pûr′kē), *adj.,* **perk·i·er, perk·i·est.** jaunty; brisk; pert. [PERK[1] + -Y[1]] **—perk′i·ly,** *adv.* **—perk′i·ness,** *n.*

perle (pûrl), *n.* a medicinal capsule that resembles a pearl in shape. [< F: lit., PEARL[1]]

Perle (pûrl), *n.* a girl's given name. Also, **Pearl.**

Per·le·a (per′lā′ə), *n.* **Jo·nel** (zhō′nel), born 1900, Rumanian conductor and composer in the U.S.

perle′ cot′ton. See **pearl cotton.**

Perl·ie (pûr′lē), *n.* a girl's given name, form of **Pearl** or **Perle.**

per·ling (pûr′ling), *n.* *Rare.* a purlin.

Per·lis (pûr′lis), *n.* a state in Malaysia, on the SW Malay Peninsula. 101,357 (est. 1961); 310 sq. mi. *Cap.:* Kangar.

per·lite (pûr′līt), *n.* *Petrog.* a volcanic glass, usually appearing as a mass of enamellike globules, formed by concentric fractures. Also, **pearlite.** [< F; see PEARL[1], -ITE[1]] **—per·lit·ic** (pər lit′ik), *adj.*

CONCISE ETYMOLOGY KEY: <, descended or derived from; >, whence; b., blend of, blended; c., cognate with; deriv., derivative; equiv., equivalent; imit., imitative; m., modification of; obl., oblique; r., replacing; s., stem; sp., spelling; trans., translation; ?, origin unknown, perhaps; *, hypothetical. See the full key inside the front cover.

per·lu·ci·dus (pər lo͞o′si dəs), *adj.* *Meteorol.* (of a cloud) having transparent spaces between the elements. [< NL; see PER-, LUCID]

perm (pûrm), *Informal.* —*n.* **1.** See **permanent wave.** —*v.t.* **2.** to give (the hair) a permanent wave. —*v.i.* **3.** to apply a permanent wave to the hair. [by shortening]

Perm (perm), *n.* a city in the RSFSR, in the E Soviet Union in Europe, on the Kama River. 763,000 (1965). Also called **Molotov.**

per·ma·frost (pûr′mə frôst′, -frost′), *n.* (in arctic or subarctic regions) perennially frozen subsoil. Also called **pergelisol.** [PERMA(NENT) + FROST]

per′mafrost ta′ble, the variable surface constituting the upper limit of permafrost. Also called **pergelisol table.** Cf. **frost line** (def. 2).

perm·al·loy (pûrm′al′oi, pûr′mə loi′), *n.* any of a class of alloys of high magnetic permeability, containing from 30 to 90 percent nickel. [PERM(ANENT) + ALLOY]

per·ma·nence (pûr′mə nəns), *n.* the condition or quality of being permanent; perpetual or continued existence. [late ME < ML *permanentia.* See PERMANENT, -ENCE]

per·ma·nen·cy (pûr′mə nən sē), *n., pl.* **-cies. 1.** permanence. **2.** something that is permanent. [< ML *permanentia.* See PERMANENT, -ENCY]

per·ma·nent (pûr′mə nənt), *adj.* **1.** existing perpetually; everlasting. **2.** intended to exist or function for a long, indefinite period without regard to unforeseeable conditions: *a permanent construction; a permanent employee; the permanent headquarters of the United Nations.* **3.** long-lasting; nonfading: *permanent pleating; permanent ink.* —*n.* **4.** See **permanent wave.** [late ME < L *permanent-* (s. of *permanēns*) remaining, prp. of *permanēre.* See PER-, REMAIN, -ENT] —**per′ma·nent·ly,** *adv.* —**per′ma·nent·ness,** *n.*
—**Syn. 1.** stable, invariable, constant. —**Ant. 1.** temporary; inconstant.

Per′manent Court′ of Arbitra′tion, official name of the **Hague Tribunal.**

Per′manent Court′ of Interna′tional Jus′tice, an international tribunal established under the Covenant of the League of Nations and replaced in 1945 by the International Court of Justice.

per′manent ech′o, *Electronics.* a radar signal reflected to a radar station on the ground by a building or other fixed object.

per′manent mag′net, a magnet that retains its magnetism after being removed from an external magnetic field. —**per′manent mag′netism.**

per′manent press′, (of a fabric) wrinkle-resistant and requiring little or no ironing after washing.

per′manent tooth′, any of the 32 adult teeth that replace the 20 milk teeth.

per′manent wave′, a wave that is set into the hair by the application of a special chemical preparation and that remains for a number of months.

per′manent way′, *Brit.* the roadbed and track of a railroad.

per·man·ga·nate (pər maŋ′gə nāt′), *n.* *Chem.* a salt of permanganic acid. Cf. **potassium permanganate.** [PERMANGAN(IC ACID) + -ATE[2]]

per·man·gan·ic (pûr′man gan′ik), *adj.* *Chem.* of or derived from permanganic acid. [PER- + MANGANIC]

per′mangan′ic ac′id, *Chem.* an acid, $HMnO_4$, known only in solution.

per·ma·tron (pûr′mə tron′), *n.* *Electronics.* a thermionic gas diode in which the flow of electrons is controlled by an external magnetic field instead of a grid. [PERMA(NENT) + -TRON]

per·me·a·bil·i·ty (pûr′mē ə bil′i tē), *n.* **1.** the property or state of being permeable. **2.** the magnetic permeance of a substance compared with that of air. **3.** *Aeron.* the rate at which gas is lost through the envelope of an aerostat, usually expressed as the number of liters thus diffused in one day through a square meter. **4.** *Naut.* the capacity of a space in a vessel to absorb water, measured with reference to its temporary or permanent contents and expressed as a percentage of the total volume of the space. [PERMEABLE + -ITY]

per·me·a·ble (pûr′mē ə bəl), *adj.* capable of being permeated. [late ME < L *permeābil(is),* equiv. to *permeā(re)* (to) PERMEATE + *-bilis* -BLE] —**per′me·a·ble·ness,** *n.* —**per′me·a·bly,** *adv.*

per·me·a·me·ter (pûr′mē ə mē′tər, pûr′mē am′i tər), *n.* an instrument for measuring magnetic permeability. [PERMEA(BILITY) + -METER]

per·me·ance (pûr′mē əns), *n.* **1.** the act of permeating. **2.** the conducting power of a magnetic circuit for magnetic flux; the reciprocal of magnetic reluctance. [PERME(ANT) + -ANCE]

per·me·ant (pûr′mē ənt), *adj.* permeating; pervading. [< L *permeant-* (s. of *permeāns*) permeating, prp. of *permeāre.* See PERMEATE, -ANT]

per·me·ate (pûr′mē āt′), *v.,* **-at·ed, -at·ing.** —*v.t.* **1.** to pass through the substance or mass of. **2.** to penetrate through the pores, interstices, etc., of. **3.** to be diffused through; pervade; saturate: *Cynicism permeated his report.* —*v.i.* **4.** to become diffused; penetrate. [< L *permeāt(us)* passed through, ptp. of *permeāre.* See PER-, MEATUS] —**per′me·a′tion,** *n.* —**per′me·a′tive,** *adj.* —**per′me·a′tor,** *n.*

per men·sem (per men′sem; *Eng.* pər men′səm), *Latin.* by the month.

Per·mi·an (pûr′mē ən), *adj.* **1.** *Geol.* noting or pertaining to a period of the Paleozoic era occurring from 220,000,000 to 270,000,000 years ago and characterized by the existence of many reptiles (formerly regarded as an epoch of the Carboniferous). See table under **era.** —*n.* **2.** *Geol.* the Permian period or system. **3.** a branch of Uralic, comprising certain Finno-Ugric languages, esp. Votyak and Zyrian, spoken in the northern Ural Mountains. [PERM + -IAN]

per mill (pər mil′), per thousand. Also, **per mil′.**

per·mil·lage (pər mil′ij), *n.* a rate or proportion per thousand. Cf. **percentage** (def. 1). [PER MILL + -AGE]

per·mis·si·ble (pər mis′ə bəl), *adj.* allowable; permitted: *a permissible amount of casualness under the circumstances.* [late ME < ML *permissibil(is).* See PERMISSION, -IBLE] —**per·mis′si·bil′i·ty, per·mis′si·ble·ness,** *n.* —**per·mis′si·bly,** *adv.*

per·mis·sion (pər mish′ən), *n.* **1.** the act of permitting; formal or express allowance or consent. **2.** liberty or license granted to do something. [late ME < L *permissiōn-* (s. of *permissiō*) a yielding, giving leave, equiv. to *permiss(us)* (ptp. of *permittere* to PERMIT) + *-iōn-* -ION] —**per·mis′sioned,** *adj.* —**per·mis·so·ry** (pər mis′ə rē), *adj.*
—**Syn. 2.** leave, consent. —**Ant. 2.** restraint, refusal.

per·mis·sive (pər mis′iv), *adj.* **1.** granting or denoting permission: *a permissive nod.* **2.** habitually or characteristically permitting or tolerating behavior that others might disapprove or forbid: *a permissive family.* [PERMISS(ION) + -IVE; cf. F *permissif*] —**per·mis′sive·ly,** *adv.* —**per·mis′sive·ness,** *n.*

per·mit[1] (*v.* pər mit′; *n.* pûr′mit, pər mit′), *v.,* **-mit·ted, -mit·ting,** *n.* —*v.t.* **1.** to allow to do something: *Permit me to explain.* **2.** to allow to be done or occur: *The law permits the sale of such drugs.* **3.** to tolerate; agree to: *a law permitting Roman Catholicism in England.* **4.** to afford opportunity for, or admit of: *vents to permit the escape of gases.* —*v.i.* **5.** to grant permission; allow liberty to do something. **6.** to afford opportunity or possibility: *Write when time permits.* **7.** to allow or admit (usually fol. by *of*): *statements that permit of no denial.* —*n.* **8.** a written order granting special permission to do something. **9.** an authoritative or official certificate of permission; license: *a fishing permit.* **10.** permission. [late ME < L *permitt(ere)* (to) let go through, give leave, equiv. to *per* PER + *mittere* to let or make (someone) go. See ADMIT, COMMIT, etc.] —**per·mit′ted·ly,** *adv.* —**per·mit·tee** (pûr′mi tē′), *n.* —**per·mit′ter,** *n.*
—**Syn. 1.** See **allow. 9.** franchise. —**Ant. 1.** refuse.

per·mit[2] (pûr′mit), *n.* a pompano, *Trachinotus falcatus,* found in the West Indies. [< Sp *palometa* (by folk etymology). See PALOMETA]

per·mit·tiv·i·ty (pûr′mi tiv′i tē), *n., pl.* **-ties.** See **dielectric constant.**

per·mon′o·sul·fu′ric ac′id (pər mon′ō sul fyo͝or′ik), *Chem.* See **persulfuric acid** (def. 1). [PER- + MONO- + SULFURIC ACID]

per·mu·tate (pûr′myə tāt′, pər myo͞o′tāt), *v.t.,* **-tat·ed, -tat·ing. 1.** to cause (something) to undergo permutation. **2.** to arrange (items) in a different sequence. [< L *permūtāt(us),* ptp. of *permūtāre* to PERMUTE; see -ATE[1]]

per·mu·ta·tion (pûr′myə tā′shən), *n.* **1.** *Math.* **a.** the act of changing the order of elements arranged in a particular order, as *abc* into *acb, bac,* etc., or of arranging a number of elements in groups made up of equal numbers of the elements in different orders, as *a* and *b* in *ab* and *ba;* a one-to-one transformation of a set with a finite number of elements. **b.** any of the resulting arrangements or groups. **2.** the act of permuting or permutating; alteration; transformation. [ME < L *permūtātiōn-* (s. of *permūtātiō*) thorough-going change. See PER-, MUTATION, PERMUTE] —**per′mu·ta′tion·al,** *adj.* —**per′mu·ta′tion·ist,** *n.*
—**Syn. 2.** arrangement, change.

permuta′tion ma′trix, *Math.* a square matrix in which 1 is an entry exactly once in each row and each column, all other entries being zero.

per·mute (pər myo͞ot′), *v.t.,* **-mut·ed, -mut·ing. 1.** to alter; change. **2.** *Math.* to subject to permutation. [< L *permūt(āre)* (to) change throughout. See PER-, MUTATE] —**per·mut′a·bil′i·ty, per·mut′a·ble·ness,** *n.* —**per·mut′a·ble,** *adj.* —**per·mut′a·bly,** *adv.* —**per·mut′er,** *n.*

Per·nam·bu·co (pûr′nam byo͞o′kō; *Port.* peʀ′nəm-bo͞o′ko͝o), *n.* Recife.

per·nan·cy (pûr′nən sē), *n.* *Law.* a taking or receiving, as of the rents or profits of an estate. [alter. of AF *pernance,* metathetic var. of OF *prenance,* lit., a taking, equiv. to *pren-,* pre-tonic s. of *prendre* to take (< L *pre(he)ndere;* see APPREHEND) + *-ance* -ANCE; see -ANCY]

per·ni·cious (pər nish′əs), *adj.* **1.** ruinous; injurious; hurtful: *pernicious teachings; a pernicious lie.* **2.** deadly; fatal: *a pernicious disease.* **3.** *Obs.* evil; wicked. [< L *perniciōs(us)* ruinous, equiv. to *pernici(ēs)* ruin (*per-* PER- + *nici-,* var. of *neci-,* s. of *nex* death + *-ēs* n. suffix) + *-ōsus* -OUS] —**per·ni′cious·ly,** *adv.* —**per·ni′cious·ness,** *n.*
—**Syn. 1.** harmful, detrimental, deleterious, destructive, damaging, baneful, noxious, malicious. **2.** lethal.

perni′cious ane′mia, *Pathol.* a severe anemia caused by the failure of the gastric mucosa to secrete the intrinsic factor necessary for the absorption of vitamin B_{12}, and characterized by a great reduction in the number of red blood cells, an increase in their size, and the presence in the blood of large, primitive cells that contain no hemoglobin.

per·nick·et·y (pər nik′i tē), *adj.* *Informal.* **1.** fastidious; fussy. **2.** requiring painstaking care. Also, **persnickety.** [orig. Scot] —**per·nick′et·i·ness,** *n.*

Per·nik (*Bulg.* peʀ′nik), *n.* former name of **Dimitrovo.**

per·ni·o (pûr′nē ō′), *n.* *Pathol.* chilblain. [< L, deriv. of *pern(a)* haunch of the leg; see -ION]

Per·nod (pâr nō′; *Fr.* peʀ nō′), *n.* *Trademark.* an anise- and licorice-flavored liqueur, originally from France.

per·nor (pûr′nər, -nôr), *n.* *Law.* one who takes or receives the rents, profits, or other benefit of an estate, lands, etc. [late ME *pernour* < AF, metathetic var. of OF *preneor* taker, equiv. to *pren-* (see PERNANCY) + *-eor* -OR[2]]

Pe·ro (pēr′ō), *n.* *Class. Myth.* a daughter of Neleus and Chloris who was given in marriage to Bias when he presented Neleus with the cattle of Phylacus.

Pe·rón (pə rōn′; *Sp.* pe ʀôn′), *n.* **1. E·va Duar·te de** (ē′və dwär′tā də; *Sp.* e′vä dwäʀ′te the), 1919–52, Argentine political figure (wife of Juan Perón). **2. Juan (Do·min·go)** (wän də miŋ′gō; *Sp.* hwän dō-miŋ′gō), 1895–1974, Argentine military and political leader: president 1946–55, 1973–74.

per·o·ne·al (per′ə nē′əl), *adj.* *Anat.* pertaining to or situated near the fibula. [< NL *peronē* the fibula (< Gk) + -AL[1]]

per·o·ne·us (per′ə nē′əs), *n., pl.* **-ne·i** (-nē′ī). *Anat.* any of several muscles on the outer side of the leg, the action of which assists in extending the foot and in turning it outward. [< NL: lit., of the fibula, equiv. to *peronē* the fibula (< Gk) + *-us* -OUS]

Pe·ro·nism (pə rō′niz əm), *n.* (*sometimes l.c.*) the principles or policies of Juan Perón. Also, **Pe·ro·nis·mo** (per′ə nēz′mō; *Sp.* pe′ʀô nēs′mô). [< Sp *peronismo(o).* See PERÓN, -ISM]

Pe·ro·nist (pə rō′nist), (*sometimes l.c.*) *n.* **1.** a supporter of Juan Perón. —*adj.* **2.** of or pertaining to Juan Perón or Peronism. [< Sp *peronist(a).* See PERÓN, -IST]

Pe·ro·nis·ta (per′ə nis′tə; *Sp.* pe′ʀô nēs′tä), *n., pl.* **-tas** (-təz; *Sp.* -täs). Peronist.

per·o·rate (per′ə rāt′), *v.i.,* **-rat·ed, -rat·ing. 1.** to speak at length; make a speech. **2.** to bring a speech to a close with a formal conclusion. [< L *perōrāt(us)* spoken fully or at the end, ptp. of *perōrāre.* See PER-, ORATE] —**per′o·ra′tor,** *n.*

per·o·ra·tion (per′ə rā′shən), *n.* *Rhet.* the concluding part of a speech or discourse, in which the speaker or writer recapitulates the principal points and urges them with greater earnestness and force. [< L *perōrātiōn-* (s. of *perōrātiō*) the closing of a speech. See PERORATE, -ION] —**per′o·ra′tion·al, per′o·ra′tive,** *adj.* —**per·or·a·tor·i·cal** (pə rôr′ə tôr′i kəl, -tor′-, -ror′-), *adj.* —**per·or′a·tor′i·cal·ly,** *adv.* —**per·or·a·tor·y** (pə rôr′ə tôr′ē, -tōr′ē), *n.*

pe·ro·sis (pə rō′sis), *n., pl.* **-ses** (-sēz). *Vet. Pathol.* a disorder of young chicks, turkeys, and other birds, caused by malnutrition and characterized by shortening and thickening of the limb bones, enlargement of the hock, and slipped tendons. Also called **slipped tendon.** [< NL < Gk *pēr(ós)* maimed, disabled + *-ōsis* -OSIS] —**pe·rot·ic** (pə rot′ik), *adj.*

Per·o·ti·nus (per′ə tī′nəs, -tē′-), *n.* (“*Magnus Magister*”) fl. late 12th to early 13th century, French composer. Also called **Per·o·tin** (per′ə tēn′), **Pé·ro·tin** (*Fr.* pā ʀô taN′).

Pe·ro·vo (pə rō′və; *Russ.* pyi ʀô′və), *n.* a former city in the W Russian Federation, incorporated into Moscow.

per·ox·i·dase (pə rok′si dās′, -dāz′), *n.* *Biochem.* any of a class of oxidoreductase enzymes that catalyze the oxidation of a compound by the decomposition of hydrogen peroxide or of an organic peroxide. [PEROXIDE + -ASE]

per·ox·i·date (pə rok′si dāt′), *v.t., v.i.,* **-dat·ed, -dat·ing.** *Chem.* peroxidize. [PER- + OXIDATE] —**per·ox′i·da′tion,** *n.*

per·ox·ide (pə rok′sīd), *n., v.,* **-id·ed, -id·ing.** —*n.* **1.** *Chem.* **a.** a compound containing the bivalent ion, -O-O-, derived from hydrogen peroxide, as sodium peroxide, NaOONa, or dimethyl peroxide, CH_3OOCH_3. **b.** that oxide of an element which contains an unusually large amount of oxygen. **c.** hydrogen peroxide, H_2O_2 or H-O-O-H. —*v.t.* **2.** to use peroxide as a bleaching agent on (esp. the hair). [PER- + OXIDE] —**per·ox·id·ic** (pûr′ok sid′ik), *adj.*

per·ox·i·dize (pə rok′si dīz′), *v.t., v.i.,* **-dized, -diz·ing.** *Chem.* to convert into a peroxide, esp. of the highest oxidation potential. [PEROXIDE + -IZE]

per·ox·y (pə rok′sē), *adj.* *Chem.* containing the peroxy group. [PER- + OXY-[2]]

peroxy-, a combining form denoting the peroxy group: *peroxyborate.*

per·ox·y·ac·id (pə rok′sē as′id), *n.* *Chem.* an acid derived from hydrogen peroxide and containing the -O-O- group, as peroxysulfuric acid, $H_2S_2O_8$.

per·ox·y·bo·rate (pə rok′sē bôr′āt, -it, -bōr′-), *n.* *Chem.* perborate. [PEROXY- + BORATE]

per·ox′y·bo′ric ac′id (pə rok′sē bôr′ik, -bōr′-, -rok′-), *Chem.* the hypothetical acid HBO_3, known only in the form of its salts, the perborates. [PEROXY- + BORIC ACID]

per·ox′y·di·sul·fu′ric ac′id (pə rok′sē dī′sul-fyo͝or′ik, -rok′-), *Chem.* See **persulfuric acid** (def. 2). [PEROXY- + DI-[1] + SULFURIC ACID]

perox′y group′, *Chem.* the bivalent group, $-O_2-$, derived from hydrogen peroxide. Also called **perox′y rad′ical.**

per·ox′y·mon·o·sul·fu′ric ac′id (pə rok′sē mon′ō sul fyo͝or′ik, -rok′-), *Chem.* See **persulfuric acid** (def. 1). [PEROXY- + MONO- + SULFURIC ACID]

per·ox′y·sul·fu′ric ac′id (pə rok′sē sul fyo͝or′ik, -rok′-), *Chem.* See **persulfuric acid** (def. 1). [PEROXY- + SULFURIC ACID]

per·pend[1] (pûr′pənd), *n.* a large stone passing through the entire thickness of a wall. Also, **parpen, perpent.** Also called **thorough stone, through stone.** [late ME < MF *perpain* < ?]

per·pend[2] (pər pend′), *Archaic.* —*v.t.* **1.** to consider. —*v.i.* **2.** to ponder; deliberate. [< L *perpend(ere)* (to) weigh carefully, ponder, equiv. to *per-* PER- + *pendere* to weigh]

per·pen·dic·u·lar (pûr′pən dik′yə lər), *adj.* **1.** vertical; upright. **2.** *Geom.* meeting a given line or surface at right angles. **3.** (*cap.*) noting or pertaining to the last style of English Gothic architecture, prevailing from the late 14th through the early 16th century and characterized by the use of predominantly vertical tracery, by an overall linear, shallow effect, by fine intricate stonework, and by such features as the four-centered arch, the lierne and tierceron, the fan vault, and the hammer-beam roof. **4.** maintaining a standing or upright position; standing up: *We engaged in a little perpendicular drinking the other night.* **5.** having a sharp pitch or slope; steep. —*n.* **6.** a perpendicular line or plane. **7.** an instrument for indicating the vertical line from any point. **8.** an upright position. **9.** moral uprightness; rectitude. **10.** *Naut.* either of two lines perpendicular to the keel line, base line, or designed water line of a vessel, the forward perpendicular line being taken through the fore part of the stem either at the uppermost strength deck or at the designed water line, the after perpendicular, being taken through the after side of the sternpost, the axis of the rudderpost or at some other point according to the type of stern. **11.** a sharply pitched or precipitously steep mountain face. [< L *perpendiculār(is)* vertical, equiv. to *perpendicul(um)* plumbline (see PERPEND[2], -I-, -CULE) + *-āris* -AR[1]; r. ME *perpendiculer* < AF] —**per′pen·dic′u·lar′i·ty, per′pen·dic′u·lar·ness,** *n.* —**per′pen·dic′u·lar·ly,** *adv.*
—**Syn. 1.** standing. See **upright.**
—**Ant. 1.** parallel.

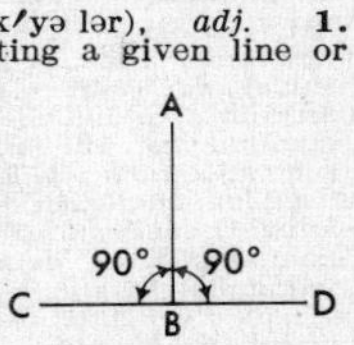

A
90° 90°
C B D
AB, Perpendicular to CD

per·pent (pûr′pənt), *n.* perpend[1].

per·pe·trate (pûr′pi trāt′), *v.t.,* **-trat·ed, -trat·ing. 1.** to perform, execute, or commit (a crime, wrong, etc.):

to perpetrate a murder. **2.** to carry out or enact (a prank, deception, etc.): *to perpetrate a hoax.* **3.** to present, execute, or do in a poor or tasteless manner: *who perpetrated this farce?* [< L *perpetrāt(us)* carried through (ptp. of *perpetrāre*), equiv. to *per-* PER- + *-petrā-* (var. s. of *patrāre* to father, bring about; see PATER) + *-tus* ptp. suffix] —**per·pe·tra·ble** (pûr′pi trə bəl), *adj.* —**per′pe·tra′tion,** *n.* —**per′pe·tra′tor,** *n.*

Per·pet·u·a (pər pech′o͞o ə), *n.* a girl's given name.

per·pet·u·al (pər pech′o͞o əl), *adj.* **1.** continuing or enduring forever. **2.** lasting an indefinitely long time: *perpetual snows.* **3.** continuing or continued without intermission or interruption: *a perpetual stream of visitors all day.* **4.** *Hort.* blooming more or less continuously throughout the season or the year. —*n.* **5.** a hybrid rose that is perpetual. [late ME *perpetuall* < L *perpetuāl(is)* permanent, equiv. to *perpetu(us)* uninterrupted (*per-* PER- + *petu-* (var. s. of *petere* to seek) + *-us* adj. suffix) + *-ālis* -AL[1]; r. ME *perpetuel* < MF] —**per·pet′u·al′i·ty, per·pet′u·al·ness,** *n.* —**per·pet′u·al·ly,** *adv.*
—**Syn. 1.** everlasting, permanent, enduring. See **eternal. 3.** continuous, ceaseless, incessant, constant, unending, uninterrupted. —**Ant. 1.** temporary. **3.** discontinuous.

perpet′ual adora′tion, *Rom. Cath. Ch.* uninterrupted adoration of the Blessed Sacrament.

perpet′ual cal′endar, a calendar devised to be used for many years, as in determining the day of the week on which a given date falls.

perpet′ual check′, *Chess.* **1.** a continuing series of checks resulting in a drawn game because they cannot be halted or evaded without resulting in checkmate or a serious disadvantage. **2.** the situation in which this occurs.

perpet′ual mo′tion, *Mech.* the motion of a theoretical mechanism that, without any losses due to friction or other forms of dissipation of energy, would continue to operate indefinitely at the same rate without any external energy being applied to it.

per·pet·u·ate (pər pech′o͞o āt′), *v.t.*, **-at·ed, -at·ing.** to make perpetual; preserve from extinction or oblivion: *to perpetuate one's name.* [< L *perpetuāt(us)* continued without interruption (ptp. of *perpetuāre*). See PERPETUAL, -ATE[1]] —**per·pet′u·a·ble,** *adj.* —**per·pet′u·a′tion, per·pet·u·ance** (pər pech′o͞o əns), *n.* —**per·pet′u·a′tor,** *n.*

per·pe·tu·i·ty (pûr′pi to͞o′i tē, -tyo͞o′-), *n., pl.* **-ties. 1.** the state or character of being perpetual (often prec. by *in*): *to desire happiness in perpetuity.* **2.** endless or indefinitely long duration or existence. **3.** something that is perpetual. **4.** an annuity paid for life. **5.** *Law.* (of property) an interest under which property is less than completely alienable for longer than the law allows. [late ME *perpetuite* < L *perpetuitās.* See PERPETUAL, -ITY]

per·phen·a·zine (pər fen′ə zēn′, -zin), *n.* *Pharm.* a crystalline, water-insoluble powder, $C_{21}H_{26}ClN_3OS$, used chiefly as a tranquilizer and in the treatment of nausea. [PER- + PHEN(OTHI)AZINE]

Per·pi·gnan (per pē nyäN′), *n.* a city in and the capital of Pyrénées-Orientales, in the S extremity of France. 86,156 (1962).

per·plex (pər pleks′), *v.t.* **1.** to cause to be puzzled or bewildered over what is not understood or certain; confuse mentally. **2.** to make complicated or confused, as a matter, question, etc. **3.** to hamper with complications, confusion, or uncertainty. [back formation from PERPLEXED] —**per·plex′er,** *n.* —**per·plex′ing·ly,** *adv.*
—**Syn. 1.** mystify, confound. **2.** tangle, snarl. **3.** vex, annoy, bother.

per·plexed (pər plekst′), *adj.* **1.** bewildered; puzzled: *a perplexed state of mind.* **2.** involved; entangled; complicated: *a perplexed question.* [ME *perplex* intricate, confused (< L *perplex(us)*; see PER-, COMPLEX) + -ED[2]] —**per·plex·ed·ly** (pər plek′sid lē), *adv.* —**per·plex′ed·ness,** *n.*

per·plex·i·ty (pər plek′si tē), *n., pl.* **-ties. 1.** the state of being perplexed; confusion; uncertainty. **2.** that which perplexes: *a case plagued with perplexities.* **3.** a tangled, involved, or confused condition or situation. [ME *perplexite* < OF < LL *perplexitāt-* (s. of *perplexitās*), equiv. to L *perplex(us)* (see PERPLEXED) + *-itāt-* -ITY]

per pro., per procurationem. Also, **per proc.**

per pro·cu·ra·ti·o·nem (pər prok′yə rā′shē ō′nem, per prok′ə rä′tē ō′nem), *Chiefly Law.* by one acting as an agent; by proxy. Also, **per procuration.** [< L]

per·qui·site (pûr′kwi zit), *n.* **1.** an incidental emolument, fee, or profit over and above fixed income, salary, or wages. **2.** Also called **perk, perq.** *Brit.* **a.** anything that has served its primary use and is then customarily allowed or given an employee, esp. a servant. **b.** a servant's customary right to claim such used or discarded items. **c.** *Informal.* any bonus or fringe benefit granted an employee, as free use of a company car. **3.** something demanded or due as a particular privilege: *homage that was once the perquisite of royalty.* [late ME < ML *perquīsīt(um)* something acquired, n. use of neut. of L *perquīsītus* diligently asked about or sought for (ptp. of *perquīrere*). See PER-, INQUISITIVE]

Per·rault (pe rō′; *Fr.* pe rō′), *n.* **1. Charles** (chärlz; *Fr.* sharl), 1628–1703, French poet, critic, and author of fairy tales. **2.** his brother, **Claude** (klōd; *Fr.* klōd), 1613–88, French architect, scientist, and physician.

Per·ret (pe rā′), *n.* **Au·guste** (ō gyst′), 1874–1954, French architect.

Per·rin (pe raN′), *n.* **Jean Bap·tiste** (zhäN ba tēst′), 1870–1942, French physicist and chemist: Nobel prize for physics 1926.

Per·rine (pûr′īn), *n.* a town in S Florida. 6424 (1960).

Per·ris (per′is), *n.* a town in S California. 2950 (1960).

per·ron (per′ən; *Fr.* pe rôN′), *n., pl.* **per·rons** (per′ənz; *Fr.* pe rôN′). *Archit.* an outside platform upon which the entrance door of a building opens, with steps leading to it. [ME < MF, equiv. to *perre* (< L *petra* rock) + *-on* aug. suffix]

Per·ron·et (pe rô ne′), *n.* **Jean Ro·dolphe** (zhäN rô dôlf′), 1708–94, French engineer

per·ru·quier (pe ro͞o kyā′; *Eng.* pə ro͞o′kē ər), *n., pl.* **-quiers** (-kyā′; *Eng.* -kē ərs). *French.* one who makes or sells perukes; wigmaker.

per·ry (per′ē), *n., pl.* **-ries.** *Brit.* a fermented beverage, similar to cider, made from the juice of pears. [ME *pereye* < MF *perey*, var. of *pere* << LL **pirātum* (L *pir(a)* pear + *-ātum*, neut. of *-ātus* -ATE[1])]

Per·ry (per′ē), *n.* **1. Antoinette,** 1888–1946, U.S. actress, theatrical manager, and producer. **2. Bliss,** 1860–1954, U.S. educator, literary critic, and editor. **3. Matthew Cal·braith** (kal′brāth), 1794–1858, U.S. commodore. **4.** his brother, **Oliver Hazard,** 1785–1819, U.S. naval officer. **5. Ralph Barton,** 1876–1957, U.S. philosopher and educator. **6.** a town in N Florida. 8030 (1960). **7.** a town in central Iowa. 6442 (1960). **8.** a town in central Georgia. 6032 (1960). **9.** a town in N Oklahoma. 5210 (1960). **10.** a boy's given name.

Per·rys·burg (per′ēz bûrg′), *n.* a town in NW Ohio. 5519 (1960).

Per·ry·ton (per′ē tən, -tᵊn), *n.* a town in N Texas. 7903 (1960).

Per·ry·ville (per′ē vil′), *n.* a town in E Missouri. 5117 (1960).

Pers, Persian.

Pers., **1.** Persia. **2.** Persian.

pers., **1.** person. **2.** personal.

Per·sa (pûr′sə), *n.* *Class. Myth.* a daughter of Oceanus and Tethys.

per·salt (pûr′sôlt′), *n.* *Chem.* **1.** (in a series of salts of a given metal or group) the salt in which the metal or group has a high, or the highest apparent, valence. **2.** (loosely) the salt of a peroxy acid. [PER- + SALT]

per se (pər sē′, sā′), by, of, for, or in itself; intrinsically.

perse (pûrs), *adj.* of a very deep shade of blue or purple. [ME *pers* < ML *pers(us)*, perh. var. of *perseus* kind of blue, itself alter. of L *Persicus* Persian]

Perse (pers, pûrs), *n.* **St.-John** (sin′jən), pen name of Alexis Saint-Léger Léger.

per′ sec′ond per′ sec′ond, a unit for expressing the rate of change of a rate of change, as of acceleration, which is the rate of change of velocity.

per·se·cute (pûr′sə kyo͞ot′), *v.t.*, **-cut·ed, -cut·ing. 1.** to pursue with harassing or oppressive treatment; harass persistently. **2.** to oppress with injury or punishment, for adherence to principles or religious faith. **3.** to annoy persistently; importune; trouble. [late ME, back formation from *persecutour* << LL *persecutor* persecutor, L: prosecutor, equiv. to *persecūt(us)* prosecuted, closely pursued (ptp. of *persequī*; see PER-, SEQUENCE) + *-or* -OR[2]] —**per′se·cut′ing·ly,** *adv.* —**per′se·cu′tive,** *adj.* —**per′se·cu′tive·ness,** *n.* —**per′se·cu′tor,** *n.* —**per·se·cu·to·ry** (pûr′sə kyo͞o′tə rē, pûr′sə kyo͞o′-; pûr′sə kyə tôr′ē, -tōr′ē, pər-sek′yə-), *adj.*
—**Syn. 1.** afflict. **2.** torture, torment. **3.** worry, badger, vex, bother, pester.

per·se·cu·tion (pûr′sə kyo͞o′shən), *n.* **1.** the act of persecuting. **2.** the state of being persecuted. **3.** a program or campaign to exterminate, drive away, or subjugate a people because of their religious, ethical, or moral beliefs or practices: *the persecutions of Christians by the Romans.* [ME *persecucio(u)n* < LL *persecūtiōn-* (s. of *persecūtiō*) persecution, L: prosecution, equiv. to *persecūt(us)* (see PERSECUTE) + *-iōn-* -ION] —**per′se·cu′tion·al,** *adj.*

Per·se·id (pûr′sē id), *n.* *Astron.* any of a shower of meteors appearing in August, and radiating from a point in the constellation Perseus. [< Gk, back formation from *Persēides* pl., taken to mean offspring of Perseus (constellation); see -ID[1]]

per·se·i·ty (pər sē′i tē, -sā′-), *n.* (in medieval philosophy) the quality of those things having substance independently of any real object. [< ML *perseitās*, equiv. to L *per sē* by itself (cf. Gk *kath' autó*) + *-itās* -ITY]

Per·seph·o·ne (pər sef′ə nē), *n.* **1.** Also, **Proserpina, Proserpine.** *Class. Myth.* a daughter of Zeus and Demeter, abducted by Pluto to be queen of Hades, but allowed to return to the surface of the earth for part of the year. **2.** a personification of spring. **3.** a girl's given name.

Per·sep·o·lis (pər sep′ə lis), *n.* an ancient capital of Persia: its imposing ruins are in S Iran, ab. 30 mi. NE of Shiraz. —**Per·se·pol·i·tan** (pûr′sə pol′i tᵊn), *adj., n.*

Per·se·us (pûr′sē əs, -so͞os), *n., gen.* **-se·i** (-sē ī′) for 3. **1.** *Class. Myth.* a hero, the son of Zeus and Danaë, who slew the Gorgon Medusa, and afterward saved Andromeda from a sea monster. **2.** (*italics.*) a representation in bronze (1545?–54?) by Benvenuto Cellini of Perseus holding aloft Medusa's head. **3.** *Astron.* a northern constellation between Cassiopeia and Taurus, containing the variable star Algol.

per·se·ver·ance (pûr′sə vēr′əns), *n.* **1.** steady persistence in a course of action, a purpose, a state, etc. **2.** *Theol.* continuance in a state of grace to the end, leading to eternal salvation. [ME *perseveraunce* < AF, MF *perseverance* < L *persevērantia.* See PERSEVERE, -ANCE] —**per′se·ver′ant,** *adj.*
—**Syn. 1.** doggedness, steadfastness. PERSEVERANCE, PERSISTENCE, TENACITY, PERTINACITY imply resolute and unyielding holding on, in following a course of action. PERSEVERANCE commonly suggests activity maintained in spite of difficulties; steadfast and long-continued application: *Endurance and perseverance combined to win in the end.* It is regularly used in a favorable sense. PERSISTENCE, which may be used in either a favorable or an unfavorable sense, implies unremitting (and sometimes annoying) perseverance: *persistence in a belief; persistence in talking when others wish to be quiet.* TENACITY, with the original meaning of adhesiveness, as of glue, is a dogged and determined holding on. Whether used literally or figuratively it has favorable implications: *a bulldog quality of tenacity; the tenacity of one's memory.* PERTINACITY, unlike its related word, is used chiefly in an unfavorable sense, that of over-insistent tenacity: *the pertinacity of the social climber.*

per·se·vere (pûr′sə vēr′), *v.*, **-vered, -ver·ing.** —*v.i.* **1.** to persist in anything undertaken; maintain a purpose in spite of difficulty or obstacles; continue steadfastly. **2.** to persist in speech, interrogation, argument, etc.; insist. —*v.t.* **3.** to bolster, sustain, or uphold: *unflagging faith that had persevered him.* [ME *persevere(n)* < MF *persever(er)* < L *persevērāre* to persist, deriv. of *persevērus* very strict. See PER-, SEVERE]
—**Syn. 1.** See **continue.**

per·se·ver·ing (pûr′sə vēr′ing), *adj.* displaying perseverance; persistent; steadfast: *a persevering student.* [PERSEVERE + -ING[2]] —**per′se·ver′ing·ly,** *adv.*

Per·shing (pûr′shing), *n.* **1. John Joseph** ("*Black-jack*"), 1860–1948, U.S. general: commander of the A.E.F. in World War I. **2.** *U.S.* a two-stage, surface-to-surface ballistic missile.

Per·sia (pûr′zhə, -shə), *n.* **1.** Also called **Per′sian Em′pire.** an ancient empire located in W and SW Asia: at its height it extended from Egypt and the Aegean to India; conquered by Alexander the Great 334–331 B.C. **2.** former official name (until 1935) of **Iran.** [< L, var. of *Persis* < Gk < OPers *Pārsa*]

Per·sian (pûr′zhən, -shən), *adj.* **1.** of or pertaining to Iran, its people, or their language. —*n.* **2.** a member of the native race of Iran, now a mixed race which is descended in part from the ancient Iranians. **3.** a citizen of ancient Persia. **4.** an Indo-European, Iranian language, the principal language of Iran, in its historical forms (Old Persian and Pahlavi) and modern form. **5.** *Archit.* a figure of a man used as a column. **6. Persians.** See **Persian blinds.** [PERSI(A) + -AN; r. ME *Persien* < MF, r. OE *Persisc*; see PERSE, -ISH[1]]

Per′sian blinds′, **1.** outside window shutters made of thin, movable horizontal slats. **2.** (loosely) Venetian blinds.

Per′sian car′pet, a handwoven carpet or rug produced in Iran and characterized by fine warp and filling yarns, a usually tight, even pile made with the Sehna knot, and a variety of floral, foliate, animal, and avian designs woven in rich, harmonious colors. Also called **Persian rug.**

Persian cat

Per′sian cat′, a long-haired variety of the domestic cat, originally raised in Persia and Afghanistan.

Per′sian Gulf′, an arm of the Arabian Sea, between SW Iran and Arabia. 600 mi. long.

Per′sian knot′. See **Sehna knot.**

Per′sian lamb′, **1.** the young lamb of the karakul sheep. **2.** the fur of this animal, of lustrous gray or dyed black or brown, used for women's coats, for hats, and for trimming on coats for both men and women; caracul.

Per′sian li′lac, an Asian lilac, *Syringa persica*, having pale reddish-purple flowers.

Per′sian mel′on, **1.** a round variety of muskmelon having a green, reticulate, unribbed rind and orange flesh. **2.** the plant bearing this fruit.

Per′sian rug′. See **Persian carpet.**

Persians, The, a tragedy (472 B.C.) by Aeschylus.

Per′sian wal′nut. See **English walnut.**

Per·si·chet·ti (pûr′sə ket′ē), *n.* **Vincent,** born 1915, U.S. composer.

per·si·ennes (pûr′zē enz′; *Fr.* per syen′), *n.* (*construed as pl.*) **1.** See **Persian blinds. 2.** (*construed as sing.*) a printed or painted fabric of cotton or silk. [< F, n. use of pl. of *persienne*, fem. of *persien*, obs. var. of *persan* PERSIAN]

per·si·flage (pûr′sə fläzh′; *Fr.* per sē flazh′), *n.* **1.** light, bantering talk. **2.** a frivolous style of treating a subject. [F, deriv. of *persifler* to banter, equiv. to *per-* PER- + *siffler* to whistle, hiss << L *sībilāre.* See SIBILANT, -AGE]
—**Syn. 1.** banter, badinage, jesting, pleasantry, frivolity.

per·sim·mon (pər sim′ən), *n.* **1.** any of several trees of the genus *Diospyros*, esp. *D. virginiana*, of North America, bearing astringent, plumlike fruit that is sweet and edible when ripe, and *D. Kaki*, of Japan and China, bearing soft, red or orange fruit. **2.** the fruit itself. [< Algonquian (Delaware) *pasimenan* (artificially) dried fruit]

Per·sis (pûr′sis), *n.* a girl's given name.

per·sist (pər sist′, -zist′), *v.i.* **1.** to continue steadily or firmly in some state, purpose, course of action, or the like, esp. in spite of opposition, remonstrance, etc.: *to persist in a belief; to persist in one's folly.* **2.** to last or endure: *The legend of Cleopatra has persisted for two thousand years.* **3.** to be insistent in a statement, request, question, etc. [< L *persist(ere)*, lit., to stand firm permanently, equiv. to *per-* PER- + *-sistere*, a comb. form of *stāre* to stand] —**per·sist′er,** *n.* —**per·sist′ing·ly,** *adv.* —**per·sis′tive,** *adj.* —**per·sis′tive·ly,** *adv.* —**per·sis′tive·ness,** *n.*
—**Syn. 1, 2.** See **continue. 3.** insist.

per·sist·ence (pər sis′təns, -zis′-), *n.* **1.** the act or fact of persisting. **2.** the quality of being persistent: *You have persistence, I'll say that for you.* **3.** continued existence or occurrence. **4.** the continuance of an effect after its cause is removed. Also, **per·sist′en·cy.** [PERSIST + -ENCE]
—**Syn. 1.** See **perseverance.**

persist′ence of vi′sion, the retention of a visual image for a short period of time after the removal of the stimulus that produced it.

per·sist·ent (pər sis′tənt, -zis′-), *adj.* **1.** persisting, esp. in spite of opposition; persevering: *a most annoyingly persistent young man.* **2.** lasting or enduring: *Walking through the house, I was aware of the persistent odor of verbena.* **3.** constantly repeated; continued: *persistent noise.* **4.** *Biol.* continuing or permanent. **5.** *Zool.* perennial; holding to morphological character, or continuing in function or activity. [< L *persistent-* (s. of *persistēns*) persisting, prp. of *persistere.* See PERSIST, -ENT] —**per·sist′ent·ly,** *adv.*
—**Syn. 1.** indefatigable, pertinacious, tenacious. See **stubborn. 3.** steady. —**Ant. 3.** sporadic.

Per·sius (pûr′shəs, -shē əs), *n.* (*Aulus Persius Flaccus*) A.D. 34–62, Roman satirist.

per·snick·e·ty (pər snik′i tē), *adj.* *Informal.* pernickety. —**per·snick′et·i·ness,** *n.*

per·son (pûr′sən), *n.* **1.** a human being, whether man, woman, or child: *Four persons saw him.* **2.** a human being as distinguished from an animal or a thing. **3.** *Sociol.* an individual human being, esp. with reference to his social relationships and behavioral patterns as conditioned by his culture. **4.** *Philos.* a self-conscious or rational being. **5.** the actual self or individual personality of a human being: *You ought not to generalize, but to consider the person you are dealing with.* **6.** the body of a living human being, sometimes including the clothes being worn: *He had no money on his person.* **7.** the body in its external aspect: *an attractive person to look at.* **8.** a character, part, or role, as in a play, story, etc. **9.** an individual of distinction or importance. **10.** one not entitled to social recognition or respect. **11.** *Law.* a human being **(natural person)** or a group of human beings, a corporation, a partnership, an estate, or other legal entity **(artificial person** or **juristic person)** recognized by law as having rights and duties. **12.** *Gram.* a category found in many languages that is used to distinguish between the speaker of an utterance and those to or about whom he is speaking. In English there are three persons in the pronouns, the first represented by *I* and *we*, the second by *you*, and the third by *he, she, it,* and *they*. Most verbs have distinct third person singular forms in the present tense, as *writes;* the verb *be* has, in addition, a first person singular form *am.* **13.** *Theol.* any of the three hypostases or modes of being in the Trinity, namely the Father, the Son, and the Holy Ghost. **14. in person,** in one's own bodily presence; personally: *Applicants are requested to apply in person.* [ME *persone* < L *persōna* role (in life, a play, a tale), LL: member (of the Trinity), orig. actor's mask]

—Syn. 1. PERSON, INDIVIDUAL, PERSONAGE are terms applied to human beings. PERSON is the most general and common word: *the average person.* INDIVIDUAL views a person as standing alone or as a single member of a group: *the characteristics of the individual;* its implication is sometimes derogatory: *a disagreeable individual.* PERSONAGE is used (sometimes ironically) of an outstanding or illustrious person: *We have a distinguished personage visiting us today.*

per·so·na (pər sō′nə), *n., pl.* **-nae** (-nē), **-nas. 1.** a person. **2. personae,** the characters in a play, novel, etc. **3.** the speaker of a poem or other literary work, not necessarily identical with the author. **4.** (in the psychology of C. G. Jung) the public personality; the mask or façade presented to satisfy the demands of the situation or the environment and not representing the inner personality of the individual (contrasted with *anima*). [< L *persōna* mask, character. See PERSON]

per·son·a·ble (pûr′sə nə bəl), *adj.* of pleasing personal appearance; handsome or comely; attractive: *a personable young woman.* [late ME; see PERSON, -ABLE] **—per′son·a·ble·ness,** *n.* **—per′son·a·bly,** *adv.*

Per·so·nae (pər sō′nē), *n.* a collection of poems (1926) by Ezra Pound.

per·son·age (pûr′sə nij), *n.* **1.** a person of distinction or importance. **2.** any person. **3.** a character in a play, story, etc. [late ME: body or image (statue, portrait) of a person (cf. ML *personagium*). See PERSON, -AGE]
—Syn. 1. See **person.**

per·so·na gra·ta (per sō′nä grä′tä; *Eng.* pər sō′nə grä′tə, grā′tə), *pl.* **per·so·nae gra·tae** (per sō′nī grä′tī; *Eng.* pər sō′nē grä′tē, grā′-). *Latin.* an acceptable person, esp. a diplomatic representative acceptable to the government to which he is accredited.

per·son·al (pûr′sə nᵊl), *adj.* **1.** of, pertaining to, or coming as from a particular person; individual; private: *a merely personal opinion, based on guesswork.* **2.** relating to, directed to, or intended for a particular person: *a personal favor; one's personal life; a letter marked "Personal."* **3.** referring or directed to a particular person in a disparaging or offensive sense or manner: *personal remarks.* **4.** making personal remarks or attacks: *to become personal in a dispute.* **5.** done, effected, held, etc., in person: *a personal conference.* **6.** pertaining to or characteristic of a person, or self-conscious being: *That is my personal belief.* **7.** of the nature of an individual rational being. **8.** pertaining to one's person, or bodily aspect: *personal cleanliness.* **9.** *Gram.* **a.** noting person: *In Latin* portō *"I carry,"* -ō *is a personal ending.* **b.** of, pertaining to, or characteristic of the personal pronoun. **10.** of or pertaining to personal property: *personal interests.* **11.** *U.S. Journalism.* **a.** a short news paragraph in a newspaper concerning a particular person, as one who is socially prominent, or a group of particular persons who are socially prominent. **b.** a brief, private notice in a newspaper or magazine, often addressed to a particular person and typically bearing an abbreviated salutation and signature to preserve its confidentiality, usually printed in a special part of the classified advertising section. [ME < LL *persōnāl(is).* See PERSON, -AL[1]] **—per′son·al·ness,** *n.*

per′sonal effects′, privately owned articles consisting chiefly of clothing, toilet items, etc., for intimate use by an individual. Cf. **household effects.**

per′sonal equa′tion, the tendency to personal bias which accounts for variation in interpretation or approach and for which allowance must be made.

per·so·na·li·a (pûr′sə nā′lē ə, -nāl′yə), *n.pl.* **1.** personal belongings. **2.** biographical data, personal reminiscences, or the like: *He could never keep the personalia out of his essays.* [< LL, neut. pl. of L *persōnālis* PERSONAL]

per·son·al·ise (pûr′sə nᵊlīz′), *v.t.,* **-ised, -is·ing.** *Chiefly Brit.* personalize. **—per′son·al·i·sa′tion,** *n.*

per·son·al·ism (pûr′sə nᵊliz′əm), *n.* a modern philosophical movement locating ultimate value and reality in persons, human or divine. Also called **per′sonal ide′alism.** [PERSONAL + -ISM] **—per′son·al·ist,** *n.* **—per′son·al·is′tic,** *adj.*

per·son·al·i·ty (pûr′sə nal′i tē), *n., pl.* **-ties. 1.** the visible aspect of one's character, as it impresses others: *He has a pleasing personality.* **2.** a person as an embodiment of a collection of qualities: *He is a curious personality.* **3.** *Psychol.* **a.** the sum total of the physical, mental, emotional, and social characteristics of an individual. **b.** the organized pattern of behavioral characteristics of the individual. **4.** the quality of being a person; existence as a self-conscious human being; personal identity. **5.** the essential character of a person. **6.** something apprehended as reflective of or analogous to a distinctive human personality, as the atmosphere of a place or thing: *This house has a warm personality, with all its chintzes and woodwork.* **7.** application or reference to a particular person or particular persons, often in disparagement or hostility. **8.** a disparaging or offensive statement referring to a particular person: *The conversation deteriorated into personalities.* **9.** a famous, notable, or prominent person; celebrity. **10.** *Geog.* the distinguishing or peculiar characteristics of a region. [ME *personalite* < LL *persōnālitās.* See PERSONAL, -ITY]
—Syn. 1. See **character.**

per·son·al·ize (pûr′sə nᵊlīz′), *v.t.,* **-ized, -iz·ing. 1.** to make personal, as by applying a general statement to oneself. **2.** to ascribe personal qualities to; personify. **3.** to have marked with one's initials, name, or monogram: *to personalize stationery.* Also, *esp. Brit.,* **personalise.** [PERSONAL + -IZE] **—per′son·al·i·za′tion,** *n.*

per′sonal lib′erty, the liberty of an individual to do his will freely except for such restraints imposed by law to safeguard the physical, moral, political, and economic welfare of others.

per·son·al·ly (pûr′sə nᵊlē), *adv.* **1.** as regards oneself: *Personally, I don't care to go.* **2.** as an individual: *to like someone personally, but not as an employee.* **3.** through direct contact; in person; directly: *I will thank him personally.* **4.** as if intended for or directed at one's own person: *to take someone's comments personally.* [ME; see PERSONAL, -LY]

per′sonal pro′noun, *Gram.* any one of the pronouns used to refer to the speaker, or to one or more to or about whom or which he is speaking, as, in English, *I, we, you, he, she, it, they.*

per′sonal prop′erty, *Law.* an estate or property consisting of movable articles both corporeal, as furniture or jewelry, or incorporeal, as stocks or bonds (distinguished from *real property*).
—Syn. chattels, effects.

per′sonal shop′per, an employee of a department store or the like who assists customers in selecting merchandise or who personally chooses items to fill mail or telephone orders.

per′sonal staff′, *Mil., Navy.* the aides of a general officer or a flag officer. Cf. **general staff, special staff.**

per·son·al·ty (pûr′sə nᵊl tē), *n., pl.* **-ties.** *Law.* personal estate or property. [< AF *personalte* < LL *persōnālitās* PERSONALITY]

per·so·na non gra·ta (per sō′nä nōn grä′tä; *Eng.* pər sō′nə non grä′tə, grā′-), *pl.* **per·so·nae non gra·tae** (per sō′nī nōn grä′tī; *Eng.* pər sō′nē non grä′tē, grā′-). *Latin.* **1.** an unacceptable person, esp. a diplomatic representative unacceptable to the government to which he is accredited. **2.** a person who is not welcome: *He has become* persona non grata *in our club since his angry outburst.*

per·son·ate[1] (pûr′sə nāt′), *v.,* **-at·ed, -at·ing.** *—v.t.* **1.** to act or portray (a character in a play, a part, etc.). **2.** to assume the character or appearance of; pass oneself off as, esp. with fraudulent intent. **3.** to represent in terms of personal properties or characteristics; personify. *—v.i.* **4.** to act or play a part. [v. use of L *persōnātus* assumed, feigned, lit., masked. See PERSON, -ATE[1]] **—per′son·a′tion,** *n.* **—per′son·a′tive,** *adj.* **—per′son·a′tor,** *n.*

per·son·ate[2] (pûr′sə nit, -nāt′), *adj.* **1.** *Bot.* **a.** (of a bilabiate corolla) masklike. **b.** having the lower lip pushed upward so as to close the gap between the lips, as in the snapdragon. **2.** *Zool.* **a.** having a masked or disguised form, as the larvae of certain insects. **b.** having masklike markings. [< NL, L. See PERSONATE[1]] **—per′son·ate·ly,** *adv.*

per·son·i·fi·ca·tion (pər son′ə fə kā′shən), *n.* **1.** the attribution of personal nature or character to inanimate objects or abstract notions, esp. as a rhetorical figure. **2.** the representation of a thing or abstraction in the form of a person, as in art. **3.** the person or thing embodying a quality or the like; an embodiment: *He is the personification of tact.* **4.** an imaginary person or creature conceived or figured to represent a thing or abstraction. **5.** the act of personifying. **6.** *Psychiatry.* a type of projection in which an individual, as a result of a frustrating experience, attributes favorable or unfavorable deeds or motives to another person. **7.** a character portrayal or representation in a dramatic or literary work. [PERSONI(FY) + -FICATION] **—per·son′i·fi·ca′tor,** *n.*

per·son·i·fy (pər son′ə fī′), *v.t.,* **-fied, -fy·ing. 1.** to attribute personal nature or character to (an inanimate object or an abstraction), as in speech or writing. **2.** to represent (a thing or abstraction) in the form of a person, as in art. **3.** to embody (a quality, idea, etc.) in a real person or a concrete thing. **4.** to be an embodiment of; typify: *He personifies the caginess and acquisitiveness of the peasant.* **5.** to personate. [PERSON + -IFY; cf. F *personnifier,* It *personificare*] **—per·son′i·fi′a·ble,** *adj.* **—per·son′i·fi′ant,** *adj.* **—per·son′i·fi′er,** *n.*

per·son·nel (pûr′sə nel′), *n.* the body of persons employed in any work, undertaking, or service (distinguished from *matériel*). [< F, n. use of *personnel* (adj.) PERSONAL; r. *personal* (n.), equiv. to G *Personal,* var. of *Personale* < LL, neut. of *persōnālis* PERSONAL; cf. It, Dan *personale*]

personnel′ a′gency, an agency for placing employable persons in jobs; employment agency.

personnel′ depart′ment, the department of a business firm that deals with problems affecting the employees of the firm and that usually interviews applicants for jobs.

per·son-to-per·son (pûr′sən tə pûr′sən), *adj.* **1.** (of a long-distance telephone call) chargeable only upon speaking with a specified person at the number called: *a person-to-person call from California.* Cf. **station-to-station. 2.** through or involving personal contact or meeting: *person-to-person diplomacy; The disease is contracted through person-to-person contacts.* *—adv.* **3.** (in making a long-distance telephone call) to one specified person: *I telephoned him person-to-person.* Cf. **station-to-station. 4.** face-to-face; in person: *They interviewed her person-to-person.*

per·sorp·tion (pər sôrp′shən, -zôrp′-), *n.* *Physical Chem.* the deep penetration of a liquid into a highly porous solid, resulting in an intimate mixture. [PER- + (AD)SORPTION]

per·spec·tive (pər spek′tiv), *n.* **1.** a technique of depicting volumes and spacial relationships on a flat surface. Cf. **aerial perspective; linear perspective. 2.** a picture employing this technique, esp. one in which it is prominent: *an architect's perspective of a house.* **3.** a visible scene, esp. one extending to a distance; vista: *a perspective on the main axis of an estate.* **4.** the state of existing in space before the eye: *The elevations look all right, but the building's composition is a failure in perspective.* **5.** the state of one's ideas, the facts known to one, etc., in having a meaningful interrelationship: *You have to live here a few years to see local conditions in perspective.* **6.** the faculty of seeing all the relevant data in a meaningful relationship: *Your work is admirably detailed but it lacks perspective.* **7.** a mental view or prospect: *the dismal perspective of one's declining years.* **8.** *Obs.* an optical glass. *—adj.* **9.** of or pertaining to the art of perspective, or represented according to its laws. [ME < ML *perspectīva (ars)* optical (science), *perspectīvum* optical glass, n. uses of fem. and neut. of *perspectīvus* optical < L *perspect(us)* seen through (see PER-, (IN)SPECT) + *-īvus* -IVE] **—per·spec′tiv·al,** *adj.* **—per·spec′tived,** *adj.* **—per·spec′tive·less,** *adj.* **—per·spec′tive·ly,** *adv.*

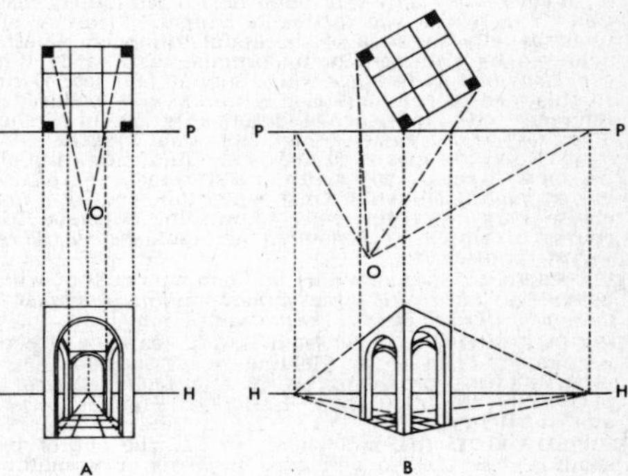

Perspective
A, One-point perspective; B, Two-point perspective; H, Horizon; O, Position of observer; P, Picture plane

per·spec·tiv·ism (pər spek′tə viz′əm), *n.* *Philos.* the doctrine that reality is known only in terms of the perspectives of it seen by individuals or groups at particular moments. [< G *Perspektivismus.* See PERSPECTIVE, -ISM] **—per·spec′tiv·ist,** *n., adj.*

Per·spex (pûr′speks), *n.* *Trademark. Chiefly Brit.* a clear plastic prepared by the polymerization of methyl methacrylate.

per·spi·ca·cious (pûr′spə kā′shəs), *adj.* **1.** having keen mental perception; discerning: *to exhibit perspicacious judgment.* **2.** *Archaic.* having keen sight. [PERSPICACI(TY) + -OUS] **—per′spi·ca′cious·ly,** *adv.* **—per′spi·ca′cious·ness,** *n.*
—Syn. 1. perceptive, acute, penetrating. **—Ant. 1.** dull, stupid.

per·spi·cac·i·ty (pûr′spə kas′i tē), *n.* **1.** keenness of mental perception; discernment; penetration. **2.** *Archaic.* keenness of sight. [earlier *perspicacite* < LL *perspicācitās* sharpness of sight, equiv. to *perspicāci-* (s. of *perspicax* sharp-sighted; see PERSPICUOUS) + *-tās* -TY[2]]
—Syn. 1. shrewdness, acuity, astuteness, insight, acumen. See **perspicuity. —Ant. 1.** obtuseness.

per·spi·cu·i·ty (pûr′spə kyōō′i tē), *n.* **1.** clearness or lucidity, as of a statement. **2.** the quality of being perspicuous. **3.** perspicacity. [late ME *perspicuitie* < L *perspicuitās.* See PERSPICU(OUS), -ITY]
—Syn. 1. clarity, plainness, intelligibility. **2.** transparency. **3.** PERSPICUITY and PERSPICACITY are not properly synonyms, but for several centuries the first has been confused with the second. Both are derived from a Latin word meaning to see through clearly. PERSPICACITY refers to the power of seeing clearly, to clearness of insight or judgment: *a man of acute perspicacity; the perspicacity of his judgment.* PERSPICUITY refers to that which can be seen through, i.e., to lucidity, clearness of style or exposition, freedom from obscurity: *the perspicuity of his argument.* **—Ant. 2.** dimness, opacity.

per·spic·u·ous (pər spik′yōō əs), *adj.* **1.** clear to the understanding. **2.** clear in expression or statement; lucid. **3.** perspicacious. [late ME < L *perspicuus* transparent, equiv. to *perspicu-* (var. of *perspici-,* s. of *perspicere* to look or see through (*per-* PER- + *-spicere,* comb. form of *specere* to look)) + *-us* -OUS] **—per·spic′u·ous·ly,** *adv.* **—per·spic′u·ous·ness,** *n.*
—Syn. 2. intelligible, plain, distinct, explicit. **—Ant. 2.** obscure, indistinct.

per·spi·ra·tion (pûr′spə rā′shən), *n.* **1.** the act or process of perspiring. **2.** that which is perspired; sweat. [< medical NL *perspīrātiōn-* (s. of *perspīrātiō*) insensible sweating, lit., a breathing through. See PERSPIRE, -ATION]
—Syn. 2. PERSPIRATION, SWEAT refer (primarily) to moisture exuded (by animals and people) from the pores of the skin. PERSPIRATION is the more refined and elegant word, and is often used overfastidiously by those who consider SWEAT coarse; but SWEAT is a strong word and in some cases obviously more appropriate: *a light perspiration; the sweat of his brow.* SWEAT is always used when referring to animals or objects: *Sweat drips from a horse's flanks.* It may also be used metaphorically of objects: *Sweat forms on apples after they are gathered.*

per·spir·a·to·ry (pər spī′rə tôr′ē, -tōr′ē), *adj.* of, pertaining to, or stimulating perspiration. [PERSPIRA-T(ION) + -ORY[1]]

per·spire (pər spīᵊr′), *v.,* **-spired, -spir·ing.** *—v.i.* **1.** to excrete watery fluid through the pores; sweat. *—v.t.* **2.** to emit through pores; exude. [< L *perspīr(āre)* (to) blow constantly (said of the wind), lit., to breathe through; in NL: to sweat insensibly. See PER-, INSPIRE] **—per·spir′a·bil′i·ty,** *n.* **—per·spir′a·ble,** *adj.* **—per·spir′ing·ly,** *adv.* **—per·spir′y,** *adj.*

per stir·pes (pər stûr′pēz), *Law.* pertaining to or noting a method of dividing an estate in which the descendants of a deceased legatee share as a group in the portion to which the deceased would have been entitled. Cf. **per capita** (def. 2). [< L: lit., by stock]

per·suade (pər swād′), *v.t.*, **-suad·ed, -suad·ing.** **1.** to prevail on (a person) to do something, as by advising, urging, etc.: *We could not persuade him to wait.* **2.** to induce to believe; convince: *Can I not persuade you that this is so?* [< L *persuād(ēre).* See PER-, DISSUADE, SUASION] —**per·suad′a·bil′i·ty, per·suad′a·ble·ness,** *n.* —**per·suad′a·ble,** *adj.* —**per·suad′a·bly,** *adv.* —**per·suad′ed·ly,** *adv.* —**per·suad′ed·ness,** *n.* —**per·suad′ing·ly,** *adv.*
—**Syn. 1.** urge, influence, move, entice, impel. PERSUADE, INDUCE, CONVINCE imply influencing someone's thoughts or actions. PERSUADE and INDUCE (followed by the infinitive) are used today mainly in the meaning of winning over a person to a certain course of action: *It was I who persuaded him to call a doctor. I induced him to do it.* They differ in that PERSUADE suggests appealing more to the reason and understanding: *I persuaded him to go back to his wife* (although it is often lightly used: *Can't I persuade you to stay to supper?*); INDUCE emphasizes only the idea of successful influence, whether achieved by argument or by promise of reward: *What can I say that will induce you to stay at your job?* Owing to this idea of compensation, INDUCE may be used in reference to the influence of factors as well as of persons: *The prospect of a raise of salary was what induced him to stay.* CONVINCE means to satisfy the understanding of a person with regard to a truth or a statement: *to convince one by quoting statistics.* Only when followed by a *that*-clause may CONVINCE refer to winning a person to a course of action: *I convinced her that she should go.* —**Ant. 1.** dissuade.

per·suad·er (pər swā′dər), *n.* one who or that which persuades: *The cool lake was a most enticing persuader for those who liked to swim.* [PERSUADE + -ER[1]]

per·sua·si·ble (pər swā′sə bəl), *adj.* capable of being persuaded; open to or yielding to persuasion. [< L *persuāsibil(is)* convincing, equiv. to *persuās(us)* (ptp. of *persuādēre* to PERSUADE) + *-ibil(is)* -IBLE] —**per·sua′si·bil′i·ty,** *n.*

per·sua·sion (pər swā′zhən), *n.* **1.** the act of persuading or seeking to persuade. **2.** power of persuading; persuasive force. **3.** the state or fact of being persuaded or convinced. **4.** a conviction or belief. **5.** a form or system of belief, esp. religious belief: *the Quaker persuasion.* **6.** a sect, group, or faction holding or advocating a particular belief, idea, ideology, etc.: *Several of the people present are of the socialist persuasion.* **7.** (*cap., italics.*) a novel (1818) by Jane Austen. **8.** *Informal.* kind or sort. [late ME < L *persuāsiōn-* (s. of *persuāsiō*; see PER-, SUASION); r. ME *persuacioun* < MF *persuacion*]
—**Syn. 1.** See **advice.**

per·sua·sive (pər swā′siv), *adj.* **1.** able, fitted, or intended to persuade: *a very persuasive argument.* —*n.* **2.** something that persuades; inducement. [ML *persuāsīv(us).* See PERSUASIBLE, -IVE] —**per·sua′sive·ly,** *adv.* —**per·sua′sive·ness,** *n.*

per·sul·fate (pər sul′fāt), *n. Chem.* a salt of persulfuric acid, as potassium persulfate, $K_2S_2O_5$ or $K_2S_2O_8$. [PER- + SULFATE]

per′sul·fu′ric ac′id (pûr′sul fyo͝or′ik, pûr′-), *Chem.* **1.** Also called **permonosulfuric acid, peroxymonosulfuric acid, peroxysulfuric acid, Caro's acid.** a white crystalline solid, H_2SO_5, used as an oxidizing agent for certain organic compounds. **2.** Also called **peroxydisulfuric acid.** a white, crystalline solid, $H_2S_2O_8$, used in the manufacture of hydrogen peroxide. [PER- + SULFURIC]

pert (pûrt), *adj.* **1.** bold; forward; impertinent; saucy. **2.** lively; sprightly; in good health. **3.** *Obs.* clever. [ME, aph. var. of *apert* < L *apert(us)* open (ptp. of *aperīre*; see APERIENT) + OF *apert* < L *expert(us)* EXPERT] —**pert′ly,** *adv.* —**pert′ness,** *n.*
—**Syn. 1.** presumptuous, impudent.

PERT (pûrt), *n.* a management method of controlling and analyzing a system or program using periodic time and money reports to determine dollar and labor status at any given time. [*P(rogram) E(ducation and) R(eview) T(echnique)*]

pert., pertaining.

per·tain (pər tān′), *v.i.* **1.** to have reference or relation; relate: *documents pertaining to the case.* **2.** to belong or be connected as a part, adjunct, possession, attribute, etc. **3.** to belong properly or fittingly; be appropriate. [ME *perte(i)ne, parte(i)ne* < MF *partenir* < L *pertinēre* to be applicable, lit., to hold through, reach, equiv. to *per-* PER- + *-tinēre,* comb. form of *tenēre* to hold]

Perth (pûrth), *n.* **1.** Also called **Perthshire.** a county in central Scotland. 127,018 (1961); 2493 sq. mi. **2.** its county seat: a port on the Tay River. 41,199 (1961). **3.** a city in and the capital of Western Australia, in SW Australia. 420,133 with suburbs (1961).

Perth′ Am′boy (am′boi), a seaport in E New Jersey. 38,007 (1960).

perth·ite (pûr′thīt), *n.* a variety of pegmatite containing irregular bands of albite in microcline. [named after *Perth,* Ontario, Canada; see -ITE[1]] —**per·thit·ic** (pər thit′ik), *adj.* —**per·thit′i·cal·ly,** *adv.*

Perth·shire (pûrth′shēr, -shər), *n.* Perth (def. 1).

per·ti·na·cious (pûr′tᵊnā′shəs), *adj.* **1.** holding tenaciously to a purpose, course of action, or opinion; stubborn. **2.** extremely persistent: *a pertinacious salesman from whom I could not escape.* [PERTINACI(TY) + -OUS] —**per′ti·na′cious·ly,** *adv.* —**per′ti·na′cious·ness,** *n.*
—**Syn. 1.** persevering. **2.** dogged.

per·ti·nac·i·ty (pûr′tᵊnas′i tē), *n.* the quality of being pertinacious; persistence. [< LL *pertinācitās* for L *pertinācia* stubbornness, perseverance, equiv. to *pertināci-* (s. of *pertināx*) steadfast, stubborn + *-tās* -TY[2]. See PER-, TENACITY]
—**Syn.** firmness, determination, resolution. See **perseverance.**

per·ti·nent (pûr′tᵊnənt), *adj.* pertaining or relating to the matter at hand; relevant: *pertinent details.* [late ME < L *pertinent-* (s. of *pertinēns*) pertaining, prp. of *pertinēre.* See PERTAIN, -ENT] —**per′ti·nence, per′ti·nen·cy,** *n.* —**per′ti·nent·ly,** *adv.*
—**Syn.** appropriate, fitting, fit, suitable, applicable. See **apt.** —**Ant.** irrelevant.

per·turb (pər tûrb′), *v.t.* **1.** to disturb or disquiet greatly in mind; agitate. **2.** to throw into great disorder; derange. **3.** *Astron.* to produce deviations in the orbit of (a celestial body) by the action of a force additional to the gravitational attraction of a spherical primary. [ME *perturbe* < L *perturb(āre)* (to) throw into confusion, equiv. to *per-* PER- + *turbāre* to disturb; see TURBID] —**per·turb′a·bil′i·ty,** *n.* —**per·turb′a·ble,** *adj.* —**per·tur·ba·tious** (pûr′tər bā′shəs), *adj.* —**per·turb·ed·ly** (pər tûr′bid lē), *adv.* —**per·turb′ed·ness,** *n.* —**per·turb′er, per·tur·ba·tor** (pûr′tər bā′tər), *n.* —**per·turb′ing·ly,** *adv.* —**per·turb′ment,** *n.*
—**Syn. 1.** trouble. **2.** confuse, addle, muddle. —**Ant. 1.** pacify.

per·tur·ba·tion (pûr′tər bā′shən), *n.* **1.** the act of perturbing. **2.** the state of being perturbed. **3.** mental disquiet or agitation. **4.** a cause of mental agitation. **5.** *Astron.* deviation of a celestial body from a regular orbit about its primary, caused by the presence of one or more other bodies that act upon the celestial body. [< L *perturbātiōn-* (s. of *perturbātiō*; see PERTURB, -ATION); r. ME *perturbacioun* < AF] —**per′tur·ba′tion·al,** *adj.*

per·tur·ba·tive (pûr′tər bā′tiv, pər tûr′bə tiv), *adj. Rare.* having a tendency to perturb; disturbing. [< LL *perturbātīv(us).* See PERTURBAT(ION), -IVE]

per·tus·sis (pər tus′is), *n. Pathol.* See **whooping cough.** [< NL, L *per-* PER- + *tussis* a cough] —**per·tus′sal,** *adj.*

Pe·ru (pə ro͞o′), *n.* a republic in W South America. 10,364,620 (1961); 496,222 sq. mi. *Cap.:* Lima. Spanish, **Pe·rú** (pe ro͞o′). —**Pe·ru·vi·an** (pə ro͞o′vē ən), *adj., n.*

Peru′ bal′sam, a dark, molasseslike, aromatic, water-insoluble liquid having a warm, bitter taste, obtained from the leguminous tree, *Myroxylon Pereirae,* of Central America: used in medicine, perfumery, and in the manufacture of chocolate. Also called **balsam of Peru, Peruvian balsam, black balsam, China oil, Indian balsam.**

Peru′ Cur′rent, a cold Pacific Ocean current flowing N along the coasts of Chile and Peru. Also called **Humboldt Current.**

Pe·ru·gia (pe ro͞o′jä; *Eng.* pə ro͞o′jə), *n.* **1.** a city in central Umbria, in central Italy. 109,596 (1961). **2. Lake of.** See **Trasimeno.** —**Pe·ru·gian** (pə ro͞o′jən, -jē ən), *adj., n.*

Pe·ru·gi·no, Il (ēl per′o͞o jē′nō; *It.* ēl pe′ro͞o jē′nō), (*Pietro Vannucci*) 1446–1524, Italian painter. —**Pe·ru·gin·esque** (pə ro͞o′jə nesk′), *adj.*

pe·ruke (pə ro͞ok′), *n.* a wig, esp. of the kind worn by men in the 17th and 18th centuries; periwig. [< MF *perruque* < It *perrucca, parrucca* wig] —**pe·ruked′,** *adj.* —**pe·ruke′less,** *adj.*

Peruke

pe·ruk·er (pə ro͞o′kər), *n.* one who makes perukes; wig-maker. Also, **pe·ru·ki·er, pe·ru·qui·er** (pə ro͞o′kē-ər). [PERUKE + -ER[1]]

pe·rus·al (pə ro͞o′zəl), *n.* **1.** a reading: *a perusal of the current books.* **2.** the act of perusing; survey; scrutiny: *A more careful perusal yields this conclusion.* [PERUSE + -AL[2]]

pe·ruse (pə ro͞oz′), *v.t.*, **-rused, -rus·ing.** **1.** to read through, as with thoroughness or care: *to peruse a report.* **2.** to read. **3.** *Archaic.* to survey or examine in detail. [late ME; orig., to use up. See PER-, USE] —**pe·rus′a·ble,** *adj.* —**pe·rus′er,** *n.*

Per·utz (per′əts), *n.* **Max Ferdinand,** born 1914, English chemist, born in Austria: Nobel prize 1962.

Peru′vian bal′sam. See **Peru balsam.**

Peru′vian bark′, cinchona (def. 2).

Peru′vian mas′tic tree′, a pepper tree, *Schinus molle.*

Peru′vian rhat′any. See under **rhatany** (def. 1).

Pe·ruz·zi (pe ro͞ot′tsē), *n.* **Bal·das·sa·re Tom·ma·so** (bäl′däs sä′re tôm mä′zô), 1481–1536, Italian architect and painter.

per·vade (pər vād′), *v.t.*, **-vad·ed, -vad·ing.** **1.** to extend its presence, activities, influence, etc., throughout: *Spring pervaded the air.* **2.** to go, pass, or spread through. **3.** *Rare.* to go everywhere throughout (a place), as a person. [< L *pervād(ere)* (to) pass through, equiv. to *per-* PER- + *vādere* to go, walk] —**per·vad′er,** *n.* —**per·vad′ing·ly,** *adv.* —**per·vad′ing·ness,** *n.* —**per·va·sion** (pər vā′zhən), *n.* —**per·va·sive** (pər-vā′siv), *adj.* —**per·va′sive·ly,** *adv.* —**per·va′sive·ness,** *n.*
—**Syn. 1.** diffuse, fill.

per·verse (pər vûrs′), *adj.* **1.** willfully determined or disposed to go counter to what is expected or desired; contrary. **2.** characterized by or proceeding from such a determination: *a perverse mood.* **3.** wayward; cantankerous. **4.** persistent or obstinate in what is wrong. **5.** turned away from what is right, good, or proper; wicked. [ME *perverse* < L *pervers(us)* askew, orig. ptp. of *pervertere.* See PERVERT] —**per·verse′ly,** *adv.* —**per·verse′ness,** *n.*
—**Syn. 1.** contumacious, disobedient. **4.** stubborn, headstrong. See **willful. 5.** evil, bad, sinful. —**Ant. 1.** agreeable. **4.** tractable.

per·ver·sion (pər vûr′zhən, -shən), *n.* **1.** the act of perverting. **2.** the state of being perverted. **3.** a perverted form of something. **4.** any of various means of attaining sexual gratification that are widely regarded as being abnormal, esp. when practiced habitually and in preference to normal heterosexual intercourse. **5.** *Pathol.* a change to what is unnatural or abnormal: *a perversion of function or structure.* [ME < L *perversiōn-* s. of *perversiō*). See PERVERSE, -ION]

per·ver·si·ty (pər vûr′si tē), *n., pl.* **-ties** for 2. **1.** the state or quality of being perverse. **2.** an instance of this. [< L *perversitās.* See PERVERSE, -ITY]

per·ver·sive (pər vûr′siv), *adj.* tending to pervert. [< L *pervers(us)* PERVERSE + -IVE]

per·vert (*v.* pər vûrt′; *n.* pûr′vərt), *v.t.* **1.** to turn away from the right course. **2.** to lead astray morally. **3.** to lead into mental error or false judgment. **4.** to bring over to a religious belief regarded as false or wrong. **5.** to turn to an improper use; misapply. **6.** to misconstrue or misinterpret, esp. deliberately; distort: *to pervert someone's statement.* **7.** to bring to a less excellent state; vitiate; debase. **8.** *Pathol.* to change to what is unnatural or abnormal. **9.** to affect with perversion. —*n.* **10.** one who practices sexual perversion. **11.** *Pathol.* one affected with perversion. **12.** one who has been perverted, esp. to a religious belief regarded as erroneous. [ME *perverte* < L *pervert(re)* to overturn, subvert, equiv. to *per-* PER- + *vertere* to turn] —**per·vert′er,** *n.* —**per·vert′i·bil′i·ty,** *n.* —**per·vert′i·ble,** *adj.* —**per·vert′i·bly,** *adv.*
—**Syn. 1.** divert. **2.** seduce, corrupt, demoralize. **3.** mislead, misguide. **7.** pollute, defile; impair, degrade.

per·vert·ed (pər vûr′tid), *adj.* **1.** *Pathol.* changed to or being of an unnatural or abnormal kind: *a perverted interest in death.* **2.** turned from what is right; wicked; misguided; distorted. **3.** affected with or caused by perversion. [PERVERT + -ED[2]] —**per·vert′ed·ly,** *adv.* —**per·vert′ed·ness,** *n.*

pervert′ed im′age. See **mirror image.**

per·vi·ca·cious (pûr′və kā′shəs), *adj.* extremely willful; obstinate; stubborn. [*pervicaci(ty)* doggedness (< LL *pervicācitās* for L *pervicācia*) + -OUS; *pervicācitās,* equiv. to *pervicāci-* (s. of *pervicāx*) dogged (*per-* PER- + *vic-,* as in *victor* + *-āci-* adj. suffix) + *-tās* -TY[2]] —**per′vi·ca′cious·ly,** *adv.* —**per′vi·ca′cious·ness,** *n.*

per·vi·ous (pûr′vē əs), *adj.* **1.** admitting of passage or entrance; permeable: *pervious soil.* **2.** accessible to reason, feeling, argument, etc. [< L *pervius* passable, equiv. to *per-* PER- + *vi(a)* way, road + *-us* -OUS] —**per′vi·ous·ness,** *n.*

Per·vou·ralsk (per′vo͞o rälsk′), *n.* a city in the central RSFSR, in the Ural Mountains in Asia. 104,000 (est. 1962).

pes (pēz), *n., pl.* **pe·des** (pē′dēz, ped′ēz). **1.** (in prescriptions) the foot. **2.** *Anat., Zool.* a foot or footlike part. [< L]

Pe·sach (pā′säkh), *n. Judaism.* Passover (def. 1). Also, **Pe′sah.** [< Heb *pesaḥ*]

pe·sade (pə säd′, -zäd′, -zäd′), *n. Dressage.* a maneuver in which the horse is made to rear, keeping its hind legs stationary and its forelegs drawn in. [< F, earlier *posade* < It *posata* a halt (see POSE[1], -ADE[1]); *pes-* by assoc. with *peser* to weigh. See POISE]

Pe·sa·ro (pe′zä rô), *n.* a seaport in E Italy, on the Adriatic Sea. 66,519 (1961).

Pes·ca·do·res (pes′kä-dôr′is, -ēz), *n.pl.* a group of small islands off the SE coast of China, in Formosa Strait: ceded to Japan 1895; returned to China 1945. 85,886 (1956); ab. 50 sq. mi. Also called **Pengu Penghutao.** Japanese, **Boko Gunto, Bokoto, Hoko Gunto, Hokoto.**

Pe·sca·ra (pes kä′rä), *n.* a city in E Italy, on the Adriatic Sea. 87,984 (1961).

pe·se·ta (pə sā′tə; *Sp.* pe se′tä), *n., pl.* **-tas** (-təz; *Sp.* -täs). **1.** a bronze coin and monetary unit of Spain and Spanish territories, equal to 100 centimos and equivalent to about .017 of a U.S. dollar. *Abbr.:* P., Pta. **2.** a former silver coin of Spain and Spanish America, equal to two reals; pistareen. [< Sp, dim. of *pesa* weight. See PESO]

Pe·sha·war (pe shä′wər), *n.* a city in N West Pakistan, near the Khyber Pass: the capital of former North-West Frontier province. 218,691 (1961).

Pe·shit·ta (pə shē′tə), *n.* the principal Syriac version of the Bible. Also, **Pe·shi·to** (pə shē′tō).

Pesh·ti·go (pesh′tə gō′), *n.* a town in NE Wisconsin. 2504 (1960).

pes·ky (pes′kē), *adj.*, **-ki·er, -ki·est.** *Informal.* annoying; troublesome: *bothered by a pesky fly.* [*pes(ty)* (deriv. of PEST) + (RI)SKY] —**pesk′i·ly,** *adv.* —**pesk′i·ness,** *n.*

pe·so (pā′sō; *Sp.* pe′sô), *n., pl.* **-sos** (-sōz; *Sp.* -sôs). **1.** a silver and copper coin and monetary unit of Mexico, equal to 100 centavos and equivalent to about .08 of a U.S. dollar. *Abbr.:* P. **2.** a silver coin and monetary unit of Cuba, equal to 100 centavos and equivalent to one U.S. dollar. *Abbr.:* P. **3.** the monetary units of Argentina, Colombia, the Dominican Republic, and Uruguay. **4.** a paper money and monetary unit of the Philippine Islands, equal to 100 centavos and equivalent to about .26 of a U.S. dollar. **5.** a zinc coin of Chile, the 1000th part of an escudo, equal to .00035 of a U.S. dollar. **6.** a former silver coin of Spain and Spanish America, equal to eight reals; dollar; piece of eight; piaster. [< Sp: lit., weight < L *pēnsum* something weighed, n. use of neut. of *pēnsus,* ptp. of *pendere* to weigh]

pes·sa·ry (pes′ə rē), *n., pl.* **-ries.** *Med.* **1.** an instrument worn in the vagina to remedy uterine displacement. **2.** a vaginal suppository. **3.** diaphragm (def. 4). [late ME *pessarie* < LL *pessāri(um)* a suppository, equiv. to L *pess(um)* for *pessus* (< Gk *pessós* oval stone used in a game) + *-ārium* -ARY]

pes·si·mism (pes′ə miz′əm), *n.* **1.** the tendency to see or anticipate only what is disadvantageous or futile in current or future conditions or actions, often when it is reasonably possible to see or anticipate advantages or gains. **2.** the doctrine that the existing world is the worst of all possible worlds, or that all things naturally tend to evil. **3.** the belief that the evil and pain in the world are not compensated for by goodness and happiness. [< L *pessim(us)* superl. of *malus* bad + -ISM; modeled on *optimism*]

pes·si·mist (pes′ə mist), *n.* **1.** a person who habitually sees or anticipates the worst, or is disposed to be gloomy. **2.** an adherent of pessimism. [PESSIM(ISM) + -IST]

pes·si·mis·tic (pes′ə mis′tik), *adj.* pertaining to or characterized by pessimism; gloomy: *a pessimistic outlook.* [PESSIMIST + -IC] —**pes′si·mis′ti·cal·ly,** *adv.*
—**Syn.** foreboding. See **cynical.**

pest (pest), *n.* **1.** a destructive or troublesome person, animal, or thing; nuisance. **2.** a deadly epidemic disease; pestilence. **3.** a disease produced by the plague bacillus. [< L *pest(is)* plague]
—**Syn. 1.** annoyance. **2.** plague, scourge, bane.

Pest (pest; *Hung.* pesht), *n.* See under **Budapest.**

Pes·ta·loz·zi (pes′tə lot′sē; *It.* pes′tä lôt′tsē), *n.* **Jo·hann Hein·rich** (*Ger.* yō′hän hīn′rikh), 1746–1827, Swiss educational reformer. —**Pes′ta·loz′zi·an,** *adj., n.* —**Pes′ta·loz′zi·an·ism,** *n.*

Peste, La (*Fr.* lᴀ pest′). See **Plague, The.**

pes·ter (pes′tər), *v.t.* to harass with petty annoyances; trouble; bother: *Don't pester me with your trivial problems.* [? aph. var. of *empester* < MF *empestrer* to hobble, entangle < LL **impāstōriāre* to hobble, equiv. to *im-* IM- + **pāstōria* a hobble, n. use of L *pāstōrius* of a herdsman or shepherd. See PASTOR, -IOUS] —**pes′ter·er,** *n.* —**pes′ter·ing·ly,** *adv.* —**pes′ter·some,** *adj.* —**Syn.** annoy, vex, tease, disturb; irritate, provoke, plague; badger, harry, hector. —**Ant.** entertain.

pes·ter·ous (pes′tər əs), *adj.* tending to vex or annoy; vexatious. [PESTER + -OUS]

pest·hole (pest′hōl′), *n.* a location prone to epidemic disease. [PEST + HOLE]

pest·house (pest′hous′), *n., pl.* **-hous·es** (-hou′ziz). a house or hospital for persons infected with pestilential disease. [PEST + HOUSE]

pest·i·cide (pes′ti sīd′), *n.* a chemical preparation for destroying pests, as flies, mosquitoes, etc. [PEST + -I- + -CIDE] —**pes′ti·cid′al,** *adj.*

pes·tif·er·ous (pe stif′ər əs), *adj.* **1.** bringing or bearing disease. **2.** pestilential. **3.** pernicious; evil. **4.** *Informal.* mischievous; troublesome or annoying. [< L *pestiferus* plague-bringing, equiv. to *pesti-* (s. of *pestis*) PEST + *-ferus* -FEROUS] —**pes·tif′er·ous·ly,** *adv.* —**pes·tif′er·ous·ness,** *n.*

pes·ti·lence (pes′tᵊ ləns), *n.* **1.** a deadly epidemic disease. **2.** See **bubonic plague. 3.** something that is considered harmful or evil. [ME < MF < L *pestilent(ia).* See PESTILENT, -ENCE]

pes·ti·lent (pes′tᵊ lənt), *adj.* **1.** producing or tending to produce infectious disease; infectious; pestilential. **2.** destructive to life; deadly; poisonous. **3.** injurious to peace, morals, etc.; pernicious. **4.** troublesome, annoying, or mischievous. [< L *pestilent-* (s. of *pestilēns*) noxious, equiv. to *pesti-* (s. of *pestis*) PEST + *-lent-* adj. suffix] —**pes′ti·lent·ly,** *adv.*

pes·ti·len·tial (pes′tᵊ len′shəl), *adj.* **1.** producing, or tending to produce, pestilence. **2.** pertaining to or of the nature of pestilence, esp. bubonic plague. **3.** pernicious; harmful; troublesome. [ME < ML *pestilentiāl(is).* See PESTILENT, -IAL] —**pes′ti·len′tial·ly,** *adv.* —**pes′ti·len′tial·ness,** *n.*

pes·tle (pes′əl, pes′tᵊl), *n., v.,* **-tled, -tling.** —*n.* **1.** an instrument for braying or triturating substances in a mortar. See illus. under **mortar**¹. **2.** any of various appliances for pounding, stamping, etc. —*v.t.* **3.** to pound or triturate with or as with a pestle. —*v.i.* **4.** to work with a pestle. [ME *pestel* < MF < L *pistillum,* deriv. of *pistum* pounded, ptp. of *pinsere*]

pet¹ (pet), *n., adj., v.,* **pet·ted, pet·ting.** —*n.* **1.** any domesticated or tamed animal that is kept as a favorite and cared for affectionately. **2.** a person especially cherished or indulged; favorite: *He was the teacher's pet.* **3.** a thing particularly cherished. —*adj.* **4.** kept or treated as a pet: *a pet lamb.* **5.** especially cherished or indulged, as a child or other person. **6.** favorite: *a pet theory.* **7.** showing affection: *to address someone with pet words.* —*v.t.* **8.** to treat as a pet; fondle or indulge. **9.** *Informal.* to fondle or caress (one of the opposite sex). —*v.i.* **10.** *Informal.* to engage in fondling and caressing a person of the opposite sex. [? back formation from *pet lamb* cade lamb, ? syncopated var. of *petty lamb* little lamb; see PETCOCK] —**pet′ta·ble,** *adj.* —**Syn. 8.** baby, humor, pamper, favor.

pet² (pet), *n.* **1.** a fit of peevishness: *to be in a pet.* —*v.i.* **2.** to be peevish; sulk. [appar. back formation from PETTISH] —**pet′ted·ly,** *adv.* —**pet′ted·ness,** *n.*

Pet., Peter.

Pé·tain (pā taɴ′), *n.* **Hen·ri Phi·lippe O·mer** (äɴ rē′ fē lēp′ ō mer′), 1856–1951, marshal of France: premier of the Vichy government 1940–44.

pet·al (pet′ᵊl), *n.* one of the often colored segments of the corolla of a flower. See diag. under **flower.** [< NL *petal(um)* petal, L: metal plate < Gk *pétalon* a thin plate, leaf, n. use of neut. of *pétalos* spread out, akin to *petannýnai* to be open. See PATENT] —**pet′al·age,** *n.* —**pet′aled, pet′alled,** *adj.* —**pet′al·less,** *adj.* —**pet′al·like′,** *adj.*

Pet·al (pet′ᵊl), *n.* a town in SE Mississippi. 4007 (1960).

-petal, a combining form meaning "seeking," used in the formation of compound words: *centripetal.* [< NL *-pet(us),* repr. L *petere* to seek, + -AL¹]

pet·al·if·er·ous (pet′ᵊlif′ər əs), *adj.* bearing petals. [PETAL + -I- + -FEROUS]

pet·al·ine (pet′ᵊlin, -ᵊlīn′), *adj.* pertaining to or resembling a petal. [< NL *petalin(us).* See PETAL, -INE¹]

pet·al·ite (pet′ᵊlīt′), *n.* a mineral, lithium aluminum silicate, $Li(AlSi_4O_{10})$, occurring in colorless or white foliated masses: an important source of lithium. [< G *Petalit.* See PETAL, -ITE¹]

pet·a·lo·dy (pet′ᵊlō′dē), *n. Bot.* a condition in flowers, in which certain organs, as the stamens in most double flowers, assume the appearance of or become metamorphosed into petals. [< Gk *petalṓd(ēs)* leaflike (see PETAL, -ODE¹) + -Y³] —**pet·a·lod·ic** (pet′ᵊlod′ik), *adj.*

pet·al·oid (pet′ᵊloid′), *adj.* having the form or appearance of a petal. [PETAL + -OID]

pet·al·ous (pet′ᵊləs), *adj.* having petals. [PETAL + -OUS]

Pet·a·lu·ma (pet′ᵊ lo͞o′mə), *n.* a city in W California, N of San Francisco. 14,035 (1960).

Pe·tar (pē′tər; *Serbo-Croatian.* pe′tär), *n.* a boy's given name, form of **Peter.**

pe·tard (pi tärd′), *n.* **1.** an engine of war or an explosive device formerly used to blow in a door or gate, form a breach in a wall, etc. **2.** a kind of firecracker. **3. hoist by or with one's own petard,** caught in one's own trap; defeated by one's own plot. [< MF, equiv. to *pet(er)* (to) break wind (deriv. of *pet* < L *pēdit(um)* a breaking wind, orig. neut. of ptp. of *pēdere* to break wind) + *-ard* -ARD]

pet·a·sus (pet′ə səs), *n., pl.* **-sus·es.** a broad-brimmed hat worn by ancient Greek travelers and hunters, often represented in art as a winged hat worn by Hermes or Mercury. Also, **pet·a·sos** (pet′ə səs, -sos′). [< L: hat with a broad brim < Gk *pétasos,* akin to *petannýnai* to spread out]

Pe·ta·vi·us (pə tā′vē əs), *n.* a walled plain in the fourth quadrant of the face of the moon: about 100 miles in diameter from crest to crest.

pet·cock (pet′kok′), *n.* a small valve or faucet, as for draining off excess or waste material from the cylinder of a steam engine or an internal-combustion engine. Also, **pet′ cock′.** [PETT(Y) + COCK¹]

Pet.E., Petroleum Engineer.

pe·te·chi·a (pi tē′kē ə, -tek′ē ə), *n., pl.* **-te·chi·ae** (-tē′kē ē′, -tek′ē ē′). *Med.* a minute hemorrhage in the skin or in a mucous or serous membrane. [< NL < It *petecchia* miser, in pl., spots on skin]

pe·te·chi·al (pi tē′kē əl, -tek′ē-), *adj. Med.* pertaining to, resembling, or characterized by petechiae. [< NL *petechiāl(is).* See PETECHIA, -AL¹]

pe·te·chi·ate (pi tē′kē it, -āt′, -tek′ē-), *adj. Med.* having or marked with petechiae. [PETECHI(A) + -ATE¹]

pete·man (pēt′mən), *n., pl.* **-men.** *Slang.* a safecracker. [*Pete* (shortened form of proper name *Peter*) + MAN¹]

pe·ter¹ (pē′tər), *v.i. Informal.* to diminish gradually and then disappear or cease (usually fol. by *out*).

pe·ter² (pē′tər), *n. Whist.* a signal for an echo. [from BLUE PETER]

pe·ter³ (pē′tər), *n. Slang (Vulgar).* penis. [from the name *Peter*]

Pe·ter (pē′tər), *n.* **1.** Also called **Simon Peter.** died A.D. 67?, one of the 12 apostles and the reputed author of two of the Epistles. **2.** either of these two Epistles in the New Testament, I Peter or II Peter. **3.** a word formerly used in communications to represent the letter P. **4.** a boy's given name. [ME; OE *Petrus* < L < Gk *Pétros* stone, trans. of Syriac *kēfā*]

Peter I, **1.** ("*the Great*") 1672–1725, czar of Russia 1682–1725. **2.** (*Peter Karageorgevich*) 1844–1921, king of Serbia 1903–21.

Peter II, born 1923, king of Yugoslavia 1934–45.

Peter III, 1728–62, czar of Russia 1762 (husband of Catherine II; father of Paul I).

Pe·ter·bor·ough (pē′tər bûr′ō, -bur′ō, -bər ə), *n.* **1.** a city in NE Northamptonshire, in central England. 62,031 (1961). **2.** a city in SE Ontario, in SE Canada. 47,185 (1961). **3. Soke of** (sōk), an administrative division in NE Northamptonshire, in central England. 74,442 (1961); 84 sq. mi.

Pe′ter Ib′bet·son (ib′it sən), a novel (1891) by George Du Maurier.

Pe·ter·lee (pē′tər lē′), *n.* a town in E Durham, in NE England. 13,792 (1961).

Pe′ter·mann Peak′ (pā′tər män′), a mountain in E Greenland. 9645 ft.

Pe′ter of Am′iens. See **Peter the Hermit.**

Pe′ter Pan′, **1.** the hero of Sir James M. Barrie's play about a boy who never grew up. **2.** (*italics.*) the play itself (1904).

Pe′ter Pan′ col′lar, a close-fitting flat collar with rounded corners that meet in front of a high, round neckline.

Pe′ter Quince′ at the Clavier′, a poem (1923) by Wallace Stevens.

Pe·ters (pē′tərz), *n.* a walled plain in the first quadrant of the face of the moon: about 10 miles in diameter.

Pe·ters·burg (pē′tərz bûrg′), *n.* **1.** a city in SE Virginia: besieged by Union forces 1864–65. 36,750 (1960). **2.** a town in SW Indiana. 2939 (1960).

pe·ter·sham (pē′tər shəm), *n.* **1.** a heavy woolen cloth for men's overcoats and other bulky outerwear. **2.** a coat or jacket made of this cloth. **3.** a corded material for hatbands, the insides of belts, etc. **4.** a narrow belting for the tops of skirts. [named after Viscount *Petersham* (1780–1851)]

Pe′ter's pence′, **1.** an annual tax or tribute, originally of a penny from each householder, formerly paid by the people of certain countries to the papal see at Rome. **2.** a voluntary contribution to the Pope, made by Roman Catholics everywhere. Also, **Pe′ter pence′.** [ME *Peteres peni*]

Pe′ter the Her′mit, c1050–1115, French monk: preacher of the first Crusade 1095–99. Also called **Peter of Amiens.**

pet·i·o·lar (pet′ē ə lər), *adj. Bot.* of, pertaining to, or growing from a petiole. [PETIOLE + -AR¹]

pet·i·o·late (pet′ē ə lāt′), *adj. Zool.* having a petiole or peduncle. Also, **pet′i·o·lat′ed.** [< NL *petiolāt(us).* See PETIOLE, -ATE¹]

pet·i·ole (pet′ē ōl′), *n.* **1.** *Bot.* the slender stalk by which a leaf is attached to the stem; leafstalk. See illus. under **leaf. 2.** *Zool.* a stalk or peduncle, as that connecting the abdomen and thorax in wasps. [< NL *petiol(us)* leafstalk, special use of L *petiolus,* unexplained var. of *pediculus* PEDICLE]

pet·i·o·lule (pet′ē əl yo͞ol′, pet′ē ol′yo͞ol), *n. Bot.* a small petiole, as of a leaflet. [< NL *petiolul(us).* See PETIOLE, -ULE] —**pet·i·ol·u·lar** (pet′ē ol′yə lər), **pet·i·ol·u·late** (pet′ē ol′yə lāt′, -lit), *adj.*

pet·it (pet′ē; *Fr.* pə tē′), *adj. Obs. exc. Law.* small; petty; minor. [ME < MF; see PETTY]

pe·tit bour·geois (pə tē′ bo͝or′zhwä, pet′ē bo͝or′zhwä; *Fr.* pə tē bo͞oʀ zhwᴀ′), *pl.* **pe·tits bour·geois** (pə tē′ bo͝or′zhwäz, pet′ē bo͝or′zhwäz; *Fr.* pə tē bo͞oʀ zhwᴀ′). **1.** a person who belongs to the petite bourgeoisie. **2.** See **petite bourgeoisie.** [< F] —**pe·tit′-bour·geois′,** *adj.*

pe·tite (pə tēt′), *adj.* (of a woman) small in stature or figure; diminutive. [< F; fem. of PETIT] —**pe·tite′ness,** *n.*

pe·tite bour·geoise (pə tēt′ bo͝or zhwäz′; *Fr.* pə tēt bo͞oʀ zhwᴀz′), *pl.* **pe·tites bour·geoises** (pə tēt′ bo͝or zhwäz′; *Fr.* pə tēt bo͞oʀ zhwᴀz′). a woman who belongs to the petite bourgeoisie. [< F; fem. of PETIT BOURGEOIS]

pe·tite bour·geoi·sie (pə tēt′ bo͝or′zhwä zē′; *Fr.* pə tēt bo͞oʀ zhwᴀ zē′), the portion of the bourgeoisie having the least wealth and lowest social status; the lower middle class. [< F]

pe·tite mar·mite (pə tēt′ mär′mīt; *Fr.* pə tēt mär mēt′), **1.** an aromatic broth made from meat, vegetables, and seasonings, served in the pot in which it has cooked. **2.** a small marmite for cooking and serving this soup. [< F]

pe·tite per·cep·tion (pə tēt′ pər sep′shən; *Fr.* pə tēt peʀ sep syôɴ′), *pl.* **pe·tites per·cep·tions** (pə tēt′ pər sep′shənz; *Fr.* pə tēt peʀ sep syôɴ′). (in the philosophy of Leibnitz) the faint and vague self-awareness of each one of the lesser monads. [< F]

pe·tit feu (*Fr.* pə tē fœ′), *Ceram.* **1.** a firing of ceramics at a low temperature. **2.** the category of ceramic colors fired in a muffle kiln at low temperature. Cf. **grand feu.** [< F: lit., small fire]

pet·it four (pet′ē fôr′, fōr′; *Fr.* pə tē fo͞oʀ′), *pl.* **pet·its fours** (pet′ē fôrz′, fōrz′; *Fr.* pə tē fo͞oʀ′). a small teacake, variously frosted and decorated. [< F: lit., small oven]

pe·ti·tion (pə tish′ən), *n.* **1.** a formally drawn request, often bearing the names of a number of petitioners, which is addressed to a person or body of persons in authority or power, soliciting some favor, right, mercy, or other benefit: *a petition for clemency; a petition for the repeal of an unfair law.* **2.** a request made for something desired, esp. a respectful or humble request, as to a superior or to one of those in authority; a supplication or prayer: *a petition for aid; a petition to God for courage and strength.* **3.** that which is sought by request or entreaty: *to receive one's full petition.* **4.** *Law.* an application for an order of court or for some judicial action. —*v.t.* **5.** to beg for or request (something). **6.** to address a formal petition to (a sovereign, a legislative body, etc.): *He received everything for which he had petitioned the king.* **7.** to ask by petition for (something). —*v.i.* **8.** to present a petition. **9.** to address or present a formal petition. **10.** to request or solicit, as by a petition: *to petition for redress of grievances.* [ME *peticioun* < L *petītiōn-* (s. of *petītiō*) a seeking out < *petīt(us)* sought (ptp. of *petere*) + *-iōn-* -ION] —**pe·ti′tion·a·ble,** *adj.* —**pe·ti′tion·er, pe·ti′tion·ist,** *n.* —**Syn. 1.** suit. **2.** entreaty, solicitation, appeal. **9.** solicit, sue. See **appeal.**

pe·ti·tion·ar·y (pə tish′ə ner′ē), *adj.* **1.** of the nature of or expressing a petition. **2.** *Archaic.* petitioning; suppliant. [PETITION + -ARY]

pe·ti·ti·o prin·ci·pi·i (pi tish′ē ō′ prin sip′ē ī′; *Lat.* pe tē′ti ō′ priɴg kip′i ē′), *Logic.* a fallacy in reasoning resulting from the assumption of that which in the beginning was set forth to be proved; begging the question. [< L, trans. of Gk *tò en archêi aiteîsthai* an assumption at the outset]

pet′it ju′ry (pet′ē), *Law.* See **petty jury.** —**pet′it ju′ror.**

pet′it lar′ceny (pet′ē), *Law.* See **petty larceny.**

pe·tit-maî·tre (pə tē me′tʀᵊ), *n., pl.* **pe·tits-maî·tres** (pə tē me′tʀᵊ). *French.* a man who is excessively interested in his clothes and appearance; fop; dandy. [lit., small master]

pe·tit mal (pə tē′ mal′; *Fr.* pə tē mᴀl′), *Pathol.* a form of epilepsy characterized by unconsciousness for periods of short duration. Cf. **grand mal.** [< F: lit., small illness]

pet·i·tor (pet′i tər, pə tī′tər), *n. Obs.* a seeker; an applicant or candidate. [< L; see PETITION, -OR²] —**pet·i·to·ry** (pet′i tôr′e, -tōr′ē), *adj.*

pet′it point′ (pet′ē), **1.** a small stitch used in embroidery. Cf. **gros point** (def. 1), **tent stitch. 2.** embroidery done on a canvas backing and resembling woven tapestry. [< F: lit., small stitch]

Pe·tit Prince, Le (*Fr.* lə pə tē pʀaɴs′). See **Little Prince, The.**

pet′it ser′jeanty (pet′ē), *Medieval Eng. Law.* serjeanty in which the tenant rendered services of an impersonal nature to the king, as providing him annually with an implement of war, as a lance or bow. Cf. **grand serjeanty.** [< AF]

pe·tits pois (pə tē pwᴀ′; *Eng.* pet′ē pwä′), *French.* small green peas.

pet′it trea′son (pet′ē), *Eng. Law.* the killing of a husband by his wife, of a lord by his servant, or of an ecclesiastic by a subordinate ecclesiastic. Also, **petty treason.** [< AF]

PETN, See **pentaerythritol tetranitrate.**

pet′ name′, a name or a term of address used to express affection for a person, thing, etc.: *His car's pet name is Betsy.*

pe·to (pā′tō), *n., pl.* **-tos,** (*esp. collectively*) **-to.** wahoo². [< AmerSp; Sp: breastplate < It *petto* breast, breastplate < L *pectus* breast]

Pe·tö·fi (pe′tœ fē), *n.* **Sán·dor** (shän′dôr), (*Sándor Petrovics*), 1823–49, Hungarian poet and patriot.

Pe·tos·key (pi tos′kē), *n.* a town in NW Michigan. 6138 (1960).

petr-, var. of **petro-** before a vowel: *petrous.*

Pe·tra (pē′trə), *n.* an ancient city in SW Jordan: many of its ruined structures are carved out of varicolored stratified rock; capital of the Nabataeans and Edomites.

Pe·trarch (pē′trärk, pe′-), *n.* (*Francesco Petrarca*) 1304–74, Italian poet and scholar.

Pe·trar·chan (pi trär′kən), *adj.* Also, **Pe·trar·chi·an** (pi trär′kē ən). **1.** of, pertaining to, or characteristic of the works of Petrarch. **2.** characteristic or imitative of the style of Petrarch. —*n.* **3.** Petrarchist. [PETRARCH + -AN]

Petrar′chan son′net, a sonnet form popularized by Petrarch, consisting of an octave with the rhyme scheme *abbaabba* and of a sestet with one of several rhyme schemes, as *cdecde* or *cdcdcd.* Also called **Italian sonnet.**

Pe·trarch·ism (pe′trär kiz′əm), *n.* the poetic style introduced by Petrarch and characteristic of his work, marked by complex grammatical structure, elaborate conceits, and conventionalized diction. Also, **Pe·trar·chi·an·ism** (pi trär′kē ə niz′əm). [PETRARCH + -ISM]

Pe·trarch·ist (pe′trär kist), *n.* a person who imitates the literary style employed by Petrarch, esp. the poets of the English Renaissance who employed the Petrarchan sonnet style. Also, **Petrarchan.** [PETRARCH + -IST]

pet·rel (pe′trəl), *n.* **1.** any of numerous sea birds of the family *Procellariidae.* **2.** See **storm petrel.** [earlier *pitteral;* present form by folk etymology: thought of as St. Peter's bird because it seems to walk on water. Matt. 14:29]

petri-, var. of **petro-** before elements of Latin origin: *petrifaction.*

pe′tri dish′ (pē′trē), a shallow, circular, glass or plastic dish with a loose-fitting cover over the top and sides, used for culturing bacteria and other microorganisms. [named after J. R. *Petri* (d. 1921), German bacteriologist]

Petri dish

Pe·trie (pē′trē), *n.* **Sir (William Matthew) Flin·ders** (flin′dərz), 1853–1942, English Egyptologist and archaeologist.

pet·ri·fac·tion (pe′trə fak′shən), *n.* **1.** the act or process of petrifying, or the state of being petrified. **2.** something petrified. Also, **pet·ri·fi·ca·tion** (pe′trə fə kā′shən). [PETRI- + -*faction* < L *factiōn-* (s. of *factiō*) a making. See PETRIFY, FACTION] —**pet′ri·fac′tive,** *adj.*

Pet′rified For′est, a national monument in E Arizona: forests turned to stone by the action of mineral-laden water. 40 sq. mi.

Pet′rified For′est, The, a play (1934) by Robert Sherwood.

pet·ri·fy (pe′trə fī′), *v.,* **-fied, -fy·ing.** —*v.t.* **1.** to convert into stone or a stony substance. **2.** to make rigid or inert; stiffen; benumb: *to petrify one's feelings.* **3.** to stupefy or paralyze with astonishment, horror, or other strong emotion: *to petrify someone with fright.* —*v.i.* **4.** to become petrified. [< MF *petrifier.* See PETRI-, -FY] —**pet′ri·fi′a·ble,** *adj.* —**pe·trif·i·cant** (pi trif′ə kənt), *adj.* —**pet′ri·fi′er,** *n.*

Pe·tril·lo (pə tril′ō), *n.* **James Caesar,** born 1892, U.S. labor leader: president of the American Federation of Musicians 1940–58.

Pe·tri·na (pə trē′nə), *n.* a girl's given name.

Pe·trine (pē′trīn, -trin), *adj.* of or pertaining to the apostle Peter or the Epistles bearing his name. [< LL *Petr(us)* (see PETER) + -INE[1]]

Pe·trin·ism (pē′trə niz′əm), *n.* the body of theological doctrine taught by, or attributed to, the apostle Peter. [PETRINE + -ISM] —**Pe′trin·ist,** *n.*

petro-, a combining form meaning "rock," "stone" (*petrology*) or "petroleum" (*petrochemical*). Also, **petr-, petri-.** [< Gk, comb. form of *pétra* rock, *pétros* stone]

Pet·ro·bru·sian (pe′trō brōō′zhən, -shən), *n.* a member of a 12th-century sect in S France that rejected the Mass, infant baptism, prayers for the dead, sacerdotalism, the veneration of the cross, and the building of churches. [< ML *petrobrusiān(us),* named after Petrus *Brusius* Pierre de Bruys, 12th-century Frenchman who founded the sect; see -AN]

pet·ro·chem·i·cal (pe′trō kem′i kəl), *n.* **1.** any substance obtained from petroleum, as gasoline, kerosene, or petrolatum. —*adj.* **2.** of or pertaining to petrochemistry or a petrochemical. [PETRO- + CHEMICAL]

pe·tro·chem·is·try (pe′trō kem′i strē), *n.* **1.** the chemistry of rocks. **2.** the branch of chemistry dealing with petroleum or its products. [PETRO- + CHEMISTRY]

pet·ro·dol·lars (pe′tro dol′ərz), *n.pl.* huge surplus revenues accumulated by petroleum-exporting countries, esp. those of the Middle East.

petrog., petrography.

pet·ro·gen·e·sis (pe′trō jen′i sis), *n.* **1.** the branch of petrology dealing with the origin and formation of rocks. **2.** the origin and formation of rocks. [< NL; see PETRO-, GENESIS] —**pet·ro·ge·net·ic** (pe′trō jə net′ik), *adj.*

pe·trog·e·ny (pi troj′ə nē), *n.* the branch of petrology dealing with the origin and formation of rocks, esp. igneous rocks. [PETRO- + -GENY] —**pet·ro·gen·ic** (pe′trə jen′ik), *adj.*

pet·ro·glyph (pe′trə glif′), *n.* a drawing or carving on rock, made by a member of a prehistoric or primitive people. Also called **petrograph.** [< F *pétroglyphe.* See PETRO-, GLYPH] —**pet′ro·glyph′ic,** *adj.* —**pe·trog·ly·phy** (pi trog′lə fē), *n.*

Pet·ro·grad (pe′trə grad′; *Russ.* pe tro grät′), *n.* former name (1914–24) of **Leningrad.**

pet·ro·gram (pe′trə gram′), *n.* a drawing or painting on rock, esp. one made by a member of a prehistoric or primitive people. Cf. **petroglyph.** [PETRO- + -GRAM[1]]

pet·ro·graph (pe′trə graf′, -gräf′), *n.* petroglyph. [PETRO- + -GRAPH]

pe·trog·ra·phy (pi trog′rə fē), *n.* the branch of petrology dealing with the description and classification of rocks. [< NL *petrographia.* See PETRO-, -GRAPHY] —**pe·trog′ra·pher,** *n.* —**pet·ro·graph·ic** (pe′trə graf′ik), **pet′ro·graph′i·cal,** *adj.* —**pet′ro·graph′i·cal·ly,** *adv.*

pet·rol (pe′trəl), *n., v.,* **-rolled, -rol·ling.** —*n.* **1.** *Brit.* gasoline. **2.** *Archaic.* petroleum. —*v.t.* **3.** *Brit.* to clean with gasoline. [< MF *petrole* < ML *petroleum* PETROLEUM]

petrol., petrology.

pet·ro·la·tum (pe′trə lā′təm), *n.* a yellowish or whitish, translucent, gelatinous, oily, semisolid, amorphous mass obtained from petroleum: used as a lubricant, rust preventive, in the manufacture of cosmetics, and in medicine as a protective dressing, emollient, and ointment base. Also called **petroleum jelly.** [< NL; see PETROLEUM, -ATE[2]]

pet·ro·lene (pe′trə lēn′), *n.* any of the constituents of a bitumen, as asphalt, that are soluble in pentane, hexane, or naphthalene. Also called **malthene.** Cf. **asphaltene.** [PETROL(EUM) + -ENE]

pe·tro·le·um (pə trō′lē əm), *n.* an oily, thick, flammable, usually dark-colored liquid that is a form of bitumen or a mixture of various hydrocarbons, occurring naturally in various parts of the world and commonly obtained by drilling: used in a natural or refined state as fuel, or separated by distillation into gasoline, naptha, benzene, kerosene, paraffin, etc. [< ML: lit., rock oil, equiv. to L *petr(a)* rock (< Gk) + *oleum* oil] —**pe·tro′le·ous,** *adj.*

petro′leum e′ther, a flammable, low-boiling hydrocarbon mixture produced by the fractional distillation of petroleum, used as a solvent.

petro′leum jel′ly, petrolatum.

pe·trol·ic (pi trol′ik), *adj.* of, pertaining to, or produced from petroleum. [PETRO(LEUM) + -IC]

Pe·tro·li·na (pi trōō lē′nə), *n.* a city in NE Brazil. 15,643 (1960).

pe·trol·o·gy (pi trol′ə jē), *n.* the scientific study of rocks, including petrography and petrogenesis. [PETRO- + -LOGY] —**pet·ro·log·ic** (pe′trə loj′ik), **pet′ro·log′i·cal,** *adj.* —**pet′ro·log′i·cal·ly,** *adv.* —**pe·trol′o·gist,** *n.*

pet·ro·nel (pe′trə nᵊl), *n.* a 15th-century firearm that was fired with the butt resting against the breast. [< MF *petrinal,* dial. var. of *poitrinal,* equiv. to *poitrine* chest (VL **pectorina,* n. use of fem. of *pectorinus* of the breast; see PECTORAL, -INE[1]) + *-al* -AL[1]]

Pe·tro·ni·us (pi trō′nē əs), *n.* **Gai·us** (gā′əs), (*Gaius Petronius Arbiter*) ("*Arbiter Elegantiae*"), died A.D. 66?, Roman satirist.

Pe·tro·pav·lovsk (pe′tro päv′lofsk), *n.* a city in N Kazakstan, in the S Soviet Union in Asia. 156,000 (est. 1964).

Pe·tro·pav·lovsk-Kam·chat·ski (pe′tro päv′lôfsk-käm chät′skē), *n.* a city in SW Kamchatka, in the E Soviet Union in Asia. 110,000 (est. 1964).

pe·tro·sal (pi trō′səl), *adj.* **1.** petrous; hard. **2.** *Anat.* of or pertaining to the petrous portion of the temporal bone. [< L *petrōs(us)* rocky (see PETR-, -OSE[1]) + -AL[1]]

Pe·trouch·ka (pə trōōsh′kə), *n.* a ballet (1911) by Stravinski.

pet·rous (pe′trəs, pē′-), *adj.* **1.** *Anat.* noting or pertaining to the hard dense portion of the temporal bone, containing the internal auditory organs; petrosal. **2.** like stone, esp. in hardness; stony; rocky. [< L *petrōs(us)* rocky. See PETR-, -OUS]

Pe·tro·za·vodsk (pe′tro zä vôtsk′), *n.* a city in the NW RSFSR, in the NW Soviet Union in Europe. 149,000 (est. 1964).

pe-tsai (bā′tsī′), *n.* a lettucelike plant, *Brassica pekinensis,* of China, having an elongated, compact head of light green leaves. Also called **Chinese cabbage.** [< Chin (Peking): white greens]

Pet·sa·mo (*Fin.* pet′sä-mô), *n.* a seaport in the NW RSFSR, in the NW Soviet Union in Europe, on the Arctic Ocean: ice-free all year; ceded by Finland 1944. Russian, **Pechenga.**

pet·ti·coat (pet′ē kōt′), *n.* **1.** an underskirt, esp. one that is wide and often trimmed and ruffled and of a decorative fabric. **2.** any skirtlike part or covering. **3.** *Informal.* a woman or girl. **4.** *Elect.* the skirt-shaped portion of a petticoat insulator. —*adj.* **5.** of or pertaining to women; female; feminine: *petticoat traits.* [late ME *petycote.* See PETTY, COAT] —**pet′ti·coat′-less,** *adj.*

pet′ticoat breech′es, men's breeches, often ornate, having loose, skirtlike legs, worn in France and England from about 1650 to 1680. Also called **Rhinegrave breeches.**

pet·ti·coat·ed (pet′ē kō′tid), *adj.* having or wearing a petticoat or petticoats: *petticoated writers of sentimental verse.* [PETTICOAT + -ED[3]]

pet′ticoat in′sulator, *Elect.* a bell-shaped insulator used for high-voltage insulation.

pet′ticoat narcis′sus, a narcissus, *Narcissus Bulbocodium,* of southern France and Morocco, having solitary, yellow or white flowers. Also called **hoop-petticoat narcissus.**

pet·ti·fog (pet′ē fog′, -fôg′), *v.i.,* **-fogged, -fog·ging.** **1.** to bicker or quibble over trifles when more important matters are to be dealt with. **2.** to carry on a petty or shifty law business. **3.** to practice chicanery of any sort. [back formation from *pettifogger,* equiv. to PETTY + *fogger* < MLG *voger* or MD *voeger* one who arranges things; akin to OE *gefōg* a joining] —**pet′ti·fog′ger,** *n.* —**pet′ti·fog′ger·y,** *n.*

pet·ti·fog·ging (pet′ē fog′ing, -fô′ging), *adj.* **1.** insignificant in comparison with other matters at hand: *pettifogging details.* **2.** dishonest in insignificant matters; petty; mean. [PETTIFOG + -ING[2]]

pet·tish (pet′ish), *adj.* peevish; petulant: *a pettish refusal.* [PET[1] + -ISH[1]; orig., like a spoiled child] —**pet′tish·ly,** *adv.* —**pet′tish·ness,** *n.*

Pet·tit (pet′it), *n.* **Robert E. Lee** (*Bob*), born 1922, U.S. basketball player.

pet·ti·toes (pet′ē tōz′), *n.pl.* **1.** the feet of a pig, esp. as food. **2.** the human toes or feet, esp. those of a child. [pl. of obs. *pettytoe* offal < MF *petite oye* giblets of a goose, equiv. to *petite* PETITE + *oye* goose < LL *av(i)ca*]

pet·tle[1] (pet′ᵊl), *v.t.,* **-tled, -tling.** *Scot. and North Eng.* to fondle; pet. [PET[1] + -LE]

pet·tle[2] (pet′ᵊl), *n. Brit. Dial.* paddle[1] (def. 9).

pet·to (pet′tô), *n., pl.* **-ti** (-tē). *Italian.* the chest or breast. Cf. **in petto.**

pet·ty (pet′ē), *adj.,* **-ti·er, -ti·est.** **1.** of small importance or consequence; trifling; trivial: *petty grievances.* **2.** of lesser or secondary importance, merit, etc.: *petty considerations.* **3.** having or showing narrow ideas, interests, etc.: *petty minds.* **4.** mean or ungenerous in small or trifling things: *a petty person.* **5.** showing or caused by meanness of spirit: *a petty revenge.* **6.** of secondary importance or rank, esp. in relation to others of the same class or kind: *petty states; a petty tyrant.* [ME *pety* small, minor, var. of PETIT] —**pet′ti·ly,** *adv.* —**pet′ti·ness,** *n.*

—**Syn. 1.** nugatory, negligible, inconsiderable, slight. PETTY, PALTRY, TRIFLING, TRIVIAL apply to that which is so insignificant as to be almost unworthy of notice. PETTY implies contemptible insignificance and littleness, inferiority and small worth: *petty quarrels.* PALTRY is applied to that which is beneath one's notice, even despicable: *a paltry amount.* That which is TRIFLING is so unimportant and inconsiderable as to be practically negligible: *a trifling error.* That which is TRIVIAL is slight, insignificant, and even in incongruous contrast to that which is significant or important: *a trivial remark; a trivial task.* **3.** small. **4.** stingy, miserly. —**Ant. 1.** important. **4.** generous.

Pet·ty (pet′ē), *n.* **William, 2nd Earl of Shel·burne** (shel′bûrn), **1st Marquis of Lans·downe** (lanz′dən, -doun), 1737–1805, British statesman: prime minister 1782–83.

pet′ty bourgeois′. See **petit bourgeois.**

pet′ty cash′, a small cash fund for paying minor charges, as for office supplies, deliveries, etc.

pet′ty ju′ry, (in a civil or criminal proceeding) a jury, usually of 12 persons, impaneled to determine the facts and render a verdict pursuant to the court's instructions on the law. Also, **petit jury.** —**pet′ty ju′ror.**

pet′ty lar′ceny, *Law.* larceny in which the value of the goods taken is below a certain amount. Also, **petit larceny.** Cf. **grand larceny.**

pet′ty of′ficer, **1.** an enlisted man in the navy holding an official rank corresponding to that of a noncommissioned officer in the army. **2.** one of the minor officers on a merchant ship, as a boatswain, carpenter, or the like.

pet′ty ses′sions, *Eng. Law.* a court of summary jurisdiction for minor offenses that is held without a jury.

pet′ty trea′son, *Eng. Law.* See **petit treason.**

pet·u·lance (pech′ə ləns), *n.* **1.** the state or quality of being petulant. **2.** a petulant speech or action. **3.** *Rare.* petulant spirit or behavior. [< L *petulantia* impudence. See PETULANT, -ANCE]

pet·u·lan·cy (pech′ə lən sē), *n., pl.* **-cies.** *Rare.* petulance. [< L *petulantia.* See PETULANCE, -CY]

pet·u·lant (pech′ə lənt), *adj.* moved to or showing sudden, impatient irritation, esp. over some trifling annoyance: *a petulant toss of the head.* [< L *petulant-* (s. of *petulāns*) impudent, akin to *petere* to attack] —**pet′u·lant·ly,** *adv.*

pe·tu·ni·a (pə tōō′nē ə, -nyə, -tyōō′-), *n.* **1.** any solanaceous herb of the genus *Petunia,* native to tropical America, having funnel-shaped flowers of various colors. **2.** a deep, reddish purple. [< NL < obs. F *petun* tobacco < Tupi *petyn;* see -IA]

pe·tun·tse (pə tōōn′tsə; *Chin.* bô′dun′dzu′), *n.* a Chinese feldspathic mineral, pulverized and used in certain porcelains. Also, **pe·tun′tze.** [< Chin, equiv. to *pe* white + *tun* mound + *tze* formative particle (akin to *tzu* offspring)]

peu à peu (pœ a pœ′), *French.* little by little.

peu de chose (pœdᵊ shōz′), *French.* a trifling or unimportant matter.

Pevs·ner (*Russ.* pefs′ner), *n.* **An·toine** (*Fr.* äN twan′), 1886–1962, French sculptor and painter, born in Russia (brother of Naum Gabo).

pew (pyōō), *n.* **1.** (in a church) one of a number of fixed, benchlike seats with backs, accessible by aisles, for the use of the congregation. **2.** an enclosed seat in a church, or an enclosure with seats, appropriated to the use of a family or other group of worshipers. **3.** those occupying pews. [ME *puwe* < MF *puie* balcony < L *podia,* pl. (taken as sing.) of *podium* balcony. See PODIUM]

pew·age (pyōō′ij), *n.* **1.** an amount or the dues paid for a church pew. **2.** the pews of a church; pews collectively. [PEW + -AGE]

pe·wee (pē′wē), *n.* **1.** See **wood pewee. 2.** the phoebe. —*adj.* **3.** See **pee wee** (def. 1). [imit.]

pew′ hinge′, a rising hinge for a small door.

pew·hold·er (pyōō′hōl′dər), *n.* one who rents or owns a pew. [PEW + HOLDER]

pe·wit (pē′wit, pyōō′it), *n.* **1.** the lapwing, *Vanellus vanellus.* **2.** the phoebe. **3.** the European black-headed gull, *Larus ridibundus.* Also, **peewit.** [imit.]

pew·ter (pyōō′tər), *n.* **1.** any of various alloys in which tin is the chief constituent, originally one of tin and lead. **2.** a vessel or utensil made of such an alloy. **3.** such utensils collectively: *a revival of interest in pewter.* **4.** *Brit. Slang.* **a.** a cup awarded as a prize or trophy, as in a sporting event. **b.** See **prize money** (def. 2). —*adj.* **5.** consisting or made of pewter: *a pewter mug.* [ME *pewtre* < MF *peutre* << LL **piltrum* (whence also It *peltro*); akin to *spelter* zinc]

pew·ter·er (pyōō′tər ər), *n.* a maker of pewter utensils or vessels. [ME *peuterer* < MF *peutrier.* See PEWTER, -ER[2]]

-pexy, a learned borrowing from Greek used, with the meaning "fixation," in the formation of compound words: *mastopexy.* [< Gk *-pēxia,* equiv. to *pêx(is)* a fixing, solidity, coagulation + *-ia* -Y[3]]

pe·yo·te (pā ō′tē, pē-; *Sp.* pe yô′te), *n., pl.* **-tes** (-tēz; *Sp.* -tes). **1.** a cactus, *Lophophora Williamsii,* containing a drug having a narcotic effect; mescal: used esp. by the Indians of Mexico and certain regions of the southwestern U.S. **2.** the drug produced by this plant; mescaline. **3.** (in Mexico) any of several related or unrelated cacti. [< MexSp < Nahuatl *peyotl*]

Pey·ton (pāt′ᵊn), *n.* a boy's given name, form of **Payton.**

pey·tral (pā′trəl), *n. Armor.* a piece for the breast and shoulders of a horse. Also, **pey′trel, poitrel.** [ME *peytrel* < MF *peitral* < L *pectorāle* PECTORAL]

pF, picofarad; picofarads. Also, **pf**

Pf., **1.** perfect. **2.** pfennig. **3.** pianoforte. **4.** (of stock) preferred. **5.** proof.

p.f., *Music.* louder. [< It *più forte*]

Pfalz (pfälts), *n.* German name of **The Palatinate.**

Pfc., *Mil.* private first class.

pfd., (of stock) preferred.

pfen·nig (fen′ig; *Ger.* pfen′iкн), *n., pl.* **pfen·nigs, pfen′ni·ge** (*Ger.* pfen′i gə). **1.** a copper-coated iron coin and monetary unit of Germany, the 100th part of a Deutsche mark. **2.** (formerly) a minor coin and monetary unit of East Germany, the 100th part of an ostmark. [< G: PENNY]

pfg., pfennig.

Pfitz·ner (pfits′nər), *n.* **Hans E·rich** (häns ā′riкн), 1869–1949, German composer and conductor.

Pforz·heim (pfôrts′hīm′, pfôrts′-), *n.* a city in W Baden-Wurttemburg, in SW West Germany. 86,100 (1963).

Pfund′ se′ries (fund, pfōōnd), *Physics.* a series of lines in the infrared spectrum of hydrogen.

Pg, Portuguese.

Pg., **1.** Portugal. **2.** Portuguese.

pg., page.

P.G., **1.** Past Grand. **2.** paying guest. **3.** Postgraduate.

PGA, Professional Golfers' Association. Also, **P.G.A.**

PGA, *Biochem.* See **folic acid.** [*p(teroyl)* + *g(lutamic) a(cid)*]

Ph, *Chem.* phenyl.

pH, *Chem.* the symbol for the logarithm of the reciprocal of hydrogen ion concentration in gram atoms per liter. For example, a pH of 5 indicates a concentration of .00001 or 10^{-5} gram atoms of hydrogen ions in one liter of solution.

ph, phot; phots.

ph., **1.** phase. **2.** phone.

P.H., Public Health.

PHA, Public Housing Administration.

phac·o·lite (fak′ə līt′), *n. Mineral.* a colorless variety of chabazite. [< Gk *phakō(s)* lentel plant + -LITE]

Phae·a (fē′ə), *n. Class. Myth.* See **Crommyonian sow.**

Phae·a·cia (fē ā′shə), *n. Class. Myth.* an island nation on the shores of which Odysseus was shipwrecked and discovered by Nausicaä. —**Phae·a′cian,** *n., adj.*

Phae·ax (fē′aks), *n. Class. Myth.* a son of Corcyra and Poseidon, and the eponymous ancestor of the Phaeacians.

Phae·do (fē′dō), *n.* a philosophical dialogue (4th century B.C.) by Plato, purporting to describe the death of Socrates, dealing with the immortality of the soul, and setting forth the theory of Ideas.

Phae·dra (fē′drə), *n. Class. Myth.* a daughter of Minos and Pasiphaë, wife of Theseus, and stepmother of Hippolytus. She fell in love with Hippolytus and eventually hanged herself.

Phae·drus (fē′drəs), *n.* fl. A.D. c40, Roman writer of fables.

Pha·ën·na (fā en′ə), *n. Class. Myth.* one of the Graces worshiped at Sparta.

phae·o·mel·a·nin (fē′ō mel′ə nin), *n. Biochem.* a reddish-brown to dull-yellow pigment related to melanin and found chiefly in birds. [< Gk *phaió(s)* dusky + MELANIN]

Phaes·tus (fē′stəs), *n.* Phaistos.

Pha·ë·thon (fā′ə thon), *n. Class. Myth.* a son of Helios who borrowed the chariot of the sun for one day and drove it so dangerously close to earth that Zeus struck him down with a thunderbolt to save the world from catching fire. Cf. **Heliades.** [< Gk: lit., shining]

pha·e·ton (fā′i tᵊn *or, esp. Brit.,* fāt′ᵊn), *n.* **1.** a light, four-wheeled carriage, with or without a top, having one or two seats facing forward, and made in various forms. **2.** an automobile of the touring-car type. [special use of L *Phaetōn*, var. of *Phaethōn* PHAETHON]

Phaeton

-phage, a learned borrowing from Greek meaning "eating," "devouring," used in biology to refer to phagocytes: *bacteriophage.* Also, **-phag.** Cf. **-phagia, phago-, -phagous, -phagy.** [< Gk *-phagos*]

phag·e·de·na (faj′i dē′nə), *n. Pathol.* a severe, destructive, eroding ulcer. Also, **phag′e·dae′na.** [< medical L *phagedaena* < Gk *phagédaina* an ulcer, akin to *phagein* to eat] —**phag·e·den·ic, phag·e·daen·ic** (faj′i den′ik, -dē′nik), **phag′e·den′i·cal, phag′e·daen′i·cal, phag·e·de·nous, phag·e·dae·nous** (faj′i dē′nəs), *adj.*

-phagia, var. of **-phagy.** [< NL < Gk]

phago-, a learned borrowing from Greek referring to eating, used in the formation of compound words: *phagocyte.* Cf. **-phage, -phagous, -phagy.** [< Gk, comb. form akin to *phagein* to eat, devour]

phag·o·cyte (fag′ə sīt′), *n. Physiol.* a blood cell that ingests and destroys foreign particles, bacteria, and other cells. [PHAGO- + -CYTE] —**phag·o·cyt·ic** (fag′ə sit′ik), *adj.*

phag′ocyt′ic in′dex, the average number of bacteria ingested per phagocyte in an incubated mixture of bacteria, phagocytes, and blood serum: used in determining the opsonic index.

phag·o·cyt·ize (fag′ə sī′tīz, -si tīz′), *v.t.,* **-ized, -iz·ing.** (of a phagocyte) to devour (material). [PHAGOCYTE + -IZE]

phag·o·cy·tol·y·sis (fag′ə sī tol′i sis), *n.* the destruction of phagocytes. [PHAGOCYTE + -O- + -LYSIS] —**phag·o·cy·to·lyt·ic** (fag′ə sīt′ᵊlit′ik), *adj.*

phag·o·cy·tose (fag′ə sī′tōs, -tōz), *v.t.,* **-tosed, -tos·ing.** phagocytize. [PHAGOCYTE + -OSE^{2}]

phag·o·cy·to·sis (fag′ə sī tō′sis), *n.* the ingestion and destruction of particlelike matter by cells, esp. of infectious microorganisms in man. [PHAGOCYTE + -OSIS]

pha·gol·y·sis (fə gol′i sis), *n.* phagocytolysis. [PHAGO- + -LYSIS] —**phag·o·lyt·ic** (fag′ə lit′ik), *adj.*

-phagous, a word element meaning "eating," "feeding on," "devouring," used to form adjectives corresponding to nouns ending in *-phage: creophagous; hylophagous; rhizophagous.* [< Gk *-phagos*]

-phagy, a word element used as a noun termination meaning "eating," "devouring," esp. as a practice or habit: *allotriophagy; anthropophagy.* Also, **-phagia.** [< Gk *-phagia;* see -PHAGE, -Y^{3}]

pha·i·no·pep·la (fā i′nō pep′lə, fā′ə-), *n.* a crested passerine bird, *Phainopepla nitens,* of the southwestern U.S. and Mexico. [< NL < Gk *phaeinó(s)* shining (verbal of *phâein* to shine) + *péplа,* pl. of *péplos* PEPLOS]

Phais·tos (fī′stəs), *n.* an ancient city in S central Crete: site of Minoan palace; Linear A tablets and important pottery objects unearthed here. Also, **Phaestus.**

phal·ange (fal′ənj, fə lanj′), *n., pl.* **pha·lan·ges** (fə lan′jēz). *Anat., Zool.* a phalanx. [back formation from PHALANGES]

pha·lan·ge·al (fə lan′jē əl), *adj.* **1.** of or pertaining to a phalanx. **2.** *Anat., Zool.* of or pertaining to a phalanx or the phalanges. [< NL *phalange(us)* + -AL^{1}]

pha·lan·ger (fə lan′jər), *n.* any of numerous arboreal marsupials of the family *Phalangeridae,* of the Australian region, having foxlike ears and a long, bushy tail. [< L *phalang-* PHALANX + -ER^{1}]

pha·lan·ges (fə lan′jēz), *n.* **1.** a pl. of **phalanx. 2.** pl. of **phalange.** [< L < Gk]

phal·an·ste·ri·an (fal′ən stēr′ē ən), *adj.* **1.** of or pertaining to a phalanstery. **2.** of or pertaining to phalansterianism. —*n.* **3.** a member of a phalanstery. **4.** an advocate of phalansterianism; a Fourierist. [PHALANSTERY + -AN]

phal·an·ste·ri·an·ism (fal′ən stēr′ē ə niz′əm), *n.* a system by which society would be reorganized into units comprising their own social and industrial elements; Fourierism. [PHALANSTERIAN + -ISM]

phal·an·ster·y (fal′ən ster′ē), *n., pl.* **-ster·ies. 1.** (in Fourierism) **a.** the buildings occupied by a phalanx. **b.** the community itself. **2.** any similar association, or the buildings they occupy. [< F *phalanstère,* b. *phalange* phalanx + *monastère* monastery]

pha·lanx (fā′langks, fal′angks), *n., pl.* **pha·lanx·es** or, for 6, **pha·lang·es** (fə lan′jēz), *v.* —*n.* **1.** (in ancient Greece) a body of heavily-armed infantry formed in ranks and files close and deep, with shields joined and long spears overlapping. **2.** any body of troops in close array. **3.** a compact or closely massed body of persons, animals, or things. **4.** a number of individuals, esp. persons, united for a common purpose. **5.** (in Fourierism) a group of about 1800 persons, living together and holding their property in common. **6.** *Anat., Zool.* any of the bones of the fingers or toes. See diag. under **skeleton. 7.** *Bot.* a bundle of stamens, joined by their filaments. —*v.i.* **8.** *Print.* to arrange the distribution of work in a shop as evenly as possible. [< L < Gk military formation, bone of finger or toe, wooden roller, etc.]

phal·a·rope (fal′ə rōp′), *n.* any of three species of small, aquatic birds of the family *Phalaropodidae,* resembling sandpipers but having lobate toes. [< F < NL *Phalărop(ūs)* genus name < Gk *phalār(is)* coot + *-o-* -o- + *poûs* foot]

phal·er·a (fal′ər ə), *n., pl.* **phal·er·ae** (fal′ə rē′). a metal disk or boss worn on a man's breast as an ornament or as a military decoration or used to adorn the harness of a horse. [< L: metal disk or boss < Gk *phálara* cheek-pieces]

Pha·le·rus (fə lēr′əs), *n. Class. Myth.* a son of Alcon who became one of the Argonauts.

phal·lic (fal′ik), *adj.* of or pertaining to the phallus or phallicism. Also, **phal′li·cal.** [< Gk *phallik(ós).* See PHALLUS, -IC]

phal·li·cism (fal′i siz′əm), *n.* worship of the phallus, esp. as symbolic of power or of the creative power of nature. Also, **phal·lism** (fal′iz əm). [PHALLIC + -ISM] —**phal′li·cist, phal′list,** *n.*

phal·lus (fal′əs), *n., pl.* **phal·li** (fal′ī), **phal·lus·es. 1.** an image of the male reproductive organ, symbolizing in certain religious systems the generative power in nature, esp. that carried in procession in ancient festivals of Dionysus, or Bacchus. **2.** *Anat.* the penis, the clitoris, or the sexually undifferentiated embryonic organ out of which either of these develops. [< L < Gk *phallós* penis]

phan·a·tron (fan′ə tron′), *n.* phanotron.

-phane, a learned borrowing from Greek indicating an apparent similarity to some particular substance: *cellophane.* Cf. **-phany.** [< Gk *phan-* (s. of *phaínein*) shine, appear (in pass.)]

phan·er·ite (fan′ə rīt′), *n.* any igneous rock of which the grains are visible to the naked eye. [< Gk *phaner(ós)* manifest, visible + -ITE^{1}] —**phan·er·it·ic** (fan′ə rit′ik), *adj.*

phan·e·ro·crys·tal·line (fan′ə rō kris′tᵊ lin, -tᵊlīn′), *adj. Mineral.* (of a rock) having the principal constituents in the form of crystals visible to the naked eye. [< Gk *phaneró(s)* visible, manifest + CRYSTALLINE]

phan·er·o·gam (fan′ər ə gam′), *n. Bot.* any of the *Phanerogamia,* a former primary division of plants comprising those having reproductive organs; a flowering plant or seed plant (opposed to *cryptogam*). [< NL *phanerogam(us),* equiv. to Gk *phaneró(s)* visible (see -PHANE) + *-gamos* -GAMOUS] —**phan′er·o·gam′ic, phan·er·og·a·mous** (fan′ə rog′ə məs), **phan·er·o·ga·mi·an** (fan′ər ə gā′mē ən), *adj.* —**phan′er·og′a·my,** *n.*

Phan·er·o·zo·ic (fan′ər ə zō′ik), *Geol.* —*n.* **1.** the eon comprising the Paleozoic, Mesozoic, and Cenozoic eras. —*adj.* **2.** of or pertaining to this eon. [< Gk *phaner(ós)* manifest, visible + -ZOIC]

phan·o (fan′ō), *n., pl.* **phan·os.** fanon.

phan·o·tron (fan′ə tron′), *n. Electronics.* a hot-cathode gas diode. Also, **phanatron.** [? < Gk *phan(ázein)* (to) appear + -TRON]

phan·tasm (fan′taz əm), *n.* **1.** an apparition or specter. **2.** a creation of the imagination or fancy. **3.** an illusive likeness of something. **4.** a mental image or representation of a real object. Also, **fantasm.** [< L *phantasm(a)* < Gk: image, vision, etc. (akin to *phantázein* to bring before the mind); r. ME *fantesme* < OF]
—**Syn. 1.** ghost, vision. See **apparition. 3.** hallucination, illusion.

phan·tas·ma (fan taz′mə), *n., pl.* **-ma·ta** (-mə tə). phantasm (defs. 1, 2). [< L]

phan·tas·ma·go·ri·a (fan taz′mə gôr′ē ə, -gōr′-), *n.* **1.** a shifting series of phantasms, illusions, or deceptive appearances, as in a dream or as created by the imagination. **2.** a changing scene made up of many elements. **3.** optical illusions that are produced by a magic lantern or the like and in which figures increase or diminish in size, pass into each other, dissolve, etc. [< NL < Gk *phántasm(a)* image, vision + (?) *agor(á)* an assembly + *-ia* -IA] —**phan·tas′ma·go′ri·al, phan·tas·ma·gor·ic** (fan taz′mə gôr′ik, -gor′-), **phan·tas′ma·gor′i·cal, phan·tas′ma·go′ri·an,** *adj.* —**phan·tas′ma·go′ri·al·ly, phan·tas′ma·gor′i·cal·ly, phan·tas′ma·go′ri·an·ly,** *adv.* —**phan·tas′ma·gor′ist,** *n.*

phan·tas·ma·go·ry (fan taz′mə gôr′ē, -gōr′ē), *n., pl.* **-ries.** phantasmagoria.

phan·tas·mal (fan taz′məl), *adj.* pertaining to or of the nature of a phantasm; unreal; illusory; spectral: *He saw himself as surrounded by the creatures of some weird, phantasmal world of his subconscious.* Also, **phan·tas′mic, phan·tas′mi·cal, phan·tas·mat·ic** (fan′taz mat′ik), **phan′tas·mat′i·cal.** [PHANTASM + -AL^{1}] —**phan·tas·mal·i·ty** (fan′taz mal′i tē), *n.* —**phan·tas′mal·ly, phan·tas′mi·cal·ly, phan′tas·mat′i·cal·ly,** *adv.*

phan·tast (fan′tast), *n.* fantast.

phan·tas·tron (fan tas′tron), *n. Electronics.* an electronic circuit utilizing a pentode that, on receiving a triggering signal, generates a sharp pulse output for an accurately adjustable time interval.

Phan·ta·sus (fan′tə səs), *n. Class. Myth.* an ancient Greek god of dreams who assumed the shapes of inanimate objects.

phan·ta·sy (fan′tə sē, -zē), *n., pl.* **-sies.** fantasy. —**phan·tas·tic** (fan tas′tik), **phan·tas′ti·cal,** *adj.*

phan·tom (fan′təm), *n.* **1.** an image appearing in a dream or formed in the mind. **2.** an apparition or specter. **3.** a thing or person that is little more than an appearance or show: *a phantom of a ruler.* **4.** an appearance without material substance. —*adj.* **5.** of, pertaining to, or of the nature of a phantom; illusory: *a phantom sea serpent; a phantom invader.* **6.** *Elect.* noting or pertaining to a phantom circuit. Also, **fantom.** [ME *fantosme* < MF, OF, < L *phantasma* PHANTASM] —**phan′tom·like′,** *adj.*
—**Syn. 1.** See **apparition. 5.** imaginary. —**Ant. 5.** real, material.

phan′tom accelera′tion, *Rocketry.* the acceleration of a missile due to Coriolis acceleration or to the earth's irregular shape.

phan′tom cir′cuit, *Elect.* a circuit derived from two suitably arranged pairs of wires, each pair being a circuit **(side circuit)** and also acting as one half of an additional derived circuit, the entire system providing the capabilities of three circuits while requiring wires for only two.

-phany, an element occurring in loan words from Greek, meaning "appearance," "manifestation" (*epiphany*); used in the formation of compound words (*Christophany; Satanophany*). Cf. **-phane.** [< Gk *-phanía*]

Pha·on (fā′ən), *n. Class. Myth.* an aged boatman who was given youth by Aphrodite.

Phar., **1.** pharmaceutical. **2.** pharmacology. **3.** pharmacopoeia. **4.** pharmacy. Also, **phar.**

Phar·aoh (fâr′ō), *n.* a title of an ancient Egyptian king. [ME *Pharao,* OE *Pharaon* < L < Gk < Heb *Par'ōh* < Egypt *per-'o* great house] —**Phar·a·on·ic** (fâr′ā on′ik), **Phar′a·on′i·cal,** *adj.*

Phar′aoh ant′, a red or yellow ant, *Monomorium pharaonis,* introduced from Europe, commonly found as a household pest, esp. in the northern U.S. Also, **Phar′aoh's ant′.**

Phar.B., Bachelor of Pharmacy.

Phar.D., Doctor of Pharmacy.

Phar·i·sa·ic (far′i sā′ik), *adj.* **1.** of or pertaining to the Pharisees. **2.** (*l.c.*) practicing or advocating strict observance of external forms and ceremonies of religion or conduct without regard to the spirit; self-righteous; sanctimonious. Also, **Phar′i·sa′i·cal.** [< LL *Pharisaic(us)* < Gk *Pharisaikós.* See PHARISEE, -IC] —**Phar′i·sa′i·cal·ly,** *adv.* —**Phar′i·sa′i·cal·ness,** *n.*

Phar·i·sa·ism (far′i sā iz′əm), *n.* **1.** the principles and practices of the Pharisees. **2.** (*l.c.*) rigid observance of external forms of religion or conduct without genuine piety; hypocrisy. Also, **Phar·i·see·ism** (far′i sē iz′əm). [< NL *Pharisaism(us).* See PHARISA(IC), -ISM] —**Phar′i·sa·ist,** *adj.*

Phar·i·see (far′i sē′), *n.* **1.** *Judaism.* a member of a Jewish sect, consisting mainly of laymen and scholars, which flourished during the 1st century B.C. and 1st century A.D. and which differed from the Sadducees chiefly in its strict observance of religious ceremonies and practices, liberal interpretation of the Scriptures, adherence to oral laws and traditions, and belief in an afterlife and the coming of a Messiah. **2.** (*l.c.*) a sanctimonious, self-righteous, or hypocritical person. [ME *Pharise, Farise,* OE *Fariséus* < LL *Pharīsēus,* var. of *Pharīsaeus* < Gk *Pharīsaîos* < Aram *p'rīshāiyā,* pl. of *p'rīsh* separated]

Pharm., **1.** pharmaceutical. **2.** pharmacology. **3.** pharmacopoeia. **4.** pharmacy. Also, **pharm.**

phar·ma·ceu·ti·cal (fär′mə sōō′ti kəl), *adj.* **1.** pertaining to pharmacy. —*n.* **2.** a pharmaceutical preparation; drug. Also, **phar′ma·ceu′tic.** [PHARMACEUTIC(S) + -AL^{1}] —**phar′ma·ceu′ti·cal·ly,** *adv.*

phar·ma·ceu·tics (fär′mə sōō′tiks), *n.* (*construed as sing.*) pharmacy (def. 1). [< L *pharmaceutic(us)* < Gk *pharmakeutikós.* See PHARMACY, -IC, -ICS]

phar·ma·cist (fär′mə sist), *n.* one skilled in and having the authorization to engage in pharmacy; druggist; apothecary; pharmaceutical chemist. Also, **phar·ma·ceu·tist** (fär′mə sōō′tist). [PHARMAC(Y) + -IST]
—**Syn.** chemist.

pharmaco-, a learned borrowing from Greek meaning "drug," used in the formation of compound words: *pharmacology.* [comb. form repr. Gk *phármakon* drug]

phar·ma·co·dy·nam·ics (fär′mə kō dī nam′iks), *n.* (*construed as sing.*) the branch of pharmacology dealing with the course of action, effect, and breakdown of drugs within the body. [PHARMACO- + DYNAMICS] —**phar′ma·co·dy·nam′ic, phar′ma·co·dy·nam′i·cal,** *adj.*

phar·ma·cog·no·sy (fär′mə kog′nə sē), *n.* See **materia medica** (def. 2). [PHARMACO- + -GNOS(IS) + -Y^{3}] —**phar′ma·cog′no·sist,** *n.* —**phar·ma·cog·nos·tic** (fär′mə kog nos′tik), *adj.*

phar·mac·o·lite (fär mak′ə līt′, fär′mə kə-), *n.* a mineral, hydrous arsenate of calcium, $2CaO \cdot As_2O_5 \cdot 5H_2O$, formed by the alteration of mineral deposits containing arsenopyrite and arsenical ores of cobalt and silver. [PHARMACO- + -LITE; modeled on G *Pharmakolith*]

phar·ma·col·o·gy (fär′mə kol′ə jē), *n.* the science dealing with the preparation, uses, and esp. the effects, of drugs. [< NL *pharmacologia.* See PHARMACO-, -LOGY] —**phar·ma·co·log·i·cal** (fär′mə kə loj′i kəl), **phar′ma·co·log′ic,** *adj.* —**phar′ma·co·log′i·cal·ly,** *adv.* —**phar′ma·col′o·gist,** *n.*

phar·ma·co·poe·ia (fär′mə kə pē′ə), *n. Pharm.* **1.** a book published usually under the jurisdiction of the government and containing a list of drugs, their formulas, methods for making medicinal preparations, requirements and tests for their strength and purity, and other related information. **2.** a stock of drugs. Also, **phar′ma·co·pe′ia.** [< NL < Gk *pharmakopoiía* drug-maker's art, equiv. to *phármako(n)* drug + *-poi(os)* maker, making (*poi(eîn)* (to) make + *-os* adj. suffix) + *-ia* -IA] —**phar′ma·co·poe′ial, phar′ma·co·poe′ic,** *adj.* —**phar′ma·co·poe′ist,** *n.*

phar·ma·co·psy·cho·sis (fär′mə kō sī kō′sis), *n. Psychiatry.* a psychosis caused by a drug. [PHARMACO- + PSYCHOSIS]

phar·ma·cy (fär′mə sē), *n., pl.* **-cies. 1.** the art and science of preparing and dispensing drugs. **2.** drugstore. [earlier *pharmacia* < LL < Gk *pharmakeía* druggist's work. See PHARMACO-, -Y^{3}]

Pharm.D., Doctor of Pharmacy.

Pharm.M., Master of Pharmacy.

Pha·ros (fâr′os), *n.* **1.** a small peninsula in the N United Arab Republic, near Alexandria: site of ancient lighthouse built by Ptolemy. **2.** the lighthouse on this peninsula. Cf. **Seven Wonders of the World. 3.** any lighthouse or beacon to direct seamen.

Phar·sa·li·a (fär sā′lē ə), *n.* a district in ancient Greece whose chief city was Pharsalus. —**Phar·sa′li·an,** *adj.*

Phar·sa·lus (fär sā′ləs), *n.* an ancient city in central Greece, in Thessaly: site of Caesar's victory over Pompey 48 B.C.

pharyng-, var. of **pharyngo-** before a vowel: *pharyngitis.*

pha·ryn·ge·al (fə rin′jē əl, -jəl, far′in jē′əl), *adj.* of, pertaining to, or situated near the pharynx. Also, **pha·ryn·gal** (fə ring′gəl). [< NL *pharynge(us)* pharyngeal (see PHARYNG-, -EOUS) + -AL[1]]

phar·yn·gec·to·my (far′in jek′tə mē), *n., pl.* **-mies.** *Surg.* excision of part or all of the pharynx. [PHARYNG- + -ECTOMY]

phar·yn·gi·tis (far′in jī′tis), *n. Pathol.* inflammation of the mucous membrane of the pharynx. [PHARYNG- + -ITIS]

pharyngo-, a learned borrowing from Greek, used as the combining form of *pharynx* in the formation of compound words: *pharyngology.* Also, *esp. before a vowel,* **pharyng-.** [< Gk, comb. form of *phárynx* throat]

phar·yn·gol·o·gy (far′ing gol′ə jē), *n.* the science of the pharynx and its diseases. [PHARYNGO- + -LOGY]

pha·ryn·go·scope (fə ring′gə skōp′), *n.* an instrument for inspecting the pharynx. [PHARYNGO- + -SCOPE] —**phar·yn·gos·co·py** (far′ing gos′kə pē), *n.*

phar·ynx (far′ingks), *n., pl.* **phar·yn·ges** (fə rin′jēz), **phar·ynx·es.** *Anat.* the tube or cavity, with its surrounding membrane and muscles, which connects the mouth and nasal passages with the esophagus. [< NL < Gk: throat, akin to *pháranx* gulf, chasm]

phase (fāz), *n., v.,* **phased, phas·ing.** —*n.* **1.** any of the major appearances or aspects in which a thing of varying modes or conditions manifests itself to the eye or mind. **2.** a stage in a process of change or development: *The adolescent phase of man is full of uncertainties.* **3.** a side, aspect, or point of view: *This is only one phase of the question.* **4.** a state of synchronous operation: *to put two mechanisms in phase.* **5.** *Astron.* **a.** the particular appearance presented by the moon or a planet at a given time. **b.** one of the recurring appearances or states of the moon or a planet in respect to the form, or the absence, of its illuminated disk: *the phases of the moon.* **6.** *Biol.* an aspect of or stage in meiosis or mitosis. **7.** *Zool.* See **color phase. 8.** *Chem.* a mechanically separate, homogeneous part of a heterogeneous system: *the solid, liquid, and gaseous phases of a system.* **9.** *Physics.* a particular stage or point of advancement in a cycle; the fractional part of the period through which the time has advanced, measured from some arbitrary origin. **10.** *Survey.* unequal illumination of the two sides of a target. —*v.t.* **11.** to schedule or order so as to be available when or as needed: *to phase the various processes in book production.* **12.** to put in phase; synchronize: *to phase one mechanism with another.* **13.** **phase in,** to put into use or incorporate gradually or by degrees: *to phase in new machinery for increased automation.* **14.** **phase out,** to ease (something) out of service; withdraw gradually: *plans to phase out obsolescent machinery.* [back formation from *phases,* pl. of PHASIS] —**phase′less,** *adj.* —**pha′sic, pha′se·al,** *adj.*
—**Syn. 1.** form, shape; facet, side.

phase′ mi′croscope, a microscope that utilizes the phase differences of light rays transmitted by different portions of an object to create an image in which the details of the object are distinct, despite their near-uniformity of refractive index. Also called **phase′-con′trast mi′croscope** (fāz′kon′trast), **phase′-dif′fer·ence mi′croscope** (fāz′dif′ər əns, -dif′rəns).

phase′ modula′tion, *Electronics.* radio transmission in which the carrier wave is modulated by changing its phase to transmit the amplitude and pitch of the signal.

phase′ rule′, *Physical Chem.* a law that the number of degrees of freedom in a system in equilibrium is equal to two plus the number of components less the number of phases. Thus, a system of ice, melted ice, and water vapor, being one component and three phases, has no degrees of freedom. Cf. **variance** (def. 4).

phase′ space′, *Physics.* a hypothetical space constructed so as to have as many coordinates as are necessary to define the state of a given substance or system.

phase′ veloc′ity, *Physics.* the velocity with which a simple harmonic wave is propagated, equal to the wavelength divided by the period of vibration. Cf. **group velocity, particle velocity.**

-phasia, a learned borrowing from Greek, used to refer to disordered speech in the formation of compound words: *aphasia.* Also, **-phasy.** [< Gk, comb. form akin to *phánai* to speak]

pha·sis (fā′sis), *n., pl.* **-ses** (-sēz). a manner, stage, or aspect of being; phase. [< NL < Gk *phásis* appearance < *pha-* (root of *phaínein* to show) + *-sis* -SIS]

phas·ma·jec·tor (faz′mə jek′tər), *n. Rare.* monoscope. [< L *phasma* apparition (see PHANTOM) + (PRO)JECTOR]

Phaye (fā), *n.* a girl's given name, form of **Fae.**

Ph.B., Bachelor of Philosophy. [< L *Philosophiae Baccalaureus*]

Ph. C., Pharmaceutical Chemist.

Ph.D., Doctor of Philosophy. [< L *Philosophiae Doctor*]

P.H.E., Public Health Engineer.

pheas·ant (fez′ənt), *n.* **1.** any of numerous large, usually long-tailed, gallinaceous birds of the family *Phasianidae,* of the Old World. **2.** *Southern U.S.* the ruffed grouse. **3.** any of various other birds that resemble or suggest a pheasant. [ME *fesaunt* < AF, OF *fesan* < L *phāsiān(us)* < Gk *phāsiānós (órnis)* (bird) of the Phasis river]

Ring-necked pheasant, *Phasianus colchicus* (Length to 3 ft.)

pheas·ant's-eye (fez′ənts ī′), *n., pl.* **-eyes.** an herb, *Adonis annua,* of Eurasia, having red flowers with a prominent dark center.

Pheb (fēb), *n.* a girl's given name, form of **Phebe** or **Phoebe.**

Phe·be (fē′bē), *n.* a girl's given name. Also, **Phoebe.**

Phè·dre (*Fr.* fe′drə), *n.* a tragedy (1677) by Racine.

Phe·ge·us (fē′jē əs, -jōōs), *n. Class. Myth.* a king of Psophis who purified Alcmaeon, gave him his daughter Arsinoë in marriage, and later murdered him for betraying her.

Phei·dip·pi·des (fī dip′i dēz′), *n.* the Athenian runner who secured aid from Sparta in the struggle between the Athenians and the Persians 490 B.C. Also, **Philippides.**

phel·lem (fel′əm, -em), *n. Bot.* cork (def. 6). [< Gk *phell(ós)* cork + (PHLO)EM]

phel·lo·derm (fel′ə dûrm′), *n. Bot.* a layer of tissue in certain plants, formed from the inner cells of phellogen and consisting usually of chlorenchyma. [< Gk *phelló(s)* cork + -DERM] —**phel′lo·der′mal,** *adj.*

phel·lo·gen (fel′ə jən), *n. Bot.* cork cambium, a layer of tissue or secondary meristem external to the true cambium, giving rise to cork tissue on the outside and phelloderm on the inside. [< Gk *phelló(s)* cork + -GEN] —**phel·lo·ge·net·ic** (fel′ə jə net′ik), **phel·lo·gen·ic** (fel′ə jen′ik), *adj.*

phe·lo·ni·on (fe lô′nē ôn; *Eng.* fə lō′nē ən), *n., pl.* **-ni·a** (-nē ä; *Eng.* -nē ə), **-ni·ons.** *Gk. Orth. Ch.* a liturgical vestment resembling the chasuble, worn by priests. Also called **phenolion.** [< Gk *phelónion* a kind of mantle]

Phelps (felps), *n.* **1. William Ly·on** (lī′ən), 1865–1943, U.S. educator and literary critic. **2.** a boy's given name.

Phem·e·rol (fem′ə rōl′, -rôl′, -rol′), *n. Pharm., Trademark.* See **benzethonium chloride.**

Phe·mi·us (fē′mē əs), *n.* (in the *Odyssey*) a bard who, against his will, entertained the suitors of Penelope.

phen-, var. of **pheno-** esp. before a vowel: *phenazine.*

phe·na·caine (fē′nə kān′, fen′ə-), *n. Pharm.* a compound, $C_{18}H_{22}N_2O_2$, usually used in the form of its hydrochloride as a local anesthetic for the eye. [PHEN- + A(CET)- + (CO)CAINE]

phe·nac·e·tin (fə nas′i tin), *n. Pharm.* acetophenetidin. [PHEN(ETIDINE) + ACET(YL) + -IN[2]]

phen·a·cite (fen′ə sīt′), *n.* a rare vitreous mineral, beryllium silicate, Be_2SiO_4, occurring in crystals, sometimes used as a gem. [< Gk *phenak-* (s. of *phénax*) a cheat, quack + -ITE[1]]

phe·nan·thra·qui·none (fə nan′thrə kwi nōn′, -kwin′ōn), *n.* (erroneously) phenanthrenequinone.

phe·nan·threne (fə nan′thrēn), *n. Chem.* a colorless, shiny, crystalline, water-insoluble isomer of anthracine, $C_{14}H_{10}$, derived from coal tar: used chiefly in dyestuffs and in the synthesis of drugs. [PHEN- + ANTHR- + -ENE]

phen·an·threne·qui·none (fi nan′thrēn kwi nōn′, -kwin′ōn), *n. Chem.* a yellowish-orange, crystalline, water-insoluble solid, $C_6H_4COCOC_6H_4$, used chiefly in organic synthesis and the manufacture of dyes. [PHENANTHRENE + QUIN(INE) + -ONE]

phen·ar′sa·zine chlo′ride (fi när′sə zēn′), *Chem.* adamsite. [PHEN- + ARS(ENIC) + AZINE]

phen·a·zine (fen′ə zēn′, -zin), *n. Chem.* a yellow, crystalline, slightly water-soluble solid, $C_6H_4N_2C_6H_4$, used in organic synthesis chiefly in the manufacture of dyes. Also called **azophenylene.** [PHEN- + AZINE]

phen·cy·cli·dine (fen sī′kli dēn′, -sik′li-), *n.* an anesthetic drug, $C_{17}H_{25}N$, used as an animal tranquilizer: also widely used in several forms as an illicit hallucinogen. Cf. **angel dust, PCP.** [PHEN- + CYCL(IC) + -ID[3] + -INE[1]]

phen·eth′yl al′cohol (fen eth′əl), *Chem.* a colorless, viscous, slightly water-soluble liquid, $C_6H_5CH_2CH_2OH$, having a faint roselike odor: used chiefly in perfumery. Also, **phenylethyl alcohol.** [PHEN- + ETHYL]

phe·net·i·dine (fə net′i dēn′, -din), *n. Chem.* a colorless organic liquid, $H_2NC_6H_4OC_2H_5$, used chiefly in its para form (**para-phenetidine**) in the synthesis of phenacetin, dyes, and other compounds. Also, **phe·net·i·din** (fə net′i din). [PHENET(OLE) + -ID[3] + -INE[2]]

phen·e·tole (fen′i tōl′, -tol′), *n. Chem.* a colorless, volatile, aromatic, water-insoluble liquid, $C_6H_5OC_2H_5$. Also called **phenyl ethyl ether.** [PHEN- + ET(HYL) + -OLE]

phen·for·min (fen fôr′min), *n. Pharm.* See **DBI.** [PHEN- + FORM(ALIN) + -IN[2]]

Phe·ni·cia (fə nish′ə, -nē′shə), *n.* Phoenicia.

phe·nix (fē′niks), *n.* phoenix.

Phe′nix Cit′y (fē′niks), a city in E Alabama, on the Chattahoochee River. 27,630 (1960).

phen·met·ra·zine (fen me′trə zēn′), *n. Pharm.* a compound, $C_{11}H_{15}NO$, used in the form of its hydrochloride chiefly to control the appetite in the treatment of obesity. [PHEN(YL) + ME(THYL + TE)TRA- + (OXA)ZINE]

pheno-, **1.** a learned borrowing from Greek meaning "shining," used in the formation of compound words: *phenocryst.* **2.** *Chem.* a combining form indicating derivation from benzene, relationship to aromatic compounds, and referring to the phenyl group and sometimes phenol; used esp. before a consonant: *phenobarbital.* Also, *esp. before a vowel,* **phen-.** [< Gk *phaino-* shining, comb. form of *phaínein* to shine, appear; in chemical senses, used orig. with reference to products from the manufacture of illuminating gas]

phe·no·bar·bi·tal (fē′nō bär′bi tal′, -tôl′, -nə-), *n. Pharm.* a white, crystalline powder, $C_{12}H_{12}N_2O_3$, available also as the sodium salt (**phenobar′bital so′dium**) for greater solubility: used as a sedative, a hypnotic, and as an antispasmodic in epilepsy. Also, *esp. Brit.,* **phenobarbitone.** Also called **phenylethylbarbituric acid, phenylethylmalonylurea.** [PHENO- + BARBITAL]

phe·no·bar·bi·tone (fē′nō bär′bi tōn′), *n. Pharm., Chiefly Brit.* phenobarbital. [PHENO- + BARBIT(URIC ACID) + -ONE]

phe·no·cryst (fē′nə krist, fen′ə-), *n. Geol.* any of the conspicuous crystals in a porphyritic rock. [PHENO- + CRYST(AL)]

phe·nol (fē′nōl, -nol), *n. Chem.* **1.** Also called **carbolic acid, hydroxybenzine, oxybenzene, phenylic acid.** a white, crystalline, water-soluble, poisonous mass, C_6H_5OH, obtained from coal tar, or a hydroxyl derivative of benzene: used chiefly as a disinfectant, as an antiseptic, and in organic synthesis. **2.** any analogous hydroxyl derivative of benzene. [PHEN- + -OL[1]] —**phe·no·lic** (fi nō′lik, -nol′-, -nol′ik), *adj.*

phe·no·late (fēn′əl āt′), *n., v.,* **-lat·ed, -lat·ing.** —*n.* **1.** Also called **phenoxide.** a salt of phenol, as sodium phenolate, C_6H_5ONa. —*v.i.* **2.** to treat, impregnate, or disinfect with phenol; carbolize. [PHENOL + -ATE[2]]

phe·no·lat·ed (fēn′əl ā′tid), *adj. Chem.* containing phenol; carbolated. [PHENOL + -ATE[1] + -ED[2]]

phe′nol coeffi′cient, *Chem.* the number indicating the effectiveness of a disinfectant as a germicide relative to phenol, arbitrarily assigned the number 1, based on the time required to kill a given quantity of a specific type of bacteria.

pheno′lic res′in, *Chem.* any of the class of thermosetting resins formed by the condensation of phenol, or of a phenol derivative, with an aldehyde, esp. formaldehyde: used chiefly in the manufacture of paints and plastics and as adhesives for sandpaper and plywood. [PHENOL + -IC]

phe·no·li·on (fe nô′lē ôn; *Eng.* fə nō′lē ən), *n., pl.* **-li·a** (-lē ä; *Eng.* -lē ə), **-li·ons.** *Gk. Orth. Ch.* phelonion.

phe·nol·o·gy (fi nol′ə jē), *n.* the science dealing with the influence of climate on the recurrence of such annual phenomena of animal and plant life as bird migrations, budding, etc. [syncopated var. of PHENOMENOLOGY, with restriction to climatic phenomena] —**phe·no·log·i·cal** (fēn′əl oj′i kəl), *adj.* —**phe′no·log′i·cal·ly,** *adv.* —**phe·nol′o·gist,** *n.*

phe·nol·phthal·ein (fē′nōl thal′ēn, -ē in, -fthal′-, -nol-), *n. Chem., Pharm.* a white, crystalline, water-insoluble compound, $C_{20}H_{14}O_4$, used as an indicator in acid-base titration and as a laxative. [PHENOL + PHTHALEIN]

phe·nom·e·na (fi nom′ə nə), *n.* a pl. of **phenomenon.**

phe·nom·e·nal (fi nom′ə nəl), *adj.* **1.** extraordinary or prodigious: *phenomenal speed.* **2.** of or pertaining to phenomena or to a phenomenon. **3.** of the nature of a phenomenon; cognizable by the senses. [PHENOMEN(ON) + -AL[1]] —**phe·nom′e·nal·i·ty** (fi nom′ə nal′i tē), *n.* —**phe·nom′e·nal·ly,** *adv.*

phe·nom·e·nal·ism (fi nom′ə nəliz′əm), *n. Philos.* **1.** a manner or habit of thinking that considers things as phenomena only. **2.** the doctrine that phenomena are the only objects of knowledge or the only form of reality. [PHENOMENAL + -ISM] —**phe·nom′e·nal·ist,** *n.* —**phe·nom′e·nal·is′tic,** *adj.* —**phe·nom′e·nal·is′ti·cal·ly,** *adv.*

phe·nom·e·nal·ize (fi nom′ə nəlīz′), *v.t.,* **-ized, -iz·ing.** *Philos.* to regard or interpret purely as a phenomenon. Also, **phenomenize.** [PHENOMENAL + -IZE]

phe·nom·e·nize (fi nom′ə nīz′), *v.t.,* **-nized, -nizing.** *Philos.* phenomenalize.

phe·nom·e·nol·o·gy (fi nom′ə nol′ə jē), *n. Philos.* **1.** the study of phenomena. **2.** the system of Husserl and his followers. It stresses the careful description of phenomena in all areas of experience. [PHENOMEN(A) + -O- + -LOGY] —**phe·nom·e·no·log·i·cal** (fi nom′ə nəloj′i kəl), **phe·nom′e·no·log′ic,** *adj.* —**phe·nom′e·no·log′i·cal·ly,** *adv.*

phe·nom·e·non (fi nom′ə non′), *n., pl.* **-na** (-nə) for 1, 3, **-nons** for 2. **1.** a fact, occurrence, or circumstance observed or observable: *to study the phenomena of nature.* **2.** something that impresses the observer as extraordinary; a remarkable thing or person. **3.** *Philos.* **a.** an appearance or immediate object of awareness in experience. **b.** *Kantianism.* a thing as it appears to and is constructed by the mind, as distinguished from a noumenon, or thing-in-itself. [< LL *phaenomenon* < Gk *phainómenon* appearance, n. use of neut. of *phainómenos,* prp. of *phaínesthai* to appear, pass. of *phaínein* to show]
—**Syn. 1.** event, incident. **2.** prodigy, marvel, wonder, miracle.

phe·no·plast (fē′nə plast′), *n. Chem.* See **phenolic resin.** [PHENO- + -PLAST]

phe·no·saf·ra·nine (fē′nə saf′rə nēn′, -nin), *n. Chem.* safranine (def. 2). [PHENO- + SAFRANINE]

phe·no·thi·a·zine (fē′nə thī′ə zin, -zēn′), *n. Chem.* a grayish-green to greenish-yellow, crystalline, water-insoluble solid, $C_{12}H_9NS$, used chiefly as an insecticide and vermifuge, and in the synthesis of pharmaceuticals. [PHENO- + THIAZINE]

phe·no·type (fē′nə tīp′), *n. Genetics.* **1.** the observable constitution of an organism. **2.** the appearance of an organism resulting from the interaction of the genotype and the environment. Cf. **genotype.** [PHENO(MENON) + TYPE; modeled on G *Phänotypus*] —**phe·no·typ·ic** (fē′nə tip′ik), **phe′no·typ′i·cal,** *adj.* —**phe′no·typ′i·cal·ly,** *adv.*

phe·nox·ide (fi nok′sīd), *n. Chem.* phenolate (def. 1). [PHEN- + OXIDE]

phe·nox·y·ben·za·mine (fi nok′sē ben′zə mēn′, -min), *n. Pharm.* a compound, $C_{18}H_{22}ClNO$, usually used in the form of its crystalline, slightly water-soluble hydrochloride to increase peripheral blood flow, esp. in the treatment of hypertension. [PHEN- + OXY-[2] + BENZAMINE]

phen·yl (fen′əl, fēn′əl), *adj. Chem.* containing the phenyl group. [PHEN- + -YL]

phen·yl·ac·e·tal·de·hyde (fen′əlas′i tal′də hīd′, fēn′-), *n. Chem.* a colorless, oily, water-insoluble liquid, $C_6H_5CH_2CHO$, having a hyacinthlike odor: used chiefly in perfumery. Also, **phen′yl·a·ce′tic al′dehyde** (fen′əl ə sē′tik, -set′ik, fēn′-, fen′-, fēn′-). Also called **hyacinthin.** [PHENYL + ACET- + ALDEHYDE]

phen′yl ac′etate, *Chem.* a colorless, water-insoluble liquid, $CH_3COOC_6H_5$, having a phenolic odor: used chiefly as a solvent.

phen·yl·al·a·nine (fen′əlal′ə nēn′, fēn′əlal′-), *n. Biochem.* a crystalline, water-soluble amino acid, $C_6H_5CH_2CH(NH_2)COOH$, essential to the nutrition of man and most animals, obtained chiefly from egg white or skim milk. Also called **phen·yl·a·mi·no·pro·pi·on′ic ac′id** (fen′əl ə mē′nō prō pē on′ik, -am′ə nō-, fēn′-). [PHENYL + ALANINE]

phen·yl·am·ine (fen′əl ə mēn′, -am′in, fēn′-), *n. Chem.* aniline. [PHENYL + AMINE]

phen·yl·ben·zene (fen′əl ben′zēn, -ben zēn′, fēn′-), *n. Chem.* biphenyl. [PHENYL + BENZENE]

phen·yl·car·bi·nol (fen′əl kär′bə nōl′, -nôl′, -nol′, fēn′-), *n. Chem.* See **benzyl alcohol.** [PHENYL + CARBINOL]

phen·yl·di·eth·a·nol·a·mine (fen′əl dī eth′ə nō′lə mēn, -nō′-, -nol′ə-, fēn′-), *n. Chem.* a white, crystalline, slightly water-soluble substance, $C_6H_5N(CH_2CH_2OH)_2$, used in the manufacture of dyes and in organic synthesis. [PHENYL + DI-[1] + ETHANOL + AMINE]

phen·yl·ene (fen′əlēn′, fēn′-), *adj. Chem.* containing a phenylene group. [PHENYL + -ENE]

phen′ylene group′, *Chem.* any of three bivalent, isomeric groups having the formula $-C_6H_4-$, derived from benzene by the removal of two hydrogen atoms. Also called **phen′ylene rad′ical.** Cf. **meta, ortho, para**[2].

phen·yl·eph·rine (fen′ᵊlef′rēn, -rin, fē′-), *n. Pharm.* an antihistaminic compound, $C_9H_{13}NO_2$, used in the form of its hydrochloride chiefly as a nasal decongestant. [PHENYL + (EPIN)EPHRINE]

phen′yl·eth′yl al′cohol (fen′ᵊl eth′əl, fēn′-, fen′-, fēn′-), *Chem.* See **phenethyl alcohol.** [PHENYL + ETHYL]

phen′yl·eth·yl·bar·bi·tu′ric ac′id (fen′ᵊleth′əl-bär′bi to͝or′ik, -tyo͝or′ik, -, fēn′-, fen′-, fēn′-), *Pharm.* phenobarbital. [PHENYL + ETHYL + BARBITURIC ACID]

phen·yl·eth·yl·ene (fen′ᵊl eth′ə lēn′, fēn′-), *n. Chem.* styrene. [PHENYL + ETHYLENE]

phen′yl eth′yl e′ther, *Chem.* phenetole.

phen·yl·eth·yl·mal·o·nyl·u·re·a (fen′ᵊl eth′əl-mal′ə nil yo͞o rē′ə, fēn′-), *n. Pharm.* phenobarbital. [PHENYL + ETHYL + *malon(ic)* (of MALONIC ESTER) + -YL + UREA]

phen′yl·for′mic ac′id (fen′ᵊl fôr′mik, fēn′-, fen′-, fēn′-), *Chem.* See **benzoic acid.** [PHENYL + FORMIC ACID]

phen′yl group′, *Chem.* the univalent group, C_6H_5-, derived from benzene. Also called **phen′yl rad′ical.**

phen·yl·hy·dra·zine (fen′ᵊl hī′drə zēn′, -zin, fēn′-), *n. Chem.* a yellow, poisonous liquid or low-melting solid, $C_6H_5NHNH_2$, used in chemical analysis and organic synthesis. [< G; see PHENYL, HYDRAZINE]

phe·nyl′ic ac′id (fə nil′ik), *Chem.* phenol (def. 1). [PHENYL + -IC]

phen′yl isocy′anate, *Chem.* a liquid reagent, C_6H_5NCO, having an unpleasant, irritating odor: used chiefly for identifying alcohols and amines. Also called **carbanil.** [ISO- + CYANATE]

phen·yl·ke·to·nu·ri·a (fen′ᵊl kēt′ᵊno͝or′ē ə, -ᵊnyo͝or′-, fēn′-), *n. Pathol.* an inherited, abnormal condition characterized by phenylketones in the urine, due to faulty metabolism of phenylalanine, and usually first characterized by signs of mental retardation in infancy. Also called **phenylpyruvic oligophrenia.** [< NL; see PHENYL, KETONE, -URIA]

phen·yl·meth·ane (fen′ᵊl meth′ān, fēn′-), *n. Chem.* toluene. [PHENYL + METHANE]

phen′yl·meth·yl·car′bi·nyl ac′etate (fen′ᵊl-meth′əl kär′bə nil, fēn′-, fen′-, fēn′-), *Chem.* See **methylphenylcarbinyl acetate.** [PHENYL + METHYL + *carbinyl* (? < obs. G *Karbin* + -YL)]

phen′yl meth′yl ke′tone, *Chem.* acetophenone.

phen′yl·pro′pyl ac′etate (fen′ᵊl prō′pil, fēn′-, fen′-, fēn′-), *Chem.* a colorless, water-insoluble liquid, $CH_3COOCH_2CH_2C_6H_5$, used chiefly in perfumery. Also, **propylphenyl acetate.** [PHENYL + PROPYL]

phen·yl·py·ru·vic ol·i·go·phre·ni·a (fen′ᵊl pī-ro͞o′vik ol′ə gō frē′nē ə, -frēn′yə, -pi-, fēn′-), *Pathol.* phenylketonuria. [PHENYL + PYRUVIC (ACID)]

phen′yl salicyl′ate, *Chem.* salol.

phen·yl·thi·o·ur·e·a (fen′ᵊl thī′ō yo͞o rē′ə, -yo͝or′ē ə, -thī′ə-, fēn′ᵊl-), *n. Biochem.* a crystalline, slightly water-soluble solid, $C_6H_5NHCSNH_2$, that is either tasteless or bitter, depending upon the heredity of the taster and is used in medical genetics and as a diagnostic. Also called **phen·yl·thi·o·car·ba·mide** (fen′ᵊl thī′ō kär′bə mid, -mīd, -thī′ə-, fēn′ᵊl-). [PHENYL + THIOUREA]

phen′yl val′er·ate (val′ə rāt′), *Chem.* a colorless, slightly water-soluble liquid, $C_4H_9COOC_6H_5$, used chiefly in flavoring and perfumery. [VALER(IC ACID) + -ATE[2]]

phe·on (fē′on), *n. Heraldry.* a charge representing an arrowhead with widely spread barbs. Also called **broad arrow.** [late ME *feon* <?]

Phe·rae (fēr′ē), *n.* (in ancient geography) a town in SE Thessaly: the home of Admetus and Alcestis.

Pher·e·clus (fer′ə kləs), *n.* (in the *Iliad*) a son of Tecton who was endowed by Athena with great skill as an artisan, and who built the fleet of ships in which Paris sailed with Helen to Troy.

Phe·res (fēr′ēz), *n. Class. Myth.* the eponymous founder and king of Pherae, and the father of Admetus, Idomene, and Periapis.

pher·o·mone (fer′ə mōn′), *n. Biochem.* any of a class of hormonal substances secreted by an individual and stimulating a physiological or behavioral response from an individual of the same species. [< Gk *phér(ein)* (to) bear + -o- + (HOR)MONE]

phew (fyo͞o, pfyo͞o), *interj.* (used as an exclamation to express disgust, exhaustion, surprise, impatience, relief, etc.): *Phew! It's hot!*

Ph. G., Graduate in Pharmacy.

phi (fī, fē), *n., pl.* **phis. 1.** the 21st letter of the Greek alphabet (Φ,φ). **2.** the consonant sound represented by this letter.

phi·al (fī′əl), *n.* vial (def. 1). **—phi·al·ine** (fī′ə lin, -līn′), *adj.*

phi·a·le (fī′ə lē), *n., pl.* **-lae** (-lē′), **-lai** (-lī′). *Gk. and Rom. Antiq.* a shallow cup resembling a saucer, having a central boss and sometimes set upon a foot, used as a drinking vessel or to pour libations. [< Gk *phiálē* PHIAL]

Phi Be·ta Kap·pa (fī′ bā′tə kap′ə, bē′tə), **1.** a national honor society founded in 1776 whose members are chosen, for lifetime membership, from among college undergraduates of high academic distinction. **2.** a member of Phi Beta Kappa.

Phi Bete (fī′ bāt′), *Informal.* **1.** a member of the Phi Beta Kappa. **2.** the Phi Beta Kappa.

Phi·chol (fī′kol), *n.* the commander of Abimelech's army. Gen. 26 : 26. Also, *Douay Bible,* **Phi′col.**

Phid·i·an (fid′ē ən), *adj.* of, associated with, or following the style of Phidias, as exemplified in the Parthenon. [PHIDI(AS) + -AN]

Phid·i·as (fid′ē əs), *n.* c500–432? B.C., Greek sculptor.

Phi·dip·pi·des (fī dip′i dēz′), *n.* Pheidippides.

Phil (fil), *n.* a boy's given name, form of Philip.

phil-, var. of **philo-** before a vowel: *philanthropy.*

-phil, var. of **-phile:** *eosinophil.*

Phil., 1. Philemon. **2.** Philip. **3.** Philippians. **4.** Philippine.

phil., 1. philosophical. **2.** philosophy.

Phila., Philadelphia.

phil·a·beg (fil′ə beg′), *n.* filiberg.

Phil·a·del·phi·a (fil′ə del′fē ə), *n.* **1.** a city in SE Pennsylvania, on the Delaware River: Declaration of Independence signed here July 4, 1776. 2,002,512 (1960). **2.** a town in central Mississippi. 5017 (1960).

Philadel′phia law′yer, a lawyer of outstanding ability in matters involving fine points and technicalities.

Philadel′phia pep′per pot′. See **pepper pot** (def. 2).

Phi·lae (fī′lē), *n.* an island in the Nile, in Upper Egypt: the site of ancient temples; submerged except during months the sluices of the Aswan dam are open.

Phi·lam·mon (fi lā′mon), *n. Class. Myth.* the musician son of Chione and Apollo.

phi·lan·der (fi lan′dər), *v.i.* (of a man) to make love without serious intentions; carry on flirtations. [< Gk *phílandr(os)* one who loves; later used in fiction as a proper name for a lover] **—phi·lan′der·er,** *n.* **—Syn.** trifle, dally.

phil·an·throp·ic (fil′ən throp′ik), *adj.* of, pertaining to, or characterized by philanthropy; benevolent. Also, **phil′an·throp′i·cal.** [PHILANTHROP(Y) + -IC] **—phil′an·throp′i·cal·ly,** *adv.*

phi·lan·thro·pise (fi lan′thrə pīz′), *v.t., v.i.,* **-pised, -pis·ing.** *Chiefly Brit.* philanthropize.

phi·lan·thro·pist (fi lan′thrə pist), *n.* one who practices philanthropy. [PHILANTHROP(Y) + -IST] **—phi·lan′thro·pis′tic,** *adj.*

phi·lan·thro·pize (fi lan′thrə pīz′), *v.,* **-pized, -piz·ing.** **—***v.t.* **1.** to treat (persons) in a philanthropic manner. **—***v.i.* **2.** to practice philanthropy. Also, *esp. Brit.,* **philanthropise.** [PHILANTHROP(Y) + -IZE]

phi·lan·thro·py (fi lan′thrə pē), *n., pl.* **-pies. 1.** affection for mankind, esp. as manifested in donations of money, property, or work to needy persons or to socially useful purposes: *works of philanthropy.* **2.** the activity of donating to such persons or purposes in this way: *to devote one's later years to philanthropy.* **3.** a particular form or instance of this activity: *A home for unwed mothers was one of his philanthropies.* **4.** a philanthropic organization. [earlier *philanthropia* < LL < Gk: love for mankind. See PHIL-, ANTHROP(O), -Y[3]]

phi·lat·e·ly (fi lat′ᵊlē), *n.* **1.** the study of postage stamps, revenue stamps, stamped envelopes, postmarks, postal cards, covers, and similar material relating to postal or fiscal history. **2.** the collecting of stamps and other postal matter. [< F *philatélie* love of postage stamps < Gk *phil-* PHIL- + *atéleia* freedom from charges (taken to mean recipient's freedom from delivery charges by virtue of the stamp which sender affixed to the letter), lit., want of taxation, equiv. to *a-* A-[6] + *tél(os)* tax + *-eia* -Y[3]] **—phil·a·tel·ic** (fil′ə tel′ik), **phil′a·tel′i·cal,** *adj.* **—phil′a·tel′i·cal·ly,** *adv.* **— phi·lat·e·list** (fi lat′ᵊlist), *n.*

Phi·la·the·a (fi lā′thē ə), *n.* a former international, interdenominational body of young women organized to study the Bible. Cf. **Baraca.**

-phile, a word element meaning "loving," "friendly," or "lover," "friend," used in the formation of nouns and adjectives: *Anglophile; bibliophile; demophile.* Also, **-phil.** [< L *-philus, -phila* < Gk *-phílos* dear, beloved (occurring in proper names). Cf. F *-phile*]

Philem., Philemon.

Phi·le·mon (fi lē′mən, fī-), *n.* **1.** *Class. Myth.* the husband of Baucis. **2.** an Epistle written by Paul. **3.** a person who was probably a convert of Paul and to whom this Epistle is addressed.

phil·har·mon·ic (fil′här mon′ik, fil′ər-), *adj.* **1.** fond of music; music-loving: used esp. in the name of certain musical societies **(Phil′harmon′ic Soci′eties)** and hence applied to their concerts **(phil′harmon′ic con′certs). 2.** of or noting a musical group or organization. **—***n.* **3.** such a group or organization; symphony orchestra. [PHIL- + HARMONIC; modeled on F *philharmonique* or It *filarmonico*]

phil′harmon′ic pitch′, *Music.* a standard of pitch in which A above middle C is established at 440 vibrations per second. Cf. **diapason normal pitch.**

phil·hel·lene (fil hel′ēn), *n.* a friend or supporter of the Greeks. Also, **phil·hel·len·ist** (fil hel′ə nist, fil′he-lē′nist). [< Gk *philéllēn* Greek-loving. See PHIL-, HELLENE] **—phil·hel·len·ic** (fil′he len′ik, -lē′nik), *adj.* **—phil·hel·len·ism** (fil hel′ə niz′əm), *n.*

Phil. I., Philippine Islands.

Phi·li·a (fi lī′ə), *n. Class. Myth.* a nymph of Daxos who watched over the infant Dionysus.

-philia, a learned borrowing from Greek used in pathological terminology to indicate an abnormal liking for or a tendency toward something: *hemophilia; necrophilia.* Cf. **-philous.** [< Gk *philía* loving; see -PHILE, -IA]

phil·i·beg (fil′ə beg′), *n.* filibeg.

Phil·ip (fil′ip), *n.* **1.** one of the 12 apostles. Mark 3:18; John 1:43–48; 6:5–7. **2.** one of the leaders of the Christian Hellenists in the early church in Jerusalem who afterwards became an evangelist and missionary. Acts 6; 8:26–40. **3. King** (*Metacomet*), died 1676, North American Indian chief: sachem of the Wampanoag tribe 1662–76; leader of the Indians in King Philip's War. **4. Prince, Duke of Edinburgh,** born 1921, consort of Elizabeth II. **5.** Also, **Phillip.** a boy's given name.

Philip II, 1. ("*Philip of Macedon*") 382–336 B.C., king of Macedonia 359–336 (father of Alexander the Great). **2.** ("*Philip Augustus*") 1165–1223, king of France 1180–1223. **3.** 1527–98, king of Spain 1556–98 (husband of Mary I).

Philip IV, ("*Philip the Fair*") 1268–1314, king of France 1285–1314.

Philip V, 1683–1746, king of Spain 1700–46.

Philip VI, 1293–1350, king of France 1328–50: first ruler of the house of Valois.

Philip., Philippians.

Phi·lip·pa (fi lip′ə), *n.* a girl's given name.

Phi·lippe·ville (*Fr.* fē lēp vēl′; *Eng.* fil′ip vil′), *n.* a seaport in NE Algeria. 48,773 (1954).

Phi·lip·pi (fi lip′ī), *n.* a ruined city in NE Greece, in Macedonia: Octavian and Mark Antony defeated Brutus and Cassius here, 42 B.C.; the site of one of the first Christian churches in Europe, founded by St. Paul. **—Phi·lip·pi·an** (fi lip′ē ən), *adj., n.*

Phi·lip·pi·ans (fi lip′ē ənz), *n.* (*construed as sing.*) an Epistle written by Paul to the Christian community in Philippi.

Phi·lip·pic (fi lip′ik), *n.* **1.** any of the orations delivered by Demosthenes, the Athenian orator, in the 4th century B.C., against Philip, king of Macedon. **2.** (*l.c.*) any discourse or speech of bitter denunciation. [< L *Philippic(us)* < Gk *Philippikós.* See PHILIP, -IC]

Phil·ip·pine (fil′ə pēn′), *adj.* of or pertaining to the Philippines or their inhabitants.

Phil′ippine fowl′ disease′, *Vet. Pathol.* See **Newcastle disease.**

Phil′ippine mahog′any, 1. any of several Philippine trees, as the almon, yielding a wood that closely resembles mahogany. **2.** the wood of any of these trees.

Phil·ip·pines (fil′ə pēnz′, fil′ə pēnz′), *n.* (*construed as pl.*) an archipelago of 7083 islands in the Pacific, SE of China: formerly under the guardianship of the U.S.; now an independent republic. 27,087,685 (1960); 114,830 sq. mi. *Cap.:* Manila. Also called **Phil′ippine Is′lands.** Formerly, **Commonwealth of the Philippines** (1935–46). Official name, **Republic of the Philippines.**

Phil·ip·pop·o·lis (fil′ə pop′ə lis), *n.* Greek name of **Plovdiv.**

phi·lip·pus (fi lip′əs), *n., pl.* **-lip·pi** (-lip′ī). a gold coin of ancient Greece, originally issued by Philip II of Macedon. [< L]

Phil·ips (fil′ips), *n.* **Ambrose,** 1675?–1749, English poet and dramatist.

Phil·ips·burg (fil′ips bûrg′), *n.* a town in central Pennsylvania. 3872 (1960).

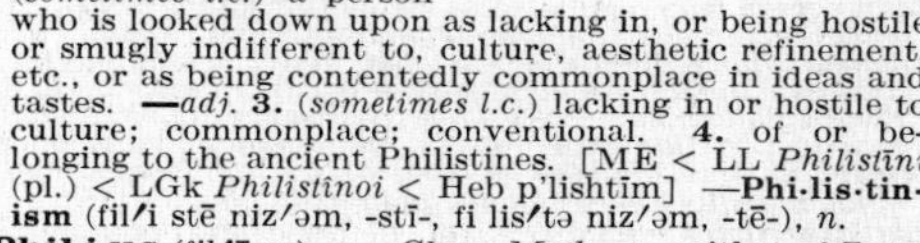

Phil′ip the Good′, 1396–1467, duke of Burgundy 1419–67.

-philism, an element used to form abstract nouns from stems ending in **-phile:** *necrophilism.* [-PHILE + -ISM]

-philist, an element used to form personal nouns from stems ending in **-phile.** [-PHILE + -IST]

Phi·lis·ti·a (fi lis′tē ə), *n.* an ancient country on the E coast of the Mediterranean. **—Phi·lis′ti·an,** *adj.*

Phil·is·tine (fil′i stēn′, -stin′, fi lis′tin, -tēn), *n.* **1.** a native or inhabitant of ancient Philistia. **2.** (*sometimes l.c.*) a person who is looked down upon as lacking in, or being hostile or smugly indifferent to, culture, aesthetic refinement, etc., or as being contentedly commonplace in ideas and tastes. **—***adj.* **3.** (*sometimes l.c.*) lacking in or hostile to culture; commonplace; conventional. **4.** of or belonging to the ancient Philistines. [ME < LL *Philistīni* (pl.) < LGk *Philistīnoi* < Heb p'lishtīm] **—Phil·is·tin·ism** (fil′i stē niz′əm, -stī-, fi lis′tə niz′əm, -tē-), *n.*

Phil·i·us (fil′ē əs), *n. Class. Myth.* an epithet of Zeus, meaning "friendly."

Phil·li·da (fil′i də), *n.* a girl's given name, form of **Phillis** or **Phyllis.**

Phil·lip (fil′ip), *n.* a boy's given name. Also, **Philip.**

Phil·lips (fil′ips), *n.* **1. David Graham,** 1867–1911, U.S. novelist. **2. Stephen,** 1868–1915, English poet and playwright. **3. Wen·dell** (wen′dᵊl), 1811–84, U.S. orator and reformer. **4.** a town in N Texas. 3605 (1960). **5.** a ring formation in the fourth quadrant of the face of the moon: about 75 miles in diameter.

Phil·lips·burg (fil′ips bûrg′), *n.* **1.** a city in NW New Jersey, on the Delaware River. 18,502 (1960). **2.** a town in N Kansas. 3233 (1960).

Phil′lips head′, a screw head having two partial slots crossed at right angles, driven by a special screwdriver. See illus. under **screw.** [after trademark *Phillips Screws*]

phil·lips·ite (fil′ip sīt′), *n.* a zeolite mineral, similar to stilbite but with potassium replacing some of the calcium. [named after J.W. *Phillips,* (1775–1828), English mineralogist; see -ITE[1]]

Phil·lis (fil′is), *n.* a girl's given name. Also, **Phyliss, Phyllis.**

Phil·ly (fil′ē), *n.* Philadelphia (used as a nickname).

Phi·lo (fī′lō), *n.* a boy's given name.

philo-, an element appearing in loan words from Greek, where it meant "loving" (*philology*); on this model, used in the formation of compound words (*philoprogenitive*). Also, *esp. before a vowel,* **phil-.** [< Gk, comb. of *phílos* loving, dear]

Phil·oc·te·tes (fil′ək tē′tēz), *n.* **1.** *Class. Myth.* the armor bearer of Hercules, and the archer whose poisoned arrow caused the death of Paris in the Trojan War. **2.** (*italics.*) a tragedy (408? B.C.) by Sophocles.

phil·o·den·dron (fil′ə den′drən), *n.* a tropical American climbing plant of the family *Araceae,* usually having smooth, shiny, evergreen leaves, often used as an ornamental house plant. [< NL < Gk, n. use of neut. of *philódendros* fond of trees. See PHILO-, -DENDRON]

Phi·loe·tius (fi lē′shəs), *n.* (in the *Odyssey*) a cowherd of Odysseus who remained loyal to his master and helped him kill the suitors of Penelope.

phi·log·y·ny (fi loj′ə nē), *n.* love of or liking for women. [< Gk *philogynía.* See PHILO-, GYNY] **—phi·log′y·nist,** *n.* **—phi·log′y·nous,** *adj.*

Phi·lo Ju·dae·us (fī′lō jo͞o dē′əs), c20 B.C.–A.D. c50, Alexandrian Jewish theologian and Hellenistic philosopher.

philol., 1. philological. **2.** philology.

Phil·o·la·us (fil′ō lā′əs), *n.* a crater in the second quadrant of the face of the moon: about 46 miles in diameter.

phil·o·lo·gi·an (fil′ə lō′jē ən), *n.* a philologist. [< L *philologi(a)* (see PHILOLOGY) + -AN]

phi·lol·o·gy (fi lol′ə jē), *n.* **1.** the study of written records, the establishment of their authenticity and their original form, and the determination of their meaning. **2.** *Chiefly Brit.* linguistics. [ME *philologie* < L *philologia*

< Gk: love of learning and literature, equiv. to *philólog(os)* literary, studious, argumentative, etc. + *-ia* -Y[3]. See PHILO-, -LOGY] —**phil·o·log·i·cal** (fil′ə loj′i-kəl), **phil′o·log′ic,** *adj.* —**phil′o·log′i·cal·ly,** *adv.* —**phi·lol′o·gist, phi·lol′o·ger,** *n.*

phil·o·mel (fil′ə mel′), *n.* *Poetic.* the nightingale. Also, **philomela.** [earlier *philomele, philomela* < L *philomēla* < Gk: nightingale (see PHILO-, MELIC); r. ME *philomene* < ML *philomēna,* dissimilated var. of *philomēla*]

Phil·o·me·la (fil′ə mē′lə), *n.* **1.** *Class. Myth.* an Athenian princess who was raped by her brother-in-law Tereus and had her tongue cut out by him. She was subsequently avenged and transformed into a nightingale. **2.** (*l.c.*) philomel.

Phil·o·me·li·des (fil′ō mə lī′dēz), *n.* *Class. Myth.* a king of Lesbos who challenged all travelers to wrestle with him and who killed every opponent until he himself was defeated by Odysseus.

Phil·o·me·na (fil′ə mē′nə), *n.* a girl's given name.

Phil·o·nis (fi lō′nis), *n.* *Class. Myth.* Chlone.

Phi·lon·o·me (fi lon′ə mē′), *n.* *Class. Myth.* Phylonome.

phil·o·pe·na (fil′ə pē′nə), *n.* **1.** a custom, presumably of German origin, in which two persons share the kernels of a nut and determine that one shall receive a forfeit from the other at a later time upon the saying of a certain word or the performance of a certain action. **2.** the thing shared. **3.** the forfeit paid. Also, **fillipeen.** [earlier *philippina* < D *philippine* < G *vielliebchen,* dim. of *vielliеb* very dear; in earlier form *vielliеb* was taken as proper name *Philippe* Philip and *-chen* was made into fem. suffix *-ina,* giving a woman's name; in later form the word was Anglicized along pseudo-classical lines. See PHILO-, PENAL]

phil·o·pro·gen·i·tive (fil′ō prō jen′i tiv), *adj.* **1.** producing offspring, esp. abundantly; prolific. **2.** of, pertaining to, or characterized by love for offspring, esp. one's own. [PHILO- + PROGENITIVE]

philos., **1.** philosopher. **2.** philosophical. **3.** philosophy.

phi·los·o·phas·ter (fi los′ə fas′tər, fi los′ə fas′tər), *n.* one who has only a superficial knowledge of philosophy or who feigns a knowledge he does not possess. [< LL: a bit of a philosopher. See PHILOSOPHER, -ASTER[1]]

phil·o·sophe (fil′ə sof′, fil′ə zof′; *Fr.* fē lô zôf′), *n., pl.* **-sophes** (-sofs′, -zofs′; *Fr.* -zôf′). **1.** any of the popular French intellectuals or social philosophers of the 18th century, as Diderot, Rousseau, Voltaire, etc. **2.** a philosophaster. [< F]

phi·los·o·pher (fi los′ə fər), *n.* **1.** a person who offers his views or theories on profound questions in ethics, metaphysics, logic, and other related fields. **2.** a person who is deeply versed in philosophy. **3.** a person who establishes the central ideas of some movement, cult, etc. **4.** a person who regulates his life, actions, judgments, utterances, etc., by the light of philosophy or reason. **5.** a person who is philosophical, esp. under trying circumstances. **6.** *Obs.* an alchemist or occult scientist. [ME, var. of *philosophre* < AF (MF *philosophe*); r. OE *philosoph* < L *philosoph(us)* < Gk *philósophos* philosopher, equiv. to *philo-* PHILO- + *soph(ía)* wisdom (see -SOPHY) + *-os* n. suffix] —**phi·los′o·pher·ship′,** *n.*

philos′opher king′, the Platonic ideal of a ruler, philosophically trained and enlightened.

philos′ophers' stone′, *Alchemy.* an imaginary substance or preparation believed capable of transmuting baser metals into gold or silver, and of prolonging life. Also, **philos′opher's stone′.**

philos′opher's wool′. See **zinc oxide.** [so called from its resemblance to wool upon formation in solution]

phil·o·soph·i·cal (fil′ə sof′i kəl), *adj.* **1.** of or pertaining to philosophy: *philosophical studies.* **2.** versed in or occupied with philosophy. **3.** proper to or befitting a philosopher. **4.** rationally or sensibly calm under trying circumstances. **5.** *Rare.* of or pertaining to natural philosophy or physical science. Also, **phil′o·soph′ic.** [L *philosophic(us)* < Gk *philosophikós* (see PHILOSOPHER, -IC) + -AL[1]] —**phil′o·soph′i·cal·ly,** *adv.* —**phil′o·soph′i·cal·ness,** *n.*

philosoph′ical anthropol′ogy, anthropology (def. 4).

philosoph′ical existen′tialism, existentialism (def. 2). —**philosoph′ical existen′tialist.**

phi·los·o·phise (fi los′ə fīz′), *v.i.,* **-phised, -phis·ing.** *Chiefly Brit.* philosophize. —**phi·los′o·phi·sa′tion,** *n.* —**phi·los′o·phis′er,** *n.*

phi·los·o·phism (fi los′ə fiz′əm), *n.* **1.** a false or contrived argument, esp. one designed to deceive. **2.** spurious or deceitful philosophy. [PHILOSOPH(Y) + -ISM]

phi·los·o·phize (fi los′ə fīz′), *v.i.,* **-phized, -phiz·ing.** **1.** to speculate or theorize in a superficial or imprecise manner. **2.** to think or reason as a philosopher. Also, *esp. Brit.,* **philosophise.** [PHILOSOPH(Y) + -IZE] —**phi·los′o·phi·za′tion,** *n.* —**phi·los′o·phiz′er,** *n.*

phi·los·o·phy (fi los′ə fē), *n., pl.* **-phies.** **1.** the rational investigation of the truths and principles of being, knowledge, or conduct. **2.** any one of the three branches, namely natural philosophy, moral philosophy, and metaphysical philosophy, that are accepted as composing this study. **3.** a system or philosophical doctrine: *the philosophy of Spinoza.* **4.** the critical study of the basic principles and concepts of a particular branch of knowledge, esp. with a view to improving or reconstituting them: *the philosophy of science.* **5.** a system of principles for guidance in practical affairs. **6.** a philosophical attitude, as one of composure and calm in the presence of troubles or annoyances. [ME *philosophie* < L *philosophia* < Gk. See PHILO-, -SOPHY]

-philous, an element used to form adjectives from stems ending in **-phile:** *dendrophilous; heliophilous.* [< L *-philus* < Gk *-philos.* See -PHILE, -OUS]

phil·ter (fil′tər), *n., v.,* **-tered, -ter·ing.** —*n.* **1.** a potion or drug that is supposed to induce the person taking it to fall in love with some other person. **2.** a magic potion for any purpose. —*v.t.* **3.** to enchant or bewitch with a philter. [16th-century *philter,* 17th-century *philtrum* < L; 17th-century *filtre* < L or F. See FILTRUM] —**phil′ter·er,** *n.*

phil·tre (fil′tər), *n., v.t.,* **-tred, -tring.** *Chiefly Brit.* philter.

phil·trum (fil′trəm), *n., pl.* **-tra** (-trə). **1.** *Anat.* the groove on the surface of the upper lip, below the septum of the nose. **2.** a philter. [< L < Gk *philtron* a love-potion, dimple in upper lip. See PHIL-, -TRON]

Phil·y·ra (fil′i rə), *n.* *Class. Myth.* a daughter of Oceanus who was changed into a linden tree after giving birth to Chiron.

phi·mo·sis (fī mō′sis, fi-), *n., pl.* **-ses** (-sēz). *Pathol.* **1.** constriction of the orifice of the prepuce so as to prevent the foreskin from being drawn back to uncover the glans penis. **2.** narrowness of the vagina. [< NL < Gk, lit., a muzzling, equiv. to *phim(oûn)* (to) muzzle + *-ōsis* -OSIS] —**phi·mot·ic** (fī mot′ik, fi-), *adj.*

Phin·e·as (fin′ē əs), *n.* a boy's given name.

Phin·e·us (fin′ē əs, fī′nōōs, -nyōōs), *n.* *Class. Myth.* **1.** the brother of Cadmus and Europa who blinded his two sons when he believed false accusations made against them by their stepmother, Idaea. He was in turn blinded by Zeus. **2.** a brother of Cepheus who was not brave enough to rescue his betrothed, Andromeda, from a sea monster and who was eventually turned to stone when Perseus, claiming Andromeda as his own, exposed him to the head of Medusa.

phi-phe·nom·e·non (fī′fi nom′ə non′), *n., pl.* **-na** (-nə). *Psychol.* motion perceived by a subject, esp. the illusion of movement produced when stationary stimuli, as pictures, lights, etc., are presented in rapid succession and are, sometimes, in slightly different positions.

Phi·thom (fī′thəm), *n.* *Douay Bible.* Pithom.

Phit·sa·nu·lok (fēt′sä nōō′lōk), *n.* a city in central Thailand. 25,000 (est. 1961).

phiz (fiz), *n.* *Slang.* face. [abbr. of PHYSIOGNOMY]

Ph.L., Licentiate in Philosophy.

phle·bi·tis (flə bī′tis), *n.* *Pathol.* inflammation of a vein. [< NL; see PHLEB-, -ITIS] —**phle·bit·ic** (flə-bit′ik), *adj.*

phlebo-, a learned borrowing from Greek meaning "vein," used in the formation of compound words: *phlebosclerosis.* Also, *esp. before a vowel,* **phleb-.** [< Gk, comb. form of *phléps* vein]

phle·boc·ly·sis (flə bok′li sis, fleb′ə klī′sis), *n.* *Med.* the injection of a large quantity of glucose, saline solution, or the like into a vein. [< NL; see PHLEBO-, CLYSIS]

phleb·oid (fleb′oid), *adj.* *Anat.* pertaining to or resembling a vein. [PHLEB- + -OID]

phleb·o·scle·ro·sis (fleb′ō skli rō′sis), *n.* *Pathol.* sclerosis, or hardening, of the walls of veins. [PHLEBO- + SCLEROSIS]

phleb·o·throm·bo·sis (fleb′ō throm bō′sis), *n.* *Pathol.* the presence of a thrombus in a vein unaccompanied by irritation of the vessel wall. Cf. **thrombophlebitis.** [< NL; see PHLEBO-, THROMBOSIS]

phleb·o·tome (fleb′ə tōm′), *n.* a cutting instrument used for phlebotomy. [back formation from PHLEBOTOMY]

phleb·o·tom·ic (fleb′ə tom′ik), *adj.* **1.** of or noting phlebotomy. **2.** (of insects) bloodsucking. Also, **phleb′o·tom′i·cal.**

phle·bot·o·mise (flə bot′ə mīz′, flē-, fle-), *v.t.,* **-mised, -mis·ing.** *Chiefly Brit.* phlebotomize. —**phle·bot′o·mi·sa′tion,** *n.*

phle·bot·o·mist (flə bot′ə mist, flē-, fle-), *n.* *Surg.* a specialist in phlebotomy. [PHLEBOTOM(Y) + -IST]

phle·bot·o·mize (flə bot′ə mīz′, flē-, fle-), *v.t.,* **-mized, -miz·ing.** to subject to phlebotomy; bleed. Also, *esp. Brit.,* **phlebotomise.** [< MF *phlebotomiser* (cf. ML *flebotomizāre*). See PHLEBOTOMY, -IZE] —**phle·bot′o·mi·za′tion,** *n.*

phle·bot·o·my (flə bot′ə mē), *n., pl.* **-mies.** *Med.* act or practice of opening a vein for letting blood; bleeding. [late ME *flebotomye,* etc. < LL *flebotomia,* var. of *phlebotomia* < Gk. See PHLEBO-, -TOMY] —**phleb·o·tom·ic** (fleb′ə tom′ik), **phleb′o·tom′i·cal,** *adj.* —**phleb′o·tom′i·cal·ly,** *adv.* —**phle·bot′o·mist,** *n.*

Phleg·e·thon (fleg′ə thon′, flej′-), *n.* **1.** Also called **Pyriphlegethon.** *Class. Myth.* a river of fire, one of five rivers surrounding Hades. **2.** (*often l.c.*) a stream of fire or fiery light. [< L < Gk, n. use of *phlegéthōn* blazing, verbid of *phlegéthein* to blaze. See PHLEGM] —**Phleg′e·thon′tal, Phleg′e·thon′tic,** *adj.*

phlegm (flem), *n.* **1.** the thick mucus secreted in the respiratory passages and discharged through the mouth, esp. that occurring in the lungs and throat passages, as during a cold. **2.** *Old Physiol.* a humor regarded as causing sluggishness or apathy. **3.** sluggishness; apathy. **4.** self-possession; coolness. [ME *fleem* < MF *flemme* < LL *phlegma* < Gk: flame, phlegmatic humor, equiv. to *phlég(ein)* (to) burn + *-ma* n. suffix] —**phlegm′less,** *adj.*
—**Syn. 3.** indifference; impassivity. **4.** calm. —**Ant. 3.** concern. **4.** warmth, passion.

phleg·mat·ic (fleg mat′ik), *adj.* **1.** not easily excited to action or display of emotion; apathetic; sluggish. **2.** self-possessed; cool. **3.** of the nature of or abounding in the humor phlegm. Also, **phleg·mat′i·cal.** [< LL *phlegmatic(us)* < Gk *phlegmatikós* pertaining to phlegm, equiv. to *phlegmat-* (s. of *phlégma*) + *-ikos* -IC] —**phleg·mat′i·cal·ly,** *adv.* —**phleg·mat′i·cal·ness, phleg·mat′ic·ness,** *n.*
—**Syn. 1.** stoical, cool, cold, uninterested, dull, torpid. **2.** calm, composed, collected, unruffled, placid, quiet.

phleg·ma·tized (fleg′mə tīzd′), *adj.* *Chem.* (of explosives) desensitized.

phlegm·y (flem′ē), *adj.,* **phlegm·i·er, phlegm·i·est.** of, pertaining to, or characterized by phlegm. [PHLEGM + -Y[1]]

Phleg·yas (flej′yəs), *n.* *Class. Myth.* a king of the Lapithae who condemned Apollo when he learned that his daughter had been violated by the god. Phlegyas was slain for his irreverence.

Phli·as (flī′əs), *n.* *Class. Myth.* a son of Dionysus who joined the Argonauts.

phlo·em (flō′em), *n.* the part of a vascular bundle consisting of sieve tubes, companion cells, parenchyma, and fibers and forming the food-conducting tissue of a plant. See diag. under **stem.** [< G < Gk *phló(os)* bark (var. of *phloiós*) + *-ēm(a)* -EME]

phlo′em ray′, *Bot.* a vascular ray extending into or located entirely within the secondary phloem.

phlo·gis·tic (flō jis′tik), *adj.* **1.** *Pathol.* inflammatory. **2.** pertaining to or consisting of phlogiston. [< Gk *phlogist(ós)* inflammable (verbid of *phlogízein* to set on fire; akin to PHLOX, PHLEGM) + -IC]

phlo·gis·ton (flō jis′ton, -tən), *n.* a nonexistent chemical that, prior to the discovery of oxygen, was thought to be released during combustion. [< NL: inflammability, n. use of Gk *phlogistón,* neut. of *phlogistós* inflammable, burnt up; see PHLOGISTIC]

phlog·o·pite (flog′ə pīt′), *n.* a mica, $KMg_3AlSi_3O_{10}(OH)_2$, usually yellowish-brown, but sometimes reddish-brown. [< Gk *phlogōp(ós)* fiery-looking + -ITE[1]]

phlo·go·sis (flə gō′sis), *n.* *Med. Obs.* inflammation, esp. of the skin; erysipelas. [< NL < Gk, lit., a burning, equiv. to *phlog-* (s. of *phlóx*) flame + *-ōsis* -OSIS] —**phlo·got·ic** (flə got′ik), *adj.*

phlor·i·zin (flôr′i zin, flor′-, flə rī′zin), *n.* *Chem.* a bitter, crystalline glucoside, $C_{21}H_{24}O_{10}$, obtained from the root bark of the apple, pear, cherry, etc.: formerly used as a tonic and as an antiperiodic for malaria; now used chiefly in biochemical research. Also, **phlo·rid·zin** (flə rid′zin), **phlo′rhi·zin, phlor′rhi·zin.** [< Gk *phló(os)* bark (var. of *phloiós*) + *rhíz(a)* root + -IN[2]]

phlor·o·glu·cin·ol (flôr′ə glōō′sə nōl′, -nôl′, -nol′, flor′-), *n.* *Chem.* a white to yellow, crystalline, slightly water-soluble powder, $C_6H_3(OH)_3·2H_2O$, used chiefly in analytical chemistry and in the preparation of pharmaceuticals. Also, **phlor·o·glu·cin** (flôr′ə glōō′sin, flor′-), **phlor·o·glu·cine** (flôr′ə glōō′sēn, -sin, flor′-). [PHLORO- + GLUC- + -IN[2] + -OL[1]]

phlox (floks), *n.* **1.** any polemoniaceous herb of the genus *Phlox,* of North America, certain species of which are cultivated for their showy flowers of various colors. **2.** the flower of this plant. [< ML, special use of L *phlox* < Gk: a flame-colored plant, lit., a flame. See PHLEGM, PHLOGISTIC]

phlyc·tae·na (flik tē′nə), *n., pl.* **-nae** (-nē). *Pathol.* phlyctena.

phlyc·te·na (flik tē′nə), *n., pl.* **-nae** (-nē). *Pathol.* a small vesicle, blister, or pustule. Also, **phlyc·tae′na.** [< NL, var. of *phlyctaena* < Gk *phlýktaina* a blister, akin to *phlýein, phlýzein* to swell, boil over]

Ph.M., Master of Philosophy.

Phnom Penh (nom′ pen′, pə nôm′ pen′), a city in and the capital of Cambodia, in the S part. 403,500 (est. 1962). Also, **Pnom Penh, Pnom-penh, Pnompenh.**

-phobe, a suffix used to form personal nouns corresponding to nouns ending in **-phobia:** *Anglophobe.* [< Gk, comb. form of *phóbos* fearing]

Pho·be·tor (fə bē′tôr), *n.* *Class. Myth.* an epithet of Icelus, meaning "terrifier."

pho·bi·a (fō′bē ə), *n.* a fear or anxiety that exceeds normal proportions or that has no basis in reality; an obsessive or irrational dread. [abstracted from nouns ending in -PHOBIA] —**pho′bic,** *adj.*
—**Syn.** aversion, hatred.

-phobia, an element occurring in loan words from Greek (*hydrophobia*); on this model used, with the meaning "fear," "dread," often abnormal, or with the implication of hatred or aversion, in the formation of compound words (*agoraphobia*). [< L < Gk, equiv. to *phób(os)* fearing + *-ia* -IA]

Pho·bos (fō′bos, fob′os), *n.* **1.** *Class. Myth.* Phobus. **2.** *Astron.* one of the two satellites of Mars, having a diameter of about 10 miles and orbiting the planet at an altitude of 3700 miles. Cf. **Deimos.**

Pho·bus (fō′bəs), *n.* *Class. Myth.* a son and attendant of Ares and the personification of that fear which possesses armies and causes their defeat. Also, **Phobos.**

Pho·cae·a (fō sē′ə), *n.* an ancient seaport in Asia Minor: northernmost of the Ionian cities; later an important maritime state.

pho·cine (fō′sin, -sin), *adj.* *Zool.* **1.** of or pertaining to seals. **2.** belonging to the subfamily *Phocinae,* comprising the earless or hair seals. [< L *phōc(a)* seal (< Gk *phṓkē*) + -INE[1]]

Pho·ci·on (fō′shē ən), *n.* 402?–317 B.C., Athenian statesman and general.

Pho·cis (fō′sis), *n.* an ancient district in central Greece, N of the Gulf of Corinth: site of Delphic oracle.

pho·co·me·li·a (fō′kō mē′lē ə, -mēl′yə), *n.* *Pathol.* a usually congenital deformity of the extremities in which the limbs are abnormally short. Also, **phokomelia, pho·com·e·ly** (fō kom′ə lē). [< NL < Gk *phṓkē* seal + *-melia* -MELIA]

Pho·cus (fō′kəs), *n.* *Class. Myth.* **1.** the favorite son of Aeacus, by Psamathe, who was killed by his jealous half brothers, Telamon and Peleus. **2.** a son of Ornytion who married Antiope after purifying her of the murder of Dirce.

Pho·cyl·i·des (fō sil′i dēz′), *n.* a crater in the third quadrant of the face of the moon: about 60 miles in diameter.

phoe·be (fē′bē), *n.* any of several small American flycatchers of the genus *Sayornis,* esp. *S. phoebe,* of eastern North America. [imit.; sp. by influence of PHOEBE]

Phoe·be (fē′bē), *n.* **1.** *Class. Myth.* a Titaness, daughter of Uranus and Gaea and mother of Leto, later identified with Artemis and with the Roman goddess Diana. **2.** *Astron.* one of the nine satellites of Saturn. **3.** *Literary.* the moon personified. **4.** Also, **Phebe.** a girl's given name.

Phoe·bus (fē′bəs), *n.* **1.** *Class. Myth.* Apollo as the sun god. **2.** *Literary.* the sun personified. [< L < Gk *Phoîbos:* lit., bright, akin to *pháos* light; r. ME *Phebus* < ML] —**Phoe·be·an** (fi bē′ən, fē′bē-), *adj.*

Phoe·ni·cia (fi nish′ə, -nē′shə), *n.* an ancient kingdom on the Mediterranean, in the region of modern Syria, Lebanon, and Israel. Also, **Phenicia.**

Phoe·ni·cian (fi nish′ən, -nē′shən), *n.* **1.** a native or inhabitant of Phoenicia. **2.** the extinct Semitic language of the Phoenicians. —*adj.* **3.** of or pertaining to Phoenicia, its people, or their language. **4.** noting or pertaining to the script used for the writing of Phoenician from the 11th century B.C. or earlier and from which were derived the Greek, Roman, and all other western alphabets. [PHOENICI(A) + -AN]

Phoe·nis·sae (fē nis′ē), *n.* a tragedy (c410 B.C.) by Euripides.

phoe·nix (fē′niks), *n., gen.* **Phoe·ni·cis** (fē nī′sis) for **2.** **1.** (*sometimes cap.*) a mythical bird of great beauty, the only one of its kind, fabled to live 500 or 600 years in the Arabian wilderness, to burn itself on a funeral pile, and to rise from its ashes in the freshness of youth and live through another cycle of years: often an emblem of immortality. **2.** (*cap.*) *Astron.* a southern constellation between Hydrus and Sculptor. **3.** a person or thing of peerless beauty or excellence; paragon. **4.** a person or thing that has become renewed or restored after suffering calamity or apparent annihilation. Also, **phenix.** [< L < Gk *phoînix* a mythical bird, purple-red color, Phoenician; r. ME, OE *fēnix* < ML]

Phoe·nix (fē′niks), *n.* **1.** *Class. Myth.* **a.** the brother of Cadmus and Europa, and eponymous ancestor of the Phoenicians. **b.** a son of Amyntor and Cleobule who became the foster father of Achilles and who fought with the Greek forces in the Trojan War. **2.** a city in and the capital of Arizona, in the central part. 764,911. **3.** a town in NE Illinois. 4203 (1960).

Phoe′nix Is′lands, a group of eight coral islands in the central Pacific: part of the British Gilbert and Ellice Islands; two of the group are under American and British control. 16 sq. mi.

pho·ko·me·li·a (fō′kō mē′lē ə, -mēl′yə), *n.* *Pathol.* phocomelia.

Phol·i·do·ta (fol′i dō′tə), *n.* the order comprising the pangolins. [< NL < Gk *pholidōt(ós)* clad in scales + NL *-a* neut. pl. ending]

Pho·lus (fō′ləs), *n.* *Class. Myth.* a centaur who guarded the wine presented to the centaurs by Dionysus.

phon (fon), *n.* a unit for measuring the apparent loudness of a sound, equal in number for a given sound to the intensity in decibels of a sound having a frequency of 1000 cycles per second when, in the judgment of a group of listeners, the two sounds are of equal loudness. [< Gk *phōn(ḗ)* voice]

phon-, var. of **phono-** before a vowel: *phonic.*

phon., phonetics.

phon·as·the·ni·a (fō′nas thē′nē ə), *n.* *Med.* difficult or abnormal voice production; vocal weakness. [PHON- + ASTHENIA]

pho·nate (fō′nāt), *v.t., v.i.,* **-nat·ed, -nat·ing.** **1.** *Phonet.* to provide (a sound source, and hence the pitch) for a given voiced continuant or vowel, through rapid, periodic glottal action. **2.** to vocalize. [PHON- + -ATE[1]]

pho·na·tion (fō nā′shən), *n.* *Phonet.* **1.** rapid, periodic opening and closing of the glottis through separation and apposition of the vocal cords which, accompanied by breath under lung pressure, constitutes a source of vocal sound. **2.** (not in technical use) voice; vocalization. Cf. **voice** (defs. 13, 14). [PHON- + -ATION] **—pho·na·to·ry** (fō′nə tôr′ē, -tōr′ē), *adj.*

phon·au·to·graph (fōn ô′tə graf′, -gräf′), *n.* **1.** a device for producing a visible record of a sound wave. **2.** the record produced by such a device. [PHON- + AUTOGRAPH] **—phon·au·to·graph·ic** (fōn ô′tə graf′ik), *adj.* **—phon·au′to·graph′i·cal·ly,** *adv.*

phone[1] (fōn), *n., v.t., v.i.,* **phoned, phon·ing.** *Informal.* telephone. [by shortening]

phone[2] (fōn), *n.* *Phonet.* a speech sound: *There are three phonetically different "t" phones in an utterance of "titillate," and two in an utterance of "tattletale."* Cf. **allophone, phoneme.** [< Gk; see PHON-] **—pho′nal,** *adj.*

-phone, var. of **phono-** as final element of compound words, esp. used in names of instruments: *megaphone; telephone; xylophone.*

phone′ book′. See **telephone book.**

pho·ne·mat·ic (fō′nə mat′ik), *adj.* phonemic. [< Gk *phōnēmat-* (s. of *phṓnēma*) utterance + -IC]

pho·ne·mat·ics (fō′nə mat′iks), *n.* (*construed as sing.*) phonemics. [see PHONEMATIC, -ICS]

pho·neme (fō′nēm), *n.* *Ling.* any of a small set of units, usually about 20 to 60 in number, and different for each language, often considered to be the basic units of sound by which morphemes, words, and sentences are represented. They are arrived at for any given language by determining which differences in sound function to indicate a difference in meaning, so that in English the difference in sound and meaning between *pit* and *bit* is taken to indicate the existence of different labial phonemes, while the difference in sound between the unaspirated *p* of *spun* and the aspirated *p* of *pun,* since it is never the only distinguishing feature between two different words, is not taken as ground for setting up two different p phonemes in English. Cf. **distinctive feature.** [< Gk *phṓnēma* sound. See PHON-, -EME]

pho·ne·mic (fə nē′mik, fō-), *adj.* **1.** of or pertaining to phonemes: *a phonemic system.* **2.** of or pertaining to phonemics. **3.** concerning or involving the discrimination of distinctive speech elements of a language: *a phonemic contrast.* [PHONEME + -IC]

pho·ne·mi·cize (fə nē′mi sīz′), *v.t.,* **-cized, -ciz·ing.** to transcribe into phonemic symbols. [PHONEMIC + -IZE]

pho·ne·mics (fə nē′miks, fō-), *n.* (*construed as sing.*) **1.** the study of phonemes and phonemic systems. **2.** the phonemic system of a language, or a discussion of this: *English phonemics.* [PHONEME + -ICS] **—pho·ne·mi·cist** (fō nē′mi sist), *n.*

pho·nes·the·mic (fō′nis thē′mik), *adj.* *Ling.* (of a speech sound) shared in common by a set of echoic or symbolic words, as the *sn-* of *sneer, snarl, snatch, snide, snitch, snoop,* etc. [b. PHONEME and ESTHETIC]

phonet., phonetics.

pho·net·ic (fə net′ik, fō-), *adj.* **1.** Also, **pho·net′i·cal.** of or pertaining to speech sounds, their production, or their transcription in written symbols. **2.** corresponding to pronunciation: *phonetic transcription.* **3.** agreeing with pronunciation: *phonetic spelling.* **4.** concerning or involving the discrimination of nondistinctive elements of a language. In English, certain phonological features, as length and aspiration, are phonetic, but not phonemic. —*n.* **5.** (in Chinese writing) a written element that represents a sound and is used in combination with a radical to form a character. [< NL *phōnētic(us)* < Gk *phōnētikós* vocal < *phōnēt(ós)* to be spoken (verbid of *phōnein* to speak) + *-ikos* -IC] **—pho·net′i·cal·ly,** *adv.*

phonet′ic al′phabet, an alphabet containing a separate character for each distinguishable speech sound.

pho·ne·ti·cian (fō′ni tish′ən), *n.* **1.** a specialist in phonetics or in some aspect of phonetics. **2.** a dialectologist. **3.** a linguist with an affinity or a special aptitude for phonology. [PHONETIC + -IAN]

phonet′ic law′, *Historical Ling.* a statement of some regular pattern of sound change in a specific language, as Grimm's law or Verner's law.

pho·net·ics (fə net′iks, fō-), *n.* (*construed as sing.*) **1.** the science or study of speech sounds and their production, transmission, and reception, and their analysis, classification, and transcription. Cf. **acoustic phonetics, articulatory phonetics, auditory phonetics, physiological phonetics.** **2.** *Linguistics.* the science or study of speech sounds in distinguishing meanings among words (sometimes opposed to *phonemics*). Cf. **phonology.** **3.** the phonetic system or the body of phonetic facts of a particular language. [see PHONETIC, -ICS]

pho·ne·tist (fō′ni tist), *n.* one who uses or advocates phonetic spelling. [< Gk *phōnēt(ós)* (see PHONETIC) + -IST]

Phone·vi·sion (fōn′vizh′ən), *n.* *Trademark.* a system of transmitting television signals over telephone lines so that people speaking to each other on the telephone can see each other on small television receivers.

pho·ney (fō′nē), *adj.,* **-ni·er, -ni·est,** *n., pl.* **-neys.** phony. **—pho′ney·ness,** *n.*

pho·ni·at·rics (fō′nē a′triks), *n.* (*construed as sing.*) *Speech Pathol.* the study and treatment of voice disorders. Also, **pho·ni·a·try** (fō nī′ə trē). [PHON- + -IATRIC; see -ICS] **—pho′ni·at′ric,** *adj.*

phon·ic (fon′ik, fō′nik), *adj.* of or pertaining to speech sounds. [PHON- + -IC]

phon·ics (fon′iks, fō′niks), *n.* (*construed as sing.*) **1.** a method of teaching reading, pronunciation, and spelling based upon the phonetic interpretation of ordinary spelling. **2.** *Obs.* phonetics. [PHON- + -ICS]

pho·no (fō′nō), *n., pl.* **-nos.** *Informal.* phonograph. [by shortening]

phono-, a learned borrowing from Greek meaning "sound," "voice," used in the formation of compound words: *phonology.* Also, *esp. before a vowel,* **phon-.** Cf. **-phone, -phony.** [< Gk, comb. form repr. *phōnḗ*]

pho·no·car·di·o·gram (fō′nə kär′dē ə gram′), *n.* *Med.* the graphic record produced by a phonocardiograph. [PHONO- + CARDIOGRAM]

pho·no·car·di·o·graph (fō′nə kär′dē ə graf′,-gräf′), *n.* *Med.* an instrument for graphically recording the sound of the heartbeat. [PHONO- + CARDIOGRAPH] **—pho·no·car·di·og·ra·phy** (fō′nə kär′dē og′rə fē), *n.*

pho·no·deik (fō′nə dīk′), *n.* a device for producing and, usually, photographing a visual representation of a sound wave. [PHONO- + *-deik* (< Gk *deik(nýnai)* (to) show)]

pho·no·gram (fō′nə gram′), *n.* a unit symbol of a phonetic writing system, standing for a speech sound, syllable, or other sequence of speech sounds without reference to meaning. [PHONO- + -GRAM[1]] **—pho′no·gram′ic, pho′no·gram′mic,** *adj.* **—pho′no·gram′i·cal·ly, pho′no·gram′mi·cal·ly,** *adv.*

pho·no·graph (fō′nə graf′, -gräf′), *n.* any sound-reproducing machine using records, whether cylinders or disks. [PHONO- + -GRAPH]

pho·no·graph·ic (fō′nə graf′ik), *adj.* **1.** of, pertaining to, or characteristic of a phonograph. **2.** of, pertaining to, or noting phonography. Also, **pho′no·graph′i·cal.** [PHONOGRAPH, PHONOGRAPH(Y) + -IC]

pho·nog·ra·phy (fō nog′rə fē), *n.* **1.** phonetic spelling, writing, or shorthand. **2.** a system of phonetic shorthand, as that invented by Sir Isaac Pitman in 1837. [PHONO- + -GRAPHY] **—pho·nog′ra·pher, pho·nog′ra·phist,** *n.*

phonol., phonology.

pho·no·lite (fōn′ᵊlīt′), *n.* a fine-grained volcanic rock composed chiefly of alkali feldspar and nepheline, some varieties of which split into pieces which ring on being struck. [< F < G *Phonolith.* See PHONO-, -LITE] **—pho·no·lit·ic** (fōn′ᵊlit′ik), *adj.*

pho·nol·o·gist (fō nol′ə jist, fə-), *n.* a phonetician and phonemicist. [PHONOLOG(Y) + -IST]

pho·nol·o·gy (fō nol′ə jē, fə-), *n., pl.* **-gies.** **1.** phonetics, phonemics, or both together. **2.** the phonetic and phonemic system or the body of phonetic and phonemic facts of a language. [PHONO- + -LOGY] **—pho·no·log·i·cal** (fōn′ᵊloj′i kəl), **pho′no·log′ic,** *adj.* **—pho′no·log′i·cal·ly,** *adv.*

pho·nom·e·ter (fə nom′i tər), *n.* a device for measuring the intensity of a sound. [PHONO- + -METER] **—pho·no·met·ric** (fō′nə me′trik), *adj.*

pho·non (fō′non), *n.* *Physics.* a quantum of sound or vibratory elastic energy, being the analogue of a photon of electromagnetic energy. [PHON- + -ON[1]]

pho·no·phore (fō′nə fōr′, -fôr′), *n.* a device permitting the simultaneous transmission of telephonic and telegraphic messages over a telegraph line. Also, **pho·no·pore** (fō′nə pōr′, -pôr′). [PHONO- + -PHORE] **—pho·no·phor·ic** (fō′nə fôr′ik, -for′-), *adj.*

pho·no·re·cep·tion (fō′nō ri sep′shən), *n.* the physiological perception of sound. [PHONO- + RECEPTION]

pho·no·re·cep·tor (fō′nō ri sep′tər), *n.* *Physiol., Biol.* a receptor stimulated by sound waves. [PHONO- + RECEPTOR]

pho·no·scope (fō′nə skōp′), *n.* **1.** an instrument for making visible the motions or properties of a sounding body. **2.** a device for testing the quality of strings for musical instruments. [PHONO- + -SCOPE]

pho·no·type (fō′nə tīp′), *n.* *Print.* **1.** a piece of type bearing a phonetic character or symbol. **2.** phonetic type or print. [PHONO- + -TYPE] **—pho·no·typ·ic** (fō′nə tip′ik), **pho′no·typ′i·cal,** *adj.* **—pho′no·typ′i·cal·ly,** *adv.*

pho·no·typ·y (fō′nə tī′pē), *n.* a system of phonetic shorthand, as the Pitman method. [PHONOTYPE + -Y[3]] **—pho′no·typ′ist, pho′no·typ′er,** *n.*

pho·ny (fō′nē), *adj.,* **-ni·er, -ni·est,** *n., pl.* **-nies.** *Informal.* —*adj.* **1.** not genuine; spurious, counterfeit, or bogus; fraudulent. —*n.* **2.** a counterfeit or fake. **3.** a faker. Also, **phoney.** [? var. of *fawney* < Ir *fáinne* finger-ring in phrase *fawney rig* confidence game in which a brass ring is sold as a gold one] **—pho′ni·ness,** *n.*

-phony, an element used in the formation of abstract nouns corresponding to nouns ending in **-phone:** *telephony.* [< Gk *-phōnia;* see -PHONE, -Y[3]]

pho′ny disease′, *Plant Pathol.* a disease of peaches, characterized by dwarfing, dark-green leaves, premature leafing and flowering, and the production of reduced numbers of small fruit, caused by a virus, *Nanus mirabilis.* Also called **pho′ny peach′.**

phoo·ey (fo͞o′ē), *interj.* *Informal.* (an exclamation indicating rejection, contempt, or disgust): *Phooey on all that sentimentality!*

THE INTERNATIONAL PHONETIC ALPHABET

(Revised to 1951)

		Bi-labial	Labio-dental	Dental and Alveolar	Retro-flex	Palato-alveolar	Alveolo-palatal	Palatal	Velar	Uvular	Pharyn-gal	Glottal
CONSONANTS	Plosive	p b		t d	ʈ ɖ			c ɟ	k g	q ɢ		ʔ
	Nasal	m	ɱ	n	ɳ			ɲ	ŋ	ɴ		
	Lateral Fricative			ɬ ɮ								
	Lateral Non-fricative			l	ɭ			ʎ				
	Rolled			r						ʀ		
	Flapped			ɾ	ɽ					ʀ		
	Fricative	ɸ β	f v	θ ð s z ɹ	ʂ ʐ	ʃ ʒ	ɕ ʑ	ç ʝ	x ɣ	χ ʁ	ħ ʕ	h ɦ
	Frictionless Continuants and Semi-vowels	w ɥ	ʋ	ɹ				j (ɥ)	(w)	ʁ		
VOWELS								Front Central	Back			
	Close	(y ʉ u)						i y ɨ ʉ	ɯ u			
	Half-close	(ø o)						e ø	ɤ o			
									ə			
	Half-open	(œ ɔ)						ɛ œ	ʌ ɔ			
								æ	ɐ			
	Open	(ɒ)						a	ɑ ɒ			

(Secondary articulations are shown by symbols in brackets.)

Other Sounds.—Palatalized consonants: ƫ, ȡ, etc.; palatalized ʃ, ʒ: ʆ, ʓ. Velarized or pharyngalized consonants: ɫ, ɗ, ƶ, etc. Ejective consonants (with simultaneous glottal stop): p', t', etc. Implosive voiced consonants: ɓ, ɗ, etc. ɼ fricative trill. σ, ϱ (labialized θ, ð, or s, z). ʆ, ʓ (labialized ʃ, ʒ). ʇ, ʗ, ʖ (clicks, Zulu *c, q, x*). ɺ (a sound between r and l). ɳ Japanese syllabic nasal. ɧ (combination of x and ʃ). ʍ (voiceless w). ɩ, ʏ, ɷ (lowered varieties of i, y, u). ɜ (a variety of ə). ɵ (a vowel between ø and o).

Affricates are normally represented by groups of two consonants (ts, tʃ, dʒ, etc.), but, when necessary, ligatures are used (ʦ, ʧ, ʤ, etc.), or the marks ⁀ or ‿ (t͡s or t‿s, etc.). ⁀ ‿ also denote synchronic articulation (m͡ŋ = simultaneous m and ŋ). c, ɟ may occasionally be used in place of tʃ, dʒ, and ʒ, ƻ for ts, dz. Aspirated plosives: ph, th, etc. r-colored vowels: eɹ, aɹ, ɔɹ, etc., or eʴ, aʴ, ɔʴ, etc., or ɚ, a˞, ɔ˞, etc.; r-colored ə : əɹ or əʴ or ɹ or ə˞ or ɚ.

Length, Stress, Pitch.— ː (full length). ˑ (half length). ˈ (stress, placed at beginning of the stressed syllable). ˌ (secondary stress). ˉ (high level pitch); ˍ (low level); ˊ (high rising); ˏ (low rising); ˋ (high falling); ˎ (low falling); ˆ (rise-fall); ˇ (fall-rise).

Modifiers.— ˜ nasality. ˳ breath (l̥ = breathed l). ˬ voice (s̬ = z). ʻ slight aspiration following p, t, etc. ̫ labialization (n̫ = labialized n). ̪ dental articulation (t̪ = dental t). ˙ palatalization (ż = ʑ). ̣ specially close vowel (ẹ = a very close e). ̨ specially open vowel (ę = a rather open e). ˔ tongue raised (e˔ or e̝ = ẹ). ˕ tongue lowered (e˕ or e̞ = ę). ˖ tongue advanced (u˖ or u̟ = an advanced u, t̟ = t̪). ˗ or ˗ tongue retracted (i- or i̠ = ɨ˖, t̠ = alveolar t). ˒ lips more rounded. ˓ lips more spread. Central vowels: ï (= ɨ), ü (= ʉ), ë (= ə˗), ö (= ɵ), ɛ̈, ɔ̈. ̩ (e.g. n̩) syllabic consonant. ̆ consonantal vowel. ʃˢ variety of ʃ resembling s, etc.

Courtesy of Association Phonétique Internationale

Phor·bas (fôr′bəs), *n. Class. Myth.* **1.** a son of Lapithes who dispelled a plague of serpents in Rhodes. **2.** a leader of the Phrygian allies of Troy, slain by Ajax. **3.** a renowned boxer who challenged pilgrims, killed them, and was eventually slain by Apollo.

Phor·cids (fôr′sidz), *n.pl. Class. Myth.* the children of Phorcys and Ceto, among them Ladon and the Gorgons.

Phor·cys (fôr′sis), *n. Class. Myth.* **1.** a sea god who fathered the Gorgons. **2.** (in the *Odyssey*) the Ithacan harbor where Odysseus was left by the Phaeacians.

-phore, a learned borrowing from Greek meaning "bearer," "thing or part bearing (something)," used in the formation of compound words: *gonophore.* Cf. **-phorous.** [< NL *-phorus* < Gk *-phoros* bearing]

phor·e·sy (fôr′i sē), *n. Zool.* (among insects and arachnids) a nonparasitic relationship in which one species is carried about by another. [< NL *phoresia* < Gk *phórēsi(s)* a being carried (*phorē-*, verbid s. of *phoreîn*, durative of *phérein* to bear, + *-sis* -SIS) + *-ia* -Y³]

Pho·ro·ne·us (fə rō′nē əs), *n. Class. Myth.* a son of Inachus and the nymph Melia who was the founder of Argos and who was considered a national hero for furthering religious, cultural, and civil causes in the Peloponnesus.

pho·ro·nid (fə rō′nid), *n.* **1.** any of several wormlike, tube-dwelling, marine invertebrates of the phylum *Phoronidea*, having a horseshoe-shaped lophophore. —*adj.* **2.** belonging or pertaining to the *Phoronidea*. [< NL *Phoronid(ea)*, equiv. to *Phoron(is)* name of genus (< L: a name of Io) + *-idea* neut. pl. n. suffix; see -ID²]

-phorous, an element used in the formation of adjectives corresponding to nouns with stems ending in **-phore:** *gonophorous.* [< NL *-phorus* < Gk *-phoros* bearing]

phos·gene (fos′jēn), *n. Chem.* a poisonous, colorless, very volatile liquid or suffocating gas, $COCl_2$, a chemical-warfare compound: used chiefly in organic synthesis. Also called **carbon oxychloride, carbonyl chloride, chloroformyl chloride.** [< Gk *phôs* light (contr. of *pháos*) + *-gene* -GEN]

phos·ge·nite (fos′jə nīt′), *n.* a mineral, lead chlorocarbonate, $Pb_2Cl_2CO_3$, occurring in crystals. [< G *Phosgenit.* See PHOSGENE, -ITE¹]

phosph-, var. of **phospho-** before a vowel: *phosphate.*

phos·pha·gen (fos′fə jin, -jen′), *n. Biochem.* phosphocreatine. [PHOSPHA(TE) + -GEN]

phos·pha·tase (fos′fə tās′), *n. Biochem.* an enzyme, found in body tissues, that breaks up compounds made of carbohydrates and phosphates. [PHOSPHATE + -ASE]

phos·phate (fos′fāt), *n.* **1.** *Chem.* **a.** (loosely) a salt or ester of phosphoric acid. **b.** a tertiary salt of orthophosphoric acid, as sodium phosphate. **2.** *Agric.* a fertilizing material containing compounds of phosphorus. **3.** a carbonated drink of water and fruit syrup containing a little phosphoric acid. [PHOSPH- + -ATE²]

phos′phate rock′, a rock consisting chiefly of calcium phosphates and calcite, used in fertilizers.

phos·phat·ic (fos fat′ik), *adj.* of, pertaining to, or containing phosphates: *phosphatic slag.* [PHOSPHATE + -IC]

phos·pha·tide (fos′fə tīd′, -tid), *n. Biochem.* any of a group of fatty compounds, as lecithin, composed of phosphoric esters, and occurring in cellular organisms. Also called **phospholipid, phospholipide, phospholipin.** [PHOSPHATE + -IDE]

phos·pha·tise (fos′fə tīz′), *v.t.*, **-tised, -tis·ing.** *Chiefly Brit.* phosphatize. —**phos′pha·ti·sa′tion,** *n.*

phos·pha·tize (fos′fə tīz′), *v.t.*, **-tized, -tiz·ing. 1.** to treat with phosphates. **2.** to change to phosphate. [PHOSPHATE + -IZE] —**phos′pha·ti·za′tion, phos·pha·tion** (fos fā′shən), *n.*

phos·pha·tu·ri·a (fos′fə to͝or′ē ə, -tyo͝or′-), *n. Pathol.* the presence of an excessive quantity of phosphates in the urine. [PHOSPHATE + -URIA] —**phos′pha·tu′ric,** *adj.*

phos·phene (fos′fēn), *n. Physiol.* a luminous image produced by mechanical stimulation of the retina, as by pressure applied to the eyeball by the finger when the lid is closed. [< Gk *phôs* light (contr. of *pháos*) + *phaín(ein)* (to) show, shine]

phos·phide (fos′fīd, -fid), *n. Chem.* a binary compound of phosphorus with a basic element or group. [PHOSPH- + -IDE]

phos·phine (fos′fēn, -fin), *n. Chem.* **1.** a colorless, poisonous, ill-smelling, flammable gas, PH_3. **2.** any of certain organic derivatives of this compound. [PHOSPH- + -INE¹]

phos·phite (fos′fīt), *n. Chem.* (loosely) a salt of phosphorous acid. [PHOSPH- + -ITE¹]

phospho-, a combining form representing **phosphorus:** *phosphoprotein.* Also, *esp. before a vowel,* **phosph-.** Cf. **phosphoro-.**

phos·pho·cre·a·tine (fos′fō krē′ə tēn′, -tin), *n. Biochem.* a compound, $C_4H_{10}O_5N_3P$, found chiefly in muscle, formed by the enzymatic interaction of an organic phosphate and creatine, the breakdown of which provides energy for muscle contraction. Also called **creatine phosphate, phosphagen.** [PHOSPHO- + CREATINE]

phos·pho·lip·ide (fos′fō lip′īd, -id, -lī′pīd, -pid), *n. Biochem.* phosphatide. Also, **phos·pho·lip·id** (fos′fō-lip′id, -lī′pid), **phos·pho·lip·in** (fos′fō lip′in, -lī′pin). [PHOSPHO- + LIP(ID) + -IDE]

phos·pho·ni·um (fos fō′nē əm), *n. Chem.* the positively charged group, PH_4^+, analogous to ammonium, NH_4^+. [PHOSPH(ORUS) + (AMM)ONIUM]

phospho′nium i′odide, *Chem.* a colorless to slightly yellowish, crystalline, water-soluble solid, PH_4I, used in chemical synthesis.

phos·pho·nu·cle·ase (fos′fō no͞o′klē ās′, -nyo͞o′-), *n. Biochem.* nucleotidase. [PHOSPHO- + NUCLE(IC ACID) + -ASE]

phos·pho·pro·tein (fos′fō prō′tēn, -tē in), *n. Biochem.* a protein composed of a molecule of protein linked with a substance other than nucleic acid or lecithin and containing phosphorous. [PHOSPHO- + PROTEIN]

phos·phor (fos′fər), *n.* **1.** any of a number of substances that exhibit luminescence when struck by light of certain wave lengths, as by ultra violet. **2.** *Literary.* a phosphorescent substance. —*adj.* **3.** *Archaic.* phosphorescent. [< F *phosphore* < NL *phosphor(us)* PHOSPHOROUS]

Phos·phor (fos′fər), *n.* the morning star, esp. Venus. Also, **Phos·phore** (fos′fōr, -fôr), **Phosphorus.** [< L *Phōsphor(us)* < Gk *Phōsphóros* the morning star; lit., the light-bringing one, equiv. to *phôs* light + *phoros* bringing; see -PHORE]

phosphor-, var. of **phosphoro-** before a vowel: *phosphorate.*

phos·pho·rate (fos′fə rāt′), *v.t.*, **-rat·ed, -rat·ing. 1.** *Chem.* to combine or impregnate with phosphorus. **2.** to cause to have phosphorescence. [PHOSPHOR- + -ATE²]

phos′phor bronze′, a bronze, composed about 80 percent of copper, 10 percent of tin, 9 percent of antimony, and 1 percent of phosphorus, having great hardness and resistance to corrosion.

phos·pho·resce (fos′fə res′), *v.i.*, **-resced, -resc·ing.** to be luminous without sensible heat, as phosphorus. [PHOSPHOR(US) + -ESCE]

phos·pho·res·cence (fos′fə res′əns), *n.* **1.** the property of being luminous at temperatures below incandescence, as from slow oxidation in the case of phosphorus or after exposure to light or other radiation. **2.** a luminous appearance resulting from this. **3.** any radiation emitted from a substance after the removal of the exciting agent. [PHOSPHORESC(ENT) + -ENCE]

phos·pho·res·cent (fos′fə res′ənt), *adj.* exhibiting phosphorescence. [PHOSPHOR(US) + -ESCENT] —**phos′pho·res′cent·ly,** *adv.*

phos·phor·et·ed (fos′fə ret′id), *adj. Chem.* phosphureted. Also, **phos′phor·et′ted.**

phos·phor·ic (fos fôr′ik, -for′-), *adj. Chem.* of or containing phosphorus, esp. in the pentavalent state. [PHOSPHOR + -IC]

phosphor′ic ac′id, *Chem.* any of three acids, orthophosphoric acid, H_3PO_4, metaphosphoric acid, HPO_3, or pyrophosphoric acid, $H_4P_2O_7$, derived from phosphorus pentoxide, P_2O_5, and various amounts of water.

phosphor′ic anhy′dride, *Chem.* See **phosphorus pentoxide.**

phos·pho·rise (fos′fə rīz′), *v.t.*, **-rised, -ris·ing.** *Chiefly Brit.* phosphorize. —**phos′pho·ri·sa′tion,** *n.*

phos·pho·rism (fos′fə riz′əm), *n. Pathol.* condition of chronic phosphorus poisoning. [PHOSPHOR- + -ISM]

phos·pho·rite (fos′fə rīt′), *n.* **1.** a massive form of the mineral apatite: the principal source of phosphate for fertilizers. **2.** any of various compact or earthy, more or less impure varieties of calcium phosphate. [PHOSPHOR- + -ITE¹] —**phos·pho·rit·ic** (fos′fə rit′ik), *adj.*

phos·pho·rize (fos′fə rīz′), *v.t.*, **-rized, -riz·ing.** *Chem.* phosphorate. Also, *esp. Brit.,* **phosphorise.** [PHOSPHOR- + -IZE] —**phos′pho·ri·za′tion,** *n.*

phosphoro-, a combining form representing **phosphorus:** *phosphoroscope.* Also, *esp. before a vowel,* **phosphor-.** Cf. **phospho-.**

phos·phor·o·scope (fos fôr′ə skōp′, -for′-), *n.* an instrument for measuring the duration of evanescent phosphorescence in different substances. [PHOSPHORO- + -SCOPE]

phos·pho·rous (fos′fər əs, fos fôr′əs, -fōr′-), *adj. Chem.* containing trivalent phosphorus. [PHOSPHOR- + -OUS]

phos′phorous ac′id, *Chem.* a colorless, crystalline, water-soluble acid of phosphorus, H_3PO_3, from which phosphites are derived.

phos·pho·rus (fos′fər əs), *n., pl.* **-pho·ri** (-fə rī′). **1.** *Chem.* a solid, nonmetallic element existing in at least two allotropic forms, one that is yellow, poisonous, flammable, and luminous in the dark, and another that is red, less poisonous, and less flammable. The element is used in forming smoke screens, its compounds are used in matches and phosphate fertilizers, and it is a necessary constituent in plant and animal life in bones, nerves, and embryos. *Symbol:* P; *at. wt.:* 30.974; *at. no.:* 15; *sp. gr.:* (yellow) 1.82 at 20°C, (red) 2.20 at 20°C. **2.** any phosphorescent substance. **3.** phosphor. [< NL < L *phosphorus.* See PHOSPHOR]

Phos·pho·rus (fos′fər əs), *n.* Phosphor.

phos′phorus pent·ox′ide (pen tok′sīd, -sid), *Chem.* a white, deliquescent, crystalline powder, P_2O_5, that, depending upon the amount of water it absorbs, forms orthophosphoric acid, metaphosphoric acid, or pyrophosphoric acid, produced by the burning of phosphorus in dry air: used in the preparation of phosphoric acids, as a drying and dehydrating agent, and in organic synthesis. Also called **phosphoric anhydride.**

phos′phorus sesquisul′fide, (not in scientific use) a yellow, crystalline, flammable substance, P_4S_3, insoluble in cold water and decomposed by hot water: used chiefly in organic synthesis and in the manufacture of matches.

phosphorus 32, *Chem.* a radioactive isotope of phosphorus, used as a chemotherapeutic agent. Also called **radiophosphorus.**

phos′phorus trichlo′ride, *Chem.* a clear, colorless, fuming liquid, PCl_3, used chiefly in organic synthesis as a chlorinating agent.

phos·pho·ryl·ase (fos′fər ə lās′, -lāz′, fos fûr′ə-lās′, -for′-), *n. Biochem.* an enzyme, occurring widely in animal and plant tissue, that in the presence of inorganic phosphate catalyzes the conversion of glycogen into sugar phosphate. [PHOSPHOR- + -YL + -ASE]

phos·pho·ryl·ate (fos fôr′ə lāt′, -for′-), *v.t.*, **-at·ed, -at·ing.** *Chem.* to introduce the phosphoryl group into (an organic compound). [PHOSPHOR- + -YL + -ATE¹] —**phos′pho·ryl·a′tion,** *n.*

phos′pho·ryl group′ (fos′fə ril), *Chem.* the trivalent group, ≡P=O. Also called **phos′phoryl rad′ical.** [PHOSPHOR- + -YL]

phos·phu·ret·ed (fos′fyə ret′id), *adj. Chem.* combined with phosphorus, esp. in its lowest valence state. Also, **phosphoreted, phosphoretted, phos′phu·ret′ted.** [*phosphuret* phosphide (see PHOSPH-, -URET) + -ED³]

phot (fot, fōt), *n. Optics.* a unit of illumination, equal to 1 lumen per square centimeter. *Abbr.:* ph [< Gk *phōt-* (s. of *phôs*) light, contr. of *pháos*]

phot., **1.** photograph. **2.** photographer. **3.** photographic. **4.** photography.

pho·tal·gi·a (fō tal′jə, -jē ə), *n. Med.* pain that is caused by intensity of light. [PHOT + -ALGIA]

pho·tic (fō′tik), *adj.* **1.** of or pertaining to light. **2.** pertaining to the generation of light by organisms, or their excitation by means of light. [PHOT + -IC]

pho·tics (fō′tiks), *n.* (*construed as sing.*) the science of light. [PHOT + -ICS]

pho·tism (fō′tiz əm), *n. Psychol.* a form of synesthesia in which a visual sensation, as of color, form, etc., is produced by sensations from another modality. [< Gk *phōtism(ós)* illumination, equiv. to *phōt(ízein)* (to) give light + *-ismós* -ISM]

Pho·ti·us (fō′shē əs), *n.* A.D. c820–891, patriarch of Constantinople 858–867, 877–882.

pho·to (fō′tō), *n., pl.* **-tos.** *Informal.* photograph. [shortened form]

photo-, a learned borrowing from Greek meaning "light," sometimes used to represent "photographic" or "photograph" in the formation of compound words: *photoelectric.* [< Gk, comb. form *phôs* (gen., *phōtós*)]

pho·to·ac·tin·ic (fō′tō ak tin′ik), *adj.* emitting radiation having the chemical effects of light and ultraviolet rays, as on a photographic film. [PHOTO- + ACTINIC]

pho′to base′, *Aerial Photogrammetry.* an air base as represented on the photographs taken.

pho·to·bath·ic (fō′tə bath′ik), *adj.* in or relating to the stratum of ocean depth penetrated by sunlight. [PHOTO- + BATH(O)- + -IC]

pho·to·bi·ot·ic (fō′tō bī ot′ik), *adj. Bot., Zool.* living or thriving only in the presence of light. [PHOTO- + BIOTIC]

pho·to·cath·ode (fō′tō kath′ōd), *n.* a cathode, typically of a cesium or sodium compound, having the property of emitting electrons when activated by light or other radiation. [PHOTO- + CATHODE]

pho·to·cell (fō′tō sel′), *n.* **1.** a phototube. **2.** See **photoelectric cell** (def. 1). [PHOTO- + CELL]

pho·to·chem·is·try (fō′tō kem′i strē), *n.* the branch of chemistry that deals with the chemical action of light. [PHOTO- + CHEMISTRY] —**pho·to·chem·i·cal** (fō′tō kem′i kəl), **pho′to·chem′ic,** *adj.* —**pho′to·chem′i·cal·ly,** *adv.* —**pho′to·chem′ist,** *n.*

pho·to·chro·my (fō′tə krō′mē), *n. Obs.* color photography. [PHOTO- + -CHROME + -Y³]

pho·to·chron·o·graph (fō′tə kron′ə graf′, -gräf′, -krō′nə-), *n.* **1.** an obsolete device for taking a series of instantaneous photographs of a rapidly moving object. **2.** a picture taken by such a device. **3.** a chronograph in which the tracing or record is made by a pencil of light on a sensitized surface. **4.** an instrument for measuring small intervals of time by the photographic trace of a pencil of light. [PHOTO- + CHRONOGRAPH] —**pho·to·chron·og·ra·phy** (fō′tə krə nog′rə fē), *n.*

pho·to·com·pose (fō′tō kəm pōz′), *v.t.*, **-posed, -pos·ing.** to set (type) on a photocomposer. [PHOTO- + COMPOSE]

pho·to·com·pos·er (fō′tō kəm pō′zər), *n.* a machine for setting type photographically. [PHOTO- + COMPOSER]

pho·to·com·po·si·tion (fō′tō kom′pə zish′ən), *n.* the technique or art of setting type by means of a photocomposer. [PHOTO- + COMPOSITION]

pho·to·con·duc·tive (fō′tō kən duk′tiv), *adj.* **1.** *Physics.* of, pertaining to, or exhibiting photoconductivity. **2.** losing an electrical charge on exposure to light. [PHOTO- + CONDUCTIVE] —**pho′to·con·duc′tion,** *n.* —**pho′to·con·duc′tor,** *n.*

pho·to·con·duc·tiv·i·ty (fō′tō kon′duk tiv′i tē), *n. Physics.* the increase of the electric conductivity of a substance, often nonmetallic, caused by the absorption of electromagnetic radiation. [PHOTO- + CONDUCTIVITY]

pho·to·cop·y (fō′tə kop′ē), *n., pl.* **-cop·ies,** *v.*, **-cop·ied, -cop·y·ing.** —*n.* **1.** a photographic copy of a document, print, or the like. —*v.t.* **2.** to copy (a document, print, or the like) photographically. [PHOTO- + COPY]

pho·to·cur·rent (fō′tō kûr′ənt, -kur′-), *n. Physics.* an electric current produced by a photoelectric effect. Also called **photoelectric current.** [PHOTO- + CURRENT]

pho·to·dis·in·te·gra·tion (fō′tō di sin′tə grā′shən), *n. Physics.* the disintegration of a nucleus, induced by its absorption of a photon. [PHOTO- + DISINTEGRATION]

pho·to·dis·so·ci·a·tion (fō′tō di sō′sē ā′shən), *n.* the dissociation or breakdown of a chemical compound by radiant energy. [PHOTO- + DISSOCIATION]

pho·to·dra·ma (fō′tə drä′mə, -dram′ə), *n.* photoplay. [PHOTO- + DRAMA] —**pho·to·dra·mat·ic** (fō′tō drə mat′ik), *adj.* —**pho′to·dra·mat′ics,** *n.* —**pho·to·dram·a·tist** (fō′tə dram′ə tist), *n.*

pho·to·du·pli·cate (fō′tō do͞o′plə kit, -dyo͞o′-), *n.* a photographic duplicate, as of a document. [PHOTO- + DUPLICATE]

pho·to·du·pli·ca·tion (fō′tō do͞o′plə kā′shən, -dyo͞o′-), *n.* the act or process of making photographic duplicates, as of documents. [PHOTO- + DUPLICATION]

pho·to·dy·nam·ics (fō′tō dī nam′iks, -di-), *n.* (*construed as sing.*) the science dealing with light in its relation to movement in plants. [PHOTO- + DYNAMICS] —**pho′to·dy·nam′ic, pho′to·dy·nam′i·cal,** *adj.* —**pho′to·dy·nam′i·cal·ly,** *adv.*

pho·to·e·las·tic·i·ty (fō′tō i las tis′i tē, -ē la stis′-), *n. Physics.* the phenomenon of double refraction of polarized light by a transparent substance under elastic stress, used to measure strain in elastic, transparent materials. [PHOTO- + ELASTICITY] —**pho·to·e·las·tic** (fō′tō i las′tik), *adj.*

pho·to·e·lec·tric (fō′tō i lek′trik), *adj.* pertaining to the electronic or other electric effects produced by light. Also, **pho′to·e·lec′tri·cal.** [PHOTO- + ELECTRIC] —**pho′to·e·lec′tri·cal·ly,** *adv.*

pho′toelec′tric cell′, *Electronics.* **1.** a device incorporated in an electric circuit to make the resistance or electromotive force of part of the circuit variable in accordance with variations in the intensity of light or similar radiation falling upon it, thus making operations controlled by the circuit dependent on variations in illumination, a beam of radiation, etc. **2.** a phototube.

pho′toelec′tric cur′rent, *Physics.* photocurrent.

pho′toelec′tric effect′, *Physics.* the phenomenon in which the absorption of electromagnetic radiation, as light, of sufficiently high frequency by a surface, usually metallic, induces the emission of electrons from the surface. Also called **photoemission.**

pho·to·e·lec·tric·i·ty (fō′tō i lek tris′i tē, -ē′lek-), *n.* *Physics.* **1.** electricity induced by electromagnetic radiation, as in certain processes, as the photoelectric and photovoltaic effects, photoconductivity, and photoionization. **2.** the branch of physics that deals with these phenomena. [PHOTO- + ELECTRICITY]

pho′toelec′tric me′ter, *Photog.* an exposure meter using a photoelectric cell for the measurement of light intensity.

pho′toelec′tric thresh′old, *Physics.* the minimum frequency or maximum wavelength of incident radiation necessary to release photons from a given surface.

pho·to·e·lec·tron (fō′tō i lek′tron), *n.* *Physics.* an electron emitted from a system by the photoelectric effect. [PHOTO- + ELECTRON]

pho·to·e·lec·tro·type (fō′tō i lek′trə tīp′), *n.* an electrotype made by photographic means. [PHOTO- + ELECTROTYPE]

pho·to·e·mis·sion (fō′tō i mish′ən), *n.* *Physics.* See **photoelectric effect.** [PHOTO- + EMISSION] —**pho·to·e·mis·sive** (fō′tō i mis′iv), *adj.*

photoeng., photoengraving.

pho·to·en·grave (fō′tō en grāv′), *v.t.,* **-graved, -grav·ing.** to make a photoengraving of. [PHOTO- + ENGRAVE] —**pho′to·en·grav′er,** *n.*

pho·to·en·grav·ing (fō′tō en grā′ving), *n.* **1.** a photographic process of preparing printing plates for letterpress printing. **2.** a process of photographic reproduction by which a relief printing surface is obtained for letterpress printing. **3.** a plate so produced. **4.** a print made from it. [PHOTO- + ENGRAVING]

pho′to fin′ish, *Sports.* a finish of a race in which two or more contestants are so close to the finish line that reference to a photograph of the finish is necessary to decide on the winner. —**pho′to-fin′ish,** *adj.*

pho·to·fin·ish·er (fō′tō fin′i shər), *n.* one who develops photographic film, makes prints, etc. [PHOTO + FINISH + -ER[1]]

pho·to·fin·ish·ing (fō′tō fin′i shing), *n.* the act or occupation of developing films, printing photographs, etc. [PHOTO + FINISHING]

pho·to·fis·sion (fō′tə fish′ən), *n.* *Physics.* nuclear fission induced by the absorption of a high-energy photon. [PHOTO- + FISSION]

pho′to·flash lamp′ (fō′tə flash′), *Photog.* a flash bulb. [PHOTO- + FLASH]

pho′toflash photog′raphy. See **flash photography.**

pho′toflash syn′chronizer, *Photog.* a device for synchronizing a camera shutter with a flash lamp.

pho·to·flight (fō′tə flīt′), *adj.* pertaining to a flight made for the purpose of aerial photography. [PHOTO- + FLIGHT[1]]

pho′to·flood lamp′ (fō′tə flud′), an incandescent tungsten lamp in which high intensity is obtained by overloading voltage: used in photography, television, etc. [PHOTO- + FLOOD]

photog., **1.** photographer. **2.** photographic. **3.** photography.

pho·to·gel·a·tin (fō′tə jel′ə tin), *adj.* pertaining to any photographic process in which gelatin is used to receive or transfer a print. [PHOTO- + GELATIN]

photogel′atin proc′ess, collotype (def. 1).

pho·to·gen (fō′tə jen′), *n.* **1.** a light oil obtained by the distillation of bituminous shale, coal, or peat: used chiefly as an illuminant and as a solvent. **2.** *Biol.* a photogenic organ, organism, or substance. [PHOTO- + -GEN]

pho·to·gene (fō′tə jēn′), *n.* *Ophthalm.* an afterimage on the retina. [PHOTO- + GENE]

pho·to·gen·ic (fō′tə jen′ik), *adj.* **1.** forming an attractive subject for photography or looking well in a photograph: *a photogenic face.* **2.** *Biol.* producing or emitting light, as certain bacteria; luminiferous; phosphorescent. **3.** *Med.* produced or caused by light, as a skin condition. [PHOTO- + GENIC] —**pho′to·gen′i·cal·ly,** *adv.*

pho·to·gram (fō′tə gram′), *n.* **1.** a silhouette photograph made by laying an object directly on sensitized paper and exposing it to light. **2.** *Rare.* a photograph. [PHOTO- + -GRAM[1]]

pho·to·gram·me·try (fō′tə gram′i trē), *n.* the process of making surveys and maps through the use of photographs. [PHOTOGRAM + -METRY] —**pho·to·gram·met·ric** (fō′tō grə me′trik), **pho′to·gram·met′ri·cal,** *adj.* —**pho′to·gram·met′ri·cal·ly,** *adv.* —**pho′to·gram′me·trist,** *n.*

pho·to·graph (fō′tə graf′, -gräf′), *n.* **1.** a picture produced by photography. —*v.t.* **2.** to take a photograph of. —*v.i.* **3.** to practice photography. **4.** to be photographed, or be suitable for being photographed, in some specified way: *The children photographed very attractively.* [PHOTO- + -GRAPH] —**pho′to·graph′a·ble,** *adj.*

pho·tog·ra·pher (fə tog′rə fər), *n.* one who takes photographs, esp. one who practices photography professionally. [PHOTOGRAPH + -ER[1]]

pho·to·graph·ic (fō′tə graf′ik), *adj.* **1.** of or pertaining to photography. **2.** used in, or produced by means of, photography: *photographic equipment; a photographic section of a newspaper.* **3.** suggestive of a photograph; extremely realistic and detailed: *photographic accuracy.* **4.** remembering, reproducing, or functioning with the precision of a photograph: *a photographic memory; photographic art.* Also, **pho′to·graph′i·cal.** [PHOTOGRAPH + -IC] —**pho′to·graph′i·cal·ly,** *adv.*

pho·tog·ra·phy (fə tog′rə fē), *n.* the process or art of producing images of objects on sensitized surfaces by the chemical action of light or of other forms of radiant energy, as x-rays, gamma rays, cosmic rays, etc. [PHOTO- + -GRAPHY]

pho·to·gra·vure (fō′tə grə vyŏŏr′, fō′tə grā′vyər), *n.* **1.** any of various processes, based on photography, by which an intaglio engraving is formed on a metal plate, from which ink reproductions are made. **2.** the plate. **3.** a print made from it. [PHOTO- + GRAVURE] —**pho′to·gra·vure′ist,** *n.*

pho·to·he·li·o·graph (fō′tə hē′lē ə graf′, -gräf′), *n.* *Astron.* an instrument for photographing the sun, consisting of a camera and a specially adapted telescope. Also called **heliograph.** [PHOTO- + HELIOGRAPH] —**pho·to·he·li·o·graph·ic** (fō′tə hē′lē ə graf′ik), *adj.* —**pho·to·he·li·og·ra·phy** (fō′tə hē′lē og′rə fē), *n.*

pho·to·i·o·ni·za·tion (fō′tō ī′ə ni zā′shən), *n.* *Physics.* the phenomenon in which the absorption of electromagnetic radiation by an atom in a gas induces the atom to emit a bound electron, thereby ionizing the atom. [PHOTO- + IONIZATION]

pho·to·jour·nal·ism (fō′tō jûr′nəliz′əm), *n.* **1.** journalism in which photography dominates written copy, as in certain magazines. **2.** news photography, esp. as conceived of as the achieving of maximum narrative significance in photographs, whether or not for primarily pictorial media, publications, or stories. [PHOTO- + JOURNALISM] —**pho′to·jour′nal·ist,** *n.*

pho·to·ki·ne·sis (fō′tō ki nē′sis, -kī-), *n.* *Physiol.* movement occurring upon exposure to light. [PHOTO- + Gk *kínēsis* movement (see KINETIC)] —**pho·to·ki·net·ic** (fō′tō ki net′ik, -kī-), *adj.*

pho′to lay′out, a picture spread. See under **spread** (def. 32).

pho·to·lith·o (fō′tə lith′ō), *n.,* *pl.* **-lith·os,** *adj.* —*n.* **1.** photolithography. **2.** photolithograph. —*adj.* **3.** photolithographic. [PHOTO- + LITHO-]

pho·to·lith·o·graph (fō′tə lith′ə graf′, -gräf′), *n.* **1.** a lithograph printed from a stone or the like upon which a picture or design has been formed by photography. —*v.t.* **2.** to make a photolithograph of. [PHOTO- + LITHOGRAPH]

pho·to·li·thog·ra·phy (fō′tō li thog′rə fē), *n.* the technique or art of making photolithographs. [PHOTO- + LITHOGRAPHY] —**pho·to·lith·o·graph·ic** (fō′tə·lith′ə graf′ik), *adj.* —**pho′to·li·thog′ra·pher,** *n.*

pho·to·lith·o·print (fō′tə lith′ə print′), *n.* a print made from a photolithograph. [PHOTOLITHO + PRINT]

pho·to·lu·mi·nes·cence (fō′tə lōō′mə nes′əns), *n.* *Physics.* luminescence induced by the absorption of infrared radiation, visible light, or ultraviolet radiation. [PHOTO- + LUMINESCENCE] —**pho′to·lu′mi·nes′cent,** *adj.*

pho·tol·y·sis (fō tol′i sis), *n.* the breakdown of materials under the influence of light. [PHOTO- + -LYSIS] —**pho·to·lyt·ic** (fōt′ᵊlit′ik), *adj.*

photom., photometry.

pho·to·mac·ro·graph (fō′tə mak′rə graf′, -gräf′), *n.* **1.** a photograph showing a subject at actual size or somewhat larger. **2.** a photograph made through a microscope of low power. [PHOTO- + MACROGRAPH]

pho·to·map (fō′tə map′), *n.,* *v.,* **-mapped, -mapping.** —*n.* **1.** a mosaic of aerial photographs marked as a map, with grid lines, place-names, etc. —*v.t.* **2.** to map by means of aerial photography. [PHOTO- + MAP]

pho·to·me·chan·i·cal (fō′tō mə kan′i kəl), *adj.* noting or pertaining to any of various processes for printing in ink from plates or surfaces prepared by the aid of photography. [PHOTO- + MECHANICAL] —**pho′to·me·chan′i·cal·ly,** *adv.*

pho·tom·e·ter (fō tom′i tər), *n.* *Optics.* an instrument that measures luminous intensity or brightness, luminous flux, light distribution, color, etc., usually by comparing the light emitted by two sources, one source having certain specified standard characteristics. [< NL *photometr(um).* See PHOTO-, -METER]

•**pho·tom·e·try** (fō tom′i trē), *n.* **1.** the measurement of the intensity of light or of relative illuminating power. **2.** the science dealing with such measurements. [< NL *photometria.* See PHOTO-, -METRY] —**pho·to·met·ric** (fō′tə me′trik), **pho′to·met′ri·cal,** *adj.* —**pho′to·met′ri·cal·ly,** *adv.* —**pho·tom′e·trist, pho·to·me·tri·cian** (fō′tə me trish′ən), *n.*

pho·to·mi·cro·graph (fō′tə mī′krə graf′, -gräf′), *n.* **1.** a photograph taken through a microscope. **2.** a microphotograph. [PHOTO- + MICROGRAPH] —**pho·to·mi·crog·ra·pher** (fō′tə mī krog′rə fər), *n.* —**pho·to·mi·cro·graph·ic** (fō′tə mī′krə graf′ik), **pho′to·mi′cro·graph′i·cal,** *adj.* —**pho′to·mi′cro·graph′i·cal·ly,** *adv.* —**pho′to·mi·crog′ra·phy,** *n.*

pho·to·mi·cro·scope (fō′tə mī′krə skōp′), *n.* a microscope having an illuminator and a camera mechanism for producing a photomicrograph. [PHOTO- + MICROSCOPE] —**pho·to·mi·cros·co·py** (fō′tə mī kros′kə pē), *n.*

pho·to·mon·tage (fō′tə mon täzh′, -môn-), *n.* *Photog.* a combination of several photographs joined together for artistic effect or to show more of the subject than can be disclosed in a single photograph. [PHOTO- + MONTAGE]

pho·to·mount (fō′tō mount′), *n.* a heavy paper or board suitable for mounting photographs.

pho·to·mul·ti·pli·er (fō′tə mul′tə plī′ər), *n.* an extremely sensitive detector of light and of other radiation, consisting of a tube in which the electrons released by radiation striking a photocathode are accelerated to successive dynodes that release several electrons for each incident electron, greatly amplifying the signal obtainable from small quantities of radiation. [PHOTO- + MULTIPLIER]

pho·to·mur·al (fō′tə myŏŏr′əl), *n.* a wall decoration consisting of a very large photograph or photographs. [PHOTO- + MURAL]

pho·ton (fō′ton), *n.* **1.** a quantum of electromagnetic radiation, usually considered as an elementary particle that is its own antiparticle and that has zero rest mass and charge and a spin of one. *Symbol:* γ **2.** Also called **troland.** *Ophthalm.* a unit of measurement of retinal response to light. [PHOT- + -ON[1]]

pho·to·neg·a·tive (fō′tə neg′ə tiv), *adj.* *Physics.* pertaining to a substance having a conductivity that decreases upon absorption of electromagnetic radiation. [PHOTO- + NEGATIVE]

pho·to·neu·tron (fō′tə nōō′tron, -nyōō′-), *n.* *Physics.* a neutron emitted from a nucleus during photodisintegration. [PHOTO- + NEUTRON]

pho·to-off·set (fō′tō ôf′set′, -of′-), *n.,* *v.,* **-set, -set·ting.** —*n.* **1.** a method of printing, based on photolithography, in which the inked image is transferred from the metal plate to a rubber surface and then to the paper. —*v.t., v.i.* **2.** to print by photo-offset.

pho·top·a·thy (fō top′ə thē), *n.* **1.** movement of an organism in response to the intensity of light, esp. away from the source of light. **2.** a condition or disease produced by the effect of light, esp. in excessive amounts. [PHOTO- + -PATHY] —**pho·to·path·ic** (fō′tə path′ik), *adj.*

pho·to·pe·ri·od (fō′tə pēr′ē əd), *n.* *Biol.* the interval in a 24-hour period during which a plant or animal is exposed to light. [PHOTO- + PERIOD] —**pho·to·pe·ri·od·ic** (fō′tə pēr′ē od′ik), **pho′to·pe′ri·od′i·cal,** *adj.* —**pho′to·pe′ri·od′i·cal·ly,** *adv.*

pho·to·pe·ri·od·ism (fō′tə pēr′ē ə diz′əm), *n.* *Biol.* the response, as affecting growth, reproduction, etc., of a plant or animal to the length of exposure to light in a 24-hour period. Also called **pho·to·pe·ri·o·dic·i·ty** (fō′tō pēr′ē ə dis′i tē). [PHOTOPERIOD + -ISM]

pho·toph·i·lous (fō tof′ə ləs), *adj.* thriving in strong light, as a plant. [PHOTO- + -PHILOUS] —**pho·toph′i·ly,** *n.*

pho·to·pho·bi·a (fō′tə fō′bē ə), *n.* *Pathol.* an abnormal dread or intolerance of light, as in iritis. [PHOTO- + -PHOBIA]

pho·to·phore (fō′tə fōr′, -fôr′), *n.* *Zool.* a luminous organ found in certain fishes and crustaceans. [PHOTO- + -PHORE]

pho·to·phos·pho·ryl·a·tion (fō′tə fos′fər ə lā′shən), *n.* *Biochem.* phosphorylation that utilizes light as a source of energy. [PHOTO- + PHOSPHORYLATION]

pho·to·pi·a (fō tō′pē ə), *n.* *Ophthalm.* vision in bright light (opposed to *scotopia*). Cf. **light adaptation.** [PHOT- + -OPIA] —**pho·top·ic** (fō top′ik, -tō′pik), *adj.*

pho·to·play (fō′tə plā′), *n.* a play presented, or written to be presented, as a motion picture; screenplay. [PHOTO- + PLAY] —**pho′to·play′er,** *n.*

pho·to·pos·i·tive (fō′tə poz′i tiv), *adj.* *Physics.* pertaining to a substance having a conductivity that increases upon absorption of electromagnetic radiation. [PHOTO- + POSITIVE]

pho·to·print (fō′tə print′), *n.* **1.** a photographic print. **2.** a print made by a photomechanical process. [PHOTO + PRINT] —**pho′to·print′er,** *n.* —**pho′to·print′ing,** *n.*

pho·to·pro·ton (fō′tə prō′ton), *n.* *Physics.* a proton emitted from a nucleus during photodisintegration. [PHOTO- + PROTON]

pho·to·re·cep·tion (fō′tō ri sep′shən), *n.* the physiological perception of light. [PHOTO- + RECEPTION] —**pho′to·re·cep′tive,** *adj.*

pho·to·re·cep·tor (fō′tō ri sep′tər), *n.* *Physiol., Biol.* a receptor stimulated by light. [PHOTO- + RECEPTOR]

pho·to·re·con·nais·sance (fō′tō ri kon′i səns), *n.* reconnaissance for the purpose of aerial photography. Also, **pho′to·re·con′nais·sance.** [PHOTO- + RECONNAISSANCE]

pho·to·re·cord·er (fō′tō ri kôr′dər), *n.* a device for making photographic records. [PHOTO- + RECORDER]

pho·to·re·cord·ing (fō′tō ri kôr′ding), *n.* the act of making photographic records, esp. of documents. [PHOTO- + RECORD + -ING[1]]

pho·to·sen·si·tive (fō′tə sen′si tiv), *adj.* sensitive to light or similar radiation. [PHOTO- + SENSITIVE] —**pho′to·sen′si·tiv′i·ty,** *n.*

pho·to·spec·tro·scope (fō′tə spek′trə skōp′), *n.* spectrograph (def. 2). [PHOTO- + SPECTROSCOPE] —**pho·to·spec·tro·scop·ic** (fō′tə spek′trə skop′ik), **pho′to·spec′tro·scop′i·cal,** *adj.* —**pho·to·spec·tros·co·py** (fō′tə spek tros′kə pē), *n.*

pho·to·sphere (fō′tə sfēr′), *n.* **1.** a sphere of light or radiance. **2.** *Astron.* the luminous visible surface of the sun, being a shallow layer of strongly ionized gases. [PHOTO- + -SPHERE] —**pho·to·spher·ic** (fō′tə sfer′ik), *adj.*

pho′to spread′, a picture spread. See under **spread** (def. 32).

Pho·to·stat (fō′tə stat′), *n.* **1.** *Trademark.* a camera for making facsimile copies of documents, drawings, etc., in the form of paper negatives on which the positions of lines, objects, etc., in the originals are maintained. **2.** (*often l.c.*) a copy made with this camera. —*v.t., v.i.* **3.** (*l.c.*) to copy with this camera. —**pho′to·stat′er, pho′to·stat′ter,** *n.* —**pho′to·stat′ic,** *adj.* —**pho′to·stat′i·cal·ly,** *adv.*

pho·to·syn·thate (fō′tə sin′thāt), *n.* *Biochem.* a compound formed by photosynthesis. [PHOTOSYNTH(ESIS) + -ATE[2]]

pho·to·syn·the·sis (fō′tə sin′thi sis), *n.* *Biol., Biochem.* (esp. in plants) the synthesis of complex organic materials, esp. carbohydrates, from carbon dioxide, water, and inorganic salts, using sunlight as the source of energy and with the aid of a catalyst, as chlorophyll. [PHOTO- + SYNTHESIS] —**pho·to·syn·thet·ic** (fō′tə·sin thet′ik), *adj.* —**pho′to·syn·thet′i·cal·ly,** *adv.*

pho·to·tax·is (fō′tə tak′sis), *n.* *Biol.* movement of an organism toward or away from a source of light. Also, **pho′to·tax′y.** [PHOTO- + -TAXIS] —**pho·to·tac·tic** (fō′tə tak′tik), *adj.* —**pho′to·tac′ti·cal·ly,** *adv.*

pho·to·tel·e·graph (fō′tə tel′ə graf′, -gräf′), *n.* a phototelegraphic reproduction. [PHOTO- + TELEGRAPH]

pho·to·te·leg·ra·phy (fō′tō tə leg′rə fē), *n.* the electric transmission of facsimiles of photographs and pictures; telephotography. [PHOTO- + TELEGRAPHY] —**pho·to·tel·e·graph·ic** (fō′tə tel′ə graf′ik), *adj.* —**pho′to·tel′e·graph′i·cal·ly,** *adv.*

pho·to·the·od·o·lite (fō′tō thē od′əlīt′), *n.* an optical tracking instrument for filming the flight of a rocket or guided missile. Also called **theodolite.** [PHOTO- + THEODOLITE]

pho·to·ther·a·peu·tics (fō′tə ther′ə pyōō′tiks), *n.* (*construed as sing.*) the branch of therapeutics which deals with the curative use of light rays. [PHOTO- + THERAPEUTICS] —**pho′to·ther′a·peu′tic,** *adj.*

pho·to·ther·a·py (fō′tə ther′ə pē), *n.* treatment of disease by means of light rays. [PHOTO- + THERAPY] —**pho·to·the·rap·ic** (fō′tō thə rap′ik), *adj.* —**pho′to·ther′a·pist,** *n.*

pho·to·ther·mic (fō′tə thûr′mik), *adj.* **1.** pertaining to the thermal effects of light. **2.** pertaining to or involving both light and heat. [PHOTO- + THERMIC]

pho·tot·o·nus (fō tot′ᵊnəs), *n.* *Biol.* **1.** the normal condition of sensitiveness to light in plants or plant organs. **2.** the irritability exhibited by protoplasm when exposed to light of a certain intensity. [PHOTO- + TONUS] —**pho·to·ton·ic** (fō′tə ton′ik), *adj.*

pho·to·pog·ra·phy (fō′tō tə pog′rə fē), *n.* topographical surveying employing photography. [PHOTO- + TOPOGRAPHY] —**pho·to·top·o·graph·ic** (fō′tō top′ə graf′ik), **pho′to·top′o·graph′i·cal,** *adj.*

pho·to·troph (fō′tə trof′), *n.* a microorganism, esp. an autotrophic bacterium, utilizing light as its source of energy. [PHOTO- + TROPH(IC)]

pho·to·trop·ic (fō′tə trop′ik), *adj.* *Bot.* **1.** taking a particular direction under the influence of light. **2.** growing toward or away from the light. [PHOTO- + -TROPIC] —**pho′to·trop′i·cal·ly,** *adv.*

pho·tot·ro·pism (fō to′trə piz′əm), *n.* *Bot.* phototropic tendency or growth. [PHOTO- + TROPISM]

pho·to·tube (fō′tə to͞ob′, -tyo͞ob′), *n.* *Electronics.* a diode in which light falling on the light-sensitive cathode causes electrons to be emitted, the electrons being collected by the plate. [PHOTO- + TUBE]

pho·to·type (fō′tə tīp′), *n.* *Print.* **1.** a plate with a relief printing surface produced by photography. **2.** any process for making such a plate. **3.** a print made from it. **4.** *Obs.* collotype. [PHOTO- + -TYPE] —**pho·to·typ·ic** (fō′tə tip′ik), *adj.* —**pho′to·typ′i·cal·ly,** *adv.*

pho·to·ty·pog·ra·phy (fō′tō tī pog′rə fē), *n.* *Obs.* the art or technique of making printing surfaces by light or photography, by any of a large number of processes. [PHOTO- + TYPOGRAPHY] —**pho·to·ty·po·graph·ic** (fō′tō tī′pə graf′ik), *adj.*

pho·to·typ·y (fō′tə tī′pē, fō tot′ə pē), *n.* *Obs.* the art or process of producing phototypes. [PHOTOTYPE + -Y[3]]

pho·to·vol·ta·ic (fō′tō vol tā′ik), *adj.* providing a source of electric current under the influence of light or similar radiation. [PHOTO- + VOLTAIC]

pho′tovolta′ic cell′, *Elect.* a cell in which an electromotive force is generated by a photovoltaic effect.

pho′tovolta′ic effect′, *Physics.* the phenomenon in which the incidence of electromagnetic radiation upon the junction of two dissimilar materials, as a metal and a semiconductor, induces the generation of an electromotive force.

pho·to·zin·cog·ra·phy (fō′tō ziŋ kog′rə fē), *n.* *Obs.* a type of photoengraving using a sensitized zinc plate. [PHOTO- + ZINCOGRAPHY]

Pho·tron·ic (fō tron′ik), *adj.* *Trademark.* pertaining to or utilizing a photovoltaic cell.

pho·tu·ri·a (fō to͝or′ē ə, -tyo͝or′-), *n.* *Med.* the passage of phosphorescent urine. [PHOT + -URIA]

phr., phrase.

phras·al (frā′zəl), *adj.* of, consisting of, or of the nature of a phrase or phrases: *phrasal construction.* [PHRASE + -AL[1]]

phrase (frāz), *n., v.,* **phrased, phras·ing.** —*n.* **1.** *Gram.* **a.** a sequence of two or more words arranged in a grammatical construction and acting as a unit in a sentence. **b.** (in English) a sequence of two or more words that does not contain a finite verb and its subject, as a preposition and a noun or pronoun, an adjective and noun, an adverb and verb, etc. **2.** *Rhet.* a word or group of spoken words that the mind focuses on momentarily as a meaningful unit and is preceded and followed by pauses. **3.** a way of speaking, mode of expression, or phraseology: *a book written in the phrase of the West.* **4.** a characteristic, current, or proverbial expression: *a hackneyed phrase.* **5.** a brief utterance or remark: *In a phrase, he's a dishonest man.* **6.** *Music.* a division of a composition, commonly a passage of four or eight measures, forming part of a period. **7.** *Dance.* a sequence of motions making up a choreographic pattern. —*v.t.* **8.** to express or word in a particular way: *to phrase an apology well.* **9.** to express in words: *to phrase one's thoughts.* **10.** *Music.* **a.** to mark off or bring out the phrases of (a piece), esp. in execution. **b.** to group (notes) into a phrase. [back formation from *phrases,* pl. of LL *phrasis* < Gk: speech, equiv. to *phrá(zein)* (to) speak + *-sis* -SIS]

phra·se·o·gram (frā′zē ə gram′), *n.* a written symbol or combination of symbols, as in shorthand, used to represent a phrase. [PHRASE + -O- + -GRAM[1]]

phra·se·o·graph (frā′zē ə graf′, -gräf′), *n.* a phrase for which there is a phraseogram. [PHRASE + -O- + -GRAPH]

phra·se·ol·o·gist (frā′zē ol′ə jist), *n.* **1.** one who treats of or is concerned with phraseology. **2.** one who affects a particular phraseology or is skilled in coining phrases. [PHRASEOLOG(Y) + -IST]

phra·se·ol·o·gy (frā′zē ol′ə jē), *n.* **1.** manner or style of verbal expression; characteristic language: *legal phraseology.* **2.** expressions; phrases: *obscure phraseology.* [< NL *phraseologia.* See PHRASE, -O-, -LOGY] —**phra·se·o·log·i·cal** (frā′zē ə loj′i kəl), **phra′se·o·log′ic,** *adj.* —**phra′se·o·log′i·cal·ly,** *adv.* —**Syn. 1.** See **diction.**

phras·ing (frā′ziŋ), *n.* **1.** the act, or a manner or method, of forming phrases; phraseology. **2.** *Music.* the grouping of the notes of a musical line into distinct phrases. [PHRASE + -ING[1]]

phra·try (frā′trē), *n., pl.* **-tries. 1.** a grouping of clans or other social units within a tribe. **2.** (in ancient Greece) a subdivision of a phyle. [< Gk *phratría*] —**phra′tric, phra′tral, phra′tri·ac′, phra′tri·al,** *adj.*

phre·at·ic (frē at′ik), *adj.* *Geol.* noting or pertaining to that layer of soil or rock through which water may enter wells or from which springs and seeps may emerge: *phreatic zone; phreatic water.* [< Gk *phreat-* (s. of *phréar*) artificial well + -IC]

phre·at·o·phyte (frē at′ə fīt′), *n.* a long-rooted plant that absorbs its water from the water table or the soil above it. [< Gk *phreat-* (see PHREATIC) + -O- + -PHYTE] —**phre·at·o·phyt·ic** (frē′at ə fit′ik), *adj.*

phren-, var. of **phreno-** before a vowel: *phrenic.*

phren., **1.** phrenological. **2.** phrenology.

phre·net·ic (fri net′ik), *adj.* Also, **phre·net′i·cal. 1.** frenetic. **2.** filled with extreme excitement; fanatic; frenzied. —*n.* **3.** a phrenetic individual. [< L *phrenēticus* < LGk *phrenētikós,* Gk *phrenītikós* frenzied (see PHRENITIS, -IC); r. ME *frenetike* < AF] —**phre·net′i·cal·ly,** *adv.* —**phre·net′ic·ness,** *n.*

-phrenia, an element used in pathological terminology to indicate mental disorder: *schizophrenia.* [< NL < Gk *phren-* (s. of *phrḗn*) mind + *-ia* -IA]

phren·ic (fren′ik), *adj.* **1.** *Anat.* of or pertaining to the diaphragm. **2.** *Physiol.* relating to the mind or mental activity. [< NL *phrenic(us).* See PHREN-, -IC]

phre·ni·tis (fri nī′tis), *n.* *Pathol.* **1.** inflammation of the brain; encephalitis. **2.** inflammation of the diaphragm. **3.** delirium; frenzy. [< LL *phrenītis* delirium, frenzy < Gk *phrenîtis.* See PHREN-, -ITIS] —**phre·nit·ic** (fri nit′ik), *adj.*

phreno-, a learned borrowing from Greek meaning "mind," "diaphragm," used in the formation of compound words: *phrenology.* Also, *esp. before a vowel,* **phren-.** [< Gk, comb. form repr. *phrḗn* mind, diaphragm]

phren·o·gas·tric (fren′ō gas′trik), *adj.* *Anat.* of, pertaining to, or involving the diaphragm and the stomach. [PHRENO- + GASTRIC]

phrenol., **1.** phrenological. **2.** phrenology.

phre·nol·o·gy (fri nol′ə jē, fre-), *n.* a psychological theory or analytical method based on the idea that certain of one's mental faculties and character traits are indicated by the configurations of one's skull. [PHRENO- + -LOGY] —**phren·o·log·ic** (fren′ə loj′ik), **phren′o·log′i·cal,** *adj.* —**phren′o·log′i·cal·ly,** *adv.* —**phre·nol′o·gist,** *n.*

phren·sy (fren′zē), *n., pl.* **-sies,** *v.t.,* **-sied, -sy·ing.** frenzy.

Phrix·us (frik′səs), *n.* *Class. Myth.* a son of Nephele and Athamas who escaped on the back of a ram with his sister Helle from a plot made against them by their stepmother, Ino, in the interests of her own children. The fleece of the ram, which he sacrificed, was the Golden Fleece.

phro·ne·sis (frō nē′sis), *n.* *Philos.* wisdom in determining ends and the means of attaining them. [< Gk: thinking, equiv. to *phronē-* (long s. of *phronein* to think) + *-sis* -SIS]

Phron·tis (fron′tis), *n.* *Class. Myth.* **1.** a son of Phrixus and Chalciope. **2.** the wife of Panthous of Troy.

Phryg·i·a (frij′ē ə), *n.* an ancient country in central and NW Asia Minor.

Phryg·i·an (frij′ē ən), *adj.* **1.** of or pertaining to Phrygia, its people, or their language. —*n.* **2.** a native or inhabitant of Phrygia. **3.** an Indo-European language that was the language of Phrygia. [< L *Phrygiān(us).* See PHRYGIA, -AN]

Phryg′ian cap′, a soft, conical cap represented in ancient Greek art as part of Phrygian or oriental dress and associated, since the late 18th and early 19th centuries, with the liberty cap.

Phryg′ian mode′, *Music.* an authentic church mode represented on the white keys of a keyboard instrument by an ascending scale from E to E.

PHS, Public Health Service. Also, **P.H.S.**

phthal·ein (thal′ēn, -ē in, fthal′-), *n.* *Chem.* any of a group of compounds formed by treating phthalic anhydride with phenols, from which certain important dyes are derived. [(NA)PHTHALE(NE) + -IN[2]]

phthal·ic (thal′ik, fthal′-), *adj.* *Chem.* of or derived from phthalic acid. [(NA)PHTHAL(ENE) + -IC]

phthal′ic ac′id, **1.** *Chem.* any of three isomeric acids having the formula $C_6H_4(COOH)_2$, esp. the ortho isomer (**ortho-phthalic acid**), a colorless, crystalline, slightly water-soluble solid used chiefly in the manufacture of dyes, medicine, and perfume. **2.** See **isophthalic acid. 3.** See **terephthalic acid.**

phthal′ic anhy′dride, *Chem.* a white, crystalline, slightly water-soluble solid, $C_6H_4(CO)_2O$, used chiefly in the manufacture of dyes, alkyd resins, and plasticizers.

phthal·in (thal′in, fthal′-), *n.* *Chem.* any of a group of compounds obtained by the reduction of the phthaleins. [(NA)PHTHAL(ENE) + -IN[2]]

phthal·o·cy·a·nine (thal′ō sī′ə nīn′, fthal′-), *n.* *Chem.* **1.** Also called **metal-free phthalocyanine.** a blue-green pigment, $C_{32}H_{18}N_8$, derived from phthalic anhydride. **2.** any of the group of blue or green pigments produced by the interaction of metal-free phthalocyanine and a metal, esp. copper: used chiefly in the manufacture of enamels, printing inks, and automotive finishes. [(NA)PHTHAL(ENE) + -O- + CYANINE]

phthal′ocy′anine blue′, a pigment used in painting, derived from copper phthalocyanine and characterized chiefly by its brilliant, dark-blue color and by permanence.

phthal′ocy′anine green′, a pigment used in painting, derived from chlorinated copper phthalocyanine and characterized chiefly by its intense green color and permanence.

Phthi·a (thī′ə), *n.* *Class. Myth.* **1.** the mother, by Apollo, of Dorus, Laodocus, and Polypoetes. **2.** (in the *Iliad*) the concubine of Amyntor who was seduced by Phoenix, Amyntor's son, at his mother's request.

phthi·o·col (thī′ə kōl′, -kol′), *n.* *Biochem.* a yellow pigment, the vitamin-K properties of which counteract hemorrhage. [PHTHI(SIS) + -O- + -c- connective + -OL[1]]

phthis·ic (tiz′ik), *Pathol.* —*n.* **1.** a wasting disease of the lungs; phthisis. **2.** asthma. **3.** one who suffers from phthisis. —*adj.* **4.** pertaining to phthisis; phthisical. [< L *phthisic(us)* < Gk *phthisikós* (see PHTHISIS, -IC); r. ME *tisike* < ML *(p)tisic(us)*]

phthis·i·cal (tiz′i kəl), *adj.* pertaining to, of the nature of, or affected by phthisis. Also, **phthis′ick·y.** [PHTHISIC + -AL[1]]

phthi·sis (thī′sis, fthī′-), *n.* *Pathol.* **1.** a wasting away. **2.** tuberculosis of the lungs; consumption. [< Gk: lung disease, lit., a wasting away, equiv. to *phthí(ein)* (to) decay + *-sis* -SIS]

phu·goid (fyo͞o′goid), *adj.* *Rocketry, Aeron.* of or pertaining to long-period oscillation in the longitudinal motion of an aircraft, rocket, or missile. [irreg. < Gk *phyg(ḗ)* flight + -OID]

Phu·ket (po͞o′ket′), *n.* an island near the W coast of Thailand. 64,637 (est. 1956); 294 sq. mi.

Phu·mi·phon A·dul·det (po͞o mi′pōn ä do͞ol′det). See **Rama IX.**

-phyceae, a learned borrowing from Greek meaning "seaweed," used in the names of algae: *rhodophyceae.* [< NL (pl.); see PHYCO-]

-phyceous, an element used to form adjectives from nouns with stems ending in **-phyceae:** *Rhodophyceous.* [-PHYCE(AE) + -OUS]

phyco-, a learned borrowing from Greek meaning "seaweed," "algae," used in the formation of compound words: *phycochrome.* [< Gk, comb. form repr. *phŷkos*]

phy·co·chrome (fī′kə krōm′), *n.* *Biochem.* a bluish-green pigment consisting of a mixture of chlorophyll and phycocyanin, found in blue-green algae. [PHYCO- + -CHROME]

phy·co·col·loid (fī′kə kol′oid), *n.* *Biochem.* any of the class of polysaccharides, derived from brown or red seaweed, that form colloidal dispersions with water. [PHYCO- + COLLOID]

phy·co·cy·an·in (fī′kō sī′ə nin), *n.* *Biochem.* a blue protein pigment, found in algae, that contributes to the process of photosynthesis. [PHYCO- + CYAN-[1] + -IN[2]]

phy·col·o·gy (fī kol′ə jē), *n.* the branch of botany dealing with algae. [PHYCO- + -LOGY] —**phy·co·log·i·cal** (fī′kə loj′i kəl), *adj.* —**phy·col′o·gist,** *n.*

Phy·co·my·ces (fī′kō mī′sēz), *n.* a genus of fungi producing a metallic mycelium. [< Gk *phŷko(s)* PHYCO- + *mýkēs* fungus]

phy·co·my·cete (fī′kō mī′sēt, -mī sēt′), *n.* a fungus of the class *Phycomycetes;* a phycomycetous fungus. [back formation from PHYCOMYCETES]

Phy·co·my·cet·es (fī′kō mī sē′tēz), *n.* the class comprising fungi of the genera *Rhizopus, Mucor,* etc., and the downy mildews. [< NL; see PHYCO-, -MYCETES]

phy·co·my·ce·tous (fī′kō mī sē′təs), *adj.* *Bot.* belonging or pertaining to the *Phycomycetes,* the lowest of the three primary subdivisions of the fungi, whose members more closely resemble algae than do the higher fungi. [< NL *Phycomycē-t(ēs)* + -OUS]

Phyfe (fīf), *n.* **Dun·can** (duŋ′kən), 1768–1854, U.S. cabinetmaker, born in Scotland.

phyl-, var. of **phylo-** before a vowel: *phylic.*

-phyl, var. of **phyllo-** as final element of compound words: *chlorophyl.* Also, **-phyll.**

phy·la (fī′lə), *n.* pl. of **phylum.**

phy·lac·ter·y (fə lak′tə rē), *n., pl.* **-ter·ies. 1.** *Judaism.* either of two small, black, leather cubes having leather straps and containing a piece of parchment inscribed with verses 4–9, 11, and 13–21 of Deut. 6 and 1–16 of Ex. 13, one cube worn strapped to the left arm and the other to the forehead during the morning religious service on days other than the Sabbath and holy days by Orthodox and Conservative Jewish males of 13 years of age and older. **2.** (in the early Christian church) a receptacle containing a holy relic. **3.** a reminder. **4.** an amulet, charm, or safeguard. [< LL *phylactēri(um)* < Gk *phylaktḗrion* outpost, safeguard, amulet; r. ME *philaterie* < ML *philatēri(um)*] —**phyl·ac·ter·ic** (fil′ak ter′ik), **phyl′ac·ter′i·cal,** *adj.* —**phy·lac′ter·ied,** *adj.*

Phylactery

phy·lac·tic (fi lak′tik), *adj.* defending or protecting, esp. from disease. [< Gk *phylaktik(ós)* preservative, equiv. to *phylaktós* guarding (verbid of *phylássein* to guard) + *-ikos* -IC. See PROPHYLACTIC]

Phy·la·ko·pi (fē lä kō pē′), *n.* an archaeological site on the Greek island of Melos, in the Cyclades group: excavations have revealed the remains of three successive ancient cities erected on a primitive Cycladic settlement.

phy·le (fī′lē), *n., pl.* **-lae** (-lē). (in ancient Greece) a tribe or clan, based on supposed kinship. [< Gk] —**phy′lic,** *adj.*

phy·let·ic (fī let′ik), *adj.* *Biol.* pertaining to race or species; phylogenic; racial. [< Gk *phyletik(ós).* See PHYLE, -TIC] —**phy·let′i·cal·ly,** *adv.*

Phy·le·us (fī′lē əs, fī′lo͞os), *n.* **1.** *Class. Myth.* a son of Augeas who was banished when he reminded his father of an unpaid debt. **2.** a king of Ephyra and the father of Astyocheia.

phyll-, var. of **phyllo-** before a vowel: *phyllite.*

-phyll, var. of **-phyl.**

phyl·la·ry (fil′ə rē), *n., pl.* **-ries.** *Bot.* one of the bracts forming the involucre or the head or inflorescence of a composite plant. [< NL *phyllari(um)* < Gk *phyllárion,* dim. of *phýllon* leaf]

Phyl·lis (fil′is), *n.* *Class. Myth.* **1.** a Thracian princess who took her own life, cursing her husband Demophon for not having returned to her as he had promised. **2.** a Thracian princess in love with Acamas. When a storm delayed his return from Troy, she died from despair and was changed into an almond tree. **3.** Also, **Phyl′iss, Phillis.** a girl's given name.

phyl·lite (fil′īt), *n.* a slaty rock with lustrous cleavage planes due to minute scales of mica. [PHYLL- + -ITE[1]] —**phyl·lit·ic** (fi lit′ik), *adj.*

phyllo-, a learned borrowing from Greek meaning "leaf," used in the formation of compound words: *phyllopod.* Also, **phyll-, -phyl, -phyll.** [< Gk, comb. form of *phýllon*]

phyl·lo·clade (fil′ə klād′), *n.* *Bot.* **1.** a flattened stem or branch having the function of a leaf. **2.** a cladophyll. [< NL *phylloclad(ium).* See PHYLLO-, CLAD-] —**phyl′lo·cla′di·oid′,** *adj.*

phyl·lo·cla·di·um (fil′ə klā′dē əm), *n., pl.* **-di·a** (-dē ə). *Bot.* phylloclade.

phyl·loc·la·dous (fi lok′lə dəs), *adj.* *Bot.* having phylloclades. [PHYLLOCLADE + -OUS]

phyl·lode (fil′ōd), *n.* *Bot.* an expanded petiole resembling and having the function of a leaf. [< Gk *phyllṓdēs* leaflike. See PHYLL-, -ODE[1]] —**phyl′lo′di·al,** *adj.*

P, Phyllode

phyl·lo·dy (fil′ə dē), *n.* *Bot.* the abnormal transformation of a floral structure into a foliage leaf. [PHYLLODE + -Y[3]]

phyl·lo·ge·net·ic (fil′ō jə net′ik), *adj.* *Bot.* of or pertaining to the development of leaves. [PHYLLO- + GENETIC]

phyl·loid (fil/oid), *adj.* leaflike. [< NL *phylloid(es)*. See PHYLL-, -OID]

phyl·lo·ma·ni·a (fil/ə mā/nē ə, -mān/yə), *n. Bot.* the production of leaves in abnormal numbers or places. [PHYLLO- + -MANIA] —**phyl/lo·ma/ni·ac/**, *adj.*

phyl·lome (fil/ōm), *n. Bot.* **1.** a leaf of a plant. **2.** a structure corresponding to it. [< NL *phyllōm(a)* < Gk: foliage. See PHYLL-, -OMA] —**phyl·lom·ic** (fi lom/ik, -lō/mik), *adj.*

phyl·lo·phore (fil/ə fōr/, -fôr/), *n. Bot.* the terminal bud of a stem, esp. of the stem of a palm. [PHYLLO- + -PHORE]

phyl·lo·pod (fil/ə pod/), *n.* **1.** any crustacean of the order *Phyllopoda*, having leaflike swimming appendages. —*adj.* **2.** belonging or pertaining to the *Phyllopoda*. Also, **phyl·lop·o·dan** (fi lop/ə dən). [< NL *Phyllopod(a)*. See PHYLLO-, -POD]

phyl·lo·qui·none (fil/ō kwə nōn/, -kwin/ōn), *n. Biochem.* See **vitamin K_1.** [PHYLLO- + QUINONE]

phyl·lo·sil·i·cate (fil/ō sil/ə kit, -kāt/), *n.* any silicate mineral having the tetrahedral silicate groups linked in sheets, each group containing four oxygen atoms, three of which are shared with other groups so that the ratio of silicon atoms to oxygen atoms is two to five. [PHYLLO- + SILICATE]

phyl·lo·tax·is (fil/ə tak/sis), *n., pl.* **-tax·es** (-tak/sēs). *Bot.* phyllotaxy. [PHYLO- + -TAXIS]

phyl·lo·tax·y (fil/ə tak/sē), *n., pl.* **-tax·ies.** *Bot.* **1.** the arrangement of leaves on a stem or axis. **2.** the study of such arrangement. [PHYLLOTAX(IS) + -Y[3]] —**phyl·lo·tac·tic** (fil/ə tak/tik), —**phyl/lo·tac/ti·cal, phyl/lo·tax/ic**, *adj.*

-phyllous, an element meaning "having leaves," "leaved," used in the formation of adjectives: *diphyllous; monophyllous.* [< Gk *-phyllos* pertaining to a leaf]

phyl·lox·e·ra (fil/ək sēr/ə, fi lok/sər ə), *n., pl.* **phyl·lox·e·rae** (fil/ək sēr/ē, fi lok/sə rē/), **phyl·lox·e·ras.** any of several plant lice of the genus *Phylloxera*, esp. *P. vitifoliae* **(grape phylloxera)**, which attacks the leaves and roots of grapevines in the U.S. and Europe. [< NL; see PHYLLO-, XER(O)-, -A]

Phy·lo (fī/lō), *n. Class. Myth.* a handmaid of Helen at the court of Menelaus.

phylo-, a learned borrowing from Greek meaning "race," "tribe," "kind": *phylogeny.* Also, *esp. before a vowel,* **phyl-.** [< Gk, comb. form of *phŷlon*]

phy·log·e·ny (fī loj/ə nē), *n.* the development or evolution of a kind or type of animal or plant; racial history. Also, **phy·lo·gen·e·sis** (fī/lə jen/i sis). Cf. **ontogeny.** [PHYLO- + -GENY] —**phy·lo·ge·net·ic** (fī/lə jə net/ik), **phy/lo·ge·net/i·cal, phy/lo·gen/ic,** *adj.* —**phy/lo·ge·net/i·cal·ly,** *adv.* —**phy·log/e·nist,** *n.*

Phy·lom·a·che (fi lom/ə kē), *n. Class. Myth.* the mother, by Pelias, of Acastus and Alcestis.

phy·lon (fī/lon), *n., pl.* **-la** (-lə). a group that has genetic relationship, as a race. [< NL < Gk *phŷlon* race, tribe, class, akin to *phŷein* to bring forth, produce]

Phy·lon·o·me (fi lon/ə mē), *n. Class. Myth.* the second wife of Cycnus, buried alive for falsely accusing her stepson, Tenes, of trying to seduce her. Also, **Philonome.**

phy·lum (fī/ləm), *n., pl.* **-la** (-lə). **1.** *Biol.* the major primary subdivision of the animal kingdom, consisting of one or more related classes. Cf. **division** (def. 12). **2.** *Ling.* a category consisting of language stocks which, because of cognates in vocabulary, are considered likely to be related by common origin. Cf. **stock** (def. 14). [< NL < Gk *phŷlon* tribe, stock]

phy·ma (fī/mə), *n., pl.* **-mas, -ma·ta** (-mə tə). *Pathol.* a nodule, swelling, or small, rounded tumor of the skin. [< L < Gk; a swelling, tumor, equiv. to *phŷ(esthai)* (to) grow + *-ma* n. suffix] —**phy·mat·ic** (fī mat/ik), *adj.*

-phyre, a combining form of **porphyry:** *granophyre.* [< Gk *-phyr*]

phys., 1. physical. **2.** physician. **3.** physics. **4.** physiological. **5.** physiology.

phys. chem., physical chemistry.

phys. ed. (fiz/ ed/), physical education.

phys. geog., physical geography.

physi-, var. of **physio-.**

phys·i·at·rics (fiz/ē a/triks), *n. (construed as sing.)* **1.** See **physical medicine. 2.** physiotherapy. [PHYS(I)- + -IATRICS] —**phys/i·at/ric, phys/i·at/ri·cal,** *adj.*

phys·i·at·rist (fiz/ē a/trist), *n.* a physician specializing in physical medicine. [PHYSIATR(ICS) + -IST]

phys·ic (fiz/ik), *n., v.,* **-icked, -ick·ing.** —*n.* **1.** a medicine that purges; a cathartic. **2.** any medicine; a drug or medicament. **3.** *Archaic.* the medical art or profession. **4.** *Obs.* See **natural science.** —*v.t.* **5.** to treat with a physic or medicine. **6.** to treat with, or act upon as, a cathartic; purge. **7.** to work upon as a medicine does; relieve or cure. [ME *fisyke* < L *physica* natural science (ML: medical science) < Gk *physikḗ* science of nature, n. use of fem. adj.: pertaining to nature] —**Syn. 1.** laxative.

phys·i·cal (fiz/i kəl), *adj.* **1.** of or pertaining to the body: *physical exercise.* **2.** of or pertaining to that which is material: *the physical universe; the physical sciences.* **3.** noting or pertaining to the properties of matter and energy other than those peculiar to living matter; pertaining to physical science. —*n.* **4.** See **physical examination.** [ME < ML *physicāl(is)* concerning medicine. See PHYSIC, -AL[1]] —**phys/i·cal·ly,** *adv.* —**phys/i·cal·ness,** *n.*

—**Syn. 1.** somatic; carnal; fleshly. PHYSICAL, BODILY, CORPOREAL, CORPORAL agree in pertaining to the body. PHYSICAL indicates connected with, pertaining to, the animal or human body as a material organism: *physical strength, exercise.* BODILY means belonging to, concerned with, the human body as distinct from the mind or spirit: *bodily pain or suffering.* CORPOREAL, a more poetic and philosophical word than BODILY, refers esp. to the mortal substance of which the human body is composed as opposed to spirit: *this corporeal habitation.* CORPORAL is now usually reserved for reference to whippings and other punishments inflicted on the human body. **2.** tangible; palpable. —**Ant. 1.** spiritual.

phys/ical anthropol/ogy, the branch of anthropology dealing with the evolutionary changes in man's bodily structure and the classification of modern races, using mensurational and descriptive techniques. Cf. **cultural anthropology.**

phys/ical chem/istry, that branch of chemistry dealing with the relations between the physical properties of substances and their chemical composition and transformations.

phys/ical dou/ble star/. See under **double star.**

phys/ical educa/tion, systematic instruction in sports, exercises, and hygiene given as part of a school or college program.

phys/ical examina/tion, an examination, usually by a physician, of a person's body in order to determine his state of health or physical fitness, as for military service, participation in a sport, etc.

phys/ical geog/raphy, the part of geography concerned with natural features and phenomena of the earth's surface, as land forms, drainage features, climates, ocean currents, soils, vegetation, and animal life.

phys·i·cal·ism (fiz/i kə liz/əm), *n. Logical Positivism.* the doctrine that every meaningful statement, other than the necessary statements of logic and mathematics, must refer directly or indirectly to observable properties of spatiotemporal things or events. [< G *Physikalism(us).* See PHYSICAL, -ISM] —**phys/i·cal·ist,** *n., adj.*

phys·i·cal·is·tic (fiz/i kə lis/tik), *adj. Logical Positivism.* **1.** of or pertaining to physicalism. **2.** (of a statement) capable of being interpreted quantitatively in terms of space and time. [PHYSICALIST + -IC]

phys·i·cal·i·ty (fiz/i kal/i tē), *n., pl.* **-ties. 1.** the physical attributes of a person, esp. when overdeveloped or overemphasized: *to be attracted by blatant physicality.* **2.** preoccupation with one's body, physical needs, or appetites. [PHYSICAL + -ITY]

phys/ical jerks/, *Brit.* physical conditioning exercises, as push-ups, knee bends, etc. Also called **jerks.**

phys/ical med/icine, the branch of medicine dealing with the diagnosis and treatment of disease and injury by means of physical agents, as manipulation, massage, exercise, heat, water, etc.

phys/ical meteorol/ogy, the branch of meteorology dealing with the study of optical, electrical, acoustical, and thermodynamic phenomena in the atmosphere, including the physics of clouds and precipitation. Cf. **dynamic meteorology.**

phys/ical op/tics, the branch of optics dealing with light as a wave motion, with energy propagated normal to the advancing wave fronts.

phys/ical pen/dulum, *Physics.* any apparatus consisting of a body of possibly irregular shape allowed to rotate freely about a horizontal axis on which it is pivoted (distinguished from *simple pendulum*). Also called **compound pendulum.**

phys/ical sci/ence, the study of natural laws and processes other than those peculiar to living matter, as in physics, chemistry, astronomy, etc.

phys/ical ther/apy, physiotherapy. —**phys/ical ther/apist.**

phy·si·cian (fi zish/ən), *n.* **1.** a person who is legally qualified to practice medicine; doctor of medicine. **2.** one engaged in general medical practice, as distinguished from one specializing in surgery. **3.** one who is skilled in the art of healing. [PHYSIC + -IAN (see -ICIAN); r. ME *fisicien* < OF]

phy·si·cian·ly (fi zish/ən lē), *adj.* appropriate for or characteristic of a physician: *a physicianly manner.* [PHYSICIAN + -LY]

phy·si·cian·ship (fi zish/ən ship/), *n.* the position, function, or office of a physician. [PHYSICIAN + -SHIP]

phys·i·cist (fiz/i sist), *n.* a scientist who specializes in physics. [PHYSIC(S) + -IST]

phys/ic nut/, **1.** an ornamental tree, *Jatropha Curcas*, of tropical America, having ivylike leaves, small, yellow or greenish-yellow flowers, and olive-shaped fruit yielding a purgative, poisonous oil. **2.** the fruit itself. Also called **Barbados nut, purging nut.**

physico-, a combining form of **physical.**

phys·i·co·chem·i·cal (fiz/ə kō kem/i kəl), *adj. Chem.* **1.** physical and chemical: *the physicochemical properties of an isomer.* **2.** pertaining to physical chemistry. [PHYSICO- + CHEMICAL] —**phys/i·co·chem/i·cal·ly,** *adv.*

phys·ics (fiz/iks), *n. (construed as sing.)* the science that deals with matter and energy in terms of motion and force. [PHYS(I)- + -ICS]

physio-, a word element representing **physical** and **physics:** *physiotherapy; physiognomy.* [< Gk *physio-* comb. form of *phýsi(s)*; see PHYSIC, -O-]

phys·i·o·crat (fiz/ē ə krat/), *n.* one of a school of political economists who followed Quesnay in holding that an inherent natural order properly governed society, regarding land as the basis of wealth and taxation, and advocating a laissez-faire economy. [< F *physiocrate.* See PHYSIO-, -CRAT] —**phys/i·o·crat/ic,** *adj.*

phys·i·og·no·my (fiz/ē og/nə mē, -on/ə mē), *n., pl.* **-mies. 1.** the face or countenance, esp. when considered as an index to the character: *a fierce physiognomy.* **2.** Also called **anthroposcopy.** the art of determining character or personal characteristics from the form or features of the body, esp. of the face. **3.** the outward appearance of anything, taken as offering some insight into its character: *the physiognomy of a nation.* [< LL **physiognōmia* < LGk, syncopated var. of Gk *physiognōmonía* art of judging a person by his features (see PHYSIO-, GNOMON, -Y[3]); r. ME *phisonomie*, etc. < ML *phisonomia*] —**phys·i·og·nom·ic** (fiz/ē og nom/ik, -ē ə nom/-), **phys/i·og·nom/i·cal, phys·i·og·no·mon·ic** (fiz/ē og/nə mon/ik, -on/ə-), **phys/i·og/no·mon/i·cal,** *adj.* —**phys/i·og·nom/i·cal·ly, phys/i·og/no·mon/i·cal·ly,** *adv.* —**phys/i·og/no·mist,** *n.*

phys·i·og·ra·phy (fiz/ē og/rə fē), *n.* **1.** the science of physical geography. **2.** *U.S.* geomorphology. **3.** the systematic description of nature in general. [PHYSIO- + -GRAPHY] —**phys/i·og/ra·pher,** *n.* —**phys·i·o·graph·ic** (fiz/ē ə graf/ik), **phys/i·o·graph/i·cal,** *adj.*

physiol., 1. physiological. **2.** physiologist. **3.** physiology.

phys·i·o·log·i·cal (fiz/ē ə loj/i kəl), *adj.* **1.** of or pertaining to physiology. **2.** consistent with the normal functioning of an organism. Also, **phys/i·o·log/ic.** [PHYSIOLOG(Y) + -ICAL] —**phys/i·o·log/i·cal·ly,** *adv.*

physiolog/ical at/mosphere, ecosphere.

physiolog/ical phonet/ics, 1. (not in technical use) speech production. **2.** the branch of phonetics that deals with the motive processes, anatomical measurements, spirometric properties, muscle and membrane tone, and any or all kinetic and kinematic aspects of the production of speech and analogous involvements and hydrodynamic and related aspects of the reception of speech.

physiolog/ical salt/ solu/tion, *Pharm.* See **isotonic sodium chloride solution.**

physiolog/ical so/dium chlo/ride solu/tion, *Pharm.* See **isotonic sodium chloride solution.**

phys·i·ol·o·gist (fiz/ē ol/ə jist), *n.* a specialist in physiology. [PHYSIOLOG(Y) + -IST]

phys·i·ol·o·gy (fiz/ē ol/ə jē), *n.* **1.** the science dealing with the functions of living organisms or their parts. **2.** the organic processes or functions in an organism or in any of its parts. [< L *physiologia* < Gk. See PHYSIO-, -LOGY]

phys·i·om·e·try (fiz/ē om/i trē), *n.* measurement of the physiological functions of the body. [PHYSIO- + -METRY]

phys·i·o·path·ol·o·gy (fiz/ē ō pə thol/ə jē), *n.* the science dealing with the disturbances of bodily function resulting from disease. [PHYSIO- + PATHOLOGY] —**phys·i·o·path·o·log·i·cal** (fiz/ē ō path/ə loj/i kəl), **phys/i·o·path/o·log/ic,** *adj.*

phys·i·o·ther·a·py (fiz/ē ō ther/ə pē), *n.* the treatment of disease or bodily weaknesses or defects by physical remedies, as massage, gymnastics, etc., rather than by drugs. [PHYSIO- + THERAPY] —**phys/i·o·ther/a·pist,** *n.*

phy·sique (fi zēk/), *n.* physical or bodily structure, organization, or development. [< F < L *physic(us).* See PHYSIC]

phy·sis (fī/sis), *n., pl.* **-ses** (-sēz). **1.** the principle of growth or change in nature. **2.** nature as the source of growth or change. **3.** that which grows, becomes, or develops. [< Gk *phýsis* origin, natural form of a thing]

physo-, a learned borrowing from Greek meaning "bladder," used in the formation of compound words: *physogastric.* [comb. form repr. Gk *phŷsa* bladder, bellows]

phy·so·clis·tous (fī/sə klis/təs), *adj. Ichthyol.* having the air bladder closed off from the mouth. Cf. **physostomous.** [< NL *Phȳsoclist(ī)* genus name (*phȳso-* PHYSO- + *kleistoí*, pl. of *kleistós*, verbid of *kleíein* to shut) + -OUS]

phy·so·gas·tric (fī/sə gas/trik), *adj.* pertaining to the swollen, membranous abdomen of certain insects, esp. termite and ant queens. [PHYSO- + GASTRIC] —**phy/so·gas/trism, phy/so·gas/try,** *n.*

phy·so·stig·mine (fī/sō stig/mēn, -min), *n. Pharm.* a colorless to pinkish, crystalline, slightly water-soluble alkaloid, $C_{15}H_{21}O_2N_3$, constituting the active principle of the Calabar bean: used in medicine chiefly in the form of its salicylate or sulfate as a miotic in glaucoma. Also called **eserine.** [< NL *Phȳsostigm(a)* genus name (see PHYSO-, STIGMA) + -INE[2]]

phy·sos·to·mous (fī sos/tə məs), *adj. Ichthyol.* having the mouth and air bladder connected by an air duct. Cf. **physoclistous.** [< NL *phȳsostomus* pertaining to the *Phȳsostomī* (genus name). See PHYSO-, -STOMOUS]

Phyt·a·lus (fit/ə ləs), *n. Class. Myth.* an Eleusinian who was given a fig tree by Demeter in return for his hospitality.

-phyte, var. of **phyto-** as final element of compound words: *lithophyte.*

Phyt·e·us (fit/ē əs), *n. Class. Myth.* an epithet of Apollo. [< L < Gk *Phyteos* (slayer) of the Python]

phy/tic ac/id (fī/tik, fit/ik), *Chem.* a white to pale-yellow, water-soluble liquid, $C_6H_6[OPO(OH)_2]_6$, found in cereal grains: used chiefly to chelate heavy metals during the manufacture of animal fats and vegetable oils and as a water-softening agent. Also called **inositol-hexaphosphoric acid.** [PHYT(O)- + -IC]

Phy·tin (fī/tin), *n. Trademark.* a white powder, $Ca_5Mg(C_6H_{12}O_{24}P_6 \cdot 3H_2O)_2$, that is a magnesium-calcium salt of phytic acid and that occurs in seeds, tubers, and rhizomes as a reserve material: used in the synthesis of inositol and as a nutrient, tonic, and calcium supplement.

phyto-, a learned borrowing from Greek meaning "plant," used in the formation of compound words: *phytogenesis.* Also, **-phyte.** [< Gk *phŷt(on)* a plant + -O-]

phy·to·bi·ol·o·gy (fī/tō bī ol/ə jē), *n.* the branch of biology dealing with plants. [PHYTO- + BIOLOGY]

phy·to·cide (fī/tə sīd/), *n.* a substance or preparation for killing plants. [PHYTO- + -CIDE] —**phy/to·cid/al,** *adj.*

phy·to·cli·ma·tol·o·gy (fī/tō klī/mə tol/ə jē), *n.* See under **microclimatology.** [PHYTO- + CLIMATOLOGY] —**phy·to·cli·ma·to·log·ic** (fī/tō klī/mə tᵊloj/ik), **phy/to·cli/ma·to·log/i·cal,** *adj.*

phy·to·coe·no·sis (fī/tō sē nō/sis), *n., pl.* **-ses** (-sēz). the plants of a given area considered as a whole. [< NL; see PHYTO-, COENO-, -SIS]

phy·to·gen·e·sis (fī/tə jen/i sis), *n.* the origin and development of plants. Also, **phy·tog·e·ny** (fī toj/ə nē). [PHYTO- + GENESIS] —**phy·to·ge·net·ic** (fī/tō jə net/ik), **phy/to·ge·net/i·cal,** *adj.* —**phy/to·ge·net/i·cal·ly,** *adv.*

phy·to·gen·ic (fī/tə jen/ik), *adj.* of plant origin. [PHYTO- + -GENIC]

phy·to·ge·og·ra·phy (fī/tō jē og/rə fē), *n.* the science dealing with the geographical relationships of plants. [PHYTO- + GEOGRAPHY] —**phy/to·ge·og/ra·pher,** *n.* —**phy·to·ge·o·graph·i·cal** (fī/tō jē/ə graf/i kəl), **phy/to·ge/o·graph/ic,** *adj.* —**phy/to·ge/o·graph/i·cal·ly,** *adv.*

phy·tog·ra·phy (fī tog/rə fē), *n.* the branch of botany dealing with the description of plants. [< NL *phytographia.* See PHYTO-, -GRAPHY] —**phy·tog/ra·pher, phy·tog/ra·phist,** *n.* —**phy·to·graph·ic** (fī/tə graf/ik), **phy/to·graph/i·cal,** *adj.*

phy·to·hor·mone (fī/tə hôr/mōn), *n.* a plant hormone. [PHYTO- + HORMONE]

phy·tol·o·gy (fī tol/ə jē), *n. Obs.* botany. [< NL *phytologia.* See PHYTO-, -LOGY] —**phy·to·log·ic** (fīt/ᵊloj/ik), **phy/to·log/i·cal,** *adj.* —**phy/to·log/i·cal·ly,** *adv.*

phy·to·na·di·one (fī/tō nə dī/ōn), *n. Biochem.* See **vitamin K_1.** [PHYT(IC ACID) + -O- + NA(PHTHOQUINONE) + DIONE]

phy·to·pa·thol·o·gy (fī′tō pə thol′ə jē), *n.* See **plant pathology.** [PHYTO- + PATHOLOGY] —**phy·to·path·o·log·i·cal** (fī′tō path′ə loj′i kəl), **phy′to·path′o·log′ic,** *adj.* —**phy′to·pa·thol′o·gist,** *n.*

phy·toph·a·gous (fī tof′ə gəs), *adj.* herbivorous. [PHYTO- + -PHAGOUS]

phy·to·plank·ton (fī′tə plangk′tən), *n.* the plant organisms in plankton. Cf. **zooplankton.** [PHYTO- + PLANKTON]

phy·to·plasm (fī′tə plaz′əm), *n.* protoplasm of a plant or plants. [PHYTO- + -PLASM]

phy·to·so·ci·ol·o·gy (fī′tō sō′sē ol′ə jē, -shē-), *n.* the branch of ecology dealing with the origin, composition, structure, and classification of plant communities. [PHYTO- + SOCIOLOGY] —**phy·to·so·ci·o·log·ic** (fī′tə-sō′sē ə loj′ik, -sō′shē-), **phy′to·so′ci·o·log′i·cal,** *adj.* —**phy′to·so′ci·o·log′i·cal·ly,** *adv.* —**phy′to·so′ci·ol′o·gist,** *n.*

phy·to·suc·civ·o·rous (fī′tō sək siv′ər əs), *adj.* feeding on sap, as certain sucking insects. [*phytosucci*-sap (PHYTO- + *succi*-, comb. form of L *succus* juice) + -VOROUS]

phy·to·tox·ic (fī′tə tok′sik), *adj.* **1.** of or pertaining to phytotoxin. **2.** inhibitory to the growth of or poisonous to plants. [PHYTO- + TOXIC] —**phy·to·tox·ic·i·ty** (fī′-tō tok sis′i tē), *n.*

phy·to·tox·in (fī′tə tok′sin), *n.* any toxin produced by a plant and having an effect similar to any of certain toxins produced by microorganisms. [PHYTO- + TOXIN]

Phyx·i·us (fik′sē əs), *n.* *Class. Myth.* an epithet of Zeus, meaning "god of escape."

pi[1] (pī), *n., pl.* **pis. 1.** the 16th letter of the Greek alphabet (Π, π). **2.** the consonant sound represented by this letter. **3.** *Math.* **a.** the letter π, used as the symbol for the ratio of the circumference of a circle to its diameter. **b.** the ratio itself; 3.141592+. [< Gk; used in mathematics to represent Gk *periphérion* periphery]

pi[2] (pī), *n., v.,* **pied, pi·ing.** *U.S.* —*n.* **1.** printing types mixed together indiscriminately. —*v.t.* **2.** to reduce (printing types) to a state of confusion. Also, **pie.** [?]

Pi., piaster. Also, **pi.**

P.I., Philippine Islands.

Pi·a (pē′ə), *n.* a girl's given name.

Pia·cen·za (pyä chen′tsä), *n.* a city in N Italy, on the Po River. 87,930 (1961). Ancient, **Placentia.**

pi·ac·u·lar (pī ak′yə lər), *adj.* **1.** expiatory; atoning; reparatory. **2.** requiring expiation; sinful; wicked. [< L *piāculār(is)* atoning, equiv. to *piācul(um)* a means of atoning (*piā(re)* (to) appease, deriv. of *pius* PIOUS, + *-culum* -CULE) + *-āris* -AR[1]] —**pi·ac′u·lar·ly,** *adv.* —**pi·ac′u·lar·ness,** *n.*

Pi·af (pē äf′, pē′äf), *n.* **Edith** (*Edith Giovanna Gassion*), 1914–63, French singer.

piaffe (pyaf), *n., v.,* **piaffed, piaff·ing.** *Dressage.* —*n.* **1.** a cadenced trot executed on one spot, with the hocks well engaged. —*v.i.* **2.** (of a horse) to execute such a movement. **3.** (of a rider) to cause a horse to piaffe. —*v.t.* **4.** to cause (a horse) to piaffe. [< F *piaff(er)*]

pi·al (pī′əl), *adj.* of or pertaining to the pia mater. [PI(A) (MATER) + -AL[1]]

pia·la (pyä′lə, pē ä′-), *v.i., v.t.* *Australian Obs.* pyalla.

pi·a ma·ter (pī′ə mā′tər), *Anat.* the delicate, fibrous, and highly vascular membrane forming the innermost of the three coverings of the brain and spinal cord. Cf. **arachnoid** (def. 6), **dura mater.** [ME < ML: lit., pious mother, imperfect trans. of Ar *umm raqīqah* tender mother]

pi·an (pē an′, -än′, pyän), *n.* *Pathol.* yaws. [< F < Tupi] —**pi·an′ic,** *adj.*

pi·a·nette (pē′ə net′), *n.* a small upright piano. [PIAN(O)[1] + -ETTE]

pi·a·nism (pē′ə niz′əm, pē an′iz-, pyan′-), *n.* **1.** the artistry and technique of a pianist. **2.** performance by a pianist: *an evening of first-rate pianism.* [PIAN(O)[1] + -ISM]

pi·a·nis·si·mo (pē′ə nis′ə mō′; *It.* pyä nēs′sē mô′), *adj., adv., n., pl.* **-mos.** *Music.* —*adj.* **1.** very soft. —*adv.* **2.** very softly. —*n.* **3.** a passage or movement played in this way. [< It, superl. of *piano* PIANO[2]]

Grand piano

pi·an·ist (pē an′ist, pyan′-, pē′ə nist), *n.* a person who plays the piano expertly, esp. one who performs professionally in public. [< F *pianiste* < It *pianista.* See PIANO[1], -IST]

pi·an·o[1] (pē an′ō, pyan′ō), *n., pl.* **-an·os.** a musical instrument in which hammers, operated from a keyboard, strike upon metal strings. Cf. **baby grand piano, concert grand piano, grand piano, spinet, square piano, upright piano.** [short for PIANOFORTE]

pi·a·no[2] (pē ä′nō; *It.* pyä′nô), *Music.* —*adj.* **1.** soft; subdued. —*adv.* **2.** softly. *Abbr.:* p, p. [< It: soft, low (of sounds), plain, flat < L *plānus* PLAIN[1]]

pian′o duet′, a musical composition for two pianists playing two pianos or playing together at one piano.

pi·an·o·for·te (pē an′ə fōr′tē, -tā, -fōr′-), *n.* piano. [< It, equiv. to *piano* soft (see PIANO[2]) + *forte* loud (see FORTE[2])]

Pi·a·no·la (pē′ə nō′lə), *n.* *Trademark.* a form of player piano.

pi·a·no no·bi·le (pyä′nô nô′bē le′), *pl.* **pia·ni no·bi·li** (pyä′nē nô′bē lē′). *Italian.* the principal story of a large building, as a palace or villa.

pian′o play′er, 1. pianist. **2.** a mechanical device which actuates the keys of a player piano.

pian′o quartet′, 1. a musical composition scored for piano and three other instruments, typically violin, viola, and cello. **2.** an instrumental group consisting of a pianist and three other musicians, typically a violinist, violist, and cellist. **3.** a group of four pianists playing music written or arranged for four pianos.

pian′o quintet′, 1. a musical composition scored for a string quartet, or other combination of four instruments, and piano. **2.** a group of five musicians playing a piano quintet.

pian′o roll′, a roll of paper containing perforations such that air passing through them actuates the keys of a player piano.

pian′o wire′, a very thin steel wire of high tensile strength.

Pi·a·rist (pī′ər ist), *n.* a member of a Roman Catholic teaching congregation founded in Rome in 1597. [< NL phrase (*patrēs scholārum*) *piār(um)* (fathers) of religious (schools); see -IST]

pias., piaster.

pi·as·sa·va (pē′ə sä′və), *n.* **1.** a coarse, woody fiber obtained from either of two palms, *Leopoldinia Piassaba* or *Attalea funifera,* of South America, used in making brooms, mats, etc. **2.** either of these trees. Also, **pi′as·sa′ba.** [< Pg < Tupi *piaçaba*]

pi·as·ter (pē as′tər), *n.* **1.** a former coin of Turkey, the 100th part of a lira: replaced by the kurus in 1933. **2.** the 100th part of a lira: replaced... the 100th part of the pounds of Lebanon, Sudan, Syria, and the United Arab Republic. **3.** Also called **dong.** a paper money and monetary unit of Vietnam, equal to 100 cents and equivalent to about .01 of a U.S. dollar. **4.** the former peso or dollar of Spain and Spanish America. Also, **pi·as′tre.** [< F *piastre* < It *piastra* thin sheet of metal, silver coin (short for *piastra d'argento,* lit., plate of silver), akin to *piastro* PLASTER]

Pia·ti·gorsk (pyä′ti gôrsk′), *n.* Pyatigorsk.

Pia·ti·gor·sky (pyä′ti gôr′skē, pyat′i-), *n.* **Greg·or** (greg′ər), 1903–76, U.S. cellist, born in Russia.

Piau·í (pyou ē′), *n.* a state in NE Brazil. 1,263,368 (1960); 96,860 sq. mi. *Cap.:* Teresina.

Pia·ve (pyä′ve), *n.* a river in NE Italy, flowing S and SE into the Adriatic. 137 mi. long.

pi·az·za (pē az′ə, -ä′zə; *Brit.* pē at′sə, -ad′zə; *It.* pyät′tsä), *n., pl.* **pi·az·zas,** *It.* **piaz·ze** (pyät′tse). **1.** an open square or public place in a city or town, esp. in Italy. **2.** *Chiefly New Eng. and Southern U.S.* a porch on a house; veranda. **3.** *Chiefly Brit.* an arcade or covered walk or gallery, as around a public square or in front of a building. [< It < L *platea* courtyard, orig., street < Gk *plateia.* See PLACE] —**pi·az′zaed,** *adj.* —**pi·az′zi·an,** *adj.*

Pi·az·zi (pē ät′sē, pə ä′zē), *n.* a walled plain in the third quadrant of the face of the moon: about 80 miles in diameter.

Piaz′zi Smyth′, a crater in the second quadrant of the face of the moon: about 6 miles in diameter.

pi·bal (pī′bəl), *n.* *Meteorol.* the measurement and computation of the speed and direction of winds by theodolitic tracking of a pilot balloon. Cf. **rabal.** [*pi(lot) bal(loon)*]

pib·gorn (pib′gôrn), *n.* a primitive wind instrument of Wales resembling the hornpipe. Also, **pib·corn** (pib′-kôrn′). Also called **stockhorn.** [< Welsh *pib gorn,* lit., pipe of horn]

pi·blok·to (pi blok′tō), *n., pl.* **-tos.** a form of manic seizure occurring among Eskimo women. Also, **pi·block′to.** [< Eskimo]

pi·broch (pē′brokh), *n.* (in the Scottish Highlands) a kind of musical piece performed on the bagpipe, comprised of a series of variations on a ground theme, usually martial in character, but sometimes used as a dirge or otherwise. [< ScotGael *piobaireachd* piper music, equiv. to *piob* PIPE[1] + *-air* -ER[1] + *-eachd,* n. suffix denoting quality or state]

pic[1] (pēk), *n.* *Piquet.* **1.** the scoring of 30 points in the declaration of hands and in the play before one's opponent scores a point. **2.** the bonus of 30 points won for so scoring. Also, **pique.** Cf. **repic.** [< F: lit., prick]

pic[2] (pik), *n., pl.* **pix** (piks), **pics.** *Slang.* **1.** a movie. **2.** *Journalism.* a photograph. Also, **pix.** [by shortening from PICTURE]

pi·ca[1] (pī′kə), *n.* *Print.* **1.** a 12-point type of a size between small pica and English. **2.** the depth of this type size as a unit of linear measurement for type, pages containing type, etc.; one sixth of an inch. **3.** a 12-point type, widely used for typewriters and having 10 characters to the inch. Cf. **elite** (def. 4). [< AL *pica* a collection of church rules; appar. special (– orig. jocular) use of L *pīca* magpie]

pi·ca[2] (pī′kə), *n.* *Pathol.* depraved or perverted appetite or craving for unnatural food, as chalk, clay, etc., common in chlorosis, pregnancy, etc. [< medical L, special use of L *pīca* magpie, with ref. to its omnivorous feeding]

pic·a·dor (pik′ə dôr′; *Sp.* pē′kä thôr′), *n., pl.* **-dors,** *Sp.* **-do·res** (-thô′res). one of the mounted assistants to a matador, who opens the bullfight by vexing and enraging the bull and by weakening its shoulder muscles with a lance. [< Sp: lit., pricker, equiv. to *pic(ar)* (to) prick (see PIQUE) + *-ador* < L *-ātor;* see -ATE[1], -OR[2]]

pic·a·nin·ny (pik′ə nin′ē), *n., pl.* **-nies.** pickaninny.

PICAO, Provisional International Civil Aviation Organization.

pic·a·ra (pik′ə rä′; *Sp.* pē′kä rä′), *n., pl.* **-ras** (-räz′; *Sp.* -räs′). a female picaro. [fem. of PICARO]

Pi·card (pē kar′ *for 1 and 2;* pik′ərd *for 3*), *n.* **1. Charles É·mile** (sharl ā mēl′), 1856–1941, French mathematician. **2. Jean** (zhäN), 1620–82, French astronomer. **3.** a crater in the first quadrant of the face of the moon: about 21 miles in diameter.

ENGLAND
BELGIUM
ENGLISH CHANNEL
Picardy
NORMANDY
ILE DE FRANCE
Paris
CHAMPAGNE
MAINE
ORLÉANAIS

Pic·ar·dy (pik′ər dē), *n.* a region in N France: formerly a province.

Pic′ardy third′, *Music.* a major third in the final tonic chord of a composition written in a minor key. [so called from its great use in the music of the *Picardy* region]

pic·a·resque (pik′ə resk′), *adj.* **1.** pertaining to, characteristic of, or characterized by a form of prose fiction, originally developed in Spain, in which the adventures of an engagingly roguish hero are described in a series of usually humorous or satiric episodes that often depict, in realistic detail, the everyday life of the common people: *picaresque novel; picaresque hero; a picaresque element.* **2.** of, pertaining to, or resembling rogues. [< Sp *picaresco.* See PICARO, -ESQUE]

pic·a·ro (pik′ə rō′; *Sp.* pē′kä rô′), *n., pl.* **-ros** (-rōz′; *Sp.* -rôs′). a rogue or vagabond. [< Sp *pícaro* rogue]

pic·a·roon (pik′ə rōōn′), *n.* **1.** a rogue, thief, or brigand. **2.** a pirate or corsair. —*v.i.* **3.** to act or operate as a pirate or brigand. [< Sp *picarón,* aug. of *pícaro* rogue]

Pi·cas·so (pi kä′sō; *Sp.* pē käs′sô), *n.* **Pa·blo** (pä′blō; *Sp.* pä′vlô), 1881–1973, Spanish painter and sculptor in France.

pic·a·yune (pik′ē yōōn′), *n.* **1.** (formerly, in Louisiana, Florida, etc.) a coin equal to half a Spanish real or six U.S. cents in value. **2.** *U.S.* any small coin, as a five-cent piece. **3.** *Informal.* an insignificant person or thing. —*adj.* Also, **pic′a·yun′ish.** *Informal.* **4.** of little value or account; small; trifling: *a picayune amount; a picayune adjustment of the machine.* **5.** petty, carping, or prejudiced: *Her objections were entirely picayune. I didn't want to seem picayune by criticizing.* [< F *picaillon* copper coin from Savoy and Piedmont < Pr *picaioun*] —**pic′a·yun′ish·ly,** *adv.* —**pic′a·yun′·ish·ness,** *n.*
—**Syn. 4.** trivial, insignificant. **5.** narrow-minded.

Pic·a·yune (pik′ə yōōn′), *n.* a town in SE Mississippi. 7834 (1960).

Pic·ca·dil·ly (pik′ə dil′ē), *n.* a street in London, England: noted for its fashionable shops, clubs, and residences. [named after *Pickadilly* Hall (early 17th century), which owed its name to some association with *pickadilly* edging, ruff, var. of *pickedil* < D < Sp **picadillo,* akin to *picado* slashed, pricked. See PICADOR]

Pic′cadilly Cir′cus, a traffic circle and open square in W London, England: theater and amusement center.

pic·ca·lil·li (pik′ə lil′ē), *n., pl.* **-lis.** a spiced pickle of East Indian origin, made of chopped vegetables, usually green peppers and onions, often with cucumbers or green tomatoes. [earlier *piccalillo* Indian pickle; akin to PICKLE]

pic·ca·nin·ny (pik′ə nin′ē), *n., pl.* **-nies.** *Chiefly Brit.* pickaninny.

Pic·card (*Fr.* pē kar′), *n.* **1. Au·guste** (*Fr.* ō gyst′), 1884–1962, Swiss physicist, aeronaut, inventor, and deep-sea explorer: designer of bathyscaphes. **2.** his son **Jacques** (zhäk), born 1922, Swiss oceanographer and bathyscaphe designer, born in Belgium. **3. Jean Fé·lix** (zhäN fā lēks′), 1884–1963, U.S. chemist and aeronautical engineer, born in Switzerland (brother of Auguste).

Pic·cin·ni (pēt chē′nē), *n.* **Nic·co·lò** (nēk′kô lô′) (or **Ni·co·la**) (nē kô′lä), 1728–1800, Italian composer. Also, **Pic·ci′ni, Picinni.**

pic·co·lo (pik′ə lō′), *n., pl.* **-los.** a small flute, sounding an octave higher than the ordinary flute. [< It: lit., small]

pic·co·lo·ist (pik′ə lō′ist), *n.* a person who plays the piccolo. [PICCOLO + -IST]

Piccolo

Pic·co·lo·mi·ni (pē′kə lō′mē nē), *n.* a walled plain in the fourth quadrant of the face of the moon: about 56 miles in diameter.

pice (pīs), *n., pl.* **pice. 1.** a former bronze coin of British India, one quarter of an anna. Cf. **pie**[5]. **2.** paisa (def. 2). [< Mahratti *paisā*]

pic·e·ous (pis′ē əs, pī′sē əs), *adj.* **1.** of, pertaining to, or resembling pitch. **2.** inflammable; combustible. **3.** *Zool.* black or nearly black as pitch. [< L *piceus* made of pitch, equiv. to *pice-* (s. of *pix*) pitch + *-us* -OUS]

pich (pich), *n.* a shrub or small tree, *Calliandra portoricensis,* of the West Indies, having numerous leaflets which fold up at evening and night-blooming, white flowers. [< AmerSp < AmerInd]

Pich·er (pich′ər), *n.* a town in NE Oklahoma. 2553 (1960).

pich·i·ci·a·go (pich′i sē ä′gō, -ā′gō), *n., pl.* **-gos.** any of several small armadillos of the genera *Chlamydophorous* and *Burmeisteria,* of southern South America. [< AmerSp *pichiciego* < Guarani *pichey* small armadillo + Sp *ciego* blind (< L *caecus*)]

Pi·cin·ni (pē chēn′nē), *n.* See **Piccinni, Niccolò.**

pick[1] (pik), *v.t.* **1.** to choose or select, esp. with care: *to pick a contestant from the audience.* **2.** to seek and find occasion for; provoke: *to pick a fight.* **3.** to attempt to find; seek out: *to pick flaws.* **4.** to steal the contents of (a person's pocket, purse, etc.). **5.** to open (a lock) with a device other than the key, as a sharp instrument, wire, etc., esp. for the purpose of burglary: *to pick a lock.* **6.** to pierce, indent, dig into, or break up (something) with a pointed instrument: *to pick rock; to pick ore.* **7.** to form (a hole) by such action: *to pick a hole in asphalt.* **8.** to use a pointed instrument, the fingers, the teeth, the beak, etc., on (a thing), in order to remove or loosen something, as a small part or adhering matter. **9.** to clear or clean by such action: *to pick one's teeth.* **10.** to prepare for use by removing a covering piece by piece, as feathers, hulls, or other parts: *to pick a fowl.* **11.** to detach or remove piece by piece with the fingers: *She daintily picked the meat from the bones.* **12.** to pluck or gather one by one: *to pick flowers.* **13.** (of birds or other animals) to take up (small bits of food) with the bill or teeth. **14.** to eat daintily or in small morsels. **15.** to separate, pull apart, or pull to pieces: *to pick fibers.* **16.** *Music.* **a.** to pluck (the strings of an instrument). **b.** to play (a stringed instrument) by plucking with the fingers.
—*v.i.* **17.** to strike with or use a pointed instrument or the like on something. **18.** (of birds or other animals) to take up small bits of food with the bill or teeth: *The hens were busily picking about in their coop.* **19.** to select carefully or fastidiously. **20.** to pilfer; steal. **21.** *Basketball.* to execute a pick. **22. pick and choose,** to be very careful or particular in choosing: *With such a limited supply of fresh fruit, you won't be able to pick and choose.* **23. pick at, a.** *Informal.* to find fault with unnecessarily or persistently; nag. **b.** to eat sparingly or daintily: *As he was ill, he only picked at his food.* **c.** to grasp at; touch; handle: *The baby loved to pick at her mother's glass frames.* **24. pick off, a.** to remove by pulling or plucking off. **b.** to single out and shoot: *The hunter picked off a duck rising from the marsh.* **c.** *Base-*

ball. to put out (a base runner) in a pick-off play. **25. pick on, a.** *Informal.* to criticize or blame; tease; harass. **b.** to make a selection of; choose: *The professor always picks on me to translate long passages.* **26. pick one's way or steps,** to walk with care and deliberation: *She picked her way across the muddy field.* **27. pick out, a.** to choose; designate: *to pick out one's successor.* **b.** to distinguish from that which surrounds or accompanies; recognize: *to pick out a well-known face in a crowd.* **c.** to discern (sense or meaning); discriminate. **d.** to play (a melody) by ear or work (it) out note by note. **e.** to extract by picking. **28. pick over,** to examine (an assortment of items) in order to make a selection: *Eager shoppers were picking over the shirts on the bargain tables.* **29. pick someone's brains.** See **brain** (def. 9). **30. pick up, a.** to lift or take up: *to pick up a stone.* **b.** to recover (one's courage, health, etc.); regain. **c.** to gain by occasional opportunity; obtain casually: *to pick up a livelihood.* **d.** to take (a person or thing) into a car or ship, etc., or along with one. **e.** to bring into range of reception, observation, etc.: *to pick up Rome on one's radio.* **f.** to accelerate; speed up: *The car picked up once it was on the open road.* **g.** to put in good order; tidy: *to pick up a room.* **h.** to make progress; improve: *Business is beginning to pick up.* **i.** *Informal.* to become acquainted with informally or casually: *He picked up a girl in the movies last night.* **j.** *Slang.* to take into custody; arrest: *They picked him up for vagrancy.* **k.** *Slang.* to obtain; find; purchase: *She picked up some nice shoes on sale.* **l.** *Slang.* to steal: *to pick up jewels and silver.* **m.** *Informal.* to accept, as in order to pay: *to pick up the check.* —*n.* **31.** act of choosing or selecting; choice; selection: *to take one's pick.* **32.** one who or that which is selected: *He is our pick for president.* **33.** the choicest or most desirable part, example, or examples: *This horse is the pick of the stable.* **34.** the right of selection: *He gave me my pick of the litter.* **35.** the quantity of a crop picked, as from trees, bushes, etc., at a particular time: *The pick was poor this season.* **36.** *Print.* **a.** a speck of dirt, hardened ink, or extra metal on set type or a plate. **b.** a small area removed from the surface of a coated paper by ink that adheres to the form. **37.** a stroke with something pointed: *The rock shattered at the first pick of the ax.* **38.** plectrum. **39.** *Basketball.* an offensive maneuver in which a player moves into a position between a defender and a teammate with the ball so as to prevent the defender from interfering with the shot. [ME *pyke* (rhyming with *thyke* thick); c. D *pikken,* G *picken,* Icel *pikka* to pick; akin to PECK[2]]
—**Syn. 1.** See **choose. 4.** rob, pilfer. **12.** reap, collect. **33.** best.

pick[2] (pik), *n.* **1.** a hand tool consisting of an iron or steel head, usually curved, tapering to a point at one or both ends, mounted on a wooden handle, and used for loosening and breaking up soil, rock, etc. **2.** a hammerlike tool for the rough dressing of stone, having two sharp, pyramidal faces. **3.** any pointed or other tool or instrument for picking (often used in combination): *a toothpick.* [ME *pikk(e);* perh. var. of PIKE[5]] —**Syn. 1.** pickax.

pick[3] (pik), *Textiles.* —*v.t.* **1.** to cast (a shuttle). —*n.* **2.** (in a loom) one passage of the shuttle. **3.** filling (def. 4). [var. of PITCH[1]]

pick·a·back (pik′ə bak′), *adv., adj.* piggyback (defs. 1, 2). [earlier *a pickback;* see PICK[1], BACK[1]]

pick′aback plane′, a powered airplane designed to be carried aloft by another airplane and released in flight.

pick·a·nin·ny (pik′ə nin′ē), *n., pl.* **-nies.** *Usually Offensive.* a Negro child. Also, **picaninny;** *esp. Brit.,* **piccaninny.** [? < Pg *pequenino* very little one]

pick·ax (pik′aks′), *n., pl.* **-ax·es,** *v.,* **-axed, -ax·ing.** —*n.* **1.** a pick, esp. a mattock. —*v.t.* **2.** to cut or clear away with a pickax. —*v.i.* **3.** to use a pickax. Also, **pickaxe.** [PICK[2] + AX; r. ME *picois* < MF, OF; akin to F *pic* PICK[2]. See PIQUE[1]]

picked[1] (pikt), *adj.* **1.** specially chosen or selected: *a crew of picked men.* **2.** cleared or cleaned by or as by picking: *picked fruit; picked bones.* [PICK[1] + -ED[3]]

pick·ed[2] (pik′id, pikt), *adj.* *Brit. and New Eng.* pointed. [PICK[2] + -ED[2]]

pick·eer (pik ēr′), *v.i.* *Obs.* **1.** to engage in skirmishes in advance of troops of an army. **2.** to reconnoiter; scout; survey. [< D *pikeer(en),* var. of *pikereien* < F *picorée* < Sp *pecorea* pillaging, lit., cattle-raiding, verbid of *pecorear* to carry off cattle, deriv. of L *pecus* cattle]

Pick·ens (pik′ənz), *n.* **1. Andrew,** 1739–1817, American Revolutionary general. **2. Fort.** See **Fort Pickens.**

pick·er[1] (pik′ər), *n.* **1.** one who or that which picks. **2.** a machine that picks fibers. **3.** a person who plucks or gathers fruit, flowers, etc. **4.** *Foundry.* a pointed rod for removing a pattern from a half mold. [PICK[1] + -ER[1]]

pick·er[2] (pik′ər), *n.* *Textiles.* **1.** a tool or instrument for picking. **2.** the piece that throws the shuttle of the loom through the warp. **3.** a person who works a weaving instrument or device for picking. [PICK[3] + -ER[1]]

pick·er·el (pik′ər əl, pik′rəl), *n., pl.* (*esp. collectively*) **-el,** (*esp. referring to two or more kinds or species*) **-els. 1.** any of several small species of pike, as *Esox niger* **(chain pickerel)** and *E. americanus americanus* **(redfin pickerel),** found in eastern North America. **2.** the walleye or pikeperch, *Stizostedion vitreum.* **3.** *Brit.* a young pike. [ME *pickerel.* See PIKE[1], -EREL]

pick′erel frog′, a meadow frog, *Rana palustris,* common in eastern North America, similar to the leopard frog but with squarish dark spots on the back.

pick·er·el·weed (pik′ər əl wēd′, pik′rəl-), *n.* any American plant of the genus *Pontederia,* esp. *P. cordata,* a blue-flowered herb common in shallow fresh water. [PICKEREL + WEED[1]]

Pick·er·ing (pik′ər ing, pik′ring), *n.* **Edward Charles,** 1846–1919, and his brother **William Henry,** 1858–1938, U.S. astronomers.

pick·er·ing·ite (pik′ər ing it′, pik′ring-), *n.* a mineral, magnesia alum, occurring usually in the form of white fibrous masses. [named after John *Pickering* (1777–1846), American linguist; see -ITE[1]]

pick·et (pik′it), *n.* **1.** a post, stake, pale, or peg which is driven vertically into the ground and used in a fence or barrier, to fasten down a tent, etc. **2.** a person or a body of persons stationed by a trade union or the like before a business establishment in order to dissuade or prevent workers or shoppers from entering the building during a strike. **3.** a person or body of persons engaged in any similar demonstration, as against a government's policies or actions, before an embassy, office building, construction project, etc. **4.** *Mil.* a soldier or group of soldiers placed on a line forward of a position to warn against an enemy advance. **5.** *Navy, Air Force.* an aircraft or ship performing similar sentinel duty. —*v.t.* **6.** to enclose within a picket fence or stockade, as for protection, imprisonment, etc.: *to picket a lawn; to picket captives.* **7.** to fasten or tether to a picket. **8.** to place pickets in front of or around (a factory, store, business, embassy, etc.), as during a strike or demonstration. **9.** *Mil.* **a.** to guard, as with pickets. **b.** to post as a picket. —*v.i.* **10.** to stand or march as a picket. [< F *piquet.* See PIKE[2], -ET] —**pick′et·er,** *n.*

pick′et fence′, a fence consisting of pickets driven vertically into the ground and fastened together.

pick′et line′, a line of strikers or other demonstrators serving as pickets.

Pick·ett (pik′it), *n.* **George Edward,** 1825–75, Confederate general in the Civil War.

Pick·ford (pik′fərd), *n.* **Mary** (*Gladys Marie Smith*), 1893–1979, U.S. motion-picture actress, born in Canada.

pick·ing (pik′ing), *n.* **1.** the act of one who or that which picks. **2.** that which is or may be picked or picked up. **3.** the amount picked. **4. pickings, a.** scraps or remains that are worth saving or appropriating: *the pickings of a feast.* **b.** profits or advantages obtained by means not strictly honest. [ME; see PICK[1], -ING[1]]

pick·le[1] (pik′əl), *n., v.,* **-led, -ling.** —*n.* **1.** a cucumber that has been preserved in brine, vinegar, or the like. **2.** Often, **pickles.** vegetables, as cucumbers, cauliflower, etc., preserved in vinegar and eaten as a relish. **3.** something preserved in a brine or marinade. **4.** a liquid prepared with salt or vinegar for preserving or flavoring fish, meat, vegetables, etc.; brine or marinade. **5.** *Metall.* an acid or other chemical solution in which metal objects are dipped to remove oxide scale or other adhering substances. **6.** *Informal.* a troublesome or awkward situation; predicament: *She was in a pretty pickle after the check bounced.* **7.** *Informal.* a sour, disagreeable person. —*v.t.* **8.** to preserve or steep in brine or marinade. **9.** to treat with a chemical solution, as for the purpose of cleaning. [late ME *pikkyll, pekille* < MD *pekel;* akin to G *Pökel* brine, pickle]
—**Syn. 6.** plight, quandary.

pick·le[2] (pik′əl), *n.* *Scot. and North Eng.* **1.** a single grain or kernel, as of barley or corn. **2.** a small amount; a little. [? n. use of *pickle* to take tiny bits of food in eating, freq. of PICK[1]]

pick·led (pik′əld), *adj.* **1.** preserved or steeped in brine or marinade. **2.** *Slang.* drunk. [PICKLE[1] + -ED[2]]

pick·le·worm (pik′əl wûrm′), *n.* the larva of a pyralid moth, *Diaphania nitidalis,* that bores into the stem and fruit of squash, cucumber, and other cucurbitaceous plants. [PICKLE[1] + WORM]

pick·lock[1] (pik′lok′), *n.* **1.** a person who picks locks. **2.** a thief. **3.** an instrument for picking locks; lock pick. [PICK[1] + LOCK[1]]

pick·lock[2] (pik′lok′), *n.* a term designating high-grade wool. [PICK[1] + LOCK[2]]

pick-me-up (pik′mē up′), *n.* *Informal.* **1.** an alcoholic drink taken to restore one's energy or good spirits. **2.** any restorative, as a snack or coffee. Also called **pickup.**

Pick·ney (pik′nē), *n.* a boy's given name.

pick-off (pik′ôf′, -of′), *n.* **1.** *Baseball.* a play in which a base runner, caught off base, is tagged out by an infielder on a quick throw from the pitcher or catcher. **2.** *Electronics.* a mechanism that senses mechanical motion and produces a corresponding electric signal. [n. use of v. phrase *pick off*]

pick·pock·et (pik′pok′it), *n.* a person who steals money, wallets, etc., from the pockets of people passing by, in public places, or the like. [PICK[1] + POCKET]

pick·thank (pik′thangk′), *n.* *Archaic.* a person who curries favor by flattery or talebearing; sycophant. [n. use of former v. phrase *pick a thank*]

pick·up (pik′up′), *n.* **1.** *Informal.* a casual, usually unintroduced acquaintance, often one made in hope of a sexual relationship. **2.** *Auto.* **a.** capacity for rapid acceleration. **b.** Also called **pick′up truck′.** a small truck having a chassis comparable to that of a passenger car and a low-sided open body, used for deliveries and light hauling. **3.** *Informal.* an improvement, as in health, work, production, etc. **4.** *Informal.* pick-me-up. **5.** *Sports.* the act of fielding a ball after it hits the ground. **6.** *Radio.* **a.** the act of receiving sound waves in the transmitting set in order to change them into electrical waves. **b.** a receiving or recording device. **c.** the place from which a broadcast is being transmitted. **d.** interference. **7.** *Television.* **a.** the change of light energy into electrical energy in the transmitting set. **b.** the device used. **c.** a telecast made directly from the scene of an action. **8.** Also called **cartridge.** a device which generates electric or acoustic impulses in accordance with the mechanical variations impressed upon a phonograph record. **9.** an instance of stopping for or taking aboard passengers or freight, as by a train, ship, taxicab, etc., esp. an instance of taking freight or a shipment of goods onto a truck. **10.** the person, freight, or shipment so taken aboard: *The cab driver had a pickup at the airport who wanted to be driven to the docks.* **11.** *Metalworking.* (in the cold-drawing of metal) the adhesion of particles of the metal to the die or plug. [n. use of v. phrase *pick up*]

pick′up arm′. See **tone arm.**

pick-up-sticks (pik′up′stiks′), *n.* jackstraws played with sticks.

pick·wick (pik′wik), *n.* a picklike implement for catching up and raising a short wick of an oil lamp. [PICK[2] + WICK[1]]

Pick·wick·i·an (pik wik′ē ən), *adj.* **1.** of, pertaining to, or characteristic of Mr. Pickwick, central character of *The Pickwick Papers.* **2.** (of the use or interpretation of an expression) intentionally or unintentionally odd or unusual. **3.** (of words or ideas) meant or understood in a sense different from the apparent or usual one. [*Pickwick* + -IAN] —**Pick·wick′i·an·ly,** *adv.*

Pick·wick·i·an·ism (pik wik′ē ə niz əm), *n.* a Pickwickian statement, expression, word, or the like.

Pick′wick Pa′pers, The, (*The Posthumous Papers of the Pickwick Club*) a novel (1837) by Charles Dickens.

pick·y (pik′ē), *adj.,* **pick·i·er, pick·i·est.** extremely fussy or finicky, usually over trifles: *He wasn't discerning, merely picky.* [PICK[1] + -Y[1]]

pic·nic (pik′nik), *n., v.,* **-nicked, -nick·ing.** —*n.* **1.** an outing or excursion, typically one in which those taking part carry food with them and share a meal in the open air. **2.** Also called **pic′nic ham′, pic′nic shoul′der.** a section of pork shoulder, usually boned, smoked, and weighing 4–6 pounds. Cf. **daisy** (def. 2). **3.** *Informal.* an enjoyable experience, time, task, etc.: *Being laid up in a hospital is no picnic.* —*v.i.* **4.** to hold, or take part in, a picnic. [< G *Pic-nic* (now *Picknick*) < F *pique-nique,* rhyming compound < ?] —**pic′nick·er,** *n.*

pico-, *Metric System.* a combining form meaning "one trillionth": *picometer.* [< Sp *pico* odd number, peak. See PIC[1]]

pi·co·cu·rie (pī′kə kyŏŏr′ē, -kyŏŏ rē′), *n.* one trillionth of a curie. *Abbr.:* pCi, pc [PICO- + CURIE]

Pi·co del·la Mi·ran·do·la (pē′kō del′ə mə ran′də lə; *It.* pē′kō del′lä mē rän′dô lä′), **Count Gio·van·ni** (jô vän′nē), 1463–94, Italian humanist and writer.

Pi·co de Te·ide (*Sp.* pē′kô ŧħe tā′ŧħe). See **Teide, Pico de.**

pi·co·far·ad (pī′kə far′əd, -ad), *n.* *Elect.* micromicrofarad. *Abbr.:* pF, pf [PICO- + FARAD]

pic·o·line (pik′ə lēn′, -lin), *n.* *Chem.* any of three isomeric methyl derivatives of pyridine having the formula $CH_3C_5H_4N$, obtained from coal tar as a colorless oily liquid with a strong odor. [< L *pic-* (s. of *pix*) PITCH[2] + -OL[2] + -INE[2]] —**pic·o·lin·ic** (pik′ə lin′ik), *adj.*

pi·com·e·ter (pī′kō mē′tər), *n.* *Metric System.* micromicron. [PICO- + -METER]

Pi·co Ri·ve·ra (pē′kō ri vâr′ə), a city in SW California, near Los Angeles. 49,150 (1960).

pi·co·sec·ond (pī′kə sek′ənd), *n.* one trillionth of a second. *Abbr.:* psec [PICO- + SECOND[2]]

pi·cot (pē′kō), *n.* one of a number of ornamental loops in embroidery, or along the edge of lace, ribbon, etc. [< F: a purl, lit., a splinter, dim. of *pic* pick < Gmc; see PIKE[2]]

pic·o·tee (pik′ə tē′), *n.* *Chiefly Brit.* a variety of carnation having an outer margin of another color, usually red. [< F *picoté* marked, pricked, ptp. of *picoter* to mark with tiny points. See PICOT]

pi′cot stitch′, a stitch that produces picots, or loops, of thread that extend beneath a row of connecting or finishing stitches.

pi·co·watt (pī′kə wot′), *n.* one trillionth of a watt. *Abbr.:* pW, pw [PICO- + WATT]

picr-, var. of **picro-** before a vowel: *picric.*

pic·ram′ic ac′id (pi kram′ik), *Chem.* a red, crystalline, sparingly water-soluble substance, $C_6H_2(NO_2)_2(NH_2)OH$, used chiefly in the manufacture of azo dyes. [PICR- + AMIC]

pic·rate (pik′rāt), *n.* *Chem.* a salt or ester of picric acid. [PICR- + -ATE[2]] —**pic·rat′ed,** *adj.*

pic·ric (pik′rik), *adj.* *Chem.* of or derived from picric acid. [PICR- + -IC]

pic′ric ac′id, *Chem.* a yellow, crystalline, water-soluble, intensely bitter, poisonous acid, $C_6H_2(NO_2)_3OH$, used chiefly as an explosive. Also called **carbazotic acid, nitroxanthic acid, pi′cro·ni′tric ac′id** (pī′krō nī′trik, pī′krō-).

pic·rite (pik′rīt), *n.* a granular igneous rock composed chiefly of olivine and augite, but containing small amounts of feldspar. [PICR- + -ITE[1]]

picro-, a learned borrowing from Greek meaning "bitter," specialized in chemical terms as a combining form of **picric acid:** *picrotoxin.* Also, *esp. before a vowel,* **picr-.** [comb. form repr. Gk *pikrós* bitter]

pic·rol (pik′rōl, -rol), *n.* *Chem.* a colorless, crystalline, water-soluble powder, $C_6H_3O_5I_2SK$, used as an antiseptic. [PICR- + -OL[1]]

pic·ro·tox·in (pik′rə tok′sin), *n.* *Pharm.* a white, crystalline, slightly water-soluble, bitter, poisonous solid, $C_{30}H_{34}O_{13}$, obtained from the seeds of *Anamirta cocculus:* used chiefly in the treatment of barbiturate poisoning to stimulate respiration and the central nervous system. [PICRO- + TOXIN] —**pic′ro·tox′ic,** *adj.*

Pict (pikt), *n.* one of an ancient people of uncertain origin who inhabited parts of northern Britain, waged war with the Romans, and in the 9th century A.D. united with the Scots. [back formation from ME *Pictes* (pl.) (< L *Pictī*); r. ME *Peghties,* OE *Peohtas* < < L *Pictī,* lit., painted ones, pl. of *pictus,* ptp. of *pingere* to paint]

Pic·tet (pik′tit), *n.* a walled plain in the third quadrant of the face of the moon: about 40 miles in diameter.

Pict·ish (pik′tish), *n.* **1.** the language of the Picts, apparently a Celtic language. —*adj.* **2.** of or pertaining to the Picts. [PICT + -ISH[1]]

pic·to·graph (pik′tə graf′, -gräf′), *n.* **1.** a record consisting of pictorial symbols, as a prehistoric cave drawing or a graph or chart with symbolic figures representing a certain number of people, cars, factories, etc. **2.** a pictorial sign or symbol. [< L *pict(us)* painted (see PICT) + -O- + -GRAPH] —**pic·to·graph·ic** (pik′tə graf′ik), *adj.* —**pic′to·graph′i·cal·ly,** *adv.*

pic·tog·ra·phy (pik tog′rə fē), *n.* the use of pictographs; picture writing. [PICTOGRAPH + -Y[3]; see -GRAPHY]

Pic·tor (pik′tər), *n., gen.* **Pic·to·res** (pik tôr′is, -tōr′-). *Astron.* the Painter, a southern constellation between Dorado and Carina.

pic·to·ri·al (pik tôr′ē əl, -tōr′ē əl), *adj.* **1.** pertaining to, expressed in, or of the nature of a picture or pictures. **2.** illustrated by or containing pictures: *a pictorial history.* **3.** of or pertaining to the art of painting and drawing pictures, the pictures themselves, or their makers: *the architectural and pictorial masterpieces of the Renaissance.* **4.** having or suggesting the visual appeal or imagery of a picture: *a pictorial description of the countryside.* —*n.* **5.** a periodical in which pictures constitute a leading feature. [< L *pictōri(us)* of a painter, equiv. to *pictōri-* (s. of *pictor,* equiv. to *pict(us)* ptp. of *pingere* to paint + *-or* -OR[2]) + *-us* -OUS + -AL[1]] —**pic·to′ri·al·ly,** *adv.* —**pic·to′ri·al·ness,** *n.*
—**Syn. 4.** picturesque, vivid, striking, telling.

pic·to·ri·al·ise (pik tōr′ē ə līz′, -tôr′-), *v.t.*, **-ised, -is·ing.** *Chiefly Brit.* pictorialize. —**pic·to′ri·al·i·sa′tion,** *n.*

pic·to·ri·al·ism (pik tōr′ē ə liz′əm, -tôr′-), *n.* the use of pictorial style or representation. [PICTORIAL + -ISM] —**pic·to′ri·al·ist,** *n.*

pic·to·ri·al·ize (pik tōr′ē ə līz′, -tôr′-), *v.t.*, **-ized, -iz·ing.** to make pictorial; illustrate or represent with or as with pictures. Also, *esp. Brit.*, **pictorialise.** [PICTORIAL + -IZE] —**pic·to′ri·al·i·za′tion,** *n.*

pic·ture (pik′chər), *n.*, *v.*, **-tured, -tur·ing.** —*n.* **1.** a representation of a person, object, or scene, as a painting, drawing, photograph, etc. **2.** any visible image, however produced: *the pictures made by reflections in a pool of water.* **3.** a mental image: *a clear picture of how he had looked that day.* **4.** a graphic or vivid description or account: *Gibbon's picture of ancient Rome.* **5.** a tableau, as in theatrical representation. **6.** See **motion picture. 7.** a person, thing, group, or scene regarded as resembling a work of pictorial art in beauty, fineness of appearance, etc.: *She was a picture in her new blue dress.* **8.** the image or counterpart of someone else: *He is the picture of his father.* **9.** a visible or concrete embodiment of some quality or condition: *the picture of health.* **10.** a situation or set of circumstances: *Recent developments have cast new light on the employment picture.* **11.** understanding of a situation: *Do you get the picture?* **12.** the viewing screen of a television set or a motion-picture theater: *Our TV has a 19-inch picture.* **13.** *Pathol.* the assemblage of conditions presented in a case of disease. —*v.t.* **14.** to represent in a picture or pictorially, as by painting or drawing. **15.** to form a mental picture of; imagine: *He couldn't picture himself doing such a thing.* **16.** to depict in words; describe graphically: *He pictured Rome so vividly that you half-believed you were there.* **17.** to convey a clear conception or reflection of: *His book pictured the world of the future.* [late ME < L *pictūra* painting, equiv. to *pict(us)* (see DEPICT) + *-ūra* -URE] —**pic′tur·a·ble,** *adj.* —**pic′tur·a·ble·ness,** *n.* —**pic′tur·a·bly,** *adv.* —**pic′tur·er,** *n.*
—**Syn. 1.** similitude, semblance, likeness. **11.** drift; meaning. **14, 16.** delineate, paint, draw, represent.

pic′ture book′, a book consisting mainly of pictures, esp. one for children who have not yet learned to read.

pic′ture hat′, a woman's hat having a very broad, flexible brim, often decorated with feathers, flowers, or the like.

pic′ture lay′out, a picture spread. See under **spread** (def. 32).

pic′ture mold′, a molding near a ceiling from which pictures can be suspended. Also called **pic′ture rail′.**

Pic′ture of Do′ri·an Gray′, The (dōr′ē ən, dôr′-), a novel (1891) by Oscar Wilde.

pic′ture plane′, the plane of a painting, drawing, or the like, that is in the extreme foreground of a picture, is coextensive with but not the same as the material surface of the work, is the point of visual contact between the viewer and the picture, and is conceived as a major structural element in the production of abstract or illusionistic forms. See diag. under **perspective.**

pic′ture sash′, a large window sash, as for a picture window.

pic′ture show′, *Dial.* **1.** See **motion picture. 2.** a motion-picture theater.

pic′ture spread′. See under **spread** (def. 32).

pic·tur·esque (pik′chə resk′), *adj.* **1.** visually charming or quaint, as if resembling or suitable for a painting: *a picturesque fishing village.* **2.** (of writing, speech, etc.) strikingly graphic or vivid. **3.** having pleasing or interesting qualities; strikingly effective in appearance: *a picturesque hat.* [PICTURE + -ESQUE, modeled (imperfectly) on F *pittoresque* < It *pittoresco*, equiv. to *pittor(e)* painter + *-esco* -ESQUE] —**pic′tur·esque′ly,** *adv.* —**pic′tur·esque′ness,** *n.*
—**Syn. 2.** PICTURESQUE, GRAPHIC, VIVID apply to descriptions that produce a strong, especially a visual, impression. PICTURESQUE is a less precise term than the other two. A PICTURESQUE account, though striking and interesting, may be inaccurate or may reflect personal ideas: *He called the landscape picturesque.* A GRAPHIC account is more objective and factual: it produces a clear, definite impression, and carries conviction. A VIVID account is told with liveliness and intenseness; the description is so interesting, or even exciting, that the hearer may be emotionally stirred.

pic′ture tube′, a cathode-ray tube forming the screen on which televised images are reproduced.

pic′ture win′dow, a large window in a house, usually dominating the room or wall in which it is located, and often designed or decorated to present an attractive view as seen from inside or outside the house.

pic′ture writ′ing, 1. the art of recording events or expressing ideas by pictures, or pictorial symbols, as practiced by preliterate peoples. **2.** pictorial symbols forming a record or communication.

pic·tur·ize (pik′chə rīz′), *v.t.*, **-ized, -iz·ing.** to represent in a picture, esp. in a motion picture; make a picture of. [PICTURE + -IZE] —**pic′tur·i·za′tion,** *n.*

pic·ul (pik′əl), *n.* (in China and southeast Asia) a weight equal to 100 catties, or from about 133 to about 143 pounds avoirdupois. [< Malay *pikul* full load (for a man), n. use of *pikul* (v.) to carry a full load]

pic·u·let (pik′yə lit), *n.* any of several small woodpeckers, chiefly of the genus *Picumnus*, which lack stiffened shafts in the tail feathers. [< L *pīcu(s)* woodpecker + -LET]

Pi·cum·nus (pi kum′nəs), *n.* one of two ancient Roman fertility gods. Cf. **Pilumnus.**

Pi·cus (pī′kəs), *n.* an ancient Italian god of agriculture.

pid·dle (pid′ᵊl), *v.*, **-dled, -dling.** —*v.i.* **1.** to spend time in a wasteful, trifling, or ineffective way; dawdle: *Stop piddling and finish your dinner!* —*v.t.* **2.** to waste (time); fail to utilize (usually fol. by *away*): *to piddle away one's leisure hours.* [?] —**pid′dler,** *n.*

pid·dling (pid′ling), *adj.* trifling; petty; negligible: *a piddling sum of money.* [PIDDLE + -ING[2]]

pid·dock (pid′ək), *n.* any bivalve mollusk of the genus *Pholas* or the family *Pholadidae*, having long, ovate shells and burrowing in soft rock, wood, etc. [? akin to OE *puduc* wart]

Pid·geon (pij′ən), *n.* **Walter,** born 1898, U.S. actor, born in Canada.

pidg·in (pij′ən), *n.* an auxiliary language that has come into existence through attempts to communicate by the speakers of two different languages and that is primarily a simplified form of one of the languages, with considerable variation in pronunciation, and with a major part of its grammatical features selected from those common to both of the native languages of its speakers. Also, **pigeon.** [perh. repr. Chin pronunciation of *business*]

pidg′in Eng′lish, 1. an English jargon used in commerce in Chinese ports. **2.** any of several similar jargons used in other areas, as Melanesia or West Africa. Also, **Pidg′in Eng′lish.**

pidg·in·ize (pij′ə nīz′), *v.t.*, **-ized, -iz·ing.** to develop (a language) into a pidgin. [PIDGIN + -IZE] —**pid′gin·i·za′tion,** *n.*

Pid·yon Ha·ben (pid yôn′ hä bän′; *Eng.* pid′yən hə ben′), *Hebrew.* the Jewish rite of redeeming the first child born, if male, to parents not descended from Aaron or Levi by the payment of money by the father to a member of the priestly class, celebrated 30 days after the child's birth. Also, **Pidyon′ ha-Ben′.** [lit., son's redemption]

pie[1] (pī), *n.* **1.** a baked food having a sweet or savory filling, prepared in a pastry-lined pan or dish and often topped with a pastry crust. **2.** a layer cake with a filling of cream, jelly, or the like. **3. pie in the sky, a.** the illusory prospect of future benefits: *Political promises are often pie in the sky meant to win votes.* **b.** a state of perfect happiness; utopia: *to promise pie in the sky.* [ME; special use of *pie* shallow pit < ONorman *pi, pis*, dial. var. of OF *puis* < L *puteus* well, pit. See PIT[1]] —**pie′like′,** *adj.*

pie[2] (pī), *n.* magpie. [ME < OF < L *pīca*, akin to *pīcus* woodpecker]

pie[3] (pī), *n.*, *v.t.*, **pied, pie·ing.** *U.S.* pi[2].

pie[4] (pī), *n.* (in England before the Reformation) a book of ecclesiastical rules for finding the particulars of the service for the day. Also, **pye.** [trans. of L *pīca* magpie; see PICA[1]]

pie[5] (pī), *n.* a former bronze coin of India, the 12th part of an anna. Cf. **naya paisa, paisa, pice.** [< Mahratti *pā′ī*, lit., a fourth]

pie·bald (pī′bôld′), *adj.* **1.** having patches of black and white or of other colors; parti-colored. —*n.* **2.** a piebald animal, esp. a horse. [PIE[2] (see PIED) + BALD] —**pie′bald′ly,** *adv.* —**pie′bald′ness,** *n.*

pie′bald skin′, *Pathol.* vitiligo.

piece (pēs), *n.*, *v.*, **pieced, piec·ing.** —*n.* **1.** a separate or limited portion or quantity of something: *a piece of land; a piece of chocolate; a piece of cotton.* **2.** a quantity of some substance or material forming a single mass or body: *a nice piece of lumber.* **3.** a more or less definite portion or quantity of a whole: *to cut a blueberry pie into six pieces.* **4.** a particular length, as of certain goods prepared for the market: *cloth sold by the piece.* **5.** an amount of work forming a single job: *to work by the piece.* **6.** an example of workmanship, esp. of artistic production, as a picture or a statue: *The museum has some interesting pieces from the Renaissance.* **7.** a literary composition, usually short, in prose or verse. **8.** a literary selection for recitation: *Each child had a chance to recite his piece.* **9.** a musical composition, usually a short one. **10.** one of the parts which, when assembled, form a whole: *the pieces of a machine.* **11.** an individual article of a set or collection: *a set of dishes containing 100 pieces.* **12.** *Chess, Checkers.* **a.** one of the figures, disks, blocks, or the like, of wood, ivory, or other material, used in playing, as on a board or table. **b.** (in chess) a superior man, as distinguished from a pawn: *to take a rook, a bishop, and other pieces.* **13.** a token, charm, or amulet: *a good-luck piece.* **14.** an individual thing of a particular class or kind: *a piece of furniture; a piece of drawing paper.* **15.** an example, specimen, or instance of something: *a fine piece of workmanship.* **16.** one of the parts into which a thing is destructively divided or broken; a part, fragment, or shred: *to tear a letter into pieces.* **17.** *Mil.* **a.** a soldier's rifle, pistol, etc. **b.** a cannon or other unit of ordnance: *field piece.* **18.** a coin: *a five-cent piece.* **19.** *Chiefly Midland U.S.* a distance: *I'm going down the road a piece. The next town is quite a piece from here.* **20.** *Slang (vulgar).* coitus or a woman considered as an object of coitus. **21. give someone a piece of one's mind.** See **mind** (def. 20). **22. go to pieces,** to lose control of oneself; become emotionally or physically upset: *When he flunked out of medical school he went to pieces.* **23. of a piece,** of the same kind; harmonious; consistent. Also, **of one piece. 24. speak one's piece,** *Informal.* to express one's opinion; reveal one's thoughts upon a subject: *I decided to speak my piece whether they liked it or not.* —*v.t.* **25.** to mend (a garment, article, etc.) by applying a piece or pieces; patch. **26.** to complete, enlarge, or extend by an added piece or something additional (often fol. by *out*): *to piece out a library with new books.* **27.** to make by or as if by joining pieces (often fol. by *together*): *to piece a quilt; to piece together a program.* **28.** to join together, as pieces or parts: *to piece together the fragments of a broken dish.* **29.** to join as a piece or addition to something: *to piece new wire into the cable.* **30.** to assemble into a meaningful whole by combining available facts, information, details, etc.: *He pieced the story together after a lot of effort.* —*v.i.* **31.** *Chiefly Dial.* to eat small portions of food between meals; snack: *Stop piecing, it's almost dinner time!* [ME *pece* < OF < Gaulish **pettia;* akin to Breton *pez* piece, Welsh, Cornish *peth* part]
—**Syn. 1.** section, segment, scrap, fragment. See **part. 26.** augment. —**Ant. 1.** whole.

pièce à thèse (pyes A tez′), *pl.* **pièces à thèse** (pyes A tez′). *French.* See **thesis play.**

pièce de ré·sis·tance (pyes də RĀ zē stäɴs′; *Eng.* pē es′ də ri zē′stäns), *pl.* **pièces de ré·sis·tance** (pyes də RĀ zē stäɴs′; *Eng.* pē es′ də ri zē′stäns). *French.* **1.** the principal dish of a meal. **2.** the principal event, incident, article, etc., of a series or group.

pièce d'oc·ca·sion (pyes dô kä zyôɴ′), *pl.* **pièces d'oc·ca·sion** (pyes dô kä zyôɴ′). *French.* something prepared or used for a special occasion.

piece-dyed (pēs′dīd′), *adj.* dyed after weaving (opposed to *yarn-dyed*).

piece′ goods′, goods, esp. fabrics, sold at retail by linear measure. Also called **yard goods.**

piece·meal (pēs′mēl′), *adv.* **1.** piece by piece; gradually: *to work piecemeal.* **2.** into pieces or fragments: *to tear a letter piecemeal.* —*adj.* **3.** done piece by piece. [ME *pecemele;* r. OE *styccemǣlum.* See PIECE, -MEAL]

piece′ of eight′, peso (def. 5).

piece′ of exchange′, a piece of plate armor for reinforcing or replacing a piece ordinarily used in a suit. Also called **double piece.**

piec·er (pē′sər), *n.* a person whose occupation is the joining together of pieces or threads, as in textile work. [PIECE + -ER[1]]

piece′ rate′, compensation based on output or production, usually a fixed sum per piece of work turned out.

piece·work (pēs′wûrk′), *n.* work done and paid for by the piece. Cf. **timework.** [PIECE + WORK] —**piece′work′er,** *n.*

pie·crust (pī′krust′), *n.* **1.** dough prepared with shortening for making the crust or shell of a pie; paste. **2.** the crust or shell of a pie. [PIE[1] + CRUST]

pie′crust ta′ble, *U.S. Furniture.* a table having a top, usually round, with a raised and intricately carved edge.

pied (pīd), *adj.* **1.** having patches of two or more colors, as various birds and other animals: *a pied horse.* **2.** wearing pied clothing. [PIE[2] (with reference to the black and white plumage of the magpie) + -ED[3]]

pied-à-terre (pyā tA teR′), *n.*, *pl.* **pied-à-terre** (pyā tA teR′). *French.* a small dwelling for temporary use, as an apartment maintained in a foreign city. [lit., foot on ground]

pied′-billed grebe′ (pīd′bild′), an American grebe, *Podilymbus podiceps*, having a whitish bill with a black band around it.

pied-de-biche (pē ā′də bēsh′; *Fr.* pyādᵊ bēsh′), *n.*, *pl.* **pieds-de-biche** (pē āz′də bēsh′; *Fr.* pyādᵊ bēsh′). *Furniture.* a termination to a leg, consisting of a slight outward curve ending in the semblance of a cloven hoof. Also called **hoof foot.** [< F: lit., doe's foot]

pied-de-biche′ spoon′, a spoon having a handle with a trifid end.

pi·ed·fort (pē ā fôr′, pyā-), *n.* *Coining.* a coin or pattern struck on a blank thicker than that used for the regular issue. Also, **piefort.** [< F, equiv. to *pied* foot + *fort* strong]

pied′ goose′. See **magpie goose.**

Pied·mont (pēd′mont), *n.* **1.** a plateau between the coastal plain and the Appalachian Mountains, including parts of Virginia, North Carolina, South Carolina, Georgia, and Alabama. **2.** Italian, **Piemonte.** a region in NW Italy. 3,889,962 (1961); 11,335 sq. mi. **3.** a town in NE Alabama. 4794 (1960). **4.** (*l.c.*) a district lying along or near the foot of a mountain range. —*adj.* **5.** (*l.c.*) lying along or near the foot of a mountain range. [< It *Piedmonte*, lit., foothill]

Pied·mon·tese (pēd′mon tēz′, -tēs′), *n.*, *pl.* **-tese,** *adj.* —*n.* **1.** a native or inhabitant of Piedmont, Italy. —*adj.* **2.** of, pertaining to, or characteristic of the people or region of Piedmont, Italy. [PIEDMONT + -ESE]

pied·mont·ite (pēd′mon tīt′), *n.* a mineral, similar to epidote but containing manganese: found in schists and manganese ores. [< G; see PIEDMONT, -ITE[1]]

pied noir (pyā nwaR′), *French.* a European, esp. a French settler or his descendant in Algeria. Also, **pied-noir′.** [lit., black foot]

Pied′ Pip′er, 1. the hero of a German folk legend, popularized in *The Pied Piper of Hamelin* (1842) by Robert Browning. **2.** (*sometimes l.c.*) a person who induces others to imitate his example, esp. by means of false or extravagant promises.

Pie·dras Ne·gras (pye′thräs ne′gräs), a city in N Mexico, on the Rio Grande. 27,578 (1950).

pie-eyed (pī′īd′), *adj.* *Slang.* drunk; intoxicated.

pie-faced (pī′fāst′), *adj.* *Informal.* having a broad, flat face and a vacuous expression.

pi·e·fort (pē ā fôr′, pyā-), *n.* piedfort.

pie′ in the sky′, pie[1] (def. 3).

Pi·e·lus (pī′ə ləs), *n.* *Class. Myth.* a son of Neoptolemus and Andromache from whom Alexander the Great claimed descent.

Pie·mon·te (pye môn′te), *n.* Italian name of **Piedmont.**

piend (pēnd), *n.* arris. Also, **pien** (pēn). [? var. of PEEN]

pie·plant (pī′plant′, -plänt′), *n.* *U.S.* the garden rhubarb: so called from its use in pies. [PIE[1] + PLANT]

pier (pēr), *n.* **1.** a structure built to extend from land out over water, used as a landing place for ships, an entertainment or amusement area, etc. **2.** (in a bridge or the like) a support for the ends of adjacent spans. **3.** a square pillar. **4.** a portion of wall between doors, windows, etc. **5.** a pillar or post on which a gate or door is hung. **6.** a support of masonry or the like for sustaining vertical pressure. See diag. under **arch.** [ME *pere*, early ME *per*, equiv. to AL *pera* pier of a bridge]

pierce (pērs), *v.*, **pierced, pierc·ing.** —*v.t.* **1.** to penetrate into or run through (something), as a sharp-pointed object or instrument does. **2.** to make a hole or opening in. **3.** to bore into or through; tunnel. **4.** to perforate. **5.** to make (a hole, opening, etc.) by or as by boring or perforating. **6.** to force or make a way into or through: *a road that pierces the jungle.* **7.** to penetrate with the eye or mind; see into or through: *She couldn't pierce his thoughts.* **8.** to affect sharply with some sensation or emotion, as of cold, pain, grief, etc.: *The sun's rays pierced her eyes. Beethoven's music pierces the soul.* **9.** to sound sharply through (the air, stillness, etc.), as a cry: *A pistol shot pierced the night.* —*v.i.* **10.** to force or make a way into or through something; penetrate: *They pierced to the heart of the forest. With brilliant logic he pierced straight to the heart of the matter.* [ME *perce(n)* < OF *perc(er)*, perh. < VL **pertiūre*, deriv. of L *pertus* gone through (hence, pierced), ptp. of *perīre.* See PERISH] —**pierce′a·ble,** *adj.* —**pierc′er,** *n.*
—**Syn. 1.** enter, puncture. PIERCE, PENETRATE suggest the action of one object passing through another or

making a way through and into another. The terms are used both concretely and figuratively. To PIERCE is to perforate quickly, as by stabbing; it suggests the use of a sharp-pointed instrument which is impelled by force: *to pierce the flesh with a knife; A scream pierces one's ears.* PENETRATE suggests a slow or difficult movement: *No ordinary bullet can penetrate an elephant's hide; to penetrate the depths of one's ignorance.* **8.** touch, move, strike, thrill.

Pierce (pērs), *n.* **1.** **Franklin,** 1804–69, 14th president of the U.S. 1853–57. **2.** Also, **Pearce.** a boy's given name.

pierced (pērsd), *adj.* **1.** punctured or perforated, as to form a decorative design: *a piece of jewelry in pierced copper.* **2.** (of the ear) having the lobe punctured, as for earrings or other jewelry. **3.** *Heraldry.* (of a charge) open at the center to reveal the field: *a lozenge pierced.* [special use of ptp. of PIERCE; see -ED[2]]

pierced′ dol′lar, *Australian.* See **holey dollar.**

Pierce′'s disease′, *Plant Pathol.* a disease of grapevines, characterized by withered, brown leaves, defoliation, dwarfed or withered fruit, and delayed growth, caused by a virus, *Morsus suffodiens.* [named after N. B. *Pierce* (d. 1917), American plant pathologist]

pierc·ing (pēr′sing), *adj.* **1.** loud or shrill, as the quality of a voice: *piercing screams.* **2.** extremely cold or bitter, as weather: *a piercing wind.* **3.** appearing to gaze deeply into an object: *piercing eyes.* **4.** perceptive or aware: *a piercing mind.* **5.** sarcastic or caustic, as a remark; cutting. [ME; see PIERCE, -ING[2]] —**pierc′ing·ly,** *adv.* —**pierc′ing·ness,** *n.*

pier′ glass′, a tall mirror, often full-length, intended to be set between windows.

pier·head (pēr′hed′), *n.* **1.** the outermost end of a pier or wharf. **2.** (in the Great Lakes area) a breakwater. [PIER + HEAD]

Pi·e·ri·a (pī ēr′ē ə), *n.* a coastal region in NE Greece, W of the Gulf of Salonika.

Pi·e·ri·an (pī ēr′ē ən), *adj.* **1.** of or pertaining to the Muses or to inspiration. **2.** of or pertaining to Pieria. **3.** of or pertaining to poetry or poetic inspiration. [< L *Pīeri(us)* of Pieria + -AN]

Pie′rian Spring′, *Class. Myth.* a fountain in Pieria, sacred to the Muses and supposedly conferring inspiration or learning on anyone who drank from it.

pi·er·id (pī er′id, pī′ər-), *adj.* **1.** belonging or pertaining to the *Pieridae,* a family of butterflies comprising the whites, sulphurs, etc. —*n.* **2.** a pierid butterfly. [back formation from NL *Pieridae* family name < Gk *Pierides* Muses; see -IDAE]

Pi·e·ri·des (pī er′i dēz′), *n.pl.* *Class. Myth.* **1.** the Muses. **2.** nine Thessalian maidens who challenged the Muses to a singing contest, lost, and were changed into magpies for insulting the victors.

Pie·ro del·la Fran·ce·sca (pyâr′ō del′ə frän ches′kə; *It.* pye′rô del′lä frän ches′kä), (*Piero de' Franceschi*). See **Francesca, Piero della.** Also called **Pie′ro.**

Pie·ro di Co·si·mo (pyâr′ō di kō′zə mō′; *It.* pye′rô dē kô′zē mô), (*Piero di Lorenzo*), 1462–1521, Italian painter.

Pierre (pēr *for 1;* pē âr′, *Fr.* pyer *for 2*), *n.* **1.** a city in and the capital of South Dakota, in the central part, on the Missouri River. 10,088 (1960). **2.** a boy's given name, form of **Peter.**

Pi·er·rette (pē′ə ret′; *Fr.* pye ret′), *n.* (*sometimes l.c.*) the female counterpart of a Pierrot, usually accompanying him, as in an entertainment or masquerade.

Pi·er·rot (pē′ə rō′; *Fr.* pye rō′), *n., pl.* **-rots** (-rōz′; *Fr.* -rō′). **1.** a male character in certain French pantomime, having a whitened face and wearing a loose white fancy costume. **2.** (*l.c.*) an actor, masquerader, or buffoon so made up. [< F, dim. of *Pierre* Peter]

Pier·rot Lu·naire (pē′ə rō′ lo͞o nâr′; *Fr.* pye rō ly ner′), a cycle of 21 songs (1912) for voice and instruments, by Arnold Schönberg, written in *Sprechgesang* style and set to poems of Albert Giraud in German translation.

pierrot′ show′, a variety show in which the entertainers wear make-up and costumes characteristic of Pierrot. Pierrot shows were popular in England during the latter part of the 19th and the early part of the 20th centuries.

Piers Plow·man (pērz′ plou′mən), (*The Vision Concerning Piers Plowman*) an alliterative poem written in three versions (1360–99), ascribed to William Langland.

pier′ ta′ble, a low table or console intended to be set between two windows, often beneath a pier glass.

pi·et (pī′it), *n.* **1.** *Scot.* a magpie. **2.** *Scot. and North Eng.* a talkative person; one who chatters. [PIE[2] + -ET; r. ME *piot* < OF *pie* PIE[2] + *-ot* dim. suffix]

Pie·tà (pē′ā tä′, pyā tä′, pē ā′tə, pyā′-), *n.* (*often cap.*) *Fine Arts.* a representation of the Virgin Mary mourning the body of the dead Christ, usually shown held on her lap. [< It: lit., pity < L *pietās* PIETY]

Pi·e·tas (pī′i tas′), *n.* the ancient Roman personification of familial affection.

Pie·ter·mar·itz·burg (pē′tər mar′its bûrg′), *n.* a city in and the capital of Natal province, in the E Republic of South Africa. 91,178 (1960).

Pi·e·tism (pī′i tiz′əm), *n.* **1.** a movement, originating in the Lutheran Church in Germany in the 17th century, that stressed personal piety over religious formality and orthodoxy. **2.** the principles and practices of the Pietists. **3.** (*l.c.*) highly intense, religious devotion or feeling: *the pietism of early Christianity.* **4.** (*l.c.*) exaggeration or affectation of piety: *the pietism of Tartuffe.* [< G *Pietism(us)* < L *piet(ās)* PIETY + *-ismus* -ISM] —**Pi′e·tist,** *n.* —**pi′e·tis′tic, pi′e·tis′ti·cal,** *adj.* —**pi′e·tis′ti·cal·ly,** *adv.*
—**Syn. 4.** sanctimony.

pi·e·ty (pī′i tē), *n., pl.* **-ties.** **1.** reverence for God or devout fulfillment of religious obligations: *a prayer full of piety.* **2.** quality or fact of being pious: *saintly piety.* **3.** dutiful respect or regard for parents, race, etc.: *filial piety.* **4.** a pious act, remark, belief, or the like: *the pieties and sacrifices of an austere life.* [ME *piete* < MF < L *pietās.* See PIOUS, -ETY]
—**Syn. 1.** respect, veneration, awe. **2.** godliness, devotion, devoutness, sanctity, holiness. —**Ant. 1.** irreverence.

pi·e·zo·e·lec·tric·i·ty (pī ē′zō i lek tris′i tē, -ē′lek-), *n.* electricity, or electric polarity, produced by mechanical pressure on a nonconducting crystal. [< Gk *piéz(ein)* (to) press + -O- + ELECTRICITY] —**pi·e·zo·e·lec·tric** (pī ē′zō i lek′trik), *adj.* —**pi·e′zo·e·lec′tri·cal·ly,** *adv.*

pi·e·zoid (pī ē′zoid), *n.* *Electronics.* a completed crystal blank, esp. after the attachment of electrodes to the faces. [< Gk *piéz(ein)* (to) press + -OID]

pi·e·zom·e·ter (pī′i zom′i tər), *n.* any of several instruments for measuring the pressure of a fluid or the compressibility of a substance when subjected to such a pressure. [< Gk *piéz(ein)* (to) press + -O- + -METER] —**pi·e·zo·met·ric** (pī ē′zə me′trik), **pi·e′zo·met′ri·cal,** *adj.*

pi·e·zom·e·try (pī′i zom′i trē), *n.* the measurement of pressure or compressibility. [< Gk *piéz(ein)* (to) press + -O- + -METRY]

pif·fle (pif′əl), *n., v.,* **-fled, -fling.** *Informal.* —*n.* **1.** nonsense, as idle talk. —*v.i.* **2.** to talk nonsense. [? akin to PUFF]

pig[1] (pig), *n., v.,* **pigged, pig·ging.** —*n.* **1.** a young swine of either sex weighing less than 120 pounds. **2.** (loosely) any wild or domestic swine. **3.** the flesh of swine; pork. **4.** *Informal.* a person of piggish character or habits. **5.** *Metall.* **a.** an oblong mass of metal that has been run while still molten into a mold of sand or the like, esp. such a mass of iron from a blast furnace. **b.** one of the molds for such masses of metal. **c.** metal in the form of such masses. **d.** pig iron. —*v.i.* **6.** to bring forth pigs; farrow. —*v.t.* **7.** to mold (metal) into pigs. **8. pig it,** *Chiefly Brit.* **a.** to live in dirt. **b.** to lead a disorganized, makeshift life; live without plan or pattern. [ME *pigge* young pig, OE *pigga (recorded from 11th century as nickname); ? akin to D *big* young pig]

pig[2] (pig), *n.* *Scot. and North Eng.* **1.** an earthenware crock, pot, pitcher, or jar. **2.** potter's clay; earthenware as a material. Also, **pigg.** [late ME *pygg*]

Pi·galle (*Fr.* pē gal′), *n.* See **Place Pigalle.**

pig′ bed′, *Metall.* a bed of sand for molding pigs into which molten metal is poured.

pig·boat (pig′bōt′), *n.* *Slang.* a submarine. [PIG[1] + BOAT]

pig′ boil′ing, *Metall.* See **wet puddling.**

pi·geon[1] (pij′ən), *n.* **1.** any bird of the family *Columbidae,* having a compact body and short legs, esp. the larger species with square or rounded tails. Cf. **dove**[1] (def. 1). **2.** a domesticated member of this family, as one of the varieties of the rock dove. **3.** a young, usually attractive, girl. **4.** *Slang.* a person who is easily fooled; dupe. **5.** *Poker Slang.* a card, acquired in the draw, that greatly improves a hand or makes it a winner. [ME *pejon* young dove < MF *pijon* < LL *pīpiōn-* (s. of *pīpiō*) squab, akin to *pīpīre, pīpāre* to chirp]

pi·geon[2] (pij′ən), *n.* (not in technical use) pidgin; pidgin English.

pi·geon·ber·ry (pij′ən ber′ē), *n., pl.* **-ries.** See **blue dogwood.** [PIGEON[1] + BERRY]

pi′geon blood′, **1.** dark red. **2.** *Informal.* soy (def. 1). Also, **pi′geon's blood′.**

pi′geon breast′, *Pathol.* See **chicken breast.** Also called **pi′geon chest′.** —**pi′geon-breast′ed, pi′geon-chest′ed,** *adj.* —**pi′geon-breast′ed·ness, pi′geon-chest′ed·ness,** *n.*

pi′geon clock′. See **pigeon timer.**

pi′geon grape′. See **summer grape.**

pi′geon hawk′, a small American falcon, *Falco columbarius,* closely related to the European merlin.

pi·geon-heart·ed (pij′ən här′tid), *adj.* timid; meek.

pi·geon·hole (pij′ən hōl′), *n., v.,* **-holed, -hol·ing.** —*n.* **1.** one of a series of small compartments in a desk, cabinet, or the like, used for filing papers, letters, etc. **2.** a hole or recess, or one of a series of recesses, for pigeons to nest in. **3.** Also called **pi′geon hole′, white hole.** *Print.* white space created by setting words or lines too far apart. —*v.t.* **4.** to lay aside for reference at some later, indefinite time: *We must pigeonhole this excellent plan until the time is ripe.* **5.** to assign to a definite place or to definite places in some orderly system: *to pigeonhole new ideas; to pigeonhole one's life.* **6.** to put aside for the present, esp. with the intention of ignoring or forgetting: *to pigeonhole an unwanted invitation.* **7.** to place in or as if in a pigeonhole or pigeonholes: *to pigeonhole papers.* **8.** to fit or provide with pigeonholes: *The desk must be pigeonholed for all my papers.* [PIGEON[1] + HOLE]
—**Syn. 4.** file. **5.** categorize, catalog. **6.** postpone, shelve.

pi·geon·ite (pij′ə nīt′), *n.* *Mineral.* a pyroxene consisting mainly of a mixture of $(Mg,Fe)SiO_3$ and $CaMg(SiO_3)_2$. [named after *Pigeon* Point, Northeast Minnesota; see -ITE[1]]

pi·geon-liv·ered (pij′ən liv′ərd), *adj.* meek-tempered; spiritless; mild.

pi′geon pea′, **1.** a tropical, leguminous shrub, *Cajanus indicus,* having showy yellow flowers. **2.** the brown, edible seed of this plant.

pi′geon pox′, *Vet. Pathol.* a disease affecting pigeons, similar to fowl pox. Also, **pi·geon·pox** (pij′ən-poks′).

pi′geon tim′er, a device for timing the arrivals of pigeons being raced, consisting of a magazine for holding the identification bands of the contestants in the order in which they are inserted and a recording clock to register the times of insertion. Also called **pigeon clock.**

pi·geon-toed (pij′ən tōd′), *adj.* having the toes or feet turned inward.

pi·geon·wing (pij′ən wing′), *n.* *U.S.* **1.** a particular figure in skating, outlining the spread wing of a pigeon. **2.** a similar fancy step or evolution in dancing. [PIGEON[1] + WING]

pig·fish (pig′fish′), *n., pl.* **-fish·es,** (*esp. collectively*) **-fish.** a grunt, *Orthopristis chrysopterus,* found off the Atlantic coast of the southern U.S. [PIG[1] + FISH]

pigg (pig), *n.* *Scot. and North Eng.* pig[2].

pig·ger·y (pig′ə rē), *n., pl.* **-ger·ies.** *Chiefly Brit.* a pigsty. [PIG[1] + -ERY]

pig·gie (pig′ē), *n., adj.,* **-gi·er, -gi·est.** piggy.

pig·gin (pig′in), *n.* **1.** *Dial.* a small wooden pail or tub with a handle formed by continuing one of the staves above the rim. **2.** See **cream pail.** [? akin to PIG[2]]

pig·gish (pig′ish), *adj.* like or befitting a pig; greedy or filthy: *piggish table manners.* [PIG[1] + -ISH[1]] —**pig′gish·ly,** *adv.* —**pig′gish·ness,** *n.*

Pig·gott (pig′ət), *n.* a town in NE Arkansas. 2776 (1960).

pig·gy (pig′ē), *n., pl.* **-gies,** *adj.,* **-gi·er, -gi·est.** —*n.* **1.** a small or young pig. **2.** *Babytalk.* an infant's finger or toe. —*adj.* **3.** (of a sow) in an advanced state of pregnancy. Also, **pig′gie.** [PIG + -Y[2]]

pig·gy·back (pig′ē bak′), *adv.* **1.** on the back or shoulders like a pack: *The little girl rode piggyback on her father.* —*adj.* **2.** astride the back or shoulders: *a piggyback ride.* **3.** noting or pertaining to the carrying of one vehicle or the like by another, as the carrying of truck trailers on flatcars. —*v.t.* **4.** to carry (truck trailers) by railroad on flatcars. —*v.i.* **5.** to carry truck trailers by railroad on flatcars. Also, **pickaback** (for defs. 1, 2). [alter. of PICKABACK]

pig′gyback car′, *Railroads.* a flatcar designed to accommodate one or more standard containers or highway truck trailers.

pig′gy bank′, **1.** a small bank, having the shape of a pig, provided with a slot to receive small coins. **2.** any small bank in which coins are kept.

pig·head·ed (pig′hed′id), *adj.* stupidly obstinate; stubborn: *pigheaded resistance to progress.* [PIG[1] + -HEADED] —**pig′head′ed·ly,** *adv.* —**pig′head′ed·ness,** *n.*

pig′ in a poke′, something purchased or acquired without a preliminary examination: *The farm was a pig in a poke that proved to be a bad buy.*

pig′ i′ron, **1.** iron tapped from a blast furnace and cast into pigs in preparation for conversion into steel, cast iron, or wrought iron. **2.** iron in the chemical state in which it is when tapped from the blast furnace, without any subsequent alloying or refinement.

Pig′ Lat′in, a form of language often used by children that is derived from ordinary language by moving the first consonant or consonant cluster of each word to the end of the word and adding the sound (ā), as in *Eakspay igpay atinlay* meaning "Speak Pig Latin."

pig′ lead′ (led), lead molded in pigs.

pig·let (pig′lit), *n.* a little pig. [PIG[1] + -LET]

pig·ling (pig′ling), *n.* a young or small pig. [PIG[1] + -LING[1]]

pig·ment (pig′mənt), *n.* **1.** a coloring matter or substance. **2.** a dry insoluble substance, usually pulverized, which when suspended in a liquid vehicle becomes a paint, ink, etc. **3.** *Biol.* any substance whose presence in the tissues or cells of animals or plants colors them. —*v.t.* **4.** to color; add pigment to: *He lightly pigmented the picture with touches of red and gold.* —*v.i.* **5.** to become pigmented; acquire color; develop pigmentation: *a poor quality of paper that doesn't pigment well.* [ME < L *pigment(um)* paint, equiv. to *pig-* (s. of *pingere* to paint) + *-mentum* -MENT]

pig·men·tar·y (pig′mən ter′ē), *adj.* of, pertaining to, having, or producing pigment. [< L *pigmentāri(us).* See PIGMENT, -ARY]

pig·men·ta·tion (pig′mən tā′shən), *n.* **1.** *Biol.* coloration with or deposition of pigment. **2.** coloration, esp. of the skin: *There was a gradual change in pigmentation over several generations.* [< LL *pigmentāt(us)* painted, colored (see PIGMENT, -ATE[1]) + -ION]

Pig·my (pig′mē), *n., pl.* **-mies,** *adj.* Pygmy.

pi·gno·li·a (pēn yō′lē ə), *n.* the edible seed of the cones of a nut pine. [< It *pignol(o)* + *-ia* -IA; cf. L *pīneus* of the pine]

pi·gnon (pēn′yon), *n.* the edible seed of the cones of certain pines, as the nut pine, *Pinus Pinea,* of southern Europe. [< Sp *piñón;* cf. L *pīneus* of the pine]

pig·nus (pig′nəs), *n., pl.* **pig·no·ra** (pig′nər ə). *Roman and Civil Law.* **1.** property held as security for a debt. **2.** the contract containing such a pledge. [< L: lit., pledge]

pig·nut (pig′nut′), *n.* **1.** the nut of the brown hickory, *Carya glabra,* of North America. **2.** the tree itself. **3.** the tuber of a European plant, *Conopodium denudatum.* [PIG[1] + NUT]

pig·pen (pig′pen′), *n.* **1.** a pen for keeping pigs. **2.** a dirty or untidy place: *Her kitchen is a pigpen.* [PIG[1] + PEN[2]]

Pigs (pigz), *n.* **Bay of,** a bay of the Caribbean Sea in SW Cuba: attempted invasion of Cuba by anti-Castro forces April 1961. Spanish, **Bahía de Cochinos.**

pigs′ in blan′kets, *sing.* **pig in a blanket.** **1.** oysters, chicken livers, etc., wrapped in bacon, skewered, and broiled or sautéed. **2.** frankfurters or small sausages wrapped in dough and baked or broiled.

pig·skin (pig′skin′), *n.* **1.** the skin of a pig. **2.** leather made from it. **3.** *Informal.* a saddle. **4.** *Informal.* a football. [PIG[1] + SKIN]

pig·stick (pig′stik′), *v.i.* to hunt for wild boar, usually on horseback and using a spear. [PIG[1] + STICK[1]] —**pig′stick′er,** *n.* —**pig′stick′ing,** *n.*

pig·sty (pig′stī′), *n., pl.* **-sties.** pigpen. [PIG[1] + STY[1]]

pig′sty bul′wark, *Naut.* a bulwark having gaps between the strakes of planking in order to allow water to escape from the decks.

pig·tail (pig′tāl′), *n.* **1.** a braid of hair hanging down the back of the head: *a little girl with blond pigtails.* **2.** tobacco in a thin, twisted roll. **3.** *Elect.* a short, flexible wire used in connecting a stationary terminal with a terminal having a limited range of motion. **4.** a short wire connected to an electric device, as a lead or ground. [PIG[1] + TAIL[1]]

pig′tail hook′, a screw hook having an eye in the form of a spiral for holding a loop, chain link, etc., at any angle.

pig·weed (pig′wēd′), *n.* **1.** any goosefoot of the genus *Chenopodium,* esp. *C. album.* **2.** any of certain amaranths, as *Amaranthus retroflexus.* [PIG[1] + WEED[2]]

pi·ka (pī′kə), *n.* any of several small mammals of the family *Ochotonidae,* closely related to the rabbits, inhabiting alpine regions of the Northern Hemisphere. [< Tungusic *piika*]

pike[1] (pīk), *n., pl.* (*esp. collectively*) **pike,** (*esp. referring to two or more kinds or species*) **pikes.** **1.** any of several large, slender, voracious, fresh-water fishes of the genus

Esox, having a long, flat snout. Cf. **northern pike.** **2.** any of various superficially similar fishes, as the walleye or pikeperch. [ME, short for *pikefish*, so called from its pointed snout. See PIKE[5]] —**pike′like′**, *adj.*

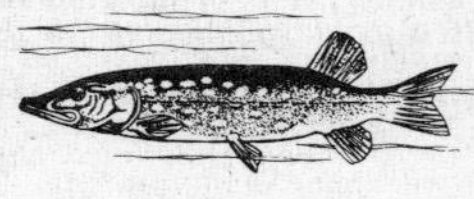

Northern pike, *Esox lucius* (Length to 4½ ft.)

pike[2] (pīk), *n., v.,* **piked, pik·ing.** —*n.* **1.** a shafted weapon having a sharp head, formerly used by the infantry. —*v.t.* **2.** to pierce, wound, or kill with or as with a pike. [< MF *pique*, fem. var. of *pic* pick < Gmc. See PIKE[5], PIQUE]

pike[3] (pīk), *n.* **1.** a toll road or highway; turnpike road. **2.** a turnpike or tollgate. **3.** the toll paid at a tollgate. [short for TURNPIKE]

pike[4] (pīk), *n.* *Chiefly Brit.* a hill or mountain with a pointed summit. [special use of PIKE[5]. Cf. OE *hornpīc* pinnacle]

pike[5] (pīk), *n.* **1.** a sharply pointed projection or spike. **2.** the pointed end of anything, as of an arrow or a spear. [ME *pīk* pick, spike, (pilgrim's) staff, OE *pīc* pointed tool. See PIKE[2]]

pike[6] (pīk), *v.i.,* **piked, pik·ing.** *Slang.* to go quickly. [ME *pyke* (reflexive); perh. orig. to equip oneself with a walking stick. See PIKE[5]]

pike[7] (pīk), *n.* **1.** *Fancy Diving.* a dive in which the diver bends at the waist, keeps his knees straight, and usually touches his toes. **2.** *Tumbling.* a body position resembling this posture. Cf. **layout** (def. 10b), **tuck**[1] (def. 2b). [? special use of PIKE[1]]

Pike (pīk), *n.* **1.** **James Albert,** born 1913, U.S. Protestant Episcopal clergyman, lawyer, and author. **2.** **Zeb·u·lon Montgomery** (zeb′yo͞o lən), 1779–1813, U.S. general and explorer.

pike·blen·ny (pīk′blen′ē), *n., pl.* (*esp. collectively*) **-ny,** (*esp. referring to two or more kinds or species*) **-nies.** any of several tropical American clinid fishes of the genus *Chaenopsis*, as *C. ocellata* (**bluethroat pikeblenny**), the male of which is noted for its aggressive behavior in defending its territory. [PIKE[1] + BLENNY]

piked′ dog′fish, *Brit.* the spiny dogfish.

pike·man (pīk′mən), *n., pl.* **-men.** a soldier armed with a pike. [PIKE[2] + MAN[1]]

pike·perch (pīk′pûrch′), *n., pl.* (*esp. collectively*) **-perch,** (*esp. referring to two or more kinds or species*) **-perch·es.** any of several pikelike fishes of the perch family, esp. the walleye, *Stizostedion vitreum.* [PIKE[1] + PERCH[2]]

pik·er (pī′kər), *n.* *Informal.* **1.** a person who gambles, speculates, etc., in a small, cautious way. **2.** a person who does anything in a contemptibly small or cheap way. [*pike*, var. of PICK[1] + -ER[1]]

Pikes′ Peak′, a mountain in central Colorado: a peak of the Rocky Mountains. 14,108 ft.

pike·staff (pīk′staf′, -stäf′), *n., pl.* **-staves** (-stāvz′). **1.** the shaft of a pike. **2.** a foot traveler's staff with a metal point or spike at the lower end. [ME *pykstaf.* See PIKE[5], STAFF[2]]

Pikes·ville (pīks′vil), *n.* a town in central Maryland, near Baltimore. 18,737 (1960).

Pike·ville (pīk′vil), *n.* a town in E Kentucky. 4754 (1960).

pil., (in prescriptions) pill. [< L *pilula*]

pi·laf (pi läf′, pē′läf), *n.* **1.** rice cooked in a meat or poultry broth. **2.** a Middle Eastern dish consisting of sautéed rice steamed in bouillon, sometimes with poultry, meat, shellfish, etc., and flavored with herbs, spice, or the like. Also, **pi·lau.** [< Turk *pilâv* < Pers *pilāw*]

pi·lar (pī′lər), *adj.* *Anat.* of, pertaining to, or covered with hair. [< NL *pilār(is)* of hair. See PILE[3], -AR[1]]

pi·las·ter (pi las′tər), *n.* *Archit.* a shallow rectangular feature projecting from a wall, having a capital and base and usually imitating the form of a column. [PILE[1] (in obs. sense pillar) + -ASTER, modeled on It *pilastro* or ML *pīlastrum*]

A B

A, Pilasters on Renaissance wall surface; B, Detail of upper end of pilaster

pi·las·tered (pi las′tərd), *adj.* having, or supported by, pilasters. [PILASTER + -ED[3]]

pilas′ter mass′, *Archit.* an engaged pier, usually plain, used as a buttress.

pilas′ter strip′, *Archit.* a pilaster mass of relatively slight projection.

pil·as·trade (pil′ə strād′, pil′ə strād′), *n.* a row of pilasters. [< It *pilastrata.* See PILASTER, -ADE[1]]

Pi·late (pī′lət), *n.* **Pon·tius** (pon′shəs, -tē əs), fl. early 1st century A.D., Roman procurator of Judea A.D. 26–36?, who tried and condemned Jesus Christ.

Pi·la·tus (*Ger.* pē lä′to͝os), *n.* a mountain in central Switzerland, near Lucerne: a peak of the Alps; cable railway. 6998 ft.

pi·lau (pi läf′, pē′läf), *n.* pilaf.

pilch (pilch), *n.* an infant's wrapper worn over a diaper. [ME *pilche* a kind of outer garment, OE *pylece* < ML *pellicea* a furred garment, fem. of L *pelliceus* of skins, hides, deriv. of *pellis* a skin]

pil·chard (pil′chərd), *n.* **1.** a small, southern European, marine fish, *Sardina pilchardus*, related to the herring but smaller and rounder. **2.** any of several related fishes, as *Sardinops caeruleus*, found off the California coast. [earlier *pilcher* < ?]

pil·cher (pil′chər), *n.* *Papermaking.* a pad of three or four felts put on top of a post for pressing. [< PILCH]

Pil·co·ma·yo (pēl′kō mä′yō), *n.* a river in S central South America, flowing SE from S Bolivia along the boundary between Paraguay and Argentina to the Paraguay River at Asunción. 1000 mi. long.

pile[1] (pīl), *n., v.,* **piled, pil·ing.** —*n.* **1.** an assemblage of things laid or lying one upon the other: *a pile of bricks; a pile of lumber.* **2.** *Informal.* a large number, quantity, or amount of anything: *a pile of work.* **3.** a heap of wood on which a dead body, a living person, or a sacrifice is burned. **4.** a lofty or large building or mass of buildings: *the noble pile of Windsor Castle.* **5.** *Informal.* a large accumulation of money: *They made a pile on Wall Street.* **6.** a bundle of pieces of iron ready to be welded and drawn out into bars; fagot. **7.** reactor (def. 4). **8.** *Elect.* See **voltaic pile.** —*v.t.* **9.** to lay or dispose in a pile (often fol. by *up*): *to pile up leaves.* **10.** to accumulate or store (often fol. by *up*): *to pile up money; to pile up food against the winter.* **11.** to cover or load with a pile or piles: *He piled the wagon with hay.* —*v.i.* **12.** to accumulate, as money, debts, evidence, etc. (usually fol. by *up*). **13.** *Informal.* to get somewhere in a more or less disorderly group: *to pile off a train; to pile into the restaurant; to pile out of a car; to pile down from a ledge.* **14.** to gather or rise in a pile or piles (often fol. by *up*): *The snow is piling up on the roofs.* [late ME < MF < L *pīla* pillar, mole of stone]
—**Syn. 1.** collection, heap, mass, accumulation.

pile[2] (pīl), *n., v.,* **piled, pil·ing.** —*n.* **1.** a cylindrical or flat member of wood, steel, concrete, etc., often tapered or pointed at the lower end, hammered vertically into soil to form part of a foundation or retaining wall. **2.** *Heraldry.* an ordinary in the form of a wedge or triangle coming from one edge of the escutcheon, from the chief unless otherwise specified. **3.** *Archery.* the head or striking end of an arrow, usually of metal and of the form of a wedge or cylinder. **4.** **in pile,** *Heraldry.* (of a number of charges) arranged in the manner of a pile. —*v.t.* **5.** to furnish, strengthen, or support with piles. **6.** to drive piles into. [ME; OE *pīl* shaft < L *pīl(um)* javelin]

pile[3] (pīl), *n.* **1.** hair. **2.** soft, fine hair or down. **3.** wool, fur, or pelage. **4.** a fabric with a surface of upright yarns, cut or looped, as corduroy, Turkish toweling, velvet, and velveteen. **5.** such a surface. **6.** one of the strands in such a surface. [late ME < L *pil(us)* hair; *-i-* short in L but long in Anglicized school pronunciation]

pile[4] (pīl), *n.* Usually, **piles.** *Pathol.* **1.** a hemorrhoid. **2.** the condition of having hemorrhoids. [late ME *pyles* (pl.) < L *pilae*, lit., balls. See PILL[1]]

pile[5] (pīl), *n.* the lower of two dies for coining by hand. Cf. **trussell.** [ME *pyl* < ML *pīla*, special use of L *pīla* PILE[1]]

pi·le·ate (pī′lē it, -āt′, pil′ē-), *adj.* *Bot., Zool.* having a pileus. [< L *pileāt(us)* capped. See PILEUS, -ATE[1]]

pi·le·at·ed (pī′lē ā′tid, pil′ē-), *adj.* *Ornith.* crested. [PILEATE + -ED[2]]

pi′leated wood′pecker, a large, black-and-white, American woodpecker, *Pryocopus pileatus*, having a prominent red crest.

Pileated woodpecker (Length 17 to 19½ in.)

piled (pīld), *adj.* having a pile, as velvet and other fabrics. [PILE[3] + -ED[3]]

pile′ driv′er, a machine for driving piles, usually composed of a tall framework in which either a weight is raised and dropped on a pile head or in which a steam hammer drives the pile.

pile′ fend′er. See **fender pile.**

pi·le·ous (pī′lē əs, pil′ē-), *adj.* hairy or furry. [PILE[3] + -OUS]

pi·le·um (pī′lē əm, pil′ē-), *n., pl.* **pi·le·a** (pī′lē ə, pil′ē ə). the top of the head of a bird, from the base of the bill to the nape. [< NL, special use of L *pīleum*, var. of *pīleus* skullcap]

pile·up (pīl′up′), *n.* **1.** an accumulation, as of chores, bills, etc. **2.** a massive collision of several or many moving vehicles. **3.** *Football.* the piling on of defensive players in an attempt to stop the ball-carrier. [n. use of v. phrase *pile up*]

pi·le·us (pī′lē əs, pil′ē-), *n., pl.* **pi·le·i** (pī′lē ī′, pil′ē ī′) for 1, 2, 4, **pi·le·us** for 3. **1.** *Bot.* the horizontal portion of a mushroom, bearing gills, tubes, etc., on its underside; a cap. See diag. under **mushroom.** **2.** *Zool.* the umbrella or bell of a jellyfish. **3.** Also called **cap cloud, scarf cloud.** a small, thin cloud just above or attached to a growing cumulus cloud. **4.** a felt skullcap worn by the ancient Romans and Greeks. [< NL, special use of L *pīleus* skullcap; akin to Gk *pîlos* felt, felt cap]

pile·wort (pīl′wûrt′), *n.* **1.** (in the New World) **a.** the amaranthaceous weed, *Amaranthus cruentus*, native to Asia. **b.** fireweed. **2.** (in the Old World) the lesser celandine, *Ranunculus Ficaria.* [PILE[4] + WORT[1], so called from its use in medicine]

pil·fer (pil′fər), *v.i., v.t.* to steal, esp. in small quantities; practice, or obtain by, petty theft. [v. use of late ME *pilfre* booty < MF *pelfre.* See PELF] —**pil′fer·er,** *n.*

pil·fer·age (pil′fər ij), *n.* **1.** the act or practice of pilfering; petty theft. **2.** that which is pilfered. [PILFER + -AGE]

pil·gar·lic (pil gär′lik), *n.* **1.** a baldheaded man. **2.** a person regarded or thought of with facetious contempt or pity. [earlier *pyllyd garleke*, lit., peeled garlic, orig. metaphor for a bald man, whose head is compared to a peeled garlic bulb. See PILL[2], GARLIC] —**pil·gar′lick·y,** *adj.*

pil·grim (pil′grim, -grəm), *n.* **1.** a person who journeys, esp. a long distance, to some sacred place as an act of devotion. **2.** a traveler or wanderer, esp. in a foreign place. **3.** an original settler in a region. **4.** (*cap.*) one of the Pilgrim Fathers. **5.** a newcomer to a region or place, esp. the western U.S. [early ME *pilegrim, pelegrim;* c. OFris *pilegrim*, MLG *pelegrim*, OHG *piligrim*, Icel *pīlagrīmr*, all < ML *pelegrinus*, dissimilated var. of L *peregrīnus* alien, deriv. of *peregrē* abroad, equiv. to *per-* PER- + *-egr-* (comb. form of *ager* field; see ACRE) + *-e* adv. suffix] —**pil′gri·mat′ic, pil′gri·mat′i·cal,** *adj.*

pil·grim·age (pil′grə mij), *n., v.,* **-aged, -ag·ing.** —*n.* **1.** a journey, esp. a long one, made to some sacred place as an act of devotion: *a pilgrimage to Lourdes.* **2.** any long journey, esp. one undertaken in quest of something for a particular purpose, as to pay homage: *a pilgrimage to the grave of Shakespeare.* —*v.i.* **3.** to make a pilgrimage. [ME *pilegrimage* (see PILGRIM, -AGE); r. earlier *pelrimage*, alter. of OF *pelerinage*]
—**Syn. 2.** excursion, tour. See **trip.**

Pil′grimage to the Is′land of Cythe′ra, A. See **Embarkation for Cythera, The.**

pil′grim bot′tle, a flat-sided water bottle having two loops at the side of a short neck for a suspending cord or chain. Also, **pil′grim's bot′tle.**

Pil′grim Fa′thers, the band of Puritans who founded the colony of Plymouth, Massachusetts in 1620.

Pil′grim's Prog′ress, an allegory (1678) by John Bunyan.

pi·li (pē lē′), *n., pl.* **-lis.** **1.** a Philippine, burseraceous tree, *Canarium ovatum*, the edible seeds of which taste like a sweet almond. **2.** Also called **pili′ nut′.** the seed of this tree. [< Tagalog]

pili-, a learned borrowing from Latin meaning "hair," used in the formation of compound words: *piliform.* [comb. form repr. L *pilus;* see -I-]

pi·lif·er·ous (pī lif′ər əs), *adj.* having or producing hair. [PILI- + -FEROUS]

pil·i·form (pil′ə fôrm′), *adj.* having the form of a hair; resembling hair. [< NL *piliform(is).* See PILI-, -FORM]

pil·ing (pī′ling), *n.* **1.** a mass of building piles considered collectively. **2.** a structure composed of piles. [late ME *pylyng.* See PILE[2], -ING[1]]

pill[1] (pil), *n.* **1.** a small globular or rounded mass of medicinal substance, usually covered with a hard coating, that is to be swallowed whole. **2.** something unpleasant that has to be accepted or endured: *Ingratitude is a bitter pill.* **3.** *Slang.* a tiresomely disagreeable person: *With her endless scruples and prohibitions, Aunt Ella was an old pill.* **4.** *Sports Slang.* a ball, esp. a baseball or golf ball. **5.** **the pill.** See **birth-control pill.** **6.** **pills,** *Brit. Slang.* billiards. —*v.t.* **7.** to dose with pills. **8.** to form or make into pills. **9.** *Slang.* to blackball. —*v.i.* **10.** to form into small, pill-like balls, as the fuzz on a wool sweater. [late ME *pille* < MFlem *pille* < L *pilula*, dim. of *pila* ball; see -ULE]

pill[2] (pil), *v.t., v.i.* **1.** *Brit.* to peel. **2.** *Obs.* to become or cause to become bald. [ME *pil(en)*, OE *pilian* to skin, peel < L *pil(āre)* (to) strip (of hair). See PILE[3]]

pill[3] (pil), *v.t.* *Archaic.* to rob, plunder, or pillage. [ME; metaphorical use of PILL[2]]

pil·lage (pil′ij), *v.,* **-laged, -lag·ing,** *n.* —*v.t.* **1.** to strip of money or goods by open violence, as in war; plunder. **2.** to take as booty. —*v.i.* **3.** to rob with open violence; take booty: *Soldiers roamed the countryside, pillaging and killing.* —*n.* **4.** act of plundering, esp. in war. **5.** booty or spoil. [ME *pilage* (see PILL[3], -AGE), modeled on MF *pillage*, deriv. of *piller* < LL *pīliāre to take] —**pil′lag·er,** *n.*
—**Syn. 1.** rob, sack, spoil, despoil, rape. **4.** rapine, depredation, spoliation. **5.** plunder.

pil·lar (pil′ər), *n.* **1.** an upright shaft or structure, of stone, brick, or other material, relatively slender in proportion to its height, and of any shape in section, used as a building support, or standing alone, as for a monument: *Gothic pillars; a pillar to commemorate Columbus.* **2.** a natural formation resembling such a construction: *a pillar of basaltic rock; a pillar of smoke.* **3.** any upright, supporting part; a post: *the pillar of a table.* **4.** *Horol.* any of several short parts for spacing and keeping in the proper relative positions two plates holding the bearings of a watch or clock movement. **5.** *Mining.* an isolated mass of mineral in a subterranean mine, usually serving as a roof support in early operations and later removed, wholly or in part. **6.** a person who is a chief supporter of a state, institution, etc.: *a pillar of the community.* **7.** *Mach.* mast[1] (def. 2). **8.** **from pillar to post, a.** aimlessly from place to place. **b.** uneasily from one situation or predicament to another: *After abandoning a promising legal career, he went from pillar to post.* —*v.t.* **9.** to provide or support with pillars. [ME *pillare* < ML *pīlāre* (see PILE[1], -AR[2]); r. earlier *piler* < OF < ML, as above] —**pil′lared,** *adj.* —**pil′lar·like′,** *adj.*
—**Syn. 1.** pilaster, pier. See **column.**

pil·lar-and-breast (pil′ər ən brest′), *adj.* room-and-pillar.

pil′lar box′, *Brit.* a pillarlike box in which letters are deposited for collection by mailmen; mailbox. Also called **pil′lar post′.**

pil·lar·et (pil′ə ret′), *n.* a small pillar. [PILLAR + -ET]

Pil′lars of Her′cules, the two promontories on either side of the eastern end of the Strait of Gibraltar: the Rock of Gibraltar in Europe and the Jebel Musa in Africa; fabled to have been raised by Hercules. Also called **Hercules' Pillars.**

Pil′lars of the Faith′, *Islam.* the duties and religious observances of a Muslim; Din: Ibadat. Also called **Pil′lars of Is′lam.**

pill·box (pil′boks′), *n.* **1.** a box, usually shallow and often round, for holding pills. **2.** a small, low structure of reinforced concrete, enclosing machine guns, and employed as a minor fortress in warfare. **3.** a short, round, brimless hat with straight sides and a flat top, worn esp. by women. [PILL[2] + BOX[1]]

pill′ bug′, any of various small terrestrial isopods, esp. of the genus *Armadillo*, which can roll themselves up into a pill-shaped ball.

pil·lion (pil′yən), *n.* **1.** a pad or cushion attached behind a saddle, esp. as a seat for a woman. **2.** a pad, cushion, saddle, or the like, used as a passenger seat on a bicycle, motor scooter, etc. **3.** a passenger's saddle or seat behind the driver's seat on a motorcycle. [< Gael *pillean* cushion, pad, kind of saddle, dim. of *peall* skin, rug < L *pellis* skin]

pil·li·winks (pil′ə wingks′), *n.* (*construed as sing. or pl.*) an old instrument of torture similar to the thumbscrew. [Scot var. of late ME *pyrwykes, pyrewinkes*]

pil·lo·ry (pil′ə rē), *n., pl.* **-ries,** *v.,* **-ried, -ry·ing.** —*n.* **1.** a wooden framework erected on a post, with holes for securing the head and hands, formerly used to expose an offender to public derision. —*v.t.* **2.** to set in the pillory. **3.** to expose to public ridicule or abuse: *The candidate mercilessly pilloried his opponent.* [ME *pyllory* < OF *pilori;* akin to Pr *espitlori* pillory]

Pillory

pil·low (pil′ō), *n.* **1.** a bag or case made of cloth, which is filled with feathers, down, or other soft ma-

terial, and is used to cushion the head during sleep or rest. 2. anything used to cushion the head; a headrest: *a pillow of moss.* 3. Also called **lace pillow.** a hard cushion or pad that supports the pattern and threads in the making of bobbin lace. 4. a supporting piece or part, as the block on which the inner end of a bowsprit rests. —*v.t.* 5. to rest on or as on a pillow. 6. to support with pillows. 7. to serve as a pillow for: *She stood below the falling child to pillow it with her body.* —*v.i.* 8. to rest as on a pillow. [ME *pilwe,* OE *pylu* < L *pulvinus* cushion, whence also G *Pfühl*] —**pil′low·less,** *adj.* —**pil′low·like′,** *adj.*
—**Syn. 1.** See **cushion.**

pil′low block′, *Mach.* a cast-iron or steel block for supporting a journal or bearing.

pil·low·case (pil′ō kās′), *n.* a removable case, usually of white cotton or linen, drawn over a pillow. Also called **pil·low·slip** (pil′ō slip′). [PILLOW + CASE[2]]

pil′low lace′. See **bobbin lace.**

pil′low sham′, an ornamental cover laid over a bed pillow.

pil′low sword′, a sword of the 17th century, having a straight blade and a straight cross guard.

pil·low·y (pil′ō ē), *adj.* pillowlike; soft; yielding: *a pillowy carpet.* [PILLOW + -Y[1]]

pilo-, a learned borrowing from Greek used, with the meaning "felt," in the formation of compound words: *pilocarpine.* [comb. form repr. Gk *pîlos* wool or hair made into felt]

pi·lo·car·pi·dine (pī′lə kär′pi dēn′, -din, pil′ə-), *n. Pharm.* a syrupy liquid, $C_{10}H_{14}N_2O_2$, obtained from jaborandi, having properties similar to those of pilocarpine. [< NL *Pilocarp(us)* name of genus of shrubs which includes jaborandi (see PILO-, -CARP) + -ID[3] + -INE[2]]

pi·lo·car·pine (pī′lə kär′pēn, -pin, pil′ō-), *n. Pharm.* an oil or crystalline alkaloid, $C_{11}H_{16}N_2O_2$, obtained from jaborandi: used in the form of its hydrochloride or nitrate chiefly to produce sweating, promote the flow of saliva, contract the pupil of the eye, and for glaucoma. [< NL *Pilocarp(us)* (see PILO-, -CARP) + -INE[1]]

pi·lo·ni·dal (pī′lə nīd′əl), *adj. Pathol.* noting or pertaining to a growth of hair in a dermoid cyst or in the deeper layers of the skin. [< NL; see PILI-, -O-, NIDUS, -AL[1]]

Pi·los (pē′lôs), *n.* Greek name of **Navarino.**

pi·lose (pī′lōs), *adj.* covered with hair, esp. soft hair; furry. Also, **pilous.** [< L *pilōs(us)* shaggy. See PILE[3], -OSE[1]] —**pi·los·i·ty** (pī los′i tē), *n.*

pi·lot (pī′lət), *n.* 1. a person duly qualified to steer ships into or out of a harbor or through certain difficult waters. 2. the steersman of a ship. 3. *Aeron.* a person duly qualified to operate an airplane, balloon, or other aircraft. 4. a guide or leader: *the pilot of the expedition.* 5. See **coast pilot.** 6. *Mach.* **a.** a smaller element acting in advance of another or principal element, and causing the latter to come into play when desired: *the pilot on a gas stove.* **b.** a guide for centering or otherwise positioning two adjacent parts, often consisting of a projection on one part fitting into a recess in the other. 7. *Railroads.* cowcatcher (def. 1). 8. *Television.* See **pilot film.** —*v.t.* 9. to steer. 10. to guide or conduct, as through unknown places, intricate affairs, etc. 11. to act as pilot on, in, or over. —*adj.* 12. serving as an experimental or trial undertaking prior to full-scale operation or use: *a pilot project.* [earlier *pylotte* < MF *pillotte* < It *pilota,* dissimilated var. of *pedota* < MGk **pēdṓtēs* steersman, equiv. to *pēd(á)* rudder (pl. of *pēdón* oar) + *-ōtēs* agent suffix] —**pi′lot·less,** *adj.*
—**Syn. 2.** helmsman. **11.** maneuver, manage.

pi·lot·age (pī′lə tij), *n.* 1. act, occupation, or skill of piloting. 2. the fee paid to a pilot for his services. 3. See **pilot station** (def. 1). 4. the process of directing the movement of a ship or aircraft by optical or electronic observations of recognizable landmarks. [< F; see PILOT, -AGE]

pi′lot balloon′, a balloon for the visual observation of upper-atmosphere wind currents. Also called **trial balloon.**

pi′lot bis′cuit, hardtack.

pi′lot boat′, a boat carrying pilots to or from large ships.

pi′lot burn′er. See **pilot light** (def. 1).

pi′lot chart′, 1. any of a number of charts issued to mariners by the U.S. Hydrographic Office and showing meteorological, hydrographic, and navigational conditions prevailing, or likely to prevail, subsequent to the date of issue in some part of the world: issued monthly for most areas. 2. a chart giving information on air conditions at various altitudes.

pi′lot en′gine, a locomotive sent on ahead of a railroad train to see that the way is clear and the track is safe.

pi′lot film′, a film serving as an example of a contemplated series of television shows, intended to attract sponsors.

pi·lot·fish (pī′lət fish′), *n., pl.* (*esp. collectively*) **-fish,** (*esp. referring to two or more kinds or species*) **-fish·es.** 1. a small, marine fish, *Naucrates ductor,* often found around sharks. 2. any of various other fishes having similar habits. [PILOT + FISH]

pi′lot flag′, *Naut.* 1. the flag symbolizing the letter "G" in the International Code of Signals, flown by itself to request a pilot from a pilot service: a flag of three yellow and three blue vertical stripes. 2. Also called **pi′lot jack′.** a union or ensign, sometimes surrounded with a white border and flown at the fore truck to indicate that a pilot is wanted.

pi·lot·house (pī′lət hous′), *n., pl.* **-hous·es** (-hou′ziz). *Naut.* an enclosed structure or space from which a vessel may be navigated. [PILOT + HOUSE]

pi·lo·ti (pi lot′ē), *n.* a column of iron, steel, or reinforced concrete supporting a building above an open ground level. [< F *piloti(s),* equiv. to *pilot* (aug. of *pile* PILE[1]) + *-is,* collective suffix]

pi·lot·ing (pī′lə ting), *n.* the determination of the course or position of a ship or airplane by any of various navigational methods or devices. [PILOT + -ING[1]]

pi′lot lad′der, *Naut.* See **Jacob's ladder** (def. 2a).

pi′lot lamp′, an electric lamp, used in association with a control, which by means of position or color indicates the functioning of the control; an indicator light or a control light.

pi′lotless air′craft, 1. an aircraft equipped for operation by radio or by robot control, without a human pilot aboard; drone. 2. *Obs.* a rocket or guided missile, esp. an air-breather. [PILOT + -LESS]

pi′lot light′, 1. Also called **pilot burner.** a small flame kept burning continuously, as in a gas stove, to relight any main gas burners whenever necessary or desired. 2. See **pilot lamp.**

pi′lot plant′, an experimental factory in which processes or techniques planned for use in full-scale manufacturing are tested in advance.

pi′lot raise′, *Mining.* a small raise intended to be enlarged later.

pi′lot sig′nal, *Naut.* 1. a signal, as a flag or light, used to request a pilot. 2. a signal to indicate that a pilot is on board.

pi′lot skiff′, an open fishing boat used off the coast of the Carolinas.

pi′lot sta′tion, *Naut.* 1. Also called **pilotage.** an onshore office or headquarters for pilots. 2. an area in which pilot boats cruise.

pi′lot tun′nel, a narrow or low tunnel intended to be enlarged into a broader or taller one.

pi′lot wa′ters, *Naut.* 1. waters in which the services of a pilot are required by law or are necessary because of navigational hazards. 2. waters in which the services of a pilot are available.

pi·lot·weed (pī′lət wēd′), *n.* the compass plant, *Silphium laciniatum.* [PILOT + WEED[1]]

pi′lot whale′. See **black whale.**

pi·lous (pī′ləs), *adj.* pilose. [< L *pilōs(us).* See PILOSE, -OUS]

pil·pul (pil′po͝ol), *n.* subtle or keen disputation among rabbinical scholars regarding the interpretation of Talmudic rules and principles as applied chiefly to religious and moral questions. [< Aram, Heb *pilpūl,* akin to *pilpēl* to search, debate] —**pil′pul·ist,** *n.* —**pil′pul·is′tic,** *adj.*

Pil·sen (pil′zən), *n.* a city in Bohemia, in W Czechoslovakia. 141,736 (1963). Czech, **Plzeň.**

Pil·sner (pilz′nər, pils′-), *n.* (*sometimes l.c.*) 1. a pale, light lager beer. 2. any lager beer of high quality. 3. Also called **pil′sner glass′.** a tall glass that is tapered at the bottom, used esp. for beer. Also, **Pil·sen·er** (pil′zə nər, -sə-, pilz′nər, pils′-). [< G: lit., of PILSEN; see -ER[1]]

Pil·sud·ski (pil so͞ot′skē), *n.* **Jó·zef** (yo͞o′zef), 1867–1935, Polish marshal and statesman: president 1918–22; premier 1926–28, 1930.

Pilt′down man′, a hypothetical early modern man whose existence, inferred from skull fragments found at Piltdown, England, in 1912, has now been completely discredited upon proof that the fragments were assembled as a hoax.

pil·u·lar (pil′yə lər), *adj.* of, pertaining to, or resembling pills. [< L *pilul(a)* PILULE + -AR[1]]

pil·ule (pil′yo͞ol), *n.* a small pill. [< L *pilula.* See PILE[4], -ULE]

pi·lum (pī′ləm), *n., pl.* **-la** (-lə). a javelin used in ancient Rome by legionaries, consisting of a three-foot-long shaft with an iron head of the same length. [< L: dart, javelin]

Pi·lum·nus (pi lum′nəs), *n.* one of two ancient Roman fertility gods protective of marriages and esp. of women in childbirth. Cf. **Picumnus.**

pi·lus (pī′ləs), *n., pl.* **-li** (-lī). *Bot., Zool.* a hair or hairlike structure. [< L]

pil·y (pī′lē), *adj. Heraldry.* (of the field of an escutcheon, or an ordinary) divided into a number of piles: *pily of seven, or and gules.* [PILE[2] + -Y[1]]

Pi·ma (pē′mə), *n., pl.* **-mas,** (*esp. collectively*) **-ma** for 1. 1. a member of an Indian people of southern Arizona and northern Mexico. 2. the Uto-Aztecan language of the Pima Indians. —**Pi′man,** *adj.*

Pi′ma cot′ton, a variety of Egyptian cotton developed in the southwestern U.S., used chiefly in the manufacture of shirts, ties, etc. Also called **Pima.**

pim·e·li·tis (pim′ə lī′tis, pī′mə-), *n. Pathol.* 1. inflammation of adipose tissue. 2. inflammation of connective tissue. [< Gk *pimel(ḗ)* fat + -ITIS]

pi·men·to (pi men′tō), *n., pl.* **-tos.** 1. the dried fruits of a tropical American, myrtaceous tree, *Pimenta officinalis;* allspice. 2. the tree itself. 3. the pimiento. 4. Also called **Chinese vermilion, Harrison red, signal red.** a vivid red color. [alter. of Sp *pimiento* pepper plant, masc. of *pimienta* pepper fruit < LL *pigmenta* spiced drink, spice, pepper, pl. (taken as sing.) of L *pigmentum* PIGMENT]

pimen′to cheese′, a processed cheese made from Neufchâtel, cream cheese, Cheddar, or other cheese, combined with pimientos. Also, **pimien′to cheese′.**

pi′ me′son, *Physics.* a meson having a mass from approximately 264 to approximately 273 times that of an electron with positive, negative, or zero charge and spin of zero. Also called **pion.**

pi·mien·to (pi myen′tō), *n., pl.* **-tos.** a garden pepper, used as a vegetable, a relish, etc. [see PIMENTO]

pim·o·la (pi mō′lə), *n.* an olive stuffed with red sweet pepper; stuffed olive. [PIM(IENTO) + OL(IVE) + *-a*]

pimp (pimp), *n.* 1. a man who solicits customers for a prostitute or a brothel, usually in return for a share of the proceeds; pander; procurer. 2. a despicable person. 3. *Australian.* an informer; stool pigeon. —*v.i.* 4. to act as a pimp. [?]

pim·per·nel (pim′pər nel′, -nəl), *n.* a primulaceous herb of the genus *Anagallis,* esp. *A. arvensis* (**scarlet pimpernel**), having scarlet, purplish, or white flowers that close at the approach of bad weather. [late ME *pympernele* < MF *pimprenelle,* nasalized var. of OF *piprenelle* < LL **piperīnella,* equiv. to *piper* PEPPER + *-īn-* -INE[1] + *-ella* dim. suffix; r. OE *pipeneale* < LL *pipinella,* syncopated var. of **piperīnella*]

pimp·ing (pim′ping), *adj.* 1. petty; insignificant; trivial. 2. *Dial.* weak; sickly. [?]

pim·ple (pim′pəl), *n. Pathol.* a small, usually inflammatory swelling or elevation of the skin; a papule or pustule. [late ME *pinple,* nasalized var. of OE **pypel* (whence *pyplian* to break out in pimples) < L *papula* pimple]

pim′ple cop′per, *Metall.* a form of copper matte about 80 percent pure, somewhat less refined than blister copper. Also called **pim′ple met′al.**

pim·ply (pim′plē), **-pli·er, -pli·est.** having many pimples. Also, **pim·pled** (pim′pəld). [PIMPLE + -Y[1]]

pin (pin), *n., v.,* **pinned, pin·ning.** —*n.* 1. a small, slender, often pointed piece of wood, metal, etc., used to fasten, support, or attach things. 2. a short, slender piece of wire with a point at one end and a head at the other, for fastening things together. 3. any of various forms of fasteners or ornaments consisting essentially or partly of a pointed or penetrating wire or shaft (often used in combination): *a jeweled pin; a tiepin.* 4. a badge having a pointed bar or pin attached, by which it is fastened to the clothing: *a lodge pin; a fraternity pin.* 5. a short metal rod, as a linchpin, driven through the holes of adjacent parts, as a hub and an axle, to keep them together. 6. a short cylindrical rod or tube, as a wristpin or crankpin, joining two parts so as to permit them to move in one plane relative to each other. 7. a short axle, as one on which a pulley rotates in a block. 8. the part of a cylindrical key stem entering a lock. 9. a clothespin. 10. a hairpin. 11. See **rolling pin.** 12. a peg, nail, or stud marking the center of a target. 13. *Bowling.* one of the rounded wooden clubs set up as the target in tenpins, ninepins, duckpins, etc. 14. *Golf.* the flag staff which identifies a hole. 15. *Informal.* a leg. 16. *Music.* peg (def. 5). 17. *Wrestling.* a fall. 18. *Naut.* **a.** an axle for a sheave of a block. **b.** See **belaying pin.** 19. *Carpentry.* a tenon in a dovetail joint; dovetail. 20. a very small amount; a trifle: *Such advice isn't worth a pin.* 21. *Chess.* the immobilization of an enemy piece by attacking with one's queen, rook, or bishop. —*v.t.* 22. to fasten or attach with or as with a pin or pins: *to pin cloth together.* 23. to hold fast in a spot or position: *The debris pinned him down.* 24. to transfix with a pin or the like: *to pin a flower as a botanical specimen.* 25. to give one's fraternity pin to (a girl) as a pledge of one's fondness or attachment (usually used in passive constructions): *She was pinned by the class president.* 26. *Chess.* to immobilize (an enemy piece) by placing one's queen, rook, or bishop in a position to check the exposed king or capture a valuable piece if the pinned piece were moved. 27. *Slang.* to seize or nab: *He was pinned by the cops for the holdup.* 28. *Wrestling.* to secure a fall over one's opponent. 29. **pin down, a.** to bind or hold to a course of action, a promise, etc. **b.** to force (someone) to deal with a situation or to come to a decision: *We tried to pin him down for a definite answer, but he was too wily for us.* 30. **pin in,** to fill (gaps in a rubble wall, etc.) with spalls. 31. **pin something on someone,** *Slang.* to ascribe the blame for something to a person; make an accusation on the basis of evidence: *He is suspected of having been an accomplice in the slaying, but they can't pin it on him.* 32. **pin up,** to make (a piece of masonry) level or plumb with wedges. [ME *pinne,* OE *pinn* peg; c. D *pin,* G *Pinne,* Icel *pinni;* ? akin to MIr *benn* (for **bend*), now *beann* peak, steeple, gable, etc.]
—**Syn. 1.** bolt, peg. **3.** brooch.

pi·ña (pē′nyä; *Eng.* pēn′yə), *n., pl.* **pi·ñas** (pē′nyäs; *Eng.* pēn′yəz). *Spanish.* 1. pineapple. 2. (esp. in Latin America) a pineapple drink.

pi·na·ceous (pī nā′shəs), *adj.* belonging to the *Pinaceae,* or pine family of trees and shrubs, comprising the pine, spruce, fir, etc. [< NL *Pīnāce(ae)* (see PINE[1], -ACEAE) + -OUS]

pi′ña cloth′, a fine, sheer fabric of pineapple-leaf fiber, used esp. for lingerie.

pin·a·coid (pin′ə koid′), *n. Crystall.* a form whose faces are parallel to two of the axes. [< Gk *pinak-* (s. of *pínax*) slab, board + -OID] —**pin′a·coi′dal,** *adj.*

pin·a·fore (pin′ə fōr′, -fôr′), *n.* 1. a child's apron, usually one large enough to cover most of the dress. 2. a woman's sleeveless dress derived from it, low-necked, tying or buttoning in back, and usually worn over a blouse, sweater, or the like. 3. *Chiefly Brit.* **a.** a large apron worn by adults. **b.** a sleeveless smock. [PIN + AFORE]

Pin·a·fore (pin′ə fōr′, -fôr′), *n.* See **H. M. S. Pinafore.**

pi·nang (pi nang′), *n.* the betel palm or its nut. [< Malay]

pi·nard (pē NAR′; *Eng.* pē när′), *n., pl.* **-nards** (-NAR′; *Eng.* -närz′). *French. Informal.* wine.

Pi·nar del Rí·o (pē när′ del rē′ô), a city in W Cuba. 38,885 (1953).

pi·nas·ter (pī nas′tər, pi-), *n.* a pine, *Pinus Pinaster,* of southern Europe, having the cones arranged around the branches in radiating clusters. [< L: wild pine. See PINE, -ASTER[1]]

pi·ña·ta (pēn yä′tə, pin yä′-; *Sp.* pē nyä′tä), *n.* (in Mexico and Central America) a gaily decorated crock or papier-mâché figure filled with toys, candy, etc., and suspended from above, esp. during Christmas festivities, so that children, who are blindfolded, may break it or knock it down with sticks and release the contents. [< Sp: lit., pot]

pin·ball (pin′bôl′), *n.* any of various games played on a sloping board, the object usually being either to shoot a ball, driven by a spring, up a side passage and cause it to roll back down against pins or bumpers and through channels which electrically record the score, or to shoot a ball into pockets at the back of the board. [PIN + BALL[1]]

pin′ball machine′, the machine on which pinball is played.

pin′ boy′, a person, usually a boy, stationed in the sunken area of a bowling alley behind the pins who places the pins in the proper positions, removes pins that have been knocked down, and returns balls to the bowlers. Also called **pinsetter.**

pince-nez (pans′nā′, pins′-; *Fr.* PANS nā′), *n., pl.* **pince-nez** (pans′nāz′, pins′-; *Fr.* PANS nā′). a pair of eyeglasses held on the face by a spring that pinches the nose. [< F: lit., pinch-nose]

pin·cers (pin′sərz), *n.* (*usually construed as pl.*) 1. a gripping tool consisting of two pivoted limbs forming a pair of jaws and a pair of handles (usually used with *pair of*). 2. *Zool.* a grasping organ or pair of organs resembling this. [ME *pinsers,* earlier *pynceours,* pl. of **pinceour* < AF *pince(r)* (to) PINCH + *-our* -OR[2]]

pin′cers move′ment, a military maneuver in which both flanks of an enemy force are attacked with the aim of attaining complete encirclement.

pinch (pinch), *v.t.* 1. to compress between the finger and thumb, the teeth, the jaws of an instrument, or the like. 2. to compress, constrict, or squeeze painfully, as a tight shoe does. **3.** to cramp within narrow bounds or quarters: *The crowd pinched him into a corner.* **4.** to render (the face, body, etc.) unnaturally thin and drawn, as pain or distress does: *Years of hardship had pinched her countenance beyond recognition.* **5.** *Hort.* to remove or shorten (buds or shoots) in order to produce a certain shape, improve the quality of the bloom or fruit, or increase the development of buds (often fol. by *out, off,* or *back*). **6.** to affect with sharp discomfort or distress, as cold, hunger, or need does. **7.** to straiten in means or circumstances: *The depression pinched them.* **8.** to stint (a person, family, etc.) in allowance of money, food, or the like: *They were severely pinched by the drought.* **9.** to hamper or inconvenience by lack of something specified: *The builders were pinched by the shortage of good lumber.* **10.** *Informal.* to stint the supply or amount of (a thing): *Foodstuffs were pinched by wartime shortages.* **11.** to put a pinch or small quantity of (a powder, spice, etc.) into something. **12.** *Slang.* to steal. **13.** *Informal.* to arrest. **14.** to roll or slide (a heavy object) with leverage from a pinch bar. **15.** *Naut.* to sail (a vessel) so close to the wind that her sails shake slightly and her speed is reduced. **16.** *Horse Racing, Brit.* to press (a horse) to the point of exhaustion. —*v.i.* **17.** to exert a sharp or painful compressing force: *This shoe pinches.* **18.** to cause sharp discomfort or distress: *Their stomachs pinched with hunger.* **19.** to economize unduly; stint oneself: *They pinched and scraped for years to save money.* **20.** *Mining.* (of a vein of ore or the like) **a.** to diminish. **b.** to diminish to nothing (sometimes fol. by *out*). **21.** *Naut.* to trim a sail too flat when sailing to windward. **22. pinch pennies,** to stint on or be frugal with expenditures; economize: *They didn't pinch pennies on the new opera house. I'll have to pinch pennies if I'm going to get through school.* —*n.* **23.** act of pinching; nip; squeeze. **24.** as much of anything as can be taken up between the finger and thumb: *a pinch of salt.* **25.** a very small quantity of anything: *a pinch of pungent wit.* **26.** sharp or painful stress, as of hunger, need, or any trying circumstances: *the pinch of conscience; the pinch of wartime shortages; to feel the pinch of poverty.* **27.** a situation or time of special stress; an emergency: *A friend is someone who will stand by you in a pinch.* **28.** See **pinch bar. 29.** *Slang.* a raid or an arrest. **30.** *Slang.* a theft. [ME *pinch(en)* < AF **pincher* (equiv. to OF *pincier,* Sp *pinchar*) < LL **pīnctiāre,* b. **piccāre* to prick and *punctiāre* to prick] —**pinch′a·ble,** *adj.*

pinch′ bar′, a kind of crowbar or lever with a projection that serves as a fulcrum. Also called **ripping bar, wrecking bar.**

pinch·beck (pinch′bek′), *n.* **1.** an alloy of copper and zinc, used in imitation of gold. **2.** something sham or counterfeit. —*adj.* **3.** made of pinchbeck. **4.** sham or counterfeit: *pinchbeck heroism.* [named after Christopher *Pinchbeck* (d. 1732), English watchmaker and its inventor]

pinch·bot·tle (pinch′bot′əl), *n.* a bottle with concave sides, as for containing liquor. [PINCH + BOTTLE[1]]

pinch·cock (pinch′kok′), *n.* a clamp for compressing a flexible pipe, as a rubber tube, in order to regulate or stop the flow of a fluid. [PINCH + COCK[1]]

pin·check (pin′chek′), *n.* **1.** a very small check woven into fabric, much used in the manufacture of men's and women's suits. **2.** a strong cotton cloth having a vertical and horizontal design of white dots on a blue ground, used in the manufacture of work clothes. —*adj.* **3.** of or pertaining to a fabric having a pincheck design. [PIN + CHECK]

pinch′ effect′, *Physics.* the tendency of an electric conductor or stream of charged particles to constrict, caused by the action of a magnetic field which is produced by a flow of electricity.

pinch·er (pin′chər), *n.* **1.** one who or that which pinches. **2. pinchers,** pincers. [late ME *pynchar* niggard. See PINCH, -ER[2]]

pin′ cher′ry, **1.** a wild, often shrubby cherry, *Prunus pensylvanica,* having white flowers. **2.** the red, acid fruit of this tree.

pinch′ hit′, *Baseball.* a hit made by a pinch hitter.

pinch-hit (pinch′hit′), *v.i.,* **-hit, -hit·ting.** *Baseball.* **1.** to serve as a pinch hitter. **2.** to substitute for someone. —*v.t.* **3.** to get, or make (a hit) in pinch-hitting. [back formation from PINCH HITTER]

pinch′ hit′ter, **1.** *Baseball.* a substitute who bats for a teammate, often at some critical moment of the game. **2.** any substitute for another, esp. in an emergency.

Pin·chot (pin′shō), *n.* **Gifford,** 1863–1946, U.S. political leader, forester, and teacher.

pinch·pen·ny (pinch′pen′ē), *n., pl.* **-nies,** *adj.* —*n.* **1.** a miser or niggard. —*adj.* **2.** stingy; miserly; niggardly. [ME; see PINCH, PENNY]

pinch′ pleat′, a narrow pleat that is usually part of a series at the top of curtains.

pinch′ roll′er, a flexible device that presses magnetic tape against the capstan in a tape recorder.

pinch′ run′ner, *Baseball.* a player sent into a game to replace a base runner. —**pinch′ run′ning.**

Pinck·ney (piŋk′nē), *n.* **Charles Cotes·worth** (kōts′wûrth), 1746–1825, and his brother **Thomas,** 1750–1828, American patriots and statesmen.

Pinck′ney's Trea′ty, an agreement in 1795 between Spain and the U.S. by which Spain recognized the 31st parallel as the southern boundary of the U.S. and permitted free navigation of the Mississippi to American ships.

Pinck·ney·ville (piŋk′nē vil′), *n.* a town in SW Illinois. 3085 (1960).

pin′ curl′, a dampened curl that is kept in place by a clip or hairpin.

pin-curl (pin′kûrl′), *v.t.* to curl (the hair) by using a clip or hairpin. [v. use of PIN CURL]

pin·cush·ion (pin′ko͝osh′ən), *n.* a small cushion into which pins are stuck until needed. [PIN + CUSHION]

pin′cushion distor′tion, *Optics.* a distortion produced by a lens in which the magnification increases toward the edge of the field. Cf. **barrel distortion.**

pin·cush·ion-flow·er (pin′ko͝osh′ən flou′ər), *n.* See **sea urchin** (def. 2).

pin·dan (pin′dən, -dan), *n. Australian.* **1.** semi-arid country; scrubland. **2.** the scrubs, grasses, and small trees covering scrublands. [< native Austral]

Pin·dar (pin′dər), *n.* 522?–443? B.C., Greek poet.

Pin·dar·ic (pin dar′ik), *adj.* **1.** of, pertaining to, or in the style of Pindar. **2.** of elaborate or regular metrical structure, as an ode or verse. —*n.* **3.** See **Pindaric ode.** [< L *Pindaric(us)* < Gk *Pindarikós.* See PINDAR, -IC] —**Pin·dar′i·cal·ly,** *adv.*

Pindar′ic ode′, *Pros.* an ode consisting of several units, each of which is composed of a strophe and an antistrophe of identical form followed by a contrasting epode. Also called **regular ode.**

pind·ling (pind′liŋ), *adj. Dial.* puny; sickly. [PINE[2] + -LING, modeled on *dwindling*]

pin′do palm′ (pin′dō), a feather palm, *Butia capitata,* of Brazil, having long, arching leaves, grayish beneath, and small, egg-shaped fruit. [*pindo* < AmerSp < Guarani]

Pin·dus (pin′dəs), *n.* a mountain range in central Greece: highest peak, 7665 ft.

pine[1] (pīn), *n.* **1.** any evergreen, coniferous tree of the genus *Pinus,* having long, needle-shaped leaves, certain species of which yield timber, turpentine, tar, pitch, etc. **2.** any of various similar coniferous trees. **3.** the wood of the pine tree. **4.** *Informal.* the pineapple. [ME; OE *pīn* < L *pīn(us)*] —**pine′like′,** *adj.*

pine[2] (pīn), *v.,* **pined, pin·ing,** *n.* —*v.i.* **1.** to yearn deeply; suffer with longing; long painfully (often fol. by *for*): *to pine for one's home and family.* **2.** to fail gradually in health or vitality from grief, regret, or longing (often fol. by *away*): *Abandoned by her lover, she pined away.* **3.** *Archaic.* to be discontented; fret. —*v.t.* **4.** *Archaic.* to suffer grief or regret over. —*n.* **5.** *Archaic.* painful longing. [ME; OE *pīn(ian)* (to) torture, deriv. of *pīn* torture < LL *pēna,* var. of L *poena* punishment. See PAIN]
—**Syn. 2.** dwindle, decline, languish, droop, waste.

pin·e·al (pin′ē əl), *adj.* **1.** resembling a pine cone in shape. **2.** of or pertaining to the pineal body. [< medical L *pīneāl(is),* equiv. to L *pīne(a)* pine cone, n. use of fem. of *pīneus* of a pine tree (*pīn(us)* PINE[1] + *-eus* -EOUS) + *-ālis* -AL[1]]

pin′eal appara′tus, **1.** a median outgrowth of the roof of the diencephalon in vertebrates which in some develops into the pineal eye and in others into the pineal body. **2.** See **parietal eye.**

pin′eal bod′y, a body of unknown function present in the brain of all vertebrates having a cranium, believed to be a vestigial sense organ. Also called **pin′eal gland′.** See diag. under **brain.**

Pineapple, *Ananas comosus*

pin′eal eye′, an eyelike structure that develops from the pineal apparatus in certain cold-blooded vertebrates.

pine·ap·ple (pīn′ap′əl), *n.* **1.** the edible, juicy, collective fruit of a tropical, bromeliaceous plant, *Ananas comosus,* which develops from a spike or head of flowers and is surmounted by a crown of leaves. **2.** the plant itself, having a short stem and rigid, spiny-margined, recurved leaves. **3.** *Mil. Slang.* a fragmentation hand grenade. [ME *pinappel* pine cone. See PINE[1], APPLE]

pine′apple cac′tus, devil's-pincushion.

pine′apple cup′, a large German standing cup having a body formed like a pineapple or cluster of pineapples.

pine′ bar′ren, *Southern U.S.* a tract of sandy or peaty soil in which pine trees are the principal growth.

Pine′ Bluff′, a city in central Arkansas, on the Arkansas River. 44,037 (1960).

Pine′ Bluff′ Southeast′, a town in central Arkansas. 2679 (1960).

pine′ cone′, the cone or strobile of a pine tree.

pine·drops (pīn′drops′), *n., pl.* **-drops.** **1.** a slender, leafless, North American, ericaceous herb, *Pterospora andromedea,* having nodding white flowers, found growing under pines. **2.** beechdrops. [PINE[1] + DROP + -S[3]]

pine′ finch′. See **pine siskin.**

pine′ gros′beak, a large grosbeak, *Pinicola enucleator,* of coniferous forests of northern North America and Eurasia, the male of which has rose and gray plumage. Also called **pine′ bull′finch.**

Pine′ Hill′, a town in SW New Jersey. 3939 (1960).

Pine·hurst (pīn′hûrst), *n.* a town in NW Washington. 3989 (1960).

Pi·nel (pē nel′), *n.* **Phil·ippe** (fē lēp′), 1745–1826, French physician: reformer in the treatment and care of the mentally ill.

Pine′ Lawn′, a town in E Missouri. 5943 (1960).

pine′ mar′ten, **1.** a marten, *Martes martes,* of Europe and western Asia. **2.** Also called **American marten.** a marten, *Martes americana,* found in forests of the U.S. and Canada.

pi·nene (pī′nēn), *n. Chem.* a liquid terpene, $C_{10}H_{16}$, the principle constituent of oil of turpentine, found in other essential oils: used chiefly in the manufacture of camphor. [PINE[1] + -ENE]

pine′ nee′dle, the needlelike leaf of a pine tree.

pine′ nut′, **1.** the seed of any of several pine trees, eaten roasted or salted or used in making candy, pastry, etc., after removing the hard seed coat. **2.** See **pine cone.**

Pi·ne·ro (pə nēr′ō, -ner′ō), *n.* **Sir Arthur Wing,** 1855–1934, English playwright and actor.

pin·er·y (pī′nə rē), *n., pl.* **-er·ies.** **1.** a place in which pineapples are grown. **2.** a forest or grove of pine trees. [PINE[1] + -ERY]

Pines (pīnz), *n.* **Isle of,** an island in the Caribbean, south of and belonging to Cuba. 1182 sq. mi.

pine·sap (pīn′sap′), *n.* either of two parasitic or saprophytic herbs of the genus *Monotropa,* esp. the tawny or reddish *M. Hypopithys* **(false beechdrops),** of eastern North America. Cf. **Indian pipe.** [PINE[1] + SAP[1]]

pine′ sis′kin, a small, North American finch, *Spinus pinus,* found in coniferous forests, having yellow markings on the wings and tail. Also called **pine finch.**

pine′ snake′, a bullsnake, *Pituophis melanoleucus,* often found in pine forests of the eastern U.S.

pine′ tar′, a very viscid, blackish-brown liquid having an odor resembling that of turpentine, obtained by the destructive distillation of pine wood, used in medicine locally, for skin infections and internally, as an expectorant.

Pine′ Tree′ State′, Maine (used as a nickname).

pi·ne·tum (pī nē′təm), *n., pl.* **-ta** (-tə). an arboretum of pines and coniferous trees. [< L: a pine wood, equiv. to *pīn(us)* PINE[1] + *-ētum* collective suffix of place]

Pine·ville (pīn′vil), *n.* **1.** a town in central Louisiana. 8636 (1960). **2.** a town in SE Kentucky. 3181 (1960).

pine′ war′bler, a warbler, *Dendroica pinus,* found principally in pine forests of the southeastern U.S.

pin·e·y (pī′nē), *adj.,* **pin·i·er, pin·i·est.** piny.

pin·feath·er (pin′feth′ər), *n. Ornith.* **1.** an undeveloped feather, before the web portions have expanded. **2.** a feather just coming through the skin. [PIN + FEATHER]

pin·fire (pin′fīər′), *adj.* **1.** of or pertaining to a cartridge fitted with a pin which, when struck by the hammer of the firearm, causes the cartridge to explode. **2.** of or pertaining to a firearm that uses such a cartridge. [PIN + FIRE]

pin·fish (pin′fish′), *n., pl.* **-fish·es,** (*esp. collectively*) **-fish.** a small fish, *Lagodon rhomboides,* of the porgy family, found in the bays of the South Atlantic and Gulf coasts of the U.S. [PIN + FISH]

pin·fold (pin′fōld′), *n.* **1.** a pound for stray animals. **2.** a fold, as for sheep or cattle. **3.** a place of confinement or restraint. —*v.t.* **4.** to confine in or as in a pinfold. [late ME *pynfold* for **pindfold,* OE *pynd(an)* (to) impound (deriv. of *pund* POUND[3]) + *f(e)ald* FOLD[2]; r. ME *po(u)n(d)fold(e),* late OE *pundfald*]

ping (piŋ), *v.i.* **1.** to produce a sharp sound like that of a bullet striking a hard object, as a sheet of metal. —*n.* **2.** a pinging sound: *His car has a soft ping in the motor.* [imit.]

pinge (pinj), *v.i.,* **pinged, ping·ing.** *Scot. and North Eng.* peenge.

Ping-Pong (piŋ′poŋ′), *n. Trademark.* See **table tennis.**

Ping·ré (piŋ′rā), *n.* a crater in the third quadrant of the face of the moon: about 12 miles in diameter.

pin·guid (piŋ′gwid), *adj.* fat; oily; greasy. [< L *pingu(is)* fat (c. Gk *pīōn*) + -ID[4]] —**pin·guid′i·ty,** *n.*

pin·head (pin′hed′), *n.* **1.** the head of a pin. **2.** something very small or insignificant. **3.** *Slang.* a stupid person. [PIN + HEAD]

pin·hole (pin′hōl′), *n.* a small hole made by or as by a pin: *The print was marred by pinholes.* [PIN + HOLE]

pin·ion[1] (pin′yən), *n. Mach.* **1.** a gear with a small number of teeth, esp. one engaging with a rack or larger gear. **2.** a shaft or spindle cut with teeth engaging with a gear. **3.** *Metalworking.* a gear driving a roll in a rolling mill. [< F *pignon* cogwheel, gable, MF also battlement, wing < LL **pinniōn-* (s. of **pinniō*), deriv. of L *pinna* battlement, pinnacle, wing, fin; see -ION] —**pin′ion·less,** *adj.* —**pin′ion·like′,** *adj.*

pin·ion[2] (pin′yən), *n.* **1.** the distal or terminal segment of the wing of a bird consisting of the carpus, metacarpus, and phalanges. See diag. under **rack**[1]. **2.** the wing of a bird. **3.** a feather. **4.** the flight feathers collectively. —*v.t.* **5.** to cut off the pinion of (a wing) or bind (the wings), as in order to prevent a bird from flying. **6.** to disable or restrain (a bird) in such a manner. **7.** to bind (a person's arms or hands) so as to deprive him of the use of them. **8.** to disable (someone) in such a manner; shackle. **9.** to bind or hold fast, as to a thing: *to be pinioned to one's bad habits.* [late ME *pynyon* < MF *pignon* wing, pinion, a now obs. sense of *pignon* PINION[1]]

pin·ite (pin′īt, pī′nīt), *n.* a micalike mineral, essentially a hydrous silicate of aluminum and potassium. [< G *Pinit,* named after *Pini,* mine in Germany; see -ITE[1]]

pi·ni·tol (pi′ni tōl′, -tôl′, -tol′, pin′i-), *n. Chem.* a white, crystalline, inositol derivative, $C_6H_6(OH)_5OCH_3$, obtained from the resin of the sugar pine. [obs. *pinite* pinitol (< F; see PINE[1], -ITE[1]) + -OL[1]]

pink[1] (piŋk), *n.* **1.** a color varying from light crimson to pale reddish purple. **2.** any of several caryophyllaceous plants of the genus *Dianthus,* as the clove pink or carnation. **3.** the flower of such a plant; a carnation. **4.** the highest type or example of excellence: *She is the pink of graciousness.* **5.** the highest form or degree: *in the pink of condition.* **6.** (*often cap.*) *U.S. Slang.* a person with left-wing, but not extreme, political opinions. **7. pinks,** *Fox Hunting.* See **pink coat. 8.** the scarlet color of this coat. —*adj.* **9.** of the color pink: *pink marble.* **10.** *U.S. Slang.* holding, or regarded as holding, mildly leftist views, esp. in politics. [?] —**pink′ness,** *n.*

pink[2] (piŋk), *v.t.* **1.** to pierce with a rapier or the like; stab. **2.** to finish at the edge with a scalloped, notched, or other ornamental pattern. **3.** to punch (cloth, leather, etc.) with small holes or figures for ornament. **4.** *Chiefly Brit. Dial.* to adorn or ornament, esp. with scalloped edges or a punched-out pattern. [ME *pynke(n)* (to) prick, deriv. of OE *pinca* point, itself deriv. of *pinn* PIN]

pink[3] (piŋk), *n.* **1.** Also, **pinky.** a kind of vessel with a narrow stern. **2.** pinky[1] (def. 1). [late ME *pynk* < MD *pinke* fishing boat]

pink′ boll′worm, the larva of a gelechiid moth, *Pectinophora gossypiella,* that feeds on the seeds of the bolls of cotton and was introduced into cotton-growing regions of the world from Asia. Also called **bollworm.**

pink′ cal′la lil′y. See **red calla lily.**

pink′ coat′, *Fox Hunting.* the coat, usually scarlet, of the hunt uniform worn by the staff and by male members of the hunt. Also called **pinks.**

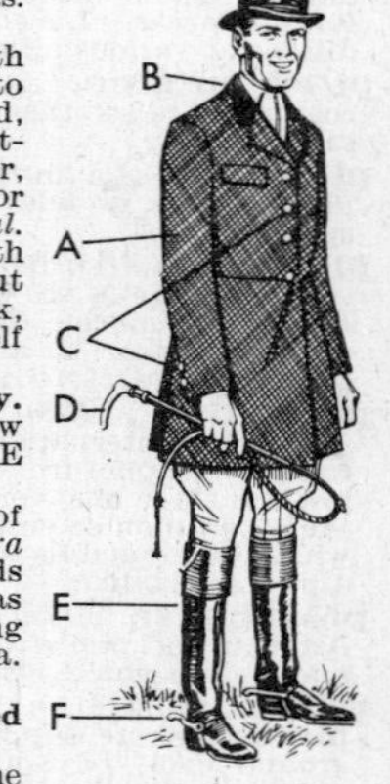

A, Pink coat; B, Hunt collar; C, Hunt buttons; D, Whip; E, Hunt boot; F, Spur

pink′ coryd′alis, an herb, *Corydalis sempervirens,* of North America, having weak, pale, bluish-green foliage and branched clusters of pink, yellow-tipped flowers. Also called **pale corydalis.**

pink′ disease′, *Pathol.* acrodynia.

Pink·er·ton (ping′kər tən), *n.* **Allan,** 1819–84, U.S. detective, born in Scotland.

pink·ey (ping′kē), *n., pl.* **-eys.** *Naut.* pinky[1].

pink·eye (pingk′ī′), *n.* *Pathol.* a contagious, epidemic form of acute conjunctivitis occurring in man and certain animals: so called from the color of the inflamed eye. [PINK[1] + EYE]

Pin·kiang (*Chin.* bin′gyäng′), *n.* Harbin.

pink·ie[1] (ping′kē), *n.* *Naut.* pinky[1] (def. 1).

pink·ie[2] (ping′kē), *n.* *Informal.* the little finger. Also, **pinky.** [< D *pinkje,* dim. of *pink* little finger]

pink·ie[3] (ping′kē), *n.* *Australian Informal.* inferior or cheap wine, esp. red wine. [PINK[1] + -IE]

pink′ing i′ron, a tool for perforating, or for notching or scalloping the edge of fabric, leather, etc.

pink′ing shears′, shears having notched blades, for cutting and simultaneously pinking fabric or for finishing garments with a notched, nonfraying edge.

pink·ish (ping′kish), *adj.* somewhat pink: *The sky at sunset has a pinkish glow.* [PINK[1] + -ISH[1]]

pink′ la′dy, a cocktail made with gin, grenadine, and the white of eggs, shaken and strained before serving.

pink′ lo′cust. See **rose acacia.**

pink·o (ping′kō), *n., pl.* **-os, -oes.** *U.S. Slang.* a person who holds leftist political views. [PINK[1] + *-o* associative suffix]

pink′ rhododen′dron, a rhododendron, *Rhododendron macrophyllum,* of the western coast of the U.S.: the State flower of Washington. Also called **California rosebay.**

pink′ root′, *Plant Pathol.* a disease of onions and other plants, characterized by pink, withered roots, caused by a fungus, *Pyrenochaeta terrestris.*

pink·root (pingk′ro͞ot′, -ro͝ot′), *n.* **1.** the root of any of various loganiaceous plants of the genus *Spigelia,* esp. that of *S. marilandica* of the U.S., which is used as a vermifuge. **2.** any of these plants. [PINK[1] + ROOT[1]]

pink′ slip′, a notice of dismissal from one's job.

Pink·ster (pingk′stər), *n.* *U.S. Dial.* Whitsuntide. Also, **Pinkster.** [< D: Easter << Gk (by alter.) *pentēkostē* PENTECOST]

pink′ster flow′er. See **pinxter flower.**

pink′ tea′, *Informal.* a formal tea or reception.

pink′ vine′. See **coral vine.**

pink·y[1] (ping′kē), *n., pl.* **pink·ies. 1.** Also called **pink.** a pink-sterned schooner, built mainly at Essex, Massachusetts, having two masts with a bald-headed fore-and-aft rig and a short bowsprit with one headsail. **2.** pink[3] (def. 1). Also, **pinkey, pinkie.** [< D *pinkje,* dim. of *pink* PINK[3]]

pink·y[2] (ping′kē), *n., pl.* **pink·ies.** pinkie[2].

pin′-lev·er escape′ment (pin′lev′ər, -lē′vər). See **pin-pallet escapement** (def. 1).

pin′ mark′, the circular indentation on the upper part of a type body, made by the pin which ejects the type from the caster. See diag. under **type.**

pin′ mon′ey, 1. any small sum set aside for nonessential minor expenditures. **2.** an allowance of money given by a husband to his wife for her personal expenditures. —**pin′-mon′ey,** *adj.*

pin·na (pin′ə), *n., pl.* **pin·nae** (pin′ē), **pin·nas. 1.** *Bot.* one of the primary divisions of a pinnate leaf. **2.** *Zool.* **a.** a feather, wing, or winglike part. **b.** a fin or flipper. **3.** *Anat.* auricle (def. 1a). [< L: feather, wing, fin] —**pin′nal,** *adj.*

pin·nace (pin′is), *n.* **1.** a light sailing vessel, esp. one formerly used in attendance on a larger vessel. **2.** any of various kinds of ship's boats. **3.** a small 17th-century ship having two or three masts and a flat stern, used in northern Europe as a warship and merchant ship and as a tender. [< MF *pinace* < It *pinaccia,* lit., something made of *pino* PINE[1]]

pin·na·cle (pin′ə kəl), *n., v.,* **-cled, -cling.** —*n.* **1.** a lofty peak. **2.** the highest or culminating point, as of success, power, fame, etc.: *to reach the pinnacle of one's profession.* **3.** any pointed, towering part or formation, as of rock. **4.** *Archit.* a relatively small, upright structure, commonly terminating in a gable, a pyramid, or a cone, rising above the roof or coping of a building, or capping a tower, buttress, or other projecting architectural member. —*v.t.* **5.** to place on or as on a pinnacle. **6.** to form a pinnacle on; crown. [ME *pinacle* < MF < LL *pinnācul(um),* dim. of *pinna* battlement, pinnacle; see -CULE]
—**Syn. 2.** apex, acme, summit, zenith. **3.** needle. —**Ant. 2.** base.

pin·nate (pin′āt, -it), *adj.* **1.** resembling a feather, as in construction or arrangement; having parts arranged on each side of a common axis: *a pinnate branch; pinnate trees.* **2.** *Bot.* (of a leaf) having leaflets or primary divisions arranged on each side of a common petiole. Also, **pin′nat·ed.** [< L *pinnāt(us)* feathered, winged. See PINNA, -ATE[1]] —**pin′nate·ly, pin′nat·ed·ly,** *adv.*

Pinnate leaf

pinnati-, a combining form of **pinnate:** *pinnatipartite.* [repr. L *pinnātus;* see -I-]

pin·nat·i·fid (pi nat′ə fid), *adj.* *Bot.* (of a leaf) pinnately cleft, with clefts reaching halfway or more to the midrib. [< NL *pinnātifid(us).* See PINNATI-, -FID]

pin·nat·i·lo·bate (pi nat′ᵊlō′bāt), *adj.* *Bot.* (of a leaf) pinnately lobed, with the divisions extending less than halfway to the midrib. Also, **pin·nat·i·lobed** (pi-nat′ᵊlōbd′). [PINNATI- + LOBATE]

pin·na·tion (pi nā′shən), *n.* *Bot.* pinnate condition or formation. [PINNATE + -ION]

pin·nat·i·par·tite (pi nat′ə pär′tīt), *adj.* *Bot.* (of a leaf) parted in a pinnate manner. [PINNATI- + PARTITE]

pin·nat·i·ped (pi nat′ə ped′), *adj.* *Ornith.* having lobate feet. [< NL *pinnātiped-* (s. of *pinnātipes*). See PINNATI-, -PED]

pin·nat·i·sect (pi nat′i sekt′), *adj.* *Bot.* (of a leaf) divided in a pinnate manner. [PINNATI- + -SECT]

pin·ner (pin′ər), *n.* **1.** one who or that which pins. **2.** a headdress with a long hanging flap pinned on at each side. **3.** a small apron fastened on by pins, as that worn by a parlormaid. [PIN + -ER[1]]

pin·ni·grade (pin′ə grād′), *adj.* **1.** moving by means of finlike parts or flippers, as the seals and walruses. —*n.* **2.** a pinnigrade animal. [< NL *pinnigrad(us).* See PINNA, -I-, -GRADE]

pin·ni·ped (pin′ə ped′), *adj.* **1.** belonging to the *Pinnipedia,* a suborder of carnivores with limbs adapted to an aquatic life, including the seals and walruses. —*n.* **2.** a pinniped animal. [< NL *pinniped-* (s. of *pinnipēs*). See PINNA, -I-, -PED] —**pin·ni·pe·di·an** (pin′ə pē′dē ən), *adj., n.*

pin·nu·la (pin′yə lə), *n., pl.* **-lae** (-lē′). **1.** a pinnule. **2.** a barb of a feather. [< L, dim. of *pinna* PINNA; see -ULE]

pin·nu·late (pin′yə lāt′), *adj.* having pinnules. Also, **pin′nu·lat′ed.** [PINNULE + -ATE[1]]

pin·nule (pin′yo͞ol), *n.* **1.** *Zool.* **a.** a part or organ resembling a barb of a feather, a fin, or the like. **b.** a finlet. **2.** *Bot.* a secondary pinna, one of the pinnately disposed divisions of a bipinnate leaf. **3.** a metal plate with a small hole in it, used as a sight in a quadrant. [see PINNULA] —**pin·nu·lar** (pin′yə lər), *adj.*

pin′ oak′, an oak, *Quercus palustris,* characterized by the pyramidal manner of growth of its branches and deeply pinnatifid leaves.

Pi·no·chet U·gar·te (pē′nô chet′ o͞o gär′te), **Au·gus·to** (ou go͞os′tô), born 1915, Chilean army general and political leader: president since 1973.

pi·noch·le (pē′nuk əl, -nok-), *n.* **1.** a card game played by two, three, or four persons, with a 48-card deck. **2.** a meld of the queen of spades and the jack of diamonds in this game. Also, **penuchle, penuckle, pi′noc·le.** [?]

pi′nochle rum′my, *Cards.* See **five hundred rummy.**

pi·no·le (pi nō′lē; *Sp.* pē nô′le), *n.* corn or wheat, dried, ground, and sweetened, usually with the flour of mesquite beans. [< AmerSp < Nahuatl *pinolli*]

Pi·nole (pə nōl′), *n.* a town in W California. 14,253.

pi·ñon (pin′yən, pēn′yōn; *Sp.* pē nyôn′), *n., pl.* **pi·ñons,** *Sp.* **pi·ño·nes** (pē nyô′nes). **1.** any of various pines, esp. of the southern Rocky Mountain region, bearing large edible seeds. **2.** the seed. [< Sp, deriv. of *piña* pine cone]

Pi·not (pē nō′), *n.* **1.** any of several varieties of purple or white vinifera grapes yielding a red or white wine. **2.** a red (**Pinot noir**) or white (**Pinot blanc**) wine made from this grape.

Pi·not blanc (pē′nō bläN′, pē nō′; *Fr.* pē nō bläN′). See under **Pinot** (def. 2).

Pi·not noir (pē′nō nwär′, pē nō′; *Fr.* pē nō NWAR′). See under **Pinot** (def. 2).

pin′-pal·let escape′ment (pin′pal′it), *Horol.* **1.** Also called **pin-lever escapement.** a lever escapement employing perpendicular steel pins as pallets rather than jewels. **2.** See **Brocot escapement.**

pin′ plate′, *Building Trades.* a bearing plate having a projection for fixing into masonry.

pin·point (pin′point′), *n.* **1.** the point of a pin. **2.** a trifle; pinhead. —*v.t.* **3.** to locate or describe exactly: *to pinpoint the problem.* —*adj.* **4.** exact; precise: *pinpoint workmanship.* [PIN + POINT]

pin·prick (pin′prik′), *n.* **1.** any minute puncture made by or as by a pin. **2.** a petty annoyance.

pin′ rail′, 1. *Theat.* a rail on a fly gallery, wall, etc., holding two rows of pins or cleats for securing lines attached to scenery. **2.** *Naut.* a strong rail at the side of the deck of a vessel, for holding the pins to which some of the running rigging is belayed. Cf. **fife rail.**

pins′ and nee′dles, 1. a tingly, prickly sensation in a limb that is recovering from numbness. **2. on pins and needles,** in a state of nervousness or anxiety, esp. in anticipation of something: *The father-to-be was on pins and needles.*

pin′ seal′, leather made of the skin of young seals.

pin·set·ter (pin′set′ər), *n.* **1.** a mechanical apparatus in a bowling alley that places all of the pins into position at one time and removes pins that have been knocked down. **2.** See **pin boy.** [PIN + SETTER]

Pinsk (pinsk; *Russ.* pēnsk), *n.* a city in SW Byelorussia, in the W Soviet Union in Europe: formerly in Poland. 39,000 (1959).

pin′ spot′, *Theat.* **1.** a spotlight that produces a narrow beam of light illuminating a very small part of a stage, esp. used to focus attention on a detail. **2.** the beam of light so produced.

pin-spot (pin′spot′), *v.t.,* **-spot·ted, -spot·ting.** *Theat.* to illuminate with a pin spot. [v. use of PIN SPOT]

pin·spot·ter (pin′spot′ər), *n.* pinsetter.

pin′ stripe′, 1. a very thin stripe, often used in fabrics. **2.** a pattern of such stripes. **3.** a fabric or garment having such stripes.

pint (pīnt), *n.* a liquid and also dry measure of capacity, equal to one half of a liquid and dry quart respectively. *Abbr.:* pt, pt. [ME *pynte* < MFlem: lit., plug; c. OFris, MLG *pint* penis. See PINTLE]

pin·ta (pin′tə; *Sp.* pēn′tä), *n.* *Pathol.* a nonvenereal treponematosis occurring chiefly in Central and South America, characterized by spots of various colors on the skin. [< AmerSp, special use of Sp *pinta* spot < VL **pincta,* fem. of **pinctus,* nasalized var. of L *pictus,* ptp. of *pingere* to paint]

Pin·ta (pin′tə; *Sp.* pēn′tä), *n.* one of the three ships under charge of Columbus when he made his first voyage to America in 1492.

pin·ta·do (pin tä′dō), *n., pl.* **-dos, -does.** the cero, *Scomberomorus regalis.* Also, **pin·ta·da** (pin tä′də). [< Pg, ptp. of *pintar* to paint < VL **pinctus* painted]

pin·tail (pin′tāl′), *n., pl.* **-tails,** (*esp. collectively*) **-tail. 1.** a long-necked river duck, *Anas acuta,* of the Old and New Worlds, having long narrow middle tail feathers. **2.** See **ruddy duck. 3.** See **sharp-tailed grouse. 4.** See **pin-tailed sand grouse.** [PIN + TAIL[1]]

pin-tailed (pin′tāld′), *adj.* *Ornith.* **1.** having a tapered tail with long, pointed central feathers. **2.** having the feathers of the tail stiff, narrow, and pointed.

pin′-tailed sand′ grouse′, an Old World sand grouse, *Pterocles alchata,* having long, narrow, middle tail feathers.

pin·ta·no (pin tä′nō), *n., pl.* **-nos.** See **Sergeant major** (def. 3). [< AmerSp]

Pin·ter (pin′tər), *n.* **Harold,** born 1930, English playwright.

pin′ the tail′ on the don′key, a children's party game in which a blindfolded player, holding a paper tail, is turned around a number of times before a large picture of a tailless donkey which he then attempts to locate with the object of pinning the tail in place.

pin·tle (pin′tᵊl), *n.* **1.** a pin or bolt, esp. one on which something turns, as the gudgeon of a hinge. **2.** a pin, bolt, or hook by which a gun or the like is attached to the rear of a towing vehicle. **3.** a cast iron or steel base for a wooden post, often cast in a single piece with a cap for a lower post. [ME, OE *pintel* penis; c. O-Dan *pintel;* see PINT]

Pintle

pin′tle boss′, *Naut.* See **rudder snug.**

pin·to (pin′tō, pēn′-), *adj., n., pl.* **-tos.** —*adj.* **1.** piebald; mottled; spotted: *a pinto horse.* —*n.* **2.** *Western U.S.* a pinto horse. **3.** See **pinto bean.** [< AmerSp (obs. Sp) < VL **pinctus* painted; see PINTA]

pin′to bean′, *Western U.S.* a variety of the common bean, *Phaseolus vulgaris,* having mottled or spotted seeds.

Pintsch′ gas′ (pinch), gas with high illuminating power made from shale oil or petroleum, used in floating buoys, lighthouses, and railroad cars. [named after Richard *Pintsch* (1840–1919), German inventor]

pint-size (pīnt′sīz′), *adj.* *Informal.* **1.** comparatively small in size: *a pint-size typewriter; a pint-size individual.* **2.** smaller than standard: *a pint-size fullback.* Also, **pint′-sized′.**

pin·up (pin′up′), *Informal.* —*n.* **1.** a picture that is suitable for pinning up on a wall, usually of an attractive and often voluptuous girl. **2.** a girl in such a picture. **3.** a device or fixture that is fastened to a wall, as a lamp. —*adj.* **4.** of, pertaining to, or appearing in a pinup: *a pinup girl.* **5.** designed or suitable for hanging or fastening on a wall: *a pinup lamp.* Also, **pin′-up′.** [n., adj. use of *pin up*]

pin·weed (pin′wēd′), *n.* any cistaceous plant of the genus *Lechea,* having slender stems and narrow leaves. [PIN + WEED[1]]

pin·wheel (pin′hwēl′, -wēl′), *n.* **1.** a child's toy consisting of a wheel or spokes of paper or plastic loosely attached by a pin to a stick, designed to revolve when blown by or as by the wind. **2.** Also called **catherine wheel.** a kind of firework supported on a pin which, when ignited, revolves rapidly and gives a dazzling display of light. **3.** a wheel having pins at right angles to its rim for engaging the teeth of a gear. Also, **pin′ wheel′.** [PIN + WHEEL]

pin′wheel escape′ment, a clock escapement in which two pallets, usually of unequal length, alternately engage and release pins set on the escape wheel perpendicular to its plane of rotation.

pin·wheel·ing (pin′hwē′ling, -wē′-), *n.* *U.S. Naut.* the act of turning a multiple-screw vessel within a minimum radius by having some engines going forward and others going in reverse. [PINWHEEL + -ING[1]]

pin·work (pin′wûrk′), *n.* (in the embroidery of needlepoint lace) crescent-shaped stitches raised from the surface of the design. [PIN + WORK]

pin·worm (pin′wûrm′), *n.* a small nematode worm, *Enterobius vermicularis,* infesting the intestine and migrating to the rectum and anus, esp. in children. [PIN + WORM]

pin′ wrench′, a wrench having a pin for insertion into the heads of certain bolts to drive them. Cf. **spanner** (def. 2).

pinx., pinxit.

pinx·it (pingk′sit), *v.* *Latin.* he painted (it); she painted (it): formerly used on paintings as part of the artist's signature.

Pinx·ter (pingk′stər), *n.* Pinkster.

pinx′ter flow′er, a wild azalea, *Rhododendron nudiflorum* **(Azalea nudiflora),** of the U.S., having pink or purplish flowers. Also, **pinkster flower.** Also called **wild honeysuckle.**

pin·y (pī′nē), *adj.,* **pin·i·er, pin·i·est. 1.** abounding in or covered with pine trees: *piny hillsides.* **2.** consisting of pine trees: *piny woodland areas.* **3.** pertaining to or suggestive of pine trees: *a piny fragrance.* Also, **piney.** [PINE[1] + -Y[1]]

Pin·yin (pin′yin′), *n.* the official system for transliterating Chinese into the Roman alphabet, adopted by the People's Republic of China in 1979. Also called **Pin′yin′ sys′tem.** [< Chin *pinyin* lit., phonetic sound]

pin′yon jay′ (pin′yən, pēn′yōn), a grayish-blue, uncrested jay, *Gymnorhinus cyanocephalus,* found in mountainous parts of the western U.S. [*pinyon* < AmerSp *piñón* PIGNON]

Pin·za (pin′zə; *It.* pēn′tsä), *n.* **E·zi·o** (et′sē ō′, ā′zē ō′; *It.* e′tsyô), 1895–1957, Italian basso, in the U.S.

Pin·zón (pēn thōn′), *n.* **Mar·tín A·lon·zo** (mär tēn′ ä lôn′thō), c1440–93?, and his brother **Vi·cen·te Yá·ñez** (bē then′te yä′nyeth), c1460–1524?, Spanish navigators with Christopher Columbus.

PIO, *U.S. Mil.* **1.** public information office. **2.** public information officer.

pi·on (pī′on), *n.* *Physics.* See **pi meson.** [by shortening]

pi·o·neer (pī′ə nēr′), *n.* **1.** one of those who first enter or settle a region, thus opening it for occupation and development by others. **2.** one of those who are first or earliest in any field of inquiry, enterprise, or progress: *pioneers in cancer research.* **3.** one of a body of foot soldiers detailed to make roads, dig intrenchments, etc., in advance of the main body. **4.** *Ecol.* a plant or animal which successfully invades and becomes established in a bare area. **5.** (*cap.*) *U.S.* one of a series of unmanned lunar probes launched by a Delta booster. **6.** (*cap.*) a member of a Communist organization in the Soviet Union for children ranging in age from 10 to 16. Cf. **Komsomol, Octobrist.** —*v.i.* **7.** to act as a pioneer. —*v.t.* **8.** to be the first to open or prepare (a way, settlement, etc.). **9.** to take part in the beginnings of; initiate: *to pioneer public education in underdeveloped countries.* **10.** to lead the way for (a group); guide. —*adj.* **11.** being the earliest, original, first of a particular kind, etc.: *to conduct pioneer research in cystic fibrosis; a pioneer method of adult education.* **12.** of, pertaining to, or characteristic of a pioneer or pioneers: *a pioneer settlement; the swiftness of pioneer justice.* **13.** being a pioneer: *a pioneer fur trader.* [< MF *pionier,* OF *peonier* foot soldier. See PEON, -EER]

Pioneers, The, a historical novel (1823) by James Fenimore Cooper. Cf. **Leather-Stocking Tales.**

pi·os·i·ty (pī os′i tē), *n.* an excessive or obvious show of piousness; sanctimoniousness. [PIOUS + -ITY; modeled on *religious, religiosity*]

pi·ous (pī′əs), *adj.* **1.** having or showing a dutiful spirit of reverence for God, or an earnest wish to fulfill religious obligations. **2.** practiced or used in the name of real or pretended religious motives, or for some ostensibly good object: *a pious deception.* **3.** characterized by a hypocritical concern with virtue; sanctimonious. **4.** sacred rather than secular: *pious literature.* **5.** *Archaic.* having or showing due respect or regard for parents or others. [< L *pius,* akin to *piāre* to propitiate] —**pi′ous·ly,** *adv.* —**pi′ous·ness,** *n.*
—**Syn. 1.** devout, godly, reverent. See **religious.**

Pi·oz·zi (pē ot′sē; *It.* pyôt′tsē), *n.* **Hester Lynch.** See **Thrale, Hester Lynch.**

pip[1] (pip), *n.* **1.** one of the spots on dice, playing cards, or dominoes. **2.** each of the small segments into which the surface of a pineapple is divided. **3.** *Slang.* metal insigne of rank on the shoulders of commissioned officers. **4.** *Hort.* **a.** an individual rootstock of a plant, esp. of the lily of the valley. **b.** a portion of the rootstock or root of several other plants, as the peony. [earlier *peep* < ?]

pip[2] (pip), *n.* **1.** *Vet. Pathol.* a contagious disease of birds, esp. poultry, characterized by the secretion of a thick mucus in the mouth and throat. **2.** *Facetious.* any minor or unspecified ailment in a person. [ME *pippe* < MD < VL **pipita* for L *pītuīta* phlegm, pip]

pip[3] (pip), *n.* **1.** a small seed, esp. of a fleshy fruit, as an apple or orange. **2.** *Slang.* someone or something wonderful: *Last night's party was a pip.* [short for PIPPIN]

pip[4] (pip), *v.,* **pipped, pip·ping.** —*v.i.* **1.** to peep or chirp. —*v.t.* **2.** (of a young bird) to crack or chip a hole through (the shell). [var. of PEEP[2]]

pip[5] (pip), *n.* *Electronics.* an image, usually a spot of light, on a radarscope, produced by a radar wave reflected by an object, indicating the presence of the object. [imit.]

pip[6] (pip), *v.t.,* **pipped, pip·ping.** *Brit. Slang.* **1.** to blackball. **2.** to defeat (an opponent). **3.** to shoot, esp. to wound or kill by a gunshot. [? special use of PIP[1], in metamorphical sense of a small ball]

Pip (pip), *n.* a boy's given name, form of **Philip.**

pip·age (pī′pij), *n.* **1.** conveyance, as of water, gas, or oil, by means of pipes. **2.** the pipes so used. **3.** the sum charged for the conveyance. [PIPE[1] + -AGE]

pi·pal (pī′pəl), *n.* a fig tree, *Ficus religiosa,* of India, somewhat resembling the banian. Also, **peepul.** [< Hindi *pīpal* < Skt *pippala*]

pipe[1] (pīp), *n., v.,* **piped, pip·ing.** —*n.* **1.** a hollow cylinder of metal, wood, or other material, used for the conveyance of water, gas, steam, petroleum, etc. **2.** any of various tubular or cylindrical objects, parts, or formations, as an eruptive passage of a volcano or geyser. **3.** a tube of wood, clay, hard rubber, or other material, with a small bowl at one end, used for smoking tobacco, opium, etc. **4.** a quantity, as of tobacco, that fills the bowl. **5.** *Music.* **a.** a tube used as, or to form an essential part of, a musical wind instrument. **b.** a musical wind instrument consisting of a single tube of straw, reed, wood, or other material, as a flute, clarinet, or oboe. **c.** one of the wooden or metal tubes from which the tones of an organ are produced. **d.** a small end-blown flute played with one hand while the other beats a small drum. **6.** *Naut.* **a.** the sound of a boatswain's pipe. **b.** See **boatswain's pipe. 7.** the call or utterance of a bird, frog, etc. **8. pipes, a.** *Music.* any woodwind instrument. **b.** the human vocal cords or the voice, esp. as used in singing. **9.** Usually, **pipes. a.** *Music.* bagpipe. **b.** a set of flutes, as Panpipes. **c.** *Informal.* a tubular organ or passage of a human or animal body, esp. a respiratory passage: *to complain of congested pipes.* **10.** *Mining.* **a.** a cylindrical vein or body of ore. **b.** (in South Africa) a vertical, cylindrical matrix, of eruptive origin, in which diamonds are found. **11.** *Metall.* a depression occurring at the center of the head of an ingot as a result of the tendency of solidification to begin at the bottom and sides of the ingot mold. **12.** *Bot.* the stem of a plant. —*v.i.* **13.** to play on a pipe. **14.** *Naut.* to signal, as with a boatswain's pipe. **15.** to speak in a high-pitched or piercing tone. **16.** to make or utter a shrill sound like that of a pipe: *to laugh and pipe with glee.* **17.** *Mining.* to excavate a cylindrical hole. **18.** *Metall.* (of an ingot or the like) to acquire a cylindrical or conical depression at the top when cooling after being cast. —*v.t.* **19.** to convey by means of pipes. **20.** to supply with pipes. **21.** to play (music) on a pipe or pipes. **22.** to summon, order, etc., by sounding the boatswain's pipe or whistle: *all hands were piped on deck.* **23.** to bring, lead, etc., by or as by playing on a pipe: *to pipe dancers.* **24.** to utter in a shrill tone: *to pipe a command.* **25.** to trim or finish with piping, as an article of clothing. **26.** *Informal.* to convey by an electrical wire or cable: *to pipe a signal from the antenna.* **27.** *Slang.* to look at: *Pipe her in that hat.* **28. pipe down,** *Slang.* to stop talking; be quiet: *He shouted at us to pipe down.* **29. pipe one's eye.** See **eye** (def. 40). **30. pipe up, a.** to begin to play (a musical instrument) or to sing. **b.** to make oneself heard; speak up, esp. as to assert oneself. **c.** to increase in velocity, as the wind. [ME *pipe(n),* OE *pīpian* (v.), ME, OE *pīpe* (n.) (c. D *pijp,* LG *pīpe,* G *Pfeife,* Icel *pípa*) < LL **pīpa,* back formation from L *pīpāre* to chirp] —**pipe′less,** *adj.* —**pipe′like′,** *adj.*

pipe[2] (pīp), *n.* **1.** a large cask, of varying capacity, esp. for wine or oil. **2.** such a cask as a measure of capacity for wine, etc., equal to 4 barrels, 2 hogsheads, or half a tun, and containing 126 wine gallons. **3.** such a cask with its contents. [ME < MF, ult. same as PIPE[1]]

pipe′ bat′ten, batten[2] (def. 5a).

pipe′ clay′, a fine, white clay used for making tobacco pipes, whitening parts of military or other dress, etc.

pipe-clay (pīp′klā′), *v.t.* to whiten with pipe clay.

pipe′ dream′, *Informal.* any fantastic notion or story: *She couldn't believe that her plans for a movie career had all been merely a pipe dream.*

pipe·fish (pīp′fish′), *n., pl.* (*esp. collectively*) **-fish,** (*esp. referring to two or more kinds or species*) **-fish·es.** any elongated, marine fish of the family *Syngnathidae,* having a tubular snout and covered with bony plates. [PIPE[1] + FISH]

pipe·ful (pīp′fo͝ol), *n., pl.* **-fuls.** a quantity sufficient to fill the bowl of a pipe: *a pipeful of tobacco.* [PIPE[1] + -FUL]

pipe′ line′, 1. a conduit of pipe, esp. underground and extending for a considerable distance, for the transportation of petroleum, petroleum products, natural gas, water, etc. **2.** a channel of information, esp. one which is direct, privileged, or confidential: *diplomatic pipelines.* Also, **pipe′line′.**

pip em·ma (pip′ em′ə), *Brit.* in, on, or during the afternoon. [phrase repr. *P.M.,* used by signalmen]

pipe′ of peace′, a calumet; peace pipe.

pipe′ or′gan, organ (def. 1).

pip·er (pī′pər), *n.* **1.** a person who plays on a pipe. **2.** a bagpiper. **3. pay the piper, a.** to pay the cost of something. **b.** to bear the unfavorable consequences of one's actions or pleasures: *Someday he'll have to pay the piper for all that gambling.* [ME; OE *pīpere.* See PIPE (v.), -ER[1]]

pip·er·a·ceous (pip′ə rā′shəs, pī′pə-), *adj.* belonging to the *Piperacae,* or pepper family of plants, which comprise the spice-bearing pepper, *Piper nigrum,* the betel and cubeb plants, etc. [< L *piper* pepper + -ACEOUS]

pi·per·a·zine (pi per′ə zēn′, -zin, pī-, pip′ər ə-), *n.* *Chem.* **1.** Also called **pip·er·az·i·dine** (pip′ə raz′i dēn′, -din, pī′pə-). a colorless, crystalline, deliquescent ring compound, $C_4H_{10}N_2$, prepared by the reaction of ethylene bromide or ethylene chloride with ammonia: used chiefly in veterinary medicine as an anthelmintic, and as an insecticide; diethylenediamine; hexahydropyrazine. **2.** any derivative of this compound. [< L *piper* pepper + -AZINE]

pi·per·i·dine (pi per′i dēn′, -din, pī-, pip′ər i-), *n.* *Chem.* a colorless, water-soluble liquid, $C_5H_{11}N$, obtained from the alkaloid piperine or from pyridine: used chiefly as a solvent. [< L *piper* pepper + -ID[3] + -INE[1]]

pip·er·ine (pip′ə rēn′, -ər in), *n.* *Chem.* a white, crystalline alkaloid, $C_{17}H_{19}NO_3$, obtained from pepper and other piperaceous plants and also prepared synthetically. [< L *piper* pepper + -INE[1]]

pi·per·o·nal (pi per′ə nal′, pī-, pip′ər ə-), *n.* *Chem.* a white, crystalline, water-insoluble aldehyde, $CH_2(O_2)C_6H_3CHO$, which darkens on exposure to light: used chiefly in perfumery and organic synthesis. Also called **piper′onyl al′dehyde, heliotropin.** [PIPER(INE) + -ONE + -AL[1]]

pi·per′o·nyl butox′ide (pi per′ə nəl, pī-, pip′ər ə nil), *Chem.* a light-brown liquid, $C_{19}H_{30}O_5$, used chiefly as a synergist in certain insecticides. [PIPERON(AL) + -YL + *but-* (from BUTYRIC) + OXIDE]

pipe′ snake′, any of several nonvenomous, burrowing snakes of the genus *Cylindrophis,* of southeastern Asia and the Malay Archipelago, having an evenly cylindrical body.

pipe·stem (pīp′stem′), *n.* **1.** the stem of a tobacco pipe. **2.** something resembling this in slenderness, as an unusually thin arm or leg. [PIPE[1] + STEM]

pipe·stone (pīp′stōn′), *n.* a reddish argillaceous stone used by North American Indians for making tobacco pipes. [PIPE[1] + STONE]

Pipe·stone (pīp′stōn′), *n.* a town in SW Minnesota. 5324 (1960).

pi·pet (pī pet′, pi-), *n., v.t.,* **-pet·ted, -pet·ting.** pipette.

pi·pette (pī pet′, pi-), *n., v.,* **-pet·ted, -pet·ting.** —*n.* **1.** a slender graduated tube for measuring and transferring liquids from one vessel to another. —*v.t.* **2.** to measure or transfer a liquid with a pipette. [< F; see PIPE[1], -ETTE]

A B

Pipettes A, Transfer pipette; B, Measuring pipette

pipe′ vine′, the Dutchman's-pipe.

pip·ing (pī′ping), *n.* **1.** pipes collectively; a system or network of pipes. **2.** material formed into a pipe or pipes. **3.** the act of one who or that which pipes. **4.** the sound of pipes. **5.** a shrill sound. **6.** the music of pipes. **7.** a cordlike ornamentation made of icing, used on pastry. **8.** a tubular band of material, sometimes containing a cord, for trimming garments, upholstery, etc., along edges and seams. —*adj.* **9.** characterized by the music of the peaceful pipe rather than by that of the martial fife or trumpet. **10.** playing on a musical pipe. **11.** that pipes. **12.** emitting a shrill sound: *a piping voice.* **13. piping hot,** (of food or drink) very hot: *Clam chowder must be served piping hot.* [ME (n.); see PIPE[1], -ING[1], -ING[2]] —**pip′ing·ly,** *adv.* —**pip′ing·ness,** *n.*

pip·i·strelle (pip′i strel′, pip′i strel′), *n.* any of numerous insectivorous bats of the genus *Pipistrellus,* esp. *P. pipistrellus* of Europe and Asia. [< F < It *pipistrello, vipistrello* < L *vespertiliōn-* (s. of *vespertiliō*) bat. See VESPERTILIONINE]

pip·it (pip′it), *n.* any of several small songbirds of the genus *Anthus,* of the family *Motacillidae,* resembling the larks in coloration, structure, and habits. [imit.]

pip·kin (pip′kin), *n.* **1.** a small, earthen pot. **2.** *Dial.* a piggin. [? PIPE[2] + -KIN]

Pip·pa (pip′ə; *It.* pēp′pä), *n.* a girl's given name, Italian form of **Philippa.**

Pip′pa Pass′es (pip′ə), a poem (1841) by Robert Browning.

pip·per (pip′ər), *n.* the center of the reticule of a gunsight. Also called **pip.** [PIP[1] + -ER[1]]

pip·pin (pip′in), *n.* **1.** any of numerous, roundish, or oblate varieties of apple. **2.** *Bot.* a seed. [ME *pipin,* var. of *pepin* < OF]

pip·sis·se·wa (pip sis′ə wə), *n.* any evergreen, ericaceous herb of the genus *Chimaphila,* esp. *C. umbellata,* the leaves of which are used medicinally for their tonic, diuretic, and astringent properties. Also called **prince's-pine.** [< Cree *pipisisikweu,* lit., it breaks it up, i.e., fragments the stone in the bladder]

pip-squeak (pip′skwēk′), *n.* *Informal.* a small or unimportant person; a twerp.

pip·to·nych·i·a (pip′tə nik′ē ə), *n.* *Pathol.* a falling out of the nails. [< NL < Gk *piptein* (to) fall + *onykh-* (s. of *ónyx*) nail + *-ia* -IA]

pip·y (pī′pē), *adj.,* **pip·i·er, pip·i·est. 1.** pipelike; tubular. **2.** piping; shrill: *a pipy voice.* [PIPE[1] + -Y[1]]

Piq·ua (pik′wä, -wə), *n.* a city in W Ohio. 19,219 (1960).

pi·quant (pē′kənt, -känt), *adj.* **1.** agreeably pungent or sharp in taste or flavor; biting; tart: *a piquant aspic.* **2.** agreeably stimulating, interesting, or attractive: *She had a delightful, piquant smile.* **3.** of a provocative or lively character: *a piquant wit.* **4.** *Archaic.* sharp or stinging, esp. to the feelings. [< F: lit., pricking (see PIQUE, -ANT); r. *pickante* < It *piccante*] —**pi′quan·cy, pi′quant·ness,** *n.* —**pi′quant·ly,** *adv.*
—**Syn. 1.** spicy. **2.** intriguing. **3.** sharp, clever. —**Ant. 1.** insipid.

pique[1] (pēk), *v.,* **piqued, piqu·ing,** *n.* —*v.t.* **1.** to affect with sharp irritation and resentment, esp. by some wound to pride: *He piqued her by refusing her invitation.* **2.** to wound (the pride, vanity, etc.). **3.** to excite (interest, curiosity, etc.): *Her curiosity was piqued by what the town gossips were saying.* **4.** to arouse an emotion or provoke to action: *to pique someone to answer a challenge.* **5.** *Archaic.* to pride (oneself) (usually fol. by *on* or *upon*): *He piqued himself on his elegant manners.* **6.** *Aeron. Obs.* to dive at. —*v.i.* **7.** to arouse pique in someone; cause anger, resentment, or sharp irritation: *an action that piqued when it was meant to soothe.* —*n.* **8.** a feeling of irritation or resentment, as from a wound to pride or self-esteem: *to be in a pique.* **9.** *Obs.* a state of irritated feeling between persons. [< MF *pique* (n.), *piquer* (v.) < VL **piccare;* see PICKAX, PIQUÉ, PIKE[2]]
—**Syn. 1.** offend, sting, nettle, vex, irritate, chafe. **2.** affront. **3.** stimulate, stir, prick, incite, goad. —**Ant. 1.** please. **2.** compliment.

pique[2] (pēk), *n.* *Piquet.* pic.

pi·qué (pi kā′, pē-; *Fr.* pē kā′), *n., pl.* **-qués** (-kāz′; *Fr.* -kā′) for 2, *adj.* —*n.* **1.** a fabric of cotton, spun rayon, or silk, woven lengthwise with raised cords. **2.** *Ballet.* a step in which the dancer steps onto the tip of the toe without bending the knee. **3.** ornamentation by means of punched or stippled patterns, sometimes inlaid with metal, ivory, tortoise shell, etc. —*adj.* **4.** (of glove seams and gloves) stitched through lapping edges. **5.** decorated with inlay: *a piqué box.* [< F, ptp. of *piquer* to quilt, prick; see PIQUE[1]]

pi·quet (pi ket′, -kā′), *n.* a card game played by two persons with a pack of 32 cards, the cards from deuces to sixes being excluded. [< F; see PIC[1], -ET]

pir (pēr), *n.* *Islam.* a religious instructor, esp. in mystical sects. [< Hindi *pīr* old man < Pers]

pi·ra·cy (pī′rə sē), *n., pl.* **-cies. 1.** practice of a pirate; robbery or illegal violence at sea. **2.** the unauthorized appropriation or use of a copyrighted or patented work, idea, etc.: *Piracy of literary works was common in the last century.* [earlier *pyracie* < ML *pīrātia* < Gk *peirāteía.* See PIRATE, -ACY]

Pi·rae·us (pī rē′əs), *n.* a seaport in SE Greece: the port of Athens. 183,877 (1961). Also, **Peiraeus.** Greek, **Peiraievs.**

pi·ra·gua (pi rä′gwə, -rag′wə), *n.* **1.** a long canoe fashioned by hollowing out a tree trunk. **2.** a flat-bottomed sailing vessel having two masts. [< Sp < Carib: dugout]

Pi·ran·del·lo (pir′ən del′ō; *It.* pē′Rän del′lô), *n.* **Lu·i·gi** (lo͞o ē′jē), 1867–1936, Italian dramatist, novelist, and poet: Nobel prize 1934.

Pi·ra·ne·si (pē′Rä ne′zē), *n.* **Giam·bat·tis·ta** (jäm′bät tēs′tä), or **Gio·van·ni Bat·tis·ta** (jô vän′nē bät tēs′tä), 1720–78, Italian architect and engraver.

Piranha, *Serrasalmus rhombeus* (Length to 1½ ft.)

pi·ra·nha (pi rän′yə, -ran′-), *n.* any of the extremely voracious, South American, characin fishes of the subfamily *Serrasalminae,* known to attack man and devour large animals which enter the water. Also called **caribe.** [< Pg < Tupi]

Pi·ra·pó·ra (pē′Rə pô′Rə), *n.* a city in E Brazil. 16,297 (1960).

pi·ra·ru·cu (pi rär′ə ko͞o′), *n.* the arapaima. [< Pg < Tupi *pirá-rucú,* lit., red fish]

pi·rate (pī′rət), *n., v.,* **-rat·ed, -rat·ing.** —*n.* **1.** a person who robs, or commits illegal violence, at sea or on the shores of the sea. **2.** a vessel employed by such persons. **3.** any plunderer, predator, etc.: *confidence men, slumlords, and other pirates.* **4.** a person who appropriates and reproduces the work or invention of another, without authorization, as for his own profit. **5.** Also called **pi′rate stream′.** *Geol.* a stream which diverts into its own flow the headwaters of another stream, river, etc. —*v.t.* **6.** to commit piracy upon; plunder; rob. **7.** to take by piracy: *to pirate gold.* **8.** to appropriate and reproduce (a book, an invention, etc.) without authorization or legal right. —*v.i.* **9.** to commit or practice piracy. [late ME < L *pīrāta* < Gk *peirātḗs,* akin to *peirân* to attack] —**pi′rate·like′,** *adj.* —**pi·rat·i·cal** (pī rat′i kəl), **pi·rat′ic,** *adj.* —**pi·rat′i·cal·ly,** *adv.*
—**Syn. 1.** freebooter, buccaneer, corsair, plunderer.

Pi′rate Coast′, former name of **Trucial Oman.**

pi′rate perch′, a purplish, North American, freshwater fish, *Aphredoderus sayanus,* the adult of which has the vent located in back of the lower jaw.

Pi′rates of Penzance′, an operetta (1897) by Sir William S. Gilbert and Sir Arthur Sullivan.

Pire (*Fr.* pēR), *n.* **Do·mi·nique Georges Hen·ri** (*Fr.* dô mē nēk′ zhôRzh äN Rē′), born 1910, Belgian priest: Nobel peace prize 1958.

Pi·ren (pī′rēn), *n.* *Class. Myth.* a son of Glaucus, believed to have been accidentally killed by his brother Bellerophon. Also, **Peiren.**

Pi·re·ne (pī rē′nē), *n. Class. Myth.* a daughter of either Achelous or Asopus who was changed into a fountain when she grieved over the death of her son, Cenchrias.

pir·i·for·mis (pir′ə fôr′mis, -fôr′-), *n., pl.* **-mes** (-mēz). *Anat.* a flat muscle in the hip region, the action of which assists in raising the thigh sideways, in rotating the front of the thigh away from the body, and in slightly extending the thigh. Also, **pyriformis.** [< NL: lit., pear-shaped < L *piri-* (comb. form of *pirum* pear) + *-formis* -FORM]

Pi·rith·o·üs (pī rith′ō əs), *n. Class. Myth.* a prince of the Lapithae and friend of Theseus, in whose company he attempted unsuccessfully to abduct Persephone from Hades.

Pir·ke A·both (piʀ kā′ ä bôt′), *Judaism.* a treatise of the Mishnah that comprises six chapters and consists chiefly of proverbs, aphorisms, and principles of ethics, law, and religion as set forth by the Mishnaic scholars. Also called **Ethics of the Fathers.**

pirn (pûrn, pirn), *n. Brit. Dial.* **1.** a weaver's bobbin, spool, or reel. **2.** a fishing reel. [late ME *pyrne* < ?]

pi·ro·gen (pi rō′gən), *n.* (*construed as pl.*) piroshki. [< Yiddish, pl. of *pirog* small stuffed pastry < Russ]

pi·rogue (pi rōg′), *n.* **1.** a canoe hollowed from the trunk of a tree. **2.** a native boat, esp. an American dugout. **3.** periauger. Also, **piragua.** [< F < Sp *piragua* PIRAGUA]

pir·o·plas·mo·sis (pir′ə plaz mō′sis), *n., pl.* **-ses** (-sēz). *Vet. Pathol.* babesiosis. [< NL; see PIRIFORMIS, -O-, PLASMA, -OSIS]

pi·rosh·ki (pi rôsh′kē, -rosh′-), *n.* (*construed as pl.*) small turnovers or dumplings with a filling, as of meat or fruit. Also, **pirogen.** [< Russ *pirozhke* small pastries, dim. of *pirog* stuffed pastry]

pir·ou·ette (pir′o͞o et′), *n., v.,* **-et·ted, -et·ting.** —*n.* **1.** a whirling about on one foot or on the points of the toes, as in dancing. **2.** *Dressage.* a complete turn in which the horse uses its hind legs as a pivot. —*v.i.* **3.** to perform a pirouette; whirl, as on the toes. [< F: a whirl, top, etc., fem. of MF *pirouet*, equiv. to *pirou-* (c. It *pirolo*, dim. of *piro* peg) + *-et* -ET]

Pi·ro·us (pī′rō əs), *n.* (in the *Iliad*) a leader of the Thracian allies of Troy.

Pi·sa (pē′zə; *It.* pē′zä), *n.* a city in NW Italy, on the Arno River: leaning tower. 91,108 (1961). —**Pi′san,** *adj., n.*

pis al·ler (pē za lā′), *French.* the last resort or resource.

Pi′san Can′tos, a section of the *Cantos* by Ezra Pound, published in 1948.

Pi·san·der (pī san′dər), *n.* (in the *Iliad*) a captain of the Myrmidons in the Trojan War.

Pi·sa·nel·lo (pē′zä nel′lô), *n.* **An·to·nio** (än tô′nyô), (*Antonio Pisano*), 1397–1455?, Italian painter and medalist.

Pi·sa·no (pē zä′nô), *n.* **1. An·dre·a** (än dʀe′ä), c1270–c1348, Italian sculptor. **2. Gio·van·ni** (jô vän′nē), c1245–c1320, and his father, **Ni·co·la** (nē kô′lä), c1220–78, Italian sculptors and architects.

pi·say (pē′zā), *n.* pisé.

pis·ca·ry (pis′kə rē), *n., pl.* **-ries.** **1.** *Law.* the right or privilege of fishing in particular waters. **2.** a place for fishing. [late ME < ML *piscāria*, neut. pl. (fishing rights), fem. sing. (fishing place) of L *piscārius* of fishing or fish. See PISCI-, -ARY]

pis·ca·tol·o·gy (pis′kə tol′ə jē), *n. Rare.* art or science of fishing. [< L *piscāt(us)* a fishing (see PISCI-, -ATE[1]) + -O- + -LOGY]

pis·ca·tor (pi skā′tər, pis′kə-), *n.* fisherman. [< L, equiv. to *piscāt(us)* (see PISCATOLOGY) + *-or* -OR[2]]

pis·ca·to·ry (pis′kə tôr′ē, -tôr′ē), *adj.* **1.** of or pertaining to fishermen or fishing: *a piscatory settlement; piscatory methods.* **2.** devoted to or dependent upon fishing: *a piscatory people; piscatory birds.* Also, **pis·ca·to·ri·al** (pis′kə tôr′ē əl, -tôr′-). [< L *piscātōri(us)*, equiv. to *piscāt(us)* (see PISCATOLOGY) + *-ōrius* -ORY[1]]

Pis·ces (pī′sēz, pis′ēz), *n., gen.* **Pis·ci·um** (pish′ē əm), for 1. **1.** *Astron.* the Fishes, a zodiacal constellation between Aries and Aquarius. **2.** the twelfth sign of the zodiac. See illus. under **zodiac.** **3.** (*italics.*) the class of vertebrates comprising the fish and sometimes including, in certain classifications, the cyclostomes. [< L *piscēs*, pl. of *piscis* a fish]

pisci-, a learned borrowing from Latin meaning "fish," used in the formation of compound words: *piscivorous.* [comb. form repr. L *pisc(is)*]

pis·ci·cul·ture (pis′i kul′chər), *n.* the breeding, rearing, and transplantation of fish by artificial means. [PISCI- + CULTURE] —**pis′ci·cul′tur·al,** *adj.* —**pis′ci·cul′tur·al·ly,** *adv.* —**pis′ci·cul′tur·ist,** *n.*

pis·ci·form (pis′ə fôrm′), *adj.* shaped like a fish. [PISCI- + FORM]

pis·ci·na (pi sī′nə, pi sē′-), *n., pl.* **-nae** (-nē). *Eccles.* a basin with a drain used for certain ablutions, now generally in the sacristy. [< eccl. L, special use of L *piscīna* a fish pond, swimming pool, equiv. to *pisci(s)* a fish + *-īna*, fem. of *-īnus* -INE[1]]

pis·cine (pis′īn, -ēn, -in), *adj.* of, pertaining to, or resembling a fish or fishes. [< L *piscīn(us)* adj. See PISC(I)-, -INE[1]]

Pis·cis Aus·tri·nus (pī′sis ô strī′nəs, pis′is), *gen.* **Pis·cis Aus·tri·ni** (pī′sis ô strī′nī, pis′is). *Astron.* the Southern Fish, a southern constellation between Aquarius and Grus, containing the bright star Fomalhaut.

pis·civ·o·rous (pi siv′ər əs), *adj.* fish-eating. [PISCI- + -VOROUS]

pis·co (pis′kō, pē′skō; *Sp.* pē′skô), *n.* a brandy made in the district near Pisco, a seaport in Peru. [< Sp]

pi·sé (pē zā′), *n.* See **rammed earth.** Also, **pisay.** Also called **pi·sé′ de terre′** (də târ′). [< F, n. use of ptp. of *piser* to beat down (earth) < L *pīsāre, pinsere* to pound, stamp down]

Pis·gah (piz′gə), *n.* **Mount,** a mountain ridge of ancient Palestine, now in Jordan, NE of the Dead Sea: from its summit (**Mt. Nebo**) Moses viewed the Promised Land. Deut. 34:1.

pish (psh; *spelling pron.* pish), *interj.* **1.** (used as an exclamation of contempt or impatience.) —*n.* **2.** an exclamation of "pish!" —*v.i.* **3.** to say "pish." —*v.t.* **4.** to say "pish" at or to. [imit.]

pi·shogue (pi shōg′), *n. Irish Eng.* **1.** sorcery; witchcraft; black magic. **2.** an evil spell; hex. [< Ir *piseog*]

Pi·sid·i·a (pi sid′ē ə, pī-), *n.* an ancient country in S Asia Minor: later a Roman province.

Pi·sid·i·an (pi sid′ē ən, pī-), *n.* the extinct language of Pisidia, not known to be related to any other language, written in a script derived from the Greek alphabet. [PISIDI(A) + -AN]

pi·si·form (pī′sə fôrm′), *adj.* **1.** having or resembling the form of a pea. **2.** *Anat., Zool.* pertaining to the pealike bone on the ulnar side of the carpus. [< NL *pisiform(is)* pea-shaped, equiv. to *pisi-* (comb. form repr. L *pisum* pea < Gk *píson* pulse) + *-formis* -FORM]

Pi·sis·trat·i·dae (pī′si strat′i dē′, pis′i-), *n.pl.* Hippias and Hipparchus, the sons of Pisistratus.

Pi·sis·tra·tus (pī sis′trə təs, pi-), *n.* c605–527 B.C., tyrant of Athens 560–527 (father of Hipparchus and Hippias). Also, **Peisistratus.**

pis·mire (pis′mīᵊr′), *n.* an ant. [ME *pissemyre*, lit., urinating ant, equiv. to *pisse* to urinate + obs. *mire* ant < Scand (cf. Dan *myre*, Sw *myra*); c. D *mier*; pejorative name from stench of formic acid proper to ants]

pi·so·lite (pī′sə līt′, piz′ə-), *n.* limestone composed of rounded concretions about the size of a pea. [< NL *pisolith(us)* < Gk *píso(s)* pea + *líthos* -LITE] —**pi·so·lit·ic** (pī′sə lit′ik), *adj.*

piss (pis), *n., v.* **pissed, piss·ing.** *Slang* (*vulgar*) —*n.* **1.** urine. —*v.i.* **2.** to urinate. [ME *pisse(n)* < OF *pissier* < VL **pisiare*, ultimately sound imit.]

Pis·sar·ro (pi sär′ō; *Fr.* pē sa ʀō′), *n.* **Ca·mille** (ka mē′yᵊ), 1830–1903, French painter.

pissed′ off′, *Slang* (*vulgar*). angry.

pis·soir (pē swar′), *n., pl.* **-soirs** (-swar′). *French.* a street urinal for public use, enclosed by a low wall, screen, or the like.

pis·ta′chi·a galls′ (pi stash′ē ə, -stä′shē ə), mastic (def. 1). [var. of *pistacia* < LL < Gk *pistákē* pistachio tree + *-ia* -IA]

pis·ta·chi·o (pi stash′ē ō′, -stä′shē ō′), *n., pl.* **-chi·os.** **1.** the nut of an anacardiaceous tree, *Pistacia vera*, of southern Europe and Asia Minor, containing an edible, greenish kernel. **2.** the kernel itself, used for flavoring. **3.** the tree itself. **4.** pistachio nut flavor. **5.** See **pistachio green.** Also, **pis·tache** (pi stash′), **pista′chio nut′** (for defs. 1, 2). [< It *pistacchio* < L *pistācium* < Gk *pistákion* pistachio nut, dim. of *pistákē* pistachio tree < Pers *pistah*; r. late ME *pistace* < MF < L, as above]

pista′chio green′, a light or medium shade of yellow green.

pis·ta·reen (pis′tə rēn′), *n.* **1.** peseta (def. 2). —*adj.* **2.** of little value or worth. [? deriv. of Sp *peseta* PESETA]

pis·til (pis′til), *n. Bot.* **1.** the ovule-bearing or seed-bearing organ of a flower, consisting when complete of ovary, style, and stigma. See diag. under **flower.** **2.** such organs collectively, where there are more than one in a flower. **3.** a gynoecium. [earlier *pistillum*, special use of L *pistillum* pestle]

pis·til·late (pis′tᵊlit, -tᵊlāt′), *adj. Bot.* **1.** having a pistil or pistils. **2.** having a pistil or pistils but no stamens. See illus. under **monoecious.** [PISTIL + -ATE[1]]

pis·til·lo·dy (pis′tᵊlō′dē), *n. Bot.* the metamorphosis of an organ, as a sepal, into a pistil. [PISTIL + -ODE[1] + -Y[3]]

Pis·to·ia (pē stô′yä), *n.* a city in N Tuscany, in N Italy. 82,401 (1961).

pis·tol (pis′tᵊl), *n., v.,* **-toled, -tol·ing** or (*esp. Brit.*) **-tolled, -tol·ling.** —*n.* **1.** a short firearm intended to be held and fired with one hand. —*v.t.* **2.** to shoot with a pistol. [< MF *pistole* (now obs.), back formation from *pistolet* the weapon] —**pis′tol·like′,** *adj.*

pis·tole (pi stōl′), *n.* **1.** a former gold coin of Spain, equal to two escudos. **2.** any of various former gold coins of Europe, as the louis d'or. [< MF, back formation from *pistolet* the coin]

pis·to·leer (pis′tᵊlēr′), *n. Obs.* a person, esp. a soldier, who uses or is armed with a pistol. Also, **pis′to·lier′.** [PISTOL + -EER]

pis′tol grip′, a handle or grip, as of a rifle or saw, shaped like the butt of a pistol.

pis′tol-han′dle knife′ (pis′tᵊl-han′dᵊl), a table knife, esp. of the 18th century, having a handle curved slightly toward the end in the direction of the edge, resembling the grip of a flintlock pistol.

pis·tol·o·gy (pi stol′ə jē), *n.* the branch of theology dealing with faith. [< Gk *píst(is)* faith (akin to *peíthein* to persuade) + -O- + -LOGY]

pis·tol-whip (pis′tᵊl hwip′, -wip′), *v.t.,* **-whipped, -whip·ping.** to hit (someone) repeatedly with a pistol, esp. in the head and shoulder area.

pis·ton (pis′tən), *n.* **1.** a disk or cylindrical part tightly fitting and moving within a cylinder, either to compress or move a fluid collected in the cylinder, as air or water, or to transform energy imparted by a fluid entering or expanding inside the cylinder, as compressed air, explosive gases, or steam, into a rectilinear motion usually transformed into rotary motion by means of a connecting rod. **2.** a pumplike valve used to change the pitch in a cornet or the like. [< F < It *pistone* piston, a learned alter. of *pestone* great pestle, equiv. to *pest(are)* (to) pound (var. of ML *pistare*, deriv. of L *pistus*, ptp. of *pinsere* to pound) + *-one* aug. suffix] —**pis′ton·like′,** *adj.*

A B C

A, Piston of automobile engine; B, Wrist pin; C, Connecting rod

Pis·ton (pis′tən), *n.* **Walter,** 1894–1976, U.S. composer.

pis′ton pin′. See **wrist pin.**

pis′ton ring′, a metallic ring, usually one of a series, and split so as to be expansible, placed around a piston in order to maintain a tight fit, as inside the cylinder of an engine. Also called **packing ring.**

pis′ton rod′, a rod communicating the rectilinear motion of a piston to the small end of a connecting rod or elsewhere.

pit[1] (pit), *n., v.,* **pit·ted, pit·ting.** —*n.* **1.** a naturally formed or excavated hole or cavity in the ground: *pits caused by erosion; clay pits.* **2.** a covered or concealed excavation in the ground, serving as a trap. **3.** *Mining.* **a.** an excavation made in digging for some mineral deposit. **b.** the shaft of a coal mine. **c.** the mine itself. **4.** the abode of evil spirits and lost souls; hell: *an evil inspiration from the pit.* **5.** a hollow or indentation in a surface: *glass flawed by pits.* **6.** a natural hollow or depression in the body: *the pit of the back.* **7.** a small, depressed scar, as one of those left on the skin after smallpox. **8.** an enclosure for combats, as of dogs or cocks. **9.** *U.S.* (in a commodity exchange) a part of the floor of the exchange where trading in a particular commodity takes place: *the corn pit.* **10.** *Archit.* **a.** all that part of the main floor of a theater behind the musicians. **b.** *Brit.* a section of the main floor of a theater behind the orchestra and in front of the parquet, parterre, or orchestra stalls, usually of unreserved seats. **c.** the group of persons occupying the pit: *The pit applauded loudly.* **11.** (in a hoistway) a space below the level of the lowest floor served. **12.** *Auto Racing.* an area at the side of a track, for servicing and refueling the cars. **13.** *Bowling.* the sunken area of a bowling alley behind the pins, for the placement or recovery of pins that have been knocked down. **14.** *Track.* the area forward of the take-off point in a jumping event, as the broad jump or pole vault, that is filled with sawdust or soft earth to lessen the force of the jumper's landing. —*v.t.* **15.** to mark with pits or depressions: *ground pitted by erosion.* **16.** to scar with pockmarks: *His forehead was pitted by chicken pox.* **17.** to place or bury in a pit, as for storage. **18.** to set in opposition or combat, as one against another. **19.** to set (animals) in a pit or enclosure, for fighting. —*v.i.* **20.** to become marked with pits or depressions. **21.** (of body tissue) to retain temporarily a mark of pressure, as by a finger, instrument, etc. [ME; OE *pytt* < L *pute(us)* well, pit, shaft]

pit[2] (pit), *n., v.,* **pit·ted, pit·ting.** *U.S.* —*n.* **1.** the stone of a fruit, as of a cherry, peach, or plum. —*v.t.* **2.** to remove the pit from (a fruit or fruits): *to pit cherries for a pie.* [< D: kernel; c. PITH]

pi·ta[1] (pē′tə), *n.* **1.** a fiber obtained from plants of the genera *Agave, Aechmea*, etc., used for cordage, mats, etc. **2.** any of these plants. [< SP < Kechua]

pi·ta[2] (pē′tä), *n.* a round, flat Middle Eastern bread. [< ModGk *pḗtta, pitta* bread, cake]

pit·a·ha·ya (pit′ə hī′ə), *n.* **1.** Also called **sweet pitahaya.** a tall cactus, *Lemaireocereus thurberi*, of southern Arizona and Mexico, having long, needlelike spines and white-margined, pinkish-purple flowers nearly three inches long. **2.** a bushy, very spiny, cactus, *Machaerocereus gummosus*, of southern California and Mexico, having purple flowers and edible, scarlet fruit. [< AmerSp < Taino]

Pit·a·ka (pit′ə kə), *n. Buddhism.* See under **Pali Canon.** [< Pali: lit., basket]

Pit′ and the Pen′dulum, The, a short story (1843) by Edgar Allan Poe.

pi·tan·ga (pə tang′gə), *n.* See **Surinam cherry.** [< Pg < Tupi]

pit·a·pat (pit′ə pat′), *adv., n., v.,* **-pat·ted, -pat·ting.** —*adv.* **1.** with a quick succession of beats or taps: *Her heart beat pitapat with excitement.* —*n.* **2.** the movement or the sound of something going pitapat: *the pitapat of hail on a roof.* —*v.i.* **3.** to go pitapat. [imit. gradational compound]

Pi·ta·tus (pi tā′təs), *n.* a walled plain in the third quadrant of the face of the moon: about 50 miles in diameter.

pit′ boss′, a person who is in charge of the gambling tables in a casino.

pit′ bull′ ter′rier, one of an American breed of strong, stocky dogs developed from the Staffordshire terrier, having wide-set forelegs and a short, stiff coat.

Pit′cairn Is′land, a small British island in the S Pacific, SE of Tuamotu Archipelago: settled 1790 by mutineers of the *Bounty.* 146 (1959); 2 sq. mi.

pitch[1] (pich), *v.t.* **1.** to erect or set up (a tent, camp, or the like). **2.** to put, set, or plant in a fixed or definite place or position. **3.** to throw, fling, hurl, or toss. **4.** *Baseball.* **a.** to deliver or serve (the ball) to the batter. **b.** to fill the position of pitcher in (a game): *He pitched a no-hitter. He pitched a good game.* **5.** to set at a certain point, degree, level, etc.: *He pitched his hopes too high.* **6.** *Music.* to set at a particular pitch, or determine the key or keynote of (a melody). **7.** *Cards.* **a.** to lead (a card of a particular suit), thereby fixing that suit as trump. **b.** to determine (the trump) in this manner. **8.** to pave or revet with small stones. **9.** *Masonry.* **a.** to square (a stone), cutting the arrises true with a chisel. **b.** to cut with a chisel. **10.** *Obs.* to set in order; to arrange, as a field of battle. **11.** *Obs.* to fix firmly as in the ground; embed.
—*v.i.* **12.** to plunge or fall forward or headlong. **13.** to lurch. **14.** to throw or toss. **15.** *Baseball.* **a.** to deliver or serve the ball to the batter. **b.** to fill the position of pitcher: *He pitched for the Mets last year.* **16.** to slope downward; dip. **17.** to plunge with alternate fall and rise of bow and stern, as a ship (opposed to *roll*). **18.** (of a rocket or guided missile) to deviate from a stable flight attitude by oscillations of the longitudinal axis in a vertical plane about the center of gravity. **19.** to fix a tent or temporary habitation; encamp: *They pitched by a mountain stream.* **20.** *Golf.* to play a pitch shot. **21.** *Rare.* to become established; settle down. **22. pitch in,** *Informal.* **a.** to contribute; join in: *When they took up a collection for the annual dinner, he promised to pitch in.* **b.** to begin to work vigorously: *If I really pitch in, I may be able to finish the paper before the deadline.* **23. pitch into,** *Informal.* **a.** to attack verbally or physically: *He apologized for pitching into me yesterday.* **b.** to begin to work on vigorously: *He pitched into the morning mail with a hopeful air.* **24. pitch on** or **upon,** to choose, esp. casually; decide on: *We pitched on a day for our picnic.*
—*n.* **25.** relative point, position, or degree: *a high pitch of excitement.* **26.** degree of inclination or slope; angle: *the pitch of an arch; the pitch of a stair.* **27.** the highest point or greatest height: *enjoying the pitch of success.* **28.** (in music, speech, etc.) degree of height or depth of a tone or of sound, depending upon the relative rapidity of the vibrations by which it is produced. **29.** a particular

tonal standard with which given tones may be compared in respect to their relative level. **30.** *Acoustics.* the apparent predominant frequency sounded by an acoustical source. **31.** act or manner of pitching. **32.** a throw or toss. **33.** *Baseball.* the serving of the ball to the batter by the pitcher, usually preceded by a windup or stretch. **34.** the pitching movement or forward plunge, as of a ship. **35.** upward or downward inclination or slope: *a road descending at a steep pitch.* **36.** a sloping part or place: *to build on the pitch of a hill.* **37.** a quantity of something pitched or placed somewhere. **38.** *Cricket.* the central part of the field; the area between the wickets. **39.** *Slang.* **a.** a high-pressure sales talk: *the pitch of television commercials.* **b.** a specific plan of action; angle: *to tackle a problem again, using a new pitch.* **40.** the specific location in which a person or object is placed or stationed; an allotted or assigned place. **41.** *Chiefly Brit.* the established location, often a street corner, of a beggar, street peddler, newspaper vendor, etc. **42.** *Aeron.* **a.** the nosing of an airplane or spacecraft up or down about a transverse axis. **b.** the distance which a given propeller would advance in one revolution. **43.** (of a rocket or guided missile) **a.** the motion due to pitching. **b.** the extent of the rotation of the longitudinal axis involved in pitching. **44.** *Geol., Mining.* the inclination of the axis of a fold from the horizontal. **45.** *Mach.* **a.** the distance between the corresponding surfaces of two adjacent gear teeth measured either along the pitch circle (**cir′cular pitch′**) or between perpendiculars to the root surfaces (**nor′mal pitch′**). **b.** the ratio of the number of teeth in a gear or splined shaft to the pitch circle diameter, expressed in inches. **c.** the distance between any two adjacent things in a series, as screw threads, rivets, etc. **46.** (in carpet weaving) the weftwise number of warp ends, usually determined in relation to 27 inches. **47.** *Cards.* **a.** See **all fours** (def. 2). **b.** See **auction pitch. 48.** *Masonry.* a true or even surface on a stone. [ME *picche(n)*; ? akin to PICK[1]] —**pitch′a·ble,** *adj.*
—**Syn. 3.** See **throw.**

pitch[2] (pich), *n.* **1.** any of various dark, tenacious, and viscous substances for calking and paving, consisting of the residue of the distillation of coal tar or wood tar. **2.** any of certain bitumens, as asphalt: *mineral pitch.* **3.** any of various resins. **4.** the sap or crude turpentine which exudes from the bark of pines. —*v.t.* **5.** to smear or cover with pitch. [ME *pich,* OE *pic* < L *pic(em)* (acc. of *pix*), whence also D *pek,* G *Pech;* akin to Gk *píssa* (for **pikia*) pitch] —**pitch′like′,** *adj.*

pitch-and-putt (pich′ən put′), *adj.* of or pertaining to a small-scale golf course, 5 to 20 acres, and usually having 9 holes of 50 yards in length from tee to cup. Cf. **par-three.**

pitch′-and-run′ shot′ (pich′ən run′), *Golf.* See **chip shot.** Also called **pitch′-and-run′.**

pitch-and-toss (pich′ən tôs′, -tos′), *n.* a game in which players toss coins at a mark, the person whose coin hits closest to the mark tossing all the coins in the air and winning all those that come down heads up. Cf. **chuck-farthing.**

pitch-black (pich′blak′), *adj.* extremely dark or black, as pitch: *a pitch-black place in the road.*

pitch·blende (pich′blend′), *n.* an impure uraninite, occurring in black pitchlike masses: the principal ore of uranium and radium. [half trans., half adoption of G *Pechblende.* See PITCH[2], BLENDE]

pitch′ board′, (in stair building) a templet for marking the outlines of steps on carriage pieces or the like. Also called **gauge board.**

pitch′ chain′. See **power chain.**

pitch′ chis′el, *Masonry.* a broad-edged chisel for cutting plane surfaces on stones.

pitch′ cir′cle, *Mach.* an imaginary circle within the profiles of the teeth of a gear, such that it rotates against a similar circle rotating at the same rate on a meshing gear.

pitch′ cone′. See under **pitch surface.**

pitch′ cyl′inder. See under **pitch surface.**

pitch-dark (pich′därk′), *adj.* black or dark as pitch: *a pitch-dark night.* —**pitch′-dark′ness,** *n.*

pitched′ bat′tle, 1. a battle in which the orderly arrangement of forces and the location have been predetermined. **2.** an encounter in which the antagonists are completely and intensely engaged: *The dispute evolved into a pitched battle between management and labor.*

pitch·er[1] (pich′ər), *n.* **1.** a container, usually with a handle and spout or lip, for holding and pouring liquids. **2.** *Bot.* **a.** a pitcherlike modification of the leaf of certain plants. **b.** an ascidium. [ME *picher* < OF *pichier* < ML *picār(ium),* var. of *bicārium* BEAKER] —**pitch′er-like′,** *adj.*

pitch·er[2] (pich′ər), *n.* **1.** a person who pitches. **2.** *Baseball.* the player who delivers or serves the ball to the batter. **3.** Also called **number seven iron.** *Golf.* a club with an iron head the face of which has more slope than a pitching niblick but less slope than a mashie niblick. **4.** sett (def. 1). [PITCH[1] + -ER[1]]

pitch·er·ful (pich′ər fo͝ol′), *n., pl.* **-fuls.** the amount held by a pitcher. [PITCHER[1] + -FUL]

pitch′er plant′, any of various plants having leaves modified into a pitcherlike receptacle, or ascidium, as the plants of the genera *Sarracenia* and *Darlingtonia.*

Pitcher plant, *Sarracenia pupurea*

pitch-faced (pich′fāst′), *adj.* *Masonry.* (of a stone) having all arrises in the same plane and the faces roughly dressed with a pick.

pitch-far·thing (pich′fär′thing), *n.* See **chuck-farthing.**

pitch·fork (pich′fôrk′), *n.* **1.** a long-handled fork for manually lifting and pitching hay, stalks of grain, etc. —*v.t.* **2.** to pitch or throw with or as with a pitchfork. [PITCH[1] + FORK]

pitch·ing (pich′ing), *n.* **1.** the act of revetting or paving with small stones. **2.** stones so used. Also called **penning, soling.** [PITCH[1] + -ING[1]]

pitch′ing nib′lick, *Golf.* a club with an iron head the face of which has more slope than a pitcher but less slope than a niblick. Also called **number eight iron.**

pitch′ing pen′nies, a gambling game in which pennies are tossed to a mark or against a wall, the winner being the person who tosses his penny closest to the mark or wall.

pitch′ing piece′. See **apron piece.**

Pitch′ Lake′, a deposit of natural asphalt in SW Trinidad, West Indies. 114 acres.

pitch′ line′, *Mach.* **1.** See **pitch circle. 2.** an imaginary line within the profiles of the teeth of a rack, such that it moves against, and at the same rate as, the pitch circle of an engaging pinion.

pitch·man (pich′mən), *n., pl.* **-men. 1.** an itinerant salesman of small wares that are usually carried in a case with collapsible legs, allowing it to be set up or removed quickly. **2.** any high-pressure salesman, as one at a concession at a fair or carnival. [PITCH[1] + MAN[1]]

Pitch·om·e·ter (pich om′i tər), *n.* *Trademark.* an instrument for measuring the pitch of a propeller blade.

pitch·out (pich′out′), *n.* **1.** *Baseball.* a ball purposely thrown by a pitcher too far outside of the plate for the batter to hit, esp. in anticipation of an attempted steal by a base runner. **2.** *Football.* a lateral pass thrown behind the line of scrimmage by one back, esp. a T-formation quarterback, to another. [n. use of v. phrase *pitch out*]

pitch′ pine′, any of several pines from which pitch or turpentine is obtained.

pitch′ pipe′, a small flue or reed pipe producing one or more pitches when blown into, used chiefly for establishing the proper pitch in singing or in tuning a musical instrument.

pitch′ plane′. See under **pitch surface.**

pitch·pole (pich′pōl′), *v.i.,* **-poled, -pol·ing.** (of a boat) to capsize end over end, as in heavy surf. [PITCH[1] + *pole,* alter. of POLL[1]]

pitch·pot (pich′pot′), *n.* a pot used by sailors for heating pitch. [PITCH[2] + POT[1]]

pitch′ ra′tio, *Mach.* the ratio of the pitch of a propeller to the diameter.

pitch′ shot′, *Golf.* a shot in which the ball is hit high into the air and with backspin to ensure little roll upon landing, used in approaching the green. Cf. **chip shot.**

pitch·stone (pich′stōn′), *n.* a glassy igneous rock having a resinous luster and resembling hardened pitch. [trans. of G *Pechstein.* See PITCH[2], STONE]

pitch′ sur′face, (in a gear or rack) an imaginary surface forming a plane (**pitch plane**), a cylinder (**pitch cylinder**), or a cone or frustrum (**pitch cone**), that moves tangent to a similar surface in a meshing gear so that both surfaces travel at the same speed.

pitch·y (pich′ē), *adj.,* **pitch·i·er, pitch·i·est. 1.** full of or abounding in pitch. **2.** smeared with pitch. **3.** resembling pitch, as in color, consistency, etc.: *pitchy mud.* **4.** black; dark as pitch. [PITCH[2] + -Y[1]] —**pitch′i·ness,** *n.*

pit′ dwell′ing, a primitive dwelling consisting of a pit excavated in the earth and roofed over. Also called **pit house.**

pit·e·ous (pit′ē əs), *adj.* **1.** evoking or deserving pity; pathetic: *piteous cries for help.* **2.** *Archaic.* compassionate. [ME *pite* PITY + *-ous;* r. ME *pitous* < OF < ML *pietōs(us).* See PITY, -OUS] —**pit′e·ous·ly,** *adv.* —**pit′e·ous·ness,** *n.*
—**Syn. 1.** affecting, moving, distressing, lamentable, woeful, sad, wretched, sorrowful. See **pitiful.** —**Ant. 1.** delightful.

pit·fall (pit′fôl′), *n.* **1.** a concealed pit prepared as a trap for men or animals. **2.** any trap or danger for the unwary: *the pitfall of pride.* [ME *pittefalle,* OE *pytt* PIT[1] + *fealle* trap]
—**Syn. 1, 2.** See **trap**[1].

pit′ grave′, *Archaeol.* a shallow grave hollowed out of a bed of rock or the floor of a tholos.

pith (pith), *n.* **1.** *Bot.* the central cylinder of parenchymatous tissue in the stems of dicotyledonous plants. See diag. under **stem. 2.** *Zool.* the soft inner part of a feather, a hair, etc. **3.** the important or essential part; essence; heart: *the pith of the matter.* **4.** weight; substance; solidity: *an argument without pith.* **5.** *Archaic.* spinal cord or bone marrow. **6.** *Archaic.* strength, force, or vigor; mettle: *men of pith.* —*v.t.* **7.** to remove the pith from (plants). **8.** to destroy the spinal cord or brain of. **9.** to slaughter, as cattle, by severing the spinal cord. [ME; OE *pitha;* c. D *pit.* See PIT[2]]

pit·head (pit′hed′), *n.* a mine entrance and the surrounding area. [PIT[1] + HEAD]

pith·e·can·thrope (pith′ə kan′thrōp, pith′ə kən thrōp′), *n.* a member of the genus *Pithecanthropus.* [short for PITHECANTHROPUS] —**pith·e·can·throp·ic** (pith′ə kən throp′ik), **pith·i·can·thro·pine** (pith′ə-kan′thrə pīn′), *adj.* —**pith·e·can·thro·pid** (pith′ə-kan′thrə pid, -kən thrō′pid, -throp′id), *n., adj.*

pith·e·can·thro·poid (pith′ə kan′thrə poid′, -kən-thrō′poid), *adj.* of, pertaining to, or resembling a *Pithecanthropus.* [PITHECANTHROP(US) + -OID]

Pith·e·can·thro·pus (pith′ə kan′thrə pəs, -kən-thrō′pəs), *n.* an extinct genus of apelike men, esp. *Pithecanthropus erectus* of the Pleistocene of Java. See illus. in next column. [< NL < Gk *píthēk(os)* ape + *ánthrōpos* man]

pith·e·coid (pith′ə koid′, pi thē′koid), *adj.* **1.** belonging or pertaining to the genus *Pithecia* and related genera, including the saki monkeys. **2.** (loosely) apelike; monkeylike. [< NL *pithēc(us)* (< Gk *píthēkos* ape) + -OID]

Pi·thom (pī′thəm), *n.* one of the two cities built for the Pharaoh by the Israelites during their bondage in Egypt. Ex. 1:11. Also, *Douay Bible,* **Phithom.** Cf. **Raamses.**

pi·thos (pith′os, pī′thos), *n., pl.* **pi·thoi** (pith′oi, pī′thoi). a very large earthenware jar having a wide mouth, used by the ancient Greeks for storing liquids, as wine, or for holding food, as grain, or for the burial of the dead. [< Gk]

pit′ house′. See **pit dwelling.**

pith·y (pith′ē), *adj.,* **pith·i·er, pith·i·est. 1.** full of vigor, substance, or meaning; terse; forcible: *a pithy observation.* **2.** of, like, or abounding in pith. [ME: see PITH, -Y[1]] —**pith′i·ly,** *adv.* —**pith′i·ness,** *n.*
—**Syn. 1.** succinct, pointed, meaty, concise.

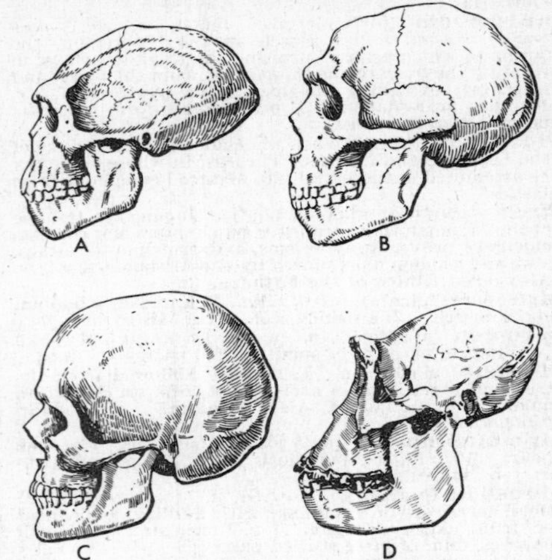

A, Pithecanthropus; B, Neanderthal man; C, Cro-Magnon; D, Gorilla

pit·i·a·ble (pit′ē ə bəl), *adj.* **1.** evoking or deserving pity; lamentable: *pitiable, homeless children.* **2.** evoking or deserving contemptuous pity; miserable; contemptible: *a pitiable lack of character.* [ME < OF *piteable,* equiv. to *pite(er)* (to) PITY + *-able* -ABLE] —**pit′i·a·ble·ness,** *n.* —**pit′i·a·bly,** *adv.*
—**Syn. 1, 2.** See **pitiful.**

pit·i·er (pit′ē ər), *n.* a person who pities. [PITY + -ER[1]]

pit·i·ful (pit′i fəl), *adj.* **1.** such as to excite or deserve pity: *a pitiful fate.* **2.** such as to excite contempt by smallness, poor quality, etc.: *pitiful attempts.* **3.** *Rare.* full of pity or compassion; compassionate. [ME; see PITY, -FUL] —**pit′i·ful·ly,** *adv.* —**pit′i·ful·ness,** *n.*
—**Syn. 1.** lamentable, deplorable, woeful, pathetic. **1, 2.** PITIFUL, PITIABLE, PITEOUS apply to that which excites pity (with compassion or with contempt). That which is PITIFUL is touching and excites pity or is mean and contemptible: *a pitiful leper; a pitiful exhibition of cowardice.* PITIABLE may mean lamentable, or wretched and paltry: *a pitiable hovel.* PITEOUS refers only to that which exhibits suffering and misery, and is therefore heart-rending: *piteous poverty.* **2.** deplorable, mean, low, base, vile, despicable. —**Ant. 1.** delightful. **2.** honorable.

pit·i·less (pit′ē lis, pit′i-), *adj.* feeling or showing no pity; merciless: *pitiless criticism.* [ME. See PITY, -LESS] —**pit′i·less·ly,** *adv.* —**pit′i·less·ness,** *n.*
—**Syn.** unmerciful, implacable, relentless. See **cruel.** —**Ant.** merciful.

Pi·tis·cus (pi tis′kəs), *n.* a crater in the fourth quadrant of the face of the moon: about 52 miles in diameter.

pit·man (pit′mən), *n., pl.* **-men** for 1, **-mans** for 2, 3. **1.** a person who works in a pit, as in coal mining. **2.** *Mach.* any of certain types of connecting rods. **3.** *Rare.* See **walking beam.** [PIT[1] + MAN[1]]

Pit·man (pit′mən), *n.* **1. Sir Isaac,** 1813–97, English inventor of a system of shorthand. **2.** a town in SW New Jersey. 8644 (1960).

Pi·to·cin (pi tō′sin), *n.* *Pharm., Trademark.* oxytocin.

pi·ton (pē′ton, -tōn; *Fr.* pē tôN′), *n., pl.* **-tons** (-tonz, -tōnz; *Fr.* -tôN′). *Mountain Climbing.* a metal spike with an eye through which a rope may be passed. [< F: ringbolt, peak (of a mountain)]

Pi′tot-stat′ic tube′ (pē′tō stat′ik, pē tō′-), (*often l.c.*) *Aeron.* a device consisting of a modified Pitot tube for measuring velocity by means of the differential pressure between the impact and static openings, often connected to an airspeed indicator in aircraft. Also called **Pitot tube.** [see PITOT TUBE]

Pi′tot tube′ (pē′tō, pē tō′), **1.** an instrument for measuring fluid velocity by means of the differential pressure between the tip (dynamic) and side (static) openings. **2.** See **Pitot-static tube.** [named after Henri *Pitot* (1695–1771), French physicist, who invented it]

Pi·tri (pi′trē), *n., pl.* **-tris, -tri.** *Hinduism.* the legendary progenitor of any family. [< Skt *pitṛ* father]

pits (pits), **the,** *Slang.* an extremely unpleasant, boring, or depressing place, condition, person, etc.; the worst: *When you're alone, Christmas is the pits. He's the pits!*

pit′ sam′ple, *Metall.* a sample of new steel taken for chemical analysis during teeming.

pit·saw (pit′sô′), *n.* a two-handed saw used in pit sawing. Also, **pit′ saw′.** [PIT[1] + SAW[1]] —**pit′ saw′yer.**

pit′ saw′ing, a method of sawing logs or timbers, as into boards, in which the piece to be cut is laid horizontally and cut by a saw operated vertically by two men, one above and one in a pit below the piece.

Pitt (pit), *n.* **1. William, 1st Earl of Chatham,** 1708–78, British statesman. **2.** his son **William,** 1759–1806, British statesman: prime minister 1783–1801, 1804–06.

pit·ta (pit′ə), *n.* any of several brilliantly colored, passerine birds of the family *Pittidae,* found in dark, Old World, tropical forests. [< Telugu: bird]

pit·tance (pit′ᵊns), *n.* **1.** a small allowance or sum for living expenses. **2.** a scanty income or remuneration. [ME *pitaunce* < OF *pitance,* var. of *pietance* piety, pity, allowance of food (in a monastery). See PITY, -ANCE]

pit·ter-pat·ter (pit′ər pat′ər), *n.* **1.** the sound of a rapid succession of light beats or taps, as of rain, footsteps, etc. —*v.i.* **2.** to produce this sound: *She pitter-pattered along the hallway.* —*adv.* **3.** with such a sound: *Mice ran pitter-patter through the deserted house.* [? imit.]

Pit·the·us (pit′thē əs, -thōōs), *n. Class. Myth.* a son of Pelops and Hippodamia, and father of Aethra. He was considered the wisest man of his time.

Pitts·burg (pits′bûrg), *n.* **1.** a city in W California. 19,062 (1960). **2.** a city in SE Kansas. 18,678 (1960). **3.** a town in NE Texas. 3796 (1960).

Pitts·burgh (pits′bûrg), *n.* a port in SW Pennsylvania, at the confluence of the Allegheny and Monongahela rivers which forms the Ohio River: steel industry. 604,332 (1960).

Pitts′burg Land′ing, a village in SW Tennessee, on the Tennessee River: battle of Shiloh in 1862.

Pitts·field (pits′fēld′), *n.* **1.** a city in W Massachusetts. 57,879 (1960). **2.** a town in W Illinois. 4089 (1960). **3.** a town in central Maine. 3232 (1960).

pi·tu·i·tar·y (pi tōō′i ter′ē, -tyōō′-), *n., pl.* **-tar·ies,** *adj.* **—***n.* **1.** See **pituitary gland. 2.** *Pharm.* the extract obtained from the lobes of the pituitaries of hogs, sheep, and other domestic animals: the posterior lobe constituent increases blood pressure, contracts stomach muscles, etc., and the anterior lobe constituent regulates growth of the skeleton. **—***adj.* **3.** of, pertaining to, or involving the pituitary gland. **4.** noting a physical type of abnormal size with overgrown extremities resulting from excessive pituitary secretion. [< L *pītuītāri(us)* pertaining to or secreting phlegm. See PIP², -ARY]

pitu′itary gland′, *Anat.* a small, oval endocrine gland attached to the base of the brain and situated in a depression of the sphenoid bone, which secretes several hormones. Also called **pitu′itary bod′y, hypophysis.** See diag. under **brain.**

pi·tu·i·tous (pi tōō′i təs, -tyōō′-), *adj. Archaic.* mucous. [< L *pītuītōs(us)* full of phlegm. See PIP², -OUS] **—pi·tu′i·tous·ness,** *n.*

pit·u·ri (pich′ə rē), *n.* **1.** a solanaceous shrub or small tree, *Duboisia hopwoodi*, of Australia. **2.** a stimulant made from the dried leaves and twigs of this plant, used by the aborigines as a narcotic. [< native Austral]

pit′ vi′per, any of numerous venomous snakes of the family *Crotalidae*, of the New World, Asia, and the Malay Archipelago, as the rattlesnake, water moccasin, and copperhead, having a heat-sensitive pit on each side of the head between the eye and nostril.

pit·y (pit′ē), *n., pl.* **pit·ies,** *v.,* **pit·ied, pit·y·ing. —***n.* **1.** sympathetic or kindly sorrow excited by the suffering or misfortune of another, often leading one to give relief or aid or to show mercy: *to weep from pity; to feel pity for someone; to have pity on someone.* **2.** a cause or reason for pity, sorrow, or regret: *What a pity you could not go!* **—***v.t.* **3.** to feel pity or compassion for; be sorry for; commiserate. **—***v.i.* **4.** to have compassion; feel pity. [ME *pite* < OF; early OF *pitet* < L *pietāt-* (s. of *pietās*) PIETY] **—pit′y·ing·ly,** *adv.*
—Syn. 1. commiseration, sympathy, compassion.

pit·y·ri·a·sis (pit′ə rī′ə sis), *n.* **1.** *Pathol.* any of various skin diseases marked by the shedding of branlike scales of epidermis. **2.** *Vet. Pathol.* a skin disease in various domestic animals marked by dry scales. [< NL < Gk: branlike eruption, equiv. to *pítyr(on)* bran, scale + *-iasis* -IASIS]

pit·y·roid (pit′ə roid′), *adj. Med.* scaly; resembling bran. [< Gk *pítyr(on)* + -OID]

Pit·ys (pit′is), *n. Class. Myth.* a nymph who was changed into a pine tree to escape the god Pan.

più (pyōō), *adv. Music.* more: *più allegro.* [< It < L *plus*]

Pius I (pī′əs), **Saint,** pope A.D. 140–155?.

Pius II, (*Enea Silvio de Piccolomini*) 1405–64, Italian ecclesiastic: pope 1458–64. Literary name, **Aeneas Silvius.**

Pius III, (*Francesco Nanni Todeschini Piccolomini*) 1439–1503, Italian ecclesiastic: pope 1503.

Pius IV, (*Giovanni Angelo Medici*) 1499–1565, Italian ecclesiastic: pope 1559–65.

Pius V, Saint (*Michele Ghislieri*), 1504–72, Italian ecclesiastic: pope 1566–72.

Pius VI, (*Giovanni Angelo,* or *Giannangelo, Braschi*) 1717–99, Italian ecclesiastic: pope 1775–99.

Pius VII, (*Luigi Barnaba Chiaramonti*) 1740–1823, Italian ecclesiastic: pope 1800–23.

Pius VIII, (*Francesco Saverio Castiglioni*) 1761–1830, Italian ecclesiastic: pope 1829–30.

Pius IX, (*Giovanni Maria Mastai-Ferretti*) 1792–1878, Italian ecclesiastic: pope 1846–78.

Pius X, Saint (*Giuseppe Sarto*), 1835–1914, Italian ecclesiastic: pope 1903–14.

Pius XI, (*Achille Ratti*) 1857–1939, Italian ecclesiastic: pope 1922–39.

Pius XII, (*Eugenio Pacelli*) 1876–1958, Italian ecclesiastic: pope 1939–58.

Pi·ute (pī ōōt′), *n., pl.* **-utes,** (*esp. collectively*) **-ute.** Paiute.

piv·ot (piv′ət), *n.* **1.** a pin or short shaft on the end of which something rests and turns, or upon and about which something rotates or oscillates. **2.** the end of a shaft or arbor, resting and turning in a bearing. **3.** that on which something turns, hinges, or depends: *He is the pivot of her life.* **4.** the person in a line, as of troops on parade, whom the others use as a point about which to wheel or maneuver. **5.** a whirling about on one foot. **6.** *Dentistry.* (formerly) dowel (def. 3). **—***v.i.* **7.** to turn on or as on a pivot. **—***v.t.* **8.** to mount on, attach by, or provide with a pivot or pivots. [< F < It *pivolo* peg (with *-ot* for *-olo*), dim. of **pivo* for *piva*, var. of *pipa* PIPE¹]

piv·ot·al (piv′ə tᵊl), *adj.* **1.** of, pertaining to, or serving as a pivot. **2.** of critical importance: *a pivotal event in his career.* [PIVOT + -AL¹] **—piv′ot·al·ly,** *adv.*

piv·ot·ing (piv′ə tiŋ), *n. Dentistry.* (formerly) the attaching of an artificial crown to the root of a tooth with a metal dowel. [PIVOT (V.) + -ING¹]

pix¹ (piks), *n.* pyx.

pix² (piks), *n., pl.* **pix** for 2. **1.** a pl. of **pic**². **2.** pic².

pix·el (pik′səl, -sel), *n. Computers, Television.* the smallest element of an image that can be individually displayed. [PIX² (def. 1) + EL(EMENT)]

pix·i·lat·ed (pik′sə lā′tid), *adj.* amusingly eccentric or prankish. [PIXY + (TITT)ILATED]

pix·y (pik′sē), *n., pl.* **pix·ies,** *adj.* **—***n.* **1.** a fairy or sprite, esp. a mischievous one. **—***adj.* **2.** playfully impish or mischievous; prankish: *pixy mood; a pixy sense of humor.* Also, **pix′ie.** [?]

pix·y·ish (pik′sē ish), *adj.* pixy. Also, **pix′ie·ish.** [PIXY + -ISH¹]

pi·zaine (pē′zān), *n. Armor.* a mail collar of the 14th century, worn with a hauberk. [appar. < OF, equiv. to *piz* breast (< L *pectus*) + *-aine* n. suffix]

Pi·zar·ro (pi zär′ō; *Sp.* pē thär′rō, -sär′-), *n.* **Fran·cis·co** (fran sis′kō; *Sp.* fʀän thēs′kō, -sēs′-), c1470–1541, Spanish conqueror of Peru.

pizz., *Music.* pizzicato.

piz·za (pēt′sə), *n.* a flat, open-faced pie of Italian origin, consisting of a crust topped with tomato sauce and cheese, often garnished with anchovies, sausage slices, mushrooms, bacon, olives, etc. [< It]

piz·ze·ri·a (pēt′sə rē′ə), *n. U.S.* a restaurant, bakery, or the like, where pizzas are sold and usually made. [PIZZ(A) + *-eria*, Italianized -ERY]

piz·zi·ca·to (pit′sə kä′tō; *It.* pēt′tsē kä′tô), *adj., n., pl.* **-ti** (-tē). *Music.* **—***adj.* **1.** played by plucking the strings with the finger instead of using the bow, as on a violin. **—***n.* **2.** a note or passage so played. [< It, ptp. of *pizzicare* to pluck, pick, twang (a stringed instrument)]

pk, peck; pecks.

pk., *pl.* **pks. 1.** pack. **2.** park. **3.** peak. **4.** peck.

pkg., *pl.* **pkgs.** package.

pkt., packet.

PKU test, a urine test for detecting phenylketonuria in infants.

pl., 1. place. **2.** plate. **3.** plural.

P.L., Poet Laureate.

plac·a·ble (plak′ə bəl, plā′kə-), *adj.* capable of being placated or appeased; forgiving. [ME < OF < L *plācābil(is).* See PLACATE¹, -ABLE] **—plac′a·bil′i·ty, plac′a·ble·ness,** *n.*

plac·age (plak′ij), *n.* a thin facing on a building. [< F; see PLAQUE, -AGE]

plac·ard (plak′ärd, -ərd), *n.* **1.** a written or printed notice to be posted in a public place; poster. **2.** *Armor.* placate². **—***v.t.* **3.** to post placards on or in. **4.** to publicize, or give notice of, by means of placards. **5.** to post as a placard. [late ME < MF. See PLAQUE, -ARD] **—plac′ard·er,** *n.*

pla·cate¹ (plā′kāt, plak′āt), *v.t.,* **-cat·ed, -cat·ing.** to appease or pacify: *to placate an outraged citizenry.* [< L *plācāt(us)*, ptp. of *plācāre* to quiet, calm, appease, akin to *placēre* to please; see -ATE¹] **—pla′cat·er,** *n.* **—pla·ca·tion** (plā kā′shən), *n.*
—Syn. conciliate, satisfy.

plac·ate² (plak′āt, -it), *n. Armor.* a piece of plate armor of the 15th to the 18th century protecting the lower part of the torso in front: used esp. as a reinforcement over a breastplate. Also, **placard, plac′cate, plackart.** [appar. var. of PLACARD]

pla·ca·tive (plā′kə tiv, plak′ə-), *adj.* placatory. [PLACATE¹ + -IVE]

pla·ca·to·ry (plā′kə tôr′ē, -tōr′ē, plak′ə-), *adj.* serving, tending, or intended to placate: *a placatory remark.* [< L *plācātōri(us).* See PLACATE¹, -ORY¹]

place (plās), *n., v.,* **placed, plac·ing. —***n.* **1.** a particular portion of space, whether of definite or indefinite extent. **2.** space in general: *time and place.* **3.** the portion of space occupied by anything: *The vase is in its place.* **4.** a space or spot, set apart or used for a particular purpose: *a place of worship.* **5.** any part or spot in a body or surface: *a decayed place in a tooth.* **6.** a particular passage in a book or writing: *to find the place where one left off reading.* **7.** a space or seat for a person, as in a theater, train, etc.: *Please save my place for me.* **8.** the space or position customarily or previously occupied by a person or thing: *Some of the books are out of place.* **9.** position, situation, or circumstances: *if I were in your place.* **10.** a proper or appropriate location or position: *A restaurant is not the place for an argument.* **11.** a job, post, or office: *persons in high places in government.* **12.** a function or duty: *It is not your place to offer criticism.* **13.** a position, situation, or circumstance: *I'd take the job if I were in your place.* **14.** high position or rank: *aristocrats of power and place.* **15.** official employment or position: *several places that have not been filled.* **16.** a region: *to travel to distant places.* **17.** an open space, or square, in a city or town. **18.** a short street, a court, etc. **19.** a portion of space used for habitation, as a city, town, or village: *Trains rarely stop in that place any more.* **20.** a building, location, etc., set aside for a specific purpose: *He will soon need a larger place for his expanding business. A nightclub is a place of entertainment.* **21.** a part of a building: *The kitchen is the sunniest place in the house.* **22.** a residence, dwelling, or house: *Please come and have dinner at my place.* **23.** lieu; substitution (usually fol. by *of*): *Use water in place of milk.* **24.** a step or point in order of proceeding: *in the first place.* **25.** a fitting opportunity: *There's a place in this town for a man of his talents.* **26.** a reasonable ground or occasion: *This is no place for such an outburst.* **27.** *Arith.* **a.** the position of a figure in a series, as in decimal notation. **b.** Usually, **places.** the figures of the series. **28.** *Drama.* one of the three unities. Cf. **unity** (def. 11). **29.** *Astron.* the position of a heavenly body at any instant. **30.** *Sports.* **a.** a position among the leading competitors, usually the first, second, or third at the finish line. **b.** *U.S.* the position of the competitor who comes in second in a horse race, harness race, etc. Cf. **show** (def. 33), **win** (def. 16). **31. places,** *Theat.* a call summoning performers for the beginning of a performance or an act. **32.** *Archaic.* room or space for entry or passage: *to make place for the gentry.* **33. give place to, a.** to give precedence or priority to: *Time passes and the old gives place to the new.* **b.** to be succeeded or replaced by: *Laissez faire has given place to the extension of government control in the nation's economic life.* **34. go places,** *Slang.* to become successful; advance in one's career: *He'll never go places if he stays in his home town.* **35. in place,** in the correct or usual position or order: *Dinner is ready, and everything is in place.* **36. know** or **keep one's place,** to recognize one's social rank, esp. if inferior, and adjust one's behavior accordingly: *They treated their servants well, but expected them always to know their place.* **37. out of place, a.** not in the correct or usual position or order: *The chairs are out of place.* **b.** unsuitable to the circumstances or surroundings; inappropriate: *He had always felt out of place in an academic environment. A green suit was out of place at the ball.* **38. put someone in his place,** to lower someone's self-esteem; humble, esp. an arrogant person: *A hitch in the army ought to put him in his place. He put her in her place by reminding her who was boss.* **39. take place,** to happen; occur: *The commencement exercises will take place outdoors, unless it rains.* **—***v.t.* **40.** to put in the proper position or order; arrange; dispose: *Place the silverware on the table for dinner.* **41.** to put in a suitable place for some purpose: *to place an advertisement in the newspaper.* **42.** to put into particular or proper hands: *to place evidence with the district attorney.* **43.** to appoint (a person) to a post or office: *The president placed him in the Department of Agriculture.* **44.** to find a place, situation, etc., for (a person): *The agency had no trouble placing him with a good firm.* **45.** to determine or indicate the place of: *to place health among the greatest gifts of life.* **46.** to assign a certain position or rank to: *The army placed him in the infantry.* **47.** to succeed in attaining a position for in an athletic or other contest: *to place players on the all-American team; to place students in the finals of the interscholastic chess tournament.* **48.** to put or set in a particular place, position, situation, or relation. **49.** to identify by connecting with the proper place, circumstances, etc.: *to be unable to place a person; to place a face; to place an accent.* **50.** to sing or speak with consciousness of the bodily point of emphasis of resonance of each tone or register. **51.** *Sports.* **a.** to finish among the first three competitors in a race. **b.** *U.S.* to finish second in a horse race, harness race, etc. **52.** to earn a specified standing with relation to others, as in an examination, competition, etc.: *He placed second in a graduation class of 90.* [ME; OE *plæce* < L *platea*, var. of *platēa* street, courtyard, area < Gk *plateia* broad street, n. use of fem. of *platýs* broad; see PLATY-] **—place′a·ble,** *adj.* **—place′less,** *adj.* **—place′less·ly,** *adv.*
—Syn. 1. location, locale, locality, site. **11.** rank, employment. See **position. 12.** charge; responsibility. **16.** area, section, sector. **40.** situate, station. See **put. 41.** locate, set, deposit, lay, seat. **43.** hire.

pla·ce·bo (plə sē′bō), *n., pl.* **-bos, -boes. 1.** *Rom. Cath. Ch.* the vespers of the office for the dead: so called from the initial word of the first antiphon, taken from Psalm 114:9 of the Vulgate. **2.** *Med., Pharm.* **a.** a substance having no pharmacological effect but given merely to satisfy a patient who supposes it to be a medicine. **b.** a substance having no pharmacological effect but administered as a control in testing experimentally or clinically the efficacy of a biologically active preparation. [ME < L: I shall be pleasing, acceptable]

place′ card′, a card with the name of a guest on it, placed on the table, indicating where he is to sit.

place′ kick′, *Football.* a kick in which the ball is held nearly upright on the ground either by means of a tee or by a teammate, as in a kickoff, an attempt at a field goal, etc. Cf. **drop kick, punt**¹ (def. 1).

place-kick (plās′kik′), *Football.* **—***v.t.* **1.** to make (a field goal or point after touchdown) by a place kick. **2.** to kick (the ball) as held for a place kick. **—***v.i.* **3.** to make a place kick. [v. use of PLACE KICK] **—place′-kick′er,** *n.*

place·man (plās′mən), *n., pl.* **-men.** *Brit.* a person who holds an office, esp. one appointed to a government office as a reward for political support of an elected officer. [PLACE + MAN¹] **—place′man·ship′,** *n.*

place′ mat′, a mat set on a dining table beneath a place setting.

place·ment (plās′mənt), *n.* **1.** act of placing. **2.** state of being placed. **3.** act of an employment office or employer in filling a position. **4.** location; arrangement: *the placement of furniture.* **5.** *Football.* **a.** the placing of the ball on the ground in attempting a place kick. **b.** the position of the ball. **c.** a place kick. **d.** a score made by a place kick: *Jones made 43 consecutive placements last season.* **6.** (in tennis, badminton, handball, etc.) a winning shot in which the ball or shuttlecock is so hit that one's opponent is unable to touch it with his racket, as in tennis, or with his hand, as in handball. [PLACE + -MENT]

place-name (plās′nām′), *n.* the name given to or held by a geographical location, as a town, city, village, etc.

pla·cen·ta (plə sen′tə), *n., pl.* **-tas, -tae** (-tē). **1.** *Anat., Zool.* the organ in most mammals, formed in the lining of the uterus by the union of the uterine mucous membrane with the membranes of the fetus, that provides for the nourishment of the fetus and the elimination of its waste products. **2.** *Bot.* **a.** the part of the ovary of flowering plants which bears the ovules. **b.** (in ferns and related plants) the tissue giving rise to sporangia. [< NL: something having a flat, circular form, L: a cake < Gk *plakóenta*, acc. of *plakóeis* flat cake, deriv. of *pláx* (gen. *plakós*) flat] **—pla·cen′tal, plac·en·tar·y** (plas′ən ter′ē, plə sen′tə rē), *adj.*

pla·cen·tate (plə sen′tāt), *adj.* having a placenta. [PLACENT(A) + -ATE¹]

plac·en·ta·tion (plas′ən tā′shən), *n.* **1.** *Anat., Zool.* **a.** the formation of a placenta. **b.** the manner of the disposition or construction of a placenta. **2.** *Bot.* the disposition or arrangement of a placenta or placentas. [< F *placentation.* See PLACENTA, -ATION]

Pla·cen·tia (plə sen′shə, -shē ə), *n.* **1.** a town in S California. 5861 (1960). **2.** ancient name of **Piacenza.**

place′ of arms′, 1. an area in a fortress or a fortified town where troops could assemble for defense. **2.** an enlarged part of the covered way in a fortification.

Place Pi·galle (plȧs pē gȧl′), a square in Paris, France: noted for its night clubs.

plac·er¹ (plas′ər), *n. Mining.* **1.** a superficial gravel or similar deposit containing particles of gold or the like. **2.** the site of a form of mining (**plac′er min′ing**) in which a placer deposit is washed to precipitate the gold. [< AmerSp: sand-bank; akin to **PLAZA.** See PLACE]

plac·er[2] (plā′sər), *n.* **1.** a person who sets things in place or arranges them. **2.** a person or animal that is among the winners of a race or other contest. [PLACE + -ER[1]]

Plac·er·ville (plas′ər vil′), *n.* a town in central California. 4439 (1960).

pla′cer·y boom′ (plā′sə rē), *Naut.* either of two booms formerly rigged out from the sides of a sailing vessel to hold out the clews of a square foresail when running before the wind. Also, **passaree boom.** [*placery* alter. of *passaree,* ? < F *passeresse,* fem. of *passeur* passer, term used for the reef point]

place′ set′ting, 1. the group of dishes and eating utensils, as knives, forks, etc., set at the place of each person at a meal. **2.** a group of such dishes or eating utensils as a selling unit.

pla·cet (plā′sit), *n.* an expression or vote of assent or sanction by the Latin word *placet* (it pleases).

plac·id (plas′id), *adj.* pleasantly calm or peaceful; unruffled; tranquil; serene: *placid waters.* [< L *placid(us)* calm, quiet, akin to *placēre* to please (orig., to calm); see -ID[4]] **—pla·cid·i·ty** (plə sid′i tē), **plac′id·ness,** *n.* **—plac′id·ly,** *adv.*
—Syn. quiet, undisturbed. See **peaceful.**

Plá′ci·do's disk′ (plä′si dōz′), *Ophthalm.* a white disk marked with concentric black rings, used as a keratoscope.

Plac·i·dyl (plas′i dil, plä′si-), *n. Pharm. Trademark.* ethchlorvynol.

plack (plak), *n.* a very small copper coin used in Scotland in the 15th and 16th centuries as a four-penny piece. [late ME *placke* < MFlem: small coin, something (beaten) flat]

plack·art (plak′ərt), *n. Armor.* placate[2].

plack·et (plak′it), *n.* **1.** the opening or slit at the top of a skirt, or in a dress or blouse, which facilitates putting it on and taking it off. **2.** a pocket, esp. one in a woman's skirt. **3.** *Archaic.* **a.** a petticoat. **b.** a woman. [< D, var. of MD *plackaet* breastplate, equiv. to ML *placca* thin plate (see PLACK) + *-āta* -ATE[1]]

plac·ode (plak′ōd), *n. Embryol.* a local thickening of the epithelial layer in the embryo, which usually constitutes the primordium of a specific structure or organ. [< Gk *plak-* (s. of *pláx*) something flat, tablet + -ODE[1]]

plac·oid (plak′oid), *adj.* platelike, as the scales or dermal investments of sharks. [< Gk *plak-* (s. of *pláx*) something flat, tablet + -OID]

pla·fond (plə fon′; *Fr.* pla fôɴ′), *n., pl.* **-fonds** (-fonz′; *Fr.* -fôɴ′). *Archit.* a ceiling, whether flat or arched, esp. one of decorative character. [< F; MF *platfond* ceiling, lit., flat bottom, i.e., underside. See PLATE[1], FUND]

pla·ga (plā′gə), *n., pl.* **pla·gae** (plā′gē). *Zool.* a spot or streak of color. [< L: stripe, wound; akin to Gk *plēgḗ* stroke]

pla·gal (plā′gəl), *adj. Music.* (of a Gregorian mode) having the final in the middle of the compass. Cf. **authentic** (def. 5a). [< ML *plagāl(is),* equiv. to *plag(a)* plagal mode (appar. back formation from *plagius* plagal; see PLAGE) + *-ālis* -AL[1]]

pla′gal ca′dence, *Modern Music.* a cadence in which the chord of the tonic is preceded by that of the subdominant.

pla·gate (plā′gāt), *adj. Zool.* marked with a plaga or plagae. [PLAG(A) + -ATE[1]]

plage (plȧzh *for 1;* plāzh *for 2*), *n., pl.* **plages** (plȧzh *for 1;* plā′zhiz *for 2*). **1.** (*italics.*) *French.* a beach on the seashore for bathing. **2.** *Astron.* the phenomenon of large, bright clouds of hydrogen and calcium often seen near sun spots on the sun's surface. [< F < It *piaggia* < LL *plagia* shore, n. use of fem. of *plagius* < Gk *plágios* slanting, sideways; see PLAGI-]

plagi-, var. of **plagio-:** *plagihedral.*

pla·gia·rise (plā′jə rīz′, -jē ə rīz′), *v.t., v.i.,* **-rised, -ris·ing.** *Chiefly Brit.* plagiarize. **—pla′gia·ris′er,** *n.*

pla·gia·rism (plā′jə riz′əm, -jē ə riz′-), *n.* **1.** the appropriation or imitation of the language, ideas, and thoughts of another author, and representation of them as one's original work. **2.** something appropriated and presented in this manner. [PLAGIAR(Y) + -ISM] **—pla′gia·rist,** *n.* **—pla′gia·ris′tic,** *adj.*

pla·gia·rize (plā′jə rīz′, -jē ə rīz′), *v.,* **-rized, -riz·ing.** **—***v.t.* **1.** to appropriate by plagiarism. **2.** to appropriate ideas, passages, etc., from (a work) by plagiarism. **—***v.i.* **3.** to commit plagiarism. Also, *esp. Brit.,* **plagiarise.** [PLAGIAR(ISM) + -IZE] **—pla′gia·riz′er,** *n.*

pla·gia·ry (plā′jə rē, -jē ə rē), *n., pl.* **-ries. 1.** plagiarism. **2.** a plagiarist. [< L *plagiāri(us)* kidnaper, equiv. to *plagi(um)* kidnaping (akin to *plagia* snare) + *-ārius* -ARY]

pla·gi·he·dral (plā′jə hē′drəl), *adj.* (of a crystal) having faces arranged obliquely in a helix. [PLAGI- + -HEDRAL]

plagio-, a learned borrowing from Greek meaning "oblique," used in the formation of compound words: *plagioclase.* Also, **plagi-.** [comb. form repr. Gk *plágios,* equiv. to *plág(os)* side + *-ios* adj. suffix]

pla·gi·o·ceph·a·ly (plā′jē ə sef′ə lē), *n. Med.* a deformity of the skull in which one side is more developed in the front, and the other side is more developed in the rear. Also, **pla′gi·o·ceph′a·lism.** [PLAGIO- + CEPHAL- + -Y[3]] **—pla·gi·o·ce·phal·ic** (plā′jē ō sə fal′ik), **pla′gi·o·ceph′a·lous,** *adj.*

pla·gi·o·clase (plā′jē ə klās′), *n.* any of the feldspar minerals varying in composition from acidic albite, $NaAlSi_3O_8$, to basic anorthite, $CaAl_2Si_2O_8$, found in most igneous rocks: shows twinning striations on good cleavage surfaces. Also called **soda-lime feldspar.** [PLAGIO- + Gk *klásis* fracture] **—pla·gi·o·clas·tic** (plā′jē ə klas′tik), *adj.*

pla·gi·o·trop·ic (plā′jē ə trop′ik), *adj. Bot.* noting, pertaining to, or exhibiting a mode of growth which is more or less divergent from the vertical. [PLAGIO- + -TROPIC] **—pla′gi·o·trop′i·cal·ly,** *adv.*

pla·gi·ot·ro·pism (plā′jē o′trə piz′əm), *n. Bot.* plagiotropic tendency or growth. [PLAGIOTROP(IC) + -ISM]

plague (plāg), *n., v.,* **plagued, pla·guing.** **—***n.* **1.** an epidemic disease of high mortality; pestilence. **2.** an infectious, epidemic disease caused by a bacterium, *Pasteurella pestis,* characterized by fever, chills, and prostration, transmitted to man from rats by means of the bites of fleas. Cf. **bubonic plague, pneumonic plague, septicemic plague. 3.** any widespread affliction, calamity, or evil, esp. one regarded as a visitation from God: *a plague of war and desolation.* **4.** any cause of trouble or vexation: *Uninvited guests are a plague.* **—***v.t.* **5.** to trouble or torment in any manner: *The question of his future plagues him with doubt.* **6.** to annoy, bother, or pester: *Ants plagued the picnickers.* **7.** to smite with a plague, pestilence, death, etc.; scourge: *those whom the gods had plagued.* **8.** to infect with a plague; cause an epidemic in or among: *diseases that still plague us.* **9.** to afflict with any evil: *He was plagued by rheumatism all his life.* [ME *plage* < L *plāga* stripe, wound, LL: pestilence; see PLAGA] **—pla′guer,** *n.*
—Syn. 4. nuisance, bother, annoyance, torment. **6.** harass, vex, harry, hector, fret, worry, badger, irritate, disturb. See **bother.**

Plague, The, a novel (1947) by Albert Camus. French, **La Peste.**

pla·guy (plā′gē), *Archaic except Dial.* **—***adj.* **1.** such as to plague, torment, or annoy; vexatious: *a plaguy pile of debts.* **—***adv.* **2.** vexatiously or excessively: *The room is plaguy hot.* Also, **pla′guey.** [PLAGUE + -Y[1]] **—pla′gui·ly,** *adv.*

plaice (plās), *n., pl.* **plaice. 1.** a European flatfish, *Pleuronectes platessa,* used for food. **2.** any of various American flatfishes or flounders. [ME, var. of *plais* < OF < LL *platessa* flatfish < Gk *platýs* flat, broad]

plaid (plad), *n.* **1.** any fabric woven of differently colored yarns in a crossbarred pattern. **2.** a pattern of this kind. **3.** a long, rectangular piece of cloth, usually with such a pattern and worn across the left shoulder by Scottish Highlanders. **—***adj.* **4.** having the pattern of a plaid. [< Gael *plaide* blanket, plaid]

plaid·ed (plad′id), *adj.* **1.** wearing a plaid. **2.** made of plaid, or having a similar pattern. [PLAID + -ED[3]]

plain[1] (plān), *adj.* **1.** clear or distinct to the eye or ear: *a plain trail to the river; to stand in plain view.* **2.** clear to the mind; evident, manifest, or obvious: *to make one's meaning plain; a dislike of the subject that was plain.* **3.** conveying the meaning clearly and simply; easily understood: *plain talk.* **4.** downright; sheer; utter: *plain folly; plain stupidity.* **5.** free from ambiguity or evasion; candid; outspoken: *the plain truth of the matter.* **6.** without special pretensions, superiority, elegance, etc.; ordinary: *plain people.* **7.** not beautiful; physically unattractive or undistinguished: *a plain face; a childhood fear that she would be plain.* **8.** without intricacies or difficulties. **9.** ordinary, simple, or unostentatious: *Although she was a duchess, her manners were attractively plain.* **10.** with little or no embellishment, decoration, or enhancing elaboration: *a plain blue suit.* **11.** without a pattern, figure, or device: *a plain fabric.* **12.** not rich, highly seasoned, or elaborately prepared, as food: *plain, fresh, substantial fare; a plain diet.* **13.** flat or level: *plain country.* **14.** unobstructed, clear, or open, as ground, a space, etc. **15.** *Cards.* being other than a face card or a trump. **—***adv.* **16.** clearly and simply: *He's just plain stupid.* **—***n.* **17.** an area of land not significantly higher than adjacent areas and with relatively minor differences in elevation, commonly less than 500 feet, within the area. **18. the Plain,** *Fr. Hist.* (in the National Assembly) the loosely organized party of moderate republicans: so called because its members occupied the lowest seats or benches. Cf. **mountain** (def. 4). **19. The Plains.** See **Great Plains.** [ME < OF < L *plān(us)* flat, level, *plān(um)* flat country] **—plain′ly,** *adv.* **—plain′ness,** *n.*
—Syn. 1, 2. lucid, understandable, intelligible, unmistakable, apparent, perspicuous. **2.** unambiguous, unequivocal, patent, transparent. **3.** direct. **5.** unreserved, straightforward, blunt, frank, ingenuous, open, sincere. **6.** unpretentious. **10.** unadorned. See **simple.**
—Ant. 1. indistinct. **2.** obscure. **13.** hilly.

plain[2] (plān), *v.i. Brit. Dial.* complain. [ME *plei(g)n-e(n)* < OF *plaign-,* s. of *plaindre* < L *plangere* to beat (the breast, etc.), lament; akin to Gk *plēssein* to strike]

plain′ bear′ing, *Mach.* any of various bearings, not containing rolling elements, that present to the shaft or axle they support broad areas of corresponding form, usually segments of a cylinder. Cf. **rolling-element bearing.**

plain·chant (plān′chant′, -chänt′), *n.* plainsong. [PLAIN[1] + CHANT, modeled on F *plain-chant*]

plain′-clothes′ man′ (plān′klōz′, -klōthz′), a police detective who wears mufti while on duty.

plain·clothes·man (plān′klōz′mən, -man′, -klōthz′-), *n., pl.* **-men** (-mən, -men′). See **plain-clothes man.**

plain′ deal′ing, direct and honest conduct in one's relations and transactions with others.

Plain·field (plān′fēld′), *n.* **1.** a city in N New Jersey. 45,330 (1960). **2.** a town in central Indiana. 5460 (1960).

plain′ knit′, the simplest knitted construction, consisting of vertical ribs visible on the front of the fabric and horizontal rows of stitches visible on the back, used in the production of hosiery and jersey fabrics. Also called **flat knit.**

plain-laid (plān′lād′), *adj. Ropemaking.* noting a rope laid right-handed with three left-handed strands, without a heart; hawser-laid.

plain′ lap′. See **lap joint.**

Plain′ Peo′ple, members of the Amish, the Mennonites, or the Dunkers: so named because they wear plain dress and stress simple living.

plain′ rail′, (in a double-hung window) a meeting rail equal in thickness to its sash. Cf. **check rail.**

plain′ sail′, 1. any of the ordinary working sails of a vessel. **2.** all these sails, taken collectively.

plain′ sail′ing, 1. *Naut.* sailing on waters that are free of hazards or obstructions. Cf. **plane sailing. 2.** an easy and unobstructed way, course, or plan: *As an heir to a large fortune, he looked forward to financial plain sailing.*

plain-saw (plān′sô′), *v.t.,* **-sawed, -sawed** or **-sawn, -saw·ing.** to reduce (a squared log) to boards with evenly spaced parallel cuts; bastard-saw; tangent-saw.

Plains′ In′dian, a member of any of the American Indian tribes, as those of the Algonquian, Athabascan, Caddoan, Kiowa, Siouan, or Uto-Aztecan linguistic stocks, which formerly inhabited the Great Plains. All were more or less nomadic, following the buffalo, and were often in touch with one another so that the development among them of common culture traits is noticeable. Also called **Buffalo Indian.**

plains·man (plānz′mən), *n., pl.* **-men.** a man or inhabitant of the plains. [PLAIN[1] + -S[3] + MAN[1]]

Plains′ of A′braham, a high plain adjoining the city of Quebec, Canada: battlefield where the English under Wolfe defeated the French under Montcalm in 1759.

plain′ song′, 1. a cantus firmus or theme chosen for contrapuntal development. **2.** any simple and unadorned melody or air.

plain·song (plān′sông′, -song′), *n.* **1.** the unisonous vocal music used in the Christian church from the earliest times. **2.** modal liturgical music; Gregorian chant. Also called **plainchant.** [trans. of ML *cantus plānus*]

plain-spo·ken (plān′spō′kən), *adj.* candid; blunt.

plain·stones (plān′stōnz′), *n.pl. Scot.* **1.** flagstones. **2.** (*construed as sing.*) a flagstone walk or passageway. Also, **plain·stanes** (plān′stānz′). [PLAIN[1] + STONE + -S[3]]

plain′ suit′, *Cards.* a suit other than the trump suit. Also called **side suit.**

plaint (plānt), *n.* **1.** a complaint. **2.** *Law.* a statement of grievance made to a court for the purpose of asking redress. **3.** *Archaic.* a lament. [ME < MF < L *planct-t(us)* (4th decl. n.) a striking or beating (the breast) in grief, equiv. to *planct-* (ptp. s. of *plangere* to beat, strike, etc.) + *-us,* u- stem suffix]

plain′ ta′ble. See **plane table.**

plain′ text′, the original message of a cryptogram expressed in ordinary language, as opposed to a coded or enciphered version. Also called **clear text.** Cf. **cryptography.**

plain·tiff (plān′tif), *n. Law.* a person who brings suit in a court (opposed to *defendant*). [late ME *plaintif* complaining person, n. use of *plaintif,* early form of PLAINTIVE] **—plain′tiff·ship′,** *n.*

plain·tive (plān′tiv), *adj.* expressing sorrow or melancholy: *a plaintive melody.* [PLAINT + -IVE; r. ME *plaintif* < MF] **—plain′tive·ly,** *adv.* **—plain′tive·ness,** *n.*
—Syn. wistful, sorrowful, sad. **—Ant.** happy, pleasant.

plain′ tripe′, the fatty, inner lining of the stomach of the steer, calf, hog, or sheep, having a bland taste and used as a food and in the preparation of such dishes as haggis, head cheese, etc. Cf. **honeycomb tripe.**

Plain·view (plān′vyōō′), *n.* **1.** a town on W Long Island, in SE New York. 27,710 (1960). **2.** a city in N Texas. 18,735 (1960).

Plain·ville (plān′vil), *n.* a town in central Kansas. 3104 (1960).

plain′ weave′, the most common and tightest of basic weave structures in which the filling threads pass over and under successive warp threads and repeat the same pattern with alternate threads in the following row, producing a checkered surface. Cf. **satin weave, twill weave.**

Plain weave

Plain·well (plān′wel′, -wəl), *n.* a town in SW Michigan. 3125 (1960).

plais·ter (plā′stər), *n., v.t. Obs.* plaster.

plait (plāt, plat), *n.* **1.** a braid, as of hair or straw. **2.** a pleat or fold, as of cloth. **—***v.t.* **3.** to braid, as hair or straw. **4.** to make, as a mat, by braiding. **5.** pleat. [ME *pleyt* < MF *pleit* < VL **plict(um),* syncopated var. of L *plicitum,* n. use of neut. of *plicitus* folded, ptp. of *plicāre;* see PLY[2]]

plait·ing (plā′ting, plat′ing), *n.* that which is braided or pleated; plaits collectively. [ME *pleyting.* See PLAIT, -ING[1]]

plan (plan), *n., v.,* **planned, plan·ning.** **—***n.* **1.** a scheme of action or procedure: *battle plans.* **2.** a design or scheme of arrangement: *an elaborate plan for seating guests.* **3.** a project or definite purpose: *plans for the future.* **4.** a drawing made to scale to represent the top view or a horizontal section of a structure or a machine, as a floor plan of a building. **5.** a representation of a thing drawn on a plane, as a map or diagram: *a plan of the dock area.* **6.** (in perspective drawing) one of several planes in front of a represented object, and perpendicular to the line between the object and the eye. **—***v.t.* **7.** to arrange a plan or scheme for (any work, enterprise, or proceeding): *to plan a new recreation center.* **8.** to project a plan, act, or course of action for: *to plan one's vacation; to plan a reception for royalty.* **9.** to draw or make a plan of, as a building. **—***v.i.* **10.** to make plans: *to plan ahead; to plan for one's retirement.* [< F: plane, plan, groundwork, scheme < L *plān(us)* level, *plānum* level ground. See PLANE[1], PLAIN[1]] **—plan′na·ble,** *adj.* **—plan′less,** *adj.* **—plan′less·ly,** *adv.* **—plan′less·ness,** *n.*
—Syn. 1. plot, formula, system. PLAN, PROJECT, DESIGN, SCHEME imply a formulated method of doing something. PLAN refers to any method of thinking out acts and purposes beforehand: *What are your plans for today?* A PROJECT is a proposed or tentative plan, often elaborate or extensive: *an irrigation project.* DESIGN suggests art, dexterity, or craft (sometimes evil and selfish) in the elaboration or execution of a plan, and often tends to emphasize the purpose in view: *a misunderstanding brought about by design.* A SCHEME is apt to be either a speculative, possibly impractical, plan, or a selfish or dishonest one: *a scheme to swindle someone.* **4.** sketch, draft, diagram, chart. **7.** design, devise, plot.
—Usage. Many teachers object to the phrase PLAN ON plus a gerund, considering it poor style for PLAN TO followed by an infinitive: *I had planned to go to the movies tonight,* (not *I had planned on going to the movies tonight*).

plan-, var. of **plano-**[1] before a vowel: *planate.*

Pla·na (plā′nə), *n.* a crater in the first quadrant of the face of the moon: about 24 miles in diameter.

pla·nar (plā′nər), *adj.* **1.** of or pertaining to a plane. **2.** flat. [< LL *plānār(is)* flat, on a level surface, equiv. to L *plān(um)* PLANE[1] + *-āris* -AR[1]]

pla·nar·i·an (plə nâr′ē ən), *n. Zool.* a free-swimming flatworm having a trifid intestine. [< NL *Plānāri(a)* the typical genus (n. use of fem. of LL *plānārius* level, flat; see PLANE[1], -ARY) + -AN]

Planarian,
Euplanaria tigrinum
(Length 1¼ inches)

pla·nate (plā′nāt), *adj.* having a plane or flat surface. [< LL *plānāt(us),* ptp. of *plānāre.* See PLANE[1], -ATE[1]]

pla·na·tion (plā nā′shən, plə-), *n.* the production of a flat or plane surface by erosion. [PLANE[1] + -ATION]

plan·cer (plan′sər), *n.* the soffit of a cornice, esp. one of wood. Also, **plan·ceer** (plan sēr′), **plan·cher** (plan′chər), **plan·cier** (plan sēr′), **plansheer.** [< obs. F, equiv. to MF *plancher.* See PLANCH, -ER[2]]

planch (planch, plänch), *n.* **1.** a flat piece of metal, stone, or baked clay, used as a tray in an enameling oven. **2.** *Brit. Dial.* **a.** a floor. **b.** a plank. Also, **planche.** [ME *plaunche* < MF *planche* < L *planca* plank]

planch·et (plan′chit), *n.* a flat piece of metal for stamping as a coin; a coin blank. [PLANCH + -ET]

plan·chette (plan chet′), *n.* a small, heart-shaped board supported by two castors and a pencil or stylus which, when moved across a surface by the light, unguided pressure of the finger tips, is supposed to trace meaningful patterns or written messages revealing subconscious thoughts, psychic phenomena, clairvoyant messages, etc. Cf. **ouija board.** [< F; see PLANCH, -ETTE]

Planck (plängk), *n.* **Max Karl Ernst** (mäks kärl ernst), 1858–1947, German physicist: Nobel prize 1918.

Planck's′ con′stant, *Physics.* the fundamental constant of quantum mechanics, expressing the ratio of the energy of one quantum of radiation to the frequency of the radiation and approximately equal to 6.624×10^{-27} erg-seconds. *Symbol:* h [named after M. K. E. PLANCK]

Planck's′ radia′tion law′, *Physics.* **1.** the law that energy associated with electromagnetic radiation, as light, is composed of discrete quanta of energy, each quantum equal to Planck's constant times the corresponding frequency of the radiation: the fundamental law of quantum mechanics. **2.** the law giving the spectral distribution of radiation from a blackbody. Also called **Planck′ radia′tion for′mula, Planck's′ law′.** [named after M. K. E. PLANCK]

Planc·tae (plangk′tē), *n.pl. Class. Myth.* rocks forming a group said to shift in the sea so as to be a menace to navigation, sometimes identified with the Clashing Rocks. [< L, fem. pl. n. use of *planctus,* ptp. of *plangere* to strike, beat, lament]

plane[1] (plān), *n., adj., v.,* **planed, plan·ing.** —*n.* **1.** a flat or level surface. **2.** *Math.* a surface generated by a line moving at a constant velocity with respect to a fixed point. **3.** *Fine Arts.* an area of a two-dimensional surface having determinate extension, and spatial direction or position: *oblique plane; horizontal plane.* **4.** a level of dignity, character, existence, development, or the like: *a high moral plane.* **5.** an airplane or a hydroplane. **6.** *Aeron.* a thin, flat or curved, extended section of an airplane or a hydroplane, affording a supporting surface. **7.** *Archit.* a longitudinal section through the axis of a column. —*adj.* **8.** flat or level, as a surface. **9.** of or pertaining to planes or plane figures. —*v.i.* **10.** to glide. **11.** (of a boat) to lift partly out of water when running at high speed. [< L *plān(um)* level ground. See PLAIN[1]] —**plane′ness,** *n.*
—**Syn. 4.** stratum, stage. **8.** smooth, even, flush.

A

B

Planes (def. 1)
A, Jack plane; B, Router

plane[2] (plān), *n., v.,* **planed, plan·ing.** —*n.* **1.** *Carpentry.* any of various woodworking instruments for paring, truing, or smoothing, or for forming moldings, chamfers, rabbets, grooves, etc., by means of an inclined, adjustable blade moved along and against the piece being worked. **2.** a trowellike tool for smoothing the surface of clay in a brick mold. —*v.t.* **3.** to smooth or dress with or as with a plane or a planer. **4.** to remove by or as by means of a plane (usually fol. by *away* or *off*). —*v.i.* **5.** to work with a plane. **6.** to function as a plane. [late ME < MF < LL *plāna* (n.), *plānāre* (v.); akin to PLAIN[1], PLANE[1]]

plane[3] (plān), *n.* See **plane tree.** [ME < MF < L *platan(us)* < Gk *plátanos,* deriv. of *platýs* broad (with reference to the leaves)]

plane′ an′gle, *Math.* an angle between two intersecting lines.

plane′ geom′etry, *Math.* the geometry of figures whose parts all lie in one plane.

plane′ i′ron, *Carpentry.* the blade of a plane.

plane′ of in′cidence, *Optics.* a plane determined by a given ray, incident on a surface, and the normal at the point where the incident ray strikes the surface.

plane′ polariza′tion, *Optics.* polarization of light in which the vibrations are confined to a single plane, that of the wave front. Also called **linear polarization.** —**plane-po·lar·ized** (plān′pō′lə rīzd′), *adj.*

plan·er (plā′nər), *n.* **1.** *Carpentry.* a power machine for removing the rough or excess surface from a board. **2.** a machine for cutting flat surfaces on metal, having a cutting tool supported by an overhead frame beneath which the work slides on a bed with a reciprocating motion. Cf. **shaper** (def. 2). **3.** a block of smooth, hard wood for leveling the type in a chase by tapping with a mallet. [PLANE[2] + -ER[1]]

plan′er saw′, *Carpentry.* a hollow-ground circular saw for ripping and cutting across grain, having raker teeth for clearing away the chips cut by the cutting teeth.

plan′er tree′, a small, ulmaceous tree, *Planera aquatica,* growing in moist ground in the southern U.S., bearing a small, ovoid, nutlike fruit and yielding a compact light-brown wood. [named after I. J. Planer, 18th-century German botanist]

plane′ sail′ing, *Navig.* sailing on a course plotted without reference to the curvature of the earth. Cf. **plain sailing** (def. 1).

plane-shear (plān′shēr′), *n.* plank-sheer. Also, **plane′-sheer′.**

plan·et (plan′it), *n.* **1.** *Astron.* **a.** Also called **major planet.** any of the nine large heavenly bodies revolving about the sun and shining by reflected light: (Mercury, Venus, Earth, Mars, Jupiter, Saturn, Uranus, Neptune, or Pluto in the order of their proximity to the sun). **b.** a similar body revolving about a star other than the sun. **c.** (formerly) a celestial body moving in the sky, as distinguished from a fixed star, formerly applied also to the sun and moon. **2.** *Astrol.* a heavenly body regarded as exerting an influence on mankind. [ME *planete* < ML *planēte,* pl. (taken as sing.) of LL *planētae* < Gk *planētai,* lit., wanderers]

plane′ ta′ble, *Surveying.* a drawing board mounted on a tripod, used in the field for obtaining and plotting survey data. Also **plain table.**

plane-ta·ble (plān′tā′bəl), *v.t., v.i.,* **-bled, -bling.** to survey with a plane table. [v. use of PLANE TABLE]

plane·ta·bler (plān′tā′blər), *n. Survey.* a person who surveys with a plane table. [PLANE TABLE + -ER]

plan·e·tar·i·um (plan′i târ′ē əm), *n., pl.* **-tar·i·ums, -tar·i·a** (-târ′ē ə). **1.** an apparatus or model representing the planetary system. **2.** a device that produces a representation of the heavens by the use of a number of moving projectors. **3.** the structure in which such a planetarium is housed. [< NL, neut. of L *planētārius* PLANETARY]

plan·e·tar·y (plan′i ter′ē), *adj.* **1.** of, pertaining to, or resembling a planet or the planets. **2.** wandering; erratic. **3.** terrestrial; global. **4.** *Mach.* noting or pertaining to an epicyclic gear train in which a sun gear is linked to one or more planet gears also engaging with an encircling ring gear. —*n.* **5.** *Mach.* a planetary gear train. [< L *planētāri(us).* See PLANET, -ARY]

plan′etary neb′ula, *Astron.* nebula (def. 1b).

plan′etary preces′sion, *Astron.* the small component of the precession of the equinoxes contributed by the motion of the ecliptic, the change in orientation of the plane of the earth's orbit being produced by the gravitational attraction of the planets.

plan·e·tes·i·mal (plan′i tes′ə məl), *Astron.* —*n.* **1.** one of the minute bodies that, hypothetically, was an original constituent of the solar system. —*adj.* **2.** of or pertaining to a planetesimal or planetesimals. [PLANET + (INFINIT)ESIMAL]

planetes′imal hypoth′esis, *Astron.* the hypothesis that the solar system or a similar system originally consisted of the sun or another star and innumerable minute bodies revolving about it, and that these minute bodies gradually united to form the planets and satellites of the system.

plan′et gear′, *Mach.* any of the gears in an epicyclic train surrounding and engaging with the sun gear. Also called **planet wheel.**

plan·et·oid (plan′i toid′), *n. Astron.* an asteroid. [PLANET + -OID] —**plan′et·oi′dal,** *adj.*

plan·e·tol·o·gy (plan′i tol′ə jē), *n.* the branch of astronomy that deals with the physical features of the planets. [PLANET + -O- + -LOGY]

plane′ tree′, any tree of the genus *Platanus,* esp. *P. orientalis,* which is found wild from Italy to Persia and is grown in Europe as an ornamental, or *P. occidentalis,* the buttonwood or sycamore of North America.

plane′ trigonom′etry, *Math.* the branch of trigonometry dealing with plane triangles.

plan·et-struck (plan′it struk′), *adj.* **1.** stricken by the supposed influence of a planet; blasted. **2.** stricken with terror; panic-stricken. Also, **plan·et-strick·en** (plan′it strik′ən).

plan′et wheel′. See **planet gear.**

plan·gent (plan′jənt), *adj.* **1.** beating or dashing, as waves. **2.** resounding loudly, esp. with a plaintive sound, as a bell. [< L *plangent-* (s. of *plangēns*) lamenting, prp. of *plangere.* See PLAIN[2], -ENT] —**plan′gen·cy,** *n.* —**plan′gent·ly,** *adv.*

planh (plä′nyᵊ), *n.* a Provençal elegiac poem. [< Pr < L *planctus* a striking, beating, lamentation. See PLAINT]

plani-, var. of **plano-**[1]: *planigraph.*

pla·ni·form (plā′nə fôrm′, plan′ə-), *adj.* having a flattened shape, as an anatomical joint. [PLANI- + -FORM]

pla·ni·graph (plā′nə graf′, -gräf′, plan′ə-), *n. Med.* an x-ray photograph in which a given plane of the body is well defined and those above and below it purposely out of focus. Also, **pla·ni·gram** (plā′nə gram′, plan′ə-). [PLANI- + -GRAPH] —**pla·nig·ra·phy** (plə nig′rə fē), *n.*

pla·nim·e·ter (plə nim′i tər), *n.* an instrument for measuring mechanically the area of plane figures. [PLANI- + -METER]

pla·nim·e·try (plə nim′i trē), *n.* the measurement of plane areas. [PLANI- + -METRY] —**plan·i·met·ric** (plan′ə me′trik), **plan′i·met′ri·cal,** *adj.*

plan′ing hull′, *Naut.* a hull that tends to rise from the water when under way so that no significant amount of water is displaced beyond a certain speed. Cf. **displacement hull.**

plan·ish (plan′ish), *v.t.* **1.** to give a smooth finish to (metal) by striking it lightly with a smoothly faced hammer or die. **2.** to give a smooth finish to (metal, paper, etc.) by passing it through rolls. [ME < OF *planiss-,* long s. of *planir* to smooth, deriv. of *plan* level < L *plān(us)* PLAIN[1]] —**plan′ish·er,** *n.*

plan·i·sphere (plan′i sfēr′), *n.* **1.** a map of half or more of the celestial sphere with a device for indicating the part visible at a given time of a given location. **2.** a projection or representation of the whole or a part of a sphere on a plane. [PLANI- + SPHERE; r. ME *planisperie* < ML *plānisphaeri(um)*] —**plan·i·spher·i·cal** (plan′i sfer′i kəl), **plan′i·spher′ic, plan·i·spher·al** (plan′i sfēr′əl), *adj.*

plank (plangk), *n.* **1.** a long, flat piece of timber, thicker than a board. **2.** lumber in such pieces; planking. **3.** something to stand on or to cling to for support. **4.** one of the expressed principles or objectives comprising the political platform of a party campaigning for election: *They fought for a plank supporting civil rights.* **5. walk the plank, a.** to be forced, as by pirates, to walk to one's death by stepping off a plank extending from the ship's side over the water. **b.** to relinquish something, as a position, office, etc., under compulsion: *We suspect that the new vice-president walked the plank because of a personality clash.* —*v.t.* **6.** to lay, cover, or furnish with planks. **7.** to bake or broil and serve (fish, chicken, etc.) on a board. **8. plank or plunk down, a.** to lay or put down with force. **b.** *Informal.* to pay (money) immediately or speedily: *He went into the camera shop and planked down his savings.* [ME *planke* < ONF < L *planca* board, plank. See PLANCH] —**plank′less,** *adj.* —**plank′like′,** *adj.*

plank·er (plangk′ər), *n. U.S. Shipbuilding.* a person who fastens planking to the frames of a wooden vessel; ceiler. [PLANK + -ER[1]]

plank′ floor′, *Shipbuilding.* a floor made from sawed, straight-grained timber.

plank-frame (plangk′frām′), *adj.* **1.** noting a type of frame construction using posts, sills, girts, and plates as bearing members, and heavy planks laid edge-to-edge to form nonbearing walls and partitions. **2.** noting a type of frame used in barns and the like, consisting entirely of nailed planks.

plank·ing (plang′king), *n.* **1.** planks collectively, as in a floor. **2.** act of laying or covering with planks. [PLANK + -ING[1]]

plank-sheer (plangk′shēr′), *n. Naut.* (in a wooden hull) a timber covering for the heads of the frames at main deck level, enclosing the deck planking. Also, **plank′-shear′, plane-shear, plane-sheer.** Also called **covering board.**

plank·ter (plangk′tər), *n.* any organism that is an element of plankton. [< Gk: roamer. See PLANKTON]

plank·ton (plangk′tən), *n.* the aggregate of passively floating or drifting organisms in a body of water. [< G, special use of Gk *planktós* drifting, equiv. to *plank-* (var. of *plang-,* s. of *plázesthai* to drift, roam, wander) + *-tos* verbal suffix; akin to L *planctus.* See PLAINT] —**plank·ton·ic** (plangk ton′ik), *adj.*

planned′ econ′omy, an economic system in which the government controls and regulates production, distribution, prices, etc. Cf. **free enterprise.**

planned′ par′enthood, the methods and practices by which parents may regulate the number and frequency of their children. Cf. **birth control.**

plan·ner (plan′ər), *n.* a person who plans. [PLAN + -ER[1]]

Pla·no (plā′nō), *n.* **1.** a town in N Texas. 3695 (1960). **2.** a town in NE Illinois. 3343 (1960).

plano-[1], a learned borrowing from Latin used, with the meaning "flat," "plane," in the formation of compound words: *planography.* Also, **plan-, plani-.** [comb. form repr. L *plānus* level, *plānum* level ground]

plano-[2], a learned borrowing from Greek used, with the meaning "moving," "capable of movement," in the formation of compound words: *planogamete.* [comb. form repr. Gk *plános* wandering, roaming. See PLANET]

plan·o·blast (plan′ə blast′), *n. Zool.* the medusa of a hydroid. [PLANO-[2] + -BLAST] —**plan′o·blas′tic,** *adj.*

pla·no-con·cave (plā′nō kon′kāv), *adj. Optics.* pertaining to or noting a lens that is plane on one side and concave on the other. See diag. under **lens.** [PLANO-[1] + CONCAVE]

pla·no-con·vex (plā′nō kon′veks), *adj. Optics.* pertaining to or noting a lens that is plane on one side and convex on the other. See diag. under **lens.** [PLANO-[1] + CONVEX]

plan·o·gam·ete (plan′ō gam′ēt, plan′ə gə mēt′), *n. Bot., Zool.* a motile gamete. [PLANO-[2] + GAMETE]

pla·no·graph (plā′nə graf′, -gräf′, plan′ə-), *Print.* —*v.t.* **1.** to print from a level surface. —*n.* **2.** an impression so produced. [PLANO-[1] + -GRAPH]

pla·nog·ra·phy (plə nog′rə fē), *n. Print.* the art or technique of printing from a level surface directly or by offset. Also called **surface-printing.** [PLANO-[1] + -GRAPHY] —**pla·no·graph·ic** (plā′nə graf′ik), *adj.* —**pla′no·graph′i·cal·ly,** *adv.*

pla·nom·e·ter (plə nom′i tər), *n.* See **surface plate.** [PLANO-[1] + -METER] —**pla·nom′e·try,** *n.*

plan·o·spore (plan′ə spôr′, -spōr′), *n. Bot.* a zoospore. [PLANO-[2] + SPORE]

plan′ posi′tion in′dicator, a radarscope on which an object reflecting radar waves shows its bearing and distance from the radar detector by causing a spot of light to appear on a screen which represents a map of the area around the detector. *Abbr.:* PPI

plan·sheer (plän′shēr), *n.* plancer.

plant (plant, plänt), *n.* **1.** any member of the vegetable group of living organisms: *A tree is a plant.* **2.** an herb or other small vegetable growth, in contrast with a tree or a shrub. **3.** a seedling or a growing slip, esp. one ready for transplanting. **4.** the equipment, including the fixtures, machinery, tools, etc., and often the buildings, necessary to carry on any industrial business: *a manufacturing plant.* **5.** the complete equipment or apparatus for a particular mechanical process or operation: *the heating plant for a home.* **6.** the buildings, equipment, etc., of an institution: *the sprawling plant of the university.* **7.** *Slang.* something intended to trap, decoy, or lure, as criminals. **8.** *Slang.* a scheme to trap, trick, swindle, or defraud. **9.** a person, placed in an audience, whose rehearsed or prepared reactions, comments, etc., appear spontaneous to the rest of the audience. **10.** *Theat.* a line of dialogue, or a character, action, etc., introducing an idea or theme that will be further developed at a later point in the play: *Afterward we remembered the suicide plant in the second act.* [ME, OE *plante* < L *planta* a shoot, sprig, scion (for planting), plant] —*v.t.* **11.** to put or set in the ground for growth, as seeds, young trees, etc. **12.** to furnish or stock (land) with plants: *to plant a section with corn.* **13.** to establish or implant (ideas, principles, doctrines, etc.): *to plant a love for learning in growing children.* **14.** to introduce (a breed of animals) into a country. **15.** to deposit (young fish, or spawn) in a river, lake, etc. **16.** to bed (oysters). **17.** to insert or set firmly in or on the ground or some other body or surface: *to plant posts along a road.* **18.** *Theat.* to insert or place (an idea, person, or thing) in a play. **19.** to place; put. **20.** *Informal.* to place with great force or firmness: *He planted his fist in the palm of his other hand.* **21.** to station; post: *to plant a policeman on every corner; to plant spies.* **22.** to locate; situate: *Branch stores are planted all over.* **23.** to establish (a colony, city, etc.); found. **24.** to settle (persons), as in a colony. **25.** to say or place (something) in order to obtain a desired result, esp. one that will seem spontaneous: *She plants stories about herself with columnists that keep her name constantly before the public.* **26.** *Carpentry.* to nail, glue, or otherwise attach (a molding or the like) to a surface. **27.** *Slang.* to hide or conceal, as stolen goods. **28.** *Slang.* to put (gold dust, ore, etc.) in a mine or the like to create a false impression of the value of the property. [ME *planten,* OE *plantian* < L *plant(āre)* (to) plant] —**plant′a·ble,** *adj.* —**plant′less,** *adj.* —**plant′like′,** *adj.*

Plan·tag·e·net (plan taj′ə nit), *n.* a member of the royal house which ruled England from the accession of Henry II in 1154 to the death of Richard III in 1485. [< F: lit., sprig of broom, nickname of the Angevin kings of England]

plan′ta genis′ta (plan′tə), *Heraldry.* a representation of a sprig of broom: used as a badge of the Plantagenets. [< NL, equiv. to *planta* plant + *genista* (< L: broom)]

plan·tain[1] (plan′tin, -tən), *n.* **1.** a tropical, herbaceous plant, *Musa paradisiaca,* resembling the banana. **2.** its fruit. [earlier *pla(n)tan* < Sp *plá(n)tano* plantain, also plane tree < ML *pla(n)tanus,* L *platanus* PLANE[3]]

plan·tain[2] (plan′tin, -tən), *n.* any plant of the genus *Plantago,* esp. *P. major,* a weed with large, spreading leaves close to the ground and long, slender spikes of small flowers. [ME *plauntein* < OF *plantein* < L *plantāgin-* (s. of *plantāgō*), deriv. of *planta* sole of the foot, lit., something flat and spread out, like the broad leaf of the plantain; akin to Gk *platýs;* see PLATY-]

plan·tain-eat·er (plan′tin ē′tər, -tən-), *n.* any of various touracos, erroneously believed to feed chiefly on plantains and bananas.

plan′tain lil′y, any liliaceous herb of the genus *Hosta,* of China and Japan, having large leaves and spikes or racemes of white, lilac, or blue flowers.

plan·tar (plan′tər), *adj. Anat., Zool.* of or pertaining to the sole of the foot. [< L *plantār(is),* equiv. to *plant(a)* sole of the foot + *-āris* -AR[1]]

plan′tar re′flex, a normal reflex flexion of the toes, esp. in persons above one year of age, resulting from stroking the sole of the foot. Cf. **Babinski's reflex.**

plan·ta·tion (plan tā′shən), *n.* **1.** a farm or estate, esp. in a tropical or semitropical country, on which cotton, tobacco, coffee, or the like is cultivated, usually by resident laborers. **2.** *Chiefly Brit.* a group of planted trees or plants. **3.** *Hist.* **a.** a colony or new settlement. **b.** the establishment of a colony or new settlement. **4.** *Rare.* the planting of seeds, young trees, etc. [late ME *plantacioune* < L *plantātiōn-* (s. of *plantātiō*) a planting. See PLANT (v.), -ATION] —**plan·ta′tion·like′,** *adj.*

Plan·ta·tion (plan tā′shən), *n.* a town in S Florida. 4772 (1960).

Planta′tion Walk′ing Horse′. See **Tennessee Walking Horse.**

plant′ bug′, any of numerous, often brightly colored hemipterous insects of the family *Miridae* that feed on the juices of plants. Also called **leaf bug.**

Plant′ Cit′y, a city in W Florida. 15,711 (1960).

plant-cut·ter (plant′kut′ər, plänt′-), *n.* any of several South American, passerine birds of the family *Phytotomidae,* superficially resembling grosbeaks but having serrated edges on the bill which aid in cutting leaves and other plant food.

plant·er (plan′tər, plän′-), *n.* **1.** a person who plants. **2.** an implement or machine for planting seeds in the ground. **3.** the owner or occupant of a plantation. **4.** *Hist.* a colonist or new settler. **5.** a decorative container, of a variety of sizes and shapes, for plants, ferns, etc. [ME *plaunter.* See PLANT, -ER[1]]

plant′er's punch′, a punch made with rum, lime juice, sugar, and water or soda.

plant′ food′, nourishment, as fertilizer, chemicals, etc., for plants.

plan·ti·grade (plan′tə grād′), *adj.* **1.** walking on the whole sole of the foot, as man, the bears, etc. —*n.* **2.** a plantigrade animal. [< NL *plantigrad(us),* equiv. to L *plant(a)* sole + *-i-* -I- + *-gradus* -GRADE]

Plan·tin (plän tan′), *n.* **Chris·tophe** (krē stôf′), c1520–1589, French typographer.

plant′ king′dom, plants collectively. Also called **vegetable kingdom.** Cf. **animal kingdom, mineral kingdom.**

plant′ louse′, **1.** aphid. **2.** any of various related insects having similar habits.

plant′ pathol′ogy, the branch of botany dealing with diseases of plants.

Plants·ville (plants′vil), *n.* a town in central Connecticut. 2793 (1960).

plan·u·la (plan′yə lə), *n., pl.* **-lae** (-lē′). *Zool.* the ciliate, free-swimming larva of a coelenterate. [< NL, dim. of L *plānum* something flat. See PLANE[1], -ULE] —**plan′u·lar, plan·u·late** (plan′yə lāt′), *adj.*

plaque (plak), *n.* **1.** a thin, flat plate or tablet of metal, porcelain, etc., intended for ornament, as on a wall, or set in a piece of furniture. **2.** a platelike brooch or ornament, esp. one worn as the badge of an honorary order. **3.** *Anat., Zool.* a small, flat formation or area. **4.** *Dentistry.* a gelatinous accumulation of bacteria and salivary mucin that forms on the teeth. [< F, back formation from *plaquier* to plate < MD *placken* to beat (metal) thin and flat. See PLACK, PLACKET]

Plaque·mine (plak′min, -ə min), *n.* a town in central Louisiana. 7689 (1960).

pla·quette (pla ket′), *n.* a small, ornamented metal panel, cast in relief in a wax mold, often inserted for decoration in the covers of books made in France during the 15th and 16th centuries. [< F, dim. of *plaque.* See PLAQUE, -ETTE]

plash[1] (plash), *n.* **1.** a splash. **2.** a pool or puddle. —*v.t., v.i.* **3.** to splash. [ME *plasch,* OE *plæsc;* c. D, LG *plas,* prob. of imit. orig.] —**plash′ing·ly,** *adv.*

plash[2] (plash), *v.t.* pleach. [late ME < MF *plaiss(ier),* deriv. of *plais* hedge < VL **plaxum* < ?] —**plash′er,** *n.*

plash·y (plash′ē), *adj.,* **plash·i·er, plash·i·est.** **1.** marshy; wet. **2.** splashing. [PLASH[1] + -Y[1]]

-plasia, an element of Greek origin used with the specialized meaning "plasmic growth": *hypoplasia.* Also, **-plasy.** [< NL < Gk *plás(is)* a molding + *-ia* -IA]

-plasm, an element meaning "something formed or molded," occurring as a noun termination in biological and other scientific terms: *bioplasm; metaplasm; neoplasm; protoplasm.* [comb. form repr. Gk *plásma.* See PLASMA]

plasm-, var. of **plasmo-** before a vowel: *plasmic.*

plas·ma (plaz′mə), *n.* **1.** *Anat., Physiol.* the liquid part of blood or lymph, as distinguished from the suspended elements. **2.** *Biol.* protoplasm. **3.** whey. **4.** a green, faintly translucent chalcedony. **5.** *Physics.* a highly-ionized gas containing an approximately equal number of positive ions and electrons. Also, **plasm** (plaz′əm). [< LL < Gk *plásma* something molded or formed, akin to *plássein* to form, mold. See PLASTIC] —**plas·mat·ic** (plaz mat′ik), **plas′mic,** *adj.*

plas′ma cell′, a plasmacyte.

plas·ma·cyte (plaz′mə sīt′), *n. Anat.* a cell occurring in bone marrow and connective tissue, which produces antibodies during certain chronic inflammations. Also, **plasmocyte.** [PLASMA + -CYTE]

plas·ma·gel (plaz′mə jel′), *n.* the gelatinous outer layer of cytoplasm of an amoeba, beneath the cell membrane. [PLASMA + GEL]

plas·mal·o·gen (plaz mal′ə jin, -jen′), *n. Biochem.* any of the class of phosphatides that contain an aldehyde of a fatty acid, found in heart and skeletal muscle, the brain, the liver, and in eggs. Also called **acetal phosphaticle.** [PLASM- + AL(KALAI) + -O- + -GEN]

plas′ma mem′brane, *Biol.* a cell membrane.

plas·ma·pher·e·sis (plaz′mə fer′i sis), *n., pl.* **-ses** (-sēz′). *Med.* a procedure in which blood is removed from the body, centrifuged, and its corpuscles resuspended and returned to the bloodstream: used for the conservation of corpuscles when only blood plasma is to be exteriorized, as by a donor. Also, **plasmaphaeresis, plasmaphoresis.**

plas·ma·sol (plaz′mə sōl′, -sôl′, -sol′), *n.* the relatively fluid, inner cytoplasm of an amoeba. [PLASMA + SOL[4]]

plas′ma thromboplas′tic compo′nent, *Biochem.* See **Christmas factor.**

plas·min (plaz′min), *n. Biochem.* fibrinolysin (def. 1). [PLASM- + -IN[2]]

plas·min·o·gen (plaz min′ə jin, -jen′), *n. Biochem.* the blood substance that when activated forms plasmin. [PLASMIN + -O- + -GEN]

plasmo-, a combining form of **plasma** or **protoplasm:** *plasmoptysis.* Also, *esp. before a vowel,* **plasm-.** [comb. form, repr. Gk *plásma.* See PLASMA]

Plas·mo·chin (plaz′mə kin), *n. Pharm., Trademark.* pamaquine.

plas·mo·cyte (plaz′mə sīt′), *n.* plasmacyte.

plas·mo·di·um (plaz mō′dē əm), *n., pl.* **-di·a** (-dē ə). **1.** *Biol.* an amoeboid, multinucleate mass or sheet of protoplasm characteristic of some stages of organisms, as a myxomycete or slime mold. **2.** any parasitic protozoan of the genus *Plasmodium,* causing malaria in man. [< NL; see PLASM-, -ODE[1]] —**plas·mo′di·al,** *adj.*

plas·mog·a·my (plaz mog′ə mē), *n. Biol.* the fusion of the protoplasts of cells. [PLASMO- + -GAMY]

plas·mol·y·sis (plaz mol′i sis), *n. Bot.* contraction of the protoplasm in a living cell when water is removed by exosmosis. [PLASMO- + -LYSIS] —**plas·mo·lyt·ic** (plaz′mə lit′ik), *adj.* —**plas′mo·lyt′i·cal·ly,** *adv.*

plas·mo·ma (plaz mō′mə), *n., pl.* **-mas, -ma·ta** (-mə tə). *Pathol.* a tumor composed of plasma cells. [PLASM- + -OMA]

plas·mop·ty·sis (plaz mop′ti sis), *n. Biol.* the bursting of protoplasm from a cell, resulting from the rupture of the cell wall because of a high osmotic pressure within the cell. [< NL, equiv. to *plasmo-* PLASMO- + Gk *ptýsis* spitting]

plas·mo·quine (plaz′mə kwīn′), *n. Pharm.* pamaquine. [PLASMO- + QU(IN)INE]

plas·mo·some (plaz′mə sōm′), *n. Biol.* a true nucleolus, as distinguished from a karyosome. [PLASMO- + -SOME[3]]

Plas·sey (plä′sē), *n.* a village in NE India, about 80 miles north of Calcutta: Clive's victory over a Bengal army here (1757) led to the establishment of British power in India.

-plast, a learned borrowing from Greek meaning "formed," "molded," used esp. in biological and botanical terms: *bioplast; chloroplast; mesoplast; protoplast.* [comb. form, repr. Gk *plastós* formed, molded, equiv. to *pláss(ein)* (to) form, mold + *-tos* verbid suffix. See PLASTIC]

plas·ter (plas′tər, plä′stər), *n.* **1.** a composition, as of lime or gypsum, sand, water, and sometimes hair, applied in a pasty form to walls, ceilings, etc., and allowed to harden and dry. **2.** powdered gypsum. **3.** See **plaster of Paris. 4.** a solid or semisolid preparation for spreading upon cloth or the like and applying to the body for some remedial or other purpose. —*v.t.* **5.** to cover (walls, ceilings, etc.) with plaster. **6.** to treat with gypsum or plaster of Paris. **7.** to lay flat like a layer of plaster. **8.** to daub or fill with plaster or something similar. **9.** to apply a plaster to (the body, a wound, etc.). **10.** to overspread with something, esp. thickly or excessively: *a wall plastered with posters.* [ME, OE < ML *plastr(um)* plaster (both medical and building senses), aph. var. of L *emplastrum* < Gk *émplastron* salve, equiv. to *em-* -EM[2] + *pláss(ein)* (to) mold, form + *-tron* -TRON] —**plas′ter·er,** *n.* —**plas′ter·i·ness,** *n.* —**plas′ter·like′, plas′ter·y,** *adj.*

plas·ter·board (plas′tər bōrd′, -bôrd′, plä′stər-), *n.* a material used for insulating or covering walls, or as a lath, consisting of paper-covered sheets of gypsum and felt. [PLASTER + BOARD]

plas′ter cast′, any piece of sculpture reproduced in plaster of Paris.

plas·tered (plas′tərd, plä′stərd), *adj. Slang.* drunk. [PLASTER + -ED[2]]

plas′ter of Par′is, calcined gypsum in white, powdery form, used as a base for gypsum plasters, as an additive of lime plasters, and as a material for making fine and ornamental casts: characterized by its ability to set rapidly when mixed with water. Also, **plas′ter of par′is.** [late ME; so called because prepared from the gypsum of *Paris,* France]

plas·ter·work (plas′tər wûrk′, plä′stər-), *n. Building Trades.* finish or ornamental work done in plaster. [PLASTER + WORK]

plas·tic (plas′tik), *adj.* **1.** capable of being molded or of receiving form: *plastic substances.* **2.** produced by molding: *plastic figures.* **3.** having the power of molding or shaping formless or yielding material: *the plastic forces of nature.* **4.** being able to create, esp. within an art form; having the power of artistic expression: *the plastic imagination of great poets and composers.* **5.** *Fine Arts.* **a.** concerned with or pertaining to molding or modeling; sculptural. **b.** relating to three-dimensional form or space, esp. on a two-dimensional surface. **c.** pertaining to the tools or techniques of drawing, painting, or sculpture: *the plastic means.* **d.** characterized by an emphasis on formal structure: *plastic requirements of a picture.* **6.** *Biol., Pathol.* formative. **7.** *Surg.* concerned with or pertaining to the remedying or restoring of malformed, injured, or lost parts. **8.** pliable; impressionable: *the plastic mind of youth.* —*n.* **9.** Often, **plastics.** any of a group of synthetic or natural organic materials which may be shaped when soft and then hardened, including many types of resins, resinoids, polymers, cellulose derivatives, casein materials, and proteins: used in place of other materials as glass, wood, and metals in construction and decoration, for making many articles, as coatings, and, drawn into filaments, for weaving. They are usually known by trademark names as *Bakelite, Vinylite, Lucite,* etc. [< L *plastic(us)* that may be molded < Gk *plastikós.* See -PLAST, -IC] —**plas′ti·cal·ly, plas′tic·ly,** *adv.*
—**Syn. 8.** pliant, flexible, amenable.

-plastic, an element forming adjectives corresponding to nouns with stems ending in *-plasm, -plast,* and *-plasty: metaplastic; chloroplastic.* [see PLASTIC]

plas′tic art′, **1.** an art, as sculpture, in which forms are carved or modeled. **2.** an art, as painting or sculpture, in which forms are rendered in or as if in three dimensions.

plas′tic bomb′, an adhesive, puttylike substance composed of explosives, as nitroglycerine and nitrocellulose, detonated electrically or by fuse: used esp. in terrorist activities, guerrilla warfare, or the like.

plas′tic flow′, deformation of a material which remains rigid under stresses of less than a certain intensity but which behaves under severer stresses approximately as a Newtonian fluid. Also called **plas′tic deforma′tion.**

Plas·ti·cine (plas′ti sēn′), *n. Trademark.* a synthetic material used as a substitute for clay or wax in modeling.

plas·ti·cise (plas′ti sīz′), *v.t., v.i.,* **-cised, -cis·ing.** *Chiefly Brit.* plasticize. —**plas′ti·ci·sa′tion,** *n.*

plas·tic·i·ty (pla stis′i tē), *n.* **1.** quality or state of being plastic. **2.** capability of being molded, receiving shape, or being made to assume a desired form: *the plasticity of social institutions; the great plasticity of clay.* [PLASTIC + -ITY]

plas·ti·cize (plas′ti sīz′), *v.t., v.i.,* **-cized, -ciz·ing.** to render or become plastic. Also, *esp. Brit.,* **plasticise.** [PLASTIC + -IZE] —**plas′ti·ci·za′tion,** *n.*

plas·ti·ciz·er (plas′ti sī′zər), *n.* **1.** any of a group of substances which are used in plastics or the like to impart viscosity, flexibility, softness, or other properties to the finished product. **2.** an admixture for making mortar or concrete workable with little water. Also, *esp. Brit.,* **plas′ti·cis′er.** [PLASTICIZE + -ER[1]]

plas′tic opera′tion, an operation in which plastic surgery is performed.

plas·tics (plas′tiks), *adj.* of or pertaining to a plastic or plastics: *a plastics firm; plastics research.* [see PLASTIC, -ICS]

plas′tic sur′gery, the branch of surgery dealing with the repair or replacement of malformed, injured, or lost organs or tissues. Also called **anaplasty.** —**plas′tic sur′geon.**

Plas′tic Wood′, *Trademark.* a compound for patching and filling woodwork.

plas·tid (plas′tid), *n. Biol.* any of certain small specialized masses of protoplasm found in plant cells and certain protozoans. See diag. under **cell.** [< G *Plastide* < Gk *plastid-,* s. of *plástis,* fem. of *plástēs* modeler, creator, equiv. to *pláss(ein)* (to) form + *-tēs* agent suffix]

plas·tique (pla stēk′; *Fr.* plᴀ stek′), *n.* **1.** a ballet technique for mastering the art of slow, controlled movement and statuelike posing. **2.** (*italics*) *French.* See **plastic bomb.** [< F: PLASTIC]

plas·ti·queur (plᴀ stē kœr′), *n., pl.* **-queurs** (-kœr′). *French.* a person who makes or explodes plastic bombs.

plasto-, a learned borrowing from Greek meaning "formed," "molded," used in the formation of compound words: *plastotype.* Cf. **-plast.** [comb. form, repr. Gk *plastós*]

plas·tom·e·ter (pla stom′i tər), *n.* an instrument for measuring the plasticity of a substance. [PLASTO- + -METER] —**plas·to·met·ric** (plas′tə me′trik), *adj.* —**plas·tom′e·try,** *n.*

plas·to·type (plas′tə tīp′), *n.* a casting of a type specimen, esp. of a fossil. [PLASTO- + -TYPE]

plas·tral (plas′trəl), *adj. Zool.* relating to the plastron. [PLASTR(ON) + -AL[1]]

plas·tron (plas′trən), *n.* **1.** a piece of plate armor for the upper part of the torso in front. **2.** *Fencing.* a quilted pad worn over part of the torso, for protection. **3.** an ornamental front piece of a woman's bodice. **4.** the starched front of a shirt. **5.** *Zool.* the ventral part of the shell of a turtle. [< MF < It *piastrone,* aug. of *piastra* metal plate, PIASTER. See PLASTER]

-plasty, an element meaning "formation," occurring in terms of the processes of plastic surgery (*dermoplasty; neoplasty*), and occasionally in other words (*galvanoplasty*). [< Gk *-plastia.* See -PLAST, -Y[3]]

-plasy, var. of **-plasia.**

plat[1] (plat), *n., v.,* **plat·ted, plat·ting.** —*n.* **1.** a plot of ground. **2.** *U.S.* a plan or map, as of land. —*v.t.* **3.** *U.S.* to make a play of; plot. [ME (in place names); c. Goth *plat* patch; akin to PLOT[2]]

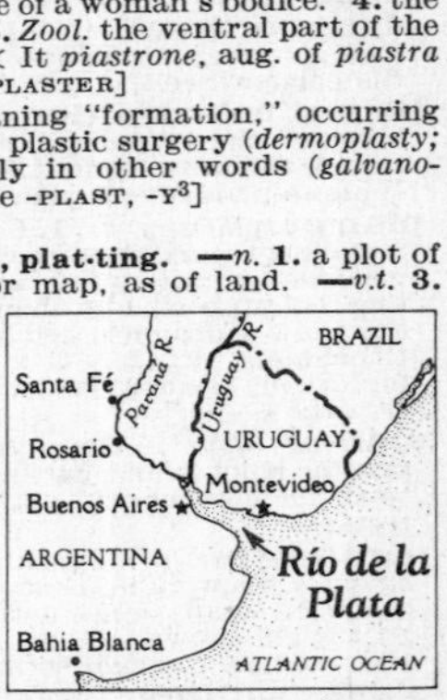

plat[2] (plat), *n., v.,* **plat·ted, plat·ting.** —*n.* **1.** a plait or braid. —*v.t.* **2.** to plait; braid. [var. of PLAIT]

plat., **1.** plateau. **2.** platoon.

plat-, var. of **platy-.**

Pla·ta (plä′tä), *n.* **Rí·o de la** (rē′ô ᵺe lä), an estuary on the SE coast of South America between Argentina and Uruguay, formed by the Uruguay and Paraná rivers, ab. 185 mi. long. Also, **La Plata.** Also called **Pla′ta Riv′er;** *Brit.* **River Plate.**

Pla·tae·a (plə tē′ə), *n.* an ancient city in Greece, in Boeotica: Greeks defeated Persians here 479 B.C.

plat·an (plat′ən), *n.* See **plane tree.** [< L *platanus* < Gk *plátanos* plane tree]

Pla·ta·nis·ti·us (plə tə nis′tē əs), *n. Class. Myth.* an epithet of Apollo meaning "god of the plane-tree grove."

plat·band (plat′band′), *n. Archit.* **1.** a flat structural member, as a lintel or flat arch. **2.** any shallow molding having a flat face. [< MF *platebande*, equiv. to *plate* flat (see PLATE[1]) + *bande* BAND[2]]

plat du jour (plä′ də zhōōr′; *Fr.* plᴀ dʏ zhōōr′), *pl.* **plats du jour** (pläz′ də zhōōr′; *Fr.* plᴀ dʏ zhōōr′). the special or featured dish of the day on a restaurant menu. [< F: dish of the day]

plate[1] (plāt), *n., v.,* **plat·ed, plat·ing.** —*n.* **1.** a shallow, usually circular dish, often of earthenware or porcelain, from which food is eaten. **2.** the contents of such a dish: *a vegetable plate.* **3.** the food and service for one person, as at a banquet, fund-raising dinner, or the like: *The wedding breakfast cost $10 a plate.* **4.** an entire course on one dish. **5.** *Chiefly Brit.* domestic dishes, utensils, etc., of gold or silver. **6.** a dish, as of metal or wood, used for collecting offerings, as in a church. **7.** a thin, flat sheet or piece of metal or other material, esp. of uniform thickness. **8.** metal in such sheets. **9.** a flat, polished piece of metal on which something may be or is engraved. **10.** a flat or curved sheet of metal, plastic, glass, or similar hard material, on which a picture or text has been engraved, etched, molded, photographically developed, or drawn. It is inked, as in a press, for printing impressions on other surfaces. **11.** a printed impression from such a piece, or from some similar piece, as a woodcut. **12.** a full-page illustration in a book, esp. an insert on paper different from the text pages. **13.** plated metallic ware: *silver plate.* **14.** a piece of armor made from a thin, flat piece or several such pieces of tough material, esp. wrought iron or steel. **15.** armor composed of thin, flat pieces; plate armor. **16.** *Dentistry.* **a.** the part of a denture that conforms to the mouth and contains the teeth. **b.** (loosely) the entire denture. **17.** *Baseball.* **a. the plate.** See **home plate. b.** rubber (def. 13). **18.** See **plate glass. 19.** *Photog.* a sheet of glass, metal, etc., coated with a sensitized emulsion, used for taking a photograph. **20.** *Anat., Zool.* a platelike part, structure, or organ. **21.** a thin piece or cut of beef from the lower end of the ribs. **22.** *Electronics.* one of the interior elements of a vacuum tube, toward which electrons are attracted by virtue of its positive charge; anode. **23.** *Carpentry.* any of various horizontal timbers or boards laid flat across the heads of studding, upon floors, etc., to support joists, rafters, or studs at or near their ends. **24.** a gold or silver cup or the like awarded as the prize in a horse race or some other contest. **25.** a horse race or some other contest for such a prize. **26.** *Heraldry.* a rounded argent. **27. plates,** *Chiefly Brit. Slang.* See **plates of meat.** —*v.t.* **28.** to coat (metal) with a thin film of gold, silver, nickel, etc., by mechanical or chemical means. **29.** to cover or overlay with metal plates for protection. **30.** *Metalworking.* **a.** to forge (a bloom or the like) into a broad piece. **b.** to hammer (cutlery) gently to produce an even surface. **31.** *Print.* to make a stereotype or electrotype plate from (type). **32.** *Papermaking.* to give a high gloss to (paper), as on supercalendered paper. [ME < OF: lit., something flat, n. use of fem. of *plat* flat < LL **platt(us)*, akin to Gk *platýs* broad, flat] —**plate′less,** *adj.* —**plate′like′,** *adj.*

plate[2] (plāt), *n. Obs.* a coin, esp. of silver. [ME < OF; special use of PLATE[1]]

plate′ ar′mor, 1. armor made of thin, flat, shaped pieces of wrought iron or steel. **2.** (loosely) any armor composed of, or having as an exterior surface, tough, stiff, flat pieces, large or small, of various materials, as iron, steel, cuir-bouilli, horn, etc.

pla·teau (pla tō′ *or, esp. Brit.,* plat′ō), *n., pl.* **-teaus, -teaux** (-tōz′, -tōz). **1.** a land area having a level surface considerably raised above adjoining land on at least one side, and often cut by deep canyons. **2.** *Psychol.* a period of little or no apparent progress in an individual's learning, marked by an inability to increase speed, reduce number of errors, etc., and indicated by a horizontal stretch in his learning curve or graph. **3.** (on a dining table) a low centerpiece having a length determined by that of the table. [< F; OF *platel* flat object, dim. of *plat* PLATE[1]]

Pla·teau's′ prob′lem (pla tōz′), *Math.* the problem in the calculus of variations of finding the surface with the least area bounded by a given closed curve in space. [named after J. A. F. *Plateau* (1801–83), Belgian physicist]

plat·ed (plā′tid), *adj.* (of a knitted fabric) made of two yarns, as wool on the face and cotton on the back. [PLAT[2] + -ED[3]]

plate-dog (plāt′dôg′, -dog′), *n.* a heavy metal plate on which plates, stereos, etc., are locked into position for printing on a rotary press.

plat′ed stem′, *Shipbuilding.* See **fashion plate stem.**

plate·ful (plāt′fo͝ol), *n., pl.* **-fuls.** as much as a plate will hold. [PLATE[1] + -FUL]

plate′ gird′er, an iron or steel beam built up from plates and shapes welded or riveted together, usually including a plate or plates for a web, four angle irons forming two flanges, and a pair of plates to reinforce the flanges.

plate′ glass′, a soda-lime-silica glass formed by rolling the hot glass into a plate which is subsequently ground and polished, used in large windows, mirrors, etc.

plate·hold·er (plāt′hōl′dər), *n.* a lightproof container for a photographic plate, loaded into the camera with the plate and having a slide that is removed before exposing. [PLATE[1] + HOLDER]

plate·lay·er (plāt′lā′ər), *n. Brit.* a person who lays or maintains railroad tracks. [PLATE[1] + LAYER]

plate·let (plāt′lit), *n.* a small platelike body, esp. a blood platelet. [PLATE[1] + -LET]

plate′ mark′, 1. hallmark. **2.** a mark made on paper by the edge of an intaglio plate during printing.

plat·en (plat′ᵊn), *n.* **1.** a flat plate in a printing press for pressing the paper against the inked type or plate to produce an impression. **2.** a rotating cylinder used for the same purpose. **3.** the roller of a typewriter. **4.** (on a planing machine or the like) the bed to which the work is fastened. **5.** (on a testing machine) a plate for applying compression to a sample. [earlier *platyne* < MF *platine.* See PLATE[1], -INE]

plate′ pail′, a paillike, wooden container for carrying plates between a kitchen and a dining room.

plat·er (plā′tər), *n.* **1.** one who or that which plates. **2.** an inferior race horse. [PLATE[1] + -ER[1]]

plate′ rail′, a rail or narrow shelf fixed along a wall to hold plates, esp. for ornament or display.

plate′ resist′ance, *Electronics.* See **anode resistance.**

plate′ shop′, *Shipbuilding.* a shop for cold-forming metal plates. Also called **structural shop.**

plates′ of meat′, *Chiefly Brit. Slang.* feet. Also called **plates.** [rhyming slang]

plate′ tecton′ics, a theory that the earth's crust is divided into plates that continuously shift, bringing the continents closer together or moving them farther apart.

plate′ trac′ery, tracery, as in early Gothic architecture, formed of cut or pierced slabs of stone set on edge with the flat side outward. Also called **perforated tracery.**

plat·form (plat′fôrm), *n.* **1.** a raised flooring or structure, as in a hall or meeting place, for use by public speakers, performers, etc. **2.** a landing in a flight of stairs. **3.** the raised area between or alongside the tracks of a railroad station, from which the cars of the train are entered. **4.** *U.S.* the open entrance area, or the vestibule, at the end of a railroad passenger car. **5.** *Building Trades.* a relatively flat member or construction for distributing weight, as a wall plate, grillage, etc. **6.** *Mil.* **a.** solid ground on which artillery pieces are mounted. **b.** a metal stand or base attached to certain types of artillery pieces. **7.** *Naut.* flat (def. 30). **8.** a flat, elevated piece of ground. **9.** a body of principles on which a person or group takes a stand in appealing to the public; program: *The Fabians developed an all-embracing platform promising utopia.* **10.** a public statement of the principles, objectives, and policy of a political party, esp. as put forth by the representatives of the party in a convention to nominate candidates for an election: *The platform contained the usual platitudes.* **11.** a set of principles; plan. **12.** *Rare.* a scheme of religious principles or doctrines. [earlier *platte forme* < MF: lit., flat form, plane figure. See PLATE[1], FORM] —**plat′form·less,** *adj.*
—**Syn. 1.** stage, dais, rostrum, pulpit.

plat′form car′, a railroad freight car having no enclosing sides or top; a flatcar.

plat′form frame′, *Carpentry.* a building frame having studs only one story high, regardless of the number of stories built, each story having a box sill. Also called **western frame.**

platin-, var. of **platino-** before a vowel: *platinate.*

plat·i·na (plat′ᵊnə, plə tē′nə), *n.* a native alloy of platinum with palladium, iridium, osmium, etc. [< Sp: lit., silverlike element, equiv. to *plat(a)* silver (< Pr: lit.; silver plate) + *-ina* -INE[1]. See PLATINUM]

plat·i·nate (plat′ᵊnāt′), *n., v.,* **-nat·ed, -nat·ing.** *Chem.* —*n.* **1.** a salt of platinic acid. —*v.t.* **2.** to platinize. [PLATIN- + -ATE[2]]

plat·ing (plā′ting), *n.* **1.** a thin coating of gold, silver, etc. **2.** an external layer of metal plates. **3.** act of one who or that which plates. [PLATE[1] + -ING[1]]

pla·tin·ic (plə tin′ik), *adj. Chem.* of or containing platinum, esp. in the tetravalent state. [PLATIN- + -IC]

platin′ic ac′id, *Chem.* a white, crystalline, water-insoluble powder, H_2PtO_3, used chiefly in platinization.

platin′ic chlo′ride, *Chem.* See **chloroplatinic acid.**

plat·in·i·rid·i·um (plat′ᵊni rid′ē əm, -ᵊnī rid′-), *n.* a natural alloy composed chiefly of platinum and iridium. [PLATIN- + IRIDIUM]

plat·i·nise (plat′ᵊnīz′), *v.t.,* **-nised, -nis·ing.** *Chiefly Brit.* platinize. —**plat′i·ni·sa′tion,** *n.*

Plat·in·ite (plat′ᵊnīt′), *n. Trademark.* an alloy of about 55 percent iron and 45 percent nickel, having the same coefficient of expansion as platinum and used as a substitute for platinum in electrical work.

plat·i·nize (plat′ᵊnīz′), *v.t.,* **-nized, -niz·ing.** to coat or plate with metallic platinum. Also, *esp. Brit.,* **platinise.** [PLATIN- + -IZE] —**plat′i·ni·za′tion,** *n.*

platino-, a combining form of **platinum:** *platinotype.* Also, *esp. before a vowel,* **platin-.**

plat·i·no·cy·an·ic (plat′ᵊnō sī an′ik), *adj. Chem.* of or derived from platinocyanic acid. [PLATINO- + -CYANIC]

plat′inocyan′ic ac′id, *Chem.* the hypothetical acid containing platinum and the cyano group, $H_2Pt(CN)_4$.

plat·i·no·cy·a·nide (plat′ᵊnō sī′ə nīd′, -nid), *n. Chem.* a salt of platinocyanic acid. Also called **cyanoplatinite.** [PLATINOCYAN(IC) + -IDE]

plat·i·noid (plat′ᵊnoid′), *adj.* **1.** resembling platinum: *the platinoid elements.* —*n.* **2.** any of the metals, as palladium, iridium, etc., with which platinum is commonly associated. **3.** an alloy of copper, zinc, and nickel, to which small quantities of such elements as tungsten or aluminum have been added. [PLATIN- + -OID]

plat·i·no·tron (plat′ᵊnō tron′), *n. Electronics.* a vacuum tube similar to a magnetron, for generating microwaves. [PLATINO- + -TRON]

plat·i·no·type (plat′ᵊnō tīp′), *n. Photog.* **1.** a process of printing positives in which a platinum salt is used, rather than the usual silver salts, in order to make a more permanent print. **2.** a print made by this process. [PLATINO- + -TYPE]

plat·i·nous (plat′ᵊnəs), *adj. Chem.* containing bivalent platinum. [PLATIN- + -OUS]

plat·i·num (plat′ᵊnəm), *n.* **1.** *Chem.* a heavy, grayish-white, highly malleable and ductile metallic element, resistant to most chemicals, practically unoxidizable except by the presence of bases, and fusible only at extremely high temperatures: used for making chemical and scientific apparatus, as a catalyst in the oxidation of ammonia to nitric acid, and in jewelry. *Symbol:* Pt; *at. wt.:* 195.09; *at. no.:* 78; *sp. gr.:* 21.5 at 20°C. **2.** a light, metallic gray with very slight bluish tinge when compared with silver. [< NL, alter. of *platina* < Sp; see PLATINA]

plat′inum black′, *Chem.* a black powder consisting of very finely divided metallic platinum, used as a catalyst, esp. in organic synthesis.

plat′inum blonde′, a girl or woman whose hair is of a pale blonde or silver color, usually colored artificially by bleaching or dyeing.

plat·i·tude (plat′i to͞od′, -tyo͞od′), *n.* **1.** a flat, dull, or trite remark, esp. one uttered as if it were fresh and profound. **2.** quality or state of being flat, dull, or trite: *the platitude of most political oratory.* [< F: lit., flatness, equiv. to *plat* flat (see PLATE[1]) + *-itude*, as in *latitude, altitude, magnitude,* etc.]
—**Syn. 1.** cliché, truism.

plat·i·tu·di·nise (plat′i to͞od′ᵊnīz′, -tyo͞od′-), *v.i.,* **-nised, -nis·ing.** *Chiefly Brit.* platitudinize. —**plat′i·tu′di·ni·sa′tion,** *n.* —**plat′i·tu′di·nis′er,** *n.*

plat·i·tu·di·nize (plat′i to͞od′ᵊnīz′, -tyo͞od′-), *v.i.,* **-nized, -niz·ing.** to utter platitudes. [PLATITUDIN(OUS) + -IZE] —**plat′i·tu′di·ni·za′tion,** *n.* —**plat′i·tu′di·niz′er,** *n.*

plat·i·tu·di·nous (plat′i to͞od′ᵊnəs, -tyo͞od′-), *adj.* **1.** characterized by or given to platitudes. **2.** of the nature of or resembling a platitude. [PLATITUDE + (MULTI-TUD)INOUS] —**plat′i·tu′di·nous·ly,** *adv.* —**plat′i·tu′di·nous·ness,** *n.*

Pla·to (plā′tō), *n.* **1.** 427–347 B.C., Greek philosopher. **2.** a walled plain in the second quadrant of the face of the moon, having a dark floor: about 60 miles in diameter.

Pla·ton·ic (plə ton′ik, plā-), *adj.* **1.** of, pertaining to, or characteristic of Plato or his doctrines: *the Platonic philosophy of ideal forms.* **2.** pertaining to, involving, or characterized by Platonic love as a striving toward love of spiritual beauty. **3.** (*usually l.c.*) purely spiritual; free from sensual desire, esp. in a relationship between a man and a woman. **4.** (*usually l.c.*) feeling or professing platonic love: *He insisted that he was completely platonic in his admiration.* [< L *platōnic(us)* < Gk *platōnikós.* See PLATO, -IC] —**Pla·ton′i·cal·ly,** *adv.*

Platon′ic love′, 1. *Platonism.* love of the idea of beauty, seen as terminating an evolution from physical desire for an individual through love of physical beauty and later of spiritual or ideal beauty. **2.** (*usually l.c.*) an intimate companionship or relationship between a man and a woman which is characterized by the apparent absence of sexual desire; a spiritual affection.

Platon′ic sol′id, *Geom.* one of the five regular polyhedrons, a tetrahedron, octahedron, hexahedron, icosahedron, or dodecahedron.

Platon′ic year′, *Astron.* the period of about 26,000 years, equal to the time required for a complete revolution of the equinoxes. Also called **great year.** Cf. **precession of the equinoxes.**

Pla·to·nise (plāt′ᵊnīz′), *v.i., v.t.,* **-nised, -nis·ing.** *Chiefly Brit.* Platonize. —**Pla′to·ni·sa′tion,** *n.* —**Pla′to·nis′er,** *n.*

Pla·to·nism (plāt′ᵊniz′əm), *n.* **1.** the philosophy or doctrines of Plato or his followers. **2.** a Platonic doctrine or saying. **3.** the belief that physical objects are impermanent representations of unchanging Ideas, and that the Ideas alone give true knowledge as they are known by the mind. **4.** (*sometimes l.c.*) the doctrine or practice of platonic love. [< NL *platōnism(us).* See PLATO, -ISM] —**Pla′to·nist,** *n., adj.*

Pla·to·nize (plāt′ᵊnīz′), *v.,* **-nized, -niz·ing.** —*v.i.* **1** to follow or adopt the doctrines of Plato. **2.** to think or reason in the manner of Plato. —*v.t.* **3.** to give a Platonic character to. **4.** to explain in accordance with Platonic principles. Also, *esp. Brit.,* **Platonise.** [< Gk *platōníz(ein).* See PLATO, -IZE] —**Pla′to·ni·za′tion,** *n.* —**Pla′to·niz′er,** *n.*

pla·toon (plə to͞on′), *n.* **1.** a military unit consisting of two or more squads or sections and a headquarters. **2.** a small unit of a police force. **3.** a company or group of persons: *a platoon of visitors.* **4.** *Football.* a group of players specially trained in one aspect of the game, as offense or defense, and used as a unit in their specialty: *a halfback on the offensive platoon.* [earlier *plotton* < F *peloton* little ball, group, platoon, dim. of *pelote* ball. See PELLET, -OON]

Platt·deutsch (plät′doich′), *n.* the informal German of northern Germany. Also called **Low German.** [< G: lit., flat (i.e., lowland) German. See PLATE[1], DUTCH]

Platte (plat), *n.* a river flowing E from the junction of the North and South Platte rivers in central Nebraska to the Missouri River S of Omaha. 310 mi. long.

Plat·ten·see (plät′ᵊn zā′), *n.* German name of **Balaton.**

plat·ter (plat′ər), *n.* **1.** a large, shallow dish, usually oval in shape, for holding and serving food. **2.** *Slang.* a phonograph record. [ME *plater* < AF, deriv. of *plat* dish. See PLATE[1], -ER[2]]

Platte·ville (plat′vil), *n.* a town in SW Wisconsin. 6957 (1960).

Platt′ Na′tional Park′ (plat), a national park in S Oklahoma: sulfur springs. 912 acres.

Platts·burgh (plats′bûrg), *n.* a city in NE New York, on Lake Champlain: battle, 1814. 20,172 (1960).

Platts·mouth (plats′məth), *n.* a town in E Nebraska. 6244 (1960).

plat·y[1] (plā′tē), *adj.,* **plat·i·er, plat·i·est.** (of a rock) split into thin, flat pieces, often resembling strata, as a result of uneven cooling. [PLATE[1] + -Y[1]]

plat·y[2] (plat′ē), *n., pl.* (*esp. collectively*) **plat·y,** (*esp. referring to two or more kinds or species*) **plat·ys, plat·ies.** any of several fishes of the genus *Xiphophorus,* esp. *X maculatus,* found in Mexico and often kept in aquariums, which in the wild state is yellowish gray and in captivity is extremely variable in color. [< NL *Platy(poecilus)* genus name, equiv. to *platy-* PLATY- + *-poecilus* < Gk *poikílos* mottled]

plat·y[3] (plā′tē), *adj. Heraldry.* semé of plates. [PLATE[2] + -Y[1]]

platy-, a learned borrowing from Greek meaning "flat," used in the formation of compound words: *platyhelminth.* Also, **plat-.** [comb. form repr. Gk *platýs* broad, flat]

plat·y·ce·phal·ic (plat′ē sə fal′ik), *adj. Cephalom.* having a head whose cranial vault is broad or flat. Also, **plat·y·ceph·a·lous** (plat′i sef′ə ləs). [PLATY- + -CEPHALIC]

plat·y·ceph·a·ly (plat′i sef′ə lē), *n.* the state of being platycephalic. [PLATY- + -CEPHAL + -Y[3]]

plat·yc·ne·mi·a (plat′ik nē′mē ə, plat′i nē′-), *n.* (in the shinbone) the state of being laterally flattened. [< NL; see PLATY-, CNEMIS, -IA]

plat·y·hel·minth (plat′i hel′minth), *n.* any worm of the phylum *Platyhelminthes,* having bilateral symmetry and a soft, solid, usually flattened body, including the planarians, tapeworms, trematodes, etc.; a flatworm. [< NL *Platyhelminth(a)* flatworm. See PLATY-, HELMINTH] —**plat′y·hel·min′thic,** *adj.*

Plat·y·hel·min·thes (plat′ē hel min′thēz), *n.* the phylum comprising the platyhelminths. [< NL; see PLATYHELMINTH]

plat·y·kur·tic (plat′i kûr′tik), *adj. Statistics.* **1.** (of a frequency distribution) less concentrated about the mean than the corresponding normal distribution. **2.** (of a frequency distribution curve) having a wide, rather flat distribution about the mode. [PLATY- + *kurt-* (var. of Gk *kyrtós* bulging, swelling) + -IC]

plat·y·kur·to·sis (plat′ē kûr tō′sis), *n. Statistics.* the state of being platykurtic. [< NL; see PLATYKURTIC, -OSIS]

plat·y·pod (plat′i pod′), *adj.* **1.** Also, **pla·typ·o·dous** (plə tip′ə dəs). having a broad foot, as certain gastropod mollusks. —*n.* **2.** a platypod animal. [PLATY- + -POD]

plat·y·pus (plat′i pəs), *n., pl.* **-pus·es, -pi** (-pī′). duckbill. [< NL < Gk *platýpous* broad-footed, equiv. to *platy-* PLATY- + *poús* foot]

plat·yr·rhine (plat′i rīn′, -rin), *adj.* **1.** *Anthropol.* having a broad, flat-bridged nose. **2.** belonging or pertaining to the group *Platyrrhini*, comprising the New World monkeys, having a broad, flat nose and a usually long, prehensile tail. —*n.* **3.** a platyrrhine animal. Also, **plat·yr·rhin·i·an** (plat′i rin′ē ən). [< NL *platyrrhīn(us)*, equiv. to *platy-* PLATY- + Gk *rhin-* (s. of *rhís*) nose]

pla·tys·ma (plə tiz′mə), *n., pl.* **-mas, -ma·ta** (-mə tə), *Anat.* a broad, thin muscle, one on each side of the neck, extending from the upper part of the shoulder to the corner of the mouth, the action of which wrinkles the skin of the neck and depresses the corner of the mouth. [< NL < Gk: a plate, lit., something wide and flat, equiv. to *platý(nein)* (to) widen + *-sis* -SIS + *-ma* resultative suffix]

plau·dit (plô′dit), *n.* Usually, **plaudits. 1.** a demonstration or round of applause, as for some approved or admired performance. **2.** any enthusiastic expression of approval: *Her cake won the plaudits of her guests.* [earlier *plaudite* (3 syllables) < L, 2nd pl. impv. of *plaudere* to APPLAUD]

Plau·en (plou′ən), *n.* a city in S central East Germany. 81,998 (est. 1955).

plau·si·ble (plô′zə bəl), *adj.* **1.** having an appearance of truth or reason; seemingly worthy of approval or acceptance; credible; believable: *a plausible excuse; a plausible alibi; a plausible plot.* **2.** well-spoken and apparently worthy of confidence: *a plausible commentator.* [< L *plausibil(is)* deserving applause, equiv. to *plaus(us)* (ptp. of *plaudere* to APPLAUD) + *-ibilis* -IBLE] —**plau′si·bil′i·ty, plau′si·ble·ness,** *n.* —**plau′si·bly,** *adv.*

—**Syn. 1.** PLAUSIBLE, SPECIOUS describe that which has the appearance of truth but might be deceptive. The person or thing that is PLAUSIBLE strikes the superficial judgment favorably; it may or may not be true: *a plausible argument* (one which cannot be verified or believed in entirely). SPECIOUS definitely implies deceit or falsehood; the surface appearances are quite different from what is beneath: *a specious pretense of honesty; a specious argument* (one deliberately deceptive, probably for selfish or evil purposes). —**Ant. 1.** honest, sincere.

plau·sive (plô′ziv, -siv), *adj.* **1.** applauding. **2.** *Obs.* plausible. [< L *plaus(us)* (ptp. of *plaudere* to APPLAUD) + -IVE]

Plau·tus (plô′təs), *n.* **Ti·tus Mac·ci·us** (tī′təs mak′sē əs), c254–c184 B.C., Roman dramatist.

play (plā), *n.* **1.** a dramatic composition or piece; drama. **2.** a dramatic performance, as on the stage. **3.** exercise or action by way of amusement or recreation. **4.** fun, jest, or trifling, as opposed to earnest: *He said it merely in play.* **5.** a pun: *a play upon the meaning of the word.* **6.** the playing or conduct of a game: *The pitcher was withdrawn in the fourth inning of play.* **7.** manner or style of playing or of doing something: *We admired his fine play all last season.* **8.** an act or instance of playing or of doing something: *a stupid play that cost him the match.* **9.** turn to play: *Whose play is it?* **10.** a playing for stakes; gambling. **11.** action, conduct, or dealing of a specified kind. **12.** action, activity, or operation: *the play of fancy.* **13.** brisk movement or action: *a fountain with a leaping play of water.* **14.** elusive change or movement, as of light or colors: *the play of a searchlight against the night sky.* **15.** a space in which something, as a part of a mechanism, can move. **16.** freedom of movement within a space, as of a part of a mechanism. **17.** freedom for action, or scope for activity: *full play of the mind.* **18.** attention in the press; coverage: *There was plenty of hard news that day, but the birth of the baby elephant got a big play, anyhow.* **19. bring into play,** to put into motion; cause to be introduced: *New evidence has been brought into play in this trial.* **20. in** or **out of play,** in or not in the state of being played with or in use in the active playing of a game, as a ball. **21. make a play for,** *Slang.* **a.** to try to attract sexually: *He made a play for his buddy's girl.* **b.** to attempt to gain by impressing favorably: *This ad will make a play for new consumer markets.* [ME *pleye*, OE *plega*]

—*v.t.* **22.** to act the part of (a person or character) in a dramatic performance; portray: *to play Lady Macbeth.* **23.** to perform (a drama, pantomime, etc.) on or as on the stage. **24.** to act or sustain (a part) in a dramatic performance or in real life: *to play the role of benefactor.* **25.** to act the part or character of in real life: *to play the fool; to play God.* **26.** to give performances in, as a theatrical company does: *to play the larger cities.* **27.** to engage in (a game, pastime, etc.). **28.** to contend against in a game. **29.** to function or perform as (a specified player) in a game or competition: *Jones will play left end.* **30.** to employ (a piece of equipment, a player, etc.) in a game: *He played his highest card.* **31.** to use as if in playing a game, as for one's own advantage: *He played his brothers against each other.* **32.** to stake or wager, as in a game. **33.** to lay a wager or wagers on (something). **34.** to represent or imitate in jest or sport: *to play cowboys and Indians; to play house.* **35.** to perform on (a musical instrument). **36.** to perform (music) on an instrument. **37.** to do, perform, or execute: *You shouldn't play tricks. Having mutual interests plays an important part in marriage.* **38.** to carry or put into operation; act upon: *to play a hunch.* **39.** to cause to move or change lightly or quickly: *to play colored lights on a fountain.* **40.** to operate, or cause to operate, esp. continuously or with repeated action: *to play a hose on a fire.* **41.** to allow (a hooked fish) to exhaust itself by pulling on the line.

—*v.i.* **42.** to exercise or employ oneself in diversion, amusement, or recreation. **43.** to do something in sport which is not to be taken seriously. **44.** to amuse oneself; toy; trifle (often fol. by *with*). **45.** to take part or engage in a game. **46.** to take part in a game for stakes; gamble. **47.** to conduct oneself or act in a specified way: *to play fair.* **48.** to act on or as on the stage; perform. **49.** to perform on a musical instrument. **50.** (of the instrument or the music) to sound in performance: *The strings are playing well this evening.* **51.** to be capable of or suitable for performance, as a television or dramatic script: *We hope this scene will play well.* **52.** to move freely within a space, as a part of a mechanism. **53.** to move about lightly or quickly: *The water of the fountain played in the air.* **54.** to present the effect of such motion, as light or the changing colors of an iridescent substance: *The lights played strangely over the faces of the actors.* **55.** to operate continuously or with repeated action. **56.** *Journalism.* to dummy in or run (a news story, photograph, etc.), as on a particular page or in a particular spot: *Play it on the split page, below the fold.* **57. play at, a.** to pretend interest in: *She plays at fishing for her boyfriend's sake.* **b.** to do something without seriousness: *He is merely playing at being a student.* **58. play both ends against the middle,** to maneuver opposing groups in order to benefit oneself. **59. play by ear,** to play music or a piece of music by memory and without a sheet of music before one, esp. with a keen sense of sound values and some practical experience, but usually without technical knowledge or preparation. **60. play down,** to treat as of little importance; belittle: *He has consistently played down his own part in the successful enterprise.* **61. played out, a.** exhausted; weary. **b.** out of fashion; hackneyed: *New styles in clothing are soon played out in New York.* **c.** used up; finished: *The original tires were played out and had to be replaced.* **62. play fast and loose,** to act in an irresponsible or inconsiderate manner, esp. to employ deception to gain one's ends: *He played fast and loose with her affections.* **63. play for time,** to prolong something in order to gain an advantage; forestall an event or decision: *Their maneuvering at the conference was obviously calculated to play for time.* **64. play into the hands of** or **into someone's hands,** to act in such a way as to give an advantage to one's opponent: *If you lose your temper when he insults you, you will be playing right into his hands.* **65. play it by ear,** to improvise, esp. in a challenging situation when confronted by unknown factors: *Faced by his two wives he had to play it by ear.* **66. play off,** to play an extra game or round in order to settle a tie. **67. play one off against another** or **the other,** to maneuver one person so that his actions will thwart or countervail those of another, esp. to gain a personal advantage: *She was always able to avoid deciding between her suitors by playing one off against the other.* **68. play one's cards.** See **card**[1] (def. 11). **69. play on** or **upon,** to exploit, as the feelings or weaknesses of another; take selfish advantage of: *She is one of those people who will go through life playing on the good nature of others.* **70. play out, a.** to bring to an end; finish. **b.** to use up; exhaust: *to play out one's supplies.* **c.** to reel or pay out, as a rope, line, etc. **71. play the game.** See **game**[1] (def. 16). **72. play up,** to magnify the importance of; publicize; emphasize: *The schools are playing up their science programs.* **73. play up to,** *Informal.* to attempt to impress in order to gain someone's favor: *Students who too obviously play up to their teachers are usually disliked by their classmates.* **74. play with fire.** See **fire** (def. 40). [ME *pleye(n)*, OE *pleg(i)an* (c. MD *pleien* to leap for joy, dance, rejoice, be glad), gradational var. of *plagian*, akin to *plōg* PLOW] —**play′ing·ly,** *adv.* —**play′less,** *adj.* —**play′like′,** *adj.*

—**Syn. 2.** show. **3.** diversion, pastime. PLAY, GAME, SPORT refer to forms of diverting activity. PLAY is the general word for any such form of activity, often undirected, spontaneous, or random: *Childhood should be a time for play.* GAME refers to a recreational contest, mental or physical, usually governed by set rules: *a game of chess.* Besides referring to an individual contest, GAME may refer to a pastime as a whole: *Golf is a good game.* If, however, the pastime is one (usually an outdoor one) depending chiefly on physical strength, though not necessarily a contest, the word SPORT is applied: *Football is a vigorous sport.* **12.** movement, exercise. **16, 17.** liberty. **23.** enact. **25.** personate, impersonate. **30.** use. **32.** bet. **33.** back. **42.** sport, frolic, romp, revel. **44.** dally. —**Ant. 3, 42.** work.

pla·ya (plī′ə; *Sp.* plä′yä), *n., pl.* **pla·yas** (plī′əz; *Sp.* plä′yäs). **1.** *Western U.S.* the sandy, salty, or mud-caked flat floor of a desert basin having interior drainage, usually occupied by a shallow lake during or after prolonged, heavy rains. Cf. **dry lake. 2.** (in Spain) a beach or seashore, esp. one having large resort areas, hotels, etc., nearby. [< Sp: shore < LL *plagia*; see PLAGE]

play·a·ble (plā′ə bəl), *adj.* **1.** capable of or suitable for being played. **2.** (of ground) fit to be played on, as for a football match. [PLAY + -ABLE] —**play′a·bil′i·ty,** *n.*

play·act (plā′akt′), *v.i.* **1.** to engage in make-believe. **2.** to be insincere or affected in speech, manner, etc.: *She was playacting again when she declared she was in love.* **3.** to perform in a play. —*v.t.* **4.** to dramatize (something): *They playacted the movements of a burglar.* [back formation from PLAYACTING]

play·act·ing (plā′ak′ting), *n.* an act or instance of a person or group that playacts. [PLAY + ACTING]

play′ a′gent, a broker representing a playwright in dealings with theater managers, producers, etc. Also called **playbroker.**

play·back (plā′bak′), *n.* **1.** the act of operating a phonograph, tape recorder, or the like, so as to hear a reproduction of the recording. **2.** (in a sound recording device) the apparatus used in producing playbacks. **3.** the recording so played, esp. the first time it is heard after being recorded. [n. use of v. phrase *play back*]

play·bill (plā′bil′), *n.* a program or announcement of a play. [PLAY + BILL[1]]

play·book (plā′bo͝ok′), *n.* **1.** (in Elizabethan drama) the script of a play, used by the actors as an acting text. **2.** a book containing the scripts of one or more plays. [PLAY + BOOK]

play·boy (plā′boi′), *n.* a wealthy, carefree man who devotes most of his time to leisure, self-amusement, and hedonistic pleasures, conventionally frequenting parties and night clubs, romancing a rapid succession of attractive young women, and racing speedboats or sports cars. [PLAY + BOY]

Play′boy of the West′ern World′, The, a satiric comedy (1907) by John Millington Synge.

play·bro·ker (plā′brō′kər), *n.* See **play agent.** [PLAY + BROKER]

play-by-play (plā′bī plā′), *adj.* pertaining to or being a detailed account of each incident or act of an event, as in sports: *a play-by-play broadcast of a baseball game.*

play·clothes (plā′klōz′, -klōthz′), *n.pl.* clothes for use on informal occasions, when relaxing at home, etc. [PLAY + CLOTHES]

play·day (plā′dā′), *n.* a day for relaxation or for participation in sports contests; a holiday. [PLAY + DAY]

play′ doc′tor, *Theat.* a person, usually a professional playwright, employed to improve a script, esp. shortly before the play opens on Broadway.

play·down (plā′doun′), *n. Chiefly Canadian.* a play-off. Also, **play′-down′.** [PLAY + DOWN[1]]

play·er (plā′ər), *n.* **1.** one who or that which plays. **2.** a person who takes part or is skilled in some game. **3.** *Brit.* a professional athlete; one whose occupation is sports. **4.** a person who plays parts on the stage; an actor. **5.** a performer on a musical instrument. **6.** a mechanical device by which a musical instrument is played automatically. **7.** a gambler. [ME *pleyer*, OE *plegere*. See PLAY, -ER[1]]

Play·er (plā′ər), *n.* **Gary,** born 1935, South African golfer.

play′er pian′o, a piano that can play automatically when the keys are actuated by a pneumatic device controlled by a piano roll.

Play·fair (plā′fâr′), *n.* a walled plain in the fourth quadrant of the face of the moon: about 28 miles in diameter.

play·fel·low (plā′fel′ō), *n.* a playmate. [PLAY + FELLOW]

play·ful (plā′fəl), *adj.* **1.** full of play; sportive; frolicsome. **2.** pleasantly humorous: *a playful remark.* [ME *pleiful*. See PLAY, -FUL] —**play′ful·ly,** *adv.* —**play′ful·ness,** *n.*

play·girl (plā′gûrl′), *n.* a girl or woman whose life is devoted to social activities for the sake of pleasure. [PLAY + GIRL]

play·go·er (plā′gō′ər), *n.* a person who attends the theater often or habitually. [PLAY + GOER]

play·ground (plā′ground′), *n.* **1.** an area used specifically for outdoor recreation, as one attached to a school. **2.** any place of outdoor recreation, as a resort: *the playgrounds of Europe.* [PLAY + GROUND[1]]

play·house (plā′hous′), *n., pl.* **-hous·es** (-hou′ziz). **1.** a theater. **2.** a small house for children to play in. **3.** a toy house. [ME; OE *pleghūs*. See PLAY, HOUSE]

play′ing card′, **1.** one of the conventional set of 52 cards in four suits, as diamonds, hearts, spades, and clubs, used in playing various games of chance and skill. **2.** one of any set or pack of cards used in playing games.

play′ing field′, *Chiefly Brit.* any official field, ground, park, or stadium where athletic contests are held, as a baseball park, soccer field, etc.

play′ing trick′, *Bridge.* a card in a hand considered as likely to take a trick, assuming that the holder of the hand or his partner is the declarer.

play·land (plā′land′), *n.* **1.** grounds that have recreational facilities, esp. for children. **2.** a town or city that relies heavily on its tourist trade to bolster its economy. [PLAY + LAND]

play·let (plā′lit), *n.* a short play. [PLAY + -LET]

play·mak·er (plā′mā′kər), *n. Sports.* an offensive player, as in basketball or ice hockey, who executes plays designed to put one or more teammates in a position to score. [PLAY + MAKER]

play·mate (plā′māt′), *n.* a child's companion in play. [PLAY + MATE[1]]

play-off (plā′ôf′, -of′), *n.* **1.** (in competitive sports) the playing of an extra game, rounds, innings, etc., in order to settle a tie. **2.** a series of games or matches, as between the leading teams of two leagues, in order to decide a championship: *In America the most exciting play-off is the World Series.* [n. use of v. phrase *play off*]

play′ on words′, a pun.

play·pen (plā′pen′), *n.* a small enclosure in which a young child can play safely by himself without constant supervision. [PLAY + PEN[2]]

play·read·er (plā′rē′dər), *n.* a person who reads and evaluates plays, as for a publisher, producer, or theatrical company. Also called **script reader.** [PLAY + READER]

play·room (plā′ro͞om′, -ro͝om′), *n.* a room set aside for children's play or adult recreation. [PLAY + ROOM]

play·suit (plā′so͞ot′), *n.* a sports costume for women and children, usually consisting of shorts and a shirt, worn as beach wear, for tennis, etc. [PLAY + SUIT]

play′ ther′apy, a form of psychotherapy used chiefly with children, in which the patient acts out situations expressive of his emotional problems.

play·thing (plā′thing′), *n.* **1.** a thing to play with; toy. **2.** a person who is used capriciously and selfishly by another: *She was a Circe who was never satisfied until she had made every man she met her plaything.* [PLAY + THING[1]]

play·time (plā′tīm′), *n.* time for play or recreation. [PLAY + TIME]

play·wright (plā′rīt′), *n.* a writer of plays; dramatist. [PLAY + WRIGHT]

play·writ·ing (plā′rī′ting), *n.* the act of writing plays; work or profession of a playwright. [PLAY + WRITING]

pla·za (plä′zə, plaz′ə), *n.* a public square or open space in a city or town. [< Sp < L *platea,* var. of *platēa* < Gk *plateia* broad street. See PLACE]

pla·za de to·ros (*Sp.* plä′thä the tô′rôs, plä′sä; *Eng.* plä′zə dā tôr′ōs, tōr′-, plaz′ə), *pl.* **pla·zas de to·ros** (*Sp.* plä′thäs the tô′rôs, plä′säs; *Eng.* plä′zəz dā tôr′ōs, tōr′-, plaz′əz). *Spanish.* a bullring.

Pla·za Las·so (plä′sä lä′sô), **Ga·lo** (gä′lô), born 1906, Ecuadorian statesman and diplomat, born in the U.S.: president 1948–52.

plea (plē), *n.* **1.** that which is alleged, urged, or pleaded in defense or justification. **2.** an excuse; pretext: *He begged off on the plea that his car wasn't working.* **3.** *Law.* **a.** an allegation made by, or on behalf of, a party to a legal suit, in support of his claim or defense. **b.** a defendant's answer to a legal declaration or charge. **c.** (in courts of equity) a plea which admits the truth of the declaration, but alleges special or new matter in avoidance. **d.** a suit or action. **4.** an appeal or entreaty: *a plea for mercy.* **5. cop a plea,** *Slang.* to plead guilty to a charge, esp. with the intention of escaping more serious punishment which might result from standing trial. [ME *ple,* earlier *plaid* < OF < early ML *placit(um)* law-court, suit, decision, decree, L: opinion (lit., that which is pleasing or agreeable), n. use of neut. of ptp. of *placēre* to please]
—Syn. 2. justification. **4.** request, petition, supplication, solicitation, suit.

pleach (plēch), *v.t.* **1.** to interweave (branches, vines, etc.), as for a hedge or arbor. **2.** to make or renew (a hedge, arbor, etc.) by such interweaving. **3.** to braid (hair). [ME *pleche(n),* var. of PLASH[2]]

plead (plēd), *v.,* **plead·ed** or **plead** (pled) or **pled; plead·ing.** **—***v.i.* **1.** to appeal or entreat earnestly: *to plead for time.* **2.** to use arguments or persuasions, as with a person, for or against something: *She pleaded with him not to go to war.* **3.** to afford an argument or appeal: *His youth pleads for him.* **4.** *Law.* **a.** to make any allegation or plea in an action at law. **b.** to put forward an answer on the part of a defendant to a legal declaration or charge. **c.** to address a court as an advocate. **d.** *Obs.* to prosecute a suit or action at law. **—***v.t.* **5.** to allege or urge in defense, justification, or excuse: *to plead ignorance.* **6.** *Law.* **a.** to maintain (a cause) by argument before a court. **b.** to allege or set forth (something) formally in an action at law. **c.** to allege or cite in legal defense: *to plead a statute of limitations.* [ME *plaide(n)* < OF *plaid(i)e(r)* (to) go to law, plead < early ML *placitāre* to litigate, deriv. of L *placitum* opinion. See PLEA]
—Syn. 1. beg, supplicate. **2.** reason. **5.** claim.

plead·a·ble (plē′də bəl), *adj.* capable of being pleaded. [ME < AF *pledable.* See PLEAD, -ABLE]

plead·er (plē′dər), *n.* a person who pleads, esp. at law. [PLEAD + -ER[1]]

plead·ing (plē′ding), *n.* **1.** act of one who pleads. **2.** *Law.* **a.** the advocating of a cause in a court of law. **b.** the art or science of setting forth or drawing pleas in legal causes. **c.** a formal statement, usually written, setting forth the cause of action or defense of a case. **d. pleadings,** the successive statements delivered alternately by plaintiff and defendant until issue is joined. [ME *pletynge.* See PLEAD, -ING[1]] **—plead′ing·ly,** *adv.* **—plead′ing·ness,** *n.*

Pleas (plez), *n.* a boy's given name, form of **Pleasant.**

pleas·ance (plez′əns), *n.* **1.** a place laid out as a pleasure garden or promenade. **2.** *Archaic.* pleasure. [ME *plesaunce* < MF *plaisance.* See PLEASANT, -ANCE]

pleas·ant (plez′ənt), *adj.* **1.** pleasing, agreeable, or enjoyable: *pleasant news.* **2.** (of persons, manners, disposition, etc.) socially acceptable or adept; polite; amiable. **3.** fair, as weather: *a pleasant summer day.* **4.** *Archaic.* gay, sprightly, or merry. **5.** *Obs.* jocular or facetious. [ME *plesaunt* < MF *plaisant,* orig. prp. of *plaisir* to PLEASE; see -ANT] **—pleas′ant·ly,** *adv.* **—pleas′ant·ness,** *n.*
—Syn. 1. welcome, gratifying. **2.** delightful, congenial, friendly. **4.** cheerful, cheery; vivacious. **5.** playful, amusing, jocose.

Pleas·ant (plez′ənt), *n.* a boy's given name.

Pleas′ant Grove′, **1.** a town in central Utah. 4772 (1960). **2.** a town in central Alabama. 3097 (1960).

Pleas′ant Hill′, **1.** a city in W California, near San Francisco Bay. 23,844 (1960). **2.** a town in W Missouri. 2689 (1960). **3.** a town in SE Virginia. 2636 (1960).

Pleas′ant Hills′, a town in SW Pennsylvania. 8573 (1960).

Pleas′ant Is′land, former name of **Nauru.**

Pleas·an·ton (plez′ən tən), *n.* **1.** a town in W California. 4203 (1960). **2.** a town in SW Texas. 3467 (1960).

Pleas′ant Ridge′, a town in SE Michigan. 3807 (1960).

pleas·ant·ry (plez′ən trē), *n., pl.* **-ries.** **1.** good-humored teasing; banter. **2.** a humorous or jesting remark. **3.** a humorous action. [< F *plaisanterie,* OF *plesanterie.* See PLEASANT, -RY]

Pleas·ant·ville (plez′ənt vil′), *n.* **1.** a city in SE New Jersey. 15,172 (1960). **2.** a town in SE New York. 5877 (1960).

pleas·ant-voiced (plez′ənt voist′), *adj.* characterized by a pleasant, agreeable voice: *He's looking for a pleasant-voiced secretary.*

please (plēz), *v.,* **pleased, pleas·ing.** **—***v.t.* **1.** to act to the pleasure or satisfaction of: *to please the public.* **2.** to be the pleasure or will of: *May it please your Majesty.* **3.** (used as a polite addition to requests, commands, etc.) if you would be so kind or obliging: *Please come here.* **4.** to like, wish, or choose: *Go where you please.* **—***v.i.* **5.** to give pleasure or satisfaction; be agreeable: *manners that please.* **6. if you please, a.** if it be your pleasure; if you like or prefer. **b.** (used as an exclamation expressing astonishment, indignation, etc.): *The missing letter was in his pocket, if you please!* [ME *plese* < MF *plais(ir)* < L *placēre* to please, seem good. See PLACID] **—pleas′a·ble,** *adj.* **—pleas·ed·ly** (plē′zid lē, plēzd′-), *adv.* **—pleas′ed·ness,** *n.* **—pleas′er,** *n.*

pleas·ing (plē′zing), *adj.* pleasure-giving; agreeable; gratifying: *a pleasing performance.* [ME *plesing.* See PLEASE, -ING[2]] **—pleas′ing·ly,** *adv.* **—pleas′ing·ness,** *n.*
—Syn. pleasant, charming, delightful, engaging. See **interesting.**

pleas·ur·a·ble (plezh′ər ə bəl), *adj.* such as to give pleasure; agreeable; pleasant: *a pleasurable experience.* [PLEASURE + -ABLE] **—pleas′ur·a·ble·ness,** *n.* **—pleas′ur·a·bly,** *adv.*

pleas·ure (plezh′ər), *n., v.,* **-ured, -ur·ing.** **—***n.* **1.** state or feeling of being pleased. **2.** enjoyment or satisfaction derived from what is to one's liking; gratification; delight. **3.** worldly or frivolous enjoyment: *the pursuit of pleasure.* **4.** sensual gratification. **5.** a cause or source of enjoyment or delight: *It was a pleasure to see you.* **6.** pleasurable quality: *the pleasure of his company.* **7.** one's will, desire, or choice: *to make known one's pleasure.* **—***v.t.* **8.** to give pleasure to; gratify; please: *It pleasures me to know you.* **—***v.i.* **9.** to take pleasure; delight: *I pleasure in your company.* **10.** *Informal.* to seek pleasure, as by taking a holiday. [late ME (see PLEASE, -URE); r. ME *plaisir* < MF < L *placēre* to please (n. use of inf.)] **—pleas′ure·less,** *adj.* **—pleas′ure·less·ly,** *adv.* **—pleas′ure·ful,** *adj.*
—Syn. 1. happiness, gladness, delectation. PLEASURE, ENJOYMENT, DELIGHT, JOY refer to the feeling of being pleased and happy. PLEASURE is the general term: *to take pleasure in beautiful scenery.* ENJOYMENT is a quiet sense of well-being and pleasurable satisfaction: *enjoyment at sitting in the shade on a warm day.* DELIGHT is a high degree of pleasure, usually leading to active expression of it: *delight at receiving a hoped-for letter.* JOY is a feeling of delight so deep and so lasting that one radiates happiness and expresses it spontaneously: *joy at unexpected good news.* **4.** luxury, voluptuousness. **7.** preference, wish, inclination, predilection.

pleas′ure prin′ciple, *Psychoanal.* an automatic mental drive or instinct seeking to avoid pain and to obtain pleasure.

pleat (plēt), *n.* **1.** a fold of definite, even width made by doubling cloth or the like upon itself, and pressing, stitching, or otherwise fastening in place. **—***v.t.* **2.** to fold or arrange in pleats. Also, **plait.** [var. of PLAIT] **—pleat′er,** *n.* **—pleat′less,** *adj.*

pleb (pleb), *n.* **1.** a member of the plebs; a plebeian or commoner. **2.** plebe (def. 1). [short for PLEBEIAN]

plebe (plēb), *n.* **1.** Also, **pleb.** (at the U.S. Military and Naval academies) a member of the lowest class. **2.** *Obs.* plebeian (def. 4). [short for PLEBEIAN]

ple·be·ian (plə bē′ən), *adj.* **1.** of, pertaining to, or belonging to the ancient Roman plebs. **2.** belonging or pertaining to the common people. **3.** common, commonplace, or vulgar: *a plebeian joke.* **—***n.* **4.** a member of the ancient Roman plebs. **5.** a member of the common people. [< L *plēbēi(us)* of the plebs (*plēbē(s)* plebs + *-ius* adj. suffix) + -AN] **—ple·be′ian·ism,** *n.* **—ple·be′ian·ly,** *adv.* **—ple·be′ian·ness,** *n.*

ple·be·ian·ise (plə bē′ə nīz′), *v.t.* **-ised, -is·ing.** *Chiefly Brit.* plebeianize. **—ple·be′ian·i·sa′tion,** *n.*

ple·be·ian·ize (plə bē′ə nīz′), *v.t.,* **-ized, -iz·ing.** to make common, trite, or coarse; vulgarize; debase: *a concept of playwriting that threatens to plebeianize the theater.* [PLEBEIAN + -IZE] **—ple·be′ian·i·za′tion,** *n.*

pleb·i·scite (pleb′i sīt′, -sit), *n.* **1.** a direct vote of the qualified electors of a state in regard to some important public question. **2.** the vote by which the people of a political unit determine autonomy or affiliation with another country. [< F < L *plēbiscīt(um)* decree of the plebs, equiv. to *plēbi* (gen. sing. of *plēbēs* PLEBS) + *scītum,* n. use of neut. of *scītus,* ptp. of *scīscere* to enact, decree, orig., to seek to know, learn, incohative of *scīre* to know]

plebs (plebz), *n., pl.* **ple·bes** (plē′bēz). **1.** (in ancient Rome) the commons as contrasted with the patricians, and later with the senatorial nobility or the equestrian order. **2.** the common people; the populace. [< L]

plec·tog·nath (plek′tog nath′), *adj.* **1.** belonging to the *Plectognathi,* a group of teleost fishes having the jaws extensively ankylosed, and including the filefishes, globefishes, etc. **—***n.* **2.** a plectognath fish. [< NL *plectognath(ī)* (pl.) < Gk *plektó(s)* plaited, twisted + *gnáthoi* jaws] **—plec′tog·nath′ic, plec·tog·na·thous** (plek tog′nə thəs), *adj.*

plec·tron (plek′tron), *n., pl.* **-tra** (-trə). plectrum.

plec·trum (plek′trəm), *n., pl.* **-tra** (-trə), **-trums.** **1.** a small piece of wood, metal, ivory, etc., for plucking strings of a lyre, mandolin, etc. **2.** *Anat., Zool.* an anatomical part resembling a plectrum in shape. [< L < Gk *plêktron*]

pled (pled), *v.* a pt. and pp. of **plead.**

pledge (plej), *n., v.,* **pledged, pledg·ing.** **—***n.* **1.** a solemn promise or agreement to do or refrain from doing something: *a pledge of aid; a pledge not to wage war.* **2.** something delivered as security for the payment of a debt or fulfillment of a promise, and subject to forfeiture on failure to pay or fulfill the promise. **3.** state of being given or held as security: *to put a thing in pledge.* **4.** *Law.* **a.** the act of delivering goods, property, etc., to another for security. **b.** the resulting legal relationship. **5.** something given or regarded as a security. **6.** a person accepted for membership in a club, fraternity, etc., but not yet formally approved. **7.** an assurance of support or good will conveyed by drinking a person's health; a toast. **8.** *Obs.* **a.** a hostage. **b.** a person who becomes bail or surety for another. **9. take the pledge,** to make a solemn, formal vow to abstain from intoxicating drink. **—***v.t.* **10.** to bind by or as by a pledge: *to pledge hearers to secrecy.* **11.** to promise solemnly: *to pledge one's support.* **12.** to give or deposit as a pledge; pawn. **13.** to stake, as one's honor. **14.** to secure by a pledge; give a pledge for. **15.** to accept as a pledge for club or fraternity membership. **16.** to drink a health or toast to. **—***v.i.* **17.** to make or give a pledge: *to pledge for someone.* **18.** to drink a pledge; toast someone's health, success, etc. [ME *plege* < AF < early ML *plev(ium), pleb(ium),* deriv. of *plebīre* to pledge < Gmc; cf. OE *plēon* to risk, G *pflegen* to look after. See PLIGHT[2]] **—pledge′a·ble,** *adj.* **—pledg′er,** *n.* **—pledge′less,** *adj.*

pledg·ee (plej ē′), *n.* a person to whom a pledge is made or with whom something is deposited as a pledge. [PLEDGE + -EE]

Pledge′ of Alle′giance, a solemn oath of allegiance or fidelity to the U.S., beginning, "I pledge allegiance to the flag" and generally forming part of the flag-saluting ceremony practiced in American schools.

pledg·et (plej′it), *n.* a small, flat mass of lint, absorbent cotton, or the like, for use on a wound, sore, etc. [?]

pledg·or (plej ôr′), *n.* *Law.* a person who deposits personal property as a pledge. [PLEDGE + -OR[2]]

-plegia, an element of Greek origin used in pathological terms denoting forms of paralysis: *paraplegia.* [< Gk, comb. form repr. *plēgē* blow, stroke]

Ple·iad (plē′əd, plī′əd), *n.* **1.** any of the Pleiades. **2.** French, **Plé·iade** (plā yad′). a group of seven French poets of the latter half of the 16th century. **3.** (*usually l.c.*) any group of eminent or brilliant persons or things, esp. when seven in number. [< Gk *Pleiad-* (s. of *Pleiás,* pl. *Pleiádes*), akin to *pleîn* to sail]

Ple·ia·des (plē′ə dēz′, plī′-), *n.pl.* **1.** *Class. Myth.* seven daughters of Atlas and half sisters of the Hyades, placed among the stars to save them from the pursuit of Orion. One of them (the **Lost Pleiad**) hides, either from grief or shame. **2.** *Astron.* a conspicuous group or cluster of stars in the constellation Taurus, commonly spoken of as seven, though only six are visible.

plein air (plān′ âr′; *Fr.* ple ner′), **1.** the open air, esp. the daylight of outdoors. **2.** *Fine Arts.* the quality of light and atmosphere out of doors, esp. this quality as rendered in painting. [< F: open (lit., full) air]

plein-air (plān′âr′; *Fr.* ple ner′), *adj.* **1.** pertaining to a manner or style of painting developed chiefly in France in the mid-19th century, characterized by the representation of the luminous effects of natural light and atmosphere as contrasted with the artificial light and absence of the sense of air or atmosphere associated with paintings produced in the studio. **2.** designating a painting executed out of doors and representing a direct response to the scene or subject in front of the artist. **3.** (of a painting) having the qualities of air and natural light. [adj. use of PLEIN AIR] **—plein′-air′ism, plein-air·isme** (*Fr.* ple ne rēs′mᵊ), *n.*

pleio-, var. of **plio-.**

Plei·o·cene (plī′ə sēn′), *adj., n.* *Geol.* Pliocene.

plei·om·er·y (plī om′ə rē), *n.* *Bot.* the state of having more than the normal number of floral structures in any whorl. [PLEIO- + -MERY] **—plei·om′er·ous,** *adj.*

Ple·i·o·ne (plē ī′ə nē′), *n.* *Class. Myth.* the mother by Atlas, of the Pleiades.

plei·o·phyl·ly (plī′ə fil′ē), *n.* *Bot.* an abnormal increase in the number of leaves or leaflets. [PLEIO- + -PHYLL + -Y[3]] **—plei′o·phyl′lous,** *adj.*

plei·o·tax·y (plī′ə tak′sē), *n.* *Bot.* an increase in the normal number of parts. Also, **plei′o·tax′is.** [PLEIO- + -TAXY]

Pleis·to·cene (plī′stə sēn′), *Geol.* **—***adj.* **1.** noting or pertaining to the epoch forming the earlier half of the Quaternary or one part of the Neogene period, originating about one million years ago, characterized by widespread glacial ice and by the appearance of man. See table under **era.** **2.** *Rare.* Quaternary. **—***n.* **3.** the Pleistocene epoch or series. **4.** *Rare.* the Quaternary period or system. [< Gk *pleisto(s)* (superl. of *polýs* much) + -CENE]

Ple·kha·nov (pli khä′nof), *n.* **Ge·or·gi** (or **Ge·or·gy**) **Va·len·ti·no·vich** (ge ôr′gi vä′len tē′no vich), 1857–1918, Russian philosopher and leader of the Mensheviks.

ple·na·ry (plē′nə rē, plen′ə-), *adj.* **1.** full; complete; entire; absolute; unqualified: *plenary powers.* **2.** attended by all qualified members; fully constituted: *a plenary session of Congress.* [< LL *plēnāri(us)* (see PLENUM, -ARY); r. ME *plener* < AF < LL *plēnār(is);* see -AR[1]]

ple′nary indul′gence, *Rom. Cath. Ch.* a remission of the total temporal punishment which is still due to sin after absolution. Cf. **indulgence** (def. 5).

ple·nip·o·tent (plə nip′ə tᵊnt), *adj.* invested with or possessing full power. [< LL *plēnipotent-* (s. of *plēnipotēns*). See PLENUM, -I-, POTENT]

plen·i·po·ten·ti·ar·y (plen′ə pə ten′shē er′ē, -shə-rē), *n., pl.* **-ar·ies,** *adj.* **—***n.* **1.** a person, esp. a diplomatic agent, invested with full power or authority to transact business on behalf of another. **—***adj.* **2.** invested with full power or authority, as a diplomatic agent. **3.** conferring or bestowing full power, as a commission. **4.** absolute or full, as power. [< ML *plēnipotentiāri(us).* See PLENIPOTENT, -I-, -ARY]

plen·ish (plen′ish), *v.t.* *Chiefly Scot.* to fill up; stock; furnish. [late ME *plenyss* < MF *pleniss-,* long s. of *plenir* to fill, deriv. of L *plēnus* full. See PLENUM, -ISH[2]] **—plen′ish·er,** *n.* **—plen′ish·ment,** *n.*

plen·i·tude (plen′i to͞od′, -tyo͞od′), *n.* **1.** fullness or adequacy in quantity, measure, or degree; abundance: *a plenitude of food, air, and sunlight.* **2.** state of being full or complete: *With this work his artistry has reached its plenitude.* [< L *plēnitūdō.* See PLENUM, -I-, TUDE]

ple·no ju·re (ple′nō yo͞o′re; *Eng.* plē′nō jo͝or′ē), *Latin.* with full authority.

plen·te·ous (plen′tē əs), *adj.* **1.** plentiful; copious; abundant: *a plenteous supply of corn.* **2.** yielding abundantly; fruitful: *a plenteous harvest.* [ME *plenteus* (see PLENTY, -OUS); r. *plentivous* < OF, equiv. to *plentif* abundant (*plent(e)* plenty + *-if* -IVE) + *-ous* -OUS] **—plen′te·ous·ly,** *adv.* **—plen′te·ous·ness,** *n.*

plen·ti·ful (plen′ti fəl), *adj.* **1.** existing in great plenty: *a woman of plentiful charm.* **2.** yielding abundantly: *a plentiful source of inspiration.* [PLENTY + -FUL] **—plen′ti·ful·ly,** *adv.* **—plen′ti·ful·ness,** *n.*
—Syn. 1. PLENTIFUL, AMPLE, ABUNDANT, BOUNTIFUL describe a more than adequate supply of something. PLENTIFUL suggests an over-adequate quantity: *a plentiful supply.* AMPLE suggests a more than adequate quality as well: *to give ample praise.* ABUNDANT implies a greater degree of plenty, and BOUNTIFUL a still more ample quality as well: *an abundant, a bountiful harvest.* **2.** fruitful, bounteous, productive; luxuriant. **—Ant. 1.** sparse, scanty. **2.** barren, fruitless, sterile.

plen·ty (plen′tē), *n., pl.* **-ties,** *adj., adv.* —*n.* **1.** a full or abundant supply: *There is plenty of time.* **2.** the state or quality of being plentiful; abundance: *resources in plenty.* **3.** an abundance, as of goods or luxuries, or a time of such abundance: *the plenty of a rich harvest; the plenty that comes with peace.* —*adj. Informal.* **4.** existing in ample quantity or number; plentiful; abundant: *Food is never too plenty in the area.* **5.** more than sufficient; ample: *We'll have plenty helpers for you. That helping is plenty for me.* —*adv.* **6.** *Informal.* fully; quite: *plenty good enough.* [ME *plente* (< OF), later form of *plenteth* < OF *plented, plentet* < L *plēnitāt-* (s. of *plēnitās*) fullness. See PLENUM, -ITY]
—**Syn. 2.** plenteousness, copiousness, luxuriance, affluence. PLENTY, ABUNDANCE, PROFUSION refer to a large quantity or supply. PLENTY suggests a supply that is fully adequate to any demands: *plenty of money.* ABUNDANCE implies a great plenty, an ample and generous oversupply: *an abundance of rain.* PROFUSION applies to such a lavish and excessive abundance as often suggests extravagance or prodigality: *luxuries in great profusion.*
—**Usage.** Note that the adjectival and adverbial uses of PLENTY are labeled *Informal.* Use instead PLENTY OF, PLENTIFUL (for adjectives) and AMPLY, QUITE (for adverbs): *Food is never too plentiful in the area. That helping is quite good enough for me.*

Plen·ty (plen′tē), *n.* **Sea of.** See **Mare Fecunditatis.**

ple·num (plē′nəm, plen′əm), *n., pl.* **ple·nums, ple·na** (plē′nə, plen′ə). **1.** the state or the space in which a gas, usually air, is contained at a pressure greater than atmospheric pressure. **2.** the whole of space regarded as being filled with matter (opposed to *vacuum*). **3.** a full assembly, as a joint legislative assembly. [< L, neut. of *plēnus* FULL]

ple′num ventila′tion, a system of mechanical ventilation in which fresh air is forced into the spaces to be ventilated from a chamber **(ple′num cham′ber)** at a pressure slightly higher than atmospheric pressure, so as to expel foul air.

pleo-, var. of **plio-.**

ple·o·chro·ic (plē′ə krō′ik), *adj.* (of a biaxial crystal) characterized by pleochroism; trichroic. [PLEO- + -CHROIC]

ple·och·ro·ism (plē ok′rō iz′əm), *n.* the property of certain crystals to exhibit different colors when viewed from different directions under transmitted light. Cf. **dichroism** (def. 1), **trichroism.** [PLEOCHRO(IC) + -ISM] —**ple·och′ro·it′ic,** *adj.*

ple·o·mor·phic (plē′ə môr′fik), *adj.* of, pertaining to, or characterized by pleomorphism; polymorphous. Also, **ple′o·mor′phous.** [PLEOMORPH(ISM) + -IC]

ple·o·mor·phism (plē′ə môr′fiz əm), *n. Zool., Bot.* existence of an animal or plant in two or more distinct forms during the life cycle; polymorphism. Also, **ple′o·mor′phy.** [PLEO- + -MORPH + -ISM]

ple·on (plē′on), *n.* the abdomen of a crustacean. [< Gk, prp. of *pleîn* to swim, sail; see PLEOPOD] —**ple·on·al** (plē′ə nəl), **ple·on′ic,** *adj.*

ple·o·nasm (plē′ə naz′əm), *n.* **1.** the use of more words than are necessary to express an idea; redundancy: *the pleonasm of sensational advertising.* **2.** an instance of this, as *free gift* or *true fact.* **3.** a redundant word or expression. [< L *pleonasm(us)* < Gk *pleonasmós* redundancy, deriv. of *pleonázein* to be or have more than enough; cf. PLEO-, -ISM] —**ple′o·nas′tic,** *adj.* —**ple′o·nas′ti·cal·ly,** *adv.*

ple·o·pod (plē′ə pod′), *n. Zool.* a swimmeret. [PLEO(N) + -POD]

pler·er·gate (pli rûr′gāt), *n. Entomol., Rare.* replete (def. 3). [< Gk *plḗr(es)* full + ERGATE]

ple·si·o·saur (plē′sē ə sôr′), *n.* any marine reptile of the extinct genus *Plesiosaurus,* from the Jurassic and Cretaceous periods, having a small head, a long neck, four paddlelike limbs, and a short tail. [< NL *plesiosaur(us)* < Gk *plēsío(s)* near + *saûros* -SAUR] —**ple′si·o·sau′roid,** *adj.*

ples·sor (ples′ər), *n. Med.* plexor. [< Gk *plḗss(ein)* (to) strike + -OR²]

pleth·o·ra (pleth′ər ə), *n.* **1.** overfullness; superabundance: *a plethora of advice and a paucity of assistance.* **2.** *Pathol., Obs.* a morbid condition due to excess of red corpuscles in the blood or increase in the quantity of blood. [< NL < Gk *plēthṓrē* fullness]

ple·thor·ic (ple thôr′ik, -thor′-, pleth′ə rik), *adj.* **1.** overfull; turgid; inflated: *a plethoric, pompous speech.* **2.** of, pertaining to, or characterized by plethora. [PLETHOR(A) + -IC] —**ple·thor′i·cal·ly,** *adv.*

pleur-, var. of **pleuro-** before a vowel: *pleurite.*

pleu·ra (plo͝or′ə), *n., pl.* **pleu·rae** (plo͝or′ē) for 1. **1.** *Anat., Zool.* a delicate serous membrane investing each lung in mammals and folded back as a lining of the corresponding side of the thorax. **2.** pl. of **pleuron.** [< NL < Gk: side, rib]

pleu·ral (plo͝or′əl), *adj.* **1.** *Anat.* of or pertaining to the pleura. **2.** of or pertaining to a pleuron or pleurite. [PLEUR(A), PLEUR(ON), PLEUR(ITE) + -AL¹]

pleu·ri·sy (plo͝or′i sē), *n. Pathol.* inflammation of the pleura, with or without a liquid effusion. [ME *pluresy* < OF *pleurisie* < LL *pleurisis,* alter. of L *pleuritis* < Gk; See PLEURA, -ITIS] —**pleu·rit·ic** (plo͝o rit′ik), *adj.*

pleu′risy root′, **1.** a North American milkweed, *Asclepias tuberosa,* whose root was used as a remedy for pleurisy. **2.** the root.

pleu·rite (plo͝or′īt), *n.* **1.** a lateral sclerite of an arthropod. **2.** a sclerite of the pleuron of an insect. [PLEUR- + -ITE¹]

pleuro-, a learned borrowing from Greek used, with the meaning "side," "rib," "lateral," or "pleura," in the formation of compound words: *pleuropneumonia.* Also, *esp. before a vowel,* **pleur-.** [see PLEURA, -O-]

pleu·ro·car·pous (plo͝or′ə kär′pəs), *adj.* (of certain mosses) bearing the fructifications along the main stem or lateral branches. Also, **pleu′ro·car′pic.** [PLEURO- + -CARPOUS]

pleu·ro·dont (plo͝or′ə dont′), *adj.* **1.** ankylosed or attached to the inner edge of the jaw, as a tooth. **2.** having teeth so ankylosed, as certain lizards. —*n.* **3.** a pleurodont animal. [PLEUR- + -ODONT]

pleu·ro·dy·ni·a (plo͝or′ə dī′nē ə), *n. Pathol.* **1.** pain in the chest or side. **2.** Also called **epidemic pleurodynia, devil's grip, Bornholm disease.** a disease characterized by sudden chest pain, mild fever, and recurrence on the third day of these symptoms. [< NL; see PLEUR-, -ODYNIA]

pleu·ron (plo͝or′on), *n., pl.* **pleu·ra** (plo͝or′ə). *Entomol.* the lateral plate or plates of a thoracic segment of an insect. [< Gk: rib, pl. side]

pleu·ro·pneu·mo·ni·a (plo͝or′ō no͞o mōn′yə, -mō′nē ə, -nyo͞o-), *n. Pathol.* pleurisy conjoined with pneumonia. [PLEURO- + PNEUMONIA] —**pleu·ro·pneu·mon·ic** (plo͝or′ō no͞o mon′ik, -nyo͞o-), *adj.*

pleu′ro·pneu·mo′nia-like or′ganism (plo͝or′ō no͞o mōn′yə līk′, -mō′nē ə-, -nyo͞o-, plo͝or′-), any minute, pleomorphic, nonmotile microorganism of the order *Mycoplasmatales,* intermediate in certain characteristics between bacteria and viruses, many species of which are saprophytic and pathogenic for man and animals. *Abbr.:* PPLO

Plev·en (plev′en), *n.* a city in N Bulgaria: siege of 143 days 1877. 57,555 (1956). Also, **Plev·na** (plev′nä).

plex·al (plek′səl), *adj.* of or pertaining to a plexus. [PLEX(US) + -AL¹]

plex·i·form (plek′sə fôrm′), *adj.* **1.** of, pertaining to, or resembling a plexus. **2.** intricate; complex. [PLEX(US) + -I- + -FORM]

Plex·i·glas (plek′sə glas′, -gläs′), *n. Trademark.* a thermoplastic polymer of methyl methacrylate having a light weight, resistant to weathering, capable of being bent when hot but returning to its original shape when reheated, and used chiefly for signs, windows, furniture, etc.

plex·im·e·ter (plek sim′i tər), *n. Med.* a small, thin plate, as of ivory, to receive the blow of a plexor. [< Gk *plêxi(s)* stroke, percussion + -METER] —**plex·i·met·ric** (plek′sə me′trik), *adj.* —**plex·im′e·try,** *n.*

Plex·ip·pus (plek sip′əs), *n. Class. Myth.* **1.** a brother of Althaea who was killed by his nephew Meleager for attempting to take the hide of the Calydonian Boar from Atalanta. **2.** Also called **Parthenius.** a son of Phineus. Cf. **Pandion** (def. 1).

plex·or (plek′sər), *n. Med.* a small hammer with a soft rubber head or the like, used in percussion for diagnostic purposes. Also, **plessor.** [< Gk *plêx(is)* stroke, percussion + -OR²]

plex·us (plek′səs), *n., pl.* **-us·es, -us. 1.** a network, as of nerves or blood vessels. **2.** any complex structure containing an intricate network of interrelated parts: *the plexus of international relations.* [< L: an interweaving, twining, equiv. to *plex-* (ptp. s. of *plectere* to turn) + *-us* n. suffix (4th decl.), akin to *plicāre* to fold] —**plex′al,** *adj.*

plf, pounds per linear foot.

plf., plaintiff. Also, **plff.**

pli, pounds per linear inch.

pli·a·ble (plī′ə bəl), *adj.* **1.** easily bent; flexible; supple: *pliable leather.* **2.** easily influenced or persuaded; yielding; adaptable: *the pliable mind of youth.* [< F, equiv. to *pli(er)* (to) PLY² + *-able* -ABLE] —**pli′a·bil′i·ty, pli′a·ble·ness,** *n.* —**pli′a·bly,** *adv.*

pli·ant (plī′ənt), *adj.* **1.** bending readily; flexible; supple: *She manipulated the pliant clay.* **2.** easily influenced; yielding; compliant: *He has a pliant nature.* [ME < OF, prp. of *plier* to PLY²; see -ANT] —**pli′an·cy, pli′ant·ness,** *n.* —**pli′ant·ly,** *adv.*
—**Syn. 1, 2.** pliable, flexile. See **flexible. 2.** manageable, tractable, docile.

pli·ca (plī′kə), *n., pl.* **pli·cae** (plī′sē). **1.** *Zool., Anat.* a fold or folding. **2.** Also called **pli′ca po·lon′i·ca** (pə lon′i kə). *Pathol.* a matted, filthy condition of the hair, caused by disease, vermin, etc. **3.** (in medieval music) a vertical mark attached to a neume, standing for an interpolated melodic ornament. [< ML: a fold, back formation from L *plicāre* to PLY²] —**pli′cal,** *adj.*

pli·cate (*adj.* plī′kāt, -kit; *v.* plī′kāt), *adj., v.,* **-cat·ed, -cat·ing.** —*adj.* **1.** Also, **pli′cat·ed.** folded like a fan; pleated. —*v.t.* **2.** *Surg.* to perform plication on. [< L *plicāt(us),* ptp. of *plicāre.* See PLY², -ATE¹] —**pli′cate·ly,** *adv.* —**pli′cate·ness,** *n.*

Plicate leaf

pli·ca·tion (plī kā′shən, pli-), *n.* **1.** the act or procedure of folding. **2.** the state or quality of being folded; a fold. **3.** *Surg.* **a.** the folding in tucks and suturing, so as to tighten weakened or stretched tissue. **b.** the folding of an organ, as a section of the intestine, and the attaching of it to another organ or tissue. **c.** an operation for plication. Also, **plic·a·ture** (plik′ə chər). [late ME *plicacioun* < L *plicātiōn-* (s. of *plicātiō*) a folding. See PLICATE, -ION]

pli·é (plē ā′), *n., pl.* **pli·és** (plē āz′; *Fr.* plē ā′). *Ballet.* a movement in which the legs are bent while the back is held straight. [< F, n. use of ptp. of *plier* to bend; see PLY²]

pli·er (plī′ər), *n.* **1. pliers,** (*sometimes construed as sing.*) small pincers with long jaws, for bending wire, holding small objects, etc. (usually used with *pair of*). **2.** one who or that which plies. Also, *esp. Brit.,* **plyer.** [PLY² + -ER¹]

plight¹ (plīt), *n.* condition, state, or situation, esp. an unfavorable one: *to find oneself in a sorry plight.* [ME *plit* < AF (c. MF *pleit* PLAIT) fold, manner of folding, condition; meaning perh. influenced by PLIGHT² in archaic sense of danger]
—**Syn.** case. See **predicament.**

plight² (plīt), *v.t.* **1.** to pledge (one's troth) in engagement to marry. **2.** to bind (someone) by a pledge, esp. of marriage. **3.** to give in pledge, as one's word, or to pledge, as one's honor. —*n.* **4.** *Archaic.* pledge. [ME; OE *pliht* danger, risk; c. D *plicht,* G *Pflicht* duty, obligation] —**plight′er,** *n.*

plim (plim), *v.t., v.i.,* **plimmed, plim·ming.** *Brit. Dial.* to enlarge; swell; grow fuller or more rounded. [akin to dial. *plum,* ME *plumen* to swell, rise]

plim·soll (plim′səl, -sôl, -sol), *n. Brit.* a canvas shoe with a rubber sole. Also, **plim′sol, plim′sole.** [? so called from fancied resemblance of the sole to a Plimsoll mark]

Plim′soll line′ (plim′səl, -sôl, -sol), *Naut.* See **load line** (def. 1). [see PLIMSOLL MARK]

Plim′soll mark′, *Naut.* See **load-line mark.** Also called **Plim′soll.** [named after Samuel *Plimsoll* (1824–98), English M. P. and reformer who brought about its adoption]

Plin·i·us (plin′ē əs), *n.* a crater in the first quadrant of the face of the moon: about 30 miles in diameter.

plink (plingk), *v.i.* **1.** to shoot, as with a rifle, at targets selected at whim: *to plink at coins tossed in the air.* **2.** to make a series of short, light, ringing sounds. —*v.t.* **3.** to shoot at for practice or amusement, as with a rifle: *to plink bottles set along a fence railing.* **4.** to cause to make a series of short, light, ringing sounds. —*n.* **5.** a plinking sound. [imit.] —**plink′er,** *n.*

plinth (plinth), *n. Archit.* **1.** a slablike member beneath the base of a column or pier. See diagram under **column. 2.** a square base or a lower block, as of a pedestal. **3.** Also called **plinth′ course′.** a projecting course of stones at the base of a wall; earth table. **4.** (in joinery) a flat member at the bottom of an architrave, dado, baseboard, or the like. [earlier *plinthus* < L < Gk *plínthos* plinth, squared stone, brick, tile; see FLINT] —**plinth′less,** *adj.* —**plinth′like′,** *adj.*

plinth′ block′, a plinth interrupting a door or window architrave at the floor or ground level.

Plin·y (plin′ē), *n.* **1.** ("*the Elder,*" *Gaius Plinius Secundus*) A.D. 23–79, Roman naturalist, encyclopedist, and writer. **2.** his nephew ("*the Younger,*" *Gaius Plinius Caecilius Secundus*) A.D. 62?–c113, Roman writer, statesman, and orator. —**Plin′i·an,** *adj.*

plio-, a learned borrowing from Greek meaning "more," and sometimes specialized to mean "Pliocene," used in the formation of compound words. Also, **pleio-, pleo-.** [comb. form repr. Gk *pleíōn* more (comp. of *polýs;* see -POLY)]

Pli·o·cene (plī′ə sēn′), *Geol.* —*adj.* **1.** noting or pertaining to an epoch either of the Tertiary or Neogene period, occurring from one million to ten million years ago, and characterized by increased size and numbers of mammals, by the growth of mountains, and by gradual cooling of the climate. See table under **era.** —*n.* **2.** the Pliocene epoch or series. Also, **Pleiocene.** [PLIO- + -CENE]

Pli·o·film (plī′ə film′), *n. Trademark.* a resinlike rubber hydrochloride that forms a clear, flexible, water-resistant, heat-sealable plastic, used for packaging, raincoats, etc.

pli·o·tron (plī′ə tron′), *n. Electronics.* any hot-cathode vacuum tube having an anode and one or more grids as control electrodes. [formerly a trademark]

plis·ky (plis′kē), *n., pl.* **-kies,** *adj. Scot. and North Eng.* —*n.* **1.** a mischievous trick; practical joke; prank. —*adj.* **2.** mischievous; playful. Also, **plis′kie.** [?]

plis·se (plē sā′, pli-), *n.* fabric chemically treated to produce a crepe effect. Also, **plis·sé′.** [< F *plissé,* n. use of ptp. of *plisser* to pleat; see PLY²]

Plis·the·nes (plis′thə nēz′), *n. Class. Myth.* a son of Atreus and Cleola.

PLO, Palestine Liberation Organization.

plo·ce (plō′sē), *n. Rhet.* the repetition of a word or phrase to gain special emphasis or to indicate an extension of meaning, as in Ex. 3:14: "I am that I am." [earlier *ploche* < LL *plocē* < Gk *plokḗ* plaiting, akin to *plékein* to plait]

plod (plod), *v.,* **plod·ded, plod·ding,** *n.* —*v.i.* **1.** to walk heavily or move laboriously; trudge: *to plod under the weight of a burden.* **2.** to work with constant and monotonous perseverance; drudge. —*v.t.* **3.** to walk heavily over or along. —*n.* **4.** the act or a course of plodding. **5.** a sound of or as of a heavy tread. [? imit.] —**plod′der,** *n.* —**plod′ding·ly,** *adv.* —**plod′ding·ness,** *n.*
—**Syn. 1.** See **pace**¹. **2.** toil, moil, labor.

Plo·eș·ti (plô yesht′), *n.* a city in S Rumania: the center of a rich oil-producing region. 133,711 (est. 1964).

-ploid, a combining form used in cytology and genetics to indicate the number of chromosomes: *haploid.* [orig. abstracted from HAPLOID, DIPLOID, etc.]

plomb (plum), *n. Surg. Obs.* any inert body, as a plastic ball, for collapsing the lung in treating pulmonary tuberculosis. [var. of PLUMB]

plonk (plongk), *n. Australian Informal.* **1.** inferior or cheap wine, originally white wine. **2.** liquor of any kind, esp. inferior or cheap liquor. [? alter. of F (*vin*) *blanc* white (wine)]

plop (plop), *v.,* **plopped, plop·ping,** *n., adv.* —*v.t.* **1.** to drop heavily: *She plopped her books on the desk.* —*v.i.* **2.** to make a sound like that of a flat object striking water without a splash. **3.** to drop or fall plump: *He plopped into a chair.* —*n.* **4.** a plopping sound or fall. **5.** act of plopping. —*adv.* **6.** with a plop: *the stone fell plop into the water.* [imit.]

plo·sion (plō′zhən), *n. Phonet.* the forced release of the occlusive phase of a plosive, whether voiceless or unvoiced, either audible due to frication or inaudible due to a contiguous following consonant. Also called **explosion.** Cf. **implosion** (def. 2). [(EX)PLOSION]

plo·sive (plō′siv), *Phonet.* —*adj.* **1.** (of a stop consonant or occlusive) characterized by release in a plosion; explosive. —*n.* **2.** Also called **explosive.** a plosive speech sound. [(EX)PLOSIVE]

plot¹ (plot), *n., v.,* **plot·ted, plot·ting.** —*n.* **1.** a secret plan or scheme to accomplish some purpose, esp. a hostile, unlawful, or evil purpose: *a plot to overthrow the government.* **2.** the plan, scheme, or main story of a play, novel, poem, or short story. **3.** *Artillery.* a point or points located on a map or chart: *target plot.* **4.** a list, timetable, or scheme dealing with any of the various arrangements for the production of a play, motion picture, etc.: *According to the property plot, there should be a lamp stage left.* —*v.t.* **5.** to plan secretly, esp. something hostile or evil: *to plot mutiny.* **6.** to mark on a plan, map, or chart, as the course of a ship or aircraft. **7.** to draw a plan or map of, as a tract of land or a building. **8.** to determine and mark (points), as on plotting paper, by means of measurements or coordinates. **9.** to draw (a curve) by means of points so marked. **10.** to represent by means of such a curve. **11.** to devise or construct the plot of (a play, novel, etc.). **12.** to prepare a list, timetable, or scheme of (production arrangements), as for a play or motion picture: *The stage manager hadn't plotted the set changes until one day before the dress rehearsal.* **13.** to make (a calculation) by graph. —*v.i.* **14.** to form secret plots; conspire. [special use of PLOT²; pejorative use by assoc. with COMPLOT] —**plot′ful,** *adj.* —**plot′less,** *adj.* —**plot′less·ness,** *n.*
—**Syn. 1.** intrigue, conspiracy, cabal. **5.** brew, hatch, frame. **14.** PLOT, CONSPIRE, SCHEME imply secret, cunning, and often unscrupulous planning to gain one's own ends. To PLOT is to contrive a secret plan of a selfish and often treasonable kind: *to plot against someone's life.* To CONSPIRE is to unite with others in an illicit or illegal machination: *to conspire to seize a govern-*

ment. To SCHEME is to plan ingeniously, subtly, and often craftily for one's own advantage: *to scheme how to gain power.*

plot[2] (plot), *n., v.,* **plot·ted, plot·ting.** —*n.* **1.** a small piece or area of ground: *a garden plot; burial plot.* **2.** *Chiefly U.S.* a plan, map, or diagram, as of land, a building, etc. —*v.t.* **3.** to divide (land) into plots. [ME, OE << Slav; cf. OSlav *platŭ* patch]

Plo·tin·i·an (plō tin′ē ən), *adj.* of, pertaining to, or in accordance with Plotinus or his philosophy. [PLOTIN(US) + -IAN]

Plo·ti·nism (plō tī′niz əm, plōt′ənīz′-), *n.* the Neo-platonism of Plotinus, holding that all existence consists of emanations from the One, and that the personal soul is perpetually reincarnated unless it can attain union with the One. [PLOTIN(US) + -ISM] —**Plo·ti′nist,** *n., adj.*

Plo·ti·nus (plō tī′nəs), *n.* A.D. 205?–270?, Roman philosopher, born in Egypt.

plot′ line′, Usually, **plot lines.** dialogue that advances the plot, as in a play or motion-picture script.

plot·tage (plot′ij), *n.* the area within or comprising a plot of land. [PLOT[2] + -AGE]

plot·ter (plot′ər), *n.* **1.** one who or that which plots. **2.** an instrument, as a protractor, for plotting lines and measuring angles on a chart. [PLOT[1] + -ER[1]]

Plott′ hound′ (plot), an American hound having a brindled coat, used esp. in hunting bears and wild boars. [prob. named after J. Plott, 18th-century American who bred dogs]

plot′ting board′, **1.** *Navig.* a transparent table on a ship, used as a plotting sheet. **2.** *Mil.* a device based on a map or other scale representation of a region against which artillery fire is to be directed, for use in directing artillery fire against a fixed or moving target.

plot′ting pa′per, paper ruled into small squares or spaces, used in plotting points, curves, etc.

plot′ting sheet′, *Navig.* a blank chart having only a compass rose and latitude lines, longitude lines, or both, marked and annotated, as required, by a navigator.

plough (plou), *n., v.t., v.i.* *Chiefly Brit.* plow. —**plough′er,** *n.*

Plough′ and the Stars′, The, a play (1926) by Sean O'Casey.

plough·boy (plou′boi′), *n.* *Chiefly Brit.* plowboy.

plough·man (plou′mən), *n., pl.* **-men.** *Chiefly Brit.* plowman. —**plough′man·ship′,** *n.*

plough·share (plou′shâr′), *n.* *Chiefly Brit.* plowshare.

Plov·div (plôv′dif), *n.* a city in S Bulgaria, on the Maritsa River. 198,200 (est. 1963). Greek, **Philippopolis.**

plov·er (pluv′ər, plō′vər), *n.* **1.** any of various limicoline birds of the family *Charadriidae*, esp. those with a short tail and a bill like that of a pigeon. Cf. **dotterel** (def. 1), **killdeer, lapwing.** **2.** any of various shore birds, as the upland plover. [ME < AF; OF *plovier* rainbird < LL **pluviār(ius)*. See PLUVIAL, -ER[2]]

plow (plou), *n.* **1.** an agricultural implement used for cutting, lifting, turning over, and partly pulverizing the soil. **2.** any of various implements resembling or suggesting this, as a kind of plane for cutting grooves or a contrivance for clearing away snow from a road or track. **3.** *Type Founding.* (formerly) an instrument for cutting the groove in the foot of type. **4.** *Bookbinding.* a device for trimming the edges of the leaves by hand. **5.** *(cap.) Astron.* **a.** the constellation Ursa Major. **b.** the Big Dipper. —*v.t.* **6.** to turn up (the soil) with a plow. **7.** to make (a furrow) with a plow. **8.** to make (a furrow, groove, etc.) as if with a plow (often fol. by *up*): *The plane plowed up an acre of trees.* **9.** to proceed through (a body of water) in the manner of a plow: *She plowed the Atlantic for 17 years.* **10.** to invest, as capital (often fol. by *into*): *to plow several hundred million into developing new oil fields.* **11.** to reinvest or reutilize (usually fol. by *back*): *to plow profits back into new plants and equipment.* **12.** *Naut.* **a.** to cleave the surface of (the water). **b.** to make (a way) or follow (a course) thus. —*v.i.* **13.** to till the soil or work with a plow. **14.** to take plowing in a specified way: *land that plows easily.* **15.** to move or proceed through something in the manner of a plow (often fol. by *through, into,* etc.): *I plowed through a stack of books. The car plowed into our house.* **16.** to move through water by cleaving the surface: *a ship plowing through a turbulent sea.* Also, *esp. Brit.,* **plough.** [ME; OE *plōh* plowland; c. G *Pflug* plow] —**plow′er,** *n.*

plow·boy (plou′boi′), *n.* **1.** a boy who leads or guides a team drawing a plow. **2.** a country boy. Also, *esp. Brit.,* **ploughboy.** [PLOW + BOY]

plow·man (plou′mən), *n., pl.* **-men.** **1.** a man who plows. **2.** a farm laborer or a rustic. Also, *esp. Brit.,* **ploughman.** [ME; see PLOW, MAN[1]] —**plow′man·ship′,** *n.*

plow·share (plou′shâr′), *n.* the cutting part of the moldboard of a plow; share. Also, *esp. Brit.,* **ploughshare.** [ME *plowghschare.* See PLOW, SHARE]

plow′ steel′, steel that contains 0.5 to 0.95 percent carbon. [? from the quality of the strong wire rope, used to attach a plow to a steam engine]

plow′ wind′ (wind), *U.S. Informal.* a wind squall with a narrow, straight path of advance.

ploy[1] (ploi), *n.* **1.** a maneuver or stratagem, as in conversation, to gain the advantage. —*v.t.* **2.** *Mil., Archaic.* to move (troops) from a line into a column. Cf. **deploy.** —*v.i.* **3.** *Mil., Archaic.* to move from a line into a column. [late ME *ploye* to bend < MF *ployer*(r), c. *plier* < L *plicāre* to PLY[2]; see DEPLOY]

ploy[2] (ploi), *n.* *Chiefly Brit.* **1.** a personal and amusing escapade; revelry; carousal. **2.** a hobby or pastime. [? aph. var. of EMPLOY]

plu., plural.

pluck (pluk), *v.t.* **1.** to pull off or out from the place of growth, as fruit, flowers, feathers, etc.: *to pluck feathers from a chicken.* **2.** to give a pull at: *to pluck someone's sleeve.* **3.** to pull with sudden force or with a jerk. **4.** to pull by force (often fol. by *away, off,* or *out*). **5.** to remove the feathers, hair, etc., from by pulling: *to pluck a chicken.* **6.** *Slang.* to rob, plunder, or fleece. **7.** to sound (the strings of a musical instrument) by pulling at them with the fingers or a plectrum. **8.** *Brit. Slang.* to reject (a candidate for a degree) in a university examination; fail or flunk (a student). —*v.i.* **9.** to pull or tug sharply (often fol. by *at*). **10.** to snatch (often fol. by *at*). **11. pluck up, a.** to eradicate; uproot. **b.** to summon up one's courage; rouse one's spirits: *He always plucked up at the approach of danger. She was a stranger in the town, but, plucking up her courage, she soon made friends.* —*n.* **12.** act of plucking; a tug. **13.** the heart, liver, and lungs, esp. of an animal used for food. **14.** courage or resolution in the face of difficulties. [ME *plukke(n)*, OE *pluccian*; c. MLG *plucken*; akin to D *plukken*, G *pflücken*] —**pluck′er,** *n.*
—**Syn. 2.** tug. **3.** yank, tear, rip. **14.** bravery, boldness, determination, mettle, nerve.

pluck·less (pluk′lis), *adj.* without courage or resolution, esp. in the face of difficulties. [PLUCK + -LESS] —**pluck′less·ness,** *n.*

pluck·y (pluk′ē), *adj.,* **pluck·i·er, pluck·i·est.** having or showing pluck or courage; brave: *The drowning swimmer was rescued by a plucky schoolboy.* [PLUCK + -Y[1]] —**pluck′i·ly,** *adv.* —**pluck′i·ness,** *n.*
—**Syn.** courageous, determined; cheerful; spunky.

plug (plug), *n., v.,* **plugged, plug·ging.** —*n.* **1.** a piece of wood or other material used to stop up a hole or aperture, to fill a gap, or to act as a wedge. **2.** *Elect.* a device to which may be attached the conductors of a cord and which by insertion in a jack, or screwing into a receptacle, establishes contact. **3.** See **spark plug** (def. 1). **4.** a fireplug. **5.** a cake of pressed tobacco. **6.** a piece of tobacco cut off for chewing. **7.** *Metalworking.* **a.** a mandrel on which tubes are formed. **b.** a punch on which a cup is drawn. **c.** a protrusion on a forging die for forming a recess in the work. **d.** a false bottom on a die. **8.** Also called **dook.** a small piece of wood inserted into masonry as a hold for a nail. **9.** *Masonry.* See under **plug and feathers.** **10.** *Chiefly U.S. Slang.* a worn-out or inferior horse. **11.** *Informal.* the favorable mention of a product, as in a lecture, radio show, etc.: *The actress was happy to give her new show a plug.* **12.** Also called **plug′ hat′.** a man's tall silk hat. **13.** *Informal.* a shopworn or unsalable article. **14.** *Slang.* punch[1] (def. 1). **15.** *Angling.* an artificial lure made of wood, plastic, or metal, and fitted with one or more gang hooks, used chiefly in casting. —*v.t.* **16.** to stop or fill with or as with a plug (often fol. by *up*): *to plug up a leak; plug a gap.* **17.** to insert or drive a plug into. **18.** to secure with or as with a plug. **19.** to insert (something) as a plug. **20.** *Informal.* to mention (a product) favorably, as in a lecture, radio show, etc.: *He says he will appear if he can plug his new TV series.* **21.** *Slang.* to punch. **22.** *Slang.* to shoot. —*v.i.* **23.** *Informal.* to work steadily or doggedly (often fol. by *along*). **24.** *Slang.* to strike; shoot. **25. plug in,** to connect (an electrical device) with an outlet: *When I plugged in the toaster the lights went out.* [< MD *plugge* (D *plug*) plug, peg; c. G *Pflock* plug, peg] —**plug′ga·ble,** *adj.* —**plug′ger,** *n.* —**plug′ging·ly,** *adv.* —**plug′less,** *adj.* —**plug′like′,** *adj.*

plug′ and feath′ers, an apparatus for splitting stone, consisting of two tapered bars **(feathers),** inserted into a hole drilled into the stone, between which a narrow wedge **(plug)** is hammered to spread them.

plug·board (plug′bōrd′, -bôrd′), *n.* **1.** *Elect.* an electric switchboard with plugs for telephones and the like. **2.** (in a computer, calculating machine, etc.) a modular board or panel containing a large number of electric terminals into which connecting wires may be plugged to complete circuits for a particular computer program. [PLUG + BOARD]

plug′ cast′ing, *Angling.* bait casting in which a plug is used as the lure.

plug·ug·ly (plug′ug′lē), *n., pl.* **-lies.** *Informal.* a ruffian; rowdy; tough. [PLUG + UGLY]

plum[1] (plum), *n.* **1.** the drupaceous fruit of any of several rosaceous trees of the genus *Prunus*, having an oblong stone. **2.** the tree itself. **3.** any of various other trees bearing a plumlike fruit. **4.** the fruit itself. **5.** a sugarplum. **6.** a raisin, as in a cake or pudding. **7.** a deep purple varying from bluish to reddish. **8.** *Slang.* an excellent or desirable thing, as a fine position: *The choicest plums went to his old cronies.* **9.** *Slang.* an unanticipated large increase in money or property, as an unexpected legacy; a windfall: *The company offered bonuses and other plums.* Cf. **melon** (def. 3). **10.** Also called **displacer.** a large stone used in massive concrete construction. [ME; OE *plūme* (c. G *Pflaume*) << Gk *proûmnon* plum, *proúmnē* plum-tree] —**plum′like′,** *adj.*

plum[2] (plum), *adj., adv.* plumb.

plum·age (plōō′mij), *n.* **1.** the entire feathery covering of a bird. **2.** feathers collectively. [late ME < MF. See PLUME, -AGE] —**plum′aged,** *adj.*

plu·mate (plōō′māt, -mit), *adj.* *Zool.* resembling a feather, as a hair or bristle which bears smaller hairs. [< L *plūmāt(us)* feathered. See PLUME, -ATE[1]]

plumb (plum), *n.* **1.** a small mass of lead or other heavy material, as that suspended by a line and used to measure the depth of water or to ascertain a vertical line. **2. out of** or **off plumb,** not corresponding to the perpendicular; out of true. —*adj.* **3.** true according to a plumb line; perpendicular. **4.** *Informal.* downright or absolute. —*adv.* **5.** in a perpendicular or vertical direction. **6.** exactly, precisely, or directly. **7.** *Informal.* completely or absolutely: *She was plumb mad. You're plumb right.* —*v.t.* **8.** to test or adjust by a plumb line. **9.** to make vertical. **10.** *Shipbuilding.* horn (def. 24). **11.** to sound with or as with a plumb line. **12.** to measure (depth) by sounding. **13.** to examine closely in order to discover or understand: *to plumb someone's thoughts.* **14.** seal with lead. Also, **plum** (for defs. 3–7). [ME *plumbe* < ML **plumba*, var. of L *plumbum* lead] —**plumb′a·ble,** *adj.* —**plumb′less,** *adj.* —**plumb′ness,** *n.*
—**Syn. 3.** vertical, straight, square.

plum·bag·i·na·ceous (plum baj′ə nā′shəs), *adj.* belonging to the *Plumbaginaceae*, or leadwort family of plants. [< L *plumbāgin-* (s. of *plumbāgō*) leadwort + -ACEOUS]

plum·bag·i·nous (plum baj′ə nəs), *adj.* *Rare.* containing graphite. [< L *plumbāgin-* (s. of *plumbāgō*) lead ore + -OUS]

plum·ba·go (plum bā′gō), *n., pl.* **-gos.** **1.** graphite. **2.** a drawing made by an instrument with a lead point. **3.** any plant of the genus *Plumbago*, comprising the leadworts. [< L, trans. of Gk *polýbdaina* lead ore, deriv. of *pólybdos* lead. See PLUMB, VIRAGO]

plumb′ bob′, plummet (def.1).

plum·be·ous (plum′bē əs), *adj.* resembling or containing lead; leaden. [< L *plumbeus*, equiv. to *plumb(um)* lead + *-eus* -EOUS]

plumb·er (plum′ər), *n.* **1.** a person who installs and repairs piping, fixtures, appliances, and appurtenances in connection with the water supply, drainage systems, etc., both in and out of buildings. **2.** *Obs.* a worker in lead or similar metals. [late ME, sp. var. of ME *plowber* << LL *plumbār(ius)*; r. ME *plummer* < AF; OF *plummier*. See PLUMB, -ER[2]]

plumb·er·y (plum′ə rē), *n., pl.* **-er·ies.** **1.** a plumber's workshop. **2.** the work or trade of a plumber. [ME < OF *plommerie*. See PLUMBER, -RY]

plum·bic (plum′bik), *adj.* *Chem.* containing lead, esp. in the tetravalent state. [< L *plumb(um)* lead + -IC]

plum·bif·er·ous (plum bif′ər əs), *adj.* yielding or containing lead. [< L *plumb(um)* lead + -I- + -FEROUS]

plumb·ing (plum′ing), *n.* **1.** the system of pipes and other apparatus for conveying water, liquid wastes, etc., as in a building. **2.** the work or trade of a plumber. **3.** act of one who plumbs, as in ascertaining depth. [PLUMB + -ING[1]]

plum·bism (plum′biz əm), *n.* *Pathol.* See **lead poisoning** (def. 1b). [< L *plumb(um)* lead + -ISM]

plumb′ joint′, (in sheet metal work) a soldered lap joint.

plumb′ line′, **1.** a cord with a metal bob attached to one end, used to determine perpendicularity, the depth of water, etc. **2.** See **plumb rule.**

plum·bous (plum′bəs), *adj.* *Chem.* containing bivalent lead. [< L *plumbōs(us)*. See PLUMB, -OUS]

plum′bous ox′ide, *Chem.* litharge.

plumb′ rule′, a device for determining perpendicularity, consisting of a narrow board with a plumb line and bob suspended from an upper edge. [ME *plomreule*]

plum·bum (plum′bəm), *n.* *Chem.* lead. *Abbr.:* Pb [< L]

plum·cot (plum′kot), *n.* **1.** a hybrid tree produced by crossing the apricot and the plum. **2.** the fruit of this tree. [PLUM[1] + (APRI)COT]

plum′ cur·cu′lio. See under **curculio.**

plum′ duff′, a duff containing raisins.

plume (plōōm), *n., v.,* **plumed, plum·ing.** —*n.* **1.** a feather. **2.** a large, long, or conspicuous feather: *the brilliant plume of a peacock.* **3.** a soft, fluffy feather: *the plume of an egret.* **4.** any plumose part or formation. **5.** a feather, a tuft of feathers, or some substitute, worn as an ornament, as on a hat, helmet, etc. **6.** a feather or featherlike token of honor or distinction, esp. one worn on a helmet. **7.** *Chiefly Literary.* plumage. —*v.t.* **8.** to furnish, cover, or adorn with plumes or feathers. **9.** (of a bird) to preen (itself or its feathers). **10.** to feel complacent satisfaction with (oneself); pride (oneself) (often fol. by *on* or *upon*): *She sat before the mirror, pluming herself upon her beauty.* [earlier *plome, plume*, ME *plume*, OE *plūm* < L *plūma* soft feather (pl., down)] —**plume′less,** *adj.* —**plume′like′,** *adj.*

plumed (plōōmd), *adj.* having or appearing to have a plume or plumes. [PLUME + -ED[3]]

plume·let (plōōm′lit), *n.* a small plume. [PLUME + -LET]

plume′ pop′py, any of several Asian papaveraceous herbs of the genus *Macleaya*, esp. *M. cordata*, having plumelike terminal clusters of small flowers. Also called **tree celandine.**

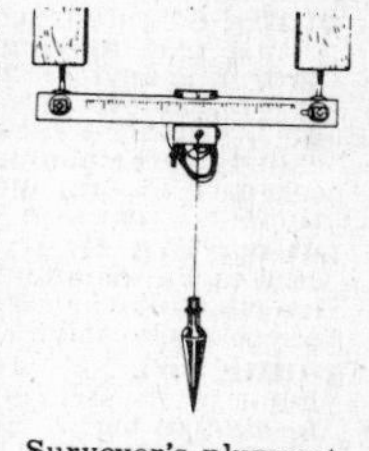

Surveyor's plummet

plum·met (plum′it), *n.* **1.** Also called **plumb bob.** a piece of lead or some other weight attached to a line, used for determining perpendicularity, for sounding, etc.; the bob of a plumb line. **2.** See **plumb rule.** **3.** something that weighs down or depresses. —*v.i.* **4.** to plunge. [ME *plommet* < MF, dim. of *plomb* lead. See PLUMB, -ET]

plum·my (plum′ē), *adj.,* **-mi·er, -mi·est.** **1.** containing or resembling plums. **2.** *Brit. Informal.* good; desirable. [PLUM[1] + -Y[1]]

plu·mose (plōō′mōs), *adj.* **1.** having feathers or plumes; feathered. **2.** feathery or plumelike. [< L *plūmōs(us)*. See PLUME, -OSE[1]] —**plu′mose·ly,** *adv.* —**plu·mos·i·ty** (plōō mos′i tē), **plu′mose·ness,** *n.*

plump[1] (plump), *adj.* **1.** well filled out or rounded in form; somewhat fleshy or fat. —*v.i.* **2.** to become plump (often fol. by *up* or *out*). —*v.t.* **3.** to make plump (often fol. by *up* or *out*): *to plump up the sofa pillows.* [late ME *plompe* dull, rude < MFlem; c. MLG *plump* blunt, thick, rude] —**plump′ly,** *adv.* —**plump′ness,** *n.*
—**Syn. 1.** portly, round. See **stout.** **2, 3.** fatten. —**Ant. 1.** thin.

plump[2] (plump), *v.i.* **1.** to drop or fall heavily or suddenly; come down abruptly or with direct impact. **2.** *Chiefly Brit.* to vote exclusively for one candidate in an election, instead of distributing or splitting one's votes among a number. —*v.t.* **3.** to drop or throw heavily or suddenly (often fol. by *down*): *He plumped himself down and fell asleep.* **4.** to utter or say bluntly (often fol. by *out*): *She plumps out the truth at the oddest times.* **5.** to praise or extol: *road signs plumping the delights of a new candy bar.* **6. plump for,** to support enthusiastically; be wholeheartedly in favor of: *to plump for a team.* —*n.* **7.** a heavy or sudden fall. **8.** the sound resulting from such a fall. —*adv.* **9.** with a heavy or sudden fall or drop. **10.** directly or bluntly, as in speaking. **11.** in a vertical direction; straight down. **12.** with sudden encounter. **13.** with direct impact. —*adj.* **14.** direct; downright; blunt. [ME *plumpe(n)*; c. D *plompen*; prob. imit.]

plump[3] (plump), *n.* *Chiefly Brit. Dial.* a group or cluster. [late ME *plumpe* < ?]

plump·er[1] (plum′pər), *n.* **1.** an act of falling heavily; a plumping. **2.** *Chiefly Brit.* the vote of one who plumps. [PLUMP[2] + -ER[1]]

plump·er[2] (plum′pər), *n.* something carried in the mouth to fill out hollow cheeks. [PLUMP[1] + -ER[1]]

plum′ pud′ding, a rich steamed or boiled pudding containing raisins, currants, citron, spices, etc.

plu·mu·la·ceous (plōōm′yə lā′shəs), *adj.* having the texture of down. [PLUMULE + -ACEOUS]

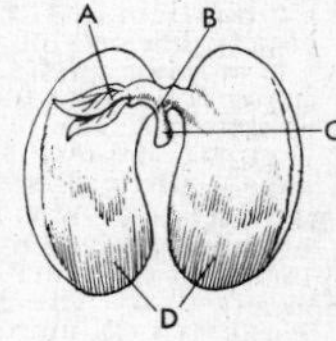

A, Plumule of a bean, *Vicia faba;* B, Hypocotyl; C, Radicle; D, Cotyledons

plu·mule (plōōm′yōōl), *n.* **1.** *Bot.* the bud of the ascending axis of a plant while still in the embryo. **2.** *Ornith.* a down feather. [< NL, L *plūmula*. See PLUME, -ULE] —**plu·mu·lar** (plōōm′yə lər), *adj.*

plu·mu·lose (plōōm′yə lōs′), *adj.* *Zool.* shaped like a downy feather or plumule. [< NL *plūmulōs(us)*. See PLUMULE, -OSE[1]]

plum·y (plo͞o′mē), *adj.*, **plum·i·er, plum·i·est. 1.** having plumes or feathers. **2.** adorned with a plume or plumes: *a plumy helmet.* **3.** plumelike or feathery. [PLUME + -Y¹]

plum′y co′conut. See **queen palm.**

plun·der (plun′dər), *v.t.* **1.** to rob of goods or valuables by open force, as in war, hostile raids, brigandage, etc.: *to plunder a town.* **2.** to rob, despoil, or fleece: *to plunder the public treasury.* **3.** to take wrongfully, as by pillage, robbery, or fraud: *to plunder a piece of property.* —*v.i.* **4.** to take plunder; pillage. —*n.* **5.** plundering, pillage, or spoliation. **6.** that which is taken in plundering; loot. **7.** anything taken by robbery, theft, or fraud. [< D *plunder(en)* (to) plunder, pillage, loot, sack] —**plun′der·a·ble,** *adj.* —**plun′der·er,** *n.* —**plun′der·ing·ly,** *adv.* —**plun′der·ous,** *adj.* —**Syn. 1.** rape, ravage, sack, devastate. **5.** rapine, robbery. **6.** booty, spoils.

plun·der·age (plun′dər ij), *n.* **1.** act of plundering; pillage. **2.** *Law.* **a.** the embezzlement of goods on board a ship. **b.** the goods embezzled. [PLUNDER + -AGE]

plunge (plunj), *v.*, **plunged, plung·ing,** *n.* —*v.t.* **1.** to cast or thrust forcibly or suddenly into a liquid, a penetrable substance, a place, etc.; immerse; submerge: *to plunge a dagger into one's heart.* **2.** to bring suddenly or forcibly into some condition, situation, etc.: *to plunge a country into war; to pull a switch and plunge a house into darkness.* **3.** *Hort.* to place (a potted plant) up to its rim in soil or in certain other materials, as sand or moss. **4.** *Survey.* to transit (the telescope of a transit or theodolite). —*v.i.* **5.** to cast oneself, or fall as if cast, into water, a hole, etc. **6.** to rush or dash with headlong haste: *to plunge through a crowd.* **7.** *Informal.* to bet or speculate recklessly: *to plunge on the stock market.* **8.** to throw oneself impetuously or abruptly into some condition, situation, matter, etc.: *to plunge into debt.* **9.** to descend abruptly or precipitously, as a cliff, road, etc. **10.** to pitch violently forward, as a horse, ship, etc. —*n.* **11.** act of plunging. **12.** a leap or dive, as into water. **13.** a headlong or impetuous rush or dash: *a plunge into danger.* **14.** a sudden, violent pitching movement. **15.** a place for plunging or diving, as a swimming pool. **16.** **take the plunge,** to enter with sudden decision upon an unfamiliar course of action, as after hesitation or deliberation: *She took the plunge and invested her entire savings in the plan.* [ME < MF *plung(i)e(r)* << LL **plumbicāre* to heave the lead. See PLUMB] —**Syn. 1.** See **dip. 5.** dive. **6.** hasten. **9.** drop.

plunge′ ba′sin, a cavity at the base of a falls or cataract, formed by the action of the falling water.

plunge′ pool′, the water in a plunge basin.

plung·er (plun′jər), *n.* **1.** *Mach.* a pistonlike reciprocating part moving within the cylinder of a pump or hydraulic device. **2.** *Auto.* a pistonlike part in the valve of a pneumatic tire. **3.** one who or that which plunges. **4.** *Informal.* a reckless better or speculator. **5.** Also called **oyster sloop.** *Naut.* any of various cat-rigged vessels used for transporting oysters on the Pacific coast of the U.S. [PLUNGE + -ER¹]

plung′ing fire′, *Mil.* artillery or other fire that strikes the ground at a steep angle, as from high ground overlooking the target or from a weapon fired at a high angle of elevation.

plunk (plungk), *v.t.* **1.** to pluck (a stringed instrument or its strings); twang: *to plunk a guitar.* **2.** *Informal.* to throw, push, put, etc., heavily or suddenly; plump (often fol. by *down*): *Plunk down your money.* —*v.i.* **3.** to give forth a twanging sound. **4.** *Informal.* to drop heavily or suddenly; plump (often fol. by *down*): *to plunk down somewhere and take a nap.* —*n.* **5.** act or sound of plunking. **6.** *Informal.* a direct, forcible blow. **7.** *Slang.* a dollar. —*adv.* **8.** *Informal.* with a plunking sound. **9.** *Informal.* squarely; exactly: *The tennis ball landed plunk in the middle of the net.* [nasalized var. of PLUCK]

plunk·er (plungk′kər), *n.* **1.** one who or that which plunks. **2.** *Angling.* a casting lure that makes a plunking sound upon hitting the surface of the water. [PLUNK + -ER¹]

plu·per·fect (plo͞o pûr′fikt), *Gram.* —*adj.* **1.** perfect with respect to a point of reference in past time, as *had done* in *He had done it when I came.* **2.** designating a tense or other verb formation or construction with such meaning, as Latin *portāveram* "I had carried." —*n.* **3.** the pluperfect tense, or other verb formation or construction with such meaning. **4.** a form in the pluperfect. [< L *plū(s quam) perfect(um)* more than perfect]

plupf., pluperfect. Also, **plup.**

plur., **1.** plural. **2.** plurality.

plu·ral (plo͝or′əl), *adj.* **1.** consisting of, containing, or pertaining to more than one. **2.** pertaining to or involving a plurality of persons or things: *plural marriage.* **3.** being one of such a plurality: *a plural wife.* **4.** *Gram.* noting or pertaining to a member of the category of number, found in many languages, indicating that a word has more than one referent, as in English *men,* or more than two referents, as in Old English *ge* "you." —*n. Gram.* **5.** the plural number. **6.** a form in the plural. [ME < L *plūrāl(is).* See PLUS, -AL¹]

plu·ral·ise (plo͝or′ə līz′), *v.t., v.i.,* **-ised, -is·ing.** *Chiefly Brit.* pluralize. —**plu′ral·i·sa′tion,** *n.* —**plu′ral·is′er,** *n.*

plu·ral·ism (plo͝or′ə liz′əm), *n.* **1.** *Philos.* **a.** a theory that there is more than one basic substance or principle. Cf. **dualism** (def. 2), **monism** (def. 1). **b.** a theory that reality consists of two or more independent elements. Cf. **monism** (def. 2). **2.** *Eccles.* **a.** the holding by one person of two or more offices at the same time. **b.** plurality (def. 7a). **3.** state or quality of being plural. [PLURAL + -ISM] —**plu′ral·ist,** *n.* —**plu′ral·is′tic,** *adj.* —**plu′ral·is′ti·cal·ly,** *adv.*

plu·ral·i·ty (plo͞o ral′i tē), *n., pl.* **-ties. 1.** the excess of votes received by the leading candidate, in an election in which there are three or more candidates, over those received by the next candidate (distinguished from *majority*). **2.** more than half of the whole; the majority. **3.** a number greater than one. **4.** fact of being numerous. **5.** a large number; multitude. **6.** state or fact of being plural. **7.** *Eccles.* **a.** the holding by one person of two or more benefices at the same time; pluralism. **b.** any of the benefices so held. [ME *pluralite* < OF < LL *plūrālitās.* See PLURAL, -ITY]

plu·ral·ize (plo͝or′ə līz′), *v.,* **-ized, -iz·ing.** —*v.t.* **1.** to express in the plural form; make plural: *to pluralize a noun.* —*v.i.* **2.** to receive or take a plural form. Also, *esp. Brit.,* **pluralise.** [PLURAL + -IZE] —**plu′ral·i·za′tion,** *n.* —**plu′ral·iz′er,** *n.*

plu·ral·ly (plo͝or′ə lē), *adv.* as a plural; in a plural sense. [ME *pluraliche.* See PLURAL, -LY]

pluri-, an element of Latin origin meaning "several," "many," used in the formation of compound words: *pluriaxial.* [< L, comb. form repr. L *plūs* (s. *plūri-*) more (pl. many). See PLUS]

plur·i·ax·i·al (plo͝or′ē ak′sē əl), *adj. Bot.* having flowers that grow from a secondary branch or stem. [PLURI- + AXIAL]

plus (plus), *prep.* **1.** more by the addition of; increased by: *ten plus two.* **2.** with the addition of; with: *He had wealth plus fame.* —*adj.* **3.** involving or noting addition. **4.** positive: *a plus quantity.* **5.** more (by a certain amount). **6.** *Elect.* pertaining to or characterized by positive electricity: *the plus terminal.* **7.** *Bot.* designating, in the absence of morphological difference, one of the two strains or mycelia in fungi which must unite in the sexual process. —*n.* **8.** a plus quantity. **9.** See **plus sign. 10.** something additional. **11.** a surplus or gain. —*adv.* **12.** *Informal.* with something in addition: *He has personality plus. Hers is a car with power plus.* [< L: more; akin to Gk *pleîon,* Icel *fleiri* more, *fjöl* much, Goth *filu,* G *viel,* OE *feolu, fela,* Gk *polý,* OIr *il*]

plus′ fours′, baggy knickers, as for sports wear. —**plus′-foured′,** *adj.*

plush (plush), *n.* **1.** a fabric, as of silk, cotton, or wool, whose pile is more than ¹/₈ inch high. —*adj.* **2.** connoting wealth or ease; luxurious: *a plush night club.* [< F *pluche,* syncopated var. of *peluche* << L *pilus* hair] —**plushed,** *adj.* —**plush′like′,** *adj.*

plus′ sight′, *Survey.* a backsight used in leveling.

plus′ sign′, *Arith.* the symbol (+) indicating summation or a positive quality.

Plu·tarch (plo͞o′tärk), *n.* **1.** A.D. c46–c120, Greek biographer. **2.** a walled plain in the first quadrant of the face of the moon: about 40 miles in diameter.

Plu·tarch·i·an (plo͞o tär′kē ən), *adj.* **1.** of or pertaining to the biographer Plutarch. **2.** characteristic of or resembling a biography by Plutarch or its subject: *a life worthy of Plutarchian description; a deed of Plutarchian splendor.* [PLUTARCH + -IAN]

Plu′tarch's Lives′, (*Parallel Lives*) a collection (A.D. 105–15) by Plutarch of 46 short biographies of the leading political figures of ancient Greece and Rome.

plu·te·us (plo͞o′tē əs), *n., pl.* **-te·i** (-tē ī′), **-te·us·es. 1.** (in ancient Roman architecture) a dwarf wall, esp. one between columns as a barrier. **2.** the free-swimming, bilaterally symmetrical larva of an echinoid or ophiuroid. [< L: breastwork, movable shelter] —**plu′te·al, plu′te·an,** *adj.*

Plu·to (plo͞o′tō), *n.* **1.** *Class. Myth.* a name given to Hades, under which he is identified by the Romans with Orcus. **2.** *Astron.* the planet ninth in order from the sun, having a diameter that is probably somewhat less than that of the earth, a mean distance from the sun of 3,671,000,000 miles, a period of revolution of 248.42 years, and having no known satellites: the outermost planet in the solar system.

plu·toc·ra·cy (plo͞o tok′rə sē), *n., pl.* **-cies. 1.** the rule or power of wealth or of the wealthy. **2.** a government or state in which the wealthy class rules. **3.** a class or group ruling, or exercising power or influence, by virtue of its wealth. [< Gk *ploutokratía.* See PLUTUS, -CRACY]

plu·to·crat (plo͞o′tə krat′), *n.* a member of a plutocracy. [back formation from Gk *ploutokratía* PLUTOCRACY]

plu·to·crat·ic (plo͞o′tə krat′ik), *adj.* of, pertaining to, or characterized by a plutocracy or plutocrats. Also, **plu′to·crat′i·cal.** [PLUTOCRAT + -IC] —**plu′to·crat′i·cal·ly,** *adv.*

plu·ton (plo͞o′ton), *n. Geol.* any body of igneous rock that solidified far below the earth's surface. [named after PLUTO]

Plu·to·ni·an (plo͞o tō′nē ən), *adj.* **1.** Also, **Plu·ton·ic** (plo͞o ton′ik). of, pertaining to, or resembling Pluto or the lower world; infernal. **2.** (*often l.c.*) *Geol.* pertaining to the theory that the present condition of the earth's crust is mainly due to igneous action. [< L *Plūtōni(us)* (< Gk *Ploutṓnios,* deriv. of *Ploútōn* PLUTO) + -AN]

plu·ton·ic (plo͞o ton′ik), *adj. Geol.* noting or pertaining to a class of igneous rocks which have solidified far below the earth's surface. [PLUTON + -IC]

plu·to·ni·um (plo͞o tō′nē əm), *n. Chem.* a radioactive element, capable of self-maintained explosive fission, isolated during research on the atomic bomb in 1940. It is formed by deuteron bombardment of neptunium, and has an isotope of major importance (Pu^{239}), which is fissionable and can be produced in chain-reacting units from uranium 238 by neutron capture followed by the spontaneous emission of two beta particles. *Symbol:* Pu; *at. no.:* 94. [< Gk *Ploútōn* PLUTO + -IUM]

Plu·tus (plo͞o′təs), *n.* **1.** *Class. Myth.* a god personifying wealth, sometimes confused with Pluto. **2.** (*italics.*) a comedy (388 B.C.) by Aristophanes.

plu·vi·al (plo͞o′vē əl), *adj.* **1.** of or pertaining to rain, esp. much rain; rainy. **2.** *Geol.* occurring through the action of rain. [< L *pluviāl(is),* equiv. to *pluvi(a)* rain + *-ālis* -AL¹]

plu·vi·om·e·ter (plo͞o′vē om′i tər), *n.* See **rain gauge.** [< L *pluvi(a)* rain + -O- + -METER] —**plu·vi·o·met·ric** (plo͞o′vē ə me′trik), **plu′vi·o·met′ri·cal,** *adj.* —**plu′vi·om′e·try,** *n.*

Plu·vi·ôse (plo͞o′vē ōs′; *Fr.* ply vyōz′), *n.* (in the French Revolutionary calendar) the fifth month of the year, extending from January 20 to February 18. [< F < L *pluviōs(us)* rainy. See PLUVIOUS]

plu·vi·ous (plo͞o′vē əs), *adj.* of or pertaining to rain; rainy. [< L *pluviōs(us).* See PLUVIAL, -OUS] —**plu·vi·os·i·ty** (plo͞o′vē os′i tē), *n.*

Plu·vi·us (plo͞o′vē əs), *n.* an ancient Roman epithet of Jupiter as rain-maker.

ply¹ (plī), *v.,* **plied, ply·ing.** —*v.t.* **1.** to work with or at; employ busily; use: *to ply the needle.* **2.** to carry on, practice, or pursue: *to ply a trade.* **3.** to treat with or apply something repeatedly: *to ply a fire with fresh fuel.* **4.** to assail persistently: *to ply horses with a whip.* **5.** to supply with or offer something pressingly: *to ply a person with drink.* **6.** to address (someone) persistently or importunately, as with questions, solicitations, etc.; importune. **7.** to pass over or along (a river, stream, etc.) steadily or on a regular basis: *boats that ply the Mississippi.* —*v.i.* **8.** to run or travel regularly over a fixed course or between certain places, as a boat, bus, etc. **9.** to perform one's work or office busily or steadily: *to ply with the oars; to ply at a trade.* [ME *plye,* aph. var. of *aplye* to APPLY] —**ply′ing·ly,** *adv.*

ply² (plī), *n., pl.* **plies,** *v.,* **plied, ply·ing.** —*n.* **1.** one thickness or layer, as in certain wood products. **2.** a unit of yarn: *single ply.* **3.** bent, bias, or inclination. —*v.t.* **4.** *Brit. Dial.* to bend, fold, or mold. —*v.i.* **5.** *Obs.* to bend, incline, or yield. [ME *plie(n)* < MF *plier* to fold, bend, var. of *ployer,* OF *pleiier* < L *plicāre* to fold]

-ply, a combining form of **ply²:** *three-ply.*

ply·er (plī′ər), *n.* *Chiefly Brit.* plier.

ply′ met′al, a composition of dissimilar metals bonded together in sheet form.

Plym·outh (plim′əth), *n.* **1.** a seaport in SW Devonshire, in SW England, on the English Channel: naval base; the departing point of the *Mayflower* 1620. 204,279 (1961). **2.** a city in SE Massachusetts: the oldest town in New England, founded by the Pilgrims 1620. 6488 (1960).

Plym′outh Breth′ren, a loosely organized body of Christians founded in Plymouth, England, about 1830, having no ordained ministry, no formal creed or ritual, and accepting the Bible as the only guide.

Plym′outh Col′ony, *Amer. Hist.* the colony established in SE Massachusetts by the Pilgrim Fathers in 1620.

Plym′outh Com′pany, a company, formed in England in 1606 to establish colonies in America and which founded a colony in Maine in 1607.

Plym′outh Rock′, **1.** a rock at Plymouth, Massachusetts on which the Pilgrims who sailed on the *Mayflower* are said to have stepped ashore when they landed in America in 1620. **2.** one of an American breed of medium-sized chickens, raised for meat and eggs.

ply′ roll′ing, *Metalworking.* See **pack rolling.**

ply·wood (plī′wo͝od′), *n.* a material used for building purposes, consisting usually of an odd number of veneers glued over each other at right angles. [PLY² + WOOD¹]

Pl·zeň (pl′zen′yᵊ), *n.* a city in Bohemia, in the W Czech Republic. 175,000. German, **Pilsen.**

Pm, *Chem.* promethium.

pm., premium.

P.M., 1. Past Master. **2.** Paymaster. **3.** See **p.m. 4.** Police Magistrate. **5.** Postmaster. **6.** post-mortem. **7.** Prime Minister. **8.** Provost Marshal.

p.m., 1. after noon; the period between 12 noon and 12 midnight. **2.** an afternoon or evening newspaper, sometimes issued before noon. Cf. **a.m.** [< L *post meridiem*]

PMA, Production and Marketing Administration.

P.M.G., 1. Paymaster General. **2.** Postmaster General. **3.** Provost Marshal General.

pmk., postmark.

PMLA, Publications of the Modern Language Association. Also, **P.M.L.A.**

PMS, *Path.* premenstrual syndrome: a complex of physical and emotional changes, including depression, irritability, water retention, breast soreness, etc., one or more of which may be experienced in the several days before the onset of menstrual flow.

PN, 1. (*often l.c.*) please note. **2.** (*often l.c.*) promissory note. **3.** psychoneurotic.

P/N, promissory note. Also, **p.n.**

PNA, *Biochem.* See **RNA.** [*p*(entose) *n*(ucleic) *a*(cid)]

pneu·drau·lic (no͞o drô′lik, nyo͞o-), *adj.* of or pertaining to a mechanism involving both pneumatic and hydraulic action. [PNEU(MATIC + HY)DRAULIC]

pneum., 1. pneumatic. **2.** pneumatics.

pneu·ma (no͞o′mə, nyo͞o′-), *n.* **1.** the vital spirit; the soul. **2.** *Theol.* the Spirit of God; the Holy Ghost. [< Gk: lit., breath, wind, akin to *pnein* to blow, breathe]

pneu·mat·ic (no͝o mat′ik, nyo͝o-), *adj.* **1.** of or pertaining to air, gases, or wind. **2.** of or pertaining to pneumatics. **3.** operated by air or by the pressure or exhaustion of air: *a pneumatic drill.* **4.** filled with or containing compressed air, as a tire. **5.** equipped with pneumatic tires. **6.** *Theol.* of or pertaining to the spirit; spiritual. **7.** *Zool.* containing air or air cavities. —*n.* **8.** a pneumatic tire. **9.** a vehicle having wheels with such tires. [< L *pneumatic(us)* < Gk *pneumatikós* pertaining to air, breath or wind, spiritual, equiv. to *pneumat-* (s. of *pneûma;* see PNEUMA) + *-ikos* -IC] —**pneu·mat′i·cal·ly,** *adv.* —**pneu·ma·tic·i·ty** (no͞o′mə tis′i tē, nyo͞o′-), *n.*

pneumat′ic duct′, the duct joining the air bladder and alimentary canal of a physostomous fish.

pneumat′ic pile′, *Building Trades.* a hollow pile, used under water, in which a vacuum is induced so that air and water pressure force it into place.

pneu·mat·ics (no͝o mat′iks, nyo͝o-), *n.* (*construed as sing.*) the branch of physics that deals with the mechanical properties of air and other gases. Also called **pneumodynamics.** [see PNEUMATIC, -ICS]

pneumat′ic trough′, *Chem.* a trough filled with liquid, esp. water, for collecting gases in bell jars or the like by displacement.

pneumato-, a learned borrowing from Greek used, with the meaning "air," "breath," "spirit," in the formation of compound words: *pneumatology; pneumatophore.* [< Gk, comb. form of *pneûma*]

pneu·ma·to·cyst (no͞o′mə tə sist′, nyo͞o′-), *n. Biol.* **1.** the cavity of a pneumatophore. **2.** pneumatophore.

pneu·ma·to·graph (no͞o′mə tə graf′, -gräf′, nyo͞o′-), *n. Med.* pneumograph.

pneu·ma·tol·o·gy (no͞o′mə tol′ə jē, nyo͞o′-), *n.* **1.** *Theol.* **a.** doctrine concerning the Holy Spirit. **b.** the belief in intermediary spirits between men and God. **2.** the doctrine or theory of spiritual beings. **3.** *Archaic.* psychology. **4.** *Obs.* pneumatics. [PNEUMATO- + -LOGY] —**pneu·ma·to·log·ic** (no͞o′mə tᵊloj′ik, nyo͞o′-), **pneu′ma·to·log′i·cal,** *adj.* —**pneu′ma·tol′o·gist,** *n.*

pneu·ma·tol·y·sis (no͞o′mə tol′i sis, nyo͞o′-), *n. Geol.* the process by which minerals and ores are formed by the action of vapors given off from igneous magmas. [PNEUMATO- + -LYSIS]

pneu·ma·to·lyt·ic (no͞o′mə tᵊ lit′ik, nyo͞o′-), *adj.* pertaining to or formed by pneumatolysis. Also, **pneu′ma·to·lit′ic.** [PNEUMATO- + -LYTIC]

pneu·ma·tom·e·ter (no͞o′mə tom′i tər, nyo͞o′-), *n.* an instrument for measuring either the quantity of air inhaled or exhaled during a single inspiration or expiration, or the force of inspiration or expiration. [PNEUMATO- + -METER]

pneu·ma·to·phore (no͞o′mə tə fōr′, -fôr′, nyo͞o′-; no͞o mat′ə fōr′, -fôr′, nyo͞o-), *n.* **1.** *Bot.* a specialized structure developed from the root in certain plants growing in swamps and marshes, serving as a respiratory organ. **2.** *Zool.* the air sac of a siphonophore, serving as a float. [PNEUMATO- + -PHORE] —**pneu·ma·toph·or·ous** (no͞o′mə tof′ər əs, nyo͞o′-), *adj.*

pneu·ma·to·ther·a·py (no͞o′mə tō ther′ə pē, nyo͞o′-), *n.* the use of compressed or rarefied air in treating disease. [PNEUMATO- + THERAPY]

pneu·mec·to·my (no͞o mek′tə mē, nyo͞o-), *n., pl.* **-mies.** *Surg.* pneumonectomy.

pneumo-, an element of Greek origin, used to refer to air, respiration, or the lungs: *pneumococcus.* Cf. **pneumato-.** [repr. Gk *pneúmōn* lung, or sometimes *pneûma* wind, air, breath]

pneu·mo·ba·cil·lus (no͞o′mō bə sil′əs, nyo͞o′-), *n., pl.* **-cil·li** (-sil′ī). a bacterium, *Klebsiella pneumoniae,* causing a type of pneumonia and associated with certain other diseases, esp. of the respiratory tract. Also called **Friedländer's bacillus, Friedländer's pneumobacillus.** [< NL; see PNEUMO-, BACILLUS]

pneu·mo·coc·cus (no͞o′mə kok′əs, nyo͞o′-), *n., pl.* **-coc·ci** (-kok′sī). a bacterium, *Diplococcus pneumoniae,* causing lobar pneumonia and associated with certain other diseases, as pericarditis and meningitis. [< NL; see PNEUMO-, -COCCUS] —**pneu·mo·coc·cal** (no͞o′mə-kok′əl, nyo͞o′-), **pneu·mo·coc·cic** (no͞o′mə kok′sik, nyo͞o′-), **pneu·mo·coc·cous** (no͞o′mə kok′əs, nyo͞o′-), *adj.*

pneu·mo·co·ni·o·sis (no͞o′mə kō′nē ō′sis, nyo͞o′-), *n.* *Pathol.* fibrous induration of the lungs due to irritation caused by the inhalation of dust, esp. in certain occupations, as coal mining, stonecutting, or the like. Also, **pneumonoconiosis, pneumonokoniosis.** [syncopated var. of *pneumonoconiosis,* equiv. to PNEUMONO- + Gk *kóni(s)* dust + -OSIS]

pneu·mo·dy·nam·ics (no͞o′mə dī nam′iks, nyo͞o′-, -di-), *n.* (*construed as sing.*) pneumatics. [PNEUMO- + DYNAMICS]

pneu·mo·en·ceph·a·li·tis (no͞o′mō en sef′ə lī′tis, nyo͞o′-), *n.* *Vet. Pathol.* See **Newcastle disease.** [< NL; see PNEUMO-, ENCEPHALITIS]

pneu·mo·en·ceph·al·o·gram (no͞o′mō en sef′ə lə-gram′, nyo͞o′-), *n.* *Med.* an encephalogram made after the replacement of the cerebrospinal fluid by air or gas. [PNEUMO- + ENCEPHALOGRAM]

pneu·mo·en·ceph·a·log·ra·phy (no͞o′mō en sef′ə-log′rə fē, nyo͞o′-), *n.* *Med.* encephalography. [PNEUMO- + ENCEPHALOGRAPHY]

pneu·mo·gas·tric (no͞o′mə gas′trik, nyo͞o′-), *Anat.* —*adj.* **1.** of or pertaining to the lungs and stomach. —*n.* **2.** See **pneumogastric nerve.** [PNEUMO- + GASTRIC]

pneu′mogas′tric nerve′, *Anat.* (formerly) the vagus nerve.

pneu·mo·graph (no͞o′mə graf′, -gräf′, nyo͞o′-), *n.* *Med.* a device for recording graphically the respiratory movements of the thorax. Also, **pneumatograph.** [PNEUMO- + -GRAPH] —**pneu·mo·graph·ic** (no͞o′mə-graf′ik, nyo͞o′-), *adj.*

pneu·mog·ra·phy (no͝o mog′rə fē, nyo͝o-), *n.* *Med.* **1.** the process of recording the movements of the thorax in respiration. **2.** the production of x-ray photographs of the lungs. [PNEUMO- + -GRAPHY]

pneumon-, var. of **pneumono-** before a vowel: *pneumonectomy.*

pneu·mo·nec·to·my (no͞o′mə nek′tə mē, nyo͞o′-), *n., pl.* **-mies.** *Surg.* excision of part or all of a lung. Also, **pneumectomy.** [PNEUMON- + -ECTOMY]

pneu·mo·nia (no͝o mōn′yə, -mō′nē ə, nyo͝o-), *n.* *Pathol.* **1.** inflammation of the lungs. **2.** Also called **croupous pneumonia, lobar pneumonia.** an acute affection of the lungs, regarded as due to the pneumococcus. [< NL < Gk *pneumonía.* See PNEUMON-, -IA]

pneu·mon·ic (no͝o mon′ik, nyo͝o-), *adj.* **1.** of, pertaining to, or affecting the lungs; pulmonary. **2.** pertaining to or affected with pneumonia. [< NL *pneumonic(us)* < Gk *pneumonikós.* See PNEUMON-, -IC]

pneumon′ic plague′, *Pathol.* a form of plague characterized by lung involvement. Cf. **plague.**

pneumono-, a learned borrowing from Greek meaning "lung," used in the formation of compound words: *pneumonoconiosis.* Also, *esp. before a vowel,* **pneumon-.** [comb. form repr. Gk *pneúmōn* lung]

pneu·mo·no·co·ni·o·sis (no͞o′mə nō kō′nē ō′sis, nyo͞o′-), *n.* *Pathol.* pneumoconiosis. Also, **pneu′mo-no·ko′ni·o′sis.**

pneu·mo·no·ul·tra·mi·cro·scop·ic·sil·i·co·vol·ca·no·co·ni·o·sis (no͞o′mə nō ul′trə mī′krə skop′ik-sil′ə kō′vol kā′nō kō′nē ō′sis, nyo͞o′-), *n.* *Pathol.* a disease of the lungs caused by the breathing of extremely fine siliceous dust particles. Also, **pneu′mo·no·ul′tra·mi′cro·scop′ic·sil′i·co·vol·ca′no·ko′ni·o′sis.** [< NL; see PNEUMONO-, ULTRAMICROSCOPIC, SILICO-, VOLCANO, CONIDIUM, -OSIS]

pneu·mo·tho·rax (no͞o′mə thōr′aks, -thôr′-, nyo͞o′-), *n.* *Pathol.* the presence of air or gas in the pleural cavity. [< NL; see PNEUMO-, THORAX]

Pnom Penh (nom′ pen′, pə nôm′ pen′). See **Phnom Penh.** Also, **Pnom′-penh′, Pnom′penh′.**

pnxt., pinxit.

Pnyx (niks, pniks), *n.* a hill in Athens, Greece, near the Acropolis: the place of assembly in ancient Athens.

Po (pō), *n.* a river in Italy, flowing E from the Alps in the NW to the Adriatic. 418 mi. long. Ancient, **Padus.**

Po, *Chem.* polonium.

po., *Baseball.* put-out; put-outs.

P.O., 1. petty officer. **2.** postal order. **3.** post office.

p.o., (in prescriptions) by mouth. [< L *per ōs*]

POA, See **primary optical area.**

po·a·ceous (pō ā′shəs), *adj.* belonging to the *Poaceae* (or *Gramineae*), the grass family of plants. [< NL *Po(a)* the typical genus (< Gk *póa* grass) + -ACEOUS]

poach[1] (pōch), *v.i.* **1.** *Chiefly Brit.* **a.** to trespass, esp. on another's game preserve, in order to steal animals or to hunt without the landowner's permission. **b.** *Informal.* to cheat in a game or sports contest. **2.** to take game or fish illegally. **3.** (of land) to become broken up or slushy by being trampled. **4.** (in tennis, squash, handball, etc.) to play a ball hit into the territory of one's partner that is properly his ball to play. —*v.t.* **5.** to break or tear up by trampling. **6.** to mix with water and reduce to a uniform consistency, as clay. [< MF *poche(r)* (to) gouge < Gmc; akin to POKE[1]] —**poach′-a·ble,** *adj.*

poach[2] (pōch), *v.t.* to cook (eggs, fish, fruits, etc.) in a hot liquid that is kept just below the boiling point. [var. of *potch,* late ME *pocche* < MF *pocher,* lit., to bag (the white of an egg being made to hold the yoke as a bag would), deriv. of *poche* bag, central F form of Picard *poque* < MD *poke* POKE[2]] —**poach′a·ble,** *adj.*

poach·er[1] (pō′chər), *n.* **1.** a person who trespasses on private property, esp. to catch fish or game illegally. **2.** Also called **sea-poacher.** any of several slender, marine fishes of the family *Agonidae,* found chiefly in deeper waters of the North Pacific, having the body covered with bony plates. [POACH[1] + -ER[1]]

poach·er[2] (pō′chər), *n.* **1.** a pan having a tight-fitting lid and metal cups for steaming or poaching eggs. **2.** any dish or pan used for poaching food, esp. a baking dish for poaching fish. [POACH[2] + -ER[1]]

poach·y (pō′chē), *adj.,* **poach·i·er, poach·i·est.** (of land) slushy; swampy. [POACH[1] + -Y[1]] —**poach′i·ness,** *n.*

POB, Post Office Box. Also, **P.O.B.**

Po·ca·hon·tas (pō′kə hon′təs), *n.* **1.** (*Rebecca Rolfe*) 1595?–1617, American Indian girl who is said to have prevented the execution of Captain John Smith. **2.** a town in NE Arkansas. 3665 (1960).

Po·ca·tel·lo (pō′kə tel′ō), *n.* a city in SE Idaho. 28,534 (1960).

po·chade (pô shȧd′), *n., pl.* **-chades** (-shȧd′). *French.* a small sketch or study, esp. one executed in oils, out of doors, and in preparation for a finished painting.

po·chard (pō′chərd, -kərd), *n., pl.* **-chards,** (*esp. collectively*) **-chard. 1.** an Old World diving duck, *Aythya ferina,* having a chestnut-red head. **2.** any of various related ducks, as the American redhead. [?]

po·ché (pō shā′), *n.* the walls, columns, and other solids of a building or the like, as indicated on an architectural plan, usually in black. [< F, ptp. of *pocher* to make a rough sketch, POACH[2]]

po·chette (pō shet′), *n.* kit[2]. [< F, dim. of *poche* pocket]

Po Chü-i (bô′ jy′ē′), *n.* A.D. 772–846, Chinese poet.

pocill., (in prescriptions) a little cup. [< L *pōcillum*]

pock (pok), *n.* **1.** a pustule on the body in an eruptive disease, as smallpox. **2.** a mark or spot left by or resembling such a pustule. **3.** *Scot.* poke[2]. [ME *pokke,* OE *poc;* c. G *Pocke;* perh. akin to OE *pocca.* See POKE[2]]

pocked (pokt), *adj.* marked with pustules or with pits left by them; pitted. [POCK + -ED[3]]

pock·et (pok′it), *n.* **1.** a shaped piece of fabric attached inside or outside a garment and forming a pouch used esp. for carrying small articles. **2.** a bag or pouch. **3.** means; financial resources: *a selection of gifts to fit every pocket.* **4.** any pouchlike receptacle, compartment, hollow, or cavity. **5.** an envelope, receptacle, etc., usually of heavy paper and open at one end, used for storing or preserving photographs, stamps, phonograph records, etc.: *Each album has 12 pockets.* **6.** a recess, as in a wall, for receiving a sliding door, sash weights, etc. **7.** a cavity in the earth, esp. one containing gold or other ore. **8.** a small ore body or mass of ore, frequently isolated. **9.** *Mining.* **a.** a bin for ore or rock storage. **b.** a raise or small slope fitted with chute gates. **10.** *Billiards, Pool.* any of the pouches or bags at the corners and sides of the table. **11.** a position in which a competitor in a race is so hemmed in by others that his progress is impeded. **12.** *Bowling.* the space between the headpin and the pin next behind to the left or right, taken as the target for a strike. **13.** *Naut.* a holder consisting of a strip of sailcloth sewed to a sail, and containing a thin wooden batten which stiffens the leech of the sail. **14.** *Anat.* any saclike cavity in the body: *a pus pocket.* **15.** See **stage pocket. 16.** an English unit of weight for hops equivalent to 168 pounds. **17. in one's pocket,** in one's possession; under one's influence: *He has the audience in his pocket.* **18. line one's pockets,** to profit, esp. at the expense of others: *While millions were fighting and dying, the profiteers were lining their pockets.* **19. out of pocket,** having suffered a financial loss; poorer: *He had made unwise land purchases, and found himself several thousand dollars out of pocket.* —*adj.* **20.** small enough or suitable for carrying in the pocket: *a pocket radio.* **21.** relatively small; smaller than usual: *a pocket war; a pocket country.* —*v.t.* **22.** to put into one's pocket: *to pocket one's keys.* **23.** to take possession of as one's own, often dishonestly: *to pocket public funds.* **24.** to submit to or endure without protest or open resentment: *to pocket an insult.* **25.** to conceal or suppress: *to pocket one's pride.* **26.** to enclose or confine in or as in a pocket: *The town was pocketed in a small valley.* **27.** *Billiards, Pool.* to drive (a ball) into a pocket. **28.** *U.S.* (of the President or a legislative executive) to retain (a bill) without action on it and thus prevent it from becoming a law. **29.** to hem in (a contestant) so as to impede progress, as in racing. [ME *poket* < MD < ONF (Picard) *poquet,* dim. of *poque* < MD *poke* POKE[2]; see -ET] —**pock′et-a·ble,** *adj.* —**pock′et·a·ble·ness,** *n.* —**pock′et·less,** *adj.* —**pock′et·like′,** *adj.*

pock′et bat′tleship, a small heavily armed and armored warship serving as a battleship because of limitations imposed by treaty.

pock′et bil′liards, pool[2] (def. 8).

pock·et·book (pok′it bo͝ok′), *n.* **1.** a small bag or case, as of leather, for papers, money, etc., usually carried by a handle or in the pocket. **2.** pecuniary resources: *The price was out of reach of his pocketbook.* **3.** Also, **pock′et book′.** a book, usually paperbound, that is small enough to fit into a pocket or purse. [POCKET + BOOK]

pock′et bor′ough, 1. (before the Reform Bill of 1832) any English borough whose representatives in Parliament were controlled by an individual or family. **2.** an election district under the control of an individual, family, or group.

pock′et chis′el, any woodworking chisel having a blade of medium length.

pock·et·ful (pok′it fo͝ol′), *n., pl.* **-fuls.** as much as a pocket will hold. [POCKET + -FUL]

pock′et go′pher, any of numerous burrowing rodents of the family *Geomyidae,* of western and southern North America and Central America, having large, external, fur-lined cheek pouches. Also called **gopher, pouched rat.**

pock·et-hand·ker·chief (pok′it haŋg′kər chif, -chēf′), *n.* handkerchief (def. 1).

pock·et·ing (pok′i ting), *n.* any of various fabrics for making the insides of pockets. [POCKET + -ING[1]]

pock·et·knife (pok′it nīf′), *n., pl.* **-knives.** a knife with one or more blades which fold into the handle, suitable for carrying in the pocket. [POCKET + KNIFE]

pock′et mon′ey, money for small, current expenses.

pock′et mouse′, any of numerous burrowing rodents, esp. of the genus *Perognathus,* found chiefly in arid parts of the southwestern U.S. and northern Mexico, having fur-lined cheek pouches and usually long tails.

pock′et piece′, (in a window frame) a removable part of a pulley stile permitting access to sash weights.

pock′et ve′to, 1. a veto brought about by the failure of the President to sign a bill presented to him within ten days of the adjournment of Congress. **2.** a similar action on the part of any legislative executive.

pock·mark (pok′märk′), *n.* **1.** Usually, **pockmarks.** marks or pits left by a pustule in smallpox or the like. —*v.t.* **2.** to mark or scar with or as with pockmarks: *gopher holes pockmarking the field.* [POCK + MARK[1]] —**pock′marked′,** *adj.*

pock·y (pok′ē), *adj.,* **pock·i·er, pock·i·est.** of, pertaining to, characterized by, or covered with pocks. [ME *pokky.* See POCK, -Y[1]] —**pock′i·ly,** *adv.*

po·co (pō′kō; *It.* pô′kô), *adv.* *Music.* somewhat; rather: *poco presto.* [< It: little < L *paucus* few]

po·co a po·co (pō′kō ä pō′kō; *It.* pô′kô ä pô′kô), *Music.* gradually; little by little: *poco a poco accelerando.* [< It]

po·co·cu·ran·te (pō′kō ko͞o ran′tē, -rän′-; *It.* pô′kô-ko͞o rän′te), *n., pl.* **-ti** (-tē), *adj.* —*n.* **1.** a careless or indifferent person. —*adj.* **2.** caring little; indifferent; nonchalant. [< It: lit., caring little. See POCO, CURE, -ANT] —**po·co·cu·ran·tism** (pō′kō ko͞o ran′tiz əm, -rän′-), **po′co·cu·ran′te·ism,** *n.*

Po′co·moke Cit′y (pō′kə mōk′), a town in SE Maryland. 3329 (1960).

Po·ços de Cal·das (pô′so͞ozh də käl′dəs), a city in E Brazil. 32,191 (1960).

po·co·sin (pə kō′sən, pō′kə sən), *n.* *Southeastern U.S.* a swamp or marsh in an upland coastal region. Also, **po·co′son, po·co′sen.** [< Algonquin (Delaware) *poquosin,* equiv. to *poquo* to break open, widen + *-(e)s* dim. suffix + *-in(g)* locative suffix]

pocul., (in prescriptions) a cup. [< L *pōculum*]

poc·u·li·form (pok′yə lə fôrm′), *adj.* cup-shaped. [< L *pōcul(um)* cup + -I- + -FORM]

pod[1] (pod), *n., v.,* **pod·ded, pod·ding.** —*n.* **1.** a somewhat elongated, two-valved seed vessel, as that of the pea or bean. **2.** a dehiscent fruit or pericarp having several seeds. **3.** a streamlined compartment, sometimes detachable, under the fuselage or wing of an airplane, for housing a jet engine, cargo, or weapons. —*v.i.* **4.** to produce pods. **5.** to swell out like a pod. [appar. back formation from *podder* peasecod gatherer. Cf. *podder,* var. of *podware,* unexplained var. of *codware* bagged vegetables (COD[2] pod, bag + *-ware* crops, vegetables)] —**pod′like′,** *adj.*

pod[2] (pod), *n.* **1.** a small herd or school, esp. of seals or whales. **2.** a small flock of birds. [? special (orig. facetious) use of POD[1]]

pod[3] (pod), *n.* **1.** the straight groove or channel in the body of certain augers or bits. **2.** pad[1] (def. 14b). [ME **pod* socket, special (technical) use of **pod,* OE *pād* covering, cloak, the socket being thought of as something that covers or hides from view what is thrust into it]

pod-, a learned borrowing from Greek meaning "foot," used in the formation of compound words: *pododynia.* Also, *esp. before a consonant,* **podo-.** [comb. form repr. Gk *poús* (gen. *podós*) FOOT]

-pod, a learned borrowing from Greek meaning "footed," used in the formation of compound words: *cephalopod.* [< Gk *-podos,* equiv. to *pod-* (s. of *poús*) foot + *-os* adj. suffix]

POD, port of debarkation.

P.O.D., 1. pay on death. **2.** pay on delivery. **3.** Post Office Department.

-poda, pl. of **-pod,** specialized in zoological terminology to denote the class of which the individual is a member: *Cephalopoda.*

po·dag·ra (pō dag′rə, pod′ə grə), *n.* *Pathol.* gout in the foot. [< L < Gk: lit., foot-trap, equiv. to *pod-* POD-[2] + *ágra* a catching, seizure] —**po·dag′ral, po·dag′ric, po·dag′ri·cal, pod·a·grous** (pod′ə grəs), *adj.*

po·dal·gia (pō dal′jə, -jē ə), *n.* *Med.* pain in the foot. Also called **pododynia.** [POD- + -ALGIA]

po·dal·ic (pō dal′ik), *adj.* *Med.* pertaining to the feet. [*podal* of the feet (see POD-, -AL[1]) + -IC]

Pod·a·li·ri·us (pod′ə lir′ē əs), *n.* *Class. Myth.* a son of Asclepius who was physician to the Greeks in the Trojan War.

Po·dar·ces (pō där′sēz), *n.* *Class. Myth.* **1.** Priam. **2.** (in the *Iliad*) a son of Iphiclus who, following the death of his brother, took command of the Pythians in the Trojan War. Cf. **Protesilaus.**

Po·dar·ge (pō där′jē), *n.* *Class. Myth.* one of the Harpies.

pod·dock (pod′ək), *n.* *Scot. and North Eng.* paddock[2].

pod·dy (pod′ē), *n., pl.* **-dies.** *Australian.* **1.** a newborn or unweaned calf. **2.** any young animal. **3.** maverick. [?]

pod·dy-dodg·er (pod′ē doj′ər), *n.* *Australian.* a person who musters wild cattle and mavericks from land other than his own.

-pode, var. of **-podium:** *megapode.*

Po·des (pō′dēz), *n.* (in the *Iliad*) a Trojan warrior killed by Menelaus in the struggle for the corpse of Patroclus.

po·des·ta (pō des′tə; *It.* pô′de stä′), *n.* **1.** any of certain magistrates in Italy, as a chief magistrate in medieval towns and republics. **2.** a person appointed to serve as mayor of an Italian city during the Fascist regime. [< It *podestà* power < L *potestās*]

po·de·ti·i·form (pə dē′shē ə fôrm′), *adj.* shaped like a podetium. [PODET(IUM) + -I- + -FORM]

po·de·ti·um (pō dē′shē əm), *n., pl.* **-ti·a** (-shē ə). *Bot.* **1.** (in certain lichens) a stalk bearing an apothecium. **2.** any stalklike elevation. [POD- + *-etium* (< ?)]

Pod·gor·ny (pod gôr′ni), *n.* **Ni·ko·lai Vik·to·ro·vitch** (ni ko lī′ vēk′to ro vich), born 1903, Russian government official: member of the Presidium 1955–65; president of the Soviet Union since 1965.

Pod·go·ri·ca (*Serbo-Croatian.* pôd′gô rē′tsä), *n.* the capital of Montenegro, in SW Yugoslavia. 132,290. Formerly (1945–92), **Titograd.**

podg·y (poj′ē), *adj.,* **podg·i·er, podg·i·est.** *Chiefly Brit.* pudgy. —**podg′i·ly,** *adv.* —**podg′i·ness,** *n.*

po·di·a·try (pə dī′ə trē, pō-), *n. Med.* the investigation and treatment of foot disorders. [POD- + -IATRY] —**po·di′a·trist,** *n.*

pod·ite (pod′īt), *n.* **1.** an arthropod limb. **2.** a podomere. [POD- + -ITE[1]] —**po·dit·ic** (pə dit′ik), *adj.*

po·di·um (pō′dē əm), *n., pl.* **-di·ums, -di·a** (-dē ə). **1.** a small platform for the conductor of an orchestra, for a public speaker, etc. **2.** *Archit.* **a.** a low wall forming a base for a construction, as a colonnade or dome. **b.** a stereobate for a classical temple, esp. one with perpendicular sides. **c.** the masonry supporting a classical temple. **d.** a raised platform surrounding the arena of an ancient Roman amphitheater, having on it the seats of privileged spectators. **3.** *Zool., Anat.* a foot. **4.** *Bot.* a footstalk or stipe. [< L: elevated place, balcony < Gk *pódion* little foot, equiv. to *pod-* POD- + *-ion* dim. suffix. See PEW]

-podium, an element meaning "footlike": *pseudopodium.* Also, **-pode.** [< NL; see PODIUM]

podo-, var. of **pod-** before a consonant: *podotheca.*

pod·o·dyn·i·a (pod′ə din′ē ə), *n. Med.* podalgia.

Po·dolsk (po dôlsk′), *n.* a city in the W RSFSR, in the central Soviet Union in Europe, S of Moscow. 144,000 (est. 1962).

pod·o·mere (pod′ə mēr′), *n. Zool.* any segment of a limb of an arthropod. [PODO- + -MERE]

pod·o·phyl·lin (pod′ə fil′in), *n.* a resin, occurring as a light brown to greenish amorphous powder, obtained from podophyllum, and used in medicine chiefly as a cathartic. Also called **pod′ophyl′lin res′in.** [PODOPHYLL(UM) + -IN[2]] —**pod′o·phyl′lic,** *adj.*

pod·o·phyl·lum (pod′ə fil′əm), *n.* the dried rhizome of the May apple, *Podophyllum peltatum.* [< NL; see PODO-, -PHYLL]

pod·o·the·ca (pod′ə thē′kə), *n., pl.* **-cae** (-sē). *Ornith.* the horny integument covering unfeathered portions of the legs and toes of most birds. [< NL; see PODO-, THECA] —**pod′o·the′cal,** *adj.*

-podous, a suffix used to form adjectives corresponding to nouns with stems in **-pod**: *cephalopodous.* [-POD + -OUS]

pod·sol (pod′sol), *n.* an infertile forest soil, notably acidic, having a grayish-white or ash-colored upper layer, depleted of colloids and of iron and aluminum compounds, and a brownish lower layer in which these colloids and compounds have accumulated: found over large areas of N North America and Eurasia. Also, **podzol** (pod′zol). [< Russ *podzol,* lit., like ashes, equiv. to *pod* near + *zola* ash] —**pod·sol′ic, pod·zol′ic,** *adj.*

pod·sol·ize (pod′sə līz′), *v.,* **-ized, -iz·ing.** —*v.t.* **1.** to make into podsol. —*v.i.* **2.** to become podsol. Also, **podzolize.** [PODSOL + -IZE] —**pod′sol·i·za′tion,** *n.*

Po·dunk (pō′dungk), *n.* any small and insignificant or inaccessible town or village: *After a year in the big city, most young men have stopped writing the girl friend back in Podunk.* [special use of *Podunk,* near Hartford, Conn.]

pod·zol·ize (pod′zə līz′), *v.t., v.i.,* **-ized, -iz·ing.** podsolize. —**pod′zol·i·za′tion,** *n.*

Poe (pō), *n.* **1. Edgar Allan,** 1809–49, U.S. poet, short-story writer, and critic. **2.** a boy's given name.

POE, port of embarkation.

Poe·as (pē′əs), *n. Class. Myth.* a Meliboean king who lit the funeral pyre of Hercules.

poe·ci·le (pē′sə lē), *n.* poikilie.

poe·cil·i·id (pē sil′ē id), *n.* **1.** any fish of the family *Poeciliidae,* comprising the livebearers. —*adj.* **2.** belonging or pertaining to the family *Poeciliidae.* [< NL *Poeciliid(ae),* equiv. to *Poecili(a)* name of genus (< Gk *poikilia* striped, marked with various colors) + *-idae* -ID[2]]

po·em (pō′əm), *n.* **1.** a composition in verse, esp. one that is characterized by a highly developed artistic form and by the use of heightened language and rhythm to express an intensely imaginative interpretation of the subject. **2.** composition which, though not in verse, is characterized by great beauty of language or expression: *a prose poem from the Scriptures; a symphonic poem.* **3.** something having qualities that are suggestive of or likened to those of poetry: *Marcel, that chicken cacciatore was an absolute poem.* [< L *poēma* < Gk *pōēma,* var. of *poíēma* poem, something made, equiv. to *poi(eîn)* (to) make + *-ēma* -EME]

Po·e·ma del Cid (pô e′mä thel thēd′), a Spanish epic poem (12th century) relating the adventures of El Cid.

Po·èmes An·tiques (*Fr.* pô em zän tēk′), a collection of poems (1852) by Leconte de Lisle.

Po·èmes Bar·bares (*Fr.* pô em bar bar′), a collection of poems (1862, 1872, 1878) by Leconte de Lisle.

Po′ems Chief′ly in the Scot′tish Di′alect, a collection of poems (1786) by Robert Burns.

Poe·na (pē′nə), *n.* an ancient Greek personification of punishment or revenge, sometimes conceived of as a monster and sometimes associated with the Furies. Also, **Poine.**

poe·nol·o·gy (pē nol′ə jē), *n.* penology.

po·e·sy (pō′i sē, -zē), *n., pl.* **-sies.** **1.** *Archaic.* **a.** poetry in general. **b.** the work or the art of poetic composition. **c.** verse or poetry in metrical form. **2.** *Obs.* **a.** a poem or verse used as a motto. Cf. **posy** (def. 2). **b.** a poem. [ME *poesie* < MF < L *poēsis* < Gk *pōēsis,* var. of *poíēsis* poetic art, poetry, lit., a making, equiv. to *poiē-* (var. s. of *poieîn* to make) + *-sis* -SIS]

po·et (pō′it), *n.* **1.** a person who composes poetry. **2.** a person who has the gift of poetic thought, imagination, and creation, together with eloquence of expression. [ME *poete* < L *poēta* < Gk *poētēs,* var. of *poiētēs* poet, lit., maker, equiv. to *poiē-* (var. s. of *poieîn* to make) + *-tēs* agent suffix] —**po′et·less,** *adj.* —**po′et·like′,** *adj.*
—**Syn. 1.** versifier, bard.

poet., **1.** poetic. **2.** poetical. **3.** poetry.

po·et·as·ter (pō′it as′tər), *n.* an inferior poet; a writer of indifferent verse. [< ML or NL; see POET, -ASTER[1]] —**po′et·as′ter·ing, po′et·as′ter·y, po′et·as′try, po′et·as′ter·ism,** *n.* —**po′et·as′tric, po′et·as′tri·cal,** *adj.*
—**Syn.** rhymester.

po·et·ess (pō′i tis), *n.* a female poet. [POET + -ESS]

po·et·ic (pō et′ik), *adj.* Also, **po·et′i·cal.** **1.** possessing the qualities or charm of poetry: *poetic descriptions of nature.* **2.** of or pertaining to a poet or poets. **3.** characteristic of or befitting a poet: *poetic feeling; poetic insight.* **4.** endowed with the faculty or feeling of a poet: *a poetic eulogist.* **5.** having or showing the sensibility of a poet: *a poetic lover.* **6.** of or pertaining to poetry: *poetic literature.* **7.** of the nature of or resembling poetry: *a poetic composition; poetic drama; poetic imagination.* **8.** celebrated in poetry, as a place. **9.** providing a subject for poetry. **10.** of or pertaining to literature in verse form. —*n.* **11.** poetics. [< L *poētic(us)* < Gk *po(i)ētikós.* See POET, -IC] —**po·et′i·cal·ly,** *adv.*

Poet′ic Ed′da. See under **Edda.**

po·et·i·cise (pō et′i sīz′), *v.t., v.i.,* **-cised, -cis·ing.** *Chiefly Brit.* poeticize.

po·et·i·cize (pō et′i sīz′), *v.,* **-cized, -ciz·ing.** —*v.t.* **1.** to make (thoughts, feelings, etc.) poetic; express in poetry. **2.** to write poetry about (an event, occasion, etc.). —*v.i.* **3.** to speak or write poetry. [POETIC + -IZE]

poet′ic jus′tice, an ideal distribution of rewards and punishments such as is common in some poetry and fiction.

poet′ic li′cense, license or liberty taken by a poet, prose writer, or other artist in deviating from rule, conventional form, logic, or fact, in order to produce a desired effect.

po·et·ics (pō et′iks), *n.* (*construed as sing.*) **1.** literary criticism treating of the nature and laws of poetry. **2.** the study of prosody. **3.** a treatise on poetry. **4.** (*cap., italics.*) a treatise or collection of notes on aesthetics (4th century B.C.) by Aristotle. [see POETIC, -ICS]

po·et·ise (pō′i tīz′), *v.i., v.t.,* **-ised, -is·ing.** *Chiefly Brit.* poetize. —**po′et·is′er,** *n.*

po·et·ize (pō′i tīz′), *v.,* **-ized, -iz·ing.** —*v.i.* **1.** to write poetry. —*v.t.* **2.** to express oneself poetically: *to poetize a story.* **3.** to make or treat as poetic; poeticize: *to poetize reality.* [POET + -IZE] —**po′et·iz′er,** *n.*

po′et lau′reate, *pl.* **poets laureate.** **1.** (in Great Britain) a poet appointed for life as an officer of the royal household, formerly expected to write poems in celebration of court and national events. **2.** a poet recognized or acclaimed as the most eminent or representative of a country or locality. **3.** (formerly) a poet officially recognized for his efforts, as by a sovereign, university, etc.

po·et·ry (pō′i trē), *n.* **1.** the art of rhythmical composition, written or spoken, for exciting pleasure by beautiful, imaginative, or elevated thoughts. **2.** literary work in metrical form; verse. **3.** prose with poetic qualities. **4.** poetic qualities however manifested: *the poetry of simple acts and things.* **5.** poetic spirit or feeling: *The pianist played the prelude with poetry.* **6.** something suggestive of or likened to poetry: *the pure poetry of a beautiful view on a clear day.* [ME *poetrie* < ML *poētria* poetic art, L: poetess < Gk *poiḗtria,* var. of *poiḗtris,* fem. of *poiētēs* POET; see -Y[3]] —**po′et·ry·less,** *adj.*
—**Syn. 2.** POETRY, VERSE agree in referring to the work of a poet. The difference between POETRY and VERSE is usually the difference between substance and form. POETRY is lofty thought or impassioned feeling expressed in imaginative words: *Elizabethan poetry.* VERSE is any expression in words which simply conforms to accepted metrical rules and structure: *the differences between prose and verse.* —**Ant. 2.** prose.

po′et's narcis′sus, a European narcissus, *Narcissus poeticus,* having white flowers with a red-margined corona.

pog·a·mog·gan (pog′ə mog′ən), *n.* a club with a knobbed head, used by various American Indian peoples. [< Algonquin: lit., that which is for striking]

Po·ga·ny (pō gä′nē), *n.* **Willy** (*William Andrew*), 1882–1955, U.S. painter, stage designer, and illustrator; born in Hungary.

po·gey (pō′gē), *n.* **1.** *Slang.* an institution maintained by private charities or government funds for the housing of the aged, sick, orphaned, or feeble-minded; an old-age home, charity hospital, orphanage, or the like. **2.** *Canadian.* **a.** any form of charity or government relief. Cf. **dole** (defs. 1, 3). **b.** unemployment insurance provided by the government. —*adj.* **3.** *Canadian.* obtained through charity or government relief: *pogey shoes.* [earlier *pogie* workhouse < ?]

pogge (pog), *n. Ichthyol.* a poacher, *Agonus cataphractus,* common near the British Isles and ranging north to Greenland and Iceland. Also called **armed bullhead.** [?]

POGO (pō′gō), Polar Orbiting Geophysical Observatory.

po·go·ni·a (pə gō′nē ə, -gōn′yə), *n.* a terrestrial orchid of the genus *Pogonia,* of North America. [< NL < Gk *pōgōnías* bearded (with reference to the lip which is frequently fringed)]

pog·o·nip (pog′ə nip), *n.* an ice fog that forms in the mountain valleys of the western U.S. [< Shoshone; said to mean white death]

po′go stick′ (pō′gō), a long stick having a pair of handles at the top and, near the bottom, a pair of footrests attached to a powerful spring, so that by standing on the footrests while grasping the handles, a person can propel himself along in a series of leaps. Also, **po′go-stick′.** [*pogo* formerly trademark]

po·grom (pə grum′, -grom′, pō-), *n.* an organized massacre, esp. of Jews. [< Russ: devastation, destruction, equiv. to *po-* perfective prefix + *-grom,* cf. *gromit* to batter, hence wreck (deriv. of *grom* thunder)]
—**Syn.** slaughter, butchery.

po·gy (pō′gē, pog′ē), *n., pl.* (*esp. collectively*) **-gy,** (*esp. referring to two or more kinds or species*) **-gies.** **1.** a porgy. **2.** a viviparous perch, *Holconotus rhodoterus,* found in the shallow waters off the Pacific coast of the U.S. **3.** the menhaden. [? syncopated var. of Algonquian *pohegan* menhaden]

Po·hai (pō′hī′; *Chin.* bô′hī′), *n.* an arm of the Yellow Sea in NE China. Formerly, **Gulf of Chihli.**

Po·hjo·la (pô′hyō lə), *n. Finnish Legend.* a region to the north of Finland, ruled by the sorceress Louhi: often identified with Lapland.

poi (poi, pō′ē), *n.* a Hawaiian dish made of the root of the taro baked, pounded, moistened, and fermented. [< Hawaiian]

-poiesis, a combining form denoting production: *hematopoiesis.* [< Gk; see POESY, -SIS]

-poietic, a combining form meaning "producing": *hematopoietic.* [< Gk *poiētik(ós).* See POETIC]

poign·ant (poin′yənt, poin′ənt), *adj.* **1.** keenly distressing to the feelings: *poignant regret.* **2.** keen or strong in mental appeal: *a subject of poignant interest.* **3.** affecting or moving the emotions: *a poignant scene.* **4.** pungent to the smell: *poignant cooking odors.* [ME *poynaunt* < MF *poignant,* prp. of *poindre* < L *pungere* to prick, pierce. See PUNGENT, -ANT] —**poign′an·cy,** *n.* —**poign′ant·ly,** *adv.*
—**Syn. 1.** intense, sincere, heartfelt. **4.** piquant, sharp. —**Ant. 1, 2.** mild.

poi·ki·lie (poi′kə lē), *n.* (in classical architecture) a portico or public building decorated with paint. Also, **poecile.** [< Gk *poikílē,* fem. of *poikílos* many-colored, dappled]

poi·ki·lit·ic (poi′kə lit′ik), *adj. Petrog.* (of igneous rocks) having small crystals of one mineral scattered irregularly in larger crystals of another mineral. [< Gk *poikíl(os)* various + -ITE[1] + -IC]

poi·ki·lo·blast (poi′kə lō blast′, poi kil′ə-), *n. Anat.* an immature and nucleate poikilocyte. [< Gk *poikílo(s)* mottled + -BLAST]

poi·kil·o·blas·tic (poi kil′ə blas′tik, poi′ki lə-), *adj. Petrog.* (of metamorphic rocks) having small crystals of one mineral embedded in larger crystals of another mineral. [POIKILOBLAST + -IC]

poi·ki·lo·cyte (poi′kə lō sīt′, poi kil′ə-), *n. Anat.* an erythrocyte having an abnormal shape. [< Gk *poikílo(s)* various + -CYTE]

poi·ki·lo·ther·mal (poi′kə lō thûr′məl, poi kil′ə-), *adj. Zool.* having a body temperature that fluctuates with the temperature of the environment; cold-blooded (opposed to *homoiothermal*). [< Gk *poikílo(s)* various + THERMAL] —**poi′ki·lo·ther′mism, poi′ki·lo·ther′my,** *n.*

poil (poil), *n.* a yarn or thread made from silk, used for ribbon, velvet, and as the core of gold, silver, and tinsel yarn. [< F < L *pil(us)* hair]

poi·lu (pwä′lo͞o; *Fr.* pwa lʏ′), *n., pl.* **-lus** (-lo͞oz; *Fr.* -lʏ′). a French common soldier. [< F: lit., hairy, haired, equiv. to *poil* POIL + *-u* ptp. suffix (< L *-utus*)]

poi·men·ics (poi men′iks), *n.* (*construed as sing.*) See **pastoral theology.** [< Gk *poimenik(ós)* of a shepherd, equiv. to *poimḗn* shepherd + *-ikos* -IC; see -ICS]

Poin·ca·ré (pwan ka rā′), *n.* **1. Jules Hen·ri** (zhʏl än rē′), 1854–1912, French mathematician. **2.** his cousin **Ray·mond** (re mōn′), 1860–1934, French statesman: president of France 1913–20.

poin·ci·an·a (poin′sē an′ə, -ä′nə), *n.* **1.** any caesalpinaceous shrub or small tree of the genus *Poinciana,* esp. *P. pulcherrima,* having showy orange or scarlet flowers. **2.** a tree, *Delonix regia,* of Madagascar, having showy, scarlet flowers. [< NL; named after M. de *Poinci,* 17th-century governor of the French Antilles]

poind (poind; *Scot. also* pynd), *Scot.* —*v.t.* **1.** to seize and sell property of a debtor under a warrant. **2.** to impound. —*n.* **3.** distraint. [ME (Scot) *poynd,* OE *pynd(an)* (to) enclose. See POUND[3]]

Poi·ne (poi′nə), *n.* Poena.

poin·set·ti·a (poin set′ē ə, -set′ə), *n.* an euphorbiaceous plant, *Euphorbia* (*Poinsettia*) *pulcherrima,* native to Mexico and Central America, having variously lobed leaves and brilliant scarlet, pink, or white bracts. [< NL; named after J.R. *Poinsett* (1799–1851), American minister to Mexico, who discovered the plant there in 1828]

point (point), *n.* **1.** a sharp or tapering end, as of a dagger. **2.** a projecting part of anything: *A point of land juts into the bay.* **3.** a tapering extremity: *the points of the fingers.* **4.** something having a sharp or tapering end: *a pen point.* **5.** a pointed tool or instrument, as an etching needle. **6.** a mark made with or as with the sharp end of something: *Her sharp heels left points in the carpet.* **7.** a mark of punctuation. **8.** period (def. 15). **9.** See **decimal point.** **10.** *Phonet.* a diacritic indicating a vowel or other modification of sound. **11.** one of the embossed dots used in certain systems of writing and printing for the blind. **12.** something that has position but not extension, as the intersection of two lines. **13.** a place of which the position alone is considered; spot: *We're leaving for Chicago and points west.* **14.** any definite position, as in a scale, course, etc.: *the boiling point.* **15.** *Navig.* any of 32 separate horizontal directions, 11° 15′ apart, as indicated on the card of a compass or gauged with reference to the heading of a vessel. **16.** *Naut.* See **point of sailing.** **17.** a degree or stage: *frankness to the point of insult.* **18.** a particular instant of time: *It was at that point that I told him he'd said enough.* **19.** a critical position in a course of affairs: *Morale had reached a low point.* **20.** a decisive state of circumstances: *He reached the point where he could no longer pay his debts.* **21.** the important or essential thing: *the point of the matter.* **22.** the salient feature of a story, epigram, joke, etc: *to miss the point.* **23.** a particular aim, end, or purpose: *He carried his point.* **24.** a hint or suggestion: *points on getting a job.* **25.** a single or separate article or item, as in an extended whole; a detail or particular: *the fine points of a contract.* **26.** an individual part or element of something: *noble points in her character.* **27.** a distinguishing mark or quality, esp. one of an animal, used as a standard in stockbreeding, judging, etc. **28. points, a.** the extremities of an animal, esp. a horse or dog. **b.** *Railroads, Brit.* a switch. **29.** a single unit, as in counting. **30.** a unit of count in the score of a game: *Our team won by five points.* **31.** (in craps) the number which must be thrown to win but not including 7 or 11 on the first roll: *Your point is 4.* **32.** *Cricket.* **a.** the position of the fielder who plays a short distance in front of and to the offside of the batsman. **b.** the fielder playing this position. **33.** *Chiefly Boxing.* the end or tip (of the chin). **34.** *Hunting.* **a.** the action of a hunting dog that indicates the presence and location of game by standing rigid and directing its head toward the game. **b.** the position taken by a hunting dog in pointing game. **35.** a branch of an antler of a deer: *an eight-point buck.* **36.** *Sports.* **a.** a cross-country run. **b.** a scoring unit in certain games and contests. **37.** one of the narrow tapering spaces marked on a backgammon board. **38.**

Educ. a single credit, usually corresponding to an hour's class work per week for one semester. **39.** *Elect.* **a.** either of a pair of contacts tipped with tungsten or platinum that make or break current flow in a distributor, as in an automobile. **b.** *Brit.* an outlet or socket. **40.** *Com.* a unit of price quotation, as in the U.S., one dollar in stock transactions, one hundredth of a cent in cotton and coffee, or one cent in oil, grain, pork, etc.: *Prices on the stock exchange advanced two points.* **41.** *Jewelry.* a unit of weight equal to 1/100 of a carat. **42.** *Mil.* **a.** a patrol or reconnaissance unit that goes ahead of the advance party of an advance guard, or follows the rear party of the rear guard. **b.** the stroke in bayonet drill or combat. **43.** *Print.* **a.** *U.S.* a unit of type measurement equal to .013835 inch (1/72 inch), or 1/12 pica. Cf. **Didot point system. b.** Also called **press point.** (in a press) one of several metal prongs for perforating the sheet so that it will be in register when the reverse is printed. **44.** a unit of measure of paper or card thickness, equal to .001 inch. **45.** See **vaccine point. 46.** See **point lace. 47.** any lace made by hand. **48.** *Heraldry.* one of the pendent parts of a label. **49.** *Railroads.* **a.** the vertex of the angle formed at a frog by two rails; the intersection of gauge lines in a switch or frog. **b.** *Brit.* a tapering movable rail, as in a railroad switch. **50.** (in the game of go) any place where lines intersect or meet. **51.** act of pointing. **52.** *Archaic.* a tagged ribbon or cord, formerly much used in dress, as for tying or fastening parts. **53.** *Obs.* an end or conclusion. **54.** *Obs.* a pointed weapon, as a dagger. **55.** *Obs.* condition. **56. at, on,** or **upon the point of,** on the verge of; close to: *on the point of death.* **57. in point,** that is pertinent; applicable: *a case in point.* **58. in point of,** as regards; in reference to: *in point of fact.* **59. make a point of,** to regard as important; insist upon: *In that country, one makes a point of bringing flowers if invited for dinner.* **60. strain** or **stretch a point,** to depart from the usual procedure or rule because of special circumstances; make a concession or exception: *Though the position required three years of previous experience, and he had only two, they stretched a point because of his outstanding record.* **61. to the point,** pertinent; fitting: *The reply was short and to the point.* [ME < OF *point* dot, mark, place, moment (< L *punctum*) + *pointe* sharp end (< L *puncta*); both L words ptp. forms of *pungere* to prick, stab]
—*v.t.* **62.** to direct (the finger, a weapon, the attention, etc.) at, to, or upon something. **63.** to indicate the presence or position of (usually fol. by *out*): *to point out an object in the sky.* **64.** to direct attention to (usually fol. by *out*): *to point out the advantages of a proposal.* **65.** to furnish with a point or points; sharpen: *to point a lead pencil.* **66.** to mark with one or more points, dots, or the like. **67.** *Sculpture.* to transfer measurements of depth from a clay, wax, or plaster model to (a block of stone) by means of an apparatus that drills holes to the required depth prior to carving. **68.** to punctuate, as writing. **69.** *Phonet.* to mark (letters) with points. **70.** to separate (figures) by dots or points (usually fol. by *off*). **71.** to give greater or added force to (often fol. by *up*): *to point up the necessity for caution.* **72.** *Hunting.* (of a hunting dog) to indicate the presence and location of (game) by standing rigid and facing toward the game. **73.** *Masonry.* **a.** to fill the joints of (brickwork, stonework, etc.) with mortar or cement treated in various ways with tools after application. **b.** to dress the surface of (a stone) with a pointed tool. **74.** to dress (a stone) with a point. **75.** *Metalworking.* **a.** to narrow the end of (a rod) for passing through the dies of a drawbench. **b.** to narrow the end of (a tube) over the head of a pin which is gripped to pull the tube through the dies of a drawbench.
—*v.i.* **76.** to indicate position or direction, as with the finger. **77.** to direct the mind or thought in some direction; call attention to: *Everything points to his guilt.* **78.** to aim. **79.** to have a tendency toward something: *Economic conditions point to further inflation.* **80.** to have a specified direction: *The sign pointed west.* **81.** to face in a particular direction, as a building. **82.** *Hunting.* (of a hunting dog) to point game. **83.** *Naut.* to sail close to the wind. **84.** (of an abscess) to come to a head. [ME *poynte* < MF *point(er)*, deriv. of *pointe* (n.)]

poin·tal (poin′t(ə)l), *n.* pointel.

point′-bear·ing pile′ (point′bâr′ing), *Engineering, Building Trades.* a pile depending on the soil or rock beneath its foot for support. Cf. **friction pile.**

point-blank (point′blangk′), *adj.* **1.** aimed or fired straight at the mark; direct. **2.** straightforward, plain, or explicit: *a point-blank denial.* —*adv.* **3.** with a direct aim; directly; straight. **4.** bluntly; frankly: *She told him point-blank that he was not welcome.*

point′ blan′ket, *Canadian.* See **Hudson Bay blanket.**

point′ boat′, *Naut.* See **Newport boat.**

point′ charge′, *Elect.* one of two charged points which have small dimensions compared with the distance between them.

point′ count′, *Bridge.* **1.** a method of evaluating the strength of a hand by assigning a numerical value to high cards and to certain combinations and distributions of cards in the hand. **2.** the total number of points in one player's hand.

Point′ Coun′ter Point′, a novel (1928) by Aldous Huxley.

point cou·pé (*Fr.* pwan ko͞o pā′), **1.** Also called **cutwork.** a process for producing lace in which predetermined threads in the ground material are cut and removed in order to provide open areas for the insertion of ornamental patterns. **2.** Also called **cutwork lace.** the lace produced by this process. [< F: cut point]

point d'Al·en·çon (*Fr.* pwan dȧ län sôn′), See **Alençon lace** (def. 1). [< F: Alençon stitch]

point d'An·gle·terre (*Fr.* pwan dän glə ter′), a bobbin lace in which the design is worked out with either a needle or bobbin. [< F: English stitch]

point d'ap·pui (pwan dȧ pwē′), *pl.* **points d'ap·pui** (pwan dȧ pwē′). *French.* **1.** a prop; stay. **2.** *Mil.* a point of support for a battle line.

point de gaze (*Fr.* pwan də gäz′). a needlepoint lace in which delicate floral designs are sewn onto a net ground. [< F: gauze stitch]

point de Hon·grie (*Fr.* pwan də ôn grē′). See **flame stitch.** [< F: Hungarian stitch]

point d'es·prit (*Fr.* pwan de sprē′). a bobbinet or tulle with oval or square dots woven in an irregular pattern. [< F: spirit (Holy Ghost) stitch]

point-de·vice (point′di vīs′), *Archaic.* —*adv.* **1.** completely; perfectly; exactly. —*adj.* **2.** perfect; precise; scrupulously nice or neat. [ME *at point devis* arranged to a point, i.e., to a nicety, to perfection; see DEVICE]

point′ du′ty, *Brit.* the directing of traffic by a policeman, as at an intersection.

pointe (*Fr.* pwant), *n., pl.* **pointes** (*Fr.* pwant). *Ballet.* **1.** the tip of the toe. **2.** a position on the extreme tips of the toes. [< F: lit., point]

Pointe-à-Pi·tre (*Fr.* pwan tȧ pē′tr(ə)), *n.* a seaport on central Guadeloupe, in the E West Indies. 45,000 (est. 1960).

point·ed (poin′tid), *adj.* **1.** having a point or points: *a pointed arch.* **2.** sharp or piercing: *pointed wit.* **3.** having direct effect, significance, or force: *pointed criticism.* **4.** directed; aimed: *a pointed gun.* **5.** directed particularly, as at a person: *a pointed remark.* **6.** marked; emphasized. **7.** *Heraldry.* (of a cross) having parallel sides with points formed by two inclined sides on each end: *a cross pointed.* [ME; see POINT, -ED[3]] —**point′ed·ly,** *adv.* —**point′ed·ness,** *n.*
—**Syn. 2.** penetrating; epigrammatic. —**Ant. 2.** blunt, dull.

point′ed arch′, an arch having a pointed apex.

point′ed fox′, a red fox fur having badger hairs glued to it near the skin to simulate silver fox.

poin·tel (poin′t(ə)l), *n.* a pavement of tile mosaic forming an abstract design. Also, **pointal, poyntell, poyntill.** [ME: stylus, pencil, pointed instrument < OF (F *pointeau*): point of a spear; c. It *puntello*, dim. of *punto* POINT]

Pointe-Noire (*Fr.* pwant nwar′), *n.* a seaport in the S Republic of Congo. 28,643 (est. 1955).

point·er (poin′tər), *n.* **1.** one who or that which points. **2.** a long, tapering stick used by teachers, lecturers, etc., in pointing things out on a map, blackboard, or the like. **3.** the hand on a watch dial, clock face, scale, etc. **4.** *Mil.* the member of an artillery crew who aims the weapon. **5.** *Naval.* the member of a gun crew responsible for bringing a gun or turret to the proper elevation. **6.** one of a breed of short-haired hunting dogs trained to point game. **7.** a piece of advice, esp. on how to succeed in a specific area: *The food expert gave some good pointers on making better salads.* **8. Pointers,** *Astron.* the two outer stars of the Big Dipper that lie on a line which passes very near Polaris and are used for finding it. [POINT + -ER[1]]

Pointer (26 in. high at shoulder)

point-e·vent (point′i vent′), *n.* (in the philosophy of Whitehead) a particular phenomenon, regarded as the intersection in space-time of certain of the eternal objects.

Point′ Four′, a program of U.S. aid providing scientific and technical assistance to underdeveloped countries: proposed by President Truman in 1949 and approved by Congress in 1950.

point′ group′, *Crystall.* a class of crystals determined by a combination of their symmetry elements, all crystals left unchanged by a given set of symmetry elements being placed in the same class. Also called **symmetry class.**

poin·til·lé (*Fr.* pwan tē yā′), *adj.* (of book covers) decorated with a tooled pattern of dots. [< F, ptp. of *pointiller* to dot, POINT]

Poin·til·lism (pwan′t(ə)liz′əm), *n.* (*often l.c.*) a theory and technique developed by the Neo-Impressionists, based on the belief that the immediate juxtaposition of pure colors, as blue and yellow, are optically mixed into the resulting hue, as green, by the viewer. [< F *pointillisme*, equiv. to *pointill(er)* (to) mark with points + *-isme* -ISM] —**poin′til·list,** *n.*

point′ lace′, lace made with a needle rather than with bobbins; needlepoint. —**point′-laced′,** *adj.*

point·less (point′lis), *adj.* **1.** without a point: *a pointless pen.* **2.** blunt, as an instrument. **3.** without force, meaning, or relevance: *a pointless remark.* **4.** without a point scored, as in a game: *a pointless inning.* [ME *point les.* See POINT, -LESS] —**point′less·ly,** *adv.* —**point′less·ness,** *n.*

point′ of articula′tion, *Phonet.* a relatively fixed speech organ, as the teeth, alveolar ridge, or hard palate, that during articulation is touched or nearly touched by a movable speech organ. Cf. **articulator.**

point′ of depar′ture, 1. *Naut.* the precise location of a vessel, established in order to set a course, especially in beginning a voyage in open water. **2.** a place to begin, as in a discussion, argument, etc. Also called **departure.**

point′ of flight′, (in architectural shades and shadows) the point upon the edge of a shadow beyond which the edge is raised or lowered on the elevation to show a projecting or receding surface.

point′ of hon′or, something that affects one's honor, reputation, etc.: *It was a point of honor with him to avenge any insult to his family.*

point′ of or′der, *Parl. Proc.* a question raised as to whether proceedings are in order, or in conformity with parliamentary law.

point′ of sail′ing, *Naut.* the bearing of a sailing vessel, considered with relation to the direction of the wind.

point′ of view′, 1. a specified or stated manner of consideration or appraisal; standpoint: *from the point of view of a doctor.* **2.** an opinion, attitude, or judgment: *He refuses to change his point of view in the matter.*

Point′ Pleas′ant, a town in W West Virginia. 5785 (1960).

Point′ Pleas′ant Beach′, a town in E New Jersey. 3873 (1960).

Point′ Rey′es li′lac (rā′is), a prostrate shrub, *Ceanothus gloriosus*, of southern California, having leathery, roundish leaves and purplish or deep-blue flowers. [named after *Point Reyes*, California]

point-set (point′set′), *adj.* *Typesetting.* (of spaces) cast in widths that conform to standard point measure.

point′-set topol′ogy, *Math.* topology (def. 2).

points·man (points′mən), *n., pl.* **-men.** *Brit.* **1.** a railway switchman. **2.** a policeman who directs traffic, as at an intersection. [POINT + -S[3] + MAN[1]]

point′ source′, *Physics, Optics.* a source of radiation sufficiently distant compared to its length and width that it can be considered as a point.

point′ sys′tem, 1. *Print.* a system for grading the sizes of type bodies, leads, etc., which employs the point as a unit of measurement. Cf. **point** (def. 43a). **2.** any of certain systems of writing and printing for the blind which employ embossed symbols for letters. **3.** a system of promoting students by an evaluation of their work on the basis of points representing quality of achievement. **4.** See **Bedaux system.**

point ti·ré (*Fr.* pwan tē rā′). See **drawn work.** [< F: drawn stitch]

point-to-point (point′tə point′), *n.* a cross-country horse race between specified points, in which each rider is often free to select his own course between the points.

point·wise (point′wīz′), *adj.* *Math.* occurring at each point of a given set: *pointwise convergence.* [POINT + -WISE]

point·y (poin′tē), *adj.,* **point·i·er, point·i·est.** having a comparatively sharp point: *The elf had pointy little ears.* [POINT + -Y[1]]

poise[1] (poiz), *n., v.,* **poised, pois·ing.** —*n.* **1.** a state of balance or equilibrium, as from equality or equal distribution of weight; equipoise. **2.** dignified, self-confident manner or bearing; composure; self-possession: *to show poise in company.* **3.** steadiness; stability: *intellectual poise.* **4.** suspense or wavering, as between rest and motion or two phases of motion: *the poise of the tides.* **5.** the way of being poised, held, or carried. **6.** the state or position of hovering: *the poise of a bird in the air.* —*v.t.* **7.** to adjust, hold, or carry in equilibrium; balance evenly. **8.** to hold supported or raised, as in position for casting, using, etc.: *to poise a spear.* **9.** to hold or carry in a particular manner: *She walked, carefully poising a water jug on her head.* **10.** *Obs.* to weigh. —*v.i.* **11.** to rest in equilibrium; be balanced. **12.** to hang supported or suspended. **13.** to hover, as a bird in the air. [late ME < MF; OF *peise*, 3rd pers. sing. pres. ind. of *peser* < L *pensāre*, freq. of *pendere* to weigh]
—**Syn. 2.** self-control; polish, grace, refinement. —**Ant. 1, 3.** instability.

poise[2] (pwäz), *n.* *Physics.* a centimeter-gram-second unit of viscosity, equal to the viscosity of a fluid in which a stress of one dyne per square centimeter is required to maintain a difference of velocity of one centimeter per second between two parallel planes in the fluid that lie in the direction of flow and are separated by a distance of one centimeter. *Abbr.:* P, p [< F; named after Jean Louis Marie *Poiseuille* (1799–1869), French physician]

poised (poizd), *adj.* **1.** (of a person) composed, dignified, and self-assured. **2.** being in balance or equilibrium: *a balloon poised on the nose of a seal.* **3.** teetering or wavering: *to be poised on the brink of disaster.* **4.** hovering or suspended in or as in midair: *a bird poised in flight; a helicopter poised overhead.* [POISE[1] + -ED[2], -ED[3]]

pois·er (poi′zər), *n.* **1.** one who or that which poises. **2.** *Obs.* halter[2]. [POISE[1] + -ER[1]]

Poi·seuille's′ law′ (pwä zwēz′), *Physics, Mech.* the law that the velocity of a liquid flowing through a capillary is directly proportional to the pressure of the liquid and the fourth power of the radius of the capillary and is inversely proportional to the viscosity of the liquid and the length of the capillary. [see POISE[2]]

poi·son (poi′zən), *n.* **1.** a liquid, solid, or gaseous substance which has an inherent property that tends to destroy life or impair health. **2.** something that is harmful or pernicious, as to happiness or well-being: *the poison of slander.* **3.** *Slang.* any variety of alcoholic liquor: *Name your poison!* —*v.t.* **4.** to administer poison to (a person or animal). **5.** to kill or injure with or as with poison. **6.** to put poison into or upon; saturate with poison: *to poison food.* **7.** to ruin, vitiate, or corrupt: *Hatred had poisoned his mind.* **8.** *Physical Chem.* to destroy or diminish the activity of (a catalyst or enzyme). —*adj.* **9.** causing poisoning; poisonous: *a poison shrub.* [ME *puisun* < OF < L *pōtiōn-* (s. of *pōtiō*) drink, potion, poisonous draught] —**poi′son·er,** *n.* —**poi′son·less,** *adj.* —**poi′son·less·ness,** *n.*
—**Syn. 1.** POISON, TOXIN, VENOM, VIRUS are terms for any substance that injures the health or destroys life when absorbed into the system, esp. of a higher animal. POISON is the general word: *a poison for insects.* A TOXIN is a poison produced in animal tissues by the action of microorganisms; it is a medical term for the albuminous secretion of microbes, which causes certain diseases: *A toxin produces diphtheria.* VENOM is esp. used of the poisons secreted by certain animals, usually injected by bite or sting: *the venom of a snake.* VIRUS is a medical term for the active organic element or poison which infects with and produces contagious disease: *the virus of scarlet fever.* **7.** contaminate, pollute, taint.

poi′son dog′wood. See **poison sumac.** Also called **poi′son el′der.**

poi′son gas′, any of various toxic gases, esp. those used in chemical warfare to kill or incapacitate on inhalation or contact, as phosgene, chlorine, etc.

Poison ivy, *Rhus radicans*

poi′son haw′, a shrub, *Viburnum molle*, of the central U.S., having white flowers and bluish-black fruit.

poi′son hem′lock, hemlock (defs. 1, 3).

poi·son·ing (poi′zə ning), *n.* *Pathol.* the condition produced by a poison or by a toxic substance. [ME *poisenynge.* See POISON, -ING[1]]

poi′son i′vy, any of several North American, anacardiaceous shrubs of the genus *Rhus*, having green flowers, white berries and shiny, trifoliate leaves, poisonous to the touch, esp. a climbing species. *R. radicans*, growing on fences, rocks, trees, etc.

poi′son oak′, 1. any of several shrubs of the genus *Rhus.* 2. See **poison sumac.** 3. a poison ivy, *Rhus diversiloba,* of the Pacific coast.

poi·son·ous (poi′zə nəs), *adj.* 1. full of or containing poison: *poisonous air; a poisonous substance.* 2. harmful; destructive: *poisonous rumors.* 3. deeply malicious; malevolent: *poisonous efforts.* [POISON + -OUS] —**poi′son·ous·ly,** *adv.* —**poi′son·ous·ness,** *n.*

poi·son-pen (poi′zən pen′), *adj.* 1. composed or sent maliciously, as a letter, usually anonymously and for the purpose of damaging another's reputation or happiness: *She received a poison-pen note telling of her husband's infidelities.* 2. characterized by or given to the sending of poison-pen letters: *a poison-pen campaign; a poison-pen writer.*

poi′son su′mac, a highly poisonous shrub or small tree, *Rhus Vernix,* having pinnate leaves and whitish berries, growing in swamps.

Pois·son (pwä sôn′; *Fr.* PWA SÔN′), *n.* **Si·mé·on De·nis** (sē mā ôN′ də nē′), 1781–1840, French mathematician.

Poisson′ distribu′tion, *Statistics.* a limiting form of the binomial probability distribution for small values of the probability of success and for large numbers of trials: particularly useful in industrial quality-control work and in radiation and bacteriological problems. [named after S. D. POISSON]

Poisson's′ ra′tio, *Physics.* the ratio, in an elastic body under longitudinal stress, of the strain normal to the stress to the strain parallel to the stress. Also, **Poisson′ ra′tio.** [named after S. D. POISSON]

Poi·tiers (pwa tyā′), *n.* a city in and the capital of Vienne, in W France: Roman ruins; battles A.D. 507, A.D. 732, 1356. 66,222 (1962).

Poi·tou (pwa to͞o′), *n.* 1. a former province in W France. *Cap.:* Poitiers. 2. **Gate of,** a wide pass near Poitiers.

poi·trel (poi′trəl), *n. Armor.* peytral.

po·kal (pō käl′), *n.* a large German glass standing cup. [< G < It *boccale* drinking-vessel < LL *baucal(is)* vessel used to cool wine < Gk *baúkalis*]

poke[1] (pōk), *v.,* **poked, pok·ing,** *n.* —*v.t.* 1. to prod or push, esp. with something narrow or pointed, as a finger, elbow, stick, etc.: *to poke someone in the ribs.* 2. to make (a hole, one's way, etc.) by or as by prodding or pushing. 3. to thrust or push: *She poked her head out of the window.* 4. to force, drive, or stir by or as by pushing or thrusting: *He poked the fire up.* 5. to thrust obtrusively: *The prosecutor kept poking his finger at the defendant.* —*v.i.* 6. to make a pushing or thrusting movement with the finger, a stick, etc. 7. to extend or project (often fol. by *out*): *His handkerchief is poking out of his back pocket.* 8. to thrust oneself obtrusively: *to poke into something that is not one's affair.* 9. to search curiously; pry (often fol. by *around* or *about*). 10. to go or proceed in a slow or aimless way (often fol. by *along*). 11. **poke fun at,** to ridicule or mock, esp. covertly or slyly: *Children love to poke fun at their teachers.* 12. **poke one's nose into something,** to meddle in another person's affairs; pry: *She simply couldn't resist poking her nose into her married children's lives.* —*n.* 13. a thrust or push. 14. *Informal.* a slow or dawdling person; slowpoke. [ME < MD, MLG *poken* to thrust. See POACH[1]] —**pok′a·ble,** *adj.*

poke[2] (pōk), *n.* 1. *Midland U.S. and Scot.* a bag or sack. 2. *Archaic.* a pocket. [ME < MD, whence also ONF *poque,* F *poche* bag, pocket. See POUCH]

poke[3] (pōk), *n.* 1. a projecting brim at the front of a bonnet, framing the face. 2. Also called **poke′ bon′net.** a bonnet or hat with such a brim. [appar. special use of POKE[1]]

Poke[3] (def. 2)

poke[4] (pōk), *n.* pokeweed. [short for Algonquian (Virginia) *puccoon* weed used for dyeing]

poke·ber·ry (pōk′ber′ē, -bə rē), *n., pl.* **-ries.** 1. the berry of the pokeweed. 2. the plant. [POKE[4] + BERRY]

poke′ check′, *Ice Hockey.* an attempt to deprive an opponent of the puck by pushing it away with one's stick. Cf. **check** (def. 41).

poke·lo·gan (pōk′lō′gən), *n. Northeastern U.S.* marshy or stagnant water which has branched off from a stream or lake. Also, **poke·lo·ken** (pōk′lō′kən). Also called **logan.** [< Algonquian]

pok·er[1] (pō′kər), *n.* 1. one who or that which pokes. 2. a metal rod for poking or stirring a fire. [POKE[1] (v.) + -ER[1]]

pok·er[2] (pō′kər), *n.* a card game played by two or more persons, in which the players bet on the value of their hands, the winner taking the pool. [? orig. braggart, bluffer; cf. MLG *poken* to brag, play, MD *poken* to bluff, brag]

pok′er dice′, 1. dice which, instead of being marked on each side with from one to six spots, carry on their faces a picture or symbol representing the six highest playing cards: ace, king, queen, jack, ten, nine. 2. any of various gambling games played with from three to six such dice, each throw usually corresponding to a hand of poker.

pok·er face′, 1. an expressionless face: *He can tell a funny story with a poker face.* 2. a person who has or deliberately assumes a poker face: *It is impossible to tell what that poker face is really thinking.*

poke·weed (pōk′wēd′), *n.* a tall herb, *Phytolacca americana,* of North America, having juicy purple berries and a purple root used in medicine, and young edible shoots resembling asparagus. Also called **poke-root** (pōk′ro͞ot′, -ro͝ot′), **scoke.** [POKE[4] + WEED[1]]

pok·ey (pō′kē), *adj.* **po·ki·er, pok·i·est,** *n., pl.* **pok·eys.** poky.

pok·y (pō′kē), *adj.,* **pok·i·er, pok·i·est,** *n., pl.* **pok·ies.** —*adj. Informal.* 1. puttering; slow; dull: *poky drivers.* 2. (of a place) small and cramped: *a poky little room.* 3. (of dress) dowdy. —*n.* 4. *Slang.* a jail: *They put him in the poky for carrying around a concealed weapon.* [POKE[1] + -Y[1]] —**pok′i·ly,** *adv.* —**pok′i·ness,** *n.*

Pol., 1. Poland. 2. Also, **Pol** Polish.

pol., 1. political. 2. politics.

Po·la (pō′lä; *It.* pô′lä), *n.* 1. Yugoslavian, **Pula, Pulj.** a seaport in NW Yugoslavia, on the Istrian Peninsula. 37,403 (1961). 2. a girl's given name.

po·lac·ca[1] (pō lak′ə), *n.* any of various sailing vessels, formerly used in the Mediterranean Sea, having some combination of square and lateen sails on two or three masts. Also, **po·la·cra** (pō lä′krə), **po·la·cre** (pō lä′kər). Cf. **polacca rig.** [< It < ?]

po·lac·ca[2] (pō lak′ə), *n.* polonaise (def. 1). [< It, fem. of *polacco* Polish. See POLACK]

polac′ca rig′, *Naut.* a square rig on a pole mast in which all yards are close together when the sails are furled. Cf. **polacca**[1]. —**po·lac′ca-rigged′,** *adj.*

Po·lack (pō′lak, -läk), *n.* 1. *Disparaging.* a person of Polish descent. 2. *Obs.* a Pole. [< Pol *Polak* a Pole]

Po·land (pō′lənd), *n.* 1. Polish, **Polska.** a republic in central Europe. 30,940,000 (est. 1963); ab. 121,000 sq. mi. (since 1946). *Cap.:* Warsaw. 2. a town in E Ohio. 2766 (1960).

Po′land Chi′na, one of an American breed of black hogs having white markings.

po·lar (pō′lər), *adj.* 1. of or pertaining to a pole, as of the earth, a magnet, an electric cell, etc. 2. opposite in character or action: *The two have personalities that are polar.* 3. capable of ionizing, as NaCl, HCl, or NaOH; electrolytic; heteropolar. 4. central; pivotal: *the polar provision of the treaty.* 5. analogous to the polestar as a guide; guiding: *a polar precept.* [< ML *polār(is).* See POLE[2], -AR[1]]

po′lar ax′is, *Math.* the fixed line, usually horizontal, from which the angle made by the radius vector is measured in a polar coordinates system.

Polar bear (4 ft. high at shoulder; length 7½ ft.)

po′lar bear′, a large white bear, *Thalarctos maritimus,* of the arctic regions.

po′lar bod′y, *Biol.* one of the minute cells arising by the very unequal meiotic divisions of the ovum at or near the time of fertilization. Also called **polocyte.**

po′lar cir′cle, either the Arctic or the Antarctic circle.

po′lar coor′dinates, *Math.* a system of coordinates for locating a point in a plane by the length of its radius vector and the angle this vector makes with a fixed line.

po′lar dis′tance, *Astron.* codeclination.

po′lar equa′tion, *Math.* an equation in which the variables are polar coordinates.

po′lar front′, the transition region, or belt, between the cold, polar easterly winds and the relatively warm southwesterly winds of the middle latitudes.

po·lar·im·e·ter (pō′lə rim′i tər), *n. Optics.* 1. an instrument for measuring the amount of polarized light, or the extent of polarization, in the light received from a given source. 2. a form of polariscope for measuring the angular rotation of the plane of polarization. [< ML *polāri(s)* POLAR + -METER]

Po·lar·is (pō lâr′is), *n.* 1. *Astron.* the polestar or North Star, a star of the second magnitude situated close to the north pole of the heavens, in the constellation Ursa Minor: the outermost star in the handle of the Little Dipper. 2. *U.S.* a two-stage ballistic missile, usually fired from a submerged submarine. [short for ML *stella polāris* Polar star]

po·lar·i·sa·tion (pō′lər i zā′shən), *n. Chiefly Brit.* polarization.

po·lar·i·scope (pō lar′i skōp′, pə-), *n. Optics.* an instrument for measuring or exhibiting the polarization of light or for examining substances in polarized light, often to determine stress and strain in glass and other substances. [< ML *polāri(s)* POLAR + -SCOPE] —**po·lar·i·scop·ic** (pə lar′i skop′ik), *adj.* —**po·lar′i·scop′i·cal·ly,** *adv.*

po·lar·ise (pō′lə rīz′), *v.t., v.i.,* **-ised, -is·ing.** *Chiefly Brit.* polarize. —**po′lar·is′a·bil′i·ty,** *n.* —**po′lar·is′a·ble,** *adj.* —**po′lar·is′er,** *n.*

po·lar·i·ty (pō lar′i tē, pə-), *n.* 1. *Physics.* **a.** the possession of a property or characteristic that produces unequal physical effects at different points in a body or system, as a magnet or storage battery. **b.** the positive or negative state in which a body reacts to a magnetic, electric, or other field. 2. the presence or manifestation of two opposite or contrasting principles or tendencies. [POLAR + -ITY]

po·lar·i·za·tion (pō′lər i zā′shən), *n.* 1. *Optics.* a state, or the production of a state, in which rays of light or similar radiation exhibit different properties in different directions. Cf. **circular polarization, elliptical polarization, plane polarization.** 2. *Elect.* **a.** the deposit of gases, produced during electrolysis, on the electrodes of a cell, increasing the resistance of the cell. **b.** a vector quantity indicating the electric dipole moment per unit of volume of a dielectric. **c.** the induction of polarity in a ferromagnetic substance. 3. the production or acquisition of polarity. Also, *esp. Brit.,* **polarisation.** [POLARIZE + -ATION]

po·lar·ize (pō′lə rīz′), *v.,* **-ized, -iz·ing.** —*v.t.* 1. to cause polarization in. 2. to give polarity to. —*v.i.* 3. to become polarized. Also, *esp. Brit.,* **polarise.** [POLAR + -IZE] —**po′lar·iz′a·bil′ity,** *n.* —**po′lar·iz′a·ble,** *adj.*

po·lar·iz·er (pō′lə rī′zər), *n.* 1. *Optics.* a device, often a crystal or prism, that produces polarized light from unpolarized light. 2. one who or that which polarizes. [POLARIZE + -ER[1]]

po′larizing an′gle, *Optics.* Brewster angle. See under **Brewster's law.**

po′larizing mi′croscope, a microscope that utilizes polarized light to reveal detail in an object, used esp. to study crystalline and fibrous structures.

po′lar lights′, the aurora borealis in the Northern Hemisphere or the aurora australis in the Southern Hemisphere.

po·lar·o·gram (pō lar′ə gram′), *n.* the record produced by the action of a Polarograph. [POLAR + -O- + -GRAM[1]]

Po·lar·o·graph (pō lar′ə graf′, -gräf′), *n. Trademark.* an instrument that automatically registers the current in electrolysis at a dropping mercury electrode. —**po·lar·o·graph·ic** (pō lar′ə graf′ik), *adj.* —**po·lar·og·ra·phy** (pō′lə rog′rə fē), *n.*

Po·lar·oid (pō′lə roid′), *n. Trademark.* 1. a material for producing polarized light from unpolarized light by dichroism, consisting typically of a stretched sheet of colorless plastic treated with an iodine solution so as to have long, thin, parallel chains of polymeric molecules containing conductive iodine atoms. It is used widely in optical and lighting devices to reduce glare. 2. Also called **Po′laroid cam′era, Po′laroid Land′ cam′era.** a portable camera that produces a finished picture in seconds after each exposure.

po′lar out′break, *Meteorol.* a vigorous thrust of cold, polar air across temperate regions.

Po′lar Re′gions, the regions within the Arctic and Antarctic circles.

po′lar va′lence, *Chem.* electrovalence (def. 1).

pol·der (pōl′dər), *n.* a tract of low land, esp. in the Netherlands, reclaimed from the sea or other body of water and protected by dikes. [< D]

pole[1] (pōl), *n., v.,* **poled, pol·ing.** —*n.* 1. a long, cylindrical, often slender piece of wood, metal, etc.: *a telephone pole; a fishing pole.* 2. a long, tapering piece of wood or other material which extends from the front axle of a vehicle between the animals drawing it. 3. *Naut.* **a.** a light spar. **b.** that part of a mast between the uppermost standing rigging and the truck. 4. the lane of a race track nearest to the infield; the inside lane. Cf. **post**[1] (def. 5). 5. a unit of length equal to 16½ feet; a rod. 6. a square rod, 30¼ square yards. 7. **under bare poles, a.** *Naut.* (of a sailing ship) with no sails set, as during a violent storm. **b.** stripped; naked; destitute: *The thugs robbed him and left him under bare poles.* —*v.t.* 8. to furnish with poles. 9. to push, strike, or propel with a pole: *to pole a raft.* 10. *Baseball Slang.* to make (an extra-base hit) by batting the ball hard and far: *He poled a triple to deep right-center.* 11. *Metall.* to stir (molten metal, as copper, tin, or zinc) with poles of green wood so as to produce carbon which reacts with the oxygen present to effect deoxidation. —*v.i.* 12. to propel a boat, raft, etc., with a pole: *to pole down the river.* [ME; OE *pāl* < L *pāl(us)* stake. See PALE[2]] —**pole′less,** *adj.*

pole[2] (pōl), *n.* 1. each of the extremities of the axis of the earth or of any spherical body. 2. *Astron.* See **celestial pole.** 3. one of two opposite or contrasted principles or tendencies: *His behavior ranges between the poles of restraint and abandon.* 4. a point of concentration of interest, attention, etc: *The beautiful actress was the pole of everyone's curiosity.* 5. *Physics.* either of the two regions or parts of an electric battery or the like, at which certain opposite forces are manifested or appear to be concentrated. 6. *Biol.* **a.** either end of an ideal axis in a nucleus, cell, or ovum, about which parts are more or less symmetrically arranged. **b.** either end of a spindle-shaped figure formed in a cell during mitosis. 7. *Anat.* the point in a nerve cell where a process or dendrite begins. 8. *Math.* **a.** a singular point at which a given function of a complex variable can be expanded in a Laurent series beginning with a specified finite, negative power of the variable. **b.** origin (def. 6b). 9. **poles apart** or **asunder,** having widely divergent or completely opposite attitudes, interests, etc.: *In education and background they were poles apart.* [ME *po(o)l* < L *pol(us)* < Gk *pólos* pivot, axis, pole]

Pole (pōl), *n.* a native or inhabitant of Poland. [< G, sing. of *Polen,* MHG *Polanc* < Pol *Poljane* Poles, lit., men of the field or plain]

Pole (pōl), *n.* **Reginald,** 1500–58, English cardinal and last Roman Catholic archbishop of Canterbury.

pole·ax (pōl′aks′), *n., pl.* **-ax·es** (-ak′siz), *v.,* **-axed, -ax·ing.** —*n.* 1. a medieval shafted weapon with blade combining ax, hammer, and apical spike, used for fighting on foot. 2. an ax, usually with a hammer opposite the cutting edge, used in stunning and slaughtering animals. 3. an ax with both a blade and a hook, formerly used in naval warfare to assist sailors in boarding vessels. —*v.t.* 4. to strike down or kill with or as with a poleax. [ME *pollax* battle-ax, lit., head-ax (see POLL[1], AX); akin to MLG *polexe*]

pole·axe (pōl′aks′), *n., pl.* **-ax·es** (-ak′siz), *v.t.,* **-axed, -ax·ing.** poleax.

pole′ bean′, any vinelike variety of bean that is trained to grow upright on a pole, trellis, fence, etc.

pole·cat (pōl′kat′), *n., pl.* **-cats,** (*esp. collectively*) **-cat.** 1. a European mammal, *Mustela putorius,* of the weasel family, having a blackish fur and ejecting a fetid fluid when attacked or disturbed. Cf. **ferret** (def. 1). 2. any of various North American skunks. [ME *polcat,* ? < MF *pol, poul* chicken (< L *pullus*); see CAT[1]]

pole′ com′pass, (formerly) a ship's compass elevated on a wooden pole to isolate it as much as possible from local magnetism.

Pol. Econ., political economy. Also, **pol. econ.**

pole′ ham′mer, a shafted weapon having a spiked hammer head. Also called **war hammer.**

pole′ horse′, a horse harnessed to the tongue of a vehicle; poler; wheeler.

pole′ jump′. See **pole vault.**

pole-jump (pōl′jump′), *v.i.* pole-vault. —**pole′-jump′er,** *n.*

pole′ mast′, *Naut.* a mast on a sailing vessel, consisting of a single piece without separate upper masts.

po·lem·ic (pə lem′ik, pō-), *n.* 1. a controversial argument, as one against some opinion, doctrine, etc. 2. a person who argues in opposition to another; controversialist. —*adj.* 3. Also, **po·lem′i·cal.** of or pertaining to disputation or controversy; controversial. [< Gk *polemik(ós)* of or for war, equiv. to *pólem(os)* war + *-ikos* -IC] —**po·lem′i·cal·ly,** *adv.*

po·lem·ics (pə lem′iks, pō-), *n.* (*construed as sing.*) 1. the art or practice of disputation or controversy: *a master of polemics.* 2. the branch of theology dealing with the history or conduct of ecclesiastical disputation and controversy. Cf. **irenics.** [see POLEMIC, -ICS]

pol·e·mist (pol′ə mist), *n.* a person who is engaged or versed in polemics. Also, **po·lem·i·cist** (pə lem′i sist, pō-). [< Gk *polemistḗs* warrior, equiv. to *pólem(os)* war + *-istēs* -IST]

pol·e·mo·ni·a·ceous (pol′ə mō′nē ā′shəs), *adj.* belonging to the *Polemoniaceae,* a family of plants comprising the Jacob's-ladder, phlox, etc. [< NL *Polemōni(um)* the typical genus (< Gk *polemṓnion* kind of plant) + -ACEOUS]

po·len·ta (pō len′tə), *n.* (esp. in Italian cooking) a thick mush of corn meal. [< It < L: peeled or pearl barley]

pole′ of cold′. See **cold pole.**

pole′ piece′, *Elect.* a piece of magnetic material at a pole of a permanent magnet or of an electromagnet, shaped to control the magnetic flux distribution in the vicinity of the pole.

pole′ plate′, *Carpentry.* (in a trussed roof) a plate resting upon tie beams and supporting common rafters near their lower ends.

pol·er (pō′lər), *n.* **1.** one who or that which poles. **2.** See **pole horse.** [POLE[1] + -ER[1]]

pole′ screen′, a fine screen mounted on a pole.

pole·star (pōl′stär′), *n.* **1.** Polaris. **2.** something that is the center of attention or attraction. **3.** something that serves as a guiding principle. [POLE[2] + STAR]

pole′ topgal′lant mast′, *Naut.* See **long topgallant mast.**

pole′ vault′, *Track.* **1.** a field event in which a leap or vault over a crossbar is performed with the aid of a long pole. **2.** a leap or vault so performed.

pole-vault (pōl′vôlt′), *v.i.* to execute a pole vault. —**pole′-vault′er,** *n.*

po·leyn (pō′lān), *n.* *Armor.* a piece for the knee, made of plate or cuir bouilli. Also called **genouillère, knee cop.** [ME *poleyn, polayne* < OF *po(u)lain* < ?]

po·li·a·nite (pō′lē ə nīt′), *n.* *Mineral.* a variety of pyrolusite, MnO_2, having well-developed crystals. [< G *Polianit,* irreg. < Gk *poliaín(esthai)* (to) grow white (with sea foam), deriv. of *poliós* grey; see -ITE[1]]

Pol·i·as (pol′ē əs), *n.* *Class. Myth.* an epithet of Athena as protectress of cities.

Po·li·a·tas (pō′lē ā′təs), *n.* *Class. Myth.* an epithet of Athena, meaning "keeper of the city."

po·lice (pə lēs′), *n., v.,* **-liced, -lic·ing.** —*n.* **1.** an organized civil force for maintaining order, preventing and detecting crime, and enforcing the laws. **2.** (*construed as pl.*) members of such a force: *Several police are patrolling the neighborhood.* **3.** the regulation and control of a community, esp. for the maintenance of public order, safety, health, morals, etc. **4.** the department of the government concerned with this, esp. with the maintenance of order. **5.** any body of men officially maintained or employed to keep order, enforce regulations, etc. **6.** *Mil.* (in the U.S. Army) **a.** the cleaning and keeping clean of a camp, post, station, etc. **b.** the condition of a camp, post, station, etc., with reference to cleanliness. —*v.t.* **7.** to regulate, control, or keep in order by or as by means of police. **8.** *Mil.* to clean and keep clean (a camp, post, etc.) [< MF: government, civil administration, police < LL *polītia,* var. of L *polītīa* POLITY]

police′ ac′tion, a relatively localized military action undertaken by regular armed forces, without a formal declaration of war, against guerrillas, insurgents, etc., held to be violating international peace and order.

police′ car′. See **squad car.**

police′ court′, an inferior court with summary jurisdiction for the trial of persons accused of any of certain minor offenses, and with power to examine those charged with more serious offenses and hold them for trial in a superior court or for a grand jury.

police′ dog′, **1.** a dog trained to assist the police. **2.** See **German shepherd.**

Police dog, German shepherd (2 ft. high at shoulder)

po·lice·man (pə lēs′mən), *n., pl.* **-men.** a member of a police force or body. [POLICE + MAN[1]] —**po·lice′man·like′,** *adj.*

police′ pow′er, the power of a nation, within the limits of its constitution, to regulate the conduct of its citizens in the interest of the common good.

police′ state′, a nation in which the police, esp. a secret police, suppresses any act by an individual or group that conflicts with governmental policy or principle.

police′ sta′tion, police headquarters for a particular district, from which policemen are dispatched and to which persons under arrest are brought. Also called **station house.**

police′ wag′on. See **patrol wagon.**

po·lice·wom·an (pə lēs′wo͝om′ən), *n., pl.* **-wom·en.** a female member of a police force. [POLICE + WOMAN]

pol·i·cli·nic (pol′ē klin′ik), *n.* a department of a hospital at which outpatients are treated. [< G *Poliklinik,* equiv. to Gk *pōli(s)* city + *klinik(ē)* clinic art]

pol·i·cy[1] (pol′i sē), *n., pl.* **-cies.** **1.** a definite course of action adopted for the sake of expediency, facility, etc.: *We have a new company policy. Honesty is the best policy.* **2.** a course of action adopted and pursued by a government, ruler, political party, etc.: *our nation's foreign policy.* **3.** action or procedure conforming to or considered with reference to prudence or expediency: *It was good policy to consent.* **4.** prudence, practical wisdom, or expediency: *Policy demands occasional compromise.* **5.** sagacity; shrewdness: *Showing great policy, he pitted his enemies against one another.* **6.** *Rare.* government; polity. [ME *policie* government, civil administration < L *polītīa* POLITY]
—**Syn. 1.** strategy, principle, rule. **5.** acumen, astuteness, skill, art. —**Ant. 5.** ingenuousness, naiveté.

pol·i·cy[2] (pol′i sē), *n., pl.* **-cies.** **1.** a document embodying a contract of insurance. **2.** *U.S.* **a.** a method of gambling in which bets are made on numbers to be drawn by lottery. **b.** See **numbers pool** (def. 1). [< MF *police* (< It *polizza* < ML *apodīxa* receipt << Gk *apódeixis* a showing or setting forth; see APODICTIC, -SIS) + -Y[3]]

pol·i·cy·hold·er (pol′i sē hōl′dər), *n.* the individual or firm in whose name an insurance policy is written; an insured. [POLICY[2] + HOLDER]

pol′icy loan′, *Insurance.* a loan made by a life-insurance company to a policyholder with the cash value of his policy serving as security.

po·li·en·ceph·a·li·tis (pō′lē en sef′ə lī′tis), *n.* *Pathol.* polioencephalitis.

po·li·en·ceph·a·lo·my·e·li·tis (pō′lē en sef′ə lō mī′ə lī′tis), *n.* *Pathol.* polioencephalomyelitis.

Pol·i·eus (pol′ē o͞os′), *n.* *Class. Myth.* an epithet of Zeus, meaning "urban."

pol·i·met·rum (pol′ē me′trəm), *n.* *Survey.* an obsolete instrument having a plumb line, a sighting tube, and graduated vertical and horizontal circles, used for leveling and for taking bearings and altitudes. [*poli-,* var. of POLY- + *-metrum,* Latinized form of -METER]

po·li·o (pō′lē ō′), *n.* poliomyelitis. [shortened form]

po·li·o·en·ceph·a·li·tis (pō′lē ō en sef′ə lī′tis), *n.* *Pathol.* a disease characterized by inflammation of the gray matter of the brain; cerebral poliomyelitis. Also, **poliencephalitis.** [< NL < Gk *poliō(s)* gray + NL *encephalitis* ENCEPHALITIS]

po·li·o·en·ceph·a·lo·my·e·li·tis (pō′lē ō en sef′ə lō mī′ə lī′tis), *n.* *Pathol.* a disease characterized by inflammation of the gray matter of the brain and spinal cord. Also, **poliencephalomyelitis.** [< NL; see POLIOENCEPHALITIS, MYELITIS]

po·li·o·my·e·li·tis (pō′lē ō mī′ə lī′tis), *n.* *Pathol.* an acute viral disease, most common in infants but often attacking older children and even adults, characterized by inflammation of the nerve cells, mainly of the anterior horns of the spinal cord, and resulting in a motor paralysis, followed by muscular atrophy, and often by permanent deformities. Also called **acute anterior poliomyelitis, infantile paralysis, polio.** [< NL < Gk *poliō(s)* gray + NL *myelitis* MYELITIS] —**po·li·o·my·e·lit·ic** (pō′lē ō mī′ə lit′ik), *adj.*

po·lis (pō′lis), *n., pl.* **-leis** (-līs). an ancient Greek city-state. [< Gk]

-polis, an element appearing in loan words from Greek (*metropolis*), and used in the formation of place names (*Annapolis*). [comb. form repr. Gk *pólis* POLIS]

pol·ish (pol′ish), *v.t.* **1.** to make smooth and glossy, esp. by rubbing or friction: *to polish a brass doorknob.* **2.** to render finished, refined, or elegant: *His speech needs polishing.* **3.** to take or bring to a different state by polishing or refining (often fol. by *away, off,* or *out*): *brook pebbles polished into roundness.* —*v.i.* **4.** to become smooth and glossy through polishing: *a flooring that polishes easily.* **5.** *Archaic.* to become refined or elegant. **6. polish off,** *Slang.* **a.** to finish or dispose of quickly: *They polished off a quart of vodka between them.* **b.** to subdue or get rid of someone: *The fighter polished off his opponent in the first round.* **7. polish up,** *Slang.* to improve; refine: *She took lessons to polish up her speech.* —*n.* **8.** a substance used to give smoothness or gloss: *shoe polish.* **9.** the act of polishing. **10.** state of being polished. **11.** smoothness and gloss of surface. **12.** superiority of manner or execution; refinement; elegance: *the polish of a professional singer.* [ME *polishe(n)* < MF *poliss-,* long s. of *polir* < L *polīre* to polish; see -ISH[2]] —**pol′ish·er,** *n.*
—**Syn. 1.** shine, brighten, burnish, buff, smooth. **11.** shine, gleam. POLISH, GLOSS, LUSTER, SHEEN refer to a smooth, shining, or bright surface from which light is reflected. POLISH suggests the smooth, bright reflection often produced by friction: *rubbed to a high polish.* GLOSS suggests a superficial, hard smoothness characteristic of lacquered, varnished, or enameled surfaces: *a gloss on oilcloth, on paper.* LUSTER denotes the characteristic quality of the light reflected from the surfaces of certain materials (pearls, silk, wax, freshly cut metals, etc.): *a pearly luster.* SHEEN, sometimes poetical, suggests a glistening brightness such as that reflected from the surface of silk or velvet, or from furniture oiled and hand-polished: *a rich velvety sheen.*

Pol·ish (pō′lish), *adj.* **1.** of, pertaining to, or characteristic of Poland, its inhabitants, or their language. —*n.* **2.** a Slavic language, the principal language of Poland. [POLE + -ISH[1]]

Pol′ish Cor′ridor, a strip of land near the mouth of the Vistula River: formerly separated Germany from East Prussia; given to Poland in the Treaty of Versailles 1919 to provide her with access to the Baltic.

pol·ished (pol′isht), *adj.* **1.** made smooth and glossy: *a figurine of polished mahogany.* **2.** naturally smooth and glossy: *polished pebbles on the beach.* **3.** refined, cultured, or elegant: *a polished manner.* **4.** flawless; skillful; excellent: *a polished conversationalist.* [ME *polist.* See POLISH, -ED[2]]

pol′ished rice′, white rice polished or buffed by leather-covered cylinders during processing.

Pol′ish sau′sage, (*sometimes l.c.*) kielbasa.

Pol′ish wheat′, a wheat, *Triticum polonicum,* grown chiefly in S Europe, N Africa, and Turkestan.

polit., **1.** political. **2.** politics.

Po·lit·bu·ro (pol′it byo͝or′ō, pō′lit-, pə lit′-), *n.* (*often l.c.*) the executive committee and chief policymaking body of a Communist party. Also, **Po′lit·bu′reau.** [< Russ *politbyuró,* shortening of *politícheskoe byuró* political bureau]

po·lite (pə līt′), *adj.* **1.** showing good manners toward others, as in behavior, speech, etc.; courteous; civil: *a polite reply.* **2.** refined or cultured: *polite society.* **3.** of a refined or elegant kind: *polite learning.* [late ME < L *polīt(us)* polished, ptp. of *polīre*] —**po·lite′ly,** *adv.* —**po·lite′ness,** *n.*
—**Syn. 1.** well-bred, gracious. See **civil. 2.** urbane, polished, poised, courtly, cultivated. —**Ant. 1, 2.** rude.

polit. econ., political economy.

Po·li·tes (pə lī′tēz), *n.* (in the *Odyssey*) a companion of Odysseus who was changed into a swine by Circe.

pol·i·tesse (pol′i tes′; *Fr.* pô lē tes′), *n.* politeness. [< F: orig. clean or polished state < It *politezza,* var. of *pulitezza* (see POLITE); *-ess,* as in PROWESS]

Po·li·tian (pō lish′ən), *n.* (*Angelo Poliziano*) 1454–94, Italian classical scholar, teacher, and poet.

pol·i·tic (pol′i tik), *adj.* **1.** sagacious; prudent. **2.** shrewd; artful. **3.** expedient; judicious. **4.** political. Cf. **body politic.** [late ME *politik* < MF *politique* < L *polīticus* < Gk *polītikós* civic, equiv. to *polīt(ēs)* citizen (see POLITY) + *-ikos* -IC] —**pol′i·tic·ly,** *adv.*
—**Syn. 1.** discreet, judicious, astute, wary. See **diplomatic. 2.** sly, cunning, clever, subtle, intriguing, crafty. —**Ant. 1.** tactless. **2.** open.

po·lit·i·cal (pə lit′i kəl), *adj.* **1.** of, pertaining to, or concerned with the science or art of politics: *political writers.* **2.** of, pertaining to, or connected with a political party: *a political campaign.* **3.** exercising or seeking power in the governmental or public affairs of a state, municipality, etc.: *a political machine; a political boss.* **4.** of or pertaining to the state or its government: *political measures.* **5.** affecting or involving the state or government: *a political offense.* **6.** engaged in or connected with civil administration: *political office.* **7.** having a definite policy or system of government: *a political community.* **8.** of or pertaining to citizens: *political rights.* [< L *polītic(us)* civic (see POLITIC) + -AL[1]] —**po·lit′i·cal·ly,** *adv.*

polit′ical econ′omy, **1.** a social science dealing with political policies and economic processes, their interrelations, and their influence on social institutions. **2.** (in the 17th–18th centuries) the art of management of communities, esp. as affecting the wealth of a government. **3.** (in the 19th century) a social science similar to modern economics but dealing chiefly with governmental policies. **4.** economics (def. 1). —**polit′ical econ′omist.**

po·lit·i·cal·ize (pə lit′i kə līz′), *v.t.,* **-ized, -iz·ing.** to cause to be political; color with politics. [POLITICAL + -IZE] —**po·lit′i·cal·i·za′tion,** *n.*

polit′ical lib′erty, the right to express oneself freely and effectually regarding the conduct, make-up, and principles of the government under which one lives.

po·lit′i·cal·ly cor·rect′, marked by or adhering to a typically progressive orthodoxy on issues involving esp. race, gender, sexual affinity, or ecology. *Abbr.:* PC, P.C. —**polit′ical correct′ness.**

polit′ical ques′tion, *Law.* a question regarded by the courts as being a matter to be determined by another department of government rather than of law and therefore one with which they will not deal, as the recognition of a foreign state.

polit′ical sci′ence, the science of politics, or of the principles and conduct of government. —**polit′ical sci′entist.**

pol·i·ti·cian (pol′i tish′ən), *n.* **1.** a person who is active in party politics. **2.** a seeker or holder of public office, who is more concerned about winning favor or retaining power than about maintaining principles. **3.** a person who holds a political office. **4.** a person skilled in political government or administration; statesman. **5.** an expert in politics or political government. **6.** a person who seeks to gain power or advancement within an organization in ways that are generally disapproved. [< F *politicien.* See POLITIC, -IAN]
—**Syn. 4.** POLITICIAN, STATESMAN refer to one skilled in politics. These terms differ particularly in their connotations; POLITICIAN is more often derogatory, and STATESMAN laudatory. POLITICIAN suggests the schemes and devices of one who engages in (esp. small) politics for party ends or his own advantage: *a dishonest politician.* STATESMAN suggests the eminent ability, foresight, and unselfish devotion to the interests of his country of one dealing with (esp. important or great) affairs of state: *a distinguished statesman.*

po·lit·i·cize (pə lit′i sīz′), *v.,* **-cized, -ciz·ing.** —*v.t.* **1.** to bring a political character or flavor to; make political: *to politicize a private dispute.* —*v.i.* **2.** to engage in or discuss politics. [POLITIC(AL) + -IZE]

pol·i·tick (pol′i tik), *v.i.* to engage in politicking. [back formation from POLITICKING]

pol·i·tick·ing (pol′i tik′ing), *n.* activity undertaken for political reasons or ends, as campaigning for votes before an election, making speeches, etc., or otherwise promoting oneself or one's policies. [*politick,* var. of POLITIC + -ING[1]]

po·lit·i·co (pə lit′i kō′), *n., pl.* **-cos.** a politician. [< It or Sp: politician]

politico-, a combining form of **political:** *politico-religious.*

pol·i·tics (pol′i tiks), *n.* (*construed as sing. or pl.*) **1.** the science or art of political government. **2.** the practice or profession of conducting political affairs. **3.** political affairs: *The advocated reforms have become embroiled in politics.* **4.** political methods or maneuvers: *We could not approve of his politics in winning passage of the bill.* **5.** political principles or opinions: *She avoided discussion of religion and politics. His politics are his own affair.* **6.** use of intrigue or strategy in obtaining any position of power or control, as in a business, university, etc. **7.** (*cap., italics.*) a treatise (4th century B.C.) by Aristotle, dealing with the structure, organization, and administration of the state, esp. the city-state as known in ancient Greece. [see POLITIC, -ICS]

pol·i·ty (pol′i tē), *n., pl.* **-ties.** **1.** a particular form or system of government: *civil polity; ecclesiastical polity.* **2.** the condition of being constituted as a state or other organized community or body: *The polity of ancient Athens became a standard for later governments.* **3.** government or administrative regulation: *The colonists demanded independence in matters concerning internal polity.* **4.** a state or other organized community or body. [< L *polītīa* < Gk *polīteía* citizenship, government, form of government, commonwealth, equiv. to *polītē(s)* citizen (see POLIS, -ITE[1]) + *-ia* -IA]

Pol·i·u·chus (pol′ē o͞o′kəs), *n.* *Class. Myth.* an epithet of Athena, meaning "city-protecting."

Polk (pōk), *n.* **1. James Knox,** 1795–1849, the 11th president of the U.S. 1845–49. **2.** a town in NW Pennsylvania. 3574 (1960).

pol·ka (pōl′kə, pō′kə), *n., pl.* **-kas,** *v.,* **-kaed, -ka·ing.** —*n.* **1.** a lively round dance of Bohemian origin, with music in duple meter. **2.** a piece of music for such a dance or in its rhythm. —*v.i.* **3.** to dance the polka. [< Czech, var. of *pulka* half (step)]

pol′ka dot′, **1.** a dot or round spot (printed, woven, or embroidered) repeated to form a pattern on a textile fabric. **2.** a pattern of or a fabric with such dots.

poll[1] (pōl), *n.* **1.** the registering of votes, as at an election. **2.** the voting at an election. **3.** the number of votes cast. **4.** the numerical result of the voting. **5.** an enumeration or a list of individuals, as for purposes of taxing or voting. **6.** Usually, **polls.** the place where votes are taken. **7.** See **poll tax. 8.** a person or individual in a number or list. **9.** a sampling or collection of opinions on a subject, taken from either a selected or a random group of persons, as for the purpose of analysis. **10.** the head, esp. the part of it on which the hair grows. **11.** the back of the head. **12.** the rear portion of the head of a horse; the nape. See diag. under **horse. 13.** the part of the head between the ears of certain animals, as the horse and cow. **14.** the broad end or face of a hammer. —*v.t.* **15.** to receive at the polls, as votes. **16.** to enroll (someone) in a list or register, as for purposes of taxing or voting. **17.** to take or register the votes of (persons). **18.** to deposit or cast at the polls, as a vote. **19.** to bring to the polls, as voters. **20.** to take a sampling of the attitudes or opinions of. **21.** to cut short or cut off the hair, wool, etc., of (an animal); crop; clip; shear. **22.** to cut short or cut off (hair, wool, etc.). **23.** to cut off the top of (a tree); pollard. **24.** to cut off or cut short the horns of (cattle). —*v.i.* **25.** to vote at the polls; give one's vote. [ME *polle* (hair of the) head < MLG: hair of the head, top of a tree or other plant; akin to Dan *puld*, Sw *pull* crown of the head] —**poll′a·ble,** *adj.*

poll² (pōl), *n.* (esp. at Cambridge University, England) **1.** the body of students who read for or obtain a degree without honors. **2.** Also called **poll degree.** the degree so awarded. [appar. < Gk *poll(oí)*, in *hoi polloí* the many; see POLY-]

pol·lack (pol′ək), *n., pl.* **-lacks,** (*esp. collectively*) **-lack.** a darkly-colored, North Atlantic food fish, *Pollachius virens*, of the cod family. Also, *esp. Brit.,* **pollock.** [assimilated var. of *podlok* (Scot); akin to Scot dial. *paddle* bumpfish; see -OCK]

Pol·lai·uo·lo (pō′lī wō′lō; *It.* pôl′lī wô′lô), *n.* **1.** **An·to·nio** (än tô′nyô), 1429–98, Italian sculptor, painter, and goldsmith. **2.** his brother **Pie·ro** (pye′rô), 1443–96, painter, sculptor, and goldsmith. Also, **Pol·lai·o·lo** (pō′lī ō′lō; *It.* pôl′lī ô′lô), **Pol·laj·uo·lo** (pō′lī wō′lō; *It.* pôl′lī wô′lô).

pol·la·ki·u·ri·a (pol′ə kē yŏŏr′ē ə, -kī-), *n. Med.* abnormally frequent urination. [< Gk *pollákis*, *pollákis* many times + -URIA]

pol·lard (pol′ərd), *n.* **1.** a tree cut back nearly to the trunk, so as to produce a dense mass of branches. **2.** an animal, as a stag, ox, or sheep, having no horns. —*v.t.* **3.** to convert into a pollard. [POLL¹ + -ARD]

poll·book (pōl′bŏŏk′), *n.* the official list of the registered voters in a given area. [POLL¹ + BOOK]

poll′ degree′ (pōl), *Brit.* poll² (def. 2). Also called **pass degree.**

polled (pōld), *adj.* **1.** hornless, as the Aberdeen Angus. **2.** *Obs.* having the hair cut off. [POLL¹ + -ED²]

poll·ee (pō lē′), *n.* a person who is asked questions in a poll. [POLL¹ + -EE]

pol·len (pol′ən), *n.* **1.** the fertilizing element of flowering plants, consisting of fine, powdery, yellowish grains or spores, sometimes in masses. —*v.t.* **2.** to pollinate. [< NL, special use of L: fine flour, mill dust] —**pol′lened,** *adj.* —**pol′len·less,** *adj.* —**pol′len·like′,** *adj.* —**pol·lin·ic** (pə lin′ik), **pol·lin′i·cal,** *adj.*

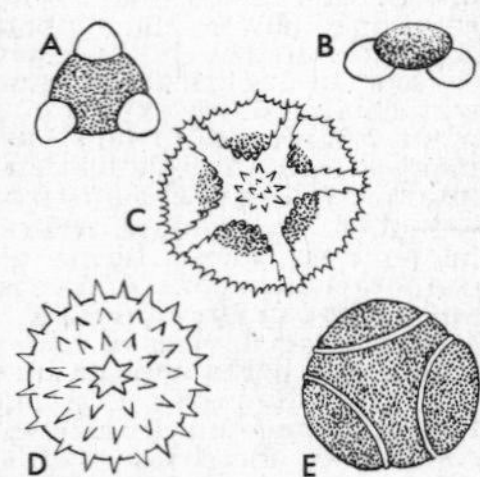

Pollen grains
A, Evening primrose, *Oenothera biennis;* B, Scotch pine, *Pinus sylvestris;* C, Chicory, *Chicorium intybus;* D, Hibiscus, *Hibiscus moscheutos;* E, Passionflower, *Passiflora caerulea*

pol′len bas′ket, (of bees) a smooth area on the hind tibia of each leg which is fringed with long hairs and serves to transport pollen. Also called **corbicula.**

pol′len brush′, the mass of stiff hairs on the legs or abdomen of an insect, for collecting pollen. Also called **scopa.**

pol′len count′, a count of the amount of pollen in the air, based on the average of the number of pollen grains that collect on slides exposed to the air for a given period of time.

poll′ end′ (pōl), the hub holding the sail arms of a windmill.

pol·len·o·sis (pol′ə nō′sis), *n. Pathol.* See **hay fever.** [POLLEN + -OSIS]

pol·le·ra (pə yâr′ə; *Sp.* pô ye′rä), *n., pl.* **pol·le·ras** (pə yâr′əz; *Sp.* pô ye′räs). a gaily colored costume worn by women during fiestas in Latin-American countries. [< AmerSp, special use of *pollera* poultry yard, chicken coop, deriv. of *pollo* chicken]

poll′ e′vil (pōl), *Vet. Med.* an acute swelling on the top of the head of a horse originating in an inflamed bursa which underlies the great neck ligament there.

pol·lex (pol′eks), *n., pl.* **pol·li·ces** (pol′i sēz′). the innermost digit of the forelimb; thumb. [< L: thumb]

pol·li·ce ver·so (pōl′li ke′ wer′sō; *Eng.* pol′i sē vûr′sō), *Latin.* with thumbs turned downward: the sign made by spectators calling for the death of a defeated gladiator in the ancient Roman circus.

pol·lic·i·ta·tion (pə lis′i tā′shən), *n. Civil Law.* an offer or promise made by one party to another before the latter's consent or acceptance. [< L *pollicitātiōn-* (s. of *pollicitātiō*) a promising, equiv. to *pollicitāt(us)* (ptp. of *pollicitārī* to promise, freq. of *pollicērī* to promise, lit., bid for, equiv. to *pol-* (assimilated var. of *por-*, c. *pro-* for) + *licērī* to bid) + *-iōn-* -ION]

pol·li·nate (pol′ə nāt′), *v.t.,* **-nat·ed, -nat·ing.** *Bot.* to convey pollen to the stigma of (a flower). [< NL *pollin-* (s. of *pollen*) POLLEN + -ATE¹] —**pol′li·na′tor,** *n.*

pol·li·na·tion (pol′ə nā′shən), *n. Bot.* the transfer of pollen from the anther to the stigma. [POLLINATE + -ION]

poll′ing booth′, a booth in which voters cast their votes.

poll′ing place′, a place at or in which votes in an election are cast.

pol·li·nif·er·ous (pol′ə nif′ər əs), *adj.* **1.** *Bot.* producing or bearing pollen. **2.** *Zool.* fitted for carrying pollen. [< NL *pollin-* (s. of *pollen*) POLLEN + -I- + -FEROUS]

pol·lin·i·um (pə lin′ē əm), *n., pl.* **-lin·i·a** (-lin′ē ə). *Bot.* an agglutinated mass or body of pollen grains, characteristic of orchidaceous and asclepiadaceous plants. [< NL, equiv. to *pollin-* (s. of *pollen*) POLLEN + *-ium* -IUM]

pol·li·nize (pol′ə nīz′), *v.t.,* **-nized, -niz·ing.** pollinate. [< NL *pollin-* (s. of *pollen*) POLLEN + -IZE] —**pol′li·ni·za′tion,** *n.*

pol·li·no·sis (pol′ə nō′sis), *n. Pathol.* See **hay fever.** [< NL; see POLLINIZE, -OSIS]

pol·li·wog (pol′ē wog′), *n.* a tadpole. Also, **pollywog.** [var. of *polliwig*, earlier *polwigge*, late ME *polwygle*. See POLL¹, WIGGLE]

pol·lock (pol′ək), *n., pl.* **-locks,** (*esp. collectively*) **-lock.** *Chiefly Brit.* pollack.

Pol·lock (pol′ək), *n.* **1.** **Sir Frederick,** 1845–1937, English legal scholar and author. **2.** **Jackson,** 1912–56, U.S. painter.

poll·ster (pōl′stər), *n. Often Derogatory.* a person whose occupation is the taking of public-opinion polls. [POLL¹ + -STER]

poll′ tax′ (pōl), a capitation tax, the payment of which is sometimes a prerequisite to exercise the right of suffrage.

poll-tax·er (pōl′tak′sər), *n.* a Congressman from a State having a poll tax.

pol·lu·tant (pə lōōt′ᵊnt), *n.* that which pollutes: *Rivers are full of pollutants from the factories and cities along their banks.* [POLLUTE + -ANT]

pol·lute (pə lōōt′), *v.t.,* **-lut·ed, -lut·ing.** **1.** to make foul or unclean; dirty: *to pollute the air with smoke.* **2.** to make morally unclean; defile. **3.** to render ceremonially impure; desecrate: *to pollute a house of worship.* [ME *polute* < L *pollūt(us)*, ptp. of *polluere* to soil, defile, equiv. to *pol-* for *por-* intensive prefix (akin to PER-) + *-luere* to let loose (something bad), akin to LUES] —**pol·lut′er,** *n.* —**pol·lu′tion,** *n.*
—**Syn. 1.** soil, befoul. **2.** taint, contaminate, vitiate, corrupt, debase, deprave. —**Ant. 1, 2.** purify.

pol·lut·ed (pə lōō′tid), *adj.* **1.** made unclean or impure; contaminated; tainted: *swimming in polluted waters.* **2.** *Slang.* drunk. [late ME; see POLLUTE, -ED²] —**pol·lut′ed·ness,** *n.*

Pol·lux (pol′əks), *n.* **1.** Greek, **Polydeuces.** *Class. Myth.* the brother of Castor. Cf. **Castor and Pollux.** **2.** *Astron.* a first-magnitude star in the constellation Gemini.

poll′ watch′er (pōl), a representative of a political party or of an organization running a candidate who is assigned to the polls on Election Day to watch for violations of the laws that regulate voting, campaigning, etc. Also called **watcher.**

Pol·ly (pol′ē), *n.* a girl's given name, form of **Mary.**

Pol·ly·an·na (pol′ē an′ə), *n.* an excessively or blindly optimistic person. [from the name of the heroine created by Eleanor Porter (1868–1920), American writer]

pol·ly·fish (pol′ē fish′), *n., pl.* (*esp. collectively*) **-fish,** (*esp. referring to two or more kinds or species*) **-fish·es.** parrotfish. [*polly* (pet name for a parrot) + FISH]

pol·ly·wog (pol′ē wog′), *n.* polliwog.

po·lo (pō′lō), *n.* **1.** a game played on horseback between two teams, each of four players, the object being to score points by driving a wooden ball into the opponents' goal using a long-handled mallet. **2.** any game broadly resembling this, esp. water polo. [< Balti (Tibetan dial. of Kashmir): ball] —**po′lo·ist,** *n.*

Po·lo (pō′lō), *n.* **1.** **Mar·co** (mär′kō), c1254–1324, Venetian traveler. **2.** a town in N Illinois. 2551 (1960).

po′lo coat′, a double-breasted, often belted overcoat made of camel's hair or a similar fabric.

po·lo·cyte (pō′lə sīt′), *n.* See **polar body.** [POLE² + -O- + -CYTE]

pol·o·naise (pol′ə nāz′, pō′lə-), *n.* **1.** Also called **polacca.** a slow dance of Polish origin, in triple meter, consisting chiefly of a march or promenade in couples. **2.** a piece of music for, or in the rhythm of, such a dance. **3.** Also, **pol·o·nese** (pol′ə nēz′, -nēs′, pō′lə-). a coatlike outer dress, combining bodice and cutaway overskirt, worn in the late 18th century over a separate skirt. [< F, fem. of *polonais* Polish, equiv. to *Polon-* (< ML *Polonia* Poland) + *-ais* -ESE]

Po·lo·nise (pō′lə nīz′), *v.t.,* **-nised, -nis·ing.** *Chiefly Brit.* Polonize. —**Po′lo·ni·sa′tion,** *n.*

po·lo·ni·um (pə lō′nē əm), *n. Chem.* a radioactive element discovered by M. and Mme. Curie in 1898; *Symbol:* Po; *at. no.:* 84; *at. wt.:* about 210. Also called **radium F.** [< NL, equiv. to *polon-* (< ML *Polonia* Poland) + *-ium* -IUM]

Po·lo·ni·us (pə lō′nē əs), *n.* the sententious father of Ophelia in Shakespeare's *Hamlet.*

Po·lo·nize (pō′lə nīz′), *v.t.,* **-nized, -niz·ing.** **1.** to cause or force to take on ways, customs, viewpoints, etc., that are characteristically Polish. **2.** to alter (a word or phrase) so that it resembles Polish. Also, *esp. Brit.,* **Polonise.** [< ML *Polon(ia)* Poland + -IZE] —**Po′lo·ni·za′tion,** *n.*

Po·lon·na·ru·wa (pō lun′ə rōō′və), *n.* a town in central Ceylon: Buddhist ruins. ab. 2300.

po′lo po′ny, a small, swift, agile horse specially trained for use in polo.

pol·os (pol′os), *n., pl.* **pol·oi** (pol′oi). a tall, cylindrical headdress represented, esp. on statues, as worn by women in ancient Greece. [< Gk: axis]

po′lo shirt′, a short-sleeved, pull-over sport shirt, usually of cotton knit, with a round neckband or a turnover collar.

Pol·ska (pôl′skä), *n.* Polish name of **Poland.**

Pol·ta·va (pol tä′vä), *n.* a city in the E Ukraine, in the SW Soviet Union in Europe: Russian defeat of Swedes 1709. 163,000 (est. 1964).

pol·ter·geist (pōl′tər gīst′), *n.* a ghost or spirit supposed to manifest its presence by noises, knockings, etc. [< G: lit., noise-ghost]

Pol·to·ratsk (*Russ.* pol to rätsk′), *n.* former name of **Ashkhabad.**

pol·troon (pol trōōn′), *n.* a wretched coward; craven. [earlier *pultrowne*, etc. < MF *poultron* < OIt *poltrone* idler, coward, lit., one who lies abed (akin to *poltrire* to lie lazily in bed), appar. deriv. of obs. *poltro* bed < OHG *polstar* BOLSTER; see -OON]
—**Syn.** dastard.

pol·troon·er·y (pol trōō′nə rē), *n.* cowardice. [POLTROON + -ERY]

poly-, an element, meaning "much," "many," occurring originally in loan words from Greek (*polyandrous; polychrome*), but now used freely as a general formative, esp. in scientific or technical words (*polyarteritis; polydomous; polyethylene*). [< Gk, comb. form repr. *polýs*; akin to OE *fela* many. See PLUS]

poly., polytechnic.

pol·y·ac·id (pol′ē as′id), *Chem.* —*adj.* **1.** having more than one replaceable hydrogen atom. **2.** capable of reacting with more than one equivalent weight of an acid. —*n.* **3.** an acid having more than one replaceable hydrogen atom. **4.** an oxyacid containing the equivalent of extra molecules of its anhydride, as the polysulfuric acids, $H_2S_2O_7$ or $H_2SO_4 \cdot SO_3$, and $H_2S_3O_{10}$ or $H_2SO_4 \cdot 2SO_3$. [POLY- + ACID]

pol′y·a·cryl′ic ac′id (pol′ē ə kril′ik, pol′-), *Chem.* a polymer of acrylic acid, $(-CH_2CH(COOH)-)_n$, used as a size in the manufacture of nylon and other synthetic textiles. [POLY- + ACRYLIC]

pol·y·ac·ry·lo·ni·trile (pol′ē ak′rə lō nī′tril, -trēl, -tril), *n. Chem.* a polymer of acrylonitrile, $(-CH_2CH(CN)-)_n$, used in the manufacture of Orlon and other synthetic textiles. [POLY- + ACRYLO- + NITRILE]

pol·y·a·del·phous (pol′ē ə del′fəs), *adj. Bot.* (of stamens) united by the filaments into three or more sets or bundles. [< Gk *polyádelph(os)* having many brothers (*poly-* POLY- + *adelphós* brother) + -OUS]

Pol·ya·kov (pôl′yä kôf′), *n.* **Va·si·ly I** (vä sē′li), born 1913, Russian journalist and government official: member of the Presidium 1962–64.

pol·y·am·ide (pol′ē am′īd, -id), *n. Chem.* a polymer in which the monomer units are linked together by the amide group –CONH–. [POLY- + AMIDE]

pol·y·a·mine (pol′ē ə mēn′, -am′in), *n. Chem.* a compound containing more than one amino group. [POLY- + -AMINE]

pol·y·an·drist (pol′ē an′drist), *n.* a woman who practices or favors polyandry. [POLYANDR(Y) + -IST]

pol·y·an·drous (pol′ē an′drəs), *adj.* **1.** of, pertaining to, characterized by, or practicing polyandry. **2.** *Bot.* having the stamens indefinitely numerous. [< Gk *polyandros* having many husbands. See POLY-, -ANDROUS]

pol·y·an·dry (pol′ē an′drē, pol′ē an′-), *n.* **1.** the practice or condition of having more than one husband at one time (distinguished from *monandry*). **2.** *Bot.* the state of being polyandrous. [< Gk *polyandría*. See POLY-, -ANDROUS, -Y³]

pol·y·an·gu·lar (pol′ē ang′gyə lər), *adj.* multangular; multiangular. [POLY- + ANGULAR]

Pol·yan·sky (pol yän′ski), *n.* **Dmi·tri Ste·pa·no·vich** (dmē′tri ste pä′no vich), born 1917, Russian government official: alternate member of the Presidium.

pol·y·an·thus (pol′ē an′thəs), *n., pl.* **-thus·es.** **1.** a hybrid primrose, *Primula polyantha.* **2.** a narcissus, *Narcissus Tazetta*, having small white or yellow flowers. [< NL < Gk *polyánthos* having many flowers. See POLY-, -ANTHOUS]

pol·y·ar·chy (pol′ē är′kē), *n., pl.* **-chies.** a form of government in which power is vested in three or more persons. [POLY- + -ARCHY] —**pol′y·ar′chic, pol′y·ar′chi·cal,** *adj.*

pol·y·ar·te·ri·tis (pol′ē är′tə rī′tis), *n. Pathol.* inflammation of the layers of an artery or of many arteries, usually caused by a severe hypersensitivity reaction, and characterized by nodules and hemorrhage along the involved vessels. Also called **periarteritis nodosa.** [< NL; see POLY-, ARTERITIS]

pol·y·ar·thri·tis (pol′ē är thrī′tis), *n. Pathol.* arthritis occurring in more than one joint. [POLY- + ARTHRITIS]

pol·y·ar·tic·u·lar (pol′ē är tik′yə lər), *adj. Anat.* pertaining to or affecting many joints. [POLY- + ARTICULAR]

pol·y·a·tom·ic (pol′ē ə tom′ik), *adj. Chem.* pertaining to a molecule containing more than two atoms. [POLY- + ATOMIC]

pol·y·ba·sic (pol′ē bā′sik), *adj. Chem.* (of an acid) having two or more atoms of replaceable hydrogen. [POLY- + BASIC] —**pol·y·ba·sic·i·ty** (pol′ē bə sis′i tē), *n.*

pol·y·ba·site (pol′ē bā′sīt, pə lib′ə sīt′), *n.* a blackish mineral, Ag_9SbS_6: a minor ore of silver. [< G *Polybasit.* See POLY-, BASE¹, -ITE¹]

Po·lyb·i·us (pə lib′ē əs), *n.* **1.** c205–c123 B.C., Greek historian. **2.** a crater in the fourth quadrant of the face of the moon: about 20 miles in diameter.

Pol·y·bo·tes (pol′ə bō′tēz), *n. Class. Myth.* one of the Gigantes.

Pol·y·bus (pol′ə bəs), *n. Class. Myth.* **1.** a Corinthian king who was the foster father of Oedipus. **2.** (in the *Iliad*) a son of Antenor and Theano who fought against the Greeks in the Trojan War.

pol·y·bu·tene (pol′ē byōō′tēn), *n. Chem.* polybutylene. [POLY- + BUTENE]

pol·y·bu·tyl·ene (pol′ē byōōt′ᵊlēn′), *n. Chem.* any of several polymers of butylene, used chiefly in the manufacture of lubricants and synthetic rubber. [POLY- + BUTYLENE]

Pol·y·carp (pol′ē kärp′), *n.* **Saint,** A.D. 69?–155, bishop of Smyrna and a Christian martyr.

pol·y·car·pel·lar·y (pol′ē kär′pə ler′ē), *adj. Bot.* consisting of two or more carpels. [POLY- + CARPELLARY]

pol·y·car·pic (pol′ē kär′pik), *adj. Bot.* **1.** producing fruit many times, as a perennial plant. **2.** having a gynoecium composed of two or more distinct ovaries. Also, **pol′y·car′pous.** [< NL *Polycarpic(us)*. See POLY-, -CARPIC] —**pol′y·car′py,** *n.*

Pol·y·cas·te (pol′ə kas′tē), *n. Class. Myth.* Perdix.

Pol·y·chae·ta (pol′ə kē′tə), *n.* the class comprising the polychaetes. [< NL, neut. pl. of *polychætus*. See POLYCHAETE]

pol·y·chaete (pol′ə kēt′), *n.* **1.** any annelid of the class *Polychaeta*, having unsegmented swimming appendages with many chaetae or bristles. —*adj.* **2.** Also, **pol′y·chae′tous.** belonging or pertaining to the *Polychaeta.* [< NL *Polychæta* < Gk *polychaítēs* having much hair. See POLY-, CHAETA]

pol·y·cha·sium (pol′ē kā′zhəm, -zhē əm, -zē əm), *n., pl.* **-sia** (-zhə, -zhē ə, -zē ə). *Bot.* a form of cymose inflorescence in which each axis produces more than two lateral axes. [< NL; see POLY-, DICHASIUM] —**pol′y·cha′si·al,** *adj.*

pol·y·chro·mat·ic (pol′ē krō mat′ik, -krə-), *adj.* having or exhibiting a variety of colors. Also, **pol·y·chro·mic** (pol′ē krō′mik). [POLY- + CHROMATIC] —**pol·y·chro·ma·tism** (pol′ē krō′mə tiz′əm), *n.*

pol·y·chrome (pol′ē krōm′), *adj.*, *v.*, **-chromed, -chrom·ing.** —*adj.* **1.** being of many or various colors. **2.** decorated or executed in many colors, as a statue, vase, mural, etc. —*v.t.* **3.** to paint in many or various colors. [earlier *polychrom* < G < Gk *polýchrōmos* many-colored. See POLY-, -CHROME]

pol·y·chro·my (pol′ē krō′mē), *n.* the art of employing many colors in decoration, as in painting or architecture. [POLYCHROME + -Y³] —**pol′y·chro′mous,** *adj.*

pol·y·clad (pol′ē klad′), *n.* any free-swimming, marine flatworm of the order *Polycladida,* having a broad, flat body and a many-branched gastrovascular cavity. [< NL *Polyclad(us)* genus name < Gk *polýklados* many-branched. See POLY-, CLADO-]

pol·y·clin·ic (pol′ē klin′ik), *n.* a clinic or a hospital dealing with various diseases. [< G *Poliklinik* (< Gk *pόli(s)* POLIS + *klīnikós;* see CLINIC); -y by assoc. with POLY-]

Pol·y·cli·tus (pol′ə klī′təs), *n.* fl. c450–c420 B.C., Greek sculptor. Also, **Pol′y·clei′tus, Pol·y·cle·tus** (pol′ə klē′təs).

pol·y·con·ic (pol′ē kon′ik), *adj.* pertaining to or utilizing two or more cones. [POLY- + CONIC]

polycon′ic projec′tion, *Cartog.* a conic projection in which the parallels are arcs of circles that are not concentric but are equally spaced along the central straight meridian, all other meridians being curves equally spaced along the parallels.

pol·y·cot·y·le·don (pol′ē kot′ᵊlēd′ᵊn), *n.* a plant having more than two cotyledons, as certain gymnosperms. [POLY- + COTYLEDON] —**pol′y·cot′y·le′don·ous,** *adj.*

Po·lyc·ra·tes (pə lik′rə tēz′), *n.* died 522? B.C., Greek tyrant of Samos.

pol·y·crys·tal·line (pol′ē kris′tᵊlēn′, -tᵊlin), *adj.* **1.** (of a rock or metal) composed of more than one crystal. **2.** having or consisting of crystals that are variously oriented. [POLY- + CRYSTALLINE]

pol·y·cy·the·mi·a (pol′ē sī thē′mē ə), *n. Pathol.* a condition of the blood characterized by an abnormally large number of red blood cells. Also, **pol′y·cy·thae′mi·a.** [< NL; see POLY-, -CYTE, -EMIA] —**pol′y·cy·the′mic, pol′y·cy·thae′mic,** *adj.*

pol·y·dac·tyl (pol′ē dak′tᵊl, -til), *adj.* **1.** having many or several digits. **2.** having more than the normal number of fingers or toes. —*n.* **3.** a polydactyl animal. [< Gk *polydáktyl(os).* See POLY-, DACTYL] —**pol′y·dac′tyl·ism,** *n.*

pol·y·dae·mon·ism (pol′ē dē′mə niz′əm), *n.* the belief in many evil spirits. Also, **pol′y·de′mon·ism.** [POLY- + DAEMON + -ISM] —**pol′y·dae′mon·ist, pol′y·de′mon·ist,** *n., adj.* —**pol′y·dae′mon·is′tic, pol′y·de′mon·is′tic,** *adj.*

Po·lyd·a·mas (pō lid′ə məs), *n.* (in the *Iliad*) a courageous warrior and adviser of Hector in the Trojan War.

Pol·y·dec·tes (pol′i dek′tēz), *n. Class. Myth.* a king of Seriphus who wanted to marry Danaë but who was turned to stone when her son Perseus showed him the head of Medusa.

Pol·y·deu·ces (pol′i dōō′sēz, -dyōō′-), *n.* Greek name of **Pollux.**

pol·y·dip·si·a (pol′ē dip′sē ə), *n. Med.* excessive thirst. [< NL < Gk *polydípsi(os)* very thirsty (*poly-* POLY- + *díps(a)* thirst + *-ios* adj. suffix) + *-ia* -IA]

pol·y·dis·perse (pol′ē di spûrs′), *adj. Physical Chem.* of or noting a sol which contains particles of different sizes. [POLY- + DISPERSE]

po·lyd·o·mous (pə lid′ə məs), *adj.* living in more than one nest, as certain ant colonies. Cf. **monodomous.** [POLY- + Gk *dóm(os)* house + -OUS]

pol·y·don·tia (pol′ē don′shə, -shē ə), *n. Dentistry.* the condition of having more than the normal number of teeth. [POLY- + -(O)DONT + -IA]

Pol·y·do·ra (pol′i dôr′ə, -dōr′ə), *n.* (in the *Iliad*) a daughter of Peleus.

Pol·y·do·rus (pol′i dôr′əs, -dōr′-), *n.* **1.** fl. 1st century B.C., Greek sculptor who, with Agesander and Athenodorus, carved the Laocoön group. **2.** (in the *Iliad*) the youngest son of Priam and Hecuba, given to Polymnestor for safekeeping during the Trojan War but murdered by him. **3.** *Class. Myth.* **a.** a son of Cadmus and Harmonia who became king of Thebes. **b.** a son of Hippomedon who was one of the Epigoni.

pol·y·em·bry·o·ny (pol′ē em′brē ə nē, -ō′nē, -em brī′ə nē), *n. Embryol.* the production of more than one embryo from one egg. [POLY- + Gk *émbryon* EMBRYO + -Y³]

pol·y·es·ter (pol′ē es′tər, pol′ē es′tər), *n. Chem.* a polymer in which the monomer units are linked together by the group -COO-, usually formed by polymerizing a polyhydric alcohol with a polybasic acid: used chiefly in the manufacture of resins, plastics, and textile fibers. [POLY- + ESTER]

pol·y·eth·nic (pol′ē eth′nik), *adj.* inhabited by or consisting of people of many ethnic backgrounds. [POLY- + ETHNIC]

pol·y·eth·yl·ene (pol′ē eth′ə lēn′), *n. Chem.* a plastic polymer of ethylene, $(-CH_2CH_2-)_n$, used chiefly for containers, electrical insulation, and packaging. Also called, *Brit.,* **polythene.** [POLY- + ETHYLENE]

polyeth′ylene gly′col, *Chem.* any of a series of polymers having the general formula $HOCH_2(CH_2OCH_2)_nCH_2OH$ or $H(OCH_2CH_2)_nOH$, having a molecular weight of from about 200 to 6,000, obtained by condensation of ethylene glycol or of ethylene oxide and water, used as an emulsifying agent and lubricant in ointments, creams, etc.

pol·y·foil (pol′ē foil′), *adj., n. Archit.* multifoil. [POLY- + FOIL²]

pol·y·func·tion·al (pol′ē fuŋgk′shə nᵊl), *adj. Chem.* containing more than one functional group. [POLY- + FUNCTIONAL]

po·lyg·a·la (pə lig′ə lə), *n.* any plant of the genus *Polygala,* comprising the milkworts. [< NL, genus name, special use of L *polygala* < Gk *polýgala,* pl. (taken as sing.) of *polýgalon* milkwort, lit., something very milky. See POLY-, GALAXY] —**pol·y·ga·la·ceous** (pol′ē gə lā′shəs, pə lig′ə-), *adj.*

po·lyg·a·mist (pə lig′ə mist), *n.* a person who practices or favors polygamy. [POLYGAM(Y) + -IST] —**po·lyg′a·mis′tic,** *adj.*

po·lyg·a·mous (pə lig′ə məs), *adj.* **1.** of, pertaining to, characterized by, or practicing polygamy. **2.** *Bot.* bearing both unisexual and hermaphrodite flowers on the same or on different plants. [< Gk *polýgamos.* See POLY-, -GAMOUS] —**po·lyg′a·mous·ly,** *adv.*

po·lyg·a·my (pə lig′ə mē), *n.* **1.** the practice or condition of having many or several spouses, esp. wives, at one time. Cf. **bigamy, monogamy** (def. 1). **2.** *Zool.* the habit of mating with more than one of the opposite sex. [< Gk *polygamía.* See POLY-, -GAMY]

pol·y·gen·e·sis (pol′ē jen′i sis), *n. Biol.* the descent of a species or race from more than one ancestral species. [POLY- + -GENESIS]

pol·y·ge·net·ic (pol′ē jə net′ik), *adj.* **1.** *Biol.* relating to or exhibiting polygenesis. **2.** having many or several different sources of origin. [POLY- + -GENETIC] —**pol′y·ge·net′i·cal·ly,** *adv.*

pol′y·gen′ic inher′itance (pol′ē jen′ik, pol′-), *Genetics.* the heredity of complex characters that are determined by a large number of genes, each one usually having a relatively small effect. [POLY- + -GENIC]

po·lyg·e·nism (pə lij′ə niz′əm), *n.* the theory that the human race has descended from two or more ancestral types. [POLY- + -GEN(Y) + -ISM] —**po·lyg′e·nist,** *n., adj.* —**po·lyg′e·nis′tic,** *adj.*

pol·y·glot (pol′ē glot′), *adj.* **1.** knowing many or several languages; multilingual. **2.** containing, composed of, or in several languages: *a polyglot Bible.* —*n.* **3.** a mixture or confusion of languages. **4.** a person who has a command of a number of languages, having either a speaking or reading knowledge or both. **5.** a book, esp. a Bible, containing the same text in several languages. [< ML *polyglōtt(us)* < Gk *polýglōttos* many-tongued. See POLY-, -GLOT]

Pol·yg·no·tus (pol′ig nō′təs), *n.* fl. c450 B.C., Greek painter.

pol·y·gon (pol′ē gon′), *n.* a figure, esp. a closed plane figure, having three or more, usually straight, sides. [< L *polygōn(um)* < Gk *polýgōnon,* neut. of *polýgōnos* many-angled. See POLY-, -GON] —**po·lyg·o·nal** (pə lig′ə nᵊl), *adj.* —**po·lyg′o·nal·ly,** *adv.*

pol·y·go·na·ceous (pol′ē gə nā′shəs), *adj.* belonging to the *Polygonaceae,* or buckwheat family of plants, comprising the knotgrass, jointweed, dock, etc. [POLYGON(UM) + -ACEOUS]

po·lyg·o·num (pə lig′ə nəm), *n.* any of several, chiefly herbaceous plants of the genus *Polygonum,* comprising the knotgrasses, bistorts, smartweeds, etc. [< NL < Gk *polýgonon* knotgrass, lit., something with many joints. See POLY-, KNEE]

pol·y·graph (pol′ē graf′, -gräf′), *n.* **1.** an apparatus for producing copies of a drawing or writing. **2.** a prolific or versatile author. **3.** an instrument for receiving and recording simultaneously tracings of variations in certain body activities. **4.** a lie detector. [< Gk *polýgraph(os)* writing much. See POLY-, -GRAPH] —**pol·y·graph·ic** (pol′ē graf′ik), *adj.* —**po·lyg·ra·phist** (pə lig′rə fist), **po·lyg′ra·pher,** *n.*

po·lyg·y·nist (pə lij′ə nist), *n.* one who practices or favors polygyny. [POLYGYN(Y) + -IST]

po·lyg·y·nous (pə lij′ə nəs), *adj.* **1.** of, pertaining to, characterized by, or practicing polygyny. **2.** *Bot.* having many pistils or styles. [POLYGYN(Y) + -OUS]

po·lyg·y·ny (pə lij′ə nē), *n.* **1.** the practice or condition of having more than one wife at one time. Cf. **monogyny.** **2.** (of a male animal) the condition of having two or more mates at a time. **3.** *Bot.* the state or condition of having many pistils or styles. [< Gk *polygýn(aios)* having many wives (see POLY-, GYN-) + -Y³]

pol·y·he·dral (pol′ē hē′drəl), *adj.* of, pertaining to, or having the shape of a polyhedron. [< Gk *polýedr(os)* many-based (see POLYHEDRON) + -AL¹]

pol·y·he·dron (pol′ē hē′drən), *n., pl.* **-drons, -dra** (-drə). a solid figure having many faces. [< Gk *polýedron,* neut. of *polýedros* having many bases. See POLY-, -HEDRON]

pol·y·his·tor (pol′ē his′tər), *n.* a person of great and varied learning. Also, **pol·y·his·tor·i·an** (pol′ē hi stôr′ē ən, -stōr′-). [< L < Gk *polyístōr* very learned. See POLY-, HISTORY] —**pol·y·his·tor·ic** (pol′ē hi stôr′ik, -stor′-), *adj.* —**pol′y·his′to·ry,** *n.*

pol·y·hy·dric (pol′ē hī′drik), *adj. Chem.* (esp. of alcohols and phenols) polyhydroxy. [POLY- + HYDRIC¹]

pol·y·hy·drox·y (pol′ē hī drok′sē), *adj. Chem.* containing two or more hydroxyl groups. [POLY- + HYDROXY]

Pol·y·hym·ni·a (pol′ə him′nē ə), *n. Class. Myth.* the Muse of sacred music and dance. Also, **Polymnia.** [< L, alter. of Gk *Polýmnia.* See POLY-, HYMN, -IA]

Pol·y·i·dus (pol′ē ī′dəs), *n. Class. Myth.* a Corinthian seer who revived the dead Glaucus.

pol·y·im·ide (pol′ē im′īd, -id), *n.* any of a class of plastics resistant to high temperatures, wear, radiation, and many chemicals. [POLY- + -IMIDE]

pol·y·i·so·bu·tyl·ene (pol′ē ī′sə byōōt′ᵊlēn′, -ᵊlin), *n. Chem.* a polymer of isobutylene, used chiefly in the manufacture of synthetic rubber. Also, **pol·y·i·so·bu·tene** (pol′ē ī′sə byōō′tēn). [POLY- + ISOBUTYLENE]

Pol·y·mas·tus (pol′ə mas′təs), *n. Class. Myth.* an epithet of Artemis, meaning "many-breasted," in reference to a many-breasted image of her at Ephesus.

Pol·y·me·la (pol′ə mē′lə), *n. Class. Myth.* **1.** Also, **Pol·y·me·le** (pol′ə mē′lē). a daughter of Phylas who bore Eudorus to Hermes. **2.** a daughter of Actor who killed herself when she was erroneously informed that her husband, Peleus, was leaving her.

Pol·y·me·lus (pol′ə mē′ləs), *n.* (in the *Iliad*) a Lycian ally of the Trojans, killed by Patroclus.

pol·y·mer (pol′ə mər), *n. Chem.* **1.** a compound of high molecular weight derived either by the addition of many smaller molecules, as polyethylene, or by the condensation of many smaller molecules with the elimination of water, alcohol, or the like, as nylon. **2.** a compound formed from two or more polymeric compounds. **3.** a product of polymerization. [< Gk *polymer(ḗs)* having many parts. See POLY-, -MER]

pol·y·mer·ic (pol′ə mer′ik), *adj. Chem.* (of compounds) having the same elements combined in the same proportions by weight, recently extended to include substances of high molecular weight. [POLYMER + -IC]

po·lym·er·i·sa·tion (pə lim′ər i zā′shən, pol′ə mər-), *n. Chiefly Brit.* polymerization.

pol·y·mer·ise (pol′ə mə rīz′, pə lim′ə-), *v.t., v.i.,* **-ised, -is·ing.** *Chiefly Brit.* polymerize.

po·lym·er·ism (pə lim′ə riz′əm, pol′ə mə-), *n.* **1.** *Chem.* a polymeric state. **2.** *Biol., Bot.* a polymerous state. [POLYMER + -ISM]

po·lym·er·i·za·tion (pə lim′ər i zā′shən, pol′ə mər-), *n. Chem.* **1.** the act or process of forming a polymer or polymeric compound. **2.** the combination of many like or unlike molecules to form a more complex product of higher molecular weight, with elimination of water, alcohol, or the like **(condensation polymerization),** or without such elimination **(addition polymerization).** **3.** the conversion of one compound into another by such a process. [POLYMERIZE + -ATION]

po·lym·er·ize (pə lim′ə rīz′, pol′ə mə rīz′), *v.,* **-ized, -iz·ing.** *Chem.* —*v.t.* **1.** to subject to polymerization. —*v.i.* **2.** to undergo polymerization. Also, *esp. Brit.,* **polymerise.** [POLYMER + -IZE]

po·lym·er·ous (pə lim′ər əs), *adj.* **1.** *Biol.* composed of many parts. **2.** *Bot.* having numerous members in each whorl. [POLYMER + -OUS]

Pol·ym·nes·tor (pol′əm nes′tər), *n. Class. Myth.* a Thracian king who murdered Polydorus and stole the treasure that Priam had given him to guard during the Trojan War.

Po·lym·ni·a (pə lim′nē ə), *n.* Polyhymnia.

pol·y·morph (pol′ē môrf′), *n.* **1.** *Zool., Bot.* a polymorphous organism or substance. **2.** *Crystall.* any of the forms assumed by a polymorphous substance. [back formation from POLYMORPHOUS]

pol·y·mor·phism (pol′ē môr′fiz əm), *n.* **1.** state or condition of being polymorphous. **2.** *Crystall.* crystallization into two or more chemically identical but crystallographically distinct forms. **3.** *Zool., Bot.* existence of an animal or plant in several form or color varieties. [POLYMORPH + -ISM] —**pol′y·mor·phis′tic,** *adj.*

pol·y·mor·pho·nu·cle·ar (pol′ē môr′fə nōō′klē ər, -nyōō′-), *adj.* (of a leukocyte) having a lobulate nucleus. [POLY- + -MORPHO(US) + NUCLEAR]

pol·y·mor·phous (pol′ē môr′fəs), *adj.* having, assuming, or passing through many or various forms, stages, or the like. Also, **pol′y·mor′phic.** [< Gk *polýmorphos* multiform. See POLY-, -MORPHOUS]

Pol·y·ne·sia (pol′ə nē′zhə, -shə), *n.* one of the three principal divisions of Oceania, comprising those island groups in the Pacific lying E of Melanesia and Micronesia and extending from the Hawaiian Islands S to New Zealand.

Pol·y·ne·sian (pol′ə nē′zhən, -shən), *adj.* **1.** of or pertaining to Polynesia, its inhabitants, or their languages. —*n.* **2.** a member of any of a number of brown-skinned peoples, variously classified as to race, of distinctive customs, speaking closely related Austronesian languages, who inhabit Polynesia. **3.** the easternmost group of Malayo-Polynesian languages, including Maori, Tahitian, Samoan, Hawaiian, and the language of Easter Island. [POLYNESI(A) + -AN]

pol·y·neu·ri·tis (pol′ē nōō rī′tis, -nyōō-), *n. Pathol.* inflammation of several nerves at the same time; multiple neuritis. [POLY- + NEURITIS] —**pol·y·neu·rit·ic** (pol′ē nōō rit′ik, -nyōō-), *adj.*

Pol·y·ni·ces (pol′ə nī′sēz), *n. Class. Myth.* a son of Oedipus and Jocasta and brother of Eteocles and Antigone, on whose behalf the Seven against Thebes were organized. He and Eteocles killed each other, and his body was left exposed by their uncle, Creon, until it was buried by Antigone. Also, **Pol′y·nei′ces.**

pol·y·no·mi·al (pol′ē nō′mē əl), *adj.* **1.** consisting of or characterized by many or several names or terms. —*n.* **2.** a polynomial name or term. **3.** *Algebra.* an expression consisting of two or more terms, as $2x^3 + 7x^2 + 4x + 2$. **4.** *Zool., Bot.* a species name containing more than two terms. [POLY- + (BI)NOMIAL]

pol′yno′mial ring′, *Math.* the set of all polynomials in an indeterminate variable with coefficients that are elements of a given ring.

pol·y·nu·cle·ar (pol′ē nōō′klē ər, -nyōō′-), *adj.* having many nuclei. Also, **pol·y·nu·cle·ate** (pol′ē nōō′klē it, -āt′, -nyōō′-). [POLY- + NUCLEAR]

pol·yp (pol′ip), *n.* **1.** *Zool.* **a.** a sedentary type of animal form characterized by a more or less fixed base, columnar body, and free end with mouth and tentacles, esp. as applied to coelenterates. **b.** an individual zooid of a compound or colonial organism. **2.** *Pathol.* a projecting growth from a mucous surface, as of the nose, being either a tumor or a hypertrophy of the mucous membrane. [ME *polip,* short for *polipus* nasal tumor (later, also cephalopod, now obs.) < ML, L *pōlypus,* in same senses. See POLYPUS] —**pol′yp·ous,** *adj.*

pol·y·par·y (pol′ə per′ē), *n., pl.* **-par·ies.** the common supporting structure of a colony of polyps, as corals. [< NL *polypāri(um).* See POLYP, -ARY] —**pol·y·par·i·an** (pol′ə pâr′ē ən), *adj.*

Pol·y·pe·mon (pol′ə pē′mon), *n. Class. Myth.* Procrustes.

pol·y·pep·tide (pol′ē pep′tīd), *n. Biochem.* one of a group of amides formed from amino acids, the simplest having the structure $H_2NCH_2CONHCH_2COOH$, with molecular weights up to about 10,000. [POLY- + PEPTIDE]

pol·y·pet·al·ous (pol′ē pet′ᵊləs), *adj. Bot.* having numerous or separate petals. [POLY- + PETALOUS] —**pol′y·pet′al·y,** *n.*

pol·y·pha·gi·a (pol′ē fā′jē ə, -jə), *n.* **1.** *Pathol.* excessive desire to eat. **2.** *Zool.* the habit of subsisting on many different kinds of food. [< NL < Gk; see POLY-, -PHAGY] —**pol′y·pha′gi·an,** *n., adj.* —**po·lyph·a·gist** (pə lif′ə jist), *n.* —**po·lyph·a·gous** (pə lif′ə gəs), **pol·y·phag·ic** (pol′ē faj′ik), *adj.*

pol·y·phase (pol′ē fāz′), *adj. Elect.* **1.** having more than one phase. **2.** of or pertaining to a set of alternating currents that have the same frequency but different phases and which enter a specified region at more than two points. [POLY- + PHASE]

Pol·y·phe·mus (pol′ə fē′məs), *n. Class. Myth.* **1.** a Cyclops who murdered Acis in jealousy over Galatea, and who was finally blinded by Odysseus. **2.** a son of Elatus who joined the Argonauts.

Pol′yphe′mus moth′, a large, yellowish-brown silkworm moth, *Antheraea polyphemus,* having a prominent eyespot on each hind wing.

Pol·y·phi·des (pol′ə fī′dēz), *n. Class. Myth.* **1.** a seer upon whom Apollo bestowed special gifts. **2.** a king of Sicyon who protected Agamemnon and Menelaus after the murder of Atreus.

pol·y·phone (pol′ē fōn′), *n. Phonet.* a polyphonic letter or symbol. [< Gk *polýphōn(os).* See POLY-, -PHONE]

pol·y·phon·ic (pol′ē fon′ik), *adj.* **1.** consisting of many voices or sounds. **2.** *Music.* **a.** having two or more voices or parts, each with an independent melody, but all harmonizing; contrapuntal (opposed to *homophonic*). **b.** pertaining to music of this kind. **c.** capable of producing more than one tone at a time, as an organ or a harp. **3.** *Phonet.* having more than one phonetic value, as the letter *s,* which is voiced (z) in *nose* and unvoiced (s) in *salt.* [POLYPHONE + -IC] —**pol′y·phon′i·cal·ly,** *adv.*

pol′yphon′ic prose′, prose characterized by the use of poetic devices, as alliteration, assonance, rhyme, etc., and esp. by an emphasis on rhythm not strictly metered.

Pol·y·phon·tes (pol′ə fon′tēz), *n. Class. Myth.* according to some accounts, the brother and murderer of Cresphontes.

po·lyph·o·ny (pə lif′ə nē), *n.* **1.** *Music.* polyphonic composition; counterpoint. **2.** *Phonet.* representation of different sounds by the same letter or symbol. [< Gk *polyphōnía* variety of tones or speech. See POLY-, -PHONY] —**po·lyph′o·nous,** *adj.* —**po·lyph′o·nous·ly,** *adv.*

pol·y·phy·let·ic (pol′ē fī let′ik), *adj.* developed from more than one ancestral type, as a group of animals. [POLY- + PHYLETIC] —**pol′y·phy·let′i·cal·ly,** *adv.*

po·lyp·i·dom (pə lip′i dəm), *n. Rare.* polypary. [< L *pōlypi-* (comb. form of *pōlypus* POLYP) + L *dom(us)* or Gk *dôm(os)* house]

pol·y·ploid (pol′ē ploid′), *adj., n. Biol.* —*adj.* **1.** having a chromosome number that is more than double the basic or haploid number. —*n.* **2.** a polyploid cell or organism. [POLY- + -PLOID] —**pol′y·ploi′dic,** *adj.* —**pol′y·ploi′dy,** *n.*

pol·yp·ne·a (pol′ip nē′ə), *n. Med.* rapid breathing; panting. Also, **pol′yp·noe′a.** [< NL, equiv. to *poly-* POLY- + *-pnea* (< Gk *pnein* to breathe)]

pol·y·po·dy (pol′ē pō′dē), *n., pl.* **-dies.** any fern of the genus *Polypodium,* as *P. vulgare,* having creeping rootstocks, deeply pinnatifid evergreen fronds, and round, naked sori. [< L *polypodi(um)* < Gk *polypódion* kind of fern, lit., something with many little feet. See POLY-, -PODIUM]

Pol·y·po·e·tes (pol′ə pō ē′tēz), *n.* **1.** *Class. Myth.* a son of Pirithous and Hippodamia, and a leader of the Greeks in the Trojan War. **2.** a son of Odysseus and Callidice. **3.** a son of Apollo and Phthia.

pol·yp·oid (pol′ə poid′), *adj. Pathol.* resembling a polyp. [POLYP + -OID]

Pol·y·por·this (pol′ə pôr′this), *n. Class. Myth.* a son of Penelope and Odysseus, born after the return of Odysseus to Ithaca.

pol·y·pro·pyl·ene (pol′ē prō′pə lēn′), *n. Chem.* a plastic polymer of propylene, $[-CH(CH_3)CH_2-]_n$, similar to polyethylene, used chiefly for containers, electrical insulation, and packaging. [POLY- + PROPYLENE]

pol·y·prot·ic (pol′ē prot′ik), *adj. Chem.* (of an acid) having two or more transferable protons. [POLY- + PROT(ON) + -IC]

pol·yp·tych (pol′ip tik), *n.* a work of art composed of several connected panels. Cf. **diptych, pentaptych, triptych.** [special use of LL *polyptychum* < Gk *polýptychon* a register, roll, n. use of neut. of *polýptychos* having many folds. See POLY-, DIPTYCH, TRIPTYCH]

pol·y·pus (pol′ə pəs), *n., pl.* **-pi** (-pī′). *Pathol.* a polyp. [< L: POLYP < Gk (Doric) *pōlypos* many-footed, equiv. to *polýpous* (Attic). See POLY-, FOOT]

pol·y·rhythm (pol′ē rith′əm), *n. Music.* the simultaneous occurrence of sharply contrasting rhythms within a composition. [POLY- + RHYTHM] —**pol′y·rhyth′mic,** *adj.* —**pol′y·rhyth′mi·cal·ly,** *adv.*

pol·y·sac·cha·ride (pol′ē sak′ə rīd′, -rid), *n. Chem.* a carbohydrate, as starch, inulin, cellulose, etc., containing more than three monosaccharide units per molecule, the units being attached to each other in the manner of acetals, and therefore capable of hydrolysis by acids or enzymes to monosaccharides. Also, **pol·y·sac·cha·rose** (pol′ē sak′ə rōs′, -rōz′). [POLY- + SACCHARIDE]

pol·y·se·my (pol′ē sē′mē), *n.* diversity of meanings. [< NL *polysēmia,* equiv. to LL *polysēm(us)* (< Gk *polýsēmos* with many significations, equiv. to *poly-* POLY- + *sêm(a)* sign + *-os* adj suffix) + *-ia* -Y³] —**pol′y·se′mous,** *adj.*

pol·y·sep·al·ous (pol′ē sep′ə ləs), *adj. Bot.* having the sepals separate or unconnected. [POLY- + -SEPALOUS]

pol·y·spast (pol′ē spast′), *n.* an ancient hoist or hauling device having a number of blocks. [< L *polyspast(on)* < Gk *polýspaston,* neut. of *polýspastos* drawn by many cords, equiv. to *poly-* POLY- + *-spastos;* see SPASM]

pol·y·sper·mi·a (pol′ē spûr′mē ə), *n. Med.* the secretion of an excessive amount of semen. [< Gk *polyspermía* abundance of seed. See POLY-, SPERM, -IA]

pol·y·sper·my (pol′ē spûr′mē), *n.* the fertilization of an ovum by several spermatozoa. [see POLYSPERMIA] —**pol·y·sper·mic** (pol′ē spûr′mik), *adj.*

pol·y·style (pol′ē stīl′), *adj.* having many columns. [< Gk *polýstyl(os)* with many columns. See POLY-, STYLITE]

pol·y·sty·rene (pol′ē stī′rēn), *n. Chem.* a clear plastic or stiff foam, $[-CH(C_6H_5)CH_2-]_n$, a polymer of styrene, used chiefly as an insulator in refrigerators and air conditioners. [POLY- + STYRENE]

pol·y·sul·fide (pol′ē sul′fīd, -fid), *n. Chem.* a sulfide containing more than the usual quantity of sulfur. [POLY- + SULFIDE]

pol·y·sul·fo·nate (pol′ē sul′fə nāt′), *n. Chem.* a sulfonated polymer. Also, **pol′y·sul′pho·nate′.** [POLY- + SULFONATE]

pol·y·sus·pen·soid (pol′ē sə spen′soid), *n. Physical Chem.* a suspensoid in which the solid particles are polydisperse. [POLY- + SUSPENSOID]

pol·y·syl·lab·ic (pol′ē si lab′ik), *adj.* **1.** consisting of three, four, or more syllables, as a word. **2.** characterized by such words, as a language, piece of writing, etc. Also, **pol′y·syl·lab′i·cal.** [< ML *polysyllab(us)* (< Gk *polysýllabos* of many syllables) + -IC. See POLY-, SYLLABIC] —**pol′y·syl·lab′i·cal·ly,** *adv.*

pol·y·syl·la·ble (pol′ē sil′ə bəl, pol′ē sil′-), *n.* a polysyllabic word. [POLY- + SYLLABLE]

pol·y·syl·lo·gism (pol′ē sil′ə jiz′əm), *n. Logic.* an argument made up of a chain of syllogisms, the conclusion of each being a premise of the one following, until the last one. [POLY- + SYLLOGISM] —**pol′y·syl′lo·gis′tic,** *adj.*

pol·y·syn·de·ton (pol′ē sin′di ton′), *n. Rhet.* the use of a number of conjunctions in close succession. Cf. **asyndeton.** [< NL; see POLY-, ASYNDETON]

pol·y·syn·the·sism (pol′i sin′thi siz′əm), *n.* **1.** the synthesis of various elements. **2.** the combining of several words of a sentence into one word. [POLY- + SYNTHESIS) + -ISM]

pol·y·syn·thet·ic (pol′ē sin thet′ik), *adj.* **1.** (of a language) characterized by a prevalence of relatively long words containing a large number of affixes to express syntactic relationships and meanings. Many American Indian languages are polysynthetic. Cf. **analytic** (def. 2), **synthetic** (def. 3). **2.** of or pertaining to polysynthesism. Also, **pol′y·syn·thet′i·cal.** [< LGk *polysýnthet(os)* much compounded. See POLY-, SYNTHETIC]

pol·y·tech·nic (pol′ē tek′nik), *adj.* **1.** of, pertaining to, or offering instruction in industrial arts or scientific or technical subjects: *a polytechnic institute.* —*n.* **2.** a school or other institution in which instruction in technical subjects is given. [POLY- + TECHNIC, modeled on F *polytechnique*]

Pol·y·tech·nus (pol′i tek′nəs), *n. Class. Myth.* the husband of Aëdon who was punished for boasting that his marital happiness excelled that of Zeus and Hera.

pol·y·tet·ra·flu·o·ro·eth·y·lene (pol′ē te′trə flo͞o′-ə rō eth′ə lēn′, -flo͝or′ō-, -flôr′-, -flōr′-), *n. Chem.* any polymer, plastic, or resin having the formula $(C_2F_4)_n$, prepared from tetrafluoroethylene, noted for its slippery, nonsticking properties, and used in the manufacture of gaskets, electrical insulation, tubing, candy molds, container linings, frying-pan coatings, etc. [POLY- + TETRAFLUOROETHYLENE]

pol·y·the·ism (pol′ē thē iz′əm, pol′ē thē′iz əm), *n.* the doctrine of or belief in more than one god or in many gods. [POLY- + THEISM; cf. F *polythéisme*] —**pol′y·the′ist,** *n.* —**pol′y·the·is′tic, pol′y·the·is′ti·cal,** *adj.* —**pol′y·the·is′ti·cal·ly,** *adv.*

pol·y·thene (pol′ə thēn′), *n. Chem. Brit.* polyethylene.

po·lyt·o·my (pə lit′ə mē), *n., pl.* **-mies. 1.** division into more than three parts. **2.** state or condition of being so divided. [POLY- + -TOMY] —**po·lyt′o·mous,** *adj.*

pol·y·ton·al (pol′ē tōn′əl), *adj. Music.* marked by or using polytonality. [POLY- + TONAL] —**pol′y·ton′al·ly,** *adv.*

pol·y·to·nal·i·ty (pol′ē tō nal′i tē), *n. Music.* the use of more than one key at the same time. Also, **pol·y·ton·al·ism** (pol′ē tōn′əliz′əm). [POLY- + TONALITY] —**pol·y·ton·al·ist** (pol′ē tōn′əlist), *n.*

pol·y·tri·glyph (pol′ē trī′glif′), *n.* (in classical architecture) an intercolumniation of at least four triglyphs. [POLY- + TRIGLYPH]

pol·y·troph·ic (pol′ē trof′ik), *adj.* (of certain bacteria) deriving nourishment from many organic substances. [POLY- + TROPHIC]

pol·y·typ·ic (pol′ē tip′ik), *adj.* having or involving many or several types. Also, **pol′y·typ′i·cal.** [POLY- + TYPIC]

pol·y·un·sat·u·rate (pol′ē un sach′ər it, -ə rāt′), *n.* a polyunsaturated substance. [back formation from POLYUNSATURATED]

pol·y·un·sat·u·rat·ed (pol′ē un sach′ə rā′tid), *adj.* of or noting a class of fats of animal or vegetable origin, esp. plant oils, whose molecules consist of carbon chains with many double bonds unsaturated by hydrogen atoms (associated with a low cholesterol content of the blood). [POLY- + UNSATURATED]

pol·y·u·re·thane (pol′ē yo͝or′ə thān′), *n. Chem.* a light polymer whose foamed texture results from carbon dioxide's evolving during its production and becoming trapped and forming pores: used for padding and insulation in furniture, clothing, and packaging, and in the manufacture of resins for adhesives and fillers. Also, **pol·y·u·re·than** (pol′ē yo͝or′ə than′). [POLY- + URETHANE]

pol·y·u·ri·a (pol′ē yo͝or′ē ə), *n. Pathol.* the passing of an excessive quantity of urine, as in diabetes, in certain nervous diseases, etc. [< NL; see POLY, -URIA] —**pol′y·u′ric,** *adj.*

pol·y·va·lent (pol′ē vā′lənt, pə liv′ə lənt), *adj.* **1.** *Chem.* having more than one valence. **2.** *Bacteriol.* (of an immune serum) containing several antibodies, each capable of reacting with a specific antigen. [POLY- + -VALENT] —**pol′y·va′lence,** *n.*

pol·y·vi·nyl (pol′ē vī′nil, -vīn′əl, -vin′il, -əl), *adj. Chem.* pertaining to or derived from a vinyl polymer. [POLY- + VINYL]

pol′yvi′nyl ac′etal, *Chem.* **1.** any of the class of thermoplastic resins derived by the condensation of an aldehyde with polyvinyl alcohol. **2.** the slightly yellow, water-insoluble resin produced from partially hydrolyzed polyvinyl acetate and formaldehyde: used chiefly in the manufacture of lacquers, photographic film, and adhesives.

pol′yvi′nyl ac′etate, *Chem.* a colorless, odorless, nontoxic, transparent, thermoplastic, water-insoluble resin, $[-(H_2C-CHOOCCH_3)-]_n$, used as an adhesive in certain paints and as an intermediate in the synthesis of polyvinyl acetal and polyvinyl alcohol.

pol′yvi′nyl al′cohol, *Chem.* a colorless, water-soluble, thermoplastic resin, $(-CH_2CHOH-)_n$, derived by the hydrolysis of polyvinyl acetate: used chiefly as an adhesive and as a size in the manufacture of textiles, paper, and plastics.

pol′yvi′nyl bu′tyral, *Chem.* a white, water-insoluble, polyvinyl acetal made with butyraldehyde, used chiefly as an interlayer in the manufacture of safety glass.

pol′yvi′nyl chlo′ride, *Chem.* a white, water-insoluble, thermoplastic resin, $(-CH_2CHCl-)_n$, derived by the polymerization of vinyl chloride: used chiefly as a coating for phonograph records, in the manufacture of floor coverings, and as an insulator for metal pipes and wire.

pol′yvi′nyl for′mal, *Chem.* a colorless, water-insoluble, polyvinyl acetal produced from partially hydrolyzed polyvinyl acetate and formaldehyde, used chiefly in the manufacture of lacquers.

pol·y·vi·nyl·i·dene (pol′ē vī nil′i dēn′), *adj. Chem.* pertaining to or derived from a polymer of a vinylidene compound. [POLYVINYL + -ID³ + -ENE]

pol′yvinyl′idene chlo′ride, *Chem.* a polymer of vinylidene chloride, used chiefly in the manufacture of saran.

pol′yvinyl′idene res′in, *Chem.* any of the class of thermoplastic resins derived by the polymerization or copolymerization of a polyvinylidene compound, used similarly to the polyvinyl resins. Also called **vinylidene resin.**

pol·y·vi·nyl·pyr·rol·i·done (pol′ē vī′nil pi rōl′i-dōn′, -rol′i-, -vīn′əl-, -vin′il-, -əl-), *n. Chem.* a white, amorphous, water-insoluble powder, $[-CH_2CH(NC_4H_6O)-]_n$, used chiefly as a vehicle in the manufacture of pharmaceuticals. Also called **PVP** [POLYVINYL + PYRROLIDONE]

pol′yvi′nyl res′in, *Chem.* any of the class of thermoplastic resins derived by the polymerization or copolymerization of a vinyl compound: used chiefly as adhesives, sizes, and coatings. Also called **vinyl resin.**

pol·y·vol·tine (pol′ē vōl′tēn, -tən), *adj.* multivoltine. [POLY- + -*voltine* < F *voltin,* equiv. to It *volt(a)* turn (cf. L *volvere* to turn) + F *-in* -INE¹]

Po·lyx·e·na (pə lik′sə nə), *n. Class. Myth.* a daughter of Priam and Hecuba, loved by Achilles and sacrificed to appease his ghost.

Po·lyx·e·nus (pə lik′sə nəs), *n. Class. Myth.* a grandson of Augeas who was an ally of the Greek forces in the Trojan War.

Po·lyx·o (pə lik′sō), *n. Class. Myth.* an old nurse who advised Hypsipyle to welcome the Argonauts and have them father sons by the Lemnian women, who had killed all the men on their island.

pol·y·zo·an (pol′ē zō′ən), *adj., n.* bryozoan. [< NL *Polyzo(a)* name of the class (see POLY-, -ZOA) + -AN]

pol·y·zo·ar·i·um (pol′ē zō âr′ē əm), *n., pl.* **-ar·i·a** (-âr′ē ə). *Zool.* a bryozoan colony, or its supporting skeleton. [< NL; see POLY-, -ZOA, -ARY] —**pol′y·zo·ar′i·al,** *adj.*

pol·y·zo·ic (pol′ē zō′ik), *adj.* **1.** (of a bryozoan colony) composed of many zooids. **2.** (of a spore) producing many sporozoites. **3.** (of a habitat) containing many animals or many different kinds of animals. [POLY- + -ZO(A) + -IC]

pom·ace (pum′is), *n.* **1.** the pulpy residue from apples or similar fruit after crushing and pressing, as in cider making. **2.** any crushed or ground, pulpy substance. [? < ML *pōmāc(ium)* cider, n. use of L **pōmāceum,* neut. of **pōmāceus* of fruit. See POMACEOUS]

po·ma·ceous (pō mā′shəs), *adj.* of, pertaining to, or of the nature of pomes. [< NL *pōmāceus.* See POME, -ACEOUS]

po·made (pə mād′, -mäd′, pō-), *n., v.,* **-mad·ed, -mad·ing.** —*n.* **1.** a scented ointment, esp. one used for the scalp or for dressing the hair. —*v.t.* **2.** to dress with pomade; apply pomade to. [earlier *pommade* < F < It *pomata* (so called because apples were orig. an ingredient), equiv. to *pom(a)* apple (< L, pl. of *pōmum* fruit) + *-ata* -ADE¹. See POMATUM]

po·man·der (pō′man dər, pō man′dər), *n.* **1.** a mixture of aromatic substances, often in the form of a ball, formerly carried on the person as a supposed guard against infection but now placed in closets, dressers, etc. **2.** the ball, box, or other case in which it was formerly carried. [late ME *pomandre,* dissimilated var. of **pomambre,* ML *pōmum ambrē* (i.e., *ambrae*), lit., pome of amber. See POME, AMBER]

po·ma·tum (pō mā′təm, -mä′-, pə-), *n.* pomade. [< NL, Latinization of POMADE; neut. (for fem.) to agree with L *pōmum* fruit]

pome (pōm), *n. Bot.* the characteristic fruit of the apple family, as an apple, pear, quince, etc., in which the edible flesh arises from the greatly swollen receptacle and not from the carpels. [late ME < MF << L *pōma,* pl. (taken as sing.) of *pōmum* fruit] —**pome′like′,** *adj.*

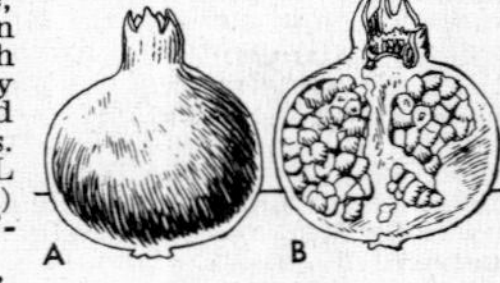

A, Pomegranate
B, Vertical section

pome·gran·ate (pom′gran′it, pom′ə-, pum′-; pom′ə gran′it, pəm-gran′-), *n.* **1.** a chambered, many-seeded, globose fruit, having a tough, usually red rind and surmounted by a crown of calyx lobes, the edible portion consisting of pleasantly acid flesh developed from the outer seed coat. **2.** the shrub or small tree, *Punica Granatum,* which bears it, native to southwestern Asia but widely cultivated in warm regions. [ME *poumgarnet,* etc. < MF *pome garnete,* etc., lit., seeded apple. See POME, GRENADE]

pom·el (pum′əl, pom′-), *n. Archit.* pommel (def. 3).

pom·e·lo (pom′ə lō′), *n., pl.* **-los. 1.** grapefruit (def. 1). **2.** shaddock (def. 1). [pseudo-Spanish alter. of *pamplemoose* < D *pompelmoes* shaddock, said to be a compound of *pomp(oen)* pumpkin + Pg *limoes,* pl. of *limão* lemon]

Pom·er·a·ni·a (pom′ə-rā′nē ə, -rān′yə), *n.* a former province of NE Germany, now mostly in NW Poland. German, **Pommern.**

Pom·er·a·ni·an (pom′ə rā′nē ən, -rān′yən), *adj.* **1.** of, pertaining to, or characteristic of Pomerania. —*n.* **2.** one of a breed of small dogs having long, straight hair, erect ears, and a tail carried over the back. 3. a native or inhabitant of Pomerania. [POMERANI(A) + -AN]

Pomeranian (14 in. high at shoulder)

Pom·er·oy (pom′ə roi′, pom′roi), *n.* a town in SE Ohio. 3345 (1960).

po·mey (pō′mē), *n.* *Heraldry.* a roundel vert. [?]

pom·fret (pom′frit), *n., pl.* (*esp. collectively*) **-fret,** (*esp. referring to two or more kinds or species*) **-frets.** **1.** any of several scombroid fishes of the family *Bramidae*, found in the North Atlantic and Pacific. **2.** any of several East Indian stromateid fishes, esp. *Stromateoides argenteus*, valued as food. [earlier *pamplee, pamflet, pomfret;* cf. F *pample,* Pg *pampo*]

po·mi·cul·ture (pō′mə kul′chər), *n.* the cultivation or growing of fruit. [< L *pōmi-* (comb. form of *pōmum* fruit) + CULTURE] —**po′mi·cul′tur·ist,** *n.*

po·mif·er·ous (pō mif′ər əs), *adj.* *Bot.* bearing pomes or pomelike fruits. [< L *pōmifer* fruit-bearing (see POME, -I-, -FER) + -OUS]

Pom·mard (pō märd′; *Fr.* pô MAR′), *n.* a dry, red wine from the Pommard parish in Burgundy.

pomme blanche (*Fr.* pôm blänsh′), *pl.* **pommes blanches** (*Fr.* pôm blänsh′). breadroot. [< F: lit., white apple]

pom·mée (po mā′, pə-, pō-; *Fr.* pô mā′), *adj.* *Heraldry.* (of a cross) having arms with knoblike ends: *a cross pommée.* [< F: lit., balled, equiv. to *pomme* apple, ball (see POME) + *-ée* -EE]

pom·mel (pum′əl, pom′əl), *n., v.,* **-meled, -mel·ing** or (*esp. Brit.*) **-melled, -mel·ling.** —*n.* **1.** a knob, as on the hilt of a sword. **2.** the protuberant part at the front and top of a saddle. See illus. under **saddle. 3.** Also, **pomel.** *Archit.* a spherical ornament or finial. **4.** *Gymnastics.* either of the two curved handles on the top surface of a side horse. —*v.t.* **5.** to beat or strike with or as if with the fists or a pommel. Also, **pummel.** [ME *pomel* < MF (equiv. to ML *pomellus* ball, knob) < VL or LL **pōmellum,* dim. of L *pōmum* fruit]

Pom·mern (pôm′ərn), *n.* German name of **Pomerania.**

pom·my (pom′ē), *n., pl.* **-mies.** *Australian Slang.* **1.** an English immigrant. **2.** an Englishman. [?]

Po·mo (pō′mō), *n., pl.* **-mos,** (*esp. collectively*) **-mo. 1.** a member of an American Indian people of northern California. **2.** any of several related languages of the Pomo Indians.

po·mol·o·gy (pō mol′ə jē), *n.* the science that deals with fruits and fruit growing. [< NL *pōmologia.* See POME, -O-, -LOGY] —**po·mo·log·i·cal** (pō′mə loj′i kəl), *adj.* —**po′mo·log′i·cal·ly,** *adv.* —**po·mol′o·gist,** *n.*

Po·mo·na (pə mō′nə), *n.* **1.** the ancient Roman goddess of fruit trees. **2.** a city in SW California, E of Los Angeles. 67,157 (1960). **3.** Also called **Mainland.** the largest of the Orkney Islands, N of Scotland. 13,352 (1951); 190 sq. mi. **4.** a girl's given name.

Pomo′na glass′, an American art glass having one of its surfaces stained a pale amber color and the other surface etched.

pomp (pomp), *n.* **1.** stately or splendid display; splendor; magnificence. **2.** ostentatious or vain display, esp. of dignity or importance. **3. pomps,** pompous displays, actions, or things: *The official was accompanied by all the pomps of his high position.* **4.** *Obs.* a stately or splendid procession; pageant. [ME < L *pompa* display, a parade, procession < Gk *pompḗ* in same senses, orig. a sending, akin to *pémpein* to send] —**pomp′less,** *adj.* —**Syn. 1.** See **show.**

pom·pa·dour (pom′pə dōr′, -dôr′, -dŏŏr′), *n.* **1.** an arrangement of a man's hair in which it is brushed up high from the forehead. **2.** an arrangement of a woman's hair in which it is raised over the forehead in a roll, sometimes over a pad. **3.** *Textiles.* any fabric, as cotton or silk, having a bright-hued design of small flowers or bouquets. [named after the Marquise de POMPADOUR]

Pom·pa·dour (pom′pə dōr′, -dôr′, -dŏŏr′; *Fr.* pôɴ pa dōōr′), *n.* **Marquise de** (*Jeanne Antoinette Poisson Le Normant d'Étioles*), 1721–64, mistress of Louis XV of France.

pom·pa·no (pom′pə nō′), *n., pl.* (*esp. collectively*) **-no,** (*esp. referring to two or more kinds or species*) **-nos. 1.** a deep-bodied food fish of the genus *Trachinotus.* **2.** a food fish, *Palometus simillimus,* of California. [< Sp *pámpano* kind of fish]

Pom′pano Beach′, a city in SE Florida. 15,992 (1960).

Pom·pe·ia (pom pē′ə), *n.* fl. 1st century B.C., second wife of Julius Caesar, divorced in 62. Cf. **Calpurnia, Cornelia** (def. 2).

Pom·pe·ian (pom pā′ən, -pē′-), *adj.* **1.** of or pertaining to Pompeii, or its culture. **2.** pertaining to or designating a style of mural painting, examples of which have been found in or near Pompeii, Herculaneum, etc., dating from about the beginning of the 1st century B.C. to 79 A.D., characterized chiefly by the illusion of three-dimensional form organized in an architectonic structure. —*n.* **3.** a native or inhabitant of Pompeii. Also, **Pom·pei′ian.** [< L *Pompeiān(us).* See POMPEII, -AN]

Pom·peii (pom pā′, -pā′ē), *n.* an ancient city in SW Italy, on the Bay of Naples: it was buried along with Herculaneum by an eruption of nearby Mount Vesuvius in A.D. 79; much of the city has been excavated.

pom·pel·mous (pom′pəl mōōs′), *n., pl.* **-mous, -mous·es.** shaddock. [< D *pompelmoes.* See POMELO]

Pom·pey (pom′pē), *n.* (*Gnaeus Pompeius Magnus*) ("*the Great*") 106–48 B.C., Roman general and statesman: a member of the first triumvirate.

Pom·pi·dou (pôɴ pē dōō′), *n.* **Georges Jean Raymond** (zhôrzh zhäɴ ʀa môɴ′), 1911–74, French political leader: president 1969–74.

pom·pom (pom′pom), *n.* an automatic antiaircraft cannon. Also, **pom′-pom.** [imit.]

pom·pon (pom′pon; *Fr.* pôɴ pôɴ′), *n., pl.* **-pons** (-ponz; *Fr.* -pôɴ′). **1.** an ornamental tuft or ball of feathers, wool, or the like, used on hats, slippers, etc. **2.** the high plume at the front of a shako. **3.** *Hort.* a form of small, globe-shaped flower head that characterizes a class or type of various flowering plants, esp. chrysanthemums and dahlias. **4.** See **black margate. 5.** a brown alga, *Pterygophora californica,* having a sticklike stem with long, flowing blades at its tip. [< F; repetitive formation, appar. based on *pompe* POMP]

pom·pos·i·ty (pom pos′i tē), *n., pl.* **-ties** for 3. **1.** the quality of being pompous. **2.** pompous parading of dignity or importance. **3.** an instance of being pompous, as by ostentatious loftiness of language, manner, or behavior. Also, **pom·pous·ness** (pom′pəs nis) (for defs. 1, 2). [late ME *pomposite* < LL *pompōsitās.* See POMPOUS, -ITY]

pomp·ous (pom′pəs), *adj.* **1.** characterized by an ostentatious display of dignity or importance: *a pompous minor official.* **2.** ostentatiously lofty or high-flown: *a pompous speech.* **3.** characterized by pomp, stately splendor, or magnificence. [late ME < LL *pompōs(us).* See POMP, -OUS] —**pomp′ous·ly,** *adv.* —**Syn. 1.** pretentious. **2.** inflated, turgid, bombastic.

Pomp′ton Lakes′ (pomp′tən, pom′-), a town in NE New Jersey. 9445 (1960).

Pon·ca (pong′kə), *n., pl.* **-cas,** (*esp. collectively*) **-ca. 1.** a member of a Siouan people of northern Nebraska. **2.** the dialect of the Ponca Indians, reciprocally intelligible with Osage and belonging to the Siouan language family.

Pon′ca Cit′y, a city in N Oklahoma. 24,411 (1960).

ponce (pons), *n.* *Brit. Slang.* a pimp. [?]

Pon·ce (pôn′se), *n.* a seaport in S Puerto Rico. 114,286 (1960).

pon·ceau (pon sō′), *n.* **1.** a vivid red to reddish-orange color. —*adj.* **2.** having the color ponceau. [< F (cf. OF *pouncel* poppy), ? dim. of *paon* peacock < L *pavōn-* (s. of *pavō*)]

Ponce de Le·ón (pons′ də lē′ən; *Sp.* pôn′the le ôn′, pôn′se), **Juan** (hwän), c1460–1521, Spanish explorer.

Pon·ce·let (pôɴsᵊ le′), *n.* **Jean Vic·tor** (zhäɴ vēk tôʀ′), 1788–1867, French mathematician.

Pon·cha·tou·la (pon′chə tōō′lə), *n.* a town in SE Louisiana. 4727 (1960).

Pon·chiel·li (pông kyel′lē), *n.* **A·mil·ca·re** (ä mēl′kä ʀe), 1834–86, Italian composer.

pon·cho (pon′chō), *n., pl.* **-chos.** a blanketlike cloak with a hole in the center to admit the head, originating in South America, now worn by soldiers and sportsmen as a raincoat. [< AmerSp < Araucanian *pantho*] —**pon′choed,** *adj.*

pond (pond), *n.* a body of water smaller than a lake, sometimes artificially formed, as by damming a stream. [ME *ponde, pande,* OE *pond* pool, akin to *pyndan* dam, *gepyndan* to impound. See POUND³]

pond-apple (pond′ap′əl), *n.* an evergreen tree, *Annona glabra,* of tropical America, having yellowish-red flowers.

pon·der (pon′dər), *v.i.* **1.** to consider something deeply and thoroughly; meditate (often fol. by *over* or *upon*). —*v.t.* **2.** to weigh carefully in the mind; consider thoughtfully: *He pondered his next words thoroughly.* [ME *pondre(n)* < MF *ponderer* < L *ponderāre* to ponder, weigh] —**pon′der·er,** *n.* —**Syn. 1.** reflect, cogitate, deliberate, ruminate.

pon·der·a·ble (pon′dər ə bəl), *adj.* **1.** capable of being considered carefully or deeply. **2.** capable of being weighed; having appreciable weight. [< LL *ponderābil(is).* See PONDER, -ABLE] —**pon′der·a·bil′i·ty, pon′der·a·ble·ness,** *n.*

pon′der·o′sa pine′ (pon′də rō′sə, pon′-), **1.** Also called **western yellow pine.** a large pine, *Pinus ponderosa,* of western North America, having yellowish-brown bark: the State tree of Montana. **2.** the light, soft wood of this tree, used for making furniture and in the construction of houses, ships, etc. [< NL *Pinus ponderōsa* heavy pine]

pon·der·ous (pon′dər əs), *adj.* **1.** of great weight; heavy; massive. **2.** awkward or unwieldy: *He carried a ponderous burden on his back.* **3.** heavy; dull; labored: *a ponderous dissertation.* [late ME, var. of *ponderose* < L *ponderōs(us).* See PONDER, -OUS] —**pon′der·ous·ly,** *adv.* —**pon′der·ous·ness, pon·der·os·i·ty** (pon′də ros′i tē), *n.*

Pon·di·cher·ry (pon′di cher′ē, -sher′ē), *n.* **1.** a former province of French India, on the Coromandel Coast; now a union territory of India. With Mahé, Karikal, and Yanaon, 369,079 (1961); 200 sq. mi. **2.** a seaport in and the capital of this territory. 58,600 (est. 1952). Also, **Pon·di·ché·ry** (pôɴ dē shā ʀē′). Cf. **French India.**

pond′ lil′y. See **water lily.**

pond′ scum′, any free-floating fresh-water alga that forms a green scum on water.

pon·dus med·i·ci·na·le (pon′dəs med′i si nal′ē), (in prescriptions) medicinal weight; apothecaries' weight. [< L]

pond·weed (pond′wēd′), *n.* any aquatic plant of the genus *Potamogeton,* most species of which grow in ponds and quiet streams. [POND + WEED¹]

pone¹ (pōn), *n.* *Southern U.S.* **1.** Also called **pone′ bread′.** a baked or fried bread made of corn meal. **2.** an oval-shaped loaf or cake of it. [< Algonquian (Va.); akin to Delaware *apān* baked]

pone² (pōn), *n.* *Cards.* **1.** the player on the dealer's right. Cf. **eldest hand. 2.** the player who opposes the dealer in a game with two players. [< L *pōne,* impv. 2nd sing. of *pōnere* to place]

pon·gee (pon jē′, pon′jē), *n.* **1.** silk of a slightly uneven weave made from filaments of wild silk woven in natural tan color. **2.** a cotton or rayon fabric imitating it. Cf. **Shantung, tussah.** [? < NChin *pun-chi,* lit., own loom (i.e. homemade), equiv. to Mandarin *pun-kī*]

pon·gid (pon′jid), *n.* any anthropoid ape of the family *Pongidae,* including the gibbon, gorilla, chimpanzee, etc. [back formation from NL *Pongidae* the family name, equiv. to *Pong(o)* typical genus (< Congo *mpungu* ape) + *-idae* -IDAE]

pon·iard (pon′yərd), *n.* **1.** a dagger. —*v.t.* **2.** to stab with a poniard. [< F *poignard,* deriv. of *poing* fist < L *pugn(us);* see -ARD]

po·no·graph (pō′nə graf′, -gräf′), *n.* *Med.* an instrument for graphically recording muscular fatigue. [< Gk *póno(s)* pain, work + -GRAPH]

Po·no·ma·rev (po no mä ʀôf′), *n.* **Bo·ris Ni·ko·la·ye·vich** (bo ʀēs′ ni ko lä′yə vich), born 1905, Russian historian and government official: member of the Presidium since 1956.

pons (ponz), *n., pl.* **pon·tes** (pon′tēz). *Anat.* **1.** Also called **pons Varolii.** a band of nerve fibers in the brain connecting the lobes of the midbrain, medulla, and cerebrum. **2.** a connecting part. [< L *pōns* bridge (gen. *pontis*)]

Pons (ponz; *Fr.* pôɴs), *n.* **Lil·y** (lil′ē; *Fr.* lē lē′), 1904–76, U.S. operatic soprano, born in France.

pons′ as·i·no·rum (as′ə nōr′əm, -nôr′-), a geometric proposition that if a triangle has two of its sides equal, the angles opposite these sides are also equal: so named from the difficulty experienced by beginners in mastering it. Euclid, 1:5. [< L: bridge of asses]

Pon·selle (pon sel′), *n.* **Rosa (Mel·ba)** (mel′bə), born 1897, U.S. soprano.

pons′ Va·ro′li·i (və rō′lē ī′), *pl.* **pon′tes Va·ro′li·i** (və rō′lē ī′). pons (def. 1). [< NL: lit., Varoli's bridge; named after Varoli, Italian anatomist (1543–75)]

Pon·ta Del·ga·da (*Port.* pôɴn′tə del gä′də), a seaport on SW São Miguel island, in the E Azores. 24,491 (1960).

pon·tage (pon′tij), *n.* *Eng. Law.* **1.** a duty or tax for the repair and maintenance of bridges. **2.** a toll for passage over a bridge. [ME < OF < ML *pontātic(um)* bridge-toll, equiv. to L *pont-* (s. of *pōns*) bridge + *-āticum* -AGE]

Pon·ta Gros·sa (pôɴn′tə gʀô′sə), a city in S Brazil. 78,557 (1960).

Pon·ta·nus (pon′tə nəs), *n.* a crater in the fourth quadrant of the face of the moon: about 28 miles in diameter.

Pont·char·train (pon′chər trān′), *n.* **Lake,** a shallow extension of the Gulf of Mexico in SE Louisiana, N of New Orleans. 41 mi. long; 25 mi. wide.

Pon·té·cou·lant (pon′tā kōō län′, -länt′), *n.* a ring formation in the fourth quadrant of the face of the moon: about 60 miles in diameter.

Pon·te·fract (pon′tə frakt′; *locally also* pum′frit, pom′-), *n.* a city in S Yorkshire, in N England, SE of Leeds: ruins of a 12th-century castle. 27,114 (1961).

Pon·ti·ac (pon′tē ak′), *n.* **1.** c1720–69, American Indian, chief of the Ottawa tribe. **2.** a city in SE Michigan. 82,233 (1960). **3.** a town in central Illinois. 8435 (1960).

Pon·tian (pon′shən, -shē ən), *n.* pope A.D. 230–235. Also, **Pon·ti·a·nus** (pon′shē ā′nəs).

Pon·ti·a·nak (pon′tē ä′näk), *n.* a seaport on W Borneo, in central Indonesia. 146,547 (1961).

pon·tic (pon′tik), *n.* *Dentistry.* an artificial tooth in a bridge. Also called **dummy.** [< L *pont-* (s. of *pōns*) bridge + -IC]

Pon·tic (pon′tik), *adj.* pertaining to the Pontus Euxinus or to Pontus.

pon·ti·cel·lo (pon′ti chel′ō), *n., pl.* **-los.** the bridge of a stringed instrument. [< It]

pon·ti·fex (pon′tə feks′), *n., pl.* **pon·tif·i·ces** (pon tif′i sēz′). *Rom. Relig.* a member of the Pontifical College, which was presided over by a chief priest (**Pon′tifex Max′imus**). [< L: lit., bridgemaker, equiv. to *ponti-* (s. of *pōns*) bridge + *-fec-* (var. s. of *facere* to make) + *-s* nom. sing. ending]

pon·tiff (pon′tif), *n.* **1.** any pontifex. **2.** any high or chief priest. **3.** *Eccles.* **a.** a bishop. **b.** the Roman Catholic Pope, the Bishop of Rome. [earlier *pontife* < F, short for L *pontifex* PONTIFEX]

pon·tif·ic (pon tif′ik), *adj.* *Archaic.* pontifical. [PONTIFF + -IC]

pon·tif·i·cal (pon tif′i kəl), *adj.* **1.** of, pertaining to, or characteristic of a pontiff; papal. —*n.* **2.** (in the Western Church) a book containing the forms for the sacraments and other rites and ceremonies to be performed by bishops. **3. pontificals,** the vestments and other insignia of a pontiff, esp. a bishop. [late ME < L *pontificāl(is),* equiv. to *pontific-* (s. of *pontifex*) PONTIFEX + *-ālis* -AL¹] —**pon·tif′i·cal·ly,** *adv.*

Pontif′ical Col′lege, the chief body of priests in ancient Rome.

Pontif′ical Mass′, (*sometimes l.c.*) *Rom. Cath. Ch.* a High Mass celebrated by a bishop or other prelate.

pon·tif·i·cate (*n.* pon tif′ə kit, -kāt′; *v.* pon tif′ə kāt′), *n., v.,* **-cat·ed, -cat·ing.** —*n.* **1.** the office or term of office of a pontiff. —*v.i.* **2.** to discharge the office or duties of a pontiff. **3.** to speak in a pompous or dogmatic manner: *Did he pontificate about the responsibilities of a good citizen?* **4.** to serve as a bishop, esp. in a Pontifical Mass. [< ML *pontificāt(us).* See PONTIFICAL, -ATE¹]

pon·tif·i·ces (pon tif′i sēz′), *n.* pl. of **pontifex.**

pon·til (pon′til), *n.* punty. [< F; see POINT, -IL]

pon·tine (pon′tīn, -tēn), *adj.* *Anat.* of or pertaining to the pons. [< L *pont-* (s. of *pōns*) PONS + -INE¹]

Pon·tine (pon′tēn, -tīn), *adj.* of or pertaining to the Pontine Marshes.

Pon′tine Marsh′es, an area in W Italy, SE of Rome: formerly marshy, now drained.

Pon·tius (pon′shəs, -tē əs), *n.* family name of **Pilate.**

Pont l'É·vêque (pont lə vek′; *Fr.* pôɴ lā vek′), a strongly flavored, pale-yellow cheese with a soft center, made from whole or skimmed milk. [after the town of the same name in northwestern France]

pont·lev·is (pont lev′is), *n.* a drawbridge. [< F, equiv. to *pont* bridge (< L *pont-,* s. of *pōns*) + *levis* (<< LL **leviticius*)]

Pon·to·caine (pon′tə kān′), *n.* *Pharm., Trademark.* tetracaine.

pon·to·nier (pon′tᵊnēr′), *n.* *Mil.* an officer or soldier in charge of bridge equipment or construction of pontoon bridges. [< F *pontonnier.* See PONTOON¹, -IER]

pon·toon¹ (pon tōōn′), *n.* **1.** *Mil.* a boat or some other floating structure used as one of the supports for a temporary bridge over a river. **2.** a float for a derrick, landing stage, etc. **3.** *Naut.* a float for raising a sunken or deeply laden vessel in the water; a camel or caisson. **4.** a seaplane float. Also, **pon·ton** (pon′tᵊn). [< F *ponton* < L *pontōn-* (s. of *pontō*) ferry-boat, floating bridge. See PONS, -OON]

pon·toon² (pen to͞on′), *n. Brit.* the card game twenty-one. [(? humorous) mispronunciation of F *vingt-et-un* the game]

pon′toon bridge′, a bridge supported by pontoons.

pon′toon hull′, *Naut.* a flat-bottomed hull having a squared-off bow.

pon′toon life′boat, a lifeboat depending for buoyancy on a watertight double bottom.

Pon·top·pi·dan (pon top′i dän′), *n.* **Hen·rik** (hen′rek), 1857–1943, Danish novelist: Nobel prize 1917.

Pon·tor·mo (pon tôr′mō; *It.* pôn tôr′mô), *n.* **Ja·co·po da** (yä′kô pô dä), (*Jacopo Carrucci*), 1494–1557, Italian painter.

Pon·tus (pon′təs), *n.* **1.** an ancient country in NE Asia Minor, bordering on the Black Sea: later a Roman province. **2.** Also, **Pon·tos** (pon′tos). the ancient Greek personification of the sea.

Pon′tus Eux·i·nus (yo͞ok sī′nəs), ancient name of the **Black Sea.**

po·ny (pō′nē), *n., pl.* **-nies,** *v.,* **-nied, -ny·ing.** —*n.* **1.** a small horse of any of several breeds, usually not more than 14 hands high. **2.** a horse of any small type or breed. **3.** *Slang.* a translation or other illicit aid, used instead of doing one's own work. Cf. **crib. 4.** something small of its kind. **5.** a small glass for liquor. **6.** the amount of liquor it will hold. **7.** *Brit. Slang.* the sum of 25 pounds. —*v.t., v.i.* **8.** *Slang.* to prepare (lessons) by means of a pony. **9.** to pay (money), as in settling an account (fol. by *up*): *They made him pony up the money he owed.* [earlier *powney* < obs. F *poulenet,* dim. of *poulain* colt < ML *pullān(us)* (L *pull(us)* foal + *-ānus* -AN); see -ET]

po′ny express′, a former system in the American West of carrying mail and express by relays of riders mounted on ponies, esp. the system operating (1860–61) between St. Joseph, Missouri, and Sacramento, California.

Po′ny League′, a baseball league similar to a Little League and having teams whose players are from 13 to 14 years of age.

po′ny shaft′, *Engineering.* a passage with an air lock connecting two pneumatic caissons below water level.

po·ny·tail (pō′nē tāl′), *n.* an arrangement of a girl's or woman's hair in which the hair, usually long and straight, is drawn back tightly and fastened at the back of the head with an elastic band, a clip, etc. [PONY + TAIL¹]

po′ny truss′, a through bridge truss having its deck between the top and bottom chords and having no top lateral bracing.

pooch (po͞och), *n. Slang.* a dog. [?]

pood (po͞od), *n.* a Russian weight equal to about 36 pounds avoirdupois. [< Russ *pud* < LG or Scand *pund* POUND¹]

poo·dle (po͞od′əl), *n.* one of a breed of active dogs, having long, thick, frizzy or curly hair usually trimmed in standard patterns, and occurring in three varieties differing only in size. [< G *Pudel,* short for *Pudelhund.* lit., splash-dog (i.e., water-dog), equiv. to *pudel(n)* (to) splash (see PUDDLE) + *Hund* HOUND¹]

Poodle (15 in. high at shoulder)

pooh¹ (po͞o, po͝o), *interj.* **1.** (used as an exclamation of disdain or contempt.) —*n.* **2.** an exclamation of "pooh."

pooh² (po͞o), *v.t.* poop².

Pooh Bah (po͞o′ bä′, bä′), (*often l.c.*) **1.** a person who holds several positions, esp. ones which give him bureaucratic importance. **2.** a pompous, self-important person. [after the character in *The Mikado*]

pooh-pooh (po͞o′po͞o′), *v.t.* **1.** to express disdain or contempt for; dismiss lightly: *He pooh-poohed all their superstitious fears.* —*v.i.* **2.** to express disdain or contempt. [v. use of redupl. of POOH¹]

poo·ka (po͞o′kə), *n.* puca.

pool¹ (po͞ol), *n.* **1.** a small body of standing water; pond. **2.** a puddle. **3.** any small collection of liquid on a surface: *a pool of blood.* **4.** a still, deep place in a stream. **5.** See **swimming pool. 6.** a subterranean reservoir of oil or gas held in porous sedimentary rock. —*v.i.* **7.** to form a pool. **8.** (of blood) to accumulate in a body part or organ. —*v.t.* **9.** to cause pools to form in. **10.** to cause (blood) to form pools. [ME; OE *pōl;* c. D *poel,* G *Pfuhl*]

pool² (po͞ol), *n.* **1.** an association of competitors who agree to control the production, market, and price of a commodity for mutual benefit, although they appear to be rivals. **2.** *Finance.* a combination of persons or organizations for the purpose of manipulating the prices of securities. **3.** a combination of interests, funds, etc., for common advantage. **4.** the combined interests or funds. **5.** a facility, resource, or service that is shared by a group of people: *a car pool; a typing pool.* **6.** the persons or parties involved. **7.** the stakes in certain games. **8.** Also called **pocket billiards.** any of various games played on a pool table with a cue ball and 15 other balls that are usually numbered, in which the object is to drive all the balls into the pockets with the cue ball. **9.** *Brit.* a billiard game. **10.** the total amount staked by a combination of bettors, as on a race, to be awarded to the successful bettor or bettors. **11.** the combination of such bettors. **12.** *Fencing.* a match in which each teammate successively plays against each member of the opposing team. —*v.t.* **13.** to put (interests, money, etc.) into a pool, or common stock or fund, as for a financial venture, according to agreement. **14.** to form a pool of. **15.** to make a common interest of. —*v.i.* **16.** to enter into or form a pool. [< F *poule* stakes, lit., hen. See PULLET]
—**Syn. 1.** corner, monopoly.

pool′ hall′, *U.S.* poolroom (def. 1). Also, **pool′hall′.**

pool·room (po͞ol′ro͞om′, -ro͝om′), *n.* **1.** an establishment or room for the playing of pool or billiards. **2.** a place where betting is carried on, esp. illegally; a bookmaker's establishment. [POOL² + ROOM]

pool′ ta′ble, a billiard table with six pockets, on which pool is played.

poon (po͞on), *n.* **1.** any of several East Indian trees of the genus *Calophyllum,* which yield a light, hard wood used for masts, spars, etc. **2.** the wood of these trees. [< Singhalese or Telugu *pūna*]

Poo·na (po͞o′nə), *n.* a city in W Maharashtra, W India, SE of Bombay. 597,600 (1961).

poop¹ (po͞op), *n.* **1.** a superstructure at the stern of a vessel. **2.** See **poop deck.** —*v.t.* **3.** (of a wave) to break over the stern of (a ship). **4.** to take (seas) over the stern. [late ME *pouppe* < MF << L *puppis* stern of a ship]

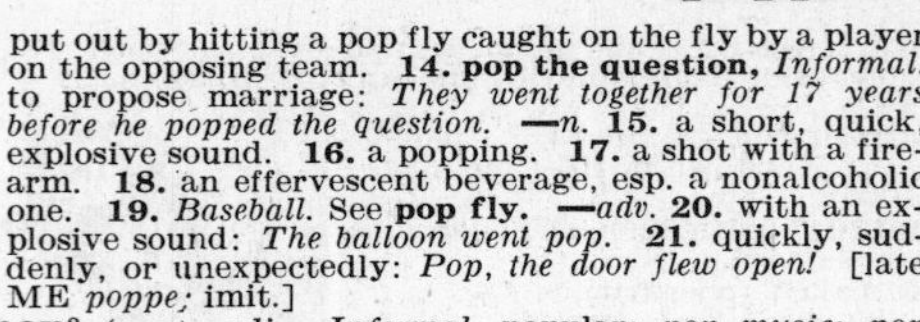

Poop

poop² (po͞op), *v.t.* **1.** *Slang.* to cause to become out of breath or fatigued; exhaust: *Climbing that mountain pooped the whole group.* **2. poop out,** *Slang.* to cease from or fail in something, as from fear, exhaustion, etc.: *When the time for action came, they all pooped out and went home instead.* [ME *poupe(n)* (to) blow; imit.]

poop³ (po͞op), *n. Slang.* information; low-down: *Send a reporter to get the poop on that accident.* [?]

poop′ cab′in, *Naut.* a cabin situated immediately beneath the poop deck of a ship.

poop′ deck′, a weather deck on top of a poop. See illus. under **quarter deck.**

Po·o·pó (pô′ô pô′), *n.* a lake in SW Bolivia, in the Andes. 60 mi. long; 12,000 ft. above sea level.

poop′ staff′. See **ensign staff.**

poor (po͝or), *adj.* **1.** having little or no money, goods, or other means of support: *a poor family living on welfare.* **2.** *Law.* dependent upon charity or public support. **3.** (of a country, institution, etc.) meagerly supplied or endowed with resources or funds. **4.** characterized by or showing poverty. **5.** deficient or lacking in something specified: *a region poor in mineral deposits.* **6.** faulty or inferior, as in construction: *poor workmanship.* **7.** deficient in desirable ingredients, qualities, or the like: *poor soil.* **8.** lean or emaciated, as cattle. **9.** of an inferior, inadequate, or unsatisfactory kind: *poor health.* **10.** lacking in skill, ability, or training: *a poor cook.* **11.** deficient in moral excellence; cowardly, abject, or mean. **12.** scanty, meager, or paltry in amount or number: *a poor audience.* **13.** humble; modest: *They shared their poor meal with a stranger.* **14.** unfortunate; hapless: *The poor dog was limping.* **15. poor as Job's turkey,** extremely poor; impoverished: *They're poor as Job's turkey, but just as proud as they come.* —*n.* **16.** (*construed as pl.*) poor persons collectively (usually prec. by *the*): *sympathy for the poor.* [ME *pov(e)re* < OF *povre* < L *pauper.* See PAUPER] —**poor′ness,** *n.*
—**Syn. 1.** needy, indigent, necessitous, straitened, destitute, penniless, poverty-stricken. POOR, IMPECUNIOUS, IMPOVERISHED, PENNILESS refer to those lacking money. POOR is the simple term for the condition of lacking means to obtain the comforts of life: *a very poor family.* IMPECUNIOUS often suggests that the poverty is a consequence of unwise habits: *an impecunious actor.* IMPOVERISHED often implies a former state of greater plenty, from which one has been reduced: *the impoverished aristocracy.* PENNILESS may mean destitute, or it may apply simply to a temporary condition of being without funds: *The widow was left penniless with three small children.* **5.** meager. **6.** unsatisfactory, shabby. **7.** sterile, barren, unfruitful, unproductive. **8.** thin, skinny, meager, gaunt. **14.** miserable, unhappy, pitiable. —**Ant. 1, 5, 7.** rich. **1, 3, 4.** wealthy.

poor′ boy′, 1. See **hero sandwich. 2.** *Slang.* (among oil-field workers) any cheap or makeshift device.

poor′ boy′ sweat′er, a snug-fitting, pullover sweater with ribbing on both the body and sleeves, worn by girls and women.

poor′ farm′, a farm maintained at public expense for the housing and support of paupers.

poor·ga (po͝or′gə), *n.* purga.

poor·house (po͝or′hous′), *n., pl.* **-hous·es** (-hou′ziz). an institution in which paupers are maintained at public expense. [POOR + HOUSE]

poor′ law′, a law or system of laws providing for the relief or support of the poor at public expense.

poor·ly (po͝or′lē), *adv.* **1.** in a poor manner or way: *The team played poorly.* —*adj.* **2.** in poor health; somewhat ill: *I hear she's been poorly.* [ME *pourely.* See POOR, -LY]

Poor′ Rich′ard's Al′manac, an almanac (1732–58) written and published by Benjamin Franklin.

Poor′ Rob′in's plan′tain, the rattlesnake weed, *Hieracium venosum.* Also called **Robin's plantain.**

poor-spir·it·ed (po͝or′spir′i tid), *adj.* having or showing a poor, cowardly, or abject spirit.

poor·tith (po͝or′tith), *n. Scot. and North Eng.* poverty; the condition of being poor. [earlier *purteth* < MF *povretet,* var. of *povrete* POVERTY]

poor′ white′, *Usually Derogatory.* a white person, esp. of the southern U.S., having low social status and little or no money, property, or education.

poor′ white′ trash′, *Derogatory.* poor whites collectively.

poor-will (po͝or′wil′), *n.* a goatsucker, *Phalaenoptilus nuttallii,* of western North America. [imit.]

pop¹ (pop), *v.,* **popped, pop·ping,** *n., adv.* —*v.i.* **1.** to make a short, quick, explosive sound: *The cork popped.* **2.** to burst open with such a sound, as chestnuts or corn in roasting. **3.** to come or go quickly, suddenly, or unexpectedly: *We promised to pop in for a short visit.* **4.** to shoot with a firearm: *to pop at a mark.* **5.** *Baseball.* **a.** to hit a pop fly (often fol. by *up*). **b.** to pop out. —*v.t.* **6.** to cause to make a sudden, explosive sound. **7.** to cause to burst open with such a sound. **8.** to put or thrust quickly, suddenly, or unexpectedly. **9.** *Informal.* to cause to fire; discharge: *He popped his rifle at the bird.* **10.** to shoot (usually fol. by *at, off,* etc.): *He popped off bottles with a slingshot.* **11.** *Brit. Slang.* to pawn. **12. pop off,** *Slang.* **a.** to die, esp. suddenly. **b.** to depart, esp. abruptly. **c.** to express oneself volubly or excitedly and sometimes irately or indiscreetly: *He popped off about the injustice of the verdict.* **13. pop out,** *Baseball.* to be put out by hitting a pop fly caught on the fly by a player on the opposing team. **14. pop the question,** *Informal.* to propose marriage: *They went together for 17 years before he popped the question.* —*n.* **15.** a short, quick, explosive sound. **16.** a popping. **17.** a shot with a firearm. **18.** an effervescent beverage, esp. a nonalcoholic one. **19.** *Baseball.* See **pop fly.** —*adv.* **20.** with an explosive sound: *The balloon went pop.* **21.** quickly, suddenly, or unexpectedly: *Pop, the door flew open!* [late ME *poppe;* imit.]

pop² (pop), *adj. Informal.* popular: *pop music; pop singers.* [by shortening]

pop³ (pop), *n. Informal.* father. [short form of POPPA]

pop., **1.** popular. **2.** popularly. **3.** population.

P.O.P., 1. See **print-out paper. 2.** point of purchase.

Pop′ Art′, (*sometimes l.c.*) *Fine Arts.* a style, esp. of figurative painting, developed in the U.S. and current in the early 1960's, characterized chiefly by magnified forms and images derived from such commercial art genres as comic strips and advertising posters.

Po·pa·yán (pô′pä yän′), *n.* a city in SW Colombia. 61,490 (est. 1961).

pop′ con′cert, a concert of popular and light classical music played by a symphony orchestra. Also, **pops concert.**

pop·corn (pop′kôrn′), *n.* **1.** any of several varieties of corn whose kernels burst open and puff out when subjected to dry heat. **2.** popped corn. [short for *popped corn.* See POP¹, -ED², CORN¹]

pope (pōp), *n.* **1.** (*often cap.*) the bishop of Rome as head of the Roman Catholic Church. **2.** (in the early Christian church) a bishop. **3.** one considered as having or assuming authority or a position similar to that of the Roman Catholic pope. **4.** the title of the Coptic patriarch of Alexandria. **5.** *Eastern Ch.* **a.** the Orthodox patriarch of Alexandria. **b.** (in certain churches) a parish priest. [ME; OE *pāpa* < eccl. L: bishop, pope < LGk *pápas* bishop, priest, var. of *páppas* father; see PAPA¹] —**pope′less,** *adj.* —**pope′like′,** *adj.*

Pope (pōp), *n.* **1. Alexander,** 1688–1744, English poet. **2. John,** 1822–92, Union general in the Civil War. **3. John Russell,** 1874–1937, U.S. architect.

pope·dom (pōp′dəm), *n.* **1.** the office or dignity of a pope. **2.** the tenure of office of a pope. **3.** the papal government. [ME *pape dom,* OE *pāpdōm.* See POPE, -DOM]

pop·e·line (pop′ə lēn′, pop′ə lēn′), *n.* a fabric, resembling broadcloth, rep, or poplin and made with silk or rayon warp and wool filling, used in the manufacture of dress goods. [< F: POPLIN]

pop·er·y (pō′pə rē), *n.* *Usually Disparaging.* the Roman Catholic Church, esp. its doctrines, ceremonies, and system of government. [POPE + -ERY]

pope's′ nose′, *Slang.* the fleshy protuberance at the posterior end of a dressed fowl, esp. the tailpiece of a cooked chicken. Also called **parson's nose.**

pop′eye catalu′fa. See under **catalufa.**

pop·eyed (pop′īd′), *adj.* marked by bulging, staring eyes: *a young boy popeyed with excitement.* [POP¹ + EYED]

pop′ fly′, *Baseball.* a high fly ball hit to the infield or immediately beyond it that can easily be caught before reaching the ground. Also called **pop-up.**

pop·gun (pop′gun′), *n.* a child's toy gun from which a pellet is shot by compressed air, producing a loud pop. [POP¹ + GUN¹]

pop·ie (pop′ē), *n. Rare.* poppyhead. [earlier *popey,* late ME *papye;* ? special use of POPPY]

pop·i·nac (pop′ə nak′), *n.* huisache. [alter. of L *opopanax* < Gk *opopánax* gum (of *Opopanax hispidus*), equiv. to *opo-,* comb. form of *opós* juice + *pánax* PANACEA]

pop·in·jay (pop′in jā′), *n.* **1.** a person given to vain displays and empty chatter; coxcomb; fop. **2.** *Brit. Dial.* a woodpecker, esp. the green woodpecker. **3.** *Archaic.* the figure of a parrot usually fixed on a pole and used as a target in archery and gun shooting. **4.** *Archaic.* a parrot. [ME *papejay, popingay,* etc. < MF *papegai, papingay,* etc., parrot < Sp *papagayo* < Ar *bab(ba)ghā′*]

pop·ish (pō′pish), *adj. Usually Disparaging.* of, pertaining to, or characteristic of the Roman Catholic Church. [POPE + -ISH¹] —**pop′ish·ly,** *adv.* —**pop′ish·ness,** *n.*

Pop′ish Plot′, an imaginary conspiracy against the crown of Great Britain on the part of English Roman Catholics, fabricated 1678 by Titus Oates as a means of gaining power.

pop·lar (pop′lər), *n.* **1.** any of the rapidly growing, salicaceous trees of the genus *Populus,* usually characterized by the columnar or spirelike manner of growth of its branches. **2.** the light, soft wood of any of these trees, used for pulp. **3.** any of various similar trees, as the yellow poplar **(tulip tree). 4.** the wood of any such tree. [ME *popler(e),* var of *populer,* equiv. to ME, OE *popul* (< L *pōpulus* poplar) + *-er* -ER²; suffix appar. added on model of MF *pouplier,* equiv. to *pouple* poplar + *-ier* -ER²] —**pop′lared,** *adj.*

Pop′lar Bluff′, a city in SE Missouri. 15,926 (1960).

Pop·lar·ism (pop′lə riz′əm), *n. Brit.* **1.** a policy of administering excessive out-relief by a local government. **2.** any similar policy of government spending that leads to unreasonably increased taxes. [after *Poplar,* East London, where such a policy was put into effect] —**Pop′lar·ist,** *n.*

pop·lin (pop′lin), *n.* a finely corded fabric of cotton, rayon, silk, or wool, for dresses, draperies, etc. [< F *popeline,* earlier *papeline* < It *papalina,* fem. of *papalino* papal; so called from being made at the papal city of Avignon. See PAPAL, -INE¹]

pop·lit·e·al (pop lit′ē əl, pop′li tē′əl), *adj. Anat.* of or pertaining to the ham, or part of the leg back of the knee. [POPLITE(US) + -AL¹]

pop·lit·e·us (pop lit′ē əs, pop′li tē′-), *n., pl.* **-lit·e·i** (-lit′ē ī′, -li tē′ī). *Anat.* a thin, flat, triangular muscle in back of the knee, the action of which assists in bending the knee and in rotating the leg toward the body. [< NL, equiv. to L *poplit-* (s. of *poples*) the ham + *-eus* -EOUS]

Po·po·cat·e·petl (pô′pô kä te′pet′əl, pō′pə kat′ə-pet′əl), *n.* a volcano in S central Mexico, SE of Mexico City. 17,887 ft.

pop·o·ver (pop′ō′vər), *n.* a puffed muffin with a hollow center, made with a batter of flour, salt, egg, and milk. [POP¹ + OVER]

pop·pa (pop′ə), *n. Informal.* father.

Pop·pae·a Sa·bi·na (po pē′ə sə bī′nə), died A.D. 65?, second wife of the Roman emperor Nero.

pop·per (pop′ər), *n.* **1.** one who or that which pops. **2.** a utensil, as a covered pan, used for popping corn. **3.** *Angling.* chugger. [POP[1] + -ER[1]]

pop·pet (pop′it), *n.* **1.** Also called **pop′pet valve′.** *Mach.* a rising and falling valve consisting of a disk at the end of a vertically set stem, used in internal-combustion and steam engines. **2.** *Brit. Dial.* a term of endearment for a girl or child. **3.** *Naut.* **a.** any of the vertical timbers bracing the bow or stern of a vessel about to be launched. **b.** a piece of wood set in the gunwales of a boat, supporting or forming part of an oarlock. **4.** poppethead. [earlier form of PUPPET]

pop·pet·head (pop′it hed′), *n.* a tailstock or headstock of a lathe. Also called **poppet, puppet.** [POPPET + HEAD]

pop·pied (pop′ēd), *adj.* **1.** covered or adorned with poppies: *poppied fields.* **2.** affected by or as if by opium; listless. [POPPY + -ED[3]]

pop′ping crease′ (pop′ing), *Cricket.* a line parallel to and in advance of a bowling crease, marking the limit of a batsman's approach in hitting the ball.

pop·ple[1] (pop′əl), *v.*, **-pled, -pling,** *n.* —*v.i.* **1.** to move in a tumbling, irregular manner, as boiling water. —*n.* **2.** a poppling motion. [ME *pople(n)*; imit.]

pop·ple[2] (pop′əl), *n. Informal.* a poplar of the genus *Populus.* [ME; OE *popul* < L *pōpulus*]

pop·py (pop′ē), *n., pl.* **-pies** for 1, 4, 5. **1.** any plant of the genus *Papaver,* having nodding, red, violet, yellow, or white flowers. **2.** an extract, as opium, from such a plant. **3.** Also called **pop′py red′.** an orangeish red resembling scarlet. **4.** *Archit.* poppyhead. **5.** an artificial flower resembling a poppy, esp. one received as evidence of a contribution to a fund for disabled war veterans. [ME; OE *popæg, papig* << VL *papāv(um)* for L *papāver*] —**pop′py·like′,** *adj.*

Poppy,
Papaver orientale

pop′py anem′one, a perennial herb, *Anemone coronaria,* of southern Europe and the U.S., having tuberous roots and solitary, poppylike, red, blue, or white flowers, grown as an ornamental.

pop·py·cock (pop′ē kok′), *n.* nonsense; bosh. [? < D *pappekak* (*pap* soft + *kak* dung)] —**pop′py·cock′·ish,** *adj.*

pop·py·head (pop′ē hed′), *n. Archit.* a finial or other ornament, often richly carved, as the top of the upright end of a bench or pew. Also called **poppy.** [POPPY + HEAD]

pop′py seed′, seed of the poppy plant, used as an ingredient or topping for breads, rolls, cakes, and cookies. [ME *popy seed*]

pops (pops), *adj.* of or pertaining to a symphony orchestra specializing in popular or light classical music. [see POP[2]]

pops′ con′cert. See **pop concert.**

pop-shop (pop′shop′), *n. Brit. Slang.* pawnshop. [POP[1] + SHOP]

Pop·si·cle (pop′si kəl, -sik′əl), *n. Trademark.* a flavored ice on a stick.

pop·u·lace (pop′yə ləs), *n.* **1.** the common people of a community, nation, etc., as distinguished from the higher classes. **2.** all the inhabitants of a place; population. [< F < It *popolaccio,* equiv. to *popol(o)* PEOPLE + *-accio* pejorative suffix]

pop·u·lar (pop′yə lər), *adj.* **1.** regarded with favor, approval, or affection by people in general: *a popular preacher.* **2.** regarded with favor, approval, or affection by an acquaintance or acquaintances: *He's not very popular with me just now.* **3.** of, pertaining to, or representing the people, esp. the common people: *popular discontent.* **4.** of the people as a whole, esp. of all citizens of a nation or state qualified to participate in an election: *popular suffrage; the popular vote; popular representation.* **5.** prevailing among the people generally: *a popular superstition.* **6.** suited to or intended for the general masses of people: *popular music.* **7.** adapted to the ordinary intelligence or taste: *popular lectures on science.* **8.** suited to the means of ordinary people; not expensive: *popular prices on all tickets.* [late ME *populer* < L *populār(is).* See PEOPLE, -AR[1]]
—**Syn. 1.** favorite, approved, liked. **5.** common, current. See **general.**

pop′ular etymol′ogy. See **folk etymology.**

pop′ular front′, a coalition, usually temporary, of leftist and sometimes centrist political parties, formed against a common opponent, as fascism, and promoting social reform, esp. such a coalition used by the Communist party to attain power. Also called **people's front.**

pop·u·lar·ise (pop′yə lə rīz′), *v.t.*, **-ised, -is·ing.** *Chiefly Brit.* popularize. —**pop′u·lar·i·sa′tion,** *n.* —**pop′u·lar·is′er,** *n.*

pop·u·lar·i·ty (pop′yə lar′i tē), *n.* **1.** the quality or fact of being popular. **2.** the favor of the general public or of a particular group of people: *His popularity with television audiences is unrivaled.* [< L *populāritās* a courting of popular favor. See POPULAR, -ITY]

pop·u·lar·ize (pop′yə lə rīz′), *v.t.*, **-ized, -iz·ing.** to make popular: *to popularize a dance.* Also, *esp. Brit.,* **popularise.** [POPULAR + -IZE] —**pop′u·lar·i·za′tion,** *n.* —**pop′u·lar·iz′er,** *n.*

pop·u·lar·ly (pop′yə lər lē), *adv.* **1.** by the people as a whole; generally; widely: *a fictitious story popularly accepted as true.* **2.** in a popular manner: *He writes popularly on many subjects.* [POPULAR + -LY]

pop′ular sing′er, a professional singer who specializes in popular songs. Cf. **jazz singer.**

pop′ular song′, a song that is written to have an immediate and wide appeal and is usually popular for only a short time, but that sometimes is of a sufficiently high quality to become part of the permanent repertoire of popular music and jazz. Cf. **standard** (def. 11).

pop′ular sov′ereignty, 1. the doctrine that sovereign power is vested in the people and that those chosen to govern, as trustees of such power, must exercise it in conformity with the general will. **2.** *Amer. Hist.* (before the Civil War) a doctrine, held chiefly by the opponents of the abolitionists, that the people living in a Territory should be free of federal interference in determining domestic policy, esp. with respect to slavery.

pop′ular vote′, 1. *U.S.* the vote for a presidential candidate made by the qualified voters, as opposed to that made by the electoral college. Cf. **electoral vote. 2.** the vote for a candidate, issue, etc., made by the qualified voters, as opposed to a vote made by elected representatives.

pop·u·late (pop′yə lāt′), *v.t.*, **-lat·ed, -lat·ing. 1.** to inhabit; live in; be the inhabitants of. **2.** to furnish with inhabitants, as by colonization; people. [< ML *populāt(us),* ptp. of *populāre* to inhabit. See PEOPLE, -ATE[1]]

pop·u·la·tion (pop′yə lā′shən), *n.* **1.** the total number of persons inhabiting a country, city, or any district or area. **2.** the body of inhabitants of a place: *The population of the city opposes the addition of fluorides to the drinking water.* **3.** the number or body of inhabitants of a particular race or class in a place: *the native population; the working-class population.* **4.** *Statistics.* any finite or infinite aggregation of individuals, not necessarily animate, subject to a statistical study. **5.** *Ecol.* **a.** the assemblage of plants or animals living in a given area. **b.** all the individuals of one species in a given area. **6.** act or process of populating: *Population of the interior was hampered by dense jungles.* [< LL *populātiōn-* (s. of *populātiō*). See POPULATE, -ION] —**pop′u·la′tion·al,** *adj.* —**pop′u·la′tion·less,** *adj.*

popula′tion param′eter, *Statistics.* a quantity or statistical measure which, for a given population, is fixed and which is used as the value of a variable in some general distribution or frequency function to make it descriptive of that population: *The mean and variance of a population are population parameters.*

popula′tion pres′sure, *Ecol.* the force exerted by a growing population upon its environment, resulting in dispersal or reduction of the population.

popula′tion pyr′amid, *Sociol.* a graph showing the distribution of a population by sex, age, etc.

Pop·u·list (pop′yə list), *n. U.S. Politics.* a member of the People's party. [< L *popul(us)* PEOPLE + -IST] —**Pop′u·lism,** *n.* —**Pop′u·lis′tic,** *adj.*

pop·u·lous (pop′yə ləs), *adj.* **1.** full of residents or inhabitants, as a region; heavily populated: *California and New York are the most populous States.* **2.** jammed or crowded with people: *There's no more populous place than Times Square on New Year's Eve.* **3.** forming or comprising a large number or quantity: *Because of epidemics they are not nearly so populous as they once were.* [late ME *populus* < L *populōs(us).* See PEOPLE, -OUS] —**pop′u·lous·ly,** *adv.* —**pop′u·lous·ness,** *n.*

pop-up (pop′up′), *n. Baseball.* See **pop fly.**

Po·quo·son (pə kō′sən), *n.* a town in E Virginia. 4278 (1960).

p.o.r., pay on return.

Por·ban·dar (pōr bun′dər), *n.* a seaport in SW Gujarat, in W India. 74,100 (1961).

por·bea·gle (pôr′bē′gəl), *n.* a shark of the genus *Lamna,* esp. *L. nasus,* a large, voracious species of the North Atlantic and North Pacific oceans. [orig. Cornish dial.]

por·ce·lain (pōr′sə lin, pôr′-; pōrs′lin, pôrs′-), *n.* **1.** a strong, vitreous, translucent ceramic material, biscuit-fired at a low temperature and glost-fired at a very high temperature. **2.** ware made from this. [< F *porcelaine* < It *porcellana* (orig. a kind of shell), deriv. of *porcella,* dim. of *porca* < ? (? akin to pork)] —**por·ce·la·ne·ous, por·cel·la·ne·ous** (pōr′sə lā′nē əs, pôr′-), *adj.*

por′celain enam′el, a glass coating, made to adhere to a metal or another enamel by fusion.

por·ce·lain·ise (pōr′sə lə nīz′, pôr′-, pōrs′lə-, pôrs′-), *v.t.*, **-ised, -is·ing.** *Chiefly Brit.* porcelainize. —**por′ce·lain·i·sa′tion,** *n.*

por·ce·lain·ize (pōr′sə lə nīz′, pôr′-, pōrs′lə-, pôrs′-), *v.t.*, **-ized, -iz·ing.** to make into or coat with porcelain or something resembling porcelain. Also, *esp. Brit.,* **porcelainise.** [PORCELAIN + -IZE] —**por′ce·lain·i·za′tion,** *n.*

porch (pōrch, pôrch), *n.* **1.** an exterior appendage to a building, forming a covered approach or vestibule to a doorway. **2.** *U.S.* a veranda. **3.** a portico. **4. the Porch,** the portico or stoa in the agora of ancient Athens, where the Stoic philosopher Zeno of Citium and his followers met. [ME *porche* < OF < L *porticus* porch, portico] —**porch′less,** *adj.* —**porch′like′,** *adj.*

Porcupine,
Erethizon dorsatum
(Total length 3 ft.; tail 8 in.)

por·cine (pôr′sīn, -sin), *adj.* **1.** of or pertaining to swine. **2.** resembling swine; hoggish; piggish. [< L *porcīn(us)*]

por·cu·pine (pôr′kyə pīn′), *n.* any of several rodents covered with stiff, sharp, erectile spines or quills, as *Erethizon dorsatum,* of the U.S. and Canada, having short spines or quills partially concealed by the hair. [late ME *porcupyne,* var. of *porcapyne;* r. *porke despyne* < MF *porc d'espine* thorny pig. See PORK, SPINE]

por′cupine ant′eater, an echidna or spiny anteater.

por·cu·pine·fish (pôr′kyə pīn fish′), *n., pl.* (*esp. collectively*) **-fish,** (*esp. referring to two or more kinds or species*) **-fish·es.** any of several fishes of the family *Diodontidae,* esp. *Diodon hystrix,* found in tropical seas, capable of inflating the body with water or air until it resembles a globe, with erection of the long spines covering the skin. [PORCUPINE + FISH]

pore[1] (pōr, pôr), *v.i.*, **pored, por·ing. 1.** to meditate or ponder intently (usually fol. by *over, on,* or *upon*): *He pored over the strange events of the preceding evening.* **2.** to gaze earnestly or steadily: *to pore over a painting.* **3.** to read or study with steady attention or application: *a scholar poring over a rare old manuscript.* [ME *poure(n)* < ?]

pore[2] (pōr, pôr), *n.* **1.** a minute opening or orifice, as in the skin or a leaf, for perspiration, absorption, etc. **2.** a minute interstice, as in a rock. [ME *poore* < L *por(us)* < Gk *pōros* passage] —**pore′like′,** *adj.*

por·gy (pôr′gē), *n., pl.* (*esp. collectively*) **-gy,** (*esp. referring to two or more kinds or species*) **-gies. 1.** a sparid food fish, *Pagrus pagrus,* found in the Mediterranean and off the Atlantic coasts of Europe and America. **2.** any of several other sparid fishes, as the scup. [*porg(o),* var. of *pargo* (< Sp or Pg < L *pag(a)rus* kind of fish < Gk *págros,* var. of *phágros*) + -Y[2]]

Por′gy and Bess′ (pôr′gē ən bes′), an opera (1935) by George Gershwin.

Po·ri (pô′ri), *n.* a seaport in W Finland, on the Gulf of Bothnia. 59,543 (est. 1965).

Po·rif·er·a (pō rif′ər ə, pô-, pə-), *n.* the phylum comprising the sponges. [< NL: lit., the porous ones, equiv. to L *por(us)* PORE[2] + *-i-* -I- + *-fera,* neut. pl. of *-fer* -FEROUS]

po·rif·er·an (pō rif′ər ən, pô-, pə-), *n.* **1.** any animal of the phylum *Porifera,* comprising the sponges. —*adj.* **2.** belonging or pertaining to the *Porifera.* [PORIFER(A) + -AN]

po·rif·er·ous (pō rif′ər əs, pô-, pə-), *adj.* bearing or having pores. [PORIFER(A) + -OUS]

po·ri·form (pōr′ə fôrm′, pôr′-), *adj.* resembling a pore in form. [< L *por(us)* PORE[2] + -I- + -FORM]

po·ri·on (pōr′ē on′, pôr′-), *n., pl.* **po·ri·a** (pōr′ē ə, pôr′-), **po·ri·ons.** *Craniom.* the most lateral point in the roof of the bony external auditory meatus. [< NL < Gk *pór(os)* passage, way + *-ion* dim. suffix]

po·rism (pōr′iz əm, pôr′-), *n. Math.* a form of proposition among the Greeks which has been variously defined, esp. a proposition affirming the possibility of finding such conditions as will render a certain problem indeterminate, or capable of innumerable solutions. [ME *porysme* < L *porisma* < Gk: corollary, akin to *porizein* to bring about, deduce. See PORE[2], -ISM]

pork (pōrk, pôrk), *n.* **1.** the flesh of hogs used as food. **2.** *U.S. Slang.* appropriations, appointments, etc., made by the government for political reasons rather than for public benefit, as for public buildings, river improvements, etc. [ME *porc* < OF < L *porc(us)* hog, pig; c. FARROW[1]] —**pork′ish, pork′like′,** *adj.* —**pork′less,** *adj.*

pork′ bar′rel, *U.S. Slang.* a government appropriation, bill, or policy which supplies funds for local improvements designed to ingratiate legislators with their constituents.

pork·chop (pōrk′chop′, pôrk′-), *n.* **1.** a chop of pork. **2.** *Journ., Print.* thumbnail (def. 4). [PORK + CHOP[1]]

pork·er (pōr′kər, pôr′-), *n.* a pig, esp. one being fattened for its meat. [PORK + -ER[1]]

pork·fish (pōrk′fish′, pôrk′-), *n., pl.* **-fish·es,** (*esp. collectively*) **-fish.** a black and gold grunt, *Anisotremus virginicus,* found in the West Indies. [PORK + FISH]

pork·pie (pōrk′pī′, pôrk′-), *n.* a snap-brimmed hat with a round, flat crown, usually made of felt. [PORK + PIE[1]]

pork·y (pōr′kē, pôr′-), *adj.*, **pork·i·er, pork·i·est. 1.** of, pertaining to, or resembling pork. **2.** fat: *a porky child.* [PORK + -Y[1]] —**pork′i·ness,** *n.*

por·nog·ra·pher (pôr nog′rə fər), *n.* a person who writes or sells pornography. [PORNOGRAPH(Y) + -ER[1]]

por·nog·ra·phy (pôr nog′rə fē), *n.* obscene literature, art, or photography, esp. that having little or no artistic merit. [< Gk *pornográph(os)* writing or writer about harlots (*porno-,* comb. form of *pórnē* harlot, + *-graphos* -GRAPH) + -Y[3]] —**por·no·graph·ic** (pôr′nə graf′ik), *adj.* —**por′no·graph′i·cal·ly,** *adv.*

po·ros·i·ty (pō ros′i tē, pô-, pə-), *n., pl.* **-ties** for 2. **1.** state or quality of being porous. **2.** the ratio, expressed as a percentage, of the volume of the pores or interstices of a substance, as a rock or rock stratum, to the total volume of the mass. [ME *porosytee* < ML *porōsitās.* See POROUS, -ITY]

po·rous (pōr′əs, pôr′-), *adj.* **1.** full of pores. **2.** permeable by water, air, etc. [late ME, var. of *porose* < ML *porōs(us).* See PORE[2], -OUS] —**po′rous·ly,** *adv.* —**po′rous·ness,** *n.*

por·phy·ri·a (pôr fēr′ē ə, -fīr′ē ə), *n. Pathol.* a defect of blood pigment metabolism in which porphyrins are produced in excess, are present in the blood, and are found in the urine. Also called **hematoporphyria.** [PORPHYR(IN) + -IA]

por·phy·rin (pôr′fə rin), *n. Biochem.* any of a group of iron-free or magnesium-free pyrrole derivatives, occurring in all plant and animal protoplasm, formed by the decomposition of hematin and chlorophyll. [< Gk *porphýr(a)* purple + -IN[2]]

Por·phy·ri·on (pôr fī′rē on′), *n. Class. Myth.* one of the Gigantes.

por·phy·ri·sa·tion (pôr′fər i zā′shən), *n. Chiefly Brit.* porphyrization.

por·phy·rise (pôr′fə rīz′), *v.t.*, **-rised, -ris·ing.** *Chiefly Brit.* porphyrize.

por·phy·rit·ic (pôr′fə rit′ik), *adj.* **1.** of, pertaining to, containing, or resembling porphyry. **2.** noting, pertaining to, or resembling the texture or structure characteristic of porphyry. [late ME *porphiritike* < ML *porphyrītic(us)* < Gk *porphyrītikós* of PORPHYRY; see -IC]

por·phy·ri·za·tion (pôr′fə ri zā′shən), *n.* reduction to a powder, formerly done on a slab of porphyry. Also, *esp. Brit.,* **porphyrisation.** [PORPHYRIZE + -ATION]

por·phy·rize (pôr′fə rīz′), *v.t.*, **-rized, -riz·ing.** to subject to porphyrization. Also, *esp. Brit.,* **porphyrise.** [PORPHYR(Y) + -IZE]

por·phy·roid (pôr′fə roid′), *n.* **1.** a rock resembling porphyry. **2.** a sedimentary rock which has been metamorphosed so as to leave some original crystals in a fine-textured, layered matrix. [PORPHYR(Y) + -OID]

por·phy·ry (pôr′fə rē), *n., pl.* **-ries. 1.** a very hard rock, anciently quarried in Egypt, having a dark, purplish-red groundmass containing small crystals of feldspar. **2.** any rock containing coarse crystals in a finer-grained groundmass. [ME *porfurie, porfirie* < ML **porphyri(um),* alter. of LL *porphyrītēs* < Gk: porphyry, short for *porphyrītēs líthos* porphyritic (i.e., purplish) stone, equiv. to *pórphyr(os)* purple + *-ītēs;* see -ITE[1]]

Por·phy·ry (pôr′fə rē), *n.* (*Malchus*) A.D. c233–c304, Greek philosopher. —**Por·phyr·e·an** (pôr fēr′ē ən), *adj.* —**Por·phyr′i·an,** *adj., n.* —**Por·phyr′i·an·ist,** *n.*

por·poise (pôr′pəs), *n., pl.* (*esp. collectively*) **-poise,** (*esp. referring to two or more kinds or species*) **-pois·es,** *v.* **-poised, -pois·ing.** —*n.* **1.** any of several small, gregarious cetaceans of the genus *Phocaena,* five to eight feet long, usually blackish above and paler beneath, and having a blunt, rounded snout, esp. the common porpoise, *P. phocaena,* of both the North Atlantic and Pacific. **2.** any of several other small cetaceans, as the common dolphin, *Delphinus delphis.* —*v.i.* **3.** (of a speeding motorboat) to leap clear of the water after striking a wave. **4.** (of a torpedo) to appear above the surface of the water. [ME *porpoys* < MF *porpois* < LL **porcus piscis* hog fish, for L *porcus marīnus* sea hog] —**por′poise·like′,** *adj.*

Porpoise, *Phocaena phocaena* (Length 5 to 8 ft.)

por·rect[1] (pə rekt′, pô-), *adj.* extending horizontally; projecting. [< L *porrect(us).* See PORRECT[2]]

por·rect[2] (pə rekt′, pô-), *v.t.* *Eccles. Law.* to submit or put forward for inspection or emendation: *to porrect a bill of costs.* [ME < L *porrect(us)* stretched out (ptp. of *porrigere*), equiv to *por-* PRO-[2] + *reg-* rule, direct, guide + *-tus* ptp. suffix] —**por·rec·tion** (pə rek′shən), *n.*

por·ridge (pôr′ij, por′-), *n.* *Chiefly Brit.* a food made of oatmeal, or some other meal or cereal, boiled to a thick consistency in water or milk. [var. of POTTAGE] —**por′ridge·like′,** *adj.*

Por·ri·ma (por′ə mə), *n.* Antevorta.

por·rin·ger (pôr′in jər, por′-), *n.* a low dish or cup, often with a handle, from which soup, porridge, or the like is eaten. [var. of late ME *potinger,* nasalized form of *potager* < MF. See POTTAGE, -ER[2]]

Por′ro prism′ (pôr′ō), *Optics.* an isosceles, right-triangular prism in which light entering one half of the hypotenuse face is reflected at the two short sides and is reversed in orientation when it leaves the other half of the hypotenuse: used in 90°-oriented pairs in binoculars to increase the length of the optical path and to erect the final image. [named after Ignazio *Porro* (1801–1875), Italian engineer]

Por·se·na (pôr′sə nə), *n.* **Lars** (lärz), a legendary Etruscan king, reputed to have attacked Rome in order to restore the banished Tarquinius Superbus to the throne. Also, **Por·sen·na** (pôr sen′ə).

port[1] (pōrt, pôrt), *n.* **1.** a city, town, or other place where ships load or unload. **2.** a place along a coast in which ships may take refuge from storms; harbor. **3.** Also called **port of entry.** *Law.* any place where persons and merchandise are allowed to pass, by water or land, into and out of a country and where customs officers are stationed to inspect or appraise imported goods. **4.** a geographical area which forms a harbor: *the largest port on the eastern seaboard.* **5.** *Informal.* an airport. [ME, OE < L *port(us)* harbor, haven] —**port′less,** *adj.*
—**Syn. 1.** See **harbor. 2.** anchorage.

port[2] (pōrt, pôrt), *n.* **1.** the left-hand side of a vessel or aircraft, facing forward. —*adj.* **2.** pertaining to port. **3.** on the left side of a vessel or aircraft. —*v.t., v.i.* **4.** to turn or shift to the port, or left, side. [special use of PORT[4]]

port[3] (pōrt, pôrt), *n.* any of a class of very sweet wines, mostly dark-red, originally from Portugal. [after *Oporto* (Pg *o porto* the port). See OPORTO]

port[4] (pōrt, pôrt), *n.* **1.** *Naut.* any of various glass-covered apertures in the side of a vessel or of a deckhouse on a vessel, used for admitting light and air, analogous to windows. **2.** *Mach.* an aperture in the surface of a cylinder, for the passage of steam, air, water, etc. **3.** a small aperture in an armored vehicle, aircraft, or fortification through which a gun can be fired or a camera directed. **4.** the raised center portion of certain bits. **5.** *Chiefly Scot.* a gate or portal, as a town or fortress. [ME, OE < L *porta* gate]

port[5] (pōrt, pôrt), *v.t.* **1.** *Mil.* to carry (a rifle or other weapon) with both hands, in a slanting direction across the front of the body, with the barrel or like part near the left shoulder. —*n.* **2.** *Mil.* the position of a rifle or other weapon when ported. **3.** manner of bearing oneself; carriage; bearing. [< F *port(er)* < L *portāre* to carry. See FARE]

Port., **1.** Portugal. **2.** Portuguese.

port·a·ble (pōr′tə bəl, pôr′-), *adj.* **1.** capable of being transported or conveyed: *a portable stage.* **2.** easily carried or conveyed by hand: *a portable typewriter.* **3.** *Obs.* endurable. —*n.* **4.** something which is portable, esp. as distinguished from a nonportable counterpart: *Of their three television sets, one is a portable.* [late ME < LL *portābil(is).* See PORT[5], -ABLE] —**port′a·bil′i·ty,** *n.*

por·tage (pōr′tij, pôr′-), *n., v.,* **-taged, -tag·ing.** —*n.* **1.** the act of carrying; carriage. **2.** the carrying of boats, goods, etc., overland from one navigable water to another. **3.** place or course over which this is done. **4.** cost of carriage. —*v.i.* **5.** to make a portage: *On this stretch of the river, we have to portage for a mile.* —*v.t.* **6.** to carry (something) on a portage; make a portage with: *We portaged our canoe around the rapids.* [late ME < MF; see PORT[5], -AGE]

Por·tage (pōr′tij, pôr′-), *n.* **1.** a town in central Wisconsin. 7822 (1960). **2.** a town in central Pennsylvania. 3933 (1960).

Por·tage·ville (pōr′tij vil′, pôr′-), *n.* a town in SE Missouri. 2505 (1960).

por·tal[1] (pōr′tᵊl, pôr′-), *n.* **1.** a door, gate, or entrance, esp. one of imposing appearance, as to a palace. **2.** Also called **por′tal frame′.** an iron or steel bent for bracing a framed structure, having curved braces between the vertical members and a horizontal member at the top. **3.** an entrance to a tunnel or mine. [ME *portale* < ML, neut. of *portālis* of a gate. See PORTAL[2]] —**por′taled, por′talled,** *adj.*

por·tal[2] (pōr′tᵊl, pôr′-), *Anat.* —*adj.* **1.** noting or pertaining to the transverse fissure of the liver. —*n.* **2.** See **portal vein.** [< ML *portāl(is)* of a gate. See PORT[4], -AL[1]]

por′tal brace′, a brace of quadrantal form for reinforcing the knee of an iron or steel bent.

Por·ta·les (pôr tä′lis), *n.* a town in E New Mexico. 9695 (1960).

Port′ Al·le·ga′ny (al′ə gā′nē, al′ə gā′-), a town in N Pennsylvania. 2742 (1960).

Port′ Al′len, a town in central Louisiana. 5026 (1960).

por′tal-to-por′tal pay′ (pōr′tᵊl tə pōr′tᵊl, pôr′tᵊl tə pôr′tᵊl), payment, as to a miner or factory worker, that includes compensation for time spent on the employer's premises in preparation, in travel from the entrance to the assigned work area and back, etc.: *Because workers must change their clothes and pick up tools prior to the work shift, they are demanding portal-to-portal pay.*

por′tal vein′, *Anat.* the large vein conveying blood to the liver from the veins of the stomach, intestine, spleen, and pancreas.

por·ta·men·to (pōr′tə men′tō, pôr′-; *It.* pôr′tä men′tō), *n., pl.* **-ti** (-tē), **-tos.** *Music.* a passing or gliding from one pitch or tone to another with a smooth progression. [< It: fingering, lit., a bearing, carrying. See PORT[5], -MENT]

port·ance (pōr′tᵊns, pôr′-), *n.* *Archaic.* bearing; behavior. [< MF; see PORT[5], -ANCE]

Port′ An′ge·les (an′jə ləs), a city in NW Washington, on the Juan de Fuca Strait. 12,653 (1960).

Port′ Ar′thur, **1.** Japanese, **Ryojunko, Ryojun.** a seaport in S Liaoning province, in Manchuria, in NE China, on the Yellow Sea: formerly a possession of Japan (1905–45); now part of Lushun municipality; nominally under joint Russian and Chinese control. 210,000 (est. 1954). **2.** a seaport in SE Texas, on Sabine Lake. 66,676 (1960). **3.** a city in S Ontario, in S Canada, on Lake Superior. 45,276 (1961).

por·ta·tive (pōr′tə tiv, pôr′-), *adj.* **1.** capable of being carried; portable. **2.** having or pertaining to the power or function of carrying. —*n.* **3.** Also called **por′tative or′gan.** a small portable pipe organ used esp. during the Middle Ages and the Renaissance. [ME *portatif* < MF. See PORT[5], -ATIVE]

Port-au-Prince (pōrt′ō prins′, pôrt′-; *Fr.* pôr tō-prans′), *n.* a seaport in and the capital of Haiti, in the S part. 240,000 (est. 1960).

port′ author′ity, a government commission that manages bridges, tunnels, airports, and other such facilities of a port or city.

Port′ Blair′ (blâr), a seaport in and the capital of the Andaman and Nicobar Islands, on S Andaman. 3496 (1951).

port′ cap′tain, *Naut.* **1.** an official in charge of the harbor activities of a seaport. **2.** See **marine superintendent.**

Port′ Car′bon, a town in central Pennsylvania. 2775 (1960).

Port′ Char′lotte, a town in SW Florida. 3197 (1960).

Port′ Ches′ter, a city in SE New York, on Long Island Sound. 24,960 (1960).

Port′ Clin′ton, a town in N Ohio. 6870 (1960).

port·cul·lis (pōrt kul′is, pôrt-), *n.* (esp. in medieval castles) a strong grating, as of iron, made to slide along vertical grooves at the sides of a gateway of a fortified place and let down to prevent passage. [ME *portecolys* < MF *porte coleice,* equiv. to *porte* PORT[4] + *coleice,* fem. of *coleis* flowing, sliding < LL *cōlāticius;* see COULEE, -ITIOUS]

Portcullis

port de bras (*Fr.* pôr də brȧ′), *Ballet.* **1.** the technique of moving the arms properly. **2.** the exercises for developing this technique. [< F: carriage of arm]

Port du Sa·lut (pôrt′ də sə lo͞o′, pōrt′; *Fr.* pôr dy sa ly′), Port-Salut.

Porte (pōrt, pôrt), *n.* the former Ottoman court or government in Turkey. Official name, **Sublime Porte.** [short for *Sublime Porte* High Gate, F trans. of the Turkish official title *Babi Ali,* with reference to the palace gate at which justice was administered]

porte-co·chere (pōrt′kō shâr′, -kə-, pôrt′-), *n.* **1.** a covered carriage entrance leading into a courtyard. **2.** a porch at the door of a building for sheltering persons entering and leaving carriages. Also, **porte′-co·chère′.** [< F: gate for coaches]

Porte E·troite, La (*Fr.* lȧ pôrt ā trwät′). See **Strait Is the Gate.**

Port′ Eliz′abeth, a seaport in the SE Cape of Good Hope province, in the S Republic of South Africa. 270,815 with suburbs (1960).

port′ engineer′, one who is responsible for the maintenance and repair of the machinery of the vessels of a shipping line and for the supervision of its engineering personnel. Also called **superintendent engineer.**

porte-mon·naie (pôrt mō ne′; *Eng.* pōrt′mun′ē, pôrt′-), *n., pl.* **-mon·naies** (-mō ne′; *Eng.* -mun′ēz), *French.* a small purse or pocketbook. [lit., money-carrier]

por·tend (pōr tend′, pôr-), *v.t.* **1.** to indicate in advance; to foreshadow or presage, as an omen does: *The street incident may portend a general uprising.* **2.** *Obs.* to signify; mean. [late ME < L *portend(ere)* (to) point out, indicate, portend, var. of *prōtendere* to extend. See PRO-[1], TEND[1]]
—**Syn. 1.** foretell, forecast, augur, promise, forebode.

por·tent (pōr′tent, pôr′-), *n.* **1.** an indication or omen of something about to happen, esp. something momentous. **2.** ominous significance: *an occurrence of dire portent.* **3.** a prodigy or marvel. [< L *portent(um)* sign, token, n. use of neut. of *portentus,* ptp. of *portendere* to PORTEND]
—**Syn. 1.** augury, warning. See **sign. 2.** import.

por·ten·tous (pōr ten′təs, pôr-), *adj.* **1.** of the nature of a portent; momentous. **2.** ominously significant or indicative: *a portentous defeat.* **3.** marvelous; amazing; prodigious. [< L *portentōs(us).* See PORTENT, -OUS] —**por·ten′tous·ly,** *adv.* —**por·ten′tous·ness,** *n.*
—**Syn. 2.** unpropitious, inauspicious, threatening.

por·ter[1] (pōr′tər, pôr′-), *n.* **1.** one employed to carry burdens or baggage, as at a railroad station or a hotel. **2.** one who does cleaning and maintenance work in a building, factory, store, etc. **3.** *U.S.* an attendant in a parlor car or sleeping car. [ME, var. of *portour* < MF *porteour* < LL *portātōr-* (s. of *portātor*). See PORT[5], -OR[2]]

por·ter[2] (pōr′tər, pôr′-), *n.* **1.** one who has charge of a door or gate; doorkeeper. **2.** *Rom. Cath. Ch.* ostiary (def. 1). [ME < AF < LL *portār(ius)* gatekeeper. See PORT[4], -ER[2]]

por·ter[3] (pōr′tər, pôr′-), *n.* a heavy, dark-brown ale made with malt browned by drying at a high temperature. [short for *porter's ale,* appar. orig. brewed for porters]

Por·ter (pōr′tər, pôr′-), *n.* **1. Cole,** 1893–1964, U.S. composer. **2. David,** 1780–1843, U.S. naval officer. **3.** his son **David Dix·on** (dik′sən), 1813–91, Union naval officer in the Civil War. **4. Gene** (*Gene Stratton Porter*), 1868–1924, U.S. novelist. **5. Katherine Anne,** 1894–1980, U.S. writer. **6. Noah,** 1811–92, U.S. educator, writer, and lexicographer. **7. William Sidney** ("*O. Henry*"), 1862–1910, U.S. short-story writer. **8.** a boy's given name.

por·ter·age (pōr′tər ij, pôr′-), *n.* **1.** the work of a porter or carrier. **2.** the charge for such work. [late ME; see PORTER[1], -AGE]

por′ter chair′, *Eng. Furniture.* a chair of the 18th century having deep wings continued to form an arch over the seat. Also called **page chair.**

por·ter·ess (pōr′tər is, pôr′-), *n.* portress.

por·ter·house (pōr′tər hous′, pôr′-), *n., pl.* **-hous·es** (-hou′ziz). **1.** Also called **por′terhouse steak′.** a choice cut of beef from between the prime ribs and the sirloin. **2.** *Archaic.* a house at which porter and other liquors are retailed. [PORTER[3] + HOUSE]

Por·ter·ville (pōr′tər vil′, pôr′-), *n.* a town in central California. 7991 (1960).

Port-E·tienne (*Fr.* pôr tā tyen′), *n.* a seaport in W Mauritania. 1300 (est. 1961).

Port′ Ew′en (yo͞o′ən), a town in SE New York. 2622 (1960).

port·fo·li·o (pōrt fō′lē ō′, pôrt-), *n., pl.* **-li·os.** **1.** a portable case for carrying loose papers, prints, etc. **2.** such a case for carrying documents of a government department. **3.** the office or post of a minister of state or member of a cabinet. Cf. **minister without portfolio.** **4.** an itemized account; the securities, discount paper, etc., of an investment organization, bank, or other investor. [< It *portafoglio,* equiv. to *porta,* impv. of *portare* to carry (< L) + *foglio* leaf, sheet (< L *folium*)]

Port Gen·til (*Fr.* pôr zhäN tē′), a seaport in W Gabon. 20,000 (est. 1961).

Port′ Gib′son, a town in SW Mississippi. 2861 (1960).

Port′ Har′court (här′kərt, -kōrt, -kôrt), a seaport in S Nigeria. 72,000 (est. 1963).

port·hole (pōrt′hōl′, pôrt′-), *n.* **1.** any of various relatively small ports in a vessel, as for light or ventilation. **2.** an opening in a wall, door, etc., as one through which to shoot. [PORT[4] + HOLE]

port′hole die′, *Metalworking.* a die having several openings for the extrusion of separate parts of an object later formed by the welding or fusing together of these parts.

Port′ Hud′son, a village in SE Louisiana, on the Mississippi, N of Baton Rouge: siege during the Civil War 1863.

Port′ Hu′ron, a port in SE Michigan, on the St. Clair River, at the S end of Lake Huron. 36,084 (1960).

Por·tia (pōr′shə, -shē ə, pôr′-), *n.* **1.** the heroine of Shakespeare's *Merchant of Venice,* who, in one scene, disguises herself as a lawyer. **2.** a woman lawyer. **3.** a girl's given name.

por·ti·co (pōr′tə kō′, pôr′-), *n., pl.* **-coes, -cos.** a structure consisting of a roof supported by columns or piers, usually attached to a building as a porch. [< It < L *porticus* porch, portico. See PORT[4]]

Portico

por·ti·coed (pōr′tə kōd′, pôr′-), *adj.* provided with a portico or porticoes. [PORTICO + -ED[3]]

por·tiere (pōr tyâr′, pôr-, pōr′tē âr′, pôr′-), *n.* a curtain hung in a doorway, either to replace the door or for decoration. Also, **portière.** [< F *portière* < ML *portāria,* n. use of fem. of LL *portārius;* see PORTER[2]] —**por·tiered′,** *adj.*

por·tière (pōr tyâr′, pôr-, pōr′tē âr′, pôr′-; *Fr.* pôr tyer′), *n., pl.* **-tières** (-tyârz′, -tē ârz′; *Fr.* -tyer′). portiere.

Por·ti·na·ri (pôr tē nä′rē), *n.* **Cân·di·do** (käN′dē-do͞o), 1903–62, Brazilian painter.

por·tion (pōr′shən, pôr′-), *n.* **1.** a part of any whole, either separated from or integrated with it: *I read a portion of the manuscript.* **2.** the part of a whole allotted to or belonging to a person or group; share. **3.** an amount of food served for one person; serving; helping: *He took a large portion of spinach.* **4.** the part of an estate that goes to an heir or a next of kin. **5.** the money, goods, or estate which a woman brings to her husband at marriage; dowry. **6.** that which is allotted to a person by God or fate. —*v.t.* **7.** to divide into or distribute in portions or shares (often fol. by *out*). **8.** to furnish with a portion, as with an inheritance or a dowry: *All of his children have been amply portioned.* **9.** to provide with a lot or fate: *She was portioned with sorrow throughout her life.* [ME *porcion* < OF < L *portiōn-* (s. of *portiō*) share, part, akin to *pars* PART] —**por′tion·a·ble,** *adj.* —**por′tion·less,** *adj.*
—**Syn. 1.** section, segment. See **part. 2.** allotment, quota, lot, dividend. **3.** ration. **4.** inheritance. **7.** allot, apportion. **8.** endow. —**Ant. 1.** whole.

por·tion·er (pōr′shə nər, pôr′-), *n.* a person who receives or holds a portion, or who divides something into portions. [PORTION + -ER[1]]

Port′ Is′abel, a town in S Texas. 3575 (1960).

Port′ Jack′son, an inlet of the Pacific in SE Australia: the harbor of Sydney.

Port′ Jer′vis (jûr′vis), a town in SE New York. 9268 (1960).

Port·land (pōrt′lənd, pôrt′-), *n.* **1.** a seaport in NW Oregon, at the confluence of the Willamette and Columbia rivers. 372,676 (1960). **2.** a seaport in SW Maine, on Casco Bay. 72,566 (1960). **3.** a town in E Indiana. 6999

(1960). **4.** a town in central Connecticut. 5587 (1960). **5.** a town in central Michigan. 3330 (1960). **6.** a town in S Texas. 2538 (1960).

Port′land cement′, a type of hydraulic cement usually made by burning a mixture of limestone and clay in a kiln. Also, **port′land cement′.** [after the Isle of *Portland*, Dorsetshire, England]

Port′land stone′, a limestone quarried on the Isle of Portland, Dorsetshire, England.

Port′ La·vac′a (lə vak′ə), a town in S Texas. 8864 (1960).

Port′ Lou′is (lo͞o′is, lo͞o′ē), a seaport in and the capital of Mauritius, in the Indian Ocean, E of Madagascar. 125,000 (est. 1963).

port·ly (pōrt′lē, pôrt′-), *adj.*, **-li·er, -li·est.** **1.** rather heavy or fat; stout; corpulent. **2.** *Archaic.* stately, dignified, or imposing. [PORT[5] (n.) + -LY] **—port′li·ness,** *n.*

port·man·teau (pōrt man′tō, pôrt-; pōrt′man tō′, pôrt′-), *n., pl.* **-teaus, -teaux** (-tōz, -tō; -tōz′, -tō′). *Chiefly Brit.* a case or bag to carry clothing in while traveling, esp. a leather trunk or suitcase which opens into two halves. [< F *portemanteau*, lit., cloak carrier. See PORT[5], MANTLE]

portman′teau word′, blend (def. 9).

Port′ Mores′by (mōrz′bē, môrz′-), a seaport in SE New Guinea: capital of the merged Australian territories of Papua and New Guinea: important Allied base in World War II. 14,250 (est. 1956).

Port′ Nech′es (nech′iz), a town in SE Texas. 8696 (1960).

Pôr·to (pôr′to͝o), *n.* Portuguese name of **Oporto.**

Pôr·to A·le·gre (pôʀ′to͝o ä le′gʀə), a seaport in S Brazil. 625,957 (1960).

Pôr·to A·mé·lia (*Port.* pôʀ′to͝o ə me′lyə), a seaport in NE Mozambique. 52,148 (est. 1955).

Por·to·bel·lo (pōr′tō bel′ō, pôr′-), *n.* a small seaport on the Caribbean coast of Panama, NE of Colón: harbor discovered and named by Columbus 1502; a principal city of Spanish colonial America.

port′ of call′, a port visited briefly by a ship, usually to take on or discharge passengers and cargo or to undergo repairs.

port′ of en′try, port[1] (def. 3).

Port-of-Spain (pōrt′əv spān′, pôrt′-), *n.* a seaport on NW Trinidad, in the SE West Indies: the capital of Trinidad and Tobago. 93,954 (1960).

por·to·la·no (pōr′tᵊlä′nō, pôr′-), *n., pl.* **-nos, -ni** (-nē). a descriptive atlas of the Middle Ages, giving sailing directions and providing charts showing rhumb lines and the location of ports and various coastal features. Also called **portulan chart, rutter.** [< It: shipmaster's guidebook; earlier, harbor master < ML *portulānus*. See PORT[1], -ULE, -AN]

Por·to No·vo (pōr′tō nō′vō, pôr′-), a seaport in and the capital of Dahomey. 69,500 (est. 1964).

Port′ Or′chard, a town in central Washington. 2778 (1960).

Port′ Or′ford ce′dar (ôr′fərd). See **white cedar.** [after *Port Orford*, Oregon]

Por·to Ri·co (pōr′tə rē′kō, pôr′-), former official name (until 1932) of **Puerto Rico.** **—Por′to Ri′can.**

Pôr·to Ve·lho (pôʀ′to͝o ve′lyo͝o), a city in and the capital of Rondônia, in W Brazil, on the Madeira River. 22,824 (1960).

Port′ Phil′lip Bay′, a bay in SE Australia: the harbor of Melbourne. 31 mi. long; 25 mi. wide.

Port′ Pir′ie (pir′ē), a city in S Australia. 14,003 (1961).

por·trait (pōr′trit, -trāt, pôr′-), *n.* **1.** a likeness of a person, esp. of the face, as a painting, drawing, photograph, etc.: *a gallery of family portraits.* **2.** a verbal picture or description, usually of a person: *a biography that provides a fascinating portrait of an 18th-century rogue.* [< MF: a drawing, image, etc., n. use of ptp. of *portraire* to PORTRAY] **—por′trait-like′,** *adj.*

por′trait flask′, a glass flask of the 19th century having a portrait molded onto the side.

por·trait·ist (pōr′tri tist, -trā-, pôr′-), *n.* one who makes portraits. [PORTRAIT + -IST]

Por′trait of a La′dy, The, a novel (1881) by Henry James.

Por′trait of the Art′ist as a Young′ Man′, a novel (1916) by James Joyce.

por·trai·ture (pōr′tri chər, pôr′-), *n.* **1.** the art of portraying. **2.** a pictorial representation; portrait. **3.** a verbal picture. [ME < MF; see PORTRAIT, -URE]

por·tray (pōr trā′, pôr-), *v.t.* **1.** to represent by a drawing, painting, carving, or the like. **2.** to represent dramatically, as on the stage: *He portrayed Napoleon in the play.* **3.** to depict in words; describe graphically. [ME *portraye* < MF *portraire* < LL *prōtrahere* to depict, L: to draw forth, equiv. to *prō-* PRO-[1] + *trahere* to draw] **—por·tray′a·ble,** *adj.* **—por·tray′er,** *n.* **—Syn. 1, 3.** picture, delineate, limn. See **depict.**

por·tray·al (pōr trā′əl, pôr-), *n.* **1.** act of portraying. **2.** a representation; portrait. [PORTRAY + -AL[2]]

por·tress (pōr′tris, pôr′-), *n.* a female porter or doorkeeper. Also, **porteress.** [ME *porteresse*. See PORTER[2], -ESS]

Port′ Roy′al, **1.** a village in S South Carolina, on Port Royal island: colonized by French Huguenots 1562. **2.** an historic town on SE Jamaica at the entrance to Kingston harbor: a former capital of Jamaica. **3.** former name of **Annapolis Royal.**

Port′ Sa·id′ (sä ēd′), a seaport in the NE United Arab Republic at the Mediterranean end of the Suez Canal. 256,100 (est. 1962). Also, **Port′ Sa·ïd′.**

Port-Sa·lut (pôr′sə lo͞o′, pôr′-; *Fr.* pôʀ sa ly′), *n.* a yellow, whole-milk cheese, esp. that made at the monastery of Port du Salut near the town of Laval, France.

Ports·mouth (pōrts′məth, pôrts′-), *n.* **1.** a seaport in S Hampshire, in S England, on the English Channel: chief British naval station. 215,198 (1961). **2.** a seaport in SE Virginia: navy yard. 114,773 (1960). **3.** a seaport in SE New Hampshire: naval base; Russian-Japanese peace treaty 1905. 25,833 (1960). **4.** a city in S Ohio, on the Ohio River. 33,637 (1960).

Port St. Joe, a town in NW Florida. 4217 (1960).

Port′ Sudan′, a seaport in the NE Sudan, on the Red Sea. 47,562 (1956).

Port′ Sul′phur, a town in SE Louisiana. 2868 (1960).

port′ superinten′dent. See **marine superintendent.**

Port′ Town′send (toun′zənd), a town in NW Washington. 5074 (1960).

Por·tu·gal (pōr′chə gəl, pôr′-; *Port.* pôʀ′to͝o gäl′), *n.* a republic in SW Europe, on the Iberian Peninsula, W of Spain. (Including the Azores and the Madeira Islands) 9,107,000 (est. 1964); 35,414 sq. mi. *Cap.:* Lisbon.

Por·tu·guese (pōr′chə gēz′, -gēs′, pôr′-; pōr′chə gēz′, -gēs′, pôr′-), *adj., n., pl.* **-guese.** **—adj. 1.** of, pertaining to, or characteristic of Portugal, its inhabitants, or their language. **—n. 2.** a native or inhabitant of Portugal. **3.** the language, a Romance language, of Portugal and Brazil. [< Pg *portuguez*, Sp *portugues*, etc. See PORTUGAL, -ESE]

Por′tuguese cher′ry lau′rel, a tree, *Laurocerasus lusitanica*, of Spain and Portugal, having clusters of fragrant, white flowers, and dark-purple fruit.

Por′tuguese cy′press, a tree, *Cupressus lusitanica*, of Mexico, having drooping main branches and bluish-green leaves.

Por′tuguese East′ Af′rica, Mozambique (def. 1).

Por′tuguese Guin′ea, a Portuguese overseas province on the W coast of Africa between Guinea and Senegal. 525,000 (est. 1964); 13,948 sq. mi. *Cap.:* Brissau.

Por′tuguese In′dia, a former Portuguese overseas territory on the W coast of India, consisting of the districts of Goa, Daman, and Diu: annexed by India December 1961. *Cap.:* Goa.

Por′tuguese man-of-war′, any of several large, oceanic hydrozoans of the genus *Physalia*, having a large, bladderlike structure by which they are buoyed up and from which are suspended numerous processes.

Portuguese man-of-war, *Physalia arethusa* (Float length about 8 in.; tentacles 40 to 60 ft.)

Por′tuguese Ti′mor, Timor (def. 3).

Por′tuguese West′ Af′rica, Angola.

por·tu·lac·a (pōr′chə lak′ə, pôr′-), *n.* any plant of the genus *Portulaca*, comprising the purslanes. [< NL, genus name, L: PURSLANE]

por·tu·la·ca·ceous (pōr′chə lə kā′shəs, pôr′-), *adj.* belonging to the *Portulacaceae*, or purslane family of plants. [PORTULAC(A) + -ACEOUS]

por′tulan chart′ (pōr′chə lən, pôr′-), portolano.

Por·tu·nus (pôr to͞o′nəs, -tyo͞o′-), *n.* the ancient Roman god of ports and harbors. Also, **Por·tum·nus** (pôr tum′nəs).

Port′ Vue′ (vyo͞o), a town in SW Pennsylvania. 6635 (1960).

Port′ Wash′ington, **1.** a town on NW Long Island, in SE New York. 15,657 (1960). **2.** a town in E Wisconsin. 5984 (1960).

Port′ Went′worth (went′wûrth′), a town in E Georgia. 3705 (1960).

pos., **1.** position. **2.** positive. **3.** possession. **4.** possessive.

po·sa·da (pô sä′thä), *n., pl.* **-das** (-thäs). *Spanish.* an inn. [lit., halting place]

Po·sa·das (pô sä′thäs), *n.* a city in NE Argentina, on the Paraná River. 77,817 (est. 1965).

pose[1] (pōz), *v.,* **posed, pos·ing,** *n.* **—v.i. 1.** to affect or assume a particular character, esp. with a view to the impression made on others: *He likes to pose as a judge of literature.* **2.** to present oneself insincerely: *He seems to be posing in all his behavior.* **3.** to assume or hold a physical attitude, as for an artistic purpose: *to pose for a painter.* **—v.t. 4.** to place in a suitable position or attitude for a picture, tableau, or the like: *to pose a group for a photograph.* **5.** to assert, state, or propound: *to pose a difficult problem.* **6.** *Archaic.* to put or place. **—n. 7.** a bodily attitude or posture: *Her pose had a note of defiance in it.* **8.** a mental attitude or posture: *a pose cultivated by the upper classes.* **9.** the act or period of posing, as for a picture. **10.** a position or attitude assumed in posing, or exhibited by a figure in a picture, sculptural work, tableau, or the like. **11.** a studied attitude; affectation: *His liberalism is merely a pose.* [ME < MF *pose(r)* < LL *pausāre* to lay down (a sense due to confusion with L *pōnere* to place, put), L: to halt, stop, deriv. of *pausa* a PAUSE] **—pos′ing·ly,** *adv.* **—Syn. 3.** sit, model. **7.** See **position.**

pose[2] (pōz), *v.t.,* **posed, pos·ing.** **1.** to embarrass or baffle, as by a difficult question or problem. **2.** *Obs.* to examine by putting questions. [aph. var. of obs. *appose*, var. of OPPOSE, used in sense of L *appōnere* to put to]

Po·sei·don (pō sīd′ᵊn, pə-), *n.* the ancient Greek god of the sea, with the power to cause earthquakes, identified by the Romans with Neptune.

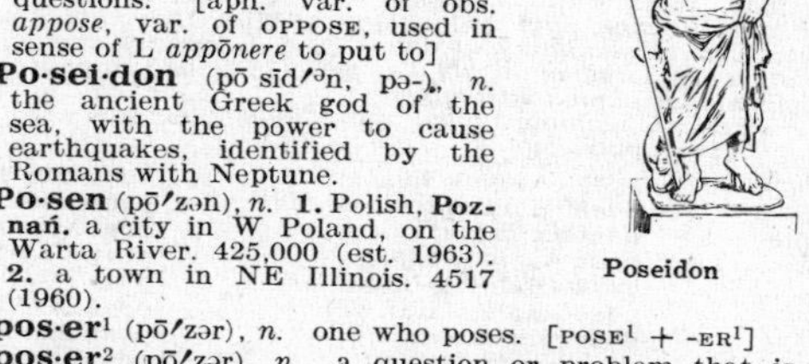

Poseidon

Po·sen (pō′zən), *n.* **1.** Polish, **Poznań.** a city in W Poland, on the Warta River. 425,000 (est. 1963). **2.** a town in NE Illinois. 4517 (1960).

pos·er[1] (pō′zər), *n.* one who poses. [POSE[1] + -ER[1]]

pos·er[2] (pō′zər), *n.* a question or problem that is puzzling or confusing. [POSE[2] + -ER[1]]

po·seur (pō zûr′; *Fr.* pō zœʀ′), *n., pl.* **-seurs** (-zûrz′; *Fr.* -zœʀ′). one who attempts to impress others by assuming or affecting a manner, degree of elegance, sentiment, etc., other than his true one. [< F; see POSE[1], -OR[2]]

posh[1] (posh), *interj.* (used as an exclamation of contempt or disgust.)

posh[2] (posh), *adj.* sumptuously comfortable or elegant; luxurious: *a posh apartment; a restaurant that's very posh and expensive.* [?]

Pos·i·do·ni·us (pos′i dō′nē əs, pō′si-), *n.* a walled plain in the first quadrant of the face of the moon: about 62 miles in diameter.

pos′i·grade rock′et (poz′ə grād′), *Rocketry.* a rocket on a multistage missile which fires in the direction of flight, usually to effect separation of a burned-out stage. [POSI(TIVE) + -GRADE (? modeled on *retrograde*)]

pos·it (poz′it), *v.t.* **1.** to place, put, or set. **2.** to lay down or assume as a fact or principle; affirm; postulate. **—n. 3.** that which is posited; assumption; postulate. [< L *posit(us)*, ptp. of *pōnere* to place, put]

po·si·tion (pə zish′ən), *n.* **1.** condition with reference to place; location; situation. **2.** a place occupied or to be occupied; site: *a fortified position.* **3.** proper, appropriate, or usual place: *out of position.* **4.** situation or condition, esp. with relation to favorable or unfavorable circumstances: *to be in an awkward position; to bargain from a position of strength.* **5.** status or standing: *He has a position to maintain in the community.* **6.** high standing, as in society; important status: *a person of wealth and position.* **7.** a post of employment: *a position in a bank.* **8.** manner of being placed, disposed, or arranged: *the relative position of the hands of a clock.* **9.** bodily posture or attitude: *to be in a sitting position.* **10.** mental attitude; stand: *one's position on a controversy.* **11.** act of positing. **12.** that which is posited. **13.** *Music.* the arrangement of tones in a chord, esp. with regard to the location of the root tone in a triad or to the distance of the tones from each other. Cf. **close position, inversion** (def. 6a), **open position, root position.** **14.** *Music.* **a.** any of the places on the fingerboard of a stringed instrument where the fingers stop the strings to produce the various pitches. **b.** any of the places to which the slide of a trombone is shifted to produce changes in pitch. **15.** *Class. Pros.* the situation of a short vowel before two or more consonants or their equivalent, making the syllable metrically long. **—v.t. 16.** to put in a particular or appropriate position; place. **17.** to determine the position of; locate. [ME *posicioun* a positing < L *positiōn-*, (s. of *positiō*) a placing, etc. See POSIT, -ION] **—po·si′tion·al,** *adj.* **—po·si′tion·less,** *adj.*

—Syn. 2. station, place, locality, spot. **5.** rank, place. **7.** POSITION, JOB, PLACE, SITUATION refer to a post of employment. POSITION is any employment, though usually above manual labor: *a position as clerk.* JOB is colloquial for POSITION, and applies to any work from lowest to highest in an organization: *a job as fireman, as manager.* PLACE and SITUATION are both mainly used today in reference to a position that is desired or being applied for; SITUATION is the general word in the business world: *Situations Wanted;* PLACE is used rather of domestic employment: *She is looking for a place as a housekeeper.* **8.** placement, disposition, array, arrangement. **9.** POSITION, POSTURE, ATTITUDE, POSE refer to an arrangement or disposal of the body or its parts. POSITION is the general word for the arrangement of the body: *in a reclining position.* POSTURE is usually an assumed arrangement of the body, esp. when standing: *a relaxed posture.* ATTITUDE is often a posture assumed for imitative effect or the like, but may be one adopted for a purpose (as that of a fencer or a tightrope walker): *an attitude of prayer.* A POSE is an attitude assumed, in most cases, for artistic effect: *an attractive pose.* **12.** proposition, hypothesis, postulate, thesis; dictum, assertion, predication, contention; doctrine, principle. **16.** situate.

posi′tional er′ror, *Horol.* error in a timepiece, esp. a watch, as a result of the position in which it is carried or placed.

posi′tion buoy′, a buoy used to mark the position of an anchored or submerged object.

posi′tion i′somer, *Chem.* any of two or more isomers that differ only in the position occupied by a substituent.

posi′tion line′, *Navig.* See **line of position.**

pos·i·tive (poz′i tiv), *adj.* **1.** explicitly stated, stipulated, or expressed: *a positive acceptance of the agreement.* **2.** determined by enactment or convention; arbitrarily laid down: *positive law.* **3.** admitting of no question: *positive proof.* **4.** stated; express; emphatic: *a positive denial.* **5.** confident in opinion or assertion, as a person; fully assured: *He is positive that he will win the contest.* **6.** overconfident or dogmatic: *The less he knows, the more positive he gets.* **7.** without relation to or comparison with other things; not relative or comparative; absolute. **8.** *Informal.* downright; out-and-out: *She's a positive idiot.* **9.** possessing an actual force, being, existence, etc. **10.** *Philos.* **a.** constructive and sure, rather than skeptical. **b.** concerned with or based on matters of experience: *positive philosophy.* **11.** not speculative or theoretical; practical: *a positive approach to the problem.* **12.** emphasizing what is laudable, hopeful, or to the good: *a positive attitude toward the future; positive things to say about a painting.* **13.** consisting in or characterized by the presence or possession of distinguishing or marked qualities or features (opposed to *negative*): *Light is positive, darkness negative.* **14.** noting the presence of such qualities, as a term. **15.** measured or proceeding in a direction assumed as beneficial, progressive, or auspicious: *a positive upturn in the stock market.* **16.** (of government) assuming control or regulation of activities beyond those involved merely with the maintenance of law and order. **17.** *Elect.* **a.** of, pertaining to, or characterized by positive electricity. **b.** indicating a point in a circuit that has a higher potential than that of another point, the current flowing from the point of higher potential to the point of lower potential. **18.** of, pertaining to, or noting the north pole of a magnet. **19.** *Chem.* (of an element or group) tending to lose electrons and become positively charged; basic. **20.** *Photog.* denoting a print or transparency showing the brightness values as they are in the subject. **21.** *Gram.* being, noting, or pertaining to the initial degree of the comparison of adjectives and adverbs as the positive form *good.* Cf. **comparative** (def. 4), **superlative** (def. 3). **22.** *Math.* noting a quantity greater than zero.

23. *Biol.* oriented or moving toward the focus of excitation: *a positive tropism.* 24. *Bacteriol.* (of blood, affected tissue, etc.) showing the presence of an organism which causes a disease. 25. *Mach.* noting or pertaining to a process or machine part having a fixed or certain operation, esp. as the result of elimination of play, free motion, etc.: *positive lubrication.* 26. *Biochem.* See **Rh factor.** —*n.* 27. something positive. 28. a positive quality or characteristic. 29. a positive quantity or symbol. 30. *Photog.* a positive image, as on a print or transparency. 31. *Gram.* a. the positive degree. b. a form in the positive, as *good* or *smooth.* [< L *positīv(us)*; r. ME *positif* < MF. See POSIT, -IVE] —**pos′i·tive·ness, pos′i tiv′i·ty,** *n.*
—**Syn.** 1. definite, unequivocal, categorical, clear, precise, sure. 3. incontrovertible, indisputable. 5. unquestioning. 5, 6. See **sure.** —**Ant.** 1. indefinite. 3. doubtful. 5. unsure, unconfident, uncertain.

pos′itive col′umn, *Physics.* the luminous region between the Faraday dark space and the anode glow in a vacuum tube, occurring when the pressure is low.

pos′itive def′initeness, *Math.* the property of a function that takes on only nonnegative values or that generates another function that takes on only nonnegative values.

pos′itive electric′ity, *Elect.* the electricity present in a body or substance which has a deficiency of electrons, as the electricity developed on glass when rubbed with silk. Cf. **negative electricity.**

pos′itive i′on, *Physics. Chem.* See under **ion** (def. 1).

pos′itive lens′, *Optics.* See **converging lens.**

pos·i·tive·ly (poz′i tiv lē; *esp. for* 3 poz′i tiv′lē), *adv.* 1. with certainty; absolutely: *The statement is positively true.* 2. undoubtedly; decidedly; unquestionably; definitely: *His conduct is positively shocking.* —*interj.* 3. (used to express strong affirmation) yes: *Do you plan to go to the party? Positively!* [POSITIVE + -LY]

pos′itive ray′, *Physics.* See **canal ray.**

pos·i·tiv·ism (poz′i tə viz′əm), *n.* 1. state or quality of being positive; definiteness; assurance. 2. a philosophical system founded by Auguste Comte, concerned with positive facts and phenomena, and excluding speculation upon ultimate causes or origins. [POSITIVE + -ISM] —**pos′i·tiv·ist,** *adj., n.* —**pos′i·tiv·is′tic,** *adj.* —**pos′i·tiv·is′ti·cal·ly,** *adv.*

pos·i·tron (poz′i tron′), *n. Physics.* an elementary particle having the same mass and spin as an electron but having a positive charge equal in magnitude to that of the electron; the antiparticle of the electron. [POSI(TIVE + ELEC)TRON]

pos·i·tro·ni·um (poz′i trō′nē əm), *n. Physics.* a short-lived atomic system consisting of a positron and an electron bound together. [POSITRON + -IUM]

po·sol·o·gy (pə sol′ə jē, pō-), *n.* the branch of pharmacology dealing with the determination of dosage. [< Gk *póso(s)* how much + -LOGY] —**pos·o·log·ic,** (pos′ə loj′ik), **pos′o·log′i·cal,** *adj.* —**po·sol′o·gist,** *n.*

poss., 1. possession. 2. possessive. 3. possible. 4. possibly.

pos·se (pos′ē), *n.* 1. See **posse comitatus.** 2. a body or force armed with legal authority. [< ML *posse* power, force, n. use of L inf.: to be able, have power, equiv. to *pot-* (see POTENT) + *-se* inf. suffix]

pos·se co·mi·ta·tus (pos′ē kom′i tä′təs, -tā′-), 1. the body of men that a peace officer of a county is empowered to call to assist him in preserving the peace, making arrests, and serving writs. 2. a body of men so called into service. [< ML: posse (of the) county]

pos·sess (pə zes′), *v.t.* 1. to have as belonging to one; have as property; own: *to possess a house and a car.* 2. to have as a faculty, quality, or the like: *to possess courage.* 3. to have knowledge of: *to possess a language.* 4. to impart to; inform; familiarize (often fol. by *of* or *with*): *to possess someone of the facts of the case.* 5. to keep or maintain (oneself, one's mind, etc.) in a certain state, as of peace, patience, etc. 6. to maintain control over (oneself, one's mind, etc.). 7. (of a spirit, esp. an evil one) to occupy, dominate, or control (a person) from within: *He thought he was possessed by devils.* 8. (of a feeling, idea, etc.) to dominate or actuate in the manner of such a spirit: *He was possessed by envy.* 9. to make (someone) owner, holder, or master, as of property, information, etc.: *He possessed them of the facts.* 10. to cause to be dominated or influenced, as by an idea, feeling, etc. 11. (of a man) to succeed in having sexual intercourse with. 12. *Archaic.* to seize or take. 13. *Archaic.* to gain or win. 14. *Obs.* to occupy or hold. [ME *possesse(n)* < MF *possess(i)er,* back formation from *possession* POSSESSION] —**pos·ses′sor,** *n.* —**pos·ses′sor·ship′,** *n.*
—**Syn.** 1. See **have.**

pos·sessed (pə zest′), *adj.* 1. spurred or moved by a strong feeling, madness, or a supernatural power (often fol. by *by, of,* or *with*): *The army fought as if possessed. As she was subject to fits, the village believed her to be possessed of the devil.* 2. self-possessed; poised: *She remained possessed despite the trying circumstances.* 3. **possessed of,** having; possessing: *He is possessed of intelligence and ambition.* [POSSESS + -ED²] —**pos·sess·ed·ly** (pə zes′id lē, -zest′lē), *adv.* —**pos·sess′ed·ness,** *n.*

Possessed, The, a novel (1871) by Dostoevski.

pos·ses·sion (pə zesh′ən), *n.* 1. act or fact of possessing. 2. state of being possessed. 3. ownership. 4. *Law.* actual holding or occupancy, either with or without rights of ownership. 5. a thing possessed: *He packed all his possessions into one trunk.* 6. **possessions,** property or wealth. 7. a territorial dominion of a state. 8. *Sports.* a. physical control of the ball or puck by a player or team: *He didn't have full possession when he was tackled.* b. the right of a team to put the ball into play: *They had possession after the other team sank a free throw.* 9. control over oneself, one's mind, etc. 10. domination, actuation, or obsession by a feeling, idea, etc. 11. the feeling or idea itself. [ME < L *possessiōn-* (s. of *possessiō*) a having or taking possession, deriv. of (1) *possessus,* ptp. of *possidēre* to have and hold (opposed to *domināri* to own absolutely); (2) *possessus,* ptp. of *possīdere* to take possession of; see -ION]
—**Syn.** 1. tenure, occupation. 1, 3. See **custody.**

pos·ses·sive (pə zes′iv), *adj.* 1. of or pertaining to possession or ownership. 2. desirous of possessing, esp. excessively so: *A young child is so possessive he will not allow another to play with his toys; a possessive wife.* 3. jealously opposed to the personal independence of, or to any influence other than one's own upon, a child, spouse, etc. 4. *Gram.* a. indicating possession, ownership, origin, etc. *His* in *his book* is a possessive adjective. *His* in *The book is his* is a possessive pronoun. b. noting or pertaining to a case that indicates possession, ownership, origin, etc., as, in English, *John's* in *John's hat.* —*n. Gram.* 5. the possessive case. 6. a form in the possessive. [< L *possessīv(us).* See POSSESS, -IVE] —**pos·ses′sive·ly,** *adv.* —**pos·ses′sive·ness,** *n.*

pos·ses·so·ry (pə zes′ə rē), *adj.* 1. of or pertaining to a possessor or to possession. 2. arising from possession: *a possessory interest.* 3. having possession. [< LL *possessōri(us),* equiv. to L *possess(us)* (ptp. of *possidēre* to POSSESS) + *-ōrius* -ORY¹] —**pos·ses′so·ri·ness,** *n.*

pos·set (pos′it), *n.* a drink made of hot milk curdled with ale, wine, or the like, often sweetened and spiced. [late ME *poshote, possot,* ? OE **poswǣt* drink good for cold, equiv. to *pos* cold in the head + *wǣt* drink]

pos·si·bil·i·ty (pos′ə bil′i tē), *n., pl.* **-ties.** 1. state or fact of being possible: *the possibility of error.* 2. something possible: *He had exhausted every possibility but one.* [ME *possibilite* < L *possibilitās.* See POSSIBLE, -ITY]

pos·si·ble (pos′ə bəl), *adj.* 1. that may or can be, exist, happen, be done, be used, etc: *no possible cure.* 2. that may be true or may be the case, as something concerning which one has no knowledge to the contrary: *It is possible that he went.* [ME < L *possibil(is)* that may be done, equiv. to *poss(e)* (to) be able (see POSSE) + *-ibilis* -IBLE]
—**Syn.** 1. POSSIBLE, FEASIBLE, PRACTICABLE refer to that which may come about or take place without prevention by serious obstacles. That which is POSSIBLE is naturally able or even likely to happen, other circumstances being equal: *Discovery of a new source of plutonium may be possible.* FEASIBLE refers to the ease with which something can be done and implies a high degree of desirability for doing it: *This plan is the most feasible.* PRACTICABLE applies to that which can be done with the means which are at hand and with conditions as they are: *We ascended the slope as far as was practicable.*

pos·si·bly (pos′ə blē), *adv.* 1. perhaps; maybe: *It may possibly rain today.* 2. in a possible manner: *She has all the money she can possibly use.* 3. by any possibility: *Could you possibly check this information for me?* [ME; see POSSIBLE, -LY]

pos·sie (pos′ē), *n. Australian.* a job; position. Also, **possy.** [shortening and alter. of POSITION]

POSSLQ (pos′əl kyōō′), *n.* a person of the opposite sex who shares another's living quarters but is not related by blood, marriage, or adoption. Also, **POSSLQU.** [*p(artner of the) o(pposite) s(ex) s(haring) l(iving) q(uarters)*]

pos·sum (pos′əm), *n.* 1. opossum. 2. *Australian.* any of various phalangers, esp. of the genus *Trichosurus.* 3. **play possum,** *U.S. Informal.* a. to feign sleep or death. b. to dissemble or pretend ignorance: *The baseball broke the window, but the boys played possum when asked who had thrown it.* [short for OPOSSUM]

pos′sum haw′, 1. a shrub, *Ilex decidua,* of the southeastern U.S., having leaves which are hairy on the upper surface and red fruit. 2. a shrub, *Viburnum nudum,* of the eastern and southern coasts of the U.S., having slightly scurfy twigs and leaves, small, white or yellowish-white flowers, and nearly round, blue-black fruit.

pos·sy (pos′ē), *n., pl.* **-sies.** *Australian.* possie.

post¹ (pōst), *n.* 1. a strong piece of timber, metal, or the like, set upright as a support, a point of attachment, a place for displaying notices, etc. 2. *Furniture.* one of the principal uprights of a piece of furniture, as one supporting a chair back or forming one corner of a chest of drawers. Cf. **stump** (def. 11). 3. *Papermaking.* a stack of 144 sheets of handmolded paper, placed on the couch, interleaved with felts, and topped with a pilcher preparatory to pressing. 4. *Horse Racing.* a pole on a race track indicating the point where a race begins or ends: *the starting post.* 5. the lane of a race track farthest from the infield; the outside lane. Cf. **pole¹** (def. 4). —*v.t.* 6. to affix (a notice, bulletin, etc.) to a post, wall, or the like. 7. to bring to public notice by or as by a placard: *to post a reward.* 8. to denounce by a public notice or declaration: *to post a person as a coward.* 9. to enter the name of in a published list: *to post a student on the dean's list.* 10. to publish the name of (a ship) as missing or lost. 11. to placard (a wall, fence, etc.) with notices or bills: *Post no bills. It is forbidden to post this building.* [ME, OE < L *post(is)* a post, door-post, whence also D, LG *post,* G *Pfosten*] —**post′less,** *adj.* —**post′like′,** *adj.*
—**Syn.** 1. column, pillar, pile, pole. 6. announce, advertise, publicize.

post² (pōst), *n.* 1. a position of duty, employment, or trust to which one is assigned or appointed: *a diplomatic post.* 2. the station or rounds of a person on duty, as a soldier, sentry, nurse, etc. 3. a military station with permanent buildings. 4. *U.S.* a local unit of a veterans' organization. 5. See **trading post.** 6. a place in the stock exchange where a particular stock is traded. 7. (in the British military services) either of two bugle calls (**first post** and **last post**) giving notice of the time to retire for the night, similar in purpose to the U.S. taps. 8. *Obs.* the body of troops occupying a military station. —*v.t.* 9. to place or station at a post. 10. *Mil., Navy.* (formerly) to appoint to a post of command. [< F *poste* < It *posto* < L *positum,* neut. of *positus,* ptp. of *pōnere* to place, put. See POSITION]
—**Syn.** 1. assignment. See **appointment.**

post³ (pōst), *n.* 1. *Chiefly Brit.* a. a single dispatch or delivery of mail. b. the mail itself. c. the letters and packages being delivered to a single recipient. d. an established mail system or service, esp. under government authority. 2. *Brit.* See **post office** (def. 1b). 3. one of a series of stations along a route, for furnishing relays of men and horses for carrying mail, currency, etc. 4. one who travels express, esp. over a fixed route, carrying mail, currency, etc. 5. *Print.* a. a size of printing paper, 15½ × 19¼ inches in England, 16 × 20 to 16½ × 21 inches in America. b. *Chiefly Brit.* a size of drawing or writing paper 15¼ × 19 to 16½ × 21 inches. 6. **post octavo,** a size of book, from about 5 × 8 to 5¼ × 8¼ inches, untrimmed, in America; 5 × 8 inches, untrimmed, in England. *Abbr.:* post 8vo 7. **post quarto,** *Chiefly Brit.* a size of book, about 8 × 10 inches, untrimmed. *Abbr.:* post 4to —*v.t.* 8. *Chiefly Brit.* to place in a post office or a mailbox for transmission; mail. 9. *Bookkeeping.* a. to transfer (an entry or item), as from the journal to the ledger. b. to enter (an item) in due place and form. c. to make all the requisite entries in (the ledger, etc.). 10. to supply with up-to-date information; inform: *Keep me posted on his activities.* —*v.i.* 11. *Manège.* (of a horseman) to rise from and descend to the saddle in accordance with the rhythm of a horse at a trot. 12. to travel with speed; go or pass rapidly; hasten. —*adv.* 13. with speed or haste; posthaste. 14. by post or courier. 15. with post horses. [< F *poste* < It *posta* < L *posita,* fem. of *positus,* ptp., placed, put. See POST²]

Post (pōst), *n.* 1. **Emily Price,** 1873?–1960, U.S. writer on social etiquette. 2. **George Browne,** 1837–1913, U.S. architect. 3. a town in NW Texas. 4663 (1960).

post-, an element, meaning "behind," "after," occurring originally in loan words from Latin (*postscript*), but now used freely in the formation of compound words (*post-Elizabethan; postfix; postgraduate; postorbital*). [< L, comb. form repr. *post* (adv. and prep.)]

post·age (pō′stij), *n.* the charge for the conveyance of a letter or other matter sent by mail, usually prepaid by means of a stamp or stamps. [POST³ + -AGE]

post′age stamp′, an official stamp on an envelope, postal card, etc., in the form of a design or printed adhesive label, used as evidence of prepayment of a designated postage or as an indication of postage due.

post·al (pōs′təl), *adj.* 1. of or pertaining to the post office or mail service: *postal delivery; postal employees.* —*n.* 2. *Informal.* See **postal card.** [POST³ + -AL¹] —**post′al·ly,** *adv.*

post′al card′, 1. a card sold by the post office with a stamp already printed on it, usually mailable at a rate lower than that for letters in envelopes. 2. See **post card** (def. 1).

post′al deliv′ery zone′, zone (def. 9).

post′al or′der, *Chiefly Brit.* See **money order.**

post′al sav′ings bank′, a savings bank operated by the U.S. Post Office Department and limited to small accounts.

post′al stor′age car′, a railroad car for transporting unsorted mail.

post·au·dit (pōst ô′dit), *n. Accounting.* an audit of accounting records, conducted at some interval of time after a transaction or a series of transactions has already occurred. Also, **post-au′dit.** Cf. **pre-audit.** [POST- + AUDIT]

post·ax·i·al (pōst ak′sē əl), *adj. Anat., Zool.* situated behind the body axis; pertaining to the posterior part of the ulnar side of the forearm and the fibular side of the leg. [POST- + AXIAL] —**post·ax′i·al·ly,** *adv.*

post·bag (pōst′bag′), *n. Brit.* mailbag.

post bel·lum (pōst′ bel′əm), after the war. [< L]

post-bel·lum (pōst bel′əm), *adj.* occurring after a war, esp. after the American Civil War: *post-bellum reforms.*

post·boat (pōst′bōt′), *n. Brit.* mailboat.

post·box (pōst′boks′), *n.* a mailbox, esp. one for public deposit of mail. [POST³ + BOX¹]

post·boy (pōst′boi′), *n.* 1. a boy or man who rides post or carries mail. 2. a postilion. [POST³ + BOY]

post·ca·non·i·cal (pōst′kə non′i kəl), *adj.* written at a later date than the books belonging to a canon, esp. the Bible. [POST- + CANONICAL]

post′ card′, 1. Also called **picture post card.** a small, commercially printed card, usually having a picture on one side, to which a postage stamp must be attached for mailing. 2. See **postal card** (def. 1). Also, **post′card′.**

post′ chaise′, a four-wheeled coach for rapid transportation of passengers and mail, used in the 18th and early 19th centuries.

post·ab′do·men, *n.*
post′ab·dom′i·nal, *adj.*
post′ac·e·tab′u·lar, *adj.*
post′act′, *n.*
post′-A·dam′ic, *adj.*
post-Ad′vent, *adj.*
post′-Al·ex·an′drine, *adj.*
post′al·lan·to′ic, *adj.*
post′am·ni·ot′ic, *adj.*
post·a′nal, *adj.*
post′an·es·thet′ic, *adj.*
post′an·ten′nal, *adj.*
post′a·or′tic, *adj.*
post′ap·o·plec′tic, *adj.*
post′ap·os·tol′ic, *adj.*
post′ap·os·tol′i·cal, *adj.*
post′ap·pen·dic′u·lar, *adj.*
post′-Ar·is·to·te′lian, *adj.*
post·ar′mi·stice, *n.*
post′ar·te′ri·al, *adj.*
post′ar·thrit′ic, *adj.*
post′ar·tic′u·lar, *adj.*
post′ar·y·te′noid, *adj.*
post′asth·mat′ic, *adj.*
post·au′di·to′ry, *adj.*
post′au·ric′u·lar, *adj.*
post′-Au·gus′tan, *adj.*
post′-Au·gus·tin′i·an, *adj.*
post·ax′il·lar′y, *adj.*
post-Az′tec, *adj.*
post′-Bab·y·lo′ni·an, *adj.*
post′bap·tis′mal, *adj.*
post-Bib′li·cal, *adj.*
post·bra′chi·al, *adj.*
post·bra′chi·um, *n.*
post·break′fast, *adj.*
post·bron′chi·al, *adj.*
post·buc′cal, *adj.*
post·bul′bar, *adj.*
post·bur′sal, *adj.*
post·cae′cal, *adj.*
post′-Cae·sar′e·an, *adj.*
post-Cam′bri·an, *adj.*
post′-Car·bon·if′er·ous, *adj.*
post·car′di·ac, *adj.*
post·car′di·nal, *adj.*
post′-Car·o·lin′gi·an, *adj.*
post′ca·rot′id, *adj.*
post′-Car·te′sian, *adj.*
post′car·ti·lag′i·nous, *adj.*
post′ca·tar′rhal, *adj.*
post′caud′al, *adj.*
post·cen′tral, *adj.*
post′ce·phal′ic, *adj.*
post′cer·e·bel′lar, *adj.*
post·cer′e·bral, *adj.*
post′-Ce·sar′e·an, *adj.*
post′-Chau·ce′ri·an, *adj.*
post-Chris′tian, *adj.*
post-Christ′mas, *adj.*
post·clas′si·cal, *adj.*
post·co′lon, *adj.*
post′-Co·lum′bi·an, *adj.*
post′col·u·mel′lar, *adj.*
post′com·mu′ni·cant, *adj.*

post·com·mun·ion (pōst/kə myōōn/yən), *n. Eccles.* the part of a communion service that follows after the congregation has received communion. [< ML *postcommūniōn-* (s. of *postcommūniō*). See POST-, COMMUNION]

post·con·so·nan·tal (pōst/kon sə nan/tᵊl), *adj. Phonet.* immediately following a consonant. [POST- + CONSONANTAL]

post·date (pōst dāt/), *v.t.*, **-dat·ed, -dat·ing. 1.** to give a date later than the true date: *to postdate the termination of one's employment.* **2.** to date (a check, invoice, letter, etc.) with a date later than the current date. **3.** to follow in time: *His recognition as an artist postdated his death.* [POST- + DATE[1]]

post·di·lu·vi·an (pōst/di lōō/vē ən), *adj.* **1.** existing or occurring after the Flood. —*n.* **2.** one who lived after the Flood. [POST- + DILUVIAN]

post·doc·tor·al (pōst dok/tər əl), *adj.* of or pertaining to study or professional work undertaken after the receipt of a doctorate: *postdoctoral courses.* [POST- + DOCTORAL]

post·em·bry·on·ic (pōst em/brē on/ik, pōst/em-), *adj.* occurring after the embryonic phase. [POST- + EMBRYONIC]

post/ en/try, a horse and rider entered in a horse show class after the catalog has been printed but before the class has begun.

post·er[1] (pō/stər), *n.* **1.** a placard or bill posted or intended for posting in a public place, as for advertising. **2.** one who posts bills, placards, etc. [POST[1] (v.) + -ER[1]]

post·er[2] (pō/stər), *n.* **1.** See **post horse. 2.** *Archaic.* one who travels rapidly. [POST[3] + -ER[1]]

poste res·tante (pōst/ re stänt/ *or, esp. Brit.,* res/tänt; *Fr.* pôst RES TÄNT/), **1.** a direction written on mail to indicate that it should be held at the post office until called for by the addressee. **2.** *Chiefly Brit.* a department in charge of such mail. [< F: lit., standing post]

pos·ter·i·ad (po stēr/ē ad/), *adv. Anat., Zool.* toward the posterior; posteriorly. [POSTERI(OR) + L *ad* to, towards]

pos·te·ri·or (po stēr/ē ər), *adj.* **1.** situated behind or at the rear of; hinder (opposed to *anterior*). **2.** coming after in order, as in a series. **3.** coming after in time; later; subsequent (sometimes fol. by *to*). **4.** pertaining to the caudal end of the body. **5.** *Anat.* of or pertaining to the dorsal side of man. **6.** *Bot.* (of an axillary flower) on the side next to the main axis. —*n.* **7.** Often, **posteriors.** the hinder parts of the body; buttocks. [< L, comp. of *posterus* coming after, deriv. of *post* after] —**pos·te/ri·or·ly,** *adv.* —**Syn. 1.** See **back**[1].

pos·te·ri·or·i·ty (po stēr/ē ôr/i tē, -or/-), *n.* state or quality of being posterior. [ME *posteriorite* < ML *posteriōritās.* See POSTERIOR, -ITY]

pos·ter·i·ty (po ster/i tē), *n.* **1.** succeeding or future generations collectively: *Judgment of this age must be left to posterity.* **2.** all descendants of one person: *His fortune was gradually dissipated by his posterity.* [ME *posterite* < L *posteritās.* See POSTERIOR, -ITY]

pos·tern (pō/stərn, pos/tərn), *n.* **1.** a back door or gate. **2.** a private entrance or any entrance other than the main one. —*adj.* **3.** of, pertaining to, or resembling a postern. [ME *posterne* < OF, var. of *posterle* < LL *posterula,* dim. of *postera* back door, n. use of fem. of *posterus* coming behind. See POSTERIOR, -ULE]

post/ exchange/, *U.S. Army.* a retail store on an army installation that sells uniforms, insignia, and miscellaneous goods.

post·ex·il·i·an (pōst/eg zil/ē ən, -zil/yən, -ek sil/-), *adj.* being or occurring subsequent to the exile of the Jews in Babylonia 597–538 B.C. Also, **post/ex·il/ic.** [POST- + EXILIAN]

post·fac·tor (pōst/fak/tər), *n. Math.* an expression, written after another expression, which is to be multiplied by it. In *a* × *b*, *a* · *b*, and *ab*, *b* is the postfactor. [POST- + FACTOR]

post·fix (*v.* pōst fiks/; *n.* pōst/fiks/), *v.t.* **1.** to affix at the end of something; append; suffix. —*n.* **2.** something postfixed. **3.** a suffix added after closure of a set of suffixes. [POST- + FIX, modeled on *prefix*] —**post·fix/al, post·fix/i·al,** *adj.*

post-free (pōst/frē/), *adj.* **1.** that may be sent free of postal charges, as government mail. **2.** *Brit.* postpaid. —*adv.* **3.** *Brit.* postpaid.

post·gla·cial (pōst glā/shəl), *adj.* after a given glacial epoch, esp. the Pleistocene. [POST- + GLACIAL]

post·grad·u·ate (pōst graj/ōō it, -āt/), *adj.* **1.** of, pertaining to, characteristic of, or consisting of postgraduates: *a postgraduate seminar.* —*n.* **2.** a student who is taking advanced work after graduation, as from a high school or college. [POST- + GRADUATE]

post·haste (pōst/hāst/), *adv.* **1.** with the greatest possible speed or promptness: *to come to a friend's aid posthaste.* —*n.* **2.** *Archaic.* great haste. [POST[3] + HASTE]

post·heat (pōst hēt/), *v.t.* to heat (a metal piece, as a weld) after working, as to relieve stresses. [POST- + HEAT]

post hoc (pōst/ hōk/; *Eng.* pōst/ hok/), *Latin.* after this; afterward. Also, **post/hoc/.**

post hoc, er·go prop·ter hoc (pōst hōk/, ER/gō PROP/tER hōk/; *Eng.* pōst hok/, ûr/gō prop/tər hok/), *Latin.* after this, therefore because of it: a formula designating an error in logic which accepts as a cause something that merely occurred earlier in time.

post/ horse/, a horse kept, as at a station on a post road, for the use of persons riding post or for hire by travelers. Also called **poster.**

post/ house/, a house or inn keeping post horses.

post·hu·mous (pos/chə məs, -chōō-), *adj.* **1.** published after the death of the author: *a posthumous novel.* **2.** born after the death of the father. **3.** arising, occurring, or continuing after one's death: *a posthumous award for bravery.* [< L *posthumus,* erroneously (by assoc. with *humus* earth, ground, as if referring to burial) for *postumus* last, superl. of *posterus.* See POSTERIOR] —**post/hu·mous·ly,** *adv.* —**post/hu·mous·ness,** *n.*

post·hyp·not·ic (pōst/hip not/ik), *adj.* **1.** of or pertaining to the period after hypnosis. **2.** (of a suggestion) made during hypnosis so as to be effective after awakening. [POST- + HYPNOTIC] —**post/hyp·not/i·cal·ly,** *adv.*

pos·tiche (pô stēsh/, po-), *adj.* **1.** superadded, esp. inappropriately, as a sculptural or architectural ornament. **2.** artificial, counterfeit, or false. —*n.* **3.** an imitation or substitute. **4.** pretense; sham. **5.** a false hairpiece. [< F < It *(ap)posticcio* < L *appositīcius* put on, factitious, false. See APPOSITE, -ITIOUS]

pos·ti·cous (po sti/kəs), *adj. Bot.* hinder; posterior. [< L *postīcus* behind, hinder, deriv. of *post* after; opposed to *antīcus* fore, deriv. of *ante* before]

pos·ti·cum (po sti/kəm), *n., pl.* **-ca** (-kə). **1.** epinaos. **2.** opisthodomos (def. 1). [< L: backdoor, back part (of a building), neut. of *postīcus.* See POSTICOUS]

pos·til·ion (pō stil/yən, po-), *n.* one who rides the horse on the left of the leading pair when four or more horses are used to draw a carriage, or one who rides the horse on the left when only one pair is used. Also, *esp. Brit.,* **pos·til/lion.** [earlier *postillon* < MF < It *postiglione,* deriv. of *posta* POST[3]] —**pos·til/ioned, pos·til/lioned,** *adj.*

Post-Im·pres·sion·ism (pōst/im presh/ə niz/əm), *n.* a varied development of Impressionism by a group of painters chiefly between 1880–1900 stressing formal structure as with Cézanne and Seurat, or the expressive possibilities of form and color, as with Van Gogh and Gauguin. Also, **post-impressionism.** [POST- + IMPRESSIONISM] —**Post/-Im·pres/sion·ist,** *n.* —**Post/-Im·pres/sion·is/tic,** *adj.*

post·ing (pō/sting), *n.* assignment to a military post. [POST[2] + -ING[1]]

post·lim·i·ny (pōst lim/ə nē), *n. Internat. Law.* the right by which persons and things taken in war are restored to their former status when coming again under the power of the nation to which they belonged. [< L *postlīmini(um),* lit., the state of being behind one's threshold, i.e., at home. See POST-, LIMINAL, -Y[3]]

post·lude (pōst/lōōd), *n. Music.* **1.** a concluding piece or movement. **2.** a voluntary at the end of a church service. [POST- + L *lūd(us)* game, modeled on *prelude*]

post·man[1] (pōst/mən), *n., pl.* **-men. 1.** a postal employee who carries and delivers mail. **2.** *Obs.* courier. [POST[3] + MAN[1]]

post·man[2] (pōst/mən), *n., pl.* **-men.** *Old Eng. Law.* a barrister in the Court of Exchequer who had precedence in motions. Cf. **tubman.** [POST[1] + MAN[1]]

post·mark (pōst/märk/), *n.* **1.** an official mark stamped on letters and other mail, serving as a cancellation of the postage stamp and indicating the place, date, and sometimes time of sending or receipt. —*v.t.* **2.** to stamp with a postmark. [POST[3] + MARK[1]]

post·mas·ter (pōst/mas/tər, -mä/stər), *n.* **1.** the official in charge of a post office. **2.** the master of a station which furnishes post horses to travelers. [POST[3] + MASTER] —**post/mas/ter·ship/,** *n.*

post/master gen/eral, *pl.* **postmasters general.** the executive head of the postal system of a country.

post·me·rid·i·an (pōst/mə rid/ē ən), *adj.* **1.** of or pertaining to the afternoon. **2.** occurring after noon: *a postmeridian lull.* [POST- + MERIDIAN]

post me·rid·i·em (pōst/ mə rid/ē əm). See **p.m.** [< L: after noon]

post·mill (pōst/mil/), *n.* a windmill the machinery of which is mounted on a frame which turns in its entirety to face the wind. [POST[1] + MILL[1]]

post·mil·len·ni·al (pōst/mi len/ē əl), *adj.* of or pertaining to the period following the millennium. [POST- + MILLENNIAL]

post·mil·len·ni·al·ism (pōst/mi len/ē ə liz/əm), *n.* the doctrine or belief that the second coming of Christ will follow the millennium. [POSTMILLENNIAL + -ISM] —**post/mil·len/ni·al·ist,** *n.*

post·mis·tress (pōst/mis/tris), *n.* a woman in charge of a post office. [POST[3] + MISTRESS]

post·mod·ern (pōst mod/ərn), *adj.* of or pertaining to any of several trends or movements in the arts or literature rejecting or reacting to modernism, esp. in reference to the architecture of the late 20th century, which is more ornate than standard modern architecture. [POST- + MODERN] —**post·mod/ern·ism,** *n.* —**post·mod/ern·ist,** *n., adj.*

post-mor·tem (pōst môr/təm), *adj.* **1.** of, pertaining to, or occurring in the time following death. **2.** of or pertaining to examination of the body after death. **3.** occurring after the end of something; after the event: *a post-mortem criticism of a television show.* —*n.* **4.** a post-mortem examination. **5.** an evaluation or discussion occurring after the end or fact of something: *to do a post-mortem on the decision of a court.* **6.** *Cards Informal.* a discussion of the bidding or playing of a previous hand. Also, **post·mor/tem.** [< L: after death]

post-mor/tem examina/tion, *Med.* an autopsy.

post·mul·ti·ply (pōst mul/tə plī/), *v.t.,* **-plied, -ply·ing.** *Math.* to multiply (a quantity) by a postfactor. [POST(FACTOR) + MULTIPLY[1]]

post·na·sal (pōst/nā/zəl), *adj.* located or occurring behind the nose or in the nasopharynx, as a flow of mucus; nasopharyngeal: *a postnasal infection.* [POST- + NASAL[1]]

post/nasal drip/, a trickling of mucus onto the pharyngeal surface from the posterior portion of the nasal cavity, usually caused by a cold or allergy.

post·na·tal (pōst nāt/ᵊl), *adj.* subsequent to childbirth: *postnatal infection.* [POST- + NATAL]

post·nup·tial (pōst nup/shəl, -chəl), *adj.* subsequent to marriage: *postnuptial adjustments; a postnuptial trip.* [POST- + NUPTIAL] —**post·nup/tial·ly,** *adv.*

post/ oak/, any of several American oaks, esp. *Quercus stellata,* the wood of which is used for posts.

post-o·bit (pōst ō/bit, -ob/it), *adj.* effective after a particular person's death. [< L *post obit(um)* after death]

post-o/bit bond/, a bond paying a sum of money after the death of some specified person.

post o·bi·tum (pōst ō/bi tōōm/; *Eng.* pōst ob/i-təm), *Latin.* after death.

post/ of/fice, 1. an office or station of a government postal system at which mail is received and sorted, from which it is dispatched and distributed, and at which stamps are sold or other services rendered. **2.** (*often cap.*) the department of a government charged with the transportation of mail. **3.** a game in which players enter a room, one at a time, ostensibly to call for a letter but instead receive a kiss from a member of the opposite sex who is designated postmaster or postmistress. —**post/-of/fice,** *adj.*

post/-office box/, (in a post office) a locked, numbered compartment into which mail is put to be called for. *Abbr.:* POB, P.O.B.

Post/ Of/fice Depart/ment, *U.S.* the department of the federal government having responsibility for postal services.

post·op·er·a·tive (pōst op/ər ə tiv, -ə rā/tiv), *adj.* occurring after a surgical operation. [POST- + OPERATIVE]

post·or·bit·al (pōst ôr/bi tᵊl), *adj.* located behind the orbit or socket of the eye. [POST- + ORBITAL]

post·paid (pōst/pād/), *adj., adv.* with the postage prepaid: *Mail the package postpaid.* [POST- + PAID]

post/ par/tum (pär/təm), *Obstet.* of or noting the period of time following childbirth; after delivery. Also

post·con/dy·lar, *adj.*
post/con·fine/ment, *n.*
post/-Con·fu/cian, *adj.*
post/con·nu/bi·al, *adj.*
post·con/quest, *adj.*
post/-Con·stan·tin/i·an, *adj.*
post·con/tract, *n.*
post/con·va·les/cent, *adj.*
post/con·vul/sive, *adj.*
post/-Co·per/ni·can, *adj.*
post·cos/tal, *adj.*
post·cox/al, *adj.*
post/cre·ta/ceous, *adj.*
post·crit/i·cal, *adj.*
post·cru/ci·ate, *adj.*
post·cru/ral, *adj.*
post/-Cru·sade/, *adj.*
post·cu/bi·tal, *adj.*
post/-Dar·win/i·an, *adj.*
post/-Da·vid/ic, *adj.*
post·den/tal, *adj., n.*
post/de·pres/sive, *adj.*
post/de·ter/mined, *adj.*
post/de·vel/op·men/tal, *adj.*
post/-De·vo/ni·an, *adj.*
post/di·ag·nos/tic, *adj.*
post/di·a·phrag·mat/ic, *adj.*
post/di·as·tol/ic, *adj.*
post/di·ges/tive, *adj.*
post·dig/i·tal, *adj.*
post/-Di·o·cle/tian, *adj.*
post/diph·the/ri·al, *adj.*
post/diph·ther/ic, *adj.*
post/diph·the·rit/ic, *adj.*
post/dis·ap·proved/, *adj.*
post/dis·coi/dal, *adj.*
post·du/ral, *adj.*
post/dys·en·ter/ic, *adj.*
post-East/er, *adj.*
post/e·lec/tion, *adj.*
post/el·e·men/tal, *adj.*
post/el·e·men/ta·ry, *adj.*
post/-E·liz/a·be/than, *adj.*
post/en·ceph·a·lit/ic, *adj.*
post-E/o·cene, *adj.*
post/ep·i·lep/tic, *adj.*
post/e·rup/tive, *adj.*
post/e·so·phag/e·al, *adj.*
post·eth/moid, *adj.*
post/ex·ist/ence, *n.*
post·fe/brile, *adj.*
post·fem/o·ral, *adj.*
post·fe/tal, *adj.*
post·foe/tal, *adj.*
post·fo/ve·al, *adj.*
post/-Gal·i·le/an, *adj.*
post/gan·gli·on/ic, *adj.*
post·gas/tric, *adj.*
post·gen/ial, *adj.*
post·gen/i·tal, *adj.*
post-Goth/ic, *adj.*
post·grip/pal, *adj.*
post/hem·i·ple/gic, *adj.*
post/hem·or·rhag/ic, *adj.*
post/he·pat/ic, *adj.*
post·hex/a·plar, *adj.*
post/hip·po·cam/pal, *adj.*
post-Hit/tite, *adj.*
post/-Ho·mer/ic, *adj.*
post·hu/mer·al, *adj.*
post·hy/oid, *adj.*
post/hys·ter/i·cal, *adj.*
post/-Ib/sen, *adj.*
post/ic·ter/ic, *adj.*
post/in·car·na/tion, *adj.*
post/in·fec/tive, *adj.*
post/in·flu·en/zal, *adj.*
post/in·tes/ti·nal, *adj.*
post/-John·so/ni·an, *adj.*
post·jug/u·lar, *adj.*
post/-Ju·ras/sic, *adj.*
post/-Jus·tin/i·an, *adj.*
post-Jut/land, *adj.*
post-Kan/san, *adj.*
post-Kant/i·an, *adj.*
post·la/bi·al, *adj.;* **-ly,** *adv.*
post·lach/ry·mal, *adj.*
post·lar/val, *adj.*
post/la·ryn/gal, *adj.*
post/la·ryn/geal, *adj.*
post·le/gal, *adj.*
post/le·git/i·ma/tion, *n.*
post/-Leib·nitz/i·an, *adj.*
post/-Leib·niz/i·an, *adj.*
post-Lent/, *adj.*
post/len·tic/u·lar, *adj.*
post/li·cen/ti·ate, *adj.*
post/-Lin·ne/an, *adj.*
post/ma·lar/i·al, *adj.*
post·mam/ma·ry, *adj.*
post·mam/mil·lar/y, *adj.*
post/man·dib/u·lar, *adj.*
post/ma·ni/a·cal, *adj.*
post·mar/i·tal, *adj.*
post·mar/riage, *n., adj.*
post-Marx/i·an, *adj.*
post·mas/toid, *adj.*
post·max/il·lar/y, *adj.*
post·max/i·mal, *adj.*
post/me·di·ae/val, *adj.*
post·me/di·al, *adj.*
post·me/di·an, *adj.*
post/me·di·e/val, *adj.*
post·med/ul·lar/y, *adj.*
post/mei·ot/ic, *adj.*
post/-Men·del/i·an, *adj.*
post/me·nin/ge·al, *adj.*
post/men·o·pau/sal, *adj.*
post·men/stru·al, *adj.*
post/mes·en·ter/ic, *adj.*
post/-Mes·o·zo/ic, *adj.*
post-Mi/o·cene/, *adj.*
post/-Mish·na/ic, *adj.*
post-Mish/nic, *adj.*
post-Mish/ni·cal, *adj.*
post/-Mo·sa/ic, *adj.*
post·mun/dane, *adj.*
post·mus/cu·lar, *adj.*
post/-My·ce/ne·an, *adj.*
post/my·cot/ic, *adj.*
post/myx·e·dem/a·tous, *adj.*
post/myx·e·dem/ic, *adj.*
post/-Na·po/le·on/ic, *adj.*
post/ne·crot/ic, *adj.*
post/ne·phrit/ic, *adj.*
post/neu/ral, *adj.*
post/neu·ral/gic, *adj.*
post/neu·rit/ic, *adj.*
post/neu·rot/ic, *adj.*
post/-New·to/ni·an, *adj.*
post·nod/al, *adj.*
post·nod/u·lar, *adj.*
post-Ol/i·go·cene/, *adj.*
post·ol/i·var/y, *adj.*
post/o·men/tal, *adj.*
post·op/tic, *adj.*
post·o/ral, *adj.*
post/or·di·na/tion, *adj.*
post/-Or·do·vi/cian, *adj.*
post/or·gas/tic, *adj.*
post·os/se·ous, *adj.*
post/-Pa·le·o·zo/ic, *adj.*
post·pal/pe·bral, *adj.*
post/pa·lu/dal, *adj.*
post/par·a·lyt/ic, *adj.*
post·pa·rot/id, *adj.*
post/par·o·tit/ic, *adj.*
post/par·ox·ys/mal, *adj.*
post/par·tu·ri·ent, *adj.*
post/pa·tel/lar, *adj.*

post-par′tum, post-par′tum, post-par′tal. Cf. **ante partum.** [< L: lit., after childbirth, equiv. to *post* POST- + *partum*, acc. of *partus* a bringing forth (4th decl.), equiv. to *part-*, ptp. s. of *parere* to bear + *-us* u-stem suffix]

post·pone (pōst pōn′), *v.t.*, **-poned, -pon·ing. 1.** to put off to a later time; defer: *He has postponed his departure until tomorrow.* **2.** to place after in order of importance or estimation; subordinate: *to postpone private ambitions to the public welfare.* [< L *postpōne(re)* (to) put after, lay aside, equiv. to *post-* POST- + *pōnere* to put] —**post·pon′a·ble,** *adj.* —**post·pone′ment,** *n.* —**post·pon′er,** *n.* —**Syn. 1.** See **defer.**

post·po·si·tion (pōst′pə zish′ən, pōst′pə zish′ən), *n.* **1.** act of placing after. **2.** state of being so placed. **3.** *Gram.* **a.** the use of words, particles, or affixes following the elements they modify or govern, as of the adjective *general* in *attorney general*, or of the particle *e* "to" in Japanese *Tokyo e* "to Tokyo." **b.** a word so used. [POST- + POSITION] —**post′po·si′tion·al,** *adj.*

post·pos·i·tive (pōst poz′i tiv), *Gram.* —*adj.* **1.** placed after. —*n.* **2.** a postposition. [< L *postposit(us)* (ptp. of *postponere*; see POSTPONE, POSITION) + -IVE] —**post·pos′i·tive·ly,** *adv.*

post·pran·di·al (pōst pran′dē əl), *adj.* after a meal, esp. after dinner: *postprandial oratory; a postprandial brandy.* [POST- + L *prandi(um)* meal + -AL[1]] —**post·pran′di·al·ly,** *adv.*

post′ race′, *Horse Racing.* a race in which the entries to compete are named by their owners at the time stipulated otherwise for confirming entries named previously.

pos·tre·mo·gen·i·ture (po strē′mō jen′i chər), *n.* *Law.* a system of inheritance under which the estate of a deceased person goes to his youngest son. Also called **ultimogeniture.** Cf. **primogeniture** (def. 2). [< L *postrēm(us)* last (superl. of *posterus* coming after) + -o- + GENITURE]

post·rid·er (pōst′rī′dər), *n.* one who rides post; a mounted mail carrier. [POST[3] + RIDER]

post′ road′, 1. a road with stations for furnishing horses for postriders, mail coaches, or travelers. **2.** a road or route over which mail is carried.

pos·trorse (pos′trôrs, po strôrs′), *adj.* directed backward. [< L *post(e)r(us)* behind + (RE)TORSE]

post·script (pōst′skript′, pōs′skript′), *n.* **1.** a paragraph, phrase, etc., added to a letter that has already been concluded and signed by the writer. **2.** any addition or supplement, as one appended by a writer to a book to supply further information. [< L *postscript(um)*, neut. of ptp. of *postscrībere* to write after]

post·scu·tel·lum (pōst′skōō tel′əm, -skyōō-), *n., pl.* **-tel·la** (-tel′ə). postnotum. [< NL; see POST-, SCUTELLUM]

post·syn·ap·tic (pōst′si nap′tik), *adj.* following a synapse. [POST- + SYNAPTIC]

post-ten·sion (pōst ten′shən), *v.t.* **1.** (in prestressed-concrete construction) to apply tension to (reinforcing strands) after the concrete has set. Cf. **pretension. 2.** to make (a concrete member) with post-tensioned reinforcement. [POST- + TENSION]

post′ time′, *Horse Racing.* the time at which the entries in a race are required to be at the starting post.

post·ton·ic (pōst ton′ik), *adj.* immediately following a stressed syllable: *a posttonic syllable; a posttonic vowel.*

post·ty·phoid (pōst tī′foid), *adj.* *Pathol.* occurring as a sequel of typhoid fever. [POST- + TYPHOID]

pos·tu·lan·cy (pos′chə lən sē), *n., pl.* **-cies.** the period or state of being a postulant, esp. in a religious order. Also, **pos′tu·lance.** [POSTULAN(T) + -CY]

pos·tu·lant (pos′chə lənt), *n.* **1.** one who asks or applies for something. **2.** a candidate, esp. for admission into a religious order. [< F < L *postulant-* (s. of *postulāns*) asking for, prp. of *postulāre* to ask for, claim, require] —**pos′tu·lant·ship′,** *n.*

pos·tu·late (*v.* pos′chə lāt′; *n.* pos′chə lit, -lāt′), *v.*, **-lat·ed, -lat·ing,** *n.* —*v.t.* **1.** to ask, demand, or claim. **2.** to claim or assume the existence or truth of, esp. as a basis for reasoning. **3.** to assume without proof, or as self-evident; take for granted. **4.** *Math., Logic.* to assume as a postulate. —*n.* **5.** something taken as self-evident or assumed without proof as a basis for reasoning. **6.** *Math., Logic.* a proposition that requires no proof, being self-evident, or that is for a specific purpose assumed true, and that is used in the proof of other propositions; axiom. **7.** a fundamental principle. **8.** a necessary condition; prerequisite. [< L *postulāt(um)* thing requested, n. use of neut. of ptp. of *postulāre* to request, demand, akin to *pōscere* to request] —**pos′tu·la′tion,** *n.* —**pos′tu·la′tion·al,** *adj.* —**Syn. 3.** hypothecate, presuppose, conjecture. **5.** hypothesis, theory; axiom; assumption, conjecture.

pos·tu·la·tor (pos′chə lā′tər), *n.* *Rom. Cath. Ch.* a priest who presents a plea for a beatification or the canonization of a beatus. Cf. **devil's advocate** (def. 2). [< L: claimant. See POSTULATE, -OR[2]]

pos·ture (pos′chər), *n., v.*, **-tured, -tur·ing.** —*n.* **1.** the relative disposition of the parts of something. **2.** the position of the limbs or the carriage of the body as a whole: *poor posture; a sitting posture.* **3.** an affected or unnatural attitude: *He struck a comic posture.* **4.** a mental or spiritual attitude: *His ideas reveal a defensive posture.* **5.** position, condition, or state, as of affairs. —*v.t.* **6.** to place in a particular posture or attitude. —*v.i.* **7.** to assume a particular posture. **8.** to assume affected or unnatural postures, as by bending or contorting the body. **9.** to act in an affected or artificial manner, as to create a certain impression. [< F < L *positūra.* See POSIT, -URE] —**pos′tur·al,** *adj.* —**pos′tur·er,** *n.* —**Syn. 2.** See **position.**

pos·tur·ise (pos′chə rīz′), *v.i.*, **-ised, -is·ing.** *Chiefly Brit.* posturize.

pos·tur·ize (pos′chə rīz′), *v.i.*, **-ized, -iz·ing.** to posture; pose. [POSTURE + -IZE]

post·vo·cal·ic (pōst′vō kal′ik, -və-), *adj.* *Phonet.* immediately following a vowel. [POST- + VOCALIC] —**post′vo·cal′i·cal·ly,** *adv.*

Post·vor·ta (pōst vôr′tə), *n.* *Class. Myth.* a nymph of the Camenae having full knowledge of the past. Cf. **Antevorta.**

post·war (pōst′wôr′), *adj.* of, pertaining to, or characteristic of a period following a war: *postwar problems; postwar removal of rationing.* [POST- + WAR[1]]

po·sy (pō′zē), *n., pl.* **-sies. 1.** a flower, nosegay, or bouquet. **2.** *Archaic.* a brief motto or the like, as one inscribed within a ring. [syncopated var. of POESY]

pot[1] (pot), *n., v.*, **pot·ted, pot·ting.** —*n.* **1.** a container of earthenware, metal, etc., usually round and deep and having a handle or handles and often a lid, used for cooking, serving, and other purposes. **2.** such a vessel with its contents: *a pot of stew.* **3.** the amount contained in or held by a pot; potful. **4.** a container of liquor or other drink: *a pot of ale.* **5.** liquor or other drink. **6.** a cagelike vessel for trapping fish, lobsters, eels, etc., typically made of wood, wicker, or wire. Cf. **lobster pot. 7.** *Metall.* **a.** a vessel for melting metal; melting pot. **b.** an electrolytic cell for reducing certain metals, as aluminum, from fused salts. **8.** *Brit.* **a.** See **chimney pot. b.** *Dial.* a basket or box used for carrying provisions or the like; a pannier. **9.** *Slang.* a large sum of money. **10.** all the money bet at a single time; pool. **11.** *Brit. Slang.* (in horse racing) the favorite. **12.** See **pot shot. 13.** a liquid measure, usually equal to a pint or quart. **14.** *Armor.* **a.** an open, broad-brimmed helmet of the 17th century. **b.** any open helmet. **15.** *Slang.* marijuana. **16.** *Slang.* a potbelly. **17. go to pot,** to become ruined; deteriorate: *With no one to care for it, the lovely old garden went to pot.* —*v.t.* **18.** to put into a pot. **19.** to preserve (food) in a pot. **20.** to cook in a pot. **21.** to transplant into a pot: *We must pot the petunias.* **22.** *Hunting.* **a.** to shoot (game birds) on the ground or water, or (game animals) at rest, instead of in flight or running: *He can't even pot a sitting duck.* **b.** to shoot for food, not for sport. **23.** *Informal.* to capture, secure, or win. —*v.i.* **24.** *Slang.* to take a pot shot; shoot. [ME; OE *pott* (see POTTER[1]); c. D, LG *pot* (? whence F *pot*)] —**pot′like′,** *adj.*

pot[2] (pot), *n.* *Scot. and North Eng.* a deep hole; pit. [ME; ? same as POT[1]]

pot., potential.

po·ta·ble (pō′tə bəl), *adj.* **1.** fit or suitable for drinking: *potable water.* —*n.* **2.** Usually, **potables.** drinkable liquids; beverages. [< LL *pōtābil(is)* drinkable, equiv. to *pōtā(re)* (to) drink + *-bilis* -BLE] —**po′ta·bil′i·ty, po′ta·ble·ness,** *n.*

po·tage (pô tazh′; *Eng.* pō täzh′), *n.* *French.* soup.

po·tam·ic (pō tam′ik, pə-), *adj.* of or pertaining to rivers. [< Gk *potam(ós)* river + -IC]

pot·a·mog·a·le (pot′ə mog′ə lē), *n.* See **otter shrew.** [< NL, equiv. to Gk *potamó(s)* river + *galê*, contr. of *galéē* weasel]

pot·a·mo·plank·ton (pot′ə mō plangk′tən), *n.* plankton living in fresh-water streams. [< Gk *potamó(s)* river + PLANKTON]

po·tance (pōt′əns), *n.* *Horol.* potence[2].

pot′ arch′, an auxiliary furnace in which pots used in melting frit are preheated.

pot·ash (pot′ash′), *n.* **1.** potassium carbonate, esp. the crude impure form obtained from wood ashes. **2.** caustic potash. **3.** the oxide of potassium, K_2O. **4.** potassium, as carbonate of potash. [back formation from *pot-ashes* (pl.), trans. of early D *potasschen.* See POT[1], ASH[1]]

pot′ash al′um, *Chem.* alum (def. 1).

pot′ash feld′spar, any of the feldspar minerals having the composition $K(AlSi_3O_8)$.

pot·ass (pot′as′), *n.* **1.** potash. **2.** potassium. [< F *potasse* < D *potasch* (pronounced and now also spelled *potas*) POTASH]

po·tas·sa (pə tas′ə), *n.* *Chem.* See **potassium hydroxide.** [< NL; see POTASS]

po·tas·sic (pə tas′ik), *adj.* of, pertaining to, or containing potassium. [POTASS(IUM) + -IC]

po·tas·si·um (pə tas′ē əm), *n.* *Chem.* a silvery-white metallic element, which oxidizes rapidly in the air, and whose compounds are used as fertilizer and in special hard glasses. *Symbol:* K; *at. wt.:* 39.102; *at. no.:* 19; *sp. gr.:* 0.86 at 20°C. [< NL; see POTASSA, -IUM]

potas′sium ac′etate, *Chem.* a white, crystalline, deliquescent, water-soluble powder, CH_3COOK, used chiefly as a reagent in analytical chemistry.

potas′sium ac′id car′bonate, *Chem.* See **potassium bicarbonate.**

potas′sium ac′id ox′alate, *Chem.* See **potassium binoxalate.**

potas′sium ac′id sul′fate, *Chem.* See **potassium bisulfate.**

potas′sium ac′id tar′trate, *Chem.* See **cream of tartar.**

potas′sium al′um, *Chem.* alum (def. 1).

potas′sium an′timonate, *Chem.* a white, crystalline, slightly water-soluble powder, $KSb(OH)_6$, used chiefly as a pigment in paints.

potas′sium an′timonyl tar′trate, *Chem.* See **tartar emetic.**

potas′sium ar′gon dat′ing, *Physics.* a method for estimating the age of a mineral by determining the ratio of argon to potassium in the mineral, based on the natural radioactive disintegration of potassium into argon. Also called **argon potassium dating.**

potas′sium bicar′bonate, *Chem., Pharm.* a white, crystalline, slightly alkaline, salty-tasting, water-soluble powder, $KHCO_3$, produced by the passage of carbon dioxide through an aqueous potassium carbonate solution: used in cookery as a leavening agent and in medicine as an antacid. Also called **potassium acid carbonate.**

potas′sium bichro′mate, *Chem.* See **potassium dichromate.**

potas′sium binox′alate, *Chem.* a white, crystalline, hygroscopic, poisonous solid KHC_2O_4, which is usually hydrated: used chiefly for removing ink stains, cleaning metal and wood, and in photography. Also called **salt of sorrel, sorrel salt, potassium acid oxalate.**

potas′sium bisul′fate, *Chem.* a colorless, crystalline, water-soluble solid, $KHSO_4$, used chiefly in the conversion of tartrates to bitartrates. Also called **potassium acid sulfate.**

potas′sium bitar′trate, *Chem.* See **cream of tartar.**

potas′sium bro′mate, *Chem.* a white, crystalline, water-soluble powder, $KBrO_3$, used chiefly as an oxidizing agent and as an analytical reagent.

potas′sium bro′mide, *Chem.* a white, crystalline, water-soluble powder, KBr, having a bitter saline taste: used chiefly in the manufacture of photographic papers and plates, in engraving, and in medicine as a sedative.

potas′sium car′bonate, *Chem.* a white, granular, water-soluble powder, K_2CO_3, used chiefly in the manufacture of soap, glass, and potassium salts.

potas′sium chlo′rate, *Chem.* a white or colorless, crystalline, water-soluble, poisonous solid, $KClO_3$, used chiefly as an oxidizing agent in the manufacture of explosives, fireworks, matches, bleaches, and disinfectants.

potas′sium chlo′ride, *Chem.* a white or colorless, crystalline, water-soluble solid, KCl, used chiefly in the manufacture of fertilizers and mineral water, and as a source of other potassium compounds.

potas′sium chrome′ al′um, *Chem.* See **chrome alum** (def. 2).

potas′sium chro′mic sul′fate, *Chem.* See **chrome alum** (def. 2).

potas′sium co·bal·ti·ni′trite (kō′bôl tə nī′trīt), *Chem.* a yellow, crystalline, slightly water-soluble powder, $K_3Co(NO_2)_6$, used as a pigment in oil and water-color paints, and for coloring surfaces of glass, porcelain, etc. Also called **cobalt potassium nitrite, cobalt yellow.** [COBALT + -I- + NITRATE]

potas′sium cy′anide, *Chem.* a white, granular, water-soluble, poisonous powder, KCN, having a faint almondlike odor, used chiefly in metallurgy and photography.

potas′sium dichro′mate, *Chem.* an orange-red, crystalline, water-soluble, poisonous powder, $K_2Cr_2O_7$, used chiefly in dyeing, photography, and as a laboratory reagent. Also called **potassium bichromate.**

potas′sium eth′yl di·thi·o·car′bon·ate (dī-thī′ō kär′bə nāt′), *Chem.* See **potassium xanthate.** [DI-[1] + THIO- + CARBONATE]

potas′sium eth′yl xan′tho·gen·ate (zan′thə-jə nāt′, zan thoj′ə-), *Chem.* See **potassium xanthate.** [XANTHO- + -GEN + -ATE[2]]

potas′sium ferricy′anide, *Chem.* a bright-red, crystalline, water-soluble, poisonous solid, $K_3Fe(CN)_6$, used chiefly in the manufacture of pigments, as Prussian blue, and of paper, esp. blueprint paper. Also called **red prussiate of potash.**

potas′sium ferrocy′anide, *Chem.* a lemon-yellow, crystalline, water-soluble solid, $K_4Fe(CN)_6 \cdot 3H_2O$, used chiefly in casehardening alloys having an iron base and in dyeing wool and silk. Also called **yellow prussiate of potash.**

potas′sium flu′oride, *Chem.* a white, crystalline, hygroscopic, toxic powder, KF, used chiefly as an insecticide, a disinfectant, and in etching glass.

---

post′path·o·log′ic, *adj.*
post′path·o·log′i·cal, *adj.*
post-Paul′ine, *adj.*
post·pec′to·ral, *adj.*
post′pe·dun′cu·lar, *adj.*
post′-Pen·te·cos′tal, *adj.*
post·per′fo·rat′ed, *adj.*
post′per·i·car′di·al, *adj.*
post-Per′mi·an, *adj.*
post-Pe′trine, *adj.*
post′pha·ryn′gal, *adj.*
post′pha·ryn′geal, *adj.*
post-Phid′i·an, *adj.*
post′phlo·gis′tic, *adj.*
post·phren′ic, *adj.*
post·phthis′ic, *adj.*
post′pi·tu′i·tar′y, *adj.*
post′-Pla·ton′ic, *adj.*
post-Pleis′to·cene′, *adj.*
post-Pli′o·cene′, *adj.*
post′pneu·mon′ic, *adj.*
post′pro·phet′ic, *adj.*
post′pro·phet′i·cal, *adj.*
post·pros′tate, *adj.*
post·pu′ber·ty, *adj.*
post′pu·bes′cent, *adj.*
post′pu·er′per·al, *adj.*
post·pul′mo·nar′y, *adj.*
post′pu·pil′lar′y, *adj.*
post′py·lor′ic, *adj.*
post′py·ram′i·dal, *adj.*
post′py·ret′ic, *adj.*
post′-Py·thag′o·re′an, *adj.*
post′ra·chit′ic, *adj.*
post·rec′tal, *adj.*
post′re·demp′tion, *n.*
post′-Ref·or·ma′tion, *n.*
post-Ren′ais·sance′, *adj.*
post·re′nal, *adj.*
post′-Res·to·ra′tion, *n.*
post′res·ur·rec′tion, *n.*
post′res·ur·rec′tion·al, *adj.*
post·ret′i·nal, *adj.*
post′-Rev·o·lu′tion·ar′y, *adj.*
post′rheu·mat′ic, *adj.*
post·rhi′nal, *adj.*
post-Ro′man, *adj.*
post′-Ro·man′tic, *adj.*
post·ros′tral, *adj.*
post′ru·be′o·lar, *adj.*
post·sac′cu·lar, *adj.*
post′scar·la·ti′noid, *adj.*
post′scho·las′tic, *adj.*
post′scor·bu′tic, *adj.*
post·sea′son, *adj.*
post′-Shake·spear′e·an, *adj.*
post′-Shake·spear′i·an, *adj.*
post·sig′moid, *adj.*
post′sig·moi′dal, *adj.*
post·sign′, *v.t.*
post·sign′er, *n.*
post′-Si·lu′ri·an, *adj.*
post′-So·crat′ic, *adj.*
post′spas·mod′ic, *adj.*
post·sphe′noid, *adj.*
post′sphyg·mic, *adj.*
post·spi′nous, *adj.*
post·splen′ic, *adj.*
post·ster′nal, *adj.*
post′ster·to′rous, *adj.*
post′sup·pu·ra′tive, *adj.*
post·sur′gi·cal, *adj.*
post′sym·phys′i·al, *adj.*
post′syph·i·lit′ic, *adj.*
post′sys·tol′ic, *adj.*
post′ta·bet′ic, *adj.*
post′-Tal·mud′ic, *adj.*
post′-Tal·mud′i·cal, *adj.*
post·tar′sal, *adj.*
post·tem′po·ral, *adj.*
post-Ter′ti·ar′y, *adj.*
post′te·tan′ic, *adj.*
post′tha·lam′ic, *adj.*
post′tho·rac′ic, *adj.*
post′thy·roi′dal, *adj.*
post·tib′i·al, *adj.*
post·tox′ic, *adj.*
post·tra′che·al, *adj.*
post′-Tran·scen·den′tal, *adj.*
post′trap′e·zoid′, *adj.*
post′trau·mat′ic, *adj.*
post′-Tri·as′sic, *adj.*
post′-Tri·den′tine, *adj.*
post′tu·ber′cu·lar, *adj.*
post·tus′sive, *adj.*
post′tym·pan′ic, *adj.*
post·ul′nar, *adj.*
post′um·bil′i·cal, *adj.*
post·um′bo·nal, *adj.*
post′u·re′ter·al, *adj.*
post′u·re·ter′ic, *adj.*
post·u′ter·ine, *adj.*
post·vac′ci·nal, *adj.*
post·var′i·o·loid′, *adj.*
post-Ve′dic, *adj.*
post′ve·ne′re·al, *adj.*
post·ve′nous, *adj.*
post·ven′tral, *adj.*
post·ver′te·bral, *adj.*
post·ves′i·cal, *adj.*
post′-Vic·to′ri·an, *adj.*
post-Vol′stead, *adj.*
post·xiph′oid, *adj.*
post′zyg·ap·o·phys′e·al, *adj.*
post′zyg·ap·o·phys′i·al, *adj.*

potas′sium hy′drate, *Chem.* See **potassium hydroxide.**

potas′sium hydrox′ide, *Chem.* a white, deliquescent, water-soluble solid, KOH, usually in the form of lumps, sticks, or pellets, which upon solution in water generates heat: used chiefly in the manufacture of soap, as a laboratory reagent, and in medicine as a caustic. Also called **caustic potash, potassa, potassium hydrate.**

potas′sium i′odide, *Chem., Pharm.* a white, crystalline, water-soluble powder, KI, having a bitter saline taste: used chiefly in the manufacture of photographic emulsions, as a laboratory reagent, in the preparation of Gram's solution for biological staining, and in medicine as an expectorant and in thyroid conditions.

potas′sium my′ron·ate (mī′rə nāt′), *Chem.* sinigrin. [< Gk *mýron* perfume + -ATE²]

potas′sium ni′trate, *Chem.* a crystalline compound, KNO_3, produced by nitrification in soil, and used in gunpowders, fertilizers, and preservatives; saltpeter; niter.

potas′sium ox′alate, *Chem.* a colorless, crystalline, water-soluble, poisonous solid, $K_2C_2O_4 \cdot H_2O$, used chiefly as a bleaching agent and in medicine.

potas′sium perman′ganate, *Chem.* a very dark purple, crystalline, water-soluble solid, $KMnO_4$, used chiefly as an oxidizing agent, disinfectant, laboratory reagent, and in medicine as an astringent and antiseptic.

potas′sium rho′da·nide (rōd′ᵊnīd′, rō dan′id), *Chem.* See **potassium thiocyanate.** [alter. of Gk *rhódon* rose (see RHODO-) + -IDE]

potas′sium so′dium tar′trate, *Chem.* See **Rochelle salt.**

potas′sium sul′fate, *Chem.* a crystalline, water-soluble solid, K_2SO_4, used chiefly in the manufacture of fertilizers, alums, and mineral water, and as a reagent in analytical chemistry.

potas′sium thiocy′anate, *Chem.* a colorless, crystalline, hygroscopic, water-soluble solid, KSCN, used chiefly in the manufacture of chemicals, dyes, and drugs. Also called **potassium rhodanide.**

potas′sium xan′thate, *Chem.* a colorless or light-yellow, water-soluble powder, $KS_2COC_2H_5$, used chiefly as a fungicide in soil treatment. Also called **potassium ethyl dithiocarbonate, potassium ethyl xanthogenate, potas′sium xan′tho·gen·ate** (zan′thə jə nāt′, zan-thoj′ə-).

po·ta·tion (pō tā′shən), *n.* **1.** act of drinking. **2.** a drink or draft, esp. of an alcoholic beverage. [late ME *potacion* < L *pōtātiōn-* (s. of *pōtātiō*) a drinking, equiv. to *pōtāt(us)* (ptp. of *pōtāre* to drink) + *-iōn-* -ION]

po·ta·to (pə tā′tō), *n., pl.* **-toes. 1.** Also called **Irish potato, white potato.** the edible tuber of a cultivated plant, *Solanum tuberosum.* **2.** the plant itself. **3.** See **sweet potato.** [< Sp *patata* white potato, var. of *batata* sweet potato < Taino]

pota′to ap′ple, the green berry of the potato.

pota′to bean′, groundnut.

pota′to bee′tle. See **Colorado potato beetle.**

pota′to bug′. See **Colorado potato beetle.**

pota′to chip′, a thin slice of potato fried until crisp, usually salted and eaten cold. Also called **Saratoga chip.**

pota′to crisp′, *Brit.* See **potato chip.**

pota′to moth′, a gelechiid moth, *Gnorimoschema operculella,* the larvae of which feed on the leaves and bore into the tubers of potatoes and other solanaceous plants.

pota′to race′, a novelty race in which each contestant must move a number of potatoes from one place to another, usually in a spoon, carrying one potato at a time.

po·ta·to·ry (pō′tə tōr′ē, -tôr′ē), *adj.* of, pertaining to, or given to drinking. [< L *pōtātōri(us).* See POTATION, -ORY¹]

pota′to tu′ber·worm (to͞o′bər wûrm′, tyo͞o′-), the larva of the potato moth. [TUBER + WORM]

pota′to vine′, a tender, woody vine, *Solanum jasminoides,* of Brazil, having showy, starlike, blue-tinged, white flowers in clusters, grown as an ornamental.

pota′to worm′. See **tomato hornworm.**

pot-au-feu (pô tō fœ′), *n. French Cookery.* a dish of boiled meat and vegetables, the broth of which is usually served separately. [< F: lit., pot on the fire]

Pot·a·wat·o·mi (pot′ə wot′ə mē), *n., pl.* **-mis,** (*esp. collectively*) **-mi.** a member of an Algonquian Indian people originally of Michigan and Wisconsin.

pot·bel·lied (pot′bel′ēd), *adj.* having or resembling a potbelly: *a potbellied stove.* [POTBELLY + -ED³]

pot·bel·ly (pot′bel′ē), *n., pl.* **-lies.** a distended or protuberant belly. [POT¹ + BELLY]

pot·boil·er (pot′boi′lər), *n. Informal.* a mediocre work of literature or art produced merely for financial gain. [POT¹ + BOILER]

pot·boy (pot′boi′), *n. Brit.* **1.** a boy or man who carries pots, bottles, glasses, or mugs of beer, ale, etc., to customers in a tavern; a waiter in a tavern. **2.** a boy or man who washes pots and pans in a tavern or restaurant; dishwasher. Also called **potman.** [POT¹ + BOY]

pot′ cheese′. See **cottage cheese.**

pot-de-fer (*Fr.* pôdᵊ fer′), *n. Armor.* an iron or steel skullcap worn above or below a coif. [< F: lit., pot of iron]

Po·teau (pə tō′), *n.* a town in SE Oklahoma. 4428 (1960).

po·teen (pō tēn′), *n.* (in Ireland) illicitly distilled whiskey. Also, **potheen.** [< Ir *poitín* small pot, dim. of *pota* pot]

Po·teet (pə tēt′), *n.* **1.** a town in SW Texas. 2811 (1960). **2.** a girl's given name.

Po·tem·kin (pō tem′kin, pə-; *Russ.* po tyôm′kin), *n.* **Prince Gri·go·ri A·le·ksan·dro·vich** (gri gô′ri ä′le-ksän′dro vich), 1739–91, Russian statesman and favorite of Catherine II.

po·tence¹ (pōt′ᵊns), *n.* potency. [ME < OF < L *potentia* POTENCY]

po·tence² (pōt′ᵊns), *n. Horol.* a bracket or shelf supporting the inner pivot of a balance staff. Also, **potance.** [ME: crutch < ML *potentia,* special use of L *potentia* POTENCY]

po·ten·cy (pōt′ᵊn sē), *n., pl.* **-cies** for 4–6. **1.** state or quality of being potent. **2.** power; authority. **3.** efficacy; effectiveness; strength. **4.** capacity to be, become, or develop; potentiality. **5.** a person or thing exerting power or influence. **6.** *Math.* See **cardinal number** (def. 2). Also, **potence.** [< L *potentia.* See POTENT¹, -ENCY]
—Syn. 1. strength, force, energy, capacity, potential.

po·tent¹ (pōt′ᵊnt), *adj.* **1.** powerful; mighty: *a potent fighting force.* **2.** cogent; persuasive: *Several potent arguments were in his favor.* **3.** producing powerful physical or chemical effects: *a potent drug.* **4.** having or exercising great power or influence: *a potent factor in the economy.* **5.** (of a male) capable of sexual intercourse. [< L *potent-* (s. of *potēns*), prp. of *posse* to be able, have power; see -ENT] **—po′tent·ly,** *adv.* **—po′tent·ness,** *n.*
—Syn. 1. strong, puissant. See **powerful. 4.** influential.
—Ant. 1. weak. **4.** ineffectual.

po·tent² (pōt′ᵊnt), *Heraldry.* **—***n.* **1.** a fur having a pattern of T-shaped forms, placed in alternate directions and having alternating tinctures, one metal and one color, so that all forms of one tincture face the same way and are between, above, and below forms of the other tincture facing the other way. Cf. **counterpotent. 2.** a T-shaped form used in potent or counterpotent. **—***adj.* **3.** (of a cross) having a crosspiece at the extremity of each arm: *a cross potent.* [ME *potente* crutch; var. of POTENCE²]

po·ten·tate (pōt′ᵊn tāt′), *n.* one who possesses great power; a sovereign, monarch, or ruler. [< LL *potentāt(us)* potentate, L: power, dominion. See POTENT¹, -ATE¹]

po·ten·tée (pōt′ᵊn tā′), *adj. Heraldry.* potenty.

po·ten·tial (pə ten′shəl), *adj.* **1.** possible, as opposed to actual: *the potential uses of nuclear energy.* **2.** capable of being or becoming: *a potential danger to safety.* **3.** *Gram.* expressing possibility: *the potential subjunctive in Latin; the potential use of* can *in* I can go. **4.** *Archaic.* potent¹. **—***n.* **5.** possibility; potentiality: *an investment that has little growth potential.* **6.** a latent excellence or ability that may or may not be developed. **7.** *Gram.* **a.** a potential aspect, mood, construction, case, etc. **b.** a form in the potential. **8.** *Elect.* a quantity associated with a point near or within an electrified substance and represented either as the potential difference between the point and some reference point, as the ground nearby or the earth in general, assumed to have a zero potential, or as the work hypothetically necessary to bring a unit of positive charge from an infinite distance to the given point. **9.** *Math., Physics.* a type of function from which the intensity of a field may be derived, usually by differentiation. [ME *potencial* < LL *potentiāl(is).* See POTENCY, -AL¹]
—Syn. 2. See **latent. 5.** capacity, potency.

poten′tial dif′ference, *Elect.* the difference between the potentials of two points in an electric field, equal to the amount of work done in moving a relatively small charge from one point to the other.

poten′tial divid′er, *Elect.* See **voltage divider.**

poten′tial en′ergy, *Physics.* the energy of a body or a system with respect to the position of the body or the arrangement of the particles of the system. Cf. **kinetic energy.**

poten′tial gra′dient, *Elect.* the rate of change of potential with respect to distance in the direction of greatest change.

po·ten·ti·al·i·ty (pə ten′shē al′i tē), *n., pl.* **-ties** for 2. **1.** the state or quality of being potential. **2.** something potential; a possibility: *Atomic destruction is a grim potentiality.* [< ML *potentiālitās.* See POTENTIAL, -ITY]

po·ten·tial·ly (pə ten′shə lē), *adv.* possibly but not yet actually: *potentially useful information.* [POTENTIAL + -LY]

po·ten·ti·ate (pə ten′shē āt′), *v.t.,* **-at·ed, -at·ing. 1.** to cause to be potent; make powerful. **2.** to increase the effectiveness of; intensify. [< L *potenti(a)* power, POTENCY + -ATE¹] **—po·ten′ti·a′tion,** *n.* **—po·ten′ti·a′tor,** *n.*

po·ten·til·la (pōt′ᵊn til′ə), *n.* any rosaceous herb or small shrub of the genus *Potentilla,* of north temperate regions. [< NL, special use of ML *potentilla* garden valerian, equiv. to *potent-* POTENT¹ + *-illa* dim. suffix]

po·ten·ti·om·e·ter (pə ten′shē om′i tər), *n. Elect.* **1.** a device for measuring electromotive force or potential difference by comparison with a known voltage. **2.** See **voltage divider.** [POTENTI(AL) + -O- + -METER] **—po·ten·ti·o·met·ric** (pə ten′shē ə me′trik), *adj.*

poten′tiomet′ric titra′tion, *Chem.* titration in which the end point is determined by measuring the voltage of an electric current of given amperage passed through the solution.

po·ten·ty (pōt′ᵊn tē), *adj. Heraldry.* a partition line or a charge, as an ordinary, having a series of T-shaped indentations: *a fess potenty.* Also, **potentée.** [POTENT² + -Y¹]

pot·ful (pot′fo͝ol), *n., pl.* **-fuls.** the amount that can be held by a pot. [POT¹ + -FUL]

poth·e·cary (poth′ə ker′ē), *n., pl.* **-car·ies.** *Chiefly Dial.* apothecary. [ME *potecarie,* aph. var. of *apothecarie* APOTHECARY]

po·theen (pō thēn′), *n.* poteen.

poth·er (poth′ər), *n.* **1.** commotion; uproar. **2.** a disturbance; fuss. **3.** a choking or suffocating cloud, as of smoke or dust. **—***v.t., v.i.* **4.** to worry; bother. [?]

pot·herb (pot′ûrb′, -hûrb′), *n.* any herb prepared as food by cooking in a pot, as spinach, or added as seasoning in cookery, as thyme. [POT¹ + HERB]

pot·hold·er (pot′hōl′dər), *n.* a thick piece of material, as a quilted or woven pad, used in handling hot pots and dishes to prevent burning the hands. [POT¹ + HOLDER]

pot·hole (pot′hōl′), *n.* **1.** a deep hole; pit. **2.** a hole formed in street or sidewalk pavement, as by excessive use or by extremes of weather. **3.** a more or less cylindrical hole formed in rock by the grinding action of the detrital material in eddying water. **4.** a cave opening vertically from the ground surface. [POT¹ + HOLE]

pot·hol·er (pot′hō′lər), *n. Chiefly Brit. Slang.* an explorer of caves; spelunker. [POTHOLE + -ER¹]

pot·hook (pot′ho͝ok′), *n.* **1.** a hook for suspending a pot or kettle over an open fire. **2.** an iron rod, usually curved, with a hook at the end, used to lift hot pots, irons, stove lids, etc. **3.** an S-shaped stroke in writing, esp. as made by children in learning to write. [late ME *pottehok.* See POT¹, HOOK]

Po·thos (pō′thos), *n. Class. Myth.* a companion of Aphrodite, regarded as the personification of desire and longing.

pot·house (pot′hous′), *n., pl.* **-hous·es** (-hou′ziz). *Brit.* a place where ale, beer, etc., are retailed; alehouse. [POT¹ + HOUSE]

pot·hunt·er (pot′hun′tər), *n.* **1.** a person who hunts for food or profit, ignoring the rules of sport. **2.** a person who takes part in contests merely to win prizes. [POT¹ + HUNTER] **—pot′hunt′ing,** *n., adj.*

po·tiche (pō tēsh′; *Fr.* pô tēsh′), *n., pl.* **-tich·es** (-tē′shiz; *Fr.* -tēsh′). a vase or jar, as of porcelain, with a rounded or polygonal body narrowing at the top. [< F; akin to POT¹]

Pot·i·dae·a (pot′i dē′ə), *n.* a city on the Chalcidice Peninsula, whose revolt against Athens in 432 B.C. was one of the causes of the Peloponnesian War.

po·tion (pō′shən), *n.* a drink or draft, esp. one having or reputed to have medicinal, poisonous, or magical powers: *a love potion; a sleeping potion.* [late ME *pocion* < L *pōtiōn-* (s. of *pōtiō*) a drinking, equiv. to *pōt(us)* drunk (var. of *pōtātus,* ptp. of *pōtāre*) + *-iōn-* -ION; r. ME *pocioun* < AF]

Pot·i·phar (pot′ə fər), *n.* the Egyptian officer whose wife tried to seduce Joseph. Gen. 39:1–20. Also, *Douay Bible,* **Putiphar.**

pot·latch (pot′lach), *n.* **1.** (among American Indians of the northern Pacific coast, esp. the Kwakiutl) a ceremonial festival at which gifts are bestowed on the guests and property is destroyed by its owner in a show of wealth which the guests later attempt to surpass. **2.** *Informal.* a celebration; party. [< Chinook, metathetic var. of Nootka *potshatl* gift]

pot′ lead′ (led), *Naut.* graphite applied to the bottom of a vessel to reduce friction.

pot·lick·er (pot′lik′ər), *n. Southern and Midland U.S.* See **pot liquor.**

pot·lik·ker (pot′lik′ər), *n. Southern and Midland U.S.* See **pot liquor.**

pot·line (pot′līn′), *n. Metall.* a row of electrolytic cells for reducing certain metals, as aluminum, from fused salts. [POT¹ + LINE¹]

pot′ liq′uor, the broth in which meat or vegetables, as salt pork or greens, have been cooked. Also, **pot-liq′uor.**

pot·luck (pot′luk′, -luk′), *n.* food or a meal that happens to be available without special preparation or purchase: *to take potluck with a friend.* [POT¹ + LUCK]

pot·man (pot′mən), *n., pl.* **-men.** *Brit.* potboy. [POT¹ + MAN¹]

pot′ mar′igold, the common marigold, *Calendula officinalis,* the flower heads of which are sometimes used in cookery for seasoning.

pot′ mar′joram, a perennial, labiate herb, *Origanum,* having aromatic foliage and small purplish-pink flowers. Also called **wild marjoram.**

pot′ met′al, 1. an alloy of copper and lead, formerly used for making plumbing fixtures, bearings, etc. **2.** cast iron of a quality suitable for making pots. **3.** *Glass-making.* **a.** glass colored by being mixed with stained glass during fusion. **b.** glass melted in a pot.

Po·to·mac (pə tō′mək), *n.* a river flowing SE from the Allegheny Mountains in West Virginia, along the boundary between Maryland and Virginia to the Chesapeake Bay. 287 mi. long.

Poto′mac long′ boat′, a two-masted, fore-and-aft-rigged barge used to carry cordwood on Chesapeake Bay and the Potomac River.

po·tom·e·ter (pə tom′i tər), *n. Meteorol.* an instrument for measuring the amount of water that a plant loses through transpiration, consisting of a sealed vessel of water and a cutting, the latter having been inserted into the vessel in such a way that moisture can escape only through absorption and transpiration. [< Gk *potó(n)* drink + -METER]

po·too (pō to͞o′), *n., pl.* **-toos.** any of several nocturnal birds of the family *Nyctibiidae,* of Mexico and Central and South America, related to the goatsuckers. [imit.]

po·to·roo (pō′tə ro͞o′), *n., pl.* **-roos.** any of several small, ratlike kangaroos of the genus *Potorous,* of the Australian region. [< native name in New South Wales]

Po·to·si (pə tō′sē), *n.* a town in central Missouri. 2805 (1960).

Po·to·sí (pô′tô sē′), *n.* a city in S Bolivia: formerly a rich silver-mining center. 52,278 (est. 1959); 13,022 ft. above sea level.

pot·pie (pot′pī′), *n.* **1.** a deep-dish pie containing meat, chicken, or the like, often combined with vegetables and topped with a pastry crust. **2.** a stew, as of chicken or veal, with dumplings, biscuits, or the like.

pot·pour·ri (pō′po͞o rē′, pō′po͞o rē′, pot po͞or′ē; *Fr.* pô po͞o rē′), *n., pl.* **-pour·ris** (-po͞o rēz′, -po͞o rēz′, -po͞or′ēz; *Fr.* -po͞o rē′). **1.** a mixture of dried petals of roses or other flowers with spices, kept in a jar for their fragrance. **2.** a musical medley. **3.** a collection of miscellaneous literary extracts. **4.** any mixture, esp. of unrelated objects, subjects, etc. [< F: lit., rotten pot, trans. of Sp *olla podrida;* see OLLA]

pot′ roast′, a dish of meat, usually of round or chuck steak or brisket of beef, stewed in one piece in a covered pot and served in its own gravy.

Pots·dam (pots′dam; *for 1 also Ger.* pôts′däm), *n.* **1.** a city in and the capital of Brandenburg, in NE Germany, SW of Berlin: formerly the residence of German emperors; wartime conference July–August 1945 of Truman, Stalin, Churchill, and later, Attlee. 142,860. **2.** a town in N New York. 10,635.

pot·sherd (pot′shûrd′), *n.* a broken pottery fragment, esp. one of archaeological value. [POT¹ + *sherd,* var. of SHARD]

pot′ shot′, 1. a shot fired at game merely for food, with little regard to skill or the rules of sport. **2.** a shot at an animal or person within easy range, as from ambush. **3.** a casual or aimless shot. **4.** a random or incidental criticism: *to take a pot shot at military spending in a speech on taxation.* Also, **pot′shot′.**

pot′ spin′ning, the spinning of rayon filaments in a centrifugal box. Also called **centrifugal spinning.**

pot′ still′, a still for making whiskey in which a flame is applied directly to the pot containing the mash.

pot·stone (pot′stōn′), *n.* a kind of soapstone, sometimes used for making pots and other household utensils. [POT[1] + STONE]

pot·sy (pot′sē), *n.* hopscotch. [?]

pott (pot), *n.* **1.** *Chiefly U.S.* a size of printing paper, 12½ × 16 inches. **2.** *Chiefly Brit.* a size of drawing or writing paper, 12½ × 15 inches. **3. pott octavo,** a size of book, about 4 × 6¾ inches, untrimmed, in America, 4 × 6¼ inches, untrimmed, in England. *Abbr.:* pott 8vo **4. pott quarto,** *Chiefly Brit.* a size of book, about 6¼ × 8 inches, untrimmed. *Abbr.:* pott 4to [var. of POT[1]; so called because it orig. bore the watermark of a pot]

pot·tage (pot′ij), *n.* a thick soup made of vegetables, with or without meat. [ME *potage* < OF: lit., something in or from a POT[1]; see -AGE]

pot·ted (pot′id), *adj.* **1.** placed or enclosed in a pot. **2.** transplanted into or grown in a pot. **3.** preserved or cooked in a pot: *potted beef.* **4.** *Brit. Slang.* (of the treatment of a subject) shallow; superficial. **5.** *Slang.* drunk. [POT[1] + -ED[2]]

pot·ter[1] (pot′ər), *n.* one who makes pottery. [ME; OE *pottere.* See POT[1], -ER[1]]

pot·ter[2] (pot′ər), *v.i., n. Chiefly Brit.* putter[1]. [freq. of obs. or dial. *pote* to push, poke, ME *poten,* OE *potian* to push, thrust. See PUT] **—pot′ter·er,** *n.* **—pot′ter·ing·ly,** *adv.*

Pot·ter (pot′ər), *n.* **Paul,** 1625–54, Dutch painter.

Pot·ter·ies (pot′ə rēz), *n.* **the,** a district in central England famous for the manufacture of pottery and china. The towns comprising this district were combined in 1910 to form Stoke-on-Trent. Also called **Five Towns.** Cf. **Stoke-on-Trent.**

pot′tern ore′ (pot′ərn), *Obs.* any ore that becomes vitreous when heated. [POTTER[1] + *-n,* as in *leathern*]

pot′ter's field′, a piece of ground reserved as a burial place for strangers and the friendless poor. Matt. 27:7.

pot′ter's wheel′, a device with a rotating horizontal disk upon which clay is molded by a potter.

pot′ter wasp′, any of several mason wasps, esp. of the genus *Eumenes,* which construct a juglike nest.

pot·ter·y (pot′ə rē), *n., pl.* **-ter·ies. 1.** ceramic ware, esp. earthenware and stoneware. **2.** the art or business of a potter; ceramics. **3.** a place where earthen pots or vessels are made. [late ME: potter's workshop (cf. F *poterie*). See POTTER[1], -Y[3]]

pot·tle (pot′əl), *n.* **1.** a former liquid measure equal to two quarts. **2.** a pot or tankard of this capacity. **3.** the wine or other liquid in it. **4.** alcoholic beverages, as wine and liquor. **5.** *Chiefly Brit.* a small container or basket, as for fruit. [ME *potel* < MF, dim. of *pot* POT[1]]

pot·to (pot′ō), *n., pl.* **-tos. 1.** any of several lorislike, African lemurs of the genera *Perodicticus* and *Arctocebus,* esp. *P. potto,* having a short tail and vestigial index fingers. **2.** the kinkajou. [< WAfr]

Pott's′ disease′ (pots), *Pathol.* caries of the bodies of the vertebrae, often resulting in marked curvature of the spine, and usually associated with a tuberculosis infection. [named after Percival *Pott* (1714–88), British surgeon, who described it]

Pott's′ frac′ture, a fracture of the lower fibula and of the malleolus of the tibia, resulting in outward displacement of the foot. [see POTT'S DISEASE]

Potts·town (pots′toun′), *n.* a borough in SE Pennsylvania. 26,144 (1960).

Potts·ville (pots′vil), *n.* a city in E Pennsylvania. 21,659 (1960).

pot·ty[1] (pot′ē), *adj.,* **-ti·er, -ti·est. 1.** *Chiefly Brit. Informal.* slightly insane; eccentric. **2.** *Brit.* paltry; trifling; petty. [POT[1] + -Y[1]]

pot·ty[2] (pot′ē), *n., pl.* **-ties. 1.** a seat of reduced size fitting over a toilet seat, for use by a small child. **2.** a small metal pot fitting under a potty-chair. **3.** a toilet (used by or in addressing a child). [POT[1] + -Y[2]]

pot·ty-chair (pot′ē châr′), *n.* a small chair with an open seat over a removable pot, for use by a child during toilet training.

po·tus (pō′təs), *n., pl.* **-ti** (-tī). (in prescriptions) a drink. [< L]

pot-val·iant (pot′val′yənt), *adj.* brave only as a result of being drunk. **—pot′-val′iant·ly,** *adv.* **—pot-val·or** (pot′val′ər), **pot-val·ian·cy** (pot′val′yən sē), *n.*

pot·wal·lop·er (pot′wol′ə pər, pot wol′-), *n. Eng. Hist.* (in some boroughs before the Reform Bill of 1832) a man who qualified as a householder, and therefore a voter, by virtue of ownership of his own fireplace at which to boil pots. Also, **pot′-wal′lop·er.** Also called **pot·wal·ler** (pot′wol′ər). [POT[1] + WALLOPER; r. *potwaller,* lit., potboiler (POT[1] + *wall,* OE *weallan* to boil, + -ER[1])]

pouch (pouch), *n.* **1.** a bag, sack, or similar receptacle, esp. one for small articles or quantities: *a tobacco pouch.* **2.** a small moneybag. **3.** a bag for carrying mail. **4.** a bag or case of leather, used by soldiers to carry ammunition. **5.** something shaped like or resembling a bag or pocket. **6.** *Chiefly Scot.* a pocket in a garment. **7.** a baggy fold of flesh under the eye. **8.** *Anat., Zool.* a baglike or pocketlike part; a sac or cyst, as the sac beneath the bill of pelicans, the saclike dilation of the cheeks of gophers, or the receptacle for the young of marsupials. **9.** *Bot.* a baglike cavity. **—***v.t.* **10.** to put into or enclose in a pouch, bag, or pocket; pocket. **11.** to arrange in the form of a pouch. **12.** (of a fish or bird) to swallow. **—***v.i.* **13.** to form a pouch or a cavity resembling a pouch. [ME *pouche* < ONF, var. of OF *poche;* also *poke, poque* bag. See POKE[2]]

pouched (poucht), *adj.* having a pouch, as the pelicans, gophers, and marsupials. [POUCH + -ED[3]]

pouched′ mole′. See **marsupial mole.**

pouched′ rat′. See **pocket gopher.**

pouch·y (pou′chē), *adj.,* **pouch·i·er, pouch·i·est.** possessing or resembling a pouch: *pouchy folds under the eyes.* [POUCH + -Y[1]]

pou·drette (po͞o dret′), *n.* a fertilizer made from dried night soil mixed with other substances, as gypsum and charcoal. [< F, equiv. to *poudre* POWDER + *-ette* -ETTE]

pou·dreuse (po͞o dro͞oz′; *Fr.* po͞o drœz′), *n., pl.* **-dreus·es** (-dro͞o′ziz; *Fr.* -drœz′). a small toilet table of the 18th century. [< F, deriv. of *poudre* POWDER]

pou·drin (po͞o′drin), *n.* See **ice crystals.** [< F *poudr(e)* POWDER + -IN[2]]

pouf (po͞of), *n.* **1.** a high headdress with the hair rolled in puffs, worn by women in the late 18th century. **2.** an arrangement of the hair over a pad; puff. **3.** a puff of material as an ornament on a dress or headdress. **4.** *Chiefly Brit.* a hassock. [< F; see PUFF]

Pough·keep·sie (pə kip′sē), *n.* a city in SE New York, on the Hudson: regatta. 38,330 (1960).

Pouil·ly (po͞o yē′), *n.* a village in central France: known for its wines. 1804 (1962). Also called **Pouil·ly-sur-Loire** (po͞o yē syr lwär′).

Pouil·ly-Fuis·sé (po͞o yē fwē sā′), *n.* a dry, white wine from Burgundy.

Pouil·ly-Fu·mé (po͞o yē′fyo͞o mā′; *Fr.* po͞o yē fy-mā′), *n.* a dry, white wine from Burgundy.

pou·laine (po͞o lān′), *n.* **1.** a shoe or boot with an elongated pointed toe, fashionable in the 15th century. **2.** the toe on such a shoe. Also called **crakow.** [< F, OF *Poulaine* Poland (in the phrase *souliers à la Poulaine* shoes of Polish style); r. AF *poleine*]

pou·lard (po͞o lärd′), *n.* a hen spayed to improve the flesh for use as food. Also, **pou·larde′.** [< F, equiv. to *poule* hen (see PULLET) + *-ard* -ARD]

poulard′ wheat′, a Mediterranean wheat, *Triticum turgidum,* grown as a forage crop in the U.S. Also called **cone wheat, rivet wheat.**

Pou·lenc (po͞o laɴk′), *n.* **Fran·cis** (fräɴ sēs′), 1899–1963, French composer and pianist.

poult (pōlt), *n.* the young of the domestic fowl, the turkey, the pheasant, or a similar bird. [late ME *pult(e);* syncopated var. of PULLET]

poult-de-soie (*Fr.* po͞odᵊ swä′), *n.* a soft, ribbed silk fabric, used esp. for dresses. [< F; see PADUASOY]

poul·ter·er (pōl′tər ər), *n. Brit.* a dealer in poultry, hares, and game; poultryman. [obs. *poulter* poultry dealer (< F *pouletier;* see PULLET, -ER[2]) + -ER[1]]

poul·tice (pōl′tis), *n., v.,* **-ticed, -tic·ing.** **—***n.* **1.** a soft, moist mass of cloth, bread, meal, herbs, etc., applied as a medicament to the body. **—***v.t.* **2.** to apply a poultice to. [earlier *pultes,* appar. pl. of L *puls* thick pap. See PULSE[2]]

poul·try (pōl′trē), *n.* domesticated fowl collectively, esp. those valued for their meat and eggs, as chickens, turkeys, ducks, geese, guinea fowl, etc. [ME *pult(e)rie* < MF *pouleterie.* See PULLET, -ERY] **—poul′try·less,** *adj.* **—poul′try·like′,** *adj.*

poul·try·man (pōl′trē mən), *n., pl.* **-men. 1.** one who raises domestic fowls, esp. chickens, to sell as meat; a chicken farmer. **2.** a poultry dealer, esp. one who sells chickens to housewives for cooking. [POULTRY + MAN[1]]

pounce[1] (pouns), *v.,* **pounced, pounc·ing,** *n.* **—***v.i.* **1.** to swoop down suddenly and grasp, as a bird does in seizing its prey. **2.** to spring, dash, or come suddenly: *Unexpectedly she pounced on the right answer.* **—***v.t.* **3.** to seize with the talons. **4.** to swoop down upon and seize suddenly, as a bird of prey does. **—***n.* **5.** the claw or talon of a bird of prey. **6.** a sudden swoop, as on an object of prey. [late ME;? akin to PUNCH[2]] **—pounc′ing·ly,** *adv.*

pounce[2] (pouns), *v.t.,* **pounced, pounc·ing.** to emboss (metal) by hammering on an instrument applied on the reverse side. [? same as POUNCE[1]]

pounce[3] (pouns), *n., v.,* **pounced, pounc·ing.** **—***n.* **1.** a fine powder, as of cuttlebone, formerly used to prevent ink from spreading in writing, as over an erasure or an unsized paper, or to prepare parchment for writing. **2.** a fine powder, often of charcoal, used in transferring a design through a perforated pattern. **3.** Also, **pounce′ bag′.** a small bag filled with pounce and struck against a perforated design. **—***v.t.* **4.** to sprinkle, smooth, or prepare with pounce. **5.** to trace (a design) with pounce. **6.** to finish the surface of (hats) by rubbing with sandpaper or the like. [< F *ponce* << L *pūmicem,* acc. of *pūmex* PUMICE] **—pounc′er,** *n.*

pounce′ box′, a small box with perforated lid for holding pounce powder for transferring designs, or for use in writing.

poun′cet box′ (poun′sit), a small perfume box with a perforated lid. [POUNCE[2] or POUNCE[3] + -ET]

pound[1] (pound), *v.t.* **1.** to strike repeatedly and with great force, as with an instrument, the fist, heavy missiles, etc. **2.** to produce or effect by striking or thumping, or in a manner resembling this (often fol. by *out*): *to pound out a tune on the piano.* **3.** to force (a way) by battering; batter (often fol. by *down*): *He pounded the door down. He pounded his way through the mob.* **4.** to crush by beating, as with an instrument; bray, pulverize, or triturate. **—***v.i.* **5.** to strike heavy blows repeatedly: *to pound on a door.* **6.** to beat or throb violently, as the heart. **7.** to give forth a thumping sound: *The drums pounded loudly.* **8.** to walk or go with heavy steps; move along with force or vigor. **—***n.* **9.** act of pounding. **10.** a heavy or forcible blow. **11.** a thump. [ME *poune(n),* OE *pūnian;* akin to D *puin* rubbish] **—pound′er,** *n.*
—Syn. 1. See **beat.**

pound[2] (pound), *n., pl.* **pounds,** (*collectively*) **pound. 1.** a unit of weight and of mass, varying in different periods and countries. **2. a.** (in English-speaking countries) an avoirdupois unit of weight equal to 7000 grains, divided into 16 ounces, used for ordinary commerce. **b.** a troy unit of weight, in the U.S. and formerly in Britain, equal to 5760 grains, divided into 12 ounces, used for gold, silver, and other precious metals. **c.** (in the U.S.) an apothecaries' unit of weight equal to 5,760 grains, divided into 12 ounces. **3.** Also called **pound sterling.** a paper money and monetary unit of the United Kingdom, equal to 20 shillings or 240 pence and equivalent to about 2.40 U.S. dollars. *Abbr.:* L; *Symbol:* £ **4.** Also called **pound Scots.** a former Scottish money of account, originally equal to the pound sterling but equal to only a twelfth of the pound sterling at the union of the crowns of England and Scotland in 1603. **5.** any of the monetary units of various countries, as Cyprus, Ireland, Israel, Lebanon, Libya, Nigeria, Sudan, Syria, and of certain British Commonwealth countries. **6.** (formerly) the Turkish lira. [ME; OE *pund* (c. D *pond,* G *Pfund,* Goth, Icel *pund*) << L *pondō* pound (indeclinable n.), orig. abl. of *pondus* weight (2nd decl.)]

pound[3] (pound), *n.* **1.** an enclosure maintained by public authorities for confining stray or homeless animals. **2.** an enclosure for sheltering, keeping, confining, or trapping animals. **3.** an enclosure or trap for fish. **4.** a place of confinement or imprisonment. **5.** reach (def. 25). **—***v.t.* **6.** *Archaic.* to shut up in or as in a pound; impound, imprison. [ME *poond,* early ME, late OE *pund-;* akin to POND]

Pound (pound), *n.* **1. Ezra Loo·mis** (lo͞o′mis), born 1885, U.S. poet. **2. Louise,** 1872–1958, U.S. scholar and linguist. **3.** her brother, **Roscoe,** 1870–1964, U.S. legal scholar and writer.

pound·age[1] (poun′dij), *n.* **1.** a tax, commission, rate, etc., of so much per pound sterling or per pound weight. **2.** weight in pounds. [ME; see POUND[2], -AGE]

pound·age[2] (poun′dij), *n.* **1.** confinement within an enclosure or within certain limits. **2.** the fee demanded to free animals from a pound. [POUND[3] + -AGE]

pound·al (poun′dᵊl), *n. Physics.* the foot-pound-second unit of force, equal to the force that produces an acceleration of one foot per second per second on a mass of one pound. *Abbr.:* pdl [POUND[2] + -AL[2]]

pound′ cake′, a rich, sweet cake made with approximately a pound each of butter, sugar, and flour.

pound·er[1] (poun′dər), *n.* one who or that which pounds, pulverizes, or beats. [POUND[1] + -ER[1]]

pound·er[2] (poun′dər), *n.* **1.** a person or thing having or associated with a weight or value of a pound or a specified number of pounds (often used in combination): *He caught only one fish, but it was an eight-pounder.* **2.** a gun that discharges a missile of a specified weight in pounds: *a ten-pounder.* **3.** a person possessing, receiving an income of, or paying a specified number of pounds. [POUND[2] + -ER[1]]

pound-fool·ish (pound′fo͞o′lish), *adj. Chiefly Brit.* foolish in regard to large sums.

pound-force (pound′fōrs′, -fôrs′), *n. Physics.* a foot-pound-second unit of force, equal to the force that produces an acceleration equal to the acceleration of gravity when acting on a mass of one pound. *Abbr.:* lbf

pound′ net′, a trap for catching fish, consisting of a system of nets staked upright in the water with a fence leading the fish out from a point offshore into a heart-shaped chamber emptying into a rectangular enclosure or pound from which escape is impossible.

pound′ Scots′, pound[2] (def. 4).

pound′ ster′ling, pound[2] (def. 3).

pour (pōr, pôr), *v.t.* **1.** to send (a liquid, fluid, or anything in loose particles) flowing or falling, as from one container to another, or into, over, or on something: *to pour a glass of milk; to pour water on a plant.* **2.** to emit or propel, esp. continuously or rapidly: *The hunter poured bullets into the moving object.* **3.** to produce or utter in or as in a stream or flood (often fol. by *out*): *to pour out one's troubles to a friend.* **—***v.i.* **4.** to issue, move, or proceed in great quantity or number: *Crowds poured from the stadium after the game.* **5.** to flow forth or along; stream: *Flood waters poured over the embankments.* **6.** to rain heavily (often used impersonally with *it* as subject): *It was pouring, but fortunately we had umbrellas.* **—***n.* **7.** act of pouring. **8.** an abundant or continuous flow or stream: *a pour of invective.* **9.** a heavy fall of rain. [ME *poure(n)*] **—pour′a·bil′i·ty,** *n.* **—pour′a·ble,** *adj.* **—pour′er,** *n.* **—pour′ing ly,** *adv.*

pour·boire (po͞or bwar′), *n., pl.* **-boires** (-bwar′). *French.* a gratuity; tip. [lit., for drinking]

pour′ing box′, *Foundry.* tundish (def. 2). Also called **pour′ing bas′ket, pour′ing ba′sin.**

pour le mé·rite (po͞or lə mā ret′), *French.* for merit.

pour·par·ler (po͞or par lā′; *Eng.* po͞or′pär lā′), *n., pl.* **-lers** (-lā′; *Eng.* -lāz′). *French.* an informal preliminary conference. [lit., for talking]

pour·par·ty (po͞or′pär′tē), *n. Law.* purparty.

pour′ point′, *Chem.* the lowest temperature at which a substance will flow under given conditions.

pour·point (po͞or′point′, -pwant′), *n.* a stuffed and quilted doublet worn by men from the 14th to 17th centuries. [< F, n. use of ptp. of *pourpoindre* to quilt, perforate, equiv. to *pour-,* for *par-* (< L *per ad*) through + *poindre* (< L *pungere* to prick, pierce); r. ME *purpont* < ML *purpunct(us)* for *perpunctum*]

pour′ test′, *Chem.* any test for determining the pour point of a substance.

pousse-ca·fé (po͞os′ka fā′; *Fr.* po͞os ka fā′), *n., pl.* **-fés** (-fāz′; *Fr.* -fā′). **1.** a small glass of liqueur served after coffee. **2.** a glass of various liqueurs arranged in layers. [< F: lit., coffee-pusher]

pous·sette (po͞o set′), *n., v.,* **-set·ted, -set·ting.** **—***n.* **1.** a dance step in which a couple or several couples dance around the ballroom, holding hands, as in country dances. **—***v.i.* **2.** to perform a poussette, as a couple in a country dance. [< F, equiv. to *pouss(er)* (to) PUSH + *-ette* -ETTE]

pous·sie (po͞o′sē), *n. Scot.* a cat of any age; pussy.

Pous·sin (po͞o saɴ′), *n.* **Ni·co·las** (nē kô lä′), 1594–1655, French painter.

Pous·sin·isme (po͞o sa nēs′mᵊ), *n. French.* (in fine arts) the doctrine, advocated in the French Academy during the latter half of the 17th century, that painting must primarily satisfy the intellect and therefore that linear drawing and design, as the chief instruments for achieving intellectual satisfaction, should be the principal criteria in evaluating the formal excellence of a work of art. Also, **Pous·sin·ism** (po͞o saɴ′iz əm). Cf. **Rubenisme.**

pou sto (po͞o′ stō′, pou′), *Greek.* **1.** a place to stand on. **2.** a basis of operation. [lit., where I may stand]

pout[1] (pout), *v.i.* **1.** to thrust out the lips, esp. in displeasure or sullenness. **2.** to look or be sullen. **3.** to swell out or protrude, as lips. **—***v.t.* **4.** to protrude (the lips). **5.** to utter with a pout. **—***n.* **6.** act of pouting; a protrusion of the lips. **7.** a fit of sullenness: *to be in a pout.* [ME *poute(n);* c. Sw (dial.) *puta* to be inflated] **—pout′ful,** *adj.* **—pout′ing·ly,** *adv.*

pout[2] (pout), *n., pl.* (*esp. collectively*) **pout,** (*esp. referring to two or more kinds or species*) **pouts. 1.** See **horned pout. 2.** See **ocean pout. 3.** a northern, marine food fish, *Gadus luscus.* [OE *-pute,* in *ǣlepūte* eel pout; c. D *puit* frog]

pout·er (pou′tər), *n.* **1.** a person who pouts. **2.** one of a breed of long-legged domestic pigeons, characterized by the habit of puffing out the distensible crop. [POUT[1] + -ER[1]]

pov·er·ty (pov′ər tē), *n.* **1.** the state or condition of having little or no money, goods, or means of support; condition of being poor; indigence. **2.** lack of something specified: *a poverty of intellect.* **3.** deficiency of desirable ingredients, qualities, etc.: *poverty of the soil.* **4.** scantiness; insufficiency: *Their efforts to stamp out disease were hampered by a poverty of medical supplies.* [ME *poverte* < OF < L *paupertāt-* (s. of *paupertās*) small means, moderate circumstances. See PAUPER, -TY[2]]
—**Syn. 1.** penury. POVERTY, DESTITUTION, NEED, WANT imply a state of privation and lack of necessities. POVERTY denotes serious lack of the means for proper existence: *living in a state of extreme poverty.* DESTITUTION, a somewhat more literary word, implies a state of having absolutely none of the necessities of life: *widespread destitution in countries at war.* NEED emphasizes the fact that help or relief is necessary: *Most of the people were in great need.* WANT emphasizes privations, esp. lack of food and clothing: *Families were suffering from want.* **4.** meagerness. —**Ant. 1.** riches, wealth, plenty.

pov·er·ty-strick·en (pov′ər tē strik′ən), *adj.* extremely poor: *poverty-stricken refugees.*

pow (pō, pou), *n. Scot. and North Eng.* the head; poll. [var. of POLL[1]]

POW, prisoner of war. Also, **P.O.W.**

pow·der[1] (pou′dər), *n.* **1.** any solid substance reduced to a state of fine, loose particles by crushing, grinding, disintegration, etc. **2.** a preparation in this form, as gunpowder, face powder, etc. **3.** Also, **powder snow.** *Skiing.* loose, usually fresh snow that is not granular, wet, or packed. —*v.t.* **4.** to reduce to powder; pulverize. **5.** to sprinkle or cover with powder: *She powdered the cookies with confectioners' sugar.* **6.** to apply powder to (the face, skin, etc.) as a cosmetic. **7.** to sprinkle or strew as if with powder: *A light snowfall powdered the landscape.* **8.** to ornament in this fashion, as with small objects scattered over a surface: *a dress lightly powdered with sequins.* —*v.i.* **9.** to use powder as a cosmetic. **10.** to become pulverized. [ME *poudre* < OF < L *pulver-* (s. of *pulvis*) dust, powder] —**pow′der·er,** *n.*

pow·der[2] (pou′dər), *v.i.* **1.** *Brit. Dial.* to rush. —*n.* **2.** *Brit. Dial.* a sudden, frantic, or impulsive rush. **3.** **take a powder,** *Slang.* to leave in a hurry; depart without taking leave, as to avoid something unpleasant: *He took a powder and left his mother to worry about his gambling debts.* Also, **take a runout powder.** [?]

pow′der blue′, a pale blue diluted with gray. —**pow′der-blue′,** *adj.*

pow′der boy′. See **powder monkey** (def. 1).

pow′der burn′, a skin burn caused by exploding gunpowder.

pow′der charge′, propellant (def. 2).

pow′der chest′, a small wooden box containing a charge of powder, old nails, scrap iron, etc., formerly secured over the side of a ship and exploded on the attempt of an enemy to board.

pow′der down′, modified down feathers which continually crumble at the tips, producing a fine powder that forms a bloom on the plumage of certain birds, as pigeons and herons.

pow′dered milk′. See **dry milk.**

pow′dered sug′ar, a sugar produced by pulverizing granulated sugar, esp. a coarser variety used for fruits or cold beverages. *Symbol:* XX Cf. **confectioners' sugar.**

pow′der flag′, *Naut.* See **red flag** (def. 3).

pow′der flask′, a small flask of gunpowder formerly carried by soldiers and hunters.

pow′der horn′, a powder flask made from the horn of a cow or ox.

pow·der·ing (pou′dər iŋ), *n.* a large number of small objects or figures; decoration of a surface with these: *She has a powdering of freckles on her nose. He painted a powdering of stars on the ceiling.* [late ME *powderynge.* See POWDER[1], -ING[1]]

pow′der keg′, **1.** a small, metal, barrellike container for gunpowder or blasting powder. **2.** a potentially dangerous situation, esp. one involving violent repercussions.

pow′der magazine′, a compartment for the storage of ammunition and explosives.

pow′der met′allurgy, the art or science of manufacturing useful articles by compacting metal and other powders in a die, followed by sintering.

pow′der mill′, a mill in which gunpowder is made.

pow′der mon′key, **1.** (formerly) a boy employed on warships to carry gun powder from the magazine to the guns. **2.** a man in charge of explosives in any operation requiring their use.

pow′der puff′, a soft, feathery ball or pad, as of cotton or down, for applying powder to the skin.

pow′der room′, **1.** a room containing toilet and washing facilities, esp. one on the ground floor of a house for the use of female guests; lavatory. **2.** (in euphemistic or whimsical use) a bathroom or ladies' room.

pow′der snow′, *Skiing.* powder[1] (def. 3).

pow·der·y (pou′də rē), *adj.* **1.** consisting of or resembling powder: *powdery sand; powdery clouds.* **2.** easily reduced to powder: *powdery plaster.* **3.** sprinkled or covered with or as with powder: *flowers powdery with pollen.* [late ME *powdry.* See POWDER[1], -Y[1]]

Pow·ell (pou′əl), *n.* **1. Cecil Frank,** born 1903, English physicist: Nobel prize 1950. **2. Lewis F(ranklin), Jr.,** born 1907, U.S. jurist: associate justice of the U.S. Supreme Court 1972–87.

pow·er (pou′ər), *n.* **1.** ability to do or act; capability of doing or accomplishing something. **2.** Usually, **powers.** particular faculties or capabilities of body or mind: *creative powers; the power of speech.* **3.** political or national strength: *the balance of power in Europe.* **4.** great or marked ability to do or act; strength; might; force. **5.** the possession of control or command over others; authority; ascendancy: *power over men's minds.* **6.** political ascendancy or control in the government of a country, state, etc.: *They attained power by overthrowing the legal government.* **7.** legal ability, capacity, or authority: *the power of attorney.* **8.** delegated authority; authority granted to a person or persons in a particular office or capacity: *the powers of the president.* **9.** a document or written statement conferring legal authority. **10.** one who or that which possesses or exercises authority or influence. **11.** a state or nation having international authority or influence: *The great powers held an international conference.* **12.** a military or naval force: *The Spanish Armada was a mighty power.* **13.** Often, **powers.** a deity; divinity: *the heavenly powers.* **14. powers,** *Theol.* an order of angels. Cf. **angel** (def. 1). **15.** *Dial.* a large number or amount: *There's a power of good eatin' at the church social.* **16.** *Physics.* **a.** work done or energy transferred per unit of time. *Symbol:* P **b.** the time rate of doing work. **17.** mechanical energy as distinguished from hand labor: *a loom driven by power.* **18.** a particular form of mechanical or physical energy: *hydroelectric power.* **19.** energy, force, or momentum: *The door slammed shut, seemingly under its own power.* **20.** *Math.* **a.** the product obtained by multiplying a quantity by itself one or more times: *The third power of 2 is 8.* **b.** See **cardinal number** (def. 2). **21.** *Optics.* **a.** the magnifying capacity of a microscope, telescope, etc., expressed as the ratio of the diameter of the image to the diameter of the object. **b.** the reciprocal of the focal length of a lens. **22. the powers that be,** those in supreme command; the authorities: *The decision is in the hands of the powers that be.* —*v.t.* **23.** to supply with electricity or other means of power: *Atomic energy powers the new submarines.* **24.** to give power to; make powerful: *An outstanding quarterback powered the team in its upset victory.* **25.** to inspire; spur; sustain: *A strong faith in divine goodness powers his life.* **26.** (of a fuel, engine, or any source able to do work) to supply force to operate (a machine): *An electric motor powers this drill.* [ME *poër* < AF, orig. inf. < LL **potēre,* r. L *posse* to be able, have power. See POTENT[1]]
—**Syn. 1.** capacity. **4.** energy. See **strength. 5, 6.** sway, rule, sovereignty. —**Ant. 1.** incapacity. **4.** weakness.

pow′er am′plifier, *Elect.* an amplifier for increasing the power of a signal.

Pow′er and the Glo′ry, The, a novel (1940) by Graham Greene.

pow′er base′, a source of authority or influence, esp. in politics, founded on support by an organized body of voters, ethnic minority, economic class, etc.: *His election as governor gives him a power base for seeking the presidency.*

pow·er·boat (pou′ər bōt′), *n.* **1.** a boat propelled by mechanical power. **2.** motorboat. [POWER + BOAT]

pow′er brake′, an automotive brake set by pressure from some power source, as a compressed-air reservoir, in proportion to a smaller amount of pressure on the brake pedal.

pow′er ca′ble, *Elect.* cable for conducting electric power.

pow′er chain′, an endless chain for transmitting motion and power between sprockets on shafts with parallel axes. Also called **pitch chain.** Cf. **roller chain, silent chain.**

pow′er dive′, *Aeron.* a dive, esp. a steep dive, by an aircraft in which the engine or engines are delivering thrust at or near full power.

pow·er-dive (pou′ər dīv′), *v.t., v.i.,* **-dived** or **-dove, -dived, -div·ing.** *Aeron.* to cause to perform or to perform a power dive.

pow′er drill′, a drill operated by a motor.

pow·ered (pou′ərd), *adj.* (of a machine, vehicle, etc.) having a specified fuel or prime mover: *a gasoline-powered engine; an engine-powered pump.* [POWER + -ED[2]]

pow·er·ful (pou′ər fəl), *adj.* **1.** having or exerting great power or force. **2.** physically strong, as a person: *a large, powerful man.* **3.** producing great physical effects, as a machine or a blow. **4.** potent; efficacious: *a powerful drug.* **5.** having great effectiveness, as a speech, speaker, description, reason, etc. **6.** having great power, authority, or influence; mighty: *a powerful nation.* **7.** *Chiefly Dial.* great in number or amount: *a powerful lot of money.* [late ME *powarfull.* See POWER, -FUL] —**pow′er·ful·ly,** *adv.* —**pow′er·ful·ness,** *n.*
—**Syn. 1.** forceful, strong. POWERFUL, MIGHTY, POTENT suggest great force or strength. POWERFUL suggests capability of exerting great force or overcoming strong resistance: *a powerful machine like a bulldozer.* MIGHTY, now chiefly rhetorical, implies uncommon or overwhelming strength of power: *a mighty army.* POTENT implies great natural or inherent power: *a potent influence.* **5.** influential, convincing, forcible, cogent, effective. —**Ant. 1.** weak.

pow·er·house (pou′ər hous′), *n., pl.* **-hous·es** (-hou′ziz). **1.** *Elect.* a generating station. **2.** *Informal.* a person, group, team, or the like, having great energy, strength, or potential for success. **3.** *Sports.* a team considered to be the best or among the best of its class on the basis of ability, manpower, style of play, and past record of performance. [POWER + HOUSE]

pow·er·less (pou′ər lis), *adj.* **1.** unable to produce an effect: *a disease against which modern medicine is virtually powerless.* **2.** lacking power to act; helpless: *His legs crumpled, and he was powerless to rise.* [POWER + -LESS] —**pow′er·less·ly,** *adv.* —**pow′er·less·ness,** *n.*

pow′er line′, *Elect.* a line for conducting electric power.

pow′er load′ing, *Aeron.* See under **loading** (def. 4).

pow′er loom′, a loom worked by machinery.

pow′er of appoint′ment, *Law.* the right granted by one person (the donor) to another (the donee) to dispose of the donor's property or create rights therein.

pow′er of attor′ney, *Law.* a written document given by one person or party to another authorizing the latter to act for the former.

pow′er pack′, *Electronics.* a device for converting the voltage from a power line or battery to the various voltages required by the components of an electronic circuit.

pow′er plant′, **1.** a plant, including engines, dynamos, etc., and the building or buildings necessary for the generation of power, as electric power. **2.** the machinery for supplying power for a particular mechanical process or operation.

pow′er play′, **1.** *Sports.* an offensive play characterized by a concentration of players at a certain point or in a certain area, as for clearing a path for the ball-carrier in football or mounting a scoring rush in ice hockey. **2.** a strategic and usually aggressive action, as in political, business, diplomatic, or military affairs, in which a concentration or manipulation of power is employed to pressure the opposition into compliance or acquiescence.

pow′er pol′itics, international diplomacy based on the use, or threatened use, of military power.

pow′er press′, a press operated by a mechanical, hydraulic, or pneumatic device.

pow′er saw′, a saw driven by a motor.

pow·er-saw (pou′ər sô′), *v.t.,* **-sawed, -sawed** or **-sawn, -saw·ing.** to cut with a power saw.

pow′er se′ries, *Math.* an infinite series in which the terms are coefficients times successive powers of a given variable, or times products of powers of two or more variables.

pow′er set′, *Math.* the collection of all subsets of a given set.

pow′er sta′tion, *Elect.* a generating station.

pow′er steer′ing, *Auto.* a steering system in which the position of the steering wheel controls a power source which in its turn guides the wheels on which the vehicle turns.

pow′er struc′ture, **1.** the system of authority or influence in government, politics, education, etc.: *The state elections threatened to upset the existing power structure.* **2.** the people who participate in such a system: *He hoped to become a part of the power structure.*

pow′er supply′, a device that provides power to electric machines, generators, etc.

pow′er train′, a train of gears and shafting transmitting power from an engine, motor, etc., to a mechanism being driven.

Pow·ha·tan (pou′hə tan′, pou hat′ən), *n.* c1550–1618, Indian chief in Virginia, father of Pocahontas.

pow·wow (pou′wou′), *n.* **1.** (among North American Indians) a ceremony, esp. one accompanied by magic, feasting, and dancing, performed for the cure of disease, success in a hunt, etc. **2.** a council or conference of or with Indians. **3.** *Informal.* any conference or meeting. —*v.i.* **4.** to hold a powwow. **5.** *Informal.* to confer. [< Algonquian (Narragansett) *pow waw* or *po-wan*]

Pow·ys (pō′is), *n.* **1. John Cowper,** 1872–1963, English author. **2.** his brother, **Llewelyn,** 1884–1939, English author. **3.** his brother, **Theodore Francis,** 1875–1953, English author.

pox (poks), *n. Pathol.* **1.** a disease characterized by multiple skin pustules, as smallpox. **2.** *Informal.* syphilis. **3.** Also called **soil rot.** *Plant Pathol.* a disease of sweet potatoes, characterized by numerous pitlike lesions on the roots, caused by a fungus, *Streptomyces ipomoea.* **4.** (used interjectionally to express distaste, rejection, aversion, etc.): *A pox on your Mr. Twiddle!* [for *pocks,* pl. of POCK]

Po·yang (pô′yäng′), *n.* a lake in E China, in Kiangsi province. 90 mi. long.

poyn·tell (poin′tel), *n.* pointel. Also, **poyn′till.**

Poz·nan (pôz′nän′yə), *n.* Polish name of **Posen.**

Po·zsony (pô′zhôn′yə), *n.* Hungarian name of **Bratislava.**

poz·zo·la·na (pot′sə lä′nə; *It.* pôt′tsô lä′nä), *n.* a porous variety of volcanic tuff or ash used in making hydraulic cement. Also, **poz·zo·lan** (pot′sə lən), **poz·zuo·la·na** (pot′swə lä′nə; *It.* pôt′tswô lä′nä), **puzzolana.** [< It << L *puteolāna,* fem. of *puteolānus* of *Pozzuoli* (deriv. of *Puteolī,* lit., little springs); see -AN]

poz·zo·la·nic (pot′sə lä′nik), *adj.* (of a cement admixture) having properties similar to those of pozzolana. Also, **poz·zu·o·la·nic** (pot′sōō ə lä′nik). [POZZOLAN(A) + -IC]

Poz·zuo·li (pot swō′lē; *It.* pôt tswô′lē), *n.* a seaport in SW Italy, near Naples: Roman ruins. 51,548 (1961).

pp., **1.** pages. **2.** past participle. **3.** pianissimo. **4.** privately printed.

P.P., **1.** parcel post. **2.** parish priest. **3.** past participle. **4.** postpaid. **5.** prepaid.

p.p., **1.** parcel post. **2.** past participle. **3.** postpaid.

ppd., **1.** postpaid. **2.** prepaid.

P.P. factor, *Biochem.* See **pellagra-preventive factor.**

pph., pamphlet.

PPI, See **plan position indicator.**

ppl., participle.

PPLO, See **pleuropneumonia-like organism.**

ppm, **1.** parts per million. **2.** pulse per minute.

p.p.m., parts per million. Also, **P.P.M., ppm., ppm**

ppr., present participle. Also, **p.pr.**

pps, pulse per second.

P.P.S., a second or additional postscript. Also, **p.p.s.** [< L *post postscriptum*]

ppt., *Chem.* precipitate.

P.Q., Province of Quebec.

p.q., previous question.

PR, **1.** payroll. **2.** public relations.

Pr, Provençal.

Pr, *Chem.* praseodymium.

Pr., **1.** (of stock) preferred. **2.** Priest. **3.** Prince. **4.** Provençal.

pr., **1.** pair; pairs. **2.** paper. **3.** power. **4.** preference. **5.** (of stock) preferred. **6.** present. **7.** price. **8.** priest. **9.** printing. **10.** pronoun.

P.R., **1.** parliamentary report. **2.** Roman people. [< L *populus Romanus*] **3.** press release. **4.** prize ring. **5.** proportional representation. **6.** public relations. **7.** Puerto Rico.

PRA, Public Roads Administration.

praam (präm), *n. Naut.* pram[2] (def. 1).

prac·tic (prak′tik), *adj.* practical. [ME *practik* < LL *practic(us)* < Gk *praktikós,* equiv. to *prak-* (verbid s. of *prássein* to do) + *-ikos* -TIC]

prac·ti·ca·ble (prak′tə kə bəl), *adj.* **1.** capable of being done, effected, or put into practice, with the available means; feasible: *a practicable solution.* **2.** capable of being used: *a practicable gift.* **3.** *Theat.* (of a stage property or part of a set) designed or constructed for actual use: *a practicable window; practicable water faucets.* [< ML *practic(āre)* (to) PRACTICE + -ABLE] —**prac′ti·ca·bil′i·ty, prac′ti·ca·ble·ness,** *n.* —**prac′ti·ca·bly,** *adv.*
—**Syn. 1.** workable, achievable, attainable. See **possible.** PRACTICABLE, PRACTICAL, though not properly synonyms, often cause confusion. PRACTICABLE means possible or feasible, able to be done, capable of being put into practice or of being used: *a practicable method of communication.* PRACTICAL (applied to persons) means

sensible and businesslike, (applied to things) efficient and workable, as contrasted with theoretical: *practical measures.* —**Ant. 1.** unfeasible.

prac·ti·cal (prak′ti kəl), *adj.* **1.** of or pertaining to practice or action: *practical mathematics.* **2.** consisting of, involving, or resulting from practice or action: *a practical application of a rule.* **3.** of, pertaining to, or concerned with ordinary activities, business, or work: *practical affairs.* **4.** adapted or designed for actual use; useful: *practical instructions.* **5.** engaged or experienced in actual practice or work: *a practical politician.* **6.** inclined toward or fitted for actual work or useful activities: *a practical man.* **7.** mindful of the results, usefulness, advantages or disadvantages, etc., of action or procedure. **8.** matter-of-fact; prosaic. **9.** being such in practice or effect; virtual: *a practical certainty.* **10.** *Theat.* practicable (def. 3). [PRACTIC + -AL[1]] —**prac′ti·cal′i·ty, prac′ti·cal·ness,** *n.*

—**Syn. 1.** See **practicable. 7.** PRACTICAL, JUDICIOUS, SENSIBLE refer to good judgment in action, conduct, and the handling of everyday matters. PRACTICAL suggests the ability to adopt means to an end or to turn what is at hand to account: *to adopt practical measures for settling problems.* JUDICIOUS implies the possession and use of discreet judgment, discrimination, and balance: *a judicious use of one's time.* SENSIBLE implies the possession and use of sound reason and shrewd common sense: *a sensible suggestion.* —**Ant. 7.** ill-advised, unwise, foolish.

prac′tical imper′ative, (in Kantian ethics) the dictum that one should treat oneself and all humanity as an end and never as a means.

prac′tical joke′, a playful trick, often involving some physical agent or means, in which the victim is placed in an embarrassing or disadvantageous position.

prac·ti·cal·ly (prak′tik lē), *adv.* **1.** in effect; virtually: *It is practically useless to protest.* **2.** in a practical manner: *to think practically.* **3.** from a practical point of view: *Practically speaking, the plan is not very promising.* **4.** almost; nearly: *Their provisions were practically gone.* [PRACTICAL + -LY]

prac′tical nurse′, one who has not graduated from an accredited school of nursing but who is skilled in caring for the sick, usually under the direction of a licensed physician or registered nurse.

prac′tical rea′son, *Kantianism.* reason applied to the problem of action and choice, esp. in ethical matters.

prac·tice (prak′tis), *n., v.,* **-ticed, -tic·ing.** —*n.* **1.** habitual or customary performance; operation: *office practice.* **2.** habit; custom: *It is not the practice here for women to appear on the street in shorts.* **3.** repeated performance or systematic exercise for the purpose of acquiring skill or proficiency: *Practice makes perfect.* **4.** skill gained by experience or exercise: *She refused to play the piano, because she was out of practice.* **5.** the action or process of performing or doing something: *to put a scheme into practice; the shameful practices of a blackmailer.* **6.** the exercise or pursuit of a profession or occupation, esp. law or medicine: *He plans to set up practice in his home town.* **7.** the business of a professional man: *The doctor wanted his son to take over his practice when he retired.* **8.** *Law.* the established method of conducting legal proceedings. **9.** *Archaic.* plotting; intrigue; trickery. **10.** Usually, **practices.** *Rare.* intrigues; plots. —*v.t.* **11.** to perform or do habitually or usually: *to practice a strict regimen.* **12.** to follow or observe habitually or customarily: *to practice one's religion.* **13.** to exercise or pursue as a profession, art, or occupation: *to practice law.* **14.** to perform or do repeatedly in order to acquire skill or proficiency: *to practice the violin.* **15.** to train or drill (a person, animal, etc.) in something in order to give proficiency. —*v.i.* **16.** to do something habitually or as a practice. **17.** to pursue a profession, esp. law or medicine. **18.** to exercise oneself by performance tending to give proficiency: *to practice at shooting.* **19.** *Archaic.* to plot or conspire. Also, **practise.** [late ME *practize, practyse* < ML *practizāre,* alter. of *practicāre,* deriv. of *practica* < Gk *praktikḗ* practical work, n. use of fem. of *praktikós* PRACTIC; see -IZE] —**prac′tic·er,** *n.*

—**Syn. 2.** See **custom. 3.** application. See **exercise.**

prac·ticed (prak′tist), *adj.* **1.** experienced; expert; proficient: *a practiced hand at politics.* **2.** acquired or perfected through practice: *a practiced English accent.* Also, **prac′tised.** [PRACTICE + -ED[2]]

prac′tice teach′er. See **student teacher.**

prac·ti·cum (prak′tə kəm), *n.* (in a college or university) the part of a course consisting of practical work in a particular field. [< L, neut. of *practicus* PRACTIC]

prac·tise (prak′tis), *v.t., v.i.,* **-tised, -tis·ing.** practice. —**prac′tis·er,** *n.*

prac·ti·tion·er (prak tish′ə nər), *n.* **1.** one engaged in the practice of a profession, occupation, etc.: *a medical practitioner.* **2.** one who practices something specified. **3.** *Christian Science.* one authorized to practice healing. [alter. of *practician* (PRACTIC + -IAN) + -ER[1]]

prad (prad), *n. Australian.* horse. [metathetic var. of D *paard* horse (c. G *Pferd*) << L *paravēred(us)* post horse for lesser highways. See PALFREY]

prae-, var. of **pre-.**

prae·cip·i·ta·ti·o (prē sip′i tā′shē ō′), *n. Meteorol.* precipitation that reaches the surface of the earth (distinguished from *virga*). [< L; see PRECIPITATION]

prae·di·al (prē′dē əl), *adj.* **1.** of, pertaining to, or consisting of land or its products; real; landed. **2.** arising from or consequent upon the occupation of land. **3.** attached to land. Also, **predial.** [< ML *praediāl(is)* landed, equiv. to L *praedi(um)* farm, estate + *-ālis* -AL[1]] —**prae′di·al′i·ty,** *n.*

prae·fect (prē′fekt), *n.* prefect.

prae·lect (pri lekt′), *v.i.* prelect. —**prae·lec′tion,** *n.* —**prae·lec′tor,** *n.*

prae·mu·ni·re (prē′myo͞o nī′rē), *n. Eng. Law.* **1.** a writ charging the offense of resorting to a foreign court or authority, as that of the pope, and thus calling in question the supremacy of the English Crown. **2.** the offense. **3.** the penalty of forfeiture, imprisonment, outlawry, etc., incurred. [short for late ME *praemūnīre faciās* < ML (for L *praemonēre faciās* that you cause (someone) to be forewarned), the operative words of the writ, deriv. of *praemūnīre* to warn (L: protect, lit., fortify). See PRAE-, MUNIMENT]

Prae·nes·te (prē nes′tē), *n.* ancient name of **Palestrina.**

Prae·nes·tine (prē nes′tin), *adj.* of or pertaining to the ancient town of Praeneste in Italy, or to the Latin dialect spoken there. [< L *Praenestīn(us).* See PRAENESTE, -INE[1]]

prae·no·men (prē nō′mən), *n., pl.* **-nom·i·na** (-nom′ə nə), **-no·mens.** the first or personal name of a Roman citizen, as "Gaius" in "Gaius Julius Caesar." Also, **prenomen.** [< L, equiv. to *prae-* PRAE- + *nōmen* NAME] —**prae·nom·i·nal** (prē nom′ə nəl), *adj.*

prae·pos·tor (prē pos′tər), *n.* a senior student at an English public school who is given authority over the other students. Also, **prepositor, prepostor.** [< ML *praepos(i)tor.* See PRAE-, POSIT, -OR[2]] —**prae·pos·to·ri·al** (prē′po stôr′ē əl, -stōr′-), *adj.*

prae·tex·ta (prē tek′stə), *n., pl.* **-tex·tae** (-tek′stē). **1.** (in ancient Rome) a white toga with a broad purple border, worn by priests and magistrates as an official costume, and by certain other Romans as ceremonial dress. **2.** a similar garment worn by a boy until he assumed the toga virilis, or by a girl until she married. Also, **pretexta.** [< L, short for *toga praetexta,* lit., bordered toga. See PRETEXT]

prae·tor (prē′tər), *n.* (in the ancient Roman republic) one of a number of elected magistrates charged chiefly with the administration of civil justice. Also, **pretor.** [late ME *pretor* < L *praetor* leader, lit., one going before, equiv. to *prae(i)t(us)* led (ptp. of *praeīre,* equiv. to *prae-* PRAE- + *īre* to go) + *-or* -OR[2]]

prae·to·ri·an (prē tôr′ē ən, -tōr′-), *adj.* **1.** of or pertaining to a praetor. **2.** (*often cap.*) noting or pertaining to the Praetorian Guard. —*n.* **3.** a person having the rank of praetor or ex-praetor. **4.** (*often cap.*) a soldier of the Praetorian Guard. Also, **pretorian.** [< L *praetōriān(us).* See PRAETOR, -IAN]

Praeto′rian Guard′, *Rom. Hist.* the bodyguard of a military commander, esp. the imperial guard stationed in Rome.

prae·to·ri·an·ism (prē tôr′ē ə niz′əm, -tōr′-), *n.* the control of a society by force or fraud, esp. when exercised through titular officials and by a powerful minority. [PRAETORIAN + -ISM]

prae·tor·ship (prē′tər ship′), *n.* the office or dignity of a praetor. Also, **pretorship.** [PRAETOR + -SHIP]

Prag (präkh), *n.* German name of **Prague.**

prag·mat·ic (prag mat′ik), *adj.* Also, **prag·mat′i·cal** (for defs. 2, 3, 6, 7). **1.** treating historical phenomena with special reference to their causes, antecedent conditions, and results. **2.** *Philos.* of or pertaining to pragmatism. **3.** of or pertaining to the practical point of view or practical considerations. **4.** of or pertaining to the affairs of a state or community. **5.** busy; active. **6.** officious; meddlesome; interfering. **7.** dogmatic; opinionated. —*n.* **8.** See **pragmatic sanction. 9.** an officious or meddlesome person. [< L *pragmatic(us)* < Gk *pragmatikós* practical, equiv. to *pragmat-* (s. of *prâgma*) deed, state business, etc. + *-ikos* -IC] —**prag·mat′i·cal′i·ty, prag·mat′i·cal·ness,** *n.* —**prag·mat′i·cal·ly,** *adv.*

prag·mat·i·cism (prag mat′i siz′əm), *n.* the pragmatist philosophy of C. S. Peirce: so called by him to distinguish it from the pragmatism of William James. [PRAGMATIC + -ISM]

prag·mat·ics (prag mat′iks), *n.* (*construed as sing.*) the branch of semiotic dealing with the causal and other relations between words, expressions, or symbols and their users. [see PRAGMATIC, -ICS]

pragmat′ic sanc′tion, **1.** any one of various imperial decrees with the effect of fundamental law. **2.** (*caps.*) *Hist.* **a.** any of several imperial or royal decrees limiting the power or privilege of the papacy, as the decree of Charles VII of France in 1438 or that of the Diet of Mainz in 1439. **b.** the imperial decree of Charles VI of Austria in 1713, by which his daughter, Maria Theresa, inherited his dominions.

pragmat′ic the′ory, the theory of truth that the truth of a statement consists in its practical consequences, esp. in its agreement with subsequent experience. Cf. **coherence theory, correspondence theory.**

prag·ma·tism (prag′mə tiz′əm), *n.* **1.** character or conduct which emphasizes practicality. **2.** a philosophical system or movement stressing practical consequences and values as standards by which concepts are to be analyzed and their validity determined. **3.** officiousness; meddlesomeness. **4.** dogmatism; arrogance. [PRAGMAT(IC) + -ISM] —**prag′ma·tis′tic,** *adj.*

prag·ma·tist (prag′mə tist), *n.* **1.** one who is oriented toward the success or failure of a particular line of action, thought, etc.; a practical person. **2.** an advocate or adherent of philosophical pragmatism. —*adj.* **3.** of, pertaining to, or characteristic of pragmatism. [PRAGMAT(IC) + -IST]

Prague (präg), *n.* **a city in and the capital of the Czech Republic, in the W central part, on the Vltava: formerly capital of Czechoslovakia. 1,211,000. Czech, Pra·ha** (prä′hä). **German, Prag.**

Prague′ School′, a school of linguistics emphasizing structure, active in the 1920's and 1930's.

prahm (präm), *n. Naut.* pram[2] (def. 1).

pra·hu (prä′ho͞o), *n.* proa (def.2). [< Malay *p(e)rahu* boat]

Prai·ri·al (prᴇ rē al′), *n.* (in the French Revolutionary calendar) the ninth month of the year, extending from May 20 to June 18. [< F; see PRAIRIE, -AL[1]]

prai·rie (prâr′ē), *n.* **1.** an extensive, level or slightly undulating, mostly treeless tract of land in the Mississippi valley, characterized by a highly fertile soil and originally covered with coarse grasses, and merging into drier plateaus in the west. **2.** a tract of grassland; meadow. **3.** (in Florida) a low, sandy tract of grassland often covered with water. **4.** *Southern U.S.* wet grassland; marsh. **5.** (*cap.*) a steam locomotive having a two-wheeled front truck, six driving wheels, and a two-wheeled rear truck. [< F: meadow << L *prāt(um)* meadow + *-āria,* fem. of *-ārius* -ARY] —**prai′rie·like′,** *adj.*

Prairie, The, a historical novel (1827) by James Fenimore Cooper. Cf. **Leather-Stocking Tales.**

prai′rie break′er, breaker[1] (def. 5).

prai′rie but′ton snake′root, a stout herb, *Liatris pycnostachya,* found in the prairies of the central U.S., having showy, rose-purple flower heads in dense spikes. Also called **Kansas gay-feather.**

prai′rie chick′en, **1.** either of two North American gallinaceous birds of western prairies, *Tympanuchus cupido* (**great′er prai′rie chick′en**), or *T. pallidicinctus* (**less′er prai′rie chick′en**), having rufous, brown, black, and white plumage. **2.** See **sharp-tailed grouse.** Also called **prairie fowl, prairie grouse.**

prai′rie clo′ver, any leguminous herb of the genus *Petalostemon,* found chiefly in western North America, having pinnately compound leaves and spikes of white, purple, or pink flowers.

prai′rie cone′flower, a rough-hairy perennial herb, *Ratibida columnaris,* found from the central U.S. to Mexico, having yellow flower heads nearly two inches wide with a columnar disk.

prai′rie crab′ ap′ple, a tree, *Malus ioensis,* of the central U.S., having downy branchlets, white or rose-tinted flowers, and round, waxy, greenish fruit.

prai′rie dock′, a North American rosinweed, *Silphium terebinthinaceum.*

prai′rie dog′, any of several gregarious, burrowing rodents of the genus *Cynomys,* of North American prairies, having a barklike cry.

Prairie dog, *Cynomys ludovicianus* (Total length 16 in.; tail 3½ in.)

Prai·rie du Chien (prâr′ē də shēn′), a town in SW Wisconsin. 5649 (1960).

prai′rie fal′con, a North American falcon, *Falco mexicanus,* grayish-brown above and white barred with brown below.

prai′rie flax′, a perennial herb, *Linum lewisi,* of western North America, having blue flowers.

prai′rie fowl′. See **prairie chicken.** Also called **prai′rie grouse′.**

prai′rie lil′y, a biennial herb, *Mentzelia decapetala,* found from South Dakota to Texas, having fragrant, white or yellow flowers that open in the evening. Also called **gumbo lily.**

prai′rie mal′low. See **red false mallow.**

prai′rie owl′, **1.** See **burrowing owl. 2.** See **short-eared owl.**

prai′rie oys′ter, **1.** a raw egg, or the yolk of a raw egg, often mixed with seasonings, as salt, pepper, Worcestershire sauce, etc., and used as a hangover remedy. **2.** the testis of a calf used as food. Cf. **mountain oyster.**

prai′rie phlox′, an erect, perennial herb, *Phlox pilosa,* of eastern North America, having clusters of flowers varying from white to purple.

prai′rie pine′, gay-feather (def. 2).

prai′rie point′er. See **shooting star** (def. 2).

Prai′rie Prov′inces, the provinces of Manitoba, Saskatchewan, and Alberta, in W Canada.

prai′rie rat′tlesnake, a rattlesnake, *Crotalus viridis viridis,* of the prairies of western North America.

prai′rie rose′, a climbing rose, *Rosa setigera,* of the central U.S., having pinkish to white flowers: the State flower of North Dakota.

prai′rie schoon′er, a type of covered wagon, similar to but smaller than the Conestoga wagon, used by pioneers in crossing the prairies and plains of North America.

prai′rie smoke′, a perennial herb, *Geum triflorum,* of North America, having purplish flowers and silky-plumed fruit. Also called **Johnny smokers.**

Prai′rie Vil′lage, a city in E Kansas, near Kansas City. 25,356 (1960).

prai′rie wake′robin, a woodland, perennial herb, *Trillium recurvatum,* of the central U.S., having purple-mottled leaves and brown-purple flowers.

prai′rie war′bler, a North American wood warbler, *Dendroica discolor,* olive-green above, yellow below, and striped with black on the face and sides.

prai′rie wolf′, coyote (def. 1).

prai·ril·lon (prə ril′yən, prə ril′ən), *n. Obs.* a small prairie. [prob. < AmerF, dim. of F *prairie*]

praise (prāz), *n., v.,* **praised, prais·ing.** —*n.* **1.** act of expressing approval or admiration; commendation; laudation. **2.** the offering of grateful homage in words or song, as an act of worship: *a hymn of praise to God.* **3.** state of being approved or admired: *The King lived in praise for many years.* **4.** *Archaic.* a ground for praise, or a merit. **5.** *Obs.* an object of praise. **6. sing someone's praises,** to praise someone publicly and enthusiastically: *He is always singing his wife's praises.* —*v.t.* **7.** to express approval or admiration of; commend; extol. **8.** to offer grateful homage to (God or a deity), as in words or song. [ME *preise(n)* < OF *preisi(er)* (to) value, prize < LL *pretiāre,* deriv. of L *pretium* price, worth, reward. See PRIZE[2]] —**praise′ful,** *adj.* —**praise′ful·ly,** *adv.* —**praise′ful·ness,** *n.* —**praise′less,** *adj.* —**prais′er,** *n.*

—**Syn. 1.** acclamation, plaudit, applause, approbation, compliment. **2.** encomium, eulogy, panegyric. **7.** laud, applaud, eulogize. See **approve. 8.** glorify, magnify, exalt, honor. —**Ant. 1.** condemnation. **7.** depreciate.

praise·wor·thy (prāz′wûr′thē), *adj.* deserving of praise; laudable: *a praiseworthy motive.* [PRAISE + WORTHY] —**praise′wor′thi·ly,** *adv.* —**praise′wor′thi·ness,** *n.*

Pra·ja·dhi·pok (prə chä′ti pok′), *n.* 1893–1941, king of Siam 1925–35.

Pra·ja·pa·ti (prə jä′put′ē), *n. Hindu Myth.* a Vedic god personifying a creative force which evolves all things from itself.

praj·na (pruj′nyä), *n. Buddhism, Hinduism.* pure and unqualified knowledge. Also called **Enlightenment.** [< Skt *prajñā*]

Praj·na-Pa·ra·mi·ta (pruj′nyä pä rum′i tä), *n. Buddhism.* a collection of Madhyamika texts, in the form of dialogues, upon the ineffability of nirvana and the unimportance of the means to it.

Pra·krit (prä′krit, -krēt), *n.* any of the vernacular Indic languages of the ancient and medieval periods, as distinguished from Sanskrit. [< Skt *prākrta* natural, common, vulgar, equiv. to *pra-* before (c. PRE-) + *kr* to do, make + *-ta* ptp. suffix. See SANSKRIT] —**Pra·krit′ic,** *adj.*

pra·kri·ti (pruk′ri tē), *n. Hinduism.* (in Sankhya philosophy) primal matter or substance from which the physical and mental universe evolves under the influence of purusha. Cf. **guna, purusha.** [< Skt *prākṛti* things made first, equiv. to *prākṛt-* (see PRAKRIT) + *-i* neut. pl. suffix]

pra·line (prä′lēn, prā′-, prä lēn′), *n.* any of various confections consisting of almonds, pecans, or other nuts, cooked in syrup, often prepared with brown sugar. [< F; named after Marshall du Plessis-*Praslin* (1598–1675), whose cook invented them]

prall·tril·ler (präl′tril′ər), *n. Music.* See **inverted mordent.** [< G: lit., rebounding trill]

pram[1] (pram), *n. Chiefly Brit. Informal.* perambulator. [by shortening]

pram[2] (präm), *n. Naut.* **1.** Also called **praam, prahm.** a flat-bottomed lighter used in Dutch and German ports. **2.** small open fishing vessel of Norway, having a pram bow. [< LG, D *praam;* c. G *Prahm* < Slav]

pram′ bow′ (bou), *Naut.* a bow in which the side planks are gathered into a narrow area terminated by a small, raking, transomlike board, well above the water, which the planking of the bottom rises to meet.

pra·na (prä′nə), *n.* **1.** *Yoga, Jainism.* the vital principle. **2.** *Yoga.* one of five vital breaths moving in the body. [< Skt: lit., breath]

pra·na·va (prun′ə və), *n. Hinduism.* the word "Om." [< Skt]

prance (prans, präns), *v.,* **pranced, pranc·ing,** *n.* —*v.i.* **1.** to spring from the hind legs; to move by springing, as a horse. **2.** to ride on a horse doing this. **3.** to ride gaily, proudly, or insolently. **4.** to move or go in an elated manner; cavort. **5.** to dance or move in a lively or spirited manner; caper. —*v.t.* **6.** to cause to prance. —*n.* **7.** act of prancing; a prancing movement. [ME *pra(u)nce;* akin to Dan (dial.) *prans(k)* spirited, said of a horse] —**pranc′er,** *n.* —**pranc′ing·ly,** *adv.*

prand., (in prescriptions) dinner. [< L *prandium*]

pran·di·al (pran′dē əl), *adj.* of or pertaining to a meal, esp. dinner. [< L *prandi(um)* luncheon, meal + -AL[1]] —**pran′di·al·ly,** *adv.*

Prandtl′ num′ber (prän′tᵊl), *Physics, Thermodynamics.* the ratio of the fluid viscosity to the thermal conductivity of a substance, a low number indicating high convection. [named after Ludwig *Prandtl* (1875–1953), German physicist]

prang (prang), *v.t. Brit. Slang.* **1.** to collide with; bump into. **2.** to destroy or severely damage by a bombing raid; bomb (an enemy target). **3.** to destroy or shoot down (an enemy aircraft). [imit.]

pran·i·dha·na (prun′i dä′nə), *n.* (in Mahayana Buddhism) the resolution not to enter nirvana until all beings are ready to enter. [< Skt]

prank[1] (prangk), *n.* **1.** a trick of an amusing or playful nature. **2.** a trick of a malicious nature. [?]

prank[2] (prangk), *v.t.* **1.** to dress or adorn in an ostentatious manner: *They were all pranked out in their fanciest clothes.* —*v.i.* **2.** to make an ostentatious show or display. [akin to D *pronken* to show off, strut, *pronk* show, finery, MLG *prank* pomp]

prank·ish (prang′kish), *adj.* **1.** of the nature of a prank: *a prankish plan.* **2.** full of pranks; playful: *a prankish boy; a prankish kitten.* [PRANK[1] + -ISH[1]] —**prank′ish·ly,** *adv.* —**prank′ish·ness,** *n.*

prank·ster (prangk′stər), *n.* a mischievous or malicious person who plays tricks, practical jokes, etc., at the expense of another. [PRANK[1] + -STER]

prao (prou), *n., pl.* **praos.** proa (def. 2).

Pra·sad (prə säd′), *n.* **Ra·jen·dra** (rä jen′drə), 1884–1963, first president of the Republic of India 1950–62.

prase (prāz), *n.* a leek-green cryptocrystalline variety of chalcedony. [< F < L *pras(ius)* leek-green stone < Gk *prásios* leek-green, equiv. to *prás(on)* leek + *-ios* -IOUS; r. ME *prassius* < L]

pra·se·o·dym·i·um (prā′zē ō dim′ē əm, prā′sē-), *n. Chem.* a rare-earth, metallic, trivalent element, named from its green salts. *Symbol:* Pr; *at. wt.:* 140.91; *at. no.:* 59; *sp. gr.:* 6.77 at 20°C. [*praseo-* (comb. form repr. PRASE) + (DI)DYMIUM]

prat (prat), *n. Slang.* the buttocks. [?]

Prat·de·sa·bá (prät′də sä bä′), *n.* a ring formation in the fourth quadrant of the face of the moon, in the libration area: about 80 miles in diameter.

prate (prāt), *v.,* **prat·ed, prat·ing,** *n.* —*v.i.* **1.** to talk excessively and pointlessly; babble: *She prated of the good old days.* —*v.t.* **2.** to utter in empty or foolish talk: *to prate absurdities with the greatest seriousness.* —*n.* **3.** act of prating. **4.** empty or foolish talk. [late ME < MD *praete(n).* See PRATTLE] —**prat′er,** *n.* —**prat′ing·ly,** *adv.*

prat·fall (prat′fôl′), *n. Slang.* **1.** a fall in which one lands on the buttocks. **2.** a humiliating blunder or defeat. [PRAT + FALL]

prat·in·cole (prat′ing kōl′, prā′tin-), *n.* any of several limicoline birds of the genus *Glareola,* of the Eastern Hemisphere, having a short bill, long, narrow, pointed wings, and a forked tail. [< NL *Prātincol(a)* genus name, equiv. to L *prāt(um)* meadow + *incola* inhabitant]

pra·tin·co·lous (prə ting′kə ləs), *adj. Zool.* living in a meadow. [< NL *prātincol(a)* meadow-dweller (see PRATINCOLE) + -OUS]

pra·tique (pra tēk′, prat′ik; *Fr.* PRA tēk′), *n. Com.* license or permission to use a port, given to a ship after quarantine or on showing a clean bill of health. [< F: practice < ML *practica.* See PRACTICE]

Pra·to (prä′tô), *n.* a city in central Italy, near Florence. 111,634 (1961). Also called **Pra′to in To·sca′na** (ēn tô skä′nä).

Pratt (prat), *n.* a town in S Kansas. 8156 (1960).

prat·tle (prat′ᵊl), *v.,* **-tled, -tling,** *n.* —*v.i.* **1.** to talk in a foolish or simple-minded way; chatter; babble. —*v.t.* **2.** to utter by chattering or babbling. —*n.* **3.** act of prattling. **4.** chatter; babble: *the prattle of children.* **5.** a babbling sound: *the prattle of water rushing over stones.* [< MLG *pratele(n)* (to) chatter, freq. of *praten* to PRATE] —**prat′tler,** *n.* —**prat′tling·ly,** *adv.*

Pratt′ truss′, a truss having vertical compression members and diagonal tension members that cross one panel. Cf. **Whipple truss.** See illus. under **truss.** [after the proper name *Pratt*]

Pratt·ville (prat′vil), *n.* a town in central Alabama. 6616 (1960).

Prat·ye·ka (prut yā′kə), *n.* (in Mahayana Buddhism) one who enters into nirvana as the intended goal of unassisted effort. Pali, **Pacceka.** [shortening of Skt *pratyekabuddha,* equiv. to *pratyeka* each one, single + *buddha* BUDDHA]

prau (prou), *n.* proa (def. 2).

Prav·da (präv′də), *n.* the official newspaper of the Communist party in the U.S.S.R. Cf. **Izvestia.**

prawn (prôn), *n.* **1.** any of various shrimplike decapod crustaceans of the genera *Palaemon, Penaeus,* etc., certain of which are used as food. —*v.t.* **2.** to catch prawns, as for food. [late ME *prane*] —**prawn′er,** *n.*

Prawn,
Palaemon serratus
(Length 3 to 4 in.)

prax·is (prak′sis), *n., pl.* **prax·is·es, prax·es** (prak′sēz). **1.** practice, as distinguished from theory; application or use, as of knowledge or skills. **2.** convention, habit, or custom. **3.** a set of examples for practice. [< ML < Gk *prâxis* deed, act, action]

Prax·is (prak′sis), *n. Class. Myth.* an epithet of Aphrodite, meaning "action."

Prax·it·e·les (prak sit′ᵊlēz′), *n.* fl. c350 B.C., Greek sculptor. —**Prax·it′e·le′an,** *adj.*

Prax·ith·e·a (prak sith′ē ə), *n. Class. Myth.* the wife of King Erechtheus.

pray (prā), *v.t.* **1.** to make earnest petition to (a person). **2.** to offer devout petition, praise, thanks, etc., to (God or an object of worship). **3.** to make petition or entreaty for; crave: *She prayed his forgiveness.* **4.** to offer (a prayer). **5.** to bring, put, etc., by praying: *to pray a soul into heaven.* —*v.i.* **6.** to make entreaty or supplication, as to a person or for a thing. **7.** to offer devout petition, praise, thanks, etc., to God or to an object of worship. **8.** to enter into spiritual communion with God or an object of worship through prayer. [ME *preie(n)* < OF *prei(er)* << L *precārī* to beg, pray, deriv. of *prex* (s. *prec-*) prayer; akin to OE *frīcgan,* D *vragen,* G *fragen,* Goth *fraíhnan* to ask] —**pray′ing·ly,** *adv.*
—**Syn. 1.** importune, entreat, supplicate, beg, beseech, implore.

prayer[1] (prâr), *n.* **1.** a devout petition to, or any form of spiritual communion with, God or an object of worship. **2.** the act or practice of praying to God or an object of worship. **3.** a spiritual communion with God or an object of worship, as in supplication, thanksgiving, adoration, or confession. **4.** a formula or sequence of words used in or appointed for praying: *the Lord's Prayer.* **5.** a religious observance, either public or private, consisting wholly or mainly of prayer. **6.** that which is prayed for. **7.** a petition; entreaty. **8.** the section of a bill in equity, or of a petition, which sets forth the complaint or the action desired. [ME *preiere* < OF < ML *precāria,* orig. neut. pl. of L *precārius* obtained by entreaty, equiv. to *prec-* (s. of *prex*) prayer + *-ārius* -ER[2]] —**prayer′less,** *adj.* —**prayer′less·ly,** *adv.* —**prayer′less·ness,** *n.*

pray·er[2] (prā′ər), *n.* one who prays. [late ME *preyare.* See PRAY, -ER[1]]

prayer′ beads′ (prâr), a rosary.

prayer′ book′ (prâr), **1.** a book containing formal prayers to be used in public or private religious devotions. **2.** (*usually caps.*) See **Book of Common Prayer. 3.** *Naut.* a small holystone.

prayer·ful (prâr′fəl), *adj.* given to, characterized by, or expressive of prayer; devout. [PRAYER + -FUL] —**prayer′ful·ly,** *adv.* —**prayer′ful·ness,** *n.*

prayer′ meet′ing (prâr), **1.** a meeting chiefly for prayer. **2.** (in certain Protestant churches) a meeting in midweek, chiefly for individual prayer and the offering of testimonies of faith. Also called **prayer′ serv′ice.**

Prayer′ of Manas′ses (prâr), a book of the Apocrypha.

prayer′ rug′ (prâr), a small rug upon which a Muslim kneels and prostrates himself during his devotions.

prayer′ shawl′ (prâr), *Judaism.* a tallith.

prayer′ wheel′ (prâr), a wheel or cylinder inscribed with or containing prayers, used chiefly by Buddhists of Tibet as a mechanical aid to continual praying, each revolution counting as an uttered prayer.

pray′ing man′tis, mantis. Also, **pray′ing man′tid.**

pre-, an element occurring originally in loan words from Latin, where it meant "before" (*preclude; prevent*); applied freely as a prefix, with the meanings "prior to," "in advance of," "early," "beforehand," "before," "in front of," and with other figurative meanings (*preschool; prewar; prepay; preoral; prefrontal*). Also, **prae-.** [< L *prae-,* comb. form repr. *prae* (prep. and adv.); akin to FIRST, FORE[1]]

P.R.E., Petroleum Refining Engineer.

preach (prēch), *v.t.* **1.** to advocate or inculcate (religious or moral truth, right conduct, etc.) in speech or writing. **2.** to proclaim or make known by sermon (the gospel, good tidings, etc.). **3.** to deliver (a sermon). —*v.i.* **4.** to deliver a sermon. **5.** to give earnest advice, as on religious or moral subjects or the like. **6.** to do this in an obtrusive or tedious way. [ME *preche(n)* < OF *pre(ë)chie(r)* < eccl. L *praedicāre* to preach (L: to assert publicly, proclaim). See PREDICATE]

preach·er (prē′chər), *n.* **1.** one whose occupation or function it is to preach the gospel. **2.** one who preaches. **3.** See **Friar Preacher.** [ME *precho(u)r* < OF *prech(e)or,* earlier *preëch(e)or* < L *praedicātor(em).* See PREACH, -ER[1]]

preach′er bird′. See **red-eyed vireo.**

preach·i·fy (prē′chə fī′), *v.i.,* **-fied, -fy·ing.** *Usually Disparaging.* to preach in an obtrusive or tedious way. [PREACH + -IFY] —**preach′i·fi·ca′tion,** *n.*

preach·ing (prē′ching), *n.* **1.** act or practice of one who preaches. **2.** the art of delivering sermons. **3.** a sermon. **4.** a public religious service with a sermon. —*adj.* **5.** of, pertaining to, or resembling preaching: *a preaching tone of voice.* [ME *preching* (n.). See PREACH, -ING[1], -ING[2]] —**preach′ing·ly,** *adv.*

preach·ment (prēch′mənt), *n.* **1.** act of preaching. **2.** a sermon or other discourse, esp. when obtrusive or tedious. [ME *prechement* < OF *preë(s)chement* < ML *praedicāment(um)* speech (L: PREDICAMENT)]

preach·y (prē′chē), *adj.,* **preach·i·er, preach·i·est.** *Informal.* tediously or pretentiously didactic. [PREACH + -Y[1]]

pre·ad·am·ite (prē ad′ə mīt′), *n.* **1.** a person supposed to have existed before Adam. **2.** a person who believes that there were men in existence before Adam. —*adj.* Also, **pre·a·dam·ic** (prē′ə dam′ik). **3.** existing before Adam. **4.** of or pertaining to the preadamites. [PRE- + ADAM + -ITE[1]]

pre·ad·mis·sion (prē′ad mish′ən), *n.* (in a reciprocating engine) admission of steam or the like to the end of the cylinder toward which the piston is traveling near the end of the stroke, as to cushion the force of the stroke or to allow full pressure at the beginning of the return stroke. [PRE- + ADMISSION]

pre·ad·o·les·cence (prē′adᵊles′əns), *n.* the period immediately preceding adolescence, usually designated as the years from 9 to 12. [PRE- + ADOLESCENCE]

pre·ad·o·les·cent (prē′adᵊles′ənt), *adj.* **1.** of or pertaining to preadolescence or a preadolescent. —*n.* **2.** one who is in the preadolescent years. [PRE- + ADOLESCENT]

pre·a·dult (prē′ə dult′, prē ad′ult), *adj.* of or pertaining to the period prior to adulthood: *preadult strivings for independence.* [PRE- + ADULT] —**pre′a·dult′hood,** *n.*

pre·al·lot·ment (prē′ə lot′mənt), *n.* an allotment given in advance. [PRE- + ALLOTMENT]

---

pre′ab·sorb′, *v.*
pre′ab·sorb′ent, *adj., n.*
pre·ab′stract, *adj.*
pre′a·bun′dance, *n.*
pre′a·bun′dant, *adj.;* **-ly,** *adv.*
pre′ac·cept′, *v.*
pre′ac·cept′ance, *n.*
pre·ac′cess, *n.*
pre′ac·ces′si·ble, *adj.*
pre′ac·ci·den′tal, *adj.;* **-ly,** *adv.*
pre′ac·com′mo·date′, *v.t.,* **-dat·ed, -dat·ing.**
pre′ac·com′mo·dat′ing·ly, *adv.*
pre′ac·com′mo·da′tion, *n.*
pre′ac·com′plish, *v.t.*
pre′ac·com′plish·ment, *n.*
pre′ac·cord′, *n., v.i.*
pre′ac·cord′ance, *n.*
pre′ac·count′, *v.*
pre′ac·cred′it, *v.t.*
pre′ac·cu′mu·late′, *v.t.,* **-lat·ed, -lat·ing.**
pre′ac·cu′mu·la′tion, *n.*
pre′ac·cu·sa′tion, *n.*
pre′ac·cuse′, *v.t.,* **-cused, -cus·ing.**
pre′ac·cus′tom, *v.t.*
pre′ac·e·tab′u·lar, *adj.*
pre′a·chieved′, *adj.*
pre′ac′id, *adj.;* **-ness,** *n.*
pre′a·cid′i·ty, *n.*
pre′ac·knowl′edge, *v.t.,* **-edged, -edg·ing.**
pre′ac·knowl′edge·ment, *n.*
pre′ac·knowl′edg·ment, *n.*
pre′ac·quaint′, *v.t.*
pre′ac·quaint′ance, *n.*
pre′ac·quire′, *v.,* **-quired, -quir·ing.**
pre′ac·qui·si′tion, *n.*
pre′ac·quis′i·tive, *adj.;* **-ly,** *adv.;* **-ness,** *n.*
pre′ac·quit′, *v.t.,* **-quit·ted, -quit·ting.**
pre′ac·quit′tal, *n.*
pre·act′, *v.t.*
pre·ac′tion, *n.*
pre·ac′tive, *adj.;* **-ly,** *adv.;* **-ness,** *n.*
pre′ac·tiv′i·ty, *n.*
pre′a·dam′ic, *adj.*
pre′a·dapt′, *v.t.*
pre′a·dapt′a·ble, *adj.*
pre′ad·ap·ta′tion, *n.*
pre′ad·di′tion, *n.*
pre′ad·di′tion·al, *adj.*
pre′ad·dress′, *n., v.t.*
pre·ad′e·qua·cy, *n.*
pre·ad′e·quate, *adj.;* **-ly,** *adv.;* **-ness,** *n.*
pre′ad·here′, *v.i.,* **-hered, -her·ing.**
pre′ad·her′ence, *n.*
pre′ad·her′ent, *adj.;* **-ly,** *adv.*
pre′ad·jec·ti′val, *adj.;* **-ly,** *adv.*
pre·ad′jec·tive, *adj.*
pre′ad·journ′, *v.t.*
pre′ad·journ′ment, *n.*
pre′ad·just′, *v.t.*
pre′ad·just′a·ble, *adj.*
pre′ad·just′ment, *n.*
pre′ad·min′is·tra′tion, *n.*
pre′ad·min′is·tra′tive, *adj.*
pre′ad·min′is·tra′tor, *n.*
pre′ad·mire′, *v.t.,* **-mired, -mir·ing.**
pre′ad·mir′er, *n.*
pre′ad·mit′, *v.t.,* **-mit·ted, -mit·ting.**
pre′ad·mon′ish, *v.t.*
pre′ad·mo·ni′tion, *n.*
pre′a·dopt′, *v.t.*
pre′a·dop′tion, *n.*
pre′a·dorn′, *v.t.*
pre′a·dorn′ment, *n.*
pre·ad′ver·tise′, *v.,* **-tised, -tis·ing.**
pre′ad·ver′tise·ment, *n.*
pre·ad′ver·tis′er, *n.*
pre′ad·vice′, *n.*
pre′ad·vis′a·ble, *adj.*
pre′ad·vise′, *v.t.,* **-vised, -vis·ing.**
pre′ad·vi′so·ry, *adj.*
pre′ad·vo·ca·cy, *n.*
pre·ad′vo·cate, *n.*
pre·ad′vo·cate′, *v.t.,* **-cat·ed, -cat·ing.**
pre·aes′ti·val, *adj.*
pre′af·fect′, *v.t.*
pre′af·fec′tion, *n.*
pre′af·fi·da′vit, *n.*
pre′af·fil′i·ate, *n.*
pre′af·fil′i·ate′, *v.,* **-at·ed, -at·ing.**
pre′af·fil′i·a′tion, *n.*
pre′af·firm′, *v.*
pre′af·fir·ma′tion, *n.*
pre′af·firm′a·tive, *adj.*
pre′af·flict′, *v.t.*
pre′af·flic′tion, *n.*
pre′af·ter·noon′, *n., adj.*
pre·age′, *v.,* **-aged, -ag·ing.**
pre·aged′, *adj.*
pre·ag′gra·vate′, *v.t.,* **-vat·ed, -vat·ing.**
pre′ag·gra·va′tion, *n.*
pre′ag·gres′sion, *n.*
pre′ag·gres′sive, *adj.;* **-ly,** *adv.;* **-ness,** *n.*
pre·ag′i·tate′, *v.t.,* **-tat·ed, -tat·ing.**
pre′ag·i·ta′tion, *n.*
pre′a·gree′, *v.i.,* **-greed, -gree·ing.**
pre′a·gree′ment, *n.*
pre·ag′ri·cul′tur·al, *adj.*
pre·ag′ri·cul′ture, *n.*
pre′a·larm′, *v.t., n.*
pre′al·co·hol′ic, *adj.*
pre·al′ge·bra, *n., adj.*
pre·al′ge·bra′ic, *adj.*
pre′al·le·ga′tion, *n.*
pre′al·lege′, *v.t.,* **-leged, -leg·ing.**
pre′al·li′ance, *n.*
pre′al·lied′, *adj.*
pre′al·lot′, *v.t.,* **-lot·ted, -lot·ting.**
pre′al·low′, *v.t.*
pre′al·low′a·ble, *adj.;* **-bly,** *adv.*
pre′al·low′ance, *n.*
pre′al·lude′, *v.i.,* **-lud·ed, -lud·ing.**
pre′al·lu′sion, *n.*
pre·al′ly, *n., pl.* **-lies.**
pre′al·ly′, *v.,* **-lied, -ly·ing.**
pre·al′pha·bet, *adj., n.*
pre′al·pha·bet′i·cal, *adj.;* **-ly,** *adv.*

---

pre·al·tar (prē ôl′tər), *adj.* in front of the altar. [PRE- + ALTAR]

pre·al′ter·nate molt′ (prē ôl′tər nit), *Ornith.* the molt by which many birds replace only some and rarely all of the feathers assumed at the prebasic molt, usually occurring prior to breeding. [PRE- + ALTERNATE]

pre·am·ble (prē′am′bəl), *n.* **1.** an introductory statement; preface; introduction. **2.** the introductory part of a statute, deed, or the like, stating the reasons and intent of what follows. **3.** a preliminary or introductory fact or circumstance: *His childhood in the slums was a preamble to a life of crime.* **4.** (*cap.*) the introductory statement of the U.S. constitution, setting forth the general principles of American government and beginning with the words, "We the people of the United States, in order to form a more perfect Union . . . ." [ME < ML *praeambul(um)*, n. use of neut. of LL *praeambulus* walking before. See PRE-, AMBLE] **—pre′am′bled,** *adj.*
—Syn. 1. opening, beginning; foreword, prologue, prelude.

pre·amp (prē′amp′), *n.* *Informal.* a preamplifier. Also, **pre′-amp′.** [by shortening]

pre·am·pli·fi·er (prē am′plə fī′ər), *n.* a device in the amplifier circuit of a radio or phonograph which increases the strength of a weak signal for detection and amplification. [PRE- + AMPLIFIER]

pre·an·es·thet·ic (prē an′is thet′ik, prē′an-), *n.* **1.** a substance that produces a preliminary or light anesthesia. **—***adj.* **2.** given prior to an anesthetic that induces total insensibility. [PRE- + ANESTHETIC]

pre·an·ti·sep·tic (prē′an ti sep′tik), *adj.* *Med.* (esp. of surgery) noting that period of time before the adoption of the principles of antisepsis (about 1867). [PRE- + ANTISEPTIC]

pre·ap·point (prē′ə point′), *v.t.* to appoint beforehand. [PRE- + APPOINT] **—pre′ap·point′ment,** *n.*

pre·ar·range (prē′ə rānj′), *v.t.*, **-ranged, -rang·ing.** to arrange in advance or beforehand. [PRE- + ARRANGE] **—pre′ar·range′ment,** *n.*

pre·a·sep·tic (prē′ā sep′tik), *adj.* *Med.* pertaining to the period before the use of aseptic practices in surgery. [PRE- + ASEPTIC]

pre·au·dit (prē ô′dit), *n.* *Accounting.* an examination of vouchers, contracts, etc., in order to substantiate a transaction or a series of transactions before they are paid for and recorded. Also, **pre·au′dit.** Cf. **postaudit.** [PRE- + AUDIT]

pre·ax·i·al (prē ak′sē əl), *adj.* *Anat., Zool.* situated before the body axis; pertaining to the radial side of the upper limb and the tibial side of the lower limb. [PRE- + -AXIAL] **—pre·ax′i·al·ly,** *adv.*

pre·ba′sic molt′ (prē bā′sik), *Ornith.* the molt by which most birds replace all of their feathers, usually occurring annually after the breeding season. [PRE- + BASIC]

preb·end (preb′ənd), *n.* **1.** a stipend allotted from the revenues of a cathedral or a collegiate church to a canon or member of the chapter. **2.** the land yielding such a stipend. **3.** a prebendary. [ME *prebende* < ML *prēbenda*, var. of *praebenda* prebend, LL: allowance, neut. pl. gerundive of L *prae(hi)bēre* to offer, furnish, equiv. to *prae-* PRE- + *hibēre*, comb. form of *habēre* to have, hold] **—pre·ben·dal** (pri ben′dəl), *adj.*

preb·en·dar·y (preb′ən der′ē), *n., pl.* **-dar·ies.** **1.** a canon or clergyman who is entitled to a prebend for special services at a cathedral or collegiate church. **2.** *Ch. of Eng.* an honorary canon having the title of a prebend but not receiving a stipend. [< ML *praebendārī(us)*. See PREBEND, -ARY]

Pre·ble (preb′əl), *n.* **Edward,** 1761–1807, U.S. naval officer.

prec., **1.** preceded. **2.** preceding.

Pre·cam·bri·an (prē kam′brē ən), *Geol.* **—***adj.* **1.** noting or pertaining to the earliest era, ending 600,000,000 years ago, during which the earth's crust was formed and the first life appeared. See table under **era.** **—***n.* **2.** the Precambrian era. Also, **Pre-Cam′bri·an.** [PRE- + CAMBRIAN]

pre·can·cel (prē kan′səl), *v.*, **-celed, -cel·ing** or (*esp. Brit.*) **-celled, -cel·ling,** *n.* *Philately.* **—***v.t.* **1.** to cancel (a stamp) before placing it on a piece of postal matter. **—***n.* **2.** a precanceled stamp. [PRE- + CANCEL] **—pre′can·cel·la′tion,** *n.*

pre·car·i·ous (pri kâr′ē əs), *adj.* **1.** dependent on circumstances beyond one's control; uncertain; unstable; insecure: *a precarious livelihood.* **2.** dependent on the will or pleasure of another; liable to be withdrawn or lost at the will of another: *He held a precarious tenure under an arbitrary administration.* **3.** exposed to or involving danger; dangerous; perilous; risky: *the precarious life of an underseas diver.* **4.** having insufficient, little, or no foundation: *a precarious assumption.* [< L *precārius* obtained by entreaty or mere favor, hence uncertain, precarious. See PRAYER[1]] **—pre·car′i·ous·ly,** *adv.* **—pre·car′i·ous·ness,** *n.*
—Syn. 1. unsure, unsteady. See **uncertain. 2.** doubtful, dubious, unreliable, undependable. **3.** hazardous. **4.** groundless, baseless, unfounded. **—Ant. 1.** secure. **2.** reliable. **3.** safe. **4.** well-founded.

pre·cast (prē kast′, -käst′), *v.t.*, **-cast, -cast·ing.** *Building Trades.* to cast (a concrete block or slab, etc.) in a place other than where it is to be installed in a structure. [PRE- + CAST]

prec·a·to·ry (prek′ə tōr′ē, -tôr′ē), *adj.* of, pertaining to, characterized by, or expressing entreaty or supplication: *precatory overtures.* Also, **prec·a·tive** (prek′ə tiv). [< LL *precātōri(us)*, equiv. to L *precāt(us)* (ptp. of *precārī* to pray, entreat) *-ōrius* -ORY[1]]

pre·cau·tion (pri kô′shən), *n.* **1.** a measure taken in advance to avert possible evil or to secure good results. **2.** caution employed beforehand; prudent foresight. **—***v.t.* **3.** to forewarn; put on guard. [< LL *praecautiōn-* (s. of *praecautiō*). See PRE-, CAUTION]

pre·cau·tion·ar·y (pri kô′shə ner′ē), *adj.* **1.** of, pertaining to, or characterized by precaution: *precautionary measures.* **2.** expressing or advising precaution: *precautionary warnings against possible tornadoes.* Also, **pre·cau′tion·al.** [PRECAUTION + -ARY]

pre·cau·tious (pri kô′shəs), *adj.* using or displaying precaution: *a precautious reply; a precautious person.* [PRECAUTIO(N) + -OUS]

pre·cede (pri sēd′), *v.*, **-ced·ed, -ced·ing,** *n.* **—***v.t.* **1.** to go before, as in place, order, rank, importance, or time. **2.** to introduce by something preliminary; preface: *to precede one's statement with a qualification.* **—***v.i.* **3.** to go or come before. **—***n.* **4.** *Journalism.* copy printed at the beginning of a news story, esp. one that has been previously set, in order to present late bulletins, editorial notes, or prefatory remarks. [ME *precede(n)* < L *praecēd(ere)*. See PRE-, CEDE] **—pre·ced′a·ble,** *adj.*

prec·e·dence (pres′i dəns, pri sēd′əns), *n.* **1.** act or fact of preceding. **2.** priority in order, rank, importance, etc. **3.** priority in time. **4.** the right to precede others in ceremonies or social formalities. **5.** the order to be observed in ceremonies by persons of different ranks, as by diplomatic protocol. [PRECED(ENT)[2] + -ENCE]

prec·e·den·cy (pres′i dən sē, pri sēd′ən sē), *n., pl.* **-cies.** precedence. [PRECED(ENCE) + -ENCY]

prec·e·dent[1] (pres′i dənt), *n.* **1.** a preceding instance or case which may serve as an example for or a justification in subsequent cases. **2.** *Law.* a legal decision or form of proceeding serving as an authoritative rule or pattern in future similar or analogous cases. [late ME; n. use of PRECEDENT[2]] **—prec′e·dent·less,** *adj.*

pre·ced·ent[2] (pri sēd′ənt, pres′i dənt), *adj.* preceding; anterior. [ME < L *praecēdent-* (s. of *praecēdēns*) going before, prp. of *praecēdere* to PRECEDE; see -ENT]

prec·e·den·tial (pres′i den′shəl), *adj.* **1.** of the nature of or constituting a precedent. **2.** having precedence. [PRECEDENT[1] + -IAL]

pre·ced·ing (pri sē′ding), *adj.* that precedes; previous: *Refer back to the footnote on the preceding page.* [PRECEDE + -ING[2]]
—Syn. foregoing, prior, former, earlier. **—Ant.** succeeding, following.

pre·cent (pri sent′), *v.t.* **1.** to lead as a precentor in singing. **—***v.i.* **2.** to act as a precentor. [back formation from PRECENTOR]

pre·cen·tor (pri sen′tər), *n.* one who leads a church choir or congregation in singing. [< LL *praecentor* leader in music, equiv. to L *praecent(us)* played before (ptp. of *praecinere*) + *-or* -OR[2]. See PRE-, CANTOR] **—pre·cen·to·ri·al** (prē′sen tōr′ē əl, -tôr′-), *adj.* **—pre·cen′tor·ship′,** *n.*

pre·cept (prē′sept), *n.* **1.** a commandment or direction given as a rule of action or conduct. **2.** an injunction as to moral conduct; maxim. **3.** a procedural directive or rule, as for the performance of some technical operation. **4.** *Law.* **a.** a writ or warrant. **b.** a written order issued pursuant to law, as a sheriff's order for an election. [ME < L *praecept(um)* maxim, n. use of neut. of *praeceptus* instructed, ptp. of *praecipere* to direct, lit., to take beforehand, equiv. to *prae-* PRE- + *-cipere*, comb. form of *capere* to take]
—Syn. 1. directive, order, guide, instruction, prescription.

pre·cep·tive (pri sep′tiv), *adj.* **1.** of the nature of or expressing a precept; mandatory. **2.** giving instructions; instructive. [late ME < L *praeceptīv(us)*. See PRECEPT, -IVE] **—pre·cep′tive·ly,** *adv.*

pre·cep·tor (pri sep′tər, prē′sep-), *n.* **1.** an instructor; teacher; tutor. **2.** the head of a preceptory. Also, *referring to a woman,* **pre·cep′tress.** [late ME < L *praeceptor.* See PRECEPT, -OR[2]] **—pre·cep·tor·ate** (pri sep′tər it), *n.* **—pre·cep·to·ri·al** (prē′sep tōr′ē əl, -tôr′-), **pre·cep′to·ral,** *adj.* **—pre′cep·to′ri·al·ly,** *adv.* **—pre·cep′tor·ship′,** *n.*

pre·cep·to·ry (pri sep′tə rē), *n., pl.* **-ries.** a subordinate house or community of the Knights Templars; commandery. [< ML *praeceptōria.* See PRECEPTOR, -Y[3]]

pre·cess (prē ses′), *v.i.* *Mech.* to undergo precession. [back formation from PRECESSION]

pre·ces·sion (prē sesh′ən), *n.* **1.** act or fact of preceding; precedence. **2.** *Astron.* **a.** See **precession of the equinoxes. b.** the related motion of the earth's axis of rotation. **3.** *Mech.* the motion of the rotation axis of a rigid body, as a spinning top, when a disturbing torque is applied while the body is rotating such that the rotation axis describes a cone with the vertical through the vertex of the body as axis of the cone and the motion of the rotation axis is perpendicular to the direction of the torque. [< LL *praecessiōn-* (s. of *praecessiō*) a going before, advance, equiv. to L *praecess(us)* (ptp. of *praecēdere* to PRECEDE) + *-iōn-* -ION]

pre·ces·sion·al (prē sesh′ə nəl), *adj.* **1.** pertaining to or resulting from the precession of the equinoxes. **2.** *Mech.* of, pertaining to, or characterized by precession. [PRECESSION + -AL[1]]

preces′sion of the e′quinoxes, *Astron.* the earlier occurrence of the equinoxes in each successive sidereal year because of a slow retrograde motion of the equinoctial points along the ecliptic, caused by the gravitational force of the sun and the moon upon the earth and by the gravitational force of the planets upon the earth's orbit: a complete revolution of the equinoxes requires about 26,000 years. Cf. **Platonic year.**

pre-Chris·tian (prē kris′chən), *adj.* of, pertaining to, or belonging to a time or period before the Christian Era. [PRE- + CHRISTIAN]

pré·cieuse (prā′sē ōōz′; *Fr.* prā syœz′), *n., pl.* **-cieus·es** (-sē ōōz′iz; *Fr.* -syœz′), *adj.* **—***n.* **1.** one of the 17th-century literary women of France who affected an extreme care in the use of language. **2.** an affected or pretentious woman, esp. one marked by preciosity in manner or speech. **—***adj.* **3.** (of a woman) marked by affectation or preciosity. [< F; fem. of PRÉCIEUX]

pré·cieux (prā′sē ōō′; *Fr.* prā syœ′), *adj., n., pl.* **-cieux** (-sē ōōz′; *Fr.* -syœ′). **—***adj.* **1.** (of a man) overly fastidious or refined; precious; affected. **—***n.* **2.** an affected or excessively fastidious man, as in dress, manner, or speech. [< F; lit., PRECIOUS]

pre·cinct (prē′singkt), *n.* **1.** a district, as of a city, marked out for governmental, administrative, or other purposes: *a police precinct.* **2.** Also called **election district.** one of a fixed number of districts, each containing one polling place, into which a city, town, etc., is divided for voting purposes. **3.** a space or place of definite or understood limits. **4.** Often, **precincts.** an enclosing boundary or limit. **5. precincts,** the parts or regions immediately surrounding a place; environs: *the precincts of a town.* **6.** *Chiefly Brit.* the ground immediately surrounding a church, temple, or the like. **7.** a walled or otherwise bounded or limited space within which a building or place is situated. [ME < ML *praecinct(um)*,

pre·al′ter, *v.t.*
pre′al·ter·a′tion, *n.*
pre′a·mal′ga·ma′tion, *n.*
pre′am·bas′sa·do′ri·al, *adj.*
pre′am·bi′tion, *n.*
pre′am·bi′tious, *adj.*; **-ly,** *adv.*
pre-Am′mon·ite′, *adj., n.*
pre·a′nal, *adj.*
pre′a·naph′o·ral, *adj.*
pre′an·nex′, *v.t.*
pre′an·nounce′, *v.t.*, **-nounced, -nounc·ing.**
pre′an·nounce′ment, *n.*
pre′an·nounc′er, *n.*
pre′an·te·pe′nult, *adj.*
pre′an·te·pe·nul′ti·mate, *adj.*
pre′an·tic′i·pate′, *v.t.*, **-pat·ed, -pat·ing.**
pre′an·tiq′ui·ty, *n.*
pre′a·or′tic, *adj.*
pre′ap·pear′ance, *n.*
pre′ap·per·cep′tion, *n.*
pre′ap·pli·ca′tion, *n.*
pre′ap·ply′, *v.t.*, **-plied, -ply·ing.**
pre′ap·pre·hen′sion, *n.*
pre′ap·prise′, *v.t.*, **-prised, -pris·ing.**
pre′ap·prize′, *v.t.*, **-prized, -priz·ing.**
pre′ap·pro·ba′tion, *n.*
pre′ap·prov′al, *n.*
pre′ap·prove′, *v.*, **-proved, -prov·ing.**
pre·ap′ti·tude′, *n.*
pre·arm′, *v.t.*
pre′ar·rest′, *v.t.*
pre′ar·rest′ment, *n.*
pre′-Ar·thu′ri·an, *adj.*
pre′ar·tic′u·late, *adj.*
pre′ar·tis′tic, *adj.*
pre-Ar′y·an, *adj.*
pre′as·cer·tain′, *v.t.*
pre′as·cer·tain′ment, *n.*
pre′as·cet′ic, *adj.*
pre′as·sem′ble, *v.t.*, **-bled, -bling.**
pre′as·sem′bly, *n.*
pre′as·sert′, *v.t.*
pre′as·sign′, *v.t.*
pre′as·signed′, *adj.*
pre′as·sume′, *v.t.*, **-sumed, -sum·ing.**
pre′as·sump′tion, *n.*
pre′as·sur′ance, *n.*
pre′as·sure′, *v.t.*, **-sured, -sur·ing.**
pre′-As·syr′i·an, *adj.*
pre′a·tax′ic, *adj.*
pre′at·tach′ment, *n.*
pre′at·tune′, *v.t.*, **-tuned, -tun·ing.**
pre·au′di·to′ry, *adj.*
pre′-Au·gus′tan, *adj.*
pre-Au′gus·tine′, *adj.*
pre′au·ric′u·lar, *adj.*
pre′a·ver′, *v.t.*, **-verred, -ver·ring.**
pre′a·vow′al, *n.*
pre′-Bab·y·lo′ni·an, *adj.*
pre·bach′e·lor, *adj., n.*
pre′-Ba·co′ni·an, *adj.*
pre·bal′ance, *v.*, **-lanced, -lanc·ing.**
pre·bal′lot, *v.t.*, **-lot·ed, -lot·ing.**
pre·bank′rupt·cy, *n.*
pre′bar·bar′ic, *adj.*
pre′bar·bar′i·cal·ly, *adv.*
pre·bar′bar·ous, *adj.*; **-ly,** *adv.*; **-ness,** *n.*
pre·bar′gain, *v.t.*
pre·ba′sal, *adj.*
pre·bas′i·lar, *adj.*
pre′be·lief′, *n.*
pre′be·lieve′, *v.*, **-lieved, -liev·ing.**
pre′be·liev′er, *n.*
pre′be·loved′, *adj., n.*
pre′ben·e·dic′tion, *n.*
pre′ben·e·fi′ci·ar′y, *n., pl.* **-ar·ies.**
pre·ben′e·fit, *v.*, **-fit·ed, -fit·ing.**
pre′be·set′, *v.t.*, **-set, -set·ting.**
pre′be·stow′, *v.t.*
pre′be·stow′al, *n.*
pre′be·tray′, *v.t.*
pre′be·tray′al, *n.*
pre′be·troth′al, *adj.*
pre·bid′, *n., v.*, **-bade** or **-bad** or **-bid, -bid·den** or **-bid, -bid·ding.**
pre·bill′, *v.t.*
pre·bless′, *v.t.*
pre′block·ade′, *n., v.t.*, **-ad·ed, -ad·ing.**
pre·bloom′ing, *adj.*
pre·boast′, *n., v.*
pre·bod′ing, *adj.*
pre·boil′, *v.t.*
pre·born′, *adj.*
pre·bor′row·ing, *n.*
pre·boy′hood, *n.*
pre·bra′chi·al, *adj.*
pre·bran′chi·al, *adj.*
pre·breathe′, *v.t.*, **-breathed, -breath·ing.**
pre·brid′al, *adj.*
pre-Brit′ish, *adj.*
pre·broad′cast′ing, *adj.*
pre′bro·mid′ic, *adj.*
pre·bron′chi·al, *adj.*
pre·bronze′, *adj.*
pre·brute′, *adj.*
pre·buc′cal, *adj.*
pre-Bud′dhist, *adj.*
pre·bud′get, *n., adj.*
pre·bud′get·ar′y, *adj.*
pre′bur·lesque′, *adj.*
pre·burn′, *v.t.*
pre-Byz′an·tine′, *adj.*
pre·cal′cu·la·ble, *adj.*
pre·cal′cu·late′, *v.t.*, **-lat·ed, -lat·ing.**
pre′cal·cu·la′tion, *n.*
pre-Cam′bridge, *adj.*
pre′cam·paign′, *n., adj.*
pre-Ca′naan·ite′, *n., adj.*
pre′-Ca·naan·it′ic, *adj.*
pre·can′cer·ous, *adj.*
pre·can′di·da·cy, *n.*
pre·can′di·da·ture, *n.*
pre·can′ning, *n., adj.*
pre·can′vass, *v.t., n.*
pre·cap′i·tal·ist, *n.*
pre′cap·i·tal·is′tic, *adj.*
pre′cap·tiv′i·ty, *n.*
pre·cap′ture, *v.t.*, **-tured, -tur·ing;** *adj.*
pre′-Car·bon·if′er·ous, *adj.*
pre·car′di·ac′, *adj.*
pre·car′ni·val, *adj.*
pre′-Car·o·lin′gi·an, *adj.*
pre′car·ti·lag′i·nous, *adj.*
pre·cau′dal, *adj.*
pre·cel′e·brant, *n.*
pre·cel′e·brate′, *v.*, **-brat·ed, -brat·ing.**
pre′cel·e·bra′tion, *n.*
pre-Celt′ic, *adj.*
pre·cen′sure, *v.t.*, **-sured, -sur·ing.**
pre·cen′sus, *n.*
pre′cen·ten′ni·al, *adj.*
pre′cer·e·bel′lar, *adj.*
pre·cer′e·bral, *adj.*
pre·cer′e·broid′, *adj.*
pre′cer·e·mo′ni·al, *adj.*
pre·cer′e·mo′ny, *n., pl.* **-nies.**
pre′cer·ti·fi·ca′tion, *n.*
pre·cer′ti·fy′, *v.t.*, **-fied, -fy·ing.**
pre·chal′lenge, *v.t.*, **-lenged, -leng·ing.**
pre·cham′pi·oned, *adj.*
pre·cham′pi·on·ship′, *n.*
pre·charge′, *v.t.*, **-charged, -charg·ing;** *n.*
pre·chart′, *v.t.*
pre·chart′ed, *adj.*
pre′-Chau·ce′ri·an, *adj.*
pre·check′, *v.t., n.*
pre·chem′i·cal, *adj.*
pre·child′hood, *n.*
pre·chill′, *v.t.*
pre′-Chi·nese′, *adj., n., pl.* **-nese.**
pre·chlo′ric, *adj.*
pre·chlo′ro·form′, *v.t.*
pre·choice′, *n.*
pre·choose′, *v.t.*, **-chose, -cho·sen, -choos·ing.**
pre·chor′dal, *adj.*
pre·cho′roid, *adj.*
pre′-Chris·ti·an′ic, *adj.*
pre-Christ′mas, *adj.*

neut. of L *praecinctus* girded about, surrounded (ptp. of *praecingere*), equiv. to *prae-* PRE- + *cing-* (s. of *cingere* to surround) + *-tus* ptp. suffix]
—**Syn. 1,** 2. ward. 3. territory. 6. compound.

pre·ci·os·i·ty (presh′ē os′i tē), *n., pl.* **-ties.** fastidious or carefully affected refinement, as in language, style, or taste. [ME *preciousite* preciousness < MF *preciosite* < L *pretiōsitās.* See PRECIOUS, -ITY]

pre·cious (presh′əs), *adj.* **1.** of high price or great value; very valuable or costly: *precious metals; precious jewels.* **2.** highly esteemed for some spiritual, nonmaterial, or moral quality: *precious faith; precious memories.* **3.** dear; beloved: *a precious child; a precious friend.* **4.** choice; fine; great (used ironically): *A precious lot of good his education did him!* **5.** flagrant; gross: *a precious fool.* **6.** *Informal.* beautiful; wonderful; great: *Her little house is just precious!* **7.** affectedly or excessively delicate, refined, or nice: *precious manners.* **8.** highly important; irreplaceable or irretrievable; necessary: *We lost precious minutes retracing our steps.* —*n.* **9.** a dearly beloved person; darling. —*adv.* **10.** *Informal.* extremely; very: *She spends precious little time working.* [ME *preciose* < L *pretiōs(us)* costly, valuable, equiv. to *preti(um)* PRICE, value + *-ōsus* -OUS] —**pre′cious·ly,** *adv.* —**pre′cious·ness,** *n.*
—**Syn. 1.** See **valuable. 3.** darling, cherished.

pre′cious cor′al. See **red coral.**

pre′cious met′al, a metal of the gold, silver, or platinum group.

pre′cious moon′stone, moonstone (def. 1).

pre′cious o′pal, any opal having a play of colors, used as a gemstone. Also called **noble opal.**

pre′cious stone′, a gem distinguished for its beauty and rarity, used in jewelry.

prec·i·pice (pres′ə pis), *n.* **1.** a cliff with a vertical, or nearly vertical, or overhanging face. **2.** a situation of great peril: *on the precipice of war.* [< MF < L *praecipit(ium)* steep place, equiv. to *praecipit-* (s. of *praeceps*) steep, lit., head before + *-ium* n. suffix. See PRE-, CAPUT] —**prec′i·piced,** *adj.*

pre·cip′i·ta·ble wa′ter (pri sip′i tə bəl), the total water vapor contained in a unit vertical column of the atmosphere. [PRECIPIT(ATE) + -ABLE]

pre·cip·i·tan·cy (pri sip′i tən sē), *n., pl.* **-cies. 1.** the quality or state of being precipitant. **2.** headlong or rash haste. **3. precipitancies,** hasty or rash acts. Also, **pre·cip′i·tance.** [PRECIPIT(ANT) + -ANCY]

pre·cip·i·tant (pri sip′i tᵊnt), *adj.* **1.** falling headlong. **2.** rushing headlong, rapidly, or hastily onward. **3.** hasty; rash. **4.** unduly sudden or abrupt. —*n.* **5.** *Chem.* anything that causes precipitation. [< L *praecipitant-* (s. of *praecipitāns*), prp. of *praecipitāre* to cast down headlong. See PRECIPITATE, -ANT] —**pre·cip′i·tant·ly,** *adv.*

pre·cip·i·tate (*v.* pri sip′i tāt′; *adj., n.* pri sip′i tit, -tāt′), *v.,* **-tat·ed, -tat·ing,** *adj., n.* —*v.t.* **1.** to hasten the occurrence of; bring about prematurely, hastily, or suddenly: *to precipitate an international crisis.* **2.** *Chem.* to separate (a substance) in solid form from a solution, as by means of a reagent. **3.** *Meteorol.* to condense moisture from a vaporous state into rain, snow, etc. **4.** to cast down headlong; fling or hurl down. **5.** to cast, plunge, or send, esp. violently or abruptly: *He precipitated himself into the struggle for the ball.* —*v.i.* **6.** to separate from a solution as a precipitate. **7.** to fall to the earth's surface as a condensed form of water; to rain, snow, hail, drizzle, etc. **8.** to be cast or thrown down headlong. —*adj.* **9.** headlong: *a precipitate fall down the stairs.* **10.** rushing headlong or rapidly onward. **11.** proceeding rapidly or with great haste: *a precipitate retreat.* **12.** exceedingly sudden or abrupt: *a precipitate stop; a precipitate decision.* **13.** done or made without sufficient deliberation; overhasty; rash: *a precipitate marriage.* —*n.* **14.** *Chem.* a substance precipitated from a solution. **15.** moisture condensed in the form of rain, snow, etc. [< L *praecipitāt(us)* (ptp. of *praecipitāre*) to cast down headlong, equiv. to *praecipit-* (s. of *praeceps* steep; see PRECIPICE) + *-ātus* -ATE¹] —**pre·cip′i·tate·ly,** *adv.* —**pre·cip′i·tate·ness,** *n.* —**pre·cip′i·ta′tive,** *adj.* —**pre·cip′i·ta′tor,** *n.*
—**Syn. 1.** accelerate; crystallize. **13.** reckless, indiscreet. —**Ant. 1.** retard. **13.** careful.

pre·cip·i·ta·tion (pri sip′i tā′shən), *n.* **1.** act of precipitating; state of being precipitated. **2.** a casting down or falling headlong. **3.** a hastening or hurrying in movement, procedure, or action. **4.** sudden haste. **5.** unwise or rash rapidity. **6.** *Chem., Physics.* the precipitating of a substance from a solution. **7.** *Meteorol.* **a.** falling products of condensation in the atmosphere, as rain, snow, or hail. **b.** the amount precipitated at a given place within a given period, usually expressed in inches of water. [< LL *praecipitātiōn-* (s. of *praecipitātiō*) a falling headlong. See PRECIPITATE, -ION]

pre·cip·i·tin (pri sip′i tin), *n.* *Immunol.* an antibody that reacts with its specific antigen to form an insoluble precipitate. [PRECIPIT(ATE) + -IN²]

pre·cip·i·tous (pri sip′i təs), *adj.* **1.** of the nature of or characterized by precipices: *a precipitous wall of rock.* **2.** extremely or impassably steep: *precipitous mountain trails.* **3.** precipitate. [PRECIPIT(ATE) (adj.) + -OUS] —**pre·cip′i·tous·ly,** *adv.* —**pre·cip′i·tous·ness,** *n.*
—**Syn. 2.** abrupt, sheer, perpendicular. —**Ant. 1, 2.** flat, level.

Pre·cip·i·tron (pri sip′i tron′), *n.* *Trademark.* a variety of electrostatic precipitator.

pré·cis (prā sē′, prā′sē), *n., pl.* **-cis** (-sēz′, -sēz), *v.* —*n.* **1.** an abstract or summary. —*v.t.* **2.** to make a précis of. [< F, n. use of adj., lit., cut short. See PRECISE]
—**Syn. 1.** digest, condensation.

pre·cise (pri sīs′), *adj.* **1.** definitely or strictly stated, defined, or fixed: *precise directions.* **2.** being exactly that and neither more nor less: *a precise temperature; a precise amount.* **3.** being just that and no other: *the precise dress she had wanted.* **4.** definite or exact in statement, as a person. **5.** carefully distinct: *precise articulation.* **6.** exact in measuring, recording, etc.: *a precise instrument.* **7.** excessively or rigidly particular: *precise observance of regulations; precise grooming.* [< L *praecīs(us)* lopped off, brief (ptp. of *praecīdere*), equiv. to *prae-* PRE- + *-cīsus,* comb. form of *caesus,* ptp. of *caedere* to cut] —**pre·cise′ly,** *adv.* —**pre·cise′ness,** *n.*
—**Syn. 1.** explicit. See **correct.** —**Ant. 1.** indefinite.

pre·ci·sian (pri sizh′ən), *n.* **1.** one who adheres punctiliously to the observance of rules or forms, esp. in matters of religion. **2.** one of the English Puritans of the 16th and 17th centuries. [PRECISE + -IAN] —**pre·ci′sian·ism,** *n.*

pre·ci·sion (pri sizh′ən), *n.* **1.** state or quality of being precise. **2.** accuracy; exactness: *to arrive at an estimate with precision.* **3.** mechanical exactness: *a lens ground with precision.* **4.** punctiliousness; strictness: *precision in one's business dealings.* **5.** *Math.* the degree to which the correctness of a quantity is expressed. Cf. **accuracy** (def. 3). **6.** *Chem., Physics.* the extent to which a given set of measurements of the same sample agree with their mean. Cf. **accuracy** (def. 2). —*adj.* **7.** of, pertaining to, or characterized by precision: *precision swimming; precision instruments for aircraft.* [< L *praecisiōn-* (s. of *praecisiō*) a cutting off. See PRECISE, -ION] —**pre·ci′sion·al,** *adj.* —**pre·ci′sion·ism,** *n.* —**pre·ci′sion·ist,** *n.*

preci′sion bomb′ing, aerial bombing in which bombs are dropped, as accurately as possible, on a specific, usually small, target. Also called **pinpoint bombing.** Cf. **area bombing, pattern bombing.**

preci′sion cast′ing, *Foundry.* See **investment casting.**

pre·ci·sive¹ (pri sī′siv), *adj.* separating or distinguishing (a person or thing) from another or others: *precisive imputation of guilt.* [< L *praecīs(us)* (see PRECISE) + -IVE]

pre·ci·sive² (pri sī′siv), *adj.* characterized by accuracy or exactness: *a precisive method of expressing oneself.* [PRECIS(ION) + -IVE]

pre·cli·max (prē klī′maks), *n.* *Ecol.* a stable community that precedes the full development of the climax of a given area and that results from local variations in soil and water. [PRE- + CLIMAX]

pre·clin·i·cal (prē klin′i kəl), *adj.* *Med.* of or pertaining to the period prior to the appearance of the symptoms. [PRE- + CLINICAL]

pre·clude (pri klōōd′), *v.t.,* **-clud·ed, -clud·ing. 1.** to prevent the presence, existence, or occurrence of; make impossible: *The insufficiency of the evidence precludes a conviction.* **2.** to exclude or debar from something: *His physical disability precludes an athletic career for him.* [< L *praeclūd(ere)* (to) shut off, close, equiv. to *prae-* PRE- + *-clūdere,* comb. form of *claudere* to shut] —**pre·clud′a·ble,** *adj.* —**pre·clu·sion** (pri klōō′zhən), *n.* —**pre·clu·sive** (pri klōō′siv), *adj.* —**pre·clu′sive·ly,** *adv.*
—**Syn. 1.** forestall; eliminate.

pre·co·cial (pri kō′shəl), *adj.* (of birds) active, down-covered, and able to move about freely when hatched. [PRECOCI(OUS) + -AL¹]

pre·co·cious (pri kō′shəs), *adj.* **1.** forward in development, esp. mental development: *a precocious child.* **2.** prematurely developed, as the mind, faculties, etc. **3.** of or pertaining to premature development. **4.** *Bot.* **a.** flowering, fruiting, or ripening early, as plants or fruit. **b.** bearing blossoms before leaves, as plants. **c.** appearing before leaves, as flowers. [PRECOCI(TY) + -OUS] —**pre·co′cious·ly,** *adv.* —**pre·co′cious·ness,** *n.*

pre·coc·i·ty (pri kos′i tē), *n.* the state, condition, or tendency of being precocious. [< F *préciosité,* equiv. to *précose* (< L *praecoci,* s. of *praecox* early ripe) + *-ité* -ITY]

pre·cog·ni·tion (prē′kog nish′ən), *n.* **1.** knowledge of a future event or situation. **2.** *Parapsychol.* the knowledge of a future event through extrasensory means. **3.** *Scot. Law.* **a.** the examination of witnesses and other related parties before a trial in order to supply a legal ground for prosecution. **b.** the evidence established in such an examination. [PRE- + COGNITION] —**pre·cog·ni·tive** (prē kog′ni tiv), *adj.*

pre-Co·lum·bi·an (prē′kə lum′bē ən), *adj.* belonging to the period before the discovery of America by Columbus: *pre-Columbian art.*

pre·com·pose (prē′kəm pōz′), *v.t.,* **-posed, -pos·ing.** to compose beforehand: *to precompose a reply to a possible question.* [PRE- + COMPOSE]

pre·con·ceive (prē′kən sēv′), *v.t.,* **-ceived, -ceiv·ing.** to form an idea or conception of in advance. [PRE- + CONCEIVE]

pre·con·cep·tion (prē′kən sep′shən), *n.* **1.** a conception or opinion formed beforehand. **2.** bias; predilection. [PRE- + CONCEPTION] —**pre′con·cep′tion·al,** *adj.*

pre·con·cert (prē′kən sûrt′), *v.t.* to arrange in advance or beforehand, as by a previous agreement. [PRE- + CONCERT] —**pre′con·cert′ed·ly,** *adv.* —**pre′con·cert′ed·ness,** *n.*

pre·con·demn (prē′kən dem′), *v.t.* to condemn in advance, esp. where objectivity is required, as in a trial. [PRE- + CONDEMN]

pre·con·di·tion (prē′kən dish′ən), *v.t.* **1.** to subject (a person or thing) to a special treatment in preparation for a subsequent experience, process, test, etc.: *to precondition a surface to receive paint.* —*n.* **2.** a condition existing before or necessary to a subsequent result: *Two years of practical experience were a precondition for that promotion.* [PRE- + CONDITION]

pre·co·nise (prē′kə nīz′), *v.t.,* **-nised, -nis·ing.** *Chiefly Brit.* preconize. —**pre′co·ni·sa′tion,** *n.* —**pre′co·nis′er,** *n.*

pre·co·nize (prē′kə nīz′), *v.t.,* **-nized, -niz·ing. 1.** to proclaim or commend publicly. **2.** to summon publicly. **3.** *Rom. Cath. Ch.* (of the pope) to declare solemnly in consistory the appointment of (a new bishop or other high ecclesiastic). [late ME < ML *praecōnīz(āre)* (to) herald, announce, equiv. to L *praecōn-* (s. of *praecō*) crier, herald + *-izāre* -IZE] —**pre′co·ni·za′tion,** *n.* —**pre′co·niz′er,** *n.*

pre·con·scious (prē kon′shəs), *adj.* **1.** *Psychoanal.* absent from but capable of being readily brought into consciousness; foreconscious. **2.** occurring prior to the development of consciousness. —*n.* **3.** the preconscious portion of the mind. [PRE- + CONSCIOUS] —**pre·con′scious·ly,** *adv.*

pre·con·so·nan·tal (prē kon′sə nan′tᵊl, prē′kon-), *adj.* *Phonet.* immediately preceding a consonant. [PRE- + CONSONANTAL]

pre·cir′cu·late′, *v.,* **-lat·ed, -lat·ing.**
pre′cir·cu·la′tion, *n.*
pre′ci·ta′tion, *n.*
pre·cite′, *v.t.,* **-cit·ed, -cit·ing.**
pre·civ′i·li·za′tion, *n.*
pre·claim′, *v.t., n.*
pre·claim′ant, *n.*
pre·claim′er, *n.*
pre·clas′sic, *adj.*
pre·clas′si·cal, *adj.;* **-ly,** *adv.*
pre·clas′si·fi·ca′tion, *n.*
pre·clas′si·fy′, *v.t.,* **-fied, -fy·ing.**
pre·clean′, *v.t.*
pre·clean′er, *n.*
pre·cler′i·cal, *adj.*
pre′clo·a′cal, *adj.*
pre·close′, *v.t.,* **-closed, -clos·ing.**
pre·clo′sure, *n.*
pre·clothe′, *v.t.,* **-clothed, -cloth·ing.**
pre′coc·cyg′e·al, *adj.*
pre·cog′i·tate′, *v.,* **-tat·ed, -tat·ing.**
pre′cog·i·ta′tion, *n.*
pre·cog′ni·za·ble, *adj.*
pre·cog′ni·zant, *adj.*
pre·cog′nize, *v.t.,* **-nized, -niz·ing.**
pre·coil′, *v.i.*
pre·coil′er, *n.*
pre′co·in′ci·dence, *n.*
pre′co·in′ci·dent, *adj.;* **-ly,** *adv.*
pre′col·laps′a·ble, *adj.*
pre′col·lapse′, *v.,* **-lapsed, -laps·ing.**
pre′col·laps′i·bil′i·ty, *n.*
pre′col·laps′i·ble, *adj.*
pre′col·lect′, *v.t.*
pre′col·lect′a·ble, *adj.*
pre′col·lec′tion, *n.*
pre′col·lec′tor, *n.*
pre·col′lege, *n., adj.*
pre′col·le′giate, *adj.*
pre′col·lude′, *v.i.,* **-lud·ed, -lud·ing.**
pre′col·lu′sion, *n.*
pre′col·lu′sive, *adj.*
pre·col′or, *n., v.*
pre·col′or·a·ble, *adj.*
pre′col·or·a′tion, *n.*
pre·col′our, *n., v.*
pre·col′our·a·ble, *adj.*
pre·col·our·a′tion, *n.*
pre·com′bat, *n., v.,* **-bat·ed, -bat·ing** or (*esp. Brit.*) **-bat·ted, -bat·ting.**
pre′com·bat′ant, *n.*
pre′com·bi·na′tion, *n.*
pre′com·bine′, *v.,* **-bined, -bin·ing.**
pre′com·bus′tion, *n.*
pre′com·mand′, *n., v.*
pre·com′ment, *n., v.*
pre′com·mer′cial, *adj.*
pre′com·mit′, *v.t.,* **-mit·ted, -mit·ting.**
pre′com·mune′, *v.i.,* **-muned, -mun·ing.**
pre′com·mu′ni·cate′, *v.,* **-cat·ed, -cat·ing.**
pre′com·mu′ni·ca′tion, *n.*
pre′com·pare′, *v.t.,* **-pared, -par·ing.**
pre′com·par′i·son, *n.*
pre·com′pass, *v.t., n.*
pre′com·pel′, *v.t.,* **-pelled, -pel·ling.**
pre·com′pen·sate′, *v.t.,* **-sat·ed, -sat·ing.**
pre′com·pen·sa′tion, *n.*
pre′com·pi·la′tion, *n.*
pre′com·pile′, *v.t.,* **-piled, -pil·ing.**
pre′com·pil′er, *n.*
pre′com·plete′ness, *n.*
pre′com·ple′tion, *n.*
pre′com·pli′ance, *n.*
pre′com·pli′ant, *adj.*
pre·com′pli·cate′, *v.t.,* **-cat·ed, -cat·ing.**
pre′com·pli·ca′tion, *n.*
pre′com·pound′, *v.*
pre′com·pre·hend′, *v.t.*
pre′com·pre·hen′sion, *n.*
pre′com·pre·hen′sive, *adj.;* **-ly,** *adv.;* **-ness,** *n.*
pre′com·press′, *v.t.*
pre′com·pres′sion, *n.*
pre′com·pul′sion, *n.*
pre·com′rade·ship′, *n.*
pre′con·ceal′, *v.t.*
pre′con·ceal′ment, *n.*
pre′con·cede′, *v.t.,* **-ced·ed, -ced·ing.**
pre·con′cen·trate′, *v.,* **-trat·ed, -trat·ing;** *n.*
pre′con·cen·tra′tion, *n.*
pre′con·cern′, *n., v.t.*
pre′con·cern′ment, *n.*
pre′con·ces′sion, *n.*
pre′con·ces′sive, *adj.*
pre′con·clude′, *v.t.,* **-clud·ed, -clud·ing.**
pre′con·clu′sion, *n.*
pre′con·cur′, *v.i.,* **-curred, -cur·ring.**
pre′con·cur′rence, *n.*
pre′con·cur′rent, *adj.;* **-ly,** *adv.*
pre′con·dem·na′tion, *n.*
pre′con·den·sa′tion, *n.*
pre′con·dense′, *v.,* **-densed, -dens·ing.**
pre′con·duct′, *v.t.*
pre′con·duc′tion, *n.*
pre′con·duc′tor, *n.*
pre·con′dy·lar, *adj.*
pre·con′dy·loid′, *adj.*
pre′con·fer′, *v.i.,* **-ferred, -fer·ring.**
pre·con′fer·ence, *n.*
pre′con·fess′, *v.t.*
pre′con·fes′sion, *n.*
pre′con·fide′, *v.,* **-fid·ed, -fid·ing.**
pre′con·fig′u·ra′tion, *n.*
pre′con·fig′ure, *v.t.,* **-ured, -ur·ing.**
pre′con·fine′, *v.t.,* **-fined, -fin·ing.**
pre′con·fin′ed·ly, *adv.*
pre′con·fine′ment, *n.*
pre′con·firm′, *v.t.*
pre′con·fir·ma′tion, *n.*
pre′con·flict′, *v.i., n.*
pre′con·form′, *v.*
pre′con·form′i·ty, *n.*
pre′con·found′, *v.t.*
pre′con·fuse′, *v.t.,* **-fused, -fus·ing.**
pre′con·fus′ed·ly, *adv.*
pre′con·fu′sion, *n.*
pre′con·gen′ial, *adj.*
pre′con·gest′ed, *adj.*
pre′con·ges′tion, *n.*
pre′con·ges′tive, *adj.*
pre′con·grat′u·late′, *v.t.,* **-lat·ed, -lat·ing.**
pre′con·grat′u·la′tion, *n.*
pre′-Con·gre·ga′tion·al·ist, *n., adj.*
pre-Con′gress, *n.*
pre′con·gres′sion·al, *adj.*
pre′con·jec′ture, *v.t.,* **-tured, -tur·ing.**
pre′con·nec′tion, *n.*
pre′con·nec′tive, *adj.*
pre′con·nu′bi·al, *adj.*
pre·con′quer, *v.t.*
pre·con′quest, *n.*
pre·con′se·crate′, *v.t.,* **-crat·ed, -crat·ing.**
pre′con·se·cra′tion, *n.*
pre′con·sent′, *n., v.i.*
pre′con·sid′er, *v.t.*
pre′con·sid′er·a′tion, *n.*
pre′con·sign′, *v.t.*
pre′con·sol′i·date′, *v.,* **-dat·ed, -dat·ing.**
pre′con·sol′i·da′tion, *n.*
pre′con·spir′a·cy, *n., pl.* **-cies.**
pre′con·spir′a·tor, *n.*
pre′con·spire′, *v.,* **-spired, -spir·ing.**
pre·con′stit′u·ent, *n.*
pre·con′sti·tute′, *v.t.,* **-tut·ed, -tut·ing.**
pre′con·struct′, *v.t.*
pre′con·struc′tion, *n.*
pre′con·sult′, *v.*
pre′con·sul·ta′tion, *n.*
pre′con·sul′tor, *n.*
pre′con·sume′, *v.t.,* **-sumed, -sum·ing.**
pre′con·sum′er, *n.*
pre′con·sump′tion, *n.*
pre′con·tain′, *v.t.*
pre′con·temn′, *v.t.*

pre·con·tract (*n.* prē kon′trakt; *v.* prē′kən trakt′), *n.* **1.** a preexisting contract which legally prevents one from making another contract of the same nature. **2.** (formerly) such an agreement constituting a legally binding betrothal. —*v.t.* **3.** to bind by means of a precontract. **4.** to contract for or agree to do (something) in advance of beginning it: *They precontracted all the terms and conditions.* —*v.i.* **5.** to make an advance contract or agreement. [PRE- + CONTRACT] —**pre′con·trac′tive,** *adj.* —**pre·con·trac·tu·al** (prē′ kən trak′cho͞o əl), *adj.*

pre·cook (prē ko͝ok′), *v.t.* to cook (food) partly or completely beforehand, so that it may be cooked or warmed and served quickly at a later time. [PRE- + COOK] —**pre·cook′er,** *n.*

pre·cool (prē ko͞ol′), *v.t.* to cool in advance; cool artificially, as meat or fresh produce, before shipping. [PRE- + COOL] —**pre·cool′er,** *n.*

pre·crit·i·cal (prē krit′i kəl), *adj.* *Med.* anteceding a crisis. [PRE- + CRITICAL]

pre·cur·sor (pri kûr′sər, prē′kûr-), *n.* **1.** one who or that which precedes, as in a job, a method, etc.; a predecessor. **2.** one who or that which goes before and indicates the approach of someone or something else; harbinger: *The first robin is a precursor of spring.* [< L *praecursor* forerunner. See PRE-, CURSIVE, -OR²]
—**Syn. 1.** forerunner. **2.** herald.

pre·cur·so·ry (pri kûr′sə rē), *adj.* **1.** of the nature of a precursor; preliminary; introductory: *precursory remarks.* **2.** indicative of something to follow: *precursory indications of disease.* Also, **pre·cur·sive** (pri kûr′siv). [< L *praecursōri(us).* See PRECURSOR, CURSORY]

pred., predicate.

preda′ceous div′ing bee′tle, any of numerous water beetles of the family *Dytiscidae* that have the body adapted for swimming and feed on small aquatic animals.

pre·da·cious (pri dā′shəs), *adj.* predatory; rapacious. Also, *esp. Biol.,* **pre·da′ceous.** [PRED(ATORY) + -ACIOUS] —**pre·da′cious·ness, pre·dac·i·ty** (pri das′i tē); *esp. Biol.,* **pre·da′ceous·ness,** *n.*

pre·date (prē dāt′), *v.t.,* **-dat·ed, -dat·ing. 1.** to date before the actual time; antedate: *He predated the check by three days.* **2.** to precede in date: *a house that predates the Civil War.* [PRE- + DATE¹]

pre·da·tion (pri dā′shən), *n.* **1.** depredation; plundering. **2.** act of plundering or robbing. **3.** predatory behavior. **4.** a relation between animals in which one organism captures and feeds on others. [< L *praedātiōn-* (s. of *praedātiō*) a taking of booty, plundering. See PREDATORY, -ION]

preda′tion pres′sure, *Ecol.* the effect of predation upon a population, resulting in the decrease in size of that population.

pre·dat·ism (pri dā′tiz əm), *n.* the state of living as a predator or by predation. [PREDAT(ION) + -ISM]

pred·a·tor (pred′ə tər), *n.* a predatory person, organism, or thing. [< L *praedātor* plunderer, equiv. to *praedāt(us)* (ptp. of *praedārī* to plunder, deriv. of *praeda* PREY) + *-or* -OR²]

pred·a·to·ry (pred′ə tōr′ē, -tôr′ē), *adj.* **1.** of, pertaining to, or characterized by plunder, pillage, robbery, or exploitation: *predatory tactics.* **2.** addicted to or living by plunder, pillage, robbery, or exploitation: *predatory bands of brigands.* **3.** *Zool.* habitually preying upon other animals. [< L *praedātōri(us).* See PREDATOR, -ORY¹] —**pred′a·to′ri·ly,** *adv.* —**pred′a·to′ri·ness,** *n.*
—**Syn. 1, 2.** rapacious.

pre·dawn (prē dôn′, prē′-), *n.* **1.** the period immediately preceding dawn. —*adj.* **2.** of or pertaining to the time immediately prior to dawn. [PRE- + DAWN]

pre·de·cease (prē′di sēs′), *v.t.,* **-ceased, -ceas·ing.** to die before (another person, the occurrence of an event, etc.). [PRE- + DECEASE]

pred·e·ces·sor (pred′i ses′ər, pred′i ses′ər *or, esp. Brit.,* prē′di ses′ər), *n.* **1.** one who precedes another in an office, position, etc. **2.** something succeeded or replaced by something else: *The new monument in the park is more beautiful than its predecessor.* **3.** *Archaic.* an ancestor; forefather. [ME *predecessour* < AF < LL *praedēcessor,* equiv. to L *prae-* PRE- + *dēcessor* retiring official, equiv. to *dēcess(us)* retired (ptp. of *dēcēdere* to withdraw; see DE-, CEDE) + *-or* -OR²]

pre·del·la (pri del′ə; *It.* pʀe del′lä), *n., pl.* **-le** (-lē; *It.* -le). *Fine Arts.* the base of an altarpiece, often decorated with small paintings or reliefs. [< It: slab < OHG or Langobardish **pret,* var. of *bret* BOARD + *-ella* dim. suffix]

pre·des·ig·nate (prē dez′ig nāt′, -des′-), *v.t.,* **-nat·ed, -nat·ing.** to designate beforehand. [PRE- + DESIGNATE] —**pre′des·ig·na′tion,** *n.* —**pre·des·ig·na·to·ry** (prē dez′ig nə tōr′ē, -tôr′ē), *adj.*

pre·des·ti·nar·i·an (pri des′tə nâr′ē ən), *adj.* **1.** of or pertaining to predestination. **2.** believing in predestination. —*n.* **3.** one who believes in predestination. [PREDESTIN(ATION) + -ARIAN] —**pre·des′ti·nar′i·an·ism,** *n.*

pre·des·ti·nate (*v.* pri des′tə nāt′; *adj.* pri des′tə nit, -nāt′), *v.,* **-nat·ed, -nat·ing,** *adj.* —*v.t.* **1.** *Theol.* to foreordain by divine decree or purpose. **2.** *Obs.* to foreordain; predetermine. —*adj.* **3.** predestined; foreordained. [ME < L *praedestināt(us),* ptp. of *praedestināre* to appoint beforehand. See PRE-, DESTINE, -ATE¹] —**pre·des′ti·nate·ly,** *adv.*

pre·des·ti·na·tion (pri des′tə nā′shən, prē′des-), *n.* **1.** act of predestinating or predestining. **2.** state of being predestinated or predestined. **3.** fate; destiny. **4.** *Theol.* **a.** the action of God in foreordaining from eternity whatever comes to pass. **b.** the decree of God by which certain souls are foreordained to salvation. Cf. **election** (def. 4), **double predestination.** [ME *predestinacioun* < LL *praedestinātiōn-* (s. of *praedestinātiō*). See PREDESTINATE, -ION]

pre·des·tine (pri des′tin), *v.t.,* **-tined, -tin·ing.** to destine in advance; foreordain; predetermine: *He seemed predestined for the ministry.* [ME *predestine(n)* < L *praedestin(āre).* See PRE-, DESTINE] —**pre·des′ti·na·ble,** *adj.*

pre·de·ter·mi·nate (prē′di tûr′mə nit, -nāt′), *adj.* determined beforehand; predetermined. [PRE- + DETERMINATE] —**pre′de·ter′mi·nate·ly,** *adv.*

pre·de·ter·mine (prē′di tûr′min), *v.t.,* **-mined, -min·ing. 1.** to settle or decide in advance: *He had predetermined his answer to the offer.* **2.** to ordain in advance; predestine: *She believed that God had predetermined her son's early death.* **3.** to direct or impel in advance to something: *His sympathy for the poor predetermined his choice of a career.* [PRE- + DETERMINE] —**pre′de·ter′mi·na′tion,** *n.* —**pre·de·ter·mi·na·tive** (prē′di tûr′mə nā′tiv, -nə tiv), *adj.* —**pre′de·ter′min·er,** *n.*

pre·di·al (prē′dē əl), *adj.* praedial.

pred·i·ca·ble (pred′ə kə bəl), *adj.* **1.** that may be predicated or affirmed; assertable. —*n.* **2.** that which may be predicated; an attribute. **3.** *Logic.* any one of the various kinds of predicate that may be used of a subject. [< L *praedicābil(is)* assertable, equiv. to *praedicā(re)* (to) declare publicly (see PREACH) + *-bilis* -BLE] —**pred′i·ca·bil′i·ty, pred′i·ca·ble·ness,** *n.* —**pred′i·ca·bly,** *adv.*

pre·dic·a·ment (pri dik′ə mənt), *n.* **1.** an unpleasantly difficult, perplexing, or dangerous situation. **2.** a class or category of logical or philosophical predication. **3.** *Archaic.* a particular state, condition, or situation. [ME < LL *praedicāment(um)* something predicated, asserted, deriv. of *praedicāre.* See PREDICATE, -MENT] —**pre·dic·a·men·tal** (pri dik′ə men′tᵊl), *adj.* —**pre·dic′a·men′tal·ly,** *adv.*

—**Syn. 1.** PREDICAMENT, DILEMMA, PLIGHT, QUANDARY refer to unpleasant or puzzling situations. PREDICAMENT and PLIGHT stress more the unpleasant nature, QUANDARY and DILEMMA the puzzling nature of the situation. PREDICAMENT and PLIGHT are sometimes interchangeable; PLIGHT, however, though originally meaning peril or danger, is seldom used today except laughingly: *When his suit failed to come back from the cleaners, he was in a terrible plight.* PREDICAMENT, though likewise capable of being used lightly, may also refer to a really crucial situation: *Stranded in a strange city without money, he was in a predicament.* DILEMMA, in popular use, means a position of doubt or perplexity in which one is faced by two equally undesirable alternatives: *the dilemma of a hostess who must choose between shocking her strait-laced guests or disappointing those who expected cocktails.* QUANDARY is the state of mental perplexity of one faced with a difficult situation: *There seemed to be no way out of the quandary.*

pred·i·cant (pred′ə kənt), *adj.* **1.** preaching: *predicant duties; a predicant religious order.* —*n.* **2.** a preacher. [< eccl. L *praedicant-* (s. of *praedicāns*) preaching. See PREACH, -ANT]

pred·i·cate (*v.* pred′ə kāt′; *adj., n.* pred′ə kit), *v.,* **-cat·ed, -cat·ing,** *adj., n.* —*v.t.* **1.** to proclaim; declare; affirm; assert. **2.** *Logic.* **a.** to affirm or assert (something) of the subject of a proposition. **b.** to make (a term) the predicate of such a proposition. **3.** to connote; imply: *His retraction predicates a change of attitude.* **4.** to found (a statement, action, etc.); base (usually fol. by *on*): *He predicated his behavior on his faith in humanity.* —*v.i.* **5.** to make an affirmation or assertion. —*adj.* **6.** predicated. **7.** *Gram.* belonging to the predicate: *a predicate noun.* —*n.* **8.** *Gram.* (in many languages, as English) a syntactic unit that functions as one of the two main constituents of a simple sentence, the other being the subject, and that consists of a verb, which in English may agree with the subject in number, and of all the words governed by the verb or modifying it, the whole often expressing the action performed by or the state attributed to the subject, as *is here* in *Larry is here.* **9.** *Logic.* that which is affirmed or denied concerning the subject of a proposition. [< L *praedicāt(us)* ptp. of *praedicāre* to declare publicly, assert, equiv. to *prae-* PRE- + *-dicāre,* comb. form of *dīcere* to say, make known; see -ATE¹] —**pred′i·ca′tion,** *n.* —**pred′i·ca′tion·al,** *adj.* —**pred′i·ca′tive,** *adj.* —**pred′i·ca′tive·ly,** *adv.*

pred′icate ad′jective, *Gram.* an adjective used in the predicate, esp. with a copulative verb and attributive to the subject, as in *He is dead,* or attributive to the direct object, as in *It made him sick.*

pred′icate cal′culus, *Logic.* See **functional calculus.**

pred′icate nom′inative, (in Latin, Greek, and certain other languages) a predicate noun, or adjective in the nominative case.

pred′icate noun′, *Gram.* a noun used in the predicate with a copulative verb or certain other verbs, as *make, choose, crown,* and having the same referent as the subject, as in *He is the king,* or *They made him king.*

pred′icate objec′tive, *Gram.* See **objective complement.**

pred·i·ca·to·ry (pred′ə kə tōr′ē, -tôr′ē), *adj.* of or pertaining to preaching. [< eccl. L *praedicatōri(us)* of preaching. See PREACH, -ORY¹]

pre·dict (pri dikt′), *v.t.* **1.** to tell in advance; prophesy: *to predict the weather; to predict the fall of a civilization.* —*v.i.* **2.** to foretell the future; make a prediction. [< L *praedict(us),* ptp. of *praedicere* to foretell, equiv. to *prae-* PRE- + *dicere* to say; see DICTUM] —**pre·dict′a·bil′i·ty,** *n.* —**pre·dict′a·ble,** *adj.* —**pre·dict′a·bly,** *adv.*
—**Syn. 1, 2.** presage, divine, augur, project, prognosticate, portend. PREDICT, PROPHESY, FORESEE, FORE-

pre′con′tem·plate′, *v.,* **-plat·ed, -plat·ing.**
pre′con·tem·pla′tion, *n.*
pre′con·tem′po·ra·ne′i·ty, *n.*
pre′con·tem′po·ra′ne·ous, *adj.;* **-ly,** *adv.*
pre′con·tend′, *v.i.*
pre′con·ten′tion, *n.*
pre′con·tent′ment, *n.*
pre′con·test′, *v.t.*
pre·con′test, *n.*
pre′con·ti·nen′tal, *adj.*
pre′con·trac′tive, *adj.*
pre′con·trac′tu·al, *adj.*
pre′con·trib′ute, *v.t.,* **-ut·ed, -ut·ing.**
pre′con·tri·bu′tion, *n.*
pre′con·trib′u·tive, *adj.*
pre′con·triv′ance, *n.*
pre′con·trive′, *v.,* **-trived, -triv·ing.**
pre′con·trol′, *n., v.t.,* **-trolled, -trol·ling.**
pre′con·tro·ver′sial, *adj.*
pre·con′tro·ver′sy, *n., pl.* **-sies.**
pre′con·ven′tion, *n.*
pre′con·ver·sa′tion, *n.*
pre′con·ver·sa′tion·al, *adj.*
pre′con·ver′sion, *n.*
pre′con·vert′, *v.t.*
pre′con·vey′, *v.t.*
pre′con·vey′ance, *n.*
pre′con·vict′, *v.t.*
pre′con·vic′tion, *n.*
pre′con·vince′, *v.t.,* **-vinced, -vinc·ing.**
pre·cook′, *v.t.*
pre′-Co·per′ni·can, *adj.*
pre′-Co·per′ni·can·ism, *n.*
pre·cop′y, *n., v.t.,* **-cop·ied, -cop·y·ing.**
pre·cor′a·coid′, *adj.*
pre·cor′dial, *adj.*
pre·cor′ne·al, *adj.*
pre′cor·o·na′tion, *n.*
pre′cor·rect′, *v.t.;* **-ly,** *adv.;* **-ness,** *n.*
pre′cor·rec′tion, *n.*
pre′cor·res·pond′, *v.i.*
pre′cor·res·pond′ence, *n.*
pre′cor·res·pond′ent, *adj.*
pre·cor′ri·dor, *n.*
pre′cor·rupt′, *v.t.;* **-ly,** *adv.;* **-ness,** *n.*
pre′cor·rup′tion, *n.*
pre′cor·rup′tive, *adj.*
pre·cos′mic, *adj.*
pre·cos′mi·cal, *adj.;* **-ly,** *adv.*
pre·cos′tal, *adj.*
pre·coun′sel, *n., v.,* **-seled, -sel·ing** or (*esp. Brit.*) **-selled, -sel·ling.**
pre·coun′sel·lor, *n.*
pre·cov′er, *v.t.*
pre·cra′ni·al, *adj.;* **-ly,** *adv.*
pre′cre·a′tion, *n.*
pre·cred′it, *v.t.*
pre·cred′i·tor, *n.*
pre·creed′, *n.*
pre·crit′i·cism, *n.*
pre·crit′i·cize′, *v.t.,* **-cized, -ciz·ing.**
pre·cru′cial, *adj.*
pre·cru′ral, *adj.*
pre′-Cru·sade′, *adj.*
pre·crys′tal·line, *adj.*
pre·cul′ti·vate′, *v.t.,* **-vat·ed, -vat·ing.**
pre′cul·ti·va′tion, *n.*
pre·cul′tur·al, *adj.;* **-ly,** *adv.*
pre·cul′ture, *n.*
pre·cure′, *n., v.t.,* **-cured, -cur·ing.**
pre·cur′rent, *adj.*
pre′cur·ric′u·lar, *adj.*
pre′cur·ric′u·lum, *n., pl.* **-lums, -la.**
pre·cur′tain, *n.*
pre·cy′clone, *n.*
pre′cy·clon′ic, *adj.*
pre·cys′tic, *adj.*
pre·dam′age, *n., v.t.,* **aged, -ag·ing.**
pre·damn′, *v.t.*
pre′dam·na′tion, *n.*
pre′-Dan′te·an, *adj.*
pre·dark′, *adj.*
pre·dark′ness, *n.*
pre′-Dar·win′i·an, *adj.*
pre·da′ta, *n.*
pre·day′, *n.*
pre·day′light, *n.*
pre·day′time, *n.*
pre·deal′er, *n.*
pre·deal′ing, *n.*
pre·death′, *n.*
pre·death′ly, *adj.*
pre′de·bate′, *n.*
pre′de·bat′er, *n.*
pre·deb′it, *n., v.t.*
pre·debt′or, *n.*
pre′de·ceive′, *v.t.,* **-ceived, -ceiv·ing.**
pre′de·ceiv′er, *n.*
pre′de·cep′tion, *n.*
pre′de·cide′, *v.t.,* **-cid·ed, -cid·ing.**
pre′de·ci′sion, *n.*
pre′de·ci′sive, *adj.;* **-ly,** *adv.*
pre′dec·la·ra′tion, *n.*
pre′de·clare′, *v.t.,* **-clared, -clar·ing.**
pre′dec·li·na′tion, *n.*
pre′de·cline′, *v.t.,* **-clined, -clin·ing.**
pre′de·cree′, *v.t.,* **-creed, -cree·ing.**
pre·ded′i·cate′, *v.t.,* **-cat·ed, -cat·ing.**
pre′ded·i·ca′tion, *n.*
pre′de·duct′, *v.t.*
pre′de·duc′tion, *n.*
pre′de·fault′, *n., v.*
pre′de·feat′, *n., v.*
pre′de·fect′, *n.*
pre′de·fec′tive, *adj.*
pre′de·fence′, *n.*
pre′de·fend′, *v.t.*
pre′de·fense′, *n.*
pre′de·fi′ance, *n.*
pre′de·fi′cien·cy, *n.*
pre′de·fi′cient, *adj.;* **-ly,** *adv.*
pre′de·fine′, *v.t.,* **-fined, -fin·ing.**
pre′def·i·ni′tion, *n.*
pre′de·fray′, *v.t.*
pre′de·fray′al, *adj.*
pre′de·fy′, *v.t.,* **-fied, -fy·ing.**
pre′de·gen′er·a·cy, *n.*
pre′de·gen′er·ate, *adj.*
pre′de·gree′, *n.*
pre′de·lay′, *n., v.*
pre·del′e·gate′, *n., v.,* **-gat·ed, -gat·ing.**
pre′del·e·ga′tion, *n.*
pre′de·lib′er·ate′, *v.t.,* **-at·ed, -at·ing.**
pre′de·lib′er·ate, *adj.;* **-ly,** *adv.*
pre′de·lib′er·a′tion, *n.*
pre′de·lin′e·ate′, *v.t.,* **-at·ed, -at·ing.**
pre′de·lin′e·a′tion, *n.*
pre′de·lin′quen·cy, *n.*
pre′de·lin′quent, *adj.;* **-ly,** *adv.*
pre′de·liv′er, *v.t.*
pre′de·liv′er·y, *n., pl.* **-er·ies.**
pre′de·lude′, *v.t.,* **-lud·ed, -lud·ing.**
pre′de·lu′sion, *n.*
pre′de·mand′, *v.t.*
pre′de·moc′ra·cy, *n.*
pre′dem·o·crat′ic, *adj.*
pre·dem′on·strate′, *v.t.,* **-strat·ed, -strat·ing.**
pre′dem·on·stra′tion, *n.*
pre′de·mon′stra·tive, *adj.*
pre′de·ni′al, *adj.*
pre′de·ny′, *v.t.,* **-nied, -ny·ing.**
pre′de·part·men′tal, *adj.*
pre′de·par′ture, *n.*
pre′de·pend′a·ble, *adj.*
pre′de·pend′ence, *n.*
pre′de·pend′ent, *adj.*
pre′de·plete′, *v.t.,* **-plet·ed, -plet·ing.**
pre′de·ple′tion, *n.*
pre′de·pos′it, *n., v.*
pre′de·pos′i·to′ry, *n.*
pre′de·pre′ci·ate′, *v.,* **-at·ed, -at·ing.**
pre′de·pre′ci·a′tion, *n.*
pre′de·pres′sion, *n., adj.*
pre′dep·ri·va′tion, *n.*
pre′de·prive′, *v.t.,* **-prived, -priv·ing.**
pre′der·i·va′tion, *n.*
pre′de·rive′, *v.t.,* **-rived, -riv·ing.**
pre′des·cend′, *v.*
pre′des·cent′, *n.*
pre′de·scribe′, *v.t.,* **-scribed, -scrib·ing.**
pre′de·scrip′tion, *n.*
pre′de·sert′, *v.t.*
pre′de·sert′er, *n.*
pre′de·ser′tion, *n.*
pre′de·serve′, *v.t.,* **-served, -serv·ing.**
pre′de·sign′, *v.t.*
pre′de·sir′ous, *adj.;* **-ly,** *adv.*
pre′de·spond′en·cy, *n.*
pre′de·spond′ent, *adj.*
pre·des′ti·tute′, *adj.*
pre′des·ti·tu′tion, *n.*
pre′de·stroy′, *v.t.*
pre′de·struc′tion, *n.*
pre′de·tach′, *v.t.*
pre′de·tach′ment, *n.*
pre′de·tail′, *v.t.*
pre′de·tain′, *v.t.*
pre′de·tain′er, *n.*
pre′de·tect′, *v.t.*
pre′de·tec′tion, *n.*
pre′de·ten′tion, *n.*
pre′det·ri·men′tal, *adj.*
pre′de·vel′op, *v.*
pre′de·vel′op·ment, *n.*
pre′de·vise′, *v.t.,* **-vised, -vis·ing.**
pre′de·vo′tion, *n.*
pre′de·vour′, *v.t.*
pre′di·ag·no′sis, *n., pl.* **-ses.**
pre′di·ag·nos′tic, *adj.*
pre′di·as·tol′ic, *adj.*
pre′di·crot′ic, *adj.*

CAST mean to know or tell (usually correctly) beforehand what will happen. To PREDICT is usually to foretell with precision of calculation, knowledge, or shrewd inference from facts or experience: *The astronomers can predict an eclipse;* it may, however, be used quite lightly: *I predict she'll be a success at the party.* PROPHESY may have the solemn meaning of predicting future events by the aid of divine or supernatural inspiration: *Merlin prophesied the two knights would meet in conflict;* this verb, too, may be used loosely: *I prophesy he'll be back in the old job.* To FORESEE refers specifically not to the uttering of predictions but to the mental act of seeing ahead; there is often (but not always) a practical implication of preparing for what will happen: *He was clever enough to foresee this shortage of materials.* FORECAST has much the same meaning as FORESEE, except that conjecture rather than real insight or knowledge is apt to be involved; it is used today particularly of the weather: *Rain and snow are forecast for tonight.*

pre·dic·tion (pri dik′shən), *n.* **1.** act of predicting. **2.** an instance of this; prophecy. [< L *praedictiōn-* (s. of *praedictiō*) a foretelling. See PREDICT, -ION] —**Syn. 2.** forecast, augury, prognostication, divination, projection.

pre·dic·tive (pri dik′tiv), *adj.* **1.** of or pertaining to prediction: *losing one's predictive power.* **2.** used or useful for predicting or foretelling the future: *to look for predictive signs among the stars.* **3.** being an indication of the future or of future conditions: *a cold wind predictive of snow.* [< LL *praedictīv(us)* foretelling. See PREDICT, -IVE] —**pre·dic′tive·ly,** *adv.* —**pre·dic′tive·ness,** *n.*

pre·dic·tor (pri dik′tər), *n.* **1.** one who or that which predicts. **2.** *Math.* a formula for determining additional values or derivatives of a function from the relationship of its given values. [< ML *praedictor.* See PREDICT, -OR[2]]

pre·dic·to·ry (pri dik′tə rē), *adj. Archaic.* predictive. [PREDICT + -ORY[1]]

pre·di·gest (prē′di jest′, -dī-), *v.t.* to treat (food) by an artificial process analogous to digestion so that, when taken into the body, it is more easily digestible. [PRE- + DIGEST] —**pre′di·ges′tion,** *n.*

pre·di·lec·tion (pred′əlek′shən, prēd′-), *n.* a preexisting tendency to think favorably of something; partiality; preference: *a predilection for Bach.* [? *predilect* loved more (< ML *praedīlect(us),* ptp. of *praedīligere*) + *dilection* love (now obs.) < L *dīlectiōn-* (s. of *dīlectiō*), lit., a choosing (for love) apart from others. See PRE-, DI-[2], ELECT, -ION] —**Syn.** bias, inclination, leaning, liking, weakness, predisposition.

pre·dis·pose (prē′di spōz′), *v.,* **-posed, -pos·ing.** —*v.t.* **1.** to give an inclination or tendency to beforehand: *Genetic factors may predispose human beings to certain metabolic diseases.* **2.** to render subject, susceptible, or liable: *The evidence predisposes him to public censure.* **3.** to dispose beforehand. **4.** *Archaic.* to dispose of beforehand, as in a will, legacy, or the like. —*v.i.* **5.** to give or furnish a tendency or inclination: *an underground job that predisposes to lung infection.* [PRE- + DISPOSE] —**pre′dis·pos′al,** *n.* —**pre·dis·pos·ed·ly** (prē′di spō′zid lē, -spōzd′-), *adv.* —**pre′dis·pos′ed·ness,** *n.* —**Syn. 1.** prearrange, prepare. **3.** bias, incline.

pre·dis·po·si·tion (prē dis′pə zish′ən, prē′dis-), *n.* **1.** condition of being predisposed: *a predisposition to think optimistically.* **2.** *Pathol.* a dormant condition which may be triggered into activity: *a predisposition to tuberculosis.* [PRE- + DISPOSITION] —**pre·dis′po·si′tion·al,** *adj.*

pre·dis·tor·tion (prē′di stôr′shən), *n. Electronics.* preemphasis. Also, **pre′-dis·tor′tion.** [PRE- + DISTORTION]

pre·dom·i·nance (pri dom′ə nəns), *n.* state, condition, or quality of being predominant: *the predominance of the rich over the poor.* Also, **pre·dom′i·nan·cy.** [PREDOMIN(ANT) + -ANCE]

pre·dom·i·nant (pri dom′ə nənt), *adj.* **1.** having ascendancy, power, authority, or influence over others; ascendant. **2.** prevailing; prominent: *Excessive pride was a predominant cause of his downfall. Green is the predominant color of a peacock feather.* [< ML *praedominant-* (s. of *praedominans*) predominating, prp. of *praedominārī.* See PRE-, DOMINANT] —**pre·dom′i·nant·ly,** *adv.* —**Syn. 1, 2.** See **dominant.**

pre·dom·i·nate (pri dom′ə nāt′), *v.,* **-nat·ed, -nat·ing.** —*v.i.* **1.** to be the stronger or leading element; preponderate; prevail: *They began to fear that the radicals might predominate in the new legislature.* **2.** to have or exert controlling power (often fol. by *over*): *Good sense predominated over his wild impulse to fight.* **3.** to surpass others in authority or influence: *He was one of the figures who predominated in the political scene.* **4.** to appear more noticeable or imposing than something else: *Blues and greens predominated in the painting.* —*v.t.* **5.** to dominate or prevail over. [< ML *praedominat(us),* ptp. of *praedominārī* to predominate. See PRE-, DOMINATE] —**pre·dom·i·nate·ly** (pri dom′ə nit lē), *adv.* —**pre·dom′i·nat′ing·ly,** *adv.* —**pre·dom′i·na′tion,** *n.* —**pre·dom′i·na′tor,** *n.* —**Syn. 1.** outweigh. **2.** overrule, dominate.

pre·dor·mi·tion (prē′dôr mish′ən), *n. Med.* the period of semiconsciousness that precedes actual sleep. [PRE- + LL *dormitiōn-* (s. of *dormitiō*) a falling asleep, L: a sleeping, equiv. to *dormit(us)* (see DORMITORY) + *-iōn-* -ION]

pre·dy·nas·tic (prē′dī nas′tik), *adj.* of, pertaining to, or belonging to a time or period before the first dynasty of a nation, esp. the period in Egypt before c3200 B.C. [PRE- + DYNASTIC]

pree (prē), *n., v.,* **preed, pree·ing.** *Scot. and North Eng.* —*n.* **1.** a test, trial, or taste; a test by sampling. —*v.t.* **2.** to try, test, or taste. **3. pree the mouth of,** *Scot.* to kiss. Also, **prie.** [shortened form of *preive,* side-form of PROVE]

pre·e·lec·tion (prē′i lek′shən), *n.* **1.** a choice or selection made beforehand. —*adj.* **2.** coming before an election: *preelection primaries.* Also, **pre′-e·lec′tion, pre′ë·lec′tion.** [PRE- + ELECTION]

pre-E·liz·a·be·than (prē′i liz′ə bē′thən, -beth′ən), *adj.* (of English culture, history, traditions, etc.) before the reign of Queen Elizabeth I; before the second half of the 16th century.

pree·mie (prē′mē), *n.* premie.

pre·em·i·nence (prē em′ə nəns), *n.* state or character of being preeminent. Also, **pre-em′i·nence, pre·ëm′i·nence.** [ME < LL *praeēminentia.* See PREEMINENT -ENCE]

pre·em·i·nent (prē em′ə nənt), *adj.* eminent above or before others; superior; surpassing: *He is preeminent in his profession.* Also, **pre-em′i·nent, pre·ëm′i·nent.** [late ME < L *praeēminent-* (s. of *praeēminēns*), prp. of *praeēminēre* to project forward, be prominent. See PRE-, EMINENT] —**pre·em′i·nent·ly, pre-em′i·nent·ly, pre·ëm′i·nent·ly,** *adv.* —**Syn.** distinguished, peerless, supreme, superior. See **dominant.**

pre·em·pha·sis (prē em′fə sis), *n. Electronics.* a process of increasing the amplitude of certain frequencies relative to others in a signal in order to help them override noise, complemented by deemphasis before final reproduction of the signal being received. Also, **pre-em′pha·sis, pre·ëm′pha·sis.** Also called **emphasis, predistortion, preequalization.** [PRE- + EMPHASIS]

pre·empt (prē empt′), *v.t.* **1.** to occupy (land) in order to establish a prior right to buy. **2.** to acquire or appropriate before someone else: *to preempt the choicest cut of meat.* —*v.i.* **3.** *Bridge.* to make a preemptive bid. —*n.* **4.** *Bridge.* a preemptive bid. Also, **pre-empt′, pre·ëmpt′.** [back formation from PREEMPTION] —**pre·emp·tor, pre-emp·tor, pre·ëmp·tor** (prē emp′tôr), *n.* —**Syn. 1.** claim, appropriate, usurp.

pre·emp·tion (prē emp′shən), *n.* act or right of claiming or purchasing before or in preference to others. Also, **pre-emp′tion, pre·ëmp′tion.** [< ML *praeēmpt(us)* brought beforehand (ptp. of *praeēmere*) + -ION. See PRE-, REDEEM]

pre·emp·tive (prē emp′tiv), *adj.* **1.** of or pertaining to preemption. **2.** *Bridge.* pertaining to, involving, or noting an opening bid or an overcall in a suit that is at an unnecessarily high level and that is essentially a defensive maneuver designed to make communication between one's opponents more difficult: *a preemptive bid; to give a preemptive response.* Also, **pre-emp′tive, pre·ëmp′tive.** [PREEMPT + -IVE] —**pre·emp′tive·ly, pre-emp′tive·ly, pre·ëmp′tive·ly,** *adv.*

preen[1] (prēn), *v.t.* **1.** (of animals, esp. birds) to trim or dress (feathers, fur, etc.) with the beak or tongue: *The peacock preened itself on the lawn.* **2.** to dress (oneself) carefully or smartly; primp: *She preened herself in front of the mirror.* **3.** to pride (oneself) on an achievement, personal quality, etc.: *He preened himself on having been graduated with honors.* —*v.i.* **4.** to make oneself appear elegant or smart: *She's been preening for hours.* **5.** to be exultant or proud. [? b. PRUNE[3] and *preen* to pierce (ME *prene,* v. use, now dial., of PREEN[2]), from the pricking action of a bird's beak in preening] —**preen′er,** *n.*

preen[2] (prēn), *n. Chiefly Brit. Dial.* a pin or brooch. [ME *prene,* OE *prēon* a pin; c. Icel *prjōnn* pin; akin to D *priem,* G *Pfreim* awl]

pre·en·gage (prē′en gāj′), *v.t., v.i.,* **-gaged, -gag·ing.** **1.** to engage beforehand. **2.** to put under obligation, esp. to marry, by a prior engagement. **3.** to win the favor or attention of beforehand: *Other matters preengaged him.* Also, **pre′-en·gage′, pre′ën·gage′.** [PRE- + ENGAGE]

preen′ gland′. See **uropygial gland.**

pre·e·qual·i·za·tion (prē ē′kwə li zā′shən), *n. Electronics.* preemphasis. Also, **pre-e′qual·i·za′tion, pre·ë′qual·i·za′tion.** [PRE- + EQUALIZATION]

pre·es·tab·lish (prē′e stab′lish), *v.t.* to establish beforehand. Also, **pre′-es·tab′lish, pre′ës·tab′lish.** [PRE- + ESTABLISH]

pre′estab′lished har′mony, (in the philosophy of Leibnitz) synchronous operation of all monads, since their simultaneous creation, in accordance with the preexisting plan of God.

pre/dic′tate, *v.t.,* **-tat·ed, -tat·ing.**
pre·di′et, *n.*
pre·di′e·tar′y, *adj.*
pre·dif′fi·cul′ty, *n.*
pre·dig′i·tal, *adj.*
pre·dil′i·gent, *adj.;* **-ly,** *adv.*
pre′di·lu′vi·al, *adj.*
pre′di·min′ish, *v.t.*
pre′di·min′ish·ment, *n.*
pre′di·mi·nu′tion, *n.*
pre·dine′, *v.i.,* **-dined, -din·ing.**
pre·din′ner, *n.*
pre′diph·the·rit′ic, *adj.*
pre′di·plo′ma, *n.*
pre′di·plo′ma·cy, *n.*
pre′dip·lo·mat′ic, *adj.*
pre′di·rect′, *v.t.*
pre′di·rec′tion, *n.*
pre′di·rec′tor, *n.*
pre′dis·a·gree′, *v.i.,* **-greed, -gree·ing.**
pre′dis·a·gree′ment, *n.*
pre′dis·ap·point′ment, *n.*
pre′dis·as′ter, *n.*
pre′dis·as′trous, *adj.;* **-ly,** *adv.*
pre′dis·cern′, *v.t.*
pre′dis·cern′ment, *n.*
pre·dis′charge, *n.*
pre′dis·charge′, *v.t.,* **-charged, -charg·ing.**
pre·dis′ci·pline, *v.t.,* **-plined, -plin·ing;** *n.*
pre′dis·close′, *v.t.,* **-closed, -clos·ing.**
pre′dis·clo′sure, *n.*
pre′dis·con·tent′, *n.*
pre′dis·con·tent′ed, *adj.*
pre′dis·con·tent′ment, *n.*
pre·dis′count, *n., v.t.*
pre′dis·count′a·ble, *adj.*
pre′dis·cour′age, *v.t.,* **-aged, -ag·ing.**
pre′dis·cour′age·ment, *n.*
pre·dis′course, *n.*
pre′dis·cov′er, *v.t.*
pre′dis·cov′er·er, *n.*
pre′dis·cov′er·y, *n., pl.* **-er·ies.**
pre′dis·crim′i·nate′, *v.t.,* **-nat·ed, -nat·ing.**
pre′dis·crim′i·na′tion, *n.*
pre′dis·crim′i·na′tor, *n.*
pre′dis·cuss′, *v.t.*
pre′dis·cus′sion, *n.*
pre′dis·grace′, *n.*
pre′dis·guise′, *n., v.t.,* **-guised, -guis·ing.**
pre′dis·gust′, *n.*
pre′dis·like′, *n., v.t.,* **-liked, -lik·ing.**
pre′dis·miss′, *v.t.*
pre′dis·mis′sal, *n.*
pre′dis·or′der, *n.*
pre′dis·or′dered, *adj.*
pre′dis·patch′, *n., v.t.*
pre′dis·patch′er, *n.*
pre′dis·perse′, *v.t.,* **-persed, -pers·ing.**
pre′dis·per′sion, *n.*
pre′dis·place′, *v.t.,* **-placed, -plac·ing.**
pre′dis·place′ment, *n.*
pre′dis·play′, *n., v.t.*
pre′dis·pu′tant, *n.*
pre′dis·pu·ta′tion, *n.*
pre′dis·pute′, *n., v.,* **-put·ed, -put·ing.**
pre′dis·rupt′, *v.t.*
pre′dis·rup′tion, *n.*
pre′dis·sat′is·fac′tion, *n.*
pre′dis·so·lu′tion, *n.*
pre′dis·solve′, *v.t.,* **-solved, -solv·ing.**
pre′dis·suade′, *v.t.,* **-suad·ed, -suad·ing.**
pre′dis·tin′guish, *v.t.*
pre′dis·tress′, *n., v.t.*
pre′dis·trib′ute, *v.t.,* **-ut·ed, -ut·ing.**
pre′dis·tri·bu′tion, *n.*
pre′dis·trib′u·tor, *n.*
pre·dis′trict, *n.*
pre′dis·trust′, *n., v.t.*
pre′dis·trust′ful, *adj.*
pre′dis·turb′, *v.t.*
pre′dis·turb′ance, *n.*
pre′di·ver′sion, *n.*
pre′di·vert′, *v.t.*
pre′di·vide′, *v.t.,* **-vid·ed, -vid·ing.**
pre′di·vid′er, *n.*
pre′di·vin′a·ble, *adj.*
pre′di·vin′i·ty, *n.*
pre′di·vi′sion, *n.*
pre′di·vorce′, *n., adj.*
pre′di·vorce′ment, *n.*
pre·doc′tor·ate, *n.*
pre′doc·u·men′tar·y, *adj.*
pre′do·mes′tic, *adj.*
pre′do·mes′ti·cal·ly, *adv.*
pre·do′nate, *v.t.,* **-nat·ed, -nat·ing.**
pre′do·na′tion, *n.*
pre·do′nor, *n.*
pre·doom′, *v.t.*
pre-Do′ri·an, *adj.*
pre-Dor′ic, *adj.*
pre·dor′sal, *adj.*
pre·doubt′, *n., v.*
pre·doubt′er, *n.*
pre·doubt′ful, *adj.;* **-ly,** *adv.*
pre·draft′, *n., v.t.*
pre′dra·mat′ic, *adj.*
pre′-Dra·vid′i·an, *adj.*
pre′-Dra·vid′ic, *adj.*
pre·draw′, *v.,* **-drew, -drawn, -draw·ing;** *n.*
pre·draw′er, *n.*
pre·dread′, *n., v.t.*
pre·drill′, *v.t.*
pre·drill′er, *n.*
pre·drive′, *v.,* **-drove, -driv·en, -driv·ing.**
pre·driv′er, *n.*
pre·dry′, *v.t.,* **-dried, -dry·ing.**
pre·du′pli·cate′, *v.t.,* **-cat·ed, -cat·ing.**
pre′du·pli·ca′tion, *n.*
pre·dusk′, *n.*
pre-Dutch′, *adj.*
pre·dwell′, *v.i.*
pre·earth′ly, *adj.*
pre·earth′quake′, *adj.*
pre-East′er, *n.*
pre′e·co·nom′ic, *adj.*
pre′e·co·nom′i·cal, *adj.;* **-ly,** *adv.*
pre·ed′it, *v.t.*
pre′e·di′tion, *n.*
pre·ed′i·tor, *n.*
pre′ed·i·to′ri·al, *adj.;* **-ly,** *adv.*
pre·ed′u·cate′, *v.t.,* **-cat·ed, -cat·ing.**
pre′ed·u·ca′tion, *n.*
pre′ed·u·ca′tion·al, *adj.;* **-ly,** *adv.*
pre′ef·fect′, *n., v.t.*
pre′ef·fec′tive, *adj.;* **-ly,** *adv.*
pre′ef·fec′tu·al, *adj.;* **-ly,** *adv.*
pre·ef′fort, *n.*
pre′e·lect′, *v.t.*
pre′e·lec′tive, *adj.*
pre′e·lec′tric, *adj.*
pre′e·lec′tri·cal, *adj.;* **-ly,** *adv.*
pre′el·e·men′tal, *adj.*
pre′el·e·men′ta·ry, *adj.*
pre′el·i·gi·bil′i·ty, *n.*
pre·el′i·gi·ble, *adj.;* **-ble·ness,** *n.;* **-bly,** *adv.*
pre′e·lim′i·nate′, *v.t.,* **-nat·ed, -nat·ing.**
pre′e·lim′i·na′tion, *n.*
pre′e·lim′i·na′tor, *n.*
pre′e·man′ci·pa′tion, *n.*
pre′em·bar′rass, *v.t.*
pre′em·bar′rass·ment, *n.*
pre′em·bod′i·ment, *n.*
pre′em·bod′y, *v.t.,* **-bod·ied, -bod·y·ing.**
pre′e·mer′gen·cy, *adj., n., pl.* **-cies.**
pre′e·mo′tion, *n.*
pre′e·mo′tion·al, *adj.;* **-ly,** *adv.*
pre-Em′pire, *adj.*
pre·em′per·or, *n.*
pre′em·ploy′, *v.t.*
pre′em·ploy′ee, *n.*
pre′em·ploy′er, *n.*
pre′em·ploy′ment, *n.*
pre′en·a′ble, *v.t.,* **-bled, -bling.**
pre′e·nact′, *v.t.*
pre′e·nac′tion, *n.*
pre′en·close′, *v.t.,* **-closed, -clos·ing.**
pre′en·clo′sure, *n.*
pre′en·coun′ter, *n., v.t.*
pre′en·cour′age, *v.t.*
pre′en·cour′age·ment, *n.*
pre′en·deav′or, *n.*
pre′en·dorse′, *v.t.,* **-dorsed, -dors·ing.**
pre′en·dorse′ment, *n.*
pre′en·dors′er, *n.*
pre′en·force′, *v.t.,* **-forced, -forc·ing.**
pre′en·force′ment, *n.*
pre′en·gi·neer′ing, *adj.*
pre-Eng′lish, *adj.*
pre′en·joy′, *v.t.*
pre′en·joy′a·ble, *adj.*
pre′en·joy′ment, *n.*
pre′en·large′, *v.t.,* **-larged, -larg·ing.**
pre′en·large′ment, *n.*
pre′en·light′en, *v.t.*
pre′en·light′en·er, *n.*
pre′en·light′en·ment, *n.*
pre′en·list′, *v.*
pre′en·list′ment, *n.*
pre′en·roll′, *v.*
pre′en·roll′ment, *n.*
pre′en·tail′, *v.t.*
pre′en·tail′ment,
pre·en′ter, *v.i.*
pre′en·ter·tain′, *v.t.*
pre′en·ter·tain′er, *n.*
pre′en·ter·tain′ment, *n.*
pre′en·thu′si·asm′, *n.*
pre′en·ti′tle, *v.t.,* **-tled, -tling.**
pre·en′trance, *n.*
pre·en′try, *n.*
pre′e·nu′mer·ate′, *v.t.,* **-at·ed, -at·ing.**
pre′e·nu′mer·a′tion, *n.*
pre′en·vel′op, *v.t.*
pre′en·vel′op·ment, *n.*
pre′en·vi′ron·men′tal, *adj.*
pre′ep·i·dem′ic, *n., adj.*
pre·ep′och·al, *adj.*
pre′e·quip′, *v.t.,* **-quipped, -quip·ping.**
pre′e·quip′ment, *n.*
pre·eq′ui·ty, *n.*
pre′e·rect′, *v.t.*
pre′e·rec′tion, *n.*
pre′e·rupt′, *v.i.*
pre′e·rup′tion, *n.*
pre′e·rup′tive, *adj.;* **-ly,** *adv.*
pre′es·cape′, *n., v.i.,* **-caped, -cap·ing.**
pre′e·soph′a·ge′al, *adj.*
pre·es′say, *n.*
pre′es·say′, *v.i.*
pre′es·sen′tial, *n., adj.;* **-ly,** *adv.*
pre′es·teem′, *v.t.*
pre·es′ti·mate′, *v.t.,* **-mat·ed, -mat·ing.**
pre·es′ti·mate, *n.*
pre′es·ti·ma′tion, *n.*
pre·es′ti·val, *adj.*
pre′e·ter′nal, *adj.*
pre′e·ter′ni·ty, *n.*
pre′e·vade′, *v.t.,* **-vad·ed, -vad·ing.**

pre·ex·il·i·an (prē′eg zil′ē ən, -zil′yən, -ek sil′-), *adj.* being or occurring prior to the exile of the Jews in Babylonia 597–538 B.C. Also, **pre′-ex·il′i·an, pre′-ëx·il′i·an, pre′ex·il′ic, pre′-ex·il′ic, pre′ëx·il′ic.** [PRE- + L *exili(um)* EXILE + -AN]

pre·ex·ist (prē′ig zist′), *v.i.* **1.** to exist beforehand. **2.** to exist in a previous state. —*v.t.* **3.** to exist prior to (something or someone else): *The Indians preexisted the first white colonists in the New World.* Also, **pre′-ex·ist′, pre′ëx·ist′.** [PRE- + EXIST] —**pre′ex·ist′ence, pre′-ex·ist′ence, pre′ëx·ist′ence,** *n.* —**pre′ex·ist′ent, pre′-ex·ist′ent, pre′ëx·ist′ent,** *adj.*

pre·ex·po·sure (prē′ik spō′zhər), *n.* **1.** exposure beforehand. **2.** *Photog.* the exposing of a film to even light, before photographing a subject, to increase its sensitivity. Also, **pre′-ex·po′sure, pre′ëx·po′sure.** [PRE- + EXPOSURE]

pref., **1.** preface. **2.** prefaced. **3.** prefatory. **4.** preference. **5.** preferred. **6.** prefix. **7.** prefixed.

pre·fab (*adj., n.* prē′fab′; *v.* prē fab′), *adj., n., v.,* **-fabbed, -fab·bing.** —*adj.* **1.** prefabricated. —*n.* **2.** something prefabricated. —*v.t.* **3.** to prefabricate. [by shortening]

pre·fab·ri·cate (prē fab′rə kāt′), *v.t.,* **-cat·ed, -cat·ing.** **1.** to fabricate or construct beforehand. **2.** to manufacture in standardized parts or sections ready for quick assembly and erection, as buildings. [PRE- + FABRICATE] —**pre′fab·ri·ca′tion,** *n.* —**pre·fab′ri·ca′tor,** *n.*

pref·ace (pref′is), *n., v.,* **-aced, -ac·ing.** —*n.* **1.** a preliminary statement by the author or editor of a book, setting forth its purpose and scope, expressing acknowledgment of assistance from others, etc. **2.** an introductory part, as of a speech. **3.** something preliminary or introductory: *The accident was the preface to a great scientific discovery.* **4.** *Eccles.* a prayer of thanksgiving, the introduction to the canon of the Mass, ending with the *Sanctus.* —*v.i.* **5.** to provide with or introduce by a preface. **6.** to serve as a preface to. [ME < MF < ML *prēfātia* for L *praefātiō* a saying beforehand, equiv. to *praefāt(us)* aforesaid (ptp. of *praefārī*) + *-iō* -ION] —**pref′ac·er,** *n.*
—**Syn. 1.** See **introduction. 2, 3.** preamble, prologue, prolegomena. —**Ant. 1.** appendix. **2, 3.** epilogue.

pre·fac·tor (prē′fak′tər), *n.* *Math.* an expression, written before another expression, which is to multiply it. In $a \times b$, $a \cdot b$, and ab, a is the prefactor. [PRE- + FACTOR]

pref·a·to·ry (pref′ə tōr′ē, -tôr′ē), *adj.* of, pertaining to, or of the nature of a preface: *prefatory explanations.* Also, **pref′a·to′ri·al.** [< L *praefāt(iō)* PREFACE + -ORY[1]] —**pref′a·to′ri·ly,** *adv.*

pre·fect (prē′fekt), *n.* **1.** a person appointed to any of various positions of command, authority, or superintendence, as a chief magistrate in ancient Rome, or the chief administrative official of a department of France and Italy. **2.** *Rom. Cath. Ch.* **a.** the dean of a Jesuit school or college. **b.** a cardinal in charge of a congregation in the Curia Romana. **3.** *Chiefly Brit.* a praeposter. Also, **praefect.** [ME < L *praefect(us)* overseer, director (n. use of ptp. of *praeficere* to make before, i.e., put in charge), equiv. to *prae-* PRE- + *-fectus* (comb. form of *factus,* ptp. of *facere* to make); see FACT]

pre′fect apostol′ic, *pl.* **prefects apostolic.** *Rom. Cath. Ch.* the administrator, usually below the rank of bishop, in charge of a prefecture apostolic.

pre·fec·to·ri·al (prē′fek tōr′ē əl, -tôr′-), *adj.* of, pertaining to, or characteristic of a prefect: *prefectorial powers.* [< LL *praefectōri(us)* (see PREFECT, -ORY[1]) + -AL[1]]

pre·fec·ture (prē′fek chər), *n.* the office, jurisdiction, territory, or official residence of a prefect. [< L *praefectūra.* See PREFECT, -URE] —**pre·fec·tur·al** (pri fek′chər əl), *adj.*

prefec′ture apostol′ic, *pl.* **prefectures apostolic.** *Rom. Cath. Ch.* a territory in the early stage of missionary development.

pre·fer (pri fûr′), *v.t.,* **-ferred, -fer·ring.** **1.** to set or hold before or above other persons or things in estimation; like better; choose rather than: *to prefer Hemingway to Steinbeck.* **2.** *Law.* to give priority, as to one creditor over another. **3.** to put forward or present (a statement, suit, charge, etc.) for consideration or sanction. **4.** to put forward or advance, as in rank or office: *to be preferred for advancement.* [ME *preferre* < L *praeferre* to bear before, set before, prefer, equiv. to *prae-* PRE- + *ferre* to BEAR[1]] —**pre·fer·red·ly** (pri fûr′id lē, -fûrd′-), *adv.* —**pre·fer′red·ness,** *n.* —**pre·fer′rer,** *n.*
—**Syn. 1.** favor, fancy. See **choose. 3.** offer, proffer, tender. **4.** promote. —**Ant. 1.** reject. **3.** retract. **4.** demote.

pref·er·a·ble (pref′ər ə bəl, pref′rə-), *adj.* **1.** worthy to be preferred. **2.** more desirable. [< F *préférable.* See PREFER, -ABLE] —**pref′er·a·bil′i·ty, pref′er·a·ble·ness,** *n.* —**pref′er·a·bly,** *adv.*

pref·er·ence (pref′ər əns, pref′rəns), *n.* **1.** the act of preferring. **2.** the state of being preferred. **3.** that which is preferred: *His preference is for simple cooking.* **4.** a practical advantage given to one over others. **5.** a prior right or claim, as to payment of dividends or to assets upon dissolution. **6.** the favoring of one country or group of countries by granting special advantages over others in international trade. [< ML *praeferentia.* See PREFER, -ENCE]
—**Syn. 3.** selection, pick. See **choice.**

pref′erence share′, *Brit.* a share of preferred stock.

pref′erence stock′, *Brit.* See **preferred stock.**

pref·er·en·tial (pref′ə ren′shəl), *adj.* **1.** of, pertaining to, or of the nature of preference: *preferential policies.* **2.** showing or giving preference: *a preferential hiring system.* **3.** receiving or enjoying preference, as a country in trade relations. [< ML *praeferenti(a)* PREFERENCE + -AL[1]] —**pref′er·en′tial·ism,** *n.* —**pref′er·en′tial·ist,** *n.* —**pref′er·en′tial·ly,** *adv.*

pref′eren′tial shop′, a shop in which union members are preferred, usually by agreement of an employer with a union.

pref′eren′tial vot′ing, a system of voting designed to permit the voter to indicate his order of preference for the candidates on the ballot.

pre·fer·ment (pri fûr′mənt), *n.* **1.** act of preferring. **2.** state of being preferred. **3.** advancement or promotion, as in rank: *They congratulated him on his preferment in the clergy.* **4.** a position or office giving social or pecuniary advancement. [late ME; see PREFER, -MENT]

preferred′ lie′, *Golf.* a position of a ball improved from the one where it landed and to which it can sometimes be moved without loss of a stroke or strokes to the player.

preferred′ posi′tion, especially desirable advertising space for which, if it is specifically requested by the advertiser, a publication charges a premium rate. Cf. **r.o.p.**

preferred′ stock′, stock which has a superior claim to that of common stock with respect to dividends and often to assets in the event of liquidation.

pre·fig·u·ra·tion (prē fig′yə rā′shən, prē′fig-), *n.* **1.** act of prefiguring. **2.** that in which something is prefigured. [ME *prefiguracioun* < LL *praefigūrātiōn-* (s. of *praefigūrātiō*), equiv. to *praefigūrāt(us)* (ptp. of *praefigūrāre* to PREFIGURE) + *-iōn-* -ION]

pre·fig·ure (prē fig′yər), *v.t.,* **-ured, -ur·ing.** **1.** to represent beforehand by a figure or type; foreshadow. **2.** to represent to oneself beforehand; imagine. [late ME < LL *praefigūrāre.* See PRE-, FIGURE (v.)] —**pre·fig·ur·a·tive** (prē fig′yər ə tiv), *adj.* —**pre·fig′ur·a·tive·ly,** *adv.* —**pre·fig′ur·a·tive·ness,** *n.* —**pre·fig′ure·ment,** *n.*

pre·fix (*n.* prē′fiks; *v.* prē fiks′, prē′fiks), *n.* **1.** *Gram.* an affix placed before a base or another prefix, as *un-* in *unkind, un-* and *re-* in *unrewarding.* **2.** something prefixed, as a title before a person's name. [< NL *praefix(um),* neut. of *praefixus.* See PRE-, FIX] —*v.t.* **3.** to fix or put before or in front. **4.** *Gram.* to add as a prefix. **5.** *Rare.* to fix, settle, or appoint beforehand. [late ME < MF *prefix(er)* < L *praefix(us),* ptp. of *praefigere* to set up in front] —**pre·fix′a·ble,** *adj.* —**pre·fix·al** (prē′fik səl, prē fik′-), *adj.* —**pre′fix·al·ly,** *adv.* —**pre·fix·ion** (prē fik′shən), *n.*

pre·form (*v.* prē fôrm′; *n.* prē′fôrm′), *v.t.* **1.** to form beforehand. **2.** to determine or decide beforehand: *to preform an opinion.* **3.** to shape or fashion beforehand: *to preform a mold.* **4.** biscuit (def. 5). —*n.* **5.** any of various uncompleted objects of manufacture after preliminary shaping. [< L *praeform(āre).* See PRE-, FORM]

pre·for·ma·tion (prē′fôr mā′shən), *n.* **1.** previous formation. **2.** *Biol.* (formerly) the theory that the individual, with all its parts, preexists in the germ and grows from microscopic to normal proportions during embryogenesis (opposed to *epigenesis*). [PRE- + FORMATION] —**pre′for·ma′tion·ar·y,** *adj.*

pre·fron·tal (prē frun′tᵊl), *adj.* *Anat.* of, pertaining to, or situated in the anterior part of a frontal structure. [PRE- + FRONTAL]

prefron′tal lobot′omy, *Surg.* a lobotomy performed in the region of the anterior portion of the frontal lobe of the brain.

Pregl (prā′gəl), *n.* **Fritz** (frits), 1869–1930, Austrian chemist: Nobel prize 1923.

pre·gla·cial (prē glā′shəl), *adj.* prior to a given glacial epoch, esp. the Pleistocene. [PRE- + GLACIAL]

preg·na·ble (preg′nə bəl), *adj.* **1.** capable of being taken or won by force: *a pregnable fortress.* **2.** open to attack; assailable: *His flimsy argument is quite pregnable.* [late ME *prenable* < MF, equiv. to *pren-* (weak s. of *prendre* < L *pre(he)ndere* to seize, take) + *-able* -ABLE; *-g-* perh. from *expugnable* (now obs.). See IMPREGNABLE] —**preg′na·bil′i·ty,** *n.*

preg·nan·cy (preg′nən sē), *n., pl.* **-cies.** state, condition, or quality of being pregnant. [PREGNAN(T) + -CY]

preg·nant (preg′nənt), *adj.* **1.** having a child or other offspring developing in the body; with child or young, as a woman or female mammal. **2.** fraught, filled, or abounding (usually fol. by *with*): *a silence pregnant with suspense.* **3.** fertile; rich (often fol. by *in*): *a mind pregnant in ideas.* **4.** full of meaning; highly significant: *a pregnant utterance.* **5.** full of possibilities; involving important issues or results; momentous: *a pregnant moment in the history of the world.* **6.** teeming with ideas or imagination: *a pregnant wit.* [late ME < L *praegnant-* (s. of *praegnāns*) heavy with young, equiv. to *prae-* PRE- + *gn-* (as in *gnatus* born) + *-ant* -ANT; see KIN] —**preg′nant·ly,** *adv.* —**preg′nant·ness,** *n.*

pre·hard·en·er (prē här′dᵊnər, -härd′nər), *n.* **1.** one who or that which prehardens. **2.** *Photog.* a solution for protecting film against the effects of the excessive warmth of a developer. [PRE- + HARDENER]

pre·heat (prē hēt′), *v.t.* to heat before using or before subjecting to some further process: *to preheat an oven before baking a cake.* [PRE- + HEAT] —**pre·heat′er,** *n.*

pre·hen·si·ble (pri hen′sə bəl), *adj.* able to be seized or grasped. [< L *prehens(us)* (see PREHENSION) + -IBLE]

pre·hen·sile (pri hen′sil, -sīl), *adj.* **1.** adapted for seizing, grasping, or taking hold of something: *a prehensile limb.* **2.** fitted for grasping by folding or wrapping around an object: *a monkey with a prehensile tail.* [PREHENS(ION) + -ILE (coined by Buffon)] —**pre·hen·sil·i·ty** (prē′hen sil′i tē), *n.*

pre·hen·sion (pri hen′shən), *n.* **1.** act of seizing or grasping. **2.** mental apprehension. [< L *prehen-siōn-* (s. of *prehensiō*) a taking hold, equiv. to *prehens(us)* (ptp. of *prehendere* to seize) + *-iōn-* -ION]

pre·his·tor·ic (prē′hi stôr′ik, -stor′-), *adj.* of or pertaining to a period prior to recorded history: *The dinosaur is a prehistoric beast.* Also, **pre′his·tor′i·cal.** [PRE- + HISTORIC] —**pre′his·tor′i·cal·ly,** *adv.*

pre·his·to·ry (prē his′tə rē, -his′trē), *n., pl.* **-ries.** **1.** the history of man in the period before recorded events, known mainly through archaeological discoveries, study, research, etc.; history of prehistoric man. **2.** a history of the events or incidents leading to a crisis, situation, or the like. [PRE- + HISTORY] —**pre·his·to·ri·an** (prē′hi stôr′ē ən, -stōr′-), *n.*

prehn·ite (prā′nīt, pren′it), *n.* a mineral, hydrous calcium aluminum silicate, occurring in light-green reniform aggregates or tabular crystals. [named after Col. Van Prehn, 18th-century Dutchman who brought it from South Africa to Europe; see -ITE[1]]

pre′e·vap′o·rate′, *v.,* **-rat·ed, -rat·ing.**
pre′e·vap′o·ra′tion, *n.*
pre′e·vap′o·ra′tor, *n.*
pre′e·va′sion, *n.*
pre·ev′i·dence, *n.*
pre·ev′i·dent, *adj.;* **-ly,** *adv.*
pre′ev·o·lu′tion·al, *adj.*
pre′ev·o·lu′tion·ar′y, *adj.*
pre′ev·o·lu′tion·ist, *n.*
pre′ex·act′, *adj., v.t.*
pre′ex·ac′tion, *n.*
pre′ex·am′i·na′tion, *n.*
pre′ex·am′ine, *v.t.,* **-ined, -in·ing.**
pre′ex·am′in·er, *n.*
pre′ex·cept′, *v.t.*
pre′ex·cep′tion, *n.*
pre′ex·cep′tion·al, *adj.;* **-ly,** *adv.*
pre′ex·change′, *v.t.,* **-changed, -chang·ing.**
pre′ex·ci·ta′tion, *n.*
pre′ex·cite′, *v.t.,* **-cit·ed, -cit·ing.**
pre′ex·clude′, *v.t.,* **-clud·ed, -clud·ing.**
pre′ex·clu′sion, *n.*
pre′ex·clu′sive, *adj.;* **-ly,** *adv.*
pre′ex·cur′sion, *n.*
pre′ex·cuse′, *v.t.,* **-cused, -cus·ing.**
pre·ex′e·cute′, *v.t.,* **-cut·ed, -cut·ing.**
pre′ex·e·cu′tion, *n.*
pre′ex·ec′u·tor, *n.*
pre′ex·empt′, *v.t.*
pre′ex·emp′tion, *n.*
pre′ex·haust′, *v.t.*
pre′ex·haus′tion, *n.*
pre′ex·hib′it, *n., v.t.*
pre′ex·hi·bi′tion, *n.*
pre′ex·hib′i·tor, *n.*
pre′ex·pand′, *v.t.*
pre′ex·pan′sion, *n.*
pre′ex·pect′, *v.t.*
pre′ex·pect′ant, *n.*
pre′ex·pec·ta′tion, *n.*
pre′ex·pe·di′tion, *n.*
pre′ex·pe·di′tion·ar′y, *adj.*
pre′ex·pend′, *v.t.*
pre′ex·pend′i·ture, *n.*
pre′ex·pense′, *n.*
pre′ex·pe′ri·ence, *n., v.t.,* **-enced, -enc·ing.**
pre′ex·per′i·ment, *n.*
pre′ex·per′i·men′tal, *adj.*
pre′ex·pi·ra′tion, *n.*
pre′ex·plain′, *v.*
pre′ex·pla·na′tion, *n.*
pre′ex·plan′a·to′ry, *adj.*
pre′ex·plode′, *v.,* **-plod·ed, -plod·ing.**
pre′e·xplo′sion, *n.*
pre′ex·pose′, *v.t.,* **-posed, -pos·ing.**
pre′ex·po·si′tion, *n.*
pre′ex·pound′, *v.t.*
pre′ex·pound′er, *n.*
pre′ex·press′, *v.t.*
pre′ex·pres′sion, *n.*
pre′ex·pres′sive, *adj.*
pre′ex·tend′, *v.*
pre′ex·ten′sive, *adj.;* **-ly,** *adv.*
pre′ex·tent′, *n.*
pre′ex·tinc′tion, *n.*
pre′ex·tin′guish, *v.t.*
pre′ex·tin′guish·ment, *n.*
pre′ex·tract′, *v.t.*
pre′ex·trac′tion, *n.*
pre′fa·mil′iar, *adj.;* **-ly,** *adv.*
pre′fa·mil′i·ar′i·ty, *n.*
pre·fa′mous, *adj.;* **-ly,** *adv.*
pre·fash′ion, *v.t., n.*
pre·fash′ioned, *adj.*
pre·fa′vor, *n., v.t.*
pre·fa′vor·a·ble, *adj.;* **-bly,** *adv.*
pre·fa′vor·ite, *n., adj.*
pre·fear′ful, *adj.;* **-ly,** *adv.*
pre·feast′, *n.*
pre′fec·un·da′tion, *n.*
pre′fer·men·ta′tion, *n.*
pre·fer′rous, *adj.*
pre·fer′tile, *adj.*
pre′fer·til′i·ty, *n.*
pre′fer·ti·li·za′tion, *n.*
pre·fer′ti·lize′, *v.t.,* **-lized, -liz·ing.**
pre·fes′ti·val, *n.*
pre·feu′dal, *adj.*
pre·feu′dal·ism, *n.*
pre·fill′er, *n.*
pre′fi·nance′, *v.t.,* **-nanced, -nanc·ing.**
pre′fi·nan′cial, *adj.*
pre·fin′ish, *v.t., n.*
pre·flag′el·late′, *adj.*
pre·flag′el·lat′ed, *adj.*
pre·flat′ter, *v.t.*
pre·fla′vor, *n., v.t.*
pre·flight′, *n.*
pre·flood′, *adj.*
pre·flow′er·ing, *adj.*
pre′for·bid′den, *adj.*
pre′for·give′, *v.t.* **-gave, -giv·en, -giv·ing.**
pre′for·give′ness, *n.*
pre·for′mu·late′, *v.t.,* **-lat·ed, -lat·ing.**
pre′for·mu·la′tion, *n.*
pre′foun·da′tion, *n.*
pre·found′er, *n.*
pre·frank′ness, *n.*
pre′fra·ter′nal, *adj.;* **-ly,** *adv.*
pre·fraud′, *n.*
pre′free′-trade′, *adj.*
pre·freeze′, *v.t.,* **-froze, -fro·zen, -freez·ing.**
pre-French′, *adj.*
pre·fresh′man, *n., pl.* **-men.**
pre·friend′ly, *adj.*
pre·friend′ship, *n.*
pre′ful·fill′, *v.t.*
pre′ful·fill′ment, *n.*
pre·func′tion, *n.*
pre·func′tion·al, *adj.*
pre·fu′ner·al, *adj.*
pre·fur′lough, *n.*
pre·fur′nish, *v.t.*
pre·gain′, *v.t.*
pre·gain′er, *n.*
pre·gal′va·nize′, *v.t.,* **-nized, -niz·ing.**
pre·game′, *adj.*
pre′gan·gli·on′ic, *adj.*
pre·gas′tru·lar, *adj.*
pre·gath′er, *v.i.*
pre·gen′er·ate′, *v.t.,* **-at·ed, -at·ing.**
pre′gen·er·a′tion, *n.*
pre·gen′i·tal, *adj.*
pre′ge·o·log′i·cal, *adj.*
pre-Geor′gian, *adj.*
pre-Ger′man, *adj., n.*
pre′-Ger·man′ic, *adj., n.*
pre·girl′hood, *n.*
pre-Goth′ic, *adj., n.*
pre·grade′, *v.t.,* **-grad·ed, -grad·ing;** *n.*
pre′grad·u·a′tion, *n.*
pre·gran′ite, *n., adj.*
pre′gra·nit′ic, *adj.*
pre′grat·i·fi·ca′tion, *n.*
pre·grat′i·fy′, *v.t.,* **-fied, -fy·ing.**
pre-Greek′, *adj., n.*
pre·greet′, *v.t.*
pre·griev′ance, *n.*
pre·growth′, *n.*
pre′guar·an·tee′, *n., v.t.,* **-teed, -tee·ing.**
pre·guar′an·tor′, *n.*
pre·guard′, *v.t.*
pre·guess′, *n., v.*
pre·guid′ance, *n.*
pre·guide′, *v.t.,* **-guid·ed, -guid·ing.**
pre·guilt′, *n.*
pre-Han′, *adj.*
pre·hand′i·cap′, *n., v.t.,* **-capped, -cap·ping.**
pre·han′dle, *v.t.,* **-dled, -dling.**
pre·hard′en, *v.t.*
pre′har·mo′ni·ous, *adj.;* **-ly,** *adv.;* **-ness,** *n.*
pre·har′mo·ny, *n.*
pre·har′vest, *n.*
pre·ha′tred, *n.*
pre·haz′ard, *adj.*
pre·heal′, *v.t.*
pre·hear′ing, *n.*
pre-He′brew, *adj., n.*
pre′-Hel·len′ic, *adj.*
pre′hem·i·ple′gic, *adj.*
pre·hes′i·tan·cy, *n.*
pre·hes′i·tate′, *v.i.,* **-tat·ed, -tat·ing.**
pre′hes·i·ta′tion, *n.*
pre′hex·am′er·al, *adj.*
pre′-Hi·e·ro·nym′i·an, *adj.*
pre′-His·pan′ic, *adj.*

CONCISE ETYMOLOGY KEY: <, descended or derived from; >, whence; b., blend of, blended; c., cognate with; deriv., derivative; equiv., equivalent; imit., imitative; m., modification of; obl., oblique; r., replacing; s., stem; sp., spelling; trans., translation; ?, origin unknown, perhaps; *, hypothetical. See the full key inside the front cover.

pre·hu·man (prē hyōō′mən *or, often,* -yōō′-), *adj.* preceding the appearance or existence of human beings: *the prehuman ages.* [PRE- + HUMAN]

pre·ig·ni·tion (prē′ig nish′ən), *n.* ignition of the charge in an internal-combustion engine earlier in the cycle than is compatible with proper operation. [PRE- + IGNITION]

pre-In·can (prē ing′kən), *adj.* of or pertaining to the period preceding the Incan empire in Peru.

pre·in·car·na·tion (prē in′kär nā′shən, prē′in-), *n.* a previous incarnation or an existence before incarnation. [PRE- + INCARNATION]

pre·in·cline (prē′in klīn′), *v.t.*, **-clined, -clin·ing.** to dispose or prepare beforehand: *Their experiences had preinclined them to think pessimistically.* [PRE- + INCLINE] —**pre·in·cli·na·tion** (prē in′klə nā′shən, prē′in-), *n.*

pre·in·di·cate (prē in′də kāt′), *v.t.*, **-cat·ed, -cat·ing.** to indicate in advance: *The early thaw preindicated an avalanche.* [PRE- + INDICATE] —**pre·in′di·ca′tion,** *n.*

pre·in·form (prē′in fôrm′), *v.t.* to supply with information beforehand: *He preinformed the newspapers of his decision.* [PRE- + INFORM[1]]

pre·in·struct (prē′in strukt′), *v.t.* to instruct in advance: *to preinstruct a child in reading.* [PRE- + INSTRUCT] —**pre′in·struc′tion,** *n.* —**pre′in·struc′tion·al,** *adj.* —**pre′in·struc′tive,** *adj.*

pre·in·va·sive (prē′in vā′siv), *adj.* *Pathol.* of or pertaining to a stage preceding invasion of the tissues. [PRE- + INVASIVE]

pre-Is·lam·ic (prē′is lam′ik, -lä′mik), *adj.* existing prior to the influence of Islam; pre-Muslim.

pre·judge (prē juj′), *v.t.*, **-judged, -judg·ing. 1.** to judge beforehand. **2.** to pass judgment on prematurely or without sufficient reflection or investigation. [< F *préjug(er)* < L *praejūdicāre.* See PRE-, JUDGE] —**pre·judg′er,** *n.* —**pre·judg′ment;** *esp. Brit.,* **pre·judge′ment,** *n.*

prej·u·dice (prej′ə dis), *n., v.,* **-diced, -dic·ing.** —*n.* **1.** an unfavorable opinion or feeling formed beforehand or without knowledge, thought, or reason. **2.** any preconceived opinion or feeling, either favorable or unfavorable. **3.** unreasonable feelings, opinions, or attitudes, esp. of a hostile nature, directed against a racial, religious, or national group. **4.** such attitudes considered collectively: *The war against prejudice is never-ending.* **5.** disadvantage resulting from some judgment or action of another: *a law that operated to the prejudice of the majority.* **6.** resulting injury or detriment. **7. without prejudice,** *Law.* without dismissing, damaging, or otherwise affecting a legal interest or demand. —*v.t.* **8.** to affect with a prejudice, either favorable or unfavorable: *His honesty and sincerity prejudiced us in his favor.* **9.** to affect to the disadvantage or detriment of; damage; injure: *Lack of education prejudiced his chances for success.* [ME < OF < L *praejūdic(ium)* prejudgment, orig. preliminary or previous judicial inquiry, equiv. to *prae-* PRE- + *jūdicium* trial, deriv. of *jūdex* (s. *jūdici-*) JUDGE] —**prej′u·diced·ly,** *adv.* —**prej′u·dice·less,** *adj.*
—**Syn. 2.** preconception, partiality, predilection, predisposition. See **bias. 8.** bias, influence.

prej·u·di·cial (prej′ə dish′əl), *adj.* causing prejudice or disadvantage; detrimental. [late ME (see PREJUDICE, -AL[1]); cf. ML *prejūdiciālis*] —**prej′u·di′cial·ly,** *adv.* —**prej′u·di′cial·ness,** *n.*

prel·a·cy (prel′ə sē), *n., pl.* **-cies. 1.** the office or dignity of a prelate. **2.** the order of prelates. **3.** the body of prelates collectively. **4.** *Often Derogatory.* the system of church government by prelates. [ME *prelacie* < AF < ML *praelātia.* See PRELATE, -Y[3]]

prel·ate (prel′it), *n.* an ecclesiastic of a high order, as an archbishop, bishop, etc.; a church dignitary. [ME *prelat* < ML *praelāt(us)* a civil or ecclesiastical dignitary, n. use of L *praelātus* (ptp. of *praeferre* to set before), equiv. to *prae-* PRE- + *lātus,* ptp. of *ferre* to bear] —**prel′ate·ship′,** *n.* —**pre·lat·ic** (pri lat′ik), *adj.*

prel·a·tism (prel′ə tiz′əm), *n.* prelacy; episcopacy. [PRELATE + -ISM] —**prel′a·tist,** *n.*

prel·a·ture (prel′ə chər), *n.* **1.** the office of a prelate. **2.** the order of prelates. **3.** prelates collectively. [< ML *praelātūra.* See PRELATE, -URE]

pre·lect (pri lekt′), *v.i.* to lecture or discourse publicly. Also, **praelect.** [< L *praelect(us),* ptp. of *praelegere* to lecture, equiv. to *prae-* PRE- + *legere* to read aloud, choose] —**pre·lec·tion** (pri lek′shən), *n.* —**pre·lec′tor,** *n.*

pre·li·ba·tion (prē′lī bā′shən), *n.* a foretaste. [< LL *praelībātiōn-* (s. of *praelībātiō*) a foretaste, equiv. to *praelībāt(us)* (ptp. of *praelībāre* to taste beforehand) + *-iōn-* -ION. See PRE-, LIBATION]

pre·lim (prē′lim, prə lim′), *n.* *Slang.* preliminary. [by shortening]

prelim., preliminary.

pre·lim·i·nar·y (pri lim′ə ner′ē), *adj., n., pl.* **-nar·ies.** —*adj.* **1.** preceding and leading up to the main part, matter, or business; introductory; preparatory: *preliminary examinations.* —*n.* **2.** something preliminary, as an introductory or preparatory step, measure, contest, etc.: *He passed the preliminary and went on to the finals.* **3.** a boxing match or other athletic contest that takes place before the main event on the program: *A preliminary was fought at 8:00.* **4.** a preliminary examination, as of a candidate for an academic degree. **5. preliminaries,** *Print.* See **front matter.** [< NL *praelīmināri(s).* See PRE-, LIMINAL, -ARY] —**pre·lim′i·nar′i·ly,** *adv.*
—**Syn. 1.** prefatory. PRELIMINARY, INTRODUCTORY both refer to that which comes before the principal subject of consideration. That which is PRELIMINARY is in the nature of preparation or of clearing away details which would encumber the main subject or problem; it often deals with arrangements and the like, which have to do only incidentally with the principal subject: *preliminary negotiations.* That which is INTRODUCTORY leads with natural, logical, or close connection directly into the main subject of consideration: *introductory steps.* —**Ant. 1.** concluding.

pre·lim·it (prē lim′it), *v.t.* to limit within bounds beforehand: *The chairman prelimited his speech to ten minutes.* [PRE- + LIMIT] —**pre·lim′i·ta′tion,** *n.*

pre·lit·er·ate (prē lit′ər it), *adj.* not leaving or having written records: *In New Guinea we find a contemporary preliterate culture.* [PRE- + LITERATE]

prel·ude (prel′yōōd, prāl′-, prē′lōōd, prā′-), *n., v.,* **-ud·ed, -ud·ing.** —*n.* **1.** a preliminary to an action, event, condition, or work of broader scope and higher importance. **2.** preliminary action, remarks, etc. **3.** *Music.* **a.** a relatively short, independent instrumental composition, free in form and of an improvised character. **b.** a piece which precedes a more important movement. **c.** the overture to an opera. **d.** an independent piece, of moderate length, sometimes used as an introduction to a fugue. **e.** music opening a church service; an introductory voluntary. [earlier *preludy* < ML *praelūdi(um)* foreplay, equiv. to *prae-* PRE- + *-lūdium* play, as in *hastilūdium* tournament (lit., spear-play); cf. L *lūdius* actor, lit., adj. of *lūdus* play, game]
—*v.t.* **4.** to serve as a prelude or introduction to. **5.** to introduce by a prelude. **6.** to play as a prelude.
—*v.i.* **7.** to serve as a prelude. **8.** to give a prelude. **9.** to play a prelude. [< L *praelūde(re)* (to) play beforehand] —**pre·lud·er** (pri lōō′dər, prel′yə dər), *n.* —**pre·lu′di·al, pre·lu′di·ous,** *adj.* —**pre·lu′di·ous·ly,** *adv.*

Prelude, The, an autobiographical poem in 14 books (1799–1805) by Wordsworth.

Pre·lu·din (pri lōōd′ən, prā-), *n.* *Pharm., Trademark.* phenmetrazine.

pre·lu·sion (pri lōō′zhən), *n.* a prelude. [< L *praelūsiōn-* (s. of *praelūsiō*) a prelude, equiv. to *praelūs(us)* (ptp. of *praelūdere;* see PRELUDE) + *-iōn-* -ION]

pre·lu·sive (pri lōō′siv), *adj.* introductory. Also, **pre·lu·so·ry** (pri lōō′sə rē). [< L *praelūs(us)* (see PRELUSION) + -IVE] —**pre·lu′sive·ly, pre·lu′so·ri·ly,** *adv.*

prem., premium.

pre·mar·i·tal (prē mar′i təl), *adj.* preceding marriage. [PRE- + MARITAL]

pre·ma·ture (prē′mə tōōr′, -tyōōr′, -chōōr′, prē′mə-chōōr′), *adj.* **1.** occurring, coming, or done too soon: *a premature announcement.* **2.** *Rare.* mature or ripe before the proper time. [< L *praemātūr(us).* See PRE-, MATURE] —**pre′ma·ture′ly,** *adv.* —**pre′ma·tu′ri·ty, pre′ma·ture′ness,** *n.*

pre′mature beat′, *Med.* extrasystole.

pre′mature contrac′tion, *Med.* extrasystole.

pre·max·il·la (prē′mak sil′ə), *n., pl.* **-max·il·lae** (-mak sil′ē). *Anat., Zool.* one of a pair of bones of the upper jaw of vertebrates, situated in front of and between the maxillary bones. [< NL *praemaxilla.* See PRE-, MAXILLA] —**pre·max·il·lar·y** (prē mak′sə ler′ē), *adj.*

pre·med (prē med′), *n.* Also, **pre·med′ic. 1.** a program of premedical study or training. **2.** a student enrolled in such a program. —*adj.* **3.** of or pertaining to premedical studies. [short for PREMEDICAL]

pre·med·i·cal (prē med′i kəl), *adj.* of or pertaining to studies in preparation for the formal study of medicine: *a premedical student; a premedical course.* [PRE- + MEDICAL]

pre·me·di·e·val (prē mē′dē ē′vəl, -med′ē-, prē′mē-dē-, prē′med ē-), *adj.* prior to the Middle Ages. [PRE- + MEDIEVAL]

pre·med·i·tate (pri med′i tāt′), *v.i., v.i.,* **-tat·ed, -tat·ing.** to meditate, consider, or plan beforehand: *The killing was proved to have been premeditated.* [< L *praemeditāt(us)* previously thought out, ptp. of *praemeditāre.* See PRE-, MEDITATE] —**pre·med′i·tat′ed·ly,**

pre·hold′er, *n.*
pre·hold′ing, *n.*
pre·hol′i·day, *adj.*
pre′-Ho·mer′ic, *adj.*
pre·hos′tile, *adj.*
pre′hos·til′i·ty, *n.*
pre·hu′mor, *n., v.t.*
pre·hun′ger, *n.*
pre′i·de′a, *n.*
pre′i·den′ti·fi·ca′tion, *n.*
pre′i·den′ti·fy′, *v.t.,* **-fied, -fy·ing.**
pre·il′i·um, *n.*
pre′il·lu′mi·nate′, *v.t.*
pre′il·lu′mi·na′tion, *n.*
pre·il′lus·trate′, *v.t.,* **-trat·ed, -trat·ing.**
pre′il·lus·tra′tion, *n.*
pre·im′age, *n.*
pre′i·mag′i·nar′y, *adj.*
pre′i·mag′i·na′tion, *n.*
pre′i·mag′ine, *v.t.,* **-ined, -in·ing.**
pre′im·bibe′, *v.t.,* **-bibed, -bib·ing.**
pre′im·bue′, *v.t.,* **-bued, -bu·ing.**
pre·im′i·tate′, *v.t.,* **-tat·ed, -tat·ing.**
pre·im′i·ta′tion, *n.*
pre·im′i·ta′tive, *adj.*
pre′im·mi·gra′tion, *n.*
pre′im·pair′, *v.t.*
pre′im·pair′ment, *n.*
pre′im·part′, *v.t.*
pre′im·pe′ri·al, *adj.*
pre′im·port′, *v.t.*
pre·im′port, *n.*
pre′im·por′tance, *n.*
pre′im·por′tant, *adj.;* **-ly,** *adv.*
pre′im·por·ta′tion, *n.*
pre′im·pose′, *v.t.,* **-posed, -pos·ing.**
pre′im·po·si′tion, *n.*
pre′im·press′, *v.t.*
pre′im·pres′sion, *n.*
pre′im·pres′sive, *adj.*
pre′im·prove′, *v.t.,* **-proved, -prov·ing.**
pre′im·prove′ment, *n.*
pre′in·au′gu·ral, *adj.*
pre′in·au′gu·rate′, *v.t.,* **-rat·ed, -rat·ing.**
pre′in·cen′tive, *n.*
pre′in·clude′, *v.t.,* **-clud·ed, -clud·ing.**
pre′in·clu′sion, *n.*
pre′in·cor′po·rate′, *v.t.,* **-rat·ed, -rat·ing;** *adj.*
pre′in·cor′po·ra′tion, *n.*
pre·in′crease, *n.*
pre′in·crease′, *v.t.,* **-creased, -creas·ing.**
pre′in·debt′ed, *adj.;* **-ly,** *adv.;* **-ness,** *n.*
pre′in·dem′ni·fi·ca′tion, *n.*
pre′in·dem′ni·fy′, *v.t.,* **-fied, -fy·ing.**
pre′in·dem′ni·ty, *n.*
pre′in·de·pend′ence, *n.*
pre′in·de·pend′ent, *adj.;* **-ly,** *adv.*
pre-In′di·an, *n., adj.*
pre′in·dis·pose′, *v.t.,* **-posed, -pos·ing.**
pre′in·dis·po·si′tion, *n.*
pre′in·duce′, *v.t.,* **-duced, -duc·ing.**
pre′in·duce′ment, *n.*
pre′in·duc′tion, *n.*
pre′in·duc′tive, *adj.*
pre′in·dulge′, *v.t.,* **-dulged, -dulg·ing.**
pre′in·dul′gence, *n.*
pre′in·dul′gent, *adj.*
pre′in·dus′tri·al, *adj.*
pre·in′dus·try, *n., adj.*
pre′in·fect′, *v.t.*
pre′in·fec′tion, *n.*
pre′in·fer′, *v.t.,* **-ferred, -fer·ring.**
pre·in′fer·ence, *n.*
pre′in·flec′tion, *n.*
pre′in·flec′tion·al, *adj.*
pre′in·flict′, *v.t.*
pre′in·flic′tion, *n.*
pre·in′flu·ence, *n.*
pre′in·hab′it, *v.t.*
pre′in·hab′it·ant, *n.*
pre′in·hab′i·ta′tion, *n.*
pre′in·here′, *v.i.,* **-hered, -her·ing.**
pre′in·her′it, *v.t.*
pre′in·her′it·ance, *n.*
pre′in·i′tial, *v.t.*
pre′in·i′ti·ate′, *v.t.,* **-at·ed, -at·ing.**
pre′in·i′ti·ate, *n.*
pre′in·i′ti·a′tion, *n.*
pre′in·ju′ri·ous, *adj.*
pre′in·qui·si′tion, *n.*
pre′in·scribe′, *v.t.,* **-scribed, -scrib·ing.**
pre′in·scrip′tion, *n.*
pre′in·sert′, *v.t.*
pre′in·ser′tion, *n.*
pre′in·sin′u·ate′, *v.,* **-at·ed, -at·ing.**
pre′in·sin′u·at′ing·ly, *adv.*
pre′in·sin′u·a′tion, *n.*
pre′in·sin′u·a′tive, *adj.*
pre′in·spect′, *v.t.*
pre′in·spec′tion, *n.*
pre′in·spec′tor, *n.*
pre′in·spire′, *v.t.,* **-spired, -spir·ing.**
pre′in·stall′, *v.t.*
pre′in·stal·la′tion, *n.*
pre′in·still′, *v.t.*
pre′in·stil·la′tion, *n.*
pre·in′su·late′, *v.t.,* **-lat·ed, -lat·ing.**
pre′in·su·la′tion, *n.*
pre′in·sult′, *v.t.*
pre′in·sur′ance, *n.*
pre′in·sure′, *v.t.,* **-sured, -sur·ing.**
pre′in·tel·lec′tu·al, *adj.;* **-ly,** *adv.*
pre′in·tel′li·gence, *n.*
pre′in·tel′li·gent, *adj.;* **-ly,** *adv.*
pre′in·tend′, *v.t.*
pre′in·ten′tion, *n.*
pre′in·ter·cede′, *v.i.,* **-ced·ed, -ced·ing.**
pre′in·ter·ces′sion, *n.*
pre′in·ter·change′, *n.*
pre·in′ter·course′, *n.*
pre·in′ter·est, *n., v.*
pre′in·ter′pret, *v.t.*
pre′in·ter′pre·ta′tion, *n.*
pre′in·ter′pre·ta′tive, *adj.*
pre·in′ter·view′, *n., v.t.*
pre·in′ti·mate, *adj.;* **-ly,** *adv.*
pre·in′ti·mate′, *v.t.,* **-mat·ed, -mat·ing.**
pre′in·ti·ma′tion, *n.*
pre′in·vent′, *v.t.*
pre′in·ven′tion, *n.*
pre′in·ven′tive, *adj.*
pre′in·ven′to′ry, *n., pl.* **-ries.**
pre′in·vest′, *v.t.*
pre′in·ves′ti·gate′, *v.,* **-gat·ed, -gat·ing.**
pre′in·ves′ti·ga′tion, *n.*
pre′in·ves′ti·ga′tor, *n.*
pre′in·vest′ment, *n.*
pre′in·vi·ta′tion, *n.*
pre′in·vite′, *v.t.,* **-vit·ed, -vit·ing.**
pre′in·vo·ca′tion, *n.*
pre′in·volve′, *v.t.,* **-volved, -volv·ing.**
pre′in·volve′ment, *n.*
pre-I′rish, *adj.*
pre′ir·ri·ga′tion, *n.*
pre′ir·ri·ga′tion·al, *adj.*
pre-Is′ra·el·ite′, *adj., n.*
pre·is′su·ance, *n.*
pre·is′sue, *n., v.t.,* **-sued, -su·ing.**
pre-Jew′ish, *adj.*
pre′jour·nal·is′tic, *adj.*
pre′ju·di′ci·a·ble, *adj.*
pre·jun′ior, *adj.*
pre′ju·ris·dic′tion, *n.*
pre′jus·ti·fi·ca′tion, *n.*
pre·jus′ti·fy′, *v.t.,* **-fied, -fy·ing.**
pre′-Jus·tin′i·an, *adj.*
pre·ju′ve·nile, *adj.*
pre-Kant′i·an, *adj.*
pre·kin′der·gar′ten, *n., adj.*
pre·kin′dle, *v.t.,* **-dled, -dling.**
pre·knit′, *v.t.,* **-knit·ted** or **-knit, -knit·ting.**
pre·know′, *v.t.,* **-knew, -known, -know·ing.**
pre·knowl′edge, *n.*
pre′-Ko·ran′ic, *adj.*
pre·la′bel, *n., v.t.,* **-beled, -bel·ing** or (*esp. Brit.*) **-belled, -bel·ling.**
pre·la′bi·al, *adj.*
pre·la′bor, *n., v.i.*
pre·lac′te·al, *adj.*
pre·lan′guage, *adj.*
pre′la·ryn′go·scop′ic, *adj.*
pre-Lat′in, *n.*
pre·launch′, *v.t.*
pre·law′ful, *adj.;* **-ly,** *adv.;* **-ness,** *n.*
pre·lease′, *n., v.,* **-leased, -leas·ing.**
pre·lec′ture, *n., adj., v.,* **-tured, -tur·ing.**
pre·le′gal, *adj.*
pre·leg′end, *n., adj.*
pre·leg′end·ar′y, *adj.*
pre·leg′is·la′tive, *adj.*
pre′li·a·bil′i·ty, *n.*
pre·li′a·ble, *adj.*
pre·lib′er·al, *adj., n.;* **-ly,** *adv.*
pre′lib·er·al′i·ty, *n.*
pre·lib′er·ate′, *v.t.,* **-at·ed, -at·ing.**
pre′lib·er·a′tion, *n.*
pre·li′cense, *n., v.t.,* **-censed, -cens·ing.**
pre·lim′i·tate′, *v.t.,* **-tat·ed, -tat·ing.**
pre·lin′gual, *adj.;* **-ly,** *adv.*
pre′-Lin·nae′an, *adj.*
pre′-Lin·ne′an, *adj.*
pre·liq′ui·date′, *v.t.,* **-dat·ed, -dat·ing.**
pre′liq·ui·da′tion, *n.*
pre·lit′er·ar′y, *adj.*
pre·lit′er·a·ture, *n.*
pre·lith′ic, *adj.*
pre′lit·i·ga′tion, *n.*
pre·loan′, *n., v.*
pre·lo′cate, *v.,* **-cat·ed, -cat·ing.**
pre·loss′, *n.*
pre·lum′bar, *adj.*
pre-Lu′ther·an, *adj.*
pre′lux·u′ri·ous, *adj.;* **-ly,** *adv.;* **-ness,** *n.*
pre·mad′ness, *n.*
pre′main·tain′, *v.t.*
pre·main′te·nance, *n.*
pre·make′, *v.t.,* **-made, -mak·ing.**
pre·mak′er, *n.*
pre-Ma′lay, *adj.*
pre′-Ma·lay′an, *adj.*
pre′-Ma·lay′sian, *adj.*
pre′man·dib′u·lar, *adj.*
pre·man′hood, *n.*
pre′ma·ni′a·cal, *adj.*
pre·man′i·fest′, *v.*
pre′man·i·fes·ta′tion, *n.*
pre′man′kind′, *n.*
pre′man·u·fac′ture, *v.t.,* **-tured, -tur·ing.**
pre·mar′riage, *n.*
pre·mar′ry, *v.t.,* **-ried, -ry·ing.**
pre-Marx′i·an, *adj.*
pre·mas′ter·y, *n.*
pre·match′, *n., v.t.*
pre·mate′, *n., v.t.,* **-mat·ed, -mat·ing.**
pre′ma·te′ri·al, *adj.*
pre′ma·ter′ni·ty, *n.*
pre′mat·ri·mo′ni·al, *adj.;* **-ly,** *adv.*
pre·meas′ure, *v.t.,* **-sured, -sur·ing.**
pre·meas′ure·ment, *n.*
pre·me′di·an, *n., adj.*
pre·med′i·cate′, *v.t.,* **-cat·ed, -cat·ing.**

adv. —**pre·med′i·tat′ed·ness,** *n.* —**pre·med′i·tat′-ing·ly,** *adv.* —**pre·med′i·ta′tive,** *adj.* —**pre·med′i-ta′tor,** *n.*
—**Syn.** See **deliberate.**

pre·med·i·ta·tion (pri med′i tā′shən), *n.* **1.** the act of premeditating. **2.** *Law.* sufficient forethought to impute deliberation and intent to commit the act. [late ME *premeditacion* < L *praemeditātiōn-* (s. of *praemeditātiō*) a considering beforehand. See PREMEDITATE, -ION]

pre·mi·ate (prē′mē āt′), *v.t.,* **-at·ed, -at·ing.** *Rare.* to grant a prize or an award to. [< ML *praemiāt(us),* ptp. of *praemiāre* to reward (L: stipulate for a reward). See PREMIUM, -ATE[1]]

pre·mie (prē′mē), *n.* *Slang.* a premature infant. Also, **preemie.** [shortening and alter. of PREMATURE]

pre·mier (pri mēr′, prim yēr′), *n.* **1.** the head of the cabinet in France and Italy and certain other countries; the first minister; prime minister. **2.** a chief officer. —*adj.* **3.** first in rank; chief; leading. **4.** first in time; earliest; oldest. [< F: lit., first < L *prīmār(ius)* of the first rank] —**pre·mier′ship,** *n.*

pre·mier dan·seur (*Fr.* prə myā dän sœr′), *n., pl.* **pre·miers dan·seurs** (*Fr.* prə myā dän sœr′). the leading male dancer in a ballet company. [< F]

pre·miere (pri mēr′, -myâr′), *n., v.,* **-miered, -mier·ing,** *adj.* —*n.* **1.** a first public performance of a play, opera, etc. **2.** the leading woman, as in a drama. —*v.t.* **3.** to present publicly for the first time: *to premiere a new foreign film.* —*v.i.* **4.** to have the first public showing: *It will premiere at the Arcadia Theatre.* **5.** to perform publicly for the first time, as in a particular role, entertainment medium, etc.: *When does he premiere as Hamlet?* —*adj.* **6.** first; initial; principal: *a premiere showing crowded with celebrities; the premiere attraction of the evening.* [< F: lit., first; fem. of PREMIER]

pre·mière (pri mēr′, -myâr′; *Fr.* prə myer′), *n., pl.* **-mières** (-mērz′, -myârz′; *Fr.* -myer′), *v.t., v.i.,* **-miered, -mier·ing,** *adj.* premiere.

pre·mière′ par·tie′ (pri mēr′ pär tē′, -myâr′; *Fr.* prə myer par tē′), *Furniture.* (in buhlwork) the primary inlay formed, in which the tortoise shell forms the ground for a design cut in brass. Cf. **contre-partie.** [< F: lit., the first part]

pre·mil·le·nar·i·an (prē′mil ə nâr′ē ən), *n.* **1.** a believer in premillennialism. —*adj.* **2.** of or pertaining to the doctrine of premillennialism or a believer in this doctrine. [PRE- + MILLENARIAN] —**pre′mil·le·nar′i·an·ism,** *n.*

pre·mil·len·ni·al (prē′mi len′ē əl), *adj.* of or pertaining to the period preceding the millennium. [PRE- + MILLENNIAL] —**pre′mil·len′ni·al·ly,** *adv.*

pre·mil·len·ni·al·ise (prē′mi len′ē ə līz′), *v.i.,* **-ised, -is·ing.** *Chiefly Brit.* premillennialize.

pre·mil·len·ni·al·ism (prē′mi len′ē ə liz′əm), *n.* the doctrine or belief that the Second Coming of Christ will precede the millennium. [PREMILLENNIAL + -ISM] —**pre′mil·len′ni·al·ist,** *n.*

pre·mil·len·ni·al·ize (prē′mi len′ē ə līz′), *v.i.,* **-ized, -iz·ing.** to support or believe in premillennialism. Also, *esp. Brit.,* **premillennialise.** [PREMILLENNIAL + -IZE]

Prem·in·ger (prem′in jər), *n.* **Otto (Ludwig),** born 1906, U.S. motion-picture actor, director, and producer, born in Austria.

prem·ise (prem′is), *n., v.,* **-ised, -is·ing.** —*n.* **1.** Also, **prem′iss.** *Logic.* a proposition supporting or helping to support a conclusion. **2. premises, a.** a tract of land including its buildings. **b.** a building together with its grounds or other appurtenances. **c.** the property forming the subject of a conveyance or bequest. **3.** *Law.* **a.** a basis, stated or assumed, on which reasoning proceeds. **b.** an earlier statement in a document. **c.** (in a bill in equity) the statement of facts upon which the complaint is based. —*v.t.* **4.** to set forth beforehand, as by way of introduction or explanation. **5.** to assume, either explicitly or implicitly, (a proposition) as a premise for a conclusion. —*v.i.* **6.** to state or assume a premise. [ME *premiss* < ML *praemissa,* n. use of fem. of L *praemissus* sent before, ptp. of *praemittere,* equiv. to *prae-* PRE- + *mittere* to send. See DISMISS, REMISS]
—**Syn. 1.** assumption, postulate. **5.** postulate, hypothecate.

pre·mi·um (prē′mē əm), *n.* **1.** a prize, bonus, or award given as an inducement, as to purchase products, enter competitions initiated by business interests, etc. **2.** a bonus, gift, or sum additional to price, wages, interest, or the like. **3.** *Insurance.* the amount paid or to be paid by the policyholder for coverage under the contract, usually in periodic installments. **4.** *Econ.* the excess value of one form of money over another of the same nominal value. **5.** a sum above the nominal or par value of a thing. **6.** the amount paid to the lender of stock by the borrower, typically a short seller. **7.** a fee paid for instruction in a trade or profession. **8.** a sum additional to the interest paid for the loan of money. **9. at a premium, a.** at an unusually high price. **b.** in short supply; in demand: *Housing in that area is at a premium.* [< L *praemium* profit, reward]
—**Syn. 2.** reward. See **bonus.**

pre′mium loan′, *Insurance.* a loan made by a life-insurance company in order that a policyholder may pay his due premium, the cash value on the policy serving as security.

pre-Mo·ham·med·an (prē′mō ham′i dᵊn), *adj.* pre-Islamic.

pre·mo·lar (prē mō′lər), *adj.* **1.** situated in front of the molar teeth. **2.** pertaining to a milk tooth which will later be supplanted by a permanent molar. —*n.* **3.** a premolar tooth. **4.** Also called **bicuspid.** (in man) any of eight teeth located in pairs on each side of the upper and lower jaws between the cuspids and molar teeth. [PRE- + MOLAR[1]]

pre·mon·ish (pri mon′ish), *v.t., v.i.* *Rare.* to warn beforehand. [PRE- + *monish,* ME *mones,* back formation from *monest* (*-t* being taken as sign of ptp.) < OF *monester,* unexplained deriv. of L *monēre* to remind, warn. See ADMONISH]

pre·mo·ni·tion (prē′mə nish′ən, prem′ə-), *n.* **1.** a forewarning. **2.** a feeling of anticipation of or anxiety over a future event; presentiment: *He had a vague premonition of danger.* [< LL *praemonitiōn-* (s. of *praemonitiō*) forewarning. See PRE-, MONITION]

pre·mon·i·to·ry (pri mon′i tōr′ē, -tôr′ē), *adj.* giving premonition; serving to warn beforehand. [< LL *praemonitōri(us).* See PRE-, MONITORY]

Pre·mont (prē mont′), *n.* a town in S Texas. 3049 (1960).

pre·morse (pri môrs′), *adj.* *Biol.* having the end irregularly truncate, as if bitten or broken off. [< L *praemors(us)* bitten off in front (ptp. of *praemordere*), equiv. to *prae-* PRE- + *morsus* bitten; see MORSEL]

pre·mul·ti·ply (prē mul′tə plī′), *v.t.,* **-plied, -ply·ing.** *Math.* to multiply (a quantity) by a prefactor. [PRE-(FACTOR) + MULTIPLY]

pre·mun·dane (prē mun′dān, prē′mən dān′), *adj.* before the creation of the world; antemundane. [PRE- + MUNDANE]

pre·na·tal (prē nāt′ᵊl), *adj.* previous to birth or to giving birth: *one's prenatal existence; prenatal care for mothers.* [PRE- + NATAL] —**pre·na′tal·ly,** *adv.*

Pren·der·gast (pren′dər gast′, -gäst′), *n.* **Maurice Braz·il** (braz′əl), 1859–1924, U.S. painter.

pre·no·men (prē nō′mən), *n., pl.* **-nom·i·na** (-nom′ə-nə, -nō′mə-), **-no·mens.** praenomen. —**pre·nom·i·nal** (prē nom′ə nᵊl), *adj.*

pre·nom·i·nate (pri nom′ə nāt′, -nit), *Obs.* —*adj.* **1.** mentioned beforehand. —*v.t.* **2.** to mention beforehand. [< L *praenōmināt(us)* named before, ptp. of *praenōmināre.* See PRE-, NOMINATE] —**pre·nom′i·na′tion,** *n.*

pre·no·tion (prē nō′shən), *n.* a preconception. [< L *praenōtiōn-* (s. of *praenōtiō*) an innate idea. See PRE-, NOTION]

pren·tice (pren′tis), *adj., n., v.* *Informal.* apprentice. [ME]

Pren·tice (pren′tis), *n.* a boy's given name.

pre·oc·cu·pan·cy (prē ok′yə pən sē), *n.* **1.** act, right, or instance of prior occupancy. **2.** state of being absorbed in thought; preoccupation. [PRE- + OCCUPANCY]

pre·oc·cu·pa·tion (prē ok′yə pā′shən, prē′ok-), *n.* **1.** act of preoccupying. **2.** state of being preoccupied. [< L *praeoccupātiōn-* (s. of *praeoccupātiō*) a taking possession beforehand. See PRE-, OCCUPATION]

pre·oc·cu·pied (prē ok′yə pīd′), *adj.* **1.** completely engrossed in thought; absorbed. **2.** previously occupied; taken; filled. **3.** *Biol.* already used as a name for some species, genus, etc., and not available as a designation for any other. [PREOCCUPY + -ED[2]] —**pre·oc′cu·pied′·ly,** *adv.* —**pre·oc′cu·pied′ness,** *n.*
—**Syn. 1.** busy; concentrating.

pre·oc·cu·py (prē ok′yə pī′), *v.t.,* **-pied, -py·ing. 1.** to absorb or engross to the exclusion of other things. **2.** to occupy beforehand or before others. [PRE- + OCCUPY] —**pre·oc′cu·pi′er,** *n.*

pre·o·ral (prē ōr′əl, -ôr′-), *adj.* *Zool.* situated in front of or before the mouth. [PRE- + ORAL] —**pre·o′ral·ly,** *adv.*

pre·or·dain (prē′ôr dān′), *v.t.* to ordain beforehand; foreordain. [PRE- + ORDAIN] —**pre·or·di·na·tion** (prē′ôr dᵊnā′shən), *n.*

prep (prep), *n., v.,* **prepped, prep·ping.** —*n.* *Informal.* **1.** See **preparatory school.** —*v.i.* **2.** to attend preparatory school. —*v.t.* **3.** to study (a subject), prepare (a person), etc., as for a course of study, campaign, operation, test, etc.: *We prepped him for the quiz.* [by shortening]

prep., **1.** preparation. **2.** preparatory. **3.** prepare. **4.** preposition.

pre·pack·age (prē pak′ij), *v.t.,* **-aged, -ag·ing.** to package (foodstuffs or manufactured goods) before retail distribution or sale. Also, **pre·pack′.** [PRE- + PACKAGE]

prep·a·ra·tion (prep′ə rā′shən), *n.* **1.** a proceeding, measure, or provision by which one prepares for something: *preparations for a journey.* **2.** any proceeding, experience, or the like, considered as a mode of preparing for the future. **3.** act of preparing; state of being prepared. **4.** something prepared, manufactured, or compounded: *a special preparation for sunbathers.* **5.** a specimen, as an animal body, prepared for scientific examination, dissection, etc. **6.** *Music.* **a.** the preparing of a dissonance, by introducing the dissonant tone as a consonant tone in the preceding chord. **b.** the tone so introduced. **7.** *New Testament.* the day before the Sabbath or a feast day. **8.** *Brit.* work done by students in preparation for class; homework. **9. the Preparation,** the introductory prayers of the Mass or other divine service. [ME *preparacion* < L *praeparātiōn-* (s. of *praeparātiō*), a preparing, equiv. to *praeparāt(us)* (ptp. of *praeparāre* to PREPARE) + *-iōn-* -ION]

pre·par·a·tive (pri par′ə tiv), *adj.* **1.** preparatory. —*n.* **2.** something that prepares. **3.** a preparation. [late ME *preparatif* < MF < ML *praeparātīv(us).* See PREPARATION, -IVE] —**pre·par′a·tive·ly,** *adv.*

pre·par·a·tor (pri par′ə tər), *n.* one who prepares a specimen, as an animal, for scientific examination or exhibition. [< LL *praeparātor* preparer. See PREPARATION, -OR[2]]

pre·par·a·to·ry (pri pâr′ə tōr′ē, -tôr′ē, -par′-, prep′ər ə-), *adj.* **1.** serving or designed to prepare: *preparatory arrangements.* **2.** preliminary; introductory: *preparatory remarks.* **3.** of or pertaining to training that prepares for more advanced education. [< ML *praeparātōri(us).* See PREPARATION, -ORY[1]] —**pre·par′a·to′ri·ly,** *adv.*

prepar′atory school′, **1.** a private secondary school, especially one boarding its students and providing a college-preparatory education. **2.** *Brit.* a private elementary school, esp. one preparing its students for public school.

pre·pare (pri pâr′), *v.,* **-pared, -par·ing.** —*v.t.* **1.** to put in proper condition or readiness: *to prepare a patient for surgery.* **2.** to get (a meal) ready for eating, as by proper assembling, cooking, etc. **3.** to manufacture, compound, or compose: *to prepare a cough syrup.* **4.** *Music.* to lead up to (a discord, an embellishment, etc.) by some preliminary tone or tones. —*v.i.* **5.** to put things or oneself in readiness; get ready: *to prepare for war.* [late ME < L *praepar(āre)* (to) make ready beforehand, equiv. to *prae-* PRE- + *parāre* to set, get ready] —**pre·par′er,** *n.*
—**Syn. 1.** provide, arrange, order. PREPARE, CONTRIVE, DEVISE imply planning for and making ready for something expected or thought possible. To PREPARE is to make ready beforehand for some approaching event, need, and the like: *to prepare a room, a speech.* CONTRIVE and DEVISE emphasize the exercise of ingenuity and inventiveness. The first word suggests a shrewdness that borders on trickery, but this is absent from DEVISE: *to contrive a means of escape; to devise a time-saving method.* **3.** make. **Ant. 1.** disorganize. **2.** destroy.

pre·pared (pri pârd′), *adj.* **1.** properly equipped; ready: *prepared for a hurricane.* **2.** (of food) processed by the manufacturer or seller as by cooking, cleaning, or the like, so as to be ready to serve or use with little or no further preparation. [PREPARE + -ED[2]] —**pre·par·ed·ly** (pri pâr′id lē), *adv.*

pre′meg·a·lith′ic, *adj.*
pre′mem·o·ran′dum, *n., pl.* **-dums, -da.**
pre·men′ace, *n., v.t.,* **-aced, -ac·ing.**
pre′-Men·de′li·an, *adj.*
pre·men′stru·al, *adj.*
pre·men′tion, *n., v.t.*
pre·mer′it, *v.t.*
pre′-Mes·si·an′ic, *adj.*
pre′me·thod′i·cal, *adj.*
pre-Meth′od·ist, *adj., n.*
pre·mid′night′, *n.*
pre·mid′sum′mer, *n., adj.*
pre·mil′i·tar′y, *adj.*
pre·min′is·ter, *v.i.*
pre·min′is·try, *n., pl.* **-tries.**
pre′mis·rep′re·sent′, *v.t.*
pre′mis·rep′re·sen·ta′tion, *n.*
pre·mix′, *v.t.*
pre·mix′er, *n.*
pre·mix′ture, *n.*
pre·mod′el, *v.i.,* **-eled, -el·ing** or (*esp. Brit.*) **-elled, -el·ling.**
pre·mod′ern, *adj.*
pre′mod·i·fi·ca′tion, *n.*
pre·mod′i·fy′, *v.t.,* **-fied, -fy·ing.**
pre·mold′, *n., v.t.*
pre·mold′er, *n.*
pre′mo·nar′chal, *adj.*
pre′mo·nar′chi·al, *adj.*
pre′mo·nar′chi·cal, *adj.*
pre·mon′e·tar′y, *adj.*
pre′-Mon·go′li·an, *adj.*
pre′mo·nop′o·lize′, *v.t.,* **-lized, -liz·ing.**
pre′mo·nop′o·ly, *n., pl.* **-lies,** *adj.*
pre′mon·u·men′tal, *adj.*
pre·mor′al, *adj.;* **-ly,** *adv.*
pre′mo·ral′i·ty, *n.*
pre·mor′bid, *adj.;* **-ly,** *adv.;* **-ness,** *n.*
pre·morn′ing, *adj.*
pre·mor′tal, *adj.;* **-ly,** *adv.*
pre·mor′ti·fi·ca′tion, *n.*
pre·mor′ti·fy′, *v.t.,* **-fied, -fy·ing.**
pre·mor′tu·ar′y, *adj.*
pre·mor′u·la, *adj.*
pre′mo·sa′ic, *adj.*
pre-Mos′lem, *adj.*
pre·mud′dle, *n., v.t.,* **-dled, -dling.**
pre′mu·nic′i·pal, *adj.*
pre·mu′si·cal, *adj.;* **-ly,** *adv.*
pre-Mus′lim, *adj.*
pre·mus′ter, *v.t.*
pre·mu′ti·ny, *n., pl.* **-nies;** *v.t.,* **-nied, -ny·ing.**
pre′-My·ce·nae′an, *adj.*
pre′my·cot′ic, *adj.*
pre·myth′i·cal, *adj.*
pre′-Na·po′le·on′ic, *adj.*
pre′nar·cot′ic, *adj.*
pre·nar′i·al, *adj.*
pre·na′sal, *adj.*
pre·na′tion·al, *adj.*
pre·nat′ur·al, *adj.*
pre·na′val, *adj.*
pre·neb′u·lar, *adj.*
pre′ne·ces′si·tate′, *v.t.,* **-tat·ed, -tat·ing.**
pre′ne·glect′, *v.t.*
pre′ne·glect′ful, *adj.*
pre·neg′li·gence, *n.*
pre·neg′li·gent, *adj.*
pre′ne·go′ti·ate′, *v.,* **-at·ed, -at·ing.**
pre′ne·go′ti·a′tion, *n.*
pre′ne·o·lith′ic, *adj.*
pre′ne·phrit′ic, *adj.*
pre·neu′ral, *adj.*
pre′neu·ral′gic, *adj.*
pre′-New·to′ni·an, *adj.*
pre·nom′i·nal, *adj.*
pre-Nor′man, *adj.*
pre-Norse′, *adj.*
pre·note′, *v.t.,* **-not·ed, -not·ing.**
pre·no′ti·fy′, *v.t.,* **-fied, -fy·ing.**
pre·num′ber, *v.t., n.*
pre·nup′tial, *adj.*
pre·nur′ser·y, *adj., n., pl.* **-ser·ies.**
pre′o·be′di·ence, *n.*
pre′o·be′di·ent, *adj.;* **-ly,** *adv.*
pre′ob·ject′, *v.i.*
pre′ob·jec′tion, *n.*
pre′ob·jec′tive, *adj.*
pre·ob′li·gate′, *v.t.,* **-gat·ed, -gat·ing.**
pre·ob′li·ga′tion, *n.*
pre′o·blige′, *v.t.,* **-liged, -lig·ing.**
pre·ob·lon·ga′ta, *n.*
pre′ob·serv′ance, *n.*
pre′ob·ser·va′tion, *n.*
pre′ob·ser·va′tion·al, *adj.*
pre′ob·serve′, *v.t.,* **-served, -serv·ing.**
pre′ob·struct′, *v.t.*
pre′ob·struc′tion, *n.*
pre′ob·tain′, *v.t.*
pre′ob·tain′a·ble, *adj.*
pre′ob·trude′, *v.t.,* **-trud·ed, -trud·ing.**
pre′ob·tru′sion, *n.*
pre′ob·tru′sive, *adj.*
pre·ob′vi·ate′, *v.t.,* **-at·ed, -at·ing.**
pre·ob′vi·ous, *adj.;* **-ly,** *adv.;* **-ness,** *n.*
pre′oc·ca′sioned, *adj.*
pre′oc·cip′i·tal, *adj.*
pre′oc·clu′sion, *n.*
pre′oc·cul·ta′tion, *n.*
pre·oc′cu·pant, *n.*
pre′oc·cur′, *v.i.,* **-curred, -cur·ring.**
pre′oc·cur′rence, *n.*
pre′o·ce·an′ic, *adj.*
pre·oc′u·lar, *adj.*
pre·o′dor·ous, *adj.*
pre′oe·soph′a·ge′al, *adj.*
pre′of·fend′, *v.t.*
pre′of·fen′sive, *adj.;* **-ly,** *adv.;* **-ness,** *n.*
pre·of′fer, *n., v.t.*
pre′of·fi′cial, *adj.;* **-ly,** *adv.*
pre′o·mis′sion, *n.*
pre′o·mit′, *v.t.,* **-mit·ted, -mit·ting.**
pre·o′pen, *v.t.*
pre·op′er·ate′, *v.i.,* **-at·ed, -at·ing.**
pre′op·er·a′tion, *n.*
pre·op′er·a′tor, *n.*
pre′o·pin′ion, *n.*
pre′op·pose′, *v.t.,* **-posed, -pos·ing.**
pre′op·posed′, *adj.*
pre′op·po·si′tion, *n.*
pre′op·press′, *v.t.*
pre′op·pres′sion, *n.*
pre′op·pres′sor, *n.*
pre·op′tic, *adj.*
pre′op·ti·mis′tic, *adj.*
pre·op′tion, *n.*
pre·or′bi·tal, *adj.*
pre·or′der, *n.*
pre·or′di·nance, *n.*
pre′or·gan′ic, *adj.*
pre′or·gan′i·cal·ly, *adv.*
pre·or′gan·i·za′tion, *n.*
pre·or′gan·ize′, *v.,* **-ized, -iz·ing.**
pre′o·rig′i·nal, *adj.;* **-ly,** *adv.*
pre′or·na·men′tal, *adj.*
pre·ot′ic, *adj.*
pre·out′fit′, *v.t.,* **-fit·ted, -fit·ting.**
pre·out′line′, *n., v.t.,* **-lined, -lin·ing.**
pre·o′ver·throw′, *n.*
pre′o·ver·throw′, *v.t.,* **-threw, -thrown, -throw·ing.**
pre′pa·lae·o·lith′ic, *adj.*
pre′-Pa·lae·o·zo′ic, *adj.*
pre·pal′a·tal, *adj.*
pre·pal′a·tine′, *adj.*
pre′pa·le·o·lith′ic, *adj.*
pre′-Pa·le·o·zo′ic, *adj.*

pre·par·ed·ness (pri pâr′id nis, -pârd′nis), *n.* **1.** state of being prepared; readiness. **2.** possession of adequate armed forces and industrial potential, esp. as a deterrent to enemy attack. [PREPARED + -NESS]

pre·pa·ren·tal (prē′pə ren′tᵊl), *adj.* prior to becoming a parent: *preparental instruction.* [PRE- + PARENTAL]

pre·pay (prē pā′), *v.t.*, **-paid, -pay·ing.** to pay the charge upon in advance; pay beforehand: *The company will prepay the postage.* [PRE- + PAY¹] —**pre·pay′a·ble,** *adj.* —**pre·pay′ment,** *n.*

pre·pense (pri pens′), *adj.* planned or intended in advance; premeditated. [PRE- + -*pense* < L *pēns(us)* weighed, considered, ptp. of *pendere* to make (scales) hang down, hence, to weigh]

pre·pol·lex (pri pol′iks), *n., pl.* **-pol·li·ces** (-pol′i sēz′). a rudimentary additional digit on the preaxial side of the thumb of certain amphibians and mammals. [< NL; see PRE-, POLLEX]

pre·pon·der·ance (pri pon′dər əns), *n.* fact or quality of being preponderant; superiority in weight, power, numbers, etc.: *The preponderance of votes is against the proposal.* Also, **pre·pon′der·an·cy.** [PREPONDER(ANT) + -ANCE]

pre·pon·der·ant (pri pon′dər ənt), *adj.* superior in weight, force, influence, numbers, etc.; preponderating: *This preponderant misconception impedes progress.* [< L *praeponderant-* (s. of *praeponderāns*), prp. of *praeponderāre* to outweigh. See PRE-, PONDER, -ANT] —**pre·pon′der·ant·ly,** *adv.*
—**Syn.** overpowering, overruling, major, dominant.

pre·pon·der·ate (pri pon′də rāt′), *v.i.*, **-at·ed, -at·ing.** **1.** to exceed something else in weight; be the heavier. **2.** to incline downward or descend, as one scale or end of a balance, because of greater weight; be weighed down. **3.** to be superior in power, force, influence, number, amount, etc.; predominate: *Evidence for the accused preponderated at the trial.* [< L *praeponderāt(us)*, ptp. of *praeponderāre* to outweigh. See PRE-, PONDER, -ATE¹] —**pre·pon′der·at′ing·ly,** *adv.* —**pre·pon′der·a′tion,** *n.*

prep·o·si·tion (prep′ə zish′ən), *n.* *Gram.* any member of a class of words found in many languages that are used before nouns or adjectives to form phrases functioning as modifiers of verbs, nouns, or adjectives, and that typically express a spatial, temporal, or other relationship, as *in, on, by, to, since.* [ME *preposicioun* < L *praepositiōn-* (s. of *praepositiō*) a putting before, a prefix, preposition. See PRE-, POSITION] —**prep′o·si′tion·al,** *adj.* —**prep′o·si′tion·al·ly,** *adv.*

prep′osi′tional phrase′, *Gram.* a phrase consisting of a preposition, its object, which may be an adjective or a noun, and any modifiers of the object, as *in the gray desk I use.*

pre·pos·i·tive (prē poz′i tiv), *adj.* **1.** put before; prefixed: *a prepositive adjective.* **2.** *Gram.* (of a word) placed before another word to modify it or to show its relation to other parts of the sentence. In "red book" "red" is a prepositive adjective. "John's" in "John's book" is a prepositive genitive. —*n.* **3.** *Gram.* a word placed before another as a modifier or to show its relation to other parts of the sentence. In "red book" "red" is an adjectival prepositive. "John's" in "John's book" is a genitival prepositive. [< LL *praepositīv(us)* prefixed. See PREPOSITION, -IVE] —**pre·pos′i·tive·ly,** *adv.*

pre·pos·i·tor (prē poz′i tər), *n.* praepostor. Also, **prepostor.**

pre·pos·sess (prē′pə zes′), *v.t.* **1.** to possess or dominate mentally beforehand, as a prejudice does. **2.** to prejudice or bias, esp. favorably. **3.** to impress favorably beforehand or at the outset. [PRE- + POSSESS]

pre·pos·sess·ing (prē′pə zes′ing), *adj.* that impresses favorably: *a prepossessing exterior; an alert, confident, and prepossessing young man.* [PREPOSSESS + -ING²] —**pre′pos·sess′ing·ly,** *adv.* —**pre′pos·sess′ing·ness,** *n.*

pre·pos·ses·sion (prē′pə zesh′ən), *n.* **1.** state of being prepossessed. **2.** a prejudice, esp. one in favor of a person or thing. [PRE- + POSSESSION] —**pre′pos·ses′sion·ar′y,** *adj.*
—**Syn. 2.** predilection, liking, bias, interest.

pre·pos·ter·ous (pri pos′tər əs, -trəs), *adj.* completely contrary to nature, reason, or common sense; absurd; senseless; utterly foolish: *a preposterous tale.* [< L *praeposterus* with the hinder part foremost. See PRE-, POSTERIOR] —**pre·pos′ter·ous·ly,** *adv.* —**pre·pos′ter·ous·ness,** *n.*
—**Syn.** unreasonable, excessive. See **absurd.**

pre·pos·tor (prē pos′tər), *n.* praeposter.

pre·po·ten·cy (pri pōt′ᵊn sē), *n.* *Genetics.* the ability of one parent to impress its hereditary characters on its progeny because it possesses more homozygous, dominant, or epistatic genes. [< L *praepotentia.* See PREPOTENT, -ENCY]

pre·po·tent (pri pōt′ᵊnt), *adj.* **1.** preeminent in power, authority, or influence; predominant: *a prepotent name in the film industry.* **2.** *Genetics.* noting, pertaining to, or having prepotency. [< L *praepotent-* (s. of *praepotēns*) prp. of *praeposse* to have greater power. See PRE-, POTENT¹] —**pre·po′tent·ly,** *adv.*

prep·pie (prep′ē), *U.S. Informal.* —*n.* **1.** a person who attends or has recently graduated from a preparatory school. **2.** Also called **prep′pie look′.** a style of casual dress favored by preppies, typically consisting of slacks or skirts, button-down shirt, pullover sweater, and loafers. —*adj.* **3.** of or pertaining to preppies or the attitudes, habits, or esp. the style of dress associated with them. Also, **prep′py.** [PREP + -IE]

pre·pran·di·al (prē pran′dē əl), *adj.* before a meal, esp. before dinner; anteprandial: *a preprandial apéritif.* [PRE- + PRANDIAL]

pre·pref·er·ence (prē pref′ər əns, -pref′rəns), *adj.* *Brit.* taking precedence over preference shares in dividends or in capital distribution at the time of dissolution or liquidation of a business. [PRE- + PREFERENCE]

pre·pri·ma·ry (prē prī′mer ē, -mə rē), *adj.* *Politics.* preceding a primary election: *preprimary endorsement.* [PRE- + PRIMARY]

pre·print (prē′print′), *n.* an advance printing, usually of a portion of a book or of an article in a periodical. [PRE- + PRINT]

pre·puce (prē′pyo͞os), *n.* *Anat.* the fold of skin which covers the head of the penis or clitoris. Cf. **foreskin.** [late ME < MF < L *praepūt(ium)* the foreskin, equiv. to *prae-* PRE- + -*pūtium* < Gk *pósthion* little penis (*pósth(ē)* penis + -*ion* dim. suffix)] —**pre·pu·tial** (pri pyo͞o′shəl), *adj.*

pre·pu·pa (prē pyo͞o′pə), *n., pl.* **-pae** (-pē), **-pas.** an insect in the nonfeeding, inactive stage between the larval period and the pupal period. [< NL; see PRE-, PUPA] —**pre·pu′pal,** *adj.*

pre·purge (prē pûrj′), *v.t.*, **-purged, -purg·ing.** *Metall.* to purge (a furnace or stove) before further use. [PRE- + PURGE]

Pre-Raph·a·el·ite (prē raf′ē ə līt′, -rā′fē-), *n.* **1.** one of a group of English artists (**Pre-Raph′aelite Broth′erhood**) formed in 1848, and including Holman Hunt, John Everett Millais, and Dante Gabriel Rossetti, who aimed to revive the style and spirit of the Italian artists before the time of Raphael. —*adj.* **2.** of, pertaining to, or characteristic of the Pre-Raphaelites. [PRE- + RAPHAEL + -ITE¹] —**Pre-Raph′a·el·it′ism,** *n.*

pre·re·cord (prē′ri kôrd′), *v.t.* to record (a radio show, television program, etc.) prior to an actual broadcast or showing: *They prerecorded the show and hoped it wouldn't be outdated by the time of its release.* [PRE- + RECORD]

pre·re·lease (prē′ri lēs′), *n.* something released beforehand, as a movie shown before its scheduled premiere. [PRE- + RELEASE]

pre·req·ui·site (pri rek′wi zit), *adj.* **1.** required beforehand: *a prerequisite fund of knowledge.* —*n.* **2.** something prerequisite: *A visa is still a prerequisite for travel in many countries.* [PRE- + REQUISITE]

pre·rog·a·tive (pri rog′ə tiv), *n.* **1.** an exclusive right, privilege, etc., exercised by virtue of rank, office, or the like: *the prerogatives of a senator.* **2.** a right, privilege, etc., limited to a specific person, or to persons of a particular category: *She said it was a woman's prerogative to change her mind. Voting is the prerogative of adult citizens.* **3.** a power, immunity, or the like restricted to a sovereign government or its representative: *Making war is a prerogative of the state. The royal prerogative exempts the king from taxation.* **4.** *Obs.* precedence. —*adj.* **5.** having or exercising a prerogative. **6.** pertaining to, characteristic of, or existing by virtue of a prerogative. [late ME < L *praerogātīv(us)* (adj.) voting first, *praerogātīva* (n. use of fem. of adj.) tribe or century with right to vote first. See PRE-, INTERROGATIVE]
—**Syn. 1.** See **privilege.**

prerog′ative court′, **1.** a former ecclesiastical court in England and Ireland for the trial of certain testamentary cases. **2.** (formerly) the court of probate in New Jersey.

Pres (pres, prez), *n.* a boy's given name, form of **Presley.**

Pres., **1.** Presbyterian. **2.** President.

pres., **1.** present. **2.** presidency.

pre·sa (prā′sə; *It.* pre′sä), *n., pl.* **-se** (-sā; *It.* -se). a mark, as :S:, +, or ※, used in a canon, round, etc., to indicate where the successive voice parts are to take up the theme. [< It: lit., a taking up, fem. of *preso*, ptp. of *prendere* to take < L *prehendere* to seize]

pres·age (*n.* pres′ij; *v.* pres′ij, pri sāj′), *n., v.*, **-aged, -ag·ing.** —*n.* **1.** a presentiment or foreboding. **2.** a prophetic impression. **3.** something that portends or foreshadows a future event; an omen, prognostic, or warning indication. **4.** prophetic significance; augury. **5.** foresight; prescience. **6.** *Archaic.* a forecast or prediction. —*v.t.* **7.** to have a presentiment of. **8.** to portend, foreshow, or foreshadow: *The incidents may presage war.* **9.** to forecast; predict. —*v.i.* **10.** to make a prediction. **11.** *Archaic.* to have a presentiment. [ME < L *praesāg(ium)* a foreboding, deriv. of *praesāgus* divining, lit., perceiving beforehand, equiv. to *prae-* PRE- + -*sāgus*, akin to *sāgīre* to perceive intuitively] —**pres′age·ful,** *adj.* —**pres′age·ful·ly,** *adv.* —**pres′ag·er,** *n.*
—**Syn. 1.** foreshadowing, indication, premonition. **3.** portent, sign, token.

pre·sanc·ti·fied (prē sangk′tə fīd′), *adj.* (of the Eucharistic elements) consecrated at a previous Mass. [trans. of ML *praesanctificātus.* See PRE-, SANCTIFIED] —**pre·sanc′ti·fi·ca′tion,** *n.*

Presb., Presbyterian.

pres·by·cu·sis (prez′bə kyo͞o′sis, pres′-), *n.* *Med.* impaired hearing due to old age. Also, **pres·by·cou·sis** (prez′bə ko͞o′sis, pres′-), **pres·by·a·cu·sia** (prez′bē ə kyo͞o′zhə, -zhē ə, -zē ə, pres′-), **pres·by·a·cou·sia** (prez′bē ə ko͞o′zhə, -zhē ə, -zē ə, pres′-). [< NL, equiv. to Gk *presby-* (comb. form of *présbys* old, old man) + (*á*)*kousis* hearing, equiv. to *akoú(ein)* (to) hear + -*sis* -SIS]

pre′par·lia·men′ta·ry, *adj.*
pre′par·ox·ys′mal, *adj.*
pre′par·take′, *v.i.*, **-took, -tak·en, -tak·ing.**
pre·par′tic′i·pa′tion, *n.*
pre·par′ti·san, *adj.*
pre′par·ti′tion, *n., v.t.*
pre·part′ner·ship′, *n.*
pre·pat′ent, *n., v.t.*
pre′pa·tri′cian, *adj.*
pre-Paul′ine, *adj.*
pre·pave′, *v.t.*, **-paved, -pav·ing.**
pre·pave′ment, *n.*
pre·pec′to·ral, *adj.*
pre′pe·dun′cle, *n.*
pre·pen′e·trate′, *v.t.*, **-trat·ed, -trat·ing.**
pre′pen·e·tra′tion, *n.*
pre′per·i·to·ne′al, *adj.*
pre-Per′mi·an, *adj.*
pre-Per′sian, *adj., n.*
pre′per·suade′, *v.t.*, **-suad·ed, -suad·ing.**
pre′per·sua′sion, *n.*
pre′per·sua′sive, *adj.*
pre′pe·rus′al, *adj.*
pre′pe·ruse′, *v.t.*, **-used, -us·ing.**
pre′pe·ti′tion, *n., v.t.*
pre-Pe′trine, *adj.*
pre′-Phar·a·on′ic, *adj.*
pre-Phid′i·an, *adj.*
pre·phthis′i·cal, *adj.*
pre′pig·men′tal, *adj.*
pre·pin′e·al, *adj.*
pre·pi′ous, *adj.*; **-ly,** *adv.*
pre′pi·tu′i·tar′y, *adj.*
pre·place′, *v.t.*, **-placed, -plac·ing.**
pre·place′ment, *n.*
pre′pla·cen′tal, *adj.*
pre·plan′, *v.*, **-planned, -plan·ning.**
pre·plant′, *v.t.*
pre·pledge′, *v.t.*, **-pledged, -pledg·ing;** *n.*
pre·plot′, *v.t.*, **-plot·ted, -plot·ting.**
pre′po·et′ic, *adj.*
pre′po·et′i·cal, *adj.*
pre′po·lice′, *adj.*
pre·pol′ish, *n., v.t.*
pre-Po′lish, *adj., n.*
pre·pol′i·tic, *adj.*
pre′po·lit′i·cal, *adj.*; **-ly,** *adv.*
pre′por·tray′, *v.t.*
pre′por·tray′al, *n.*
pre·prac′ti·cal, *adj.*
pre·prac′tice, *v.*, **-ticed, -tic·ing.**
pre·prac′tise, *v.*, **-tised, -tis·ing.**
pre′prep·a·ra′tion, *n.*
pre·price′, *v.t.*, **-priced, -pric·ing;** *n.*
pre·prim′er, *n.*
pre·prim′i·tive, *adj.*
pre′pro·fess′, *v.t.*
pre′pro·hi·bi′tion, *n.*
pre·prom′ise, *n., v.t.*, **-ised, -is·ing.**
pre′pro·mote′, *v.t.*, **-mot·ed, -mot·ing.**
pre′pro·mo′tion, *n.*
pre′pro·nounce′, *v.t.*, **-nounced, -nounc·ing.**
pre′pro·nounce′ment, *n.*
pre′pro·phet′ic, *adj.*
pre′pro·stat′ic, *adj.*
pre·prove′, *v.t.*, **-proved, -proved** or **-prov·en, -prov·ing.**
pre′pro·vide′, *v.t.*, **-vid·ed, -vid·ing.**
pre′pro·vi′sion, *n.*
pre′prov·o·ca′tion, *n.*
pre′pro·voke′, *v.t.*, **-voked, -vok·ing.**
pre·pru′dent, *adj.*; **-ly,** *adv.*
pre′psy·cho·log′i·cal, *adj.*
pre′psy·chol′o·gy, *n.*
pre·pu′bis, *n.*
pre′pub·li·ca′tion, *n.*
pre·pub′lish, *v.t.*
pre·pueb′lo, *adj.*
pre·punc′tu·al, *adj.*
pre·pun′ish, *v.t.*
pre·pun′ish·ment, *n.*
pre·pur′chase, *n., v.t.*, **-chased, -chas·ing.**
pre·pur′chas·er, *n.*
pre·pur′pose, *v.t.*, **-posed, -pos·ing.**
pre·pur′po·sive, *adj.*
pre′py·lor′ic, *adj.*
pre′qual·i·fi·ca′tion, *n.*
pre·qual′i·fy′, *v.*, **-fied, -fy·ing.**
pre·quar′an·tine′, *n., v.t.*, **-tined, -tin·ing.**
pre·ques′tion, *v.t.*
pre′quo·ta′tion, *n.*
pre·quote′, *v.t.*, **-quot·ed, -quot·ing.**
pre·rac′ing, *adj.*
pre·ra′di·o′, *adj.*
pre·rail′road′, *adj.*
pre·rail′way′, *adj.*
pre·ra′tion·al, *adj.*
pre·read′i·ness, *n.*
pre·read′y, *adj.*
pre·re′al·i·za′tion, *n.*
pre·re′al·ize′, *v.t.*, **-ized, -iz·ing.**
pre′re·bel′lion, *adj.*
pre′re·ceipt′, *v.t.*
pre′re·ceive′, *v.t.*, **-ceived, -ceiv·ing.**
pre′re·ceiv′er, *n.*
pre′re·cit′al, *n.*
pre′re·cite′, *v.t.*, **-cit·ed, -cit·ing.**
pre·reck′on, *v.t.*
pre·reck′on·ing, *n.*
pre′rec·og·ni′tion, *n.*
pre·rec′og·nize′, *v.t.*, **-nized, -niz·ing.**
pre′rec·om·mend′, *v.t.*
pre′rec·om·men·da′tion, *n.*
pre·rec′on·cile′, *v.t.*, **-ciled, -cil·ing.**
pre·rec′on·cile′ment, *n.*
pre′rec·on·cil′i·a′tion, *n.*
pre′-Re·con·struc′tion, *n., adj.*
pre·rec′tal, *adj.*
pre′re·deem′, *v.t.*
pre′re·demp′tion, *n.*
pre′re·fer′, *v.t.*, **-ferred, -fer·ring.**
pre·ref′er·ence, *n.*
pre′re·fine′, *v.t.*, **-fined, -fin·ing.**
pre′re·fine′ment, *n.*
pre′re·form′, *adj.*
pre′-Ref·or·ma′tion, *n.*
pre′ref·or·ma′tion, *adj.*
pre′re·form′a·to′ry, *adj.*
pre′re·fus′al, *n.*
pre′re·fuse′, *v.t.*, **-fused, -fus·ing.**
pre·re′gal, *adj.*
pre·reg′is·ter, *v.t., v.i.*
pre′reg·is·tra′tion, *n.*
pre·reg′u·late′, *v.t.*, **-lat·ed, -lat·ing.**
pre′re·ject′, *v.t.*
pre′re·jec′tion, *n.*
pre′re·joice′, *v.t.*, **-joiced, -joic·ing.**
pre′re·late′, *v.t.*, **-lat·ed, -lat·ing.**
pre′re·la′tion, *n.*
pre′re·la′tion·ship′, *n.*
pre′re·li′gious, *adj.*
pre′re·luc′tance, *n.*
pre′re·mit′, *v.t.*, **-mit·ted, -mit·ting.**
pre′re·mit′tance, *n.*
pre′re·morse′, *n.*
pre′re·mov′al, *n.*
pre′re·move′, *v.t.*, **-moved, -mov·ing.**
pre′re·mu′ner·ate′, *v.t.*, **-at·ed, -at·ing.**
pre′re·mu′ner·a′tion, *n.*
pre-Ren′ais·sance, *adj.*
pre·re′nal, *adj.*
pre·rent′, *v.t.*
pre·rent′al, *n.*
pre′re·port′, *n., v.*
pre′rep·re·sent′, *v.t.*
pre′rep·re·sen·ta′tion, *n.*
pre′re·pub′li·can, *adj.*
pre′re·quest′, *n., v.t.*
pre′re·quire′, *v.t.*, **-quired, -quir·ing.**
pre′re·quire′ment, *n.*
pre′re·sem′blance, *n.*
pre′re·sem′ble, *v.*, **-bled, -bling.**
pre′res·o·lu′tion, *n.*
pre′re·solve′, *v.*, **-solved, -solv·ing.**
pre′re·sort′, *v.i.*
pre′re·spect′a·bil′i·ty, *n.*
pre′re·spect′a·ble, *adj.*
pre′res·pi·ra′tion, *n.*
pre′re·spire′, *v.t.*
pre′re·spon′si·bil′i·ty, *n.*
pre′re·spon′si·ble, *adj.*
pre′-Res·to·ra′tion, *adj.*
pre′res·to·ra′tion, *adj.*
pre′re·strain′, *v.t.*
pre′re·straint′, *n.*
pre′re·strict′, *v.t.*
pre′re·stric′tion, *n.*
pre′re·turn′, *n., v.i.*
pre′re·veal′, *v.t.*
pre′rev·e·la′tion, *n.*
pre′re·venge′, *n., v.t.*, **-venged, -veng·ing.**
pre′re·ver′sal, *n.*
pre′re·verse′, *n., v.t.*, **-versed, -vers·ing.**
pre′re·view′, *n., v.t.*
pre′re·vise′, *v.t.*, **-vised, -vis·ing.**
pre′re·vi′sion, *n.*
pre′re·viv′al, *n., adj.*
pre′-Rev·o·lu′tion, *adj.*
pre′rev·o·lu′tion·ar′y, *adj.*
pre′rheu·mat′ic, *adj.*
pre·right′eous, *adj.*; **-ly,** *adv.*; **-ness,** *n.*
pre-Ro′man, *adj.*
pre′ro·man′tic, *adj.*
pre′ro·man′ti·cism, *n.*
pre·route′, *v.t.*, **-rout·ed, -rout·ing.**
pre·roy′al, *adj.*; **-ly,** *adv.*
pre·roy′al·ty, *n.*
pre·sa′cral, *adj.*
pre·sac′ri·fice′, *n., v.*, **-ficed, -fic·ing.**
pre′sac·ri·fi′cial, *adj.*
pre·sanc′ti·fy′, *v.t.*, **-fied, -fy·ing.**
pre·san′guine, *adj.*
pre·san′i·tar′y, *adj.*
pre′sar·to′ri·al, *adj.*
pre′sat·is·fac′tion, *n.*
pre′sat·is·fac′to·ry, *adj.*
pre·sat′is·fy′, *v.t.*, **-fied, -fy·ing.**
pre·sav′age, *adj.*
pre·sav′age·ry, *n.*
pre-Sax′on, *adj., n.*

pres·by·ope (prez′bē ōp′, pres′-), *n.* *Ophthalm.* a presbyopic person. [back formation from PRESBYOPIA]

pres·by·o·pi·a (prez′bē ō′pē ə, pres′-), *n.* *Ophthalm.* a defect of vision incident to advancing age, in which near objects are seen with difficulty; farsightedness. [< Gk *presby-* (comb. form of *présbys* old, old man) + -OPIA] —**pres·by·op·ic** (prez′bē op′ik, pres′-), *adj.*

Presbyt., Presbyterian.

pres·by·ter (prez′bi tər, pres′-), *n.* **1.** (in the early Christian church) an office bearer who exercised teaching, priestly, and administrative functions. **2.** (in hierarchical churches) a priest. **3.** an elder in a Presbyterian church. [< eccl. L < Gk *presbýter(os)* elder, equiv. to *présby(s)* old + *-teros* comp. suffix] —**pres·byt·er·al** (prez bit′ər əl, pres-), *adj.*

pres·byt·er·ate (prez bit′ər it, -ə rāt′, pres-), *n.* **1.** the office of a presbyter or elder. **2.** a body of presbyters or elders. [< ML *presbyterāt(us).* See PRESBYTER, -ATE[1]]

pres·by·te·ri·al (prez′bi tēr′ē əl, pres′-), *adj.* **1.** of or pertaining to a presbytery. **2.** presbyterian (def. 1). [PRESBYTERY + -AL[1]]

pres·by·te·ri·an (prez′bi tēr′ē ən, pres′-), *adj.* **1.** pertaining to or based on the principle of ecclesiastical government by presbyters or presbyteries. **2.** (*cap.*) designating or pertaining to various churches having this form of government and holding more or less modified forms of Calvinism. —*n.* **3.** (*cap.*) a member of a Presbyterian church; one who supports Presbyterianism. [PRESBYTERY + -AN]

Pres·by·te·ri·an·ism (prez′bi tēr′ē ə niz′əm, pres′-), *n.* **1.** church government by presbyters or elders, equal in rank and organized into graded administrative courts. **2.** the doctrines of Presbyterian churches. [PRESBYTERIAN + -ISM]

pres·by·ter·y (prez′bi ter′ē, pres′-), *n., pl.* **-ter·ies.** **1.** a body of presbyters or elders. **2.** (in Presbyterian churches) an ecclesiastical court consisting of all the ministers and one or two presbyters from each congregation in a district. **3.** the churches under the jurisdiction of a presbytery. **4.** the part of a church appropriated to the clergy. **5.** *Rom. Cath. Ch.* a rectory. [late ME *presbetory, -bitory* < LL *presbyteri(um)* < Gk *presbytérion.* See PRESBYTER, -IUM]

pre·school (*adj.* prē′skōōl′; *n.* prē′skōōl′), *adj.* **1.** of, pertaining to, or intended for a child between infancy and school age: *new methods of preschool education.* —*n.* **2.** a school or nursery for preschool children. [PRE- + SCHOOL[1]]

pre·sci·ence (prē′shē əns, -shəns, presh′ē-, presh′-əns), *n.* knowledge of things before they exist or happen; foreknowledge; foresight. [ME < LL *praescientia* foreknowledge. See PRE-, SCIENCE] —**pre′sci·ent,** *adj.* —**pre′sci·ent·ly,** *adv.*

pre·scind (pri sind′), *v.t.* **1.** to separate in thought; abstract. **2.** to remove. —*v.i.* **3.** to withdraw the attention (usually fol. by *from*). **4.** to turn aside in thought. [< L *praescind(ere)* (to) cut off in front. See PRE-, RESCIND]

pre·score (prē skōr′, -skôr′), *v.t.,* **-scored, -scor·ing.** to record the sound of (a motion picture) before filming. [PRE- + SCORE]

Pres·cott (pres′kət), *n.* **1. William Hick·ling** (hik′-ling), 1796–1859, U.S. historian. **2.** a city in central Arizona. 12,861 (1960). **3.** a town in SW Arkansas. 3533 (1960).

pre·scribe (pri skrīb′), *v.,* **-scribed, -scrib·ing.** —*v.t.* **1.** to lay down, in writing or otherwise, as a rule or a course to be followed; appoint, ordain, or enjoin. **2.** *Med.* to designate or order for use (a remedy, treatment, etc.). **3.** *Law.* to render invalid by prescription. —*v.i.* **4.** to lay down rules; direct; dictate. **5.** *Med.* to designate remedies, treatment, etc., to be used. **6.** *Law.* **a.** to claim a right or title by virtue of long use and enjoyment (usually fol. by *for* or *to*). **b.** to become invalid or outlawed by negative prescription, or through lapse of time, as a claim or action. [late ME < legal L *praescrībe(re)* (to) hold (property) by legal prescription, lit., to write before or above, equiv. to *prae-* PRE- + *scrībere* to write; see SHRIVE] —**pre·scrib′a·ble,** *adj.* —**pre·scrib′er,** *n.*
—**Syn. 1.** direct, dictate, decree.

pre·script (*adj.* pri skript′, prē′skript; *n.* prē′skript), *adj.* **1.** prescribed. —*n.* **2.** that which is prescribed or laid down, as a rule, precept, or order. [< L *praescrip-t(um)* an order, rule, lit., something written before or above, n. use of neut. of ptp. of *praescrībere* to PRESCRIBE. See PRE-, SCRIPT]

pre·scrip·ti·ble (pri skrip′tə bəl), *adj.* **1.** subject to or suitable for prescription. **2.** depending on or derived from prescription, as a claim or right. [< ML *prescriptibil(is).* See PRESCRIPTION, -IBLE] —**pre·scrip′ti·bil′i·ty,** *n.*

pre·scrip·tion (pri skrip′shən), *n.* **1.** *Med.* **a.** a direction, usually written, by the physician to the pharmacist for the preparation and use of a medicine or remedy. **b.** the medicine prescribed: *Take this prescription three times a day.* **2.** act of prescribing. **3.** that which is prescribed. **4.** *Law.* **a.** a long or immemorial use of some right with respect to a thing so as to give a right to continue such use. **b.** the process of acquiring rights by uninterrupted assertion of the right over a long period of time. —*adj.* **5.** (of drugs) sold only upon medical prescription; ethical. Cf. **over-the-counter** (def. 2). [ME < legal L *praescrīptiōn-* (s. of *praescrīptiō*) legal possession (of property), law, order, lit., a writing before, hence, a heading. See PRESCRIPT, -ION]

pre·scrip·tive (pri skrip′tiv), *adj.* **1.** that prescribes; giving directions or injunctions: *a prescriptive letter from an anxious father; a prescriptive method of writing a dictionary.* **2.** depending on or arising from effective legal prescription, as a right or title established by a long unchallenged tenure: *the prescriptive rights of the landed gentry.* [PRESCRIPT + -IVE, modeled on *descriptive,* etc.] —**pre·scrip′tive·ly,** *adv.* —**pre·scrip′tive·ness,** *n.*

prescrip′tive gram′mar, grammar that is considered in terms of what is correct, and therefore good usage, and that points out what is incorrect or substandard, and therefore bad usage.

pre·scrip·tiv·ist (pri skrip′tə vist), *n.* a writer, teacher, or supporter of prescriptive grammar. [PRESCRIPTIVE + -IST]

pre·scu·tum (prē skyōō′təm), *n., pl.* **-ta** (-tə), **-tums.** the anterior dorsal sclerite of a thoracic segment of an insect. [< NL; see PRE-, SCUTUM]

pre·se·lect (prē′si lekt′), *v.t.* to select in advance; choose beforehand: *Preselect a roasting time, and the oven will shut off automatically when the roast is done.* [PRE- + SELECT] —**pre′se·lec′tion,** *n.*

pre·se·lec·tor (prē′si lek′tər), *n.* a preamplifier between the antenna and receiving circuit of a radio to improve reception. [PRESELECT + -OR[2]]

pres·ence (prez′əns), *n.* **1.** state or fact of being present, as with others or in a place. **2.** attendance or company: *Your presence is requested.* **3.** immediate vicinity; close proximity: *in the presence of witnesses.* **4.** *Chiefly Brit.* the immediate personal vicinity of a great personage giving audience or reception. **5.** the ability to project a sense of ease, poise, or self-assurance, esp. the quality or manner of a person's bearing before an audience: *The speaker had a good deal of stage presence.* **6.** personal appearance or bearing, esp. of a dignified or imposing kind: *a man of fine presence.* **7.** a person, esp. of dignified or fine appearance: *He is a real presence, even at a private party.* **8.** a divine or supernatural spirit felt to be present: *He felt a presence with him in the room.* **9.** *Brit. Obs.* See **presence chamber.** [ME < MF < L *praesentia.* See PRESENT[1], -ENCE]
—**Syn. 3.** neighborhood. **5.** carriage, mien. —**Ant. 1.** absence.

pres′ence cham′ber, *Chiefly Brit.* the special room in which a great personage, as a sovereign, receives guests, holds audiences, etc.

pres′ence of mind′, a calm state of mind that allows one to act effectively in emergencies: *When he heard someone enter the house, he had the presence of mind to call the police.*

pre·se·nile (prē sē′nīl, -nil, -sen′īl), *adj.* pertaining to or exhibiting the characteristics of presenility; prematurely old. [PRE- + SENILE]

pre·se·nil·i·ty (prē′sə nil′i tē), *n.* premature old age. [PRE- + SENILITY]

pres·ent[1] (prez′ənt), *adj.* **1.** being, existing, or occurring at this time or now: *the present ruler.* **2.** at this time: *articles for present use.* **3.** *Gram.* **a.** noting an action or state occurring at the moment of speaking. *Knows* is a present form in *He knows that.* **b.** noting or pertaining to a tense or other verb formation with such meaning. **4.** being with one or others, or in the specified or understood place (opposed to *absent*): *to be present at a wedding.* **5.** being here or there, rather than elsewhere: *Is everyone present?* **6.** existing in a place, thing, combination, or the like: *Carbon is present in many minerals.* **7.** being actually here or under consideration: *the present document; the present topic.* **8.** being before the mind. **9.** *Obs.* mentally alert and calm, esp. in emergencies. **10.** *Obs.* immediate or instant. —*n.* **11.** the present time. **12.** *Gram.* **a.** the present tense. **b.** a verb formation or construction with present meaning. **c.** a form in the present. **13. presents,** *Law.* the present writings, or this document, used in a deed of conveyance, a lease, etc., to denote the document itself: *Know all men by these presents.* **14.** *Obs.* the matter in hand. **15. at present,** at the present time or moment; now: *There are no job openings here at present.* **16. for the present,** for now; temporarily: *For the present, we must be content with matters as they stand.* [ME < L *praesent-* (s. of *praesēns*) there, here, special use of prp. of *praeësse* to be before (others), i.e., to preside, be in charge. See PRE-, ESSE, -ENT] —**pres′ent·ness,** *n.*
—**Syn. 1.** extant. See **current.** —**Ant. 1.** absent.

pre·sent[2] (*v.* pri zent′; *n.* prez′ənt), *v.t.* **1.** to furnish or endow with a gift or the like, esp. by formal act: *to present someone with a gold watch.* **2.** to bring, offer, or give, often in a formal or ceremonious way: *to present one's card.* **3.** afford or furnish (an opportunity, possibility, etc.). **4.** to hand or send in, as a bill or a check, for payment: *The waiter presented our bill for lunch.* **5.** to introduce (a person) to another, esp. in a formal manner: *Mrs. Smith, may I present Mr. Jones?* **6.** to bring before or introduce to the public: *to present a new play.* **7.** to come to show (oneself) before a person, in or at a place, etc. **8.** to show or exhibit: *This theater will present films on a larger screen.* **9.** to bring before the mind; offer for consideration: *to present an alternative plan.* **10.** to set forth in words: *to present arguments.* **11.** to represent, impersonate, or act, as on the stage. **12.** to direct, point, or turn (something) to something or someone: *He presented his back to the audience.* **13.** to level or aim (a weapon, esp. a firearm). **14.** *Law.* **a.** to bring a formal charge against, as a person. **b.** to bring formally to the notice of the proper authority, as an offense. **15.** *Eccles. Brit.* to offer or recommend (a clergyman) to the bishop for institution to a benefice. —*n.* **16.** a thing presented as a gift; gift: *Christmas presents.* [ME *presente(n)* < OF *presente(r)* < L *praesentāre* to make (someone or something) present, i.e., to exhibit, bring into the presence of (someone) (ML: to make as a gift). See PRESENT[1]] —**pre·sent′er,** *n.*
—**Syn. 1.** bestow, donate. See **give. 2.** proffer. **3.** yield. **5.** See **introduce. 9.** introduce. **11.** enact. **16.** benefaction, grant, tip, gratuity. PRESENT, GIFT, DONATION, BONUS refer to something freely given. PRESENT and GIFT are both used of something given as an expression of affection, friendship, interest, or respect. PRESENT is the less formal; GIFT is generally used of something conferred (esp. with ceremony) on an individual, a group, or an institution: *a birthday present; a gift to a bride.* DONATION applies to an important gift, usually of considerable size, though the term is often used, to avoid the suggestion of charity, in speaking of small gifts to or for the needy: *a donation to an endowment fund, to the Red Cross.* BONUS applies to something given in addition to what is due, esp. to employees who have worked for a long time or particularly well: *a bonus at the end of the year.*

pre·sent·a·ble (pri zen′tə bəl), *adj.* **1.** that may be presented. **2.** suitable, as in appearance, dress, manners, etc., for being introduced into society or company: *a presentable young man.* **3.** of sufficiently good appearance, or fit to be seen: *Are you presentable now?* [PRESENT[2] + -ABLE] —**pre·sent′a·bil′i·ty, pre·sent′a·ble·ness,** *n.* —**pre·sent′a·bly,** *adv.*

present′ arms′, *Mil.* **1.** a position of salute in the manual of arms in which the rifle is held in both hands vertically in front of the body, with the muzzle upward and the trigger side forward. **2.** (for troops in formation not under arms) the hand salute.

pres·en·ta·tion (prez′ən tā′shən, prē′zən-), *n.* **1.** the act of presenting. **2.** the state of being presented. **3.** introduction, as of a person at court. **4.** exhibition or representation, as of a play or film. **5.** offering, delivering, or bestowal, as of a gift. **6.** a gift. **7.** *Com.* the presentment of a bill, note, or the like. **8.** *Obstet.* the appearance of a particular part of the fetus at the mouth of the uterus during labor: *a breech presentation.* **9.** *Eccles.* the act or the right of presenting a clergyman to the bishop for institution to a benefice. [ME < eccl. L *praesentātiōn-* (s. of *praesentātiō*) nomination (of a priest) to a benefice, religious dedication (of a person) by bringing him before God. See PRESENT[2], -ATION]

pres·en·ta·tion·al (prez′ən tā′shə nəl, prē′zən-), *adj.* **1.** of or pertaining to presentation. **2.** pertaining to or characterized by presentationalism. **3.** presentive. [PRESENTATION + -AL[1]]

pres·en·ta·tion·al·ism (prez′ən tā′shə nəliz′əm, prē′zən-), *n.* *Theat.* a style of production in which the story, skit, scene, etc., is presented directly to the audience, with little or no attempt at realism. [PRESENTATIONAL + -ISM]

pres·en·ta·tion·ism (prez′ən tā′shə niz′əm, prē′-zən-), *n.* *Epistemology.* the doctrine that in perception, or in all forms of knowledge, there is an immediate awareness of the things perceived. Also called **presentative realism.** [PRESENTATION + -ISM] —**pres′en·ta′tion·ist,** *n., adj.*

pre·sent·a·tive (pri zen′tə tiv), *adj.* **1.** (of an image, idea, etc.) presented, known, or capable of being known directly. **2.** *Eccles.* admitting of or pertaining to presentation. **3.** *Philos.* immediately knowable; capable of being known without thought or reflection. [PRESENT[2] + -ATIVE]

present′ative re′alism, *Epistemology.* presentationism. —**present′ative re′alist.**

pres·ent-day (prez′ənt dā′), *adj.* current; modern: *present-day techniques; present-day English.*

pres·en·tee (prez′ən tē′), *n.* **1.** one to whom something is presented. **2.** one who is presented, as to a benefice. [late ME < AF; see PRESENT[2], -EE]

pre·sen·ti·ment (pri zen′tə mənt), *n.* a feeling or impression of something about to happen, esp. something evil; foreboding. [< F, obs. spelling of *pressentiment.* See PRE-, SENTIMENT] —**pre·sen′ti·ment′al,** *adj.*

pres·en·tist (prez′ən tist), *n.* *Theol.* a person who maintains that the prophecies in the Apocalypse are now being fulfilled. Cf. **futurist, preterist.** [PRESENT[1] + -IST]

pre·sen·tive (pri zen′tiv), *adj.* *Semantics.* notional (def. 7). [PRESENT[2] + -IVE] —**pre·sen′tive·ly,** *adv.* —**pre·sen′tive·ness,** *n.*

pres·ent·ly (prez′ənt lē), *adv.* **1.** in a little while; soon: *They will be here presently.* **2.** at the present time: *He is presently out of the country.* **3.** *Archaic.* immediately. [ME; see PRESENT[1], -LY]
—**Syn. 1.** shortly, forthwith. See **immediately.** —**Ant. 1.** later.

pre·sent·ment (pri zent′mənt), *n.* **1.** act of presenting, esp. to the mind, as an idea, view, etc. **2.** state of being presented. **3.** a presentation. **4.** the manner or mode in which something is presented. **5.** a representation, picture, or likeness. **6.** *Com.* the presenting of a bill, note, or the like, as for acceptance or payment. **7.** *Law.* the written statement of an offense by a grand jury, of their own knowledge or observation, when no indictment has been laid before them. **8.** a theatrical or dramatic presentation. [ME *presentement* < MF. See PRESENT[2], -MENT]

pres′ent par′ticiple, a participle with present meaning, as *growing* in *a growing boy.*

pres′ent per′fect, **1.** (in English) the tense form consisting of the present tense of *have* with a past participle and noting that the action of the verb was completed prior to the present, as *I have finished.* **2.** a tense of similar construction found in certain other languages. **3.** a form in this tense.

pre·serv·a·tive (pri zûr′və tiv), *n.* **1.** something that preserves or tends to preserve. **2.** a chemical substance used to preserve foods from decomposition or fermentation. **3.** a medicine that preserves health or prevents disease. —*adj.* **4.** tending to preserve. [ME < MF *preservatif* < ML *praeservātīv(us).* See PRESERVE, -ATIVE]

pre·serve (pri zûrv′), *v.,* **-served, -serv·ing,** *n.* —*v.t.* **1.** to keep alive or in existence; make lasting: *to preserve our liberties as free men.* **2.** to keep safe from harm or injury; save. **3.** to keep up; maintain: *to preserve historical monuments.* **4.** to keep possession of; retain: *to preserve one's composure.* **5.** to prepare (food or any perishable substance) so as to resist decomposition or fermentation. **6.** to prepare (fruit, vegetables, etc.) by cooking with sugar. **7.** to maintain and reserve (game, fish, etc.) for private use in hunting or fishing. —*v.i.* **8.** to preserve fruit, vegetables, etc.; make preserves. **9.** to maintain a preserve for game or fish, esp. for sport. —*n.* **10.** something that preserves. **11.** that which is preserved. **12.** Usually, **preserves.** fruit, vegetables, etc., prepared by cooking with sugar. **13.** a place set apart for the protection and propagation of game or fish, esp. for sport. [ME *preserve(n)* < ML *praeservā(re)* (to) guard, (LL: to observe), L *prae-* PRE- + *servāre* to watch over, keep, preserve, observe] —**pre·serv′a·bil′i·ty,** *n.* —**pre·serv′a·ble,** *adj.* —**pres·er·va·tion** (prez′ər vā′shən), *n.* —**pre·serv′er,** *n.*
—**Syn. 1.** conserve. **2.** safeguard, shelter, shield. See **defend. 3.** continue, uphold, sustain. —**Ant. 1, 4.** forgo, lose.

pre·set (prē set′), *v.,* **-set, -set·ting,** *adj.* —*v.t.* **1.** to set beforehand. —*adj.* **2.** set in advance: *This preset*

pre′scho·las′tic, *adj.*
pre′sci·en·tif′ic, *adj.*
pre·scout′, *adj.*
pre·seal′, *n., v.t.*
pre·search′, *n., v.t.*
pre·sea′son, *n.*
pre·sea′son·al, *adj.*
pre·sec′u·lar, *adj.*
pre′se·cure′, *v.t.,* -cured, -cur·ing.
pre·sed′en·tar′y, *adj.*
pre·see′, *v.t.,* -saw, -seen, -see·ing.
pre′sem·i·lu′nar, *adj.*
pre·sem′i·nal, *adj.*
pre·sem′i·nar′y, *adj., n.*
pre′-Se·mit′ic, *adj., n.*
pre·sen′tence, *v.t.,* -tenced, -tenc·ing.
pre·sep′a·rate′, *v.t.,* -rat·ed, -rat·ing.
pre′sep·a·ra′tion, *n.*
pre·sep′a·ra′tor, *n.*
pre·sep′tal, *adj.*
pre·ses′sion, *n.*

radio has been adjusted at the factory to receive certain stations. 3. (of the guidance system of a missile or the course of flight it determines) set before launching to reach a specific destination without any alteration in response to signals from the ground. [PRE- + SET]

pre′set board′, a control board for setting up theatrical lighting switches and dimmer readings in advance so that during a performance the lights can be automatically operated for one or several scenes. Also called **pre′set control′ board′, multi-scene control board, pre′set switch′board.**

pre-shrunk (prē shrungk′), *adj.* of or pertaining to a fabric or garment that has been subjected to a shrinking process in order to reduce contraction when the apparel is washed or laundered. Also, **pre·shrunk′.**

pre·side (pri zīd′), *v.i.*, **-sid·ed, -sid·ing.** 1. to occupy the place of authority or control, as in an assembly, meeting, etc.; act as president or chairman. 2. to exercise management or control (usually fol. by *over*): *The lawyer presided over the estate.* [< L *praesid(ēre)* (to) preside over, lit., sit in front of, equiv. to *prae-* PRE- + *-sidēre*, comb. form of *sedēre* to sit] —**pre·sid′er,** *n.*

Pre·si·den·cia Ro·que Sá·enz Pe·ña (pre′se-then′syä rō′ke sä′ens pe′nyä), a city in N Argentina. 23,100 (1947).

pres·i·den·cy (prez′i dən sē), *n., pl.* **-cies.** 1. the office, function, or term of office of a president. 2. (*often cap.*) the office of President of the United States. 3. *Mormon Ch.* a. a local governing body consisting of a council of three. b. (*often cap.*) Also called **First Presidency.** the highest administrative body, composed of the prophet and his two councilors. 4. the former designation of any of the three original provinces of British India: Bengal, Bombay, and Madras. [< ML *praesidentia.* See PRESIDENT, -ENCY]

pres·i·dent (prez′i dənt), *n.* 1. (*often cap.*) the highest executive officer of a modern republic. 2. an officer appointed or elected to preside over an organized body of persons. 3. the chief officer of a college, university, society, corporation, etc. 4. one who presides. [ME < L *praesident-* (s. of *praesidēns*), n. use (in pl.) of prp. of *praesidēre* to PRESIDE, govern; see -ENT]

pres·i·dent-e·lect (prez′i dənt i lekt′), *n.* a president after election but before induction into office.

Pre·si·den·te Pru·den·te (pre′zi denn′tə prōō-denn′tə), a city in central Brazil. 72,782 (1960).

pres·i·den·tial (prez′i den′shəl), *adj.* 1. of or pertaining to a president or presidency. 2. of the nature of a president. [< ML *praesidentiāl(is).* See PRESIDENCY, -AL[1]] —**pres′i·den′tial·ly,** *adv.*

pres′iden′tial pri′mary, *U.S.* a direct primary for the choice of State delegates to a national party convention and the expression of preference for a presidential nominee.

pres·i·dent·ship (prez′i dənt ship′), *n. Brit.* presidency. [PRESIDENT + -SHIP]

pre·sid·i·o (pri sid′ē ō′; *Sp.* pre sē′thyō), *n., pl.* **-sid·i·os** (-sid′ē ōz′; *Sp.* -sē′thyōs). 1. a garrisoned fort; military post. 2. a Spanish penal settlement. [< Sp < L *praesidium* guard, garrison, post, lit., defense, protection. See PRESIDIUM] —**pre·sid′i·al, pre·sid·i·ar·y** (pri sid′ē er′ē), *adj.*

pre·sid·i·um (pri sid′ē əm), *n.* (*often cap.*) (in the Soviet Union) an administrative committee, usually permanent and governmental, acting when its parent body is in recess but exercising full powers: *He was elevated to a position on the Presidium of the Supreme Soviet.* [< L *praesidium*, deriv. of *praes(es)* (s. *praesid-*), lit., sitting before, i.e., guarding (adj.), defender, ruler, leader (n.). See PRESIDE, PRESIDENT]

pre·sig·ni·fy (prē sig′nə fī′), *v.t.*, **-fied, -fy·ing.** to signify or indicate beforehand; foretell. [< L *praesignificāre* (to) show beforehand. See PRE-, SIGNIFY]

pre·sin·ter (prē sin′tər), *v.t.* (in powder metallurgy) to heat a compact in preparation for sintering. [PRE- + SINTER]

Pres·ley (pres′lē, prez′-), *n.* a boy's given name.

pre-So·crat·ic (prē′sə krat′ik, -sō-), *adj.* 1. of or pertaining to the philosophers or philosophical systems of the period before the Socratic period. —*n.* 2. any philosopher of this period.

pres. part., present participle.

Presque Isle (presk′ īl′), a city in NE Maine. 12,886 (1960).

press[1] (pres), *v.t.* 1. to act upon with steadily applied weight or force. 2. to move by weight or force in a certain direction or into a certain position: *The crowd pressed him into a corner.* 3. to compress or squeeze, as to alter in shape or size: *He pressed the clay into the figure of a horse.* 4. to weigh heavily upon; subject to pressure. 5. to hold closely, as in an embrace; clasp: *He pressed her in his arms.* 6. to flatten; make smooth: *to press clothes; to press flowers in the leaves of a book.* 7. to extract juice, sugar, etc., from by pressure: *to press grapes.* 8. to squeeze out or express, as juice: *to press the juice from grapes.* 9. to beset or harass: *He was pressed by problems on all sides.* 10. to trouble or oppress; put into a difficult position, as by lack of something: *Poverty pressed them hard.* 11. to urge or impel, as to a particular course; constrain or compel: *pressed him for payment of the debt.* 12. to urge onward; hasten: *He pressed his horse to go faster.* 13. to urge, importune, insist, or entreat: *They pressed me for an immediate answer.* 14. to emphasize or insist upon: *He pressed his own ideas on us.* 15. to plead with insistence: *to press a claim.* 16. to push forward. —*v.i.* 17. to exert weight, force, or pressure. 18. to iron clothing, curtains, etc. 19. to bear heavily, as upon the mind. 20. to compel haste: *Time presses.* 21. to demand immediate attention. 22. to use urgent entreaty: *to press for an answer.* 23. to push forward or advance with force, eagerness, or haste: *The army pressed to reach the river by dawn.* 24. to crowd or throng. —*n.* 25. printed publications collectively, esp. newspapers and periodicals. 26. all the media and agencies that print, broadcast, or gather and transmit news, including newspapers, news magazines, radio and television news bureaus, wire services, etc. 27. the editorial employees, taken collectively, of these media and agencies. 28. (*often construed as pl.*) a group of news reporters, or of news reporters and news photographers: *The press are in the outer office, waiting for a statement.* 29. the consensus of the critical commentary, or the amount of coverage accorded a person, thing, or event, esp. in newspapers and periodicals (often prec. by *good* or *bad*): *Despite a good press, the play closed after eight performances. Poorly timed politically, the Foreign Minister's visit got a bad press in general.* 30. *Print.* a. See **cylinder press.** b. See **rotary press.** 31. an establishment for printing books, magazines, etc. 32. the process or art of printing. 33. any of various devices or machines for exerting pressure. 34. a wooden or metal viselike device for preventing a tennis or other racket from warping when not in use. 35. act of pressing; pressure. 36. a pressing or pushing forward. 37. a crowding, thronging, or pressing together: *The press of the crowd drove them on.* 38. a crowd, throng, or multitude. 39. state of being pressed. 40. the desired smooth or creased effect caused by ironing or pressing: *He was unkempt and unshaven, and his suit was out of press.* 41. pressure or urgency, as of affairs or business. 42. an upright case, or piece of furniture, for holding clothes, books, pamphlets, etc. 43. **go to press,** to begin being printed: *The last edition has gone to press.* [ME *presse(n)*, v. use of n. *presse* (but cf. OF *presser* < L *pressāre*, freq. of *premere*, ptp. *pressus*, to press) OE *press* clothespress < ML *pressa*, n. use of fem. ptp. of L *premere*] —**press′a·ble,** *adj.*
—**Syn.** 9. annoy, worry, torment, assail, besiege. 11. push. 13. induce, persuade, beg, implore. 37. crush.

press[2] (pres), *v.t.* 1. to force into service, esp. naval or military service; impress. 2. to make use of in a manner different from that intended or desired: *French taxis were pressed into service as troop transports.* —*n.* 3. impressment into service, esp. naval or military service. [back formation from *prest*, ptp. of obs. *prest* to take (men) for military service, v. use of PREST[2] in sense of enlistment money]

Press (pres), *n.* a boy's given name.

press′ a′gent, a person employed to promote the interests of an individual, organization, etc., by obtaining favorable publicity through advertisements, mentions in columns, and other publicity in the press.

press′ associa′tion, 1. an organization formed for the purpose of gathering news for transmittal to its members. Cf. **news agency.** 2. an association of publishers in a particular area, usually statewide.

press′ bed′, a bed enclosed within a closet, cupboard, etc.

press·board (pres′bōrd′, -bôrd′), *n.* a kind of millboard or pasteboard. [PRESS[1] + BOARD]

press′ box′, a press section, esp. at a sports event.

press′ brake′, brake[1] (def. 5).

press′ bu′reau, an organization or a department that acts as a press agent.

Press·burg (pres′bo͝orkh′), *n.* German name of **Bratislava.**

press′ con′ference, a prearranged interview with newsmen, held to elicit publicity or, as granted by a dignitary, public official, research scientist, etc., to fulfill a request from the press.

press′ cup′board, *Eng. Furniture.* a cupboard of the 16th and 17th centuries having an overhanging top above a recessed cabinet beneath which is a section of drawers or cabinets. Cf. **court cupboard.**

pressed′ brick′, face brick molded under pressure to a desired finish.

pressed′ glass′, molded glass that has been shaped or given its pattern, while molten, by the action of a plunger thrust into its mold.

press·er (pres′ər), *n.* 1. one who or that which presses or applies pressure. 2. a person whose occupation is pressing or ironing clothes in a laundry or dry-cleaning establishment. [PRESS[1] + -ER[1]]

press′er foot′, a forked, metal device on a sewing machine used for holding the fabric in place while stitching.

press′ fas′tener, *Brit.* See **snap fastener.**

press′ fit′, *Mach.* assembly of two tightly fitting parts, as a hub on a shaft, made by a press or the like. Also called **drive fit, force fit.**

press′ gal′lery, 1. a press section, esp. in a legislative chamber. 2. the group of newsmen present or qualified to be present in this section.

press′ gang′, a body of men under the command of an officer, formerly employed to impress other men for service, esp. in the navy or army. Also, **press′gang′.**

press·ing (pres′ing), *adj.* 1. urgent; demanding immediate attention: *a pressing engagement; a pressing need.* —*n.* 2. any phonograph record produced in a record-molding press from a master or a stamper. 3. a number of such records produced at one time: *The fifth pressing of his hit song has sold out.* [ME *presing* (n.). See PRESS[1], -ING[2], -ING[1]] —**press′ing·ly,** *adv.* —**press′ing·ness,** *n.*

press·man (pres′mən), *n., pl.* **-men.** 1. a man who operates or has charge of a printing press. 2. *Brit.* a writer or reporter for the press. [PRESS[1] + MAN[1]]

press·mark (pres′märk′), *n. Library Science, Brit.* a class number for a book. [PRESS[1] + MARK[1]]

press′ mon′ey, *Brit. Obs.* See **prest money.**

press′ of sail′, *Naut.* as much sail as the wind or other conditions will permit a ship to carry. Also called **press′ of can′vas.**

pres·sor (pres′ər), *adj. Physiol.* causing an increase in blood pressure; causing vasoconstriction. [attributive use of LL *pressor* presser, equiv. to L *press(us)* (ptp. of *premere* to press) + *-or* -OR[2]]

pres·so·re·cep·tor (pres′ō ri sep′tər), *n. Physiol.* a proprioceptor responding to changes of blood pressure. [PRESS(URE) + -O- + RECEPTOR]

press′ par′ty, a party given for reporters and photographers exclusively or particularly to get publicity, as for the introduction of a new product, the maiden voyage of a liner, or the like. Cf. **press conference.**

press-point (pres′point′), *n. Print.* point (def. 43b).

press′ proof′, *Print.* the last proof examined before matter goes to press.

press′ release′, *Journalism.* a statement prepared and distributed to the press by a public relations firm, governmental agency, etc. Also called **news release, release.**

press·room (pres′ro͞om′, -ro͝om′), *n.* the room in a printing or newspaper publishing establishment where the printing presses are installed. [PRESS[1] + ROOM]

press·run (pres′run′), *n.* 1. the running of a printing press for a specific job: *The pressrun will take about an hour.* 2. the quantity that is run: *a pressrun of more than 5000.* Also called **run.** [PRESS[1] + RUN]

press′ sec′tion, a section or part of an area, as at the scene of a public event, reserved for reporters.

press′ stud′, *Chiefly Brit.* See **snap fastener.**

press′ time′, the time at which a pressrun begins, esp. that of a newspaper. Cf. **edition time.**

pres·sure (presh′ər), *n., v.,* **-sured, -sur·ing.** —*n.* 1. the exertion of force upon a surface by an object, fluid, etc., in contact with it: *the pressure of earth against a wall.* 2. *Physics.* force per unit area. *Symbol:* P Cf. **stress** (def. 5). 3. *Meteorol.* See **atmospheric pressure.** 4. *Elect.* See **electromotive force.** 5. the state of being pressed or compressed. 6. harassment; oppression: *the pressures of daily life.* 7. a state of trouble or embarrassment: *He is under financial pressure from his debts.* 8. a constraining or compelling force or influence: *the social pressures of city life.* 9. urgency, as of affairs or business: *He works well under pressure.* 10. *Obs.* that which is impressed. —*v.t.* 11. to force (someone) toward a particular end: *They pressured him into accepting the contract.* 12. to make deliberate use of public opinion, personal ties, or the like, to create psychological pressure on; influence: *Through planted news stories, they pressured the director into changing his policy.* 13. pressurize. [ME < L *pressūr(a).* See PRESS[1], -URE] —**pres′sure·less,** *adj.*

pres′sure altim′eter, *Meteorol.* an aneroid barometer adapted for measuring altitude by converting the indicated atmospheric pressure to altitude according to a standard relationship. Cf. **standard atmosphere.**

pres′sure al′titude, *Meteorol.* the altitude for a given pressure in a standard atmosphere, such as that registered by a pressure altimeter.

pres′sure cab′in, *Aeron.* a pressurized cabin.

pres′sure cen′ter, *Meteorol.* the central point of an atmospheric high or low. Cf. **high** (def. 40), **low**[1] (def. 48).

pres·sure-cook (presh′ər ko͝ok′), *v.t.* to cook in a pressure cooker.

pres′sure cook′er, a reinforced pot, usually of steel or aluminum, in which soups, meats, vegetables, etc., may be cooked quickly in heat above boiling point by steam maintained under pressure.

pres′sure gauge′, 1. an instrument for measuring the pressure of a gas or liquid. 2. an instrument used to determine the pressure in the bore or chamber of a gun when the charge explodes.

pres′sure gra′dient, *Meteorol.* the decrease in atmospheric pressure per unit of horizontal distance in the direction in which pressure decreases most rapidly.

pres′sure group′, any group, esp. a special interest group, which attempts to influence legislation through the use of lobbying techniques and propaganda.

pres′sure head′, *Physics.* head (def. 30).

pres′sure point′, 1. a point on the skin which is extremely sensitive to pressure because of the presence of pressure-sensing organs. 2. a point on the body where relatively slight pressure serves to press an artery lying close to the surface against underlying bony tissue, so as to arrest the flow of blood into a part.

pres′sure-vac′u·um valve′ (presh′ər vak′yo͞o-əm, -yo͞om), a valve for relieving a sealed tank of any pressure or vacuum exceeding acceptable limits.

pres′sure weld′ing, the welding together of two objects by holding them together under pressure.

pres·sur·i·za·tion (presh′ər i zā′shən), *n.* 1. the process or act of pressurizing. 2. the state of being pressurized. [PRESSURIZE + -ATION]

pres·su·rize (presh′ə rīz′), *v.t.,* **-rized, -riz·ing.** 1. to maintain normal air pressure in (the cockpit or cabin of) an airplane designed to fly at high altitudes. 2. to apply pressure to (a gas or liquid); supercharge. 3. to pressure-cook. [PRESSURE + -IZE]

---

pre·set′tle, *v.t.,* **-tled, -tling.**
pre·set′tle·ment, *n.*
pre·shad′ow, *n., v.t.*
pre-Shake′speare, *adj.*
pre′-Shake·spear′e·an, *adj.*
pre′-Shake·spear′i·an, *adj.*
pre·shape′, *n., v.t.,* **-shaped, -shap·ing.**
pre·share′, *n., v.t.,* **-shared, -shar·ing.**
pre·sharp′en, *v.t.*
pre·ship′, *v.t.,* **-shipped, -ship·ping.**
pre·ship′ment, *n.*
pre·short′age, *n.*
pre·short′en, *v.t.*
pre·show′, *v.t.,* **-showed, -shown** or **-showed, -show·ing;** *adj., n.*
pre·sift′, *v.t.*
pre·sig′nal, *n., v.t.,* **-naled, -nal·ing** or (*esp. Brit.*) **-nalled, -nal·ling.**
pre′-Si·lu′ri·an, *adj., n.*
pre·slav′er·y, *adj., n.*
pre·smooth′, *v.t.*
pre·so′cial, *adj.*
pre·so′cial·ism, *n.*
pre·so′cial·ist, *n.*
pre·so′lar, *adj.*
pre′so·lic′it, *v.t.*
pre′so·lic′i·ta′tion, *n.*
pre′-Sol·o·mon′ic, *adj.*
pre′-So·lo′ni·an, *adj.*
pre′so·lu′tion, *n.*
pre·solve′, *v.t.,* **-solved, -solv·ing.**
pre·soph′o·more′, *adj.*
pre·sound′, *n., v.*
pre-Span′ish, *adj.*
pre·spe′cial·ist, *n.*
pre·spe′cial·ize′, *v.i.,* **-ized, -iz·ing.**
pre′spe·cif′ic, *adj.*
pre′spe·cif′i·cal·ly, *adv.*
pre′spec·i·fi·ca′tion, *n.*
pre·spec′i·fy′, *v.t.,* **-fied, -fy·ing.**
pre·spec′u·late′, *v.i.,* **-lat·ed, -lat·ing.**
pre′spec·u·la′tion, *n.*
pre·sphe′noid, *adj.*
pre·spi′nal, *adj.*
pre′spi·rac′u·lar, *adj.*
pre·spread′, *v.t.,* **-spread, -spread·ing.**
pre·sprin′kle, *v.t.,* **-kled, -kling.**
pre·spur′, *v.t.,* **-spurred, -spur·ring.**

pres′surized suit′, *Aeron.* an airtight suit that can be inflated to maintain approximately normal atmospheric pressure on a flyer at high altitudes.

press·work (pres′wûrk′), *n.* **1.** the working or management of a printing press. **2.** the work done by it. [PRESS[1] + WORK]

prest[1] (prest), *adj.* *Obs.* ready. [ME < OF < LL *praest(us)* ready. See PRESTO]

prest[2] (prest), *n.* *Obs.* **1.** a loan. **2.** an advance payment on wages. **3.** See **prest money.** [late ME *preste* < MF *prest,* OF, back formation from *prester* to lend < L *praestāre* to perform, vouch for, excel (ML: to lend), lit., to stand in front. See PRE-, STAND]

Pres′ter John′ (pres′tər), a legendary Christian monk and potentate of the Middle Ages, supposed to have had a kingdom in some remote part of Asia or Africa and associated with fabulous narratives of travel.

pres·ti·dig·i·ta·tion (pres′ti dij′i tā′shən), *n.* sleight of hand; legerdemain. [< F, lit., ready-fingerness, alter. of L *praestigiae* (see PRESTIGE) juggler's tricks. See PREST[1], DIGIT, -ATION] —**pres′ti·dig′i·ta′tor,** *n.* —**pres·ti·dig·i·ta·to·ry** (pres′ti dij′i tə tôr′ē, -tōr′ē), **pres·ti·dig·i·ta·to·ri·al** (pres′ti dij′i tə tôr′ē əl, -tōr′-), *adj.*

pres·tige (pre stēzh′, -stēj′, pres′tij), *n.* **1.** reputation or influence arising from success, achievement, rank, or other favorable attributes. **2.** distinction or reputation attaching to a person or thing and dominating the mind of others or of the public: *The new discothèque has great prestige with the jet set.* —*adj.* **3.** having or showing success, rank, wealth, etc. [< F, orig. pl. < L *praestigiae* juggler's tricks, dissimilated var. of *praestrigiae, akin to *praestringere* to blunt (sight or mind), lit., to press in front. See PRE-, STRIGIL]
—**Syn. 1.** weight, importance. —**Ant. 1.** disrepute.

pres·tig·ious (pre stij′əs, -stij′ē əs, -stē′jəs, -stē′jē-əs), *adj.* having a high reputation; honored; esteemed: *Faulkner is one of the most prestigious authors of our time.* [< LL *praestigiōs(us)* full of tricks, deceitful, equiv. to L *praestigi(um)* (see PRESTIGE) + *-ōsus* -OUS]

pres·tis·si·mo (pre stis′ə mō′; *It.* pre stēs′sē mō′), *adv.* (a musical direction) in the most rapid tempo. [< It: most quickly, superl. of *presto* PRESTO]

prest′ mon′ey, *Brit. Obs.* a sum of money advanced to men enlisting in the navy or the army, given to bind the bargain and as an inducement. Also called **press money, prest.**

pres·to (pres′tō), *adv., adj., n., pl.* **-tos.** —*adv.* **1.** quickly, rapidly, or immediately. **2.** at a rapid tempo (used as a musical direction). —*adj.* **3.** quick or rapid. **4.** executed at a rapid tempo (used as a musical direction). —*n.* **5.** *Music.* a movement or piece in quick tempo. [< It: quick, quickly < LL *praestus* (adj.) ready, L *praestō* (adv.) at hand]

pres′to chan′go (chān′jō), **1.** change at once (usually used imperatively, as in a magician's command). **2.** a change occurring suddenly and as if by magic: *There is always an element of presto chango in international relations.* [rhyming alter. of CHANGE]

Pres·ton (pres′tən), *n.* **1.** a seaport in W Lancashire, in NW England. 113,208 (1961). **2.** a town in SE Idaho. 3640 (1960). **3.** a boy's given name.

Pres·ton·pans (pres′tən panz′), *n.* a seaside resort in SE Scotland, E of Edinburgh: battle 1745. 3183 (est. 1964).

Pres·tons·burg (pres′tənz bûrg′), *n.* a town in E Kentucky. 3133 (1960).

pre·store (prē stôr′, -stōr′), *v.t.,* **-stored, -stor·ing.** **1.** to store beforehand for future use. **2.** *Computer Technol.* to fix an opening value for (the address of an operand or of a cycle index). [PRE- + STORE]

pre·stress (prē stres′), *v.t.* **1.** (in certain concrete construction) to apply stress to (reinforcing strands) before they assume a load. **2.** to make (a concrete member) with prestressed reinforcing strands. [PRE- + STRESS]

pre′stressed con′crete, concrete reinforced with wire strands, pretensioned or post-tensioned within their elastic limit to give an active resistance to loads.

Prest·wick (prest′wik), *n.* international airport in W Scotland.

pre·sum·a·ble (pri zo͞o′mə bəl), *adj.* capable of being taken for granted; probable. [PRESUME + -ABLE]

pre·sum·a·bly (pri zo͞o′mə blē), *adv.* by assuming reasonably; probably: *Since he is a consistent winner, he is presumably a superior player.* [PRESUMABLE + -LY]

pre·sume (pri zo͞om′), *v.,* **-sumed, -sum·ing.** —*v.t.* **1.** to take for granted, assume, or suppose: *I presume you're tired after your drive.* **2.** *Law.* to assume as true in the absence of proof to the contrary. **3.** to undertake with unwarrantable boldness. **4.** to undertake or venture (to do something), as by taking a liberty: *to presume to speak for another.* —*v.i.* **5.** to take something for granted; suppose. **6.** to act or proceed with unwarrantable or impertinent boldness. **7.** to rely in acting unwarrantably or in taking liberties (usually fol. by *on* or *upon*): *Do not presume upon his tolerance.* [ME < L *praesūme(re)* (to) take beforehand (LL: take for granted, assume, dare), equiv. to *prae-* PRE- + *sūmere* to take up, suppose (*su-* SUB- + -(*e*)*mere* to take)] —**pre·sum·ed·ly** (pri zo͞o′mid lē), *adv.* —**pre·sum′er,** *n.* —**pre·sum′ing·ly,** *adv.*
—**Syn. 1.** presuppose. **6.** overstep.

pre·sump·tion (pri zump′shən), *n.* **1.** the act of presuming. **2.** assumption of something as true. **3.** belief on reasonable grounds or probable evidence. **4.** that which is presumed; an assumption. **5.** a ground or reason for presuming or believing. **6.** *Law.* an inference required or permitted by law as to the existence of one fact from proof of the existence of other facts. **7.** *Logic.* an assumption, often not fully established, which is taken for granted in some piece of reasoning. **8.** unwarrantable, unbecoming, or impertinent boldness. [ME: effrontery, supposition < L *praesūmptiōn-* (s. of *praesūmptiō*) anticipation, supposition, LL: presumptuousness, equiv. to *praesūmpt(us)* (ptp. of *praesūmere* to undertake beforehand; see PRESUME) + *-iōn-* -ION]

presump′tion of fact′, *Law.* a presumption based on experience or knowledge of the relationship between a known fact and a fact inferred from it. Also called **logical presumption.**

presump′tion of in′nocence, *Law.* the rebuttable presumption of the innocence of the defendant in a criminal action in Anglo-Saxon jurisprudence, placing upon the prosecution the burden of proof of his guilt.

presump′tion of law′, *Law.* a presumption based upon a policy of law or a general rule and not upon the facts or evidence in an individual case.

presump′tion of survi′vorship, *Law.* a presumption based upon such factors as age, health, or the like, and not upon direct evidence, that determines which one of connected persons dying in the same disaster survived longer and whose heirs will therefore inherit.

pre·sump·tive (pri zump′tiv), *adj.* **1.** affording ground for presumption: *presumptive evidence.* **2.** based on presumption: *a presumptive title.* **3.** regarded as such by presumption; based on inference. **4.** *Embryol.* pertaining to the part of an embryo that in the course of normal development will predictably become a particular structure or region. [< LL *praesūmptīv(us).* See PRESUMPTION, -IVE] —**pre·sump′tive·ly,** *adv.*

presump′tive heir′, *Law.* See **heir presumptive.**

pre·sump·tu·ous (pri zump′cho͞o əs), *adj.* **1.** full of, characterized by, or showing presumption or readiness to presume in conduct or thought. **2.** unwarrantedly or impertinently bold; forward. **3.** *Obs.* presumptive. [ME < LL *praesūmptuōs(us),* var. of L *praesūmptiōsus.* See PRESUMPTION, -OUS] —**pre·sump′tu·ous·ly,** *adv.* —**pre·sump′tu·ous·ness,** *n.*
—**Syn. 1, 2.** impertinent, audacious; fresh; arrogant. See **bold.** —**Ant. 1, 2.** modest, unassuming.

pre·sup·pose (prē′sə pōz′), *v.t.,* **-posed, -pos·ing.** **1.** to suppose or assume beforehand; take for granted in advance. **2.** (of a thing, condition, or state of affairs) to require or imply as an antecedent condition: *An effect presupposes a cause.* [ME < MF *présuppose(r).* See PRE- SUPPOSE] —**pre·sup·po·si·tion** (prē′sup ə zish′ən), *n.* —**pre′sup·po·si′tion·less,** *adj.*
—**Syn. 1.** presume.

pre·sup·pu·ra·tive (prē sup′yə rā′tiv, -yər ə tiv), *adj.* *Pathol.* noting or pertaining to the stage of inflammation before the formation of pus. [PRE- + SUPPURATIVE]

pre·sur·mise (prē′sər mīz′), *n., v.,* **-mised, -mis·ing.** —*n.* **1.** a surmise previously formed. —*v.t.* **2.** to surmise beforehand. [PRE- + SURMISE]

pret., preterit.

pre·ta (prā′tə), *n.* *Hindu Myth.* a wandering or disturbed ghost. [< Skt, equiv. to *pra-* PRE- + *ita* gone]

pre·tar·sus (prē tär′səs), *n., pl.* **-si** (-sī). the terminal outgrowth of the tarsus of an arthropod. [< NL; see PRE-, TARSUS]

pre·tence (pri tens′, prē′tens), *n.* *Chiefly Brit.* pretense. —**pre·tence′ful,** *adj.* —**pre·tence′less,** *adj.*

pre·tend (pri tend′), *v.t.* **1.** to cause or attempt to cause (what is not so) to seem so: *to pretend illness; to pretend that nothing is wrong.* **2.** to appear falsely, as to deceive; feign: *to pretend to go to sleep.* **3.** to allege or profess, esp. insincerely or falsely: *He pretended to have no knowledge of her whereabouts.* —*v.i.* **4.** to make believe. **5.** to lay claim to (usually fol. by *to*): *He pretended to the throne when his brother, the crown prince, died.* **6.** to make pretensions (usually fol. by *to*): *He pretends to great knowledge.* **7.** *Obs.* to aspire, as a suitor or candidate (fol. by *to*). [ME *pretende(n)* < L *praetendere* to stretch forth, put forward, pretend. See PRE-, TEND[1]]
—**Syn. 1.** simulate, fake, sham, counterfeit. PRETEND, AFFECT, ASSUME, FEIGN imply an attempt to create a false appearance. To PRETEND is to create an imaginary characteristic or to play a part: *to pretend sorrow.* To AFFECT is to make a consciously artificial show of having qualities which one thinks would look well and impress others: *to affect shyness.* To ASSUME is to take on or put on a specific outward appearance, often (but not always) with intent to deceive: *to assume an air of indifference.* To FEIGN implies using ingenuity in pretense, and some degree of imitation of appearance or characteristics: *to feign surprise.*

pre·tend·ed (pri ten′did), *adj.* **1.** insincerely or falsely professed; alleged; so-called: *a pretended interest in art.* **2.** feigned, fictitious, or counterfeit: *His pretended wealth was proved to be nonexistent.* **3.** alleged or asserted; reputed. [late ME; see PRETEND, -ED[2]] —**pre·tend′ed·ly,** *adv.*

pre·tend·er (pri ten′dər), *n.* **1.** one who pretends, esp. for a dishonest purpose. **2.** an aspirant or claimant (often fol. by *to*): *a pretender to the throne.* **3.** one who makes unjustified or false claims, statements, etc., as about personal status, abilities, intentions, or the like: *a pretender to literary genius.* [PRETEND + -ER[1]]

pre·tense (pri tens′, prē′tens), *n.* **1.** pretending or feigning; make-believe: *My sleepiness was all pretense.* **2.** a false show of something: *a pretense of friendship.* **3.** a piece of make-believe. **4.** act of pretending or alleging falsely. **5.** a false allegation or justification: *He excused himself from the lunch on a pretense of urgent business.* **6.** insincere or false profession: *His pious words were mere pretense.* **7.** the putting forth of an unwarranted claim. **8.** the claim itself. **9.** any allegation or claim: *to obtain money under false pretenses.* **10.** pretension (usually fol. by *to*): *destitute of any pretense to wit.* **11.** pretentiousness. **12. in pretense,** *Heraldry.* on an escutcheon of pretense: *a wife's family arms worn in pretense.* Also, *esp. Brit.,* **pretence.** [late ME < LL *praetensa, n. use of fem. of *praetensus,* ptp. (r. L *praetentus*) of *praetendere* to PRETEND] —**pre·tense′ful,** *adj.* —**pre·tense′less,** *adj.*
—**Syn. 1.** shamming. **2.** semblance. **3.** mask, veil.

pre·ten·sion[1] (pri ten′shən), *n.* **1.** laying of a claim to something. **2.** a claim or title to something. **3.** Often, **pretensions.** a claim made, esp. indirectly or by implication, to some quality, merit, or the like: *Her pretensions to superior judgment have no basis in fact.* **4.** a claim to dignity, importance, or merit. **5.** pretentiousness. **6.** act of pretending or alleging. **7.** an allegation of doubtful veracity. **8.** a pretext. [< ML *praetensiōn-* (s. of *praetensiō*). See PRETENSE, -ION]

pre·ten·sion[2] (prē ten′shən), *v.t.* **1.** (in prestressed-concrete construction) to apply tension to (reinforcing strands) before the concrete is poured. **2.** to make (a concrete member) with pretensioned reinforcement. [PRE- + TENSION]

pre·ten·tious (pri ten′shəs), *adj.* **1.** full of pretense or pretension. **2.** characterized by assumption of dignity or importance. **3.** making an exaggerated outward show; ostentatious. [earlier *pretensious.* See PRETENSION, -OUS] —**pre·ten′tious·ly,** *adv.* —**pre·ten′tious·ness,** *n.*
—**Syn. 2.** pompous. **3.** showy.

preter-, an element, meaning "beyond," "more than," "by," "past," occurring originally in loan words from Latin (*preterit*), and used in the formation of compound words (*preterlegal*). [< L *praeter-,* repr. *praeter* (adv. and prep.)]

pre·ter·hu·man (prē′tər hyo͞o′mən *or, often,* -yo͞o′-), *adj.* beyond what is human: *preterhuman experience.* [PRETER- + HUMAN]

pret·er·ist (pret′ər ist), *Theol.* —*n.* **1.** one who maintains that the prophecies in the Apocalypse have already been fulfilled. Cf. **futurist** (def. 3), **presentist.** —*adj.* **2.** of or pertaining to the preterists. [PRETER- + -IST]

pret·er·it (pret′ər it), *n.* *Gram.* **1.** past (def. 12). **2.** a preterit tense. **3.** a verb form in this tense. —*adj.* **4.** *Gram.* noting a past action or state. **5.** *Archaic.* bygone; past. Also, **pret′er·ite.** [ME < L *praeterit(us)* past, ptp. of *praeterīre* to go by, equiv. to *praeter-* PRETER- + *īre* to go] —**pret′er·it·ness, pret′er·ite·ness,** *n.*

pret·er·i·tion (pret′ə rish′ən), *n.* **1.** act of passing by or over; omission; disregard. **2.** *Law.* the passing over by a testator of an heir otherwise entitled to a portion. **3.** *Calvinistic Theol.* the passing over by God of those not elected to salvation or eternal life. **4.** *Rhet.* paralipsis. [< LL *praeteritiōn-* (s. of *praeteritiō*) a passing by. See PRETERIT, -ION]

pre·ter·i·tive (pri ter′i tiv), *adj.* *Gram.* (of verbs) limited to past tenses. [PRETERIT + -IVE]

pre·ter·le·gal (prē′tər lē′gəl), *adj.* being beyond the scope or limits of law. [PRETER- + LEGAL]

pre·ter·mit (prē′tər mit′), *v.t.,* **-mit·ted, -mit·ting.** **1.** to let pass without notice; disregard. **2.** to leave undone; neglect; omit. **3.** to suspend or interrupt: *The government temporarily pretermitted its repayments of foreign aid.* [< LL *praetermitt(ere)* (to) let pass, equiv. to *praeter-* PRETER- + *mittere* to let go] —**pre·ter·mis·sion** (prē′tər mish′ən), *n.* —**pre′ter·mit′ter,** *n.*

pre·ter·nat·u·ral (prē′tər nach′ər əl), *adj.* **1.** out of the ordinary course of nature; exceptional or abnormal: *With his preternatural eyesight he could make out the distant mountains.* **2.** outside of nature; supernatural. [< ML *praeternātūrāl(is),* adj. for L phrase *praeter*

pre·stamp′, *n., v.t.*
pre·stand′ard, *n., adj.*
pre·stand′ard·i·za′tion, *n.*
pre·stand′ard·ize′, *v.t.,* **-ized, -iz·ing.**
pre′sta·tis′ti·cal, *adj.*
pre·steam′, *adj., v.t.*
pre·steel′, *n., adj.*
pre·stim′u·late′, *v.t.,* **-lat·ed, -lat·ing.**
pre′stim·u·la′tion, *n.*
pre′stim′u·lus, *n., pl.* **-li.**
pre·stock′, *n., v.t.*
pre·stor′age, *n.*
pre·straight′en, *v.t.*
pre·strain′, *n., v.t.*
pre·strength′en, *v.t.*
pre·stretch′, *v.t., n.*
pre·strick′en, *adj.*
pre·strug′gle, *n., v.i.,* **-gled, -gling.**
pre·stub′born, *adj.*
pre·stu′di·ous, *adj.;* **-ly,** *adv.;* **-ness,** *n.*
pre·stud′y, *v.t.,* **-stud·ied, -stud·y·ing;** *n.*
pre′sub·due′, *v.t.,* **-dued, du·ing.**
pre′sub·ject′, *v.t.*
pre′sub·jec′tion, *n.*
pre′sub·mis′sion, *n.*
pre′sub·mit′, *v.t.,* **-mit·ted, -mit·ting.**
pre′sub·or′di·nate′, *v.t.,* **-nat·ed, -nat·ing.**
pre′sub·or′di·na′tion, *n.*
pre′sub·scribe′, *v.,* **-scribed, -scrib·ing.**
pre′sub·scrib′er, *n.*
pre′sub·scrip′tion, *n.*
pre′sub·sist′, *v.i.*
pre′sub·sist′ence, *n.*
pre′sub·sist′ent, *adj.*
pre′sub·stan′tial, *adj.*
pre·sub′sti·tute′, *v.t.,* **-tut·ed, -tut·ing.**
pre′sub·sti·tu′tion, *n.*
pre′suc·cess′, *n.*
pre′suc·cess′ful, *adj.;* **-ly,** *adv.*
pre·suf′fer, *v.*
pre′suf·fi′cien·cy, *n.*
pre′suf·fi′cient, *adj.;* **-ly,** *adv.*
pre·suf′frage, *n.*
pre′sug·gest′, *v.t.*
pre′sug·ges′tion, *n.*
pre′sug·ges′tive, *adj.*
pre′suit′a·bil′i·ty, *n.*
pre·suit′a·ble, *adj.;* **-bly,** *adv.*
pre′-Su·me′ri·an, *adj., n.*
pre′su·per·in·tend′ence, *n.*
pre′su·per·in·tend′en·cy, *n.*
pre·su′per·vise′, *v.t.,* **-vised, -vis·ing.**
pre′su·per·vi′sion, *n.*
pre·su′per·vi′sor, *n.*
pre′sup·ple·men′tal, *adj.*
pre′sup·ple·men′ta·ry, *adj.*
pre·sup′pli·cate′, *v.t.,* **-cat·ed, -cat·ing.**
pre′sup·pli·ca′tion, *n.*
pre′sup·ply′, *n., v.t.,* **-plied, -ply·ing.**
pre′sup·port′, *n., v.t.*
pre′sup·press′, *v.t.*
pre′su·prem′a·cy, *n.*
pre·sur′ger·y, *adj.*
pre·sur′gi·cal, *adj.*
pre′sur·ren′der, *n.*
pre′sur·round′, *v.t.*
pre·sur′vey, *n.*
pre′sur·vey′, *v.t.*
pre′sus·cep′ti·bil′i·ty, *n.*
pre′sus·cep′ti·ble, *adj.*
pre′sus·pect′, *v.t.*
pre′sus·pend′, *v.t.*
pre′sus·pen′sion, *n.*
pre′sus·pi′cion, *n.*
pre′sus·pi′cious, *adj.;* **-ly,** *adv.;* **-ness,** *n.*
pre′sus·tain′, *v.t.*
pre·su′tur·al, *adj.*
pre·swal′low, *n., v.t.*
pre·sym′pa·thize′, *v.i.,* **-thized, -thiz·ing.**
pre·sym′pa·thy, *n.*
pre′sym·phon′ic, *adj.*
pre·sym′pho·ny, *n.*
pre′sym·phys′i·al, *adj.*
pre·symp′tom, *n.*
pre′symp·to·mat′ic, *adj.*
pre′syn·sa′cral, *adj.*
pre-Syr′i·ac, *adj.*
pre-Syr′i·an, *adj., n.*
pre′sys·tem·at′ic, *adj.*
pre′sys·tem·at′i·cal·ly, *adv.*
pre·sys′tole′, *n.*
pre′sys·tol′ic, *adj.*
pre·tab′u·late′, *v.t.,* **-lat·ed, -lat·ing.**
pre′tab·u·la′tion, *n.*
pre·tan′gi·ble, *adj.;* **-bly,** *adv.*
pre·tar′iff, *n., adj.*
pre·taste′, *n., v.t.,* **-tast·ed, -tast·ing.**
pre·tast′er, *n.*
pre·teach′, *v.,* **-taught, -teach·ing.**
pre·tech′ni·cal, *adj.;* **-ly,** *adv.*
pre·tel′e·graph′, *adj.*
pre′tel·e·graph′ic, *adj.*
pre·tel′e·phone′, *adj.*
pre′tel·e·phon′ic, *adj.*
pre·tell′, *v.,* **-told, -tell·ing.**
pre·tem′per·ate, *adj.;* **-ly,** *adv.*
pre·tempt′, *v.t.*
pre′temp·ta′tion, *n.*
pre·ten′ta·tive, *adj.*
pre·ter′mi·nal, *adj.*
pre′ter·res′tri·al, *adj.*
pre′ter·ri·to′ri·al, *adj.*
pre-Ter′ti·ar′y, *adj.*

CONCISE ETYMOLOGY KEY: <, descended or derived from; >, whence; b., blend of, blended; c., cognate with; deriv., derivative; equiv., equivalent; imit., imitative; m., modification of; obl., oblique; r., replacing; s., stem; sp., spelling; trans., translation; ?, origin unknown, perhaps; *, hypothetical. See the full key inside the front cover.

natūram beyond nature. See PRETER-, NATURAL] —**pre′ter·nat′u·ral·ism, pre·ter·nat·u·ral·i·ty** (prē′tər naCH′ə ral′i tē), **pre′ter·nat′u·ral·ness,** *n.* —**pre′ter·nat′u·ral·ly,** *adv.*
—**Syn. 1.** unusual, extraordinary, unnatural. See **miraculous.** —**Ant. 1.** ordinary, usual.

pre·test (*n.* prē′test; *v.* prē test′), *n.* **1.** a test given to determine if a student is sufficiently prepared to begin a new course of study. **2.** a test taken for practice, as a trial, etc. —*v.t.* **3.** to give a pretest to (a student, product, etc.). —*v.i.* **4.** to conduct a pretest: *The company is pretesting for consumer acceptance.* [PRE- + TEST]

pre·text (prē′tekst), *n.* **1.** that which is put forward to conceal a true purpose or object; an ostensible reason: *The leaders used the insults as a pretext to declare war.* **2.** the misleading appearance or behavior assumed with this intention: *His many lavish compliments were a pretext for subtle mockery.* [< L *praetext(um)* pretext, ornament, n. use of neut. ptp. of *praetexere* to pretend, lit., to weave in front, hence, adorn. See PRE-, TEXTURE]
—**Syn. 2.** subterfuge, evasion.

pre·tex·ta (prē tek′stə), *n., pl.* **-tex·tae** (-tek′stē). praetexta.

pre·tor (prē′tər), *n.* praetor. —**pre·to·ri·al** (prē tôr′ē əl, -tōr′-), *adj.* —**pre·to′ri·an,** *adj., n.*

Pre·to·ri·a (pri tôr′ē ə, -tōr′-), *n.* a city in and the administrative capital of the Republic of South Africa, in the NE part: also the capital of Transvaal. 420,053 (1960).

Pre·to·ri·us (pri tôr′ē əs, -tōr′-; *Du.* prā tō′rē ōōs′), *n.* **An·dries Wil·hel·mus Ja·co·bus** (än′drēs vil hel′mōōs yä kô′bōōs), 1799–1853, and his son **Mar·thi·nus Wes·sels** (mär tē′nōōs ves′əls), 1819–1901, Boer soldiers and statesmen in South Africa.

pre·tri·al (prē trī′əl, -trīl′), *Law.* —*n.* **1.** a proceeding held by a judge, arbitrator, etc., before a trial to simplify the issues of law and fact and stipulate certain matters between the parties, in order to expedite justice and curtail costs at the trial. —*adj.* **2.** of or pertaining to such a proceeding. [PRE- + TRIAL]

pret·ti·fy (prit′ə fī′), *v.t.,* **-fied, -fy·ing. 1.** *Often Disparaging.* to make pretty: *to prettify a natural beauty.* **2.** to minimize or gloss over (something unpleasant): *to prettify the current international crisis; an attempt to prettify his rude behavior.* [PRETT(Y) + -IFY] —**pret′ti·fi·ca′tion,** *n.* —**pret′ti·fi′er,** *n.*

pret·ty (prit′ē), *adj.,* **-ti·er, -ti·est,** *n., pl.* **-ties,** *adv., v.,* **-tied, -ty·ing.** —*adj.* **1.** pleasing or attractive to the eye in a feminine or childlike way, as by delicacy, gracefulness, etc.: *a pretty face.* **2.** (of things, places, etc.) pleasing to the eye, esp. without grandeur. **3.** pleasing to the ear: *a pretty tune.* **4.** pleasing to the mind or aesthetic taste: *He writes pretty little stories.* **5.** (often used ironically) fine; grand: *This is a pretty mess!* **6.** *Informal.* considerable, fairly great: *This accident will cost him a pretty sum.* **7.** *Archaic or Scot.* brave; hardy. —*n.* **8.** Usually, **pretties.** a pretty thing, as an ornament. **9.** (used in address) a pretty person: *Sit down, my pretty.* —*adv.* **10.** moderately: *Her work was pretty good.* **11.** quite; very: *The wind blew pretty hard.* **12.** *Chiefly Dial.* prettily. **13. sitting pretty,** *Slang.* **a.** in an advantageous position. **b.** well-to-do; successful. —*v.t.* **14.** to make pretty; improve the appearance of (sometimes fol. by *up*): *to pretty oneself for a party; to pretty up a room.* [ME *prety, praty,* OE *prættig,* cunning, wily, deriv. of *prætt* a trick, wile; c. D *part* trick, prank, Icel *prettr* trick, *prettugr* tricky] —**pret′ti·ly,** *adv.* —**pret′ti·ness,** *n.* —**pret′ty·ish,** *adj.*
—**Syn. 1.** See **beautiful. 2.** pleasant. **11.** fairly, somewhat. —**Ant. 1.** ugly.

pret·ty-face (prit′ē fās′), *n.* an herb, *Brodiaea ixiodes,* of the western coast of the U.S., having purple-streaked, salmon or salmon-yellow flowers.

pre·typ·i·fy (prē tip′ə fī′), *v.t.,* **-fied, -fy·ing.** to foreshadow or prefigure the type of: *The father's personality pretypified his son's.* [PRE- + TYPIFY]

pret·zel (pret′səl), *n.* a crisp, dry biscuit, usually in the form of a knot or stick, salted on the outside. [< G *Pretzel,* var. of *Bretzel;* cf. ML *bracellus* bracelet]

Preus·sen (proi′sən), *n.* German name of **Prussia.**

pre·vail (pri vāl′), *v.i.* **1.** to be widespread or current; exist everywhere or generally: *Dead silence prevailed along the funeral route.* **2.** to appear or occur as the more important or frequent feature or element; predominate: *Green tints prevail in the upholstery.* **3.** to be or prove superior in strength, power, or influence (usually fol. by *over*): *They prevailed over their enemies in the battle.* **4.** to succeed; become dominant; win out: *to wish that the right side might prevail.* **5.** to use persuasion or inducement successfully: *He prevailed upon us to accompany him.* [ME *prevaylle(n)* (to) grow very strong < L *praevalē(re)* (to) be more able, equiv. to *prae-* PRE- + *valēre* to be strong] —**pre·vail′er,** *n.*
—**Syn. 2.** preponderate. **3.** overcome. —**Ant. 3.** lose.

pre·vail·ing (pri vā′liNG), *adj.* **1.** predominant: *prevailing winds.* **2.** generally current: *the prevailing opinion.* **3.** having superior power or influence. **4.** effectual. [PREVAIL + -ING²] —**pre·vail′ing·ly,** *adv.* —**pre·vail′ing·ness,** *n.*
—**Syn. 1.** preponderant, preponderating, dominant; prevalent. **2.** common. See **current. 4.** effective. —**Ant. 2.** rare.

prev·a·lent (prev′ə lənt), *adj.* **1.** widespread; of wide extent or occurrence; in general use or acceptance. **2.** having the superiority or ascendancy. **3.** *Archaic.* effectual or efficacious. [< L *praevalent-* (s. of *praevalēns*), prp. of *praevalēre* to PREVAIL. See PRE-, -VALENT] —**prev′a·lence, prev′a·lent·ness,** *n.* —**prev′a·lent·ly,** *adv.*
—**Syn. 1.** common, extensive. See **current.** —**Ant. 1.** rare.

pre·var·i·cate (pri var′ə kāt′), *v.i.,* **-cat·ed, -cat·ing.** to speak falsely or misleadingly; deliberately misstate or create an incorrect impression; lie. [< L *praevāricāt(us),* ptp. of *praevāricārī* to walk as if straddling, (legal L: engage in collusion, eccl. L: transgress), equiv. to *prae-* PRE- + *vāricāre* to straddle, deriv. of *vāricus* straddling (*vār(us)* crooked, bent + *-icus* -IC)] —**pre·var′i·ca′tion,** *n.* —**pre·var′i·ca′tive, pre·var·i·ca·to·ry** (pri var′ə kə tôr′ē, -tōr′ē), *adj.*
—**Syn.** evade, shift.

pre·var·i·ca·tor (pri var′ə kā′tər), *n.* **1.** one who prevaricates. **2.** a Cambridge University student formerly delegated to give a satirical oration at commencement. Cf. **terrae filius** (def. 1). [< L; see PREVARICATE, -OR²]

pré·ve·nance (prāvᵊ näNs′), *n., pl.* **-nances** (-näNs′) for 2. *French.* **1.** assiduity in anticipating or catering to the pleasures of others. **2.** an instance of this.

pre·ven·ient (pri vēn′yənt), *adj.* **1.** coming before; antecedent. **2.** anticipatory. [< L *praevenient-* (s. of *praeveniēns*) coming before, prp. of *praevenīre* to anticipate. See PRE-, CONVENIENT] —**prev·e·nance** (prev′ə nəns), **pre·ven·ience** (pri vēn′yəns), *n.* —**pre·ven′ient·ly,** *adv.*

preven′ient grace′, divine grace operating on the human will prior to its turning to God.

pre·vent (pri vent′), *v.t.* **1.** to keep from occurring; hinder: *He intervened to prevent bloodshed.* **2.** to hinder, as from doing something: *There is nothing to prevent us from going.* **3.** *Archaic.* to act ahead of; forestall. **4.** *Archaic.* to precede. **5.** *Archaic.* to anticipate. —*v.i.* **6.** to interpose a hindrance: *He will come if nothing prevents.* [ME < L *praevent(us)* started beforehand (ptp. of *praevenīre* to anticipate), equiv. to *prae-* PRE- + *ven-* (s. of *venīre* to come) + *-tus* ptp. suffix] —**pre·vent′a·bil′i·ty,** *n.* —**pre·vent′a·ble, pre·vent′i·ble,** *adj.* —**pre·vent′ing·ly,** *adv.*
—**Syn. 1.** obstruct, forestall, preclude, obviate, thwart. PREVENT, HAMPER, HINDER, IMPEDE refer to different degrees of stoppage of action or progress. To PREVENT is to stop something effectually by forestalling action and rendering it impossible: *to prevent the sending of a message.* To HAMPER is to clog or entangle or put an embarrassing restraint upon: *to hamper preparations for a trip.* To HINDER is to keep back by delaying or stopping progress or action: *to hinder the progress of an expedition.* To IMPEDE is to make difficult the movement or progress of anything by interfering with its proper functioning: *to impede a discussion by demanding repeated explanations.* —**Ant. 1.** help, assist.

pre·vent·er (pri ven′tər), *n.* **1.** one who or that which prevents. **2.** *Naut.* **a.** any of various lines set up to reinforce or relieve ordinary running or standing rigging. **b.** a line for preventing a sail from jibing. [PREVENT + -ER¹]

prevent′er back′stay, *Naut.* See **jumper stay.** Also called **prevent′er stay′.**

pre·ven·tion (pri ven′shən), *n.* **1.** the act of preventing; effectual hindrance. **2.** a preventive: *This serum is a prevention against disease.* [< LL *praeventiōn-* (s. of *praeventiō*) a forestalling. See PREVENT, -ION]

pre·ven·tive (pri ven′tiv), *adj.* **1.** *Med.* of or noting a drug, vaccine, etc., for preventing disease; prophylactic. **2.** serving to prevent or hinder: *preventive medicine.* —*n.* **3.** *Med.* a drug or other substance for preventing disease. **4.** a preventive agent or measure. Also, **pre·vent·a·tive** (pri ven′tə tiv) (for defs. 2, 4). [PREVENT + -IVE] —**pre·ven′tive·ly,** *adv.* —**pre·ven′tive·ness,** *n.*

preven′tive deten′tion, *Eng. Law.* imprisonment of a habitual criminal for periods ranging from 5–14 years during which he is given corrective training or placed under psychiatric and medical care.

preven′tive law′, *Law.* that part of office practice that attempts to anticipate and prevent future disappointment or controversy.

pre·ven·to·ri·um (prē′vən tôr′ē əm, -tōr′-, -ven-), *n., pl.* **-to·ri·a** (-tôr′ē ə, -tōr′-), **-to·ri·ums.** an institutional home for persons, esp. children, who might otherwise be exposed at their own homes to relatives having contagious or infectious diseases. [PREVENT + -ORIUM]

pre·view (prē′vyōō′), *n.* **1.** an earlier or previous view. **2.** an advance showing of a motion picture, play, etc., before its public opening. **3.** an advance showing of brief scenes in a motion picture, television show, etc., to advertise its coming performance. **4.** anything that gives an advance idea or impression of something to come. —*v.t.* **5.** to view or show beforehand or in advance. Also, **prevue.** [PRE- + VIEW]

pre·vi·ous (prē′vē əs), *adj.* **1.** coming or occurring before something else; prior: *the previous owner.* **2.** *Informal.* done, occurring, etc., before the proper time; premature: *Aren't you a little previous with that request?* **3. previous to,** before; prior to: *Previous to her marriage she was a fashion model.* [< L *praevius* going before, equiv. to *prae-* PRE- + *vi(a)* way + *-us* adj. suffix] —**pre′vi·ous·ly,** *adv.* —**pre′vi·ous·ness,** *n.*
—**Syn. 1.** earlier, former, preceding, foregoing. —**Ant. 1.** later.

pre′vious ques′tion, *Parl. Proc.* the question whether a vote shall be taken at once on a main question: moved before the main question is put and resorted to, esp. in the U.S., in order to cut off debate.

pre·vise (pri vīz′), *v.t.,* **-vised, -vis·ing. 1.** to foresee. **2.** to forewarn. [< L *praevīs(us)* foreseen, ptp. of *praevidēre.* See PRE-, VISA] —**pre·vi′sor,** *n.*

pre·vi·sion (pri vizh′ən), *n.* **1.** foresight, foreknowledge, or prescience. **2.** a prophetic or anticipatory vision or perception. [PRE- + VISION] —**pre·vi′sion·al,** *adj.*

pre·vo·cal·ic (prē′vō kal′ik), *adj.* *Phonet.* immediately preceding a vowel. [PRE- + VOCALIC] —**pre′vo·cal′i·cal·ly,** *adv.*

pre·vo·ca·tion·al (prē′vō kā′shə nᵊl), *adj.* of, pertaining to, or constituting preliminary vocational training. [PRE- + VOCATIONAL]

Pré·vost (prā vō′), *n.* **Mar·cel** (mar sel′), 1862–1941, French novelist and dramatist.

Pré·vost d'Ex·iles (prā vō′ deg zēl′), **An·toine Fran·çois** (äN twan′ fräN swa′), ("*Abbé Prévost*"), 1697–1763, French novelist.

pre·vue (prē′vyōō′), *n., v.t.,* **-vued, -vu·ing.** preview.

Prew (prōō), *n.* a boy's given name.

pre·war (prē′wôr′), *adj.* before the war: *prewar prices.* [PRE- + WAR¹]

Prew·ett (prōō′it), *n.* a boy's given name, form of **Prew.** Also, **Prew′itt, Pruett, Pruitt.**

prex·y (prek′sē), *n., pl.* **prex·ies.** *Slang.* a president, esp. of a college or university. Also, **prex.** [*prex* (by shortening and alter. of president) + -Y²]

prey (prā), *n.* **1.** an animal hunted or seized for food, esp. by a carnivorous animal. **2.** a person or thing that is the victim of an enemy, a swindler, a disease, or the like. **3.** the action or habit of preying: *beast of prey.* **4.** *Archaic.* booty or plunder. —*v.i.* **5.** to seize and devour prey, as an animal does (usually fol. by *on* or *upon*): *Foxes prey on rabbits.* **6.** to make raids or attacks for booty or plunder: *The Vikings preyed on coastal settlements.* **7.** to exert a harmful or destructive influence: *His worries preyed upon his mind.* **8.** to victimize a class of persons (usually fol. by *on* or *upon*): *loan sharks that prey upon the poor.* [ME *preye* < OF < L *praeda* booty, prey] —**prey′er,** *n.*

Pri·am (prī′əm), *n.* *Class. Myth.* **1.** a king of Troy, the son of Laomedon, husband of Hecuba, and father of Paris, Cassandra, Hector, Polyxena, and many others. He was killed during the capture of Troy. **2.** the grandson of King Priam.

Pri·a·mid (prī′ə mid), *n.* *Class. Myth.* any of the 50 sons of Priam.

pri·a·pe·an (prī′ə pē′ən), *adj.* priapic. [< F *priapéen* < L *Priāpē(ius)* < Gk *Priāpeios.* See PRIAPUS, -AN]

pri·ap·ic (prī ap′ik), *adj.* **1.** (*sometimes cap.*) of or pertaining to Priapus; phallic. **2.** characterized by or emphasizing a phallus: *priapic figurines used in fertility rites.* **3.** (of an image) suggestive of or resembling a phallus by its shape. **4.** exaggeratedly concerned with masculinity and male sexuality. [PRIAP(US) + -IC]

pri·a·pism (prī′ə piz′əm), *n.* **1.** *Pathol.* continuous erection of the penis, esp. due to disease. **2.** prurient behavior or display. [PRIAP(US) + -ISM] —**pri′a·pis′mic,** *adj.*

pri·a·pi·tis (prī′ə pī′tis), *n.* *Pathol.* inflammation of the penis. [PRIAP(US) + -ITIS]

Pri·a·pus (prī ā′pəs), *n.* **1.** *Class. Myth.* a god of male procreative power, the son of Dionysus and Aphrodite. **2.** (*l.c.*) a phallus.

Prib·i·lof Is′lands (prib′ə lof′), a group of islands in the Bering Sea, SW of Alaska, and belonging to the U.S.: the breeding ground of fur seals.

pre·tes′ti·fy′, *v.t.,* **-fied, -fy·ing.**
pre·tes′ti·mo′ny, *n., pl.* **-nies.**
pre′-Thanks·giv′ing, *adj.*
pre′the·o·log′i·cal, *adj.*
pre·tho·rac′ic, *adj.*
pre·threat′en, *v.t.*
pre·thrust′, *n., v.t.*
pre·thy′roid, *adj.*
pre·tib′i·al, *adj.*
pre·time′li·ness, *n.*
pre·time′ly, *adj.*
pre·tinc′ture, *n.*
pre·tire′, *v.t.,* **-tired, -tir·ing.**
pre·to′ken, *n., v.t.*
pre·ton′ic, *n., adj.*
pre·tor′ture, *n., v.t.,* **-tured, -tur·ing;** *n.*
pre·tour′na·ment, *n.*
pre·trace′, *n., v.t.,* **-traced, -trac·ing.**
pre·tra′che·al, *adj.*
pre′tra·di′tion·al, *adj.*
pre·train′, *v.t.*
pre·train′ing, *n.*
pre′trans·act′, *v.t.*
pre′trans·ac′tion, *n.*
pre′tran·scribe′, *v.t.,* **-scribed, -scrib·ing.**
pre′tran·scrip′tion, *n.*
pre′trans·late′, *v.t.,* **-lat·ed, -lat·ing.**
pre′trans·la′tion, *n.*
pre′trans·mis′sion, *n.*
pre′trans·mit′, *v.t.,* **-mit·ted, -mit·ting.**
pre′trans·port′, *v.t.*
pre′trans·por·ta′tion, *n.*
pre·trav′el, *n., v.,* **-eled, -el·ing.** or (*esp. Brit.*) **-elled, -el·ling.**
pre·trib′al, *adj.*
pre′-Tri·den′tine, *adj.*
pre·tro′chal, *adj.*
pre·try′, *v.t.,* **-tried, -try·ing.**
pre-Tu′dor, *adj.*
pre′tym·pan′ic, *adj.*
pre·ty′phoid, *adj.*
pre′ty·po·graph′i·cal, *adj.*
pre′ty·ran′ni·cal, *adj.*
pre·tyr′an·ny, *n.*
pre·um′bo·nal, *adj.*
pre′un·der·stand′, *v.,* **-stood, -stand·ing.**
pre′un·der·take′, *v.t.,* **-took, -tak·en, -tak·ing.**
pre·un′ion, *adj.*
pre′u·nite′, *v.t.,* **-nit·ed, -nit·ing.**
pre·u′ti·liz′a·ble, *adj.*
pre·u′ti·li·za′tion, *n.*
pre·u′ti·lize′, *v.t.,* **-lized, -liz·ing.**
pre·va′cate, *v.t.,* **-cat·ed, -cat·ing.**
pre′va·ca′tion, *n., adj.*
pre·vac′ci·nate′, *v.t.,* **-nat·ed, -nat·ing.**
pre′vac·ci·na′tion, *n.*
pre·val′id, *adj.;* **-ly,** *adv.*
pre′va·lid′i·ty, *n.*
pre·val′u·a′tion, *n.*
pre·val′ue, *v.t.,* **-ued, -u·ing;** *n.*
pre′var·i·a′tion, *n.*
pre′veg·e·ta′tion, *n.*
pre·ven′tral, *adj.*
pre·ven′ture, *n., v.,* **-tured, -tur·ing.**
pre·ver′bal, *adj.*
pre′ver·i·fi·ca′tion, *n.*
pre·ver′i·fy′, *v.t.,* **-fied, -fy·ing.**
pre·ver′sion, *n.*
pre·ver′te·bral, *adj.*
pre·ve′to, *n., pl.* **-toes;** *v.t.,* **-toed, -to·ing.**
pre′-Vic·to′ri·an, *adj.*
pre′vic·to′ri·ous, *adj.*
pre·vig′i·lance, *n.*
pre·vig′i·lant, *adj.;* **-ly,** *adv.*
pre·vi′o·late′, *v.t.,* **-lat·ed, -lat·ing.**
pre′vi·o·la′tion, *n.*
pre′-Vir·gil′i·an, *adj.*
pre′vis·i·bil′i·ty, *n.*
pre·vis′i·ble, *adj.;* **-bly,** *adv.*
pre·vis′it, *n., v.*
pre·vis′i·tor, *n.*
pre·vogue′, *n.*
pre·void′, *v.t.*
pre·void′ance, *n.*
pre′-Vol·i′tion·al, *adj.*
pre′-Vol′stead, *n.*
pre′vol·un·teer′, *n., v.*
pre·vote′, *n., v.,* **-vot·ed, -vot·ing.**
pre·warm′, *v.t.*
pre·warn′, *v.t.*
pre·war′rant, *n., v.t.*
pre·wash′, *n., v.t.*
pre·weigh′, *v.t.*
pre·wel′come, *n., v.t.,* **-comed, -com·ing.**
pre·whip′, *v.t.,* **-whipped, -whip·ping.**
pre·will′ing, *adj.;* **-ly,** *adv.;* **-ness,** *n.*
pre·wire′, *v.t.,* **-wired, -wir·ing.**
pre·wire′less, *adj.*
pre·wit′ness, *n., v.t.*
pre·world′li·ness, *n.*
pre·world′ly, *adj.*
pre·wor′ship, *n., v.,* **-shiped** or **-shipped, -ship·ing** or **-ship·ping.**
pre·wor′thi·ly, *adv.*
pre·wor′thi·ness, *n.*
pre·wor′thy, *adj.*
pre·wound′, *n., v.t.*
pre·wrap′, *v.t.,* **-wrapped, -wrap·ping.**
pre·youth′ful, *adj.*
pre′zy·go·mat′ic, *adj.*

price (prīs), *n., v.,* **priced, pric·ing.** —*n.* **1.** the sum or amount of money or its equivalent for which anything is bought, sold, or offered for sale. **2.** a sum offered for the capture of a person alive or dead: *The authorities put a price on his head.* **3.** the sum of money, or other consideration, for which a person's support, consent, etc., may be obtained, esp. in cases involving sacrifice of integrity: *They claimed that every man has his price.* **4.** that which must be given, done, or undergone in order to obtain a thing: *He gained the victory, but at a heavy price.* **5.** odds (def. 2). **6.** *Archaic.* value or worth: *The price of an honest man is beyond measure.* **7.** *Archaic.* great value or worth (usually prec. by *of*): *Among the inventory were many articles of price.* **8. at any price,** at any cost, no matter how great: *There were no bananas to be had at any price. He would have his own way at any price.* **9. beyond** or **without price,** of incalculable value; priceless: *The crown jewels are beyond price.* —*v.t.* **10.** to fix the price of. **11.** to ask or determine the price of: *We spent the day pricing furniture at various stores.* [ME *pris* < OF < L *pret(ium)* price, value, worth] —**price′a·ble,** *adj.*

—**Syn. 1, 4.** PRICE, CHARGE, COST, EXPENSE refer to outlay or expenditure required in buying or maintaining something. PRICE is used mainly of single, concrete objects offered for sale; CHARGE, of services: *What is the price of that coat? There is a small charge for mailing packages.* COST is mainly a purely objective term, often used in financial calculations: *The cost of building a new annex was estimated at $10,000.* EXPENSE suggests cost plus incidental expenditure: *The expense of a journey was more than the contemplated cost.* Only CHARGE is not used figuratively. PRICE, COST, and sometimes EXPENSE may be used to refer to the expenditure of mental energy, what one "pays" in anxiety, suffering, etc.

Price (prīs), *n.* **1. Bruce,** 1845–1903, U.S. architect. **2. (Mary) Le·on·tyne** (lē′ən tēn′), born 1927, U.S. soprano. **3.** a town in central Utah. 6802 (1960). **4.** a boy's given name.

price′ cut′ting, selling an article at a price under the usual or advertised price.

price′ discrimina′tion, the practice of offering identical goods to different buyers at different prices, the costs being equal to the seller.

price′-earn′ings ra′tio (prīs′ûr′niṅgz), the ratio of the market price of a share of common stock to the earnings per share.

price′ fix′ing, the establishing of prices at a determined level, either by a government or by mutual consent among producers of a commodity, product, etc.

price·less (prīs′lis), *adj.* **1.** having a value beyond all price; invaluable: *She was a priceless help to him.* **2.** *Informal.* delightfully amusing; absurd: *That was a priceless anecdote!* [PRICE + -LESS] —**price′less·ness,** *n.*

price′ list′, a list giving the prices of items for sale.

pric·er (prī′sər), *n.* **1.** (esp. in retail stores) an employee who establishes prices at which articles will be sold, or one who affixes price tags to merchandise. **2.** one who inquires prices, as from a competitor. [PRICE + -ER[1]]

price′ range′, the highest and lowest price of a commodity, security, etc., over a given period of time.

price′ support′, the maintenance of the price of a commodity, product, etc., esp. by means of a public subsidy or government purchase.

price′ tag′, a label or tag that shows the price of the item to which it is attached.

price′ war′, *Com.* intensive competition, esp. among retailers, in which prices are repeatedly cut in order to undersell competitors or sometimes to force smaller competitors out of business.

pric·ey (prī′sē), *adj.,* **pric·i·er, pric·i·est.** *Informal.* expensive or unduly expensive: *a pricey wine.* Also, **pricy.** [PRICE + -Y[1]] —**pric′i·ly,** *adv.* —**pric′i·ness,** *n.*

Prich·ard (prich′ərd), *n.* a city in S Alabama. 47,371 (1960).

prick (prik), *n.* **1.** a puncture made by a needle, thorn, or the like. **2.** act of pricking: *the prick of a needle.* **3.** the state or sensation of being pricked. **4.** the pointed end of a prickspur. **5.** *Slang (vulgar).* penis. **6.** *Archaic.* a goad for oxen. **7.** *Obs.* a small or minute mark, a dot, or a point. **8.** *Obs.* any pointed instrument or weapon. **9. kick against the pricks,** to resist incontestable facts or authority; protest uselessly: *In appealing the case again, you will just be kicking against the pricks.* —*v.t.* **10.** to pierce with a sharp point; puncture. **11.** to affect with sharp pain, as from piercing. **12.** to cause sharp mental pain to; sting, as with remorse, anger, etc.: *His conscience pricked him suddenly.* **13.** to urge on with or as with a goad or spur: *My duty pricks me on.* **14.** to mark (a surface) with pricks or dots in tracing something. **15.** to mark or trace (something) on a surface by pricks or dots. **16.** to cause to stand erect or point upward: *to prick up one's ears.* **17.** *Farriery.* **a.** to lame (a horse) by driving a nail improperly into its hoof. **b.** to nick: *to prick a horse's tail.* **18.** to measure (distance, the size of an area, etc.) on a chart with dividers (usually fol. by *off*). **19.** *Hort.* to transplant (a seedling) into a container that provides more room for growth (usually fol. by *out* or *off*). —*v.i.* **20.** to perform the action of piercing or puncturing something. **21.** to have a sensation of being pricked. **22.** *Archaic.* to spur or urge a horse on; ride rapidly. **23. prick up,** to rise erect or point upward, as the ears of an animal. **24. prick up one's ears,** to become very alert; listen attentively: *She pricked up her ears at the prospect of some juicy gossip.* [ME *prike* (n.), *prike(n)* (v.), OE *prica, price* dot, point, *prician* (v.); c. D, LG *prik* point] —**prick′er,** *n.* —**prick′ing·ly,** *adv.*

prick-eared (prik′ērd′), *adj.* **1.** having the ears upright and pointed: *a prick-eared dog.* **2.** *Brit.* **a.** *Informal.* (of a man) having the hair cut short. **b.** *Archaic.* following or sympathetic to the Puritans or Roundheads. **c.** *Archaic.* priggish.

prick·et (prik′it), *n.* **1.** a sharp metal point on which to stick a candle. **2.** a candlestick with one or more such points. **3.** a buck in his second year. [ME; see PRICK, -ET]

prick·ing (prik′iṅg), *n.* **1.** act of one who or that which pricks. **2.** a prickly or smarting sensation. [ME; see PRICK, -ING[1]]

prick·le (prik′əl), *n., v.,* **-led, -ling.** —*n.* **1.** a sharp point. **2.** a small, pointed process growing from the bark of a plant. **3.** a sharp process or projection, as from the skin of an animal; a spine. **4.** a pricking sensation. —*v.t.* **5.** to prick lightly. **6.** to cause a pricking or tingling sensation in. —*v.i.* **7.** to tingle as if pricked. [ME *prykel,* OE *pricel.* See PRICK, -LE]

prick·le·back (prik′əl bak′), *n.* **1.** any of several blennioid fishes of the family *Stichaeidae,* found in arctic seas, having spiny rays in the dorsal fin. **2.** stickleback. [PRICKLE + BACK[1]]

prick·ly (prik′lē), *adj.,* **-li·er, -li·est. 1.** full of or armed with prickles. **2.** full of troublesome points: *a prickly problem.* **3.** prickling; smarting: *a prickly sensation.* [PRICKLE + -Y[1]] —**prick′li·ness,** *n.*

prick′ly ash′, 1. Also called **angelica tree.** a rutaceous shrub or small tree, *Zanthoxylum americanum,* having aromatic leaves and usually prickly branches. **2.** Hercules'-club (def. 1).

prick′ly com′frey, a hardy perennial herb, *Symphytum asperum,* found from Russia to Persia, having stiff, hairy leaves and rose-colored flowers that turn blue, grown as forage.

prick′ly glass′wort, glasswort (def. 2).

prick′ly heat′, *Pathol.* a cutaneous eruption accompanied by a prickling and itching sensation, due to an inflammation of the sweat glands.

prick′ly pear′, 1. the pear-shaped or ovoid, often prickly and sometimes edible, fruit of any cactus of the genus *Opuntia.* **2.** the plant itself.

prick′ly phlox′, a perennial herb or woody shrub, *Gilia californica,* of California, having fingerlike leaves and rose-pink or lilac-colored flowers.

prick′ly pop′py, any tropical American plant of the genus *Argemone,* esp. *A. mexicana* (**Mexican poppy**), having prickly pods and leaves and yellow or white, poppylike flowers.

prick′ly shield′ fern′, a hardy fern, *Polystichum brauni,* of North America and Europe, having hairlike scales on the leafstalk.

prick′ly thrift′, any of several evergreen, plumbaginaceous herbs of the genus *Acantholimon,* having prickly, rigid leaves.

prick-post (prik′pōst′), *n.* (in a framed structure) a secondary post, as a queen post.

prick′ song′, 1. *Archaic.* written music. **2.** descant (def. 1a). [short for *pricked song*]

prick·spur (prik′spûr′), *n.* a spur having a single sharp goad or point. [PRICK + SPUR]

prick-tim·ber (prik′tim′bər), *n.* See **spindle tree.**

pric·y (prī′sē), *adj.,* **pric·i·er, pric·i·est.** *Informal.* pricey.

pride (prīd), *n., v.,* **prid·ed, prid·ing.** —*n.* **1.** a high or inordinate opinion of one's own dignity, importance, merit, or superiority, whether as cherished in the mind or as displayed in bearing, conduct, etc. **2.** the state or feeling of being proud. **3.** becoming or dignified sense of what is due to oneself or one's position or character; self-respect; self-esteem. **4.** pleasure or satisfaction taken in something done by or belonging to oneself or believed to reflect credit upon oneself: *civic pride.* **5.** that of which a person or a body of persons is proud: *His art collection was the pride of the family.* **6.** the best of a group, class, society, etc.: *This bull is the pride of the herd.* **7.** the most flourishing state or period: *in the pride of manhood.* **8.** mettle in a horse. **9.** *Literary.* splendor, magnificence, or pomp. **10.** a company or group of lions. **11.** *Dial.* sexual desire, esp. in a female animal. **12.** *Archaic.* ornament or adornment. —*v.t.* **13.** to indulge or plume (oneself) in a feeling of pride (usually fol. by *on* or *upon*): *She prides herself on her cooking.* [ME; OE *prȳde* (c. Icel *prȳthi* bravery, pomp), deriv. of *prūd* PROUD] —**pride′ful,** *adj.* —**pride′ful·ly,** *adv.* —**pride′ful·ness,** *n.* —**pride′less,** *adj.* —**pride′less·ly,** *adv.*

—**Syn. 1.** PRIDE, CONCEIT, SELF-ESTEEM, EGOTISM, VANITY, VAINGLORY imply an unduly favorable idea of one's own appearance, advantages, achievements, etc., and often apply to offensive characteristics. PRIDE is a lofty and often arrogant assumption of superiority in some respect: *Pride must have a fall.* CONCEIT implies an exaggerated estimate of one's own abilities or attainments, together with pride: *blinded by conceit.* SELF-ESTEEM may imply an estimate of oneself that is higher than that held by others: *a ridiculous self-esteem.* EGOTISM implies an excessive preoccupation with oneself or with one's own concerns, usually but not always accompanied by pride or conceit: *His egotism blinded him to others' difficulties.* VANITY implies self-admiration and an excessive desire to be admired by others: *His vanity was easily flattered.* VAINGLORY, somewhat literary, implies an inordinate and therefore empty or unjustified pride: *puffed up by vainglory.* **5.** boast. —**Ant. 1.** humility.

Pride (prīd), *n.* **Thomas,** died 1658, English soldier and regicide.

Pride′ and Prej′udice, a novel (1813) by Jane Austen (written 1796–97).

pride-of-Cal·i·for·nia (prīd′əv kal′ə fôr′nyə, -nē ə), *n.* a shrubby, perennial herb, *Lathyrus splendens,* of southern California, having showy clusters of pale rose-pink, violet, or magenta flowers and smooth, beaked pods from two to three inches long. Also called **campo pea.**

pride′ of Chi′na, the chinaberry, *Melia Azedarach.* Also called **pride′ of In′dia.**

pride-of-In·di·a (prīd′əv in′dē ə), *n.* a tree, *Koelreuteria paniculata,* of eastern Asia, having showy clusters of yellow flowers from 12 to 18 inches long, and papery, brilliantly colored pods with black seeds, grown as an ornamental. Also called **China tree, varnish tree.**

pride′ of the morn′ing, light mist or precipitation observed at sea in the morning and regarded as indicating a fine day.

Pride's′ Purge′, *Eng. Hist.* the forceful exclusion from the House of Commons, carried out by Col. Thomas Pride in December, 1648, of about 100 members who favored compromise with the Royalist party.

prie (prē), *n., v.t. Scot. and North Eng.* pree.

prie-dieu (prē′dyœ′; *Fr.* prē dyœ′), *n., pl.* **-dieus, -dieux** (-dyœz′), *Fr.* **-dieu.** a piece of furniture for kneeling on during prayer, having a rest above, as for a book. [< F: lit., pray God]

pri·er (prī′ər), *n.* one who looks or searches curiously or inquisitively into something. Also, **pryer.** [PRY + -ER[1]]

priest (prēst), *n.* **1.** one whose office it is to perform religious rites, and esp. to make sacrificial offerings. **2.** (in Christian use) **a.** a person ordained to the sacerdotal or pastoral office; clergyman; minister. **b.** (in hierarchical churches) a clergyman of the order next below that of bishop, authorized to carry out the Christian ministry. **c.** any Christian. **3.** a minister of any religion. —*v.t.* **4.** to ordain as a priest. [ME *preest,* OE *prēost,* unexplained alter. of PRESBYTER] —**priest′less,** *adj.* —**priest′like′,** *adj., adv.*

priest·craft (prēst′kraft′, -kräft′), *n.* the training, knowledge, and abilities necessary to a priest. [PRIEST + CRAFT]

priest·ess (prē′stis), *n.* a girl or woman who officiates in sacred rites, esp. of a pagan religion. [PRIEST + -ESS]

priest·fish (prēst′fish′), *n., pl.* **-fish·es,** (*esp. collectively*) **-fish.** See **blue rockfish.** [PRIEST + FISH; so called from its dark color]

priest·hood (prēst′ho͝od), *n.* **1.** the condition or office of a priest. **2.** priests collectively. [ME, OE *prēosthād.* See PRIEST, -HOOD]

Priest·ley (prēst′lē), *n.* **1. J(ohn) B(oyn·ton)** (boin′-tən, -tᵊn), born 1894, English novelist. **2. Joseph,** 1733–1804, English chemist, author, and clergyman.

priest·ly (prēst′lē), *adj.,* **-li·er, -li·est. 1.** of or pertaining to a priest; sacerdotal: *priestly vestments.* **2.** characteristic of or befitting a priest. [ME; OE *prēostlic.* See PRIEST, -LY] —**priest′li·ness,** *n.*

priest-rid·den (prēst′rid′ᵊn), *adj.* objectionably controlled, influenced, or dominated by priests.

prig[1] (prig), *n.* one who displays or demands of others pointlessly precise conformity, fussiness about trivialities, or exaggerated propriety, esp. in a self-righteous or irritating manner. [formerly, coxcomb; perh. akin to PRINK]

prig[2] (prig), *v.,* **prigged, prig·ging,** *n.* —*v.t.* **1.** *Chiefly Brit.* to steal. —*v.i.* **2.** *Scot. and North Eng.* to haggle or argue over price. **3.** *Brit. Informal.* to beg or entreat; ask a favor. —*n.* **4.** *Chiefly Brit.* a thief. [orig. cant]

prig·ger·y (prig′ə rē), *n., pl.* **-ger·ies** for 2. **1.** the conduct or character of a prig. **2.** an act or remark characteristic of a prig. [PRIG[1] + -ERY]

prig·gish (prig′ish), *adj.* characteristic of or resembling a prig: *a priggish remark; a priggish person.* [PRIG[1] + -ISH[1]] —**prig′gish·ly,** *adv.* —**prig′gish·ness,** *n.*

prig·gism (prig′iz əm), *n.* priggish character or ideas; priggishness. [PRIG[1] + -ISM]

prim[1] (prim), *adj.,* **prim·mer, prim·mest,** *v.,* **primmed, prim·ming.** —*adj.* **1.** formally precise or proper, as persons, behavior, etc.; stiffly neat. —*v.i.* **2.** to draw up the mouth in an affectedly nice or precise way. —*v.t.* **3.** to make prim, as in appearance. **4.** to draw (one's face, lips, etc.) into a prim expression. [?] —**prim′ly,** *adv.* —**prim′ness,** *n.*

—**Syn. 1.** starched, formal, rigid. —**Ant. 1.** flexible.

prim[2] (prim), *n.* privet (def. 1). [shortening of *primprint,* PRIVET]

prim., 1. primary. **2.** primitive.

pri′ma balleri′na (prē′mə), the principal ballerina in a ballet company. [< It]

Pri′ma Balleri′na, The, a pastel (1876?) by Edgar Degas.

pri·ma·cy (prī′mə sē), *n., pl.* **-cies. 1.** state of being first in order, rank, importance, etc. **2.** Also called **primateship.** *Eng. Eccles.* the office, rank, or dignity of a primate. **3.** *Rom. Cath. Ch.* the jurisdiction of the pope as supreme bishop. [ME *primacie* < ML *prīmatia,* alter. of L *prīmātus* (*prīm(us)* PRIME + *-ātus* -ATE[1]); see -Y[3]]

pri·ma don·na (prē′mə don′ə, prim′ə; *It.* prē′mä dôn′nä), *pl.* **pri·ma don·nas,** *It.* **pri·me don·ne** (prē′me dôn′ne). **1.** a first or principal female singer of an operatic company. **2.** a temperamental person; a person who takes adulation and privileged treatment as a right and reacts with petulance to criticism or inconvenience. [< It: lit., first lady]

pri·mae·val (prī mē′vəl), *adj.* primeval.

pri·ma fa·ci·e (prī′mə fā′shē ē′, fā′shē, fā′shə), **1.** at first appearance; at first view, before investigation. **2.** plain or clear; self-evident; obvious. [< L]

pri′ma fa′cie case′, *Law.* a case in which the evidence produced is sufficient to enable a decision or verdict to be made unless the evidence is rebutted.

pri′ma fa′cie ev′idence, *Law.* evidence sufficient to establish a fact, or to raise a presumption of fact, unless rebutted.

pri·mage (prī′mij), *n.* a small allowance formerly paid by a shipper to the master and crew of a vessel for the loading and care of the goods: now charged with the freight and retained by the shipowner. [< AL *prīmāg(ium)* < ?]

pri·ma in·ter pa·res (prē′mä in′ter pä′res; *Eng.* prī′mə in′tər pâ′rēz), *Latin.* (of a female) first among equals.

pri·mal (prī′məl), *adj.* **1.** first; original; primeval: *primal eras before the appearance of life on earth.* **2.** of first importance; fundamental: *the primal resources of a nation.* [ML *prīmāl(is).* See PRIME, -AL[1]]

pri·ma·quine (prī′mə kwēn′), *n.* *Pharm.* a viscous liquid, $C_{15}H_{21}N_3O$, used chiefly in the form of its phosphate in the treatment of malaria. [< It *prima* PRIME + QUIN(OLIN)E]

pri·ma·ri·ly (prī mâr′ə lē, prī′mer ə lē, -mər ə-), *adv.* **1.** essentially; mostly; chiefly; principally: *They live primarily from farming.* **2.** in the first instance; at first; originally: *Primarily a doctor, he later became a lawyer.* [PRIMARY + -LY]

pri·ma·ry (prī′mer ē, -mə rē), *adj., n., pl.* **-ries.** —*adj.* **1.** first or highest in rank or importance; chief; principal: *his primary goals in life.* **2.** first in order in any series, sequence, etc. **3.** first in time; earliest; primitive. **4.** of, pertaining to, or characteristic of primary school: *the primary grades.* **5.** constituting or belonging to the first stage in any process. **6.** of the nature of the ultimate or simpler constituents of which something complex is made up: *Animals have a few primary instincts.* **7.** original; not derived or subordinate; fundamental; basic. **8.** immediate or direct, or not involving intermediate agency: *primary perceptions.* **9.** *Sociol.* (of social values or ideals) conceived as derived from the primary group and culturally defined as being necessary to the welfare of the individual and society. **10.** *Ornith.* pertaining to any of the set of flight feathers situated on the distal segment of a bird's wing. **11.** *Elect.* noting or pertaining to the circuit, coil, winding, or current that induces current in secondary windings in an induction coil, transformer, or the like. **12.** *Chem.* **a.** involving or obtained by replacement of one atom or group. **b.** noting or containing a carbon atom united to no other

or to only one other carbon atom in a molecule. **13.** *Gram.* **a.** (of derivation) with a root or other unanalyzable element as underlying form. **b.** (of Latin, Greek, Sanskrit tenses) having reference to present or future time. Cf. **secondary** (def. 9). **—***n.* **14.** that which is first in order, rank, or importance. **15.** *U.S. Politics.* **a.** a meeting of the voters of a political party in an election district for nominating candidates for office, choosing delegates for a convention, etc.; caucus. **b.** Also called **primary election.** a preliminary election in which voters of each party nominate candidates for office, party officers, etc. Cf. **closed primary, open primary, direct primary, indirect primary.** **16.** See **primary color.** **17.** *Ornith.* a primary feather. **18.** *Elect.* a winding in a transformer or the like which carries a current and which induces a current in secondary windings. **19.** *Astron.* **a.** a body in relation to a smaller body or smaller bodies revolving around it, as a planet in relation to its satellites. **b.** the brighter of the two stars comprising a double star. Cf. **companion**[1] (def. 6). [late ME < L *prīmāri(us)* of the first rank. See PRIME, -ARY] **—pri′ma·ri·ness,** *n.*
—Syn. 1. main, prime. **3.** original; primeval. **5.** beginning, opening. See **elementary.** **—Ant. 1, 2.** last. **2.** final.

pri′mary ac′cent, the principal or strongest stress of a word.

pri′mary cell′, *Elect.* a cell designed to produce electric current through an electrochemical reaction which is not efficiently reversible, so that the cell when discharged cannot be efficiently recharged by an electric current.

pri′mary col′or, a color, as red, yellow, or blue, which in mixture yields other colors. Cf. **complementary color, secondary color, tertiary color.**

pri′mary con′tact, *Sociol.* a communication or relationship between people that is characterized by intimacy and personal familiarity. Cf. **secondary contact.**

pri′mary elec′tion, primary (def. 15b).

pri′mary group′, *Sociol.* a group of individuals living in close, intimate, and personal relationship. Cf. **secondary group.**

pri′mary let′ter, *Print.* a lower-case character having neither a descender nor an ascender, as *a, c, e, i, m, n, o, r, s, u, v, w, x, z.*

pri′mary o′ocyte. See under **oocyte.**

pri′mary op′tical a′rea, *Graphic Design.* a point in or toward the upper left-hand corner of a printed page, advertisement, or the like, looked at first in reading. *Abbr.:* POA

pri′mary phlo′em, *Bot.* phloem derived directly from the growth of an apical meristem.

pri′mary qual′ity, *Epistemology.* any of the qualities inherent in an object, namely quantity, extent, figure, solidity, and motion or rest. Cf. **secondary quality.**

pri′mary school′, **1.** See **elementary school.** **2.** a school covering the first three or four years of public school.

pri′mary sex′ characteris′tic, *Med.* any of the body structures directly concerned in reproduction, as the testes, ovaries, and external genitalia. Also called **pri′mary sex′ char′acter.**

pri′mary spermat′ocyte. See under **spermatocyte.**

pri′mary syph′ilis, *Pathol.* the first stage of syphilis, characterized by the formation of a chancre at the site of infection.

pri′mary type′, *Biol.* a specimen used in the original description or illustration of a species.

pri′mary wave′. See **P wave.**

pri′mary xy′lem, *Bot.* xylem derived directly from the growth of an apical meristem.

pri·mate (prī′māt *or, esp. for 1,* prī′mit), *n.* **1.** *Eccles.* an archbishop or bishop ranking first among the bishops of a province, country, etc. **2.** any mammal of the order *Primates,* including man, the apes, monkeys, lemurs, tarsiers, and marmosets. **3.** *Archaic.* a chief or leader. [ME *primat* < eccl. L *prīmāt-* (s. of *prīmās*) of first rank (adj.), archbishop (n.), deriv. of *prīmus* first. See PRIME] **—pri·ma′tal,** *adj., n.* **—pri·ma·tial** (prī mā′shəl), **pri·mat·i·cal** (prī mat′i kəl), *adj.*

Pri′mate of All′ Eng′land (prī′mit), *Ch. of Eng.* a title of the archbishop of Canterbury.

Pri′mate of Eng′land, *Ch. of Eng.* a title of the archbishop of York.

Pri·ma·tes (prī mā′tēz), *n.* the order comprising the primates. [< NL, pl. of L *prīmāt-* (s. of *prīmās*) one of the first, chief, principal. See PRIMATE]

pri·mate·ship (prī′mit ship′, -māt-), *n.* primacy (def. 2). [PRIMATE + -SHIP]

pri·ma·tol·o·gy (prī′mə tol′ə jē), *n.* the branch of zoology dealing with the primates. [PRIMATE + -O- + -LOGY] **—pri′ma·tol′o·gist,** *n.*

pri·ma·ve·ra (prē′mə ver′ə), *n.* **1.** a bignoniaceous tree, *Cybistax Donnell-Smithi,* of Central America, having showy, yellow flowers. **2.** Also called **white mahogany.** the hard, yellowish-white wood of this tree, used for making furniture. [< Sp: lit., spring; so called from its early flowering]

prime (prīm), *adj., n., v.,* **primed, priming.** **—***adj.* **1.** of the first importance; demanding the fullest consideration: *a prime requisite.* **2.** of the greatest relevance or significance: *a prime example.* **3.** of the highest eminence or rank: *the prime authority on Chaucer.* **4.** of the greatest commercial value: *prime building lots.* **5.** first-rate: *This ale is absolutely prime!* **6.** (of meat, esp. of beef) noting or pertaining to the first grade or best quality: *prime ribs of beef.* **7.** first in order of time, existence, or development; earliest; primitive. **8.** basic; fundamental: *These are the prime axioms of his philosophy.* **9.** *Math.* **a.** not divisible without remainder by any number except itself and unity: *The number 5 is a prime number.* **b.** having no common divisor except unity: *The number 2 is prime to 9.* [late ME < L *prīm(us)* first (superl. of *prior* PRIOR[1])]
—*n.* **10.** the most flourishing stage or state. **11.** the time of early manhood or womanhood: *the prime of youth.* **12.** the period or state of greatest perfection or vigor of human life: *He was a fine man in his prime.* **13.** the choicest or best part of anything. **14.** (esp. in the grading of U.S. beef) a grade, classification, or designation indicating the highest or most desirable quality. **15.** the beginning or earliest stage of any period. **16.** the spring of the year. **17.** the first hour or period of the day, after sunrise. **18.** *Eccles.* the second of the seven canonical hours or the service for it, originally fixed for the first hour of the day. **19.** *Math.* **a.** a prime number. **b.** one of the equal parts into which a unit is primarily divided. **c.** the mark (′) indicating such a division: *a, a′.* **20.** *Fencing.* the first of eight defensive positions. **21.** *Music.* **a.** unison. **b.** (in a scale) the tonic or keynote. **22.** *Metall.* a piece of tin plate free from visible defects. [ME; OE *prīm* < L *prīma* (*hōra*) first (hour)]
—*v.t.* **23.** to prepare or make ready for a particular purpose or operation. **24.** to supply (a firearm) with powder for communicating fire to a charge. **25.** to lay a train of powder to (a charge, mine, etc.). **26.** to pour or admit liquid into (a pump) to expel air and make it ready for action. **27.** to put fuel into (a carburetor) before starting an engine, in order to insure a sufficiently rich mixture at the start. **28.** to cover (a surface) with a preparatory coat or color, as in painting. **29.** to supply or equip with information, words, etc., for use: *The politician was primed by his aides for the press conference.* **—***v.i.* **30.** (of a boiler) to deliver or discharge steam containing an excessive amount of water. [?, special use of n.] **—prime′ness,** *n.*
—Syn. 1. primary. **7.** PRIME, PRIMEVAL, PRIMITIVE have reference to that which is first. PRIME means first in numerical order or order of development: *prime meridian; prime cause.* PRIMEVAL means belonging to the first or earliest ages: *the primeval forest.* PRIMITIVE suggests the characteristics of the origins or early stages of a development, and hence implies the simplicity of original things: *primitive tribes, conditions, ornaments, customs, tools.*

prime′ cost′, that part of the cost of a commodity deriving from the labor and materials directly utilized in its manufacture.

prime′ field′, *Math.* a field which contains no proper subset that is itself a field.

prime′ ide′al, *Math.* an ideal in a ring with a multiplicative identity, having the property that when the product of two elements of the ring results in an element of the ideal, at least one of the elements is an element of the ideal.

prime·ly (prīm′lē), *adv. Informal.* excellently. [PRIME + -LY]

prime′ merid′ian, a meridian from which longitude east and west is reckoned, usually that of Greenwich, England.

prime′ min′ister, the first or principal minister of certain governments; chief of the cabinet or ministry: *the British prime minister.* **—prime-min·is·te·ri·al** (prīm′min′i stēr′ē əl), *adj.* **—prime′-min′is·ter·ship′,** *n.* **—prime′ min′istry.**

prime′ mov′er, **1.** *Mech.* **a.** the initial agent, as wind, electricity, etc., which puts a machine in motion. **b.** a machine, as a water wheel or steam engine, which receives and modifies energy as supplied by some natural source. **2.** means of towing a cannon, as an animal, truck, or tractor. **3.** Also called **unmoved mover.** *Aristotelianism.* that which is the first cause of all movement and does not itself move.

prime′ num′ber the′orem, *Math.* the theorem that the number of prime numbers less than or equal to a given number is approximately equal to the given number divided by its natural logarithm.

prim·er[1] (prim′ər *or, esp. Brit.,* prī′mər), *n.* **1.** an elementary book for teaching children to read. **2.** any book of elementary principles: *a primer of phonetics.* **3.** See **great primer.** **4.** See **long primer.** [ME < ML *prīmār(ium),* n. use of neut. of *prīmārius* PRIMARY]

prim·er[2] (prī′mər), *n.* **1.** one who or that which primes. **2.** a cap, cylinder, etc., containing a compound that may be exploded by percussion or other means, used for firing a charge of powder. See diag. under **cartridge.** [PRIME (v.) + -ER[1]]

pri·me·ro (pri mâr′ō), *n.* a card game fashionable in England in the 16th and 17th centuries. [< Sp: lit., first < L *prīmārius* PRIMARY]

prime′ time′, *Radio and Television.* the evening broadcasting hours, generally between 8 and 11 P.M., considered as drawing the largest available audience.

pri·me·val (prī mē′vəl), *adj.* of or pertaining to the first age or ages, esp. of the world: *primeval forms of life.* Also, **primaeval.** [< L *prīmaev(us)* young (*prīm(us)* PRIME + *aev(um)* age) + -AL[1]] **—pri·me′val·ly,** *adv.*
—Syn. primary, primordial, pristine. See **prime.**

pri·mi·ge·ni·al (prī′mi jē′nē əl, -jēn′yəl), *adj.* **1.** of a primitive type; primordial. **2.** *Obs.* first generated or produced. Also, **primogenial.** [< L *prīmigeni(us)* original (*prīmi-,* comb. form of *prīmus* PRIME, + *geni-* old s. of *gignere* to beget + *-us* adj. suffix) + -AL[1]]

pri·mine (prī′min), *n. Bot.* the outer integument of an ovule. Cf. **secundine.** [< L *prīm(us)* first (see PRIME) + -INE[2]]

prim·ing (prī′ming), *n.* **1.** the powder or other material used to ignite a charge. **2.** act of one who or that which primes. **3.** a first coat or layer of paint, size, etc., given to any surface as a ground. [PRIME + -ING[1]]

pri·mip·a·ra (prī mip′ər ə), *n., pl.* **-a·rae** (-ə rē′). *Obstet.* a woman who has borne but one child or who is parturient for the first time. [< L *prīmi-* (comb. form of *prīmus* first) + *-para,* fem. of *-parus.* See PRIME, -PAROUS] **—pri·mi·par·i·ty** (prī′mi par′i tē), *n.* **—pri·mip′ar·ous,** *adj.*

prim·i·tive (prim′i tiv), *adj.* **1.** being the first or earliest of the kind or in existence; esp. in an early age of the world: *primitive forms of life.* **2.** early in the history of the world or of mankind. **3.** characteristic of early ages or of an early state of human development: *primitive art.* **4.** *Anthropol.* of or pertaining to a race, group, etc., having cultural or physical similarities with their early ancestors. **5.** unaffected or little affected by civilizing influences; uncivilized; savage: *primitive passions.* **6.** being in its or the earliest period; early: *the primitive phase of the history of a town.* **7.** old-fashioned: *primitive ideas and habits.* **8.** simple; unsophisticated: *a primitive farm implement.* **9.** crude; unpolished: *primitive living conditions.* **10.** original or radical, as distinguished from derivative. **11.** primary, as distinguished from secondary. **12.** *Biol.* **a.** rudimentary; primordial. **b.** noting species, varieties, etc., only slightly evolved from early antecedent types. **c.** of early formation and temporary, as a part that subsequently disappears. **—***n.* **13.** someone or something primitive. **14.** *Fine Arts.* **a.** an artist of a preliterate culture. **b.** a naïve or unschooled artist. **c.** an artist belonging to the early stage in the development of a style. **d.** a work of art by a primitive artist. **15.** *Math.* **a.** a geometric or algebraic form or expression from which another is derived. **b.** a function of which the derivative is a given function. **16.** the form from which a given word or other linguistic form has been derived, by either morphological or historical processes, as *take* in *undertake.* [< L *prīmitīv(us)* first of its kind; r. ME *primitif* < MF. See PRIME, -ITIVE] **—prim′i·tive·ly,** *adv.* **—prim′i·tive·ness, prim′i·tiv′i·ty,** *n.*
—Syn. 1, 2. prehistoric, primal, primary, primordial, original, aboriginal, antediluvian, pristine. See **prime.**

Prim′itive Bap′tist, (esp. in the Southern U.S.) one belonging to a highly conservative, loosely organized Baptist group, characterized by extreme fundamentalism and by opposition to missionary work, Sunday Schools, and the use of musical instruments in church.

prim′itive cell′, *Crystall.* a unit cell containing no points of the lattice except at the corners of the cell.

prim′itive church′, **1.** the early Christian church, esp. in reference to its earliest form and organization. **2.** this church, esp. as representative of Christianity in its supposedly purest form.

Prim′itive Friends′, a group of Quakers, noted for their extreme conservatism, who withdrew from the Wilburites in 1861.

Prim′itive Meth′odist, **1.** a member of a Protestant denomination **(Prim′itive Meth′odist Church′)** founded in England in 1812 and later established in the U.S., characterized by its adherence to the basic doctrines, principles, and practices taught by John Wesley. **2.** a member of a Protestant denomination **(Prim′itive Meth′odist Church′ in Great′ Brit′ain)** that united with other British Methodist groups in 1932 to form the Methodist Church. **—Prim′itive Meth′odism.**

prim′itive polyno′mial, *Math.* a polynomial which has content equal to 1. Cf. **content**[1] (def. 8).

prim·i·tiv·ism (prim′i ti viz′əm), *n.* a recurrent theory or belief, as in philosophy, art, etc., that the qualities of primitive or chronologically early cultures are superior to those of contemporary civilization. [PRIMITIVE + -ISM] **—prim′i·tiv·ist,** *n.* **—prim′i·tiv·is′tic,** *adj.*

pri·mo (prē′mō; *It.* prē′mô), *n., pl.* **-mos,** *It.* **-mi** (-mē). *Music.* **1.** the part of a piano duet played on the upper half of the keyboard. **2.** the first or leading part in an ensemble. [< It: lit., first < L *prīmus.* See PRIME]

Pri·mo (prī′mō, prē′-), *n.* a boy's given name.

Pri·mo de Ri·ve·ra (prē′mô the rē ve′rä), **Mi·guel** (mē gel′), **Marqués de Es·te·lla** (es te′lyä), (*Miguel Prima de Rivera y Orbanja*), 1870–1930, Spanish general and political leader: dictator of Spain 1923–29.

pri·mo·ge·ni·al (prī′mə jē′nē əl, -jēn′yəl), *adj.* primigenial.

pri·mo·gen·i·tor (prī′mə jen′i tər), *n.* **1.** a first parent or earliest ancestor: *Adam and Eve are the primogenitors of mankind.* **2.** a forefather or ancestor. [< LL: lit., first begetter, equiv. to L *prīmō* at first + *genitor* (*genit(us)* begotten, ptp. of *gignere* to beget, + *-or* -OR[2])]

pri·mo·gen·i·ture (prī′mə jen′i chər), *n.* **1.** state or fact of being the first-born of children of the same parents. **2.** *Law.* the system of inheritance or succession by the first-born, specifically the eldest son. Cf. **postremogeniture.** [< LL *prīmōgenitūra* a first birth, equiv. to L *prīmō* at first + *genitūra,* equiv. to *genit(us)* begotten (ptp. of *gignere*) + *-ūra* -URE] **—pri·mo·gen′i·tar′y, pri′mo·gen′i·tal,** *adj.* **—pri′mo·gen′i·ture·ship′,** *n.*

pri·mor·di·al (prī môr′dē əl), *adj.* **1.** constituting a beginning; giving origin to something derived or developed; original; elementary: *primordial forms of life.* **2.** *Biol.* primitive; initial; first formed. **3.** pertaining to or existing at or from the very beginning: *primordial matter existing before the earth was formed.* [ME < LL *prīmōrdiāl(is)* of the beginning. See PRIMORDIUM, -AL[1]] **—pri·mor·di·al·i·ty** (prī môr′dē al′i tē), *n.* **—pri·mor′di·al·ly,** *adv.*

pri·mor·di·um (prī môr′dē əm), *n., pl.* **-di·a** (-dē ə). *Embryol.* the first recognizable, histologically undifferentiated stage in the development of an organ. [< L, n. use of neut. of *prīmōrdius* original, equiv. to *prīm(us)* PRIME + *ōrdi-* (s. of *ōrdīrī* to begin) + *-us* adj. suffix]

primp (primp), *v.t.* **1.** to dress or adorn with care. **—***v.i.* **2.** to groom oneself carefully: *She spends hours primping in front of the mirror.* [akin to PRIM[1]]

prim·rose (prim′rōz′), *n.* **1.** any perennial herb of the genus *Primula,* as *P. vulgaris* **(English primrose),** of Europe, having yellow flowers, or *P. sinensis* **(Chinese primrose),** of China, having variously colored flowers. **2.** See **evening primrose.** **3.** pale yellow. **—***adj.* **4.** of or pertaining to the primrose. **5.** Also, **prim′rosed′.** abounding in primroses: *a primrose garden.* **6.** of a pale yellow. [ME *primerose* < ML *prīma rosa* first rose]

Prim·rose (prim′rōz′), *n.* **Archibald Philip, 5th Earl of Rosebery.** See **Rosebery, Archibald Philip Primrose, 5th Earl of.**

prim′rose jas′mine, an evergreen shrub, *Jasminum mesnyi,* of China, having thick, shiny leaflets and yellow flowers with a darker eye.

prim′rose path′, **1.** a way of life devoted to irresponsible hedonism, often of a sensual nature: *treading the primrose path while she still had her youth.* **2.** a course of action that is easy or tempting but hazardous: *the primrose path to insolvency.*

prim·sie (prim′sē, -zē), *adj. Scot.* prim[1]. [PRIM[1] + *-sie* adj. suffix]

prim·u·la (prim′yə lə), *n.* primrose (def. 1). [< ML *prīmula,* short for *prīmula vēris,* lit., first (flower) of spring. See PRIME, -ULE]

prim·u·la·ceous (prim′yə lā′shəs), *adj.* belonging to the *Primulaceae,* or primrose family of plants. [PRIMUL(A) + -ACEOUS]

pri·mum mo·bi·le (prē′mŏŏm mō′bi le′; *Eng.* prī′məm mob′ə lē′), *Latin.* **1.** (in Ptolemaic astronomy) the outermost of the 10 concentric spheres of the universe, making a complete revolution every 24 hours and causing all the others to do likewise. **2.** See **prime mover.** [lit.: first moving (thing)]

pri·mus[1] (prī′məs), *n., pl.* **-mus·es.** (*often cap.*) *Scot. Episc. Ch.* a bishop who is elected to represent the body of his church and to summon and preside at synods but possesses no metropolitan power. [< ML, n. use of L adj.; see PRIME]

pri·mus[2] (prī′mēs), *adj.* (in prescriptions) first. [< L]

pri·mus in·ter pa·res (prē′mo͝os in′ter pä′res; *Eng.* prī′məs in′tər pâ′rēz), *Latin.* (of males) first among equals.

Pri′mus stove′, *Trademark.* a portable oil stove used by campers and the like.

prin., 1. principal. 2. principally. 3. principle.

prince (prins), *n.* 1. a nonreigning male member of a royal family. 2. *Hist.* a sovereign or monarch; king. 3. (in Great Britain) a son or grandson (if the child of a son) of a king or queen. 4. the English equivalent of any of various titles of nobility in other countries. 5. a holder of such a title. 6. the ruler of a small state, as one actually or nominally subordinate to a suzerain: *Monaco is ruled by a prince.* 7. one who or that which is chief or preeminent in any class, group, etc.: *a merchant prince; a prince among men.* 8. a person possessing admirably fine and genial characteristics: *He is a prince of a man.* [ME < OF < L *princip-* (s. of *princeps*) first, principal (adj.), principal person, leader (n.), equiv. to *prīn-* PRIME + *-cep-* (comb. form of *capere* to take) + *-s* nom. sing. ending] —**prince′less,** *adj.* —**prince′ship,** *n.*

Prince (prins), *n.* a boy's given name.

Prince, The, a treatise on statecraft (1513) by Niccolò Machiavelli. Italian, **Il Principe.**

Prince′ Al′bert, 1. a city in central Saskatchewan, in S Canada. 24,168 (1961). 2. a long, double-breasted frock coat.

Prince′ Al′bert Na′tional Park′, a national park in W Canada, in central Saskatchewan. 1869 sq. mi.

Prince′ and the Pau′per, The, a historical romance (1882) by Mark Twain.

prince′ con′sort, a prince who is the husband of a reigning female sovereign.

prince·dom (prins′dəm), *n.* 1. the position, rank, or dignity of a prince. 2. the territory of a prince; principality. 3. **princedoms,** (in medieval angelology) principalities. Cf. **angel** (def. 1). [PRINCE + -DOM]

Prince′ Ed′ward Is′land, an island in the Gulf of St. Lawrence, forming a province of Canada: fox farms. 104,629 (1961); 2184 sq. mi. *Cap.:* Charlottetown.

Prince′ George′, a city in central British Columbia, in W Canada. 13,877 (1961).

prince·kin (prins′kin), *n.* a small, young, or minor prince. Also, **prince·let** (prins′lit). [PRINCE + -KIN]

prince·ling (prins′ling), *n.* 1. a young prince. 2. a subordinate, minor, or insignificant prince. [PRINCE + -LING[1]]

prince·ly (prins′lē), *adj.*, **-li·er, -li·est.** 1. greatly liberal; lavish; magnificent: *a princely entertainment.* 2. like or befitting a prince; magnificent: *princely manners.* 3. of or pertaining to a prince; royal; noble: *princely blood.* 4. that is a prince: *his princely self.* [PRINCE + -LY] —**prince′li·ness,** *n.*

Prince′ of Dark′ness, Satan.

Prince′ of Peace′, Jesus Christ, regarded by Christians as the Messiah. Isa. 9:6.

Prince′ of Wales′, 1. a title conferred on the eldest son, or heir apparent, of the British sovereign. 2. **Cape,** a cape in W Alaska, on Bering Strait opposite the Soviet Union: the westernmost point of North America.

Prince′ of Wales′ Is′land′, 1. the largest island in the Alexander Archipelago, in SE Alaska. 1500 sq. mi. 2. an island in N Canada, in the Northwest Territories. ab. 14,000 sq. mi.

prince′ re′gent, a prince who is regent of a country.

prince′ roy′al, the eldest son of a king or queen.

Prince′ Ru′pert, a seaport and railway terminus in W British Columbia, in W Canada. 11,987 (1961).

Prince′ Ru′pert's met′al, a brass composed of from about 60 to 85 percent copper and about 15 to 40 percent zinc, used to imitate gold. Also called **Prince′'s met′al.**

prince's-feath·er (prin′siz feth′ər), *n.* 1. a tall, showy plant, *Amaranthus hybridus hypochondriacus,* having reddish foliage and thick spikes of small, red flowers. 2. a hairy, much-branched, annual herb, *Polygonum orientale,* of Asia and Australia, having pink or rose-colored flower spikes.

Prince′'s Is′land, former name of **Principe.**

prince's-pine (prin′siz pīn′), *n.* pipsissewa.

prince′'s pipe′, the pipsissewa, *Chimaphila umbellata.*

prin·cess (prin′sis, -ses), *n.* 1. a nonreigning female member of a royal family. 2. *Hist.* a female sovereign or monarch; queen. 3. the consort of a prince. 4. (in Great Britain) a daughter or granddaughter (if the child of a son) of a king or queen. —*adj.* 5. Also, **prin′cesse.** (of a woman's dress, coat, or the like) styled with a close-fitting bodice and flared skirt, cut in single pieces, as gores, from shoulder to hem. [ME *princesse* < F. See PRINCE, -ESS] —**prin′cess-like′,** *adj.* —**prin′cess·ly,** *adj.*

Prin′cess Cas·a·mas′si·ma, The (kaz′ə mas′ə mə), a novel (1886) by Henry James.

Prin·cesse de Clèves, La (*Fr.* LA PRAN ses′ də klev′). See **La Princesse de Clèves.**

prin′cess post′, (in a queen truss) one of two vertical suspension members supplementing the queen posts nearer to the ends of the span.

prin′cess re′gent, 1. a princess who is regent of a country. 2. the wife of a prince regent.

prin′cess roy′al, 1. the eldest daughter of a king or queen. 2. (in Great Britain and, formerly, Prussia) an eldest princess to whom this title has been granted for life by the sovereign.

prin′cess tree′, a Chinese tree, *Paulownia tomentosa,* having pubescent leaves and violet flowers, naturalized in the eastern U.S. Also called **karri-tree, empress tree.**

Prince·ton (prins′tən), *n.* 1. a borough in central New Jersey: battle 1777. 11,890 (1960). 2. a town in S West Virginia. 8393 (1960). 3. a town in SW Indiana. 7906 (1960). 4. a town in N Illinois. 6250 (1960). 5. a town in W Kentucky. 5618 (1960).

prin·ci·pal (prin′sə pəl), *adj.* 1. first or highest in rank, importance, value, etc.; chief; foremost. 2. of, of the nature of, or constituting principal or capital: *a principal investment.* 3. *Geom.* (of an axis of a conic) passing through the foci. —*n.* 4. a chief or head. 5. the head or director of a school or, esp. in England, a college. 6. a person who takes a leading part in any activity, as a play; chief actor or doer. 7. the first player of a division of instruments in an orchestra (excepting the leader of the first violins). 8. something of principal or chief importance. 9. *Law.* a. a person authorizing another, as an agent, to represent him. b. a person directly responsible for a crime, either as an actual perpetrator or as an abettor present at its commission. Cf. **accessory** (def. 3). 10. a person primarily liable for an obligation, in contrast with an endorser, or the like. 11. the main body of an estate, or the like, as distinguished from income. 12. *Finance.* a capital sum, as distinguished from interest or profit. 13. *Music.* a. Also called **diapason.** an organ stop. b. the subject of a fugue (opposed to *answer*). 14. (in a framed structure) a member, as a truss, upon which adjacent or similar members depend for support or reinforcement. 15. each of the combatants in a duel, as distinguished from the seconds. [ME < L *prīncipāl(is)* first, chief, equiv. to *princip-* (see PRINCE) + *-ālis* -AL[1]] —**prin′ci·pal·ship′,** *n.*
—**Syn.** 1. prime, paramount, leading, main, cardinal, preeminent. See **capital**[1]. 4. leader. 5. headmaster, dean, master. —**Ant.** 1. secondary, ancillary.

prin′cipal ar′gument, *Math.* the radian measure of the argument between $-\pi$ and π of a complex number. Cf. **argument** (def. 6c).

prin′cipal ax′is, 1. *Optics.* a line passing through the center of the surface of a lens or spherical mirror and through the centers of curvature of all segments of the lens or mirror. 2. *Physics.* one of three mutually perpendicular axes of a body about which the moment of inertia is maximum or minimum.

prin′cipal clause′, the main clause.

prin′cipal diag′onal. See under **diagonal** (def. 9).

prin′cipal fo′cus, *Optics.* See **focal point.**

prin′cipal ide′al, *Math.* the smallest ideal containing a given element in a ring; an ideal in a ring with a multiplicative identity, obtained by multiplying each element of the ring by one specified element.

prin′cipal ide′al domain′, *Math.* a commutative integral domain with multiplicative identity in which every ideal is principal. Also called **prin′cipal ide′al ring′.**

prin·ci·pal·i·ty (prin′sə pal′i tē), *n., pl.* **-ties.** 1. a state ruled by a prince, usually a relatively small state or a state that falls within a larger state such as an empire. 2. the position or authority of a prince or chief ruler; sovereignty; supreme power. 3. the rule of a prince of a small or subordinate state. 4. (*sometimes cap.*) **the principality,** *Brit.* Wales. 5. **principalities,** *Theol.* a. an order of angels. Cf. **angel** (def. 1). b. supramundane powers often in conflict with God. Ephes. 6:12. 6. *Obs.* preeminence. [ME *principalite* < OF < LL *prīncipālitāt-* (s. of *prīncipālitās*) first place, superiority (ML: authority or territory of a prince). See PRINCIPAL, -ITY]

prin·ci·pal·ly (prin′sə pə lē, -sip lē), *adv.* chiefly; mainly. [ME; see PRINCIPAL, -LY]
—**Syn.** primarily. See **especially.**

prin′cipal parts′, *Gram.* a set of inflected forms of a form class from which all the other inflected forms can be derived, as *sing, sang, sung; smoke, smoked.*

prin′cipal plane′, *Optics.* a plane that is perpendicular to the axis of a lens, mirror, or other optical system and at which rays diverging from a focal point are deviated parallel to the axis or at which rays parallel to the axis are deviated to converge to a focal point.

prin′cipal point′, *Optics.* the point where a principal plane intersects the axis.

prin′cipal quan′tum num′ber, *Physics.* the nonnegative, integral quantum number that defines the stationary orbits in the Bohr model of the atom. Also called **total quantum number.**

prin′cipal raft′er, a diagonal member of a roof principal, usually forming part of a truss and supporting the purlins on which the common rafters rest.

prin′cipal se′ries, *Math.* See **composition series.**

prin′cipal sum′, *Insurance.* See **capital sum.**

prin′cipal val′ue, *Math.* a value selected at a point in the domain of a multiple-valued function, chosen so that the function has a single value at the point.

prin·ci·pate (prin′sə pāt′), *n.* supreme power or office. [ME < L *prīncipāt(us),* equiv. to *princip-* (see PRINCE) + *-ātus* -ATE[1]]

prin·ci·pe (prēn′chē pe), *n., pl.* **-pi** (-pē). *Italian.* a prince.

prín·ci·pe (*Port.* prēNn′sē pə; *Sp.* prēn′thē pe′, -sē-), *n., pl.* **-pes** (*Port.* -pesh′; *Sp.* -pes′). *Portuguese, Spanish.* a prince.

Prin·ci·pe (prin′si pē; *Port.* prēNn′sē pə), *n.* an island in the Gulf of Guinea, off the W coast of Africa: one of the two components of the republic of St. Thomas and Principe. 4305; 54 sq. mi. Also, **Prín′ci·pe.** Formerly, **Prince's Island.**

prin·cip·i·um (prin sip′ē əm), *n., pl.* **-cip·i·a** (-sip′ē ə). a principle. [< L: lit., that which is first, equiv. to *princip-* (see PRINCE) + *-ium* n. suffix]

prin·ci·ple (prin′sə pəl), *n.* 1. an accepted or professed rule of action or conduct: *a person of good moral and ethical principles.* 2. a fundamental, primary, or general law or truth from which others are derived: *the principles of modern physics.* 3. a fundamental doctrine or tenet; a distinctive ruling opinion: *the principles of the Stoics.* 4. **principles,** a personal or specific basis of conduct or management: *to adhere to one's principles; a kindergarten run on modern principles.* 5. guiding sense of the requirements and obligations of right conduct: *a man of principle.* 6. an adopted rule or method for application in action: *a working principle for general use.* 7. a rule or law exemplified in natural phenomena, the construction or operation of a machine, the working of a system, or the like: *the principle of capillary attraction.* 8. the method of formation, operation, or procedure exhibited in a given case: *a community organized on the ancient patriarchal principle.* 9. a determining characteristic of something; essential quality. 10. an originating or actuating agency or force: *the interacting principles of Yin and Yang.* 11. an actuating agency in the mind or character, as an instinct, faculty, or natural tendency: *the principles of human behavior.* 12. *Chem.* a constituent of a substance, esp. one giving to it some distinctive quality or effect. 13. *Obs.* beginning or commencement. 14. **in principle,** in essence or substance; fundamentally: *to accept a plan in principle.* 15. **on principle, a.** according to a fixed rule, method, or practice: *He drank hot milk every night on principle.* b. according to personal rules for right conduct; as a matter of moral principle: *He refused on principle to agree to the terms of the treaty.* [ME, alter. of MF *principe* or L *prīncipium,* on analogy of *manciple.* See PRINCIPIUM]
—**Syn.** 1, 2, 3. PRINCIPLE, CANON, RULE imply something established as a standard or test, for measuring, regulating, or guiding conduct or practice. A PRINCIPLE is a general and fundamental truth which may be used in deciding conduct or choice: *to adhere to principle.* CANON, originally referring to an edict of the Church (a meaning which it still retains), is used of any principle, law, or critical standard which is officially approved, particularly in aesthetics and scholarship: *canons of literary criticism.* A RULE, usually something adopted or enacted, is often the specific application of a principle: *the golden rule.* 2. theorem, axiom, postulate, proposition. 5. integrity, probity, rectitude, honor.

prin·ci·pled (prin′sə pəld), *adj.* imbued with or having principles (often used in combination): *high-principled.* [PRINCIPLE + -ED[3]]

prin′ciple of com·ple·men·tar′i·ty (kom′plə men tar′i tē), *Physics.* See **correspondence principle.** [COMPLEMENTARY + -TY[2]]

prin′ciple of correspond′ence, *Physics.* See **correspondence principle.**

prin′ciple of mathemat′ical induc′tion, *Math.* a law in set theory which states that if a set is a subset of the set of all positive integers and if for each number in the given set the succeeding natural number is in the set, then the given set is identical to the set of all positive integers.

prin′ciple of superposi′tion, *Physics.* any of several physical laws that the resultant of similar vector quantities at a point is a function of the sum of the individual quantities, esp. the law that the displacement at a point in a medium undergoing simple harmonic motion is equal to the sum of the displacements of each individual wave. Also called **superposition principle.**

prin′ciple of vir′tual work′, *Mech.* the principle that the total work done by all forces on a system in static equilibrium is zero for a set of infinitesimally small displacements.

prin·cox (prin′koks, pring′-), *n.* *Archaic.* a self-confident young fellow; coxcomb. Also, **prin·cock** (prin′kok, pring′-). [?]

Prine·ville (prīn′vil), *n.* a town in central Oregon. 3263 (1960).

prink (pringk), *v.t.* 1. to deck or dress for show. —*v.i.* 2. to deck oneself out. 3. to fuss over one's dress, esp. before the looking glass. [appar. akin to PRANK[2] (v.)] —**prink′er,** *n.*

print (print), *v.t.* 1. to produce (a text, picture, etc.) by applying inked types, plates, blocks, or the like, to paper or other material either by direct pressure or indirectly by offsetting an image onto an intermediate roller. 2. to reproduce (a design or pattern), as one engraved on a plate or block. 3. to form a design or pattern upon, as by stamping with an engraved plate or block: *to print calico.* 4. to cause (a manuscript, text, etc.) to be published in print. 5. to write in letters like those commonly used in print: *Print your name on these forms.* 6. *Computer Technol.* to produce (data) in legible alphanumeric form. 7. to indent or mark by pressing something into or upon (something). 8. to produce or fix (an indentation, mark, etc.), as by pressure. 9. to impress on the mind, memory, etc. 10. to apply (a thing) with pressure so as to leave an indentation, mark, etc.: *The horses printed their hoofs on the wet grass.* 11. *Photog.* to produce a positive picture from (a negative) by the transmission of light. —*v.i.* 12. to take impressions from type, an engraved plate, etc., as in a press. 13. to produce by means of a reproduction process: *to print in color; to print unevenly.* 14. to make an image by means of ink, chemical action, etc., as type, engraved plates, etc.: *This type is too worn to print cleanly.* 15. to write in characters such as are used in print: *He prints, rather than using longhand.* 16. to follow the vocation of a printer. 17. **print out,** *Computer Technol.* to print (output), usually on paper moving continuously through a printer. —*n.* 18. state of being printed. 19. printed lettering, esp. with reference to character, style, or size: *This print is too large for footnotes.* 20. printed matter. 21. a printed publication, as a newspaper or magazine. 22. newsprint. 23. a picture, design, or the like, printed from an engraved or otherwise prepared block, plate, etc. 24. an indentation, mark, etc., made by the pressure of one body or thing on another. 25. something with which an impression is made; a stamp or die. 26. *Textiles.* a. a design or pattern on cloth made by dyeing, weaving, or printing with engraved rollers, blocks of wood, stencils, etc. b. a cloth so treated. c. an article of apparel made of this cloth. 27. something that has been subjected to impression, as a pat of butter. 28. *Photog.* a picture, esp. a positive made from a negative. 29. any reproduced image, as a blueprint. 30. **in print, a.** in printed form; published. b. (of a book) still available for purchase from the publisher. 31. **out of print,** (of a book) no longer available for purchase from the publisher. [ME *priente* < OF: impression, print, n. use of fem. ptp. of *preindre* < L *premere* to press]

print., printing.

print·a·ble (prin′tə bəl), *adj.* 1. capable of being printed. 2. suitable for publication; fit to print. [PRINT + -ABLE] —**print′a·bil′i·ty, print′a·ble·ness,** *n.*

prin·ta·nier (*Fr.* PRAN TA nyā′), *adj.* (of food) prepared or garnished with mixed fresh vegetables. Also, **prin·ta·nière** (*Fr.* PRAN TA NYER′). [< F, lit., of spring, equiv. to *printan-* (var. of *printemps* spring, equiv. to *prin-* PRIME + *temps* time) + *-ier* -ARY]

print·back (print′bak′), *n.* *Photog.* an enlarged print from a microfilm copy. [n. use of v. phrase *print back*]

print′ed cir′cuit, (in electronic equipment) a circuit in which the interconnecting wires have been replaced by conductive strips printed, etched, etc., onto a dielectric sheet.

print·er (prin′tər), *n.* 1. one who or that which prints, esp. one whose occupation is printing. 2. *Computer Technol.* a mechanism or machine that produces an output of printed alphanumeric characters. 3. an instrument that automatically records telegraphic messages by means of a printing mechanism activated by incoming signals. [PRINT + -ER[1]] —**prin′ter-like′,** *adj.*

print′er's dev′il, devil (def. 4).

print′er's er′ror, an error introduced into typeset copy by the compositor, so that the printer cannot charge for correcting it. *Abbr.:* P.E., p.e. Cf. **author's alteration.**

print′er's ream′. See under **ream**[1] (def. 1).

print·er·y (prin′tə rē), *n., pl.* **-er·ies. 1.** (formerly) an establishment for typographic printing. **2.** an establishment where printing, as of books, newspapers, etc., is done. [PRINT + -ERY]

print·ing (prin′ting), *n.* **1.** the art, process, or business of producing books, newspapers, etc., by impression from movable types, plates, etc. **2.** the act of one who or that which prints. **3.** words, symbols, etc., in printed form. **4.** printed matter. **5.** the whole number of copies of a book, etc., printed at one time: *The book had a first printing of 10,000.* **6.** writing in which the letters resemble printed ones. [ME; see PRINT, -ING[1]]

print′ing frame′, *Photog.* a shallow, boxlike device with a glass plate on one side and an opaque, removable back, for holding a negative firmly against print paper in contact printing.

print′ing pa′per, *Photog.* sensitized paper for printing positives.

print′ing press′, a machine for printing on paper or the like from type, plates, etc.

print·less (print′lis), *adj.* making, retaining, or showing no print or impression. [PRINT + -LESS]

print·mak·er (print′mā′kər), *n.* a person who makes prints, esp. an artist working in one of the graphic mediums. [PRINT + MAKER]

print·mak·ing (print′mā′king), *n.* the art or technique of making prints, esp. as practiced in engraving, etching, drypoint, woodcut, serigraphy, etc. [PRINT + MAKING]

print-out (print′out′), *n. Computer Technol.* the printed output of a computer, usually produced on continuously moving paper. [n. use of v. phrase *print out*]

print′-out pa′per, *Photog.* sensitized paper for prints that darkens under light and requires treatment to fix an image. *Abbr.:* P.O.P. Also called **print′ing-out′ pa′per.** Cf. **developing-out paper.**

print′ shop′, 1. a shop where prints or graphics are sold. **2.** a shop where printing is done.

Prinz (prinz), *n.* a walled plain in the second quadrant of the face of the moon: about 28 miles in diameter.

pri·on (prī′on), *n.* any of several petrels of the genus *Pachyptila,* located in the oceans of the Southern Hemisphere and having serrated edges on the bill. [< NL < Gk: saw]

pri·or[1] (prī′ər), *adj.* **1.** preceding in time or in order; earlier or former; anterior or antecedent: *A prior agreement prevents me from accepting this.* **2. prior to,** preceding; before: *Prior to that time, buffalo had roamed the Great Plains in tremendous numbers.* [< L: former, elder, superior (adj.), before (adv.), comp. of OL *pri* before; akin to PRIME, PRE-]
—Syn. 1. previous.

pri·or[2] (prī′ər), *n.* **1.** an officer in a monastic order or religious house, sometimes next in rank below an abbot. **2.** a chief magistrate, as in the medieval republic of Florence. [ME, OE < ML, LL: superior, head; n. use of PRIOR[1]] **—pri′or·ship′,** *n.*

Pri·or (prī′ər), *n.* **Matthew,** 1664–1721, English poet.

pri·or·ate (prī′ər it), *n.* **1.** the office, rank, or term of office of a prior. **2.** a priory. [ME < LL *priōrāt(us)* priority, preference (ML: office of prior). See PRIOR[2], -ATE[1]]

pri·or·ess (prī′ər is), *n.* a woman holding a position corresponding to that of a prior, sometimes ranking next below an abbess. [ME *prioresse* < OF. See PRIOR[2], -ESS]

pri·or·i·ty (prī or′i tē, -ôr′-), *n., pl.* **-ties. 1.** the state or quality of being earlier in time, occurrence, etc. **2.** precedence in order, rank, privilege, etc. **3.** the right to take precedence in obtaining certain supplies, services, facilities, etc., esp. during a shortage. [ME < MF *priorite* < ML *priōritās.* See PRIOR[2], -ITY]

pri·o·ry (prī′ə rē), *n., pl.* **-ries.** a religious house governed by a prior or prioress, often dependent upon an abbey. [ME *priorie* < ML *priōria.* See PRIOR[2], -Y[3]]

Pri·pet (prē′pet), *n.* a river in the W Soviet Union in Europe flowing E through the Pripet Marshes to the Dnieper River in NW Ukraine. 500 mi. long. Also, **Pripyat.**

Pri′pet Marsh′es, an extensive wooded marshland in the W Soviet Union in Europe: dense network of rivers, lakes, and canals. 33,500 sq. mi.

Pri·pyat (*Russ.* prē pyät′yə), *n.* Pripet.

pri·sage (prī′zij), *n. Old Eng. Law.* the right of the king to take a certain quantity of every cargo of wine imported. Cf. **butlerage.** [PRISE + -AGE; cf. ML *prisāgium*]

Pris·ci·an (prish′ē ən, prish′ən), *n.* fl. A.D. c500, Latin grammarian.

Pris·cil·la (pri sil′ə), *n.* a girl's given name.

prise (prīz), *v.t.,* **prised, pris·ing,** *n.* prize[3].

pris·iad·ka (pris yäd′kə), *n.* a step in Slavic folk-dancing in which the dancer squats on his haunches and kicks out each foot alternately; the characteristic step of the kazachok. [< Russ *prisyadka*]

prism (priz′əm), *n.* **1.** *Optics.* a transparent, solid polygonal body, often having triangular bases, used for dispersing light into a spectrum or for reflecting rays of light. **2.** *Geom.* a solid having bases or ends that are parallel, congruent polygons and sides that are parallelograms. **3.** *Crystall.* a form having faces parallel to the vertical axis and intersecting the horizontal axes. [< LL *prisma* < Gk *prîsma,* lit., something sawed, akin to *prīzein* to saw, *prīstēs* sawyer]

Prisms

pris·mat·ic (priz mat′ik), *adj.* **1.** of, pertaining to, or like a prism. **2.** formed by or as if by a transparent prism. **3.** spectral in color; brilliant: *prismatic colors.* **4.** highly varied or faceted: *a prismatic representation of events; a prismatic existence.* Also, **pris·mat′i·cal.** [< Gk *prismat-* (s. of *prîsma*) PRISM + -IC] **—pris·mat′i·cal·ly,** *adv.*

prismat′ic coeffi′cient, *Naval Archit.* See **longitudinal coefficient.**

prismat′ic com′pass, a hand compass equipped with sights and prisms to permit aiming the instrument at a point and at the same time reading the compass direction of the point.

prismat′ic lay′er, the middle layer of the shell of certain mollusks, consisting chiefly of crystals of calcium carbonate.

prismat′ic tel′escope, *Survey.* a telescope having an eyepiece at the side or top equipped with a reflecting prism, used for taking sights at steep angles.

pris·ma·toid (priz′mə toid′), *n. Geom.* a polyhedron having its vertices lying on two parallel planes. [< Gk *prismat-* (s. of *prîsma*) PRISM + -OID]

prism′ binoc′ular, Sometimes, **prism binoculars.** *Optics.* binocular (def. 2).

prism′ diop′ter, *Optics.* a unit of prismatic deviation, in which the number one represents a prism which deflects a beam of light a distance of one centimeter on a plane placed normal to the initial direction of the beam and one meter away from the prism.

pris·moid (priz′moid), *n. Geom.* a solid having bases or ends that are parallel and similar but not congruent, and polygons and sides that are trapezoids. Cf. **prism** (def. 2). [PRISM + -OID] **—pris·moi′dal,** *adj.*

prism′ spectrom′eter, *Optics.* See under **spectrometer.**

pris·on (priz′ən), *n.* **1.** a building for the confinement of persons held while awaiting trial, persons sentenced after conviction, etc. **2.** See **State prison. 3.** any place of confinement or involuntary restraint. **4.** imprisonment. [ME < OF, var. of *preson* < L *pre(he)nsiōn-* (s. of *prehensiō*) a seizure, arrest, equiv. to *prehens(us)* (ptp. of *prehendere*) + *-iōn-* -ION. See APPREHEND] **—pris′on·like′,** *adj.*

pris·on·er (priz′ə nər, priz′nər), *n.* **1.** a person who is confined in prison or kept in custody, esp. as the result of legal process. **2.** Also called **pris′oner of war′.** a person who is captured and held by an enemy during war, esp. a member of the armed forces. *Abbr.:* POW **3.** one who or that which is deprived of liberty or kept in restraint. [ME < MF *prisonier.* See PRISON, -ER[2]]

pris′oner's base′, any of various children's games in which each of two teams has a home base where members of the opposing team are kept prisoner after being tagged or caught and from which they can be freed only in specified ways. Also called **pris′on base′.**

pris′on psycho′sis, *Psychiatry.* a state of mental confusion, transitory or permanent, brought on by incarceration or by the anticipation of imprisonment.

pris′on rus′tic work′, rustication having a deeply pitted surface.

Pris·sie (pris′ē), *n.* a girl's given name, form of **Priscilla.** Also, **Pris′sy.**

pris·sy (pris′ē), *adj.,* **-si·er, -si·est.** excessively proper; affectedly correct; prim. [b. PRI(M[1] + SI)SSY] **—pris′si·ly,** *adv.* **—pris′si·ness,** *n.*

pris·tine (pris′tēn, -tin, -tīn), *adj.* **1.** of or pertaining to the earliest period or state; primitive. **2.** having its original purity; uncorrupted or unsullied. [< L *prīstin(us)* early; akin to PRIME]

prith·ee (prith′ē), *interj. Archaic.* (I) pray thee.

Pri·thi·vi (pri tē′vi), *n. Hindu Myth.* a Vedic goddess personifying the earth and fertility.

pri·us (prī′əs), *adj.* (in prescriptions) before; former. [< L]

priv., 1. private. **2.** privative.

pri·va·cy (prī′və sē; *also Brit.* priv′ə sē), *n., pl.* **-cies. 1.** the state of being private; retirement or seclusion. **2.** secrecy. **3.** *Archaic.* a private place. [late ME *privace.* See PRIVATE, -ACY]

pri·vat·do·cent (prē vät′dō tsent′), *n.* (in German and certain other universities) a private teacher or lecturer recognized by the university but receiving no compensation from it, being remunerated by fees. Also, **pri·vat′do·zent′.** Also called **docent.** [< G; see PRIVATE, DOCENT]

pri·vate (prī′vit), *adj.* **1.** belonging to some particular person or persons: *private property.* **2.** pertaining to or affecting a particular person or a small group of persons; individual; personal: *for your private satisfaction.* **3.** confined to or intended only for the person or persons immediately concerned; confidential: *a private meeting.* **4.** personal and not publicly expressed: *one's private feelings in a controversy.* **5.** not holding public office or employment: *a group of private citizens.* **6.** not of an official or public character: *to retire to private life.* **7.** removed from or out of public view or knowledge; secret: *the private papers of President Wilson.* **8.** not open or accessible to the general public: *a private beach.* **9.** without the presence of others; alone; secluded. **10.** intimate; most personal: *private behavior.* **11.** of, having, or receiving special hospital facilities, privileges, and services, esp. a room of one's own and liberal visiting hours: *a private room; a private patient.* **12.** of lowest military rank. —*n.* **13.** a soldier of one of the three lowest enlisted ranks. **14. privates.** Also called **private parts.** the external genitals. **15. in private,** not publicly; secretly: *The hearing will be conducted in private.* [ME *pryvat* < L *prīvāt(us)* private, lit., taken away (from public affairs), special use of ptp. of *prīvāre* to rob). See DEPRIVE, -ATE[1]] **—pri′vate·ly,** *adv.* **—pri′vate·ness,** *n.*
—Syn. 2. singular, particular, peculiar. **9.** sequestered, retired. **—Ant. 2.** general, public.

pri′vate bill′, a congressional or parliamentary bill involving the private interests of a particular individual, corporation, or local unit. Cf. **public bill.**

pri′vate com′pany, *Brit.* a company whose shareholders may not exceed 50 in number and whose shares may not be offered for public subscription. Cf. **public company.**

pri·va·teer (prī′və tēr′), *n.* **1.** an armed ship that is privately owned and manned, commissioned by a government to fight or harass enemy shipping. **2.** privateersman. —*v.i.* **3.** to cruise as a privateer. [PRIVATE + -EER, modeled on *volunteer*]

pri·va·teers·man (prī′və tērz′mən), *n., pl.* **-men.** an officer or seaman of a privateer. [PRIVATEER + -S[1] + MAN[1]]

pri′vate eye′, *Slang.* a private detective.

pri′vate interna′tional law′, the law governing the rights of private persons as dependent on different laws and jurisdictions of different states or nations (distinguished from *public international law*).

pri′vate judg′ment, personal opinion formed independently of the expressed position of an institution, as in matters of religion or politics.

pri′vate law′, 1. a branch of law dealing with the legal relationships of private individuals. Cf. **public law** (def. 2). **2.** a statute affecting only one person or a small number of persons directly.

pri′vate-line car′ (prī′vit līn′), a freight car owned by a company other than a railroad but operated over the tracks of railroads.

Pri′vate Mem′ber, (*sometimes l.c.*) *Brit.* a member of a legislative body, esp. of the House of Commons, who has no special duties and is not a member of the ministry.

pri′vate prac′tice, the practice of one's profession as an independent rather than as an employee.

pri′vate school′, a school founded, conducted, and maintained by a private group rather than by the government, usually charging tuition and often following a particular philosophy, viewpoint, etc.

pri′vate sec′retary, a person who attends to the individual or confidential correspondence, files, etc., of a business executive, official, or the like.

pri·va·tion (prī vā′shən), *n.* **1.** lack of the usual comforts or necessaries of life: *His life of privation at length began to affect his health.* **2.** an instance of this. **3.** act of depriving. **4.** state of being deprived. [< F < L *prīvātiōn-* (s. of *prīvātiō*) a taking away. See PRIVATE, -ION]
—Syn. 1. deprivation, want, need, distress. See **hardship.**

priv·a·tive (priv′ə tiv), *adj.* **1.** causing, or tending to cause, deprivation. **2.** consisting in or characterized by the taking away, loss, or lack of something. **3.** *Gram.* indicating negation or absence. —*n.* **4.** *Gram.* a privative element, as *a-* in *asymmetric.* **5.** something that is deprived. [< L *prīvātīv(us).* See PRIVATE, -IVE] **—priv′a·tive·ly,** *adv.*

priv·et (priv′it), *n.* **1.** a European, oleaceous shrub, *Ligustrum vulgare,* having evergreen leaves and small white flowers, used for hedges. **2.** any of various other plants of the genus *Ligustrum.* **3.** See **swamp privet.** [?]

priv′et androm′eda. See **swamp andromeda.**

priv·i·lege (priv′ə lij, priv′lij), *n., v.,* **-leged, -leg·ing.** —*n.* **1.** a right, immunity, or benefit enjoyed only by a person or persons beyond the advantages of most: *the privileges of the very rich.* **2.** a special right, immunity, or exemption granted to persons in authority or office to free them from certain obligations or liabilities: *the privilege of a Senator to speak in Congress without danger of a libel suit.* **3.** a grant to an individual, corporation, etc., of a special right or immunity, under certain conditions: *Possession of this license is a privilege revokable at any time.* **4.** the principle or condition of enjoying special rights or immunities. **5.** any of the rights common to all citizens under a modern constitutional government: *We enjoy the privileges of free men.* **6.** *Stock Exchange.* an option to buy or sell stock at a stipulated price for a limited period of time, including puts, calls, spreads, and straddles. —*v.t.* **7.** to grant a privilege to. **8.** to exempt (usually fol. by *from*). **9.** to authorize or license (something otherwise forbidden). [ME *privileg(i)e* < L *prīvilēgi(um),* orig., a law for or against an individual, equiv. to *prīvi-* (comb. form of *prīvus* one's own) + *lēg-* (see LEGAL) + *-ium* -IUM] **—priv′i·leg·er,** *n.*
—Syn. 1. PRIVILEGE, PREROGATIVE refer to a special advantage or right possessed by an individual or group. A PRIVILEGE is a right or advantage gained by birth, social position, effort, or concession. It can have either legal or personal sanction: *the privilege of paying half fare; the privilege of calling whenever one wishes.* PREROGATIVE refers to an exclusive right claimed and granted, often officially or legally, on the basis of social status, heritage, sex, etc.: *the prerogatives of a king; the prerogatives of management.* **4.** license, freedom, liberty.

priv·i·leged (priv′ə lijd, priv′lijd), *adj.* **1.** belonging to a class which enjoys a special privilege or privileges; favored: *the privileged few.* **2.** entitled to or exercising a privilege: *a privileged person; a privileged group.* **3.** restricted to a select group or individual: *privileged information; a privileged position.* **4.** *Law.* (of utterances or communications) **a.** not rendering the person making them liable to prosecution for libel or slander, in view of the attendant circumstances. **b.** not requiring any testimony concerning them to be presented in court. **5.** *Navig.* (of a vessel) having the right of way. Cf. **burdened.** [ME; see PRIVILEGE, -ED[3]]

priv′ileged al′tar, *Rom. Cath. Ch.* an altar at which a plenary indulgence for a departed soul may be granted upon celebration of a Mass.

priv′ileged communica′tion, *Law.* See **confidential communication.**

priv·i·ly (priv′ə lē), *adv.* in a privy manner; secretly. [ME; see PRIVY, -LY]

priv·i·ty (priv′i tē), *n., pl.* **-ties. 1.** private or secret knowledge. **2.** participation in the knowledge of something private or secret, esp. as implying concurrence or consent. **3.** *Law.* the relation between privies. **4.** *Obs.* privacy. [ME *privete, privite* < OF. See PRIVY, -ITY]

priv. pr., privately printed.

priv·y (priv′ē), *adj.,* **priv·i·er, priv·i·est,** *n., pl.* **priv·ies.** —*adj.* **1.** participating in the knowledge of something private or secret (usually fol. by *to*): *Many persons were privy to the plot.* **2.** private; assigned to private uses. **3.** belonging or pertaining to some particular person or persons, esp. with reference to a sovereign. **4.** *Archaic.* secret, concealed, hidden, or secluded. **5.** *Archaic.* acting or done in secret. —*n.* **6.** an outhouse serving as a toilet. **7.** *Law.* a person participating directly in or having a derivative interest in a legal transaction. [ME *prive* < OF: private (adj.), close friend, private place (n.) < L *prīvāt(us)* PRIVATE]

priv′y cham′ber, 1. a private apartment in a royal residence. **2.** *Archaic.* a room reserved for the private or exclusive use of some particular person or persons. [ME]

priv′y coat′, a mail shirt worn under ordinary clothing as a defense against swords or daggers.

priv′y coun′cil, 1. a board or select body of personal advisers, as of a sovereign. 2. *(caps.)* (in Great Britain) a body of advisers, theoretically selected by the sovereign, whose function it is to advise the sovereign in matters of state. 3. *(sometimes caps.)* any similar body, as one appointed to assist the governor of a British dominion. [ME *prive counseil* privy counsel] —**priv′y coun′cilor.**

priv′y purse′, *Brit.* 1. a sum from the public revenues allotted to the sovereign for personal expenses. 2. a member of the royal household in charge of paying these expenses.

priv′y seal′, (in Great Britain) the seal affixed to grants, documents, etc., that are to pass the great seal, and to documents of less importance that do not require the great seal. [ME *prive seal*]

prix fixe (prē′ fiks′; *Fr.* prē fēks′), *pl.* **prix fixes** (prē′ fiks′; *Fr.* prē fēks′). a fixed price charged for any meal chosen from the variety listed on the menu: *This restaurant has a prix fixe of $10.* Cf. **à la carte, table d'hôte.** [< F]

Prix Gon·court (prē′ gon ko͝or′; *Fr.* prē gôɴ ko͞or′), Goncourt (def. 2).

prize[1] (prīz), *n.* 1. a reward for victory or superiority, as in a contest or competition. 2. something that is won in a lottery or the like. 3. anything striven for, worth striving for, or much valued. 4. something seized or captured, esp. an enemy's ship and cargo captured at sea according to the laws of war. 5. the act of taking or capturing, esp. a ship at sea. 6. *Archaic.* a contest or match. —*adj.* 7. having won a prize: *a prize bull; a prize play.* 8. worthy of a prize. 9. given or awarded as a prize. [ME *prise* < MF: a seizing, capturing < L *pre(he)nsa,* n. use of fem. ptp. of *pre(he)ndere* to take + ME *prise,* var. of *pris* reward. See PRICE] —**Syn.** 1. premium. See **reward.**

prize[2] (prīz), *v.t.,* **prized, priz·ing.** 1. to value or esteem highly. 2. to estimate the worth or value of. [ME *prise* < MF *pris(ier),* var. of *preisier* to PRAISE] —**Syn.** 1. See **appreciate.**

prize[3] (prīz), *v.,* **prized, priz·ing,** *n.* —*v.t.* 1. *Chiefly Brit. Dial.* pry[2]. —*n.* 2. leverage. 3. a lever. Also, **prise.** [ME *prise* < MF: a hold, grasp < L *pre(he)nsa.* See PRIZE[1]]

prize′ court′, a court whose function it is to adjudicate on prizes taken in war.

prize′ fight′, a contest between boxers for a prize, a sum of money, etc.; a professional boxing match. Also, **prize′fight′.** —**prize′ fight′er.** —**prize′fight′er,** *n.* —**prize′ fight′ing.** —**prize′fight′ing,** *n.*

prize′ flag′, a flag hoisted by a yachtsman upon learning that his vessel has won a prize in a race.

prize′ mon′ey, 1. money offered, won, or received in prizes. 2. a portion of the money realized from the sale of a prize, esp. an enemy's vessel, divided among the captors.

priz·er (prī′zər), *n. Archaic.* a competitor for a prize. [PRIZE[1] + -ER[1]]

prize′ ring′, 1. a ring where prize fights take place; boxing ring. 2. the sport of prize fighting.

prize·win·ner (prīz′win′ər), *n.* one who or that which wins a prize or is deserving of a prize: *a Nobel prizewinner; a new toothpaste that's a real prizewinner.* [PRIZE[1] + WINNER]

p.r.n., (in prescriptions) as occasion arises; as needed. [< L *prō rē nāta*]

pro[1] (prō), *adv., n., pl.* **pros.** —*adv.* 1. in favor of a proposition, opinion, etc. Cf. **con**[1]. —*n.* 2. a proponent of an issue; a person who upholds the affirmative in a debate. 3. an argument, consideration, vote, etc., for something. [< L *prō,* prep., in favor of, FOR; akin to Gk *prō,* Skt *pra*]

pro[2] (prō), *n., pl.* **pros,** *adj. Informal.* professional. [shortened form]

pro[3] (prō), *n. Slang.* prophylactic. [shortened form]

pro[4] (prō; *Eng.* prō), *prep. Latin.* for.

pro-[1], 1. a prefix indicating favor for some party, system, idea, etc., without identity with the group (*pro-British; pro-Communist; proslavery*), having *anti-* as its opposite. 2. a prefix of priority in space or time having especially a meaning of advancing or projecting forward or outward, and also used to indicate substitution, attached widely to stems not used as words: *provision; prologue; proceed; produce; protract; procathedral; proconsul.* [comb. form repr. L *prō* PRO[1]]

pro-[2], a prefix identical in meaning with **pro-**[1], occurring in words borrowed from Greek (*prodome*) or formed of Greek (and occasionally Latin) elements. [comb. form repr. Gk *prō* for, before, in favor of]

Proa (def. 1)

PRO, *U.S. Mil.* (formerly) public relations officer.

pro·a (prō′ə), *n.* 1. any of various types of South Pacific boat. 2. a swift Malay sailing boat built with the lee side flat and balanced by a single outrigger. Also, **prahu, prao, prau.** [< Malay *prāu,* var. of *perahu* boat]

pro·ac·cel·er·in (prō′ak sel′ər in), *n. Biochem.* See **accelerator globulin.** [PRO-[1] + ACCELER(ATE) + -IN[2]]

pro·ag·on (prō ag′ōn, -on), *n., pl.* **pro·a·go·nes** (prō′ə-gō′nēz). *Greek.* (in ancient Greek comedy) a disputatious exchange, sometimes of a slapstick nature, between the chorus and the characters, or among the characters themselves, usually following the *parodos* and preceding the *agon.* [lit., before the contest]

prob., 1. probable. 2. probably. 3. problem.

prob·a·bi·lism (prob′ə bə liz′əm), *n.* 1. *Philos.* the doctrine, introduced by the Skeptics, that certainty is impossible and that probability suffices to govern faith and practice. 2. *Rom. Cath. Theol.* a theory that in cases of doubt as to the lawfulness or unlawfulness of an action, it is permissible to follow a soundly probable opinion favoring its lawfulness. Cf. **equiprobabilism.** [< F *probabilisme.* See PROBABLE, -ISM] —**prob′a·bi·list,** *n., adj.* —**prob′a·bi·lis′tic,** *adj.*

prob·a·bil·i·ty (prob′ə bil′i tē), *n., pl.* **-ties.** 1. quality or fact of being probable. 2. a strong likelihood or chance of something: *The probability of the book's success makes us optimistic.* 3. a probable event, circumstance, etc.: *Our going to Ceylon is a probability.* 4. *Statistics.* a. the relative possibility that an event will occur, as expressed by the ratio of the number of actual occurrences to the total number of possible occurrences. b. the relative frequency with which an event occurs or is likely to occur. 5. **in all probability,** very probably; quite likely: *The plant will in all probability be relocated somewhere in the South.* [< L *probābilitās.* See PROBABLE, -ITY]

probabil′ity curve′, *Statistics.* 1. a curve which describes the distribution of probability over the values of a variate. 2. See **normal curve.**

prob·a·ble (prob′ə bəl), *adj.* 1. likely to occur or prove true: *He foresaw a probable business loss. He is the probable writer of the article.* 2. having more evidence for than against, or evidence which inclines the mind to belief but leaves some room for doubt. 3. affording ground for belief. [late ME < L *probābil(is)* likely, lit., capable of standing a test, equiv. to *probā(re)* to test (see PROBE) + *-bilis* -BLE]

prob′able cause′, *Law.* reasonable ground for a belief, as, in a criminal case, that the accused was guilty of the crime, or, in a civil case, that grounds for the action existed: used esp. as a defense to an action for malicious prosecution.

prob′able er′ror, *Statistics Obsolesc.* a measure of variability equal to .6745 times the standard deviation. A normally distributed population has half its elements within one probable error of the mean.

prob·a·bly (prob′ə blē), *adv.* in all likelihood; very likely: *The case will probably be dropped for lack of evidence.* [PROBABLE + -LY]

pro·bang (prō′baŋ), *n. Surg.* a long, slender, elastic rod with a sponge, ball, or the like, at the end, to be introduced into the esophagus or larynx, as for removing foreign bodies, or for introducing medication. [alter. (by assoc. with PROBE) of *provang,* unexplained coinage of the inventor]

pro·bate (prō′bāt), *n., adj., v.,* **-bat·ed, -bat·ing.** —*n.* 1. *Law.* the official proving of a will as authentic or valid in a court of probate. 2. an officially certified copy of a will so proved. —*adj.* 3. of or pertaining to probate or a court of probate. —*v.t.* 4. to establish the authenticity or validity of (a will). [late ME *probat* < L *probāt(um)* a thing approved, neut. ptp. of *probāre* to test and find good; see -ATE[1]]

pro′bate court′, a special court with power over administration of estates of deceased persons, the probate of wills, etc.

pro·ba·tion (prō bā′shən), *n.* 1. act of testing. 2. the testing or trial of a person's conduct, character, qualifications, or the like. 3. the state or period of such testing or trial. 4. *Law.* a. a method of dealing with offenders, esp. young persons guilty of minor crimes or first offenses, by allowing them to go at large under supervision, as that of a person **(proba′tion of′ficer)** appointed for such duty. b. the state of having been conditionally released. 5. *Educ.* a trial period or condition of students in certain educational institutions who are being permitted to redeem failures, misconduct, etc. 6. the testing or trial of a candidate for membership in a religious body or order, for holy orders, etc. 7. *Archaic.* proof. [late ME *probacion* < L *probātiōn-* (s. of *probātiō*). See PROBATE, -ION] —**pro·ba′tion·al, pro·ba′tion·ar·y** (prō bā′shə ner′ē), *adj.* —**pro·ba′tion·ship′,** *n.*

pro·ba·tion·er (prō bā′shə nər), *n.* a person undergoing probation or trial. [PROBATION + -ER[1]] —**pro·ba′tion·er·ship′,** *n.*

pro·ba·tive (prō′bə tiv, prob′ə-), *adj.* 1. serving or designed for testing or trial. 2. affording proof or evidence. Also, **pro·ba·to·ry** (prō′bə tôr′ē, -tōr′ē). [late ME *probatiffe* < L *probātīv(us)* of proof. See PROBATE, -IVE] —**pro′ba·tive·ly,** *adv.*

probe (prōb), *v.,* **probed, prob·ing,** *n.* —*v.t.* 1. to search into or examine thoroughly; question closely: *to probe one's conscience.* 2. to examine or explore with a probe. —*v.i.* 3. to examine or explore with or as with a probe. —*n.* 4. act of probing. 5. a slender surgical instrument for exploring the depth or direction of a wound, sinus, or the like. 6. *U.S.* an investigation, esp. by a legislative committee, of suspected illegal activity. 7. *Rocketry.* a space vehicle for exploring outer space and transmitting the data recorded by instruments on board. 8. a projecting, pipelike device on a receiving aircraft used to make connection with and receive fuel from a tanker aircraft during refueling in flight. [< ML *proba* examination, LL: test. See PROOF] —**probe′a·ble,** *adj.* —**prob′er,** *n.* —**Syn.** 1. investigate, scrutinize.

pro·ben·e·cid (prō ben′i sid), *n. Pharm.* a white, crystalline, water-insoluble powder, $C_{13}H_{19}NO_4S$, used chiefly in the treatment of gouty arthritis. [PRO(PYL) + BEN(ZEN)E + (A)CID]

prob·it (prob′it), *n. Statistics.* a normal equivalent deviate increased by five. [PROB(ABILITY + UN)IT]

pro·bi·ty (prō′bi tē, prob′i-), *n.* integrity; uprightness; honesty. [< L *probitās* uprightness, equiv. to *prob(us)* upright + *-itās* -ITY] —**Syn.** rectitude. —**Ant.** dishonesty.

prob·lem (prob′ləm), *n.* 1. any question or matter involving doubt, uncertainty, or difficulty. 2. a question proposed for solution or discussion. 3. *Math.* a statement requiring a solution, usually by means of a mathematical operation or geometric construction. —*adj.* 4. difficult to train or guide; unruly: *a problem child.* 5. *Literature.* dealing with choices of action difficult either for an individual or for society at large: *a problem play.* [ME *probleme* < L *problēma* < Gk *próblēma,* akin to *probállein* to lay before, equiv. to *pro-* PRO-[2] + *bállein* to throw] —**Syn.** 1, 2. puzzle, riddle, enigma. —**Ant.** 1. certitude.

prob·lem·at·ic (prob′lə mat′ik), *adj.* of the nature of a problem; doubtful; uncertain; questionable. Also, **prob′lem·at′i·cal.** [< LL *problēmatic(us)* < Gk *problēmatikós,* equiv. to *problēmat-* (s. of *próblēma*) PROBLEM + *-ikos* -IC] —**prob′lem·at′i·cal·ly,** *adv.* —**Syn.** unsure, indeterminate, unsettled, dubious, ambiguous.

pro bo·no pu·bli·co (prō bō′nō po͞o′bli kō′; *Eng.* prō bō′nō pub′lə kō′), *Latin.* for the public good or welfare.

pro·bos·ci·date (prō bos′i dāt′), *adj.* having a proboscis. [< L *proboscid-* (s. of *proboscis*) + -ATE[1]]

Pro·bos·cid·e·a (prō′bə sid′ē ə, prō bə sid′ē ə), *n.* the order comprising the elephants. [< NL, equiv. to L *proboscid-* (s. of *proboscis*) + *-ea* neut. pl. ending]

pro·bos·cid·e·an (prō′bə sid′ē ən, -bo-, prō bos′i-dē′ən), *adj.* 1. pertaining to or resembling a proboscis. 2. having a proboscis. 3. belonging or pertaining to the mammals of the order *Proboscidea,* consisting of the elephants and extinct related animals. —*n.* 4. a proboscidean animal. Also, **pro′bos·cid′i·an.** [PROBOSCIDE(A) + -AN]

pro·bos·cid·i·form (prō′bə sid′ə fôrm′, -bo-), *adj. Zool.* shaped like a proboscis. [< L *proboscid-* (s. of *proboscis*) + -I- + -FORM]

pro·bos·cis (prō bos′is), *n., pl.* **-bos·cis·es, -bos·ci·des** (-bos′i dēz′). 1. the trunk of an elephant. 2. any long flexible snout, as of the tapir. 3. Also called **beak.** the elongate, protruding mouth parts of certain insects, adapted for sucking or piercing. 4. *Zool.* any elongate or snoutlike feeding organ. 5. *Facetious.* the human nose, esp. when unusually long or prominent. [< L < Gk *proboskís* elephant's trunk, lit., feeder, equiv. to *pro-* PRO-[2] + *bósk(ein)* (to) feed + *-is* (s. *-id-*) n. suffix]

probos′cis mon′key, a reddish, arboreal monkey, *Nasalis larvatus,* of Borneo, the male of which has a long, flexible nose.

proc., 1. procedure. 2. proceedings. 3. process. 4. proclamation. 5. proctor.

pro·caine (prō kān′, prō′kān), *n. Pharm.* a compound, $C_6H_4NH_2COOCH_2CH_2N(C_2H_5)_2$, used in the form of its hydrochloride chiefly as a local and spinal anesthetic. [PRO-[1] + (CO)CAINE]

procaine′ am′ide, *Pharm.* a compound, $C_{13}H_{21}ON_3$, used in the form of its white, crystalline, water-soluble hydrochloride in the treatment of abnormal rhythms of the heart.

pro·cam·bi·um (prō kam′bē əm), *n. Bot.* the meristem from which vascular bundles are developed. [< NL; see PRO-[1] + CAMBIUM] —**pro·cam′bi·al,** *adj.*

pro·carp (prō′kärp), *n. Bot.* (in red algae) a carpogonium with its associated cells. [< NL *procarp(ium)* < Gk *pro-* PRO-[2] + *karpíon,* dim. of *karpós* fruit]

pro·ca·the·dral (prō′kə thē′drəl), *n.* a church used temporarily as a cathedral. [PRO-[1] + CATHEDRAL]

pro·ce·dure (prə sē′jər), *n.* 1. act or manner of proceeding in any action or process; conduct. 2. a particular course or mode of action. 3. mode of conducting legal, parliamentary, or other business, esp. litigation and judicial proceedings. [< F; see PROCEED, -URE] —**pro·ce′dur·al,** *adj.* —**Syn.** 1. management. 2. operation, maneuver, transaction. See **process.**

pro·ceed (*v.* prə sēd′; *n.* prō′sēd), *v.i.* 1. to move or go forward or onward, esp. after stopping. 2. to carry on or continue any action or process. 3. to go on to do something. 4. to continue one's discourse.

pro′a·bo·li′tion, *adj.*
pro′ab·o·li′tion·ist, *n., adj.*
pro·ab′so·lut′ism, *adj., n.*
pro·ab′so·lut′ist, *adj., n.*
pro·ab′sti·nence, *adj.*
pro′-Ab·ys·sin′i·an, *adj., n.*
pro′ac·a·dem′ic, *adj.*
pro′ac·cept′ance, *adj.*
pro′ac·qui·si′tion, *adj.*
pro′ac·quit′tal, *adj.*
pro·act′ing, *adj.*
pro·ac′tion, *adj.*
pro′ad·journ′ment, *adj.*
pro′ad·min′is·tra′tion, *adj.*
pro′ad·mis′sion, *adj.*
pro′a·dop′tion, *adj.*
pro·ad′ver·tis′ing, *adj.*
pro·ad′ver·tiz′ing, *adj.*
pro-Af′ri·can, *adj., n.*
pro′ag·i·ta′tion, *adj.*
pro′a·grar′i·an, *adj.*
pro′a·gree′ment, *adj.*
pro·air′plane′, *adj.*
pro′-Al·a·bam′an, *adj., n.*
pro′-A·las′kan, *adj.*
pro′-Al·ge′ri·an, *adj., n.*
pro·al′ien, *adj.*
pro′al·li′ance, *adj.*
pro′al·lot′ment, *adj.*
pro′-Al·sa′tian, *adj., n.*
pro′al·ter·a′tion, *adj.*
pro·am′a·teur′, *adj.*
pro′a·mend′ment, *adj.*
pro′-A·mer′i·can, *adj., n.*
pro′-A·mer′i·can·ism, *n.*
pro′an·ar′chic, *adj.*
pro·an′ar·chism, *n.*
pro·an′ar·chy, *adj.*
pro-An′gli·can, *adj., n.*
pro′an·nex·a′tion, *adj.*
pro′ap·os·tol′ic, *adj.*
pro′ap·point′ment, *adj.*
pro′ap·por′tion·ment, *adj.*
pro′ap·pro′pri·a′tion, *adj.*
pro′ap·prov′al, *adj.*
pro-Ar′ab, *adj.*
pro′-A·ra′bi·an, *adj., n.*
pro-Ar′a·bic, *adj.*
pro′ar·bi·tra′tion, *adj.*
pro′ar·bi·tra′tion·ist, *n.*
pro′-Ar·gen·ti′na, *adj.*
pro-Ar′i·an, *adj.*
pro′ar·is·toc′ra·cy, *adj.*
pro′a·ris′to·crat′ic, *adj.*
pro′-Ar·is·to·te′li·an, *adj.*
pro′-Ar·me′ni·an, *adj., n.*
pro·ar′my, *adj.*
pro·art′, *adj.*
pro-A′sian, *adj.*
pro′-A·si·at′ic, *adj.*
pro′as·sess′ment, *adj.*
pro′as·so′ci·a′tion, *adj.*
pro·a′the·ism, *adj., n.*
pro·a′the·ist, *n., adj.*
pro′-A·the′ni·an, *adj., n.*
pro′at·tack′, *adj.*
pro′at·tend′ance, *adj.*
pro·auc′tion, *adj.*
pro·au′di·ence, *adj.*
pro′-Aus·tra′li·an, *adj., n.*
pro-Aus′tri·an, *adj., n.*
pro·au′thor, *adj.*
pro′au·to·ma′tion, *adj.*
pro-Ba·co′ni·an, *adj.*
pro·ban′ish·ment, *adj.*
pro·bank′rupt·cy, *adj.*
pro-Bap′tist, *adj., n.*
pro·bar′gain·ing, *adj.*
pro·base′ball′, *adj.*
pro·bas′ket·ball′, *adj.*
pro-Bel′gian, *adj., n.*
pro-Bib′li·cal, *adj.*
pro·birth′-con·trol′, *adj.*
pro′block·ade′, *adj.*
pro′-Bo·he′mi·an, *adj., n.*
pro′-Bo·liv′i·an, *adj., n.*
pro-Bol′she·vik, *adj., n.*
pro-Bol′she·vism, *n.*
pro-Bol′she·vist, *n., adj.*
pro·box′ing, *adj.*
pro·boy′cott, *adj.*
pro′-Bra·zil′ian, *adj., n.*
pro-Brit′ish, *adj.*
pro-Bud′dhist, *n., adj.*
pro·bud′get·ing, *adj.*
pro′-Bul·gar′i·an, *adj., n.*
pro-Bur′man, *adj.*
pro·busi′ness, *adj.*
pro′-Cam·bo′di·a, *adj.*
pro′-Came·roun′, *adj., n.*
pro′-Ca·na′di·an, *adj., n.*
pro·cap′i·tal·ism, *adj.*
pro·cap′i·tal·ist, *n., adj.*
pro-Cath′o·lic, *adj.*
pro′-Ca·thol′i·cism, *n.*

5. *Law.* **a.** to begin and carry on a legal action. **b.** to take legal action (usually fol. by *against*). **6.** to be carried on, as an action, process, etc. **7.** to go or come forth; issue (often fol. by *from*). **8.** to arise, originate, or result (usually fol. by *from*). —*n.* **9. proceeds, a.** that which results or accrues. **b.** the total sum derived from a sale or other transaction: *The proceeds from the deal were divided equally among us.* **c.** the profits or returns from a sale, investment, etc.: *After the costs were deducted, the proceeds from the bazaar came to $985.* **10.** *Archaic.* proceeds. [ME *procede* < L *prōcēdere.* See PRO-[1], CEDE] —**pro·ceed′er,** *n.*
—**Syn. 1.** progress, continue, pass on. See **advance. 7.** emanate. **8.** spring, ensue. —**Ant. 1.** recede.

pro·ceed·ing (prə sē′ding), *n.* **1.** a particular action, or course of action. **2.** action, course of action, or conduct. **3.** act of one who or that which proceeds. **4. proceedings,** records of the doings of a fraternal, academic, etc., society. **5.** *Law.* **a.** the instituting or carrying on of an action at law. **b.** a legal step or measure: *to institute proceedings against a person.* [PROCEED + -ING[1]]
—**Syn. 1, 2, 4.** See **process.**

proc·e·leus·mat·ic (pros′ə lo͞os mat′ik), *adj.* **1.** inciting, animating, or inspiriting. **2.** *Pros.* **a.** noting a metrical foot of four short syllables. **b.** pertaining to or consisting of feet of this kind. —*n.* **3.** *Pros.* a proceleusmatic foot. [< LL *proceleusmatic(us)* < Gk *prokeleusmatikós,* lit., calling for incitement, equiv. to *pro* PRO-[2] + *keleusmat-* (s. of *kéleusma* summons, akin to *keleúein* to rouse to action) + *-ikos* -IC]

Pro·cel·la·rum (prō sə lär′əm), *n.* **Oceanus.** See **Oceanus Procellarum.**

pro·cel·las (prō sel′əs), *n.* pucellas. [alter. of It *procello*]

pro·cel·lous (prō sel′əs), *adj.* stormy, as the sea. [< L *procellōs(us)* stormy, equiv. to *procell(a)* storm + *-osus* -OUS]

pro·ce·phal·ic (prō′sə fal′ik), *adj.* of or pertaining to the front of the head. [PRO-[1] + CEPHALIC]

proc·ess (pros′es *or, esp. Brit.,* prō′ses), *n.* **1.** a systematic series of actions directed to some end: *to devise a process for homogenizing milk.* **2.** a continuous action, operation, or series of changes taking place in a definite manner: *the process of decay.* **3.** *Law.* **a.** the summons, mandate, or writ by which a defendant or thing is brought before court for litigation. **b.** the whole course of the proceedings in an action at law. **4.** *Photog.* **a.** photomechanical or photoengraving methods collectively. **b.** a system of superimposing background in motion pictures, or otherwise creating a picture by combining elements not ordinarily united. **5.** *Biol., Anat.* a natural outgrowth, projection, or appendage: *a process of a bone.* **6.** the action of going forward or on. **7.** the condition of being carried on. **8.** course or lapse, as of time. —*v.t.* **9.** to treat or prepare by some particular process, as in manufacturing. **10.** to handle (papers, records, etc.) by systematically organizing them, recording or making notations on them, following up with appropriate action, or the like: *He processed the early-morning mail first and then went on to the rest of his chores.* **11.** to require (someone) to answer questionnaires, perform various tasks, and sometimes to undergo physical and aptitude classification examinations before the beginning or termination of a period of service: *The army processes all personnel entering or leaving the service.* **12.** to convert (an agricultural commodity) into marketable form by some special process. **13.** to institute a legal process against. **14.** to serve a process or summons on. —*v.i.* **15.** to undergo the activities involved in processing personnel: *The recruits expected to process in four days.* —*adj.* **16.** prepared or modified by an artificial process: *process cheese.* **17.** noting, pertaining to, or involving photomechanical or photoengraving methods: *process printing.* **18.** *Motion Pictures.* created by or used in a process: *a moving background on a process screen.* [ME *proces* < MF < L *prōcess(us)* a going forward, equiv. to ptp. s. of *prōcēdere* to proceed + *-us* 4th decl. suffix]
—**Syn. 1.** operation. PROCESS, PROCEDURE, PROCEEDING apply to something which goes on or takes place. A PROCESS is a series of progressive and interdependent steps by which an end is attained: *a chemical process.* PROCEDURE usually implies a formal or set order of doing a thing, a method of conducting affairs: *parliamentary procedure.* PROCEEDING (usually pl.) applies to what goes on or takes place on a given occasion or to the records of the occasion: *Proceedings of the Royal Academy of Sciences.*

proc′ess cost′ing, *Accounting.* a method of assigning costs to production processes where products must of necessity be produced in one continuous process, with unit cost arrived at by averaging units produced to the total cost of the process. Cf. **job-order costing.**

proc′essing tax′, a tax levied by the government at an intermediate stage in the production of goods.

pro·ces·sion (prə sesh′ən), *n.* **1.** the act of moving along or proceeding in orderly succession or in a formal and ceremonious manner, as a line of people, animals, vehicles, etc. **2.** the line or body of persons or things moving along in such a manner. **3.** *Eccles.* an office, litany, etc., said or sung in a religious procession. **4.** *Theol.* the emanation of the Holy Spirit from the Father and later, in the Western Church, from the Son: distinguished from the "generation" of the Son and the "unbegottenness" of the Father. **5.** the act of coming forth from a source. —*v.i.* **6.** to go in procession. [early ME < ML *prōcessiōn-* (s. of *prōcessiō*) a religious procession, lit., a marching on. See PROCESS, -ION]

pro·ces·sion·al (prə sesh′ə nəl), *adj.* **1.** of, pertaining to, or characteristic of a procession or processions. **2.** of the nature of a procession; moving in an orderly or regular succession, sequence, or the like. **3.** of a style, design, etc., customarily used in processions: *processional regalia.* **4.** sung or played during a procession, as a hymn, march, etc. —*n.* **5.** a piece of music, as a hymn or slow march, suitable for accompanying a procession. **6.** a book containing hymns, litanies, etc., for use in religious processions. [< ML *prōcessiōnāl(is).* See PROCESSION, -AL[1]] —**pro·ces′sion·al·ly,** *adv.*

pro·ces·sive (prə ses′iv), *adj.* advancing or going forward; progressive: *the processive quality of language.* [< L *prōcess(us)* (see PROCESS) + -IVE]

proc′ess print′ing, a method of printing almost any color by using a limited number of separate color plates, as red, yellow, and blue, in combination.

proc′ess serv′er, *Law.* a person who serves legal documents, as subpoenas, writs, or warrants, esp. those requiring appearance in court.

proc′ess shot′, *Motion Pictures.* a shot in which images are introduced by various artificial means, as by projecting them onto the rear of a translucent screen to form the background of a scene being photographed.

pro·cès-ver·bal (prō sā′ver bäl′; *Fr.* prô se ver-bal′), *n., pl.* **-baux** (-bō′). **1.** a report of proceedings, as of an assembly. **2.** *Fr. Law.* an authenticated written account of facts in connection with a criminal or other charge. [< F; see PROCESS, VERBAL]

pro·chein a·mi (prō′shen ə mē′), *Law.* See **next friend.** Also, **pro′chein a·my′.** [< AF]

pro·chlo·rite (prō klōr′īt, -klôr′-), *n.* *Mineral.* a dark green member of the chlorite group, usually foliated. [PRO-[1] + CHLORITE[1]]

pro-choice (prō chois′), *adj.* advocating or sympathetic to legalized abortion. Cf. **pro-life.**

pro·cho·os (prō′kō os′, prok′ō-), *n., pl.* **pro·cho·oi** (prō′kō oi′, prok′ō-). *Gk. and Rom. Antiq.* an elongated form of the oinochoe. [< Gk, equiv. to *pro-* PRO-[2] + *choös* pitcher, lit., measure of quantity, akin to *chein* to pour. See OINOCHOE]

Pro·cho·rov (prô′cho rôf′), *n.* **A·le·ksan·dr Mi·khai·lo·vich** (ä le ksän′dər mi khī′lo vich), born 1916, Russian physicist: Nobel prize 1964.

pro·chro·nism (prō′krə niz′əm, prok′rə-), *n.* a chronological error in which a person, event, etc., is assigned a date earlier than the actual one; prolepsis. Cf. **anachronism, parachronism.** [PRO-[2] + Gk *chrón(os)* time + -ISM. See ANACHRONISM]

pro·claim (prō klām′, prə-), *v.t.* **1.** to announce or declare in an official or formal manner: *The king proclaimed war on the French.* **2.** to announce or declare publicly or officiously: *to proclaim one's opinions.* **3.** to indicate or make known publicly or openly. **4.** to extol or praise publicly: *Let them proclaim the Lord.* **5.** to declare (a territory, district, etc.) subject to particular legal restrictions. **6.** to declare to be an outlaw, evildoer, or the like. **7.** to denounce or prohibit publicly. —*v.i.* **8.** to make proclamation. [late ME *proclame(n)* < L *prōclāmāre* to cry out. See PRO-[1], CLAIM] —**pro·claim′er,** *n.*
—**Syn. 1.** advertise. See **announce. 2.** promulgate.

proc·la·ma·tion (prok′lə mā′shən), *n.* **1.** that which is proclaimed; a public and official announcement. **2.** act of proclaiming. [late ME *proclamacyon* < L *prōclāmātiōn-* (s. of *prōclāmātiō*), equiv. to *prōclāmāt(us)* (ptp. of *prōclāmāre* to PROCLAIM) + *-iōn-* -ION]

Pro·cle·a (prō klē′ə), *n.* *Class. Myth.* the first wife of Cycnus of Colonae.

Pro·cles (prō′klēz), *n.* *Class. Myth.* the twin brother of Eurysthenes.

pro·cli·nate (prok′lə nāt′), *adj.* *Zool.* (of a part) directed or inclined forward. [< L *prōclīnāt(us)* bent forward, ptp. of *prōclīnāre.* See PRO-[1], RECLINE, -ATE[1]]

pro·clit·ic (prō klit′ik), *Gram.* —*adj.* **1.** (of a word) closely connected with the following word and not having an independent accent or phonological status. —*n.* **2.** a proclitic word. [< NL *proclitic(us)*; modeled on *enclitic*; see PRO-[2]]

pro·cliv·i·ty (prō kliv′i tē), *n., pl.* **-ties.** natural or habitual inclination or tendency; propensity; predisposition: *a proclivity to meticulousness.* [< L *prōclīvitās* tendency, lit., a steep descent, steepness, equiv. to *prōclīv(is)* sloping forward, steep (*prō-* PRO-[1] + *clīv(us)* slope + *-is* adj. suffix) + *-itās* -ITY]

Pro·clus (prō′kləs, prok′ləs), *n.* **1.** A.D. c411–485, Greek philosopher and theologian. **2.** a walled plain in the first quadrant of the face of the moon: about 18 miles in diameter.

Proc·ne (prok′nē), *n.* *Class. Myth.* an Athenian princess, the sister of Philomela and wife of Tereus. She fed the flesh of their son to Tereus to punish him for raping Philomela. She was later turned into a swallow.

pro·con·sul (prō kon′səl), *n.* **1.** *Rom. Hist.* an official, usually a former consul, who acted as governor or military commander of a province, and who had powers similar to those of a consul. **2.** any appointed administrator over a dependency or an occupied area. [ME < L; see PRO-[1], CONSUL] —**pro·con′su·lar,** *adj.* —**pro·con′su·lar·ly,** *adv.*

pro·con·su·late (prō kon′sə lit), *n.* *Hist.* the office or term of office of a proconsul. Also, **pro·con′sul·ship′.** [< L *prōconsulāt(us).* See PROCONSUL, -ATE[1]]

Pro·co·pi·us (prō kō′pē əs), *n.* A.D. c490–c562, Greek historian.

pro·cras·ti·nate (prō kras′tə nāt′, prə-), *v.,* **-nat·ed, -nat·ing.** —*v.i.* **1.** to defer action; delay: *to procrastinate until an opportunity is lost.* —*v.t.* **2.** to put off till another day or time; defer; delay. [< L *prōcrāstināt(us)* (ptp. of *prōcrāstināre* to put off till the morrow), equiv. to *prō-* PRO-[1] + *crās* tomorrow + *-tin(us)* adj. suffix + *-ātus* -ATE[1]] —**pro·cras′ti·nat′ing·ly, pro·cras′ti·na′tive·ly,** *adv.* —**pro·cras′ti·na′tion,** *n.* —**pro·cras′ti·na′tive, pro·cras·ti·na·to·ry** (prō kras′tə nə tōr′ē, -tôr′ē, prə-), *adj.* —**pro·cras′ti·na′tive·ness,** *n.* —**pro·cras′ti·na′tor,** *n.*

pro·cre·ant (prō′krē ənt), *adj.* **1.** procreating or generating: *a sufficiently procreant breed of fish; a procreant cause.* **2.** pertaining to procreation. [< L *prōcreant-* (s. of *prōcreāns*), prp. of *prōcreāre* to breed. See PROCREATE, -ANT]

pro·cre·ate (prō′krē āt′), *v.t.,* **-at·ed, -at·ing. 1.** to beget or generate (offspring). **2.** to produce; bring into being. [< L *prōcreāt(us),* ptp. of *prōcreāre* to breed. See PRO-[1], CREATE] —**pro′cre·a′tion,** *n.* —**pro′cre·a′tive,** *adj.* —**pro′cre·a′tive·ness,** *n.* —**pro′cre·a′tor,** *n.*

Pro·cris (prō′kris, prok′ris), *n.* *Class. Myth.* **1.** a daughter of the Athenian king Erechtheus who was killed, while spying on her husband Cephalus, when he mistook her for a concealed animal, and threw at her a spear fated never to miss. **2.** a daughter of Thespius who bore twin sons to Hercules.

Pro·crus·te·an (prō krus′tē ən), *adj.* **1.** pertaining to or suggestive of Procrustes. **2.** tending to produce conformity by violent or arbitrary means. [PROCRUSTE(S) + -AN]

Pro·crus·tes (prō krus′tēz), *n.* *Class. Myth.* a robber who stretched or amputated the limbs of travelers to make them conform to the length of his bed. He was killed by Theseus. Also called **Damastes, Polypemon.**

pro·cryp·tic (prō krip′tik), *adj.* *Zool.* serving to conceal an animal from predators. Cf. **anticryptic.** [PRO(TECTIVE) + CRYPTIC] —**pro·cryp′ti·cal·ly,** *adv.*

proc·tec·to·my (prok tek′tə mē), *n., pl.* **-mies.** *Surg.* excision of the anus and rectum. Also called **rectectomy.** [PROCT- + -ECTOMY]

procto-, a learned borrowing from Greek meaning "anus," "rectum," used in the formation of compound words: *proctoscope.* Also, *esp. before a vowel,* **proct-.** [< Gk *prōkto-,* comb. form of *prōktós*]

proc·toc·ly·sis (prok tok′li sis), *n.* *Med.* the slow, continuous introduction of a solution into the rectum. [< NL; see PROCTO-, CLYSIS]

proc·to·dae·um (prok′tə dē′əm), *n., pl.* **-dae·a** (-dē′ə). proctodeum. —**proc′to·dae′al,** *adj.*

proc·to·de·um (prok′tə dē′əm), *n., pl.* **-de·a** (-dē′ə), **-de·ums.** *Embryol.* a depression in the ectoderm of the anal region of a young embryo, which develops into part of the anal canal. [< NL < Gk *prōkt-* PROCT- + *hodaî(on),* neut. of *hodaîos* that is on or by the way; see -ODE[2], -EOUS] —**proc′to·de′al,** *adj.*

proc·tol·o·gy (prok tol′ə jē), *n.* the branch of medicine dealing with the rectum and anus. [PROCTO- + -LOGY] —**proc·to·log·ic** (prok′tᵊloj′ik), **proc′to·log′i·cal,** *adj.* —**proc·tol′o·gist,** *n.*

proc·tor (prok′tər), *n.* **1.** (in a university or college) **a.** a person appointed to keep watch over students at examinations. **b.** *Chiefly Brit.* an official charged with various duties, esp. with the maintenance of good order. **2.** *Law.* a person employed to manage another's cause, esp. in admiralty and ecclesiastical courts. —*v.t., v.i.* **3.** to supervise or monitor. [contracted var. of PROCURATOR] —**proc·to·ri·al** (prok tōr′ē əl, -tôr′-), *adj.* —**proc·to′ri·al·ly,** *adv.* —**proc′tor·ship′,** *n.*

Proc·tor (prok′tər), *n.* **1.** a town in NE Minnesota. 2963 (1960). **2.** a walled plain in the third quadrant of the face of the moon: about 35 miles in diameter.

proc·to·scope (prok′tə skōp′), *n.* an instrument for visual examination of the interior of the rectum. [PROCTO- + -SCOPE] —**proc·to·scop·ic** (prok′tə skop′ik), *adj.* —**proc·tos·co·py** (prok tos′kə pē), *n.*

pro·cum·bent (prō kum′bənt), *adj.* **1.** lying on the face; prone; prostrate. **2.** *Bot.* (of a plant or stem) lying along the ground, but not putting forth roots. [< L *prōcumbent-* (s. of *prōcumbēns*) bending forward, prp. of *prōcumbere.* See PRO-, INCUMBENT]

pro·cur·a·ble (prō kyo͝or′ə bəl), *adj.* obtainable. [PROCURE + -ABLE]

proc·u·ra·cy (prok′yər ə sē), *n., pl.* **-cies.** *Archaic.* the office of a proctor or procurator. [ME *procuracie* < ML *prōcūrātia* for L *prōcūrātiō* PROCURATION; see -ACY]

pro·cur·ance (prō kyo͝or′əns), *n.* act of bringing something about; agency. [PROCURE + -ANCE]

proc·u·ra·tion (prok′yə rā′shən), *n.* **1.** act of obtaining or getting; procurement. **2.** act of procuring women for purposes of prostitution. **3.** the appointment of a procurator, agent, or attorney. **4.** the authority given. **5.** a document whereby the authority is given. **6.** *Archaic.* management for another; agency. [ME *procuracion* < L *prōcūrātiōn-* (s. of *prōcūrātiō*) management, equiv. to *prōcūrāt(us)* (ptp. of *prōcūrāre* to take care of; see PROCURE) + *-iōn-* -ION]

proc·u·ra·tor (prok′yə rā′tər), *n.* **1.** *Rom. Hist.* any of various imperial officials with fiscal or administrative powers. **2.** a cellarer. **3.** a person, as a deputy, attorney, or agent, employed to manage the affairs of another. [ME *procurat(o)ur* < L *prōcūrātor* manager. See PROCURATION, -OR[2]] —**proc·u·ra′tor·ate, proc′u·ra′tor·ship′,** *n.* —**proc·u·ra·to·ri·al** (prok′yər ə tōr′ē əl, -tôr′-), **proc′u·ra′to·ry,** *adj.*

pro·cure (prō kyo͝or′), *v.,* **-cured, -cur·ing.** —*v.t.* **1.** to obtain or get by care, effort, or the use of special means: *to procure evidence.* **2.** to bring about, esp. by unscrupulous and indirect means: *to procure secret documents.* **3.** to obtain (women or girls) for the purpose of prostitution. —*v.i.* **4.** to act as a procurer or pimp. [ME *procure(n)* < L *prōcūr(āre)* (to) take care of. See PRO-[1], CURE] —**pro·cure′ment,** *n.*
—**Syn. 1.** gain, win. See **get. 2.** contrive. **4.** pander, pimp. —**Ant. 1.** lose.

pro·cur·er (prō kyo͝or′ər), *n.* a person who procures, esp. a pander or pimp. Also, *referring to a woman,* **pro·cur·ess** (prō kyo͝or′is). [late ME (see PROCURE, -ER[1]); r. ME *procurour* < AF << L *prōcūrātōr-* (s. of *prōcūrātor*) PROCURATOR]

Pro·cy·on (prō′sē on′), *n.* *Astron.* a first-magnitude star in the constellation Canis Minor. [< L < Gk

pro·cen′sor·ship′, *adj.*
pro·cen′sure, *adj.*
pro′cen·tral·i·za′tion, *adj.*
pro′-Cey·lon′, *adj.*
pro·char′i·ty, *adj.*
pro-Chil′e·an, *adj., n.*
pro′-Chi·nese′, *adj., n.*
pro·church′, *adj.*
pro·cit′y, *adj.*
pro·civ′ic, *adj.*
pro′ci·vil′ian, *adj.*
pro·clas′si·cal, *adj.*
pro·cler′gy, *adj.*
pro·cler′i·cal, *adj.*
pro′co·er′cion, *adj.*
pro′col·lec′tiv·ism, *n.*
pro′col·lec′tiv·ist, *adj., n.*
pro′col·lec′tiv·is′tic, *adj.*
pro′col·le′giate, *adj.*
pro′-Co·lom′bi·an, *adj., n.*
pro′co·lo′ni·al, *adj., n.*
pro·com′e·dy, *adj.*
pro′com·mer′cial, *adj.*
pro·com′mu·nism, *n., adj.*
pro·com′mu·nist, *adj., n.*
pro′com·mu′ni·ty, *adj.*
pro′com·mu·ta′tion, *adj.*
pro′com·pen·sa′tion, *adj.*
pro′com·pe·ti′tion, *adj.*
pro·com′pro·mise′, *adj.*
pro′con·ces′sion, *adj.*
pro′con·cil′i·a′tion, *adj.*
pro′-Con·fed′er·ate, *adj.*
pro′con·fis·ca′tion, *adj.*
pro′-Con·go·lese′, *adj., n., pl.* **-lese.**
pro′-Con·gres′sion·al, *adj.*
pro′con·scrip′tion, *adj.*
pro′con·ser·va′tion, *adj.*
pro′con·ser·va′tion·ist, *adj., n.*
pro′con·sol·i·da′tion, *adj.*
pro′con·sti·tu′tion·al, *adj.*
pro′con·sti·tu′tion·al·ism, *n.*
pro′con·sul·ta′tion, *adj.*
pro′con·tin′u·a′tion, *adj.*
pro′con·ven′tion, *adj.*
pro′con·vic′tion, *adj.*
pro′-Cu′ban, *adj., n.*
pro-Cy′prus, *adj.*
pro-Czech′, *adj., n.*

Prokyōn name of a star, lit., before (*pro-* PRO-[2]) the dog (*kyōn*), so called because it rises just before Sirius, the dog-star]

prod (prod), *v.*, **prod·ded, prod·ding,** *n.* —*v.t.* **1.** to poke or jab with or as with something pointed: *I prodded him with my elbow.* **2.** to rouse or incite as if by poking; nag; goad. —*n.* **3.** act of prodding; a poke or jab. **4.** any of various pointed instruments, as a goad. [?] —**prod′der,** *n.*

prod., **1.** produce. **2.** produced. **3.** product.

prodd (prod), *n.* a crossbow for hurling stones or balls: used for sport. [? sp. var. of PROD]

prod·i·gal (prod′ə gəl), *adj.* **1.** wastefully or recklessly extravagant: *prodigal expenditure.* **2.** giving or yielding profusely; lavish (usually fol. by *of* or *with*): *prodigal of smiles; prodigal with money.* **3.** lavishly abundant; profuse: *nature's prodigal sources of beauty.* —*n.* **4.** a person who spends, or has spent, his money or substance with wasteful extravagance; spendthrift. [back formation from PRODIGALITY] —**prod′i·gal·ly,** *adv.*
—**Syn. 1.** profligate. See **lavish. 2, 3.** copious, bounteous. **4.** waster, wastrel. —**Ant. 1.** cautious, provident.

prod·i·gal·i·ty (prod′ə gal′i tē), *n., pl.* **-ties. 1.** quality or fact of being prodigal; wasteful extravagance in spending. **2.** an instance of it. **3.** lavish abundance. [ME *prodigalite* < LL *prōdigālitās* wastefulness, equiv. to L *prōdig(us)* wasteful + *-āl(is)* -AL[1] + *-itās* -ITY]

pro·di·gious (prə dij′əs), *adj.* **1.** extraordinary in size, amount, extent, degree, force, etc.: *a prodigious research grant.* **2.** wonderful or marvelous: *a prodigious feat.* **3.** abnormal; monstrous. **4.** *Obs.* ominous. [< L *prōdigiōs(us)* marvelous. See PRODIGY, -OUS] —**pro·di′gious·ly,** *adv.* —**pro·di′gious·ness,** *n.*
—**Syn. 1.** enormous, immense, huge, gigantic, tremendous. **2.** amazing, stupendous, astounding, wondrous, miraculous. —**Ant. 1.** tiny. **2.** ordinary.

prod·i·gy (prod′i jē), *n., pl.* **-gies. 1.** a person, esp. a child or young person, having extraordinary talent or ability: *a musical prodigy.* **2.** a marvelous example (usually fol. by *of*): *that prodigy of learning.* **3.** something wonderful or marvelous; a wonder. **4.** something abnormal or monstrous. **5.** *Archaic.* something extraordinary regarded as of prophetic significance. [< L *prōdigi(um)* prophetic sign, equiv. to *prōd-* PRO-[1] + *-igium,* akin to *-agium* in *adāgium* ADAGE]

pro·do·mos (prō dō′mos), *n., pl.* **-moi** (-moi). *Archit.* an open vestibule, as a pronaos. [< Gk: lit., before-house, equiv. to *pro-* PRO-[2] + *dómos* house]

pro·drome (prō′drōm), *n.* *Pathol.* a premonitory symptom. [< F < NL *prodrom(us)* < Gk *pródromos* running before. See PRO-[2], -DROME] —**prod·ro·mal** (prod′rə məl), *adj.*

Pro·dro·mi·a (prə drō′mē ə), *n.* *Class. Myth.* an epithet of Hera, meaning "pioneer."

pro·duce (*v.* prə do͞os′, -dyo͞os′; *n.* prod′o͞os, -yo͞os, prō′do͞os, -dyo͞os), *v.* **-duced, -duc·ing,** *n.* —*v.t.* **1.** to bring into existence; give rise to; cause: *to produce steam; to produce a reaction.* **2.** to bring into existence by intellectual or creative ability: *to produce a novel; to produce a great painting.* **3.** *Econ.* to create (something having exchange value): *to produce goods for sale.* **4.** to bring forth; give birth to; bear: *to produce a litter of puppies.* **5.** to provide, furnish, or supply; yield: *a mine producing silver.* **6.** *Finance.* to cause to accrue: *stocks producing unexpected dividends.* **7.** to bring forward; present to view or notice; exhibit: *to produce one's credentials.* **8.** to bring (a play, movie, opera, etc.) before the public. **9.** to extend or prolong, as a line. —*v.i.* **10.** to create, bring forth, or yield offspring, products, etc.: *Their mines are closed because they no longer produce.* **11.** *Econ.* to create economic value; bring crops, goods, etc., to a point at which they will command a price. —*n.* **12.** that which is produced; yield; product. **13.** agricultural products collectively, esp. vegetables and fruits. **14.** offspring, esp. of a female animal: *the produce of a mare.* [ME < L *prōdūce(re)* (to) lead or bring forward, extend, prolong, bring forth, produce, equiv. to *prō-* PRO-[1] + *dūcere* to lead] —**pro·duc′i·bil′i·ty, pro·duct·i·bil·i·ty** (prə duk′tə bil′i tē), *n.* —**pro·duc′i·ble·ness, pro·duce′a·ble·ness,** *n.* —**pro·duc′i·ble, pro·duce′a·ble, pro·duct′i·ble,** *adj.*
—**Syn. 1.** generate, create. **3.** make, manufacture. **4.** afford, yield. **7.** show. **12.** See **crop.** —**Ant. 1.** destroy, ruin. **7.** conceal.

pro·duc·er (prə do͞o′sər, -dyo͞o′-), *n.* **1.** a person who produces. **2.** *Econ.* a person who creates economic value, or produces goods and services. **3.** a person responsible for the financial and administrative aspects of a stage, film, television, or radio production; the person who exercises general supervision of a production and is responsible chiefly for raising money, hiring technicians and artists, etc., required to stage a play, make a motion picture, or the like. Cf. **director** (def. 3). **4.** *Theat. Brit.* a director of theatrical productions; stage director. **5.** an apparatus for making producer gas. **6.** *Ecol.* an organism, as a plant, that is able to produce its own food from inorganic substances. [PRODUCE + -ER[1]]

prod′uce race′, *Horse Racing.* a race for the offspring of parents identified or characterized at the time of nomination.

produc′er gas′, a gas composed of carbon monoxide, hydrogen, and nitrogen, obtained by passing air and steam through incandescent coke: used as an industrial fuel, in certain gas engines, and in the manufacture of ammonia.

produc′er goods′, *Econ.* goods, as machinery, raw materials, etc., that are used in the process of creating consumer goods.

prod·uct (prod′əkt, -ukt), *n.* **1.** a thing produced by labor: *products of farm and factory; the product of his thought.* **2.** a person or thing produced by or resulting from a process, as a natural, social, or historical one; result: *He is a true product of his time.* **3.** *Chem.* a substance obtained from another substance through chemical change. **4.** *Math.* **a.** the result obtained by multiplying two or more quantities together. **b.** intersection (def. 2). [late ME < L *prōduct(um)* (thing) produced, neut. of ptp. of *prōdūcere* to PRODUCE]

pro·duc·tile (prə duk′til), *adj.* *Rare.* capable of being lengthened out; extensile. [< LL *prōductil(is)* prolongable, equiv. to L *prōduct(us)* prolonged (ptp. of *prōdūcere* to PRODUCE) + *-ilis* -ILE]

pro·duc·tion (prə duk′shən), *n.* **1.** act of producing; creation; manufacture. **2.** that which is produced; a product. **3.** *Econ.* the creation of value; the producing of articles having exchange value. **4.** the total amount produced: *Production is up this month.* **5.** a work of literature or art. **6.** act of presenting for display; presentation; exhibition: *He demanded the production of evidence in support of the allegation.* **7.** *Informal.* an unnecessarily or exaggeratedly complicated situation or activity: *She can make a production out of having one guest to dinner.* **8.** the concerted application of financial, artistic, and managerial resources in organizing and presenting a play, opera, circus, or any other theatrical spectacle: *It was an expensive production. The show is now in production.* [late ME < L *prōductiōn-* (s. of *prōductiō*) a lengthening. See PRODUCT, -ION] —**pro·duc′tion·al,** *adj.*

produc′tion num′ber, *Theat.* a specialty number or routine, usually performed by the entire cast consisting of musicians, singers, dancers, stars, etc., of a musical comedy, vaudeville show, or the like.

pro·duc·tive (prə duk′tiv), *adj.* **1.** having the power of producing; generative; creative: *a productive effort.* **2.** producing readily or abundantly; fertile: *a productive vineyard.* **3.** causing; bringing about (usually fol. by *of*): *conditions productive of crime and sin.* **4.** *Econ.* producing or tending to produce goods and services having exchange value. [< ML *productīv(us).* See PRODUCT, -IVE] —**pro·duc′tive·ly,** *adv.* —**pro·duc·tiv·i·ty** (prō′duk tiv′i tē, prod′ək-), **pro·duc′tive·ness,** *n.*
—**Syn. 2.** fecund. PRODUCTIVE, FERTILE, FRUITFUL, PROLIFIC apply to the generative aspect of something. PRODUCTIVE refers to a generative source of continuing activity: *productive soil; a productive influence.* FERTILE applies to that in which seeds, literal or figurative, take root: *fertile soil; a fertile imagination.* FRUITFUL refers to that which has already produced and is capable of further production: *fruitful soil, discovery, theory.* PROLIFIC means highly productive: *a prolific farm, writer.* —**Ant. 2.** sterile.

pro·em (prō′em), *n.* an introductory discourse; introduction; preface; preamble. [< L *prooem(ium)* < Gk *prooímion* prelude (*pro-* PRO-[2] + *oím(ē)* song + *-ion* dim. suffix); r. ME *proheme* < MF] —**pro·e·mi·al** (prō ē′mē əl), *adj.*

pro·en·zyme (prō en′zīm), *n.* *Biochem., Biol.* zymogen. [PRO-[1] + ENZYME]

Pro·e·tus (prō ē′təs), *n.* *Class. Myth.* a son of Abas who was a lifelong enemy of his twin, Acrisius. In their warfare, the brothers invented the shield.

prof (prof), *n.* (*often cap.*) *Informal.* professor. [by shortening]

Prof., Professor.

prof·a·na·tion (prof′ə nā′shən), *n.* act of profaning; desecration; defilement; debasement. [< LL *profānātiōn-* (s. of *profānātiō*) desecration, equiv. to L *profānāt(us)* desecrated (ptp. of *profānāre*) + *-iōn-* -ION; r. *prophanation* < MF. See PROFANE]
—**Syn.** sacrilege, blasphemy.

pro·fan·a·to·ry (prə fan′ə tōr′ē, -tôr′ē, prō-), *adj.* tending to desecrate; profaning. [PROFANAT(ION) + -ORY[1]]

pro·fane (prə fān′, prō-), *adj., v.,* **-faned, -fan·ing.** —*adj.* **1.** characterized by irreverence or contempt for God or sacred principles or things; irreligious. **2.** not devoted to holy or religious purposes; unconsecrated; secular (opposed to *sacred*). **3.** unholy; heathen; pagan: *profane rites.* **4.** not initiated into religious rites or mysteries, as persons. **5.** common or vulgar. [< L *profān(us),* lit., before (outside of) the temple; r. late ME *prophane* < ML *prophān(us)* desecrated. See PRO-[1], FANE]
—*v.t.* **6.** to misuse (anything that should be held in reverence or respect); defile; debase; employ basely or unworthily. **7.** to treat (anything sacred) with irreverence or contempt; violate the sanctity of: *to profane a shrine.* [< L *profān(āre),* deriv. of *profānus;* r. ME *prophane(n)* < ML *profān(āre)* (to) desecrate] —**pro·fane′ly,** *adv.* —**pro·fane′ness,** *n.* —**pro·fan′er,** *n.*
—**Syn. 1.** blasphemous, sacrilegious, impious, ungodly. **2.** temporal. **3.** unhallowed. **5.** low, mean, base. **7.** desecrate. —**Ant. 1.** sacred. **2.** spiritual. **3.** holy.

pro·fan·i·ty (prə fan′i tē, prō-), *n., pl.* **-ties** for **2. 1.** quality of being profane; irreverence. **2.** profane conduct or language; a profane act or utterance. [< LL *profānitās.* See PROFANE, -ITY]
—**Syn. 1, 2.** blasphemy, sacrilege. **2.** swearing, malediction; curse.

Prof. Eng., Professional Engineer.

pro·fer·ment (prō fûr′mənt), *n.* *Biochem.* zymogen. [PRO-[1] + FERMENT]

pro·fert (prō′fərt), *n.* *Law.* an exhibition of a record or paper in open court. [< L: lit., he brings forward]

pro·fess (prə fes′), *v.t.* **1.** to lay claim to, often insincerely; pretend to: *He professed extreme regret.* **2.** to declare openly; announce or affirm; avow or acknowledge: *to profess one's satisfaction.* **3.** to affirm faith in or allegiance to (a religion, God, etc.). **4.** to declare oneself skilled or expert in; claim to have knowledge of; make (a thing) one's profession or business. **5.** to receive or admit into a religious order. —*v.i.* **6.** to make a profession, avowal, or declaration. **7.** to take the vows of a religious order. [back formation from PROFESSED]

pro·fessed (prə fest′), *adj.* **1.** avowed; acknowledged. **2.** professing to be qualified; professional, rather than amateur. **3.** having taken the vows of, or been received into, a religious order. **4.** alleged; pretended. [ME (in religious sense) < ML *profess(us)* (special use of L *professus,* ptp. of *profitērī* to declare publicly, equiv. to *pro-* PRO-[1] + *-fitērī,* comb. form of *fatērī* to acknowledge) + -ED[2]]

pro·fess·ed·ly (prə fes′id lē), *adv.* **1.** allegedly; pretendedly: *He is only professedly poor.* **2.** avowedly; by open declaration: *He is professedly guilty of the crime.* [PROFESSED + -LY]

pro·fes·sion (prə fesh′ən), *n.* **1.** a vocation requiring knowledge of some department of learning or science: *the profession of teaching.* Cf. **learned profession. 2.** any vocation or business. **3.** the body of persons engaged in an occupation or calling: *to be respected by the medical profession.* **4.** act of professing; avowal; a declaration, whether true or false: *professions of dedication.* **5.** the declaration of belief in or acceptance of religion or a faith: *the profession of Christianity.* **6.** a religion or faith professed. **7.** the declaration made on entering into membership of a church or religious order. [ME < ML *professiōn-* (s. of *professiō*) the taking of the vows of a religious order. See PROFESS, -ION] —**pro·fes′sion·less,** *n.*
—**Syn. 1.** calling, employment. See **occupation. 4.** asseveration, assertion, protestation.

pro·fes·sion·al (prə fesh′ə nəl), *adj.* **1.** following an occupation as a means of livelihood or for gain: *He is not a professional builder.* **2.** pertaining or appropriate to a profession: *professional studies; the professional objectivity of a doctor.* **3.** engaged in one of the learned professions: *a professional man.* **4.** following as a business an occupation ordinarily engaged in as a pastime: *a professional golfer.* **5.** making a business or constant practice of something not properly to be regarded as a business: *"A salesman," he said, "is a professional optimist."* **6.** undertaken or engaged in as a means of livelihood or for gain: *professional baseball.* —*n.* **7.** a person who belongs to one of the professions, esp. one of the learned professions. **8.** a person who makes a business of an occupation, practice, etc., esp. of an art or sport in which amateurs engage for amusement or recreation. **9.** an expert player, as of golf or tennis, hired by a club, community, etc., to serve as a teacher or consultant in his specialty; pro. [PROFESSION + -AL[1]] —**pro·fes′sion·al·ly,** *adv.*

pro·fes·sion·al·ise (prə fesh′ə nəlīz′), *v.t., v.i.,* **-ised, -is·ing.** *Chiefly Brit.* professionalize. —**pro·fes′sion·al·i·sa′tion,** *n.*

pro·fes·sion·al·ism (prə fesh′ə nəliz′əm), *n.* **1.** professional character, spirit, or methods. **2.** the standing, practice, or methods of a professional, as distinguished from an amateur. [PROFESSIONAL + -ISM]

pro·fes·sion·al·ize (prə fesh′ə nəlīz′), *v.,* **-ized, -iz·ing.** —*v.t.* **1.** to give a professional character to; make into or establish as a profession. —*v.i.* **2.** to become professional. Also, *esp. Brit.,* **professionalise.** [PROFESSIONAL + -IZE] —**pro·fes′sion·al·i·za′tion,** *n.*

pro·fes·sor (prə fes′ər), *n.* **1.** a teacher of the highest academic rank in a college or university, who has been awarded the title *Professor* in a particular branch of learning; a full professor: *a professor of Spanish literature.* **2.** any teacher who has the rank of professor, associate professor, or assistant professor. **3.** a teacher. **4.** an instructor in some art or skilled sport: *a professor of singing; a professor of boxing.* **5.** a person who professes his sentiments, beliefs, etc. [ME < ML: one who has taken the vows of a religious order + L: a public lecturer. See PROFESS, -OR[2]] —**pro·fes·so·ri·al** (prō′fə sōr′ē əl, -sôr′-, prof′ə-), *adj.* —**pro′fes·so′ri·al·ism,** *n.* —**pro′fes·so′ri·al·ly,** *adv.*

pro·fes·sor·ate (prə fes′ər it), *n.* **1.** the office or the period of service of a professor. **2.** a group of professors. [PROFESSOR + -ATE[1]]

pro·fes·so·ri·ate (prō′fi sōr′ē it, -sôr′-, prof′i-), *n.* **1.** a group of professors. **2.** the office or post of professor. [PROFESSORI(AL) + -ATE[1]]

pro·fes·sor·ship (prə fes′ər ship′), *n.* the office or post of a professor. [PROFESSOR + -SHIP]

prof·fer (prof′ər), *v.t.* **1.** to put before a person for acceptance; offer. —*n.* **2.** act of proffering. **3.** an offer or proposal for one's acceptance: *a proffer of hospitality.* [ME *profre(n)* < AF *profre(r),* var. of OF *poroffrir,* equiv. to *por-* PRO-[1] + *offrir* to OFFER] —**prof′fer·er,** *n.*
—**Syn. 1.** volunteer, propose, suggest. See **offer.**

pro·fi·cien·cy (prə fish′ən sē), *n.* state of being proficient; skill; expertness: *proficiency in music.* [< L *prōfici(ēns)* PROFICIENT + -ENCY]

pro·fi·cient (prə fish′ənt), *adj.* **1.** well-advanced or expert in any art, science, or subject; skilled: *a proficient swimmer.* —*n.* **2.** an expert. [< L *prōficient-* (s. of *prōficiēns*) prp. of *prōficere* to advance, make progress, equiv. to *prō-* PRO-[1] + *-ficere,* comb. form of *facere* to make, do. See -ENT, EFFICIENT] —**pro·fi′cient·ly,** *adv.* —**pro·fi′cient·ness,** *n.*
—**Syn. 1.** adept, competent, experienced, accomplished, able, finished. —**Ant. 1.** unskilled, inept.

pro·file (prō′fīl), *n., v.,* **-filed, -fil·ing.** —*n.* **1.** the outline or contour of the human face, esp. the face viewed from one side. **2.** a picture or representation of the side view of a head. **3.** an outlined view, as of a city or mountain. **4.** *Archit.* **a.** an outline of an object, as a molding, formed on a vertical plane passed through the object at right angles to one of its principal horizontal dimensions. **b.** a drawing or the like representing this. **5.** a verbal, arithmetical, or graphic summary or analysis of the history, status, etc., of a process or relationship: *a profile of national consumer spending;*

pro′-Czech·o·slo·va′ki·an, *n. adj.*
pro-Dan′ish, *adj.*
pro-Dar′win, *adj.*
pro′-Dar·win′i·an, *adj., n.*
pro-Dar′win·ism, *n.*
pro·dem′o·crat′, *adj., n.*
pro′dem·o·crat′ic, *adj.*
pro′de·moc′ra·cy, *adj.*
pro-Den′mark, *adj.*
pro′de·por·ta′tion, *adj.*
pro′dis·ar′ma·ment, *adj.*
pro′dis·so·lu′tion, *adj.*
pro′dis·tri·bu′tion, *adj.*
pro′di·vi′sion, *adj.*
pro′di·vorce′, *adj.*
pro′-Do·min′i·can, *adj., n.*
pro-East′, *adj.*
pro-East′ern, *adj.*
pro-Ec′ua·dor, *adj.*
pro′ed·u·ca′tion, *adj.*
pro′-E·gyp′tian, *adj., n.*
pro′e·lec′tri·fi·ca′tion, *adj.*
pro′e·lim′i·na′tion, *adj.*
pro′-E·liz′a·be′than, *adj.*
pro′-Em·er·so′ni·an, *adj., n.*
pro·em′pire, *adj.*
pro′em·pir′i·cism, *n.*
pro′em·pir′i·cist, *n.*
pro′em·ploy′ee, *adj.*
pro′em·ploy′er, *adj.*
pro′em·ploy′ment, *adj.*
pro′en·force′ment, *adj.*
pro-Eng′lish, *adj.*
pro′en·large′ment, *adj.*
pro′e·qual′i·ty, *adj.*
pro-Es′ki·mo′, *adj., n.*
pro′-E·thi·o′pi·an, *adj., n.*
pro′-Eu·ro·pe′an, *adj., n.*
pro′ev·o·lu′tion, *adj.*
pro′ev·o·lu′tion·ar′y, *adj.*
pro′ev·o·lu′tion·ist, *adj., n.*
pro′ex·ec′u·tive, *adj.*
pro′ex·per′i·ment, *adj.*
pro′ex·per′i·men·ta′tion, *adj.*
pro·ex′pert, *adj.*
pro′ex·ten′sion, *adj.*
pro·fac′ul·ty, *adj.*
pro·farm′er, *adj.*
pro·fas′cism, *n.*
pro·fas′cist, *adj., n.*
pro′fed·er·a′tion, *adj.*
pro·fem′i·nism, *n.*
pro·fem′i·nist, *n., adj.*
pro·fic′tion, *adj.*

CONCISE ETYMOLOGY KEY: <, descended or derived from; >, whence; b., blend of, blended; c., cognate with; deriv., derivative; equiv., equivalent; imit., imitative; m., modification of; obl., oblique; r., replacing; s., stem; sp., spelling; trans., translation; ?, origin unknown, perhaps; *, hypothetical. See the full key inside the front cover.

a profile of an employee's work record. **6.** a vivid and concisely written sketch of the life and characteristics of a person. **7.** *Theat.* a flat stage property or scenic piece cut from a firm, thin material, as of beaverboard or plywood, and having an irregular edge resembling the silhouette of a natural object. **8.** (in a gear) the outline of either end of a tooth. **9.** *Naval Archit.* a longitudinal elevation or section of a vessel. Cf. **inboard profile, outboard profile.** —*v.t.* **10.** to draw a profile of. **11.** to write a profile of. [< It *profilo* (n.), *profilare* (v.) < L *pro-* PRO-[1] + *fīlum* contour; see FILE[1]] —**Syn. 1.** silhouette.

pro′file mi′croscope, an instrument for measuring the contour of a ground surface, consisting of a light source that projects a ray at an angle of 45° to the surface being measured and a microscope having its principal axis aligned at 90° to this ray. Also called **Schmaltz profile microscope.**

pro′file plan′, *Naval Archit.* See **sheer plan.**

pro·fil·er (prō′fī lər), *n.* any of several types of machine tools for reproducing shapes in metal or other materials from a master form. Also called **duplicating machine.** [PROFILE + -ER[1]]

Pro·fi·lom·e·ter (prō′fə lom′i tər), *n. Trademark.* a device for measuring the roughness of a surface. [PROFILE + -O- + -METER]

prof·it (prof′it), *n.* **1.** Often, **profits.** *Econ.* **a.** pecuniary gain resulting from the employment of capital in any transaction. Cf. **gross profit, net profit. b.** the ratio of such pecuniary gain to the amount of capital invested. **c.** returns, proceeds, or revenue, as from property or investments. **2.** the monetary surplus left to a producer or employer after deducting wages, rent, cost of raw materials, etc.: *He worked on a small margin of profit.* **3.** Usually, **profits.** additional charges, as interest on capital, insurance, etc. **4.** advantage; benefit; gain. —*v.i.* **5.** to gain an advantage or benefit: *He profited greatly from his schooling.* **6.** to make profit. **7.** to take advantage: *He profits from the weaknesses of others.* **8.** to be of service or benefit. **9.** *Obs.* to make progress. —*v.t.* **10.** to be of advantage or profit to: *Nothing profits one so much as a sound education.* [ME < MF < L *prōfect(us)* progress, profit, equiv. to *prōfect-* (ptp. s. of *prōficere* to make headway) + *-us* 4th decl. suffix. See PROFICIENT] —**prof′it·er,** *n.* —**prof′it·less,** *adj.* —**prof′it·less·ly,** *adv.* —**prof′it·less·ness,** *n.*
—**Syn. 1.** return. **2.** net income. **4.** good, welfare, advancement, improvement. See **advantage. 5, 10.** advance, improve. —**Ant. 1.** loss. **5.** lose.

prof·it·a·ble (prof′i tə bəl), *adj.* **1.** yielding profit; remunerative: *a profitable deal.* **2.** beneficial or useful. [ME; see PROFIT, -ABLE] —**prof′it·a·bil′i·ty, prof′it·a·ble·ness,** *n.* —**prof′it·a·bly,** *adv.*
—**Syn. 2.** advantageous, valuable, helpful.

prof′it and loss′, the gain and loss arising from commercial or other transactions, applied esp. to an account or statement of account in bookkeeping showing gains and losses in business. —**prof′it-and-loss′,** *adj.*

prof′it and loss′ account′. See **income account** (def. 2).

prof·it·eer (prof′i tēr′), *n.* **1.** a person who seeks or exacts exorbitant profits, as by taking advantage of public necessity. —*v.i.* **2.** to act as a profiteer. [PROFIT + -EER]

pro·fit·er·ole (prə fit′ə rōl′), *n.* a small cream puff with a sweet or savory filling, as of ice cream and chocolate sauce. [< F, said to be dim. of *profit* PROFIT]

prof′it shar′ing, the sharing of profits, as between employer and employee, esp. in such a way that the employee receives, in addition to his wages, a share in the profits of the business. —**prof′it-shar′ing,** *adj.*

prof′it squeeze′, a sharp narrowing of the gap between cost and revenue.

prof′it tak′ing, *Stock Exchange.* the selling of securities that have risen in price above costs; selling in order to realize a profit.

prof·li·ga·cy (prof′lə gə sē), *n.* **1.** shameless dissoluteness. **2.** reckless extravagance. **3.** great abundance. [PROFLIGA(TE) + -CY]

prof·li·gate (prof′lə git, -gāt′), *adj.* **1.** utterly and shamelessly immoral; thoroughly dissolute. **2.** recklessly prodigal or extravagant. —*n.* **3.** a profligate person. [< L *prōflīgāt(us)* broken down in character, degraded, lit., struck down, overthrown, ptp. of *prōflīgāre* to shatter, debase, equiv. to *pro-* PRO-[1] + *-flīgāre*, comb. form of *flīgere* to strike; see -ATE[1]] —**prof′li·gate·ly,** *adv.* —**prof′li·gate·ness,** *n.*
—**Syn. 1.** abandoned, licentious.

prof·lu·ent (prof′lo͞o ənt), *adj.* flowing smoothly or abundantly forth. [ME < L *prōfluent-* (s. of *prōfluēns*), prp. of *prōfluere* to flow forth. See PRO-[1], FLUENT]

pro for·ma (prō fôr′mä; *Eng.* prō fôr′mə), *Latin.* according to form; as a matter of form.

pro·found (prə found′), *adj.* **1.** penetrating or entering deeply into subjects of thought or knowledge: *a profound theologian.* **2.** intense; extreme: *profound anxiety.* **3.** being or going far beneath what is superficial, external, or obvious: *profound insight.* **4.** of deep meaning; of great and broadly inclusive significance: *a profound book.* **5.** extending, situated, or originating far down, or far beneath the surface: *the profound depths of the ocean.* **6.** low: *a profound bow.* **7.** deep. —*n. Archaic.* **8.** that which is profound. **9.** the deep sea; ocean. **10.** depth; abyss. [< ME < AF < L *prōfund(us)* deep, vast, equiv. to *prō-* PRO-[1] + *fundus* bottom] —**pro·found′ly,** *adv.* —**pro·found′ness,** *n.*
—**Syn. 1.** deep, sagacious. —**Ant. 1.** shallow, superficial.

pro·fun·da (prə fun′də), *n., pl.* **-dae** (-dē). *Anat.* an artery or vein extending far beneath the surface of the body. [< NL, n. use of fem. of L *prōfundus* deep. See PROFOUND]

pro·fun·di·ty (prə fun′di tē), *n., pl.* **-ties. 1.** quality of being profound; depth. **2.** a profoundly deep place; abyss. **3.** Usually, **profundities.** profound or deep matters. [ME *profundite* < LL *prōfunditās.* See PROFOUND, -ITY]

pro·fuse (prə fyo͞os′), *adj.* **1.** spending or giving freely and in large amount, often to excess; extravagant (often fol. by *in*): *He was profuse in his praise of her singing.* **2.** made or done freely and abundantly: *profuse apologies.* **3.** abundant; in great amount. [late ME < L *profūs(us)*, ptp. of *prōfundere* to pour out or forth. See PRO-[1], FUSE[2]] —**pro·fuse′ly,** *adv.* —**pro·fuse′ness,** *n.*
—**Syn. 1.** See **lavish. 3.** See **ample.** —**Ant. 1.** thrifty.

pro·fu·sion (prə fyo͞o′zhən), *n.* **1.** abundance; abundant quantity. **2.** a great quantity or amount (often fol. by *of*). **3.** lavish spending; extravagance. [< L *prōfūsiōn-* (s. of *prōfūsiō*). See PROFUSE, FUSION]
—**Syn. 1.** copiousness, bounty. See **plenty. 3.** prodigality, profligacy, excess, waste. —**Ant. 1.** scarcity.

pro·fu·sive (prə fyo͞o′siv), *adj.* profuse; lavish; prodigal: *profusive generosity.* [PROFUSE + -IVE] —**pro·fu′sive·ly,** *adv.* —**pro·fu′sive·ness,** *n.*

prog (prog), *v.,* **progged, prog·ging,** *n. Brit. Slang.* —*v.i.* **1.** to search or prowl about, as for plunder or food; forage. —*n.* **2.** food or victuals. [perh. b. PROD and BEG]

Prog., Progressive.

prog., **1.** progress. **2.** progressive.

pro·gen·i·tive (prō jen′i tiv), *adj.* capable of having offspring; reproductive. [PROGENIT(OR) + -IVE] —**pro·gen′i·tive·ness,** *n.*

pro·gen·i·tor (prō jen′i tər), *n.* **1.** a biologically or nonbiologically related ancestor; forefather: *a progenitor of the race.* **2.** one who or that which first indicates a direction, originates something, or serves as a model; predecessor: *The late-medieval conciliar movement was a progenitor of the Reformation. Manet is the progenitor of much of contemporary painting.* [ME *progenitour* < L *prōgenitor* the founder of a family. See PRO-[1], PRIMOGENITOR] —**pro·gen·i·to·ri·al** (prō jen′i tôr′ē əl, -tōr′-), *adj.* —**pro·gen′i·tor·ship′,** *n.*

prog·e·ny (proj′ə nē), *n., pl.* **-ny,** for plants or animals **-nies. 1.** a descendant or offspring, as a child, plant, or animal. **2.** such descendants or offspring collectively. [ME *progenie* < MF < L *prōgeniēs* offspring, equiv. to *pro-* PRO-[1] + *geni(tus)*, ptp. of *gignere* to beget + *-ēs* n. suffix]

pro·ges·ta·tion·al (prō′jes tā′shə nəl), *adj. Med.* **1.** prepared for pregnancy, as the lining of the uterus prior to menstruation or in the early stages of gestation itself; progravid. **2.** of, noting, or characteristic of the action of progesterone; inducing a progravid state. [PRO-[1] + GESTATIONAL]

pro·ges·ter·one (prō jes′tə rōn′), *n.* **1.** *Biochem.* a hormone, $C_{21}H_{30}O_2$, that prepares the uterus for the fertilized ovum and maintains pregnancy. **2.** *Pharm.* a commercial form of this compound, obtained from the corpus luteum of pregnant sows or synthesized: used in the treatment of functional bleeding, dysmenorrhea, threatened or recurrent abortion, etc. Also, **pro·ges·tin** (prō jes′tin). [PRO-[1] + GE(STATION) + STER(OL) + -ONE]

pro·glot·tis (prō glot′is), *n., pl.* **-glot·ti·des** (-glot′i dēz′). *Zool.* one of the segments or joints of a tapeworm, containing complete reproductive systems, usually both male and female. Also, **pro·glot·tid** (prō glot′id). [< NL < Gk *proglōttís* point of the tongue. See PRO-[2], GLOTTIS] —**pro·glot′tic, pro′glot·tid′e·an,** *adj.*

prog·na·thous (prog′nə thəs, prog nā′-), *adj. Craniom.* having protrusive jaws; having a gnathic index over 103. Also, **prog·nath·ic** (prog nath′ik). See diag. under **facial angle.** [PRO-[2] + -GNATHOUS] —**prog·na·thism** (prog′nə thiz′əm), **prog′na·thy,** *n.*

prog·nose (prog nōs′, -nōz′), *v.t., v.i.,* **-nosed, -nos·ing.** *Med.* to subject to or make a prognosis. [back formation from PROGNOSIS]

prog·no·sis (prog nō′sis), *n., pl.* **-ses** (-sēz). **1.** *Med.* a forecasting of the probable course and termination of a disease. **2.** a forecast or prognostication. [< LL < Gk *prógnōsis* foreknowledge. See PRO-[2], GNOSIS]

prog·nos·tic (prog nos′tik), *adj.* **1.** of or pertaining to prognosis. **2.** predictive of something in the future: *prognostic signs and symbols.* [< ML *prognōstic(us)* < Gk *prognōstikós* of foreknowledge, equiv. to *pro(gi)gnṓs(kein)* (to) know beforehand + *-tikos* -TIC. See PRO-[2], GNOSTIC]
—*n.* **3.** a forecast or prediction. **4.** an omen or portent; sign. [< L *prognōstic(on)* < Gk *prognōstikón*, neut. of *prognōstikós*] —**prog·nos′ti·ca·ble,** *adj.* —**prog·nos′ti·cal·ly,** *adv.*

prog·nos·ti·cate (prog nos′tə kāt′), *v.,* **-cat·ed, -cat·ing.** —*v.t.* **1.** to forecast or predict (something future) from present indications or signs; prophesy. **2.** to foretoken; presage: *The arrival of the summer birds prognosticated fair weather.* —*v.i.* **3.** to make a forecast; prophesy. [< ML *prognōsticāt(us)*, ptp. of *prognōsticāre.* See PROGNOSTIC, -ATE[1]] —**prog·nos′ti·ca′tive, prog·nos·ti·ca·to·ry** (prog nos′tə kə tôr′ē, -tōr′ē), *adj.* —**prog·nos′ti·ca′tor,** *n.*
—**Syn. 1.** foretell, foresee, project.

prog·nos·ti·ca·tion (prog nos′tə kā′shən), *n.* **1.** act of prognosticating. **2.** a forecast or prediction. [late ME *pronosticacion* < ML *prognōsticātiōn-* (s. of *prognōsticātiō*). See PROGNOSTICATE, -ION]

prognos′tic chart′, a chart showing the predicted state of the atmosphere for a given time in the future.

pro·gram (prō′gram, -grəm), *n., v.,* **-gramed, -gram·ing** or (*esp. Brit. and Computer Technol.*) **-grammed, -gram·ming.** —*n.* Also, *esp. Brit.,* **pro′gramme. 1.** a plan or schedule to be followed. **2.** a list of items, pieces, performers, etc., in a musical, theatrical, or other entertainment. **3.** an entertainment with reference to its pieces or numbers: *a program of American and French music.* **4.** a radio or television performance or production. **5.** a prospectus or syllabus: *the program of courses now being offered.* **6.** *Computer Technol.* **a.** a systematic plan for the automatic solution of a problem by a computer. **b.** the precise sequence of instructions enabling a computer to solve a problem. —*v.i.* **7.** to plan a program. —*v.t.* **8.** to schedule as part of a program. **9.** *Computer Technol.* to prepare a program for. [< LL *programm(a)* < Gk *prógramma* public notice in writing. See PRO-[2], -GRAM[1]]

pro·gram·mat·ic (prō′grə mat′ik), *adj.* **1.** of, pertaining to, consisting of, or resembling program music. **2.** of, having, advocating, or following a plan, policy, or program: *programmatic art.* [< Gk *programmat-* (s. of *prógramma*) PROGRAM + -IC] —**pro′gram·mat′i·cal·ly,** *adv.*

pro·gram·mer (prō′gram ər), *n.* a person who prepares a program, esp. for a computer. [PROGRAM + -ER[1]]

pro′gram mu′sic, music intended to convey an impression of a definite series of images, scenes, or events.

pro′gram pic′ture, a motion picture produced on a low budget, usually shown as the second film of a double feature.

pro·grav·id (prō grav′id), *adj. Med.* progestational (def. 1). [PRO-[1] + GRAVID]

Pro·gre·so (prô gre′sô), *n.* a city in NW Honduras. 13,797 (1961).

prog·ress (*n.* prog′res or, *esp. Brit.,* prō′gres; *v.* prə gres′), *n.* **1.** a movement toward a goal or to a further or higher stage: *the progress of a scholar in his studies.* **2.** developmental activity in science, technology, etc., esp. with reference to the commercial opportunities created thereby or to the promotion of the material well-being of the public through the goods, techniques, or facilities created. **3.** advancement in general. **4.** growth or development; continuous improvement: *He shows progress in his muscular coordination.* **5.** *Sociol.* the development of an individual or group in a direction considered more beneficial than and superior to the previous level. **6.** *Biol.* increasing differentiation and perfection in the course of ontogeny or phylogeny. **7.** forward or onward movement: *the progress of the planets.* **8.** the forward course of action, events, time, etc. **9. in progress,** going on; under way; being done; happening: *The meeting was already in progress.* —*v.i.* **10.** to advance. **11.** to go forward or onward. [late ME *progresse* < L *prōgress(us)* a going forward, equiv. to *prōgress-* (ptp. s. of *prōgredī* to step forward, advance (*pro-* PRO-[1] + *gredī*, comb. form of *gradī* to step; see GRADE)) + *-us* 4th decl. suffix]
—**Syn. 1.** advance, progression. **3.** increase; betterment. **11.** proceed; develop, improve, grow, increase. —**Ant. 1.** regression. **11.** regress.

pro·gres·sion (prə gresh′ən), *n.* **1.** act of progressing; forward or onward movement. **2.** a passing successively from one member of a series to the next; succession; sequence. **3.** *Astron.* direct motion. **4.** *Math.* a succession of quantities in which there is a constant relation between each member and the one succeeding it. Cf. **arithmetic progression, geometric progression, harmonic progression. 5.** *Music.* the manner in which chords or melodic tones follow one another. [late ME < L *prōgressiōn-* (s. of *prōgressiō*). See PROGRESS, -ION] —**pro·gres′sion·al,** *adj.* —**pro·gres′sion·al·ly,** *adv.*

pro·gres·sion·ist (prə gresh′ə nist), *n.* a person who believes in progress, as of mankind or society. [PROGRESSION + -IST] —**pro·gres′sion·ism,** *n.*

prog·ress·ist (prog′res ist, prō′gres ist), *n.* a person favoring progress, as in politics; progressive. [PROGRESS + -IST] —**prog′ress·ism,** *n.*

pro·gres·sive (prə gres′iv), *adj.* **1.** favoring or advocating progress, change, improvement, or reform, as opposed to wishing to maintain things as they are, esp. in political matters: *a progressive mayor.* **2.** progressing or advancing; making progress toward better conditions, more enlightened or liberal ideas, the use of new and advantageous methods, etc.: *a progressive community.* **3.** characterized by such progress, or by continuous improvement. **4.** (*cap.*) of or pertaining to the Progressive party. **5.** going forward or onward; passing successively from one member of a series to the next; proceeding step by step. **6.** *Govt.* noting or pertaining to a form of taxation in which the rate increases with certain increases in taxable income. **7.** *Gram.* noting a verb aspect, or other verb category, which indicates action or state going on at a temporal point of reference: *the progressive form of "is doing" in "He is doing it."* **8.** *Med.* continuously increasing in extent or severity, as a disease. —*n.* **9.** a person who is progressive, or who favors progress or reform, esp. in political matters. **10.** (*cap.*) a member of the Progressive party. [PROGRESS + -IVE] —**pro·gres′sive·ly,** *adv.* —**pro·gres′sive·ness,** *n.*
—**Syn. 1, 9.** liberal. **5.** successive.

progres′sive jazz′, 1. a style of modern jazz marked by the combination of jazz and nonjazz elements in dissonant big-band arrangements. **2.** See **modern jazz.**

Progres′sive par′ty, 1. a party formed in 1912 under the leadership of Theodore Roosevelt, advocating popular control of government, direct primaries, the initiative, the referendum, woman suffrage, etc. **2.** a similar party formed in 1924 under the leadership of Robert M. La Follette. **3.** a political party formed in 1948 under the leadership of Henry A. Wallace.

progres′sive tri′als, *Naut.* trials made of the efficiency of the propulsion machinery of a vessel at various speeds, all other pertinent factors being equal. Also called **standardization trials.**

pro·gres·siv·ism (prə gres′ə viz′əm), *n.* **1.** the principles and practices of progressives. **2.** (*cap.*) the doctrines and beliefs of the Progressive party. [PROGRESSIVE + -ISM] —**pro·gres′siv·ist,** *n.*

pro·hib·it (prō hib′it), *v.t.* **1.** to forbid (an action, activity, etc.) by authority: *Smoking is prohibited here.* **2.** to forbid the action of (a person). **3.** to prevent; hinder. [late ME *prohibite* < L *prohibit(us)*, ptp. of *prohibēre* to hold before, hold back, restrain, hinder, forbid, equiv. to *pro-* PRO-[1] + *-hibēre*, comb. form of *habēre* to have, hold] —**pro·hib′it·er, pro·hib′i·tor,** *n.*
—**Syn. 1.** interdict. See **forbid. 3.** obstruct. —**Ant. 1.** permit.

pro·hi·bi·tion (prō′ə bish′ən), *n.* **1.** the interdiction by law of the manufacture and sale of alcoholic drinks for common consumption. **2.** the period from 1920 to 1933, when the sale of alcoholic beverages in the U.S. was forbidden by an amendment to the Constitution. **3.** the act of prohibiting. **4.** a law or decree that forbids. [ME *prohibicion* < L *prohibitiōn-* (s. of *prohibitiō*). See PROHIBIT, -ION] —**pro′hi·bi′tion·ar′y,** *adj.*
—**Syn. 4.** interdiction.

pro·hi·bi·tion·ist (prō′ə bish′ə nist), *n.* **1.** a person who favors or advocates prohibition. **2.** (*cap.*) a member of the Prohibition party. [PROHIBITION + -IST]

pro-Fin′nish, *adj.*
pro-Flor′en·tine′, *adj.*
pro-for′eign, *adj.*
pro-France′, *adj.*
pro-French′, *adj.*
pro-Freud′, *adj.*
pro-Freud′i·an, *adj., n.*
pro-Gael′ic, *adj.*
pro·gam′bling, *adj.*
pro-Gen′tile, *adj., n.*
pro-Ger′man, *adj., n.*
pro-Gha′na, *adj.*
pro-Goth′ic, *adj.*
pro·gov′ern·ment, *adj.*
pro-Gre′cian, *adj.*
pro-Greek′, *adj., n.*
pro′-Gua·te·ma′lan, *adj., n.*
pro-Hai′tian, *adj.*
pro-Ha·wai′ian, *adj.*
pro′-Hel·len′ic, *adj.*

Prohi·bi′tion par′ty, *U.S.* a party organized in 1869, advocating the prohibition of the manufacture and sale of alcoholic beverages.

pro·hib·i·tive (prō hib′i tiv), *adj.* **1.** that prohibits or forbids something. **2.** sufficing to prevent the use, purchase, etc., of something: *prohibitive prices on luxuries.* [< LL *prohibitīv(us).* See PROHIBIT, -IVE] —**pro·hib′i·tive·ly,** *adv.* —**pro·hib′i·tive·ness,** *n.*

pro·hib·i·to·ry (prō hib′i tōr′ē, -tôr′ē), *adj.* prohibitive. [< L *prōhibitōri(us)* restraining. See PROHIBIT, -ORY[1]] —**pro·hib′i·to′ri·ly,** *adv.*

proj·ect (*n.* proj′ekt; *v.* prə jekt′), *n.* **1.** something that is contemplated, devised, or planned; plan; scheme. **2.** a large or major undertaking, esp. one involving considerable money, personnel, and equipment. **3.** a specific task of investigation, esp. in scholarship. **4.** *Educ.* an educational assignment necessitating personal initiative on the part of a student. [< L *prōject(um),* neut. of *prōjectus* (ptp.)] —*v.t.* **5.** to propose, contemplate, or plan. **6.** to throw, cast, or impel forward or onward. **7.** to set forth or calculate (some future thing): *They projected the building costs for the next five years.* **8.** to throw or cause to fall upon a surface or into space, as a ray of light, a shadow, etc. **9.** to cause (a figure or image) to appear, as on a background. **10.** to regard (something within the mind, as a feeling, thought, or attitude) as having some form of reality outside the mind: *The subject projected his hostilities upon others, whom he then regarded as enemies.* **11.** to cause to jut out or protrude. **12.** *Geom.* **a.** to throw forward an image of (a figure or the like) by straight lines or rays, either parallel, converging, or diverging, which pass through all its points and reproduce it on another surface or figure. **b.** to transform the points (of one figure) into those of another by a correspondence between points. **13.** to present (an idea, program, etc.) for consideration or action: *They made every effort to project the notion of world peace.* **14.** *Theat.* **a.** to use (one's voice, gestures, etc.) forcefully enough to carry throughout the theater and be perceived by all members of the audience. **b.** to produce a compelling image of: *He projected the character of the king with expertise and finesse.* **c.** to cause (the voice) to appear to come from a source other than oneself, as in ventriloquism; throw. —*v.i.* **15.** to extend or protrude beyond something else. **16.** to make clear one's thoughts, role, etc., to an audience, as by using correct techniques of speaking, singing, acting, or the like. [v. use of late ME *projecte* extended, projected < L *prōject(us),* ptp. of *prōicere* to throw forward, extend, equiv. to *prō-* PRO-[1] + *-icere,* comb. form of *jacere* to throw] —**pro·ject′a·ble,** *adj.* —**pro·ject′ing·ly,** *adv.*
—**Syn. 1.** proposal. See **plan. 5.** contrive, scheme, plot, devise. **7.** predict. **15.** bulge, obtrude, overhang.

project′ed win′dow, a casement window in which the inner end of the sash slides along a track on the sill as the sash swings outward.

pro·jec·tile (prə jek′til, -tīl), *n.* **1.** *Mil.* an object fired from a gun with an explosive propelling charge, such as a bullet, shell, rocket, or grenade. **2.** a body projected or impelled forward, as through the air. —*adj.* **3.** impelling or driving forward, as a force. **4.** caused by impulse, as motion. **5.** capable of being impelled forward, as a missile. **6.** *Zool.* protrusile, as the jaws of a fish. [< NL, neut. of adj. *prōjectilis* projecting. See PROJECT, -ILE]

pro·jec·tion (prə jek′shən), *n.* **1.** a projecting or protruding part. **2.** state or fact of jutting out or protruding. **3.** a causing to jut or protrude. **4.** act, process, or result of projecting. **5.** *Cartog.* a systematic construction of lines drawn on a plane surface representative of and corresponding to the meridians and parallels of the curved surface of the earth or celestial sphere. **6.** *Photog.* **a.** the act of reproducing on a surface, by optical means, a remote image on a film, lantern slide, etc. **b.** an image so reproduced. **7.** the act of visualizing and regarding an idea or the like as an objective reality. **8.** that which is so visualized and regarded. **9.** calculation of some future thing: *They fell short of their projection for the rate of growth.* **10.** act of communicating distinctly and forcefully to an audience. **11.** *Psychol.* **a.** the tendency to ascribe to another person feelings, thoughts, or attitudes present in oneself, or to regard external reality as embodying such feelings, etc. in some way. **b.** *Psychoanal.* such an ascription relieving the ego of a sense of guilt or other intolerable feeling. **12.** the act of planning or scheming. **13.** *Alchemy.* the casting of the powder of philosophers' stone upon metal in fusion, to transmute it into gold or silver. [< L *prōjectiōn-* (s. of *prōjectiō*) a throwing forward. See PROJECT, -ION] —**pro·jec·tion·al** (prə jek′shə nəl), *adj.*
—**Syn. 1.** jut, overhang, protrusion. **9.** prediction.

projec′tion booth′, **1.** a soundproof compartment in a theater where a motion-picture projector is housed and from which the picture is projected on the screen. **2.** a compartment at the rear of or above an auditorium, in which spotlights and other lighting units are operated.

pro·jec·tion·ist (prə jek′shə nist), *n.* a person who operates a motion-picture or slide projector. [PROJECTION + -IST]

projec′tion machine′, an apparatus which projects motion pictures.

projec′tion pa′per, *Photog.* sensitized paper for recording a projected image.

projec′tion print′, *Photog.* a print made by the projection of an image onto sensitized paper.

projec′tion print′ing, *Photog.* the act or process of making projection prints Cf. **contact printing.**

pro·jec·tive (prə jek′tiv), *adj.* **1.** of or pertaining to projection. **2.** produced, or capable of being produced, by projection. **3.** *Psychol.* of, pertaining to, or noting a test or technique for revealing the hidden motives or underlying personality structure of an individual by the use of test materials, as ink blots, cloud pictures, or cartoons, that allow him to express himself freely rather than restrict him to set responses. [PROJECT + -IVE] —**pro·jec′tive·ly,** *adv.* —**pro·jec·tiv·i·ty** (prō′jek tiv′i tē), *n.*

projec′tive geom′etry, the geometric study of projective properties.

projec′tive prop′erty, a geometric property which is unaltered by projection; a property of relative position, as coincidence or length, but not of magnitude.

Proj′ect Mer′cury, *U.S.* the project sponsored by NASA to launch satellites carrying human passengers into orbit about the earth. It produced the first orbital flight of an American, Col. John H. Glenn, Jr., February 20, 1962. Cf. **mercury** (def. 8).

pro·jec·tor (prə jek′tər), *n.* **1.** an apparatus for throwing an image on a screen, as a magic lantern, a motion-picture projector, etc. **2.** a device for projecting a beam of light. **3.** a person who forms projects or plans; schemer. [PROJECT + -OR[2]]

Proj′ect Plow′share, *U.S.* a program instituted by the Atomic Energy Commission to examine the possible peaceful uses of nuclear explosions.

pro·jet (prō zhā′; *Fr.* prô zhe′), *n., pl.* **-jets** (-zhāz′; *Fr.* -zhe′). **1.** a project. **2.** a draft of a proposed treaty or other instrument. [< F < L *prōject(um).* See PROJECT]

Pro·ko·fiev (prō kō′fē əf, -ef′, prə-; *Russ.* pro kô′fyef), *n.* **Ser·gei Ser·ge·e·vich** (ser gā′ ser ge′yə vich), 1891–1953, Russian composer.

Pro·ko·pyevsk (pro kô′pyefsk′), *n.* a city in the S central RSFSR, in the S Soviet Union in Asia, SE of Novosibirsk. 292,000 (est. 1962).

pro·lac·tin (prō lak′tin), *n.* *Biochem.* luteotropin. [PRO-[1] + LACT- + -IN[2]]

pro·lam·in (prō lam′in, prō′lə min), *n.* *Biochem.* any of the class of simple proteins, as gliadin, hordein, or zein, found in grains, soluble in dilute acids, alkalis, and alcohols, and insoluble in water, neutral salt solutions, and absolute alcohol. Also, **pro·lam·ine** (prō lam′in, -ēn, prō′lə min, -mēn′). [PROL(INE) + AM(MONIA) + -IN[2]]

pro·lan (prō′lan), *n.* *Biochem.* a sex hormone found in high concentration in pregnancy urine, making possible the early diagnosis of pregnancy. [contr. of PROLACTIN]

pro·lapse (prō laps′), *n., v.,* **-lapsed, -laps·ing.** —*n.* **1.** *Pathol.* a falling down of an organ or part, as the uterus, from its normal position. —*v.i.* **2.** to fall or slip down or out of place. Also, **pro·lap·sus** (prō lap′səs). [< LL *prōlaps(us)* a slipping forth. See PRO-[1], LAPSE]

A B

A, Prolate spheroid; B, Oblate

pro·late (prō′lāt), *adj.* elongated along the polar diameter, as a spheroid generated by the revolution of an ellipse about its longer axis (opposed to *oblate*). [< L *prōlāt(us),* ptp. of *prōferre* to bring forward, extend] —**pro′late·ly,** *adv.* —**pro′late·ness,** *n.*

pro·la·tion (prō lā′shən), *n.* *Medieval Music.* the time relationship between a semibreve and a minim in mensural notation. [ME *prolacion* < L *prōlātiōn-* (s. of *prōlātiō*) a bringing forward. See PROLATE, -ION]

prole (prōl, prō′lē), *n.* *Chiefly Brit. Informal.* **1.** a member of the proletariat. **2.** a person who performs routine tasks in a society. [shortened form of PROLETARIAT]

P

P, Prolegs of larva of monarch butterfly, *Danaus plexippus*

pro·leg (prō′leg′), *n.* one of the abdominal ambulatory processes of caterpillars and other larvae, as distinct from the true or thoracic legs. [PRO-[1] + LEG]

pro·le·gom·e·non (prō′lə gom′ə non′, -nən), *n., pl.* **-na** (-nə). **1.** a preliminary discussion; introductory essay, as prefatory matter in a book; a prologue. **2.** Usually, **prolegomena.** (*sometimes construed as sing.*) a treatise serving as a preface or introduction to a book. [< NL < Gk *prolegómenon* being said beforehand, neut. of pass. prp. of *prolégein,* equiv. to *pro-* PRO-[2] + *légein* to say]

pro·le·gom·e·nous (prō′lə gom′ə nəs), *adj.* **1.** prefatory; preliminary; introductory. **2.** characterized by unnecessary or lengthy prologuizing. [PROLEGOMEN(ON) + -OUS]

pro·lep·sis (prō lep′sis), *n., pl.* **-ses** (-sēz). **1.** *Rhet.* the anticipation of possible objections in order to answer them in advance. **2.** the assigning of a person, event, etc., to a period earlier than the actual one; prochronism. **3.** the use of an epithet in anticipation of its becoming applicable. **4.** *Pathol.* the return of an attack of a periodic disease or of a paroxysm before the expected time or at progressively shorter intervals. [< L < Gk *prólēpsis* anticipation, preconception, equiv. to *prolēp-* (verbal s. of *prolambánein* to anticipate (*pro-* PRO-[2] + *lambánein* to take)) + *-sis* -SIS] —**pro·lep·tic** (prō lep′tik), **pro·lep′ti·cal,** *adj.* —**pro·lep′ti·cal·ly,** *adv.*

pro·le·tar·i·an (prō′li târ′ē ən), *adj.* **1.** pertaining or belonging to the proletariat. **2.** (in ancient Rome) belonging to the lowest or poorest class of the people. —*n.* **3.** a member of the proletariat. [see PROLETARY, -AN] —**pro′le·tar′i·an·ly,** *adv.* —**pro′le·tar′i·an·ness,** *n.*

pro·le·tar·i·an·ise (prō′li târ′ē ə nīz′), *v.t.,* **-ised, -is·ing.** *Chiefly Brit.* to proletarianize. —**pro′le·tar′i·an·i·sa′tion,** *n.*

pro·le·tar·i·an·ism (prō′li târ′ē ə niz′əm), *n.* the practices, attitudes, or social status of a proletarian. [PROLETARIAN + -ISM]

pro·le·tar·i·an·ize (prō′li târ′ē ə nīz′), *v.t.,* **-ized, -iz·ing. 1.** to convert or transform into a member of the proletariat: *Rapid fluctuations in the economy proletarianized the small businessman.* **2.** to change to or adopt (the language, manners, etc.) of the proletariat: *There is increasing tendency to proletarianize language and behavior.* Also, *esp. Brit.,* **proletarianise.** [PROLETARIAN + -IZE] —**pro′le·tar′i·an·i·za′tion,** *n.*

pro·le·tar·i·at (prō′li târ′ē ət), *n.* **1.** the unpropertied class; the class that is dependent for support on daily or casual employment. **2.** the working class. **3.** (in theory) the class of manual workers who do not possess capital or property and must sell their labor to survive. [< F; see PROLETARY, -ATE[1]]

pro·le·tar·ise (prō′li târ′īz), *v.t.,* **-ised, -is·ing.** *Chiefly Brit.* to proletarize.

pro·le·tar·ize (prō′li târ′īz), *v.t.,* **-ized, -iz·ing.** to proletarianize. —**pro′le·tar′i·za′tion,** *n.*

pro·le·tar·y (prō′li ter′ē), *adj., n., pl.* **-tar·ies.** proletarian. [adj. use of L *prōlētāri(us)* a Roman citizen who contributed to the state only through his offspring, equiv. to *prōlēt-* (akin to *prōlēs* offspring; see PRO-[1], ADULT) + *-ārius* -ARY]

pro·li·cide (prō′li sīd′), *n.* the killing of one's child or children. [< ML *prōli-* (comb. form repr. L *prōlēs* offspring; see PROLETARY) + -CIDE] —**pro′li·cid′al,** *adj.*

pro-life (prō līf′), *adj.* of or supporting a movement that strongly opposes unnecessary abortions or euthanasia: *pro-life demonstrators.* —**pro-lif′er,** *n.*

pro·lif·er·ate (prō lif′ə rāt′), *v.i., v.t.,* **-at·ed, -at·ing. 1.** to grow or produce by multiplication of parts, as in budding or cell division. **2.** to spread excessively and rapidly. [PROLIFER(OUS) + -ATE[1]] —**pro·lif′er·a′tive,** *adj.*

pro·lif·er·a·tion (prō lif′ə rā′shən), *n.* **1.** the growth or production of cells by multiplication of parts. **2.** an excessive, rapid spread: *nuclear proliferation.* [PROLIFERATE + -ION]

pro·lif·er·ous (prō lif′ər əs), *adj.* **1.** proliferating. **2.** *Bot.* **a.** producing new individuals by budding or the like. **b.** producing an organ or shoot from an organ which is itself normally the last, as a shoot or a new flower from the midst of a flower. [< ML *prōlifer* bearing offspring + -OUS. See PROLICIDE, -FEROUS]

pro·lif·ic (prō lif′ik), *adj.* **1.** producing offspring, young, fruit, etc., abundantly; highly fruitful: *a prolific pear tree.* **2.** producing in large quantities: *a prolific writer.* **3.** profusely productive or fruitful (often fol. by *in* or *of*): *It was an ambiguously worded bequest, likely to be prolific of litigations.* **4.** characterized by abundant production: *a prolific year for tomatoes.* [< ML *prōlific(us)* fertile. See PROLICIDE, -FIC] —**pro·lif·i·ca·cy** (prō lif′ə kə sē), **pro·lif′ic·ness, pro·lif′i·cal·ness,** *n.* —**pro·lif′i·cal·ly, pro·lif′ic·ly,** *adv.*
—**Syn 1, 2.** teeming, fecund, abundant. See **productive.**
—**Ant. 1.** barren.

pro·line (prō′lēn, -lin), *n.* *Biochem.* an alcohol-soluble amino acid found in all proteins. [alter. of PYRROLIDINE]

pro·lix (prō liks′, prō′liks), *adj.* **1.** extended to great, unnecessary, or tedious length; long and wordy. **2.** (of a person) given to speaking or writing at great or tedious length. [late ME < L *prōlix(us)* extended, long, equiv. to *prō-* PRO-[1] + *-lixus,* akin to *liquī* to flow; see LIQUOR] —**pro·lix·i·ty** (prō lik′si tē), **pro·lix′ness,** *n.* —**pro·lix′ly,** *adv.*
—**Syn. 2.** verbose, prolonged, protracted, extended.

pro·loc·u·tor (prō lok′yə tər), *n.* **1.** a presiding officer of an assembly; chairman. **2.** *Ch. of Eng.* the chairman of the lower house of a convocation. [< L *prōlocūtor* one who speaks out, equiv. to *prōlocūt(us)* (ptp. of *prōloquī,* equiv. to, *prō-* PRO-[1] + *loquī* to speak) + *-or* -OR[2]] —**pro·loc′u·tor·ship′,** *n.*

pro·log·ise (prō′lô gīz′, -lo-, prō′lə jīz′), *v.i.,* **-ised, -is·ing.** *Chiefly Brit.* prologize.

pro·log·ize (prō′lô gīz′, -lo-, prō′lə jīz′), *v.i.,* **-ized, -iz·ing.** prologuize.

pro·lo·gos (prō lô′gos, -gōs, -log′os), *n., pl.* **-lo·goi** (-lô′goi, -log′oi). *Greek.* (in ancient Greek drama) an introductory speech or scene, esp. in tragedy: usually opening the drama, preceding the *parodos,* and performed by the principal characters. Also, **prologus.**

pro·logue (prō′lôg, -log), *n., v.,* **-logued, -logu·ing.** —*n.* **1.** a preliminary discourse; a preface or introductory part of a discourse, poem, or novel. **2.** an introductory speech, often in verse, calling attention to the theme of a play. **3.** the actor who delivers it. **4.** an introductory scene, preceding the first act of a play, opera, etc. **5.** any introductory proceeding, event, etc.: *Appetizing delicacies were only the prologue to a long dinner.* —*v.t.* **6.** to introduce with or as with a prologue. Also, **pro′log.** [ME *prologe,* OE *prologa* (masc.) < L *prōlog(us)* < Gk *prólogos.* See PRO-[2], -LOGUE] —**pro′logue·ist, pro′log·ist,** *n.* —**pro′logue·like′, pro′log·like′,** *adj.*
—**Syn. 4.** preamble; beginning, opening; prelude.

pro·logu·ise (prō′lô gīz′, -lo-), *v.i.,* **-ised, -is·ing.** *Chiefly Brit.* prologuize. —**pro′logu·is′er,** *n.*

pro·logu·ize (prō′lô gīz′, -lo-), *v.i.,* **-ized, -iz·ing.** to compose or deliver a prologue. Also, **prologize;** *esp. Brit.,* **prologuise, prologise.** [PROLOGUE + -IZE] —**pro′logu·iz′er,** *n.*

pro·lo·gus (prō lō′gəs, -log′əs), *n., pl.* **-lo·gi** (-lō′jī, -loj′ī). prologos.

pro·long (prə lông′, -long′), *v.t.* **1.** to lengthen out in time; extend the duration of; cause to continue longer: *to prolong one's stay abroad.* **2.** to make longer in spatial extent: *to prolong a line.* [late ME *prolonge* < LL *prōlongāre* to lengthen, equiv. to *prō-* PRO-[1] + *long(us)* LONG[1] + *-ā-* v. suffix + *-re* inf. ending] —**pro·long′a·ble,** *adj.* —**pro·long′a·ble·ness,** *n.* —**pro·long′a·bly,** *adv.* —**pro·long′er,** *n.* —**pro·long′ment,** *n.*
—**Syn. 1.** See **lengthen.** —**Ant. 1.** abbreviate.

pro·lon·gate (prə lông′gāt, -long′-), *v.t.,* **-gat·ed, -gat·ing.** to prolong. [< LL *prōlongāt(us),* ptp. of *prōlongāre* to PROLONG; see -ATE[1]]

pro·lon·ga·tion (prō′lông gā′shən, -long-), *n.* **1.** act of prolonging: *the prolongation of a line.* **2.** state of being prolonged. **3.** a prolonged or extended form: *Every abbreviation has its prolongation in the complete word.* **4.** an added part. [< LL *prōlongātiōn-* (s. of *prōlongātiō*) extension. See PROLONGATE, -ION]

pro·longe (prō lonj′; *Fr.* prô lônzh′), *n., pl.* **-long·es** (-lon′jiz; *Fr.* -lônzh′). *Mil.* a rope having a hook at one end and a toggle at the other, used for various purposes, as to draw a gun carriage. [< F, back formation from *prolonger* to PROLONG]

pro-Hin′du, *adj.*
pro-Hit′ler, *adj.*
pro′-Hon·du′ran, *adj., n.*
pro′-Hun·gar′i·an, *adj., n.*
pro′-Ice·lan′dic, *adj.*
pro′im·mi·gra′tion, *adj.*
pro·in′crease, *adj.*
pro-In′di·an, *adj.*
pro′-In·do·ne′sian, *adj.*
pro′in·dus′tri·al·i·sa′tion, *adj.*
pro′in·dus′tri·al, *adj.*
pro′in·dus′tri·al·i·za′tion, *adj.*
pro·in′dus·try, *adj.*
pro′in·sur′ance, *adj.*
pro′in·te·gra′tion, *adj.*
pro′in·ter·ven′tion, *adj.*
pro′in·vest′ment, *adj.*
pro′-I·ra′ni·an, *adj., n.*
pro′-I·raq′, *adj.*
pro′-I·ra′qi, *n., adj.*
pro-I′rish, *adj.*
pro′ir·ri·ga′tion, *adj.*
pro-Is′ra·el, *adj.*
pro′-Is·rae′li, *n., adj.*
pro′-I·tal′ian, *adj., n.*
pro′-Jac·o·be′an, *adj.*
pro′-Jap·a·nese′, *adj., n., pl.* -nese.
pro′-Jef·fer·so′ni·an, *adj.*
pro-Jew′ish, *adj.*
pro-Jor′dan, *adj.*
pro′-Ko·re′an, *adj., n.*
pro′-Ko·weit′, *adj.*
pro′-Ku·wait′, *adj.*
pro·la′bor, *adj.*
pro′-La·o′tian, *adj., n.*
pro-Lat′in, *adj.*
pro′-Leb·a·nese′, *adj., n., pl.* -nese.
pro′-Li·be′ri·an, *adj., n.*

prolonge′ knot′, a knot consisting of three overlapping loops formed by a single rope passed alternately over and under itself at crossings. Also called **sailor's breastplate.** See illus. under **knot.**

pro·lu·sion (prō lo͞o′zhən), *n.* **1.** a preliminary written article. **2.** an essay of an introductory nature, preliminary to a more profound work. [< L *prōlūsiōn-* (s. of *prōlūsiō*) preliminary excercise, prelude, equiv. to *prōlūs(us)*, ptp. of *prōlūdere* (*prō-* PRO-[1] + *lūdere* to play) + *-iōn-* -ION]

pro·lu·so·ry (prō lo͞o′sə rē), *adj.* **1.** serving for prolusion. **2.** of the nature of a prolusion. [< ML *prōlūsōri(us)*. See PROLUSION, -ORY[1]]

prom (prom), *n.* *U.S. Informal.* a formal dance, esp. at an American school or college. [short for PROMENADE]

prom., promontory.

Pro·ma·chor·ma (prō′mə kôr′mə), *n.* *Class. Myth.* an epithet of Athena, meaning "protectress of the anchorage."

Prom·a·chus (prom′ə kəs), *n.* *Class. Myth.* **1.** an epithet of Athena, meaning "defender." **2.** any deity who protects or defends an army or person by force of arms. **3.** one of the Epigoni. **4.** (in the *Iliad*) a Boeotian military leader.

pro·ma·zine (prō′mə zēn′), *n.* *Pharm.* a compound, $C_{17}H_{20}N_2S$, used in the form of its hydrochloride as a tranquilizer. [PRO(PYL) + M(ETHYL) + (THI)AZINE]

Prome (prōm), *n.* a city in central Burma, on the Irrawaddy River: location of several noted pagodas. 36,997 (1953).

pro me·mo·ri·a (prō me mō′ri ä; *Eng.* prō mə mōr′ē ə, -môr′-), *Latin.* for memory (used in diplomacy to recall rights which have lapsed for a long time).

prom·e·nade (prom′ə nād′, -näd′), *n., v.,* **-nad·ed, -nad·ing.** —*n.* **1.** a stroll or walk, esp. in a public place, as for pleasure or display. **2.** an area used for leisurely walking. **3.** a prom. **4.** a march of guests into a ballroom constituting the opening of a formal ball. **5.** a march of dancers in folk or square dancing. —*v.i.* **6.** to take a promenade. —*v.t.* **7.** to take a promenade through or about. **8.** to conduct or display in or as in a promenade; parade: *He promenaded her before the jealous eyes of her suitors.* [< F, deriv. of *promener* to lead out, take for a walk or airing < L *prōmināre* to drive (beasts) forward (*prō-* PRO-[1] + *mināre* to drive); see -ADE[1]] —**prom′e·nad′er,** *n.*

promenade′ deck′, a deck used as a promenade on a passenger vessel, usually covered with a light shade deck.

promenade′ tile′. See **quarry tile.**

pro·met·a·cen·ter (prō met′ə sen′tər), *n.* *Naval Archit.* the intersection between two lines, each drawn vertically through the center of buoyancy of a hull at a certain angle of heel. [PRO-[1] + METACENTER]

Pro·me′the·a moth′ (prə mē′thē ə), a silkworm moth, *Callosamia promethea*, having reddish-brown wings, each with a border of white or yellow, the larvae of which feed on spicebush and other lauraceous plants. Also called **spicebush silk moth.** [< NL, fem. of L *Prometheus* PROMETHEUS]

Pro·me·the·an (prə mē′thē ən), *adj.* **1.** of or suggestive of Prometheus. **2.** creative; boldly original. —*n.* **3.** a person who resembles Prometheus in spirit or action. **4.** (formerly) a matchlike device usually consisting of a small glass tube of sulfuric acid surrounded by inflammable material. [PROMETHE(US) + -AN]

Pro·me·the·us (prə mē′thē əs, -thyo͞os), *n.* *Class. Myth.* a Titan, the father of Deucalion and brother of Atlas and Epimetheus. He taught mankind various arts and confined all its troubles in the box that Zeus treacherously gave to Epimetheus as the dowry of Pandora. For having stolen fire from Olympus and given it to mankind in defiance of Zeus, he was chained to a rock where an eagle daily tore at his liver, until he was finally released by Hercules.

Prome′theus Bound′, a tragedy (c465 B.C.) by Aeschylus.

Prome′theus Unbound′, a drama in verse (1820) by Shelley.

pro·me·thi·um (prə mē′thē əm), *n.* *Chem.* a rare-earth, metallic, trivalent element. *Symbol:* Pm; *at. no.:* 61. [< NL; see PROMETHEUS, -IUM]

Pro·min (prō′min), *n.* *Pharm., Trademark.* glucosulfone.

prom·i·nence (prom′ə nəns), *n.* **1.** Also, **prom′i·nen·cy.** state of being prominent; conspicuousness. **2.** that which is prominent; a projection or protuberance: *a prominence high over a ravine; the prominences of a face.* **3.** *Astron.* a cloud of gas that rises high above the surface of the sun, seen during an eclipse or by means of a helioscope. [< L *prōminentia* a jutting out, protuberance. See PROMINENT, -ENCE]

prom·i·nent (prom′ə nənt), *adj.* **1.** standing out so as to be easily seen; conspicuous; particularly noticeable: *Her eyes are her most prominent feature.* **2.** standing out beyond the adjacent surface or line; projecting. **3.** leading, important, or well-known: *He is a prominent citizen.* [< L *prōminent-* (s. of *prōminēns*), prp. of *prōminēre* to jut out, stand out, equiv. to *prō-* PRO-[1] + *minēre* to project]
—**Syn. 1.** manifest, chief, principal, important, main. **2.** protruding, jutting, protuberant. **3.** eminent, celebrated, famous, famed, distinguished. —**Ant. 1.** inconspicuous. **2.** recessed. **3.** unknown.

prom·is·cu·i·ty (prom′i skyo͞o′i tē, prō′mi-), *n., pl.* **-ties. 1.** state of being promiscuous. **2.** a promiscuous sexual union. **3.** indiscriminate mixture. [PROMISCU(OUS) + -ITY; cf. F *promiscuité*]

pro·mis·cu·ous (prə mis′kyo͞o əs), *adj.* **1.** characterized by or involving indiscriminate mingling or association, esp. having sexual relations with a number of partners on an informal or casual basis. **2.** consisting of parts, elements, or individuals of different kinds brought together without order. **3.** indiscriminate; without discrimination. **4.** casual; irregular; haphazard. [< L *prōmiscuus* mixed up, equiv. to *prō-* PRO-[1] + *miscu-* (perf. s. of *miscēre* to mix) + *-us* -OUS] —**pro·mis′cu·ous·ly,** *adv.* —**pro·mis′cu·ous·ness,** *n.*
—**Syn. 1.** unchaste. **2.** hodgepodge, confused, mixed, jumbled. See **miscellaneous. 3.** careless. —**Ant. 1, 2.** pure. **3.** selective.

prom·ise (prom′is), *n., v.,* **-ised, -is·ing.** —*n.* **1.** a declaration that something will or will not be done, given, etc., by one: *a promise to sin no more; a promise of a toy.* **2.** an express assurance on which expectation is to be based: *promises that an enemy will not win.* **3.** something that has the effect of an express assurance; indication of what may be expected. **4.** indication of future excellence or achievement: *a writer who shows promise.* **5.** that which is promised. —*v.t.* **6.** to engage or undertake by promise (usually used with an infinitive or a clause as object): *She promised to go tomorrow.* **7.** to make a promise of (some specified act, gift, etc.): *to promise help.* **8.** to make a promise of something to (a specified person): *Promise me that you will come.* **9.** to afford ground for expecting: *The sky promised a storm.* **10.** to engage to join in marriage. **11.** *Informal.* to assure (used in emphatic declarations): *I won't go there again, I promise you that!* —*v.i.* **12.** to afford ground for expectation (often foll. by *well* or *fair*): *His forthcoming novel promises well.* **13.** to make a promise. [late ME *promis(se)* < ML *prōmissa*, n. use of fem. ptp. of *prōmittere* to promise] —**prom′is·a·ble,** *adj.* —**prom′ise·ful,** *adj.* —**prom′is·er,** *n.*
—**Syn. 2.** word, pledge. **6.** pledge, covenant, agree.

Prom′ised Land′, 1. Heaven. **2.** Canaan, the land promised by God to Abraham and his descendants. Gen. 12:7.

prom·is·ee (prom′i sē′), *n.* *Law.* a person to whom a promise is made. [PROMISE + -EE]

prom·is·ing (prom′i sing), *adj.* giving favorable promise; likely to turn out well: *a promising young man; a promising situation.* [PROMISE + -ING[2]] —**prom′is·ing·ly,** *adv.* —**prom′is·ing·ness,** *n.*

prom·i·sor (prom′i sôr′, prom′i sôr′), *n.* *Law.* a person who makes a promise. [PROMISE + -OR[2]]

prom·is·so·ry (prom′i sōr′ē, -sôr′ē), *adj.* **1.** containing or implying a promise. **2.** of the nature of a promise. **3.** *Insurance.* of or noting agreements or representations stipulating what is required to take place after the issuance of a policy. [< ML *prōmissōri(us)*. See PROMISE, -ORY[1]] —**prom′is·so′ri·ly,** *adv.*

prom′issory note′, a written promise to pay a specified sum of money to a designated person or to his order, or to the bearer of the note, at a fixed time or on demand.

prom·on·to·ry (prom′ən tōr′ē, -tôr′ē), *n., pl.* **-ries. 1.** a high point of land or rock projecting into the sea or other water beyond the line of coast; a headland. **2.** a bluff, or part of a plateau, overlooking a lowland. **3.** *Anat.* a prominent or protuberant part. [< ML *prōmontōri(um)*, L *prōmunturium*, akin to *mentum* chin; see PRO-[1]]

pro·mote (prə mōt′), *v.t.,* **-mot·ed, -mot·ing. 1.** to help or encourage to exist or flourish; further: *to promote world peace; to promote the development of the resources of backward countries.* **2.** to advance in rank, dignity, position, etc. (opposed to *demote*). **3.** *Educ.* to put ahead to the next higher stage or grade of a course or series of classes. **4.** to aid in organizing (business undertakings). **5.** to present (a product) for consumer acceptance, esp. through advertising. **6.** *Slang.* to obtain (something) by cunning or trickery; wangle. [ME < L *prōmōt(us)*, ptp. of *prōmovēre* to move forward, advance. See PRO-[1], MOTIVE] —**pro·mot′able,** *adj.*
—**Syn. 1.** abet, back, forward, advance, assist, help, support. **2.** elevate, raise, exalt. —**Ant. 1.** discourage, obstruct. **2.** demote, degrade, abase.

pro·mot·er (prə mō′tər), *n.* **1.** a person who initiates or takes part in the organizing of a company, development of a project, etc. **2.** one who or that which promotes. **3.** *Chem.* any substance that in small amounts is capable of increasing the activity of a catalyst. **4.** Also called **collector.** *Metall.* a water-repellent reagent enhancing the ability of certain ores to float for extraction by the flotation process. **5.** *Obs.* an informer. [PROMOTE + -ER[1]; r. earlier *promotour* < AF]

promot′er of the faith′. See **devil's advocate** (def. 2).

pro·mo·tion (prə mō′shən), *n.* **1.** advancement in rank or position. **2.** furtherance or encouragement. **3.** act of promoting. **4.** state of being promoted. **5.** material issued in behalf of some product, cause, institution, etc.: *The professor's mailbox was full of promotions for textbooks.* **6.** Also called **queening.** *Chess.* the replacement of a pawn that has reached the enemy's first rank by a more powerful piece of the same color, usually a queen. [late ME < LL *prōmōtiōn-* (s. of *prōmōtiō*). See PROMOTE, -ION] —**pro·mo′tion·al,** *adj.*

pro·mo·tive (prə mō′tiv), *adj.* tending to promote. [PROMOTE + -IVE] —**pro·mo′tive·ness,** *n.*

prompt (prompt), *adj.* **1.** done, performed, delivered, etc., at once or without delay: *a prompt reply.* **2.** ready in action; quick to act as occasion demands. **3.** quick or alert: *prompt to take offense.* [late ME < L *prompt(us)* ready, prompt, special use of ptp. of *prōmere*] —*v.t.,* **4.** to move or induce to action: *What prompted him to say that?* **5.** to occasion or incite; inspire: *What prompted his resignation from the club?* **6.** to assist (a person speaking) by suggesting something to be said. **7.** *Theat.* to supply (an actor or reciter) with his cue from off-stage if he has missed it, or with his line if he has forgotten it. —*v.i.* **8.** *Theat.* to supply cues from off-stage. —*n.* **9.** *Com.* **a.** a limit of time given for payment for merchandise purchased, the limit being stated on a note of reminder (**prompt′ note′**). **b.** the contract setting the time limit. **10.** act of prompting. **11.** something serving to suggest or remind. **12. take a prompt,** (in acting) to move or speak in response to a cue. [ME < ML *prōmpt(āre)* (to) incite, L: to distribute, freq. of *prōmere* to bring out, equiv. to *prō-* PRO- + *(e)mere* to take] —**prompt′ly,** *adv.* —**prompt′ness,** *n.*
—**Syn. 4.** urge, spur, instigate, impel.

prompt·book (prompt′bo͝ok′), *n.* *Theat.* a copy of the script of a play, containing cues and notes, used by the prompter, stage manager, etc. [PROMPT + BOOK]

prompt·er (promp′tər), *n.* **1.** *Theat.* a person who is offstage and follows a play in progress from the book, repeating missed cues and supplying actors with forgotten lines. **2.** one who or that which prompts. [PROMPT + -ER[1]]

promp·ti·tude (promp′ti to͞od′, -tyo͞od′), *n.* promptness. [late ME < LL *prōmptitūdō*. See PROMPT, -I-, -TUDE]

prompt′ side′, *Theat., Chiefly Brit.* the part of the stage to the left as one faces the audience. *Abbr.:* P.S. Also, **prompt′-side′.**

prom·ul·gate (prom′əl gāt′; prō mul′gāt), *v.t.,* **-gat·ed, -gat·ing. 1.** to make known by open declaration; publish; proclaim formally or put into operation (a law, decree of a court, etc.). **2.** to set forth or teach publicly (a creed, doctrine, etc.). [< L *prōmulgāt(us)*, ptp. of *prōmulgāre* to PROMULGE; see -ATE[1]] —**prom·ul·ga·tion** (prom′əl gā′shən, prō′məl-), *n.* —**prom′ul·ga′tor,** *n.*
—**Syn. 1.** announce, issue, declare. **2.** advocate.

pro·mulge (prō mulj′), *v.t.,* **-mulged, -mulg·ing.** *Archaic.* to promulgate. [< L *prōmulg(āre)*, unexplained var. of *prōvulgāre* to make publicly known. See PRO-[1], DIVULGE] —**pro·mulg′er,** *n.*

pro·my·ce·li·um (prō′mī sē′lē əm), *n., pl.* **-li·a** (-lē ə). *Bot.* a short filament produced in the germination of a spore, which bears small spores and then dies. [< NL; see PRO-[1], MYCELIUM] —**pro′my·ce′li·al,** *adj.*

pron., 1. pronominal. **2.** pronoun. **3.** pronounced. **4.** pronunciation.

pro·na·os (prō nā′os), *n., pl.* **-na·oi** (-nā′oi). (in a classical temple) an open vestibule before the cella. Also called **anticum.** Cf. **epinaos.** [< Gk *prónaos*, lit., before the temple. See PRO-[2], NAOS]

pro·nate (prō′nāt), *v.,* **-nat·ed, -nat·ing.** —*v.t.* **1.** to turn into a prone position; to rotate (the hand or forearm) so that the surface of the palm is downward or toward the back. —*v.i.* **2.** to become pronated. [< LL *prōnāt(us)*, ptp. of *prōnāre* to bend forward. See PRONE, -ATE[1]] —**pro·na′tor,** *n.*

pro·na·tion (prō nā′shən), *n.* **1.** rotation of the hand or forearm so that the surface of the palm is facing downward or toward the back (opposed to *supination*). **2.** a comparable motion of the foot consisting of abduction followed by eversion. **3.** the position assumed as the result of this rotation. [PRONATE + -ION]

Pro·na·us (prō nā′əs), *n.* *Class. Myth.* an epithet of Athena, meaning "of the pronaos."

prone[1] (prōn), *adj.* **1.** having a natural inclination or tendency to something; disposed; liable: *to be prone to anger.* **2.** having the front or ventral part downward; lying face downward. **3.** lying flat; prostrate. **4.** having a downward direction or slope. **5.** having the palm downward, as the hand. [ME < L *prōn(us)* turned or leaning forward, inclined downward, disposed, prone] —**prone′ly,** *adv.* —**prone′ness,** *n.*
—**Syn. 1.** apt, subject, tending. **3.** recumbent.

prone[2] (prōn), *n.* a sermon or a brief hortatory introduction to a sermon, usually delivered at a service at which the Eucharist is celebrated. [< F *prône* grill, grating (separating chancel from nave); so called because notices and addresses were delivered there]

prone′ float′. See **dead-man's float.**

pro·neph·ros (prō nef′ros), *n., pl.* **-roi** (-roi), **-ra** (-rə). *Embryol.* one of the three embryonic excretory organs of vertebrates, which becomes the functional kidney of certain lower fishes, and which is vestigial in the embryos of higher vertebrates. Cf. **mesonephros, metanephros.** [< NL < Gk *pro-* PRO-[2] + *nephrós* kidney] —**pro·neph·ric** (prō nef′rik), *adj.*

prone′ pres′sure meth′od, a method of artificial respiration in which the patient is placed face downward, pressure then being rhythmically applied with the hands to the lower part of the thorax. Also called **Schafer method, Schafer's method.**

prong (prông, prong), *n.* **1.** one of the pointed tines of a fork. **2.** any pointed, projecting part, as of an antler. **3.** a branch of a stream. —*v.t.* **4.** to pierce or stab with a prong. **5.** to supply with prongs. [late ME *pronge*, var. of *prange* kind of fork; akin to OSw *prang* gorge, narrow street, MLG *prange* stake, *prangen* to press, Goth *(ana)prangan* to oppress, Gk *brónchos* windpipe. See BRONCHUS]

prong·horn (prông′hôrn′, prong′-), *n., pl.* **-horns,** (*esp. collectively*) **-horn.** a fleet antelope-like ruminant, *Antilocapra americana*, of the plains of western North America. Also called **prong′horn an′telope.** [PRONG + HORN]

Pronghorn
(3 ft. high at shoulder; horns 12 to 15 in.; length 5½ ft.)

Pro·noe·a (prə nē′ə), *n.* *Class. Myth.* an epithet of Athena, meaning "forethought."

pro·nom·i·nal (prō nom′ə nəl), *adj.* **1.** *Gram.* pertaining to, having the nature of, similar in meaning to, or derived from a pronoun: "*His*" in "*his book*" is a *pronominal adjective.* "*There*" is a *pronominal adverb.* **2.** *Heraldry.* noting the coat of arms on a quartered

pro-Lyb′i·an, *adj., n.*
pro′-Mad·a·gas′can, *adj., n.*
pro-Ma·lay′an, *adj., n.*
pro′-Ma·lay′sian, *adj., n.*
pro-mar′riage, *adj.*
pro-merg′er, *adj.*
pro-Meth′o·dist, *adj., n.*
pro-Mex′i·can, *adj., n.*
pro-mil′i·ta·rism, *adj.*
pro-mil′i·ta·rist, *adj., n.*
pro-mil′i·tar′y, *adj.*
pro′mi·nor′i·ty, *adj.*
pro′mod·er·a′tion, *adj.*
pro′mod·er·a′tion·ist, *adj., n.*
pro-mod′ern, *adj.*
pro-mod′ern·ist, *adj., n.*
pro′mod·ern·is′tic, *adj.*
pro-Mon′a·co, *adj.*
pro-mon′ar·chist, *n., adj.*
pro-mon′ar·chy, *adj.*
pro′mo·nop′o·lis′tic, *adj.*
pro′mo·nop′o·ly, *adj.*
pro′-Mo·roc′can, *adj., n.*
pro-Mos′lem, *adj., n.*
pro-Mus′lem, *adj., n.*
pro-Mus′lim, *adj., n.*
pro-na′tion·al, *adj.*
pro-na′tion·al·ism, *n.*
pro-na′tion·al·ist, *adj., n.*
pro-na′tion·al·is′tic, *adj.*
pro-na′tive, *adj.*
pro-na′val, *adj.*
pro-na′vy, *adj.*
pro′ne·go′ti·a′tion, *adj.*
pro-Ne′gro, *adj., n.*
pro′-Ni·ge′ri·an, *adj., n.*
pro-Nor′dic, *adj.*
pro-North′, *adj.*
pro-North′ern, *adj.*
pro-Nor·we′gian, *adj., n.*

escutcheon: customarily occupying the first quarter and being the original coat of arms of the paternal line. —*n.* **3.** *Gram.* a pronominal word. [< LL *prōnōmināl(is).* See PRONOUN, -AL[1]] —**pro·nom/i·nal·ly,** *adv.*

pro·no·tum (prō nō/təm), *n., pl.* **-ta** (-tə). the dorsal sclerite of the prothorax of an insect. [< NL; see PRO-[1], NOTUM]

pro·noun (prō/noun/), *n.* *Gram.* any number of a small class of words found in many languages that are used as replacements or substitutes for a wide variety of nouns and noun phrases, and that have very general reference, as *I, you, he, this, who, what.* Pronouns are sometimes formally distinguished from nouns, as in English by the existence of special objective forms, as *him* for *he,* or *me* for *I,* and by nonoccurrence with an article or adjective. [< F *pronom* < L *prōnōmen* (s. *prōnōmin-*). See PRO-[1], NOUN]

pro·nounce (prə nouns/), *v.,* **-nounced, -nounc·ing.** —*v.t.* **1.** to enunciate or articulate (words, sentences, etc.). **2.** to utter or sound in a particular manner in speaking: *He pronounces his words indistinctly.* **3.** to declare (a person or thing) to be as specified: *Some persons pronounced it the best mulled claret they had ever tasted.* **4.** to utter or deliver formally or solemnly: *to pronounce sentence.* **5.** to announce authoritatively or officially: *The judge pronounced the man guilty.* **6.** to indicate the pronunciation of (words) by providing a phonetic transcription: *This dictionary pronounces all of the important English words.* —*v.i.* **7.** to pronounce words, phrases, etc. **8.** to make a statement or assertion, esp. an authoritative statement (often fol. by *on*): *The intern was required to pronounce on the findings of his research.* **9.** to give an opinion or decision (usually fol. by *on*): *I will not pronounce on a matter I know nothing of.* **10.** to indicate the pronunciation of words: *a spelling book that pronounces.* [ME < MF *prononc(ier)* < L *prōnuntiāre* to proclaim, announce, recite, utter. See PRO-[1], ANNOUNCE] —**pro·nounce/a·ble,** *adj.* —**pro·nounce/a·ble·ness,** *n.* —**pro·nounc/er,** *n.*

pro·nounced (prə nounst/), *adj.* **1.** strongly marked: *a pronounced taste of peppermint.* **2.** clearly indicated: *a pronounced contrast.* **3.** decided; unequivocal: *to have very pronounced views.* [PRONOUNCE + -ED[2]] —**pro·nounc·ed·ly** (prə noun/sid lē), *adv.* —**pro·nounc/ed·ness,** *n.*

pro·nounce·ment (prə nouns/mənt), *n.* **1.** a formal or authoritative statement. **2.** an opinion or decision. **3.** act of pronouncing. [PRONOUNCE + -MENT]

pron·to (pron/tō), *adv.* *Slang.* promptly; quickly. [< Sp (adj. and adv.): quick < L *promptus* PROMPT (adj.)]

Pro·nu·ba (prō/nōō bə), *n.* *Class. Myth.* an epithet of Juno as goddess of marriage.

pro·nu·cle·us (prō nōō/klē əs, -nyōō/-), *n., pl.* **-cle·i** (-klē ī/). *Embryol.* either of the gametic nuclei which unite in fertilization to form the nucleus of the zygote. [< NL; see PRO-[1], NUCLEUS] —**pro·nu/cle·ar,** *adj.*

pro·nu·mer·al (prō nōō/mər əl, -nyōō/-), *n.* *Math.* an unknown; a variable. [PRO-[1] + NUMERAL]

pro·nun·ci·a·men·to (prə nun/sē ə men/tō, -shē ə-), *n., pl.* **-tos.** a proclamation; manifesto. [< Sp *pronunciamiento* < L *prōnuntiā(re)* (to) PRONOUNCE + *-mentum* -MENT]

pro·nun·ci·a·tion (prə nun/sē ā/shən), *n.* **1.** act or result of producing the sounds of speech, including articulation, vowel formation, accent, and inflection, often with reference to some standard of correctness or acceptability. **2.** an accepted standard of the sound and stress patterns of a sound, syllable, word, etc.: *He said the pronunciation of "curl" is* (kûrl), *not* (koil). **3.** the conventional patterns of treatment of the sounds of a language: *the pronunciation of French.* **4.** a phonetic transcription of a given word, phoneme, etc.: *The pronunciation of "pheasant" is* (fez/ənt). [late ME *pronunciacion* < L *prōnuntiātiōn-* (s. of *prōnuntiātiō*) delivery (of a speech), equiv. to *prōnuntiāt(us)* (ptp. of *prōnuntiāre* to PRONOUNCE) + *-iōn-* -ION] —**pro·nun/ci·a/tion·al, pro·nun·ci·a·to·ry** (prə nun/sē ə tôr/ē, -tōr/ē), **pro·nun/ci·a/tive,** *adj.*

pro/ny brake/ (prō/nē), a friction brake serving as a dynamometer for measuring torque. [named after G.C.F.M. Riche, Baron de *Prony* (d. 1839), French engineer]

proof (prōōf), *n.* **1.** evidence sufficient to establish a thing as true, or to produce belief in its truth. **2.** anything serving as such evidence: *What proof have you?* **3.** act of testing or making trial of anything; test; trial: *to put a thing to the proof.* **4.** the establishment of the truth of anything; demonstration. **5.** *Law.* (in judicial proceedings) evidence having probative weight. **6.** the effect of evidence in convincing the mind. **7.** an arithmetical operation serving to check the correctness of a calculation. **8.** *Math., Logic.* a sequence of steps, statements, or demonstrations that leads to a valid conclusion. **9.** a test to determine the quality, durability, etc., of materials used in manufacture. **10.** state of having been tested and approved. **11.** proved strength, as of armor. **12.** *Distilling.* **a.** the arbitrary standard strength, as of an alcoholic liquor. **b.** strength with reference to this standard, indicated on a scale on which "100 proof" signifies a proof spirit. **13.** *Photog.* a trial print from a negative. **14.** *Print.* **a.** a trial impression, as of composed type, taken to correct errors and make alterations. **b.** one of a number of early and superior impressions taken before the printing of the ordinary issue: *to pull a proof.* **15.** (in printmaking) an impression taken from a plate or the like to show the quality or condition of work during the process of execution; a print pulled for examination while working on a plate, block, stone, etc. **16.** *Numis.* one of a limited number of coins of a new issue struck from polished dies on a blank having a polished or mat surface. **17.** *Scot. Law.* the trial of a case by a judge alone, without a jury. —*adj.* **18.** impenetrable, impervious, or invulnerable: *proof against outside temperature changes.* **19.** of tested or proved strength or quality: *proof armor.* **20.** able to withstand; successful in not being overcome: *proof against temptation.* **21.** used for testing or proving; serving as proof. **22.** of standard strength, as an alcoholic liquor. **23.** referring to pieces of pure gold and silver which the U.S. assay and mint offices use as standards. —*v.t.* **24.** to test; examine for flaws, errors, etc.; check against a standard or standards. **25.** *Print.* prove (def. 6). **26.** to proofread. **27.** to treat or coat for the purpose of rendering resistant to deterioration, damage, etc. (often used in combination): *to proof a house against termites; to shrink-proof a shirt.* [ME *prove,* etc., alter. (by assoc. with PROVE) of *preove* < OF *prueve* < LL *proba* a test, akin to L *probāre* to test and find good]
—**Syn. 1.** confirmation, demonstration, corroboration, support. See **evidence. 3.** examination, assay. **20.** firm, steadfast.

-proof, a combining form of **proof:** *foolproof; waterproof.*

proof·ing (prōō/fing), *n.* **1.** the act or process of making a thing resistant, as in waterproof fabrics or fireproof material. **2.** any chemical used in the manufacture of a substance to make it proof against water, fire, etc. [PROOF + -ING[1]]

proof·read (prōōf/rēd/), *v.i., v.t.,* **-read** (-red/), **-read·ing.** to read (printers' proofs, copy, etc.) in order to detect and mark errors to be corrected. [back formation from *proofreader*] —**proof/read/er,** *n.*

proof/ sheet/, a printer's proof.

proof/ spir/it, 1. an alcoholic liquor, or mixture of alcohol and water, containing a standard amount of alcohol. In the U.S. proof spirit has a specific gravity of .93353 (containing one half of its volume of alcohol of a specific gravity of .7939 at 60° F). **2.** *Brit.* liquor with a specific gravity of .91984.

proof/ stress/, the load per unit area that a structure can withstand without being permanently deformed by more than a specified amount.

prop[1] (prop), *v.,* **propped, prop·ping,** *n.* —*v.t.* **1.** to support, or prevent from falling, with or as if with a prop: *to prop an old fence.* **2.** to rest (a thing) against a support: *He propped his cane against the wall.* **3.** to support or sustain. —*n.* **4.** a stick, rod, pole, beam, or other rigid support. **5.** a person or thing serving as a support or stay: *His father is his financial prop.* [ME *proppe;* c. MD *proppe* prop, support]

prop[2] (prop), *n.* *Theat. Informal.* property (def. 8a). [by shortening] —**prop/less,** *adj.*

prop[3] (prop), *n.* *Informal.* a propeller. [by shortening]

prop., 1. properly. **2.** property. **3.** proposition.

pro·pae·deu·tic (prō/pi dōō/tik, -dyōō/-), *adj.* Also **pro/pae·deu/ti·cal. 1.** pertaining to or of the nature of preliminary instruction. **2.** introductory to some art or science. —*n.* **3.** a propaedeutic subject or study. **4. propaedeutics,** (*construed as sing.*) the preliminary body of knowledge and rules necessary for the study of some art or science. [PRO-[2] + Gk *paideutik(ós)* pertaining to teaching, equiv. to *paideú(ein)* (to) teach + *-tikos* -TIC]

prop·a·ga·ble (prop/ə gə bəl), *adj.* capable of being propagated. [< ML *propāgābil(is).* See PROPAGATE, -BLE] —**prop/a·ga·bil/i·ty, prop/a·ga·ble·ness,** *n.*

prop·a·gan·da (prop/ə gan/də), *n.* **1.** information, rumors, etc., deliberately spread widely to help or harm a person, group, movement, institution, nation, etc.: *Communist propaganda about French foreign policy; profascist propaganda.* **2.** the deliberate spreading of such information, rumors, etc. **3.** the particular doctrines or principles propagated by an organization or movement. **4.** *Rom. Cath. Ch.* **a.** a committee of cardinals, established in 1622 by Pope Gregory XV, having supervision over foreign missions and the training of priests for these missions. **b.** a school **(College of Propaganda)** established by Pope Urban VIII for the education of priests for foreign missions. **5.** *Archaic.* an organization or movement for the spreading of propaganda. [< NL, short for *congregātiō dē propāgandā fidē* congregation for propagating the faith]

prop·a·gan·dise (prop/ə gan/dīz), *v.t., v.i.,* **-dised, -dis·ing.** *Chiefly Brit.* propagandize.

prop·a·gan·dism (prop/ə gan/diz əm), *n.* zealous propagation of particular doctrines or principles. [PROPAGAND(A) + -ISM]

prop·a·gan·dist (prop/ə gan/dist), *n.* **1.** a person devoted to the propagation of particular doctrines or principles. **2.** a member or agent of a propaganda. —*adj.* **3.** Also, **prop/a·gan·dis/tic.** pertaining to propaganda or propagandists. [PROPAGAND(A) + -IST] —**prop/a·gan·dis/ti·cal·ly,** *adv.*

prop·a·gan·dize (prop/ə gan/dīz), *v.,* **-dized, -diz·ing.** —*v.t.* **1.** to propagate or publicize (principles, dogma, etc.) by means of propaganda. **2.** to subject to propaganda: *The government attempted to propagandize neighboring countries.* —*v.i.* **3.** to carry on or disseminate propaganda. Also, *esp. Brit.,* **propagandise.** [PROPAGAND(A) + -IZE]

prop·a·gate (prop/ə gāt/), *v.,* **-gat·ed, -gat·ing.** —*v.t.* **1.** to cause (a plant or animal) to multiply by any process of natural reproduction from the parent stock. **2.** to reproduce (itself, its kind, etc.), as a plant or an animal does. **3.** to transmit (hereditary features or elements) to, or through, offspring. **4.** to spread (a report, doctrine, practice, etc.) from person to person; disseminate. **5.** to cause to increase in number or amount. **6.** to create (an effect) at a distance, as by electromagnetic waves, compression waves, etc., traveling through space or a physical medium: *to propagate sound.* —*v.i.* **7.** to multiply, by any process of natural reproduction, as plants or animals; breed. **8.** to increase in extent, as a structural flaw: *The crack will propagate only to this joint.* [< L *propāgāt(us)* propagated (ptp. of *propāgāre* to fasten (cuttings of plants) out, spread for sprouting, propagate), equiv. to *propāg(ēs)* something set out, scion, slip (*pro-* PRO-[1] + *pāg-,* base of *pangere* to fasten + *-ēs* n. suffix) + *-ātus* -ATE[1]] —**prop/a·ga/tive, prop·a·ga·to·ry** (prop/ə gə tôr/ē, -tōr/ē), *adj.* —**prop/a·ga/tor,** *n.*

prop·a·ga·tion (prop/ə gā/shən), *n.* **1.** act of propagating. **2.** fact of being propagated. **3.** multiplication by natural reproduction. **4.** transmission or dissemination. [late ME *propagacyon* < L *propāgātiōn-* (s. of *propāgātiō*). See PROPAGATE, -ION] —**prop/a·ga/tion·al,** *adj.*

pro·pag·u·lum (prō pag/yə ləm), *n., pl.* **-la** (-lə). *Bot.* a propagative part, as a bud or shoot. Also, **prop·a·gule** (prop/ə gyōōl/). [< NL, dim. of L *propāgo* shoot, runner; see -ULE]

pro·pane (prō/pān), *n.* *Chem.* a colorless, flammable gas, $CH_3CH_2CH_3$, of the alkane series, occurring in petroleum and natural gas: used chiefly as a fuel and in organic synthesis. Also called **dimethylmethane.** [PROP(IONIC) + -ANE]

pro·pane·di·o·ic (prō/pān dī ō/ik), *adj.* *Chem.* malonic. [PROPANE + DI-[1] + -O- + -IC]

pro/pa·no/ic ac/id (prō/pə nō/ik, prō/-), *Chem.* See **propionic acid.** [PROPANE + -O- + -IC]

pro·par·ox·y·tone (prō/pa rok/si tōn/), *Class. Gk. Gram.* —*adj.* **1.** having an accent or heavy stress on the antepenultimate syllable. —*n.* **2.** a proparoxytone word. [< Gk *proparoxýton(os).* See PRO-[2], PAROXYTONE] —**pro·par·ox·y·ton·ic** (prō/pa rok/si ton/ik), *adj.*

pro pa·tri·a (prō pä/trē ä/; *Eng.* prō pā/trē ə), *Latin.* for one's country.

pro·pel (prə pel/), *v.t.,* **-pelled, -pel·ling. 1.** to drive, or cause to move, forward: *to propel a boat by rowing.* **2.** to impel or urge onward: *Urgent need of money propelled him to take a job.* [late ME *propelle(n)* (to) expel < L *prōpell(ere)* (to) drive forward, equiv. to *pro-* PRO-[1] + *pellere* to drive]
—**Syn. 1.** compel, project, move. —**Ant.** repel.

pro·pel·lant (prə pel/ənt), *n.* **1.** a propelling agent. **2.** *Mil.* the charge of explosive used in a cannon to fire the projectile. **3.** a substance, usually a mixture of fuel and oxidizer, for propelling a rocket. [PROPEL + -ANT]

pro·pel·lent (prə pel/ənt), *adj.* **1.** serving or tending to propel or drive forward. —*n.* **2.** a propellant. [< L *prōpellent-* (s. of *prōpellēns*), prp. of *prōpellere* to drive forward. See PROPEL, -ENT]

pro·pel·ler (prə pel/ər), *n.* **1.** one who or that which propels. **2.** a device having a revolving hub with radiating blades, for propelling a steamship, an airplane, etc. **3.** the bladed rotor of a pump that drives the fluid axially. [PROPEL + -ER[1]]

propel/ler horse/power, a measure of the power actually available for driving a propeller after all wasted energy is deducted.

propel/ler post/, *Naut.* a vertical framing member through which the tailshaft passes. Also called **screw post.**

propel/ler wash/, *Aeron.* the backwash from a propeller.

pro·pend (prō pend/), *v.i.* *Obs.* to incline or tend. [< L *prōpend(ēre)* (to) hang down, be inclined. See PRO-[1], PEND]

pro·pene (prō/pēn), *n.* *Chem.* propylene (def. 2). [PROP(IONIC) + -ENE]

pro·pe·nol (prō/pə nōl/, -nôl/, -nol/), *n.* *Chem.* See **allyl alcohol.**

pro·pense (prō pens/), *adj.* *Archaic.* having a tendency toward; prone; inclined. —**pro·pense/ly,** *adv.* —**pro·pense/ness,** *n.* [< L *propens(us)* inclined, ptp. of *prōpendēre* to PROPEND]

pro·pen·sion (prə pen/shən), *n.* *Archaic.* propensity. [< L *prōpensiōn-* (s. of *prōpensiō*) inclination. See PROPENSE, -ION]

pro·pen·si·ty (prə pen/si tē), *n., pl.* **-ties. 1.** a natural inclination or tendency, often toward something not considered admirable: *His propensity for drinking too much was his major problem.* **2.** *Obs.* favorable disposition or partiality. [PROPENSE + -ITY]
—**Syn. 1.** bent, leaning, disposition, penchant, proclivity.

pro·pe·nyl (prō/pə nil), *adj.* *Chem.* containing the propenyl group. [PROPENE + -YL]

pro/penyl al/cohol, *Chem.* See **allyl alcohol.** Also called **propenol.**

pro/penyl group/, *Chem.* the univalent group, $CH_3CH{=}CH{-}$, derived from propylene. Also called **pro/penyl rad/ical.**

pro·pe·nyl·ic (prō/pə nil/ik), *adj.* of, pertaining to, or characteristic of the propenyl group. [PROPENYL + -IC]

prop·er (prop/ər), *adj.* **1.** adapted or appropriate to the purpose or circumstances; fit; suitable: *the proper time to plant strawberries.* **2.** conforming to established standards of behavior or manners; correct or decorous: *a proper young lady.* **3.** fitting; right: *It was only proper to wear a hat.* **4.** strictly belonging or applicable: *the proper place for a stove.* **5.** belonging or pertaining exclusively or distinctly to a person or thing. **6.** strict; accurate. **7.** strictly so-called; in the strict sense of the word (usually used postpositively): *Shellfish do not belong to the fishes proper.* **8.** *Gram.* **a.** (of a name, noun, or adjective) designating a particular person or thing, written in English with an initial capital letter, as *John, Chicago, Monday, American.* **b.** having the force or function of a proper name: *a proper adjective.* **9.** normal or regular. **10.** *Heraldry.* (of a device) depicted in its natural colors: *an oak tree proper.* **11.** *Eccles.* used only on a particular day or festival: *the proper introit.* **12.** *Chiefly Brit. Informal.* complete or thorough: *a proper thrashing.* **13.** *Informal.* **a.** excellent; capital; fine. **b.** good-looking or handsome. **14.** belonging to oneself or itself; own. **15.** *Math.* (of a subset of a set) not equal to the whole set. **16.** *Archaic.* of good character; respectable. —*n.* **17.** *Eccles.* a special office or special parts of an office appointed for a particular day or time. [ME *propre* < OF < L *propr(ius)* one's own] —**prop/er·ness,** *n.*
—**Syn. 1.** suited. **2.** meet, befitting, becoming, decent, polite. **5.** special, individual, peculiar. **6.** precise, exact, just, formal.

prop/er frac/tion, *Math.* a fraction having the numerator less, or lower in degree, than the denominator.

prop/er func/tion, *Math.* eigenfunction.

prop·er·ly (prop/ər lē), *adv.* **1.** in a proper manner. **2.** correctly. **3.** appropriately. **4.** decorously. **5.** accurately. **6.** justifiably. **7.** thoroughly; completely: *He got himself properly drunk.* [ME; see PROPER, -LY]

prop/er mo/tion, 1. *Astron.* the angular motion of a star relative to a suitably defined frame of reference, expressed in seconds of arc per year. Cf. **tangential motion. 2.** *Brit. Naut.* the true motion of an object observed at sea.

pro-op/er-a, *adj.*
pro/-O·ri·en/tal, *adj., n.*
pro-or/tho·dox/, *adj.*
pro-or/tho·dox/y, *adj.*
pro·pac/i·fism, *n.*
pro·pac/i·fist, *n., adj.*
pro-Pan/a·ma, *adj.*
pro/-Pan/a·ma/ni·an, *adj., n.*
pro·pa/pist, *n., adj.*
pro/-Par/a·guay, *adj.*
pro/-Par·a·guay/an, *adj., n.*
pro/pa·tri·ot/ic, *adj.*
pro·pa/tri·ot·ism, *n.*
pro·pa/tron·age, *adj.*
pro·pay/ment, *adj.*

prop′er noun′, a noun that is not normally preceded by an article or other limiting modifier, as *any, some,* and that refers to only one person or thing or to several persons or things which constitute a unique class only because they have the same name, as *Lincoln, Richard, Pittsburgh.* Also called **prop′er name′.** Cf. **common noun.**

prop·er·tied (prop′ər tēd), *adj.* owning property: *the propertied class.* [PROPERTY + -ED[3]]

Pro·per·ti·us (prō pûr′shē əs, -shəs), *n.* **Sextus** (seks′təs), c50–c15 B.C., Roman poet.

prop·er·ty (prop′ər tē), *n., pl.* **-ties. 1.** that which a person owns; the possession or possessions of a particular owner: *He lost all his property in the fire.* **2.** goods, land, etc., considered as possessions: *The corporation is a satisfactory means for the common ownership of property.* **3.** a piece of land or real estate: *property on Main Street.* **4.** ownership; right of possession, enjoyment, or disposal of anything, esp. of something tangible: *to have property in land.* **5.** something at the disposal of a person, a group of persons, or the community or public: *The secret of the invention became common property.* **6.** an essential or distinctive attribute or quality of a thing: *the chemical and physical properties of an element.* **7.** *Logic.* **a.** any attribute or characteristic. **b.** (in Aristotelian usage) an attribute not essential to a species but necessarily connected with it. **8.** *Theat.* **a.** an item of furniture, an ornament, or a decoration in a stage setting; any object handled or used by an actor in a performance. **b.** *Informal.* a play or stage adaptation of a literary work, esp. for the commercial theater: *He just bought a new property and hoped it would make a hit.* [ME *proprete* possession, attribute, what is one's own, equiv. to *propre* PROPER + *-te* -TY[2]. See PROPRIETY] —**prop′er·ty·less,** *n.*

—**Syn. 1.** belongings. PROPERTY, CHATTELS, EFFECTS, ESTATE, GOODS are terms for material things which are owned. PROPERTY is the general word: *He owns a great deal of property. He said that the umbrella was his property.* CHATTELS is a term for pieces of personal property or movable possessions; it may be applied to livestock, automobiles, etc.: *a mortgage on chattels.* EFFECTS is a term for any form of personal property, including even things of the least value: *All his effects were insured against fire.* ESTATE refers to property of any kind which has been, or is capable of being, handed down to descendants or otherwise disposed of in a will: *He left most of his estate to his nephew.* It may consist of personal estate (money, valuables, securities, chattels, etc.), or real estate (land and buildings). GOODS refers to household possessions or other movable property, esp. that comprising the stock in trade of a business: *A store arranges its goods conveniently.* **3.** acreage. **7.** feature. See **quality.**

prop′erty man′, a person responsible for securing, handling, and storing the properties used in a theatrical, motion-picture, or television production. Also called **propman, prop man.**

prop′er val′ue, *Math.* See **characteristic root.**

pro·phase (prō′fāz′), *n.* *Biol.* the first stage in mitosis, in which the chromosomes contract and become more stainable and the nuclear membrane disappears. [PRO-[1] + PHASE]

proph·e·cy (prof′i sē), *n., pl.* **-cies. 1.** the foretelling or prediction of what is to come. **2.** that which is declared by a prophet, esp. divinely inspired prediction, instruction, or exhortation. **3.** a divinely inspired utterance or revelation: *oracular prophecies.* **4.** the action, function, or faculty of a prophet. [ME *prophecie* < OF < LL *prophētīa* < Gk *prophēteía.* See PROPHET, -Y[3]]

proph·e·sy (prof′i sī′), *v.,* **-sied, -sy·ing.** —*v.t.* **1.** to foretell or predict. **2.** to indicate beforehand. **3.** to declare or foretell by or as if by divine inspiration. **4.** to utter in prophecy or as a prophet. —*v.i.* **5.** to make predictions. **6.** to make inspired declarations of what is to come. **7.** to speak as a mediator between God and man or in God's stead. **8.** to teach religious subjects. [v. use and var. of PROPHECY] —**proph′e·si′a·ble,** *adj.* —**proph′e·si′er,** *n.*

—**Syn. 1.** augur, prognosticate. See **predict. 3.** divine.

proph·et (prof′it), *n.* **1.** a person who speaks for God or a deity, or by divine inspiration. **2.** (in the Old Testament) **a.** a person chosen to speak for God and to guide the people of Israel: *Moses was the greatest of Old Testament prophets.* **b.** (*often cap.*) one of the Major or Minor Prophets. **c.** one of a band of ecstatic visionaries claiming divine inspiration and, according to popular belief, possessing magical powers. **d.** a person who practices divination. **3.** one of a class of persons in the early church, next in order after the apostles, recognized as inspired to utter special revelations and predictions. 1 Cor. 12:28. **4. the Prophet,** Muhammad, the founder of Islam. **5.** a person regarded as, or claiming to be, an inspired teacher or leader. **6.** a person who foretells or predicts what is to come: *a weather prophet.* **7.** a spokesman or proclaimer of some doctrine, cause, or the like. [early ME *prophete* < LL *prophēta* < Gk *prophḗtēs,* equiv. to *pro-* PRO-[2] + *-phētēs* speaker, action n. of *phánai* to speak] —**proph′et·hood′,** *n.* —**proph′et·less,** *adj.* —**proph′et·like′,** *adj.*

proph·et·ess (prof′i tis), *n.* **1.** a female prophet. **2.** the wife or female companion of a prophet. [ME *prophetesse* < OF < LL *prophētissa.* See PROPHET, -ESS]

proph·et-flow·er (prof′it flou′ər), *n.* a perennial herb, *Arnebia echioides,* of southeastern Europe and Armenia, having one-sided clusters of purple-spotted, yellow flowers.

pro·phet·ic (prə fet′ik), *adj.* **1.** of or pertaining to a prophet: *prophetic inspiration.* **2.** of the nature of or containing prophecy: *prophetic writings.* **3.** having the function or powers of a prophet, as a person. **4.** predictive; presageful or portentous; ominous: *prophetic signs; prophetic warnings.* Also, **pro·phet′i·cal.** [< LL *prophēticus* < Gk *prophētikós.* See PROPHET, -IC] —**pro·phet′i·cal′i·ty, pro·phet′i·cal·ness,** *n.* —**pro·phet′i·cal·ly,** *adv.*

Proph·ets (prof′its), *n.* (*construed as sing.*) the canonical group of books that forms the second of the three Jewish divisions of the Old Testament, comprising Joshua, Judges, I and II Samuel, I and II Kings, Isaiah, Jeremiah, Ezekiel, Hosea, Joel, Amos, Obadiah, Jonah, Micah, Nahum, Habakkuk, Zephaniah, Haggai, Zechariah, and Malachi. Cf. **law** (def. 16), **Hagiographa.**

pro·phy·lac·tic (prō′fə lak′tik, prof′ə-), *adj.* **1.** defending or protecting from disease, as a drug. **2.** preventive or protective. —*n.* **3.** *Med.* a prophylactic medicine or measure. **4.** a preventive. **5.** a device, usually a rubber sheath, used to prevent conception or venereal infection; condom. [< Gk *prophylaktik(ós)* of guarding, equiv. to *prophylak-* (verbid s. of *prophylássein* to guard beforehand) + *-tikos* -TIC. See PROPHYLAXIS] —**pro′phy·lac′ti·cal·ly,** *adv.*

prophylac′tic kit′, a tube or packet containing medication for the prevention of venereal disease.

pro·phy·lax·is (prō′fə lak′sis, prof′ə-), *n.* *Med.* **1.** the preventing of disease. **2.** the prevention of a specific disease, as by studying the biological behavior, transmission, etc., of its causative agent and applying a series of measures against it. **3.** prophylactic treatment. [< NL < Gk *pro-* PRO-[2] + *phýlaxis* a watching, guarding, equiv. to *phylak-* (verbid s. of *phylássein* to guard) + *-sis* -SIS]

pro·pine (*v.* prō pēn′; *n.* prō pēn′, -pīn′), *v.,* **-pined, -pin·ing,** *n.* —*v.t.* **1.** *Archaic.* to offer as a present. —*n.* **2.** *Scot.* a present; gift. [late ME < MF *propine(r)* (to) give to drink, drink one's health < L *propīnāre* < Gk *propínein* to drink first, equiv. to *pro-* PRO-[2] + *pínein* to drink]

pro·pin·qui·ty (prō ping′kwi tē), *n.* **1.** nearness in place; proximity. **2.** nearness of relation; kinship. **3.** affinity of nature; similarity. **4.** nearness in time. [ME *propinquite* < L *propinquitās* nearness, equiv. to *propinqu(us)* near (*prop(e)* near + *-inquus* adj. suffix) + *-itās* -ITY]

pro·pi·on·al·de·hyde (prō′pē on al′də hīd′), *n.* *Chem.* a colorless, water-soluble liquid, C_2H_5CHO, having a pungent odor: used chiefly in the manufacture of plastics. Also called **propyl aldehyde.** [PROPION(IC) + ALDEHYDE]

pro·pi·o·nate (prō′pē ə nāt′), *n.* *Chem.* an ester or salt of propionic acid. [PROPION(IC) + -ATE[2]]

pro·pi·on·i·bac·te·ri·um (prō′pē on′ə bak tēr′ē əm, -ō′nə-), *n., pl.* **-te·ri·a** (-tēr′ē ə). *Bacteriol.* any of several aerobic or anaerobic bacteria of the genus *Propionibacterium,* found in dairy products, esp. hard cheeses where certain species are associated with the ripening process. [< NL; see PROPIONIC, BACTERIUM]

pro·pi·on·ic (prō′pē on′ik, -ō′nik), *adj.* *Chem.* of or derived from propionic acid. [PRO-[2] + Gk *píon-* (s. of *píōn*) fat + -IC]

pro′pion′ic ac′id, *Chem., Pharm.* a colorless, oily, water-soluble liquid, CH_3CH_2COOH, having a pungent odor: used in making bread-mold-inhibiting propionates, in perfumery, etc., and in medicine as a topical fungicide. Also, **propanoic acid.** Also called **methylacetic acid.**

pro·pi·ti·ate (prə pish′ē āt′), *v.t.,* **-at·ed, -at·ing.** to make favorably inclined; appease; conciliate. [< L *propitiāt(us),* ptp. of *propitiāre* to appease. See PROPITIOUS, -ATE[1]] —**pro·pi·ti·a·ble** (prə pish′ē ə bəl), *adj.* —**pro·pi′ti·at′ing·ly,** *adv.* —**pro·pi′ti·a′tive,** *adj.* —**pro·pi′ti·a′tor,** *n.*

—**Syn.** See **appease.** —**Ant.** anger, arouse.

pro·pi·ti·a·tion (prə pish′ē ā′shən), *n.* **1.** act of propitiating; conciliation: *the propitiation of the wrathful gods.* **2.** that which propitiates. [ME *propiciacioun* < LL *propitiātiōn-* (s. of *propitiātiō*) appeasement. See PROPITIATE, -ION]

pro·pi·ti·a·to·ry (prə pish′ē ə tôr′ē, -tōr′ē), *adj.* **1.** serving or intended to propitiate. **2.** making propitiation; conciliatory. —*n.* **3.** See **mercy seat.** [ME *propiciatori* the mercy seat < LL *propitiātōri(um),* n. use of neut. of *propitiātōrius* atoning. See PROPITIATE, -ORY[1]] —**pro·pi′ti·a·to′ri·ly,** *adv.*

pro·pi·tious (prə pish′əs), *adj.* **1.** presenting favorable conditions; favorable: *propitious weather.* **2.** indicative of favor: *propitious omens.* **3.** favorably inclined; disposed to bestow favors or forgive: *if the gods be propitious.* [late ME *propicius* < L *propitius* favorable, equiv. to *prop(e)* near + *-itius* -ITIOUS] —**pro·pi′tious·ly,** *adv.* —**pro·pi′tious·ness,** *n.*

—**Syn. 2.** auspicious.

prop·jet (prop′jet′), *n.* *Aeron.* an airplane equipped with turboprops. [PROP[3] + JET[1]]

prop′jet en′gine. See **turbo-propeller engine.**

prop·man (prop′man′), *n., pl.* **-men.** *Theat.* See **property man.** Also, **prop′ man′.** [PROP[2] + MAN[1]]

pro·pneus·tic (prō nōō′stik, -nyōō′-), *adj.* *Entomol.* having only the first pair of spiracles open, as the tracheal systems of certain insects. [PRO- + Gk *pneustik(ós)* of, for breathing, akin to *pnein* to breathe; see -IC]

Pro·po·e·ti·des (prō′pō ē′ti dēz′), *n. pl.* *Class. Myth.* Cyprian maidens made wanton and later changed into stone for denying the divinity of Aphrodite.

prop·o·lis (prop′ə lis), *n.* a reddish resinous cement collected by bees from the buds of trees, used to stop up crevices in the hives, strengthen the cells, etc. Also called **bee glue.** [< L < Gk *própolis* suburb. See PRO-[2], -POLIS]

pro·pone (prə pōn′), *v.t.,* **-poned, -pon·ing.** *Scot.* **1.** to suggest for consideration; propose. **2.** to present before a jury or judge; plead for or request (an official decision). [ME *propone(n)* < L *prōpōne(re).* See PROPOSE]

pro·po·nent (prə pō′nənt), *n.* **1.** a person who puts forward a proposition or proposal; advocate. **2.** *Law.* **a.** a person who argues in favor of something. **b.** a person who seeks to obtain probate of a will. **3.** a person who supports a cause or doctrine; adherent. [< L *prōpōnent-* (s. of *prōpōnēns*). See PROPONE, -ENT]

pro·por·tion (prə pōr′shən, -pôr′-), *n.* **1.** comparative relation between things or magnitudes as to size, quantity, number, etc.; ratio. **2.** proper relation between things or parts: *Your expensive tastes and your financial means are way out of proportion.* **3.** relative size or extent. **4. proportions,** dimensions: *a rock of gigantic proportions.* **5.** a portion or part in its relation to the whole: *A large proportion of the debt remains.* **6.** symmetry, harmony, or balance: *an architect with a sense of proportion.* **7.** the significance of a thing or event that an objective view reveals: *You must try to see these mishaps in proportion.* **8.** *Math.* **a.** a relation of four quantities such that the first divided by the second is equal to the third divided by the fourth; the equality of ratios. **b.** See **rule of three. 9.** *Archaic.* analogy; comparison. —*v.t.* **10.** to adjust in proper proportion or relation, as to size, quantity, etc. **11.** to adjust the proportions of. [ME *proporcio(u)n* < L *prōportiōn-* (s. of *prōportiō*) symmetry, analogy. See PRO-[1], PORTION] —**pro·por′tion·er,** *n.* —**pro·por′tion·less,** *adj.*

—**Syn. 1.** comparison. **5.** share. **6.** distribution, arrangement. See **symmetry. 10.** regulate, arrange, balance, harmonize.

pro·por·tion·a·ble (prə pōr′shə nə bəl, -pôr′-), *adj.* being in due proportion; proportional. [ME *proporcionable* < LL *prōportiōnābil(is).* See PROPORTION, -ABLE] —**pro·por′tion·a·bil′i·ty, pro·por′tion·a·ble·ness,** *n.* —**pro·por′tion·a·bly,** *adv.*

pro·por·tion·al (prə pōr′shə nəl, -pôr′-), *adj.* **1.** having due proportion; corresponding. **2.** being in or characterized by proportion. **3.** of or pertaining to proportion; relative. **4.** *Math.* having the same or a constant ratio or relation. [ME *proporcional* < L *prōportiōnāl(is).* See PROPORTION, -AL[1]] —**pro·por′tion·al′i·ty,** *n.* —**pro·por′tion·al·ly,** *adv.*

—**Syn. 1.** harmonious, comparative, accordant, consonant, proportionate.

propor′tional count′er, *Physics.* a radiation counter in which the strength of each electric pulse generated per count is proportional to the energy of the particle or photon producing the pulse, alpha particles producing a different electric pulse from beta rays.

propor′tional lim′it, *Physics.* See **elastic limit.**

propor′tional representa′tion, a method of voting by which political parties are given legislative representation in proportion to their popular strength.

pro·por·tion·ate (*adj.* prə pōr′shə nit, -pôr′-; *v.* prə pōr′shə nāt′, -pôr′-), *adj., v.,* **-at·ed, -at·ing.** —*adj.* **1.** proportioned; being in due proportion; proportional. —*v.t.* **2.** to make proportionate. [ME *proporcionate* < LL *prōportiōnāt(us).* See PROPORTION, -ATE[1]] —**pro·por′tion·ate·ly,** *adv.* —**pro·por′tion·ate·ness,** *n.*

—**Syn. 1.** according, accordant, consonant, harmonious, balanced.

pro·por·tioned (prə pōr′shənd, -pôr′-), *adj.* **1.** adjusted to proper proportion or relation. **2.** having proportions as specified: *a badly proportioned room.* [ME *proporcioned.* See PROPORTION, -ED[2]]

pro·por·tion·ment (prə pōr′shən mənt, -pôr′-), *n.* **1.** act of proportioning. **2.** state of being proportioned. [PROPORTION + -MENT]

pro·pos·al (prə pō′zəl), *n.* **1.** act of offering or suggesting something for acceptance, adoption, or performance. **2.** a plan or scheme proposed. **3.** an offer or suggestion of marriage, made by a man to a woman. [PROPOSE + -AL[2]]

—**Syn. 1.** recommendation. **2.** suggestion, design. PROPOSAL, OVERTURE, PROPOSITION refer to something in the nature of an offer. A PROPOSAL is a plan, a scheme, an offer to be accepted or rejected: *to make proposals for peace.* An OVERTURE is a friendly approach, an opening move (perhaps involving a proposal) tentatively looking toward the settlement of a controversy, or else preparing the way for a proposal or the like: *to make overtures to an enemy.* PROPOSITION, used in mathematics to refer to a formal statement of truth, and often including the proof or demonstration of the statement, has something of this same meaning when used nontechnically (particularly in business). A PROPOSITION is a PROPOSAL in which the terms are clearly stated and their advantageous nature emphasized: *His proposition involved a large discount to the retailer.*

pro·pose (prə pōz′), *v.,* **-posed, -pos·ing.** —*v.t.* **1.** to offer or suggest (a matter, subject, case, etc.) for consideration, acceptance, or action: *to propose a new method; to propose a toast.* **2.** to suggest: *He proposed that a messenger be sent.* **3.** to present or nominate (a person) for some position, office, membership, etc. **4.** to put before oneself as something to be done; design; intend. **5.** to present to the mind or attention; state. **6.** to propound (a question, riddle, etc.). —*v.i.* **7.** to make an offer or suggestion, esp. of marriage. **8.** to form or consider a purpose or design. [ME < MF *propose(r)* (see PRO-[1], POSE[1]), by assoc. with derivatives of L *prōpositus,* ptp. of *prōpōnere* to set forth. See PROPOSITION] —**pro·pos′a·ble,** *adj.* —**pro·pos′er,** *n.*

—**Syn. 1.** proffer, tender, suggest, recommend, present. **3.** name. **4.** plan. See **intend. 5.** pose, posit. —**Ant. 1.** withdraw.

prop·o·si·tion (prop′ə zish′ən), *n.* **1.** the act of offering or suggesting something to be considered, accepted, adopted, or done. **2.** a plan or scheme proposed. **3.** an offer of terms for a transaction, as in business: *He listened to the salesman's proposition.* **4.** *Informal.* a thing, matter, or person considered as something to be dealt with or encountered: *Keeping diplomatic channels open is a serious proposition.* **5.** anything stated or affirmed for discussion or illustration. **6.** *Rhet.* a statement of the subject of an argument or a discourse, or of the course of action or essential idea to be advocated. **7.** *Logic.* a statement in which something is affirmed or denied, so that it can therefore be significantly characterized as either true or false. **8.** *Math.* a formal statement of either a truth to be demonstrated or an operation to be performed; a theorem or a problem. **9.** a proposal of illicit sexual relations. —*v.t.* **10.** to propose a plan, deal, etc., to. **11.** to propose illicit sexual relations to. [ME *proposicio(u)n* < L *prōpositiōn-* (s. of *prōpositiō*) a setting forth. See PROPOSITUS, -ION] —**prop′o·si′tion·al,** *adj.* —**prop′o·si′tion·al·ly,** *adv.*

—**Syn. 2.** See **proposal.**

proposi′tional cal′culus, *Logic.* See **sentential calculus.**

proposi′tional func′tion, *Logic.* See **sentential function.**

pro·pos·i·tus (prə poz′i təs), *n., pl.* **-ti** (-tī′). *Law.* the person from whom a line of descent is derived on a genealogical table. [< NL, special use of ptp. of L *prōpōnere* to set forth]

pro·pound (prə pound′), *v.t.* to put forward for consideration, acceptance, or adoption: *to propound a theory.* [later var. of ME *propone* (see PROPONE) < L *prōpōn(ere)* (to) set forth, equiv. to *prō-* PRO-[1] + *pōnere* to put, place, set. See COMPOUND, EXPOUND] —**pro·pound′er,** *n.*

pro′-Pe·ru′vi·an, *adj., n.* pro-Phil′ip·pine′, *adj.* pro-Pol′ish, *adj.* pro·pol′i·tics, *adj.* pro-Por′tu·guese′, *adj., n.*

pro·pox·y·phene (prō pok′sə fēn′), *n. Pharm.* See **dextro propoxyphene.** [PROP(IONATE) + OXY-² + (DI)-PHEN(YL)]

propr., proprietor.

pro·prae·tor (prō prē′tər), *n. Rom. Hist.* an officer who, after having served as praetor in Rome, was sent to govern a province with praetorial authority. Also, **pro·pre′tor.** [< L; see PRO-¹, PRAETOR] —**pro·prae·to·ri·al, pro·pre·to·ri·al** (prō′pri tōr′ē əl, -tôr′-), **pro′prae·to′ri·an, pro′pre·to′ri·an,** *adj.*

pro·pri·e·tar·y (prə prī′i ter′ē), *adj., n., pl.* **-tar·ies.** —*adj.* **1.** belonging to a proprietor or proprietors. **2.** being a proprietor or proprietors; holding property: *the proprietary class.* **3.** pertaining to property or ownership: *proprietary wealth.* **4.** belonging or controlled as property. **5.** manufactured and sold only by the owner of the patent, formula, brand name, or trademark associated with the product: *proprietary medicine.* —*n.* **6.** an owner or proprietor. **7.** a body of proprietors. **8.** *Amer. Hist.* the grantee or owner, or one of the grantees or owners, of a proprietary colony. **9.** ownership. **10.** something owned, esp. a piece of real estate. **11.** a proprietary medicine. [late ME < ML *proprietāri(us)* owner, LL: of an owner, of ownership, equiv. to L *propriet(ās)* ownership, thing owned (see PROPRIETY) + *-ārius* -ARY] —**pro·pri·e·tar·i·ly** (prə prī′i târ′i lē, -prī′i ter′-), *adv.*

propri′etary col′ony, *Amer. Hist.* any of certain colonies, as Maryland and Pennsylvania, that were granted to an individual or group by the British crown and that were granted full rights of self-government. Cf. **charter colony, royal colony.**

pro·pri·e·tor (prə prī′i tər), *n.* **1.** the owner of a business establishment, a hotel, etc. **2.** a person who has the exclusive right or title to something; an owner, as of real property. **3.** a group of proprietors; proprietary. [PROPRIET(ARY) + -OR²] —**pro·pri·e·to·ri·al** (prə prī′i tōr′ē əl, -tôr′-), *adj.* —**pro·pri′e·to′ri·al·ly,** *adv.* —**pro·pri′e·tor·ship′,** *n.*

pro·pri·e·tress (prə prī′i tris), *n.* a woman proprietor. Also, **pro·pri·e·trix** (prə prī′i triks). [PROPRIET(O)R + -ESS]

pro·pri·e·ty (prə prī′i tē), *n., pl.* **-ties. 1.** conformity to established standards of good or proper behavior or manners. **2.** appropriateness to the purpose or circumstances; suitability. **3.** rightness or justness. **4. the proprieties,** the conventional standards of proper behavior in polite society; manners: *to observe the proprieties.* **5.** *Obs.* a property. **6.** *Obs.* a peculiarity or characteristic of something. [ME *propriete* < L *proprietās* peculiarity, ownership, equiv. to *propri(us)* PROPER + *-etās,* var. of *-itās* -ITY]
—**Syn. 1.** decency, modesty. See **etiquette. 2.** aptness, fitness, seemliness. **3.** correctness.

proprio-, a learned borrowing from Latin, where it meant "one's own," used in the formation of compound words: *proprioceptive.* [comb. form repr. L *proprius* one's own, special, particular, proper]

pro·pri·o·cep·tive (prō′prē ə sep′tiv), *adj. Physiol.* pertaining to proprioceptors, the stimuli acting upon them, or the nerve impulses initiated by them. [PROPRIO- + (RE)CEPTIVE]

pro·pri·o·cep·tor (prō′prē ə sep′tər), *n. Physiol.* a receptor located in subcutaneous tissues, as muscles, tendons, and joints, that responds to stimuli produced within the body. [PROPRIO- + (RE)CEPTOR]

pro·pri·o mo·tu (prō′pri ō′ mō′tōō; *Eng.* prō′prē ō′ mō′tōō), *Latin.* by one's own volition; on one's own initiative.

prop′ root′, *Bot.* an adventitious root that supports the plant, as the aerial roots of the mangrove tree or of corn.

prop·ter hoc (prōp′ter hōk′; *Eng.* prop′tər hok′), *Latin.* because of this. Cf. **post hoc.**

prop·to·sis (prop tō′sis), *n. Pathol.* **1.** the forward displacement of an organ. **2.** exophthalmos. [< NL < Gk *próptōsis* a fall forward. See PRO-², PTOSIS] —**prop′tosed,** *adj.*

pro·pul·sion (prə pul′shən), *n.* **1.** act of propelling or driving forward or onward. **2.** state of being propelled. **3.** a means of propelling; propelling force, impulse, etc. [< L *prōpuls(us)* (ptp. of *prōpellere* to PROPEL) + -ION] —**pro·pul·sive** (prə pul′siv), **pro·pul′so·ry,** *adj.*

prop′ wash′, *Informal.* See **propeller wash.**

pro·pyl (prō′pil), *adj. Chem.* containing a propyl group. [PROP(IONIC) + -YL]

prop·y·lae·a (prop′ə lē′ə), *n.* **1.** pl. of **propylaeum. 2.** (*construed as sing.*) propylaeum.

prop·y·lae·um (prop′ə lē′əm), *n., pl.* **-lae·a** (-lē′ə). a vestibule or entrance to a temple area or other enclosure, esp. when elaborate or of architectural importance. Also, **prop·y·lon** (prop′ə lon′). [< L < Gk *propýlaion* gateway, neut. of *propýlaios* before the gate, equiv. to *pro-* PRO-² + *pýl(ē)* gate + *-aios* adj. suffix]

pro′pyl al′cohol, *Chem.* a colorless, water-soluble liquid, $CH_3CH_2CH_2OH$, used chiefly in organic synthesis and as a solvent.

pro′pyl al′dehyde, *Chem.* propionaldehyde.

pro·pyl·ene (prō′pə lēn′), *Chem.* —*adj.* **1.** containing the propylene group. —*n.* **2.** Also, **propene.** a colorless, flammable gas, $CH_3CH{=}CH_2$, of the olefin series: used chiefly in organic synthesis. [PROPYL + -ENE]

pro′pylene gly′col, *Chem.* a colorless, viscous, hygroscopic liquid, $CH_3CHOHCH_2OH$, used chiefly as a lubricant, as an antifreeze, and as a solvent for fats, oils, waxes, and resins.

pro′pylene group′, *Chem.* the bivalent group, $-CH(CH_3)CH_2-$, derived from propylene or propane. Also called **pro′pylene rad′ical.**

pro′pyl group′, *Chem.* any of two univalent, isomeric groups having the formula C_3H_7-. Also called **pro′pyl rad′ical.** Cf. **isopropyl group.**

pro·pyl·hex·e·drine (prō′pil hek′si drēn′), *n. Pharm.* a colorless, slightly water-soluble liquid, $C_6H_{11}CH_2CH(NHCH_3)CH_3$, used chiefly as an inhalant to produce nasal vasoconstriction. Cf. **Benzedrex Inhaler.** [PROPYL + HEX- + (EPH)EDRINE]

pro·pyl·ic (prō pil′ik), *adj.* of, pertaining to, or characteristic of the propyl group. [PROPYL + -IC]

prop·y·lite (prop′ə līt′), *n. Petrog.* a hydrothermally altered andesite or allied rock containing secondary minerals, as calcite, chlorite, serpentine, or epidote. [PROPYL + -ITE¹]

pro′pyl·phen′yl ac′etate (prō′pəl fen′il, -fē′nil, prō′-), *Chem.* See **phenylpropyl acetate.** [PROPYL + PHENYL]

pro ra·ta (prō rā′tə, rä′-), in proportion; according to a certain rate. [< ML]

pro-ra·ta (prō rā′tə, -rä′-), *adj.* proportionately determined: *a pro-rata share of the author's royalties.*

pro·rate (prō rāt′, prō′rāt′), *v.,* **-rat·ed, -rat·ing.** —*v.i.* **1.** to make an arrangement on a basis of proportional distribution. —*v.t.* **2.** to divide or distribute proportionately. [back formation from PRO RATA] —**pro·rat′a·ble,** *adj.* —**pro·ra′tion,** *n.*

pro re na·ta (prō re nä′tä; *Eng.* prō rē nā′tə), *Latin.* for an unforeseen need or contingency. [lit., for a thing born]

pro·rogue (prō rōg′), *v.t.,* **-rogued, -ro·guing. 1.** to discontinue a session of (the British Parliament or a similar body). **2.** to defer; postpone. [late ME *proroge* < L *prōrog(āre)* (to) prolong, protract, defer, lit., to ask publicly, equiv. to *prō-* PRO-¹ + *rogāre* to ask, propose] —**pro·ro·ga·tion** (prō′rə gā′shən), *n.*
—**Syn. 1.** suspend.

Pror·sa (prôr′sə), *n.* Antevorta.

pros., 1. proscenium. **2.** prosody.

pro·sa·ic (prō zā′ik), *adj.* **1.** commonplace or dull; matter-of-fact or unimaginative: *the prosaic type of mind.* **2.** of or having the character or form of prose rather than poetry. Also, **pro·sa′i·cal.** [< early ML *prōsaic(us).* See PROSE, -IC] —**pro·sa′i·cal·ly,** *adv.* —**pro·sa′ic·ness,** *n.*
—**Syn. 1.** vapid, humdrum, tedious, tiresome, uninteresting.

pro·sa·ism (prō zā′iz əm), *n.* **1.** prosaic character or style. **2.** a prosaic expression. Also, **pro·sa·i·cism** (prō-zā′i siz′əm). [< F *prosaïsme* < L *prōsa* PROSE; see -ISM]

pro·sa·ist (prō zā′ist), *n.* **1.** a person who writes prose. **2.** a prosaic, dull, or commonplace person. [< L *prōsa* PROSE + -IST]

Pros. Atty., prosecuting attorney.

pro·sce·ni·um (prō sē′nē əm), *n., pl.* **-ni·a** (-nē ə). *Theat.* **1.** (in the modern theater) **a.** Also called **prosce′nium arch′,** a decorative arch, sometimes including the wall, that separates a stage from the auditorium. **b.** Also called **prosce′nium o′pening.** the opening framed by this arch. *Abbr.:* pros. **2.** (formerly) the forestage. [< L < Gk *proskḗnion* (also LGk: stage curtain), equiv. to *pro-* PRO-² + *skēn(ē)* (see SCENE) + *-ion* neut. n. suffix]

pro·sciut·to (prō shōō′tō; *It.* prô shōōt′tô), *n.* spiced ham, often smoked, that has been cured by drying, always sliced paper-thin for serving. [< It: ham]

Pros·clys·ti·us (pros klis′tē əs), *n. Class. Myth.* an epithet of Poseidon, meaning "flooder."

pro·scribe (prō skrīb′), *v.t.,* **-scribed, -scrib·ing. 1.** to denounce or condemn (a thing) as dangerous or harmful; prohibit. **2.** to put outside the protection of the law; outlaw. **3.** to banish or exile. **4.** to announce the name of (a person) as condemned to death and subject to confiscation of property: *Roman rulers proscribed their enemies.* [< L *prōscrīb(ere)* (to) publish in writing, confiscate, outlaw. See PRO-¹, PRESCRIBE] —**pro·scrib′a·ble,** *adj.* —**pro·scrib′er,** *n.*

pro·scrip·tion (prō skrip′shən), *n.* **1.** act of proscribing. **2.** state of being proscribed. **3.** outlawry, interdiction, or prohibition. [ME *proscripcioun* < L *prōscrīptiōn-* (s. of *prōscrīptiō*) public notice of confiscation or outlawry, equiv. to *prōscrīpt(us)* (ptp. of *prōscrībere* to PROSCRIBE) + *-iōn-* -ION] —**pro·scrip·tive** (prō-skrip′tiv), *adj.* —**pro·scrip′tive·ly,** *adv.*

prose (prōz), *n., adj., v.,* **prosed, pros·ing.** —*n.* **1.** the ordinary form of spoken or written language, without metrical structure, as distinguished from poetry or verse. **2.** matter-of-fact, commonplace, or dull expression, quality, discourse, etc. **3.** *Liturgy.* a hymn sung after the gradual, originating from a practice of setting words to the jubilatio of the alleluia. —*adj.* **4.** of, in, or pertaining to prose. **5.** commonplace; dull; prosaic. —*v.t.* **6.** to turn into or express in prose. —*v.i.* **7.** to write or talk in a dull, matter-of-fact manner. [ME < MF < L *prōsa* (*ōrātiō*), lit., straightforward (speech), fem. of *prōsus* for *prōrsus,* var. of *prōversus,* ptp. of *prōvertere* to turn forward, equiv. to *prō-* PRO-¹ + *vertere* to turn] —**prose′like′,** *adj.*

pro·sect (prō sekt′), *v.t. Med.* to dissect (a cadaver or part) for anatomical demonstration. [back formation from PROSECTOR]

pro·sec·tor (prō sek′tər), *n.* **1.** a person who dissects cadavers for the illustration of anatomical lectures or the like. **2.** a person who performs autopsies to establish the cause of death or the nature and seat of disease. **3.** a person who performs a preliminary gross dissection prior to further dissection and study by a superior. [< LL: anatomist, lit., one who cuts in public (or beforehand), equiv. to L *prōsect(us)* (ptp. of *prōsecāre* to cut out (body organs) in public sacrifice) + *-or* -OR²] —**pro·sec·to·ri·al** (prō′sek tōr′ē əl, -tôr′-), *adj.* —**pro·sec′tor·ship′,** *n.*

pros·e·cute (pros′ə kyōōt′), *v.,* **-cut·ed, -cut·ing.** —*v.t.* **1.** *Law.* **a.** to institute legal proceedings against (a person). **b.** to seek to enforce or obtain by legal process. **c.** to conduct criminal proceedings in court against. **2.** to follow up or carry forward something undertaken or begun, usually to its completion: *to prosecute a war.* **3.** to carry on or practice. —*v.i.* **4.** *Law.* **a.** to institute and carry on a legal prosecution. **b.** to act as prosecutor. [late ME: to follow up, go on with < L *prōsecūt(us),* ptp. of *prōsequī* to pursue, proceed with, equiv. to *prō-* PRO-¹ + *sequī* to follow] —**pros′e·cut′a·ble,** *adj.*

pros′ecuting attor′ney, *U.S.* (in some States) a local prosecutor for a county or district.

pros·e·cu·tion (pros′ə kyōō′shən), *n.* **1.** *Law.* **a.** the institution and carrying on of legal proceedings against a person. **b.** the body of officials by whom such proceedings are instituted and carried on. **2.** the following up of something undertaken or begun, usually to its completion. [< LL *prōsecūtiōn-* (s. of *prōsecūtiō*) a following up. See PROSECUTE, -ION]

pros·e·cu·tor (pros′ə kyōō′tər), *n.* **1.** *Law.* **a.** a person who institutes and carries on legal proceedings in a court of justice, esp. in a criminal court. **b.** a public prosecutor or prosecuting attorney. **2.** a person who prosecutes. [< ML, LL: pursuer. See PROSECUTE, -OR²]

Prose′ Ed′da. See under **Edda.**

pros·e·lyte (pros′ə līt′), *n., v.,* **-lyt·ed, -lyt·ing.** —*n.* **1.** a person who has changed from one opinion, religious belief, sect, or the like, to another; convert. —*v.i., v.t.* **2.** to convert as a proselyte. [ME < LL *prosēlyt(us)* < Gk *prosḗlytos* newcomer, proselyte, equiv. to *prosēl-uth-* (s. of *proserchesthai* to approach) + *-os* n. suffix] —**pros′e·lyt′er,** *n.*
—**Syn. 1.** neophyte, disciple.

pros·e·lyt·ise (pros′ə li tīz′, -lī-), *v.t., v.i.,* **-ised, -is·ing.** *Chiefly Brit.* proselytize. —**pros′e·lyt·i·sa′tion,** *n.* —**pros′e·lyt·is′er,** *n.*

pros·e·lyt·ism (pros′ə li tiz′əm, -lī-), *n.* **1.** act or fact of becoming a proselyte; conversion. **2.** state or condition of a proselyte. **3.** practice of making proselytes. [PROSELYTE + -ISM] —**pros·e·lyt·i·cal** (pros′ə lit′i-kəl), *adj.*

pros·e·lyt·ize (pros′ə li tīz′, -lī-), *v.t., v.i.,* **-ized, -iz·ing.** to proselyte. Also, *esp. Brit.,* **proselytise.** [PROSELYTE + -IZE] —**pros·e·lyt·is·tic** (pros′ə li tis′tik, -lī-), *adj.* —**pros′e·lyt·i·za′tion,** *n.* —**pros′e·lyt·iz′er,** *n.*

pros·en·ceph·a·lon (pros′en sef′ə lon′), *n., pl.* **-las, -la** (-lə). *Anat.* the forebrain. [< NL < Gk *prós(ō)* forward + *enképhalon* ENCEPHALON] —**pros·en·ce·phal·ic** (pros′en sə fal′ik), *adj.*

pros·en·chy·ma (pros eng′kə mə), *n. Bot.* the tissue characteristic of the woody and bast portions of plants, consisting typically of long, narrow cells with pointed ends. [< NL < Gk *pros-* toward, to + *énchyma* infusion; modeled on *parenchyma*] —**pros·en·chym·a·tous** (pros′eng kim′ə təs), *adj.*

prose′ po′em, a composition written as prose but having the concentrated, rhythmic, figurative language characteristic of poetry.

pros·er (prō′zər), *n.* **1.** a person who talks or writes in prose. **2.** a person who talks or writes in a dull or tedious fashion. [PROSE + -ER¹]

Pro·ser·pi·na (prō sûr′pə nə), *n.* **1.** Also, **Pro·ser·pi·ne** (prō sûr′pə nē). Persephone. **2.** a girl's given name.

pro·sim·i·an (prō sim′ē ən), *adj.* **1.** belonging or pertaining to the *Prosimii,* a suborder of primates including the lemurs and lorises. —*n.* **2.** a prosimian animal. [< NL *Prosimi(ī)* lemuroids + -AN. See PRO-¹, SIMIAN]

pro·sit (prō′sit; *Eng.* prō′sit), *interj. Latin.* (used esp. by Germans and Austrians as a toast) may it do good.

pros·ko·mi·de (prôs kô′mē thē′; *Eng.* pros′kə mīd′), *n. Gk. Orth. Ch.* prothesis (def. 2a). [< Gk *proskomidḗ* oblation, equiv. to *pros-* toward + *komidḗ* conveyance, a bringing to a place; cf. *komízein* to provide, bring]

pro·slav·er·y (prō slā′və rē), *adj.* **1.** favoring slavery. **2.** *U.S. Hist.* favoring the continuance of the institution of Negro slavery, or opposed to interference with it. —*n.* **3.** the favoring or support of slavery. [PRO-¹ + SLAVERY] —**pro·slav′er,** *n.* —**pro·slav′er·y·ism,** *n.*

pros·o·dem·ic (pros′ə dem′ik), *adj.* noting or pertaining to a disease that is spread by means of personal contagion, as opposed to such infection transmitted by milk, water, or the like. [< Gk *prósō* forward + (EN)-DEMIC]

pros·o·dist (pros′ə dist), *n.* an expert in prosody. [PROSOD(Y) + -IST]

pros·o·dy (pros′ə dē), *n.* **1.** the science or study of poetic meters and versification. **2.** a particular or distinctive system of metrics and versification: *Milton's prosody.* **3.** *Ling.* the stress and intonation patterns of an utterance. [late ME < L *prosōdia* < Gk *prosōidía* tone or accent, modulation of voice, song sung to music, equiv. to *prós* toward + *ōidḗ* ODE + *-ia* -Y³] —**pro·sod·ic** (prə sod′ik), **pro·sod′i·cal,** *adj.*

pro·so·po·poe·ia (prō sō′pə pē′ə), *n. Rhet.* **1.** personification, as of inanimate things. **2.** a representation of an imaginary, absent, or deceased person as speaking or acting. Also, **pro·so′po·pe′ia.** [< L *prosōpopoeia* < Gk *prosōpopoiía* personification, equiv. to *prósōpo(n)* face, person + *poi(eîn)* (to) make + *-ia* -IA] —**pro·so′po·poe′ial, pro·so′po·pe′ial,** *adj.*

pros·o·pyle (pros′ə pīl′), *n.* (in sponges) a pore through which water is drawn from the outside into one of the saclike chambers formed by the evagination of the body wall. Cf. **apopyle.** [< Gk *prósō* forward + *pýlē* gate]

pros·pect (pros′pekt), *n.* **1.** Usually, **prospects. a.** an apparent probability of advancement, success, profit, etc. **b.** the outlook for the future: *good business prospects.* **2.** anticipation; expectation; a looking forward. **3.** something in view as a source of profit. **4.** a potential or likely customer, client, etc. **5.** a potential or likely candidate. **6.** a view, esp. of scenery; potential or likely candidate. **7.** outlook or view over a region or in a particular direction. **8.** a mental view or survey, as of a subject or situation. **9.** *Mining.* **a.** an apparent indication

pro′-Pres·by·te′ri·an, *adj., n.*
pro·priv′i·lege, *adj.*
pro·prof′it, *adj.*
pro-Prot′es·tant, *adj., n.*
pro-Prus′sian, *adj., n.*
pro′pub·li·ca′tion, *adj.*
pro′pub·lic′i·ty, *adj.*
pro·pun′ish·ment, *adj.*
pro-Qua′ker, *adj.*
pro·rac′ing, *adj.*
pro·rail′road, *adj.*
pro·re′al·ism, *n.*
pro·re′al·ist, *adj., n.*
pro′re·al·is′tic, *adj.*
pro′re·al′i·ty, *n.*
pro·reb′el, *adj.*
pro′rec·on·cil′i·a′tion, *adj.*
pro′re·duc′tion, *adj.*
pro′re·form′, *adj.*
pro′ref·u·gee′, *adj.*
pro-Ren′ais·sance′, *adj.*
pro′re·pub′li·can, *adj., n.*
pro′re·search′, *adj.*
pro′res·ig·na′tion, *adj.*
pro′res·to·ra′tion, *adj.*
pro′re·stric′tion, *adj.*
pro′re·vi′sion, *adj.*
pro′rev·o·lu′tion, *adj.*
pro′rev·o·lu′tion·ar′y, *adj.*
pro′rev·o·lu′tion·ist, *adj., n.*
pro·rit′u·al, *adj.*
pro′ro·man′tic, *adj.*
pro′ro·man′ti·cism, *n.*
pro′-Ru·ma′ni·an, *adj., n.*
pro-Rus′sian, *adj., n.*
pro′-Scan·di·na′vi·an, *adj.*
pro′scho·las′tic, *adj.*
pro′scho·las′ti·cism, *n.*
pro·sci′ence, *adj.*
pro′sci·en·tif′ic, *adj.*
pro-Scrip′tur·al, *adj.*
pro-Scrip′ture, *adj.*
pro·se′cre·cy, *adj.*
pro·slave′, *adj.*
pro′-So·ma′li·a, *adj.*
pro-South′, *adj.*
pro-South′ern, *adj.*
pro-So′vi·et, *adj.*
pro-Spain′, *adj.*
pro-Span′ish, *adj.*

of ore or native metal. **b.** a spot giving such indications. **c.** workings, or an excavation, in a mine. **10.** *Archaic.* sight; range of vision. **11.** **in prospect,** under consideration; expected; in view: *He had no other alternative in prospect.* —*v.t.* **12.** to search or explore (a region), as for gold. **13.** to work (a mine or claim) experimentally in order to test its value. —*v.i.* **14.** to search or explore a region for gold or the like. [late ME *prospecte* < L *prōspect(us)* outlook, view. See PROSPECTUS] —**pros′pect·less,** *adj.* —**pros·pec·tor** (pros′pek tər, prə spek′tər), *n.*
—**Syn. 7, 8.** perspective.

pro·spec·tive (prə spek′tiv), *adj.* **1.** of or in the future: *prospective earnings.* **2.** potential, likely, or expected: *a prospective partner.* [< LL *prōspectīv(us).* See PROSPECTUS, -IVE] —**pro·spec′tive·ly,** *adv.* —**pro·spec′tive·ness,** *n.*

Pros′pect Park′, **1.** a town in SE Pennsylvania. 6596 (1960). **2.** a town in NE New Jersey. 5201 (1960).

pro·spec·tus (prə spek′təs), *n., pl.* **-tus·es.** a report or statement which describes or advertises a forthcoming literary work, a flotation of stock, etc. [< L: outlook, view, u-stem deriv. of *prōspectus,* ptp. of *prōspicere* to look forward, equiv. to *prō-* PRO-¹ + *-spicere,* comb. form of *specere* to look]

pros·per (pros′pər), *v.i.* **1.** to be successful or fortunate, esp. in financial respects; thrive; flourish. —*v.t.* **2.** to make successful or fortunate. [late ME < L *prosper(āre)* (to) make happy. See PROSPEROUS]
—**Syn. 1.** See **succeed.** —**Ant. 1.** fail.

pros·per·i·ty (pro sper′i tē), *n., pl.* **-ties.** **1.** successful, flourishing, or thriving condition, esp. in financial respects; good fortune. **2.** **prosperities,** prosperous circumstances. [ME *prosperite* < OF < L *prosperitās.* See PROSPEROUS, -ITY]

Pros·per·o (pros′pə rō′), *n.* (in Shakespeare's *The Tempest*) the exiled Duke of Milan, who is a magician.

pros·per·ous (pros′pər əs), *adj.* **1.** having or characterized by good fortune; flourishing; successful: *a prosperous business.* **2.** well-to-do or well-off: *a prosperous family.* **3.** favorable or propitious. [late ME < L *prosperus,* var. of *prosper* favorable, lit., according to hope, equiv. to *pro-* PRO-¹ + *-sper,* akin to *spēs* hope] —**pros′per·ous·ly,** *adv.* —**pros′per·ous·ness,** *n.*
—**Syn. 1.** thriving. **2.** wealthy, rich. **3.** fortunate, lucky, auspicious.

pros·pho·ra (pros′fə rä′, -fər ə), *n.* *Eastern Ch.* antidoron. [< Gk: an offering, lit., a bringing to, applying, equiv. to *pros-* toward + *-phor-* (s. of *phérein* to bring) + *-a* nom. fem. n. suffix]

pros·pho·ron (*Gk.* prôs′fô rôn; *Eng.* pros′fə ron′, -fər ən), *n.* *Eastern Ch.* an uncut loaf of altar bread before it is consecrated. [< Gk, n. use of neut. of *prósphoros* (adj.). See PROSPHORA]

pross (pros), *Scot. and North Eng.* —*n.* **1.** prose. —*v.i.* **2.** to exhibit pride or haughtiness; put on airs. [? short for PROSPEROUS] —**pross′er,** *n.* —**pross′y,** *adj.*

Pros·ser (pros′ər), *n.* a town in S Washington. 2763 (1960).

pro·stas (prō′stas), *n., pl.* **pro·sta·des** (prō stā′dēz). **1.** (in classical architecture) an antechamber or vestibule. **2.** (in a classical temple) the area included between parastades. [< Gk: lit., that which stands before]

pro·sta·sis (prō stā′sis), *n., pl.* **-ses** (-sēz). (in a classical temple) a pronaos or prostas before a cella. [< Gk; see PRO-², STASIS]

prostat-, a combining form of **prostate:** *prostatitis.*

pros·tate (pros′tāt), *Anat.* —*adj.* **1.** Also, **pro·stat·ic** (prō stat′ik). of or pertaining to the prostate gland. —*n.* **2.** See **prostate gland.** [< ML *prostata* < Gk *prostátēs* one standing before. See PRO-², -STAT]

pros·ta·tec·to·my (pros′tə tek′tə mē), *n., pl.* **-mies.** *Surg.* excision of part or all of the prostate gland. [PROSTAT- + -ECTOMY]

pros′tate gland′, *Anat.* the muscular, glandular organ which surrounds the urethra of males at the base of the bladder.

pros·ta·ti·tis (pros′tə tī′tis), *n.* *Pathol.* inflammation of the prostate gland. [PROSTAT- + -ITIS]

pro·ster·num (prō stûr′nəm), *n., pl.* **-na** (-nə), **-nums.** the ventral sclerite of the prothorax of an insect. [< NL; see PRO-¹, STERNUM] —**pro·ster′nal,** *adj.*

pros·the·sis (pros′thi sis *or, for 1,* pros thē′sis), *n., pl.* **-ses** (-sēz′ *or, for 1,* -sēz). **1.** Also, **prothesis.** *Surg.* **a.** the addition of an artificial part to supply a defect of the body. **b.** the artificial part added. **2.** *Gram., Prosody.* the addition of one or more sounds or syllables to a word or line of verse, esp. at the beginning. [< LL < Gk *prósthesis* a putting to, addition, equiv. to *prós* to + *thésis* a placing; see THESIS] —**pros·thet·ic** (pros thet′ik), *adj.* —**pros·thet′i·cal·ly,** *adv.*

prosthet′ic den′tistry, prosthodontics.

pros·thet·ics (pros thet′iks), *n.* (*construed as sing. or pl.*) the branch of surgery or of dentistry that deals with the replacement of missing parts with artificial structures. Cf. **prosthodontics.** [see PROSTHETIC, -ICS]

pros·the·tist (pros′thi tist), *n.* a person skilled in making or fitting prosthetic devices. [PROSTHET(ICS) + -IST]

pros·thi·on (pros′thē on′), *n.* *Craniom.* the most forward projecting point of the anterior surface of the upper jaw, in the midsagittal plane. [< Gk, neut. of *prósthios* frontal, akin to *prósthen* forward] —**pros′thi·on′ic,** *adj.*

pros·tho·don·tics (pros′thə don′tiks), *n.* (*construed as sing.*) the branch of dentistry that deals with the restoration and maintenance of oral function by the replacement of missing teeth and other oral structures by artificial devices. Also, **pros·tho·don·tia** (pros′thə don′shə, -shē ə). [PROSTH(ESIS) + -ODONT + -ICS]

pros·tho·don·tist (pros′thə don′tist), *n.* a specialist in prosthodontics. [PROSTHODONT(ICS) + -IST]

Pro·stig·min (prō stig′min), *n.* *Pharm., Trademark.* neostigmine.

pros·ti·tute (pros′ti to͞ot′, -tyo͞ot′), *n., v.,* **-tut·ed, -tut·ing.** —*n.* **1.** a person, usually a woman, who engages in sexual intercourse for money; whore; harlot. **2.** a person who willingly uses his talent or ability in a base and unworthy way, usually for money. —*v.t.* **3.** to hire (oneself) out as a prostitute. **4.** to put to any base or unworthy use: *to prostitute one's talents.* [< L *prōstitūt(a)* harlot, n. use of fem. of *prōstitūtus,* ptp. of *prōstituere* to expose (for sale), equiv. to *prō-* PRO-¹ + *-stituere,* comb. form of *statuere* to cause to stand; see STATUS] —**pros′ti·tu′tor,** *n.*
—**Syn. 1.** call girl, street walker, courtesan; trollop, strumpet.

pros·ti·tu·tion (pros′ti to͞o′shən, -tyo͞o′-), *n.* **1.** act or practice of engaging in sexual intercourse for money. **2.** base or unworthy use, as of talent or ability. [< LL *prōstitūtiōn-* (s. of *prōstitūtiō*). See PROSTITUTE, -ION]

pro·sto·mi·ate (prō stō′mē āt′), *adj.* having a prostomium. [PROSTOMI(UM) + -ATE¹]

pro·sto·mi·um (prō stō′mē əm), *n., pl.* **-mi·a** (-mē ə). the unsegmented, preoral portion of the head of certain lower invertebrates. [< NL < Gk *prostómion,* lit., little afore-mouth, equiv. to *pro-* PRO-² + *stóm(a)* mouth + *-ion* dim. suffix] —**pro·sto′mi·al,** *adj.*

pro·sto·on (prō stō′on), *n., pl.* **-sto·a** (-stō′ə). (in classical architecture) a portico. [< Gk; see PRO-², STOA]

pros·trate (pros′trāt), *v.,* **-trat·ed, -trat·ing,** *adj.* —*v.t.* **1.** to cast (oneself) face down on the ground in humility, submission, or adoration. **2.** to lay flat, as on the ground. **3.** to throw down level with the ground. **4.** to overthrow, overcome, or reduce to helplessness. **5.** to reduce to physical weakness or exhaustion. —*adj.* **6.** lying flat or at full length, as on the ground. **7.** lying face down on the ground, as in token of humility, submission, or adoration. **8.** overthrown, overcome, or helpless: *a country left prostrate by natural disasters and political ferment.* **9.** physically weak or exhausted. **10.** submissive. **11.** utterly dejected or depressed; disconsolate. **12.** *Bot.* (of a plant or stem) lying flat on the ground. [ME *prostrat* < L *prōstrāt(us),* ptp. of *prōsternere* to throw prone, equiv. to *prō-* PRO-¹ + *sternere* to stretch out] —**pros·tra·tive** (pros′trə tiv), *adj.* —**pros′tra·tor,** *n.*
—**Syn. 6.** prone, supine, recumbent.

pros·tra·tion (pro strā′shən), *n.* **1.** act of prostrating. **2.** state of being prostrated. **3.** extreme mental or emotional depression or dejection: *nervous prostration.* **4.** extreme physical weakness or exhaustion: *heat prostration.* [< LL *prōstrātiōn-* (s. of *prōstrātiō*) a lying prone. See PROSTRATE, -ION]

pro·style (prō′stīl), *Archit.* —*adj.* **1.** (of a classical temple) having a portico on one front. —*n.* **2.** a prostyle building. [< L < Gk *próstyl(os)* (adj.), *próstyl(on),* n. use of neut. of adj., equiv. to *pro-* PRO-² + *stŷlos* pillar]

pros·y (prō′zē), *adj.,* **pros·i·er, pros·i·est.** **1.** of the nature of or resembling prose. **2.** prosaic; dull, tedious, wearisome, or commonplace. [PROSE + -Y¹] —**pros′i·ly,** *adv.* —**pros′i·ness,** *n.*

pro·syl·lo·gism (prō sil′ə jiz′əm), *n.* *Logic.* a syllogism the conclusion of which is used as a premise of another syllogism; any of the syllogisms included in a polysyllogism except the last. Cf. **episyllogism.** [< ML *prosyllogism(us)* < Gk *prosyllogismós.* See PRO-², SYLLOGISM]

prot-, var. of **proto-** before a vowel: *protamine.*

Prot., Protestant.

pro·tac·tin·i·um (prō′tak tin′ē əm), *n.* *Chem.* a radioactive, metallic element. *Symbol:* Pa; *at. no.:* 91. Also, **protoactinium.** [PROT- + ACTINIUM]

pro·tag·o·nist (prō tag′ə nist), *n.* **1.** the leading character or hero of a drama or other literary work. **2.** a spokesman or advocate of an idea, political or social program, etc.; a person who champions a cause. **3.** the leader or principal person in a movement, cause, etc. [< Gk *prōtagōnist(ēs)* actor who plays the first part, lit., first combatant, equiv. to *prô(tos)* first + *agōnistēs* one who contends for a prize, combatant, actor. See PROTO-, ANTAGONIST] —**pro·tag′o·nism,** *n.*

Pro·tag·o·ras (prō tag′ər əs), *n.* **1.** c480–c410 B.C., Greek philosopher. **2.** a crater in the first quadrant of the face of the moon: about 15 miles in diameter. —**Pro·tag·o·re·an** (prō tag′ə rē′ən), *adj.* —**Pro·tag′o·re′an·ism,** *n.*

pro·ta·mine (prō′tə mēn′, -min), *n.* *Biochem.* any of a group of basic, simple proteins that do not coagulate by heat, are soluble in ammonia, and upon hydrolysis form amino acids. [PROT- + AMINE]

prot·an·drous (prō tan′drəs), *adj.* exhibiting or characterized by protandry. Also, **prot·an′dric.** [PROT- + -ANDROUS] —**prot·an′drous·ly,** *adv.*

prot·an·dry (prō tan′drē), *n.* (in a hermaphrodite animal or plant) a condition in which the development of male organs or maturation of their products occurs before the development or maturation of those of the female. Also, **proterandry.** Cf. **protogyny.** [PROTANDR(OUS) + -Y³]

prot·a·nom·a·ly (prōt′ᵊnom′ə lē), *n.* *Ophthalm.* a defect of vision characterized by a diminished response of the retina to red. [PROT- + ANOMALY] —**prot′a·nom′a·lous,** *adj.*

prot·a·nope (prōt′ᵊnōp′), *n.* *Ophthalm.* a person who has protanopia. [back formation from PROTANOPIA]

prot·an·o·pi·a (prōt′ᵊnō′pē ə), *n.* *Ophthalm.* a defect of vision in which the retina fails to respond to red. [< NL; see PROT-, AN-¹, -OPIA] —**prot·a·nop·ic** (prōt′ᵊnop′ik), *adj.*

prot·a·sis (prot′ə sis), *n., pl.* **-ses** (-sēz′). **1.** the clause expressing the condition in a conditional sentence in English, usually beginning with *if.* Cf. **apodosis.** **2.** the first part of an ancient drama, in which the characters are introduced and the subject is proposed. Cf. **catastasis, catastrophe** (def. 3), **epitasis.** **3.** (in Aristotelian logic) a proposition, esp. one used as a premise in a syllogism. [< LL < Gk *prótasis* proposition, lit., a stretching forward, equiv. to *pro-* PRO-² + *tásis* a stretching (*ta-,* verbid s. of *teínein* to stretch, + *-sis* -SIS)]

pro·te·an (prō′tē ən, prō tē′-), *adj.* **1.** readily assuming different forms or characters; extremely variable. **2.** *Zool.* changeable in shape or form, as an amoeba. **3.** (of an actor) versatile; able to play many kinds of roles. **4.** (*cap.*) of, pertaining to, or suggestive of Proteus. [PROTE(US) + -AN]

pro·te·ase (prō′tē ās′), *n.* *Biochem.* any enzyme that acts upon proteins. [PROTE(IN) + -ASE]

pro·tect (prə tekt′), *v.t.* **1.** to defend or guard from attack, invasion, loss, annoyance, insult, etc.; cover or shield from injury or danger. **2.** *Econ.* to guard (the industry or an industry of a nation) from foreign competition by imposing import duties. **3.** *Com.* to provide funds for the payment of (a draft, note, etc.). —*v.i.* **4.** to provide, or be capable of providing, protection: *a floor wax that protects as well as shines.* [< L *prōtēct(us),* ptp. of *prōtegere* to cover in front, equiv. to *pro-* PRO-¹ + *tegere* to cover; akin to TOGA, THATCH]
—**Syn. 1.** screen, shelter. See **defend.** —**Ant. 1.** attack.

pro·tect·ing (prə tek′ting), *adj.* providing protection or shelter. [PROTECT + -ING²] —**pro·tect′ing·ly,** *adv.* —**pro·tect′ing·ness,** *n.*

pro·tec·tion (prə tek′shən), *n.* **1.** act of protecting; state of being protected; preservation from injury or harm. **2.** a thing, person, or group that protects: *This vaccine is a protection against disease.* **3.** patronage. **4.** *Insurance.* coverage (def. 1). **5.** *Informal.* **a.** money paid to racketeers for a guarantee against threatened violence. **b.** bribe money paid to the police, politicians, or other authorities for overlooking criminal activity. **6.** *Econ.* **a.** Also called **protective system.** the system of fostering or developing home industries by protecting them from foreign competition through duties imposed on importations from foreign countries. **b.** Also called **protectionism.** the theory or practice of this system. **7.** a document which assures safety from harm, delay, or the like, for the person, persons, or property specified in it. **8.** *Archaic.* a document given by the U.S. customs authorities to a seaman traveling abroad certifying that the holder is a citizen of the United States. [ME *proteccio(u)n* < LL *prōtectiōn-* (s. of *prōtectiō*) a covering in front. See PROTECT, -ION] —**pro·tec′tion·al,** *adj.*
—**Syn. 1.** security, refuge, safety. **2.** guard, defense, shield, bulwark. See **cover.** **3.** aegis, sponsorship. **7.** pass, permit.

pro·tec·tion·ism (prə tek′shə niz′əm), *n.* protection (def. 6b). [PROTECTION + -ISM] —**pro·tec′tion·ist,** *n.*

pro·tec·tive (prə tek′tiv), *adj.* **1.** having the quality or function of protecting: *a protective covering.* **2.** tending to protect. **3.** of, pertaining to, or designed for economic protection. [PROTECT + -IVE] —**pro·tec′tive·ly,** *adv.* —**pro·tec′tive·ness,** *n.*

protec′tive col′loid, *Physical Chem.* a lyophilic colloid added to a lyophobic sol to lessen its sensitivity to the precipitating effect of an electrolyte.

protec′tive colora′tion, coloration or anything likened to it that is assumed, organically or otherwise, so as to eliminate or reduce visibility or conspicuousness.

protec′tive slope′, a slope given to a yard or the like to drain surface water away from a building.

protec′tive sys′tem, *Econ.* protection (def. 6a).

protec′tive tar′iff, a tariff for the protection of domestic production, rather than for revenue.

pro·tec·tor (prə tek′tər), *n.* **1.** one who or that which protects; defender; guardian. **2.** *Eng. Hist.* **a.** a person in charge of the kingdom during the sovereign's minority, incapacity, or absence. **b.** (*cap.*) Also called **Lord Protector.** the title of the head of the government during the period of the Protectorate, held by Oliver Cromwell (1653–58) and by Richard Cromwell, his son (1658–59). Also, *referring to a woman,* **pro·tec·tress** (prə tek′tris). [< LL (see PROTECT, -OR²); r. ME *protectour* < MF] —**pro·tec′tor·al,** *adj.* —**pro·tec′tor·less,** *adj.* —**pro·tec′tor·ship′,** *n.*

pro·tec·tor·ate (prə tek′tər it), *n.* **1.** the relation of a strong state toward a weaker state or territory which it protects and partly controls. **2.** a state or territory so protected. **3.** the office or position, or the term of office, of a protector. **4.** the government of a protector. **5.** (*cap.*) *Eng. Hist.* the period (1653–59) during which Oliver and Richard Cromwell held the title of Lord Protector, sometimes extended to include the period of the restoration of the Rump Parliament (1659–60). [PROTECTOR + -ATE¹]

pro·tec·to·ry (prə tek′tə rē), *n., pl.* **-ries.** an institution for the care of destitute or delinquent children. [PROTECT + -ORY²]

pro·té·gé (prō′tə zhā′, prō′tə zhā′), *n.* a person under the patronage, protection, or care of someone interested in his career or welfare. Also, *referring to a woman,* **pro′té·gée′.** [< F, n. use of ptp. of *protéger* to protect < L *prōtegere.* See PROTECT]

pro·te·i·form (prō tē′ə fôrm′), *adj.* protean (def. 3). [PROTE(US) + -I- + -FORM]

pro·tein (prō′tēn, -tē in), *n.* **1.** *Biochem.* any of a group of nitrogenous organic compounds of high molecular weight, synthesized by plants and animals, that upon hydrolysis by enzymes yield amino acids, and that in animal metabolism are required for all life processes. **2.** (formerly) a substance thought to be the essential nitrogenous component of all organic bodies. —*adj.* **3.** *Biochem.* of the nature of or containing protein. Also, **pro·teid** (prō′tēd, -tē id). [< G *Protein* < Gk *prōtei(os)* primary + G *-in* -IN²; r. *proteine* < F] —**pro·tein·a·ceous** (prō′tē nā′shəs, -tē i nā′-), **pro·tein′ic, pro·tei′nous,** *adj.*

pro·tein·ase (prō′tē nās′, -tē i-), *n.* *Biochem.* any of a group of enzymes that are capable of hydrolyzing proteins. [PROTEIN + -ASE]

pro tem (prō tem′). See **pro tempore.**

pro tem·po·re (prō tem′pō re′; *Eng.* prō tem′pə rē′), *Latin.* **1.** temporarily; for the time being. **2.** temporary.

pro·te·ol·y·sis (prō′tē ol′i sis), *n.* *Biochem.* the hydrolysis, or breaking down, of proteins into simpler compounds, as in digestion. [*proteo-* (comb. form repr. PROTEIN) + -LYSIS] —**pro·te·o·lyt·ic** (prō′tē ə lit′ik), *adj.*

pro·te·ose (prō′tē ōs′), *n.* *Biochem.* any of a class of soluble compounds derived from proteins by the action of the gastric juices, pancreatic juices, etc. [PROTE(IN) + -OSE²]

prot·er·an·drous (prot′ə ran′drəs, prō′tə-), *adj.* protandrous. Also, **prot′er·an′dric.** —**prot′er·an′drous·ly,** *adv.* —**prot′er·an′drous·ness,** *n.*

pro-strike′, *adj.*
pro′sub·scrip′tion, *adj.*
pro′sub·sti·tu′tion, *adj.*
pro′-Su·da·nese′, *adj., n., pl.* **-nese.**
pro·suf′frage, *adj.*
pro′su·per·vi′sion, *adj.*
pro′sup·port′, *adj.*
pro·sur′gi·cal, *adj.*
pro′sur·ren′der, *adj.*
pro-Swe′den, *adj.*
pro-Swed′ish, *adj.*
pro-Swiss′, *adj.*
pro-Switz′er·land, *adj.*
pro·syn′di·cal·ism, *n.*
pro·syn′di·cal·ist, *n., adj.*
pro-Syr′i·an, *adj.*
pro·tar′iff, *adj.*
pro·tax′, *adj.*
pro′tax·a′tion, *adj.*

prot·er·an·dry (prot′ə ran′drē, prō′tə-), *n.* protandry.

protero-, a learned borrowing from Greek meaning "earlier," "before," "former," used in the formation of compound words: *proterotype.* Also, *esp. before a vowel,* **proter-.** Cf. **proto-.** [< Gk, comb. form repr. *próteros,* comp. formed from *pró;* see PRO-[2]]

prot·e·rog·y·nous (prot′ə roj′ə nəs), *adj.* protogynous.

prot·e·rog·y·ny (prot′ə roj′ə nē), *n.* protogyny.

prot·er·o·type (prot′ər ə tīp′, prō′tər-), *n.* a primary type. [PROTERO- + TYPE]

Prot·er·o·zo·ic (prot′ər ə zō′ik, prō′tər-), *Geol.* —*adj.* **1.** Algonkian (def. 1). **2.** (in some classification systems) Precambrian. —*n.* **3.** Algonkian (def. 3). **4.** (in some classification systems) the Precambrian era. See table under **era.** [PROTERO- + ZO- + -IC]

Pro·tes·i·la·us (prō tes′ə lā′əs), *n. Class. Myth.* a son of Iphiclus and brother of Podarces who, in accordance with a prophecy, was killed when he became the first to step on Trojan ground at the landing of the Greek forces.

pro·test (*n.* prō′test; *v.* prə test′), *n.* **1.** an expression or declaration of objection, disapproval, or dissent, often in opposition to something a person is powerless to prevent or avoid: *a protest against increased taxation.* **2.** *Com.* **a.** a formal notarial certificate attesting the fact that a check, note, or bill of exchange has been presented for acceptance or payment and that it has been refused. **b.** the action taken to fix the liability for a dishonored bill of exchange or note. **3.** *Law.* **a.** (upon one's payment of a tax or other state or city exaction) a formal statement disputing the legality of the demand. **b.** a written and attested declaration made by the master of a ship stating the circumstances under which some damage has happened to the ship or cargo, or other circumstances involving the liability of the officers, crew, etc. **4.** *Sports.* a formal objection or complaint made to an official: *to lodge a protest with the league president; to play under protest.* [ME < ML *protest(um)* declaration] —*v.i.* **5.** to give formal expression to objection or disapproval; remonstrate. **6.** to make solemn or earnest declaration. —*v.t.* **7.** to make a protest or remonstrance against; object to. **8.** to say in protest or remonstrance. **9.** to declare solemnly or earnestly; affirm; assert. **10.** to make a formal declaration of the nonacceptance or nonpayment of (a bill of exchange or note). **11.** *Obs.* to call to witness. [late ME *protest(e)* (< F *protester*) < L *prōtestārī* to declare publicly, equiv. to *pro-* PRO-[1] + *testārī* to testify, deriv. of *testis* a witness] —**pro·test′a·ble,** *adj.* —**pro·test′er,** *n.* —**pro·test′ing·ly,** *adv.* —**pro·test′ive,** *adj.*
—**Syn. 5.** complain. **6.** asseverate, avow, aver, attest. See **declare.** —**Ant. 1.** approval. **5.** approve.

Prot·es·tant (prot′i stənt), *n.* **1.** any Western Christian not an adherent of the Roman Catholic Church. **2.** an adherent of any of those Christian bodies that separated from the Church of Rome during the Reformation, or of any group descended from them. **3.** (originally) any of the German princes who protested against the decision of the Diet of Speyer in 1529, which had denounced the Reformation. **4.** (*l.c.*) a person who protests. —*adj.* **5.** belonging or pertaining to Protestants or their religion. **6.** (*l.c.*) protesting. [sing. of *protestants* for L *prōtestantēs,* pl. of prp. of *prōtestārī* to bear public witness. See PROTEST, -ANT]

Prot′estant Epis′copal Church′, the church in the U.S. that inherited the doctrine, discipline, and forms of worship of the Church of England from which it became an independent body within the Anglican communion.

Prot·es·tant·ism (prot′i stən tiz′əm), *n.* **1.** the religion of Protestants. **2.** the Protestant churches collectively. **3.** adherence to Protestant principles. [PROTESTANT + -ISM]

Prot′estant Reforma′tion, reformation (def. 2).

prot·es·ta·tion (prot′i stā′shən, prō′ti-), *n.* **1.** act of protesting or affirming. **2.** a solemn or earnest declaration or affirmation. **3.** formal expression or declaration of objection, dissent, or disapproval; protest. [ME *protestacio(u)n* < LL *prōtestātiōn-* (s. of *prōtestātiō*) declaration. See PROTEST, -ATION]

pro′test flag′, a flag hoisted by a racing yacht to advise the judges of a violation of the rules by another yacht.

Pro·te·us (prō′tē əs, -tyo͞os), *n.* **1.** *Class. Myth.* a sea god, son of Oceanus and Tethys, noted for his ability to assume different forms and to prophesy. **2.** a king of Egypt and the husband of Psamathe. During the Trojan War, in Euripides' version of the story, Proteus kept Helen in Egypt while a phantom Helen joined Paris. **3.** a person or thing that readily changes appearance, character, principles, etc. **4.** (*l.c.*) *Bacteriol.* any of several rod-shaped, aerobic bacteria of the genus *Proteus,* sometimes found as pathogens in the gastrointestinal and genitourinary tracts of man.

pro·tha·la·mi·on (prō′thə lā′mē on′, -ən), *n., pl.* **-mi·a** (-mē ə). a song or poem written to celebrate a marriage. [PRO-[2] + (EPI)THALAMION; coined by Edmund Spenser]

pro·tha·la·mi·um (prō′thə lā′mē əm), *n., pl.* **-mi·a** (-mē ə). prothalamion.

pro·thal·li·um (prō thal′ē əm), *n., pl.* **-thal·li·a** (-thal′ē ə). **1.** *Bot.* the gametophyte of ferns and related plants. **2.** the analogous rudimentary gametophyte of seed-bearing plants. [< NL < Gk *pro-* PRO-[2] + *thallion,* dim. of *thallós* young shoot] —**pro·thal′li·al, pro·thal′lic, pro·thal·line** (prō thal′ēn, -īn), *adj.* —**pro·thal′loid,** *adj.*

pro·thal·lus (prō thal′əs), *n., pl.* **-thal·li** (-thal′ī). *Bot.* prothallium. [< NL; see PRO-, THALLUS]

proth·e·sis (proth′i sis), *n., pl.* **-ses** (-sēz′) for 2b, c, 3. **1.** the addition of a sound or syllable at the beginning of a word, as in Spanish *escala* "ladder" from Latin *scala.* **2.** *Eastern Ch.* **a.** Also called **proskomide.** the preparation and preliminary oblation of the Eucharistic elements. **b.** the table on which this is done. **c.** the part of the sanctuary or bema where this table stands. **3.** (*often cap.*) *Gk. Antiq.* a representation of a dead person lying in state: *The prothesis was a common theme on geometric vases.* [< LL < Gk *próthesis* a putting before. See PRO-[2], THESIS] —**pro·thet·ic** (prə thet′ik), *adj.* —**pro·thet′i·cal·ly,** *adv.*

Pro·tho·ë·nor (prō′thō ē′nôr), *n.* (in the *Iliad*) a Boeotian leader in the Trojan War.

pro·thon·o·tar·y (prō thon′ə ter′ē, prō′thə nō′tə rē), *n., pl.* **-tar·ies. 1.** a chief clerk or official in certain courts of law. **2.** *Rom. Cath. Ch.* **a.** any of the seven members of the College of Prothonotaries Apostolic, charged chiefly with the registry of pontifical acts and canonizations. **b.** an honorary title for certain other prelates. **3.** *Gk. Orth. Ch.* the chief secretary of the patriarch of Constantinople. Also, **protonotary.** [< ML *prōthonotāri(us),* LL *prōtonotārius* < Gk *prōtonotários.* See PROTO-, NOTARY] —**pro·thon·o·tar·i·al** (prō thon′ə târ′ē əl), *adj.*

prothon′otary war′bler, a wood warbler, *Protonotaria citrea,* of the eastern U.S., having an orange-yellow head and underparts, and bluish-gray wings and tail.

pro·tho·rax (prō thōr′aks, -thôr′-), *n., pl.* **-tho·rax·es, -tho·ra·ces** (-thōr′ə sēz′, -thôr′-). the anterior division of the thorax of an insect, bearing the first pair of legs. [< NL; see PRO-[1], THORAX] —**pro·tho·rac·ic** (prō′thō ras′ik, -thō-), *adj.*

pro·throm·bin (prō throm′bin), *n. Biochem.* one of the clotting factors in the blood, believed to be the protein changed by the body into thrombin. Also called **thrombogen.** [PRO-[1] + THROMBIN]

pro·tist (prō′tist), *n.* any organism of the group Protista. [< NL *Protist(a)* (pl.) < Gk *prṓtist(os)* the very first, superl. of *prôtos* first] —**pro·tis·tan** (prō tis′tən), *adj., n.* —**pro·tis′tic,** *adj.*

Pro·tis·ta (prə tis′tə), *n.pl.* a group of organisms including all the unicellular animals and plants. [< NL; see PROTIST]

pro·tis·tol·o·gy (prō′ti stol′ə jē), *n.* the biology of the Protista. [PROTIST + -O- + -LOGY] —**pro·tis·to·log·i·cal** (prə tis′tᵊloj′i kəl), *adj.* —**pro′tis·tol′o·gist,** *n.*

pro·ti·um (prō′tē əm, -shē əm), *n. Chem.* the common isotope of hydrogen, of atomic weight 1.008. *Symbol:* H[1] [PROT- + -IUM]

proto-, a learned borrowing from Greek meaning "first," "foremost," "earliest form of," used in the formation of compound words (*protomartyr; protolithic; protoplasm*), specialized in chemical terminology to denote the first of a series of compounds, or the one containing the minimum amount of an element. Also, *esp. before a vowel,* **prot-.** [< Gk, comb. form repr. *prôtos,* superl. formed from *pró;* see PRO-[2]]

pro·to·ac·tin·i·um (prō′tō ak tin′ē əm), *n. Chem.* protactinium.

pro·to·chor·date (prō′tō kôr′dāt), *n. Zool.* any of the nonvertebrate chordates, as the tunicates, cephalochordates, and hemichordates. [< NL; see PROTO-, CHORDATE]

pro·to·col (prō′tə kôl′, -kol′, -kōl′), *n.* **1.** the customs and regulations dealing with the ceremonies and etiquette of the diplomatic corps, others at a court or capital, the military, etc. **2.** an original draft, minute, or record from which a document, esp. a treaty, is prepared. **3.** a supplementary international agreement. **4.** an agreement between states. **5.** an annex to a treaty giving data relating to it. **6.** Also called **pro′tocol state′ment, basic proposition, pro′tocol sen′tence.** a statement reporting an observation exactly and without attempting an interpretation. —*v.i.* **7.** to draft or issue a protocol. [earlier *protocoll* < ML *prōtocoll(um)* < LGk *prōtókollon,* orig., a first leaf glued to the front of a manuscript and containing notes as to contents. See PROTO-, COLLOID] —**pro·to·col·ar** (prō′tə kol′ər), **pro′to·col′a·ry, pro′to·col′ic,** *adj.*

pro·to·dea·con (prō′tō dē′kən), *n.* a chief deacon in the Greek Church. [PROTO- + DEACON]

pro·to-Dor·ic (prō′tō dôr′ik, -dor′-), *adj.* of or pertaining to architecture, as in certain Egyptian tombs, supposedly anticipating the Grecian Doric order.

pro·to-E·lam·ite (prō′tō ē′lə mīt′), *n.* the indigenous script of Elam, found on inscriptions and tablets from the fourth millennium B.C.

Pro·to·ge·ni·a (prō′tə jə nī′ə), *n. Class. Myth.* the first woman born after the great flood of Zeus, daughter of Deucalion and Pyrrha. Also, **Pro·to·ge·ne·a** (prō′tə jə nē′ə).

Pro·to·ge·o·met·ric (prō′tō jē′ə me′trik), *adj.* (*sometimes l.c.*) pertaining to or designating a style of vase painting developed in Greece chiefly during the 10th century B.C. and characterized by use of abstract geometrical motifs. Also, **Pro′to·ge′o·met′ric, pro′to·ge′o·met′ric, Pro′to-Ge′o·met′ric.** Cf. **geometric** (def. 4). [PROTO- + GEOMETRIC]

pro·to·gine (prō′tə jin, -jēn′), *n.* a gneissoid granite, occurring chiefly in the Alps. [< F, irreg. < Gk *prōto-* PROTO- + *gī́ne(sthai)* (to) be born or produced]

Pro·to·go·ni·a (prō′tə gə nī′ə), *n. Class. Myth.* a daughter of Erechtheus and Praxithea, who, when her sister Otionia was sacrificed, fulfilled a vow by taking her own life.

pro·to·gy·nous (prō′tə jī′nəs, -gī′-), *adj.* exhibiting or characterized by protogyny. Also, **proterogynous.** [PROTO- + -GYNOUS]

pro·tog·y·ny (prō toj′ə nē), *n.* (in a hermaphrodite animal or plant) a condition in which the development of female organs or maturation of their products occurs before the development or maturation of those of the male. Also, **proterogyny.** Cf. **protandry.** [PROTOGYN(OUS) + -Y[3]]

pro·to·hu·man (prō′tō hyo͞o′mən *or, often,* -yo͞o′-), *adj.* **1.** of, pertaining to, or like the earliest prehistoric men, esp. with reference to primates that had some but not all of the features of a human. —*n.* **2.** a protohuman animal. [PROTO- + HUMAN]

pro·to-I·on·ic (prō′tō ī on′ik), *adj.* of or pertaining to architecture supposedly anticipating the Grecian Ionic order.

pro·to·lan·guage (prō′tō lang′gwij, -lang′-), *n. Ling.* the hypothetically reconstructed or postulated parent form of a language or a group of related languages. [PROTO- + LANGUAGE]

pro·to·lith·ic (prōt′ᵊlith′ik), *adj. Anthropol.* noting or pertaining to stone implements selected according to suitability of the form to a particular purpose without definite shaping on the part of the user. [PROTO- + LITHIC]

pro·to·log (prōt′ᵊlôg′, -ᵊlog′), *n. Biol.* the original description of a species, genus, etc. Also, **pro′to·logue′.** [PROTO- + (CATA)LOG]

pro·to·lyt·ic (prōt′ᵊlit′ik), *adj. Chem.* involving the transfer of a proton. [PROTO- + -LYTIC]

pro·to·mar·tyr (prō′tō mär′tər), *n.* **1.** the first Christian martyr, Saint Stephen. **2.** the first martyr in any cause. [late ME *prothomartyr* < ML *prōtomartyr* < Gk. See PROTO-, MARTYR]

pro·to·mor·phic (prō′tə môr′fik), *adj. Biol.* having a primitive character or structure. [PROTO- + -MORPHIC] —**pro′to·morph′,** *n.*

pro·ton (prō′ton), *n. Physics, Chem.* an elementary particle that is a fundamental constituent of all atomic nuclei, having a positive charge equal in magnitude to that of the electron. The atomic number, or the number of protons, in a nucleus is different for each element. [< Gk, neut. of *prôtos* first] —**pro·ton′ic,** *adj.*

pro·to·ne·ma (prō′tə nē′mə), *n., pl.* **-ma·ta** (-mə tə). *Bot.* a primary, usually filamentous structure produced by the germination of the spore in mosses and certain related plants, and upon which the leafy plant which bears the sexual organs arises as a lateral or terminal shoot. [< NL < Gk, equiv. to *prōto-* PROTO- + *nêma* thread] —**pro′to·ne′mal, pro·to·nem·a·tal** (prō′tə nem′ə tᵊl), *adj.* —**pro′to·nem′a·toid′,** *adj.*

pro·ton·o·tar·y (prō ton′ə ter′ē, prōt′ᵊnō′tə rē), *n., pl.* **-tar·ies.** prothonotary. —**pro·ton′o·tar′y·ship′,** *n.*

pro·to·path·ic (prō′tə path′ik), *adj. Physiol.* **1.** noting or pertaining to a general, nondiscriminating responsiveness to pain or temperature stimuli (opposed to *epicritic*). **2.** primitive; primary. [PROTO- + -PATHIC] —**pro·top·a·thy** (prə top′ə thē), *n.*

pro·to·pec·tin (prō′tə pek′tin), *n. Biochem.* any of the class of water-insoluble pectic substances that are found in the rind of citrus fruits or in apple peels and that are hydrolyzed to pectin or pectic acid. Also called **pectinogen, pectose.** [PROTO- + PECTIN]

pro·to·phlo·em (prō′tə flō′em), *n. Bot.* the part of the primary phloem that develops first, consisting of narrow, thin-walled cells. [PROTO- + PHLOEM]

pro·to·plasm (prō′tə plaz′əm), *n. Biol.* **1.** a typically translucent, colorless, semifluid, complex substance regarded as the physical basis of life, having the powers of growth, reproduction, etc.; the living matter of all vegetable and animal cells and tissues. **2.** (formerly) cytoplasm. [< NL *prōtoplasma.* See PROTO-, -PLASM] —**pro′to·plas′mic, pro′to·plas′mal, pro·to·plas·mat·ic** (prō′tō plaz mat′ik), *adj.*

pro·to·plast (prō′tə plast′), *n.* **1.** *Biol.* **a.** the protoplasm within a cell considered as a fundamental entity. **b.** the primordial living unit or cell. **2.** one who or that which is formed first; original; prototype. **3.** the hypothetical first individual or one of the supposed first pair of a species or the like. [< LL *prōtoplast(us)* the first man < Gk *prōtóplastos* formed first. See PROTO-, -PLAST] —**pro′to·plas′tic,** *adj.*

pro·top·o·dite (prō top′ə dīt′), *n. Zool.* the basal portion of a biramous crustacean appendage. Also, **pro·to·pod** (prō′tə pod′). Cf. **endopodite, exopodite.** [PROTO- + POD- + -ITE[1]] —**pro·top·o·dit·ic** (prə top′ə dit′ik), *adj.*

pro·to·pope (prō′tə pōp′), *n.* the ranking priest in a cathedral of the Eastern Church. Also called **protopresbyter.** [< Russ *protopop* < eccl. Gk *protopapâs.* See PROTO-, POPE]

pro·to·pres·by·ter (prō′tō prez′bi tər, -pres′-), *n. Eastern Ch.* **1.** a title given to distinguished priests. **2.** protopope. [< NGk *prōtopresbýter(os).* See PROTO-, PRESBYTER]

pro·to·ste·le (prō′tə stē′lē, -stēl′), *n. Bot.* the solid stele of most roots, having a central core of xylem enclosed by phloem. [PROTO- + STELE] —**pro·to·ste·lic** (prō′tə stē′lik), *adj.*

pro·to·the·ri·an (prō′tə thēr′ē ən), *adj.* **1.** belonging or pertaining to the group *Prototheria,* comprising the monotremes. —*n.* **2.** a prototherian animal. [< NL *Prototheri(a)* (< Gk *prōto-* PROTO- + *thēría,* pl. of *thḗrion* beast) + -AN]

pro·to·troph·ic (prō′tə trof′ik), *adj.* **1.** (esp. of certain bacteria) requiring only inorganic substances for growth. **2.** (of certain microorganisms) requiring no specific nutriments for growth. [PROTO- + -TROPHIC]

pro·to·type (prō′tə tīp′), *n.* **1.** the original or model on which something is based or formed. **2.** someone or something that serves to illustrate the typical qualities of a class; model; exemplar: *She is the prototype of a suburban housewife.* **3.** something analogous to another thing of a later period: *a Renaissance prototype of our modern public housing.* **4.** *Biol.* an archetype; a primitive form regarded as the basis of a group. [< NL *prōtotyp(on)* < Gk, n. use of neut. of *prōtótypos* original. See PROTO-, TYPE] —**pro′to·ty′pal, pro·to·typ·i·cal** (prō′tə tip′i kəl), **pro′to·typ′ic,** *adj.* —**pro′to·typ′i·cal·ly,** *adv.*
—**Syn. 1.** pattern.

pro·tox·ide (prō tok′sīd, -sid), *n. Chem.* the one of a series of oxides having the smallest proportion of oxygen. Also, **pro·tox·id** (prō tok′sid). [PROT- + OXIDE]

pro·to·xy·lem (prō′tə zī′lem), *n. Bot.* the part of the primary xylem that develops first, consisting of narrow, thin-walled cells. [PROTO- + XYLEM]

Pro·to·zo·a (prō′tə zō′ə), *n.* the phylum comprising the protozoans. [< NL; see PROTO-, -ZOA]

pro·to·zo·al (prō′tə zō′əl), *adj.* of, pertaining to, or characteristic of a protozoan. [PROTOZO(A) + -AL[1]]

pro·to·zo·an (prō′tə zō′ən), *adj.* **1.** Also, **pro′to·zo′ic.** belonging or pertaining to the phylum *Protozoa,* comprising animals consisting of one cell or of a colony of like or similar cells. —*n.* **2.** any animal of the phylum *Protozoa.* [PROTOZO(A) + -AN]

pro·to·zo·ol·o·gy (prō′tō zō ol′ə jē), *n.* the branch of zoology dealing with the protozoa. Also, **pro′to·zo·öl′o·gy.** [PROTOZOO(N) + -LOGY] —**pro·to·zo·o·log·i·cal, pro·to·zo·ö·log·i·cal** (prō′tə zō′ə loj′i kəl), *adj.* —**pro′to·zo·ol′o·gist, pro′to·zo·öl′o·gist,** *n.*

pro·to·zo·on (prō′tə zō′on, -ən), *n., pl.* **-zo·a** (-zō′ə). protozoan. [sing. of Protozoa] —**pro′to·zo′on·al,** *adj.*

pro·tract (prō trakt′), *v.t.* **1.** to draw out or lengthen in time; extend the duration of; prolong. **2.** *Anat.* to extend or protrude. **3.** (in surveying, mathematics, etc.) to plot and draw (lines) with a scale and a protractor. [< L *protract(us)* drawn forth, prolonged (ptp. of *protrahere*). See pro-[1], tract[1]] —**pro·tract′ed·ly,** *adv.* —**pro·tract′ed·ness,** *n.* —**pro·tract′i·ble,** *adj.* —**pro·trac′tive,** *adj.*
—**Syn. 1.** continue. See **lengthen.** —**Ant. 1.** curtail.

pro·trac·tile (prō trak′til), *adj.* capable of being protracted, lengthened, or protruded. [protract + -ile] —**pro′trac·til′i·ty,** *n.*

pro·trac·tion (prō trak′shən), *n.* **1.** act of protracting; prolongation; extension. **2.** protrusion. **3.** that which is protracted. [< LL *prōtractiōn-* (s. of *prōtractiō*) prolongation. See protract, -ion]

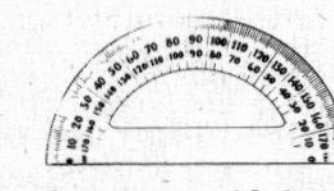
Protractor (def. 2)

pro·trac·tor (prō trak′tər), *n.* **1.** one who or that which protracts. **2.** (in surveying, mathematics, etc.) an instrument having a graduated arc for plotting or measuring angles on paper. **3.** *Anat.* a muscle which causes a part to protrude. [< ML; see protract, -or[2]]

pro·trude (prō trōōd′), *v.,* **-trud·ed, -trud·ing.** —*v.i.* **1.** to project. —*v.t.* **2.** to thrust forward; cause to protrude. [< L *prōtrūde(re)* (to) thrust forward, equiv. to *prō-* pro-[1] + *trūdere* to thrust] —**pro·trud′ent,** *adj.* —**pro·tru·si·ble** (prō trōō′sə bəl), **pro·trud′a·ble,** *adj.*

pro·tru·sile (prō trōō′sil), *adj.* capable of being thrust forth or extended, as the tongue of a hummingbird. [< L *prōtrūs(us)* (ptp. of *prōtrūdere* to protrude) + -ile]

pro·tru·sion (prō trōō′zhən), *n.* **1.** act of protruding; state of being protruded. **2.** that which protrudes or projects. [< L *prōtrūs(us)* (ptp. of *prōtrūdere* to protrude) + -ion]
—**Syn. 2.** jut, projection, bulge, protuberance.

pro·tru·sive (prō trōō′siv), *adj.* **1.** projecting or protuberant; thrusting forward, upward, or outward. **2.** obtrusive. **3.** *Archaic.* pushing forward; having propulsive force. [< L *prōtrūs(us)* (ptp. of *prōtrūdere* to protrude) + -ive] —**pro·tru′sive·ly,** *adj.* —**pro·tru′sive·ness,** *n.*

pro·tu·ber·ance (prō tōō′bər əns, -tyōō′-), *n.* **1.** condition, state, or quality of being protuberant. **2.** a protuberant part or thing; projection or bulge. [protuber(ant) + -ance] —**pro·tu·ber·an·tial** (prō tōō′bə ran′shəl, -tyōō′-), *adj.*
—**Syn. 2.** protrusion, swelling.

pro·tu·ber·an·cy (prō tōō′bər ən sē, -tyōō′-), *n., pl.* **-cies.** protuberance. [protuber(ant) + -ancy]

pro·tu·ber·ant (prō tōō′bər ənt, -tyōō′-), *adj.* bulging out beyond the surrounding surface; protruding; projecting: *protuberant eyes.* [< LL *prōtūberant-* (s. of *prōtūberāns*), prp. of *prōtūberāre* to swell. See pro-[1], tuber, -ant] —**pro·tu′ber·ant·ly,** *adv.*

pro·tu·ber·ate (prō tōō′bə rāt′, -tyōō′-), *v.i.,* **-at·ed, -at·ing.** to bulge out, forming a rounded projection. [< LL *protuberāt(us),* ptp. of *prōtūberāre.* See protuberant, -ate[1]]

pro·tu·ran (prə tŏŏr′ən, -tyŏŏr′-), *n.* **1.** a small, primitive insect of the order *Protura,* characterized by the absence of eyes, antennae, and wings, found living in damp soil and humus. —*adj.* **2.** belonging or pertaining to the order *Protura.* [< NL *Protur(a)* (see prot-, uro-[2]) + -an]

pro·tyle (prō′tīl, -til), *n.* the hypothetical, primordial substance that supposedly differentiated into the chemical elements. Also, **pro·tyl** (prō′til). [irreg. < Gk *prōt-* prot- + *hȳlē* material, matter]

proud (proud), *adj.* **1.** feeling pleasure or satisfaction over something regarded as highly honorable or creditable to oneself (often fol. by *of,* an infinitive, or a clause). **2.** having, proceeding from, or showing a high opinion of one's own dignity, importance, or superiority. **3.** having or showing self-respect or self-esteem. **4.** highly gratifying to the feelings or self-esteem: *It was a proud day for him when his son entered college.* **5.** highly honorable or creditable: *a proud achievement.* **6.** stately, majestic, or magnificent: *proud cities.* **7.** of lofty dignity or distinction: *a proud name; proud nobles.* **8.** full of vigor and spirit: *a proud young stallion.* **9.** *Obs.* brave. —*adv.* **10. do one proud, a.** to be a source of pride or credit to a person: *His conduct in such a difficult situation did him proud.* **b.** to treat someone generously or lavishly: *Mother really did us proud with this supper.* [ME; late OE *prūd* arrogant (c. Icel *prūthr* stately, fine), appar. < VL; cf. OF *prud, prod* gallant, LL *prōde* useful, L *prōdesse* to be of worth] —**proud′ly,** *adv.* —**proud′ness,** *n.*
—**Syn. 1.** contented, self-satisfied. **2.** overbearing, self-important, disdainful, imperious, presumptuous. Proud, arrogant, haughty imply a consciousness of, or a belief in, one's superiority in some respect. Proud implies sensitiveness, lofty self-respect, or jealous preservation of one's dignity, station, and the like. It may refer to an affectionate admiration or a justifiable pride concerning someone else: *proud of his son.* Arrogant applies to insolent or overbearing behavior, arising from an exaggerated belief in one's importance: *arrogant rudeness.* Haughty implies lofty reserve and confident, often disdainful assumption of superiority over others: *the haughty manner of an ill-bred debutante.* **6.** noble, imposing, splendid. —**Ant. 1.** dissatisfied. **2.** humble. **5.** dishonorable. **6.** mean; impoverished; lowly.

proud′ flesh′, *Pathol.* See **granulation tissue.**

Prou·dhon (prōō dôN′), *n.* **Pierre Jo·seph** (pyer zhô zef′), 1809–65, French socialist and writer.

Proust (prōōst), *n.* **Mar·cel** (mar sel′), 1871–1922, French novelist.

Proust·i·an (prōō′stē ən), *adj.* of, pertaining to, or resembling Marcel Proust, his writings, or the middle-class and aristocratic worlds he described: *a Proustian obsession with the past; a Proustian complexity of social relationships.* [Proust + -ian]

proust·ite (prōō′stīt), *n. Mineral.* a mineral, silver arsenic sulfide, Ag_3AsS_3, occurring in scarlet crystals and masses: a minor ore of silver; ruby silver. [named after J. L. *Proust* (1754–1826), French chemist; see -ite[1]]

Prov., **1.** Provençal. **2.** Provence. **3.** Proverbs. **4.** Province. **5.** Provost.

prov., **1.** province. **2.** provincial. **3.** provisional. **4.** provost.

pro·vas/cu·lar tis/sue (prō vas′kyə lər), procambium. [pro-[1] + vascular]

prove (prōōv), *v.,* **proved, proved** or **prov·en, prov·ing.** —*v.t.* **1.** to establish the truth or genuineness of, as by evidence or argument: *to prove one's claim.* **2.** *Law.* to establish the authenticity or validity of (a will); probate. **3.** to give demonstration of by action. **4.** to subject to a test, experiment, comparison, analysis, or the like, to determine quality, amount, acceptability, characteristics, etc.: *to prove ore.* **5.** to show (oneself) to have the character or ability expected of one, esp. through one's actions. **6.** *Math.* to verify the correctness or validity of by mathematical demonstration or arithmetical proof. **7.** Also, **proof.** *Print.* to take a trial impression of (type, a cut, etc.). **8.** to cause (dough) to rise to the necessary lightness. **9.** *Archaic.* to experience. —*v.i.* **10.** to turn out: *The experiment proved to be successful.* **11.** to be found by trial or experience to be: *His story proved false.* **12.** (of (dough) to rise to a specified lightness: *Leave covered until it has proved.* [ME < OF *prove(r)* < L *probāre* to try, test, prove, approve, deriv. of *probus* good. See probity] —**prov′a·bil′i·ty, prov′a·ble·ness,** *n.* —**prov′a·ble,** *adj.* —**prov′a·bly,** *adv.* —**prov′en·ly,** *adv.* —**prov′er,** *n.*
—**Syn. 1.** demonstrate, confirm, substantiate, verify. —**Ant. 1.** disprove.

prov·e·nance (prov′ə nəns), *n.* place or source of origin: *The provenance of the ancient manuscript has never been determined.* [< F: orig., deriv. of *provenant,* prp. of *provenir* < L *prōvenīre* to come forth; see -ance, -ant]

Pro·ven·çal (prō′vən säl′, prov′ən-; *Fr.* prô väN-sal′), *adj.* **1.** of or pertaining to Provence, its people, or their language. —*n.* **2.** a native or inhabitant of Provence. **3.** a Romance language formerly widely spoken and written in southeastern France from the Alps to the Atlantic, still in use in some rural areas, and characterized by *oc* as the word for "yes," distinct word stress (usually on the last or next-to-last syllable), less vowel apocope than French, and the lack of distinctively nasalized vowels. Cf. **langue d'oc. 4.** the dialect of Provençal used in Provence. [< F < L *prōvinciāl(is)* provincial. See Provence, -al[1]]

Pro·ven·çale (prō′vən säl′, prov′ən-; *Fr.* prô väN-sal′), *Cookery.* —*adj.* **1.** (*sometimes l.c.*) prepared with garlic or garlic and tomato. —*n.* **2.** Also called **Provençale′ sauce′.** a thick sauce of tomatoes, garlic, and seasonings cooked in oil. [< F; fem. of provençal]

Pro·vence (prô väNs′; *Eng.* prə väNs′), *n.* a region in SE France, bordering on the Mediterranean: formerly a province; famous for medieval poetry and courtly traditions.

Provence′ rose′, an erect shrub, *Rosa gallica,* of Eurasia, having a creeping rootstock, densely prickly and bristly stems, and solitary, pink or crimson flowers nearly three inches wide. Also called **French rose.**

prov·en·der (prov′ən dər), *n.* **1.** dry food, as hay or oats, for livestock or other domestic animals; fodder. **2.** food; provisions. [ME *provendre* < OF, var. of *provende* prebend, provender < LL *prōbenda,* b. *praebenda* prebend and *prōvidēre* to look out for. See prebend, provide]
—**Syn. 1.** See **feed.**

pro·ve·ni·ence (prō vē′nē əns, -vēn′yəns), *n.* provenance; origin; source. [< L *prōveni(ent)-* (s. of *prōveniēns,* prp. of *prōvenīre* to come forth, arise) + -ence. See provenance]

pro·ven·tric·u·lus (prō′ven trik′yə ləs), *n., pl.* **-tric·u·li** (-trik′yə lī′). **1.** the glandular portion of the stomach of birds, in which food is partially digested before passing to the ventriculus or gizzard. **2.** a similar enlargement in the alimentary tract of several invertebrates, variously modified for maceration and digestion. [pro-[1] + ventriculus] —**pro′ven·tric′u·lar,** *adj.*

prov·erb (prov′ərb), *n.* **1.** a short popular saying, usually of unknown and ancient origin, that expresses effectively some commonplace truth or useful thought; adage; saw. **2.** a wise saying or precept; a didactic sentence. **3.** a person or thing that is commonly regarded as an embodiment or representation of some quality; byword. **4.** *Bible.* a profound saying, maxim, or oracular utterance requiring interpretation. —*v.t.* **5.** to utter in the form of a proverb. **6.** to make (something) the subject of a proverb. **7.** to make a byword of. [ME *proverbe* < MF < L *prōverb(ium)* adage, equiv. to *prō-* pro-[1] + *verb(um)* word + *-ium* collective suffix] —**prov′erb·like′,** *adj.*
—**Syn. 1.** aphorism, apothegm. Proverb, maxim are terms for short, pithy sayings. A proverb is such a saying popularly known and repeated, usually expressing simply and concretely, though often metaphorically, a truth based on common sense or the practical experience of mankind: *"A stitch in time saves nine."* A maxim is a brief statement of a general and practical truth, esp. one that serves as a rule of conduct or a precept: *"It is wise to risk no more than one can afford to lose."*

pro·ver·bi·al (prə vûr′bē əl), *adj.* **1.** of, pertaining to, or characteristic of a proverb: *proverbial brevity.* **2.** expressed in a proverb or proverbs: *proverbial wisdom.* **3.** of the nature of or resembling a proverb: *proverbial sayings.* **4.** having been made the subject of a proverb: *the proverbial barn door which is closed too late.* **5.** having become an object of common mention or reference: *her proverbial inability to get anywhere on time.* [< LL *prōverbiāl(is).* See proverb, -al[1]] —**pro·ver′bi·al·ly,** *adv.*

Prov·erbs (prov′ərbz), *n.* (*construed as sing.*) a book of the Bible, containing the sayings of sages.

pro·vide (prə vīd′), *v.,* **-vid·ed, -vid·ing.** —*v.t.* **1.** to furnish, supply, or equip. **2.** to afford or yield. **3.** *Law.* to arrange for or stipulate beforehand, as by a provision or proviso. **4.** *Archaic.* to prepare or procure beforehand. —*v.i.* **5.** to take measures with due foresight (usually fol. by *for* or *against*). **6.** to make arrangements for supplying means of support, money, etc. (usually fol. by *for*): *He provided for his children in his will.* **7.** to supply means of support (often fol. by *for*): *able to provide for a wife.* [late ME *provide(n)* < L *prōvidē(re)* (to) foresee, look after, provide for, equiv. to *prō-* pro-[1] + *vidēre* to see] —**pro·vid′a·ble,** *adj.* —**pro·vid′er,** *n.*
—**Syn. 1.** contribute. **2.** produce, give.

pro·vid·ed (prə vī′did), *conj.* on the condition or understanding: *any dress, provided it is black; I'll go, provided that the others go, too.* [provide + -ed[2]]
—**Syn.** in case, granted. See **if.** —**Ant.** lest.

prov·i·dence (prov′i dəns), *n.* **1.** the foreseeing care and guardianship of God over His creatures. **2.** (*cap.*) God, esp. when conceived as omnisciently directing the universe and the affairs of man with wise benevolence. **3.** a manifestation of divine care or direction. **4.** provident or prudent management of resources; prudence. **5.** foresight; provident care. [ME < L *prōvidentia* foresight, forethought. See provident, -ence]

Prov·i·dence (prov′i dəns), *n.* **1.** a seaport in and the capital of Rhode Island, in the NE part, at the head of Narragansett Bay. 207,498 (1960). **2.** a town in W Kentucky. 3771 (1960).

Prov′idence Riv′er boat′, *Naut.* See **Newport boat.** Also called **Prov′idence boat′.**

prov·i·dent (prov′i dənt), *adj.* **1.** having or showing foresight; providing carefully for the future. **2.** characterized by or proceeding from foresight: *provident care.* **3.** mindful in making provision (usually fol. by *of*). **4.** economical; frugal; thrifty. [ME < L *prōvident-* (s. of *prōvidēns*), prp. of *prōvidēre* to look for, provide] —**prov′i·dent·ly,** *adv.* —**prov′i·dent·ness,** *n.*
—**Syn. 1.** cautious, prudent. —**Ant. 1.** careless.

prov·i·den·tial (prov′i den′shəl), *adj.* **1.** of, pertaining to, or resulting from divine providence: *providential care.* **2.** opportune, fortunate, or lucky: *a providential event.* [< L *prōvidenti(a)* providence + -al[1]] —**prov′i·den′tial·ly,** *adv.*
—**Syn. 2.** happy.

Pro·vi·den·tis·si·mus De·us (prō′vē den tē′sē mōōs′ dā′ōōs), *Latin.* The Most Provident God (opening words and the title of an encyclical of Pope Leo XIII issued in 1893 on the study of the Bible).

pro·vid·ing (prə vī′ding), *conj.* on the condition or understanding; provided: *He can stay here providing he works.* [ME *provydyng.* See provide, -ing[2]]
—**Syn.** See **if.**

prov·ince (prov′ins), *n.* **1.** an administrative division or unit of a country: *the provinces of Spain.* **2. the provinces, a.** the parts of a country outside of the capital or the largest cities. **b.** (in England) all parts of the country outside of London. **3.** a country, territory, district, or region. **4.** *Geog.* an area lower in rank than a region. **5.** a department or branch of learning or activity: *the province of mathematics.* **6.** sphere or field of activity or authority, as of a person; office, function, or business: *Such decisions do not lie within his province.* **7.** a major subdivision of British India. **8.** an ecclesiastical territorial division, as that within which an archbishop or a metropolitan exercises jurisdiction. **9.** *Hist.* **a.** any of the North American colonies now forming major administrative divisions of Canada. **b.** any of certain colonies of Great Britain which are now part of the U.S. **10.** *Rom. Hist.* a country or territory outside of Italy, brought under the ancient Roman dominion and administered by a governor sent from Rome. **11.** *U.S. Mining.* an individual mineral-producing area. [ME < MF < L *prōvincia* province, official charge]
—**Syn. 5.** area.

Prov·ince·town (prov′ins toun′), *n.* a resort town at the tip of Cape Cod, in SE Massachusetts. 3346 (1960).

pro·vin·cial (prə vin′shəl), *adj.* **1.** belonging or peculiar to some particular province or provinces; local: *the provincial newspaper.* **2.** of or pertaining to the provinces: *provincial customs; provincial dress.* **3.** having or showing the manners, viewpoints, etc., characteristic of unsophisticated inhabitants of a province; countrified; rustic; narrow or illiberal; parochial: *a provincial point of view.* **4.** (*cap.*) *Fine Arts.* noting or pertaining to the styles of architecture, furniture, etc., found in the provinces, esp. when imitating styles currently or formerly in fashion in or around the capital: *French Provincial; Italian Provincial.* **5.** *Hist.* of or pertaining to any of the American provinces of Great Britain. —*n.* **6.** a person who lives in or comes from the provinces. **7.** a person who lacks sophistication, urbanity, breadth of interest, broad-mindedness, etc. **8.** *Eccles.* **a.** the head of an ecclesiastical province. **b.** a member of a religious order presiding over his order in a given district or province. [ME < L *prōvinciāl(is).* See province, -al[1]] —**pro·vin′cial·ly,** *adv.*

pro·vin·cial·ism (prə vin′shə liz′əm), *n.* **1.** narrowness of mind, ignorance, or the like resulting from provincial life without exposure to cultural or intellectual activity. **2.** a trait, habit of thought, etc., characteristic of a provincial, a province, or the provinces. **3.** a word, expression, or mode of pronunciation peculiar to a province. **4.** devotion to one's own province before the nation as a whole. [provincial + -ism]

pro·vin·ci·al·i·ty (prə vin′shē al′i tē), *n., pl.* **-ties.** **1.** provincial character. **2.** provincial characteristic: *Her provincialities reflect a refreshing naturalness.* [provincial + -ity]

pro·trade′, *adj.*
pro′tra·di′tion, *adj.*
pro′tra·di′tion·al, *adj.*
pro·trag′e·dy, *adj.*
pro′-Tu·ni′sian, *adj., n.*
pro-Tur′key, *adj.*
pro-Tur′kish, *adj.*
pro′u·ni·form′i·ty, *adj.*
pro·un′ion, *adj.*
pro·un′ion·ism, *n.*
pro·un′ion·ist, *adj., n.*
pro′-U·ni·tar′i·an, *adj., n.*
pro′-U·nit′ed States′, *adj.*
pro′u·ni·ver′si·ty, *adj.*
pro′-U·ru·guay′an, *adj., n.*
pro′vac·ci·na′tion, *adj.*
pro·vac′cine, *adj.*
pro′-Ven·e·zue′lan, *adj., n.*
pro′-Vi·et′nam·ese′, *adj., n., pl.* **-ese.**

prov′ing ground′, any place, context, or area for testing something, as a piece of scientific equipment, a theory, etc.

pro·vi·sion (prə vizh′ən), *n.* **1.** a clause in a legal instrument, a law, etc., providing for a particular matter; stipulation; proviso. **2.** the providing or supplying of something, esp. of food or other necessities. **3.** arrangement or preparation beforehand, as for the doing of something, the meeting of needs, the supplying of means, etc. **4.** something provided; a measure or other means for meeting a need. **5.** a supply or stock of something provided. **6. provisions,** supplies of food. **7.** *Eccles.* **a.** an appointment to an ecclesiastical office. **b.** appointment by the pope to a see or benefice not yet vacant. —*v.t.* **8.** to supply with provisions, or stores of food. [ME < L *prōvīsiōn-* (s. of *prōvīsiō*) a foreseeing, equiv. to *prōvīs(us)* (ptp. of *prōvidēre* to PROVIDE) + *-iōn-* -ION] —**pro·vi′sion·er,** *n.* —**pro·vi′sion·less,** *adj.*
—**Syn. 1.** condition. **2.** catering, purveying. **6.** store, provender, stock.

pro·vi·sion·al (prə vizh′ə nəl), *adj.* Also, **pro·vi·sion·ar·y** (prə vizh′ə ner′ē). **1.** providing or serving for the time being only; existing only until permanently or properly replaced; temporary: *a provisional treaty; a provisional government.* **2.** accepted or adopted tentatively; conditional; probationary. —*n.* **3.** *Philately.* a stamp that serves temporarily, pending the appearance of the regular issue, or during a temporary shortage of the regular stamps. [PROVISION + -AL[1]] —**pro·vi′sion·al′i·ty, pro·vi′sion·al·ness,** *n.* —**pro·vi′sion·al·ly,** *adv.*

pro·vi·so (prə vī′zō), *n., pl.* **-sos, -soes. 1.** a clause in a statute, contract, or the like, by which a condition is introduced. **2.** a stipulation or condition. [late ME < ML *prōvīsō (quod)* it being provided (that), n. use of abl. neut. sing. of L *prōvīsus,* ptp. of *prōvidēre* to PROVIDE]

pro·vi·so·ry (prə vī′zə rē), *adj.* **1.** provisional. **2.** containing a proviso or condition; conditional. [< ML *prōvīsōri(us).* See PROVISO, -ORY[1]] —**pro·vi′so·ri·ly,** *adv.*

pro·vi·ta·min (prō vī′tə min), *n.* *Biochem.* a substance that an organism can transform into a vitamin, as carotene, which is converted to Vitamin A in the liver. [PRO-[1] + VITAMIN]

Pro·vo (prō′vō), *n.* a city in central Utah. 36,047 (1960).

prov·o·ca·tion (prov′ə kā′shən), *n.* **1.** act of provoking. **2.** something that incites, instigates, angers, or irritates. **3.** *Crim. Law.* words or conduct leading to killing in hot passion and without deliberation. [ME < L *prōvocātiōn-* (s. of *prōvocātiō*) a calling forth, equiv. to *prōvocāt(us)* (ptp. of *prōvocāre* to call forth) + *-iōn-* -ION] —**prov′o·ca′tion·al,** *adj.*

pro·voc·a·tive (prə vok′ə tiv), *adj.* **1.** tending or serving to provoke; inciting, stimulating, irritating, or vexing. —*n.* **2.** something provocative. [late ME < LL *prōvocātīv(us).* See PROVOCATION, -IVE] —**pro·voc′a·tive·ly,** *adv.* —**pro·voc′a·tive·ness,** *n.*

pro·voke (prə vōk′), *v.t.,* **-voked, -vok·ing. 1.** to anger, enrage, exasperate, or vex. **2.** to stir up, arouse, or call forth (feelings, desires, or activity): *The mishap provoked a hearty laugh.* **3.** to incite or stimulate (a person, animal, etc.) to action. **4.** to give rise to, induce, or bring about: *What could have provoked such an incident?* **5.** *Obs.* to summon. [late ME < L *prōvoc(āre)* (to) call forth, challenge, provoke] —**pro·vok′er,** *n.* —**pro·vok′ing·ly,** *adv.* —**pro·vok′ing·ness,** *n.*
—**Syn. 1.** irk, annoy, aggravate, exacerbate, infuriate. See **irritate. 2.** rouse, instigate. —**Ant. 1.** calm, propitiate.

pro·vo·lo·ne (prō′və lō′nē), *n.* a mellow light-colored, Italian cheese, usually smoked after drying. Also called **pro′volo′ne cheese′.** [< It, equiv. to *provol(a)* kind of cheese + *-one* aug. suffix]

prov·ost (prov′əst, prō′vōst *or, esp. in military usage,* prō′vō), *n.* **1.** a person appointed to superintend or preside. **2.** an administrative officer in any of various colleges and universities who holds high rank and is concerned with the curriculum, faculty appointment, etc. **3.** *Eccles.* the chief dignitary of a cathedral or collegiate church. **4.** the steward or bailiff of a medieval manor. **5.** the mayor of a municipality in Scotland. **6.** *Obs.* a prison warden. [ME; OE *profost* < ML *prōposit-(us),* lit., (one) placed before, president. See PRO-[1], POSIT] —**prov′ost·ship′,** *n.*

pro′vost court′ (prō′vō), a military court convened in occupied territory under military government, usually composed of one officer and empowered to try military personnel and civilians for minor offenses.

pro′vost guard′ (prō′vō), a detachment of soldiers assigned to police duties under the provost marshal. Cf. **military police.**

pro′vost mar′shal (prō′vō), **1.** *Army.* an officer on the staff of a commander, charged with the maintaining of order and with other police functions within a command. **2.** *Navy.* an officer charged with the safekeeping of a prisoner pending trial by court-martial.

pro′vost ser′geant (prō′vō), *Mil.* the senior noncommissioned officer of a prison or other confinement facility whose chief duty is the supervision of prisoners and of the military police unit.

prow[1] (prou), *n.* **1.** the forepart of a ship or boat; bow. **2.** the front end of an airship. **3.** *Poetic.* a ship. [< MF *proue* < dial. It (Genoese) *proa* < L *prōra* < Gk *prōira*] —**prowed,** *adj.*

prow[2] (prou), *adj.* *Archaic.* valiant. [ME < OF *prou* < LL **prōdis.* See PROUD]

prow·ess (prou′is), *n.* **1.** exceptional valor, bravery, or ability, esp. in combat or battle. **2.** exceptional or superior ability: *his prowess as a public speaker.* **3.** a valiant or daring deed. [ME *prowesse* < OF *proesse, proece* goodness, bravery, equiv. to *prou,* earlier *prod* (see PROUD) + *-esse* < L *-itia* -ICE] —**prow′essed,** *adj.*
—**Syn. 2.** audacity, heroism; might, accomplishment.

prow·fish (prou′fish′), *n., pl.* **-fish·es,** (*esp. collectively*) **-fish.** a fish, *Zaprora silensus,* found in the North Pacific. [PROW[1] + FISH]

prowl (proul), *v.i.* **1.** to rove or go about stealthily, as in search of prey, plunder, etc. —*v.t.* **2.** to rove over or through in search of what may be found: *The cat prowled the alleys in search of food.* —*n.* **3.** act of prowling. **4. on the prowl,** in the act of prowling; searching stealthily: *The cat is on the prowl for mice.* [ME *proll(en)* < ?] —**prowl′ing·ly,** *adv.*
—**Syn. 1.** roam. See **lurk.**

prowl′ car′. See **squad car.**

prowl·er (prou′lər), *n.* **1.** one who or that which prowls. **2.** a person who goes stealthily about with some unlawful intention, as burglary or theft. [PROWL + -ER[1]]

prox., proximo.

prox·i·mal (prok′sə məl), *adj.* situated toward the point of origin or attachment, as of a limb or bone. Cf. **distal** (def. 1). [< L *proxim(us)* next (superl. of *prope* near) + -AL[1]] —**prox′i·mal·ly,** *adv.*

prox′imal con′voluted tu′bule, *Anat.* the part of a nephron between the Malpighian corpuscle and the loop of Henle that reabsorbs chiefly glucose, water, sodium chloride, and phosphates from the glomerular filtrate. Cf. **distal convoluted tubule.**

prox·i·mate (prok′sə mit), *adj.* **1.** next; nearest; immediately before or after in order, place, occurrence, etc. **2.** close; very near. **3.** approximate; fairly accurate. **4.** forthcoming; imminent. [< LL *proximāt(us),* ptp. of *proximāre* to near, approach. See PROXIMAL, -ATE[1]] —**prox′i·mate·ly,** *adv.* —**prox′i·mate·ness,** *n.* —**prox·i·ma·tion** (prok′sə mā′shən), *n.*

prox·im·i·ty (prok sim′i tē), *n.* nearness in place, time, order, occurrence, or relation. [late ME *proxymite* < L *proximitās* nearness, vicinity. See PROXIMAL, -ITY]

proxim′ity fuze′, a fuze for detonating a projectile, mine, or other charge when actuated by an external influence within a predesignated radius of it but not necessarily in contact with it. Also called **variable time fuze, VT fuze.**

prox·i·mo (prok′sə mō′), *adv.* in, of, or during the next month: *on the 10th proximo.* Cf. **ultimo.** [< L, abl. of *proximus* next. See PROXIMAL]

prox·y (prok′sē), *n., pl.* **prox·ies. 1.** the agency, function, or power of a person authorized to act as the deputy or substitute for another. **2.** the person so authorized; substitute; agent. **3.** a written authorization empowering another person to vote or act for the signer, as at a meeting of stockholders. [ME *prokesye, procusie,* contr. of *procuracy* procuration. See PROCURE, -ACY]
—**Syn. 2.** deputy.

prox′y state′ment, a statement containing information, frequently exhaustive, about a corporation, its officers, and any propositions to be voted on, sent to stockholders when their proxies are being solicited for an annual or a special stockholders' meeting.

Pro·zess, Der (*Ger.* dər prō tses′). See **Trial, The.**

prs., pairs.

Pru (pro͞o), *n.* a girl's given name, form of **Prudence.** Also, **Prue.**

prude (pro͞od), *n.* a person who is excessively proper or modest in speech, conduct, dress, etc. [< F *prude* a prude (n.), prudish (adj.), short for *prudefemme,* OF *prodefeme* worthy or respectable woman. See PROUD, FEME] —**prude′like′,** *adj.*

pru·dence (pro͞od′əns), *n.* **1.** the quality or fact of being prudent. **2.** cautious practical wisdom; good judgment; careful forethought; discretion. **3.** regard for one's own interests. **4.** provident care in the management of resources; economy; frugality. [ME < MF < L *prūdentia.* See PRUDENT, -ENCE]
—**Syn. 1.** PRUDENCE, CALCULATION, FORESIGHT, FORETHOUGHT imply attempted provision against possible contingencies. PRUDENCE is care, caution, and good judgment, as well as wisdom in looking ahead: *sober prudence in handling one's affairs.* CALCULATION suggests (literally or figuratively) a disposition to get a large return for as small an outlay as possible and willingness to benefit at the expense of others: *cold calculation.* FORESIGHT implies a prudent looking ahead rather far into the future: *admirable foresight in planning.* FORETHOUGHT emphasizes the adequacy of preparation for the future: *complete forethought.* —**Ant. 1.** rashness.

Pru·dence (pro͞od′əns), *n.* a girl's given name.

pru·dent (pro͞od′ənt), *adj.* **1.** wise, judicious, or wisely cautious in practical affairs; sagacious; discreet or circumspect; sober. **2.** careful in providing for the future, for one's own interests, etc.; provident. **3.** characterized by or proceeding from prudence, as conduct, action, etc.: *a prudent decision.* [ME < L *prūdent-* (s. of *prūdēns*), contr. of *prōvidēns* PROVIDENT] —**pru′dent·ly,** *adv.*
—**Syn. 1.** sensible. **2.** economical, thrifty, frugal, saving. —**Ant. 1.** foolish. **2.** prodigal.

pru·den·tial (pro͞o den′shəl), *adj.* **1.** of, pertaining to, characterized by, or resulting from prudence. **2.** exercising prudence. **3.** having discretionary or advisory authority, as in business matters. [< L *prūdenti(a)* PRUDENCE + -AL[1]] —**pru·den′tial·ly,** *adv.* —**pru·den′tial·ness, pru·den·ti·al·i·ty** (pro͞o den′shē al′i tē), *n.*

prud·er·y (pro͞o′də rē), *n., pl.* **-er·ies** for 2. **1.** excessive propriety or modesty in speech, conduct, etc. **2. pruderies,** prudish actions or speeches. [< F *pruderie.* See PRUDE, -ERY]

Pru·d'hon (prʏ dôN′), *n.* **Pierre Paul** (pyer pôl), (*Pierre Prudon*), 1758–1823, French painter.

prud·ish (pro͞o′dish), *adj.* **1.** excessively proper or modest in speech, conduct, dress, etc. **2.** characteristic of a prude. [PRUDE + -ISH[1]] —**prud′ish·ly,** *adv.* —**prud′ish·ness,** *n.*
—**Syn. 1.** reserved, coy. See **modest.** —**Ant. 1.** immodest.

Prue (pro͞o), *n.* a girl's given name, form of **Prudence.** Also, **Pru.**

Pru·ett (pro͞o′it), *n.* a boy's given name. Also, **Prewett, Prewitt, Pru′itt.**

pru·i·nose (pro͞o′ə nōs′), *adj.* *Bot., Zool.* covered with a frostlike bloom or powdery secretion, as a plant surface. [< L *pruīnōs(us)* frosty, equiv. to *pruīn(a)* frost + *-ōsus* -OSE[1]]

prune[1] (pro͞on), *n.* **1.** a variety of plum which dries without spoiling. **2.** such a plum when dried, eaten either cooked or uncooked. **3.** any plum. [late ME < MF < L *prūna,* pl, (taken as sing.) of *prūnum* plum (*prūnus* plum tree) < Gk *proúnon,* var. of *proúmnon* PLUM]

prune[2] (pro͞on), *v.t.,* **pruned, prun·ing. 1.** to cut or lop off (twigs, branches, or roots). **2.** to cut or lop superfluous or undesired twigs, branches, or roots from; trim. **3.** to rid or clear of (anything superfluous or undesirable). **4.** to remove (anything considered superfluous or undesirable). [late ME *prouyne(n)* < MF *proognie(r)* (to) prune (vines)] —**prun′a·bil′i·ty, prun′a·ble·ness,** *n.* —**prun′a·ble,** *adj.* —**prun′er,** *n.*

prune[3] (pro͞on), *v.t.,* **pruned, prun·ing.** *Archaic.* to preen. [ME *prune(n), pruyne(n), proyne(n).* See PREEN] —**prun′a·ble,** *adj.*

pru·nel·la (pro͞o nel′ə), *n.* **1.** a strong, lightweight worsted constructed in a twill weave, used in the manufacture of women's and children's apparel. **2.** a smooth-faced fabric made of mixed fibers or wool, formerly used in the manufacture of women's dresses and of robes for clerics, scholars, and lawyers. Also, **prunelle, pru·nel·lo** (pro͞o nel′ō). [? special use of PRUNELLE, from the dark color of the cloth]

Pru·nel·la (pro͞o nel′ə), *n.* a girl's given name.

pru·nelle (pro͞o nel′), *n.* **1.** a sweet, brown, French liqueur distilled from plums. **2.** prunella. [< F, dim. of *prune* PRUNE[1]]

prunes′ and prisms′, (esp. in Victorian England) affectedly elegant, proper, or prudish speech or manners.

prun′ing hook′, an implement with a hooked blade, used for pruning vines, branches, etc.

prun′ing shears′, small, sturdy shears used for pruning shrubbery.

prunt (prunt), *n.* a small mass of glass fused to the body of a glass piece. [? var. of PRINT] —**prunt′ed,** *adj.*

pru·ri·ent (pro͝or′ē ənt), *adj.* **1.** having, inclined to have, or characterized by lascivious or lustful thoughts, desires, etc. **2.** causing lasciviousness or lust. **3.** having a restless desire or longing. [< L *prūrient-* (s. of *prūriēns*), prp. of *prūrīre* to itch] —**pru′ri·ence, pru′ri·en·cy,** *n.* —**pru′ri·ent·ly,** *adv.*

pru·rig·i·nous (pro͝o rij′ə nəs), *adj.* *Med.* itching. [< LL *prūrīginōs(us)* itchy, lascivious, equiv. to *prūrīgin-* (s. of *prūrīgo*) PRURIGO + *-ōsus* -OUS]

pru·ri·go (pro͝o rī′gō), *n.* *Pathol.* a skin affection characterized by itching papules. [< L: an itching; see PRURIENT]

pru·ri·tus (pro͝o rī′təs), *n.* *Pathol.* itching. [< L *prūrītus* an itching, u-stem (4th decl.), deriv. of ptp. of *prūrīre* to itch] —**pru·rit·ic** (pro͝o rit′ik), *adj.*

Prus., 1. Prussia. **2.** Prussian. Also, **Pruss., Pruss.**

Prus·sia (prush′ə), *n.* a former state in N Europe: developed from a small kingdom to a powerful military empire in the 17th and 18th centuries; the central state in formation of the German Empire in 1871; partitioned by the Polish Corridor in the Treaty of Versailles 1919; formally dissolved as an administrative unit March 1947. *Cap.:* Berlin. German, **Preussen.** Cf. **East Prussia, West Prussia.**

Prus·sian (prush′ən), *adj.* **1.** of or pertaining to Prussia or its inhabitants. **2.** characterized by, exemplifying, or resembling Prussianism. —*n.* **3.** a native or inhabitant of Prussia. **4.** (originally) one of a Lettic people formerly inhabiting territory along and near the coast at the southeastern corner of the Baltic Sea. **5.** a Baltic language formerly spoken in Prussia; Old Prussian. [PRUSSI(A) + -AN]

Prus′sian blue′, 1. a moderate to deep greenish blue. **2.** a dark-blue, crystalline, water-insoluble pigment, $Fe_4[Fe(CN)_6]_3$, produced by reacting ferrocyanic acid or a ferrocyanide with a ferric compound; used in painting, fabric printing, and laundry bluing.

prus·sian·ise (prush′ə nīz′), *v.t.,* **-ised, -is·ing.** (*sometimes cap.*) *Chiefly Brit.* prussianize. —**prus′sian·i·sa′tion,** *n.* —**prus′sian·is′er,** *n.*

Prus·sian·ism (prush′ə niz′əm), *n.* the spirit, system, policy, or methods of the Prussians, esp. the militarism and stern discipline attributed to the Prussians since Frederick the Great. [PRUSSIAN + -ISM]

prus·sian·ize (prush′ə nīz′), *v.t.,* **-ized, -iz·ing.** (*sometimes cap.*) to make Prussian, as in character, method, organization, etc. [PRUSSIAN + -IZE] —**prus′sian·i·za′tion,** *n.* —**prus′sian·iz′er,** *n.*

prus·si·ate (prush′ē āt′, -it, prus′-), *n.* *Chem.* **1.** a ferricyanide or ferrocyanide. **2.** a salt or prussic acid; a cyanide. [< F; see PRUSSIAN BLUE, -ATE[2]]

prus·sic (prus′ik), *adj.* *Chem.* of or derived from prussic acid. [< F *prussique,* lit., Prussian, equiv. to *Prusse* PRUSSIA + *-ique* -IC]

prus′sic ac′id, *Chem.* hydrocyanic acid.

Prut (pro͞ot), *n.* a river in E Europe, flowing SE from the Carpathian Mountains in Ukraine along the boundary between Moldavia (Moldova) and Rumania into the Danube. 500 mi. long. German, **Pruth** (pro͞ot).

pru·ta (pro͞o tä′), *n., pl.* **-toth** (-tôt′). prutah.

pru·tah (pro͞o tä′), *n., pl.* **-toth** (-tôt′). a former aluminum coin of Israel, the thousandth part of a pound, replaced as the fractional unit by the agora in 1960. [< NHeb *perūṭāh*]

pry[1] (prī), *v.,* **pried, pry·ing,** *n., pl.* **pries.** —*v.i.* **1.** to inquire impertinently or unnecessarily into something: *to pry into the personal affairs of others.* **2.** to look closely or curiously; peer; peep. —*n.* **3.** act of prying. **4.** an inquisitive person. [ME *prye(n), prie(n)* < ?]

pry[2] (prī), *v.,* **pried, pry·ing,** *n., pl.* **pries.** —*v.t.* **1.** to raise, detach, or move by leverage. **2.** to get, separate, or ferret out with difficulty: *to pry a secret out of someone; He finally pried her away from the TV.* —*n.* **3.** a tool, as a crowbar for raising, moving, or opening something by leverage. **4.** the leverage exerted. [back formation from PRIZE[3], n. (taken as pl.)]

Pry·de·ri (pri dâr′ē), *n.* *Welsh Legend.* the son of Pwyll and Rhiannon who was stolen by Gwawl shortly after his birth and was restored to his parents a few years later. Cf. **Kicva.**

pry·er (prī′ər), *n.* prier.

---

pro-war′, *adj.* **pro-West′,** *adj.* **pro-West′ern,** *adj.* **pro-West′ern·er,** *n.* **pro-Whig′,** *adj.* **pro-Yu′go·slav′,** *n., adj.* **pro′-Yu·go·sla′vi·an,** *adj., n.* **pro-Zi′on·ism,** *n., adj.* **pro-Zi′on·ist,** *n., adj.*

pry·ing (prī′ing), *adj.* **1.** that pries; looking or searching curiously. **2.** impertinently or unnecessarily curious or inquisitive. [PRY[1] + -ING[2]] —**pry′ing·ly,** *adv.* —**pry′ing·ness,** *n.*
—**Syn. 1.** peeping, peering, peeking. **2.** nosy. See **curious.**

Pry·lis (prī′lis, pril′is), *n. Class. Myth.* a son of Hermes who is sometimes believed to have suggested, through the inspiration of Athena, the use of the wooden horse in the Trojan War.

Prynne (prin), *n.* **William,** 1600–69, English Puritan leader and pamphleteer.

Pry′or Creek′ (prī′ər), a town in NE Oklahoma. 6476 (1960).

pryt·a·ne·um (prit′ənē′əm), *n.* a public building in ancient Greece, containing the symbolic hearth of the community and commonly resembling a private dwelling in plan, used as a meeting place for the administrative body of the community, as a place for entertainments, and as a lodging for guests of the community. [< L < Gk *prytaneîon*, akin to *prýtanis* prince, ruler, chief]

Pryt·a·nis (prit′ənis), *n.* (in the *Iliad*) a Lycian ally of Sarpedon, slain by Odysseus.

pryth·ee (prith′ē), *interj. Archaic.* prithee.

Prze·myśl (pshe′mish əl), *n.* a city in SE Poland: occupied by the Russians 1915. 49,000 (est. 1963).

Prze·wal′ski's horse′ (pshə väl′skēz), tarpan. [named after N. M. *Przevalski* (1839–88), Russian explorer who discovered it]

Ps., Psalm; Psalms. Also, **Psa.**

ps., **1.** pieces. **2.** pseudonym.

P.S., **1.** passenger steamer. **2.** permanent secretary. **3.** postscript. **4.** Privy Seal. **5.** *Theat.* See **prompt side. 6.** Public School.

p.s., postscript.

psalm (säm), *n.* **1.** a sacred song or hymn. **2.** (*cap.*) any of the songs, hymns, or prayers contained in the Book of Psalms. **3.** a metric version or paraphrase of any of these. **4.** a poem of a similar nature. —*v.t.* **5.** to sing, celebrate, or praise in psalms. [ME *psalme*, OE *ps(e)alm, sealm* < LL *psalm(us)* < Gk *psalmós* song sung to the harp, orig., a plucking as of strings, akin to *psállein* to twitch, play (the harp)] —**psalm′ic,** *adj.*

psalm·book (säm′bo͝ok′), *n.* a book containing psalms for liturgical or devotional use. [ME *salm boc.* See PSALM, BOOK]

psalm·ist (sä′mist), *n.* **1.** the author of a psalm or psalms. **2. the Psalmist,** David, the traditional author of the Psalms. [< LL *psalmist(a).* See PSALM, -IST]

psal·mo·dy (sä′mə dē, sal′mə-), *n., pl.* **-dies. 1.** the act, practice, or art of setting psalms to music. **2.** psalms or hymns collectively. **3.** the act, practice or art of singing psalms or hymns. [ME < LL *psalmōdia* < Gk *psalmōidía* singing to the harp. See PSALM, ODE, -Y[3]] —**psal·mod·ic** (sä mod′ik, sal-), **psal·mod′i·cal, psal·mo·di·al** (sä mō′dē əl, sal-), *adj.* —**psal′mo·dist,** *n.*

Psalms (sämz), *n.* (*construed as sing.*) a book of the Bible, composed of 150 songs, hymns, and prayers.

Psal·ter (sôl′tər), *n.* **1.** the Biblical book of Psalms. **2.** (*sometimes l.c.*) a book containing the Psalms for liturgical or devotional use. [< LL *psaltēr(ium)* the Psalter, L: a psaltery < Gk *psaltḗrion* stringed instrument; r. ME *sauter* (< AF) and OE *saltere* (< LL, as above)]

psal·te·ri·um (sôl tēr′ē əm, sal-), *n., pl.* **-te·ri·a** (-tēr′ē ə). *Zool.* the omasum. [< LL: the PSALTER, the folds of the omasum being likened to the leaves of a book] —**psal·te′ri·al,** *adj.*

Psaltery (def. 1)

psal·ter·y (sôl′tə rē), *n., pl.* **-ter·ies. 1.** an ancient musical instrument consisting of a flat sounding box with numerous strings which are plucked with the fingers or with a plectrum. **2.** (*cap.*) the Psalter. [< L *psaltērium* (see PSALTER); r. ME *sautrie* < OF]

Psam·a·the (sam′ə thē′), *n. Class. Myth.* **1.** a Nereid, the mother of Phocus, by Aeacus, and of Theoclymenus and Theonoë, by King Proteus. **2.** a princess, the mother of Linus, by Apollo.

psam·me·ad (sam′ē ad′), *n.* (in children's fiction) a spiderlike creature having the power to grant wishes that are often regretted. [? coined from Gk *psámmē*, var. of *psámmos* sand + -AD]

psam·mite (sam′īt), *n. Geol.* any sandstone. [< Gk *psámm(os)* sand + -ITE[1]] —**psam·mit·ic** (sa mit′ik), *adj.*

psam·mo·phyte (sam′ə fīt′), *n.* a plant that grows in sand or sandy soil. [< Gk *psammo-* (comb. form of *psámmos* sand) + -PHYTE] —**psam·mo·phyt·ic** (sam′ə fit′ik), *adj.*

psam·mo·sere (sam′ə sēr′), *n. Ecol.* a sere originating on sand or sandy soil. [< Gk *psammo-* (comb. form of *psámmos* sand) + SERE]

Psam·tik I (sam′tik), king of Egypt 663–609 B.C. (son of Necho I).

p's and q's, manners; behavior; conduct (usually prec. by *mind* or *watch*): *You'd better mind your p's and q's while Grandmother is here.* [? from children's difficulty in distinguishing the two letters]

PSAT, Preliminary Scholastic Aptitude Test.

PSC, Public Service Commission.

pschent (skent, pskent), *n.* the double crown worn by ancient Egyptian kings, symbolic of dominion over Upper and Lower Egypt, which had previously been separate kingdoms. [< Egypt *p-shrenk*, lit., the double crown]

psec, picosecond; picoseconds.

psel·lism (sel′iz əm), *n. Pathol.* the condition or a case of stuttering; stammering. [< Gk *psellism(ós)* stammering, equiv. to *psell(ízein)* (to) stammer + *-ismos* -ISM]

pse·phite (sē′fīt, psē′-), *n. Geol.* any coarse rock, as breccia or conglomerate. [< Gk *psêph(os)* pebble + -ITE[1]]

pse·phit·ic (sē fit′ik), *adj.* **1.** noting or pertaining to metamorphic rocks derived from psephite. **2.** of or pertaining to psephite. [PSEPHITE + -IC]

pse·phol·o·gy (sē fol′ə jē), *n.* the study of elections. [< Gk *psêpho(s)* pebble + -LOGY; so called from the Athenian custom of casting votes by means of pebbles] —**pse·pho·log·i·cal** (sē′fə loj′i kəl), *adj.* —**pse·phol′o·gist,** *n.*

pseud-, var. of **pseudo-** before a vowel: *pseudaxis.*

pseud., pseudonym.

pseud·am·pho·ra (so͞o dam′fər ə), *n., pl.* **-pho·rae** (-fə rē′). a Mycenaean vase having a spherical body, a spout on the shoulder, and a handle, curving across the top, supported by a solid conical neck. Also called **stirrup jar.** [PSEUD- + AMPHORA]

pseud·ax·is (so͞o dak′sis), *n. Bot.* sympodium. [PSEUD- + AXIS]

pseud·e·pig·ra·pha (so͞o′də pig′rə fə), *n.* (*construed as pl.*) certain writings (other than the canonical books and the Apocrypha) professing to be Biblical in character, but not considered canonical or inspired. [< NL < Gk, neut. pl. of *pseudepígraphos* falsely inscribed, bearing a false title. See PSEUD-, EPIGRAPH, -OUS] —**pseud·ep·i·graph·ic** (so͞o′dep ə graf′ik), **pseud′ep·i·graph′i·cal, pseud′e·pig′ra·phous, pseud′e·pig′ra·phal,** *adj.*

pseud·e·pig·ra·phy (so͞o′də pig′rə fē), *n.* the false ascription of a piece of writing to an author. [PSEUDEPIGRAPH(A) + -Y[3]]

pseu·di·so·dom·ic (so͞o′di sə dom′ik), *adj. Archit.* (of ashlar) composed of stones having the same length, laid in courses of different heights. [< Gk *pseudisódom(os).* See PSEUD-, ISODOMIC]

pseu·do (so͞o′dō), *adj.* false; counterfeit; spurious; sham; pretended. [ME: pretender; independent use of PSEUDO-]

pseudo-, a learned borrowing from Greek meaning "false," "pretended," used in the formation of compound words (*pseudoclassic; pseudo-intellectual; pseudosentence*): in scientific use, denoting close or deceptive resemblance to the following element (*pseudomorph; pseudoparalysis*), and used sometimes in chemical names of isomers (*pseudoephedrine*). Also, *esp. before a vowel,* **pseud-.** [< Gk, comb. form of *pseudḗs* false]

pseu·do·a·quat·ic (so͞o′dō ə kwat′ik, -kwot′-), *adj.* not aquatic but indigenous to moist regions. [PSEUDO- + AQUATIC]

pseu·do·carp (so͞o′də kärp′), *n. Bot.* a fruit which includes parts in addition to the mature ovary and its contents, as the apple, pineapple, etc. [PSEUDO- + -CARP] —**pseu′do·car′pous,** *adj.*

pseu·do·cer·cus (so͞o′dō sûr′kəs, -ker′-), *n., pl.* **-cer·ci** (-sûr′sī, -ker′kē). the median jointed caudal appendage of certain insects, as the bristletails. Also called **urogomphus.** [PSEUDO- + CERCUS]

pseu·do·clas·sic (so͞o′dō klas′ik), *adj.* **1.** falsely or spuriously classic. **2.** imitating or affecting that which is classic: *the pseudoclassic style of some modern authors.* [PSEUDO- + CLASSIC] —**pseu·do·clas·si·cism** (so͞o′dō klas′i siz′əm), **pseu′do·clas′si·cal′i·ty,** *n.*

pseu·do·code (so͞o′dō kōd′), *n. Computer Technol.* a program code unrelated to the hardware of a particular computer and requiring conversion to the code used by the computer before the program can be used. Also called **symbolic code.**

pseu·do·coel (so͞o′dō sēl′), *n. Zool.* the body cavity of certain invertebrate metazoan animals between the body wall and the intestine, which is not lined with a mesodermal epithelium. Also, **pseu′do·cele′, pseu′do·coele′, pseu·do·coe·lom** (so͞o′dō sē′ləm), **pseu·do·coe·lome** (so͞o′dō sē′lōm, -ləm), **pseu·do·ce·lom** (so͞o′dō sē′ləm). [PSEUDO- + *-coel* (var. of -COELE)]

pseu·do·coe·lo·mate (so͞o′dō sē′lə māt′, -sē lō′mit), *adj. Zool.* having a pseudocoel. [PSEUDO- + COELOM + -ATE[1]]

pseu·do·de·men·tia (so͞o′dō di men′shə, -shē ə), *n. Psychol.* a temporary inability to use one's intelligence, caused by extreme apathy or other emotional factors. [PSEUDO- + DEMENTIA]

Pseu·do-Di·o·ny·si·us (so͞o′dō dī′ə nish′ē əs, -nis′-), *n.* fl. c 4th or 5th century A.D., author of a number of mystical works: identified, during the Middle Ages, with Dionysius the Areopagite.

pseu·do·dip·ter·al (so͞o′dō dip′tər əl), *adj. Archit.* having an arrangement of columns suggesting a dipteral structure but without the inner colonnade. [< Gk *pseudodípter(os)* (see PSEUDO-, DIPTERAL) + -AL[1]]

pseu·do·e·phed·rine (so͞o′dō i fed′rin, -ef′i drēn′, -drin), *n. Pharm.* a dextrorotatory, isomeric compound, $C_6H_5CHOHCH(NHCH_3)CH_3$, used in the form of its hydrochloride as a nasal decongestant. [PSEUDO- + EPHEDRINE]

pseu·do·he·mo·phil·i·a (so͞o′dō hē′mə fil′ē ə, -fēl′yə, -hem′ə-), *n. Pathol.* a condition caused by a defect in the quality of blood platelets and characterized by a prolonged bleeding time but without the delayed coagulation time of hemophilia. Also called **hemogenia.** [PSEUDO- + HEMOPHILIA]

pseu·do·her·maph·ro·dite (so͞o′dō hûr maf′rə dīt′), *n.* an individual having male and female external sex organs and internal reproductive organs of one sex. Cf. **hermaphrodite** (def. 1). [PSEUDO- + HERMAPHRODITE] —**pseu·do·her·maph·ro·dit·ic** (so͞o′dō hûr maf′rə dit′ik), *adj.* —**pseu·do·her·maph·ro·dit·ism** (so͞o′dō hûr maf′rə dī tiz′əm), **pseu·do·her·maph·ro·dism** (so͞o′dō hûr maf′rə diz′əm), *n.*

pseu·do·hi·er·o·glyph·ic (so͞o′dō hī′ər ə glif′ik, -hī′rə-), *adj.* noting or pertaining to a script dating from the second millennium B.C. that appears to be syllabic and to represent the Phoenician language and that is inscribed on objects found at Byblos.

pseu′do·ac′a·dem′ic, *adj.*
pseu′do·ac′a·dem′i·cal·ly, *adv.*
pseu′do·ac′ci·den′tal, *adj.*; -ly, *adv.*
pseu′do·ac·quaint′ance, *n.*
pseu′do·ac′ro·meg′a·ly, *n.*
pseu′do·aes·thet′ic, *adj.*
pseu′do·aes·thet′i·cal·ly, *adv.*
pseu′do·af·fec′tion·ate, *adj.*; -ly, *adv.*
pseu′do-Af′ri·can, *adj.*
pseu′do·ag·gres′sive, *adj.*; -ly, *adv.*
pseu′do·al′le·go·ris′tic, *adj.*
pseu′do·al·ve′o·lar, *adj.*
pseu′do·am′a·teur′ish, *adj.*; -ly, *adv.*
pseu′do·am′a·teur′ism, *n.*
pseu′do·am′a·to′ri·al, *adj.*
pseu′do·am′a·to′ry, *adj.*
pseu′do·am′bi·dex′trous, *adj.*; -ly, *adv.*
pseu′do·a·me′boid, *adj.*
pseu′do-A·mer′i·can, *adj.*
pseu′do·a·nach′ro·nis′tic, *adj.*
pseu′do·a·nach′ro·nis′ti·cal, *adj.*
pseu′do·an′a·phy·lac′tic, *adj.*
pseu′do·an′ar·chis′tic, *adj.*
pseu′do·an′a·tom′ic, *adj.*
pseu′do·an′a·tom′i·cal, *adj.*; -ly, *adv.*
pseu′do·an·ces′tral, *adj.*; -ly, *adv.*
pseu′do·a·ne′mi·a, *n.*
pseu′do·a·ne′mic, *adj.*
pseu′do·an·gel′ic, *adj.*
pseu′do·an·gel′i·cal, *adj.*; -ly, *adv.*
pseu′do·an′gu·lar, *adj.*; -ly, *adv.*
pseu′do·an′thro·poid′, *adj.*
pseu′do·an′thro·po·log′i·cal, *adj.*
pseu′do·an·tique′, *adj.*
pseu′do·a·pol′o·get′ic, *adj.*
pseu′do·a·pol′o·get′i·cal·ly, *adv.*
pseu′do·ap′o·plec′tic, *adj.*
pseu′do·ap′o·plec′ti·cal, *adj.*; -ly, *adv.*
pseu′do·ap·pen′di·ci′tis, *n.*
pseu′do·ap′pli·ca′tive, *adj.*
pseu′do·ap′pre·hen′sive, *adj.*; -ly, *adv.*
pseu′do·ar·cha′ic, *adj.*
pseu′do·ar·cha′i·cal·ly, *adv.*
pseu′do-Ar′gen·tin′e·an, *adj.*
pseu′do-Ar′gen·tin′i·an, *adj.*
pseu′do·a·ris′to·crat′ic, *adj.*
pseu′do·a·ris′to·crat′i·cal, *adj.*; -ly, *adv.*
pseu′do-Ar′is·to·te′li·an, *adj.*
pseu′do·ar·tic′u·late, *adj.*; -ly, *adv.*
pseu′do·ar·tis′tic, *adj.*
pseu′do·ar·tis′ti·cal·ly, *adv.*
pseu′do-Ar′y·an, *adj.*
pseu′do·as·cet′ic, *adj.*
pseu′do·as·cet′i·cal, *adj.*; -ly, *adv.*
pseu′do·as·ser′tive, *adj.*; -ly, *adv.*
pseu′do·as·so′ci·a′tion·al, *adj.*
pseu′do-As·syr′i·an, *adj.*
pseu′do·a′sym·met′ric, *adj.*
pseu′do·a′sym·met′ri·cal, *adj.*; -ly, *adv.*
pseu′do-Aus·tral′ian, *adj.*
pseu′do-Aus′tri·an, *adj.*
pseu′do-Bab′y·lo′ni·an, *adj.*
pseu′do·bank′rupt, *adj.*
pseu′do·bap·tis′mal, *adj.*
pseu′do-Bap′tist, *adj.*
pseu′do-Bel′gian, *adj.*
pseu′do·ben′e·fac′to·ry, *adj.*
pseu′do·be·nev′o·lent, *adj.*; -ly, *adv.*
pseu′do·bi′o·graph′ic, *adj.*
pseu′do·bi′o·graph′i·cal, *adj.*; -ly, *adv.*
pseu′do·bi′o·log′i·cal, *adj.*; -ly, *adv.*
pseu′do-Bo·he′mi·an, *adj.*
pseu′do-Bo·liv′i·an, *adj.*
pseu′do·bra′chi·al, *adj.*
pseu′do·bra′chi·um, *n., pl.* **-chi·a.**
pseu′do-Brah′man, *adj.*
pseu′do-Bra·zil′ian, *adj.*
pseu′do·broth′er·ly, *adv.*
pseu′do-Bud′dhist, *adj.*
pseu′do-Bul·gar′i·an, *adj.*
pseu′do-Ca·na′di·an, *adj.*
pseu′do·can′did, *adj.*; -ly, *adv.*
pseu′do·cap′tive, *adj.*
pseu′do-Car′tha·gin′i·an, *adj.*
pseu′do·car′ti·lag′i·nous, *adj.*
pseu′do-Cath′o·lic, *adj.*
pseu′do·ca·thol′i·cal·ly, *adv.*
pseu′do·cen′tric, *adj.*
pseu′do·cer·car′i·a, *n., pl.* **-i·ae.**
pseu′do·char′i·ta·ble, *adj.*; -bly, *adv.*
pseu′do·chem′i·cal, *adj.*
pseu′do-Chil′e·an, *adj.*
pseu′do-Chi·nese′, *adj.*
pseu′do-Chris′tian, *adj.*
pseu′do·chy′lous, *adj.*
pseu′do-Cic′e·ro′ni·an, *adj.*
pseu′do·cler′i·cal, *adj.*; -ly, *adv.*
pseu′do·col′le′giate, *adj.*
pseu′do·col′u·mel′lar, *adj.*
pseu′do·com·mis′su·ral, *adj.*
pseu′do·com·pet′i·tive, *adj.*; -ly, *adv.*
pseu′do·con′cha, *n.*
pseu′do·con·fes′sion·al, *adj.*
pseu′do·con·glom′er·ate, *adj.*
pseu′do·con·serv′a·tive, *adj.*; -ly, *adv.*
pseu′do·cor′ne·ous, *adj.*
pseu′do·cos′ta, *n.*
pseu′do·cot′y·le′don·al, *adj.*
pseu′do·cot′y·le′don·ar′y, *adj.*
pseu′do·cour′te·ous, *adj.*; -ly, *adv.*
pseu′do·crit′i·cal, *adj.*; -ly, *adv.*
pseu′do·crys′tal·line, *adj.*
pseu′do·cu′bic, *adj.*
pseu′do·cu′bi·cal, *adj.*; -ly, *adv.*
pseu′do·cul′ti·vat′ed, *adj.*
pseu′do·cul′tur·al, *adj.*; -ly, *adv.*
pseu′do·cy·clo′sis, *n.*
pseu′do·cy·e′sis, *n.*
pseu′do·cy·phel′la, *n.*
pseu′do-Dan·tesque′, *adj.*
pseu′do-Dem′o·crat′ic, *adj.*
pseu′do·dem′o·crat′ic, *adj.*
pseu′do·dem′o·crat′i·cal·ly, *adv.*
pseu′do·derm′, *n.*
pseu′do·di·as·tol′ic, *adj.*
pseu′do·diph′the′ri·al, *adj.*
pseu′do·diph·ther′ic, *adj.*
pseu′do·diph′the·rit′ic, *adj.*
pseu′do·di·vine′, *adj.*
pseu′do·dra·mat′ic, *adj.*
pseu′do·dra·mat′i·cal·ly, *adv.*
pseu′do-Dutch′, *adj.*
pseu′do-East′In′di·an, *adj.*
pseu′do·e′co·nom′i·cal, *adj.*; -ly, *adv.*
pseu′do·e·de′ma, *n., pl.* **-ma·ta.**
pseu′do·ed′i·to′ri·al, *adj.*; -ly, *adv.*
pseu′do·ed′u·ca′tion·al, *adj.*; -ly, *adv.*
pseu′do-E·gyp′tian, *adj.*
pseu′do·e·lec′tor·al, *adj.*
pseu′do-E·liz′a·be′than, *adj.*
pseu′do·em′bry·on′ic, *adj.*
pseu′do·e·mo′tion·al, *adj.*; -ly, *adv.*
pseu′do·en·ceph′a·lit′ic, *adj.*
pseu′do-Eng′lish, *adj.*
pseu′do·en·thu′si·as′tic, *adj.*
pseu′do·en·thu′si·as′ti·cal·ly, *adv.*
pseu′do·e·pis′co·pal, *adj.*
pseu′do-E·pis′co·pa′lian, *adj.*
pseu′do·e·qual′i·tar′i·an, *adj.*
pseu′do·e·rot′ic, *adj.*
pseu′do·e·rot′i·cal·ly, *adv.*
pseu′do·er′y·si·pel′a·tous, *adj.*
pseu′do·eth′i·cal, *adj.*; -ly, *adv.*
pseu′do·et′y·mo·log′i·cal, *adj.*; -ly, *adv.*
pseu′do-Eu′ro·pe′an, *adj.*
pseu′do·e′van·gel′ic, *adj.*
pseu′do·e′van·gel′i·cal, *adj.*; -ly, *adv.*
pseu′do·ex·per′i·men′tal, *adj.*; -ly, *adv.*
pseu′do·faith′ful, *adj.*; -ly, *adv.*
pseu′do·fa′mous, *adj.*; -ly, *adv.*
pseu′do·fa′ther·ly, *adv.*
pseu′do·fem′i·nine, *adj.*
pseu′do·fe′ver·ish, *adj.*; -ly, *adv.*
pseu′do·fi′nal, *adj.*; -ly, *adv.*
pseu′do-French′, *adj.*
pseu′do·gas′e·ous, *adj.*
pseu′do·gen′er·al, *adj.*
pseu′do·ge·ner′ic, *adj.*
pseu′do·ge·ner′i·cal, *adj.*; -ly, *adv.*
pseu′do·gen·teel′, *adj.*
pseu′do·gen′tle·man·ly, *adv.*
pseu′do·ge′nus, *n., pl.* **-gen·er·a, -gen·us·es.**
pseu′do-Geor′gian, *adj.*
pseu′do-Ger′man, *adj.*
pseu′do-Ger·man′ic, *adj.*
pseu′do-Goth′ic, *adj.*
pseu′do-Gre′cian, *adj.*
pseu′do-Greek′, *adj.*
pseu′do·gy′rate, *adj.*
pseu′do·he′mal, *adj.*
pseu′do·he·ro′ic, *adj.*
pseu′do·he·ro′i·cal, *adj.*; -ly, *adv.*
pseu′do·hex·ag′o·nal, *adj.*; -ly, *adv.*

pseu·do·in·tel·lec·tu·al (so͞o′dō in′tᵊlek′cho͞o əl), *n.* **1.** a person who pretends to be an intellectual. **—*adj.* 2.** of, pertaining to, or characterized by fraudulent intellectuality; unscholarly: *a pseudointellectual book.* [PSEUDO- + INTELLECTUAL] **—pseu′do·in′tel·lec′tu·al·ly,** *adv.*

Pseu·do-Is·i·do·ri·an (so͞o′dō iz′i dôr′ē ən, -dōr′-), *adj.* of or pertaining to the collection of documents of the 9th century A.D. that consist chiefly of the Decretals, attributed to Isidore, archbishop of Seville, A.D. 600–36, and that were rejected as spurious in the 15th century.

pseu·do·mem·o·ry (so͞o′dō mem′ə rē), *n.* paramnesia. [PSEUDO- + MEMORY]

pseu·do·met·ric (so͞o′dō me′trik), *n.* *Math.* a function similar to a metric but having the property that two points that do not coincide may have functional value zero. [PSEUDO- + METRIC[1]]

pseu′domet′ric space′, *Math.* a topological space with a pseudometric defined on it.

pseu·dom·o·nas (so͞o dom′ə nəs, -nas′), *n., pl.* **pseu·do·mon·a·des** (so͞o′də mon′ə dēz′). *Bacteriol.* any of several rod-shaped bacteria of the genus *Pseudomonas,* certain species of which are pathogenic for plants and, sometimes, animals. [PSEUDO- + *-monas* unit (< LL; see MONAD)]

pseu·do·morph (so͞o′də môrf′), *n.* **1.** an irregular or unclassifiable form. **2.** a mineral having the outward appearance of another mineral which it has replaced by chemical action. [PSEUDO- + -MORPH] **—pseu′do·mor′phic, pseu′do·mor′phous,** *adj.* **—pseu′do·mor′phism,** *n.*

pseu·do·nym (so͞od′ᵊnim), *n.* a fictitious name used by an author to conceal his identity; pen name. Cf. **allonym** (def. 1). [< Gk *pseudṓnym(on)* false name] **—Syn.** alias, nom de plume.

pseu·do·nym·i·ty (so͞od′ᵊnim′i tē), *n.* **1.** pseudonymous character. **2.** use of a pseudonym. [PSEUDONYM + -ITY]

pseu·don·y·mous (so͞o don′ə məs), *adj.* **1.** bearing a false or fictitious name. **2.** writing or written under a fictitious name. [< Gk *pseudṓnymos*] **—pseu·don′y·mous·ly,** *adv.* **—pseu·don′y·mous·ness,** *n.*

pseu·do·pa·ral·y·sis (so͞o′dō pə ral′i sis), *n.* *Med.* the inability to move a part of the body owing to factors, as pain, other than those causing actual paralysis. [PSEUDO- + PARALYSIS] **—pseu·do·par·a·lyt·ic** (so͞o′-də par′ə lit′ik), *adj.*

pseu·do·pe·rip·ter·al (so͞o′dō pə rip′tər əl), *adj.* *Archit.* having a freestanding colonnade at each end, with engaged columns at the sides. [PSEUDO- + PERIPTERAL]

pseu·do·phone (so͞o′də fōn′), *n.* an instrument for producing illusory auditory localization by changing the relationship between the receptor and the actual direction of the sound. [PSEUDO- + -PHONE]

pseu·do·po·di·um (so͞o′də pō′dē əm), *n., pl.* **-di·a** (-dē ə). a temporary protrusion of the protoplasm of a protozoan, serving as an organ of locomotion, prehension, etc. Also, **pseu·do·pod** (so͞o′də pod′). See diag. under **amoeba.** [< NL; see PSEUDO-, -PODIUM] **—pseu·dop·o·dal** (so͞o dop′ə dᵊl), **pseu′do·po′di·al, pseu·do·pod·ic** (so͞o′də pod′ik), *adj.*

pseu·do·pro·style (so͞o′dō prō′stīl), *adj.* *Archit.* having a colonnade at each end, either very close to the front wall or engaged in it. [PSEUDO- + PROSTYLE]

pseu·do·sca·lar (so͞o′də skā′lər), *adj.* *Physics, Math.* a scalar quantity that changes sign when the sense of the orientation of the coordinate system is changed. [PSEUDO- + SCALAR]

pseu·do·scope (so͞o′də skōp′), *n.* an optical instrument for producing an image in which the depth or relief of an object is reversed. Cf. **stereoscope.**

pseu·dos·co·py (so͞o dos′kə pē), *n.* the use of a pseudoscope. [PSEUDOSCOPE + -Y[3]]

pseu·do·scor·pi·on (so͞o′dō skôr′pē ən), *n.* any of several small arachnids of the order *Chelonethida* that resemble a tailless scorpion and that feed chiefly on small insects. Also called **book scorpion.** [< NL *Pseudoscorpion(es).* See PSEUDO-, SCORPION]

pseu·do·sen·tence (so͞o′dō sen′tᵊns), *n.* *Logical Positivism.* a sentence rejected as meaningless because it does not express anything verifiable in experience.

pseu·do·so·lu·tion (so͞o′dō sə lo͞o′shən), *n.* *Physical Chem.* a colloidal suspension in which the finely divided particles appear to be dissolved because they are so widely dispersed in the surrounding medium. [PSEUDO- + SOLUTION]

pseu·do·sphere (so͞o′də sfēr′), *n.* *Geom.* a surface generated by revolving a tractrix about its asymptote. [PSEUDO- + SPHERE] **—pseu·do·spher·i·cal** (so͞o′də-sfer′i kəl), *adj.*

pseu·do·trip·ter·al (so͞o′dō trip′tər əl), *adj.* *Archit.* having an arrangement of columns suggesting a tripteral structure but without the inner colonnades. [PSEUDO- + TRIPTERAL]

psf, pounds per square foot. Also, **p.s.f.**

pshaw (shô), *interj.* **1.** (used to express impatience, contempt, disbelief, etc.) **—*n.* 2.** an exclamation of "pshaw!" **—*v.i.* 3.** to say "pshaw." **—*v.t.* 4.** to say "pshaw" at or to.

psi (sī, psē), *n., pl.* **psis. 1.** the 23rd letter of the Greek alphabet (Ψ, ψ). **2.** the group of consonant sounds represented by this letter. [< Gk]

psi, pounds per square inch. Also, **p.s.i.**

psia, pounds per square inch, absolute.

psid, pounds per square inch, differential.

psig, pounds per square inch, gauge.

psi·lan·thro·pism (sī lan′thrə piz′əm), *n.* the doctrine that Jesus Christ was only a human being. Also, **psi·lan′thro·py.** [< Gk *psīlánthrōp(os)* merely human (*psīl(ós)* mere + *ánthrōp(os)* man + *-os* -OUS) + -ISM] **—psi·lan·throp·ic** (sī′lən throp′ik), *adj.* **—psi·lan′thro·pist,** *n.*

psil·o·cy·bin (sil′ə sī′bin, sī′lə-), *n.* *Pharm.* a crystalline solid, $C_{13}H_{18}O_3N_2P_2$, obtained from the mushroom *Psilocybe mexicana,* having a psychedelic effect: used in psychological experimentation as a hallucinogen. [< NL *Psilocyb(e)* kind of mushroom (< Gk *psīló(s)* bare + *kýbē* head) + -IN[2]]

psi·lom·e·lane (sī lom′ə lān′), *n.* a common mineral consisting of various impure manganese compounds, usually found in black, rounded masses: an ore of manganese. [< Gk *psīló(s)* bare, smooth + *mélan,* neut. of *mélas* black]

Psi·lo·ri·ti (*Gk.* psē′lô rē′tē), *n.* **Mount,** modern name of Mount Ida.

psi·lo·sis (sī lō′sis), *n.* *Pathol.* **1.** a falling out of the hair. **2.** sprue[2]. [< NL < Gk: lit., a stripping bare, verbal of *psīloûn* to strip, deriv. of *psīlós* bare, smooth; see -OSIS] **—psi·lot·ic** (sī lot′ik, -lō′tik), *adj.*

psit·ta·cin·ite (sit′ə si nīt′), *n.* a mineral, lead and copper vanadate and hydroxide, occurring in the form of orthorhombic crystals. [< L *psittacīn(us)* parrotlike (*psittac(us)* parrot + *-īnus* -INE[1]) + -ITE[1]; see PSITTACOSIS]

psit·ta·cism (sit′ə siz′əm), *n.* mechanical, repetitive, and meaningless speech. [< L *psittac(us)* parrot (see PSITTACOSIS) + -ISM] **—psit′ta·cis′tic,** *adj.*

psit·ta·co·sis (sit′ə kō′sis), *n.* *Pathol.* a severe infectious disease characterized by high fever and pulmonary involvement, recently introduced into the U.S. by parrots and easily transmissible to man; parrot fever. [< L *psittac(us)* parrot (< Gk *psittakós*) + -OSIS]

Pskov (pskôf), *n.* **1.** a lake in the W Soviet Union in Europe, forming the S part of Lake Peipus. **2.** a city near this lake. 105,000 (est. 1964).

pso·as (sō′əs), *n.* (*construed as sing.*) *Anat.* either of two muscles, one on each side of the loin, extending internally from the sides of the spinal column to the upper end of the femur, which assist in bending either the thigh or the lumbar portion of the trunk on the pelvis. [< NL < Gk *psóas,* acc. pl. (taken as nom. sing.) of *psóa* a muscle of the loins] **—pso·at·ic** (sō at′ik), *adj.*

pso·cid (sō′sid, sos′id), *n.* a small insect of the family *Psocidae* (order *Psocoptera*), having mouth parts adapted for chewing and feeding on fungi, lichens, decaying plant material, etc. [< NL *Psōcid(ae),* equiv. to *Psōc(us)* name of a genus (< Gk *psṓchos* dust) + *-idae* -ID[2]] **—psoc·ine** (sos′īn, -in), *adj.*

pso·ra (sōr′ə, sôr′ə), *n.* *Pathol.* **1.** psoriasis. **2.** scabies. [< L < Gk: itch] **—pso·ric** (sôr′ik, sor′-), *adj.*

pso·ra·le·a (sə rā′lē ə, sō-), *n.* any leguminous plant of the genus *Psoralea,* esp. the breadroot, *P. esculenta.* [< NL (genus name) < Gk *psōraléa,* neut. pl. of *psōraléos* mangy, with reference to the glandular dots on the plant; see PSORIASIS]

pso·ri·a·sis (sə rī′ə sis), *n.* *Pathol.* a common chronic skin disease characterized by scaly patches. Also called **psora.** [< NL < Gk, verbid of *psōriân* to have the itch. See PSORA, -IASIS] **—pso·ri·at·ic** (sôr′ē at′ik, sōr′-), *adj.*

pso·ro·sis (sə rō′sis), *n.* *Plant Pathol.* a disease of citrus trees, characterized by a scaly, rough bark, yellowing of leaves, and stunting, caused by a virus. [< NL; see PSORA, -OSIS]

P.SS., postscripts. Also, **p.ss.** [< L *postscripta*]

PST, Pacific Standard Time. Also, **P.S.T., p.s.t.**

P-state (pē′stāt′), *n.* *Physics.* the energy state of an electron in an atom having an orbital angular momentum of one unit: so called because spectral lines from such states in alkali spectra were originally considered principal in that they are produced with little energy.

psych (sīk), *v.t.,* **psyched, psych·ing.** *Slang.* to intimidate or frighten psychologically, or make nervous (often fol. by *out*): *to psych out the competition.*

psych-, var. of **psycho-** before some vowels: *psychasthenia.*

psych., **1.** psychological. **2.** psychology.

psy·cha·nal·y·sis (sī′kə nal′i sis), *n.* psychoanalysis. **—psy·chan·a·lyt·ic** (sī′kanᵊlit′ik), **psy′chan·a·lyt′i·cal,** *adj.* **—psy′chan·a·lyt′i·cal·ly,** *adv.*

psy·chas·the·ni·a (sī′kas thē′nē ə, -thə nī′ə), *n.* **1.** *Psychiatry Obs.* a neurosis marked by fear, anxiety, phobias, etc. **2.** *Pathol.* mental weakness or exhaustion. [< NL; see PSYCH-, ASTHENIA] **—psy·chas·then·ic** (sī′kas-then′ik), *adj.*

psy·cha·tax·i·a (sī′kə tak′sē ə), *n.* *Psychiatry.* inability to concentrate. [< NL, equiv. to *psycha-,* var. of PSYCHO- + *-taxia* (see -TAXY)]

Psy·che (sī′kē), *n.* **1.** *Class. Myth.* a personification of the soul, which in the form of a beautiful girl was loved by Eros. **2.** (*l.c.*) the human soul, spirit, or mind. **3.** (*l.c.*) *Psychol., Psychoanal.* the mental or psychological structure of a person, esp. as a motive force. **4.** *Neoplatonism.* the second emanation of the One, regarded as a universal consciousness and as the animating principle of the world. **5.** a girl's given name. [< L < Gk: lit., breath, deriv. of *psýchein* to breathe, blow, hence, live]

psych·e·del·ic (sī′ki del′ik), *adj.* **1.** of or noting a mental state characterized by a profound sense of intensified sensory perception, sometimes accompanied by severe perceptual distortion and hallucinations and by extreme feelings of either euphoria or despair. **2.** of or noting any of various drugs producing this state, as LSD, mescaline, or psilocybin. **3.** resembling, characteristic of, or reproducing images, sounds, or the like, experienced while in such a state: *psychedelic painting.* Also, **psychodelic.** [PSYCHE + Gk *dēl(os)* visible, manifest, evident + -IC] **—psych′e·del′i·cal·ly,** *adv.*

Psy′che knot′, a woman's hairdo in which a knot or coil of hair projects from the back of the head.

psy·chi·a·trist (si kī′ə trist, sī-), *n.* a physician who practices psychiatry. [PSYCHIATR(Y) + -IST]

psy·chi·a·try (si kī′ə trē, sī-), *n.* the practice or the science of treating mental diseases. [PSYCH- + -IATRY] **—psy·chi·at·ric** (sī′kē a′trik), **psy′chi·at′ri·cal,** *adj.* **—psy′chi·at′ri·cal·ly,** *adv.*

psy·chic (sī′kik), *adj.* Also, **psy′chi·cal. 1.** of or pertaining to the human soul or mind; mental (opposed to *physical*). **2.** *Psychol.* pertaining to or noting mental phenomena that cannot be explained otherwise than as originating outside of or independently of normal physiological processes. **3.** outside of natural or scientific knowledge; spiritual. **4.** of, pertaining to, associated with, attributed to, or caused by some nonphysical force or agency: *psychic research; psychic phenomena.* **5.** specially sensitive to influences or forces of a nonphysical, apparently supernatural nature. **—*n.* 6.** a person who is specially sensitive to psychic influences or forces; medium. [< Gk *psychik(ós)* of the soul. See PSYCHE, -IC] **—psy′chi·cal·ly,** *adv.*

psy′chic bid′, *Bridge.* a bid designed to mislead one's opponents that is not based on the strength of one's hand or of the suit named but rather on one's feeling that not bidding would be more costly.

pseu′do-Hin′du, *adj.*
pseu′do·his·tor′ic, *adj.*
pseu′do·his·tor′i·cal, *adj.;* **-ly,** *adv.*
pseu′do-Ho·mer′ic, *adj.*
pseu′do·hu′man, *adj.*
pseu′do·hu′man·is′tic, *adj.*
pseu′do-Hun·gar′i·an, *adj.*
pseu′do·hy′per·troph′ic, *adj.*
pseu′do·i·den′ti·cal, *adj.*
pseu′do·im·par′tial, *adj.;* **-ly,** *adv.*
pseu′do-In′can, *adj.*
pseu′do·in′de·pend′ent, *adj.;* **-ly,** *adv.*
pseu′do-In′di·an, *adj.*
pseu′do·in·sane′, *adj.*
pseu′do·in′spi·ra′tion·al, *adj.*
pseu′do·in·spir′ing, *adj.*
pseu′do·in′ter·na′tion·al, *adj.*
pseu′do·in′ter·na′tion·al·is′tic, *adj.*
pseu′do·in′va·lid, *adj.*
pseu′do·in·val′id, *adj.;* **-ly,** *adv.*
pseu′do-I·ra′ni·an, *adj.*
pseu′do-I′rish, *adj.*
pseu′do·i′so·met′ric, *adj.*
pseu′do-I·tal′ian, *adj.*
pseu′do-Jap′a·nese′, *adj.*
pseu′do·la′bi·al, *adj.*
pseu′do·la′bi·um, *n., pl.* **-bi·a.**
pseu′do·lam′i·nat′ed, *adj.*
pseu′do·lat′er·al, *adj.*
pseu′do·le′gal, *adj.*
pseu′do·le·gal′i·ty, *n.*
pseu′do·leg′end·ar′y, *adj.*
pseu′do·leg′is·la′tive, *adj.*
pseu′do·leu′cite, *n.*
pseu′do·leu′co·cyte′, *n.*
pseu′do·lib′er·al, *adj.;* **-ly,** *adv.*
pseu′do·lin·guis′tic, *adj.*
pseu′do·lin·guis′ti·cal·ly, *adv.*
pseu′do·lit′er·ar′y, *adj.*
pseu′do·lo′bar, *adj.*
pseu′do·lu′nu·la, *n., pl.* **-lae.**
pseu′do·lu′nule, *n.*
pseu′do·ma·lar′i·a, *n.*
pseu′do·mas′cu·line, *adj.*
pseu′do-Ma′yan, *adj.*
pseu′do·med′i·cal, *adj.;* **-ly,** *adv.*
pseu′do·me′di·e′val, *adj.;* **-ly,** *adv.*
pseu′do-Mes′si·an′ic, *adj.*
pseu′do-Meth′o·dist, *adj.*
pseu′do-Mex′i·can, *adj.*
pseu′do·mil′i·tar′i·ly, *adv.*
pseu′do·mil′i·ta·ris′tic, *adj.*
pseu′do·mil′i·tar′y, *adj.*
pseu′do-Mil·ton′ic, *adj.*
pseu′do·min′is·te′ri·al, *adj.*
pseu′do·min′is·try, *n.*
pseu′do·mi·rac′u·lous, *adj.;* **-ly,** *adv.*
pseu′do·mod′ern, *adj.*
pseu′do·mod′est, *adj.;* **-ly,** *adv.*
pseu′do-Mo·ham′med·an, *adj.*
pseu′do·mo·nas′tic, *adj.*
pseu′do·mo·nas′ti·cal, *adj.;* **-ly,** *adv.*
pseu′do-Mon·go′li·an, *adj.*
pseu′do·mon′o·clin′ic, *adj.*
pseu′do·mon′o·cy′clic, *adj.*
pseu′do·mor′al, *adj.*
pseu′do·mor′al·is′tic, *adj.*
pseu′do·mor′u·lar, *adj.*
pseu′do-Mos′lem, *adj.*
pseu′do·mul′ti·loc′u·lar, *adj.*
pseu′do·mul′ti·sep′tate, *adj.*
pseu′do-Mus′lem, *adj.*
pseu′do-Mus′lim, *adj.*
pseu′do·myth′i·cal, *adj.;* **-ly,** *adv.*
pseu′do·nar·cot′ic, *adj.*
pseu′do·na′tion·al, *adj.;* **-ly,** *adv.*
pseu′do·no′ble, *adj.*
pseu′do-Nor·we′gian, *adj.*
pseu′do·oc′ci·den′tal, *adj.*
pseu′do·of·fi′cial, *adj.;* **-ly,** *adv.*
pseu′do·or·gan′ic, *adj.*
pseu′do·or·gan′i·cal·ly, *adv.*
pseu′do·o′ri·en′tal, *adj.;* **-ly,** *adv.*
pseu′do·or′tho·rhom′bic, *adj.*
pseu′do·o′val, *adj.;* **-ly,** *adv.*
pseu′do·pa′gan, *adj.*
pseu′do-Pan′a·ma′ni·an, *adj.*
pseu′do·pa′pal, *adj.*
pseu′do·par′al·lel′, *adj.*
pseu′do·par′a·sit′ic, *adj.*
pseu′do·pa′tri·ot′ic, *adj.*
pseu′do·pa′tri·ot′i·cal·ly, *adv.*
pseu′do·ped′i·form′, *adj.*
pseu′do·per′ma·nent, *adj.*
pseu′do-Per′sian, *adj.*
pseu′do·phal′lic, *adj.*
pseu′do·phil′an·throp′ic, *adj.*
pseu′do·phil′an·throp′i·cal, *adj.;* **-ly,** *adv.*
pseu′do·phil′o·soph′i·cal, *adj.*
pseu′do·pi′ous, *adj.;* **-ly,** *adv.*
pseu′do·po·et′ic, *adj.*
pseu′do·po·et′i·cal, *adj.*
pseu′do-Pol′ish, *adj.*
pseu′do·pol′i·tic, *adj.*
pseu′do·po·lit′i·cal, *adj.*
pseu′do·pop′u·lar, *adj.*
pseu′do·por′phy·rit′ic, *adj.*
pseu′do·preg′nant, *adj.*
pseu′do-Pres′by·te′ri·an, *adj.*
pseu′do·priest′ly, *adj.*
pseu′do·prim′i·tive, *adj.*
pseu′do·prince′ly, *adv.*
pseu′do·pro·fes′sion·al, *adj.*
pseu′do·prof′es·so′ri·al, *adj.*
pseu′do·pro·phet′ic, *adj.*
pseu′do·pro·phet′i·cal, *adj.*
pseu′do·pros′per·ous, *adj.;* **-ly,** *adv.*
pseu′do·psy′cho·log′i·cal, *adj.*
pseu′do·py′ri·form′, *adj.*
pseu′do·re′al·is′tic, *adj.*
pseu′do·re·form′a·to′ry, *adj.*
pseu′do·re·formed′, *adj.*
pseu′do·re′gal, *adj.;* **-ly,** *adv.*
pseu′do·re·li′gious, *adj.;* **-ly,** *adv.*
pseu′do-Re·pub′li·can, *adj.*
pseu′do·re·pub′li·can, *adj.*
pseu′do·res′i·dent, *adj.*
pseu′do·res′i·den′tial, *adj.*
pseu′do·rheu·mat′ic, *adj.*
pseu′do·rhom′bo·he′dral, *adj.*
pseu′do-Ro′man, *adj.*
pseu′do·ro·man′tic, *adj.*
pseu′do·ro·man′ti·cal·ly, *adv.*
pseu′do·roy′al, *adj.;* **-ly,** *adv.*
pseu′do-Rus′sian, *adj.*
pseu′do·sa′cred, *adj.*
pseu′do·sac′ri·le′gious, *adj.;* **-ly,** *adv.*
pseu′do·sa·tir′i·cal, *adj.;* **-ly,** *adv.*
pseu′do·schol′ar·ly, *adj.*
pseu′do·scho·las′tic, *adj.*
pseu′do·scho·las′ti·cal·ly, *adv.*
pseu′do·sci′en·tif′ic, *adj.*
pseu′do·sci′en·tif′i·cal·ly, *adv.*
pseu′do·se·man′tic, *adj.*
pseu′do·se·man′ti·cal·ly, *adv.*
pseu′do-Se·mit′ic, *adj.*
pseu′do·sen·sa′tion·al, *adj.*
pseu′do-Ser′bi·an, *adj.*
pseu′do·ser′vile, *adj.;* **-ly,** *adv.*
pseu′do·ses′sile, *adj.*
pseu′do-Shake·spear′e·an, *adj.*
pseu′do-Shake·spear′i·an, *adj.*
pseu′do·si·phon′al, *adj.*
pseu′do·si·phon′ic, *adj.*
pseu′do·skel′e·tal, *adj.*
pseu′do·so′cial, *adj.;* **-ly,** *adv.*
pseu′do·so′cial·is′tic, *adj.*
pseu′do-So·crat′ic, *adj.*
pseu′do-Span′ish, *adj.*
pseu′do·spec′tral, *adj.*
pseu′do·spir′i·tu·al, *adj.;* **-ly,** *adv.*
pseu′do·squa′mate, *adj.*
pseu′do·stal′ac·tit′ic, *adj.*
pseu′do·stal′ag·mit′ic, *adj.*
pseu′do·stig′mat′ic, *adj.*
pseu′do·stu′di·ous, *adj.;* **-ly,** *adv.*
pseu′do·sub′tle, *adj.;* **-tly,** *adv.*
pseu′do·su′i·ci′dal, *adj.*
pseu′do-Swed′ish, *adj.*
pseu′do·symp′to·mat′ic, *adj.*
pseu′do·syph′il·it′ic, *adj.*
pseu′do·te·trag′o·nal, *adj.*
pseu′do·trib′al, *adj.;* **-ly,** *adv.*
pseu′do-Turk′ish, *adj.*
pseu′do·var′i·an, *adj.*
pseud·o·va·ry, *n., pl.* **-ries.**
pseu′do·ve′lar, *adj.*
pseu′do-Ver·gil′i·an, *adj.*
pseu′do-Vic·to′ri·an, *adj.*
pseu′do·vi′per·ine, *adj.*
pseu′do·vi′per·ous, *adj.;* **-ly,** *adv.*
pseu′do-Vir·gil′i·an, *adj.*
pseu′do·vis′cous, *adj.*
pseu′do·zeal′ous, *adj.;* **-ly,** *adv.*
pseu′do·zo′o·gloe′al, *adj.*
pseu′do·zo′o·log′i·cal, *adj.*

psy′chic deaf′ness, *Pathol.* See **word deafness.**

psy′chic dis′tance, the degree of detachment maintained toward something or someone. Also, **psy′chical dis′tance.**

psy′chic en′ergizer, *Med.* any of a class of drugs used in the treatment of mental depression; antidepressant.

psy′chic in′come, the personal or subjective benefits, rewards, or satisfactions derived from a job or undertaking as separate from its objective or financial ones.

psy·cho (sī′kō), *n., pl.* **-chos,** *adj. Slang.* **—***n.* **1.** a psychopathic or neurotic person. **—***adj.* **2.** psychopathic; psychoneurotic. [shortened form]

psycho-, a learned borrowing from Greek, used to represent **psyche** (*psychological*) and **psychological** (*psychoanalysis*) in compound words. Also, *esp. before a vowel,* **psych-.** [< Gk, comb. form of *psȳchḗ* breath, spirit, soul, mind]

psychoanal., psychoanalysis.

psy·cho·a·nal·y·sis (sī′kō ə nal′i sis), *n.* **1.** a systematic structure of theories concerning the relation of conscious and unconscious psychological processes. **2.** a technical procedure for investigating unconscious mental processes and for treating psychoneuroses. Also, **psychanalysis.** [< G *Psychoanalyse.* See PSYCHO-, ANALYSIS] **—psy·cho·an·a·lyt·ic** (sī′kō an′əlit′ik), **psy′cho·an′a·lyt′i·cal,** *adj.* **—psy′cho·an′a·lyt′i·cal·ly,** *adv.*

psy·cho·an·a·lyst (sī′kō an′əlist), *n.* a person trained to practice psychoanalysis. [PSYCHO- + ANALYST]

psy·cho·an·a·lyze (sī′kō an′əlīz′), *v.t.,* **-lyzed, -lyzing.** to investigate or treat by psychoanalysis. [PSY-CHO- + ANALYZE] **—psy′cho·an′a·lyz′er,** *n.*

psy·cho·bi·ol·o·gy (sī′kō bī ol′ə jē), *n.* **1.** the branch of biology dealing with the relations or interactions between body and mind, esp. as exhibited in the nervous system, receptors, effectors, or the like. **2.** psychology as studied by biological methods or in terms of biology. [< G *Psychobiologie.* See PSYCHO-, BIOLOGY] **—psy·cho·bi·o·log·i·cal** (sī′kō bī′ə loj′i kəl), **psy′cho·bi′o·log′ic,** *adj.* **—psy′cho·bi·ol′o·gist,** *n.*

psy·cho·del·ic (sī′kō del′ik), *adj.* psychedelic.

psy·cho·di·ag·no·sis (sī′kō dī′əg nō′sis), *n.* a psychological examination using psychodiagnostic techniques. [< NL; see PSYCHO-, DIAGNOSIS]

psy·cho·di·ag·nos·tic (sī′kō dī′əg nos′tik), *adj.* of, pertaining to, characteristic of, or using the techniques developed in psychodiagnostics. [PSYCHO- + DIAGNOSTIC]

psy·cho·di·ag·nos·tics (sī′kō dī′əg nos′tiks), *n.* (*construed as sing.*) the study and evaluation of character or personality in terms of behavioral and anatomical traits, as gesture, posture, physiognomy, etc. [see PSYCHODIAGNOSTIC, -ICS]

psy·cho·dra·ma (sī′kō drä′mə, -dram′ə), *n. Psychiatry.* a method of group psychotherapy taking the form of a play in which the patients assume and dramatize roles relevant to their problems. [PSYCHO- + DRAMA] **—psy·cho·dra·mat·ic** (sī′kō drə mat′ik), *adj.*

psy·cho·dy·nam·ics (sī′kō dī nam′iks), *n.* (*construed as sing.*) *Psychol.* the systematic study of personality in terms of past and present experiences as related to motivation. [PSYCHO- + DYNAMICS]

psy·cho·gal·van·ic (sī′kō gal van′ik), *adj. Med.* pertaining to or involving electric changes in the body resulting from reactions to mental or emotional stimuli. [PSYCHO- + GALVANIC]

psy·cho·gal·va·nom·e·ter (sī′kō gal′və nom′i tər), *n. Med.* a type of galvanometer for detecting and measuring psychogalvanic currents. [PSYCHO- + GALVANOMETER]

psy·cho·gen·e·sis (sī′kō jen′i sis), *n.* **1.** genesis of the psyche. **2.** *Psychol.* the origin of physical or psychological states, normal or abnormal, out of the interplay of conscious and unconscious psychological forces. **3.** *Pathol.* the origin of symptoms as a result of emotional causes. [< NL; see PSYCHO-, GENESIS] **—psy·cho·ge·net·ic** (sī′kō jə net′ik), *adj.* **—psy′cho·ge·net′i·cal·ly,** *adv.*

psy·cho·gen·ic (sī′kō jen′ik), *adj. Psychol.* having origin in the mind or in a mental condition or process: *a psychogenic disorder.* [PSYCHOGEN(ESIS) + -IC]

psy·chog·no·sis (sī kog′nə sis, sī′kəg nō′sis), *n. Psychiatry Rare.* a complete examination of the mind. [PSYCHO- + GNOSIS] **—psy·chog·nos·tic** (sī′kəg-nos′tik), *adj.*

psy·cho·graph (sī′kə graf′, -gräf′), *n.* **1.** *Psychol.* a graph indicating the relative strength of the personality traits of an individual. **2.** a psychologically oriented biography. [PSYCHO- + -GRAPH] **—psy·cho·graph·ic** (sī′kə graf′ik), *adj.* **—psy′cho·graph′i·cal·ly,** *adv.*

psy·chog·ra·pher (sī kog′rə fər), *n.* a person who writes a psychograph; a psychological or psychographic biographer. [PSYCHOGRAPH + -ER[1]]

psychol., **1.** psychological. **2.** psychology.

psy·cho·lin·guis·tics (sī′kō liŋ gwis′tiks), *n.* (*construed as sing.*) the study of the relationships between language and the behavioral characteristics of those who use it. [PSYCHO- + LINGUISTICS] **—psy′cho·lin·guis′tic,** *adj.*

psy·cho·log·i·cal (sī′kə loj′i kəl), *adj.* **1.** of or pertaining to psychology. **2.** pertaining to the mind or to mental phenomena as the subject matter of psychology. **3.** of, pertaining to, dealing with, or affecting the mind, esp. as a function of awareness, feeling, or motivation: *psychological play; psychological effect.* Also, **psy′cho·log′ic.** [PSYCHOLOG(Y) + -ICAL] **—psy′cho·log′i·cal·ly,** *adv.*

psycholog′ical mo′ment, the time for achieving a desired effect; the critical time for action: *a child skilled in discovering the psychological moment to make requests.*

psycholog′ical nov′el, a novel that focuses on the complex mental and emotional lives of its characters and explores the various levels of mental activity.

psy·chol·o·gise (sī kol′ə jīz′), *v.i.,* **-gised, -gis·ing.** *Chiefly Brit.* psychologize.

psy·chol·o·gism (sī kol′ə jiz′əm), *n. Usually Disparaging.* **1.** emphasis upon psychological factors in the development of a theory, esp. of a philosophical theory. **2.** a term or concept of psychology or psychoanalysis, esp. when used in ordinary conversation or a nontechnical context. [PSYCHOLOG(Y) + -ISM]

psy·chol·o·gist (sī kol′ə jist), *n.* **1.** a specialist in psychology. **2.** *Philos.* an adherent to or advocate of psychologism. **—***adj.* **3.** Also, **psy·chol′o·gis′tic.** *Philos.* of or pertaining to psychologism. [PSYCHOLOG(Y) + -IST]

psy·chol·o·gize (sī kol′ə jīz′), *v.i.,* **-gized, -giz·ing.** to make psychological investigations or speculations. Also, *esp. Brit.,* **psychologise.** [PSYCHOLOG(Y) + -IZE]

psy·chol·o·gy (sī kol′ə jē), *n., pl.* **-gies. 1.** the science of the mind or of mental states and processes; the science of human nature. **2.** the science of human and animal behavior. **3.** the sum of the mental states and processes of a person or of a number of persons, esp. as determining action: *the psychology of a soldier at the battle front.* [< NL *psȳchologia.* See PSYCHO-, -LOGY]

psy·cho·man·cy (sī′kō man′sē), *n.* occult communication between souls or with spirits. [PSYCHO- + -MANCY]

psy·cho·met·rics (sī′kō me′triks), *n.* (*construed as sing.*) psychometry (def. 1).

psy·chom·e·try (sī kom′i trē), *n.* **1.** Also, **psychometrics.** *Psychol.* the measurement of mental traits, abilities, and processes. **2.** the alleged art or faculty of divining facts concerning an object or a person associated with it, by contact with or proximity to the object. [PSYCHO- + -METRY] **—psy′cho·met′ric, psy′cho·met′ri·cal,** *adj.* **—psy′cho·met′ri·cal·ly,** *adv.* **—psy·chom·e·tri·cian** (sī kom′i trish′ən), **psy·chom′e·trist,** *n.*

psy·cho·mo·tor (sī′kō mō′tər), *adj.* of or pertaining to a motor response caused by psychic processes. [PSYCHO- + MOTOR]

psy·cho·neu·ro·sis (sī′kō nŏŏ rō′sis, -nyŏŏ-), *n.* an emotional disorder in which feelings of anxiety, obsessional thoughts, compulsive acts, and physical complaints without objective evidence of disease, in various patterns, dominate the personality. [< NL; see PSYCHO-, NEUROSIS]

psy·cho·neu·rot·ic (sī′kō nŏŏ rot′ik, -nyŏŏ-), *adj.* **1.** of or pertaining to psychoneurosis. **—***n.* **2.** a person who suffers from psychoneurosis. [< NL; see PSYCHO-, NEUROTIC]

psy·cho·path (sī′kə path′), *n.* **1.** a person who is mentally ill or unstable. **2.** See **psychopathic personality** (def. 2). [PSYCHO- + -PATH]

psy·cho·path·ic (sī′kə path′ik), *adj.* of, pertaining to, or affected with psychopathy. [PSYCHOPATH(Y) + -IC]

psychopath′ic personal′ity, *Psychiatry.* **1.** a type of personality characterized by amoral and antisocial behavior, lack of ability to love or establish meaningful personal relationships, extreme egocentricity, failure to learn from experience, etc. **2.** a person who has such a personality.

psy·chop·a·thist (sī kop′ə thist), *n.* a specialist in treating psychopathology. [PSYCHOPATH(Y) + -IST]

psy·cho·pa·thol·o·gy (sī′kō pə thol′ə jē), *n.* the science of diseases of the mind; mental pathology. [PSYCHO- + PATHOLOGY] **—psy·cho·path·o·log·i·cal** (sī′kō path′ə loj′i kəl), **psy′cho·path′o·log′ic,** *adj.* **—psy′cho·pa·thol′o·gist,** *n.*

psy·chop·a·thy (sī kop′ə thē), *n.* mental disease. [PSYCHO- + -PATHY]

psy·cho·phar·ma·col·o·gy (sī′kō fär′mə kol′ə jē), *n.* the branch of pharmacology dealing with the psychological effects of drugs. [PSYCHO- + PHARMACOLOGY] **—psy·cho·phar·ma·co·log·ic** (sī′kō fär′mə kə loj′ik), **psy′cho·phar′ma·co·log′i·cal,** *adj.*

psy·cho·phys·ics (sī′kō fiz′iks), *n.* (*construed as sing.*) the branch of psychology that deals with the measurement of relationships between the physical attributes of stimuli and resulting sensations. [< G *Psychophysik.* See PSYCHO-, PHYSICS] **—psy·cho·phys·i·cal** (sī′kō-fiz′i kəl), **psy′cho·phys′ic,** *adj.* **—psy′cho·phys′i·cal·ly,** *adv.* **—psy·cho·phys·i·cist** (sī′kō fiz′i sist), *n.*

psy·cho·phys·i·o·log·i·cal (sī′kō fiz′ē ə loj′i kəl), *adj.* of or pertaining to psychophysiology. Also, **psy′cho·phys′i·o·log′ic.** [PSYCHOPHYSIOLOG(Y) + -ICAL] **—psy′cho·phys′i·o·log′i·cal·ly,** *adv.*

psy·cho·phys·i·ol·o·gy (sī′kō fiz′ē ol′ə jē), *n.* the branch of physiology which deals with the interrelation of mental and physical phenomena. [PSYCHO- + PHYSIOLOGY] **—psy′cho·phys′i·ol′o·gist,** *n.*

psy·cho·pomp (sī′kō pomp′), *n.* a person who conducts spirits or souls to the other world, as Hermes or Charon. [< Gk *psychopomp(ós).* See PSYCHO-, POMP]

Psy·cho·pom·pus (sī′kə pom′pəs), *n. Class. Myth.* an epithet of Hermes in his role as guide of souls to the underworld.

psy·cho·pro·phy·lax·is (sī′kō prō′fə lak′sis, -prof′ə-), *n. Obstet.* a method by which an expectant mother is prepared for childbirth by psychological and physical conditioning, including education concerning labor and delivery, and breathing exercises. Also called **Lamaze′ technique′.** [PSYCHO- + PROPHYLAXIS] **—psy·cho·pro·phy·lac·tic** (sī′kō prō′fə lak′tik), *adj.*

psy·cho·sex·u·al (sī′kō sek′shŏŏ əl), *adj.* of or pertaining to the relationship of psychological and sexual phenomena. [PSYCHO- + SEXUAL] **—psy′cho·sex′u·al′i·ty,** *n.* **—psy′cho·sex′u·al·ly,** *adv.*

psy·cho·sis (sī kō′sis), *n., pl.* **-ses** (-sēz). any major, severe form of mental disorder or disease. [< LGk *psȳ́chōsis* animation, principle of life. See PSYCHO-, -SIS] **—psy·chot·ic** (sī kot′ik), *adj., n.*

—Syn. insanity.

psy·cho·so·mat·ic (sī′kō sō mat′ik, -sə-), *adj.* noting a physical disorder that is caused by or notably influenced by the emotional state of the patient. [PSYCHO- + SOMATIC]

psy′chosomat′ic med′icine, the application of the principles of psychology in the study and treatment of physical diseases.

psy·cho·so·mat·ics (sī′kō sō mat′iks, -sə-), *n.* (*construed as sing.*) See **psychosomatic medicine.** [see PSYCHOSOMATIC, -ICS]

psy·cho·sur·ger·y (sī′kō sûr′jə rē), *n.* treatment of mental diseases by means of brain surgery. Cf. **lobotomy.** [PSYCHO- + SURGERY]

psy·cho·tech·nics (sī′kō tek′niks), *n.* (*construed as sing.*) the use of psychological techniques for controlling and modifying human behavior, esp. for practical ends. Cf. **psychotechnology.** [PSYCHO- + TECHNICS]

psy·cho·tech·nol·o·gy (sī′kō tek nol′ə jē), *n.* the body of knowledge, theories, and techniques developed and available for use in controlling human behavior for practical purposes; the study of psychotechnics. [PSYCHO- + TECHNOLOGY] **—psy·cho·tech·no·log·i·cal** (sī′kō tek′nəloj′i kəl), *adj.* **—psy′cho·tech·nol′o·gist,** *n.*

psy·cho·ther·a·peu·tics (sī′kō ther′ə pyōō′tiks), *n.* (*construed as sing.*) therapeutics concerned with the treatment of disease by psychic influence, as by mental suggestion. [PSYCHO- + THERAPEUTICS] **—psy′cho·ther′a·peu′tic,** *adj.* **—psy′cho·ther′a·peu′ti·cal·ly,** *adv.* **—psy′cho·ther′a·peu′tist,** *n.*

psy·cho·ther·a·py (sī′kō ther′ə pē), *n.* the science or method of curing psychological abnormalities and disorders by psychological techniques. [PSYCHO- + THERAPY] **—psy′cho·ther′a·pist,** *n.*

psychro-, a learned borrowing from Greek meaning "cold," used in the formation of compound words: *psychrometer.* [comb. form repr. Gk *psȳchrós* cold]

psy·chrom·e·ter (sī krom′i tər), *n.* an instrument for determining atmospheric humidity by the reading of two thermometers, the bulb of one being kept moist and ventilated. [PSYCHRO- + -METER] **—psy·chro·met·ric** (sī′krə me′trik), **psy′chro·met′ri·cal,** *adj.*

psy′chromet′ric chart′, a chart for calculating values of relative humidity, absolute humidity, and dew point from psychrometer readings.

psy·chrom·e·try (sī krom′i trē), *n.* **1.** the employment of the psychrometer. **2.** the science of measuring the water-vapor content of the air. [PSYCHRO- + -METRY]

psy·chro·phile (sī′krə fīl′, -fil), *Bacteriol.* **—***adj.* **1.** psychrophilic. **—***n.* **2.** a psychrophilic bacterium. [PSYCHRO- + -PHILE]

psy·chro·phil·ic (sī′krə fil′ik), *adj.* (of bacteria) capable of growing at or near a temperature of 0°C. [PSYCHRO- + -PHILIC]

psyk·ter (sik′tər), *n., pl.* **-ters.** *Gk. and Rom. Antiq.* a wine jar, characterized by an ovoid body tapering at the neck, and set on a high foot: used for cooling wine. Also, **psyc′ter.** [< Gk, deriv. of *psȳ́chein* to blow (cool)]

Pt, *Chem.* platinum.

Pt., **1.** point. **2.** port.

pt, pint; pints.

pt., **1.** part. **2.** payment. **3.** pint; pints. **4.** point. **5.** port. **6.** preterit.

P.T., **1.** Pacific time. **2.** physical training. **3.** postal telegraph. **4.** post town. **5.** pupil teacher.

p.t., **1.** Pacific time. **2.** past tense. **3.** post town. **4.** pro tempore.

Pta., *pl.* **Ptas.** peseta.

P.T.A., Parent-Teacher Association.

Ptah (ptä, ptäkh), *n.* an ancient Egyptian deity, believed to be a universal creator and sometimes identified with other gods: worshiped esp. at Memphis when it was the royal residence.

Ptarmigan, *Lagopus lagopus* (Length 15 in.)

ptar·mi·gan (tär′mə gən), *n., pl.* **-gans,** (*esp. collectively*) **-gan.** any of several grouses of the genus *Lagopus,* of mountainous and cold northern regions, having feathered feet. [< Gael *tarmarchan,* appar. var. of Ir *tarmanach*]

PT boat, *U.S.* a small, fast, lightly armed, unarmored, and highly maneuverable boat used chiefly for torpedoing enemy shipping. Also called **mosquito boat, motor torpedo boat.** [*p*(*ropeller*) *t*(*orpedo*)]

Ptel·e·on (tel′ē on′), *n. Class. Myth.* Cephalus.

pter-, var. of **ptero-** before a vowel: *pteranodon.*

-pter, var. of **ptero-** as final element of compound words: *hymenopter.*

pter·an·o·don (tə ran′ə don′), *n.* a flying reptile of the extinct order *Pterosauria,* from the Cretaceous period, having a wingspread of about 25 feet. [< NL, equiv. to *pter-* PTER- + Gk *anódōn* toothless (see AN-[1], -ODONT)]

Pter·e·la·us (ter′ə lā′əs), *n. Class. Myth.* a descendant of Poseidon whose immortality depended upon his preserving a lock of golden hair. Cf. **Comaetho** (def. 1).

pter·i·dol·o·gy (ter′i dol′ə jē), *n.* the branch of botany dealing with ferns and related plants, as horsetails, club mosses, etc. [*pterido-* (comb. form repr. Gk *pterid-,* s. of *pterís* fern) + -LOGY] **—pter·i·do·log·i·cal** (ter′i dəloj′i kəl), *adj.* **—pter′i·dol′o·gist,** *n.*

pte·rid·o·phyte (tə rid′ə fīt′, ter′i dō fīt′), *n.* any plant of the division *Pteridophyta,* characterized by vascular tissue and differentiation into root, stem, and leaves, comprising the ferns, horsetails, and club mosses. [< NL *Pteridophyt(a),* equiv. to Gk *pterido-* (comb. form repr. Gk *pterís* fern) + *-phyta,* pl. of *-phyton* -PHYTE] **—pte·rid·o·phyt·ic** (tə rid′ə fit′ik, ter′i dō-), **pter·i·doph·y·tous** (ter′i dof′i təs), *adj.*

pte·ri·on (tēr′ē on′, ter′-), *n. Craniom.* the craniometric point at the side of the sphenoidal fontanelle. [< NL, alter. of Gk *pterón* wing, on model of INION]

ptero-, a learned borrowing from Greek meaning "wing," "feather," used in the formation of compound words: *pterodactyl.* Also, **pter-, -pter.** [< NL, comb. form repr. Gk *pterón*]

Pterodactyl, Genus *Pterodactylus* (Wingspread 1 to 20 ft.)

pter·o·car·pous (ter′ə kär′pəs), *adj. Bot.* having winged fruit. [< NL; see PTERO-, -CARPOUS]

pter·o·dac·tyl (ter′ə dak′til), *n.* any flying reptile of the extinct order *Pterosauria,* from the Jurassic and Cretaceous periods, having the outside digit of the forelimb greatly elongated and supporting a wing membrane. [< NL *Pterodactyl(us),* genus name, equiv. to Gk *pteró(n)* wing + *dáktylos* digit] **—pter′o·dac·tyl′ic, pter′o·dac′tyl·id, pter′o·dac′tyl·ous,** *adj.* **—pter′o·dac′tyl·oid′,** *adj.*

pte·ro·ma (tə rō′mə, te-), *n., pl.* **-ma·ta** (-mə tə). pteron. [< L < Gk]

pte·ron (ter′on), *n. Archit.* **1.** (in a classical temple) a colonnade parallel to, but apart from, the cella. **2.** the space between this and the cella. [< L < Gk: lit., wing]

pter·o·pod (ter′ə pod′), *adj.* **1.** belonging or pertaining to the *Pteropoda,* a group of mollusks which have the lateral portions of the foot expanded into winglike lobes. —*n.* 2. a pteropod mollusk. [< NL *Pteropod(a)* (pl.) < Gk. See PTERO-, -POD]

pter·o·po·di·um (ter′ə pō′dē əm), *n., pl.* **-po·di·a** (-pō′dē ə). the foot of a pteropod. [< NL; see PTERO-, -IUM]

pter·o·saur (ter′ə sôr′), *n.* a pterodactyl. [< NL *Pterosaur(us).* See PTERO-, -SAUR]

-pterous, an element meaning "winged," used in the formation of adjectives: *dipterous.* [< Gk *-pteros,* comb. form akin to *pterón* wing. See PTERO-, -OUS]

pter′o·yl·glu·tam′ic ac′id (ter′ō il glo͞o tam′ik, ter′-), *Biochem.* See **folic acid.** Also called **pter′o·yl·mono·glu·tam′ic ac′id** (ter′ō il mon′ō glo͞o tam′ik, ter′-). [PTERO- + -YL + GLUTAMIC ACID]

pte·ryg·i·um (tə rij′ē əm), *n., pl.* **-ryg·i·ums, -ryg·i·a** (-rij′ē ə). *Anat.* a triangular mass of thickened conjunctiva that extends usually from the inner canthus of the eye to the cornea. [< NL < Gk *pterýgion* little wing or fin, equiv. to *pteryg-* (s. of *ptéryx*) wing, fin + *-ion* dim. suffix] —**pte·ryg′i·al,** *adj.*

pter·y·goid (ter′ə goid′), *adj.* 1. winglike. 2. *Anat.* of, pertaining to, or situated near the pterygoid process. —*n.* 3. *Anat.* a pterygoid part, as a muscle, nerve, etc. [< Gk *pterygoeid(ḗs),* equiv. to *pteryg-* (s. of *ptéryx*) wing, fin + *-oeidēs* -OID]

pter′ygoid proc′ess, *Anat.* 1. a process on each side of the sphenoid bone, consisting of two plates separated by a notch. 2. either of these two plates.

pter·y·gote (ter′ə gōt′), *adj.* belonging or pertaining to the subclass *Pterygota,* comprising the winged insects. Also, **pte·ryg·o·tous** (tə rig′ə təs). [< NL *Pterygota* < Gk, neut. pl. of *pterygōtós,* deriv. of *pteryg-* (s. of *ptéryx*) wing]

pter·y·la (ter′ə lə), *n., pl.* **-lae** (-lē′, -lī′). *Ornith.* one of the feathered areas on the skin of a bird. Also called **feather tract.** Cf. **apterium.** [< NL < Gk *pteró(n)* feather + *hýlē* wood]

pter·y·log·ra·phy (ter′ə log′rə fē), *n.* the study of the pterylae of birds. [PTERLY(A) + -O- + -GRAPHY] —**pter·y·lo·graph·ic** (ter′ə lō graf′ik), **pter′y·lo·graph′i·cal,** *adj.*

pter·y·lol·o·gy (ter′ə lol′ə jē), *n.* the study of the pterylosis of birds. [PTERYL(OSIS) + -O- + -LOGY] —**pter·y·lo·log·i·cal** (ter′ə lō loj′i kəl), *adj.*

pter·y·lo·sis (ter′ə lō′sis), *n. Ornith.* the distribution of feathers in definite tracts or areas of growth. [< NL; see PTERYLA, -OSIS]

ptg., printing.

pti·lo·sis (ti lō′sis), *n. Ophthalm.* a falling out of the eyelashes. [< NL < Gk *ptílōsis* eyelid disease, equiv. to *ptíl(os)* sore-eyed + *-ōsis* -OSIS]

ptis·an (tiz′ən, ti zan′), *n.* a nourishing decoction, originally one made from barley, supposedly having a slight medicinal quality. [< L *ptisana* < Gk *ptisánē* peeled barley, barley water; r. ME *tisane* < F]

P.T.O., please turn over (a page or leaf). Also, **p.t.o.**

Ptol·e·mae·us (tol′ə mā′əs), *n.* a walled plain in the third quadrant of the face of the moon: about 90 miles in diameter.

Ptol·e·ma·ic (tol′ə mā′ik), *adj.* 1. of or pertaining to Ptolemy or his conception of the universe. 2. of or pertaining to the dynastic house of the Ptolemies and to the period of their rule in Egypt. [< Gk *Ptolemaïk(ós)* of Ptolemy, equiv. to *Ptolemai(os)* PTOLEMY + *-ikos* -IC]

Ptol′ema′ic sys′tem, *Astron.* a system elaborated by Ptolemy and subsequently modified by others, according to which the earth was the fixed center of the universe, with the heavenly bodies moving about it.

Ptol·e·ma·ist (tol′ə mā′ist), *n.* an adherent or advocate of the Ptolemaic system of astronomy. [PTOLEMA(IC) + -IST]

Ptol·e·my (tol′ə mē), *n., pl.* **-mies** for 2. 1. (*Claudius Ptolemaeus*) fl. A.D. 127–151, Greek mathematician, astronomer, and geographer. 2. any of the kings of the Macedonian dynasty which ruled Egypt 323–30 B.C.

Ptolemy I, (surnamed *Soter*) 367?–283 B.C., king of Egypt 306–285: founder of Macedonian dynasty in Egypt.

Ptolemy II, (surnamed *Philadelphus*) 309?–247? B.C., king of Egypt 285–247? (son of Ptolemy I).

pto·maine (tō′mān, tō mān′), *n.* any of a class of basic nitrogenous substances, some of them very poisonous, produced during putrefaction of animal or plant protein and, unlike contaminants which cause food poisoning, usually easily detectable because of their appearance and odor. [< It *ptomaina* < Gk *ptôma* dead body + *-ina* -INE[2]] —**pto·main′ic,** *adj.*

pto′maine poi′soning, 1. a toxic condition caused by the eating of ptomaine. 2. (erroneously) food poisoning.

pto·sis (tō′sis), *n. Pathol.* 1. a drooping of the upper eyelid. 2. prolapse or drooping of any organ. [< NL < Gk: a falling] —**pto·tic** (tō′tik), *adj.*

Pto·üs (tō′əs), *n. Class. Myth.* a son of Athamas and Themisto for whom Mount Ptoüs in Boeotia was named.

ptp., past participle.

pts., 1. parts. 2. payments. 3. pints. 4. points. 5. ports.

pty·a·lec·ta·sis (tī′ə lek′tə sis), *n., pl.* **-ses** (-sēz′). dilatation of a salivary duct that occurs spontaneously or is produced by surgery. [< Gk *ptýal(on)* + ECTASIS]

pty·a·lin (tī′ə lin), *n. Biochem.* an enzyme in the saliva of man and certain lower animals, possessing the property of converting starch into dextrin and maltose. [< Gk *ptýal(on)* spittle, saliva + -IN[2]]

pty·a·lism (tī′ə liz′əm), *n. Pathol.* excessive secretion of saliva. [< Gk *ptyalism(ós)* expectoration, equiv. to *ptýal(on)* spittle + *-ismos* -ISM]

Pu, *Chem.* plutonium.

pub (pub), *n. Chiefly Brit. Informal.* a tavern. [short for PUBLIC HOUSE]

pub., 1. public. 2. publication. 3. published. 4. publisher. 5. publishing.

pu·ber·ty (pyo͞o′bər tē), *n.* the period or age at which a person is first capable of sexual reproduction of offspring: in common law, presumed to be 14 years in the male and 12 years in the female. [ME *puberte* < L *pūbertās* adulthood, equiv. to *pūber* grown-up + *-tās* -TY[2]]

pu·ber·u·lent (pyo͞o ber′yə lənt, -ber′ə-), *adj. Bot., Zool.* minutely pubescent. Also, **pu·ber·u·lous** (pyo͞o ber′yə ləs, -ber′ə-). [< L *pūber* downy, adult + -ULENT]

pu·bes[1] (pyo͞o′bēz), *n., pl.* **pu·bes.** *Anat.* 1. the lower part of the abdomen, esp. the region between the right and left iliac regions. 2. the hair appearing on the lower part of the abdomen at puberty. [< L *pūbēs* pubic hair, groin]

pu·bes[2] (pyo͞o′bēz), *n.* pl. of **pubis.**

pu·bes·cent (pyo͞o bes′ənt), *adj.* 1. arriving or arrived at puberty. 2. *Bot., Zool.* covered with down or fine short hair. [< L *pūbescent-* (s. of *pūbescēns*), prp. of *pūbēscere* to attain puberty, reach puberty, become hairy or downy. See PUBES[1], -ESCENT] —**pu·bes′cence, pu·bes′cen·cy,** *n.*

pu·bic (pyo͞o′bik), *adj.* of, pertaining to, or situated near the pubes or the pubis. [PUB(ES)[1] + -IC]

pu·bis (pyo͞o′bis), *n., pl.* **-bes** (-bēz). *Anat.* that part of either innominate bone that, with the corresponding part of the other, forms the front of the pelvis. See diag. under **pelvis.** [short for NL *os pūbis* bone of the PUBES[1]]

publ., 1. published. 2. publisher.

pub·lic (pub′lik), *adj.* 1. of, pertaining to, or affecting the people as a whole or the community, state, or nation: *public funds; a public nuisance.* 2. done, made, acting, etc., for the people or community as a whole: *public prosecution.* 3. open to all the people: *a public meeting.* 4. pertaining to or engaged in the affairs or service of the community or nation: *a public official.* 5. maintained at the public expense and under public control and open to the public generally: *a public library or road.* 6. open to the view or knowledge of all; existing, done, etc., in public: *The fact became public.* 7. widely known to the public; prominent: *public figures.* 8. *Rare.* of or pertaining to all mankind; universal. —*n.* 9. the people constituting a community, state, or nation. 10. a particular group of people with a common interest, aim, etc.: *the book-buying public.* 11. *Brit. Informal.* a tavern. 12. **go public,** (of a corporation) to issue stock for sale to the general public. 13. **in public,** in public view or access: *It was the first time that she had sung in public.* [< L *pūblic(us)* (earlier *pōblicus, pŏplicus;* see PEOPLE, -IC); r. late ME *publique* < MF]

pub′lic account′ant, an accountant who offers his services to the public at large in contrast to one employed on a full-time basis by a company. —**pub′lic account′ing.**

pub′lic act′. See **public law** (def. 1).

pub′lic-ad·dress′ sys′tem (pub′lik ə dres′), a combination of electronic devices designed to transmit, amplify, and reproduce speech or music, or both, so as to make it audible, via loudspeakers, to many people, as in an arena or auditorium or out of doors. Also called **PA system, P.A. system, p.a. system.**

pub·li·can (pub′lə kən), *n.* 1. *Brit. Informal.* a person who owns or manages a tavern; the keeper of a pub. 2. *Rom. Hist.* a person who collected public taxes. 3. any collector of taxes, tolls, tribute, or the like. [ME < L *pūblicān(us).* See PUBLIC, -AN]

pub·li·ca·tion (pub′lə kā′shən), *n.* 1. the act of publishing a book, periodical, map, piece of music, engraving, or the like. 2. act of bringing before the public; announcement. 3. state or fact of being published. 4. that which is published, esp. serially, as a magazine or learned journal. [ME *publicacioun* < L *pūblicātiōn-* (s. of *pūblicātiō*) a making public, confiscation, equiv. to *pūblicāt(us)* made public, confiscated (ptp. of *pūblicāre*) + *-iōn-* -ION]

pub′lic bar′, *Brit.* (in a tavern or pub) the common section of a bar or barroom, not as exclusive, as quiet, or as comfortably furnished as the saloon section.

pub′lic bill′, a congressional or parliamentary bill involving the general interests of the people at large or of the whole community. Cf. **private bill.**

pub′lic charge′, a person who is in economic distress and is supported by government expense: *He was much concerned to assure the American consul that the prospective immigrant would not become a public charge.*

pub′lic com′pany, *Brit.* a company that has more than 50 shareholders and whose shares are offered for public subscription. Cf. **private company.**

pub′lic conven′ience, *Chiefly Brit.* a rest room, esp. at a large public place, as at a railroad station.

pub′lic corpora′tion, a corporation, owned and operated by a government, established for the administration of certain public programs.

pub′lic debt′. See **national debt.**

pub′lic defend′er, *U.S.* a lawyer appointed or elected by a city or county as a full-time, official defender to represent indigents in criminal cases at public expense. Cf. **assigned counsel.**

pub′lic domain′, *Law.* 1. the status of productions of authorship upon which the copyrights have expired and of works which have been published without copyright protection. 2. land owned by the government.

pub′lic en′emy, 1. a person who is a danger or menace to the public, usually as shown by his criminal record. 2. a nation or government with which one's own is at war.

pub′lic house′, 1. *Brit.* a tavern. 2. an inn or hostelry.

pub′lic interna′tional law′, the law governing the legal relationships between independent states or nations (distinguished from *private international law*). Also called **public law.**

pub·li·cist (pub′li sist), *n.* 1. a press agent or public-relations man. 2. a person who is expert in or writes on current public or political affairs. 3. an expert in public or international law. [< G; see PUBLIC, -IST]

pub·lic·i·ty (pu blis′i tē), *n.* 1. public notice resulting from mention in the press, on the radio, or through any other medium or means of communication, including word of mouth. 2. the measures, process, or business of securing public notice. 3. information, articles, etc., issued to secure public notice or attention. 4. public notice or attention resulting from advertising. 5. the state of being public, or open to general observation or knowledge. [< F *publicité* < ML *pūblicitās.* See PUBLIC, -ITY]

pub·li·cize (pub′li sīz′), *v.t.,* **-cized, -ciz·ing.** to give publicity to; bring to public notice; advertise: *They publicized the meeting as best they could.* [PUBLIC + -IZE]

pub′lic law′, 1. Also called **public act, public statute.** a law or statute of a general character that applies to the people of a whole state or nation. 2. a branch of law dealing with the legal relationships of individuals and the state and with the relations among governmental agencies. Cf. **private law.** 3. See **public international law.**

pub′lic-li·a·bil′i·ty insur′ance (pub′lik lī′ə bil′i tē), insurance covering the insured against risks involving liability to the public for damages arising from negligence.

pub·lic·ly (pub′lik lē), *adv.* 1. in a public or open manner. 2. by the public. 3. in the name of the community. 4. by public action or consent. [PUBLIC + -LY]

pub·lic·ness (pub′lik nis), *n.* quality or state of being public or being owned by the public. [PUBLIC + -NESS]

pub′lic opin′ion, the collective opinion of many people on some issue, problem, etc., esp. as a guide to action, decision, or the like.

pub′lic-o·pin′ion poll′ (pub′lik ə pin′yən), a poll taken by sampling a cross section of the public in an effort to predict election results or to estimate public attitudes on issues.

pub′lic pol′icy, 1. the fundamental policy on which laws rest, used esp. as to policy not yet specifically enunciated in statutes. 2. the principle of law by which acts considered injurious to the public good are held to be unlawful.

pub′lic pros′ecutor, an officer charged with the conduct of criminal prosecution in the interest of the public.

pub′lic rela′tions, 1. the actions of a corporation, store, government, individual, etc., in promoting good will between itself and the public, the community, employees, customers, etc. 2. the art or technique of promoting such good will.

pub′lic school′, 1. (in the U.S.) a school that is maintained at public expense for the education of the children of a community or district and that constitutes a part of a system of free public education commonly including primary and secondary schools. 2. (in England) any of a number of endowed boarding schools, esp. for boys, that are equivalent to high school in the U.S. and that prepare students chiefly for the English universities or for public service. —**pub′lic-school′,** *adj.*

pub′lic serv′ant, a person holding a government office by election or appointment; person in public service.

pub′lic serv′ice, 1. the business of supplying an essential commodity, as gas or electricity, or a service, as transportation, to the general public. 2. the system of employment maintained by a government or, sometimes, the systems of employment maintained by the various governments within a country, taken collectively: *As mayor of his city and later as a congressman he spent more than 40 years in public service.* 3. service or a service to the public rendered without charge by a profit-making organization: *This radio program has been brought to you as a public service.*

pub′lic-serv′ice corpora′tion (pub′lik sûr′vis), a private or quasi-private corporation chartered to provide an essential commodity or service to the public.

pub·lic-spir·it·ed (pub′lik spir′i tid), *adj.* having or showing an unselfish interest in the public welfare: *a public-spirited citizen.*

pub′lic stat′ute. See **public law** (def. 1).

pub′lic util′ity, 1. a business enterprise, as a public-service corporation, performing an essential public service and regulated by the federal, State, or local government. Cf. **utility.** 2. Usually, **public utilities.** stocks or bonds of public-utilities companies, excluding railroads. —**pub′lic-u·til′i·ty,** *adj.*

pub′lic works′, structures, as roads, dams, post offices, etc., paid for by government funds for public use.

Pub′lic Works′ Administra′tion, *U.S.* the federal agency (1933–44) that instituted and administered projects for the construction of public works. *Abbr.:* PWA

pub·lish (pub′lish), *v.t.* 1. to issue, or cause to be issued, in copies made by printing or other processes, for sale or distribution to the public, as a book, periodical, map, piece of music, engraving, or the like. 2. to issue publicly the work of: *Random House publishes Faulkner.* 3. to announce formally or officially; proclaim; promulgate. 4. to make publicly or generally known. 5. *Law.* to communicate (a defamatory statement) to some person or persons other than the person defamed. —*v.i.* 6. to issue printed editions, as newspapers, books, etc.; engage in publishing: *The new house will start to publish next month. We publish every day except Sunday.* 7. to have one's work published or accepted for publication: *He has decided to publish with another house.* [ME *publisshe* < AF *publiss-, long s. of *publir for MF *publier* < L *pūblicāre* to make PUBLIC] —**pub′lish·a·ble,** *adj.*
—**Syn.** 3. disclose, reveal, declare. See **announce.**
—**Ant.** 3. conceal.

pub·lish·er (pub′li shər), *n.* 1. a person or company whose business is the publishing of books, periodicals, engravings, or the like. 2. the business head of a newspaper organization, commonly the owner or the representative of the owner. [PUBLISH + -ER[1]]

pub·lish·ing (pub′li shing), *n.* the activities or business of a publisher: *He plans to go into publishing after college.* [ME *publyssynge.* See PUBLISH, -ING[1]]

pub′lishing house′, a company that publishes books, pamphlets, engravings, or the like: *a venerable publishing house in Boston.*

pub·lish·ment (pub′lish mənt), *n. Archaic.* publication. [PUBLISH + -MENT]

pu·ca (po͞o′kə), *n.* a legendary Irish spirit, mischievous but not malevolent, corresponding to the English Puck. Also, **pooka.** [< IrGael *púca.* See PUCK]

Puc·ci·ni (po͞o chē′nē; *It.* po͞ot chē′nē), *n.* **Gia·co·mo** (jä′kô mô), 1858–1924, Italian operatic composer.

puc·coon (pə ko͞on′), *n.* 1. any of certain plants that yield a red dye, as the bloodroot and certain boraginaceous herbs of the genus *Lithospermum.* 2. the dye itself. [< Algonquian (Va.); see POKE[4]]

puce (pyo͞os), *adj.* 1. of a dark or purplish brown. —*n.* 2. dark or purplish brown. [< F: lit., flea < L *pūlicem,* acc. of *pūlex*]

pu·cel·las (pyə sel′əs), *n.* (*construed as sing.*) a tool resembling tongs or shears for handling and shaping molten glass. Also, **procellas.** [alter. of PROCELLAS]

puck (puk), *n. Ice Hockey.* a black disk of vulcanized rubber for use in passing and shooting. [alter. of POKE[1]]

Puck (puk), *n.* **1.** Also called **Hobgoblin, Robin Goodfellow.** a particularly mischievous sprite or fairy who appears as a character in Shakespeare's *A Midsummer Night's Dream.* **2.** (*l.c.*) a malicious or mischievous demon or spirit; a goblin. [ME *pouke,* OE *pūca;* c. Icel *pūki* a mischievous demon]

puck·a (puk′ə), *adj.* pukka.

puck-car·ri·er (puk′kar′ē ər), *n.* *Ice Hockey.* the player who has the puck and moves it along.

puck·er (puk′ər), *v.t., v.i.* **1.** to draw or gather into wrinkles or irregular folds. **2.** *Naut.* (in sailmaking) to gather in the excess on (the edge of a piece of sailcloth) in order to make the edge the same length as that of the piece of cloth to which it is to be sewn; eat in. **—*n.*** **3.** a wrinkle; an irregular fold. **4.** a puckered part, as of cloth tightly or crookedly sewn. **5.** *Archaic.* a state of agitation or perturbation. [appar. a freq. form connected with POKE²; see -ER⁶ and for the meaning cf. PURSE] **—puck′er·er,** *n.*

puck·er·y (puk′ə rē), *adj.* **1.** puckered. **2.** puckering. **3.** tending to pucker. [PUCKER + -Y¹]

puck·ish (puk′ish), *adj.* (*often cap.*) mischievous; impish. [PUCK + -ISH¹]

pud (po͝od), *n.* *Chiefly Brit. Informal.* pudding. [by apocope]

pud·ding (po͝od′ing), *n.* **1.** a dish made in many forms and of various ingredients, as flour, rice, tapioca, or the like, together with milk, eggs, and either fruit or condiments or other seasoning, usually sweetened. **2.** Also called **pud·den·ing** (po͝od′ᵊning). *Naut.* **a.** a pad or fender for preventing scraping or chafing or for lessening shock between vessels or other objects. **b.** material for filling such a pad or fender, including old rope, oakum, canvas, or the like. [ME *poding* kind of sausage; cf. OE *puduc* wen, sore (? orig. swelling), LG *puddewurst* black pudding] **—pud′ding-like′,** *adj.*

pud′ding boom′, *Naut.* a horizontal spar, lashed to a pair of davits, to which a boat is griped. Also called **pud′ding spar′, strongback.**

pud′ding-pipe tree′ (po͝od′ing pīp′), a tree, *Cassia fistula,* of India, having yellow flowers in clusters 12 inches long. Also called **canafistula, drumstick tree, golden shower.**

pud′ding stone′, *Geol.* conglomerate (def. 2).

pud·ding·wife (po͝od′ing wīf′), *n., pl.* **-wives** (-wīvz′). a bluish and bronze wrasse, *Halichoeres radiatus,* found along the Atlantic coast from the Florida Keys to Brazil. [ME *podyngwyf.* See PUDDING, WIFE]

pud·dle (pud′ᵊl), *n., v.,* **-dled, -dling.** **—*n.*** **1.** a small pool of water, esp. dirty water, as in a road after rain. **2.** a small pool of any liquid. **3.** clay or the like mixed with water and tempered, used as a waterproof lining for the walls of canals, ditches, etc. **—*v.t.*** **4.** to mark or fill with puddles. **5.** to wet with dirty water, mud, etc. **6.** to make (water) muddy or dirty. **7.** to muddle or confuse. **8.** to make (clay or the like) into puddle. **9.** to cover with pasty clay or puddle. **10.** *Metall.* to subject (molten iron) to the process of puddling. **11.** to destroy the granular structure of (soil) by agricultural operations on it when it is too wet. **12.** *Hort.* to dip the roots of (a tree, shrub, etc.) into a thin mixture of loam and water to retard drying out during transplanting. **—*v.i.*** **13.** to wade in a puddle: *The children were puddling.* **14.** to be or become puddled: *The backyard was puddling.* [ME *puddel, podel,* appar. dim. of OE *pudd* ditch, furrow; akin to LG *pudel* puddle] **—pud′dler,** *n.* **—pud′dly,** *adj.*

pud·dling (pud′ling), *n.* **1.** act of a person who puddles. **2.** *Metall.* the act or process of melting pig iron in a reverberatory furnace (**pud′dling fur′nace**) in an oxidizing atmosphere, stirring the melted iron, and raking off slag until the iron, in a purer state, becomes pasty, after which it is beaten and rolled to expel more slag and to convert it into wrought iron. **3.** the act or method of making puddle. **4.** puddle (def. 3). [PUDDLE + -ING¹]

pud·dock (pud′ək), *n.* *Scot. and North Eng.* paddock².

pu·den·cy (pyo͞od′ᵊn sē), *n.* modesty; bashfulness; shamefacedness. [< LL *pudentia* shame, equiv. to *pudent-* (s. of *pudēns,* prp. of *pudēre* to be ashamed) + *-ia* -Y³; see -ENCY]

pu·den·dum (pyo͞o den′dəm), *n., pl.* **-da** (-də). Usually, **pudenda.** *Anat.* the external genital organs, esp. those of the female; vulva. [< NL, special use of neut. of *pudendus,* gerundive of *pudēre* to be ashamed]

pudg·y (puj′ē), *adj.,* **pudg·i·er, pudg·i·est.** short and fat or thick: *an infant's pudgy fingers.* Also, *esp. Brit.,* **podgy.** [?] **—pudg′i·ly,** *adv.* **—pudg′i·ness,** *n.*

Pu·dov·kin (po͞o dôf′kin), *n.* **Vse·vo·lod I·la·rio·no·vich** (fse′vo lot ē′lä ʀyô′no vich), 1893–1953, Russian motion-picture director.

Pue·bla (pwe′blä), *n.* **1.** a state in S central Mexico. 1,973,837 (1960); 13,124 sq. mi. **2.** the capital of this state, in the N part. 285,284 (1960).

pueb·lo (pweb′lō; *for 3, 4, also Sp.* pwe′blô), *n., pl.* **pueb·los** (pweb′lōz; *Sp.* pwe′blôs). **1.** *U.S.* **a.** a communal structure for multiple dwelling and defensive purposes of certain agricultural Indians of the Southwest. Built of adobe or stone, typically many-storied and terraced, the structures were often placed against cliff walls and ground-floor entry was usually through the roof by ladder. **b.** (*cap.*) a member of a group of Indian peoples living in pueblo villages in New Mexico and Arizona since prehistoric times. **2.** an Indian village. **3.** (in Spanish America) a town or village. **4.** (in the Philippines) a town or a township. [< Sp: town, people < L *populus* people]

Pueb·lo (pweb′lō), *n.* a city in central Colorado. 91,181 (1960).

pu·er·ile (pyo͞o′ər il, -ə rīl′, pyo͞or′il, -īl), *adj.* **1.** of or pertaining to a child. **2.** childishly foolish; immature or trivial: *a puerile piece of writing.* [< L *puerīl(is)* boyish, equiv. to *puer* boy + *-īlis* -ILE] **—pu′er·ile·ly,** *adv.*
—Syn. 1. boyish, youthful, juvenile. **2.** juvenile, silly.

pu·er·il·ism (pyo͞o′ər ə liz′əm, pyo͞or′ə-), *n.* *Psychiatry.* childishness in the behavior of an adult. [PUERILE + -ISM]

pu·er·il·i·ty (pyo͞o′ə ril′i tē), *n., pl.* **-ties.** **1.** state or quality of being a child. **2.** quality of being puerile; childish foolishness or triviality. **3.** a puerile act, idea, remark, etc.: *an inexcusable puerility.* [earlier *puerilit(i)e* < L *puerīlitās.* See PUERILE, -ITY]

pu·er·per·a (pyo͞o ûr′pər ə), *n., pl.* **-per·ae** (-pə rē′). *Obstet.* a woman who has recently given birth to a child. [< L: woman in labor]

pu·er·per·al (pyo͞o ûr′pər əl), *adj.* **1.** of or pertaining to a woman in childbirth. **2.** pertaining to or connected with childbirth. [< NL *puerperāl(is)* of childbirth. See PUERPERA, -AL¹]

puer′peral fe′ver, *Pathol.* an infection occurring during the puerperium. Also called **childbed fever.**

pu·er·pe·ri·um (pyo͞o′ər pēr′ē əm), *n.* *Obstet.* the state of a woman during and just after childbirth. [< L: childbirth, childbed, equiv. to *puerper(us)* of a woman in labor (*puer* boy, child + *-perus* bringing forth, akin to *parere* to bear, breed) + *-ium* n. suffix of result]

Puer·to A·ya·cu·cho (pweʀ′tô ä′yä ko͞o′chô), a city in S Venezuela, on the Orinoco River. 7000 (1951).

Puer·to Bar·rios (pweʀ′tô bäʀ′ʀyôs), a seaport in E Guatemala. 19,268 (est. 1957).

Puer·to Ca·bel·lo (pweʀ′tô kä bel′yô), a seaport in N Venezuela. 34,382 (1950).

Puer·to Cor·tés (pweʀ′tô kôʀ tes′), a seaport in NW Honduras. 17,048 (1961).

Puer·to Li·món (pweʀ′tô lē mōn′), Limón (def. 1).

Puer·to Montt (pweʀ′tô mônt′), a city in S Chile. 28,944 (1951).

Puer′to Ri′can roy′al palm′, a feather palm, *Roystonea borinquena,* of Puerto Rico and St. Croix, having leaves about 10 feet long and egg-shaped, yellowish-brown fruit.

Puer·to Ri·co (pwer′tə rē′kō, pôr′-, pōr′-; *Sp.* pweʀ′tô ʀē′kô), an island in the central West Indies: a commonwealth associated with the U.S. 2,349,544 (1960); 3435 sq. mi. *Cap.:* San Juan. Formerly (until 1932), **Porto Rico.** **—Puer′to Ri′can.**

Puer·to Val·lar·ta (pweʀ′tô vä yäʀ′tä), a city in W Mexico. 15,462 (1960).

Pu·fen·dorf (po͞o′fən dôrf′, -dôrf′), *n.* **Sa·mu·el von** (zä′mo͞o əl fən), ("*Severinus de Monzambano*"), 1632–94, German jurist and historian.

puff (puf), *n.* **1.** a short, quick blast, as of wind or breath. **2.** an abrupt emission of air, vapor, etc. **3.** a whiff, as on a tobacco pipe. **4.** the sound of an abrupt emission of air, vapor, etc. **5.** a small quantity of vapor, smoke, etc., emitted at one blast. **6.** an inflated or distended part of a thing; swelling; protuberance. **7.** a form of light pastry with a filling of cream, jam, or the like. **8.** a portion of material gathered and held down at the edges but left full in the middle, as in a dress. **9.** a cylindrical roll of hair. **10.** a quilted bed covering, usually filled with down. **11.** a commendation, esp. an exaggerated one, of a book, an actor's performance, etc. **12.** exaggerated praise, esp. when given for selfish motives. **13.** See **powder puff.** **14.** puffball. **15.** *Chiefly Brit. Slang.* a homosexual. [ME; OE *pyff*]
—*v.i.* **16.** to blow with short, quick blasts, as the wind. **17.** to be emitted in a puff. **18.** to emit a puff or puffs; breathe quick and hard, as after violent exertion. **19.** to go with puffing or panting. **20.** to emit puffs or whiffs of vapor or smoke. **21.** to move with such puffs: *The locomotive puffed into the station.* **22.** to take puffs at a cigar, cigarette, etc. **23.** to become inflated, distended, or swollen (usually fol. by *up*). **24.** (esp. of an auctioneer's accomplice) to bid on an item at an auction solely to increase the price that the final bidder must pay. **—*v.t.*** **25.** to send forth (air, vapor, etc.) in short, quick blasts. **26.** to drive or impel by puffing, or with a short, quick blast. **27.** to extinguish by means of a puff (usually fol. by *out*): *to puff a match out.* **28.** to smoke (a cigar, cigarette, etc.). **29.** to inflate, distend, or swell, esp. with air. **30.** to inflate with pride, vanity, etc. (often fol. by *up*): *Their applause puffed him up.* **31.** to praise unduly or with exaggeration. **32.** to advertise with exaggerated commendation. **33.** to apply powder to (the cheeks, neck, etc.) with a powder puff. **34.** to apply (powder) with a powder puff. **35.** to arrange in puffs, as the hair. [ME *puffe(n),* OE *pyffan;* imit.] **—puff′ing·ly,** *adv.*

puff′ ad′der, a large, thick-bodied, African viper, *Bitis arientans,* that inflates its body and hisses when disturbed.

puff·ball (puf′bôl′), *n.* any of various basidiomycetous fungi, esp. of the genus *Lycoperdon* and allied genera, characterized by a ball-like fruit body which emits a cloud of spores when broken. [PUFF + BALL¹]

puff·bird (puf′bûrd′), *n.* any of several tropic American birds of the family *Bucconidae,* related to the barbets, having a large head. [PUFF + BIRD]

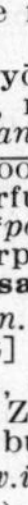
Atlantic puffin, *Fratercula arctica* (Length 1 ft.)

puff·er (puf′ər), *n.* **1.** one who or that which puffs. **2.** any of various fishes of the family *Tetraodontidae,* capable of inflating the body with water or air until it resembles a globe, the spines in the skin becoming erected. [PUFF + -ER¹]

puff·er·y (puf′ə rē), *n., pl.* **-er·ies.** **1.** undue or exaggerated praise. **2.** publicity, acclaim, etc., that is full of undue or exaggerated praise. [PUFF + -ERY]

puf·fin (puf′in), *n.* any of several alcidine sea birds of the genera *Fratercula* and *Lunda,* having a short neck and a large, compressed, grooved bill, as *F. arctica* **(Atlantic puffin),** of the North Atlantic. [ME *poffin, puffyn* < ?]

puff′ing ad′der. See **hognose snake.**

puff′ paste′, a dough used in making very light, flaky, rich pastry for pies, tarts, and the like.

puff′ pipe′, (in plumbing) a vent pipe for preventing siphonage in a trapped waste pipe.

puff·y (puf′ē), *adj.,* **puff·i·er, puff·i·est.** **1.** gusty. **2.** short-winded; panting. **3.** inflated, distended, or swollen. **4.** fat; plump. **5.** conceited. **6.** bombastic. [PUFF + -Y¹] **—puff′i·ly,** *adv.* **—puff′i·ness,** *n.*

Pug¹ (def. 1) (1 ft. high at shoulder)

pug¹ (pug), *n.* **1.** one of a breed of small, short-haired dogs having a tightly curled tail, a deeply wrinkled face, and a smooth coat that is black or silver or fawn marked with black. **2.** See **pug nose.** **3.** a fox. **4.** See **rainbow parrotfish.** [?] **—pug′gi·ness,** *n.* **—pug′gish, pug′gy,** *adj.*

pug² (pug), *v.t.,* **pugged, pug·ging.** **1.** to knead (clay or the like) with water to make it plastic, as for brickmaking. **2.** to fill or stop with clay or the like. **3.** to pack or cover with mortar or the like, as to deaden sound. **4.** to mix with water so as to form a paste.

pug³ (pug), *n.* *Slang.* a boxer; pugilist. [short for PUGILIST]

pug⁴ (pug), *n., v.,* **pugged, pug·ging.** *Anglo-Indian.* **—*n.*** **1.** a footprint, esp. of a game animal. **—*v.t.*** **2.** to track (esp. game) by following footprints or another spoor. [< Hindi *pag*]

pug·a·ree (pug′ə rē), *n.* pugree.

pug·dog (pug′dôg′, -dog′), *n.* pug¹ (def. 1). [PUG¹ + DOG]

Pu′get Sound′ (pyo͞o′jit), an arm of the Pacific, in NW Washington.

pug·ga·ree (pug′ə rē), *n.* pugree.

pug·ging (pug′ing), *n.* **1.** the act of a person who pugs. **2.** coarse mortar or the like for deadening sound. [PUG² + -ING¹]

pug·gree (pug′rē), *n.* pugree.

pugh (po͞o, pyo͞o, pē′yo͞o′), *interj.* (used as an exclamation of disgust, as at an offensive odor.)

pu·gil·ism (pyo͞o′jə liz′əm), *n.* the art or practice of fighting with the fists; boxing. [< L *pugil* boxer (akin to *pugnus* fist and *pugnāre* to fight) + -ISM]

pu·gil·ist (pyo͞o′jə list), *n.* a person who fights with his fists; a boxer, usually a professional. [< L *pugil* boxer + -IST] **—pu′gil·is′tic, pu′gil·is′ti·cal,** *adj.* **—pu′gil·is′ti·cal·ly,** *adv.*

Pu·gin (pyo͞o′jin), *n.* **1. Augustus Charles,** 1762–1832, French architectural draftsman and archaeologist in England. **2.** his son **Augustus Wel·by North·more** (wel′bē nôrth′mōr, -môr), 1812–52, English architect and designer.

Pu·glia (po͞o′lyä), *n.* Italian name of **Apulia.**

pug′ mill′, a mill for grinding and mixing materials, as clay or the ingredients of cement, to a desired condition.

pug·na·cious (pug nā′shəs), *adj.* inclined to quarrel or fight readily; quarrelsome; belligerent; combative. [*pugnaci(ty)* (< L *pugnācitās* combativeness, equiv. to *pugnāci-,* s. of *pugnāx* combative, + *-tās* -TY²) + -OUS] **—pug·na′cious·ly,** *adv.* **—pug·nac·i·ty** (pug nas′i tē), **pug·na′cious·ness,** *n.*
—Syn. argumentative, contentious, bellicose. **—Ant.** agreeable.

pug′ nose′, a short, broad, somewhat turned-up nose. **—pug-nosed** (pug′nōzd′), *adj.*

pug·ree (pug′rē), *n.* **1.** a light turban worn by natives in India. **2.** a scarf of silk or cotton, usually colored or printed, wound round a hat or helmet and falling down behind as a protection against the sun. Cf. **havelock.** Also, **pugaree, puggaree, puggree.** [< Hindi *pagrī* turban]

P'u-i (po͞o′ē′), *n.* Pu-yi.

puir (po͞oʀ, pyo͞oʀ), *adj.* *Scot.* **1.** poor. **2.** pure. **—puir′ness,** *n.*

puis·ne (pyo͞o′nē), *adj.* **1.** *Law.* younger; inferior in rank; junior, as in appointment. **—*n.*** **2.** an associate judge as distinguished from a chief justice. [< AF, equiv. to OF *puis* after (< L *posteā*) + *ne* born, ptp. of *naistre* to be born (< L *nascere*)]

Pui·seux (pi zœ′), *n.* a walled plain in the third quadrant of the face of the moon: about 15 miles in diameter.

pu·is·sance (pyo͞o′i səns, pyo͞o is′əns, pwis′əns), *n.* *Literary.* power, might, or force. [late ME < MF, equiv. to *puiss(ant)* + *-ance.* See PUISSANT, -ANCE]

pu·is·sant (pyo͞o′i sənt, pyo͞o is′ənt, pwis′ənt), *adj.* *Literary.* powerful; mighty; potent. [late ME < MF << VL **possent-* (s. of **possēns*) for L *potent-* (s. of *potēns*), prp. of *posse* to be able, have power; see -ANT] **—pu′is·sant·ly,** *adv.*

pu·ja (po͞o′jä), *n.* *Hinduism.* the worship of a particular god. [< Skt]

pu·ka (po͞o′kə), *n.* a shrub or small tree, *Griselinia lucida,* of New Zealand, having flower clusters nearly six inches long, but without petals. [< Maori]

puke (pyo͞ok), *v.i., v.t.,* **puked, puk·ing.** vomit. [?]

puk·ka (puk′ə), *adj.* *Anglo-Indian.* genuine, reliable, or good. Also, **pucka.** [< Hindi *pakkā* cooked, ripe, mature]

puk′ka sa′hib, *Anglo-Indian.* a term of respectful address formerly used by natives of India to British colonial authorities. Cf. **pukka, sahib.**

pu·ku (po͞o′ko͞o), *n.* an African antelope, *Adenota vardonii,* closely related to the waterbuck. [< some Afr language]

pul (po͞ol), *n., pl.* **puls, pu·li** (po͞o′lē). a copper coin of Afghanistan, the 100th part of an afghani, equivalent to about .0002 of a U.S. dollar. [< Pers *pūl* < Turk *pul*]

Pu·la (po͞o′lä), *n.* a seaport in W Croatia, on the Istrian Peninsula. 77,057. Also, **Pulj. Italian, Pola.**

Pu·las·ki (po͞o las′kē, -kī, pə-), *n.* **1. Count Cas·i·mir** (kaz′ə mir), 1748–79, Polish patriot; general in the American Revolutionary army. **2.** a town in SW Virginia. 10,469 (1960). **3.** a town in S Tennessee. 6616 (1960). **4. Fort.** See **Fort Pulaski.**

pul·chri·tude (pul′kri to͞od′, -tyo͞od′), *n.* physical beauty; comeliness. [ME < L *pulchritūdō* beauty, equiv. to *pulchri-* (comb. form of *pulcher* beautiful) + *-tūdō* -TUDE]

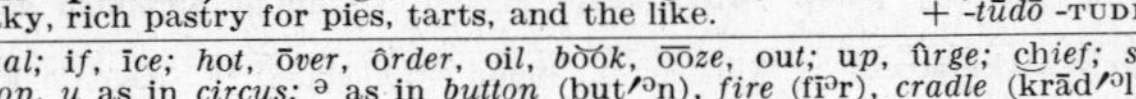

pul·chri·tu·di·nous (pul′kri to͞od′ənəs, -tyo͞od′-), *adj.* physically beautiful; comely. [< L *pulchritūdin-* (s. of *pulchritūdō*) + -OUS]

Pul·ci·nel·la (po͞ol′chə nel′ə), *n.* a ballet (1919) by Stravinsky.

pule (pyo͞ol), *v.i.*, **puled, pul·ing.** to cry in a thin voice; whine; whimper. [? imit.] —**pul′er,** *n.*

Pu·le·sa·ti (po͞o′li sä′tē, pyo͞o′-), *n.pl.* the ancient Assyrian name of the Philistines.

pu·li (po͝ol′ē, pyo͞o′lē), *n., pl.* **pu·lik** (po͝ol′ēk, pyo͞o′lēk), **pu·lis.** one of a Hungarian breed of medium-sized sheep dogs having long, fine hair that often mats, giving the coat a corded appearance. [< Hung]

pul·ing (pyo͞o′ling), *adj.* whining; whimpering: *a puling child.* [PULE + -ING²] —**pul′ing·ly,** *adv.*

Pu·litz·er (po͝ol′it sər, pyo͞o′lit-), *n.* **Joseph,** 1847–1911, U.S. journalist and publisher, born in Hungary.

Pu′litzer Prize′, *U.S.* one of a group of annual prizes in journalism, literature, music, etc., established by Joseph Pulitzer: administered by Columbia University.

Pulj (po͞ol′yə), *n.* Yugoslavian name of **Pola.**

pul·ka (pul′kə), *n.* a canoe-shaped sleigh used by the Lapps. [< Lapp *pulkke*]

pull (po͝ol), *v.t.* **1.** to draw or haul toward oneself or itself, in a particular direction, or into a particular position: *to pull a sled up a hill.* **2.** to draw or tug at with force. **3.** to draw, rend, or tear in the manner specified: *to pull a cloth to pieces.* **4.** to draw or pluck away from a place of growth, attachment, etc.: *to pull a tooth.* **5.** to strip of feathers, hair, etc., as a bird, a hide, etc. **6.** *Informal.* to draw out (as a knife or gun) for ready use (usually fol. by *on*): *Do you know what to do when someone pulls a knife on you?* **7.** *Informal.* to put or carry through (something attempted) (often fol. by *off*): *Police believe the men pulled all three robberies. We'll be rich if we can pull the deal off.* **8.** to put on or affect: *He pulled a long face when I reprimanded him.* **9.** to withdraw or remove: *to pull a wild pitcher.* **10.** to attract or win: *to pull many votes in the industrial areas.* **11.** to bring (a horse) to a stand by pulling on the reins. **12.** *Print., Graphics.* to take (an impression or proof) from type, a cut or plate, etc.: *to pull a print.* **13.** to be provided with or rowed with (a certain number of oars): *This boat pulls 12 oars.* **14.** to propel by rowing, as a boat. **15.** to strain (a muscle, ligament, or tendon). **16.** to hold in or check (a race horse), esp. so as to prevent from winning. **17.** *Cricket.* to hit (a ball pitched on the wicket or on the off side) to the one side. —*v.i.* **18.** to exert a drawing, tugging, or hauling force (often fol. by *at*). **19.** to inhale through a pipe, cigarette, etc. **20.** to become or come as specified, by pulling: *A rope pulls apart.* **21.** to row. **22.** to proceed by rowing. **23.** (of an advertisement) **a.** to have effectiveness, as specified: *The ad pulled badly.* **b.** to be effective: *That spot announcement really pulled!* **24. pull apart,** to analyze critically, esp. to point out errors: *The professor proceeded to pull apart the student's paper.* **25. pull down, a.** to draw downward: *to pull down a shade.* **b.** to demolish; wreck. **c.** to lower; reduce. **d.** *Slang.* to receive as a salary; earn: *It wasn't long before he was pulling down more than ten thousand a year.* **26. pull for,** *Informal.* to support actively; encourage: *They were pulling for the Republican candidate.* **27. pull in, a.** to reach a place; arrive: *The train pulled in early.* **b.** to tighten; curb: *to pull in the reins.* **c.** *Slang.* to arrest (someone): *The police pulled him in for questioning.* **28. pull off,** *Slang.* to perform successfully, esp. something requiring courage, daring, or shrewdness: *We pulled off a spectacular coup.* **29. pull oneself together,** to recover one's self-control; regain command of one's emotions: *It was only a minor accident, but the driver couldn't seem to pull himself together.* **30. pull out, a.** to leave; depart: *The ship pulled out of the harbor.* **b.** to abandon abruptly: *to pull out of an agreement.* **31. pull over,** to direct one's automobile or other vehicle to the curb; move out of a line of traffic: *The motorcycle policeman ordered the wild driver to pull over.* **32. pull someone's leg,** to chide or tease a person: *They always pulled his leg about his interest in insects.* **33. pull through,** to come safely through (a crisis, illness, etc.); survive: *The patient eventually pulled through after having had a close brush with death.* **34. pull up, a.** to bring or come to a halt. **b.** to bring or draw closer. **c.** to root up; pull out: *She pulled up all the crab grass in the lawn, but it soon reappeared.* —*n.* **35.** act of pulling or drawing. **36.** force used in pulling; pulling power. **37.** a drawing in of a liquid or of smoke through the mouth: *He took a long, thoughtful pull on his pipe; a refreshing pull from the scout's canteen.* **38.** *Slang.* influence, as with persons able to grant favors. **39.** a part or thing to be pulled; a handle or the like. **40.** an instrument or device for pulling something. **41.** a spell, or turn, at rowing. **42.** a stroke of an oar. **43.** a pulling of the ball in cricket or golf. **44.** *Informal.* an advantage over another or others. [ME *pulle(n),* OE *pullian* to pull, pluck; cf. MLG *pūlen* to strip off husks, pick, Icel *pūla* to work hard] —**pull′a·ble,** *adj.* —**pull′er,** *n.*
—**Syn. 2.** See **draw.** —**Ant. 2.** push.

pull·back (po͝ol′bak′), *n.* **1.** the act of pulling back. **2.** that which pulls something back or impedes its forward movement. **3.** *Mach.* a device for pulling a moving part to its original position. [n. use of v. phrase *pull back*]

pul·let (po͝ol′it), *n.* a young hen, less than one year old. [ME *polet* < MF *poulet,* dim. of *poul* cock < L *pull(us)* chicken, young of an animal; akin to FOAL]

pul·ley (po͝ol′ē), *n., pl.* **-leys. 1.** a wheel, with a grooved rim for carrying a line, that turns in a frame or block and serves to change the direction of or to transmit force, as when one end of the line is pulled to raise a weight at the other end. **2.** a combination of such wheels in a block, or of such wheels or blocks in a tackle, to increase the force applied. **3.** a wheel driven by or driving a belt or the like, used to deliver force to a machine, another belt, etc., at a certain speed and torque. [ME *poley, puly* < MF *po(u)lie* << Gk **polidion* little pivot, equiv. to *pól(os)* POLE² + *-idion* dim. suffix] —**pul′ley·less,** *adj.*

pul′ley stile′, (in a window frame) a stile against which a window sash slides. Also called **hanging stile.**

pull-in (po͝ol′in′), *n., adj. Brit.* drive-in. [n., adj. use of v. phrase *pull in*]

pull′ing boat′, a boat propelled by oars alone.

Pull·man (po͝ol′mən), *n., pl.* **-mans** for 1. **1.** (*sometimes l.c.*) *Trademark.* a railroad sleeping car or parlor car. **2. George Mortimer,** 1831–97, U.S. inventor and railroad car designer.

Pull·man (po͝ol′mən), *n.* a city in SE Washington. 12,957 (1960).

pull-on (*n.* po͝ol′on′, -ôn′; *adj.* po͝ol′on′, -ôn′), *n.* **1.** an item of apparel that is pulled onto oneself, as a sweater, glove, etc. —*adj.* **2.** that is made to be pulled on: *a pull-on jersey.* [n., adj. use of v. phrase *pull on*]

pul·lo′rum disease′ (pə lôr′əm, -lōr′-), *Vet. Pathol.* a highly contagious disease caused by the bacterium *Salmonella pullorum,* frequently a cause of death in very young poultry, transmitted esp. by the infected hen to its offspring during egg production, and characterized by depression, loss of appetite, and diarrhea. [< L *pullōrum,* gen. pl. of *pullus* cockerel, chicken]

pull-out (po͝ol′out′), *n.* a flight maneuver in which an aircraft levels into horizontal flight following a dive. [n. use of v. phrase *pull out*]

pull·o·ver (po͝ol′ō′vər), *n.* **1.** Also called **slipover.** a garment, esp. a sweater, which must be drawn over the head to be put on. —*adj.* **2.** designed to be put on by being drawn over the head. [n., adj. use of v. phrase *pull over*]

pul·lu·late (pul′yə lāt′), *v.i.*, **-lat·ed, -lat·ing. 1.** to send forth sprouts, buds, etc.; germinate; sprout. **2.** to breed, produce, or create rapidly. **3.** to increase rapidly; multiply. **4.** to exist abundantly; swarm; teem. **5.** to be produced as offspring. [< L *pullulāt(us)* (ptp. of *pullulāre* to sprout), deriv. of *pullulus* a sprout, young animal, dim. of *pullus;* see PULLET] —**pul′lu·la′tion,** *n.*

pull-up (po͝ol′up′), *n.* **1.** an exercise consisting of chinning oneself, as on a horizontal bar attached at each end to a doorpost. **2.** a flight maneuver in which an aircraft climbs sharply from level flight. [n. use of v. phrase *pull up*]

pul·lus (pul′əs), *n., pl.* **pul·li** (pul′ī). a young bird; a chick. [< NL, L: a young animal]

pul·mo·nar·y (pul′mə ner′ē, po͝ol′-), *adj.* **1.** of or pertaining to the lungs. **2.** of the nature of a lung; lunglike. **3.** affecting the lungs. **4.** having lungs or lunglike organs. **5.** pertaining to or affected with disease of the lungs. [< L *pulmōnāri(us)* of the lungs, equiv. to *pulmōn-* (s. of *pulmō* lung; akin to Gk *pleúmōn,* later *pneúmōn* lung) + *-ārius* -ARY]

pul′monary ar′tery, an artery conveying venous blood from the right ventricle of the heart to the lungs. See diag. under **heart.**

pul′monary valve′, *Anat.* a semilunar valve between the pulmonary artery and the right ventricle of the heart that prevents the blood from flowing back into the right ventricle.

pul′monary vein′, a vein conveying arterial blood from the lungs to the left atrium of the heart. See diag. under **heart.**

pul·mo·nate (pul′mə nāt′, -nit), *adj.* **1.** *Zool.* having lungs or lunglike organs. **2.** belonging to the *Pulmonata,* an order or group of gastropod mollusks usually breathing by means of a lunglike sac, and including most of the terrestrial snails and the slugs and certain aquatic snails. —*n.* **3.** a pulmonate gastropod. [< NL *pulmōnāt(us).* See PULMONARY, -ATE¹]

pul·mon·ic (pul mon′ik), *adj.* **1.** pulmonary. **2.** pneumonic. [< F *pulmonique.* See PULMONARY, -IC]

Pul·mo·tor (pul′mō′tər, po͝ol′-), *n. Trademark.* a mechanical device for artificial respiration that forces oxygen into the lungs when respiration has ceased because of asphyxiation, drowning, etc.

pulp (pulp), *n.* **1.** the succulent part of a fruit. **2.** the pith of the stem of a plant. **3.** a soft or fleshy part of an animal body. **4.** Also called **dental pulp.** the inner substance of the tooth, containing arteries, veins, and lymphatic and nerve tissue that communicate with their respective vascular, lymph, and nerve systems. See diag. under **tooth. 5.** any soft, moist, slightly cohering mass, as that into which linen, wood, etc., are converted in the making of paper. **6.** a magazine or book printed on rough, low-quality paper made of wood pulp, usually containing sensational and lurid stories, articles, etc. Cf. **slick**¹ (def. 9). **7.** *Mining.* **a.** ore pulverized and mixed with water. **b.** dry crushed ore. —*v.t.* **8.** to reduce to pulp. **9.** to remove the pulp from. —*v.i.* **10.** to become reduced to pulp. [earlier *pulpe* < L *pulpa* flesh, later pulp of fruit] —**pulp′less,** *adj.* —**pulp′like′,** *adj.*

pulp·board (pulp′bôrd′, -bōrd′), *n.* a board made from pulpwood. [PULP + BOARD]

pulp′ canal′, *Dentistry.* See **root canal.**

pulp′ canal′ ther′apy, endodontics. Also called **pulp′ canal′ treat′ment.**

pulp′ cav′ity, *Dentistry.* the entire space occupied by pulp, composed of the root canal and pulp chamber.

pulp′ cham′ber, *Dentistry.* the crown portion of the pulp cavity.

pul·pit (po͝ol′pit, pul′-), *n.* **1.** a platform or raised structure in a church, from which the clergyman delivers the sermon or conducts the service. **2. the pulpit, a.** the clerical profession; the ministry. **b.** clergymen collectively: *In attendance were representatives of medicine, the pulpit, and the bar.* **3.** (esp. in Protestantism and Judaism) the position of the pastor at any particular church, synagogue, etc.: *A vestryman told him of a pulpit in Chicago that was about to be vacated.* **4.** preaching. **5.** (in small craft) **a.** a safety rail rising about 18 to 30 inches from the deck near the bow and extending around it. **b.** a similar rail at the stern. [ME < LL *pulpit(um)* pulpit, L: platform, stage] —**pul′pit·al,** *adj.* —**pul′pit·less,** *adj.*

P, Pulpit

pul·pit·eer (po͝ol′pi tēr′, pul′-), *n. Usually Disparaging.* a preacher by profession. Also, **pul·pit·er** (po͝ol′pi tər, pul′-). [PULPIT + -EER]

pul·pi·tum (po͝ol′pi təm, pul′-), *n. Rare.* a lectern. [< LL: PULPIT]

pulp′ plas′ter, plaster containing shredded wood fiber.

pulp·wood (pulp′wo͝od′), *n.* spruce or other soft wood suitable for making paper. [PULP + WOOD¹]

pulp·y (pul′pē), *adj.*, **pulp·i·er, pulp·i·est.** of, characteristic of, or resembling pulp; fleshy or soft. [PULP + -Y¹] —**pulp′i·ly,** *adv.* —**pulp′i·ness,** *n.*

pul·que (po͝ol′kē; *Sp.* po͞ol′ke), *n.* a fermented milkish drink made from the juice of certain species of agave in Mexico. [< MexSp]

pul·sar (pul′sär), *n.* a source of rapidly pulsating radio energy within the local galaxy, believed to be either a white dwarf or a neutron star. [*puls(ating radio source)* + *-ar,* by analogy with QUASAR]

pul·sate (pul′sāt), *v.i.*, **-sat·ed, -sat·ing. 1.** to expand and contract rhythmically, as the heart; beat; throb. **2.** to vibrate; quiver. [< L *pulsāt(us),* ptp. of *pulsāre* to batter, strike, make (strings) vibrate. See PULSE¹]
—**Syn. 1.** pulse. PULSATE, BEAT, PALPITATE, THROB refer to the recurrent vibratory movement of the heart, the pulse, etc. To PULSATE is to move in a definite rhythm, temporarily or for a longer duration: *Blood pulsates in the arteries.* To BEAT is to repeat a vibration or pulsation regularly for some time: *One's heart beats many times a minute.* To PALPITATE is to beat at a rapid rate, often producing a flutter: *to palpitate with excitement.* To THROB is to beat with so much force as often to cause pain: *to throb with terror.*

pul·sa·tile (pul′sə til, -tīl′), *adj.* pulsating; throbbing. [< ML *pulsātil(is).* See PULSATE, -ILE] —**pul·sa·til·i·ty** (pul′sə til′i tē), *n.*

pul·sa·tion (pul sā′shən), *n.* **1.** act of pulsating; beating or throbbing. **2.** a beat or throb, as of the pulse. **3.** vibration or undulation. **4.** a single vibration. [< L *pulsātiōn-* (s. of *pulsātiō*). See PULSATE, -ION]

pul·sa·tive (pul′sə tiv), *adj.* throbbing; pulsating. [PULSATE + -IVE] —**pul′sa·tive·ly,** *adv.*

pul·sa·tor (pul′sā tər, pul sā′-), *n.* **1.** something that pulsates, beats, or throbs. **2.** pulsometer (def. 2). [< L: a striker. See PULSATE, -OR²]

pul·sa·to·ry (pul′sə tôr′ē, -tōr′ē), *adj.* pulsating or throbbing. [PULSAT(ION) + -ORY¹]

pulse¹ (puls), *n., v.,* **pulsed, puls·ing.** —*n.* **1.** the regular throbbing of the arteries, caused by the successive contractions of the heart, esp. as may be felt at an artery in the wrist, as by a physician in checking one's pulse rate. **2.** a single pulsation, or beat or throb, of the arteries or heart. **3.** the rhythmic recurrence of strokes, vibrations, or undulations. **4.** a single stroke, vibration, or undulation. **5.** *Elect.* a momentary, sudden fluctuation in an electrical quantity, as in voltage or current. **6.** a throb of life, emotion, etc. **7.** vitality. **8.** the general attitude, sentiment, preference, etc., as of the public. —*v.i.* **9.** to beat or throb; pulsate. **10.** to beat, vibrate, or undulate. [< L *puls(us)* a beat, *u*-stem (4th decl.) deriv. of *pulsus,* ptp. of *pellere* to set in motion by beating or striking; r. ME *pous* < MF]

pulse² (puls), *n.* **1.** the edible seeds of certain leguminous plants, as peas, beans, lentils, etc. **2.** a plant producing such seeds. [ME *puls* < L: thick pap of meal, pulse. See POULTICE]

pulse·beat (puls′bēt′), *n.* a hint or intimation of feeling, desires, etc.: *the pulsebeat of a town; the pulsebeat of an audience.* [PULSE¹ + BEAT]

pulse′jet en′gine (puls′jet′), *Aeron.* a jet engine equipped with valves that continuously open to admit air, then close during combustion, giving a pulsating thrust. Also, **pulse′-jet en′gine, pulse′jet′, pulse′-jet′, pulsojet.** [PULSE¹ + JET¹]

pulse′ pres′sure, the pressure of the pulse; the difference between the systolic and diastolic pressures.

pulse′ rate′, *Med.* the rate of the pulse: stated in pulsations per minute.

pulse′-time modula′tion (puls′tīm′), *Electronics.* radio transmission in which the carrier is modulated to produce a series of pulses timed to transmit the amplitude and pitch of a signal.

pul·sim·e·ter (pul sim′i tər), *n.* an instrument for measuring the strength or quickness of the pulse. [*pulsi-* (comb. form repr. PULSE¹) + -METER]

pul·so·jet (pul′sō jet′), *n.* See **pulsejet engine.** [*pulso* (comb. form repr. PULSE¹) + JET¹]

pul·som·e·ter (pul som′i tər), *n.* **1.** a pulsimeter. **2.** a pump without pistons, utilizing the pressure of steam and the partial vacuum caused by the condensation of steam alternately in two chambers. [*pulso-* (comb. form repr. PULSE¹) + -METER]

pul·sus al·ter·nans (pul′səs ôl tûr′nanz), a pulse in which there is a succession of alternating weak and strong beats. [< NL: alternating pulse]

pu·lu (po͞o′lo͞o), *n.* a soft, elastic vegetable fiber of yellow-brown hue obtained from the young fronds of Hawaiian tree ferns, used for mattress and pillow stuffing. Also called **pu′lu fi′ber.** [< Hawaiian: lit., something wet]

pulv., (in prescriptions) powder. [< L *pulvis*]

pul·ver·a·ble (pul′vər ə bəl), *adj.* that can be pulverized; pulverizable. [obs. *pulver* (< L *pulverāre* to pulverize) + -ABLE; see PULVERIZE]

pul·ver·ise (pul′və rīz′), *v.t., v.i.*, **-ised, -is·ing.** *Chiefly Brit.* pulverize. —**pul′ver·is′a·ble,** *adj.* —**pul′ver·i·sa′tion,** *n.* —**pul′ver·is′er,** *n.*

pul·ver·ize (pul′və rīz′), *v.*, **-ized, -iz·ing.** —*v.t.* **1.** to reduce to dust or powder, as by pounding, grinding, etc. **2.** to demolish or crush completely. **3.** *Slang.* to defeat, hurt badly, or, figuratively, render helpless: *The Kid pulverized Jackson with a series of brutal lefts. He's a veteran nightclub comic who can pulverize any audience in seconds.* —*v.i.* **4.** to become reduced to dust. [< LL *pulveriz(āre)* (to) reduce to powder, equiv. to L *pulver-* (s. of *pulvis*) dust + *-izāre* -IZE] —**pul′ver·iz′a·ble,** *adj.* —**pul′ver·i·za′tion,** *n.* —**pul′ver·iz′er,** *n.*

pul·ver·u·lent (pul ver′yə lənt, -ə lənt), *adj.* **1.** consisting of dust or fine powder. **2.** crumbling to dust or powder. **3.** covered with dust or powder. [< L *pulverulent(us)* dusty, equiv. to *pulver-* (s. of *pulvis*) dust + *-ulentus* -ULENT] —**pul·ver′u·lence,** *n.* —**pul·ver′u·lent·ly,** *adv.*

pul·vil·lus (pul vil′əs), *n., pl.* **-vil·li** (-vil′ī). *Entomol.* a soft, padlike structure located at the base of each claw on the feet of certain insects. [< L, dim. of *pulvinus* cushion]

pul·vi·nar (pul vī′nər), *n., pl.* **pul·vi·nar·i·a** (pul′və nâr′ē ə), *adj.* —*n.* **1.** (in ancient Rome) **a.** a cushioned couch kept in readiness for any visitation of a god. **b.** a cushioned seat at a circus. **2.** Also called **pulvinus.**

(on an Ionic capital) either of two convex forms having on their ends two of the volutes. See diag. under **volute.** —*adj.* **3.** pulvinate (def. 3). [< L: cushioned couch, equiv. to *pulvīn(us)* cushion + *-ar* -AR² (n.), -AR¹ (adj.)]

pul·vi·nate (pul′və nāt′), *adj.* **1.** cushion-shaped. **2.** having a pulvinus. **3.** Also, **pulvinar.** *Archit.* (of a frieze or the like) having a convex surface from top to bottom. Also, **pul′vi·nat′ed.** [< L *pulvīnāt(us)* cushioned, equiv. to *pulvīn(us)* cushion + *-ātus* -ATE¹] —**pul′vi·nate′ly,** *adv.*

pul·vi·nus (pul vī′nəs), *n., pl.* **-ni** (-nī). **1.** *Bot.* a cushionlike swelling at the base of a leaf or leaflet, at the point of junction with the axis. **2.** *Archit.* pulvinar (def. 2). [< L: cushion]

pu·ma (pyo͞o′mə), *n.* **1.** cougar. **2.** its fur. [< Sp < Quechuan]

pum·ice (pum′is), *n., v.,* **-iced, -ic·ing.** —*n.* **1.** Also called **pum′ice stone′,** a porous or spongy form of volcanic glass, used, esp. when powdered, as an abrasive, a polish, etc. —*v.t.* **2.** to rub, smooth, clean, etc., with pumice. [< L *pūmice(m),* acc. of *pūmex* pumice stone; r. late ME *pomyce, pomeys,* etc. < MF *pomis* < L; r. OE *pūmic* < L. See POUNCE³] —**pu·mi·ceous** (pyo͞o-mish′əs), *adj.* —**pum′ic·er,** *n.*

pum·mel¹ (pum′əl), *v.t.,* **-meled, -mel·ing** or (*esp. Brit.*) **-melled, -mel·ling.** to beat or thrash with or as if with the fists. Also, **pommel.** [alter. of POMMEL¹]

pump¹ (pump), *n.* **1.** an apparatus or machine for raising, driving, exhausting, or compressing fluids, as by means of a piston, plunger, or set of rotating vanes. **2.** *Engineering, Building Trades.* a shore having a jackscrew in its foot for adjusting the length or for bearing more firmly against the structure to be sustained. **3. prime the pump, a.** to increase government expenditure in an effort to stimulate the economy. **b.** to support or promote the operation or improvement of something: *His gifts of money hadn't been sufficient to prime the pump, and they went bankrupt.* —*v.t.* **4.** to raise, drive, etc., with a pump. **5.** to free from water or other liquid by means of a pump. **6.** to inflate by pumping (often fol. by *up*): *to pump up a tire.* **7.** to operate by action like that on a pump handle. **8.** to supply with air, as an organ, by means of a pumplike device. **9.** to drive, force, etc., as if from a pump: *He rapidly pumped a dozen shots into the bull's-eye.* **10.** to question artfully or persistently to elicit information: *to pump someone for confidential information.* **11.** to elicit (information) by questioning. —*v.i.* **12.** to work a pump; raise or move water, oil, etc., with a pump. **13.** to operate as a pump does. **14.** to move up and down like a pump handle. **15.** to exert oneself in a manner likened to pumping: *He pumped away at his homework all evening.* **16.** to seek to elicit information from a person. **17.** to come out in spurts. [late ME *pompe;* c. G *Pumpe,* D *pomp*] —**pump′a·ble,** *adj.* —**pump′er,** *n.* —**pump′less,** *adj.* —**pump′like′,** *adj.*

pump² (pump), *n.* **1.** a lightweight, low-cut shoe for women, without a fastening, in any of various fabrics and leathers and with a high or flat heel. **2.** a similar, low, flat-heeled shoe for men, of black patent leather, worn with formal dress. [?]

pump-ac·tion (pump′ak′shən), *adj.* (of a shotgun or rifle) having an action that extracts the empty case, loads, and cocks the piece by means of a hand-operated lever that slides backward and forward; slide-action.

pump′ box′, a chamber of a pump in which a piston operates.

pum·per·nick·el (pum′pər nik′əl), *n.* a coarse, slightly sour bread made of unbolted rye. [< G]

pump′ gun′, a shotgun or rifle having a pump-action mechanism.

pump·ing (pum′ping), *n.* **1.** the act or process of pumping or the action of a pump. **2.** *Meteorol.* rapid change in the height of the column in a mercury barometer, resulting from fluctuations in the surrounding air pressure. [PUMP¹ + -ING¹]

pump′ing plan′, a plan of a vessel showing all bilges, tanks, and other areas containing water, petroleum, etc., as well as plans and information relating to lines and machinery for pumping these.

pump·kin (pump′kin *or, commonly,* pung′kin), *n.* **1.** a large orange-yellow fruit borne by a coarse, decumbent vine, *Cucurbita Pepo,* used for making pies and as food for cattle. **2.** the vine itself. **3.** any of certain varieties of this plant. [alter. of *pumpion* (see -KIN), var. of *pompon* < MF, nasalized var. of *popon* melon, earlier *pepon* < L *pepōn-* (s. of *pepō*) < Gk *pépōn* kind of melon]

pump′kin head′, a slow or dim-witted person; dunce. —**pump′kin-head′ed,** *adj.*

pump·kin·seed (pump′kin sēd′ *or, commonly,* pung′-kin-), *n.* **1.** the seed of the pumpkin. **2.** a fresh-water sunfish, *Lepomis gibbosus,* found in eastern North America. **3.** a butterfish, *Poronotus triacanthus.* [PUMPKIN + SEED]

pump·man (pump′mən), *n., pl.* **-men.** a person who runs a power-operated pump. [PUMP¹ + MAN¹]

pump′ prim′ing, *U.S.* the spending of government funds in commercial enterprises, to stimulate the national economy.

pump′ room′, a room at a spa for drinking mineral waters.

Pump·sie (pump′sē), *n.* a boy's given name.

pump′ well′, *Naut.* **1.** a casing around the pumping machinery of certain vessels. **2.** the opening at the head of this casing.

pump·well (pump′wel′), *n.* a well from which the liquid is taken by the use of a pump. [PUMP¹ + WELL²]

pun¹ (pun), *n., v.,* **punned, pun·ning.** —*n.* **1.** the humorous use of a word so as to emphasize different meanings or applications, or the use of words that are alike or nearly alike in sound but different in meaning; a play on words. **2.** the word used in this way. —*v.i.* **3.** to make puns. [? special use of *pun,* var. (now dial.) of POUND¹; i.e., to mistreat (words)] —**pun′less,** *adj.*

pun² (pun), *v.t.,* **punned, pun·ning.** to compact (earth or fresh concrete) with a rammer. [cf. ME *pounen.* See POUND¹]

pu·na (po͞o′nä), *n.* **1.** a high, cold, arid plateau, as in the Peruvian Andes. **2.** *Pathol.* See **mountain sickness.** [< AmerSp < Quechuan]

Pu·nan (po͞o nän′), *n., pl.* **-nans,** (*esp. collectively*) **-nan.** a member of a food-gathering people living in the forests of interior Borneo.

punch¹ (punch), *n.* **1.** a thrusting blow, esp. with the fist. **2.** *Informal.* a vigorous, telling effect or force. **3. pull punches, a.** to lessen deliberately the force of one's blows. **b.** *Informal.* to act with restraint or hold back the full force or implications of something: *He wasn't going to pull any punches when he warned them of what they would be up against.* —*v.t.* **4.** to give a sharp thrust or blow to, esp. with the fist. **5.** *Western U.S. and Western Canada.* to drive (cattle). **6.** to poke or prod, as with a stick. **7.** *Informal.* to deliver (lines in a play, a musical passage, or the like) with vigor. **8.** to strike or hit vigorously in operating: *to punch the typewriter keys.* **9.** to put into operation with or as if with a vigorous blow: *to punch a time clock.* —*v.i.* **10.** to give a sharp blow to a person or thing, as with the fist: *The boxer punches well.* [perh. var. of POUNCE¹] —**punch′er,** *n.* —**Syn. 4.** strike, hit; drub, pummel.

punch² (punch), *n.* **1.** a tool or machine for piercing, perforating or stamping materials, impressing a design, forcing nails beneath a surface, driving bolts out of holes, etc. **2.** the solid upper die of a punch press, used with a hollow die to blank out shaped pieces of sheet metal or the like. —*v.t.* **3.** to cut, stamp, pierce, perforate, form, or drive with a tool or machine that punches. —*v.i.* **4.** to work at or on something with or as if with a mechanical punch. [short for PUNCHEON²] —**punch′a·ble,** *adj.*

punch³ (punch), *n.* **1.** a beverage consisting of wine or spirits mixed with water, milk, etc., and flavored with sugar, lemon, spices, etc. **2.** a beverage of two or more fruit juices, sugar, and water, often carbonated. [perh. short for PUNCHEON¹; if so, a metonymic use]

Punch (punch), *n.* **1.** the chief character in a Punch-and-Judy show. **2. pleased as Punch,** highly pleased; delighted: *They were pleased as Punch at having been asked to come along.* [short for PUNCHINELLO]

Punch′-and-Ju′dy show′ (punch′ən jo͞o′dē), a puppet show having a conventional plot consisting chiefly of slapstick humor and the tragicomic misadventures of a grotesque, hook-nosed, humpback buffoon (Punch) and his wife (Judy).

punch·ball (punch′bôl′), *n.* a form of baseball played in the streets, on playgrounds, etc., in which a rubber ball and the fist are used in place of a baseball and bat and the batter tosses the ball into the air and hits it on the way down. [PUNCH¹ + BALL¹]

punch·board (punch′bōrd′, -bôrd′), *n.* a small board, used for gambling, containing holes filled with slips of paper printed with concealed numbers that are punched out by a player in an attempt to win a prize. Also called **pushcard.** [PUNCH¹ + BOARD]

punch′ bowl′, a large bowl from which a beverage, as punch, lemonade, or the like, is served by means of a ladle.

punch′ card′, a card having holes punched in specific positions and patterns so as to represent data to be stored or processed mechanically, electrically, or photoelectrically. Also, **punched′ card′.**

punch-drunk (punch′drungk′), *adj.* **1.** (esp. of a boxer) having cerebral concussion caused by repeated blows to the head and consequently exhibiting unsteadiness of gait, hand tremors, slow muscular movement, hesitant speech, and dulled mentality. **2.** *Informal.* befuddled; dazed.

punched′ tape′, *Computer Technol.* a paper tape for coding data by means of a row or a series of rows of holes punched across its width.

pun·cheon¹ (pun′chən), *n.* **1.** a large cask of varying capacity, but usually 80 gallons. **2.** its volume as a measure. [late ME *poncion* < MF *ponçon* < ?]

pun·cheon² (pun′chən), *n.* **1.** a heavy slab of timber, roughly dressed, for use as a floorboard. **2.** a short, upright framing timber. **3.** (in goldsmith work) **a.** any of various pointed instruments; a punch. **b.** a stamping tool. [ME *ponson* < MF *ponçon* < L *punctiōn-* (s. of *punctiō*) a pricking, hence, pricking tool, equiv. to *punct(us)* (ptp. of *pungere* to prick) + *-iōn-* -ION]

pun·chi·nel·lo (pun′chə nel′ō), *n., pl.* **-los, -loes. 1.** the grotesque or absurd chief character in a puppet show of Italian origin: the prototype of Punch. **2.** any similarly grotesque or absurd person or thing. [var. of *Polichinello* < It *Pollechinella* (Naples dial.), dim. of *pollecena* turkey-cock chick; akin to PULLET]

punch′ing bag′, **1.** an inflated or stuffed bag, usually suspended, punched with the fists as an exercise. **2.** a person as an object to abuse or of abuse; scapegoat: *I told him that I wasn't going to be a punching bag for anyone.*

punch′ lift′er, a bottle-shaped vessel (used mainly c1800) for serving punch, with a capacity of one glassful, having a hole at each end, the upper one being stopped with the thumb during the transfer of punch from the bowl to a glass. Also called **grog lifter.**

punch′ line′, a phrase, sentence, or the like, as in a speech, advertisement, or humorous story, without which the desired effect cannot be produced: *to forget the punch line of a joke.*

punch′ mat′, *Naut.* See **paunch mat.**

punch′ press′, *Mach.* a power-driven machine used to cut, draw, or otherwise shape material, esp. metal sheets, with dies, under pressure or by heavy blows.

punch′ spoon′, a spoon having a pierced bowl and a barbed end for removing fruit, ice, etc., from punch.

punch·y (pun′chē), *adj.,* **punch·i·er, punch·i·est.** *Informal.* **1.** punch-drunk. **2.** being or appearing vigorously effective; forceful. [PUNCH¹ + -Y¹]

punc·tate (pungk′tāt), *adj.* marked with points or dots; having minute spots or depressions. Also, **punc′tat·ed.** [< NL *punctāt(us)* dotted, equiv. to L *punct(um)* point, dot + *-ātus* -ATE¹]

punc·ta·tim (po͝ongk tä′tim; *Eng.* pungk tā′tim), *adv. Latin.* point for point.

punc·ta·tion (pungk tā′shən), *n.* **1.** punctate condition or marking. **2.** one of the marks or depressions. [< ML *punctāt(us)* marked, punctuated (ptp. of *punctāre;* see POINT) + *-iōn-* -ION]

punc·ti·form (pungk′tə fôrm′), *adj.* shaped like or of the nature of a point or dot. [< L *punct(um)* POINT + -I- + -FORM]

punc·til·i·o (pungk til′ē ō′), *n., pl.* **-til·i·os** for **1. 1.** a fine point, particular, or detail, as of conduct, ceremony, or procedure. **2.** strictness or exactness in the observance of formalities or amenities. [< It *puntiglio* < Sp *puntillo,* dim. of *punto* < L *punctum* POINT]

punc·til·i·ous (pungk til′ē əs), *adj.* extremely attentive to punctilios; strict or exact in the observance of all formalities or amenities of conduct or actions. [PUNCTILI(O) + -OUS] —**punc·til′i·ous·ly,** *adv.* —**punc·til′i·ous·ness,** *n.*
—**Syn.** precise, demanding; careful, conscientious. See **scrupulous.** —**Ant.** careless.

punc·tu·al (pungk′cho͞o əl), *adj.* **1.** strictly observant of an appointed or regular time; not late; prompt. **2.** made, occurring, etc., at the scheduled or proper time: *punctual payment.* **3.** pertaining to or of the nature of a point. **4.** *Obs.* punctilious. [late ME < ML *punctuāl(is)* of a point, equiv. to L *punctu(s)* a point, a pricking (u-stem 4th decl.) deriv. of *punctus* (ptp. of *pungere* to prick) + *-ālis* -AL¹] —**punc′tu·al·ly,** *adv.* —**punc′tu·al·ness,** *n.*

punc·tu·al·i·ty (pungk′cho͞o al′i tē), *n.* **1.** quality or state of being punctual. **2.** strict observance in keeping engagements; promptness. [PUNCTUAL + -ITY]

punc·tu·ate (pungk′cho͞o āt′), *v.,* **-at·ed, -at·ing.** —*v.t.* **1.** to mark or divide with punctuation marks, as a sentence, in order to make the meaning clear. **2.** to interrupt at intervals: *Cheers punctuated the mayor's speech.* **3.** to give emphasis or force to; emphasize; underline. —*v.i.* **4.** to insert or use marks of punctuation. [< ML *punctuāt(us)* (ptp. of *punctuāre* to point), deriv. of L *punctus* a point; see PUNCTUAL] —**punc′tu·a′tor,** *n.*

punc·tu·a·tion (pungk′cho͞o ā′shən), *n.* **1.** the practice, art, or system of using certain conventional marks or characters, as periods, commas, etc., in writing or printing in order to make the meaning clear, as in ending a sentence, separating clauses, etc. **2.** act of punctuating. [< ML *punctuātiōn-* (s. of *punctuātiō*) a marking, pointing. See PUNCTUATE, -ION] —**punc′tu·a′tive,** *adj.*

punctua′tion mark′, any of a group of conventional marks or characters used in punctuation, as the period, comma, semicolon, question mark, or dash.

punc·ture (pungk′chər), *n., v.,* **-tured, -tur·ing.** —*n.* **1.** act of piercing or perforating, as with a pointed instrument or object. **2.** a hole or mark so made. **3.** *Zool.* a small pointlike depression. —*v.t.* **4.** to pierce or perforate, as with a pointed instrument: *to puncture leather with an awl.* **5.** to make (a hole, perforation, etc.) by piercing or perforating: *He punctured a row of holes in the cardboard.* **6.** to make a puncture in: *A piece of glass punctured the tire.* —*v.i.* **7.** to become punctured: *These tires do not puncture easily.* [< LL *punctūra* a pricking, equiv. to L *punct(us)* (ptp. of *pungere* to pierce), + *-ūra* -URE] —**punc′tur·a·ble,** *adj.* —**punc′ture·less,** *adj.* —**punc′tur·er,** *n.*

pun·dit (pun′dit), *n.* **1.** (in India) a Brahman with profound knowledge of Sanskrit, Hindu law, etc. **2.** a very learned man; an expert or authority. **3.** a person who makes comments or judgments in a solemnly authoritative manner. [< Hindi *pandit* < Skt *pandita* learned man; as adj., learned] —**pun·dit′ic,** *adj.* —**pun·dit′i·cal·ly,** *adv.*

pung (pung), *n. U.S. and Canada.* a sleigh with a box-like body on runners. [short for *tom-pung,* alter. of TOBOGGAN]

pun·gent (pun′jənt), *adj.* **1.** sharply affecting the organs of taste or smell, as if by a penetrating power; biting; acrid. **2.** acutely distressing to the feelings or mind; poignant. **3.** caustic, biting, or sharply expressive: *pungent remarks.* **4.** mentally stimulating or appealing: *pungent wit.* **5.** *Biol.* piercing or sharp-pointed. [< L *pungent-* (s. of *pungēns*), prp. of *pungere* to prick. See POIGNANT, POINT, PUNCHEON², etc.] —**pun′gen·cy,** *n.* —**pun′gent·ly,** *adv.*
—**Syn. 1.** hot, peppery, piquant, sharp. **3.** sarcastic, mordant, cutting; acrimonious, bitter. **4.** keen, sharp. —**Ant. 1.** mild, bland. **3.** soothing. **4, 5.** dull.

pung·y (pung′gē), *n., pl.* **pung·ies.** *Naut.* a schooner, built on Chesapeake Bay for fishing, oystering, and trading, having a broad, shoal hull with a greatly raking stem and a broad, shallow transom stern, fore-and-aft-rigged on two masts with a gaff foresail and mainsail, a gaff main topsail, a jib, and a main topmast staysail. Also, **pung′ey, pung′ie.** [?]

Pu·nic (pyo͞o′nik), *adj.* **1.** of or pertaining to the ancient Carthaginians. **2.** treacherous; perfidious: originally applied by the Romans to the Carthaginians. —*n.* **3.** the language of ancient Carthage, a form of late Phoenician. [< L *Pūnic(us),* var. of *Poenicus* Carthaginian, orig. Phoenician < Gk *Phoînix*]

Pu′nic Wars′, the three wars waged by Rome against Carthage, 264–241, 218–201, and 149–146 B.C., resulting in the overthrow of Carthage and its annexation by Rome.

pun·ish (pun′ish), *v.t.* **1.** to subject to pain, loss, confinement, death, etc., as a penalty for some offense, transgression, or fault: *to punish a criminal.* **2.** to inflict a penalty for (an offense, fault, etc.): *to punish theft.* **3.** to handle severely or roughly, as in a fight. **4.** to put to painful exertion, as a horse in racing. **5.** *Informal.* to make a heavy inroad on; deplete: *to punish a quart of whiskey.* —*v.i.* **6.** to inflict punishment. [ME *punische(n)* < MF *puniss-,* long s. of *punir* < L *pūnīre*] —**pun′ish·er,** *n.*
—**Syn. 1.** chastise, castigate. PUNISH, CORRECT, DISCIPLINE refer to making evident public or private disapproval of violations of law, wrongdoing, or refusal to obey rules or regulations by imposing penalties. To PUNISH is chiefly to inflict penalty or pain as a retribution for misdeeds, with little or no expectation of correction or improvement: *to punish a thief.* To CORRECT is to reprove or inflict punishment for faults, specifically with the idea of bringing about improvement: *to correct a rebellious child.* To DISCIPLINE is to give a kind of punishment which will educate or will establish useful habits: *to discipline a careless driver.* **1, 2.** penalize. —**Ant. 1.** reward.

pun·ish·a·ble (pun′i shə bəl), *adj.* liable to or deserving punishment. [PUNISH + -ABLE] —**pun′ish·a·bil′i·ty,** *n.*

pun·ish·ment (pun′ish mənt), *n.* **1.** act of punishing. **2.** fact of being punished, as for an offense or fault. **3.** a penalty inflicted for an offense, fault, etc. **4.** severe handling or treatment. [ME *punysshement* < AF *punisement,* equiv. to OF *punissement.* See PUNISH, -MENT]

pu·ni·tive (pyo͞o′ni tiv), *adj.* serving for, concerned with, or inflicting punishment: *punitive laws; punitive action.* Also, **pu·ni·to·ry** (pyo͞o′ni tôr′ē, -tōr′ē). [< ML *pūnītī-v(us)* of punishment, equiv. to L *pūnīt(us)* (ptp. of *pūnīre* to punish) + *-īvus* -IVE] —**pu′ni·tive·ly,** *adv.* —**pu′ni·tive·ness,** *n.*

pu′nitive dam′ages, *Law.* See **exemplary damages.**

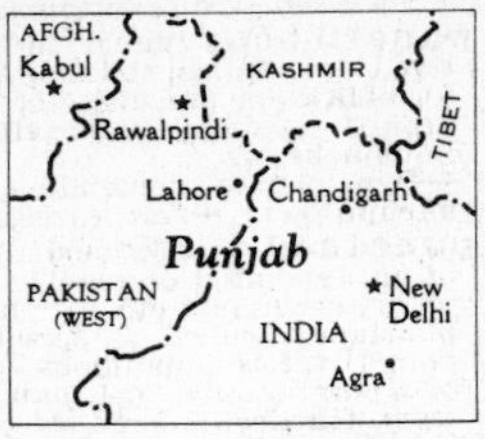

Pun·jab (pun jäb′, pun′-jäb), *n.* **1.** a former province in NW India: now divided between Punjab (in India) and West Punjab (in Pakistan). **2.** a state in NW India. 20,306,812 (1961); 47,456 sq. mi. *Cap.:* Chandigarh.

Pun·ja·bi (pun jä′bē), *n.* **1.** a native of Punjab, India. **2.** Panjabi. [< Hindi *Panjābī* < Pers *Panjab* PUNJAB + *-ī-* suffix of appurtenance]

Pun′jab States′, a former group of states in NW India; amalgamated with Punjab state (in India) in 1956.

punk[1] (pungk), *n.* **1.** any prepared substance, usually in stick form, that will smolder and can be used to light fireworks, fuses, etc. **2.** dry, decayed wood that can be used as tinder. **3.** conk[2]. **4.** amadou; touchwood. [? sandhi var. of SPUNK]

punk[2] (pungk), *n.* **1.** *Slang.* **a.** something or someone worthless or unimportant. **b.** a petty criminal or hoodlum. **c.** an inexperienced boy. **d.** the boy partner of a homosexual. **2.** *Archaic.* a prostitute. —*adj.* **3.** *Informal.* poor in quality or condition. [?]

pun·kah (pung′kə), *n.* **1.** (esp. in India) a fan, esp. a large, swinging, screenlike fan hung from the ceiling and kept in motion by a servant or by machinery. —*adj.* **2.** of, pertaining to, used on, or working a punkah: *a punkah coolie; punkah wallah; punkah ropes.* Also, **pun′ka.** [< Hindi *pankhā* a fan < Skt *pakshaka*]

punk·ie (pung′kē), *n.* any of the minute biting gnats of the family *Ceratopogonidae.* Also called **biting midge.** [< New York D *punki,* appar. deriv. of Delaware *punk* ashes, dust]

punk′ rock′, rock-'n'-roll having loud, insistent music and violent protest lyrics. —**punk′ rock′er.**

punk′ tree′, cajuput.

pun·ner[1] (pun′ər), *n.* a person who puns; punster.

pun·ner[2] (pun′ər), *n.* a rammer for compacting earth or fresh concrete. [PUN[2] + -ER[1]]

pun·ster (pun′stər), *n.* a person who makes puns frequently. [PUN[1] + -STER]

punt[1] (punt), *n.* **1.** *Football.* a kick in which the ball is dropped and then kicked before it touches the ground. Cf. **drop kick, place kick. 2.** *Chiefly Brit.* a small, shallow boat having a flat bottom and square ends, usually used for short outings on rivers or lakes and propelled by poling. —*v.t.* **3.** *Football.* to kick (a dropped ball) before it touches the ground. **4.** to propel (a small boat) by thrusting against the ground beneath, esp. with a pole. **5.** to convey in or as in a punt. —*v.i.* **6.** to punt a football. **7.** *Chiefly Brit.* **a.** to propel a boat by thrusting a pole against the bottom of a river, stream, or lake. **b.** to travel or have an outing in a punt. [OE *punt* < L *pontō* punt, PONTOON] —**punt′er,** *n.*

punt[2] (punt), *v.i.* **1.** *Cards.* to lay a stake against the bank, as at faro. **2.** *Brit.* to gamble; wager. —*n.* **3.** *Cards.* a person who lays a stake against the bank. [< F *pont(er),* deriv. of *ponte* punter, point in faro < Sp] —**punt′er,** *n.*

Punt (po͝ont), *n.* an ancient Egyptian name of an area not absolutely identified but believed to be Somaliland.

Pun·ta A·re·nas (po͞on′tä ä re′näs), a seaport in S Chile, on the Strait of Magellan: the southernmost city in the world. 64,000. Also called **Magallanes.**

Pun·ta·re·nas (po͞on′tä re′näs), *n.* a seaport in W Costa Rica. 17,069 (est. 1958).

pun·til·la (po͞on tē′ə; *Sp.* po͞on tē′lyä, -yä), *n., pl.* **-til·las** (-tē′əz; *Sp.* -tē′lyäs, -yäs). (in bullfighting) a short dagger used for cutting the spinal cord of the bull. [< Sp, dim. of *punta* POINT]

pun·til·le·ro (po͞on′tē âr′ō; *Sp.* po͞on′tē lye′rô, -ye′-), *n., pl.* **-til·le·ros** (-tē âr′ōz; *Sp.* -tē lye′rôs, -ye′-). (in bullfighting) a worker, or assistant, who gives the coup de grâce to the fallen bull with a puntilla. [< Sp, equiv. to *puntill(a)* PUNTILLA + *-ero;* see -ER[2]]

pun·ty (pun′tē), *n., pl.* **-ties.** an iron rod used in glassmaking for handling the hot glass. Also called **pontil.** [var. of PONTIL]

Punx·su·taw·ney (pungk′sə tô′nē), *n.* a town in central Pennsylvania. 8805 (1960).

pu·ny (pyo͞o′nē), *adj.,* **-ni·er, -ni·est. 1.** of less than normal size and strength; weak. **2.** unimportant; insignificant; petty or minor: *a puny excuse for a major error.* **3.** *Obs.* puisne. [sp. var. of PUISNE] —**pu′ni·ness,** *n.*

pup (pup), *n., v.,* **pupped, pup·ping.** —*n.* **1.** a young dog; puppy. **2.** a young seal. —*v.i.* **3.** to give birth to pups. [apocopated var. of PUPPY]

pu·pa (pyo͞o′pə), *n., pl.* **-pae** (-pē), **-pas.** an insect in the nonfeeding, usually immobile, transformation stage between the larva and the imago. [< NL, special use of L *pūpa* girl, doll, puppet. See PUPIL, PUPPET] —**pu′pal,** *adj.*

pu·par·i·um (pyo͞o pâr′ē əm), *n., pl.* **-par·i·a** (-pâr′ē ə). *Entomol.* a pupal case formed of the cuticula of a preceding larval instar. [< NL; see PUPA, -ARIUM] —**pu·par′i·al,** *adj.*

pu·pate (pyo͞o′pāt), *v.i.,* **-pat·ed, -pat·ing.** to become a pupa. [PUP(A) + -ATE[1]] —**pu·pa′tion,** *n.*

pup·fish (pup′fish), *n., pl.* (*esp. collectively*) **-fish,** (*esp. referring to two or more kinds or species*) **-fish·es.** any of several tiny, stout killifishes of the genus *Cyprinodon,* found in warm, fresh waters of Nevada. [PUP + FISH]

pu·pil[1] (pyo͞o′pəl), *n.* **1.** a person, usually young, who is learning under the close supervision of a teacher at school, a private tutor, or the like; student. **2.** *Civil Law.* an orphaned or emancipated minor under the care of a guardian. **3.** *Roman Law.* a person under the age of puberty orphaned or emancipated, and under the care of a guardian. [ME *pupille* < MF < L *pūpillus* (masc.), *pūpilla* (fem.) orphan, ward, diminutives of *pūpus* boy, *pūpa* girl] —**pu′pil·less,** *adj.*

—**Syn. 1.** apprentice, novice. PUPIL, DISCIPLE, SCHOLAR, STUDENT refer to one who is studying, usually in a school. A PUPIL is one under the close supervision of a teacher, either because of his youth or of specialization in some branch of study: *a grade-school pupil; the pupil of a famous musician.* A DISCIPLE is one who follows the teachings or doctrines of a person whom he considers to be a master or authority: *a disciple of Swedenborg.* SCHOLAR, once meaning the same as PUPIL, is today usually applied to one who has acquired wide erudition in some field of learning: *a great Latin scholar.* A STUDENT is one attending an institution of higher learning, or one who has devoted much attention to a particular problem: *a college student; a student of politics.* —**Ant. 1.** teacher, expert.

pu·pil[2] (pyo͞o′pəl), *n. Anat.* the expanding and contracting opening in the iris of the eye, through which light passes to the retina. See diag. under **eye.** [< L *pūpilla,* lit., little doll. See PUPA] —**pu′pil·less,** *adj.*

pu·pil·age (pyo͞o′pə lij), *n.* the state or period of being a pupil. [PUPIL + -AGE]

pu·pil·lar·i·ty (pyo͞o′pə lar′i tē), *n. Civil Law, Scots Law.* the period between birth and puberty, or until attaining majority. Also, **pu′pi·lar′i·ty.** [<L *pūpillāri(s)* of an orphan or ward (see PUPIL[1], -AR[1]) + -TY[2]]

pu·pil·lar·y[1] (pyo͞o′pə ler′ē), *adj.* of or pertaining to a pupil or student. [< L *pūpillāri(s).* See PUPIL[1], -ARY]

pu·pil·lar·y[2] (pyo͞o′pə ler′ē), *adj. Anat.* pertaining to the pupil of the eye. [< L *pūpill(a)* PUPIL[2] + -ARY]

Pu·pin (pyo͞o pēn′, po͞o′pēn), *n.* **Michael Id·vor·sky** (id vôr′skē), 1858–1935, U.S. inventor, physicist, and author, born in Hungary.

pu·pip·a·rous (pyo͞o pip′ər əs), *adj.* (of an insect) bearing fully developed larvae that are ready to pupate. [< NL *pūpiparus.* See PUPA, -I-, -PAROUS]

pup·pet (pup′it), *n.* **1.** an artificial figure representing a human being or an animal, manipulated by rods, the hand, wires, etc., as on a miniature stage. Cf. **marionette. 2.** a person whose actions are prompted and controlled by another or others. **3.** a small doll. **4.** *Mach.* poppethead. [earlier *poppet,* ME *popet,* appar. deriv. of MLG *poppe* doll < LL *puppa,* var. of L *pūpa* doll; see -ET] —**pup′pet·like′,** *adj.*

pup·pet·eer (pup′i tēr′), *n.* **1.** a person who manipulates puppets, as in a puppet show. —*v.i.* **2.** to work as a puppeteer, by making puppets perform. [PUPPET + -EER]

pup·pet·ry (pup′i trē), *n., pl.* **-ries. 1.** the art of making puppets perform. **2.** the action of puppets. **3.** mummery; mere show. **4.** puppets collectively. [PUPPET + -RY]

pup′pet show′, an entertainment, as a play or musical revue, in which the performers are puppets. Also called **pup′pet play′.**

Pup·pis (pup′is), *n., gen.* **Pup·pis.** *Astron.* the Stern, a southern constellation: one of the subordinate constellations into which Argo is divided. [< L: hinder part of a ship, stern, poop]

pup·py (pup′ē), *n., pl.* **-pies. 1.** a young dog, esp. one less than a year old. **2.** *Fox Hunting.* a foxhound that has hunted regularly for less than one season. **3.** the young of certain other animals, as the shark. **4.** a presuming, conceited, or empty-headed young man. [late ME *popi.* See PUPPET, -Y[2]] —**pup′py·hood′, pup′py·dom,** *n.* —**pup′py·ish,** *adj.* —**pup′py·like′,** *adj.*

pup·py·foot (pup′ē fo͝ot′), *n., pl.* **-feet.** *Cards Slang.* **1.** the ace of clubs. **2.** any card of the club suit. [PUPPY + FOOT; so called from fancied resemblance]

pup′py love′. See **calf love.**

pup′ tent′. See **shelter tent.**

pur (pûr), *v.t., v.i.,* **purred, pur·ring.** purr.

Pu·ra·na (po͞o rä′nə), *n.* any of a large number of traditional collections of epics, myths, popular lore, etc., embodying the principles of popular Hindu religion and ethics, originally transmitted orally and later written down. The most famous *Puranas* are the *Mahabharata* and the *Ramayana.* [< Skt: of old] —**Pu·ra′nic,** *adj.*

Pur·bach (po͝or′bäk), *n.* a walled plain in the third quadrant of the face of the moon: about 75 miles in diameter.

pur·blind (pûr′blīnd′), *adj.* **1.** nearly or partially blind; dim-sighted. **2.** slow or deficient in understanding, imagination, or vision. **3.** *Obs.* totally blind. [ME *pur blind* completely blind. See PURE, formerly used as adv., entirely] —**pur′blind′ly,** *adv.* —**pur′blind′ness,** *n.*

—**Syn. 1, 2.** See **blind.**

Pur·cell (pûr sel′ *for 1, 3;* pûr′səl *for 2*), *n.* **1. Edward Mills** (milz), born 1912, U.S. physicist: Nobel prize 1952. **2. Henry,** 1658?–95, English composer. **3.** a town in central Oklahoma. 3729 (1960).

Purcell′ Moun′tains, a range in SE British Columbia and NW Montana. Highest peak, Mt. Farnham, 11,340 ft.

Pur·chas (pûr′chəs), *n.* **Samuel,** 1575?–1626, English writer and editor of travel books.

pur·chas·a·ble (pûr′chə sə bəl), *adj.* **1.** capable of being bought. **2.** that may be influenced by bribery; venal. [PURCHASE + -ABLE] —**pur′chas·a·bil′i·ty,** *n.*

pur·chase (pûr′chəs), *v.,* **-chased, -chas·ing,** *n.* —*v.t.* **1.** to acquire by the payment of money or its equivalent; buy. **2.** to acquire by effort, sacrifice, flattery, etc. **3.** to influence by a bribe. **4.** (of things) to be sufficient to buy: *One dollar purchases a subscription.* **5.** *Law.* to acquire land or other property other than by inheritance. **6.** to move, haul, or raise, esp. by applying mechanical power. **7.** to get a leverage on; apply a lever, pulley, or other aid to. **8.** *Obs.* to procure, acquire, or obtain. —*n.* **9.** acquisition by the payment of money or its equivalent; buying, or a single act of buying. **10.** something which is purchased or bought. **11.** something purchased, with respect to the comparative degree of value it has in relation to its price; buy: *At three for a dollar they seemed like a good purchase.* **12.** *Law.* the acquisition of land or other property by other means than inheritance. **13.** acquisition by means of effort, labor, etc.: *the purchase of comfort at the price of freedom.* **14.** a lever, pulley, or other device that provides mechanical advantage or power for moving or raising a heavy object. **15.** an effective hold or position for applying power in moving or raising a heavy object; leverage. **16.** any means of applying or increasing power, influence, etc. **17.** the annual return or rent from land. **18.** a firm grip or grasp, footing, etc., on something. **19.** *Obs.* booty. [ME < AF *purchase(r)* (to) seek to obtain, procure, equiv. to *pur-* (< L *prō* for) + *chacer* to CHASE] —**pur′chas·er,** *n.*

—**Syn. 1.** get, obtain, procure. See **buy. 14.** winch, capstan. —**Ant. 1.** sell.

pur′chase tax′, *Brit.* a sales tax on nonessential and luxury goods.

pur′chasing pow′er, 1. Also called **buying power.** the ability to purchase goods and services. **2.** Also called **pur′chasing pow′er of the dol′lar.** the value of money in terms of what it can buy at a specified time compared to what it could buy at some period established as a base.

pur·dah (pûr′də), *n.* (in India, Pakistan, etc.) **1.** a screen, curtain, or veil, used for hiding women from the sight of men or strangers. **2.** seclusion in this manner: *They wanted to do away with the practice of purdah. The women were in purdah.* Also, **pur′da, pardah.** [< Hindi (Urdu) *pardah* curtain < Pers]

pure (pyo͝or), *adj.,* **pur·er, pur·est. 1.** free from anything of a different, inferior, or contaminating kind; free from extraneous matter: *pure gold; pure water.* **2.** unmodified by an admixture; simple or homogeneous. **3.** of unmixed descent or ancestry: *a pure breed of dog.* **4.** free from foreign or inappropriate elements: *pure Attic Greek.* **5.** clear; free from blemishes: *pure skin.* **6.** (of literary style) straightforward; unaffected. **7.** abstract or theoretical (opposed to *applied*): *pure science.* **8.** without any discordant quality; clear and true: *pure tones in music.* **9.** absolute; utter; sheer: *to sing for pure joy.* **10.** being that and nothing else; mere: *a pure accident.* **11.** clean, spotless, or unsullied: *pure hands.* **12.** untainted with evil; innocent: *pure in heart.* **13.** physically chaste; virgin. **14.** ceremonially or ritually clean. **15.** free of or without guilt; guiltless. **16.** independent of sense or experience: *pure knowledge.* **17.** *Biol., Genetics.* **a.** homozygous. **b.** containing only one characteristic for a trait. **18.** *Phonet.* monophthongal. [ME *pur* < OF < L *pūr(us)* clean, unmixed, plain, pure] —**pure′ness,** *n.*

—**Syn. 1.** unmixed, unadulterated, unalloyed, uncontaminated, untainted, unstained, undefiled, untarnished, immaculate, unpolluted, uncorrupted. See **clean. 4.** genuine, faultless, perfect. **12.** modest, virtuous, undefiled.

pure·bred (*adj.* pyo͝or′bred′; *n.* pyo͝or′bred′), *adj.* **1.** of or pertaining to an animal, all the ancestors of which derive over many generations from a recognized breed. —*n.* **2.** a purebred animal, esp. one of registered pedigree. [PURE + BRED]

pure′ cul′ture, the growth of only one microorganism in a culture.

pu·rée (pyo͝o rā′, -rē′, pyo͝or′ā; *Fr.* PY RĀ′), *n., v.,* **-réed, -ré·ing.** —*n.* **1.** a cooked and sieved food, esp. a vegetable or fruit. **2.** a soup made with ingredients that have been puréed. —*v.t.* **3.** to make a purée of. [< F, n. use of fem. ptp. of *purer* to strain, lit., make pure; see PURE]

pure·heart·ed (pyo͝or′här′tid), *adj.* (of a person) without malice, treachery, or evil intent; honest; sincere; guileless. [PURE + -HEARTED]

pure′ imag′inary num′ber, *Math.* a complex number of the form *iy* where *y* is a real number.

Pure′ Land′, *Buddhism.* a paradise believed by the followers of a Mahayana sect (**Pure′ Land′ sect′**) to be ruled over by a Buddha (**Amida**), whose hope it was to bring all beings into it. Chinese, **Ching-t'u.** Japanese, **Jodo.**

pure′ line′, *Genetics.* a uniform strain of organisms which is relatively pure genetically because of continued inbreeding along with selection.

pure·ly (pyo͝or′lē), *adv.* **1.** in a pure manner; without admixture. **2.** merely; only; solely: *purely accidental.* **3.** entirely; completely. **4.** innocently, virtuously, or chastely. [ME *purliche.* See PURE, -LY]

pure′ rea′son, *Kantianism.* reason based on a priori principles and providing a unifying ground for the perception of the phenomenal world.

pur·fle (pûr′fəl), *v.,* **-fled, -fling,** *n.* —*v.t.* **1.** to finish with an ornamental border. **2.** to decorate (a shrine or tabernacle) with architectural forms in miniature. —*n.* **3.** Also called **pur′fling.** an ornamental border, esp. the inlaid border near the outer edge of the table and back of a stringed instrument. [ME *purfile(n)* < MF *porfile(r)* (to) make or adorn a border, equiv. to *por-* PRO-[1] + *filer* to spin, deriv. of *fil* thread < L *fīl(um).* See PROFILE] —**pur′fler,** *n.*

pur·ga (po͝or′gə), *n.* a violent, snow-bearing storm blowing in the north Siberian tundra during the winter. Also, **poorga.** [< Russ]

pur·ga·tion (pûr gā′shən), *n.* act of purging. [ME *purgacioun* < L *pūrgātiōn-* (s. of *pūrgātiō*) a cleansing, purging, equiv. to *pūrgāt(us)* (ptp. of *pūrgāre* to make clean or pure) + *-iōn-* -ION]

pur·ga·tive (pûr′gə tiv), *adj.* **1.** purging or cleansing, esp. by causing evacuation of the bowels. —*n.* **2.** a purgative medicine or agent; cathartic. [< LL *pūrgātīv(us)* (see PURGATION, -IVE); r. late ME *purgatyf* < MF] —**pur′ga·tive·ly,** *adv.*

pur·ga·to·ri·al (pûr′gə tôr′ē əl, -tōr′-), *adj.* **1.** removing or purging sin; expiatory: *The priestess performed the purgatorial rites in seclusion.* **2.** of, pertaining to, or like purgatory. [PURGATORY + -AL[1]]

pur·ga·to·ry (pûr′gə tôr′ē, -tōr′ē), *n., pl.* **-ries,** *adj.* —*n.* **1.** (in the belief of Roman Catholics and others) a condition or place in which the souls of those dying penitent are purified from venial sins, or undergo the temporal punishment which, after the guilt of mortal sin has been remitted, still remains to be endured by the sinner. **2.** (*cap., italics*) the second part of Dante's *Divine Comedy,* in which the repentant sinners are depicted. Italian, **Purgatorio.** Cf. **inferno** (def. 3), **paradise** (def. 7). **3.** any condition or place of temporary punishment, suffering, expiation, or the like. —*adj.* **4.** serving to cleanse, purify, or expiate. [ME *purgatorie* < ML *purgātōri(um),* n. use of neut. of LL *pūrgātōrius* purging, equiv. to *pūrgā(us)* (ptp. of *pūrgāre* to PURGE) + *-ōrius* -ORY[1]]

purge (pûrj), *v.,* **purged, purg·ing,** *n.* —*v.t.* **1.** to rid of whatever is impure or undesirable; cleanse; purify. **2.** to rid, clear, or free (usually fol. by *of* or *from*): *to purge a political party of disloyal members.* **3.** to clear of imputed guilt or ritual uncleanliness. **4.** to clear away or wipe out legally (an offense, accusation, etc.) by atonement or other suitable action. **5.** to remove by cleansing or purifying (often fol. by *away, off,* or *out*). **6.** to clear or empty (the bowels) by causing evacuation. **7.** to cause evacuation of the bowels of (a person). **8.** to put to death or otherwise eliminate (a member of a political organization, nation, etc.) in the course of a purge. **9.** *Metall.* **a.** to drive off (undesirable gases) from a furnace or stove. **b.** to free (a furnace or stove) of undesirable gases. —*v.i.* **10.** to become cleansed or purified. **11.** to undergo or cause purging of the bowels. —*n.* **12.** act or process of purging. **13.** the removal or elimination of members of a political organization, nation, etc., who are considered disloyal or otherwise undesirable. **14.** something that purges, as a purgative medicine or dose. [ME < OF *purg(i)er* < L *purgāre* to cleanse] —**purge′a·ble,** *adj.* —**purg′er,** *n.*

purg′ing nut′. See **physic nut.**

Pu·ri (po͝or′ē, po͞o rē′), *n.* a seaport in E India, on the Bay of Bengal: temple of Krishna; Hindu pilgrimage center. 49,057 (1951). Cf. **Juggernaut** (def. 2).

pu·ri·fi·ca·tor (pyo͝or′ə fə kā′tər), *n.* *Eccles.* **1.** the linen cloth used by the celebrant for wiping the chalice after each communicant has drunk from it. **2.** a sponge wrapped in cloth used by the celebrant for wiping his hands. [< L *purificāt(us),* ptp. of *purificāre* (see PURIFY) + -OR²]

pu·ri·form (pyo͝or′ə fôrm′), *adj.* *Med.* resembling pus; purulent. [< L *pūr-* (s. of *pūs*) PUS + -I- + -FORM]

pu·ri·fy (pyo͝or′ə fī′), *v.,* **-fied, -fy·ing.** —*v.t.* **1.** to make pure; free from anything that debases, pollutes, adulterates, or contaminates: *to purify metals.* **2.** to free from foreign or objectionable elements: *to purify a language.* **3.** to free from guilt or evil. **4.** to clear or purge (usually fol. by *of* or *from*). **5.** to make clean for ceremonial or ritual use. —*v.i.* **6.** to become pure. [ME *purifie(n)* < MF *purifie(r)* < L *pūrificāre.* See PURE, -IFY] —**pu′ri·fi·ca′tion,** *n.* —**pu·rif·i·ca·to·ry** (pyo͝o rif′ə kə tôr′ē, -tōr′ē), *adj.* —**pu′ri·fi′er,** *n.*

Pu·rim (po͝or′im; *Heb.* po͞o rēm′), *n.* a Jewish festival, marked chiefly by the reading in the synagogue of the Book of Esther and the eating of hamantaschen, that is celebrated on the 14th day of the month of Adar and that commemorates the deliverance of the Jews in Persia from destruction by Haman. Also called **Feast of Lots.** [< Heb, pl. of *pūr* lot]

pu·rine (pyo͝or′ēn, -in), *n.* *Chem.* a white, crystalline compound, $C_5H_4N_4$, from which is derived a group of compounds including uric acid, xanthine, and caffeine. [alter. of G *Purin.* See PURE, URIC, -INE²]

pur·ism (pyo͝or′iz əm), *n.* **1.** strict observance of or insistence on purity in language, style, etc. **2.** an instance of this. **3.** (*often cap.*) *Fine Arts.* a style of art developed in France in the early 20th century, characterized by the use of simple geometric forms and images evocative of objects produced by machine. [PURE + -ISM] —**pur′ist,** *n.* —**pu·ris′tic, pu·ris′ti·cal,** *adj.* —**pu·ris′ti·cal·ly,** *adv.*

Pu·ri·tan (pyo͝or′i tᵊn), *n.* **1.** one of a class of Protestants that arose in the 16th century within the Church of England, demanding reforms in doctrine and worship, and greater strictness in religious discipline. During part of the 17th century the Puritans became a powerful political party. **2.** (*l.c.*) a person who is strict in moral or religious matters, often excessively so. —*adj.* **3.** of or pertaining to the Puritans. **4.** (*l.c.*) of, pertaining to, or characteristic of a moral puritan; puritanical. [< LL *pūrit(ās)* purity + -AN] —**pu′ri·tan·like′,** *adj.* —**pu′ri·tan·ly,** *adv.*

pu·ri·tan·i·cal (pyo͝or′i tan′i kəl), *adj.* **1.** very strict in moral or religious matters, often excessively so; rigidly austere. **2.** (*sometimes cap.*) of, pertaining to, or characteristic of Puritans or Puritanism. Also, **pu′ri·tan′ic.** [PURITAN + -ICAL] —**pu′ri·tan′i·cal·ly,** *adv.* —**pu′ri·tan′i·cal·ness,** *n.*

Pu·ri·tan·ism (pyo͝or′i tᵊniz′əm), *n.* **1.** the principles and practices of the Puritans. **2.** (*sometimes l.c.*) extreme strictness in moral or religious matters, often to excess; rigid austerity. [PURITAN + -ISM]

Pu′ritan spoon′, a silver spoon having an ovoid bowl and a straight, flat, completely plain stem.

pu·ri·ty (pyo͝or′i tē), *n.* **1.** the condition or quality of being pure; freedom from anything that debases, contaminates, pollutes, etc.: *the purity of drinking water.* **2.** freedom from any admixture or modifying addition. **3.** freedom from foreign or inappropriate elements; careful correctness: *purity of language.* **4.** *Optics.* the chroma, saturation, or degree of freedom from white of a given color. **5.** cleanness or spotlessness, as of garments. **6.** ceremonial or ritual cleanness. **7.** freedom from guilt or evil; innocence. **8.** physical chastity; virginity. [< LL *pūritās* (see PURE, -ITY); r. ME *pur(e)te* < AF]

Pur·kin′je fi′ber (pər kin′jē), any of the specialized cardiac muscle fibers forming a network in the ventricular walls that conduct electric impulses responsible for the contractions of the heart to all parts of the ventricular muscles. [named after J. E. *Purkinje* (1787–1869), Czech physiologist]

purl¹ (pûrl), *v.t., v.i.* **1.** to knit with inversion of the stitch. **2.** to finish with loops or a looped edging. —*n.* **3.** a stitch used in hand knitting to make a rib effect. **4.** one of a series of small loops along the edge of lace braid. **5.** thread made of twisted gold or silver wire. Also, **pearl.** [var. of obs. or dial. *pirl* to twist (threads, etc.) into a cord]

purl² (pûrl), *v.i.* **1.** to flow with curling or rippling motion, as a shallow stream does over stones. **2.** to flow with a murmuring sound. **3.** to pass in a manner or with a sound likened to this. —*n.* **4.** the action or sound of purling. **5.** a circle or curl made by the motion of water; ripple; eddy. [akin to Norw *purla* to bubble up, gush]

pur·lieu (pûr′lo͞o, pûrl′yo͞o), *n.* **1.** a piece of land on the border of a forest. **2.** an outlying district or region, as of a town or city. **3.** *Brit.* a piece of land which, after having been included in a royal forest, was restored to private ownership, though still subject, in some respects, to the operation of the forest laws. **4. purlieus,** environs or neighborhood. **5.** a place where one may range at large; one's bounds. **6.** one's haunt or resort. [alter. (simulating F *lieu* place) of earlier *parlewe, parley, paraley* purlieu of a forest < AF *purale(e)* a going through, equiv. to *pur* (< L *prō* for; confused with *per* through) + *aller* (see ALLEY)]

pur·lin (pûr′lin), *n.* a longitudinal member in a roof frame, usually for supporting common rafters or the like between the plate and the ridge. Also, **pur′line.** See diag. under **king post.** [?]

pur′lin plate′, *Carpentry.* (in a curb roof) a purlin at the top of a lower slope supporting the ends of the upper rafters at the curb. Also called **curb.**

pur·loin (pər loin′, pûr′loin), *v.t.* **1.** to take dishonestly; steal; filch. —*v.i.* **2.** to commit theft; steal. [late ME *purloyne(n)* < AF *purloigne(r)* (to) put off, remove, equiv. to *pur-* (< L *prō* for) + *loin* far off (< L *longē*)] —**pur·loin′er,** *n.*
—**Syn. 1.** pilfer.

Pur′loined Let′ter, The, a detective story (1845) by Edgar Allan Poe.

pur·part (pûr′pärt), *n.* *Law.* a purparty. [< ML *purpart-* (s. of *purpars*) < OF *pur* for + L *part-* PART]

pur·par·ty (pûr′pär′tē), *n.* *Law.* a share of an estate held by coparceners that is apportioned to one upon the division of the estate among them. Also, **pourparty.** [ME *purpartie* < AF, c. OF *purpartie,* equiv. to *pur, pour* for + *partie* partition, share; see PARTY]

pur·ple (pûr′pəl), *n., adj., v.,* **-pled, -pling.** —*n.* **1.** any color having components of both red and blue, such as lavender, esp. one deep in tone. **2.** cloth or clothing of this hue, esp. as formerly worn distinctively by persons of imperial, royal, or other high rank. **3.** the rank or office of a cardinal. **4.** the office of a bishop. **5.** imperial, regal, or princely rank or position. **6.** deep red; crimson. **7.** any of several nymphalid butterflies, as *Basilarchia astyanax* **(red-spotted purple),** having blackish wings spotted with red, or *Basilarchia arthemis* **(banded purple** or **white admiral),** having brown wings banded with white. **8. born in** or **to the purple,** of royal or exalted birth: *Those born to the purple are destined to live in the public eye.* —*adj.* **9.** of the color purple. **10.** imperial, regal, or princely. **11.** brilliant or gorgeous. **12.** full of exaggerated literary devices and effects; marked by excessively ornate rhetoric: *purple prose.* —*v.t., v.i.* **13.** to make or become purple. [ME *purpel,* OE *purpl(e),* var. of *purpur(e)* < L *purpura* < Gk *porphýra* kind of shellfish yielding purple dye]

pur′ple bone′set. See **joe-pye weed** (def. 1).

pur′ple ces′trum. See **coral jasmine.**

pur′ple choke′berry. See under **chokeberry** (def. 1).

pur′ple dai′sy, a perennial herb, *Echinacea angustifolia,* of central and western North America, having rose-purple or rose-colored, cone-shaped flowers.

pur′ple finch′, a North American finch, *Carpodacus purpureus,* having a raspberry red head, breast, and rump. See illus. under **finch.**

pur′ple fox′glove, a medicinal herb, *Digitalis purpurea,* of western Europe, having finger-shaped, spotted, purple flowers and leaves from which digitalis is obtained. Also called **fairy glove, fingerflower.**

pur′ple-fringed or′chid (pûr′pəl frinjd′), either of two orchids of genus *Habenaria* (*Blephariglottis*), of eastern North America, the smaller, *H. psychodes,* having dark-purple, cut, fringed flowers, and the larger, *H. fimbriata,* having similar but lighter-colored flowers.

pur′ple gal′linule, **1.** a purple, blue, green, and white gallinule, *Porphyrula martinica,* having a bright red, yellow, and blue bill, and lemon-yellow legs and feet, and inhabiting warmer parts of the New World. **2.** any of several large, Old World gallinules of the genus *Porphyrio.*

pur′ple grack′le, a North American grackle, *Quiscalus quiscula,* having iridescent, purplish-black plumage.

pur′ple granadil′la. See under **granadilla** (def. 1).

Pur′ple Heart′, *U.S. Armed Forces.* a medal awarded for wounds received in action against an enemy or as a direct result of an act of the enemy.

pur·ple·heart (pûr′pəl härt′), *n.* the hard, purplish wood of any of several leguminous South American trees of the genus *Peltogyne,* used for making furniture. [PURPLE + HEART]

pur′ple her′on, an Old World heron, *Ardea purpurea,* having maroon, buff, and black plumage.

pur′ple loose′strife. See under **loosestrife** (def. 2).

pur′ple mar′tin, a large, American swallow, *Progne subis,* the male of which is blue-black.

pur′ple med′ic, alfalfa.

pur′ple mom·bin′ (mōm bēn′), a tree, *Spondias purpurea,* of tropical America, having greenish flowers and yellowish-red or red fruit that is edible either raw or cooked. Also called **red mombin, Spanish plum.** [*mombin* < AmerSp < Carib]

pur′ple mul′lein, a biennial herb, *Verbascum phoeniceum,* of southeastern Europe and Asia, having hairy leaves and reddish-purple flowers with purplish, wooly hairs.

pur·ple·ness (pûr′pəl nis), *n.* quality or state of being purple. [PURPLE + -NESS]

pur′ple of Cas′sius (kash′əs, kash′ē əs, kä′sē-əs), a purple pigment precipitated as a sol by the interaction of gold chloride and a solution of stannic acid and stannous chloride: used chiefly in the manufacture of ruby glass, ceramic glazes, and enamels. [named after A. *Cassius,* 17th-century German physician]

pur′ple rag′wort, a tender annual herb, *Senecio elegans,* of South Africa, having red or purple flowers with yellow disks.

pur′ple rock′ cress′, a perennial herb, *Ausbrieta deltoidea,* of Italy and Greece, having purple or violet flowers.

pur′ple sage′, **1.** an herb, *Salvia leucophylla,* of California, having silvery leaves and purple flowers. **2.** a sagebrush, *Artemisia tridentata,* having silvery leaves.

pur′ple sand′piper, a North American sandpiper, *Erolia maritima,* having a slate-gray back and breast and a white abdomen.

pur′ple shore′ crab′. See under **shore crab.**

pur′ple tril′lium, birthroot (def. 1).

pur′ple wil′low herb′, the purple loosestrife. See under **loosestrife** (def. 2).

pur′ple wood′ sor′rel. See **violet wood sorrel.**

pur′ple wreath′, a tropical American, woody vine, *Petrea volubilis,* having racemes of violet or blue flowers.

pur·plish (pûr′plish), *adj.* of or having a somewhat purple hue. Also, **pur′ply.** [PURPLE + -ISH¹] —**pur′plish·ness,** *n.*

pur·port (*v.* pər pōrt′, -pôrt′, pûr′pōrt, -pôrt; *n.* pûr′pōrt, -pôrt), *v.t.* **1.** to profess or claim, often falsely: *a document purporting to be official.* **2.** to convey to the mind as the meaning or thing intended; express or imply. —*n.* **3.** the meaning, import, or sense: *the main purport of his letter.* **4.** purpose; intention; object: *the main purport of his visit to France.* [late ME < AF *purport(er)* (to) convey, equiv. to *pur-* PRO-¹ + *porter* to carry (< L *portāre*)] —**pur′port·less,** *adj.*
—**Syn. 2.** mean, intend, signify. **3.** implication, drift, trend, gist. See **meaning.**

pur·pose (pûr′pəs), *n., v.,* **-posed, -pos·ing.** —*n.* **1.** the reason for which something exists or is done, made, used, etc. **2.** an intended or desired result; end; aim; goal. **3.** determination; resoluteness. **4.** the subject in hand; the point at issue. **5.** practical result, effect, or advantage: *to act to good purpose.* **6. of set purpose,** with intention; deliberately: *The insult was made of set purpose.* **7. on purpose,** by design; intentionally: *How could he do such a thing on purpose?* **8. to the purpose,** relevant; to the point: *None of her objections were to the purpose.* —*v.t.* **9.** to set as an aim, intention, or goal for oneself; purpose. **10.** to intend; design. **11.** to resolve (to do something): *He purposed to change his way of life radically.* —*v.i.* **12.** to have a purpose. [ME *purpos* < OF, deriv. of *purposer,* var. of *proposer* to PROPOSE] —**pur′pose·less,** *adj.* —**pur′pose·less·ly,** *adv.* —**pur′pose·less·ness,** *n.*
—**Syn. 1.** See **intention. 10.** mean, contemplate, plan.

pur·pose·ful (pûr′pəs fəl), *adj.* **1.** having a purpose. **2.** determined; resolute. **3.** full of meaning; significant. [PURPOSE + -FUL] —**pur′pose·ful·ly,** *adv.* —**pur′pose·ful·ness,** *n.*

pur·pose·ly (pûr′pəs lē), *adv.* **1.** intentionally; deliberately: *He tripped me purposely.* **2.** with the particular purpose specified; expressly: *He wore that suit purposely to make a nice impression.* [PURPOSE + -LY]

pur·pos·ive (pûr′pə siv), *adj.* **1.** having, showing, or acting with a purpose, intention, or design. **2.** adapted to a purpose or end. **3.** serving some purpose. **4.** determined; resolute. **5.** of or characteristic of purpose. [PURPOSE + -IVE] —**pur′pos·ive·ly,** *adv.* —**pur′pos·ive·ness,** *n.*

pur·pres·ture (pər pres′chər), *n.* *Law.* the wrongful enclosure of or intrusion upon lands, waters, or other property rightfully belonging to the public at large. [ME < OF *pourpres(t)ure, porpresure* enclosure, occupied space, equiv. to *pourprise, porprise* (ptp. of *purprendre* to seize upon, encroach upon, enclose, equiv. to *pur, por,* for + *prendre* to take) + *-ure* -URE]

pur·pu·ra (pûr′pyo͝o rə), *n.* *Pathol.* a disease characterized by purple or livid spots on the skin or mucous membrane, caused by the extravasation of blood. [< NL, special use of L *purpura.* See PURPLE] —**pur·pu·ric** (pûr pyo͝or′ik), *adj.*

pur·pure (pûr′pyo͝or), *Heraldry.* —*n.* **1.** the tincture or color purple. —*adj.* **2.** of the tincture or color purple. [ME, OE < L *purpura* PURPLE]

pur·pu·rin (pûr′pyə rin), *n.* *Chem.* a reddish, crystalline, anthraquinone dye, $C_{14}H_5O_2(OH)_3$, isomeric with flavopurpurin. [< L *purpur(a)* PURPLE + -IN²]

purr (pûr), *v.i.* **1.** to utter a low, continuous, murmuring sound expressive of satisfaction, as a cat does. **2.** (of things) to make a sound suggestive of the purring of a cat: *The new motor of the car purred.* —*v.t.* **3.** to express by or as if by purring. —*n.* **4.** act of purring. **5.** sound of purring. Also, **pur.** [imit.] —**purr′ing·ly,** *adv.*

pur·ree (po͝or′ē, pûr′ē), *n.* **1.** See **Indian yellow** (defs. 1, 2a). —*adj.* **2.** having the color Indian yellow. [< Hindi *piūrī*]

pur sang (pyr säɴ′), *adj.* *French.* being beyond question the thing specified; full-blooded; genuine: *He had become a dictator* pur sang. [lit., pure blood]

purse (pûrs), *n., v.,* **pursed, purs·ing.** —*n.* **1.** a small bag, pouch, or case for carrying money. **2.** a woman's handbag or pocketbook. **3.** anything resembling a purse in appearance, use, etc. **4.** a sum of money collected as a present or the like. **5.** a sum of money offered as a prize or reward. **6.** money, resources, or wealth. —*v.t.* **7.** to contract into folds or wrinkles; pucker: *to purse one's lips.* **8.** *Archaic.* to put into a purse. [ME, OE *purs,* b. *pusa* bag (c. Icel *posi*) and ML *bursa* bag (<< Gk *býrsa* hide, leather)] —**purse′less,** *adj.* —**purse′like′,** *adj.*

purse′ boat′, an open boat used to close a purse seine around a school of fish.

purse′ crab′. See **coconut crab.**

purse-proud (pûrs′proud′), *adj.* proud of one's wealth, esp. in an arrogant or showy manner.

purs·er (pûr′sər), *n.* an officer, esp. on a merchant vessel, who handles accounts and various documents relating to the vessel and who keeps money and valuables for passengers. [late ME; see PURSE, -ER¹]

purse′ seine′, a large seine for use generally by two boats, that is drawn around a school of fish and then closed at the bottom by means of a line passing through rings attached along the lower edge of the net.

purse′ sein′er, a boat used in fishing with a purse seine.

purse-string (pûrs′string′), *adj.* **1.** resembling purse strings in appearance, use, operation, or the like: *a purse-string belt about the waist.* **2.** having or exercising financial control: *He had purse-string authority as chairman.*

purse′ strings′, **1.** the right to manage the disposition of money: *His father's will left him in control of the family purse strings.* **2. hold the purse strings,** to have the power to determine how money shall be spent: *Mother held the purse strings in our family.* **3. loosen** or **tighten the purse strings,** to increase or decrease expenditures: *The budget committee is in the process of tightening the purse strings.* [ME *purse strynges*]

purse′-string su′ture, *Surg.* a suture for a circular opening, stitched around the edge, that closes it when pulled.

purs·lane (pûrs′lān, -lin), *n.* **1.** a low, trailing herb, *Portulaca oleracea,* having yellow flowers, used as a salad plant and potherb. **2.** any other portulacaceous plant. [ME *purcelan(e)* < MF *porcelaine* < LL *porcillāgin-* (s. of *porcillāgō*) for L *porcilāca,* var. of *portulāca*]

pur·su·ance (pər so͞o′əns), *n.* the following or carrying out of some plan, course, injunction, or the like. [PURSUE + -ANCE]

pur·su·ant (pər so͞o′ənt), *adj.* **1.** proceeding after (usually fol. by *to*): *Pursuant to his studies he took a job in* an office. **2.** pursuing. —*adv.* Also, **pur·su′ant·ly.** **3.** according (usually fol. by *to*): *to do something pursuant to an agreement.* **4.** in a manner conformable (usually fol. by *to*): *to act pursuant to the dictates of one's conscience.* [PURSUE + -ANT; r. ME *poursuivant* < MF]

pur·sue (pər sōō′), *v.*, **-sued, -su·ing.** —*v.t.* **1.** to follow in order to overtake, capture, kill, etc.; chase. **2.** to follow close upon; go with; attend: *Bad luck pursued him.* **3.** to strive to gain; seek to attain or accomplish (an end, object, purpose, etc.). **4.** to proceed in accordance with (a method, plan, etc.). **5.** to carry on or continue (a course of action, a train of thought, an inquiry, studies, etc.). **6.** to continue to annoy, afflict, or trouble. **7.** to practice (an occupation, pastime, etc.). **8.** to continue to discuss (a subject, topic, etc.). **9.** to follow: *He pursued the river to its source. He felt their eyes pursuing him.* **10.** to continue; go on with (one's course, a journey, etc.). —*v.i.* **11.** to follow in pursuit. **12.** to continue. [ME *pursue(n)* < AF *pursue(r)* << L *prōsequī* to pursue, follow, continue. See PRO-[1], SUE, PROSECUTE] —**pur·su′a·ble,** *adj.*
—**Syn. 1.** trail, hunt. **2.** dog.

pur·su·er (pər sōō′ər), *n.* **1.** one who or that which pursues. **2.** *Scots Law, Eccles. Law.* a plaintiff or complainant. [ME; see PURSUE, -ER[1]]

pur·suit (pər sōōt′), *n.* **1.** act of pursuing: *in pursuit of the fox.* **2.** the effort to secure; quest: *the pursuit of happiness.* **3.** any occupation, pastime, or the like, in which one is engaged regularly or customarily: *literary pursuits.* [ME < AF *purseute* << LL **prōsequita* for L *prōsecūta*, fem. of *prōsecūtus*, ptp. of *prōsequī* to PURSUE]
—**Syn. 1.** chase, hunt. **2.** search. **3.** activity, preoccupation, inclination.

pursuit′ plane′, *Mil.* (formerly) an armed airplane designed for speed and maneuverability in fighting enemy aircraft.

pur·sui·vant (pûr′swi vənt), *n.* **1.** a heraldic officer of the lowest class, ranking below a herald. **2.** an official attendant on heralds. **3.** any attendant or follower. [< F *poursuivant* (prp. of *poursuivre* to pursue, follow << L *prōsequī*); r. ME *pursevant* < MF *pursivant*]

pur·sy (pûr′sē), *adj.*, **-si·er, -si·est.** **1.** short-winded, esp. from corpulence or fatness. **2.** corpulent or fat. [late ME *purcy*, var. of ME *pursif* < AF *porsif*, var. of OF *polsif*, deriv. (see -IVE) of *polser* to pant, heave. See PUSH] —**pur′si·ly,** *adv.* —**pur′si·ness,** *n.*

pur·te·nance (pûr′tᵊnəns), *n.* *Archaic.* the heart, liver, and lungs of an animal. [ME; aph. var. of APPURTENANCE]

pu·ru·lence (pyŏŏr′ə ləns, pyŏŏr′yə-), *n.* **1.** the condition of containing or forming pus. **2.** pus. Also, **pu′ru·len·cy.** [< LL *purulentia.* See PURULENT, -ENCE]

pu·ru·lent (pyŏŏr′ə lənt, pyŏŏr′yə-), *adj.* **1.** full of, containing, forming, or discharging pus; suppurating: *a purulent sore.* **2.** attended with suppuration: *purulent appendicitis.* **3.** of the nature of or like pus: *purulent matter.* [< L *pūrulent(us)*, equiv. to *pūr-* (comb. form of *pūs*) PUS + *-ulentus* -ULENT] —**pu′ru·lent·ly,** *adv.*

pu·ru·loid (pyŏŏr′ə loid′, pyŏŏr′yə-), *adj. Med.* resembling pus. [PURUL(ENT) + -OID]

Pu·rús (*Sp.* pōō rōōs′; *Port.* pōō rōōs′), *n.* a river in NW central South America, flowing NE from E Peru through W Brazil to the Amazon. 2000 mi. long.

pu·ru·sha (pŏŏr′ə shə), *n.* *Hinduism.* (in Sankhya and Yoga) one's true self, regarded as eternal and unaffected by external happenings. Cf. **prakriti.** [< Skt: lit., man]

pur·vey (pər vā′), *v.t.* to provide, furnish, or supply (esp. food or provisions). [ME *purveie(n)* < AF *purveie(r)* < L *prōvidēre* to foresee, provide for. See PROVIDE]

pur·vey·ance (pər vā′əns), *n.* **1.** act of purveying. **2.** that which is purveyed, as provisions. **3.** *Eng. Law.* a prerogative of the crown, abolished in 1660, allowing provisions, supplies, or services for the sovereign or the royal household to be purchased or acquired at an appraised value. [PURVEY + -ANCE; r. ME *purvea(u)nce, purvya(u)nce*, etc. < OF *purveance* < L *providentia.* See PROVIDENCE]

pur·vey·or (pər vā′ər), *n.* **1.** a person who purveys, provides, or supplies. **2.** *Old Eng. Law.* an officer who provided or acquired provisions for the sovereign under the prerogative of purveyance. [PURVEY + -OR[2]; r. ME *pourveour* < AF]

pur·view (pûr′vyōō), *n.* **1.** the range of operation, authority, control, concern, etc. **2.** the range of vision, insight, or understanding. **3.** *Law.* **a.** that which is provided or enacted in a statute, as distinguished from the preamble. **b.** the purpose or scope of a statute. **4.** the full scope or compass of any document, statement, subject, book, etc. [ME *purveu* < AF < VL **prōvidutus* for L *prōvīsus*, ptp. of *prōvidēre* to PROVIDE]

pus (pus), *n.* a yellow-white, more or less viscid substance produced by suppuration and found in abscesses, sores, etc., consisting of a liquid plasma in which leukocytes are suspended. [< L; akin to Gk *pýon* pus. See PYO-] —**pus′like′,** *adj.*

Pu·san (pōō′sän′), *n.* a seaport in SE South Korea. 1,419,808 (est. 1965). Formerly, **Fusan.**

Pu·sey (pyōō′zē), *n.* **1. Edward Bou·ve·rie** (bōō′və-rē), 1800–82, English clergyman. **2. Nathan Marsh,** born 1907, U.S. educator: president of Harvard University since 1953.

Pu·sey·ism (pyōō′zē iz′əm), *n.* Tractarianism. [E. B. PUSEY + -ISM] —**Pu′sey·is′ti·cal, Pu′sey·is′tic,** *adj.* —**Pu·sey·ite** (pyōō′zē īt′), *n.*

push (pŏŏsh), *v.t.* **1.** to press upon or against (a thing) with force in order to move it away. **2.** to move (something) in a specified way by exerting force; shove; drive: *to push something aside; to push something off the table; to push the door open.* **3.** to make by thrusting obstacles aside: *to push one's way through the crowd.* **4.** to press or urge to some action or course: *His mother pushed him to do his homework.* **5.** to press (an action, proposal, etc.) with energy and insistence: *to push a bill through Congress.* **6.** to carry (an action or thing) toward a conclusion or extreme: *He pushed his project to completion.* **7.** to depend excessively upon; use beyond capacity: *to push one's luck.* **8.** to press the adoption, use, sale, etc., of: *The salesman tried to push inferior merchandise on his customers.* **9.** to press or bear hard upon, as in dealings with someone: *The prosecutor pushed him for an answer.* **10.** to put into difficulties because of the lack of (usually fol. by *for*): *to be pushed for time.* **11.** *Slang.* to peddle (narcotics). —*v.i.* **12.** to exert a thrusting force upon something. **13.** to use steady force in moving a thing away; shove. **14.** to make one's way with effort or persistence, as against difficulty or opposition. **15.** to put forth vigorous or persistent efforts. **16.** to move on being pushed: *a swinging door that pushes easily.* **17. push off,** *Informal.* to go away; depart: *We stopped at Denver for the night and were ready to push off again the following morning.* **18. push on,** to press forward; continue; proceed: *The pioneers, despite overwhelming obstacles, pushed on across the plains.* —*n.* **19.** act of pushing; a shove or thrust. **20.** a contrivance or part to be pushed in order to operate a mechanism. **21.** a vigorous onset or effort. **22.** a determined advance against opposition, obstacles, etc. **23.** a vigorous and determined military attack or campaign: *The big push began in April.* **24.** the pressure of circumstances, activities, etc. **25.** *Informal.* persevering energy; enterprise. **26.** *Informal.* a crowd, company, or set of persons. **27.** *Brit. Slang.* dismissal from a job; sack. **28.** *Australian Slang.* a gang of hoodlums. [ME *posshe(n)* < MF *pousse(r)*, OF *po(u)lser* < L *pulsāre.* See PULSATE]
—**Syn. 3.** shoulder. **4.** persuade, impel.

push·ball (pŏŏsh′bôl′), *n.* **1.** a game played with a large, heavy ball, usually about six feet in diameter, which two sides attempt to push to opposite goals. **2.** the ball used in this game. [PUSH + BALL[1]]

push-bike (pŏŏsh′bīk′), *n.* *Brit.* a standard bicycle, operated by pedals rather than a motor. Also, **push′ bi′cycle, push cycle.**

push′ broom′, a wide broom with a long handle, pushed by hand and used for sweeping large areas.

push′ but′ton, **1.** a device designed to close or open an electric circuit when a button or knob is depressed, and to return to a normal position when it is released. **2.** the button or knob depressed.

push-but·ton (pŏŏsh′but′ᵊn), *adj.* **1.** operated by or as by push buttons: *push-button tuning.* **2.** using complex, automated weapons, as long-range missiles, that require only simple initial steps to put them into action: *push-button warfare.*

push·card (pŏŏsh′kärd′), *n.* punchboard. [PUSH + CARD[1]]

push·cart (pŏŏsh′kärt′), *n.* a light cart to be pushed by hand, used esp. by street venders. [PUSH + CART]

push′ cy′cle, *Brit.* push-bike.

push-down (pŏŏsh′doun′), *n.* *Aeron.* a sudden, downward shift by an aircraft in the direction of the flight path. Also called **pushover.** [n. use of v. phrase *push down*]

push·er (pŏŏsh′ər), *n.* **1.** one who or that which pushes. **2.** *Aeron.* an airplane that has its propellers behind the wings, the propellers pushing rather than pulling the airplane. **3.** *Naut.* one of the masts abaft the mizzen on a sailing vessel having more than three masts, either the sixth or seventh from forward. Cf. **driver** (def. 8b), **spanker** (def. 1b). **4.** *Slang.* a peddler of narcotics. —*adj.* **5.** *Naut.* **a.** of or pertaining to a pusher. **b.** noting or pertaining to a sail, yard, boom, etc., or to any rigging belonging to a lower or upper mast of a pusher. **c.** noting any stay running aft and upward to the head of a lower mast or some specified upper mast of a pusher: *pusher topmast stay.* [PUSH + -ER[1]]

push′er propel′ler, a propeller located on the trailing edge of an aircraft wing.

push·ing (pŏŏsh′ing), *adj.* **1.** that pushes. **2.** enterprising; energetic. **3.** tactlessly or officiously aggressive; forward; intrusive. [PUSH + -ING[2]] —**push′ing·ly,** *adv.* —**push′ing·ness,** *n.*
—**Syn. 2.** ambitious. **3.** offensive.

Push·kin (pŏŏsh′kin), *n.* **A·le·xan·der Ser·ge·e·vich** (ä′le ksän′dər ser ge′yə vich), 1799–1837, Russian poet, short-story writer, and dramatist.

push·o·ver (pŏŏsh′ō′vər), *n.* **1.** *Slang.* anything done easily. **2.** *Slang.* an easily defeated person or team. **3.** *Rocketry.* a displacement in a horizontal direction of the trajectory of a missile or rocket. **4.** *Aeron.* push-down. [n. use of v. phrase *push over*]

push·pin (pŏŏsh′pin′), *n.* **1.** an early children's game. **2.** child's play; triviality. [PUSH + PIN]

push-pull (pŏŏsh′pŏŏl′), *n.* **1.** *Radio.* a two-tube symmetrical arrangement in which the grid excitation voltages are opposite in phase. —*adj.* **2.** of or pertaining to electronic devices having components with balanced signals opposite in phase.

push′ shot′, **1.** *Basketball.* a shot with one hand from a point relatively distant from the basket, in which a player shoots the ball from shoulder level or above. **2.** *Golf.* a shot, played with an iron, in which a player with his weight forward on his front foot and with his wrists firm strikes the ball a sharp, descending blow in hitting a low ball with backspin.

Push·tu (push′tōō), *n.* Pashto. Also, **Push·to** (push′tō).

push-up (pŏŏsh′up′), *n.* an exercise in which a person, keeping a prone position with the hands palms down under the shoulders, the balls of the feet on the ground, and the back straight, pushes himself up and lets himself down by an alternate straightening and bending of the arms. [n. use of v. phrase *push up*]

push·y (pŏŏsh′ē), *adj.*, **push·i·er, push·i·est.** *Informal.* obnoxiously self-assertive. [PUSH + -Y[1]] —**push′i·ness,** *n.*

pu·sil·la·nim·i·ty (pyōō′sə lə nim′i tē), *n.* state or condition of being pusillanimous; timidity; cowardliness. [late ME < eccl. L *pusillanimitās.* See PUSILLANIMOUS, -ITY]

pu·sil·lan·i·mous (pyōō′sə lan′ə məs), *adj.* **1.** lacking courage or resolution; cowardly; faint-hearted; timid. **2.** proceeding from or indicating a cowardly spirit. [< LL *pusillanim(is)* petty-spirited, equiv. to L *pusill(us)* very small, petty + *-anim(is)* -spirited, -minded (*anim(us)* spirit + *-is* adj. suffix) + -OUS] —**pu′sil·lan′i·mous·ly,** *adv.*
—**Syn. 1.** timorous, fearful, frightened.

puss[1] (pŏŏs), *n.* **1.** a cat. **2.** a girl or woman. **3.** *Brit.* a hare. [akin to D *poes*, LG *puus-katte*, dial. Sw *kattepus*, Norw *puse(kat)*, etc.] —**puss′like′,** *adj.*

puss[2] (pŏŏs), *n.* *Slang.* **1.** face: *She smacked him in the puss.* **2.** mouth: *Shut your puss before I shut it for you.* [< Ir *pus* lip, mouth]

Puss (pŏŏs), *n.* a girl's given name. Also, **Puss·y** (pŏŏs′ē).

puss′ in the cor′ner, a parlor game for children in which one player in the middle of a room tries to occupy any of the positions along the walls that become vacant as other players dash across to exchange places at a signal. Also, **puss′y wants′ a cor′ner.**

puss·ley (pus′lē), *n.* *Informal.* purslane.

puss·y[1] (pŏŏs′ē), *n.*, *pl.* **puss·ies.** **1.** a cat, esp. a kitten. **2.** the game of tipcat. **3.** the tapering piece of wood used in tipcat. [PUSS[1] + -Y[2]]

pus·sy[2] (pus′ē), *adj.*, **-si·er, -si·est.** *Med.* puslike. [PUS + -Y[1]]

puss·y·foot (pŏŏs′ē fŏŏt′), *v.*, *n.*, *pl.* **-foots.** —*v.i.* **1.** to go or move in a stealthy or cautious manner. **2.** to act cautiously or timidly, as if afraid to commit oneself on a point at issue. —*n.* **3.** a person with a catlike, or soft and stealthy, tread. **4.** *Chiefly Brit.* a teetotaler or prohibitionist. [PUSSY[1] + FOOT]

puss′y's toe′ (pŏŏs′ēz), Usually, **puss·y's toes.** any of numerous woolly, composite herbs of the genus *Antennaria*, having heads of gray or white flowers that are sometimes used for everlastings. Also called **puss′y·toe′, ladies'-tobacco.**

puss′y wil′low (pŏŏs′ē), **1.** a small, American willow, *Salix discolor*, having silky catkins. **2.** any of various similar willows.

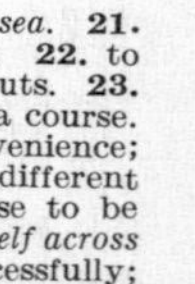

Pussy willow, *Salix discolor*

pus·tu·lant (pus′chə lənt), *adj.* **1.** causing the formation of pustules. —*n.* **2.** a medicine or agent causing pustulation. [< LL *pūstulant-* (s. of *pūstulāns*), prp. of *pūstulāre* to blister. See PUSTULE, -ANT]

pus·tu·lar (pus′chə lər), *adj.* **1.** of, pertaining to, or of the nature of pustules. **2.** characterized by pustules. [< NL *pūstulār(is).* See PUSTULE, -AR[1]]

pus·tu·late (*v.* pus′chə lāt′; *adj.* pus′chə lit, -lāt′), *v.*, **-lat·ed, -lat·ing,** *adj.* *Pathol.* —*v.t.* **1.** to cause to form pustules. **2.** to become pustular. —*adj.* **3.** covered with pustules. [< L *pūstulāt(us)*, ptp. of *pūstulāre* to blister. See PUSTULE, -ATE[1]]

pus·tu·la·tion (pus′chə lā′shən), *n.* the formation or breaking out of pustules. [< LL *pūstulātiōn-* (s. of *pūstulātiō*) a blistering. See PUSTULATE, -ION]

pus·tule (pus′chōōl), *n.* **1.** *Pathol.* a small elevation of the skin containing pus. **2.** any pimplelike or blisterlike swelling or elevation. [ME < L *pūstula* a pimple, blister, appar. var. of *pūsula*; akin to Gk *phȳsallís* bladder, *phȳsaléos* inflated] —**pus′tuled,** *adj.*

pus·tu·lous (pus′chŏŏ ləs), *adj.* pustular. [PUSTULE + -OUS]

put (pŏŏt), *v.*, **put, put·ting,** *n.* —*v.t.* **1.** to move or place (anything) so as to get it into or out of some place or position: *to put a book on the shelf.* **2.** to bring into some relation, state, etc.: *to put everything in order.* **3.** to place in the charge or power of a person, institution, etc.: *to put a child in a special school.* **4.** to subject to the endurance or suffering of something: *to put a person to trial.* **5.** to set to a duty, task, action, etc.: *I put her to setting the table.* **6.** to force or drive to some course or action: *to put an army to flight.* **7.** to render or translate, as into another language: *He put the novel into French.* **8.** to provide (words) with music as accompaniment; set: *to put a poem to music.* **9.** to assign or attribute: *He puts a political interpretation on anything social.* **10.** to set at a particular place, point, amount, etc., in a scale of estimation: *He puts the distance at five miles.* **11.** to bet or wager: *to put two dollars on a horse.* **12.** to express or state: *To put it concisely, I don't understand.* **13.** to apply, as to a use or purpose: *to put one's knowledge to practical use.* **14.** to set, give, or make: *to put an end to a practice.* **15.** to propose or submit for answer, consideration, deliberation, etc.: *to put a question before a committee.* **16.** to impose, as a burden, charge, or the like: *to put a tax on luxury articles.* **17.** to invest (often fol. by *in* or *into*): *to put one's money in real estate; to put one's savings into securities.* **18.** to lay the blame of (usually fol. by *on, to,* etc.): *He put her failure to lack of experience.* **19.** to throw or cast, esp. with a forward motion of the hand when raised close to the shoulder: *to put the shot.*
—*v.i.* **20.** to go, move, or proceed: *to put out to sea.* **21.** *Informal.* to begin to travel: *to put for home.* **22.** to shoot out or grow, or send forth shoots or sprouts. **23. put about, a.** *Naut.* to change direction, as on a course. **b.** to start (a rumor); circulate. **c.** to inconvenience; trouble. **d.** to disturb; worry. **e.** to turn in a different direction. **24. put across,** *Slang.* **a.** to cause to be understood or received favorably: *He puts himself across well. She put across her new idea.* **b.** to do successfully; accomplish: *to put a project across.* **c.** to be successful in (a form of deception): *It was obviously a lie, but he put it across.* **25. put aside, a.** to store up; save. **b.** Also, **set aside.** to put out of the way; place to one side: *Put aside your books and go for a walk.* **26. put down, a.** to write down; register; record. **b.** to suppress; check. **c.** to attribute; ascribe. **d.** *Slang.* to humble, humiliate, or embarrass (someone). **e.** to dig or sink, as a well. **f.** *Brit.* to destroy (an animal). **g.** to land an aircraft or in an aircraft: *We put down at Orly after six hours.* **27. put forth, a.** to bring out; bear; grow: *The trees are putting forth new green shoots.* **b.** to propose; present: *No one has put forth a workable solution.* **c.** to bring to public notice; publish: *A new interpretation of the doctrine has been put forth.* **d.** to exert; exercise: *We will have to put forth our best efforts to win.* **e.** to set out; depart: *Dark clouds threatened as we put forth from the shore.* **28. put forward, a.** to propose; advance: *He hesitated to put forward his plan.* **b.** to nominate, promote, or support, as for a position: *We put him forward for treasurer.* **29. put in, a.** *Naut.* to enter a port or harbor, esp. for shelter, repairs, or provisions. **b.** to interpose; intervene. **c.** to spend (time) as indicated. **d.** to apply for or request something: *The captain put in for a transfer to another post.* **30. put off, a.** to postpone; defer. **b.** to rebuff; repel. **c.** to get rid of by delay or evasion. **d.** to lay aside; take off. **e.** to start out, as on a voyage. **f.** to launch (a boat)

from shore or from another vessel: *They began to put off the lifeboats as the fire spread.* **31. put on, a.** to assume insincerely or falsely; pretend. **b.** to clothe (oneself); dress. **c.** to assume; adopt. **d.** to inflict; impose. **e.** to produce; stage. **f.** *Slang.* to act in a pretentious or ostentatious manner; exaggerate: *She is basically a nice girl, although she puts on a great deal.* **32. put oneself out,** to take pains; go to trouble or expense: *She has certainly put herself out to see that everyone is comfortable.* **33. put out, a.** to extinguish, as a fire. **b.** to confuse; embarrass. **c.** to be disturbed or annoyed: *He was put out about my promotion.* **d.** to subject to inconvenience. **e.** *Baseball, Softball, Cricket.* to cause to be removed from an opportunity to reach base or score; retire. **f.** to publish. **g.** to go out to sea. **h.** to manufacture; prepare; produce. **i.** to exert; apply: *They were putting out their best efforts.* **j.** *Slang (vulgar).* (of a woman) to indulge in coitus. **34. put over, a.** *Informal.* to succeed in; accomplish: *It will take an exceptional administrator to put over this reorganization.* **b.** to postpone; defer: *Discussion of this point will be put over until new evidence is introduced.* **35. put someone on,** *Slang.* to tease a person, esp. by pretending the truth of something that is untrue: *The astronomer told her with a perfectly straight face that the moon was inhabited, and she didn't even know he was putting her on.* **36. put something over on,** *Informal.* to take advantage of; deceive: *He suspected that his friend had put something over on him, but he had no proof.* **37. put through, a.** to complete successfully; execute: *He was not able to put through his call.* **b.** to bring about; effect: *The proposed revisions have not as yet been put through.* **38. put to it,** to be confronted with a problem; have difficulty: *We were put to it to find the missing notebook.* **39. put up, a.** to construct; erect. **b.** to can (vegetables, fruits, etc.); preserve (jam, jelly, etc.). **c.** to set or arrange (the hair). **d.** to provide (money); contribute. **e.** *Informal.* to accommodate; lodge. **f.** to display; show. **g.** *Informal.* to stake money in a wager. **h.** to propose as a candidate; nominate: *Someone is going to put him up for president.* **i.** *Archaic.* to sheathe one's sword; stop fighting. **40. put upon,** to take unfair advantage of; impose upon: *Some of the employees felt put upon when they were asked to work late.* **41. put up to,** *Informal.* to provoke; prompt; incite: *Someone put him up to calling us.* **42. put up with,** *Informal.* to endure; tolerate; bear: *I couldn't put up with the noise any longer.* **43. stay put,** *Informal.* to remain in the same position; refuse to move: *The baby wouldn't stay put, and kept trying to climb out of his playpen.*
—*n.* **44.** a throw or cast, esp. one made with a forward motion of the hand when raised close to the shoulder. **45.** *Finance.* an option that gives the right to sell a fixed amount of a particular stock at a predetermined price within a given time, purchased by a person who expects the stock may decline. Cf. **call** (def. 59). [ME *putte(n), puten* to push, thrust, put; akin to OE *putung* an impelling, inciting, *potian* to push, goad; c. Icel *pota* to thrust, poke]
—**Syn. 1.** PUT, PLACE, LAY, SET mean to bring or take an object (or cause it to go) to a certain location or position, there to leave it. PUT is the general word: *to put the dishes on the table; to put one's hair up.* PLACE is a more formal word, suggesting precision of movement or definiteness of location: *He placed his hand on the Bible.* LAY, meaning originally to cause to lie, and SET, meaning originally to cause to sit, are used particularly to stress the position in which an object is put: LAY usually suggests putting an object rather carefully into a horizontal position: *to lay a pattern out on the floor.* SET usually means to place upright: *to set a child on a horse.* **16.** levy, inflict.

pu·ta·men (pyo͞o tā′min), *n., pl.* **-tam·i·na** (-tam′ə nə). **1.** *Bot.* a hard or stony endocarp, as a peach stone. **2.** *Obs.* a shell membrane. [< L *putāmen* that which is removed in pruning, equiv. to *putā(re)* (to) trim + *-men* resultative suffix] —**pu·tam·i·nous** (pyo͞o tam′ə nəs), *adj.*

put-and-take (po͝ot′ən tāk′), *n.* any of various games of chance played with a teetotum or other special type of top, in which each player puts in an equal stake before starting to spin the top.

pu·ta·tive (pyo͞o′tə tiv), *adj.* commonly regarded as such; reputed; supposed. [late ME < LL *putātīvus* reputed, equiv. to *putāt(us)* (ptp. of *putāre* to think, consider, reckon, orig. to cut, trim, prune, akin to *pavīre* to beat, ram down; see PAVE) + *-īvus* -IVE] —**pu′ta·tive·ly,** *adv.*

pu′tative mar′riage, *Law.* a marriage contracted in violation of an impediment, but in good faith on the part of one or both of the contracting persons.

put-down (po͝ot′doun′), *n.* **1.** a landing of an aircraft. **2.** *Slang.* **a.** a snubbing remark or retort. **b.** an act intended to humiliate or embarrass someone. [n. use of v. phrase *put down*]

Pu·ti·phar (pyo͞o′tə fər), *n.* *Douay Bible.* Potiphar.

put·log (po͝ot′lôg′, -log′, put′-), *n.* any of the short horizontal timbers supporting the floor of a builder's scaffold. [alter. (by assoc. with LOG[1]) of *putlock,* appar. PUT (ptp.) + LOCK[1]]

Put·nam (put′nəm), *n.* **1. Israel,** 1718–90, American Revolutionary general. **2. Rufus,** 1738–1824, American Revolutionary officer: engineer and colonizer in Ohio. **3.** a town in NE Connecticut. 6952 (1960).

put-on (*adj.* po͝ot′on′, -ôn′; *n.* po͝ot′on′, -ôn′), *adj.* **1.** assumed, feigned, pretended, or disguised: *a put-on manner that didn't fool anyone.* —*n.* **2.** affected manner or behavior; pretentiousness: *She usually drops the put-on when she's with us.* [adj., n. use of v. phrase *put on*]

put-out (po͝ot′out′), *n.* *Baseball.* an instance of putting out a batter or base runner. [n. use of v. phrase *put out*]

put-put (put′put′, -put′ *for 1;* put′put′ *for 2*), *n.* **1.** the sound made by a small internal-combustion engine or imitative of its operation. **2.** a small internal-combustion engine, or something, as a boat, model airplane, etc., equipped with one: *the sound of distant put-puts on the lake.* Also, **putt′-putt′.** [imit.]

Pu·tre·di·nis (po͞o trād′ə nis), *n.* **Palus.** See **Palus Putredinis.**

pu·tre·fac·tion (pyo͞o′trə fak′shən), *n.* the act or process of putrefying; the decomposition of organic matter by bacteria and fungi which results in obnoxiously odorous products; rotting. [late ME < LL *putrefactiōn-* (s. of *putrefactiō*) a rottening, equiv. to L *putrefact(us)* (ptp. of *putrefacere* to PUTREFY) + *-iōn-* -ION] —**pu′tre·fac′tive, pu·tre·fa·cient** (pyo͞o′trə fā′shənt), *adj.*

pu·tre·fy (pyo͞o′trə fī′), *v.,* **-fied, -fy·ing.** —*v.t.* **1.** to render putrid; cause to rot or decay with an offensive odor. —*v.i.* **2.** to become putrid; rot. **3.** to become gangrenous. [late ME *putrefie(n)* < MF *putrefie(r)* < VL **putreficāre,* r. L *putrefacere* to make rotten] —**pu′tre·fi′a·ble,** *adj.* —**pu′tre·fi′er,** *n.*
—**Syn. 2.** decompose, spoil.

pu·tres·cent (pyo͞o tres′ənt), *adj.* **1.** becoming putrid; in process of putrefaction. **2.** of or pertaining to putrefaction. [< L *putrescent-* (s. of *putrescēns*), prp. of *putrescere* to grow rotten] —**pu·tres′cence, pu·tres′cen·cy,** *n.*

pu·tres·ci·ble (pyo͞o tres′ə bəl), *adj.* **1.** liable to become putrid. —*n.* **2.** a putrescible substance. [< L *putresc(ere)* (to) grow rotten + -IBLE] —**pu·tres′ci·bil′i·ty,** *n.*

pu·tres·cine (pyo͞o tres′ēn, -in), *n.* *Biochem.* a colorless liquid ptomaine, $NH_2(CH_2)_4NH_2$, having a disagreeable odor, usually produced by decayed animal tissue and occurring also in abnormal urine. [< L *putresc(ere)* (to) grow rotten + -INE[2]]

pu·trid (pyo͞o′trid), *adj.* **1.** in a state of foul decay or decomposition, as animal or vegetable matter; rotten. **2.** of, pertaining to, or attended by putrefaction. **3.** having the odor of decaying flesh. **4.** thoroughly corrupt, depraved, or evil. **5.** offensively or disgustingly objectionable or bad. [< L *putrid(us)* rotten, equiv. to *putr(ēre)* (to) rot + *-idus* -ID[4]] —**pu·trid′i·ty, pu′trid·ness,** *n.* —**pu′trid·ly,** *adv.* —**Syn. 3.** fetid. **4.** immoral.

pu·tri·lage (pyo͞o′trə lij), *n.* putrid or putrescent matter. [< L *putrilāgin-* (s. of *putrilāgō*) putrefaction] —**pu·tri·lag·i·nous** (pyo͞o′trə laj′ə nəs), *adj.* —**pu′tri·lag′i·nous·ly,** *adv.*

Putsch (po͝och), *n.* *German.* a revolt or uprising, esp. one that depends upon suddenness and speed.

putt (put), *Golf.* —*v.t., v.i.* **1.** to strike (the ball) gently so as to make it roll along the green into the hole. —*n.* **2.** an act of putting. **3.** a stroke made in putting. [var. of PUT]

put·tee (put′ē), *n.* **1.** a long strip of cloth wound spirally round the leg from ankle to knee, worn by sportsmen, soldiers, etc., formerly, as a protection. **2.** a gaiter or legging of leather or other material, as worn by soldiers, riders, etc. Also, **putty, puttie.** [< Hindi *paṭṭī* bandage; akin to Skt *paṭṭa* strip of cloth, bandage]

put·ter[1] (put′ər), *v.i.* **1.** to busy or occupy oneself in an ineffective manner: *to putter over a task.* **2.** to move or go in a specified manner with ineffective action or little energy or purpose: *to putter about the house on a rainy day.* **3.** to move or go slowly or aimlessly; loiter. —*n.* **4.** puttering or ineffective action; dawdling. Also, *esp. Brit.,* **potter.** [var. of POTTER[2]] —**put′ter·er,** *n.* —**put′ter·ing·ly,** *adv.*

putt·er[2] (put′ər), *n.* *Golf.* **1.** a person who putts. **2.** a club with a relatively short, stiff shaft and a wooden or iron head, used in putting. [PUTT + -ER[1]]

put·ter[3] (po͝ot′ər), *n.* **1.** one who or that which puts. **2.** *Track.* a shot-putter. [ME; see PUT, -ER[1]]

put·tie (put′ē), *n.* puttee.

put·ti·er (put′ē ər), *n.* a person who putties, as a glazier. [PUTTY[1] (v.) + -ER[1]]

putt′ing green′, *Golf.* the area of closely cropped grass surrounding the hole.

put·to (po͞o′tō; *It.* po͞ot′tô), *n., pl.* **-ti** (-tē). *Fine Arts.* a representation of a cherubic infant, often shown winged. [< It: lit., boy < L *putus*]

put·ty[1] (put′ē), *n., pl.* **-ties,** *v.,* **-tied, -ty·ing.** —*n.* **1.** a compound of whiting and linseed oil, of a doughlike consistency when fresh, used to secure window panes, patch woodwork defects, etc. **2.** any of various other compounds used for similar purposes. **3.** any of various substances for sealing the joints of tubes or pipes, composed of linseed oil with red lead, white lead, iron oxide, etc. **4.** a creamy mixture of lime and water, partially dried and mixed with sand and plaster of Paris to make a finish plaster coat. **5.** See **putty powder. 6.** any person or thing easily molded, influenced, etc.: *She was putty in his hands.* **7.** light brownish- or yellowish-gray. —*v.t.* **8.** to secure, cover, etc., with putty. [< F *potée,* lit., (something) potted. See POT[1], -EE]

put·ty[2] (put′ē), *n., pl.* **-ties.** puttee.

put′ty knife′, a tool for puttying, having a broad flexible blade.

put′ty pow′der, an abrasive consisting chiefly of stannic oxide, used for polishing hard surfaces. Also called **putty, jeweler's putty.**

put·ty·root (put′ē ro͞ot′, -ro͝ot′), *n.* an American, orchidaceous plant, *Aplectrum hyemale,* having a slender naked rootstock which produces each spring a scape with a loose raceme of brownish flowers. [PUTTY[1] + ROOT[1]]

Pu·tu·ma·yo (po͞o′to͞o mä′yô), *n.* a river in NW South America, flowing SE from S Colombia into the Amazon in NW Brazil. 900 mi. long. Portuguese, **Içá.**

put-up (po͝ot′up′), *adj.* *Informal.* planned beforehand in a secret or crafty manner: *a put-up job.* [adj. use of v. phrase *put up*]

put-up·on (po͝ot′ə pon′), *adj.* ill-used; maltreated: *a most put-upon husband.*

Pu·u·ne·ne (po͞o′o͞o nā′nā), *n.* a town on N Maui, in central Hawaii. 3054 (1960).

Pu·vis de Cha·vannes (pʏ vē′ də shȧ van′), **Pierre Cé·cile** (pyer sā sēl′), 1824–98, French painter.

Puy·al·lup (pyo͞o al′əp), *n.* a city in W Washington, SE of Tacoma. 12,063 (1960).

Puy-de-Dôme (pwē də dōm′), *n.* **1.** a mountain in central France. 4805 ft. **2.** a department in central France. 508,928 (1962); 3095 sq. mi. *Cap.:* Clermont-Ferrand.

Pu·yi (po͞o′yē′), *n.* **Henry,** 1906–67, as Hsüan T'ung, last emperor of China 1908–12; as K'ang Tē, puppet emperor of Manchukuo 1934–45. Also, **P'u-i.**

puz·zle (puz′əl), *n., v.,* **-zled, -zling.** —*n.* **1.** a toy or other contrivance designed to amuse by presenting difficulties to be solved by ingenuity or patient effort. **2.** something puzzling; a puzzling question, matter, or person. **3.** a puzzled or perplexed condition; bewilderment. —*v.t.* **4.** to put (someone) at a loss; mystify; confuse; baffle: *You puzzle me.* **5.** to frustrate or confound, as the understanding; perplex: *The problem puzzled him.* **6.** to exercise (oneself, one's brain, etc.) over some problem or matter. **7.** *Archaic.* to make intricate or complicated. —*v.i.* **8.** to be in perplexity. **9.** to ponder or study over some perplexing problem or matter. **10. puzzle out,** to solve by careful study or effort: *I was unable to puzzle out the message.* [late ME *poselet* puzzled, confused] —**puz′zled·ly,** *adv.* —**puz′zled·ness,** *n.* —**puz′zling·ly,** *adv.* —**puz′zling·ness,** *n.*
—**Syn. 2.** PUZZLE, RIDDLE, ENIGMA refer to something baffling or confusing which is to be solved. A PUZZLE is a question or problem, intricate enough to be perplexing to the mind; it is sometimes a contrivance made purposely perplexing to test one's ingenuity: *a crossword puzzle; The reason for their behavior remains a puzzle.* A RIDDLE is an intentionally obscure statement or question, the meaning of or answer to which is to be arrived at only by guessing: *the famous riddle of the Sphinx.* ENIGMA, originally meaning riddle, now refers to some baffling problem with connotations of mysteriousness: *He will always be an enigma to me.* **4.** confound.

puz′zle glass′, a glass made so as to cause the drinker to spill the contents upon himself unless he knows the trick of using it.

puz′zle jug′, a drinking jug of the 17th and 18th centuries, so made as to challenge the drinker to drink without spilling or spraying the contents over himself.

puz·zle·ment (puz′əl mənt), *n.* **1.** puzzled state; perplexity. **2.** something puzzling. [PUZZLE + -MENT]

puz·zler (puz′lər), *n.* **1.** a person who puzzles. **2.** a baffling thing or problem. **3.** a person who occupies or amuses himself by solving puzzles. [PUZZLE + -ER[1]]

puz·zo·la·na (po͞ot′sə lä′nə; *It.* po͞ot′tsô lä′nä), *n.* pozzolana. Also, **puz·zo·lan** (po͞ot′sə lən).

PVC, polyvinyl chloride.

PVP, polyvinylpyrrolidone.

Pvt., Private.

PW, 1. prisoner of war. **2.** public works.

pW, picowatt; picowatts. Also, **pw**

PWA, Public Works Administration. Also, **P.W.A.**

P wave, a longitudinal earthquake wave that travels through the interior of the earth and is usually the first conspicuous wave to reach a seismograph. Also called **primary wave.** Cf. **L wave, S wave.**

P.W.D., Public Works Department. Also, **PWD**

pwr, power.

pwt., pennyweight. Also, **pwt**

Pwyll (po͞ol), *n.* *Welsh Legend.* a prince who steals his wife, Rhiannon, from her suitor, Gwawl, and is the father of Pryteri.

PX, *pl.* **PXs.** post exchange.

P.X., please exchange.

pxt., pinxit.

py-, var. of **pyo-** before a vowel: *pyemia.*

pya (pyä, pē ä′), *n.* a copper coin of Burma, the 100th part of a kyat, equivalent to about .0021 of a U.S. dollar. [< Burmese]

py·ae·mi·a (pī ē′mē ə), *n.* *Pathol.* pyemia. —**py·ae′mic,** *adj.*

pyal·la (pyä′lə, pē ä′-), *v.i., v.t.* *Australian Obs.* to talk. Also, **piala.** [< native Austral]

Py·a·nep·si·a (pī′ə nep′sē ə), *n.* (*sometimes construed as pl.*) an annual festival held in ancient Athens in honor of Apollo and the Horae.

Pya·ti·gorsk (pyä′ti gôrsk′), *n.* a city in the SW RSFSR, in the S Soviet Union in Europe, in Caucasia. 69,000 (1959). Also, **Piatigorsk.**

pycn-, var. of **pycno-** before a vowel: *pycnium.*

pyc·nid·i·um (pik nid′ē əm), *n., pl.* **-nid·i·a** (-nid′ē ə). *Bot.* (in certain ascomycetes and *Fungi Imperfecti*) a globose or flask-shaped fruiting body bearing conidia on conidiophores. [< NL < Gk *pykn(ós)* close, thick, dense + *-idion* dim. suffix] —**pyc·nid′i·al,** *adj.*

pyc·ni·o·spore (pik′nē ə spōr′, -spôr′), *n.* *Bot.* the spore produced in a pycnium. [PYCNI(UM) + -O- + SPORE]

pyc·ni·um (pik′nē əm), *n., pl.* **-ni·a** (-nē ə). *Bot.* a flask-shaped or conical sporangium of a rust fungus, which develops below the epidermis of the host and bears pycniospores. [< NL; see PYCN-, -IUM] —**pyc′ni·al,** *adj.*

pycno-, a learned borrowing from Greek meaning "dense," "close," "thick," used in the formation of compound words: *pycnometer.* Also, *esp. before a vowel,* **pycn-.** [< NL, comb. form repr. Gk *pyknós*]

pyc·nom·e·ter (pik nom′i tər), *n.* a container for determining the density of a liquid or solid, having a specific volume and often provided with a thermometer to indicate the temperature of the contained substance. [PYCNO- + -METER]

pyc·no·style (pik′nə stīl′), *adj.* *Archit.* having an intercolumniation of 1½ diameters. See illus. under **intercolumniation.** [< L *pycnostȳl(us)* < Gk *pyknóstȳlos,* equiv. to *pyknós* PYCNO- + *stŷlos* pillar]

Pyd·na (pid′nə), *n.* a town in ancient Macedonia, W of the Gulf of Salonika: decisive Roman victory over the Macedonians 186 B.C.

pye (pī), *n.* *Eccles.* pie[4].

py·e·li·tis (pī′ə lī′tis), *n.* *Pathol.* inflammation of the pelvis or outlet of the kidney. [< NL; see PYEL-, -ITIS] —**py·e·lit·ic** (pī′ə lit′ik), *adj.*

pyelo-, a learned borrowing from Greek, used with the meaning "pelvis" in the formation of compound words: *pyelogram.* Also, *esp. before a vowel,* **pyel-.** [< NL, comb. form repr. Gk *pýelos* basin. Cf. L *pelvis* basin, PELVIS]

py·e·lo·gram (pī′ə lə gram′), *n.* a roentgenograph produced by pyelography. Also, **py·e·lo·graph** (pī′ə lə graf′, -gräf′). [PYELO- + -GRAM[1]]

py·e·log·ra·phy (pī′ə log′rə fē), *n.* the science or technique of making photographs of the kidneys, renal pelves, and ureters by means of x-rays, after the injection of an opaque solution or of a radiopaque dye. [PYELO- + -GRAPHY] —**py·e·lo·graph·ic** (pī′ə lə graf′ik), *adj.*

py·e·lo·ne·phri·tis (pī′ə lō nə frī′tis), *n.* *Pathol.* inflammation of the kidney and its pelvis. [PYELO- + NEPHRITIS] —**py·e·lo·ne·phrit·ic** (pī′ə lō′ni frit′ik), *adj.*

py·e·lo·ne·phro·sis (pī′ə lō nə frō′sis), *n.* *Pathol.* any disease of the kidney and its pelvis. [PYELO- + NEPHROSIS]

py·e·mi·a (pī ē′mē ə), *n.* *Pathol.* a diseased condition in which pyogenic bacteria are circulating in the blood, characterized by the development of abscesses in various organs. Also, **pyaemia.** [< NL; see PYO-, -EMIA] —**py·e′mic,** *adj.*

py·gid·i·um (pī jid′ē əm), *n.*, *pl.* **-gid·i·a** (-jid′ē ə). *Zool.* any of various structures or regions at the caudal end of the body in certain invertebrates. [< NL < Gk *pȳg(ḗ)* rump + *-idion* dim. suffix] —**py·gid′i·al,** *adj.*

pyg·mae·an (pig mē′ən), *adj.* pygmy. Also, **pyg·me′an.** [< L *pygmae(us)* dwarfish (see PYGMY) + -AN]

Pyg·ma·li·on (pig mā′lē ən, -māl′yən), *n.* **1.** *Class. Myth.* a sculptor and king of Cyprus who carved an ivory statue of a maiden and fell in love with it. It was brought to life, in response to his prayer, by Aphrodite, and was called Galatea. **2.** (*italics*) a comedy (1912) by George Bernard Shaw.

Pyg·my (pig′mē), *n.*, *pl.* **-mies,** *adj.* —*n.* **1.** *Anthropol.* **a.** a member of an equatorial African Negroid race of small stature. **b.** a Negrito of southeastern Asia, or of the Andaman or Philippine Islands. **2.** (*l.c.*) a small or dwarfish person. **3.** (*l.c.*) anything very small of its kind. **4.** (*l.c.*) a person who is of small importance, or who has some quality, attribute, etc., in very small measure. **5.** one of a race of dwarfs in ancient history and tradition. —*adj.* **6.** (*often l.c.*) of or pertaining to the Pygmies. **7.** (*l.c.*) of very small size, capacity, power, etc. Also, **Pigmy.** [ME *pigmeis,* pl. of *pigme* < L *Pygmae(us)* < Gk *pygmaîos* dwarfish (adj.), Pygmy (n.), equiv. to *pygm(ḗ)* distance from elbow to knuckles + *-aios* -EOUS] —**pyg′moid,** *adj.* —**pyg′my·ish,** *adj.* —**pyg′my·ism,** *n.*
—**Syn. 1.** See **dwarf.**

pyg′my glid′er, any of several flying phalangers of the genus *Acrobates,* growing to about the size of a mouse and having a featherlike tail. Also called **feather-tail glider.**

pyg′my owl′, any of several small, diurnal owls of the genus *Glaucidium,* that feed chiefly on insects.

pyg′my wea′sel. See **least weasel.**

py·go·style (pī′gə stīl′), *n.* *Ornith.* the bone at the posterior end of the spinal column in birds, formed by the fusion of several caudal vertebrae. [< Gk *pygo-* (comb. form repr. *pygḗ* rump) + *stȳlos* pillar] —**py′go·styled′,** *adj.* —**py′go·sty′lous,** *adj.*

py·in (pī′in), *n.* *Biochem.* an albuminous constituent of pus. [PY- + -IN^2] —**py′ic,** *adj.*

py·jam·as (pə jä′məz, -jam′əz), *n.* (*construed as pl.*) *Chiefly Brit.* pajamas.

pyk·nic (pik′nik), *Psychol.* —*adj.* **1.** (of a physical type) having a fat, rounded build or body structure. Cf. **athletic** (def. 4), **asthenic** (def. 2). —*n.* **2.** a person of the pyknic type. [< Gk *pykn(ós)* thick + -IC]

Pyl·a·des (pil′ə dēz′), *n.* *Class. Myth.* a son of Strophius who befriended Orestes, accompanied him in his wanderings, and eventually married Electra, sister of Orestes.

Py·lae·me·nes (pi lē′mə nēz′), *n.* (in the *Iliad*) a king of the Paphlagonians, slain by Menelaus in the Trojan War.

Py·lae·us (pi lē′əs), *n.* (in the *Iliad*) a captain of the Pelasgian allies of Troy.

Py·las (pī′ləs), *n.* *Class. Myth.* a king of Megara who gave his throne to Pandion the Younger.

Pyle (pīl), *n.* **1. Ernest** ("*Ernie*"), 1900–45, U.S. war correspondent and journalist. **2. Howard,** 1853–1911, U.S. illustrator and author.

py·lon (pī′lon), *n.* **1.** a marking post or tower for guiding aviators, frequently used in races. **2.** a relatively tall structure at the side of a gate, bridge, or avenue, marking an entrance or approach. **3.** a monumental tower forming the entrance to an ancient Egyptian temple, consisting either of a pair of tall quadrilateral masonry masses with sloping sides and a doorway between them or of one such mass pierced with a doorway. **4.** a steel tower or mast carrying high-tension, telephonic or other cables and lines. **5.** *Aeron.* a finlike device used to attach engines, auxiliary fuel tanks, bombs, etc., to an aircraft wing or fuselage. [Gk: gateway]

py·lo·rec·to·my (pī′lə rek′tə mē), *n.*, *pl.* **-mies.** *Surg.* removal of the pylorus. [PYLOR(US) + -ECTOMY]

py·lo·rus (pi lôr′əs, -lōr′-, pī-), *n.*, *pl.* **-lo·ri** (-lôr′ī, -lōr′ī). *Anat.* the opening between the stomach and the duodenum of the intestine. See diag. under **intestine.** [< LL < Gk *pylōrós,* lit., gatekeeper] —**py·lor·ic** (pi lôr′ik, -lor′-, pī-), *adj.*

Py·los (pē′lôs; *Eng.* pī′los, -lōs), *n.* Greek name of **Navarino.**

Pym (pim), *n.* **John,** 1584–1643, English statesman.

Pyn·chon (pin′chən), *n.* **William,** 1590?–1662, English colonist in America.

pyo-, a learned borrowing from Greek meaning "pus," used in the formation of compound words: *pyogenesis.* Also, *esp. before a vowel,* **py-.** [< Gk, comb. form of *pýon*]

py·o·der·ma (pī′ō dûr′mə), *n.* *Pathol.* any disease of the skin characterized by the formation of pus. [< NL; see PYO-, DERMA]

py·o·gen·e·sis (pī′ə jen′i sis), *n.* *Pathol.* the generation of pus; the process of the formation of pus. [PYO- + GENESIS]

py·o·gen·ic (pī′ə jen′ik), *adj.* *Pathol.* **1.** producing or generating pus. **2.** attended with or pertaining to the formation of pus. [PYO- + GENIC]

py·oid (pī′oid), *adj.* *Pathol.* pertaining to pus; puslike. [< Gk *pyoeid(ḗs).* See PY-, -OID]

py·o·me·tra (pī′ō mē′trə), *n.* *Pathol.* an accumulation of pus in the uterus. [< NL, equiv. to *pyo-* PYO- + Gk *mḗtra* uterus]

py·o·ne·phri·tis (pī′ō nə frī′tis), *n.* *Pathol.* suppurative inflammation of the kidney. [PYO- + NEPHRITIS]

Pyong·yang (pyung′yäng′), *n.* a city in and the capital of North Korea, in the SW part. 653,100 (est. 1960). Japanese, **Heijo.**

py·o·per·i·car·di·um (pī′ō per′ə kär′dē əm), *n.* *Pathol.* accumulation of pus in the pericardium. [PYO- + PERICARDIUM]

py·oph·thal·mi·a (pī′of thal′mē ə), *n.* *Pathol.* suppurative inflammation of the eye. Also, **py·oph·thal·mi·tis** (pī′of thal mī′tis). [PY- + OPHTHALMIA]

pyopneumo-, a combining form indicating the presence of pus and gas: *pyopneumothorax.* [< NL; see PYO-, PNEUMO-]

py·o·pneu·mo·tho·rax (pī′ō nōō′mō thôr′aks, -thōr′-, -nyōō′-), *n.* *Pathol.* the presence of gas and pus in the pleural cavity. [PYO- + PNEUMOTHORAX]

py·or·rhe·a (pī′ə rē′ə), *n.* **1.** *Pathol.* a discharge of pus. **2.** Also called **pyorrhe′a al·ve·o·lar′is** (al vē′ə lar′is), **Riggs' disease.** *Dentistry.* a disease occurring in various forms and degrees of severity, characterized in its severe forms by the formation of pus in the pockets between the roots of the teeth and their surrounding tissues, and frequently accompanied by the loosening and subsequent loss of the teeth. Also, **py′or·rhoe′a.** [< NL; see PYO-, -RHEA] —**py′or·rhe′al, py′or·rhoe′al, py′or·rhe′ic, py′or·rhoe′ic,** *adj.*

py·o·sal·pinx (pī′ō sal′pingks), *n.* *Pathol.* the accumulation of pus in an oviduct. [< NL; see PYO-, SALPINX]

py·o·sep·ti·ce·mi·a (pī′ō sep′ti sē′mē ə), *n.* *Pathol.* **1.** any condition involving both pyemia and septicemia. **2.** *Vet. Pathol.* See **joint ill.** [PY(EMIA) + -O- + SEPTICEMIA] —**py′o·sep′ti·ce′mic,** *adj.*

py·o·sis (pī ō′sis), *n.* *Pathol.* the formation of pus; suppuration. [< NL < Gk; see PY-, -OSIS]

py·o·tho·rax (pī′ō thôr′aks, -thōr′-), *n.* *Pathol.* empyema. [PYO- + THORAX]

py·o·u·re·ter (pī′ō yŏŏ rē′tər), *n.* *Pathol.* distention of a ureter with pus. [PYO- + URETER]

pyr-, var. of **pyro-,** used before *h* or a vowel: *pyran.*

Pyr·aech·mes (pi rek′mēz), *n.* (in the *Iliad*) a captain of the Paeonian allies of Troy.

pyr·a·lid (pir′ə lid), *n.* **1.** any of numerous slender-bodied moths of the family *Pyralidae,* having elongated triangular forewings, the larvae of which include many crop pests. —*adj.* **2.** belonging or pertaining to the family *Pyralidae.* [< NL *Pyralid(ae),* equiv. to *Pyral(is)* type genus (< L *pyralis,* Gk *pyralís* an insect thought to live in fire; akin to *pŷr* fire) + *-idae* -ID^2]

pyr·a·mid (pir′ə mid), *n.* **1.** *Archit.* **a.** (in ancient Egypt) a quadrilateral masonry mass having smooth, steeply sloping sides meeting at an apex, used as a tomb. **b.** (in ancient Egypt and pre-Columbian Central America) a quadrilateral masonry mass, stepped and sharply sloping, used as a tomb or a platform for a temple. **2.** anything of such form. **3.** a number of persons or things arranged or heaped up in this manner: *a pyramid of acrobats; a pyramid of boxes.* **4.** *Geom.* a solid having a polygonal base, and triangular sides which meet in a point. **5.** *Crystall.* any form the planes of which intersect all three of the axes. **6.** *Anat., Zool.* any of various parts or structures of pyramidal form. **7.** *Stock Exchange.* the series of transactions in which a speculator increases his holdings by using the rising market value of those holdings as margin for further purchases. **8.** a tree pruned or trained to grow in pyramidal form. **9. pyramids,** (*construed as sing.*) *Brit.* a form of pocket billiards for two or four players in which 15 colored balls, initially placed in the form of a triangle, are pocketed with one white cue ball. —*v.i.* **10.** to take, or become disposed in, the form of a pyramid. **11.** *Stock Exchange.* (in speculating on margin) to enlarge one's operations in a series of transactions, as on a continued rise or decline in price, by using profits in transactions not yet closed, and consequently not yet in hand, as margin for additional buying or selling in the next transaction. —*v.t.* **12.** to arrange in the form of a pyramid. **13.** to raise or increase (costs, wages, etc.) by adding amounts gradually. **14.** *Stock Exchange.* (in speculating on margin) to operate in, or employ in, pyramiding. [< L *pyramid-* (s. of *pyramis*) < Gk *pyramís* (gen. *pyramídos*) < Egypt; r. ME *pyramis* < L] —**pyr′a·mid·like′,** *adj.*

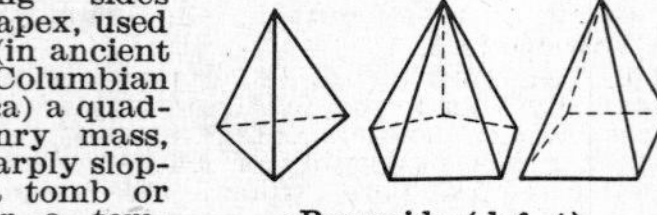
Pyramids (def. 4)

py·ram·i·dal (pi ram′i dəl), *adj.* **1.** of or pertaining to a pyramid: *the pyramidal form.* **2.** of the nature of a pyramid; pyramidlike. [PYRAMID + -AL^1] —**py·ram′i·dal·ly,** *adv.*

pyr·a·mid·i·cal (pir′ə mid′i kəl), *adj.* pyramidal. Also, **pyr′a·mid′ic.** [< Gk *pyramidik(ós)* of a pyramid (*pyramid-,* s. of *pyramís* PYRAMID, + *-ikos* -IC) + -AL^1] —**pyr′a·mid′i·cal·ly,** *adv.*

pyr·a·mid·i·on (pir′ə mid′ē on), *n.*, *pl.* **-mid·i·a** (-mid′ē ə). a miniature pyramid, as at the apex of an obelisk. [< NL, equiv. to *pyramid-* PYRAMID + *-ion* dim. suffix < Gk]

Py·ram·i·don (pi ram′i don′), *n.* *Pharm., Trademark.* aminopyrine.

Pyr′a·mus and This′be (pir′ə məs), *Class. Myth.* two young lovers of Babylon who held conversations clandestinely, and in defiance of their parents, through a crack in a wall. On believing Thisbe dead, Pyramus killed himself. When Thisbe discovered his body she committed suicide.

py·ran (pī′ran, pī ran′), *n.* *Chem.* either of two compounds having the formula C_5H_6O, containing one oxygen and five carbon atoms arranged in a six-membered ring. [PYR- + -AN]

pyr·ar·gy·rite (pī rär′jə rīt′), *n.* a blackish mineral, silver antimony sulfide, $AgSbS_3$, showing, when transparent, a deep ruby-red color by transmitted light: an ore of silver; ruby silver. [PYR- + Gk *árgyr(on)* silver + -ITE^1]

pyr·a·zole (pir′ə zōl′, -zôl′, -zol′), *n.* *Chem.* **1.** any of the group of heterocyclic compounds containing three carbon atoms, two adjacent nitrogen atoms, and two double bonds in the ring. **2.** the parent compound, $C_3H_4N_2$. [PYR- + AZOLE]

py·raz·o·line (pi raz′ə lēn′, -lin, pī-), *n.* *Chem.* **1.** any of the group of heterocyclic compounds containing three carbon atoms, two adjacent nitrogen atoms, and one double bond in the ring. **2.** the parent compound, $C_3H_6N_2$. [PYRAZOLE + -INE^2]

py·raz·o·lone (pi raz′ə lōn′, pī-), *n.* *Chem.* **1.** any of the group of heterocyclic compounds containing the pyrazoline ring in which one carbon atom is doubly linked to an oxygen atom not in the ring. **2.** the parent compound, $C_3H_4N_2O$. [PYRAZOLE + -ONE]

pyraz′olone dye′, *Chem.* any of the group of dyes, as tartrazine, derived from a pyrazolone: used chiefly to dye silk and wool.

pyre (pīᵊr), *n.* **1.** a pile or heap of wood or other combustible material. **2.** such a pile for burning a dead body: *a funeral pyre.* [< L *pyra* < Gk: hearth, funeral pile]

py·rene (pī′rēn), *n.* *Bot.* a putamen or stone, esp. when there are several in a single fruit; a nutlet. [< NL *pȳrēna* < Gk *pȳrḗn* fruit-stone]

Py·re·ne (pī rē′nē), *n.* *Class. Myth.* **1.** a princess who, ravished by Hercules, gave birth to a serpent. **2.** the mother, by Ares, of the Cycnus who fought with Hercules.

Pyr·e·nees (pir′ə nēz′), *n.* a mountain range between Spain and France. Highest peak, Pic de Néthou, 11,165 ft. —**Pyr′e·ne′an,** *adj.*

Py·ré·nées-O·ri·en·tales (pē rā nā′zô rē än tal′), *n.* a department in S France. 251,231 (1962); 1600 sq. mi. *Cap.:* Perpignan.

Py·re·ne·us (pī′rə nē′əs), *n.* *Class. Myth.* a king who offered shelter to the Muses, and then tried to assault them. Driven mad for his arrogance, he jumped from a tower to his death. Also, **Py′re·nae′us.**

py·re·no·carp (pī rē′nə kärp′), *n.* *Bot.* **1.** a perithecium. **2.** a drupe. [PYRENE + -O- + -CARP] —**py·re′no·car′pic, py·re′no·car′pous,** *adj.*

py·re·thrin (pī rē′thrin), *n.* *Chem.* **1.** Also called **pyrethrin I.** a viscous, water-insoluble liquid, $C_{21}H_{28}O_3$, extracted from pyrethrum flowers, used as an insecticide. **2.** Also called **pyrethrin II.** a like compound, $C_{22}H_{28}O_5$, obtained and used similarly. [PYRETHR(UM) + -IN^2]

py·re·thrum (pī rē′thrəm), *n.* **1.** any of several chrysanthemums, as *Chrysanthemum coccineum,* having finely divided leaves and showy red, pink, lilac, or white flowers, cultivated as an ornamental. **2.** any of several chrysanthemums, as *Chrysanthemum cinerariaefolium, C. coccineum,* or *C. Marschallii,* cultivated as a source of insecticides. **3.** *Pharm.* the dried flower heads of these plants, used chiefly as an insecticide and sometimes in medicine for certain skin disorders. [< L < Gk *pýrethron* feverfew, akin to *pyretós* fever]

py·ret·ic (pī ret′ik), *adj.* of, pertaining to, affected by, or producing fever. [< NL *pyretic(us),* equiv. to Gk *pyret(ós)* fever + L *-icus* -IC]

pyr·e·tol·o·gy (pir′i tol′ə jē, pī′ri-), *n.* the branch of medicine that treats of fevers. [< Gk *pyretó(s)* fever + -LOGY] —**pyr′e·tol′o·gist,** *n.*

pyr·e·to·ther·a·py (pir′i tō ther′ə pē, pī′ri-), *n.* *Med.* therapy by raising the body temperature, as by diathermy or by artificially inducing fever. [< Gk *pyretó(s)* fever + THERAPY]

Py·rex (pī′reks), *n.* *Trademark.* any of a class of heat and chemical-resistant glassware products of varying composition, for baking, frying, etc.

py·rex·i·a (pī rek′sē ə), *n.* *Pathol.* **1.** fever. **2.** feverish condition. [< NL < Gk *pýrex(is)* feverishness + *-ia* -IA] —**py·rex′i·al, py·rex′ic,** *adj.*

pyr·he·li·om·e·ter (pīᵊr′hē lē om′i tər, pir′-), *n.* *Astrophysics.* an instrument for measuring the total intensity of the sun's energy radiation. [PYR- + HELIO- + -METER] —**pyr·he·li·o·met·ric** (pīᵊr′hē lē ə me′trik, pir′-), *adj.*

Pyr·i·ben·za·mine (pir′ə ben′zə mēn′, pī′rə-), *n.* *Pharm., Trademark.* tripelennamine.

pyrid-, a combining form of **pyridine:** *pyridoxine.*

pyr·i·dine (pir′i dēn′, -din), *n.* *Chem.* a colorless, flammable, liquid organic base, C_5H_5N, having a disagreeable odor, usually obtained from coal or synthesized from acetaldehyde and ammonia: used chiefly as a solvent and in organic synthesis. [PYR- + -ID^2 + -INE^2] —**pyr·id·ic** (pī rid′ik), *adj.*

Py·rid·i·um (pī rid′ē əm), *n.* *Pharm., Trademark.* a compound used chiefly as a urinary antiseptic.

pyr·i·dox·ine (pir′i dok′sēn, -sin), *n.* *Biochem.* a derivative of pyridine, $CH_3C_5N(CH_2OH)_2OH$, occurring in whole-grain cereals, meats, fish, etc., and also made synthetically, known to counteract nutritional dermatitis in rats, and prescribed for human beings for the prevention of pellagra, for the formation of hemoglobin, and often, for women during pregnancy. vitamin B_6. Also, **pyr·i·dox·in** (pir′i dok′sin). [PYRID(INE) + OX(YGEN) + -INE^2]

pyr·i·form (pir′ə fôrm′), *adj.* pear-shaped. [< NL *pyriform(is)* pear-shaped, equiv. to *pyri-* (for *piri-* pear) + *-formis* -FORM]

Py·rig·e·nes (pī rij′ə nēz′), *n.* *Class. Myth.* an epithet of Dionysus, meaning "born of fire."

py·rim·i·dine (pī rim′i dēn′, pir′ə mi dēn′, -din), *n.* *Chem.* **1.** Also called **miazine.** a liquid or crystalline, water-soluble mass, $C_4H_4N_2$, a heterocyclic ring compound that is an important constituent of several biochemical substances, as thiamine. **2.** any of the group of compounds derived from this heterocyclic ring. [alter. of PYRIDINE]

Pyr·i·phleg·e·thon (pir′ə fleg′ə thon′), *n.* *Class. Myth.* Phlegethon (def. 1).

py·rite (pī′rīt), *n.* a very common brass-yellow mineral, iron disulfide, FeS_2, with a metallic luster, burned to sulfur dioxide in the manufacture of sulfuric acid: chemically similar to marcasite, but crystallizing in the isometric system. Also, **pyrites.** Also called **iron pyrites.** [< L *pyrītē(s)* < Gk *pyrítēs,* orig. adj. of or in fire. See PYR-, -ITE^1] —**py·rit·ic** (pī rit′ik, pə-), **py·rit′i·cal, py·ri·tous** (pə rī′təs, pī-), *adj.*

py·ri·tes (pī rī′tēz, pə-, pī′rīts), *n.*, *pl.* **-tes.** *Mineral.* **1.** pyrite. **2.** marcasite. **3.** any of various other metallic sulfides, as of copper, tin, etc. [< L; see PYRITE]

py·ri·to·he·dron (pī rī′tə hē′drən, pī′rī-), *n.* *Crystall.* a crystal form of 12 pentagonal faces. Also called **pentagonal dodecahedron.** [*pyrito-* (comb. form of PYRITE) + -HEDRON] —**py·ri′to·he′dral,** *adj.*

pyr·i·tol·o·gy (pir′i tol′ə jē, pī′ri-), *n.* *Obs.* pyrology. [*pyrito-* (comb. form of PYRITE) + -LOGY]

pyro-, **1.** a learned borrowing from Greek used, with the meaning "fire," "heat," "of, relating to, or concerned with fire or heat," in the formation of compound words: *pyrogen; pyrolysis; pyromancy.* **2.** *Chem.* a word element used before the name of an inorganic acid, indicating that its water content is intermediate between that of the corresponding ortho-

(more water) and meta- (least water) acids (*pyroantimonic*, $H_4Sb_2O_7$, *pyroarsenic*, $H_4As_2O_7$, and *pyrosulfuric*, $H_2S_2O_7$, *acids*). The element is also applied to the salts of these acids. If the acid ends in *-ic*, the corresponding salt ends in *-ate* (*pyroboric acid*, $H_2B_4O_7$, and *potassium pyrobate*, $K_2B_4O_7$, or *pyrosulfuric*, $H_2S_2O_7$, and *pyrosulfate*, $N_2S_2O_7$); if the acid ends in *-ous*, the corresponding salt ends in *-ite* (*pyrophosphorous acid*, $H_4P_2O_5$, *potassium pyrophosphite*, $K_4P_2O_5$). **3.** *Geol.* used in the names of minerals, rocks, etc., indicating a quality produced by the action of fire: *pyrolusite*. Also, **pyr-.** [comb. form of Gk *pȳr* fire]

py·ro·bi·tu·men (pī′rō bi to͞o′mən, -tyo͞o′-, -bich′-o͞o-), *n.* any of the dark, solid hydrocarbons including peat, coal, and bituminous shale. [PYRO- + BITUMEN] —**py′ro·bi·tu′mi·nous, py′ro·bi·tu′mi·noid′,** *adj.*

py·ro·bo·rate (pī′rə bôr′āt, -bōr′-), *n.* borax.

py·ro·cat·e·chol (pī′rō kat′ə chōl′, -chôl′, -chol′, -kōl′, -kôl′, -kol′, pir′ə-), *n.* *Chem.* catechol. Also, **py·ro·cat·e·chin** (pī′rə kat′ə chin, -kin, pir′ə-). [PYRO- + CATECHOL]

py·ro·chem·i·cal (pī′rə kem′i kəl), *adj.* pertaining to or producing chemical change at high temperatures. [PYRO- + CHEMICAL] —**py′ro·chem′i·cal·ly,** *adv.*

py·ro·chlore (pī′rə klôr′, -klōr′), *n.* a mineral, chiefly composed of niobates of the cerium metals, occurring in syenites in the form of brown crystals. [< G *Pyrochlor.* See PYRO-, CHLOR-[1]]

py·ro·clas·tic (pī′rə klas′tik), *adj.* *Geol.* composed chiefly of fragments of volcanic origin, as agglomerate, tuff, and certain other rocks. [PYRO- + CLASTIC]

py·ro·con·duc·tiv·i·ty (pī′rō kon′duk tiv′i tē), *n.* *Elect.* conductivity brought about by the application of heat, esp. in solids that are not conductors at normal temperatures. [PYRO- + CONDUCTIVITY]

py·ro·crys·tal·line (pī′rə kris′tᵊlin, -tᵊlīn′, -tᵊlēn′), *adj.* *Petrog.* crystallized from a molten magma or highly heated solution. [PYRO- + CRYSTALLINE]

py·ro·e·lec·tric (pī′rō i lek′trik), *adj.* **1.** pertaining to, subject to, or manifesting pyroelectricity. —*n.* **2.** a substance manifesting pyroelectricity. [back formation from PYROELECTRICITY]

py·ro·e·lec·tric·i·ty (pī′rō i lek tris′i tē, -ē′lek-), *n.* electrification or electrical polarity produced in certain crystals by temperature changes. [PYRO- + ELECTRICITY]

py·ro·gal·late (pī′rə gal′āt), *n.* *Chem.* a salt or ether of pyrogallol. [PYROGALL(OL) + -ATE[2]]

py·ro·gal·lol (pī′rə gal′ōl, -ôl, -ol, -gə lōl′, -lôl′, -lol′), *n.* a white, crystalline, water-soluble, poisonous, solid, phenolic compound, $C_6H_3(OH)_3$, obtained by heating gallic acid and water: used chiefly as a developer in photography, a mordant for wool, in dyeing, and in medicine in the treatment of certain skin conditions. Also called **pyrogal′lic ac′id.** [PYRO- + GALL(IC)[2] + -OL[1]] —**py′ro·gal′lic,** *adj.*

py·ro·gen (pī′rə jen′), *n.* a substance, as a thermostable bacterial toxin, which produces a rise in temperature in a man or animal. [PYRO- + -GEN]

py·ro·gen·ic (pī′rə jen′ik), *adj.* **1.** producing or produced by heat or fever. **2.** produced by fire, as igneous rock. [PYRO- + GENIC]

py·rog·e·nous (pī roj′ə nəs), *adj.* *Geol.* produced by the action of heat, hot solutions, etc. [PYRO- + -GENOUS]

py·rog·nos·tics (pī′rəg nos′tiks), *n.pl.* those properties of a mineral that it exhibits when heated, alone or with fluxes, in the blowpipe flame, as the fusibility, intumescence, or other phenomena of fusion, flame coloration, etc. [PYRO- + GNOSTIC; see -ICS]

py·ro·graph (pī′rə graf′, -gräf′), *n.* **1.** an object ornamented by pyrography. —*v.t., v.i.* **2.** to decorate or work with pyrography. [back formation from PYROGRAPHY]

py·rog·ra·phy (pī rog′rə fē), *n., pl.* **-phies** for 2. **1.** the process of burning designs on wood, leather, etc., with a heated tool. **2.** a design made by this process. Also called **py·ra·gra·vure** (pī′rə grə vyo͝or′, -grā′-vyər). [PYRO- + -GRAPHY] —**py·rog′ra·pher,** *n.* —**py·ro·graph·ic** (pī′rə graf′ik), *adj.*

py·ro·lig·ne·ous (pī′rə lig′nē əs), *adj.* produced by the distillation of wood. Also, **py′ro·lig′nic.** [PYRO- + LIGNEOUS]

pyrolig′neous ac′id, *Chem.* a yellowish, acidic, water-soluble liquid, containing about 10 percent acetic acid, obtained by the destructive distillation of wood: used for smoking meats. Also called **wood vinegar.**

pyrolig′neous al′cohol. See **methyl alcohol.** Also called **py′rolig′neous spir′it.**

py·rol·o·gy (pī rol′ə jē), *n.* *Obs.* the branch of mineralogy dealing with pyrognostics. Also called **pyritology.** [PYRO- + -LOGY] —**py·ro·log·i·cal** (pī′rə loj′i kəl), *adj.* —**py·rol′o·gist,** *n.*

py·ro·lu·site (pī′rə lo͞o′sīt, pī rol′yə sīt′), *n.* a common mineral, manganese dioxide, MnO_2, the principal ore of manganese, used in various manufactures, as a decolorizer of brown or green tints in glass, as a depolarizer in dry-cell batteries, etc. [PYRO- + Gk *loûs(is)* washing + -ITE[1]]

py·rol·y·sis (pī rol′i sis), *n.* *Chem.* **1.** the subjection of organic compounds to very high temperatures. **2.** the resulting decomposition. [PYRO- + -LYSIS] —**py·ro·lyt·ic** (pī′rə lit′ik), *adj.*

py·ro·mag·net·ic (pī′rō mag net′ik), *adj.* *Physics.* (no longer current) thermomagnetic (def. 1). [PYRO- + MAGNETIC]

py·ro·man·cy (pī′rə man′sē), *n.* divination by fire, or by forms appearing in fire. [ME *piromancie* < ML *pyromantīa* < Gk *pyromanteía* divination by fire. See PYRO-, -MANCY] —**py′ro·man′cer,** *n.* —**py′ro·man′tic,** *adj.*

py·ro·ma·ni·a (pī′rə mā′nē ə), *n.* a mania or compulsion to set things on fire. [PYRO- + -MANIA] —**py′ro·ma′ni·ac,** *n.* —**py·ro·ma·ni·a·cal** (pī′rō mə nī′ə-kəl), *adj.*

py·ro·met·al·lur·gy (pī′rə met′ᵊlûr′jē), *n.* the process or technique of refining ores with heat so as to accelerate chemical reactions or to melt the metallic or nonmetallic content. [PYRO- + METALLURGY]

py·rom·e·ter (pī rom′i tər), *n.* *Thermodynamics.* an apparatus for determining high temperatures by the observation of the color produced by a substance upon heating or by the comparison of electric currents produced by heating dissimilar metals. [PYRO- + -METER] —**py·ro·met·ric** (pī′rə me′trik), **py′ro·met′ri·cal,** *adj.* —**py′ro·met′ri·cal·ly,** *adv.* —**py·rom′e·try,** *n.*

py′romet′ric bead′, (in a kiln) a ball of material which indicates by changing color that a certain temperature has been reached.

py′romet′ric cone′, (in a kiln) a triangular piece of material that indicates by bending or melting that a certain temperature has been reached.

py·ro·mor·phite (pī′rə môr′fīt), *n.* a mineral, lead chlorophosphate, $Pb_5P_3O_{12}Cl$, occurring in crystalline and massive forms, and of a green, yellow, or brown color: a minor ore of lead; green lead ore. [< G *Pyromorphit.* See PYRO-, MORPH-, -ITE[1]]

py′ro·mu′cic al′dehyde (pī′rə myo͞o′sik, pī′-), *Chem.* furfural. [PYRO- + MUCIC (ACID)]

py·rone (pī′rōn, pī rōn′), *n.* *Chem.* either of two heterocyclic ketones having the formula $C_5H_4O_2$. [PYR- + -ONE]

Py·ro·ni·a (pī rō′nē ə), *n.* *Class. Myth.* an epithet of Artemis, meaning "fire goddess."

py·rope (pī′rōp), *n.* a mineral, magnesium-aluminum garnet, $Mg_3Al_2Si_3O_{12}$, occurring in crystals of varying shades of red, and frequently used as a gem. [ME *pirope* < L *pyrōp(us)* gold-bronze < Gk *pyrōpós*, lit., fire-eyed, equiv. to *pȳr* fire + *ōp-* (s. of *ṓps*) eye + *-os* adj. suffix]

py·ro·pho·bi·a (pī′rə fō′bē ə), *n.* an abnormal fear of fire. [PYRO- + -PHOBIA] —**py′ro·pho′bic,** *adj.*

py·ro·phor·ic (pī′rə fôr′ik, -for′-), *adj.* *Chem.* capable of igniting spontaneously in air. [< Gk *pyrophór(os)* fire-bearing (see PYRO-, -PHOROUS) + -IC]

py·ro·phos·phate (pī′rə fos′fāt), *n.* *Chem.* a salt or ester of pyrophosphoric acid. [PYROPHOSPH(ORIC ACID) + -ATE[2]]

py′ro·phos·phor′ic ac′id (pī′rō fos fôr′ik, -for′-, pī′-), *Chem.* a crystalline, water-soluble powder, $H_4P_2O_7$, formed by the union of one molecule of phosphorus pentoxide with two molecules of water. [PYRO- + PHOSPHORIC]

py·ro·pho·tom·e·ter (pī′rō fō tom′i tər), *n.* *Physics.* a form of pyrometer that measures temperature by optical or photometric means. [PYRO- + PHOTOMETER]

py·ro·phyl·lite (pī′rə fil′īt), *n.* a micalike mineral, hydrous aluminum silicate, $AlSi_2O_2(OH)_4$, usually having a white or greenish color, and occurring in either foliated or compact masses, the latter variety being used like soapstone. [< G *Pyrophyllit;* so called from its exfoliating when heated. See PYRO-, -PHYLL, -ITE[1]]

py′ro·ra·ce′mic ac′id (pī′rō rā sē′mik, -sem′ik, -rō rə-, pī′rō-), *Chem.* See **pyruvic acid.** [PYRO- + RACEMIC ACID]

py·ro·sis (pī rō′sis), *n.* *Pathol.* heartburn (def. 1). [< NL < Gk; see PYR, -OSIS]

py·ro·stat (pī′rə stat′), *n.* **1.** a thermostat for high temperatures. **2.** a safety device that, when a fire breaks out in its vicinity, automatically causes a mechanism to sound a warning alarm. [PYRO- + -STAT]

py·ro·sul·fate (pī′rə sul′fāt), *n.* *Chem.* a salt of pyrosulfuric acid. [PYROSULF(URIC) + -ATE[2]]

py·ro·sul·fu·ric (pī′rō sul fyo͝or′ik), *adj.* *Chem.* of or derived from pyrosulfuric acid; disulfuric. Also, **py′ro·sul·phu·ric.** [PYRO- + SULFURIC]

py′rosulfu′ric ac′id, *Chem.* an oily, hygroscopic, corrosive liquid, $H_2S_2O_7$, that, depending on purity, is colorless or dark brown: used chiefly as a dehydrating agent in the manufacture of explosives and as a sulfating or sulfonating agent in the manufacture of dyes. Also called **fuming sulfuric acid, oleum.**

py·ro·tech·nic (pī′rə tek′nik), *adj.* **1.** of or pertaining to pyrotechnics. **2.** pertaining to, resembling, or suggesting fireworks. Also, **py′ro·tech′ni·cal.** [PYRO- + TECHNIC] —**py′ro·tech′ni·cal·ly,** *adv.*

py·ro·tech·nics (pī′rə tek′niks), *n.* (*construed as sing. or pl.*) **1.** the art of making fireworks. **2.** the use of fireworks for display, military purposes, etc. **3.** a brilliant or sensational display, as of rhetoric, musicianship, etc. **4.** *Mil.* ammunition containing chemicals for producing smoke or light, as for signaling, illuminating, or screening. Also, **py′ro·tech′ny** (for defs. 1, 2). [PYRO- + TECHNICS]

py·ro·tech·nist (pī′rə tek′nist), *n.* one skilled in pyrotechnics. [PYROTECHN(ICS) + -IST]

py·ro·tox·in (pī′rə tok′sin), *n.* pyrogen. [PYRO- + TOXIN]

py·rox·ene (pī rok′sēn′), *n.* a very common group of minerals of many varieties, silicates of magnesium, iron, calcium, and other elements, occurring as important constituents of many kinds of rocks, esp. basic igneous rocks. [< F; see PYRO-, XENO-; orig. supposed to be a foreign substance when found in igneous rocks] —**py·rox·en·ic** (pī′rok sen′ik), *adj.*

py·rox·e·nite (pī rok′sə nīt′), *n.* any rock composed essentially, or in large part, of pyroxene of any kind. [PYROXENE + -ITE[1]]

py·rox·y·lin (pī rok′sə lin), *n.* a nitrocellulose compound containing fewer nitrate groups than guncotton, used in the manufacture of artificial silk, leather, oilcloth, etc. Also, **py·rox·y·line** (pī rok′sə lin, -lēn′). [PYRO- + XYL- + -IN[2]]

Pyr·rha (pir′ə), *n.* *Class. Myth.* a daughter of Epimetheus and the wife of Deucalion.

pyr·rhic[1] (pir′ik), *Pros.* —*adj.* **1.** consisting of two short or unaccented syllables. **2.** composed of or pertaining to pyrrhics. —*n.* **3.** Also called **dibrach.** a pyrrhic foot. [< L *pyrrhich(ius)* < Gk *pyrrhíchios* pertaining to the *pyrrhíchē* PYRRHIC[2]]

pyr·rhic[2] (pir′ik), *n.* **1.** an ancient Grecian warlike dance in which the motions of actual warfare were imitated. —*adj.* **2.** of, pertaining to, or denoting this dance. [< L *pyrrhicha* < Gk *pyrrhíchē* a dance; said to be named after Pyrrhichus, the inventor]

Pyr·rhic (pir′ik), *adj.* of, pertaining to, or resembling Pyrrhus, king of Epirus, or his costly victory. [PYRRH(US) + -IC]

Pyr′rhic vic′tory, a victory gained at too great a cost.

Pyr·rho (pir′ō), *n.* c365–c275 B.C., Greek philosopher.

Pyr·rho·nism (pir′ə niz′əm), *n.* **1.** the Skeptic doctrines of Pyrrho and his followers. **2.** extreme or absolute skepticism. [< Gk *Pýrrhōn* PYRRHO + -ISM] —**Pyr′rho·nist,** *n.* —**Pyr′rho·nis′tic,** *adj.*

pyr·rho·tite (pir′ə tīt′), *n.* a common mineral, iron sulfide, approximately FeS, occurring in massive and in crystal forms with a bronze color and metallic luster: generally slightly magnetic; iron pyrites. Also, **pyr·rho·tine** (pir′ə tēn′, -tin). [< Gk *pyrrhót(ēs)* redness + -ITE[1]]

pyr·rhu·lox·i·a (pir′ə lok′sē ə), *n.* a cardinallike grosbeak, *Pyrrhuloxia sinuata*, of the southwestern U.S. and Mexico, having a bill superficially resembling that of a parrot. [< NL *Pyrrhu(la)* finch genus (< Gk *pyrrhoúlas* a red bird, deriv. of *pyrrhós* red) + *Loxia* crossbill genus, equiv. to Gk *lox(ós)* oblique + *-ia* -IA]

Pyr·rhus (pir′əs), *n.* **1.** c318–272 B.C., king of Epirus c300–272. **2.** *Class. Myth.* Neoptolemus.

pyr·role (pi rōl′, pir′ōl), *n.* *Chem.* a colorless, toxic, liquid, five-membered ring compound, C_4H_5N, that is a component of chlorophyll, hemin, and many other important naturally occurring substances. [< Gk *pyr-r(hós)* red + -OLE] —**pyr·rol·ic** (pi rol′ik), *adj.*

pyr·rol·i·dine (pi rō′li dēn′, -din, -rol′i-), *n.* *Chem.* a colorless, water-soluble, unpleasant smelling, poisonous liquid, C_4H_9N, from which proline and certain alkaloids are derived, prepared by reducing pyrrole: used chiefly in organic synthesis. Also called **tetrahydropyrrole.** [PYRROLE + -ID[3] + -INE[2]]

py·ru·vic (pī ro͞o′vik, pi-), *adj.* *Chem.* of or derived from pyruvic acid. [PYR- + L *ūv(a)* grape + -IC]

pyru′vic ac′id, *Chem., Biochem.* a water-soluble liquid, $CH_3COCOOH$, important in many metabolic and fermentative processes, having an odor resembling that of acetic acid, prepared by the dehydration of tartaric acid: used chiefly in biochemical research. Also called **acetylformic acid, pyroracemic acid.**

pyru′vic al′dehyde, *Chem.* a yellow, liquid compound, CH_3COCHO, containing both an aldehyde and a ketone group, usually obtained in a polymeric form: used chiefly in organic synthesis. Also, **py·ruv·al·de·hyde** (pī ro͞o val′də hīd′, pir′o͞o-). Also called **methylglyoxal.**

Py·thag·o·ras (pi thag′ər əs), *n.* **1.** c582–c500 B.C., Greek philosopher, mathematician, and religious reformer. **2.** a walled plain in the second quadrant of the face of the moon: about 75 miles in diameter.

Py·thag·o·re·an (pi thag′ə rē′ən), *adj.* **1.** of or pertaining to Pythagoras, to his school, or to his doctrines. —*n.* **2.** a follower of Pythagoras. [< L *Pȳthagorē(us)* (< Gk *Pȳthagóreios* of Pythagoras) + -AN]

Py·thag·o·re·an·ism (pi thag′ə rē′ə niz′əm), *n.* the group of doctrines of Pythagoras and his followers, esp. that the universe is the manifestation of various combinations of mathematical ratios. [PYTHAGOREAN + -ISM]

Pythag′ore′an scale′, *Music.* the major scale as derived acoustically by Pythagoras from the perfect fifth.

Pythag′ore′an the′orem, *Geom.* the theorem that the square of the hypotenuse of a right triangle is equal to the sum of the squares of the other two sides.

Pyth·e·as (pith′ē əs), *n.* a crater in the second quadrant of the face of the moon: about 12 miles in diameter.

Pyth·i·a (pith′ē ə), *n.* *Gk. Myth.* the priestess of Apollo at Delphi who delivered the oracles. [< L < Gk, fem. of *Pȳ́thios* Pythian]

Pyth·i·ad (pith′ē ad′), *n.* the four-year period between two celebrations of the Pythian Games. [< Gk *Pythiad-* (s. of *Pythiás*)]

Pyth·i·an (pith′ē ən), *adj.* Also, **Pyth′ic.** **1.** of or pertaining to Delphi, in ancient Greece. **2.** of or pertaining to Apollo, with reference to his oracle at Delphi. —*n.* **3.** a Pythian priestess. [< L *Pȳthi(us)* (< Gk *Pȳ́thios* of Delphi and the oracle) + -AN]

Pyth′ian Games′, one of the great national festivals of ancient Greece, held every four years at Delphi in honor of Apollo.

Pyth·i·as (pith′ē əs), *n.* See **Damon and Pythias.**

Pyth·i·us (pith′ē əs), *n.* *Class. Myth.* Apollo: so called because he was the slayer of Python.

Py·tho (pī′thō), *n.* *Class. Myth.* Delphi (def. 1).

pyth·o·gen·ic (pī′thə jen′ik, pith′ə-), *adj.* originating from filth or putrescence. Also, **py·thog·e·nous** (pī thoj′ə nəs, pi-). [< Gk *pȳ́th(ein)* (to) rot + -o- + -GENIC] —**py′tho·gen′e·sis,** *n.*

py·thon[1] (pī′thon, -thən), *n.* **1.** a spirit or demon. **2.** a person who is possessed by a spirit and prophesies by its aid. [< LGk *pȳ́thon;* relation to PYTHON not clear]

py·thon[2] (pī′thon, -thən), *n.* any of several Old World constrictors of the family *Boidae*, of the subfamily *Pythoninae*, often growing to a length of more than 20 feet. [< NL; special use of PYTHON]

Py·thon (pī′thon, -thən), *n.* *Class. Myth.* a large dragon who guarded the chasm at Delphi from which prophetic vapors emerged. He was finally killed by Apollo, who established his oracle on the site.

py·tho·ness (pī′thə nis, pith′ə-), *n.* **1.** a woman supposed to be possessed by a soothsaying spirit, as the priestess of Apollo at Delphi. **2.** a woman with power of divination; a witch. [PYTHON[1] + -ESS; r. ME *phytonesse* < MF]

py·thon·ic[1] (pī thon′ik, pi-), *adj.* prophetic; oracular. [< L *pythōnic(us)* < Gk *pythōnikós* prophetic. See PYTHON[1], -IC]

py·thon·ic[2] (pī thon′ik, pi-), *adj.* **1.** of or pertaining to pythons. **2.** pythonlike. **3.** gigantic or monstrous. [PYTHON[2] + -IC]

py·u·ri·a (pī yo͝or′ē ə), *n.* *Pathol.* the presence of pus in the urine. [PY- + URIA]

pyx (piks), *n.* **1.** *Eccles.* **a.** the box or vessel in which the reserved Eucharist or Host is kept. **b.** a watch-shaped container for carrying the Eucharist to the sick. **2.** Also called **pyx′ chest′.** a box or chest at a mint, in which specimen coins are deposited and reserved for trial by weight and assay. Also, **pix.** [late ME *pyxe* < L *pyx(is)* < Gk *pyxís* a box, orig. made of boxwood]

Pyxidium of purslane

pyx·id·i·um (pik sid′ē əm), *n., pl.* **pyx·id·i·a** (pik sid′ē ə). *Bot.* a seed vessel which dehisces transversely, the top part acting as a lid, as in the purslane. [< NL < Gk *pyxídion* a little box, equiv. to *pyxid-* (s. of *pyxís*) a box + *-ion* dim. n. suffix]

pyx·ie (pik′sē), *n.* either of two trailing, shrubby, evergreen plants, *Pyxidanthera barbulata* or *P. brevifolia,* of the eastern U.S., having numerous small, starlike blossoms. [short for NL *Pyxidanthera,* equiv. to L *pyxid-* (s. of *pyxis*) box (see PYX) + NL *-anthera* ANTHER]

pyx·is (pik′sis), *n., pl.* **pyx·i·des** (pik′si dēz′). **1.** *Gk. and Rom. Antiq.* a box of a usually cylindrical shape having a lid with a knob in the center, used for toilet articles. **2.** pyx (def. 1). **3.** *Bot.* a pyxidium. [ME < L < Gk *pyxís* a box]

Pyx·is (pik′sis), *n., gen.* **Pyx·i·dis** (pik′si dis). *Astron.* the Compass, a southern constellation: one of the subordinate constellations into which Argo is now divided. [< L < Gk *pyxís* a box, PYX]

Pyx′is Nau′ti·ca (nô′ti kə), *gen.* **Pixidis Nau·ti·cae** (nô′ti kē′). Pyxis.

Q

Q, q (kyōō), *n., pl.* **Q's** or **Qs, q's** or **qs.** **1.** the seventeenth letter of the English alphabet, a consonant. **2.** any spoken sound represented by the letter *Q* or *q*, as in *quick, acquit, Iraq*, etc. **3.** something having the shape of a Q. **4.** a written or printed representation of the letter *Q* or *q*. **5.** a device, as a printer's type, for reproducing the letter *Q* or *q*.

Q, *Chess.* queen.

Q, **1.** the 17th in order or in a series, or, when *I* is omitted, the 16th. **2.** (*sometimes l.c.*) the medieval Roman numeral for 500. Cf. **Roman numerals. 3.** *Physics.* heat. **4.** *Electronics.* a measure of the effective operation of an electric circuit or component. **5.** *Biblical Criticism.* the symbol for material common to the Gospels of Matthew and Luke that was not derived from the Gospel of Mark. Also called **Q-factor** (for defs. 3, 4).

Q., **1.** quarto. **2.** Quebec. **3.** Queen. **4.** question. **5.** quetzal.

q., **1.** farthing. [< L *quadrans*] **2.** quart; quarts. **3.** query. **4.** question. **5.** quintal. **6.** quire.

q.2h., (in prescriptions) every two hours. [< L *quāque secundā hōrā*]

q.3h., (in prescriptions) every three hours. [< L *quāque tertiā hōrā*]

Qad·a·rite (kad′ə rīt′), *n. Islam.* a member of the Qadiriya. [< Ar *qadar(ī)* Qadarite (*qadar* fate + -*ī* suffix of appurtenance) + -ITE[1]]

Qa·dha·fi (kə dä′fē), *n.* **Mu·am·mar al-** (mōō ä′mär al), born 1942, Libyan army colonel; chief of state since 1969.

Qa·di·a·nis (kä′dē ä′nis), *n.* See under **Ahmadiya.**

Qa·dir·i·ya (kä′di rē′yä), *n. Islam.* a Sufi order founded in the 12th century, heretical in that it believed in freedom of the will. [< Ar, collective of *qadarī* Qadarite]

qāf (käf), *n.* the 21st letter of the Arabic alphabet, representing a uvular stop consonant sound. [< Ar]

qa·id (kä ēth′, kīth), *n.* caid.

Qa·ra Qum (kä rä′ kŏŏm′). See **Kara Kum.**

qa·si·da (kə sē′də), *n., pl.* **-da, -das.** *Pros.* an Arabic poem, usually in monorhyme, that may be satirical, elegiac, threatening, or laudatory. [< Ar *qaṣīdah*]

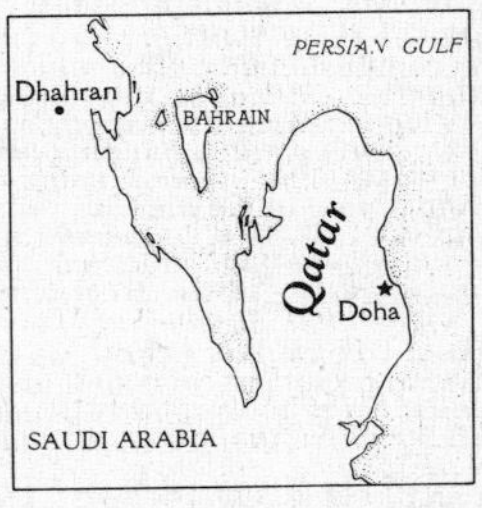

qat (kät), *n.* kat.

Qa·tar (kä′tär), *n.* **1.** a peninsula in E Arabia, in the Persian Gulf. **2.** a state coextensive with this peninsula: formerly under British protection. 100,000 (est. 1970); ab. 6000 sq. mi. *Cap.:* Doha. Also, **Katar.**

QB, *Chess.* queen's bishop.

Q.B., Queen's Bench.

Q.b., *Football.* quarterback.

QBP, *Chess.* queen's bishop's pawn.

Q.C., **1.** Quartermaster Corps. **2.** Queen's Counsel.

Q-Celt·ic (kyōō′sel′tik; *esp. Brit.*, kyōō′kel′tik), *n., adj.* Goidelic.

Q clearance, (in the Atomic Energy Commission) the highest level of security clearance, permitting access to secret information, documents, etc.

q.e., which is. [< L *quod est*]

Q.E.D., which was to be shown or demonstrated (used esp. in mathematical proofs). [< L *quod erat demonstrandum*]

Q.E.F., which was to be done. [< L *quod erat faciendum*]

Q.F., quick-firing.

Q-fac·tor (kyōō′fak′tər), *n.* Q (defs. 3, 4).

Q-fe·ver (kyōō′fē′vər), *n. Pathol.* a fever exhibiting pneumonialike symptoms, caused by the rickettsia *Coxiella burnetti.*

Q gauge. See **O gauge** (def. 2).

q.h., (in prescriptions) each hour; every hour. [< L *quāque hōrā*]

qib·la (kib′lə), *n.* kiblah.

q.i.d., (in prescriptions) four times a day. [< L *quater in die*]

qin·tar (kin tär′), *n.* a money of account of Albania, the 100th part of a lek. Also, **qin·dar** (kin där′). [< Albanian]

Qishm (kish′əm), *n.* an island S of and belonging to Iran, in the Strait of Hormuz. ab. 25,000; 68 mi. long.; ab. 510 sq. mi.

qi·yas (ki yäs′), *n. Islam.* judgment of an act or belief by application of established principles governing some analogous act or belief. Also, **kiyas.** [< Ar: analogy]

Qi·zil Qum (ki zil′ kŏŏm′). See **Kyzyl Kum.**

QKt, *Chess.* queen's knight.

QKtP, *Chess.* queen's knight's pawn.

ql., quintal.

q.l., (in prescriptions) as much as is desired. [< L *quantum libet*]

QM, Quartermaster. Also, **Q.M.**

QMC, Quartermaster Corps. Also, **Q.M.C.**

QMG, Quartermaster-General. Also, **Q.M.G., Q.M.Gen.**

QNP, *Chess.* queen's knight's pawn.

qoph (kôf), *n.* koph.

QP, *Chess.* queen's pawn.

q.p., (in prescriptions) as much as you please. Also, **q. pl.** [< L *quantum placet*]

Qq., quartos.

qq. hor., (in prescriptions) every hour. [< L *quāque hōrā*]

qq. v., which (words, things, etc.) see. [< L *quae vidē*]

QR, *Chess.* queen's rook.

qr., *pl.* **qrs.** **1.** farthing. [< L *quadrans*, pl. *quadrantes*] **2.** quarter. **3.** quire.

q.r., (in prescriptions) the quantity is correct. [< L *quantitum rectum*]

QRP, *Chess.* queen's rook's pawn.

q.s., **1.** (in prescriptions) as much as is sufficient; enough. [< L *quantum sufficit*] **2.** See **quarter section.**

qt., **1.** quantity. **2.** *pl.* **qt., qts.** quart.

q.t., **1.** *Slang.* quiet. **2. on the q.t.,** stealthily; secretly: *to meet someone on the q.t.*

qto., quarto.

qtr., **1.** quarter. **2.** quarterly.

qu., **1.** quart. **2.** quarter. **3.** quarterly. **4.** queen. **5.** query. **6.** question.

qua (kwā, kwä), *adv.* as; as being; in the character or capacity of: *The work of art qua art can be judged by aesthetic criteria only.* [< L, fem. abl. sing. of *qui* WHO]

quack[1] (kwak), *n.* **1.** the harsh, throaty cry of a duck or any similar sound. —*v.i.* **2.** to utter the cry of a duck or a sound resembling it. [imit. Cf. D *kwakken*, G *quacken*]

quack[2] (kwak), *n.* **1.** a fraudulent or ignorant pretender to medical skill. **2.** a person who pretends, professionally or publicly, to skill, knowledge, or qualifications that he does not possess; a charlatan. —*adj.* **3.** being a quack: *a quack psychologist who complicates everyone's problems.* **4.** presented falsely as having curative powers: *quack medicine.* **5.** of, pertaining to, or befitting a quack: *a quack prophet.* **6.** involving quackery: *quack methods.* —*v.i.* **7.** to play the quack. —*v.t.* **8.** to treat in the manner of a quack. **9.** to advertise or sell with fraudulent claims. [short for QUACKSALVER] —**quack′ish,** *adj.* —**quack′ish·ly,** *adv.* —**quack′ish·ness,** *n.* —**Syn. 2.** mountebank, phony.

quack·er·y (kwak′ə rē), *n., pl.* **-er·ies.** **1.** the practice or methods of a quack. **2.** an instance of this. [QUACK[2] + -ERY]

quack′ grass′, a couch grass, *Agropyron repens*, a pernicious weed in cultivated fields.

quack·sal·ver (kwak′sal′vər), *n.* **1.** a quack doctor. **2.** *Archaic.* a charlatan. [< early D; see QUACK[1] SALVE, -ER[1]]

quad[1] (kwod), *n. Informal.* a quadrangle, as on a college campus. [shortened form]

quad[2] (kwod), *n., v.,* **quad·ded, quad·ding.** *Print.* —*n.* **1.** Also called **quadrat.** a piece of type metal of less height than the lettered types, serving to cause a blank in printed matter, used for spacing. —*v.t.* **2.** to space out (matter) by means of quads. [short for QUADRAT]

quad[3] (kwod), *n. Chiefly Brit. Slang.* quod.

quad[4] (kwod), *n. Informal.* a quadruplet. [shortened form]

quad., quadrangle.

quadr-, var. of **quadri-** before a vowel: *quadrennial.*

quad·ra (kwod′rə), *n., pl.* **-rae** (-rē). *Archit.* a small molding, as a fillet. [< L: fillet]

quad·ra·ge·nar·i·an (kwod′rə jə nâr′ē ən), *adj.* **1.** 40 years of age. **2.** between the ages of 40 and 50. —*n.* **3.** a person who is 40 years old or whose age falls between 40 and 50. [< L *quadrāgēnāri(us)* consisting of forty (*quadrāgēn(i)* forty each + -*ārius* -ARY) + -AN]

Quad·ra·ges·i·ma (kwod′rə jes′ə mə), *n.* **1.** Also called **Quadrages′ima Sun′day.** the first Sunday in Lent. **2.** *Obs.* the 40 days of Lent. [< ML, short for L *quadrāgēsima dies* fortieth day]

Quad·ra·ges·i·mal (kwod′rə jes′ə məl), *adj.* **1.** of, pertaining to, or suitable for Lent; Lenten. **2.** (*sometimes l.c.*) lasting 40 days, as the fast of Lent. [QUADRAGESIM(A) + -AL[1]]

Quad·ra·ges·i·mo An·no (kwä′drä jā′sē mō′ ä′nō), *Latin.* Forty Years Later: opening words and the title of an encyclical of Pope Pius XI issued in 1931 on reconstructing the social order.

quad·ran·gle (kwod′raŋ′gəl), *n.* **1.** a plane figure having four angles and four sides, as a square. **2.** a square or quadrangular space or court that is surrounded by a building or buildings, as on a college campus. **3.** the building or buildings around such a space or court. **4.** the area shown on one of the standard topographic sheets of the U.S. Geological Survey (approximately 17 miles north to south and from 11 to 15 miles east to west). [ME < LL *quadrangul(um)* (neut.), lit., four-cornered (thing). See QUADR-, ANGLE] —**quad′ran′gled,** *adj.*

quad·ran·gu·lar (kwo draŋ′gyə lər), *adj.* having four angles and four sides; having the shape of a quadrangle. [< LL *quadrangulār(is)*, equiv. to *quadrangul(um)* QUADRANGLE + -*āris* -AR[1]] —**quad·ran′gu·lar·ly,** *adv.* —**quad·ran′gu·lar·ness,** *n.*

quad·rans (kwod′ranz), *n., pl.* **quad·ran·tes** (kwod-ran′tēz). a bronze coin of ancient Rome, the fourth part of an as. [< L: lit., fourth part]

quad·rant (kwod′rənt), *n.* **1.** a quarter of a circle; an arc of 90°. **2.** the area included between such an arc and two radii drawn one to each extremity. **3.** something shaped like a quarter of a circle, as a part of a machine. **4.** *Geom.* one of the four parts into which a plane is divided by two perpendicular lines. **5.** an instrument, usually containing a graduated arc of 90°, used in astronomy, navigation, etc., for measuring altitudes. **6.** *Furniture.* one of two metal sliding pieces, of quadrant form, used to support the fall front of a desk from above. [ME < L *quadrant-* (s. of *quadrāns*) fourth part] —**quad·ran·tal** (kwo dran′tᵊl), *adj.* —**quad′rant·like′,** *adj.*

quad·ra·phon·ic (kwod′rə fon′ik), *adj.* of, noting, or pertaining to the recording and reproduction of sound over four separate transmission channels instead of the customary two of the stereo system: *quadraphonic records.* Also, **quad·ri·phon·ic** (kwod′rə fon′ik), **quad·ro·phon·ic** (kwod′rə fon′ik). [alter. QUADRI + PHONIC]

quad·rat (kwod′rət), *n.* **1.** *Print.* quad[2] (def. 1). **2.** *Ecol.* a square or rectangular plot of land marked off for the study of plants and animals. [var. of QUADRATE]

quad·rate (*adj., n.* kwod′rit, -rāt; *v.* kwod′rāt), *adj., n., v.,* **-rat·ed, -rat·ing.** —*adj.* **1.** square or rectangular. **2.** *Zool.* of or pertaining to the quadrate. **3.** *Heraldry.* (of a cross) having an enlarged square at the junction of the limbs: *a cross quadrate.* —*n.* **4.** a square. **5.** something square or rectangular. **6.** *Zool.* one of a pair of bones in the skulls of many lower vertebrates, to which the lower jaw is articulated. —*v.t.* **7.** to cause to conform or harmonize; adapt. —*v.i.* **8.** to agree; conform. [ME *quadrat* < L *quadrāt(us)* (ptp. of *quadrāre* to make square)]

quad·rat·ic (kwo drat′ik), *adj.* **1.** square. **2.** *Algebra.* involving the square and no higher power of the unknown quantity; of the second degree. —*n.* **3.** a quadratic polynomial or equation. [QUADRATE + -IC] —**quad·rat′i·cal·ly,** *adv.*

quadrat′ic form′, *Math.* a polynomial of second degree with no constant term.

quadrat′ic for′mula, *Math.* the formula for determining the roots of a quadratic equation from its coefficients: $x = \frac{-b \pm \sqrt{b^2 - 4ac}}{2a}$ for the general equation $ax^2 + bx + c = 0$.

quadrat′ic res′idue, *Math.* a number x that is relatively prime to a given integer y and for which a number z exists whose square gives the same remainder as x when divided by y.

quad·rat·ics (kwo drat′iks), *n.* (*construed as sing.*) the branch of algebra that deals with quadratic equations. [see QUADRATIC, -ICS]

quad·ra·ture (kwod′rə chər), *n.* **1.** the act of squaring. **2.** *Math.* **a.** the act or process of finding a square equal in area to a given surface, esp. a surface bounded by a curve. **b.** the act or process of finding an area or calculating an integral, esp. by numerical methods. **c.** a definite integral. **3.** *Astron.* **a.** the situation of two heavenly bodies when their longitudes differ by 90°. **b.** either of the two points in the orbit of a body, as the moon, midway between the syzygies. **c.** (of the moon) those points or moments at which a half moon is visible. [< L *quadrātūra,* equiv. to *quadrāt(us)* (ptp. of *quadrāre;* see QUADRATE) + *-ūra* -URE]

quad′rature of the cir′cle, *Math.* the insoluble problem of constructing, by the methods of Euclidean geometry, a square equal in area to a given circle. Also called **squaring the circle.**

quad·rel (kwod′rəl), *n.* a square stone, brick, or tile. [< It *quadrello* < VL **quadrellum,* equiv. to L *quadr(um)* square + *-ellum* dim. suffix]

quad·ren·ni·al (kwo dren′ē əl), *adj.* **1.** occurring every four years: *a quadrennial festival.* **2.** of or for four years: *a quadrennial period.* —*n.* **3.** an event occurring every four years, as an anniversary or its celebration. [earlier *quadriennial* < L *quadrienni(s)* + -AL[1]] —**quad·ren′ni·al·ly,** *adv.*

quad·ren·ni·um (kwo dren′ē əm), *n., pl.* **quad·ren·ni·ums, quad·ren·ni·a** (kwo dren′ē ə). a period of four years. [< NL, alter. of L *quadriennium*]

quadri-, a learned borrowing from Latin meaning "four," used in the formation of compound words: *quadriceps.* Also, *esp. before a vowel,* **quadr-.** [< L; cf. *quattuor* four]

quad·ric (kwod′rik), *Math.* —*adj.* **1.** of the second degree (said esp. of functions with more than two variables). —*n.* **2.** a quadric function. **3.** a surface such as an ellipsoid or paraboloid as defined by a second-degree equation in three real variables. [QUADR- + -IC]

quad·ri·cen·ten·ni·al (kwod′ri sen ten′ē əl), *adj.* **1.** of, pertaining to, or marking the completion of, a period of four hundred years. —*n.* **2.** a quadricentennial anniversary. **3.** its celebration. [QUADRI- + CENTENNIAL]

quad·ri·ceps (kwod′ri seps′), *n., pl.* **-ceps·es** (-sep′siz), **-ceps.** *Anat.* a large muscle in front of the thigh, the action of which extends the leg or bends the hip joint. [< NL, equiv. to *quadri-* QUADRI- + *-ceps* (as in *biceps*)] —**quad·ri·cip·i·tal** (kwod′ri sip′i tᵊl), *adj.*

quad′ric sur′face, a three-dimensional surface whose equation is a quadratic equation.

quad·ri·cy·cle (kwod′ri sī′kəl), *n.* a vehicle similar to the bicycle and tricycle but having four wheels. [QUADRI- + CYCLE] —**quad′ri·cy′cler, quad′ri·cy′clist,** *n.*

quad·ri·fid (kwod′rə fid), *adj.* cleft into four parts or lobes. [< L *quadrifid(us).* See QUADRI-, -FID]

quad·ri·ga (kwo drī′gə), *n., pl.* **-gae** (-jē). *Class. Antiq.* a two-wheeled chariot drawn by four horses harnessed abreast. Cf. **biga, triga.** [< L, earlier pl. *quadrigae,* contr. of *quadrijugae* a team of four; cf. QUADRI-, YOKE]

quad·ri·ga·tus (kwod′rə gā′təs), *n., pl.* **-ti** (-tī). a silver coin of ancient Rome, bearing an image of Jupiter in a quadriga on the reverse. [< L, equiv. to *quadrīg(a)* QUADRIGA + *-ātus;* see -ATE[1]]

quad·ri·lat·er·al (kwod′rə lat′ər əl), *adj.* **1.** having four sides. —*n.* **2.** a plane figure having four sides and four angles. **3.** something of this form. **4.** *Geom.* **a.** a figure formed by four straight lines which have six points of intersection. **b.** a polygon with four sides. **5.** the space enclosed between and defended by four fortresses. [< L *quadrilater(us)* four-sided + -AL[1]. See QUADRI-, LATERAL] —**quad′ri·lat′er·al·ly,** *adv.* —**quad′ri·lat′er·al·ness,** *n.*

A B

Quadrilaterals
A, Simple (def. 2)
B, Complete (def. 4a)

quad′rilat′eral spin′naker, *Naut.* shadow (def. 16).

quad·ri·lin·gual (kwod′rə ling′gwəl), *adj.* using or involving four languages: *a quadrilingual person; a quadrilingual translation of the Bible.* [QUADRI- + LINGUAL]

qua·drille[1] (kwə dril′, kə-), *n.* **1.** a square dance for four couples, consisting of five parts or movements, each complete in itself. **2.** the music for such a dance. [< F < Sp *cuadrilla* company, troop, dim. of *cuadra* square < L *quadra*]

qua·drille[2] (kwə dril′, kə-), *n.* a game at cards played by four persons. [< F < Sp *cuartillo,* dim. of *cuarto* fourth < L *quartus*]

quad·ril·lion (kwo dril′yən), *n., pl.* **-lions,** (*as after a numeral*) **-lion,** *adj.* —*n.* **1.** a cardinal number represented in the U.S. and France by one followed by 15 zeros, and, in Great Britain and Germany, by one followed by 24 zeros. —*adj.* **2.** amounting to one quadrillion in number. [QUADR- + *-illion* (as in *million*)] —**quad·ril′lionth,** *n., adj.*

quad·ri·no·mi·al (kwod′rə nō′mē əl), *Algebra.* —*adj.* **1.** consisting of four terms. —*n.* **2.** a quadrinomial expression. [QUADRI- + (BI)NOMIAL]

quad·ri·par·tite (kwod′rə pär′tīt), *adj.* **1.** divided into or consisting of four parts. **2.** involving four participants: *a quadripartite treaty.* [ME < L *quadripartīt(us).* See QUADRI-, PARTITE] —**quad′ri·par′tite·ly,** *adv.*

quad·ri·ple·gi·a (kwod′rə plē′jē ə), *n.* *Pathol.* paralysis of all four limbs. Also called **tetraplegia.** [< NL; see QUADRI-, -PLEGIA]

quad·ri·pleg·ic (kwod′rə plē′jik, -plej′ik), *n.* *Pathol.* a person with quadriplegia. [QUADRIPLEG(IA) + -IC]

quad·ri·reme (kwä′drə rēm′), *n.* (in classical antiquity) a galley having four banks of oars. [< L *quadrirem(is),* equiv. to *quadri-* QUADRI- + *-rēmis* (deriv. of *remus* oar)]

quad·ri·sect (kwod′ri sekt′), *v.t.* to divide (something) into four equal parts. [QUADRI- + -SECT] —**quad′ri·sec′tion,** *n.*

quad·ri·syl·la·ble (kwod′ri sil′ə bəl), *n.* a word of four syllables. [QUADRI- + SYLLABLE] —**quad·ri·syl·lab·ic** (kwod′ri si lab′ik), **quad′ri·syl·lab′i·cal,** *adj.*

quad·ri·va·lent (kwod′rə vā′lənt, kwo driv′ə-), *adj.* *Chem.* **1.** having a valence of four; tetravalent. **2.** exercising four different valences, as antimony with valences of 5, 4, 3, and −3. [QUADRI- + -VALENT] —**quad′ri·va′lence, quad′ri·va′len·cy,** *n.* —**quad′ri·va′lent·ly,** *adv.*

quad·riv·i·al (kwo driv′ē əl), *adj.* **1.** having four ways or roads meeting in a point. **2.** (of ways or roads) leading in four directions. [ME < ML *quadriviāl(is),* equiv. to L *quadrivi(um)* QUADRIVIUM + *-ālis* -AL[1]]

quad·riv·i·um (kwo driv′ē əm), *n., pl.* **quad·riv·i·a** (kwo driv′ē ə). (during the Middle Ages) the more advanced division of the seven liberal arts, comprising arithmetic, geometry, astronomy, and music. Cf. **trivium.** [< LL, special use of L *quadrivium* place where four ways meet]

quad·roon (kwo dro͞on′), *n.* a person who is one-fourth Negro, one of the grandparents being Negro and the three others white; the offspring of a mulatto and a white person. [< Sp *cuarterón,* deriv. of *cuarto* fourth < L *quartus*]

quad·ru·mane (kwod′ro͝o mān′), *n.* a quadrumanous animal, as a monkey. [< NL *quadrumana,* equiv. to *quadru-* (see QUADRI-) + *-mana* (< L *manus* hand)]

quad·ru·ma·nous (kwo dro͞o′mə nəs), *adj.* four-handed; having all four feet adapted for use as hands, as animals of the monkey kind. [< NL *quadrumanus*]

quad·rum·vi·rate (kwo drum′və rit, -rāt′), *n.* a governing or managing group, coalition, or the like, of four men. [QUADR- + *-umvirate* (as in TRIUMVIRATE)]

quad·ru·ped (kwod′ro͝o ped′), *adj.* **1.** four-footed. —*n.* **2.** an animal, esp. a mammal, having four feet. [< L *quadruped-* (s. of *quadrupēs*), equiv. to *quadru-* (see QUADRI-) + *-ped-* -PED] —**quad·ru·pe·dal** (kwo dro͞o′pi dᵊl, kwod′ro͝o ped′ᵊl), *adj.* —**quad′ru·ped′ism,** *n.*

quad·ru·ple (kwo dro͞o′pəl, kwod′ro͝o-), *adj., n., v.,* **-pled, -pling.** —*adj.* **1.** fourfold; consisting of four parts: *a quadruple alliance.* **2.** four times as great. **3.** *Music.* having four beats to a measure. —*n.* **4.** a number, amount, etc., four times as great as another. —*v.t., v.i.* **5.** to make or become four times as great: *For an extra large cake, quadruple the ingredients. My savings quadrupled in 20 years.* [ME < L *quadrupl(us)*] —**quad·ru′ple·ness,** *n.* —**quad·ru′ply,** *adv.*

quadru′ple coun′terpoint, *Music.* invertible counterpoint involving four transposable voices.

quad·ru·ple-ex·pan·sion (kwo dro͞o′pəl ik span′shən, kwod′ro͝o-), *adj.* noting a power source, esp. a steam engine, using the same fluid at four successive stages of expansion to do work in four or more cylinders.

quadru′ple fugue′, *Music.* **1.** a fugue having four subjects developed simultaneously. **2.** a fugue having a subject and three countersubjects developed at first individually and finally together.

quad·ru·plet (kwo drup′lit, -dro͞o′plit, kwod′ro͝o plit), *n.* **1.** any group or combination of four. **2. quadruplets,** four children born of one pregnancy. **3.** one of four such children. **4.** *Music.* a group of four notes of equal value performed in the time normally taken for three. [QUADRUPLE + -ET (modeled on *triplet*)]

quadru′ple time′, **1.** a measure consisting of four beats or pulses with accent on the first and third. **2.** the rhythm created by use of this measure.

quad·ru·plex (kwod′ro͝o pleks′, kwo dro͞o′pleks), *adj.* **1.** fourfold; quadruple. **2.** noting or pertaining to a system of telegraphy by which four messages may be transmitted simultaneously over one wire or communications channel. [< L; see QUADRI-, PLEXUS] —**quad·ru·plic·i·ty** (kwod′ro͝o plis′i tē), *n.*

quad·ru·pli·cate (*v.* kwo dro͞o′plə kāt′; *adj., n.* kwo dro͞o′plə kit, -kāt′), *v.,* **-cat·ed, -cat·ing,** *adj., n.* —*v.t.* **1.** to make fourfold; quadruple. —*adj.* **2.** fourfold; quadruple. —*n.* **3.** one of four identical things. [< L *quadruplicāt(us)* (ptp. of *quadruplicāre*), equiv. to *quadruplic-* (s. of *quadruplex* QUADRUPLEX) + *-ātus* -ATE[1]] —**quad·ru′pli·ca′tion, quad·ru·pli·ca·ture** (kwo dro͞o′plə kə chər), *n.*

quae·re (kwēr′ē), *v. imperative.* **1.** ask; inquire (used to introduce or suggest a question). —*n.* **2.** a query or question. [< L, 2nd person sing. impv. of *quaerere* to seek, ask]

quaes·tor (kwes′tər, kwē′stər), *n.* *Rom. Hist.* **1.** one of two subordinates of the consuls serving as public prosecutors in certain criminal cases. **2.** (later) one of the public magistrates in charge of the state funds, as treasury officers or those attached to the consuls and provincial governors. Also, **questor.** [ME *questor* < L *quaestor,* equiv. to *quaest(us)* (ptp. of *quaerere* to seek) + *-or* -OR[2]] —**quaes·to·ri·al** (kwe stōr′ē əl, -stôr′-, kwē-), *adj.* —**quaes′tor·ship′,** *n.*

quaff (kwäf, kwaf, kwôf), *v.i.* **1.** to drink a beverage, esp. an intoxicating one, copiously and with hearty enjoyment. —*v.t.* **2.** to drink (a beverage) copiously and heartily: *We spent the whole evening quaffing ale.* —*n.* **3.** act or instance of quaffing. **4.** the beverage quaffed. [?] —**quaff′er,** *n.*

quag (kwag, kwog), *n.* a quagmire. [?]

quag·ga (kwag′ə), *n.* an extinct, equine mammal, *Equus quagga,* of southern Africa, related to and resembling the zebra, but striped only on the fore part of the body and the head. [< SAfrD (now obs.) < Zulu, ?, deriv. of *quag* striped]

quag·gy (kwag′ē, kwog′ē), *adj.,* **-gi·er, -gi·est.** **1.** of the nature of or resembling a quagmire; marshy; boggy. **2.** soft or flabby: *quaggy flesh.* [QUAG + -Y[1]] —**quag′gi·ness,** *n.*

quag·mire (kwag′mīᵊr′, kwog′-), *n.* **1.** an area of miry or boggy ground whose surface yields under the tread; a bog. **2.** a situation from which extrication is very difficult: *a quagmire of financial indebtedness.* **3.** anything soft or flabby. [QUAG + MIRE] —**quag′mir′y,** *adj.*

qua·hog (kwô′hog, -hôg, kwə hog′, -hôg′), *n.* an edible clam, *Venus mercenaria,* found along the Atlantic coast, having a relatively thick shell. Also, **qua′haug.** [< AmerInd (Narragansett), aph. var. of *poquauhock*]

quaich (kwāᴋʜ), *n.* a Scottish drinking cup of the 17th and 18th centuries having a shallow bowl with two or three flat handles. [< ScotGael *cuach*]

Quai d'Or·say (ke dôr se′), **1.** the quay along the south bank of the Seine in Paris, on which are located the department of foreign affairs and other French government offices. **2.** the Foreign Office of the French government.

quail[1] (kwāl), *n., pl.* **quails,** (*esp. collectively*) **quail.** **1.** a small, migratory, gallinaceous game bird, *Coturnix coturnix,* of the Old World. **2.** any of several other birds of the genus *Coturnix* and allied genera. **3.** any of various New World, gallinaceous game birds of the genus *Colinus* and allied genera, esp. the bobwhite. [ME *quaille* < OF < Gmc; cf. D *kwakkel* quail, MD, MLG *quackele;* akin to QUACK[1]] —**quail′like′,** *adj.*

Bobwhite quail,
Colinus virginianus
(Length 9 in.)

quail[2] (kwāl), *v.i.* to lose heart or courage in difficulty or danger; shrink with fear. [ME: to fail] —**Syn.** recoil, flinch, blench, cower.

quail-brush (kwāl′brush′), *n.* a salt-tolerant, silvery gray shrub, *Atriplex breweri,* of southern California.

quail′ clock′, a clock which announces the hours by a sound resembling that of a quail.

quail′ dove′, any of several tropical American pigeons of the genera *Starnoenas, Oreopelia,* or *Geotrygon.*

quaint (kwānt), *adj.* **1.** strange, peculiar, or unusual in an interesting, pleasing, or amusing way: *a quaint sense of humor.* **2.** having an old-fashioned attractiveness or charm; oddly picturesque: *a quaint old house.* **3.** skillfully or cleverly made. **4.** *Archaic.* wise; skilled. **5.** *Obs.* sly; crafty. [ME *queinte* < OF, var. of *cointe* clever, pleasing << L *cognitus* known (ptp. of *cognoscere*)] —**quaint′ly,** *adv.* —**quaint′ness,** *n.* —**Syn. 1.** curious, unusual, uncommon. **2.** antiquated, archaic. —**Ant. 1.** ordinary.

quake (kwāk), *v.,* **quaked, quak·ing,** *n.* —*v.i.* **1.** (of persons) to shake or tremble from cold, weakness, fear, anger, or the like: *He spoke boldly even though his legs were quaking.* **2.** (of things) to shake or tremble, as from shock, internal convulsion, or instability: *The earth suddenly began to quake.* —*n.* **3.** an earthquake. **4.** a trembling or tremulous agitation. [ME; OE *cwacian* to shake, tremble] —**quak′ing·ly,** *adv.* —**Syn. 1.** shudder, tremble. See **shiver. 2.** quiver. **3.** temblor.

quake′ grass′, a Eurasian grass, *Bromus brizaeformis,* naturalized in the U.S., having many oblong, flattened spikelets.

Quak·er (kwā′kər), *n.* a member of the Society of Friends. (The term *Quaker* is not used by members of the group). Also, *referring to a woman,* **Quak·er·ess** (kwā′kər is). [QUAKE + -ER[1]] —**Quak′er·ish, Quak′er·like′,** *adj.*

Quak′er gun′, a dummy gun, as on a ship or fort (so called in allusion to the Quakers' opposition to war).

Quak·er·ism (kwā′kə riz′əm), *n.* the beliefs, principles, and practices of Quakers. [QUAKER + -ISM]

Quak·er-la·dies (kwā′kər lā′dēz), *n.* (*construed as pl.*) bluet (def. 2).

Quak·er·ly (kwā′kər lē), *adj.* **1.** like a Quaker. —*adv.* **2.** in the manner of the Quakers. [QUAKER + -LY]

Quak′er meet′ing, **1.** a meeting of Quakers, at which all members, except those moved to speak, remain silent. **2.** *Informal.* a gathering at which there is considerable silence.

Quak·er·town (kwā′kər toun′), *n.* a town in SE Pennsylvania. 6305 (1960).

quak′ing as′pen. See under **aspen** (def. 1).

quak·y (kwā′kē), *adj.,* **quak·i·er, quak·i·est.** tending to quake; shaky or tremulous. [QUAKE + -Y[1]] —**quak′i·ly,** *adv.* —**quak′i·ness,** *n.*

qual·i·fi·ca·tion (kwol′ə fə kā′shən), *n.* **1.** a quality, accomplishment, etc., which fits a person for some function, office, or the like. **2.** a circumstance or condition required by law or custom for getting, having, or exercising a right, holding an office, or the like. **3.** act of qualifying; state of being qualified. **4.** modification, limitation, or restriction: *to endorse a plan without qualification.* **5.** an instance of this: *He protected his argument with several qualifications.* [< ML *quālificātiōn-* (s. of *quālificātio*), equiv. to *quālificāt(us)* (ptp. of *quālificāre* to QUALIFY) + *-iōn-* -ION]

qual·i·fi·ca·tor (kwol′ə fə kā′tər), *n.* *Rom. Cath. Ch.* (in an ecclesiastical court) an officer charged with examining cases and preparing them for trial. [< ML, equiv. to *quālificāt(us)* (ptp. of *quālificāre* to QUALIFY) + *-or* -OR[2]]

qual·i·fied (kwol′ə fīd′), *adj.* **1.** having the qualities, accomplishments, etc., which fit one for some function, office, or the like. **2.** having the qualities, accomplishments, etc., required by law or custom for getting, having, or exercising a right, holding an office, or the like. **3.** modified, limited, or restricted in some way: *a qualified endorsement.* [QUALIFY + -ED[2]] —**qual′i·fied′ly,** *adv.* —**qual′i·fied′ness,** *n.* —**Syn. 1.** able, capable, competent, fitted. —**Ant.** unqualified.

qual·i·fi·er (kwol′ə fī′ər), *n.* **1.** one who or that which qualifies. **2.** *Gram.* a word which qualifies the meaning of another, as an adjective or adverb; a modifier. [QUALIFY + -ER[1]]

qual·i·fy (kwol′ə fī′), *v.,* **-fied, -fy·ing.** —*v.t.* **1.** to provide with proper or necessary skills, knowledge, credentials, etc.; make competent: *to qualify oneself for a job.* **2.** to attribute some quality or qualities to; characterize, call, or name: *She cannot qualify his attitude as either rational or irrational.* **3.** to modify or limit in some way; make less strong or positive: *to qualify an endorsement.* **4.** *Gram.* to modify. **5.** to make less violent, severe, or unpleasant; moderate; mitigate. **6.** to modify or alter

the flavor or strength of: *He qualified his coffee with a few drops of brandy.* —*v.i.* **7.** to be fitted or competent for something. **8.** to get authority, license, power, etc., as by fulfilling required conditions, taking an oath, etc. **9.** *Sports.* to demonstrate the required ability in an initial or preliminary contest: *He qualified in the heat races.* **10.** to fire a rifle or pistol on a target range for a score high enough to achieve a rating of marksman, sharpshooter, or expert. **11.** *Mil.* to pass a practical test in gunnery. **12.** *Law.* to perform the actions necessary to acquire legal power or capacity: *By filing a bond and taking an oath he qualified as executor.* [< ML *quālificāre*, equiv. to L *quāl(is)* of what sort + *-ificāre* -IFY] —**qual′i·fi′a·ble,** *adj.* —**qual·i·fi·ca·to·ry** (kwol′ə fə kā′tə rē, -kə tôr′ē, -tôr′ē), *adj.* —**qual′i·fy′ing·ly,** *adv.*
—**Syn. 1.** fit, suit, adapt, prepare, equip. **2.** designate, label. **4.** narrow, restrict. See **modify. 6.** meliorate, soften, temper, reduce, diminish.

qua·lim·e·ter (kwə lim′i tər), *n.* penetrometer (def. 1). [QUALI(TY) + -METER]

qual·i·ta·tive (kwol′i tā′tiv), *adj.* pertaining to or concerned with quality or qualities. [< LL *quālitātīv(us)*, equiv. to *quālitāt-* (s. of *quālitās*) QUALITY + *-īvus* -IVE] —**qual′i·ta′tive·ly,** *adv.*

qual′itative anal′ysis, *Chem.* the analysis of a substance in order to ascertain the nature of its constituents. Cf. **quantitative analysis.**

qual·i·ty (kwol′i tē), *n., pl.* **-ties.** **1.** a characteristic, property, or attribute: *the chemical qualities of alcohol.* **2.** character or nature, as belonging to or distinguishing a thing: *the quality of sound.* **3.** character with respect to excellence, fineness, etc., or grade of excellence: *food of poor quality; silks of fine quality.* **4.** high grade; superior excellence: *wood grain of quality.* **5.** native excellence or superiority. **6.** an accomplishment or attainment. **7.** good or high social position: *a man of quality.* **8.** the superiority or distinction associated with high social position. **9.** *Acoustics.* the texture of a tone, dependent on its overtone content, which distinguishes it from others of the same pitch and loudness. **10.** *Phonet.* the tonal color, or timbre, that characterizes a particular vowel sound. **11.** *Logic.* the character of a proposition as affirmative or negative. **12.** (in saturated steam) the percentage of vapor by weight. **13.** *Archaic.* **a.** social status or position. **b.** a person of high social position: *He's quality, that one is.* —*adj.* **14.** of or having superior quality: *quality paper.* **15.** of or occupying high social status: *quality ladies.* [ME *qualite* < OF < L *quālitās*, equiv. to *quāl(is)* of what sort + *-itās* -ITY] —**qual′i·ty·less,** *adj.*
—**Syn. 1.** trait, character, feature. QUALITY, ATTRIBUTE, PROPERTY agree in meaning a particular characteristic (of a person or thing). A QUALITY is a characteristic, innate or acquired, which, in some particular, determines the nature and behavior of a person or thing: *naturalness as a quality; the quality of meat.* An ATTRIBUTE was originally a quality attributed, usually to a person or something personified; more recently it has meant a fundamental or innate characteristic: *an attribute of God; attributes of a logical mind.* PROPERTY applies only to things; it means a characteristic belonging specifically in the constitution of, or found (invariably) in, the behavior of a thing: *physical properties of uranium or of limestone.* **3.** nature, kind, grade, sort, condition.

qual′ity control′, a system for verifying and maintaining a desired level of quality in a product or process by careful planning, use of proper equipment, continued inspection, and corrective action where required.

qualm (kwäm, kwôm), *n.* **1.** an uneasy feeling or pang of conscience as to conduct; compunction: *He has no qualms about lying.* **2.** a sudden feeling of apprehensive uneasiness; misgiving: *a sudden qualm about the success of the venture.* **3.** a sudden sensation or onset of faintness or illness, esp. of nausea. [?]

qualm·ish (kwä′mish, kwô′-), *adj.* **1.** tending to have, or having, qualms. **2.** nauseous; nauseated. **3.** of the nature of a qualm. **4.** likely to cause qualms. [QUALM + -ISH[1]] —**qualm′ish·ly,** *adv.* —**qualm′ish·ness,** *n.*

quam·ash (kwom′ash, kwə mash′), *n.* camass.

quam lib·et (kwäm′ lib′et), (in prescriptions) as much as you wish. [< L]

Qua·nah (kwä′nə), *n.* a town in N Texas. 4564 (1960).

quan·da·ry (kwon′də rē, -drē), *n., pl.* **-ries.** a state of perplexity or uncertainty, esp. as to what to do; a dilemma. [? < L *quand(ō)* when + *-āre* inf. suffix]
—**Syn.** See **predicament.**

quand même (käɴ mem′), *French.* nevertheless; all the same.

quan·dong (kwon′dong′), *n.* **1.** a santalaceous tree, *Fusanus acuminatus*, of Australia, bearing an edible drupaceous fruit whose seed has an edible kernel. **2.** the fruit, or the seed or nut. Also, **quan′dang′, quantong.** [< native Austral]

quan·do·que bo·nus dor·mi·tat Ho·me·rus (kwän-dō′kwe bō′nōōs dôʀ mē′tät hō mā′rōōs), *Latin.* even good Homer sometimes nods. Horace, *Ars Poetica.*

quant (kwant, kwont), *Brit.* —*n.* **1.** a pole having a flange near its tip, used for punting. —*v.t., v.i.* **2.** to punt. [late ME < L *cont(us)* < Gk *kontós* kind of pole]

quan·ta (kwon′tə), *n.* pl. of **quantum.**

quan·tic (kwon′tik), *n.* *Math.* a rational, integral, homogeneous function of two or more variables. [< L *quant(us)* how much + -IC]

quan·ti·fi·er (kwon′tə fī′ər), *n.* **1.** *Logic.* an expression, as "all" or "some," that indicates the quantity of a proposition. Cf. **existential quantifier, universal quantifier. 2.** a word, esp. a modifier, that indicates the quantity of something. [QUANTIFY + -ER[1]]

quan·ti·fy (kwon′tə fī′), *v.t.,* **-fied, -fy·ing.** **1.** to determine, indicate, or express the quantity of. **2.** *Logic.* to make explicit the quantity of (a proposition). **3.** to give quantity to (something previously regarded as having only quality). [< ML *quantificāre*, equiv. to *quant(us)* how much + *-ificāre* -IFY] —**quan′ti·fi′a·ble,** *adj.* —**quan′ti·fi′a·bly,** *adv.* —**quan′ti·fi·ca′tion,** *n.*

quan·tile (kwon′tīl, -til), *n.* *Statistics.* one of the class of values of a variate that divides the total frequency of a sample or population into a given number of equal proportions. Cf. **percentile, quartile.** [QUANT(ITY) + *-ile* n. suffix]

quan·ti·ta·tive (kwon′ti tā′tiv), *adj.* **1.** that is or may be estimated by quantity. **2.** of or pertaining to the describing or measuring of quantity. **3.** of or pertaining to a metrical system, as that of classical verse, based on the alternation of long and short, rather than accented and unaccented, syllables. **4.** of or pertaining to the length of a spoken vowel or consonant. [< ML *quantitātīv(us)*, equiv. to L *quantitāt-* (s. of *quantitās*) QUANTITY + *-īvus* -IVE] —**quan′ti·ta′tive·ly,** *adv.* —**quan′ti·ta′tive·ness, quan′ti·tive·ness,** *n.*

quan′titative anal′ysis, *Chem.* the analysis of a substance to determine the amounts and proportions of its constituents. Cf. **qualitative analysis.**

quan·ti·ty (kwon′ti tē), *n., pl.* **-ties.** **1.** a particular, indefinite, or considerable amount of anything: *a small quantity of milk; the ocean's vast quantity of fish.* **2.** amount or measure: *She mixed the ingredients in the quantities called for.* **3.** considerable or great amount: *to extract ore in quantity.* **4.** *Math.* **a.** the property of magnitude involving comparability with other magnitudes. **b.** something having magnitude, or size, extent, amount, or the like. **c.** magnitude, size, volume, area, or length. **5.** *Music.* the length or duration of a note. **6.** *Logic.* the character of a proposition as singular, universal, particular, or mixed, according to the presence or absence of certain kinds of quantifiers. **7.** that amount, degree, etc., in terms of which another is greater or lesser. **8.** *Pros., Phonet.* (of sounds or syllables) character as to being longer or shorter, with respect to the time spent in pronouncing them. **9.** *Law.* the nature of an estate as affected by its duration in time. [ME *quantite* < OF < L *quantitās*, equiv. to *quant(us)* how much + *-itās* -ITY]

quan′tity the′ory of mon′ey, *Econ.* the theory that the general price level varies with the amount of money in circulation. Also called **quan′tity the′ory.**

quan·tize (kwon′tīz), *v.t.,* **-tized, -tiz·ing.** **1.** *Math., Physics.* to restrict (a variable quantity) to discrete values that are integral multiples of some basic, finite value rather than of a continuous set of values. **2.** to restrict (a variable) to discrete values, each of which is an integral multiple of the same number. [QUANT(UM) + -IZE] —**quan′ti·za′tion,** *n.*

quan·tong (kwon′tong′), *n.* quandong.

Quan·trill (kwon′tril), *n.* **William Clarke,** 1837–65, U.S. Confederate guerilla leader.

quan·tum (kwon′təm), *n., pl.* **-ta** (-tə). **1.** quantity or amount: *the least quantum of evidence.* **2.** a particular amount. **3.** a share or portion. **4.** a large quantity; bulk. **5.** *Physics.* **a.** the smallest quantity of radiant energy, equal to Planck's constant times the frequency of the associated radiation. **b.** the fundamental unit of a quantized physical magnitude, as angular momentum. [< L, neut. of *quantus* how much]

quan′tum field′ the′ory, *Physics.* See under **quantum mechanics** (def. 1).

quan′tum mechan′ics, *Physics.* **1.** the branch of mechanics that is applicable to systems at the atomic and nuclear level and that is composed of a theory **(nonrelativistic quantum mechanics)** for systems in which velocities are small compared to the speed of light, a theory **(relativistic quantum mechanics)** for systems in which velocities approach or equal the speed of light, and a theory **(quantum field theory)** for systems in which particles are created and destroyed (distinguished from *classical mechanics*). **2.** the mechanics of the phenomena described by this theory. —**quan′tum-me·chan′i·cal,** *adj.*

quan′tum num′ber, *Physics.* one of a set of integers or half-integers that describes an energy level **(quan′tum state′)** of a particle or system of particles.

quan′tum op′tics, the branch of optics dealing with light as a stream of photons, each possessing a quantum of energy proportional to the frequency of light when it is considered as a wave motion.

quan′tum statis′tics, *Physics.* statistics dealing with the distribution of similar kinds of elementary particles among their quantized energy levels. Cf. **Bose-Einstein statistics, Fermi-Dirac statistics.**

quan·tum suf·fi·cit (kwän′tōōm sōōf′i kit; *Eng.* kwon′təm suf′i sit), *Latin.* as much as suffices; enough.

quan′tum the′ory, *Physics.* the theory, based on Planck's radiation law, that changes of energy in atoms and molecules occur only in discrete quantities, each of which is an integral multiple of a fundamental quantity or quantum.

Quantz (kvänts), *n.* **Jo·hann Jo·a·chim** (yō′hän yō′ä-ḵim), 1697–1773, German flutist; teacher of Frederick the Great.

qua·qua·ver·sal (kwā′kwə vûr′səl), *adj.* (of a geological formation) sloping downward from the center in all directions. [< L *quāquā vers(us)*, lit., wheresoever turned, turned everywhere + -AL[1]] —**qua′qua·ver′sal·ly,** *adv.*

quar., **1.** quarter. **2.** quarterly.

quar·an·tine (kwôr′ən tēn′, kwor′-), *n., v.,* **-tined, -tin·ing.** —*n.* **1.** a strict isolation imposed to prevent the spread of disease: *The children were kept in quarantine when they had measles.* **2.** a period, orig. forty days, of detention or isolation imposed upon ships, persons, etc., on arrival at a port or place, when suspected of carrying some infectious or contagious disease. **3.** a system of measures maintained by governmental authority at ports, on frontiers, etc., for preventing the spread of disease. **4.** the branch of the governmental service concerned with such measures. **5.** a place or station at which such measures are carried out. **6.** the detention or isolation enforced. **7.** the port or place where the ships are detained. **8.** the place, esp. a hospital, where people are detained. **9.** a period of forty days. **10.** social or political isolation imposed as a punishment, as in ostracizing an individual or enforcing sanctions against a foreign state. —*v.t.* **11.** to put in or subject to quarantine. **12.** to exclude, detain, or isolate for political, social, or hygienic reasons. [< It *quarantina*, equiv. to *quarant(a)* forty (< L *quadrāgintā*) + *-ina* -INE[2]] —**quar′an·tin′a·ble,** *adj.* —**quar′an·tin′er,** *n.*

quar′antine an′chorage, an anchorage for vessels awaiting a pratique.

quar′antine flag′, *Naut.* a yellow flag, designating the letter "Q" in the International Code of Signals, flown by itself to signify that a vessel has no disease on board and requests a pratique: flown with another flag to signify that there is disease on board ship. Also called **yellow flag.**

quark (kwôrk), *n.* any one of three types of elementary particles that are believed by some physicists to form the basis of all matter in the universe. [applied by M. Gell-Mann after a coinage in *Finnegans Wake* by James Joyce]

Quarles (kwôrlz, kwärlz), *n.* **Francis,** 1592–1644, English poet.

Quar·ne·ro (kwäʀ ne′ʀô), *n.* **Gulf of,** an arm of the Adriatic Sea, in NW Yugoslavia.

quar·rel[1] (kwôr′əl, kwor′-), *n., v.,* **-reled, -rel·ing** or (*esp. Brit.*) **-relled, -rel·ling.** —*n.* **1.** an angry dispute or altercation; a disagreement marked by a temporary or permanent break in friendly relations. **2.** a cause of dispute, complaint, or hostile feeling: *He has no quarrel with his present salary.* —*v.i.* **3.** to disagree angrily; squabble; fall out. **4.** to dispute angrily; wrangle. **5.** to make a complaint; find fault. [ME *querele* < OF < L *querēl(l)a* complaint, akin to *querī* to complain] —**quar′rel·er;** *esp. Brit.,* **quar′rel·ler,** *n.* —**quar′rel·ing·ly;** *esp. Brit.,* **quar′rel·ling·ly,** *adv.*
—**Syn. 1.** argument, contention, controversy, difference, fight. QUARREL, DISSENSION refer to disagreement and conflict. QUARREL applies chiefly to a verbal disagreement between individuals or groups and is used with reference to a large variety of situations, from a slight and petty difference of opinion to a violent altercation: *It was little more than a domestic quarrel. Their quarrel led to the barroom brawl.* DISSENSION usually implies a profound disagreement and bitter conflict. It also applies chiefly to conflict within a group or to members of the same group: *dissension within the union; dissension among the Democrats.* **3.** bicker, argue, brawl, fight.

quar·rel[2] (kwôr′əl, kwor′-), *n.* **1.** a square-headed bolt or arrow, formerly used with a crossbow. **2.** Also, **quarry.** a small, square or diamond-shaped pane of glass, as used in latticed windows. **3.** any of various tools with pyramidal heads. [ME *quarel* < OF < ML *quadrellus*, dim. of L *quadrus* square]

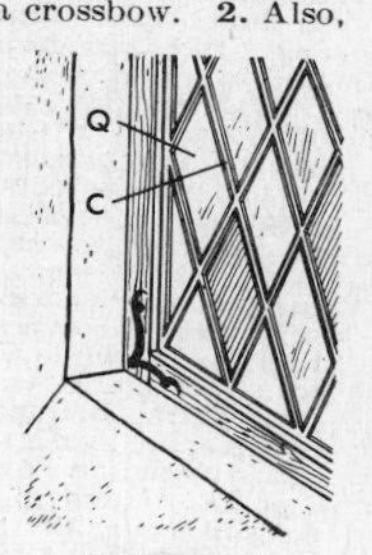

Q, Quarrel[2]
C, Came

quar·rel·some (kwôr′əl səm, kwor′-), *adj.* inclined to quarrel; argumentative; contentious. [QUARREL + -SOME[1]] —**quar′rel·some·ly,** *adv.* —**quar′rel·some·ness,** *n.*

quar·ri·er (kwôr′ē ər, kwor′-), *n.* a person who quarries stone. Also called **quarryman.** [ME *quaryer*, *quarriour* < OF *quarrier*, equiv. to **quarre* QUARRY[1] + *-ier* -ER[1]]

quar·ry[1] (kwôr′ē, kwor′ē), *n., pl.* **-ries,** *v.,* **-ried, -ry·ing.** —*n.* **1.** an excavation or pit, usually open to the air, from which building stone, slate, or the like, is obtained by cutting, blasting, etc. —*v.t.* **2.** to obtain (stone) from or as from a quarry. **3.** to make a quarry in. [ME *quarey* < ML *quareia*, var. of *quareria* < VL *quadrāria* place where stone is squared, deriv. of L *quadrāre* to square] —**quar′ri·a·ble, quar′ry·a·ble,** *adj.*

quar·ry[2] (kwôr′ē, kwor′ē), *n., pl.* **-ries.** **1.** an animal or bird hunted or pursued. **2.** game, esp. game hunted with hounds or hawks. **3.** any object of search, pursuit, or attack. [ME *querre* < OF *cuiree*, deriv. of *cuir* skin, hide < L *corium*]

quar·ry[3] (kwôr′ē, kwor′ē), *n., pl.* **-ries.** **1.** a square stone or tile. **2.** quarrel[2] (def. 2). [n. use of obs. *quarry* (*adj.*) square < OF *quarre*]

quar·ry-faced (kwôr′ē fāst′, kwor′-), *adj.* *Masonry.* rock-faced.

quar·ry·man (kwôr′ē mən, kwor′-), *n., pl.* **-men.** quarrier. [QUARRY[1] + MAN[1]]

quar′ry tile′, a machine-made, unglazed, ceramic floor tile. Also called **promenade tile.**

quart[1] (kwôrt), *n.* **1.** a unit of liquid measure of capacity, equal to one fourth of a gallon, or 57.749 cubic inches in the U.S. and 69.355 cubic inches in Great Britain. **2.** a unit of dry measure of capacity, equal to one eighth of a peck, or 67.201 cubic inches. **3.** a container holding, or capable of holding, a quart. [ME < OF *quarte* < ML *quarta* fourth (fem.)]

quart[2] (kärt), *n.* **1.** *Piquet.* a sequence of four cards of the same suit, as an ace, king, queen, and jack **(quart major),** or king, queen, jack, and ten **(quart minor). 2.** *Fencing Rare.* quarte. [< F *quarte* fourth < L *quarta*]

quart., **1.** quarter. **2.** quarterly.

quar′tal har′mony (kwôr′təl), *Music.* harmony based on chords constructed of fourths instead of thirds. [QUART(ER) + -AL[1]]

quar·tan (kwôr′tən), *adj.* **1.** (of a fever, ague, etc.) characterized by paroxysms that recur every fourth day, both days of consecutive occurrence being counted. —*n.* **2.** a quartan fever or ague. [ME *quartaine* < OF < L (*febris*) *quartāna* (fever) of the fourth]

quarte (kärt; *Fr.* KART), *n., pl.* **quartes** (kärts; *Fr.* KART). *Fencing.* the fourth of eight defensive positions. [< F < It *quarta* fourth]

quar·ter (kwôr′tər), *n.* **1.** one of the four equal or equivalent parts into which anything is or may be divided: *a quarter of an apple; a quarter of a book.* **2.** one fourth of a U.S. or Canadian dollar, equivalent to 25 cents. **3.** a silver coin of this value. **4.** one fourth of an hour: *He stayed there for an hour and a quarter.* **5.** the moment marking this period: *The clock struck the quarter.* **6.** one fourth of a year: *The bank sends out a statement each quarter.* **7.** *Astron.* **a.** a fourth of the moon's period or monthly revolution, being that portion of its period or orbital course between a quadrature and a syzygy. **b.** either quadrature of the moon. Cf. **first quarter, last quarter. 8.** (in schools, colleges, and universities) one of the terms or periods into which instruction is organized, generally 10 to 12 weeks in length. **9.** *Sports.* any of the four periods that make up certain games, as football and basketball. Cf. **half** (def. 2). **10.** one fourth of a pound. **11.** one fourth of a mile; two furlongs. **12.** one fourth of a yard; 9 inches. **13.** a unit of weight: one fourth of a hundredweight. In the U.S. this equals 25 lbs. and in Britain 28 lbs. **14.** *Brit.* a measure of capacity for grain, etc., equal to 8 bushels, or, locally, to approximately this. **15.** the region of any of the four principal points of the compass or divisions of the horizon. **16.** such a point or division. **17.** any point or direction of the compass: *The wind is blowing in that* quarter. **18.** a region, district, or place. **19.** a particular district of a city or town, esp. one generally occupied by a particular class or group of people: *the Turkish quarter; an artists' quarter.* **20.** Usually, **quarters. a.** housing accommodations, as a place of residence; lodgings. **b.** *Mil.* the buildings, houses, barracks, or rooms occupied by military personnel or their families. **21.** a part or member of a community, government, etc., that is not specified: *He received secret information from a high quarter.* **22.** mercy or indulgence, esp. as shown to a vanquished enemy in sparing his life and accepting his surrender: *to give quarter; to cry quarter.* **23.** one of the four parts, each including a leg, of the body or carcass of a quadruped. **24.** *Vet. Med.* either side of a horse's hoof, between heel and toe. **25.** *Shoemaking.* the part of a boot or shoe on each side of the foot, from the middle of the back to the vamp. **26.** *Naut.* **a.** the after part of a ship's side, usually from about the aftermost mast to the stern. **b.** the general horizontal direction 45° from the stern of a ship on either side: *Another boat is coming near on the port quarter.* **c.** one of the stations to which crew members are called for battle, emergencies, or drills. **d.** the part of a yard between the slings and the yardarm. **e.** See **quarter point.** **27.** *Heraldry.* **a.** any of the four equal areas into which an escutcheon may be divided by a vertical and a horizontal line passing through the center. **b.** any of the variously numbered areas into which an escutcheon may be divided for the marshaling of different arms. **c.** any of the arms marshaled on an escutcheon. **d.** a charge occupying one quarter of an escutcheon, esp. that in dexter chief. Cf. **canton** (def. 3). **28.** each half of a cask, consisting of the portion from the bilge to the top chime and the portion from the bilge to the bottom chime. —*v.t.* **29.** to divide into four equal or equivalent parts. **30.** to divide into parts fewer or more than four: *Quarter the pie into six pieces.* **31.** to cut the body of (a person) into quarters, esp. in executing for treason or the like. **32.** *Mach.* to make holes in, fix, etc., a quarter of a circle apart. **33.** to furnish with lodging in a particular place. **34.** to impose (soldiers) on persons, towns, etc., to be lodged and fed: *He quartered his men with the farmer.* **35.** to assign to a particular place for service, action, etc., as on a battleship. **36.** to traverse (the ground) from left to right and right to left while advancing, as dogs in search of game. **37.** *Heraldry.* **a.** to divide (an escutcheon) into four or more parts. **b.** to place or bear quarterly (different coats of arms, etc.) on an escutcheon. **c.** to display (a coat of arms) with one's own on an escutcheon. —*v.i.* **38.** to take up, or be in quarters; lodge: *to quarter in a cheap hotel.* **39.** to range to and fro, as dogs in search of game. **40.** *Naut.* to sail so as to have the wind or sea on the quarter. —*adj.* **41.** being one of four equal, or approximately equal, parts into which anything is or may be divided. **42.** being equal to only about one fourth of the full measure. [ME < OF < L *quartār(ius)*, equiv. to *quart(us)* fourth + *-ārius* -ARY] —**quar′ter·er,** *n.*

quar·ter·age (kwôr′tər ij), *n.* **1.** the act of providing troops with living accommodations. **2.** the cost of such accommodations. **3.** a shelter or lodging. **4.** a quarterly payment, charge, or allowance. [QUARTER + -AGE]

quar·ter·back (kwôr′tər bak′), *Football.* —*n.* **1.** a back who usually lines up immediately behind the center and directs the offense of the team. **2.** the position played by this back. —*v.t.* **3.** to direct the offense of (a team). —*v.i.* **4.** to play the position of quarterback. [QUARTER + BACK[1]]

quar′terback sneak′, *Football.* a play in which the quarterback charges into the middle of the line, usually immediately after receiving the ball from the center.

quar′ter badge′, either of the ornamental features used on the quarters of sailing ships consisting of a name, emblem, or window within a carved and painted frame.

quar′ter bar′, a strut for bracing the central post of a windmill.

quar′ter bend′, a 90° bend, as in a plumbing pipe.

quar′ter bind′ing, a style of bookbinding in which the spine is leather and the sides are cloth or paper. Cf. **full binding, half binding, three-quarter binding.** —**quar·ter-bound** (kwôr′tər bound′), *adj.*

quar′ter blan′ket, a horse blanket, usually placed under a saddle or harness and extending to the horse's tail.

quar′ter board′, *Naut.* **1.** either of two carved boards on the quarters of a vessel that bear the ship's name. **2. quarter boards,** boards forming a light wooden bulwark around the quarter and stern of a sailing vessel.

quar·ter-breed (kwôr′tər brēd′), *n.* a person with one white grandparent, esp. a person of American Indian ancestry.

quar′ter crack′, *Vet. Pathol.* See **sand crack.**

quar′ter day′, **1.** (in England, Ireland, and Wales) one of the four days, Lady Day, Midsummer Day, Michaelmas, or Christmas, regarded as marking off the quarters of the year, on which quarterly payments are due, tenancies begin and end, etc. **2.** (in Scotland) one of the four days, Candlemas, Whitsunday, Lammas, or Martinmas, regarded as marking off the quarters of the year.

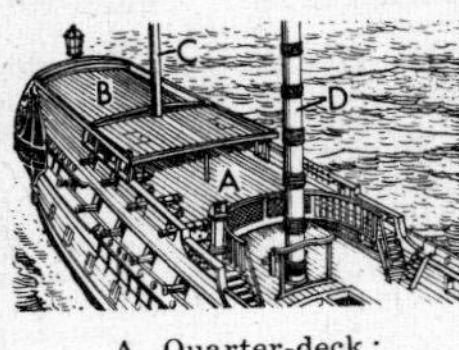

A, Quarter-deck; B, Poop deck; C, Mizzenmast; D, Mainmast

quar·ter-deck (kwôr′tər dek′), *n.* *Naut.* the part of a weather deck that runs aft from the midship area or the main mast to the stern or poop of a vessel. Also, **quar′ter-deck′.**

quar′ter dol′lar, quarter (def. 3).

quar′ter ea′gle, a gold coin of the U.S. (issued 1796–1929), one fourth of an eagle, that is equal to $2.50.

quar·tered (kwôr′tərd), *adj.* **1.** divided into quarters. **2.** furnished with quarters or lodging. **3.** (of oak, sycamore, gum, etc.) quartersawed. **4.** *Heraldry.* **a.** (of an escutcheon) divided into four or more parts. **b.** (of a cross) having the central square portion removed. [QUARTER + -ED[2]]

Quartered arms (def. 4a)

quar·ter·fi·nal (kwôr′tər fīn′ᵊl), *Sports.* —*adj.* **1.** of or pertaining to the contest or round preceding the semifinal one. —*n.* **2.** a quarterfinal contest or round. [QUARTER + FINAL]

quar·ter·fi·nal·ist (kwôr′tər fīn′ᵊlist), *n.* *Sports.* a participant in a quarterfinal contest. [QUARTER + FINALIST]

quar′ter gal′lery, *Naut.* an open or closed structure projecting from each quarter of a vessel, esp. a sailing vessel with a square stern. —**quar′ter-gal′ler·y,** *adj.*

quar′ter grain′, the grain appearing in quartersawed wood.

quar′ter hol′low, *Archit.* a deep cove or cavetto.

quar·ter-hoop (kwôr′tər hoop′), *n.* a hoop, esp. of steel, fastened around a cask between the bilge-hoop and chime-hoop of either of the two quarters of the cask.

quar′ter horse′, **1.** one of a breed of strong horses developed in the United States for short-distance races, usually a quarter of a mile. **2.** a horse of this breed now used as a stock horse.

quar·ter-hour (kwôr′tər our′, -ou′ər), *n.* **1.** a period of fifteen minutes. **2.** a point fifteen minutes after or before the hour.

quar·ter·ing (kwôr′tər ing), *n.* **1.** act of one who or that which quarters. **2.** the assignment of quarters or lodgings. **3.** *Heraldry.* **a.** the division of an escutcheon into quarters. **b.** the marshaling of various coats of arms on an escutcheon. **c.** any of the coats of arms so marshaled. —*adj.* **4.** that quarters. **5.** lying at right angles. **6.** *Naut.* (of a wind) blowing on a ship's quarter. [QUARTER + -ING[1], -ING[2]]

quar′ter line′, *Naut.* an echelon formation of vessels, each having the next vessel forward at a specified angle on the bow and the next vessel aft at a specified angle on the quarter. Also called **bow-and-quarter line.**

quar·ter·ly (kwôr′tər lē), *adj., n., pl.* **-lies,** *adv.* —*adj.* **1.** occurring, done, paid, issued, etc., at the end of every quarter of a year: *a quarterly report; quarterly interest.* **2.** pertaining to or consisting of a quarter. —*n.* **3.** a periodical issued every three months. —*adv.* **4.** by quarters; once each quarter of a year: *The bank pays interest quarterly.* **5.** *Heraldry.* **a.** with division into four quarters. **b.** in the four quarters of an escutcheon. [ME; see QUARTER, -LY]

quar·ter·mas·ter (kwôr′tər mas′tər, -mä′stər), *n.* **1.** *Mil.* an officer charged with providing quarters, clothing, fuel, transportation, etc., for a body of troops. **2.** *Navy.* a petty officer having charge of signals, navigating apparatus, etc. [ME *quarter maister.* See QUARTER, MASTER] —**quar′ter·mas′ter·like′,** *adj.* —**quar′ter·mas′ter·ship′,** *n.*

Quar′termaster Corps′, *Mil.* the branch of the U.S. Army responsible for supplying food, clothing, fuel, and equipment and for the operation of commissaries, laundries, etc.

quar′termaster gen′eral, *pl.* **quartermasters general, quartermaster generals.** *U.S. Mil.* a general in command of the Quartermaster Corps.

quar·tern (kwôr′tərn), *n.* *Chiefly Brit.* a quarter, or a fourth part, esp. of certain weights and measures, as of a pound, ounce, peck, or pint. [ME *quarteroun* < OF *quarteron,* deriv. of *quart* fourth. See QUART[1]]

quar′ter nel′son, *Wrestling.* a hold in which a wrestler, from a kneeling position beside his opponent, puts one hand on the opponent's head, passes the free arm under the far arm of the opponent, and locks the free arm to his other arm by clasping the wrist. Cf. **nelson.**

quar′ter note′, *Music.* a note equivalent to one fourth of a whole note; a crotchet. See illus. under **note.**

quar·ter·pace (kwôr′tər pās′), *n.* a landing for a quarter-turn stair. [QUARTER + PACE[1]]

quar·ter-phase (kwôr′tər fāz′), *adj.* *Elect.* differing in phase by a quarter of a cycle; two-phase.

quar·ter-pierced (kwôr′tər pērst′), *adj.* *Heraldry.* (of a cross) voided at the junction of the arms: *a cross quarter-pierced.*

quar′ter point′, the fourth part of the distance between any two adjacent points of the 32 marked on a compass, being 2° 48′ 45″. Also called **quarter.**

quar′ter round′, a molding, as on an ovolo, whose section is a quarter circle.

quar′ter rud′der, either of two oarlike rudders near the stern of various ancient or native boats.

quar·ter·saw (kwôr′tər sô′), *v.t.,* **-sawed, -sawed** or **-sawn, -saw·ing.** to saw (lumber) from quarter sections of logs so that the annual rings in any board form at least a 45° angle with the faces of the board. [QUARTER + SAW[1]]

quar′ter screw′, *Horol.* (on a balance wheel) one of four evenly spaced, radially set screws, used as weights in regulating the period of oscillation. Also called **mean-time screw.**

quar′ter sec′tion, (in surveying and homesteading) a square tract of land, half a mile on each side, thus containing ¼ sq. mi. or 160 acres. *Abbr.:* q.s.

quar′ter ses′sions, *Law.* **1.** an English court of general criminal jurisdiction for crimes less than homicide, held quarterly. **2.** *U.S.* a court with limited criminal jurisdiction, having local administrative powers in some States.

quar·ter·staff (kwôr′tər staf′, -stäf′), *n., pl.* **-staves** (-stāvz′, -stavz′, -stävz′). **1.** a former English weapon consisting of a stout pole six to eight feet long, tipped with iron. **2.** exercise or fighting with this weapon. [QUARTER + STAFF[1]]

quar′ter tone′, *Music.* an interval equivalent to half of a semitone.

quar′ter-turn stair′ (kwôr′tər tûrn′), a staircase requiring a quarter turn at each landing for continued ascent and descent.

quar·ter-wit·ted (kwôr′tər wit′id), *adj.* half as intelligent as a half-wit.

quar·tet (kwôr tet′), *n.* **1.** any group of four persons or things. **2.** an organized group of four singers or players. **3.** a musical composition for four voices or instruments. Also, *esp. Brit.,* **quar·tette′.** [< It *quartetto,* dim. of *quarto* fourth < L *quartus*]

quar·tic (kwôr′tik), *Algebra.* —*adj.* **1.** of or pertaining to the fourth degree. —*n.* **2.** Also called **biquadratic.** a quartic polynomial or equation. [QUART[1] + -IC]

quar·tile (kwôr′tīl, -til), *adj.* **1.** *Astrol.* of or pertaining to the aspect of two heavenly bodies when their longitudes differ by 90°. —*n.* **2.** *Astrol.* a quartile aspect. **3.** *Statistics.* (in a frequency distribution) one of the values of a variable which divides the distribution of the variable into four groups having equal frequencies. [< ML *quartīl(is),* equiv. to L *quart(us)* fourth + *-īlis* -ILE]

quart′ ma′jor. See under **quart²** (def. 1).

quart′ mi′nor. See under **quart²** (def. 1).

quar·to (kwôr′tō), *n., pl.* **-tos,** *adj.* —*n.* **1.** a book size of about 9½ × 12 inches, determined by folding printed sheets twice to form four leaves or eight pages. *Abbr.:* 4to, 4° **2.** a book of this size. —*adj.* **3.** bound in quarto. [short for NL *in quartō* in fourth].

quar·tus (kwôr′təs), *adj.* (in prescriptions) fourth. [<L]

quartz (kwôrts), *n.* one of the commonest minerals, silicon dioxide, SiO_2, having many varieties which differ in color, luster, etc., and occurring either in masses (as agate, bloodstone, chalcedony, jasper, etc.) or in crystals

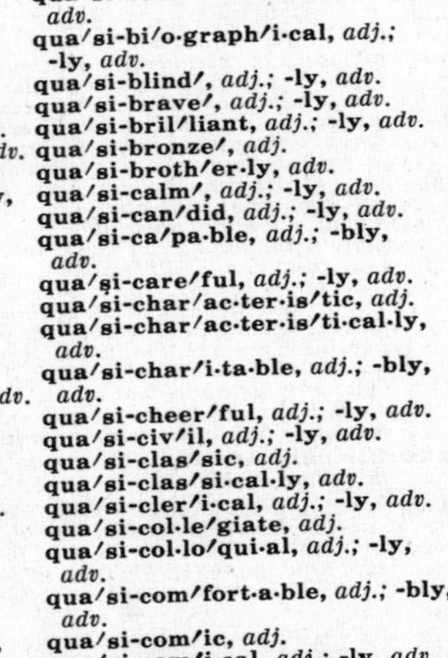

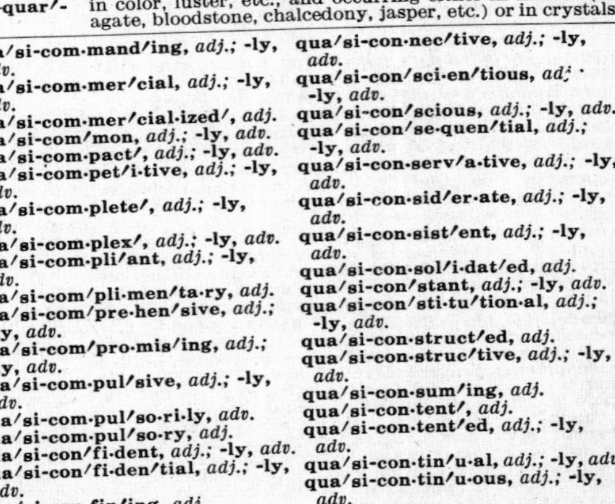

qua′si-ab′so·lute′, *adj.;* **-ly,** *adv.*
qua′si-ac′a·dem′ic, *adj.*
qua′si-ac′a·dem′i·cal·ly, *adv.*
qua′si-ac·cept′ed, *adj.*
qua′si-ac′ci·den′tal, *adj.;* **-ly,** *adv.*
qua′si-ac·quaint′ed, *adj.*
qua′si-ac′tive, *adj.;* **-ly,** *adv.*
qua′si-ad′e·quate, *adj.;* **-ly,** *adv.*
qua′si-ad·just′ed, *adj.*
qua′si-ad·mire′, *v.,* **-mired, -mir·ing.**
qua′si-a·dopt′, *v.t.*
qua′si-a·dopt′ed, *adj.*
qua′si-a·dult′, *adj.*
qua′si-ad′van·ta′geous, *adj.;* **-ly,** *adv.*
qua′si-af·fec′tion·ate, *adj.;* **-ly,** *adv.*
qua′si-af·firm′a·tive, *adj.;* **-ly,** *adv.*
qua′si-al′ter·nat′ing, *adj.;* **-ly,** *adv.*
qua′si-al·ter′na·tive, *adj.;* **-ly,** *adv.*
qua′si-am′a·teur′ish, *adj.;* **-ly,** *adv.*
qua′si-A·mer′i·can, *adj.*
qua′si-A·mer′i·can·ized′, *adj.*
qua′si-a′mi·a·ble, *adj.;* **-bly,** *adv.*
qua′si-a·mus′ing, *adj.;* **-ly,** *adv.*
qua′si-an′cient, *adj.;* **-ly,** *adv.*
qua′si-an·gel′ic, *adj.*
qua′si-an·gel′i·cal·ly, *adv.*
qua′si-an·tique′, *adj.*
qua′si-anx′ious, *adj.;* **-ly,** *adv.*
qua′si-a·pol′o·get′ic, *adj.*
qua′si-a·pol′o·get′i·cal·ly, *adv.*
qua′si-ap·peal′ing, *adj.;* **-ly,** *adv.*
qua′si-ap·point′ed, *adj.*
qua′si-ap·pro′pri·ate, *adj.;* **-ly,** *adv.*
qua′si-ar·tis′tic, *adj.*
qua′si-ar·tis′ti·cal·ly, *adv.*
qua′si-a·side′, *adv.*
qua′si-a·sleep′, *adj., adv.*
qua′si-ath·let′ic, *adj.*
qua′si-ath·let′i·cal·ly, *adv.*
qua′si-at·tempt′, *v.*
qua′si-au′di·ble, *adj.;* **-bly,** *adv.*
qua′si-au·then′tic, *adj.*
qua′si-au·then′ti·cal·ly, *adv.*
qua′si-au′thor·ized′, *adj.*
qua′si-au′to·mat′ic, *adj.*
qua′si-au′to·mat′i·cal·ly, *adv.*
qua′si-aw′ful, *adj.;* **-ly,** *adv.*
qua′si-bad′, *adj.*
qua′si-bank′rupt, *adj.*
qua′si-ba′sic, *adj.*
qua′si-ba′si·cal·ly, *adv.*
qua′si-ben′e·fi′cial, *adj.;* **-ly,** *adv.*
qua′si-be·nev′o·lent, *adj.;* **-ly,** *adv.*
qua′si-bi′o·graph′i·cal, *adj.;* **-ly,** *adv.*
qua′si-blind′, *adj.;* **-ly,** *adv.*
qua′si-brave′, *adj.;* **-ly,** *adv.*
qua′si-bril′liant, *adj.;* **-ly,** *adv.*
qua′si-bronze′, *adj.*
qua′si-broth′er·ly, *adv.*
qua′si-calm′, *adj.;* **-ly,** *adv.*
qua′si-can′did, *adj.;* **-ly,** *adv.*
qua′si-ca′pa·ble, *adj.;* **-bly,** *adv.*
qua′si-care′ful, *adj.;* **-ly,** *adv.*
qua′si-char′ac·ter·is′tic, *adj.*
qua′si-char′ac·ter·is′ti·cal·ly, *adv.*
qua′si-char′i·ta·ble, *adj.;* **-bly,** *adv.*
qua′si-cheer′ful, *adj.;* **-ly,** *adv.*
qua′si-civ′il, *adj.;* **-ly,** *adv.*
qua′si-clas′sic, *adj.*
qua′si-clas′si·cal·ly, *adv.*
qua′si-cler′i·cal, *adj.;* **-ly,** *adv.*
qua′si-col·le′giate, *adj.*
qua′si-col·lo′qui·al, *adj.;* **-ly,** *adv.*
qua′si-com′fort·a·ble, *adj.;* **-bly,** *adv.*
qua′si-com′ic, *adj.*
qua′si-com′i·cal, *adj.;* **-ly,** *adv.*
qua′si-com·mand′ing, *adj.;* **-ly,** *adv.*
qua′si-com·mer′cial, *adj.;* **-ly,** *adv.*
qua′si-com·mer′cial·ized′, *adj.*
qua′si-com′mon, *adj.;* **-ly,** *adv.*
qua′si-com·pact′, *adj.;* **-ly,** *adv.*
qua′si-com·pet′i·tive, *adj.;* **-ly,** *adv.*
qua′si-com·plete′, *adj.;* **-ly,** *adv.*
qua′si-com·plex′, *adj.;* **-ly,** *adv.*
qua′si-com·pli′ant, *adj.;* **-ly,** *adv.*
qua′si-com′pli·men′ta·ry, *adj.*
qua′si-com′pre·hen′sive, *adj.;* **-ly,** *adv.*
qua′si-com′pro·mis′ing, *adj.;* **-ly,** *adv.*
qua′si-com·pul′sive, *adj.;* **-ly,** *adv.*
qua′si-com·pul′so·ri·ly, *adv.*
qua′si-com·pul′so·ry, *adj.*
qua′si-con′fi·dent, *adj.;* **-ly,** *adv.*
qua′si-con′fi·den′tial, *adj.;* **-ly,** *adv.*
qua′si-con·fin′ing, *adj.*
qua′si-con·form′ing, *adj.*
qua′si-con·gen′ial, *adj.;* **-ly,** *adv.*
qua′si-con·grat′u·la·to′ry, *adj.*
qua′si-con·nec′tive, *adj.;* **-ly,** *adv.*
qua′si-con′sci·en′tious, *adj.;* **-ly,** *adv.*
qua′si-con′scious, *adj.;* **-ly,** *adv.*
qua′si-con′se·quen′tial, *adj.;* **-ly,** *adv.*
qua′si-con·serv′a·tive, *adj.;* **-ly,** *adv.*
qua′si-con·sid′er·ate, *adj.;* **-ly,** *adv.*
qua′si-con·sist′ent, *adj.;* **-ly,** *adv.*
qua′si-con·sol′i·dat′ed, *adj.*
qua′si-con′stant, *adj.;* **-ly,** *adv.*
qua′si-con′sti·tu′tion·al, *adj.;* **-ly,** *adv.*
qua′si-con·struct′ed, *adj.*
qua′si-con·struc′tive, *adj.;* **-ly,** *adv.*
qua′si-con·sum′ing, *adj.*
qua′si-con·tent′, *adj.*
qua′si-con·tent′ed, *adj.;* **-ly,** *adv.*
qua′si-con·tin′u·al, *adj.;* **-ly,** *adv.*
qua′si-con·tin′u·ous, *adj.;* **-ly,** *adv.*
qua′si-con′tra·ri·ly, *adv.*
qua′si-con′tra·ry, *adj.*
qua′si-con·trast′ed, *adj.*

(continued on next page)

(as rock crystal, amethyst, citrine, etc.): the chief constituent of sand and sandstone, and an important constituent of many other rocks. It is piezoelectric and used to control the frequencies of radio transmitters. [< G *Quarz* < ?] —**quartz·ose** (kwôrt/sōs), **quartz·ous** (kwôrt/səs), *adj.*

quartz/ clock/, an extremely accurate electric clock utilizing the oscillations of a quartz crystal to control the frequency of alternating current supplied to the clock motor.

quartz/ glass/, lechatelierite.

quartz·if·er·ous (kwôrt sif/ər əs), *adj.* consisting of or containing quartz: *quartziferous rock.* [QUARTZ + -I- + -FEROUS]

quartz·ite (kwôrt/sīt), *n.* a granular metamorphic rock consisting essentially of quartz in interlocking grains. [QUARTZ + -ITE[1]] —**quartz·it·ic** (kwôrt sit/ik), *adj.*

quartz/ lamp/, a lamp consisting of an ultraviolet light source, as mercury vapor, contained in a fused-silica bulb that transmits ultraviolet light with little absorption.

quartz/ plate/, *Elect.* a carefully cut quartz crystal which is piezoelectrically active. Cf. **crystal** (def. 9).

qua·sar (kwā/zär, -zər, -sär, -sər), *n. Astron.* one of about 40 celestial objects, from four to ten billion light-years distant, that are powerful sources of radio energy. Also called **quasi-stellar radio source.** [*quas*(*i-stell*)*ar* (*radio source*)]

quash[1] (kwosh), *v.t.* to put down or suppress completely; quell; subdue: *to quash a rebellion.* [ME *quasche*(*n*) < OF *quasser* < L *quassāre* to shake (freq. of *quatere*)]

quash[2] (kwosh), *v.t.* to make void, annul, or set aside (a law, indictment, decision, etc.). [ME *quasche*(*n*) < OF *quasser* < L *quassāre* shake, but influenced by LL *cassāre* to annul, deriv. of L *cassus* empty, void]

qua·si (kwā/zī, -sī, kwä/sē, -zē), *adj.* **1.** resembling; as it were: *a quasi governmental agency.* —*adv.* **2.** seemingly but not actually (usually used in combination): *quasi-scientific; quasi-public.* [ME < L, equiv. to *quam* as + *si* if]

quasi-, a combining form of **quasi:** *quasi-official, quasi-serious.*

qua/si con/tract, *Law.* an obligation imposed by law in the absence of a contract to prevent unjust enrichment.

qua·si-ju·di·cial (kwā/zī jōō dish/əl, kwā/sī-, kwä/sē-, -zē-), *adj.* having characteristics of a judicial act but performed by an administrative agency or official.

Qua·si·mo·do (kwä/sə mō/dō; *It.* kwä/zē mô/dô), *n.* **Sal·va·to·re** (säl/vä tô/re), 1901–68, Italian poet: Nobel prize 1959.

qua/si-stel/lar ra/dio source/ (kwā/zī stel/ər, kwā/sī-, kwä/sē-, -zē-), quasar.

quass (kväs, kwäs), *n.* a Russian beer made from barley, malt, and rye. Also, **kvass.** [< Russ *kvas*]

quas·sia (kwosh/ə, -ē ə), *n.* **1.** any of several tropical, simaroubaceous trees or shrubs of the genera *Quassia* and *Picrasma.* **2.** Also called **bitter wood.** *Chem., Pharm.* a prepared form of the heartwood of any of these trees, used as an insecticide and in medicine as a tonic to dispel intestinal worms. [< NL, named after *Quassi* 18th-century slave in Dutch Guiana who discovered its medicinal properties; see -IA]

quat., (in prescriptions) four. [< L *quattuor*]

quat·er (kwat/ər), *adv.* (in prescriptions) four times. [< L]

qua·ter·nar·y (kwä/tər ner/ē, kwə tûr/nə rē), *adj., n., pl.* **-nar·ies.** —*adj.* **1.** consisting of four. **2.** arranged in fours. **3.** (*cap.*) *Geol.* noting or pertaining to the present period, forming the latter part of the Cenozoic era, originating about 1,000,000 years ago and including the Recent and Pleistocene epochs. Cf. **Neocene.** See table under **era. 4.** *Metall.* (of an alloy) having four principal constituents. —*n.* **5.** a group of four. **6.** the number four. **7.** (*cap.*) *Geol.* the Quaternary period or system. [ME < L *quaternāri*(*us*), equiv. to *quatern*(*ī*) four at a time + *-ārius* -ARY]

qua/ternary ammo/nium com/pound, *Chem.* any of a class of salts derived from ammonium in which the nitrogen atom is attached to four organic groups, as benzalkonium chloride, that are cationic surface-active compounds, and that are used as antiseptics and disinfectants. Also called **quaternary, qua/ternary ammo/nium salt/.**

qua·ter·nate (kwä/tər nāt/, kwə tûr/nit), *adj.* arranged in or consisting of four parts, as the leaves of certain plants. [< NL **quaternāt*(*us*), equiv. to L *quatern*(*ī*) four at a time + *-ātus* -ATE[1]]

qua·ter·ni·on (kwə tûr/nē ən), *n.* **1.** a group or set of four persons or things. **2.** *Bookbinding.* four gathered sheets folded in two for binding together. **3.** *Math.* a quantity or operator expressed as the sum of a real number and three complex numbers, equivalent to the quotient of two vectors. The field of quaternions is not commutative under multiplication. [ME *quaternioun* < LL *quaterniōn-* (s. of *quaterniō*), equiv. to L *quatern*(*ī*) four at a time + *-iōn-* -ION]

Quath·lam·ba (kwät läm/bä), *n.* Drakensberg.

qua·torze (kə tôrz/; *Fr.* KA TÔRZ/), *n., pl.* **-torz·es** (-tôr/ziz; *Fr.* -tôrz/). *Piquet.* a set of four cards of the same denomination, aces, kings, queens, jacks, or tens, scoring 14 points. [< F: fourteen << L *quattuordecim,* equiv. to *quattuor* four + *-decim,* comb. form of *decem* ten]

quat·rain (kwo/trān), *n.* a stanza or poem of four lines, usually with alternate rhymes. [< F << L *quattuor* four]

qua·tre (kä/tər; *Fr.* KA/TRə), *n.* the four at cards, dice, or the like. [< F]

Qua·tre Bras (kä/trə brä/; *Fr.* KA/TRə BRÄ/), a village in central Belgium, near Brussels: a battle preliminary to the battle of Waterloo was fought here in 1815.

quat·re·foil (kat/ər foil/, ka/trə-), *n.* **1.** a leaf composed of four leaflets. **2.** *Archit.* a panellike ornament composed of four lobes, divided by cusps, radiating from a common center. [< OF *quatre* four + *-foil* (as in TREFOIL); r. ME *quaterfoil*] —**quat/re·foiled/,** *adj.*

Quatrefoils

quat·tro·cen·to (kwo/trō chen/tō; *It.* kwät/trô chen/tô), *n.* (*often cap.*) the 15th century, used in reference to the Italian art of that time. [< It: lit. four hundred (short for fourteen hundred)] —**quat/tro·cen/tist,** *n.*

quat·tu·or·de·cil·lion (kwot/ōō ôr/di sil/yən), *n., pl.* **-lions,** (*as after a numeral*) **-lion,** *adj.* —*n.* **1.** a cardinal number represented in the United States and France by one followed by 45 zeros, and, in Great Britain and Germany by one followed by 84 zeros. —*adj.* **2.** amounting to one quattuordecillion in number. [< L *quattuordec*(*im*) fourteen + *-illion* (as in million)] —**quat/tu·or/de·cil/lionth,** *adj., n.*

qua·ver (kwā/vər), *v.i.* **1.** to shake tremulously; quiver or tremble: *He stood there quavering with fear.* **2.** to sound, speak, or sing tremulously: *Her voice quavered a moment and then she began to cry.* **3.** to perform trills in singing or on a musical instrument. —*v.t.* **4.** to utter, say, or sing with a quavering or tremulous voice. —*n.* **5.** a quavering or tremulous shake, esp. in the voice. **6.** a quavering tone or utterance. **7.** *Music, Chiefly Brit.* an eighth note. See illus. under **note.** [ME, b. QUAKE and WAVER[1]] —**qua/ver·er,** *n.* —**qua/ver·ing·ly,** *adv.* —**qua/ver·y, qua/ver·ous,** *adj.*

quay (kē), *n.* a landing place, esp. one of solid masonry, constructed along the edge of a body of water; wharf. [sp. var. (after F *quai*) of earlier *kay,* also *key* (whence the mod. pronunciation) < OF *kay, cay;* akin to Sp *cayo* shoal. See KEY[2]] —**quay/like/,** *adj.*

quay·age (kē/ij), *n.* **1.** quays collectively. **2.** space appropriated to quays. **3.** a charge for the use of a quay or quays. [< F, equiv. to *quay* QUAY + *-age* -AGE]

Quayle (kwāl), *n.* **James Dan·forth** (dan/fôrth) (*Dan*), born 1947, U.S. politician: senator 1981–89; vice-president of the U.S. since 1989.

qub·ba (ko͝ob/ə), *n.* a small Moslem shrine. [< Ar]

Que., Quebec.

quean (kwēn), *n.* **1.** a bold, impudent woman; shrew; hussy. **2.** a prostitute. **3.** *Brit. Dial.* a girl or young woman, esp. a robust one. [ME *quene,* OE *cwene;* akin to OE *cwēn,* woman, queen] —**quean/ish,** *adj.*

quea·sy (kwē/zē), *adj.,* **-si·er, -si·est. 1.** inclined to or feeling nausea, as the stomach, a person, etc.; nauseous; nauseated. **2.** tending to cause nausea; nauseating. **3.** uneasy or uncomfortable, as feelings, the conscience, etc. **4.** squeamish; excessively fastidious. [late ME < ?] —**quea/si·ly,** *adv.* —**quea/si·ness,** *n.*

Que·bec (kwi bek/), *n.* **1.** a province in E Canada. 6,141,491; 594,860 sq. mi. **2.** a seaport in and the capital of this province, on the St. Lawrence: capital of New France from 1663 to 1759, when it was taken by the English; wartime conferences 1943, 1944. 177,082. **3.** a word used in communications to represent the letter Q. French, **Qué·bec** (kā bek/) (for 1, 2).

Que·bec·er (kwi bek/ər), *n.* a native or inhabitant of Quebec, esp. the city of Quebec. Also **Que·beck/er, Que·becois, Québecois.** [QUEBEC + -ER[1]]

Que·bec·ois (kā/be kwä/), *n., pl.* **Que·bec·ois.** Quebecer. Also, **Qué/bec·ois/.** [< F; see QUEBEC, -ESE]

que·bra·cho (kā brä/chō; *Sp.* ke VRä/chô), *n., pl.* **-chos** (-chōz; *Sp.* -chôs). **1.** either of two anacardiaceous trees, *Schinopsis Lorentzii* or *S. Balansae,* the wood and bark of which are important in tanning and dyeing. **2.** an apocynaceous tree, *Aspidosperma quebrachoblanco,* yielding a medicinal bark. **3.** any of several hard-wooded, South American trees. **4.** the wood or bark of any of these trees. [< AmerSp, var. of *quiebracha,* equiv. to Sp *quiebra* (s. of *quebrar* to break) + *hacha* ax]

que·bra·da (kā brä/də), *n.* **1.** *Southwestern U.S.* a ravine. **2.** a brook. [< Sp, n. use of fem. ptp. of *quebrar* to break]

Quech·ua (kech/wä, -wə), *n., pl.* **-uas,** (*esp. collectively*) **-ua** for 2. **1.** a language spoken by about 4,000,000 people of the Andean plateaus from Quito to Tucumán and formerly an official language of the Inca civilization. **2.** a member of an Indian people of Peru speaking Quechua. Also, **Kechua, Kechuan.**

Quech·uan (kech/wən), *adj., n., pl.* **-uans,** (*esp. collectively*) **-uan.** —*adj.* **1.** of or pertaining to the language of the Quechua. —*n.* **2.** Quechua. [QUECHU(A) + -AN]

qua/si-con·trolled/, *adj.*
qua/si-con·trol/ling, *adj.*
qua/si-con·ven/ient, *adj.;* **-ly,** *adv.*
qua/si-con·ven/tion·al, *adj.;* **-ly,** *adv.*
qua/si-con·vert/ed, *adj.*
qua/si-con·veyed/, *adj.*
qua/si-con·vinced/, *adj.*
qua/si-cor/dial, *adj.;* **-ly,** *adv.*
qua/si-cor·rect/, *adj.;* **-ly,** *adv.*
qua/si-cour/te·ous, *adj.;* **-ly,** *adv.*
qua/si-craft/i·ly, *adv.*
qua/si-craft/y, *adj.*
qua/si-crim/i·nal, *adj.;* **-ly,** *adv.*
qua/si-crit/i·cal, *adj.;* **-ly,** *adv.*
qua/si-cul/ti·vat/ed, *adj.*
qua/si-cun/ning, *adj.;* **-ly,** *adv.*
qua/si-cyn/i·cal, *adj.;* **-ly,** *adv.*
qua/si-dam/aged, *adj.*
qua/si-dan/ger·ous, *adj.;* **-ly,** *adv.*
qua/si-dar/ing, *adj.;* **-ly,** *adv.*
qua/si-deaf/, *adj.;* **-ly,** *adv.*
qua/si-deaf/en·ing, *adj.*
qua/si-dec/o·rat/ed, *adj.*
qua/si-de·feat/ed, *adj.*
qua/si-de·fi/ant, *adj.;* **-ly,** *adv.*
qua/si-def/i·nite, *adj.;* **-ly,** *adv.*
qua/si-de·ject/ed, *adj.;* **-ly,** *adv.*
qua/si-de·lib/er·ate, *adj.;* **-ly,** *adv.*
qua/si-del/i·cate, *adj.;* **-ly,** *adv.*
qua/si-de·light/ed, *adj.;* **-ly,** *adv.*
qua/si-de·mand/ing, *adj.;* **-ly,** *adv.*
qua/si-dem/o·crat/ic, *adj.*
qua/si-dem/o·crat/i·cal·ly, *adv.*
qua/si-de·pend/ent, *adj.;* **-ly,** *adv.*
qua/si-de·pressed/, *adj.*
qua/si-des/o·late, *adj.;* **-ly,** *adv.*
qua/si-des/per·ate, *adj.;* **-ly,** *adv.*
qua/si-des·pond/ent, *adj.;* **-ly,** *adv.*
qua/si-de·ter/mine, *v.*
qua/si-de·vot/ed, *adj.;* **-ly,** *adv.*
qua/si-dif/fi·cult/, *adj.;* **-ly,** *adv.*
qua/si-dig/ni·fied/, *adj.*
qua/si-dig/ni·fy/ing, *adj.*
qua/si-dip/lo·mat/ic, *adj.*
qua/si-dip/lo·mat/i·cal·ly, *adv.*
qua/si-dis·ad/van·ta/geous, *adj.;* **-ly,** *adv.*
qua/si-dis·as/trous, *adj.;* **-ly,** *adv.*
qua/si-dis·creet/, *adj.;* **-ly,** *adv.*
qua/si-dis·crim/i·nat/ing, *adj.;* **-ly,** *adv.*
qua/si-dis·graced/, *adj.*
qua/si-dis·gust/ed, *adj.;* **-ly,** *adv.*
qua/si-dis/tant, *adj.;* **-ly,** *adv.*
qua/si-dis·tressed/, *adj.*
qua/si-di·verse/, *adj.;* **-ly,** *adv.*
qua/si-di·ver/si·fied/, *adj.*
qua/si-di·vid/ed, *adj.;* **-ly,** *adv.*
qua/si-dou/ble, *adj.;* **-bly,** *adv.*
qua/si-doubt/ful, *adj.;* **-ly,** *adv.*
qua/si-dra·mat/ic, *adj.*
qua/si-dra·mat/i·cal·ly, *adv.*
qua/si-dread/ful, *adj.;* **-ly,** *adv.*
qua/si-dumb/, *adj.;* **-ly,** *adv.*
qua/si-du/pli·cate, *adj.*
qua/si-du/ti·ful, *adj.;* **-ly,** *adv.*
qua/si-ea/ger, *adj.;* **-ly,** *adv.*
qua/si-e/co·nom/ic, *adj.*
qua/si-e/co·nom/i·cal, *adj.;* **-ly,** *adv.*
qua/si-ed/u·cat/ed, *adj.*
qua/si-ed/u·ca/tion·al, *adj.;* **-ly,** *adv.*
qua/si-ef·fec/tive, *adj.;* **-ly,** *adv.*
qua/si-ef·fi/cient, *adj.;* **-ly,** *adv.*
qua/si-e·lab/o·rate, *adj.;* **-ly,** *adv.*
qua/si-el/e·men/ta·ry, *adj.*
qua/si-el/i·gi·ble, *adj.;* **-bly,** *adv.*
qua/si-el/o·quent, *adj.;* **-ly,** *adv.*
qua/si-em/i·nent, *adj.;* **-ly,** *adv.*
qua/si-e·mo/tion·al, *adj.;* **-ly,** *adv.*
qua/si-emp/ty, *adj.*
qua/si-end/less, *adj.;* **-ly,** *adv.*
qua/si-en/er·get/ic, *adj.*
qua/si-en/er·get/i·cal·ly, *adv.*
qua/si-en·forced/, *adj.*
qua/si-en·gag/ing, *adj.;* **-ly,** *adv.*
qua/si-Eng/lish, *adj.*
qua/si-en/ter·tain/ing, *adj.*
qua/si-en·thused/, *adj.*
qua/si-en·thu/si·as/tic, *adj.*
qua/si-en·thu/si·as/ti·cal·ly, *adv.*
qua/si-en/vi·ous, *adj.;* **-ly,** *adv.*
qua/si-e·pis/co·pal, *adj.;* **-ly,** *adv.*
qua/si-e/qual, *adj.;* **-ly,** *adv.*
qua/si-eq/ui·ta·ble, *adj.;* **-bly,** *adv.*
qua/si-e·quiv/a·lent, *adj.;* **-ly,** *adv.*
qua/si-e·rot/ic, *adj.*
qua/si-e·rot/i·cal·ly, *adv.*
qua/si-es·sen/tial, *adj.;* **-ly,** *adv.*
qua/si-es·tab/lished, *adj.*
qua/si-e·ter/nal, *adj.;* **-ly,** *adv.*
qua/si-ev/er·last/ing, *adj.;* **-ly,** *adv.*
qua/si-e/vil, *adj.;* **-ly,** *adv.*
qua/si-ex·act/, *adj.;* **-ly,** *adv.*
qua/si-ex·cep/tion·al, *adj.;* **-ly,** *adv.*
qua/si-ex·ces/sive, *adj.;* **-ly,** *adv.*
qua/si-ex·empt/, *adj.*
qua/si-ex/iled, *adj.*
qua/si-ex·ist/ent, *adj.*
qua/si-ex·pect/ant, *adj.;* **-ly,** *adv.*
qua/si-ex·pe/di·ent, *adj.;* **-ly,** *adv.*
qua/si-ex·pen/sive, *adj.;* **-ly,** *adv.*
qua/si-ex·pe/ri·enced, *adj.*
qua/si-ex·per/i·men/tal, *adj.;* **-ly,** *adv.*
qua/si-ex·plic/it, *adj.;* **-ly,** *adv.*
qua/si-ex·posed/, *adj.*
qua/si-ex·pressed/, *adj.*
qua/si-ex·ter/nal, *adj.;* **-ly,** *adv.*
qua/si-ex/tra·ter/ri·to/ri·al, *adj.;* **-ly,** *adv.*
qua/si-ex·treme/, *adj.*
qua/si-fab/ri·cat/ed, *adj.*
qua/si-fair/, *adj.;* **-ly,** *adv.*
qua/si-faith/ful, *adj.;* **-ly,** *adv.*
qua/si-false/, *adj.;* **-ly,** *adv.*
qua/si-fa·mil/iar, *adj.;* **-ly,** *adv.*
qua/si-fa/mous, *adj.;* **-ly,** *adv.*
qua/si-fas/ci·nat/ed, *adj.*
qua/si-fas/ci·nat/ing, *adj.;* **-ly,** *adv.*
qua/si-fash/ion·a·ble, *adj.;* **-bly,** *adv.*
qua/si-fa/tal, *adj.;* **-ly,** *adv.*
qua/si-fa/tal·is/tic, *adj.*
qua/si-fa/tal·is/ti·cal·ly, *adv.*
qua/si-fa/vor·a·ble, *adj.;* **-bly,** *adv.*
qua/si-fa/vour·a·ble, *adj.;* **bly,** *adv.*
qua/si-fed/er·al, *adj.;* **-ly,** *adv.*
qua/si-feu/dal, *adj.;* **-ly,** *adv.*
qua/si-fic·ti/tious, *adj.;* **-ly,** *adv.*
qua/si-fi/nal, *adj.*
qua/si-fi·nan/cial, *adj.;* **-ly,** *adv.*
qua/si-fire/proof, *adj.*
qua/si-fis/cal, *adj.;* **-ly,** *adv.*
qua/si-fit/, *adj.*
qua/si-fool/ish, *adj.;* **-ly,** *adv.*
qua/si-forced/, *adj.*
qua/si-for/eign, *adj.*
qua/si-for·get/ful, *adj.;* **-ly,** *adv.*
qua/si-for·got/ten, *adj.*
qua/si-for/mal, *adj.;* **-ly,** *adv.*
qua/si-for/mi·da·ble, *adj.;* **-bly,** *adv.*
qua/si-for/tu·nate, *adj.;* **-ly,** *adv.*
qua/si-frank/, *adj.;* **-ly,** *adv.*
qua/si-fra·ter/nal, *adj.;* **-ly,** *adv.*
qua/si-free/, *adj.;* **-ly,** *adv.*
qua/si-French/, *adj.*
qua/si-ful·fill/ing, *adj.*
qua/si-full/, *adj.*
qua/si-ful/ly, *adv.*
qua/si-gal/lant, *adj.;* **-ly,** *adv.*
qua/si-gas/e·ous, *adj.*
qua/si-gay/, *adj.*
qua/si-gen/er·ous, *adj.;* **-ly,** *adv.*
qua/si-gen·teel/, *adj.;* **-ly,** *adv.*
qua/si-gen/tle·man·ly, *adv.*
qua/si-gen/u·ine, *adj.;* **-ly,** *adv.*
qua/si-Ger/man, *adj.*
qua/si-glad/, *adj.;* **-ly,** *adv.*
qua/si-glo/ri·ous, *adj.;* **-ly,** *adv.*
qua/si-good/, *adj.*
qua/si-gra/cious, *adj.;* **-ly,** *adv.*
qua/si-grate/ful, *adj.;* **-ly,** *adv.*
qua/si-grave/, *adj.;* **-ly,** *adv.*
qua/si-great/, *adj.;* **-ly,** *adv.*
qua/si-Gre/cian, *adj.*
qua/si-Greek/, *adj.*
qua/si-guar/an·teed/, *adj.*
qua/si-guilt/i·ly, *adv.*
qua/si-guilt/y, *adj.*
qua/si-ha·bit/u·al, *adj.;* **-ly,** *adv.*
qua/si-hap/py, *adj.*
qua/si-harm/ful, *adj.;* **-ly,** *adv.*
qua/si-health/ful, *adj.;* **-ly,** *adv.*
qua/si-heart/i·ly, *adv.*
qua/si-heart/y, *adj.*
qua/si-help/ful, *adj.;* **-ly,** *adv.*
qua/si-he·red/i·tar/y, *adj.*
qua/si-he·ro/ic, *adj.*
qua/si-he·ro/i·cal·ly, *adv.*
qua/si-his·tor/ic, *adj.*
qua/si-his·tor/i·cal, *adj.;* **-ly,** *adv.*
qua/si-hon/est, *adj.;* **-ly,** *adv.*
qua/si-hon/or·a·ble, *adj.;* **-bly,** *adv.*
qua/si-hu/man, *adj.;* **-ly,** *adv.*
qua/si-hu/man·is/tic, *adj.*
qua/si-hum/ble, *adj.;* **-bly,** *adv.*
qua/si-hu/mor·ous, *adj.;* **-ly,** *adv.*
qua/si-i·de/al, *adj.;* **-ly,** *adv.*
qua/si-i·de/al·is/tic, *adj.*
qua/si-i·de/al·is/ti·cal·ly, *adv.*
qua/si-i·den/ti·cal, *adj.;* **-ly,** *adv.*
qua/si-ig/no·rant, *adj.;* **-ly,** *adv.*
qua/si-im·me/di·ate, *adj.;* **-ly,** *adv.*
qua/si-im·mor/tal, *adj.;* **-ly,** *adv.*
qua/si-im·par/tial, *adj.;* **-ly,** *adv.*
qua/si-im·por/tant, *adj.;* **-ly,** *adv.*
qua/si-im·proved/, *adj.*
qua/si-in·clined/, *adj.*
qua/si-in·clu/sive, *adj.;* **-ly,** *adv.*
qua/si-in·creased/, *adj.*
qua/si-in/de·pend/ent, *adj.;* **-ly,** *adv.*
qua/si-in·dif/fer·ent, *adj.;* **-ly,** *adv.*
qua/si-in·duced/, *adj.*
qua/si-in·dulged/, *adj.*
qua/si-in·dus/tri·al, *adj.;* **-ly,** *adv.*
qua/si-in·ev/i·ta·ble, *adj.;* **-bly,** *adv.*
qua/si-in·fe/ri·or, *adj.*
qua/si-in·ferred/, *adj.*
qua/si-in/fi·nite, *adj.;* **-ly,** *adv.*
qua/si-in/flu·en/tial, *adj.;* **-ly,** *adv.*
qua/si-in·for/mal, *adj.;* **-ly,** *adv.*
qua/si-in·formed/, *adj.*
qua/si-in·her/it·ed, *adj.*
qua/si-in·i/ti·at/ed, *adj.*
qua/si-in/jured, *adj.*
qua/si-in·ju/ri·ous, *adj.;* **-ly,** *adv.*
qua/si-in/no·cent, *adj.;* **-ly,** *adv.*
qua/si-in·nu/mer·a·ble, *adj.;* **-bly,** *adv.*
qua/si-in·sist/ent, *adj.;* **-ly,** *adv.*
qua/si-in·spect/ed, *adj.*
qua/si-in/spi·ra/tion·al, *adj.*

(*continued in next page*)

queen (kwēn), *n.* **1.** the wife or consort of a king. **2.** a female sovereign or monarch. **3.** a woman, or something personified as a woman, that is foremost or preeminent in any respect: *She was a movie queen. She was crowned beauty queen of the campus.* **4.** *Slang.* a male homosexual, esp. one who assumes the female role. **5.** a playing card bearing a picture of a queen. **6.** *Chess.* the most powerful piece of each color, moved any unobstructed distance in any direction. **7.** *Entomol.* a fertile female ant, bee, termite, or wasp. **8.** a word formerly used in communications to represent the letter *Q.* **9.** *Naut.* See **queen staysail.** —*v.i.* **10.** to reign as queen. **11.** to behave in an imperious or pretentious manner (usually fol. by *it*). [ME *quene, quen,* OE *cwēn* woman, queen; akin to Gk *gynē* wife, Skt *jani*] —**queen′less,** *adj.* —**queen′like′,** *adj.*

Queen′ Anne′, **1.** noting or pertaining to the style of architecture, furnishings, and decoration prevailing in England in the early 18th century, characterized by simplicity and refinement of forms, with increasing attention to French and Italian models. **2.** noting or pertaining to the style of architecture, furnishings, and decoration prevailing in England from c1865 to c1885, imitated in the U.S. from c1875 to c1890, characterized by imitation of English vernacular work of the middle and late 17th century, often with an eclectic mixture of medieval, 18th century, and Japanese motifs.

Queen′ Anne′s′ lace′, an umbelliferous plant, *Daucus Carota,* having large, lacy umbels of minute, white flowers, the central one usually dark purple; the common, weedy form of the cultivated carrot.

Queen′ Anne′s′ War′, the war (1702–13) in which England and its American colonies opposed France and its Indian allies. It constituted the American phase of the War of the Spanish Succession.

queen′ bee′, a fertile female bee. See illus. under **bee.**

queen′ bolt′, (in a roof truss) an iron or steel rod serving as a queen post. Also called **queen rod.**

Queen′ Char′lotte Is′lands, a group of islands in British Columbia off the W coast of Canada. 3014 (1961); 3970 sq. mi.

queen′ clos′er, *Masonry.* **1.** a brick of normal length and thickness but of half normal width, used to complete a course or to space regular bricks. **2.** a brick of half the usual length, for completing a course or for spacing regular bricks. Also called **queen′ clo′sure.**

queen′ con′sort, the wife of a ruling king.

queen-cup (kwēn′kup′), *n.* a North American, liliaceous herb, *Clintonia uniflora,* having downy, white flowers.

queen·dom (kwēn′dəm), *n.* **1.** the position or status of a queen. **2.** the realm of a queen. [QUEEN + -DOM]

queen′ dow′ager, the widow of a king.

queen·fish (kwēn′fish′), *n., pl.* **-fish·es,** (*esp. collectively*) **-fish.** *Ichthyol.* a silvery and bluish drum, *Seriphus politus,* found in the shallow waters along the coast of California. [QUEEN + FISH]

queen·hood (kwēn′ho͝od′), *n.* the state, dignity, or rank of a queen. [QUEEN + -HOOD]

Queen·ie (kwē′nē), *n.* a girl's given name.

queen·ing (kwē′ning), *n.* *Chess.* promotion (def. 5). [QUEEN + -ING[1]]

queen·ly (kwēn′lē), *adj.,* **-li·er, -li·est,** *adv.* —*adj.* **1.** belonging or proper to a queen: *queenly propriety.* **2.** befitting, or suggestive of, a queen: *queenly grace.* —*adv.* **3.** in a queenly manner. [QUEEN + -LY] —**queen′li·ness,** *n.*

Queen′ Mab′ (mab), **1.** *Irish and English Folklore.* a mischievous, tantalizing fairy who governs and produces the dreams of men. **2.** (*italics.*) a poem (1813) by Shelley.

Queen′ Maud′ Land′ (môd), a coastal region of Antarctica, S of Africa: Norwegian explorations.

Queen′ Maud′ Range′, a mountain range in Antarctica, in Ross Dependency, S of the Ross Sea.

queen′ moth′er, a queen dowager who is also mother of a reigning sovereign.

Queen′ of Heav′en, **1.** a designation of the Virgin Mary. **2.** (*l.c.*) an ancient Semitic goddess, variously identified with other ancient goddesses, as Isis and Ashtoreth. **3.** an epithet of Ishtar.

Queen′ of Spades′, The, **1.** a short story (1834) by Alexander Pushkin. **2.** an opera (1890) by Tschaikovsky, based on Pushkin's story.

queen′ of the mead′ow, **1.** a rosaceous herb, *Filipendula ulmaria,* of Europe and North America, having white flowers. **2.** a spiraea, *Spiraea salicifolia,* of Eurasia, having panicles of pink flowers. **3.** the joe-pye weed, *Eupatorium purpureum.* Also, **queen′-of-the-mead′ow.**

queen′ of the prai′rie, a tall, perennial herb, *Filipendula rubra,* found in meadows and prairies. Also, **queen′-of-the-prai′rie.**

queen′ ol′ive, **1.** any large, meaty olive suitable for pickling or processing. **2.** such an olive grown esp. in the area of Seville, Spain.

queen′ palm′, a feather palm, *Arecastrum romanzoffianum,* of South America, having leaves from 7 to 12 feet in length, and large, hanging clusters of small fruit. Also called **plumy coconut.**

queen′ post′, either of a pair of timbers or posts extending vertically upward from the tie beam of a roof truss or the like, one on each side of the center.

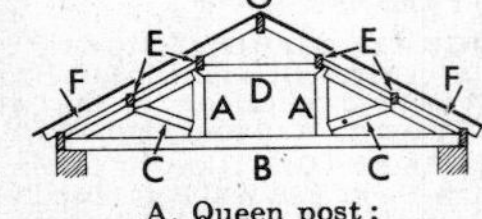

A, Queen post; B, Tie beam; C, Strut; D, Straining piece; E, Purlin; F, Common rafter; G, Ridgepole

queen′ re′gent, **1.** a queen who reigns in behalf of another. **2.** See **queen regnant.**

queen′ reg′nant, a queen who reigns in her own right. Also, **queen regent.**

queen′ rod′. See **queen bolt.**

Queens (kwēnz), *n.* a borough of E New York City, on Long Island. 1,809,578 (1960); 113.1 sq. mi.

Queen's′ Bench′. See **King's Bench.**

Queens′ber·ry rules′ (kwēnz′ber′ē, -bə rē). See **Marquis of Queensberry rules.**

Queen's′ Birth′day. See **King's Birthday.**

queen's′ boun′ty, *Brit.* See **king's bounty.** Also, **Queen's′ boun′ty, Queen's′ Boun′ty.**

Queen's′ Cham′pion. See under **Champion of England.**

queen's′ col′our. See **king's colour.** Also, **Queen's′ col′our, Queen's′ Col′our.**

Queen's′ Coun′sel. See **King's Counsel.**

queen's′ Eng′lish. See **king's English.**

queen's′ ev′idence. See **king's evidence.**

Queen's-flow·er (kwēnz′flou′ər), *n.* a tree, *Lagerstroemia speciosa,* found from India to Australia, having showy, purplish flowers three inches wide.

Queens·land (kwēnz′land′, -lənd), *n.* a state in NE Australia. 1,518,828 (1961); 670,500 sq. mi. *Cap.:* Brisbane.

Queens′land nut′, macadamia.

Queen's′ pat′tern, **1.** a pattern of ceramic decoration consisting of bands of swirling radial lines, white on blue alternating with red on white. **2.** an early 19th-century silver pattern having a shell at the stem terminal and an ornament resembling a fleur-de-lis on the stem enclosed by elaborate scrolls.

queen's′-pawn o′penings (kwēnz′pôn′), (*construed as sing.*) a class of chess openings in which the pawn in front of the queen is advanced two squares on the first move.

Queen's′ Proc′tor. See **King's Proctor.**

Queen's′ Remem′brancer. See **King's Remembrancer.**

queen's′ scout′. See **king's scout.**

queen's′ shil′ling. See **king's shilling.**

Queen's′ speech′. See **King's speech.**

queen′ stay′sail, *Naut.* a triangular sail set on the main-topmast stay of a schooner-rigged yacht.

Queens·town (kwēnz′toun′), *n.* former name of **Cóbh.**

queen's′ ware′, a hard, cream-colored earthenware, perfected c1765 by Wedgwood. Also, **queens′-ware′.**

queen's′ wreath′. See **purple wreath.**

queen′ truss′, a truss having queen posts with no king post.

queer (kwēr), *adj.* **1.** strange or odd from a conventional viewpoint; unusually different; singular: *a queer notion of justice.* **2.** of a questionable nature or character; suspicious; shady: *Something queer about the language of the prospectus kept investors away.* **3.** not feeling physi-

qua′si-in·stalled′, *adj.*
qua′si-in·struct′ed, *adj.*
qua′si-in·sult′ed, *adj.*
qua′si-in′tel·lec′tu·al, *adj.;* **-ly,** *adv.*
qua′si-in·tel′li·gent, *adj.;* **-ly,** *adv.*
qua′si-in·tend′ed, *adj.*
qua′si-in′ter·est·ed, *adj.;* **-ly,** *adv.*
qua′si-in·ter′nal, *adj.;* **-ly,** *adv.*
qua′si-in·ter′nal·ized′, *adj.*
qua′si-in′ter·na′tion·al, *adj.;* **-ly,** *adv.*
qua′si-in′ter·na′tion·al·is′tic, *adj.*
qua′si-in′ter·viewed′, *adj.*
qua′si-in′ti·mate, *adj.;* **-ly,** *adv.*
qua′si-in′ti·mat′ed, *adj.*
qua′si-in·tol′er·a·ble, *adj.;* **-bly,** *adv.*
qua′si-in·tol′er·ant, *adj.;* **-ly,** *adv.*
qua′si-in′tro·duced′, *adj.*
qua′si-in·tu′i·tive, *adj.;* **-ly,** *adv.*
qua′si-in·vad′ed, *adj.*
qua′si-in·ves′ti·gat′ed, *adj.*
qua′si-in·vis′i·ble, *adj.;* **-bly,** *adv.*
qua′si-in·vit′ed, *adj.*
qua′si-ir·reg′u·lar, *adj.;* **-ly,** *adv.*
qua′si-Jac′o·be′an, *adj.*
qua′si-Jap′a·nese′, *adj.*
qua′si-jo·cose′, *adj.;* **-ly,** *adv.*
qua′si-jo·cund′, *adj.;* **-ly,** *adv.*
qua′si-joint′ly, *adv.*
qua′si-kind′, *adj.;* **-ly,** *adv.*
qua′si-knowl′edge·a·ble, *adj.;* **-bly,** *adv.*
qua′si-la·bo′ri·ous, *adj.;* **-ly,** *adv.*
qua′si-la·ment′ed, *adj.*
qua′si-Lat′in, *adj.*
qua′si-law′ful, *adj.;* **-ly,** *adv.*
qua′si-le′gal, *adj.;* **-ly,** *adv.*
qua′si-leg′end·ar′y, *adj.*
qua′si-leg′is·lat′ed, *adj.*
qua′si-leg′is·la′tive, *adj.;* **-ly,** *adv.*
qua′si-le·git′i·mate, *adj.;* **-ly,** *adv.*
qua′si-lib′er·al, *adj.;* **-ly,** *adv.*
qua′si-lit′er·ar′y, *adj.*
qua′si-liv′ing, *adj.*
qua′si-log′i·cal, *adj.;* **-ly,** *adv.*
qua′si-loy′al, *adj.;* **-ly,** *adv.*
qua′si-lux·u′ri·ous, *adj.;* **-ly** *adv.*
qua′si-mad′, *adj.;* **-ly,** *adv.*
qua′si-mag′ic, *adj.*
qua′si-mag′i·cal, *adj.;* **-ly,** *adv.*
qua′si-ma·li′cious, *adj.;* **-ly,** *adv.*
qua′si-man′aged, *adj.*
qua′si-man′a·ge′ri·al, *adj.;* **-ly,** *adv.*
qua′si-ma·te′ri·al, *adj.;* **-ly,** *adv.*
qua′si-ma·ter′nal, *adj.;* **-ly,** *adv.*
qua′si-me·chan′i·cal, *adj.;* **-ly,** *adv.*
qua′si-med′i·cal, *adj.;* **-ly,** *adv.*
qua′si-me′di·e′val, *adj.*
qua′si-men′tal, *adj.;* **-ly,** *adv.*
qua′si-mer′can·tile, *adj.*
qua′si-met′a·phys′i·cal, *adj.;* **-ly,** *adv.*
qua′si-me·thod′i·cal, *adj.;* **-ly,** *adv.*
qua′si-might′y, *adj.*
qua′si-mil′i·ta·ris′tic, *adj.*
qua′si-mil′i·ta·ris′ti·cal·ly, *adv.*
qua′si-mil′i·tar′y, *adj.*
qua′si-min′is·te′ri·al, *adj.*
qua′si-mi·rac′u·lous, *adj.;* **-ly,** *adv.*
qua′si-mis′er·a·ble, *adj.;* **-bly,** *adv.*
qua′si-mod′ern, *adj.*
qua′si-mod′est, *adj.;* **-ly,** *adv.*
qua′si-mor′al, *adj.;* **-ly,** *adv.*
qua′si-mor′al·is′tic, *adj.*
qua′si-mor′al·is′ti·cal·ly, *adv.*
qua′si-mu·nic′i·pal, *adj.;* **-ly,** *adv.*
qua′si-mu′si·cal, *adj.;* **-ly,** *adv.*
qua′si-mu′tu·al, *adj.;* **-ly,** *adv.*
qua′si-mys·te′ri·ous, *adj.;* **-ly,** *adv.*
qua′si-myth′i·cal, *adj.;* **-ly,** *adv.*
qua′si-name′less, *adj.*
qua′si-na′tion·al, *adj.;* **-ly,** *adv.*
qua′si-na′tion·al·is′tic, *adj.*
qua′si-na′tive, *adj.*
qua′si-nat′u·ral, *adj.;* **-ly,** *adv.*
qua′si-neb′u·lous, *adj.;* **-ly,** *adv.*
qua′si-nec′es·sar′y, *adj.*
qua′si-neg′a·tive, *adj.;* **-ly,** *adv.*
qua′si-neg·lect′ed, *adj.*
qua′si-neg′li·gent, *adj.*
qua′si-neg′li·gi·ble, *adj.;* **-bly,** *adv.*
qua′si-neu′tral, *adj.;* **-ly,** *adv.*
qua′si-new′, *adj.;* **-ly,** *adv.*
qua′si-nor′mal, *adj.;* **-ly,** *adv.*
qua′si-no·tar′i·al, *adj.*
qua′si-nup′tial, *adj.*
qua′si-o·be′di·ent, *adj.;* **-ly,** *adv.*
qua′si-ob·jec′tive, *adj.;* **-ly,** *adv.*
qua′si-ob′li·gat′ed, *adj.*
qua′si-ob·served′, *adj.*
qua′si-of·fen′sive, *adj.;* **-ly,** *adv.*
qua′si-of·fi′cial, *adj.;* **-ly,** *adv.*
qua′si-op·posed′, *adj.*
qua′si-or′di·nar′y, *adj.*
qua′si-or·gan′ic, *adj.*
qua′si-or·gan′i·cal·ly, *adv.*
qua′si-o′ri·en′tal, *adj.;* **-ly,** *adv.*
qua′si-o·rig′i·nal, *adj.;* **-ly,** *adv.*
qua′si-par′ti·san, *adj.*
qua′si-pas′sive, *adj.;* **-ly,** *adv.*
qua′si-pa·thet′ic, *adj.*
qua′si-pa·thet′i·cal·ly, *adv.*
qua′si-pa′tient, *adj.;* **-ly,** *adv.*
qua′si-pa′tri·ar′chal, *adj.*
qua′si-pa′tri·ot′ic, *adj.*
qua′si-pa′tri·ot′i·cal·ly, *adv.*
qua′si-pa′tron·iz′ing, *adj.;* **-ly,** *adv.*
qua′si-peace′ful, *adj.;* **-ly,** *adv.*
qua′si-per′fect, *adj.;* **-ly,** *adv.*
qua′si-pe′ri·od′ic, *adj.*
qua′si-pe′ri·od′i·cal·ly, *adv.*
qua′si-per′ma·nent, *adj.;* **-ly,** *adv.*
qua′si-per·pet′u·al, *adj.;* **-ly,** *adv.*
qua′si-per′son·a·ble, *adj.;* **-bly,** *adv.*
qua′si-per′son·al, *adj.;* **-ly,** *adv.*
qua′si-per·us′a·ble, *adj.*
qua′si-phil′o·soph′i·cal, *adj.;* **-ly,** *adv.*
qua′si-phys′i·cal, *adj.;* **-ly,** *adv.*
qua′si-pi′ous, *adj.;* **-ly,** *adv.*
qua′si-pleas′ur·a·ble, *adj.;* **-bly,** *adv.*
qua′si-pledge′, *v.,* **-pledged, -pledg·ing.**
qua′si-plen′ti·ful, *adj.;* **-ly,** *adv.*
qua′si-po·et′ic, *adj.*
qua′si-po·et′i·cal, *adj.;* **-ly,** *adv.*
qua′si-pol′i·tic, *adj.*
qua′si-po·lit′i·cal, *adj.;* **-ly,** *adv.*
qua′si-poor′, *adj.;* **-ly,** *adv.*
qua′si-pop′u·lar, *adj.;* **-ly,** *adv.*
qua′si-pos′i·tive, *adj.;* **-ly,** *adv.*
qua′si-pow′er·ful, *adj.;* **-ly,** *adv.*
qua′si-prac′ti·cal, *adj.;* **-ly,** *adv.*
qua′si-pre′ce·dent, *adj.*
qua′si-pref′er·en′tial, *adj.;* **-ly,** *adv.*
qua′si-prej′u·diced, *adj.*
qua′si-prep′o·si′tion·al, *adj.;* **-ly,** *adv.*
qua′si-pre·vent′ed, *adj.*
qua′si-pri′vate, *adj.;* **-ly,** *adv.*
qua′si-priv′i·leged, *adj.*
qua′si-prob′a·ble, *adj.;* **-bly,** *adv.*
qua′si-prob′lem·at′ic, *adj.*
qua′si-pro·duc′tive, *adj.;* **-ly,** *adv.*
qua′si-pro·gres′sive, *adj.;* **-ly,** *adv.*
qua′si-prom′ised, *adj.*
qua′si-prompt′, *adj.;* **-ly,** *adv.*
qua′si-pro·phet′ic, *adj.*
qua′si-pro·phet′i·cal, *adj.;* **-ly,** *adv.*
qua′si-pros′e·cut′ed, *adj.*
qua′si-pros′per·ous, *adj.;* **-ly,** *adv.*
qua′si-pro·tect′ed, *adj.*
qua′si-proud′, *adj.;* **-ly,** *adv.*
qua′si-pro·vin′cial, *adj.;* **-ly,** *adv.*
qua′si-pro·voc′a·tive, *adj.;* **-ly,** *adv.*
qua′si-pub′lic, *adj.;* **-ly,** *adv.*
qua′si-pun′ished, *adj.*
qua′si-pu′pil·lar′y, *adj.*
qua′si-pur′chased, *adj.*
qua′si-qual′i·fied′, *adj.*
qua′si-rad′i·cal, *adj.;* **-ly,** *adv.*
qua′si-ra′tion·al, *adj.;* **-ly,** *adv.*
qua′si-re′al·is′tic, *adj.*
qua′si-re′al·is′ti·cal·ly, *adv.*
qua′si-rea′son·a·ble, *adj.;* **-bly,** *adv.*
qua′si-re·bel′lious, *adj.;* **-ly,** *adv.*
qua′si-re′cent, *adj.;* **-ly,** *adv.*
qua′si-rec′og·nized′, *adj.*
qua′si-rec′on·ciled′, *adj.*
qua′si-re·duced′, *adj.*
qua′si-re·fined′, *adj.*
qua′si-re·formed′, *adj.*
qua′si-re·fused′, *adj.*
qua′si-reg′is·tered, *adj.*
qua′si-reg′u·lar, *adj.;* **-ly,** *adv.*
qua′si-reg′u·lat′ed, *adj.*
qua′si-re·ject′ed, *adj.*
qua′si-re·li′a·ble, *adj.;* **-bly,** *adv.*
qua′si-re·lieved′, *adj.*
qua′si-re·li′gious, *adj.;* **-ly,** *adv.*
qua′si-re·mark′a·ble, *adj.;* **-bly,** *adv.*
qua′si-re·newed′, *adj.*
qua′si-re·paired′, *adj.*
qua′si-re·placed′, *adj.*
qua′si-re·port′ed, *adj.*
qua′si-rep′re·sent′ed, *adj.*
qua′si-re·quired′, *adj.*
qua′si-res′cued, *adj.*
qua′si-res′i·den′tial, *adj.;* **-ly,** *adv.*
qua′si-re·sist′ed, *adj.*
qua′si-re·spect′a·ble, *adj.;* **-bly,** *adv.*
qua′si-re·spect′ed, *adj.*
qua′si-re·spect′ful, *adj.;* **-ly,** *adv.*
qua′si-re·spon′si·ble, *adj.;* **-bly,** *adv.*
qua′si-re·spon′sive, *adj.;* **-ly,** *adv.*
qua′si-re·stored′, *adj.*
qua′si-re·tired′, *adj.*
qua′si-rev′o·lu′tion·ized′, *adj.*
qua′si-re·ward′ing, *adj.*
qua′si-ri·dic′u·lous, *adj.;* **-ly,** *adv.*
qua′si-right′eous, *adj.;* **-ly,** *adv.*
qua′si-ro·man′tic, *adj.*
qua′si-ro·man′ti·cal·ly, *adv.*
qua′si-roy′al, *adj.;* **-ly,** *adv.*
qua′si-ru′ral, *adj.;* **-ly,** *adv.*
qua′si-sad′, *adj.;* **-ly,** *adv.*
qua′si-safe′, *adj.;* **-ly,** *adv.*
qua′si-sa·ga′cious, *adj.;* **-ly,** *adv.*
qua′si-saint′ly, *adv.*
qua′si-sanc′tioned, *adj.*
qua′si-san′guine, *adj.;* **-ly,** *adv.*
qua′si-sar·cas′tic, *adj.*
qua′si-sar·cas′ti·cal·ly, *adv.*
qua′si-sa·tir′i·cal, *adj.;* **-ly,** *adv.*
qua′si-sat′is·fied′, *adj.*
qua′si-sav′age, *adj.;* **-ly,** *adv.*
qua′si-schol′ar·ly, *adj.*
qua′si-scho·las′tic, *adj.*
qua′si-scho·las′ti·cal·ly, *adv.*
qua′si-sci′en·tif′ic, *adj.*
qua′si-sci′en·tif′i·cal·ly, *adv.*
qua′si-se′cret, *adj.;* **-ly,** *adv.*
qua′si-se·cre′tive, *adj.;* **-ly,** *adv.*
qua′si-se·cure′, *adj.;* **-ly,** *adv.*
qua′si-sen′ti·men′tal, *adj.;* **-ly,** *adv.*
qua′si-se′ri·ous, *adj.;* **-ly,** *adv.*
qua′si-set′tled, *adj.*
qua′si-sim′i·lar, *adj.;* **-ly,** *adv.*
qua′si-sin·cere′, *adj.;* **-ly,** *adv.*
qua′si-sin′gle, *adj.;* **-gly,** *adv.*
qua′si-skill′ful, *adj.;* **-ly,** *adv.*
qua′si-slan′der·ous, *adj.;* **-ly,** *adv.*
qua′si-so′ber, *adj.;* **-ly,** *adv.*
qua′si-so′cial·is′tic, *adj.*
qua′si-so′cial·is′ti·cal·ly, *adv.*
qua′si-sov′er·eign, *adj.*
qua′si-Span′ish, *adj.*
qua′si-spa′tial, *adj.;* **-ly,** *adv.*
qua′si-spher′i·cal, *adj.;* **-ly,** *adv.*
qua′si-spir′it·ed, *adj.;* **-ly,** *adv.*
qua′si-spir′it·u·al, *adj.;* **-ly,** *adv.*
qua′si-stand′ard·ized′, *adj.*
qua′si-sta′tion·ar′y, *adj.*
qua′si-stren′u·ous, *adj.;* **-ly,** *adv.*
qua′si-stu′di·ous, *adj.;* **-ly,** *adv.*
qua′si-styl′ish, *adj.;* **-ly,** *adv.*
qua′si-sub·jec′tive, *adj.;* **-ly,** *adv.*
qua′si-sub·mis′sive, *adj.;* **-ly,** *adv.*
qua′si-suc·cess′ful, *adj.;* **-ly,** *adv.*
qua′si-suf·fi′cient, *adj.;* **-ly,** *adv.*
qua′si-su′per·fi′cial, *adj.;* **-ly,** *adv.*
qua′si-su·pe′ri·or, *adj.*
qua′si-su′per·vised′, *adj.*
qua′si-sup·port′ed, *adj.*
qua′si-sup·pressed′, *adj.*
qua′si-sym′pa·thet′ic, *adj.*
qua′si-sym′pa·thet′i·cal·ly, *adv.*
qua′si-sys′tem·at′ic, *adj.*
qua′si-sys′tem·at′i·cal·ly, *adv.*

(*continued on next page*)

cally right or well; giddy, faint, or qualmish: *to feel queer.* **4.** mentally unbalanced or deranged. **5.** *Slang.* **a.** homosexual. **b.** bad, worthless, or counterfeit. **—***v.t.* **6.** to spoil; ruin. **7.** to put (a person) in a hopeless or disadvantageous situation as to success, favor, etc. **8.** to jeopardize. **—***n. Slang.* **9.** a homosexual. **10.** counterfeit money. [< G *quer* oblique, cross, adverse] **—queer′ly,** *adv.* **—queer′ness,** *n.*
—Syn. 1. unconventional, curious, freakish, eccentric, weird. See **strange. —Ant. 1.** ordinary.

Queer′ Street′, a condition of financial instability or embarrassment: *Such extravagance will surely put them in Queer Street.*

Quel·i·ma·ne (kel′ə mä′nə), *n.* a seaport in E Mozambique. 151,618 (est. 1958).

quell (kwel), *v.t.* **1.** to suppress (a disorder, mutiny, etc.); put an end to; extinguish: *The troops quelled the rebellion quickly.* **2.** to vanquish; subdue. **3.** to quiet or allay (emotions, anxieties, etc.): *The child's mother quietly quelled his fears of the thunder.* [ME *quelle(n),* OE *cwellan* to kill; akin to Icel *kvelja* to torment, G *quälen* to vex] **—quell′a·ble,** *adj.* **—quell′er,** *n.*
—Syn. 1, 2. crush, quash, overpower, overcome, defeat, conquer, quench. **3.** calm, pacify, compose, hush. **—Ant. 1, 2.** foster. **3.** agitate.

Quel·part (kwel′pärt′), *n.* Cheju.

quel·que chose (kel′kə shōz′), kickshaw. [< F: something]

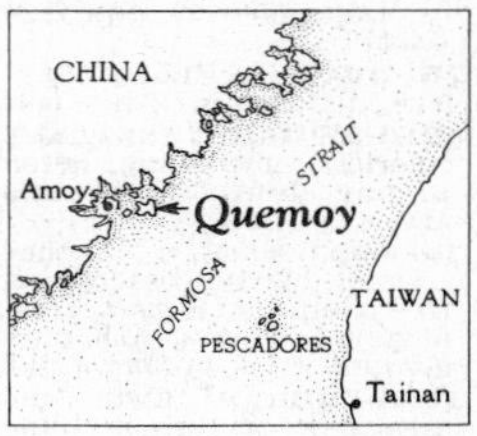

Que·moy (ki moi′), *n.* an island off the SE coast of China, in the Formosa Strait: remained with Nationalist China after the Communist conquest of the mainland. 45,347 (est. 1956); 50 sq. mi. Cf. **Matsu.**

quench (kwench), *v.t.* **1.** to slake, satisfy, or allay (thirst, desires, passion, etc.). **2.** to put out or extinguish (fire, flames, etc.). **3.** to cool suddenly by plunging into a liquid, as in tempering steel by immersion in water. **4.** to subdue or destroy; overcome; quell: *to quench an uprising.* **5.** *Electronics.* to terminate (the flow of electrons in a vacuum tube) by application of a voltage. [ME *quenche(n),* OE *-cwencean*] **—quench′a·ble,** *adj.* **—quench′a·ble·ness,** *n.* **—quench′er,** *n.*

quench·less (kwench′lis), *adj.* that cannot be quenched; unquenchable. [QUENCH + -LESS] **—quench′less·ly,** *adv.* **—quench′less·ness,** *n.*

que·nelle (kə nel′), *n.* a small ball of forcemeat mixture, usually boiled and served with a sauce or used as a garnish. [< F < G *Knödel* dumpling]

Quen·tin (kwen′tᵊn), *n.* a boy's or girl's given name. Also, **Quenton, Quinton.**

Quen′tin Dur′ward (dûr′wərd), a historical novel (1823) by Sir Walter Scott.

Quen·ton (kwen′tᵊn), *n.* a boy's or girl's given name. Also, **Quentin, Quinton.**

quer·ce·tin (kwûr′si tin), *n. Chem.* a yellow, crystalline, slightly water-soluble powder, $C_{15}H_{10}O_7$, obtained from the bark of quercitron and other vegetable substances, used as a yellow dye; flavin. Also called **meletin.** [< L *quercēt(um)* an oak-wood + -IN²] **—quer·cet·ic** (kwər set′ik, -sē′tik), *adj.*

Quer·cia (kwer′chä), *n.* **Ja·co·po Del·la** (yä′kô pô del′lä), 1374?–1438, Italian sculptor.

quer·cine (kwûr′sin, -sīn), *adj.* of or pertaining to an oak. [< L *querc(us)* oak + -INE²]

quer·ci·tol (kwûr′si tōl′, -tôl′, -tol′), *n. Chem.* a colorless, crystalline, sweet, water-soluble solid, $C_6H_7(OH)_5$, obtained from acorns or oak bark: used chiefly in medicine. Also called **acorn sugar.** [QUERCET(IN) + -OL¹]

quer·ci·tron (kwûr′si trən), *n.* **1.** an oak, *Quercus velutina,* of eastern North America, the inner bark of which yields a yellow dye. **2.** the bark itself. **3.** the dye obtained from this bark. [< L *querc(us)* oak + CITRON]

Que·ré·ta·ro (ke re′tä rô′), *n.* **1.** a state in central Mexico. 355,045 (1960); 4432 sq. mi. **2.** a city in and the capital of this state, in the SW part: republican forces executed Emperor Maximilian here 1867. 66,225 (1960).

que·rist (kwēr′ist), *n.* a person who puts a query. [QUER(Y) + -IST]

quern (kwûrn), *n.* a primitive, hand-operated mill for grinding grain. [ME; OE *cweorn;* akin to Icel *kvern* hand-mill]

quer·sprung (kver′shpro͝ong′), *n. Skiing.* a jump turn in which a skier lands at right angles to the pole or poles. [< G: diagonal jump]

quer·u·lous (kwer′ə ləs, kwer′yə-), *adj.* **1.** full of complaints; complaining. **2.** characterized by, or uttered in, complaint; peevish: *a querulous tone; constant querulous reminders of things to be done.* [late ME < L *querulus,* equiv. to *quer(ī)* to complain + *-ulus* -ULOUS] **—quer′u·lous·ly,** *adv.* **—quer′u·lous·ness,** *n.*
—Syn. 1, 2. petulant, testy; caviling, carping, discontented. **—Ant. 1.** contented.

que·ry (kwēr′ē), *n., pl.* **-ries,** *v.,* **-ried, -ry·ing.** **—***n.* **1.** a question; an inquiry. **2.** doubt; mental uncertainty or reservation. **3.** *Print.* a question mark (?), esp. as added on a manuscript, proof sheet, or the like, with reference to some point in the text. **4.** an inquiry from a writer to an editor of a magazine, newspaper, etc., regarding the acceptability of or interest in an idea for an article, news story, or the like: usually presented in the form of a letter that outlines or describes the projected piece. **—***v.t.* **5.** to ask or inquire about: *No one queried his presence.* **7.** to question as doubtful or obscure: *to query a statement.* **8.** *Print.* to mark with a query. **9.** to ask questions of. [alter. of earlier *quere* < L *quaere,* impv. of *quaerere* to ask, seek; see -Y³] **—que′ry·ing·ly,** *adv.*

ques., question.

Ques·nay (ke ne′), *n.* **Fran·çois** (fräɴ swa′), 1694–1774, French economist and physician.

Ques·nel (kwə nel′; *Fr.* ke nel′), *n.* a city in central British Columbia, in SW Canada. 4673 (1961).

quest (kwest), *n.* **1.** a search or pursuit made in order to find or obtain something: *a quest for uranium mines; a quest for knowledge.* **2.** *Medieval Romance.* an adventurous expedition undertaken by a knight or knights to secure or achieve something: *the quest of the Holy Grail.* **3.** those engaged in such an expedition. **4.** *Brit. Dial.* inquest. **5.** *Archaic.* a jury of inquest. **—***v.i.* **6.** to search; seek (often fol. by *for* or *after*): *to quest after hidden treasure.* **7.** to go on a quest. **8.** *Hunting.* (of a dog) **a.** to search for game. **b.** to bay or give tongue in pursuit of game. **—***v.t.* **9.** to search or seek for; pursue. [ME *queste* < MF << L *quaesita,* fem. ptp. of *quaerere* to seek] **—quest′er,** *n.* **—quest′ing·ly,** *adv.*

ques·tion (kwes′chən, -kwesh′-), *n.* **1.** a sentence in an interrogative form, addressed to someone in order to get information in reply. **2.** a problem for discussion or under discussion; a matter for investigation. **3.** a matter of some uncertainty or difficulty; problem (usually fol. by *of*): *It was simply a question of time.* **4.** a subject of dispute or controversy. **5.** a proposal to be debated or voted on, as in a meeting or a deliberative assembly. **6.** the procedure of putting a proposal to vote. **7.** *Politics.* a problem of public policy submitted to the voters for an expression of opinion. **8.** *Law.* **a.** a controversy which is submitted to a judicial tribunal or administrative agency for decision. **b.** the interrogation by which information is secured. **c.** *Obs.* judicial examination or trial. **9.** act of asking or inquiring; interrogation; query. **10.** inquiry into, or discussion of, some problem or doubtful matter. **11. beyond question,** beyond dispute; without doubt: *It was, beyond question, a magnificent performance.* Also, **beyond all question. 12. call in** or **into question, a.** to dispute; challenge. **b.** to cast doubt upon; question: *This report calls in question all previous research on the subject.* **13. in question, a.** under consideration. **b.** in dispute. **14. out of the question,** not to be considered; unthinkable; impossible: *She thought about a fur coat but dismissed it as out of the question.* **—***v.t.* **15.** to ask (someone) a question; ask questions of; interrogate. **16.** to ask or inquire. **17.** to make a question of; doubt: *He questioned her sincerity.* **18.** to challenge or dispute: *She questioned the judge's authority in the case.* **—***v.i.* **19.** to ask a question or questions. [ME *questiun* < AF < L *quaestiōn-* (s. of *quaestiō*), equiv. to *quaest(us)* (ptp. of *quaerere* to ask) + *-iōn-* -ION] **—ques′tion·er,** *n.*
—Syn. 1. inquiry, query, interrogation. **15.** query, examine. **16.** See **inquire. —Ant. 1, 15.** answer, reply.

ques·tion·a·ble (kwes′chə nə bəl), *adj.* **1.** of doubtful propriety, honesty, morality, respectability, etc.: *questionable activities; in questionable taste.* **2.** open to question or dispute; doubtful or uncertain: *a statement of questionable accuracy.* **3.** open to question as to being of the nature or value suggested: *a questionable privilege.* [QUESTION + -ABLE] **—ques′tion·a·ble·ness, ques′tion·a·bil′i·ty,** *n.* **—ques′tion·a·bly,** *adv.*
—Syn. 2. debatable, disputable, controvertible, dubitable, dubious. **—Ant. 1.** certain.

ques·tion·ar·y (kwes′chə ner′ē), *n., pl.* **-ar·ies.** a questionnaire. [QUESTION + -ARY]

ques·tion·ing (kwes′chə ning), *adj.* **1.** indicating or implying a question: *a questioning tone in her voice.* **2.** characterized by or indicating intellectual curiosity; inquiring: *an alert and questioning mind.* **—***n.* **3.** an inquiry or interrogation. [QUESTION + -ING², -ING¹] **—ques′tion·ing·ly,** *adv.*

ques·tion·less (kwes′chən lis), *adj.* **1.** unquestionable; doubtless: *a questionless fact.* **2.** unquestioning: *questionless faith in God.* **—***adv.* **3.** without question; unquestionably. [QUESTION + -LESS] **—ques′tion·less·ly,** *adv.*

ques′tion mark′, 1. Also called **interrogation point, interrogation mark.** a mark indicating a question: usually, as in English, the mark (?) placed after a question. **2.** something unanswered or unknown: *His identity is still a question mark to most of us.* **3.** an anglewing butterfly, *Polygonia interrogationis,* having silver spots shaped like a question mark on the underside or each hind wing.

ques·tion·naire (kwes′chə nâr′), *n.* a list of questions, usually printed, submitted for replies that can be analyzed for usable information: *a questionnaire on new trends in teaching music.* [< F, equiv. to *question-n(er)* (to) question + *-aire;* see -ARY]

ques′tion of fact′, a question concerning the reality of an alleged event or circumstance in a trial by jury, usually determined by the jury. Cf. **question of law.**

ques′tion of law′, a question concerning a rule or the legal effect or consequence of an event or circumstance, usually determined by a court or judge. Cf. **question of fact.**

ques·tor (kwes′tər, kwē′stər), *n. Rom. Hist.* quaestor. **—ques·to·ri·al** (kwe stōr′ē əl, -stôr′-, kwē-), *adj.* **—ques′tor·ship′,** *n.*

quetsch (kwech, kvech), *n.* **1.** *Hort.* **a.** a variety of plum. **b.** the tree bearing this fruit, grown in Europe. **2.** a dry, white, unaged brandy distilled from quetsch plums in Alsace. [< G *Quetsch(e)* plum]

Quet·ta (kwet′ä), *n.* a city in W central West Pakistan, in Pakistan: formerly the capital of British Baluchistan; almost totally destroyed by an earthquake 1935. 106,633 (1961).

quet·zal (ket säl′), *n.* **1.** a Central and South American bird, *Pharomachrus mocinna,* having golden-green and scarlet plumage, the male of which has long, flowing upper tail coverts: the national bird of Guatemala. **2.** a paper money and monetary unit of Guatemala, equal to 100 centavos and equivalent to one U.S. dollar. *Abbr.:* Q. Also, **que·zal** (ke säl′). [< AmerSp < Nahuatl *quetzalli* tailfeather of the bird *quetzaltototl*]

Quetzal (Total length 3 ft; tail plumes 2 ft.)

Quet·zal·co·a·tl (ket säl′kô ät′ᵊl), *n.* the feathered serpent god of the Aztec and Toltec cultures.

queue (kyo͞o), *n., v.,* **queued, queu·ing.** **—***n.* **1.** a braid of hair worn hanging down behind. **2.** a file or line, esp. of people waiting their turn. **—***v.i., v.t.* **3.** to form in a line while waiting. [< F << L *cōda* tail, r. *cauda*] **—queu′er,** *n.*

queue′ fourché′, *Heraldry.* (of a lion) having a single tail divided in two partway along its length so as to have two complete ends. Cf. **double-tailed.** [< F: lit., tail forked]

quey (kwā), *n., pl.* **queys.** *Scot. and North Eng.* a heifer. [ME *quy* < Scand; cf. Icel *kvīga*]

Que·zal·te·nan·go (ke säl′te näng′gô), *n.* a city in SW Guatemala: earthquake 1902. 33,726 (est. 1957).

Que′zon Cit′y (kā′zon), a city on S Luzon Island, in the Philippines, NE of Manila; designated the national capital in 1948 though Manila remains the traditional capital and center of administration. 475,400 (est. 1965).

Que·zon y Mo·li·na (kā′zon ē mō lē′nə; *Sp.* ke′sôn e mô lē′nä, -thôn), **Ma·nuel Lu·is** (mä nwel′ lo͞o ēs′), 1878–1944, Philippine political leader; 1st president of the Philippine Commonwealth 1933–44.

quib·ble (kwib′əl), *n., v.,* **-bled, -bling.** **—***n.* **1.** a use of ambiguous, prevaricating, or irrelevant language or arguments to evade a point at issue. **2.** the use of such arguments. **3.** petty or carping criticism; a minor objection. **—***v.i.* **4.** to use a quibble or quibbles; evade the point or the truth by a quibble. [?, deriv. of *quib* gibe, appar. var. of QUIP] **—quib′bler,** *n.*
—Syn. 1. evasion, equivocation, sophism, shift, ambiguity. **4.** equivocate, cavil.

quib·bling (kwib′ling), *adj.* **1.** characterized by or consisting of quibbles; carping; niggling: *quibbling debates among the salvationists.* **—***n.* **2.** the act of a person who quibbles. **3.** an instance of quibbling: *a relationship marked by frequent quibblings.* [QUIBBLE + -ING², -ING¹] **—quib′bling·ly,** *adv.*

Quib·dó (kēb dô′), *n.* a city in W Colombia. 9013 (1951).

Qui·be·ron (kēbᵊ rôɴ′), *n.* a peninsula in NW France, on the S coast of Brittany: British naval victory over the French 1759. 6 mi. long.

quib·us (kwib′əs), *pron.* (in prescriptions) from which. [< L]

quiche (kēsh), *n. French Cookery.* a pielike dish consisting of an unsweetened pastry shell filled with a custard and usually flavored with cheese, onion, bacon, etc.: *quiche Lorraine.* [< F < G (dial.) *Küche,* dim. of *Küche(n)* cake]

Qui·ché (kē chā′), *n.* a Mayan language of Guatemala.

quick (kwik), *adj.* **1.** done, proceeding, or occurring with promptness or rapidity, as an action, process, etc.; prompt; immediate: *a quick response.* **2.** that is over or completed within a short interval of time: *a quick shower.* **3.** moving, or able to move, with speed: *a quick fox; a quick train.* **4.** swift or rapid, as motion: *a quick flick of the wrist.* **5.** hasty; impatient: *a quick temper.* **6.** lively or keen, as feelings. **7.** acting with swiftness or rapidity: *a quick worker.* **8.** prompt or swift to do something: *quick to respond.* **9.** prompt to perceive: *a quick eye.* **10.** prompt to understand, learn, etc.; of ready intelligence: *a quick student.* **11.** (of a bend or curve) sharp: *a quick bend in the road.* **12.** consisting of living plants: *a quick pot of flowers.* **13.** brisk, as fire, flames, heat, etc. **14.** *Finance.* readily convertible into cash; liquid: *quick assets.* **15.** *Mining.* containing ore; productive. **16.** *Archaic.* **a.** endowed with life. **b.** having a high degree of vigor, energy, or activity. **—***n.* **17.** living persons: *the quick and the dead.* **18.** *Chiefly Brit.* **a.** a line of shrubs or plants, esp. of hawthorn, forming a hedge. **b.** a single shrub or plant in such a hedge. **19.** the tender, sensitive flesh of the living body, esp. that under the nails: *nails bitten down to the quick.* **20.** the vital or most important part. **21. cut to the quick,** to injure deeply; hurt the feelings of: *Their callous treatment cut her to the quick.* **—***adv.* **22.** quickly. [ME; OE *cwic, cwicu* living; c. OS *quik,* G *queck, keck,* Icel *kvikr;* akin to L *vīvus* living] **—quick′ness,** *n.*
—Syn. 1. fleet, expeditious. QUICK, FAST, SWIFT, RAPID describe speedy tempo. QUICK applies particularly to something practically instantaneous, an action or reaction, perhaps, of very brief duration: *to give a quick look around; to take a quick walk.* FAST and SWIFT refer to actions, movements, etc., which continue for a time, and usually to those which are uninterrupted; when used of communication, transportation, and the like, they suggest a definite goal and a continuous trip. SWIFT, the more formal word, suggests the greater speed: *a fast train; a swift message.* RAPID, less speedy than the others, applies to a rate or movement or action, and usually to a series of actions or movements, related or unrelated: *rapid calculation; a rapid walker.* **5.** abrupt, curt, short, precipitate, unceremonious. **6.** acute, sensi-

qua′si-sys′tem·a·tized′, *adj.*
qua′si-tan′gent, *adj.*
qua′si-tan′gi·ble, *adj.;* **-bly,** *adv.*
qua′si-tech′ni·cal, *adj.;* **-ly,** *adv.*
qua′si-tem′po·ral, *adj.;* **-ly,** *adv.*
qua′si-ter′ri·to′ri·al, *adj.;* **-ly,** *adv.*
qua′si-the·at′ri·cal, *adj.;* **-ly,** *adv.*
qua′si-thor′ough, *adj.;* **-ly,** *adv.*
qua′si-tol′er·ant, *adj.;* **-ly,** *adv.*
qua′si-to′tal, *adj.;* **-ly,** *adv.*
qua′si-tra·di′tion·al, *adj.;* **-ly,** *adv.*
qua′si-trag′ic, *adj.*
qua′si-trag′i·cal·ly, *adv.*
qua′si-tri′bal, *adj.;* **-ly,** *adv.*
qua′si-truth′ful, *adj.;* **-ly,** *adv.*
qua′si-typ′i·cal, *adj.;* **-ly,** *adv.*
qua′si-ty·ran′ni·cal, *adj.;* **-ly,** *adv.*
qua′si-u·nan′i·mous, *adj.;* **-ly,** *adv.*
qua′si-un·con′scious, *adj.;* **-ly,** *adv.*
qua′si-u′ni·fied′, *adj.*
qua′si-u′ni·ver′sal, *adj.;* **-ly,** *adv.*
qua′si-u′til·ized′, *adj.*
qua′si-val′id, *adj.;* **-ly,** *adv.*
qua′si-val′ued, *adj.*
qua′si-ven′er·a·ble, *adj.;* **-bly,** *adv.*
qua′si-vic·to′ri·ous, *adj.;* **-ly,** *adv.*
qua′si-vi′o·lat′ed, *adj.*
qua′si-vi′o·lent, *adj.;* **-ly,** *adv.*
qua′si-vir′tu·ous, *adj.;* **-ly,** *adv.*
qua′si-vi′tal, *adj.;* **-ly,** *adv.*
qua′si-vo·ca′tion·al, *adj.;* **-ly,** *adv.*
qua′si-war′rant·ed, *adj.*
qua′si-wealth′y, *adj.*
qua′si-whis′pered, *adj.*
qua′si-wick′ed, *adj.;* **-ly,** *adv.*
qua′si-will′ing, *adj.;* **-ly,** *adv.*
qua′si-wrong′, *adj.*
qua′si-young′, *adj.*
qua′si-zeal′ous, *adj.;* **-ly,** *adv.*

tive, alert. **7.** nimble, agile, brisk. **10.** See **sharp.** **—Ant. 1, 6, 10.** slow.

quick′ as′sets, *Accounting.* liquid assets including cash, receivables, and marketable securities.

quick′ bread′, bread, muffins, biscuits, etc., made with a leavening agent that acts quickly, permitting immediate baking.

quick′-change′ art′ist (kwik′chānj′), a person adept at changing from one thing to another, as an entertainer who changes costumes quickly during a performance.

quick·en (kwik′ən), *v.t.* **1.** to make more rapid; accelerate; hasten: *She quickened her pace.* **2.** to give or restore vigor or activity to; stir up, rouse, or stimulate: *to quicken the imagination.* **3.** to animate; revive; restore life to: *The spring rains quickened the earth.* **4.** *Shipbuilding.* to lessen the radius or radii of (a curve) so as to make the curve more pronounced or abrupt. **—*v.i.*** **5.** to become more active, sensitive, etc.: *This drug causes the pulse to quicken.* **6.** to become alive; receive life. **7.** (of the mother) to enter that stage of pregnancy in which the child gives indications of life. **8.** (of a child in the womb) to begin to manifest signs of life. [ME *quiken(en).* See QUICK, -EN[1]] **—quick′en·er,** *n* **—Syn. 2.** animate, vitalize, enliven. **3.** vivify.

quick′ fire′, a single shot or several shots fired at a rapid rate from small arms at a target, esp. one presented unexpectedly.

quick-fire (kwik′fīər′), *adj.* firing rapidly, esp. at moving targets. Also, **quick′-fir′ing.**

quick-freeze (kwik′frēz′), *v.t.*, **-froze, -fro·zen, -freez·ing.** to subject (cooked or uncooked food) to rapid refrigeration, permitting it to be stored almost indefinitely at freezing temperatures. Also called **sharp-freeze.**

quick′ grass′, the couch grass, *Agropyron repens.*

quick·hatch (kwik′hach′), *n.* a wolverine. [< Cree *kwekwukao*]

quick·ie (kwik′ē), *n. Slang.* **1.** a book, story, movie, etc., usually trivial in quality, requiring only a short time to produce. **2.** anything taking only a short time esp. a quickly consumed alcoholic drink. [QUICK + -IE]

quick′ie strike′. See **wildcat strike.**

quick′ kick′, *Football.* a punt, usually on second or third down, made from an offensive formation not usually used for kicking, intended to go beyond the opposing safety men in order to prevent a possible runback.

quick·lime (kwik′līm′), *n.* lime[1] (def. 1). [QUICK + LIME[1]]

quick·ly (kwik′lē), *adv.* with speed; rapidly; very soon. [ME *quikly.* See QUICK, -LY]

quick′ march′, a march in quick time.

quick·sand (kwik′sand′), *n.* a bed of soft or loose sand saturated with water and having considerable depth, yielding under weight and therefore apt to engulf persons, animals, etc., coming upon it. [ME *qwykkesand.* See QUICK, SAND] **—quick′sand′y,** *adj.*

quick·set (kwik′set′), *n. Chiefly Brit.* **1.** a plant or cutting, esp. of hawthorn, set to grow, as in a hedge. **2.** such plants collectively. **3.** a hedge of such plants. **—*adj.*** **4.** formed of quickset, or of growing plants. [late ME; see QUICK, SET]

quick-set·ting (kwik′set′ing), *adj.* setting quickly, as a cement, paint, gelatin, etc.

quick·sil·ver (kwik′sil′vər), *n.* **1.** the metallic element mercury. **—*v.t.*** **2.** to amalgamate (metal) with mercury. [ME *qwyksilver,* OE *cwicseolfor* (after L *argentum vīvum*) lit., living silver] **—quick′sil′ver·y,** *adj.*

quick·step (kwik′step′), *n.* **1.** (formerly) a lively step used in marching. **2.** music adapted to such a march, or in a brisk march rhythm. **3.** a lively step or combination of steps in ballroom dancing. [QUICK + STEP]

quick-tem·pered (kwik′tem′pərd), *adj.* easily angered.

quick′ time′, **1.** a quick rate of marching. **2.** *U.S. Mil.* a normal rate of marching in which 120 paces, each of 30 inches, are taken in a minute.

quick′ trick′, *Bridge.* a card, or group of cards, that will probably win the first or second trick in a suit, regardless of who plays it or at what declaration.

quick·wa·ter (kwik′wô′tər, -wot′ər), *n.* the part of a river or other stream having a strong current. [QUICK + WATER]

quick-wit·ted (kwik′wit′id), *adj.* having a nimble, alert mind. [QUICK + WIT[1] + -ED[3]] **—quick′-wit′ted·ly,** *adv.* **—quick′wit′ted·ness,** *n.*

quick·work (kwik′wûrk′), *n. Naut.* **1.** *Rare.* the immersed portion of a vessel when fully laden. **2.** *Obs.* planking readily attached to the upper works of a vessel being built. [QUICK + WORK]

quid[1] (kwid), *n.* a portion of something, esp. tobacco, that is to be chewed but not swallowed. [OE *cwidu* CUD]

quid[2] (kwid), *n., pl.* **quid.** *Brit.* **1.** *Slang.* a one-pound banknote. **2.** *Informal.* the sum of £1. **3.** *Archaic.* a sovereign. [?]

Quid·de (kvid′ə), **Lud·wig** (lo͞ot′viKH, lo͞od′-), 1858–1941, German historian and pacifist: Nobel peace prize 1927.

quid·di·ty (kwid′i tē), *n., pl.* **-ties. 1.** that which makes a thing what it is; the essential nature. Cf. **haecceity. 2.** a trifling nicety of subtle distinction, as in argument. [< ML *quidditās,* equiv. to L *quid* what + *-itās* -ITY]

quid·nunc (kwid′nungk′), *n.* a person who is eager to know the latest news and gossip; a gossip or busybody. [< L *quid nunc* what now?]

quid pro quo (kwid′ prō kwō′), *pl.* **quid pro quos, quids pro quo** for 2. **1.** (*Italics*) *Latin.* one thing in return for another. **2.** that which is given or taken in return for something else; substitute. [lit., something for something]

quién sa·be? (kyen sä′ve), *Spanish.* who knows?

qui·es·cent (kwē es′ənt), *adj.* being at rest; quiet; still; inactive or motionless: *a quiescent mind.* [< L *quiescent-* (s. of *quiescēns,* prp. of *quiescere*), equiv. to *quiesc-* be quiet + *-ent-* -ENT] **—qui·es′cent·ly,** *adv.* **—qui·es′cence, qui·es′cen·cy,** *n.* **—Syn.** dormant, latent.

qui·et[1] (kwī′it), *n.* **1.** freedom from noise, unwanted sound, etc.: *At least there's quiet here.* **2.** freedom from disturbance or tumult; tranquility; rest; repose: *to live in quiet.* **3.** peace; peaceful condition of affairs. [ME < L *quiēt-* (s. of *quies*)] **—Syn. 1.** silence. **2.** calm, stillness. **—Ant. 1.** noise. **2.** disturbance.

qui·et[2] (kwī′it), *adj.* **1.** making no disturbance or trouble; not turbulent; peaceable: *The factions remained quiet for twenty years.* **2.** free from disturbance or tumult; tranquil; peaceful: *a quiet life.* **3.** free from disturbing thoughts, emotions, etc.; mentally peaceful: *a quiet conscience.* **4.** being at rest. **5.** refraining or free from activity, esp. busy or vigorous activity: *a quiet Sunday afternoon.* **6.** motionless or still; moving gently: *quiet waters.* **7.** making no noise or sound, esp. no disturbing sound: *quiet neighbors.* **8.** free, or comparatively free, from noise: *a quiet street.* **9.** silent: *Be quiet!* **10.** restrained in speech, manner, etc.; saying little: *a quiet person.* **11.** said, expressed, done, etc., in a restrained or unobtrusive way: *a quiet reproach; a quiet admonition.* **12.** not showy or obtrusive; subdued: *quiet colors.* **13.** not busy or active: *The stock market was quiet last week.* **—*v.t.*** **14.** to make quiet. **15.** to make tranquil or peaceful; pacify: *to quiet a crying baby.* **16.** to calm mentally, as a person. **17.** to allay (tumult, doubt, fear, etc.). **18.** to silence. **—*v.i.*** **19.** to become quiet (often fol. by *down*). [ME < L *quiēt(us),* ptp. of *quiescere* to be quiet] **—qui′et·er,** *n.* **—qui′et·ly,** *adv.* **—qui′et·ness,** *n.* **—Syn. 2.** calm, serene. **6.** unmoving. **8.** See **still**[1]. **14.** still, hush, silence. **17.** lull, soothe. **—Ant. 2.** perturbed. **6.** active. **8.** noisy.

qui·et·en (kwī′i tən), *Chiefly Brit.* **—*v.i.*** **1.** to become quiet. **—*v.t.*** **2.** to make quiet. [QUIET[2] + -EN[1]] **—qui′et·en·er,** *n.*

qui·et·ism (kwī′i tiz′əm), *n.* **1.** a form of religious mysticism taught by Molinos, a Spanish priest, in the latter part of the 17th century, requiring extinction of the will, withdrawal from worldly interests, and passive meditation on God and divine things; Molinism. **2.** some similar form of religious mysticism. **3.** mental or bodily repose or passivity. [< It *quietismo.* See QUIET[2], -ISM] **—qui′et·ist,** *n., adj.* **—qui′et·is′tic,** *adj.*

qui·e·tude (kwī′i to͞od′, -tyo͞od′), *n.* state of being quiet; tranquillity; calmness; stillness; quiet. [< LL *quiētūdō,* deriv. of L *quiēt(us)* QUIET[2]; see -TUDE]

qui·e·tus (kwī ē′təs), *n., pl.* **-tus·es. 1.** a finishing stroke; anything that effectually ends or settles: *Having given a quietus to the argument, he left.* **2.** discharge or release from life. **3.** a period of retirement or inactivity: *After a quietus of ten years he returned.* [< ML: quit (in *quiētus est* he is quit, a formula of acquittance), L: he is quiet, at rest. (See QUIET[2], adj.); cf. QUIT[1] (adj.)]

quiff[1] (kwif), *n., pl.* **quiff, quiffs.** *Slang.* a girl or woman, esp. one of loose morals. [?]

quiff[2] (kwif), *n. Brit.* a lock or curl of hair brought forward over the forehead. [?]

quill (kwil), *n.* **1.** one of the large feathers of the wing or tail of a bird. **2.** the hard, hollow, basal part of a feather. **3.** a feather, as of a goose, formed into a pen for writing. **4.** one of the hollow spines on a porcupine or hedgehog. **5.** a device for plucking the strings of a musical instrument, as a harpsichord, made from the quill of a feather. **6.** a roll of bark, as of cinnamon, formed in drying. **7.** a reed or other hollow stem on which yarn is wound. **8.** a bobbin or spool. **9.** a toothpick. **10.** *Mach.* **a.** a hollow shaft or sleeve through which another independently rotating shaft may pass. **b.** a shaft, joined to and supported by two other shafts or machines, for transmitting motion from one to the other. **c.** a rotating toolholder used in boring or facing internal angles. **11.** *Archaic.* a musical pipe, esp. one made from a hollow reed. **—*v.t.*** **12.** *Textiles.* **a.** to arrange (fabric) in flutes or cylindrical ridges, as along the edge of a garment, hem, etc. **b.** to wind on a quill, as yarn. **13.** to penetrate with, or as with, a quill or quills. **14.** to extract a quill or quills from: *to quill a duck before cooking it.* [ME *quil;* cf. LG *quiele,* G *Kiel*] **—quill′-like′,** *adj.*

Quill (kwil), *n.* **Michael Joseph,** 1905–66, U.S. labor leader, born in Ireland: president of the Transport Workers Union of America 1935–66.

quil·lai (ki lī′), *n.* soapbark (def. 1). [< AmerSp < Chilean (Araucanian)]

quillai′ bark′, soapbark (def. 2).

quill·back (kwil′bak′), *n., pl.* **-backs,** (*esp. collectively*) **-back.** a carpsucker, *Carpiodes cyprinus,* found in the central and eastern U.S., having one ray of the dorsal fin greatly elongated. Also called **quill′back carp′sucker.** [QUILL + BACK[1]]

quill′ driv′er, *Slang.* one who does a great deal of writing, esp. an author or clerk. **—quill′ driv′ing.**

quill·er (kwil′ər), *n.* **1.** a machine for quilling yarn. **2.** one who operates such a machine. [QUILL + -ER[1]]

Quil·ler-Couch (kwil′ər ko͞och′), *n.* **Sir Arthur Thomas** ("Q"), 1863–1944, English novelist and critic.

quil·let (kwil′it), *n. Archaic.* a subtlety or quibble. [earlier *quillity,* var. of QUIDDITY] **—quil′let·ed,** *adj.*

quill·fish (kwil′fish′), *n., pl.* **-fish·es,** (*esp. collectively*) **-fish.** a fish, *Ptilichthys goodei,* found in the Bering Sea having an eellike body with long, many-rayed fins. [QUILL + FISH]

quill·ing (kwil′ing), *n.* **1.** the flutes or ridges in quilled material. **2.** quilled fabric, lace, ribbon, etc. **3.** coping. [QUILL + -ING[1]]

quil·lon (kē yôN′), *n., pl.* **quil·lons** (kē yôN′). either of two transverse projecting members forming the cross guard of a sword. [< F, deriv. of *quille* pin, club < MHG *kegel* club]

quill·wort (kwil′wûrt′), *n.* any aquatic and paludal, pteridophytic plant of the genus *Isoëtes,* characterized by clustered, quill-like leaves bearing sporangia in their bases. [QUILL + WORT[2]]

Quil·mes (kēl′mes), *n.* a city in E Argentina, near Buenos Aires. 318,144 (1960).

quilt (kwilt), *n.* **1.** a coverlet for a bed, made of two layers of fabric with some soft substance, as wool or down, between them and stitched in patterns or tufted through all thicknesses in order to prevent the filling from shifting. **2.** anything quilted or resembling a quilt. **3.** a bedspread or counterpane, esp. a thick one. **4.** *Obs.* a mattress. **—*v.t.*** **5.** to stitch together (two pieces of cloth and a soft interlining), usually in an ornamental pattern. **6.** to sew up between pieces of material. **7.** to pad or line with material. **—*v.i.*** **8.** to make quilts or quilted work. [ME *quilte* < OF *cuilte* < L *culcita* mattress, cushion] **—quilt′er,** *n.*

quilt·ed (kwil′tid), *adj.* **1.** resembling a quilt, as in texture, design, stitching, etc. **2.** padded or filled in the manner of a quilt. [QUILT + -ED[2]]

quilt·ing (kwil′ting), *n.* **1.** act of a person who quilts. **2.** material for making quilts. **3.** *Naut.* a heavily padded wrapping, as for fragile cargo, made of woven rope. [QUILT + -ING[1]]

quilt′ing bee′, *U.S.* a social gathering where women make quilts.

Quim·per (kaN per′), *n.* a port in and the capital of Finistère, in NW France: noted for pottery manufacture. 50,670 (1962).

quin·a·crine (kwin′ə krēn′), *n. Pharm.* an alkaloid, $C_{23}H_{30}ClN_3O$, similar in its properties to pamaquine, used in the treatment of malaria, esp. in the form of its hydrochloride. Also called **atebrin.** [QUIN(INE) + ACR(ID) + -INE[2]]

qui·nar·i·us (kwi nâr′ē əs), *n., pl.* **-nar·i·i** (-nâr′ē ī′). a denomination of ancient Roman coinage, issued in silver or gold at various times and undergoing many changes of value. [< L; see QUINARY]

qui·na·ry (kwī′nə rē), *adj., n., pl.* **-ries.** **—*adj.*** **1.** pertaining to or consisting of five. **2.** arranged in fives. **3.** of, pertaining to, or noting a numerical system based on the number 5. **—*n.*** **4.** a number in a quinary system. [< L *quīnāri(us),* equiv. to *quīn(ī)* five each + *-ārius* -ARY]

qui·nate (kwī′nāt), *adj. Bot.* arranged in groups of five. [< L *quīn(ī)* five each + -ATE[1]]

quin·az·o·line (kwi naz′ə lēn′, -lin), *n. Chem.* **1.** a colorless, crystalline, heterocyclic compound, $C_8H_6N_2$. **2.** any derivative of this compound. [QUIN(INE) + AZOLE + -INE[2]]

quince (kwins), *n.* **1.** the hard, yellowish, acid fruit of a small, hardy, rosaceous tree, *Cydonia oblonga.* **2.** the tree itself. [ME *qwince,* appar. orig. pl. (taken as sing.) of *quyne, coyn* < MF *cooin* < L *cotōneum,* var. of *cydōnium* < Gk *kydṓnion* quince, lit., (apple) of Cydonia]

quin·cun·cial (kwin kun′shəl), *adj.* **1.** consisting of, arranged, or formed like a quincunx or quincunxes. **2.** *Bot.* noting a five-ranked arrangement of leaves. [< L *quincunciāl(is),* equiv. to *quincunci-* (s. of *quincunx*) + *-ālis* -AL[1]] **—quin·cun′cial·ly,** *adv.*

quin·cunx (kwing′kungks, kwin′-), *n.* **1.** an arrangement of five objects, as trees, in a square or rectangle, one at each corner and one in the middle. **2.** *Bot.* an imbricated arrangement of five petals or leaves, in which two are interior, two are exterior, and one is partly interior and partly exterior. [< L: five twelfths (*quinque-* QUINQUE- + *uncia* twelfth; (see OUNCE[1]); orig. a Roman coin worth five twelfths of an as and marked with a quincunx of spots]

quin·cy (kwin′sē, -zē), *n., pl.* **-cies.** a small, flat-bottomed rowboat having sides that flare increasingly from the bow to a raking transom stern, used on the lower Mississippi River. [?]

Quin·cy (kwin′zē *for 1, 2;* kwin′sē *for 3–7*), *n.* **1. Josiah,** 1744–75, American patriot and writer. **2.** a city in E Massachusetts, near Boston. 87,409 (1960). **3.** a city in W Illinois, on the Mississippi. 43,793 (1960). **4.** a town in NW Florida. 8874 (1960). **5.** a town in central Washington. 3269 (1960). **6.** a town in NE California. 2723 (1960). **7.** a boy's given name.

quin·dec·a·gon (kwin dek′ə gon′), *n. Geom.* a polygon having 15 angles and 15 sides. [< L *quindec(im)* fifteen + *-agon* (abstracted from *decagon*)]

quin·de·cen·ni·al (kwin′di sen′ē əl), *adj.* **1.** of or pertaining to a period of 15 years or the 15th occurrence of a series, as an anniversary. **—*n.*** **2.** a 15th anniversary. [< L *quindec(im)* fifteen + *-ennial* (as in *decennial*)]

quin·de·cil·lion (kwin′di sil′yən), *n., pl.* **-lions,** (*as after a numeral*) **-lion,** *adj.* **—*n.*** **1.** a cardinal number represented in the United States and France by one followed by 48 zeros, and, in Great Britain and Germany, by one followed by 90 zeros. **—*adj.*** **2.** amounting to one quindecillion in number. [< L *quindec(im)* fifteen + *-illion* (as in *million*)] **—quin′de·cil′lionth,** *adj. n.*

quin·hy·drone (kwin hī′drōn, kwin′hī′drōn), *n. Chem.* a dark green, crystalline, slightly water-soluble solid, $C_6H_4O_2C_6H_4(OH)_2$, used in solution, together with a platinum wire, as an electrode (**quinhy′drone elec′trode**). [QUIN(INE) + HYDR(OQUIN)ONE]

quin·i·a (kwin′ē ə), *n. Chem.* quinine. [< NL; see QUININE, -IA]

quin′ic ac′id (kwin′ik), *Chem.* a white, crystalline, water-soluble, solid cyclic compound, $C_6H_7(OH)_4COOH$, present in cinchona bark, coffee beans, and the leaves of many plants. Also, **chinic acid.** [< Sp *quin(a)* quinine + -IC]

quin·i·dine (kwin′i dēn′, -din), *n. Pharm.* a colorless, crystalline alkaloid isomeric with quinine, $C_{20}H_{24}N_2O_2$, obtained from the bark of certain species of cinchona trees or shrubs: used esp. as the sulfate, chiefly to regulate the heart rhythm and to treat malaria. [QUIN(INE) + -ID[3] + -INE[2]]

qui·nine (kwī′nīn *or, esp. Brit.,* kwi nēn′), *n. Chem., Pharm.* **1.** a white, bitter, slightly water-soluble alkaloid, $C_{20}H_{24}N_2O_2$, having needlelike crystals, obtained from cinchona bark: used in medicine chiefly in the treatment of malaria and as a tonic to stimulate the appetite. **2.** a salt of this alkaloid, esp. the sulfate. Also, **qui·ni·na** (kē nē′nə). [< Sp *quin(a)* < Quechua *kina* bark + -INE[2]]

Quinn (kwin), *n.* a boy's given name, form of **Quentin.**

quin′nat salm′on (kwin′at). See **chinook salmon.** [< AmerInd (Salishan) *t′ kwinnat*]

qui·no·a (kē nō′ə), *n.* a goosefoot, *Chenopodium quinoa,* of South America, the seeds of which are used whole or ground for food. Also, **quinua.** [< Sp < Quechua *quinua*]

quin·oid (kwin′oid), *Chem.* **—*n.*** **1.** a quinonoid substance. **—*adj.*** **2.** quinonoid; quinoidal. [QUIN(ONE) + -OID] **—qui·noi′dal,** *adj.*

qui·noi·dine (kwi noi′dēn, -din), *n. Pharm.* a brownish-black, resinous substance consisting of a mixture of alkaloids, obtained as a by-product in the manufacture of quinine and used as a cheap substitute for it. Also, **chinoidine, chinoidin.** [QUIN(INE) + -OID + -INE[2]]

quin·ol (kwin′ōl, -ôl, -ol), *n. Chem.* hydroquinone. [QUIN(INE) + -OL[1]]

quin·o·line (kwin′əlēn′, -əlin), *n. Chem.* a colorless, liquid, water-immiscible, nitrogenous base, C_9H_7N, having a disagreeable odor, occurring in coal tar, and usually prepared by oxidizing a mixture of glycerol and aniline: used as a solvent, reagent, and to make dyes.

Also, **chinoline.** Also called **leucoline.** [QUINOL + -INE²]

qui·none (kwi nōn′, kwin′ōn), *n. Chem.* **1.** a yellow, crystalline, cyclic unsaturated diketone, $C_6H_4O_2$, the para isomer, formed by oxidizing aniline or hydroquinone: used chiefly in photography and in tanning leather. **2.** any of a class of compounds of this type. Also, **chinone.** [QUIN(IC ACID) + -ONE]

quinone′ di′i·mine (dī′ə mēn′), *Chem.* a colorless, crystalline solid, HN=C_6H_4=NH, the parent of the indamine dyes. Cf. **quinonimine.** [DI-¹ + -IMINE]

qui·non·i·mine (kwi non′ə mēn′, -min), *n. Chem.* a colorless, crystalline compound, O=C_6H_4=NH, the parent of the indophenol dyes, derived from quinone. Cf. **quinone diimine.** [QUIN(ONE) + -IMINE]

quin·o·noid (kwin′ə noid′, kwi nō′noid), *adj. Chem.* of or resembling quinone. Also, **quinoid.** [QUINONE + -OID]

quin·ox·a·line (kwi nok′sə lēn′, -lin), *n. Chem.* a colorless, crystalline, water-soluble powder, $C_8H_6N_2$, used chiefly in organic synthesis. Also, **quin·ox·a·lin** (kwi nok′sə lin). [QUIN(INE) + (GLY)OXAL + -INE²]

quinq., (in prescriptions) five. [< L *quinque*]

quin·qua·ge·nar·i·an (kwiŋ′kwə jə nâr′ē ən, kwin′-), *adj.* **1.** 50 years of age. **2.** between the ages of 50 and 60. —*n.* **3.** one who is 50 years old or whose age is between 50 and 60. [< L *quinquāgēnāri(us)* consisting of fifty + -AN]

quin·quag·e·nar·y (kwin kwä′jə ner′ē, kwiŋ-), *n., pl.* **-nar·ies.** a 50th anniversary. [< L *quinquāgēnārius*]

Quin·qua·ges·i·ma (kwiŋ′kwə jes′ə mə, kwin′-), *n.* the Sunday before Lent; Shrove Sunday. Also called **Quinquages′ima Sun′day.** [ME < ML, short for L *quinquāgēsima diēs* fiftieth day] —**Quin′qua·ges′i·mal,** *adj.*

quinque-, an element meaning "five," occurring in loan words from Latin (*quinquereme*); on this model, used in the formation of compound words: *quinquevalent.* [< L, comb. form of *quinque*]

quin·que·fid (kwin′kwə fid, kwiŋ′-), *adj.* cleft into five parts or lobes. [QUINQUE- + -FID]

quin·que·foil (kwin′kwə foil′, kwiŋ′-), *n.* cinquefoil (def. 2). [QUINQUE- + *-foil* (as in *trefoil*)]

quin·quen·ni·al (kwin kwen′ē əl, kwiŋ-), *adj.* **1.** of or for five years. **2.** occurring every five years. —*n.* **3.** something that occurs every five years. **4.** a fifth anniversary. **5.** a five-year term in office. **6.** a quinquennium. [late ME < L *quinquenni(s)* of five years + -AL¹] —**quin·quen′ni·al·ly,** *adv.*

quin·quen·ni·um (kwin kwen′ē əm, kwiŋ-), *n., pl.* **-quen·ni·ums, -quen·ni·a** (-kwen′ē ə). a period of five years. Also, **quin·quen·ni·ad** (kwin kwen′ē ad′, kwiŋ-). [< L]

quin·que·par·tite (kwiŋ′kwə pär′tīt, kwin′-), *adj.* divided into or consisting of five parts. [QUINQUE- + PARTITE]

quin·que·reme (kwiŋ′kwə rēm′, kwin′-), *n.* an ancient galley, believed either to have had five banks of oars or to have had each oar rowed by five men. [< L *quinquerēm(is)*, equiv. to *quinque* five + *rēm(us)* oar + *-is* adj. suffix]

quin·que·va·lent (kwiŋ′kwə vā′lənt, kwin′-, kwin-kwev′ə lənt, kwiŋ-), *adj. Chem.* **1.** pentavalent. **2.** exhibiting five different valences, as phosphorus with valences 5, 4, 3, 1, and -3. [QUINQUE- + -VALENT] —**quin·que·va·lence** (kwiŋ′kwə vā′ləns, kwin′-, kwin-kwev′ə ləns, kwiŋ-), **quin′que·va′len·cy,** *n.*

quin·sy (kwin′zē), *n. Pathol.* a suppurative inflammation of the tonsils; suppurative tonsillitis; tonsillar abscess. [ME *quin(e)sie* < ML *quinancia*, LL *cynanchē* < Gk *kynánchē* sore throat] —**quin′sied,** *adj.*

quint¹ (kwint, kint), *n.* **1.** an organ stop sounding a fifth higher than the corresponding digitals. **2.** *Piquet.* a sequence of five cards of the same suit, as an ace, king, queen, jack, and ten (**quint major**), or a king, queen, jack, ten, and nine (**quint minor**). [< F *quinte* (fem.) < L *quinta* fifth]

quint² (kwint), *n. Informal.* a quintuplet. [shortened form]

quint., (in prescriptions) fifth. [< L *quintus*]

quin·tain (kwin′tən), *n.* **1.** an object mounted on a post or attached to a movable crossbar mounted on a post, used as a target in the medieval sport of tilting. **2.** the sport of tilting at a quintain. [ME *quyntain* < MF *quintaine* < ML *quintāna* (L: street in a camp)]

Quintain

quin·tal (kwin′təl), *n.* **1.** *Metric System.* a unit of weight equal to 100 kilograms and equivalent to 220.462 avoirdupois pounds. **2.** hundredweight. [late ME < L *quintāle* < Ar *qinṭār* weight of a hundred pounds, prob. << L *centēnārius.* Cf. CENTENARY, KANTAR]

quin·tan (kwin′tən), *adj.* **1.** (of a fever, ague, etc.) characterized by paroxysms which recur every fifth day. —*n.* **2.** a quintan fever or ague. [< L *quintāna (febris)* (fever) belonging to the fifth]

Quin·ta·na Ro·o (kēn tä′nä rô′ô), a sparsely populated territory in SE Mexico, on the E Yucatán peninsula. *Cap.:* Chetumal. 19,435 sq. mi.

quin·tant (kwin′tənt), *n. Navig.* a sextant having an arc equal to one fifth of a circle. [*quint-* (< L *quintus* fifth) + *-ant* (as in *quadrant*)]

quinte (kant), *n. Fencing.* the fifth of eight defensive positions. [< F]

quinte·foil (kwint′foil′), *n.* cinquefoil (def. 2). [*quinte-* five, fifth (< F) + *-foil* (as in *trefoil*)]

quin·ter·ni·on (kwin tûr′nē ən), *n. Bookbinding.* five gathered sheets folded in two for binding together. [*quint-* five (< L *quintus* fifth) + *-ternion* (abstracted from *quaternion*)]

Quin·te·ro (kēn te′rô), *n.* See **Álvarez Quintero.**

quin·tes·sence (kwin tes′əns), *n.* **1.** the pure and concentrated essence of a substance. **2.** the most perfect embodiment of something. **3.** (in ancient and medieval philosophy) the fifth essence or element, ether, supposed to be the constituent matter of the heavenly bodies, the others being air, fire, earth, and water. [ME < ML *quinta essentia* fifth essence] —**quin·tes·sen·tial** (kwin′ti sen′shəl), *adj.* —**quin′tes·sen′tial·ly,** *adv.*

quin·tet (kwin tet′), *n.* **1.** any set or group of five persons or things. **2.** an organized group of five singers or players. **3.** a musical composition scored for five voices or instruments. Also, **quin·tette′.** [< F *quintette* < It *quintetto*, dim. of *quinto* fifth < L *quintus*]

quin·tic (kwin′tik), *Math.* —*adj.* **1.** of the fifth degree. —*n.* **2.** a quantity of the fifth degree. [< L *quint(us)* fifth + -IC]

quin·tile (kwin′til), *Astrol.* —*adj.* **1.** of or pertaining to the aspect of two heavenly bodies which are one fifth of the zodiac, or 72°, apart. —*n.* **2.** a quintile aspect. **3.** *Statistics.* a quantile for the special case of five equal proportions. [< L, neut. of *quintīlis* fifth]

Quin·til·ian (kwin til′yən, -ē ən), *n.* (*Marcus Fabius Quintilianus*) A.D. c35–c95, Roman rhetorician.

quin·til·lion (kwin til′yən), *n., pl.* **-lions,** (*as after a numeral*) **-lion,** *adj.* —*n.* **1.** a cardinal number represented in the U.S. and France by 1 followed by 18 zeros, and, in Great Britain and Germany, by 1 followed by 30 zeros. —*adj.* **2.** amounting to one quintillion in number. [< L *quint(us)* fifth + *-illion* (as in *million*)] —**quin·til′lionth,** *n., adj.*

quint′ ma′jor. See under **quint**¹ (def. 2).

quint′ mi′nor. See under **quint**¹ (def. 2).

quin·ton (kan tôN′), *n., pl.* **-tons** (-tôN′). an 18th-century violin with five strings. [< F, deriv. of *quint* fifth]

Quin·ton (kwin′tən), *n.* a boy's or girl's given name. Also, **Quentin, Quenton.**

quin·tu·ple (kwin to͞o′pəl, -tyo͞o′-, -tup′əl, kwin′to͞o-pəl, -tyo͞o-), *adj., n., v.,* **-pled, -pling.** —*adj.* **1.** fivefold; consisting of five parts. **2.** five times as great or as much. —*n.* **3.** a number, amount, etc., five times as great as another. —*v.t., v.i.* **4.** to make or become five times as great. [< F, equiv. to *quint* fifth + *-uple* (abstracted from *quadruple*)]

quintu′ple coun′terpoint, *Music.* invertible counterpoint involving five transposable voices.

quin·tu·plet (kwin tup′lit, -to͞o′plit, -tyo͞o′-, kwin′-to͞o plit, -tyo͞o-), *n.* **1.** any group or combination of five, esp. of the same kind. **2. quintuplets,** five children or offspring born of one pregnancy. **3.** one of five such children or offspring. **4.** *Music.* a group of five notes of equal value performed in the time normally taken for four. [QUINTUPLE + -ET]

quin·tu·pli·cate (*v.* kwin to͞o′plə kāt′, -tyo͞o′-; *adj., n.* kwin to͞o′plə kit, -tyo͞o′-), *v.,* **-cat·ed, -cat·ing,** *adj., n.* —*v.t.* **1.** to make fivefold; quintuple: *to quintuplicate a letter.* —*adj.* **2.** fivefold; quintuple. —*n.* **3.** one of five things. [< L *quintuplicāt(us)* (ptp. of *quintuplicāre*), equiv. to *quintuplic-* (s. of *quintuplex*) fivefold + *-ātus* -ATE¹] —**quin·tu′pli·ca′tion,** *n.*

qui·nua (kē′nwä), *n.* quinoa.

quip (kwip), *n., v.,* **quipped, quip·ping.** —*n.* **1.** a sharp, sarcastic remark; a cutting jest. **2.** a clever or witty remark or comment. **3.** a quibble. **4.** an odd or fantastic action or thing. —*v.i.* **5.** to utter quips. [back formation from *quippy* quip < L *quippe* indeed] —**quip′pish,** *adj.* —**quip′pish·ness,** *n.*
—**Syn. 1.** gibe, sally, jape. **2.** joke, witticism.

quip·ster (kwip′stər), *n.* a person who frequently makes quips. [QUIP + -STER]

qui·pu (kē′po͞o, kwip′o͞o), *n.* (among the ancient Peruvians) a device consisting of a cord with knotted strings of various colors attached, for recording events, keeping accounts, etc. [< Peruvian (Quechua): lit., knot]

quire¹ (kwīᵊr), *n.* **1.** a set of 24 uniform sheets of paper. **2.** *Bookbinding.* a section of printed leaves in proper sequence after folding; gathering. [ME *quayer* < MF *quaier* < VL **quaternum* set of four sheets, L *quaternī* four each]

quire² (kwīᵊr), *n., v.i., v.t.,* **quired, quir·ing.** *Archaic.* choir.

Quir·i·nal (kwir′ə nᵊl), *n.* **1.** one of the seven hills on which ancient Rome was built. **2.** the Italian civil authority and government (distinguished from the *Vatican*). —*adj.* **3.** noting or pertaining to the Quirinal. **4.** of or pertaining to Quirinus. [< L *Quirīnāl(is).* See QUIRINUS, -AL¹]

Qui·ri·nus (kwi rī′nəs), *n.* an ancient Roman god of war, identified with the deified Romulus; a personification of the Roman nation.

Qui·ri·tes (kwi rī′tēz), *n.pl.* the citizens of ancient Rome considered in their civil capacity. [< L, pl. of *Quirīs,* orig. an inhabitant of the Sabine town *Cures,* later a Roman citizen]

quirk (kwûrk), *n.* **1.** a peculiarity in action, behavior, or personality; mannerism: *He is full of strange quirks.* **2.** a shift, subterfuge, or evasion; a quibble. **3.** a sudden twist or turn: *He lost his money by a quirk of fate.* **4.** a flourish or showy stroke, as in writing. **5.** *Archit.* **a.** an acute angle or channel, as one dividing two parts of a molding or one dividing a flush bead from the adjoining surfaces. **b.** an area taken from a larger area, as a room or a plot of ground. **c.** an enclosure for this area. **6.** *Obs.* a quip. —*adj.* **7.** formed with a quirk or channel, as a molding. [?]

quirk·y (kwûr′kē), *adj.,* **quirk·i·er, quirk·i·est.** having, or full of, quirks. [QUIRK + -Y¹] —**quirk′i·ly,** *adv.* —**quirk′i·ness,** *n.*

quirt (kwûrt), *n.* **1.** a riding whip consisting of a short, stout stock and a lash of braided leather. —*v.t.* **2.** to strike with a quirt. [? < Sp *cuerda* cord]

quis cus·to·di·et ip·sos cus·to·des? (kwis ko͞o-stō′dē et′ ip′sōs ko͞o stō′des; *Eng.* kwis kə stō′dē-it ip′sōs kə stō′dēz), *Latin.* who shall keep watch over the guardians?

qui s'ex·cuse s'ac·cuse (kē sek skyz′ sa kyz′), *French.* whoever makes excuses for himself is incriminating himself; excuses are born of a guilty conscience.

quis·ling (kwiz′liŋ), *n.* a person who betrays his own country by aiding an invading enemy, often serving later in a puppet government; fifth columnist. [after Vidkun *Quisling* (1887–1945), pro-Nazi Norwegian leader]

quis se·pa·ra·bit? (kwis se′pä rä′bit; *Eng.* kwis sep′-ə rā′bit), *Latin.* who shall separate (us)?

quit (kwit), *v.,* **quit** or **quit·ted, quit·ting,** *adj.* —*v.t.* **1.** to stop, cease, or discontinue: *He quit what he was doing to help me paint the house.* **2.** to depart from; leave: *He quits the city for the seashore each summer.* **3.** to give up; let go; abandon; relinquish: *He quit his claim to the throne. He quit his job for a better position.* **4.** to release one's hold of (something grasped). **5.** *Archaic.* to acquit or conduct (oneself). —*v.i.* **6.** to cease from doing something; stop. **7.** to give up or resign one's job or position: *He keeps threatening to quit.* **8.** to depart or leave. **9.** to stop trying, struggling, or the like; accept or acknowledge defeat. —*adj.* **10.** released from obligation, penalty, etc.; free, clear, or rid (usually fol. by *of*): *quit of all further responsibilities.* [ME *quitte(n), quite(n)* < OF *quit(t)er* < ML *quittāre, quiētāre* to release, discharge, LL: QUIET²] —**quit′ta·ble,** *adj.*
—**Syn. 3.** resign, surrender, release. **10.** acquitted, discharged. —**Ant. 1, 6.** start. **2.** enter.

quitch (kwich), *n.* See **couch grass.** Also, **quitch′ grass′.** [OE *cwice,* c. D *kweek,* Norw *kvike;* akin to QUICK (adj.)]

quit·claim (kwit′klām′), *n. Law.* **1.** a transfer of all one's interest, as in a parcel of real estate, esp. without a warranty of title. —*v.t.* **2.** to quit or give up claim to (a possession, right, etc.). [ME *quitclayme* < AF *quiteclame,* deriv. of *quiteclamer* to declare quit. See QUIT (adj.), CLAIM]

quit′claim deed′, *Law.* a deed which conveys to the grantee only such interests in property as the grantor may have, the grantee assuming responsibility for any claims brought against the property. Cf. **warranty deed.**

quite (kwīt), *adv.* **1.** completely, wholly, or entirely: *quite the reverse; not quite finished.* **2.** actually, really, or truly: *quite a sudden change.* **3.** to a considerable extent or degree: *quite small; quite objectionable.* [ME, adv. use of *quite* (adj.) QUIT]

Quit·man (kwit′mən), *n.* a town in S Georgia. 5071 (1960).

Qui·to (kē′tô), *n.* a city in and the capital of Ecuador, in the N part. 368,217 (est. 1963); 9348 ft. above sea level.

qui trans·tu·lit sus·ti·net (kwē träns′to͞o lit so͞os′-ti net′; *Eng.* kwī trans′to͞o lit sus′tə net′, -tyo͞o lit), *Latin.* He who transplanted (it) sustains (it): motto of Connecticut.

quit·rent (kwit′rent′), *n.* rent paid by a freeholder or copyholder in lieu of services which might otherwise have been required of him. [QUIT + RENT¹]

quits (kwits), *adj.* **1.** on equal terms by repayment or retaliation. **2. call it quits, a.** to end one's activity, esp. temporarily: *At 10 o'clock he decided to call it quits for the day.* **b.** to abandon an effort: *They could not agree on policy, but finally called it quits and compromised.* **3. cry quits,** to agree to end competition and consider both sides equal: *It became too dark to continue play and they decided to cry quits.* [cf. QUIT (adj.); -s < ?]

quit·tance (kwit′ᵊns), *n.* **1.** recompense or requital. **2.** discharge from a debt or obligation. **3.** a document certifying discharge from debt or obligation, as a receipt. [ME *quitaunce* < OF *quittance,* equiv. to *quitt(er)* (to) QUIT + *-ance* -ANCE]

quit′ted trick′, *Cards.* a trick the cards of which have been collected by the taker and turned face down, further examination being prohibited.

quit·ter (kwit′ər), *n. Informal.* a person who quits or gives up easily, esp. in the face of some difficulty, danger, etc. [QUIT + -ER¹]

quit·tor (kwit′ər), *n. Vet. Pathol.* any of various infections of the foot in which tissues degenerate and form a slough, sometimes involving tendons and bone as well as skin. [ME *quittere* < OF *cuiture* cooking < L *coctūra,* equiv. to *coct(us)* (ptp. of *coquere* to cook) + *-ūra* -URE]

qui va là? (kē va lä′), *French.* Who goes there?

quiv·er¹ (kwiv′ər), *v.t., v.i.* **1.** to shake with a slight but rapid motion; vibrate tremulously; tremble. —*n.* **2.** act or state of quivering; a tremble; a tremor. [ME; c. MD *quiveren* to tremble] —**quiv′er·er,** *n.* —**quiv′er·ing·ly,** *adv.* —**quiv′er·y,** *adj.*
—**Syn. 1.** quake, shudder, shiver. See **shake. 2.** shudder, shiver, shake.

quiv·er² (kwiv′ər), *n.* **1.** a case for holding or carrying arrows. **2.** the arrows in such a case. [ME < AF *quiveir,* var. of OF *quivre;* ? < Gmc; cf. OE *cocer* quiver]

quiv·er³ (kwiv′ər), *adj. Archaic.* nimble; active. [ME *cwiver, quiver;* OE **cwifer* < ?]

quiv′er leg′, a round, tapered chair leg used in the Louis Quinze style and similar styles.

qui vive (kē vēv′), **1.** (*italics.*) *French.* Who goes there? **2. on the qui vive,** on the alert; watchful: *Special guards were on the qui vive for trespassers.*

Qui·xo·te (ki hō′tē, kwik′sət; *Sp.* kē hô′te), *n.* **Don.** See **Don Quixote.**

quix·ot·ic (kwik sot′ik), *adj.* **1.** (*sometimes cap.*) resembling or befitting Don Quixote. **2.** extravagantly chivalrous or romantic; visionary, impractical, or impracticable. Also, **quix·ot′i·cal.** [(DON) QUIXOTE + -IC] —**quix·ot′i·cal·ly,** *adv.*
—**Syn. 2.** fanciful, fantastic, imaginary. —**Ant. 2.** realistic, practical.

quix·ot·ism (kwik′sə tiz′əm), *n.* **1.** (*sometimes cap.*) quixotic character or practice. **2.** a quixotic idea or act. [(DON) QUIXOTE + -ISM]

quiz (kwiz), *v.,* **quizzed, quiz·zing,** *n., pl.* **quiz·zes.** —*v.t.* **1.** to examine or test (a student or class) informally by questions. **2.** to question closely: *The police quizzed several suspects.* **3.** *Chiefly Brit.* to make fun of; ridicule; mock; chaff. —*n.* **4.** an informal test or examination of a student or class. **5.** a questioning. **6.** a practical joke; a hoax. [?] —**quiz′za·ble,** *adj.* —**quiz′zer,** *n.*

quiz′ kid′, *Informal.* an unusually intelligent child.

quiz·mas·ter (kwiz′mas′tər, -mä′stər), *n.* a person who asks questions of contestants in a game, esp. as part of a radio or television program. [QUIZ + MASTER]

quiz′ pro′gram, a radio or television program in which contestants compete, often for prizes, by answering questions. Also called **quiz′ show′.**

quiz·zi·cal (kwiz′i kəl), *adj.* **1.** odd, queer, or comical. **2.** questioning or puzzled: *a quizzical expression on her face.* **3.** derisively questioning, ridiculing, or chaffing. [QUIZ + -ICAL] —**quiz′zi·cal′i·ty, quiz′zi·cal·ness,** *n.* —**quiz′zi·cal·ly,** *adv.*

Qum·ran (ko͝om′rän), *n.* See **Khirbet Qumran.** Also, **Qûm′ran.**

quo (kwō), *v.t. Archaic.* quoth.

quo·ad hoc (kwō′äd hōk′; *Eng.* kwō′ad hok′), *Latin.* as much as this; to this extent.

quo a·ni·mo? (kwō ä′ni mō′; *Eng.* kwō an′ə mō′), *Latin.* with what spirit or intention?

quod (kwod), *n. Chiefly Brit. Slang.* jail. Also, **quad.** [?]

quod′dy boat′ (kwod′ē), a double-ended keel boat, formerly used for lobstering and fishing along the coast of Maine, having a gaff mainsail and sometimes a jib set on a detachable bowsprit. [after (*Passama*)*quoddy Bay* between New Brunswick, Canada, and Maine]

quod e·rat de·mon·stran·dum (kwōd e′rät dem′-ōn strän′dōōm; *Eng.* kwod er′at dem′ən stran′dəm), *Latin.* which was to be shown or demonstrated.

quod e·rat fa·ci·en·dum (kwōd e′rät fä′kē en′-dōōm; *Eng.* kwod er′at fā′shē en′dəm), *Latin.* which was to be done.

quod·li·bet (kwod′lə bet′), *n.* **1.** a subtle or elaborate argument or point of debate, usually on a theological or scholastic subject. **2.** *Music.* a humorous composition consisting of two or more independent and harmonically complementary melodies, usually quotations of well-known tunes, played or sung together in a polyphonic arrangement. [ME < < L *quod libet,* lit., what pleases, as you please] —**quod′li·bet′ic, quod′li·bet′i·cal,** *adj.* —**quod′li·bet′i·cal·ly,** *adv.*

quod·li·betz (kwod′lə bets′), *n.* a painted decorative motif, as on ceramics, showing letters, playing cards, and various other small ordinary objects. [appar. var. of L *quod libet;* see QUODLIBET]

quod vi·de (kwod vī′dē). See **q.v.** [< L: which see]

quoin (koin, kwoin), *n.* **1.** an external solid angle of a wall or the like. **2.** one of the stones forming it; cornerstone. **3.** any of various bricks of standard shape for forming corners of brick walls or the like. **4.** a wedge-shaped piece of wood, stone, or other material, used for any of various purposes. **5.** *Print.* a wedge of wood or metal for securing type in a chase. —*v.t.* **6.** to provide with quoins, as a corner of a wall. **7.** to secure or raise with a quoin or wedge. Also, **coign, coigne.** [var. of COIN]

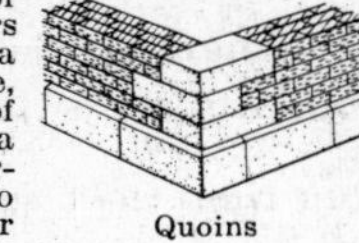
Quoins

quoit (kwoit), *n.* **1. quoits,** (*construed as sing.*) a game in which rings of rope or flattened metal are thrown at an upright peg, the object being to encircle it or come as close to it as possible. **2.** a ring used in the game of quoits. —*v.t.* **3.** to throw as or like a quoit. —*v.i.* **4.** to play quoits. [ME *coyte* < ?] —**quoit′er,** *n.* —**quoit′-like′,** *adj.*

quo ju·re? (kwō yōō′re; *Eng.* kwō jŏŏr′ē), *Latin.* by what right?

quo mo·do (kwō mō′dō), *Latin.* **1.** in what way? how? **2.** in the same manner that; as.

quon·dam (kwon′dam), *adj.* that formerly was or existed; former: *his quondam partner.* [< L]

Quon′set hut′ (kwon′sit), *Trademark.* a semicylindrical metal shelter having end walls, usually serving as a barracks, storage shed, or the like.

quor., (in prescriptions) of which. [< L *quōrum*]

quo·rum (kwôr′əm, kwōr′-), *n.* **1.** the number of members of a group or organization required to be present to transact business legally, usually a majority. **2.** a particularly chosen group. [< L *quōrum* of whom; from a use of the word in commissions written in Latin]

quot., quotation.

quo·ta (kwō′tə), *n.* **1.** the share or proportional part of a total which is required from, or is due or belongs to, a particular district, state, person, group, etc. **2.** a proportional part or share of a fixed total amount or quantity. **3.** the number of persons of a specified kind permitted to enter a college, join a club, immigrate to a country, etc. [< ML, short for L *quota pars* how great a part?]

quot·a·ble (kwō′tə bəl), *adj.* **1.** able to be quoted or easily quoted, as by reason of effectiveness, succinctness, or the like: *the most quotable book of the season.* **2.** suitable or appropriate for quotation: *His comments were hilarious but unfortunately not quotable.* [QUOTE + -ABLE] —**quot′a·bil′i·ty, quot′a·ble·ness,** *n.* —**quot′-a·bly,** *adv.*

quo·ta·tion (kwō tā′shən), *n.* **1.** that which is quoted; a passage quoted from a book, speech, etc.: *a speech full of quotations from Lincoln's letters.* **2.** act or practice of quoting. **3.** *Com.* **a.** the statement of the current or market price of a commodity or security. **b.** the price so stated. [< ML *quotātiōn-* (s. of *quotātiō*), equiv. to *quotāt(us)* (ptp. of *quotāre;* see QUOTE) + *-iōn-* -ION]

quota′tion mark′, one of the marks used to indicate the beginning and end of a quotation, in English usually shown as " at the beginning and " at the end, or, for a quotation within a quotation, of single marks of this kind, as "*He said, 'I will go.'* " Frequently, esp. in Great Britain, single marks are used instead of double, the latter being then used for a quotation within a quotation. Also, **quote mark.**

quote (kwōt), *v.,* **quot·ed, quot·ing,** *n.* —*v.t.* **1.** to repeat (a passage, phrase, etc.) from a book, speech, or the like, as by way of authority, illustration, etc. **2.** to repeat words from (a book, author, etc.). **3.** to cite, offer, or bring forward as evidence or support. **4.** to enclose (words) within quotation marks. **5.** *Com.* **a.** to state (a price). **b.** to state the current price of. —*v.i.* **6.** to make a quotation or quotations, as from a book or author. —*n.* **7.** a quotation. **8.** See **quotation mark.** [ME < ML *quotāre* to divide into chapters and verses, deriv. of L *quot* how many] —**quot′er,** *n.*

quote′ mark′. See **quotation mark.**

quote·wor·thy (kwōt′wûr′thē), *adj.* quotable. [QUOTE + WORTHY] —**quote′wor′thi·ness,** *n.*

quoth (kwōth), *v. Archaic.* said (used with nouns, and with first and third person pronouns, and always placed before the subject): *Quoth the raven, "Nevermore."* Also, **quo.** [preterit of *quethe* (otherwise obs.), OE *cwethan* to say. Cf. BEQUEATH]

quoth·a (kwō′thə), *interj. Archaic.* indeed! (used ironically or contemptuously in quoting another). [from *quoth a* quoth he]

quotid., (in prescriptions) daily. [< L *quotīdiē*]

quo·tid·i·an (kwō tid′ē ən), *adj.* **1.** daily: *a quotidian report.* **2.** everyday; ordinary. **3.** (of a fever, ague, etc.) characterized by paroxysms that recur daily. —*n.* **4.** something recurring daily. **5.** a quotidian fever or ague. [< L *quotīdiān(us)* daily; r. ME *cotidien* < OF] —**quo·tid′i·an·ly,** *adv.* —**quo·tid′i·an·ness,** *n.*

quo·tient (kwō′shənt), *n. Math.* the result of division; the number of times one quantity is contained in another. [ME < L *quotiens* how many times]

quo′tient group′, *Math.* a group, the elements of which are cosets with respect to a normal subgroup of a given group. Also called **factor group.**

quo′tient ring′, *Math.* a ring, the elements of which are cosets with respect to a given ideal. Also called **difference ring.**

quo′tient space′, *Math.* See **identification space.**

quot·i·es (kwot′ē ēz′), *conj.* (in prescriptions) as often as. [< L]

Quo Va·dis (kwō vä′dis), a historical novel (1895) by Henryk Sienkiewicz.

quo war·ran·to (kwō wô ran′tō, wo-), *Law.* **1.** (formerly, in England) a writ calling upon a person to show by what authority he claims an office, franchise, or liberty. **2.** (in England and the U.S.) a trial, hearing or other legal proceeding initiated to determine by what authority one has an office, franchise, or liberty. **3.** the pleading initiating such a proceeding. [ME < ML: by what warrant]

Qu·ran (kŏŏ rän′, -ran′), *n.* Koran.

Qutb (kōōt′əb), *n. Islam.* (in Sufi mysticism) a man believed to have been endowed by Allah with special powers. [< Ar]

q.v., **1.** (in prescriptions) as much as you wish. [< L *quantum vīs*] **2.** *pl.* **qq.v.** which see. [< L *quod vidē*]

Qy., query. Also, **qy.**

CONCISE ETYMOLOGY KEY: <, descended or derived from; >, whence; b., blend of, blended; c., cognate with; deriv., derivative; equiv., equivalent; imit., imitative; m., modification of; obl., oblique; r., replacing; s., stem; sp., spelling; trans., translation; ?, origin unknown, perhaps; *, hypothetical. See the full key inside the front cover.

R

R, r (är), *n., pl.* **R's** or **Rs, r's** or **rs. 1.** the 18th letter of the English alphabet, a consonant. **2.** any spoken sound represented by the letter *R* or *r*, as in *ran, carrot, rhyme,* etc. **3.** something having the shape of R. **4.** a written or printed representation of the letter *R* or *r*. **5.** a device, as a printer's type, for reproducing the letter *R* or *r*. **7.** See **three R's.**

R, 1. *Chem.* radical. **2.** *Math.* ratio. **3.** *Elect.* resistance. **4.** *Theat.* stage right. **5.** *Physics.* roentgen. **6.** *Chess.* rook.

R, 1. the 18th in order or in a series, or, when *I* is omitted, the 17th. **2.** (*sometimes l.c.*) the medieval Roman numeral for 80. Cf. **Roman numerals. 3.** *Physics.* See **universal gas constant. 4.** *Informal.* are: *Oysters R in season.*

r, 1. *Elect.* resistance. **2.** *Physics.* roentgen. **3.** royal. **4.** ruble. **5.** *pl.* **rs,** rupee.

R., 1. rabbi. **2.** Radical. **3.** radius. **4.** railroad. **5.** railway. **6.** rand[2]. **7.** Réaumur. **8.** Also, **R** (in prescriptions) take. [< L *recipe*] **9.** rector. **10.** redactor. **11.** regina. **12.** Republican. **13.** response. **14.** rex. **15.** river. **16.** road. **17.** royal. **18.** ruble. **19.** rupee. **20.** stage right.

r., 1. rabbi. **2.** radius. **3.** railroad. **4.** railway. **5.** range. **6.** rare. **7.** *Com.* received. **8.** recipe. **9.** replacing. **10.** residence. **11.** right. **12.** rises. **13.** river. **14.** road. **15.** rod. **16.** royal. **17.** rubber. **18.** ruble. **19.** *Baseball.* run; runs. **20.** *pl.* **rs.** rupee.

rā (rä), *n.* the 10th letter of the Arabic alphabet. [< Ar]

Ra (rä), *n.* *Egyptian Religion.* a sun god of Heliopolis, a universal creator worshiped throughout Egypt (typically represented as a hawk-headed man bearing on his head the solar disk and the uraeus). Also, **Re.**

RA, regular army.

Ra, *Chem.* radium.

R.A., 1. rear admiral. **2.** *Astron.* right ascension. **3.** royal academician. **4.** Royal Academy.

Raab (rab), *n.* **Julius,** born 1891, Austrian engineer and statesman.

R.A.A.F., Royal Australian Air Force.

Ra·am·ses (rā am′sēz), *n.* a city which was built for the Pharaoh by the Israelites and from which the Exodus began. Ex. 1:11. Also, **Rameses;** *Douay Bible,* **Ramesse, Ramesses.** Cf. **Pithom.**

rab (rab), *n.* a wooden beater for mixing plaster or mortar. [< F *rab(ot)* plane]

Rab (rab), *n.* a boy's given name, form of **Rob.**

ra·bal (rā′bəl), *n.* *Meteorol.* the measurement and computation of the speed and direction of winds aloft by theodolitic tracking of a radiosonde. Cf. **pibal.** [*ra(diosonde) bal(loon wind data)*]

ra·bat[1] (rab′ē, rə bat′), *n.* *Eccles.* a sleeveless, backless, vestlike garment extending to the waist, worn by a cleric beneath the clerical collar. Also called **rabbi.** [< MF; see REBATE[1]]

rab·at[2] (rab′ət), *n.* a piece of unglazed and imperfectly fired pottery, used for polishing hard surfaces. [< F, MF. See REBATE[1]]

Ra·bat (rä bät′), *n.* a seaport in and the capital of Morocco, in the NW part. 227,445 (1960).

ra·ba·to (rə bä′tō, -bā′-), *n., pl.* **-tos. 1.** a wide stiff collar of the 17th century, worn flat over the shoulders or open in front and standing at the back. **2.** a stiff frame of wire or wood worn in the 17th century as a support for a ruff or stand-up collar. Also, **rebato.** [< F (obs.) *rabateau;* cf. RABAT[1]]

Ra·baul (rä boul′, rä′boul), *n.* a seaport on NE New Briton island, in the Bismarck Archipelago. 36,043 indigenous (est. 1963).

rab·ban (rab′ən, rə bän′; *Heb.* RÄ bän′), *n., pl.* **rab·ba·nim** (rə bä′nim, rä′bə nēm′; *Heb.* RÄ bä nēm′). *Judaism.* master; teacher (used as a term of address and title of respect for a person ranking higher than a rabbi). [< Heb *rabbān* < Aram]

Rab·bath Am·mon (rab′əth am′ən), Amman.

rab·bet (rab′it), *n., v.,* **-bet·ed, -bet·ing.** —*n.* **1.** a deep notch formed in one edge of a board, framing timber, etc., so that something else can be fitted into it or so that a door or the like can be closed against it. **2.** a broad groove let into the surface of a board or the like; dado. —*v.t.* **3.** to cut a rabbet in (a board or the like). **4.** to join (boards or the like) by means of a rabbet or rabbets. —*v.i.* **5.** to join by a rabbet (usually fol. by *on* or *over*). Also, **rebate.** [ME *rabet* < OF *rabat;* see REBATE[1]]

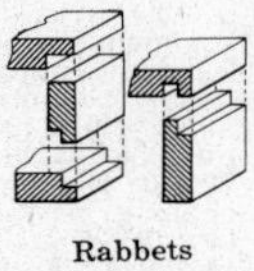

Rabbets

rab′bet draft′, *Naval Archit.* See **molded draft.**

rab′bet plane′, *Carpentry.* a plane for cutting rabbets or the like, having a blade set to one side at right angles or diagonally to the direction of motion.

rab′bet plank′, *Shipbuilding.* See **hog piece.**

rab·bi[1] (rab′ī), *n., pl.* **-bis. 1.** the chief religious official of a synagogue, trained usually in a theological seminary and duly ordained, who delivers the sermon at a religious service and performs ritualistic, pastoral, educational, and other functions in and related to his capacity as a spiritual leader of Judaism and the Jewish community. Cf. **cantor** (def. 2). **2.** a title of respect for a Jewish scholar or teacher. **3.** a Jewish scholar qualified to rule on questions of Jewish law. **4.** any of the Jewish scholars of the 1st to 6th centuries A.D. who contributed to the writing, editing, or compiling of the Talmud. [< LL *rabbī* < Gk *rhabbī* < Heb *rabbī* my master (*rabh* master + *-ī* my)]

rab·bi[2] (rab′ē), *n.* *Eccles.* rabat[1].

Rab·bi Le·vi (rab′ī lē′vī), a walled plain in the fourth quadrant of the face of the moon: about 50 miles in diameter.

rab·bin (rab′in), *n.* *Archaic.* rabbi[1]. [< F << Aram *rabbīn* masters (pl. of *rab*)]

rab·bin·ate (rab′ə nit), *n.* **1.** the office or term of office of a rabbi. **2.** a group of rabbis: *the Orthodox rabbinate.* [RABBIN + -ATE[1]]

Rab·bin·ic (rə bin′ik), *n.* the Hebrew language as used by rabbis in post-Biblical times. [RABBIN + -IC]

rab·bin·i·cal (rə bin′i kəl), *adj.* **1.** of or pertaining to rabbis or their learning, writings, etc. **2.** for the rabbinate: *a rabbinical school.* Also, **rab·bin′ic.** [< ML *rabbīn(us)* of a RABBI[1] + -ICAL]

rab·bin·ism (rab′ə niz′əm), *n.* the beliefs, practices, and precepts of the rabbis of the Talmudic period. [RABBIN + -ISM]

Rab·bin·ite (rab′ə nīt′), *n.* *Judaism.* a proponent of the Talmud and the teachings and traditions of the rabbis in the face of rejection by the Karaites. Also, **Rab·bin·ist** (rab′ə nist). Cf. **Karaite.** [RABBIN + -ITE[1]] —**rab·bin·it·ic** (rab′ə nit′ik), **rab′bin·is′tic, rab′bin·is′ti·cal,** *adj.*

rab·bit (rab′it), *n., pl.* **-bits,** (*esp. collectively*) **-bit** for 1–3. **1.** any of several rodentlike lagomorph mammals of the genus *Sylvilagus,* esp. the cottontail. **2.** a small, long-eared, burrowing lagomorph, *Lepus cuniculus,* of the hare family. **3.** the fur of any member of the rabbit family, usually processed to imitate another fur. **4.** See **Welsh rabbit. 5.** *Brit. Informal.* one who is poor at sports, esp. golf, tennis, or cricket. [ME *rabet,* prob. < ONF; cf. Walloon *robett,* Flem *robbe*] —**rab′bit-like′, rab′bit·y,** *adj.*

rab′bit ball′, a lively baseball, esp. the ball used in present-day baseball: *The pitchers keep complaining about the rabbit ball.*

rab′bit ban′dicoot, any of several bandicoots of the genus *Macrotis* (or *Thylacomys*), esp. *M. lagotis,* of the Australian region, having leathery, rabbitlike ears and a long, pointed snout. Also called **bilby.**

rab′bit ears′, 1. an indoor television antenna consisting of two telescoping, swivel-based aerials. **2.** *Sports Slang.* acute sensitivity to gibes, insults, or sarcasm: *Players with rabbit ears are the favorite targets of bench jockeys.*

rab′bit fe′ver, *Pathol., Vet. Pathol.* tularemia.

rab·bit·fish (rab′it fish′), *n., pl.* (*esp. collectively*) **-fish,** (*esp. referring to two or more kinds or species*) **-fish·es. 1.** a puffer, *Lagocephalus laevigatus.* **2.** a chimaera, *chimaera monstrosa.* [RABBIT + FISH, from the resemblance of its nose to a rabbit's]

rab′bit punch′, a short, sharp blow to the nape of the neck or the lower part of the skull.

rab·bit·ry (rab′i trē), *n., pl.* **-ries. 1.** a collection of rabbits. **2.** a place where rabbits are kept. [RABBIT + -RY]

rab′bit's foot′, 1. the foot of a rabbit, esp. the left hind foot carried as a good-luck charm. **2.** Also called **rab′bit's-foot clo′ver.** a clover, *Trifolium arvense.* Also, **rab′bit foot′, rab′bit-foot′.**

rab·ble[1] (rab′əl), *n., v.,* **-bled, -bling.** —*n.* **1.** a disorderly crowd; mob. **2. the rabble,** the lower classes; the common people: *The nobility held the rabble in complete contempt.* —*v.t.* **3.** to beset as a rabble does; mob. [ME *rabel;* ? akin to RABBLE[3]]

rab·ble[2] (rab′əl), *n., v.,* **-bled, -bling.** *Metall.* —*n.* **1.** a tool or mechanically operated device used for stirring or mixing a charge in a roasting furnace. —*v.t.* **2.** to stir (a charge) in a roasting furnace. [< F *râble* fire-shovel, tool, MF *raable* < L *rutābul(um)* fire-rake, equiv. to *rut(us)* (ptp. of *ruere* to upset, dig up) + *-ā-* thematic vowel + *-bulum* dim. suffix] —**rab′bler,** *n.*

rab·ble[3] (rab′əl), *v.t., v.i.,* **-bled, -bling.** *Brit. Dial.* to speak or read in a rapid, confused way. [late ME *rable;* cf. D *rabbelen* < Norw *rable;* ? imit.; see BABBLE]

rab·ble·ment (rab′əl mənt), *n.* a tumult; disturbance. [RABBLE[1] + -MENT]

rab·ble-rouse (rab′əl rouz′), *v.i.,* **-roused, -rousing.** to stir up the emotions or prejudices of the public; agitate. [back formation from RABBLE-ROUSER]

rab·ble-rous·er (rab′əl rou′zər), *n.* a person who stirs up the passions or prejudices of the public, usually for his own interests; demagogue.

rab·ble-rous·ing (rab′əl rou′zing), *adj.* of, pertaining to, or characteristic of a rabble-rouser.

Rab·e·lais (rab′ə lā′; *Fr.* RA ble′), *n.* **Fran·çois** (FRÄN SWA′), c1490–1553, French satirist and humorist.

Rab·e·lai·si·an (rab′ə lā′zē ən, -zhən), *adj.* **1.** of, pertaining to, or suggesting François Rabelais, whose work is characterized by broad, coarse humor and keen satire. —*n.* **2.** a person who admires or studies the works of Rabelais. [RABELAIS + -IAN] —**Rab′e·lai′si·an·ism,** *n.*

Ra·bi (rä′bē), *n.* **Is·a·dor Isaac** (iz′ə dôr′), born 1898, U.S. physicist: Nobel prize 1944.

Ra·bi·a (rə bē′ə), *n.* either of two successive months of the Islamic calendar, the third **(Rabia I)** or the fourth **(Rabia II).** [< Ar *rabī′* spring]

rab·id (rab′id), *adj.* **1.** irrationally extreme in opinion or practice: *a rabid isolationist; a rabid baseball fan.* **2.** furious or raging; violently intense: *a rabid hunger.* **3.** affected with or pertaining to rabies; mad. [< L *rabid(us)* raving, furious, mad, equiv. to *rab(ere)* (to) rave, be mad + *-idus* -ID[4]] —**rab·id′i·ty, rab′id·ness,** *n.* —**rab′id·ly,** *adv.*

ra·bies (rā′bēz, -bē ēz′), *n.* *Pathol.* an infectious disease of dogs, cats, other animals, and esp. of man, usually fatal if prophylactic treatment is not administered, caused by the virus *Formido inexoribilis,* and usually transmitted to man by the bite of an infected animal, chiefly a dog; hydrophobia. [< L *rabiēs* rage, madness, deriv. of *rabere* to be mad, rave] —**rab·ic** (rab′ik), *adj.*

Ra·bi·no·witz (rə bin′ə vits; *Russ.* RÄ′bi nô′vits), *n.* **Solomon** ("*Sholom Aleichem*"), 1859–1916, Russian author of novels, plays, and short stories in Yiddish.

ra·bi·ru·bi·a (rä′bə rōō′bē ə), *n.* yellowtail (def. 2). [< AmerSp *rabirrubia,* equiv. to Sp *rabo* tail + *rubia* golden]

Ra·born (rā′bərn), *n.* **William F.,** born 1905, U.S. admiral and government official: director of the CIA 1965–66.

rab·ot (rab′ət), *n.* a hardwood block used for rubbing marble before polishing. [< F: plane]

rac·coon (ra kōōn′), *n., pl.* **-coons,** (*esp. collectively*) **-coon. 1.** a small nocturnal carnivore, *Procyon lotor,* of North America, arboreal in habit, and having a sharp snout and a bushy ringed tail. 2. the thick gray to brown underfur of the raccoon, with silver gray guard hairs tipped with black. Also, **ra-coon.** [< AmerInd (Algonquian, Virginia) *ärähkunem* he scratches with the hands]

raccoon′ dog′, a small wild dog of the genus *Nycterentis,* of eastern Asia, having dark marks around the eyes resembling those of a raccoon.

Raccoon (Total length about 3 ft.; tail 1 ft.)

raccoon′ grape′. See **river-bank grape.**

race[1] (rās), *n., v.,* **raced, rac·ing.** —*n.* **1.** a contest of speed, as in running, riding, driving, sailing, etc. **2. races,** a series of races, usually of horses or dogs, run at a set time over a regular course: *They spent a day at the races.* **3.** any contest or competition: *an armament race; the race for the presidency.* **4.** onward movement; an onward or regular course. **5.** the course of time. **6.** the course of life or a part of life. **7.** *Geol.* **a.** a strong or rapid current of water, as in the sea or a river. **b.** the channel or bed of such a current or of any stream. **8.** an artificial channel leading water to or from a place where its energy is utilized. **9.** the current of water in such a channel. **10.** Also called **raceway.** *Mach.* a channel, groove, or the like, for sliding or rolling a part or parts, as the balls of a ball bearing. **11.** *Aeron. Obs.* the air projected to the rear by a propeller; slipstream. **12.** *Textiles.* **a.** the float between adjacent rows of pile. **b.** See **race plate.** —*v.i.* **13.** to engage in a contest of speed; run a race. **14.** to run horses or dogs in races; engage in or practice horse racing or dog racing. **15.** to run, move, or go swiftly. **16.** (of an engine, wheel, etc.) to run with undue or uncontrolled speed when the load is diminished without corresponding diminution of fuel, force, etc. —*v.t.* **17.** to run a race against; try to beat in a contest of speed. **18.** to cause to run in a race or races. **19.** to cause to run, move, or go at high speed: *to race a motor.* [ME *ras(e)* < Scand; cf. OIcel *rās* a running, race, rush of liquid; c. OE *rǣs* a running]

race[2] (rās), *n.* **1.** a group of persons related by common descent, blood, or heredity. **2.** a population so related. **3.** *Ethnol.* a subdivision of a stock, characterized by a more or less distinctive combination of physical traits that are transmitted in descent: *the Caucasian race; the Mongoloid race.* **4.** a group of tribes or peoples forming an ethnic stock. **5.** the condition of belonging to a certain ethnic stock. **6.** the distinguishing characteristics of various ethnic stocks. **7.** the human race or family; mankind: *Nuclear weapons pose a threat to the race.* **8.** *Zool.* a variety; a subspecies. **9.** a natural kind of living creature: *the race of fishes.* **10.** any group, class, or kind, esp. of persons: *Journalists are an interesting race.* **11.** (of speech, writing, etc.) characteristic quality, esp. liveliness or piquancy. **12.** the characteristic taste or flavor of wine. [< F < It *razz(a),* ? < Ar]
—**Syn. 1.** tribe, clan, family, stock, line, breed. Race, nation, people are terms for a large body of persons who may be thought of as a unit because of common characteristics. Race refers to a large body of persons, animals, or plants characterized by similarity of descent: *the white race.* Nation considers a body of persons as living under an organized government, occupying a fixed area, and dealing as a unit in matters of peace and war with other similar groups: *the English nation.* Whereas race and nation are objective, people has emotional connotations similar to those of *family.* People refers to the persons composing a race, nation, tribe, etc., as members of a body with common interests and a unifying culture: *We are one people; any people on any continent; the peoples of the world.* **7.** man.

race[3] (rās), *n.* a ginger root. [< MF *rais* < L *radic-* (s. of *radix*) root]

Race (rās), *n.* **Cape,** a cape at the SE extremity of Newfoundland.

race·a·bout (rās′ə bout′), *n.* a small, sloop-rigged racing yacht with a short bowsprit. [n. use of v. phrase *race about*]

race′ board′, *Naut.* a gangplank.

race·course (rās′kōrs′, -kôrs′), *n.* **1.** racetrack. **2.** a current of water, as a millrace. [RACE[1] + COURSE]

race′ horse′, a horse bred or kept for racing, esp. in flat races or steeplechases. Also, **race′-horse′, race′horse′.**

Race·land (rās′lənd), *n.* a town in SE Louisiana. 3666 (1960).

ra·ceme (rā sēm′, rə-), *n. Bot.* **1.** a simple indeterminate inflorescence in which the flowers are borne on short pedicels lying along a common axis, as in the lily of the valley. **2.** a compound inflorescence in which the short pedicels with single flowers of the simple raceme are replaced by racemes. [< L *racēm(us)* cluster of grapes, bunch of berries] —**ra·cemed′,** *adj.*

ra·ce·mic (rā sē′mik, -sem′ik, rə-), *adj. Chem.* noting or pertaining to any of various organic compounds in which racemism occurs. [< F *racémique* < L *racēm(us)* RACEME + F *-ique* -IC]

race′mic ac′id, *Chem.* an isomeric modification of tartaric acid that is sometimes found in the juice of grapes in conjunction with the common dextrorotatory form and is optically inactive but can be separated into the two usual isomeric forms, dextrorotatory and levorotatory.

ra·ce·mi·form (rā sē′mə fôrm′), *adj. Bot.* having the form of a raceme. [RACEME + -I- + -FORM]

rac·e·mism (ras′ə miz′əm, rā sē′miz əm), *n. Chem.* (of a compound) the state of being optically inactive and separable into two other substances of the same chemical composition as the original substance, one of which is dextrorotatory and the other levorotatory, as racemic acid. [RACEME + -ISM]

rac·e·mi·za·tion (ras′ə mi zā′shən), *n. Chem.* the conversion of an optically active substance into an optically inactive mixture of equal amounts of the dextrorotatory and levorotatory forms. [RACEME + -IZATION]

rac·e·mose (ras′ə mōs′), *adj.* **1.** *Bot.* **a.** having the form of a raceme. **b.** arranged in racemes. **2.** *Anat.* (of a gland) resembling a bunch of grapes; having branching ducts that end in acini. [< L *racēmōs(us)* full of clusters, clustering. See RACEME, -OSE[1]]

rac·e·mous (ras′ə məs), *adj.* racemose. —**rac′e·mous·ly,** *adv.*

rac·e·mule (ras′ə myōōl′), *n. Bot.* a small raceme. [RACEME + -ULE]

ra·cem·u·lose (ra sem′yə lōs′), *adj. Bot.* **1.** pertaining to or resembling a racemule. **2.** arranged in racemules. [RACEMULE + -OSE[1]]

race′ plate′, a metallic, plastic, or wooden strip directly in front of the reed on the lay of the loom, along which the shuttle travels in its passage through the shed. Also, **race′plate′.** Also called **race.**

rac·er (rā′sər), *n.* **1.** one who or that which races or takes part in a race, as a race horse, bicycle, yacht, etc. **2.** anything having great speed. **3.** See **racing skate. 4.** a turntable on which a heavy gun is turned. **5.** any of several slender, active snakes of the genera *Coluber* and *Masticophis.* [RACE[1] + -ER[1]]

race′ ri′ot, a riot resulting from racial animosity.

race·run·ner (rās′run′ər), *n.* a whiptail lizard, *Cnemidophorus sexlineatus,* common in the eastern and central U.S., that runs with great speed. [RACE[1] + RUNNER]

race′ su′icide, the extinction of a race or people that tends to result when, through the unwillingness or forbearance of its members to have children, the birth rate falls below the death rate.

race′ track′, **1.** a plot of ground, usually oval, laid out for horse racing. **2.** the course for any race. Also, **race′-track′, race′track′.**

race·way (rās′wā′), *n.* **1.** *Chiefly Brit.* a passage or channel for water, as a millrace. **2.** a race track on which harness races are held. **3.** *Elect.* a channel for protecting and holding electrical wires and cables, esp. a metal rectangular tube used for such purposes. **4.** *Mach.* race[1] (def. 10). [RACE[1] + WAY]

Ra·chel (rā′chəl *for 1, 3;* RA shel′ *for 2*), *n.* **1.** Jacob's favorite wife, the mother of Joseph and Benjamin. Gen. 29–35. **2.** (*Elisa Félix*) c1820–58, French actress. **3.** a girl's given name.

ra·chi·form (rā′kə fôrm′), *adj. Bot.* having the form of a rachis. [RACHI(S) + -FORM]

ra·chil·la (rə kil′ə), *n., pl.* **-chil·lae** (-kil′ē). *Bot.* a small or secondary rachis, as the axis of a spikelet in a grass inflorescence. [< NL; dim. of RACHIS]

ra·chis (rā′kis), *n., pl.* **ra·chis·es, rach·i·des** (rak′i dēz′, rā′ki-). **1.** *Bot.* **a.** the axis of an inflorescence when somewhat elongated, as in a raceme. **b.** (in a pinnately compound leaf or frond) the prolongation of the petiole along which the leaflets are disposed. **c.** any of various axial structures. **2.** *Ornith.* the part of the shaft of a feather bearing the web. See illus. under **feather. 3.** *Anat.* See **spinal column.** Also, **rhachis.** [< NL < Gk *rháchis* spine, ridge] —**ra·chid·i·an** (rə kid′ē ən), **ra·chi·al** (rā′kē-əl), **ra·chid′i·al,** *adj.*

R, Rachis (def. 1b)

ra·chi·tis (rə kī′tis), *n. Pathol.* rickets. [< NL < Gk *rhachītis* inflammation of the spine. See RACHIS, -ITIS] —**ra·chit·ic** (rə kit′ik), *adj.*

Rach·ma·ni·noff (räk mä′nə nôf′; *Russ.* RÄKH mä′ni-nôf′), *n.* **Ser·gei Was·si·lie·vitch** (seʀ gā′ väs sē′lyə-vich), 1873–1943, Russian pianist and composer. Also, **Rach·ma′ni·nov′.**

ra·cial (rā′shəl), *adj.* of, pertaining to, or characteristic of race, a race, or races: *racial prejudice; racial conflict.* [RACE[2] + -IAL] —**ra′cial·ly,** *adv.*

ra·cial·ism (rā′shə liz′əm), *n.* the belief in or the practice of the doctrine of racism. [RACIAL + -ISM] —**ra′cial·ist,** *n.* —**ra′cial·is′tic,** *adj.*

ra·ci·nage (ras′ə näzh′; *Fr.* RA sē NAZH′), *n.* decorative treatment of leather with colors and acids to produce a branchlike effect. [< F, equiv. to *racine* root + *-age* -AGE]

Ra·cine (RA sēn′ *for 1;* rə sēn′, rā- *for 2*), *n.* **1. Jean Bap·tiste** (zhäɴ BA tēst′), 1639–99, French dramatist. **2.** a city in SE Wisconsin. 89,144 (1960).

rac′ing flag′, a distinguishing flag flown by a yacht during the period of its participation in a race.

rac′ing form′, a sheet that provides detailed information about horse races, including background data on the horses, jockeys, etc.

rac′ing gig′, a light, narrow racing boat for two or more oarsmen.

rac′ing skate′, a tubular ice skate having a long blade extending beyond the heel and toe. Also called **racer, speed skate.** Cf. **figure skate, hockey skate, tubular skate.**

rac′ing skiff′, a very narrow racing boat for a single oarsman, having oarlocks on outriggers. Also called **single shell.**

rac·ism (rā′siz əm), *n.* **1.** a belief that human races have distinctive characteristics that determine their respective cultures, usually involving the idea that one's own race is superior and has the right to rule others. **2.** a policy of enforcing such asserted right. **3.** a system of government and society based upon it. [< F *racisme.* See RACE[2], -ISM] —**rac′ist,** *n., adj.*

rack[1] (rak), *n.* **1.** a framework of bars, wires, or pegs on which articles are arranged or deposited: *a clothes rack.* **2.** a spreading framework set on a wagon for carrying hay, straw, or the like, in large loads. **3.** *Pool.* **a.** a wooden frame of triangular shape within which the balls are arranged before play. **b.** the balls so arranged: *He took aim at the rack.* **4.** *Mach.* **a.** a bar, with teeth on one of its sides, adapted to engage with the teeth of a pinion or the like, as for converting circular into rectilinear motion or vice versa. **b.** a bar having a series of notches engaging with a pawl or the like. **5.** a former instrument of torture consisting of a framework on which a victim was tied, often spread-eagled, by his wrists and ankles, to be slowly stretched by spreading the parts of the framework. **6.** a cause or state of intense suffering of body or mind. **7.** torment; anguish. **8.** violent strain. **9. on the rack, a.** under pressure or strain. **b.** in a state of distress or anxiety: *He was on the rack during the entire examination.* —*v.t.* **10.** to torture; distress acutely; torment. **11.** to strain in mental effort: *to rack one's brains.* **12.** to strain by physical force or violence. **13.** to strain beyond what is normal or usual. **14.** to stretch the body of (a person) in torture by means of a rack. **15.** *Naut.* to seize (two ropes) together side by side. **16.** *Pool.* to put (the balls) in a rack (often fol. by *up*). [ME *rekke, rakke* < MD *rec, reck-* or MLG *rek, rekke*] —**rack′ing·ly,** *adv.*
—**Syn. 1.** crib. **7.** torture, pain, agony. **10.** See **torment. 12.** wrench.

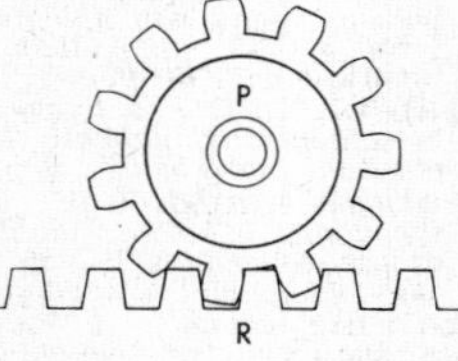

R, Rack[1] (def. 4a); P, Pinion

rack[2] (rak), *n.* **1.** *Obs.* wreck; destruction. **2. go to rack and ruin,** to decay, decline, or become destroyed: *His property went to rack and ruin in his absence.* [var. of WRACK[1]]

rack[3] (rak), *n.* **1.** the fast pace of a horse in which the legs move in lateral pairs but not simultaneously. —*v.i.* **2.** (of horses) to move in a rack. **3.** to pace. [? var. of ROCK[2]]

rack[4] (rak), *n.* **1.** Also called **cloud rack.** a group of drifting clouds. —*v.i.* **2.** to drive or move, esp. before the wind. **3.** a route or path, esp. of storm clouds. **4.** a mark or trace. Also, **wrack.** [ME *wrak,* OE *wræc* what is driven (by wind or wave); c. MD, MLG *wrak* wreckage, a wreck; akin to OE *wrecan,* Icel *reka* to drive. See WREAK]

rack[5] (rak), *v.t.* to draw off (wine, cider, etc.) from the lees. [late ME < OF; cf. obs. F *raqué* (of wine) pressed from the dregs of grapes]

rack[6] (rak), *n.* **1.** the neck portion of mutton, pork, or veal. **2.** See **hotel rack.** [ME; OE *hrace;* c. G *Rachen,* MD *rake*]

rack·board (rak′bōrd′, -bôrd′), *n.* a board with holes into which organ pipes are fitted. [RACK[1] + BOARD]

rack′ car′, *Railroads.* a flatcar containing a frame or frames for carrying various objects, as automobiles, logs, girders, etc.

rack′ clock′, a clock descending a rack and driven by its own weight. Also called **ratchet clock.**

rack·et[1] (rak′it), *n.* **1.** a loud noise, esp. of a disturbing or confusing kind; din; uproar; clamor or noisy fuss: *The traffic made a terrible racket in the street below.* **2.** social excitement, gaiety, or dissipation. **3.** an organized illegal activity, such as bootlegging or the extortion of money from legitimate businessmen by threat or violence. **4.** *Informal.* a dishonest scheme, trick, business, activity, etc.: *the latest weight-reducing racket.* **5.** Usually, **rackets** (prec. by *the*). organized illegal activities: *Some say that the revenue from legalized gambling supports the rackets.* **6.** *Slang.* source of livelihood; business: *He practices engineering as his racket.* —*v.i.* **7.** to make a racket or noise. **8.** to take part in social gaiety or dissipation. [metathetic var. of dial. *rattick;* see RATTLE[1]]
—**Syn. 1.** tumult, disturbance, outcry. See **noise.** —**Ant. 1, 2.** tranquillity.

rack·et[2] (rak′it), *n.* **1.** a light bat having a netting of catgut or nylon stretched in a more or less oval frame and used for striking the ball in tennis, the shuttlecock in badminton, etc. **2.** the short-handled paddle used to strike the ball in table tennis. **3. rackets,** (*construed as sing.*) racquet (def. 2). **4.** a snowshoe made in the form of a tennis racket. Also, **racquet.** [< MF *raquette, rachette,* ? < Ar *rāḥat* palm of the hand] —**rack′et-like′,** *adj.*

Rackets[2] A, Tennis; B, Court tennis; C, Squash; D, Squash tennis; E, Badminton; F, Paddle tennis; G, Table tennis

rack·et·eer (rak′i tēr′), *n.* **1.** a person engaged in a racket. —*v.i.* **2.** to engage in a racket. [RACKET[1] + -EER]

rack·ett (rak′it), *n.* ranket.

rack·e·ty (rak′i tē), *adj.* **1.** making or causing a racket; noisy. **2.** fond of excitement or dissipation. [RACKET[1] + -Y[1]]

rack·ing (rak′ing), *n. Masonry.* the stepping back of the ends of courses successively from bottom to top in an unfinished wall to facilitate resumption of work or bonding with an intersecting wall. [RACK[1] + -ING[1]]

rack′ locomo′tive, a locomotive designed for operation on a rack railway. Also called **cog locomotive.**

rack′ rail′, (in an inclined-plane or mountain-climbing railway) a rail between the running rails having cogs or teeth with which cogwheels on the locomotive engage.

rack′ rail′way. See **cog railway.**

rack-rent (rak′rent′), *n.* **1.** Also, **rack′ rent′.** rent equal to or nearly equal to the full annual value of a property. —*v.t.* **2.** to exact the highest possible rent for. **3.** to demand rack-rent from. —**rack′-rent′er,** *n.*

rack′ saw′, *Carpentry.* a saw with wide teeth.

rack·work (rak′wûrk′), *n.* a mechanism utilizing a rack, as a rack and pinion. [RACK[1] + WORK]

ra·con (rā′kon), *n.* See **radar beacon.** [*ra(dar bea)con*]

rac·on·teur (rak′on tûr′), *n.* a person who is skilled in relating anecdotes interestingly. [< F, equiv. to *racont(er)* (OF, equiv. to *re-* RE- + *aconter* to tell, ACCOUNT) + *-eur* -OR[2]]

rac·on·teuse (rak′on tōōz′; *Fr.* RA kôɴ tœz′), *n., pl.* **-teus·es** (-tōō′ziz; *Fr.* -tœz′). a female raconteur. [< F]

ra·coon (ra kōōn′), *n., pl.* **-coons,** (*esp. collectively*) **-coon.** raccoon.

rac·quet (rak′it), *n.* **1.** racket[2]. **2. racquets,** (*construed as sing.*) a game played with rackets and a ball by two or four persons on a four-walled court. [var. of RACKET[2]]

rac·quet·ball (rak′it bôl′), *n.* an indoor game played on a handball court in which a rubber ball is hit against the front wall by two or four players using short-handled strung racquets.

rac·y (rā′sē), *adj.,* **rac·i·er, rac·i·est. 1.** vigorous; lively; spirited. **2.** sprightly; piquant; pungent: *a* racy literary style. **3.** having an agreeably peculiar taste or flavor, as wine, fruit, etc. **4.** suggestive; risqué: *a racy story.* [RACE[1] + -Y[1]] —**rac′i·ly,** *adv.* —**rac′i·ness,** *n.*

—**Syn. 1.** animated. **2.** strong. —**Ant. 1.** slow.

rad (rad), *n.* a unit of absorbed radiation dose, equal to the radiation dose that contains 100 ergs of energy per gram of the absorbing material. [shortened form of RADIATION]

rad, radian; radians.

rad., **1.** *Math.* radical. **2.** radix.

ra·dar (rā′där), *n.* *Electronics.* a device for determining the presence and location of an object by measuring the time for the echo of a radio wave to return from it and the direction from which it returns. [*ra(dio) d(etecting) a(nd) r(anging)*]

ra′dar bea′con, a radar device at a fixed location which, on receiving a radar signal, automatically transmits a particular radar signal in reply, identifying itself and enabling navigators of ships and aircraft to determine their distance and direction from it. Also called **racon.**

ra·dar·man (rā′där mən, -man′), *n., pl.* **-men** (-mən, -men′). a person who operates or helps to operate radar equipment. [RADAR + MAN[1]]

ra·dar·scope (rā′där skōp′), *n.* the viewing screen of radar equipment. [RADAR + -SCOPE]

rad·dle[1] (rad′əl), *v.t.,* **-dled, -dling.** *Brit. Dial.* to interweave; wattle. [v. use of *raddle* lath < AF *reidele* pole, rail of a cart (OF *redelle;* cf. F *ridelle*)]

rad·dle[2] (rad′əl), *n., v.,* **-dled, -dling.** —*n.* **1.** ruddle. —*v.t.* **2.** ruddle. **3.** to color coarsely.

rad·dle·man (rad′əl mən), *n., pl.* **-men.** ruddleman.

ra·deau (rə dō′), *n., pl.* **-deaux** (-dō′, -dōz′). an armed scow, variously rigged, used as a floating battery during the American Revolution. [< F: raft < Pr *radel* < VL *ratell(us), dim. of L *ratis* raft]

ra·dec·to·my (rə dek′tə mē), *n., pl.* **-mies.** *Dentistry, Surg.* excision of part or all of the root of a tooth. [RAD(IX) + -ECTOMY]

Ra·dek (rä′dyək), *n.* **Karl** (kärl), born 1885, Russian writer and politician.

Ra·detz·ky (rä dets′kē), *n.* **Count Jo·seph** (yō′zef), 1766–1858, Austrian field marshal.

Rad·ford (rad′fərd), *n.* **1. Arthur William,** born 1896, U.S. admiral: chairman of Joint Chiefs of Staff 1953–57. **2.** a town in SW Virginia. 9371 (1960).

Ra·dha (rä′dä), *n.* *Hindu Legend.* the milkmaid who became the consort of Krishna.

Ra·dha·krish·nan (rä də krish′nən), *n.* **Sar·ve·pal·li** (sär ve päl′lē), born 1888, president of India since 1962.

ra·di·al (rā′dē əl), *adj.* **1.** arranged like radii or rays. **2.** having spokes, bars, lines, etc., arranged like radii, as a machine. **3.** made in the direction of a radius; going from the center outward or from the circumference inward along a radius: *a radial cut.* **4.** *Zool.* pertaining to structures that radiate from a central point, as the arms of a starfish. **5.** of, like, or pertaining to a radius or a ray. **6.** *Mach.* **a.** having pistons moving inward and outward from a central point or shaft: *a radial engine; a radial pump.* **b.** noting a bearing designed primarily to take thrusts radial to the center of rotation. **7.** *Anat.* of, pertaining to, or situated near the radius. **8.** acting along or in the direction of the radius of a circle: *radial motion; radial velocity.* **9.** *Entomol.* pertaining to, involving, or situated near the radius. **10.** *Naut.* (of a paddle wheel) having floats radially mounted with no provision for feathering. [< ML *radiāl(is),* equiv. to L *radi(us)* RADIUS + *-ālis* -AL[1]] —**ra′di·al′i·ty,** *n.* —**ra′di·al·ly,** *adv.*

Radial arrangement of lines
C, Center

ra′dial mo′tion, *Astron.* the component of the motion of a star away from or toward the earth along its line of sight, expressed in miles or kilometers per second and determined by the shift in the wave length of light emitted by the star. Cf. **red shift, tangential motion.**

ra′dial saw′, a cantilevered circular saw adjustable at various angles to the length of the work and to the perpendicular.

ra′dial triangula′tion, *Photogrammetry.* triangulation based upon lines radiating from the center of each of two overlapping photographs to certain objects appearing on each photograph.

ra·di·an (rā′dē ən), *n.* *Math.* an angle at the center of a circle, subtending an arc of the circle equal in length to the radius: equal to 57.2958°. *Abbr.:* rad [RADI(US) + -AN]

ra·di·ance (rā′dē əns), *n.* **1.** radiant brightness or light: *the radiance of the tropical sun.* **2.** warm, cheerful brightness: *the radiance of her expression.* **3.** *Archaic.* radiation. Also, **radiancy.** [RADI(ANT) + -ANCE]

ra·di·an·cy (rā′dē ən sē), *n., pl.* **-cies.** radiance. [RADIANT + -CY]

ra·di·ant (rā′dē ənt), *adj.* **1.** emitting rays of light; shining; bright: *the radiant sun; radiant colors.* **2.** bright with joy, hope, etc.: *radiant smiles; a radiant future.* **3.** *Physics.* emitted or propagated by radiation. **4.** *Heraldry.* **a.** noting a partition line having a series of flamelike indentations formed by ogees joined in zigzags; rayonny. **b.** (of a charge, as an ordinary) having an edge or edges so formed. —*n.* **5.** a point or object from which rays proceed. **6.** *Astron.* the point in the heavens from which a shower of meteors appears to radiate. **7.** a refractory absorbing and radiating heat from the flames of a gas fireplace or the like. [ME < L *radiant-* (s. of *radiāns,* prp. of *radiāre*) emitting beams, equiv. to *rad(ius)* beam, ray (see RADIUS) + *-ant-* -ANT] —**ra′di·ant·ly,** *adv.*

—**Syn. 1.** beaming, refulgent, resplendent. See **bright.** —**Ant. 1.** dim.

ra′diant emit′tance, *Optics.* radiant flux emitted per unit area.

ra′diant en′ergy, **1.** *Physics.* energy transmitted in wave motion, esp. electromagnetic wave motion. **2.** light (def. 2a).

ra′diant flux′, *Physics.* the time rate of flow of radiant energy.

ra′diant heat′, *Thermodynamics.* heat energy transmitted by electromagnetic waves in contrast to heat transmitted by conduction or convection.

ra′diant heat′ing, **1.** the means of heating objects or persons by radiation in which the intervening air is not heated. Cf. **convection** (def. 1). **2.** a system for heating by radiation from a surface, esp. from a surface heated by means of electric resistance, hot water, etc.

ra·di·ate (*v.* rā′dē āt′; *adj.* rā′dē it, -āt′), *v.,* **-at·ed, -at·ing,** *adj.* —*v.i.* **1.** to spread or move like rays or radii from a center. **2.** to emit rays, as of light or heat; irradiate. **3.** to issue or proceed in rays. **4.** (of persons) to project cheerfulness, joy, etc.: *She simply radiates with good humor.* —*v.t.* **5.** to emit in rays; disseminate, as from a center. **6.** (of persons) to project (joy, good will, etc.). —*adj.* **7.** radiating from a center. **8.** represented with rays proceeding from it, as a head on a coin, in art, etc. [< L *radiāt(us)* (ptp. of *radiāre*). See RADIANT, -ATE[1]] —**ra′di·a·bil′i·ty, ra′di·a·ble·ness,** *n.* —**ra′di·a·ble,** *adj.* —**ra′di·a·bly,** *adv.*

ra·di·a·tion (rā′dē ā′shən), *n.* **1.** *Physics.* **a.** the process in which energy is emitted as particles or waves. **b.** the complete process in which energy is emitted by one body, transmitted through an intervening medium or space, and absorbed by another body. **c.** the energy transferred by these processes. **2.** the act or process of radiating. **3.** something that is radiated. **4.** radial arrangement of parts. [< L *radiātiōn-* (s. of *radiātiō*) a glittering, shining. See RADIATE, -ION] —**ra′di·a′tion·al,** *adj.*

radia′tion belt′, *Physics.* See **Van Allen belt.**

radia′tion fog′, fog produced by the nocturnal cooling of the surface boundary layer to a temperature at which its content of water vapor condenses. Also called **ground fog.**

radia′tion poten′tial, *Physics.* the potential in volts that must be applied to an atom or molecule to cause it to emit radiation at one of its characteristic frequencies.

radia′tion sick′ness, *Pathol.* sickness caused by irradiation with x-rays or radioactive materials as a result of therapeutic treatment, accidental exposure, or an atomic-bomb explosion and characterized by nausea, vomiting, headache, cramps, diarrhea, loss of hair and teeth, decrease in blood cells, and prolonged hemorrhage.

ra·di·a·tive (rā′dē ā′tiv), *adj.* giving off radiation. Also, **ra·di·a·to·ry** (rā′dē ə tôr′ē). [RADIAT(ION) + -IVE]

ra′diative cap′ture, *Physics.* the capture of a particle, as a neutron, by a nucleus, inducing the emission of electromagnetic radiation, as a gamma ray.

ra·di·a·tor (rā′dē ā′tər), *n.* **1.** one who or that which radiates. **2.** any of various heating devices, as a series or coil of pipes through which steam or hot water passes. **3.** a device constructed from thin-walled tubes and metal fins, used for cooling circulating water, as in an automobile engine. **4.** *Radio.* a transmitting antenna. [RADIATE + -OR[2]]

ra′diator grille′, a grille in an automobile or the like for air cooling of the water in the cooling system.

ra·di·a·tus (rā′dē ā′təs), *adj.* *Meteorol.* (of a cloud) having bands that appear to converge toward a point on the horizon. [< NL; see RADIATE]

rad·i·cal (rad′i kəl), *adj.* **1.** of or pertaining to the root or origin; fundamental: *a radical difference.* **2.** thoroughgoing or extreme, esp. as regards change from accepted or traditional forms: *a radical change in the policy of a company.* **3.** (*often cap.*) favoring drastic political, economic, or social reforms: *radical ideas; the Radical Right.* **4.** forming a basis or foundation. **5.** existing inherently in a thing or person: *radical defects of character.* **6.** *Math.* **a.** pertaining to or forming a root. **b.** denoting or pertaining to the radical sign. **c.** irrational (def. 5b). **7.** *Gram.* of or pertaining to a root. **8.** *Bot.* of or arising from the root or the base of the stem. —*n.* **9.** a person who holds or follows strong convictions or extreme principles; extremist. **10.** (*often cap.*) a person who advocates fundamental political, economic, and social reforms by direct and often uncompromising methods. **11.** *Math.* **a.** a quantity expressed as a root of another quantity. **b.** the set of elements of a ring, some power of which is contained in a given ideal. **c.** See **radical sign.** **12.** Chem. **a.** group (def. 4). **b.** See **free radical.** **13.** *Gram.* root (def. 11). **14.** (in Chinese writing) one of 214 ideographic elements used in combination with phonetics to form thousands of different characters. [ME < LL *rādīcāl(is)* having roots, equiv. to L *rādīc-* (s. of *rādīx*) root + *-ālis* -AL[1]] —**rad′i·cal·ness,** *n.*

—**Syn. 1.** basic, essential; original, innate, ingrained. **2.** complete, unqualified, thorough; drastic, excessive, immoderate, violent. RADICAL, EXTREME, FANATICAL denote that which goes beyond moderation or even to excess in opinion, belief, action, etc. RADICAL emphasizes the idea of going to the root of a matter, and this often seems immoderate in its thoroughness or completeness: *radical ideas; radical changes or reforms.* EXTREME applies to excessively biased ideas, intemperate conduct, or repressive legislation: *to use extreme measures.* FANATICAL is applied to a person who has extravagant views, esp. in matters of religion or morality, which render him incapable of sound judgments; and excessive zeal which leads him to take violent action against those who have differing views: *fanatical in persecuting others.* —**Ant. 1, 2.** superficial.

rad′ical ax′is, *Geom.* the line such that tangents drawn from any point of the line to two given circles are equal in length.

rad′ical empir′icism, *Philos.* a doctrine, expounded chiefly by William James, that pure experience is the ground and source of the subject and object in any relationship. —**rad′ical empir′icist.**

rad·i·cal·ism (rad′i kə liz′əm), *n.* **1.** the holding or following of radical or extreme views or principles. **2.** the principles or practices of radicals. [RADICAL + -ISM]

rad·i·cal·ly (rad′ik lē), *adv.* **1.** with regard to origin or root. **2.** in a complete or basic manner; thoroughly; fundamentally. [RADICAL + -LY]

rad′ical sign′, *Math.* the symbol $\surd$ or $\sqrt{\ }$ indicating extraction of a root of the following quantity: $\sqrt{25}=5$; $\sqrt[3]{a^3b^3}=ab$.

rad·i·cand (rad′ə kand′), *n.* *Math.* the quantity under a radical sign. [< L *rādīcand(um),* neut. ger. of *rādīcāre,* equiv. to *rādīc-* (s. of *rādīx*) root]

rad·i·cant (rad′ə kənt), *adj.* *Bot.* rooting from the stem, as ivy. [< L *rādīcant-* (s. of *rādīcāns,* prp. of *rādīcāre*), equiv. to *rādīc-* (s. of *rādīx*) root + *-ant-* -ANT]

rad·i·cel (rad′i sel′), *n.* *Bot.* a minute root; a rootlet. [< NL *radicell(a)* small root, rootlet, equiv. to L *rādīc-* (s. of *rādīx*) root + *-cella* dim. suffix]

rad·i·ces (rad′i sēz′, rā′di-), *n.* pl. of **radix.**

rad·i·cle (rad′i kəl), *n.* **1.** *Bot.* **a.** the lower part of the axis of an embryo; the primary root. See illus. under **plumule.** **b.** a rudimentary root; a radicel or rootlet. **2.** *Chem.* radical. **3.** *Anat.* a small rootlike part or structure, as the beginning of a nerve or vein. [< L *rādīcul(a)* small root, equiv. to *rādīc-* (s. of *rādīx*) root + *-cula* -CLE]

ra·dic·u·lar (rə dik′yə lər, rā-), *adj.* **1.** *Bot.* of or pertaining to a radicle or root. **2.** *Anat.* of, pertaining to, or involving a radicle. [< L *rādīcul(a)* RADICLE + -AR[1]]

ra·dic·u·li·tis (rə dik′yə lī′tis), *n.* *Pathol.* inflammation of a spinal nerve root. [< NL; see RADICLE, -ITIS]

ra·dic·u·lose (rə dik′yə lōs′, rā-), *adj.* *Bot.* having many rootlets. [< L *rādīcul(a)* RADICLE + -OSE[1]]

ra·di·i (rā′dē ī′), *n.* a pl. of **radius.**

ra·di·o (rā′dē ō′), *n., pl.* **-di·os,** *adj., v.,* **-di·oed, -di·o·ing.** —*n.* **1.** wireless telegraphy or telephony: *speeches broadcast by radio.* **2.** an apparatus for receiving or transmitting radio broadcasts. **3.** a message transmitted by radio. —*adj.* **4.** pertaining to, used in, or sent by radio. **5.** pertaining to or employing radiations, as of electrical energy. —*v.t.* **6.** to transmit (a message, music, etc.) by radio. **7.** to send a message to (a person) by radio. —*v.i.* **8.** to transmit music, a message, etc., by radio. [short for *radiotelegraphic* (or *-telephonic*) *instrument, message,* or *transmission*]

radio-, **1.** a combining form representing "radio," "radium," "radioactive," "radiant energy": *radioteletype; radiogram; radiotracer; radiometer.* **2.** a combining form meaning "radial": *radiosymmetrical.* [orig. < F, comb. form repr. L *radius* beam, ray, RADIUS]

ra·di·o·a·cous·tics (rā′dē ō ə ko͞o′stiks), *n.* (*construed as sing.*) the science and technology of the production, transmission, and reproduction of sounds carried by radio waves. [RADIO- + ACOUSTICS]

ra·di·o·ac·tin·i·um (rā′dē ō ak tin′ē əm), *n.* *Chem.* the radioactive isotope of thorium having a mass number 227 and a half life of 18.8 days. *Symbol:* RdAc, Th 227 [RADIO- + ACTINIUM]

ra·di·o·ac·ti·vate (rā′dē ō ak′tə vāt′), *v.t.,* **-vat·ed, -vat·ing.** *Physics.* to make (a substance) radioactive. [RADIO- + ACTIVATE]

ra·di·o·ac·tive (rā′dē ō ak′tiv), *adj.* *Physics, Chem.* of, pertaining to, exhibiting, or caused by radioactivity. [RADIO- + ACTIVE] —**ra′di·o·ac′tive·ly,** *adv.*

ra′dioac′tive decay′, *Physics.* decay (def. 8).

ra′dioac′tive fall′out, fallout.

ra′dioac′tive se′ries, *Physics, Chem.* a succession of elements initiated in the radioactive decay of a parent, as thorium or uranium, each of which decays into the next until a stable element, usually lead, is produced. Also called **decay series.**

ra·di·o·ac·tiv·i·ty (rā′dē ō ak tiv′i tē), *n.* *Physics, Chem.* the phenomenon, exhibited by and being a property of certain elements, of spontaneously emitting radiations resulting from changes in the nuclei of atoms of the element. Also called **activity.** [RADIO- + ACTIVITY]

ra′dio astron′omy, the branch of astronomy that utilizes extraterrestrial radiation in radio wave lengths rather than visible light for the study of the universe.

ra·di·o·au·to·graph (rā′dē ō ô′tə graf′, -gräf′), *n.* autoradiograph. [RADIO- + AUTOGRAPH]

ra·di·o·au·tog·ra·phy (rā′dē ō ô tog′rə fē), *n.* autoradiography. [RADIO- + AUTOGRAPHY]

ra′dio bea′con, a radio station that sends a characteristic signal so as to enable ships or airplanes to determine their position or bearing by means of a radio compass.

ra′dio beam′, beam (def. 13).

ra·di·o·bi·ol·o·gy (rā′dē ō bī ol′ə jē), *n.* the branch of biology dealing with the effects of radiation on living matter. [RADIO- + BIOLOGY] —**ra·di·o·bi·o·log·i·cal** (rā′dē ō bī′ə loj′i kəl), **ra′di·o·bi′o·log′ic,** *adj.* —**ra′di·o·bi·ol′o·gist,** *n.*

ra·di·o·broad·cast (*n.* rā′dē ō brôd′kast′, -käst′; *v.* rā′dē ō brôd′kast′, -käst′), *n., v.,* **-cast** or **-cast·ed, -cast·ing.** —*n.* **1.** a broadcast by radio. —*v.t., v.i.* **2.** to broadcast by radio. [RADIO- + BROADCAST] —**ra′di·o·broad′cast′er,** *n.*

ra′dio car′, an automobile, esp. a police car, equipped with a two-way radio for communication.

ra·di·o·car·bon (rā′dē ō kär′bən), *n.* *Chem.* **1.** Also called **carbon 14, carbon-14.** a radioactive isotope of carbon with mass number 14 and a half life of about 5,568 years: widely used in the dating of organic materials. **2.** any radioactive isotope of carbon. [RADIO- + CARBON]

radiocar′bon dat′ing, the determination of the age of objects of plant or animal origin by measurement of the radioactivity of their radiocarbon content. Also called **carbon-14 dating.**

ra·di·o·chem·i·cal (rā′dē ō kem′i kəl), *adj.* *Chem.* pertaining to or involving radiochemistry. [RADIO- + CHEMICAL]

ra·di·o·chem·is·try (rā′dē ō kem′i strē), *n.* the chemical study of radioactive elements, both natural and artificial, and their use in the study of chemical processes. [RADIO- + CHEMISTRY] —**ra′di·o·chem′ist,** *n.*

ra′dio com′pass, a radio receiver with a directional antenna for determining the bearing of the receiver from a radio transmitter.

ra·di·o·di·ag·no·sis (rā′dē ō dī′əg nō′sis), *n., pl.* **-ses** (-sēz). *Med.* diagnosis by means of radiography or radioscopy. [RADIO- + DIAGNOSIS]

ra′dio direc′tion find′er, a navigational aid establishing a fix by means of the bearings of two known radio stations. *Abbr.:* RDF Also called **radio compass.**

ra·di·o·el·e·ment (rā′dē ō el′ə mənt), *n.* *Chem.* a radioactive element. [RADIO- + ELEMENT]

ra·di·o·fre·quen·cy (rā′dē ō frē′kwən sē), *n., pl.* **-cies.** **1.** the frequency of the transmitting waves of a given radio message or broadcast. **2.** a frequency within the range of radio transmission, from about 15,000 to 10^{11} cycles per second. Also, **ra′dio fre′quency.** [RADIO- + FREQUENCY]

ra·di·o·gen·ic (rā′dē ō jen′ik), *adj.* **1.** *Physics.* produced by radioactive decay: *radiogenic lead; radiogenic heat.* **2.** having qualities or characteristics that broadcast well; suitable for presentation on the radio. [RADIO- + -GENIC]

ra·di·o·gram[1] (rā′dē ō gram′), *n.* **1.** a message transmitted by radiotelegraphy. **2.** *Brit.* **a.** an x-ray. **b.** a telegram. [RADIO- + -GRAM[1]]

ra·di·o·gram[2] (rā′dē ō gram′), *n.* *Brit.* a combination radio and record player. [RADIO + GRAM(OPHONE)]

ra·di·o·graph (rā′dē ō graf′, -gräf′), *n.* **1.** a photographic image produced by the action of x-rays or rays from radioactive substances; shadowgraph. —*v.t.* **2.** to make a radiograph of. [RADIO- + -GRAPH]

ra·di·og·ra·phy (rā′dē og′rə fē), *n.* the production of radiographs. [RADIO- + -GRAPHY] —**ra′di·og′ra·pher,** *n.* —**ra·di·o·graph·ic** (rā′dē ō graf′ik), **ra′di·o·graph′i·cal,** *adj.* —**ra′di·o·graph′i·cal·ly,** *adv.*

ra′dio hori′zon, the locus of points on the earth's surface where rays from a transmitting antenna are tangent to the surface. The radio horizon for a fixed antenna varies with varying refraction by the atmosphere of radio waves.

ra′dio interferom′eter, *Astron.* any of several different types of instrumentation designed to observe interference patterns of electromagnetic radiation at radio wavelengths: used in the discovery and measurement of radio sources in the atmosphere.

ra·di·o·i·o·dine (rā′dē ō ī′ə dēn′), *n.* *Chem.* See **iodine 131.** [RADIO- + IODINE]

ra·di·o·i·ron (rā′dē ō ī′ərn), *n.* *Chem.* the radioactive isotope of iron, with atomic weight 59 and a half life of 46 days: used chiefly as a tracer in biochemistry. [RADIO- + IRON]

ra·di·o·i·so·tope (rā′dē ō ī′sə tōp′), *n.* a radioactive isotope, usually artificially produced: used in physical and biological research, therapeutics, etc. [RADIO- + ISOTOPE] —**ra·di·o·i·so·top·ic** (rā′dē ō ī′sə top′ik), *adj.*

ra′dio knife′, *Surg.* an electrical instrument for cutting tissue and that by searing severed blood vessels seals them and prevents bleeding.

ra·di·o·lar·i·an (rā′dē ō lâr′ē ən), *n.* any minute, marine protozoan of the group or order *Radiolaria,* having an amoebalike body with radiating pseudopodia and a usually elaborate skeleton. [< NL *Radiolari(a)* name of the class (L *radiol(us)* a feeble sunbeam, small beam, equiv. to *radi(us)* RADIUS + *-olus* dim. suffix, + *-aria* -ARIA) + -AN]

ra·di·o·lo·ca·tion (rā′dē ō lō kā′shən), *n.* the method or process of determining the position and velocity of an object by radar. [RADIO- + LOCATION]

ra·di·o·lo·ca·tor (rā′dē ō lō′kā tər, -lō kā′tər), *n.* *Brit.* radar. [RADIO- + LOCATOR]

ra·di·o·log·i·cal (rā′dē ō loj′i kəl), *adj.* involving radioactive materials: *radiological warfare.* Also, **ra′di·o·log′ic.** [RADIOLOG(Y) + -ICAL] —**ra′di·o·log′i·cal·ly,** *adv.*

ra·di·ol·o·gy (rā′dē ol′ə jē), *n.* **1.** the science dealing with x-rays or rays from radioactive substances, esp. for medical uses. **2.** the examination or photographing of organs, bones, etc., with such rays. **3.** the interpretation of medical x-ray photographs. [RADIO- + -LOGY] —**ra′di·ol′o·gist,** *n.*

ra·di·o·lu·cent (rā′dē ō lo͞o′sənt), *adj.* almost entirely transparent to radiation; almost entirely invisible in x-ray photographs and under fluoroscopy. Cf. **radiopaque, radiotransparent.** [RADIO- + LUCENT] —**ra′di·o·lu′cence, ra′di·o·lu′cen·cy,** *n.*

ra·di·o·lu·mi·nes·cence (rā′dē ō lo͞o′mə nes′əns), *n.* *Physics.* luminescence induced by radiation emitted by a radioactive substance. [RADIO- + LUMINESCENCE] —**ra′di·o·lu′mi·nes′cent,** *adj.*

ra·di·o·man (rā′dē ō man′), *n., pl.* **-men.** one who operates a radio. [RADIO + MAN[1]]

ra·di·o·me·te·or·o·graph (rā′dē ō mē′tē ər ə graf′, -gräf′), *n.* radiosonde. [RADIO- + METEOROGRAPH]

ra·di·om·e·ter (rā′dē om′i tər), *n.* **1.** an instrument for demonstrating the transformation of radiant energy into mechanical work, consisting of an exhausted glass vessel containing vanes that revolve about an axis when exposed to radiant energy. **2.** an instrument for detecting and measuring small amounts of radiant energy. [RADIO- + -METER] —**ra·di·o·met·ric** (rā′dē ō me′trik), *adj.* —**ra′di·om′e·try,** *n.*

Radiometer (def. 1)

ra·di·o·mi·crom·e·ter (rā′dē ō mī krom′i tər), *n.* an instrument for measuring small amounts of radiant energy, consisting of a sensitive thermocouple connected to a galvanometer. [RADIO- + MICROMETER]

ra·di·o·nu·clide (rā′dē ō no͞o′klīd, -nyo͞o′-), *n.* *Physics.* a radioactive nuclide. [RADIO- + NUCLIDE]

ra·di·o·paque (rā′dē ō pāk′), *adj.* opaque to radiation; visible in x-ray photographs and under fluoroscopy (opposed to *radiotransparent*). Cf. **radiolucent.** [RADI(O)- + OPAQUE] —**ra·di·o·pac·i·ty** (rā′dē ō pas′i tē), *n.*

ra·di·o·phare (rā′dē ō fâr′), *n.* a radiotelegraphic station used by vessels to determine their positions; radio beacon. [RADIO- + L *phar(us)* lighthouse, sp. var. of *pharos* < Gk *phā́ros*]

ra·di·o·phone (rā′dē ō fōn′), *n.* **1.** a radiotelephone. **2.** *Obs.* any of various devices for producing sound by the action of radiant energy. —*v.t., v.i.* **3.** to radiotelephone. [RADIO- + -PHONE] —**ra·di·o·phon·ic** (rā′dē ō fon′ik), *adj.* —**ra·di·oph·o·ny** (rā′dē of′ə nē), *n.*

ra·di·o·phos·pho·rus (rā′dē ō fos′fər əs), *n.* *Chem.* See **phosphorus 32.** [RADIO- + PHOSPHORUS]

ra·di·o·pho·to·graph (rā′dē ō fō′tə graf′, -gräf′), *n.* a photograph or other image transmitted by radio. Also called **ra′di·o·pho′to, ra·di·o·pho·to·gram** (rā′dē ō fō′tə gram′). [RADIO- + PHOTOGRAPH] —**ra·di·o·pho·tog·ra·phy** (rā′dē ō fə tog′rə fē), *n.*

ra′dio range′ bea′con, a radio transmitter that utilizes two or more directional antennas and transmits signals differing with direction, permitting a flier receiving a signal to determine his approximate bearing from the transmitter without a radio compass.

ra·di·os·co·py (rā′dē os′kə pē), *n.* the examination of objects opaque to light by means of another form of radiation, usually x-rays. [RADIO- + -SCOPY] —**ra·di·o·scop·ic** (rā′dē ō skop′ik), **ra′di·o·scop′i·cal,** *adj.*

ra·di·o·sen·si·tive (rā′dē ō sen′si tiv), *adj.* *Pathol.* (of certain tissues or organisms) sensitive to or destructible by various types of radiant energy, as x-rays, rays from radioactive material, or the like. [RADIO- + SENSITIVE] —**ra′di·o·sen′si·tiv′i·ty, ra′di·o·sen′si·bil′i·ty,** *n.*

ra′dio shack′, *Informal.* a room or structure for use by a radio operator, as on a ship.

ra·di·o·so·di·um (rā′dē ō sō′dē əm), *n.* *Chem.* the radioactive isotope of sodium having an atomic mass of 24 and a half life of 14.9 hours: used as a tracer in biochemistry. [RADIO- + SODIUM]

ra·di·o·sonde (rā′dē ō sond′), *n.* *Meteorol.* an instrument that is carried aloft by a balloon to send back information on atmospheric temperature, pressure, and humidity by means of a small radio transmitter. Also called **radiometeorograph.** [RADIO- + SONDE]

ra′dio source′, *Astron.* a cosmic object or phenomenon, as a galaxy or the remnant of a supernova or of a galactic collision, that emits radio waves.

ra′dio spec′trum, the wavelength range of electromagnetic waves: approximately 30,000 meters to 1 millimeter or 10 kilocycles to 300,000 megacycles.

ra′dio star′, *Astron. Obs.* a radio source.

ra′dio sta′tion, **1.** a combination of devices for transmitting or receiving radio signals. **2.** a complete installation for radio broadcasting, including transmitting apparatus, broadcasting studios, etc. **3.** an organization or unit in an organization whose business it is to carry on commercial broadcasting on an officially assigned radiofrequency.

ra·di·o·stron·ti·um (rā′dē ō stron′shē əm, -tē əm), *n.* *Chem.* See **strontium 90.** [RADIO- + STRONTIUM]

ra·di·o·sur·ger·y (rā′dē ō sûr′jə rē), *n.* therapeutic use of radioactive materials by surgical insertion. [RADIO- + SURGERY]

ra·di·o·sym·met·ri·cal (rā′dē ō si me′tri kəl), *adj.* *Bot.* radially symmetrical. [RADIO- + SYMMETRICAL]

ra·di·o·tech·nol·o·gy (rā′dē ō tek nol′ə jē), *n.* **1.** the technical application of any form of radiation to industry. **2.** the technical application of x-rays to industry. **3.** the technology of radio. [RADIO- + TECHNOLOGY]

ra·di·o·tel·e·gram (rā′dē ō tel′ə gram′), *n.* a message transmitted by radiotelegraphy. [RADIO- + TELEGRAM]

ra·di·o·tel·e·graph (rā′dē ō tel′ə graf′, -gräf′), *n.* **1.** a telegraph in which messages or signals are sent by means of radio waves rather than through wires or cables. —*v.t., v.i.* **2.** to telegraph by radiotelegraphy. [RADIO- + TELEGRAPH] —**ra′di·o·tel′e·graph′ic,** *adj.*

ra·di·o·te·leg·ra·phy (rā′dē ō tə leg′rə fē), *n.* the constructing or operating of radiotelegraphs. [RADIO- + TELEGRAPHY]

ra·di·o·tel·e·phone (rā′dē ō tel′ə fōn′), *n., v.,* **-phoned, -phon·ing.** —*n.* **1.** a telephone in which sound or speech is transmitted by means of radio waves instead of through wires or cables. —*v.t., v.i.* **2.** to telephone by radiotelephony. [RADIO- + TELEPHONE] —**ra·di·o·tel·e·phon·ic** (rā′dē ō tel′ə fon′ik), *adj.*

ra·di·o·te·leph·o·ny (rā′dē ō tə lef′ə nē), *n.* the constructing or operating of radiotelephones. [RADIO- + TELEPHONY]

ra′dio tel′escope, *Astron.* a reflector of radio waves, usually a paraboloid, used to gather radio waves emitted by celestial sources and bring them to a receiver placed in the focus.

ra·di·o·tel·e·type (rā′dē ō tel′i tīp′), *n.* **1.** Also called **ra′di·o·tel′e·type′writ′er.** a teletypewriter equipped for transmitting or receiving messages by radio instead of by wire. **2.** the equipment relating to transmission by radioteletypes, taken as a whole. [RADIO- + TELETYPE]

ra·di·o·ther·a·py (rā′dē ō ther′ə pē), *n.* treatment of disease by means of x-rays or of radioactive substances. [RADIO- + THERAPY] —**ra′di·o·ther′a·pist,** *n.*

ra·di·o·ther·my (rā′dē ō thûr′mē), *n.* therapy that utilizes the heat from a short-wave radio apparatus or diathermy machine. [RADIO- + -THERMY]

ra·di·o·tho·ri·um (rā′dē ō thôr′ē əm, -thōr′-), *n.* *Chem.* a disintegration product of thorium. [< NL; see RADIO-, THORIUM]

ra·di·o·trac·er (rā′dē ō trā′sər), *n.* *Chem.* a radioactive isotope used as a tracer. [RADIO- + TRACER]

ra·di·o·trans·par·ent (rā′dē ō trans pâr′ənt, -par′-), *n.* transparent to radiation; invisible in x-ray photographs and under fluoroscopy (opposed to *radiopaque*). Cf. **radiolucent.** [RADIO- + TRANSPARENT] —**ra′di·o·trans·par′en·cy,** *n.*

ra′dio tube′, a vacuum tube used in a radio receiving set.

ra·di·o·vi·sion (rā′dē ō vizh′ən), *n.* *Obs.* television. [RADIO- + VISION]

ra′dio wave′, *Elect.* an electromagnetic wave propagated through the atmosphere with the speed of light and having wavelength of from .5 centimeters to 30,000 meters.

rad·ish (rad′ish), *n.* **1.** the crisp, pungent, edible root of a cruciferous plant, *Raphanus sativus,* usually eaten raw. **2.** the plant itself. [late ME; OE *rǣdic* < L *rādīc-* (s. of *rādīx*); cf. OHG *rātih,* G *Rettich*] —**rad′ish-like′,** *adj.*

ra·di·um (rā′dē əm), *n.* **1.** *Chem.* a highly radioactive metallic element that upon disintegration produces the element radon **(radium emanation)** and alpha rays, the latter regarded as positively charged particles of helium. The disintegration of radium is understood to be a process by which an atom of radium breaks down into an atom of helium, the material of alpha rays, and into an atom of radon, the material of the radium emanation, and by which an atom of radon loses an atom of helium and becomes radium A, and by which subsequent products are formed. *Symbol:* Ra; *at. wt.:* 226; *at. no.:* 88. Cf. **Curie** (defs. 2, 3). **2.** a lustrous rayon or silk fabric constructed in plain weave and used in women's apparel, lining, and drapery. [< NL, equiv. to L *rad(ius)* RADIUS + *-ium* -IUM]

radium A, *Chem.* a substance, formed from radon by disintegration, which gives rise to radium B.

radium B, *Chem.* an isotope of lead, formed from radium A by disintegration, that gives rise to radium C, which is an isotope of bismuth, from which radium D, radium E, and radium F, or polonium, are derived.

radium F, *Chem.* polonium.

ra′dium sul′fate, *Chem.* a white, crystalline, water-insoluble, poisonous, radioactive solid, $RaSO_4$, used chiefly in radiotherapy.

ra′dium ther′apy, treatment of disease by means of radium.

ra·di·us (rā′dē əs), *n., pl.* **-di·i** (-dē ī′), **-di·us·es.** **1.** a straight line extending from the center of a circle or sphere to the circumference or surface: *The radius of a circle is half the diameter.* **2.** the length of such a line. **3.** any radial or radiating part. **4.** a circular area of an extent indicated by the length of the radius of its circumscribing circle: *every house within a radius of 50 miles.* **5.** field or range of operation or influence. **6.** extent of possible operation, travel, etc., as under a single supply of fuel: *the flying radius of an airplane.* **7.** *Anat.* the bone of the forearm on the thumb side. Cf. **ulna** (def. 1). **8.** *Zool.* a corresponding bone in the forelimb of other vertebrates. **9.** *Mach. Obs.* the throw of an eccentric wheel or cam. **10.** a rounded corner or edge on a machined or cast piece of metal. **11.** *Entomol.* one of the principal longitudinal veins in the anterior portion of the wing of an insect. [< L: staff, rod, spoke, beam; see RAY[1]]

Radii
CA, CB, CD, CE, CF

ra′dius of conver′gence, *Math.* a positive number so related to a given power series that for every number whose absolute value is less than this particular number the power series converges.

ra′dius of cur′vature, *Math.* the absolute value of the reciprocal of the curvature at a point on a curve. Cf. **circle of curvature.**

ra′dius of gyra′tion, *Physics.* the distance from an axis at which the mass of a body may be assumed to be concentrated and at which the moment of inertia will be equal to the moment of inertia of the actual mass about the axis, equal to the square root of the quotient of the moment of inertia and the mass.

ra′dius rod′, (in a feathering paddle wheel) any of the rods, meeting in a hub mounted eccentrically with the paddle-wheel shaft, for feathering the paddles while in the water. See illus. under **paddle wheel.**

ra′dius vec′tor, *pl.* **radii vec·to·res** (vek tôr′ēz, -tōr′-), **radius vectors.** **1.** *Math.* the length of the line segment joining a fixed point or origin to a given point. **2.** *Astron.* **a.** the straight line joining two bodies in relative orbital motion, as the line from the sun to a planet at any point in its orbit. **b.** the distance between two such bodies at any point in the orbit.

ra·dix (rā′diks), *n., pl.* **rad·i·ces** (rad′i sēz′, rā′di-), **ra·dix·es.** **1.** *Math.* a number taken as the base of a system of numbers, logarithms, or the like. **2.** *Anat., Bot.* a root; a radical. **3.** *Gram.* root (def. 11). [< L *rādīx* root; c. Gk *rhíza;* cf. Gk *rhā́dix* a shoot, twig]

RAdm, rear admiral.

Rad·nor (rad′nər), *n.* **1.** a town in SE Pennsylvania, near Philadelphia. 21,697 (1960). **2.** Radnorshire.

Rad·nor·shire (rad′nər shēr′, -shər), *n.* a county in E Wales. 18,431 (1961); 471 sq. mi. *Co. seat:* Presteigne. Also called **Radnor.**

Ra·dom (rä′dôm), *n.* a city in E Poland. 117,000 (est. 1955).

ra·dome (rā′dōm), *n.* a dome-shaped device used to house a radar antenna, esp. on aircraft. [RA(DAR) + DOME]

ra·don (rā′don), *n.* *Chem.* a chemically inert, radioactive gaseous element produced by the decay of radium: considered a serious health hazard. *Symbol:* Rn; *at. no.:* 86; *at. wt.:* 222. Also called **ra′dium emana′tion.** [RAD(IUM) + -ON[2]]

rad/s, radians per second. Also, **rad/sec**

rad·u·la (raj′o͝o lə), *n., pl.* **-lae** (-lē′). a chitinous band in the mouth of most mollusks, set with numerous, minute, horny teeth and drawn backward and forward over the odontophore in the process of breaking up food. [< NL, L: scraper, equiv. to *rād(ere)* (to) scrape, rub, scratch + *-ula* -ULE] —**rad′u·lar,** *adj.*

Rae (rā), *n.* **1.** a boy's given name, form of **Raymond** or **Ray.** **2.** a girl's given name, form of **Rachel.** Also, **Ray, Raye.**

Rae·burn (rā′bərn), *n.* **Sir Henry,** 1756–1823, Scottish painter.

Rae·ford (rā′fərd), *n.* a town in central North Carolina. 3058 (1960).

Rae·nell (rā nel′), *n.* a girl's given name. Also, **Raynelle.**

Rae·tic (rē′tik), *n.* **1.** an extinct language of uncertain affinities that was spoken in Rhaetia and written with the Etruscan alphabet. —*adj.* **2.** of or pertaining to Raetic. Also, **Rhaetian.** [< L *rhaetic(us).* See RHAETIA, -IC]

RAF, Royal Air Force. Also, **R.A.F.**

Ra·fer (rā′fər), *n.* a boy's given name.

raff (raf), *n.* **1.** the riffraff; the rabble. **2.** *Brit. Dial.* trash; refuse. [ME *raf;* appar. abstracted from RIFF-RAFF]

raf·fee (ra fē′), *n.* *Naut.* a triangular sail set in the manner of a square sail above the uppermost yard of a topsail schooner. Also **raffe** (raf), **raf·fie′.** [?]

raf·fer·ty (raf′ər tē), *adj.* *Brit., Australian.* confused; disorganized. [? var. of *raffery.* See RAFF, -ERY]

raf·fi·a (raf′ē ə), *n.* **1.** a palm, *Raphia pedunculata,* of the Malagasy Republic, having long, plumelike, pinnate leaves, the leafstalks of which yield an important fiber. **2.** the fiber of this palm used for tying plants, cut flowers, small packages, etc., and for making matting, baskets, hats, or the like. **3.** any other palm of the genus *Raphia.* **4.** its fiber. [< Malagasy]

raf·fi·nate (raf′ə nāt′), *n. Chem.* the part of a liquid, esp. an oil, remaining after its more soluble components have been extracted by a solvent. [< F *raffin(er)* (to) refine (*re-* RE- + *affiner* to AFFINE) + -ATE[1]]

raf·fi·nose (raf′ə nōs′), *n. Chem.* a colorless, crystalline trisaccharide, $C_{18}H_{32}O_{16}\cdot 5H_2O$, with little or no sweetness, occurring in the sugar beet, cottonseed, etc., and breaking down to fructose, glucose, and galactose on hydrolysis. Also called **gossypose, melitose, militriose.** [< F *raffin(er)* (to) refine + -OSE[2]]

raff·ish (raf′ish), *adj.* **1.** vulgar; low-class; tawdry. **2.** disreputable, rakish, or libertarian. [RAFF + -ISH[1]] —**raff′ish·ly,** *adv.* —**raff′ish·ness,** *n.*

raf·fle[1] (raf′əl), *n., v.,* **-fled, -fling.** —*n.* **1.** a form of lottery in which a number of persons buy one or more chances to win a prize. —*v.t.* **2.** to dispose of by a raffle (often fol. by *off*): *to raffle off a watch.* —*v.i.* **3.** to take part in a raffle. [ME *rafle* < MF, deriv. of *rafler* to snatch; cf. RAFF] —**raf′fler,** *n.*

raf·fle[2] (raf′əl), *n.* **1.** rubbish. **2.** *Naut.* a tangle, as of ropes, canvas, etc. [RAFF + -LE]

raf·fles (raf′əlz), *n.* (*often cap.*) a gentlemanly burglar, amateur housebreaker, or the like. [after *Raffles,* hero of *The Amateur Cracksman,* by E.W. Hornung (1866–1921), English novelist]

raf·fle·sia (rə flē′zhə, -zhē ə, -zē ə, ra-), *n.* any stemless, leafless, parasitic plant of the genus *Rafflesia,* of the Malay Peninsula and Republic of Indonesia, characterized by apetalous flowers, measuring three inches to three feet in diameter, that exude a putrid odor. [< NL, named after Sir T. Stamford *Raffles* (1781–1826), English governor in Sumatra who discovered it]

raf·fle·si·a·ceous (rə flē′zē ā′shəs, -zhē-), *adj.* belonging or pertaining to the *Rafflesiaceae,* a family of stemless, leafless, parasitic plants of the Malay Peninsula and Republic of Indonesia. [< NL *Rafflesiace(ae)* (see RAFFLESIA, -ACEAE) + -OUS]

ra·fraî·chis·soir (RA fre shē swAR′), *n. Fr. Furniture.* a table of the 18th century having a cooler for bottles and shelves for plates. [< F: lit., refresher]

raft[1] (raft, räft), *n.* **1.** a more or less rigid floating platform made of buoyant materials: *an inflatable rubber raft.* **2.** a collection of logs, planks, casks, etc., fastened together for floating on water. **3.** See **life raft. 4.** a slab of reinforced concrete providing a footing on yielding soil, usually for a whole building, so that the weight of the soil that would be displaced by the settlement of the building exceeds the weight of the building itself; mat. —*v.t.* **5.** to transport on a raft. **6.** to form (logs or the like) into a raft. **7.** to travel or cross by raft. **8.** (of an ice floe) to transport (embedded organic or rock debris) from the shore out to sea. —*v.i.* **9.** to use a raft; go or travel on a raft. **10.** (of an ice floe) to overlap another ice floe. [ME *rafte* < Scand; cf. OIcel *raptr* RAFTER[1]]

raft[2] (raft, räft), *n. Informal.* a great quantity; a lot: *a raft of trouble.* [var. of RAFF large number (ME: abundance)]

raft·er[1] (raf′tər, räf′-), *n.* **1.** any of a series of timbers or the like, usually having a pronounced slope, for supporting the sheathing and covering of a roof. —*v.t.* **2.** *Brit. Dial.* to plow (a field) so that the soil of a furrow is pushed over onto an unplowed adjacent strip. [ME; OE *ræfter;* c. MLG *rafter,* OIcel *raptr.* See RAFT[1]]

raft·er[2] (raf′tər, räf′-), *n.* a flock, esp. of turkeys. [RAFT[2] + -ER[1]]

raft′er ta′ble, *Carpentry.* a table for determining the lengths and angles of cut of the various rafters in any given roof. Also called **framing table.**

raft′ ice′, ice in cakes or sheets overlapping or piled on top of one another. Also called **raft′ed ice′.**

Raft′ of the Medu′sa, The, a painting (1818–19) by Théodore Géricault.

rafts·man (rafts′mən, räfts′-), *n., pl.* **-men.** a man who manages or is employed on a raft. [RAFT[1] + -'S[1] + MAN[1]]

rag[1] (rag), *n.* **1.** a worthless piece of cloth, esp. one that is torn or worn. **2. rags,** ragged or tattered clothing: *The tramp was dressed in rags.* **3.** a shred, scrap, or fragmentary bit of anything. **4.** *Informal.* **a.** something of very low value or in very poor condition. **b.** a newspaper or magazine regarded with contempt or distaste: *Are you still subscribing to that rag?* **5.** a person of shabby or exhausted appearance. **6.** *Bot.* the axis and carpellary walls of a citrus fruit. **7.** one of the stuffed balls of cloth raising water in a rag-and-chain pump. **8.** a large roofing slate that has one edge untrimmed. **9. chew the rag.** See **chew** (def. 10). **10. from rags to riches,** from extreme proverty to great wealth: *He went from rags to riches in only three years.* [ME *ragge* < Scand; cf. OIcel *rögg* tuft, shag]

rag[2] (rag), *v.,* **ragged, rag·ging,** *n. Informal.* —*v.t.* **1.** to scold. **2.** to subject to a teasing, esp. a strong teasing: *Some of the boys were ragging him about his haircut.* **3.** *Brit.* to torment with jokes; play crude practical jokes on. —*n.* **4.** *Brit.* an act of ragging. [? special use of RAG[1]; but cf. OIcel *ragna* to curse]

rag[3] (rag), *v.t.,* **ragged, rag·ging.** to break up (lumps of ore) for sorting. [?]

rag[4] (rag), *n., v.,* **ragged, rag·ging.** —*n.* **1.** a musical composition in ragtime. —*v.t.* **2.** to play (music) in ragtime. [shortened form of RAGTIME]

Rag (rag), *n.* a boy's given name.

ra·ga (rä′gə), *n.* one of the melodic formulas of Hindu music having the melodic shape, rhythm, and ornamentation prescribed by tradition. [< Skt *rāga* color, tone]

rag·a·muf·fin (rag′ə muf′in), *n.* **1.** a ragged, disreputable person; tatterdemalion. **2.** a child in ragged, ill-fitting, dirty clothes. [ME *Ragamoffyn,* name of a demon in the poem *Piers Plowman*]

rag′-and-bone′ man′ (rag′ən bōn′), *Chiefly Brit.* a peddler who buys and sells used clothes, old newspapers, rags, broken household items, etc.; junk peddler.

rag′-and-chain′ pump′ (rag′ən chān′), a chain pump for forcing water upward between a series of stuffed balls of cloth moving in a cylinder.

rag′ bolt′. See **barb bolt.**

rag′ doll′, a stuffed doll, esp. of cloth.

rage (rāj), *n., v.,* **raged, rag·ing.** —*n.* **1.** angry fury; violent anger: *to fall into a rage.* **2.** fury or violence of wind, waves, fire, disease, etc. **3.** violence of feeling, desire, or appetite: *the rage of thirst.* **4.** a violent desire or passion. **5.** ardor; fervor; enthusiasm: *poetic rage.* **6.** the object of widespread enthusiasm: *Raccoon coats were the rage on campus.* **7.** *Obs.* insanity. **8. all the rage,** widely in style or popular. [ME < OF < LL *rabia,* L *rabiēs* madness, rage, deriv. of *rabere* to rage] —*v.i.* **9.** to act or speak with fury; show or feel violent anger. **10.** to move, rush, dash, or surge furiously. **11.** to proceed, continue, or prevail with great violence: *The battle raged ten days.* **12.** (of feelings, opinions, etc.) to hold sway with unabated violence. [ME *rage(n)* < OF *ragie(r),* deriv. of *rage* (n.)] —**rag′ing·ly,** *adv.*
—**Syn. 1.** wrath, frenzy, passion, ire, madness. See **anger. 2.** turbulence. **5.** eagerness, vehemence. **6.** vogue, fad, fashion, craze. **9, 10.** rave, fume, storm. —**Ant. 1.** calm.

rag·fish (rag′fish′), *n., pl.* (*esp. collectively*) **-fish,** (*esp. referring to two or more kinds or species*) **-fish·es.** a deep-sea fish of the family *Icosteidae,* found in the North Pacific, having a very flexible body owing to its soft, cartilaginous skeleton. [RAG[1] + FISH]

rag·ged (rag′id), *adj.* **1.** clothed in tattered garments: *a ragged old man.* **2.** torn or worn to rags; tattered: *ragged clothing.* **3.** shaggy, as an animal, its coat, etc. **4.** having loose or hanging shreds or fragmentary bits: *a ragged wound.* **5.** full of rough or sharp projections; jagged: *ragged stones.* **6.** *Heraldry.* raguly. **7.** in a wild or neglected state: *a ragged garden.* **8.** rough, imperfect, or faulty: *a ragged piece of work.* **9.** harsh, as sound, the voice, etc. [ME *ragget.* See RAG[1], -ED[3]] —**rag′ged·ly,** *adv.* —**rag′ged·ness,** *n.*
—**Syn. 1.** shabby, poor. **2.** shredded, rent. —**Ant. 1.** neat.

rag′ged edge′, **1.** the brink, as of a cliff. **2.** any extreme edge; verge. **3. on the ragged edge,** in a dangerous or precarious position; on the verge of: *on the ragged edge of despair.*

rag′ged rob′in, a caryophyllaceous plant, *Lychnis Flos-cuculi,* having pink or white flowers with dissected petals.

rag·ged·y (rag′i dē), *adj.* characterized by raggedness; somewhat ragged, tattered, or shaggy: *a raggedy old coat; a raggedy sheep dog.* [RAGGED + -Y[1]]

rag·ging (rag′ing), *n. Metalworking.* (in the rolls of a rolling mill) corrugations affording a grip on a piece being roughed. [RAG[3] + -ING[1]]

rag·gle (rag′əl), *n.* **1.** a groove cut in masonry to receive flashing. **2.** Also called **rag′gle block′.** a manufactured masonry unit, usually of terra cotta, having a groove for receiving flashing. [?]

rag·gle-tag·gle (rag′əl tag′əl), *adj.* made up of odds and ends; motley: *an embarrassing, raggle-taggle floor show.* [alter. of *ragtag.* See RAG[1], TAG[1]]

rag′ gourd′, luffa (def. 1).

ra·gi (rag′ē), *n.* a cereal grass, *Eleusine coracana,* cultivated in the Old World for its grain. Also, **rag′gee, rag′gy.** [< Hindi *rāgī*]

rag·lan (rag′lən), *n.* a loose overcoat with raglan sleeves. [after Lord *Raglan* (1788–1855), British field marshal]

rag′lan sleeve′, a sleeve that begins at the neck and has a long, slanting seam line from the neck to the armhole, giving the garment a relatively undefined shoulder. Cf. **set-in sleeve.**

rag·man (rag′man′, -mən), *n., pl.* **-men** (-men′, -mən). a man who gathers or deals in rags. [RAG[1] + MAN[1]]

rag′man roll′, **1.** Usually, **ragman rolls.** a series of documents in which the Scottish nobles acknowledged their allegiance to Edward I of England, 1291–92 and 1296. **2.** *Obs.* a long list or record; register; catalogue. [ME *ragmane roelle* < ?]

Rag·na·rok (räg′nə rok′), *n. Scand. Myth.* the destruction of the gods and of all things in a final battle with evil powers: corresponds to the Germanic Götterdämmerung; Twilight of the Gods. Also, **Rag·na·rök** (räg′nə rœk′).

ra·gout (ra gōō′), *n., v.,* **-gouted** (-gōōd′), **-gout·ing** (-gōō′ing). —*n.* **1.** *French Cookery.* a highly seasoned stew of meat or fish, with or without vegetables. —*v.t.* **2.** to make into a ragout. [< F *ragoût,* deriv. of *ragoûter* to restore the appetite of, equiv. to *re-* RE- + *à* (< L *ad* to) + *goût* (< L *gustus* taste)]

rag′ pa′per, a high-quality paper made from cotton or linen pulp.

rag·pick·er (rag′pik′ər), *n.* a person who picks up rags and other waste material from the streets, refuse heaps, etc., for a livelihood. [RAG[1] + PICKER[1]]

rag′tag and bob′tail (rag′tag′), *Contemptuous.* the riffraff; the rabble: *The ragtag and bobtail of every nation poured into the frontier in search of gold.* Also, **rag′, tag′, and bob′tail.**

rag·time (rag′tīm′), *n. Music.* **1.** rhythm in which the accompaniment is strict two-four time and the melody, with improvised embellishments, is in steady syncopation. **2.** music, esp. for piano, in this rhythm. [prob. RAG(GED) + TIME] —**rag′time′y,** *adj.*

rag·u·ly (rag′yə lē), *adj. Heraldry.* noting a partition line or a charge, as an ordinary, similar to the embattled but with the indentations sloping in one direction. [? cf. GULES]

Ra·gu·sa (rä gōō′zä), *n.* Italian name of **Dubrovnik.**

rag·weed (rag′wēd′), *n.* **1.** any of the composite herbs of the genus *Ambrosia,* the air-borne pollen of which is the most prevalent cause of autumnal hay fever, as the common North American species, *A. trifida* (**great ragweed** or **giant ragweed**) and *A. artemisiifolia.* **2.** *U.S. Dial.* the marsh elder. **3.** *Brit.* the ragwort. [RAG[1] + WEED[1], so called from its ragged appearance]

rag·work (rag′wûrk′), *n.* masonry of thin, undressed rubble. [RAG[1] + WORK]

rag·wort (rag′wûrt′), *n.* any of various composite plants of the genus *Senecio,* as *S. Jacobaea,* of the Old World, having yellow flowers and irregularly lobed leaves, or *S. aureus* (**golden ragwort**), of North America, also having yellow flowers. [RAG[1] + WORT[2]]

rah (rä), *interj.* an exclamation of encouragement to a player or team. [short for HURRAH]

Ra·hab (rā′hab), *n.* a harlot of Jericho who gave shelter to the two agents sent by Joshua to spy on the city. Josh. 2.

Rah·man (rä′män), *n.* **Prince Ab·dul** (äb′dōōl), born 1903, Malayan political leader: prime minister of Malaya 1957–63; premier of Malaysia since 1963.

rah-rah (rä′rä′), *adj.* **1.** *Informal.* marked by or expressive of ardently enthusiastic spirit: *a group of rah-rah undergraduates; a rah-rah attitude.* —*v.i.* **2.** to shout "rah," "hurrah," or the like; cheer. [redupl. of RAH]

Rah·way (rô′wā), *n.* a city in NE New Jersey. 27,699 (1960).

ra·ia (rä′yə, rī′ə), *n. Obs.* rayah.

raid (rād), *n.* **1.** a sudden onset or attack, as upon something to be seized or suppressed: *a police raid on a gambling ring.* **2.** *Mil.* a sudden attack on the enemy, as by air or by a small land force. **3.** a vigorous, large-scale effort to lure away a competitor's employees, members, etc. **4.** *Finance.* a concerted attempt of speculators to force stock prices down. —*v.t.* **5.** to make a raid on. —*v.i.* **6.** to engage in a raid. [ME *raide* (north dial.), var. of OE *rād* expedition, lit., riding (whence ROAD); c. OIcel *reith*] —**raid′er,** *n.*
—**Syn. 1.** seizure. **2.** incursion, invasion, inroad.

rail[1] (rāl), *n.* **1.** a bar of wood or metal fixed horizontally for any of various purposes, as for a support, barrier, fence, or railing. **2.** a fence; railing. **3.** one of a pair of steel bars that provide the running surfaces for the wheels of locomotives and railroad cars. **4.** the railroad as a means of transportation: *to travel by rail.* **5. rails,** stocks or bonds of railroad companies. **6.** *Naut.* a horizontal member capping a bulwark. **7.** *Carpentry, Furniture.* any of various horizontal members framing panels or the like, as in a system of paneling, paneled door, window sash, or chest of drawers. Cf. **stile**[2]. **8. ride** (someone) **out on a rail,** to punish (someone) severely, as to banish from a community because of a crime. —*v.t.* **9.** to furnish or enclose with a rail or rails. [ME *raile* < OF *raille* bar, beam < L *rēgula* bar, straight piece of wood, REGULA] —**rail′less,** *adj.* —**rail′like′,** *adj.*

rail[2] (rāl), *v.i.* **1.** to utter bitter complaint or vehement denunciation (often fol. by *at* or *against*): *to rail at fate.* —*v.t.* **2.** to bring, force, etc., by railing. [ME *rail(en)* < MF *railler* (to) deride < Pr *ralhar* to chatter << L *ragere* to shriek] —**rail′er,** *n.* —**rail′ing·ly,** *adv.*

rail[3] (rāl), *n.* any of numerous birds of the subfamily *Rallinae,* of the family *Rallidae,* that have short wings, a narrow body, long toes, and a harsh cry and are found in grasslands, forests, and in marshes in most parts of the world. [ME *rale* < OF *raale* (c. Pr *rascla*), prob. << L *rād(ere)* (to) scratch]

Virginia rail, *Rallus limicola* (Length 9½ in.)

rail′ bead′, a long, straight, cock bead.

rail·head (rāl′hed′), *n.* **1.** the farthest point to which the rails of a railroad have been laid. **2.** *Railroads.* the upper part of a rail, used for supporting and guiding the wheels of railroad cars. **3.** *Mil.* a railroad depot at which supplies are unloaded to be distributed or forwarded by truck or other means. [RAIL[1] + HEAD]

rail·ing (rā′ling), *n.* **1.** a fencelike barrier composed of one or more horizontal rails supported by widely spaced uprights; balustrade. **2.** bannister. **3.** rails collectively. [RAIL[1] + -ING[1]]

rail·ler·y (rā′lə rē), *n., pl.* **-ler·ies. 1.** good-humored ridicule; banter. **2.** a bantering remark. [< F *raillerie* equiv. to MF *raill(er)* (to) RAIL[2] + *-erie* -ERY]

rail·road (rāl′rōd′), *n.* **1.** a permanent road laid with rails, commonly in one or more pairs of continuous lines forming a track or tracks, on which locomotives and cars are run for the transportation of passengers, freight, express, and mails. **2.** such a road together with its rolling stock, buildings, etc.; the entire railway plant, including fixed and movable property. **3.** the company of persons owning or operating such a plant. **4.** *Bowling.* a split. **5. railroads,** stocks or bonds of railroad companies. —*v.t.* **6.** to transport by means of a railroad. **7.** to supply with railroads. **8.** to send or push forward with great or undue speed: *to railroad a bill through a legislature.* **9.** *Informal.* to convict (a person) in a hasty manner by means of false charges or insufficient evidence: *The prisoner insisted he had been railroaded.* [RAIL[1] + ROAD]

rail·road·er (rāl′rō′dər), *n.* a person employed in the operation or management of a railroad. [RAILROAD + -ER[1]]

rail′road flat′, an apartment with no corridor and two or more rooms arranged like cars in a train so that one must pass through one room to enter the next.

rail·road·ing (rāl′rō′ding), *n.* the construction or operation of railroads. [RAILROAD + -ING[1]]

rail′road pen′, a ruling pen for drawing two parallel lines.

rail-split·ter (rāl′split′ər), *n.* **1.** one who or that which splits rails, esp. for fences. **2.** (*cap.*) nickname of Abraham Lincoln. [RAIL[1] + SPLITTER]

rail·way (rāl′wā′), *n.* **1.** a rail-line with lighter-weight equipment and roadbed than a main-line railroad. **2.** a railroad, esp. one operating over relatively short distances. **3.** any line or lines of rails forming a road of flanged-wheel equipment. **4.** Also called **tramway.** *Naut.* a rail of H or T section running along a mast, boom, gaff, or other spar and having a slide that guides the parrel of a yard or the heel of a gaff being raised or lowered or guides a hank of a sail; a mast track or sail track. [RAIL[1] + WAY] —**rail′wayed′,** *adj.* —**rail′-way′less,** *adj.*

rai·ment (rā′mənt), *n. Chiefly Literary.* clothing; apparel; attire. [ME *rayment,* aph. var. of *arrayment.* See ARRAY, -MENT]

Rai·mon·di (rī mōn′dē, -mon′-; *It.* Rī mōn′dē), *n.* **Marc·an·to·nio** (mäR′kän tō′nyō), c1480–c1534, Italian engraver. Also called **Marcantonio.**

rain (rān), *n.* **1.** water that is condensed from the aqueous vapor in the atmosphere and falls in drops from the sky to the earth. **2.** a rainfall, rainstorm, or shower: *We had a light rain this afternoon.* **3. rains,** the rainy season; seasonal rainfall, as in India. **4.** weather marked by steady rainfall: *We had rain most of last summer.* **5.** a heavy and continuous descent of anything: *a rain of blows; a rain of vituperation.* —*v.i.* **6.** (of rain) to fall (usually used impersonally with *it* as subject): *It rained all night.* **7.** to fall like rain: *Tears rained from her eyes.* **8.** to send down rain: *The lightning flashed and the sky rained on us in torrents.* —*v.t.* **9.** to send down: *People on the roof rained confetti on the paraders.* **10.** to offer, bestow, or give abundantly: *to rain favors upon a person.* **11.** to deal, hurl, fire, etc., repeatedly: *to rain blows on someone's head.* **12. rain cats and dogs,** *Informal.* to rain very heavily or steadily: *We canceled our picnic in the country because it rained cats and dogs.* **13. rain out,** (of rain) to cause the cancellation or postponement of, a contest, performance, or the like: *The double-header was rained out yesterday.* [ME *rein,* OE *regn;* c. D, G *regen,* OIcel *regn*] —**rain′less,** *adj.* —**rain′less·ness,** *n.*

rain·band (rān′band′), *n.* a dark band in the solar spectrum caused by water vapor in the atmosphere. [RAIN + BAND[2]]

rain·bow (rān′bō′), *n.* **1.** a bow or arc of prismatic colors appearing in the heavens opposite the sun and caused by the refraction and reflection of the sun's rays in drops of rain. **2.** a similar bow of colors, esp. one appearing in the spray of a waterfall. **3.** any brightly multicolored arrangement or display. **4.** a wide variety or range; gamut. **5.** See **rainbow trout.** [ME *reinbowe,* OE *regnboga;* c. OIcel *regnbogi,* G *Regenbogen.* See RAIN, BOW[2]] —**rain′bow′y, rain′bow′like′,** *adj.*

Rainbow, The, a novel (1915) by D. H. Lawrence.

Rain′bow Bridge′, a natural stone bridge in S Utah: a national monument. 309 ft. high; 278-ft. span.

rain′bow cac′tus, an erect stiff cactus, *Echinocereus rigidissimus,* of Arizona and Mexico, having a cylindrical body, numerous interlocking spines, and pink flowers.

rain′bow dart′er, a stout darter, *Etheostoma caeruleum,* found in the Greak Lakes and Mississippi River drainages, the spawning male of which has the sides marked with oblique blue bars with red interspaces. Also called **soldierfish.**

rain′bow dress′, *Naut.* the array of flags and pennants used in dressing a vessel rainbow fashion.

rain′bow fash′ion, *Naut.* with all code flags displayed from stem to stern by way of all mastheads: *The ship was dressed rainbow fashion.*

rain′bow par′rotfish, a parrotfish, *Scarus guacamaia,* of the tropical Atlantic Ocean.

Rain·bows (rān′bōz′), *n.* **Bay of.** See **Sinus Iridum.**

rain′bow sea′perch, an embiotocid fish, *Hypsurus caryi,* found off the Pacific coast of North America, having red, orange, and blue stripes on the body.

rain′bow snake′, a burrowing, bluish-black colubrid snake, *Abastor erythrogrammus,* of the southeastern U.S., having red or yellow stripes along the body, and having a red belly.

rain′bow trout′, a trout, *Salmo gairdnerii,* native in the coastal waters and streams from Lower California to Alaska.

rain′ check′, **1.** a ticket for future use given to spectators at an outdoor event, as a baseball game or concert, that has been postponed or interrupted by rain. **2.** an offered or requested postponement of an invitation until a more convenient, usually unspecified time: *Since you can't join us for dinner, we'll give you a rain check.*

rain·coat (rān′kōt′), *n.* a waterproof coat worn as protection against rain. [RAIN + COAT]

rain′ dance′, (esp. among American Indians) a ritualistic dance performed to bring rain.

rain·drop (rān′drop′), *n.* a drop of rain. [RAIN + DROP]

Rai·ner (rā′nər), *n.* a boy's given name. Also **Rayner.**

Rain·ey (rā′nē), *n.* **Gertrude** ("*Ma*"), 1886–1939, U.S. blues singer.

rain·fall (rān′fôl′), *n.* **1.** a fall or shower of rain. **2.** the amount of water falling in rain, snow, etc., within a given time and area, usually expressed as a hypothetical depth of coverage: *a rainfall of 70 inches a year.* [RAIN + FALL]

rain′ gauge′, an instrument for measuring rainfall.

Rai·nier (rā nēr′, rā′nēr, rə nēr′), *n.* **Mount,** a mountain in W Washington, in the Cascade Range. 14,408 ft. Also called **Mount Tacoma.**

Rai·nier III (rā nēr′, re-, rə-; *Fr.* RE nyā′), *n.* **Rainier Louis Hen·ri Max·ence Ber·trand de Gri·mal·di** (lwē äN rē′ mȧk säNs′ beR träN′ də grē mȧl dē′), **Prince of Monaco,** born 1923, reigning prince of Monaco since 1949.

rain·mak·er (rān′mā′kər), *n.* **1.** (among American Indians) a medicine man who by various rituals and incantations seeks to cause rain. **2.** a person who induces rain to fall by using various scientific techniques, as the seeding of clouds with silver iodide crystals from an airplane. [RAIN + MAKER] —**rain′mak′ing,** *n.*

rain′ or shine′, regardless of the weather or circumstances; in any event: *We'll be there tomorrow, rain or shine. He's always a reliable friend, rain or shine.*

rain·out (rān′out′), *n.* **1.** a contest, performance, or the like, that has been rained out. **2.** *Physics.* atomic fallout occurring in precipitation. [n. use of v. phrase *rain out*]

rain·proof (rān′pro͞of′), *adj.* **1.** impervious to rain; keeping out or unaffected by rain: *a rainproof cover; a rainproof coat.* —*v.t.* **2.** to make impervious to rain. [RAIN + -PROOF]

Rains (rānz), *n.* **Sea of.** See **Mare Imbrium.**

rain′ show′er, a brief rainfall, usually of variable intensity.

rain·storm (rān′stôrm′), *n.* a storm of rain. [RAIN + STORM]

rain′ wa′ter, water fallen as rain. [ME *rayn watir,* OE *regn-, rēnwæter*]

rain·wear (rān′wâr′), *n.* waterproof or water-repellent clothing. [RAIN + WEAR]

rain·y (rā′nē), *adj.,* **rain·i·er, rain·i·est. 1.** characterized by rain: *rainy weather; a rainy region.* **2.** wet with rain: *rainy streets.* **3.** bringing rain: *rainy clouds.* [ME *reyny,* OE *rēnig.* See RAIN, -Y[1]] —**rain′i·ly,** *adv.* —**rain′i·ness,** *n.*

rain′y day′, a time of need or emergency, esp. one that might arise in the future: *saving money for a rainy day.*

raise (rāz), *v.,* **raised, rais·ing,** *n.* —*v.t.* **1.** to move to a higher position; lift up; elevate: *to raise one's hand; sleepy birds raising their heads and looking about.* **2.** to set upright: *The chair fell over so he raised it again.* **3.** to cause to rise or stand up rouse: *The sound of the bugle raised him from his bed.* **4.** to build; erect: *to raise a monument; towering apartment houses raised along the avenue.* **5.** to set up the framework of: *to raise a house.* **6.** to set in motion; activate: *to raise a storm of protest.* **7.** to care for and promote the growth of: *to raise corn; to raise prize-winning terriers.* **8.** to serve in the capacity of parent to; rear: *to raise children.* **9.** to give rise to; bring up or about: *to raise a question; to raise one's hopes.* **10.** to put forward; bring into question: *He raised the issue of his opponent's eligibility.* **11.** *Law.* to make (an issue at law). **12.** to restore to life: *to raise the dead.* **13.** to stir up: *to raise a rebellion with stirring speeches.* **14.** to give vigor to; animate: *The news raised his spirits.* **15.** to advance in rank, dignity, etc.: *to raise a man to the peerage.* **16.** to gather together; collect: *to raise an army; to raise $30 for a charity.* **17.** to increase in height: *The blocks raise the table three inches.* **18.** to increase in degree, intensity, pitch, or force: *to raise the volume of a radio.* **19.** to utter (a cry, shout, etc.) in a loud voice. **20.** to cause (the voice) to be heard: *to raise one's voice in opposition.* **21.** to cause (dough or bread) to rise by expansion and become light, as by the use of yeast. **22.** to increase in amount: *to raise rents; to raise salaries.* **23.** to increase (the value or price) of a commodity, stock, bond, etc. **24.** *Poker.* **a.** to increase (another player's bet). **b.** to bet at a higher level than (a preceding bettor). **25.** *Bridge.* to increase (the bid for a contract) by repeating one's partner's bid at a higher level. **26.** to increase the amount specified in (a check, money order, or the like) by fraudulent alteration. **27.** *Mil.* to end (a siege) by withdrawing the besieging forces or by compelling the besieging forces to withdraw. **28.** *Naut.* **a.** to cause (something) to rise above the visible horizon by approaching nearer to it. **b.** to come in sight of (land, a whale, etc.). **29.** to establish communication with by radio: *The radioman was able to raise shore headquarters after three tries.* **30.** *Mining.* to dig (a shaft) upward from below. —*v.i.* **31.** *Dial.* to rise up; arise. **32. raise Cain.** See **Cain** (def. 3). —*n.* **33.** an increase in amount, as of wages: *a raise in pay.* **34.** the amount of such an increase: *His raise was five dollars.* **35.** a raising, lifting, etc.: *a raise in spirits.* **36.** a raised place. **37.** *Mining.* a shaft excavated upward from below. [ME *reise(n)* < Scand; cf. OIcel *reisa,* Goth *-raisjan* (causative of root in OE *rīsan* to RISE), OE *rǣran* to REAR[2]] —**rais′a·ble, raise′a·ble,** *adj.* —**rais′er,** *n.*

—**Syn. 1, 2.** loft. RAISE, LIFT, HEAVE, HOIST imply bringing something up above its original position. RAISE, the most general word, may mean to bring something to or toward an upright position with one end resting on the ground; or it may be used in the sense of LIFT, moving an object a comparatively short distance upward but breaking completely its physical contact with the place where it had been: *to raise a ladder; to lift a package.* HEAVE implies lifting with effort or exertion: *to heave a huge box onto a truck.* HOIST implies lifting slowly and gradually something of considerable weight, usually with mechanical help, such as given by a crane or derrick: *to hoist steel beams to the top of the framework of a building.* See **rise. 3.** arouse, awaken. **4.** construct, rear. **7.** cultivate, grow. **9.** originate, produce, effect. **13.** excite. **14.** invigorate, inspirit. **15.** elevate, promote, exalt. **16.** assemble. **17.** heighten, enlarge. **18.** aggravate, amplify, augment. —**Ant. 1.** lower.

raised (rāzd), *adj.* **1.** fashioned or made as a surface design in relief. **2.** *Cookery.* made light by the use of yeast or other ferment but not with baking powder, soda, or the like. [RAISE + -ED[2]]

raised′-deck′ boat′, *Naut.* a small vessel in which the roof of the cabin is extended to the sides of the hull to form one integrated unit.

raised′ fore′deck, *Naut.* the weather deck of a vessel between the bridge house and the forecastle or stem, raised somewhat with relation to the weather deck aft of the bridge house.

raised′ girt′, *Carpentry.* See **flush girt.**

raised′ quar′ter-deck, *Naut.* a slightly raised after portion of the weather deck of a cargo vessel (**raised′ quar′ter-deck ves′sel**), provided to compensate for loss of cargo space due to the presence of the propeller shaft alley and thereby to give the vessel its proper trim when fully loaded.

rai·sin (rā′zin), *n.* **1.** a grape of any of various sweet varieties dried in the sun or by artificial means and used in cookery. **2.** dark purplish blue. [ME *raisin, reisin* < OF < VL *racīm(us),* var. of L *racēmus*] —**rai′sin·y,** *adj.*

rais′ing plate′. See **wall plate** (def. 1).

rai·son d'é·tat (RE zôN′ dā tȧ′), *French.* for the good of the country. [lit., reason of state]

rai·son d'ê·tre (rā′zōn de′trə; *Fr.* RE zôN′ de′tR[ə]), *pl.* **rai·sons d'ê·tre** (rā′zōnz de′trə; *Fr.* RE zôN′ de′tR[ə]). reason or justification for being or existence: *Art is the artist's raison d'être.*

rai·son·né (RE zô nā′), *adj. French.* ordered; systematized. [lit., reasoned]

raj (räj), *n.* (in India) rule; reign; dominion: *the British raj.* [< Hindi *rāj* < Skt *rājya,* deriv. of *rājati* he rules]

Raj (raj), *n.* a boy's given name.

Ra·jab (rə jab′), *n.* the seventh month of the Islamic calendar. [< Ar]

ra·jah (rä′jə), *n.* **1.** a king or prince in India. **2.** a minor chief or dignitary. **3.** an honorary title conferred on Hindus in India. **4.** a title of rulers, princes, or chiefs in Java, Borneo, etc. Also, **ra′ja.** [< Hindi *rājā;* c. L *rex* king]

ra·jas (rä′jəs), *n.* *Hinduism.* See under **guna.** [< Skt: lit., dim or colored space] —**ra·jas·ic** (ru jas′ik), *adj.*

Ra·ja·sthan (rä′jə stän′), *n.* a state in NW India; formerly Rajputana and a group of small states. 20,155,602 (1961); 132,078 sq. mi. *Cap.:* Jaipur.

Ra·ja·stha·ni (rä′jə stä′nē), *n.* **1.** an Indic language, the vernacular of Rajasthan. —*adj.* **2.** of, pertaining to, or characteristic of Rajasthan, its people, culture, or language.

Raj·kot (räj′kōt), *n.* a city in S Gujarat, in W India. 193,500 (1961).

Raj·put (räj′po͝ot), *n.* a member of a Hindu people claiming descent from the ancient Kshatriya, or warrior caste, and noted for their military spirit. [< Hindi, equiv. to Skt *rāj* king (see RAJ) + *putra* son]

Raj·pu·ta·na (räj′po͝o tä′nə), *n.* a former region in NW India, now making up the principal part of Rajasthan.

ra·k'ah (ruk′ə), *n.* *Islam.* a complete set of devotions consisting of prayers and verses recited in prescribed attitudes of the body, repeated several times, and concluded in a prescribed manner. Also, **ra'k'a.** [< Ar]

rake[1] (rāk), *n., v.,* **raked, rak·ing.** —*n.* **1.** an agricultural implement with teeth or tines for gathering cut grass, hay, or the like, or for smoothing the surface of the ground. **2.** any of various implements having a similar form, as a croupier's implement for gathering in money on a gaming table. —*v.t.* **3.** to gather, draw, or remove with a rake: *to rake dead leaves from a lawn.* **4.** to clear, smooth, or prepare with a rake: *to rake a garden bed.* **5.** to clear (a fire, embers, etc.) by stirring with a poker or the like. **6.** to gather or collect abundantly (usually fol. by *in*): *He marketed his invention and has been raking money in ever since.* **7.** to bring to light, usually for discreditable reasons (usually fol. by *up*): *to rake up an old scandal.* **8.** to search thoroughly through: *They raked the apartment for the missing jewels.* **9.** to scrape; scratch: *The sword's tip raked his face lightly.* **10.** to scoop out (a masonry joint) to a given depth while the mortar is still green. **11.** to fire guns along the length of (a position, body of troops, ship, etc.). **12.** to sweep with the eyes: *He raked the horizon with his gaze.* —*v.i.* **13.** to use a rake: *The gardener raked along the border of the garden.* **14.** to search, as with a rake: *His gaze raked over the room.* **15.** to scrape; search: *She frantically raked through her belongings.* [ME; OE *raca;* c. G *Rechen,* OIcel *reka* shovel] —**rak′er,** *n.*

rake[2] (rāk), *n.* a dissolute or profligate person, esp. a man who is licentious; roué. [short for RAKEHELL]

rake[3] (rāk), *v.,* **raked, rak·ing,** *n.* —*v.i.* **1.** to incline from the vertical, as a mast, or from the horizontal. —*v.t.* **2.** to cause (something) to incline from the vertical or the horizontal. —*n.* **3.** inclination or slope away from the perpendicular or the horizontal. **4.** a board or molding placed along the sloping sides of a frame gable to cover the ends of the siding. **5.** *Aeron.* the angle measured between the tip edge of an aircraft or missile wing or other lifting surface and the plane of symmetry. **6.** *Mach.* the angle between the cutting face of a tool and a plane perpendicular to the surface of the work at the cutting point. [? var. of OE *racian, racode* to take a direction; see RAKE[4]]

rake[4] (rāk), *v.i.,* **raked, rak·ing. 1.** *Hunting* **a.** (of a hawk) to fly after game. **b.** (of a dog) to hunt with the nose close to the ground instead of in the wind. **2.** *Chiefly Scot.* to go or proceed, esp. with speed. [ME *rake(n),* OE *racian* to take a course or direction]

raked (rākt), *adj.* inclining from the vertical or from the horizontal: *raked masts; a raked stage.* [RAKE[3] + -ED[2]]

raked′ bow′ (bou), *Naut.* a bow having a straight stem inclined from the perpendicular.

ra·kee (rə kē′, rak′ē), *n.* raki.

rake·hell (rāk′hel′), *n.* **1.** a licentious or dissolute man; rake. —*adj.* **2.** dissolute; profligate. [RAKE[2] + HELL; r. ME *rakel* (adj.) rash, rough, coarse, hasty (see RAKE[4]); cf. OIcel *reikall* wandering, unsettled]

rake·hell·y (rāk′hel′ē), *adj.* rakehell. (def. 2).

rake-off (rāk′ôf′, -of′), *n.* **1.** a share or amount taken or received illicitly, as in connection with a public enterprise. **2.** a share, as of profits. **3.** a discount in the price of a commodity: *She got a 20% rake-off on the dishwasher.* [n. use of v. phrase *rake off*]

rak·er[1] (rā′kər), *n.* **1.** one who or that which rakes. **2.** See **raker tooth.** [RAKE[1] + -ER[1]]

rak·er[2] (rā′kər), *n.* *Building Trades.* an inclined member, as a pile or shore. [RAKE[3] + -ER[1]]

rak′er tooth′, a saw tooth for cleaning loose chips from a kerf. Also called **raker, cleaner tooth.**

Rake's′ Prog′ress, The, **1.** a series of paintings and engravings by William Hogarth. **2.** an opera (1951) by Igor Stravinsky.

ra·ki (rä kē′, rak′ē), *n.* a spirituous liquor distilled from grain, grapes, plums, etc., in southeastern Europe and the Near East. Also, **rakee.** [< Turk]

rak′ing bond′, a brickwork bond in which concealed courses of diagonally laid bricks are used to bond exposed brickwork to the wall structure. Cf. **clip bond, diagonal bond, herringbone bond.**

rak′ing cor′nice, *Archit.* either of two straight, sloping cornices on a pediment following or suggesting the slopes of a roof.

rak′ing course′, a concealed course of bricks laid diagonally to the wall surface in a raking bond.

rak′ing piece′, **1.** a sloping piece of scenery, as on a television or stage set, esp. such a piece used for masking the side of a ramp. **2.** a wedge used for leveling scenery on a sloping stage.

rak·ish[1] (rā′kish), *adj.* like a rake; dissolute. [RAKE[2] + -ISH[1]] —**rak′ish·ly,** *adv.* —**rak′ish·ness,** *n.*

rak·ish[2] (rā′kish), *adj.* **1.** smart; jaunty; dashing: *a hat worn at a rakish angle.* **2.** (of a vessel) having an appearance suggesting speed. [RAKE[3] + -ISH[1]]

rale (ral, räl), *n.* *Pathol.* an abnormal crackling or rattling sound heard upon auscultation of the chest, caused by disease or congestion of the lungs. [< F, deriv. of *râler* to make a rattling sound in the throat; cf. RAIL[3]]

Ra·leigh (rô′lē, rä′-), *n.* **1. Sir Walter.** Also, **Ral′egh.** 1552?–1618, English explorer and writer, a favorite of Elizabeth I. **2.** a city in and the capital of North Carolina, in the central part. 93,931 (1960). **3.** a boy's given name.

rall., rallentando.

ral·len·tan·do (rä′lən tän′dō; *It.* räl′len tän′dô), *adj.* slackening; becoming slower (used as a musical direction). [< It, prp. of *rallentare* to abate]

CONCISE ETYMOLOGY KEY: <, descended or derived from; >, whence; b., blend of, blended; c., cognate with; deriv., derivative; equiv., equivalent; imit., imitative; m., modification of; obl., oblique; r., replacing; s., stem; sp., spelling; trans., translation; ?, origin unknown, perhaps; *, hypothetical. See the full key inside the front cover.

ral·li·form (ral′ə fôrm′), *adj. Zool.* raillike in shape, anatomy, etc. [< NL *Rall(us)* name of genus (see RAIL³) + -I- + -FORM]

ral·line (ral′īn, -in), *adj.* belonging or pertaining to the subfamily *Rallinae,* comprising the rails and allied species. [< NL *Rall(us)* name of genus (see RAIL³) + -INE¹]

ral·ly¹ (ral′ē), *v.,* **-lied, -ly·ing,** *n., pl.* **-lies.** —*v.t.* **1.** to bring into order again; gather and organize anew: *The general rallied his scattered army.* **2.** to draw or call (persons) together for a common action: *He rallied his friends to help him.* **3.** to concentrate or revive, as one's strength, spirits, etc.: *They rallied their energies for the counterattack.* —*v.i.* **4.** to come together for common action: *The disunited party rallied in time for the election campaign.* **5.** to come together or into order again: *The captain ordered his small force to rally at the next stream.* **6.** to come to the assistance of a person, party, or cause (often fol. by *to* or *around*): *to rally around a political candidate.* **7.** to recover partially from illness: *He spent a bad night but began to rally by morning.* **8.** to acquire fresh strength or vigor: *The runner seemed to be rallying for a final sprint.* **9.** *Finance.* **a.** (of securities) to rise sharply in price after a drop. **b.** (of the persons forming a stock market) to begin to trade with increased activity after a slow period. **10.** (in tennis, badminton, etc.) to engage in a rally. **11.** *Baseball.* (of a team) to score one or more runs in one inning. —*n.* **12.** a recovery from dispersion or disorder, as of troops. **13.** a renewal or recovery of strength, activity, etc. **14.** a partial recovery of strength during illness. **15.** a drawing or coming together of persons, as for common action, as in a mass meeting: *A political rally that brought together hundreds of the faithful.* **16.** *Finance.* a sharp rise in price or active trading after a declining market. **17.** (in tennis, badminton, etc.) **a.** an exchange of strokes between players before a point is scored. **b.** the hitting of the ball back and forth prior to the start of a match. **18.** *Boxing.* an exchange of blows. **19.** *Baseball.* the scoring of one or more runs in one inning. **20.** *Theat. Brit.* a quickening of pace for heightening the dramatic effect in a scene or act. **21.** *Shipbuilding.* a series of blows with battering rams, made in order to drive wedges under a hull to raise it prior to launching. **22.** Also, **ral′lye.** a long-distance automobile race, esp. for sports cars, held over public roads unfamiliar to the drivers and marked off by numerous checkpoints along the route. [< F *rallі(er);* OF, equiv. to *re-* RE- + *alier* to join; see ALLY] —**ral′li·er,** *n.*
—**Syn. 2, 4.** muster. **3.** reanimate, reinvigorate. **4.** assemble. **5.** reassemble.

ral·ly² (ral′ē), *v.t.,* **-lied, -ly·ing.** to ridicule in a good-natured way; banter. [< F *raill(er)* (to) RAIL²]

ral·lye (ral′ē), *n.* rally (def. 22).

Ralph (ralf), *n.* a boy's given name.

Ralph Rois·ter Dois·ter (ralf′ rois′tər dois′tər *or, esp. Brit.,* rāf′, rāf′), a play (1553?) by Nicholas Udall: the earliest known English comedy.

ram (ram), *n., v.,* **rammed, ram·ming.** —*n.* **1.** a male sheep. **2.** (*cap.*) *Astron., Astrol.* the constellation or sign of Aries. **3.** any of various devices for battering, crushing, driving, or forcing something, esp. a battering ram. **4.** a heavy beak or spur projecting from the bow of a warship for penetrating the hull of an enemy's ship. **5.** a warship so equipped, esp. one used primarily for ramming enemy vessels. **6.** the heavy weight that strikes the blow in a pile driver or the like. **7.** a piston, as on a hydraulic press. **8.** a reciprocating part of certain machine tools, as the toolholder of a slotter or shaper. **9.** See **hydraulic ram. 10.** Also called **ram schooner.** a three-masted schooner used for carrying lumber on Chesapeake Bay and on the Chesapeake and Delaware Canal. —*v.t.* **11.** to drive or force by heavy blows. **12.** to strike with great force; dash violently against: *The car went out of control and rammed the truck.* **13.** to cram; stuff: *They rammed the gag in his mouth.* **14.** to push firmly: *to ram a bill through the Senate.* **15.** to force (a charge) into a firearm, as with a ramrod. [ME, OE; c. D, LG *ram,* G *Ramme*] —**ram′like′,** *adj.*

RAM (ram), *n.* a type of computer memory that allows the user to create, load, and run new programs and to store and manipulate data temporarily. Cf. **ROM** [*r(andom)- a(ccess) m(emory)*]

ram-, an intensive prefix: *rambunctious.* [< Scand; cf. Icel *ram-* very, special use of *rammr* strong, sharp; akin to RAM]

Ra·ma (rä′mə), *n.* (in the *Ramayana*) any of the three avatars of Vishnu: Balarama, Parashurama, or Ramachandra.

Rama IX, (*Phumiphon Aduldet* or *Bhumibol-Adulyadej*) born 1927, king of Thailand since 1950.

Ra·ma·chan·dra (rä′mə chun′drə), *n.* the hero of the *Ramayana,* and a character in the *Mahabharata.*

Ram·a·dan (ram′ə dän′), *n. Islam.* **1.** the ninth month of the Islamic calendar. **2.** the daily fast that is rigidly enjoined from dawn until sunset during this month. [< Ar]

Ra·ma·krish·na (rä mə krish′nə), *n.* **Sri** (srē, shrē), 1834–86, Hindu religious reformer and mystic.

ra·mal (rā′məl), *adj.* of or pertaining to ramus. [< L *rām(us)* branch, bough, twig + -AL¹]

Ra·man (rä′mən), *n.* **Sir Chan·dra·se·kha·ra Ven·ka·ta** (chun′drə shä′kər ə veng′kə tə), 1888–1970, Indian physicist: Nobel prize 1930.

Ra′man effect′ (rä′mən), *Optics.* the change in wavelength of light scattered while passing through a transparent medium, the collection of new wavelengths **(Ra′man spec′trum)** being characteristic of the scattering medium and differing from the fluorescent spectrum in being much less intense and in being unrelated to an absorption band of the medium. [named after Sir C. RAMAN]

Ra·ma·nu·jan (rä mä′nŏŏ jən), *n.* **Sri·ni·va·sa** (shrē′ni vä′sə, srē′-), 1887–1920, Indian mathematician.

ra·mark (rā′märk), *n.* a radar beacon developed by the U.S. Coast Guard as a marine navigational aid. [RA(DAR) + MARK(ER)]

Ra·mat Gan (rə mät′ gän′), a city in central Israel, near Tel-Aviv. 95,800 (est. 1963).

Ra·ma·ya·na (rä mä′yə nə), *n.* an epic of India, one of the *Puranas* attributed to Valmiki and concerned with the life and adventures of Ramachandra and his wife Sita.

Ram·a·zan (ram′ə zän′), *n.* (in India) Ramadan.

Ram·bam (räm bäm′), *n.* Maimonides.

ram·bla (räm′blə), *n.* a dry ravine. [< Sp < Ar *ramlah*]

ram·ble (ram′bəl), *v.,* **-bled, -bling,** *n.* —*v.i.* **1.** to wander around in a leisurely, aimless manner: *They rambled through the shops until closing time.* **2.** to take a course with many turns or windings, as a stream or path. **3.** to grow in a random, unsystematic fashion: *The vine rambled over the walls and tree trunks.* **4.** to talk or write in a discursive, aimless way: *The speaker rambled on with anecdote after anecdote.* —*v.t.* **5.** to walk aimlessly over or through: *They spent the spring afternoon rambling woodland paths.* —*n.* **6.** a walk without a definite route, taken merely for pleasure. [? ROAM + -LE]
—**Syn. 1.** stroll, saunter, amble, stray, straggle. See **roam. 6.** excursion, tour.

ram·bler (ram′blər), *n.* **1.** one who or that which rambles. **2.** See **ranch house** (def. 2). **3.** any of several climbing roses having clusters of small flowers. [RAMBLE + -ER¹]

ram·bling (ram′bling), *adj.* **1.** aimlessly wandering. **2.** taking an irregular course; straggling: *a rambling brook.* **3.** spread out irregularly in various directions: *a rambling mansion.* **4.** straying from one subject to another: *a rambling novel.* [RAMBLE + -ING²] —**ram′bling·ly,** *adv.* —**ram′bling·ness,** *n.*
—**Syn. 4.** discursive.

Ram·bouil·let (ram′bŏŏ lā′; *Fr.* räN bōō ye′), *n.* one of a breed of hardy sheep, developed from the Merino, that yield good mutton and a fine grade of wool. [named after *Rambouillet,* France, source of the breed]

ram′ bow′ (bou), *Naut.* a bow having a stem receding from the forefoot to a point above the water line.

ram·bunc·tious (ram bungk′shəs), *adj.* **1.** difficult to control or handle; wildly boisterous: *a rambunctious child.* **2.** turbulently active and noisy: *a social gathering that became rambunctious and out of hand.* [RAM- + var. of BUMPTIOUS] —**ram·bunc′tious·ly,** *adv.* —**ram·bunc′tious·ness,** *n.*

ram·bu·tan (ram bōōt′ən), *n.* **1.** the bright-red oval fruit of a Malayan, sapindaceous tree, *Nephelium lappaceum,* covered with soft spines, or hairs, and having a subacid taste. **2.** the tree itself. [< Malay]

Ra·meau (RA mō′), *n.* **Jean Phi·lippe** (zhäN fē lēp′), 1683–1764, French composer and musical theorist.

Ra·mée (rə mā′), *n.* **Louise de la** ("*Ouida*"), 1839–1908, English novelist.

ram·e·kin (ram′ə kin), *n.* **1.** a small, separately cooked portion of a cheese preparation or other food mixture baked in a small dish without a lid. **2.** a small dish in which food can be baked and served. Also, **ram′e·quin.** [< F *ramequin* < Gmc; cf. Flem *rammeken*]

ram·en·ta·ceous (ram′ən tā′shəs), *adj. Bot.* resembling or covered with ramenta. [RAMENT(UM) + -ACEOUS]

ra·men·tum (rə men′təm), *n., pl.* **-ta** (-tə). **1.** a scraping, shaving, or particle. **2.** *Bot.* one of the thin, chafflike scales covering the shoots or leaves of certain ferns. [< L, equiv. to *rā(dere)* (to) scrape + *-mentum* -MENT]

Ram·e·ses (ram′i sēz′), *n.* **1.** Ramses (def. 1). **2.** Raamses.

ra·met (rā′mit), *n.* an individual plant of a clone. [< L *rām(us)* branch + -ET]

ra·mi (rā′mī), *n.* pl. of **ramus.**

ram·ie (ram′ē), *n.* **1.** an Asian, urticaceous shrub, *Boehmeria nivea,* yielding a fiber used esp. in making textiles. **2.** the fiber itself. [< Malay *rāmī*]

ram·i·fi·ca·tion (ram′ə fə kā′shən), *n.* **1.** the act or process of ramifying. **2.** a branch: *ramifications of a nerve.* **3.** a related or derived subject, problem, etc.; outgrowth; consequence: *The new tax law proved to have many ramifications not foreseen by the lawmakers.* **4.** *Bot.* **a.** a structure formed of branches. **b.** a configuration of branching parts. [< MF < ML *rāmificāt-* (s. of *rāmificātus*) (ptp. of *rāmificāre* to RAMIFY) + MF *-ion* -ION]

ram·i·form (ram′ə fôrm′), *adj.* **1.** having the form of a branch; branchlike. **2.** branched. [< L *rām(us)* branch + -I- + -FORM]

ram·i·fy (ram′ə fī′), *v.t., v.i.,* **-fied, -fy·ing.** to divide or spread out into branches or branchlike parts; extend into subdivisions. [< MF *ramifi(er)* < ML *rāmificāre,* equiv. to L *rām(us)* branch + *-ificāre* -IFY]

Ra·mil·lies (*Fr.* RA mē yē′), *n.* a village in central Belgium: Marlborough's defeat of the French 1706.

ram·jet (ram′jet′), *n.* a jet engine operated by the injection of fuel into a stream of air compressed by the forward speed of the aircraft. Also called **ram′jet en′gine.** [RAM + JET¹]

rammed′ earth′, a mixture of sand, loam, clay, and other ingredients rammed hard within forms as a building material. Also called **pisé, pisé de terre, pisay.**

ram·mels·berg·ite (ram′əlz bûr′gīt), *n.* a mineral, essentially nickel diarsenide, $NiAs_2$. [named after Karl Friedrich *Rammelsberg* (1813–99), German chemist; see -ITE¹]

ram·mer (ram′ər), *n.* one who or that which rams. [RAM + -ER¹]

ram·mish (ram′ish), *adj.* **1.** resembling a ram. **2.** having a disagreeable taste or smell; rank. [ME; see RAM, -ISH¹] —**ram′mish·ness,** *n.*

ra·mon (rə mōn′), *n.* any of several tropical American, moraceous trees of the genus *Brosimum,* the leaves of which are used as forage, esp. *B. Alicastrum,* which bears the breadnut. Also, **ra·moon** (rə mōōn′). [< Sp *ramón* browse, aug. of *ramo* branch (< L *rāmus*)]

Ra·mon (rā′mən), *n.* a boy's given name, form of **Raymond.**

Ra·mo·na (rə mō′nə), *n.* a girl's given name.

Ra·món y Ca·jal (rä mōn′ ē kä häl′), **San·tia·go** (sän tyä′gô), 1852–1934, Spanish histologist: Nobel prize for medicine 1906.

ra·mose (rā′mōs, rə mōs′), *adj.* **1.** having many branches. **2.** branching. [< L *rāmōs(us)* full of boughs, equiv. to *rām(us)* branch + *-ōsus* -OSE¹] —**ra′mose·ly,** *adv.* —**ra·mos·i·ty** (rə mos′i tē), *n.*

ra·mous (rā′məs), *adj.* **1.** ramose. **2.** resembling or pertaining to branches. [< L *rāmōs(us).* See RAMOSE, -OUS]

ramp (ramp), *n.* **1.** a sloping surface connecting two levels. **2.** a short concave slope or bend, as one connecting the higher and lower parts of a staircase railing at a landing. **3.** any extensive sloping walk or passageway. **4.** the act of ramping. **5.** Also called **boarding ramp.** *U.S.* a movable staircase for entering or leaving a cabin door of an airplane. **6.** Also called **parking ramp.** *U.S.* apron (def. 6). [< F *rampe*]
—*v.i.* **7.** (of a lion or other large quadruped on a coat of arms) to rise or stand on the hind legs. **8.** to rear as if to spring. **9.** to leap or dash with fury (often fol. by *about*). **10.** to act violently; rage; storm: *ramping and raging in a great fury.* **11. ramp along,** *Naut.* to sail on a tack with all sails filled. [ME *ramp(en)* < OF *ramp(er)* (to) creep, crawl, climb < ?] —**ramp′ing·ly,** *adv.*

ram·page (*n.* ram′pāj; *v.* ram pāj′), *n., v.,* **-paged, -pag·ing.** —*n.* **1.** violent or excited behavior. **2.** a state of violent anger or agitation: *The smallest mistake sends him into a rampage. The river has gone on a rampage and flooded the countryside.* —*v.i.* **3.** to rush, move, or act furiously or violently: *a bull elephant rampaging through the jungle.* [RAMP + -AGE] —**ram·pag′er,** *n.*

ram·pa·geous (ram pā′jəs), *adj.* violent; unruly; boisterous. [RAMPAGE + -OUS] —**ram·pa′geous·ly,** *adv.* —**ram·pa′geous·ness,** *n.*

ramp·an·cy (ram′pən sē), *n.* a rampant condition or position. [RAMPANT + -CY]

ramp·ant (ram′pənt), *adj.* **1.** violent in action or spirit; raging; furious: *a rampant leopard.* **2.** in full sway; prevailing unbridled: *anarchy reigning rampant; a rampant rumor.* **3.** standing on the hind legs; ramping. **4.** *Heraldry.* (of a beast used as a charge) represented in profile facing the dexter side, with the body upraised and resting on the left hind leg, the tail and other legs elevated, the right foreleg highest, and the head in profile unless otherwise specified: *a lion rampant.* **5.** *Archit.* (of an arch or vault) springing at one side from one level of support and resting at the other on a higher level. [ME < OF, prp. of *ramper* to RAMP] —**ramp′ant·ly,** *adv.*

Rampant (Heraldic lion)

ram·part (ram′pärt, -pərt), *n.* **1.** *Fort.* **a.** a broad elevation or mound of earth raised as a fortification around a place and usually capped with a stone or earth parapet. **b.** such an elevation together with the parapet. **2.** anything serving as a bulwark or defense. —*v.t.* **3.** to furnish with or as if with a rampart. [< MF, deriv. of *remparer,* equiv. to *re-* RE- + *emparer* to take possession of < Pr *amparar* < L *ante-* ANTE- + *parāre* to PREPARE]
—**Syn. 2.** fortification, breastwork, barricade, guard.

ram·pike (ram′pīk′), *n. Chiefly Canadian.* a dead tree, esp. the bleached skeleton or splintered trunk of a tree killed by fire, lightning, or wind. Also called **ram·pick** (ram′pik), **ram·pole** (ram′pōl′). [?]

ram·pi·on (ram′pē ən), *n.* **1.** a European campanula, *Campanula Rapunculus,* having an edible white tuberous root used in Europe for salad. **2.** any campanulaceous plant of the genus *Phyteuma,* having heads or spikes of blue flowers. [cf. It *ramponzolo*]

ram·rod (ram′rod′), *n., v.,* **-rod·ded, -rod·ding.** —*n.* **1.** a rod for ramming down the charge of a muzzle-loading firearm. **2.** a cleaning rod for the barrel of a firearm. **3.** a strict disciplinarian; martinet. —*v.t.* **4.** to exert discipline and authority on. [RAM + ROD]

Ram·say (ram′zē), *n.* **1. Allan,** 1686–1758, Scottish poet. **2. George.** See **Dalhousie** (def. 1). **3. James Andrew Broun.** See **Dalhousie** (def. 2). **4. Sir William,** 1852–1916, English chemist: Nobel prize 1904.

ram′ schoon′er, ram (def. 10).

Rams·den (ramz′dən), *n.* a walled plain in the third quadrant of the face of the moon: about 16 miles in diameter.

Rams′den eye′piece (ramz′dən), *Optics.* an eyepiece consisting of two plano-convex crown-glass lenses of equal focal length, placed with the convex sides facing each other and with a separation between the lenses of about two-thirds of the focal length of each. [named after Jesse *Ramsden* (1735–1800), English maker of astronomical instruments]

Ram·ses (ram′sēz), *n.* **1.** the name of several kings of ancient Egypt. **2.** Raamses. Ex. 12:37; Num. 33:3–5. Also, **Rameses.**

Ramses I, 1324?–1258 B.C., king of ancient Egypt.

Ramses II, 1292–1225 B.C., king of ancient Egypt.

Ramses III, 1198–1167 B.C., king of ancient Egypt.

Ram·sey (ram′zē), *n.* **1. Arthur Michael,** born 1904, English clergyman and scholar: archbishop of Canterbury since 1961. **2.** a town in NE New Jersey. 9527 (1960). **3.** a boy's given name.

Rams·gate (ramz′gāt′; *Brit.* ramz′git), *n.* a seaport in E Kent, in SE England: resort. 36,906 (1961).

ram·shack·le (ram′shak′əl), *adj.* loosely made or held together; rickety; shaky: *a ramshackle house.* [earlier *ramshackled,* equiv. to RAM- + *shackled,* ptp. of *shackle* (var. of SHAKE); see -LE] —**ram′shack′le·ness,** *n.*

ram's′-head la′dy's-slipper (ramz′hed′), a slender-stemmed orchid, *Cypripedium arietinum,* of northeastern North America and China, that has crimson-streaked, whitish-lipped flowers with purple sepals and grows in moist soil.

ram·son (ram′zən, -sən), *n.* **1.** a garlic, *Allium ursinum,* having broad leaves. **2.** Usually, **ramsons.** its bulbous root, used as a relish. [ME *ramsyn* (orig. pl., taken as sing.) OE *hramsan,* pl. of *hramsa* broad-leafed garlic; c. Gk *krómmyon* onion]

ram·stam (ram′stam), *Scot. and North Eng.* —*adj.* **1.** obstinate; headstrong. —*n.* **2.** a stubborn or thoughtless person. [perh. rhyming compound based on RAM + *stam* to STAMP]

ram·til (ram′til), *n.* See **niger seed.** [< Bengali]

ram·u·lose (ram′yə lōs′), *adj. Bot., Zool.* having many small branches. Also, **ram·u·lous** (ram′yə ləs). [< L *rāmulōs(us)* full of branching veins, equiv. to *rāmul(us)* little branch, twig (*rām(us)* branch + *-ul-* -ULE) + *-ōsus* -OSE¹]

ra·mus (rā′məs), *n., pl.* **-mi** (-mī). *Bot., Zool., Anat.* a branch, as of a plant, vein, bone, etc. [< L: branch, twig, bough]

ran (ran), *v.* pt. of **run.**

Ran (rän), *n. Scand. Myth.* a sea-goddess who drags down ships and drowns sailors: the wife of Aegir.

Ran·ca·gua (räng kä′gwä), *n.* a city in central Chile. 50,719 (est. 1959).

rance[1] (rans), *n.* a variety of Belgian marble that is dull red with white and blue graining. [< F]

rance[2] (rans), *n.* any kind of prop. [? < F *ranche* round (of a ladder), peg]

ranch (ranch), *n.* **1.** an establishment maintained for raising livestock under range conditions. **2.** the persons employed or living on it. **3.** *Chiefly Western U.S.* any farm or farming establishment. **4.** a dude ranch. —*v.i.* **5.** to conduct or work on a ranch. [< Sp *ranch(o)* RANCHO] —**ranch′less,** *adj.* —**ranch′like′,** *adj.*

ranch·er (ran′chər), *n.* a person who owns or works on a ranch. [RANCH + -ER[1]]

ran·che·ro (ran châr′ō; *Sp.* rän che′rô), *n., pl.* **-che·ros** (-châr′ōz; *Sp.* -che′rôs). (in Spanish America and the southwestern U.S.) rancher. [< Sp]

ranch′ house′, **1.** the house of the owner of a ranch, usually of one story and with a low-pitched roof. **2.** any one-story house of the same general form, esp. one built in the suburbs.

Ran·chi (rän′chē), *n.* a city in S Bihar, in E India. 122,400 (1961).

ranch·man (ranch′mən), *n., pl.* **-men.** a rancher. [RANCH + MAN[1]]

ran·cho (ran′chō, rän′-; *Sp.* rän′chô), *n., pl.* **-chos** (-chōz; *Sp.* -chôs). **1.** a ranch. **2.** a hut or collection of huts for herdsmen, laborers, or travelers. [< AmerSp: small farm, camp (Sp: camp) < OSp *rancharse* to lodge, be billeted < MF *(se) ranger* to be arranged, be installed; see RANGE]

Ran·cho Cor·do·va (ran′chō kôr′də və), a town in central California. 7429 (1960).

Ranch′ Wag′on, *Trademark.* See **station wagon.**

ran·cid (ran′sid), *adj.* **1.** having a rank, unpleasant, stale smell or taste, as through decomposition: *rancid butter.* **2.** (of an odor or taste) rank, unpleasant, and stale: *a rancid smell.* [< L *rancid(us)* rank, stinking, equiv. to **ranc(ēre)* (to) stink, be rancid + *-idus* -ID[4]] —**ran′cid·ly,** *adv.* —**ran′cid·ness,** *n.*

ran·cid·i·ty (ran sid′i tē), *n.* **1.** a rancid state or quality. **2.** a rancid odor or taste. [RANCID + -ITY]

ran·cor (rang′kər), *n.* bitter, rankling resentment or ill will; hatred; malice: *The rancor of sworn enemies.* Also, *esp. Brit.,* **ran′cour.** [ME *rancour* < MF < LL *rancōr-* (s. of *rancor*) rancidity, equiv. to **ranc(ēre)* (see RANCID) + *-ōr* -OR[1]] —**ran′cored;** *esp. Brit.,* **ran′coured,** *adj.*
—**Syn.** bitterness, spite, venom, animosity. See **malevolence.** —**Ant.** benevolence.

ran·cor·ous (rang′kər əs), *adj.* full of or showing rancor. [RANCOR + -OUS] —**ran′cor·ous·ly,** *adv.* —**ran′cor·ous·ness,** *n.*

rand[1] (rand), *n.* **1.** (in shoemaking) a strip of leather set in a shoe at the heel before the lifts are attached. **2.** *Brit. Dial.* **a.** a strip or long slice. **b.** a border or margin. —*v.t.* **3.** to provide (footwear) with rands. [ME, OE; c. D, G *rand* border, margin]

rand[2] (rand), *n.* the monetary unit of Lesotho, Botswana, the Republic of South Africa, South-West Africa, and Swaziland, equal to 100 cents and equivalent to about 1.40 U.S. dollars. *Abbr.:* R. [< SAfrD: shield, monetary unit; special use of RAND[1]]

Rand, The (rand), Witwatersrand. —**Rand′ite,** *n.*

R & D, research and development.

Rand·ers (rän′əRs), *n.* a seaport in E Jutland, in Denmark. 54,780 (1960).

R. & I., **1.** queen and empress. [< L *Regina et Imperatrix*] **2.** king and emperor. [< L *Rex et Imperator*]

ran·die (ran′dē), *adj., n. Brit. Dial.* randy.

Ran·dolph (ran′dolf, -dəlf), *n.* **1. A(sa) Philip,** born 1889, U.S. labor leader: president of the Brotherhood of Sleeping Car Porters since 1925. **2. Edmund Jen·nings** (jen′ingz), 1753–1813, U.S. statesman: first U.S. Attorney General 1789–94; Secretary of State 1794–95. **3. John,** 1773–1833, U.S. statesman and author. **4.** a town in E Massachusetts, S of Boston. 18,900 (1960). **5.** a boy's given name.

ran·dom (ran′dəm), *adj.* **1.** proceeding, made, or occurring without definite aim, purpose, or reason: *the random selection of numbers.* **2.** *Statistics.* of or characterizing a process of selection in which each item of a set has an equal probability of being chosen. **3.** *Building Trades.* **a.** (of building materials) lacking uniformity of dimensions: *random shingles.* **b.** (of ashlar) laid without continuous courses. **c.** constructed or applied without regularity: *random bond.* **4.** *Chiefly Brit.* bank[3] (def. 6b). —*adv.* **5.** *Building Trades.* without uniformity: *random-sized slates.* **6. at random,** without definite aim, purpose, method, or adherence to a prior arrangement; in a haphazard way: *Contestants were chosen at random from the studio audience.* [ME *raundon, random* < OF *randon,* deriv. of *randir* to gallop < Gmc] —**ran′dom·ly,** *adv.* —**ran′dom·ness,** *n.*
—**Syn. 1.** haphazard, chance, fortuitous.

ran′dom ac′cess, *Computer Technol.* equal access to any location in the memory of a computer irrespective of previous registers consulted.

ran′dom line′, *Survey.* **1.** a tentative, approximate survey line from a station toward a predetermined, invisible point. **2.** a traverse run to a certain point to determine its direction.

ran′dom sam′pling, *Statistics.* a method of selecting a sample from a statistical population in such a way that every possible sample that could be selected has the same probability of being selected.

ran′dom var′iable, *Statistics.* variate.

ran′dom walk′, *Physics.* the tendency of particles in random motion to achieve a net displacement or to drift in a particular direction.

R and R, **1.** rest and recuperation. **2.** rock-'n'-roll. Also, **R & R**

rand·y (ran′dē), *adj., n., pl.* **rand·ies.** —*adj.* **1.** *Brit. Dial.* disorderly; unruly. **2.** *Scot.* rude and aggressive; obnoxious. **3.** sexually aroused; lustful. —*n.* **4.** *Scot.* a rude and aggressive person, esp. an obnoxious beggar or a coarse woman. Also, **randie.** [*rand* (obs. var. of RANT) + -Y[1]]

Ran·dy (ran′dē), *n.* a boy's given name, form of **Randel** or **Randolph.**

ra·nee (rä′nē), *n.* (in India) **1.** the wife of a rajah. **2.** a reigning queen or princess. Also, **rani.** [< Hindi *rānī* < Skt *rājñī* queen (fem. of *rājan*)]

rang (rang), *v.* pt. of **ring**[2].

range (rānj), *n., adj., v.,* **ranged, rang·ing.** —*n.* **1.** the extent to which or the limits between which variation is possible: *the range of prices for steel.* **2.** the extent or scope of the operation or action of something: *within range of vision.* **3.** the distance to which a projectile is or may be sent by a weapon. **4.** the distance of the target from the weapon. **5.** an area equipped with targets for practice in shooting weapons: *a rifle range.* **6.** an area used for flight-testing missiles. **7.** the distance of something to be located from some point of operation, as in sound ranging. **8.** the distance that can be covered by an aircraft, ship, or other vehicle, carrying a normal load without refueling. **9.** *Statistics.* the difference between the smallest and largest varieties in a statistical distribution. **10.** a continuous course of masonry of the same height from end to end. **11.** *Music.* compass (def. 4). **12.** *Survey.* **a.** the horizontal direction or extension of a survey line established by two or more marked points. **b.** a line established by markers or lights on shore for the location of soundings. **13.** *Navig.* an imaginary line projected seaward from two or more navigational aids or landmarks and indicating a navigable channel. **14.** (in U.S. public-land surveys) one of a series of divisions numbered east or west from the principal meridian of the survey and consisting of a row of townships, each six miles square, which are numbered north or south from a base line. **15.** a rank, class, or order: *in the higher ranges of society.* **16.** a row, line, or series, as of persons or things. **17.** an act of ranging or moving around, as over an area or region. **18.** an area or tract that is or may be ranged over, esp. an open region for the grazing of livestock. **19.** the region over which something is distributed: *the range of a weed.* **20.** *Math.* the set of all values attained by a given function throughout its domain. **21.** a chain of mountains: *the Catskill Range.* **22.** a large portable or stationary cooking stove having burners built into the top surface and containing one or sometimes two ovens and often storage drawers. **23.** *Physics.* the maximum distance that a charged particle, as a proton, can penetrate a given medium and still maintain sufficient kinetic energy to produce ionization in the medium. **24.** *Naut.* **a.** a large cleat for securing various lines, esp. the tacks and sheets of courses. **b.** a length of anchor cable laid on deck. **25. in range,** (of two or more objects observed from a vessel) located one directly behind the other.
—*adj.* **26.** working or grazing on a range: *range horses; range animals like steer and sheep.* [ME < OF *renge,* deriv. of *renc* line; see RANK[1]]
—*v.t.* **27.** to draw up or arrange (persons or things) in rows or lines or in a specific position, company, or group: *The sergeant ranged the men in columns of six across.* **28.** to place or arrange systematically; set in order; dispose: *The members of the cast were ranged in their proper places on stage.* **29.** to place in a particular class; classify: *They ranged themselves with the progressive group.* **30.** to make straight, level, or even, as lines of type. **31.** to pass over or through (an area or region) in all directions, as in exploring or searching: *They ranged the entire countryside.* **32.** to pasture (cattle) on a range. **33.** to direct or train, as a telescope, upon an object. **34.** to obtain the range of (something aimed at or to be located). **35.** *Naut.* to lay out (an anchor cable) so that the anchor may descend smoothly.
—*v.i.* **36.** to vary within certain limits: *prices ranging from $5 to $10.* **37.** to have range of operation. **38.** to have a particular range, as a gun, missile, etc. **39.** to find the range, as of something aimed at or to be located. **40.** to stretch out or extend in a line, as things: *The shabby houses ranged along the road.* **41.** to extend, run, or go in a certain direction: *a boundary ranging east and west.* **42.** to lie or extend in the same line or plane, as one thing with another or others. **43.** to take up a position in a line or in order. **44.** to have a certain variety of things somehow related: *Emotions ranging from smugness to despair appeared on the faces of the crowd.* **45.** to move around or through a region in all directions, as persons, animals, etc. **46.** to rove, roam, or wander: *The talk ranged over a variety of matters.* **47.** to extend, be found, or occur over an area or throughout a period, as animals, plants, etc.: *a plant which ranges from Canada to Mexico.* **48.** *Naut.* (of an anchored vessel) to swerve or sheer (often fol. by *about*). [ME *range(n)* < MF *rang(er)* < OF *rengier,* deriv. of *renc* (n.)]
—**Syn. 1.** sweep, reach. RANGE, COMPASS, LATITUDE, SCOPE refer to extent or breadth, with or without limits. RANGE emphasizes extent and diversity: *the range of one's interests.* COMPASS suggests definite limits: *within the compass of one's mind.* LATITUDE emphasizes the idea of freedom from narrow confines; thus breadth or extent: *granted latitude of action.* SCOPE suggests great freedom but a proper limit: *the scope of one's activities or of one's obligations.* **15.** kind, sort. **16.** tier, file. **27.** align, rank. **28.** array. **40.** lie. **45.** See **roam.**

ranged (rānjd), *adj. Masonry.* coursed. [RANGE + -ED[2]]

range′ find′er, any of various instruments for determining the distance from the observer to a particular object, as for sighting a gun, adjusting the focus of a camera, etc.

Range′ley Lakes′ (rānj′lē), a group of lakes in W Maine.

range′ light′, *Naut.* **1.** Also called **leading light.** a light for indicating a channel: either provided with a shield so as to be visible only from the channel or used as one of a pair of such lights that appear in line when seen from the channel. **2.** either of two lights, one on the foremost and one above and behind, carried by certain kinds of commercial vessels when under way at night.

range′ line′, one of two parallel lines running north and south that define the east and west borders of a township. Cf. **township** (def. 2), **township line.**

range′ mark′er, *Naut.* one of two or more markers on shore that, when in line or forming a specified pattern, serve as a guide for navigating a narrow channel, esp. at the entrance to a harbor, or that delineate the extremes of a certain course when sighted at specified bearings from a vessel. Also called **range′ mark′.** Cf. **range** (def. 13).

range′ of accommoda′tion, *Ophthalm.* the range of distance over which an object can be accurately focused on the retina by accommodation of the eye.

range′ of stabil′ity, *Naval Archit.* the angle to the perpendicular through which a vessel may be heeled without losing the ability to right itself.

range′ oil′, oil suitable for burning as the fuel of a kitchen stove.

range′ pole′, *Survey.* a conspicuously painted pole held upright to show the position of a survey mark.

rang·er (rān′jər), *n.* **1.** a warden employed to patrol a tract of forest. **2.** one of a body of armed men who patrol a region as guards. **3.** *(cap.)* a U.S. soldier in World War II specially trained for making surprise raids and attacks in small groups. Cf. **commando** (def. 1). **4.** a soldier specially trained in the techniques of guerrilla warfare, esp. in jungle terrain. **5.** *Brit.* a keeper of a royal forest or park. **6.** *Building Trades.* wale[1] (def. 5). **7.** *(cap.) U.S.* one of a series of instrumented satellites for crashing on the moon and communicating observations of the moon's surface. [RANGE + -ER[1]]

Rang·er (rān′jər), *n.* **1.** a town in central Texas. 3313 (1960). **2.** a boy's given name.

range′ ta′ble, one of a number of identical small tables that can be used together to form a single table.

range′ wool′. See **territory wool.**

Ran·goon (rang go͞on′), *n.* a seaport in and the capital of Burma, in the S part. 821,800 (1957).

rang·pur (rung′po͝or, rung po͝or′), *n.* a variety of mandarin orange, bearing a tart fruit. [after *Rangpur,* region of East Bengal, Pakistan]

rang·y (rān′jē), *adj.,* **rang·i·er, rang·i·est.** **1.** slender and long-limbed, as animals or persons. **2.** given to or fitted for ranging or moving about, as animals. **3.** mountainous. [RANGE + -Y[1]] —**rang′i·ness,** *n.*

ra·ni (rä′nē), *n., pl.* **-nis.** ranee.

Ra′ni·khet disease′ (rä′nə ket′), *Vet. Pathol.* See **Newcastle disease.** [after *Ranikhet,* town in northern India]

Ran·jit Singh (run′jit sing), (*"Lion of the Punjab"*) 1780–1839, Indian maharaja: founder of the Sikh kingdom of Punjab.

rank[1] (rangk), *n.* **1.** a number of persons forming a separate class in a social hierarchy or in any graded body. **2.** a social or official position or standing: *the rank of vice-president.* **3.** high position or station in the social or some similar scale: *pride of rank.* **4.** a class in any scale of comparison. **5.** relative position or standing: *a writer of the highest rank.* **6.** a row, line, or series of things or persons: *orchestra players arranged in ranks.* **7. ranks, a.** the people comprising a military force. **b.** military enlisted men as a group. **8.** Usually, **ranks.** the general body of any party, society, or organization apart from the officers or leaders. **9.** orderly arrangement; array. **10.** a line of persons, esp. soldiers, standing abreast in close-order formation (distinguished from *file*). **11.** *Chess.* one of the horizontal lines of squares on a chessboard. **12.** a set of organ pipes of the same kind and tonal color. **13.** Also called **determinant rank.** the order of the nonzero determinant of greatest order which can be selected from a given matrix by the elimination of rows and columns. **14. pull one's rank (on),** *Slang.* to make unexpected use of one's superior rank in demanding respect, obedience to orders, etc., from those in a subordinate position. Also, **pull rank (on).** —*v.t.* **15.** to arrange in ranks or in regular formation: *The men were ranked according to height. He ranked the chessmen on the board.* **16.** to assign to a particular position, station, class, etc.: *She was ranked among the best-dressed women.* **17.** to outrank: *The colonel ranks all other officers in the squadron.* —*v.i.* **18.** to form a rank or ranks. **19.** to take up or occupy a place in a particular rank, class, etc.: *He ranks well ahead of the rest of his family in tact.* **20.** to have rank or standing. **21.** to be the senior in rank: *The colonel ranks at this camp.* [< F *ranc* (obs.), OF *renc, ranc, rang* row, line < Gmc; cf. OE *hrinc* RING[1]] —**rank′less,** *adj.*
—**Syn. 3.** distinction, eminence, dignity. **6.** range, tier. **9.** alignment. **15.** align, range, array.

rank[2] (rangk), *adj.* **1.** growing with excessive luxuriance; vigorous and tall of growth: *tall rank grass.* **2.** producing an excessive and coarse growth, as land. **3.** having an offensively strong smell or taste: *a rank cigar.* **4.** offensively strong, as a smell or taste. **5.** utter; absolute: *a rank outsider; rank treachery.* **6.** highly offensive; disgusting: *a rank sight of carnage.* **7.** grossly coarse, vulgar, or indecent: *rank language.* [ME; OE *ranc* bold, proud; c. Icel *rakkr* straight, bold] —**rank′ish,** *adj.* —**rank′ly,** *adv.* —**rank′ness,** *n.*
—**Syn. 1.** abundant, exuberant. **3.** gamy, pungent. **5.** complete, sheer, entire. **6.** repulsive, repellent. **7.** foul.

Rank (rängk), *n.* **Ot·to** (ôt′ō), 1884–1939, Austrian psychoanalyst.

rank′ and file′, the general membership of an organization, nation, etc., exclusive of its leaders.

rank-and-fil·er (rangk′ən fī′lər), *n.* a member of the rank and file.

Ran·ke (räng′kə), *n.* **Le·o·pold von** (lā′ō pôlt′ fən), 1795–1886, German historian.

rank·er (rang′kər), *n.* **1.** a person who ranks. **2.** *Brit.* a soldier in the ranks or a commissioned officer promoted from the ranks. [RANK[1] + -ER[2]]

ran·ket (rang′kit), *n.* **1.** Also, **ran′kett, rackett.** Also called **sausage bassoon.** a double-reed wind instrument of the 16th and 17th centuries consisting of a short wood or ivory cylinder pierced by several vertical channels connected to form a continuous tube and having finger holes in the cylinder wall. **2.** a stop common in reed organs until the 17th century. [< G *Rankett*]

Ran·kin (rang′kin), *n.* a town in SW Pennsylvania. 5164 (1960).

Ran·kine (rang′kin), *n.* **1. William John Mac·quorn** (mə kwôrn′), 1820–70, Scottish engineer and physicist. —*adj.* **2.** *Physics.* pertaining to an absolute scale of temperature (**Ran′kine scale′**) in which the degree intervals are equal to those of the Fahrenheit scale and in which 0° Rankine equals −459.7° Fahrenheit. Cf. **absolute scale, Kelvin** (def. 2).

Ran′kine cy′cle, *Thermodynamics.* the hypothetical cycle of a steam engine in which all heat transfers take place at constant pressure and in which expansion and compression occur adiabatically. Also called **Clausius cycle.** [named after W. J. M. RANKINE]

ran·kle (rang′kəl), *v.*, **-kled, -kling.** —*v.i.* **1.** (of unpleasant feelings, experiences, etc.) to continue to cause keen irritation or bitter resentment within the mind; fester; be painful. —*v.t.* **2.** to cause keen irritation or bitter resentment in: *Her remark rankled him for days.* [ME *rancle(n)* < MF *rancler,* OF *(d)raoncler* to fester, deriv. of *draoncle* a sore < LL *dracunculus,* dim. of L *dracō* serpent, DRAGON] —**ran′kling·ly,** *adv.*

ran·sack (ran′sak), *v.t.* **1.** to search thoroughly or vigorously through (a house, receptacle, etc.): *He ransacked the house for the missing letter.* **2.** to search through for plunder; pillage: *The enemy ransacked the entire town.* [ME *ransake(n)* < Scand; cf. Icel *rannsaka* to search (a house), equiv. to *rann* house + *-saka,* akin to *sōkja* to seek] —**ran′sack·er,** *n.*

ran·seur (rän sûr′), *n.* a medieval shafted weapon having a pointed head with two branches curving outward from its base. [< MF, equiv. to *rance* (irreg. < L *rāmex* forked stick) + *-eur* -OR[2]]

ran·som (ran′səm), *n.* **1.** the redemption of a prisoner, slave, or kidnapped person, of captured goods, etc., for a price. **2.** the sum or price paid or demanded. **3.** a means of deliverance or rescue from punishment for sin, esp. the payment of a redemptive fine. [ME *ransoun* < OF *rançon* < L *redemptiōn-* (s. of *redemptiō*) REDEMPTION] —*v.t.* **4.** to redeem from captivity, bondage, detention, etc., by paying a demanded price. **5.** to release or restore on receipt of a ransom. **6.** to deliver or redeem from punishment for sin. [ME *ransoun(en)* < OF *rançonner*] —**ran′som·er,** *n.*
—**Syn. 1.** deliverance, liberation, release. **4.** See **redeem.**

Ran·som (ran′səm), *n.* **John Crowe** (krō), born 1888, U.S. poet, critic, and teacher.

rant (rant), *v.i.* **1.** to speak or declaim extravagantly or violently; talk in a wild or vehement way: *a demagogue ranting for hours at his audience.* —*v.t.* **2.** to utter or declaim in a ranting manner. —*n.* **3.** ranting, extravagant, or violent declamation. **4.** a ranting utterance. [< MD *rant(en)* (to) rave; c. G *ranzen* to frolic] —**rant′er,** *n.* —**rant′ing·ly,** *adv.*
—**Syn. 3.** bombast, extravagance.

ran·u·la (ran′yə lə), *n. Pathol.* a cystic tumor formed beneath the tongue and caused by obstruction and dilatation of the sublingual or submaxillary gland or of a mucous gland. [< L *rānula* little frog, swelling, equiv. to *rān(a)* frog + *-ula* -ULE] —**ran′u·lar,** *adj.*

ra·nun·cu·la·ceous (rə nung′kyə lā′shəs), *adj.* belonging to the *Ranunculaceae,* the crowfoot or buttercup family of plants, including the marsh marigold, aconite, black hellebore, anemone, hepatica, clematis, columbine, larkspur, peony, etc. [< NL *Ranunculace(ae)* name of family. See RANUNCULUS, -ACEOUS]

ra·nun·cu·lus (rə nung′kyə ləs), *n., pl.* **-lus·es, -li** (-lī′). any plant of the genus *Ranunculus;* a buttercup or crowfoot. [< L *rānunculus* little frog, tadpole, equiv. to *rān(a)* frog + *-unculus* double dim. suffix]

ra·ob (rā′ob), *n.* meteorological observations conducted by means of radio signals received from a radiosonde. Cf. **rawin, rawinsonde.** [*ra(diosonde) ob(servation)*]

Ra·oult's′ law′ (rä o͞olz′), *Physical Chem.* the principle that the fraction by which the vapor pressure of a solvent is lowered by the addition of a nonvolatile, nonelectrolytic solute is equal to the mole fraction of the solute in the solution. [named after François *Raoult* (1830–1901), French chemist and physicist]

rap[1] (rap), *v.*, **rapped, rap·ping,** *n.* —*v.t.* **1.** to strike, esp. with a quick, smart, or light blow: *He rapped the door with his cane.* **2.** (of a spirit summoned by a medium) to communicate (a message) by raps (often fol. by *out*). **3.** to utter sharply or vigorously: *to rap out a command.* **4.** *Foundry.* to jar (a pattern) loose from a sand mold. —*v.i.* **5.** to knock smartly or lightly, esp. so as to make a noise: *to rap on a door.* **6.** *Slang.* **a.** to talk, chat, or converse. **b.** to discuss or argue. —*n.* **7.** a quick, smart, or light blow: *a rap on the knuckles with a ruler.* **8.** the sound produced by such a blow: *They heard a loud rap at the door.* **9.** *Informal.* blame or punishment, esp. for a crime: *He took the rap for the burglary.* **10.** *Slang.* a criminal charge: *a murder rap.* **11.** *Slang.* **a.** a talk, chat, or conversation. **b.** a discussion or argument. **c.** popular music featuring a rhyming patter of urban slang intoned over a steady and insistent beat. **12. a bum rap,** *Slang.* a conviction for a crime that one did not commit; a frame-up. **13. beat the rap,** *Slang.* to succeed in evading the penalty for a crime; be acquitted: *The defendant calmly insisted that he would beat the rap.* **14. take the rap,** *Slang.* to take the blame and punishment for a crime committed by another. [ME *rappe,* akin to Sw *rappa* to beat, drub, G *rappeln* to rattle]

rap[2] (rap), *n.* **1.** the least bit: *I don't care a rap.* **2.** a counterfeit halfpenny formerly passed in Ireland. [cf. G *Rappe* small coin]

rap[3] (rap), *v.t.*, **rapped** or **rapt, rap·ping. 1.** *Archaic.* **a.** to carry off; transport. **b.** to transport with rapture. **2.** *Obs.* to seize for oneself; snatch. [back formation from RAPT]

ra·pa·cious (rə pā′shəs), *adj.* **1.** given to seizing for plunder or the satisfaction of greed. **2.** inordinately greedy; predatory; extortionate: *a rapacious disposition.* **3.** (of animals) subsisting by the capture of living prey; predacious. [< L *rapāci-* (s. of *rapāx* greedy, akin to *rapere* to seize; see RAPE[1]) + -OUS] —**ra·pa′cious·ly,** *adv.* —**ra·pac·i·ty** (rə pas′i tē), **ra·pa′cious·ness,** *n.*
—**Syn. 2.** ravenous, voracious, grasping; preying.
—**Ant. 2.** generous.

Ra·pal·lo (rä päl′lō), *n.* a seaport in NW Italy, on the Gulf of Genoa: treaties 1920, 1922. 20,762 (1961).

Ra·pa Nu·i (rä′pə no͞o′ē). See **Easter Island.**

rape[1] (rāp), *n., v.,* **raped, rap·ing.** —*n.* **1.** the act of seizing and carrying off by force. **2.** the act of physically forcing a woman to have sexual intercourse. **3.** See **statutory rape.** —*v.t.* **4.** to seize, take, or carry off by force. **5.** to plunder (a place). **6.** to force (a woman) to have sexual intercourse. —*v.i.* **7.** to commit rape. [ME *rape(n)* < L *rapere* to seize, snatch] —**rap′ist,** *n.*

rape[2] (rāp), *n.* a brassicaceous plant, *Brassica Napus,* whose leaves are used for food for hogs, sheep, etc., and whose seeds yield rape oil. [ME < L *rāp-* (s. of *rāpum,* *rāpa*) turnip; c. Gk *rháhys*]

rape[3] (rāp), *n.* the residue of grapes, after the juice has been extracted, used as a filter in making vinegar. [< F *râpe* < Gmc; cf. OHG *raspōn* to scrape]

Rape′ of Lu·crece′, The (lo͞o krēs′, lo͞o′krēs), a narrative poem (1594) by Shakespeare.

Rape′ of the Daugh′ters of Leu·cip′pus (lo͞o sip′əs), a painting (1615) by Peter Paul Rubens.

Rape′ of the Lock′, The, a mock-epic poem (1712) by Alexander Pope.

Rape′ of the Ring′lets, The, Perikeiromene.

Rape′ of the Sa′bine Wom′en, The, a painting (1636?–37?) by Nicolas Poussin.

rape′ oil′, *Chem.* a brownish-yellow oil obtained by expression from rapeseed and used chiefly as a lubricant, an illuminant, and in the manufacture of rubber substitutes. Also called **rape′seed oil′, colza oil.**

rape·seed (rāp′sēd′), *n.* **1.** the seed of the rape. **2.** the plant itself. [RAPE[2] + SEED]

rap′ full′, *Naut.* **1.** (of a sail or sails) filled with wind; clean full. **2.** with all sails full of wind. Also, **rapt full.**

Raph·a·el (raf′ē əl, rā′fē-, rä′fī el′), *n.* **1.** (*Raffaello Santi* or *Sanzio*) 1483–1520, Italian painter. **2.** one of the archangels. **3.** a boy's given name.

ra·phe (rā′fē), *n., pl.* **-phae** (-fē). **1.** *Anat.* a seamlike union between two parts or halves of an organ or the like. **2.** *Bot.* **a.** (in certain ovules) a ridge connecting the hilum with the chalaza. **b.** a median line or slot on a cell wall of a diatom. [< NL < Gk *raphḗ* seam, suture, akin to *rháptein* to sew, stitch together]

raph·i·des (raf′i dēz′), *n.pl. Bot.* acicular crystals, usually composed of calcium oxalate, that occur in bundles in the cells of many plants. [< NL < Gk: pl. of *rhaphís* needle]

-raphy, var. of **-rrhaphy.**

rap·id (rap′id), *adj.* **1.** occurring within a short time; happening speedily: *rapid growth.* **2.** moving or acting with great speed; swift: *a rapid worker.* **3.** characterized by speed: *rapid motion.* —*n.* **4.** Usually, **rapids.** a part of a river where the current runs very swiftly. [< L *rapid(us)* tearing away, seizing, swift. See RAPE[1], -ID[4]] —**rap′id·ly,** *adv.*
—**Syn. 2.** See **quick.**

Rap·i·dan (rap′i dan′), *n.* a river in N Virginia, flowing E from the Blue Ridge Mountains into the Rappahannock River: Civil War battle 1862.

Rap′id Cit′y, a city in SW South Dakota. 42,399 (1960).

rap′id fire′, *Mil.* a rate of firing small arms that is intermediate between slow fire and quick fire.

rap·id-fire (rap′id fīər′), *adj.* **1.** characterized by or delivered or occurring in rapid succession: *rapid-fire questions; rapid-fire events.* **2.** *Mil.* discharging in rapid fire: *rapid-fire rifles.*

ra·pid·i·ty (rə pid′i tē), *n.* a rapid state or quality; quickness; celerity. Also, **rap·id·ness** (rap′id nis). [< L *rapiditās.* See RAPID, -ITY]
—**Syn.** swiftness, fleetness. See **speed.**

ra·pi·do (rä′pē dō′; *Sp.* rä′pē t̸hō′; *It.* rä′pē dô), *n., pl.* **-dos** (-dōz′; *Sp.* -t̸hōs′), *It.* **-di** (-dē). (esp. in Spain, Italy, and Latin America) an express train. [< It *rapido,* Sp *rápido* (n. use of adj.). See RAPID]

rap′id trans′it, a means of rapid transportation in a metropolitan area, esp. a subway or elevated train system.

ra·pi·er (rā′pē ər), *n.* **1.** a sword that is used for thrusting and has a long, narrow blade and an elaborate guard. **2.** *Obs.* a sword that is used for slashing and thrusting and has a long, double-edged blade. [< MF *(espee) rapiere,* lit., rasping (sword); see RAPE[3]] —**ra′pi·ered,** *adj.*

Rapier and scabbard (17th century)

rap·ine (rap′in), *n.* the violent seizure and carrying off of another's property; plunder. [ME *rapine* < L *rapīna* robbery, pillage. See RAPE[1], -INE[2]]

rap·loch (rap′ləkh), *Scot.* —*n.* **1.** homespun woolen cloth, esp. if coarse and undyed. —*adj.* **2.** homely; crude. [?]

Rapp (rap; *Ger.* räp), *n.* **George,** 1757–1847, U.S. religious preacher, born in Germany: leader of the Harmonists.

Rap·pa·han·nock (rap′ə han′ək), *n.* a river flowing SE from N Virginia into the Chesapeake Bay: battle 1863. 185 mi. long.

rap·pa·ree (rap′ə rē′), *n.* **1.** an armed Irish freebooter or plunderer, esp. of the 17th century. **2.** any freebooter or robber. [< Ir *rapaire*]

rap·pee (ra pē′), *n.* a strong snuff made from dark, rank tobacco leaves. [< F *râpé* grated (ptp. of *râper*); see RAPE[3]]

rap·pel (ra pel′, rə-), *n., v.,* **-pelled, -pel·ling.** —*n.* **1.** (in mountaineering) the act or method of moving down a steep incline or past an overhang by means of a double rope secured above and placed around the body, usually under the left thigh and over the right shoulder, and paid out gradually in the descent. —*v.i.* **2.** to descend by means of a rappel. [< F: mountaineering term, lit., a recall. See REPEAL]

rap·per (rap′ər), *n.* **1.** the knocker of a door. **2.** one who or that which raps or knocks. [RAP[1] + -ER[1]]

rap·ping (rap′ing), *n.* **1.** the act or sound of one who or that which raps. **2.** communication by the sound of taps or knocks, as between medium and spirit during a séance. [RAP[1] + -ING[1]]

Rapp·ist (rap′ist), *n.* Harmonist. Also, **Rappite** (rap′īt). [after George RAPP; see -IST]

rap·port (ra pôr′, -pōr′; *Fr.* RA pôr′), *n.* relation; connection, esp. harmonious or sympathetic relation: *a teacher trying to establish close rapport with his students.* Cf. **en rapport.** [< F, deriv. of *rapporter,* equiv. to *re-* RE- + *apporter,* OF *aporter* < L *apportāre,* equiv. to *ap-* AP- + *portāre* to carry]

rap·por·teur (rap′ôr to͞or′; *Fr.* RA pôr tœr′), *n., pl.* **-teurs** (-to͞orz′; *Fr.* -tœr′). one responsible for compiling reports and presenting them, as to a governing body. [< F, deriv. of *rapporter* to bring back. See RAPPORT, -OR[2]]

rap·proche·ment (*Fr.* RA prôsh män′), *n.* an establishment or reestablishment of harmonious relations: *a rapprochement reached between warring factions.* [< F, equiv. to *rapproche(r)* (to) bring near, bring together (*re-* RE- + *approcher;* see APPROACH) + *-ment* -MENT]

rap·scal·lion (rap skal′yən), *n.* a rascal; rogue; scamp. [earlier *rascallion,* based on RASCAL]

Rap′son's slide′ (rap′sənz), *Naut.* a device for controlling a tiller by means of force applied to a block fitted so as to slide along the tiller and also along a transverse guide so that as the tiller is put farther over from the amidships position the block moves farther toward its outer end, thus increasing the leverage. [after proper name *Rapson*]

rapt (rapt), *adj.* **1.** deeply engrossed or absorbed: *rapt in thought.* **2.** transported with emotion; enraptured: *rapt with joy.* **3.** showing or proceeding from rapture: *a rapt smile.* **4.** carried off spiritually to another place, sphere of existence, etc. [ME (ptp.) < L *rapt(us)* seized, carried off (ptp. of *rapere*), equiv. to *rap-* (see RAPE[1]) + *-tus* ptp. suffix] —**rapt′ly,** *adv.* —**rapt′ness,** *n.*
—**Syn. 2.** ecstatic.

Raptorial bird
Head and foot of golden eagle, *Aquila chrysaëtos*

rapt′ full′, *Naut.* See **rap full.**

rap·to·ri·al (rap tôr′ē əl, -tōr′-), *adj.* **1.** preying upon other animals; predatory. **2.** adapted for seizing prey, as the bill or claws of a bird. **3.** belonging or pertaining to the *Raptores,* a former order in which the falconiform and strigiform birds were erroneously grouped together. [< L *raptōr-* (s. of *raptor* one who seizes by force, robber; *rapt(us)* RAPT + *-or* -OR[2]) + -IAL]

rap·ture (rap′chər), *n.* **1.** ecstatic joy or delight; joyful ecstasy. **2.** Often, **raptures.** an utterance or expression of ecstatic delight. **3.** the carrying of a person to another place or sphere of existence. **4.** *Archaic.* the act of carrying off. —*v.t.* **5.** *Literary.* to enrapture. [RAPT + -URE] —**rap′ture·less,** *adj.*
—**Syn. 1.** bliss, beatitude; transport, exaltation. —**Ant. 1.** misery.

rap·tur·ous (rap′chər əs), *adj.* **1.** full of, feeling, or manifesting ecstatic joy or delight. **2.** characterized by, attended with, or expressive of such rapture: *rapturous surprise.* [RAPTURE + -OUS] —**rap′tur·ous·ly,** *adv.* —**rap′tur·ous·ness,** *n.*

rap·tus (rap′təs), *n.* a state of intense or overwhelming excitement; rapture; ecstasy. [< L: a seizing, n. use of *raptus* RAPT]

ra·ra a·vis (râr′ə ā′vis; *Lat.* rä′rä ä′wis), *pl.* **ra·rae a·ves** (râr′ē ā′vēz; *Lat.* rä′rī ä′wēs). a rare person or thing. [< L: rare bird]

rare[1] (râr), *adj.,* **rar·er, rar·est. 1.** coming or occurring far apart in time; unusual; uncommon: *a rare disease; His visits are rare occasions.* **2.** thinly distributed over an area; few and widely separated: *Lighthouses are rare on that part of the coast.* **3.** having the component parts not closely compacted together: *rare gases; lightheaded from the rare mountain air.* **4.** unusually great: *sympathetic to a rare degree.* **5.** unusually excellent; admirable; fine: *She showed rare tact in inviting them.* [ME < L *rār(us)* loose, wide apart, thin] —**rare′ness,** *n.*
—**Syn. 1.** exceptional, extraordinary, singular. **2.** sparse, infrequent. **5.** choice, exquisite, incomparable, inimitable. —**Ant. 1.** common. **2.** frequent. **5.** inferior.

rare[2] (râr), *adj.,* **rar·er, rar·est.** (of meat) cooked just slightly: *He likes his steak rare.* [ME *rere,* OE *hrēr* lightly boiled]

rare·bit (râr′bit), *n.* See **Welsh rabbit.**

rare′ book′, a book that is distinguished by its early printing date, by its limited issue, by the special character of the edition or binding, by its historical interest, or the like.

rare′ earth′, *Chem.* the oxide of any of the rare-earth elements, contained in various minerals.

rare′-earth′ el′ement (râr′ûrth′), *Chem.* any of a group of closely related metallic elements of atomic number 57 to 71 inclusive often divided into three subgroups: the cerium metals that are comprised of lanthanum, cerium, praseodymium, neodymium, promethium, and samarium; the terbium metals that are comprised of europium, gadolinium, and terbium; and the yttrium metals that are comprised of dysprosium, holmium, erbium, thulium, yttrium, ytterbium, and lutetium. Also called **rare′-earth′ met′al.**

rar′ee show′ (râr′ē), **1.** See **peep show. 2.** a carnival. [RARE[1] + -EE]

rar·e·fac·tion (râr′ə fak′shən), *n.* the act or process of rarefying; the state of being rarefied. [< ML *rārēfactiōn-* (s. of *rārēfactiō*), equiv. to L *rārēfact(us)* (ptp. of *rārēfacere;* see RAREFY) + *-iōn-* -ION] —**rar′e·fac′tion·al,** *adj.* —**rar·e·fac·tive** (râr′ə fak′tiv), *adj.*

rar·e·fied (râr′ə fīd′), *adj.* **1.** extremely high or elevated; lofty; exalted: *rarefied thinking; rarefied art.* **2.** of or belonging to an exclusive group; select: *the rarefied company of Nobel prizewinners.* [RAREFY + -ED[2]]

rar·e·fy (râr′ə fī′), *v.,* **-fied, -fy·ing.** —*v.t.* **1.** to make rare or rarer; make less dense: *to rarefy a gas.* **2.** to make less gross; refine: *to rarefy one's spiritual life.* —*v.i.* **3.** to become rare or less dense; become thinned: *Moisture rarefies when heated.* [ME *rarefie(n)* < MF *rarefie(r)* < L *rārēfacere,* equiv. to *rār(us)* RARE[1] + *facere* to make; see -FY] —**rar′e·fi′a·ble,** *adj.* —**rar′e·fi′er,** *n.*

rare·ly (râr′lē), *adv.* **1.** on rare occasions; infrequently; seldom: *He is rarely late for appointments.* **2.** exceptionally; in an unusual degree. **3.** unusually or remarkably well; excellent. [RARE[1] + -LY]

rare·ripe (râr′rīp′), *Bot.* —*adj.* **1.** ripening early. —*n.* **2.** a fruit or vegetable that ripens early. [*rare* early (obs. except dial.; var. of RATHE) + RIPE]

Rar·i·tan (rar′i tən, -tən), *n.* **1.** a town in NE New Jersey. 15,324 (1960). **2.** a town in central New Jersey. 6137 (1960).

rar·i·ty (râr′i tē), *n., pl.* **-ties. 1.** something rare, unusual, or uncommon: *Snowstorms are a rarity in the South.* **2.** something esteemed or interesting in being rare, uncommon, or curious: *That folio is a rarity that will bring a good price.* **3.** the state or quality of being rare. **4.** rare occurrence; infrequency: *Volcanic eruptions on the island occur with great rarity.* **5.** unusual excellence. **6.** thinness, as of air or a gas. [< L *rāritās,* equiv. to *rār(us)* RARE[1] + *-itās* -ITY]

Ra·ro·tong·a (rar′ə tong′gə), *n.* one of the Cook Islands, in the S Pacific. 8676 (1961); 26 sq. mi.

ra·sa (rus′ə), *n.* (in Hindu aesthetics) flavor, sentiment, or emotion: regarded as one of the fundamental qualities of classical music, dance, and poetry. [< Skt *rāsa* sap, fluid, essence]

Ras Ad·dar (räs′ a där′). See **Bon, Cape.**

ras·bo·ra (raz bôr′ə, -bōr′ə, raz′bər ə), *n.* any of several minnows of the genus *Rasbora,* found in southeastern Asia and the Malay Archipelago, esp. the silvery *R. heteromorpha,* that has a black triangular marking near the tail and is often kept in aquariums. [< NL < EInd native name]

ras·cal (ras′kəl), *n.* **1.** a base, dishonest, or unscrupulous person. **2.** any mischievous person or animal: *Both the child and the puppy are rascals.* **3.** *Archaic.* a person belonging to the rabble. —*adj.* **4.** knavish; dishonest. **5.** *Archaic.* belonging to or being the rabble. [ME *rascaile, raskaille* < OF *rascaille* rabble; akin to RASH[2]] —**ras′cal·like′,** *adj.*
—**Syn. 1.** rapscallion, scamp, villain, miscreant, scapegrace. See **knave. 4.** base, low.

ras·cal·i·ty (ra skal′i tē), *n., pl.* **-ties. 1.** rascally or knavish character or conduct. **2.** a rascally act. [RASCAL + -ITY]

ras·cal·ly (ras′kə lē), *adj.* **1.** being, characteristic of, or befitting a rascal or knave; dishonest; mean: *a rascally trick.* **2.** *Obs.* rascal (def. 5). —*adv.* **3.** in a rascally manner. [RASCAL + -LY]

ras·casse (ra skas′), *n.* any of several scorpionfishes, as *Scorpaena scrofa* or *S. porcus,* found in the Mediterranean Sea, used in making bouillabaise. [< F < Pr *rascass(o),* deriv. of *rasca* to scrape < VL **rasicāre*]

rase (rāz), *v.t.,* **rased, ras·ing.** raze. —**ras′er,** *n.*

rash[1] (rash), *adj.* **1.** acting too hastily or without due consideration: *a rash young man.* **2.** characterized by or showing too great haste or lack of consideration: *rash promises.* [ME; c. D, G *rasch* quick, brisk, OIcel *rǫskr* brave] —**rash′ly,** *adv.* —**rash′ness,** *n.*
—**Syn. 1.** hasty, impetuous, reckless, incautious, precipitate, indiscreet, foolhardy. —**Ant. 1.** cautious.

rash[2] (rash), *n.* **1.** an eruption or efflorescence on the skin. **2.** a multitude of instances of something occurring more or less during the same period of time: *a rash of robberies last month.* [< F *rache* (obs.), OF *rasche* skin eruption, deriv. of *raschier* to scratch << L *rās(us),* ptp. of *rādere* to scratch] —**rash′like′,** *adj.*

rash·er[1] (rash′ər), *n.* **1.** a thin slice of bacon or ham for frying or broiling. **2.** a portion or serving of bacon, usually three or four slices. [? akin to RASH[2]]

rash·er[2] (rash′ər), *n.* See **vermilion rockfish.** [? < Sp *rascacio;* see RASCASSE]

Ra·shi (rä′shē), *n.* (*Solomon ben Isaac*) 1040–1105, French Hebrew scholar.

Ra·shō·mon (rä′shō mon′; *Jap.* rä′shô môn′), *n.* a short story (1915) by Ryūnosuke Akutagawa.

Rask (rask; *Dan.* räsk), *n.* **Ras·mus Christian** (ras′məs; *Dan.* räs′mŏŏs), 1787–1832, Danish philologist.

Ras·kol·nik (rə skôl′nik), *n., pl.* **-niks, -ni·ki** (-nə kē′). a member of any of several sects founded by dissenters from the Russian Orthodox Church, who opposed the liturgical reforms of Nikon in the 17th century. Also called **Old Believer, Old Ritualist.** [< Russ *raskol′nik* separatist, equiv. to *raskol* separation + *-nik* agent suffix]

Ras·mus·sen (räs′mōō sən), *n.* **Knud Jo·han Vic·tor** (knōōth yō hän′ vēk′tôr), 1879–1933, Danish arctic explorer.

ra·son (rä′sôn; *Eng.* ras′on), *n., pl.* **-sa** (-sä; *Eng.* -sə). *Gk. Orth. Ch.* a long, loose, black gown with wide sleeves, worn by the clergy. [< MGk *rhāson* a woolen cloth]

ras·o·phore (raz′ə fôr′, -fōr′), *n.* *Gk. Orth. Ch.* a monk authorized to wear the rason. [< MGk *rhasophór(os).* See RASON, -PHORE]

ra·so·ri·al (rə sôr′ē əl, -sōr′-), *adj.* given to scratching the ground for food, as poultry; gallinaceous. [< NL *Rasor(es)* name of the order, LL, pl. of *rāsor* scratcher, equiv. to L *rās(us)* (ptp. of *rādere* to scrape, scratch) + *-or* -OR[2] + -IAL]

Rasorial bird's foot

rasp (rasp, räsp), *v.t.* **1.** to scrape or abrade with a rough instrument. **2.** to scrape or rub roughly: *The glacier rasps the valley floor.* **3.** to grate upon or irritate: *The sound rasped his nerves.* **4.** to utter with a grating sound: *He rasped his answer.* —*v.i.* **5.** to scrape or grate. **6.** to make a grating sound. —*n.* **7.** an act of rasping. **8.** a rasping sound. **9.** a coarse file, used mainly on wood, having separate conical teeth. **10.** (in an insect) a roughened surface used in stridulation. [ME *rasp(en)* < OF *rasp(er)* (to) scrape, grate < Gmc; see RAPE[3]] —**rasp′ish,** *adj.*

rasp·ber·ry (raz′ber′ē, -bə rē, räz′-), *n., pl.* **-ries. 1.** the fruit of any of several rosaceous shrubs of the genus *Rubus,* consisting of small and juicy red, black, or pale-yellow drupelets forming a detachable cap about a convex receptacle. **2.** any shrub bearing this fruit. **3.** a dark reddish-purple color. **4.** *U.S.* See **Bronx cheer.** [earlier *rasp(is)* raspberry (< ?) + BERRY]

rasp·er (ras′pər, rä′spər), *n.* one who or that which rasps, as a machine for rasping sugarcane. [RASP + -ER[1]]

rasp′head rock′fish (rasp′hed′, räsp′-), a red rockfish, *Sebastodes ruberrimus,* found along the Pacific coast of North America, having sawlike, bony ridges on the head. Also called **tambor.** [RASP + HEAD]

rasp·ing (ras′ping, rä′sping), *adj.* harsh; grating: *a rasping voice.* [RASP + -ING[2]] —**rasp′ing·ly,** *adv.* —**rasp′ing·ness,** *n.*

Ras·pu·tin (ra spyōō′tin; *Russ.* räs pōō′tin), *n.* **Gri·go·ri E·fi·mo·vich** (gri gô′ri e fē′mo vich), 1871–1916, Siberian peasant monk who was very influential at the court of Czar Nicholas II and Czarina Alexandra.

rasp·y (ras′pē, rä′spē), *adj.,* **rasp·i·er, rasp·i·est. 1.** harsh; grating; rasping. **2.** easily annoyed; irritable. [RASP + -Y[1]]

Ras Sham·ra (räs sham′rə), a locality in W Syria, near the Mediterranean Sea: site of ancient Ugarit; many archaeologically important objects dating to the Bronze Age.

ras·sle (ras′əl), *v.i., v.t.,* **-sled, -sling,** *n.* *Dial.* wrestle.

Ras·ta·far·i·an (ras′tə fâr′ē ən), *n.* **1.** a follower of Rastafarianism. —*adj.* **2.** of or pertaining to Rastafarianism.

Ras·ta·far·i·an·ism (ras′tə fâr′ē ə niz′əm), *n.* a militant black religious cult, originally of Jamaica, that regards Africa as the Promised Land, to which all blacks will someday return, and the late Haile Selassie I, former emperor of Ethiopia, as the messiah. [< *Ras* prince *Tafari* (precoronation name of Haile Selassie) + -AN + -ISM]

ras·ter (ras′tər), *n.* *Television.* a pattern of scanning lines covering the area upon which the image is projected in the cathode ray tube of a television set. [< G < L: toothed hoe, rake, deriv. of *rādere* to scratch, scrape]

ras·tle (ras′əl), *v.i., v.t.,* **-tled, -tling,** *n.* *Dial.* wrestle.

Ras·tus (ras′təs), *n.* a boy's given name.

ra·sure (rā′zhər), *n.* an erasure. [< MF < LL *rāsūra,* equiv. to L *rās(us)* (ptp. of *rādere* to scratch, scrape) + *-ūra* -URE]

rat (rat), *n., interj., v.,* **rat·ted, rat·ting.** —*n.* **1.** any of several long-tailed rodents of the family *Muridae,* of the genus *Rattus* and related genera, distinguished from the mouse by being larger. **2.** any of various similar or related animals. **3.** *Slang.* a scoundrel. **4.** *Slang.* **a.** a person who abandons his party or associates, esp. in a time of trouble. **b.** an informer. **c.** a scab laborer. **5.** *U.S.* a pad with tapered ends used in women's hair styles to give the appearance of greater thickness. **6. smell a rat,** to suspect or surmise treachery; have suspicion: *After noting several discrepancies in his client's story, the attorney began to smell a rat.* —*interj.* **7. rats,** *Slang.* (an exclamation of disappointment, disgust, or disbelief.) —*v.i.* **8.** *Slang.* **a.** to desert one's party or associates, esp. in a time of trouble. **b.** to turn informer; squeal: *He ratted on the gang, and the police picked up the lot of them.* **c.** to work as a scab. **9.** to hunt or catch rats. —*v.t.* **10.** to dress (the hair) with or as if with a rat. [ME *ratte,* OE *rǣt;* c. G *Ratz, Ratte*] —**rat′like′,** *adj.*

ra·ta (rä′tə), *n.* a round-headed tree, *Metrosideros robusta,* of New Zealand, having fruit and dark red flowers in dense clusters. [< Maori]

rat·a·ble (rā′tə bəl), *adj.* **1.** capable of being rated or appraised. **2.** proportional: *ratable distribution of wealth.* **3.** *Brit.* liable to rates or local taxes. Also, **rateable.** [RATE[1] + -ABLE] —**rat′a·bil′i·ty, rat′a·ble·ness,** *n.* —**rat′a·bly,** *adv.*

rat·a·fi·a (rat′ə fē′ə), *n.* a liqueur flavored with fruit kernels, fruit, or the like. Also, **rat·a·fee** (rat′ə fē′). [< F]

ratafi′a bis′cuit, *Brit.* a macaroon.

rat·al (rāt′əl), *n.* *Brit.* the amount on which rates or taxes are assessed. [RATE[1] + -AL[1]]

ra·tan (ra tan′), *n.* rattan.

rat·a·plan (rat′ə plan′), *n., v.,* **-planned, -plan·ning.** —*n.* **1.** a sound of or as of the beating of a drum; rub-a-dub. —*v.i.* **2.** to produce such a sound. [< F; imit.]

rat·a·tat (rat′ə tat′), *n.* a sound imitative of knocking or rapping: *a sharp rat-a-tat on the window.* Also, **rat′-a-tat′-tat′.**

rat′bite fe′ver (rat′bīt′), *Pathol.* a relapsing fever, widely distributed geographically, caused by infection with a spirillum transmitted by rats. Also called **rat′-bite disease′.** [RAT + BITE]

rat·catch·er (rat′kach′ər), *n.* **1.** one who or that which catches and exterminates rats, esp. a person whose business it is to rid a property of rats. **2.** *Chiefly Brit.* an informal fox-hunting costume, as a tweed jacket and tan riding breeches. [RAT + CATCHER]

ratch (rach), *n.* a ratchet.

ratch·et (rach′it), *n.* **1.** a toothed bar with which a pawl engages. **2.** (not in technical use) a pawl or the like used with a ratchet or ratchet wheel. **3.** a mechanism consisting of such a bar or wheel with the pawl. **4.** See **ratchet wheel.** [alter. of F *rochet* < MF *rocquet* a blunt lance-head < Gmc]

ratch′et clock′. See **rack clock.**

ratch′et jack′, a screw jack rotated by a ratchet mechanism.

ratch′et wheel′, a wheel, with teeth on the edge, into which a pawl drops or catches, as to prevent reversal of motion or convert reciprocating motion into rotatory motion.

Ratchet wheel

rat′ claw′ foot′, *Furniture.* an elongated foot having the form of a thin claw grasping a ball.

rate[1] (rāt), *n., v.,* **rat·ed, rat·ing.** —*n.* **1.** the amount of a charge or payment with reference to some basis of calculation: *a high rate of interest on loans.* **2.** a certain quantity or amount of one thing considered in relation to a unit of another thing and used as a standard or measure: *at the rate of 60 miles an hour.* **3.** a fixed charge per unit of quantity: *a rate of 10 cents a pound.* **4.** price; cost: *to cut rates on all household items.* **5.** degree of speed, progress, etc.: *to work at a rapid rate.* **6.** degree or comparative extent of action or procedure: *the rate of increase in work output.* **7.** relative condition or quality; grade, class, or sort. **8.** assigned position in any of a series of graded classes; rating. **9.** *Insurance.* the premium charge per unit of insurance. **10.** a charge by a common carrier for transportation, sometimes including certain services involved in rendering such transportation. **11.** a wage paid on a specified time basis: *a salary figured on an hourly rate.* **12.** a charge or price established in accordance with a scale or standard: *hotel rates varying with the number of rooms in the suite.* **13.** *Horol.* the relative adherence of a timepiece to perfect timekeeping, measured in terms of the amount of time gained or lost within a certain period. **14.** Usually, **rates.** *Brit.* **a.** a tax on property for some local purpose. **b.** any tax assessed and paid to a local government, as any city tax, district tax, etc. **15. at any rate,** at all events; at least: *It was a mediocre film, but at any rate there was one outstanding individual performance.* —*v.t.* **16.** to estimate the value or worth of; appraise: *to rate a student's class performance.* **17.** to esteem, consider, or account: *He was rated one of the rich men of the city.* **18.** to fix at a certain rate, as of charge or payment. **19.** to value for purposes of taxation or the like. **20.** to make subject to the payment of a certain rate or tax. **21.** to place in a certain rank, class, etc., as a ship or a seaman; give a specific rating to. **22.** to arrange for the conveyance of (goods) at a certain rate. —*v.i.* **23.** to have value, standing, etc.: *Her performance didn't rate very high in the competition.* **24.** to have position in a certain class. [ME *rate(n)* < ML *rata* < L (*prō*) *ratā* (*parte*), fem. of *ratus,* ptp. of *rērī* to judge]
—**Syn. 5.** pace.

rate[2] (rāt), *v.t., v.i.,* **rat·ed, rat·ing.** to chide vehemently; scold. [ME *(a)rate(n)* < Scand; cf. Sw *rata* to reject] —**rat′er,** *n.*

rate·a·ble (rā′tə bəl), *adj.* ratable. —**rate′a·bil′i·ty, rate′a·ble·ness,** *n.* —**rate′a·bly,** *adv.*

ra·tel (rāt′əl, rät′-), *n.* a badgerlike carnivore, *Mellivora capensis,* of Africa and India. [< SAfrD]

Ratel (11 in. high at shoulder; total length 3 ft.; tail 9 in.)

rate′-of-climb′ in′dicator (rāt′əv klīm′), *Aeron.* a flight instrument that indicates the rate of climb or of descent of an aircraft.

rate′ of exchange′, the ratio at which the unit of currency of one country can be exchanged for the unit of currency of another country. Also called **exchange rate.**

rate·pay·er (rāt′pā′ər), *n.* *Brit.* a person who pays rates; a taxpayer of the local government. [RATE[1] + PAYER] —**rate′pay′ing,** *adj., n.*

rat·er (rā′tər), *n.* **1.** a person who makes rates or ratings. **2.** one who or that which is of a specific rating (usually used in combination): *The show's star is a first rater.* **3.** *Slang.* any of various small, popular yachts belonging to standard classes. [RATE[1] + -ER[1]]

rat·fink (rat′fingk′), *n.* *Slang.* fink (def. 4). [RAT + FINK]

rat·fish (rat′fish′), *n., pl.* (*esp. collectively*) **-fish,** (*esp. referring to two or more kinds or species*) **-fish·es.** a chimaera, *Hydrolagus colliei,* that is found in the Pacific Ocean from Alaska to Lower California and has a ratlike tail. [RAT + FISH]

rat′ guard′, a disk of sheet metal fitted around a hawser to prevent rats from boarding a vessel moored at a dock.

rath[1] (rät), *n.* a Dravidian cave temple in India. [< EInd]

rath[2] (rath), *adj.* rathe.

Rat·haus (rät′hous′, rat′-; *Pol.* rät′hous′), *n.* **Karol** (kar′əl; *Pol.* kä′rôl), 1895–1954, Polish composer, in the U.S. after 1938.

Rat·haus (rät′hous′), *n., pl.* **-häu·ser** (-hoi′zər). *German.* a town hall. [lit., counsel house]

Rath·bone (rath′bōn), *n.* **Basil,** 1892–1967, English actor, born in South Africa.

rathe (rāth), *adj.* **1.** Also, **rath.** *Archaic.* growing, blooming, or ripening early in the year or season. —*adv.* **2.** *Brit. Dial.* early. [ME; OE *hræth, hræd* quick, active; c. D *rad,* OIcel *hrathr*] —**rathe′ly,** *adv.* —**rathe′ness,** *n.*

Ra·the·nau (rät′ənou′), *n.* **Wal·ther** (väl′tər), 1867–1922, German industrialist, writer, and statesman.

rath·er (*adv.* rath′ər, rä′thər; *interj.* rath′ûr′, rä′thûr′), *adv.* **1.** in a measure; to a certain extent; somewhat: *rather good.* **2.** in some degree: *I rather thought you would regret it.* **3.** more properly or justly; with better reason: *The contrary is rather to be supposed.* **4.** sooner; more readily or willingly: *to die rather than yield; I would rather go today.* **5.** more properly or correctly speaking; more truly: *He is a painter or, rather, a watercolorist.* **6.** on the contrary: *It's not generosity, rather self-interest.* —*interj.* **7.** *Chiefly Brit.* emphatically yes; assuredly; without doubt: *Is the book worth reading? Rather!* **8. had rather.** See **have** (def. 20). [ME; OE *hrather,* comp. of *hrathe* quickly, RATHE]

Rath′ke's pouch′ (rät′kəz), *Embryol.* an invagination of stomodeal ectoderm developing into the anterior lobe of the pituitary gland. Also called **Rath′ke's pock′et.** [named after Martin Heinrich *Rathke* (1793–1860), German anatomist]

rat·hole (rat′hōl′), *n.* **1.** a hole made by a rat, as into a room, barn, etc.: *The first chore in the old building is to plug up the ratholes.* **2.** the burrow or shelter of a rat. **3.** any small and uncomfortable room, office, apartment, etc., esp. one that is dirty or disordered: *He lives in a rathole near the docks.* **4. down the rathole,** for a worthless purpose or purposes: *seeing his inheritance disappear down the rathole.* [RAT + HOLE]

raths·kel·ler (rät′skel′ər, rat′-, rath′-), *n.* **1.** (in Germany) the cellar of a town hall, often used as a beer hall or restaurant. **2.** a restaurant patterned on the German rathskeller, usually located below street level. [< G, equiv. to *Rat(h)* counsel (abstracted from *Rathaus*) + *-s* 's[1] + *Keller* cellar]

rat·i·cide (rat′i sīd′), *n.* a substance or preparation for killing rats. [RAT + -I- + -CIDE] —**rat′i·cid′al,** *adj.*

rat·i·fi·ca·tion (rat′ə fə kā′shən), *n.* **1.** the act of ratifying; confirmation; sanction. **2.** the state of being ratified. [< ML *ratificātiōn-* (s. of *ratificātiō*), equiv. to *ratificāt(us)* (ptp. of *ratificāre* to RATIFY) + *-iōn-* -ION] —**rat′i·fi·ca′tion·ist,** *n., adj.*

rat·i·fy (rat′ə fī′), *v.t.,* **-fied, -fy·ing. 1.** to confirm by expressing consent, approval, or formal sanction: *to ratify an amendment to a constitution.* **2.** to confirm (something done or arranged by an agent or by representatives) by such action. [ME *ratifie(n)* < MF *ratifi(er)* < ML *ratificāre),* equiv. to L *rat(us)* calculated (see RATE[1]) + *-ificāre* -IFY] —**rat′i·fi′er,** *n.*
—**Syn. 1.** corroborate, approve. **2.** substantiate, validate, establish. —**Ant. 1.** veto, disapprove.

ra·ti·né (rat′ənā′; *Fr.* ra tē nā′), *n.* a loosely woven fabric made with nubby or knotty yarns. Also, **ra·ti·ne** (rat′ənā′, ra tēn′). [< F, ptp. of *ratiner* to make a nap on cloth]

rat·ing[1] (rā′ting), *n.* **1.** classification according to grade or rank. **2.** *Naut.* **a.** assigned position in a particular class or grade, or relative standing, as of a ship or a seaman. **b. ratings,** crew members having certain ratings, esp. the enlisted personnel in the British Navy. **3.** the credit standing of a person or firm. **4.** a percentage derived from a sampling of radio or television set owners and indicating the number of listeners to or viewers of a specific program. **5.** an amount fixed as a rate. **6.** *Brit.* apportioning of a tax. **7.** *Elect.* a designated limit, for a machine, apparatus, etc., of operating characteristics, as voltage, load, frequency, etc., based on specified conditions. [RATE[1] + -ING[1]]

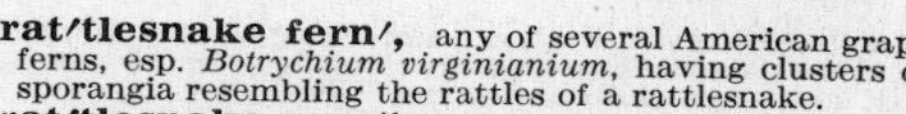

rat·ing[2] (rā′ting), *n.* an angry reprimand or rebuke; scolding. [RATE[2] + -ING[1]]

rat′ing badge′, *U.S. Navy.* a badge that indicates the rank and specialty of a petty officer and is worn on the upper left sleeve.

rat′ing nut′, *Horol.* a nut that screws onto the lower end of the rod of a clock pendulum for raising or lowering the weight to alter the rate of the clock.

ra·tio (rā′shō, -shē ō′), *n., pl.* **-tios. 1.** the relation between two similar magnitudes in respect to the number of times the first contains the second: *the ratio of 5 to 2, written 5:2 or 5/2.* **2.** proportional relation; rate: *the ratio between acceptances and rejections.* **3.** *Finance.* the relative value of gold and silver in a bimetallic currency system. [< L *ratiō* a reckoning, account, calculation; see REASON]

ra·ti·oc·i·nate (rash′ē os′ə nāt′), *v.i.,* **-nat·ed, -nat·ing.** to reason; carry on a process of reasoning. [< L *ratiōcināt(us)* reckoned, calculated, concluded (ptp. of *ratiōcinārī*), deriv. of *ratiō* reason] **—ra′ci·oc′i·na′·tor,** *n.*

ra·ti·oc·i·na·tion (rash′ē os′ə nā′shən), *n.* the process of logical reasoning. [< L *ratiōcinātiōn-* (s. of *ratiōcinātiō*), equiv. to *ratiōcināt(us)* (see RATIOCINATE) + *-iōn-* -ION] **—ra′ti·oc′i·na′tive,** *adj.*

ra·ti·om·e·ter (rā′shē om′i tər), *n.* (in three-color photography) a device for determining the exposure factors of the filters to be used. [RATIO + -METER]

ra·tion (rash′ən, rā′shən), *n.* **1.** a fixed allowance of provisions or food, esp. for a soldier or sailor: *a daily ration of meat and bread.* **2.** an allotted amount: *They finally saved up enough gas rations for the trip.* **3. rations,** provisions: *Enough rations were brought along to feed all the marchers.* **—*v.t.* 4.** to supply, apportion, or distribute as rations: *to ration food to an army.* **5.** to supply or provide with rations: *to ration an army with food.* **6.** to restrict the consumption of (a commodity, food, etc.): *to ration meat during war.* **7.** to restrict the consumption of (a consumer): *The civilian population was rationed while the war lasted.* [< F < L *ratiōn-* (s. of *ratiō*) REASON]
—Syn. 1. portion, allotment. **4.** mete, dole, allot.

ra·tion·al (rash′ə nəl), *adj.* **1.** agreeable to reason; reasonable; sensible: *a rational plan for limiting traffic congestion.* **2.** having or exercising reason, sound judgment, or good sense: *a rational, poised statesman.* **3.** being in or characterized by full possession of one's reason; sane; lucid: *The patient appeared perfectly rational.* **4.** endowed with the faculty of reason: *Man is a rational animal.* **5.** of, pertaining to, or constituting reasoning powers: *the rational faculty.* **6.** proceeding or derived from reason or based on reasoning: *a rational explanation.* **7.** *Math.* **a.** capable of being expressed exactly by a ratio of two integers. **b.** (of a function) capable of being expressed exactly by a ratio of two polynomials. **8.** *Class. Pros.* capable of measurement in terms of the metrical unit or mora. **—*n.* 9.** *Math.* See **rational number.** [ME *racional* < L *ratiōnāl(is),* equiv. to *ratiōn-* (s. of *ratiō*) reason + *-ālis* -AL[1]] **—ra′tion·al·ly,** *adv.* **—ra′·tion·al·ness,** *n.*
—Syn. 2. intelligent, wise, judicious, sagacious, enlightened. **6.** See **reasonable. —Ant. 2.** stupid. **3.** insane.

ra·tion·ale (rash′ə nal′), *n.* **1.** a statement of reasons. **2.** a reasoned exposition of principles. **3.** the fundamental reasons serving to account for something. [< L *ratiōnāle,* neut. of *ratiōnālis* RATIONAL]

ra′tional form′, *Math.* a quotient of two polynomials with integral coefficients.

ra′tional func′tion, *Math.* a function that can be written as the quotient of two polynomials with integral coefficients.

ra·tion·al·ise (rash′ə nəlīz′), *v.t., v.i.,* **-ised, -is·ing.** *Chiefly Brit.* rationalize. **—ra′tion·al·i·sa′tion,** *n.* **—ra′tion·al·is′er,** *n.*

ra·tion·al·ism (rash′ə nəliz′əm), *n.* **1.** the principle or habit of accepting reason as the supreme authority in matters of opinion, belief, or conduct. **2.** *Philos.* **a.** the doctrine that reason alone is a source of knowledge and is independent of experience. **b.** (in the philosophies of Descartes, Spinoza, etc.) the doctrine that all knowledge is expressible in self-evident propositions or their consequences. **3.** *Theol.* the doctrine that human reason, unaided by divine revelation, is an adequate or the sole guide to all attainable religious truth. [RATIONAL + -ISM] **—ra′tion·al·ist,** *n.* **—ra′tion·al·is′tic, ra′·tion·al·is′ti·cal,** *adj.* **—ra′tion·al·is′ti·cal·ly,** *adv.*

ra·tion·al·i·ty (rash′ə nal′i tē), *n., pl.* **-ties. 1.** the state or quality of being rational. **2.** the possession of reason. **3.** agreeableness to reason; reasonableness. **4.** the exercise of reason. **5.** a reasonable view, practice, etc. [< LL *ratiōnālitās* reasonableness. See RATIONAL, -ITY]

ra·tion·al·ize (rash′ə nəlīz′, rash′nəlīz′), *v.,* **-ized, -iz·ing. —*v.t.* 1.** *Psychol.* to ascribe (one's acts, opinions, etc.) to causes that superficially seem reasonable and valid but that actually are unrelated to the true, possibly unconscious causes: *The patient rationalized his compulsive acts as consciously controlled behavior.* **2.** to remove unreasonable elements from. **3.** to make rational or conformable to reason. **4.** to treat or explain in a rational or rationalistic manner. **5.** *Math.* to eliminate radicals from (an equation or expression): *to rationalize the denominator of a fraction.* **6.** *Brit.* to reorganize and integrate (an industry). **—*v.i.* 7.** to employ reason; think in a rational or rationalistic manner. **8.** to invent plausible explanations for acts, opinions, etc., that are actually based on other causes: *He tried to prove that he was not at fault, but he was obviously rationalizing.* Also, *esp. Brit.,* **rationalise.** [RATIONAL + -IZE] **—ra′tion·al·i·za′tion,** *n.* **—ra′tion·al·iz′er,** *n.*

ra′tional num′ber, *Math.* a number that can be expressed exactly by a ratio of two integers.

ra′tio test′, *Math.* the theorem that a given infinite series converges if the absolute value of the ratio of the term succeeding the *n*th term to the *n*th term approaches a limit less than 1 as *n* increases without bound. Also called **d'Alembert's test.**

Rat·is·bon (rat′is bon′, -iz-), *n.* Regensburg.

rat·ite (rat′īt), *adj.* **1.** having a flat, unkeeled sternum, as an ostrich, cassowary, emu, moa, etc. **—*n.* 2.** a bird having a ratite breastbone. [< L *rat(is)* raft, float + -ITE[2]]

rat-kan·ga·roo (rat′kang′gə ro͞o′), *n., pl.* **-roos.** any of several rabbit-sized, ratlike, Australian kangaroos of the genera *Bettongia, Petorous,* etc.

rat·line (rat′lin), *n.* *Naut.* **1.** any of the small ropes or lines that traverse the shrouds horizontally and serve as steps for going aloft. **2.** Also, **rat′line stuff′.** three-stranded, right-laid, tarred hemp stuff of from 6 to 24 threads, used for ratlines, lashings, etc. Also, **rat′lin, rat′-lin, rattling.** [late ME *ratling, radelyng* < ?]

R, Ratline

RATO (rā′tō), *n.* *Rocketry.* rocket-assisted takeoff.

Ra·ton (rə tōn′), *n.* a town in NE New Mexico. 8146 (1960).

ra·toon (ra to͞on′), *n.* **1.** a sprout or shoot from the root of a plant, esp. a sugarcane, after it has been cropped. **—*v.i., v.t.* 2.** to put forth or cause to put forth ratoons. Also, **rattoon.** [< Sp *retoño* sprout < Hindi *ratun*] **—ra·toon′er,** *n.*

rat′-poi·son plant′ (rat′poi′zən), a stout shrub, *Hamelia erecta,* of Central America, having grayish, hairy twigs, scarlet or orange flowers, and reddish-purple, egg-shaped fruit.

rat′ race′, *Informal.* any exhausting, unremitting activity or routine, esp. one that leaves no time for relaxation, contemplation, etc.: *the suburban rat race of keeping up with one's neighbors in a show of affluence.*

rats·bane (rats′bān′), *n.* **1.** rat poison. **2.** the trioxide of arsenic. [RAT + 'S[1] + BANE]

rat′ snake′, any of several New and Old World colubrid snakes, of the genus *Elaphe,* that feed chiefly on small mammals and birds. Also called **chicken snake.**

rat-strip·per (rat′strip′ər), *n.* a low shrub, *Pachistima canbyi,* of E central U.S., having trailing, rooting branches and tiny, reddish flowers, grown as an ornamental.

rat-tail (rat′tāl′), *n.* grenadier (def. 4). Also, **rat′tail′.**

rat′-tail cac′tus, a cactus, *Aporocactus flagelliformis,* of Mexico, having slim, cylindrical stems that are easily trained into strange designs, and crimson flowers.

rat′tail comb′, a comb for the hair having a narrow, pointed handle used in setting the hair.

rat′-tail file′, a long, narrow file having a circular cross section.

rat′-tailed mag′got (rat′tāld′), the aquatic larva of any of several syrphid flies of the genus *Eristalis,* that breathes through a long, thin tube at the posterior end of its body.

rat′-tail spoon′, a spoon having a tapered rib running beneath the bowl as a continuation of the stem.

rat·tan (ra tan′), *n.* **1.** any of various climbing palms of the genus *Calamus* or allied genera. **2.** the tough stems of such palms, used for wickerwork, canes, etc. **3.** a stick or switch of this material. Also, **ratan.** [< Malay *rōtan*]

rat·teen (ra tēn′), *n.* *Obs.* ratiné.

rat·ten (rat′ən), *v.t.* *Brit. Informal.* to molest (workers) or inflict damage on (a factory or machinery) during a labor dispute. [perh. back formation from RATTENING]
—rat′ten·er, *n.*

rat·ten·ing (rat′əning), *n.* *Brit. Informal.* the causing of injury or damage to workers, a factory, machinery, etc., during a labor dispute. [? akin to RATTON]

rat·ter (rat′ər), *n.* one who or that which catches rats, as a terrier or a cat. [RAT + -ER[1]]

rat′ ter′rier, a terrier of any of several breeds developed esp. for catching rats, as the Manchester terrier.

Rat·ti·gan (rat′ə gən), *n.* **Terence,** born 1911, English playwright.

rat·tish (rat′ish), *adj.* **1.** of, pertaining to, characteristic of, or resembling a rat. **2.** infested with rats. [RAT+-ISH[1]]

rat·tle[1] (rat′əl), *v.,* **-tled, -tling,** *n.* **—*v.i.* 1.** to give out or cause a rapid succession of short, sharp sounds, as in consequence of agitation and repeated concussions: *The windows rattled in their frames.* **2.** to move or go, esp. rapidly, with such sounds: *The car rattled along the highway.* **3.** to talk rapidly; chatter: *She rattled on for an hour about her ailments.* **—*v.t.* 4.** to cause to rattle: *He rattled the doorknob violently.* **5.** to drive, send, bring, etc., esp. rapidly, with rattling: *The wind rattled the metal can across the roadway.* **6.** to utter or perform in a rapid or lively manner: *to rattle off a speech.* **7.** to disconcert or confuse (a person): *A sudden noise rattled the speaker.* **8.** *Hunting.* to stir up (a cover). **—*n.* 9.** a rapid succession of short, sharp sounds, as from the collision of hard bodies. **10.** an instrument contrived to make a rattling sound, as a child's toy. **11.** the series of horny, interlocking elements at the end of the tail of a rattlesnake, with which it produces a rattling sound. **12.** a rattling sound in the throat, as the death rattle. [ME *ratele(n)* (c. D *ratelen,* G *rasseln*); imit.]
—Syn. 1. clatter, knock. **7.** discompose. **9.** clatter.

rat·tle[2] (rat′əl), *v.t.,* **-tled, -tling.** *Naut.* to furnish with ratlines (usually fol. by *down*). [back formation from RATLINE (taken as verbal n.)]

rat·tle·brain (rat′əl brān′), *n.* a giddy, empty-headed, talkative person. [RATTLE[1] + BRAIN]

rat·tle·brained (rat′əl brānd′), *adj.* foolish; flighty; scatterbrained. [RATTLEBRAIN + -ED[2]]

rat·tle-bush (rat′əl bo͝osh′), *n.* See **blue false indigo.**

rat·tle·head (rat′əl hed′), *n.* a rattlebrain. [RATTLE[1] + HEAD] **—rat′tle·head′ed,** *adj.*

rat·tle·pate (rat′əl pāt′), *n.* a rattlebrain. [RATTLE[1] + PATE] **—rat′tle·pat′ed,** *adj.*

rat·tler (rat′lər), *n.* **1.** a rattlesnake. **2.** one who or that which rattles. **3.** *Informal.* a fast freight train. [late ME; see RATTLE[1], -ER[1]]

rat·tle·snake (rat′əl snāk′), *n.* any of several New World pit vipers of the genera *Crotalus* and *Sistrurus,* having a rattle composed of a series of horny, interlocking elements at the end of the tail. [RATTLE[1] + SNAKE]

Timber rattlesnake, *Crotalus horridus* (Length 3½ to 6 ft.)

rat′tlesnake fern′, any of several American grape ferns, esp. *Botrychium virginianium,* having clusters of sporangia resembling the rattles of a rattlesnake.

rat′tlesnake mas′ter, **1.** gay-feather (def. 1). **2.** the blazing star, *Liatris squarrosa.* **3.** See **false aloe.**

rat′tlesnake plan′tain, any of several low, terrestrial orchids, as *Goodyera repens,* of northern temperate regions.

rat′tlesnake root′, **1.** any of certain plants of the genus *Prenanthes,* whose roots or tubers have been regarded as a remedy for snake bites, as *P. serpentaria* or *P. alba.* **2.** the root or tuber. **3.** the snakeroot, *Polygala Senega.* **4.** its root. **5.** the liliaceous plant, *Trillium cernuum.*

rat′tlesnake weed′, **1.** a hawkweed, *Hieracium venosum,* of eastern North America, whose leaves and root are thought to possess medicinal properties. **2.** a carrotlike weed, *Daucus pusillus,* of southern and western North America. **3.** any of certain other plants, as an umbelliferous plant, *Eryngium aquaticum.* **4.** See **rattlesnake plantain.**

rat·tle·trap (rat′əl trap′), *n.* a shaky, rattling object, as a rickety vehicle. [RATTLE[1] + TRAP[1]]

rat·tling[1] (rat′ling), *adj.* **1.** that rattles: *a rattling door.* **2.** remarkably good, lively, or fast: *a rattling talk; a rattling gallop.* **—*adv.* 3.** very: *a rattling good time.* [ME *rateling.* See RATTLE[1], -ING[2]] **—rat′tling·ly,** *adv.*

rat·tling[2] (rat′lin), *n.* ratline.

rat·tly (rat′lē), *adj.* tending to rattle; making or having a rattling sound. [RATTLE[1] + -Y]

rat·ton (rat′ən), *n.* *Brit. Dial.* a rat. [ME *ratoun* < OF *raton,* dim. of *rat* RAT, ? < Gmc]

rat·toon (ra to͞on′), *n., v.i., v.t.* ratoon.

rat·trap (rat′trap′), *n.* **1.** a device for catching rats. **2.** a run-down, filthy, or dilapidated place. **3.** a difficult, involved, or entangling situation. [RAT + TRAP[1]]

rat·ty (rat′ē), *adj.,* **-ti·er, -ti·est. 1.** full of rats. **2.** of or characteristic of a rat. **3.** wretched; shabby: *a ratty, old overcoat.* [RAT + -Y[1]]

Rau·schen·busch (rou′shən bo͝osh′), *n.* **Walter,** 1861–1918, U.S. clergyman and social reformer.

rau·cous (rô′kəs), *adj.* harsh; strident; grating: *raucous voices; raucous laughter.* [< L *rauc(us)* hoarse, harsh, rough + -OUS] **—rau′cous·ly,** *adv.* **—rau′cous·ness, rau·ci·ty** (rô′si tē), *n.*

raught (rôt; *Scot.* RÔKHT), *v.i.* *Brit. Obs.* to reach. [ME *raughte* (past tense) *raught* (ptp.), OE *rǣhte, geræht,* ptp. of *rǣcan* to REACH]

raun·chy (rôn′chē, roun′-, rän′-), *adj.* *Slang.* **1.** slovenly; careless: *a raunchy army outfit.* **2.** obscene; smutty: *a raunchy joke.* **3.** lecherous. [?]

Rau·rich (rou′rik), *n.* a ring formation in the fourth quadrant of the face of the moon: about 30 miles in diameter.

Rau·schen·burg (rou′shən bûrg′), *n.* **Robert,** borr 1925, U.S. artist.

rau·wol·fi·a (rô wo͝ol′fē ə), *n.* **1.** any tropical tree or shrub of the genus *Rauwolfia,* as *R. serpentina,* of India. **2.** an extract from the roots of the rauwolfia, *R. serpentina,* containing alkaloids the most important of which is reserpine: used in medicine chiefly for the treatment of hypertension and as a sedative. [< NL, named after L. *Rauwolf,* 16th-century German botanist; see -IA]

rav·age (rav′ij), *n., v.,* **-aged, -ag·ing. —*n.* 1.** devastating or destructive action. **2.** havoc; ruinous damage: *the ravages of war.* **—*v.t.* 3.** to work havoc upon; damage or mar by ravages: *a face ravaged by grief.* **—*v.i.* 4.** to work havoc; do ruinous damage. [< F, MF; equiv. to *rav(ir)* (to) RAVISH + *-age* -AGE] **—rav′age·ment,** *n.* **—rav′ag·er,** *n.*
—Syn. 1. ruin, waste, desolation. **3.** ruin, despoil, plunder, pillage, sack. RAVAGE, DEVASTATE, LAY WASTE all refer, in their literal application, to the wholesale destruction of a countryside by an invading army (or something comparable). LAY WASTE has remained the closest to the original meaning of destruction of land: *The invading army laid waste the towns along the coast.* But RAVAGE and DEVASTATE (the Latin equivalent of LAY WASTE) are used in reference to other types of violent destruction and may also have a purely figurative application. RAVAGE is often used of the results of epidemics: *The Black Plague ravaged 14th-century Europe;* and even of the effect of disease or suffering on the human countenance: *a face ravaged by despair.* DEVASTATE, in addition to its concrete meaning (*vast areas devastated by bombs*), may be used figuratively: *a devastating wit.* **—Ant. 1.** creation. **3.** build, repair.

Ra·va·na (rä′və nə), *n.* (in the *Ramayana*) the king of Ceylon who abducts Sita, the wife of Ramachandra, and is later defeated by Ramachandra.

rave[1] (rāv), *v.,* **raved, rav·ing,** *n.* **—*v.i.* 1.** to talk wildly, as in delirium. **2.** (of wind, water, storms, etc.) to make a wild or furious sound; rage. **3.** to talk or write with extravagant enthusiasm: *The critics raved over the play. She raved about her child's intelligence.* **—*v.t.* 4.** to utter as if in madness. **—*n.* 5.** an act of raving. **6.** an extravagantly enthusiastic appraisal or review of something, esp. a play. [ME *rave(n),* prob. < MF *re(s)v(er)* (to) wander, be delirious] **—rav′er,** *n.*

rave[2] (rāv), *n.* a vertical sidepiece of a wagon or other vehicle. [alter. of dial. *rathe* (ME) < ?]

rave′ hook′, *Naut.* a hooklike tool for picking old oakum out of seams in planking. Also called **reef hook, reefing hook, reef iron, reefing iron, ripping iron.** [? obs. *rave* to drag, pull (ME *raven*) < ?]

rav·el (rav′əl), *v.,* **-eled, -el·ing** or (*esp. Brit.*) **-elled, -el·ling,** *n.* **—*v.t.* 1.** to disentangle or unravel the threads or fibers of (a woven or knitted fabric, rope, etc.). **2.** to tangle or entangle. **3.** to involve; confuse; perplex. **4.** to make clear; unravel (often fol. by *out*). **—*v.i.* 5.** to become disjoined thread by thread or fiber by fiber; fray. **6.** to become tangled. **7.** to become confused or perplexed. **8.** (of a road surface) to lose aggregate. **—*n.* 9.** a tangle or complication. [appar. < MD *ravel(en)* (to) entangle] **—rav′el·er;** *esp. Brit.,* **rav′el·ler,** *n.* **—rav′el·ly,** *adj.*

Ra·vel (rə vel′; *Fr.* RA vel′), *n.* **Mau·rice Jo·seph** (mō rēs′ zhō zef′), 1875–1937, French composer.

rave·lin (rav′lin), *n.* *Fort.* a V-shaped outwork outside the main ditch and covering the works between two bastions. [< F, earlier *revelin* < D *regeling* framework]

rav·el·ing (rav′ə liŋ), *n.* something raveled out, as a thread drawn from a knitted or woven fabric. Also, *esp. Brit.,* **rav′el·ling.** [RAVEL + -ING[1]]

rav·el·ment (rav′əl mənt), *n.* entanglement; confusion. [RAVEL + -MENT]

ra·ven[1] (rā′vən), *n.* **1.** any of several large, corvine birds having lustrous, black plumage and a loud, harsh call, esp. *Corvus corax,* of the New and Old Worlds. **2.** the divine culture hero and trickster of the North Pacific coast Indians. **3.** (*cap.*) *Astron.* the constellation Corvus. —*adj.* **4.** lustrous black: *raven locks of hair.* [ME; OE *hræfn;* c. G *Rabe,* OIcel *hrafn*] —**ra′ven·like′,** *adj.*

Raven, *Corvus corax* (Length 26 in.)

rav·en[2] (rav′ən), *v.i.* **1.** to seek plunder or prey. **2.** to eat or feed voraciously or greedily: *to raven like an animal.* **3.** to have a ravenous appetite. —*v.t.* **4.** to seize as spoil or prey. **5.** to devour voraciously. —*n.* **6.** rapine; robbery. **7.** plunder or prey. Also, **ravin.** [ME *ravine* < MF < L *rapīn(a)* RAPINE]

Ra·ven (rā′vən), *n.* a boy's given name.

Raven, The, a lyric poem (1845) by Edgar Allan Poe.

rav·en·ing (rav′ə niŋ), *adj.* **1.** rapacious; voracious. —*n.* **2.** rapacity. [RAVEN[2] + -ING[2], -ING[1]] —**rav′en·ing·ly,** *adv.*
—**Syn. 1.** See **ravenous.**

Ra·ven·na (rə ven′ə; *It.* rä ven′nä), *n.* a city in NE Italy: the capital of Italy in the period of the Byzantine Empire; tomb of Dante. 115,205 (1961).

rav·en·ous (rav′ə nəs), *adj.* **1.** extremely rapacious: *a ravenous jungle beast.* **2.** voracious or gluttonous: *feeling ravenous after a hard day's work.* [ME < OF *ravineux,* equiv. to *ravin(er)* (to) RAVEN[2] + *-eux* -OUS] —**rav′en·ous·ly,** *adv.* —**rav′en·ous·ness,** *n.*
—**Syn. 1.** predatory. **2.** greedy, starved, famished, devouring. RAVENOUS, RAVENING, VORACIOUS suggest a greediness for food and usually intense hunger. RAVENOUS implies extreme hunger, or a famished condition: *ravenous wild beasts.* RAVENING adds the idea of fierceness and savagery, esp. as shown in a violent manner of acquiring food: *ravening wolves.* VORACIOUS implies the eating of a great deal of food, or the disposition to eat a great deal, without reference to the degree of hunger (*a voracious small boy incessantly eating*) or figuratively (*a voracious reader*). —**Ant. 1.** sated.

Ra·vens·wood (rā′vənz wŏŏd′), *n.* a town in W West Virginia. 3410 (1960).

ra·vi·gote (*Fr.* RA vē gôt′), *n.* **1.** a highly seasoned velouté with white wine and vinegar, butter, cream, and mushrooms cooked in liquor, usually served hot with variety meats and poultry. **2.** a sauce of oil, vinegar, chopped capers, parsley, chervil, tarragon, and onion, served cold with vegetables or seafood or warm with meat. [< F, deriv. of *ravigoter* to refresh; MF, equiv. to *ra-* (alter. < L *re-* RE-) + *vigoter* (alter. of *vigorer* VIGOR)]

rav·in (rav′in), *v.i., v.t., n.* raven[2].

ra·vine (rə vēn′), *n.* a narrow steep-sided valley commonly eroded by running water. [ME < MF: torrent, OF: a violent rushing; see RAVEN[2]] —**ra·vine′y,** *adj.*

rav·ing (rā′viŋ), *adj.* **1.** that raves; delirious; frenzied: *a raving maniac.* **2.** *Informal.* extraordinary or remarkable: *She's a raving beauty.* —*n.* **3.** irrational, incoherent talk. **4.** wildly extravagant or outrageous talk; bombast. [RAVE + -ING[2], -ING[1]] —**rav′ing·ly,** *adv.*

ra·vi·o·li (rav′ē ō′lē, rä′vē-; *It.* rä vyô′lē), *n.* (*construed as sing. or pl.*) small squares of pasta stuffed with a filling, usually of meat or cheese, and often served with grated cheese and a sauce or butter. [< It, pl. of dial. *raviolo* little turnip, dim. of *rava* < L *rāpa;* see RAPE[2]]

rav·ish (rav′ish), *v.t.* **1.** to fill with strong emotion, esp. joy. **2.** to seize and carry off by force. **3.** to carry off (a woman) by force. **4.** to rape (a woman). [ME *ravish(en)* < MF *raviss-* long s. of *ravir* to seize << L *rapere;* see RAPE[1]] —**rav′ished·ly,** *adv.* —**rav′ish·er,** *n.*

rav·ish·ing (rav′i shiŋ), *adj.* entrancing; enchanting: *her ravishing beauty.* [ME; see RAVISH, -ING[2]] —**rav′ish·ing·ly,** *adv.*

rav·ish·ment (rav′ish mənt), *n.* **1.** rapture or ecstasy. **2.** violent removal. **3.** the forcible abduction of a woman. **4.** rape[1] (def. 2). [< MF *ravissement,* equiv. to *raviss-* (see RAVISH) + *-ment* -MENT]

Ra·vo·nelle (rā′və nel′), *n.* a girl's given name.

raw (rô), *adj.* **1.** uncooked, as articles of food: *a raw carrot.* **2.** not having undergone processes of preparing, dressing, finishing, refining, or manufacture: *raw silk.* **3.** unnaturally or painfully exposed, as flesh, by removal of the skin or natural integument. **4.** painfully open, as a sore, wound, etc. **5.** crude in quality or character; not tempered or refined by art or taste: *rather raw humor.* **6.** ignorant, inexperienced, or untrained: *a raw recruit.* **7.** brutally or grossly frank: *a raw portrayal of human passions.* **8.** brutally harsh or unfair: *a raw deal; receiving raw treatment from his friends.* **9.** disagreeably damp and chilly, as the weather, air, etc.: *a raw, foggy day at the beach.* **10.** not diluted, as alcoholic spirits: *raw whiskey.* —*n.* **11.** a sore or irritated place, as on the flesh. **12.** unrefined sugar, oil, etc. **13. in the raw, a.** in the natural, uncultivated, or unrefined state: *nature in the raw.* **b.** *Slang.* in the nude; naked: *The explorers found the natives living in the raw.* [ME; OE *hrēaw, hrǣw;* c. D *rauw,* G *roh;* akin to L *crūdus* raw, *cruor* blood, Gk *kréas* raw flesh] —**raw′ish,** *adj.* —**raw′ish·ness,** *n.* —**raw′ly,** *adv.* —**raw′ness,** *n.*
—**Syn. 1.** fresh. **2.** unprepared, rough, makeshift. RAW, CRUDE, RUDE refer to something not in a finished or highly refined state. RAW applies particularly to material not yet changed by a process, by manufacture, or by preparation for consumption: *raw cotton, leather.* CRUDE refers to that which still needs refining: *crude petroleum.* RUDE refers to what is still in a condition of rough simplicity or in a makeshift or roughly made form: *rude agricultural implements; the rude bridge that arched the flood.* **6.** undisciplined, green, unskilled, unpracticed. **9.** cold, wet. **10.** straight, neat. —**Ant. 1.** prepared.

Ra·wal·pin·di (rä′wəl pin′dē), *n.* a city in N West Pakistan. 343,000 (est. 1961).

raw·boned (rô′bōnd′), *adj.* having little flesh; gaunt. [RAW + BONED]

raw′ fi′bers, textile fibers, as cotton or wool, or textile filaments, as silk or nylon, that have received no manipulation or treatment.

raw·hide (rô′hīd′), *n., v.,* **-hid·ed, -hid·ing.** —*n.* **1.** untanned skin of cattle or other animals. **2.** a rope or whip made of rawhide. —*v.t.* **3.** to whip with a rawhide. [RAW + HIDE[2]]

ra·win (rā′win), *n.* an observation of upper-air winds conducted by means of a weather balloon tracked by radar or a radio direction finder. Cf. **raob, rawinsonde.** [*ra(dio)* + *win(ds-aloft)*]

ra·win·sonde (rā′win sond′), *n.* meteorological, upper-atmosphere observations conducted by means of a radiosonde tracked by radar. Cf. **raob, rawin.** [*ra(dar)* + *win(d)* + *(radio)sonde*]

Raw·lings (rô′liŋz), *n.* **Marjorie Kin·nan** (kin′ən), 1896–1953, U.S. novelist and journalist.

Raw·lins (rô′linz), *n.* a town in S Wyoming. 8968 (1960).

Raw·lin·son (rô′lin sən), *n.* **1. George,** 1812–1902, English historian. **2.** his brother, **Sir Henry Cres·wicke** (krez′ik), 1810–95, English archaeologist, diplomat, and soldier.

Rawl·plug (rôl′plug′), *n.* *Trademark.* a device for anchoring objects to masonry, consisting of a fiber tube expanded inside a drilled hole by a screw driven into its center.

raw′ mate′rial, material before being processed or manufactured into a final form.

raw′-pack meth′od (rô′pak′). See **cold pack** (def. 2).

raw′ score′, the original score, as of a test, before it is statistically adjusted.

raw′ sien′na. See under **sienna** (def. 1).

raw′ silk′, reeled silk that has not had the sericin removed.

rax (raks), *Scot. and North Eng.* —*v.i.* **1.** to stretch oneself, as after sleeping. **2.** to extend the hand. —*v.t.* **3.** to elongate; stretch. [ME (north) *rax(en),* OE *raxan;* akin to OE *reccean* to stretch, G *recken*]

ray[1] (rā), *n.* **1.** a narrow beam of light. **2.** a gleam or slight manifestation: *a ray of hope.* **3.** a raylike line or stretch of something. **4.** light or radiance. **5.** a line of sight. **6.** *Physics, Optics.* **a.** any of the lines or streams in which light appears to radiate from a luminous body. **b.** the straight line normal to the wave front in the propagation of radiant energy. **c.** a stream of material particles all moving in the same straight line. **7.** *Math.* **a.** one of a system of straight lines emanating from a point. **b.** the part of a straight line considered as originating at a point on the line and as extending in one direction from that point. **8.** any of a system of parts radially arranged. **9.** *Zool.* **a.** one of the branches or arms of a starfish or other radiate animal. **b.** one of the bony or cartilaginous rods in the fin of a fish. **10.** *Bot.* **a.** See **ray flower. b.** one of the branches of an umbel. **c.** See **vascular ray. d.** (in certain composite plants) the marginal part of the flower head. **11.** *Astron.* one of many long, bright streaks radiating from the large lunar craters, conspicuous in a telescopic view or photograph of the moon within a few days before or after a full moon. **12.** a prominent upright projection from the circlet of a crown or coronet, having a pointed or ornamented termination. —*v.i.* **13.** to emit rays. **14.** to issue in rays. —*v.t.* **15.** to send forth in rays. **16.** to throw rays upon; irradiate. **17.** to subject to the action of rays, as in radiotherapy. **18.** *Informal.* to make a radiograph of; x-ray. **19.** to furnish with rays or radiating lines. [ME *raie, raye* < OF *rai* < L *rad(ius)* RADIUS]
—**Syn. 1.** See **gleam.**

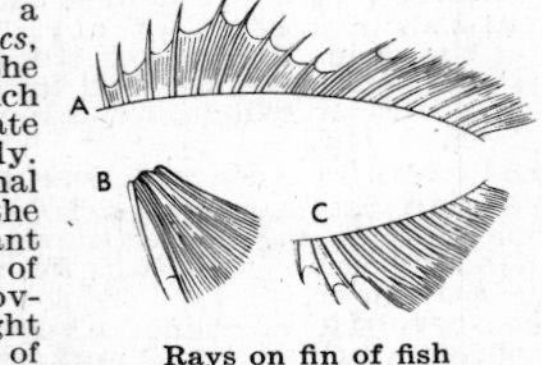

Rays on fin of fish
A, Dorsal, with ten spines
B, Ventral, with one spine
C, Anal, with three spines

ray[2] (rā), *n.* any of numerous elasmobranch fishes having a flattened body adapted for life on the sea bottom and greatly enlarged pectoral fins with the gills on the undersides. [ME *raye* < L *rāia*]

Ray (rā), *n.* **1. Man** (man), born 1890, U.S. painter and photographer. **2.** Also, **Roy.** a boy's given name, form of **Raymond. 3.** Also, **Rae, Raye.** a girl's given name, form of **Rachel.**

ra·yah (rā′yə, rī′ə), *n.* a Christian subject of an Ottoman ruler. Also, **ra′ya.** [< Turk *râiyye* < Ar *ra'īyah* herd]

Ray·burn (rā′bûrn), *n.* **1. Sam,** 1882–1961, U.S. lawyer and political leader: Speaker of the House 1940–47, 1949–53, 1955–61. **2.** a boy's given name.

ray′ flow′er, *Bot.* one of the marginal florets surrounding the disk of tubular florets in the flower heads of certain composite plants. Also called **ray′ flo′ret.**

ray′ grass′, the perennial ryegrass. See under **ryegrass.**

Ray·leigh (rā′lē), *n.* **John William Strutt** (strut), **3rd Baron,** 1842–1919, English physicist: Nobel prize 1904.

Ray′leigh disk′, *Acoustics, Mech.* a small circular disk, usually of mica, that is suspended from a fiber and tends to be deflected at right angles to a stream of air, indicating by its deflection the intensity of a sound wave. [named after J. W. S. RAYLEIGH]

Ray′leigh scat′tering, *Optics.* the scattering of light by particles that are very small in relation to the wavelength of the light, and in which the intensity of the scattered light varies inversely with the fourth power of the wavelength. [named after J. W. S. RAYLEIGH]

Ray′leigh wave′, *Mech.* a wave along the surface of a solid, elastic body, esp. along the surface of the earth. [named after J. W. S. RAYLEIGH]

ray·less (rā′lis), *adj.* **1.** lacking rays or raylike parts. **2.** unlit, dark, or gloomy: *a rayless cave.* [RAY[1] + -LESS] —**ray′less·ness,** *n.*

Ray·mond (rā′mənd), *n.* **1. Henry Jarvis,** 1820–69, U.S. publicist: founder of *The New York Times.* **2.** a town in SW Washington. 3301 (1960). **3.** a boy's given name.

Ray·mond·ville (rā′mənd vil, -mən-), *n.* a town in S Texas. 9385 (1960).

Rayne (rān), *n.* a town in S Louisiana. 8634 (1960).

Ray·nelle (rā nel′), *n.* a girl's given name. Also, **Raenell.**

Ray·ner (rā′nər), *n.* a boy's given name. Also, **Rainer.**

ray·on (rā′on), *n.* **1.** a regenerated textile filament made from cellulose, cotton linters, or chips of hemlock, pine, or spruce by passing an appropriate solution of any of these through spinnerets. **2.** fabric made of this filament. —*adj.* **3.** made of rayon. [< F, equiv. to OF *rai* RAY[1] + *-on* dim. n. suffix]

ray·on·ny (rā′ə nē), *adj.* *Heraldry.* radiant (def. 4). [< F *rayonné,* ptp. of *rayonner,* equiv. to *rayon* (see RAYON) + *-er* inf. suffix]

Ray·town (rā′toun′), *n.* a city in W Missouri, near Kansas City. 17,083 (1960).

Ray·ville (rā′vil), *n.* a town in NE Louisiana. 4052 (1960).

raze (rāz), *v.t.,* **razed, raz·ing.** to tear down; demolish; level to the ground. Also, **rase.** [ME *rase(n)* < MF *ras(er)* < *VL *rāsāre,* L *rās(us)* scraped, ptp. of *rādere*] —**raz′er,** *n.*
—**Syn.** See **destroy.**

ra·zee (ra zē′), *n., v.,* **-zeed, -zee·ing.** —*n.* **1.** a ship, esp. a warship, reduced in height by the removal of the upper deck. —*v.t.* **2.** to cut down (a ship) by removing the upper deck. [< F (*vaisseau*) *rasé* razed (ship), ptp. of *raser* to RAZE]

razee′ plane′, *Carpentry.* a plane having a wooden body cut down at the rear to permit the handle to be set low.

ra·zor (rā′zər), *n.* **1.** a sharp-edged instrument used esp. for shaving the face or trimming the hair. **2.** an electrically powered instrument used for the same purpose. —*v.t.* **3.** to shave, cut, or remove with or as if with a razor. **4. on the razor's edge,** in a difficult or precarious position. [ME *rasour* < OF *rasor,* equiv. to *ras(er)* (to) RAZE + *-or* OR[2]] —**ra′zor·less,** *adj.*

ra·zor·back (rā′zər bak′), *n.* **1.** a finback or rorqual. **2.** a wild or semiwild hog with a ridgelike back, common in the southern U.S. **3.** a sharp narrow ridge or range of hills. [RAZOR + BACK[1]]

ra′zor-billed auk′ (rā′zər bild′), a black and white auk, *Alca torda,* of the American and European coasts of the northern North Atlantic, having a compressed black bill encircled by a white band. Also called **ra′zor·bill′.** See illus. under **auk.**

ra′zor clam′, any bivalve mollusk of the family *Solenidae,* esp. of the genus *Ensis,* as *E. directus* (**Atlan′tic ra′zor clam′**), having a long, rectangular, slightly curved shell. Also called **jackknife clam.**

ra·zor·fish (rā′zər fish′), *n., pl.* (*esp. collectively*) **-fish,** (*esp. referring to two or more kinds or species*) **-fish·es.** any of several wrasses of the genus *Xyrichthys,* having a compressed, sharp-edged head, as *X. psittacus* (**pearly razorfish**), found in the West Indies and the Mediterranean Sea. [RAZOR + FISH]

razz (raz), *Slang.* —*v.t.* **1.** to deride; make fun of; tease. —*n.* **2.** raspberry (def. 4). [short for RASPBERRY]

raz·zi·a (raz′ē ə), *n.* a plundering raid. [< F < Ar (Algerian) *ghāzya* military raid (< Ar *ghazwa*)]

raz·zle-daz·zle (raz′əl daz′əl), *n.* *Informal.* **1.** confusion, commotion, or riotous gaiety. **2.** *Chiefly Football.* deceptive action typically consisting of a series of complex maneuvers, as a double reverse or hand-off, usually executed in a flashy manner: *a team relying more on power and speed than razzle-dazzle.* **3.** showy and diverting but often meretricious activity: *The show has plenty of razzle-dazzle but not much talent.* [rhyming compound based on DAZZLE]

razz·ma·tazz (raz′mə taz′), *n.* *Informal.* razzle-dazzle (def. 3). [by alter.]

Rb, *Chem.* rubidium.

R.B.I., *Baseball.* run batted in; runs batted in. Also, **RBI, rbi, r.b.i.**

R.C., 1. Red Cross. **2.** Reserve Corps. **3.** Roman Catholic. Also, **RC**

R.C.A.F., Royal Canadian Air Force. Also, **RCAF**

R.C.Ch., Roman Catholic Church.

rcd., received.

R.C.M.P., Royal Canadian Mounted Police.

r-col·or (är′kul′ər), *n.* *Phonet.* a particular phonetic quality resulting from a retroflex articulation. Also called **r-quality.**

r-col·ored (är′kul′ərd), *adj.* *Phonet.* pronounced with an articulation, usually retroflex, that produces the quality of an *r*-sound.

R.C.P., Royal College of Physicians.

rcpt., receipt.

R.C.S., Royal College of Surgeons.

Rct, 1. receipt. **2.** *Mil.* recruit.

rcvr, receiver.

Rd, *Chem. Obs.* radium.

rd, rod; rods.

Rd., Road.

rd., 1. rendered. **2.** road. **3.** rod; rods. **4.** round.

R/D, *Banking.* refer to drawer.

R.D., Rural Delivery.

RdAc, *Chem.* radioactinium.

RD&E, research, development, and engineering.

RDB, *Mil.* Research and Development Board.

RDF, See **radio direction finder.**

r-drop·ping (är′drop′iŋ), *adj.* *Phonet.* (of certain pronunciations of English) characterized by the absence of the sound *r* in postvocalic position in the same syllable, as often encountered in speech identified with the southern and eastern United States and with most of England; r-less.

RDT&E, research, development, testing, and engineering.

RDX, a white, crystalline, water-insoluble, powerful high explosive, $C_3H_6N_6O_6$, used chiefly in bombs and shells. Also called **cyclonite, cyclotrimethylenetrinitramine.**

Re (rā), *n. Egyptian Religion.* Ra.

Re, *Chem.* rhenium.

re[1] (rā, rē), *n. Music.* **1.** the syllable used for the second tone of a diatonic scale. **2.** (in the fixed system of solmization) the tone D. Cf. **sol-fa** (def. 1). [see GAMUT]

re[2] (rē), *prep. Chiefly Law and Com.* in the case of; with reference to; in re. [< L *rē* (in) the matter, affair, thing (abl. of *rēs*)]

're (ər), contraction of *are: How're you? Where're you going?*

re-, a prefix, occurring originally in loan words from Latin, used with the meaning "again" or "again and again" to indicate repetition, or with the meaning "back" or "backward" to indicate withdrawal or backward motion: *revert; regenerate; refurbish; retrace; retype.* Also, **red-.** [ME < L *re-, red-*]

Re., rupee. Also, **re.**

R.E., 1. Reformed Episcopal. **2.** Right Excellent.

r.e., *Football.* right end.

REA, Rural Electrification Administration. Also, **R.E.A.**

reach (rēch), *v.t.* **1.** to get to or get as far as in moving, going, traveling, etc.: *The boat reached the shore.* **2.** to come to or arrive at in some course of progress, action, etc.: *His letter reached me.* **3.** to succeed in touching or seizing with an outstretched hand, a pole, etc.: *to reach a book on a high shelf.* **4.** to stretch or hold out; extend: *reaching out his hand in greeting.* **5.** to stretch or extend so as to touch or meet: *The bookcase reaches the ceiling.* **6.** to establish communication with: *I called but couldn't reach you.* **7.** to amount to, as in the sum or total: *The cost will reach millions.* **8.** to penetrate to: *distant stars the eye cannot reach.* **9.** to succeed in striking or hitting, as with a weapon or missile: *The artillery fire reached the shore.* **10.** to succeed in influencing, impressing, interesting, convincing, etc.: *advertising used as a means of reaching an audience.* —*v.i.* **11.** to make a stretch, as with the hand or arm. **12.** to become outstretched, as the hand or arm. **13.** to make a movement or effort as if to touch or seize something: *to reach for a weapon.* **14.** to extend in operation or effect: *power that reaches throughout the land.* **15.** to stretch in space; extend in direction, length, distance, etc.: *a coat reaching to the knee; a tower reaching to the skies.* **16.** to extend or continue in time. **17.** to get or come to a specified place, person, condition, etc. (often fol. by *to*). **18.** to amount (often fol. by *to*): *sums reaching to a considerable total.* **19.** to penetrate: *Fields of brightly colored flowers stretched out as far as the eye could reach.* **20.** *Naut.* **a.** to sail on a reach. **b.** to sail with the wind forward of the beam but so as not to require sailing close-hauled. —*n.* **21.** act or instance of reaching: *to make a reach for a gun.* **22.** the extent or distance of reaching: *within reach of his voice.* **23.** range of effective action, power, or capacity. **24.** a continuous stretch or extent of something: *a reach of woodland.* **25.** Also called **pound.** a level portion of a canal, between locks. **26.** *Naut.* a point of sailing in which the wind is within a few points of the beam, either forward of the beam **(close reach),** directly abeam **(beam reach),** or abaft the beam **(broad reach).** **27.** the pole connecting the rear axle of a wagon to the transverse bar or bolster over the front axle supporting the wagon bed. **28.** a straight portion of a river between two bends. [ME *reche,* OE *rǣcan;* c. G *reichen,* D *reiken*] —**reach′a·ble,** *adj.* —**reach′er,** *n.*
—**Syn. 1.** attain. **23.** area, sphere, scope.

reach′ boat′, a small, double-ended fishing boat used along the Maine coast and moved by one or two spritsails or by rowing.

reach′ing fore′sail, a large triangular sail set on the forestay of a racing yacht and overlapping the mainsail: similar to a genoa but set on a different stay. Also called **genoa foresail.**

reach′ing jib′, *Naut.* genoa.

reach·me·down (rēch′mē doun′), *n., adj. Brit.* hand-me-down.

reach′ rod′, a rod for operating a remote piece of machinery, as a valve.

re-act (rē akt′), *v.t.* to act or perform again. [RE- + ACT]

re·act (rē akt′), *v.i.* **1.** to act in return on an agent or influence; act reciprocally upon each other, as two things: *How did the audience react to his remarks?* **2.** to act in a reverse direction or manner. **3.** to act in opposition, as against some force. **4.** to respond to a stimulus in a particular manner: *reacting to a shock by jumping.* [RE- + ACT, prob. modeled on L *reagere*]

re·ac·tance (rē ak′təns), *n.* **1.** *Elect.* the opposition of inductance and capacitance to alternating current, equal to the product of the sine of the angular phase difference between current and voltage and the ratio of the effective voltage to the effective current. *Symbol:* X Cf. **capacitive reactance, inductive reactance. 2.** *Acoustics.* See **acoustic reactance.** [REACT + -ANCE]

re·ac·tant (rē ak′tənt), *n.* **1.** one who or that which reacts. **2.** *Chem.* any substance that undergoes a chemical change in a given reaction. [REACT + -ANT]

re·ac·tion (rē ak′shən), *n.* **1.** a reverse movement or tendency; an action in a reverse direction or manner. **2.** movement in the direction of political conservatism or extreme rightism. **3.** action in response to some influence, event, etc.: *the nation's reaction to the President's speech.* **4.** *Physiol.* action in response to a stimulus, as of the system or of a nerve, muscle, etc. **5.** *Med.* **a.** the action caused by the resistance to another action. **b.** a return to the opposite physical condition, as after shock, exhaustion, or chill. **6.** *Bacteriol., Immunol.* the specific cellular effect produced by a foreign matter, as in testing for allergies. **7.** *Chem.* the reciprocal action of chemical agents upon each other; chemical change. **8.** Also called **nuclear reaction.** a process in which a nucleus that is bombarded by a photon, particle, or other nucleus, produces a nucleon, alpha particle, or the like, and a nucleus having approximately the same atomic weight as the original nucleus. **9.** *Mech.* the instantaneous response of a system to an applied force, manifested as the exertion of a force equal in magnitude but opposite in direction to the applied force. **10.** *Com.* a decline in the market after an advance in prices. [RE- + ACTION, modeled on *react*] —**re·ac′tion·al,** *adj.* —**re·ac′tion·al·ly,** *adv.*

re·ac·tion·ar·y (rē ak′shə ner′ē), *adj., n., pl.* **-ar·ies.** —*adj.* **1.** of, pertaining to, marked by, or favoring reaction, as in politics. —*n.* **2.** a person who favors or inclines to reaction. Also, **re·ac′tion·ist.** [REACTION + -ARY; cf. F *réactionnaire*] —**re·ac′tion·ism, re·ac′tion·ar′y·ism, re·ac′tion·ar·ism,** *n.*
—**Syn. 1, 2.** ultra-conservative. —**Ant. 1, 2.** radical.

reac′tion en′gine, *Aeron., Rocketry.* any engine which produces power as a reaction to the momentum given by substances ejected from it, as a rocket or jet engine. Also called **reac′tion mo′tor.**

reac′tion forma′tion, *Psychoanal.* a behavioral tendency developed in direct opposition to a repressed impulse.

reac′tion time′, *Psychol.* the interval between stimulation and response.

reac′tion tur′bine, a turbine driven by the reactive force of a fluid passing through the rotor blades. Cf. **impulse turbine.**

re·ac·ti·vate (rē ak′tə vāt′), *v.,* **-vat·ed, -vat·ing.** —*v.t.* **1.** to render active again. —*v.i.* **2.** to be active again. [RE- + ACTIVATE] —**re·ac′ti·va′tion,** *n.*

re·ac·tive (rē ak′tiv), *adj.* **1.** tending to react. **2.** pertaining to or characterized by reaction. **3.** *Elect.* pertaining to or characterized by reactance. [REACT + -IVE] —**re·ac′tive·ly,** *adv.* —**re′ac·tiv′i·ty, re·ac′tive·ness,** *n.*

re·ac·tor (rē ak′tər), *n.* **1.** a substance or person undergoing a reaction. **2.** *Elect.* a device whose primary purpose is to introduce reactance into a circuit. **3.** *Immunol., Vet. Med.* a patient or animal that reacts positively towards a foreign material. **4.** Also called **atomic pile, barocyclonometer, chain reactor, nuclear reactor, pile.** *Physics.* An apparatus in which a nuclear-fission chain reaction can be initiated, sustained, and controlled, for generating heat or producing useful radiation. **5.** *Chem.* (esp. in industry) a large container, as a vat, for processes in which the substances involved undergo a chemical reaction. [REACT + -OR[2]]

read[1] (rēd), *v.,* **read** (red), **read·ing** (rē′ding). —*v.t.* **1.** to peruse and apprehend the meaning of (something written, printed, etc.): *to read a book.* **2.** to utter aloud or render in speech (something written, printed, etc.): *reading a story to his children.* **3.** to have such knowledge of (a language) as to be able to understand things written in it: *to be able to read French.* **4.** to apprehend the meaning of (signs, characters, etc.) otherwise than with the eyes, as by means of the fingers: *to read Braille.* **5.** to make out the significance of by scrutiny or observation: *to read the dark and cloudy sky as the threat of a storm.* **6.** to foresee, foretell, or predict: *to read a person's fortune in tea leaves.* **7.** to make out the character, motivations, desires, etc., of (a person or persons), as by the interpretation of outward signs. **8.** to infer (something not expressed or directly indicated) from what is read or considered (usually fol. by *into*): *He read an underlying sarcasm into her letter.* **9.** to adopt or give as a reading in a particular passage: *For "one thousand" another version reads "ten thousand."* **10.** to register or indicate, as a thermometer, clock, etc. **11.** (in an electronic computer) **a.** to obtain (information) esp. from external units, as punch cards. **b.** to read (data) in or out. **12.** *Chiefly Brit.* to study, as by perusing books: *to read law.* **13.** to learn by or as if by perusal: *to read a person's thoughts.* **14.** to bring, put, etc., by reading: *to read oneself to sleep.* **15.** to give one (a lecture or lesson) by way of admonition or rebuke. **16.** to discover or explain the meaning of (a riddle, dream, etc.). —*v.i.* **17.** to read or peruse written or printed matter. **18.** to utter aloud or render in speech written or printed words that one is perusing: *to read to a person.* **19.** to give a public reading or recital. **20.** to inspect and apprehend the meaning of written or other signs or characters. **21.** to occupy oneself seriously with reading or study. **22.** to obtain knowledge or learn of something by reading. **23.** to admit of being read, esp. properly or well. **24.** to have a certain wording. **25.** to admit of being interpreted: *a rule that reads two different ways.* **26.** (of an electronic computer) to read data. **27. read in,** to introduce information into a computer. **28. read out, a.** to oust (a member of a political party or other group) by a public announcement of dismissal: *He was read out of the association because of alleged subversive activities.* **b.** to retrieve information from a computer. [ME *rede(n),* OE *rǣdan* to counsel, read; c. D *raden,* G *raten,* OIcel *rāutha;* akin to Skt *rādhnōti* makes right]

read[2] (red), *adj.* having knowledge gained by reading (usually used in combination): *a well-read person.* [ptp. of READ[1]]

Read (rēd), *n.* **1. George,** 1733–98, American political leader, pres. Continental Congress 1777–78. **2. Sir Herbert,** 1893–1968, English critic and poet. **3.** Also, **Reade.** a boy's given name.

read·a·bil·i·ty (rē′də bil′i tē), *n.* **1.** Also, **read′a·ble·ness.** the state or quality of being readable. **2.** *Typography.* the property of type that affects the ease with which printed matter can be read for a sustained period. Cf. **legibility** (def. 2). [READABLE + -ITY]

read·a·ble (rē′də bəl), *adj.* **1.** easy or interesting to read. **2.** capable of being read; legible: *readable handwriting.* [READ[1] + -ABLE] —**read′a·bly,** *adv.*

Reade (rēd), *n.* **Charles,** 1814–84, English novelist.

read·er (rē′dər), *n.* **1.** a person who reads. **2.** a schoolbook for instruction and practice in reading: *a second-grade reader.* **3.** a person employed to read and evaluate manuscripts offered for publication. **4.** a person who reads or recites before an audience; elocutionist. **5.** a person authorized to read the lessons, Bible, etc., in a church service. **6.** a lecturer or instructor, esp. in some British universities: *appointed reader in English history.* **7.** an assistant to a professor, who grades examinations, papers, etc. **8.** a playing card marked on its back so that the suit or denomination of the card can be identified. [ME *reder(e), redar(e),* OE *rǣdere.* See READ[1], -ER[1]]

read·er·ship (rē′dər ship′), *n.* **1.** the people who read or are thought to read a particular book, newspaper, magazine, etc.: *The periodical has a dwindling readership.* **2.** the duty, status, or profession of a reader. **3.** (esp. in British universities) the position of instructor or lecturer. **4.** the state or quality of being a reader: *appealing to a higher level of readership.* [READER + -SHIP]

read·i·ly (red′ə lē), *adv.* **1.** promptly; quickly; easily: *The information is readily available.* **2.** in a ready manner; willingly: *He readily agreed to help us.* [ME *redily.* See READY, -LY]

read·i·ness (red′ē nis), *n.* **1.** the condition of being ready. **2.** ready action or movement; promptness; quickness; ease; facility. **3.** willingness; inclination; cheerful consent: *a readiness to help others.* **4.** a developmental stage at which a child has the capacity to receive instruction at a given level of difficulty or to engage in a particular activity. [ME *redyness(e).* See READY, -NESS]

read·ing (rē′ding), *n.* **1.** the action or practice of one who reads. **2.** *Speech.* the oral interpretation of written language. **3.** the interpretation given in the performance of a dramatic part, musical composition, etc.: *an interesting reading of the Beethoven 5th.* **4.** the extent to which one has read; literary knowledge: *a man of wide reading.* **5.** matter read or for reading: *a novel that makes good reading.* **6.** the form or version of a given passage in a particular text: *the various readings of a line in Shakespeare.* **7.** an interpretation given to anything: *What is your reading of the situation?* **8.** the indication of a graduated instrument: *The thermometer reading is 101.2°.* —*adj.* **9.** pertaining to or used for reading. **10.** given to reading: *the reading public.* [ME *redyng* (n.), OE *rǣdinge.* See READ, -ING[1], -ING[2]]

Read·ing (red′ing), *n.* **1. Rufus Daniel Isaacs, 1st Marquis of,** 1860–1935, Lord Chief Justice of England 1913–21; viceroy of India 1921–26. **2.** a city in and the county seat of Berkshire, in S England. 119,810 (1961). **3.** a city in SE Pennsylvania. 98,177 (1960). **4.** a town in E Massachusetts, near Boston. 19,259 (1960).

read′ing chair′, a chair of the 18th century, designed to be sat on backwards, having a crest rail continued forward on both sides and supporting an adjustable reading stand.

read′ing desk′, 1. a desk for use in reading, esp. by a person standing. **2.** a lectern in a church.

read′ing no′tice, a short advertisement placed at the bottom of a column, as on the front page of a newspaper, and often set in the same print as other matter.

read′ing room′, a room set aside for reading, as in a library or club.

re·ad·just (rē′ə just′), *v.t.* to adjust again or anew; rearrange. [RE- + ADJUST] —**re′ad·just′a·ble,** *adj.* —**re′ad·just′er,** *n.*

re·ad·just·ment (rē′ə just′mənt), *n.* **1.** an act of readjusting or the state of being readjusted. **2.** *Finance.* a rearrangement in the financial structure of a corporation, usually less drastic than a reorganization. [RE-ADJUST + -MENT]

read·y (red′ē), *adj.,* **read·i·er, read·i·est,** *v.,* **read·ied, read·y·ing,** *n., interj.* —*adj.* **1.** completely prepared or in fit condition for immediate action or use: *troops ready for battle; Dinner is ready.* **2.** duly equipped, completed, adjusted, or arranged, as for an occasion or purpose: *The mechanic called to say that the car is ready.* **3.** willing: *ready to forgive.* **4.** prompt or quick in perceiving, comprehending, speaking, writing, etc. **5.** proceeding from or showing such quickness: *a ready reply.* **6.** prompt or quick in action, performance, manifestation, etc.: *a keen mind and ready wit.* **7.** inclined; disposed; apt: *too ready to criticize others.* **8.** in such a condition as to be imminent; likely at any moment: *a tree ready to fall.* **9.** immediately available for use: *ready money.* **10.** pertaining to prompt payment. **11.** present or convenient: *to lie ready to one's hand.* **12. get ready!** (in calling the start of a race) be prepared to start: *Get ready! Get set! Go!* **13. make ready, a.** to bring to a state of readiness or completion; prepare. **b.** *Print.* to ready a press for printing. —*v.t.* **14.** to make ready; prepare. **15. ready about!** *Naut.* prepare to tack! **16. ready up,** *Brit. and Australian Slang.* to swindle. —*n.* **17.** *Informal.* ready money. **18.** condi-

re′a·ban′don, *v.t.*
re′a·bridge′, *v.t.,* **-bridged, -bridg·ing.**
re′ab·sorb′, *v.t.*
re′ab·sorp′tion, *n.*
re′ac·cede′, *v.t.,* **-ced·ed, -ced·ing.**
re′ac·cel′er·ate′, *v.t.,* **-at·ed, -at·ing.**
re·ac′cent, *v.t.*
re′ac·cen′tu·ate′, *v.t.,* **-at·ed, -at·ing.**
re′ac·cept′, *v.t.*
re′ac·cept′ance, *n.*
re′ac·ces′sion, *n.*
re′ac·claim′, *v.t.*
re′ac·cli′mate, *v.,* **-mat·ed, -mat·ing.**
re′ac·cli′ma·ti·za′tion, *n.*
re′ac·cli′ma·tize′, *v.,* **-tized, -tiz·ing.**
re′ac·com′mo·date′, *v.,* **-dat·ed, -dat·ing.**
re′ac·com′pa·ny, *v.t.,* **-nied, -ny·ing.**
re′ac·cred′it, *v.t.*
re′ac·cu′mu·late′, *v.,* **-lat·ed, -lat·ing.**
re′ac·cu′mu·la′tion, *n.*
re′ac·cu·sa′tion, *n.*
re′ac·cuse′, *v.t.,* **-cused, -cus·ing.**
re′ac·cus′tom, *v.t.*
re′a·cid′i·fi·ca′tion, *n.*
re′a·cid′i·fy′, *v.,* **-fied, -fy·ing.**
re′ac·knowl′edge, *v.t.,* **-edged, -edg·ing.**
re′ac·knowl′edg·ment, *n.*
re′ac·quaint′, *v.t.*
re′ac·quaint′ance, *n.*
re′ac·quire′, *v.t.,* **-quired, -quir·ing.**
re′ac·qui·si′tion, *n.*
re′a·dapt′, *v.t.*
re′a·dap′ta·bil′i·ty, *n.*
re′a·dap′ta·ble, *adj.*
re′ad·ap·ta′tion, *n.*
re′a·dap′tive, *adj.;* **-ness,** *n.*
re·add′, *v.t.*
re′ad·di′tion, *n.*
re′ad·dress′, *v.t.,* **-dressed** or **-drest, -dres·sing.**
re′ad·journ′, *v.*
re′ad·journ′ment, *n.*
re′ad·ju′di·cate′, *v.,* **-cat·ed, -cat·ing.**
re′ad·ju′di·ca′tion, *n.*
re′ad·mis′sion, *n.*
re′ad·mit′, *v.,* **-mit·ted, -mit·ting.**
re′ad·mit′tance, *n.*
re′a·dopt′, *v.t.*
re′a·dop′tion, *n.*
re′a·dorn′, *v.t.*
re′a·dorn′ing, *adj.*
re′a·dorn′ment, *n.*
re·ad′ver·tise, *v.,* **-tised, -tis·ing.**
re′ad·ver·tise′ment, *n.*
re·ad′ver·tize′, *v.,* **-tized, -tiz·ing.**
re′ad·vise′, *v.,* **-vised, -vis·ing.**
re·ad′vo·cate′, *v.t.,* **-cat·ed, -cat·ing.**
re′ad·vo·ca′tion, *n.*

CONCISE PRONUNCIATION KEY: *act, āble, dâre, ärt; ebb, ēqual; if, īce; hot, ōver, ôrder, oil, bo͝ok, o͞oze, out; up, ûrge; chief; sing; shoe; thin, that;* zh *as in measure.* ə = *a* as in *alone, e* as in *system, i* as in *easily, o* as in *gallop, u* as in *circus;* ə as in *button* (but′ən), *fire* (fīər), *cradle* (krād′əl). See the full key inside the front cover.

tion or position of being ready for use: *to bring a rifle to the ready.* —*interj.* **19.** (in calling the start of a race) be prepared to start: *Ready! Set! Go!* [ME *redy,* early ME *rǣdig,* equiv. to OE *rǣde* prompt + *-ig* -Y[1]]
—Syn. 1. fitted, fit, set. **3.** agreeable, glad, happy. **4.** alert, acute, sharp, keen, adroit, facile, clever, skillful, nimble, adaptable. **—Ant. 1.** unfit. **3.** unwilling.

read·y-made (red′ē mād′), *adj.* **1.** made in advance for sale to any purchaser, rather than to order: *a ready-made coat.* **2.** made for immediate use. **3.** unoriginal; conventional. —*n.* **4.** a manufactured object exhibited as being aesthetically satisfying. Cf. **found object. 5.** something that is ready-made, esp. a garment.

read·y-mix (red′ē miks′, -miks′), *n.* **1.** a commercial preparation in which the principal ingredients have already been mixed for easy use: *a bride's reliance on ready-mixes.* —*adj.* **2.** Also, **read′y-mixed′.** being a ready-mix; consisting of ingredients that are already mixed: *ready-mix pancakes.*

read′y reck′oner, reckoner (def. 2).

read′y room′, a room in which members of an aircrew await their orders for takeoff.

read·y-to-wear (red′ē tə wâr′), *n.* **1.** clothing made in standard sizes. —*adj.* **2.** pertaining to or dealing in such clothing: *the ready-to-wear business; a ready-to-wear shop.* Cf. **made-to-measure, made-to-order.**

read·y-wit·ted (red′ē wit′id), *adj.* having a quick wit or intelligence. —**read′y-wit′ted·ly,** *adv.* —**read′y-wit′ted·ness,** *n.*

Rea·gan (rā′gən), *n.* **Ronald (Wilson),** born 1911, U.S. motion-picture actor and political leader: governor of California 1967–75; 40th president of the U.S. 1981–89.

re·a·gent (rē ā′jənt), *n. Chem.* a substance which, because of the reactions it causes, is used in analysis and synthesis. [RE- + AGENT, modeled on REACT]

re·al[1] (rē′əl, rēl), *adj.* **1.** true; not merely ostensible, nominal, or apparent: *the real reason for an act.* **2.** existing or occurring as fact; actual rather than imaginary, ideal, or fictitious: *a story taken from real life.* **3.** being an actual thing; having objective existence; not imaginary: *The events you will see in the film are real and not just made up.* **4.** being actually such; not merely so-called: *a real victory.* **5.** genuine; not counterfeit, artificial, or imitation: *a real antique; a real diamond; real silk.* **6.** unfeigned or sincere: *real sympathy; a real friend.* **7.** *Philos.* **a.** existent or pertaining to the existent as opposed to the nonexistent. **b.** actual as opposed to possible or potential. **c.** independent of experience as opposed to phenomenal or apparent. **8.** of or pertaining to real property. **9.** *Optics.* (of an image) formed by the actual convergence of rays, as the image produced in a camera (opposed to *virtual*). **10.** *Math.* **a.** of, pertaining to, or having the value of a real number. **b.** using real numbers: *real analysis; real vector space.* —*adv.* **11.** *Informal.* very: *You did a real nice job painting the house.* —*n.* **12.** See **real number. 13. for real,** *Slang.* in reality; in actuality: *You mean she dyed her hair green for real?* **14. the real, a.** something that actually exists, as a particular quantity. **b.** reality in general. [ME < LL *reāl(is),* equiv. to L *rē(s)* thing + *-ālis* -AL[1]] —**re′al·ness,** *n.*
—Syn. 2. REAL, ACTUAL, TRUE suggest a faithful rendering of facts, whether those existing in nature or those created by human action. REAL applies particularly to facts rooted in nature: *Sunshine and rain are real.* ACTUAL applies to facts as they now are or have become, implying that one may have previously had a different idea of them or that the facts themselves may have been changed by circumstances: *The actual facts of natural science are different today since new elements have been created.* TRUE may be used of that which conforms to either the real or the actual. **5.** authentic.

re·al[2] (rē′əl, rēl; *Sp.* re äl′), *n., pl.* **re·als** (rē′əlz, rēlz), *Sp.* **re·a·les** (re ä′les). **1.** a former silver coin of Spain and Spanish America, the eighth part of a peso. **2.** a former monetary unit of Spain equal to a quarter of a peseta. [< Sp: royal < L *rēgāl(is)* REGAL]

re·al[3] (rā äl′; *Port.* re äl′), *n.* sing. of **reis.**

re′al ax′is (rē′əl, rēl), *Math.* the horizontal axis in an Argand diagram.

re′al estate′ (rē′əl, rēl), **1.** property, esp. in land: *three acres of real estate.* **2.** See **real property.** —**re′al-es·tate′,** *adj.*

re·al·gar (rē al′gər), *n.* arsenic disulfide, As_2S_2, found native as an orange-red mineral and also produced artificially: used in pyrotechnics. Also called **red orpiment.** [< ML *realger* << Ar *rahj al-ghar* powder of the mine or cave]

re·a·li·a (rē ā′lē ə, rā ä′lē ə), *n.pl.* **1.** *Educ.* objects, as coins, tools, etc., used by a teacher to illustrate everyday living. **2.** *Philos.* things that are real. [< LL: real things (neut. pl.); see REAL[1]]

re′al in′come (rē′əl, rēl), the amount of goods and services that money income will buy.

re·al·i·sa·tion (rē′ə li zā′shən), *n. Chiefly Brit.* realization.

re·al·ise (rē′ə līz′), *v.,* **-ised, -is·ing.** *Chiefly Brit.* realize. —**re′al·is′a·ble,** *adj.* —**re′al·is′er,** *n.*

re·al·is·ing (rē′ə lī′zing), *adj. Chiefly Brit.* realizing.

re·al·ism (rē′ə liz′əm), *n.* **1.** interest in or concern for the actual or real, as distinguished from the abstract, speculative, etc. **2.** the tendency to view or represent things as they really are. **3.** *Fine Arts.* **a.** treatment of forms, colors, space, etc., in such a manner as to emphasize their correspondence to actuality or to ordinary visual experience. Cf. **idealism** (def. 4), **naturalism** (def. 2). **b.** (*usually cap.*) a style of painting and sculpture developed about the mid-19th century in which figures and scenes are depicted as they are experienced or might be experienced in everyday life. **4.** *Literature.* **a.** a manner of treating subject matter that presents a careful description of everyday life, usually of the lower and middle classes. **b.** a theory of writing in which the ordinary, familiar, or mundane aspects of life are represented in a straightforward or matter-of-fact manner that is presumed to reflect life as it actually is. Cf. **naturalism** (def. 1b). **5.** *Philos.* **a.** the doctrine that universals have a real objective existence. Cf. **conceptualism, nominalism. b.** the doctrine that objects of sense perception have an existence independent of the act of perception. Cf. **idealism.** [REAL[1] + -ISM; cf. F *réalisme*]

re·al·ist (rē′ə list), *n.* **1.** a person who tends to view or represent things as they really are. **2.** an artist or a writer whose work is characterized by realism. **3.** *Philos.* an adherent of realism. [REAL[1] + -IST; cf. F *réaliste*]

re·al·is·tic (rē′ə lis′tik), *adj.* **1.** interested in, concerned with, or based on what is real or practical: *a realistic estimate of costs; a realistic planner.* **2.** pertaining to, characterized by, or given to the representation in literature or art of things as they really are: *a realistic novel.* **3.** *Philos.* of or pertaining to realists or realism. [REALIST + -IC] —**re′al·is′ti·cal·ly,** *adv.*

re·al·i·ty (rē al′i tē), *n., pl.* **-ties** for 3–6. **1.** the state or quality of being real. **2.** resemblance to what is real. **3.** a real thing or fact. **4.** *Philos.* **a.** something that exists independently of ideas concerning it. **b.** something that exists independently of all other things and from which all other things derive. **5.** something that is real. **6.** something that constitutes a real or actual thing, as distinguished from something that is merely apparent. **7. in reality,** in fact or truth; actually: *brave in appearance, but in reality a coward.* [< ML *reālitāt-* (s. of *reālitās*). See REAL[1], -ITY]

re·al·i·za·tion (rē′ə li zā′shən), *n.* **1.** the making or being made real of something imagined, planned, etc. **2.** the result of such a process: *The new church was the realization of a ten-year dream.* **3.** the act of realizing or the state of being realized. **4.** an instance or result of realizing. **5.** *Music.* **a.** the act of realizing a figured bass. **b.** a printed score of a realized figured bass. [< F *réalisation,* MF, equiv. to *realis(er)* (to) REALIZE + *-ation* -ATION]

re·al·ize (rē′ə līz′), *v.,* **-ized, -iz·ing.** —*v.t.* **1.** to grasp or understand clearly. **2.** to make real; give reality to (a hope, fear, plan, etc.). **3.** to bring vividly to the mind: *She suddenly realized the significance of his remark.* **4.** to convert into cash or money: *to realize securities.* **5.** to obtain as a profit or income for oneself by trade, labor, or investment. **6.** to bring as proceeds, as from a sale: *The goods realized $1000.* **7.** *Music.* to sight-read on a keyboard instrument or write out in notation the full harmony and ornamentation indicated by (a figured bass). —*v.i.* **8.** to convert property or goods into cash or money. [< F *réalise(r),* MF, equiv. to *real* REAL[1] + *-iser* -IZE] —**re′al·iz′a·bil′i·ty,** *n.* —**re′al·iz′a·ble·ness,** *n.* —**re′al·iz′a·ble,** *adj.* —**re′al·iz′a·bly,** *adv.* —**re′al·iz′er,** *n.*
—Syn. 1. conceive, comprehend. **2.** accomplish, effect. **3.** See **imagine. —Ant. 1.** misunderstand.

re·al·iz·ing (rē′ə lī′zing), *adj.* **1.** that realizes. **2.** clear in apprehending or understanding. [REALIZE + -ING[2]] —**re′al·iz′ing·ly,** *adv.*

re′al line′ (rē′əl, rēl), *Math.* the set of all real numbers.

re·al·ly[1] (rē′ə lī′), *v.t., v.i.,* **-lied, -ly·ing.** to ally again or anew. [ME *realy.* See RE-, ALLY]

re·al·ly[2] (rē′ə lē, rē′lē), *adv.* **1.** in reality; actually: *to see things as they really are.* **2.** genuinely or truly: *a really honest man.* **3.** indeed: *Really, this is too much.* [ME; see REAL[1], -LY]

realm (relm), *n.* **1.** a royal domain; kingdom: *the realm of England.* **2.** the region, sphere, or domain within which anything occurs, prevails, or dominates: *the realm of dreams.* **3.** the special province or field of something or someone: *the realm of physics; facts within the realm of political scientists.* [ME *realme, reaume* < OF < *reialme,* deriv. of *reial* < L *rēgāl(is)* REGAL]
—Syn. 1. See **kingdom.**

re′al num′ber (rē′əl, rēl), *Math.* a rational number or the limit of a sequence of rational numbers, as opposed to a complex number. Also called **real.**

re·al·po·li·tik (rē äl′pō′li tēk′), *n.* political realism, esp. policy based on power rather than on ideals. [< G]

re′al pres′ence (rē′əl, rēl), *Theol.* the doctrine that the substance of the body and blood of Christ are present in the Eucharist.

re′al prop′erty (rē′əl, rēl), *Law.* an estate or property consisting of lands and of all appurtenances to lands, as buildings, crops, or mineral rights (distinguished from *personal property*).

re′al time′ (rē′əl, rēl), *Computer Technol.* the actual time elapsed in the performance of a computation by a computer, the result of the computation being required for the continuation of a physical process.

Re·al·tor (rē′əl tər, -tôr′), *n. Trademark.* a person who works in the real estate business and is a member of the National Association of Real Estate Boards, or one of its constituent boards, and abides by its Code of Ethics.

re·al·ty (rē′əl tē), *n.* real property or real estate. [ME *realte.* See REAL[1], -TY[2]]

re′al var′iable (rē′əl, rēl), *Math.* a variable to which only real numbers are assigned as values.

re′al wag′es (rē′əl, rēl), wages estimated not in money but in purchasing power. Cf. **nominal wages.**

ream[1] (rēm), *n.* **1.** a standard quantity of paper, consisting of 20 quires or 500 sheets (formerly 480 sheets), or 516 sheets **(printer's ream** or **perfect ream). 2.** Usually, **reams.** a large quantity: *He has written reams of poetry.* [ME *rem(e)* < MF *reime, rame* < Sp *rezma* < Ar *rizmah* bale]

ream[2] (rēm), *v.t.* **1.** to enlarge to desired size (a previously bored hole) by means of a reamer. **2.** Also, **reem.** *Naut.* to enlarge (the seams of planking) before calking with oakum. [ME *reme,* OE *rēman* to open up (? var. of *rȳman* to widen); see ROOM]

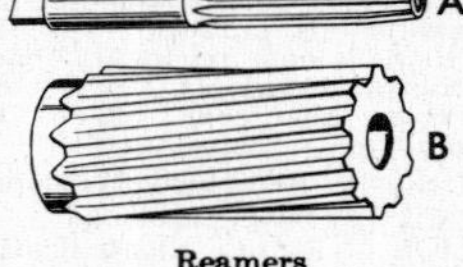

Reamers
A, Parallel hand reamer
B, Shell reamer

ream·er (rē′mər), *n.* **1.** any of various rotary tools, with helical or straight flutes, for finishing or enlarging holes drilled in metal. **2.** *Dentistry.* a drill with a spiral blade, for enlarging root canals. [REAM[2] + -ER[1]]

re·an·i·mate (rē an′ə māt′), *v.t.,* **-mat·ed, -mat·ing. 1.** to restore to life; resuscitate. **2.** to give fresh vigor, spirit, or courage to. **3.** to stimulate to renewed activity. [RE- + ANIMATE] —**re·an′i·ma′tion,** *n.*

reap (rēp), *v.t.* **1.** to cut (wheat, rye, etc.) with a sickle or other implement or a machine, as in harvest. **2.** to gather or take (a crop, harvest, etc.). **3.** to get as a return, recompense, or result: *to reap large profits.* —*v.i.* **4.** to reap a crop, harvest, etc. [ME *rep(en),* OE *repan, riopan;* c. MLG *repen* to ripple (flax); akin to RIPE] —**reap′a·ble,** *adj.*

reap·er (rē′pər), *n.* **1.** a machine for cutting standing grain; reaping machine. **2.** a person who reaps. **3.** Also called **Grim Reaper. the Reaper,** the personification of death as a man holding a scythe. [ME *reper,* OE *ripere.* See REAP, -ER[1]]

reap′ing machine′, any of various machines for reaping grain, often fitted with a device for automatically throwing out bundles of the cut grain.

re·ap·por·tion (rē′ə pōr′shən, -pôr′-), *v.t.* to apportion or distribute anew. [RE- + APPORTION]

re·ap·por·tion·ment (rē′ə pōr′shən mənt, -pôr′-), *n.* **1.** the act of redistributing or changing the apportionment of something. **2.** the redistribution of representation in a legislative body. [REAPPORTION + -MENT]

rear[1] (rēr), *n.* **1.** the back of something, as distinguished from the front: *The porch is at the rear of the house.* **2.** the space or position behind something: *The bus driver asked the passengers to move to the rear.* **3.** the buttocks; rump. **4.** the hindmost portion of an army, fleet, etc. **5. bring up the rear,** to be at the end; follow behind: *The army retreated, and the fleeing civilian population brought up the rear.* —*adj.* **6.** pertaining to or situated at the rear of something: *the rear door of a bus.* [aph. var. of ARREAR]
—Syn. 6. See **back.**

rear[2] (rēr), *v.t.* **1.** to take care of and support up to maturity: *to rear a child.* **2.** to raise by building; erect. **3.** to raise to an upright position: *to rear a ladder.* **4.** to lift or hold up; elevate; raise. —*v.i.* **5.** to rise on the hind legs, as a horse or other animal. **6.** (of a person) to start up in angry excitement, hot resentment, or the like (usually fol. by *up*). **7.** to rise high or tower aloft: *The skyscraper rears high over the neighboring buildings.* [ME *rere(n),* OE *rǣran* to RAISE; c. Goth *-raisjan,* OIcel *reisa*]
—Syn. 1. nurture, raise. **2.** construct. **4.** loft.

Rear Adm., Rear Admiral.

rear′ ad′miral, a naval officer next in rank below a vice-admiral.

rear′ end′, 1. the hindmost part of something. **2.** *Informal.* the buttocks; behind. Also called **tail end.**

rear′ guard′, a part of an army or military force detached from the main body to bring up and guard the rear from surprise attack, esp. in a retreat. [late ME *rier garde* < AF *reregard,* OF *rereguarde*]

re·arm (rē ärm′), *v.t.* **1.** to arm again. **2.** to furnish with new or better weapons: *As soon as the new rifle was in production, the troops were rearmed.* [RE- + ARM[2]] —**re·ar·ma·ment** (rē är′mə mənt), *n.*

rear·most (rēr′mōst′), *adj.* farthest in the rear; last. [REAR[1] + -MOST]

rear′ projec′tion. See **background projection.**

rear′ sight′, the sight nearest the breech of a firearm.

rear·ward (rēr′wərd), *adj., adv.* **1.** Also, **rear′wards.** toward or in the rear. —*n. Archaic.* **2.** a position at the rear: *in the rearward of fashion.* **3.** the rear division of a military unit. [ME *rerewarde* < AF. See REAR[1], -WARD] —**rear′ward·ness,** *n.*

Re′a Sil′via (rē′ə), *Rom. Legend.* See **Rhea Silvia.**

re′af·fect′, *v.t.*
re′af·fil′i·ate′, *v.,* **-at·ed, -at·ing.**
re′af·fil′i·a′tion, *n.*
re′af·firm′, *v.t.*
re′af·fir·ma′tion, *n.*
re′af·front′, *n., v.t.*
re·ag′gre·gate′, *v.,* **-gat·ed, -gat·ing.**
re′ag·gre·ga′tion, *n.*
re·ag′i·tate′, *v.,* **-tat·ed, -tat·ing.**
re′ag·i·ta′tion, *n.*
re·al′ien·ate′, *v.t.,* **-at·ed, -at·ing.**
re·al′ien·a′tion, *n.*
re′a·lign′, *v.*
re′a·lign′ment, *n.*
re·al′le·ga′tion, *n.*
re′al·lege′, *v.t.,* **-leged, -leg·ing.**
re′al·li′ance, *n.*
re·al′lo·cate′, *v.t.,* **-cat·ed, -cat·ing.**
re·al′lo·ca′tion, *n.*
re′al·lot′, *v.t.,* **-lot·ted, -lot·ting.**
re′al·lot′ment, *n.*
re·al′ter, *v.*
re·al′ter·a·ble, *adj.;* **-ble·ness,** *n.;* **-bly,** *adv.*
re·al′ter·a′tion, *n.*
re′a·mal′gam·ate′, *v.,* **-at·ed, -at·ing.**
re′a·mal′gam·a′tion, *n.*
re′a·mass′, *v.t.*
re′a·mass′ment, *n.*
re′a·mend′, *v.*
re′a·mend′ment, *n.*
re′a·nal′y·sis, *n., pl.* **-ses.**
re·an′a·lyz′a·ble, *adj.*
re·an′a·lyze′, *v.t.,* **-lyzed, -lyz·ing.**
re·an′chor, *v.*
re′an·nex′, *v.t.*
re′an·nex·a′tion, *n.*
re·an′no·tate′, *v.,* **-tat·ed, -tat·ing.**
re′an·no·ta′tion, *n.*
re′an·nounce′, *v.t.,* **-nounced, -nounc·ing.**
re′an·nounce′ment, *n.*
re′a·noint′, *v.t.*
re′a·noint′ment, *n.*
re′an·tag′o·nize′, *v.t.,* **-nized, -niz·ing.**
re′a·pol′o·gize′, *v.i.,* **-gized, -giz·ing.**
re′a·pol′o·gy, *n., pl.* **-gies.**
re′ap·peal′, *v.*
re′ap·pear′, *v.i.*
re′ap·pear′ance, *n.*
re′ap·plaud′, *v.*
re′ap·pli′ance, *n.*
re′ap·pli·ca′tion, *n.*
re′ap·ply′, *v.,* **-plied, -ply·ing.**
re′ap·point′, *v.t.*
re′ap·point′ment, *n.*
re′ap·prais′al, *n.*
re′ap·praise′, *v.t.,* **-praised, -prais·ing.**
re′ap·pre·hend′, *v.*
re′ap·pre·hen′sion, *n.*
re′ap·proach′, *v.*
re′ap·proach′a·ble, *adj.*
re′ap·pro′pri·ate′, *v.t.,* **-at·ed, -at·ing.**
re′ap·pro′pri·a′tion, *n.*
re′ap·prov′al, *n.*
re′ap·prove′, *v.,* **-proved, -prov·ing.**
re·ar′bi·trate′, *v.,* **-trat·ed, -trat·ing.**
re′ar·bi·tra′tion, *n.*
re′ar·gue′, *v.,* **-gued, -gu·ing.**
re·ar′gu·ment, *n.*
re′a·rise′, *v.i.,* **-rose, -ris·en, -ris·ing.**
re′a·rous′al, *n.*
re′a·rouse′, *v.,* **-roused, -rous·ing.**
re′ar·range′, *v.,* **-ranged, -rang·ing.**
re′ar·range′a·ble, *adj.*
re′ar·range′ment, *n.*
re′ar·rest′, *v.t., n.*
re′ar·tic′u·late′, *v.,* **-lat·ed, -lat·ing.**
re′ar·tic′u·la′tion, *n.*
re′as·cend′, *v.*
re′as·cent′, *n.*

rea·son (rē′zən), *n.* **1.** a basis or cause, as for some belief, action, fact, event, etc.: *the reason for declaring war.* **2.** a statement in justification or explanation of a belief or action. **3.** the mental powers concerned with forming conclusions, judgments, or inferences. **4.** sound judgment; good sense. **5.** normal or sound powers of mind; sanity. **6.** *Logic.* a premise of an argument. **7.** *Philos.* **a.** the faculty or power of acquiring intellectual knowledge, either by direct understanding of first principles or by argument. **b.** the power of intelligent and dispassionate thought, or of conduct influenced by such thought. **c.** *Kantianism.* the faculty by which the ideas of pure reason are created. **8. bring (someone) to reason,** to induce a change of opinion in (someone) through presentation of arguments; convince: *The mother tried to bring her rebellious daughter to reason.* **9. by reason of,** on account of; because of: *He was consulted regarding such problems by reason of his long experience.* **10. in** or **within reason,** in accord with reason; justifiable; proper: *She tried to keep her demands in reason.* **11. stand to reason,** to be clear, obvious, or logical: *With such an upbringing it stands to reason that the child will be spoiled.* **12. with reason,** with justification; properly: *The government is concerned about the latest crisis, and with reason.* —*v.i.* **13.** to think or argue in a logical manner. **14.** to form conclusions, judgments, or inferences from facts or premises. **15.** to urge reasons which should determine belief or action. —*v.t.* **16.** to think through logically, as a problem (often fol. by *out*). **17.** to conclude or infer (usually fol. by *that*). **18.** to convince, persuade, etc., by reasoning. **19.** to support with reasons. [ME *resoun, reisun* < OF *reisun, reson* < L *ratiōn-* (s. of *ratiō*) RATIO] —**rea′soned·ly,** *adv.* —**rea′son·er,** *n.*
—**Syn. 1.** purpose, end, aim, object, objective. REASON, CAUSE, MOTIVE are terms for a circumstance (or circumstances) which brings about or explains certain results. A REASON is an explanation of a situation or circumstance which made certain results seem possible or appropriate: *The reason for the robbery was the victim's display of his money.* The CAUSE is the way in which the circumstances produce the effect, that is, make a specific action seem necessary or desirable: *The cause was the robber's extreme need of money.* A MOTIVE is the hope, desire, or other force which starts the action (or an action) in an attempt to produce specific results: *The motive was to get money to buy food for his family.* **2.** excuse, rationalization. **3.** understanding, intellect, mind, intelligence. **15.** persuade.
—**Usage.** Careful writers and speakers avoid the redundant expression "the reason is because." Instead, use "the reason is that": *He said that the reason he isn't coming is that (not because) his mother won't let him.*

Rea·son (rē′zən), *n.* a boy's given name.

rea·son·a·ble (rē′zə nə bəl, rēz′nə-), *adj.* **1.** agreeable to reason or sound judgment; logical: *a reasonable choice for chairman.* **2.** not exceeding the limit prescribed by reason; not excessive: *reasonable terms.* **3.** moderate, esp. in price; not expensive: *The coat was reasonable but not cheap.* **4.** endowed with reason. [ME *resonable* < MF *raisonnable* < LL *ratiōnābil(is).* See REASON, -ABLE] —**rea′son·a·ble·ness, rea′son·a·bil′i·ty,** *n.* —**rea′son·a·bly,** *adv.*
—**Syn. 1.** sensible, intelligent, judicious, wise, equitable. REASONABLE, RATIONAL refer to the faculty of reasoning. RATIONAL is the more technical or more abstract term, concerned always with pure reason. It is applied to statements which reflect or satisfy highly logical thinking: *Her conclusions are always of a rational, never an emotional, nature.* REASONABLE has taken on more and more the pragmatic idea of simple common sense: *A reasonable supposition is one which appeals to our common sense.* **2.** equitable, fair, just.

rea·soned (rē′zənd), *adj.* **1.** based on reason: *a carefully reasoned decision.* **2.** containing reasons: *a long, reasoned reply.* [REASON + -ED²]

rea·son·ing (rē′zə niŋ), *n.* **1.** the act or process of a person who reasons. **2.** the process of forming conclusions, judgments, or inferences from facts or premises. **3.** the reasons, arguments, proofs, etc., resulting from this process. [ME *resoninge.* See REASON, -ING²] —**rea′son·ing·ly,** *adv.*

rea·son·less (rē′zən lis), *adj.* **1.** not having any reason or sense: *an utterly reasonless display of anger.* **2.** not having a natural capacity for reason. [ME *resonles.* See REASON, -LESS] —**rea′son·less·ly,** *adv.* —**rea′son·less·ness,** *n.*

re·as·sure (rē′ə sho͝or′), *v.t.,* **-sured, -sur·ing. 1.** to restore to assurance or confidence: *His praise reassured me.* **2.** to assure again. **3.** to reinsure. [RE- + ASSURE] —**re′as·sur′ance,** *n.* —**re·as·sur·ed·ly** (rē′ə sho͝or′id lē), *adv.* —**re′as·sure′ment,** *n.* —**re′as·sur′er,** *n.* —**re′as·sur′ing·ly,** *adv.*
—**Syn. 1.** encourage, hearten, comfort, inspirit.

re·a·ta (rē ä′tə), *n.* riata.

Réaum., Réaumur (thermometer).

Ré·au·mur (rā′ə myo͝or′; *Fr.* RĀ Ō MYR′), *n.* **1. Re·né An·toine Fer·chault de** (RƏ NĀ′ ÄN TWAN′ FER SHŌ′ də), 1683–1757, French physicist and inventor. **2.** a walled plain in the fourth quadrant of the face of the moon: about 30 miles in diameter. —*adj.* **3.** Also, **Re′au·mur′,** noting or pertaining to a temperature scale (**Ré′aumur scale′**) in which 0° represents the ice point and 80° represents the steam point. See illus. under **thermometer.**

reave¹ (rēv), *v.t.,* **reaved** or **reft, reav·ing.** *Archaic.* to take away by or as by force; plunder; rob. [ME *reve(n),* OE *rēafian;* c. G *rauben,* D *rooven* to ROB]

reave² (rēv), *v.t., v.i.,* **reaved** or **reft, reav·ing.** to rend; break; tear. [appar. special use of REAVE¹ (by assoc. with RIVE)]

reb (reb), *n.* *U.S. Informal.* a Confederate soldier. [shortened form of REBEL]

Reb (reb), *n.* *Yiddish.* Mister (used as a title of respect). [lit., rabbi]

Re·ba (rē′bə), *n.* a girl's given name, form of **Rebecca.**

re·bab (ri bäb′), *n.* a Near Eastern fiddle having one to three strings and played with a bow. [< Ar]

re·bar·ba·tive (rē bär′bə tiv), *adj.* causing annoyance, irritation, or aversion; repellent. [< F, fem. of *rébarbatif,* deriv. of *rébarber* to be unattractive, equiv. to *ré-* RE- + *barbe* beard (< L *barba*) + *-atif* -ATIVE]

re·bate¹ (rē′bāt, ri bāt′), *n., v.,* **-bat·ed, -bat·ing.** —*n.* **1.** a return of part of the original payment for some service or merchandise; partial refund. —*v.t.* **2.** to allow as a discount. **3.** to deduct (a certain amount), as from a total. **4.** to return (part of an original payment): *He rebated five dollars to me.* **5.** to blunt (an edged or pointed weapon). **6.** to cover the edge or point of (an edged or pointed weapon) in order to make it incapable of cutting or piercing. —*v.i.* **7.** to allow rebates, esp. as the policy or practice of a company, store, etc. [ME *rebate(n)* < OF *rabat(re)* (to) beat, put down, equiv. to *re-* RE- + *abbatre;* see ABATE] —**re·bat′a·ble, re·bate′a·ble,** *adj.* —**re·bat·er** (rē′bā tər, ri-bā′tər), *n.*

re·bate² (rē′bāt, rab′it), *n., v.,* **-bat·ed, -bat·ing.** rabbet.

re·bat·ed (ri bā′tid), *adj.* *Heraldry.* cut off or abridged in some way, as a cross potent formed as a swastika. [REBATE¹ + -ED²]

re·bate·ment (rē bāt′mənt), *n.* abatement. [REBATE¹ + -MENT]

re·ba·to (rə bä′tō), *n., pl.* **-tos.** rabato.

reb·be (reb′ə), *n.* *Yiddish.* **1.** a teacher in a Jewish school. **2.** a title of respect for the leader of a Hasidic group.

re·bec (rē′bek), *n.* a Renaissance fiddle with a pear-shaped body tapering into a neck that ends in a sickle-shaped or scroll-shaped pegbox. Also, **re′beck.** [MF; r. ME *ribibe* < OF *rebebe* << Ar *rebāb* REBAB]

Rebec

Re·bec·ca (ri bek′ə), *n.* **1.** *Douay Bible.* Rebekah. **2.** a girl's given name.

Re·bek·ah (ri bek′ə), *n.* **1.** Also, *Douay Bible,* **Re·bec′ca.** the sister of Laban, wife of Isaac, and mother of Esau and Jacob. Gen. 24–27. **2.** a girl's given name.

reb·el (*n., adj.* reb′əl; *v.* ri bel′), *n., adj., v.,* **-belled, -bel·ling.** —*n.* **1.** a person who refuses allegiance to, resists, or rises in arms against the government or ruler of his country. **2.** a person who resists any authority, control, or tradition. —*adj.* **3.** rebellious; defiant. **4.** of or pertaining to rebels. —*v.i.* **5.** to reject, resist, or rise in arms against one's government or ruler. **6.** to resist or rise against some authority, control, or tradition. **7.** to show or feel utter repugnance: *His very soul rebelled at spanking the child.* [ME < OF *rebelle* < L *rebell(is)* renewing a war, equiv. to *re-* RE- + *bellum* war] —**reb′el·like′,** *adj.*
—**Syn. 1.** insurrectionist, mutineer, traitor. **1, 3.** insurgent. **3.** mutinous. **5.** revolt, mutiny.

reb·el·dom (reb′əl dəm), *n.* **1.** a region or territory controlled by rebels. **2.** rebels collectively. **3.** rebellious conduct. [REBEL + -DOM]

re·bel·lion (ri bel′yən), *n.* **1.** open, organized, and armed resistance to one's government or ruler. **2.** resistance to or defiance of any authority, control, or tradition. **3.** the act of rebelling. [ME *rebellioun* < OF < L *rebelliōn-* (s. of *rebelliō*), equiv. to *rebell(āre)* (to) REBEL + *-iōn-* -ION]
—**Syn. 1.** mutiny, sedition. See **revolt. 2.** insubordination, disobedience.

re·bel·lious (ri bel′yəs), *adj.* **1.** defying or resisting some established authority, government, or tradition; insubordinate; inclined to rebel. **2.** pertaining to or characteristic of rebels or rebellion. **3.** (of things) resisting treatment; refractory. [ME < ML *rebelliōs(us),* equiv. to L *rebelli(ō)* REBELLION + *-ōsus* -OUS] —**re·bel′lious·ly,** *adv.* —**re·bel′lious·ness,** *n.*
—**Syn. 1.** defiant, insurgent, mutinous, seditious, rebel, refractory, disobedient, contumacious.

re·bid (*v.* rē bid′; *n.* rē′bid′), *v.,* **-bid, -bid·den** or **-bid, -bid·ding,** *n.* *Bridge.* —*v.t.* **1.** to make a second bid in (a suit that one bid previously): *He opened a spade and then rebid spades on the three level.* —*v.i.* **2.** to make a second bid: *He had enough points to open the bidding but not enough to rebid after his partner's pass.* —*n.* **3.** a second bid: *a rebid to keep the auction open.* [RE- + BID]

re·bid·da·ble (rē bid′ə bəl), *adj.* *Bridge.* (of a suit) able to be bid twice, owing to length or strength, without support from one's partner. [REBID + -ABLE]

re·birth (rē bûrth′, rē′bûrth′), *n.* **1.** a new or second birth: *the rebirth of the soul.* **2.** a renewed existence, activity, or growth; renaissance or revival: *the rebirth of conservatism.* [RE- + BIRTH]

reb·o·ant (reb′ō ənt), *adj.* resounding or reverberating loudly. [< L *reboant-* (s. of *reboāns,* prp. of *reboāre*), equiv. to *re-* RE- + *bo(āre)* (to) cry aloud (< Gk *boân*) + *-ant-* -ANT]

re·bop (rē′bop′), *n.* bop¹. [imit.]

re·born (rē bôrn′), *adj.* having undergone rebirth. [RE- + BORN]

re·bo·so (ri bō′sō), *n., pl.* **-sos.** rebozo. Also, **re·bo·sa** (rā bō′sə).

re·bo·te (ri bō′tē), *n.* **1.** the rear wall of a cancha or jai alai court. Cf. **frontis. 2.** a shot in which the ball is played as it comes off this wall. [< Sp: a rebound, equiv. to *re-* RE- + *bote,* cf. *botar* to hurl, throw]

re·bound (*v.* ri bound′; *n.* rē′bound′, ri bound′), *v.i.* **1.** to bound or spring back from force of impact. **2.** *Basketball.* to gain hold of rebounds: *a forward who rebounds well off the offensive board.* —*v.t.* **3.** to cause to bound back; cast back. **4.** *Basketball.* to gain hold of (a rebound): *The guard rebounded the ball in backcourt.* —*n.* **5.** the act of rebounding; recoil. **6.** *Basketball.* **a.** a ball that bounces off the backboard or the rim of the basket. **b.** an instance of gaining hold of such a ball. **7.** *Ice Hockey.* a puck that bounces off the gear or person of a goalkeeper attempting to make a save. **8. on the rebound, a.** after bouncing off the ground, a wall, etc.: *He hit the ball on the rebound.* **b.** after being rejected by another: *She didn't really love him: she married him on the rebound.* [ME *rebound(en)* < MF *rebond(ir),* equiv. to OF *re-* RE- + *bondir* to BOUND²]

re·bound·er (rē′boun′dər), *n.* *Basketball.* a player who excels in gaining hold of rebounds. [REBOUND + -ER¹]

re·bo·zo (ri bō′zō; *Sp.* re bô′thô, -sô), *n., pl.* **-zos** (-zōz; *Sp.* -thôs, -sôs). a long woven scarf, often of fine material, worn over the head and shoulders by Spanish and Mexican women. Also, **reboso, rebosa, riboza.** [< Sp: scarf, shawl, equiv. to *re-* RE- + *bozo,* akin to *boca* mouth]

re·broad·cast (rē brôd′kast′, -käst′), *v.,* **-cast** or **-cast·ed, -cast·ing,** *n.* —*v.t.* **1.** to broadcast again from the same station. **2.** to relay (a radio program, speech, etc.) received from another station. —*n.* **3.** a program that is rebroadcast. [RE- + BROADCAST]

re·buff (*n.* ri buf′, rē′buf; *v.* ri buf′), *n.* **1.** a blunt or abrupt rejection, as of a person making advances. **2.** a peremptory refusal of a request, offer, etc.; snub. **3.** a check to action or progress. —*v.t.* **4.** to give a rebuff to; check; repel; refuse; drive away. [< MF *rebuff(er)* < It *ribuffare* to disturb, reprimand, deriv. of *ribuffo* (n.), equiv. to *ri-* RE- + *buffo* puff] —**re·buff′a·ble,** *adj.* —**re·buff′a·bly,** *adv.*

re·build (rē bild′), *v.,* **-built** or (*Archaic*) **-build·ed; -build·ing.** —*v.t.* **1.** to repair, esp. to dismantle and reassemble with new parts: *to rebuild an old car.* **2.** to replace, restrengthen, or reinforce: *to rebuild an army.* **3.** to revise, reshape, or reorganize: *to rebuild a shattered career.* —*v.i.* **4.** to build again or afresh: *With the insurance money we can rebuild.* [RE- + BUILD] —**re·build′er,** *n.*

re·buke (ri byo͞ok′), *v.,* **-buked, -buk·ing,** *n.* —*v.t.* **1.** to express sharp, stern disapproval of; reprove; reprimand. —*n.* **2.** sharp, stern disapproval; reproof; reprimand. [ME *rebuke(n)* < AF *rebuk(er)* (OF *rebuchier*) (to) beat back, equiv. to *re-* RE- + *bucher* to beat, strike < Gmc] —**re·buk′a·ble,** *adj.* —**re·buk′er,** *n.* —**re·buk′ing·ly,** *adv.*
—**Syn. 1.** censure, upbraid, chide, admonish. See **reproach. 2.** reproach, remonstration, censure.

re·bus (rē′bəs), *n., pl.* **-bus·es. 1.** a representation of a word or phrase by pictures, symbols, etc., that suggest that word or phrase or its syllables: *Two gates and a head is a rebus for Gateshead.* **2.** a piece of writing containing many such representations. [< L *rēbus* by things (abl. pl. of *rēs;* from phrase *nōn verbīs sed rēbus* not by words but by things)]

re·bus′ sic stan·ti·bus (rē′bəs sik stan′tə bəs), *Internat. Law.* (of the duration of the binding force treaty) for as long as the relevant facts and circumstances remain basically the same. [< L: with things remaining thus]

re·but (ri but′), *v.,* **-but·ted, -but·ting.** —*v.t.* **1.** to refute by evidence or argument. **2.** to oppose by contrary proof. —*v.i.* **3.** to provide some evidence or argument that refutes or opposes. [ME *reb(o)ut(en)* < OF *rebout(er),* equiv. to *re-* RE- + *bo(u)ter* to BUTT³] —**re·but′ta·ble,** *adj.*
—**Syn. 1.** disprove, confute.

re·but·tal (ri but′əl), *n.* an act of rebutting, as in a debate. [REBUT + -AL²]

re·but·ter¹ (ri but′ər), *n.* a person who rebuts. [REBUT + -ER¹]

re·but·ter² (ri but′ər), *n.* *Law.* a defendant's answer to a plaintiff's surrejoinder. [< AF *rebuter* REBUT (n. use of inf.)]

rec., 1. receipt. **2.** (in prescriptions) fresh. [< L *recens*] **3.** recipe. **4.** record. **5.** recorder.

re·cal·ci·trant (ri kal′si trənt), *adj.* **1.** resisting authority or control; not obedient or compliant; refractory. **2.** hard to deal with, manage, or operate. —*n.* **3.** a recalcitrant person. [< L *recalcitrant-* (s. of *recalcitrāns,* prp. of *recalcitrāre*), equiv. to *re-* RE- + *calcitr(āre)* (to) strike with the heels, kick (*calc-,* s. of *calx* heel + *-i-* -I- + *-t-* freq. suffix) + *-ant-* -ANT] —**re·cal′ci·trance, re·cal′ci·tran·cy,** *n.*
—**Syn. 1.** resistant, rebellious, opposed.

re·cal·ci·trate (ri kal′si trāt′), *v.i.,* **-trat·ed, -trat·ing.** to resist or oppose; show strong objection or

re′as·sem′ble, *v.,* **-bled, -bling.**
re′as·sem′bly, *n., pl.* **-blies.**
re′as·sent′, *v.i.*
re′as·sert′, *v.t.*
re′as·ser′tion, *n.*
re′as·sess′, *v.t.*
re′as·sess′ment, *n.*
re′as·sign′, *v.t.*
re′as·sig·na′tion, *n.*
re′as·sign′ment, *n.*
re′as·sim′i·late′, *v.,* **-lat·ed, -lat·ing.**
re′as·sim′i·la′tion, *n.*
re′as·sist′, *v.t.*
re′as·sist′ance, *n.*
re′as·so′ci·ate′, *v.,* **-at·ed, -at·ing.**
re′as·so′ci·a′tion, *n.*
re′as·sort′, *v.*
re′as·sort′ment, *n.*
re′as·sume′, *v.t.,* **-sumed, -sum·ing.**
re′as·sump′tion, *n.*
re′at·tach′, *v.*
re′at·tach′a·ble, *adj.*
re′at·tach′ment, *n.*
re′at·tack′, *v.*
re′at·tain′, *v.t.*
re′at·tain′ment, *n.*
re′at·tempt′, *v.t.*
re′at·test′, *v.t.*
re′at·tire′, *v.t.,* **-tired, -tir·ing.**
re′at·tract′, *v.t.*
re′at·trac′tion, *n.*
re·au′dit, *n., v.*
re′au·di′tion, *n.*
re′au·then′ti·cate′, *v.t.,* **-cat·ed, -cat·ing.**
re′au·then′ti·ca′tion, *n.*
re′au·thor·i·za′tion, *n.*
re·au′thor·ize′, *v.t.,* **-ized, -iz·ing.**
re′a·vow′, *v.t.*
re′a·vow′al, *n.*
re′a·wake′, *v.,* **-woke** or **-waked, wak·ing.**
re′a·wak′en, *v.*
re′a·wak′en·ing, *n.*
re·bait′, *v.t.*
re·bake′, *v.t.,* **-baked, -bak·ing.**
re·bal′ance, *v.,* **-anced, -anc·ing.**
re·bale′, *v.t.,* **-baled, -bal·ing.**
re·bal′lot, *n., v.i.,* **-lot·ed, -lot·ing.**
re·band′age, *v.t.,* **-aged, -ag·ing.**
re·bank′, *v.*
re·bap′tism, *n.*
re·bap·tize′, *v.,* **-tized, -tiz·ing.**
re·bathe′, *v.,* **-bathed, -bath·ing.**
re·bend′, *v.t.,* **-bent, -bend·ing.**
re·bill′, *v.t.*
re·bind′, *v.,* **-bound, -bind·ing.**
re·bleach′, *v.*
re·blend′, *v.,* **-blend·ed** or **-blent, -blend·ing.**
re·blis′ter, *v.*
re·block′, *v.t.*
re·bloom′, *v.i.*
re·blos′som, *v.i.*
re·blown′, *adj.*
re·board′, *v.t.*
re·boil′, *v.*
re·bolt′, *v.*
re·brace′, *v.t.,* **-braced, -brac·ing.**
re·brand′, *v.t.*
re·breed′, *v.,* **-bred, -breed·ing.**
re·brew′, *v.*
re·bright′en, *v.*
re·broad′en, *v.*
re·brush′, *v.t.*
re·buck′le, *v.,* **-led, -ling.**
re·budg′et, *v.t.,* **-et·ed, -et·ing.**
re·bur′i·al, *n.*
re·bur′y, *v.t.,* **-bur·ied, -bur·y·ing.**
re·but′ton, *v.t.*
re·ca′ble, *v.,* **-bled, -bling.**
re·cage′, *v.t.,* **-caged, -cag·ing.**

repugnance. [< L *recalcitrāt(us)* (ptp. of *recalcitrāre;* see RECALCITRANT); see -ANT] —**re·cal′ci·tra′tion,** *n.*

re·cal·cu·late (rē kal′kyə lāt′), *v.t.,* **-lat·ed, -lat·ing.** to calculate again, esp. for the purpose of finding an error or confirming a previous computation. [RE- + CALCULATE] —**re′cal·cu·la′tion,** *n.*

re·ca·lesce (rē′kə les′), *v.i.,* **-lesced, -lesc·ing.** *Metall.* to become hot again (said esp. of cooling iron, which glows with increased brilliancy upon passing certain temperatures). [< L *recalēsc(ere)* (to) become warm again, equiv. to *re-* RE- + *calesc-* grow warm (*cal(ēre)* (to) be warm + *-esc-* inceptive suffix)] —**re′ca·les′cence,** *n.* —**re′ca·les′cent,** *adj.*

re·call (*v.* ri kôl′; *n.* ri kôl′, rē′kôl′), *v.t.* **1.** to bring back from memory; recollect; remember: *Can you recall what she said?* **2.** to call back; summon to return: *The army recalled many former servicemen.* **3.** to bring (one's thoughts, attention, etc.) back to matters previously considered: *He recalled his mind from pleasant daydreams to the dull task at hand.* **4.** *Internat. Law.* to summon back and withdraw the office from (a diplomat). **5.** to revoke or withdraw: *to recall a promise.* **6.** to revive. —*n.* **7.** an act of recalling. **8.** recollection; remembrance. **9.** the act or possibility of revoking something. **10.** the removal or the right of removal of a public official from office by a vote of the people taken upon petition of a specified number of the qualified electors. **11.** a signal made by a vessel to recall one of its boats. **12.** a signal displayed to direct a racing yacht to sail across the starting line again because of a violation of a rule, as for having crossed the line prematurely. [RE- + CALL] —**re·call′a·ble,** *adj.*
—**Syn. 1.** See **remember. 5.** rescind, retract, recant repeal; annul. **7.** memory. **9.** revocation, retraction, repeal, withdrawal, recantation; nullification. —**Ant. 1.** forget.

Re·ca·mier (rā′kə myā′), *n.* a backless day bed of the Directoire and Empire periods, having raised ends of equal height. [after Madame RÉCAMIER]

Ré·ca·mier (rā ka myā′), *n.* **Madame** (*Jeanne Françoise Julie Adélaïde Bernard*), 1777–1849, French social leader in the literary and political circles of Paris.

re·cant (ri kant′), *v.t.* **1.** to withdraw or disavow (a statement, opinion, etc.), esp. formally; retract. —*v.i.* **2.** to withdraw or disavow a statement, opinion, etc., esp. formally. [< L *recant(āre)* (to) sing back, sing again, equiv. to *re-* RE- + *cant-* sing; see CHANT] —**re·can·ta·tion** (rē′kan tā′shən), *n.* —**re·cant′er,** *n.* —**re·cant′ing·ly,** *adv.*
—**Syn. 1.** revoke, recall, rescind, deny.

re·cap[1] (*v.* rē′kap′, rē kap′; *n.* rē′kap′), *v.,* **-capped, -cap·ping,** *n.* —*v.t.* **1.** to recondition (a worn automobile tire) by cementing on a strip of prepared rubber and vulcanizing by subjecting to heat and pressure in a mold. —*n.* **2.** a recapped tire. [RE- + CAP] —**re·cap′pa·ble,** *adj.*

re·cap[2] (rē′kap′), *n., v.,* **-capped, -cap·ping.** —*n.* **1.** a recapitulation. —*v.t.* **2.** to recapitulate. [by shortening]

re·cap·i·tal·i·za·tion (rē kap′i tᵊli zā′shən), *n.* a revision of a corporation's capital structure by an exchange of securities. [RE- + CAPITALIZATION]

re·cap·i·tal·ize (rē kap′i tᵊlīz′), *v.t.,* **-ized, -iz·ing.** to renew or change the capital of. [RE- + CAPITALIZE]

re·ca·pit·u·late (rē′kə pich′ə lāt′), *v.,* **-lated, -lat·ing.** —*v.t.* **1.** to review by a brief summary, as at the end of a speech or discussion; summarize. **2.** *Biol.* (of an organism) to repeat (ancestral evolutionary stages) in its development. **3.** *Music.* to restate (the exposition) in a sonata-form movement. —*v.i.* **4.** to sum up statements or matters. [< LL *recapitulāt(us)* (ptp. of *recapitulāre*), equiv. to *re-* RE- + *capitulātus;* see CAPITULATE]
—**Syn. 1.** See **repeat.**

re·ca·pit·u·la·tion (rē′kə pich′ə lā′shən), *n.* **1.** the act of recapitulating or the state of being recapitulated. **2.** a brief review or summary, as of a speech. **3.** *Biol.* the theory that an organism during its embryonic development passes through stages in which certain ancestral structures are repeated. **4.** *Music.* the modified restatement of the exposition following the development section in a sonata-form movement. [ME *recapitulacioun* < LL *recapitulātiōn-* (s. of *recapitulātiō*), equiv. to *recapitulāt(us)* RECAPITULATE + *-iōn-* -ION] —**re′ca·pit′u·la′tive, re·ca·pit·u·la·to·ry** (rē′kə pich′ə lə tôr′ē, -tōr′ē), *adj.*

re·cap·tion (rē kap′shən), *n.* *Law.* the taking back without violence of one's property or a member of one's family or household unlawfully in the possession or custody of another. [RE- + CAPTION]

re·cap·ture (rē kap′chər), *v.,* **-tured, -tur·ing,** *n.* —*v.t.* **1.** to capture again; recover by capture; retake. **2.** (of a government) to take by recapture. —*n.* **3.** recovery or retaking by capture. **4.** the taking by the government of a fixed part of all earnings in excess of a certain percentage of property value, as in the case of a railroad. **5.** *Internat. Law.* the lawful reacquisition of a former possession. **6.** fact of being recaptured. [RE- + CAPTURE]

re·car·bu·rize (rē kär′byə rīz′), *v.t.,* **-rized, -riz·ing.** *Metall.* to add carbon to (steel), as in an open-hearth furnace, as by adding pig iron. [RE- + CARBURIZE] —**re′car·bu·ri·za′tion,** *n.* —**re·car′bu·riz′er,** *n.*

re·cast (*v.* rē kast′, -käst′; *n.* rē′kast′, -käst′), *v.,* **-cast, -cast·ing,** *n.* —*v.t.* **1.** to cast again or anew. **2.** to form, fashion, or arrange again. **3.** to remodel or reconstruct (a literary work, document, sentence, etc.). **4.** to supply (a theater or opera work) with a new cast. —*n.* **5.** a recasting. **6.** a new form produced by recasting. [RE- + CAST] —**re·cast′er,** *n.*

rec·ce (rek′ē), *n.* (esp. in British military use) reconnaissance: *a pilot who spent three months on recce.* Also, **rec·co** (rek′ō), **rec·cy** (rek′ē). [by shortening]

recd., received. Also, **rec'd.**

re·cede[1] (ri sēd′), *v.i.,* **-ced·ed, -ced·ing. 1.** to go or move away; retreat; go to or toward a more distant point; withdraw. **2.** to become more distant. **3.** (of a color, form, etc., on a flat surface) to move away or be perceived as moving away from an observer, esp. as giving the illusion of space. Cf. **advance** (def. 12). **4.** to slope backward: *a chin that recedes.* **5.** to draw back or withdraw from a conclusion, viewpoint, undertaking, promise, etc. [< L *recēd(ere)* (to) go, fall back, equiv. to *re-* RE- + *cēd-* go; see CEDE]
—**Syn. 5.** retire, retreat.

re·cede[2] (rē sēd′), *v.t.,* **-ced·ed, -ced·ing.** to cede back; yield or grant to a former possessor. [RE- + CEDE]

re·ceipt (ri sēt′), *n.* **1.** a written acknowledgment of having received a specified amount of money, goods, etc. **2. receipts,** the amount or quantity received. **3.** the act of receiving or the state of being received. **4.** something that is received. **5.** a recipe. —*v.t.* **6.** to acknowledge in writing the payment of (a bill). **7.** to give a receipt for (money, goods, etc.). —*v.i.* **8.** to give a receipt, as for money or goods. [ME *receite* < AF (OF *recoite*) < L *recepta,* fem. ptp. of *recipere* to RECEIVE]

re·ceipt·or (ri sē′tər), *n.* **1.** a person who receipts. **2.** *Law.* a person to whom attached property is delivered for safekeeping in return for a bond to produce it when the litigation ends. [RECEIPT + -OR[2]]

re·ceiv·a·ble (ri sē′və bəl), *adj.* **1.** fit for acceptance; acceptable. **2.** awaiting receipt of payment: *accounts receivable.* **3.** capable of being received. —*n.* **4. receivables,** business assets in the form of obligations due from others. [RECEIVE + -ABLE; r. ME *rescevable* < AF *receivable* (OF *recevable*)] —**re·ceiv′a·bil′i·ty, re·ceiv′a·ble·ness,** *n.*

re·ceive (ri sēv′), *v.,* **-ceived, -ceiv·ing.** —*v.t.* **1.** to take into one's possession (something offered or delivered): *to receive many gifts.* **2.** to have (something) bestowed, conferred, etc.: *to receive an honorary degree.* **3.** to have delivered or brought to one: *to receive a letter.* **4.** to get or be informed of: *to receive instructions; to receive news.* **5.** to be burdened with; sustain: *to receive a heavy load.* **6.** to hold or contain. **7.** to take into the mind; apprehend mentally: *to receive an idea.* **8.** to accept from another by hearing or listening: *A priest received his confession.* **9.** to meet with; experience: *to receive attention.* **10.** to suffer or undergo: *to receive an insult.* **11.** to have inflicted upon one: *to receive a broken arm.* **12.** to be at home to (visitors): *They received their neighbors on Sunday.* **13.** to greet or welcome (guests, visitors, etc.) upon arriving: *They received us at the front door.* **14.** to admit (a person) to a place: *The butler received him and asked him to wait in the drawing room.* **15.** to admit into an organization, membership, etc.: *to receive someone into the group.* **16.** to accept as authoritative, valid, true, or approved: *a principle universally received.* —*v.i.* **17.** to receive something. **18.** to receive visitors or guests. **19.** *Radio.* to convert incoming electromagnetic waves into the original signal, as sound waves or light on a kinescope screen. **20.** to receive the Eucharist: *He receives every Sunday.* [ME *receve* < ONF *receiv(re)* < L *recipere,* equiv. to *re-* RE- + *-cipere,* comb. form of *capere* to take] —**Ant. 1.** give.

Received′ Stand′ard, the form of educated English spoken generally in southern England and specifically in the English public schools and at Oxford and Cambridge universities.

re·ceiv·er (ri sē′vər), *n.* **1.** one who or that which receives. **2.** a device or apparatus that receives electrical signals, waves, or the like, and renders them perceptible to the senses, as the part of a telephone held to the ear, a radio receiving set, or a television receiving set. **3.** *Law.* a person appointed by a court to take charge of a business or property of others, pending litigation. **4.** *Com.* a person appointed to receive money due. **5.** a person who knowingly receives stolen goods for an illegal purpose; a dealer in stolen merchandise. **6.** a device or apparatus for receiving or holding something; receptacle; container. **7.** (in a firearm) the basic metal unit housing the action and to which the barrel and other components are attached. **8.** *Chem.* a vessel for collecting and containing a distillate. See illus. under **alembic. 9.** *Football.* a player on the offensive team who catches, is eligible to catch, or is noted for his ability to catch a forward pass: *Jones was the receiver of the first pass thrown. He sent all his receivers downfield.* **10.** *Baseball.* the catcher. [RECEIVE + -ER[1]; r. ME *receyvere* < AF *receivour, recevour,* c. OF *recevere*]

re·ceiv·er·ship (ri sē′vər ship′), *n.* *Law.* **1.** the condition of being in the hands of a receiver. **2.** the position or function of being a receiver in charge of administering the property of others. [RECEIVER + -SHIP]

receiv′ing blan′ket, a small blanket, usually of cotton, for wrapping an infant, esp. following a bath.

receiv′ing line′, a row formed by the hosts, guests of honor, or the like, for receiving guests formally at a ball, reception, etc.

receiv′ing pal′let, *Horol.* the pallet first touched by a tooth of the escape wheel. Also called **entrance pallet.** Cf. **discharging pallet.**

receiv′ing set′, *Radio.* a mechanism for the reception of electromagnetic waves.

re·cen·sion (ri sen′shən), *n.* **1.** an editorial revision of a literary work, esp. on the basis of critical examination of the text and the sources used. **2.** a version of a text resulting from such revision. [< L *recensiōn-* (s. of *recensiō*) a reviewing, equiv. to *recens(ēre)* (*re-* RE- + *censēre* to estimate, assess) + *-iōn-* -ION] —**re·cen′sion·ist,** *n.*

re·cent (rē′sənt), *adj.* **1.** of late occurrence, appearance, or origin; lately happening, done, made, etc.: *recent events; a recent trip.* **2.** not long past: *in recent years.* **3.** of or belonging to a time not long past. **4.** (*cap.*) *Geol.* noting or pertaining to the present epoch, originating at the end of the glacial period and forming the latter half of the Quaternary or the latest part of the Neocene period; Holocene. See table under **era.** —*n.* **5.** Also called **Holocene.** (*cap.*) *Geol.* the Recent epoch or series. [< L *recent-* (s. of *recēns*) fresh, new] —**re′cen·cy, re′cent·ness,** *n.* —**re′cent·ly,** *adv.*
—**Syn. 1.** fresh, new. See **modern.** —**Ant. 1.** early, old.

re·cept (rē′sept), *n.* *Psychol.* an idea formed by the repetition of similar percepts, as successive percepts of the same object. [< L *recept(um)* taken back, ptp. of *recipere* to RECEIVE] —**re·cep·tu·al** (ri sep′cho͞o əl), *adj.* —**re·cep′tu·al·ly,** *adv.*

re·cep·ta·cle (ri sep′tə kəl), *n.* **1.** a container, device, etc., that receives or holds something: *a receptacle for trash.* **2.** *Bot.* the modified or expanded portion of an axis that bears the organs of a single flower or the florets of a flower head. **3.** *Elect.* a contact device installed at an outlet for the connection of a portable lamp, appliance, or other electric device by means of a plug and flexible cord. [< L *receptācul(um)* reservoir, equiv. to *receptā(re)* (to) take again, receive back (freq. of *recipere* to RECEIVE) + *-culum* -CLE]

R, Receptacle (Longitudinal section)

re·cep·ti·ble (ri sep′tə bəl), *adj.* adapted to or suitable for reception. [< LL *receptibil(is)* that may be acquired again, equiv. to L *recept(us)* (ptp. of *recipere* to RECEIVE) + *-ibilis* -IBLE] —**re·cep′ti·bil′i·ty,** *n.*

re·cep·tion (ri sep′shən), *n.* **1.** the act of receiving or the state of being received. **2.** a manner of being received: *The book met with a favorable reception.* **3.** a function or occasion when persons are formally received: *a wedding reception.* **4.** the quality or fidelity attained in receiving radio or television broadcasts under given circumstances. [ME *recepcion* < L *receptiōn-* (s. of *receptiō*), equiv. to *recept(us)* (ptp. of *recipere* to RECEIVE) + *-iōn-* -ION]

re·cep·tion·ism (ri sep′shə niz′əm), *n.* *Theol.* the doctrine that in the communion service the communicant receives the body and blood of Christ but that the bread and wine are not transubstantiated. [RECEPTION + -ISM]

re·cep·tion·ist (ri sep′shə nist), *n.* **1.** a person employed to receive callers, as in an office. **2.** *Theol.* a person who advocates receptionism. [RECEPTION + -IST]

recep′tion room′, a room for receiving visitors, clients, patients, etc.

re·cep·tive (ri sep′tiv), *adj.* **1.** having the quality of receiving, taking in, or admitting. **2.** able or quick to receive knowledge, ideas, etc.: *a receptive mind.* **3.** willing or inclined to receive suggestions, offers, etc., with favor: *a receptive listener.* **4.** of or pertaining to reception or receptors: *a receptive end organ.* [< ML *receptīv(us)* RECEPTION, -IVE] —**re·cep′tive·ly,** *adv.* —**re·cep·tiv·i·ty** (rē′sep tiv′i tē), **re·cep′tive·ness,** *n.*

re·cep·tor (ri sep′tər), *n.* **1.** *Physiol.* an end organ or a group of end organs of sensory or afferent neurons, specialized to be sensitive to stimulating agents. **2.** the panlike base of a stall shower. [late ME *receptour* < OF < L *receptor.* See RECEPTION, -OR[2]]

re·cer·ce·lée (ri sûr′sə lā′), *adj.* *Heraldry.* (of a cross) having the end of each limb divided and curved outward so as to form two partial spirals: *a cross recercelée.* Also, **cercelé, cercelée, re·cer′ce·lé′.** Cf. **moline.** [< MF: curled, fem. ptp. of *recerceler,* equiv. to *re-* RE- + *cerceler* to CIRCLE]

re·cess (ri ses′, rē′ses), *n.* **1.** temporary withdrawal or cessation from the usual work or activity. **2.** a period of such withdrawal. **3.** a receding part or space, as a bay or alcove in a room. **4.** an indentation in a line or extent of coast, hills, forest, etc. **5. recesses,** a secluded or inner area or part: *in the recesses of the palace.* —*v.t.* **6.** to place or set in a recess. **7.** to set or form as or like a recess; make a recess or recesses in: *to recess a wall.* —*v.i.* **8.** to take a recess. [< L *recess(us)* n. use of ptp. of *recēdere* to RECEDE[1]]

re·ces·sion[1] (ri sesh′ən), *n.* **1.** the act of receding or withdrawing. **2.** a receding part of a wall, building, etc. **3.** a withdrawing procession, as at the end of a religious service. **4.** the short period centering on the peak of a business cycle; the start of business contraction. [< L *recessiōn-* (s. of *recessiō*). See RECESS, -ION]

re·ces·sion[2] (ri sesh′ən), *n.* a return of ownership to a former possessor. [RE- + CESSION]

re·ces·sion·al (ri sesh′ə nᵊl), *adj.* **1.** of or pertaining to a recession of the clergy and choir after the service. **2.** of or pertaining to a recess, as of a legislative body. —*n.* **3.** a hymn or other piece of music played at the end of a service while the congregation is filing out. [RECESSION[1] + -AL[1]]

reces′sional hymn′, a hymn sung at the close of a church service while the clergy and choir retire from the chancel to the vestry.

re·ces·sive (ri ses′iv), *adj.* **1.** tending to go, move, or slant back; receding. **2.** *Genetics.* of or pertaining to a recessive. **3.** *Phonet.* (of an accent) showing a tendency to recede from the end toward the beginning of a word. —*n.* *Genetics.* **4.** that one of a pair of alternative alleles whose effect is masked by the activity of the second when both are present in the same cell or organism. **5.** the trait or character determined by such an allele. Cf. **dominant** (def. 6). [< L *recess(us)* (see RECESS) + -IVE] —**re·ces′sive·ly,** *adv.* —**re·ces′sive·ness,** *n.*

re·charge·a·ble (rē chär′jə bəl), *adj.* (of a storage battery) capable of being charged repeatedly. Cf. **cordless** (def. 2). [RE- + CHARGEABLE]

ré·chauf·fé (*Fr.* rā shō fā′), *n., pl.* **-fés** (*Fr.* -fā′). **1.** a warmed-up dish of food. **2.** anything old or stale brought into service again. [< F, ptp. of *réchauffer,* re- RE- + *échauffer* to warm; see CHAFE]

re·cher·ché (rə shâr′shā; *Fr.* rə sher shā′), *adj.* **1.** sought out with care. **2.** very rare, exotic, or choice; arcane; obscure. **3.** of studied refinement or elegance; precious. [< F: sought after, ptp. of *rechercher;* see RESEARCH]

re·cid·i·vate (ri sid′ə vāt′, rē-), *v.i.* **-vat·ed, -vat·ing.** to engage in recidivism; relapse. [< ML *recidīvāt(us)* relapsed, ptp. of *recidīvāre.* See RECIDIVISM, -ATE[1]]

re·cid·i·vism (ri sid′ə viz′əm), *n.* **1.** repeated or habitual relapse, as into crime. **2.** *Psychiatry.* the chron-

re·calk′, *v.t.*
re′cam·paign′, *v.*
re·can′cel, *v.t.,* **-celed, -cel·ing** or (*esp. Brit.*) **-celled, -cel·ling.**
re·can′cel·la′tion, *n.*
re·cane′, *v.t.,* **-caned, -can·ing.**
re·car′pet, *v.t.*
re·car′ry, *v.t.,* **-ried, -ry·ing.**
re·carve′, *v.,* **-carved, -carv·ing.**
re·cat′a·log′, *v.t.*
re·cat′a·logue′, *v.t.,* **-logued, -logu·ing.**
re·cat′e·gor·ize′, *v.t.,* **-ized, -iz·ing.**
re·cau′tion, *v.t.*
re·cel′e·brate′, *v.,* **-brat·ed, -brat·ing.**
re′cel·e·bra′tion, *n.*
re·ce·ment′, *v.*
re·cen′sor, *v.t.*
re′cen·tral·i·za′tion, *n.*
re·cen′tral·ize′, *v.,* **-ized, -iz·ing.**
re′cer·ti·fi·ca′tion, *n.*
re·cer′ti·fy′, *v.t.,* **-fied, -fy·ing.**
re·chal′lenge, *v.t.,* **-lenged, -leng·ing.**
re·chan′nel, *v.t.,* **-neled, -nel·ing** or (*esp. Brit.*) **-nelled, -nel·ling.**
re·charge′, *v.,* **-charged, -charg·ing.**
re·charg′er, *n.*
re·chart′, *v.t.*
re·char′ter, *v.t.*
re·check′, *v.*
re′check, *n.*
re·choose′, *v.,* **-chose, -chos·en, -choos·ing.**
re·chris′ten, *v.t.*

ic tendency toward repetition of criminal or antisocial behavior patterns. [< L *recidīv(us)* relapsing, equiv. to *recid(ere)* (*re-* RE- + *cid-* fall, sp. var. of *cad-*) + *-īv(us)* -IVE + -ISM] **—re·cid′i·vist,** *n.* **—re·cid′i·vis′tic, re·cid′i·vous,** *adj.*

Re·ci·fe (re sē′fə), *n.* a seaport in E Brazil. 788,569 (1960). Also called **Pernambuco.**

rec·i·pe (res′ə pē′), *n.* **1.** a set of instructions for making or preparing something, esp. a food dish: *a recipe for a cake.* **2.** a medical prescription. **3.** a method to attain a desired end: *a recipe for success.* [ME < L: take, impv. sing. of *recipere* to RECEIVE]

re·cip·i·ence (ri sip′ē əns), *n.* **1.** the act of receiving; reception. **2.** the state or quality of being receptive; receptiveness. Also, **re·cip′i·en·cy.** [RECIPI(ENT) + -ENCE]

re·cip·i·ent (ri sip′ē ənt), *n.* **1.** one who or that which receives; receiver: *the recipient of a prize.* **—adj. 2.** receiving or capable of receiving. [< L *recipient-* (s. of *recipiēns*) prp. of *recipere* to RECEIVE; see -ENT]

re·cip·ro·cal (ri sip′rə kəl), *adj.* **1.** given or felt by each toward the other; mutual: *reciprocal respect.* **2.** given, performed, felt, etc., in return: *reciprocal aid.* **3.** *Gram.* expressing mutual relation: *"Each other" and "one another" are reciprocal pronouns.* **4.** *Math.* noting expressions, relations, etc., involving reciprocals: *a reciprocal function.* **5.** *Navig.* bearing in a direction 180° to a given direction; back. **—n. 6.** something that is reciprocal to something else; equivalent; counterpart; complement. **7.** *Math.* the ratio of unity to a given quantity or expression; that by which the given quantity or expression is multiplied to produce unity: *The reciprocal of x is* $^1/_x$. [< L *reciproc(us)* returning, reciprocal + -AL[1]] **—re·cip′ro·cal′i·ty, re·cip′ro·cal·ness,** *n.* **—re·cip′ro·cal·ly,** *adv.*
—Syn. 1. See **mutual.**

recip′rocal exchange′, an unincorporated association formed so that its members can participate in reciprocal insurance.

recip′rocal insur′ance, insurance in which members of a reciprocal exchange, acting through an attorney-in-fact, insure themselves and each other.

recip′rocal lev′eling, *Survey.* leveling between two widely separated marks in which observations are made in both directions to eliminate the effects of atmospheric refraction and the curvature of the earth.

recip′rocal ohm′, *Elect.* mho.

recip′rocal transloca′tion, *Genetics.* an exchange of segments between two nonhomologous chromosomes.

re·cip·ro·cate (ri sip′rə kāt′), *v.,* **-cat·ed, -cat·ing.** **—v.t. 1.** to give, feel, etc., in return. **2.** to give and receive reciprocally; interchange: *to reciprocate favors.* **3.** to cause to move alternately backward and forward. **—v.i. 4.** to make a return, as for something given. **5.** to make interchange. **6.** to be correspondent. **7.** to move alternately backward and forward. [< L *reciprocāt(us)* moved back and forth (ptp. of *reciprocāre*). See RECIPROCAL, -ATE[1]] **—re·cip′ro·ca′tive, re·cip·ro·ca·to·ry** (ri sip′rə kə tōr′ē, -tôr′ē), *adj.* **—re·cip′ro·ca′tor,** *n.*

recip′rocating en′gine, any engine employing the rectilinear motion of one or more pistons in cylinders.

re·cip·ro·ca·tion (ri sip′rə kā′shən), *n.* **1.** an act or instance of reciprocating. **2.** a returning, usually for something given. **3.** a mutual giving and receiving. **4.** the state of being reciprocal or corresponding. [< L *reciprocātiōn-* (s. of *reciprocātiō*). See RECIPROCATE, -ION]

rec·i·proc·i·ty (res′ə pros′i tē), *n.* **1.** a reciprocal state or relation. **2.** reciprocation; mutual exchange. **3.** the relation or policy in commercial dealings between countries by which corresponding advantages or privileges are granted by each country to the citizens of the other. [< L *reciproc(us)* (see RECIPROCAL) + -ITY]

re·ci·sion (ri sizh′ən), *n.* an act of canceling or voiding; cancellation. [< L *recīsiōn-* (s. of *recīsiō*), equiv. to *recīs(us)* (ptp. of *recīdere* to cut back; *re-* RE- + *cīdere* to cut) + *-iōn-* -ION]

Recit., *Music.* recitative.

re·cit·al (ri sīt′ᵊl), *n.* **1.** a musical entertainment given usually by a single performer or by a performer and one or more accompanists. **2.** a similar entertainment in a field other than music: *a dance recital.* **3.** an act or instance of reciting. **4.** a detailed statement. **5.** an account, narrative, or description: *He gave a recital of the things he'd been doing since we'd last seen him.* [RECITE + -AL[2]]
—Syn. 5. See **narrative.**

rec·i·ta·tif (res′i tə tēf′), *n.* recitative[2].

rec·i·ta·tion (res′i tā′shən), *n.* **1.** an act of reciting. **2.** a reciting or repeating of something from memory, esp. formally or publicly. **3.** oral response by a pupil or pupils to a teacher on a prepared lesson. **4.** a period of classroom instruction. **5.** an elocutionary delivery of a piece of poetry or prose, without the text, before an audience. **6.** a piece so delivered or for such delivery. [< L *recitātiōn-* (s. of *recitātiō*), equiv. to *recitāt(us)* (ptp. of *recitāre* to RECITE) + *-iōn-* -ION]

rec·i·ta·tive[1] (res′i tā′tiv, ri sīt′tə-), *adj.* pertaining to or of the nature of recital. [RECITE + -ATIVE]

rec·i·ta·tive[2] (res′i tə tēv′), *Music.* **—adj. 1.** of the nature of or resembling recitation or declamation. **—n. 2.** a style of vocal music intermediate between speaking and singing. **3.** a passage, part, or piece in this style. [< It *recitativ(o).* See RECITE, -IVE]

rec·i·ta·ti·vo (res′i tə tē′vō; *It.* Re′che tä tē′vô), *n., pl.* **-vi** (*Eng., It.* -vē), **-vos.** *Music.* recitative[2].

rec·i·ta·ti·vo ac·com·pa·gna·to (res′i tə tē′vō ə kum′pən yä′tō; *It.* Re′che tä tē′vô äk kôm′pä-nyä′tô), *pl.* **rec·i·ta·ti·vi ac·com·pa·gna·ti** (res′i tə tē′vē ə kum′pən yä′tē; *It.* Re′che tä tē′vē äk kôm′pä nyä′tē). See **recitativo stromentato.** [< It: accompanied recitative]

rec·i·ta·ti·vo sec·co (res′i tə tē′vō sek′ō; *It.* Re′che tä tē′vô sek′kô), *pl.* **re·ci·ta·ti·vi sec·chi** (res′i tə tē′vē sek′ē; *It.* Re′che tä tē′vē sek′kē). *Music.* operatic recitative, generally in simple, declamatory style, accompanied by a keyboard instrument. [< It: dry recitative]

re·ci·ta·ti·vo stro·men·ta·to (res′i tə tē′vō strō′mən tä′tō; *It.* Re′che tä tē′vô stRô′men tä′tô), *pl.* **re·ci·ta·ti·vi stro·men·ta·ti** (res′i tə tē′vē strō′mən tä′tē; *It.* Re′che tä tē′vē stRô′men tä′tē). *Music.* dramatic, expressive recitative with orchestral accompaniment. Also called **recitativo accompagnato.** [< It: instrumentalized recitative]

re·cite (ri sīt′), *v.,* **-cit·ed, -cit·ing.** **—v.t. 1.** to repeat the words of, as from memory, esp. in a formal manner: *to recite a lesson.* **2.** to repeat (a piece of poetry or prose) before an audience, as for entertainment. **3.** to give an account of: *to recite one's adventures.* **4.** to enumerate. **—v.i. 5.** to recite a lesson or part of a lesson for a teacher. **6.** to recite or repeat something from memory. [ME *recite(n)* < L *recit(āre)* (to) read aloud, equiv. to *re-* RE- + *citāre* to summon, CITE] **—re·cit′a·ble,** *adj.* **—re·cit′er,** *n.*
—Syn. 3. narrate, describe. See **relate. 4.** count, number, detail.

reck (rek), *v.i.* **1.** to have care, concern, or regard (often fol. by *of, with,* or a clause). **2.** to take heed. **3.** *Archaic.* to be of concern or importance; matter: *It recks not.* **—v.t. 4.** to have regard for; mind; heed. [ME *rekk(en),* OE *reccan;* c. OE *rēcan,* OIcel *roekja* to have care, G *(ge)ruhen* to deign]

reck·less (rek′lis), *adj.* **1.** utterly unconcerned about the consequences of some action; without caution; careless (usually fol. by *of*): *reckless of the danger.* **2.** characterized by or proceeding from such carelessness: *reckless extravagance.* [ME *rekles,* OE *recceleās* careless, var. of *rēceleās;* c. G *ruchlos*] **—reck′less·ly,** *adv.* **—reck′less·ness,** *n.*
—Syn. 1. rash, heedless, incautious, negligent, imprudent. **—Ant. 1.** careful.

Reck·ling·hau·sen (rek′ling hou′zən), *n.* a city in NW West Germany. 130,100 (1963).

reck·on (rek′ən), *v.t.* **1.** to count, compute, or calculate, as in number or amount. **2.** to esteem or consider; regard as: *to be reckoned a wit.* **3.** *Informal. Chiefly Midland and Southern U.S.* to think or suppose. **—v.i. 4.** to count; make a computation or calculation. **5.** to settle accounts, as with a person (often fol. by *up*). **6.** to count, depend, or rely, as in expectation (often fol. by *on*). **7. reckon with, a.** to include in consideration or planning; anticipate: *He hadn't reckoned with so many obstacles.* **b.** to deal with: *I have to reckon with many problems every day.* **8. reckon without one's host.** See **host**[1] (def. 4). [ME *reken(en),* OE *(ge)recenian* to report, pay; c. G *rechnen* to compute] **—reck′on·a·ble,** *adj.*
—Syn. 1. enumerate. **2.** account, deem, estimate, judge.

reck·on·er (rek′ə nər), *n.* **1.** a person who reckons. **2.** Also called **ready reckoner.** a collection of mathematical and other tables for ready calculation. [ME; see RECKON, -ER[1]]

reck·on·ing (rek′ə ning), *n.* **1.** count; computation; calculation. **2.** the settlement of accounts, as between two businessmen. **3.** a statement of an amount due; bill. **4.** an accounting, as for things received or done. **5.** *Navig.* See **dead reckoning. 6.** See **day of reckoning** (def. 1). [ME; see RECKON, -ING[1]]

re-claim (rē klām′), *v.t.* **1.** to claim or demand the return or restoration of, as a right, possession, etc. **2.** to claim again. [RE- + CLAIM]

re·claim (ri klām′), *v.t.* **1.** to bring (wild, waste, or marshy land) into a condition for cultivation or other use. **2.** to recover (substances) in a pure or usable form from refuse, discarded articles, etc. **3.** to bring back to a preferable manner of living, sound principles, ideas, etc. **4.** *Archaic.* to tame. **—v.i. 5.** *Archaic.* to protest; object. **—n. 6.** reclamation: *beyond reclaim.* [ME *recla(i)m(en)* < OF *reclam(er)* (tonic s. *reclaim-*) < L *reclāmāre,* equiv. to *re-* RE- + *clāmāre* to CLAIM] **—re·claim′a·ble,** *adj.* **—re·claim′er,** *n.*
—Syn. 2. regain, restore. See **recover.**

re·claim·ant (ri klā′mənt), *n.* a person who makes appeals to reclaim. [RECLAIM + -ANT]

rec·la·ma·tion (rek′lə mā′shən), *n.* **1.** the reclaiming of waste, desert, marshy, or submerged land for cultivation or other use. **2.** the act or process of reclaiming. **3.** the state of being reclaimed. **4.** the process or industry of deriving usable materials from waste, by-products, etc. [< MF < L *reclāmātiōn-* (s. of *reclāmātiō*) crying out against, equiv. to *reclāmāt(us)* (ptp. of *reclāmāre;* see RECLAIM) + *-iōn-* -ION]

ré·clame (*Fr.* Ra klam′), *n.* **1.** publicity; self-advertisement; notoriety. **2.** hunger for publicity; talent for getting attention. [< F, deriv. of *réclamer;* see RECLAIM]

re·clas·si·fy (rē klas′ə fī′), *v.t.,* **-fied, -fy·ing. 1.** to classify anew. **2.** to change the security classification of (information, a document, etc.). [RE- + CLASSIFY] **—re·clas′si·fi·ca′tion,** *n.*

rec·li·nate (rek′lə nāt′, -nit), *adj. Bot., Zool.* bending or curved downward. [< L *reclīnāt(us)* (ptp. of *reclīnāre* to RECLINE); see -ATE[1]]

re·cline (ri klīn′), *v.,* **-clined, -clin·ing. —v.i. 1.** to lean or lie back; rest in a recumbent position. **—v.t. 2.** to cause to lean back on something; place in a recumbent position. [ME *recline(n)* < L *reclīn(āre),* equiv. to *re-* RE- + *clīnāre* to LEAN[1]] **—re·clin′a·ble,** *adj.* **—rec·li·na·tion** (rek′lə nā′shən), *n.*

re·clin·er (ri klī′nər), *n.* **1.** one who or that which reclines. **2.** See **reclining chair.** [RECLINE + -ER[1]]

reclin′ing chair′, an easy chair with the back and footrest adjustable up or down to the comfort of the user.

rec·li·vate (rek′lə vāt′), *adj. Entomol.* (of an organ or part) sigmoid. [< LL *recliv(is)* or *recliv(us)* bending backwards (*re-* RE- + *clīvus* incline, hill) + -ATE[1]]

rec·luse (*n.* rek′lo͞os, ri klo͞os′; *adj.* ri klo͞os′), *n.* **1.** a person who lives in seclusion or apart from society, often for religious meditation. **2.** Also, **incluse.** a religious voluntary immured in a cave, hut, or the like, or one remaining within a cell for life. **—adj. 3.** shut off or apart from the world; living in seclusion, often for religious reasons. **4.** characterized by seclusion. [ME < OF *reclus* < L *reclūs(us),* ptp. of *reclūdere* to shut up (earlier, to unclose), equiv. to *re-* RE- + *-clūd-,* var. of *claud-* CLOSE] **—re·clu′sive,** *adj.*

re·clu·sion (ri klo͞o′zhən), *n.* **1.** the condition or life of a recluse. **2.** a shutting or a being shut up in seclusion. [ME < LL *reclūsiōn-* (s. of *reclūsiō*) a shutting off, equiv. to L *reclūs(us)* RECLUSE + *-iōn-* -ION]

rec·og·nise (rek′əg nīz′), *v.t.,* **-nised, -nis·ing.** *Chiefly Brit.* recognize. **—rec′og·nis′a·ble,** *adj.* **—rec′og·nis′er,** *n.*

rec·og·ni·tion (rek′əg nish′ən), *n.* **1.** an act of recognizing or the state of being recognized. **2.** the identification of something as having been previously seen, heard, known, etc. **3.** the perception of something as existing or true; realization. **4.** the acknowledgment of something as valid or as entitled to consideration: *the recognition of a claim.* **5.** the acknowledgment of achievement, service, merit, etc. **6.** the expression of this in the form of some token of appreciation: *This promotion constitutes our recognition of her exceptional ability.* **7.** formal acknowledgment conveying approval or sanction. **8.** acknowledgment of right to be heard or given attention: *The chairman refused recognition to any delegate until order could be restored.* **9.** *Internat. Law.* an official act by which one state acknowledges the existence of another state or government, or of belligerency or insurgency. [< L *recognitiōn-* (s. of *recognitiō*), equiv. to *recognit(us)* (ptp. of *recognōscere;* see RECOGNIZE) + *-iōn-* -ION] **—rec′og·ni′tion·al,** *adj.* **—re·cog·ni·tive** (ri kog′ni tiv), **re·cog·ni·to·ry** (ri kog′ni tōr′ē, -tôr′ē), *adj.*

re·cog·ni·zance (ri kog′ni zəns, -kon′i-), *n.* **1.** *Law.* **a.** a bond or obligation of record entered into before a court of record or a magistrate, binding a person to do a particular act. **b.** the sum pledged as surety on such a bond. **2.** *Archaic.* recognition. **3.** *Archaic.* a token; badge. [ME *reconissaunce, recognisaunce* < OF *reconuissance.* See RECOGNIZE, -ANCE]

rec·og·nize (rek′əg nīz′), *v.t.,* **-nized, -niz·ing. 1.** to identify as something or someone previously seen, known, etc.: *He had changed so much that one could scarcely recognize him.* **2.** to identify from knowledge of appearance or characteristics: *I recognized him from the description. He recognized her as a fraud.* **3.** to perceive as existing or true; realize: *to be the first to recognize a fact.* **4.** to acknowledge as the person entitled to speak at a particular time: *The Speaker recognized the Congressman from Maine.* **5.** to acknowledge formally as entitled to treatment as a political unit: *The United States refused to recognize Red China.* **6.** to acknowledge or accept formally a specified factual or legal situation: *to recognize a successful revolutionary regime as the de facto government of the country.* **7.** to acknowledge or treat as valid: *to recognize a claim.* **8.** to acknowledge acquaintance with, as by a greeting, handshake, etc. **9.** to show appreciation of (achievement, service, merit, etc.), as by some reward, public honor, or the like. **10.** *Law.* to acknowledge (an illegitimate child) as one's own. [RECOGN(ITION) + -IZE; r. ME *racunnys, recognis* < OF *reconuiss-,* s. of *reconuistre* < L *recognōscere,* equiv. to *re-* RE- + *cognōscere* to know; see COGNITION] **—rec′og·niz′a·bil′i·ty,** *n.* **—rec·og·niz·a·ble** (rek′əg-nī′zə bəl, rek′əg nī′-), *adj.* **—rec′og·niz′a·bly,** *adv.* **—rec′og·niz′er,** *n.*

re·cog·ni·zee (ri kog′ni zē′, -kon′i-), *n. Law.* the person to whom an obligation is owed in a recognizance. [RECOGNIZE + -EE]

re·cog·ni·zor (ri kog′ni zôr′, -kon′i-), *n. Law.* a person who enters into a recognizance. [RECOGNIZE + -OR[2]]

re·coil (*v.* ri koil′; *n.* rē koil, rē′koil′ *for 5,* rē′koil′ *for 6*), *v.i.* **1.** to draw back; start or shrink back, as in alarm, horror, or disgust. **2.** to spring or fly back, as in consequence of force of impact or the force of the discharge, as a firearm. **3.** to spring or come back; react (usually fol. by *on* or *upon*): *Plots frequently recoil upon the plotters.* **4.** *Physics.* (of an atom, a nucleus, or a particle) to undergo a change in momentum as a result either of a collision with an atom, a nucleus, or a particle or of the emission of a particle. **—n. 5.** an act of recoiling. **6.** the length through which a weapon moves backward after its discharge. [ME *recoil(en), recul(en)* < OF *recul(er)* < L *re-* RE- + *cūlus* rump] **—re·coil′ing·ly,** *adv.*
—Syn. 1. withdraw, quail, flinch, falter. **2.** rebound.

re′coil escape′ment, *Horol.* See **anchor escapement.**

re·coil·less (ri koil′lis, rē′koil′-), *adj.* having little or no recoil: *a recoilless rifle.* [RECOIL + -LESS]

re-col·lect (rē′kə lekt′), *v.t.* **1.** to collect, gather, or assemble again (something scattered). **2.** to rally (one's faculties, powers, spirits, etc.); recover or compose (oneself). [< L *recollect(us),* taken as RE- + COLLECT]

rec·ol·lect (rek′ə lekt′), *v.t.* **1.** to recall to mind; recover knowledge of by memory; remember. **2.** to absorb (oneself) in spiritual meditation, esp. during prayer. **—v.i. 3.** to have a recollection; remember. [< ML *recollect(us)* (n. use of ptp. of L *recolligere* to collect again), equiv. to L *re-* RE- + *collectus* COLLECT] **—rec′ol·lec′tive,** *adj.* **—rec′ol·lec′tive·ly,** *adv.* **—rec′ol·lec′tive·ness,** *n.*
—Syn. 1. See **remember. —Ant. 1.** forget.

rec·ol·lect·ed (rek′ə lek′tid), *adj.* **1.** calm; composed. **2.** remembered; recalled. **3.** characterized by or given to contemplation. [RECOLLECT + -ED[2]] **—rec′ol·lect′ed·ly,** *adv.* **—rec′ol·lect′ed·ness,** *n.*

re-col·lec·tion (rē′kə lek′shən), *n.* the act of re-collecting or the state of being re-collected. [RE- + COLLECTION]

rec·ol·lec·tion (rek′ə lek′shən), *n.* **1.** the act or power of recollecting, or recalling to mind; remembrance. **2.** something that is recollected: *recollections of one's childhood.* [< F *récollection* or ML *recollēctiōn-* (s. of *recollēctiō*), equiv. to *recollēct(us)* (see RECOLLECT) + *-iōn-* -ION; taken as RE- + COLLECTION]
—Syn. 1. recall. **1, 2.** memory. **2.** memoir.

re·cir′cle, *v.,* **-cled, -cling.**
re·cir′cu·late′, *v.,* **-lat·ed, -lat·ing.**
re′cir·cu·la′tion, *n.*
re·clasp′, *v.t.*
re·class′, *v.t.*
re′clas·si·fi·ca′tion, *n.*
re·clean′, *v.t.*
re·cleanse′, *v.t.,* **-cleansed, -cleans·ing.**
re·climb′, *v.t.,* **-climbed, -climb·ing.**
re·clos′a·ble, *adj.*
re·close′a·ble, *adj.*
re·clothe′, *v.t.,* **-clothed** or **-clad, -cloth·ing.**
re′co·ag′u·late′, *v.,* **-lat·ed, -lat·ing.**
re′co·ag′u·la′tion, *n.*
re·coat′, *v.t.*
re·code′, *v.t.,* **-cod·ed, -cod·ing.**
re′cod·i·fi·ca′tion, *n.*
re·cod′i·fy′, *v.t.,* **-fied, -fy·ing.**
re·coin′, *v.t.*
re·coin′age, *n.*

re·com·bi·nant (rē kom′bə nənt), *adj.* of or resulting from new combinations of genetic material.

recom′binant DNA, *Biochem.* any of various techniques for inserting DNA fragments from the genes of one organism directly into the chromosomes of another so as to change genetic makeup: used in basic research and to produce vaccines, hormones, etc. Also called **gene-splicing.**

re·com·bi·na·tion (rē′kom bə nā′shən), *n. Genetics.* the formation of new combinations of genes either by crossing over at meiosis or by segregation. [RE- + COMBINATION]

rec·om·mend (rek′ə mend′), *v.t.* **1.** to present as worthy of confidence, acceptance, use, etc.; commend; mention favorably: *to recommend an applicant for a job; to recommend a book.* **2.** to represent or urge as advisable or expedient: *to recommend caution.* **3.** to advise, as an alternative; suggest (a choice, course of action, etc.) as appropriate, beneficial, or the like: *He recommended the blue-plate special. The doctor recommended special exercises for her.* **4.** to make desirable or attractive: *a plan that has very little to recommend it.* [ME *recommend(en)* < ML *recommend(āre),* equiv. to L *re-* RE- + *commendāre* to COMMEND] —**rec′om·mend′a·ble,** *adj.* —**rec′om·mend′er,** *n.*
—**Syn. 1.** approve, condone. **3.** counsel. —**Ant. 1.** condemn.

rec·om·men·da·tion (rek′ə men dā′shən), *n.* **1.** an act of recommending. **2.** a letter or the like recommending a person or thing. **3.** representation in favor of a person or thing. **4.** anything that serves to recommend a person or thing, or induce acceptance or favor. [ME *recommendacion* < ML *recommendātiōn-* (s. of *recommendātiō*), equiv. to *recommendāt(us)* (ptp. of *recommendāre* to RECOMMEND) + *-iōn-* -ION]
—**Syn. 1.** See **advice.**

rec·om·mend·a·to·ry (rek′ə men′də tōr′ē, -tôr′ē), *adj.* **1.** serving to recommend; recommending. **2.** serving as or being a recommendation. [< ML *recommendāt(us)* (see RECOMMENDATION) + -ORY[1]]

re·com·mit (rē′kə mit′), *v.t.,* **-mit·ted, -mit·ting. 1.** to commit again. **2.** to refer again to a committee. [RE- + COMMIT] —**re′com·mit′ment, re′com·mit′tal,** *n.*

rec·om·pense (rek′əm pens′), *v.,* **-pensed, -pens·ing,** *n.* —*v.t.* **1.** to repay; remunerate; reward, as for service, aid, etc. **2.** to pay or give compensation for; make restitution or requital for (damage, injury, or the like). —*v.i.* **3.** to make compensation for something; repay someone: *no attempt to recompense for our trouble.* —*n.* **4.** compensation, as for an injury, wrong, etc.: *to make recompense for the loss one's carelessness has caused.* **5.** a repayment or requital, as for favors, gifts, etc. **6.** a remuneration or reward, as for services, aid, or the like. [ME *recompense(n)* < MF *recompens(er)* < LL *recompens(āre),* equiv. to L *re-* RE- + *compensāre;* see COMPENSATE] —**rec′om·pen′sa·ble,** *adj.* —**rec′om·pens′er,** *n.*
—**Syn. 1.** reimburse, recoup. **4.** payment, amends, indemnification, satisfaction.

re·com·pose (rē′kəm pōz′), *v.t.,* **-posed, -pos·ing. 1.** to compose again; reconstitute; rearrange. **2.** to restore to composure or calmness. [RE- + COMPOSE] —**re·com·po·si·tion** (rē′kom pə zish′ən), *n.*

re·con (ri kon′), *n. Informal.* reconnaissance. [by shortening]

re·con·cen·tra·tion (rē′kon sən trā′shən), *n.* the act or state of concentrating again. [RE- + CONCENTRATION]

rec·on·cil·a·ble (rek′ən sī′lə bəl, rek′ən sī′lə bəl), *adj.* capable of being reconciled. [RECONCILE + -ABLE] —**rec′on·cil′a·bil′i·ty, rec′on·cil′a·ble·ness,** *n.* —**rec′on·cil′a·bly,** *adv.*

rec·on·cile (rek′ən sīl′), *v.t.,* **-ciled, -cil·ing. 1.** to render no longer opposed; bring to acquiescence or acceptance (usually fol. by *to*): *to reconcile someone to his fate.* **2.** to win over to friendliness; cause to become amicable: *to reconcile hostile persons.* **3.** to compose or settle (a quarrel, dispute, etc.). **4.** to bring into agreement or harmony; make compatible or consistent: *to reconcile differing statements.* **5.** to reconsecrate (a desecrated church, cemetery, etc.). **6.** to restore (an excommunicate or penitent) to communion in a church. [ME *reconcile(n)* < L *reconcili(āre)* (to) make good again, repair. See RE-, CONCILIATE] —**rec′on·cile′ment,** *n.* —**rec′on·cil′er,** *n.* —**rec′on·cil′ing·ly,** *adv.*
—**Syn. 2.** pacify, propitiate, placate. **4.** harmonize.

rec·on·cil·i·a·tion (rek′ən sil′ē ā′shən), *n.* **1.** an act of reconciling or the state of being reconciled. **2.** the process of making consistent or compatible. [ME *reconsiliacion* < L *reconciliātiōn-* (s. of *reconciliātiō*), equiv. to *reconciliāt(us)* (see RECONCILE, -ATE[1]) + *-iōn-* -ION]

rec·on·cil·i·a·to·ry (rek′ən sil′ē ə tōr′ē, -tôr′ē), *adj.* tending to reconcile. [< L *reconciliāt(us)* (see RECONCILE, -ATE[1]) + -ORY[1]]

rec·on·dite (rek′ən dīt′, ri kon′dīt), *adj.* **1.** dealing with very profound, difficult, or abstruse subject matter: *a recondite treatise.* **2.** beyond ordinary knowledge or understanding; esoteric: *recondite principles.* **3.** little known; obscure: *a recondite fact.* [earlier *recondit* < L *recondit(us)* hidden (ptp. of *recondere*), equiv. to *re-* RE- + *cond(ere)* to bring together (*con-* CON- + *-dere* put) + *-itus* -ITE[2]] —**rec′on·dite′ly,** *adv.* —**rec′on·dite′ness,** *n.*
—**Syn. 2.** deep. **3.** mysterious, occult, secret. —**Ant. 2.** superficial. **3.** clear.

re·con·di·tion (rē′kən dish′ən), *v.t.* to restore to a good or satisfactory condition; repair; make over. [RE- + CONDITION]

re·con·nais·sance (ri kon′i səns), *n.* **1.** act of reconnoitering. **2.** *Mil.* a search made for useful military information in the field, esp. by examining the ground. **3.** *Survey, Civ. Eng.* a general examination or survey of a region, usually followed by a detailed survey. **4.** *Geol.* an examination or survey of the general geological characteristics of a region. Also, **re·con′nois·sance.** [< F; MF *reconoissance* RECOGNIZANCE]

recon′naissance car′, a specially equipped and armed car used for making military reconnaissance.

re·con·noi·ter (rē′kə noi′tər, rek′ə-), *v.t.* **1.** to inspect, observe, or survey (the enemy, the enemy's strength or position, a region, etc.) in order to gain information for military purposes. **2.** to examine or survey (a region, area, etc.) for engineering, geological, or other purposes. —*v.i.* **3.** to make a reconnaissance. [< obs. F *reconnoître* to explore < MF *reconoistre.* See RECOGNIZE] —**re′con·noi′ter·er,** *n.*

re·con·noi·tre (rē′kə noi′tər, rek′ə-), *v.t., v.i.,* **-tred, -tring.** *Chiefly Brit.* reconnoiter. —**re′con·noi′trer,** *n.*

Re·con·qui·sta (re′kông kē′stä), *n.* a city in NE Argentina, on the Paraná River. 12,729 (1947).

re·con·sid·er (rē′kən sid′ər), *v.t.* **1.** to consider again, esp. with a view to change of decision or action: *to reconsider a refusal.* **2.** *Parl. Proc.* to take up for consideration a second time, as a motion or a vote, as with the view of reversing or modifying action taken. —*v.i.* **3.** to reconsider a matter. [RE- + CONSIDER] —**re′con·sid′er·a′tion,** *n.*

re·con·sign·ment (rē′kən sīn′mənt), *n.* **1.** a consigning again. **2.** *Com.* a change in the route, point of delivery, or consignee as stated in the original bill of lading. [RE- + CONSIGNMENT]

re·con·sti·tute (rē kon′sti to͞ot′, -tyo͞ot′), *v.t.,* **-tut·ed, -tut·ing.** to constitute again; reconstruct; recompose. [RE- + CONSTITUTE] —**re·con·sti·tu·ent** (rē′kən stich′o͞o ənt), *adj., n.* —**re′con·sti·tu′tion,** *n.*

re·con·sti·tut·ed (ri kon′sti to͞o′tid, -tyo͞o′-), *adj.* constituted again, esp. of a liquid product made by adding water to dry solids from which the water has been evaporated: *reconstituted orange juice.* [RECONSTITUTE + -ED[2]]

re·con·struct (rē′kən strukt′), *v.t.* **1.** to construct again; rebuild; make over. **2.** to recreate in the mind from given or available information: *to reconstruct the events of the murder.* **3.** *Historical Ling.* to arrive at (hypothetical earlier forms of words, phonemic systems, etc.) by comparison of data from a later language or group of related languages. [RE- + CONSTRUCT] —**re′con·struc′ti·ble,** *adj.*

re·con·struct·ed (rē′kən struk′tid), *adj.* **1.** constructed again; rebuilt. **2.** noting a gem, esp. a ruby, made by an obsolete process from fused fragments of natural gems. [RECONSTRUCT + -ED[2]]

re·con·struc·tion (rē′kən struk′shən), *n.* **1.** an act of reconstructing. **2.** (*cap.*) *U.S. Hist.* **a.** the process by which the States that had seceded were reorganized as part of the Union after the Civil War. **b.** the period during which this took place, 1865–77. [RE- + CONSTRUCTION] —**re′con·struc′tion·al, re′con·struc′tion·ar′y,** *adj.*

Reconstruc′tion Acts′, *U.S. Hist.* the acts of Congress during the period from 1867 to 1877 providing for the reorganization of the former Confederate States and setting forth the process by which they were to be restored to representation in Congress, esp. the acts passed in 1867 and 1868.

Reconstruc′tion Finance′ Corpora′tion, a public corporation that was created by an act of Congress in 1932 to provide loans and other financial as sistance to industrial, commercial, and banking organizations. Abolished in 1957. *Abbr.:* RFC

Re·con·struc·tion·ism (rē′kən struk′shə niz′əm), *n.* a 20th-century movement among U.S. Jews, founded by Rabbi Mordecai M. Kaplan, advocating that Judaism, being a culture and way of life as well as a religion, is in sum a religious civilization requiring constant adaptation to contemporary conditions so that Jews can identify more readily and meaningfully with the Jewish community. [RECONSTRUCTION + -ISM]

Re·con·struc·tion·ist (rē′kən struk′shə nist), *n.* **1.** an advocate or supporter of Reconstruction or Reconstructionism. —*adj.* **2.** of or pertaining to Reconstruction or Reconstructionism. [RECONSTRUCTION + -IST]

re·con·struc·tive (rē′kən struk′tiv), *adj.* tending to reconstruct. [RE- + CONSTRUCTIVE] —**re′con·struc′tive·ly,** *adv.* —**re′con·struc′tive·ness,** *n.*

re·con·ven·tion (rē′kən ven′shən), *n. Civil Law.* an action brought by the defendant in pending litigation against the plaintiff: the defendant's claim must be connected in some way with the subject matter of the plaintiff's action. [< MF; see RE-, CONVENTION]

re·con·vey (rē′kən vā′), *v.t.* **1.** to convey again. **2.** to convey back to a previous position or place. [RE- + CONVEY] —**re′con·vey′ance,** *n.*

re·cord (*v.* ri kôrd′; *n., adj.* rek′ərd), *v.t.* **1.** to set down in writing or the like, as for the purpose of preserving evidence. **2.** to cause to be set down or registered: *to record one's vote.* **3.** to state or indicate: *He recorded his protest, but it was disregarded.* **4.** to serve to relate or to tell of: *The document records that the battle took place six years earlier.* **5.** to set down or register in some permanent form, as on a seismograph. **6.** to set down, register, or fix by characteristic marks, incisions, magnetism, etc., for the purpose of reproduction by a phonograph or magnetic reproducer. **7.** to make a recording of: *The orchestra recorded the 6th Symphony. The company has recorded most of Shakespeare's plays.* —*v.i.* **8.** to record something; make a record. —*n.* **9.** an act of recording. **10.** the state of being recorded, as in writing. **11.** an account in writing or the like preserving the memory or knowledge of facts or events. **12.** information or knowledge preserved in writing or the like. **13.** a report, list, or aggregate of actions or achievements: *He made a good record in college. The ship has a fine sailing record.* **14.** a criminal record: *They discovered that the suspect had a record.* **15.** something or someone serving as a remembrance; memorial: *Keep this souvenir as a record of your visit.* **16.** the tracing, marking, or the like, made by a recording instrument. **17.** a cylinder, disk, or other device having characteristic markings or the like for reproducing sound, as in a phonograph. **18.** the highest or best rate, amount, etc., ever attained, esp. in sports: *to hold the record for home runs; to break the record in the high jump.* **19.** *Sports.* the standing of a team or individual with respect to contests won, lost, and tied. **20.** an official writing intended to be preserved. **21.** *Law.* **a.** the commitment to writing, as authentic evidence, of something having legal importance, esp. as evidence of the proceedings or verdict of a court. **b.** evidence preserved in this manner. **c.** an authentic or official written report of proceedings of a court of justice. **22. go on record,** to issue a public statement of one's opinion or stand: *He went on record as advocating immediate integration.* **23. off the record,** not intended for publication; unofficial; confidential: *The President's comment was strictly off the record.* **24. on record, a.** existing as a matter of public knowledge; known. **b.** existing in a publication, document, file, etc.: *There was no birth certificate on record to reveal her age.* —*adj.* **25.** making or affording a record. **26.** surpassing or superior to all others: *a record year for automobile sales.* [ME *record(en)* < OF *record(er)* < L *recordārī* to remember, recollect, equiv. to *re-* RE- + *cord-* (s. of *cors*) heart] —**re·cord′a·ble,** *adj.* —**rec′ord·less,** *adj.*
—**Syn. 1.** register, enroll, enter, note. **11.** chronicle, history, journal; note, memorandum.

rec′ord chang′er, a device that automatically places each of a stack of records in succession onto the turntable of a phonograph.

Re·cor·de (ri kôr′dē), *n.* a walled plain in the first quadrant of the face of the moon: about 80 miles in diameter.

re·cord·er (ri kôr′dər), *n.* **1.** one who records, esp. as an official duty. **2.** *Eng. Law.* **a.** a judge in a city or borough court. **b.** (formerly) the legal advisor of a city or borough, with responsibility for keeping a record of legal actions and local customs. **3.** a recording or registering apparatus or device. **4.** a device for recording sound by varying the magnetism in a moving tape. The sound is recorded by moving the tape past a head incorporating an inductor and may be erased by demagnetizing. **5.** an end-blown flute having a fipple mouthpiece and a soft, mellow tone. [RECORD + -ER[1]; r. ME: an official < AF *recordour,* OF *recordeur*]

Recorder (def. 5)

re·cord·ing (ri kôr′ding), *n.* **1.** the act or practice of one who or that which records. **2.** something that is recorded, as a musical work. **3.** something used for making a record. [ME; see RECORD, -ING[1]]

rec′ord play′er, phonograph.

re-count (*v.* rē kount′; *n.* rē′kount′, rē kount′), *v.t.* **1.** to count again. —*n.* **2.** a second or additional count, as of votes in an election. [RE- + COUNT[1]]

re·count (ri kount′), *v.t.* **1.** to relate or narrate; tell in detail; give the facts or particulars of. **2.** to narrate in order. **3.** to tell one by one; enumerate. [ME *recount(en)* < MF *recont(er),* equiv. to *re-* RE- + *conter* to tell, COUNT[1]] —**Syn. 1.** describe. See **relate.**

re·count·al (rē koun′təl), *n.* an act of recounting. [RECOUNT + -AL[2]]

re·coup (ri ko͞op′), *v.t.* **1.** to get back the equivalent of: *to recoup one's losses by a lucky investment.* **2.** to regain or recover. **3.** to reimburse or indemnify; pay back: *to recoup a person for expenses.* **4.** *Law.* to withhold (a portion of something due), having some rightful claim to do so. —*v.i.* **5.** to get back an equivalent, as of something lost. **6.** *Law.* to plead in defense a claim arising out of the same subject matter as the plaintiff's claim. —*n.* **7.** an act of recouping. [ME < MF *recoup(er)* (to) cut back, again, equiv. to *re-* RE- + *couper* to cut; see COUP[1]] —**re·coup′a·ble,** *adj.* —**re·coup′ment,** *n.*
—**Syn. 1.** recover, restore, retrieve, balance. **3.** recompense, remunerate.

re·course (rē′kōrs, -kôrs, ri kōrs′, -kôrs′), *n.* **1.** access or resort to a person or thing for help or protection: *to have recourse to the courts for justice.* **2.** a person or thing resorted to for help or protection. **3.** the right to collect from a maker or endorser of a negotiable instrument. The endorser may add the words "with-

re′col·o·ni·sa′tion, *n.*
re′col′o·nise, *v.t.,* -nised, -nis·ing.
re′col·o·ni·za′tion, *n.*
re·col′o·nize′, *v.t.,* -nized, -niz·ing.
re·col′or, *v.t.*
re′col·or·a′tion, *n.*
re·col′our, *v.t.*
re′col·our·a′tion, *n.*
re·comb′, *v.*
re′com·bine′, *v.,* -bined, -bin·ing.
re′com·mence′, *v.,* -menced, -menc·ing.
re′com·mence′ment, *n.*
re′com·mis′sion, *n., v.t.*
re′com·pare′, *v.t.,* -pared, -par·ing.
re′com·par′i·son, *n.*
re′com′pen·sate′, *v.t.,* -sat·ed, -sat·ing.
re′com·pen′sa·to′ry, *adj.*
re′com·pi·la′tion, *n.*
re′com·pile′, *v.t.,* -piled, -pil·ing.
re′com·pound′, *v.*
re′com·pu·ta′tion, *n.*
re′com·pute′, *v.t.,* -put·ed, -put·ing.
re′con·ceal′, *v.t.*
re′con·ceal′ment, *n.*
re·con′cen·trate′, *v.,* -trat·ed, -trat·ing.
re′con·demn′, *v.t.*
re′con·dem·na′tion, *n.*
re′con·den·sa′tion, *n.*
re′con·dense′, *v.,* -densed, -dens·ing.
re′con·duct′, *v.t.*
re′con·fer′, *v.,* -ferred, -fer·ring.
re′con·fine′, *v.t.,* -fined, -fin·ing.
re′con·firm′, *v.t.*
re′con·fir·ma′tion, *n.*
re·con′fis·cate′, *v.t.,* -cat·ed, -cat·ing.
re′con·form′, *v.*
re′con·front′, *v.t.*
re′con·fron·ta′tion, *n.*
re′con·fuse′, *v.t.,* -fused, -fus·ing.
re′con·fu′sion, *n.*
re′con·nect′, *v.t.*
re′con·nec′tion, *n.*
re·con′quer, *v.t.*
re·con′quest, *n.*
re·con′se·crate′, *v.t.,* -crat·ed, -crat·ing.
re′con·se·cra′tion, *n.*
re′con·sent′, *v.i.*
re′con·sign′, *v.t.*
re′con·sole′, *v.t.,* -soled, -sol·ing.
re′con·sol′i·date′, *v.,* -dat·ed, -dat·ing.
re′con·sol′i·da′tion, *n.*
re′con·sult′, *v.*
re′con·sul·ta′tion, *n.*
re·con′tact, *n., v.*
re·con′tem·plate′, *v.,* -plat·ed, -plat·ing.
re′con·tem·pla′tion, *n.*
re′con·tend′, *v.i.*
re′con·test′, *v.*
re′con·tract′, *v.t.*
re′con·trac′tion, *n.*
re′con·vene′, *v.,* -vened, -ven·ing.
re′con·verge′, *v.i.,* -verged, -verg·ing.
re′con·ver′gence, *n.*
re′con·ver′sion, *n.*
re′con·vert′, *v.t.*
re′con·vert′er, *n.*
re′con·vict′, *v.t.*
re′con·vic′tion, *n.*
re·cook′, *v.*
re·cool′, *v.*
re·cop′y, *v.t.,* -cop·ied, -cop·y·ing.
re′cor·o·na′tion, *n.*
re′cor·rect′, *v.t.*
re·cost′, *v.t.*
re′cos·tume′, *v.t.,* -tumed, -tum·ing.
re·coun′sel, *v.t.,* -seled, -sel·ing or (*esp. Brit.*) -selled, -sel·ling.

out recourse" on the instrument, thereby transferring the instrument without assuming any liability. [ME *recours* < OF < LL *recurs(us)*, L: return, retreat, n. use of ptp. of *recurrere* to run back; see RECUR]

re·cov·er (rē kuv′ər), *v.t.* to cover again or anew. [ME; see RE-, COVER]

re·cov·er (ri kuv′ər), *v.t.* **1.** to get back or regain (something lost or taken away): *to recover a stolen watch.* **2.** to make up for or make good (loss, damage, etc., to oneself). **3.** to regain the strength, composure, balance, etc., of (oneself). **4.** *Law.* **a.** to obtain by judgment in a court of law, or by legal proceedings: *to recover damages for a wrong.* **b.** to acquire title to through judicial process: *to recover land.* **5.** to reclaim from a bad state, practice, etc. **6.** to regain (a substance) in usable form, as from refuse material or from a waste product or by-product of manufacture; reclaim. **7.** *Mil.* to return (a weapon) to a previously held position in the manual of arms. **8.** *Football.* to gain or regain possession of (a fumble): *They recovered the ball on their own 20-yard line.* —*v.i.* **9.** to regain health after being sick, wounded, or the like (often fol. by *from*): *to recover from an illness.* **10.** to regain a former and better state or condition: *The city soon recovered from the effects of the earthquake.* **11.** to regain one's strength, composure, balance, etc. **12.** *Law.* to obtain a favorable judgment in a suit for something. **13.** *Football.* to gain or regain possession of a fumble: *The Giants recovered in the end zone for a touchdown.* **14.** to make a recovery in fencing or rowing. [ME *recover(en)* < MF *recover(er)* < L *recuperāre* to regain, RECUPERATE] —**re·cov′er·er,** *n.*

—**Syn. 1.** restore. RECOVER, RECLAIM, RETRIEVE are to regain literally or figuratively something or someone. To RECOVER is to obtain again what one has lost possession of: *to recover a stolen jewel.* To RECLAIM is to bring back from error or wrongdoing, or from a rude or undeveloped state: *to reclaim desert land by irrigation.* To RETRIEVE is to bring back or restore, esp. something to its former, prosperous state: *to retrieve one's fortune.* **9.** heal, mend, recuperate; rally.

re·cov·er·a·ble (ri kuv′ər ə bəl), *adj.* able to recover or be recovered: *a patient now believed to be recoverable; recoverable losses on his investments.* [ME; see RECOVER, -ABLE] —**re·cov′er·a·ble·ness,** *n.*

re·cov·er·y (ri kuv′ə rē), *n., pl.* **-er·ies.** **1.** an act of recovering. **2.** the regaining of or possibility of regaining something lost or taken away. **3.** restoration or return to health from sickness. **4.** restoration or return to any former and better state or condition. **5.** time required for recovering. **6.** something that is gained in recovering. **7.** the regaining of substances in usable form, as from refuse material or waste products. **8.** *Law.* the obtaining of right to something by verdict or judgment of a court of law. **9.** *Football.* an act or instance of recovering a fumble. **10.** *Fencing.* the movement to the position of guard after a lunge. **11.** *Rowing.* a return to a former position for making the next stroke. [ME < AF *recoverie.* See RECOVER, -Y[3]]

recov′ery peg′, *Survey.* a peg driven in some known position relative to that of another peg, permitting the latter to be replaced if disturbed. Also called **reference peg.**

recov′ery room′, a room near the operating or delivery room of a hospital, equipped with specific apparatus and staffed by specially trained personnel for emergencies, used for the recovery from anesthesia of a postoperative or obstetrical patient before being brought to a hospital room or ward.

recpt, receipt.

rec·re·ant (rek′rē ənt), *adj.* **1.** cowardly or craven. **2.** unfaithful, disloyal, or traitorous. —*n.* **3.** a coward. **4.** an apostate, traitor, or renegade. [ME < OF, prp. of *recreire* to yield in a contest, *re-* RE- + *creire* < L *crēdere* to believe] —**rec′re·ance, rec′re·an·cy,** *n.* —**rec′re·ant·ly,** *adv.*

—**Syn. 1.** dastardly, pusillanimous, base, faint-hearted, yellow. **2.** faithless, untrue, apostate. **3.** dastard. —**Ant. 1.** brave. **2.** loyal. **3.** hero.

re-cre·ate (rē′krē āt′), *v.t.,* **-at·ed, -at·ing.** to create anew. [RE- + CREATE] —**re′-cre·a′tor,** *n.*
—**Syn.** reproduce, remake.

rec·re·ate (rek′rē āt′), *v.,* **-at·ed, -at·ing.** —*v.t.* **1.** to refresh by means of relaxation and enjoyment, as after work. **2.** to restore or refresh physically or mentally. —*v.i.* **3.** to take recreation. [< L *recreāt(us)* (ptp. of *recreāre* to create again, revive), equiv. to *re-* RE- + *creāt(us)*; see CREATE] —**rec′re·a′tive,** *adj.* —**rec′re·a′tive·ly,** *adv.* —**rec′re·a′tive·ness,** *n.* —**rec′re·a′tor,** *n.*

re-cre·a·tion (rē′krē ā′shən), *n.* **1.** the act of creating anew. **2.** something created anew. [RE- + CREATION]

rec·re·a·tion (rek′rē ā′shən), *n.* **1.** refreshment by means of some pastime, agreeable exercise, or the like, as after work. **2.** a pastime, diversion, exercise, or other resource affording relaxation and enjoyment. **3.** an act of recreating or the state of being recreated. [ME *recreacion* < MF *recreation* or L *recreātiōn-* (s. of *recreātiō*) restoration, recovery, equiv. to *recreāt(us)* (see RECREATE) + *-iōn-* -ION] —**rec′re·a′tion·al,** *adj.* **rec·re·a·to·ry** (rek′rē ə tôr′ē, -tōr′ē), *adj.*

recrea′tion room′, (in a home or public building) a room for informal entertaining, as for dancing, games, cards, etc.

rec·re·ment (rek′rə mənt), *n.* **1.** *Physiol.* a secretion, as saliva, that is reabsorbed by the body. **2.** refuse separated from anything; dross. [< MF < L *recrēment(um)* dross, refuse, equiv. to *re-* RE- + *crē-* separate (s. of *cernere*; see SHEAR) + *-mentum* -MENT] —**rec′re·men′tal,** *adj.*

re·crim·i·nate (ri krim′ə nāt′), *v.,* **-nat·ed, -nat·ing.** —*v.i.* **1.** to bring a countercharge against an accuser. —*v.t.* **2.** to accuse in return. [< ML *recrīmināt(us)* accused in turn (ptp. of *recrīminārī*), equiv. to *re-* RE- + *crīmin-* CRIME + *-ātus* -ATE[1]] —**re·crim′i·na′tion,** *n.* —**re·crim′i·na′tive, re·crim·i·na·to·ry** (ri krim′ə nə tôr′ē, -tōr′ē), *adj.* —**re·crim′i·na′tor,** *n.*

rec′ room′ (rek), *Informal.* a recreation room.

re·cru·desce (rē′krōō des′), *v.i.,* **-desced, -desc·ing.** to break out afresh, as a sore, a disease, or anything else that has been quiescent. [< L *recrūdesc(ere)* (to) become raw again, equiv. to *re-* RE- + *crūdescere* to grow harsh, worse (*crūd(us)* bloody (see CRUDE) + *-escere* inceptive suffix)]
—**Syn.** erupt, revive.

re·cru·des·cence (rē′krōō des′əns), *n.* breaking out afresh or into renewed activity; revival or reappearance in active existence. Also, **re′cru·des′cen·cy.** [< L *recrūdesc(ere)* (to) RECRUDESCE + -ENCE] —**re′cru·des′cent,** *adj.*

re·cruit (ri krōōt′), *n.* **1.** a newly enlisted or drafted member of the armed forces. **2.** a new member of a group, organization, or the like. **3.** *Archaic.* a fresh supply of something. —*v.t.* **4.** to enlist (persons) for service in one of the armed forces. **5.** to raise (a force) by enlistment. **6.** to strengthen or supply (an armed force) with new men. **7.** to furnish or replenish with a fresh supply; renew. **8.** to renew or restore (the health, strength, etc.). —*v.i.* **9.** to enlist men for service in one of the armed forces. **10.** to recover health, strength, etc. **11.** to gain new supplies of anything lost or wasted. [< F, s. of *recruter,* deriv. of *recrue* new growth, ptp. of *recroître* (*re-* RE- + *croître* < L *crescere* to grow)] —**re·cruit′a·ble,** *adj.* —**re·cruit′er,** *n.*

re·cruit·ment (ri krōōt′mənt), *n.* **1.** the act or process of recruiting. **2.** *Physiol.* an increase in the response to a stimulus owing to the activation of additional receptors, resulting from the continuous application of the stimulus with the same intensity. [RECRUIT + -MENT]

re·crys·tal·lise (rē kris′t^{ə}līz′), *v.i., v.t.,* **-lised, -lis·ing.** *Chiefly Brit.* recrystallize.

re·crys·tal·lize (rē kris′t^{ə}līz′), *v.,* **-lized, -liz·ing.** —*v.i.* **1.** to become crystallized again. **2.** *Metall.* (of a metal) to acquire a new granular structure with new crystals because of plastic deformation, as when hot-worked. —*v.t.* **3.** to crystallize again. [RE- + CRYSTALLIZE] —**re′crys·tal·li·za′tion,** *n.*

Rec. Sec., Recording Secretary. Also, **rec. sec.**

rect-, var. of **recti-** before a vowel: *rectangle.*

rect., **1.** receipt. **2.** (in prescriptions) rectified. [< L *rectificātus*] **3.** rector. **4.** rectory.

rec·ta (rek′tə), *n.* a pl. of **rectum.**

rec·tal (rek′t^{ə}l), *adj.* of or pertaining to the rectum. [RECT(O) + -AL[1]] —**rec′tal·ly,** *adv.*

rec·tan·gle (rek′tang′gəl), *n.* a parallelogram having four right angles. [< ML *rectangulum,* LL *rectiangul(um)* right-angled triangle (neut. of *rectiangulus* having a right angle), equiv. to *recti-* RECT- + *angulum* ANGLE]

Rectangle

rec·tan·gu·lar (rek tang′gyə lər), *adj.* **1.** shaped like a rectangle. **2.** having the base or section in the form of a rectangle: *a rectangular pyramid.* **3.** having one or more right angles. **4.** forming a right angle. [< ML *rectangul(um)* RECTANGLE + -AR[1]] —**rec·tan·gu·lar·i·ty** (rek tang′gyə lar′i tē), **rec·tan′gu·lar·ness,** *n.* —**rec·tan′gu·lar·ly,** *adv.*

rectan′gular coor′dinates, *Math.* a coordinate system in which the axes meet at right angles.

rectan′gular hyper′bola, *Geom.* a hyperbola with transverse and conjugate axes equal to each other. Also called **equiangular hyperbola, equilateral hyperbola.**

rec·tec·to·my (rek tek′tə mē), *n., pl.* **-mies.** *Surg.* proctectomy. [RECT(O)- + -ECTOMY]

rec·ti (rek′tī), *n.* pl. of **rectus.**

recti-, a learned borrowing from Latin meaning "right," "straight," used in the formation of compound words: *rectilinear.* Also, *esp. before a vowel,* **rect-.** [< L, comb. form of *rectus* RIGHT]

rec·ti·fi·a·ble (rek′tə fī′ə bəl), *adj.* **1.** able to be rectified. **2.** *Math.* of or pertaining to a curve or arc that has finite length. [RECTIFY + -ABLE]

rec·ti·fi·er (rek′tə fī′ər), *n.* **1.** one who or that which rectifies. **2.** *Elect.* an apparatus in which current more readily flows in one direction than in the reverse direction, for changing an alternating current into a direct current. **3.** the apparatus that in distillation separates the most volatile material by condensing it; condenser. [RECTIFY + -ER[1]]

rec·ti·fy (rek′tə fī′), *v.t.,* **-fied, -fy·ing.** **1.** to make, put, or set right; remedy; correct: *He sent them a check to rectify his account.* **2.** to put right by adjustment or calculation, as an instrument or a course at sea. **3.** *Chem.* to purify (esp. a spirit or liquor) by repeated distillation. **4.** *Elect.* to change (an alternating current) into a direct current. **5.** to determine the length of (a curve). **6.** *Astron., Geog.* to adjust (a globe) for the solution of any proposed problem. [ME *rectifie(n)* < MF *rectifi(er)* < ML *rectific(āre),* equiv. to L *rect(us)* RECT- + *-ificāre* -IFY] —**rec′ti·fi·ca′tion,** *n.*

—**Syn. 1.** mend, emend, amend; better, ameliorate, improve. **2.** adjust, regulate, straighten. —**Ant. 1.** worsen.

rec·ti·lin·e·ar (rek′t^{ə}lin′ē ər), *adj.* **1.** forming a straight line. **2.** formed by straight lines. **3.** characterized by straight lines. **4.** moving in a straight line. Also, **rec′ti·lin′e·al.** [< LL *rectilīne(us)* (*rect(us)* RECT- + *līnea* LINE[1]) + -AR[1]] —**rec′ti·lin′e·ar·ly,** *adv.*

rec·ti·ros·tral (rek′tə ros′trəl), *adj.* (of a bird) having a straight bill. [RECTI- + ROSTRAL]

rec·ti·tude (rek′ti tōōd′, -tyōōd′), *n.* **1.** rightness of principle or practice; moral virtue: *the rectitude of his motives.* **2.** correctness: *rectitude of judgment.* **3.** straightness. [ME < MF < LL *rectitūdin-* (s. of *rectitūdō*) straightness, equiv. to L *rect(us)* RECTI- + *-tūdin-* -TUDE]

rec·to (rek′tō), *n., pl.* **-tos.** *Print.* a right-hand page of an open book or manuscript; the front of a leaf (opposed to *verso*). [< LL *rectō* (*foliō*) on the right-hand (leaf or page), abl. of L *rectus* right]

recto-, a combining form of **rectum:** *rectocele.*

rec·to·cele (rek′tə sēl′), *n.* a hernia of the rectum into the vagina. [RECTO- + -CELE[1]]

rec·tor (rek′tər), *n.* **1.** a clergyman in charge of a parish in the Protestant Episcopal Church. **2.** *Rom. Cath. Ch.* an ecclesiastic in charge of a college, religious house, or congregation. **3.** *Anglican Ch.* a clergyman who has the charge of a parish with full possession of all its rights, tithes, etc. **4.** the head of certain universities, colleges, and schools. [ME *rectour* < L *rector* ruler, leader, equiv. to *rect(us)* ruled (ptp. of *regere*) + *-or* -OR[2]] —**rec·to·ri·al** (rek tôr′ē əl, -tōr′-), *adj.*

rec·tor·ate (rek′tər it), *n.* the office, dignity, or term of a rector. [< ML *rectorāt(us)* office of rector, equiv. to L *rectōr-* (s. of *rector*) RECTOR + *-ātus* -ATE[1]]

rec·to·ry (rek′tə rē), *n., pl.* **-ries.** **1.** a rector's house; parsonage. **2.** *Brit.* a benefice held by a rector. [< ML *rectoria,* equiv. to L *rectōr-* (s. of *rector*) RECTOR + *-ia* -Y[3]]

rec·trix (rek′triks), *n., pl.* **rec·tri·ces** (rek trī′sēz). *Ornith.* one of the tail feathers of a bird. [< L *rectrīx,* fem. of *rector* RECTOR] —**rec·tri·cial** (rek trish′əl), *adj.*

rec·tum (rek′təm), *n., pl.* **-tums, -ta** (-tə). *Anat.* the comparatively straight, terminal section of the intestine, ending in the anus. See diag. under **intestine.** [< NL *rectum* (*intestinum*) the straight (intestine)]

rec·tus (rek′təs), *n., pl.* **-ti** (-tī). *Anat.* any of several straight muscles, as of the abdomen, thigh, eye, etc. [< NL *rectus* (*musculus*) the straight (muscle)]

re·cum·bent (ri kum′bənt), *adj.* **1.** lying down; reclining; leaning. **2.** inactive; idle. **3.** *Zool., Bot.* noting a part that leans or reposes upon anything. —*n.* **4.** a recumbent person, animal, plant, etc. [< L *recumbent-* (s. of *recumbēns,* prp. of *recumbere*) lying back, equiv. to *re-* RE- + *cumb-* (cf. *cubāre* to lie down) + *-ent-* -ENT] —**re·cum′ben·cy, re·cum′bence,** *n.* —**re·cum′bent·ly,** *adv.*

—**Syn. 1.** prone, supine; prostrate; inclined.

re·cu·per·ate (ri kōō′pə rāt′), *v.,* **-at·ed, -at·ing.** —*v.i.* **1.** to recover from sickness or exhaustion; regain health or strength. **2.** to recover from financial loss. —*v.t.* **3.** to restore to health, vigor, etc. [< L *recuperāt(us)* recovered (ptp. of *recuperāre,* sp. var. of *reciperāre*), equiv. to *re-* RE- + *cuper-* get, take + *-ātus* -ATE[1]] —**re·cu′per·a′tion,** *n.*

—**Syn. 1.** heal, mend.

re·cu·per·a·tive (ri kōō′pə rā′tiv, -pər ə tiv, -kyōō′-), *adj.* **1.** that recuperates. **2.** having the power of recuperating. **3.** pertaining to recuperation: *recuperative powers.* Also, **re·cu·per·a·to·ry** (ri kōō′pər ə tôr′ē, -tōr′ē, -kyōō′-). [< L *recuperātīv(us)* that can be regained, equiv. to *recuperāt(us)* (see RECUPERATE) + *-īvus* -IVE] —**re·cu′per·a′tive·ness,** *n.*

recu′perative fur′nace, a furnace having its incoming air heated by exhaust gases, the passage of air and gases through the furnace being always in the same direction. Cf. **regenerative furnace.**

re·cu·per·a·tor (ri kōō′pə rā′tər, -kyōō′-), *n.* **1.** one who or that which recuperates. **2.** (in a recuperative furnace) a system of thin-walled ducts through which incoming air and exhausted gases pass separately so that the air is heated by the gases. [< L: regainer, equiv. to *recuperāt(us)* (see RECUPERATE) + *-or* -OR[2]]

re·cur (ri kûr′), *v.i.,* **-curred, -cur·ring.** **1.** to occur again, as an event, experience, etc. **2.** to return to the mind: *recurring ideas.* **3.** to come up again for consideration, as a question. **4.** to return in action, thought, etc.: *to recur to a subject.* **5.** to have recourse. [< L *recurr(ere)* (to) run back, equiv. to *re-* RE- + *currere* to run] —**re·cur′ring·ly,** *adv.*

—**Syn. 4.** refer, revert.

re·cur·rence (ri kûr′əns, -kur′-), *n.* **1.** an act or instance of recurring. **2.** return to a previous condition, habit, subject, etc. **3.** recourse. [RECUR + -ENCE]

recur′rence for′mula, *Math.* See **recursion formula.**

re·cur·rent (ri kûr′ənt, -kur′-), *adj.* **1.** that recurs; occurring or appearing again, esp. repeatedly or periodically. **2.** *Anat.* turned back so as to run in a reverse direction, as a nerve, artery, branch, etc. [< L *recurrent-* (s. of *recurrēns,* prp. of *recurrere*) running back, equiv. to *recurr-* RECUR + *-ent-* -ENT] —**re·cur′rent·ly,** *adv.*

—**Syn. 1.** repeated; persistent, intermittent.

recur′rent fe′ver, *Pathol.* See **relapsing fever.**

recur′ring dec′imal. See **circulating decimal.**

re·cur′sion for′mula (ri kûr′zhən), *Math.* a formula for determining the next term of a sequence from one or more of the preceding terms. Also called **recurrence formula.** [< L *recursiōn-* (s. of *recursiō*) a running back, equiv. to *recurs(us)* (see RECOURSE) + *-iōn-* -ION]

recur′sive defini′tion, *Logic.* a definition consisting of a set of rules such that by repeated application of the rules the meaning of the definiendum is uniquely determined in terms of ideas that are already familiar. [RECURS(ION) + -IVE]

re·cur·vate (ri kûr′vit, -vāt), *adj.* bent back or backward; recurved. [< L *recurvāt(us)* bent backwards (ptp. of *recurvāre;* *re-* RE- + *curv-* CURVE + *-ātus* -ATE[1])]

re·curve (ri kûrv′), *v.t., v.i.,* **-curved, -curv·ing.** to curve or bend back or backward. [< L *recurv(āre),* equiv. to *re-* RE- + *curvāre* to curve]

re·curved (rē kûrvd′), *adj.* curved upward, as the bill of a bird. [RE- + CURVED]

rec·u·san·cy (rek′yə zən sē, ri kyōō′-), *n.* **1.** the state of being recusant. **2.** obstinate refusal or opposition. [RECUS(ANT) + -ANCY]

rec·u·sant (rek′yə zənt, ri kyōō′zənt), *adj.* **1.** refusing to submit, comply, etc. **2.** obstinate in refusal. **3.** *Eng. Hist.* refusing to attend services of the Church of England. —*n.* **4.** one who is recusant. **5.** *Eng. Hist.* a person, esp. a Roman Catholic, who refused to attend the services of the Church of England. [< L *recūsant-* (s. of *recūsāns,* prp. of *recūsāre* to refuse, object), equiv. to *re-* RE- + *-cūs-* cause (var. of *causa*) + *-ant-* -ANT]

re·cuse (ri kyōōz′), *v.t.,* **-cused, -cus·ing.** *Rare.* to reject or challenge (a judge or juror) as disqualified to act, esp. because of interest or bias. [ME *recuse(n)* < MF *recus(er)* < L *recūs(āre)*; see RECUSANT] —**rec·u·sa·tion** (rek′yōō zā′shən), *n.*

re·cy·cle (rē sī′kəl), *v.t.,* **-cled, -cling.** to pass through or undergo again, as for further treatment, change, use, etc. [RE- + CYCLE]

red[1] (red), *adj.,* **red·der, red·dest,** *n.* —*adj.* **1.** of the color red. **2.** distinguished by being red, wearing red, etc.: *the red numbers on the chart.* **3.** radically left politically. **4.** (*often cap.*) communist. —*n.* **5.** any of various colors resembling the color of blood; a color at the extreme end of the visible spectrum. **6.** something

re·crate′, *v.t.,* **-crat·ed, -crat·ing.**
re·crit′i·cize′, *v.t.,* **-cized, -ciz·ing.**
re·cross′, *v.*
re·crown′, *v.t.*
re·cul′ti·vate′, *v.t.,* **-vat·ed, -vat·ing.**
re′cul·ti·va′tion, *n.*
re·cut′, *v.,* **-cut, -cut·ting.**

red. **7.** (*often cap.*) an ultraradical leftist in politics, esp. a communist. **8.** the condition of operating at a loss or being in debt (opposed to *black*): *The newspaper strike put many businesses in the red and bankrupted others.* **9. paint the town red.** See **paint** (def. 14). **10. see red,** *Informal.* to become very angry; become enraged: *Snobs of a particular type make her see red.* [ME *red*, OE *rēad*; c. G *rot*, D *rood*, OIcel *raudhr*, L *rūfus*, *ruber*, Gk *erathrós*; see RUBELLA, RUFESCENT, ERYSIPELAS]

red[2] (red), *v.t.*, **red, red·ding.** redd[1].

Red (red), *n.* a boy's or girl's given name.

red-, var. of **re-** before a vowel in some words: *redintegrate.*

-red, a native English suffix, denoting condition, formerly used in the formation of nouns: *hatred; kindred.* [ME *-rede*, OE *-rǣden*]

re·dact (ri dakt′), *v.t.* **1.** to put into suitable literary form; revise; edit. **2.** to draw up or frame (a statement, proclamation, etc.). [< L *redāct(us)* led back (ptp. of *redigere; red-* RED- + *actus*); see ACT] **—re·dac′tion,** *n.* **—re·dac′tion·al,** *adj.* **—re·dac′tor,** *n.*

red′ ad′miral. See under **admiral** (def. 6).

red′ al′der, 1. an alder, *Alnus rubra*, of western North America. **2.** the hard, red wood of this tree, used for making furniture. **—red′-al′der,** *adj.*

red′ alert′, 1. (in military or civilian defense) the most urgent form of alert, signaling that an enemy attack is believed to be imminent. **2.** the signal or alarm sounded for this alert. Cf. **blue alert, white alert, yellow alert.**

red′ al′ga, an alga of the class *Rhodophyceae*, in which the chlorophyll is masked by a red or purplish pigment.

re·dan (ri dan′), *n.* *Fort.* a V-shaped work, usually projecting from a fortified line. [< F, var. of *redent* a double notching or jagging, equiv. to *re-* RE- + *dent* tooth < L *dent-* (s. of *dēns*)]

Red′ and the Black′, The, a novel (1832) by Stendhal. French, **Le Rouge et le Noir.**

red′ ant′, any of various reddish ants, esp. the Pharaoh ant.

Red′ Ar′my, the official name of the Soviet army.

Red′ Badge′ of Cour′age, The, a novel (1895) by Stephen Crane.

red·bait (red′bāt′), *v.i.* to denounce or deprecate as a political radical, esp. to accuse of being communist. [back formation from *redbaiter, redbaiting*. See RED[1], BAIT] **—red′bait′er,** *n.*

red′ balm′, a bee balm, *Monarda didyma.*

red′ bay′, an evergreen tree, *Persea Borbonia*, of the eastern coast of the U.S., having faintly bluish-green leaves and blue or blue-black, red-stalked fruit, grown as an ornamental. Also called **bull bay.**

red′-bel·lied tur′tle (red′bel′ēd), a fresh-water turtle, *Pseudemys rubiventris*, of coastal regions of the Eastern U.S., having red markings on the shell.

red·bird (red′bûrd′), *n.* **1.** the cardinal, *Richmondena cardinalis.* **2.** any of various other birds having red plumage, as the scarlet tanager. [RED[1] + BIRD]

red′ blood′ cell′, an erythrocyte. Also called **red′ blood′ cor′puscle.**

red-blood·ed (red′blud′id), *adj.* vigorous; virile. **—red′-blood′ed·ness,** *n.*

Red′ Bluff′, a town in N California. 7202 (1960).

red·bone (red′bōn′), *n.* an American hound having a red coat, used in hunting raccoons, bears, cougars, and wildcats. [RED[1] + BONE[1]]

Red′ Branch′, *Irish Legend.* the warriors of Conchobar, alienated from him after his treachery to Deirdre and Naoise.

red′ brass′, an alloy of from 77 to 86 percent copper with the balance zinc; Mannheim gold.

red·breast (red′brest′), *n.* **1.** a robin. **2.** any of various other birds, as a dowitcher or knot. **3.** a fresh-water sunfish, *Lepomis auritus*, found in the eastern U.S. [RED[1] + BREAST]

red′-breast·ed mergan′ser (red′bres′tid), a merganser, *Mergus serrator*, of the Northern Hemisphere, having a chestnut band of color on its breast.

red′-brick univer′sity (red′brik′), *Brit. Informal.* **1.** any new or little-known university, esp. one built since World War II to educate students in industrial regions, emphasizing technical subjects rather than the classics, and often partially supported by government funds. **2.** any university lacking the prestige of Oxford and Cambridge. Also, **red′brick univer′sity.**

red·bud (red′bud′), *n.* **1.** an American, leguminous tree, *Cercis canadensis*, resembling the Eurasian Judas tree and having small, budlike, pink flowers: the State tree of Oklahoma. **2.** any of various related trees. [RED[1] + BUD[1]]

red·bug (red′bug′), *n.* chigger (def. 1). [RED + BUG]

red′ cal′la lil′y, an herb, *Zantedeschia rehmanni*, of South Africa, having white-spotted leaves and rose-red, trumpet-shaped flowers. Also called **pink calla lily.**

red·cap (red′kap′), *n.* **1.** *U.S.* a baggage porter whose work is confined to a railroad station. **2.** *Brit. Informal.* a military policeman. **3.** *Brit. Dial.* the European goldfinch, *Carduelis carduelis.* [RED[1] + CAP]

red′ car′pet, 1. a red strip of carpet placed on the ground for high-ranking dignitaries to walk on when entering or leaving a building, vehicle, or the like. **2.** a display of courtesy or deference, as that shown to persons of high station: *The visiting princess was treated to the red carpet in Rome.* **—red′-car′pet,** *adj.*

red′ ce′dar, 1. Also called **eastern red cedar, savin.** an American, coniferous tree, *Juniperus virginiana*, yielding a fragrant, reddish wood used for making lead pencils, etc. **2.** the western red cedar, *Thuja plicata.* **3.** the wood of these trees.

red′ cent′, *U.S. Informal.* a cent, as representative of triviality: *His promise isn't worth a red cent!*

Red′ Cham′ber, *Canadian Informal.* the Canadian Senate chamber.

Red′ Chi′na. See **China, People's Republic of.**

red′ choke′berry. See under **chokeberry** (def. 1).

red′ clay′, *Geol.* a brown to red, widely distributed, deep-sea deposit consisting chiefly of inorganic materials, as iron oxides and manganese. **—red′-clay′,** *adj.*

red′ clo′ver, a clover, *Trifolium pratense*, having red flowers, grown for forage: the State flower of Vermont.

red′ clus′ter pep′per, a tropical, woody plant, *Capsicum frutescens fasciculatum*, having erect, very pungent, red fruit in small clusters.

red·coat (red′kōt′), *n.* (esp. during the American Revolution) a British soldier. [RED[1] + COAT]

red′ cor′al, any of several alcyonarian corals of the genus *Corallium*, as *C. nobile*, of the Mediterranean Sea, having a red or pink skeleton, used for jewelry. Also called **precious coral.**

red′ count′, a count of the red cells in a person's blood. Cf. **blood count.**

Red′ Cres′cent, an organization functioning as the Red Cross in Turkey, having as its insignia a red crescent.

Red′ Cross′, 1. an international philanthropic organization (**Red′ Cross′ Soci′ety**), formed in consequence of the Geneva Convention of 1864, to care for the sick and wounded in war, secure neutrality of nurses, hospitals, etc., and help relieve suffering caused by pestilence, floods, fires, and other calamities. **2.** a branch of this organization: *the American Red Cross.* **3.** the English national emblem of St. George's cross. **4.** See **Geneva cross.** Also, **red′ cross′** (for defs. 3, 4).

red′ cur′rant, 1. any of various currants of the genus *Ribes*, bearing an edible, red fruit. **2.** the fruit itself.

redd[1] (red), *v.t.*, **redd** or **redd·ed, redd·ing.** *Northern and Midland U.S.* **1.** to put in order; tidy: *to redd a room for company.* **2.** to clear: *to redd the way.* Also, **red.** [special use of obs. *redd* to free, rescue, OE *hreddan*, confused with *rede*, deriv. of OE *rǣdan* to put in order; see READY]

redd[2] (red), *n.* the spawning area or nest of trout or salmon. [?]

red′ dead′ net′tle, a Eurasian, weedy herb, *Lamium purpureum*, naturalized in North America, having purple-red flowers. Also called **French nettle.**

red′ deer′, 1. a deer, *Cervus elaphus*, of Europe and Asia, having a reddish-brown summer coat. **2.** the white-tailed deer, *Odocoileus virginianus*, in its summer coat. [late ME]

red·den (red′ən), *v.t.* **1.** to make or cause to become red. **—***v.i.* **2.** to become red. **3.** to blush; flush. [RED[1] + -EN[1]]

Red′ Des′ert. See **Nefud Desert.**

red′ dev′il, a wrymouth, *Lyconectes aleutensis*, found in the northeastern Pacific Ocean.

Red·ding (red′ing), *n.* a city in N California. 12,773 (1960).

red·dish (red′ish), *adj.* somewhat red; tending to red; tinged with red. [ME *redische*. See RED[1], -ISH[1]] **—red′dish·ness,** *n.*

red·dle (red′əl), *n., v.t.*, **-dled, -dling.** raddle[2].

red·dle·man (red′əl mən), *n., pl.* **-men.** ruddleman.

red-dog (red′dôg′, -dog′), *v.*, **-dogged, -dog·ging.** *Football.* (esp. of linebackers) **—***v.t.* **1.** to charge directly for (the passer) as soon as the ball is snapped. **—***v.i.* **2.** to red-dog the passer. **—red′-dog′ger,** *n.*

red′ dog′wood, 1. a Eurasian dogwood, *Cornus sanguinea*, having greenish-white flowers and dark red branches. **2.** a variety of flowering dogwood, *Cornus florida rubra*, having red or pink bracts.

red′ drum′, *Ichthyol.* a large, edible drum, *Sciaenops ocellata*, found off the Atlantic coast of the U.S.

red′ dust′er, a red ensign having the Union Jack as a canton, flown by most British merchant ships.

rede (rēd), *v.*, **red·ed, red·ing,** *n.* *Chiefly Brit. Dial.* **—***v.t.* **1.** to counsel; advise. **2.** to explain. **—***n.* **3.** counsel; advice. **4.** a plan; scheme. **5.** a tale; story. [ME *rede(n)*, OE *rǣdan*; see READ[1]]

red′ear sun′fish (red′ēr′), a fresh-water sunfish, *Lepomis microlophos*, found in the lower Mississippi valley and southeastern States, having the gill cover margined with scarlet. Also called **red′ear shell′-cracker.** [RED + EAR[1]]

re·deem (ri dēm′), *v.t.* **1.** to buy or pay off; clear by payment: *to redeem a mortgage.* **2.** to buy back, as after a tax sale or a mortgage foreclosure. **3.** to recover (something pledged or mortgaged) by payment or other satisfaction: *to redeem a pawned watch.* **4.** to convert (paper money) into specie. **5.** to discharge or fulfill (a pledge, promise, etc.). **6.** to make up for; make amends for; offset (some fault, shortcoming, etc.): *His bravery redeemed his youthful idleness.* **7.** to obtain the release or restoration of, as from captivity, by paying a ransom. **8.** *Theol.* to deliver from sin and its consequences by means of a sacrifice offered for the sinner. [ME *redem(en)* < MF *redim(er)* < L *redimere*, equiv. to *red-* RE- + *-imere* to buy, var. of *emere* to purchase]

—Syn. 1, 2, 7, 8. repurchase; free, liberate, rescue, save. REDEEM, RANSOM mean literally to buy back. REDEEM is wider in its application than RANSOM, and means to buy back, regain possession, or improve the condition of anything; as by money, endeavor, devotion, sacrifice, or the like: *to redeem one's property.* To RANSOM is to redeem a person from captivity by paying a stipulated price, or to redeem from sin by sacrifice: *to ransom a kidnapped child.* **—Ant. 1.** abandon.

re·deem·a·ble (ri dē′mə bəl), *adj.* **1.** capable of being redeemed. **2.** that is to be redeemed: *bonds redeemable in 1975.* Also, **re·demp·ti·ble** (ri demp′tə bəl). [REDEEM + -ABLE] **—re·deem′a·bil′i·ty, re·deem′a·ble·ness,** *n.* **—re·deem′a·bly,** *adv.*

re·deem·er (ri dē′mər), *n.* **1.** one who redeems. **2.** (*cap.*) Jesus Christ. [ME; see REDEEM, -ER[1]]

re·deem·ing (ri dē′ming), *adj.* offsetting or counterbalancing some fault, defect, or the like: *a redeeming quality.* [REDEEM + -ING[2]]

red′ eft′. See under **eft**[1] (def. 1).

re·de·liv·er (rē′di liv′ər), *v.t.* **1.** to deliver again. **2.** to deliver back; return. [RE- + DELIVER] **—re′de·liv′er·er,** *n.*

re·de·mand (rē′di mand′, -mänd′), *v.t.* **1.** to demand again. **2.** to demand back; demand the return of. [RE- + DEMAND] **—re′de·mand′a·ble,** *adj.*

re·demp·tion (ri demp′shən), *n.* **1.** an act of redeeming or the state of being redeemed. **2.** deliverance; rescue. **3.** *Theol.* deliverance from sin; salvation. **4.** atonement for guilt. **5.** repurchase, as of something sold. **6.** paying off, as of a mortgage, bond, or note. **7.** recovery by payment, as of something pledged. **8.** conversion of paper money into specie. [ME *redempcioun* < MF < LL *redemptiōn-* (s. of *redemptiō*), equiv. to L *redempt(us)* (ptp. of *redimere* to REDEEM) + *-iōn-* -ION] **—re·demp′tion·al,** *adj.* **—re·demp′tion·less,** *adj.*

redemp′tion cen′ter, a commercial establishment at which trading stamps of a specific brand may be exchanged for merchandise.

re·demp·tion·er (ri demp′shə nər), *n.* *Amer. Hist.* an emigrant from Europe to America who obtained passage by becoming an indentured servant for a specified period of time. [REDEMPTION + -ER[1]]

re·demp·tive (ri demp′tiv), *adj.* **1.** serving to redeem. **2.** of, pertaining to, or centering on redemption or salvation: *redemptive religions.* [REDEMPT(ION) + -IVE] **—re·demp′tive·ly,** *adv.*

Re·demp·tor·ist (ri demp′tər ist), *n.* *Rom. Cath. Ch.* a member of the "Congregation of the Most Holy Redeemer," founded by St. Alphonsus Liguori in 1732. [< F *rédemptoriste* < LL *redemptor*, equiv. to L *redempt(us)* (see REDEMPTION) + *-or* -OR[2] + F *-iste* -IST]

re·demp·to·ry (ri demp′tə rē), *adj.* **1.** of or pertaining to redemption; redemptive. **2.** redeeming; saving: *a redemptory act.* [REDEMPT(ION) + -ORY[1]]

re·de·ploy (rē′di ploi′), *Mil.* **—***v.t.* **1.** to transfer (a unit, a person, supplies, etc.) from one theater of operations to another. **—***v.i.* **2.** to execute a redeployment. [RE- + DEPLOY] **—re′de·ploy′ment,** *n.*

re·de·vel·op (rē′di vel′əp), *v.t.* **1.** to develop (something) again. **2.** *Photog.* to submit (a film or the like) to a second development, as to intensify or tone it. **—***v.i.* **3.** to develop again. [RE- + DEVELOP] **—re′de·vel′op·er,** *n.* **—re′de·vel′op·ment,** *n.*

redevel′opment com′pany, a private corporation or a public agency that stimulates the improvement of land, as through a building project subject to certain designs and controls, by financing, selling, or leasing such real estate to interested buyers or lessees.

red·eye (red′ī′), *n., pl.* **-eyes,** (*esp. collectively*) **-eye. 1.** any of several fishes having red eyes, as the rock bass. **2.** See **red-eyed vireo. 3.** *U.S.* cheap, strong whiskey. [RED[1] + EYE]

red′-eyed vir′eo (red′īd′), an American vireo, *Vireo olivaceus*, having olive-green and white plumage and red irises. Also called **preacher bird.** See illus. under **vireo.**

red-faced (red′fāst′), *adj.* **1.** having a red face. **2.** blushing or flushed with embarrassment, anger, resentment, or the like. **—red-fac·ed·ly** (red′fā′sid lē, -fāst′lē), *adv.*

red′ false′ mal′low, a woody-based, perennial herb, *Sphaeralcea coccinea*, of central North America, having brick-red flowers in dense, terminal clusters. Also called **prairie mallow.**

Red′ Feath′er, of, pertaining to, or maintained by a community chest: *working for a Red Feather organization.*

red′ fes′cue, a perennial grass, *Festuca rubra*, of the meadows of the North Temperate Zone, having green, reddish, or bluish-green flower clusters. Also called **creeping fescue.**

Red·field (red′fēld′), *n.* **1. Robert,** 1897–1958, American anthropologist. **2.** a town in central South Dakota. 2952 (1960).

red-fig·ure (red′fig′yər), *adj.* pertaining to or designating a style of vase painting developed in Greece in the latter part of the 6th and the 5th century B.C., characterized chiefly by figurative representations in red against a black-slip background, details painted in the design, and the introduction of three-dimensional illusion in the rendering of form and space. Also, **red′-fig′ured.** Cf. **black-figure.**

red·fin (red′fin′), *n.* any of various small fresh-water minnows with red fins, esp. a shiner, *Notropis umbratilis*, found in eastern and central North America. [RED[1] + FIN]

red′fin pick′erel. See under **pickerel** (def. 1).

red′ fir′, 1. any of several firs, as *Abies magnifica*, of the western U.S., having a reddish bark. **2.** the light, soft wood of these trees. **3.** See **Douglas fir.**

---

re·dam′age, *v.t.*, **-aged, -ag·ing.**
re·dare′, *v.t.*, **-dared, -dar·ing.**
re·darn′, *v.t.*
re·date′, *v.*, **-dat·ed, -dat·ing.**
re·deal′, *n., v.*, **-dealt, -deal·ing.**
re′de·bate′, *n., v.*, **-bat·ed, -bat·ing.**
re·deb′it, *v.t.*
re′de·cay′, *v.*
re′de·ceive′, *v.t.*, **-ceived, -ceiv·ing.**
re′de·cide′, *v.*, **-cid·ed, -cid·ing.**
re′de·ci′sion, *n.*
re′dec·la·ra′tion, *n.*
re′de·clare′, *v.t.*, **-clared, -clar·ing.**
re′de·cline′, *v.*, **-clined, -clin·ing.**
re·dec′o·rate′, *v.*, **-rat·ed, -rat·ing.**
re′dec·o·ra′tion, *n.*
re·ded′i·cate′, *v.t.*, **-cat·ed, -cat·ing.**
re′ded·i·ca′tion, *n.*
re·deed′, *v.t.*
re′de·feat′, *v., n.*
re′de·fine′, *v.t.*, **-fined, -fin·ing.**
re′def·i·ni′tion, *n.*
re′de·fy′, *v.t.*, **-fied, -fy·ing.**
re·del′e·gate′, *v.t.*, **-gat·ed, -gat·ing.**
re′del·e·ga′tion, *n.*
re′de·lete′, *v.t.*, **-let·ed, -let·ing.**
re′de·lib′er·ate′, *v.*, **-at·ed, -at·ing.**
re′de·lib′er·a′tion, *n.*
re′de·liv′er·y, *n., pl.* **-er·ies.**
re·dem′on·strate′, *v.*, **-strat·ed, -strat·ing.**
re′dem·on·stra′tion, *n.*
re′de·ni′al, *n.*
re′de·ny′, *v.t.*, **-nied, -ny·ing.**
re′de·pend′, *v.i.*
re′de·pos′it, *v., n.*
re′de·pre′ci·ate′, *v.*, **-at·ed, -at·ing.**
re′de·pre′ci·a′tion, *n.*
re′de·scend′, *v.*
re′de·scent′, *n.*
re′de·scribe′, *v.t.*, **-scribed, -scrib·ing.**
re′de·scrip′tion, *n.*
re′de·sert′, *v.*
re′de·sign′, *v.*
re·des′ig·nate′, *v.t.*, **-nat·ed, -nat·ing.**
re′des·ig·na′tion, *n.*
re′de·ter′mine, *v.*, **-mined, -min·ing.**

CONCISE ETYMOLOGY KEY: <, descended or derived from; >, whence; b., blend of, blended; c., cognate with; deriv., derivative; equiv., equivalent; imit., imitative; m., modification of; obl., oblique; r., replacing; s., stem; sp., spelling; trans., translation; ?, origin unknown, perhaps; *, hypothetical. See the full key inside the front cover.

red′ fire′, any of various combustible preparations, as one containing strontium nitrate, that burn with a vivid red light: used chiefly in pyrotechnic displays and in signaling.

red·fish (red′fish′), *n., pl.* (*esp. collectively*) **-fish,** (*esp. referring to two or more kinds or species*) **-fish·es.** **1.** Also called **ocean perch, rosefish.** a North Atlantic rockfish, *Sebastes marinus,* used for food. **2.** See **red drum.** **3.** sheephead. [RED[1] + FISH]

red′ flag′, **1.** the symbol or banner of a left-wing revolutionary party. **2.** a danger signal. **3.** Also called **powder flag.** *Naut.* a red burgee, designating in the International Code of Signals the letter "B," flown by itself to show that a vessel is carrying, loading, or discharging explosives or highly inflammable material.

red′ flash′, *Astron.* a red coloration of the lower portion of the sun, occasionally seen as the sun rises above or sinks to the horizon.

red′ flour′ bee′tle, a reddish-brown flour beetle, *Tribolium castaneum,* that feeds on stored grain, dried fruit, etc.

red′ fox′, a fox, *Vulpes vulpes,* usually having orangish-red to reddish-brown fur. See illus. under **fox.**

red′ gi′ant, *Astron.* a star in an intermediate stage of evolution, characterized by a large volume, low surface temperature, and reddish hue.

red′ goat′fish, a goatfish, *Mullus auratus.*

Red·grave (red′grāv), *n.* **Sir Michael (Scud·a·more)** (skud′ə mōr′, -môr′, sko͞o′də-), born 1908, English actor.

red′ grouse′, a grouse, *Lagopus scoticus,* of the British Isles, having reddish-brown plumage, closely related to the ptarmigans.

red′ gum′, **1.** a gum tree, *Eucalyptus rostrata,* having smooth, gray bark. **2.** the hard, reddish wood of this tree, used for making railroad ties, fence posts, etc. **3.** See **sweet gum** (defs. 1, 2).

red′ gum′, *Pathol.* strophulus.

red-hand·ed (red′han′did), *adj., adv.* in the very act of a crime, wrongdoing, etc., or in possession of self-incriminating evidence: *They caught him red-handed dipping into the till.* —**red′-hand′ed·ly,** *adv.* —**red′-hand′ed·ness,** *n.*

red′ hat′, **1.** the broad-brimmed official hat of a Roman Catholic cardinal, symbolic of his office or dignity. **2.** a cardinal. Also called **scarlet hat.**

Red′ Hats′, the original sect of Tibetan Buddhist monks, whose doctrines were much influenced by the earlier Bön sect. Cf. **Yellow Hats.**

red·head (red′hed′), *n.* **1.** a person having red hair. **2.** an American diving duck, *Aythya americana,* the male of which has a bright chestnut-red head. [RED[1] + HEAD]

red-head·ed (red′hed′id), *adj.* **1.** having red hair, as a person. **2.** having a red head, as an animal, esp. a bird. Also, **red′head′ed.**

red′-headed wood′pecker, a black and white, North American woodpecker, *Melanerpes erythrocephalus,* having a red head and neck.

red′ heart′, a treelike shrub, *Ceanothus spinosus,* of California, having pale blue or white flowers.

red′ heat′, **1.** the temperature of a red-hot body. **2.** condition of being red-hot.

red′ her′ring, **1.** a smoked herring. **2.** something intended to divert attention from the real problem or matter at hand; a misleading clue. **3.** Also called **red′-her′ring prospec′tus.** *Finance Informal.* a tentative prospectus circulated by the underwriters of a new issue of stocks or bonds which is pending approval by the U.S. Securities and Exchange Commission: so called because the front cover of such a prospectus must carry a special notice printed in red. [ME]

red·hi·bi·tion (red′i bish′ən, red′hi-), *n.* *Civil Law.* the nullification of a sale because of a defect in the article sold of such nature as to make it totally or virtually unusable or as to have prevented the purchase if known to the buyer. [< L *redhibitiōn-* (s. of *redhibitiō*), equiv. to *redhibit(us),* ptp. of *redhibēre* (*red-* RED- + *-hib(ēre),* comb. form of *habēre* to have + *-itus* -ITE[2]) + *-iōn-* -ION] —**red·hib·i·to·ry** (red hib′i tôr′ē, -tōr′ē), *adj.*

red′ hind′ (hīnd), a serranoid food fish, *Epinephelus guttatus,* of Florida, the West Indies, etc.

red·horse (red′hôrs′), *n.* any of several suckers of the genus *Moxostoma,* found in the fresh waters of North America, often having reddish fins. Also, **red′-horse suck′er.** [RED[1] + HORSE]

red-hot (red′hot′), *adj.* **1.** red with heat; very hot. **2.** very excited or enthusiastic. **3.** violent; furious: *red-hot anger.* **4.** very fresh or new; most recent: *red-hot tips on the stock market.* [ME *red het*]

Re·di (RE′dē), *n.* **Fran·ces·co** (frän ches′kô), 1626?–98, Italian biologist.

Red′ In′dian, Indian (def. 1).

red·in·gote (red′ing gōt′), *n.* **1.** a dress or lightweight coat, usually belted, open along the entire front to reveal a dress or petticoat worn underneath it. **2.** a coatdress with a contrasting gore in front. **3.** a long, double-breasted overcoat worn by men in the 18th century. [< F < E *riding coat*]

red·in·te·grate (red in′tə grāt′), *v.t.,* **-grat·ed, -grat·ing.** to make whole again; restore to a perfect state; renew; reestablish. [ME *redintegrate(n)* < L *redintegrāt(us)* made whole again (ptp. of *redintegrāre*), equiv. to *red-* RED- + *integr-* (s. of *integer*) whole, entire + *-ātus* -ATE[1]] —**red·in·te·gra′tive,** *adj.*

red·in·te·gra·tion (red in′tə grā′shən), *n.* **1.** the act or process of redintegrating. **2.** *Psychol.* the tendency to repeat the response made to a complex stimulus on later experiencing any part of the stimulus. [< L *redintegrātiōn-* (s. of *redintegrātiō*), equiv. to *redintegrāt(us)* (see REDINTEGRATE) + *-iōn-* -ION]

re·di·rect (rē′də rekt′, -dī-), *v.t.* **1.** to direct again. —*adj.* **2.** *Law.* pertaining to the examination of a witness by the party calling him, after cross-examination. [RE- + DIRECT] —**re′di·rec′tion,** *n.*

re·dis·count (rē dis′kount), *v.t.* **1.** to discount again. —*n.* **2.** an act of rediscounting. **3.** Usually, **rediscounts.** commercial paper discounted a second time. [RE- + DISCOUNT]

re·dis·trict (rē dis′trikt), *v.t.* to divide anew into districts, as for administrative or electoral purposes. [RE- + DISTRICT]

red·i·vi·vus (red′ə vī′vəs), *adj.* living again; revived. [< LL: that lives again, L: renewed, renovated, equiv. to *red-* RED- + *vīvus* alive (deriv. of *vīvere* to be alive)]

red′ jas′mine, a shrubby tree, *Plumeria rubra,* found from Mexico to Venezuela, having fragrant, pink or reddish-purple flowers.

red′ jun′gle fowl′. See under **jungle fowl.**

red′ kau′ri, a kauri tree, esp. *Agathis australis.*

red′ ko′whai (kō′wī), parrot's-bill. [*kowhai* < Maori]

red′ la′bel, *U.S.* the phrase warning against fire hazards required by the Interstate Commerce Commission to be shown on the containers and shipping documents of inflammable materials while in transit.

Red·lands (red′ləndz), *n.* a city in SW California, near Los Angeles. 26,829 (1960).

red′ lark′spur, a perennial herb, *Delphinium nudicaule,* of the western coast of the U.S., having red flowers with yellow petals.

red′ lat′tice, *Obs.* an alehouse.

red′ lead′ (led), *n.* an orange to red, heavy, earthy, water-insoluble, poisonous powder, Pb_3O_4, obtained by heating litharge in the presence of air: used chiefly as a paint pigment, in the manufacture of glass and glazes, and in storage batteries. Also called **minium.** Cf. **litharge.**

red′ lead′ ore′ (led), crocoite.

red′-lead put′ty (red′led′), a compound for calking pipe joints, made of red lead, white lead, and boiled linseed oil.

Red·leg (red′leg′), *n.* *U.S. Hist.* a member of a secret organization, formed in Kansas in 1862, that engaged in guerrilla activities during the Civil War. [so called from the red leggings worn by the members]

red-let·ter (red′let′ər), *adj.* **1.** marked by red letters, as festival days in the church calendar. **2.** memorable; especially important or happy: *a red-letter day* [ME]

red′ light′, **1.** a red lamp, used as a traffic signal to mean "stop." **2.** an order or directive to halt an action, project, etc.: *Send out a red light on all unnecessary expenses.* **3.** a children's game in which, typically, a number of players starting at a line advance on the leader, who stands with his back to the others, counts ten, and calls "Red light!," whereupon he turns abruptly and penalizes any player still in motion by sending him back to the starting line, the winner being the player who reaches the leader, tags him, and runs back to the line without being caught. **4.** a signal of danger; warning. —**red′-light′,** *adj.*

red′-light′ dis′trict, a neighborhood with many houses of prostitution sometimes, esp. formerly, identified by a red light at the door or in one of the windows.

red′ line′, *Ice Hockey.* a line of the color red that is parallel to and equidistant from the goal lines and divides the rink in half. See diag. under **ice hockey.**

red·line (red′līn′), *v.,* **-lined, -lin·ing.** —*v.t.* **1.** to establish the recommended safe speed of (an airplane): *The bomber is redlined at 650 miles an hour.* **2.** to draw a canceling red line through (an item on a list). **3.** to cause (an airplane) to be grounded. **4.** to subject (an area) to redlining. —*v.i.* **5.** to practice redlining. [RED[1] + LINE[1]]

red·lin·ing (red′lī′ning), *n.* an arbitrary practice by which banks limit or refuse to grant mortgage loans for properties in blighted urban areas. [so called because such areas are said to be encircled by red pencil on maps]

Red′ Li′on, a town in S Pennsylvania. 5594 (1960).

red′ liq′uor. See **mordant rouge.**

red′ maids′, a fleshy shrub, *Calandrinia ciliata menziesi,* of the western U.S., having rose-colored or crimson flowers.

red′ man′, a North American Indian.

red′ ma′ple, any of several American maples, esp. *Acer rubrum,* having crimson flowers.

red′ meat′, any meat that is dark-colored before cooking, as beef, lamb, venison, or mutton (distinguished from *white meat*).

red′ mercu′ric ox′ide. See under **mercuric oxide.**

red′ mercu′ric sul′fide. See under **mercuric sulfide.**

red′ mombin′. See **purple mombin.**

Red·mond (red′mənd), *n.* **1. John Edward,** 1856–1918, Irish political leader. **2.** a town in central Oregon. 3340 (1960).

red′ mul′berry. See under **mulberry** (def. 2).

red′ mul′let, a goatfish or surmullet.

red·neck (red′nek′), *n.* (in the southern U.S.) *Disparaging.* an uneducated, white farm laborer. [RED[1] + NECK]

red·ness (red′nis), *n.* the quality or state of being red. [ME *rednesse,* OE *readnis.* See RED[1], -NESS]

red′ oak′, **1.** any of several oak trees, as *Quercus velutina* or *Q. borealis,* of North America. **2.** the hard, cross-grained wood of these trees.

Red′ Oak′, a town in SW Iowa. 6421 (1960).

red′ o′cher, any of the red natural earths that are mixtures of hematites and are used as pigments.

red·o·lent (red′ələnt), *adj.* **1.** having a pleasant odor; fragrant. **2.** odorous or smelling (usually fol. by *of*): *a kitchen redolent of garlic.* **3.** suggestive; reminiscent (usually fol. by *of*): *a speech redolent of one by Shakespeare.* [ME < L *redolent-* (s. of *redolēns,* prp. of *redolēre* to emit odor), equiv. to *red-* RED- + *ol(ere)* (to) smell + *-ent-* -ENT] —**red′o·lence, red′o·len·cy,** *n.* —**red′o·lent·ly,** *adv.*
—**Syn. 1.** odorous, aromatic, odoriferous.

Re·don (rə don′; *Fr.* Rə dôN′), *n.* **O·di·lon** (ō′də lon; *Fr.* ô dē lôN′), 1840–1916, French painter and etcher.

Re·don′do Beach′ (rə don′dō), a city in SW California. 46,986 (1960).

red′ or′piment, realgar.

red′ o′sier, **1.** a willow, *Salix purpurea,* having tough, flexible twigs or branches used for wickerwork. **2.** any willow having reddish branches. **3.** *U.S.* a dogwood, *Cornus stolonifera,* having red bark and sending up osierlike shoots.

re·dou·ble (rē dub′əl), *v.,* **-bled, -bling,** *n.* —*v.t.* **1.** to double; make twice as great: *to redouble one's efforts.* **2.** to echo or reecho. **3.** *Bridge.* to double the double of (an opponent). **4.** to go back over: *to redouble one's footsteps.* **5.** *Archaic.* to repeat. —*v.i.* **6.** to be doubled; become twice as great. **7.** to be echoed; resound. **8.** *Bridge.* to double the double of an opponent. —*n.* **9.** *Bridge.* the act of doubling one's opponent's double. **10.** *Fencing.* an attack in a line other than that of the previous attack, made after the failure of the opponent to follow his parry of the previous attack with a riposte. [late ME < MF *redoubl(er).* See RE-, DOUBLE] —**re·dou′bler,** *n.*

re·doubt (ri dout′), *n.* *Fort.* **1.** an isolated work forming a complete enclosure of any form, used to defend a prominent point. **2.** an independent earthwork built within a permanent fortification to reinforce it. [< F *redoute* < It *ridott(o)* < LL *reduct(us)* a refuge n. use of ptp. of L *redūcere* to lead back; see REDUCE]

re·doubt·a·ble (ri dou′tə bəl), *adj.* **1.** that is to be feared; formidable. **2.** commanding or evoking respect, reverence, or the like. [ME *redoutable* < MF, equiv. to *redout(er)* (to) fear (*re-* RE- + *douter* to fear, DOUBT) + *-able* -ABLE] —**re·doubt′a·ble·ness,** *n.* —**re·doubt′a·bly,** *adv.*

re·doubt·ed (ri dou′tid), *adj.* **1.** dreaded; formidable. **2.** respected; renowned. [ME, ptp. of *redouten* to fear, dread. See REDOUBTABLE, -ED[2]]

re·dound (ri dound′), *v.i.* **1.** to have an effect or result, as to the advantage, disadvantage, credit, or discredit, of a person or thing. **2.** to result or accrue, as to a person. **3.** to come back or recoil, as upon a person. **4.** to proceed, issue, or arise. [ME *redound(en)* < MF *redond(er)* < L *redundāre* to overflow, equiv. to *red-* RED- + *undāre* to surge (deriv. of *unda* wave)]

red·o·wa (red′ə wə, -və), *n.* a Bohemian dance in two forms, one resembling the waltz or the mazurka, the other resembling the polka. [< F *rédowa,* G *Redowa* < Czech *reydovák* deriv. of *reydovati* to whirl around]

red-pen·cil (red′pen′səl), *v.t.,* **-ciled, -cil·ing** or (*esp. Brit.*) **-cilled, -cil·ling.** to delete, censor, correct, or abridge (written material) with or as if with a pencil having a red lead: *His talk was heavily red-penciled before it got clearance.*

red′ pep′per, **1.** cayenne. **2.** a pepper, *Capsicum frutescens,* cultivated in many varieties, the yellow or red pods of which are used for flavoring, sauces, etc.

red′ per′iwinkle. See **Cape periwinkle.**

Red′ Poll′, one of a breed of red, hornless, dual-purpose cattle, raised originally in England. Also, **Red′ Polled′.**

red·poll (red′pōl′), *n.* any of various small fringilline birds of the genus *Acanthis,* the adults of which usually have a crimson crown patch. [RED[1] + POLL[1]]

red′ prus′siate of pot′ash. See **potassium ferricyanide.**

re·draft (rē′draft′, -dräft′), *n.* **1.** a second draft or drawing. **2.** *Finance.* a draft on the drawer or endorsers of a protested bill of exchange for the amount of the bill plus the costs and charges. [RE- + DRAFT]

red′ rag′, something that arouses anger; a provocation: *A mere mention of the incident is a red rag to him.*

red′ rat′ snake′. See **corn snake.**

re-dress (rē dres′), *v.t.* to dress again. [RE- + DRESS]

re·dress (*n.* rē′dres, ri dres′; *v.* ri dres′), *n.* **1.** the setting right of what is wrong: *redress of abuses.* **2.** relief from wrong or injury. **3.** compensation or satisfaction for a wrong or injury. —*v.t.* **4.** to set right; remedy or repair (wrongs, injuries, etc.). **5.** to correct or reform (abuses, evils, etc.). **6.** to remedy or relieve (suffering, want, etc.). **7.** to adjust evenly again, as a balance. [ME *redress(en)* < MF *redress(er),* OF *redrecier,* equiv. to *re-* RE- + *drecier* to straighten; see DRESS] —**re·dress′a·ble, re·dress′i·ble,** *adj.* —**re·dress′er, re·dres′sor,** *n.*
—**Syn. 1.** indemnity, restoration, remedy, atonement. REDRESS, REPARATION, RESTITUTION suggest making amends or giving indemnification for a wrong. REDRESS may refer either to the act of setting right an unjust situation (as by some power), or to satisfaction sought or gained for a wrong suffered: *the redress of grievances.* REPARATION means compensation or satisfaction for a wrong or loss inflicted. The word may have the moral idea of amends: *to make reparation for one's neglect;* but more frequently it refers to financial compensation (which is asked for, rather than given): *the reparations demanded of the aggressor nations.* RESTITUTION means literally the restoration of what has been taken from the lawful owner: *He demanded restitution of his land;* it

re·dic′tate, *v.,* **-tat·ed, -tat·ing.**
re′dif·fer·en′ti·ate′, *v.,* **-at·ed, -at·ing.**
re′dif·fer·en′ti·a′tion, *n.*
re′dif·fuse′, *v.,* **-fused, -fus·ing.**
re′dif·fu′sion, *n.*
re·dig′, *v.,* **-dug** or **-digged, -dig·ging.**
re′di·gest′, *v.t.*
re′di·ges′tion, *n.*
re′di·late′, *v.,* **-lat·ed, -lat·ing.**
re·dip′, *v.,* **-dipped** or **-dipt, -dip·ping.**
re′dis·burse′, *v.t.,* **-bursed, -burs·ing.**
re′dis·burse′ment, *n.*
re′dis·charge′, *v.,* **-charged, -charg·ing.**
re·dis′ci·pline, *v.t.,* **-plined, -plin·ing.**
re′dis·cov′er, *v.t.*
re′dis·cov′er·y, *n., pl.* **-er·ies.**
re′dis·cuss′, *v.t.*
re′dis·cus′sion, *n.*
re′dis·in·fect′, *v.t.*
re′dis·miss′, *v.t.*
re′dis·miss′al, *n.*
re′dis·patch′, *v.t.*
re′dis·per′sal, *n.*
re′dis·perse′, *v.,* **-persed, -pers·ing.**
re′dis·play′, *v.t.*
re′dis·pose′, *v.t.,* **-posed, -pos·ing.**
re′dis·po·si′tion, *n.*
re′dis·pute′, *v.,* **-put·ed, -put·ing.**
re′dis·sect′, *v.t.*
re′dis·sec′tion, *n.*
re′dis·sol′u·ble, *adj.;* **-ble·ness,** *n.;* **-bly,** *adv.*
re′dis·so·lu′tion, *n.*
re′dis·solve′, *v.,* **-solved, -solv·ing.**
re′dis·till′, *v.t.*
re′dis·till′a·ble, *adj.;* **-ness,** *n.*
re′dis·til·la′tion, *n.*
re′dis·tin′guish, *v.*
re′dis·trib′ute, *v.t.,* **-ut·ed, -ut·ing.**
re′dis·tri·bu′tion, *n.*
re′di·vert′, *v.t.*
re′di·vide′, *v.,* **-vid·ed, -vid·ing.**
re′di·vi′sion, *n.*
re′di·vorce′, *n., v.,* **-vorced, -vorc·ing.**
re·do′, *v.t.,* **-did, -done, -do·ing.**
re·dock′, *v.*
re·dock′et, *v.t.,* **-et·ed, -et·ing.**
re·doc′u·ment′, *v.t.*
re·dom′i·nate′, *v.,* **-nat·ed, -nat·ing.**
re·draw′, *v.* **-drew, -drawn, -draw·ing;** *n.*
re·draw′er, *n.*

may also refer to restoring the equivalent of what has been taken: *The servant convicted of robbery made restitution to his employer.* **5.** amend, mend, emend, right, rectify, adjust. **6.** ease.

red′ rib′bon, an herb, *Eucharidium Concinnum*, of California, having rose-purple flowers.

Red′ Riv′er, 1. a river flowing E from NW Texas along the S boundary of Oklahoma into the Mississippi River in Louisiana. ab. 1300 mi. long. **2.** Also called **Red′ Riv′er of the North′.** a river flowing N along the boundary between Minnesota and North Dakota to Lake Winnipeg in S Canada. 533 mi. long. **3.** Songka.

Red′ Riv′er War′, a punitive campaign (1874–75) led by General Sheridan against hostile Indians in the region of the Red River and the Llano Estacado.

Red·roe (red′rō), *n.* a boy's given name.

red·root (red′ro͞ot′, -ro͝ot′), *n.* **1.** a North American plant, *Lachnanthes tinctoria*, having sword-shaped leaves, woolly flowers, and a red root. **2.** any of various other plants having red roots, as the alkanet, *Alkanna tinctoria*, pigweed, *Amaranthus retroflexus*, and New Jersey tea, *Ceanothus americanus*. [RED[1] + ROOT[1]]

red′ rose′, *Eng. Hist.* the emblem of the royal house of Lancaster. Cf. **Wars of the Roses, white rose.**

red′ rot′, *Plant Pathol.* **1.** a disease of sugarcane, characterized by a red discoloration within the affected stalks, caused by a fungus, *Colletotrichum falcatum*. **2.** a similar disease of sorgo, caused by *Colletotrichum graminicolum*.

red′ rov′er, a children's game in which two teams, some distance apart, face each other and take turns designating an opposing player to run toward their line. If he fails to break through their clasped hands he becomes a member of that team.

red′ sage′, a showy, rank-smelling shrub, *Lantana Camara*, of tropical America, having yellow flowers that turn orange or red. Also called **yellow sage.**

red′ Sal′ly, the purple loosestrife. See under **loosestrife** (def. 2).

red′ sal′mon. See **sockeye salmon.**

red′ san′dalwood, 1. See under **sandalwood** (def. 3). **2.** See **Barbados pride** (def. 1).

Red′ Sea′, an arm of the Indian Ocean, extending NW between Africa and Arabia: connected to the Mediterranean by the Suez Canal. 1450 mi. long; 170,000 sq. mi.; greatest depth, 7254 ft.

red·shank (red′shangk′), *n.* an Old World sandpiper, *Totanus totanus*, having red legs and feet. [RED[1] + SHANK]

red′ shanks′. See **herb Robert.**

red′ shift′, *Physics, Astron.* the systematic shift toward longer wave lengths in the spectra of light from distant galaxies, assumed to be caused by the Doppler effect and indicating that the galaxies are receding. Cf. **Einstein shift.**

red-short (red′shôrt′), *adj.* *Metall.* brittle when at red heat, as iron or steel containing too much sulfur. [< Sw *rödskör* (*jern* iron), neut. of *rödskör*, equiv. to *röd* red + *skör* brittle]

red′-shoul·dered hawk′ (red′shōl′dərd), a North American hawk, *Buteo lineatus*, having rufous shoulders.

red·skin (red′skin′), *n.* *Often Offensive.* a North American Indian. [RED[1] + SKIN]

red′ snap′per, any of several snappers of the genus *Lutjanus*, esp. *L. blackfordi*, a large food fish found in the Gulf of Mexico.

red′-spot·ted pur′ple (red′spot′id). See under **purple** (def. 6).

Red′ Springs′, a town in S North Carolina. 2767 (1960).

red′ spruce′, a spruce, *Picea rubens*, of eastern North America, having reddish-brown bark and cones and yielding a light, soft wood used for pulp, in the construction of boxes, etc.

red′ squill′, a variety of squill whose bulbs are red, used chiefly as a rat poison.

red′ squir′rel, a reddish squirrel, *Tamiasciurus hudsonius*, of North America. Also called **chickaree.**

red·start (red′stärt′), *n.* **1.** any of several small, Old World thrushes, usually with reddish-brown tails, esp. *Phoenicurus phoenicurus* **(European redstart). 2.** any of several fly-catching, New World warblers, esp. *Setophaga ruticilla* **(American redstart),** having black and white plumage with reddish-orange patches. [RED[1] + obs. *start* tail, ME *start, stert* tail, handle, OE *steort* tail; akin to OHG *sterz*, ON *stertr*, OE *starian* to stare]

Red·stone (red′stōn′), *n.* *U.S.* a surface-to-surface ballistic missile powered by a single rocket engine. [after *Redstone* Arsenal, Huntsville, Alabama]

red′ stuff′, a compound of oil and sesquioxide of iron used for polishing brass, steel, silver, etc.; crocus or rouge.

red′ tai′. See under **tai.**

red′-tailed hawk′ (red′tāld′), a North American hawk, *Buteo jamaicensis*, dark brown above, whitish with black streaking below, and having a reddish-brown tail. See illus. under **hawk.**

red′ tape′, excessive formality and routine, as in multiplicity of forms, records, and often unnecessarily detailed information required before action can be taken. —**red′tap′ism,** *n.*

red′ tas′sel flow′er, a perennial herb, *Petalostemon purpureum*, of central North America, having dense clusters of purple or violet-colored flowers.

red′ tide′, a brownish-red discoloration of marine waters caused by the presence of enormous numbers of certain microscopic flagellates, esp. the dinoflagellates. Also called **red water.**

red·top (red′top′), *n.* a grass, *Agrostis alba*, certain forms of which have a reddish panicle. Also called **fiorin.** [RED[1] + TOP[1]]

red′ tril′lium, a hardy, perennial herb, *Trillium sessile*, found from New York to Georgia and westward, having stalkless, purple or green flowers. Also called **bloody butchers, nosebleed.**

red′ tur′tlehead, a perennial herb, *Chelone lyoni*, of the mountainous regions of the southeastern U.S., having rose-purple flowers.

re·duce (ri do͞os′, -dyo͞os′), *v.*, **-duced, -duc·ing.** —*v.t.* **1.** to bring down to a smaller extent, size, amount, number, etc.: *to reduce one's weight by 10 pounds.* **2.** to lower in degree, intensity, etc.: *to reduce the speed of a car.* **3.** to bring down to a lower rank, dignity, etc. **4.** to lower in price. **5.** to bring to a certain state, condition, arrangement, etc.: *to reduce glass to powder.* **6.** to bring under control or authority. **7.** *Cookery.* to evaporate water from (a sauce, soup, or other liquid), usually by boiling, esp. to concentrate the flavor. **8.** *Photog.* to lessen the density of (an exposed negative). **9.** to adjust or correct by making allowances, as an astronomical observation. **10.** *Math.* to change the denomination or form of (a fraction, polynomial, etc.). **11.** *Chem.* **a.** to deoxidize. **b.** to add hydrogen to. **c.** to change (a compound) so that the valence of the positive element is lower. **12.** *Chem., Metall.* to bring into the metallic state by separating from nonmetallic constituents; smelt. **13.** to thin or dilute: *to reduce paint with oil or turpentine.* **14.** to lower the alcoholic concentration of (spirits) by diluting with water. **15.** *Surg.* to restore to the normal place, relations, or condition, as a dislocated organ or a fractured bone with separation of the fragment ends. —*v.i.* **16.** to become reduced. **17.** *Biol.* to undergo meiosis. [ME *reduce(n)* (to) lead back < L *redūc(ere)* (to) lead back, bring back, equiv. to *re-* RE- + *dūcere* to lead] —**re·duc′i·bil′i·ty,** *n.* —**re·duc′i·ble,** *adj.* —**re·duc′i·bly,** *adv.*

—**Syn. 1.** diminish, decrease, shorten, abridge, curtail, contract, retrench. **1, 2.** lessen, attenuate, abate. **3.** degrade, demote, humble. **6.** subdue, subjugate, conquer, subject, vanquish, overcome, overpower. —**Ant. 1.** increase. **3.** elevate, exalt.

re·duced (ri do͞ost′, -dyo͞ost′), *adj.* **1.** that is or has been reduced. **2.** *Math.* noting a polynomial equation in which the second highest power is missing: *The cubic equation* $x^3 - 4x + 4 = 0$ *is reduced.* [REDUCE + -ED[2]]

reduced′ he′moglobin, *Biochem.* See under **hemoglobin.**

reduced′ mass′, *Physics.* a quantity obtained when one particle is moving about another, larger particle that is also moving, equivalent to the mass of the smaller particle, were the larger particle not moving, and equal to the quotient of the product of the two masses divided by their sum.

reduced′ paid′-up′ insur′ance (pād′up′), life insurance in which a nonforfeiture value is used to purchase a reduced amount of fully paid-up insurance of the same kind as the surrendered policy.

re·ducer (ri do͞o′sər, -dyo͞o′-), *n.* **1.** one who or that which reduces. **2.** *Photog.* **a.** an oxidizing solution for lessening the density of an exposed negative. **b.** a developing agent. **3.** (in plumbing) a coupling decreasing in diameter at one end. Cf. **increaser** (def. 2). [REDUCE + -ER[1]]

re·duc·i·ble (ri do͞o′sə bəl, -dyo͞o′-), *adj.* **1.** capable of being reduced. **2.** *Math.* **a.** of or pertaining to a polynomial that can be factored into the product of polynomials, each of lower degree. **b.** of or pertaining to a group that can be written as the direct product of two of its subgroups. **c.** of or pertaining to a set whose set of accumulation points is countable. [REDUCE + -IBLE] —**re·duc′i·bil′i·ty, re·duc′i·ble·ness,** *n.* —**re·duc′i·bly,** *adv.*

reduc′ing a′gent, *Chem.* a substance that causes another substance to undergo reduction and that is oxidized in the process.

reduc′ing glass′, a lens or mirror that produces a virtual image of an object smaller than the object itself.

re·duct (ri dukt′), *n.* a small area partitioned off from the general area of a room for the sake of balance with a fireplace, vestibule, etc. [< ML *rēduct(us)* a retreat, n. use of L ptp. of *rēdūcere* to REDUCE; cf. F *réduit* a retreat]

re·duc·tase (ri duk′tās, -tāz), *n.* *Biochem.* any enzyme acting as a reducing agent. [REDUCT(ION) + -ASE]

reduc′tase test′, a test for the bacterial content in milk to determine its fitness for drinking.

re·duc·ti·o ad ab·sur·dum (re do͝ok′ti ō äd äb so͝or′do͝om; *Eng.* ri duk′shē ō′ ad ab sûr′dəm), *Latin.* a reduction to an absurdity; the refutation of a proposition by demonstrating the inevitably absurd conclusion to which it would logically lead.

re·duc·tion (ri duk′shən), *n.* **1.** the act of reducing or the state of being reduced. **2.** the amount by which something is reduced or diminished. **3.** a form produced by reducing; a copy on a smaller scale. **4.** *Biol.* meiosis, esp. the first meiotic cell division in which the chromosome number is reduced. **5.** *Chem.* **a.** the removal of oxygen from. **b.** the addition of hydrogen to. **c.** the lowering of the valence of a positive element in a compound. **6.** a village or settlement established in South America by Spanish Jesuit missionaries for religious and cultural education of the Indians. [late ME *reduccion* < MF *reduction* < L *rēductiōn-* (s. of *rēductiō*) a bringing back, equiv. to *rēduct(us)* (ptp. of *rēdūcere;* see REDUCE) + *-iōn-* -ION] —**re·duc′tion·al,** *adj.*

reduc′tion poten′tial, *Physical Chem.* (in a galvanic cell) the potential of the electrode at which reduction occurs. Cf. **oxidation potential.**

re·duc·tive (ri duk′tiv), *adj.* **1.** of, pertaining to, characterized by, or producing reduction or abridgment: *an urgent need for reductive measures.* **2.** of or pertaining to change from one form to another. —*n.* **3.** something causing or inducing a reductive process. [REDUCT(ION) + -IVE] —**re·duc′tive·ly,** *adv.*

re·duc·tor (ri duk′tər), *n.* a tube with a stopcock at one end, usually filled with a metal, for reducing a constituent in a solution. [REDUCT(ION) + -OR[2]]

re·dun·dan·cy (ri dun′dən sē), *n., pl.* **-cies. 1.** the state of being redundant. **2.** superfluous repetition or overlapping, esp. of words. **3.** a redundant thing, part, or amount; superfluity. Also, **re·dun′dance.** [< L *redundantia* an overflowing, excess, deriv. of *redundant-*. See REDUNDANT, -CY]

re·dun·dant (ri dun′dənt), *adj.* **1.** characterized by verbosity or unnecessary repetition in expressing ideas; prolix: *a redundant style.* **2.** being in excess; exceeding what is usual or natural: *a redundant part.* **3.** having some unusual or extra part or feature. **4.** characterized by superabundance or superfluity: *lush, redundant vegetation of the African jungles.* **5.** *Engineering.* **a.** (of a structural member) not necessary for resisting statically determined stresses. **b.** (of a structure) having members designed to resist other than statically determined stresses; hyperstatic. Cf. **indeterminate** (def. 6). **c.** noting a complete truss having additional members for resisting eccentric loads. [< L *redundant-* (s. of *redundāns*), prp. of *redundāre.* See REDOUND, -ANT] —**re·dun′dant·ly,** *adv.*

—**Syn. 1.** wordy, verbose, repetitive. **2.** excessive; useless; superfluous, tautologous.

redun′dant check′, *Computer Technol.* See **parity check.**

redun′dant verb′, *Gram.* a verb that has a variant for one or more of its inflected forms, as *light,* whose past can be *lit* or *lighted.*

redupl., reduplication.

re·du·pli·cate (*v.* ri do͞o′plə kāt′, -dyo͞o′-; *adj.* ri do͞o′plə kit, -kāt′, -dyo͞o′-), *v.*, **-cat·ed, -cat·ing,** *adj.* —*v.t.* **1.** to double; repeat. **2.** *Gram.* to form (a derivative or inflected form) by doubling a specified syllable or other portion of the primitive, sometimes with fixed modifications, as in Greek *léloipa* "I have left," *leípo* "I leave." —*v.i.* **3.** to become doubled. **4.** *Gram.* to become reduplicated. —*adj.* **5.** doubled. **6.** *Bot.* valvate, with the edges folded back so as to project outward. [< LL *reduplicāt(us)* (ptp. of *reduplicāre*), equiv. to L *re-* RE- + *duplic(āre)* (to) double + *-ātus* -ATE[1]]

re·du·pli·ca·tion (ri do͞o′plə kā′shən, -dyo͞o′-), *n.* **1.** the act of reduplicating; the state of being reduplicated. **2.** something resulting from reduplicating. **3.** *Gram.* **a.** reduplicating as a grammatical pattern. **b.** the added element in a reduplicated form. **c.** a form containing a reduplicated element. [< LL *reduplicātiōn-* (s. of *reduplicātiō*). See REDUPLICATE, -ION]

re·du·pli·ca·tive (ri do͞o′plə kā′tiv, -dyo͞o′-), *adj.* **1.** tending to reduplicate. **2.** pertaining to or marked by reduplication. **3.** *Bot.* reduplicate. [REDUPLICATE + -IVE] —**re·du′pli·ca′tive·ly,** *adj.*

re·u·zate (rej′o͞o zāt′), *n.* *Geochem.* a sediment that has not undergone oxidation, as of coal, oil, sulfur, and sulfides. [< G *Reduzat* reduction]

red′ valer′ian, a perennial, bushy herb, *Centranthus ruber*, of Europe and southwestern Asia, having many fragrant red, crimson, or white flowers. Also called **Jupiter's-beard, scarlet lightning.**

red·ware[1] (red′wâr′), *n.* a utilitarian, early American earthenware made from red clay. [RED[1] + WARE[1]]

red·ware[2] (red′wâr′), *n.* a large brown seaweed, *Laminaria digitata*, common off northern Atlantic coasts. [RED[1] + dial. *ware* (ME; OE *wār* seaweed; see WIRE)]

red-wat (red′wat′), *adj.* *Scot.* stained with blood; bloody. [RED[1] + *wat,* Scot var. of WET]

red′ wa′ter. See **red tide.**

red′ whor′tleberry, the cowberry, *Vaccinium Vitis-Idaea.*

red′ wine′, wine having a predominantly red color derived from the skin pigment in the red or other dark-colored grapes used in making it.

red·wing (red′wing′), *n.* **1.** a European thrush, *Turdus musicus*, having chestnut-red flank and axillary feathers. **2.** See **red-winged blackbird.** [RED[1] + WING]

red′-winged black′bird (red′wingd′), a North American blackbird, *Agelaius phoeniceus*, the male of which is black with scarlet patches, usually bordered with buff or yellow, on the bend of the wing.

red·wood[1] (red′wo͝od′), *n.* **1.** Also called **California redwood.** a coniferous tree, *Sequoia sempervirens*, of California, noted for its height of from 200 to over 300 feet: the State tree of California. **2.** its valuable brownish-red timber. **3.** a red-colored wood. **4.** any of various trees yielding a reddish wood. **5.** any tree whose wood produces a red dyestuff. [RED[1] + WOOD[1]]

red·wood[2] (red′wo͝od′), *adj.* *Scot.* **1.** raving mad; insane. **2.** distracted with anger; furious. Also, **red′-wud′.** [RED[1] + WOOD[2]]

Red′wood Cit′y (red′wo͝od′), a city in W California. 46,290 (1960).

Red′wood Falls′, a town in SW Minnesota. 4285 (1960).

ree[1] (rē), *n.* reeve[3].

ree[2] (rē, rā), *v.t.*, **reed, ree·ing.** *Eng. Dial.* to sift (grain, peas, beans, etc.). [ME < ?]

re·ech·o (rē ek′ō), *v.*, **-ech·oed, -ech·o·ing,** *n., pl.* **-ech·oes.** —*v.i.* **1.** to echo back, as a sound. **2.** to give back an echo; resound. —*v.t.* **3.** to echo back. **4.** to repeat like an echo. —*n.* **5.** a repeated echo. Also, **re-ech′o, re·ëch′o.** [RE- + ECHO]

reed (rēd), *n.* **1.** the straight stalk of any of various tall grasses, esp. of the genera *Phragmites* and *Arundo*, growing in marshy places. **2.** any of the plants themselves. **3.** such stalks or plants collectively. **4.** anything made from such a stalk or from something similar, as an arrow. **5.** *Music.* **a.** a pastoral or rustic musical pipe made from a reed or from the hollow stalk of some other plant. **b.** a small, flexible piece of cane or metal which, attached to the mouth of any of various wind instruments **(reed instruments),** is set into vibration by a stream of air and, in turn, sets into vibration the air column enclosed in the tube of the instrument. **c.** any instrument with such a device, as the oboe, clarinet, etc. **6.** Also, **reeding.** (in architecture, carpentry, etc.) a small convex molding. **7.** *Textiles.* the series of parallel strips of wires in a loom that force the weft up to the web and separate the threads of the warp. **8.** a unit of length, equal to 6 cubits. Ezek. 40:5. **9. a broken reed,** a person or thing too frail or weak to be relied on for support: *Under stress she showed herself to be a broken reed.* —*v.t.* **10.** to decorate with reed. **11.** to thatch with or as if with reed. **12.** *Shipbuilding.* to

re·drill′, *v.*
re·drive′, *v.*, **-drove, -dri·ven, -driv·ing.**
re·droop′, *v.i.*
re·drug′, *v.t.*, **-drugged, -drug·ging.**
re·dry′, *v.*, **-dried, -dry·ing.**
re·dust′, *v.t.*
re·dye′, *v.t.*, **-dyed, -dy·ing.**
re·earn′, *v.t.*

smooth (the edges of plates) after calking. **13.** to make vertical grooves on (the edge of a coin, medal, etc.). [ME; OE *hrēod;* c. G, D *riet*] —**reed′like′,** *adj.*

Reed (rēd), *n.* **1. John,** 1887–1920, U.S. journalist and poet. **2. Stanley For·man** (fôr′mən), 1884–1980, U.S. jurist: associate justice of the U.S. Supreme Court 1938–57. **3. Walter C.,** 1851–1902, U.S. army surgeon who identified the mosquito that transmits the yellow fever virus. **4.** a boy's given name, form of **Read.**

Ree·da (rē′də), *n.* a girl's given name.

reed·bird (rēd′bûrd′), *n.* *Southern U.S.* bobolink. [REED + BIRD]

reed·buck (rēd′buk′), *n., pl.* **-bucks,** *(esp. collectively)* **-buck.** any of several yellowish African antelopes of the genus *Redunca,* found near lakes and rivers, the male of which has short, forward-curving horns. [trans. of SAfrD *rietbok*]

reed′ bunt′ing, an Old World bunting, *Emberiza schoeniclus,* found in marshy areas.

reed′ canar′y grass′. See under **canary grass.**

reed′ grass′, any of several reeds or reedy grasses, as those of the genera *Calamagrostis, Phragmites,* or *Arundo.*

reed·ing (rē′ding), *n.* *Archit.* **1.** reed (def. 6). **2.** a set of reed moldings, as on a column, resembling small convex fluting. **3.** ornamentation consisting of such moldings. **4.** a number of narrow, vertical grooves on the edge of a coin, medal, etc. [REED + -ING[1]]

reed′ in′strument, *Music.* a wind instrument with a single or double reed.

Reed·ley (rēd′lē), *n.* a town in central California. 5850 (1960).

reed·ling (rēd′ling), *n.* *Brit. Dial.* the bearded tit. [REED + -LING[1]]

reed′ mace′, cattail (def. 1).

reed′ or′gan, a musical keyboard instrument, as the harmonium or American organ, having small metal reeds through which air is forced to produce the sound.

reed′ pipe′, an organ pipe having a reed that is vibrated by air to produce the sound.

Reeds·burg (rēdz′bûrg), *n.* a town in central Wisconsin. 4371 (1960).

Reeds·port (rēdz′pōrt′, -pôrt′), *n.* a town in W Oregon. 2998 (1960).

reed′ stop′, a set of reed pipes in a pipe organ.

re·ed·u·cate (rē ej′o͝o kāt′, -ed′yo͝o-), *v.t.,* **-cat·ed, -cat·ing. 1.** to educate again, as for new purposes. **2.** to educate for resumption of normal activities, as a disabled person. Also, **re-ed′u·cate′, re·ëd′u·cate′.** [RE- + EDUCATE] —**re·ed′u·ca′tion, re-ed′u·ca′tion, re·ëd′u·ca′tion,** *n.*

reed′ warb′ler, a small Old World warbler, *Acrocephalus scirpaceus,* inhabiting marshy places.

reed·y (rē′dē), *adj.,* **reed·i·er, reed·i·est. 1.** full of reeds: *a reedy marsh.* **2.** consisting or made of a reed or reeds: *a reedy pipe.* **3.** like a reed or reeds: *reedy grass.* **4.** having a sound like that of a reed instrument. [ME *reeddy.* See REED, -Y[1]] —**reed′i·ness,** *n.*

reef[1] (rēf), *n.* **1.** a ridge of rocks or sand, often of coral debris, at or near the surface of the water. **2.** *Mining.* a lode or vein. [earlier *riff(e)* < D or LG *rif;* c. OIcel *rif* RIB, reef]

reef[2] (rēf), *Naut.* —*n.* **1.** a part of a sail that is rolled and tied down to reduce the area exposed to the wind. —*v.t.* **2.** to shorten (sail) by tying in one or more reefs. **3.** to reduce the length of (a topmast, a bowsprit, etc.), as by lowering, sliding inboard, or the like. **4.** to pull (old oakum) out of seams, as with a rave hook (often fol. by *out*). [ME *riff* ? < MD or MLG *rif* or ? < Scand *rif;* see REEF[1]]

reef′ band′, *Naut.* a horizontal band on a square sail, reinforcing the sail and reef points.

reef·er[1] (rē′fər), *n.* **1.** *Naut.* one who reefs. **2.** *Clothing.* **a.** a short coat or jacket of thick cloth. **b.** a woman's tailored, fitted, single- or double-breasted coat of durable material with a collar. [REEF[2] + -ER[1]]

reef·er[2] (rē′fər), *n.* a marijuana cigarette. [REEF[2] + -ER[1] (in generalized sense of rolled object)]

ree·fer[3] (rē′fər), *n.* **1.** *Slang.* a refrigerator, esp. one large enough to be walked into. **2.** *Railroad Slang.* a refrigerator car. [alter. and shortening of REFRIGERATOR]

reef·fish (rēf′fish′), *n., pl.* *(esp. collectively)* **-fish,** *(esp. referring to two or more kinds or species)* **-fish·es.** any of several damselfishes, as *Chromis insolatus,* that live among reefs. [REEF[1] + FISH]

reef′ hook′, *Naut.* See **rave hook.** Also called **reef′ing hook′, reef′ i′ron, reef′ing i′ron.**

reef′ing bat′ten, *Naut.* any of a number of vertical battens used for reefing fore-and-aft sails in certain small boats.

reef′ing bow′sprit, *Naut.* See **running bowsprit.**

reef′ knot′, *Naut.* a square knot used in tying reef points.

reef′ point′, *Naut.* a short piece of line fastened through a sail for tying in a reef.

reek (rēk), *n.* **1.** a strong, unpleasant smell. **2.** vapor or steam. —*v.i.* **3.** to smell strongly and unpleasantly. **4.** to be strongly pervaded with something unpleasant or offensive. **5.** to give off steam, smoke, etc. **6.** to be wet with sweat, blood, etc. —*v.t.* **7.** to expose to or treat with smoke. **8.** to emit (smoke, fumes, etc.). [ME *rek(e),* OE *rēc;* c. G *rauch,* D *rook,* OIcel *reykr*] —**reek′er,** *n.* —**reek′ing·ly,** *adv.* —**reek′y,** *adj.*

reel[1] (rēl), *n.* **1.** a cylinder, frame, or other device that turns on an axis and is used to wind up or pay out something. **2.** a rotatory device attached to a fishing rod at the butt, for winding up or letting out the line. **3.** *Chiefly Brit.* a spool of sewing thread; a roller or bobbin of sewing thread. **4.** a quantity of something wound on a reel. **5.** *Photog.* **a.** a spool on which film, esp. motion-picture film, is wound. **b.** a roll of motion-picture film. **c.** a holder for roll film in a developing tank. **6. off the reel, a.** without pause; continuously. **b.** without delay or hesitation; immediately. Also, **right off the reel.** —*v.t.* **7.** to wind on a reel, as thread, yarn, etc. **8.** to unwind (silk filaments) from a cocoon. **9.** to pull or draw by winding a line on a reel: *to reel in a fish.* **10. reel off,** to say, write, or produce quickly and easily: *The old sailor reeled off one story after another.* [ME *rele,* OE *hrēol;* c. OIcel *hræll* weaver's rod] —**reel′a·ble,** *adj.*

reel[2] (rēl), *v.i.* **1.** to sway or rock under a blow, shock, etc.: *The boxer reeled and fell.* **2.** to waver or fall back: *The troops reeled and then ran in disorder.* **3.** to sway about in standing or walking, as from dizziness, intoxication, etc.; stagger. **4.** to turn round and round; whirl. **5.** to have a sensation of whirling: *His brain reeled.* —*v.t.* **6.** to cause to reel. —*n.* **7.** an act of reeling; a reeling or staggering movement. [ME *rel(en),* deriv. of *rele* REEL[1]]
—**Syn. 3.** See **stagger.**

reel[3] (rēl), *n.* **1.** a lively dance popular in Scotland. **2.** See **Virginia reel. 3.** music for either of these. [special use of REEL[2]]

reel′ and bead′. See **bead and reel.**

reeled′ silk′, a long strand made of silk reeled from a number of cocoons and not twisted or thrown. Cf. **spun silk** (def. 1).

reel·er (rē′lər), *n.* **1.** one who or that which reels. **2.** a machine for burnishing the exterior and interior of seamless tubing. [REEL[1] + -ER[1]]

reem (rēm), *v.t.* *Naut.* ream[2] (def. 2).

re·en·force (rē′en fōrs′, -fôrs′), *v.t.,* **-forced, -forc·ing.** reinforce. Also, **re′-en·force′, re′ën·force′.** —**re′en·force′ment, re′-en·force′ment, re′ën·force′ment,** *n.* —**re′en·forc′er, re′-en·forc′er, re′ën·forc′er,** *n.*

re·en·list (rē′ən list′), *v.i., v.t.* to enlist again: *The sergeant reenlisted for three years. They hoped to reenlist many of last year's volunteers.* Also, **re′-en·list′, re′ën·list′.** [RE- + ENLIST]

re·en·list·ment (rē′ən list′mənt), *n.* **1.** an act of reenlisting. **2.** a person who reenlists: *We've gained 3000 reenlistments this month.* **3.** the period of service following a reenlistment: *His reenlistment is three years.* Also, **re′-en·list′ment, re′ën·list′ment.** [RE- + ENLISTMENT]

re·en·ter (rē en′tər), *v.t.* **1.** to enter again: *The guests reentered the reception room after dinner.* **2.** to record again, as in a list or account. —*v.i.* **3.** to enter again: *The butler exits and reenters at stage left.* Also, **re-en′ter, re·ën′ter.** [late ME; see RE-, ENTER] —**re·en·trance, re-en·trance, re·ën·trance** (rē en′trəns), *n.*

reen′tering an′gle, *Geom.* an interior angle of a polygon that is greater than 180°. See diag. under **salient.**

reen′tering pol′ygon, a polygon having one or more reentering angles.

re·en·trant (rē en′trənt), *adj.* **1.** reentering: *a reentrant angle.* —*n.* **2.** a reentering angle or part. [RE- + ENTRANT]

re·en·try (rē en′trē), *n., pl.* **-tries. 1.** an act of reentering. **2.** the return from outer space into the earth's atmosphere of an artificial satellite, a rocket, etc. **3.** *Law.* the retaking of possession under a right reserved in a prior conveyance. **4.** Also, **reen′try card′.** *Bridge, Whist.* a card that will win a trick enabling one to regain the lead previously lost, esp. the lead from a particular hand. [late ME; see RE-, ENTRY]

reest[1] (rēst), *v.t.* *Scot. and North Eng.* to cure, smoke, or dry (meat or fish). [? < Scand; cf. D, Norw *riste* to boil, grill, *røste* to ROAST]

reest[2] (rēst), *v.i.* *Scot. and North Eng.* (of a horse) to stop or refuse to go; balk. Also, **reist.** [dial. var. of REST[2]]

reeve[1] (rēv), *n.* **1.** an administrative officer of a town or district. **2.** *Brit.* an overseer or superintendent of workers, tenants, or an estate. **3.** *Brit.* (formerly) a person of high rank representing the crown. **4.** *Canada.* the presiding officer of a village or town council. [ME *(i)reve,* OE *gerēfa* high official, lit., head of a *rōf* array, number (of soldiers)]

reeve[2] (rēv), *v.t.,* **reeved** or **rove, reeved** or **rov·en, reev·ing.** *Naut.* **1.** to pass (a rope or the like) through a hole, ring, or the like. **2.** to fasten by placing through or around something. **3.** to pass a rope through (the swallow of a block). [? < D *reve(n);* see REEF[2]]

reeve[3] (rēv), *n.* the female of the ruff, *Philomachus pugnax.* Also called **ree.** [?]

re·ex·am·ine (rē′ig zam′in), *v.t.,* **-ined, -in·ing. 1.** to examine again. **2.** *Law.* to examine (a witness) again after having questioned him previously. Also, **re′-ex·am′ine, re′ëx·am′ine.** [RE- + EXAMINE] —**re′ex·am′in·a·ble, re′-ex·am′in·a·ble, re′ëx·am′in·a·ble,** *adj.* —**re′ex·am′i·na′tion, re′-ex·am′i·na′tion, re′ëx·am′i·na′tion,** *n.* —**re′ex·am′in·er, re′-ex·am′in·er, re′ëx·am′in·er,** *n.*

re·ex·port (*v.* rē′ik spōrt′, -spôrt′, rē eks′pōrt, -pôrt; *n.* rē eks′pōrt, -pôrt), *v.t.* **1.** to export again, as imported goods. —*n.* **2.** the act of reexporting. **3.** a commodity that is reexported. Also, **re′-ex·port′, re′ëx·port′.** [RE- + EXPORT] —**re′ex·por·ta′tion, re′-ex·por·ta′tion, re′ëx·por·ta′tion,** *n.* —**re′ex·port′er, re′-ex·port′er, re′ëx·port′er,** *n.*

ref (ref), *n., v.t., v.i.,* **reffed, ref·fing.** *Sports Slang.* referee. [by shortening]

ref., **1.** referee. **2.** reference. **3.** referred. **4.** reformation. **5.** reformed. **6.** refund.

re·face (rē fās′), *v.t.,* **-faced, -fac·ing. 1.** to renew, restore, or repair the face or surface of (buildings, stone, etc.). **2.** to provide with a new facing, as a garment. [RE- + FACE]

Ref. Ch., Reformed Church.

re·fect (ri fekt′), *v.t.* *Archaic.* to refresh, esp. with food or drink. [< L *refect(us)* made again, renewed (ptp. of *reficere*), equiv. to *re-* RE- + *fec-* make (comb. form of *facere* to make, do) + *-t-* ptp. suffix]

re·fec·tion (ri fek′shən), *n.* **1.** refreshment, esp. with food or drink. **2.** a portion of food or drink; repast. [ME *refeccioun* < L *refectiōn-* (s. of *refectiō*) restoration, equiv. to *refect(us)* (see REFECT) + *-iōn-* -ION] —**re·fec′tive,** *adj.*

re·fec·to·ri·al (rē′fek tōr′ē əl, -tôr′-), *adj.*

Refectory table (Italy, 16th century)

re·fec·to·ry (ri fek′tə rē), *n., pl.* **-ries.** a dining hall in a religious house, a college, or other institution. [< ML *refectōri(um),* equiv. to L *refect(us)* renewed, restored (see REFECT) + *-ōrium* -ORY[2]]

refec′tory ta′ble, **1.** a long, narrow table having a single stretcher between trestlelike supports at the ends. **2.** a narrow dining table having extensible ends.

re·fer (ri fûr′), *v.,* **-ferred, -fer·ring.** —*v.t.* **1.** to direct the attention or thoughts of: *The asterisk refers the reader to a footnote.* **2.** to direct for information or anything required: *He referred me to books on astrology.* **3.** to hand over or submit for information, consideration, decision, etc.: *to refer the argument to arbitration.* **4.** to assign to a class, period, etc.; regard as belonging or related. —*v.i.* **5.** to direct attention, as a reference mark does. **6.** to direct anyone for information, esp. about one's character, abilities, etc.: *to refer to a former employer for a recommendation.* **7.** to have relation; relate; apply. **8.** to have recourse or resort; turn, as for aid or information: *to refer to one's notes.* **9.** to make or direct a remark; make reference or allusion; mention: *The author referred to his teachers twice in his article.* [ME *referr(en)* < L *refer(re)* (to) bring back, equiv. to *re-* RE- + *ferre* to bring, BEAR[1]] —**ref·er·a·ble** (ref′ər ə bəl), **re·fer·ra·ble, re·fer·ri·ble** (ri fûr′ə bəl), *adj.* —**re·fer′ral,** *n.* —**re·fer′rer,** *n.*
—**Syn. 4.** attribute, ascribe, impute. **7.** pertain, belong. **9.** advert, allude.

ref·er·ee (ref′ə rē′), *n., v.,* **-eed, -ee·ing.** —*n.* **1.** one to whom something is referred, esp. for decision or settlement; arbitrator. **2.** (in certain games and sports) a judge having functions fixed by the rules of the game or sport; umpire. **3.** *Law.* a person selected by a court to take testimony in a case and return it to the court with recommendations as to the decision. —*v.t.* **4.** to preside over as referee; act as referee in. —*v.i.* **5.** to act as referee. [REFER + -EE]
—**Syn. 1.** arbiter. See **judge. 4.** judge, umpire, arbitrate.

re′ed′i·fy′, *v.t.,* **-fied, -fy·ing.**
re·ed′it, *v.t.*
re′e·ject′, *v.t.*
re′e·lect′, *v.t.*
re′e·lec′tion, *n.*
re·el′e·vate′, *v.t.,* **-vat·ed, -vat·ing.**
re′el·e·va′tion, *n.*
re·el′i·gi·bil′i·ty, *n.*
re·el′i·gi·ble, *adj.;* **-ble·ness,** *n.;* **-bly,** *adj.*
re·em′a·nate′, *v.i.,* **-nat·ed, -nat·ing.**
re′em·bar·ca′tion, *n.*
re′em·bark′, *v.*
re′em·bar·ka′tion, *n.*
re′em·bel′lish, *v.t.*
re′em·bod′y, *v.t.,* **-bod·ied, -bod·y·ing.**
re′em·brace′, *v.t.,* **-braced, -brac·ing.**
re′e·merge′, *v.i.,* **-merged, -merg·ing.**
re′e·mer′gence, *n.*
re′e·mer′gent, *adj.*
re′e·mer′sion, *n.*
re·em′i·grate′, *v.i.,* **-grat·ed, -grat·ing.**
re′em·i·gra′tion, *n.*
re′e·mis′sion, *n.*
re′e·mit′, *v.t.,* **-mit·ted, -mit·ting.**
re·em′pha·sis, *n., pl.* **-ses.**
re·em′pha·size′, *v.t.,* **-sized, -siz·ing.**
re′em·ploy′, *v.t.*
re′em·ploy′ment, *n.*
re′en·act′, *v.t.*
re′en·ac′tion, *n.*
re′en·act′ment, *n.*
re′en·close′, *v.t.,* **-closed, -clos·ing.**
re′en·coun′ter, *v., n.*
re′en·cour′age, *v.t.,* **-aged, -ag·ing.**
re′en·cour′age·ment, *n.*
re′en·dorse′, *v.t.,* **-dorsed, -dors·ing.**
re′en·dorse′ment, *n.*
re′en·dow′, *v.t.*
re′en·dow′ment, *n.*
re·en′er·gize′, *v.t.,* **-gized, -giz·ing.**
re′en·gage′, *v.,* **-gaged, -gag·ing.**
re′en·gage′ment, *n.*
re′en·grave′, *v.t.,* **-graved, -grav·ing.**
re′en·gross′, *v.t.*
re′en·join′, *v.t.*
re′en·joy′, *v.t.*
re′en·joy′ment, *n.*
re′en·large′, *v.,* **-larged, -larg·ing.**
re′en·large′ment, *n.*
re′en·light′en, *v.t.*
re′en·light′en·ment, *n.*
re′en·slave′, *v.t.,* **-slaved, -slav·ing.**
re′en·trance′, *v.t.,* **-tranced, -tranc·ing.**
re′e·nu′mer·ate′, *v.t.,* **-at·ed, -at·ing.**
re′e·nu′mer·a′tion, *n.*
re′e·nun′ci·ate′, *v.,* **-at·ed, -at·ing.**
re′e·nun′ci·a′tion, *n.*
re′e·quip′, *v.t.,* **-quipped, -quip·ping.**
re′e·rect′, *v.t.*
re′e·rec′tion, *n.*
re′e·rupt′, *v.i.*
re′e·rup′tion, *n.*
re′es·tab′lish, *v.t.*
re′es·tab′lish·ment, *n.*
re·es′ti·mate′, *v.t.,* **-mat·ed, -mat·ing.**
re·es′ti·mate, *n.*
re′es·ti·ma′tion, *n.*
re′e·vac′u·ate′, *v.,* **-at·ed, -at·ing.**
re′e·vac′u·a′tion, *n.*
re′e·val′u·ate′, *v.t.,* **-at·ed, -at·ing.**
re′e·val′u·a′tion, *n.*
re′e·va′sion, *n.*
re·ev′i·dence, *v.t.,* **-denced, -denc·ing.**
re·ex′ca·vate′, *v.t.,* **-vat·ed, -vat·ing.**
re′ex·ca·va′tion, *n.*
re′ex·change′, *v.,* **-changed, -chang·ing.**
re·ex′e·cute′, *v.t.,* **-cut·ed, -cut·ing.**
re′ex·e·cu′tion, *n.*
re·ex′er·cise′, *v.,* **-cised, -cis·ing.**
re′ex·hib′it, *v.t.*
re′ex·hi·bi′tion, *n.*
re′ex·pand′, *v.*
re′ex·pan′sion, *n.*
re′ex·pel′, *v.t.,* **-pelled, -pel·ling.**
re′ex·pe′ri·ence, *v.,* **-enced, -enc·ing.**
re′ex·per′i·ment, *v.t., n.*
re′ex·plain′, *v.t.*
re′ex·pla·na′tion, *n.*
re·ex′pli·cate′, *v.t.,* **-cat·ed, -cat·ing.**
re′ex·pli·ca′tion, *n.*
re′ex·plo·ra′tion, *n.*
re′ex·plore′, *v.,* **-plored, -plor·ing.**
re′ex·pose′, *v.t.,* **-posed, -pos·ing.**
re′ex·po·si′tion, *n.*
re′ex·po′sure, *n.*
re′ex·press′, *v.t.*
re′ex·pres′sion, *n.*
re′fa·mil′iar·i·za′tion, *n.*
re′fa·mil′iar·ize′, *v.t.,* **-ized, -iz·ing.**
re·fash′ion, *v.t.*
re·fas′ten, *v.t.*
re·fed′er·al·i·za′tion, *n.*
re·fed′er·al·ize′, *v.,* **-ized, -iz·ing.**
re·fed′er·ate′, *v.,* **-at·ed, -at·ing.**
re′fed·er·a′tion, *n.*
re·feed′, *v.,* **-fed, -feed·ing.**
re·feel′, *v.,* **-felt, -feel·ing.**

ref·er·ence (ref′ər əns), *n., v.,* **-enced, -enc·ing.** —*n.* **1.** an act or instance of referring. **2.** direction of the attention: *marks of reference.* **3.** a mention; allusion. **4.** something for which a name or designation stands; denotation. **5.** a direction in a book or writing to some other book, passage, etc.: *to look up a reference.* **6.** a note indicating this: *The asterisk is a reference to a footnote.* **7.** direction or a direction to some source of information: *Do not omit any necessary references.* **8.** use or recourse for purposes of information: *a library for public reference.* **9.** a person to whom one refers for testimony as to one's character, abilities, etc. **10.** a statement, usually written, as to a person's character, abilities, etc. **11.** relation, regard, or respect: *all persons, without reference to age.* —*v.t.* **12.** to furnish (a book, dissertation, etc.) with references: *Each new volume is thoroughly referenced.* **13.** to arrange (notes, data, etc.) for easy reference: *Statistical data is referenced in the glossary.* [REFER + -ENCE]
—**Syn. 5.** note, citation. **10.** endorsement. **11.** consideration, concern.

ref′erence book′, a publication consulted for facts or background information, as an encyclopedia, dictionary, atlas, yearbook, etc.

ref′erence elec′trode, *Physical Chem.* an electrode of known oxidation potential used in determining the electromotive force of a galvanic cell.

ref′erence frame′, *Physics.* See **frame of reference** (def. 2).

ref′erence group′, *Sociol.* a group with which an individual identifies and whose values he accepts as guiding principles.

ref′erence mark′, *Survey.* a permanent mark set at a specific distance in a specific direction from a survey station so as to permit accurate reestablishment of the station.

ref′erence peg′, *Survey.* See **recovery peg.**

ref·er·en·dum (ref′ə ren′dəm), *n., pl.* **-dums, -da** (-də). **1.** the principle or practice of referring measures proposed or passed by a legislative body to the vote of the electorate for approval or rejection. Cf. **initiative** (def. 3a). **2.** a vote on a measure thus referred. [< L: thing to be carried back (neut. ger. of *referre* to REFER)]

ref·er·ent (ref′ər ənt), *n.* **1.** the object or event to which a term or symbol refers. **2.** *Logic.* the first term in a proposition to which succeeding terms relate. [< L *referent-* (s. of *referēns*), prp. of *referre.* See REFER, -ENT]

ref·er·en·tial (ref′ə ren′shəl), *adj.* **1.** having reference: *referential to something.* **2.** containing a reference. **3.** used for reference. [REFERENT + -IAL] —**ref′er·en′tial·ly,** *adv.*

re·fer·ral (ri fûr′əl), *n.* **1.** an act of referring; the state of being referred. **2.** an instance of referring. **3.** a person recommended to someone or for something. [REFER + -AL[2]]

referred′ pain′, *Pathol.* pain felt in an area remote from the site of origin. Also called **synalgia.**

ref·fo (ref′ō), *n., pl.* **-fos.** *Australian Informal.* an immigrant, esp. one who has been in Australia only a short time. [shortening and alter. of REFUGEE]

re·fill (*v.* rē fil′; *n.* rē′fil′), *v.t.* **1.** to fill again. —*n.* **2.** a material, supply, or the like, to replace something that has been used up: *a refill for a prescription.* [RE- + FILL] —**re·fill′a·ble,** *adj.*

re·fi·nance (rē fī′nans, rē′fī nans′), *v.i., v.t.,* **-nanced, -nanc·ing.** to sell securities in order to redeem (existing bonds or other indebtedness or preferred stock). [RE- + FINANCE]

re·fine (ri fīn′), *v.,* **-fined, -fin·ing.** —*v.t.* **1.** to bring to a fine or a pure state; free from impurities: *to refine metal, sugar, or petroleum.* **2.** to purify from what is coarse, vulgar, or debasing; make elegant or cultured. **3.** to bring to a finer state or form by purifying. **4.** to make more fine, subtle, or precise: *to refine one's writing style.* —*v.i.* **5.** to become pure. **6.** to become more fine, elegant, or polished. **7.** to make fine distinctions in thought or language. **8. refine on** or **upon,** to improve by inserting finer distinctions, superior elements, etc.: *After 30 years, the mature author was able to refine on the work of his youth.* [RE- + FINE[1]] —**re·fin′a·ble,** *adj.* —**re·fin′er,** *n.*

re·fined (ri fīnd′), *adj.* **1.** having or showing well-bred feeling, taste, etc.: *refined people.* **2.** freed or free from coarseness, vulgarity, etc.: *refined taste.* **3.** freed from impurities: *refined sugar.* **4.** very subtle, precise, or exact: *refined distinctions.* [REFINE + -ED[2]] —**re·fin·ed·ly** (ri fī′nid lē, -fīnd′-), *adv.* —**re·fin′ed·ness,** *n.*
—**Syn. 1.** cultivated, polished, polite, courteous, civilized, courtly, genteel, elegant. **3.** clarified, distilled, purified. —**Ant. 1.** rude, coarse, crude.

re·fine·ment (ri fīn′mənt), *n.* **1.** fineness or elegance of feeling, taste, manners, language, etc. **2.** an instance of refined feeling, manners, etc. **3.** the act or process of refining. **4.** quality or state of being refined. **5.** a subtle point or distinction. **6.** subtle reasoning. **7.** an improved, higher, or extreme form of something: *a house that is the ultimate refinement of civilized living; the refinements found in a luxury car.* **8.** *Math.* a set whose elements include the elements of a given set. [REFINE + -MENT]

re·fin·er·y (ri fī′nə rē), *n., pl.* **-er·ies.** an establishment for refining something, as metal, sugar, or petroleum. [REFINE + -ERY]

re·fin·ish (rē fin′ish), *v.t.* to give a new surface to (wood, furniture, etc.): *refinishing a table to show the natural wood.* [RE- + FINISH] —**re·fin′ish·er,** *n.*

re·fit (rē fit′), *v.,* **-fit·ted, -fit·ting,** *n.* —*v.t.* **1.** to fit, prepare, or equip again. —*v.i.* **2.** to renew supplies or equipment. **3.** to get refitted. —*n.* **4.** an act of refitting. [RE- + FIT[1]]

refl., **1.** reflection. **2.** reflective. **3.** reflex. **4.** reflexive.

re·flate (ri flāt′), *v.,* **-flat·ed, -flat·ing.** —*v.i.* **1.** to increase again the amount of money and credit in circulation. —*v.t.* **2.** to increase (money and credit) again. [back formation from REFLATION]

re·fla·tion (ri flā′shən), *n.* the increasing of the quantity of currency of a country in order to restore a price level. [RE- + (IN)FLATION]

re·flect (ri flekt′), *v.t.* **1.** to cast back (light, heat, sound, etc.) from a surface: *He pointed the mirror so that it would reflect light on the wall behind him.* **2.** to give back or show an image of; mirror. **3.** to serve to cast or bring (credit, discredit, etc.). **4.** to reproduce; show: *followers reflecting the views of the leader.* **5.** to throw or cast back; cause to return or rebound: *Her bitterness reflects gloom on all her family.* —*v.i.* **6.** to be turned or cast back, as light. **7.** to cast back light, heat, etc. **8.** to be reflected or mirrored. **9.** to give back or show an image. **10.** to think, ponder, or meditate: *to reflect on one's virtues and faults.* **11.** to serve or tend to bring reproach or discredit: *His crimes reflected on the whole community.* **12.** to serve to give a particular aspect or impression: *His poor speeches reflected unfavorably on his desirability as a candidate.* [ME *reflect(en)* < L *reflect(ere)* (to) bend back, equiv. to *re-* RE- + *flectere* to bend] —**re·flect′ed·ly,** *adv.* —**re·flect′ed·ness,** *n.* —**re·flect′i·bil′i·ty,** *n.* —**re·flect′i·ble,** *adj.* —**re·flect′ing·ly,** *adv.*
—**Syn. 10.** ruminate, deliberate, muse, consider, cogitate, contemplate. See **study. 4.** manifest. **6.** rebound.

re·flect·ance (ri flek′təns), *n.* *Physics, Optics.* the ratio of the intensity of reflected radiation to that of the radiation incident on a surface. Cf. **albedo.** [REFLECT + -ANCE]

reflect′ed plan′, a plan, as of a room, taken as seen from above but having the outlines of some upper surface, as a vault or compartmented ceiling, projected downward upon it so that a part that would appear at the right when seen from below appears on the plan at the left.

reflect′ing tel′escope. See under **telescope** (def. 1). Also called **reflector.**

re·flec·tion (ri flek′shən), *n.* **1.** the act of reflecting or the state of being reflected. **2.** an image; representation; counterpart. **3.** a fixing of the thoughts on something; careful consideration. **4.** a thought occurring in consideration or meditation. **5.** an unfavorable remark or observation. **6.** the casting of some imputation or reproach. **7.** *Physics, Optics.* **a.** the return of light, heat, sound, etc., after striking a surface. **b.** something so reflected, as heat or, esp., light. **8.** *Anat.* the bending or folding back of a part upon itself. Also, *esp. Brit.,* **reflexion.** [ME < LL *reflexiōn-* (s. of *reflexiō*) a bending back, equiv. to L *reflex(us)* (see REFLEX) + *-iōn-* -ION] —**re·flec′tion·al,** *adj.* —**re·flec′tion·less,** *adj.*
—**Syn. 3.** meditation, rumination, deliberation, cogitation, study, thinking. **5.** imputation, aspersion, reproach, criticism. —**Ant. 3.** heedlessness. **5.** praise.

reflec′tion plane′, *Crystall.* a plane through a crystal which divides the crystal into two halves that are mirror images of each other. Also called **symmetry plane.** Cf. **symmetry element.**

re·flec·tive (ri flek′tiv), *adj.* **1.** that reflects; reflecting. **2.** of or pertaining to reflection. **3.** cast by reflection. **4.** given to or concerned with meditation: *a reflective man.* [REFLECT + -IVE] —**re·flec′tive·ly,** *adv.* —**re·flec′tive·ness, re·flec·tiv·i·ty** (rē′flek tiv′i tē), *n.*
—**Syn. 4.** contemplative, thoughtful. See **pensive.**

re·flec·tom·e·ter (rē′flek tom′i tər), *n.* *Optics.* a device for measuring reflectance. [REFLECT + -O- + -METER]

re·flec·tor (ri flek′tər), *n.* **1.** one who or that which reflects. **2.** a body, surface, or device that reflects light, heat, sound, or the like. **3.** a reflecting telescope. **4.** *Physics.* a substance, as graphite or heavy water, used to prevent the escape of neutrons from the core of a reactor. [REFLECT + -OR[2]]

re·flec·tor·ize (ri flek′tə rīz′), *v.t.,* **-ized, -iz·ing.** to treat something so that it reflects light: *to reflectorize license plates.* [REFLECTOR + -IZE]

re·flet (rə flā′), *n.* an effect of brilliance or luster due to the reflection of light on a surface, esp. of pottery; iridescence. [< F, earlier *reflès* < It *riflesso*) reflection; see REFLEX]

re·flex (*adj., n.* rē′fleks; *v.* ri fleks′), *adj.* **1.** *Physiol.* noting or pertaining to an involuntary response to a stimulus, the nerve impulse from a receptor being transmitted inward to a nerve center that in turn transmits it outward to an effector. **2.** occurring in reaction; responsive. **3.** designating a radio apparatus in which the same part performs two functions, as in a reflex klystron, in which one resonator acts as buncher and catcher. **4.** cast back; reflected, as light, color, etc. **5.** bent or turned back. —*n.* **6.** *Physiol.* **a.** Also called **re′flex act′.** movement caused by a reflex response. **b.** Also called **re′flex ac′tion.** the entire physiological process activating such movement. **7.** the reflection or image of an object, as exhibited by a mirror or the like. **8.** a reproduction, as if in a mirror. **9.** a copy; adaptation. **10.** reflected light, color, etc. **11.** a reflex radio receiving apparatus or set. **12.** a reflex camera. —*v.t.* **13.** to subject to a reflex process. **14.** to bend, turn, or fold back. **15.** to arrange in a reflex system. [< L *reflex(us)* bent back, ptp. of *reflectere* to REFLECT] —**re′flex·ly,** *adv.* —**re′flex·ness,** *n.*

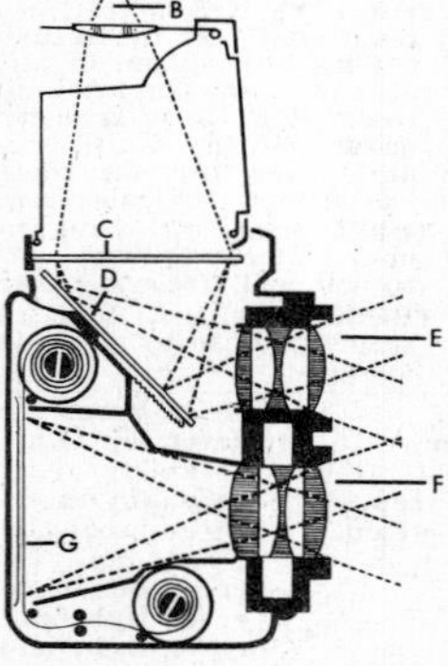

Reflex camera (twin-lens)
A, Eye; B, Lens magnifying image on ground glass; C, Ground glass; D, Reflecting mirror; E, Focusing lens; F. Photographic lens; G, Film

re′flex an′gle, *Geom.* an angle greater than 180°.

re′flex arc′, *Physiol.* the nerve pathways followed by an impulse in the production of a reflex.

re′flex cam′era, a camera in which the image appears on a ground-glass viewer after being reflected by a mirror or after passing through a prism or semi-transparent glass. In one type (**single′-lens re′flex cam′era**), the image passes through the same lens to both the ground glass and the film. In another type (**twin′-lens re′flex cam′era**), the image passes through one lens to the ground glass and through a second lens to the film, the lenses being coupled together for focusing.

re·flexed (ri flekst′), *adj.* bent backward or downward, as a leaf. [ME; see REFLEX, -ED[3]]

re·flex·ion (ri flek′shən), *n.* *Chiefly Brit.* reflection. [ME] —**re·flex′ion·al,** *adj.*

re·flex·ive (ri flek′siv), *adj.* **1.** *Gram.* **a.** (of a verb) taking a subject and object with identical referents, as *shave* in *I shave myself.* **b.** (of a pronoun) used as an object to refer to the subject of a verb, as *myself* in *I shave myself.* **2.** reflex; responsive. **3.** able to reflect; reflective. **4.** *Math.* **a.** noting a relation in which each element is in relation to itself, as the relation "less than or equal to." Cf. **antireflexive. b.** (of a vector space) having the property that the dual space of the dual space of the given vector space equals the given vector space. —*n.* **5.** *Gram.* a reflexive verb or pronoun. [< ML *reflexīv(us)* turned back, reflected. See REFLEX, -IVE] —**re·flex′ive·ly,** *adv.* —**re·flex′ive·ness, re·flex·iv·i·ty** (rē′flek siv′i tē), *n.*

ref·lu·ent (ref′lo͞o ənt), *adj.* flowing back; ebbing, as the waters of a tide. [< L *refluent-* (s. of *refluēns*), prp. of *refluere.* See RE-, FLUENT] —**ref′lu·ence,** *n.*

re·flux (rē′fluks′), *n.* a flowing back; ebb. [< ML *reflux(us).* See RE-, FLUX]

re·for·est (rē fôr′ist, -for′-), *v.t.* to replant trees in a forest that has been affected by cutting, fire, or the like. [RE- + FOREST] —**re′for·est·a′tion,** *n.*

re-form (rē fôrm′), *v.t., v.i.* to form again. [RE- + FORM] —**re-form′er,** *n.*

re·form (ri fôrm′), *n.* **1.** the improvement or amendment of what is wrong, corrupt, unsatisfactory, etc.: *social reform; spelling reform.* **2.** an instance of this. **3.** the amendment of conduct, belief, etc. **4.** (*cap.*) See **Reform Judaism.** [< F *réforme,* deriv. of *reformer*] —*v.t.* **5.** to change to a better state, form, etc.; improve by alteration, substitution, abolition, etc. **6.** to cause (a person) to abandon wrong or evil ways of life or conduct. **7.** to put an end to (abuses, disorders, etc.). —*v.i.* **8.** to abandon evil conduct or error: *The drunkard promised to reform.* [ME *reform(en)* < MF, OF *reform(er)* < L *reformāre.* See RE-, FORM] —**re·form′a·bil′i·ty, re·form′a·ble·ness,** *n.* —**re·form′a·ble,** *adj.* —**re·form′a·tive,** *adj.* —**re·form′a·tive·ly,** *adv.* —**re·form′a·tive·ness,** *n.* —**re·form′ing·ly,** *adv.*
—**Syn. 1.** correction, reformation, betterment, amelioration. **5.** better, rectify, correct, amend, emend, ameliorate, repair, restore. —**Ant. 1.** deterioration.

ref·or·ma·tion (ref′ər mā′shən), *n.* **1.** the act of reforming; state of being reformed. **2.** (*cap.*) the religious movement in the 16th century which had for its object the reform of the Roman Catholic Church, and which led to the establishment of the Protestant churches. [ME *reformacion* < L *reformātiōn-* (s. of *reformātiō*), equiv. to *reformāt(us)* (ptp. of *reformāre* to REFORM) + *-iōn-* -ION] —**ref′or·ma′tion·al,** *adj.*
—**Syn. 1.** improvement, betterment, correction, reform.

re·form·a·to·ry (ri fôr′mə tôr′ē, -tōr′ē), *adj., n., pl.* **-ries.** —*adj.* **1.** serving or designed to reform: *reformatory lectures; reformatory punishments.* —*n.* **2.** Also called **reform school.** a penal institution for reforming young offenders, esp. minors. [< L *reformāt(us)* (see REFORMATION) + -ORY[2]]

Reform′ Bill′, *Eng. Hist.* any of the bills passed by Parliament (1832, 1867, 1884) providing for an increase in the number of voters in elections for the House of Commons, esp. the bill of 1832 by which many rotten boroughs were disfranchised. Also called **Reform′ Act′.**

re·formed (ri fôrmd′), *adj.* **1.** amended by removal of faults, abuses, etc. **2.** improved in conduct, morals, etc. **3.** (*cap.*) noting or pertaining to Protestant churches, esp. Calvinist as distinguished from Lutheran. [REFORM + -ED[2]] —**re·form·ed·ly** (ri fôr′mid lē), *adv.*

Reformed′ Church′ in Amer′ica, a Protestant denomination having a Calvinist theology and originally called the Dutch Reformed Church.

reformed′ spell′ing, a revised orthography intended to simplify the spelling of English words, esp. to eliminate unpronounced letters, as by substituting *thru* for *through, tho* for *though, slo* for *slow,* etc.

Reform′ flask′, an English salt-glazed stoneware flask of the early 19th century formed as an effigy of one of the figures connected with the Reform Bill of 1832.

re·form·ist (ri fôr′mist), *n.* **1.** one who advocates or practices reform; reformer. **2.** a member of any reformed denomination. —*adj.* **3.** Also, **re·form·is·tic** (re′fər mis′tik). of or belonging to a movement for reform. [REFORM + -IST] —**re·form′ism,** *n.*

Reform′ Jew′, a Jew who adheres to a system of ethics and religious worship taken to reflect the needs of modern Jewry and based on only those Biblical and rabbinical laws, liturgical practices, and ritualistic observances of traditional Judaism that are considered meaningful in the light of contemporary conditions. Cf. **Conservative Jew, Orthodox Jew.**

Reform′ Ju′daism, Judaism as observed by Reform Jews.

reform′ school′, reformatory (def. 2).

Ref. Pres., Reformed Presbyterian.

re·fract (ri frakt′), *v.t.* **1.** to subject to refraction. **2.** to determine the refractive condition of (an eye). [< L *refract(us)* broken up, weakened (ptp. of *refringere*), equiv. to *re-* RE- + *frac-* (perf. s. of *frangere* to BREAK)] —**re·fract′a·ble,** *adj.* —**re·fract′ed·ly,** *adv.* —**re·fract′ed·ness,** *n.*

refract′ing tel′escope. See under **telescope** (def. 1). Also called **refractor.**

re′fer·ti·li′za·ble, *adj.*
re′fer·ti·li·za′tion, *n.*
re·fer′ti·lize′, *v.t.,* -lized, -liz·ing.
re·file′, *v.,* -filed, -fil·ing.
re·film′, *v.t.*
re·fil′ter, *v.t.*
re·find′, *v.t.,* -found, -find·ing.
re·fire′, *v.,* -fired, -fir·ing.
re·fix′, *v.t.,* -fixed, -fix·ing.
re·float′, *v.*
re′flo·res′cence, *n.*
re′flow′, *v.*
re·flow′er, *n.*
re·fo′cus, *v.,* -cused, -cus·ing or (*esp. Brit.*) -cussed, -cus·sing.
re·fold′, *v.*
re·fore′cast, *v.t.,* -cast or -cast·ed, -cast·ing.
re·for′feit, *v.t.*
re·for′fei·ture, *n.*
re·forge′, *v.t.,* -forged, -forg·ing.
re·forge′a·ble, *adj.*
re·for′mu·late′, *v.t.,* -lat·ed, -lat·ing.
re′for·mu·la′tion, *n.*
re′for·ti·fi·ca′tion, *n.*
re·for′ti·fy′, *v.t.,* -fied, -fy·ing.
re·for′ward, *v.t.*

CONCISE ETYMOLOGY KEY: <, descended or derived from; >, whence; b., blend of, blended; c., cognate with; deriv., derivative; equiv., equivalent; imit., imitative; m., modification of; obl., oblique; r., replacing; s., stem; sp., spelling; trans., translation; ?, origin unknown, perhaps; *, hypothetical. See the full key inside the front cover.

re·frac·tion (ri frak′shən), *n.* **1.** *Physics.* the change of direction of a ray of light, sound, heat, or the like, in passing obliquely from one medium into another in which its speed is different. **2.** *Optics.* **a.** the ability of the eye to refract light which enters it so as to form an image on the retina. **b.** the determining of the refractive condition of the eye. **3.** *Astron.* **a.** Also called **astronomical refraction.** the amount, in angular measure, by which the altitude of a celestial body is increased by the refraction of its light in the earth's atmosphere, being zero at the zenith and a maximum at the horizon. **b.** the observed altered location, as seen from the earth, of another planet or the like due to diffraction by the atmosphere. [< LL *refractiōn-* (s. of *refractiō*) a breaking up, open. See REFRACT, -ION] —**re·frac′tion·al,** *adj.*

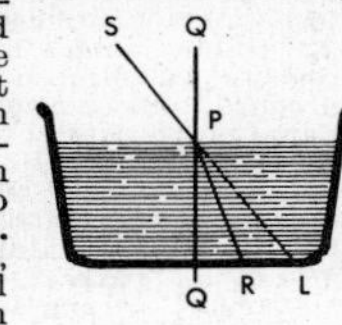

Refraction
SP, Ray of light;
SPL, Original direction of ray;
SPR, Refracted ray;
QQ, Perpendicular

re·frac·tive (ri frak′tiv), *adj.* **1.** of or pertaining to refraction. **2.** having power to refract. [< LL *refractīv(us)* breaking back. See REFRACT, -IVE] —**re·frac′tive·ly,** *adv.* —**re·frac′tive·ness,** *n.* —**re·frac·tiv·i·ty** (rē′frak tiv′i tē), *n.*

refrac′tive in′dex, *Optics.* See **index of refraction.**

re·frac·tom·e·ter (rē′frak tom′i tər), *n.* *Optics.* an instrument for determining the refractive index of a substance. [REFRACT + -O- + -METER] —**re·frac·to·met·ric** (ri frak′tə me′trik), *adj.* —**re′frac·tom′e·try,** *n.*

re·frac·tor (ri frak′tər), *n.* **1.** one who or that which refracts. **2.** See **refracting telescope.** [REFRACT + -OR[2]]

re·frac·to·ry (ri frak′tə rē), *adj., n., pl.* **-ries.** —*adj.* **1.** hard or impossible to manage; stubbornly disobedient: *a refractory child.* **2.** resisting ordinary methods of treatment. **3.** difficult to fuse, reduce, or work, as an ore or metal. —*n.* **4.** a material having the ability to retain its physical shape and chemical identity when subjected to high temperatures. **5. refractories,** bricks of various shapes used in lining furnaces. **6.** *Physiol.* a momentary state of reduced irritability following a response: *the refractory period of a nerve.* [var. of *refractary* (by analogy with adjectives in -ORY[1]) < L *refractāri(us)* stubborn, obstinate, equiv. to *refract(us)* (see REFRACT) + *-ārius* -ARY] —**re·frac′to·ri·ly,** *adv.* —**re·frac′to·ri·ness,** *n.*
—**Syn. 1.** obstinate, perverse, mulish, headstrong, intractable, disobedient, recalcitrant, ungovernable, unruly. —**Ant. 1.** obedient, tractable.

re·frain[1] (ri frān′), *v.i.* **1.** to keep oneself from doing, thinking, or saying something; abstain (often fol. by *from*). —*v.t.* **2.** *Archaic.* to curb. [ME *refrein(en)* < OF *refren(er)* < L *refrēnāre* to bridle, equiv. to *re-* RE- + *frēn(um)* bridle] —**re·frain′er,** *n.* —**re·frain′ment,** *n.*
—**Syn. 1.** cease, desist.

re·frain[2] (ri frān′), *n.* **1.** a phrase or verse recurring at intervals in a song or poem, esp. at the end of each stanza; chorus. **2.** *Music.* **a.** a musical setting for the refrain of a poem. **b.** any melody. **3.** the principal, recurrent section of a rondo. [ME *refreyne* < OF *refrain,* deriv. of *refraindre* < VL *refrangere,* r. L *refringere* to REFRACT]

re·fran·gi·ble (ri fran′jə bəl), *adj.* capable of being refracted, as rays of light. [RE- + FRANGIBLE] —**re·fran′gi·ble·ness, re·fran′gi·bil′i·ty,** *n.*

re·fresh (ri fresh′), *v.t.* **1.** to provide new vigor and energy by rest, food, etc. (often used reflexively). **2.** to stimulate (the memory). **3.** to make fresh again; reinvigorate or cheer (a person, the mind, spirits, etc.). **4.** to freshen in appearance, color, etc., as by a restorative. —*v.i.* **5.** to take refreshment, esp. food or drink. **6.** to become fresh or vigorous again; revive. [ME *refresch(en)* < MF, OF *refresch(ir).* See RE-, FRESH] —**re·fresh′ful,** *adj.* —**re·fresh′ful·ly,** *adv.*
—**Syn. 1.** revive. **3.** freshen, enliven, reanimate. **4.** restore, repair, renovate, renew, retouch. —**Ant. 3.** dispirit, discourage.

re·fresh·er (ri fresh′ər), *n.* **1.** one who or that which refreshes. **2.** *Brit.* a partial or interim fee paid to a lawyer during a prolonged case. [ME *refressher.* See REFRESH, -ER[1]]

refresh′er course′, a study course serving as a review of previous education.

re·fresh·ing (ri fresh′ing), *adj.* **1.** having the power to restore freshness, vitality, energy, etc.: *a refreshing nap.* **2.** arousing uncommon or exceptional interest; exhilarating; stimulating: *the most refreshing play this season.* [REFRESH + -ING[2]] —**re·fresh′ing·ly,** *adv.* —**re·fresh′ing·ness,** *n.*

re·fresh·ment (ri fresh′mənt), *n.* **1.** something that refreshes, esp. food or drink. **2. refreshments,** articles or portions of food or drink, esp. for a light meal. **3.** act of refreshing; state of being refreshed. [ME *refresshement* < MF *refreschement.* See REFRESH, -MENT]

re·frig·er·ant (ri frij′ər ənt), *adj.* **1.** refrigerating; cooling. **2.** reducing bodily heat or fever. —*n.* **3.** a refrigerant agent, as a drug. **4.** a liquid capable of vaporizing at a low temperature, as ammonia, used in mechanical refrigeration. **5.** a cooling substance, as ice or solid carbon dioxide, used in a refrigerator. [< L *refrīgerant-* (s. of *refrīgerāns*), prp. of *refrīgerāre.* See REFRIGERATE, -ANT]

re·frig·er·ate (ri frij′ə rāt′), *v.t.,* **-at·ed, -at·ing.** **1.** to make or keep cold or cool. **2.** to chill or freeze (food) for preservation. [< L *refrīgerāt(us)* made cool, ptp. of *refrīgerāre,* equiv. to *re-* RE- + *frīgerāre* to make cool, deriv. of *frīgor-* (s. of *frīgus*) cold; see -ATE[1]] —**re·frig′er·a′tive, re·frig·er·a·to·ry** (ri frij′ər ə tôr′ē, -tōr′ē), *adj.*

re·frig·er·a·tion (ri frij′ə rā′shən), *n.* **1.** the act or process of refrigerating. **2.** the state of being refrigerated. [ME *refrigeracion* < L *refrīgerātiōn-* (s. of *refrīgerātiō*). See REFRIGERATE, -ION]

re·frig·er·a·tor (ri frij′ə rā′tər), *n.* **1.** a box, room, or cabinet in which food, drink, etc., are kept cool by means of ice or mechanical refrigeration. **2.** the part of a distilling apparatus that cools the volatile material, causing it to condense; condenser; rectifier. [REFRIGERATE + -OR[2]]

refrig′erator car′, a freight car having either an ice chest or machinery for chilling perishables and sometimes having a heating unit to keep perishables from freezing.

re·frin·gent (ri frin′jənt), *adj.* refracting; refractive. [< L *refringent-* (s. of *refringēns*), prp. of *refringere* to break up. See REFRACT, -ENT] —**re·frin′gen·cy, re·frin′gence,** *n.*

Ref. Sp., reformed spelling.

reft (reft), *v.* a pt. and pp. of **reave.**

re·fu·el (rē fyo͞o′əl), *v.,* **-eled, -el·ing** or (*esp. Brit.*) **-elled, -el·ling.** —*v.t.* **1.** to supply again with fuel: *to refuel an airplane.* —*v.i.* **2.** to take on a fresh supply of fuel: *The plane refueled at Paris and flew on.* [RE- + FUEL]

ref·uge (ref′yo͞oj), *n., v.,* **-uged, -ug·ing.** —*n.* **1.** shelter or protection from danger, trouble, etc.: *to take refuge from a storm.* **2.** a place of shelter, protection, or safety. **3.** anything to which one has recourse for aid, relief, or escape. **4.** *Brit.* a platform in the center of a street for the use of pedestrians in crossing; island. —*v.t.* **5.** *Archaic.* to afford refuge to. —*v.i.* **6.** *Archaic.* to take refuge. [ME < MF < L *refug(ium),* deriv. of *refugere* to flee away (*re-* RE- + *fugere* to flee); see FUGITIVE]
—**Syn. 1.** security, safety. **2.** asylum, retreat, sanctuary, haven, stronghold.

ref·u·gee (ref′yo͞o jē′), *n.* one who flees for refuge or safety, esp. to a foreign country, as in time of political upheaval, war, etc. [< F *réfugié,* ptp. of *réfugier* to take refuge. See REFUGE, -EE] —**ref′u·gee′ism,** *n.*

Re·fu·gi·o (ri fyo͞o′zhē ō′, -fyo͞o′zhē ō′), *n.* a town in S Texas. 4944 (1960).

re·fu·go (rə fyo͞o′gō), *n.* cork of inferior quality, used for insulating materials, etc. [< Pg: refuse, dross]

re·ful·gent (ri ful′jənt), *adj.* shining; radiant; glowing. [< L *refulgent-* (s. of *refulgēns,* prp. of *refulgēre*). See RE-, FULGENT] —**re·ful′gence, re·ful′gen·cy, re·ful′gent·ness,** *n.* —**re·ful′gent·ly,** *adv.*

re·fund[1] (*v.* ri fund′; *n.* rē′fund), *v.t.* **1.** to give back or restore (esp. money); repay. **2.** to make repayment to; reimburse. —*v.i.* **3.** to make repayment. —*n.* **4.** a repayment. [ME *refund(en)* < L *refund(ere)* (to) pour back, equiv. to *re-* RE- + *fund-* pour; see FOUND[3]] —**re·fund′a·ble,** *adj.* —**re·fund′er,** *n.* —**re·fund′ment,** *n.*

re·fund[2] (rē fund′), *v.t.* **1.** to fund anew. **2.** *Finance.* **a.** to meet (a matured debt structure) by new borrowing, esp. through issuance of bonds. **b.** to replace (an old issue) with a new one. [RE- + FUND]

re′fund annu′ity, *Insurance.* an annuity providing for a lump-sum payment or installment payments to the beneficiary for the amount remaining of the purchase price at the death of the annuitant.

re·fur·bish (rē fûr′bish), *v.t.* to furbish again; renovate; polish up again; brighten: *The theater lobby was fully refurbished.* [RE- + FURBISH] —**re·fur′bish·ment,** *n.*
—**Syn.** refurnish, redecorate.

re·fus·al (ri fyo͞o′zəl), *n.* **1.** an act or instance of refusing. **2.** priority in refusing or taking something; option. **3.** complete resistance of a driven pile to further driving. [ME *refusell.* See REFUSE[1], -AL[2]]

re·fuse[1] (ri fyo͞oz′), *v.,* **-fused, -fus·ing.** —*v.t.* **1.** to decline to accept (something offered): *to refuse the nomination for mayor.* **2.** to decline to give; deny (a request, demand, etc.): *to refuse permission.* **3.** to express a determination not to (do something): *to refuse to discuss the question.* **4.** to decline to submit to. **5.** (of a horse) to decline to leap over (a barrier). **6.** *Mil.* to bend or curve back (the flank units of a military force) so that they face generally to the flank rather than the front. **7.** *Obs.* to renounce. —*v.i.* **8.** to decline acceptance, consent, or compliance. [ME *refuse(n)* < MF, OF *refus(er)* << L *refūs(us),* ptp. of *refundere* to pour back; see REFUND[1]] —**re·fus′a·ble,** *adj.* —**re·fus′er,** *n.*
—**Syn. 1.** rebuff. REFUSE, DECLINE, REJECT, SPURN all imply nonacceptance of something. TO DECLINE is milder and more courteous than to REFUSE, which is direct and often emphatic in expressing determination not to accept what is offered or proposed: *to refuse a bribe; to decline an invitation.* TO REJECT is even more positive and definite than REFUSE: *to reject a suitor.* TO SPURN is to reject with scorn: *to spurn a bribe.* **2.** repudiate. —**Ant. 1.** accept, welcome.

ref·use[2] (ref′yo͞os), *n.* **1.** something that is discarded as worthless or useless; rubbish; trash; garbage. —*adj.* **2.** rejected as worthless; discarded: *refuse matter.* [ME < MF, OF *refus* denial, rejection, deriv. of *refuser* to REFUSE[1]]

ref·u·ta·tion (ref′yo͞o tā′shən), *n.* an act of refuting a statement, charge, etc.; disproof. Also, **re·fut·al** (ri fyo͞ot′əl). [< L *refūtātiōn-* (s. of *refūtātiō*), equiv. to *refūtāt(us)* checked, resisted (ptp. of *refūtāre* to REFUTE) + *-iōn-* -ION]

re·fut·a·tive (ri fyo͞o′tə tiv), *adj.* tending to refute; pertaining to refutation: *a refutative point of view.* Also, **re·fut′a·to′ry.** [REFUTAT(ION) + -IVE]

re·fute (ri fyo͞ot′), *v.t.,* **-fut·ed, -fut·ing.** **1.** to prove to be false or erroneous, as an opinion, charge, etc. **2.** to prove (a person) to be in error. [< L *refūt(āre)* (to) check, rebut, equiv. to *re-* RE- + *-fūtāre* to beat] —**re·fu·ta·bil·i·ty** (ri fyo͞o′tə bil′i tē, ref′yə-), *n.* —**re·fu·ta·ble** (ri fyo͞o′tə bəl, ref′yə tə-), *adj.* —**ref·u·ta·bly** (ref′yə tə blē), *adv.* —**re·fut′er,** *n.*
—**Syn. 1.** disprove, rebut. **1, 2.** confute.

Reg (rej), *n.* a boy's given name, form of **Reginald.**

Reg., **1.** queen. [< L *rēgīna*] **2.** regiment.

reg., **1.** regent. **2.** regiment. **3.** region. **4.** register. **5.** registered. **6.** registrar. **7.** registry. **8.** regular. **9.** regularly. **10.** regulation. **11.** regulator.

re·gain (ri gān′), *v.t.* **1.** to get again; recover: *to regain one's health.* **2.** to succeed in reaching again; get back to: *to regain the shore.* —*n.* **3.** (in a moisture-free fabric) the percentage of the weight that represents the amount of moisture the material is expected to absorb under normal conditions. [RE- + GAIN] —**re·gain′a·ble,** *adj.* —**re·gain′er,** *n.*

Re·gain (*Fr.* rə gaN′), *n.* a novel (1930) by Jean Giono. English, **Harvest.**

re·gal[1] (rē′gəl), *adj.* **1.** of or pertaining to a king; royal: *the regal power.* **2.** befitting or resembling a king. **3.** stately; splendid. [ME < L *rēgāl(is)* ROYAL] —**re′gal·ly,** *adv.* —**re′gal·ness,** *n.*
—**Syn. 2.** See **kingly.** —**Ant. 3.** base.

re·gal[2] (rē′gəl), *n.* a portable reed organ of the 16th and 17th centuries. [< MF *regale* < ?]

re·gale[1] (ri gāl′), *v.,* **-galed, -gal·ing,** *n.* —*v.t.* **1.** to entertain lavishly or agreeably; delight. **2.** to entertain with choice food or drink. —*v.i.* **3.** to feast. —*n.* *Archaic.* **4.** a sumptuous feast. **5.** a choice article of food or drink. **6.** refreshment. [< F *régal(er),* deriv. of OF *regale* feast, var. of *gale* pleasure < MD *wale* wealth] —**re·gale′ment,** *n.* —**re·gal′er,** *n.*

re·ga·le[2] (ri gā′lē), *n., pl.* **-ga·li·a** (-gā′lē ə, -gāl′yə). **1.** the right claimed by kings, esp. in the Middle Ages, by which they were to receive the revenue from a vacant bishopric or benefice. **2. regalia, a.** the rights or privileges of a king. **b.** the ensigns or emblems of royalty, as the crown, scepter, etc. **c.** the decorations or insignia of any office or order. [< ML: king's prerogative, n. use of L neut. of *rēgālis* REGAL[1]]

re·gal·i·ty (ri gal′i tē), *n., pl.* **-ties.** **1.** royalty, sovereignty, or kingship. **2.** a right or privilege pertaining to a king. **3.** a kingdom. **4.** (in Scotland) **a.** territorial jurisdiction of a royal nature formerly conferred by the king. **b.** a territory subject to such jurisdiction. [ME *regalite* < MF < ML *rēgālitāts* (s. of *rēgālitās*). See REGAL[1], -ITY]

Re·gan (rē′gən), *n.* (in Shakespeare's *King Lear*) the younger of Lear's two faithless daughters. Cf. **Cordelia** (def. 1), **Goneril.**

re·gard (ri gärd′), *v.t.* **1.** to look upon or think of with a particular feeling: *to regard a person with favor.* **2.** to have or show respect or concern for. **3.** to think highly of; esteem. **4.** to take into account; consider. **5.** to look at; observe: *She regarded him with amusement.* **6.** to relate to; concern: *The news does not regard the explosion.* **7.** to see, look at, or conceive of in a particular way; judge (usually fol. by *as*): *I regard every assignment as a challenge. They regarded his behavior as childish.* **8.** *Obs.* to show attention to; guard. —*v.i.* **9.** to pay attention. **10.** to look or gaze. **11. as regards.** See **as**[1] (def. 21). —*n.* **12.** reference; relation: *to err with regard to facts.* **13.** an aspect, point, or particular: *quite satisfactory in this regard.* **14.** thought; attention; concern. **15.** look; gaze. **16.** respect, esteem, or deference: *a high regard for scholarship.* **17.** kindly feeling; liking. **18. regards,** sentiments of esteem or affection: *Give them my regards.* **19.** *Obs.* aspect. [ME *regard* (n.) < MF *regard(er)* (to) look at. See RE-, GUARD] —**re·gard′a·ble,** *adj.*
—**Syn. 3.** respect, honor, revere, value. **5.** notice, note, see, remark, mark. **16.** concern, estimation, consideration, reverence.

re·gard·ant (ri gär′dᵊnt), *adj.* *Heraldry.* (of a beast) looking backward: *a stag regardant.* Also, **reguardant.** [ME < MF, prp. of *regarder* to REGARD]

re·gard·ful (ri gärd′fəl), *adj.* **1.** observant; attentive; heedful (often fol. by *of*): *a man regardful of the feelings of others.* **2.** showing or feeling regard or esteem; respectful. [REGARD + -FUL] —**re·gard′ful·ly,** *adv.* —**re·gard′ful·ness,** *n.*

re·gard·ing (ri gär′ding), *prep.* with regard to; respecting; concerning: *He knew nothing regarding the lost watch.* [REGARD + -ING[2]]

re·gard·less (ri gärd′lis), *adj.* **1.** having or showing no regard; heedless; unmindful; careless (often fol. by *of*): *regardless of the advice of his elders.* **2.** without regard to expense, danger, etc. —*adv.* **3.** without concern as to advice, warning, hardship, etc.; anyway: *I must make the decision regardless.* **4.** in spite of; without regard for: *We won regardless of our injuries.* [REGARD + -LESS] —**re·gard′less·ly,** *adv.* —**re·gard′less·ness,** *n.*
—**Syn. 1.** inattentive, negligent, neglectful, indifferent, unconcerned. —**Ant. 1.** attentive, mindful.

re·gat·ta (ri gat′ə, -gä′tə), *n.* **1.** a boat race, as of rowboats, yachts, or other vessels. **2.** an organized series of such races. **3.** (originally) a gondola race in Venice. **4.** a strong, striped cotton fabric that is of twill weave. [< It (Venetian) *regatta, regata*]

re·ge·late (rē′jə lāt′, rē′jə lāt′), *v.i.,* **-lat·ed, -lat·ing.** to freeze by regelation. [back formation from REGELATION]

re·ge·la·tion (rē′jə lā′shən), *n.* *Physics.* a phenomenon in which the freezing point of water is lowered by the application of pressure; the melting and refreezing of ice, at constant temperature, caused by varying the pressure. [RE- + GELATION]

Ré·gence (rē′jəns; *Fr.* rā zhäNs′), *adj.* noting or pertaining to the style of French furnishings and decoration of c1700–20, in which a transition occurs from the Baroque style of Louis XIV to the Rococo of Louis XV. [< F, MF < ML *regentia* REGENCY]

re·gen·cy (rē′jən sē), *n., pl.* **-cies,** *adj.* —*n.* **1.** the office, jurisdiction, or control of a regent or body of regents exercising the ruling power during the minority, absence, or disability of a sovereign. **2.** a body of regents. **3.** a government consisting of regents. **4.** a territory under the control of a regent or regents. **5.** the term of office of a regent. **6.** (*cap.*) *Brit. Hist.* the period (1811–20) during which George, Prince of Wales, later George IV, was regent. **7.** (*cap.*) *Fr. Hist.* the period of the minority of Louis XV. **8.** the office or function of a regent or ruler. —*adj.* **9.** of or pertaining to a regency. **10.** *Hist.* of or pertaining to the Regencies in England or France. **11.** (*cap.*) of or pertaining to the style of architecture prevailing during the period of the Regency in Britain, characterized by extreme simplicity of

re·frac′tur·a·ble, *adj.*
re·frac′ture, *v.,* -tured, -tur·ing.
re·frame′, *v.t.,* -framed, -fram·ing.
re·freeze′, *v.,* -froze, -fro·zen, freez·ing.
re·fresh′en, *v.t.*
re·frus′trate, *v.t.,* -trat·ed, -trat·ing.
re·fry′, *v.,* -fried, -fry·ing.
re·func′tion, *v.i.*
re·fur′nish, *v.t.*
re/gal′va·ni·za′tion, *n.*
re·gal′va·nize′, *v.t.,* -nized, -niz·ing.
re·gam′ble, *v.,* -bled, -bling.
re·gar′ment, *v.t.*
re·gar′nish, *v.t.*
re·gar′ri·son, *v.t.*
re·gath′er, *v.*
re·gauge′, *v.t.,* -gauged, -gaug·ing.
re·gear′, *v.*
re·gel′, *v.i.,* -gelled, -gel·ling.

appearance in buildings of all types, the frequent use of stucco, the presence of such features as the bow window and the iron balcony and veranda, the tendency in cities to build large rows of uniform houses, the close imitation of ancient Greek forms and the less common adaptation of Gothic forms, and the occasional fanciful use of Hindu, Islamic, and ancient Egyptian motifs. **12.** of or pertaining to the style of furnishings and decoration of the British Regency, somewhat similar to the French Directoire and Empire styles and characterized by close imitation of ancient Greek forms as well as by less frequent and looser adaptations of ancient Roman, Gothic, Chinese, and ancient Egyptian forms, the progress of the style being generally from simplicity and elegance to lavishness and coarseness. [< ML *regentia.* See REGENT, -CY]

re·gen·er·a·cy (ri jen′ər ə sē), *n.* a regenerate state. [REGENER(ATE) + -ACY]

re·gen·er·ate (*v.* ri jen′ə rāt′; *adj.* ri jen′ər it), *v.*, **-at·ed, -at·ing,** *adj.* —*v.t.* **1.** to effect a complete moral reform in. **2.** to re-create, reconstitute, or make over, esp. in a better form or condition. **3.** to revive or produce anew; bring into existence again. **4.** *Biol.* to renew or restore (a lost, removed, or injured part). **5.** *Physics.* to restore (a substance) to a favorable state or physical condition. **6.** *Electronics.* to magnify the amplification of, by relaying part of the output circuit power into the input circuit. **7.** *Theol.* to cause to be born again spiritually. —*v.i.* **8.** to come into existence or be formed again. **9.** to reform; become regenerate. **10.** to produce a regenerative effect. **11.** to undergo regeneration. —*adj.* **12.** reconstituted or made over in a better form. **13.** reformed. **14.** *Theol.* born again spiritually. [< L *regenerāt(us)* brought forth again (ptp. of *regenerāre*), equiv. to *re-* RE- + *generātus* GENERATE] —**re·gen′er·a·ble,** *adj.* —**re·gen′er·ate·ness,** *n.*

re·gen·er·a·tion (ri jen′ə rā′shən), *n.* **1.** act of regenerating; state of being regenerated. **2.** *Electronics.* a feedback process in which energy from the output of an amplifier is fed back to the grid circuit to reinforce the input. **3.** *Biol.* the restoration or new growth by an organism of organs, tissues, etc., which have been lost, removed, or injured. **4.** *Theol.* spiritual rebirth; religious conversion. [ME *regeneracion* < LL *regenerātiōn-* (s. of *regenerātiō*). See REGENERATE, -ION]

re·gen·er·a·tive (ri jen′ə rā′tiv, -ər ə tiv), *adj.* **1.** of, pertaining to, or characterized by regeneration. **2.** tending to regenerate. [ME < ML *regenerātīv(us).* See REGENERATE, -IVE] —**re·gen·er·a·tive·ly** (ri jen′ə-rā′tiv lē, -ər ə tiv-), *adv.*

regen′erative cool′ing, **1.** *Physics.* a method of liquefying a gas, utilizing the rapid expansion of a portion of the gas to cool the remainder. **2.** the cooling of a reaction engine by circulating around it the liquid propellant prior to its use in the combustion chamber of the engine, the heat energy absorbed by the propellant contributing to the total thrust of the exhaust.

regen′erative feed′back, *Electronics.* See under **feedback** (def. 1).

regen′erative fur′nace, a furnace in which the incoming air is heated by regenerators. Cf. **recuperative furnace.**

re·gen·er·a·tor (ri jen′ə rā′tər), *n.* **1.** one who or that which regenerates. **2.** (in a regenerative furnace) either of two chambers filled with checkerwork through which incoming air and hot exhaust gases pass alternately so that heat from the gases is stored in the checkerwork and given off to the air.

Re·gens·burg (rā′gəns bo͝orkh′), *n.* a city in central Bavaria, in SE West Germany: battle 1809. 125,300 (1963). Also called **Ratisbon.**

re·gent (rē′jənt), *n.* **1.** one who exercises the ruling power in a kingdom during the minority, absence, or disability of the sovereign. **2.** a member of the governing board of a state university or a state educational system. **3.** *U.S.* a university officer who exercises general supervision over the conduct and welfare of the students. **4.** (in certain Catholic universities) a member of the religious order who is associated in the administration of a school or college with a layman who is its dean or director. **5.** (in old universities) a member of certain governing and teaching bodies. **6.** a ruler or governor. —*adj.* **7.** acting as regent of a country; exercising ruling authority in behalf of a sovereign during his minority, absence, or disability (usually used postpositively): *a prince regent.* **8.** *Archaic.* holding the position of a regent in a university. **9.** *Archaic.* ruling; governing. [ME < L *regent-* (s. of *regēns*), prp. of *regere* to rule] —**re′gent·al,** *adj.* —**re′gent·ship′,** *n.*

Re·ger (rā′gər), *n.* **Max** (mäks), 1873–1916, German composer and pianist.

reg·gae (reg′ā), *n.* a style of popular Jamaican music, blending calypso and rock-'n'-roll, and characterized by a syncopated rhythm and lyrics with a social message. [< Jamaican E, var. of *reggay* (introduced in the song "Do the Reggay" (1968) by Frederick "Toots" Hilbert), a dance name based on *rege,* **strege* a dowdy or raggedy fellow; cf. *rege-rege* ragged clothing, quarrel, row]

Reg·gio Ca·la·bria (red′jô kä lä′bryä), a seaport in S Italy, on the Strait of Messina: almost totally destroyed by an earthquake 1908. 150,334 (1961). Also, **Reg·gio di Ca·la·bria** (red′jô dē′ kä lä′bryä).

Reg·gio E·mi·lia (red′jô e mē′lyä), a city in N Italy. 116,515 (1961). Also, **Reg·gio nel·l' E·mi·lia** (red′jô nel′le mē′lyä).

reg·i·cide (rej′i sīd′), *n.* **1.** the killing of a king. **2.** one who kills a king or is in any way responsible for his death, esp. one of the judges who condemned Charles I of England to death. [< L *rēgi-* king (comb. form of *rēg-,* s. of *rēx*) + -CIDE] —**reg′i·cid′al,** *adj.*

re·gime (rə zhēm′, rā-), *n.* **1.** a mode or system of rule or government: *a dictatorial regime.* **2.** a ruling or prevailing system. **3.** the period during which a particular government or ruling system is in power. **4.** *Med.* regimen (def. 1). Also, **ré·gime′.** [< F *régime* < L *regimen* REGIMEN]

reg·i·men (rej′ə men′, -mən), *n.* **1.** *Med.* a regulated course of diet, exercise, or manner of living, intended to preserve or restore health or to attain some result. **2.** rule or government. **3.** a particular form or system of government. **4.** a prevailing system. **5.** *Gram.* government: *the regimen of the verb by its subject.* [< L: rule, government, guidance, equiv. to *reg(ere)* (to) rule + *-i-* -I- + *-men* act of, result of (n. suffix)]

reg·i·ment (*n.* rej′ə mənt; *v.* rej′ə ment′), *n.* **1.** *Mil.* a unit of ground forces, consisting of two or more battalions or battle groups, a headquarters unit, and certain supporting units. **2.** *Obs.* government. —*v.t.* **3.** to manage or treat in a rigid, uniform manner; subject to strict discipline. **4.** to form into a regiment or regiments. **5.** to assign to a regiment or group. **6.** to form into an organized group, usually for the purpose of rigid or complete control. [ME < MF < LL *regiment(um),* equiv. to L *reg(ere)* (to) rule + *-i-* -I- + *-mentum* -MENT] —**reg′i·men·ta′tion,** *n.*

reg·i·men·tal (rej′ə men′tᵊl), *adj.* **1.** of or pertaining to a regiment. —*n.* **2. regimentals,** the uniform of a regiment. [REGIMENT + -AL¹] —**reg′i·men′tal·ly,** *adv.*

Re·gin (rā′gin), *n.* (in the *Volsunga Saga*) a smith, the brother of Fafnir, who raises Sigurd and encourages him to kill Fafnir in the hope of gaining the gold he guards.

re·gi·na (ri jī′nə *for 1;* ri jē′nə, -jī′- *for 2*), *n.* **1.** queen. **2.** (*usually cap.*) the official title of a queen: *Elizabeth Regina.* **3.** (*cap.*) a girl's given name. [< L] —**re·gi′nal,** *adj.*

Re·gi·na (ri jī′nə), *n.* a city in and the capital of Saskatchewan, in the S part, in SW Canada. 112,141 (1961).

Reg·i·nald (rej′ə nəld), *n.* a boy's given name.

Re·gi·o·mon·ta·nus (rē′jē ō mon tā′nəs, -tä′-, -tan′-əs, rej′ē-; *for 1 also Ger.* rā′gē ō mōn tä′no͞os), *n.* **1.** See **Müller, Johann. 2.** an elliptical walled plain in the third quadrant of the face of the moon: about 80 miles long and 65 miles wide.

re·gion (rē′jən), *n.* **1.** an extensive, continuous part of a surface, space, or body: *a region of the earth.* **2.** Usually, **regions.** the vast or indefinite entirety of a space or area, or something compared to one: *the regions of the firmament; the regions of the mind.* **3.** a part of the earth's surface (land or sea) of considerable and usually indefinite extent: *a tropical region.* **4.** a district without respect to boundaries or extent: *a charming region in Connecticut.* **5.** a part or division of the universe, as the heavens: *a galactic region.* **6.** a large indefinite area or range of something specified; sphere: *a region of authority.* **7.** an area of interest, activity, pursuit, etc.; field: *a study of the entire region of logic.* **8.** an administrative division of a city or territory. **9.** *Zoogeog.* a major faunal area of the earth's surface, sometimes one regarded as a division of a larger area. **10.** *Anat.* a place in or a division of the body or a part of the body: *the abdominal region.* [ME < AF *regiun* < L *regiōn-* (s. of *regiō*) direction, line, boundary, equiv. to *reg(ere)* (to) rule + *-iōn-* -ION]
—**Syn. 1.** area, section, portion. **4.** locale, site, tract, quarter.

re·gion·al (rē′jə nᵊl), *adj.* **1.** of or pertaining to a region of considerable extent; not merely local: *a regional meeting of the Boy Scouts.* **2.** of or pertaining to a particular region, district, area, or part, as of a country; sectional; local: *regional differences in pronunciation.* **3.** *Anat.* of, pertaining to, or localized in a particular area or part of the body. **4.** having, exhibiting, or characterized by regionalism: *He writes regional novels.* [< L *regiōnāl(is).* See REGION, -AL¹] —**re′gion·al·ly,** *adv.*

re·gion·al·ism (rē′jə nᵊliz′əm), *n.* **1.** *Govt.* the principle or system of dividing a city, state, etc., into separate administrative regions. **2.** advocacy of such a principle or system. **3.** a quality or characteristic peculiar to a certain area, as of an expression or speech pattern. **4.** devotion to the interests of one's own region. **5.** *Literature.* the theory or practice of emphasizing the regional characteristics of locale or setting, as by stressing local speech. **6.** (*often cap.*) a style of American painting developed chiefly 1930–40 in which subject matter was derived principally from rural areas. [REGIONAL + -ISM] —**re′gion·al·ist,** *n., adj.* —**re′-gion·al·is′tic,** *adj.*

re·gion·al·ize (rē′jə nᵊlīz′), *v.t.*, **-ized, -iz·ing.** to separate into or arrange by regions: *to regionalize ambulance service.* [REGIONAL + -IZE]

Re·gis (rē′jis), *n.* a boy's given name.

ré·gis·seur (rā zhē sœr′), *n., pl.* **-seurs** (-sœr′). *French.* a director, as of a theatrical or motion-picture production.

reg·is·ter (rej′i stər), *n.* **1.** a book in which records of acts, events, names, etc., are kept. **2.** a list or record of such acts, events, etc. **3.** an entry in such a book, record, or list. **4.** an official document issued to a merchant ship as evidence of its nationality. **5.** registration or registry. **6.** a mechanical device by which certain data are automatically recorded. **7.** See **cash register. 8.** *Music.* **a.** the compass or range of a voice or an instrument. **b.** a particular series of tones, esp. of the human voice, produced in the same way and having the same quality: *the head register.* **c.** (in an organ) a stop. **9.** a device for controlling the flow of warmed air or the like through an opening, as from a duct to an interior, composed of a number of narrow, parallel blades, usually behind a grating, that may be adjusted so as to overlap and close the opening. **10.** *Photog.* proper relationship between two plane surfaces in photography, as corresponding plates in photoengraving. **11.** *Print.* **a.** a precise adjustment or correspondence, as of lines, columns, etc., esp. on the two sides of a leaf. **b.** correct relation or exact superimposition, as of colors in color printing. **12.** a bookmark, esp. a ribbon attached to the spine of a book. [ME *registre* < MF, OF < ML *registr(um),* alter. of LL *regesta* catalogue (pl.), n. use L neut. pl. of *regestus* carried back (ptp. of *regerere,* equiv. to *re-* RE- + *gerere* to carry, bear)]
—*v.t.* **13.** to enter or cause to be entered formally in a register. **14.** to cause (mail) to be recorded upon delivery to a post office for safeguarding against loss, theft, damage, etc., during transmission. **15.** to enroll (a student, voter, etc.) in a school or course of study, on the voting rolls, etc.: *It took three days to register all the new students.* **16.** to indicate by a record, as instruments do: *The thermometer registered 102 degrees today.* **17.** to indicate or show, as on a scale. **18.** *Print.* to adjust so as to secure exact correspondence; cause to be in register. **19.** *Mil.* to adjust (fire) on a known point. **20.** to show (surprise, joy, anger, etc.) by facial expression or by actions. **21.** to document (a merchant ship engaged in foreign trade) by issuing a certificate of registry. —*v.i.* **22.** to enter one's name or cause it to be entered in a register; enroll: *to register with a draft board; to register at a motel.* **23.** to apply for and obtain inclusion of one's name on the list of voters. **24.** to enroll in a school or course of study: *I've registered for three English classes for next fall.* **25.** *Print.* to be in register. **26.** to show: *A broad smile registered on his face.* **27.** to have some effect; make some impression: *My plea didn't register on him at all.* [ME *registre(n)* << ML *registrāre,* deriv. of *registrum*] —**reg′is·ter·er,** *n.* —**reg′is·tra·bil′i·ty,** *n.* —**reg′is·tra·ble, reg′is·ter·a·ble,** *adj.*
—**Syn. 1.** record, ledger, archive. **2.** roll, roster, catalogue, chronicle, schedule, annals. **13.** enroll, list, record, catalogue, chronicle. **20.** demonstrate, evince.

reg·is·tered (rej′i stərd), *adj.* **1.** recorded, as in a register or book; enrolled. **2.** *Com.* officially listing the owner's name with the issuing corporation and suitably inscribing the certificate, as with bonds to evidence title. **3.** officially or legally certified by a government officer or board: *a registered patent.* **4.** denoting cattle, horses, dogs, etc., having pedigrees verified and filed by authorized associations of breeders. [REGISTER + -ED²]

reg′istered bond′, a bond recorded in the name of the owner.

reg′istered breadth′, *Naut.* the breadth of a hull as officially measured, equal to the extreme distance between opposite points on the exterior of the hull. Also, **reg′ister breadth′.**

reg′istered depth′, *Naut.* the depth of a hull as officially measured for purposes of tonnage assessment, equal to the vertical dimension amidships from the top of the floors, of a double bottom, or from a certain height above the floors if a wooden ceiling is fitted, to the upper edge of the beam of the tonnage deck above the keel, as well as the vertical dimension of the clear space of any shelter deck or spar deck forming part of the hull above the tonnage deck. Also, **reg′ister depth′.** Also called **depth of hold.**

reg′istered length′, *Naut.* the length of a hull as officially measured, equal to the length along the uppermost continuous deck from the foremost part of the stem, excluding bowsprit, to the after side of the sternpost, or to the center of the rudderstock if the vessel has a cruiser stern. Also, **reg′ister length′.**

reg′istered nurse′, a graduate nurse who has passed a state board examination and been registered and licensed to practice nursing. *Abbr.:* R.N.

reg′istered represent′ative, *Stock Exchange.* an employee of a member firm of a stock exchange, authorized to execute orders for the clients of the firm. Also called **customer's man.**

reg′ister of wills′, *U.S.* (in some States) the official charged with the probate of wills or with the keeping of the records of the probate court.

reg′ister ton′. See under **ton**¹ (def. 6).

reg′ister ton′nage, *Naut.* the volume of a vessel, esp. the net tonnage as measured officially and registered for purposes of taxation.

reg·is·trant (rej′i strənt), *n.* one who registers. [< ML *registrant-* (s. of *registrāns*) prp. of *registrāre.* See REGISTER, -ANT]

reg·is·trar (rej′i strär′, rej′i strär′), *n.* **1.** one who keeps a record; an official recorder. **2.** an agent of a bank, trust company, or other corporation, who is responsible for certifying and registering issues of securities. **3.** an official at a school or college who maintains students' personal and academic records, issues reports of grades, mails out official publications, etc. [< ML *registrār(ius);* r. ME *registrer* < AF < ML *registrātor,* equiv. to *registrāt(us)* (see REGISTRATE) + *-or* -OR²] —**reg′is·trar·ship′,** *n.*

reg·is·trate (rej′i strāt′), *v.i.*, **-trat·ed, -trat·ing.** to select and combine pipe organ stops. [< ML *registrāt(us)* (ptp. of *registrāre*). See REGISTER, -ATE¹]

reg·is·tra·tion (rej′i strā′shən), *n.* **1.** the act of registering. **2.** an instance of this. **3.** an entry in a register. **4.** the group or number registered. **5.** an official act of registering one's name in the list of qualified voters. **6.** a certificate attesting to the fact that someone or something has been registered: *a boat registration.* **7.** *Music.* **a.** the act or technique of registrating. **b.** the selection of stops made by an organist for a particular piece. [< MF < ML *registrātiōn-* (s. of *registrātiō*). See REGISTRATE, -ION] —**reg′is·tra′tion·al,** *adj.*

reg·is·try (rej′i strē), *n., pl.* **-tries. 1.** the act of registering; registration. **2.** a place where a register is kept; an office of registration. **3.** a register. **4.** the state of being registered. **5.** the nationality of a merchant ship as shown on its register. [REGIST(ER) + -RY]

reg′istry of′fice, *Brit.* **1.** a government office and depository in which records and civil registers are kept and civil marriages performed. **2.** an employment agency for domestic help, as maids, cooks, etc.

re·gi·us (rē′jē əs, -jis), *adj.* **1.** of or belonging to a king. **2.** (of a professor in a British university) holding a chair founded by or dependent on the sovereign. —*n.* **3.** (*cap.*) the Greek uncial codex of the four Gospels, dating from the 8th century A.D. [< L, equiv. to *rēg-* (s. of *rēx*) king + *-ius* of, belonging to (adj. suffix)]

re·gle (rē′gəl), *n.* a groove or channel for guiding a sliding door. [< F *règle* straight-edge, rule]

reg·let (reg′lit), *n.* **1.** *Archit.* **a.** a groove for guiding or holding a panel, window sash, etc. **b.** a narrow, flat molding; fillet. **2.** *Print.* **a.** a thin strip, usually of wood, less than type-high, used to produce a blank in or about a page of type. **b.** such strips collectively. [< F, dim. of *règle* RULE (< L *rēgula*)]

reg·ma (reg′mə), *n., pl.* **-ma·ta** (-mə tə). *Bot.* a dry fruit consisting of three or more carpels which separate from the axis at maturity. [< NL < Gk *rhēgma* fracture, break, equiv. to *rhēg(nýmai)* (to) break, shatter + *-ma* result of (n. suffix)]

reg·nal (reg′nᵊl), *adj.* of or pertaining to a sovereign, sovereignty, or reign: *the second regnal year of Louis XIV.* [< ML *regnāl(is),* equiv. to L *rēgn(um)* rule, kingdom + *-ālis* -AL¹; see REIGN]

reg·nant (reg′nənt), *adj.* **1.** reigning; ruling (usually used following the noun it modifies): *a queen regnant.* **2.**

re·ger′mi·nate′, *v.*, **-nat·ed, -nat·ing.**
re′ger·mi·na′tion, *n.*
re·ger′mi·na′tive, *adj.;* **-ly,** *adv.*
re·gild′, *v.t.*, **-gild·ed** or **-gilt, -gild·ing.**
re·gird′, *v.t.*, **-girt** or **-gird·ed, -gird·ing.**
re·give′, *v.*, **-gave, -giv·en, -giv·ing.**
re·glaze′, *v.t.*, **-glazed, -glaz·ing.**
re′glo·ri·fi·ca′tion, *n.*
re·glo′ri·fy′, *v.t.*, **-fied, -fy·ing.**
re·glue′, *v.t.*, **-glued, -glu·ing.**

exercising authority, rule, or influence. **3.** prevalent; widespread. [< L *rēgnant-* (s. of *rēgnāns,* prp. of *regnāre*). See REIGN, -ANT] —**reg·nan·cy** (reg′nən sē), *n.*

reg·nat po·pu·lus (reg′nät pō′po͝o lo͞os′; *Eng.* reg′nat pop′yə ləs), *Latin.* let the people rule: motto of Arkansas.

Ré·gnault (rān′yəlt), *n.* a crater in the second quadrant of the face of the moon: about 35 miles in diameter.

reg·o·lith (reg′ə lith), *n.* See **mantle rock.** [< Gk *rhêgo(s)* rug, blanket + -LITH]

re·gorge (ri gôrj′), *v.* **-gorged, -gorg·ing.** —*v.t.* **1.** to disgorge; cast up again. —*v.i.* **2.** to rush back again; gush: *The waters regorged.* [< F, MF *regorg(er).* See RE-, GORGE]

regr., registrar.

re·grate[1] (ri grāt′), *v.t.,* **-grat·ed, -grat·ing. 1.** to buy up (grain, provisions, etc.) in order to sell again at a profit in or near the same market. **2.** to sell again (commodities so bought); retail. [ME *regrate(n)* < OF *regrat(er),* equiv. to *re-* RE- + *grater,* ? GRATE[2]] —**re·grat′er,** *n.*

re·grate[2] (ri grāt′), *v.t.,* **-grat·ed, -grat·ing.** to dress or tool (existing stonework) anew. [< F *regratt(er),* equiv. to *re-* RE- + *gratter* to scratch, scrape]

re·greet (rē grēt′), *v.t., v.i.* **1.** to greet in return or again. **2.** *Obs.* a return greeting. [RE- + GREET[1]]

re·gress (*v.* ri gres′; *n.* rē′gres), *v.i.* **1.** to move in a backward direction; go back. **2.** to revert to an earlier or less advanced state or form. —*n.* **3.** the act of going back; return. **4.** the right to go back. **5.** backward movement or course; retrogression. [ME *regresse* (n.) < L *regress(us)* gone back, turned back, returned (ptp. of *regredī*), equiv. to *re-* RE- + *gress(us),* ptp. of *gradī* (*gre-* go + *-ss* ptp. suffix)] —**re·gres′sor,** *n.*

re·gres·sion (ri gresh′ən), *n.* **1.** the act of going back to a previous place or state; return or reversion. **2.** retrogradation; retrogression. **3.** *Biol.* reversion to an earlier or less advanced state or form or to a common or general type. **4.** *Psychoanal.* the reversion to a chronologically earlier or less adapted pattern of behavior and feeling. **5.** a progressive subsidence of a disease: *an apparent regression of symptoms shortly after treatment was begun.* [< L *regressiōn-* (s. of *regressiō*). See REGRESS, -ION]

regres′sion coeffi′cient, *Statistics.* the coefficient of the independent variable in an equation designed to estimate the values of a corresponding dependent variable.

re·gres·sive (ri gres′iv), *adj.* **1.** regressing or tending to regress; retrogressive. **2.** *Biol.* of, pertaining to, or effecting regression. **3.** (of a tax rate) decreasing proportionately with an increase in the tax base. **4.** *Logic.* obtained from or characterized by backward reasoning. [REGRESS + -IVE] —**re·gres′sive·ly,** *adv.* —**re·gres′sive·ness,** *n.*

re·gret (ri gret′), *v.,* **-gret·ted, -gret·ting,** *n.* —*v.t.* **1.** to feel sorrow or remorse for (an act, fault, disappointment, etc.): *to regret the decline in good manners; He no sooner spoke than he regretted it.* **2.** to think of with a sense of loss: *to regret one's vanished youth.* —*n.* **3.** a sense of loss, disappointment, dissatisfaction, etc. **4.** a feeling of sorrow or remorse for a fault, act, loss, disappointment, etc. **5. regrets,** a polite, usually formal refusal of an invitation: *I sent her my regrets.* **6.** a note expressing regret at one's inability to accept an invitation: *I have had four acceptances and one regret.* [ME *regrett(en)* (v.) < MF, OF *regret(er),* equiv. to *re-* RE- + *-greter* < ? Gmc] —**re·gret′ta·ble, re·gret′a·ble,** *adj.* —**re·gret′ta·ble·ness, re·gret′a·ble·ness,** *n.* —**re·gret′ta·bly, re·gret′a·bly,** *adv.* —**re·gret′ter,** *n.* —**re·gret′ting·ly,** *adv.*

—**Syn. 1.** deplore, lament, bewail, bemoan, mourn, sorrow, grieve. REGRET, PENITENCE, REMORSE imply a sense of sorrow about events in the past, usually wrongs committed or errors made. REGRET is distress of mind, sorrow for what has been done: *to have no regrets.* PENITENCE implies a sense of sin or misdoing, a feeling of contrition and determination not to sin again: *a humble sense of penitence.* REMORSE implies pangs, qualms of conscience, a sense of guilt, regret, and repentance for sins committed, wrongs done, or duty not performed: *a deep sense of remorse.* —**Ant. 1.** rejoice. **4.** joy.

re·gret·ful (ri gret′fəl), *adj.* full of regret; sorrowful because of what is lost, gone, or done. [REGRET + -FUL] —**re·gret′ful·ly,** *adv.* —**re·gret′ful·ness,** *n.*

Regt., **1.** regent. **2.** regiment.

re·guard·ant (ri gär′dᵊnt), *adj. Heraldry.* regardant.

reg·u·la (reg′yə lə), *n., pl.* **-lae** (-lē′). (in a Doric entablature) a fillet, continuing a triglyph beneath the taenia, from which guttae are suspended. Also called **guttae band.** [< L *rēgula* ruler, pattern]

reg·u·la·ble (reg′yə lə bəl), *adj.* that can be regulated; controllable. [REGUL(ATE) + -ABLE]

reg·u·lar (reg′yə lər), *adj.* **1.** usual; normal; customary: *to put something in its regular place.* **2.** evenly or uniformly arranged; symmetrical: *regular teeth.* **3.** characterized by fixed principle, uniform procedure, etc.: *regular income.* **4.** recurring at fixed times; periodic: *regular bus departures; regular meals.* **5.** rhythmical: *regular breathing.* **6.** adhering to a rule or procedure; methodical: *regular habits; to be regular in one's diet.* **7.** observing fixed times or habits: *a regular customer.* **8.** orderly; well-ordered: *a regular life.* **9.** conforming to some accepted rule, discipline, etc. **10.** carried out in accordance with an accepted principle or rule; formally correct: *a regular session of the court.* **11.** properly qualified for or engaged in an occupation. **12.** *Informal.* **a.** real; genuine: *a regular fellow.* **b.** thoroughgoing; utter: *a regular rascal.* **c.** full-scale; fully deserving of its specified designation: *That was a regular downpour.* **13.** (of a flower) having the members of each of its floral circles or whorls normally alike in form and size. **14.** *Gram.* conforming to the most prevalent pattern of formation, inflection, construction, etc. **15.** *Math.* **a.** governed by one law throughout. **b.** (of a polygon) having all sides and angles equal. **c.** (of a polyhedron) having all faces congruent regular polygons, and all solid angles congruent. **d.** (of a topological space) having the property that, corresponding to each point and a closed set not containing the point, there are two disjoint open sets, one containing the point, the other containing the closed set. **e.** (of a function of a complex variable) analytic (def. 5). **16.** *Mil.* noting or belonging to the permanently organized, or standing, army of a state. **17.** *Internat. Law.* noting soldiers recognized as legitimate combatants in warfare. **18.** *Eccles.* subject to a religious rule, or belonging to a religious or monastic order (opposed to *secular*): *regular clergy.* **19.** *U.S. Politics.* of, pertaining to, or selected by the recognized agents of a political party: *the regular ticket.* —*n.* **20.** a habitual customer or client: *He's one of the regulars here.* **21.** *Eccles.* a member of a duly constituted religious order under a rule. **22.** *Mil.* a professional soldier. **23.** *U.S. Politics.* a party member who faithfully stands by his party. **24.** a size of garment designed for men of average build: *The regulars are hanging over here.* **25.** a garment, as a suit or overcoat, in this size. **26.** an athlete who plays in most of the games, usually from the start. [ME *reguler* < MF < LL, L *rēgulār(is).* See REGULA, -AR[1]] —**reg′u·lar′i·ty, reg′u·lar·ness,** *n.*

—**Syn. 2.** even, formal, orderly, uniform. **4.** habitual, established, fixed. **6.** systematic. **7.** habitual.

Reg′ular Ar′my, *U.S.* the permanent army maintained in peace as well as in war; the standing army: one of the major components of the Army of the United States.

reg′ular bev′el, the bevel of a bolt or lock on a door opening into the building, room, etc., to which the doorway leads (opposed to *reverse bevel*).

reg′ular check′ing account′, *U.S.* a checking account for which the monthly fee is based on the average balance maintained and the number of transactions recorded. Cf. **special checking account.**

reg·u·lar·ise (reg′yə lə rīz′), *v.t.,* **-ised, -is·ing.** *Chiefly Brit.* regularize. —**reg′u·lar·i·sa′tion,** *n.*

reg·u·lar·ize (reg′yə lə rīz′), *v.t.,* **-ized, -iz·ing.** to make regular. [REGULAR + -IZE] —**reg′u·lar·i·za′tion,** *n.* —**reg′u·lar·iz′er,** *n.*

reg′ular lay′, *Ropemaking.* a right-handed lay, as of a plain-laid rope.

reg·u·lar·ly (reg′yə lər lē), *adv.* **1.** at regular times or intervals. **2.** according to plan, custom, etc. [REGULAR + -LY]

reg′ular ode′, *Pros.* See **Pindaric ode.**

reg′ular ter′tiaries. See under **tertiary** (def. 5).

reg′ular year′. See under **Jewish calendar.**

reg·u·late (reg′yə lāt′), *v.t.,* **-lat·ed, -lat·ing. 1.** to control or direct by a rule, principle, method, etc.: *to regulate household expenses.* **2.** to adjust to some standard or requirement, as amount, degree, etc.: *to regulate the temperature.* **3.** to adjust so as to ensure accuracy of operation: *to regulate a watch.* **4.** to put in good order: *to regulate the digestion.* [< LL *rēgulāt(us)* (ptp. of *rēgulāre*). See REGULA, -ATE[1]] —**reg·u·la·tive** (reg′yə lā′tiv, -yə lə tiv), **reg·u·la·to·ry** (reg′yə lə tôr′ē, -tōr′ē), *adj.* —**reg′u·la′tive·ly,** *adv.*

—**Syn. 1.** rule, govern, manage, order, adjust, arrange, dispose, conduct. **2.** set. **4.** systematize.

reg·u·la·tion (reg′yə lā′shən), *n.* **1.** a rule or order prescribed by authority, as to regulate conduct; a governing direction or law. **2.** the act of regulating; state of being regulated. **3.** *Elect.* the percentage difference in some quantity related to the operation of an apparatus or machine, as the voltage output of a transformer or the speed of a motor, between the value of the quantity at no-load operation and its value at full-load operation. **4.** *Electronics.* the difference between maximum and minimum voltage drops between the anode and the cathode of a gas tube for a specified range of values of the anode current. —*adj.* **5.** prescribed by or conforming to regulation: *regulation army equipment.* **6.** usual; normal; customary: *They decorated the room with all the regulation decorations for a Halloween party.* [REGULATE + -ION]

—**Syn. 2.** direction, management, control, disposition, adjustment.

Regulation T, *U.S.* a federal law governing the amount of credit that may be advanced by brokers and dealers to customers for the purchase of securities.

Regulation U, *U.S.* a federal law governing the amount of credit that may be advanced by a bank for the purchase of securities.

reg·u·la·tor (reg′yə lā′tər), *n.* **1.** one who or that which regulates. **2.** *Horol.* **a.** an adjustable device in a clock or a watch for making it go faster or slower. **b.** a master clock, usually of great accuracy, against which other clocks are checked. **3.** *Mach.* **a.** a governor mechanism for regulating the flow of fuel, steam, etc., to an engine in order to maintain constant speed under varying load or resistance. **b.** a valve for regulating the pressure of flowing gas or liquid to maintain a predetermined pressure. **c.** any of various mechanisms for maintaining a temperature, a level of liquid in a tank, etc. **4.** *Elect.* a device for maintaining a designated characteristic, as voltage or current, at a predetermined value, or for varying it according to a predetermined plan. **5.** a device on scuba equipment for regulating the amount of compressed air fed through a breathing tube in proportion to its depth under water. **6.** a device for maintaining a constant gas pressure. **7.** (*cap.*) *Amer. Hist.* **a.** a member of any of several bands or committees in North Carolina (1767–71), formed to resist certain abuses, as extortion by officials. **b.** (in newly settled areas) a member of any band or committee organized to preserve order before the establishment of regular legal authority. [REGULATE + -OR[2]]

reg′ulator pin′, either of two pins on the regulators of certain timepieces, one on each side of the hairspring, that can be moved toward or away from the stud to increase or decrease the virtual length of the spring and thus adjust the rate of the timepiece. Also called **curb pin.**

reg·u·line (reg′yə lin, -līn′), *adj. Metall.* of, pertaining to, or of the nature of, a regulus. [REGUL(US) + -INE[1]]

reg·u·lus (reg′yə ləs), *n., pl.* **-lus·es, -li** (-lī′). **1.** (*cap.*) *Astron.* a first magnitude star in the constellation Leo. **2.** *Metall.* **a.** the metallic mass which forms beneath the slag at the bottom of the crucible or furnace in smelting ores. **b.** an impure intermediate product obtained in smelting ores. [< L: lit., little king (dim. of *rēx*); in early chemistry, antimony, so called because it readily combines with gold (the king of metals)]

Reg·u·lus (reg′yə ləs), *n.* **Marcus A·til·i·us** (ə til′ē əs), died 250? B.C., Roman general.

re·gur·gi·tate (ri gûr′ji tāt′), *v.,* **-tat·ed, -tat·ing.** —*v.i.* **1.** to surge or rush back, as liquids, gases, undigested food, etc. —*v.t.* **2.** to cause to surge or rush back. [< ML *regurgitāt(us)* (ptp. of *regurgitāre*), equiv. to *re-* RE- + *gurgit-* engulf, flood (deriv. of *gurgit-,* s. of *gurges* whirlpool) + *-ātus* -ATE[1]] —**re·gur·gi·tant** (ri gûr′ji tənt), *n.*

re·gur·gi·ta·tion (ri gûr′ji tā′shən), *n.* **1.** the act of regurgitating. **2.** *Med.* voluntary or involuntary return of partly digested food from the stomach to the mouth. **3.** *Physiol.* the reflux of blood through defective heart valves. [< ML *regurgitātiōn-* (s. of *regurgitātiō*). See REGURGITATE, -ION]

re·ha·bil·i·tate (rē′hə bil′i tāt′), *v.t.,* **-tat·ed, -tat·ing. 1.** to restore to a condition of good health, ability to work, or the like. **2.** to restore to good operation or management, as a bankrupt business. **3.** to reestablish the good reputation of (a person, one's character or name, etc.). **4.** to restore formally to former capacity, standing, rank, rights, or privileges. [< ML *rehabilitāt(us)* restored (ptp. of *rehabilitāre*). See RE-, HABILITATE] —**re′ha·bil′i·ta′tion,** *n.* —**re′ha·bil′i·ta′tive,** *adj.*

re·hash (*v.* rē hash′; *n.* rē′hash′), *v.t.* **1.** to work up (old material) in a new form. —*n.* **2.** the act of rehashing. **3.** something rehashed. [RE- + HASH]

re·hear·ing (rē hēr′ing), *n. Law.* a second presentation of the evidence and arguments of a case before the court of original presentation. [RE- + HEARING]

re·hears·al (ri hûr′səl), *n.* **1.** a session of exercise, drill, or practice, usually private, in preparation for a public performance, ceremony, etc.: *a play rehearsal; a wedding rehearsal.* **2.** the act of practicing, usually in private, for a public performance, formal occasion or ceremony, etc.: *We had four days of rehearsal.* **3.** a repeating or relating: *a rehearsal of grievances.* [ME *rehersaille.* See REHEARSE, -AL[2]]

re·hearse (ri hûrs′), *v.,* **-hearsed, -hears·ing.** —*v.t.* **1.** to practice (a musical composition, a part in a play, a speech, etc.) in private prior to a public presentation: *We are rehearsing the last act of* Macbeth. *We must rehearse the symphony once more before tomorrow's performance.* **2.** to drill or train (an actor, musician, etc.) by rehearsal, as for some performance or part. **3.** to relate the facts or particulars of; recount. —*v.i.* **4.** to rehearse a play, part, etc.; participate in a rehearsal. [ME *rehers(en), reherc(en)* < MF *reherc(ier)* (to) repeat, equiv. to *re-* RE- + *hercier* to strike, harrow (deriv. of *herce, herse* a harrow); see HEARSE] —**re·hears′a·ble,** *adj.* —**re·hears′er,** *n.*

—**Syn. 3.** delineate, describe, portray; narrate, recapitulate. See **relate.**

re·heat·ing (rē hē′ting), *n.* **1.** heating again. **2.** *Aeron.* a process in certain turbojet engines in which gases are expanded by turbines after combustion, burned again in a second chamber, expanded again by additional turbines, and released through the exhaust nozzle. [RE- + HEATING]

Rehn·quist (ren′kwist), *n.* **William H(ubbs),** born 1924, U.S. jurist: associate justice of the U.S. Supreme Court 1972–86: Chief Justice since 1986.

Re·ho·bo·am (rē′ə bō′əm), *n.* the successor of Solomon and the first king of Judah, reigned 922?–915? B.C. I Kings 11:43. Also, *Douay Bible,* **Roboam.**

Re·ho′both Beach′ (rə hō′bəth, -bōth), a town in SE Delaware: beach resort. 1507 (1960).

Re·ho·vot (rə hō′vōt), *n.* a town in N Israel, S of Tel Aviv. 31,300 (1963). Also, **Re·ho′voth, Re·ho·both** (rə hō′bōt).

Reich (rīk; *Ger.* RĪKH), *n.* **1.** (with reference to Germany) empire; realm; nation. **2.** the German state, esp. during the Nazi period. Cf. **First Reich, Second Reich, Third Reich.** [< G: kingdom]

Reich (RĪKH), *n.* **Wil·helm** (vil′helm), 1897–1957, Austrian psychoanalyst in U.S.

Rei·chen·berg (RĪ′KHən berKH′), *n.* German name of **Liberec.**

Reichs·bank (rīks′bangk′; *Ger.* RĪKHS′bängk′), *n.* the German national bank. [< G; see REICH, 's[1], BANK[2]]

Reichs·füh·rer (RĪKHS′fY′RəR), *n. German.* the title of the chief of the Schutzstaffel. [lit., Reich leader]

reichs·mark (rīks′märk′; *Ger.* RĪKHS′märk′), *n., pl.* **-marks, -mark.** the German mark having a value

re·gov′ern, *v.t.*
re·gov′ern·ment, *n.*
re·grab′, *v.t.,* **-grabbed, -grab·bing.**
re·gra′date, *v.,* **-dat·ed, -dat·ing.**
re′gra·da′tion, *n.*
re·grade′, *v.t.,* **-grad·ed, -grad·ing.**
re·graft′, *v.*
re·grant′, *v.t., n.*
re·graph′, *v.t.*
re·grasp′, *v.t.*
re·grease′, *v.t.,* **-greased, -greas·ing.**
re·grind′, *v.,* **-ground, -grind·ing.**
re·grip′, *v.,* **-gripped** or **-gript, -grip·ping.**
re·group′, *v.*
re·grow′, *v.,* **-grew, -grown, -grow·ing.**
re·growth′, *n.*
re′guar·an·tee′, *n., v.t.,* **-teed, -tee·ing.**
re·guar′an·ty′, *n., pl.* **-ties.**
re·guide′, *v.t.,* **-guid·ed, -guid·ing.**
re·ham′mer, *v.t.*
re·han′dle, *v.t.,* **-dled, -dling.**
re·hang′, *v.t.,* **-hung, -hanged, -hang·ing.**
re·hard′en, *v.*
re·har′mo·nize′, *v.t.,* **-nized, -niz·ing.**
re·har′ness, *v.t.*
re·har′vest, *v.*
re·haul′, *v.*
re·hear′, *v.,* **-heard, -hear·ing.**
re·heat′, *v.t.*
re·heat′er, *n.*
re·heel′, *v.t.*
re·hem′, *v.t.,* **-hemmed, -hem·ming.**
re·hide′, *v.,* **-hid, -hid·den** or **-hid, -hid·ing.**
re·hinge′, *v.t.,* **-hinged, -hing·ing.**
re·hire′, *v.t.,* **-hired, -hir·ing,** *n.*
re·hone′, *v.t.,* **-honed, -hon·ing.**
re·hon′or, *v.t.*
re′hos·pi·tal·i·za′tion, *n.*
re·hos′pi·tal·ize′, *v.t.,* **-ized, -iz·ing.**
re′hu·man·i·za′tion, *n.*
re·hu′man·ize′, *v.,* **-ized, -iz·ing.**
re′hu·mil′i·ate′, *v.t.,* **-at·ed, -at·ing.**
re′hu·mil′i·a′tion, *n.*
re·hyp′no·tize′, *v.t.,* **-tized, -tiz·ing.**
re′hy·poth′e·cate′, *v.t.,* **-cat·ed, -cat·ing.**
re·ice′, *v.,* **-iced, -ic·ing.**

equivalent to .238 of a U.S. dollar: the monetary unit of Germany from November, 1924, until 1948. Cf. **Deutsche mark, mark**², (def. 1). **ostmark.** [< G: Reich mark]

reichs·pfen·nig (rīкнs′pfen′iкн), *n.* a former bronze coin of Germany, the 100th part of a reichsmark. [< G: Reich penny]

Reichs·rat (rīкнs′rät′), *n.* **1.** *Ger. Hist.* the upper house of the parliament during the period of the Second Reich and the Weimar Republic. **2.** *Hist.* the legislature or parliament in the Austrian division of Austria-Hungary. Also, **Reichs′rath′.** [< G: Reich council]

Reichs·tag (rīks′täg′; *Ger.* rīкнs′täкн′), *n.* *Ger. Hist.* the lower house of the parliament during the period of the Second Reich and the Weimar Republic. [< G: Reich diet]

Reich·stein (rīk′stīn′; *Ger.* rīкн′shtīn′), *n.* **Ta·de·us** (tä dā′o͞os), born 1897, Swiss chemist, born in Poland: Nobel prize for medicine 1950.

reichs·tha·ler (rīks′tä′lər; *Ger.* rīкнs′tä′lər), *n.*, *pl.* **-ler.** a silver thaler of Germany, originally issued in 1566; rix-dollar. [< G: Reich thaler]

Reid (rēd), *n.* **1. Sir George Huston,** 1845–1918, Australian statesman, born in Scotland: prime minister 1904–05. **2. Thomas,** 1710–96, Scottish philosopher. **3. White·law** (hwīt′lô′, wīt′-), 1837–1912, U.S. diplomat and journalist. **4.** a boy's given name, form of **Read.**

reif (rēf), *n.* *Scot. Obs.* **1.** plunder; booty; loot. **2.** robbery, piracy. **3.** act of seizing booty. [ME (north) *ref,* OE *rēaf;* akin to REAVE¹, BEREAVE]

Reif (rāf, rīf), *n.* a boy's given name.

re·i·fy (rē′ə fī′), *v.t.*, **-fied, -fy·ing.** to convert into or regard as a concrete thing: *to reify an abstract concept.* [< L *rē(s)* thing + -IFY] **—re′i·fi·ca′tion,** *n.*

reign (rān), *n.* **1.** the period during which a sovereign occupies the throne. **2.** royal rule or authority; sovereignty. **3.** dominating power or influence: *the reign of law.* **—***v.i.* **4.** to possess or exercise sovereign power or authority. **5.** to hold the position and name of sovereign without exercising the ruling power. **6.** to have control, rule, or influence of any kind. **7.** to predominate; be prevalent. [ME *reine, regne* < OF *reigne* < L *rēgn(um)* realm, reign, deriv. of *rēg-* (s. of *rēx*) king]
—Syn. 2. dominion, suzerainty. **4.** rule, govern, prevail.
—Ant. 4. obey.

Reign′ of Ter′ror, a period of the French Revolution, from about March, 1793, to July, 1794, during which many persons were ruthlessly executed by the ruling faction.

Reik (rīk; *Ger.* rīk), *n.* **The·o·dor** (thē′ə dôr′, -dōr′; *Ger.* te′ō dôr′), born 1888, U.S. psychologist and author, born in Austria.

Rei·ma·rus (rī′mər əs), *n.* a crater in the fourth quadrant of the face of the moon: about 29 miles in diameter.

re·im·burse (rē′im bûrs′), *v.t.*, **-bursed, -burs·ing.** **1.** to make repayment to for expense or loss incurred: *The insurance company reimbursed him for his losses in the fire.* **2.** to pay back; refund; repay. [RE- + obs. *imburse* < ML *imburs(āre),* equiv. to L *in-* IN-² + ML *bursa* purse, bag] **—re′im·burs′a·ble,** *adj.* **—re′im·burse′ment,** *n.* **—re′im·burs′er,** *n.*
—Syn. 1. recompense, remunerate, indemnify, redress, recoup.

re·im·port (rē′im pōrt′, -pôrt′), *v.t.* to import back into the country of exportation. [RE- + IMPORT] **—re′im·por·ta′tion,** *n.*

re·im·pres·sion (rē′im presh′ən), *n.* **1.** a second or repeated impression. **2.** a reprinting or a reprint. [RE- + IMPRESSION]

Reims (rēmz; *Fr.* raɴs), *n.* a city in NE France: cathedral; unconditional surrender of Germany May 7, 1945. 121,145 (1954). Also, **Rheims.**

rein (rān), *n.* **1.** a leather strap, fastened to each end of the bit of a bridle, by which the rider or driver controls a horse or other animal by pulling so as to exert pressure on the bit. See illus. under **harness.** **2.** any of certain other straps or thongs forming part of a harness, as a checkrein. **3.** any means of curbing, controlling, or directing; check; restraint. **4. reins,** the controlling or directing power: *the reins of government.* **5. draw rein,** to curtail one's speed or progress; halt: *The rider saw the snake and drew rein sharply.* **6. give rein to,** to give full scope or play to; indulge freely: *to give rein to one's imagination.* **—***v.t.* **7.** to check or guide (a horse or other animal) by exerting pressure on a bridle bit by means of the reins. **8.** to curb; restrain; control. **—***v.i.* **9.** to obey the reins: *a horse that reins well.* **10.** to rein a horse or other animal. [ME *rene* < OF *re(s)ne* < VL **retina;* cf. L *retinēre* to hold back, RETAIN] **—rein′less,** *adj.*

re·in·car·nate (*v.* rē′in kär′nāt; *adj.* rē′in kär′nit), *v.*, **-nat·ed, -nat·ing,** *adj.* **—***v.t.* **1.** to given another body to; incarnate again. **—***adj.* **2.** incarnate anew. [RE- + INCARNATE]

re·in·car·na·tion (rē′in kär nā′shən), *n.* **1.** the belief that the soul, upon death of the body, comes back to earth in another body or form. **2.** rebirth of the soul in a new body. **3.** a new incarnation or embodiment, as of a person. [RE- + INCARNATION] **—re′in·car·na′tion·ist,** *n.*

European reindeer,
Rangifer tarandus
(4½ ft. high at shoulder;
length 5½ ft.)

rein·deer (rān′dēr′), *n.*, *pl.* **-deer,** *(occasionally)* **-deers.** any of several large deer of the genus *Rangifer,* of northern and arctic regions of Europe, Asia, and North America, both male and female of which have antlers. [ME *rayndere(e)* < Scand; cf. OIcel *hreindȳri,* equiv. to *hreinn* reindeer + *dȳr* animal, C. DEER]

Rein′deer Lake′, a lake in central Canada, in NE Saskatchewan and NW Manitoba. 2444 sq. mi.

rein′deer moss′, any of several lichens of the genus *Cladonia,* esp. the gray, many-branched *C. rangiferina,* of arctic and subarctic regions, eaten by reindeer and caribou.

Rei·neck·e (rī′nə kə), *n.* **Carl Hein·rich Car·sten** (kärl hīn′riкн kär′stən), 1824–1910, German pianist, conductor, composer, and teacher.

Rei·ner (rī′nər), *n.* **1. Fritz,** 1888–1963, Hungarian conductor, in the U.S. **2.** a crater in the second quadrant of the face of the moon: about 20 miles in diameter.

re·in·force (rē′in fōrs′, -fôrs′), *v.t.*, **-forced, -forc·ing.** **1.** to strengthen with some added piece, support, or material: *to reinforce a wall.* **2.** to strengthen (a military force) with additional men, ships, or aircraft: *to reinforce a garrison.* **3.** to strengthen; make more forcible or effective: *to reinforce efforts.* **4.** to augment; increase: *to reinforce a supply.* **5.** *Psychol.* to strengthen the probability of (a response) to a given stimulus by giving or withholding a reward. **—***n.* **6.** *Obs.* something that reinforces; specifically, the metal band on the rear part of the bore of a gun, where the explosion occurs. Also, **reenforce, re-enforce, reënforce.** [RE- + *inforce,* alter. of ENFORCE] **—re′in·forc′er,** *n.*

re′inforced con′crete, concrete containing steel bars, strands, mesh, etc., to absorb tensile and shearing stresses.

re·in·force·ment (rē′in fōrs′mənt, -fôrs′-), *n.* **1.** the act of reinforcing. **2.** the state of being reinforced. **3.** something that reinforces or strengthens. **4.** Often, **reinforcements.** an additional supply of men, ships, aircraft, etc., for a military force. **5.** a system of steel bars, strands, wires, or mesh for absorbing the tensile and shearing stresses in concrete work. [REINFORCE + -MENT]

Rein·hardt (rīn′härt), *n.* **Max** (mäks), (*Max Goldman*), 1873–1943, German theatrical director, producer, and actor; born in Austria.

Rein·hold (rīn′hōld), *n.* **1.** a walled plain in the second quadrant of the face of the moon: about 30 miles in diameter. **2.** a boy's given name.

reins (rānz), *n.pl.* *Archaic.* **1.** the kidneys. **2.** the region of the kidneys, or the lower part of the back. **3.** the seat of the feelings or affections, formery identified with the kidneys (esp. in Biblical use). [ME < OF; r. ME *reenes,* OE *rēnys* < L *rēnēs* kidneys, loins (pl.)]

re·in·state (rē′in stāt′), *v.t.*, **-stat·ed, -stat·ing.** to put back or establish again, as in a former position or state: *to reinstate the ousted chairman.* [RE- + INSTATE] **—re′in·state′ment, re′in·sta′tion,** *n.* **—re′in·sta′tor,** *n.*

re·in·sure (rē′in sho͝or′), *v.t.*, **-sured, -sur·ing.** **1.** to insure again. **2.** *Insurance.* to insure under a contract by which a first insurer relieves himself from a part or all of the risk and devolves it upon another insurer. [RE- + INSURE] **—re′in·sur′ance,** *n.* **—re′in·sur′er,** *n.*

reis (rās; *Port.* rās), *n.pl.*, *sing.* **re·al** (rā äl′; *Port.* re äl′). a former money of account of Portugal and Brazil. Cf. **milreis.** [< Pg, pl. of *rei* king]

reist (rēst), *v.i.* *Scot. and North Eng.* reest².

re·it·er·ant (rē it′ər ənt), *adj.* reiterating or repeating, esp. to an intensified degree: *reiterant chatter.* [< L *reiterant-* (s. of *reiterāns*), prp. of *reiterāre.* See REITERATE, -ANT]

re·it·er·ate (rē it′ə rāt′), *v.t.*, **-at·ed, -at·ing.** to say or do again or repeatedly; repeat, often endlessly and tediously. [< L *reiterāt(us)* repeated, ptp. of *reiterāre,* equiv. to *re-* RE- + *iterāre* to repeat, deriv. of *iterum* again; see -ATE¹] **—re·it′er·a·ble,** *adj.* **—re·it′er·a′tion,** *n.* **—re·it·er·a·tive** (rē it′ə rā′tiv, -ər ə tiv), *adj.*
—Syn. See **repeat.**

reive (rēv), *v.t.*, *v.i.*, **reived, reiv·ing.** *Chiefly Scot.* to rob; plunder. [var. of REAVE¹] **—reiv′er,** *n.*

Ré·jane (rā zhaɴ′), *n.* (*Gabrielle-Charlotte Réju*) 1856–1920, French actress.

re·ject (*v.* ri jekt′; *n.* rē′jekt), *v.t.* **1.** to refuse to have, take, recognize, etc.: *to reject the offer of a better job.* **2.** to refuse to grant (a request, demand, etc.): *The company rejected his request for a transfer.* **3.** to refuse to accept (a person); rebuff: *The other children in his class rejected him.* **4.** to throw away or discard as useless or unsatisfactory: *His latest literary effort has been rejected by critics and public alike.* **5.** to cast out or eject; vomit. **6.** to cast out or off. **—***n.* **7.** something rejected, as an imperfect article. [ME *reject(en)* (v.) < L *rēject(us)* thrown back (ptp. of *rējicere*), equiv. to *re-* RE- + *jec-* throw (ptp. s. of *jacere*) + *-t-* ptp. suffix] **—re·ject′a·ble,** *adj.* **—re·ject′er,** *n.* **—re·jec′tive,** *adj.*
—Syn. 1. See **refuse**¹. **1, 2.** repudiate, deny. **3.** repel, renounce. **4.** eliminate, jettison. **7.** second.
—Ant. 1. accept.

re·jec·ta·men·ta (ri jek′tə men′tə), *n.pl.* things or matter rejected as useless or worthless. [< NL: things thrown back (pl. of *rejectamentum*), equiv. to L *rējectā(re)* (intensive of *rejicere* to REJECT) + *-mentum* -MENT]

re·ject·ee (ri jek tē′, -jek′tē, rē′jek tē′), *n.* one who is or has been rejected, esp. for military service. [REJECT + -EE]

re·jec·tion (ri jek′shən), *n.* **1.** the act of rejecting. **2.** the state of being rejected. **3.** that which is rejected. [< L *rējectiōn-* (s. of *rējectiō*) a throwing back, equiv. to *rēject(us)* (see REJECT) + *-iōn-* -ION]

rejec′tion slip′, a slip of paper, printed with a notification of rejection, attached by a publisher to a manuscript before returning it to its author or his agent.

re·jig·ger (rē jig′ər), *v.t.* *Informal.* to change or rearrange in a new or different way, esp. by the use of techniques not always considered ethical. [RE- + JIGGER¹]

re·joice (ri jois′), *v.*, **-joiced, -joic·ing.** **—***v.i.* **1.** to be glad; take delight (often fol. by *in*): *to rejoice in another's happiness.* **—***v.t.* **2.** to make joyful; gladden: *a song to rejoice the heart.* [ME *rejoic(en)* < OF *rejouiss-,* long s. of *rejouir,* equiv. to *re-* RE- + *jouir;* see JOY] **—re·joice′ful,** *adj.* **—re·joic′er,** *n.*

re·joic·ing (ri joi′siŋ), *n.* **1.** the act of one who rejoices. **2.** the feeling or the expression of joy. **3.** Often, **rejoicings.** an occasion for expressing joy. [ME; see REJOICE, -ING¹] **—re·joic′ing·ly,** *adv.*

re·join¹ (rē join′), *v.t.* **1.** to come again into the company of: *to rejoin a party after a brief absence.* **2.** to join together again; reunite. **—***v.i.* **3.** to become joined together again. [RE- + JOIN]

re·join² (ri join′), *v.t.* **1.** to say in answer; reply, esp. to counterreply. **—***v.i.* **2.** to answer; reply, esp. to counterreply. **3.** *Law.* to answer a plaintiff's replication. [ME *rejoin(en)* < AF *rejoyn(er),* var. of MF *rejoindre,* equiv. to *re-* RE- + *joindre* to JOIN]
—Syn. 2. respond, retort.

re·join·der (ri join′dər), *n.* **1.** an answer to a reply; response. **2.** *Law.* a defendant's answer to a plaintiff's replication. [ME *rejoiner* < MF *rejoindre* (n. use of inf.); see REJOIN²]
—Syn. 1. reply, riposte. See **answer.**

re′i·den′ti·fi·ca′tion, *n.*
re′i·den′ti·fy′, *v.t.*, **-fied, -fy·ing.**
re′ig·nite′, *v.t.*, **-nit·ed, -nit·ing.**
re′ig·ni′tion, *n.*
re′il·lu′mi·nate′, *v.*, **-nat·ed, -nat·ing.**
re′il·lu′mi·na′tion, *n.*
re·il′lus·trate′, *v.t.*, **-trat·ed, -trat·ing.**
re′il·lus·tra′tion, *n.*
re·im′age, *v.t.*, **-aged, -ag·ing.**
re′im·plant′, *v.t.*
re′im·plan·ta′tion, *n.*
re·im′ple·ment′, *v.t.*
re′im·ply′, *v.t.*, **-plied, -ply·ing.**
re′im·pose′, *v.*, **-posed, -pos·ing.**
re′im·po·si′tion, *n.*
re′im·preg′nate, *v.t.*, **-nat·ed, -nat·ing.**
re′im·press′, *v.t.*
re′im·print′, *v.t.*
re′im·pris′on, *v.t.*
re′im·pris′on·ment, *n.*
re′in·au′gu·rate′, *v.t.*, **-rat·ed, -rat·ing.**
re′in·au′gu·ra′tion, *n.*
re′in·cite′, *v.t.*, **-cit·ed, -cit·ing.**
re′in·cline′, *v.*, **-clined, -clin·ing.**
re′in·clude′, *v.t.*, **-clud·ed, -clud·ing.**
re′in·clu′sion, *n.*
re′in·cor′po·rate′, *v.*, **-rat·ed, -rat·ing.**
re′in·cor′po·rate, *adj.*
re′in·crease′, *v.*, **-creased, -creas·ing,** *n.*
re′in·cur′, *v.t.*, **-curred, -cur·ring.**
re·in′dex, *v.t.*
re·in′di·cate′, *v.t.*, **-cat·ed, -cat·ing.**
re′in·di·ca′tion, *n.*
re′in·dict′, *v.t.*
re′in·dict′ment, *n.*
re′in·doc′tri·nate′, *v.t.*, **-nat·ed, -nat·ing.**
re′in·doc′tri·na′tion, *n.*
re′in·dorse′, *v.t.*, **-dorsed, -dors·ing.**
re′in·dorse′ment, *n.*
re′in·duce′, *v.t.*, **-duced, -duc·ing.**
re′in·duce′ment, *n.*
re′in·duct′, *v.t.*
re′in·duc′tion, *n.*
re′in·dulge′, *v.*, **-dulged, -dulg·ing.**
re′in·dul′gence, *n.*
re′in·dus′tri·al·i·za′tion, *n.*
re′in·dus′tri·al·ize′, *v.t.*, **-ized, -iz·ing.**
re′in·fect, *v.t.*
re′in·fec′tion, *n.*
re·in·fer′, *v.t.*, **-ferred, -fer·ring.**
re′in·fest′, *v.t.*
re′in·fes·ta′tion, *n.*
re′in·fil′trate, *v.*, **-trat·ed, -trat·ing.**
re′in·fil·tra′tion, *n.*
re′in·flame′, *v.*, **-flamed, -flam·ing.**
re·in·flat′a·ble, *adj.*
re′in·flate′, *v.*, **-flat·ed, -flat·ing.**
re′in·fla′tion, *n.*
re′in′flu·ence, *v.t.*, **-enced, -enc·ing.**
re′in·form′, *v.t.*
re′in·fuse′, *v.t.*, **-fused, -fus·ing.**
re′in·fu′sion, *n.*
re′in·hab′it, *v.t.*
re′in·her′it, *v.*
re′in·ject′, *v.t.*
re·in′jure, *v.t.*, **-jured, -jur·ing.**
re·in′ju·ry, *n.*, *pl.* **-ju·ries.**
re·ink′, *v.t.*
re′in·oc′u·late′, *v.t.*, **-lat·ed, -lat·ing.**
re′in·oc′u·la′tion, *n.*
re′in·quire′, *v.*, **-quired, -quir·ing.**
re′in·quir′y, *n.*, *pl.* **-quir·ies.**
re′in·scribe′, *v.t.*, **-scribed, -scrib·ing.**
re′in·sert′, *v.t.*
re′in·ser′tion, *n.*
re′in·sist′, *v.i.*
re′in·spect′, *v.t.*
re′in·spec′tion, *n.*
re′in·spi·ra′tion, *n.*
re′in·spire′, *v.*, **-spired, -spir·ing.**
re′in·stall′, *v.t.*
re′in·stal·la′tion, *n.*
re′in·stall′ment, *n.*
re′in·stal′ment, *n.*
re·in′sti·tute′, *v.t.*, **-tut·ed, -tut·ing.**
re′in·sti·tu′tion, *n.*
re′in·struct′, *v.t.*
re′in·struc′tion, *n.*
re·in′su·late′, *v.t.*, **-lat·ed, -lat·ing.**
re·in′te·grate′, *v.*, **-grat·ed, -grat·ing.**
re′in·te·gra′tion, *n.*
re′in·ter′, *v.t.*, **-terred, -ter·ring.**
re·in′ter·est, *n.*, *v.t.*
re′in·ter′ment, *n.*
re′in·ter′pret, *v.*
re′in·ter′pre·ta′tion, *n.*
re′in·ter′ro·gate′, *v.*, **-gat·ed, -gat·ing.**
re′in·ter·ro·ga′tion, *n.*
re′in·ter·rupt′, *v.*
re′in·ter·rup′tion, *n.*
re′in·ter·vene′, *v.i.*, **-vened, -ven·ing.**
re′in·ter·ven′tion, *n.*
re·in′ter·view′, *n.*, *v.t.*
re′in·trench′, *v.t.*
re′in·trench′ment, *n.*
re′in·tro·duce′, *v.t.*, **-duced, -duc·ing.**
re′in·tro·duc′tion, *n.*
re′in·vade′, *v.t.*, **-vad·ed, -vad·ing.**
re′in·va′sion, *n.*
re′in·vent′, *v.t.*
re′in·ven′tion, *n.*
re′in·vest′, *v.t.*
re′in·ves′ti·gate′, *v.*, **-gat·ed, -gat·ing.**
re′in·ves·ti·ga′tion, *n.*
re′in·vest′ment, *n.*
re′in·vig′or·ate′, *v.t.*, **-at·ed, -at·ing.**
re′in·vig′or·a′tion, *n.*
re′in·vi·ta′tion, *n.*
re′in·vite′, *v.*, **-vit·ed, -vit·ing.**
re′in·voke′, *v.t.*, **-voked, -vok·ing.**
re′in·volve′, *v.t.*, **-volved, -volv·ing.**
re′in·volve′ment, *n.*
re·ir′ri·gate′, *v.t.*, **-gat·ed, -gat·ing.**
re′ir·ri·ga′tion *n.*
re·i′so·late′, *v.t.*, **-lat·ed, -lat·ing.**
re′i·so·la′tion, *n.*
re·is′su·a·ble, *adj.*; **-bly,** *adj.*
re·is′sue, *v.*, **-sued, -su·ing.**
re·i′tem·ize′, *v.t.*, **-ized, -iz·ing.**
re·jail′, *v.t.*
re·jeop′ard·ize′, *v.t.*, **-ized, -iz·ing.**

re·ju·ve·nate (ri jo͞o′və nāt′), *v.t.*, **-nat·ed, -nat·ing.** 1. to make young again; restore to youthful vigor, appearance, etc.: *That vacation has certainly rejuvenated him.* 2. *Phys. Geog.* **a.** to renew the activity, erosive power, etc., of (a stream) by the uplifting of the region it drains, or by removal of a barrier in the bed of the stream. **b.** to impress again the characters of youthful topography on (a region) by the action of rejuvenated streams. [RE- + L *juven(is)* young + -ATE[1]] —**re·ju′ve·na′tion,** *n.* —**re·ju′ve·na′tive,** *adj.* —**re·ju′ve·na′tor,** *n.*
—**Syn. 1.** refresh, renew, freshen.

re·ju·ve·nes·cent (ri jo͞o′və nes′ənt), *adj.* 1. becoming young again. 2. making young again; rejuvenating. [< ML *rejuvenesc(ere)* (to) become young again (L *re-* RE- + *juven(is)* young + *-esc-* inceptive suffix) + -ENT] —**re·ju′ve·nes′cence,** *n.*

re·ju·ve·nise (ri jo͞o′və nīz′), *v.t.*, **-nised, -nis·ing.** *Chiefly Brit.* rejuvenize.

re·ju·ve·nize (ri jo͞o′və nīz′), *v.t.*, **-nized, -niz·ing.** to rejuvenate. [RE- + L *juven(is)* young + -IZE]

-rel, a noun suffix having a diminutive or pejorative force: *wastrel.* Also, **-erel.** [ME < OF *-erel, -erelle*]

rel., 1. relating. 2. relative. 3. relatively. 4. religion. 5. religious.

re·la·dle (rē lād′əl), *v.t.*, **-dled, -dling.** *Metall.* to mix (molten alloy steel) by pouring it from ladle to ladle. [RE- + LADLE]

re·laid (rē lād′), *v.* pt. and pp. of **re-lay.**

re·lapse (*v.* ri laps′; *n.* ri laps′, rē′laps), *v.*, **-lapsed, -laps·ing,** *n.* —*v.i.* 1. to fall or slip back into a former state, practice, etc.: *to relapse into silence.* 2. to fall back into illness after convalescence or apparent recovery. 3. to fall back into vice, wrongdoing, or error; backslide: *to relapse into heresy.* —*n.* 4. the act of relapsing. 5. a return of a disease or illness after partial recovery from it. [< L *relaps(us)* slid back, sunk back (ptp. of *relābī*), equiv. to *re-* RE- + *lap-* slide, fall (var. of *lāb-*) + *-sus* ptp. suffix] —**re·laps′a·ble,** *adj.* —**re·laps′er,** *n.*

relaps′ing fe′ver, *Pathol.* one of a group of fevers characterized by relapses, occurring in many tropical countries, and caused by several species of spirochetes transmitted by several species of lice and ticks. Also called **recurrent fever.**

re·late (ri lāt′), *v.*, **-lat·ed, -lat·ing.** —*v.t.* 1. to tell; give an account of (an event, circumstance, etc.). 2. to bring into or establish association, connection, or relation: *to relate events to probable causes.* —*v.i.* 3. to have reference (often fol. by *to*). 4. to have some relation (often fol. by *to*). 5. to establish a social or sympathetic relationship with a person or thing: *an individual unable to relate to his environment.* [< L *relāt(us)* carried back (ptp. of *referre*); see REFER] —**re·lat′a·bil′i·ty,** *n.* —**re·lat′a·ble,** *adj.* —**re·lat′er,** *n.*
—**Syn. 1.** narrate, delineate, detail, repeat. RELATE, RECITE, RECOUNT, REHEARSE mean to tell, report, or describe in some detail an occurrence or circumstance. To RELATE is to give an account of happenings, events, circumstances, etc.: *to relate one's adventures.* To RECITE may mean to give details consecutively, but more often applies to the repetition from memory of something learned with verbal exactness: *to recite a poem.* To RECOUNT is usually to set forth consecutively the details of an occurrence, argument, experience, etc., to give an account in detail: *to recount an unpleasant experience.* REHEARSE implies some formality and exactness in telling, sometimes with repeated performance as for practice before final delivery: *to rehearse one's side of a story.* 2. ally. —**Ant. 2.** dissociate.

re·lat·ed (ri lā′tid), *adj.* 1. associated; connected. 2. allied by nature, origin, kinship, marriage, etc. 3. narrated. 4. *Music.* (of tones) belonging to a melodic or harmonic series, so as to be susceptible of close connection. [RELATE + -ED[2]] —**re·lat′ed·ness,** *n.*
—**Syn. 1.** relevant, affiliated. 2. linked, united, joined.

re·la·tion (ri lā′shən), *n.* 1. an existing connection; a significant association between or among things: *the relation between cause and effect.* 2. **relations, a.** the various connections between peoples, countries, etc.: *foreign relations.* **b.** the various connections in which persons are brought together: *business and social relations.* **c.** sexual intercourse. 3. the mode or kind of connection between one person and another, between man and God, etc. 4. connection between persons by blood or marriage. 5. a person who is related by blood or marriage; relative: *He can't stand his wife's relations.* 6. reference; regard; respect: *to plan with relation to the future.* 7. the act of relating, narrating, or telling; narration. 8. a narrative; account. 9. *Law.* a principle whereby effect is given to an act done at one time as if it had been done at a previous time. 10. *Math.* **a.** a property which associates two quantities in a definite order, as equality or inequality. **b.** a many-valued function. [ME *relacion* < L *relātiōn-* (s. of *relātiō*). See RELATE, -ION] —**re·la′tion·less,** *adj.*
—**Syn. 1.** relationship; tie, link. **2a, b.** association. 4. relationship, kinship. 7. recitation, recital, description. 8. report, story, chronicle, tale, history. —**Ant. 1.** independence.

re·la·tion·al (ri lā′shə nəl), *adj.* 1. of or pertaining to relations. 2. indicating or specifying some relation. 3. *Gram.* serving to indicate relations between various elements in a sentence, as prepositions, conjunctions, etc. Cf. **notional** (def. 7). [RELATION + -AL[1]]

re·la·tion·ship (ri lā′shən ship′), *n.* 1. a connection, association, or involvement. 2. connection by blood or marriage. 3. an emotional or other connection between people: *a good father-son relationship; the relationship between teachers and students.* [RELATION + -SHIP]
—**Syn. 1.** dependence, alliance, kinship. 2. affinity, consanguinity. RELATIONSHIP, KINSHIP refer to connection with others by blood or by marriage. RELATIONSHIP can be applied to connection either by birth or by marriage: *relationship to a ruling family.* KINSHIP generally denotes common descent, and implies a more intimate connection than relationship: *the ties and obligations of kinship.*

rel·a·tive (rel′ə tiv), *n.* 1. one who is connected with another or others by blood or marriage. 2. something having, or standing in, some relation to something else. 3. something dependent upon external conditions for its specific nature, size, etc. (opposed to *absolute*). 4. *Gram.* a relative pronoun, adjective, or adverb. —*adj.* 5. considered in relation to something else; comparative: *the relative merits of democracy and monarchy.* 6. existing or having its specific nature only by relation to something else; not absolute or independent: *Happiness is relative.* 7. having relation or connection: *to study magnetism and relative phenomena.* 8. having reference or regard; relevant; pertinent (usually fol. by *to*): *to determine the facts relative to an accident.* 9. correspondent; proportionate: *Value is relative to demand.* 10. (of a term, name, etc.) depending for significance upon something else: *"Better" is a relative term.* 11. *Gram.* noting or pertaining to a word or other element which constitutes or introduces a subordinate clause of which it is, or is a part of, the subject or predicate and which refers to some element of the principal clause (the antecedent), as the relative pronoun *who* in *He's the man who saw you,* where *who saw you* is a relative clause. [< LL *relātīv(us).* See RELATE, -IVE]

rel′ative ap′erture, *Optics.* the ratio of the diameter of a lens, esp. a camera lens, to the focal length; the reciprocal of the f number or focal ratio of the lens.

rel′ative bear′ing, *Navig.* the bearing of an object, relative to the heading of a vessel or aircraft.

rel′ative clause′, a clause that modifies an antecedent, as *who saw us* in the sentence *It was she who saw us.*

rel′ative com′plement, *Math.* the set of elements contained in a given set which are not elements of another specified set. Also called **difference.**

rel′ative den′sity, *Physics.* See **specific gravity.**

rel′ative disper′sion, *Optics.* See **Abbe number.**

rel′ative fre′quency, *Statistics.* the ratio of the number of times an event occurs to the number of occasions on which it might occur in the same period.

rel′ative humid′ity, the amount of water vapor in the air, expressed as a percentage of the maximum amount that the air could hold at the given temperature; the ratio of the actual water vapor pressure to the saturation vapor pressure. Also called **humidity.** Cf. **absolute humidity, dew point, humidity, mixing ratio, specific humidity.**

rel′ative imped′iment, *Law.* a fact or circumstance that disqualifies from lawful marriage persons who are closely related.

rel′ative in′dex of refrac′tion, *Optics.* See under **index of refraction.**

rel·a·tive·ly (rel′ə tiv lē), *adv.* 1. in a relative manner: *a relatively small difference.* 2. *Archaic.* **a.** with reference (usually fol. by *to*). **b.** in proportion (usually fol. by *to*). [RELATIVE + -LY]

rel′atively prime′ num′bers, *Math.* two numbers whose greatest common divisor is 1. Cf. **greatest common divisor.**

rel′ative ma′jor, *Music.* the major key whose tonic is the third degree of a given minor key.

rel′ative max′imum, *Math.* maximum (def. 2a).

rel′ative min′imum, *Math.* minimum (def. 4a).

rel′ative mi′nor, *Music.* the minor key whose tonic is the sixth degree of a given major key.

rel·a·tive·ness (rel′ə tiv nes), *n.* the state or fact of being relative. [RELATIVE + -NESS]

rel′ative per·mit·tiv′i·ty (pûr′mi tiv′i tē), *Elect.* See **dielectric constant.** [PERMIT + -IVE + -ITY]

rel′ative pitch′, *Music.* 1. the pitch of a tone as determined by its relationship to other tones in a scale. 2. the ability to identify or sing a tone by mentally determining the distance of its pitch from that of a tone already sounded. Cf. **absolute pitch.**

rel′ative pro′noun, a pronoun that refers to an antecedent, as *who* in *It was I who told you.*

rel′ative topol′ogy, *Math.* a topology of a subset of a topological space, obtained by intersecting the subset with every open set in the topology of the space. Also called **induced topology, subspace topology.**

rel·a·tiv·ism (rel′ə ti viz′əm), *n.* *Philos.* any theory holding that criteria of judgment are relative, varying with individuals and their environments. [RELATIVE + -ISM]

rel·a·tiv·ist (rel′ə ti vist), *n.* an adherent or advocate of relativism or of the principle of relativity. [RELATIVE + -IST]

rel·a·tiv·is·tic (rel′ə ti vis′tik), *adj.* 1. of or pertaining to relativity or relativism. 2. *Physics.* having a value that varies with velocity, in classical mechanics being equivalent to the value obtained when the velocity is appreciably smaller than the speed of light: *relativistic mass; relativistic momentum.* [RELATIVIST + -IC]

relativis′tic quan′tum mechan′ics, *Physics.* See under **quantum mechanics** (def. 1).

rel·a·tiv·i·ty (rel′ə tiv′i tē), *n.* 1. the state or fact of being relative. 2. *Physics.* a theory, formulated essentially by Albert Einstein, that all motion must be defined relative to a frame of reference and that space and time are relative, rather than absolute concepts: it consists of two principal parts. The theory dealing with uniform motion **(special theory of relativity** or **restricted theory of relativity)** is based on the two postulates that physical laws have the same mathematical form when expressed in any inertial system, and the velocity of light is independent of the motion of its source and will have the same value when measured by observers moving with constant velocity with respect to each other. Derivable from these postulates are the conclusions that there can be no motion at a speed greater than that of light in a vacuum, mass increases as velocity increases, mass and energy are equivalent, and time is dependent on the relative motion of an observer measuring the time. The theory dealing with gravity **(general theory of relativity)** is based on the postulate that the local effects of a gravitational field and of acceleration of an inertial system are identical. 3. dependence of a mental state or process upon the nature of the human mind: *relativity of values; relativity of knowledge.* [RELATIVE + -ITY]

re·la·tor (ri lā′tər), *n.* 1. one who relates or tells; narrator. 2. *Law.* a private person on whose suggestion or complaint an action or special proceeding in the name of the state is brought, to try a question involving both public and private right. [< L: a proposer, mover. See RELATE, -OR[2]]

re·lax (ri laks′), *v.t.* 1. to make less tense, rigid, or firm; make lax: *to relax the muscles.* 2. to diminish the force of. 3. to slacken or abate, as effort, attention, etc. 4. to make less strict or severe, as rules, discipline, etc.: *to relax the requirements for a license.* 5. to release or bring relief from the effects of tension, anxiety, etc.: *He has to take a tranquilizer to relax himself. Smoking a cigarette relaxes me.* —*v.i.* 6. to become less tense, rigid, or firm. 7. to become less strict or severe; grow milder: *The social rules at our colleges and universities have relaxed considerably in the past twenty years.* 8. to reduce or stop work, effort, application, etc., esp. for the sake of rest or recreation. 9. to release oneself from inhibition, worry, tension, etc. [ME *relax(en)* < L *relax(āre)* (to) stretch out again, loosen, equiv. to *re-* RE- + *laxāre* to loosen, deriv. of *laxus* slack, LAX] —**re·lax′a·tive, re·lax·a·to·ry** (ri lak′sə tôr′ē, -tōr′ē), *adj.* —**re·lax·ed·ly** (ri lak′sid lē), *adv.* —**re·lax′ed·ness,** *n.* —**re·lax′er,** *n.*
—**Syn. 1, 6.** loosen, slacken. 2. mitigate, weaken, lessen, reduce. 4. ease. 6. unbend. 7. relent, soften. —**Ant. 1, 6** tighten, tense.

re·lax·ant (ri lak′sənt), *adj.* 1. of, pertaining to, or causing a relaxation. —*n.* 2. *Med.* a drug that relaxes, esp. one that lessens strain in muscle. [< L *relaxant-* (s. of *relaxāns*), prp. of *relaxāre.* See RELAX, -ANT]

re·lax·a·tion (rē′lak sā′shən), *n.* 1. abatement or relief from bodily or mental work, effort, application, etc. 2. an activity or recreation that provides such relief; diversion; entertainment. 3. a loosening or slackening. 4. diminution or remission of strictness or severity. 5. *Math.* a numerical procedure for solving systems of equations by successive approximations of the variables. [< L *relaxātiōn-* (s. of *relaxātiō*), equiv. to *relaxāt(us)* (ptp. of *relaxāre* to RELAX) + *-iōn-* -ION]

re-lay (rē lā′), *v.t.*, **-laid, -lay·ing.** to lay again. Also, **relay.** [RE- + LAY[1]]

re·lay[1] (*n.* rē′lā; *v.* rē′lā, ri lā′), *n., v.*, **-layed, -lay·ing.** —*n.* 1. a series of persons relieving one another or taking turns; shift. 2. a fresh set of dogs or horses posted in readiness for use in a hunt, on a journey, etc. 3. *Sports.* **a.** See **relay race. b.** a length or leg in a relay race. 4. *Mach.* an automatic control device in which the settings of valves, switches, etc., are regulated by a powered element, as a motor, solenoid, or pneumatic mechanism actuated by a smaller, sensitive element. 5. *Elect.* a device, usually consisting of an electromagnet and an armature, by which a change of current or voltage in one circuit can be made to produce a change in the electric condition of another circuit or to affect the operation of other devices in the same or another electric circuit. 6. *(cap.) U.S.* one of a series of low-altitude, active communications satellites for receiving and transmitting radio and television signals. —*v.t.* 7. to carry forward by or as by relays: *to relay a message.* 8. to provide with or replace by fresh relays. 9. *Elect.* to retransmit (a signal, message, etc.) by or as by means of a telegraphic relay. —*v.i.* 10. *Elect.* to relay a message. [ME *relai* (n.), *relai(en)* (v.) < MF *relais* (n.), *relai(er)* (v.), OF: to leave behind, equiv. to *re-* RE- + *laier* to leave, alter. of *laissier* < L *laxāre*; see RELAX]

re·lay[2] (rē lā′), *v.t.*, **-laid, -lay·ing.** re-lay.

re′lay race′, *Sports.* a race between two or more teams of contestants, each contestant being relieved by a teammate after running part of the distance. Cf. **medley relay.**

re-lease (rē lēs′), *v.t.*, **-leased, -leas·ing.** 1. to lease again. 2. *Law.* to make over (land, property, etc.), as to another. [RE- + LEASE]

re·lease (ri lēs′), *v.*, **-leased, -leas·ing,** *n.* —*v.t.* 1. to free from confinement, bondage, obligation, pain, etc.; let go: *to release a prisoner; to release someone from a debt.* 2. to free from anything that restrains, fastens, etc.: *to release a catapult.* 3. to allow to be known, issued, done, or exhibited: *to release an article for publication.* 4. *Law.* to give up, relinquish, or surrender (a right, claim, etc.). —*n.* 5. a freeing or releasing from confinement, obligation, pain, etc. 6. liberation from anything that restrains or fastens. 7. some device or agency for effecting such liberation. 8. the releasing of something for publication, performance, use, exhibition, or sale, as a written article for newspapers. 9. an article, statement, or the like, issued to newspapers, radio stations, etc., for publication. 10. *Law.* **a.** the surrender of a right or the like to another. **b.** a document embodying such a surrender. 11. *Obs. exc. Law.* a remission, as of a debt, tax, or tribute. 12. a control mechanism for starting or stopping a machine, esp. by removing some restrictive apparatus. 13. *Mach.* **a.** the opening of an exhaust port or valve at or near the working stroke of an engine so that the working fluid can be exhausted on the return stroke. **b.** the point in the stroke of an engine at which the exhaust port or valve is opened. 14. (in jazz or popular music) a bridge. 15. See **press release.** [ME *reles(s)e(n)* (v.) < OF *relesser, relaissier* < L *relaxāre* to loosen; see RELAX] —**re·leas′a·bil′i·ty,** *n.* —**re·leas′a·ble, re·leas′i·ble,** *adj.* —**re·leas′er,** *n.*
—**Syn. 1.** loose, deliver. RELEASE, FREE, DISMISS, DISCHARGE, LIBERATE, EMANCIPATE may all mean to set at liberty, let loose, or let go. RELEASE and FREE, when applied to persons, suggest a helpful action. Both may be used (not always interchangeably) of delivering a person from confinement or obligation: *to free or release prisoners.* FREE (less often, RELEASE) is also used for delivering a person from pain, sorrow, etc.: *to free from fear.* DISMISS, meaning to send away, usually has the meaning of forcing to go unwillingly (*to dismiss a servant*), but may refer to giving permission to go: *The teacher dismissed the class early.* DISCHARGE, meaning originally to relieve of a burden (*to discharge a gun*), has come to

re·judge′, *v.*, **-judged, -judg·ing.**
re·judge′ment, *n.*
re·judg′ment, *n.*
re′jus·ti·fi·ca′tion, *n.*
re·jus′ti·fy′, *v.t.*, **-fied, -fy·ing.**
re·kin′dle, *v.*, **-dled, -dling.**
re·knead′, *v.t.*
re·knit′, *v.*, **-knit·ted** or **-knit, -knit·ting.**
re·knock′, *v.*
re·knot′, *v.*, **-knot·ted, -knot·ting.**
re·la′bel, *v.t.*, **-beled, -bel·ing** or (*esp. Brit.*) **-belled, -bel·ling.**
re·lace′, *v.*, **-laced, -lac·ing.**
re·lac′quer, *v.t.*
re·lance′, *v.t.*, **-lanced, -lanc·ing.**
re·land′, *v.*
re·latch′, *v.t.*
re·launch′, *v.t.*
re·laun′der, *v.t.*
re·lead′, *v.*
re·learn′, *v.*, **-learned** or **-learnt, -learn·ing.**

refer to that which is sent away, and is often a close synonym to DISMISS; it is used in the meaning permit to go, in connection with courts and the armed forces: *The court discharged a man accused of robbery.* LIBERATE and EMANCIPATE, more formal synonyms for RELEASE and FREE, also suggest action intended to be helpful. LIBERATE suggests particularly the release from unjust punishment, oppression, and the like, and often means to set free through forcible action or military campaign: *They liberated the prisoners, the occupied territories, etc.* EMANCIPATE also suggests a release of some size and consequence, but one that is less overt, a more formal or legal freedom; and it sometimes connotes an inner liberation: *Lincoln emancipated the slaves. John emancipated himself.* **2.** loose, extricate, disengage. **3.** announce, publish. **5.** liberation, deliverance, emancipation. **—Ant. 1.** bind. **2.** fasten.

release′ cop′y, *Journalism.* **1.** an article, notice, announcement, or the like, issued in advance for publication or broadcast, bearing a release date. **2.** the contents of such an advance.

release′ date′, *Journalism.* **1.** the time, as the day, part of the day, and sometimes the hour, on or at which release copy may be published or broadcast. **2.** the printed notation of this time on a press release or other advance.

release′ ther′apy, *Psychiatry.* psychotherapy in which the patient finds emotional release in the expression of his hostilities and emotional conflicts.

rel·e·gate (rel′ə gāt′), *v.t.*, **-gat·ed, -gat·ing. 1.** to send or consign to an inferior position, place, or condition: *He has been relegated to a post at the fringes of the diplomatic service.* **2.** to consign or commit (a matter, task, etc.), as to a person: *He relegates the less pleasant tasks to his assistant.* **3.** to assign or refer (something) to a particular class or kind. **4.** to send into exile; banish. [< L *relēgāt(us)* sent away, dispatched, ptp. of *relēgāre.* See RE-, LEGATE] **—rel·e·ga·ble** (rel′ə gə bəl), *adj.* **—rel′e·ga′tion,** *n.*
—Syn. 2. confide, entrust.

re·lent (ri lent′), *v.i.* **1.** to soften in feeling, temper, or determination; become more mild, compassionate, or forgiving. **2.** to become less severe; slacken: *Finally the winds relented.* **—v.t. 3.** *Obs.* to cause to soften in feeling, temper, or determination. **4.** *Obs.* to cause to slacken; abate. **5.** *Obs.* to abandon; relinquish. [ME *relent(en),* ? << RE- + L *lent(us)* tough, viscous, slow] **—re·lent′ing·ly,** *adv.*
—Syn. 1. bend, yield.

re·lent·less (ri lent′lis), *adj.* that does not relent; unyieldingly severe, strict, or harsh; unrelenting; *a relentless enemy.* [RELENT + -LESS] **—re·lent′less·ly,** *adv.* **—re·lent′less·ness,** *n.*
—Syn. rigid, stern, undying, unbending, unforgiving, merciless, ruthless, unmerciful, pitiless, unpitying, hard, obdurate, adamant, unyielding, remorseless. **—Ant.** merciful.

rel·e·vant (rel′ə vənt), *adj.* bearing upon or connected with the matter in hand; to the purpose; pertinent: *a relevant remark.* [< ML *relevant-* (s. of *relevāns*), prp. of *relevāre* to raise, lift up. See RELIEVE, -ANT] **—rel′e·vance, rel′e·van·cy,** *n.* **—rel′e·vant·ly,** *adv.*
—Syn. applicable, germane, apposite, appropriate, suitable, fitting. See **apt.**

re·le·vé (rel′ə vā′; *Fr.* Rəl° vā′), *n. Ballet.* a rising up onto full point or half point from the flat of the feet. [< F: lit., raised, ptp. of *relever;* see RELIEVE]

re·li·a·ble (ri lī′ə bəl), *adj.* that may be relied on; trustworthy; dependable in achievement, accuracy, honesty, etc.: *reliable sources of information.* [RELY + -ABLE] **—re·li′a·bil′i·ty, re·li′a·ble·ness,** *n.* **—re·li′a·bly,** *adv.*
—Syn. trusty, authentic, consistent. RELIABLE, INFALLIBLE, TRUSTWORTHY apply to persons, objects, ideas, or information that can be depended upon with confident certainty. RELIABLE suggests consistent dependability of judgment, character, performance, or result: *a reliable formula, judge, car, meteorologist.* INFALLIBLE suggests the complete absence of error, breakdown, or poor performance: *an infallible test, system, marksman.* TRUSTWORTHY emphasizes the steady and honest dependability which encourages one's confidence, belief, or trust: *trustworthy and accurate reports.* **—Ant.** undependable, questionable, deceitful.

re·li·ance (ri lī′əns), *n.* **1.** confident or trustful dependence. **2.** confidence. **3.** something or someone relied on. [RELY + -ANCE]

re·li·ant (ri lī′ənt), *adj.* **1.** having or showing dependence: *He is working now and no longer reliant on money from home.* **2.** confident; trustful. **3.** self-reliant. [RELY + -ANT] **—re·li′ant·ly,** *adv.*

rel·ic (rel′ik), *n.* **1.** a surviving memorial of something past. **2.** an object having interest by reason of its age or its association with the past: *a museum of historic relics.* **3.** a surviving trace of something: *a custom which is a relic of paganism.* **4. relics, a.** remaining parts or fragments. **b.** the remains of a deceased person. **5.** something kept in remembrance; souvenir; memento. **6.** *Eccles.* (esp. in the Roman Catholic and Greek churches) the body, a part of the body, or some personal memorial of a saint, martyr, or other sacred person, preserved as worthy of veneration. [ME *relik* < OF *relique* < L *reliquae* (pl.) remains (> OE *reliquias*), equiv. to *reliqu(us)* remaining + *-iae* pl. n. suffix] **—rel′ic·like′,** *adj.*

rel·ict (rel′ikt), *n.* **1.** *Ecol.* a plant or animal species living in an environment that has changed from that which is typical for it. **2.** a remnant or survivor. **3.** *Archaic.* a widow. [late ME < ML *relicta* widow (L *relictus,* ptp. of *relinquere* to RELINQUISH)]

re·lief[1] (ri lēf′), *n.* **1.** alleviation, ease, or deliverance through the removal of pain, distress, oppression, etc. **2.** a means or thing that relieves pain, distress, anxiety, etc. **3.** money, food, or other help given to those in poverty or need. **4.** something affording a pleasing change, as from monotony. **5.** release from a post of duty, as by the arrival of a substitute or replacement. **6.** the person or persons acting as replacement. **7.** the rescue of a besieged town, fort, etc., from an attacking force. **8.** the freeing of a closed space, as a tank or boiler, from more than a desirable amount of pressure or vacuum. **9.** *Feudal Law.* a fine or composition which the heir of a feudal tenant paid to the lord for the privilege of succeeding to the estate. **10.** *Literature.* **a.** a distinct or abrupt change in mood, scene, action, etc., resulting in a reduction of intensity, as in a play or novel. **b.** See **comic relief. 11. on relief,** receiving financial assistance from a municipal, state, or federal government because of poverty or need. [ME *relef* < OF *relief,* deriv. of *relever* to raise; see RELIEVE] **—re·lief′less,** *adj.*
—Syn. 1. mitigation, assuagement, comfort. **3.** succor, aid, redress, remedy. **—Ant. 1.** intensification.

Relief [2]
A, Bas-relief; B, High relief

re·lief[2] (ri lēf′), *n.* **1.** prominence, distinctness, or vividness due to contrast. **2.** the projection of a figure or part from the ground or plane on which it is formed, as in sculpture or similar work. **3.** a piece or work in such projection: *a high relief.* **4.** an apparent projection of parts in a painting, drawing, etc., giving the appearance of the third dimension. **5.** *Phys. Geog.* a contour variation of the land surface in relation to the surrounding land. **6.** *Print.* any printing process by which the printing ink is transferred to paper or another printed surface from areas that are higher than the rest of the block. [< F *relief,* It *rilievo;* see RELIEF[1]]

re·lief·er (ri lē′fər), *n.* **1.** *Baseball.* See **relief pitcher. 2.** one who, because of old age, indigence, physical disability, or the like, receives welfare benefits from the state. **3.** one who temporarily replaces someone else. [RELIEF[1] + -ER[1]]

relief′ map′, a map showing the relief of an area, usually by generalized contour lines.

relief′ pitch′er, *Baseball.* **1.** a pitcher brought into a game to replace another pitcher, often in a critical situation. **2.** a pitcher regularly so used, as opposed to one who regularly starts games. Also called **reliever, reliefer.**

relief′ tube′, *Rocketry.* a tube for carrying urine from the body to a waste container, during manned space flights.

relief′ valve′, a device that, when actuated by static pressure above a predetermined level, opens in proportion to the excess above this level and reduces the pressure to it. Cf. **safety valve** (def. 1).

re·li·er (ri lī′ər), *n.* one who or that which relies. [RELY + -ER[1]]

re·lieve (ri lēv′), *v.,* **-lieved, -liev·ing. —v.t. 1.** to ease or alleviate (pain, distress, anxiety, need, etc.). **2.** to free from anxiety, fear, pain, etc. **3.** to free from need, poverty, etc. **4.** to bring effective aid to (a besieged town, military position, etc.). **5.** to ease (a person) of any burden, wrong, or oppression, as by legal means. **6.** to reduce (a pressure, load, weight, etc., on a device or object under stress): *to remove the lid of a pot to relieve the steam pressure; to add a column to relieve the stress on the others.* **7.** to make less tedious, unpleasant, or monotonous; break or vary the sameness of: *to relieve the tension of a drama with comic episodes.* **8.** to bring into relief or prominence; heighten the effect of. **9.** to release (one on duty) by coming as or providing a substitute or replacement. **10.** *Mach.* **a.** to free (a closed space, as a tank, boiler, etc.) of more than a desirable pressure or vacuum. **b.** to reduce (the pressure or vacuum in such a space) to a desirable level. **11.** *Baseball.* to replace (a pitcher): *Jones relieved the starting pitcher in the eighth inning.* **—v.i. 12.** *Baseball.* to act as a relief pitcher: *He relieved in 52 games for the Pirates last season.* **13. to relieve oneself,** to urinate or defecate. [ME *releve(en)* < MF *relev(er)* (to) raise < L *relevāre* to lift, raise up again, lighten, equiv. to *re-* RE- + *levāre* to raise] **—re·liev′a·ble,** *adj.* **—re·liev·ed·ly** (ri lē′vid lē), *adv.*
—Syn. 1. mitigate, assuage, allay, lighten, lessen, abate, diminish. See **comfort. 1–4.** aid, help, assist. **3.** support, sustain. **4.** succor. **—Ant. 1.** intensify.

re·liev·er (ri lē′vər), *n.* **1.** one who or that which relieves. **2.** *Baseball.* See **relief pitcher.** [late ME; see RELIEVE, -ER[1]]

reliev′ing arch′. See **discharging arch.**

reliev′ing tack′le, *Naut.* a tackle for absorbing from a rudder shocks that in heavy weather would otherwise be transmitted to the steering gear. Also called **kicking tackle, rudder tackle.**

re·lie·vo (ri lē′vō, -lyev′ō), *n., pl.* **-vos.** *Obs.* relief[2] (defs. 2, 3). [< It]

relig., religion.

re·li·gieuse (Rə lē zhyœz′), *n., pl.* **-gieuses** (-zhyœz′). *French.* a woman belonging to a religious order, congregation, etc.

re·li·gieux (Rə lē zhyœ′), *adj., n., pl.* **-gieux.** *French.* **—adj. 1.** religious; devout; pious. **—n. 2.** a person under monastic vows.

re·li·gion (ri lij′ən), *n.* **1.** concern over what exists beyond the visible world, differentiated from philosophy in that it operates through faith or intuition rather than reason, and generally including the idea of the existence of a single being, a group of beings, an eternal principle, or a transcendent spiritual entity that has created the world, that governs it, that controls its destinies, or that intervenes occasionally in the natural course of its history, as well as the idea that ritual, prayer, spiritual exercises, certain principles of everyday conduct, etc., are expedient, due, or spiritually rewarding, or arise naturally out of an inner need as a human response to the belief in such a being, principle, etc. **2.** a specific fundamental set of beliefs and practices generally agreed upon by a number of persons or sects: *the Christian religion.* **3.** the body of persons adhering to a particular set of beliefs and practices: *a world council of religions.* **4.** a deep conviction of the validity of religious beliefs and practices: *to get religion.* **5.** the life or state of a monk, nun, etc.: *to enter religion.* **6.** the practice of religious beliefs; ritual observance of faith. **7.** a point or matter of ethics or conscience: *to make a religion of fighting prejudice.* **8. religions,** *Archaic.* religious rites. **9.** *Archaic.* strict faithfulness; devotion: *a religion to one's vow.* [ME *religioun* < L *religiōn-* (s. of *religiō*) conscientiousness, piety, ?, equiv. to *relig(āre)* to tie, fasten (*re-* RE- + *lig-* bind, tie) + *-iōn-* -ION] **—re·li′gion·less,** *adj.*

re·li·gion·ism (ri lij′ə niz′əm), *n.* **1.** excessive or exaggerated religious zeal. **2.** affected or pretended religious zeal. [RELIGION + -ISM] **—re·li′gion·ist,** *n.* **—re·li′gion·is′tic,** *adj.*

re·li·gi·ose (ri lij′ē ōs′), *adj.* characterized by religiosity. [< L *religiōsus;* see RELIGIOUS]

re·lig·i·os·i·ty (ri lij′ē os′i tē), *n.* **1.** the quality of being religious; piety; devoutness. **2.** affected or excessive devotion to religion. [ME *religiosite* < LL *religiōsitās* = L *religiōs(us)* RELIGIOUS + *-itās* -ITY]

re·li·gious (ri lij′əs), *adj., n., pl.* **-gious. —adj. 1.** of, pertaining to, or concerned with religion: *a religious holiday.* **2.** imbued with or exhibiting religion; pious; devout; godly: *a religious man.* **3.** scrupulously faithful; conscientious: *religious care.* **4.** pertaining to or connected with a monastic or religious order. **5.** appropriate to religion or to sacred rites or observances. **—n. 6.** a member of a religious order, congregation, etc.; a monk, friar, or nun. **7. the religious,** devout or religious persons: *Each year, thousands of the religious make pilgrimages to the shrine.* [ME < L *religiōs(us),* equiv. to *religi(ō)* RELIGION + *-ōsus* -OUS] **—re·li′gious·ly,** *adv.* **—re·li′gious·ness,** *n.*
—Syn. 2. reverent. RELIGIOUS, DEVOUT, PIOUS indicate a spirit of reverence toward God. RELIGIOUS is a general word, applying to whatever pertains to faith or worship: *a religious ceremony.* DEVOUT indicates a fervent spirit, usually genuine and often independent of outward observances: *a deeply devout though unorthodox church member.* PIOUS implies such constant attention to, and extreme conformity with, outward observances as often to suggest sham or hypocrisy: *a pious hypocrite.* **—Ant. 2.** impious.

reli′gious house′, a convent or monastery.

Reli′gious of the Cen′acle, *Rom. Cath. Ch.* a member of the "Society of Our Lady of the Cenacle," engaged in directing retreats for women.

Reli′gious of the Sa′cred Heart′, *Rom. Cath. Ch.* a member of the congregation of the "Society of the Sacred Heart," founded in France in 1800 and engaged in the education of girls.

Reli′gious Soci′ety of Friends′, a sect founded by George Fox in England about 1650, opposed to oath-taking and all war; commonly called Quakers.

re·lin·quish (ri liŋg′kwish), *v.t.* **1.** to renounce or surrender (a possession, right, etc.): *to relinquish the throne.* **2.** to give up; put aside or desist from: *to relinquish a plan.* **3.** to let go; release: *to relinquish one's hold.* [late ME < MF *relinquiss-,* extended s. of *relinquir* < L *relinquere* to leave behind, equiv. to *re-* RE- + *linquere* to leave] **—re·lin′quish·er,** *n.* **—re·lin′quish·ment,** *n.*
—Syn. 2. yield, cede, waive, forego, abdicate, leave, quit, forswear, desert, resign. See **abandon**[1].

rel·i·quar·y (rel′ə kwer′ē), *n., pl.* **-quar·ies.** a repository or receptacle for a relic or relics. [< MF *reliquaire* < ML *reliquiār(ium),* equiv. to L *reliqui(ae)* remains (see RELIC) + *-ārium* -ARY]

rel·ique (rel′ik; *Fr.* Rə lēk′), *n., pl.* **rel·iques** (rel′iks; *Fr.* Rə lēk′). *Archaic.* relic.

re·liq·ui·ae (ri lik′wē ē′), *n.* (*construed as pl.*) remains, as those of fossil organisms. [< L; see RELIC]

rel·ish (rel′ish), *n.* **1.** liking or enjoyment of the taste of something. **2.** pleasurable appreciation of anything; liking: *He has no relish for obscene jokes.* **3.** *Cookery.* **a.** something savory or appetizing added to a meal, as pickles or olives. **b.** a sweet pickle made of various vegetables, usually chopped or minced. **c.** an appetizer or hors d'oeuvre. **4.** a pleasing or appetizing flavor. **5.** a pleasing or enjoyable quality. **6.** a taste or flavor. **7.** a smack, trace, or touch of something. **—v.t. 8.** to take pleasure in; like; enjoy: *I don't relish the long drive home.* **9.** to make pleasing to the taste. **10.** to like the taste or flavor of. **—v.i. 11.** to have taste or flavor. **12.** to be agreeable or pleasant. [alter. of ME *reles* aftertaste, scent < OF, var. of *relais* remainder, that left behind; see RELEASE] **—rel′ish·a·ble,** *adj.* **—rel′ish·ing·ly,** *adv.* **—Syn. 1, 2.** gusto, zest. **2.** inclination, partiality, predilection, preference. **3.** condiment, appetizer. **6.** savor. **8.** appreciate. **—Ant. 1, 2.** distaste, disfavor.

rel. pron., relative pronoun.

re·lu·cent (ri lo͞o′sənt), *adj.* shining; bright. [< L *relūcent-* (s. of *relūcēns*), prp. of *relūcēre.* See RE-, LUCENT]

re·luct (ri lukt′), *v.i. Archaic.* **1.** to struggle (against something); rebel. **2.** to object; show reluctance. [< L *reluct(ārī),* equiv. to *re-* RE- + *luct-* strive, struggle]

re·luc·tance (ri luk′təns), *n.* **1.** unwillingness; disinclination: *reluctance to speak in public.* **2.** *Elect.* the resistance to magnetic flux offered by a magnetic circuit,

re·lend′, *v.t.,* **-lend, -lend·ing.**
re·let′, *v.,* **-let, -let·ting.**
re·let′ter, *v.t.*
re·lev′el, *v.,* **-eled, -el·ing** or (*esp. Brit.*) **-elled, -el·ling.**
re·lev′er, *v.t.*
re·lev′y, *v.t.,* **-lev·ied, -lev·y·ing.**
re·lib′er·ate′, *v.t.,* **-at·ed, -at·ing.**
re·li′cense, *v.t.,* **-censed, -cens·ing.**
re·light′, *v.,* **-light·ed** or **-lit, -light·ing.**
re·lim′it, *v.t.*
re·line′, *v.t.,* **-lined, -lin·ing.**
re·link′, *v.t.*
re·liq′ue·fy′, *v.,* **-fied, -fy·ing.**
re·liq′ui·date′, *v.,* **-dat·ed, -dat·ing.**
re′liq·ui·da′tion, *n.*
re·list′, *v.t.*
re·lis′ten, *v.*
re·lit′i·gate′, *v.t.,* **-gat·ed, -gat·ing.**
re′lit·i·ga′tion, *n.*
re·liv′a·ble, *adj.*
re·live′, *v.,* **-lived, -liv·ing.**
re·load′, *n., v.*
re·loan′, *n., v.t.*
re·lo′cate, *v.t.,* **-cat·ed, -cat·ing.**
re′lo·ca′tion, *n.*
re·lose′, *v.t.,* **-lost, -los·ing.**
re·low′er, *v.t.*
re·lu′bri·cate′, *v.t.,* **-cat·ed, -cat·ing.**

numerically equal to the magnetomotive force divided by the magnetic flux. Also, **re·luc′tan·cy.** [RELUCT(ANT) + -ANCE]

re·luc·tant (ri luk′tənt), *adj.* **1.** unwilling; disinclined: *a reluctant candidate for the governorship.* **2.** struggling in opposition. [< L *reluctant-* (s. of *reluctāns*), prp. of *reluctārī.* See RELUCT, -ANT] —**re·luc′tant·ly,** *adv.*
—**Syn. 1.** RELUCTANT, LOATH, AVERSE describe disinclination toward something. RELUCTANT implies some sort of mental struggle, as between disinclination and sense of duty: *reluctant to expel students.* LOATH describes extreme disinclination: *loath to part from a friend.* AVERSE, used with *to* and a noun or a gerund, describes a long-held dislike or unwillingness, though not a particularly strong feeling: *averse to an idea; averse to getting up early.* —**Ant. 1.** willing.

rel·uc·tiv·i·ty (rel′ək tiv′i tē), *n. Elect.* the tendency of a magnetic circuit to conduct magnetic flux, equal to the reciprocal of the permeability of the circuit. [RELUCT + -IVE + -ITY]

re·lume (ri lo͞om′), *v.t.,* **-lumed, -lum·ing.** to light or illuminate again; relumine. [< LL *relūm(ināre).* See RELUMINE]

re·lu·mine (ri lo͞o′min), *v.t.,* **-mined, -min·ing.** to relume. [< LL *relūmin(āre),* equiv. to L *re-* RE- + *(il)lūmināre* to ILLUMINE]

re·ly (ri lī′), *v.i.,* **-lied, -ly·ing.** to depend confidently; put trust in (usually fol. by *on* or *upon*): *You can rely on her work.* [ME *relie(n)* < MF *relie(r)* < L *religāre* to tie back. See RE, LIGAMENT]

rem (rem), *n.* the quantity of ionizing radiation whose biological effect is equal to that produced by one roentgen of x-rays. Cf. **rep**³. [*r(oentgen) e(quivalent in) m(an)*]

re·main (ri mān′), *v.i.* **1.** to continue in the same state; continue to be as specified: *to remain at peace.* **2.** to stay behind or in the same place: *to remain at home; I'll remain here when you go to the airport.* **3.** to be left after the removal, loss, destruction, etc., of all else: *The front wall is all that remains of the fort.* **4.** to be left to be done, told, shown, etc.: *Only the dishwashing remains.* **5.** to be reserved or in store. —*n.* **6.** Usually, **remains.** that which remains or is left; remnants. **7. remains, a.** miscellaneous, fragmentary, or other writings still unpublished at the time of the author's death. **b.** traces of some quality, condition, etc. **c.** that which remains of a person after death; a dead body. **d.** parts or substances remaining from animal or plant life that occur in the earth's crust or strata: *fossil remains; organic remains.* [ME *remain(en)* < AF *remain-,* stressed s. of MF *remanoir* < L *remanēre,* equiv. to *re-* RE- + *manēre* to stay; see MANOR]
—**Syn. 1.** abide, stay. See **continue. 2.** wait, tarry, rest. **3.** endure, abide. —**Ant. 2.** depart.

re·main·der (ri mān′dər), *n.* **1.** that which remains or is left: *the remainder of the day.* **2.** a remaining part. **3.** *Arith.* **a.** the quantity that remains after subtraction. **b.** the portion of the dividend that is not evenly divisible by the divisor. **4.** *Law.* a future interest so created as to take effect at the end of another estate, as when property is conveyed to one person for life and then to another. **5. remainders,** *Philately.* the quantities of stamps on hand after they have been demonetized or otherwise voided for postal use. **6.** a copy of a book remaining in the publisher's stock when its sale has practically ceased, frequently sold at a reduced price. —*adj.* **7.** remaining; leftover. —*v.t.* **8.** to dispose of or sell as a remainder. [ME < AF, n. use of MF *remaindre* to remain]
—**Syn. 1.** residuum, remnant, excess, rest, overage. **2.** REMAINDER, BALANCE, RESIDUE, SURPLUS refer to a portion left over. REMAINDER is the general word (*the remainder of one's life*); it may refer in particular to the mathematical process of subtraction: *7 minus 5 leaves a remainder of 2.* BALANCE, originally a bookkeeper's term referring to the amount of money left to one's account (*a bank balance*), is often used colloquially as a synonym for REMAINDER: *the balance of the day.* RESIDUE is used particularly to designate what remains as the result of a process; this is usually a chemical process, but the word may also refer to a legal process concerning inheritance: *a residue of ash left from burning leaves.* SURPLUS suggests that what remains is in excess of what was needed: *a surplus of goods.*

re·main·der·man (ri mān′dər mən), *n., pl.* **-men.** *Law.* a person who owns a remainder. [REMAINDER + MAN¹]

re·make (*v.* rē māk′; *n.* rē′māk′), *v.,* **-made, -mak·ing,** *n.* —*v.t.* **1.** to make again or anew. **2.** *Motion Pictures.* to film again, as a picture or screenplay. —*n.* **3.** a screenplay or motion picture that is to be, or has been, filmed again. [RE- + MAKE] —**re·mak′er,** *n.*

re·man (rē man′), *v.t.,* **-manned, -man·ning. 1.** to man again; furnish with a fresh supply of men. **2.** to restore the manliness or courage of. [RE- + MAN¹]

re·mand (ri mand′, -mänd′), *v.t.* **1.** to send back, remit, or consign again. **2.** *Law.* **a.** to send back (a case) to a lower court from which it was appealed, with instructions as to what further proceedings should be had. **b.** (of a court or magistrate) to send back (a prisoner or accused person) into custody, as to await further proceedings. —*n.* **3.** the act of remanding. **4.** the state of being remanded. **5.** a person remanded. [ME *remaund(en)* < OF *remand(er)* < LL *remandāre* to repeat a command, send back word, equiv. to *re-* RE- + *mandāre* to entrust, enjoin; see MANDATE]

remand′ home′, *Brit.* a detention home for juvenile offenders aged 8–16 years. Cf. **borstal.**

rem·a·nence (rem′ə nəns), *n. Elect.* the magnetic flux that remains in a magnetic circuit after an applied magnetomotive force has been removed. [REMAN(ENT) + -ENCE]

rem·a·nent (rem′ə nənt), *adj.* remaining; left behind. [< L *remanent-* (s. of *remanēns*), prp. of *remanēre.* See REMAIN, -ENT]

re·mar·gin (rē mär′jin), *v.i.* to provide additional cash or collateral to a broker in order to keep secure stock bought on margin. [RE- + MARGIN]

re·mark (ri märk′), *v.t.* **1.** to say casually, as in making a comment: *Someone remarked that tomorrow would be a warm day.* **2.** to note; perceive; observe: *I remarked a slight accent in her speech.* **3.** *Obs.* to mark distinctively. —*v.i.* **4.** to make a remark or observation (usually fol. by *on* or *upon*): *He remarked on her lack of wit or intelligence.* —*n.* **5.** the act of remarking; notice. **6.** comment or mention: *to let a thing pass without remark.* **7.** a casual or brief expression of thought or opinion. **8.** *Fine Arts.* remarque. [< F, MF *remarqu(er)* (to) note, heed, equiv. to *re-* RE- + *marquer* to MARK¹] —**re·mark′er,** *n.*
—**Syn. 2.** heed, regard, notice. **4.** comment. **5.** regard. **7.** REMARK, COMMENT, NOTE, OBSERVATION imply giving special attention, an opinion, or a judgment. A REMARK is usually a casual and passing expression of opinion: *a remark about a play.* A COMMENT expresses judgment or explains a particular point: *a comment on the author's scholarship.* A NOTE is a memorandum or explanation, as in the margin of a page: *a note explaining a passage.* OBSERVATION suggests a note based on judgment and experience: *an observation on customary usages.* —**Ant. 2.** ignore.

re·mark·a·ble (ri mär′kə bəl), *adj.* **1.** notably or conspicuously unusual; extraordinary: *a remarkable change.* **2.** worthy of notice or attention. [< F *remarquable.* See REMARK, -ABLE] —**re·mark′a·bil′i·ty, re·mark′a·ble·ness,** *n.* —**re·mark′a·bly,** *adv.*
—**Syn. 2.** notable, noteworthy, striking, extraordinary, wonderful, unusual, singular, uncommon. —**Ant. 1, 2.** common, ordinary.

re·marque (ri märk′), *n. Fine Arts.* **1.** a distinguishing mark or peculiarity indicating a particular stage of a plate. **2.** a small sketch engraved in the margin of a plate, and usually removed after a number of early proofs have been printed. **3.** a plate so marked. Also, **remark.** [< F; see REMARK]

Re·marque (ri märk′; *Ger.* rə märk′), *n.* **E·rich Ma·ri·a** (er′ik mə rē′ə; *Ger.* ā′rĭKH mä rē′ä), born 1898, German novelist in the U.S.

Rem·brandt (rem′brant, -bränt; *Du.* rem′bränt), *n.* (*Rembrandt Harmenszoon van Rijn* or *van Ryn*) 1606–69, Dutch painter. —**Rem′brandt·esque′, Rem′brandt·ish,** *adj.*

re·me·di·a·ble (ri mē′dē ə bəl), *adj.* capable of being remedied. [ME < MF < LL *remediābil(is)* curable. See REMEDY, -ABLE] —**re·me′di·a·ble·ness,** *n.* —**re·me′di·a·bly,** *adv.*

re·me·di·al (ri mē′dē əl), *adj.* **1.** affording remedy; tending to remedy something. **2.** intended to correct or improve one's skill in a specified field: *remedial English.* [< LL *remediāl(is).* See REMEDY, -AL¹] —**re·me′di·al·ly,** *adv.*

reme′dial read′ing, instruction in reading aimed at increasing speed and comprehension by correcting poor reading habits.

re·me·di·a·tion (ri mē′dē ā′shən), *n.* the correction of something bad or defective.

rem·e·di·less (rem′i dē lis), *adj.* not admitting of remedy, as disease, trouble, damage, etc.; unremediable. [ME; see REMEDY, -LESS]

rem·e·dy (rem′i dē), *n., pl.* **-dies,** *v.,* **-died, -dy·ing.** —*n.* **1.** something that cures or relieves a disease or bodily disorder; a healing medicine, application, or treatment. **2.** something that corrects or removes an evil of any kind. **3.** *Law.* legal redress; the legal means of enforcing a right or redressing a wrong. **4.** *Coinage.* a certain allowance at the mint for deviation from the standard weight and fineness of coins; tolerance. —*v.t.* **5.** to cure, relieve, or heal. **6.** to restore to the natural or proper condition; put right: *to remedy a matter.* **7.** to counteract or remove: *to remedy an evil.* [ME *remedie* < AF < L *remedi(um),* equiv. to *remed(ērī)* (*re-* RE- + *med-* heal) + *-ium* -Y³]
—**Syn. 1.** cure, restorative, specific, medicament, medication. **2.** corrective, antidote. **5.** See **cure. 6.** repair, correct, redress, renew. —**Ant. 5.** worsen.

re·mem·ber (ri mem′bər), *v.t.* **1.** to recall to the mind by an act or effort of memory; think of again: *I'll try to remember the exact date.* **2.** to retain in the memory; keep in mind; remain aware of: *Remember your appointment with the dentist.* **3.** to have (something) come into the mind again: *I just remembered that it's your birthday today.* **4.** to bear (a person) in mind as deserving a gift, reward, or fee: *The company always remembers us at Christmas.* **5.** to reward; tip: *Don't forget to remember the doorman.* **6.** to mention to another as sending kindly greetings: *Remember me to your family.* **7.** *Archaic.* to remind. —*v.i.* **8.** to possess or exercise the faculty of memory. **9.** to have recollection (often fol. by *of*): *I'm getting too old to remember very well of my boyhood.* [ME *remembre(n)* < OF *remembr(er)* < LL *rememorārī,* equiv. to *re-* RE- + L *memor* mindful; see MEMORY] —**re·mem′ber·er,** *n.*
—**Syn. 1.** REMEMBER, RECALL, RECOLLECT refer to bringing back before the conscious mind things which exist in the memory. REMEMBER implies that a thing exists in the memory, though not actually present in the thoughts at the moment: *to remember the days of one's childhood.* RECALL, a rather conversational word, implies a voluntary effort, though not a great one: *to recall the words of a song.* RECOLLECT implies an earnest voluntary effort to remember some definite, desired fact or thing: *I cannot recollect the exact circumstances.* —**Ant. 1, 2.** forget.

re·mem·brance (ri mem′brəns), *n.* **1.** a retained mental impression; memory. **2.** the act or fact of remembering. **3.** the power or faculty of remembering. **4.** the length of time over which recollection or memory extends. **5.** the state of being remembered; commemoration: *to hold someone's name in remembrance.* **6.** something that serves to bring to mind or keep in mind some place, person, event, etc.; memento. **7.** a gift given as a token of love or friendship: *I sent her a small remembrance on Mother's Day.* **8. remembrances,** greetings; respects. [ME < OF; see REMEMBER, -ANCE]
—**Syn. 1.** recollection, reminiscence. **3.** memory. **6.** keepsake, trophy, souvenir, token, memorial.

Remem′brance Day′, (in Canada) November 11, set apart for observances in memory of those who died in World War I, similar to the U.S. Armistice Day.

Remem′brance of Things′ Past′, a novel (1913–27) by Marcel Proust. French, **À la Recherche du Temps Perdu.**

re·mem·branc·er (ri mem′brən sər), *n.* **1.** one who reminds another of something. **2.** one engaged to do this. **3.** a reminder; memento; souvenir. **4.** (*usually cap.*) **a.** See **King's Remembrancer, Queen's Remembrancer. b.** (formerly) any of certain officials of the Court of Exchequer. **5.** an officer of the corporation of the City of London. [ME < AF; see REMEMBRANCE, -ER¹]

re·mex (rē′meks), *n., pl.* **rem·i·ges** (rem′i jēz′). *Ornith.* one of the flight feathers of the wing. [< L: oarsman, equiv. to *rēm(us)* oar + *-ex* agent suffix] —**re·mig·i·al** (ri mij′ē əl), *adj.*

remi-, a learned borrowing from Latin meaning "oar," used in the formation of compound words: *remiform.* [< L, comb. form of *rēmus* oar]

rem·i·form (rem′ə fôrm′), *adj.* shaped like an oar. [REMI- + -FORM]

rem·i·grant (rem′ə grənt), *n.* one who or that which returns. [< L *remigrant-* (s. of *remigrāns*), prp. of *remigrāre.* See RE-, MIGRATE, -ANT]

re·mind (ri mīnd′), *v.t.* to cause (a person) to remember: *Remind me to phone him tomorrow.* [RE- + MIND] —**re·mind′er,** *n.*

re·mind·ful (ri mīnd′fəl), *adj.* **1.** reviving memory of something; reminiscent. **2.** retaining memory of something; mindful. [REMIND + -FUL]

Rem·ing·ton (rem′ing tən), *n.* **Frederic,** 1861–1909, U.S. painter and sculptor.

rem·i·nisce (rem′ə nis′), *v.i.,* **-nisced, -nisc·ing.** to recall past experiences, events, etc.; indulge in reminiscence. [back formation from REMINISCENCE]
—**Syn.** remember, recollect, muse.

rem·i·nis·cence (rem′ə nis′əns), *n.* **1.** the act or process of recalling past experiences, events, etc. **2.** a mental impression retained and revived. **3.** Often, **reminiscences.** a recollection narrated or told: *reminiscences of an American soldier.* **4.** something that recalls or suggests something else. **5.** (in Platonic philosophy) anamnesis (def. 2). [< MF < LL *reminiscentia.* See REMINISCENT, -ENCE]
—**Syn. 1.** recollection. **2.** memory. **3.** anecdote, tale, memoir. **4.** reminder.

rem·i·nis·cent (rem′ə nis′ənt), *adj.* **1.** awakening memories of something else; suggestive (usually fol. by *of*): *His style of writing is reminiscent of Melville's.* **2.** characterized by or of the nature of reminiscence or reminiscences. **3.** given to reminiscence: *a reminiscent old sailor.* [< L *reminiscent-* (s. of *reminiscēns*) remembering, prp. of *reminiscī,* equiv. to *re-* RE- + *-minisc-* (deriv. of *ment-,* s. of *mēns* mind) + *-ent-* -ENT] —**rem′i·nis′cent·ly,** *adv.*

rem·i·ped (rem′ə ped′), *Zool.* —*adj.* **1.** having feet adapted for use as oars. —*n.* **2.** a remiped animal. [< F *rémipède.* See REMI-, -PED]

re·mise (ri mīz′), *v.t.,* **-mised, -mis·ing.** *Law.* to give up a claim to; surrender by deed. [ME < MF, ptp. (fem.) of *remettre* to put back, deliver < L *remittere* to REMIT]

re·miss (ri mis′), *adj.* **1.** negligent, careless, or slow in performing one's duty, business, etc.: *He's terribly remiss in his work.* **2.** characterized by negligence or carelessness. **3.** lacking force or energy; languid; sluggish. [ME < L *remiss(us)* sent back, relaxed (ptp. of *remittere*); see REMIT] —**re·miss′ly,** *adv.* —**re·miss′ness,** *n.*
—**Syn. 1, 2.** derelict, thoughtless, lax, slack, neglectful. **3.** dilatory, slothful, slow.

re·mis·si·ble (ri mis′ə bəl), *adj.* that may be remitted. [< MF < LL *remissibil(is).* See REMISS, -IBLE] —**re·mis′si·bil′i·ty, re·mis′si·ble·ness,** *n.*

re·mis·sion (ri mish′ən), *n.* **1.** the act of remitting. **2.** pardon; forgiveness, as of sins or offenses. **3.** abatement or diminution, as of diligence, labor, intensity, etc. **4.** the relinquishment of a payment, obligation, etc. **5.** a temporary or permanent decrease or subsidence of manifestations of a disease. [ME < OF < L *remissiōn-* (s. of *remissiō*). See REMISS, -ION]
—**Syn. 2.** absolution. **3.** lessening, relaxation. **4.** release. **5.** pause, interruption, hiatus, suspension, abatement. —**Ant. 2.** blame, censure. **3.** intensification.

re·mis·sive (ri mis′iv), *adj.* **1.** characterized by remission or decrease. **2.** producing or granting pardon or remission. [< ML *remissīv(us).* See REMISS, -IVE] —**re·mis′sive·ly,** *adv.* —**re·mis′sive·ness,** *n.*

re·mit (ri mit′), *v.,* **-mit·ted, -mit·ting,** *n.* —*v.t.* **1.** to transmit or send (money) to a person or place, usually in payment. **2.** to refrain from inflicting or enforcing, as a punishment, sentence, etc. **3.** to refrain from exacting, as a payment or service. **4.** to pardon or forgive (a sin, offense, etc.). **5.** to slacken; abate; relax: *to remit watchfulness.* **6.** to give back: *to remit a fine.* **7.** *Law.* to send back (a case) to an inferior court for further action. **8.** to put back into a previous position or condition. **9.** to put off; postpone; defer. **10.** *Obs.* to set free; release. **11.** *Obs.* to send back to prison or custody. **12.** *Obs.* to give up; surrender. —*v.i.* **13.** to transmit money, a check, etc., as in payment. **14.** to abate for a time or at intervals, as a fever. **15.** to slacken; abate. —*n.* **16.** *Law.* a transfer of the record

re′mag·net·i·za′tion, *n.*
re·mag′net·ize′, *v.t.,* **-ized, -iz·ing.**
re·mag′ni·fy′, *v.t.,* **-fied, -fy·ing.**
re·mail′, *v.t.*
re·maim′, *v.t.*
re·man′i·fest′, *v.t.*
re′man·i·fes·ta′tion, *n.*
re′man·u·fac′ture, *v.t.,* **-tured, -tur·ing.**
re·map′, *v.t.,* **-mapped, -map·ping.**
re·mar′ket, *v.t.*
re·mar′riage, *n.*
re·mar′ry, *v.,* **-ried, -ry·ing.**
re·mar′shal, *v.t.,* **-shaled, -shal·ing** or (*esp. Brit.*) **-shalled, -shal·ing.**
re·mas′ter, *v.t.*
re·mas′ter·y, *n., pl.* **-ter·ies.**
re·mas′ti·cate′, *v.,* **-cat·ed, -cat·ing.**
re′mas·ti·ca′tion, *n.*
re·match′, *v.t.*
re′ma·te′ri·al·i·za′tion, *n.*
re′ma·te′ri·al·ize′, *v.,* **-ized, -iz·ing.**
re′ma·tric′u·late′, *v.,* **-lat·ed, -lat·ing.**
re·meas′ure, *v.t.,* **-ured, -ur·ing.**
re·meas′ure·ment, *n.*
re·me′di·ate′, *v.t.,* **-at·ed, -at·ing.**
re·melt′, *v.t.*
re·mem′o·rize′, *v.t.,* **-rized, -riz·ing.**
re·mend′, *v.*
re·men′tion, *v.t.*
re·merge′, *v.,* **-merged, -merg·ing.**
re·mi′grate, *v.i.,* **-grat·ed, -grat·ing.**
re′mi·gra′tion, *n.*
re′mil′i·ta·ri·za′tion, *n.*
re·mil′i·ta·rize′, *v.t.,* **-rized, -riz·ing.**
re·mill′, *v.t.*
re·mill′a·ble, *adj.*
re·min′gle, *v.,* **-gled, -gling.**
re·mint′, *v.t.*

of an action from one tribunal to another, particularly from an appellate court to the court of original jurisdiction. [ME *remitt(en)* < L *remitt(ere)* (to) send back, let go back, concede, allow, equiv. to *re-* RE- + *mittere* to send] —**re·mit′ta·ble,** *adj.*
—**Syn. 1.** forward. **4.** excuse, overlook. **5.** diminish. **6.** return, restore. —**Ant. 1.** retain. **4.** condemn. **5.** increase.

re·mit·tal (ri mit′əl), *n.* a remission. [REMIT + -AL[2]]

re·mit·tance (ri mit′əns), *n.* **1.** the sending of money, checks, etc., to a recipient at a distance. **2.** money or its equivalent sent from one place to another. [REMIT + -ANCE]

remit′tance man′, one who is supported abroad chiefly by remittances from home.

re·mit·tee (ri mi tē′, -mit′ē), *n. Law.* a person or company to which a remittance is made. [REMIT + -EE]

re·mit·tent (ri mit′ənt), *adj.* **1.** abating for a time or at intervals: *remittent symptoms.* **2.** of, pertaining to, or characterized by a remittent fever. —*n.* **3.** a remittent fever. [< L *remittent-* (s. of *remittēns*) sending back (prp. of *remittere*). See REMIT, -ENT] —**re·mit′tence, re·mit′ten·cy,** *n.* —**re·mit′tent·ly,** *adv.*

re·mit·ter (ri mit′ər), *n. Law.* **1.** the principle or operation by which a person who enters on an estate by a defective title, and who previously had an earlier and more valid title to it, is adjudged to hold it by the earlier and more valid one. **2.** the act of remitting a case to another court for decision. **3.** restoration, as to a former right or condition. [REMIT + -ER[3]]

re·mit·tor (ri mit′ər), *n. Law.* a person or company that makes a remittance. [REMIT + -OR[2]]

rem·nant (rem′nənt), *n.* **1.** a remaining, usually small part, quantity, number, or the like. **2.** a fragment or scrap. **3.** a small, unsold or unused piece of cloth, lace, etc., as at the end of a bolt. **4.** a trace; vestige: *remnants of former greatness.* —*adj.* **5.** remaining; leftover. [ME *remna(u)nt,* contr. of *remenant* < OF, prp. of *remenoir* to REMAIN] —**rem′nant·al,** *adj.*
—**Syn. 1.** remainder, residue, residuum; rest, remains.

re·mod·el (rē mod′əl), *v.t.,* **-eled, -el·ing** or (*esp. Brit.*) **-elled, -el·ling. 1.** to model again. **2.** to reconstruct; make over. [RE- + MODEL] —**re·mod′el·er;** *esp. Brit.,* **re·mod′el·ler,** *n.*
—**Syn. 2.** renew, renovate, recreate, repair.

re·mo·lade (rē′mə läd′), *n.* rémoulade.

re·mon·e·tise (rē mon′i tīz′, -mun′-), *v.t.,* **-tised, -tis·ing.** *Chiefly Brit.* remonetize. —**re·mon′e·ti·sa′tion,** *n.*

re·mon·e·tize (rē mon′i tīz′, -mun′-), *v.t.,* **-tized, -tiz·ing.** to restore to use as legal tender: *to remonetize silver.* [RE- + MONETIZE] —**re·mon′e·ti·za′tion,** *n.*

re·mon·strance (ri mon′strəns), *n.* **1.** the act of remonstrating; expostulation. **2.** a protest: *deaf to remonstrances.* [< MF, equiv. to *remonstr(er)* (< ML *remonstrāre* to point out; see REMONSTRATE) + *-ance* -ANCE]

re·mon·strant (ri mon′strənt), *adj.* **1.** remonstrating; expostulatory. —*n.* **2.** one who remonstrates. **3.** (*cap.*) one of the Dutch Arminians whose doctrinal differences from strict Calvinists were set forth in 1610. [< ML *remonstrant-* (s. of *remonstrāns,* prp. of *remonstrāre*). See REMONSTRATE, -ANT] —**re·mon′strant·ly,** *adv.*

re·mon·strate (ri mon′strāt), *v.,* **-strat·ed, -strat·ing.** —*v.t.* **1.** to say or plead in protest, objection, or disapproval. **2.** *Obs.* to point out; show. —*v.i.* **3.** to present reasons in complaint; plead in protest. [< ML *remonstrāt(us)* exhibited, demonstrated, ptp. of *remonstrāre,* equiv. to *re-* RE- + *monstrāre* to show; see -ATE[1]] —**re·mon′strat·ing·ly,** *adv.* —**re·mon·stra·tion** (rē′mon strā′shən, rem′ən-), *n.* —**re·mon·stra·tive** (ri mon′strə tiv), *adj.* —**re·mon′stra·tive·ly,** *adv.* —**re·mon·stra·tor** (ri mon′strā tər), *n.*
—**Syn. 3.** argue, object, expostulate.

re·mon·tant (ri mon′tənt), *adj.* **1.** (of certain roses) blooming more than once in a season. —*n.* **2.** a remontant rose. [< F, prp. of *remonter* to REMOUNT]

rem·on·toire (rem′ən twär′), *n. Horol.* **1.** a device for periodically raising the weight or winding the spring driving a clock mechanism. **2.** an escapement for giving a uniform impulse to a pendulum or balance. Also, **rem′on·toir′.** [< F: winder, deriv. of *remonter* to raise, wind up, REMOUNT; see -ORY[2]]

Remora, *Echeneis naucrates* (Length 3 ft.)

rem·o·ra (rem′ər ə), *n.* **1.** any of several fishes of the family *Echeneididae,* having on the top of the head a sucking disk by which they can attach themselves to sharks, turtles, ships, and other moving objects. **2.** *Archaic.* an obstacle, hindrance, or obstruction. [< L: lit., delay, hindrance, equiv. to *re-* RE- + *mora* delay]

re·morse (ri môrs′), *n.* **1.** deep and painful regret for wrongdoing; compunction. **2.** *Obs.* pity; compassion. [ME < MF *remors* < LL *remors(um),* L: bitten again, harassed (ptp. of *remordēre*), equiv. to *re-* RE- + *mord-* bite, sting, attack; see MORDANT]
—**Syn. 1.** contrition. See **regret.**

re·morse·ful (ri môrs′fəl), *adj.* **1.** full of remorse. **2.** characterized by or due to remorse: *a remorseful mood.* [REMORSE + -FUL] —**re·morse′ful·ly,** *adv.* —**re·morse′ful·ness,** *n.*
—**Syn. 1, 2.** contrite, regretful, penitent.

re·morse·less (ri môrs′lis), *adj.* without remorse; merciless; pitiless; relentless. [REMORSE + -LESS] —**re·morse′less·ly,** *adv.* —**re·morse′less·ness,** *n.*
—**Syn.** ruthless, unrelenting, implacable, inexorable, cruel.

re·mote (ri mōt′), *adj.,* **-mot·er, -mot·est,** *n.* —*adj.* **1.** far apart; far distant in space; situated at some distance away: *the remote corners of the earth; a remote house.* **2.** out-of-the-way; secluded: *a remote village; a remote mountain top.* **3.** distant in time: *remote antiquity.* **4.** distant in relationship or connection: *a remote ancestor.* **5.** far off; abstracted; removed: *principles remote from actions.* **6.** not direct, primary, or proximate; not directly involved or influential: *the remote causes of the war.* **7.** slight or faint; unlikely: *not the remotest idea; a remote chance.* **8.** reserved and distant in manner; aloof; not warmly cordial. —*n.* **9.** Also called **nemo.** *Radio and Television.* a program originating outside of a studio, as a sports event or a political convention. [< L *remōt(us)* moved back, ptp. of *removēre;* see REMOVE] —**re·mote′ly,** *adv.* —**re·mote′ness,** *n.*
—**Syn. 2.** sequestered, isolated, removed, apart, solitary. **7.** inconsiderable. **8.** withdrawn. —**Ant. 1.** close, near.

remote′ control′, control of the operation or performance of an apparatus from a distance, as the control of a guided missile by radio signals. —**re·mote′-con·trol′,** *adj.*

re·mo·tion (ri mō′shən), *n.* **1.** the act of removing; removal. **2.** *Obs.* departure. [ME *remosion* < L *remōtiōn-* (s. of *remōtiō*) a putting back, removing. See REMOTE, -ION]

ré·mou·lade (rā′mə läd′; *Fr.* rā mo͞o lȧd′), *n.* a cold sauce made with mayonnaise and various condiments and herbs, as chopped pickles, capers, mustard, parsley, chervil, and tarragon. Also, **remolade.** [< F < It *remolata,* alter. of L *armoracea* horseradish; see -ADE[1]]

re·mount (*v.* rē mount′; *n.* rē′mount′, rē mount′), *v.t., v.i.* **1.** to mount again; reascend. —*n.* **2.** a fresh horse or supply of fresh horses. [ME *remounten* < OF *remonter.* See RE-, MOUNT[1]]

re·mov·a·ble (ri mo͞o′və bəl), *adj.* **1.** that may be removed. **2.** *Math.* **a.** (of a singularity of a function of a complex variable) noting that the function is not analytic at the point but that the function can be redefined so as to be analytic at the point. **b.** (of a discontinuity) noting that the function is discontinuous at the point but that the function can be redefined so as to be continuous at the point. Cf. **essential** (def. 5). [REMOVE + -ABLE] —**re·mov′a·bil′i·ty, re·mov′a·ble·ness,** *n.* —**re·mov′a·bly,** *adv.*

re·mov·al (ri mo͞o′vəl), *n.* **1.** the act of removing. **2.** change of residence, position, etc. **3.** dismissal, as from an office. [REMOVE + -AL[2]]

re·move (ri mo͞ov′), *v.,* **-moved, -mov·ing.** *n.* —*v.t.* **1.** to move from a place or position; take away or off: *to remove the napkins from the table.* **2.** to take off or shed (an article of clothing): *to remove one's jacket.* **3.** to move or shift to another place or position; transfer: *She removed the painting to another wall.* **4.** to put out; send away: *to remove a tenant.* **5.** to dismiss or force from a position or office; discharge: *They removed him for embezzling.* **6.** to take away, withdraw, or eliminate: *to remove the threat of danger.* **7.** to do away with; put an end to: *to remove a stain; to remove the source of disease.* **8.** to kill; assassinate. —*v.i.* **9.** to move from one place to another, esp. to another locality or residence: *We remove to Newport early in July.* **10.** to go away; depart; disappear. —*n.* **11.** the act of removing. **12.** a removal from one place, as of residence, to another. **13.** the distance by which one person, place, or thing is separated from another: *to see something at a remove.* **14.** a distance from the reality of something as a result of psychological detachment or lack of experience: *to criticize something at a remove.* **15.** a degree of difference or of time or distance: *a folk survival, at many removes, of a druidic rite.* **16.** a step or degree, as in a graded scale. **17.** *Brit.* a promotion of a pupil to a higher class or division at school. [ME *remove(n)* < OF *remouv(oir)* < L *removēre.* See RE-, MOVE]
—**Syn. 1.** dislodge. **3.** displace, transport. **6.** extract, abstract. **8.** destroy, murder. —**Ant. 1.** leave. **9.** remain.

re·moved (ri mo͞ovd′), *adj.* **1.** remote; separate; not connected with; distinct from. **2.** (of a cousin) distant by a given number of degrees of descent or kinship: *A first cousin twice removed could be a first cousin's grandchild.* [REMOVE + -ED[2]] —**re·mov·ed·ly** (ri mo͞o′vid lē, -mo͞ovd′-), *adv.* —**re·mov′ed·ness,** *n.*
—**Syn. 1.** withdrawn, abstracted; isolated, solitary, apart.

re·mov·er (ri mo͞o′vər), *n.* **1.** one who or that which removes. **2.** *Law.* the transfer of a case from one court to another, as by a writ of error. [REMOVE + -ER[1]]

Rem·scheid (rem′shīt), *n.* a city in W West Germany, in the Ruhr region. 128,600 (1963).

Rem·sen (rem′sən), *n.* **Ira,** 1846–1927, U.S. chemist and educator.

re·mu·da (ri mo͞o′də; *Sp.* re mo͞o′ᵺä), *n., pl.* **-das** (-dəz; *Sp.* -ᵺäs). a group of saddle horses from which ranch hands choose mounts for the day. [< Amer Sp: a change (of horses), Sp: exchange, deriv. of *remudar,* equiv. to *re-* RE- + *mudar* to change (< L *mūtāre*); see MOTT]

re·mu·ner·ate (ri myo͞o′nə rāt′), *v.t.,* **-at·ed, -at·ing. 1.** to pay, recompense, or reward for work, trouble, etc. **2.** to yield a recompense for (work, services, etc.). [< L *remūnerāt(us)* repaid, rewarded (ptp. of *remūnerārī*), equiv. to *re-* RE- + *mūnerare* to give, bestow (deriv. of *mūner-,* s. of *munus* gift) + *-ātus* -ATE[1]] —**re·mu′ner·a·bil′i·ty,** *n.* —**re·mu′ner·a·ble,** *adj.* —**re·mu′ner·a·bly,** *adv.* —**re·mu′ner·a′tor,** *n.*
—**Syn. 1.** reimburse, requite, compensate.

re·mu·ner·a·tion (ri myo͞o′nə rā′shən), *n.* **1.** the act of remunerating. **2.** that which remunerates; reward; pay: *He received little remuneration for his services.* [late ME *remuneracion* < L *remūnerātiōn-* (s. of *remūnerātiō*), equiv. to *remūnerāt(us)* (see REMUNERATE) + *-iōn-* -ION]

re·mu·ner·a·tive (ri myo͞o′nə rā′tiv, -nər ə tiv), *adj.* **1.** affording remuneration; profitable: *remunerative work.* **2.** that remunerates. [REMUNERATE + -IVE] —**re·mu·ner·a·tive·ly** (ri myo͞o′nə rā′tiv lē, -nər ə tiv-), *adv.* —**re·mu′ner·a′tive·ness,** *n.*

Re·mus (rē′məs), *n.* **1.** *Rom. Legend.* See under **Romulus. 2. Uncle.** See **Uncle Remus.**

Re·na (rē′nə), *n.* a girl's given name. Also, **Rina.**

Ren·ais·sance (ren′i säns′, -zäns′, ren′i säns′, -zäns′, ri nā′səns; *Fr.* rə ne säɴs′), *n.* Also, **Renascence. 1.** the activity, spirit, or time of the great revival of art, literature, and learning in Europe beginning in the 14th century and extending to the 17th century, marking the transition from the medieval to the modern world. **2.** the forms and treatments in art used during this period. **3.** (*sometimes l.c.*) any similar revival in the world of art and learning. **4.** (*l.c.*) a renewal of life, vigor, interest, etc.; rebirth; revival: *a moral renaissance.* —*adj.* **5.** of, pertaining to, or suggestive of the European Renaissance of the 14th through the 17th centuries: *Renaissance attitudes.* **6.** noting or pertaining to the group of styles of architecture existing in Italy in the 15th and 16th centuries as adaptations of ancient Roman architectural details or compositional forms to contemporary uses, characterized at first by the free and inventive use of isolated details, later by the more imitative use of whole orders and compositional arrangements, with great attention to the formulation of compositional rules after the precepts of Vitruvius and the precedents of existing ruins, and at all periods by an emphasis on symmetry, exact mathematical relationships between parts, and a general effect of simplicity and repose. **7.** noting or pertaining to any of the various adaptations of this group of styles in foreign architecture characterized typically by the playful or grotesque use of isolated details in more or less traditional buildings. **8.** noting or pertaining to the furnishings or decorations of the Renaissance, in which motifs of classical derivation frequently appear. [< F MF: rebirth, equiv. to *renaiss-* (s. of *renaistre* to be born again < L *renascī,* equiv. to *re-* RE- + *nascī* to be born) + *-ance* -ANCE]

Renaissance chest (Florence, 16th century)

Ren′aissance man′, 1. the typical educated, cultured man of the Renaissance, who, because the knowledge of the world was generally limited, was able to know everything there was to know about a great variety of given subjects. **2.** a present-day man with many broad interests who has the opportunity to indulge himself in them so as to acquire a knowledge of each that is more than superficial.

re·nal (rēn′əl), *adj.* of or pertaining to the kidneys or the surrounding regions. [< LL *rēnāl(is),* equiv. to L *rēn(ēs)* kidneys (pl.) + *-ālis* -AL[1]]

re′nal cal′culus, *Pathol.* See **kidney stone.**

Re·nan (ri nan′; *Fr.* rə näɴ′), *n.* **Er·nest** (ûr′nist; *Fr.* er nest′), 1823–92, French philologist, historian, and critic.

Ren·ard (ren′ərd), *n.* Reynard. —**Ren·ard·ine** (ren′ər din), *adj.*

Re·nas·cence (ri nas′əns), *n.* (*sometimes l.c.*) Renaissance. [RENASC(ENT) + -ENCE]

re·nas·cent (ri nas′ənt), *adj.* being reborn; springing again into being or vigor: *a renascent interest in Henry James.* [< L *renascent-* (s. of *renascēns*), prp. of *renascī.* See RENAISSANCE, -ENT]

Re·na·ta (rə nä′tə; *It.* re nä′tä), *n.* a girl's given name.

Re·nault (rə nōlt′; *Fr.* rə nō′), *n.* **Lou·is** (lo͞o′ē; *Fr.* lwē), 1843–1918, French jurist: Nobel peace prize 1907.

ren·con·tre (ren kon′tər; *Fr.* räɴ kôɴ′trᵊ), *n., pl.* **-tres** (-tərz; *Fr.* -trᵊ). rencounter. [< F]

ren·coun·ter (ren koun′tər), *n.* Also, **rencontre. 1.** a hostile meeting; battle. **2.** a contest of any kind. **3.** a casual meeting. —*v.t., v.i.* **4.** to encounter casually. **5.** *Obs.* to meet hostilely. [< MF *rencontr(er).* See RE-, ENCOUNTER]

rend (rend), *v.,* **rent, rend·ing.** —*v.t.* **1.** to separate into parts with force or violence: *The storm rent the ship to pieces.* **2.** to tear apart, split, or divide: *a racial problem which is rending the nation.* **3.** to pull or tear violently (often fol. by *away, off, up,* etc.). **4.** to tear (one's garments or hair) in grief, rage, etc. **5.** to disturb (the air) sharply with loud noise. **6.** to harrow or distress (the heart) with painful feelings. —*v.i.* **7.** to render or tear something. **8.** to become torn, split, or divided. [ME *rende(n),* OE *rendan;* c. OFris *renda*] —**rend′i·ble,** *adj.*
—**Syn. 2.** rive, sunder, sever, cleave, chop, fracture, rupture. See **tear**[2].

ren·der[1] (ren′dər), *v.t.* **1.** to cause to be or become; make: *to render someone helpless.* **2.** to do; perform: *to render a service.* **3.** to furnish; provide: *to render aid.* **4.** to exhibit or show (obedience, attention, etc.). **5.** to present for consideration, approval, payment, action, etc., as an account. **6.** *Law.* to return; to make (a payment in money, kind, or service) as by a tenant to his superior. **7.** to pay as due (a tax, tribute, etc.): "*Render unto Caesar the things that are Caesar's.*" **8.** to deliver formally or officially; hand down: *to render a verdict.* **9.** to translate into another language: *The effect of the original Russian was lost when they rendered his poems into English.* **10.** to represent; depict, as in painting: *He renders landscapes with great skill and artistry.* **11.** to represent (a perspective view of a projected building) in drawing or painting. **12.** to bring out the meaning of by performance or execution; interpret, as a part in a drama, a piece of music, etc. **13.** to give in return or requital. **14.** to give back; restore (often fol. by *back*). **15.** to give up; surrender. **16.** *Building Trades.* to cover (masonry) with a first coat of plaster. **17.** *Naut.* **a.** to pass (a rope) through a block or the like. **b.** to ease the tension on (a line, chain, etc.). **18.** to melt, as fat; clarify or extract by melting; try out: *to render lard.* —*v.i.* **19.** to provide due reward. **20.** *Naut.* (of a line, chain, etc.) to pass readily through a block, the holes of a deadeye, etc. **21.** to try out oil from fat, blubber, etc., by melting. —*n.* **22.** *Building Trades.* a first coat of plaster for a masonry surface. [ME *rendre(n)* < MF *rendre* < VL *rendere, alter. (formed by analogy with *prendere* to take) of *reddere* to give back, equiv. to *red-* RE- + *dare* to give] —**ren′der·a·ble,** *adj.* —**ren′der·er,** *n.*
—**Syn. 3.** give, supply, contribute, afford. **4.** demonstrate. **15.** cede, yield.

re·mix′, *v.,* **-mixed** or **-mixt, -mix·ing.**
re/mo·bi·li·za′tion, *n.*
re·mo′bi·lize′, *v.,* **-lized, -liz·ing.**
re/mod·i·fi·ca′tion, *n.*
re·mod′i·fy′, *v.,* **-fied, -fy·ing.**
re·mod′u·late′, *v.t.,* **-lat·ed, -lat·ing.**
re·mold′, *v.*
re·mol′li·fy′, *v.t.,* **-fied, -fy·ing.**
re·mort′gage, *v.t.,* **-gaged, -gag·ing.**
re·mould′, *v.*
re/mul·ti·pli·ca′tion, *n.*
re·mul′ti·ply′, *v.,* **-plied, -ply·ing.**
re·nail′, *v.t.*
re·name′, *v.t.,* **-named, -nam·ing.**
re·na′tion·al·ize′, *v.,* **-ized, -iz·ing.**
re·nav′i·gate′, *v.t.,* **-gat·ed, -gat·ing.**
re/nav·i·ga′tion, *n.*

rend·er[2] (ren′dər), *n.* one who or that which rends. [REND + -ER[1]]

ren·der·ing (ren′dər ing), *n.* **1.** an instance of or the act of interpretation, rendition, or depiction, as of a dramatic part, a musical composition, an idea, etc.: *Her rendering of the part of Hedda was one of the triumphs of her career.* **2.** a translation: *I prefer Chapman's rendering of Homer.* **3.** a representation of a building, interior, etc., executed in perspective and usually done for purposes of presentation. **4.** *Building Trades.* render[1] (def. 22). [ME; see RENDER, -ING[1]]

ren′dering works′, (*construed as sing.*) a factory or plant that renders and processes livestock carcasses into tallow, hides, fertilizer, etc. Also called **ren′dering plant′.**

ren·dez·vous (rän′də vo͞o′, -dā-; *Fr.* rän de vo͞o′), *n., pl.* **-vous** (-vo͞oz′; *Fr.* -vo͞o′), *v.,* **-voused** (vo͞od′), **-vous·ing** (-vo͞o′ing). —*n.* **1.** an agreement between two or more persons to meet at a certain time and place. **2.** a place for meeting or assembling, esp. of troops or ships. —*v.t., v.i.* **3.** to assemble at an agreed time and place. [< MF, n. use of v. phrase *rendez-vous* present or betake yourselves; see RENDER[1]]

ren·di·tion (ren dish′ən), *n.* **1.** the act of rendering. **2.** a translation. **3.** an interpretation, as of a role or a piece of music. **4.** *Archaic.* surrender. [< obs., F, MF, alter. of *reddition* (> ME *reddicion*) < LL *redditiōn-* (s. of *redditiō*), equiv. to L *reddit(us)* (ptp. of *reddere;* see RENDER[1]) + *-iōn-* -ION]

ren·du (rän dY′; *Eng.* rän′do͞o), *n. French.* an architectural rendering.

Re·née (rə nā′; *Fr.* rə nā′), *n.* a girl's given name, French form of **Renata.**

ren·e·gade (ren′ə gād′), *n.* **1.** a person who deserts a party or cause for another. **2.** an apostate from a religious faith. —*adj.* **3.** of or like a renegade; traitorous. [< Sp *renegad(o)* < ML *renegāt(us)* (ptp. of *renegāre*), equiv. to *re-* RE- + *neg-* deny + *-ātus* -ADE[1]]

ren·e·ga·do (ren′ə gā′dō), *n., pl.* **-dos.** *Archaic.* a renegade.

re·nege (ri nig′, -neg′, -neg′), *v.,* **-neged, -neg·ing,** *n.* —*v.i.* **1.** *Cards.* to play a card that is not of the suit led when one can follow suit; break a rule of play. **2.** to go back on one's word: *He has reneged on his promise.* —*v.t.* **3.** *Archaic.* to deny; disown; renounce. —*n.* **4.** *Cards.* an act or instance of reneging. [< ML *reneg(āre),* equiv. to *re-* RE- + *negāre* to deny] —**re·neg′er,** *n.*

re·ne·go·ti·ate (rē′ni gō′shē āt′), *v.t., v.i.,* **-at·ed, -at·ing.** **1.** to negotiate again. **2.** *Govt.* to reexamine (a contract, esp. one involving matériel for defense) with a view to eliminating or modifying those provisions found to represent excessive profits to the contractor. [RE- + NEGOTIATE] —**re·ne·go·ti·a·ble** (rē′ni gō′shē ə bəl), *adj.* —**re′ne·go′ti·a′tion,** *n.*

re·new (ri no͞o′, -nyo͞o′), *v.t.* **1.** to begin or take up again, as an acquaintance, a conversation, etc.; resume. **2.** to make effective for an additional period: *to renew a lease.* **3.** to restore or replenish: *to renew a stock of goods.* **4.** to make, say, or do again. **5.** to revive; reestablish. **6.** to recover (youth, strength, etc.). **7.** to restore to a former state; make new or as if new again. —*v.i.* **8.** to begin again; recommence. **9.** to renew a lease, note, etc. **10.** to be restored to a former state; become new or as if new again. [ME *renew(en).* See RE-, NEW] —**re·new′a·bil′i·ty,** *n.* —**re·new′a·ble,** *adj.* —**re·new′a·bly,** *adv.* —**re·new·ed·ly** (ri no͞o′id lē, -nyo͞o′-), *adv.* —**re·new′er,** *n.*

—**Syn. 3.** restock. **7.** recreate, rejuvenate, regenerate, reinstate, mend. RENEW, RENOVATE, REPAIR, RESTORE suggest making something the way it formerly was. To RENEW means to bring back to an original condition of freshness and vigor: *to renew one's enthusiasm.* RENOVATE means to do over or make good any dilapidation of something: *to renovate an old house.* To REPAIR is to put into good or sound condition; to make good any injury, damage, wear and tear, decay, etc.; to mend: *to repair the roof of a house.* To RESTORE is to bring back to its former place or position something which has faded, disappeared, been lost, etc., to reinstate a person in rank or position: *to restore a king to his throne.*

re·new·al (ri no͞o′əl, -nyo͞o′-), *n.* **1.** the act of renewing. **2.** the state of being renewed. **3.** an instance of this. [RENEW + -AL[2]]

Ren·frew (ren′fro͞o), *n.* a county in SW Scotland. 338,815 (1961); 225 sq. mi. *Co. seat:* Renfrew. Also called **Ren·frew·shire** (ren′fro͞o shēr′, -shər).

ren·ga (reng′gə), *n. Pros.* See **linked verse.** [< Jap]

Re·ni (rē′nē), *n.* **Gui·do** (gwē′dô), 1575–1642, Italian painter.

reni-, a learned borrowing from Latin meaning "kidney," used in the formation of compound words: *reniform.* [< L, comb. form of *rēnēs* kidneys]

re·ni·fleur (ren′ə flûr′), *n. Psychiatry.* one who is sexually aroused or gratified by odors. [< F, equiv. to *renifl(er)* (to) sniff + *-eur* -OR[2]]

ren·i·form (ren′ə fôrm′, rē′nə-), *adj.* kidney-shaped: *a reniform leaf; hematite in reniform masses.* [< NL *rēniform(is).* See RENI-, -FORM]

Reniform leaf

re·nin (rē′nin), *n. Biochem.* an enzyme found in ischemic kidneys, serving to convert hypertensinogen to hypertensin. [REN(I)- + -IN[2]]

re·ni·tent (ri nīt′ənt, ren′i tənt), *adj.* **1.** resisting pressure; resistant. **2.** persistently opposing; recalcitrant. [< L *renītent-* (s. of *renītēns,* prp. of *renītī*), equiv. to *re-* RE- + *nīt(ī)* (to) strive, make an effort + *-ent-* -ENT] —**re·ni′ten·cy, re·ni′tence,** *n.*

Rennes (ren), *n.* a city in and the capital of Ille-et-Vilaine, in NW France: former capital of Brittany; scene of trial of Alfred Dreyfus, 1899. 157,692 (1962).

ren·net (ren′it), *n.* **1.** the lining membrane of the fourth stomach of a calf or of the stomach of certain other young animals. **2.** *Biochem.* the rennin-containing substance from the stomach of the calf. **3.** a preparation or extract of the rennet membrane, used to curdle milk, as in making cheese, junket, etc. [ME; cf. OE *(ge)rennan,* G *gerinnen* to coagulate; akin to RUN]

Ren·nie (ren′ē), *n.* **John,** 1761–1821, Scottish engineer.

ren·nin (ren′in), *n. Biochem.* a coagulating enzyme occurring in the gastric juice of the calf, forming the active principle of rennet and able to curdle milk. [RENN(ET) + -IN[2]]

Re·no (rē′nō), *n.* a city in W Nevada. 51,470 (1960).

Re·noir (ren′wär; *Fr.* rə nwar′), *n.* **Pierre Au·guste** (pyer ō gyst′), 1841–1919, French painter.

re·nounce (ri nouns′), *v.,* **-nounced, -nounc·ing,** *n.* —*v.t.* **1.** to give up or put aside voluntarily: *to renounce all worldly pleasures.* **2.** to give up by formal declaration: *to renounce a claim.* **3.** to repudiate; disown: *How could he renounce his own son?* —*v.i.* **4.** *Cards.* **a.** to play a card of a different suit from that led. **b.** to abandon or give up a suit led. **c.** to fail to follow the suit led. —*n.* **5.** *Cards.* an act or instance of renouncing. [ME *renounce(n)* < MF *renonc(er)* < L *renuntiāre* to bring back word, disclaim, equiv. to *re-* RE- + *nuntiāre* to announce, deriv. of *nuntius* messenger, news] —**re·nounce′a·ble, re·nun·ci·a·ble** (ri nun′shē ə bəl, -sē-), *adj.* —**re·nounce′ment,** *n.* —**re·nounc′er,** *n.*

—**Syn. 1.** forsake, forgo, forswear, leave, quit. See **abandon**[1]. **2.** resign, abdicate. **3.** disclaim, reject, disavow, deny. —**Ant. 1.** claim. **3.** accept.

ren·o·vate (ren′ə vāt′), *v.,* **-vat·ed, -vat·ing,** *adj.* —*v.t.* **1.** to restore to good condition; make new or as if new again; repair. **2.** to reinvigorate; refresh; revive. —*adj.* **3.** *Archaic.* renovated. [< L *renovāt(us)* (ptp. of *renovāre*), equiv. to *re-* RE- + *nov(us)* NEW + *-ātus* -ATE[1]] —**ren′o·vat′ing·ly,** *adv.* —**ren′o·va′tion,** *n.* —**ren′o·va′tive,** *adj.* —**ren′o·va′tor,** *n.*

—**Syn. 1.** See **renew.**

Re·no·vo (rə nō′vō), *n.* a town in central Pennsylvania. 3316 (1960).

re·nown (ri noun′), *n.* **1.** widespread and high repute; fame. **2.** *Obs.* report or rumor. [ME *renoun* < AF, OF *renom,* deriv. of *renomer* to make famous < L *re-* RE- + *nōmināre* to NAME] —**re·nown′less,** *adj.*

—**Syn. 1.** celebrity, glory, distinction, note, eminence, reputation, name, honor. —**Ant. 1.** disrepute.

re·nowned (ri nound′), *adj.* celebrated; famous. [ME; see RENOWN, -ED[2]] —**re·nown·ed·ly** (ri nou′nid lē, -nound′-), *adv.* —**re·nown′ed·ness,** *n.*

—**Syn.** famed, distinguished, honored, notable.

Rens·se·laer (ren′sə lēr′, rens lēr′, ren′sə lər, rens′lər), *n.* **1.** a town in E New York. 10,506 (1960). **2.** a town in NW Indiana. 4740 (1960).

rens·se·laer·ite (ren′sə lə rīt′, ren′sə lâr′īt), *n.* a variety of talc. [named after Stephen Van *Rensselaer* (1764–1839), American politician and army officer; see -ITE[1]]

rent[1] (rent), *n.* **1.** a payment made periodically by a tenant to an owner or landlord in return for the use of land, a building, an apartment, an office, or other property. **2.** a payment or series of payments made by a lessee to an owner in return for the use of machinery, equipment, etc. **3.** *Econ.* the excess of the produce or return yielded by a given piece of cultivated land over the cost of production; the yield from a piece of land or real estate. **4.** profit or return derived from any differential advantage in production. **5.** *Obs.* revenue or income. **6. for rent,** available for tenancy or use: *There are no apartments for rent in this building.* —*v.t.* **7.** to grant the possession and enjoyment of (property) in return for a payment or payments to be made at agreed times. **8.** to take and hold (property) in return for a payment or payments to be made at agreed times. —*v.i.* **9.** to be leased or let for rent: *This apartment rents cheaply.* [ME *rente* < OF < VL **rendita,* fem. ptp. of **rendere;* see RENDER[1]] —**rent′a·bil′i·ty,** *n.* —**rent′a·ble,** *adj.*

—**Syn. 8.** lease, let. See **hire.**

rent[2] (rent), *n.* **1.** an opening made by rending or tearing; slit; fissure. **2.** a breach of relations or union between individuals or groups; schism. —*v.* **3.** pt. and pp. of **rend.** [n. use of *rent* (v.), var. of REND]

—**Syn. 1.** tear, split, rift, cleft, rip, rupture, fracture. **2.** division, separation.

rent·al (ren′təl), *n.* **1.** an amount received or paid as rent. **2.** an apartment, house, or other property offered or given for rent. **3.** an income arising from rents received. **4.** a rent-roll. —*adj.* **5.** pertaining to rent. [ME < AL *rentāle.* See RENT[1], -AL[2]]

rent′al collec′tion, a group of books, in a public or other free library, for which a borrower must pay a small daily fee.

rent′al li′brary. See **lending library.**

rente (ränt), *n., pl.* **rentes** (ränt). *French.* **1.** revenue or income, or the instrument evidencing a right to such periodic receipts. **2. rentes.** Also called **rentes sur l'é·tat** (ränt syr lā ta′). perpetual bonds issued by the French government.

rent·er (ren′tər), *n.* a person who or organization which holds, or has the use of, property by payment of rent. [ME; see RENT, -ER[1]]

rent-free (rent′frē′), *adv.* **1.** without payment of rent: *We lived rent-free for six months because my wife's father owned the house.* —*adj.* **2.** not subject to rent: *a rent-free apartment.*

ren·tier (rän tyā′), *n., pl.* **-tiers** (-tyā′). *French.* one who has a fixed income, as from lands, bonds, etc.

Ren·ton (ren′tən), *n.* a city in W Washington, near Seattle. 18,453 (1960).

rent′ par′ty, a party that is thrown to raise money for the host's rent and that, in traditionally featuring a jazz pianist as entertainment, has been an important factor in the development of various jazz piano styles.

rent-roll (rent′rōl′), *n.* an account or schedule of rents, the amount due from each tenant, and the total received.

rent′ seck′, *pl.* **rents seck.** a right to rent in which the renter does not have the usual power of collection by seizure of the tenant's goods. Also called **dry rent.** [ME *rent sek* < AF *rente seque,* lit., dry rent]

rent′ ta′ble, *Eng. Furniture.* a drum table of the 18th century, having six drawers and originally used by landlords to keep rent money and papers pertaining to their estates.

Rent table (18th century)

re·nun·ci·a·tion (ri nun′sē ā′shən, -shē-), *n.* an act or instance of relinquishing, abandoning, repudiating, or sacrificing something, as a right, title, person, ambition, etc.: *His renunciation of the throne stunned the world.* [ME < L *renunciātiōn-* (s. of *renunciātiō*) proclamation, equiv. to *renunciāt(us)* (ptp. of *renunciāre* to RENOUNCE) + *-iōn-* -ION] —**re·nun′ci·a′tive, re·nun·ci·a·to·ry** (ri nun′sē ə tôr′ē, -tōr′ē, -shē ə-), *adj.*

ren·ver·sé (rän′ver sā′; *Fr.* rän ver sā′), *adj. Ballet.* performed with the body bent from the waist: *a pirouette renversé.* [< F: lit., turned back]

ren·voi (ren voi′), *n.* **1.** the expulsion by a government of an alien, esp. a foreign diplomat, from the country. **2.** the referral of a case involving a jurisdictional dispute in international law to a law other than the local one. [< F: a sending back, deriv. of *renvoyer.* See RE-, ENVOY]

re·o·pen (rē ō′pən), *v.t., v.i.* **1.** to open again. **2.** to start again; resume: *to reopen an argument; to reopen an attack.* [RE- + OPEN]

re·or·der (rē ôr′dər), *v.t.* **1.** to put in order again: *It will take me an hour to reorder this file.* **2.** *Com.* to give a reorder for: *Remember to reorder those books before we're completely sold out.* —*n.* **3.** *Com.* a second or repeated order for the same goods from the same dealer: *Did you put through a reorder for those lamps?* [RE- + ORDER]

re·or·di·na·tion (rē′ôr dənā′shən), *n.* **1.** a second ordination. **2.** *Rom. Cath. Ch.* the ordination of a priest whose first orders have been held invalid. **3.** *Eccles.* the second ordination of a priest whose first orders were received from another church. **4.** the sacrament elevating a deacon, priest or bishop to a higher grade or order. [< ML *reordinātiōn-* (s. of *reordinātiō*). See RE-, ORDINATION]

re·or·gan·ise (rē ôr′gə nīz′), *v.t., v.i.,* **-ised, -is·ing.** *Chiefly Brit.* reorganize. —**re·or′gan·is′er,** *n.*

re·or·gan·i·za·tion (rē′ôr gə ni zā′shən), *n.* **1.** the act or process of reorganizing; state of being reorganized. **2.** *Finance.* a thorough or drastic reconstruction of a business corporation, including a marked change in capital structure, often following a failure and receivership or bankruptcy trusteeship. [RE- + ORGANIZATION]

re·or·gan·ize (rē ôr′gə nīz′), *v.t., v.i.,* **-ized, -iz·ing.** to organize again. [RE- + ORGANIZE] —**re·or′gan·iz′er,** *n.*

re·o·ri·ent (rē ôr′ē ent′, -ôr′-), *v.t., v.i.* **1.** to orient again or anew. —*adj.* **2.** *Rare.* rising anew. [RE- + ORIENT]

re·o·ri·en·ta·tion (rē ôr′ē en tā′shən, -ôr′-), *n.* the act or state of reorienting or of being reoriented. [RE- + ORIENTATION]

rep[1] (rep), *n.* a transversely corded fabric of wool, silk, rayon, or cotton. Also, **repp.** [< F *reps*] —**repped,** *adj.*

rep[2] (rep), *n. Slang.* reputation. [by shortening]

rep[3] (rep), *n.* the quantity of ionizing radiation, which on absorption by living tissues, produces an energy gain equal to that produced by one roentgen of x-ray or of gamma radiation. Cf. **rem.** [*r(oentgen) e(quivalent) p(hysical)*]

Rep., 1. Representative. **2.** Republic. **3.** Republican.

rep., 1. repeat. **2.** (in prescriptions) let it be repeated. [< L *repetātur*] **3.** report. **4.** reported. **5.** reporter.

re·paint (*v.* rē pānt′; *n.* rē′pānt′, rē pānt′), *v.t.* **1.** to paint again: *We are repainting the house this spring.* —*n.* **2.** a part repainted, esp. a part of a picture by a restorer. **3.** the act of repainting. [RE- + PAINT]

re·pair[1] (ri pâr′), *v.t.* **1.** to restore to a good or sound condition after decay or damage; mend: *to repair a motor.* **2.** to restore or renew by any process of making good, strengthening, etc.: *to repair one's health by resting.* **3.** to remedy; make good; make up for: *to repair damage; to repair a deficiency.* **4.** to make amends for; compensate: *to repair a wrong done.* —*n.* **5.** an act, process, or work of repairing: *to order the repair of a building.* **6.** Usually, **repairs. a.** an instance or operation of repairing: *to lay up a boat for repairs.* **b.** a repaired part or an addition made in repairing: *17th-century repairs in brick are conspicuous in parts of the medieval stonework.* **7. repairs,** (in bookkeeping, accounting, etc.) the part of maintenance expense which has been paid out to keep fixed assets in usable condi-

re′ne·gate′, *v.t.,* **-gat·ed, -gat·ing.**
re′ne·ga′tion, *n.*
re·neu′tral·ize′, *v.,* **-ized, -iz·ing.**
re·nom′i·nate′, *v.t.,* **-nat·ed, -nat·ing.**
re′nom·i·na′tion, *n.*
re·nor′mal·i·za′tion, *n.*
re·nor′mal·ize′, *v.t.,* **-ized, -iz·ing.**
re·no′ta·rize′, *v.t.,* **-rized, -riz·ing.**
re′no·ta′tion, *n.*
re·no′tice, *v.t.,* **-ticed, -tic·ing.**
re′no·ti·fi·ca′tion, *n.*
re·no′ti·fy′, *v.t.,* **-fied, -fy·ing.**
re·nour′ish, *v.t.*
re·nour′ish·ment, *n.*
re·nul′li·fi·ca′tion, *n.*
re·nul′li·fy′, *v.t.,* **-fied, -fy·ing.**
re·num′ber, *v.t.*
re·nu′mer·ate′, *v.t.,* **-at·ed, -at·ing.**
re′ob·ject′, *v.t.*
re·ob′li·gate′, *v.t.,* **-gat·ed, -gat·ing.**
re′ob·li·ga′tion, *n.*
re′ob·lige′, *v.t.,* **-liged, -lig·ing.**
re′ob·ser·va′tion, *n.*
re′ob·serve′, *v.,* **-served, -serv·ing.**
re′ob·tain′, *v.t.*
re′ob·tain′a·ble, *adj.*
re′oc·cu·pa′tion, *n.*
re·oc′cu·py′, *v.t.,* **-pied, -py·ing.**
re′oc·cur′, *v.i.,* **-curred, -cur·ring.**
re′oc·cur′rence, *n.*
re′of·fend′, *v.*
re·of′fer, *v., n.*
re·oil′, *v.*
re·op′er·ate′, *v.t.,* **-at·ed, -at·ing.**
re′op·er·a′tion, *n.*
re′op·pose′, *v.t.,* **-posed, -pos·ing.**
re′op·press′, *v.t.*
re·or′ches·trate′, *v.,* **-trat·ed, -trat·ing.**
re′or·ches·tra′tion, *n.*
re′or·dain′, *v.t.*
re·o′ri·en·tate′, *v.t.,* **-tat·ed, -tat·ing.**
re·or′na·ment′, *v.t.*
re·out′fit, *v.t.,* **-fit·ted, -fit·ting.**
re·out′line, *v.t.,* **-lined, -lin·ing.**
re·ox′i·dise′, *v.,* **-dised, -dis·ing.**
re·ox′i·dize′, *v.,* **-dized, -diz·ing.**
re·pac′i·fy′, *v.t.,* **-fied, -fy·ing.**
re·pack′, *v.*
re·pack′age, *v.t.,* **-aged, -ag·ing.**
re·pad′, *v.t.,* **-pad·ded, -pad·ding.**
re·pag′i·nate′, *v.t.,* **-nat·ed, -nat·ing.**
re′pag·i·na′tion, *n.*

tion, as distinguished from amounts used for renewal or replacement. **8.** the good condition resulting from continued maintenance and repairing: *to keep in repair.* [ME *repair(en)* < MF *repar(er)* < L *reparāre,* equiv. to *re-* RE- + *parāre* to prepare; see PARE] —**re·pair′a·ble,** *adj.* —**re·pair′a·ble·ness,** *n.*
—**Syn. 1.** remodel, renovate. **2.** patch, fix, amend. See **renew. 3.** retrieve, recoup. **4.** redress. —**Ant. 1–3.** break, destroy.

re·pair[2] (ri pâr′), *v.i.* **1.** to betake oneself; go, as to a place: *He repaired in haste to Washington.* **2.** to go frequently or customarily. —*n.* **3.** a resort or haunt. **4.** the act of going or going customarily; resort: *to have repair to the country.* **5.** *Scot. Obs.* a meeting, association, or crowd of people. [ME *repaire(n)* < OF *repair(ier)* (to) return < LL *repatriāre* to return to one's fatherland; see REPATRIATE]

re·pair·er (ri pâr′ər), *n.* **1.** one who or that which repairs. **2.** *Ceramics.* a person who assembles the modeled parts of a piece and finishes the whole. [REPAIR[1] + -ER[1]]

re·pair·man (ri pâr′man′, -mən), *n., pl.* **-men** (-men′, -mən). a man whose occupation is the making of repairs, readjustments, etc. [REPAIR[1] + MAN[1]]

re·pand (ri pand′), *adj.* **1.** *Bot.* having a wavy margin, as a leaf. **2.** slightly wavy. [< L *repand(us)* bent backwards, turned up, equiv. to *re-* RE- + *pandus* bent, curved, deriv. of *pandere* to spread out, extend] —**re·pand′ly,** *adv.*

Repand leaf

rep·a·ra·ble (rep′ər ə bəl), *adj.* capable of being repaired or remedied. [< L *reparābil(is),* REPAIR[1] -ABLE] —**rep′a·ra·bly,** *adv.*

rep·a·ra·tion (rep′ə rā′shən), *n.* **1.** the making of amends for wrong or injury done: *There can be no reparation for so great an injustice.* **2.** Usually, **reparations.** compensation in money, material, labor, etc., payable by a defeated country to another country or to an individual for damages or loss suffered during or as a result of war. **3.** restoration to good condition. **4.** repair[1] (def. 7). [ME *reparacion* < MF < LL *reparātiōn-* (s. of *reparātiō*), equiv. to L *reparāt(us)* (ptp. of *reparāre* to REPAIR[1]) + *-iōn-* -ION]
—**Syn. 1.** indemnification, atonement, satisfaction. compensation. See **redress. 3.** renewal, renovation; repair. —**Ant. 3.** destruction.

re·par·a·tive (ri par′ə tiv), *adj.* **1.** tending to repair; repairing; mending. **2.** pertaining to or involving reparation. Also, **re·par·a·to·ry** (ri par′ə tōr′ē, -tôr′ē). [< LL *reparātīv(us).* See REPARATION, -IVE]

rep·ar·tee (rep′ər tē′, -tā′), *n.* **1.** a quick, witty reply. **2.** conversation full of quick, witty replies. **3.** skill in making quick, witty replies. [< F *repartie* retort. n. use of fem. ptp. of *repartir,* MF, equiv. to *re-* RE- + *partir* to PART]
—**Syn. 2.** banter; sparring, fencing.

re·par·ti·tion (rē′pär tish′ən, -pər-), *n.* **1.** distribution; partition. **2.** redistribution. —*v.t.* **3.** to divide up. [RE- + PARTITION]

re·pass (rē pas′, -päs′), *v.t., v.i.* to pass back or again. [ME *repass(en)* < MF, OF *repass(er),* equiv. to *re-* RE- + *passer* to PASS] —**re·pas·sage** (rē pas′ij), *n.*

re·past (ri past′, -päst′), *n.* **1.** a quantity of food taken or provided for one occasion of eating: *to eat a light repast.* **2.** a meal: *the evening repast.* **3.** the time during which a meal is eaten; mealtime. **4.** *Archaic.* the taking of food, as at a meal. **5.** *Obs.* food. —*v.i.* **6.** to eat or feast (often fol. by *on* or *upon*). [ME < OF < LL *repast(us),* ptp. of *repāscere* to feed regularly, equiv. to L *re-* RE- + *pāscere* to feed]

Re Pas·to·re, Il (*It.* ēl re′ päs tô′re), an opera (1775) by Mozart.

re·pa·tri·ate (*v.* rē pā′trē āt′; *n.* rē pā′trē it), *v.t.,* **-at·ed, -at·ing,** *n.* —*v.t.* **1.** to bring or send back (a person, esp. a prisoner of war, a refugee, etc.) to his country or the land of his citizenship. —*n.* **2.** one who has been repatriated. [< LL *repatriāt(us)* returned to one's fatherland (ptp. of *repatriāre*), equiv. to L *re-* RE- + *patri(a)* native country (n. use of fem. of *patrius* paternal, deriv. of *pater* FATHER) + *-ātus* -ATE[1]] —**re·pa·tri·a·ble** (rē pā′trē ə bəl), *adj.* —**re·pa′tri·a′tion,** *n.*

re·pay (ri pā′), *v.,* **-paid, -pay·ing.** —*v.t.* **1.** to pay back or refund, as money. **2.** to make return for: *She repaid the compliment with a smile.* **3.** to make return to in any way: *We can never repay you for your help.* **4.** to return: *to repay a visit.* —*v.i.* **5.** to make repayment or return. [< MF *repaier.* See RE-, PAY] —**re·pay′a·ble,** *adj.* —**re·pay′ment,** *n.*
—**Syn. 1.** reimburse, indemnify.

re·peal (ri pēl′), *v.t.* **1.** to revoke or withdraw formally or officially: *to repeal a grant.* **2.** to revoke or annul (a law, tax, duty, etc.) by express legislative enactment; abrogate. —*n.* **3.** the act of repealing; revocation; abrogation. [ME *repele(n)* < AF *repel(er),* equiv. to *re-* RE- + *apeler* to APPEAL] —**re·peal′a·bil′i·ty, re·peal′a·ble·ness,** *n.* —**re·peal′a·ble,** *adj.* —**re·peal′er,** *n.*
—**Syn. 2.** nullify, abolish, rescind, invalidate.

re·peat (ri pēt′), *v.t.* **1.** to say or utter again (something already said): *to repeat a word for emphasis.* **2.** to say or utter in reproducing the words, inflections, etc., of another: *to repeat a sentence after the teacher.* **3.** to reproduce (utterances, sounds, etc.) as an echo, a phonograph, or the like does. **4.** to tell (something heard) to another or others. **5.** to do, make, or perform again: *to repeat an action; to repeat a passage of music.* **6.** to go through or undergo again: *to repeat an experience.* —*v.i.* **7.** to do or say something again. **8.** to cause a slight regurgitation: *All those onions and potato chips repeated on me.* **9.** *U.S.* to vote illegally by casting more than one vote in the same election. —*n.* **10.** the act of repeating. **11.** something repeated; repetition. **12.** a duplicate or reproduction of something. **13.** a decorative pattern repeated, usually by printing, on a textile or the like. **14.** *Music.* **a.** a passage to be repeated. **b.** a sign, as a vertical arrangement of dots, calling for the repetition of a passage. **15.** a radio or television program that has been broadcast at least once before. [ME *repete(n)* < MF *repet(er)* < L *repetere* to attack again, demand return of, equiv. to *re-* RE- + *petere* to reach towards, seek] —**re·peat′a·bil′i·ty,** *n.* —**re·peat′a·ble,** *adj.*
—**Syn. 1.** iterate, recite, rehearse. **1, 5.** REPEAT, RECAPITULATE, REITERATE refer to saying a thing more than once. To REPEAT is to do or say something over again: *to repeat a question, an order.* To RECAPITULATE is to restate in brief form, to summarize, often by repeating the principal points in a discourse: *to recapitulate an argument.* To REITERATE is to do or say something over and over again, to repeat insistently: *to reiterate a refusal, a demand.* **3.** echo, reecho.

re·peat·ed (ri pē′tid), *adj.* done, made, or said again and again: *repeated attempts.* [REPEAT + -ED[2]] —**re·peat′ed·ly,** *adv.*

re·peat·er (ri pē′tər), *n.* **1.** one who or that which repeats. **2.** a repeating firearm. **3.** *Horol.* a timepiece, esp. a watch, which may be made to strike the hour or part of the hour. Cf. **clock watch. 4.** *Educ.* a pupil who repeats a course or group of courses which he has failed. **5.** *U.S.* one who votes illegally by casting more than one vote in the same election. **6.** *Metalworking.* (in a looping mill) a fairlead for guiding hot or flexible lengths of metal between successive stands placed side by side. **7.** *Math.* See **circulating decimal. 8.** a device capable of receiving one-way or two-way communications signals and delivering corresponding signals that are either amplified, reshaped, or both. **9.** Also called **substitute.** *Naut.* any one of three distinctive signal flags raised in a hoist with letter or number flags to indicate that the first, second, or third letter or number from the top is being repeated. **10.** *Navig.* See **gyro repeater.** [REPEAT + -ER[1]]

repeat′ing dec′imal, *Math.* See **circulating decimal.**

repeat′ing fire′arm, a firearm capable of discharging a number of shots without reloading.

repeat′ing theod′olite, *Survey.* a theodolite having a horizontal circle able to rotate freely or to be secured either to the alidade or to its support so as to permit cumulative readings. Cf. **direction theodolite.**

repeat′ing watch′, a watch built as a repeater.

re·pel (ri pel′), *v.,* **-pelled, -pel·ling.** —*v.t.* **1.** to drive or force back (an assailant, invader, etc.). **2.** to thrust back or away: *He repelled the idea because it was useless.* **3.** to resist effectively (an attack, onslaught, etc.): *to repel the army's assault.* **4.** to keep off or out; fail to mix with: *Water and oil repel each other.* **5.** to resist the absorption or passage of (water or other liquid): *This coat repels rain.* **6.** to refuse to have to do with; resist involvement in: *to repel temptation.* **7.** to refuse to accept or admit; reject: *to repel a suggestion.* **8.** to discourage the advances of (a person): *He repelled her with his harshness.* **9.** to cause distaste or aversion in: *Her untidy appearance repelled him.* **10.** to push back or away by a force, as one body acting upon another (opposed to *attract*): *The north pole of one magnet will repel the north pole of another.* —*v.i.* **11.** to act with a force that drives or keeps away something. **12.** to cause distaste or aversion. [ME *repelle(n)* < L *repell(ere)* (to) drive back, equiv. to *re-* RE- + *pellere* to drive, push; see REPULSE] —**re·pel′lence, re·pel′len·cy,** *n.* —**re·pel′ler,** *n.* —**re·pel′ling·ly,** *adv.* —**re·pel′ling·ness,** *n.*
—**Syn. 1.** repulse, parry, ward off. **3.** withstand, oppose, rebuff. **7.** decline, rebuff. —**Ant. 1.** attract.

re·pel·lent (ri pel′ənt), *adj.* **1.** causing distaste or aversion; repulsive. **2.** repelling; driving back. —*n.* **3.** something that repels: *insect repellent.* **4.** a medicine that serves to prevent or reduce swellings, tumors, etc. **5.** any of various durable or nondurable solutions applied to a fabric or garment to increase its resistance, as to water, moths, mildew, etc. Also, **re·pel′lant.** [< L *repellent-* (s. of *repellēns,* prp. of *repellere*) driving back. See REPEL, -ENT] —**re·pel′lent·ly, re·pel′lant·ly,** *adv.*

re·pent[1] (ri pent′), *v.i.* **1.** to feel sorry, self-reproachful, or contrite for past conduct; regret or be conscience-stricken about a past action, attitude, etc. (often fol. by *of*): *A man who repents of a thoughtless act is better loved than one who never committed one.* **2.** to feel such sorrow for sin or fault as to be disposed to change one's life for the better; be penitent (often fol. by *of*). —*v.t.* **3.** to remember or regard with self-reproach or contrition: *to repent one's injustice to another.* **4.** to feel sorry for; regret: *to repent an imprudent act.* [ME *repente(n)* < OF *repent(ir),* equiv. to *re-* RE- + *pentir* to feel sorrow (< L *paenitēre* to regret, be sorry); see PENITENT] —**re·pent′er,** *n.* —**re·pent′ing·ly,** *adv.*

re·pent[2] (ri pent′), *adj.* **1.** *Bot.* creeping. **2.** *Zool.* reptant. [< L *rēpent-* (s. of *rēpēns,* prp. of *rēpere*), equiv. to *rēp-* creep, crawl + *-ent-* -ENT]

re·pent·ance (ri pen′tᵊns), *n.* **1.** deep sorrow, compunction, or contrition for a past sin, wrongdoing, or the like. **2.** regret for any past action. [ME *repentaunce* < OF *repentance.* See REPENT[1], -ANCE]
—**Syn. 1.** contriteness, penitence, remorse. **2.** sorrow, regret. —**Ant. 1.** impenitence.

re·pent·ant (ri pen′tᵊnt, -pen′tənt), *adj.* **1.** repenting; penitent; experiencing repentance. **2.** characterized by or showing repentance: *a repentant mood.* [ME *repentaunt* < OF *repentant* (prp. of *repentir*). See REPENT[1], -ANT] —**re·pent′ant·ly,** *adv.*

re·peo·ple (rē pē′pəl), *v.t.,* **-pled, -pling. 1.** to furnish again with people. **2.** to restock with animals. [< MF, OF *repeupl(er).* See RE-, PEOPLE]

re·per·cus·sion (rē′pər kush′ən), *n.* **1.** an effect or result, often indirect or remote, of some event or action: *The widespread repercussions of the ambassador's speech were unexpected.* **2.** the state of being driven back by a resisting body. **3.** a rebounding or recoil of something after impact. **4.** reverberation; echo. **5.** *Music.* (in a fugue) the point after the development of an episode at which the subject and answer appear again. [< L *repercussiōn-* (s. of *repercussiō*) a rebounding, equiv. to *repercuss(us)* struck back (ptp. of *repercutere*) + *-iōn-* -ION. See RE-, PERCUSSION]

re·per·cus·sive (rē′pər kus′iv), *adj.* **1.** causing repercussion; reverberating. **2.** reflected; reverberated. [ME *repercussif* < OF < L *repercuss(us).* See REPERCUSSION, -IVE] —**re′per·cus′sive·ly,** *adv.* —**re′per·cus′sive·ness,** *n.*

re·per·fo·ra·tor (rē pûr′fə rā′tər), *n.* (esp. in teletype transmission) a machine for punching a duplicate perforated paper tape of incoming messages so that they may later be retransmitted: used for automatic typesetting. [RE- + PERFORATOR]

rep·er·toire (rep′ər twär′, -twôr′), *n.* **1.** the list of dramas, operas, parts, pieces, etc., which a company, actor, singer, or the like, is prepared to perform. **2.** the entire stock of works existing in a particular artistic field: *A new play has been added to the theatrical repertoire.* Also, **rép·er·toire′.** [< F < LL *repertōr(ium)* catalogue, inventory; see REPERTORY]

rep·er·to·ry (rep′ər tōr′ē, -tôr′ē), *n., pl.* **-ries. 1.** repertoire. **2.** a theatrical company that performs regularly and in alternate sequence several plays, operas, or the like. **3.** a store or stock of things available. **4.** storehouse. [< LL *repertōri(um)* inventory, equiv. to L *repert(us)* found, ascertained, ptp. of *reperīre* (*re-* RE- + *parīre* to bring forth, sp. var. of *parere*) + *-ōrium* -ORY[2]] —**rep′er·to′ri·al,** *adj.*

rep′ertory cat′alog. See **union catalog.**

rep·e·tend (rep′i tend′, rep′i tend′), *n.* **1.** *Math.* the part of a circulating decimal that is repeated, as 1234 in .123412341234 . . . . **2.** *Music.* a phrase or sound which is repeated. **3.** *Pros.* a word, phrase, line or longer element that is repeated, sometimes with variation, at irregular intervals in a poem. [< L *repetend(um)* that which is to be repeated, neut. ger. of *repetere* to REPEAT]

ré·pé·ti·teur (rā pā tē tûr′; *Fr.* rā pā tē tœr′), *n., pl.* **-teurs** (-tûrz′; *Fr.* -tœr′). the vocal coach of an opera chorus. [< F: tutor, coach < L *repetīt(us)* (ptp. of *repetere* to REPEAT) + F *-eur* -OR[2]]

rep·e·ti·tion (rep′i tish′ən), *n.* **1.** the act of repeating; repeated action, performance, production, or presentation. **2.** repeated utterance; reiteration. **3.** something made by or resulting from repeating. **4.** a reproduction, copy, or replica. **5.** *Civil Law.* an action or demand for the recovery of a payment or delivery made by error or upon failure to fulfill a condition. [< L *repetītiōn-* (s. of *repetītiō*), equiv. to *repetīt(us)* (ptp. of *repetere* to REPEAT) + *-iōn-* -ION]

ré·pé·ti·tion gé·né·rale (rā pā tē syôN′ zhā nā ral′), *French.* a theatrical performance or dress rehearsal not open to the general public. [lit., general repetition]

rep·e·ti·tious (rep′i tish′əs), *adj.* full of repetition, esp. unnecessary and tedious repetition: *a repetitious account of their vacation trip.* [< L *repetīt(us)* (ptp. of *repetere* to REPEAT) + -IOUS] —**rep′e·ti′tious·ly,** *adv.* —**rep′e·ti′tious·ness,** *n.*

re·pet·i·tive (ri pet′i tiv), *adj.* pertaining to or characterized by repetition. [< L *repetīt(us)* (ptp. of *repetere* to REPEAT) + -IVE] —**re·pet′i·tive·ly,** *adv.* —**re·pet′i·tive·ness,** *n.*

re·phrase (rē frāz′), *v.t.,* **-phrased, -phras·ing.** to phrase again or differently: *He rephrased the statement to give it less formality.* [RE- + PHRASE]

re·pic (ri pēk′), *n.* *Piquet.* **1.** the scoring of 30 points in the declaration of hands before one's opponent scores a point. **2.** the bonus of 60 points won for so scoring. Cf. **pic.** Also, **re·pique′.** [< F, deriv. of *repiquer* to prick, punch again. See RE-, PIQUER]

re·pine (ri pīn′), *v.i.,* **-pined, -pin·ing.** to be fretfully discontented; fret; complain. [RE- + PINE[2]] —**re·pin′er,** *n.*

re·place (ri plās′), *v.t.,* **-placed, -plac·ing. 1.** to assume the former role, position or function of; substitute for (a person or thing): *Electricity has replaced gas as a means of illumination.* **2.** to provide a substitute or equivalent in the place of: *to replace a broken vase or dish.* **3.** to restore; return; make good: *to replace a sum of money borrowed.* **4.** to restore to a former or the proper place: *She washed the ashtray and replaced it on the table.* [RE- + PLACE] —**re·place′a·bil′i·ty,** *n.* —**re·place′a·ble,** *adj.* —**re·plac′er,** *n.*
—**Syn. 1.** succeed. REPLACE, SUPERSEDE, SUPPLANT refer to putting one thing or person in place of another. To REPLACE is to take the place of, to succeed: *Mr. A. will replace Mr. B. as president.* SUPERSEDE implies that that which is replacing another is an improvement: *The typewriter has superseded the pen.* SUPPLANT implies that that which takes the other's place has ousted the former holder, and usurped the position or function esp. by art or fraud: *to supplant a former favorite.* **3.** refund, repay.

re·place·ment (ri plās′mənt), *n.* **1.** the act of replacing. **2.** a person or thing that serves to replace another: *We will be hiring summer replacements for our vacationing staff. I bought this dish as a replacement for the one I broke.* **3.** *Mil.* a sailor, soldier, or airman assigned to fill a vacancy in a military unit. **4.** Also called **metasomatism, metasomatosis.** *Geol.* the process of practically simultaneous removal and deposition by which a new mineral of partly or wholly differing chemical composition grows in the body of an old mineral or mineral aggregate. **5.** *Crystall.* substitution of one or more faces for an angle or edge. [REPLACE + -MENT]

re·pan′el, *v.t.,* **-eled, -el·ing** or (*esp. Brit.*) **-elled, -el·ling.**
re·pa′per, *v.t.*
re·park′, *v.*
re·paste′, *v.t.,* **-past·ed, -past·ing.**
re·patch′, *v.*
re′pa·trol′, *v.t.,* **-trolled, -trol·ling.**
re·pa′tron·ize′, *v.t.,* **-ized, -iz·ing.**
re·pat′tern, *v.t.*
re·pave′, *v.t.,* **-paved, -pav·ing.**
re·pawn′, *v.t.*
re·ped′dle, *v.t.,* **-dled, -dling.**
re·pen′, *v.t.,* **-penned, -pen·ning.**
re·pe′nal·ize′, *v.t.,* **-ized, -iz·ing.**
re′per·ceive′, *v.t.,* **-ceived, -ceiv·ing.**
re′per·cep′tion, *n.*
re′per·form′, *v.t.*
re′per·form′ance, *n.*
re′pe·ru′sal, *n.*
re′pe·ruse′, *v.t.,* **-rused, -rus·ing.**
re′pe·ti′tion, *v.t.*
re·pho′to·graph′, *v.t., n.*
re·pick′, *v.t.*
re·pin′, *v.t.,* **-pinned, -pin·ning.**
re·plan′, *v.t.,* **-planned, -plan·ning.**
re·plane′, *v.t.,* **-planed, -plan·ing.**

re·plead·er (rē plē′dər), *n. Law.* **1.** a second pleading. **2.** the right or privilege of pleading again. [RE- + PLEADER]

re·plen·ish (ri plen′ish), *v.t.* **1.** to make full or complete again, as by supplying what is lacking, used up, etc.: *to replenish one's stock of food.* **2.** to supply (a fire, stove, etc.) with fresh fuel. **3.** to fill again or anew. [ME *replenisshe(n)* < MF *repleniss-*, long s. of *replenir* to fill, OF, equiv. to *re-* RE- + *plenir* to fill (deriv. of *plein* < L *plēnus* FULL[1])] —**re·plen′ish·er,** *n.* —**re·plen′ish·ment,** *n.*

re·plete (ri plēt′), *adj.* **1.** abundantly supplied or provided; filled (usually fol. by *with*): *a speech replete with sentimentality.* **2.** stuffed or gorged with food and drink. **3.** complete: *a scholarly survey, replete in its notes and citations.* —*n.* **4.** *Entomol.* (among honey ants) a worker with a distensible crop in which honeydew and nectar are stored for the use of the colony. [ME *repleet* < MF *replet* < L *replēt(us)* filled up, ptp. of *replēre* (*re-* RE- + *plēre* to fill)] —**re·plete′ly,** *adv.* —**re·plete′ness,** *n.* —**re·ple′tive,** *adj.* —**re·ple′tive·ly,** *adv.*
—**Syn. 2.** sated, satiated, glutted, surfeited.

re·ple·tion (ri plē′shən), *n.* **1.** the condition of being abundantly supplied or filled; fullness. **2.** overfullness resulting from excessive eating or drinking; surfeit. [ME *replecioun* surfeit < MF < LL *replētiōn-* (s. of *replētiō*), equiv. to L *replēt(us)* filled up (see REPLETE) + *-iōn-* -ION]

re·plev·in (ri plev′in), *Law.* —*n.* **1.** an action for the recovery of goods or chattels wrongfully taken or detained. **2.** the common-law action or writ by which goods are replevied. —*v.t.* **3.** to replevy. [ME < AF, deriv. of *replevir* to bail out, admit to bail, OF. See RE-, PLEDGE]

re·plev·i·sa·ble (ri plev′i sə bəl), *adj. Law.* capable of being replevied. Also, **re·plev·i·a·ble** (ri plev′ē ə bəl). [< AF, equiv. to *repleviss-* (long s. of *replevir;* see REPLEVIN) + *-able* -ABLE]

re·plev·y (ri plev′ē), *v.*, **-plev·ied, -plev·y·ing,** *n., pl.* **-plev·ies.** *Law.* —*v.t.* **1.** to recover possession of by an action of replevin. —*v.i.* **2.** to take possession of goods or chattels under a replevin order. —*n.* **3.** a seizure in replevin. [late ME < OF *replevi(r);* see REPLEVIN]

rep·li·ca (rep′lə kə), *n.* **1.** a copy or reproduction of a work of art produced by the maker of the original or under his supervision. **2.** a copy or reproduction. [< It: reply, repetition, deriv. of *replicare* to repeat < LL *replicāre* to REPLY]
—**Syn. 2.** duplicate, facsimile; imitation.

rep·li·cate (rep′lə kit), *adj.* folded; bent back on itself. Also, **rep·li·cat·ed** (rep′lə kā′tid). [< LL *replicāt(us)* folded back, ptp. of *replicāre.* See RE-, PLY[2], -ATE[1]]

rep·li·ca·tion (rep′lə kā′shən), *n.* **1.** a reply; answer. **2.** a reply to an answer. **3.** *Law.* the reply of the plaintiff or complainant to the defendant's plea or answer. **4.** reverberation; echo. **5.** a copy. **6.** duplication of an experiment, esp. to expose or reduce error. [ME *replicacioun* < MF *replication* < L *replicātiōn-* (s. of *replicātiō*) a rolling back, equiv. to *replicāt(us)* (see REPLICATE) + *-iōn-* -ION]

re·ply (ri plī′), *v.*, **-plied, -ply·ing,** *n., pl.* **-plies.** —*v.i.* **1.** to make answer in words or writing; answer; respond: *to reply to a question.* **2.** to respond by some action, performance, etc.: *to reply to the enemy's fire.* **3.** to return a sound; echo; resound. **4.** *Law.* to answer a defendant's plea. —*v.t.* **5.** to return as an answer (usually used in a negative combination or fol. by a clause with *that*): *Not a syllable did he reply. He replied that no one would go.* —*n.* **6.** an answer or response in words or writing. **7.** a response made by some action, performance, etc. [ME *replie(n)* < MF *repli(er)* (to) fold back, reply < L *replicāre* to unroll, fold back; see REPLICATE] —**re·pli′er,** *n.*
—**Syn. 1.** rejoin. **6.** rejoinder, riposte. See **answer.**

ré·pon·dez s'il vous plaît (rā pôn dā′ sēl vōō plā′; *Fr.* rā pôn dā′ sēl vōō ple′). See **R.S.V.P.**

re·port (ri pōrt′, -pôrt′), *n.* **1.** an account or statement describing in detail an event, situation, or the like, usually as the result of observation, inquiry, etc.: *a report on the peace conference; a medical report on the patient.* **2.** a statement or announcement. **3.** a widely circulated statement or item of news; rumor; gossip. **4.** an account of a speech, debate, meeting, etc., esp. as taken down for publication. **5.** a loud noise, as from an explosion: *the report of a distant cannon.* **6.** a statement of a student's grades, level of achievement, or academic standing for or during a prescribed period of time. **7.** a statement of a judicial opinion or decision, or of a case argued and determined in a court of justice. **8.** **reports,** *Law.* a collection of adjudications. **9.** repute; reputation; fame: *a man of bad report.* —*v.t.* **10.** to carry and repeat, as an answer or message; repeat, as what one has heard. **11.** to relate, as what has been learned by observation or investigation. **12.** to give or render a formal account or statement of: *to report a deficit.* **13.** to make a formal report on (a bill, amendment, etc., officially referred), often with revisions, deletions, or the like. **14.** to make a charge against (a person), as to a superior: *I intend to report him to the Dean for cheating.* **15.** to make known the presence, condition, or whereabouts of: *to report a ship missing.* **16.** to present (oneself) to a person in authority, as in accordance with requirements. **17.** to take down (a speech, lecture, etc.) in writing. **18.** to write an account of (an event, situation, etc.), as for publication in a newspaper. **19.** to relate or tell. —*v.i.* **20.** to prepare, make, or submit a report of something observed, investigated, or the like. **21.** to serve or work as a reporter, as for a newspaper. **22.** to make one's condition or whereabouts known, as to a person in authority: *to report sick.* **23.** to present oneself duly, as at a place: *Report to Room 101 at 8:30 A.M. tomorrow.* [ME *report(en)* < MF, OF *report(er)* < L *reportāre* to carry back, equiv. to *re-* RE- + *portāre* to carry] —**re·port′a·ble,** *adj.*
—**Syn. 1.** description, story. **2.** bulletin, dispatch. **5.** shot, detonation. **10, 11.** relay. **14.** accuse. **19.** narrate, rehearse, recount, describe, detail, repeat.

re·port·age (ri pōr′tij, -pôr′-, rə pōr täzh′, -pôr-), *n.* **1.** the act or technique of reporting news. **2.** reported news collectively: *an anthology of poetry, fiction, and reportage.* **3.** a written account of an act, event, history, etc., based on direct observation or on thorough research and documentation. [< F; see REPORT, -AGE]

report′ card′, a written report containing an evaluation of a pupil's scholarship and behavior, sent periodically to his parents or guardian, usually on a card containing marks and comments together with a record of attendance.

re·port·ed·ly (ri pōr′tid lē), *adv.* according to report or rumor: *He is reportedly a billionaire.* [REPORT + -ED[2] + -LY]

re·port·er (ri pōr′tər, -pôr′-), *n.* **1.** one who reports. **2.** a person employed to gather and report news, as for a newspaper, wire service, or radio station. **3.** one who prepares official reports, as of legal or legislative proceedings. [ME *reportour* < AF. See REPORT, -ER[1]]

report′ing pay′. See **call-in pay.**

rep·or·to·ri·al (rep′ər tōr′ē əl, -tôr′-, rē′pōr-, -pôr-), *adj.* **1.** of or pertaining to a reporter. **2.** of, noting, or characteristic of a report: *His lecture was more reportorial than analytical.* [irreg. (-OR[2] r. -ER[1]) REPORTER + -IAL] —**rep′or·to′ri·al·ly,** *adv.*

re·pos·al (ri pō′zəl), *n.* act of reposing. [REPOSE[1] + -AL[2]]

re·pose (rē pōz′), *v.t., v.i.*, **-posed, -pos·ing.** to pose again. [RE- + POSE[1]]

re·pose[1] (ri pōz′), *n., v.*, **-posed, -pos·ing.** —*n.* **1.** the state of reposing or being at rest; rest; sleep. **2.** peace; tranquillity; calm. **3.** dignified calmness, as of manner; composure. **4.** absence of movement, animation, etc.: *When in repose, her little face is sad and knowing beyond her years.* —*v.i.* **5.** to lie or be at rest, as from work, activity, etc. **6.** to lie dead: *His body will repose in the chapel for two days.* **7.** to be peacefully calm and quiet: *The sea reposed under the tropical sun.* **8.** to lie or rest on something: *We could see festive, holiday cakes reposing on the sideboard.* **9.** to depend or rely on a person or thing. —*v.t.* **10.** to lay to rest; rest; refresh by rest (often used reflexively). [ME *repose(n)* < MF, OF *repos(er)* < LL *repausāre,* equiv. to L *re-* RE- + LL *pausāre* to rest (deriv. of L *pausa* PAUSE)] —**re·pos·ed·ly** (ri pō′zid lē), *adv.* —**re·pos′ed·ness,** *n.* —**re·pos′er,** *n.*

re·pose[2] (ri pōz′), *v.t.*, **-posed, -pos·ing.** **1.** to put (confidence, trust, etc.) in a person or thing. **2.** to put under the authority or at the disposal of a person or persons. **3.** *Archaic.* to deposit. [ME *repose(n)* (to) replace, irreg. (modeled after DISPOSE, etc.) < L *repos-,* perfect s., as in *reposuī, repositus* of *repōnere* to put back, replace]

re·pose·ful (ri pōz′fəl), *adj.* full of or suggesting repose; calm; quiet. [REPOSE[1] + -FUL] —**re·pose′ful·ly,** *adv.* —**re·pose′ful·ness,** *n.*
—**Syn.** restful, tranquil, peaceful, undisturbed.

re·pos·it (ri poz′it), *v.t.* **1.** to put back; replace. **2.** to lay up or store; deposit. [< L *reposit(us)* put back, replaced (ptp. of *repōnere*), equiv. to *re-* RE- + *posit(us)* placed (ptp. of *pōnere*); see POSIT]

re·po·si·tion (rē′pə zish′ən, rep′ə-), *n.* **1.** the act of depositing or storing. **2.** replacement, as of a bone. [< LL *repositiōn-* (s. of *repositiō*) a laying up, equiv. to L *reposit(us)* (see REPOSIT) + *-iōn-* -ION]

re·pos·i·to·ri·um (ri poz′i tōr′ē əm, -tôr′-), *n., pl.* **-to·ri·a** (-tōr′ē ə, -tôr′-). a place for the storage of valuables, as in an ancient Roman temple or a church. [< L: REPOSITORY]

re·pos·i·tor·y (ri poz′i tōr′ē, -tôr′ē), *n., pl.* **-tor·ies.** **1.** a receptacle or place where things are deposited, stored, or offered for sale. **2.** a burial place; sepulcher. **3.** a person to whom something is entrusted or confided. **4.** *Chiefly Brit.* warehouse. [< L *repositōri(um)* that in which anything is placed, equiv. to *reposit(us)* (see REPOSIT) + *-ōrium* -ORY[2]]

re·pos·sess (rē′pə zes′), *v.t.* **1.** to possess again; regain possession of, esp. for nonpayment of money due: *She couldn't meet the payments, so they repossessed the furniture.* **2.** to put again in possession of something: *to repossess the Bourbons of their throne.* [RE- + POSSESS] —**re·pos·ses·sion** (rē′pə zesh′ən), *n.* —**re′pos·ses′sor,** *n.*

re·pous·sage (rə pōō säzh′), *n.* **1.** the art or process of working in repoussé. **2.** the flattening of the hollow areas of an etching or engraving plate by hammering it gently on the reverse side. [< F, equiv. to *repouss(er)* (see REPOUSSÉ) + *-age* -AGE]

re·pous·sé (rə pōō sā′), *adj.* **1.** (of a design) raised in relief by hammering on the reverse side. **2.** ornamented or made in this kind of raised work. —*n.* **3.** the art or process of producing repoussé designs. [< F, ptp. of *repousser.* See RE-, PUSH]

re·pous·soir (rə pōō swär′), *n. Painting.* a figure or object in the extreme foreground: used as a contrast and to increase the illusion of depth. [< F, equiv. to *repouss(er)* (to) push back (see REPOUSSÉ) + *-oir* -ORY[2]]

repp (rep), *n.* rep[1].

Rep·plier (rep′lēr), *n.* **Agnes,** 1855–1950, U.S. essayist.

repr., **1.** represented. **2.** representing. **3.** reprint. **4.** reprinted.

rep·re·hend (rep′ri hend′), *v.t.* to reprove or find fault with; rebuke; censure; blame. [ME *reprehend(en)* < L *reprehend(ere)* (to) hold back, restrain, equiv. to *re-* RE- + *prehendere* to seize; see GET] —**rep′re·hend′a·ble,** *adj.* —**rep′re·hend′er,** *n.*
—**Syn.** reproach, upbraid, chide, admonish.

rep·re·hen·si·ble (rep′ri hen′sə bəl), *adj.* deserving of reproof, rebuke, or censure; blameworthy. [ME < LL *reprehensibil(is),* equiv. to L *reprehens(us)* (ptp. of *reprehendere* to REPREHEND) + *-ibilis* -IBLE] —**rep′re·hen′si·bil′i·ty, rep′re·hen′si·ble·ness,** *n.* —**rep′re·hen′si·bly,** *adv.*
—**Syn.** culpable. —**Ant.** praiseworthy.

rep·re·hen·sion (rep′ri hen′shən), *n.* the act of reprehending; reproof; censure. [ME < L *reprehensiōn-* (s. of *reprehensiō*), equiv. to *reprehens(us)* (ptp. of *reprehendere* to REPREHEND) + *-iōn-* -ION] —**rep·re·hen·sive** (rep′ri hen′siv), *adj.* —**rep′re·hen′sive·ly,** *adv.*

re·pre·sent (rē′pri zent′), *v.t.* to present again or anew. [RE- + PRESENT[2]]

rep·re·sent (rep′ri zent′), *v.t.* **1.** to serve to express, designate, stand for, or denote, as a word, symbol, or the like does; symbolize: *In this painting the cat represents evil and the bird, good.* **2.** to express or designate by some term, character, symbol, or the like: *to represent musical sounds by notes.* **3.** to stand or act in the place of, as a substitute, proxy, or agent does: *He represents the company in Ashtabula.* **4.** to speak and act for by delegated authority: *to represent one's government in a foreign country.* **5.** to act for or in behalf of (a constituency, State, etc.) by deputed right in exercising a voice in legislation or government: *He represents Chicago's third Congressional District.* **6.** to portray or depict; present the likeness of, as a picture does: *The painting represents him as a man 22 years old.* **7.** to present or picture to the mind. **8.** to present in words; set forth; describe; state. **9.** to set forth or describe as having a particular character (usually fol. by *as, to be,* etc.): *The article represented the dictator as a benevolent despot.* **10.** to set forth clearly or earnestly with a view to influencing opinion or action or making protest. **11.** to present, produce, or perform, as on a stage. **12.** to impersonate, as in acting. **13.** to serve as an example or specimen of; exemplify: *a genus represented by two species.* **14.** to be the equivalent of; correspond to: *The llama of the New World represents the camel of the Old World.* [ME *represent(en)* < MF *represent(er)* < L *repraesentāre,* equiv. to *re-* RE- + *praesentāre* to PRESENT[2]] —**rep′re·sent′a·bil′i·ty,** *n.* —**rep′re·sent′a·ble,** *adj.*
—**Syn. 1.** exemplify. **6.** delineate. **9.** state. **12.** personate.

rep·re·sen·ta·tion (rep′ri zen tā′shən), *n.* **1.** the act of representing. **2.** the state of being represented. **3.** the expression or designation by some term, character, symbol, or the like. **4.** action or speech on behalf of a person, group, business house, state, or the like by an agent, deputy, or representative. **5.** the state or fact of being so represented: *to demand representation on a board of directors.* **6.** *Govt.* the state, fact, or right of being represented by delegates having a voice in legislation or government. **7.** the body or number of representatives, as of a constituency. **8.** *Diplomacy.* **a.** the act of speaking or negotiating on behalf of a state. **b.** an utterance on behalf of a state. **9.** presentation to the mind, as of an idea or image. **10.** a mental image or idea so presented; concept. **11.** the act of portrayal, picturing, or other rendering in visible form. **12.** a picture, figure, statue, etc. **13.** the production or a performance of a play or the like, as on the stage. **14.** Often, **representations.** a description or statement, as of things true or alleged. **15.** a statement of facts, reasons, etc., made in appealing or protesting; a protest or remonstrance. **16.** *Law.* an implication or statement of fact to which legal liability may attach if material: *a representation of authority.* [ME *representacion* < L *repraesentātiōn-* (s. of *repraesentātiō*), equiv. to *repraesentāt(us)* (ptp. of *repraesentāre* to REPRESENT) + *-iōn-* -ION] —**rep′re·sen·ta′tion·al,** *adj.*

rep·re·sen·ta·tion·al·ism (rep′ri zen tā′shə nᵊliz′əm), *n.* **1.** Also called **represen′tative re′alism.** *Epistemology.* a Lockean form of subjective idealism in which the perception of an object represents exactly the primary qualities of the object itself. **2.** *Fine Arts.* the practice or principle of representing or depicting an object in a recognizable manner, esp. the portrayal of the surface characteristics of an object as they appear to the eye. [REPRESENTATIONAL + -ISM] —**rep′re·sen·ta′tion·al·ist,** *n.* —**rep′re·sen·ta′tion·al·is′tic,** *adj.*

rep·re·sent·a·tive (rep′ri zen′tə tiv), *n.* **1.** one who or that which represents another or others. **2.** an agent or deputy: *a legal representative.* **3.** a person who represents a constituency or community in a legislative body, esp. a member of the U.S. House of Representatives or a lower house in certain State legislatures. **4.** a typical example or specimen of a group, quality, or kind. —*adj.* **5.** serving to represent; representing. **6.** standing or acting for another or others. **7.** representing a constituency, community, or the people generally in legislation or government: *a representative assembly.* **8.** characterized by, founded on, or pertaining to representation of the people in government: *a representative government.* **9.** exemplifying a group or kind; typical: *a representative selection of Elizabethan plays.* **10.** corresponding to or replacing some other species or the like, as in a different locality. **11.** of, pertaining to, or characteristic of representationalism. **12.** pertaining to or of the nature of a mental image or representation. [ME < ML *repraesentātīv(us),* equiv. to *repraesentāt(us)* (see REPRESENTATION) + *-īvus* -IVE] —**rep′re·sent′a·tive·ly,** *adv.* —**rep′re·sent′a·tive·ness,** *n.*

re·press (rē′pres′), *v.t., v.i.* to press again or anew. [RE- + PRESS[1]]

re·press (ri pres′), *v.t.* **1.** to keep under control, check, or suppress (desires, feelings, actions, tears, etc.). **2.** to keep down or suppress (anything objectionable). **3.** to put down or quell (sedition, disorder, etc.). **4.** to reduce (persons) to subjection. **5.** *Psychoanal.* to reject (painful or disagreeable ideas, memories, feelings, or impulses) from the conscious mind. [ME *repress(en)* < L *repress(us)* kept back, restrained (ptp. of *reprimere*), equiv. to *re-* RE- + *pressus;* see PRESS[1]] —**re·press′er, re·pres′sor,** *n.* —**re·press′i·ble,** *adj.*
—**Syn. 1.** bridle, control. See **check. 3.** subdue, quash. **4.** crush. —**Ant. 1–4.** foster.

re·plant′, *v.t.*
re·plas′ter, *v.t.*
re·plate′, *v.t.*, **-plat·ed, -plat·ing.**
re·play′, *v.t.*
re′play, *n.*
re·plead′, *v.*
re·pledge′, *v.t.*, **-pledged, -pledg·ing;** *n.*
re·plot′, *v.t.*, **-plot·ted, -plot·ting.**
re·plow′, *v.t.*, **-plowed, -plow·ing.**
re·plume′, *v.t.*, **-plumed, -plum·ing.**
re·plunge′, *v.*, **-plunged, -plung·ing.**
re′po·lar·i·za′tion, *n.*
re·po′lar·ize′, *v.t.*, **-ized, -iz·ing.**
re·pol′ish, *v., n.*
re·pon′der, *v.i.*
re′pop·u·lar·i·za′tion, *n.*
re·pop′u·lar·ize′, *v.t.*, **-ized, -iz·ing.**
re·pop′u·late′, *v.t.*, **-lat·ed, -lat·ing.**
re′pop·u·la′tion, *n.*
re·por′tion, *v.t.*
re·post′, *v.t.*
re′post·pone′, *v.t.*, **-poned, -pon·ing.**
re·pos′tu·late′, *v.t.*, **-lat·ed, -lat·ing;** *n.*
re′pos·tu·la′tion, *n.*
re·pour′, *v.t.*
re·prac′tice, *v.t.*, **-ticed, -tic·ing.**
re·praise′, *v.t.*, **-praised, -prais·ing.**
re·prem′ise, *v.*, **-ised, -is·ing.**
re′pre·pare′, *v.t.*, **-pared, -par·ing.**
re′pre·scribe′, *v.t.*, **-scribed, -scrib·ing.**

re·pres·sion (ri presh′ən), *n.* **1.** the act of repressing; state of being repressed. **2.** *Psychoanal.* the rejection from consciousness of painful or disagreeable ideas, memories, feelings, or impulses. [ME *repressioun* < ML *repressiōn-* (s. of LL *repressiō*), equiv. to L *repress(us)* (see REPRESS) + *-iōn-* -ION]

re·pres·sive (ri pres′iv), *adj.* tending or serving to repress. [< ML *repressīv(us)* < L *repress(us)* (see REPRESS) + *-īvus* -IVE] **—re·pres′sive·ly,** *adv.* **—re·pres′sive·ness,** *n.*

re·prieve (ri prēv′), *v.,* **-prieved, -priev·ing,** *n.* **—***v.t.* **1.** to respite (a person) from impending punishment, esp. to grant a stay of execution to (a condemned person). **2.** to relieve temporarily from any evil. **—***n.* **3.** respite from impending punishment, esp. from execution of a sentence of death. **4.** a warrant authorizing this. **5.** any respite or temporary relief. [b. ME *reprieven* to REPROVE, appar. taken in literal sense of to test again (involving postponement) and ME *repried* (ptp.) < OF *reprit* (see REPRISE)] **—re·priev′er,** *n.*

rep·ri·mand (rep′rə mand′, -mänd′), *n.* **1.** a severe reproof or rebuke, esp. a formal one by a person in authority. **—***v.t.* **2.** to reprove or rebuke severely, esp. in a formal way. [< F *réprimande,* MF *reprimend* < L *reprimenda* that is to be repressed (fem. ger. of *reprimere*), equiv. to *re-* RE- + *prim-* PRESS[1]] **—rep′ri·mand′er,** *n.* **—rep′ri·mand′ing·ly,** *adv.* **—Syn. 1.** condemnation, reprehension. **1, 2.** censure. **2.** condemn, reprehend.

re·print (*v.* rē print′; *n.* rē′print′), *v.t.* **1.** to print again; print a new impression of. **—***n.* **2.** a reproduction in print of matter already printed. **3.** *Philately.* an impression from the original plate after the issuance of the stamps has ceased and their use for postage has been voided. **4.** a new impression, without alteration, of any printed work. [RE- + PRINT] **—re·print′er,** *n.*

re·pris·al (ri prī′zəl), *n.* **1.** (in warfare) retaliation against an enemy, for injuries received, by the infliction of equal or greater injuries. **2.** an act or an instance of retaliation. **3.** the action or practice of using force, short of war, against another nation, to secure redress of a grievance. **4.** the forcible seizure of property or subjects in retaliation. [ME *reprisail* < OF *reprisaille.* See REPRISE, -AL[2]] **—Syn. 1.** redress. See **revenge.**

re·prise (ri prīz′ *for 1;* ri prīz′, rə prēz′ *for 2, 3*), *n., v.,* **-prised, -pris·ing.** **—***n.* **1.** Usually, **reprises.** *Law.* an annual deduction, duty, or payment out of a manor or estate, as an annuity or the like. **2.** *Music.* **a.** a repetition. **b.** a return to the first theme or subject. **—***v.t.* **3.** to execute a repetition of; repeat: *They reprised the elaborate dance number in the third act.* [ME < MF: a taking back, OF, n. use of fem. ptp. of *reprendre* to take back < L *reprehendere* to REPREHEND]

re·pro (rē′prō), *n., pl.* **-pros.** *Informal.* **1.** reproduction (def. 3). **2.** See **reproduction proof.** [by shortening]

re·proach (ri prōch′), *v.t.* **1.** to find fault with (a person, group, etc.); blame; censure. **2.** to upbraid (usually fol. by *with*). **3.** to be a cause of blame or discredit to. **—***n.* **4.** blame or censure conveyed in disapproval: *a term of reproach.* **5.** an expression of upbraiding, censure, or reproof. **6.** disgrace, discredit, or blame incurred: *to bring reproach on one's family.* **7.** a cause or occasion of disgrace or discredit. **8. the Reproaches.** Also called **Improperia.** *Rom. Cath. Ch., Anglican Ch.* a series of antiphons sung in church on Good Friday, consisting of words addressed by Christ to His people, reminding them of His mercies and of their ingratitude. **9.** an object of scorn or contempt. [ME *reproche* (n.) < OF, deriv. of *reprochier* < VL **repropiāre,* equiv. to L *re-* RE- + LL **propiāre* (< L *prope* near); see APPROACH] **—re·proach′a·ble,** *adj.* **—re·proach′a·ble·ness,** *n.* **—re·proach′a·bly,** *adv.* **—re·proach′er,** *n.* **—re·proach′ing·ly,** *adv.*
—Syn. 1. chide, abuse, reprimand, reprehend, condemn, criticize. REPROACH, REBUKE, SCOLD, REPROVE imply calling one to account for something done or said. REPROACH is censure (often about personal matters, obligations, and the like) given with an attitude of fault finding and some intention of shaming: *to reproach one for neglect.* REBUKE suggests sharp or stern reproof given usually formally or officially and approaching *reprimand* in severity: *He rebuked him strongly for laxness in his accounts.* SCOLD suggests that censure is given at some length, harshly, and more or less abusively; it implies irritation, which may be with or without justification: *to scold a boy for jaywalking.* A word of related meaning, but suggesting a milder or more kindly censure, often intended to correct the fault in question, is REPROVE: *to reprove one for inattention.* **3.** shame. **4, 5.** reprehension, rebuke, criticism, remonstrance, condemnation, disapproval. **6.** dishonor, shame, disrepute, odium, obloquy, opprobrium, ignominy, infamy, scorn. **—Ant. 1, 4, 5.** praise. **6.** honor.

re·proach·ful (ri prōch′fəl), *adj.* **1.** full of or expressing reproach or censure: *a reproachful look.* **2.** *Obs.* deserving reproach; shameful. [REPROACH + -FUL] **—re·proach′ful·ly,** *adv.* **—re·proach′ful·ness,** *n.*

re·proach·less (ri prōch′lis), *adj.* irreproachable. [REPROACH + -LESS] **—re·proach′less·ness,** *n.*

rep·ro·bate (rep′rə bāt′), *n., adj., v.,* **-bat·ed, -bat·ing.** **—***n.* **1.** a depraved, unprincipled, or wicked person: *a penniless, drunken reprobate.* **2.** a person rejected by God and beyond hope of salvation. **—***adj.* **3.** morally depraved; unprincipled; bad. **4.** rejected by God and beyond hope of salvation. **—***v.t.* **5.** to disapprove, condemn, or censure. **6.** (of God) to reject (a person), as for sin; exclude from the number of the elect or from salvation. [ME *reprobate(n)* (v.) < L *reprobāt(us)* disapproved, rejected, ptp. of *reprobāre* to REPROVE] **—rep·ro·ba·cy** (rep′rə bə sē), **rep′ro·bate′ness,** *n.* **—rep′ro·bat′er,** *n.*
—Syn. 1. tramp, scoundrel, wastrel, miscreant, wretch, rascal, cad, rogue. **2.** outcast, pariah. **3.** wicked, sinful, evil, corrupt. **5.** reprehend, blame, rebuke, reprove.

rep·ro·ba·tion (rep′rə bā′shən), *n.* **1.** disapproval, condemnation, or censure. **2.** rejection. **3.** *Theol.* rejection by God, as of persons excluded from the number of the elect or from salvation. [ME *reprobacion* < LL *reprobātiōn-* (s. of *reprobātiō*) rejection, equiv. to *reprobāt(us)* (see REPROBATE) + *-iōn-* -ION] **—rep′ro·ba′tion·ar′y,** *adj.*

rep·ro·ba·tive (rep′rə bā′tiv), *adj.* reprobating; expressing reprobation. [REPROBATE + -IVE] **—rep′ro·ba′tive·ly,** *adv.*

re·proc·essed (rē pros′est), *adj.* (of wool) previously spun and woven but not used, as tailors' clippings. [RE- + PROCESSED]

re·pro·duce (rē′prə dōōs′, -dyōōs′), *v.,* **-duced, -duc·ing.** **—***v.t.* **1.** to make a copy, representation, duplicate, or close imitation of: *to reproduce a picture.* **2.** to produce again or anew by natural process: *to reproduce a torn claw.* **3.** *Biol.* to produce one or more other individuals of (a given kind of animal or plant) by some process of generation or propagation, sexual or asexual. **4.** to cause or foster the reproduction of (animals or plants). **5.** to produce, form, make, or bring about again or anew in any manner. **6.** to recall to the mind or have a mental image of (a past incident, scene, etc.), as by the aid of memory or imagination. **7.** to produce again, as a play produced at an earlier time. **—***v.i.* **8.** to reproduce its kind, as a plant or an animal; propagate; bear offspring. **9.** to turn out in a given manner when copied: *This picture will reproduce well.* [RE- + PRODUCE] **—re′pro·duc′er,** *n.* **—re′pro·duc′i·bil′i·ty,** *n.* **—re′pro·duc′i·ble,** *adj.* **—Syn. 3.** generate, propagate, beget. **5.** repeat. See **imitate.**

re·pro·duc·tion (rē′prə duk′shən), *n.* **1.** the act or process of reproducing. **2.** the state of being reproduced. **3.** something made by reproducing an original; copy; duplicate: *a photographic reproduction; a reproduction of a Florentine cassone.* **4.** *Biol.* the natural process among animals and plants by which new individuals are generated and the species perpetuated. [RE- + PRODUCTION]
—Syn. 3. replica, facsimile. **4.** generation, propagation.

reproduc′tion proof′. See **repro proof.**

re·pro·duc·tive (rē′prə duk′tiv), *adj.* **1.** serving to reproduce. **2.** concerned with or pertaining to reproduction: *a reproductive process; reproductive organs.* **—***n.* **3.** *Entomol.* a sexually mature male or female termite; a member of the reproductive caste. [RE- + PRODUCTIVE] **—re′pro·duc′tive·ly,** *adv.* **—re′pro·duc′tive·ness,** *n.*

reproduc′tive imagina′tion. See under **imagination** (def. 3).

re·prog·ra·phy (ri prog′rə fē), *n.* the reproduction and duplication of documents, written materials, drawings, designs, etc., by any process making use of light rays or photographic means, including offset printing, microfilming, photography, office duplicating, etc. [REPRO(DUCTION) + (PHOTO)GRAPHY]

re·proof (ri prōōf′), *n.* **1.** the act of reproving, censuring, or rebuking. **2.** an expression of censure or rebuke. [ME *reprof* < OF *reprove,* deriv. of *reprover* to REPROVE] **—re·proof′less,** *adj.*

re′pro proof′, *Print.* a proof, usually pulled on glossy paper, of a fidelity suitable for reproduction by photography for making a plate. Also called **repro, reproduction proof.**

re·prov·a·ble (ri prōō′və bəl), *adj.* deserving of reproof. [ME < MF, equiv. to *reprov(er)* (to) REPROVE + *-able* -ABLE] **—re·prov′a·ble·ness,** *n.*

re·prov·al (ri prōō′vəl), *n.* **1.** the act of reproving. **2.** a reproof. [REPROVE + -AL[2]]

re-prove (rē prōōv′), *v.t., v.i.,* **-proved, -proved** or **-prov·en, -prov·ing.** to prove again. [RE- + PROVE]

re·prove (ri prōōv′), *v.,* **-proved, -prov·ing.** **—***v.t.* **1.** to address words of disapproval to; rebuke. **2.** to express disapproval of (actions, words, etc.). **3.** *Obs.* to disprove or refute. **—***v.i.* **4.** to speak in reproof; administer a reproof. [ME *reprov(en)* < OF *reprov(er)* < LL *reprobāre,* equiv. to *re-* RE- + *probāre* to test, PROVE] **—re·prov′er,** *n.* **—re·prov′ing·ly,** *adv.*
—Syn. 1. censure, reprimand, upbraid, chide, reprehend, admonish. See **reproach. —Ant. 1.** praise.

Rep·sold (rep′səld), *n.* a walled plain in the second quadrant of the face of the moon: about 70 miles in diameter.

rept., **1.** (in prescriptions) let it be repeated. [< L *repetātur*] **2.** report.

rep·tant (rep′tənt), *adj.* **1.** *Zool.* creeping. **2.** *Bot.* repent[2]. [< L *reptant-* (s. of *reptāns,* prp. of *reptāre*) creeping, equiv. to *rept-* (freq. s. of *rēpere* to creep) + *-ant-* -ANT]

rep·tile (rep′til, -tīl), *n.* **1.** any cold-blooded vertebrate of the class *Reptilia,* comprising the turtles, lizards, snakes, crocodilians, and the tuatara. **2.** (loosely) any of various animals that crawl or creep. **3.** a groveling, mean, or despicable person. **—***adj.* **4.** creeping or crawling. **5.** groveling, mean, or despicable. [ME *reptil* < LL *reptile,* neut. of *reptilis* creeping, equiv. to L *rept(us)* (ptp. of *rēpere* to creep) + *-ilis* -ILE] **—rep′tile·like′,** *adj.* **—rep·ti·loid** (rep′tᵊloid′), *adj.*

Rep·til·i·a (rep til′ē ə), *n.* the class comprising the reptiles. [< NL; see REPTILIAN]

rep·til·i·an (rep til′ē ən, -til′yən), *adj.* **1.** belonging or pertaining to the *Reptilia.* **2.** groveling, debased or despicable; contemptible. **3.** mean; treacherous; harmful. **—***n.* **4.** a reptile. [< NL *Reptili(a)* reptiles (pl. of *reptile,* neut. of LL *reptilis;* see REPTILE) + -AN]

Repub., **1.** Republic. **2.** Republican.

re·pub·lic (ri pub′lik), *n.* **1.** a state in which the supreme power rests in the body of citizens entitled to vote and is exercised by representatives chosen directly or indirectly by them. **2.** any body of persons viewed as a commonwealth. **3.** a state, esp. a democratic state, in which the head of government is an elected or nominated president and not a monarch or other hereditary head of state. **4.** any of the five periods of republican government in France. Cf. **First Republic, Second Republic, Third Republic, Fourth Republic, Fifth Republic. 5.** (*cap., italics.*) a philosophical dialogue (4th century B.C.) by Plato dealing with the composition and structure of the ideal state. [< F *république,* MF < L *rēs publica,* equiv. to *rēs* thing, matter + *publica* PUBLIC]

re·pub·li·can (ri pub′li kən), *adj.* **1.** of, pertaining to, or of the nature of a republic. **2.** favoring a republic. **3.** fitting or appropriate for the citizen of a republic: *That is certainly a very republican notion.* **4.** (*cap.*) of or pertaining to the Republican party. **—***n.* **5.** one who favors a republican form of government. **6.** (*cap.*) a member of the Republican party. [< F *républicain* < MF. See REPUBLIC, -AN]

re·pub·li·can·ise (ri pub′li kə nīz′), *v.t.,* **-ised, -is·ing.** *Chiefly Brit.* republicanize. **—re·pub′li·can·i·sa′tion,** *n.* **—re·pub′li·can·is′er,** *n.*

re·pub·li·can·ism (ri pub′li kə niz′əm), *n.* **1.** republican government. **2.** republican principles or adherence to them. **3.** (*cap.*) the principles or policy of the Republican party. [REPUBLICAN + -ISM]

re·pub·li·can·ize (ri pub′li kə nīz′), *v.t.,* **-ized, -iz·ing.** to make republican. Also, *esp. Brit.,* **republicanise.** [< F *républicanis(er),* equiv. to *républicain* REPUBLICAN + *-iser* -IZE] **—re·pub′li·can·i·za′tion,** *n.* **—re·pub′li·can·iz′er,** *n.*

Repub′lican par′ty, **1.** one of the two major political parties in the U.S.: originated 1854–56. **2.** *U.S. Hist.* See **Democratic-Republican party.**

Repub′lican Riv′er, a river flowing E from E Colorado through Nebraska and Kansas into the Kansas River. 422 mi. long.

re·pub·li·ca·tion (rē′pub lə kā′shən), *n.* **1.** publication anew. **2.** a book or the like published again. [RE- + PUBLICATION]

repub′lic of let′ters, **1.** the collective body of literary people. **2.** literature.

Ré·pu·blique Mal·gache (rā py blēk′ mal gash′), French name of **Malagasy Republic.**

re·pu·di·ate (ri pyōō′dē āt′), *v.t.,* **-at·ed, -at·ing.** **1.** to reject as having no authority or binding force: *to repudiate a claim.* **2.** to cast off or disown: *to repudiate a son.* **3.** to reject with disapproval or condemnation: *to repudiate a new doctrine.* **4.** to reject with denial: *to repudiate a charge as untrue.* **5.** to refuse to acknowledge and pay (a debt), as a state, municipality, etc. [< L *repudiāt(us)* cast off, put away (ptp. of *repudiāre*), equiv. to *repudi(um)* a casting off, divorce (*re-* RE- + *pud(ere)* to make ashamed, feel shame; see PUDENDUM) + *-ātus* -ATE[1]] **—re·pu′di·a·ble,** *adj.* **—re·pu′di·a′tive,** *adj.* **—re·pu′di·a′tor,** *n.*
—Syn. 1. disavow, renounce, discard, disclaim. **3.** condemn, disapprove. **—Ant. 1.** accept. **3.** approve.

re·pu·di·a·tion (ri pyōō′dē ā′shən), *n.* **1.** the act of repudiating. **2.** the state of being repudiated. **3.** refusal, as by a state or municipality, to pay a debt lawfully contracted. [< L *repudiātiōn-* (s. of *repudiātiō*) equiv. to *repudiāt(us)* (see REPUDIATE) + *-iōn-* -ION] **—re·pu·di·a·to·ry** (ri pyōō′dē ə tôr′ē, -tōr′ē), *adj.*

re·pugn (ri pyōōn′), *v.t.* **1.** to oppose or refute. **—***v.i.* **2.** *Archaic.* to resist. [ME *repugnen* < MF *repugn(er)* < L *repugnāre* to resist, equiv. to *re-* RE- + *pugnāre* to fight]

re·pug·nance (ri pug′nəns), *n.* **1.** the state of being repugnant. **2.** strong distaste, aversion, or objection; antipathy. **3.** contradictoriness or inconsistency. Also, **re·pug′nan·cy.** [ME *repugnance* < MF < L *repugnantia,* equiv. to *repugn(āre)* to REPUGN + *-antia* -ANCE]
—Syn. 2. reluctance, hatred, hostility. See **dislike. 3.** contrariety, incompatibility, irreconcilability. **—Ant. 2.** attraction, liking. **3.** compatibility.

re·pug·nant (ri pug′nənt), *adj.* **1.** distasteful, objectionable, or offensive: *the repugnant smell of rotten eggs.* **2.** making opposition; objecting; averse. **3.** opposed or contrary, as in nature or character. [ME *repugnaunt* < MF < L *repugnant-* (s. of *repugnāns,* prp. of *repugnāre*), equiv. to *repugn-* REPUGN + *-ant-* -ANT] **—re·pug′nant·ly,** *adv.*
—Syn. 3. antagonistic, adverse, hostile.

re·pulse (ri puls′), *v.,* **-pulsed, -puls·ing,** *n.* **—***v.t.* **1.** to drive back; repel: *to repulse an assailant.* **2.** to repel with denial, discourtesy, or the like; refuse or reject. **—***n.* **3.** the act of repelling. **4.** the fact of being repelled, as in hostile encounter. **5.** a refusal or rejection. [< L *repuls(us),* ptp. of *repellere* to REPEL] **—re·puls′er,** *n.*

re·pul·sion (ri pul′shən), *n.* **1.** the act of repelling or driving back. **2.** the state of being repelled. **3.** the feeling of being repelled, as by the thought or presence of something; distaste, repugnance, or aversion. **4.** *Physics.* the force that acts between bodies of like electric charge or magnetic polarity, tending to separate them. [< MF < ML *repulsiōn-* (s. of LL *repulsiō*), equiv. to L *repuls(us)* (see REPULSE) + *-iōn-* -ION]

re·pul·sive (ri pul′siv), *adj.* **1.** causing repugnance or aversion: *a repulsive mask.* **2.** tending to repel by denial, discourtesy, or the like. **3.** *Physics.* of the nature of or characterized by physical repulsion. [REPULSE + -IVE] **—re·pul′sive·ly,** *adv.* **—re·pul′sive·ness,** *n.*

re·pur·chase (rē pûr′chəs), *v.,* **-chased, -chas·ing,** *n.* **—***v.t.* **1.** to buy again; regain by purchase. **—***n.* **2.** the act of repurchasing. [RE- + PURCHASE] **—re·pur′chas·er,** *n.*

rep·u·ta·ble (rep′yə tə bəl), *adj.* **1.** held in good repute; honorable; respectable; estimable: *a reputable organization.* **2.** considered to be good or acceptable usage; standard: *reputable speech.* [REPUTE + -ABLE] **—rep′u·ta·bil′i·ty, rep′u·ta·ble·ness,** *n.* **—rep′u·ta·bly,** *adv.*

rep·u·ta·tion (rep′yə tā′shən), *n.* **1.** the estimation in which a person or thing is held, esp. by the community or the public generally; repute: *a man of good reputation.* **2.** favorable repute; good name: *to ruin one's reputation by misconduct.* **3.** a favorable and publicly recognized name or standing for merit, achievement, etc.: *to build up a reputation.* **4.** the estimation or name of being, having, having done, etc., something specified: *He has the reputation of being a shrewd businessman.* [ME *reputacioun* < L *reputātiōn-* (s. of *reputātiō*) computation, consideration, equiv. to *reputāt(us)* (ptp. of *reputāre;* see REPUTE) + *-iōn-* -ION] **—rep′u·ta′tion·less,** *adj.*
—Syn. 1. regard, name. REPUTATION, CHARACTER are

re·price′, *v.t.,* **-priced, -pric·ing.**
re·prime′, *v.t.,* **-primed, -prim·ing.**
re·probe′, *v.,* **-probed, -prob·ing.**
re′pro·ceed′, *v.i.*
re·proc′ess, *v.t.*
re′pro·claim′, *v.t.*
re′proc·la·ma′tion, *n.*
re·pro′gram, *v.t.*
re′pro·ject′, *v.*
re·prom′ise, *v.,* **-ised, -is·ing.**
re·prom′ul·gate′, *v.t.,* **-gat·ed, -gat·ing.**
re′pro·mul·ga′tion, *n.*
re′pro·por′tion, *v.t.*
re′pro·pose′, *v.,* **-posed, -pos·ing.**
re·pros′e·cute′, *v.t.,* **-cut·ed, -cut·ing.**
re·pro′test, *n.*
re′pro·test′, *v.*
re′pro·vi′sion, *v.*
re·prune′, *v.t.,* **-pruned, -prun·ing.**
re·pub′lish, *v.t.*
re·pub′lish·a·ble, *adj.*
re·punc′tu·ate′, *v.t.,* **-at·ed, -at·ing.**
re′punc·tu·a′tion, *n.*
re·pun′ish, *v.*
re·pun′ish·a·ble, *adj.*
re·pun′ish·ment, *n.*
re·pu′ri·fi·ca′tion, *n.*
re·pu′ri·fy′, *v.,* **-fied, -fy·ing.**
re·pur′pose, *v.,* **-posed, -pos·ing.**
re′pur·sue′, *v.t.,* **-sued, -su·ing.**

often confused. REPUTATION, however, is the word which refers to the position one occupies or the standing that he has in the opinion of others, in respect to attainments, integrity, and the like: *a fine reputation; a reputation for honesty.* CHARACTER is the combination of moral and other traits which make one the kind of person he actually is (as contrasted with what others think of him): *Honesty is an outstanding trait of his character.* **2.** fame, distinction, renown, esteem, honor. **3.** See **credit.** —**Ant. 2.** disrepute.

re·pute (ri pyo͞ot′), *n., v.,* **-put·ed, -put·ing.** —*n.* **1.** estimation in the view of others; reputation: *persons of good repute.* **2.** favorable reputation; good name; public respect. —*v.t.* **3.** to consider or esteem (a person or thing) to be as specified; account or regard (usually used in the passive): *He was reputed to be a millionaire.* [ME *repute(n)* (v.) < MF *reput(er)* < L *reputāre* to compute, consider, equiv. to *re-* RE- + *putāre* to think] —**Syn. 2.** distinction, honor. See **credit. 3.** hold, deem, reckon. —**Ant. 2.** dishonor.

re·put·ed (ri pyo͞o′tid), *adj.* accounted or supposed to be such: *the reputed author of a book.* [REPUTE + -ED[2]] —**re·put′ed·ly,** *adv.*

req., **1.** required. **2.** requisition.

re·quest (ri kwest′), *n.* **1.** the act of asking for something to be given, or done, esp. as a favor or courtesy; solicitation or petition: *I have a request to make.* **2.** an instance of this: *There have been many requests for the product.* **3.** a written statement of petition: *If you need supplies, send in a request.* **4.** that which is asked for: *to obtain one's request.* **5.** the state of being much asked for; demand: *to be in much request as an after-dinner speaker.* **6. at** or **by request,** in response or accession to a request: *The orchestra played numbers by request.* —*v.t.* **7.** to ask for, esp. politely or formally: *He requested permission to speak.* **8.** to ask or beg (usually fol. by a clause or an infinitive): *to request that he leave; to request to be excused.* **9.** to ask or beg (someone) to do something: *He requested me to go.* [ME *requeste* (n.) < OF < VL *requaesita things asked for, n. use of neut. pl. ptp. of LL *requaerere* to seek, r. L *requīrere.* See REQUIRE, QUEST] —**re·quest′er,** *n.*
—**Syn. 1.** entreaty, supplication, prayer. **7.** petition, supplicate. **8.** See **beg. 9.** entreat, beseech.

Req·ui·em (rek′wē əm, rē′kwē-), *n.* **1.** *Rom. Cath. Ch.* **a.** Also called **Req′uiem Mass′.** the Mass celebrated for the repose of the souls of the dead. **b.** a celebration of this Mass. **c.** a plainsong setting for this Mass. **2.** any musical service, hymn, or dirge for the repose of the dead. Also, **req′ui·em.** [ME < L, acc. of *requiēs* rest, (the first word of the introit of the mass for the dead)]

req′uiem shark′, any of numerous, chiefly tropical sharks of the family *Carcharhinidae,* including the tiger shark and soupfin shark.

req·ui·es·cat (rek′wē es′kat), *n.* a wish or prayer for the repose of the dead. [< L: short for REQUIESCAT IN PACE]

re·qui·es·cat in pa·ce (re′kwē es′kät in pä′chā), *Latin.* may he (or she) rest in peace.

re·quire (ri kwīər′), *v.,* **-quired, -quir·ing.** —*v.t.* **1.** to have need of; need: *He requires medical care.* **2.** to call on authoritatively; order or enjoin to do something: *to require an agent to account for money spent.* **3.** to ask for authoritatively or imperatively; demand. **4.** to impose need or occasion for; make necessary or indispensable: *The work required infinite patience.* **5.** to call for or exact as obligatory: *The law requires annual income-tax returns.* **6.** to place under an obligation or necessity: *The situation requires me to take immediate action.* **7.** *Chiefly Brit.* to desire; wish to have: *Will you require tea at four o'clock?* —*v.i.* **8.** to demand; impose obligation: *to do as the law requires.* [ME *require(n)* < L *requīr(ere),* equiv. to *re-* RE- + *-quīrere,* comb. form of *quaerere* to seek, search for] —**re·quir′a·ble,** *adj.* —**re·quir′er,** *n.*
—**Syn. 3.** See **demand. 6.** obligate, necessitate. —**Ant. 3.** forgo.

re·quire·ment (ri kwīər′mənt), *n.* **1.** that which is required; a thing demanded or obligatory: *One of the requirements of a reporter is accuracy.* **2.** an act or instance of requiring. **3.** a need or necessity: *to meet the requirements of daily life.* [REQUIRE + -MENT]
—**Syn. 1.** REQUIREMENT, REQUISITE refer to that which is necessary. A REQUIREMENT is some quality or performance demanded of a person in accordance with certain fixed regulations: *requirements for admission to college.* A REQUISITE is nothing imposed from outside; it is a factor which is judged necessary according to the nature of things, or to the circumstances of the case: *This system combines the two requisites of efficacy and economy.* REQUISITE may also refer to a concrete object judged necessary: *the requisites for perfect grooming.* **2.** order, command, injunction, directive, demand, claim.

req·ui·site (rek′wi zit), *adj.* **1.** required or necessary for a particular purpose, position, etc.; indispensable: *the requisite skills of an engineer.* —*n.* **2.** something requisite; a necessary quality, thing, etc. [ME < L *requīsīt(us)* sought again, demanded, ptp. of *requīrere;* see REQUIRE] —**req′ui·site·ly,** *adv.* —**req′ui·site·ness,** *n.*
—**Syn. 1.** needed, needful. See **necessary. 2.** necessity. See **requirement.** —**Ant. 1.** dispensable. **2.** luxury.

req·ui·si·tion (rek′wi zish′ən), *n.* **1.** the act of requiring or demanding. **2.** a demand made. **3.** an authoritative or formal demand for something to be done, given, supplied, etc.: *The general issued a requisition to the townspeople for eight trucks. You'll have to submit a requisition for a new typewriter.* **4.** a written request or order for something, as supplies. **5.** the form on which such an order is drawn up. **6.** an authoritative or official demand, as of one nation on another for extradition of a criminal. **7.** the state of being required for use or called into service: *to put something in requisition.* **8.** a requirement or essential condition. —*v.t.* **9.** to require or take for use; press into service. **10.** to demand or take, as by authority, for military purposes, public needs, etc.: *to requisition supplies.* [< ML *requīsītiōn-* (s. of *requīsītiō*) a searching, equiv. to L *requīsīt(us)* REQUISITE + *-iōn-* -ION] —**req′ui·si′tion·ar′y,** *adj.* —**req′ui·si′tion·ist, req′ui·si′tion·er,** *n.*

re·quit·al (ri kwīt′əl), *n.* **1.** the act of requiting. **2.** a return or reward for service, kindness, etc. **3.** a retaliation for a wrong, injury, etc. **4.** something given or done as repayment, reward, punishment, etc., in return. [REQUITE + -AL[2]]

re·quite (ri kwīt′), *v.t.,* **-quit·ed, -quit·ing.** **1.** to make repayment or return for (service, benefits, etc.). **2.** to make retaliation for (a wrong, injury, etc.); avenge. **3.** to make return to (a person) for service, benefits, etc. **4.** to retaliate on (a person) for a wrong, injury, etc. **5.** to give or do in return. [RE- + obs. *quite,* var. of QUIT] —**re·quit′a·ble,** *adj.* —**re·quite′ment,** *n.* —**re·quit′er,** *n.*
—**Syn. 1.** repay, reward, recompense, compensate, pay, remunerate, reimburse. **2.** revenge. —**Ant. 2.** forgive.

re·ra·di·a·tion (rē′rā dē ā′shən), *n.* *Physics.* radiation emitted as a consequence of a previous absorption of radiation. [RE- + RADIATION]

rere·brace (rēr′brās′), *n.* *Armor.* a piece of plate armor for the upper arm; an upper cannon. Cf. **vambrace** (def. 1). [ME, equiv. to *rere-* comb. form < MF *rere, riere* behind, backward < L *retrō-* RETRO- + BRACE]

re-re·cord (rē′ri kôrd′), *v.t.* **1.** to record (something) another time: *Because of recent technical advances the pianist wants to re-record the Chopin nocturnes.* **2.** to transfer (a recording) from one process to another, as from shellac to long-playing record.

rere·dos (rēr′dos, rēr′i-, râr′i-), *n.* **1.** a screen or a decorated part of the wall behind an altar in a church. **2.** the back of a fireplace or of a medieval open hearth. [ME, m. AF *areredos* < MF *arere* behind (see ARREAR) + *dos* back < L *dors(um)* DORSUM]

rere·mouse (rēr′mous′), *n., pl.* **-mice.** *Archaic.* a bat. [ME *reremous,* OE *hrēremūs,* prob. equiv. to *hrēr-(an)* (to) move + *mūs* MOUSE]

Re·rum No·va·rum (rār′o͝om nō vär′o͝om), *Latin.* Of New Things (opening words and the title of an encyclical of Pope Leo XIII issued in 1891 on the condition of the working class).

re·run (*v.* rē run′; *n.* rē′run′), *v.,* **-ran, -run, -running,** *n.* —*v.t.* **1.** to run again. —*n.* **2.** the act of rerunning. **3.** a reshowing of a film. **4.** the film being reshown. [RE- + RUN]

res (rēz, rās), *n., pl.* **res.** *Chiefly Law.* an object or thing; matter. [< L]

res., **1.** reserve. **2.** residence. **3.** resigned.

Re·sa·ca de la Pal·ma (rä sä′kə dā lä päl′mə, də, rə-), a locality in S Texas, near Brownsville: battle 1846.

res ad·ju·di·ca·ta (rēz′ ə jo͞o′də kā′tə, rās), *Law.* See **res judicata.**

re·sail (rē sāl′), *v.i.* to sail back or again. [RE- + SAIL]

re·sal·a·ble (rē sā′lə bəl), *adj.* able to be resold; suitable for resale.

re·sale (rē′sāl′, rē sāl′), *n.* **1.** the act of selling a second time. **2.** the act of selling something secondhand. [RE- + SALE]

re·saw (rē′sô′), *v.,* **-sawed, -sawed** or **-sawn, -sawing,** *n.* —*v.t.* **1.** to saw again. —*n.* **2.** a saw for cutting logs into lumber. [RE- + SAW[1]] —**re·saw·yer** (rē sô′yər), **re·saw′er,** *n.*

re·scind (ri sind′), *v.t.* **1.** to abrogate; annul; revoke; repeal. **2.** to invalidate (an act, measure, etc.) by a later action or a higher authority. [< L *rescind(ere)* (to) tear off again, cut away, equiv. to *re-* RE- + *scindere* to tear, divide, destroy; see SCHISM] —**re·scind′a·ble,** *adj.* —**re·scind′er,** *n.* —**re·scind′ment,** *n.*
—**Syn. 1.** nullify; retract, withdraw. **2.** countermand, repeal, veto.

re·scis·si·ble (ri sis′ə bəl), *adj.* able to be rescinded. [< L *resciss(us)* cut off, repealed (see RESCISSION) + -IBLE]

re·scis·sion (ri sizh′ən), *n.* the act of rescinding. [< LL *rescissiōn-* (s. of *rescissiō*) a making void, rescinding, equiv. to *resciss(us)* (ptp. of *rescindere* to RESCIND) + *-iōn-* -ION]

re·scis·so·ry (ri sis′ə rē, -siz′-), *adj.* serving to rescind. [< LL *rescissōri(us)* pertaining to revoking or rescinding, equiv. to L *resciss(us)* (see RESCISSION) + *-ōrius* -ORY[1]]

re·script (rē′skript′), *n.* **1.** a written answer, as of a Roman emperor or a pope, to a query or petition in writing. **2.** any edict, decree, or official announcement. **3.** the act of rewriting. **4.** something rewritten. [< L *rescript(um)* an imperial rescript (n. use of neut. ptp. of *rescrībere* to write back, reply). See RE-, SCRIPT]

res·cue (res′kyo͞o), *v.,* **-cued, -cu·ing,** *n.* —*v.t.* **1.** to free or deliver from confinement, violence, danger, or evil. **2.** *Law.* to liberate or take by forcible or illegal means from lawful custody. —*n.* **3.** act of rescuing. [ME *rescue(n)* (v.) < OF *resour(re),* equiv. to *re-* RE- + *escourre* to shake, drive out, remove < L *excutere* (*ex-* EX-[1] + *-cutere,* comb. form of *quatere* to shake)] —**res′cu·a·ble,** *adj.* —**res′cue·less,** *adj.* —**res′cu·er,** *n.*
—**Syn. 1.** liberate, release, save, redeem, ransom, extricate, recover. **3.** liberation, deliverance, release, redemption, recovery.

res′cue grass′, a grass, *Bromus catharticus,* of tropical America, having clusters of flattened spikelets. [*rescue* (? alter. of FESCUE)]

re-search (rē sûrch′), *v.t., v.i.* to search or search for again. [RE- + SEARCH]

re·search (ri sûrch′, rē′sûrch), *n.* **1.** diligent and systematic inquiry or investigation into a subject in order to discover or revise facts, theories, applications, etc.: *recent research in medicine.* **2.** a particular instance or piece of research. —*v.i.* **3.** to make researches; investigate carefully. —*v.t.* **4.** to make an extensive investigation into: *to research a matter thoroughly.* [< MF *recerch(er)* (v.) (to) seek, OF, equiv. to *re-* RE- + *cercher* to SEARCH] —**re·search′er, re·search′ist,** *n.*
—**Syn. 1.** scrutiny, study. See **investigation. 4.** study, inquire, examine, scrutinize.

research′ li′brary, a reference library that collects materials in one or more specialized fields for use in intensive research projects.

re·seat (rē sēt′), *v.t.* **1.** to provide with a new seat or new seats. **2.** to seat again. [RE- + SEAT]

re·seau (rā zō′, rə-), *n., pl.* **-seaux** (-zōz′, -zō′), **-seaus.** **1.** a network. **2.** a netted or meshed ground in lace. **3.** *Astron.* a network of fine lines on a glass plate, used in a photographic telescope to produce a corresponding network on photographs of the stars. **4.** *Meteorol.* a system of weather stations under the direction of a single agency or cooperating for common goals. **5.** *Photog.* a screen having minute colored filters, used in some forms of color photography. Also, **ré·seau′.** [< F *réseau,* OF *resel,* dim. of *rais* net < L *rēt-* (s. of *rēte*)]

re·sect (ri sekt′), *v.t.* *Surg.* to do resection on. [< L *resect(us)* cut loose (ptp. of *resecāre*), equiv. to *re-* RE- + *secāre* to cut]

re·sec·tion (ri sek′shən), *n.* **1.** *Survey.* a technique of ascertaining the location of a point by taking bearings from the point on two other points of known location. **2.** *Surg.* the excision of part of an organ or tissue, esp. bone. [< L *resectiōn-* (s. of *resectiō*) a cutting off, trimming, equiv. to *resect(us)* (ptp. of *resecāre* to cut off) + *-iōn-* -ION] —**re·sec′tion·al,** *adj.*

re·se·da (ri sē′də), *n.* **1.** any plant of the genus *Reseda,* esp. *R. odorata,* the garden mignonette. **2.** a grayish green. —*adj.* **3.** grayish green, like the flowers of the mignonette plant. [< NL, L *resēdā,* lit., heal (impv. of *resēdāre* to heal, assuage)]

res·e·da·ceous (res′i dā′shəs), *adj.* belonging to the *Resedaceae,* or mignonette family of plants. [< NL *Resedace(ae)* type genus. See RESEDA, -ACEOUS]

re·sem·blance (ri zem′bləns), *n.* **1.** the state or fact of resembling; similarity. **2.** a degree, kind, or point of likeness. **3.** a likeness, appearance, or semblance of something. [ME < AF, equiv. to *resembl(er)* (to) RESEMBLE + *-ance* -ANCE]
—**Syn. 1.** RESEMBLANCE, SIMILARITY imply that there is a likeness between two or more people or things. RESEMBLANCE indicates primarily a likeness in appearance, either a striking one or one which merely serves as a reminder to the beholder: *The boy has a strong resemblance to his father.* SIMILARITY may imply a surface likeness, but usually suggests also a likeness in other characteristics: *There is a similarity in their tastes and behavior.* **2.** analogy, similitude. **3.** image. —**Ant. 1.** difference.

re·sem·blant (ri zem′blənt), *adj.* **1.** having a resemblance or similarity (sometimes fol. by *to*): *two persons with resemblant features; a mastery resemblant to that of Phidias.* **2.** that produces or deals in representations: *sculpture considered as a resemblant art.* [ME < OF, equiv. to *resembl(er)* (to) RESEMBLE + *-ant* -ANT]

re·sem·ble (ri zem′bəl), *v.t.,* **-bled, -bling.** **1.** to be like or similar to. **2.** *Archaic.* to liken or compare. [ME *resemble(n)* < MF *resembl(er)* < OF, equiv. to *re-* RE- + *sembler* to seem, be like < L *similāre,* deriv. of *similis* like; see SIMILAR] —**re·sem′bling·ly,** *adv.*

re·send (rē send′), *v.t.,* **-sent, -send·ing.** **1.** to send again. **2.** to send back. [RE- + SEND]

re·sent (ri zent′), *v.t.* to feel or show displeasure or indignation at (a person, act, remark, etc.) from a sense of injury or insult. [< F *ressent(ir)* (to) be angry < OF *resentir,* equiv. to *re-* RE- + *sentir* to feel < L *sentīre;* see SENSE] —**re·sent′ing·ly,** *adv.* —**re·sent′ive,** *adj.*

re·sent·ful (ri zent′fəl), *adj.* full of or marked by resentment. [RESENT + -FUL] —**re·sent′ful·ly,** *adv.* —**re·sent′ful·ness,** *n.*

re·sent·ment (ri zent′mənt), *n.* the feeling of displeasure or indignation at some act, remark, person, etc., regarded as causing injury or insult. [< F *ressentiment* < MF, equiv. to *resent(ir)* (to) RESENT + *-ment* -MENT]
—**Syn.** dudgeon, pique, irritation, envy, jealousy.

res·er·pine (res′ər pin, -pēn′, rə sûr′pin, -pēn), *n.* *Pharm.* an alkaloid, $C_{33}H_{40}N_2O_9$, obtained from the root of *Rauwolfia serpentina,* used in medicine for the alleviation of the symptoms of hypertension and as a tranquilizer for the relief of anxiety. [< G *Reserpin,* deriv. of *reserp-* (prob. irreg.) < NL *Rauwolfia serpentina,* equiv. to *Rauwolfia* RAUWOLFIA + LL *serpentīna* (fem. of *serpentīnus* SERPENTINE) + G *-in* -INE[2]]

res·er·va·tion (rez′ər vā′shən), *n.* **1.** the act of keeping back, withholding, or setting apart. **2.** the act of making an exception or qualification. **3.** an exception or qualification made expressly or tacitly: *to accept something, but with inner reservations.* **4.** *U.S.* a tract of public land set apart for a special purpose, as for the use of an Indian tribe. **5.** Often, **reservations.** the allotting or the securing of accommodations at a hotel, on a train or boat, etc., as for a traveler: *to write for reservations; to make a reservation.* **6.** the

re′qual·i·fi·ca′tion, *n.*
re·qual′i·fy′, *v.,* **-fied, -fy·ing.**
re·ques′tion, *v.t.*
re·quick′en, *v.*
re·quote′, *v.t.,* **-quot·ed, -quot·ing.**
re·ra′di·ate′, *v.,* **-at·ed, -at·ing.**
re·ra′di·a′tion, *n.*
re·rank′, *v.*
re·rate′, *v.,* **-rat·ed, -rat·ing.**
re·read′, *v.,* **-read, -read·ing.**
re·reel′, *v.*
re·reg′is·ter, *v.*
re′reg·is·tra′tion, *n.*
re·reg′u·late′, *v.t.,* **-lat·ed, -lat·ing.**
re′reg·u·la′tion, *n.*
re·rent′, *v.t.*
re·rent′al, *n.*
re·rise′, *v.,* **-rose, -ris·en, -ris·ing.**
re·roll′, *v.*
re·route′, *v.,* **-rout·ed, -rout·ing.**
re·sad′dle, *v.,* **-dled, -dling.**
re·salt′, *v.t.*
re′sa·lute′, *v.,* **-lut·ed, -lut·ing.**
re·sam′ple, *v.t.,* **-pled, -pling.**
re·sanc′tion, *v.t.*
re·sched′ule, *v.t.,* **-uled, -ul·ing.**
re·school′, *v.t.*
re·scrub′, *v.,* **-scrubbed, -scrub·bing.**
re·scru′ti·nize′, *v.t.,* **-nized, -niz·ing.**
re·scru′ti·ny, *n., pl.* **-nies.**
re·seal′, *v.t.*
re·seal′a·ble, *adj.*
re·sea′son, *v.*
re·seat′, *v.t.*
re′se·cure′, *v.,* **-cured, -cur·ing.**
re·seed′, *v.*
re·seek′, *v.t.,* **-sought, -seek·ing.**
re·seg′re·gate′, *v.,* **-gat·ed, -gat·ing.**
re′seg·re·ga′tion, *n.*
re·seize′, *v.t.,* **-seized, -seiz·ing.**
re·sei′zure, *n.*
re′se·lect′, *v.t.*
re′se·lec′tion, *n.*
re·sell′, *v.,* **-sold, -sell·ing.**
re·sell′er, *n.*
re′sen·sa′tion, *n.*
re·sen′si·ti·za′tion, *n.*
re·sen′si·tize′, *v.t.,* **-tized, -tiz·ing.**
re·sen′tence, *n., v.t.,* **-tenced, -tenc·ing.**
re·sep′a·rate′, *v.,* **-rat·ed, -rat·ing.**
re′sep·a·ra′tion, *n.*

record or assurance of such an arrangement. [ME *reservacioun* < MF *reservation* equiv. to *reserv(er)* (to) RESERVE + *-ation* -ATION]

re-serve (rē sûrv′), *v.t., v.i.,* **-served, -serv·ing.** to serve again. [RE- + SERVE]

re·serve (ri zûrv′), *v.,* **-served, -serv·ing,** *n., adj.* —*v.t.* **1.** to keep back or save for future use, disposal, treatment, etc. **2.** to retain or secure by express stipulation. **3.** to set apart for a particular use, purpose, service, etc.: *ground reserved for gardening.* **4.** to keep for some fate, lot, experience, etc. **5.** to retain (the original color) of a surface, as on a painted ceramic piece. **6.** to save or set aside (a portion of the Eucharistic elements) to be administered, as to the sick, outside of the Mass or communion service. —*n.* **7.** *Finance.* **a.** cash, or assets readily convertible into cash, held aside, as by a corporation, bank, state or national government, etc., to meet expected or unexpected demands. **b.** uninvested cash held to comply with legal requirements. **8.** something reserved, as for some purpose or object; a store or stock: *to use up one's reserve of supplies.* **9.** a resource not normally called upon but available if needed. **10.** a tract of public land set apart for a special purpose: *a forest reserve.* **11.** an act of reserving; reservation, exception, or qualification: *I will do what you ask, but with one reserve.* **12.** *Mil.* **a.** a fraction of a military force held in readiness to sustain the attack or defense made by the rest of the force. **b.** the part of a country's fighting force not in active service. **c.** **reserves,** the enrolled but not regular components of the Army of the U.S. **13.** formality and self-restraint in manner and relationship; avoidance of familiarity or intimacy with others: *His natural reserve made people think he was stand-offish.* **14.** reticence or silence. **15.** **in reserve,** put aside or withheld for a future need; reserved: *money in reserve.* **16.** **without reserve, a.** without restraint; frankly; freely. **b.** (of articles at auction) without limitation as to the terms of sale, esp. with no stipulated minimum price. —*adj.* **17.** kept in reserve; forming a reserve: *a reserve fund; a reserve supply.* [ME *reserve(n)* (v.) < MF *reserv(er)* < L *reservāre* to keep back, retain, equiv. to *re-* RE- + *servāre* to save] —**re·serv′a·ble,** *adj.* —**re·serve′less,** *adj.*
—**Syn. 1.** husband, hold, store. See **keep. 8.** supply. **14.** taciturnity, constraint, coldness. —**Ant. 1.** squander. **13, 14.** warmth.

Re·serve (ri zûrv′), *n.* a town in SE Louisiana. 5297 (1960).

reserve′ bank′, *U.S.* one of the 12 principal banks of the Federal Reserve System.

reserve′ buoy′ancy, *Naut.* the difference between the volume of a hull below the designed waterline and the volume of the hull below the lowest opening incapable of being made watertight.

re·served (ri zûrvd′), *adj.* **1.** kept or set apart for some particular use or purpose. **2.** kept by special arrangement for some person or persons: *a reserved seat.* **3.** formal or self-restrained in manner and relationship; avoiding familiarity or intimacy with others: *He is a very quiet, reserved man who is hard to know.* **4.** characterized by reserve, as the disposition, manner, etc.: *His comments were reserved and sparing.* **5.** retaining the original color of a surface, esp. when decorating portions of the surface with other colors. [late ME; see RESERVE, -ED[2]] —**re·serv·ed·ly** (ri zûr′vid lē), *adv.* —**re·serv′ed·ness,** *n.*
—**Syn. 3, 4.** composed, controlled, reticent, constrained, taciturn, withdrawn, distant, cold.

re·serv·ist (ri zûr′vist), *n.* one who belongs to a reserve military force of a country. [RESERVE + -IST]

res·er·voir (rez′ər vwär′, -vôr′, rez′ə-), *n.* **1.** a natural or artificial place where water is collected and stored for use, esp. water for supplying a community, irrigating land, furnishing power, etc. **2.** a receptacle or chamber for holding a liquid or fluid, as oil or gas. **3.** *Biol.* a cavity or part which holds some fluid or secretion. **4.** a place where anything is collected or accumulated in great amount. **5.** a large or extra supply or stock; reserve: *a great reservoir of knowledge.* [< F *réservoir,* equiv. to *réserv(er)* (to) RESERVE + *-oir* -ORY[2]]

re·set (*v.* rē set′; *n.* rē′set′), *v.,* **-set, -set·ting,** *n.* —*v.t.* **1.** to set again. —*n.* **2.** the act of resetting. **3.** that which is reset. **4.** a plant which is replanted. **5.** a device used in resetting an instrument or control mechanism. [RE- + SET] —**re·set′ter,** *n.*

res ges·tae (rēz jes′tē, rās), **1.** things done; accomplishments; deeds. **2.** *Law.* the acts, circumstances, and statements that are incidental to the principal fact of a litigated matter and are admissible in evidence in view of their relevant association with that fact. [< L]

resh (räsh), *n.* **1.** the 20th letter of the Hebrew alphabet. **2.** the consonant sound represented by this letter. [< Heb *rēsh,* lit., head]

re·shape (rē shāp′), *v.t.,* **-shaped, -shap·ing.** to shape again or into different form. [RE- + SHAPE]

Re·shev·sky (rə shef′skē), *n.* **Samuel,** born 1911, U.S. chess player, born in Poland.

re·ship (rē ship′), *v.,* **-shipped, -ship·ping.** —*v.t.* **1.** to ship again. **2.** to transfer from one ship to another. —*v.i.* **3.** to go on a ship again. **4.** (of a member of a ship's crew) to sign up for another voyage. [RE- + SHIP] —**re·ship′ment,** *n.*

Resht (resht), *n.* a city in NW Iran, near the Caspian Sea. 118,634 (est. 1963).

re·side (ri zīd′), *v.i.,* **-sid·ed, -sid·ing. 1.** to dwell permanently or for a considerable time: *He resides in Boston.* **2.** (of things, qualities, etc.) to abide, lie, or be present habitually; exist or be inherent (usually fol. by *in*). **3.** to rest or be vested, as powers, rights, etc. (usually fol. by *in*). [ME *reside(n)* < MF *resid(er)* < L *residēre,* equiv. to *re-* RE- + *sid-* sit (var. of *sedēre*)] —**re·sid′er,** *n.*
—**Syn. 1.** live, abide, sojourn, stay, lodge, remain.

res·i·dence (rez′i dəns), *n.* **1.** the place, esp. the house, in which one lives or resides; dwelling place; home: *Their residence is in New York City.* **2.** a structure serving as a dwelling or home, esp. one of large proportion and superior quality: *They have a summer residence in Connecticut.* **3.** the act or fact of residing: *during his residence in Spain.* **4.** the act of living or staying in a specified place while performing official duties, carrying on studies or research, awaiting a divorce, etc. **5.** the time during which one resides in a place: *a residence in Spain of five years.* **6.** the location of the main offices or principal center of business activity of a commercial enterprise, esp. a large corporation, as registered under law. [ME < MF < ML *residentia,* equiv. to L *resid(ēre)* (to) RESIDE + *-entia* -ENCE]
—**Syn. 1.** habitation, domicile. **1, 2.** See **house. 2.** mansion. **5.** stay, abode, sojourn.

res·i·den·cy (rez′i dən sē), *n., pl.* **-cies. 1.** residence. **2.** (formerly) the official residence of a representative of the British governor general at a native Indian court. **3.** an administrative division of the Dutch East Indies. **4.** the position or tenure of a medical resident. [RESID(ENT) + -ENCY]

res·i·dent (rez′i dənt), *n.* **1.** one who resides in a place. **2.** a diplomatic representative, inferior in rank to an ambassador, residing at a foreign court. **3.** (formerly) a representative of the British governor general at a native court in India. **4.** the governor of a residency in the Dutch East Indies. **5.** a physician who joins the medical staff of a hospital as a salaried employee for a specified period to gain advanced training usually in a particular field, being in full-time attendance at the hospital and often living on the premises. —*adj.* **6.** residing; dwelling in a place. **7.** living or staying at a place in discharge of duty. **8.** (of qualities) existing; intrinsic. **9.** (of birds) not migratory. [< L *resident-* (s. of *residēns*), prp. of *residēre* to RESIDE; see -ENT] —**res′i·dent·ship′,** *n.*

res′ident commis′sioner, *U.S.* a representative from a dependency who is entitled to speak, but not to vote, in the national House of Representatives.

res·i·den·tial (rez′i den′shəl), *adj.* **1.** of or pertaining to residence or to residences: *a residential requirement for a doctorate.* **2.** adapted or used for residence: *a residential neighborhood.* [RESIDENCE + -IAL] —**res·i·den·ti·al·i·ty** (rez′i den′shē al′i tē), *n.* —**res′i·den′tial·ly,** *adv.*

res·i·den·ti·ar·y (rez′i den′shē er′ē, -shə rē), *adj., n., pl.* **-ar·ies.** —*adj.* **1.** residing; resident. **2.** bound to or involving official residence. —*n.* **3.** a resident. **4.** an ecclesiastic bound to official residence. [< ML *residentiāri(us),* equiv. to *residenti(a)* RESIDENCE + *-ārius* -ARY]

re·sid·u·al (ri zij′o͞o əl), *adj.* **1.** pertaining to or constituting a residue or remainder; remaining; leftover. **2.** *Math.* **a.** formed by the subtraction of one quantity from another: *a residual quantity.* **b.** (of a set) having complement of first category. **3.** of or pertaining to the payment of residuals. **4.** *Med.* remaining in an organ or part following normal discharge or expulsion: *residual air.* **5.** *Geol.* remaining after the soluble elements have been dissolved: *residual soil.* —*n.* **6.** a residual quantity; remainder. **7.** Often, **residuals.** that which remains to discomfort or disable a person following an illness, injury, operation, or the like; disability: *His residuals are a weak heart and light-headedness. She recovered with no residuals.* **8.** *Math.* **a.** the deviation of one of a set of observations or numbers from the mean of the set. **b.** the deviation between an empirical and a theoretical result. **9.** *Navig.* a slight deviation of an adjusted compass on a certain heading. **10.** Usually, **residuals.** additional pay given to a performer by a sponsor or sponsors of a television program for repeated use of a film in which the performer appears. [< L *residu(um)* what is left over (neut. of *residuus,* equiv. to *re-* RE- + *sid-* sit (var. of *sed-*) + *-u(um)* adj. suffix + -AL[1]]

re·sid·u·al·ly (ri zij′o͞o ə lē), *adv.* **1.** in a residual manner. **2.** *Math.* with an element in the directed set such that for every element in the directed set in relation to the given element, the corresponding element of the net is in some given set; eventually. [RESIDUAL + -LY]

resid′ual stress′, *Metall.* a stress in a metal, on a microscopic scale and resulting from nonuniform thermal changes, plastic deformation, or other causes aside from temporary external forces or applications of heat.

re·sid·u·ar·y (ri zij′o͞o er′ē), *adj.* **1.** entitled to the residue of an estate: *a residuary legatee.* **2.** pertaining to or of the nature of a residue, remainder, or residuum. [< L *residu(um)* what is left over (see RESIDUAL) + -ARY]

res·i·due (rez′i do͞o′, -dyo͞o′), *n.* **1.** that which remains after a part is taken, disposed of, or gone; remainder; rest. **2.** *Chem.* **a.** a quantity of matter remaining after evaporation, combustion, or some other process; residuum. **b.** an atom or group of atoms considered as a group or part of a molecule. **c.** that part remaining as a solid on a filter paper after a liquid passes through in the filtration procedure. **3.** *Law.* the part of a testator's estate that remains after the payment of all debts, charges, special devises, and bequests. **4.** *Math.* **a.** the coefficient of the term with exponent −1 in a Laurent series of a function of a complex variable. **b.** a number related to a given number by a congruence. [ME < MF *residu* < L *residu(um)* what is left over; see RESIDUAL]
—**Syn. 1.** remains, residuum. See **remainder.**

re·sid·u·um (ri zij′o͞o əm), *n., pl.* **-sid·u·a** (-zij′o͞o ə). **1.** the residue, remainder, or rest of something. **2.** *Chem.* a quantity or body of matter remaining after evaporation, combustion, distillation, etc. **3.** any residual product. **4.** *Law.* the residue of an estate. [< L; see RESIDUAL]

re·sign (ri zīn′), *v.i.* **1.** to give up an office or position, often formally (often fol. by *from*): *to resign from the chairmanship of a committee.* **2.** to submit; yield: *to resign to the inevitability of death.* —*v.t.* **3.** to give up (an office, position, etc.), often formally: *to resign the presidency of a college.* **4.** to relinquish (a right, claim, agreement, etc.). **5.** to give or sign over, as to the control or care of another: *She resigned her child to an adoption agency. The ad agency resigned one of its most lucrative accounts.* **6.** to submit (oneself, one's mind, etc.) without resistance. [ME *resign(en)* < MF *resign(er)* < L *resignāre* to open, release, cancel, equiv. to *re-* RE- + *signāre* to mark, seal, SIGN]
—**Syn. 1.** withdraw. **3.** abdicate, renounce; quit, leave. **4.** give up, surrender, cede, forgo.

res·ig·na·tion (rez′ig nā′shən), *n.* **1.** the act of resigning. **2.** a formal statement, document, etc., stating that one gives up an office, position, etc. **3.** a submissive attitude, state, etc.; submission; unresisting acquiescence: *to meet one's fate with resignation.* [ME < MF < ML *resignātiōn-* (s. of *resignātiō*) a canceling, rescinding, equiv. to L *resignāt(us)* (ptp. of *resignāre* to RESIGN) + *-iōn-* -ION]
—**Syn. 1, 2.** abdication. **3.** meekness, patience, compliance, forbearance. —**Ant. 3.** recalcitrance.

re·signed (ri zīnd′), *adj.* **1.** submissive or acquiescent. **2.** characterized by or indicative of resignation. [RESIGN + -ED[2]] —**re·sign·ed·ly** (ri zī′nid lē), *adv.* —**re·sign′ed·ness,** *n.*

re·sile (ri zīl′), *v.i.,* **-siled, -sil·ing. 1.** to spring back; rebound; resume the original form or position, as an elastic body. **2.** to shrink back; recoil. [< MF *resil(ir)* < L *resilīre* to spring back; see RESILIENT] —**re·sile′ment,** *n.*

re·sil·ience (ri zil′yəns, -zil′ē əns), *n.* **1.** the power or ability to return to the original form, position, etc., after being bent, compressed, or stretched; elasticity. **2.** ability to recover readily from illness, depression, adversity, or the like; buoyancy. Also, **re·sil′ien·cy.** [< L *resil(īre)* (to) spring back, rebound + -ENCE]

re·sil·ient (ri zil′yənt, -zil′ē ənt), *adj.* **1.** springing back; rebounding. **2.** returning to the original form or position after being bent, compressed, or stretched. **3.** recovering readily from illness, depression, adversity, or the like; buoyant. [< L *resilient-* (s. of *resiliēns,* prp. of *resilīre* springing back; *re-* RE- + *sal(īre)* (to) leap, jump); see SALIENT] —**re·sil′ient·ly,** *adv.*

res·in (rez′in), *n.* **1.** any of a class of nonvolatile, solid or semisolid organic substances, as copal, mastic, etc., obtained directly from certain plants as exudations or prepared by polymerization of simple molecules: used in medicine and in the making of varnishes and plastics. **2.** a substance of this type obtained from certain pines; rosin. —*v.t.* **3.** to treat or rub with resin. [ME < MF *resine* < L *rēsīna* < Gk *rhētínē* pine resin] —**res′in·like′,** *adj.*

Res·in (rez′in), *n.* a boy's given name.

res·in·ate (rez′ə nāt′), *v.t.,* **-at·ed, -at·ing.** to treat with resin, as by impregnation. [RESIN + -ATE[1]]

res·in·if·er·ous (rez′ə nif′ər əs), *adj.* yielding resin. [RESIN + -I- + -FEROUS]

res·in·i·fy (re zin′ə fī′), *v.,* **-fied, -fy·ing.** *Chem.* —*v.t.* **1.** to convert into a resin. **2.** to treat with a resin. —*v.i.* **3.** to become a resin. [< F *résiniifi(er).* See RESIN, -IFY] —**re·sin′i·fi·ca′tion,** *n.*

res′in jack. See **rosin jack.**

res·in·oid (rez′ə noid′), *adj.* **1.** resinlike. —*n.* **2.** a resinoid substance. **3.** a resinous substance synthetically compounded. **4.** a gum resin. [RESIN + -OID]

res·in·ous (rez′ə nəs), *adj.* **1.** full of or containing resin. **2.** of the nature of or resembling resin. **3.** pertaining to or characteristic of resin. Also, **res·in·y** (rez′ə nē). [< L *rēsinōs(us).* See RESIN, -OUS] —**res′in·ous·ly,** *adv.* —**res′in·ous·ness,** *n.*

re·sist (ri zist′), *v.t.* **1.** to withstand, strive against, or oppose: *to resist infection; to resist temptation.* **2.** to withstand the action or effect of: *a watchcase that resists water.* **3.** to refrain or abstain from, esp. with difficulty or reluctance: *It was so ludicrous, she could scarcely resist a smile.* —*v.i.* **4.** to make a stand or make efforts in opposition; act in opposition; offer resistance. —*n.* **5.** a substance that prevents or inhibits some effect from taking place, as a coating on a surface of a metallic printing plate that prevents or inhibits corrosion of the metal by acid. **6.** *Textiles.* a chemically inert substance used in resist printing. [ME *resist(en)* < L *resist(ere)* (to) remain standing, equiv. to *re-* RE- + *sistere* to cause to stand] —**re·sist′er,** *n.* —**re·sist′ing·ly,** *adv.*
—**Syn. 1.** confront, counteract, rebuff. See **oppose.**

re·sist·ance (ri zis′təns), *n.* **1.** the act or power of resisting, opposing, or withstanding. **2.** the opposition offered by one thing, force, etc., to another. **3.** *Elect.* **a.** Also called **ohmic resistance.** a property of a conductor by virtue of which the passage of current is opposed, causing electric energy to be transformed into heat: equal to the voltage across the conductor divided by the current flowing in the conductor: usually measured in ohms. **b.** a conductor or coil offering such opposition; a resistor. **4.** *Psychiatry.* opposition to an attempt to bring repressed thoughts or feelings into consciousness. **5.** (*often cap.*) an underground organization composed of groups of private individuals working as an opposition force in a conquered country to overthrow the occupying power, usually by acts of sabotage, guerrilla warfare, etc.: *He worked as a member of the Resistance during the French occupation in World War II.* [ME < MF. See RESIST, -ANCE]

resist′ance thermom′eter, *Metall.* an instrument for measuring the temperature of a metal, utilizing the principle that the electrical resistance of the metal varies with the temperature.

resist′ance weld′ing, welding utilizing pressure and heat that is generated in the pieces to be welded by resistance to an electrical current.

re·sist·ant (ri zis′tənt), *adj.* **1.** resisting. —*n.* **2.** one who or that which resists. [< MF *resistant* < L *resistent-* (s. of *resistēns,* prp. of *resistere*). See RESIST, -ENT] —**re·sist′ant·ly,** *adv.*

ré·si·stant (rā zē stäN′), *n., pl.* **-stants** (-stäN′). *French.* a member of a resistance movement or group.

ré·si·stante (rā zē stäNt′), *n., pl.* **-stantes** (-stäNt′). *French.* a female member of a resistance movement or group.

re·sist·ate (ri zis′tāt), *n.* *Geochem.* any of the class of sediments, as sand or sandstone, consisting chiefly of minerals resistant to weathering. [RESIST + -ATE[1]]

re·serv′ice, *v.t.,* **-iced, -ic·ing.**
re·set′tle, *v.,* **-tled, -tling.**
re·set′tle·ment, *n.*
re·sew′, *v.t.*
re·shake′, *v.,* **-shook, -shak·en, -shak·ing.**
re·share′, *v.t.,* **-shared, -shar·ing.**
re·sharp′en, *v.*
re·shave′, *v.* **-shaved, -shav·ing.**
re·shew′, *v.*
re·shift′, *v.*
re·shine′, *v.,* **-shined, -shin·ing.**
re·shin′gle, *v.t.,* **-gled, -gling.**
re·shoe′, *v.t.,* **-shod, -shoe·ing.**
re·shoot′, *v.,* **-shot, -shoot·ing;** *n.*
re·short′en, *v.*
re·shoul′der, *v.t.*
re·show′, *v.*
re·show′er, *v.*
re·shuf′fle, *v.* **-fled, -fling;** *n.*
re·shut′, *v.,* **-shut, -shut·ting.**
re·sick′en, *v.*
re·sift′, *v.t.*
re·sight′, *v.t.*
re·sig′nal, *v.* **-naled, -nal·ing** or (*esp. Brit.*) **-nalled, -nal·ling.**
re·sil′ver, *v.t.*
re·sim′mer, *v.*

Re·sis·ten·cia (re′sēs ten′syä), *n.* a city in NE Argentina, on the Paraná River. 80,000 (est. 1965).

re·sist·i·ble (ri zis′tə bəl), *adj.* that can be resisted. [RESIST + -IBLE] —**re·sist′i·bil′i·ty, re·sist′i·ble·ness,** *n.* —**re·sist′i·bly,** *adv.*

re·sis·tive (ri zis′tiv), *adj.* resisting; capable of or inclined to resistance. [RESIST + -IVE] —**re·sis′tive·ly,** *adv.* —**re·sis′tive·ness,** *n.*

re·sis·tiv·i·ty (rē′zis tiv′i tē), *n.* **1.** the power or property of resistance. **2.** Also called **specific resistance.** *Elect.* the resistance between opposite faces of a one-centimeter cube of a given material; ratio of electric intensity to cross-sectional area; reciprocal of conductivity. [RESISTIVE + -ITY]

re·sist·less (ri zist′lis), *adj.* **1.** irresistible. **2.** unresisting. [RESIST + -LESS] —**re·sist′less·ly,** *adv.* —**re·sist′less·ness,** *n.*

re·sis·tor (ri zis′tər), *n.* *Elect.* a device, the primary purpose of which is to introduce resistance into an electric circuit. [RESIST + -OR[2]]

resist′ print′ing, a fabric-printing method in which a dye-resistant substance is applied to certain specified areas of the material prior to immersion in a dye bath and subsequently removed so as to permit the original hue to act as a pattern against the colored ground. Cf. **discharge printing.**

res ju·di·ca·ta (rēz′ jo͞o′ di kā′tə, rās), *Law.* a thing adjucated; a case that has been decided. [< L]

res·na·tron (rez′nə tron′), *n.* *Electronics.* a tetrode with the grid connected to form a drift space for the electrons, for generating large power at very high frequency. [RES(O)NA(TOR) + Gk *-tron* suffix referring to instrument or device]

re·soil (rē soil′), *v.t.* to replace topsoil, esp. that lost by erosion. [RE- + SOIL[1]]

res′o·jet en′gine (rez′ō jet′), *Aeron.* a type of pulsejet engine which burns a continuous flow of fuel, but delivers a pulsating thrust due to the resonance of shock waves traveling through it. Also called **resonant-jet engine.** [RESO(NANCE) + JET[1]]

re·sole (rē sōl′), *v.t.,* **-soled, -sol·ing.** to put a new sole on (a shoe, boot, etc.). [RE- + SOLE]

re·sol·u·ble[1] (ri zol′yə bəl, rez′əl-), *adj.* capable of being resolved. [< LL *resolubil(is),* equiv. to L *resolv(ere)* (to) RESOLVE + *-bilis* -BLE] —**re·sol′u·bil′i·ty, re·sol′u·ble·ness,** *n.*

re·sol·u·ble[2] (rē sol′yə bəl), *adj.* able to be redissolved. [RE- + SOLUBLE]

res·o·lute (rez′ə lo͞ot′), *adj.* **1.** firmly resolved or determined; set in purpose or opinion. **2.** characterized by firmness and determination, as the temper, spirit, actions, etc. [< L *resolūt(us),* ptp. of *resolvere* to RESOLVE] —**res′o·lute′ly,** *adv.* —**res′o·lute′ness,** *n.*
—**Syn. 1.** firm, steadfast, fixed. See **earnest**[1]. **2.** unwavering, undaunted.

res·o·lu·tion (rez′ə lo͞o′shən), *n.* **1.** a formal expression of opinion or intention made, usually after voting, by a formal organization, a legislature, a club, or other group. Cf. **concurrent resolution, joint resolution. 2.** a resolve or determination: *to make a firm resolution to do something.* **3.** the act of resolving or determining, as upon an action or course of action, method, procedure, etc. **4.** the mental state or quality of being resolved or resolute; firmness of purpose. **5.** the act or process of resolving or separating into constituent or elementary parts. **6.** the resulting state. **7.** *Optics.* the act, process, or capability of distinguishing between two separate but adjacent objects or sources of light or between two nearly equal wavelengths. Cf. **resolving power. 8.** a solution or explanation, as of a problem, controversy, etc. **9.** *Music.* **a.** the progression of a voice part or of the harmony as a whole from a dissonance to a consonance. **b.** the tone or chord to which a dissonance is resolved. **10.** reduction to a simpler form; conversion. **11.** *Med.* the reduction or disappearance of a swelling or inflammation without suppuration. [ME < L *resolūtiōn-* (s. of *resolūtiō*), equiv. to *resolūt(us)* RESOLUTE + *-iōn-* -ION]
—**Syn. 4.** resolve, determination, perseverance, tenacity; strength, fortitude.

A B
Resolution (def. 9)
A, Dissonance
B, Consonance

res·o·lu·tion·er (rez′ə lo͞o′shə nər), *n.* one joining in or subscribing to a resolution. Also, **res′o·lu′tion·ist.** [RESOLUTION + -ER[1]]

re·sol·u·tive (ri zol′yə tiv, rez′ə lo͞o′-), *adj.* **1.** having the ability to dissolve or terminate. **2.** serving to resolve or dispel. [ME *resolutif* < ML **resolūtīv(us).* See RESOLUTE, -IVE]

re·solv·a·ble (ri zol′və bəl), *adj.* that may be resolved. [RESOLVE + -ABLE] —**re·solv′a·bil′i·ty, re·solv′a·ble·ness,** *n.*

re·solve (ri zolv′), *v.,* **-solved, -solv·ing,** *n.* —*v.t.* **1.** to fix or settle on by deliberate choice and will; determine (to do something): *I have resolved that I shall live to the full, not just exist.* **2.** to separate into constituent or elementary parts; break up; cause to disintegrate (usually fol. by *into*). **3.** to reduce or convert by, or as by, breaking up or disintegration (usually fol. by *to* or *into*). **4.** to convert or transform by any process (often used reflexively). **5.** to reduce by mental analysis (often fol. by *into*). **6.** to settle, determine, or state formally in a vote or resolution, as of a deliberative assembly. **7.** to deal with (a question, a matter of uncertainty, etc.) conclusively; explain; solve: *Has the board resolved the question of how to get funds for this project?* **8.** to clear away or dispel (doubts, fears, etc.): *His actions over the past months have resolved any doubts we may have had as to his capabilities.* **9.** *Chem.* to separate (a racemic mixture) into its optically active components. **10.** *Music.* to cause (a voice part or the harmony as a whole) to progress from a dissonance to a consonance. **11.** *Optics.* to separate and make visible the individual parts of (an image); to distinguish between. **12.** *Med.* to cause (swellings, inflammation, etc.) to disappear without suppuration. —*v.i.* **13.** to come to a determination; make up one's mind; determine (often fol. by *on* or *upon*): *to resolve on a plan of action.* **14.** to break up or disintegrate. **15.** to be reduced or changed by breaking up or otherwise (usually fol. by *to* or *into*). **16.** *Music.* to progress from a dissonance to a consonance. —*n.* **17.** a resolution or determination made, as to follow some course of action. **18.** determination; firmness of purpose. [ME < L *resolv(ere)* (to) unfasten, loosen, release, equiv. to *re-* RE- + *solvere* to loosen; see SOLVE] —**re·solv′er,** *n.*
—**Syn. 1.** confirm. See **decide. 2.** analyze, reduce. **8.** scatter, disperse. **17, 18.** decision.

re·solved (ri zolvd′), *adj.* determined; firm in purpose; resolute. [RESOLVE + -ED[2]] —**re·solv·ed·ly** (ri zol′vid lē), *adv.* —**re·solv′ed·ness,** *n.*

re·sol·vent (ri zol′vənt), *adj.* **1.** resolving; causing solution; solvent. —*n.* **2.** something resolvent. **3.** *Med.* a remedy that causes resolution of a swelling or inflammation. [< L *resolvent-* (s. of *resolvēns,* prp. of *resolvere*). See RESOLVE, -ENT]

resolv′ing pow′er, *Optics.* the ability of an optical device to produce separate images of close objects.

res·o·nance (rez′ə nəns), *n.* **1.** the state or quality of being resonant. **2.** the prolongation of sound by reflection; reverberation. **3.** *Phonet.* **a.** amplification of the range of audibility of any source of speech sounds, esp. of phonation, by various couplings of the cavities of the mouth, nose, sinuses, larynx, pharynx, and upper thorax, and, to some extent, by the skeletal structure of the head and upper chest. **b.** the distribution of amplitudes among interrelated cavities in the head, chest, and throat that are characteristic for a particular speech sound and relatively independent of variations in pitch. **4.** *Physics.* **a.** the state of a system in which an abnormally large vibration is produced in response to an external stimulus, occurring when the frequency of the stimulus is the same, or nearly the same, as the original frequency of the system. **b.** the vibration produced in such a state. **5.** *Elect.* that condition of a circuit with respect to a given frequency or the like in which the total reactance is zero and the current flow a maximum. **6.** *Chem.* the condition exhibited by a molecule when the actual arrangement of its valence electrons is intermediate between two or more arrangements having nearly the same energy, and the positions of the atomic nuclei are identical. **7.** *Med.* (in percussing for diagnostic purposes) a sound produced when air is present. [< MF < L *resonantia* echo, equiv. to *reson(āre)* (to) RESOUND + *-antia* -ANCE]

res′onance radia′tion, *Physics.* radiation emitted by an atom or molecule, having the same frequency as that of an incident particle, as a photon, and usually involving a transition to the lowest energy level of the atom or molecule.

res·o·nant (rez′ə nənt), *adj.* **1.** resounding or reechoing, as sounds: *the resonant thundering of cannons being fired.* **2.** deep and full of resonance: *a resonant voice.* **3.** pertaining to resonance. **4.** producing resonance; causing amplification or sustention of sound. **5.** pertaining to a system in a state of resonance, esp. with respect to sound. —*n.* **6.** *Phonet.* a vowel; a voiced consonant or semivowel that is neither a stop nor an affricate, as, in English, (m, ng, n, l, r, y, w). [< L *resonant-* (s. of *resonāns,* prp. of *resonāre*). See RESOUND, -ANT] —**res′o·nant·ly,** *adv.*

res′o·nant-jet′ en′gine (rez′ə nənt jet′). See **resojet engine.**

res·o·nate (rez′ə nāt′), *v.,* **-nat·ed, -nat·ing.** —*v.i.* **1.** to resound. **2.** to act as a resonator; exhibit resonance. **3.** *Electronics.* to reinforce oscillations because the natural frequency of the device is the same as the frequency of the source. **4.** to amplify vocal sound by the sympathetic vibration of air in certain cavities and bony structures. —*v.t.* **5.** to cause to resound. [< L *resonāt(us)* (ptp. of *resonāre*). See RESOUND, -ATE[1]] —**res′o·na′tion,** *n.*

res·o·na·tor (rez′ə nā′tər), *n.* **1.** anything that resonates. **2.** an appliance for increasing sound by resonance. **3.** an instrument for detecting the presence of a particular frequency by means of resonance. **4.** *Electronics.* **a.** a hollow enclosure made of conducting material of such dimensions that electromagnetic radiation of a certain frequency will resonate. **b.** any circuit having this frequency characteristic. [< NL, equiv. to L *resonāt(us)* (see RESONATE) + *-or* -OR[2]]

re·sorb (ri sôrb′, -zôrb′), *v.t.* to absorb again, as an exudation. [< L *resorb(ēre),* equiv. to *re-* RE- + *sorbēre* to swallow, suck up] —**re·sorb′ence,** *n.* —**re·sorb′ent,** *adj.* —**re·sorp·tion** (ri sôrp′shən), *n.* —**re·sorp·tive** (ri sôrp′tiv), *adj.*

res·or·cin·ol (rez ôr′si nōl′, -nôl′, -nol′, ri zôr′-), *n.* *Chem., Pharm.* a white, needlelike, water-soluble solid, $C_6H_4(OH)_2$, a benzene derivative originally obtained from certain resins, now usually synthesized: used chiefly in making dyes, as a reagent, in tanning, in the synthesis of certain resins, and in medicine in treating certain skin conditions; meta-dihydroxybenzene. Also, **res·or′cin.** [< NL; see RESIN, ORCINOL]

res·or·cin·ol·phthal·e·in (ri zôr′si nōl thal′ēn, -ē in, -fthal′-, -nōl-, -nol-), *n.* *Chem.* fluorescein. [RESORCINOL + PHTHALEIN]

re-sort (rē sôrt′), *v.t.* to sort or arrange (cards, papers, etc.) again. [RE- + SORT]

re·sort (ri zôrt′), *v.i.* **1.** to have recourse for use, service, or help, often as a final, available resource: *to resort to war.* **2.** to go, esp. frequently or customarily: *a beach to which many people resort.* —*n.* **3.** a place to which people frequently or generally go, esp. one providing rest and recreation facilities for people on vacation: *Sarasota is a popular winter resort.* **4.** habitual or general going, as to a place or person. **5.** use of or appeal to some person or thing for aid, service, etc.; recourse: *to have resort to force; a court of last resort.* **6.** a person or thing resorted to for aid, service, etc. [ME *resort(en)* < OF *resort(ir),* equiv. to *re-* RE- + *sortir* to go out, leave, escape < ?]

re-sound (rē sound′), *v.i., v.t.* to sound again. [RE- + SOUND[1]]

re·sound (ri zound′), *v.i.* **1.** to reecho or ring with sound, as a place. **2.** to make an echoing sound, or sound loudly, as a thing: *A gong resounded loudly as the signal that the king was approaching.* **3.** to ring or be echoed, as sounds. **4.** to be famed or celebrated: *His name resounds in the pages of history.* —*v.t.* **5.** to reecho (a sound). **6.** to give forth or utter loudly. **7.** to proclaim loudly (praise, disapproval, etc.). [ME *resounen* < MF *reson(er)* < L *resonāre,* equiv. to *re-* RE- + *sonāre* to SOUND[1]] —**re·sound′ing·ly,** *adv.*

re·source (rē′sōrs, -sôrs, ri sōrs′, -sôrs′), *n.* **1.** a source of supply, support, or aid, esp. one held in reserve. **2. resources,** the collective wealth of a country or its means of producing wealth. **3.** Usually, **resources.** money, or any property which can be converted into money; assets. **4.** Often, **resources.** an available means afforded by the mind or the personal capabilities: *He has no inner resources against loneliness.* **5.** an action or measure to which one may have recourse in an emergency; expedient: *Woman's most frequently used resource is undoubtedly tears.* **6.** capability in dealing with a situation or in meeting difficulties: *a man of unlimited resource.* [< F *ressource* < OF *ressourse,* deriv. of *ressourdre* to rise up, equiv. to *re-* RE- + *sourdre* < L *surgere* to rise up, lift] —**re·source′less,** *adj.* —**re·source′less·ness,** *n.*
—**Syn. 1, 5.** resort. **5.** means, contrivance, shift. **6.** inventiveness, adaptability, ingenuity, cleverness.

re·source·ful (ri sōrs′fəl, -sôrs′-), *adj.* able to deal skillfully and promptly with new situations, difficulties, etc. [RESOURCE + -FUL] —**re·source′ful·ly,** *adv.* —**re·source′ful·ness,** *n.*

resp., 1. respective. **2.** respectively. **3.** respondent.

re·spect (ri spekt′), *n.* **1.** a particular, detail, or point (usually prec. by *in*): *to differ in some respect.* **2.** relation or reference: *inquiries with respect to a route.* **3.** esteem for or a sense of the worth or excellence of a person, a personal quality or trait, or something considered as a manifestation of a personal quality or trait: *I have no respect for cowards. I have great respect for his judgment on most matters.* **4.** deference to a right, privilege, privileged position, or to someone or something considered as having certain rights or privileges: *respect for a suspect's right to counsel; to show respect for the flag; respect for the elderly.* **5.** the condition of being esteemed or honored: *to be held in respect.* **6. respects,** a formal expression or gesture of esteem, deference, or friendship: *We called on the new neighbors to pay our respects. My respects to your dear parents! The Hibernia Hose Company paid its respects to the deceased with an impressive floral tribute.* **7.** discrimination or partiality in regard to persons or things: *hiring policy without respect to race, color, or creed.* **8.** *Archaic.* a consideration. **9. in respect of,** with regard to; in reference to. **10. in respect that,** *Archaic.* because of; since. —*v.t.* **11.** to hold in esteem or honor: *I cannot respect a cheat.* **12.** to show regard or consideration for: *to respect someone's rights.* **13.** to refrain from interfering with: *to respect a person's privacy.* **14.** to relate or have reference to. [< L *respect(us)* looked back on, looked at (ptp. of *respicere*), equiv. to *re-* RE- + *spec-* look + *-t-* ptp. suffix]
—**Syn. 1.** regard, feature, matter. **2.** regard, connection. **3.** estimation, reverence, homage, honor. RESPECT, ESTEEM, VENERATION imply recognition of personal qualities by approbation, deference, and more or less affection. RESPECT is commonly the result of admiration and approbation, together with deference: *to feel respect for a great scholar.* ESTEEM is deference combined with admiration and often with affection: *to hold a friend in great esteem.* VENERATION is an almost religious attitude of deep respect, reverence, and love, such as we feel for persons or things of outstanding superiority, endeared by long association: *veneration for one's grandparents, for noble traditions.* **7.** bias, preference. **11.** revere, venerate, consider, admire. **12.** heed.

re·spect·a·bil·i·ty (ri spek′tə bil′i tē), *n., pl.* **-ties** for **4. 1.** the state or quality of being respectable. **2.** respectable social standing, character, or reputation. **3.** a respectable person or persons. **4. respectabilities,** things accepted as respectable. [RESPECTABLE + -ITY]

re·spect·a·ble (ri spek′tə bəl), *adj.* **1.** worthy of respect or esteem; estimable; worthy: *a respectable citizen.* **2.** of good social standing, reputation, etc.: *a respectable neighborhood.* **3.** pertaining or appropriate to such standing; proper or decent: *respectable language; respectable gowns.* **4.** of moderate excellence; fairly good; fair: *a respectable but undistinguished performance of a play.* **5.** considerable in size, number, or amount: *a respectable navy.* [RESPECT + -ABLE] —**re·spect′a·ble·ness,** *n.* —**re·spect′a·bly,** *adv.*
—**Syn. 1.** honorable. **4.** middling, passable.

re·spect·ant (ri spek′tənt), *adj.* *Heraldry.* aspectant. [RESPECT + -ANT]

re·spect·er (ri spek′tər), *n.* someone or something that is influenced by the social standing, importance, power, or any deterrent put forth by persons or things (used chiefly in negative constructions): *Death is no respecter of wealth.*

re·spect·ful (ri spekt′fəl), *adj.* full of, characterized by, or showing politeness or deference: *a respectful reply.* [RESPECT + -FUL] —**re·spect′ful·ly,** *adv.* —**re·spect′ful·ness,** *n.*
—**Syn.** courteous, polite, decorous, civil, deferential. —**Ant.** discourteous, disrespectful.

re·spect·ing (ri spek′ting), *prep.* regarding; concerning. [RESPECT + -ING[2]]

re·spec·tive (ri spek′tiv), *adj.* pertaining individually or severally to each of a number of persons, things, etc.; particular: *I will now discuss the respective merits of the candidates.* [< LL *respectīv(us),* equiv. to L *respect(us)* (see RESPECT) + *-īvus* -IVE] —**re·spec′tive·ness,** *n.*
—**Syn.** separate, individual; own; corresponding. —**Ant.** irrespective.

re·spec·tive·ly (ri spek′tiv lē), *adv.* with respect to each of a number in the order given: *three samples labeled, respectively, A, B, and C.* [RESPECTIVE + -LY]

re·spell (rē spel′), *v.t.* to spell again or anew. [RE- + SPELL[1]]

Res. Phys., Resident Physician.

Re·spi·ghi (re spē′gē), *n.* **Ot·to·ri·no** (ôt′tô rē′nô), 1879–1936, Italian composer.

re·spir·a·ble (res′pər ə bəl, ri spīr′ə bəl), *adj.* **1.** capable of being respired. **2.** capable of respiring. [< LL *respīrābil(is).* See RESPIRE, -ABLE] —**re·spir′a·bil′i·ty, re·spir′a·ble·ness,** *n.*

res·pi·ra·tion (res′pə rā′shən), *n.* **1.** the act of respiring; inhalation and exhalation of air; breathing.

re·sit′, *v.,* **-sat, -sit·ting.**
re·sit′u·ate′, *v.t.,* **-at·ed, -at·ing.**
re·sketch′, *v.t.*
re·slan′der, *v.t.*
re·smooth′, *v.t.*
re·soak′, *v.*
re·sof′ten, *v.*
re·sol′der, *v.*
re′so·lic′it, *v.*
re′so·lic·i·ta′tion, *n.*
re′so·lid′i·fi·ca′tion, *n.*
re′so·lid′i·fy′, *v.*
re·sow′, *v.*
re·space′, *v.t.,* **-spaced, -spac·ing.**
re·spade′, *v.t.,* **-spad·ed, -spad·ing.**
re′spec·i·fi·ca′tion, *n.*
re·spec′i·fy′, *v.,* **-fied, -fy·ing.**
re·spice′, *v.t.,* **-spiced, -spic·ing.**

2. *Biol.* **a.** the sum total of the physical and chemical processes in an organism by which oxygen and carbohydrates are assimilated into the system and the oxidation products, carbon dioxide and water, are given off. **b.** a similar chemical process, as in muscle cells or in anaerobic bacteria, occurring in the absence of oxygen. [ME *respiracioun* < L *respīrātiōn-* (s. of *respīrātiō*) a breathing out, equiv. to *respīrāt(us)* (ptp. of *respīrāre* to RESPIRE) + *-iōn-* -ION] —**res/pi·ra/tion·al,** *adj.*

res·pi·ra·tor (res/pə rā/tər), *n.* **1.** a device, usually of gauze, worn over the mouth, or nose and mouth, to prevent the inhalation of noxious substances or the like. **2.** *Brit.* See **gas mask. 3.** an apparatus to produce artificial respiration. [< L *respīrāt(us)* (see RESPIRATION) + -OR²]

res·pi·ra·to·ry (res/pər ə tōr/ē, -tôr/ē, ri spīər/ə-), *adj.* pertaining to or serving for respiration: *the respiratory system of mammals.* [< LL *respīrātōri(us),* equiv. to L *respīrāt(us)* (see RESPIRATION) + *-ōrius* -ORY¹]

re·spire (ri spīər/), *v.,* **-spired, -spir·ing.** —*v.i.* **1.** to inhale and exhale air for the purpose of maintaining life; breathe. **2.** to breathe freely again, after anxiety, trouble, etc. —*v.t.* **3.** to breathe; inhale and exhale. **4.** to exhale. [ME *respire(n)* < L *respīrāre,* equiv. to *re-* RE- + *spīrāre* to breathe; see SPIRIT]

res·pi·rom·e·try (res/pə rom/i trē), *n.* the branch of medical science dealing with the measurement and analysis of breathing. [RESPIRE + -O- + -METRY]

res·pite (res/pit), *n., v.,* **-pit·ed, -pit·ing.** —*n.* **1.** a delay or cessation for a time, esp. of anything distressing or trying; an interval of relief: *to toil without respite.* **2.** temporary suspension of the execution of a person condemned to death; reprieve. —*v.t.* **3.** to relieve temporarily, esp. from anything distressing or trying; give an interval of relief from. **4.** to grant delay in the carrying out of (a punishment, obligation, etc.). [ME *respit* < OF < L *respect(us)*; see RESPECT]
—**Syn. 1.** hiatus, interval, rest, recess. **2.** postponement, stay. **3.** alleviate. **4.** postpone, suspend.

re·splend·ence (ri splen/dəns), *n.* a resplendent quality or state; splendor. Also, **re·splend/en·cy.** [ME < LL *resplendentia.* See RESPLENDENT, -ENCE]

re·splend·ent (ri splen/dənt), *adj.* shining brilliantly; gleaming; splendid: *hussars resplendent in white uniforms; resplendent virtues.* [< L *resplendent-* (s. of *resplendēns,* prp. of *resplendēre*) shining brightly, equiv. to *re-* RE- + *splend-* shine (see SPLENDOR) + *-ent-* -ENT] —**re·splend/ent·ly,** *adv.*
—**Syn.** radiant; dazzling, gorgeous, magnificent.

re·spond (ri spond/), *v.i.* **1.** to reply or answer in words: *to respond briefly to a question.* **2.** to make a return by some action as if in answer: *to respond generously to a charity drive.* **3.** *Physiol.* to exhibit some action or effect as if in answer; react: *Nerves respond to a stimulus.* **4.** to correspond (usually fol. by *to*). **5.** *Bridge.* to make a response. —*v.t.* **6.** to say in answer; reply. —*n.* **7.** *Archit.* a half pier, pilaster, or the like, projecting from a wall as a support for a lintel or an arch, the other side of which is supported on a freestanding pier or column. **8.** *Eccles.* **a.** a short anthem chanted at intervals during the reading of a lection. **b.** responsory. **c.** response. [ME (n.) < eccl. L *respondēre* to sing a responsory (L: to promise in return, reply, answer), equiv. to *re-* RE- + *spondēre* to pledge, promise; see SPONSOR]
—**Syn. 1.** rejoin. **2.** rise, react, reply. **4.** match.

re·spond·ence (ri spon/dəns), *n.* the act of responding; response: *respondence to a stimulus.* Also, **re·spond/en·cy.** [< obs. F; see RESPOND, -ENCE]

re·spond·ent (ri spon/dənt), *adj.* **1.** answering; responsive. **2.** *Obs.* corresponding. —*n.* **3.** a person who responds or makes reply. **4.** *Law.* a defendant, esp. in appellate and divorce cases. [< L *respondent-* (s. of *respondēns*), prp. of *respondēre.* See RESPOND, -ENT]

re·spond·er (ri spon/dər), *n.* **1.** one who or that which responds. **2.** *Electronics.* the part of a transponder that transmits the reply. [RESPOND + -ER¹]

Re·spon·sa (ri spon/sə), *n.* the branch of rabbinical literature comprised of authoritative replies in letter form made by noted rabbis or Jewish scholars to questions sent to them concerning Jewish law. [< NL; pl. of RESPONSUM]

re·sponse (ri spons/), *n.* **1.** an answer or reply, as in words or in some action. **2.** *Biol.* any behavior of a living organism which results from stimulation. **3.** *Eccles.* **a.** a verse, sentence, phrase, or word said or sung by the choir or congregation in reply to the officiant. Cf. **versicle** (def. 2). **b.** responsory. **4.** *Bridge.* a bid based on an evaluation of one's hand relative to the previous bid of one's partner. [< L *respons(um),* n. use of neut. ptp. of *respondēre* to RESPOND; r. ME *respounse* < MF *respons*] —**re·sponse/less,** *adj.*
—**Syn. 1.** rejoinder. See **answer.**

response/ generaliza/tion, *Psychol.* generalization (def. 4b).

re·spons·er (ri spon/sər), *n.* responsor.

response/ time/, *Psychol.* the time consumed in making a response.

re·spon·si·bil·i·ty (ri spon/sə bil/i tē), *n., pl.* **-ties. 1.** the state or fact of being responsible. **2.** an instance of being responsible: *The responsibility for this mess is yours!* **3.** a particular burden of obligation upon one who is responsible: *to feel the responsibilities of one's position.* **4.** something for which one is responsible: *A child is a responsibility to its parents.* **5.** reliability or dependability, esp. in meeting debts or payments. **6. on one's own responsibility,** on one's own initiative or authority: *He left the factory and on his own responsibility founded a new industry.* [RESPONSIBLE + -ITY]
—**Syn. 1.** answerability, accountability.

re·spon·si·ble (ri spon/sə bəl), *adj.* **1.** answerable or accountable, as for something within one's power, control, or management (often fol. by *to* or *for*): *You will henceforth be responsible only to the president for your decisions.* **2.** involving accountability or responsibility: *a responsible position.* **3.** chargeable with being the author, cause, or occasion of something (usually fol. by *for*): *Termites are often responsible for the collapse of wooden foundations.* **4.** having a capacity for moral decisions and therefore accountable; capable of rational thought or action: *The defendant is not responsible for his actions.* **5.** able to discharge obligations or pay debts. **6.** reliable or dependable, as in meeting debts, conducting business dealings, etc. —*n.* **7. responsibles,** *Theat.* **a.** (*construed as pl.*) small, but important, roles. **b.** (*construed as sing.*) an actor who plays such roles. [< L *respons(us)* (see RESPONSE) + -IBLE] —**re·spon/si·ble·ness,** *n.* —**re·spon/si·bly,** *adv.*
—**Syn. 1.** liable. **4.** competent. **5.** solvent. **6.** honest, capable, reliable, trustworthy.

re·spon·sion (ri spon/shən), *n.* **1.** the act of responding or answering. **2. responsions,** the first examination at Oxford University which candidates for the degree of B.A. have to pass. [ME < L *respōnsiōn-* (s. of *respōnsiō*) an answer. See RESPONSE, -ION]

re·spon·sive (ri spon/siv), *adj.* **1.** making answer or reply, esp. responding or reacting readily to influences, appeals, efforts, etc. **2.** *Physiol.* acting in response, as to some stimulus. **3.** characterized by the use of responses: *responsive worship.* [< LL *respōnsīv(us).* See RESPONSE, -IVE] —**re·spon/sive·ly,** *adv.*

re·spon·sive·ness (ri spon/siv nis), *n.* **1.** the quality or state of being responsive. **2.** *Mach.* the ability of a machine or system to adjust quickly to suddenly altered external conditions, as of speed, load, or temperature, and to resume stable operation without undue delay. [RESPONSIVE + -NESS]

re·spon·sor (ri spon/sər), *n.* *Electronics.* the portion of an interrogator-responsor that receives and interprets the signals from a transponder. Also, **responser.** [RESPONSE + -OR²]

re·spon·so·ry (ri spon/sə rē), *n., pl.* **-ries.** *Eccles.* an anthem sung after a lection by a soloist and choir alternately. [< LL *respōnsōri(um).* See RESPONSE, -ORY²]

re·spon·sum (ri spon/səm), *n., pl.* **-sa** (-sə). the reply of a noted rabbi or Jewish scholar as rendered in the Responsa. [< NL, L: a reply; see RESPONSE]

res pu·bli·ca (res pōō/bli kä/; *Eng.* rēz pub/li kə, rās), *Latin.* the state; republic; commonwealth. [lit., public matter]

res·sen·ti·ment (*Fr.* rə sän tē män/), *n.* **1.** any cautious, defeatist, or cynical attitude based on the belief that the individual and human institutions exist in a hostile or indifferent universe or society. **2.** an oppressive awareness of the futility of trying to improve one's status in life or in society.

rest¹ (rest), *n.* **1.** the refreshing quiet or repose of sleep: *a good night's rest.* **2.** refreshing ease or inactivity after exertion or labor: *to allow an hour for rest.* **3.** relief or freedom, esp. from anything that wearies, troubles, or disturbs. **4.** a period or interval of inactivity, repose, or tranquillity: *I need a long rest. Go away and give me a rest.* **5.** mental or spiritual calm; tranquillity. **6.** the repose of death: *eternal rest.* **7.** cessation or absence of motion: *to bring a machine to rest.* **8.** *Music.* **a.** an interval of silence between tones. **b.** a mark or sign indicating it. **9.** *Pros.* a short pause within a line; caesura. **10.** a place that provides shelter or lodging for travelers; an inn, hotel, or motel. **11.** a piece or thing for something to rest on: *a foot rest.* **12.** a supporting device; support. **13.** *Billiards, Pool.* bridge¹ (def. 10). **14. at rest, a.** in a state of repose, as in sleep. **b.** dead. **c.** quiescent; inactive; not in motion: *the inertia of an object at rest.* **d.** free from worry; tranquil: *Nothing could put his mind at rest.* **15. lay to rest,** to inter (a dead body); bury: *He was laid to rest last Thursday.* [ME, OE; akin to G *Rast*]

A B C D E F G H

Rest¹ (def. 8b)
A, Double whole;
B, Whole; C, Half;
D, Quarter; E, Eighth;
F, Sixteenth; G, Thirty-second; H, Sixty-fourth

—*v.i.* **16.** to refresh oneself, as by sleeping, lying down, or relaxing. **17.** to relieve weariness by cessation of exertion or labor. **18.** to be at ease; have tranquillity or peace. **19.** to repose in death. **20.** to be quiet or still. **21.** to cease from motion, come to rest; stop. **22.** to become or remain inactive. **23.** to remain without further action or notice: *to let a matter rest.* **24.** to lie, sit, lean, or be set: *His arm rested on the table.* **25.** *Agric.* to lie fallow or unworked: *to let land rest.* **26.** to be imposed as a burden or responsibility (usually fol. by *on* or *upon*). **27.** to rely (usually fol. by *on* or *upon*). **28.** to be based or founded (usually fol. by *on* or *upon*). **29.** to be or be found where specified: *The blame rests with them.* **30.** to be present; dwell; linger (usually fol. by *on* or *upon*): *A sunbeam rests upon the altar.* **31.** to be fixed or directed on something, as the gaze, eyes, etc. **32.** *Law.* to terminate voluntarily the introduction of evidence in a case. —*v.t.* **33.** to give rest to; refresh with rest: *to rest oneself.* **34.** to lay or place for rest, ease, or support: *to rest one's back against a tree.* **35.** to direct (as the eyes): *to rest one's eyes on someone.* **36.** to base, or let depend, as on some ground of reliance. **37.** to bring to rest; halt; stop. **38.** *Law.* to terminate voluntarily the introduction of evidence on: *to rest one's case.* [ME *rest(en),* OE *restan;* akin to G *rasten*] —**rest/er,** *n.*

rest² (rest), *n.* **1.** the part that is left or remains; remainder: *The rest of the students are in the corridor.* **2.** the others: *All the rest are going.* **3.** *Banking. Brit.* surplus (defs. 1, 2). —*v.i.* **4.** to continue to be; remain as specified: *Rest assured that all is well.* [ME < MF *rest(er)* (to) remain < L *restāre* to remain standing, equiv. to *re-* RE- + *stāre* to STAND]

rest³ (rest), *n.* *Armor.* a support for a lance; lance rest. [ME; aph. var. of ARREST]

re·state (rē stāt/), *v.t.,* **-stat·ed, -stat·ing.** to state again or in a new way. [RE- + STATE] —**re·state/ment,** *n.*

res·tau·rant (res/tər ənt, -tə ränt/), *n.* a place where meals are served to customers. [< F, n. use of prp. of *restaurer* < L *restaurāre* to RESTORE]

res/taurant car/, *Brit.* See **dining car.**

res·tau·ra·teur (res/tər ə tûr/; *Fr.* res tô ra tœr/), *n., pl.* **-teurs** (-tûrz/; *Fr.* -tœr/). the owner or manager of a restaurant. [< F < LL *restaurātor,* equiv. to *restaurāt(us)* (ptp. of *restaurāre* to RESTORE) + *-or* -OR²]

rest/ cure/, *Med.* a treatment for nervous disorders, consisting of a complete rest, usually combined with systematic diet, massage, etc. [REST¹ + CURE]

rest/ en/ergy, *Physics.* the energy equivalent to the mass of a particle at rest in an inertial frame of reference, equal to the rest mass times the square of the speed of light.

rest·ful (rest/fəl), *adj.* **1.** full of or giving rest. **2.** being at rest; quiet; tranquil; peaceful. [ME; see REST¹, -FUL] —**rest/ful·ly,** *adv.* —**rest/ful·ness,** *n.*
—**Syn. 2.** calm, serene, undisturbed. —**Ant. 1.** disturbing. **2.** agitated.

rest·har·row (rest/har/ō), *n.* a low, pink-flowered, European, leguminous shrub, *Ononis spinosa,* having tough roots which hinder the plow or harrow. [REST¹ + HARROW]

rest/ home/, a residential establishment that provides special care for convalescents and aged or infirm persons.

res/ti·form bod/y (res/tə fôrm/), *Anat.* a cordlike bundle of nerve fibers lying on each side of the medulla oblongata and connecting it with the cerebellum. [< NL *restiform(is),* equiv. to L *resti-* comb. form of *restis* rope + *-formis* -FORM]

rest·ing (res/ting), *adj.* **1.** that rests; not active. **2.** *Bot.* dormant: applied esp. to spores or seeds which germinate after a period of dormancy. [REST¹ + -ING²]

res·ti·tu·tion (res/ti tōō/shən, -tyōō/-), *n.* **1.** reparation made by giving an equivalent or compensation for loss, damage, or injury caused; indemnification. **2.** the restoration of property or rights previously taken away, conveyed, or surrendered. **3.** restoration to the former or original state or position. **4.** *Physics.* the return to an original physical condition, esp. after elastic deformation. [ME < OF < L *restitūtiōn-* (s. of *restitūtiō*) a calling back again, equiv. to *restitūt(us)* (ptp. of *restituere* to replace, restore; *re-* RE- + *statuere* to cause to stand; see STATUE) + *-iōn-* -ION] —**res/ti·tu/tive, res·ti·tu·to·ry** (res/ti tōō/tə rē, -tyōō/-), *adj.*
—**Syn. 1.** recompense, amends, compensation, requital, satisfaction, repayment. See **redress.**

res·tive (res/tiv), *adj.* **1.** restless; uneasy; impatient of control, restraint, or delay, as persons. **2.** refractory; stubborn. **3.** refusing to go forward; balky: *a restive horse.* [REST² + -IVE; r. ME *restif* stationary, balking < OF: inert] —**res/tive·ly,** *adv.* —**res/tive·ness,** *n.*
—**Syn. 1.** nervous, unquiet. **2.** recalcitrant, disobedient, obstinate. —**Ant. 1.** patient, quiet. **2.** obedient, tractable.

rest·less (rest/lis), *adj.* **1.** characterized by or showing inability to remain at rest: *a restless mood.* **2.** unquiet or uneasy, as a person, the mind, the heart, etc. **3.** never at rest; perpetually agitated or in motion: *the restless sea.* **4.** without rest; without restful sleep: *a restless night.* **5.** unceasingly active; averse to quiet or inaction, as persons: *a restless crowd.* [ME *restles.* See REST¹, -LESS] —**rest/less·ly,** *adv.* —**rest/less·ness,** *n.*

rest/less ca/vy, a wild guinea pig.

rest/ mass/, *Physics.* the mass of a particle at rest in an inertial frame of reference and equal to the mass in classical mechanics.

re·stock (rē stok/), *v.t., v.i.* to stock again; replenish. [RE- + STOCK]

Res·ton (res/tən), *n.* **James (Barrett),** born 1909, U.S. journalist, born in Scotland.

res·to·ra·tion (res/tə rā/shən), *n.* **1.** the act of restoring; renewal, revival, or reestablishment. **2.** the state or fact of being restored. **3.** a return of something to a former, original, normal, or unimpaired condition. **4.** restitution of something taken away or lost. **5.** something which is restored. **6.** a representation or reconstruction of an ancient building, extinct animal, or the like, showing it in its original state. **7.** a putting back into a former position, dignity, etc. **8. the Restoration, a.** the reestablishment of the monarchy in England with the return of Charles II in 1660. **b.** the period of the reign of Charles II (1660–85), sometimes extended to include the reign of James II (1685–88). [ME *restauracion* < LL *restaurātiōn-* (s. of *restaurātiō*), equiv. to L *restaurāt(us)* (ptp. of *restaurāre* to RESTORE) + *-iōn-* -ION]

re·stor·a·tive (ri stōr/ə tiv, -stôr/-), *adj.* **1.** serving to restore; pertaining to restoration. **2.** capable of renewing health or strength. —*n.* **3.** a restorative agent, means, or the like. **4.** a means of restoring a person to consciousness: *Smelling salts serve as a restorative.* [ME *restoratif* < MF *restauratif* < L *restaurāt(us)* (ptp. of *restaurāre* to RESTORE) + MF *-if* -IVE]

re·store (ri stōr/, -stôr/), *v.t.,* **-stored, -stor·ing. 1.** to bring back into existence, use, or the like; reestablish: *to restore order.* **2.** to bring back to a former, original, or normal condition, as a building, statue, or painting. **3.** to bring back to a state of health, soundness, or vigor. **4.** to put back to a former place, or to a former position, rank, etc.: *to restore the king to his throne.* **5.** to give back; make return or restitution of (anything taken away or lost). **6.** to reproduce, reconstruct, or represent (an ancient building, extinct animal, etc.) in the original state. [ME *restore(n)* < OF *restor(er)* < L *restaurāre,* equiv. to *re-* RE- + **staurāre;* see STORE] —**re·stor/a·ble,** *adj.* —**re·stor/a·ble·ness,** *n.* —**re·stor/er,** *n.*
—**Syn. 2.** mend. See **renew. 4.** replace, reinstate. **6.** rebuild.

restor/ing spring/, *Mach.* a spring so located that it returns a displaced part to its normal position.

restr., restaurant.

re·strain (rē strān/), *v.t., v.i.* to strain again. [RE- + STRAIN¹]

re·strain (ri strān/), *v.t.* **1.** to hold back from action; keep in check or under control; repress: *to restrain a man from committing suicide; to restrain one's temper.* **2.** to

re·splice/, *v.t.,* **-spliced, -splic·ing.**
re·spray/, *v.*
re·spread/, *v.,* **-spread, -spread·ing.**
re·spring/, *v.,* **-sprang** or **-sprung, -spring·ing.**
re·sprin/kle, *v.,* **-kled, -kling.**
re·squan/der, *v.t.*
re·stab/, *v.,* **-stabbed, -stab·bing.**
re/sta·bi·li·za/tion, *n.*
re·sta/bi·lize/, *v.t.,* **-lized, -liz·ing.**
re·sta/ble, *v.t.,* **-bled, -bling.**
re·stack/, *v.t.*
re·staff/, *v.t.*
re·stage/, *v.t.,* **-staged, -stag·ing.**
re·stain/, *v.*
re·stamp/, *v.t.*
re·start/, *v., n.*
re·sta/tion, *v.t.*
re/ster·i·li·za/tion, *n.*
re·ster/i·lize/, *v.t.,* **-lized, -liz·ing.**
re·stim/u·late/, *v.t.,* **-lat·ed, -lat·ing.**
re/stim·u·la/tion, *n.*
re·sting/, *v.,* **-stung, -sting·ing.**
re·stip/u·late/, *v.,* **-lat·ed, -lat·ing.**
re/stip·u·la/tion, *n.*
re·stir/, *v.,* **-stirred, -stir·ring.**
re·stitch/, *v.t.*
re·straight/en, *v.*

deprive of liberty, as by arrest or the like. **3.** to limit or hamper the activity, growth, or effect of: *to restrain trade with Cuba.* [ME *restreyn(en)* < MF *restreind(re)* < L *restringere* to bind back, bind fast, equiv. to *re-* RE- + *stringere* to draw together; see STRAIN¹] —**re·strain′a·bil′i·ty,** *n.* —**re·strain′a·ble,** *adj.* —**re·strain·ed·ly** (ri strā′nid lē), *adv.* —**re·strain′ing·ly,** *adv.*
—**Syn. 1.** bridle, suppress, constrain. See **check. 2.** restrict, circumscribe, confine, hinder, hamper. —**Ant. 1.** unbridle. **2.** free, liberate.

re·strain·er (ri strā′nər), *n.* **1.** one who or that which restrains. **2.** *Photog.* a chemical added to a developer to retard its action. [RESTRAIN + -ER¹]

restrain′ing or′der, *Law.* a judicial order to forbid a particular act until a decision is reached on an application for an injunction.

re·straint (ri strānt′), *n.* **1.** a restraining action or influence: *freedom from restraint.* **2.** a means of restraining. **3.** the act of restraining, or holding back, controlling, or checking. **4.** the state or fact of being restrained; deprivation of liberty; confinement. **5.** constraint or reserve in feelings, behavior, etc. [ME *restreinte* < MF *restrainte,* n. use of fem. ptp. of *restraindre* to RESTRAIN]
—**Syn. 4.** circumscription, restriction, imprisonment, incarceration. —**Ant. 4.** liberty.

restraint′ of trade′, action tending to interrupt the free flow of goods and services, as by price fixing and other practices that have the effect of reducing competition.

re·strict (ri strikt′), *v.t.* to confine or keep within limits, as of space, action, choice, quantity, etc. [< L *restrict(us)* drawn back, tightened, bound (ptp. of *restringere;* see RESTRAIN), equiv. to *re-* RE- + *strictus* STRICT]
—**Syn.** curb, circumscribe, abridge, restrain. —**Ant.** free.

re·strict·ed (ri strik′tid), *adj.* **1.** confined; limited. **2.** *U.S. Govt., Mil.* (of information, a document, etc.) **a.** designated with the classification *restricted.* **b.** limited to persons authorized to use information, documents, etc., so classified. Cf. **classification** (def. 3). **3.** limited to or admitting only members of a particular group or class, esp. white Gentiles: *a restricted neighborhood; a restricted hotel.* [RESTRICT + -ED²] —**re·strict′ed·ly,** *adv.* —**re·strict′ed·ness,** *n.*

restrict′ed class′, a class of yachts that, although differing somewhat in design and rigging, are deemed able to race together because of conformity to certain standards.

restrict′ed propel′lant, *Rocketry.* a solid propellant which burns in a plane perpendicular to its longitudinal axis. Also called **end burner.** Cf. **unrestricted propellant.**

restrict′ed the′ory of relativ′ity, *Physics.* See under **relativity** (def. 2).

re·stric·tion (ri strik′shən), *n.* **1.** something that restricts; a restrictive condition or regulation; limitation. **2.** the act of restricting. **3.** the state of being restricted. **4.** *Math.* a function related to a given function defined on a set, which takes on the values of the original function on a specified subset of the given set. [ME *restriccioun* < eccl. L *restrictiōn-* (s. of *restrictiō*), equiv. to L *restrict(us)* (see RESTRICT) + *-iōn-* -ION] —**re·stric′tion·ist,** *n.*

restric′tion play′, *Checkers.* a limited number of opening moves that are predetermined by their chance selection from an accepted list.

re·stric·tive (ri strik′tiv), *adj.* **1.** tending or serving to restrict. **2.** of the nature of a restriction. **3.** expressing or implying restriction or limitation of application, as terms, expressions, etc. **4.** *Gram.* limiting the meaning of a modified element: *a restrictive adjective.* [ME < MF *restrictif* < L *restrict(us)* (see RESTRICT) + MF *-if* -IVE] —**re·stric′tive·ly,** *adv.* —**re·stric′tive·ness,** *n.*

restric′tive clause′, *Gram.* a relative clause that identifies the antecedent and that is usually not set off by commas in English. In *The year that just ended was bad for crops* the clause *that just ended* is a restrictive clause. Cf. **descriptive clause.**

re·strike (*v.* rē strīk′; *n.* rē′strīk′), *v.,* **-struck, -struck** or **-strick·en, -strik·ing,** *n.* —*v.t., v.i.* **1.** to strike again. —*n.* **2.** a coin freshly minted from dies of an earlier issue. [RE- + STRIKE]

rest′ room′, a room or rooms having washbowl, toilet, and other facilities for use by employees, visitors, etc., as in a store, theater, office, or the like.

re·sult (ri zult′), *n.* **1.** that which results; outcome; consequence; effect. **2.** *Math.* a quantity, expression, etc., obtained by calculation. —*v.i.* **3.** to spring, arise, or proceed as a consequence from actions, circumstances, premises, etc.; be the outcome. **4.** to terminate or end in a specified manner or thing. [ME *result(en)* < L *resul(āre)* (to) spring back, rebound, equiv. to *resil(īre)* (to) spring back + *-t* freq. suffix; or *re-* RE- + *saltāre* to dance (*sal(īre)* (to) leap, spring + *-t* freq. suffix)]
—**Syn. 1.** conclusion, issue, end, product, fruit. See **effect. 3.** flow, come, issue. See **follow. 4.** resolve, eventuate. —**Ant. 1.** cause.

re·sult·ant (ri zul′tənt), *adj.* **1.** that results; following as a result or consequence. **2.** resulting from the combination of two or more agents: *a resultant force.* —*n.* **3.** *Math., Physics.* a single vector, often representing a force or velocity, equivalent to two or more other such vectors, being their vector sum. **4.** *Math.* a determinant, the entries of which are the coefficients of each of two polynomials in a specified arrangement and the value of which determines whether the polynomials have a common factor. **5.** that which results. [< L *resultant-* (s. of *resultāns*), prp. of *resultāre.* See RESULT, -ANT]

result′ant tone′, *Music.* See **combination tone.**

re·sult·ing·ly (ri zul′ting lē), *adv.* as a result. [RESULT + -ING² + -LY]

re·sume (ri zōōm′), *v.,* **-sumed, -sum·ing.** —*v.t.* **1.** to take up or go on with again after interruption: *to resume a journey.* **2.** to take or occupy again: *to resume one's seat.* **3.** to take or assume again: *to resume her maiden name.* **4.** to take back: *to resume the title to a property.* —*v.i.* **5.** to go on or continue after interruption: *The dancing is about to resume.* **6.** to begin again. [ME *resume(n)* < MF *resum(er)* or L *resūm(ere)* (to) take back, take again, equiv. to *re-* RE- + *sūmere* to take (*sub-* SUB- + *emere* to acquire, obtain, take)] —**re·sum′a·ble,** *adj.* —**re·sum′er,** *n.*

ré·su·mé (rez′ōō mā′, rez′ōō mā′), *n.* **1.** a summing up; summary. **2.** a brief account of personal, educational, and professional qualifications and experience, as of an applicant for a job. Also, **re′su·me′.** [< F, n. use of ptp. of *résumer* to RESUME, sum up]

re·sump·tion (ri zump′shən), *n.* **1.** the act of resuming; a reassumption, as of something previously granted. **2.** the act or fact of taking up or going on with again, as of something interrupted. **3.** the act of taking again or recovering something given up or lost. [ME < MF < LL *resumptiōn-* (s. of *resumptiō*), equiv. to L *resumpt(us)* (ptp. of *resūmere* to RESUME) + *-iōn-* -ION]

re·sump·tive (ri zump′tiv), *adj.* **1.** that summarizes: *a resumptive statement of his business experience.* **2.** that tends to resume or repeat: *a speech so digressive and resumptive that its point was lost.* [RESUMPT(ION) + -IVE; r. ME: a restorative < L *resumptīv(us)*] —**re·sump′tive·ly,** *adv.*

re·su·pi·nate (ri sōō′pə nāt′), *adj.* **1.** bent backward. **2.** *Bot.* inverted; appearing as if upside down. [< L *resupīnāt(us)* bent backward, turned back (ptp. of *resupīnāre*), equiv. to *re-* RE- + *supīn-* (see SUPINE) + *-ātus* -ATE¹]

re·su·pi·na·tion (ri sōō′pə nā′shən), *n.* a resupinate condition. [< L *resupīnāt(us)* (see RESUPINATE) + -ION]

re·su·pine (rē′sōō pīn′), *adj.* lying on the back; supine. [< L *resupīn(us)* bent back, lying back. See RE-, SUPINE]

re·sur·face (rē sûr′fis), *v.t.,* **-faced, -fac·ing.** to give a new surface to. [RE- + SURFACE]

re·sur·gam (re sōōr′gäm; *Eng.* ri sûr′gam), *Latin.* I shall rise again.

re·surge (ri sûrj′), *v.i.,* **-surged, -surg·ing.** to rise again, as from death or from virtual extinction. [< L *resurg(ere)* (to) rise again, appear again, equiv. to *re-* RE- + *surgere* to lift up, raise, var. of *surrigere,* equiv. to *sur-* up (var. of *sub-* SUB-) + *regere* to direct]

re·sur·gent (ri sûr′jənt), *adj.* rising or tending to rise again; reviving. [< L *resurgent-* (s. of *resurgēns,* prp. of *resurgere*). See RESURGE, -ENT] —**re·sur′gence,** *n.*

res·ur·rect (rez′ə rekt′), *v.t.* **1.** to raise from the dead; bring to life again. **2.** to bring back into use, practice, etc.: *to resurrect an ancient custom.* —*v.i.* **3.** to rise from the dead. [back formation from RESURRECTION] —**res′ur·rec′tor,** *n.*

res·ur·rec·tion (rez′ə rek′shən), *n.* **1.** the act of rising again from the dead. **2.** (*cap.*) the rising again of Christ after His death and burial. **3.** (*cap.*) the rising again of men on the judgment day. **4.** the state of those risen from the dead. **5.** a rising again, as from decay, disuse, etc.; revival. **6.** *Christian Science.* the ultimate awareness that spirit is the source and constituent of life, substances, and thought. [ME < eccl. L *resurrectiōn-* (s. of *resurrectiō*) the Easter church-festival, equiv. to *resurrect(us)* (ptp. of *resurgere* to rise again; see RESURGE) + *-iōn-* -ION] —**res′ur·rec′tion·al,** *adj.* —**res′ur·rec′tive,** *adj.*

res·ur·rec·tion·ar·y (rez′ə rek′shə ner′ē), *adj.* **1.** pertaining to or of the nature of resurrection. **2.** pertaining to resurrectionism. [RESURRECTION + -ARY]

resurrec′tion fern′, a drought-resistant, evergreen, epiphytic fern, *Polypodium polypodioides,* found from the southeastern U.S. to tropical America, which appears to be a ball of coiled, dead leaves in the dry season, but revives with moisture.

resurrec′tion gate′. See **lich gate.**

res·ur·rec·tion·ism (rez′ə rek′shə niz′əm), *n.* the exhumation and stealing of dead bodies, esp. for dissection. [RESURRECTION + -ISM]

res·ur·rec·tion·ist (rez′ə rek′shə nist), *n.* **1.** a person who brings something to life or view again. **2.** a believer in resurrection. **3.** *Rom. Cath. Ch.* a member of the "Congregation of the Resurrection," founded in 1836. **4.** Also called **resurrec′tion man′.** a person who exhumes and steals dead bodies, esp. for dissection; body snatcher. [RESURRECTION + -IST]

resurrec′tion plant′, **1.** a desert, perennial herb, *Selaginella lepidophylla,* found from Texas to South America, having stems that curl inward when dry. **2.** See **Rose of Jericho.**

re·sur·vey (*v.* rē′sər vā′; *n.* rē sûr′vā, rē′sər vā′), *v., n., pl.* **-veys.** —*v.t., v.i.* **1.** to survey again. —*n.* **2.** a new survey. [RE- + SURVEY]

re·sus·ci·tate (ri sus′i tāt′), *v.t.,* **-tat·ed, -tat·ing.** to revive, esp. from apparent death or from unconsciousness. [< L *resuscitāt(us)* raised up again, revived (ptp. of *resuscitāre*), equiv. to *re-* RE- + *sus-* up (var. of *sub-* SUB-) + *citāre* to move, arouse; see CITE] —**re·sus·ci·ta·ble** (ri sus′i tə bəl), *adj.* —**re·sus′ci·ta′tion,** *n.* —**re·sus′ci·ta′tive,** *adj.*

re·sus·ci·ta·tor (ri sus′i tā′tər), *n.* **1.** one who or that which resuscitates. **2.** a device used in the treatment of asphyxiation that, by forcing oxygen or a mixture of oxygen and carbon dioxide into the lungs, initiates respiration. [RESUSCITATE + -OR²]

Resz·ke (*Pol.* resh′ke), *n.* **Jean de** (*Fr.* zhäN də), 1850–1925, Polish tenor.

ret (ret), *v.t.,* **ret·ted, ret·ting.** to soak in water or expose to moisture, as flax or hemp, to facilitate the removal of the fiber from the woody tissue by partial rotting. [ME *ret(en), rett(en);* c. D *reten* (cf. D *roten.* G *rössen,* Sw *röta*); akin to ROT]

ret., **1.** retired. **2.** returned.

re·ta·ble (ri tā′bəl), *n.* a decorative structure raised above an altar at the back, often forming a frame for a picture, bas-relief, or the like, and sometimes including a shelf or shelves, as for ornaments. [< F, equiv. to OF *rere* at the back (< L *retrō*) + *table* TABLE]

re·tail (rē′tāl *for 1–4, 6;* ri tāl′ *for 5*), *n.* **1.** the sale of goods to ultimate consumers, usually in small quantities (opposed to *wholesale*). —*adj.* **2.** pertaining to, connected with, or engaged in sale at retail: *the retail price.* —*adv.* **3.** in a retail quantity or at a retail price. —*v.t.* **4.** to sell at retail; sell directly to the consumer. **5.** to relate or repeat in detail to others: *to retail scandal.* —*v.i.* **6.** to be sold at retail: *It retails at 50 cents.* [late ME < AF: a cutting, deriv. of *retailler* to cut, equiv. to *re-* RE- + *tailler* to cut; see TAIL²] —**re′tail·er,** *n.*

re·tain (ri tān′), *v.t.* **1.** to keep possession of. **2.** to continue to use, practice, etc.: *to retain an old custom.* **3.** to continue to hold or have: *to retain a prisoner in custody; This cloth retains its color.* **4.** to keep in mind; remember. **5.** to hold in place or position. **6.** to engage, esp. by payment of a preliminary fee: *to retain a lawyer.* [ME *retein(en)* < OF *reten(ir)* < L *retinēre* to hold back, hold fast, equiv. to *re-* RE- + *tinēre* to hold] —**re·tain′a·bil′i·ty, re·tain′a·ble·ness,** *n.* —**re·tain′a·ble,** *adj.* —**re·tain′ment,** *n.*
—**Syn. 1.** hold, preserve. See **keep.** —**Ant. 1.** loose, lose. **4.** forget.

retained′ earn′ings, the accumulated, undistributed earnings of a corporation. Also called **retained′ in′come, earned surplus.**

retained′ ob′ject, *Gram.* an object in a passive construction identical with the direct or indirect object in the active construction from which it is derived, as *me* in *the picture was shown me,* which is also the indirect object in the active construction *they showed me the picture.*

retained′ objec′tive com′plement, *Gram.* an objective complement that is kept in its predicative position following the verb when the verb is transformed into the passive voice, as *genius* in *He was considered a genius* from (*They*) *considered him a genius.*

re·tain·er¹ (ri tā′nər), *n.* **1.** one who or that which retains. **2.** *Hist.* one attached to a noble household and owing it occasional service. **3.** Also called **cage, separator.** *Mach.* a ring separating, and moving with, balls or rollers in a bearing. **4.** *Dentistry.* **a.** a device for holding the teeth in position: used in orthodontic correction. **b.** a part on a bridge or the like by which the bridge is attached to the natural teeth. [RETAIN + -ER¹]

re·tain·er² (ri tā′nər), *n.* **1.** the act of retaining in one's service. **2.** the fact of being so retained. **3.** a fee paid to secure services, as of a lawyer. [ME *reteinir,* prob. n. use of MF *retenir* to RETAIN]

retain′ing wall′, a wall for holding in place a mass of earth or the like, as at the edge of a terrace or excavation. Cf. **breast wall.**

Retaining wall

re·take (*v.* rē tāk′; *n.* rē′tāk′), *v.,* **-took, -tak·en, -tak·ing,** *n.* —*v.t.* **1.** to take again; take back. **2.** to recapture. **3.** *Photog., Motion Pictures.* to photograph or film again. —*n.* **4.** the act of photographing or filming again. **5.** a picture, scene, sequence, etc., which is to be or has been photographed or filmed again. [RE- + TAKE] —**re·tak′er,** *n.*

re·tal·i·ate (ri tal′ē āt′), *v.,* **-at·ed, -at·ing.** —*v.i.* **1.** to return like for like, esp. evil for evil: *to retaliate for an injury.* —*v.t.* **2.** to requite or make return for (a wrong or injury) with the like. [< LL *retaliāt(us)* (ptp. of *retaliāre*), equiv. to *re-* RE- + *tāl-* (s. of *tālis*) such, of such a nature + *-i-* -I- + *-ātus* -ATE¹] —**re·tal′i·a′tive, re·tal·i·a·to·ry** (ri tal′ē ə tôr′ē, -tōr′ē), *adj.* —**re·tal′i·a′tor,** *n.*

re·tal·i·a·tion (ri tal′ē ā′shən), *n.* the act of retaliating; return of like for like; reprisal. [RETALIATE + -ION]

re·tard (ri tärd′), *v.t.* **1.** to make slow; delay the progress of (an action, process, etc.); hinder or impede. —*v.i.* **2.** to be delayed. —*n.* **3.** retardation; delay. [< L *retard(āre)* (to) delay, protract, equiv. to *re-* RE- + *tardāre* to loiter, be slow, deriv. of *tardus* slow; see TARDY] —**re·tard′ing·ly,** *adv.*
—**Syn. 1.** obstruct, check. —**Ant. 1.** accelerate.

re·tard·ant (ri tär′dᵊnt), *n.* *Chem.* any substance capable of reducing the speed of a given reaction. [RETARD + -ANT]

re·tard·ate (ri tär′dāt), *n., v.,* **-at·ed, -at·ing,** *adj.* —*n.* **1.** a person who is mentally retarded. —*v.t.* **2.** *Obs.* to retard. —*adj.* **3.** *Obs.* retarded. [< L *retardāt(us)* (ptp. of *retardāre*). See RETARD, -ATE¹]

re·tar·da·tion (rē′tär dā′shən), *n.* **1.** the act of retarding, or the state of being retarded. **2.** that which retards; hindrance. **3.** slowness or limitation in intellectual understanding and awareness, emotional development, academic progress, etc. **4.** *Music.* a form of suspension which is resolved upward. Also,

re·strap′, *v.t.,* **-strapped, -strap·ping.**
re·strength′en, *v.*
re·stress′, *v.t.*
re·string′, *v.,* **-strung, -string·ing.**
re·string′er, *n.*
re·strive′, *v.i.,* **-strove, -striv·en, -striv·ing.**
re·struc′ture, *v.,* **-tured, -tur·ing.**
re·stud′y, *n., pl.* **-stud·ies;** *v.,* **-stud·ied, -stud·y·ing.**
re·stuff′, *v.t.*
re·style′, *v.,* **-styled, -styl·ing.**
re′sub·ject′, *v.t.*
re′sub·jec′tion, *n.*
re·sub′li·mate′, *v.t.,* **-mat·ed, -mat·ing.**
re′sub·li·ma′tion, *n.*
re′sub·merge′, *v.,* **-merged, -merg·ing.**
re′sub·mis′sion, *n.*
re′sub·mit′, *v.,* **-mit·ted, -mit·ting.**
re′sub·scribe′, *v.,* **-scribed, -scrib·ing.**
re′sub·scrip′tion, *n.*
re′sub·stan′ti·ate′, *v.t.,* **-at·ed, -at·ing.**
re′sub·stan′ti·a′tion, *n.*
re·suit′, *n., v.t.*
re·sul′fu·rize, *v.t.,* **-rized, -riz·ing.**
re·sul′phu·rize, *v.t.,* **-rized, -riz·ing.**
re·sum′mon, *v.t.*
re·sum′mon·a·ble, *adj.*
re·sum′mons, *n.*
re′sup·ply′, *v.t.,* **-plied, -ply·ing;** *n., pl.* **-plies.**
re′sup·press′, *v.t.*
re′sup·pres′sion, *n.*
re′sus·pend′, *v.*
re′sus·pen′sion, *n.*
re·swal′low, *v.*
re·swear′, *v.,* **-swore, -swear·ing.**
re·sweep′, *v.,* **-swept, -sweep·ing.**
re·sweet′en, *v.*
re·swell′, *v.*
re′sym·bol·i·za′tion, *n.*
re·sym′bol·ize′, *v.,* **-ized, -iz·ing.**
re·syn′the·sis, *n., pl.* **-ses.**
re·syn′the·size′, *v.t.,* **-sized, -siz·ing.**
re·syn′the·tize′, *v.t.,* **-tized, -tiz·ing.**
re·sys′te·ma·tize′, *v.t.,* **-tized, -tiz·ing.**
re·tab′u·late′, *v.t.,* **-lat·ed, -lat·ing.**
re·tack′, *v.t.*
re·tal′ly, *n., pl.* **-lies;** *v.,* **-lied, -ly·ing.**
re·tan′, *v.t.,* **-tanned, -tan·ning.**
re·tape′, *v.t.,* **-taped, -tap·ing.**
re·tar′, *v.t.,* **-tarred, -tar·ring.**

re·tard·ment (ri tärd′mənt). [ME *retardacion* < L *retardātiōn-* (s. of *retardātiō*), equiv. to *retardāt(us)* (see RETARDATE) + *-iōn-* -ION] —**re·tard·a·tive** (ri tär′də tiv), **re·tard·a·to·ry** (ri tär′də tôr′ē, -tōr′ē), *adj.*

re·tard·ed (ri tär′did), *adj.* characterized by retardation: *a retarded child.* [RETARD + -ED[2]]

re·tard·er (ri tär′dər), *n.* **1.** one who or that which retards. **2.** *Chem.* **a.** any substance added to rubber to delay or prevent vulcanization. **b.** any substance added to cement or plaster to delay setting. **c.** any substance added to delay the process. **3.** *Building Trades.* an admixture of concrete or plaster that retards its set. [RETARD + -ER[1]]

retch (rech), *v.i.* to make efforts to vomit. [OE *hrǣc(an)* (to) clear the throat, deriv. of *hrāca* a clearing of the throat; cf. OIcel *hrǣkja* to hawk, spit]

retd., **1.** retained. **2.** returned.

re·te (rē′tē), *n., pl.* **re·ti·a** (rē′shē ə, -shə, -tē ə). **1.** a pierced plate on an astrolabe, having projections whose points correspond to the fixed stars. **2.** a network, as of fibers, nerves, or blood vessels. [ME *riet* < L *rēte* net] —**re·ti·al** (rē′shē əl), *adj.*

re·tem (rē′tem), *n.* a shrub, *Genista raetam,* of Syria and Arabia, having white flowers: said to be the juniper of the Old Testament. [< Ar *ratam*]

re·tene (rē′tēn, ret′ēn), *n. Chem.* a crystalline hydrocarbon, $C_{18}H_{18}$, obtained chiefly from the tar of resinous woods and certain fossil resins. [< Gk *rhēt(ínē)* resin + -ENE]

re·ten·tion (ri ten′shən), *n.* **1.** the act of retaining. **2.** the state of being retained. **3.** the power to retain; capacity for retaining. **4.** act or power of remembering things; memory. [ME *retencion* < L *retentiōn-* (s. of *retentiō*) a keeping back, equiv. to *retent(us)* (ptp. of *retinēre* to RETAIN) + *-iōn-* -ION]

re·ten·tive (ri ten′tiv), *adj.* **1.** tending or serving to retain something. **2.** having power or capacity to retain. **3.** having power or ability to remember; having a good memory. [ME *retentif* < MF < ML *retentīv(us),* equiv. to L *retent(us)* (see RETENTION) + *-īvus* -IVE] —**re·ten′tive·ly,** *adv.* —**re·ten′tive·ness,** *n.*

re·ten·tiv·i·ty (rē′ten tiv′i tē), *n.* **1.** the power to retain; retentiveness. **2.** the ability to retain magnetization after the removal of the magnetizing force. [RETENTIVE + -ITY]

re·te·pore (rē′tə pōr′, -pôr′), *n.* any bryozoan of the family *Reteporidae* which forms colonies that have a networklike structure. [< NL *Retepora* name of genus, equiv. to < L *rēte* net + *por(us)* passage, PORE[2] + *-a* n. suffix]

re·ti·ar·i·us (rē′shē âr′ē əs), *n., pl.* **-ar·i·i** (-âr′ē ī′). *Rom. Hist.* a gladiator equipped with a net for casting over his opponent. [< L, equiv. to *rēt-* (s. of *rēte*) + *-i-* -I- + *-ārius* -ARIUS]

re·ti·ar·y (rē′shē er′ē), *adj.* **1.** using a net or any entangling device. **2.** netlike. **3.** making a net or web, as a spider. [< L *rēt-* (s. of *rēte*) net + -I- + -ARY]

ret·i·cent (ret′i sənt), *adj.* disposed to be silent; not inclined to speak freely; reserved. [< L *reticent-* (s. of *reticēns,* prp. of *reticēre* to be silent), equiv. to *re-* RE- + *tac(ēre)* (to) be silent + *-ent-* -ENT] —**ret′i·cence, ret′i·cen·cy,** *n.* —**ret′i·cent·ly,** *adv.*
—**Syn.** taciturn, quiet, uncommunicative. —**Ant.** talkative, voluble.

ret·i·cle (ret′i kəl), *n. Optics.* a network of fine lines, wires, or the like, placed in the focus of the objective of a telescope. [< L *rēticul(um)* little net, equiv. to *rēt-* (s. of *rēte*) net + *-i-* -I- + *-culum* -CLE]

re·tic·u·lar (ri tik′yə lər), *adj.* **1.** having the form of a net; netlike. **2.** intricate or entangled. [< NL *rēticulār(is),* equiv. to L *rēticul(um)* RETICLE + *-āris* -AR[1]] —**re·tic′u·lar·ly,** *adv.*

re·tic·u·late (*adj.* ri tik′yə lit, -lāt′; *v.* ri tik′yə lāt′), *adj., v.,* **-lat·ed, -lat·ing.** —*adj.* **1.** netted; covered with a network. **2.** netlike. **3.** *Bot.* having the veins or nerves disposed like the threads of a net. —*v.t.* **4.** to form into a network. **5.** to cover or mark with a network. —*v.i.* **6.** to form a network. [< L *rēticulāt(us)* net-like, equiv. to *rēticul(um)* RETICLE + *-ātus* -ATE[1]] —**re·tic′u·late·ly,** *adv.*

retic′ulate py′thon, a python, *Python reticulatus,* of southeastern Asia and the East Indies, sometimes growing to a length of 32 feet: usually considered to be the largest snake in the world.

re·tic·u·la·tion (ri tik′yə lā′shən), *n.* a reticulated formation, arrangement, or appearance; network. [RETICULATE + -ION]

ret·i·cule (ret′ə kyōōl′), *n.* **1.** a small purse or bag, originally of network but later of silk, rayon, etc. **2.** *Optics.* a reticle. [< F *réticule* < L *rēticul(um)* RETICLE]

re·tic·u·lo·en·do·the·li·al (ri tik′yə lō en′dō thē′lē əl, -thēl′yəl), *adj. Anat.* of or pertaining to the system of reticular and endothelial cells that are found in certain tissues and organs and that help maintain resistance and immunity to infection. [< L *rēticulo-* (comb. form of *rēticulum* RETICLE) + ENDOTHELIAL]

re·tic·u·lum (ri tik′yə ləm), *n., pl.* **-la** (-lə) for 1–3, *gen.* **-li** (-lī′) for 4. **1.** a network; any reticulated system or structure. **2.** *Anat.* **a.** a network of intercellular fibers in certain tissues. **b.** a network of structures in the endoplasm or nucleus of certain cells. **3.** *Zool.* the second stomach of ruminating animals, between the rumen and the omasum. See diag. under **ruminant.** **4.** (*cap.*) *Astron.* the Net, a southern constellation between Dorado and Hydrus. [< L: little net; see RETICLE]

re·ti·form (rē′tə fôrm′, ret′ə-), *adj.* netlike; reticulate. [< NL *rētiform(is),* equiv. to L *rēt-* (s. of *rēte*) net + *-i-* -I- + *-formis* -FORM]

ret·i·na (ret′ᵊnə, ret′nə), *n., pl.* **ret·i·nas, ret·i·nae** (ret′ᵊnē′). *Anat.* the innermost coat of the posterior part of the eyeball that receives the image produced by the crystalline lens, is continuous with the optic nerve, and consists of several layers, one of which contains the rods and cones which are sensitive to light. See diag. under **eye.** [ME *ret(h)ina* < ML *rētina,* prob. equiv. to L *rēt-* (s. of *rēte*) net + *-ina* -INE[1]] —**ret′i·nal,** *adj.*

ret·i·nene (ret′ᵊnēn′), *n. Biochem.* either of the two carotenoids that are found in the vertebrate retina, the light-yellow crystalline compound, $C_{19}H_{27}CHO$, derived from rhodopsin or iodopsin by the action of light, or the orange-red crystalline compound, $C_{19}H_{25}CHO$, derived from porphyropsin by the action of light. [RETIN(A) + -ENE]

ret·i·nite (ret′ᵊnīt′), *n.* any of various fossil resins, esp. one derived from brown coal. [< F *rétinite,* equiv. to *rétin-* (comb. form of Gk *rhētínē* RESIN) + *-ite* -ITE[1]]

ret·i·ni·tis (ret′ᵊnī′tis), *n. Pathol.* inflammation of the retina. [< NL; see RETINA, -ITIS]

ret·i·nol (ret′ᵊnōl′, -ᵊnôl′, -ᵊnol′), *n.* a yellowish oil, $C_{32}H_{16}$, obtained by the distillation of resin, used as a solvent and as an antiseptic. [< Gk *rhētín(ē)* RESIN + -OL[1]]

ret·i·no·scope (ret′ᵊnə skōp′), *n. Ophthalm.* skiascope. [RETIN(A) + -O- + -SCOPE]

ret·i·nos·co·py (ret′ᵊnos′kə pē, ret′ᵊnə skō′pē), *n. Ophthalm.* an objective method of determining the refractive error of an eye. [RETIN(A) + -O- + -SCOPY] —**ret·i·no·scop·ic** (ret′ᵊnə skop′ik), *adj.* —**ret′i·no·scop′i·cal·ly,** *adv.* —**ret′i·nos′co·pist,** *n.*

ret·i·nue (ret′ᵊnōō′, -ᵊnyōō′), *n.* a body of retainers in attendance upon an important personage; suite. [ME *retinue* < MF, n. use of fem. ptp. of *retenir* to RETAIN] —**ret′i·nued′,** *adj.*

re·tire (ri tīᵊr′), *v.,* **-tired, -tir·ing,** *n.* —*v.i.* **1.** to withdraw, or go away or apart, to a place of abode, shelter, or seclusion: *He retired to his study to think out the problem.* **2.** to go to bed: *He retired at midnight.* **3.** to withdraw from office, business, or active life: *to retire at the age of sixty.* **4.** to fall back or retreat in an orderly fashion and according to plan, as from battle, an untenable position, danger, etc. **5.** to withdraw, go away, or remove oneself: *After announcing the arrival of the guests, the butler retired to the pantry.* —*v.t.* **6.** to withdraw from circulation by taking up and paying, as bonds, bills, etc.; redeem. **7.** to withdraw or lead back (troops, ships, etc.), as from battle or danger; retreat. **8.** to remove from active service or the usual field of activity, as an officer in the army or the navy. **9.** to withdraw (a machine, ship, etc.) permanently from its normal service, usually for scrapping. **10.** *Sports.* to put out (a batter, side, etc.). —*n. Rare.* **11.** a place of withdrawal or retirement; retreat: *a cool retire from summer's heat.* **12.** retirement or withdrawal, as from worldly matters or the company of others. [< MF *retir(er)* (to) withdraw, equiv. to *re-* RE- + *tirer* to draw] —**re·tir′er,** *n.*
—**Syn. 5.** leave. See **depart.**

re·ti·ré (*Fr.* rə tē rā′), *n., pl.* **-ti·rés** (*Fr.* -tē rā′). *Ballet.* a movement in which the dancer brings one foot to the knee of the supporting leg and then returns it to the fifth position. [< F, ptp. of *retirer* to RETIRE]

re·tired (ri tīᵊrd′), *adj.* **1.** withdrawn from or no longer occupied with one's business or profession: *a retired banker.* **2.** due or given a retired person: *retired pay.* **3.** withdrawn; secluded or sequestered: *a retired little village.* [RETIRE + -ED[2]] —**re·tired′ly,** *adv.* —**re·tired′ness,** *n.*
—**Syn. 3.** isolated, removed, solitary.

re·tir·ee (ri tī rē′, -tīᵊr′ē), *n.* a person who has retired from his occupation or profession. [RETIRE + -EE]

re·tire·ment (ri tīᵊr′mənt), *n.* **1.** the act of retiring, or the state of being retired. **2.** removal or withdrawal from service, office, or business. **3.** the portion of a person's life during which he is retired. **4.** withdrawal into privacy or seclusion. **5.** privacy or seclusion. **6.** a private or secluded place. **7.** *Mil.* orderly withdrawal of a military force, according to plan, without pressure from the enemy. **8.** withdrawal of securities from the market by a corporation, as through payment at maturity, repurchase, or exchange. —*adj.* **9.** noting or pertaining to retirement: *retirement plan; retirement pay.* [< MF; see RETIRE, -MENT]

re·tir·ing (ri tīᵊr′ing), *adj.* **1.** that retires. **2.** withdrawing from contact with others; reserved; shy. [RETIRE + -ING[2]] —**re·tir′ing·ly,** *adv.* —**re·tir′ing·ness,** *n.*

re·took (rē tŏŏk′), *v.* pt. of **retake.**

re·tool (rē tōōl′), *v.t.* **1.** to replace or rearrange the tools and machinery of (a factory). **2.** to reorganize or rearrange, usually for the purpose of updating: *to retool the entire industrial organization.* —*v.i.* **3.** to replace or rearrange the tools of a factory. **4.** to replace the stamping machinery of a factory, esp. to make a remodeled product. [RE- + TOOL]

re·tor·sion (ri tôr′shən), *n. Internat. Law.* retaliation or reprisal by one state identical or similar to an act by an offending state, such as high tariffs or discriminating duties. Also, **retortion.** [< ML *retorsiōn-* (s. of *retorsiō*); see RETORTION]

re·tort[1] (ri tôrt′), *v.t.* **1.** to reply to, usually in a sharp or retaliatory way; reply in kind to. **2.** to return (an accusation, epithet, etc.) upon the person uttering it. **3.** to answer (an argument or the like) by another to the contrary. —*n.* **4.** a severe, incisive, or witty reply, esp. one that counters a first speaker's statement, argument, etc. **5.** the act of retorting. [< L *retort(us)* bent back (ptp. of *retorquēre*), equiv. to *re-* RE- + *torquēre* to twist, bend] —**re·tort′er,** *n.*
—**Syn. 1.** retaliate. **4.** riposte, rejoinder. See **answer.**

re·tort[2] (ri tôrt′), *n.* **1.** *Chem.* a vessel, commonly a glass bulb with a long neck bent downward, used for distilling or decomposing substances by heat. **2.** *Metall.* a vessel, generally cylindrically shaped, within which an ore is heated so that the metal may be removed by distillation or sublimation. **3.** an airtight, usually cylindrical vessel of fire clay or iron, used in the destructive distillation chiefly of coal and wood in the manufacture of illuminating gas. **4.** a sterilizer for food cans. —*v.t.* **5.** to sterilize canned food after it is sealed, by steam or other heating methods. [< MF *retorte* < ML *retorta,* fem. of *retortus* bent back (ptp. of L *retorquēre*); see RETORT[1]]

R, Retort

re·tor·tion (ri tôr′shən), *n.* **1.** the act of turning or bending back. **2.** retaliation. **3.** *Internat. Law.* retorsion. [< ML *retortiōn-* (s. of *retortiō*), equiv. to L *retort(us)* (see RETORT[1]) + *-iōn-* -ION]

re·touch (rē tuch′), *v.t.* **1.** to improve by new touches or the like; touch up or rework, as a painting, make-up, etc. **2.** *Photog.* to alter (a negative or positive) after development by adding or removing lines, lightening areas, etc., with a pencil, brush, or knife. **3.** to dye, tint, or bleach (a new growth of hair) to match or blend with the color of an earlier and previously dyed growth. —*n.* **4.** an added touch to a picture, painting, etc., by way of improvement or alteration. **5.** an act or instance of dyeing the new growth of hair to blend with previously dyed growth. [< MF *retouch(er),* equiv. to *re-* RE- + *toucher* to TOUCH] —**re·touch′a·ble,** *adj.* —**re·touch′er,** *n.*

re-trace (rē trās′), *v.t.,* **-traced, -trac·ing.** to trace again, as lines in writing or drawing. Also, **retrace.** [RE- + TRACE[1]]

re·trace (ri trās′), *v.t.,* **-traced, -trac·ing.** **1.** to trace backward; go back over: *to retrace one's steps.* **2.** to go back over with the memory. **3.** to go over again with the sight or attention. **4.** re-trace. [< F *retrac(er),* MF *retracier,* equiv. to *re-* RE- + *tracier* to TRACE[1]] —**re·trace′a·ble,** *adj.* —**re·trace′ment,** *n.*

re·tract[1] (ri trakt′), *v.t.* to draw back or in: *to retract fangs.* [ME *retract(en)* < L *retract(us)* drawn back (ptp. of *retrahere*), equiv. to *re-* RE- + *tractus;* see TRACT[1]]

re·tract[2] (ri trakt′), *v.t.* **1.** to withdraw (a statement, opinion, etc.) as inaccurate or unjustified. **2.** to withdraw or revoke (a decree, promise, etc.). —*v.i.* **3.** to draw or shrink back. **4.** to withdraw a promise, vow, etc. **5.** to make disavowal of a statement, opinion, etc.; recant. [< L *retract(āre)* (to) reconsider, withdraw, equiv. to *re-* RE- + *tractāre* to drag, pull, take in hand (*trac-,* ptp. s. of *trahere* to pull + *-t-* freq. suffix)] —**re·tract′a·bil′i·ty, re·tract′i·bil′i·ty,** *n.* —**re·tract′a·ble, re·tract′i·ble,** *adj.* —**re·trac·ta·tion** (rē′trak tā′shən), *n.*
—**Syn. 1, 2.** deny, renounce, recant, abrogate, nullify, annul.

re·trac·tile (ri trak′til), *adj. Zool.* capable of being drawn back or in, as the head of a tortoise; exhibiting the power of retraction. [RETRACT[1] + -ILE] —**re′trac·til′i·ty,** *n.*

re·trac·tion (ri trak′shən), *n.* **1.** the act of retracting, or the state of being retracted. **2.** withdrawal of a promise, statement, opinion, etc.: *His retraction of the libel came too late.* **3.** retractile power. [ME *retraccioun* < LL *retractiōn-* (s. of *retractiō*), equiv. to L *retract(us)* (see RETRACT[1]) + *-iōn-* -ION]

re·trac·tive (ri trak′tiv), *adj.* tending or serving to retract. [ME *retractif* < ML *retractīv(us), equiv. to L *retract(us)* (see RETRACT[1]) + *-īvus* -IVE] —**re·trac′tive·ly,** *adv.* —**re·trac′tive·ness,** *n.*

re·trac·tor (ri trak′tər), *n.* **1.** one who or that which retracts. **2.** *Anat.* a muscle that retracts an organ or protruded part. **3.** *Surg.* an instrument or appliance for drawing back an impeding part, as the edge of an incision. [RETRACT[1] + -OR[2]]

re·trad (rē′trad), *adv. Anat., Zool.* toward the back; backward. [RETR(O)- + L *ad* to, towards]

re·tral (rē′trəl), *adj.* at or toward the back; posterior. [RETR(O)- + -AL[1]] —**re′tral·ly,** *adv.*

re·tread (rē tred′), *v.t., v.i.,* **-trod, -trod·den** or **-trod, -tread·ing.** to tread again. [RE- + TREAD[1]]

re·tread (*v.* rē tred′; *n.* rē′tred′), *v.,* **-tread·ed, -tread·ing,** *n.* —*v.t.* **1.** to put a new tread on (a worn pneumatic tire casing) either by recapping or by cutting fresh treads in the smooth surface. —*n.* **2.** a retreaded tire. [RE- + TREAD[2]]

re·treat (rē trēt′), *v.t., v.i.* to treat again. [RE- + TREAT]

re·treat (ri trēt′), *n.* **1.** the forced or strategic withdrawal of an armed force before an enemy, or the withdrawing of a naval force from action. **2.** the act of withdrawing, as into safety or privacy; retirement; seclusion. **3.** a place of refuge, seclusion, or privacy: *The library was his retreat from the noise of the children.* **4.** an asylum, as for the insane. **5.** a retirement or a period of retirement for religious exercises and meditation. **6.** *Mil.* **a.** a flag-lowering ceremony held at sunset on a military post. **b.** the bugle call or drumbeat played at this ceremony. **7.** the recession of a surface, as a wall or panel, from another surface beside it. **8.** **beat a retreat,** to withdraw or retreat. esp. hurriedly or in dis-

re·tar′iff, *v.t.*
re·taste′, *v.,* **-tast·ed, -tast·ing.**
re·tax′, *v.t.*
re′tax·a′tion, *n.*
re·teach′, *v.,* **-taught, -teach·ing.**
re·tear′, *v.,* **-tore, -torn, -tear·ing.**
re·tel′e·graph′, *v.*
re·tel′e·phone′, *v.*
re·tel′e·vise′, *v.t.*
re·tell′, *v.,* **-told, -tell·ing.**
re·tem′per, *v.t.*
re·test′, *v.t.*
re·test′, *n.*
re·tes′ti·fy′, *v.,* **-fied, -fy·ing.**
re·tes′ti·mo′ny, *n., pl.* **-nies.**
re·thank′, *v.t.*
re·thatch′, *v.t.*
re·thaw′, *v.*
re·thick′en, *v.*
re·think′, *v.,* **-thought, -think·ing.**
re·thread′, *v.*
re·threat′en, *v.*
re·thresh′, *v.t.*
re·tie′, *v.t.,* **-tied, -ty·ing.**
re·tight′en, *v.*
re·tile′, *v.t.,* **-tiled, -til·ing.**
re·till′, *v.t.*
re·time′, *v.t.,* **-timed, -tim·ing.**
re·tin′, *v.t.,* **-tinned, -tin·ning.**
re·tinge′, *v.t.,* **-tinged, -tinge·ing** or **-ting·ing.**
re·tint′, *v.t.*
re·ti′tle, *v.t.,* **-tled, -tling.**
re·toast′, *v.*
re·to′tal, *v.t.,* **-taled, -tal·ing** or (*esp. Brit.*) **-talled, -tal·ling;** *n.*
re·track′, *v.*
re·trade′, *v.,* **-trad·ed, -trad·ing.**
re·train′, *v.*
re′tran·scribe′, *v.t.,* **-scribed, -scrib·ing.**
re′tran·scrip′tion, *n.*
re′trans·fer′, *v.t.,* **-ferred, -fer·ring.**
re′trans′fer, *n.*
re′trans·fer′ence, *n.*
re′trans·late′, *v.t.,* **-lat·ed, -lat·ing.**
re′trans·la′tion, *n.*
re′trans·mis′sion, *n.*
re′trans·mit′, *v.t.,* **-mit·ted, -mit·ting.**
re′trans·plant′, *v.t.*
re′trans·plan·ta′tion, *n.*
re·trav′erse, *v.,* **-ersed, -ers·ing.**

grace. —*v.i.* **9.** to withdraw, retire, or draw back, esp. for shelter or seclusion. **10.** to make a retreat: *Napoleon retreated from Moscow.* **11.** to slope backward; recede: *a retreating chin.* **12.** to draw or lead back. [ME *retret* < OF, var. of *retrait,* n. use of ptp. of *retraire* to draw back < L *retrahere* (*re-* RE- + *trahere* to draw); see RETRACT[1]] —**re·treat′al,** *adj.* —**re·treat′ing·ness,** *n.* —**re·treat′ive,** *adj.*

—**Syn. 2.** departure, withdrawal. **3.** shelter. **9.** leave, draw back, pull back. See **depart.** —**Ant. 1, 9, 10.** advance.

re·trench (ri trench′), *v.t.* **1.** to cut down, reduce, or diminish; curtail (expenses). **2.** to cut off or remove. **3.** *Mil.* to protect by a retrenchment. —*v.i.* **4.** to economize; reduce expenses: *They retrenched by eliminating half of the workers.* [< F *retrench(er)* (obs. var. of *retrancher*), MF *retrenchier,* equiv. to *re-* RE- + *trenchier* to TRENCH] —**re·trench′a·ble,** *adj.* —**re·trench′er,** *n.*

—**Syn. 1.** decrease, abridge, cut.

re·trench·ment (ri trench′mənt), *n.* **1.** the act of retrenching; a cutting down or off, as by the reduction of expenses. **2.** *Fort.* an interior work that cuts off a part of a fortification from the rest, and to which a garrison may retreat. [< F *retrenchement.* See RETRENCH, -MENT]

ret·ri·bu·tion (re′trə byo͞o′shən), *n.* **1.** requital according to merits or deserts, esp. for evil. **2.** something given or inflicted in such requital. **3.** *Theol.* the distribution of rewards and punishments in a future life. [ME *retribucioun* < MF < eccl. L *retribūtiōn-* (s. of *retribūtiō,* equiv to L *retribūt(us)* restored, given back (ptp. of *retribuere;* see RE-, TRIBUTE) + *-iōn-* -ION]

—**Syn. 2.** retaliation, repayment, recompense. See **revenge.** —**Ant. 1, 2.** pardon.

re·trib·u·tive (ri trib′yə tiv), *adj.* characterized by or involving retribution: *retributive justice.* Also, **re·trib·u·to·ry** (ri trib′yə tôr′ē, -tōr′ē). [*retribute* (< L *retribūt(us);* see RETRIBUTION) + -IVE] —**re·trib′u·tive·ly,** *adv.*

re·triev·al (ri trē′vəl), *n.* **1.** the act of retrieving. **2.** the chance of recovery or restoration: *lost beyond retrieval.* [RETRIEVE + -AL[2]]

re·trieve (ri trēv′), *v.,* **-trieved, -triev·ing,** *n.* —*v.t.* **1.** to recover or regain: *He had to run to the end of the block before he could retrieve the ball.* **2.** to bring back to a former and better state; restore: *to retrieve one's fortunes.* **3.** to make amends for: *to retrieve an error.* **4.** to make good; repair: *to retrieve a loss.* **5.** *Hunting.* (of hunting dogs) to fetch (killed or wounded game). **6.** to draw back or reel in (a fishing line). **7.** to rescue or save. **8.** (in tennis, squash, handball, etc.) to make an in-bounds return of (a shot requiring a hand run to reach. —*v.i.* **9.** *Hunting.* to retrieve game. **10.** to retrieve a fishing line. —*n.* **11.** the act of retrieving; recovery. **12.** the possibility of recovery. [ME *retrev(en)* < tonic s. of MF *retrouver* to find again, equiv. to *re-* RE- + *trouver* to find; see TROVER] —**re·triev′a·ble,** *adj.*

—**Syn. 1.** See **recover.**

re·triev·er (ri trē′vər), *n.* **1.** one who or that which retrieves. **2.** one of any of several breeds of dogs having a coarse, thick, oily coat, trained to retrieve game. **3.** any dog trained to retrieve game. [RETRIEVE + -ER[1]]

Labrador retriever (2 ft. high at shoulder)

retro-, a prefix occurring in loan words from Latin meaning "backward" (*retrogress*); on this model, used in the formation of compound words (*retrorocket*). [< L, repr. *retrō* (adv.), backward, back, behind]

ret·ro·act (re′trō akt′), *v.i.* **1.** to act in opposition; react. **2.** to have reference to or influence on past occurrences. [RETRO- + ACT]

ret·ro·ac·tion (re′trō ak′shən), *n.* action which is opposed or contrary to the preceding action. [RETRO- + ACTION]

ret·ro·ac·tive (re′trō ak′tiv), *adj.* **1.** operative with respect to past occurrences, as a statute; retrospective: *a retroactive law.* **2.** pertaining to a pay raise effective as of a past date. [RETRO- + ACTIVE] —**ret′ro·ac′tive·ly,** *adv.* —**ret′ro·ac·tiv′i·ty,** *n.*

retroac′tive inhibi′tion, *Psychol.* impairment or cancellation of learning of given information or activity by immediately following similar and confusing information or activity.

ret·ro·bul·bar (re′trō bul′bər), *adj.* *Anat.* situated behind the eyeball. [RETRO- + BULBAR]

ret·ro·cede[1] (re′trə sēd′), *v.i.,* **-ced·ed, -ced·ing.** to go back; recede; retire. [< L *retrōcēd(ere)* (to) go back, retire, equiv. to *retrō-* RETRO- + *cēdere* to go, move; see CEDE] —**ret·ro·ces·sion** (re′trə sesh′ən), **ret′ro·ced′ence,** *n.* —**ret′ro·ces′sive,** *adj.*

ret·ro·cede[2] (re′trə sēd′), *v.t.,* **-ced·ed, -ced·ing.** to cede back: *to retrocede a territory.* [RETRO- + CEDE] —**ret·ro·ces·sion** (re′trə sesh′ən), **ret′ro·ced′ence,** *n.*

ret·ro·choir (re′trə kwīᵊr′), *n.* that part of a church behind the choir or the main altar. [< ML *retrōchor(us).* See RETRO-, CHOIR]

ret·ro·di·rec·tive (re′trō di rek′tiv), *adj.* *Optics.* (of a mirror, reflector, etc.) having three reflecting surfaces so oriented that a ray of light is reflected in a direction parallel but opposite to its original direction. [RETRO- + DIRECTIVE]

ret·ro·fit (re′trō fit′, re′trō fit′), *v.,* **-fit·ted** or **-fit, -fit·ting,** *n.* —*v.t.* **1.** to modify equipment (in airplanes, automobiles, etc.) that is already in service using parts developed or made available after the time of original manufacture. —*n.* **2.** something that has been retrofitted. [RETRO + FIT[1]]

ret·ro·flex (re′trə fleks′), *adj.* **1.** bent backward; exhibiting retroflexion. **2.** *Phonet.* articulated with the tip of the tongue curled upward and back against or near the juncture of the hard and soft palates; cacuminal; cerebral; coronal. Also, **ret·ro·flexed** (re′trə flekst′). [< LL *retrōflex(us)* bent back (ptp. of *retrōflectere*). See RETRO-, FLEX]

ret·ro·flex·ion (re′trə flek′shən), *n.* **1.** a bending backward. **2.** *Pathol.* a bending backward of the body of the uterus upon the cervix. **3.** *Phonet.* **a.** retroflex articulation. **b.** the acoustic quality resulting from retroflex articulation; r-color. Also, **ret′ro·flec′tion.** [< NL *retrōflexiōn-* (s. of *retrōflexiō*), equiv. to L *retrōflex(us)* RETROFLEX + *-iōn-* -ION]

ret·ro·gra·da·tion (re′trō grā dā′shən), *n.* **1.** backward movement. **2.** decline or deterioration. [< LL *retrōgradātiōn-* (s. of *retrōgradātiō*), equiv. to L *retrōgradāt(us)* (ptp. of *retrōgradāre;* see RETROGRADE) + *-iōn-* -ION] —**ret·ro·gra·da·to·ry** (re′trə grā′də tôr′ē, -tōr′ē), *adj.*

ret·ro·grade (re′trə grād′), *adj., v.,* **-grad·ed, -grad·ing.** —*adj.* **1.** moving backward; having a backward motion or direction; retiring or retreating. **2.** inverse or reversed, as order. **3.** *Chiefly Biol.* exhibiting degeneration or deterioration. **4.** *Astron.* **a.** moving in an orbit in the direction opposite to that of the earth in its revolution around the sun. **b.** appearing to move on the celestial sphere in the direction opposite to the natural order of the signs of the zodiac, or from east to west. Cf. **direct** (def. 25). **5.** *Music.* proceeding from the last note to the first: *a melody in retrograde motion.* —*v.i.* **6.** to move or go backward; retire or retreat. **7.** *Chiefly Biol.* to decline to a worse condition; degenerate. **8.** *Astron.* to have a retrograde motion. —*v.t.* **9.** *Archaic.* to turn back. [ME < L *retrōgrad(us)* going back, deriv. of *retrōgradī,* equiv. to *retrō-* RETRO- + *gradī* to step, go; see GRADE] —**ret′ro·grade′ly,** *adv.* —**ret′ro·grad′ing·ly,** *adv.*

ret·ro·gress (re′trə gres′, re′trə gres′), *v.i.* **1.** to go backward into an earlier and usually worse condition: *to retrogress to infantilism.* **2.** to move backward. [< L *retrōgress(us)* having gone back or backwards, ptp. of *retrōgradī,* collateral form of *retrogradāre;* see RETROGRADE]

ret·ro·gres·sion (re′trə gresh′ən), *n.* **1.** the act of retrogressing; movement backward. **2.** *Biol.* degeneration; retrograde metamorphosis; passing from a more complex to a simpler structure. [< L *retrōgress(us)* (see RETROGRESS) + -ION]

ret·ro·gres·sive (re′trə gres′iv), *adj.* characterized by retrogression; degenerating. [< L *retrōgress(us)* (see RETROGRESS) + -IVE] —**ret′ro·gres′sive·ly,** *adv.*

ret·ro·len′tal fibropla′sia (re′trō len′t[ə]l), *Pathol.* an eye disease of premature infants, caused by abnormal formation of fibrous tissue behind the lens and resulting in blindness. [RETRO- + *lental* < NL *lent-* (s. of *lens* < L; see LENS) + -AL[1]]

ret·ro·rock·et (re′trō rok′it), *n.* a small, auxiliary rocket engine, forming a part of a larger rocket vehicle, that has its exhaust nozzle pointed toward the direction of flight, for decelerating the larger rocket, separating one stage from another, etc. Also, **ret′ro-rock′et.** [RETRO- + ROCKET]

re·trorse (ri trôrs′), *adj.* turned backward. [< L *retrōrs(us),* syncopated form of *retrōversus* bent backwards, equiv. to *retrō-* RETRO- + *versus* (ptp. of *vertere* to turn); see RETROVERSION] —**re·trorse′ly,** *adv.*

ret·ro·ser·rate (re′trō ser′it, -āt), *adj.* *Bot., Zool.* having retrorse teeth or barbs. [RETRO- + SERRATE]

ret·ro·ser·ru·late (re′trō ser′yə lit, -lāt′, -ser′ə-), *adj.* *Bot., Zool.* having small retrorse teeth or barbs. [RETRO- + SERRULATE]

ret·ro·spect (re′trə spekt′), *n.* **1.** contemplation of the past; a survey of past time, events, etc. **2. in retrospect,** in looking back on past events: *It was, in retrospect, the happiest day of her life.* —*v.i.* **3.** to look back in thought; refer back (often fol. by *to*): *to retrospect to a period in one's youth.* —*v.t.* **4.** to look back upon; contemplate retrospectively. [< L *retrōspect(us)* having looked back at (ptp. of *retrōspicere*), equiv. to *retrō-* RETRO- + *spec(ere)* (to) look, behold + *-t-* ptp. suffix]

ret·ro·spec·tion (re′trə spek′shən), *n.* **1.** the action, process, or faculty of looking back on things past. **2.** a survey of past events or experiences. [< L *retrōspect(us)* RETROSPECT + -ION]

ret·ro·spec·tive (re′trə spek′tiv), *adj.* **1.** directed to the past; contemplative of past situations, events, etc. **2.** looking or directed backward. **3.** retroactive, as a statute. —*n.* **4.** an art exhibit showing an entire phase or representative examples of an artist's life work. [< L *retrōspect(us)* RETROSPECT + -IVE] —**ret′ro·spec′tive·ly,** *adv.* —**ret′ro·spec′tive·ness,** *n.*

ret·rous·sage (re′trə säzh′; *Fr.* rə tro͞o säzh′), *n.* the technique or action, in etching or engraving, of drawing up ink from within the incised lines of an inked plate by deftly passing a soft cloth across its surface in order to spread ink to the adjacent areas. [< F: a turning up, equiv. to *retrouss(er)* (see RETROUSSÉ) + *-age* -AGE]

ret·rous·sé (re′tro͞o sā′; *Fr.* rə tro͞o sā′), *adj.* (esp. of the nose) turned up. [< F, ptp. of *retrousser,* MF, equiv. to *re-* RE- + *trousser* to turn, tuck up; see TRUSS]

ret·ro·ver·sion (re′trə vûr′zhən, -shən), *n.* **1.** a looking or turning back. **2.** the resulting state or condition. **3.** *Pathol.* a tilting or turning backward of an organ or part: *retroversion of the uterus.* [< L *retrōvers(us)* bent backwards (*retro-* RETRO- + *versus* turned, ptp. of *vertere*) + -ION] —**ret′ro·verse′,** *adj.* —**ret′ro·vert′ed,** *adj.*

ret·ro·vi·rus (re′trə vī′rəs), *n.* a type of RNA virus that invades the body's cells, where it produces more such RNA viruses: includes the AIDS virus and many cancer-causing viruses. [RETRO- + VIRUS] —**ret′ro·vi′ral,** *adj.*

re·trude (ri tro͞od′), *v.t.,* **-trud·ed, -trud·ing.** *Dentistry.* to produce retrusion in. [< L *retrūd(ere)* (to) thrust back, equiv. to *re-* RE- + *trūdere* to thrust]

re·tru·sion (ri tro͞o′zhən, -shən), *n.* *Dentistry.* **1.** the act of moving teeth backward. **2.** a condition characterized by the backward displacement of the teeth. [< L *retrūs(us)* removed, concealed (ptp. of *retrūdere;* see RETRUDE) + -ION] —**re·tru·sive** (ri tro͞o′siv), *adj.*

ret·si·na (ret′sə nə; *Gk.* re tsē′nä), *n.* a strong, resinated white or red wine of Greece and Cyprus. [< NGk, ? < It *resina* RESIN]

re·turn (ri tûrn′), *v.i.* **1.** to go or come back, as to a former place, position, state, etc.: *to return from abroad; to return to public office; to return to work.* **2.** to revert to a former owner: *The money I gave him returns to me in the event of his death.* **3.** to revert or recur, as in thought, discourse, etc.: *Her mind returned to that happy day. He returned to his story.* **4.** to make a reply or retort: *She taunted him, but he returned with a witty sally.* —*v.t.* **5.** to put, bring, take, give, or send back to the original place, position, etc.: *to return a book to a shelf; to return a child to her mother; to return a door to its closed position.* **6.** to send or give back in reciprocation, recompense, or requital: *to return evil for good.* **7.** to reciprocate, repay, or requite (something sent, given, done, etc.) with something similar: *to return the enemy's fire; to return a favor.* **8.** *Law.* **a.** to give to a judge or official (a statement or a writ of actions done). **b.** to render (a verdict, decision, etc.). **9.** to reflect (light, sound, etc.). **10.** to yield (a profit, revenue, etc.), as in return for labor, expenditure, or investment. **11.** to report or announce officially: *to return a list of members.* **12.** to elect, as to a legislative body: *The voters returned him by a landslide.* **13.** *Mil.* to put (a weapon) back into its holder. **14.** *Cards.* to respond to (a suit led) by a similar lead: *She returned diamonds.* **15.** to turn back or in the reverse direction, as a served ball in tennis: *Only an expert could have returned that ball.* **16.** *Chiefly Archit.* to turn away from, or at an angle to, the previous line of direction: *The architect decided to return the cornice at each end of the façade.* —*n.* **17.** the act or fact of returning as by going or coming back or bringing, sending, or giving back: *We should appreciate your return of the book immediately.* **18.** a recurrence: *many happy returns of the day; the return of the moon each month.* **19.** reciprocation, repayment, or requital: *profits in return for outlay.* **20.** response or reply. **21.** one who or that which is returned: *returns of mill goods.* **22.** the gain realized on an exchange of goods. **23.** Often, **returns.** a yield or profit, as from labor, land, business, investment, etc.: *He received a quick return on his money.* **24.** a report, esp. a formal or official report: *a tax return; the election returns.* **25.** the report or statement of financial condition. **26.** *Chiefly Brit.* a round-trip ticket. **27.** *Archit.* **a.** the continuation of a molding, projection, etc., in a different direction. **b.** a side or part which falls away from the front of any straight or flat member or area. **28.** *Sports.* **a.** the act of returning a ball. **b.** the ball which is returned. **29.** *Football.* a runback of a kick, intercepted pass, or fumble recovery. **30.** *Econ.* yield per unit as compared to the cost per unit involved in a specific industrial process. **31.** *Law.* **a.** the bringing or sending back of various documents, such as a writ, summons, or subpoena, with a brief written report usually indorsed upon it, by a sheriff, to the court from which it issued. **b.** a certified document by a great variety of officers, such as assessors, collectors, and election officers. **c.** the report or certificate indorsed in such documents. **32.** *Cards.* a lead which responds to a partner's lead. **33.** *Theat.* a flat or drapery parallel to the tormentor for masking the offstage area and often completing the downstage part of a set. **34. returns, a.** merchandise shipped back to a supplier from a retailer or distributor as unsold or unsalable. **b.** merchandise returned to a retailer by a consumer. —*adj.* **35.** of or pertaining to return or returning: *a return trip.* **36.** sent, given, or done in return: *a return shot.* **37.** done or occurring again: *a return engagement of the opera.* **38.** noting a person or thing which is returned or returning to a place: *return cargo.* **39.** changing in direction, doubling or returning on itself: *a return bend in a road.* **40.** used for returning, recirculating, etc.: *the return road; a return pipe.* **41.** (of a game) played in order to provide the loser of an earlier game with the opportunity to win from the same opponent: *return match.* **42.** adequate, necessary, or provided to enable the return of a mailed package or letter to its sender: *return postage guaranteed; return address; return envelope.* [ME *retorn(en)* < MF *retorn(er).* See RE-, TURN]

—**Syn. 4.** rejoin. **5.** replace. **6.** exchange. **10.** pay, repay. **23.** revenue, income.

re·turn·a·ble (ri tûr′nə bəl), *adj.* **1.** that may be returned: *returnable merchandise.* **2.** requiring a return, as a writ to the court from which it is issued. [ME *retournable.* See RETURN, -ABLE] —**re·turn′a·bil′i·ty,** *n.*

return′ bend′, a 180° bend, as in a plumbing pipe.

re·turn-cocked (ri tûrn′kokt′), *adj.* (of a cock bead) situated at an angle or arris.

re·turn·ee (ri tûr nē′, -tûr′nē), *n.* **1.** a person who has returned, as from travels, internment, etc. **2.** a serviceman returning from duty overseas. [RETURN + -EE]

return′-flue′ boil′er (ri tûrn′flo͞o′), a fire-tube boiler having flues which collect the combustion gases at the end of the boiler opposite the fire door and pass them through the boiler to an uptake above the fire door. Also called **re·turn′-tu′bu·lar boil′er** (ri tûrn′to͞o′byə lər, -tyo͞o′-).

return′ing of′ficer, *Brit.* a public official appointed to conduct and preside at an election.

Return′ of the Na′tive, The, a novel (1878) by Thomas Hardy.

return′ receipt′, a card bearing the signature of the recipient of registered postal matter, for return to the sender as proof of receipt.

return′ tick′et, 1. *Chiefly Brit.* a round-trip ticket. **2.** a ticket for the return portion of a trip.

re·tuse (ri to͞os′, -tyo͞os′), *adj.* having an obtuse or rounded apex with a shallow notch, as leaves. [< L *retūs(us)* blunted, dull (ptp. of *retundere*), equiv. to *re-* RE- + *tund-* beat, strike (see STUTTER) + *-s-* ptp. suffix]

Retuse leaf

Reu·ben (ro͞o′bin), *n.* **1.** the eldest son of Jacob and Leah. Gen. 29, 30. **2.** one of the 12 tribes of Israel. **3.** a boy's given name. Also, *Douay Bible,* **Ruben** (for defs. 1,2).

Reu·ben·ite (ro͞o′bə nīt′), *n.* a member of the tribe of Reuben. [REUBEN + -ITE[1]]

Reuch·lin (roikн′lēn, roikн lēn′), *n.* **Jo·hann** (yō′hän), 1455–1522, German humanist scholar.

re·un·ion (rē yo͞on′yən), *n.* **1.** the act of uniting again. **2.** the state of being united again. **3.** a gathering of relatives, friends, or associates after separation: *a family reunion.* [RE- + UNION]

Ré·u·nion (rē yo͞on′yən; *Fr.* rā ʏ nyôɴ′), *n.* an island in the Indian Ocean, E of Madagascar: a department of France. 335,000 (est. 1960); 970 sq. mi. *Cap.:* St. Denis.

re·un·ion·ist (rē yo͞on′yə nist), *n.* one who advocates the reunion of the Anglican Church with the Roman

re·tri′al, *n.*
re·try′, *v.,* **-tried, -try·ing.**
re·tune′, *v.t.,* **-tuned, -tun·ing.**
re·turf′, *v.t.*
re·twine′, *v.,* **-twined, -twin·ing.**
re·twist′, *v.*
re·type′, *v.t.,* **-typed, -typ·ing.**
re′u·ni·fi·ca′tion, *n.*
re·u′ni·fy′, *v.t.,* **-fied, -fy·ing.**

Catholic Church. [REUNION + -IST] —**re·un′ion·ism,** *n.* —**re·un′ion·is′tic,** *adj.*

re·u·nite (rē′yo͞o nīt′), *v.t., v.i.,* **-nit·ed, -nit·ing.** to unite again, as after separation. [< ML *reūnīt(us)* reunited (ptp. of *reūnīre*). (L *re-* RE- + *ūnītus* joined together; see UNITE[1])] —**re′u·nit′a·ble,** *adj.* —**re′u·nit′·er,** *n.*

re-up (rē up′), *v.i., v.t.,* **-upped, -up·ping.** *Mil. Informal.* to reenlist.

re·used (rē yo͞ozd′), *adj.* noting wool that previously has been spun, woven, and used. [RE- + USED]

Reu·ter (roi′tər), *n.* **Paul Julius, Baron de,** 1816–99, English founder of an international news agency, born in Germany.

Reu·ther (ro͞o′thər), *n.* **Walter Philip,** born 1907, U.S. labor leader: president of the UAW since 1946; president of the CIO 1952–55.

rev (rev), *n., v.,* **revved, rev·ving.** *Informal.* —*n.* **1.** a revolution (in an engine or the like). —*v.t.* **2.** to accelerate sharply the speed of (an engine or the like) (often fol. by *up*). —*v.i.* **3.** (of an engine or the like) to be revved. [short for REVOLUTION]

Rev., **1.** Revelation; Revelations. **2.** Reverend.

rev., **1.** revenue. **2.** reverse. **3.** review. **4.** revise; revised. **5.** revision. **6.** revolution. **7.** revolving.

Re·val (rā′väl), *n.* German name of **Tallinn.**

re·val·ue (rē val′yo͞o), *v.t.,* **-ued, -u·ing.** to value again. [RE- + VALUE]

re·vamp (rē vamp′), *v.t.* to renovate, redo, or revise: *We've decided to revamp the entire show.* [RE- + VAMP[1]] —**re·vamp′er,** *n.* —**re·vamp′ment,** *n.*

re·vanche (ri vänch′), *n.* the policy of a state intent on regaining areas of its original territory that have been lost to other states as a result of war, a treaty signed under duress, etc. [< F: REVENGE]

re·vanch·ist (ri vän′chist), *n.* **1.** an advocate or supporter of a political policy of revanche, esp. in order to seek vengeance for a previous military defeat. —*adj.* **2.** of or pertaining to a political policy of revanche. **3.** of or pertaining to revanchists or revanchism. [REVANCHE + -IST] —**re·vanch′ism,** *n.*

re·veal (ri vēl′), *v.t.* **1.** to make known; disclose; divulge: *to reveal a secret.* **2.** to lay open to view; display; exhibit. —*n.* **3.** an act or instance of revealing; revelation; disclosure. **4.** *Archit.* **a.** that part of the jamb of a window or door opening between the outer wall surface and the window or door frame. **b.** the whole jamb of an opening between the outer and inner surfaces of a wall. **5.** the framework or edge of an automobile window. [ME *revel(en)* < MF *revel(er)* < L *revēlāre* to unveil. See RE-, VEIL] —**re·veal′a·bil′i·ty, re·veal′a·ble·ness,** *n.* —**re·veal′a·ble,** *adj.* —**re·veal·ed·ly** (ri vē′lid lē, -vēld′-), *adv.* —**re·veal′er,** *n.* —**re·veal′ing·ly,** *adv.* —**re·veal′ing·ness,** *n.* —**re·vel·a·tive** (ri vel′ə tiv, rev′ə lā′-), *adj.*

—**Syn. 1, 2.** unveil, publish, impart, tell, announce, proclaim. REVEAL, DISCLOSE, DIVULGE is to make known something previously concealed or secret. To REVEAL is to uncover as if by drawing away a veil: *The fog lifted and revealed the harbor.* To DISCLOSE is to lay open and thereby invite inspection: *to disclose the plans of an organization.* To DIVULGE is to communicate, sometimes to a large number, what was at first intended to be private, confidential, or secret: *to divulge the terms of a contract.* —**Ant. 1, 2.** conceal, hide.

revealed′ relig′ion, religion based chiefly on the revelations of God to man, esp. as described in Scripture. Cf. **natural religion.**

revealed′ theol′ogy, theology based on the doctrine that all religious truth is derived exclusively from the revelations of God to man. Cf. **natural theology.**

re·veal·ment (ri vēl′mənt), *n.* the act of revealing; revelation. [REVEAL + -MENT]

re·veg·e·tate (rē vej′i tāt′), *v.i.,* **-tat·ed, -tat·ing.** **1.** to grow again, as plants. **2.** to put forth vegetation again, as plants. [RE- + VEGETATE] —**re·veg′e·ta′tion,** *n.*

rev·eil·le (rev′ə lē), *n.* a signal, as of a drum or bugle, sounded early in the morning after first call to alert military personnel for assembly. [< F *réveillez,* pl. impv. of *réveiller* to awaken, equiv. to *re-* RE- + *eveiller,* OF *esveillier* << L *ēvigilāre* to watch, be vigilant (*ē-* EX-[1] + *vigilāre* to watch; see VIGIL)]

rev·el (rev′əl), *v.,* **-eled, -el·ing** or (*esp. Brit.*) **-elled, -el·ling,** *n.* —*v.i.* **1.** to take great pleasure or delight (usually fol. by *in*): *She just revels in all that attention.* **2.** to make merry; indulge in boisterous festivities. —*n.* **3.** boisterous merrymaking or festivity; revelry. **4.** Often, **revels.** an occasion of merrymaking or noisy festivity with dancing, masking, etc. [ME *revel(en)* < MF *revel(er)* (to) raise tumult, make merry < L *rebellāre* to REBEL] —**rev′el·er;** *esp. Brit.,* **rev′el·ler,** *n.* —**rev′el·ment,** *n.*

Re·vel (re′vel yə), *n.* Russian name of **Tallinn.**

rev·e·la·tion (rev′ə lā′shən), *n.* **1.** the act of revealing or disclosing; disclosure. **2.** something revealed or disclosed, esp. a striking disclosure, as of something not before realized. **3.** *Theol.* **a.** God's disclosure of Himself and His will to His creatures. **b.** an instance of such communication or disclosure. **c.** something thus communicated or disclosed. **d.** that which contains such disclosure, as the Bible. **4.** (*cap.*) Often, **Revelations.** See **Revelation of St. John the Divine.** [ME *revelacion* < MF < LL *revēlātiōn-* (s. of *revēlātiō*), equiv. to L *revēlāt(us)* (ptp. of *revēlāre* to REVEAL) + *-iōn-* -ION] —**rev′e·la′tion·al,** *adj.*

rev·e·la·tion·ist (rev′ə lā′shə nist), *n.* a person who believes in divine revelation. [REVELATION + -IST]

Revela′tion of St. John′ the Divine′, The, the last book in the New Testament; the Apocalypse.

rev·e·la·tor (rev′ə lā′tər), *n.* a person who makes a revelation. [< LL, equiv. to L *revēlāt(us)* (see REVELATION) + *-or* -OR[2]]

rev·el·a·to·ry (ri vel′ə tôr′ē, -tōr′ē, rev′ə lə-), *adj.* **1.** of, pertaining to, or having the characteristics of revelation. **2.** showing or disclosing an emotion, belief, quality, or the like (fol. by *of*): *a poem revelatory of the author's deep, personal sorrow.* [< L *revēlāt(us)* (See REVELATION) + -ORY[1]]

rev·el·ry (rev′əl rē), *n., pl.* **-ries.** reveling; boisterous festivity: *The sound of their revelry could be heard across the river.* [ME *revelrie.* See REVEL, -RY]

rev·e·nant (rev′ə nənt), *n.* **1.** a person who returns. **2.** a person who returns as a spirit after death; ghost. [< F: ghost, prp. of *revenir* to return, equiv. to *re-* RE- + *venir* to come < L *venīre;* see -ANT]

re·venge (ri venj′), *v.,* **-venged, -veng·ing,** *n.* —*v.t.* **1.** to exact punishment or expiation for a wrong on behalf of, esp. in a resentful or vindictive spirit: *He revenged his dead brother.* **2.** to take vengeance for; inflict punishment for: *He revenged his brother's death.* —*v.i.* **3.** *Obs.* to take revenge. —*n.* **4.** the act of revenging; retaliation for injuries or wrongs; vengeance. **5.** something done in vengeance. **6.** the desire to revenge; vindictiveness. **7.** an opportunity of retaliation or satisfaction: *We'll have another game to give you your revenge.* [ME, *revenge(n)* < MF, OF *reveng(er),* equiv. to *re-* RE- + *vengier* to avenge < L *vindicāre;* see VINDICATE] —**re·venge′less,** *adj.* —**re·veng′er,** *n.* —**re·veng′·ing·ly,** *adv.*

—**Syn. 1.** See **avenge. 4.** requital. REVENGE, REPRISAL, RETRIBUTION, VENGEANCE suggest a punishment, or injury inflicted in return for one received. REVENGE is the carrying out of a bitter desire to injure another for a wrong done to oneself or to those who are felt to be like oneself: *to plot revenge.* REPRISAL, formerly any act of retaliation, is used specifically in warfare for retaliation upon the enemy for his (usually unlawful) actions: *to make a raid in reprisal for one by the enemy.* RETRIBUTION suggests just or deserved punishment, often without personal motives, for some evil done: *a just retribution for wickedness.* VENGEANCE is usually wrathful, vindictive, furious revenge: *implacable vengeance.*

re·venge·ful (ri venj′fəl), *adj.* full of revenge. [REVENGE + -FUL] —**re·venge′ful·ly,** *adv.* —**re·venge′ful·ness,** *n.*

—**Syn.** malevolent, malicious, malignant. See **spiteful.** —**Ant.** forgiving.

rev·e·nue (rev′ən yo͞o′, -ə no͞o′), *n.* **1.** the income of a government from taxation, excise duties, customs, or other sources, appropriated to the payment of the public expenses. **2.** the government department charged with the collection of such income. **3. revenues,** the collective items or amounts of income of a person, a state, etc. **4.** the return or yield from any kind of property, patent, service, etc.; income. **5.** an amount of money regularly coming in. **6.** a particular item or source of income. [ME < MF, n. use of fem. ptp. of *revenir* < L *revenīre,* equiv. to *re-* RE- + *venīre* to come] —**rev·e·nu·al** (rev′ən yo͞o′əl, -ə no͞o′-, ri ven′yo͞o-), *adj.* —**rev′e·nued′,** *adj.*

rev′enue cut′ter, cutter (def. 4).

rev·e·nu·er (rev′ə no͞o′ər, -nyo͞o′-), *n.* *U.S.* an agent of the Treasury Department whose responsibility is to discover and destroy illegal liquor stills and to arrest the operators. [REVENUE + -ER[1]]

rev′enue stamp′, a stamp showing that a governmental tax has been paid.

re·verb (ri vûrb′), *v.t., v.i.* to reverberate. [irreg. < L *reverb(erāre)* (to) cause to rebound]

re·ver·ber·ant (ri vûr′bər ənt), *adj.* reverberating; reechoing: *the reverberant booms of cannons being fired.* [< L *reverberant-* (s. of *reverberāns,* prp. of *reverberāre*), equiv. to *re-* RE- + *verber-* beat, last (deriv. of *verber* whip) + *-ant-* -ANT] —**re·ver′ber·ant·ly,** *adv.*

re·ver·ber·ate (*v.* ri vûr′bə rāt′; *adj.* ri vûr′bə rit), *v.,* **-at·ed, -at·ing,** *adj.* —*v.i.* **1.** to reecho or resound: *Her yelling reverberated through the house.* **2.** *Physics.* to be reflected many times, as sound waves from the walls of a confined space. **3.** to rebound or recoil. **4.** to be deflected, as flame in a reverberatory furnace. —*v.t.* **5.** to echo back or reecho (sound). **6.** to cast back or reflect (light, heat, etc.). **7.** to subject to reflected heat, as in a reverberatory furnace. —*adj.* **8.** reverberant. [< L *reverberāt(us)* struck back (ptp. of *reverberāre*). See REVERBERANT, -ATE[1]] —**re·ver′ber·a·tive,** *adj.* —**re·ver′ber·a′tor,** *n.*

re·ver·ber·a·tion (ri vûr′bə rā′shən), *n.* **1.** a reechoed sound. **2.** the fact of being reverberated or reflected. **3.** that which is reverberated: *Reverberations from the explosion reached a radius of six miles.* **4.** the act or an instance of reverberating. **5.** *Physics.* the persistence of a sound after its source has stopped, caused by multiple reflection of the sound within a closed space. **6.** the act or process of subjecting something to reflected heat, as in a reverberatory furnace. [ME *reverberacioun* < LL *reverberātiōn-* (s. of *reverberātiō*). See REVERBERATE -ION]

reverbera′tion time′, the time it takes for a sound made in a room to diminish by 60 decibels.

re·ver·ber·a·to·ry (ri vûr′bər ə tôr′ē, -tōr′ē), *adj., n., pl.* **-ries.** —*adj.* **1.** characterized or produced by reverberation. **2.** noting a furnace, kiln, or the like, in which the fuel is not in direct contact with the ore, metal, etc., to be heated, but furnishes a flame that plays over the material, esp. by being deflected downward from the roof. **3.** deflected, as flame. —*n.* **4.** any device, as a furnace, embodying reverberation. [REVERBERATE + -ORY[1]]

Reverberatory furnace (Section)

re·vere[1] (ri vēr′), *v.t.,* **-vered, -ver·ing.** to regard with respect tinged with awe; venerate: *The children revered the saintly old man.* [< L *rever(ērī),* equiv. to *re-* RE- + *verērī* to stand in awe of, fear, feel reverence] —**re·ver′a·ble,** *adj.* —**re·ver′er,** *n.*

—**Syn.** respect, reverence, honor, adore.

re·vere[2] (ri vēr′), *n.* revers.

Re·vere (ri vēr′), *n.* **1. Paul,** 1735–1818, American silversmith and patriot, famous for his night horseback ride, April 18, 1775, to warn Massachusetts colonists of the coming of British troops. **2.** a city in E Massachusetts, on Massachusetts Bay, near Boston: seaside resort. 40,080 (1960).

rev·er·ence (rev′ər əns, rev′rəns), *n., v.,* **-enced, -enc·ing.** —*n.* **1.** a feeling or attitude of deep respect tinged with awe; veneration. **2.** the outward manifestation of this feeling: *to pay reverence.* **3.** a gesture indicative of deep respect; an obeisance, bow, or curtsy. **4.** the state of being revered. **5.** (*cap.*) a title used in addressing or mentioning a clergyman (usually prec. by *your* or *his*). —*v.t.* **6.** to regard or treat with reverence; venerate: *One should reverence God and His laws.* [ME < L *reverentia* respect, fear, awe. See REVERE[1], -ENCE] —**rev′er·enc·er,** *n.*

—**Syn. 1.** awe. REVERENCE, WORSHIP imply sentiments of respect and homage. REVERENCE is a strong feeling of deference, respect, and esteem: *reverence shown to the venerable and wise.* WORSHIP, which is associated with an exalted religious feeling of reverence and love, refers primarily not to the feeling itself but to its manifestation in certain practices: *the worship of idols.* Thus, even in such expressions as *worship of beauty,* there is the suggestion of a way of behavior. **6.** revere, honor, adore. —**Ant. 1.** contempt.

rev·er·end (rev′ər ənd, rev′rənd), *adj.* **1.** (*often cap.*) an epithet of respect applied to or prefixed to the name (of a clergyman): *the Reverend Timothy Cranshaw.* **2.** worthy to be revered; entitled to reverence. **3.** pertaining to or characteristic of the clergy. —*n.* **4.** a clergyman. [late ME < L *reverend(us)* ought to be revered, ger. of *reverērī* to REVERE[1]] —**rev′er·end·ship′,** *n.*

rev·er·ent (rev′ər ənt, rev′rənt), *adj.* feeling, exhibiting, or characterized by reverence; deeply respectful: *a reverent greeting.* [ME < L *reverent-* (s. of *reverēns*), prp. of *reverērī* to REVERE[1]; see -ENT] —**rev′er·ent·ly,** *adv.* —**rev′er·ent·ness,** *n.*

rev·er·en·tial (rev′ə ren′shəl), *adj.* of the nature of or characterized by reverence; reverent: *reverential awe.* [REVERENT + -IAL] —**rev·er·en·ti·al·i·ty** (rev′ə ren′shē al′i tē), **rev′er·en′tial·ness,** *n.* —**rev′er·en′tial·ly,** *adv.*

rev·er·ie (rev′ə rē), *n.* **1.** a state of dreamy meditation or fanciful musing: *lost in reverie.* **2.** a daydream. **3.** a fantastic, visionary, or unpractical idea: *Your plans are reveries that will never come to fruition.* **4.** *Music.* an instrumental composition of a vague and dreamy character. Also, **revery.** [< F *rêverie,* deriv. of *rêver* to speak wildly. See RAVE, -ERY]

re·vers (ri vēr′, -vâr′), *n., pl.* **-vers** (-vērz′, -vârz′). **1.** a part of a garment turned back to show the lining or facing, as a lapel. **2.** a trimming simulating such a part. **3.** the facing used. Also, **revere.** [< F]

re·ver·sal (ri vûr′səl), *n.* **1.** the act of reversing. **2.** an instance of this. **3.** the state of being reversed. **4.** *Law.* the overthrow of a decision of a lower court by an appellate court. [REVERSE + -AL[2]]

rever′sal film′, *Photog.* film developed by the reversal process.

rever′sal plate′, *Photog.* a plate developed by the reversal process.

rever′sal proc′ess, *Photog.* a process for converting the negative on a film or plate to a positive by bleaching and redeveloping.

re·verse (ri vûrs′), *adj., n., v.,* **-versed, -vers·ing.** —*adj.* **1.** opposite or contrary in position, direction, order, or character: *an impression reverse to what was intended; in reverse sequence.* **2.** acting in a manner opposite or contrary to that which is usual, as an appliance or apparatus. **3.** with the back or rear part toward the observer: *the reverse side of a fabric.* **4.** pertaining to or producing movement in a mechanism opposite to that made under ordinary running conditions: *a reverse gear; a reverse turbine.* **5.** noting or pertaining to printed matter in which what is normally white, as the page of a book, appears as black, and vice versa. **6.** noting or pertaining to an image like that seen in a mirror; backward; reversed. —*n.* **7.** the opposite or contrary of something. **8.** the back or rear of anything. **9.** *Numis.* **a.** the side of a coin, medal, etc., which does not bear the principal design (opposed to *obverse*). **b.** the side of an ancient coin that was struck by the upper die. **10.** an adverse change of fortune; a misfortune, check, or defeat: *to meet with an unexpected reverse.* **11.** *Football.* a play on offense in which one back running laterally hands the ball to another back who is running in the opposite direction and who then makes either an end run or a cutback. **12.** *Mach.* **a.** the condition of being reversed: *to throw an engine into reverse.* **b.** a reversing mechanism. **13.** *Bridge.* See **reverse bid. 14.** *Print.* printed matter in which areas that normally appear as white are printed in black, and vice versa. [ME *revers* < MF < L *reversus,* ptp. of *revertere* to REVERT] —*v.t.* **15.** to turn in an opposite position; transpose: *In the American edition, the printer accidently reversed those two chapters of the book.* **16.** to turn inside out or upside down. **17.** to turn in the opposite direction; send on the opposite course. **18.** to turn in the opposite order: *to reverse the process of evolution.* **19.** to alter to the opposite in character or tendency; change completely. **20.** to revoke or annul (a decree, judgment, etc.): *to reverse a verdict.* **21.** to change the direction of running of (a mechanism). **22.** to cause (a mechanism) to run in a direction opposite to that in which it commonly runs. **23.** *Print.* to print as a reverse. —*v.i.* **24.** to turn or move in the opposite or contrary direction, as in dancing. **25.** (of a mechanism) to be reversed. **26.** to shift into reverse gear: *The driver drove forward, then reversed and backed into a wall.* **27.** *Bridge.* to make a reverse bid. [ME *reverse(n)* < MF *revers(er)* < LL *reversāre,*

re′up·hol′ster, *v.t.*
re′up·hol′ster·er, *n.*
re′up·hol′ster·y, *n., pl.* -ster·ies.
re′us·a·bil′i·ty, *n.*
re·us′a·ble, *adj.;* -ness, *n.*
re·use′, *v.,* -used, -us·ing; *n.*
re·use′a·ble, *adj.;* -ness, *n.*
re·u′ti·lise′, *v.t.,* -lised, -lis·ing.
re′u·ti·li·za′tion, *n.*
re·u′ti·lize′, *v.t.,* -lized, -liz·ing.
re·ut′ter, *v.t.*
re·ut′ter·ance, *n.*
re·va′cate, *v.t.,* -cat·ed, -cat·ing.
re·vac′ci·nate′, *v.t.,* -nat·ed, -nat·ing.
re′vac·ci·na′tion, *n.*
re·val′i·date′, *v.t.,* -dat·ed, -dat·ing.
re′val·i·da′tion, *n.*
re·val′u·ate′, *v.t.,* -at·ed, -at·ing.
re′val·u·a′tion, *n.*
re′va·por·i·za′tion, *n.*
re·va′por·ize′, *v.,* -ized, -iz·ing.
re·var′nish, *v.t.*
re·vend′, *v.t.*
re·ven′ti·late′, *v.t.,* -lat·ed, -lat·ing.
re′ven·ti·la′tion, *n.*
re·ver′i·fi·ca′tion, *n.*
re·ver′i·fy′, *v.t.,* -fied, -fy·ing.

freq. of *revertere* to REVERT] —**re·vers·ed·ly** (ri vûr′sid lē, -vûrst′lē), *adv.* —**re·verse′ly,** *adv.* —**re·vers′er,** *n.*
—**Syn. 1.** converse. See **opposite. 7.** converse, counterpart. **10.** mishap, misadventure, affliction. **15, 16.** REVERSE, INVERT agree in meaning to change into a contrary position, order, or relation. To REVERSE is to place or move something so that it is facing in the opposite direction from the one faced previously: *to reverse from right to left; to reverse a decision.* To INVERT is to turn upside down: *to invert a stamp in printing; to invert a bowl over a plate.* **20.** repeal, veto, countermand, rescind, overthrow. —**Ant. 1.** same.

reverse′ bar′, an angle iron having one leg welded or riveted to a leg of another angle iron to make a member similar to a z-bar.

reverse′ bev′el, the bevel of a bolt or lock on a door opening outward from the building, room, closet, etc., to which the doorway leads (opposed to *regular bevel*).

reverse′ bid′, *Bridge.* a bid of a higher ranking suit at the two level or higher by a player whose previous bid was of a lower ranking suit.

reverse′ curve′, an S-shaped curve, as on highways and railroad tracks, produced by the joining of two curves that turn in opposite directions.

reversed′ col′lar. See **clerical collar.**

reverse′ discrimina′tion, the unfair treatment of majority groups (whites, men, etc.) resulting from preference, as in college admissions or employment practices, intended to remedy earlier discrimination against minorities (blacks, women, etc.).

reverse′ Eng′lish, 1. Also called **reverse′ side′.** *Billiards U.S.* a spinning motion imparted to a cue ball in such a manner as to prevent it from moving in a certain direction. Cf. **running English. 2.** words which, because of their misuse or careless syntax, convey an opposite meaning from the one intended or leave their exact meaning in doubt: *"Don't miss it if you can" is reverse English.*

reverse′ plate′, *Print.* a plate for printing a reverse.

re·vers·i·ble (ri vûr′sə bəl), *adj.* **1.** capable of being reversed or of reversing. **2.** capable of reestablishing the original condition after a change by the reverse of the change. **3.** (of a fabric) woven or printed so that either side may be exposed. **4.** that can be worn with either side out: *a reversible jacket.* —*n.* **5.** a garment, esp. a coat, that may be worn with either side exposed. [REVERSE + -IBLE] —**re·vers′i·bil′i·ty, re·vers′i·ble·ness,** *n.* —**re·vers′i·bly,** *adv.*

revers′ing prism′, *Optics.* See **Dove prism.**

re·ver·sion (ri vûr′zhən, -shən), *n.* **1.** the act of turning something the reverse way. **2.** the state of being so turned; reversal. **3.** the act of reverting; return to a former practice, belief, condition, etc. **4.** *Biol.* **a.** reappearance of ancestral characters that have been absent in intervening generations. **b.** return to an earlier or primitive type; atavism. **5.** *Law.* **a.** the returning of an estate to the grantor or his heirs after the interest granted expires. **b.** an estate which so returns. **c.** the right of succeeding to an estate. **6.** *Archaic.* the remains, esp. of food or drink after a meal. [ME < legal L *reversiōn-* (s. of *reversiō*) a turning back. See REVERSE, -ION] —**re·ver′sion·al·ly,** *adv.*

re·ver·sion·ar·y (ri vûr′zhə ner′ē, -shə-), *adj.* of, pertaining to, or involving a reversion. Also, **re·ver′sion·al.** [REVERSION + -ARY]

rever′sionary annu′ity, *Insurance.* an annuity payable to a beneficiary during the period of time he survives the insured.

re·ver·sion·er (ri vûr′zhə nər, -shə-), *n.* *Law.* a person who possesses a reversion. [REVERSION + -ER[1]]

re·vert (ri vûrt′), *n.* **1.** one who or that which reverts. **2.** *Law.* a reversion. —*v.i.* **3.** to return to a former habit, practice, belief, condition, etc.: *Once away from civilization, they reverted to the primitive ways of their forefathers.* **4.** to go back in thought or discussion: *He constantly reverted to his impoverished childhood.* **5.** *Biol.* to return to an earlier or primitive type. **6.** *Law.* to go back to or return to the former owner or his heirs. [ME *revert(en)* < legal L *revertere* to turn back, equiv. to *re-* RE- + *vertere* to turn] —**re·vert′i·bil′i·ty,** *n.* —**re·vert′i·ble,** *adj.* —**re·ver′tive,** *adj.* —**re·ver′tive·ly,** *adv.*
—**Syn. 3, 5.** retrogress.

re·vert·er[1] (ri vûr′tər), *n.* one who or that which reverts. [REVERT + -ER[1]]

re·vert·er[2] (ri vûr′tər), *n.* *Law.* a future interest in property that rests in a grantor. [ME < AF, n. use of *reverter* (inf.). See REVERT, -ER[3]]

rev·er·y (rev′ə rē), *n., pl.* **-er·ies.** reverie.

re·vest (rē vest′), *v.t.* **1.** to vest (as a person) again, as with ownership or office; reinvest; reinstate. **2.** to vest (powers, office, etc.) again. —*v.i.* **3.** to become vested again in a person; go back again to a former owner. [ME *revest(en)* < eccl. L *revestīre* to reclothe. See RE-, VEST]

re·vet (ri vet′), *v.t.,* **-vet·ted, -vet·ting.** to face, as an embankment, with masonry or other material. [< F *revêt(ir),* lit., to reclothe; see REVEST]

re·vet·ment (ri vet′mənt), *n.* **1.** a facing of masonry or the like, esp. for protecting an embankment. **2.** an ornamental facing, as on a common masonry wall, of marble, face brick, tiles, etc. [< F *revêtement.* See REVET, -MENT]

re·view (ri vyōō′), *n.* **1.** a critical article or report, as in a periodical, on a recent book, play, recital, or the like; critique; evaluation. **2.** a periodical publication containing articles on current events or affairs, books, art, etc.: *a literary review.* **3.** a second or repeated view of something. **4.** the process of going over a subject again in study or recitation in order to fix it in the memory or summarize the facts. **5.** an exercise designed or intended for study of this kind. **6.** an inspection or examination by viewing, esp. a formal inspection of any military or naval force, parade, or the like. **7.** a viewing of the past; contemplation or consideration of past events, circumstances, or facts. **8.** a general survey of something, esp. in words; a report or account of something. **9.** *Bridge.* a recapitulation of the bids made by all players. **10.** a judicial reexamination, as by a higher court, of the decision or proceedings in a case. **11.** *Theat.* revue. —*v.t.* **12.** to view, look at, or look over again. **13.** to go over (lessons, studies, work, etc.) in review. **14.** to inspect, esp. formally or officially: *The President reviewed the troops.* **15.** to look back upon; view retrospectively. **16.** to survey mentally; take a survey of: *to review the situation.* **17.** to present a survey of in speech or writing. **18.** to discuss (a book, play, etc.) in a critical review; write a critical report upon: *The Times reviewed her book favorably.* **19.** *Bridge.* to repeat and summarize (all bids made by the players): *to review the bidding.* **20.** *Law.* to reexamine judicially: *a decision to review the case.* —*v.i.* **21.** to write reviews; review books, movies, etc., as for some periodical: *He reviews for some small-town newspaper.* [< MF *revue,* n. use of fem. ptp. of *revoir* to see again < L *revidēre,* equiv. to *re-* RE- + *vidēre;* see VIEW] —**re·view′a·bil′i·ty,** *n.* —**re·view′a·ble,** *adj.* —**re·view′less,** *adj.*
—**Syn. 1.** REVIEW, CRITICISM imply carefully examining something, making a judgment, and putting the judgment into (usually) written form. A REVIEW is a survey over a whole subject or division of it, or esp. an article making a critical reconsideration and summary of something written: *a review of the latest book on Chaucer.* A CRITICISM is a judgment, usually in an article, either favorable or unfavorable or both: *a criticism of a proposed plan.* The words are freely interchanged when referring to motion pictures or theater, but REVIEW implies a somewhat less formal approach than CRITICISM in referring to literary works: *movie reviews; play reviews; book reviews.* Thus, one expects to find REVIEWS in newspapers and popular periodicals; CRITICISM is confined to more learned periodicals and books. **3.** reconsideration, reexamination. **18.** criticize.

re·view·al (ri vyōō′əl), *n.* the act of reviewing. [REVIEW + -AL[2]]

re·view·er (ri vyōō′ər), *n.* **1.** a person who reviews. **2.** a person who writes reviews of new books, plays, etc. [REVIEW + -ER[1]]

re·vile (ri vīl′), *v.,* **-viled, -vil·ing.** —*v.t.* **1.** to assail with contemptuous or opprobrious language; address or speak of abusively: *He constantly reviles his employees and consequently has a high turnover.* —*v.i.* **2.** to speak abusively. [ME *revile(n)* < MF *reviler.* See RE-, VILE] —**re·vile′ment,** *n.* —**re·vil′er,** *n.* —**re·vil′ing·ly,** *adv.*
—**Syn. 1.** abuse, vilify, vituperate, berate, asperse, disparage.

re·vis·al (ri vī′zəl), *n.* the act of revising; revision. [REVISE + -AL[2]]

re·vise (ri vīz′), *v.,* **-vised, -vis·ing,** *n.* —*v.t.* **1.** to amend or alter: *to revise one's opinion.* **2.** to alter after one or more typings or printings: *to revise a manuscript.* **3.** *Brit.* to review (previously studied materials) in preparation for an examination. —*n.* **4.** an act of revising. **5.** a revised form of something; revision. **6.** *Print.* a proof sheet taken after alterations have been made, for further examination or correction. [< L *revīse(re)* (to) look back at, revisit, freq. of *revidēre* to see again; see REVIEW] —**re·vis′a·bil′i·ty,** *n.* —**re·vis′a·ble, re·vis′i·ble,** *adj.* —**re·vis′er, re·vi′sor,** *n.*
—**Syn. 1.** change; emend, correct.

Revised′ Stand′ard Ver′sion, a revision of the Bible, based on the American Standard Version and the King James Version, prepared by American scholars, published in its completed form in 1952. *Abbr.:* RSV

Revised′ Ver′sion of the Bi′ble, a recension of the Authorized Version, prepared by British and American scholars, the Old Testament being published in 1885, and the New Testament in 1881. Also called **Revised′ Ver′sion.**

re·vi·sion (ri vizh′ən), *n.* **1.** the act or work of revising. **2.** a process of revising. **3.** a revised form or version, as of a book. [< LL *revīsiōn-* (s. of *revīsiō*), equiv. to L *revīs(us)* (see REVISE) + *-iōn-* -ION] —**re·vi′sion·al, re·vi′sion·ar′y,** *adj.*

re·vi·sion·ism (ri vizh′ə niz′əm), *n.* **1.** advocacy or approval of revision. **2.** (among Marxists) any departure from a Marxist doctrine, theory, or practice held by the one making judgment to be authoritative. **3.** a departure from any authoritative or generally accepted doctrine, theory, practice, etc. [REVISION + -ISM]

re·vi·sion·ist (ri vizh′ə nist), *n.* **1.** an advocate of revision, esp. of some political or religious doctrine. **2.** a reviser. **3.** a supporter of revisionism. —*adj.* **4.** of or pertaining to revisionists or revisionism. **5.** attempting to reevaluate and restate the past based on newly acquired standards. [REVISION + -IST]

re·vi·so·ry (ri vī′zə rē), *adj.* pertaining to or for the purpose of revision. [REVISE + -ORY[1]]

re·viv·al (ri vī′vəl), *n.* **1.** the act of reviving. **2.** the state of being revived. **3.** restoration to life, consciousness, vigor, strength, etc. **4.** restoration to use, acceptance, or currency: *the revival of old customs.* **5.** a new production of an old play or motion picture. **6.** an awakening, in a church or community, of interest in and care for matters relating to personal religion. **7.** an evangelistic service or a series of services for the purpose of effecting a religious awakening: *to hold a revival.* **8.** *Law.* the reestablishment of legal force and effect. [REVIVE + -AL[2]]

re·viv·al·ism (ri vī′və liz′əm), *n.* **1.** the tendency to revive what belongs to the past. **2.** that form of religious activity which manifests itself in revivals. [REVIVAL + -ISM]

re·viv·al·ist (ri vī′və list), *n.* **1.** a person who revives former customs, methods, etc. **2.** a person, esp. a clergyman, who promotes or holds religious revivals. [REVIVAL + -IST] —**re·viv′al·is′tic,** *adj.*

Reviv′al of Learn′ing, the Renaissance in its relation to learning, esp. in literature (**Reviv′al of Lit′erature** or **Reviv′al of Let′ters**).

re·vive (ri vīv′), *v.,* **-vived, -viv·ing.** —*v.t.* **1.** to activate, set in motion, or take up again; renew: *to revive old feuds.* **2.** to make operative or valid again. **3.** to bring back into notice, use, or currency: *to revive a subject of discussion.* **4.** to produce (an old play or motion picture) again. **5.** to restore to life or consciousness: *We revived him with artificial respiration.* **6.** to reanimate or cheer (the spirit, heart, etc., or a person). **7.** to quicken or renew in the mind; bring back: *to revive memories.* **8.** *Chem.* to restore or reduce to its natural or uncombined state, as a metal. —*v.i.* **9.** to return to life, consciousness, vigor, strength, or a flourishing condition. **10.** to recover from financial depression. **11.** to be quickened, restored, or renewed, as hope, confidence, suspicions, memories, etc. **12.** to return to notice, use, or currency, as a subject, practice, doctrine, etc. **13.** to become operative or valid again. **14.** *Chem.* to recover its natural or uncombined state, as a metal. [ME *revive(n)* < L *revīvere* to live again, equiv. to *re-* RE- + *vīvere* to live, be alive] —**re·viv′a·bil′i·ty,** *n.* —**re·viv′a·ble,** *adj.* —**re·viv′a·bly,** *adv.* —**re·viv′er,** *n.* —**re·viv′ing·ly,** *adv.*
—**Syn. 1, 2.** reactivate. **5.** revitalize, reanimate, resuscitate. **7.** rouse, refresh. —**Ant. 5.** kill.

re·viv·i·fy (ri viv′ə fī′), *v.t.,* **-fied, -fy·ing.** to restore to life; give new life to; revive; animate anew. [< F *révivifi(er)* < LL *revīvificāre.* See RE-, VIVIFY] —**re·viv·i·fi·ca·tion** (ri viv′ə fə kā′shən), *n.*

rev·i·vis·cence (rev′ə vis′əns), *n.* the act or state of being revived; revival; reanimation. Also, **rev′i·vis′cen·cy.** [< L *reviviscere*) (to) come to life again (*re-* RE- + *vīviscere,* inceptive of *vīvere* to live) + -ENCE] —**rev′i·vis′cent,** *adj.*

re·vi·vor (ri vī′vər), *n.* *Eng. Law.* the revival of a legal suit that has been nullified by some circumstance, as the death of one of the parties. [REVIVE + -OR[2]]

rev·o·ca·ble (rev′ə kə bəl), *adj.* that may be revoked. Also, **re·vok·a·ble** (ri vō′kə bəl). [late ME < L *revocābil(is).* See REVOKE, -ABLE] —**rev′o·ca·bil′i·ty, rev′o·ca·ble·ness,** *n.* —**rev′o·ca·bly,** *adv.*

rev·o·ca·tion (rev′ə kā′shən), *n.* **1.** the act of revoking; annulment. **2.** *Law.* nullification or withdrawal, esp. of an offer to contract. [ME *revocacion* < L *revocātiōn-* (s. of *revocātiō*) a calling back, equiv. to *revocāt(us)* (ptp. of *revocāre* to REVOKE) + *-iōn-* -ION] —**rev·o·ca·tive** (rev′ə kā′tiv, ri vok′ə-), **rev·o·ca·to·ry** (rev′ə kə tôr′ē, -tōr′ē), *adj.*

re·voice (rē vois′), *v.t.,* **-voiced, -voic·ing. 1.** to voice again or in return; echo. **2.** to readjust the tone of: *to revoice an organ pipe.* [RE- + VOICE]

re·voke (ri vōk′), *v.,* **-voked, -vok·ing,** *n.* —*v.t.* **1.** to take back or withdraw; annul, cancel, or reverse; rescind or repeal: *to revoke a decree.* **2.** *Archaic.* to bring or summon back. —*v.i.* **3.** *Cards.* to fail to follow suit when one can and should do so; renege. —*n.* **4.** *Cards.* an act or instance of revoking. [ME *revoke(n)* < L *revocāre* to call again, equiv. to *re-* RE- + *vocāre* to call] —**re·vok′er,** *n.* —**re·vok′ing·ly,** *adv.*
—**Syn. 1.** retract, recall; nullify, countermand.

re·volt (ri vōlt′), *v.i.* **1.** to break away from or rise against constituted authority, as by open rebellion; cast off allegiance or subjection to those in authority; rebel; mutiny: *There is a movement afoot among the populace to revolt against the present government.* **2.** to turn away in mental rebellion, utter disgust, or abhorrence (usually fol. by *from*): *He revolts from eating meat.* **3.** to rebel in feeling (usually fol. by *against*): *to revolt against parental authority.* **4.** to feel horror or disgust (usually fol. by *at*): *to revolt at coarse language.* —*v.t.* **5.** to affect with disgust or abhorrence: *Such low behavior revolts me.* —*n.* **6.** the act of revolting; an insurrection or rebellion. **7.** aversion, disgust, or loathing. **8.** the state of those revolting: *to be in revolt.* [< MF *revolt(er)* (v.) < It *rivoltare* to turn around < VL **revolvitāre,* freq. of L *revolvere* to roll back, unroll, REVOLVE] —**re·volt′er,** *n.*

re·volt·ing (ri vōl′ting), *adj.* **1.** disgusting; repulsive: *She served an absolutely revolting concoction for dessert.* **2.** rebellious. [REVOLT + -ING[2]] —**re·volt′ing·ly,** *adv.*

rev·o·lute (rev′ə lōōt′), *adj.* *Biol.* rolled backward or downward; rolled backward at the tip or margin, as a leaf. [< L *revolūt(us),* ptp. of *revolvere* to REVOLVE]

A

B

A, Revolute margined leaf; B, Transverse section

rev·o·lu·tion (rev′ə lōō′shən), *n.* **1.** a complete and forcible overthrow of an established government or political system. **2.** *Sociol.* a radical and pervasive change in society and the social structure, esp. one made suddenly and often accompanied by violence. Cf. **social evolution. 3.** a complete or marked change in something: *the present revolution in church architecture.* **4.** procedure or course as if in a circuit, as back to a starting point in time. **5.** a single turn of this kind. **6.** *Mech.* **a.** a turning round or rotating, as on an axis. **b.** a moving in a circular or curving course, as about a central point. **c.** a single cycle in such a course. **7.** *Astron.* **a.** (not in technical use) the turning of a heavenly body on its axis: *The earth completes one revolution each day.* **b.** the orbiting of one heavenly body around another. **c.** a single course of such movement. Cf. **rotation. 8.** round or cycle of events in time or a recurring period of time. **9.** *Geol.* a time of world-wide orogeny and mountain-building. [ME *revolucion* < LL *revolūtiōn-* (s. of *revolūtiō*), equiv. to *revolūt(us)* (see REVOLUTE) + *-iōn-* -ION]
—**Syn. 1.** See **revolt. 5.** cycle, circuit, round, rotation.

rev·o·lu·tion·ar·y (rev′ə lōō′shə ner′ē), *adj., n., pl.* **-ar·ies.** —*adj.* **1.** pertaining to, characterized by, or of the nature of a revolution, or complete or marked change: *a revolutionary junta.* **2.** subversive to or exclusive of established procedure, principles, etc.: *a revolutionary discovery.* **3.** (*cap.*) of or pertaining to the American Revolution or to the period contemporaneous with it in U.S. history: *Revolutionary heroes; Revolutionary weapons.* **4.** revolving. —*n.* **5.** a revolutionist. [REVOLUTION + -ARY] —**rev′o·lu′tion·ar′i·ly,** *adv.* —**rev′o·lu′tion·ar′i·ness,** *n.*

Revolu′tionary cal′endar, the calendar of the first French republic, adopted in 1793 and abandoned in 1805, consisting of 12 months, each of 30 days, and 5 intercalary days added at the end of the year (6 every fourth year). The months are Vendémiaire, Brumaire,

re·ve′to, *v.t.,* **-toed, -to·ing.**
re·vi′brant, *adj.*
re·vi′brate, *v.,* **-brat·ed, -brat·ing.**
re′vi·bra′tion, *n.*
re·vict′ual, *v.,* **-ualed, -ual·ing** or (*esp. Brit.*) **-ualled, -ual·ling.**
re·vin′di·cate′, *v.t.,* **-cat·ed, -cat·ing.**
re·vin′di·ca′tion, *n.*
re·vi′o·late′, *v.t.,* **-lat·ed, -lat·ing.**
re′vi·o·la′tion, *n.*
re·vis′it, *v.*
re·vis′it·a·ble, *adj.*
re′vis·it·a′tion, *n.*
re·vis′u·al·i·za′tion, *n.*
re·vis′u·al·ize′, *v.,* **-ized, -iz·ing.**
re·vi′tal·i·sa′tion, *n.*
re·vi′tal·ise′, *v.t.,* **-ised, -is·ing.**
re·vi′tal·i·za′tion, *n.*
re·vi′tal·ize′, *v.t.,* **-ized, -iz·ing.**

Frimaire, Nivôse, Pluviôse, Ventôse, Germinal, Floréal, Prairial, Messidor, Thermidor, and Fructidor.

Revolu′tionary War′. See **American Revolution.**

revolu′tion coun′ter, a device for counting or recording the number of revolutions made by a rotating shaft, as of a motor or engine.

rev·o·lu·tion·ise (rev′ə lo͞o′shə nīz′), *v.t.*, **-ised, -is·ing.** *Chiefly Brit.* revolutionize. —**rev′o·lu′tion·is′er,** *n.*

rev·o·lu·tion·ist (rev′ə lo͞o′shə nist), *n.* a person who advocates or takes part in a revolution. [REVOLUTION + -IST]

rev·o·lu·tion·ize (rev′ə lo͞o′shə nīz′), *v.t.*, **-ized, -iz·ing. 1.** to bring about a revolution in; effect a radical change in: *a plan to revolutionize petroleum refining methods.* **2.** to subject to a political revolution. Also, *esp. Brit.,* **revolutionise.** [REVOLUTION + -IZE] —**rev′o·lu′tion·iz′er,** *n.*

re·volve (ri volv′), *v.*, **-volved, -volv·ing.** —*v.i.* **1.** to turn around or rotate, as on an axis: *The earth revolves on its axis.* **2.** to move in a circular or curving course or orbit: *The earth revolves around the sun.* **3.** to proceed or occur in a round or cycle; come around again in the process of time; recur. **4.** to be revolved in the mind. —*v.t.* **5.** to cause to turn around, as on an axis. **6.** to cause to move in a circular or curving course, as about a central point. **7.** to think about; consider. [ME *revolve(n)* < L *revolv(ere)* (to) roll back, equiv. to *re-* RE- + *volvere* to roll, turn round. See WALLOW] —**re·volv′a·ble,** *adj.* —**re·volv′a·bly,** *adv.*
—**Syn. 1.** See **turn. 2.** orbit, circle. **7.** ponder, study.

re·volv·er (ri vol′vər), *n.* **1.** a pistol having a revolving chambered cylinder for holding a number of cartridges, which may be discharged in succession without reloading. **2.** one who or that which revolves. [REVOLVE + -ER[1]]

Revolver

re·volv·ing (ri vol′ving), *adj.* **1.** that revolves: *a revolving table top.* **2.** *Mach.* noting or pertaining to a radial engine the cylinders of which revolve around a stationary crankshaft, as the engine of a helicopter. [REVOLVE + -ING[2]] —**re·volv′ing·ly,** *adv.*

revolv′ing cred′it, credit automatically available up to a predetermined limit while payments are periodically made. Cf. **credit line** (def. 2).

revolv′ing door′, an entrance door for excluding drafts from the interior of a building, consisting of four leaves usually set in the form of a cross and rotating about a central, vertical pivot in the doorway.

revolv′ing fund′, 1. any loan fund intended to be maintained by the repayment of past loans. **2.** a U.S. government fund, with loans and repayments equalized, used to aid business affecting the public interest, as public utilities.

Rev. Stat., Revised Statutes.

re·vue (ri vyo͞o′), *n.* **1.** a form of theatrical entertainment in which recent events, popular fads, etc., are parodied. **2.** any group of skits, dances, and songs. Also, **review.** [< F: REVIEW] —**re·vu′ist,** *n.*

re·vul·sant (ri vul′sənt), *Med.* —*adj.* **1.** causing or tending to revulsion. —*n.* **2.** an agent that draws blood from one region of the body to another region. [? < F, prp. of *révulser* to pull back, tear away; see REVULSION]

re·vul·sion (ri vul′shən), *n.* **1.** a sudden and violent change of feeling or response in sentiment, taste, etc. **2.** a strong feeling of repugnance, distaste, or dislike: *Poor eating habits always fill me with revulsion.* **3.** *Med.* the diminution of morbid action in one part of the body by irritation in another. **4.** the act of drawing something back or away. **5.** the fact of being so drawn. [< L *revulsiōn-* (s. of *revulsiō*) a tearing away, equiv. to *revuls(us)* (ptp. of *revellere* to tear away, equiv. to *re-* RE- + *vellere* to pluck) + *-iōn-* -ION] —**re·vul′sion·ar′y,** *adj.*
—**Syn. 1.** disgust, repulsion, loathing, repugnance, aversion.

re·vul·sive (ri vul′siv), *Med.* —*adj.* **1.** tending to alter the distribution of blood by causing congestion, esp. in the intestine. —*n.* **2.** a revulsive agent, esp. one that causes revulsion. [< L *revuls(us)* (see REVULSION) + -IVE] —**re·vul′sive·ly,** *adv.*

Rev. Ver., Revised Version (of the Bible).

re·ward (ri wôrd′), *n.* **1.** something given or received in return or recompense for service, merit, hardship, etc. **2.** a sum of money offered for the detection or capture of a criminal, the recovery of lost or stolen property, etc. —*v.t.* **3.** to recompense or requite (a person or animal) for service, merit, achievement, etc. **4.** to make return for or requite (service, merit, etc.); recompense. [ME *reward(en)* < ONF *reward(er)* (to) look at, var. of OF *regarder*; see REGARD] —**re·ward′a·ble,** *adj.* —**re·ward′a·ble·ness,** *n.* —**re·ward′a·bly,** *adv.* —**re·ward′er,** *n.* —**re·ward′less,** *adj.*
—**Syn. 1.** desert, pay, remuneration; requital; bounty, premium, bonus. REWARD, PRIZE, RECOMPENSE imply something given in return for good. A REWARD is something given or done in return for good (or, more rarely, evil) received; it may refer to something abstract or concrete: *a 50-dollar reward; Her devotion was his reward.* PRIZE refers to something concrete offered as a reward of merit, or to be contested for and given to the winner: *to win a prize for an essay.* A RECOMPENSE is something given or done, whether as reward or punishment, for acts performed, services rendered, etc.; or it may be something given in compensation for loss or injury suffered, etc.: *Renown was his principal recompense for years of hard work.* **3.** compensate, pay, remunerate.

re·win (rē win′), *v.t.*, **-won** or (*Obs.*) **-wan; -won; -win·ning.** to win back or again. [RE- + WIN[1]]

re·wire (rē wīər′), *v.t.*, **-wired, -wir·ing.** to provide with new wiring: *to rewire the electrical system in a house.* [RE- + WIRE] —**re·wir′a·ble,** *adj.*

re·word (rē wûrd′), *v.t.* **1.** to put into other words: *to reword a contract.* **2.** to repeat. [RE- + WORD]

re′worked wool′ (rē′wûrkt′), used wool which is reprocessed for additional use. [RE- + WORKED]

re·write (*v.* rē rīt′; *n.* rē′rīt′), *v.*, **-wrote, -writ·ten, -writ·ing,** *n.* —*v.t.* **1.** to write in a different form or manner; revise: *He has to rewrite the entire second act before the play opens on Broadway.* **2.** to write again. **3.** *U.S.* to write (news submitted by a reporter) for inclusion in a newspaper. —*n.* **4.** *U.S.* the news story written. **5.** something written in a different form or manner; revision. [RE- + WRITE] —**re·writ′er,** *n.*

rex (reks; *Eng.* reks), *n., pl.* **re·ges** (re′ges; *Eng.* rē′jēz). *Latin.* king.

Rex (reks), *n.* a Belgian fascist party founded in 1935. [after *Christus Rex,* title of a publication put out by its founders] —**Rex′ist,** *n.*

Rex (reks), *n.* a boy's given name

Rex·ane (rek san′) *n.* a girl's given name. Also, **Rex·an·a** (rek san′ə).

Rex·burg (reks′bûrg), *n.* a town in E Idaho. 4767 (1960).

Rex·mond (reks′mənd), *n.* a boy's given name.

Rex·roth (reks′rôth), *n.* **Kenneth,** born 1905, U.S. poet, critic, and translator.

Rey·kja·vik (rā′kyə vēk′), *n.* a seaport in and the capital of Iceland, in the SW part. 78,800 (est. 1966).

Rey·mont (rā′mônt), *n.* **Wła·dy·sław Sta·ni·sław** (vwä dē′swäf stä nē′swäf), ("*Ladislas Regmont*"), 1868–1925, Polish novelist: Nobel prize 1924.

Reyn·ard (ren′ərd, rā′närd), *n.* a name given to the fox, originally in the medieval beast epic, *Reynard the Fox.* Also, **Renard.**

Rey·naud (re nō′), *n.* **Paul** (pôl), 1878–1966, French statesman: premier 1940.

Reyn·old (ren′əld), *n.* a boy's given name, form of **Reginald.**

Reyn·olds (ren′əldz), *n.* **Sir Joshua,** 1723–92, English painter.

Reyn·olds·burg (ren′əldz bûrg′), *n.* a town in central Ohio. 7793 (1960).

Reyn·olds·ville (ren′əldz vil), *n.* a town in central Pennsylvania. 3158 (1960).

Re·za Shah Pah·la·vi (ri zä′ shä′ pä lä vē′, pal′ə vē). See **Riza Shah Pahlavi.** Also, **Re·za′ Shah′ Pah·le·vi′** (pä le vē′, pal′ə vē).

rez-de-chaus·sée (rād° shō sā′), *n., pl.* **rez-de-chaus·sées** (rād° shō sā′). *French.* street level; ground floor.

rf., *Baseball.* right fielder.

R.F., Reserve Force.

r.f., 1. radio frequency. **2.** range finder. **3.** rapid-fire. **4.** reducing flame. **5.** *Baseball.* right field.

R.F.A., Royal Field Artillery.

r.f.b., *Football.* right fullback. Also, **R.F.B.**

RFC, See **Reconstruction Finance Corporation.**

R.F.D., See **rural free delivery.** Also, **RFD**

r.g., *Football.* right guard.

Rh, *Chem.* rhodium.

Rh, *Biochem.* See **Rh factor.** Also, **Rh.**

R.H., Royal Highness.

r.h., right hand.

rhab·do·man·cy (rab′də man′sē), *n.* divination by means of a rod or wand, esp. in discovering ores, springs of water, etc. [< LL *rhabdomantīa* < Gk *rhabdomanteía,* equiv. to *rhábdo(s)* rod, wand + *manteía* -MANCY] —**rhab′do·man′tist,** *n.*

rhab·do·my·o·ma (rab′dō mī ō′mə), *n., pl.* **-ma·ta** (-mə tə), **-mas.** *Pathol.* a tumor made up of striated muscular tissue. Cf. **leiomyoma.** [< Gk *rhábdo(s)* rod + MYOMA]

rha·chis (rā′kis), *n., pl.* **rha·chis·es, rha·chi·des** (rak′i dēz′, rā′ki-). rachis.

Rhad·a·man·thys (rad′ə man′thəs), *n.* **1.** *Class. Myth.* a son of Zeus and Europa, rewarded for the justice he exemplified on earth by being made, after his death, a judge in the lower world, where he served with his brothers Minos and Aeacus. **2.** an inflexibly just or severe judge. Also, **Rhad′a·man′thus.** —**Rhad·a·man·thine** (rad′ə man′thin), *adj.*

Rhae·ti·a (rē′shē ə), *n.* an ancient Roman province in central Europe, comprising what is now E Switzerland and a part of the Tyrol: later extended to the Danube.

Rhae·tian (rē′shən), *adj.* **1.** of or pertaining to Rhaetia. **2.** Rhaeto-Romanic. **3.** Raetic. **4.** *Stratig.* Rhaetic. —*n.* **5.** Raetic. [RHAETI(A) + -AN]

Rhae′tian Alps′, a chain of the Alps in E Switzerland and W Austria. Highest peak, Mt. Bernina, 13,295 ft.

Rhae·tic (rē′tik), *adj. Geol.* pertaining to certain strata, extensively developed in the Rhaetian Alps, having features of the Triassic and Jurassic but generally classed as belonging to the former. Also, **Rhetic.** [< L *Rhaetic(us).* See RHAETIA, -IC]

Rhae·to-Ro·man·ic (rē′tō rō man′ik), *n.* **1.** a Romance language consisting of Friulian, Tyrolese Ladino, and the Romansh dialects. —*adj.* **2.** of or pertaining to Rhaeto-Romanic. Also, **Rhae′to-Ro·mance′, Rhetian.** [*rhaeto-* (repr. L *rhaetus* Rhaetian) + ROMANIC (modeled on G *Rätoromanisch*)]

-rhagia, var. of **-rrhagia.** Also, **-rhage, -rhagy.**

rha·gon (rā′gon, rag′on), *n.* a developmental stage of many leuconoid sponges, characterized by a conical shape with an osculum at the apex. [< Gk *rhag-* (s. of *rhā́x*) grape, berry + (LEUC)ON]

rha·go·noid (rā′gə noid′, rag′ə-), *adj.* resembling or pertaining to a rhagon. [RHAGON + -OID]

rham·na·ceous (ram nā′shəs), *adj.* belonging to the *Rhamnaceae,* or buckthorn family of plants. [< Gk *rhámn(os)* thorn, prickly shrub + -ACEOUS]

Rham·nes (ram′nēz), *n. Rom. Legend.* an arrogant Rutulian chief and prophet.

rham·pho·the·ca (ram′fə thē′kə), *n.* the horny covering of a bird's bill. [< Gk *rhámpho(s)* beak + THECA]

rhap·sod·ic (rap sod′ik), *adj.* **1.** pertaining to, characteristic of, or of the nature or form of rhapsody. **2.** extravagantly enthusiastic; ecstatic. Also, **rhap·sod′i·cal.** [< Gk *rhapsōidik(ós).* See RHAPSODY, -IC] —**rhap·sod′i·cal·ly,** *adv.*

rhap·so·dise (rap′sə dīz′), *v.t., v.i.,* **-dised, -dis·ing.** *Chiefly Brit.* rhapsodize.

rhap·so·dist (rap′sə dist), *n.* **1.** a person who rhapsodizes. **2.** (in ancient Greece) a person who recited epic poetry, esp. professionally. [< Gk *rhapsōid(ós)* rhapsodist (*rhaps-,* var. s. of *rháptein* to stitch, + *-ōid(e)* ODE + *-os* n. suffix) + -IST] —**rhap′so·dis′tic,** *adj.*

rhap·so·dize (rap′sə dīz′), *v.*, **-dized, -diz·ing.** —*v.i.* **1.** to speak or write rhapsodies. **2.** to talk with extravagant enthusiasm. —*v.t.* **3.** to recite as a rhapsody. [RHAPSOD(Y) + -IZE]

rhap·so·dy (rap′sə dē), *n., pl.* **-dies. 1.** an exalted or exaggerated expression of feeling or enthusiasm. **2.** an epic poem, or a part of such a poem, as a book of the *Iliad,* suitable for recitation at one time. **3.** a similar piece of modern literature. **4.** an unusually intense or irregular poem or piece of prose. **5.** *Music.* an instrumental composition irregular in form and suggestive of improvisation: *Liszt's Hungarian Rhapsodies.* **6.** *Archaic.* a miscellaneous collection; jumble. [< L *rhapsōdia* < Gk *rhapsōidía* recital of epic poetry, equiv. to *rhapsōid(ós)* RHAPSODIST + *-ia* -Y[3]]

rhat·a·ny (rat′°nē), *n., pl.* **-nies. 1.** either of two South American, leguminous shrubs of the genus *Krameria, K. tiandra* **(knotty rhatany** or **Peruvian rhatany),** or *K. argentea* **(Brazilian rhatany** or **Pará rhatany). 2.** the root of either of these plants, used as an astringent and tonic in medicine and also to color port wine. [< NL *rhatāni(a)* << Quechua *ratánya*]

rha·thy·mi·a (rə thī′mē ə), *n. Psychiatry, Psychol.* carefree behavior; light-heartedness. [< Gk *rhāithymía* easiness of temper, amusement, indifference, equiv. to *rhā́ithym(os)* easy-going + *-ia* -IA]

r.h.b., *Football.* right halfback. Also, **R.H.B.**

rhe·a (rē′ə), *n.* the ramie plant or fiber. [< Assamese *rihā*]

Rhe·a (rē′ə), *n.* **1.** *Class. Myth.* a Titaness, the daughter of Uranus and Gaea, the wife and sister of Cronus, and the mother of Zeus, Poseidon, Hera, Hades, Demeter, and Hestia: identified with Cybele and, by the Romans, with Ops. **2.** *Astron.* one of the nine satellites of Saturn. **3.** (*l.c.*) either of two South American, ratite birds, *Rhea americana* or *Pterocnemia pennata,* resembling the African ostrich but smaller and having three toes. **4.** a girl's given name.

Rhea, *Rhea americana* (Height 4 to 5 ft.; length 4¼ ft.)

-rhea, var. of **-rrhea.** Cf. **rheo-.**

Rhe·a Sil·vi·a (rē′ə sil′vē ə), *Rom. Legend.* a Vestal virgin who became the mother, by Mars, of Romulus and Remus. Also, **Rea Silvia.**

rhe·da (rē′də, rā′-), *n., pl.* **-das, -dae** (-dē, -dī). an elaborate Roman cart drawn by mules or oxen. [< L *rhēda,* var. *raeda, rēda* traveling-carriage, prob. < Celt]

Rhee (rē), *n.* **Syng·man** (sing′mən), 1875–1965, president of Korea 1948–60.

Rheims (rēmz; *Fr.* RANS), *n.* Reims.

Rheims′-Dou′ay Bi′ble (rēmz′dōō′ā). See **Douay Bible.** Also called **Rheims′-Dou′ay Ver′sion.**

Rhein (rīn), *n.* German name of the **Rhine.**

Rhein·gau (rīn′gou), *n.* a small wine-growing region in Hesse, in central West Germany, on the Rhine.

Rhein·gold (rīn′gōld′), *n.* See **Ring of the Nibelung.** Also, **Rhinegold.**

Rhein·hes·sen (rīn′hes′ən), *n.* a former Prussian province, now part of Hesse, West Germany. Also, **Rhenish Hesse.**

Rhein·land (RīN′länt′), *n.* German name of **Rhineland.**

Rhein·land-Pfalz (RīN′länt′pfälts′), *n.* German name of **Rhineland-Palatinate.**

Rhei·ta (rī′tə), *n.* a crater in the fourth quadrant of the face of the moon: about 42 miles in diameter.

Rhei′ta Val′ley, a valley in the fourth quadrant of the face of the moon near the crater Rheita: about 115 miles long and 15 miles wide at its widest point.

rhe·mat·ic (ri mat′ik), *adj.* **1.** pertaining to the formation of words. **2.** pertaining to or derived from a verb. [< Gk *rhēmatik(ós)* belonging to a word, equiv. to *rhēmat-* (s. of *rhēma*) word + *-ikos* -IC]

Rhe·ne (rē′nē), *n.* (in the *Iliad*) the mistress of Oileus and the mother of Medon.

rhe·nic (rē′nik), *adj. Chem.* of or containing rhenium. [RHEN(IUM) + -IC]

Rhen·ish (ren′ish), *adj.* **1.** of the river Rhine or the regions bordering on it. —*n.* **2.** *Brit.* See **Rhine wine.** [< L *Rhēn(us)* RHINE + -ISH[1]; r. ME *Rhinisch* < OHG]

Rhen′ish Hes′se, Rheinhessen.

rhe·ni·um (rē′nē əm), *n. Chem.* a rare metallic element of the manganese subgroup: used, because of its high melting point, in platinum-rhenium thermocouples. *Symbol:* Re; *at. no.:* 75; *at. wt.:* 186.2. [< NL, equiv. to L *Rhēn(us)* RHINE + *-ium* -IUM]

rheo-, a learned borrowing from Greek meaning "flow," "current," "stream," used in the formation of compound words: *rheoscope.* Cf. **-rrhea.** [comb. form repr. Gk *rhéos* anything flowing]

re·vote′, *v.*, **-vot·ed, -vot·ing.**
re′vote, *n.*
re·voy′age, *n., v.*, **-aged, -ag·ing.**
re·wa′ger, *v., n.*
re·wake′, *v.*, **-waked** or **-woke, -wak·ing.**
re·wak′en, *v.*
re·warm′, *v.*
re·warn′, *v.t.*
re·war′rant, *v.t.*
re·wash′, *v.*
re·wa′ter, *v.*
re·wax′, *v.*
re·weak′en, *v.*
re·wear′, *v.*, **-wore, -wear·ing.**
re·weave′, *v.*, **-wove** or (*Rare*) **-weaved; -weav·ing.**
re·wed′, *v.*, **-wed·ded, -wed·ding.**
re·weigh′, *v.*
re·weld′, *v.*
re·wet′, *v.* **-wet** or **-wet·ted, -wet·ting.**
re·wid′en, *v.*
re·wind′, *v.*, **-wound** or (*Rare*) **-wind·ed; -wind·ing.**
re·work′, *v.*, **-worked** or **-wrought, -work·ing.**
re·wound′, *v.t.*
re·wrap′, *v.*, **-wrapped** or **-wrapt, -wrap·ping.**
re·yoke′, *v.t.*, **-yoked, -yok·ing.**
re·zone′, *v.t.*, **-zoned, -zon·ing.**

rheo., rheostat; rheostats.

rhe·ol·o·gy (rē ol′ə jē), *n.* the study of the deformation and flow of matter. [RHEO- + -LOGY] —**rhe·o·log·ic** (rē′ə loj′ik), **rhe′o·log′i·cal,** *adj.* —**rhe·ol′o·gist,** *n.*

rhe·om·e·ter (rē om′i tər), *n.* an instrument for measuring the flow of fluids, esp. blood. [RHEO- + -METER] —**rhe·o·met·ric** (rē′ə me′trik), *adj.* —**rhe·om′e·try,** *n.*

rhe·o·pex·y (rē′ə pek′sē), *n.* *Physical Chem.* the property exhibited by certain slow-gelling, thixotropic sols of gelling more rapidly when the containing vessel is shaken gently. [RHEO- + *-pexy* < Gk *-pēxia,* deriv. of *pêxis* a fixing, solidity; see -Y³] —**rhe·o·pec·tic** (rē′ə-pek′tik), *adj.*

rhe·o·re·cep·tor (rē′ō ri sep′tər), *n.* a receptor of fishes and aquatic amphibians stimulated by water currents. [RHEO- + RECEPTOR]

rhe·o·scope (rē′ə skōp′), *n.* an instrument which indicates the presence of an electric current. [RHEO- + -SCOPE] —**rhe·o·scop·ic** (rē′ə skop′ik), *adj.*

rhe·o·stat (rē′ə stat′), *n.* *Elect.* an adjustable resistor so constructed that its resistance may be changed without opening the circuit in which it is connected, thereby controlling the current in the circuit. [RHEO- + -STAT] —**rhe′o·stat′ic,** *adj.*

rhe·o·tax·is (rē′ə tak′sis), *n.* *Biol.* oriented movement of an organism in response to a current of fluid, esp. water. [RHEO- + -TAXIS] —**rhe·o·tac·tic** (rē′ə-tak′tik), *adj.*

rhe·o·tron (rē′ə tron′), *n.* *Physics.* (formerly) a betatron. [RHEO- + -TRON]

rhe·o·trope (rē′ə trōp′), *n.* *Elect.* a commutator. [RHEO- + -TROPE]

rhe·ot·ro·pism (rē o′trə piz′əm), *n.* the effect of a current of water upon the direction of plant growth. [RHEO- + -TROPISM] —**rhe·o·trop·ic** (rē′ə trop′ik), *adj.*

rhe·sus (rē′səs), *n.* **1.** a macaque, *Macaca mulatta,* of India, used in experimental medicine. **2.** (*cap.*) *Class. Myth.* a Thracian ally of Troy whose horses were captured by Odysseus and Diomedes to prevent them from eating Trojan fodder or drinking from the Xanthus, since it was foretold that if the horses did so, Troy would not fall. —**rhe·sian** (rē′shən), *adj.*

Rhe′sus fac′tor (rē′səs). See **Rh factor.**

rhet., **1.** rhetoric. **2.** rhetorical.

Rhe·tian (rē′shən, -shē ən), *n., adj.* Rhaeto-Romanic.

Rhe·tic (rē′tik), *adj.* *Stratig.* Rhaetic.

rhe·tor (rē′tər), *n.* **1.** a master or teacher of rhetoric. **2.** an orator. [< L *rhētor* < Gk *rhḗtōr;* r. ME *rethor* < ML]

rhet·o·ric (ret′ər ik), *n.* **1.** the study of the effective use of language. **2.** the ability to use language effectively. **3.** the art or science of all specialized literary uses of language in prose or verse, including the figures of speech. **4.** the art of prose in general as opposed to verse. **5.** (in prose or verse) the undue use of exaggeration or display; bombast. **6.** (formerly) the study of the composition and delivery of persuasive speeches; the art of oratory. **7.** (in classical oratory) the art of influencing the thought and conduct of one's hearers. **8.** a work on rhetoric. [< L *rhētoric(a)* < Gk *rhētorikḗ* (*téchnē*) rhetorical (art); r. ME *rethorik* < ML *rēthorica*]

rhe·tor·i·cal (ri tôr′i kəl, -tor′-), *adj.* **1.** of, concerned with, or having the nature of rhetoric. **2.** used for, belonging to, or concerned with mere style or effect. **3.** marked by or tending to use bombast. [late ME < L *rhētoric(us)* (< Gk *rhētorikós*) + -AL¹] —**rhe·tor′i·cal·ly,** *adv.* —**rhe·tor′i·cal·ness,** *n.*

rhetor′ical ques′tion, a question asked solely to produce an effect or to make an asseveration and not to elicit a reply, as, "What is so rare as a day in June?"

rhetor′ical stress′, stress required by the meaning of a line, as distinguished from that required by the meter.

rhet·o·ri·cian (ret′ə rish′ən), *n.* **1.** an expert in the art of rhetoric. **2.** a person who writes or speaks in an elaborate or exaggerated style. **3.** a person who teaches rhetoric. [ME *rethoricien* < MF *rethorique* RHETORIC + *-ien* -IAN]

rheum (ro͞om), *n.* **1.** a thin, serous or catarrhal discharge. **2.** catarrh; cold. [ME *reume* < L *rheuma* < Gk *rheûma* (*rhé(ein)* (to) flow + *-ma* n. suffix of result)] —**rheum′ic,** *adj.*

rheu·mat·ic (ro͞o mat′ik), *Pathol.* —*adj.* **1.** pertaining to or of the nature of rheumatism. **2.** affected with or subject to rheumatism. —*n.* **3.** one affected with or subject to rheumatism. [ME *reumatik* < LL *rheumaticus* < Gk *rheumatikós,* equiv. to *rheumat-* (s. of *rheûma;* see RHEUM) + *-ikos* -IC] —**rheu·mat′i·cal·ly,** *adv.*

rheumat′ic fe′ver, *Pathol.* a serious disease, usually affecting children, characterized by fever, swelling and pain in the joints, sore throat, and cardiac involvement.

rheumat′ic heart′ disease′, *Pathol.* damage to the heart, esp. to the valves, as a result of rheumatic fever, characterized by inflammation of the myocardium or scarring and malfunction of the heart valves.

rheu·ma·tism (ro͞o′mə tiz′əm), *n.* *Pathol.* **1.** any disorder of the extremities or back, characterized by pain and stiffness. **2.** See **rheumatic fever.** [< LL *rheumatism(us)* catarrh, rheum < Gk *rheumatismós,* equiv. to *rheumat-* (s. of *rheûma;* see RHEUM) + *-ismos* -ISM]

rheu·ma·tism-root (ro͞o′mə tiz′əm ro͞ot′, -ro͝ot′), *n.* See **spotted wintergreen.**

rheu·ma·toid (ro͞o′mə toid′), *adj.* **1.** resembling rheumatism. **2.** rheumatic. Also, **rheu′ma·toi′dal.** [< Gk *rheumat-* (s. of *rheûma;* see RHEUM) + -OID] —**rheu′ma·toi′dal·ly,** *adv.*

rheu′matoid arthri′tis, *Pathol.* a chronic disease marked by signs and symptoms of inflammation of the joints, frequently accompanied by marked deformities, and ordinarily associated with manifestations of a general, or systemic, affliction.

rheum·y (ro͞o′mē), *adj.,* **rheum·i·er, rheum·i·est.** pertaining to, causing, full of, or affected with rheum. [RHEUM + -Y¹] —**rheum′i·ly,** *adv.* —**rheum′i·ness,** *n.*

rhex·is (rek′sis), *n., pl.* **rhex·es** (rek′sēz). *Med.* rupture, as of a blood vessel, organ, cell, etc. [< NL < Gk: a breaking, cleft, deriv. of *rhḗgnynai* to break, break loose]

Rheydt (rīt), *n.* a city in W West Germany, adjacent to Mönchen-Gladbach. 96,000 (1963).

Rh factor, *Biochem.* any one of a group of inheritable antigens in the red blood cells of most persons, who are therefore said to be Rh-positive. On repeated transfusion into an Rh-negative person, one whose blood cells lack the factor, it causes severe hemolysis of the erythrocytes, that may be transferred to an Rh-negative mother by an Rh-positive fetus and returned to subsequent fetuses to produce erythroblastosis fetalis, and that may cause a severe blood reaction in the mother upon receiving Rh-positive blood. Also called **Rh, Rh., Rhesus factor.** [so called because first found in the blood of rhesus monkeys]

Rhi·an·non (rē′an ən), *n.* *Welsh Legend.* the wife of Pwyll and mother of Pryderi. Accused of having eaten her son, she was forced to do penance until his return. After Pwyll's death she married Manawyddan.

Rhig·mus (rig′məs), *n.* (in the *Iliad*) a Thracian ally of the Trojans, slain by Achilles.

rhig·o·lene (rig′ə lēn′), *n.* *Chem.* an extremely volatile liquid obtained from petroleum: used to produce local anesthesia by freezing. [< Gk *rhîg(os)* frost, cold + -OL² + -ENE]

rhin-, var. of **rhino-** before a vowel: *rhinencephalon.*

rhi·nal (rīn′əl), *adj.* of or pertaining to the nose; nasal. [RHIN- + -AL¹]

rhi·nar·i·um (rī nâr′ē əm), *n., pl.* **-nar·i·a** (-nâr′ē ə). *Zool.* the area of naked, glandular skin surrounding the nostrils of certain mammals. [< NL; see RHIN-, -ARY]

Rhine (rīn), *n.* a river flowing from SE Switzerland through West Germany and the Netherlands into the North Sea: branches off into the Waal, Lek, and IJssel in its lower course. 820 mi. long. German, **Rhein.** French, **Rhin** (RAN). Dutch, **Rijn.**

Rhine·gold (rīn′gōld′), *n.* Rheingold.

Rhine′grave breech′es (rīn′grāv′). See **petticoat breeches.** [named after the *Rhinegrave* of Salm, who introduced the fashion in Paris about 1650]

Rhine·land (rīn′land′, -lənd), *n.* **1.** that part of Germany W of the Rhine. **2.** See **Rhine Province.** German, **Rheinland.**

Rhine·land·er (rīn′lan dər), *n.* a town in N Wisconsin. 8790 (1960).

Rhine·land-Pa·lat·i·nate (rīn′land pə lat′ənāt′, -ənit), *n.* a state in W West Germany; formerly part of Rhine Province. 3,493,000 (1963); 7655 sq. mi. *Cap.:* Mainz. German, **Rheinland-Pfalz.**

rhi·nen·ceph·a·lon (rī′nen sef′ə lon′), *n., pl.* **-lons, -la** (-lə). *Anat.* the part of the cerebrum containing the olfactory structures. [RHIN- + ENCEPHALON] —**rhi·nen·ce·phal·ic** (rī′nen sə fal′ik), **rhi′nen·ceph′a·lous,** *adj.*

Rhine′ Palat′inate, Palatinate (def. 1).

Rhine′ Prov′ince, a former province in W Germany, mostly W of the Rhine: now divided between Rhineland-Palatinate and North Rhine-Westphalia. Also called **Rhineland.** German, **Rheinland.**

rhine·stone (rīn′stōn′), *n.* an artificial gem of paste. [RHINE + STONE (trans. of F *caillou du Rhin*)]

Rhine′ wine′, **1.** any of numerous varieties of wine produced in the Rhine valley. **2.** any of a class of white wines, mostly light, still, and dry.

rhi·ni·tis (rī nī′tis), *n.* *Pathol.* inflammation of the nose or its mucous membrane. [RHIN- + -ITIS]

rhi·no¹ (rī′nō), *n., pl.* **-nos,** (*esp. collectively*) **-no.** a rhinoceros. [by shortening]

rhi·no² (rī′nō), *n.* *Chiefly Brit. Slang.* money; cash. [?]

rhino-, a learned borrowing from Greek meaning "nose," used in the formation of compound words: *rhinology.* Also, *esp. before a vowel,* **rhin-.** [< Gk, comb. form of *rhís* (s. *rhīn-*)]

Rhinoceros (Indian), *Rhinoceros unicornis* (5½ ft. high at shoulder; horn to 2 ft.; total length 13 ft.; tail 2 ft.)

rhi·noc·er·os (rī nos′ər əs), *n., pl.* **-os·es,** (*esp. collectively*) **-os. 1.** any of several large, thick-skinned, perissodactyl mammals of the family *Rhinocerotidae,* of Africa and India, having one or two upright horns on the snout. **2.** *Douay Bible.* unicorn (def. 4). [ME *rinoceros* < LL *rhīnoceros* < Gk *rhīnókerōs,* equiv. to *rhīno-* RHINO- + *kéras* horn (of an animal)]

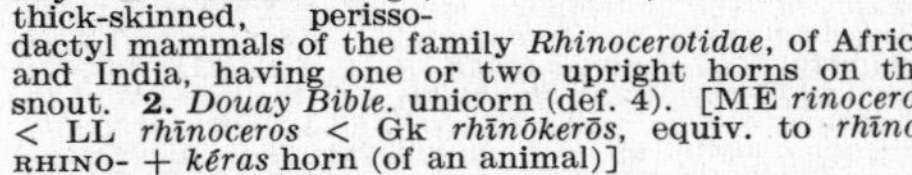

rhinoc′eros bee′tle, any of several scarabaeid beetles, esp. of the genus *Dynastes,* characterized by one or more horns on the head and prothorax.

rhi·noc·er·ot·ic (rī nos′ə rot′ik), *adj.* of, pertaining to, or resembling a rhinoceros. Also, **rhi·no·ce·ri·al** (rī′nō sēr′ē əl), **rhi·noc·er·ine** (rī nos′ər in). [< LL *rhīnocerōtic(us),* equiv. to *rhīnocerōt-* (s. of *rhīnocerōs*) RHINOCEROS + *-icus* -IC]

rhi·no·la·li·a (rī′nəlā′lē ə, -əlāl′yə), *n.* *Speech Pathol.* a voice disorder characterized by defective nasal resonance, esp. when excessive **(rhinolalia aperta),** or insufficient **(rhinolalia clausa).** [RHINO- + -LALIA]

rhinola′lia a·per′ta (ə pûr′tə). See under **rhinolalia.** [< NL: open rhinolalia]

rhinola′lia clau′sa (klô′zə). See under **rhinolalia.** [< NL: closed rhinolalia]

rhi·nol·o·gy (rī nol′ə jē), *n.* the science dealing with the nose and its diseases. [RHINO- + -LOGY] —**rhi·no·log·ic** (rī′nə loj′ik), **rhi′no·log′i·cal,** *adj.* —**rhi·nol′o·gist,** *n.*

rhi·no·plas·ty (rī′nō plas′tē), *n.* *Surg.* plastic surgery of the nose. [RHINO- + -PLASTY] —**rhi′no·plas′tic,** *adj.*

rhi·nor·rhe·a (rī′nō rē′ə), *n.* *Med.* an excessive discharge of mucus from the nose. Also, **rhi′nor·rhoe′a.**

rhi·no·scope (rī′nə skōp′), *n.* *Med.* an instrument for examining the nasal passages. [RHINO- + -SCOPE]

rhi·nos·co·py (rī nos′kə pē), *n.* *Med.* the investigation of the nasal passages. [RHINO- + -SCOPY] —**rhi·no·scop·ic** (rī′nə skop′ik), *adj.*

-rhiza, var. of **-rrhiza.**

rhi·zan·thous (rī zan′thəs), *adj.* flowering directly from the root of the host plant, as a rafflesiaceous plant. [RHIZ- + -ANTHOUS]

rhizo-, a learned borrowing from Greek meaning "root," used in the formation of compound words: *rhizophagous.* Also, *esp. before a vowel,* **rhiz-.** Cf. **-rhiza, -rrhiza.** [< Gk, comb. form of *rhíza*]

rhi·zo·bi·um (rī zō′bē əm), *n., pl.* **-bi·a** (-bē ə). *Bacteriol.* any of several rod-shaped bacteria of the genus *Rhizobium,* found as symbiotic nitrogen fixers in nodules on the roots of the bean, clover, etc. [< NL, equiv. to *rhizo-* RHIZO- + Gk *bí(os)* life + L *-um* n. suffix]

rhi·zo·car·pous (rī′zō kär′pəs), *adj.* *Bot.* having the root perennial but the stem annual, as perennial herbs. Also, **rhi·zo·car·pic** (rī′zō kär′pik). [RHIZO- + -CARPOUS]

rhi·zo·ceph·a·lous (rī′zō sef′ə ləs), *adj.* *Zool.* belonging to the *Rhizocephala,* a group of degenerate hermaphrodite crustaceans which are parasitic chiefly on crabs. [RHIZO- + -CEPHALOUS]

rhi·zo·gen·ic (rī′zō jen′ik), *adj.* *Bot.* producing roots, as certain cells. Also, **rhi·zog·e·nous** (rī zoj′ə nəs). [RHIZO- + -GENIC]

rhi·zoid (rī′zoid), *adj.* **1.** rootlike. —*n.* **2.** (in mosses, ferns, etc.) one of the rootlike filaments by which the plant is attached to the substratum. [RHIZ- + -OID] —**rhi·zoi′dal,** *adj.*

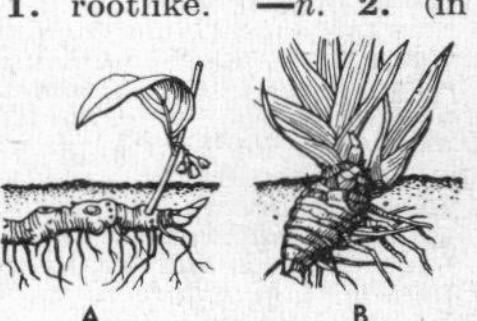

Rhizomes
A, Solomon's seal, *Polygonatum commutatum*
B, Iris. *Iris versicolor*

rhi·zome (rī′zōm), *n.* *Bot.* a rootlike subterranean stem, commonly horizontal in position, which usually produces roots below and sends up shoots progressively from the upper surface. [< NL *rhizom(a)* < Gk *rhízōma* root, stem, deriv. of *rhíza* root] —**rhi·zom·a·tous** (rī zom′ə təs, -zō′mə-), *adj.*

rhi·zo·mor·phous (rī′zō môr′fəs), *adj.* *Bot.* rootlike in form. Also, **rhi′zo·mor′phoid.** [RHIZO- + -MORPHOUS]

rhi·zoph·a·gous (rī zof′ə gəs), *adj.* feeding on roots. [RHIZO- + -PHAGOUS]

rhi·zo·pod (rī′zə pod′), *n.* any protozoan of the class *Rhizopoda,* having pseudopodia. [< NL *Rhizopod(a)* name of the class. See RHIZO-, -POD] —**rhi·zop·o·dan** (rī zop′ə dən), *adj., n.* —**rhi·zop′o·dous,** *adj.*

Rhi·zo·pus (rī′zō pəs, -zə-), *n.* a genus of phycomycetous fungi including the bread mold *R. nigricans.* [< NL, equiv. to *rhizo-* RHIZO- + Gk *poûs* foot]

rhi·zot·o·my (rī zot′ə mē), *n., pl.* **-mies.** *Surg.* the surgical section or cutting of the spinal nerve roots, usually posterior or sensory roots, to eliminate pain or paralysis. [RHIZO- + -TOMY]

Rh-neg·a·tive (är′āch′neg′ə tiv), *adj.* lacking the Rh factor.

rho (rō), *n., pl.* **rhos. 1.** the 17th letter of the Greek alphabet (Ρ, ρ). **2.** the consonant sound represented by this letter. [< Gk]

Rho., Rhodesia. Also, **Rhod.**

rhod-, var. of **rhodo-** before a vowel: *rhodamine.*

Rho·da (rō′də), *n.* a girl's given name.

rho·da·mine (rō′də mēn′, -min), *n.* *Chem.* **1.** a red dye obtained by heating an alkyl aminophenol with phthalic anhydride. **2.** any of various related dyes. [RHOD- + AMINE]

Rho·de (rō′dē), *n.* *Class. Myth.* a nymph born to Halia and Poseidon. She bore eight children by Helius.

Rhode′ Is′land (rōd), a State of the NE United States, on the Atlantic coast: a part of New England; the smallest State in the U.S. 859,488 (1960); 1214 sq. mi. *Cap.:* Providence. *Abbr.:* R.I. —**Rhode′ Is′lander.**

Rhode′ Is′land bent′, a perennial, European pasture grass, *Agrostis capillaris,* naturalized in North America, having red flower clusters.

Rhode′ Is′land Red′, one of an American breed of chickens having dark reddish-brown feathers.

Rhodes (rōdz), *n.* **1. Cecil John,** 1853–1902, English colonial capitalist and government administrator in S Africa. **2. James Ford,** 1848–1927, U.S. historian. **3.** a Greek island in the SE Aegean, off the SW coast of Turkey: the largest of the Dodecanese Islands. 58,946 (1951); 542 sq. mi. **4.** a seaport on this island. 27,393 (1961). Italian, **Rodi.** Greek, **Rhodos. 5. Colossus of,** a huge bronze statue of Apollo that stood at the entrance to the harbor of Rhodes. Cf. **Seven Wonders of the World.**

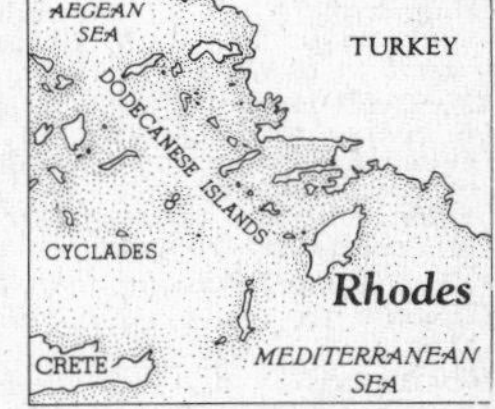

Rho·de·sia (rō dē′zhə), *n.* **1.** Formerly, **Southern Rhodesia.** former name of **Zimbabwe. 2.** a region in S Africa, that comprised the British territories of Northern Rhodesia (now Zambia) and Southern Rhodesia (now Zimbabwe), forming part of the Federation of Rhodesia and Nyasaland. —**Rho·de′sian,** *adj., n.*

Rhode′sia and Nya′saland, Federa′tion of, a former grouping of British territories in S Africa for administrative purposes: comprised of Southern Rhodesia, Zambia, and Malawi. Also called **Central African Federation.**

Rhode′sian man′, an extinct primitive man, *Homo rhodesiensis,* of the Late Pleistocene epoch, whose skeletal remains were found in Northern Rhodesia. —**Rho·de·soid** (rō dē′zoid), *adj.*

Rhodes′ schol′arship, one of a number of scholarships at Oxford University, established by the will of Cecil Rhodes, for selected students (**Rhodes′ schol′ars**) from the British Commonwealth and the United States.

Rho·di·an (rō′dē ən), *adj.* **1.** of or pertaining to the island Rhodes. —*n.* **2.** a native or inhabitant of Rhodes. [Rhod(es) + -ian]

rho·dic (rō′dik), *adj. Chem.* of or containing rhodium, esp. in the tetravalent state. [rhod(ium) + -ic]

rho·di·um (rō′dē əm), *n. Chem.* a silvery-white metallic element of the platinum family, forming salts which give rose-colored solutions: used to electroplate microscopes and instrument parts to prevent corrosion. *Symbol:* Rh; *at. wt.:* 102.905; *at. no.:* 45; *sp. gr.:* 12.5 at 20°C. [< NL; see rhod-, -ium]

rhodo-, a learned borrowing from Greek meaning "rose," used in the formation of compound words: *rhodolite.* Also, *esp. before a vowel,* **rhod-.** [< Gk, comb. form of *rhódon*]

rho·do·chro·site (rō′də krō′sīt), *n.* a mineral, manganese carbonate, $MnCO_3$, commonly containing some iron and calcium, and usually rose-red in color: a minor ore of manganese; manganese spar. Also called **dialogite.** [< Gk *rhodóchrōs* rose-colored (*rhódo(n)* rhodo- + *chrṓs* color) + -ite[1]]

rho·do·den·dron (rō′də den′drən), *n.* any evergreen or deciduous, ericaceous shrub or tree of the genus *Rhododendron,* having showy, pink, purple, or white flowers and oval or oblong leaves. [< L < Gk *rhodódendron* (*rhódo(n)* rhodo- + *déndron* tree)]

rho·do·lite (rōd′ᵊlīt′), *n.* a rose or reddish-violet garnet, similar to pyrope, used as a gem. [rhodo- + -lite]

rho·do·nite (rōd′ᵊnīt′), *n.* a mineral, manganese metasilicate, $MnSiO_3$, occurring usually in rose-red masses, sometimes used as an ornamental stone; manganese spar. [< G *Rhodonit* < Gk *rhódon* rose + G *-it* -ite[1]]

Rhod·o·pe (rod′ə pē, ro dō′-), *n.* **1.** a mountain range in SW Bulgaria. Highest peak, Mus Allah, 9595 ft. **2.** *Class. Myth.* a maiden skilled in hunting, the companion of Artemis.

Rho·do·pis (ro dō′pis), *n. Class. Myth.* a maiden whose sandal was snatched by an eagle and carried to King Psammetichus. Considering this an omen, the king married Rhodopis.

rho·dop·sin (rō dop′sin), *n. Biochem.* a bright-red photosensitive pigment found in the rod-shaped cells of the retina of certain fishes and most vertebrates. It is broken down by the action of dim light into vetinene and opsin. Also called **visual purple, erythropsin.** [rhod- + opsin]

rho·do·ra (rō dōr′ə, -dôr′ə, rə-), *n.* a low, ericaceous shrub, *Rhododendron canadensis,* of North America, having rose-colored flowers which appear before the leaves. [< L *rhodōra* name of a plant]

Rho·dos (rô′thôs), *n.* Greek name of **Rhodes.**

Rho·dus (rō′dəs), *n. Class. Myth.* a son of Aphrodite and Poseidon.

-rhoea, var. of **-rrhea.**

Rhoe·cus (rē′kəs), *n.* **1.** fl. 6th century B.C., Greek sculptor and architect. **2.** *Class. Myth.* a youth blinded for not taking seriously the love offered to him by a dryad.

Rhoe·o (rē′ō), *n. Class. Myth.* a daughter of Chrysothemis and Staphylus who was set adrift in a chest by her father when he learned that she had been seduced by Apollo.

Rhoe·tus (rē′təs), *n. Class. Myth.* one of the Gigantes who made war on the gods.

rhomb (rom, romb), *n.* rhombus. [< L *rhomb(us)*; cf. F *rhombe*]

rhom·ben·ceph·a·lon (rom′ben sef′ə lon′), *n., pl.* **-lons, -la** (-lə). *Anat.* the hindbrain. [rhomb + encephalon]

rhom·bic (rom′bik), *adj.* **1.** having the form of a rhombus. **2.** having a rhombus as base or cross section. **3.** bounded by rhombuses, as a solid. **4.** *Crystall.* orthorhombic. Also, **rhom′bi·cal.** [rhomb + -ic]

rhom·bo·he·dron (rom′bə hē′drən), *n., pl.* **-drons, -dra** (-drə). a solid bounded by six rhombic planes. [< Gk *rhómbo(s)* rhombus + -hedron] —**rhom′bo·he′dral,** *adj.*

rhom·boid (rom′boid), *n.* **1.** an oblique-angled parallelogram with only the opposite sides equal. —*adj.* **2.** Also, **rhom·boi′dal.** having a form like or similar to that of a rhombus; shaped like a rhomboid. [< LL *rhomboī-d(es)* < Gk *rhomboeidḗs* (*schêma*) rhomboid (form, shape). See rhombus, -oid] —**rhom·boi′dal·ly,** *adv.*

Rhomboid

rhom·bus (rom′bəs), *n., pl.* **-bus·es, -bi** (-bī). **1.** an oblique-angled equilateral parallelogram. **2.** a rhombohedron. [< L < Gk *rhómbos* anything that may be spun around, deriv. of *rhémbein* to revolve]

Rhombus

rhon·chus (roŋ′kəs), *n., pl.* **-chi** (-kī). a coarse rattling noise in the bronchial tubes, caused by an accumulation of mucus or other material; râle. [< L: a snoring, croaking < Gk **rhónchos,* var. of *rhénchos*] —**rhon·chi·al** (roŋ′kē əl), **rhon·chal** (roŋ′kəl), *adj.*

Rhon·da (ron′də), *n.* a girl's given name.

Rhon·dda (ron′də), *n.* a city in S Wales. 100,314 (1961).

Rhone (rōn), *n.* **1.** a river flowing from the Alps in S Switzerland through the Lake of Geneva and SE France into the Mediterranean. 504 mi. long. **2.** a department in E central France: wine-growing region. 1,116,664 (1962); 1104 sq. mi. *Cap.:* Lyons. French, **Rhône** (rōn).

Rhone′ wine′, any of numerous varieties of wine produced in the Rhone River valley, between Lyons and the Mediterranean.

rho·ta·cism (rō′tə siz′əm), *n. Phonet.* excessive use of the sound *r,* its misarticulation, or the substitution of another sound for it. [< NL *rhotacism(us)* < Gk **rhōtakismós,* deriv. of *rhōtakízein* to use the letter rho too much] —**rho′ta·cis′tic,** *adj.*

Rh-pos·i·tive (är′āch′poz′i tiv), *adj.* possessing the Rh factor.

rhu·barb (ro͞o′bärb), *n.* **1.** any polygonaceous herb of the genus *Rheum,* as *R. officinale,* having a medicinal rhizome, and *R. Rhaponticum,* having edible leafstalks. **2.** the rhizome of any medicinal species of this plant, forming a combined cathartic and astringent. **3.** the edible fleshy leafstalks of any of the garden species, used in making pies, preserves, etc. **4.** *U.S. Slang.* a quarrel or squabble. [ME *rubarb, reubarb* < OF *r(e)ubarbe* < ML *reubarb(arum)* < Gk *rhêon bárbaron* foreign rhubarb]

rhu′barb and so′da mix′ture, a mild laxative consisting of rhubarb, ipecac, sodium bicarbonate, peppermint spirit, and water, and used esp. for colic in infants.

rhumb (rum, rumb), *n.* **1.** See **rhumb line. 2.** a point of the compass. [< Sp *rumb(o)* < L *rhombus* rhombus]

rhum·ba (rum′bə, ro͝om′-), *n., pl.* **-bas** (-bəz), *v.i.,* **-baed** (bəd), **-ba·ing** (bə iŋ). rumba.

rhum·ba·tron (rum′bə tron′), *n. Electronics.* a cavity resonator. See under **resonator** (def. 4a). [rhumba + -tron]

rhumb′ line′, a curve on the surface of a sphere which cuts all meridians at the same angle. It is the path taken by a vessel or aircraft which maintains a constant compass direction. Also called **loxodrome, rhumb.**

rhy·ac·o·lite (rī ak′ə līt′), *n. Mineral.* a glassy variety of orthoclase found in lava. [< Gk *rhýak-* (s. of *rhýax*) stream of lava + -o- + -lite]

rhyme (rīm), *n., v.,* **rhymed, rhym·ing.** —*n.* **1.** identity in sound of some part, esp. of the end, of words or lines of verse. **2.** a word agreeing with another in terminal sound: Find *is a rhyme for* mind *and* kind. **3.** verse or poetry having correspondence in the terminal sounds of the lines. **4.** a poem or piece of verse having such correspondence. **5.** verse (def. 4). **6. rhyme or reason,** logic, sense, or plan: *After reviewing the dispute the following day, there seemed to be neither rhyme nor reason to it. What rhyme or reason could he have for doing that?* —*v.t.* **7.** to treat in rhyme, as a subject; turn into rhyme, as something in prose. **8.** to compose (verse or the like) in metrical form with rhymes. **9.** to use (a word) as a rhyme to another word; use (words) as rhymes. —*v.i.* **10.** to make rhyme or verse; versify. **11.** to use rhyme in writing verse. **12.** to form a rhyme, as one word or line with another: *I must find some word to rhyme with orange.* **13.** to be composed in metrical form with rhymes, as verse: *He prefers poetry that rhymes.* Also, **rime.** [ME *rime* < OF, deriv. of *rimer* to rhyme < Gallo-Roman *rimāre* to put in a row < OHG *rīm* series, row; prob. not connected with L *rhythmus* rhythm] —**rhym′er,** *n.*

rhyme′ roy′al, *Pros.* a form of verse introduced into English by Chaucer, consisting of seven-line stanzas of iambic pentameter in which there are three rhymes, the first line rhyming with the third, the second with the fourth and fifth, and the sixth with the seventh.

rhyme′ scheme′, the pattern of rhymes used in a poem, usually marked by letters to symbolize correspondences, as rhyme royal, *ababbcc.*

rhyme·ster (rīm′stər), *n.* a writer of inferior verse; poetaster. Also, **rimester.** [rhyme + -ster] —**Syn.** versifier.

rhym′ing slang′, **1.** a form of slang in which a rhyming word or phrase is substituted for the word intended, as *Kate and Sidney* for *steak and kidney* or *khaki rocks* for *army socks.* **2.** a further removal from the original word intended by ellipsis of the rhyming part, as *titfer* for *tit for tat* for *hat.*

rhyn·cho·ce·pha·lian (riŋ′kō sə fāl′yən), *adj.* **1.** belonging or pertaining to the *Rhynchocephalia,* an order of lizardlike reptiles that are extinct except for the tuatara. —*n.* **2.** a rhynchocephalian reptile. [< NL *Rhynchocephali(a)* name of the order < Gk *rhýncho(s)* snout; see cephal-, -ian]

rhy·o·lite (rī′ə līt′), *n.* a fine-grained igneous rock rich in silica: the volcanic equivalent of granite. [*rhyo-* (irreg. < Gk *rhýax* stream of lava) + -lite] —**rhy·o·lit·ic** (rī′ə lit′ik), *adj.*

rhythm (riŧħ′əm), *n.* **1.** movement or procedure with uniform or patterned recurrence of a beat, accent, or the like. **2.** measured movement, as in dancing. **3.** *Music.* **a.** the pattern of regular or irregular pulses caused in music by the occurrence of strong and weak melodic and harmonic beats. **b.** a particular form of this: *duple rhythm; triple rhythm.* **4.** the pattern of recurrent strong and weak accents, vocalization and silence, and the distribution and combination of these elements in speech. **5.** *Pros.* **a.** metrical or rhythmical form; meter. **b.** a particular kind of metrical form. **c.** metrical movement. **6.** *Art, Literature.* a patterned repetition of a motif, formal element, etc., at regular or irregular intervals in the same or a modified form. **7.** the effect produced in a play, film, novel, etc., by the combination or arrangement of formal elements, as length of scenes, speech and description, timing, recurrent themes, etc., to create movement, tension, and emotional value in the development of the plot. **8.** procedure marked by the regular recurrence of particular elements, phases, etc.: *the rhythm of the seasons.* **9.** regular recurrence of elements in a system of motion. **10.** *Physiol.* the regular recurrence of an action or function, as of the beat of the heart, the menstrual cycle, etc. [< L *rhythm(us)* < Gk *rhythmós,* cf. *rheîn* to flow] —**rhythm′less,** *adj.*

rhythm-and-blues (riŧħ′əm ən blo͞oz′), *n.* a folk-based but urbanized form of Negro popular music that is marked by strong, repetitious rhythms and simple melodies and was developed, in a commercialized form, into rock-'n'-roll.

rhyth·mic (riŧħ′mik), *adj.* **1.** cadenced; rhythmical. —*n.* **2.** rhythmics. [< LL *rhythmic(us)* < Gk *rhythmikós.* See rhythm, -ic]

rhyth·mi·cal (riŧħ′mi kəl), *adj.* **1.** periodic, as motion, a drumbeat, etc. **2.** having a flowing rhythm. **3.** of or pertaining to rhythm: *an excellent rhythmical sense.* [rhythmic + -al[1]] —**ryth′mi·cal·ly,** *adv.*

rhyth·mic·i·ty (riŧħ mis′i tē), *n.* the state or quality of being rhythmical. [rhythmic + -ity]

rhyth·mics (riŧħ′miks), *n.* (*construed as sing.*) the science of rhythm and rhythmic forms. Also, **rhythmic.** [rhythm + -ics]

rhyth·mist (riŧħ′mist), *n.* **1.** a person versed in or having a fine sense of rhythm. **2.** a person who uses rhythm in a certain way: *a good rhythmist.* [rhythm + -ist]

rhythm′ meth′od, a method for preventing fertilization by the avoidance of sexual intercourse on the days when conception is most likely to occur. Cf. **safe period.**

rhythm′ stick′, a small wooden stick used, esp. by a child, as a simple percussive instrument in learning the rudiments of musical rhythm.

rhy·ton (rī′ton), *n., pl.* **-ta** (-tə). an ancient Greek drinking horn, made of pottery or bronze, having a base in the form of the head of a woman or animal. [< Gk *rhytón,* neut. of *rhytós* flowing, akin to *rhein* to flow]

Rhyton

R.I., **1.** Queen and Empress. [< L *Regina et Imperātrix*] **2.** King and Emperor. [< L *Rēx et Imperātor*] **3.** Rhode Island.

ri·a (rē′ə), *n.* a long, narrow inlet of a river that gradually decreases in depth from mouth to head. [< Sp *ría* river]

ri·al[1] (rī′əl), *n.* a silver or cupronickel coin and monetary unit of Iran, equal to 100 dinars and equivalent to about .013 of a U.S. dollar. [< Pers < Ar *riyāl* riyal]

ri·al[2] (rī′əl), *n.* ryal.

ri·al[3] (rē ôl′, -äl′), *n.* riyal.

ri·al·to (rē al′tō), *n., pl.* **-tos.** an exchange or mart. [after the Rialto in Venice]

Ri·al·to (rē al′tō; *also for 1, 2, It.* rē äl′tô), *n.* **1.** a commercial center in Venice, Italy, consisting of an island and the surrounding district. **2.** a bridge spanning the Grand Canal in Venice, Italy: constructed of marble in 1590. **3.** a city in SW California, near Los Angeles. 18,567 (1960). **4.** the theater district of a city or town, esp. the area around Broadway in New York City.

ri·ant (rī′ənt), *adj.* laughing; smiling; cheerful; gay. [< F, prp. of *rire* to laugh < L *ridēre*] —**ri′ant·ly,** *adv.*

ri·a·ta (rē ä′tə), *n.* a lariat. Also, **reata.** [< Sp *reata,* deriv. of *reatar* to tie again, equiv. to *re-* re- + *atar* < L *aptāre* to fit]

rib[1] (rib), *n., v.,* **ribbed, rib·bing.** —*n.* **1.** one of a series of curved bones that are articulated with the vertebrae and occur in pairs, 12 in man, on each side of the vertebrate body, certain pairs being connected with the sternum and forming the thoracic wall. See diag. under **skeleton. 2.** a cut of meat, as beef, containing a rib. **3.** some thing or part resembling a rib in form, position, or use, as a supporting or strengthening part. **4.** *Archit.* **a.** any of several archlike members of a vault supporting it at the groins, defining its distinct surfaces, or dividing these surfaces into panels: including ogives and tiercerons. **b.** any of several molded members or moldings, including ridge ribs and liernes, on the surface of a vault accenting the ridges or dividing the surface into panels. **5.** a stiffening beam cast as part of a concrete slab. **6.** a structural member which supports the shape of something: *an umbrella rib.* **7.** *Naut.* any of the curved framing members in a ship's hull that rise upward and outward from the keel; frame. **8.** a primary vein of a leaf. **9.** a vertical ridge in knitted fabrics. **10.** a ridge, as in poplin or rep, caused by heavy yarn. **11.** a wife (in humorous allusion to the creation of Eve. Gen. 2:21–22). **12.** *Ceram.* a scraper for smoothing clay being thrown on a potter's wheel. **13.** a metal ridge running along the top of the barrel of a firearm to simplify aligning the sights. **14.** a longitudinal strip of metal joining the barrels of a double-barreled gun. —*v.t.* **15.** to furnish or strengthen with ribs. **16.** to enclose as with ribs. **17.** to mark with riblike ridges or markings. [ME, OE *rib(b)*; c. G *Rippe*] —**rib′less,** *adj.* —**rib′like′,** *adj.*

rib[2] (rib), *v.t.,* **ribbed, rib·bing.** to tease; make fun of. [appar. short for *rib-tickle* (v.)]

R.I.B.A. See **Royal Institute of British Architects.**

rib·ald (rib′əld), *adj.* **1.** vulgar or indecent in speech, language, etc.; coarsely mocking, abusive, or irreverent; scurrilous. —*n.* **2.** a ribald person. [ME *ribald, ribaud* < OF *ribau(l)d,* deriv. of *riber* to dissipate < MHG *rīben* to rub, be in heat, copulate] —**rib′ald·ly,** *adv.*

—**Syn. 1.** loose, low, indecent, obscene, gross.
—**Ant. 1.** pure.

rib·ald·ry (rib′əl drē), *n.* **1.** ribald character, as of language; scurrility. **2.** ribald speech. [ME *ribaudrie* < OF. See ribald, -ry]

rib·and (rib′ənd), *n.* **1.** Also, **ribband.** *Heraldry.* a diminutive of the bend, about one-eighth the usual width. **2.** *Archaic.* ribbon. [ME: ribbon]

ri·bat (ri bät′), *n. Islam.* a building housing a community of Sufis. [< Ar *ribāṭ* hostelry]

rib·band[1] (rib′band′, rib′ənd, -ən), *n.* **1.** *Shipbuilding.* a strip of wood or metal running fore-and-aft along newly erected frames to keep them in the proper position until the shell planking or plating is in place. **2.** *Carpentry.* ribbon (def. 7). **3.** *Naut.* ribbon (def. 9). [rib[1] + band[2]]

rib·band[2] (rib′ənd), *n. Heraldry.* riband.

ribbed′ toad′. See **tailed frog.**

Rib·ben·trop (rib′ən trŏp′), *n.* **Jo·a·chim von** (yō′ä ḵʜim fən), 1893–1946, German leader in the Nazi party: minister of foreign affairs 1938–45.

rib·bing (rib′iŋ), *n.* **1.** ribs collectively. **2.** an assemblage or arrangement of ribs. [rib[1] + -ing[1]]

rib·ble-rab·ble (rib′əl rab′əl), *n.* **1.** a disorderly crowd; rabble. **2.** loose or offensive chatter. [gradational redupl. of rabble[1]]

rib·bon (rib′ən), *n.* **1.** a woven strip or band of fine material, as silk or rayon, varying in width and finished off at the edges, used for ornament, tying, etc. **2.** material in such strips. **3.** anything resembling or suggesting a ribbon or woven band. **4. ribbons,** torn or ragged strips; shreds: *clothes torn to ribbons.* **5.** a long, thin flexible band of metal, as for a spring, a band saw, a tapeline, etc. **6.** a band of inked material used in a typewriter, adding machine, etc., that supplies ink for printing the figure on the striking typeface onto the paper beneath. **7.** Also, **ribband.** Also called **ledger, ledger board, rib′bon strip′.** *Carpentry.* a thin horizontal piece let into studding to support the ends of joists. **8.** *Archit.* came[2]. **9.** Also, **ribband.** *Naut.* a distinctive narrow band or stripe painted along the exterior of a hull. **10.** *Shipbuilding.* ribband[1] (def. 1). **11.** a strip of material, as satin or rayon, being or representing a medal or similar decoration, esp. a military one: *an overseas ribbon.* **12. ribbons,** reins for driving. **—*v.t.*** **13.** to adorn with ribbon. **14.** to streak or mark with something suggesting ribbon. **15.** to separate into or reduce to ribbonlike strips. **—*v.i.*** **16.** to form in ribbonlike strips. Also **riband** (for defs. 7, 9). [ME *riban* < OF, var. of *r(e)uban*, ? < Gmc. See RUDDY, BAND[2]] **—rib′bon·like′, rib′-bon·y,** *adj.*

rib′bon build′ing, *Brit.* the construction of ribbon developments.

rib′bon bush′. See **centipede plant.**

rib′bon cop′y, the original copy of a number of typewritten copies (distinguished from *carbon copy*).

rib′bon devel′opment, *Brit.* a group of stores and homes, usually unplanned, along a highway leading into a town or city; a subdivision built along a highway.

rib·bon·fish (rib′ən fish′), *n., pl.* (*esp. collectively*) **-fish,** (*esp. referring to two or more kinds or species*) **-fish·es. 1.** any of several marine fishes of the family *Trachipteridae*, having a long, compressed, ribbonlike body. **2.** any of several related fishes, as the oarfish and crestfish. **3.** any of several unrelated but similar fishes, as the cutlassfish and jackknife-fish. [RIBBON + FISH]

rib′bon mi′crophone, a microphone having a thin, metallic ribbon mounted in the field of a permanent magnet so that motion imparted to the ribbon by sound waves causes corresponding changes in the voltage across it.

rib′bon snake′, a slender, long-tailed garter snake, *Thamnophis sauritus*, of eastern and central North America, having a brownish body marked with longitudinal yellow or orange stripes.

rib·bon·wood (rib′ən wo͝od′), *n.* a tree, *Plagianthus betulinus*, of New Zealand, having coarsely toothed leaves and clusters of small, yellowish white flowers. [RIBBON + WOOD[1]]

rib′bon worm′, a nemertean.

Ri·bei·rão Prê·to (rē′bā ROUN′ pre′to͞o), a city in SE Brazil. 119,429 (1960).

Ri·be·ra (rē ve′rä), *n.* **Jo·sé** (hô se′), ("*Lo Spagnoletto*"), 1588–1656, Spanish painter.

Ri·be·ral·ta (rē′ve räl′tä), *n.* a city in N Bolivia. 6549 (1950).

Rib·i·coff (rib′ə kôf′, -kof′), *n.* **Abraham A.,** born 1910, U.S. politician: Secretary of Health, Education, and Welfare 1961–62.

ri·bo·fla·vin (rī′bō flā′vin, rī′bō flā′vin), *n.* *Biochem.* an orange-yellow, crystalline compound derived from ribose, $C_{17}H_{22}N_4O_6$, a factor of the vitamin-B complex essential for growth, found in milk, fresh meat, eggs, leafy vegetables, etc., or made synthetically, and used in enriching flour, in vitamin preparations, and in treating facial lesions. Also, **ri·bo·fla·vine** (rī′bō flā′vin, -vēn). Also called **lactoflavin, vitamin B_2, vitamin G.** [RIBO(SE) + FLAVIN]

ri·bo·nu·cle·ase (rī′bō no͞o′klē ās′, -nyo͞o′-), *n.* *Biochem.* any of the class of enzymes that catalyze the hydrolysis of RNA. [RIBONUCLE(IC ACID) + -ASE]

ri′bo·nu·cle′ic ac′id (rī′bō no͞o klē′ik, -nyo͞o-, rī′-), *Biochem.* See **RNA.** Also, **ri′bose nucle′ic ac′id.** [RIBO(SE) + NUCLEIC]

ri·bose (rī′bōs), *n.* *Chem.* a white, crystalline, water-soluble, slightly sweet solid, $HOCH_2(CHOH)_3CHO$, a pentose sugar obtained by the hydrolysis of RNA. [alter. of ARABINOSE]

ri·bo·so (ri bō′sō), *n., pl.* **-sos.** rebozo.

ri·bo·some (rī′bə sōm′), *n.* *Biol.* (in the cytoplasm of a cell) any of several minute, angular or spherical particles that are composed of protein and RNA. [RIBO(SE) + -SOME[3]]

ri·bo·zo (ri bō′zō), *n., pl.* **-zos.** rebozo.

rib·wort (rib′wûrt′), *n.* **1.** a plantain, *Plantago lanceolata*, having narrow leaves with prominent ribs. **2.** any of various similar plantains. [RIB[1] + WORT[2]]

Ri·car·do (ri kär′dō), *n.* **David,** 1772–1823, English economist.

ri·cas·so (ri kas′ō), *n., pl.* **-sos.** a flat, squared area of a sword blade next to the hilt. [< It: lit., heel]

Ric·ca′ti equa′tion (ri kä′tē; *It.* Rēk kä′tē), *Math.* a differential equation, $\frac{dy}{dx} + fy^2 + gy + h = 0$, where f, g, and h are functions of x. [named after J. F. *Riccati* (1676–1754), Italian mathematician]

Ric·ci (Rēt′chē), *n.* **Se·bas·tia·no** (se′bäs tyä′nô), 1660?–1734, Italian painter.

Ric·cio (*It.* Rēt′chō), *n.* **Da·vid** (*It.* dä′vēd). See **Rizzio.**

Ric·ci·o·li (rich′ē ō′lē), *n.* a walled plain in the third quadrant of the face of the moon: about 100 miles in diameter.

Ric·ci·us (rich′ē əs, rik′-), *n.* a crater in the fourth quadrant of the face of the moon: about 50 miles in diameter.

rice (rīs), *n., adj., v.,* **riced, ric·ing.** **—*n.*** **1.** the starchy seeds or grain of a grass, *Oryza sativa*, cultivated in warm climates and used for food. **2.** the plant itself. **—*adj.*** **3.** noting a size of anthracite whose longest dimension is more than 3/16 of an inch and less than 5/16 of an inch. **—*v.t.*** **4.** to reduce to a form resembling rice: *to rice potatoes.* [ME *ris* < OF < It *riso* << Gk *óryzon*, var. of *óryza*; of Eastern orig.]

Rice (rīs), *n.* **1. Elmer,** 1892–1967, U.S. playwright. **2. Grant·land** (grant′lənd), 1880–1954, U.S. journalist. **3.** a boy's or girl's given name.

rice′ bean′, a weakly climbing, annual herb, *Phaseolus calcaratus*, of Asia, having yellow flowers, grown for its edible red, black, brown, or straw-colored seeds.

rice·bird (rīs′bûrd′), *n.* **1.** *Southern U.S.* the bobolink. **2.** See **Java sparrow. 3.** any of several other birds that frequent rice fields. [RICE + BIRD]

Rice′ Lake′, a town in NW Wisconsin. 7303 (1960).

rice′ pa′per, 1. a thin paper made from the straw of rice, as in China. **2.** a Chinese paper consisting of the pith of certain plants cut and pressed into thin sheets.

rice′-pa·per tree′ (rīs′pā′pər), an Asiatic, araliaceous shrub or small tree, *Tetrapanax papyriferum*, the pith of which is used in making rice paper, cultivated as an ornamental in the warmer parts of the U.S.

ric·er (rī′sər), *n.* an implement for ricing potatoes, squash, etc., by pressing them through small holes. [RICE + -ER[1]]

ri·cer·car (rē′chər kär′), *n.* **1.** *Music.* a chiefly polyphonic instrumental form of the 16th and 17th centuries closely resembling the vocal motet in structure and style. **2.** a composition, esp. for a keyboard instrument, having this form. Also, **ricercare, ri·cer·ca·ta** (rē′chər kä′tə). [apocopated var. of RICERCARE]

ri·cer·ca·re (rē′chər kär′ā; *It.* Rē′cher kä′Re), *n., pl.* **-ca·ri** (-kär′ē; *It.* -kä′Rē). ricercar. [< It, n. use of *ricercare* to seek; see RESEARCH]

rice′ wee′vil, a brown weevil, *Sitophilus oryzae*, that infests, breeds in, and feeds on stored grains, esp. rice.

ric·ey (rī′sē), *adj.,* **-ey·er, -ey·est.** pertaining to, resembling, or containing rice: *a ricey dish; ricey flavor.* [RICE + -Y[1]]

rich (rich), *adj.* **1.** having wealth or great possessions; abundantly supplied with resources, means, or funds: *a rich man; a rich nation.* **2.** abounding in natural resources: *a rich territory.* **3.** having wealth or valuable resources (usually fol. by *in*): *a country rich in traditions.* **4.** abounding (usually fol. by *in* or *with*): *a countryside rich in beauty; a design rich with colors.* **5.** of great value or worth; valuable: *a rich harvest.* **6.** (of food) delectably and perhaps unhealthfully spicy, as a gravy, or sweet and abounding in butter or cream, as a pastry. **7.** costly, expensively elegant, or fine, as dress, jewels, etc. **8.** sumptuous; elaborately abundant: *a rich feast.* **9.** of valuable materials or elaborate workmanship, as buildings, furniture, etc. **10.** abounding in desirable elements or qualities: *a man rich in kindness.* **11.** (of wine) strong and finely flavored. **12.** (of color) deep, strong, or vivid: *rich purple.* **13.** full and mellow in tone: *rich sounds; a rich voice.* **14.** strongly fragrant; pungent: *a rich odor.* **15.** producing or yielding abundantly: *a rich soil.* **16.** abundant, plentiful, or ample: *a rich supply.* **17.** *Informal.* **a.** highly amusing. **b.** ridiculous; absurd. **—*n.*** (*construed as pl.*) **18.** rich persons collectively (usually prec. by *the*): *the rich.* [ME; OE *rīce* (adj.) < Gmc < Celt; c. G *reich* wealthy; akin to L *rēx*, Skt *rāj-* king] **—rich′ly,** *adv.* **—rich′ness,** *n.*

—Syn. 1. well-to-do, moneyed. RICH, AFFLUENT, OPULENT, WEALTHY agree in indicating abundance of possessions. RICH is the general word; it may imply that possessions are newly acquired: *a rich oilman.* WEALTHY suggests permanence, stability, and appropriate surroundings: *a wealthy banker.* AFFLUENT and OPULENT both suggest the possession of great wealth; AFFLUENT especially connoting a handsome income and free expenditure of resources; OPULENT suggesting display or luxuriousness: *an affluent family; opulent circumstances.* **5.** valued. **7.** precious, high-priced, dear. **12.** intense, vibrant. **14.** aromatic. **15.** fruitful, productive, prolific, luxuriant. **16.** bountiful, copious, abounding, bounteous. **—Ant. 1.** poor.

Rich (rich), *n.* a boy's given name, form of **Richard.**

Ri·chard (ri shärd′; *Fr.* Rē shar′), *n.* **Mau·rice** (mô-rēs′; *Fr.* mō Rēs′), ("*the Rocket*"), born 1921, Canadian hockey player.

Rich·ard (rich′ərd), *n.* Also, **Rychard.** a boy's given name.

Richard I, ("*Richard the Lion-Hearted,*" "*Richard Coeur de Lion*") 1157–99, king of England 1189–99.

Richard II, 1. 1367–1400, king of England 1377–99 (successor to and grandson of Edward III; son of Edward, Prince of Wales). **2.** (*italics*) a drama (1595?) by Shakespeare.

Richard III, 1. (*Duke of Gloucester*) 1452–85, king of England 1483–85. **2.** (*italics*) a drama (1592–93?) by Shakespeare.

Rich′ard Coeur′ de Li′on (kûr′də lē′ən; *Fr.* kœR də lē ôN′). See **Richard I.**

Rich′ard Co′ry (kôr′ē, kōr′ē), a poem (1897) by Edwin Arlington Robinson.

Rich·ar·dine (rich′ər dēn′), *n.* a girl's given name.

Rich′ard Roe′ (rō), a fictitious personage in legal proceedings, used esp. as the second such name when there are involved two persons whose real names cannot be ascertained. Cf. **Jane Doe, John Doe.**

Rich·ards (rich′ərdz), *n.* **1. Dickinson Wood·ruff** (wo͝od′ruf), 1895–1973, U.S. physician: Nobel prize 1956. **2. I(vor) A(rmstrong)** (ī′vər, ē′vər), 1893–1979, English literary critic in the U.S. **3. Theodore William,** 1868–1928, U.S. chemist: Nobel prize 1914.

Rich·ard·son (rich′ərd sən), *n.* **1. Henry Handel** (*Henrietta Richardson Robertson*), 1870–1946, Australian novelist. **2. Henry Hob·son** (hob′sən), 1838–86, U.S. architect. **3. Sir Owen Williams,** 1879–1959, English physicist: Nobel prize 1928. **4. Sir Ralph (David),** born 1902, English actor. **5. Samuel,** 1689–1761, English novelist. **6. Tony,** born 1928, English motion-picture and theatrical director. **7. Walter Hart,** 1880–1961, U.S. journalist. **8.** a city in NE Texas, near Dallas. 16,810 (1960).

Rich′ardson ground′ squir′rel, a ground squirrel, *Citellus richardsoni*, of the northwestern U.S. and adjacent regions in Canada. Also called **flickertail.** [named after Sir John *Richardson* (1787–1865), Scottish naturalist]

Rich·e·bourg (rish′ə bo͝org′, rē′shə-; *Fr.* Rēshə-bo͞oR′), *n.* a red wine from Burgundy.

Rich·e·lieu (rish′ə lo͞o′; *Fr.* Rēshə lyœ′), *n.* **1. Armand Jean du Ples·sis** (äR mäN′ zhäN dY ple sē′), **Duc de,** 1585–1642, French cardinal and statesman. **2.** a river in SE Canada, in Quebec, flowing N from Lake Champlain to the St. Lawrence. 210 mi. long.

rich·es (rich′iz), *n.pl.* abundant and valuable possessions; wealth. [late ME, pl. of ME *riche* wealth, power (OE *rīce* power, rule; c. G *Reich* realm); confused with ME *richesse* wealth < OF, equiv. to *riche* wealthy (< Gmc; see RICH) + *-esse* -ESS]

Ri·chet (ri shā′; *Fr.* Rē she′), *n.* **Charles Ro·bert** (sharl Rô beR′), 1850–1935, French physician: Nobel prize 1913.

Rich·field (rich′fēld′), *n.* **1.** a city in E Minnesota, near Minneapolis. 42,523 (1960). **2.** a town in central Utah. 4412 (1960).

Rich·ie (rich′ē), *n.* a boy's given name, form of **Richard.**

Ri·chier (Rē shyā′), *n.* **Ger·maine** (zheR men′), 1904–59, French sculptor.

Rich·land (rich′lənd), *n.* a city in SE Washington, on the Columbia River: residential and administrative quarters for the Hanford Works. 23,548 (1960). Cf. **Hanford** (def. 2).

Rich′land Cen′ter, a town in central Wisconsin. 4746 (1960).

Rich′land Hills′, a town in central Texas. 7804 (1960).

Rich·lands (rich′ləndz), *n.* a town in SW Virginia. 4963 (1960).

Rich·mond (rich′mənd), *n.* **1.** a port in and the capital of Virginia, in the E part, on the James River: capital of the Confederacy 1861–65. 219,958 (1960). **2.** a borough of SW New York City, comprising Staten Island. 221,991 (1960); 60.3 sq. mi. **3.** a seaport in W California, on San Francisco Bay. 71,854 (1960). **4.** a city in E Indiana. 44,149 (1960). **5.** a city in N Surrey, SE England, on the Thames, near London: site of Kew Gardens. 41,002 (1961). **6.** a town in NW Missouri. 4604 (1960). **7.** a town in S Texas. 3668 (1960). **8.** a town in SE Michigan. 2667 (1960). **9.** a boy's given name.

Rich′mond Heights′, 1. a city in E Missouri, near St. Louis. 15,622 (1960). **2.** a town in N Ohio. 5068 (1960). **3.** a town in S Florida. 4311 (1960).

Rich′mond Hill′, a town in central North Carolina. 2943 (1960).

rich′ rhyme′, *Pros.* See **rime riche.**

Rich·ter (rik′tər; *Ger., Russ.* RIKH′tər), *n.* **1. Conrad,** 1890–1968, U.S. novelist. **2. Jean Paul Frie·drich** (zhäN poul fRē′dRikh), ("*Jean Paul*"), 1763–1825, German author. **3. Svia·to·slav (Te·o·fi·lo·vich)** (svyä′to släf te′o fē′lo vich), born 1915, Russian pianist.

Rich′ter scale′, a scale, ranging from 1 to 10, for indicating the intensity of an earthquake. [named after C. F. *Richter* (born 1900), U.S. seismologist]

Rich·ter und sein Hen·ker, Der (*Ger.* der RIKH′-tər o͝ont zīn heng′kər). See **Judge and His Hangman, The.**

Richt·ho·fen (RIKHt′hō′fən), *n.* **Baron Man·fred von** (män′fRāt fən), 1892–1918, German aviator.

rich-voiced (rich′voist′), *adj.* having a full, mellow voice: *The rich-voiced preacher stirred his congregation.*

rich·weed (rich′wēd′), *n.* See **white snakeroot.** [RICH + WEED[1]]

Rich·wood (rich′wo͝od′), *n.* a town in central West Virginia. 4110 (1960).

ri·cin (rī′sin, ris′in), *n.* *Chem.* a white, poisonous, protein powder from the bean of the castor-oil plant. [< NL *Ricin(us)* name of genus, L: castor-oil plant]

ric·in·o·le·ic (ris′ə nō lē′ik, -nō′lē ik), *adj.* *Chem.* of or derived from ricinoleic acid. [< L *ricin(us)* castor-oil plant + OLEIC]

ric′inole′ic ac′id, *Chem.* a colorless to yellow, viscous, liquid, water-insoluble, unsaturated hydroxyl acid, $C_{17}H_{32}(OH)COOH$, occurring in castor oil in the form of the glyceride: used chiefly in soaps and textile finishing.

ric·in·o·le·in (ris′ə nō′lē in), *n.* *Chem.* the glyceride of ricinoleic acid, the chief constituent of castor oil. [RICINOLE(IC) + -IN[2]]

ric′i·nus oil′ (ris′ə nəs), *Chem.* See **castor oil.** [< L *ricinus* castor-oil plant]

rick[1] (rik), *n.* **1.** a large stack or pile of hay, straw, corn, or the like, in a field, esp. when thatched or covered by a tarpaulin; an outdoor or makeshift mow. **2.** a frame of horizontal bars and vertical supports, as used to hold barrels in a distillery, boxes in a warehouse, etc. **—*v.t.*** **3.** to form grain into a stack or pile. [ME *rek(e), reek,* OE *hrēac;* akin to Icel *hraukr,* OFris *reak,* MD *rooc, roke*]

rick[2] (rik), *v.t., v.i., n.* *Brit. Dial.* wrick.

Rick (rik), *n.* a boy's given name, form of **Eric** or **Richard.**

rick′ cloth′, *Brit. Dial.* a canvas cover; tarpaulin.

Rick·en·back·er (rik′ən bak′ər), *n.* **Edward Vernon** ("*Eddie*"), 1890–1973, U.S. aviator and aviation executive.

rick·ets (rik′its), *n.* *Pathol.* a disease of childhood, characterized by softening of the bones as a result of malnutrition, ordinarily lack of Vitamin D, or of insufficient ingestion of calcium, or both, and often resulting in deformities. [?]

rick·ett·si·a (ri ket′sē ə), *n., pl.* **-si·ae** (-sē ē′), **-si·as** (-sē əz). any of several bacterialike microorganisms of the genus *Rickettsia*, parasitic on arthropods and pathogenic for man and animals. [named after Howard T. *Ricketts* (1871–1910), American pathologist; see -IA] **—rick·ett′si·al,** *adj.*

rick·et·y (rik′i tē), *adj.* **1.** likely to fall or collapse; shaky: *a rickety chair.* **2.** feeble in the joints; tottering; infirm: *a rickety old man.* **3.** old, dilapidated, or in disrepair. **4.** irregular, as motion or action. **5.** affected with or suffering from rickets. **6.** pertaining to or of the nature of rickets. [RICKET(S) + -Y[1]] **—rick′et·i·ness,** *n.*

rick·ey (rik′ē), *n., pl.* **-eys.** a drink made with lime juice, carbonated water, and a spirituous liquor, esp. gin. [after a Colonel *Rickey*]

rick·le (rik′əl), *Scot. and North Eng.* **—*n.*** **1.** a loose heap, pile, or stack, as of hay, peat, or odds and ends. **—*v.t.*** **2.** to form a pile or heap; stack loosely. [? < Scand]

Rick·o·ver (rik′ō vər), *n.* **Hyman George,** 1900–86, U.S. naval officer, born in Poland.

rick·rack (rik′rak′), *n.* a narrow, zigzag braid or ribbon used as a trimming on clothing, linens, etc. Also, **ricrac.** [gradational redupl. of RACK[1]]

rick·shaw (rik′shô′), *n.* jinrikisha. Also, **rick′sha, rikisha, rikshaw.** [by shortening and contr.]

Rick·wood (rik′wo͝od′), *n.* a boy's given name.

Rick·y (rik′ē), *n.* a boy's given name, form of **Rick.** Also, **Rick′ie.**

ric·o·chet (rik′ə shā′ *or, esp. Brit.,* -shet′), *n., v.,* **-cheted** (-shād′), **-chet·ing** (-shā′ing) or (*esp. Brit.*) **-chet·ted** (-shet′id), **-chet·ting** (-shet′ing). —*n.* **1.** the motion of an object or a projectile in rebounding or deflecting one or more times from the surface over which it is passing or against which it hits a glancing blow. —*v.i.* **2.** to move in this way, as a projectile. [< F < ?] —**Syn. 2.** rebound, deflect, glance.

ri·cot·ta (ri kot′ə, -kô′tə; *It.* rē kôt′tä), *n.* a soft, Italian cottage cheese. [< It < L *recocta,* fem. of *recoctus,* ptp. of *recoquere* to re-cook. See RE-, COOK[1]]

ric·rac (rik′rak′), *n.* rickrack.

ric′tal bris′tle, a bristlelike feather growing from the base of a bird's bill.

ric·tus (rik′təs), *n., pl.* **-tus, -tus·es. 1.** the gape of the mouth of a bird. **2.** the gaping or opening of the mouth. [< L: wide open mouth, ptp. of *ringī* to open the mouth wide] —**ric′tal,** *adj.*

rid[1] (rid), *v.t.,* **rid** or **rid·ded, rid·ding. 1.** to clear, disencumber, or free of something objectionable (usually fol. by *of*): *I want to rid the house of mice. In my opinion, you're well rid of her.* **2.** to relieve or disembarrass (usually fol. by *of*): *to rid the mind of doubt.* **3.** *Archaic.* to deliver or rescue: *to rid them out of bondage; to rid him from his enemies.* [ME *ridd(en),* OE *(ge)ryddan* to clear (land); c. OIcel *rhydhja* to clear, empty] —**rid′der,** *n.*

rid[2] (rid), *v.* *Archaic.* a pt. and pp. of **ride.**

rid·a·ble (rī′də bəl), *adj.* **1.** capable of being ridden, as a horse. **2.** capable of being ridden over, through, etc., as a road or a stream. [RIDE + -ABLE] —**rid′a·bil′i·ty,** *n.*

rid·dance (rid′ᵊns), *n.* **1.** the act or fact of clearing away or out, as anything undesirable. **2.** relief or deliverance from something. **3. good riddance,** a welcome relief or deliverance from something: *We finally disposed of that old furniture, and good riddance!* [RID[1] + -ANCE]

rid·den (rid′ᵊn), *v.* a pp. of **ride.**

rid·dle[1] (rid′ᵊl), *n., v.,* **-dled, -dling.** —*n.* **1.** a question or statement so framed as to exercise one's ingenuity in answering it or discovering its meaning; conundrum. **2.** a puzzling question, problem, or matter. **3.** a puzzling thing or person. **4.** any enigmatic or dark saying or speech. —*v.i.* **5.** to propound riddles; speak enigmatically. [ME *redele,* OE *rǣdelle,* var. of *rǣdels(e)* (*rǣd* counsel (see REDE) + *-sel,* with loss of *-s-* through confusion with -LE); c. G *Rätsel,* D *raadsel*] —**Syn. 1.** See **puzzle.**

rid·dle[2] (rid′ᵊl), *v.,* **-dled, -dling,** *n.* —*v.t.* **1.** to pierce with many holes suggesting those of a sieve: *to riddle the target.* **2.** to sift through a riddle, as gravel; screen. **3.** to fill or affect with (something undesirable, weakening, etc.): *a government riddled with graft.* **4.** to impair or refute completely by persistent verbal attacks: *to riddle a person's reputation.* —*n.* **5.** a coarse sieve, as one for sifting sand in a foundry. [ME *riddil,* OE *hriddel,* var. of *hridder, hrīder;* c. G *Reiter,* L *crībrum* sieve]

rid′dle can′on, *Music.* a canon for which only part of the notes are given, with the rest of the notes and the entrances and pitches of the succeeding parts indicated by cryptic inscriptions and clues. Also called **enigma canon, enigmatic canon.**

ride (rīd), *v.,* **rode** or (*Archaic*) **rid; rid·den** or (*Archaic*) **rid; rid·ing;** *n.* —*v.i.* **1.** to sit on and manage a horse or other animal in motion; be carried on the back of an animal. **2.** to be carried on something, as a litter, a person's shoulders, or the like. **3.** to be borne along on or in a vehicle or any kind of conveyance. **4.** to move along in any way; be carried or supported: *He is riding along on his friend's success. Distress is riding among the people.* **5.** to move or float on the water: *the surfboarders riding the crests of the waves.* **6.** to lie at anchor, as a ship. **7.** to appear to float in space, as a heavenly body: *A blood-red moon rode in the cloudless sky.* **8.** to turn or rest on something: *the great globe of the world riding on its axis.* **9.** to extend or project over something, as the edge of one thing over the edge of another thing. **10.** to work or move up from the proper place or position (usually fol. by *up*): *Her skirt rode up above her knees.* **11.** to have a specified character for riding purposes: *The car rides smoothly.* **12.** to continue without interruption or interference: *He decided to let the bet ride.* **13.** to be conditioned by; depend upon: *All his hopes are riding on getting that promotion. His future success rides on this merger's going through.* —*v.t.* **14.** to sit on and manage (a horse, bicycle, etc.) so as to be carried along. **15.** to sit or move along on (something); be carried or borne along on: *The ship rode the waves. We ride a bus.* **16.** to rest on, esp. by overlapping. **17.** to control, dominate, or tyrannize over: *a man ridden by fear; a country that is ridden by a power-mad dictator.* **18.** to ridicule or harass persistently: *The boys keep riding him about his poor grades.* **19.** to ride over, along, or through (a road, boundary, region, etc.); traverse. **20.** to execute by riding: *to ride a race.* **21.** to cause to ride. **22.** to carry (a person) on something as if on a horse: *He rode the child about on his back.* **23.** to keep (a vessel) at anchor or moored. **24.** *Jazz.* to play improvisations on (a melody). **25. ride down, a.** to trample or overturn by riding upon or against. **b.** to ride up to; overtake: *The posse rode down the escaping bank robber.* **c.** *Naut.* to bear down upon (a rope of a tackle) with all one's weight. **26. ride for a fall,** to conduct oneself so as to invite misfortune or injury: *Ever since he started going with those hoodlums he's been riding for a fall.* **27. ride gain,** to control the intensity of sound, maintaining the volume suitable for transmission, as in a radio, television, or motion-picture studio. **28. ride herd on,** to have charge or control of; maintain order or discipline over: *The new teacher rode herd on the children with the air of a professional.* **29. ride out, a.** to sustain (a gale, storm, etc.) without damage, as while riding at anchor. **b.** to sustain or endure successfully. **30. ride the beam,** *Aeron.* to fly along the course indicated by a radio beam. —*n.* **31.** a journey or excursion on a horse, camel, etc., or on or in a vehicle. **32.** a way, road, etc., made esp. for riding. **33.** a vehicle or device, as a Ferris wheel, roller coaster, merry-go-round, or the like, on which people ride for amusement. **34. take for a ride,** *Slang.* **a.** to murder, esp. by abducting the victim for that purpose. **b.** to deceive; trick: *It was obvious to everyone but the victim that he was being taken for a ride.* [ME *ride(n),* OE *rīdan;* c. OIcel *rītha,* G *reiten.* See ROAD] —**Syn. 3.** See **drive.**

ri·dent (rīd′ᵊnt), *adj.* laughing; smiling; cheerful. [< L *rīdent-* (s. of *rīdens,* prp. of *rīdēre*) equiv. to *rīd-* laugh + *-ent-* -ENT]

rid·er (rī′dər), *n.* **1.** a person who rides a horse or other animal, a bicycle, or the like. **2.** that which rides. **3.** any object or device that straddles, is mounted upon, or is attached to something else. **4.** a rail or stake used to brace the corners in a snake fence. **5.** an additional clause, usually unrelated to the main body, attached to a legislative bill in passing it. **6.** an addition or amendment to a document, testament, etc. **7.** *Shipbuilding.* any of various members following and reinforcing primary framing members, esp. a plate or timber running along the top of a keel. **8.** *Numis.* **a.** a former gold coin of Scotland, first issued by James III in 1475, whose obverse bears an equestrian figure of the king. **b.** any of several gold or silver coins of the Netherlands bearing the figure of a horseman. **9.** *Mining.* a small seam of a mineral, esp. coal, lying not far above a larger seam. [ME, OE *ridere.* See RIDE, -ER[1]] —**rid′er·less,** *adj.*

Ri·der (rī′dər), *n.* a boy's given name. Also, **Ryder.**

rid·ered (rī′dərd), *adj.* braced or reinforced with riders, as a snake fence. [RIDER + -ED[3]]

rid′er plate′, *Shipbuilding.* **1.** a metal plate reinforcing the upper or inner surface of a metal keelson or stringer. **2.** (in a composite-built hull) any of a series of diagonally set plates connecting the outsides of the framing and reinforcing the hull longitudinally.

Rid′ers to the Sea′, a one-act play (1904) by Synge.

ridge (rij), *n., v.,* **ridged, ridg·ing.** —*n.* **1.** a long, narrow elevation of land; a chain of hills or mountains. **2.** the long and narrow upper edge, angle, or crest of something, as a hill, wave, vault, etc. **3.** the back of an animal. **4.** any raised, narrow strip, as on cloth. **5.** the horizontal line in which the tops of the rafters of a roof meet. **6.** (on a weather chart) a narrow, elongated area of high pressure. —*v.t.* **7.** to provide with or form into a ridge or ridges. **8.** to mark with or as with ridges. —*v. i.* **9.** to form ridges. [ME *rigge,* OE *hrycg* spine, crest, ridge; c. OIcel *hryggr,* D *rug,* G *Rücken,* L *crux*] —**ridge′like′,** *adj.*

Ridge·crest (rij′krest′), *n.* a town in central California. 5099 (1960).

Ridge·field (rij′fēld′), *n.* a town in SW Connecticut. 2954 (1960).

ridge·ling (rij′ling), *n.* *Vet. Med.* a colt with undescended testicles. Also, **ridg′ling.** Also called **ridg·el, ridg·il** (rij′əl). [? RIDGE + -LING[2], from the belief that the undescended organs were in the animal's back]

ridge·pole (rij′pōl′), *n.* the horizontal timber or member at the top of a roof, to which the upper ends of the rafters are fastened. Also, **ridge′ pole′.** Also called **ridge·piece** (rij′pēs′), **ridge′ board′.** [RIDGE + POLE[1]] —**ridge′poled′,** *adj.*

ridge′ rib′, *Archit.* a molded member following the ridge of a vault.

ridge′ rope′, *Naut.* **1.** either of a pair of life lines along the sides of a bowsprit. **2.** a rope supporting the center or sides of an awning covering the deck of a vessel. **3.** a rope rove through stanchions to serve as a railing.

Ridge·wood (rij′wo͝od′), *n.* a city in NE New Jersey. 25,391 (1960).

Ridg·way (rij′wā), *n.* **1. Matthew Bunker,** born 1895, U.S. army general. **2.** a town in central Pennsylvania. 6387 (1960).

ridg·y (rij′ē), *adj.,* **ridg·i·er, ridg·i·est.** rising in a ridge or ridges. [RIDGE + -Y[1]]

rid·i·cule (rid′ə kyo͞ol′), *n., v.,* **-culed, -cul·ing.** —*n.* **1.** speech or action intended to cause contemptuous laughter at a person or thing; derision. —*v.t.* **2.** to deride; make fun of. [< L *rīdicul(um)* that excites laughter, a jest, equiv. to *rīd(ēre)* (to) laugh + *-i-* -I- + *-culum* -CLE] —**rid′i·cul′er,** *n.*
—**Syn. 1.** mockery, raillery, sarcasm, satire, irony. **2.** banter, chaff, rally, twit, burlesque, satirize, lampoon. RIDICULE, DERIDE, MOCK, TAUNT imply making game of a person, usually in an unkind, jeering way. To RIDICULE is to make fun of, either sportively and good-humoredly, or unkindly with the intention of humiliating: *to ridicule a pretentious person.* To DERIDE is to assail one with scornful laughter: *to deride a statement of belief.* To MOCK is sometimes playfully, sometimes insultingly, to imitate and caricature the appearance or actions of another: *She mocked the seriousness of his expression.* To TAUNT is maliciously and exultingly to press upon one's attention (and often on the notice of others) some annoying or humiliating fact: *to taunt a person defeated in a contest.* —**Ant. 1.** praise.

ri·dic·u·lous (ri dik′yə ləs), *adj.* causing or worthy of ridicule or derision; absurd; preposterous; laughable: *a ridiculous plan.* [< L *rīdiculōs(us)* laughable, droll, equiv. to *rīdicul(us)* that excites laughter (see RIDICULE) + *-ōsus* -OUS] —**ri·dic′u·lous·ly,** *adv.* —**ri·dic′u·lous·ness, ri·dic·u·los·i·ty** (ri dik′yə los′i tē), *n.*
—**Syn.** nonsensical, ludicrous, funny, droll, comical, farcical. See **absurd.** —**Ant.** sensible.

rid·ing[1] (rī′ding), *n.* **1.** the act of one who or that which rides. —*adj.* **2.** used in traveling or in riding: *riding clothes.* [ME (n., adj.); OE *ridende* (adj.). See RIDE, -ING[1], -ING[2]]

rid·ing[2] (rī′ding), *n.* **1.** any of the three administrative divisions into which Yorkshire, England, is divided, namely North Riding, East Riding, and West Riding. **2.** any similar administrative division elsewhere. [ME *triding,* OE **thriding* < Scand; cf. OIcel *thrīdjungr* third part; *t-* (of ME), var. of *th-* (of OE) by assimilation to *-t* in *east, west* which commonly preceded]

rid′ing bitt′, *Naut.* a bitt for making fast the cable of a dropped anchor.

rid′ing boot′, a knee-high boot of black or brown leather, without fastenings, forming part of a riding habit.

rid′ing breech′es, calf-length trousers of whipcord or other durable fabric, flaring at the sides of the thighs and fitting snugly at and below the knees, worn with riding boots for horseback riding, hunting, etc. Also called **breeches.** Cf. **jodhpurs.**

rid′ing crop′, crop (def. 7).

rid′ing light′. See **anchor light.**

rid′ing mas′ter, a person who teaches equitation.

rid′ing sail′, *Naut.* a triangular sail set on the aftermost mast of a vessel, esp. a fishing vessel, to head it into the wind; trysail.

rid′ing school′, a place where equitation is taught.

rid·ley (rid′lē), *n., pl.* **-leys.** a sea turtle, *Lepidochelys olivacea kempi,* found chiefly in the Gulf of Mexico. Also called **bastard turtle.** [? after *Ridley,* proper name]

Rid·ley (rid′lē), *n.* **1. Nicholas,** c1500–55, English bishop, reformer, and martyr. **2.** a town in SE Pennsylvania, near Philadelphia. 35,738 (1960).

Rid′ley Park′, a town in SE Pennsylvania. 7387 (1960).

ri·dot·to (ri dot′ō), *n., pl.* **-tos.** a public ball or dance with music and often in masquerade, popular in the 18th century. [< It: retreat, resort; see REDOUBT]

rie·beck·ite (rē′be kīt′), *n.* an amphibolic mineral, silicate of sodium and iron, occurring usually in feldspathoid rocks. [named after Emil *Riebeck* (d. 1885), German explorer; see -ITE[1]]

Rieg·ger (rē′gər), *n.* **Wal·ling·ford** (wô′ling fərd), 1885–1961, U.S. composer.

Rie·ka (rē ek′ə; *Serbo-Croatian.* RYE′kä), *n.* Rijeka.

riel (rēl), *n.* a paper money and monetary unit of Cambodia, equal to 100 sen and equivalent to about .03 of a U.S. dollar. [?]

Ri·el (rē el′), *n.* **Louis,** 1844–85, Canadian revolutionary.

Rie·mann (rē′män; *Eng.* rē′män, -mən), *n.* **Ge·org Frie·drich Bern·hard** (gā ôRKH′ frē′dRiKH bern′härt), 1826–66, German mathematician. —**Rie·mann′i·an,** *adj.*

Riemann′ian geom′etry, *Geom.* **1.** Also called **elliptic geometry.** the branch of non-Euclidean geometry which replaces the parallel postulate of Euclidean geometry with the postulate that in a plane every pair of distinct lines intersects. Cf. **hyperbolic geometry. 2.** the differential geometry of a metric space that generalizes a Euclidean space.

Rie′mann in′tegral, *Math.* integral (def. 8a). [named after G. F. B. RIEMANN]

Rie′mann sphere′, *Math.* a sphere used for a stereographic projection. [named after G. F. B. RIEMANN]

Rie′mann-Stiel′tjes in′tegral (rē′män stēl′chiz), *Math.* the limit, as the norm of partitions of a given interval approaches zero, of the sum of the product of the first of two functions evaluated at some point in each subinterval multiplied by the difference in functional values of the second function at the endpoints of the subinterval. [named after G. F. B. RIEMANN and T. J. *Stieltjes*]

Rie′mann sur′face, *Math.* a geometric representation of a function of a complex variable in which a multiple-valued function is depicted as a single-valued function on several planes, the planes being connected at some of the points at which the function takes on more than one value. Cf. **branch cut, branch point.** [named after G. F. B. RIEMANN]

Rie′mann ze′ta func′tion, *Math.* See **zeta function.** [named after G. F. B. RIEMANN]

rien ne va plus (RYAN′ nə VA plY′), *French.* (in roulette) no further bets. [lit., nothing goes any more]

Ri·en·zi (rē en′zē; *It.* ryen′dzē), *n.* **Co·la di** (kô′lä dē), (*Nicholas Gabrini*), 1313?–54, Roman orator and tribune. Also, **Ri·en·zo** (rē en′zō; *It.* ryen′dzō).

Ries·ling (rēz′ling, rēs′-), *n.* **1.** *Hort.* **a.** a variety of grape. **b.** the vine bearing this grape, grown in Europe and California. **2.** a fragrant, white, dry or sweet wine made from this grape. [< G]

Riesz′ space′ (rēs), *Math.* a topological space in which sets containing one point are closed.

Rie·ti (rē et′ē; *It.* RYE′tē), *n.* **Vit·to·rio** (vēt tô′Ryô), born 1898, Italian composer, in the U.S. after 1939.

Riet·veld (rēt′felt), *n.* **Ger·rit Tho·mas** (KHe Rēt′ tô′məs), born 1888, Dutch architect.

rif (rif), *v.t.,* **riffed, rif·fing.** *Informal.* to discharge (a person) from military or civil service, esp. as part of an economy program. Also, **riff.** [special use of RIF]

Rif (rif), *n.* **Er** (er), a mountainous coastal region in N Morocco. Also called **Riff.**

RIF, *U.S.* Reduction in Force (the reduction of the staff of a government organization, esp. for budgetary reasons).

ri·fa·ci·men·to (ri fä′chi men′tō; *It.* rē fä′chē men′tô), *n., pl.* **-ti** (-tē). a recast or adaptation, as of a literary or musical work. [< It, deriv. of *rifare* to make over, equiv. to *ri-* RE- + *fare* (< L *facere* to do) + *-mento* -MENT]

rife (rīf), *adj.* **1.** of common or frequent occurrence; prevalent; in widespread existence, activity, or use: *Crime is rife in the slum areas of our cities.* **2.** current in speech or report: *Rumors are rife that the government is in financial difficulty.* **3.** abundant, plentiful, or numerous. **4.** abounding (usually fol. by *with*). [ME; OE *rīfe;* c. OIcel *rīfr* abundant, MD *rijf*] —**rife′ly,** *adv.* —**rife′ness,** *n.*
—**Syn. 3.** plenteous, multitudinous. —**Ant. 3.** scarce.

riff (rif), *Jazz.* —*n.* **1.** a melodic phrase, often constantly repeated, forming an accompaniment or part of an accompaniment for a soloist. —*v.i.* **2.** to perform riffs. [alter. and shortening of REFRAIN[2]]

Riff (rif), *n., pl.* **Riffs, Riff·i** (rif′ē), (*esp. collectively*) **Riff. 1.** a member of a group of Berber-speaking tribes living in northern Morocco. **2.** Rif.

rif·fle (rif′əl), *n., v.,* **-fled, -fling.** —*n.* **1.** *U.S.* **a.** a rapid, as in a stream. **b.** a ripple, as upon the surface of water. **2.** *Mining.* **a.** the lining at the bottom of a sluice or the like, made of blocks or slats of wood, or stones, arranged in such a manner that grooves or openings are left between them for catching and collecting particles of gold. **b.** any of the slats of wood or the like so used. **c.** any of the grooves or openings formed. **3.** a hopper for distributing bulk material. **4.** the method of riffling cards. —*v.t., v.i.* **5.** to cause or become a riffle. **6.** to turn hastily; flutter and shift: *to riffle a stack of letters;*

to riffle through a book. **7.** *Cards.* to shuffle by dividing the deck in two, raising the corners slightly, and allowing them to fall alternately together. [b. RIPPLE[1] and RUFFLE[1]]

riff·raff (rif′raf′), *n.* **1.** the worthless or disreputable element of society; rabble: *the riffraff of the city.* **2.** worthless or low persons: *a pack of riffraff.* **3.** trash; rubbish. [ME *rif and raf* every particle, things of small value < OF *rif et raf,* formed on *rifler* to spoil (see RIFLE[2]), *raffler* to ravage, snatch away]

ri·fle[1] (rī′fəl), *n., v.,* **-fled, -fling.** —*n.* **1.** a shoulder firearm with spiral grooves cut in the inner surface of the gun barrel to give the bullet a rotatory motion and thus render its flight more accurate. **2.** one of the grooves. **3.** a cannon with such grooves. **4.** **rifles,** (*often cap.*) any of certain military units or bodies equipped with rifles. —*v.t.* **5.** to cut spiral grooves within (a gun barrel, pipe, etc.). **6.** *Informal.* to propel (a ball) at high speed, as by throwing or hitting with a bat. [< LG *rīfel(n)* (to) groove, deriv. of *rīve, riefe* groove, flute, furrow; akin to OE *rifelede* wrinkled, *rīf* violent]

Rifle (Garand)

ri·fle[2] (rī′fəl), *v.t.,* **-fled, -fling.** **1.** to ransack and rob (a place, receptacle, etc.). **2.** to search and rob (a person). **3.** to plunder or strip bare. **4.** to steal or take away. [ME *rifle* < OF *rifl(er)* (to) scrape, graze, plunder < D *riffel(en)* (to) scrape; c. RIFLE[1]] —**ri′fler,** *n.* —**Syn. 1.** See **rob.**

ri′fle bird′, any of several birds of paradise having a long bill, dark plumage, and elaborate courtship displays, as *Craspedophora magnifica* (**magnificent rifle bird**).

ri′fled slug′, a shotgun projectile with helical grooves on its sides for imparting a spin to it when it is fired through the smooth bore of the shotgun.

ri′fle grenade′, *Mil.* a grenade designed to be fired from a grenade launcher attached to the muzzle of a rifle or carbine.

ri·fle·man (rī′fəl mən), *n., pl.* **-men.** **1.** a soldier armed with a rifle. **2.** an expert in the use of the rifle. [RIFLE[1] + MAN[1]] —**ri′fle·man·ship′,** *n.*

ri′fle pit′, a pit or short trench affording shelter to riflemen in firing at an enemy.

ri′fle range′, **1.** a firing range for practice with rifles. **2.** the range of, or distance coverable by, a bullet fired from a rifle: *The enemy was within rifle range.*

ri·fle·ry (rī′fəl rē), *n.* the art, practice, or sport of shooting at targets with rifles. [RIFLE[1] + -RY]

ri·fling (rī′fling), *n.* **1.** the act or process of cutting spiral grooves in a gun barrel, pipe, etc. **2.** the system of spiral grooves so cut. [RIFLE[1] + -ING[1]]

rift[1] (rift), *n.* **1.** an opening made by splitting, cleaving, etc.; fissure; cleft; chink. **2.** an open space, as in a forest or cloud mass, or a clear interval. **3.** a break in friendly relations: *a rift between two people; a rift between two nations.* **4.** a difference in opinion, belief, or interest that causes such a break in friendly relations. **5.** *Geol.* **a.** a fault. **b.** a valley along the trace of a fault. **6.** the plane or direction along which a log or mass of granite can most easily be split. **7.** wood or a piece of wood that has been split radially from a log. —*v.t., v.i.* **8.** to burst open; split. [ME < Scand; cf. Dan *rift* cleft; akin to RIVE] —**rift′less,** *adj.*

rift[2] (rift), *v.i. Dial.* **1.** to belch. **2.** to break wind. [ME *rift(en)* < ON *rypta;* cf. Icel *ropa* to belch]

rift′ saw′, a saw used for cutting wood radially from a log.

rift-sawed (rift′sôd′), *adj.* **1.** (of lumber) sawed radially so that the broader sides of the boards or timbers are approximately perpendicular to the annual rings. **2.** quartersawed. Also, **rift-sawn** (rift′sôn′).

rig[1] (rig), *v.,* **rigged, rig·ging,** *n.* —*v.t.* **1.** *Chiefly Naut.* **a.** to put in proper order for working or use. **b.** to fit (a vessel, a mast, etc.) with the necessary shrouds, stays, etc. **c.** to fit (shrouds, stays, sails, etc.) to the mast, yard, or the like. **2.** to furnish or provide with equipment, clothing, etc.; fit (usually fol. by *out* or *up*). **3.** to assemble, install, or prepare (often fol. by *up*). **4.** to manipulate fraudulently: *to rig prices.* **5.** **rig down,** *Naut.* to place in an inactive state, stowing all lines, tackles, and other removable parts: *to rig down a donkey engine.* **6.** **rig up,** to equip or set up for use: *to rig up a donkey engine.* —*n.* **7.** the arrangement of the masts, spars, sails, etc., on a boat or ship. **8.** apparatus for some purpose; equipment; outfit; gear: *a hi-fi rig; Bring your rod and reel and all the rest of your fishing rig.* **9.** a carriage, buckboard, sulky, or wagon together with the horse or horses that draw it. **10.** the equipment used in drilling an oil well. **11.** *Informal.* costume or dress, esp. when odd or conspicuous, or when designated for a particular purpose: *That was quite a rig she wore to the party. He looks quite nifty in a butler's rig.* [ME *rigge(n)* ? < Scand; cf Dan *rigge,* Sw *rigga* (*på*) to harness (up)]

rig[2] (rig), *n. Scot. and North Eng.* ridge. [ME (north), OE *hrycg* RIDGE]

rig[3] (rig), *n. Brit. Dial.* a tempest; storm. [ME *ryg(e)* < Scand; cf. OIcel *hregg* storm, blast]

Ri·ga (rē′gə), *n.* **1.** a seaport in and the capital of Latvia, on the Gulf of Riga. 915,000. **2.** **Gulf of,** an arm of the Baltic between Latvia and Estonia. 90 mi. long.

rig·a·doon (rig′ə do͞on′), *n.* **1.** a lively dance, formerly popular, for one couple, characterized by a peculiar jumping step and usually in quick duple meter. **2.** a piece of music for this dance or in its rhythm. Also, **rigaudon.** [< F *rigaudon,* perh. from name *Rigaud*]

rig·a·ma·role (rig′ə mə rōl′), *n.* rigmarole.

rig·a·ree (rig′ə rē′, rig′ə rē′), *n. Glassmaking.* decoration consisting of glass filaments applied to a glass vessel in parallel vertical lines and fused into contiguous bands. [?]

rig·a·to·ni (rig′ə tō′nē), *n. Italian Cookery.* a tubular pasta in short, ribbed pieces. [< It (n.pl.), equiv. to *rigato* furrowed, lined, striped (ptp. of *rigare,* deriv. of *riga* a line)]

ri·gau·don (*Fr.* rē gō dôN′),*n., pl.* **-dons** (*Fr.* -dôN′). rigadoon.

Ri·gel (rī′jəl, -gəl), *n. Astron.* a first-magnitude star in the constellation Orion. [< Ar *rijl* foot, so called from its position in the left foot of the figure of Orion]

rigged′ oar′, *Naut.* an oar mounted in an oarlock, becket, etc., at the stern of a small boat for sculling or steering.

rig·ger (rig′ər), *n.* **1.** one who rigs. **2.** one whose occupation is the fitting of the rigging of ships. **3.** one who works with hoisting tackle, cranes, scaffolding, etc. **4.** a protective structure around a construction site. **5.** *Aeron.* a mechanic skilled in the assembly, adjustment, and alignment of aircraft control surfaces, wings, and the like. [RIG[1] + -ER[1]]

rig·ging[1] (rig′ing), *n.* **1.** the ropes, chains, etc., employed to support and work the masts, yards, sails, etc., on a ship. **2.** lifting or hauling tackle. **3.** *Informal.* clothing. [RIG[1] + -ING[1]]

rig·ging[2] (rig′ing), *n. Scot. and North Eng.* ridge. [ME (north); see RIG[2], -ING[1]]

rig′ging bat′ten, *Naut.* a batten seized to a shroud or stay to prevent chafing. Also called **scotchman.**

rig′ging loft′, a covered area where the rigging of vessels is prepared.

rig′ging plan′, *Naval Archit.* a side elevation of a vessel showing all standing and running rigging, all booms, yards, etc., as if set directly fore-and-aft: often combined with a sail plan.

Riggs′′ disease′ (rigz), *Dentistry.* pyorrhea (def. 2). [named after John M. Riggs (1810–85), American dentist]

right (rīt), *adj.* **1.** in accordance with what is good, proper, or just: *right conduct.* **2.** in conformity with fact, reason, or some standard or principle; correct: *the right solution.* **3.** correct in judgment, opinion, or action. **4.** sound or normal, as the mind: *to be in one's right mind.* **5.** sane, as persons: *She wasn't right in her head when she made the will.* **6.** in good health or spirits: *He is all right again.* **7.** in a satisfactory state; in good order: *to put things right.* **8.** principal, front, or upper: *the right side of cloth.* **9.** most convenient, desirable, or favorable: *Chicago is the right location for a meat-packing firm.* **10.** fitting or appropriate; suitable: *to say the right thing at the right time.* **11.** genuine; authentic: *the right owner.* **12.** noting, of, near, or pertaining to the side of a person or thing that is turned toward the east when the face is toward the north (opposed to *left*). **13.** (*often cap.*) noting, of, or pertaining to political conservatives and their beliefs. **14.** straight: *a right line.* **15.** formed by or with reference to a perpendicular: *a right angle.* **16.** *Geom.* having an axis perpendicular to the base: *a right cone.* **17.** *Math.* pertaining to an element of a set which has a given property when placed on the right of an element or set of elements of the given set: *a right identity.* **18.** **too right,** *Australian Slang.* **a.** (used as an expression of emphatic agreement.) **b.** okay: *"Can we meet tonight?" "Too right."*
—*n.* **19.** a just claim or title, whether legal, prescriptive, or moral: *He has a right to say what he pleases.* **20.** Sometimes, **rights.** that which is due to anyone by just claim, legal guarantees, moral principles, etc.: *Freedom of speech is a right of all Americans.* **21.** adherence or obedience to moral and legal principles and authority. **22.** that which is morally, legally, or ethically proper: *He was taught to do right.* **23.** a moral, ethical, or legal principle considered as an underlying cause of truth, justice, morality, or ethics. **24.** Sometimes, **rights.** the interest or ownership a person, group, or business has in property: *He has a 50-percent right in a silver mine. The author controls the screen rights for the book.* **25.** the property itself or its value. **26.** *Finance.* **a.** the privilege, usually preemptive, that accrues to the owners of the stock of a corporation to subscribe to additional shares of stock or securities convertible into stock at an advantageous price. **b.** Often, **rights.** the privilege of subscribing to a specified amount of a stock or bond issue, or the document certifying this privilege. **27.** that which is in accord with fact, reason, propriety, the correct way of thinking, etc. **28.** the state or quality or an instance of being correct. **29.** the side that is normally opposite to that where the heart is; the direction toward that side: *to turn to the right.* **30.** a right-hand turn: *Make a right at the top of the hill.* **31.** the portion toward the right, as of troops in battle formation: *Our right crumbled.* **32.** (in a pair) the member that is shaped for, used by, or situated on the right side: *Is this shoe a left or a right?* **33.** the right hand: *Jab with your left and punch with your right.* **34.** (*usually cap.*) the part of a legislative assembly, esp. in continental Europe, that is situated on the right side of the presiding officer and that is customarily assigned to members of the legislature who hold more conservative or reactionary views than the rest of the members. **35.** the members of such an assembly who sit on the Right. **36.** **the Right, a.** the complex of individuals or organized groups opposing any change in a liberal direction and usually advocating rigid maintenance of the established social, political, or economic order, often by authoritarian means. **b.** the position held by these people: *The Depression led to a movement away from the Right.* Cf. **left**[1] (defs. 7a, b). **c.** See **right wing** (def. 3). **37.** *Boxing.* a blow delivered by the right hand: *a right to the jaw.* **38.** *Baseball.* See **right field.** **39.** **by rights,** in fairness; justly: *The people should by rights have been given a voice in their government.* **40.** **in one's own right,** by reason of one's own ability, ownership, etc.; in or of oneself, as independent of others: *He is a rich man in his own right.* **41.** **in the right,** having the support of reason or law; correct: *It pays to be stubborn when one is in the right.* **42.** **Mr. Right,** *U.S. Informal.* the suitable man for a woman to marry: *She'll know what to do when Mr. Right comes along.* **43.** **to rights,** into proper condition or order: *to set a room to rights.*
—*adv.* **44.** in a straight line; straight; directly: *right to the bottom; to come right home.* **45.** quite, or completely; all the way: *His hat was knocked right off.* **46.** immediately; promptly: *right after dinner.* **47.** exactly; precisely: *right here.* **48.** uprightly or righteously: *to obey one's conscience and live right.* **49.** correctly or accurately: *to guess right.* **50.** properly or fittingly: *to behave right.* **51.** advantageously, favorably, or well: *to turn out right.* **52.** toward the right hand; on or to the right: *to keep right; to turn right.* **53.** *Chiefly Dial.* extremely: *I was right glad to be there.* **54.** very (used in certain titles): *the right reverend.* **55.** **right and left,** on every side; in all directions: *throwing his clothes right and left; members resigning right and left.* **56.** **right away** or **off,** without hesitation; immediately: *She made a bad impression right off.*
—*v.t.* **57.** to put in or restore to an upright position: *to right a fallen lamp.* **58.** to put in proper order, condition, or relationship: *to right a crookedly hung picture.* **59.** to bring into conformity with fact; correct: *to right one's point of view.* **60.** to do justice to; avenge: *to be righted in court.* **61.** to redress, as a wrong.
—*v.i.* **62.** to resume an upright or the proper position: *After the storm the saplings righted.* [ME; OE *reht, riht;* c. D, G *recht,* Icel *rett(r),* Goth *raiht(s);* akin to L *rectus*]
—**Syn. 1.** equitable, fair, honest, lawful. **2.** accurate, true. **8.** obverse. **9.** proper. **10.** fit, seemly. **11.** rightful. **22.** morality, virtue, justice, fairness, integrity, equity, rectitude. **48.** rightfully, lawfully, rightly, justly, fairly, equitably. **50.** appropriately, suitably. —**Ant. 1.** wrong.

right·a·bout (rīt′ə bout′), *n.* **1.** the position assumed by turning about to the right so as to face in the opposite direction. **2.** the act of turning so as to face the opposite direction. —*adv.* **3.** facing or in the opposite direction: *Move that chair rightabout.* Also, **right′-a·bout′.** [RIGHT + ABOUT]

right′ about′ face′, **1.** *Mil.* **a.** a command, given to a soldier or soldiers at attention, to turn the body about toward the right so as to face in the opposite direction. **b.** the act of so turning in a prescribed military manner. **2.** rightabout (def. 2). **3.** any complete reversal, as of conduct, opinion, etc. Also, **right′a·bout′-face′, right′-a·bout′-face′.**

right′ an′gle, the angle formed by two radii of a circle that are drawn to the extremities of an arc equal to one quarter of the circle; an angle of 90°. —**right′-an′gled,** *adj.*

right′ ascen′sion, *Astron.* the arc of the celestial equator measured eastward from the vernal equinox to the foot of the great circle passing through the celestial poles and a given point on the celestial sphere, expressed in degrees or hours.

Right′ Bank′, a part of Paris, France, on the N bank of the Seine. Cf. **Left Bank.**

right′ cir′cular cone′, *Geom.* a cone whose surface is generated by lines joining a fixed point to the points of a circle, the fixed point lying on a perpendicular through the center of the circle. Cf. **oblique circular cone.**

right′ cir′cular cyl′inder, *Geom.* a cylinder generated by the revolution of a rectangle about one of its sides. Cf. **oblique circular cylinder.**

right·eous (rī′chəs), *adj.* **1.** characterized by uprightness or morality: *a righteous observance of the law.* **2.** morally right or justifiable: *righteous indignation.* **3.** acting in an upright, moral way; virtuous: *a righteous and godly man.* —*n.* **4.** **the righteous,** (*construed as pl.*) righteous persons collectively (usually prec. by *the*). [earlier *rightwos, rightwis* (remodeled with -OUS), OE *rihtwīs.* See RIGHT, WISE[2]] —**right′eous·ly,** *adv.*
—**Syn. 3.** good, honest, fair, right. —**Ant. 3.** evil, wicked.

right·eous·ness (rī′chəs nis), *n.* **1.** the quality or state of being righteous. **2.** righteous conduct. **3.** the quality or state of being just or rightful: *They came to realize the righteousness of his position on the matter.* [ME *rightwisnes(se),* OE *rihtwīsnes.* See RIGHTEOUS, -NESS]

right·er (rī′tər), *n.* one who rights or redresses: *a righter of wrongs.* [ME *rightar* executioner, OE *rihtere* one who regulates. See RIGHT, -ER[1]]

right′-eyed floun′der (rīt′īd′), any of several flatfishes of the family *Pleuronectidae,* having both eyes on the right side of the head. Also, **right′eye floun′der.**

right′ face′, *Mil.* **1.** a command, given to a soldier or soldiers at attention, to turn the body 90° toward the right. **2.** the act of so turning in a prescribed military manner.

right′ field′, *Baseball.* **1.** the area of the outfield to the right of center field, as viewed from home plate. **2.** the position of the player covering this area.

right′ field′er, *Baseball.* the player whose position is right field.

right·ful (rīt′fəl), *adj.* **1.** having a valid or just claim, as to some property or position; legitimate: *The rightfu owner of the farm.* **2.** belonging or held by a valid or just claim: *one's rightful property.* **3.** equitable or just, as actions, a cause, etc. [ME; see RIGHT, -FUL] —**right′ful·ly,** *adv.* —**right′ful·ness,** *n.*

right′ hand′, **1.** the hand that is on the right side, or the side opposite that where the heart is. **2.** the right side, as of a person, esp. this side considered as the side of precedence or courtesy. **3.** a position of honor or special trust: *All important matters had to be cleared with him, for he sat on the right hand of the committee chairman.* **4.** an extremely efficient or reliable person or, sometimes, tool, esp. a person considered as one's assistant: *Through the years his wife had been his right hand in his office.* [ME *riht hond,* OE *ryht handa*]

right-hand (rīt′hand′), *adj.* **1.** on the right. **2.** of, for, or with the right hand. **3.** most efficient or useful, as a helper or assistant. **4.** plain-laid. [adj. use of RIGHT HAND]

right′-hand buoy′, *Navig.* a distinctive buoy marking the side of a channel regarded as the right, or starboard, side.

right-hand·ed (rīt′han′did), *adj.* **1.** having the right hand or arm more serviceable than the left; using the right hand by preference: *a right-handed painter.* **2.** adapted to or performed by the right hand: *a right-handed lever; right-handed penmanship.* **3.** *Mach.* **a.** rotating clockwise. **b.** noting a helical, or spiral, member, as a gear tooth or screw thread, that twists clockwise as it recedes from an observer. **4.** *Building Trades.* **a.** (of a door) having the hinges on the right when seen from the exterior of the building, room, closet, etc., to which the doorway leads. **b.** (of a casement sash) having the hinges on the right when seen from inside the window. —*adv.* Also, **right′-hand′ed·ly.** **5.** in a right-handed manner or fashion: *The door opens right-*

handed. **6.** with the right hand: *She writes right-handed.* **7.** toward the right hand or in a clockwise direction: *The strands of the rope are laid right-handed.* [ME] —**right′-hand′ed·ness,** *n.*

right-hand·er (rīt′han′dər), *n.* **1.** one who is right-handed, esp. a baseball pitcher who throws with his right hand. **2.** *Informal.* **a.** a slap or punch delivered with the right hand. **b.** a throw or toss, as in basketball, made with the right hand.

right′-hand man′, an indispensable or invaluable assistant; right hand.

right′ing lev′er, *Naval Archit.* the horizontal distance in a heeling vessel between the center of gravity, acting downward, and the center of buoyancy, acting upward, when they are so placed as to form a couple **(right′ing cou′ple)** tending to restore the vessel to an upright position. Also called **right′ing arm′.** Cf. **upsetting lever.**

right′ing mo′ment, *Naval Archit.* the moment of a righting couple. Also called **moment of stability.**

right·ism (rī′tiz əm), *n.* **1.** conservatism, esp. in politics. **2.** reactionary principles, attitudes, or behavior. [RIGHT + -ISM]

right·ist (rī′tist), *adj.* **1.** noting, of, or pertaining to conservative or reactionary political views. —*n.* **2.** a conservative or reactionary. [RIGHT + -IST]

right-laid (rīt′lād′), *adj.* noting a rope, strand, etc., laid in a right-handed, or clockwise, direction as one looks away along it (opposed to *left-laid*).

right·ly (rīt′lē), *adv.* **1.** in accordance with truth or fact; correctly: *to see rightly; to understand rightly.* **2.** in accordance with morality or equity; uprightly. **3.** properly, fitly, or suitably: *to be rightly dressed.* [ME; OE *rihtlīce.* See RIGHT, -LY]

right-mind·ed (rīt′mīn′did), *adj.* having correct, honest, or good opinions or principles. [RIGHT + MINDED] —**right′-mind′ed·ly,** *adv.* —**right′-mind′ed·ness,** *n.*

right·ness (rīt′nis), *n.* **1.** correctness or accuracy. **2.** propriety or fitness. **3.** moral integrity. **4.** *Obs.* straightness or directness. [ME; OE *rihtnes.* See RIGHT, -NESS]

right·o (rīt′ō′, rīt′ō′; rī′tō′, -tō′), *interj.* *Chiefly Brit. Informal.* right-oh.

right′ of search′, *Internat. Law.* the privilege of a nation at war to search neutral ships on the high seas for contraband or other matter carried in violation of neutrality which may subject the ship to seizure.

right′ of way′, **1.** a common law or statutory right granted to a vehicle, as an airplane, boat, etc., to proceed ahead of another. **2.** a path or route that may lawfully be used. **3.** a right of passage, as over another's land. **4.** the strip of land acquired for use by a railroad for tracks. **5.** land covered by a public road. **6.** land over which a power line passes. Also, **right′-of-way′,** *n.*

right′-of-way′ sig′nal, *Naut.* any of various signals used to give individual vessels the right of way in confined waters, as those of a harbor.

right-oh (rīt′ō′, rīt′ō′; rī′tō′, -tō′), *interj.* *Chiefly Brit. Informal.* (used to express cheerful consent or understanding.)

rights (rīts), *Informal.* —*n.* **1.** (*construed as pl.*) See **civil rights.** —*adj.* **2.** civil-rights: *a rights worker.*

right′ sec′tion, a representation of an object as it would appear if cut by a plane perpendicular to its longest axis. Cf. **cross section.**

right′ stage′. See **stage right.**

right-to-life (rīt′tə līf′), *adj.* pro-life: *right-to-life movement.* —**right′-to-lif′er,** *n.*

right′-to-work′ law′ (rīt′tə wûrk′), *U.S.* a State law that makes a closed shop illegal.

right′ tri′angle, a triangle having a right angle.

right′ whale′, any of several large whalebone whales of the genera *Balaena* and *Eubalaena,* of circumpolar seas.

right′ wing′, **1.** members of a conservative or reactionary political party, or those opposing extensive political reform. **2.** such a political party, or a group of such parties. **3.** that part of a political or social organization advocating a conservative or reactionary position: *The union's right wing favored a moderate course of action.* —**right′-wing′,** *adj.* —**right′-wing′er,** *n.*

right·y (rī′tē), *adv., adj., n., pl.* **right·ies.** *Informal.* —*adv.* **1.** with the right hand; right-handed: *He sketches righty.* —*adj.* **2.** right-handed (def. 1): *He's a righty pitcher.* —*n.* **3.** a right-handed person; right-hander: *He's a righty.* [RIGHT + -Y[1]]

Ri·gi (rē′gē), *n.* a mountain in central Switzerland, near the Lake of Lucerne. 5906 ft.

rig·id (rij′id), *adj.* **1.** stiff or unyielding; not pliant or flexible; hard: *a rigid strip of metal.* **2.** firmly fixed or set. **3.** inflexible, strict, or severe: *a rigid disciplinarian; rigid rules of social behavior.* **4.** exacting; thorough; rigorous: *a rigid examination.* **5.** so as to meet precise standards; stringent: *lenses ground to rigid specifications.* **6.** *Mech.* of, pertaining to, or noting a body in which the distance between any pair of points remains fixed under all forces; having infinite values for its shear modulus, bulk modulus, and Young's modulus. **7.** *Aeron.* **a.** (of an airship or dirigible) having a form maintained by a stiff, unyielding structure contained within the envelope. **b.** pertaining to a helicopter rotor which is held fixedly at its root. [< L *rigid(us),* equiv. to *rig(ēre)* (to) be stiff, stiffen + *-idus* -ID[4]] —**ri·gid′i·ty, rig′id·ness,** *n.* —**rig′id·ly,** *adv.*
—**Syn. 1.** unbending, firm, inflexible. **2.** immovable, static. **3.** austere, stern, unyielding. See **strict. 5.** demanding. —**Ant. 1.** elastic. **3.** lax.

rig′id frame′, (in iron, steel, and reinforced-concrete construction) a bent having absolutely rigid connections at the knees. —**rig′id-frame′,** *adj.*

ri·gid·i·fy (ri jid′ə fī′), *v.t., v.i.,* **-fied, -fy·ing.** to make or become rigid. [RIGID + -IFY]

rig′id mo′tion, *Math.* any transformation, as a translation or rotation, of a set such that the distance between points is preserved.

Ri·gil Ken·tau·rus (rī′jəl ken tôr′əs, -gəl). See **Alpha Centauri.**

rig·ma·role (rig′mə rōl′), *n.* **1.** confused, incoherent, foolish, or meaningless talk. **2.** an elaborate or complicated procedure: *to go through the rigmarole of a formal dinner.* Also, **rigamarole.** [alter. of RAGMAN ROLL]

rig·ol (rig′əl), *n.* *Obs.* a ring or circle. [< F *rigole* trench, gutter]

rig·o·let (rig′ə let′), *n.* *Southern U.S.* a small stream; rivulet. [< colonial AmerF. See RIGOL, -ET]

Rig·o·let·to (rig′ə let′ō; *It.* rē′gô let′tô), *n.* an opera (1851) by Giuseppe Verdi.

rig·or (rig′ər), *n.* **1.** strictness, severity, or harshness, as in dealing with persons. **2.** the full or extreme severity of laws, rules, etc. **3.** severity of living conditions; hardship; austerity: *the rigor of wartime existence.* **4.** a severe or harsh act, circumstance, etc. **5.** scrupulous or inflexible accuracy or adherence: *the logical rigor of mathematics.* **6.** severity of weather or climate or an instance of this: *the rigors of winter.* **7.** *Pathol.* a sudden coldness, as that preceding certain fevers; chill. **8.** *Physiol.* a state of rigidity in muscle tissues during which they are unable to respond to stimuli due to the coagulation of muscle protein. **9.** *Obs.* stiffness or rigidity. Also, *esp. Brit.,* **rigour.** [ME *rigour* < L *rigor* stiffness, equiv. to *rig(ēre)* (to) be stiff + *-or* -OR[1]]
—**Syn. 1.** inflexibility, stringency. **4.** cruelty.

rig·or·ism (rig′ə riz′əm), *n.* **1.** extreme strictness. **2.** (in Roman Catholic moral philosophy) the theory that in doubtful cases of conscience no course may be followed that is contrary to Catholic law and doctrine. Also, *esp. Brit.,* **rigourism.** [< F *rigorisme.* See RIGOR, -ISM] —**rig′or·ist,** *n.* —**rig′or·is′tic,** *adj.*

rig·or mor·tis (rig′ər môr′tis, rī′gôr), the stiffening of the body after death. [< L: lit., stiffness of death]

rig·or·ous (rig′ər əs), *adj.* **1.** characterized by rigor; rigidly severe or harsh, as persons, rules, discipline, etc.: *rigorous laws.* **2.** severely exact or accurate; precise. **3.** (of weather or climate) uncomfortably severe or harsh; extremely inclement. **4.** *Logic, Math.* logically valid. [ME < ML *rigorōs(us).* See RIGOR, -OUS] —**rig′or·ous·ly,** *adv.* —**rig′or·ous·ness,** *n.*
—**Syn. 1.** stern, austere, hard, inflexible, stiff, unyielding. See **strict. 2.** demanding, finical. **3.** hard, bitter. —**Ant. 1.** flexible, soft. **2.** inaccurate. **3.** mild.

rig·our (rig′ər), *n.* *Chiefly Brit.* rigor.

rig·our·ism (rig′ə riz′əm), *n.* *Chiefly Brit.* rigorism. —**rig′our·ist,** *n.* —**rig′our·is′tic,** *adj.*

Rigs·dag (rigz′däg′), *n.* the former parliament of Denmark, consisting of an upper house and a lower house: replaced in 1953 by the unicameral Folketing. [see REICHSTAG]

rigs·da·ler (rigz′dä′lər), *n.* a former silver coin of Denmark, equal to 16 skillings; rix-dollar. [see RIX-, DOLLAR]

Rig-Ve·da (rig vā′də, -vē′də), *n.* *Hinduism.* one of the Samhitas, a collection of 1028 hymns, dating from not later than the second millennium B.C. Also, **Rig-ve′da.** Cf. **Veda.** [< Skt, equiv. to *ric* praise + *veda* knowledge] —**Rig-ve·dic** (rig vā′dik, -vē′-), *adj.*

R.I.I.A., Royal Institute of International Affairs.

Riis (rēs), *n.* **Jacob August,** 1849–1914, U.S. journalist and social reformer, born in Denmark.

Ri·je·ka (rē ek′ə; *Serbo-Croatian.* rē ye′kä), *n.* a seaport in W Croatia, at the head of the Gulf of Quarnero. Also, **Rieka.** Italian, **Fiume.**

rijks·daal·der (rīks′däl′dər), *n.* **1.** a former silver coin of Holland, equal to 48 stivers; rix-dollar. **2.** a silver coin of Holland, equal to 2½ gulden and equivalent to about .68 of a U.S. dollar. [< D; see RIX-DOLLAR]

Rijn (rīn), *n.* Dutch name of the **Rhine.**

Rijs·wijk (rīs′vīk), *n.* Dutch name of **Ryswick.**

rik·i·sha (rik′shô), *n.* jinrikisha. Also, **rik′shaw.**

Riks·dag (riks′däg′), *n.* the parliament of Sweden, consisting of an upper house and a lower house. [see REICHSTAG]

Riks·mål (riks′môl; *Norw.* rēks′môl′), *n.* Bokmål. Formerly, **Riks′maal.**

rile (rīl), *v.t.,* **riled, ril·ing.** *Chiefly U.S.* **1.** to irritate or vex. **2.** to roil (water or the like). [var. of ROIL]
—**Syn. 1.** irk, annoy, provoke, chafe, nettle.

ri·ley (rī′lē), *adj.* *U.S.* **1.** turbid; roily. **2.** angry; vexed. [RILE + -Y[1]]

Ri·ley (rī′lē), *n.* **1. James Whit·comb** (hwit′kəm, wit′-), 1849–1916, U.S. poet. **2.** Also, **Ryley.** a boy's given name.

ri·lie·vo (rē lye′vô; *Eng.* ril yev′ō), *n., pl.* **-lie·vi** (-lye′vē; *Eng.* -yev′ē). *Italian.* relief[2] (defs. 2, 3).

ri·lie·vo schiac·cia·to (rē lye′vô skyät chä′tô), *pl.* **ri·lie·vi schiac·cia·ti** (rē lye′vē skyät chä′tē). *Italian.* sculpture in extremely low relief, having less projection than in bas-relief. Also, **rilievo stiacciato.**

ri·lie·vo stiac·cia·to (rē lye′vô styät chä′tô), *pl.* **ri·lie·vi stiac·cia·ti** (rē lye′vē styät chä′tē). *Italian.* See **rilievo schiacciato.** [lit., flattened relief]

Ril·ke (ril′kə), *n.* **Rai·ner Ma·ri·a** (rī′nər mä rē′ä), 1875–1926, Austrian poet, born in Prague.

rill[1] (ril), *n.* a small rivulet or brook. [cf. D, Fris, LG *ril,* G *Rille*]

rill[2] (ril), *n.* *Astron.* any of certain long, narrow trenches or valleys observed on the surface of the moon. Also, **rille.** [< G *Rille;* see RILL[1]]

rill·et (ril′it), *n.* a little rill; streamlet. [RILL[1] + -ET]

ril·lette (ri let′; *Fr.* rē yet′), *n., pl.* **ril·lettes** (ri lets′; *Fr.* rē yet′). *French Cookery.* a preparation of minced pork, rabbit, or goose, pounded in a mortar, seasoned, and served cold as an appetizer. [< F, dim. of *rille* piece of pork. See RAIL[1], -ETTE]

rim (rim), *n., v.,* **rimmed, rim·ming.** —*n.* **1.** the outer edge, border, margin, or brink of something, esp. of a circular object. **2.** any edge, margin, or frame added to or around a central object or area. **3.** the outer circle of a wheel, attached to the hub by spokes. **4.** a circular strip of metal forming the connection between an automobile wheel and tire, either permanently attached to or removable from the wheel. **5.** a drive wheel or flywheel, as on a spinning mule. **6.** *Basketball.* the metal ring from which the net is suspended to form the basket. **7.** See **copy desk. 8.** *Metall.* (in an ingot) an outer layer of metal having a composition different from that of the center. —*v.t.* **9.** to furnish with a rim, border, or margin. **10.** (of a golf ball or putt) to roll around the edge of (a hole) but not go in. **11.** *Basketball.* (of a basketball) to roll around (the rim of the basket) and not go in. [ME; OE *rima;* c. Icel *rimi* raised strip of land, ridge] —**rim′less,** *adj.*
—**Syn. 1.** lip, verge. RIM, BRIM refer to the boundary of a circular or curved area. A RIM is a line or surface bounding such an area; an edge or border: *the rim of a glass.* BRIM usually means the inside of the rim, at the top of a hollow object (except of a hat), and is used particularly when the object contains something: *The cup was filled to the brim.* —**Ant. 1.** center.

Ri·ma (rē′mə), *n.* a girl's given name.

Rim·baud (ram bō′; *Fr.* ran bō′), *n.* **(Jean Ni·co·las) Ar·thur** (zhän nē kô lä′ ar tyr′), 1854–91, French poet.

rime[1] (rīm), *n., v.t., v.i.,* **rimed, rim·ing.** rhyme. —**rim′er,** *n.*

rime[2] (rīm), *n., v.,* **rimed, rim·ing.** —*n.* **1.** Also, **rime′ ice′.** an opaque coating of tiny, white, granular ice particles, caused by the rapid freezing of supercooled water droplets on impact with an object. Cf. **glaze, hoarfrost.** —*v.t.* **2.** to cover with rime or hoarfrost. [ME *rim,* OE *hrīm;* c. D *rijm,* OIcel *hrīm*] —**rime′less,** *adj.*

rime[3] (rīm), *v.t.,* **rimed, rim·ing.** *Naut.* to enlarge a hole in (a sail or the like) by driving a fid through it (sometimes fol. by *up*). [dial. var. of REAM[2]]

rime riche (rēm rēsh′), *pl.* **rimes riches** (rēm rēsh′). *Pros.* rhyme created by the use of two different words, or groups of words, of which both the stressed syllables and any following syllables are identical, as in *lighted, delighted.* Also called **identical rhyme, perfect rhyme, rich rhyme.** [< F: lit., rich rhyme]

rime·ster (rīm′stər), *n.* rhymester.

rime suf·fi·sante (rēm sy fē zänt′), *pl.* **rimes suf·fi·santes** (rēm sy fē zänt′). *French.* See **full rhyme.** [lit., sufficient rhyme]

rim·fire (rim′fīᵊr′), *adj.* **1.** (of a cartridge) having the primer in a rim encircling the base. Cf. **center-fire** (def. 1). **2.** (of a firearm) designed for the use of such cartridges. [RIM + FIRE]

rim′ing stool′, a stoollike device having holes of varying sizes in the top, over which sailmakers lay sails to rime them.

Rim·i·ni (rim′ə nē; *It.* rē′me nē), *n.* a seaport in NE Italy, on the Adriatic. 94,075 (1961). Ancient, **Ariminum.**

rim′ light′ing, backlighting.

rim′ lock′, a lock nailed or screwed to one face of a door, gate, etc., as opposed to one built into its edge.

rim′ man′, copyreader (def. 2). [so called because he sits at the outer rim of a U-shaped copy desk]

rimmed′ steel′, a low-carbon steel containing enough iron oxide so that there is continuous generation of carbon monoxide during solidification.

ri·mose (rī′mōs, rī mōs′), *adj.* full of crevices, chinks, or cracks. Also, **ri·mous** (rī′məs). [< L *rīmōs(us)* full of cracks, equiv. to *rīm(a)* cleft, crack, chink + *-ōsus* -OSE[1]] —**ri′mose·ly,** *adv.* —**ri·mos·i·ty** (rī mos′i tē), *n.*

Ri·mous·ki (ri mōōs′kē), *n.* a city in SE Quebec, in SE Canada, on the St. Lawrence River. 17,739 (1961).

rim·ple (rim′pəl), *n., v.,* **-pled, -pling.** —*n.* **1.** a wrinkle. —*v.t., v.i.* **2.** to wrinkle; crumple; crease. [ME; OE *hrympel;* see RUMPLE]

rim·rock (rim′rok′), *n.* *Geol.* **1.** rock forming the natural boundary of a plateau or other rise. **2.** bedrock forming the natural boundary of a placer or of a gravel deposit. [RIM + ROCK[1]]

Rim·sky-Kor·sa·kov (rim′skē kôr′sə kôf′; *Russ.* rēm′skē kor sä kôf′), *n.* **Ni·co·lai An·dre·e·vich** (ni ko lī′ än dre′yə vich), 1844–1908, Russian composer. Also, **Rim′ski-Kor′sa·kov′, Rim′sky-Kor′sa·koff′.**

rim·stone (rim′stōn′), *n.* *Geol.* a calcareous deposit forming a dam at the edge or outlet of an overflowing pool of water, often in a cavern. [RIM + STONE]

rim′stone pool′, an underground pool of water dammed by a rimstone.

ri·mu (rē′mōō), *n.* a tall tree, *Dacrydium cupressinum,* of New Zealand, having drooping branches and needlelike leaves when young, the leaves becoming scalelike on old twigs. [< Maori]

rim·y (rī′mē), *adj.,* **rim·i·er, rim·i·est.** covered with rime ice. [OE *hrīmig.* See RIME[2], -Y[1]]

rin (rin), *n., pl.* **rin.** a money of account of Japan, the thousandth part of a yen or the tenth part of a sen, equivalent to about .0000028 of a U.S. dollar. [< Jap]

Ri·na (rē′nə), *n.* a girl's given name. Also, **Rena.**

rin·ceau (*Fr.* ran sō′), *n., pl.* **-ceaux** (*Fr.* -sō′). an ornamental foliate or floral motif. [< F, irreg. var. of MF *rainsel* << L *rāmuscul(us),* dim. of *rāmus* branch]

rind[1] (rīnd), *n.* a thick and firm outer coat or covering, as of animals, plants, fruits, cheeses, etc. [ME, OE *rind(e);* c. G *Rinde*] —**rind′less,** *adj.* —**rind′y,** *adj.*

rind[2] (rīnd, rind), *n.* a piece of iron running across an upper millstone as a support. Also, **rynd.** Also called **millrind.** [ME *rynd;* c. MD *rijn,* MLG *rīn*]

rin·der·pest (rin′dər pest′), *n.* *Vet. Pathol.* an acute, usually fatal, infectious disease of cattle, sheep, etc., caused by a virus, and characterized by high fever, diarrhea, and lesions of the skin and mucous membranes. Also called **cattle plague.** [< G, equiv. to *Rinder* cattle (pl. of *Rind*) + *Pest* pestilence]

Rine·hart (rīn′härt), *n.* **Mary Roberts,** 1876–1958, U.S. novelist and playwright.

rin·for·zan·do (*It.* rēn′fôr tsän′dô), *adj., adv.* sforzando. [< It: reinforcing (prp. of *rinforzare,* equiv. to *ri-* RE- + *inforzare* to ENFORCE)]

ring[1] (ring), *n., v.,* **ringed, ring·ing.** —*n.* **1.** a typically circular band of metal or other durable material for use or adornment, esp. one of gold or other precious metal, often set with gems, for wearing on the finger as an ornament, a token of betrothal or marriage, etc. **2.** anything having the form of such a band: *a ring of water; a ring of smoke.* **3.** a circular or surrounding line or mark: *dark rings around the eyes.* **4.** a circular course: *to dance in a ring.* **5.** the outside edge of a circular body, as a wheel; rim. **6.** a single turn in a spiral or helix or in a spiral course. **7.** *Geom.* the area or space between two concentric circles. **8.** *Archit.* rowlock (def. 1). **9.** *Bot.* See **annual ring. 10.** a circle of bark cut from around a tree. **11.** a number of persons or things placed in a circle or in an approximately circular arrangement: *a ring of stones; a ring of hills.* **12.** an enclosed area, often circular, as for a sports contest or exhibition: *a circus ring.* **13.** a bullring. **14.** an enclosure in which boxing and wrestling matches take place, usually consisting of

a square, canvas-covered platform with surrounding ropes that are supported at each corner by posts. **15.** the sport of boxing; prize fighting: *the heyday of the ring.* **16.** (formerly in the U.S., now only in Brit.) an area in a racetrack where bookmakers take bets. **17.** a public competition or contest considered as an arena, esp. for political election: *to toss one's hat in the ring.* **18.** a group of persons cooperating for unethical, illicit, or illegal purposes, as to control stock-market prices, manipulate politicians, elude the law, etc.: *a ring of dope smugglers.* **19.** *Chem.* a number of atoms so united that they may be graphically represented in cyclic form. Cf. **chain** (def. 7). **20.** a bowlike or circular piece at the top of an anchor, to which the chain or cable is secured. **21.** *Astron.* See **ring formation.** **22.** Also called **spinning ring.** *Textiles.* (in the ring-spinning frame) a circular track of highly polished steel on which the traveler moves and which imparts twists to the yarn by variations in its vertical movement. **23. run rings around,** to be obviously superior to; surpass; outdo: *As an artist, she can run rings around her brother.* **24.** *Math.* a set that is closed under the operations of addition and multiplication and that is an Abelian group with respect to addition and an associative semigroup with respect to multiplication and in which the distributive laws relating the two operations hold.
—*v.t.* **25.** to surround with a ring; encircle. **26.** to form into a ring. **27.** to insert a ring through the nose of (an animal). **28.** to hem in (animals) by riding or circling about them. **29.** to cut away the bark in a ring about (a tree, branch, etc.). **30.** (in horseshoes, ringtoss, etc.) to encircle (a stake or peg) with a ring, horseshoe, etc.
—*v.i.* **31.** to form a ring or rings. **32.** to move in a ring or a constantly curving course: *The road rings around the mountain.* **33. ring up,** (of a bird of prey) to fly upward in spirals. [ME; OE *hring;* c. D, G *ring,* OIcel *hring(r).* See RANK[1]] —**ring′less,** *adj.* —**ring′like′,** *adj.*
—**Syn. 2.** circle, circlet, hoop; annulus. **12.** arena, rink, circle. **18.** bloc, coterie, confederacy, league; gang, mob, syndicate. RING, CLIQUE are terms applied with disapproving connotations to groups of persons. RING suggests a small and intimately related group, combined for selfish and often dishonest purposes: *a gambling ring.* A CLIQUE is a small group which prides itself on its congeniality and exclusiveness: *cliques in a school.*

ring[2] (ring), *v.,* **rang, rung, ring·ing,** *n.* —*v.i.* **1.** to give forth a clear resonant sound, as a bell when struck: *The bell rang twice.* **2.** to have a given effect on the mind: *His words ring true.* **3.** to cause a bell or bells to sound, esp. as a summons: *Just ring if you need anything.* **4.** to sound loudly; be loud or resonant; resound (often fol. by *out*): *His brave words rang out.* **5.** to be filled with sound; re-echo with sound, as a place. **6.** (of the ears) to have the sensation of a continued humming sound. —*v.t.* **7.** to cause (a bell or device with a bell) to ring; sound by striking: *to ring a bell.* **8.** to produce (sound) by or as by ringing: *The bell rang a low tone.* **9.** to announce or proclaim, usher in or out, summon, signal, etc., by or as by the sound of a bell: *The bell rang the hour; to ring a person's praises.* **10.** to test (a coin or other metal object) by the sound it produces when struck against something. **11.** *Chiefly Brit.* to telephone. **12. ring a bell.** See **bell**[1] (def. 9). **13. ring down the curtain, a.** to direct that the curtain of a theater be lowered or closed. **b.** to lower or close the curtain in front of a stage. **14. ring down the curtain on,** to bring to an end: *The accident rang down the curtain on his law career.* **15. ring in, a.** to indicate one's arrival at work by punching in on a time clock. **b.** *Slang.* to introduce artfully or fraudulently: *to ring in an imposter.* **16. ring off, a.** to terminate a telephone conversation. **b.** *Brit. Slang.* to stop talking. **c.** *Brit. Slang.* to go away. **17. ring out, a.** to indicate one's departure from work by punching out on a time clock. **b.** to make a sound or noise; resound: *The church bells rang out.* **18. ring the bell.** See **bell**[1] (def. 10). **19. ring the changes.** See **change** (def. 36). **20. ring true,** to appear to be true and correct: *Even though he's a criminal, his story rings true.* **21. ring up, a.** *Chiefly Brit.* to telephone. **b.** to register (the amount of a sale) on a cash register. **22. ring up the curtain, a.** to direct that the curtain of a theater be raised or opened. **b.** to raise or open the curtain in front of a stage. **23. ring up the curtain on,** to begin; inaugurate; initiate: *The $100-a-plate dinner rang up the curtain on the hospital's fund-raising drive.* —*n.* **24.** a ringing sound, as of a bell or bells: *the ring of sleigh bells.* **25.** a sound or tone likened to the ringing of a bell: *Rings of laughter issued from the school.* **26.** any loud sound; sound continued, repeated, or reverberated: *the ring of iron upon stone.* **27.** a set or peal of bells. **28.** a telephone call: *Give me a ring tomorrow.* **29.** the act or an instance of ringing a bell: *A maid answered his ring.* **30.** a characteristic sound, as of a coin. **31.** the aspect or impression presented by a statement, an action, etc., taken as revealing a specified inherent quality: *a ring of assurance in his voice; the ring of truth; a false ring.* [ME *ring(en),* OE *hringan;* c. OIcel *hringja,* G *ringen*] —**ring′ing·ly,** *adv.* —**ring′ing·ness,** *n.*

Ring (ring), *n.* a boy's given name.

ring-a-lie·vi·o (ring′ə lē′vē ō′), *n.* a game played usually between two teams in which the members of one team attempt to find, capture, and imprison the members of the other, who can be freed only by a teammate not yet captured. [var. of *ring relievo,* prob. RELIEVE + -O]

Ring′ and the Book′, The, a narrative poem (1868–69) by Robert Browning.

ring′-billed gull′ (ring′bild′), a North American gull, *Larus delawarensis,* having a black ring around the bill.

ring′ bind′er, a loose-leaf binder in which the sheets are held in by two or more rings which can be made to snap open.

ring·bolt (ring′bōlt′), *n.* a bolt with a ring fitted in an eye at its head. [RING[1] + BOLT[1]]

ring·bone (ring′bōn′), *n.* *Vet. Pathol.* a morbid bony growth on the pastern bones of a horse, often resulting in lameness. [RING[1] + BONE[1]]

Ring′ Cy′cle. See **Ring of the Nibelung, The.**

ring′ dol′lar, *Australian.* See **holey dollar.**

ring·dove (ring′duv′), *n.* **1.** a European pigeon, *Columba palumbus,* having a whitish patch on each side of the neck. **2.** a small, Old World dove, *Streptopelia risoria,* having a black half ring around the nape of the neck. [RING[1] + DOVE[1]]

ringed (ringd), *adj.* **1.** having or wearing a ring or rings. **2.** marked or decorated with or as if with a ring or rings. **3.** surrounded by or as if by a ring or rings. **4.** formed of or with rings; ringlike or annular: *a ringed growth.* **5.** *Armor.* noting armor having rings sewn side by side to a flexible backing. [ME; see RING[1], -ED[3]]

ringed′ plain′. See **walled plain.**

ringed′ plov′er, any of several cosmopolitan plovers of the genus *Charadrius,* esp. *C. hiaticula,* brownish above and white below with a black band around the breast.

ringed′ snake′. See **ring snake.**

rin·gent (rin′jənt), *adj.* **1.** gaping. **2.** *Bot.* having widely spread lips, as some corollas. [< L *ringent-* (s. of *ringēns,* prp. of *ringī* to gape), equiv. to *ring-* open the mouth + *-ent-* -ENT]

ring·er[1] (ring′ər), *n.* **1.** one who or that which encircles, rings, etc. **2.** a quoit or horseshoe so thrown as to encircle the peg. **3.** the throw itself. [RING[1] + -ER[1]]

ring·er[2] (ring′ər), *n.* **1.** one who or that which rings or makes a ringing noise: *a ringer of bells; a bell that is a loud ringer.* **2.** *Slang.* a race horse, athlete, or the like entered in a competition under false representation as to identity or ability. **3.** *Slang.* a person or thing that closely resembles another: *He sure is a ringer for my uncle.* **4.** Also, **ring′ers.** Also called **ring taw.** *Marbles.* a game in which players place marbles in a cross marked in the center of a circle, the object being to knock as many marbles as possible outside of the circle by using another marble as a shooter. **5.** *Australian.* a highly skilled sheep shearer. [late ME; see RING[2], -ER[1]]

Ring′er's solu′tion (ring′ərz), *Pharm.* an aqueous solution of the chlorides of sodium, potassium, and calcium, isotonic with blood and tissue fluid, used chiefly for sustaining tissue in physiological experimentation and for parenteral purposes. Cf. **isotonic sodium chloride solution.** [named after Sydney *Ringer* (1835–1910), English physician]

ring′ fin′ger, the third finger, esp. of the left hand, on which an engagement ring, wedding band, etc., is traditionally worn. [ME *ringe finger,* OE *hring fingre*]

ring′ forma′tion, any circular or almost circular area of the moon completely or partially surrounded by elevations; ring; ringed plain; walled plain; crater.

ring′ frame′. See **ring-spinning frame.**

ring′ gage′, a gage for checking the diameters of circular manufactured objects, consisting of a ring having a hole which is of either the maximum or minimum allowable diameter.

ring′ gate′, *Foundry.* a gate having a widened opening containing a centered disk to prevent the metal from falling in a direct vertical stream.

ring′ gear′, *Mach.* a gear in the form of a ring with internal teeth.

ring·hals (ring′hals), *n., pl.* **-hals, -hals·es.** an African cobra, *Hemachatus haemachatus,* that squirts or "spits" its venom at a victim. [< SAfrD, equiv. to *ring* RING[1] + *hals* neck]

ring·lead·er (ring′lē′dər), *n.* one who leads others, esp. in opposition to authority, law, etc.: *a ringleader of revolutionary activities.* [RING[1] + LEADER]

ring·let (ring′lit), *n.* **1.** a small ring or circle. **2.** a curled lock of hair. [RING[1] + -LET] —**ring′let·ed,** *adj.*

ring′ machine′, *Print.* a Linotype used primarily for making corrections.

ring′ man′, *Print.* an operator of a ring machine.

ring·mas·ter (ring′mas′tər, -mä′stər), *n.* one in charge of the performances in the ring of a circus. [RING[1] + MASTER]

ring·neck (ring′nek′), *n.* a ring-necked bird. [RING[1] + NECK]

ring-necked (ring′nekt′), *adj.* *Zool.* having a ring of distinctive color around the neck.

ring′-necked duck′, a North American scaup duck, *Aythya collaris,* having a chestnut ring around the neck.

ring′-necked pheas′ant, a gallinaceous Asian bird, *Phasianus colchicus,* now introduced into Great Britain and the U.S.

ring′-neck snake′, any of several small, nonvenomous North American snakes of the genus *Diadophis,* usually having a conspicuous yellow or orange ring around the neck. Also, **ring′-necked snake′.** Also called **ring snake.**

Ring′ of the Ni′be·lung, The (nē′bə lo͝ong′), **1.** (*italics*) Richard Wagner's tetralogy of music dramas: *Das Rheingold* (completed 1869), *Die Walküre* (completed 1870), *Siegfried* (completed 1876), and *Götterdämmerung* (completed 1876): the cycle was first performed at Bayreuth, 1876. **2.** (in the *Nibelungenlied*) a magic ring stolen by Alberich, who put a curse on it when it was later stolen from him.

ring′ ou′zel. See under **ouzel** (def. 1).

ring′ rot′, *Plant Pathol.* a disease of potatoes, characterized by wilted foliage and rotting of the ring of vascular bundles in the tubers, caused by a bacterium, *Corynebacterium sepedonicum.*

Ring′ Round′ the Moon′, a comedy (1948) by Jean Anouilh. French, **L'Invitation au Château.**

ring·sail (ring′sāl′), *n.* ringtail (def. 3).

ring′ seiz′ing. See **cuckold's knot.**

ring′ shout′, a group dance of West African origin introduced into parts of the southern U.S. by Negro revivalists, performed by shuffling counterclockwise in a circle while answering shouts of a preacher with corresponding shouts, and held to be, in its vigorous antiphonal patterns, a source in the development of jazz.

ring·side (ring′sīd′), *n.* **1.** the area immediately surrounding a ring, esp. the area occupied by the first row of seats on all sides of a boxing or wrestling ring. **2.** any place providing a close view. —*adj.* **3.** in or pertaining to the area immediately surrounding a ring or arena. **4.** close to the point of action; having a close view. [RING[1] + SIDE[1]]

ring′ snake′, **1.** See **grass snake** (def. 1). **2.** See **ring-neck snake.** Also, **ringed snake.**

ring′ spin′ning, a process of spinning in which the yarn is twisted and drawn while passing through a small metal device traveling rapidly around a ring in the operation of winding the yarn onto a bobbin. Cf. **mule spinning.**

ring′-spin·ning frame′ (ring′spin′ing), a machine containing the ring, traveler, and bobbin used in spinning yarn. Also called **ring frame, ring′ spin′ner.**

ring·ster (ring′stər), *n.* *U.S. Informal.* a member of a ring, esp. a political or price-fixing ring. [RING[1] + -STER]

ring′ stone′, a voussoir appearing on a face of an arch.

ring-streaked (ring′strēkt′), *adj.* having streaks or bands of color around the body.

ring·tail (ring′tāl′), *n.* **1.** any phalanger of the genus *Pseudocheirus,* related by the structure of the molar teeth to the koala. **2.** cacomistle. **3.** Also called **ringsail.** *Naut.* a narrow studdingsail set abaft a gaff sail, esp. a spanker, upon spears extending beyond the gaff and boom. Cf. **ringtail topsail.** [RING[1] + TAIL[1]]

ring-tailed (ring′tāld′), *adj.* having the tail ringed with alternating colors, as a raccoon.

ring′-tailed cat′, cacomistle.

ring′tail top′sail, *Naut.* a triangular topsail set abaft and above a mutton spanker, from the end of the boom to the head of the topmast. Cf. **ringtail** (def. 3).

ring′ taw′, *Marbles.* ringer[2] (def. 4).

ring·toss (ring′tôs′, -tos′), *n.* a game in which rings, often made of rope, are tossed to encircle an upright peg. [RING[1] + TOSS]

Ring·wood (ring′wo͝od′), *n.* a town in N New Jersey. 4182 (1960).

ring·worm (ring′wûrm′), *n.* *Pathol.* any of a number of contagious skin diseases caused by certain parasitic fungi and characterized by the formation of ring-shaped eruptive patches. [ME; see RING[1], WORM]

rink (ringk), *n.* **1.** a smooth expanse of ice for ice skating, often artificially prepared and inside a building or arena. **2.** a smooth floor, usually of wood, for roller skating. **3.** a building or enclosure for ice skating or roller skating; skating arena. **4.** an area of ice marked off for the game of curling. **5.** a section of a bowling green where a match can be played. **6.** a set of players on one side in a lawn-bowling or curling match. [orig. Scot; ME *renk,* appar. < MF *renc* RANK[1]]

rinse (rins), *v.,* **rinsed, rins·ing,** *n.* —*v.t.* **1.** to wash lightly, as by pouring water into or over or by dipping in water: *to rinse a cup.* **2.** to douse or drench in clean water as a final stage in washing. **3.** to remove (soap, dirt, etc.) by such a process (often fol. by *off*). —*n.* **4.** the act or an instance of rinsing. **5.** the water used for rinsing. **6.** any preparation that may be used on the hair after washing, esp. to remove all the soap or shampoo, increase manageability and luster, or to tint the hair. **7.** the act or an instance of using such a preparation on the hair. [ME *rynce(n)* < MF *rincer,* OF *recincier* < ?] —**rins′a·bil′i·ty, rins′i·bil′i·ty,** *n.* —**rins′a·ble, rins′i·ble,** *adj.*

rins·ing (rin′sing), *n.* **1.** the act of one who rinses or an instance of rinsing. **2.** Usually, **rinsings.** the liquid with which anything has been rinsed. [ME *rinsynge.* See RINSE, -ING[1]]

ri·o·bit·su (rē′ō bit′so͞o, -bēt′-; *Jap.* RYÔ bē′tso͞o), *n., pl.* **-su.** (on the tsuba of a Japanese sword or knife) an opening, often one of two, beside the seppa dai for a kogai or kozuka. [< Jap]

Ri·o Bran·co (rē′o͞o bRäNNG′ko͞o), a city in W Brazil. 18,147 (1960).

Rí·o Bra·vo (rē′ô brä′vô), Mexican name of **Rio Grande** (def. 1).

Rí·o Cuar·to (rē′ô kwär′tô), a city in central Argentina. 59,900 (est. 1956).

Ri·o de Ja·nei·ro (rē′ō dā zhə nâr′ō, jə-, dē, də; *Port.* Rē′o͞o də zhə ne′Ro͞o), a seaport in SE Brazil: former capital. 3,223,408 (1960). Also called **Ri·o.**

Rí·o de la Pla·ta (*Sp.* Rē′ô the lä plä′tä). See **Plata, Rio de la.**

Ri′o Dell′ (rē′ō), a town in NW California. 3222 (1960).

Rí·o de O·ro (Rē′ô the ô′Rô), **1.** the S part of Spanish Sahara: formerly a Spanish colony. ab. 70,000 sq. mi. *Cap.:* Villa Cisneros. **2.** former name of **Spanish Sahara.**

Rí·o Ga·lle·gos (Rē′ô gä ye′gôs), a seaport in S Argentina, in S Patagonia. 5888 (est. 1965). Also called **Gallegos.**

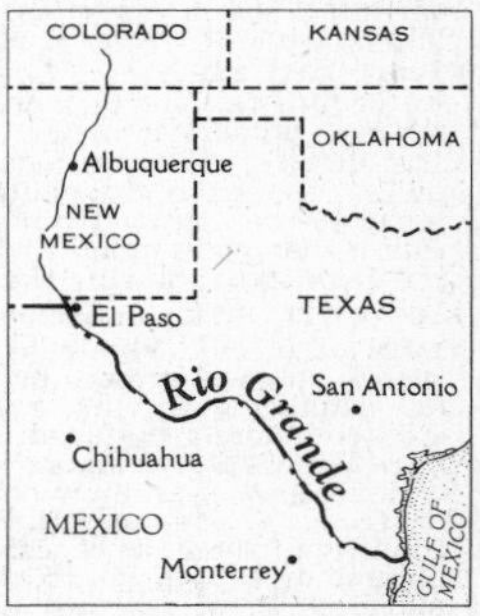

Ri·o Grande (rē′ō grand′, gran′dē, grän′dā *for 1; Port.* Rē′o͞o gRäNN′də *for 2, 3*), **1.** Mexican, **Río Bravo.** a river flowing from SW Colorado through central New Mexico and along the boundary between Texas and Mexico into the Gulf of Mexico. 1800 mi. long. **2.** a river flowing W from SE Brazil into the Paraná River. 650 mi. long. **3.** Also called **Rio Grande do Sul.** See **São Pedro de Rio Grande do Sul.**

Ri′o Grande′ Cit′y, a town in S Texas. 5835 (1960).

Ri·o Gran·de do Nor·te (Rē′o͞o gRäNN′də do͞o nôR′tə), a state in E Brazil. 1,157,258 (1960); 20,464 sq. mi. *Cap.:* Natal.

Ri·o Gran·de do Sul (Rē′o͞o gRäNN′də do͞o so͞ol′), **1.** a state in S Brazil. 5,448,823 (1960); 107,923 sq. mi. *Cap.:* Pôrto Alegre. **2.** See **São Pedro de Rio Grande do Sul.**

Rí·o Mu·ni (Rē′ô mo͞o′nē), the mainland province of Equatorial Guinea on the Guinea coast; formerly the mainland portion of Spanish Guinea. 183,377 (1960); 10,040 sq. mi. See map under **Fernando Po.**

Rí·o Ne·gro (rē′ō nā′grō; *Sp.* Rē′ô ne′gRô). See **Negro, Río.**

Ri′on Strait′ (rē′on; *Gk.* Rē′ôn), Lepanto (def. 3).

ri·ot (rī′ət), *n.* **1.** a noisy, violent public disorder caused by a group or crowd of persons, as by a group fighting in a tavern or a crowd protesting against another group, a government policy, etc., in the streets. **2.** *Law.* a disturbance of the public peace by three or more persons

acting together in a disrupting and tumultuous manner in carrying out their private purposes. **3.** violent or wild disorder or confusion. **4.** loose, wanton living; profligacy. **5.** unrestrained revelry. **6.** an unbridled outbreak, as of emotions, passions, etc. **7.** a brilliant display: *a riot of color.* **8.** *Informal.* something or someone hilariously funny: *He was a riot at the party.* **9.** **run riot, a.** to act without control or restraint: *The neighbors let their children run riot.* **b.** to grow luxuriantly or abundantly: *Crab grass is running riot in our lawn.* **—v.i. 10.** to take part in a riot or disorderly public outbreak. **11.** to live in a loose or wanton manner; indulge in unrestrained revelry: *Many of the Roman emperors rioted notoriously.* **12.** *Hunting.* (of a hound or pack) to pursue an animal other than the intended quarry. **13.** to indulge unrestrainedly; run riot. **—v.t. 14.** to spend (money, time, etc.) in riotous living (usually fol. by *away* or *out*). [ME < OF *riote* debate, dispute, quarrel, deriv. of *r(u)iohter* to quarrel, dim. of *ruir* to make an uproar < L *rugīre* to roar] **—ri′ot·er,** *n.* **—ri′ot·ing·ly,** *adv.* **—ri′ot·ist,** *n.* **—ri′ot·is′tic,** *adj.*
—Syn. 1. outbreak, brawl, fray, melee. **3.** uproar, tumult, disturbance. **10.** brawl, fight. **11.** carouse.

Ri′ot Act′, 1. an English statute of 1715 providing that if 12 or more persons assemble unlawfully and riotously, to the disturbance of the public peace, and refuse to disperse upon proclamation they shall be considered guilty of felony. **2. read the riot act, a.** to give a command to cease an activity; threaten with penalties. **b.** to reprimand; censure: *The principal read them the riot act for their behavior at the assembly.*

ri′ot gun′, a gun, esp. a shotgun with a short barrel, for quelling riots rather than inflicting serious injury.

ri·ot·ous (rī′ə təs), *adj.* **1.** (of an act) characterized by or of the nature of rioting or a disturbance of the peace. **2.** (of a person) inciting or taking part in a riot. **3.** given to or marked by unrestrained revelry; loose; wanton: *riotous living.* **4.** boisterous or uproarious: *riotous laughter.* **5.** *Informal.* hilariously funny. [ME; see RIOT, -OUS] **—ri′ot·ous·ly,** *adv.* **—ri′ot·ous·ness,** *n.*

ri′ot squad′, a group of police officers having special training and equipment for quelling riots and other public disturbances.

Ri′o Vis′ta (vis′tə), a town in central California. 2616 (1960).

rip[1] (rip), *v.*, **ripped, rip·ping,** *n.* **—v.t. 1.** to cut or tear apart in a rough or vigorous manner: *to rip open a seam; to rip up a sheet.* **2.** to cut or tear away in a rough or vigorous manner: *to rip bark from a tree.* **3.** to saw (wood) in the direction of the grain. **—v.i. 4.** to become torn apart or split open: *Cheap cloth rips easily.* **5.** *Informal.* to move with violence or great speed: *The roadster ripped along in a cloud of dust and exhaust fumes.* **6. let rip,** *Chiefly Brit. Slang.* **a.** to utter a series of oaths; swear. **b.** to speak or write violently, rapidly, or at great length: *Hamlet lets rip some magnificent poetry.* **7. rip into,** *Informal.* to attack physically or verbally; assail. **8. rip off,** *Slang.* to steal or pilfer. **9. rip out,** *Informal.* to utter angrily, as with an oath or exclamation. **—n. 10.** a rent made by ripping; tear. [late ME; c. Fris *rippe,* Flem *rippen;* cf. dial. E *ripple* to scratch] **—rip′pa·ble,** *adj.*
—Syn. 1. See **tear**[2]. **10.** laceration, cut.

rip[2] (rip), *n.* a stretch of turbulent water at sea or in a river. [see RIP[1], RIPPLE[1]]

rip[3] (rip), *n.* *Informal.* **1.** a dissolute or worthless person. **2.** a worthless or worn-out horse. **3.** something of little or no value. [prob. alter. of *rep,* shortened form of REPROBATE]

Rip (rip), *n.* a boy's given name, form of **Robert.**

R.I.P., 1. may he (or she) rest in peace. [< L *requiescat in pace*] **2.** may they rest in peace. [< L *requiescant in pace*] Also, **RIP**

ri·par·i·an (ri pâr′ē ən, rī-), *adj.* **1.** of, pertaining to, or situated or dwelling on the bank of a river or other body of water: *riparian villas.* **—n. 2.** *Law.* one who owns land on the bank of a natural watercourse or body of water. [< L *rīpāri(us)* that frequents river banks (*rīp(a)* bank of a river + *-ārius* -ARY) + -AN]

ripar′ian right′, *Law.* a right, as fishing or use of water for irrigation or power, enjoyed by one who owns riparian property.

rip′ cord′, 1. *Aeron.* a cord on a parachute that, when pulled, opens the parachute for descent. **2.** a cord fastened in the bag of a passenger balloon or dirigible so that a sharp pull upon it will rip or open the bag and let the gas escape, causing the balloon to descend rapidly.

rip′ cur′rent, undertow (def. 1).

ripe[1] (rīp), *adj.*, **rip·er, rip·est. 1.** having arrived at such a stage of growth or development as to be ready for reaping, gathering, eating, or use, as grain, fruit, etc.; completely matured. **2.** resembling such fruit, as in ruddiness and fullness: *ripe, red lips.* **3.** fully grown or developed, as animals when ready to be killed and used for food. **4.** advanced to the point of being in the best condition for use, as cheese, beer, etc. **5.** arrived at the highest or a high point of development or excellence; mature. **6.** of mature judgment or knowledge: *ripe scholars; a ripe mind.* **7.** characterized by full development of body or mind: *of ripe years.* **8.** (of time) advanced: *a ripe old age.* **9.** (of ideas, plans, etc.) ready for action, execution, etc. **10.** (of people) fully prepared, ready, or mature enough to do or undergo something: *He was ripe for college.* **11.** ready for some operation or process: *a ripe abscess.* **12.** fully or sufficiently advanced; ready enough; auspicious: *The time is ripe for a new foreign policy.* **13.** *Archaic.* drunk: *reeling ripe.* [ME; OE *rīpe;* c. D *rijp,* G *reif;* akin to OE *rīpan* to REAP] **—ripe′ly,** *adv.* **—ripe′ness,** *n.*
—Syn. 1. grown, aged. RIPE, MATURE, MELLOW refer to that which is no longer in an incomplete stage of development. RIPE implies completed growth beyond which the processes of decay begin: *a ripe harvest.* MATURE means fully grown and developed as used of living organisms: *a mature animal or tree.* MELLOW denotes complete absence of sharpness or asperity, with sweetness and richness such as characterize ripeness or age: *mellow fruit or flavor.*

ripe[2] (rīp), *v.t.*, **riped, rip·ing.** *Brit. Dial.* **1.** to search (a place); ransack. **2.** to investigate; examine. [ME *ripe(n),* OE *rȳpan;* prob. akin to Goth *raupjan,* G *raufen, rupfen* to pull, pluck]

rip·en (rī′pən), *v.t., v.i.* **1.** to make or become ripe. **2.** to bring or come to maturity, the proper condition, etc.; mature. [RIPE[1] + -EN[1]] **—rip′en·er,** *n.*

ripe′ rot′, *Plant Pathol.* a disease of ripe fruits or vegetables characterized by spotting and rapid decay, caused by any of several fungi or bacteria.

ri·pid·o·lite (ri pid′ᵊlīt′, rī-), *n.* *Mineral.* a mineral of the chlorite group, essentially hydrated magnesium and aluminum silicate with some ferrous iron. [< G *Ripidolith* < Gk *rhīpid-* (s. of *rhīpís*) fan + G *-lith* -LITE]

ri·pie·no (ri pyā′nō; *It.* RE pye′nô), *n., pl.* **-nos;** *It.* **-ni** (-nē), *adj.* *Music.* **—n. 1.** tutti (defs. 3, 4). **—adj. 2.** tutti (def. 2). [< It: full]

Rip·ley (rip′lē), *n.* **1. George,** 1802–80, U.S. literary critic, author, and social reformer: associated with the founding of Brook Farm. **2.** a town in W Tennessee. 3782 (1960). **3.** a town in W West Virginia. 2756 (1960). **4.** a town in N Mississippi. 2668 (1960).

Rip·on (rip′ən), *n.* a town in central Wisconsin. 6163 (1960).

ri·poste (ri pōst′), *n., v.,* **-post·ed, -post·ing. —n. 1.** *Fencing.* a quick thrust given after parrying a lunge. **2.** a quick, sharp return in speech or action; counterstroke: *a brilliant riposte to an insult.* **—v.i. 3.** to make a riposte. **4.** to reply or retaliate. Also, **ri·post′.** [< F, alter. of *risposte* < It *risposta* response, deriv. of *rispondere* to RESPOND]

rip·per (rip′ər), *n.* **1.** one who or that which rips. **2.** Also, **rip′per bill′, rip′per act′.** *U.S.* a legislative bill or act for taking powers of appointment to and removal from office away from the usual holders of these powers and conferring them unrestrictedly on a chief executive, as a governor or mayor, or on a board of officials. **3.** a double-ripper. **4.** a killer, esp. a madman, who dispatches and often mutilates his victims with a knife or similar weapon. **5.** *Chiefly Brit. Slang.* something especially strong, fine, or good of its kind. [RIP[1] + -ER[1]]

rip·ping (rip′ing), *adj.* **1.** of or pertaining to tearing. **2.** *Chiefly Brit. Slang.* excellent, splendid, or fine. [RIP[1] + -ING[2]] **—rip′ping·ly,** *adv.* **—rip′ping·ness,** *n.*

rip′ping bar′. See **pinch bar.**

rip′ping i′ron, *Naut.* See **rave hook.**

rip·ple[1] (rip′əl), *v.,* **-pled, -pling,** *n.* **—v.i. 1.** (of a liquid surface) to form small waves or undulations, as water agitated by a breeze. **2.** to flow with a light rise and fall or ruffling of the surface. **3.** (of a solid surface) to form or have small undulations, ruffles, or folds. **4.** (of sound) to undulate or rise and fall in tone, inflection, or magnitude. **—v.t. 5.** to form small waves or undulations on; agitate lightly. **6.** to mark as if with ripples; give a wavy form to. **—n. 7.** a small wave or undulation, as on water. **8.** any similar movement or appearance; a small undulation or wave, as in hair. **9.** *U.S.* a small rapid. **10.** See **ripple mark. 11.** a sound, as of water flowing in ripples: *a ripple of laughter.* [?] **—rip′ple·less,** *adj.* **—rip′pling·ly,** *adv.*
—Syn. 1. wave, undulate, purl. **5.** ruffle, curl, dimple. **7.** wavelet, ruffling. See **wave.**

rip·ple[2] (rip′əl), *n., v.,* **-pled, -pling. —n. 1.** a toothed or comblike device for removing seeds or capsules from flax, hemp, etc. **—v.t. 2.** to remove the seeds or capsules from (flax or hemp) with a ripple. [ME *ripel;* c. D *repel,* G *riffel*]

rip′ple mark′, one of the wavy lines or ridges produced, esp. on sand, by the action of waves, wind, or the like.

rip·pler (rip′lər), *n.* **1.** one who ripples flax, hemp, etc. **2.** an instrument for rippling; ripple. [RIPPLE[2] + -ER[1]]

rip·plet (rip′lit), *n.* a small ripple. [RIPPLE[1] + -ET]

rip·ply (rip′lē), *adj.* **1.** characterized by ripples; rippling. **2.** sounding like rippling water. [RIPPLE[1] + -Y[1]]

rip·rap (rip′rap′), *n., v.,* **-rapped, -rap·ping. —n. 1.** a quantity of broken stone for foundations, revetments of embankments, etc. **2.** a foundation or wall of stones thrown together irregularly. **—v.t. 3.** to construct with or strengthen by stones, either loose or fastened with mortar. [gradational redupl. of RAP[1]]

rip-roar·ing (rip′rōr′ing, -rôr′-), *adj.* *Informal.* boisterously wild and exciting; riotous: *Have a rip-roaring good time.* [RIP[1] + ROARING, alter. of *rip-roarious,* modeled on *uproarious*]

rip·saw (rip′sô′), *n.* a saw for cutting wood with the grain. [RIP[1] + SAW[1]]

rip·snort·er (rip′snôr′tər), *n.* *Informal.* **1.** something or someone exceedingly strong or violent: *a ripsnorter of a gale.* **2.** something or someone remarkably good or exciting. [RIP[1] + SNORTER]

rip·tide (rip′tīd′), *n.* a tide that opposes another or other tides, causing a violent disturbance in the sea. [RIP[2] + TIDE[1]]
—Syn. See **undertow.**

Rip·u·ar·i·an (rip′yo͞o âr′ē ən), *adj.* **1.** designating or pertaining to the group of Franks who dwelt along the Rhine in the neighborhood of Cologne during the 4th century or the code of laws observed by them. **—n. 2.** a Ripuarian Frank. [< ML *Ripuāri(us)* (sp. var. of *Ribuārius,* ? equiv. to L *rīp(a)* river bank + *-ārius* -ARY) + -AN]

Rip Van Win·kle (rip′ van wing′kəl), **1.** (in a story by Washington Irving) a ne'er-do-well who sleeps 20 years and upon waking is startled to find how much the world has changed. **2.** (*italics.*) the story itself, published in *The Sketch Book* (1819).

rise (rīz), *v.,* **rose, ris·en** (riz′ən), **ris·ing,** *n.* **—v.i. 1.** to get up from a lying, sitting, or kneeling posture; assume an upright position: *He rose and walked over to greet me. With great effort he rose to his knees.* **2.** to get up from bed, esp. to begin the day after a night's sleep: *to rise early.* **3.** to become erect and stiff, as the hair in fright. **4.** to get up after falling or being thrown down. **5.** to become active in opposition or resistance; revolt or rebel. **6.** to be built up, erected, or constructed. **7.** to spring up or grow, as plants: *Weeds rose overnight.* **8.** to become prominent on or project from a surface, as a blister. **9.** to come into existence; appear. **10.** to come into action, as a wind, storm, etc. **11.** to occur: *A quarrel rose between them.* **12.** to originate, issue, or be derived; to have a source. **13.** to move from a lower to a higher position; move upward; ascend: *A bird rises in the air.* **14.** to ascend above the horizon, as a heavenly body. **15.** to extend directly upward; project vertically: *The tower rises to a height of 60 feet. The Empire State Building rises above the other skyscrapers.* **16.** to have an upward slant or curve: *The path rises as it approaches the woods.* **17.** to attain higher rank, status, or importance or a higher economic level: *to rise in the world.* **18.** to advance to a higher level of action, thought, feeling, etc.: *to rise above the commonplace.* **19.** *Angling.* (of fish) to come up toward the surface of the water in pursuit of food or bait. **20.** to prove oneself equal to a demand, emergency, etc. (fol. by *to*): *to rise to the occasion; to rise to one's responsibilities.* **21.** to become animated, cheerful, or heartened, as the spirits. **22.** to become roused or stirred: *to feel one's temper rising.* **23.** to increase in height, as the level of water: *The river rose thirty feet in eight hours.* **24.** to swell or puff up, as dough from the action of yeast. **25.** to increase in amount, as prices. **26.** to increase in price or value, as commodities. **27.** to increase in degree, intensity, or force, as fever, color, etc. **28.** to become louder or of higher pitch, as the voice. **29.** to adjourn or close a session, as a deliberative body or court. **30.** to return from the dead: *Christ rose from the dead and on the third day He ascended into heaven.*
—v.t. 31. to cause to rise. **32.** *Naut.* to cause (something) to rise above the visible horizon by approaching nearer to it; raise.
—n. 33. the act or an instance of rising. **34.** appearance above the horizon, as of the sun or moon. **35.** elevation or increase in rank, fortune, influence, power, etc.: *the rise and fall of ancient Rome.* **36.** an increase in height, as of the level of water. **37.** the amount of such increase. **38.** an increase in amount, as of prices. **39.** an increase in price or value, as of commodities. **40.** *Chiefly Brit.* raise (defs. 33–36). **41.** an increase in degree or intensity as of temperature. **42.** an increase in loudness or in pitch, as of the voice. **43.** *Archit., Building Trades.* **a.** the measured height of any of various things, as a roof, a flight of steps, a stair step, the crown of a road, etc. **b.** the measured height of an arch from the springing line to the highest point of the intrados. **44.** the vertical distance through which the floor of an elevator or the like passes. **45.** origin, source, or beginning: *the rise of a stream in a mountain.* **46.** a coming into existence or notice: *the rise of a new talent.* **47.** extension upward. **48.** the amount of such extension. **49.** upward slope, as of ground or a road. **50.** a piece of rising or high ground: *a house built upon a gentle rise.* **51.** *Angling.* the coming up of a fish toward the surface in pursuit of food or bait. **52. get a rise out of,** *Informal.* to provoke, as to action or anger; evoke the expected or desired response: *You'll always get a rise out of her if you mention her Southern accent.* **53. give rise to,** to originate; produce; cause: *The industrial revolution gave rise to accelerated urbanization.* [ME *rise(n),* OE *rīsan;* c. Goth *reisan,* OHG *rīsan,* D *rijzen.* See RAISE, REAR[2]]
—Syn. 12. arise, proceed. **13.** mount. **17.** succeed, advance. **31.** RISE, RAISE are not synonyms, although the forms of RAISE are commonly and mistakenly used as if they also meant RISE. RISE, the verb with irregular forms, seldom takes an object: *A person rises from a chair.* RAISE, with regular forms (*raised, have raised, raising*), originally meaning to cause something to rise, has to have an object, either a concrete one or an abstract one: *One raises his hat. He had raised a question.* **—Ant. 1.** sink. **4.** fall. **13.** descend. **17.** fail.

rise′ of floor′, *Naut.* deadrise. Also called **rise′ of bot′tom.**

Rise′ of Si′las Lap′ham, The (sī′ləs lap′əm), a novel (1885) by William Dean Howells.

ris·er (rī′zər), *n.* **1.** one who rises, esp. from bed: *to be an early riser.* **2.** the vertical face of a stair step. **3.** a vertical pipe, duct, or conduit. **4.** *Foundry.* a chamber or enlarged opening at the top of a mold for allowing air to escape or adding extra metal. **5.** *Naut.* **a.** a heavy strake of planking in the vicinity of the garboard strake in a wooden vessel. **b.** rising (def. 11). [ME; see RISE, -ER[1]]

rish·i (rish′ē), *n.* *Hinduism.* **1.** an inspired sage or poet. **2.** (*cap.*) one of seven of these to whom the *Vedas* supposedly were revealed. [< Skt *ṛṣi*]

ris·i·bil·i·ty (riz′ə bil′i tē), *n., pl.* **-ties. 1.** Often, **risibilities.** the ability or disposition to laugh; humorous awareness of the ridiculous and absurd: *Risibility is an indication of a cheerful nature.* **2.** laughter. [< LL *rīsibil(itās).* See RISIBLE, -ITY]

ris·i·ble (riz′ə bəl), *adj.* **1.** having the ability, disposition, or readiness to laugh. **2.** pertaining to or connected with laughing. **3.** causing or capable of causing laughter; laughable; ludicrous. [LL *rīsibil(is)* that can laugh, equiv. to L *rīs(us)* (ptp. of *rīdēre* to laugh) + *-ibilis* -IBLE]
—Syn. 3. funny, humorous, comical.

ris·ing (rī′zing), *adj.* **1.** advancing, ascending, or mounting: *rising smoke.* **2.** growing or advancing to adult years: *the rising generation.* **3.** *Heraldry.* (of a bird) represented as about to take flight; rousant: *an eagle rising.* Cf. **soaring. —adv. 4.** *U.S. Dial.* somewhat more than: *The crop came to rising 6000 bushels.* **5.** in approach of; almost; well-nigh: *a lad rising sixteen.* **—n. 6.** the act of one who or that which rises. **7.** an insurrection; rebellion; revolt. **8.** something that rises; projection or prominence. **9.** a period of leavening of dough preceding baking. **10.** *Chiefly Dial.* a morbid swelling, as an abscess or boil. **11.** Also called **riser.** *Naut.* a stringer supporting the thwarts of an open boat. [ME *riseng* (n.). See RISE, -ING[2], ING[1]]

ris′ing diph′thong, *Phonet.* a diphthong in which the first of two apparent vocalic elements is of lesser stress or sonority than the second, as in *guava* (go͞o ä′və, go͞o ä′və, *or* gwä′və). Cf. **falling diphthong.**

ris′ing floor′, *Naut.* See **deep floor.**

ris′ing hinge′, a gravity hinge causing a door, shutter, etc., to rise slightly when opened.

ris′ing line′, *Naval Archit.* a line drawn on the sheer plan of a vessel to indicate the upper edges of the ends of the floors.

ris′ing rhythm′, *Pros.* a rhythmic pattern created by a succession of metrical feet each of which is composed of one accented syllable preceded by one or more unaccented ones.

risk (risk), *n.* **1.** exposure to the chance of injury or loss; a hazard or dangerous chance: *He decided to take the risk.* **2.** *Insurance.* **a.** the hazard or chance of loss. **b.** the degree of probability of such loss. **c.** the amount

which the insurance company may lose. **d.** a person or thing with reference to the hazard involved in insuring him or it. **e.** the type of loss, as life, fire, marine disaster, earthquake, etc., against which an insurance policy is drawn. **3. run a risk,** to put oneself in danger; hazard; venture: *a generation that refuses to run a risk and makes security its idol.* —*v.t.* **4.** to expose to the chance of injury or loss; hazard: *to risk one's life to save another.* **5.** to venture upon; take or run the chance of: *to risk a fall in climbing; to risk a battle.* [< F *risque* < It *risc(hi)o,* deriv. of *risicare* to dare, risk < Gk *rhiza* cliff, root (through meaning of to sail round a cliff)] —**risk′er,** *n.* —**risk′less,** *adj.*
—**Syn. 1.** venture, peril, jeopardy. **4.** imperil, endanger, jeopardize. **5.** dare.

risk′ cap′ital. See **venture capital.**

risk·y (ris′kē), *adj.,* **risk·i·er, risk·i·est.** attended with or involving risk; hazardous: *a risky undertaking.* —**risk′i·ly,** *adv.* —**risk′i·ness,** *n.* [RISK + -Y¹]
—**Syn.** dangerous, perilous.

Ri·sor·gi·men·to (rē sôr′jē men′tô), *n.* the period of or the movement for the liberation and unification of Italy 1750–1870. [< It, equiv. to *risorg(ere)* (to) rise again (< L *resurgere*) + -*i-* -I- + -*mento* -MENT]

ri·sot·to (ri sô′tō, -sot′ō; *It.* rē zôt′tô), *n.* *Italian Cookery.* a dish of rice cooked with broth and flavored with grated cheese and other seasonings. [< It]

ris·qué (ri skā′; *Fr.* rēs kā′), *adj.* daringly close to indelicacy or impropriety; off-color: *a risqué story.* [< F, ptp. of *risquer* to RISK]
—**Syn.** broad, gross, indecent, ribald.

Riss (ris), *n.* the third stage of the glaciation of Eurasia during the Pleistocene. Cf. **Illinoian** (def. 1). [named after the *Riss,* river in southwestern Germany]

ris·sole (ri sōl′, ris′ōl; *Fr.* rē sôl′), *n., pl.* **ris·soles** (ri sōlz′, ris′ōlz; *Fr.* rē sôl′). a small pastry, often in turnover form, filled with a sweet or savory mixture and usually fried in deep fat. [< F; MF *roissole, rousole* ? << VL **russeola* (fem. adj.) reddish]

ris·so·lé (ris′ə lē, ris′ə lā′; *Fr.* rē sô lā′), *adj.* (of foods) browned in deep fat. [< F, ptp. of *rissoler* to brown, deriv. of *rissole* RISSOLE]

rit., *Music.* ritardando. Also, **ritard.**

rit·a (rit′ə), *n.* *Hinduism.* the Vedic concept of cosmic and social order. [< Skt *ṛta* true]

Ri·ta (rē′tə), *n.* a girl's given name, shortened form of **Margarita.**

ri·tar·dan·do (rē′tär dän′dō; *It.* rē′tär dän′dô), *adj.* *Music.* becoming gradually slower. [< It, prp. of *ritardare;* see RETARD]

rite (rīt), *n.* **1.** a formal or ceremonial act or procedure prescribed or customary in religious or other solemn use: *rites of baptism; sacrificial rites.* **2.** a particular form or system of religious or other ceremonial practice: *the Roman rite; the Scottish rite in Freemasonry.* **3.** (*often cap.*) one of the historical versions of the Eucharistic service: *the Anglican Rite.* **4.** (*often cap.*) liturgy. **5.** (*sometimes cap.*) *Eastern Ch., Western Ch.* a division or differentiation of churches according to liturgy. **6.** any customary observance or practice: *the elegant rite of afternoon tea; the white-collar rite of the 10 a.m. coffee break.* [ME < L *rīt(us)*] —**rite′less,** *adj.* —**rite′less·ness,** *n.*
—**Syn. 1.** observance, form, usage. See **ceremony.**

ri·te·nu·to (rēt′ᵊnōō′tō; *It.* rē′te nōō′tô), *adv., adj.* (of a passage in a musical score) immediately slower. [< It: lit., held back, ptp. of *ritenere;* see RETAIN]

rite′ of intensifica′tion, *Anthropol.* a ritual or ceremony performed by a community in a time of crisis that affects all members, as a rain dance during a drought.

rite′ of pas′sage, *Anthropol.* a ceremony performed to facilitate a person's change in status upon any of several highly important occasions, as at the onset of puberty, upon entry into marriage or into a clan, etc.

Rite′ of Spring′, The, a ballet suite (1913) for orchestra by Igor Stravinsky.

ri·tor·nel·lo (rit′ər nel′ō; *It.* rē′tôr nel′lô), *n., pl.* **-los,** *It.* **-li** (-lē). *Music.* **1.** an orchestral interlude between arias, scenes, or acts in 17th-century opera. **2.** a tutti section in a concerto grosso, aria, etc. [< It, dim. of *ritorno* RETURN]

Ritsch·li·an (rich′lē ən), *adj.* **1.** of or pertaining to or to the theology of Albrecht Ritschl (1822–89), who developed a liberal Christian theology and maintained that religious faith is based on value judgments. —*n.* **2.** a supporter of Ritschlian theology. [*Ritschl* + -IAN] —**Ritsch′li·an·ism,** *n.*

rit·ter (rit′ər), *n., pl.* **rit·ter, rit·ters.** **1.** a knight. **2.** a member of the lowest order of nobility in Germany or Austria. [< G; MHG *riter* rider]

Rit·ter (rit′ər), *n.* **Joseph Elmer,** 1891–1967, U.S. cardinal.

Ritt·man (rit′mən), *n.* a town in central Ohio. 5410 (1960).

rit·u·al (rich′ōō əl), *n.* **1.** an established or prescribed procedure for a religious or other rite. **2.** a system of religious or other rites. **3.** observance of set forms in public worship. **4.** a book of rites or ceremonies. **5.** a book containing the offices to be used by priests in administering the sacraments and for visitation of the sick, burial of the dead, etc. **6.** a prescribed or established rite, ceremony, proceeding or service: *the ritual of the dead.* **7.** prescribed, established, or ceremonial acts or features collectively, as in religious services. **8.** a prescribed code of behavior regulating social conduct, as that exemplified by the raising of one's hat or the shaking of hands in greeting. —*adj.* **9.** of the nature of or practiced as a rite or rites: *a ritual dance.* **10.** of or pertaining to rites: *ritual laws.* [< L *rītuāl(is).* See RITE, -AL¹] —**rit′u·al·ly,** *adv.*
—**Syn. 1.** See **ceremony. 9.** ceremonial, formal, sacramental. —**Ant. 9.** informal.

rit·u·al·ise (rich′ōō ə līz′), *v.i., v.t.,* **-ised, -is·ing.** *Chiefly Brit.* ritualize. —**rit′u·al·i·sa′tion,** *n.*

rit·u·al·ism (rich′ōō ə liz′əm), *n.* **1.** adherence to or insistence on ritual. **2.** the study of ritual practices or religious rites. **3.** excessive fondness for ritual. [RITUAL + -ISM] —**rit′u·al·is′tic,** *adj.* —**rit′u·al·is′ti·cal·ly,** *adv.*

rit·u·al·ist (rich′ōō ə list), *n.* **1.** a student of or authority on ritual practices or religious rites. **2.** one who practices or advocates observance of ritual, as in religious services. **3.** (*cap.*) *Anglican Ch.* **a.** one who supports High Church principles. **b.** a supporter of the Oxford movement. [RITUAL + -IST]

rit·u·al·ize (rich′ōō ə līz′), *v.,* **-ized, -iz·ing.** —*v.i.* **1.** to practice ritualism. —*v.t.* **2.** to make into a ritual: *to ritualize the serving of tea.* **3.** to convert (someone) to ritualism; impose ritualism upon: *By degrees he has ritualized his congregation.* Also, *esp. Brit.,* **ritualise.** [RITUAL + -IZE] —**rit′u·al·i·za′tion,** *n.*

rit′ual mur′der, a human sacrifice made to appease the gods or a god.

ritz (rits), *n.* **1.** ostentatious or pretentious display. **2. put on the ritz,** *Slang.* to live in elegance and luxury, esp. to make an ostentatious show of one's wealth: *They put on the ritz, but only impressed other nouveaux riches.* Also, **put on the Ritz.** —*v.t.* **3.** *Slang.* to treat with condescension; snub: *The star ritzed the reporters and got a bad press.* [after the sumptuous hotels founded by César *Ritz* (d. 1918), Swiss entrepreneur]

Ritz′ combina′tion prin′ciple (rits), *Physics.* the principle that the frequencies of lines in atomic spectra can be represented as differences of a smaller number of terms, all characteristic of the emitting system, interpreted in quantum theory as the emission of exactly one photon in a transition between energy levels. Also **Ritz′s combina′tion prin′ciple.** Also called **combination principle.**

ritz·y (rit′sē), *adj.,* **ritz·i·er, ritz·i·est.** *Slang.* swanky; elegant: *a ritzy neighborhood; a ritzy hotel.* [RITZ + -Y¹] —**ritz′i·ly,** *adv.* —**ritz′i·ness,** *n.*

riv., river.

riv·age (riv′ij, rī′vij), *n.* *Archaic.* a bank, shore, or coast. [ME < MF, equiv. to *rive* river (< L *rīpa* river bank) + -*age* -AGE]

ri·val (rī′vəl), *n., adj., v.,* **-valed, -val·ing** or (*esp. Brit.*) **-valled, -val·ling.** —*n.* **1.** a person who is competing for the same object or goal as another, or who tries to equal or outdo another; competitor. **2.** one who or that which is in a position to dispute another's preeminence or superiority: *a stadium without a rival.* **3.** *Obs.* a companion in duty. —*adj.* **4.** competing or standing in rivalry: *rival suitors; rival businesses,* —*v.t.* **5.** to compete with in rivalry; strive to win from, equal, or outdo. **6.** to prove to be a worthy rival of: *He soon rivaled the others in skill.* **7.** to equal (something) as if in carrying on a rivalry: *The Hudson rivals any European river in beauty.* —*v.i.* **8.** *Archaic.* to engage in rivalry; compete. [< L *rīvāl(is),* orig. one who uses a stream in common with another, equiv. to *rīv(us)* stream + -*ālis* -AL¹] —**ri′val·less,** *adj.*
—**Syn. 1.** contestant, emulator, antagonist. See **opponent. 4.** competitive, opposed. **5.** oppose. **7.** match, emulate. —**Ant. 1.** ally.

ri·val·rous (rī′vəl rəs), *adj.* characterized by rivalry; competitive: *the rivalrous aspect of their friendship.* [RIVALR(Y) + -OUS] —**ri′val·rous·ness,** *n.*

ri·val·ry (rī′vəl rē), *n., pl.* **-ries.** **1.** the action, position, or relation of a rival or rivals; competition; emulation: *rivalry between Yale and Harvard.* **2.** an instance of this. [RIVAL + -RY]
—**Syn. 1.** opposition, antagonism; jealousy.

Rivals, The, a comedy of manners (1775) by Richard Brinsley Sheridan.

rive (rīv), *v.,* **rived, rived** or **riv·en, riv·ing.** —*v.t.* **1.** to tear or rend apart: *to rive meat from a bone.* **2.** to separate by striking; split; cleave. **3.** to rend, harrow, or distress (the feelings, heart, etc.). **4.** to split (wood) radially from a log. —*v.i.* **5.** to become rent or split apart: *stones that rive easily.* [ME *rive(n)* < Scand; cf. OIcel *rīfa.* See RIFT¹]

riv·en (riv′ən), *v.* **1.** a pp. of **rive.** —*adj.* **2.** rent or split apart. **3.** split radially, as a log.

riv·er¹ (riv′ər), *n.* **1.** a natural stream of water of fairly large size flowing in a definite course or channel or series of diverging and converging channels. **2.** a similar stream of something other than water: *a river of lava; a river of ice.* **3.** any abundant stream or copious flow; outpouring: *rivers of tears; rivers of words.* **4.** (*cap.*) *Astron.* the constellation Eridanus. **5.** *Print.* a vertical channel of white space resulting from the alignment in several lines of spaces between words. **6. sell down the river,** to betray; desert; mislead: *to sell one's friends down the river.* **7. up the river,** *Slang.* **a.** to prison: *He was sent up the river for a bank robbery.* **b.** in prison: *Thirty years up the river had made him a stranger to society.* [ME < OF *rivere, riviere* < VL **rīpāria,* n. use of L fem. of *rīpārius* RIPARIAN] —**riv′er·less,** *adj.* —**riv′er·like′,** *adj.*

riv·er² (rī′vər), *n.* a person who rives. [RIVE + -ER¹]

Ri·ve·ra (ri vâr′ə; *Sp.* rē ve′rä), *n.* **1. Die·go** (dye′gô), 1886–1957, Mexican painter. **2. Jo·sé E·us·ta·sio** (hô se′ e′ōōs tä′syô), 1889–1928, Colombian poet and novelist. **3. Ju·lio A·dal·ber·to** (hōō′lyô ä′thäl ver′tô), born 1921, president of El Salvador since 1962. **4. Mi·guel Pri·mo de** (mē gel′ prē′mô the). See **Primo de Rivera, Miguel. 5.** a city in N Uruguay. 23,600 (est. 1954).

riv·er·bank (riv′ər baŋgk′), *n.* the slopes bordering a river. [RIVER¹ + BANK¹]

Riv·er·bank (riv′ər baŋgk′), *n.* a town in central California. 2786 (1960).

riv′erbank grape′, a high-climbing vine, *Vitis vulpina,* of eastern North America, having fragrant flowers and nearly black fruit. Also called **chicken grape, frost grape, raccoon grape, white grape.**

riv′er ba′sin, *Phys. Geog.* the area of land drained by a river and its branches.

riv·er·bed (riv′ər bed′), *n.* the channel in which a river flows or formerly flowed. [RIVER¹ + BED]

riv′er carp′sucker, a carpsucker, *Carpiodes carpio,* found in silty rivers of the central U.S. south to Mexico.

Riv·er·dale (riv′ər dāl′), *n.* **1.** a town in central Maryland. 4389 (1960). **2.** a town in N New Jersey. 2596 (1960).

Riv′er Falls′, a town in W Wisconsin. 4857 (1960).

Riv′er Grove′, a town in NE Illinois. 8464 (1960).

riv·er·head (riv′ər hed′), *n.* the source or spring of a river. [RIVER¹ + HEAD]

Riv·er·head (riv′ər hed′), *n.* a town on E Long Island, in SE New York. 5830 (1960).

riv′er horse′, a hippopotamus.

riv·er·ine (riv′ə rīn′, -ər in), *adj.* **1.** of or pertaining to a river. **2.** situated or dwelling beside a river. [RIVER¹ + -INE¹]

Riv′er Oaks′, a town in N Texas. 8444 (1960).

Riv′er Plate′, *Brit.* See **Plata, Río de la.**

Riv′er Rouge′, a city in SE Michigan, near Detroit. 18,147 (1960).

Riv·ers (riv′ərz), *n.* **William Halse** (hôls), 1865–1922, English physiologist and anthropologist.

riv·er·side (riv′ər sīd′), *n.* **1.** a bank of a river. —*adj.* **2.** on or near a bank of a river. [ME *river-syde.* See RIVER¹, SIDE¹]

Riv·er·side (riv′ər sīd′), *n.* **1.** a city in SW California. 84,332 (1960). **2.** a town in NE Illinois. 9750 (1960). **3.** a town in SW New Jersey. 8474 (1960).

riv′er sun′flower, a perennial herb, *Helianthus decapetalus,* of eastern North America, having numerous yellow flower heads.

Riv·er·ton (riv′ər tən, -tᵊn), *n.* **1.** a town in central Wyoming. 6845 (1960). **2.** a town in SE New Jersey. 3324 (1960).

Riv·er·view (riv′ər vyōō′), *n.* a town in SE Michigan. 7237 (1960).

riv·et (riv′it), *n., v.,* **-et·ed, -et·ing** or (*esp. Brit.*) **-et·ted, -et·ting.** —*n.* **1.** a metal pin for passing through holes in two or more plates or pieces to hold them together, usually made with a head at one end, the other end being hammered into a head after insertion. —*v.t.* **2.** to fasten with a rivet or rivets. **3.** to hammer or spread out the end of (a pin, bolt, etc.) in order to form a head and secure something; clinch. **4.** to fasten or fix firmly. **5.** to hold (the eye, attention, etc.) firmly. [ME *revette,* deriv. of MF *river* to attach] —**riv′et·er,** *n.* —**riv′et·less,** *adj.*

riv′et set′, a tool for forming a head on a rivet after driving.

riv′et wheat′. See **poulard wheat.**

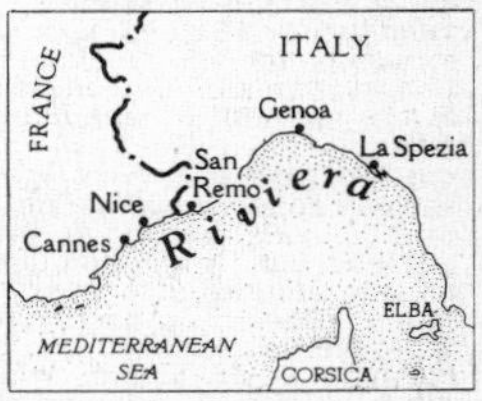

Riv·i·er·a (riv′ē âr′ə; *It.* rē vye′rä), *n.* a resort area along the Mediterranean coast, extending from Marseilles, in SE France, to La Spezia, in NW Italy. French, **Côte d'Azur.**

Ri·vier′a Beach′ (ri vēr′ə), a town in central Maryland. 4902 (1960).

ri·vière (riv′ē âr′, ri vyâr′; *Fr.* rē vyer′), *n., pl.* **ri·vières** (riv′ē ârz′, ri vyârz′; *Fr.* rē vyer′). a necklace of diamonds or other gems, esp. in more than one string. [< F: lit., river]

riv·u·let (riv′yə lit), *n.* a small stream; streamlet; brook. [earlier *rivolet* < It *rivolett(o),* dim. of *rivolo* < L *rīvulus* small stream]

riv·u·lus (riv′yə ləs), *n., pl.* **-lus.** any of several killifishes of the genus *Rivulus,* found in the mountain brooks of tropical America, often kept in aquariums. [< NL, L: RIVULET]

rix-dol·lar (riks′dol′ər), *n.* any of various silver coins, as the Scandinavian rigsdaler, the Dutch rijksdaalder, or the German reichsthaler, of about equal value. [partial trans. of obs. D *rijksdaler;* c. G *Reichsthaler* national dollar]

Ri·yadh (rē yäd′), *n.* a city in Nejd, in central Saudi Arabia: one of the two capitals of Saudi Arabia. 169,185 (1962).

ri·yal (rē yôl′, -yäl′), *n.* the monetary unit of Saudi Arabia, equal to 22 gurshes and equivalent to about .22 of a U.S. dollar. Also, **rial.** [< Ar < Sp *real* REAL²]

Ri·za (rē′zə), *n.* a girl's given name.

Ri·zal (rē säl′), *n.* **Jo·sé** (hô se′), 1861–96, Philippine patriot, novelist, poet, and physician.

Rizal′ Day′ (ri zäl′, rē säl′), (in the Philippines) a legal holiday, falling on December 30, commemorating the death of José Rizal.

Ri·za Shah Pah·la·vi (ri zä′ shä′ pä lä vē′, pal′ə vē), 1877–1944, shah of Iran 1925–41. Also, **Reza Shah Pahlavi, Reza Shah Pahlevi.**

riz·zar (riz′ər), *Scot.* —*v.t.* **1.** to dry or cure (meat, fish, etc., esp. haddock) in the sun. —*n.* **2.** a haddock dried or cured in the sun. Also, **riz·ar** (riz′ər). [prob. < obs. F *ressoré* sun-dried]

Riz·zio (rit′sē ō′, rēt′-; *It.* rēt′tsyô), *n.* **Da·vid** (dä′vēd), 1533?–66, Italian musician: private foreign secretary to Mary, Queen of Scots 1564–66. Also, **Riccio.**

RJ, *Mil.* road junction.

R.L.D., retail liquor dealer.

r-less (är′lis), *adj.* *Phonet.* r-dropping.

RM, reichsmark. Also, **r.m.**

rm., *pl.* **rms. 1.** ream. **2.** room.

R.M.A., *Brit.* **1.** Roya Marine Artillery. **2.** Royal Military Academy. **3.** Royal Military Asylum.

R.M.C., *Brit.* Royal Military College.

rms, (*often cap.*) See **root mean square.** Also, **r.m.s.**

R.M.S., **1.** Railway Mail Service. **2.** *Brit.* Royal Mail Service. **3.** *Brit.* Royal Mail Steamship.

Rn, *Chem.* radon.

R.N., **1.** registered nurse. **2.** *Brit.* Royal Navy.

RNA, *Biochem.* any of the class of nucleic acids that contains ribose, found chiefly in the cytoplasm of cells; pentose nucleic acid; PNA; yeast nucleic acid. Also called **ribonucleic acid, ribose nucleic acid.** Cf. **DNA.**

R.N.A.S., *Brit.* Royal Naval Air Service.

R.N.R., *Brit.* Royal Naval Reserve.

R.N.W.M.P., *Canadian.* Royal Northwest Mounted Police.

ro., **1.** recto. **2.** roan. **3.** rood.

R.O., **1.** Receiving Office. **2.** Receiving Officer. **3.** Regimental Order. **4.** *Brit.* Royal Observatory.

roach¹ (rōch), *n.* **1.** a cockroach. **2.** *Slang.* a cigarette butt, esp. the butt of a marijuana cigarette that has been smoked down as short as possible. [short form]

roach² (rōch), *n., pl.* **roach·es,** (*esp. collectively*) **roach.** **1.** a European, fresh-water fish, *Rutilus rutilus,* of the carp family. **2.** any of various similar fishes, as the golden shiner, *Notemigonus crysoleucas,* found in eastern North America. **3.** a fresh-water sunfish of the genus *Lepomis,* found in eastern North America. [ME *roche* < OF < ?]

roach[3] (rōch), *n. Naut.* **1.** the upward curve at the foot of a square sail. **2.** (loosely) a convexity given to any of the edges of a sail; round. —*v.t.* **3.** to clip or cut off (the mane of a horse); hog. [?]

road (rōd), *n.* **1.** a long, narrow stretch with a smoothed or paved surface, made for traveling by motor vehicle, carriage, etc., between two or more points; street or highway. **2.** *U.S.* a railroad. **3.** a way or course: *the road to peace.* **4.** Often, **roads.** Also called **roadstead.** *Naut.* a partly sheltered area of water near a shore in which vessels may ride at anchor. **5.** *Mining.* any tunnel in a mine used for hauling. **6. burn up the road,** *Slang.* to drive or move very fast: *The getaway car burned up the road, leaving the pursuing sheriff far behind.* **7. hit the road,** *Slang.* to begin or resume traveling: *We hit the road before sunrise.* **8. one for the road,** a final alcoholic drink, consumed often by way of fond farewell. **9. on the road, a.** traveling, esp. as a salesman. **b.** on tour, as a theatrical company: *The musical ends its New York run next week to go on the road.* **10. take to the road,** to begin a journey or tour. Also, **take the road. 11. the road,** the places, usually outside of New York City, at which theatrical companies on tour generally give performances. **12. to be on the road,** to be a traveling salesman: *He's on the road for one of the major dress manufacturers.* [ME *rod,* OE *rād* a riding, journey on horseback, akin to *rīdan* to RIDE] —**road′less,** *adj.* —**road′less·ness,** *n.*

road·a·bil·i·ty (rō′də bil′i tē), *n.* the ability of an automobile to ride smoothly and comfortably under adverse road conditions. [ROAD + ABILITY]

road′ a′gent, *U.S.* (formerly) a highwayman, esp. along stagecoach routes.

road·bed (rōd′bed′), *n.* **1.** the bed or foundation structure for the track of a railroad. **2.** the layer of ballast immediately beneath the ties of a railroad track. **3.** the material of which a road is composed. [ROAD + BED]

road·block (rōd′blok′), *n.* **1.** an obstruction placed across a road, esp. of barricades or police cars, for halting or hindering traffic, as to facilitate the capture of a pursued car, inspection for safety violations, etc. **2.** an obstruction on a road, as a fallen tree or a pile of fallen rocks. **3.** a hastily built barricade, as of barbed wire, erected across a road to hold up the advance of an enemy. **4.** an action, condition, etc., that obstructs progress toward an objective: *Nationalism is a roadblock to European unity.* —*v.t.* **5.** to effect a roadblock [ROAD + BLOCK]

road′ com′pany, a theatrical group that tours cities and towns, usually performing a single play which is or has been a success in New York City.

road′ gang′, **1.** a group of men employed to repair or build roads. **2.** (in the U.S.) a detail of prisoners set to repairing a road.

road′ hog′, a driver who obstructs traffic by occupying parts of two lanes. —**road′-hog′gish,** *adj.* —**road′-hog′gism,** *n.*

road·house (rōd′hous′), *n., pl.* **-hous·es** (-hou′ziz). an inn, dance hall, tavern, night club, etc., located on a highway, esp. one established beyond city limits chiefly to take advantage of milder county laws pertaining to the sale of alcoholic beverages. [ROAD + HOUSE]

road′ met′al, *Brit.* broken stone, cinders, etc., used for making roads.

Road′ Not′ Tak′en, The, a poem (1916) by Robert Frost.

road′ roll′er, **1.** one who rolls roads. **2.** any machine for rolling road materials flat.

road·run·ner (rōd′run′ər), *n.* a terrestrial cuckoo, *Geococcyx californianius,* of America. Also called **chaparral cock.** [ROAD + RUNNER]

Roadrunner (Length 2 ft.)

road′ show′, a show, as a play, musical comedy, etc., performed by a touring group of actors.

road·side (rōd′sīd′), *n.* **1.** the side or border of the road; wayside. —*adj.* **2.** on or near the side of a road. [ROAD + SIDE[1]]

road·stead (rōd′sted′), *n. Naut.* road (def. 4). [ME *radestede.* See ROAD, STEAD]

road·ster (rōd′stər), *n.* **1.** an automobile having an open body, a single seat for two or more persons, a large trunk, and often a rumble seat. **2.** a horse for riding or driving on the road. [ROAD + -STER]

Road′ Town′, a town on SE Tortola, in the NE West Indies: capital of the British Virgin Islands. 900 (1960).

road-train (rōd′trān′), *n.* **1.** a convoy of motor vehicles. **2.** a fleet of motor vehicles traveling together in line.

road·way (rōd′wā′), *n.* **1.** the land over which a road is built; a road together with the land at its edge. **2.** the part of a road over which vehicles travel; road. [ROAD + WAY]

road·work (rōd′wûrk′), *n.* the exercise of running considerable distances in areas that are reasonably free of obstructions or traffic, as fields or country roads: performed chiefly by boxers in training for a bout. [ROAD + WORK]

roak (rōk), *n. Metall.* roke.

roam (rōm), *v.i.* **1.** to walk, go, or travel without a fixed purpose or direction; ramble; wander; rove: *to roam about the world.* —*v.t.* **2.** to wander over or through: *to roam the countryside.* —*n.* **3.** the act or an instance of roaming; a ramble. [ME *rome(n)* < ?] —**roam′er,** *n.*

—**Syn. 1.** stray, stroll, prowl. ROAM, RAMBLE, RANGE, ROVE imply wandering about over (usually) a considerable amount of territory. ROAM implies a wandering or traveling over a large area, esp. as prompted by restlessness or curiosity: *to roam through a forest.* RAMBLE implies pleasant, carefree moving about, walking with no specific purpose and for a limited distance: *to ramble through fields near home.* RANGE usually implies wandering over a more or less defined but extensive area in search of something: *Cattle range over the plains.* ROVE sometimes implies wandering with specific incentive or aim, as an animal for prey: *Bandits rove through these mountains.*

roan (rōn), *adj.* **1.** (chiefly of horses) of the color sorrel, chestnut, or bay, sprinkled with gray or white. **2.** prepared from leather of this color. —*n.* **3.** a roan horse or other animal. **4.** a soft, flexible sheepskin leather, used in bookbinding, often made in imitation of morocco. [< MF < OSp *roano;* akin to L *rāvidus* yellow-gray]

Ro·a·noke (rō′ə nōk′), *n.* **1.** a city in SW Virginia. 97,110 (1960). **2.** a river flowing SE from western Virginia to Albermarle Sound in North Carolina. 380 mi. long. **3.** a town in E Alabama. 5288 (1960).

Ro′anoke bells′. See **Virginia cowslip.**

Ro′anoke Is′land, an island off the NE coast of North Carolina, S of Albemarle Sound: site of Raleigh's unsuccessful colonizing attempts 1585, 1587.

Roan′ Stal′lion, a narrative poem (1925) by Robinson Jeffers.

roar (rōr, rôr), *v.i.* **1.** to utter a loud, deep cry or howl, as in excitement, distress, anger, etc. **2.** to laugh loudly or boisterously: *to roar at a joke.* **3.** to make a loud sound or din, as thunder, cannon, waves, wind, etc. **4.** to function or move with a loud, deep sound, as a vehicle: *The automobile roared away.* **5.** to make a loud noise in breathing, as a horse. —*v.t.* **6.** to utter or express in a roar: *to roar denials.* **7.** to bring, put, make, etc., by roaring: *to roar oneself hoarse.* —*n.* **8.** a loud, deep cry or howl, as of an animal or a person: *the roar of a lion.* **9.** a loud, deep sound from an inanimate source: *the roar of the surf.* **10.** a loud outburst of laughter. [ME *rore(n),* OE *rārian;* c. OHG *rēren* to bellow] —**roar′er,** *n.*

—**Syn. 1.** bawl, yell. See **cry. 3.** resound, boom, thunder, peal.

roar·ing (rōr′ing, rôr′-), *n.* **1.** the act of one who or that which roars. **2.** a loud, deep cry or sound or a series of such sounds. **3.** *Vet. Pathol.* a disease of horses causing them to make a loud noise in breathing under exertion. —*adj.* **4.** making or causing a roar, as an animal, thunder, etc. **5.** brisk or highly successful, as trade: *He did a roaring business selling watches to tourists.* **6.** characterized by noisy, disorderly behavior; boisterous; riotous: *roaring revelry.* —*adv.* **7.** very; extremely: *roaring drunk.* [ME *roryng* (n., adj.), OE *rarung* (n.). See ROAR, -ING[1], -ING[2]] —**roar′ing·ly,** *adv.*

roar′ing for′ties, either of two areas in the ocean between 40° and 50° N or S latitude, noted for high winds and rough seas.

Roar′ing Spring′, a town in central Pennsylvania. 2937 (1960).

roast (rōst), *v.t.* **1.** to bake (meat or other food) uncovered, esp. in an oven. **2.** to cook (meat or other food) by direct exposure to dry heat, as on a spit. **3.** to brown, dry, or parch by exposure to heat, as coffee beans. **4.** to cook or heat by embedding in hot coals, embers, etc.: *to roast chestnuts.* **5.** to heat (any material) more or less violently: *The fiery sun roasted the air.* **6.** *Metall.* to heat (ore or the like) in such a way that it is exposed to air and oxidizes. **7.** to warm at a hot fire: *She roasted her hands over the fire.* **8.** *Informal.* to ridicule or criticize severely or mercilessly. —*v.i.* **9.** to roast meat or other food. **10.** to undergo the process of becoming roasted. —*n.* **11.** roasted meat or a piece of roasted meat, esp. a piece of beef or veal of a quantity and shape for slicing into more than one portion. **12.** a piece of meat for roasting. **13.** something that is roasted. **14.** the act or process of roasting. **15.** *Informal.* severe criticism. **16.** an outdoor get-together, as a picnic or barbecue, at which food is roasted and eaten: *a corn roast.* —*adj.* **17.** roasted: *roast beef.* [ME *rost(en)* < OF *rost(ir)* < Gmc; cf. D *roosten*] —**roast′a·ble,** *adj.*

roast·er (rō′stər), *n.* **1.** a contrivance for roasting something, as an oven, a pan for roasting meat, or a machine for roasting coffee beans. **2.** a pig, chicken, or other animal or article of a size convenient and grade suitable for roasting. **3.** one who or that which roasts. [ME; see ROAST, -ER[1]]

roast·ing (rō′sting), *adj.* **1.** used or suitable to roast. **2.** exceedingly hot; scorching: *a roasting July.* [ROAST + -ING[2]] —**roast′ing·ly,** *adv.*

rob (rob), *v.,* **robbed, rob·bing.** —*v.t.* **1.** to take something from (someone) by unlawful force or threat of violence; steal from. **2.** to deprive (someone) of some right or something legally due: *They robbed her of her inheritance.* **3.** to plunder or rifle (a house, shop, etc.). **4.** to deprive of something unjustly or injuriously: *The umpire called the home run a foul ball and we lost the game—we were robbed! The shock robbed him of his speech.* **5.** *Mining.* to remove mineral from (a pillar). —*v.i.* **6.** to commit or practice robbery. **7. rob Peter to pay Paul,** to take something from one person or thing to pay one's debt or hypothetical debt to another, as to sacrifice one's health by overworking. [ME *robb(en)* < OF *robb(er)* < Gmc; c. OHG *roubōn.* See REAVE]

—**Syn. 1.** ROB, RIFLE, SACK refer to seizing possessions which belong to others. ROB is the general word for taking possessions by unlawful force or violence: *to rob a bank, a house, a train.* A term with a more restricted meaning is RIFLE, to make a thorough search for what is valuable or worthwhile, usually within a small space: *to rifle a safe.* On the other hand, SACK is a term for robbery on a huge scale, during war; it suggests destruction accompanying pillage, and often includes the indiscriminate massacre of civilians: *to sack a town or district.* **2.** defraud, cheat.

Rob (rob), *n.* a boy's given name, form of **Robert.**

rob·a·lo (rob′ə lō′, rō′bə-), *n., pl.* **-los,** (*esp. collectively*) **-lo.** snook[2] (def. 1). [< Pg, m. Catalan *elobarro* << L *lupus* wolf]

rob·and (rob′ənd), *n. Naut.* a short piece of spun yarn or other material, used to secure a sail to a yard, gaff, or the like. Also, **robbin, robin, roving.** [southern form answering to northern *raband* < D *ra* sailyard + *band* BAND[2]]

Robbe-Gril·let (rôb grē ye′), *n.* **A·lain** (A laN′), born 1922, French novelist.

rob·ber (rob′ər), *n.* one who robs. [ME *robbere* < OF *robere.* See ROB, -ER[1]]

—**Syn.** highwayman, bandit, brigand; burglar. See **thief.**

rob′ber bar′on, **1.** *Hist.* a noble who robbed travelers passing through his lands. **2.** *U.S.* a capitalist or industrialist in the latter part of the 19th century considered to have become wealthy by exploiting natural resources, corrupting legislators, or other unethical means.

rob′ber fly′, any of numerous swift-flying, often large, dipterous insects of the family *Asilidae* that are predaceous on other insects.

Robber fly, *Promachus vertebratus* (Length 1 in.)

rob′ber frog′, any of numerous frogs of the genus *Eleutherodactylus,* found chiefly in the American tropics.

rob·ber·y (rob′ə rē), *n., pl.* **-ber·ies. 1.** the act, the practice, or an instance of robbing. **2.** *Law.* the felonious taking of the property of another from his person or in his immediate presence, against his will, by violence or intimidation. Cf. **theft.** [ME *robberie* < OF. See ROB, -ERY]

—**Syn. 1.** plunder, pillage; theft, burglary.

Rob·bia (rō′bē ə; *It.* RÔB′byä), *n.* **Andrea della** (än dRe′ä del′lä), 1435–1525, and his uncle, **Lu·ca del·la** (lōō′kä del′lä), c1400–82, Italian sculptors.

rob·bin (rob′in), *n. Naut.* roband.

Rob·bins (rob′inz), *n.* **1. Frederick C(hapman),** born 1916, U.S. physician: Nobel prize 1954. **2. Jerome,** born 1918, U.S. dancer and choreographer. **3.** a town in NE Illinois. 7511 (1960).

Rob·bins·dale (rob′inz dāl′), *n.* a city in SE Minnesota, near Minneapolis. 16,381 (1960).

Rob·by (rob′ē), *n.* **1.** a boy's given name, form of **Robert** or **Robin. 2.** a girl's given name, form of **Roberta** or **Robin.** Also, **Rob′bie, Rob′bye.**

robe (rōb), *n., v.,* **robed, rob·ing.** —*n.* **1.** a long, loose or flowing gown or outer garment worn by men or women as ceremonial dress, an official vestment, garb of office, etc. **2.** any long, loose garment, esp. one for wear while dressing or lounging, as a bathrobe or dressing gown. **3.** a woman's gown or dress, esp. of a more elaborate kind: *a robe for the evening.* **4. robes,** apparel in general; dress; costume. **5.** a piece of fur, cloth, knitted work, etc., used as a blanket, covering, or wrap: *a buffalo robe; a lap robe.* —*v.t.* **6.** to clothe or invest with a robe or robes; dress; array. —*v.i.* **7.** to put on a robe. [ME < OF: orig., spoil, booty < Gmc; cf. OHG *roub* < G *Raub*] —**robe′less,** *adj.* —**rob′er,** *n.*

robe-de-cham·bre (RôB də shäN′bRᵊ), *n., pl.* **robes-de-cham·bre** (RôB də shäN′bRᵊ). *French.* a dressing gown.

Rob·ert (rob′ərt), *n.* a boy's given name.

Robert I, **1.** Also called **Robert the Bruce, Robert Bruce.** 1274–1329, king of Scotland 1306–29. **2.** ("*Robert the Devil*") died 1035, duke of Normandy 1028–35 (father of William I of England).

Ro·ber·ta (rə bûr′tə), *n.* a girl's given name.

Ro·bert Guis·card (Rô beR′ gē skAR′). See **Guiscard, Robert.**

Rob·ert-John (rob′ərt jon′), *n.* a boy's given name.

Rob·erts (rob′ərts), *n.* **1. Sir Charles George Douglas,** 1860–1943, Canadian poet and novelist. **2. Elizabeth Mad·ox** (mad′əks), 1886–1941, U.S. poet and novelist. **3. Frederick Sleigh** (slā), **Earl** ("*Bobs Bahadur*"), 1832–1914, British field marshal. **4. Kenneth (Lewis),** 1885–1957, U.S. novelist and essayist. **5. Owen Jo·se·phus** (jō sē′fəs), 1875–1955, U.S. jurist: associate justice of the U.S. Supreme Court 1930–45.

Rob·ert·son (rob′ərt sən), *n.* **1. William,** 1721–93, Scottish historian. **2. Sir William Robert,** 1860–1933, British field marshal.

Rob′ert the Bruce′. See **Robert I.**

Ro·ber·val (*Fr.* RÔ beR VAL′), *n.* a city in S central Quebec, in E Canada. 7739 (1961).

Robe·son (rōb′sən), *n.* **Paul,** born 1898, U.S. singer and actor.

Robes·pierre (rōbz′pēr, -pē âr′; *Fr.* RÔ bes pyeR′), *n.* **Max·i·mil·ien Fran·çois Ma·rie I·si·dore de** (mAk sē mē lyaN′ fRäN swA′ mA Rē′ ē zē dôR′ də), 1758–94, French lawyer and revolutionary leader.

Ro·bi·go (rō bī′gō), *n.* an ancient Roman goddess who protected grain from blight.

Ro·bi·gus (rō bī′gəs), *n.* **1.** an ancient Roman god who protected grain from blight. **2.** the personification of grain blight.

rob·in[1] (rob′in), *n.* **1.** any of several small, Old World birds having a red or reddish breast, esp. *Erithacus rubecula,* of Europe. **2.** a large, American thrush, *Turdus migratorius,* having a chestnut-red breast and abdomen. Also called **rob′in red′breast.** [ME *Robyn* < OF *Robin,* dim. of *Robert* Robert]

Robin, *Turdus migratorius* (Length 10 in.)

rob·in[2] (rob′in), *n. Naut.* roband.

Rob·in (rob′in), *n.* **1.** a boy's given name, form of **Robert. 2.** a girl's given name.

Ro·bi·na (rō bē′nə, rə-), *n.* a girl's given name, form of **Robin.**

Rob·i·nette (rob′ə net′), *n.* a girl's given name, form of **Robin.**

Rob′in Good′fel·low (gŏŏd′fel′ō), Puck (def. 1).

Rob′in Hood′, a legendary English outlaw of the 12th century, hero of many ballads, who robbed the rich to give to the poor: a popular model of courage, generosity and justice, as well as of skill in archery, he lived and presided over his band of followers chiefly in Sherwood Forest.

ro·bin·i·a (rō bin′ē ə), *n.* any North American tree or shrub of the genus *Robinia,* comprising the locusts. [< NL, named after Jean *Robin* (d. 1629), French botanist; see -IA]

rob′in's-egg blue′ (rob′inz eg′), a pale green to a light greenish blue color.

Rob·in·son (rob′in sən), *n.* **1. Board·man** (bôrd′mən, bōrd′-), 1876–1952, U.S. painter and illustrator, born

CONCISE ETYMOLOGY KEY: <, descended or derived from; >, whence; b., blend of, blended; c., cognate with; deriv., derivative; equiv., equivalent; imit., imitative; m., modification of; obl., oblique; r., replacing; s., stem; sp., spelling; trans., translation; ?, origin unknown, perhaps; *, hypothetical. See the full key inside the front cover.

in Nova Scotia. **2. Edward G.** (*Emanuel Goldenberg*), 1893–1973, U.S. actor, born in Rumania. **3. Edwin Arlington,** 1869–1935, U.S. poet. **4. Frederick John, Viscount Goderich, 1st Earl of Ripon,** 1782–1859, British statesman: prime minister 1827–28. **5. Jack Roosevelt** (*Jackie*), 1919–72, U.S. baseball player. **6. James Harvey,** 1863–1936, U.S. historian. **7. Ray** (*Walker Smith*) ("Sugar Ray"), born 1921, U.S. boxer. **8. Sir Robert,** 1886–1975, English chemist: Nobel prize 1947. **9.** a town in SE Illinois. 7226 (1960). **10.** a crater in the second quadrant of the face of the moon: about 13 miles in diameter. **11.** a boy's given name.

Rob′inson Cru′soe (kro͞o′sō), **1.** (in a novel by Defoe) a mariner of York who is shipwrecked and lives adventurously for years on a small island. **2.** (*italics.*) the novel itself (1719).

Rob′in's plan′tain. See **Poor Robin's plantain.**

ro·ble (rō′blā), *n.* **1.** a Californian white oak, *Quercus lobata.* **2.** any of several other trees, esp. of the oak and beech families. [< Sp, Pg << L *rōbur* oak tree]

Ro·bo·am (rō bō′əm), *n.* *Douay Bible.* Rehoboam.

ro·bomb (rō′bom′), *n.* See **robot bomb.** [RO(BOT) + BOMB]

rob·o·rant (rob′ər ənt), *Med.* **—adj. 1.** strengthening. **—n. 2.** a tonic. [< L *rōborant-* (s. of *rōborāns*, prp. of *rōborāre*) < *rōbor-* (s. of *rōbur*) oak, hardness + *-ant-* -ANT]

ro·bot (rō′bət, -bot, rob′ət), *n.* **1.** a machine that resembles a man and does mechanical, routine tasks on command as though it were alive. **2.** a person who acts and responds in a mechanical, routine manner, usually subject to another's will; automaton. **3.** any machine or mechanical device that operates automatically with humanlike skill. [first used in the play *R.U.R.* (by Čapek), appar. back formation from Czech *robotnik* serf] **—ro′bot·ism,** *n.* **—ro·bot·is·tic** (rō′bə tis′tik, rob′ə-), *adj.* **—ro′bot·like′,** *adj.*

ro′bot bomb′, a rocket-propelled, gyroscopically steered bomb equipped with wings and control surfaces, usually launched from the ground. Also called **flying bomb, robomb.**

ro·bot·ics (rō bot′iks), *n.* (*construed as sing.*) the use of computer-controlled robots to perform manipulative tasks, esp. on an assembly line. [ROBOT + -ICS; coined by Isaac Asimov]

ro·bot·ize (rō′bə tīz′, rob′ə-), *v.t.*, **-ized, -iz·ing. 1.** to turn (someone) into a robot. **2.** to make automatic, as a factory, plant, etc.; automate. [ROBOT + -IZE] **—ro′bot·i·za′tion,** *n.*

ro′bot pi′lot, *Aeron.* See **automatic pilot.**

Rob Roy (rob′ roi′), a cocktail made with Scotch whisky, sweet vermouth, and bitters, and sometimes garnished with a maraschino cherry. [? after *Rob Roy*, nickname of Robert Macgregor (1671–1734), Scottish freebooter]

Rob·son (rob′sən), *n.* **Mount,** a mountain in SW Canada, in E British Columbia: highest peak in the Canadian Rockies, 12,972 ft.

ro·bur·ite (rō′bə rīt′), *n.* *Chem.* a smokeless, flameless explosive consisting of ammonium nitrate and dinitrobenzene or dinitrochlorobenzene, used chiefly in mining. [L *rōbur* strength + -ITE[1]]

Ro·bus (rō′bəs), *n.* **Hugo,** 1885–1963, U.S. sculptor.

ro·bust (rō bust′, rō′bust), *adj.* **1.** strong and healthy; hardy; vigorous: *a robust young man; a robust faith; a robust mind.* **2.** strongly or stoutly built: *his robust frame.* **3.** suited to or requiring bodily strength or endurance: *robust exercise.* **4.** rough, rude, or boisterous: *robust drinkers and dancers.* **5.** rich and full-bodied: *the robust flavor of freshly brewed coffee.* [< L *robust(us)* of oak, hard, strong, deriv. of *rōbur* oak, strength] **—ro·bust′ly,** *adv.* **—ro·bust′ness,** *n.*
—Syn. 1. powerful, sound. **4.** coarse, rambunctious.

ro·bus·tious (rō bus′chəs), *adj.* **1.** rough, rude, or boisterous. **2.** robust, strong, or stout. [ROBUST + -IOUS] **—ro·bus′tious·ly,** *adv.*

Rob·yn (rob′in), *n.* a girl's given name.

roc (rok), *n.* *Arabian Myth.* a fabulous bird of enormous size and strength. [< Ar *rukhkh*, prob. < Pers]

Ro·ca (rō′kə; *Port.* RÔ′kä), *n.* **Cape,** a cape in W Portugal, near Lisbon: the western extremity of continental Europe.

ro·caille (rō kī′; *Fr.* RÔ kä′yᵊ), *n.* *Fine Arts.* any of the fantastic ornamental, often asymmetrical, combinations characteristic of the Rococo period, consisting of rock, shell, and plant forms combined with artificial forms, esp. C-curves. [< F < *roc* < MF *roche* ROCK[1]]

roc·am·bole (rok′əm bōl′), *n.* a European, liliaceous plant, *Allium Scorodoprasum*, used like garlic. Also called **giant garlic.** [< F < G *Rockenbolle*, lit., distaff bulb (from its shape)]

Roc·co (rok′ō), *n.* a boy's given name.

Ro·cham·beau (RÔ shäN bō′), *n.* **Jean Bap·tiste Do·na·tien de Vi·meur** (zhäN BA tēst′ dô NA syaN′ də vē mœR′), **Count de,** 1725–1807, French general: marshal of France 1791–1807; commander of the French army in the American Revolution.

Roch·dale (roch′dāl′), *n.* a city in SE Lancashire, in N England, near Manchester: one of the earliest cooperative societies was formed here 1844. 87,758 (1961).

roche′ al′um (rōch), *Chem.* an alumlike substance derived from alunite. [obs. E *roche* cliff, rocky height < ME (see ROCK[1]) + ALUM; appar. partial trans. of MF *alum en roque, alun de roche*]

Ro·chelle (*Fr.* RÔ shel′ *for 1;* rō shel′, rə- *for 2, 3*), *n.* **1. La.** See **La Rochelle. 2.** a town in N Illinois. 7008 (1960). **3.** a girl's given name.

Rochelle′ Park′, a town in NE New Jersey. 6119 (1960).

Rochelle′ pow′ders, (not in technical use) See **Seidlitz powders.** [named after LA ROCHELLE]

Rochelle′ salt′, *Chem., Pharm.* a colorless or white, water-soluble solid, $KNaC_4H_4O_6 \cdot 4H_2O$, used in silvering mirrors, in the manufacture of Seidlitz powders and baking powder, and in medicine as a laxative. Also called **potassium sodium tartrate.** [named after LA ROCHELLE]

roche mou·ton·née (rôsh mo͞o tô nā′; *Eng.* rōsh′ mo͞ot′ᵊnā′), *pl.* **roches mou·ton·nées** (rôsh mo͞o tô nā′; *Eng.* rōsh′ mo͞ot′ᵊnāz′). *French.* a knob or rock rounded and smoothed by glacial action. [lit., woolly rock]

Roch·es·ter (roch′es tər, -i stər), *n.* **1.** a city in W New York, on the Genesee River. 318,611 (1960). **2.** a town in SE Minnesota. 40,663 (1960). **3.** a city in N Kent, in SE England. 50,121 (1961). **4.** a city in SE New Hampshire. 15,927 (1960). **5.** a town in W Pennsylvania. 5952 (1960). **6.** a town in SE Michigan. 5431 (1960). **7.** a town in N Indiana. 4883 (1960).

roch·et (roch′it), *n.* a vestment of linen or lawn, resembling a surplice, worn esp. by bishops and abbots. [ME < OF *roc* outer garment < Gmc; cf. OE *rocc* outer garment]

Ro·ci·nan·te (RÔ thē nän′te), *n.* Rosinante.

rock[1] (rok), *n.* **1.** a large mass of stone forming a hill, cliff, promontory, or the like. **2.** *Geol.* **a.** mineral matter of various composition, consolidated or unconsolidated, assembled in masses or considerable quantities in nature, as by the action of heat or water. **b.** a particular kind of such matter: *igneous rock.* **3.** stone in the mass: *buildings that stand upon rock.* **4.** a stone of any size. **5.** something resembling or suggesting a rock. **6.** a firm foundation or support: *The Lord is my rock.* **7.** *Chiefly Brit.* a kind of hard candy, variously flavored. **8.** See **rock candy. 9.** Often, **rocks.** *Slang.* **a.** a piece of money. **b.** a dollar bill. **10.** *Slang.* **a.** a diamond. **b.** any gem. **11. on the rocks, a.** *Informal.* in or into a state of disaster or ruin. **b.** *Informal.* without funds; destitute; bankrupt. **c.** (of a beverage, esp. liquor or a cocktail) with, or containing, ice cubes: *Scotch on the rocks; a vodka martini on the rocks.* [ME *rokk(e)* < OE *-rocc* < ML *rocca*] **—rock′less,** *adj.* **—rock′like′,** *adj.*

rock[2] (rok), *v.i.* **1.** to move or sway to and fro or from side to side. **2.** to be moved or swayed powerfully with excitement, emotion, etc. **3.** *Mining.* (of sand or gravel) to be washed in a cradle. **4.** rock-'n'-roll (def. 4). **—v.t. 5.** to move or sway to and fro or from side to side, esp. gently and soothingly. **6.** to lull in security, hope, etc. **7.** to affect deeply; stun; move or sway powerfully, as with emotion: *Everyone in the courtroom was rocked by the verdict.* **8.** to shake or disturb violently: *A thunderous explosion rocked the waterfront.* **9.** *Graphic Arts.* to roughen the surface of (a copperplate) with a rocker preparatory to scraping a mezzotint. **10.** *Mining.* cradle (def. 20). **—n. 11.** a rocking movement: *the gentle rock of the boat.* **12.** rock-'n'-roll (defs. 1, 2). **13.** Also, **rocker.** (in Britain) a teenager who is devoted to motorcycling, typically wears a leather jacket, tight pants, and boots, and strives to attain a tough, unsentimental personality. Cf. **mod. —adj. 14.** rock-'n'-roll (def. 3). [ME *rock(en)* < OE *roccian;* c. MD *rocken;* akin to G *rücken;* OIcel *rykkja* r. jerk] **—rock′a·ble,** *adj.* **—rock′ing·ly,** *adv.*
—Syn. 1. roll, shake. See **swing**[1].

rock[3] (rok), *n.* See **striped bass.** [short for ROCKFISH]

Rock (rok), *n.* a boy's given name.

rock·a·bil·ly (rok′ə bil′ē), *n.* a style of popular music combining the features of rock-'n'-roll and hillbilly music. [ROCK (-'N'-ROLL) + *-a-* connective + HILLBILLY]

rock-and-roll (rok′ən rōl′), *n.* rock-'n'-roll.

rock′ and rye′, a bottled drink made with rye whiskey, rock candy, and fruit.

rock′ as′ter, a perennial herb, *Aster alpinus*, of the mountainous regions of the western U.S. and Eurasia, having blue or violet ray flowers.

Rockaway

rock·a·way (rok′ə wā′), *n.* a light, four-wheeled carriage having two or three seats and a fixed top. [appar. named after ROCKAWAY]

Rock·a·way (rok′ə wā′), *n.* a town in N New Jersey. 5413 (1960).

rock′ bar′nacle. See under **barnacle**[1] (def. 1).

rock′ bass′ (bas), **1.** a game fish, *Ambloplites rupestris*, of the sunfish family, found in the fresh-water streams of the eastern U.S. **2.** See **striped bass.**

rock′ beau′ty, a gold and black butterflyfish, *Holocanthus tricolor*, found from the West Indies to Brazil.

rock′ blen′ny, *Ichthyol.* a prickleback, *Xiphister mucosus*, found along the Pacific coast from southern California to Alaska. Also called **rock-eel.**

rock′ bot′tom, the very lowest level: *He went bankrupt and touched rock bottom.*

rock-bot·tom (rok′bot′əm), *adj.* at the lowest possible limit or level; extremely low: *rock-bottom prices.*

rock-bound (rok′bound′), *adj.* hemmed in, enclosed, or covered by rocks; rocky: *the rock-bound coast of Maine.*

rock′ brake′, a fern of the genus *Pellaea.*

rock′ can′dy, sugar in large, hard, cohering crystals.

rock′ cod′, 1. rockfish. **2.** any of various other marine fishes found about rocks.

Rock′ Corn′ish, a hybrid chicken produced by mating Cornish and White Rock chickens, marketed as a roaster.

rock′ crab′, any of several crabs that live along rocky beaches, esp. those of the genus *Cancer*, as *C. irroratus*, of the eastern coast of North America, having the rear legs modified for running.

rock′ cress′, any of several cruciferous plants of the genus *Arabis*, grown as an ornamental in rock gardens.

rock′ crys′tal, transparent quartz, esp. when colorless.

rock′ cy′cle, *Geol.* See **metamorphic cycle.**

Rock·dale (rok′dāl′), *n.* a town in central Texas. 4481 (1960).

rock′ dove′, a European pigeon, *Columba livia*, from which most domestic pigeons have been developed. Also called **rock pigeon.**

rock-eel (rok′ēl′), *n.* See **rock blenny.**

Rock·e·fel·ler (rok′ə fel′ər), *n.* **1. John D(a·vi·son)** (dā′vi sən), 1839–1937, and his son **John D(avison), Jr.,** 1874–1960, U.S. oil magnates and philanthropists. **2. Nelson A(ldrich),** 1908–79, governor of New York 1959–73, vice-president 1974–76 (son of John D. Rockefeller, Jr.).

rock′ elm′, 1. an elm, *Ulmus Thomasi*, of eastern North America, having deeply furrowed, grayish-brown bark. **2.** the hard, heavy wood of this tree, used for making furniture and in the manufacture of various types of containers.

rock·er (rok′ər), *n.* **1.** Also called **runner.** one of the curved pieces on which a cradle or a rocking chair rocks. **2.** See **rocking chair. 3.** any of various devices that operate with a rocking motion. **4.** *Graphic Arts.* a small steel plate with one curved and toothed edge for roughening a copperplate to make a mezzotint. **5.** *Mining.* cradle (def. 6). **6.** an ice skate which has a curved blade. **7.** (in Britain) rock[2] (def. 13). **8. off one's rocker,** *Slang.* insane; crazy: *You're off your rocker if you think I'm going to climb that mountain.* [ROCK[2] + -ER[1]]

rock′er arm′, *Mach.* a rocking or oscillating arm or lever rotating with a moving shaft or pivoted on a stationary shaft.

rock·ered (rok′ərd), *adj.* *Naut.* (of a keel) rounded at the bottom. [ROCKER + -ED[2]]

rock′er pan′el, body paneling below the passenger compartment of a vehicle.

rock·er·y (rok′ə rē), *n., pl.* **-er·ies.** See **rock garden.** [ROCK[1] + -ERY]

rock·et[1] (rok′it), *n.* **1.** any of various simple or complex tubelike devices containing combustibles which on being ignited liberate gases whose action propels the tube through the air: used for pyrotechnic effect, signaling, carrying a life line, hurling explosives at an enemy, for putting a space capsule into orbit, etc. **2.** a space capsule or vehicle put into orbit by such devices. **3.** See **rocket engine. —v.t. 4.** to move or transport by means of a rocket. **—v.i. 5.** to move like a rocket. **6.** (of game birds) to fly straight up rapidly when flushed. [< F *roquet* < It *rocchetta*, appar. dim. of *rocca* ROCK[1], with reference to its shape] **—rock′et·like′,** *adj.*

rock·et[2] (rok′it), *n.* **1.** Also called **rocket salad.** a European plant, *Eruca sativa*, used for making salads. **2.** any cruciferous plant of the genus *Hesperis*, having showy, purple or white, fragrant flowers. Cf. **dame's rocket. 3.** a noxious weed, *Barbarea vulgaris*, of the U.S. [< F *roquette* < Pg *rouqueto* << L *ērūca* kind of colewort]

rock′et air′plane, 1. an airplane propelled wholly or mainly by a rocket engine. **2.** a military airplane armed with rockets.

rock′et bomb′, 1. an aerial bomb equipped with a rocket for added velocity after being dropped from an aircraft. **2.** (loosely) any rocket-propelled missile launched from the ground.

rock·e·teer (rok′i tēr′), *n.* **1.** a person who discharges, rides in, or pilots a rocket. **2.** a technician or scientist whose work pertains to rocketry. Also, **rock·et·er** (rok′i tər). [ROCKET[1] + -EER]

rock′et en′gine, a reaction engine that produces a thrust due to an exhaust consisting entirely of material, as oxidizer, fuel, and inert matter, which has been carried with the engine in the vehicle it propels, none of the propellant being derived from the medium through which the vehicle moves. Also called **rocket, rock′et mo′tor.**

rock′et gun′, any weapon which uses a rocket as a projectile, as a rocket launcher or bazooka.

rock′et lark′spur, an herb, *Delphinium Ajacis*, of southern Europe, having variously colored flowers. See illus. under **larkspur.**

rock′et launch′er, *Mil.* **1.** a tube used by infantrymen to fire rockets. **2.** a vehicle equipped with many such tubes for the simultaneous firing of rockets.

rock·et-pro·pelled (rok′it prə peld′), *adj.* using rocket power as the chief motive force.

rock′et propul′sion, propulsion of an object by thrust developed by a rocket.

rock·et·ry (rok′i trē), *n.* the science of rocket design, development, and flight. [ROCKET[1] + -RY]

rock′et sal′ad, rocket[2] (def. 1).

rock′et sled′, a sled propelled along a long track by rocket engines, for testing the effects of high rates of acceleration and deceleration.

rock·et·sonde (rok′it sond′), *n.* *Meteorol.* a telemeter for measuring atmospheric quantities at very high altitudes, carried aloft by rocket and returned to earth by parachute. [ROCKET[1] + SONDE]

rock-faced (rok′fāst′), *adj.* **1.** (of a person) having a stiff, expressionless face. **2.** having a rocky surface. **3.** *Masonry.* noting a stone or stonework the visible face of which is dressed with a hammer, with or without a chiseled draft at the edges; quarry-faced.

Rock′ fe′ver, *Pathol.* brucellosis. [so called from the *Rock* of Gibraltar, where it is prevalent]

rock·fish (rok′fish′), *n., pl.* (*esp. collectively*) **-fish,** (*esp. referring to two or more kinds or species*) **-fish·es. 1.** any of various fishes found about rocks. **2.** See **striped bass. 3.** any of the North Pacific marine fishes of the genus *Sebastodes.* **4.** any other fish of the family *Scorpaenidae.* Also called **rock cod.** [ROCK[1] + FISH]

rock′ flour′. See **glacial meal.**

rock′ flow′er, any shrub of the genus *Crossosoma*, native to the arid regions of the southwestern U.S.

Rock·ford (rok′fərd), *n.* a city in N Illinois. 126,706 (1960).

rock′ gar′den, 1. a garden on rocky ground or among rocks, for the growing of alpine or other plants. **2.** a garden decorated with rocks, usually a wide variety of interestingly shaped, multicolored rocks, esp. quartz. Also called **rockery.**

rock′ gla′cier, a mass of rock resembling a valley glacier which moves or is moved down a slope by its own weight or by the action of frost and interstitial ice.

rock′ gold′enrod, a tall herb, *Solidago canadensis*, of eastern North America, having large, terminal, one-sided clusters of yellow flowers.

rock′ gun′nel. See under **gunnel**[1].

Rock·hamp·ton (rok hamp′tən, -ham′-), *n.* a city in E Queensland, in E Australia. 44,128 (1961).

Rock′ Hill′, 1. a city in N South Carolina. 29,404 (1960). **2.** a town in E Missouri. 6523 (1960).

rock′ hound′, *Informal.* **1.** a geologist. **2.** a person who collects rocks as a hobby.

rock′ hy′rax, an African hyrax of the genus *Heterohyrax*, that lives in rocky places.

Rock·ies (rok′ēz), *n.* See **Rocky Mountains.**

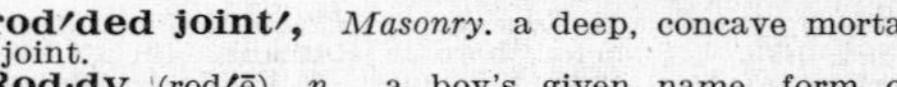

rock′ing chair′, a chair mounted on rockers or springs so as to permit a person to rock back and forth while sitting. Also called **rocker.**

Rock·ing·ham (rok′ing ham′), *n.* a town in N North Carolina. 5512 (1960).

rock′ing horse′, a toy horse, as of wood, mounted on rockers, on which children play at riding; hobbyhorse.

rock′ing rhythm′, *Pros.* a rhythmic pattern created by a succession of metrical feet each of which consists of one accented syllable between two unaccented ones.

rock′ing shear′, a shear having a curved blade that cuts with a rocking motion.

rock′ing stone′, any fairly large rock so situated on its base that slight forces can cause it to move or sway. Also called **logan stone, loggan stone, logging stone.**

rock′ing valve′, (on a steam engine) a valve mechanism oscillating through an arc to open and close.

Rock′ Is′land, a port in NW Illinois, on the Mississippi: government arsenal. 51,863 (1960).

rock′ jas′mine, any of several alpine, primulaceous plants of the genus *Androsace,* having tufted leaves often in basal rosettes, and pink, red, purple, or white flowers.

Rock·land (rok′lənd), *n.* a town in S Maine. 8769 (1960).

Rock·ledge (rok′lij), *n.* a town in SE Pennsylvania. 2587 (1960).

rock·ling (rok′ling), *n., pl.* **-lings,** (*esp. collectively*) **-ling.** any of several small cods of the genera *Enchalyopus* and *Gaidropsarus,* found in the North Atlantic. [ROCK[1] + -LING[1]]

rock′ lob′ster. See **spiny lobster.**

rock′ ma′ple, the sugar maple, *Acer saccharum.*

Rock·mart (rok′märt′), *n.* a town in NW Georgia. 3938 (1960).

rock′ milk′, glacial water carrying finely ground rock (**rock′ meal′**). Also called **agaric mineral.**

Rock·ne (rok′nē), *n.* **Knute (Kenneth)** (no͞ot), 1888–1931, U.S. football coach born in Norway.

rock-'n'-roll, (rok′ən rōl′), *n.* **1.** a style of popular music that derives in part from blues and folk music and is marked by a heavily accented beat and a simple, repetitious phrase structure. **2.** a dance performed to this music, usually with vigorous, exaggerated movements. —*adj.* **3.** of or pertaining to this music. —*v.i.* **4.** to dance to or play rock-'n'-roll. Also, **rock-and-roll, rock′'n roll′.** [contr. of phrase *rock and roll;* see ROCK[2]]

rock′ oil′, *Chiefly Brit.* petroleum. [trans. of ML *petroleum*]

rock·oon (rok′o͞on), *n.* a rocket launched from a balloon at a high altitude. [ROCK(ET[1] + BALL)OON]

rock′ pi′geon. See **rock dove.**

rock′ plant′, a plant found among rocks or in rock gardens.

Rock·port (rok′pōrt′, -pôrt′), *n.* **1.** a town in NE Massachusetts. 3511 (1960). **2.** a town in S Texas. 2989 (1960).

rock′ rab′bit, **1.** See **rock hyrax. 2.** pika.

Rock′ Rap′ids, a town in NW Iowa. 2780 (1960).

rock-ribbed (rok′ribd′), *adj.* **1.** having ribs or ridges of rock: *the rock-ribbed coast of Maine.* **2.** unyielding; confirmed and uncompromising: *a rock-ribbed conservative.*

rock·rose (rok′rōz′), *n.* **1.** any plant of the genus *Cistus* or some allied genus, as *Helianthemum.* **2.** any cistaceous plant. [ROCK[1] + ROSE]

rock′ salt′, common salt occurring in extensive, irregular beds in rocklike masses.

rock′ sax′ifrage. See **early saxifrage.**

rock·shaft (rok′shaft′, -shäft′), *n. Brit. Mach.* an oscillating shaft. [ROCK[2] + SHAFT]

rock′ speed′well, a low, woody, branched, perennial herb, *Veronica fruticans,* of Europe, having small, blue flowers with a red eye.

rock′ spray′, a low, evergreen shrub, *Cotoneaster microphylla,* of the Himalayas, having shiny leaves with grayish-hairy undersides, white flowers, and scarlet fruit.

Rock′ Springs′, a city in SW Wyoming. 10,371 (1960).

rock′ thrush′, any of several Old World thrushes of the genus *Monticola,* usually having bluish plumage, esp. *M. saxatilis,* of Europe.

Rock·ville (rok′vil), *n.* **1.** a city in central Maryland. 26,090 (1960). **2.** a town in central Connecticut. 9478 (1960). **3.** a town in W Indiana. 2756 (1960).

Rock′ville Cen′tre, a city on W Long Island, in SE New York. 26,355 (1960).

rock·weed (rok′wēd′), *n.* a ducoid seaweed growing on rocks exposed at low tide. [ROCK[1] + WEED[1]]

Rock·well (rok′wel′, -wəl), *n.* **1. Norman,** 1894–1978, U.S. illustrator. **2.** a boy's given name.

Rock′well num′ber, *Metall.* a numerical expression of the hardness of a metal as determined by a test (**Rock′well test′**) made by indenting a test piece with a Brale, or with a steel ball of specific diameter, under two successive loads and measuring the resulting permanent indentation. [named after Stanley P. *Rockwell,* 20th-century American metallurgist]

Rock·wood (rok′wo͝od′), *n.* a town in E Tennessee. 5345 (1960).

rock′ wool′. See **mineral wool.**

rock′ wren′, an American wren, *Salpinctes obsoletus,* found in the foothills, badlands, and mesa country of the western U.S. and Mexico.

rock·y[1] (rok′ē), *adj.,* **rock·i·er, rock·i·est. 1.** full of or abounding in rocks. **2.** consisting of rock. **3.** rocklike: *wood with a rocky hardness.* **4.** full of difficulties or hazards: *the rocky road to stardom.* **5.** firm; steadfast: *rocky endurance.* **6.** unfeeling; without sympathy or emotion: *my rocky heart.* [ROCK[1] + -Y[1]] —**rock′i·ness,** *n.*

rock·y[2] (rok′ē), *adj.,* **rock·i·er, rock·i·est. 1.** inclined or likely to rock; tottering; shaky; unsteady. **2.** uncertain. **3.** *Informal.* physically unsteady or weak, as from sickness. [ROCK[2] + -Y[1]]

Rock·y (rok′ē), *n.* a boy's given name, form of **Rock.**

Rock′y Ford′, a town in central Colorado. 4929 (1960).

Rock′y Grove′, a town in NW Pennsylvania. 3168 (1960).

Rock′y Mount′, a city in NE North Carolina. 32,147 (1960).

Rock′y Moun′tain bee′-plant (bē′plant′, -plänt′), a rank-smelling herb, *Cleome serrulata,* of the western U.S., having pink or white flowers, frequented by bees. Also called **stinking clover.**

Rock′y Moun′tain big′-horn, bighorn.

Rock′y Moun′tain flow′ering rasp′berry. See **boulder raspberry.**

Rock′y Moun′tain goat′, a long-haired, white, goatlike, bovid ruminant, *Oreamnos americanus,* of mountainous regions of western North America, having short, black horns.

Rocky Mountain goat, *Oreamnos americanus* (3½ ft. high at shoulder; horns 10 in.; length 5 ft.)

Rock′y Moun′tain ju′niper, a juniper, *Juniperus scopulorum,* of western North America, that yields a soft, reddish wood used for making fences, pencils, etc., and that is also grown as an ornamental. Also called **Rocky Mountain red cedar.**

Rock′y Moun′tain Na′tional Park′, a national park in N Colorado. 405 sq. mi.

Rock′y Moun′tain red′ ce′dar. See **Rocky Mountain juniper.**

Rock′y Moun′tains, the chief mountain system in North America, extending from central New Mexico to N Alaska. Highest peak, Mount McKinley, 20,300 ft. Also called **Rockies.**

Rock′y Moun′tain sheep′, bighorn.

Rock′y Moun′tain spot′ted fe′ver, *Pathol.* a disease characterized by high fever, pains in joints, bones, and muscles, and a cutaneous eruption, caused by Rickettsia transmitted by ticks: first found in the Rocky Mountain area, but now more widely distributed.

Rock′y Moun′tain States′, those States in the region of the Rocky Mountains, including Colorado, Idaho, Montana, Nevada, Utah, and Wyoming, and sometimes Arizona and New Mexico.

Rock′y Moun′tain white′fish. See **mountain whitefish.**

Rock′y Moun′tain white′ pine′. See **limber pine.**

Rock′y Riv′er, a city in NE Ohio, near Cleveland. 18,097 (1960).

ro·co·co (rə kō′kō; *Fr.* rô kô kô′), *n.* **1.** a style of architecture and decoration, originating in France about 1720, evolved from Baroque types and distinguished by its elegant refinement in using different materials (stucco, metal, wood, mirrors, tapestries) for a delicate overall effect and by its ornament of shellwork, foliage, etc. **2.** a homophonic musical style of the middle 18th century, marked by a generally superficial elegance and charm and by the use of elaborate ornamentation and stereotyped devices. —*adj.* **3.** (*cap.*) *Fine Arts.* **a.** noting or pertaining to a style of painting developed simultaneously with the rococo in architecture and decoration, characterized chiefly by smallness of scale, delicacy of color, freedom of brushwork, and the selection of gay and playful subjects as thematic material. **b.** designating a corresponding style of sculpture, chiefly characterized by diminutiveness of Baroque forms and playfulness of theme. **4.** of, pertaining to, in the manner of, or suggested by rococo architecture, decoration, or music or the general atmosphere and spirit of the rococo: *rococo charm.* **5.** ornate or florid in speech, literary style, etc. **6.** antiquated; outmoded: *old ladies with elegant, rococo manners.* [< F, irreg. < *rocaille* ROCAILLE]

Rococo mirror

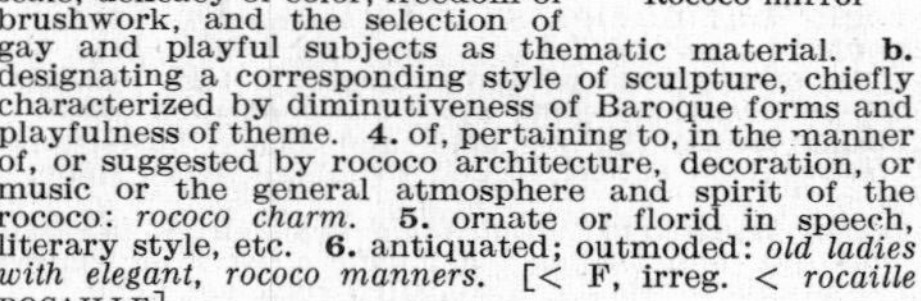

rod (rod), *n., v.,* **rod·ded, rod·ding.** —*n.* **1.** a stick, wand, staff, or the like, of wood, metal, or other material. **2.** a straight, slender shoot or stem of any woody plant, whether growing upon or cut from the plant. **3.** See **fishing rod. 4.** (in plastering or mortaring) a straightedge moved along screeds to even the plaster between them. **5.** a stick used for measuring. **6.** a unit of linear measure, 5½ yards or 16½ feet; linear perch or pole. **7.** a unit of square measure, 30¼ square yards; square perch or pole. **8.** a stick or a bundle of sticks or switches bound together for use as a whip, as an instrument of punishment. **9.** punishment or discipline: *Not one to spare the rod, I sent him to bed without T.V.* **10.** a wand, staff, or scepter carried as a symbol of office, authority, power, etc. **11.** authority, sway, or rule, esp. when tyrannical. **12.** See **lightning rod. 13.** a slender bar or tube for draping towels over, suspending curtains, etc. **14.** *Bible.* a branch of a family; tribe. **15.** a pattern, drawn on wood in full size, of one section of a piece of furniture. **16.** *U.S. Slang.* a pistol or revolver. **17.** *Anat.* one of the rodlike cells in the retina of the eye, sensitive to low intensities of light. Cf. **cone** (def. 8). **18.** *Bacteriol.* a rod-shaped microorganism. **19.** *Survey.* Also called **leveling rod, stadia rod.** a light pole, conspicuously marked with graduations, held upright and read through a surveying instrument in leveling or stadia surveying. **20.** *Metall.* round metal stock for drawing and cutting into slender bars. —*v.t.* **21.** to furnish or equip with a rod or rods, esp. lightning rods. **22.** to even (plaster or mortar) with a rod. **23.** *Foundry.* to reinforce (the core of a mold) with metal rods. [ME, OE *rodd;* akin. to OIcel *rudda* a kind of club] —**rod′less,** *adj.* —**rod′like′,** *adj.*

Rod (rod), *n.* a boy's given name, form of **Roderick** or **Rodney.**

rod′ bolt′, a long, double-ended bolt.

rod·ded (rod′id), *adj.* made of or fitted with rods (often used in combination): *a rodded bin for storing hay; a house well-rodded against electrical storms.* [ROD + -ED[3]]

rod′ded joint′, *Masonry.* a deep, concave mortar joint.

Rod·dy (rod′ē), *n.* a boy's given name, form of **Roderick** or **Rodney.** Also, **Rod′die.**

rode[1] (rōd), *v.* a pt. of **ride.**

rode[2] (rōd), *n.* (in New England and E Canada) a rope by which a boat is anchored. [?]

ro·dent (rōd′ənt), *adj.* **1.** belonging or pertaining to the gnawing or nibbling mammals of the order *Rodentia,* including the mice, squirrels, beavers, etc. **2.** (of such an animal) gnawing; biting; nibbling: *the rodent teeth of a rabbit.* —*n.* **3.** a rodent mammal. [< L *rōdent-* (s. of *rōdēns,* prp. of *rōdere* to eat away, gnaw) < *rōd-* gnaw + *-ent-* -ENT] —**ro′dent·like′,** *adj.*

Ro·den·tia (rō den′shə, -shē ə, -tē ə), *n.* the order comprising the rodents. [< NL; see RODENT, -IA]

ro·den·ti·cide (rō den′ti sīd′), *n.* a substance or preparation for killing rodents. [RODENT + -I- + -CIDE]

ro·de·o (rō′dē ō′, rō dā′ō), *n., pl.* **-de·os. 1.** a public exhibition of cowboy skills, as bronco riding and calf roping. **2.** a roundup of cattle. [< Sp: cattle ring < *rode(ar)* (to) go round < *rueda* wheel << L *rota*]

Rod·e·ri·ca (rod′ə rē′kə), *n.* a girl's given name.

Rod·er·ick (rod′ə rik), *n.* a boy's given name.

Rod′erick Hud′son, a novel (1876) by Henry James.

Ro·dez (rô dez′), *n.* a town in and the capital of Aveyron, in S France. 24,352 (1962).

Rodg·er (roj′ər), *n.* a boy's given name, form of **Roger.**

Rodg·ers (roj′ərz), *n.* **Richard,** born 1902, U.S. composer of popular music.

Ro·di (rô′dē), *n.* Italian name of **Rhodes.**

Ro·din (rō dan′, -daN′; *Fr.* rô daN′), *n.* **(Fran·çois) Au·guste (Re·né)** (fräN swa′ ō gyst′ rə nā′), 1840–1917, French sculptor.

rod·man (rod′mən), *n., pl.* **-men. 1.** a person who works with rods, as in making reinforced concrete. **2.** a person who carries the leveling rod in surveying. [ROD + MAN]

rod′ mill′, **1.** *Metalworking.* a mill for making metal rods. **2.** a mill for grinding ores or the like by means of steel rods.

Rod·ney (rod′nē), *n.* **1. George Brydg·es** (brij′iz), **Baron,** 1718–92, British admiral. **2.** a boy's given name.

rod·o·mon·tade (rod′ə mon tād′, -täd′, rō′də-, -mən-), *n., adj., v.,* **-tad·ed, -tad·ing.** —*n.* **1.** vainglorious boasting or bragging; pretentious, blustering talk. —*adj.* **2.** bragging. —*v.i.* **3.** to boast; brag; talk big. [< MF < It *Rodomonte,* the boastful king of Algiers in *Orlando Innamorato* and *Orlando Furioso* + MF *-ade* -ADE[1]]

rod′ rig′ging, *Naut.* standing rigging of thin steel rods or bars, used esp. on sailing yachts. Also called **bar rigging.**

Ro·dzin·ski (rə jin′skē), *n.* **Ar·tur** (är′to͝or), 1894–1958, U.S. orchestra conductor.

roe[1] (rō), *n.* **1.** the mass of eggs, or spawn, within the ovarian membrane of the female fish. **2.** the milt or sperm of the male fish. **3.** the eggs of any of various crustaceans, as the coral of the lobster. [ME *rowe;* c. OHG *rogo*]

roe[2] (rō), *n., pl.* **roes,** (*esp. collectively*) **roe.** See **roe deer.** [ME *roo* < OE *rā, rāha;* c. G *Reh*]

Roeb·ling (rō′bling), *n.* **1. John Augustus,** 1806–69, U.S. engineer, born in Germany: pioneer of wire-rope suspension bridges, designer of the Brooklyn Bridge. **2.** a town in W New Jersey. 3272 (1960).

roe·buck (rō′buk′), *n., pl.* **-bucks,** (*esp. collectively*) **-buck.** a male roe deer. [ME *robucke.* See ROE[2], BUCK[1]]

roe′ deer′, a small, agile Old World deer, *Capreolus capreolus,* the male of which has three-pointed antlers. Also called **roe.** [OE *rāhdēor.* See *roe*[2], deer]

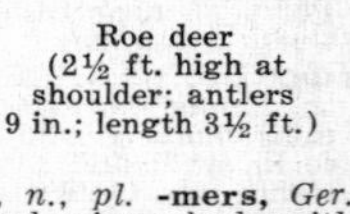

Roe deer (2½ ft. high at shoulder; antlers 9 in.; length 3½ ft.)

Roe′land Park′ (rō′lənd), a town in E Kansas. 8949 (1960).

roe·mer (rā′mər; *Ger.* RŒ′məR), *n., pl.* **-mers,** *Ger.* **-mer** (-məR). a German wineglass having a body with a globular top and a cylindrical bottom often decorated with prunts, supported by a conical foot. [< G, orig. a glass for toasting; c. D *roemer;* akin to G *rühmen* to praise]

Roent·gen (rent′gən, -jən, runt′-), *n.* **1. Wil·helm Kon·rad** (wil′helm kon′rad; *Ger.* vil′helm kôn′rät), 1845–1923, German physicist: discoverer of x-rays 1895; Nobel prize 1901. **2.** (*l.c.*) the unit of radiation equal to the amount of x- or gamma-radiation that will produce ions in air containing a quantity of positive or negative electricity equal to one electrostatic unit in 0.001293 grams of air. *Abbr.:* R, r —*adj.* **3.** (*sometimes l.c.*) of or pertaining to Wilhelm Roentgen, the Roentgen unit, or esp. to x-rays. Also, **Röntgen.**

roent·gen·ize (rent′gə nīz′, -jə-, runt′-), *v.t.,* **-ized, -iz·ing.** (formerly) to subject to the action of x-rays. Also, **röntgenize.** [ROENTGEN + -IZE] —**roent′gen·i·za′tion,** *n.*

roentgeno-, a combining form of **roentgen:** *roentgenometer.*

roent·gen·o·gram (rent′gə nə gram′, -jə-, runt′-), *n.* a photograph made with x-rays. Also, **röntgenogram.** [ROENTGENO- + -GRAM[1]]

roent·gen·o·graph (rent′gə nə graf′, -gräf′, -jə-, runt′-), *n.* (no longer current) roentgenogram. Also, **röntgenograph.** [ROENTGENO- + -GRAPH] —**roent·gen·o·graph·ic** (rent′gə nə graf′ik, -jə-, runt′-), *adj.* —**roent′gen·o·graph′i·cal·ly,** *adv.* —**roent·gen·og·ra·phy** (rent′gə nog′rə fē, -jə-, runt′-), *n.*

roent·gen·ol·o·gy (rent′gə nol′ə jē, -jə-, runt′-), *n.* the branch of medicine dealing with diagnosis and therapy through x-rays. Also, **röntgenology.** [ROENTGENO- + -LOGY] —**roent·gen·o·log·ic** (rent′gə nəloj′ik, -jə-, runt′-), **roent′gen·o·log′i·cal,** *adj.* —**roent′gen·o·log′i·cal·ly,** *adv.* —**roent′gen·ol′o·gist,** *n.*

roent·gen·om·e·ter (rent′gə nom′i tər, -jə-, runt′-), *n.* an instrument for measuring the intensity of x-rays. [ROENTGENO- + -METER] —**roent′gen·om′e·try,** *n.*

roent·gen·o·paque (rent′gə nō pāk′, -jə-, runt′-), *adj.* not permitting the passage of x-rays. [ROENTGEN + OPAQUE]

roent·gen·o·par·ent (rent′gə nō pâr′ənt, -jə-, runt′-), *adj.* visible by means of x-rays. [ROENTGENO- + (AP)PARENT]

roent·gen·o·scope (rent′gə nə skōp′, -jə-, runt′-), *n.* *Physics.* a fluoroscope. Also, **röntgenoscope.** [ROENTGENO- + -SCOPE] —**roent·gen·o·scop·ic** (rent′gə nə skop′ik, -jə-, runt′-), *adj.* —**roent·gen·os·co·py** (rent′gə nos′kə pē, -jə-, runt′-), *n.*

roent·gen·o·ther·a·py (rent′gə nō ther′ə pē, -jə-, runt′-), *n.* treatment of disease by means of x-rays. [ROENTGENO- + THERAPY]

Roent′gen ray′, (*sometimes l.c.*) x-ray.

Roe·rich (rûr′ik; *Russ.* RŒ′RIKH), *n.* **Nich·o·las Kon·stan·ti·no·vich** (nik′ə ləs kon′stən tē′nə vich; *Russ.* kon stän tē′no vich), 1874–1947, Russian painter, archaeologist, and author; in the U.S. after 1920.

Roeth·ke (ret′kə), *n.* **Theodore,** 1908–63, U.S. poet and teacher.

R.O.G., receipt of goods. Also, **ROG, r.o.g.**

ro·ga·tion (rō gā′shən), *n.* **1.** Usually, **rogations.** *Eccles.* solemn supplication, esp. as chanted during procession on the three days (**Roga′tion Days′**) before Ascension Day. **2.** *Rom. Hist.* **a.** the proposing by the consuls or tribunes of a law to be passed by the people. **b.** a law so proposed. [ME *rogacio(u)n* < L *rogātiōn-* (s. of *rogātiō*) < *rogāt(us)* (ptp. of *rogāre* to ask, beg) + *-iōn-* -ION]

rog·a·to·ry (rog′ə tōr′ē, -tôr′ē), *adj.* pertaining to asking or requesting: *a rogatory commission.* [< ML *rogātōri(us)* < L *rogāt(us)* (see ROGATION) + *-ōrius* -ORY[1]]

rog·er (roj′ər), *interj.* **1.** *Informal.* all right; O.K. **2.** message received and understood (a response to radio communications). **3.** (*often cap.*) See **Jolly Roger. 4.** (formerly used in communications to represent the letter R.) [from the name *Roger*]

Rog·er (roj′ər), *n.* a boy's given name.

Ro·ger-Du·casse (rō zhā′dy kas′), *n.* **Jean Jules A·ma·ble** (zhäN zhyl A MA′bl[ə]), 1873–1954, French composer. Also called **Ducasse.**

Rog·ers (roj′ərz), *n.* **1. Bernard,** 1893–1968, U.S. composer. **2. Bruce,** 1870–1957, U.S. book designer and printer. **3. Ginger** (*Virginia Katherine McMath*), born 1911, U.S. actress and dancer. **4. James Gamble,** 1867–1947, U.S. architect. **5. Samuel,** 1763–1855, English poet. **6. Will(iam Penn A·dair)** (ə dâr′), 1879–1935, U.S. actor and humorist. **7. William P(ierce),** born 1913, U.S. lawyer: Attorney General 1957–61; Secretary of State 1969–73. **8.** a town in NW Arkansas. 5700 (1960).

Rog′ers Cit′y, a town in NE Michigan. 4722 (1960).

Rog·ers·ville (roj′ərz vil), *n.* a town in NE Tennessee. 3121 (1960).

Ro·get (rō zhā′, rō′zhā, rozh′ā), *n.* **Peter Mark,** 1779–1869, English lexicographer and physician.

rogue (rōg), *n., v.,* **rogued, ro·guing.** —*n.* **1.** a dishonest, knavish person; scoundrel. **2.** a playfully mischievous person; scamp: *The youngest boys are little rogues.* **3.** a tramp or vagabond. **4.** a rogue elephant or other animal of similar disposition. **5.** *Biol.* a usually inferior organism, esp. a plant, varying markedly from the normal. —*v.i.* **6.** to live or act as a rogue. —*v.t.* **7.** to cheat. **8.** to uproot or destroy (as plants which do not conform to a desired standard). **9.** to perform this operation upon: *to rogue a field.* [appar. short for obs. *roger* begging vagabond, b. ROA(MER + BEG)GAR]
—**Syn. 1.** villain, trickster, swindler, cheat, mountebank, quack. See **knave.**

rogue′ el′ephant, an elephant that has been exiled from the herd and is characterized by its savage disposition.

ro·guer·y (rō′gə rē), *n., pl.* **-guer·ies. 1.** roguish conduct; rascality. **2.** playful mischief. [ROGUE + -RY]

rogues′ gal′lery, a collection of portraits of criminals, maintained for purposes of identification, or of suspects to be watched for and apprehended, as at police headquarters.

rogue's′ march′, a derisive tune played to accompany a person's expulsion from a regiment, community, etc.

rogue's′ yarn′, a yarn of distinctive color, material, or twist, laid in a strand or stands of a rope to identify the owner or the maker. Also called **identification thread.**

ro·guish (rō′gish), *adj.* **1.** pertaining to, characteristic of, or acting like a rogue; knavish or rascally. **2.** playfully mischievous: *a roguish smile.* [ROGUE + -ISH[1]] —**ro′guish·ly,** *adv.* —**ro′guish·ness,** *n.*

roil (roil), *v.t.* **1.** to render (water, wine, etc.) turbid by stirring up sediment. **2.** to disturb or disquiet; irritate; vex: *to be roiled by a delay* [?]
—**Syn. 2.** annoy, fret, ruffle, exasperate, provoke.

roil·y (roi′lē), *adj.,* **roil·i·er, roil·i·est.** turbid; muddy. [ROIL + -Y[1]]

roist·er (roi′stər), *v.i.* **1.** to act in a swaggering, boisterous, or uproarious manner. **2.** to revel noisily or without restraint. [v. use of *roister* (n.) < MF *ru(i)stre* ruffian, boor < *ru(i)ste* RUSTIC (n.)] —**roist′er·er,** *n.* —**roist′er·ous,** *n.* —**roist′er·ous·ly,** *adv.*

Ro·jas (rō′häs; *Sp.* RÔ′häs), *n.* **Fer·nan·do de** (feR nän′dô de), c1475–1541?, Spanish writer.

Rok (rok), *n.* a soldier in the army of the Republic of Korea. [after *R(epublic) o(f) K(orea)*]

ROK, Republic of Korea.

roke (rōk), *n.* *Metall.* a seam or scratch filled with scale or slag on the surface of an ingot or bar. Also, **roak.** [north dial. *roke, rawk* to scratch, flaw, etc.]

Ro·land (rō′lənd), *n.* **1.** the greatest of the paladins in the Charlemagne cycle of the *chansons de geste,* renowned for his prowess and the manner of his death in the battle of Roncesvalles (A.D. 778), also for his five days' combat with Oliver in which neither was the victor. Italian, **Orlando. 2. a Roland for an Oliver,** retaliation or a retort equal to its provocation; a blow for a blow. **3.** a boy's given name.

role (rōl), *n.* **1.** a part or character to be played by an actor. **2.** proper or customary function: *the teacher's role in society.* Also, **rôle.** [< F *rôle* ROLL (as of paper) containing the actor's part]

Rolf (rolf), *n.* **1.** Also called **Rolf′ the Gang′er** (gang′ər). Rollo (def. 1). **2.** Also, **Rolph.** a boy's given name.

Rolfe (rolf), *n.* **John,** 1585–1622, English colonist in Virginia (husband of Pocahontas).

roll (rōl), *v.i.* **1.** to move along a surface by revolving or turning over and over, as a ball or a wheel. **2.** to move or be moved on wheels, as a vehicle or its occupants. **3.** to flow or advance in a stream or with an undulating motion, as water, waves, or smoke. **4.** to extend in undulations, as land. **5.** to elapse, pass, or move, as time (often fol. by *on, away,* or *by*). **6.** to move as in a cycle (usually fol. by *round* or *around*): *as soon as summer rolls round again.* **7.** to perform a periodical revolution in an orbit, as a heavenly body. **8.** to emit or have a deep, prolonged sound, as thunder, drums, etc. **9.** to trill, as a bird. **10.** to revolve or turn over, once or repeatedly, as a wheel on an axis or a person or animal lying down. **11.** to turn around in different directions or from side to side and top to bottom, as the eyes in their sockets. **12.** (of a vessel) **a.** to rock from side to side in open water. Cf. **heave** (def. 15b), **pitch**[1] (def. 17). **b.** to sail with a side-to-side rocking motion. **13.** to walk with a swinging or swaying gait. **14.** *Slang.* to begin; start; commence: *Let's roll at sunrise.* **15.** to curl up so as to form a tube or cylinder. **16.** to admit of being formed into a tube or cylinder by curling up. **17.** to be spread out after being curled up (usually fol. by *out*). **18.** to spread out as under a roller: *The paint rolls easily.* **19.** (of a rocket or guided missile) to deviate from a stable flight attitude by rotation about its longitudinal axis.
—*v.t.* **20.** to cause to move along a surface by revolving or turning over and over, as a cask, a ball, or a hoop. **21.** to move along on wheels or rollers; to convey in a wheeled vehicle. **22.** to drive, impel, or cause to flow onward with a sweeping or undulating motion: *The wind rolled the waves high on the beach.* **23.** to utter or give forth with or cause to give forth a full, flowing, continuous sound. **24.** to trill: *to roll one's r's.* **25.** to cause to revolve or turn over or over and over: *to roll oneself on one's face.* **26.** to turn around in different directions or from side to side and top to bottom: *He smirked and rolled his eyes.* **27.** to cause to sway or rock from side to side, as a ship. **28.** to wrap (something) around an axis, around upon itself, or into a cylindrical shape, ball, or the like: *to roll string.* **29.** to make by forming a tube or cylinder: *to roll a cigarette.* **30.** to spread out flat (something curled up) (often fol. by *out*): *He rolled the map out on the table.* **31.** to wrap, infold, or envelop, as in some covering: *to roll a child in a blanket.* **32.** to spread out, level, smooth, compact, or the like, as with a rolling pin, roller, the hands, etc.: *to roll dough; to roll a tennis court.* **33.** to form (metal) in a rolling mill. **34.** to tumble (metal pieces and abrasives) in a box or barrel in such a way that their relative positions remain the same. **35.** to beat (a drum) with rapid, continuous strokes. **36.** (in certain games, as craps) to cast, or throw (dice). **37.** *Print.* to apply ink with a roller or series of rollers. **38.** *Slang.* to rob, esp. by going through the victim's pockets while he is drunk or sleeping. **39. roll back,** to reduce (the price or a commodity) to a former level, usually in response to government action. **40. roll in,** *Informal.* **a.** to luxuriate in; abound in: *rolling in money.* **b.** to go to bed; retire: *They would roll in later and later every night.* **41. roll out, a.** to spread out or flatten: *to roll out dough.* **b.** *Slang.* to arise from bed; get up: *It was nearly impossible to roll out on the first day back after vacation.* **c.** *Football.* to execute a roll-out. **42. roll up, a.** to accumulate; collect: *to roll up a large vote.* **b.** to increase. **c.** *Informal.* to arrive in a conveyance: *Returning to his home after many years, he rolled up to the front door in a chauffeur-driven limousine.*
—*n.* **43.** a document of paper, parchment, or the like, that is or may be rolled up, as for storing; scroll. **44.** a list, register, or catalogue, esp. one containing the names of the persons belonging to a company, class, society, etc. **45.** anything rolled up in a ringlike or cylindrical form: *a roll of wire.* **46.** a number of papers or other items rolled up together. **47.** a length of cloth, wallpaper, or the like, rolled up in cylindrical form (often forming a definite measure). **48.** a cylindrical or rounded mass of something: *rolls of fat.* **49.** some article of cylindrical or rounded form, as a molding. **50.** a cylindrical piece upon which something is rolled along to facilitate moving. **51.** a cylinder serving as a core upon which something is rolled up. **52.** a roller with which something is spread out, leveled, crushed, smoothed, compacted, or the like. **53.** *Cookery.* **a.** thin cake spread with jelly or the like and rolled up. **b.** a small cake of bread, originally and still often rolled or doubled on itself before baking. **c.** meat rolled up and cooked. **54.** the act, process, or an instance of rolling. **55.** undulation, as of surface: *the roll of a prairie.* **56.** a sonorous or rhythmical flow of words. **57.** a deep, prolonged sound, as of thunder: *the deep roll of a breaking wave.* **58.** the trill of certain birds, esp. of the roller canary. **59.** the continuous sound of a drum rapidly beaten. **60.** a rolling motion, as of a ship. **61.** a rolling or swaying gait. **62.** *Aeron.* a single, complete rotation of an airplane about the axis of the fuselage with little loss of altitude or change of direction. **63.** (of a rocket or guided missile) **a.** the act of rolling. **b.** the angular displacement caused by rolling. **64.** *Slang.* **a.** paper currency carried folded or rolled up: *He took out an impressive roll and paid the check with a 20-dollar bill.* **b.** bankroll; funds: *People were encouraged to shoot their rolls on mining speculation.* **65.** (in various dice games) **a.** a single cast of or turn at casting the dice. **b.** the total number of pips or points made by a single cast; score or point. **66. strike off** or **from the rolls,** to remove from membership or practice, as to disbar: *He will surely be struck off the rolls if this conduct continues.* [ME *roll(en)* < OF *roll(er)* << L *rotula,* dim. of *rota* wheel] —**roll′a·ble,** *adj.*
—**Syn. 1.** revolve, rotate. **3.** wave, undulate. **4.** undulate. **12.** swing, tilt. **44.** See **list**[1]. **51.** spindle.

Rol·land (RÔ läN′), *n.* **Ro·main** (RÔ MAN′), 1866–1944, French novelist, music critic, and dramatist: Nobel prize 1915.

roll′ and fil′let mold′ing, a roll molding having a projecting fillet along its length.

roll·a·way (rōl′ə wā′), *adj.* designed to be rolled out of the way or out of sight when not in use: *rollaway bed.* [adj. use of v. phrase *roll away*]

roll·back (rōl′bak′), *n.* a return to a lower level of prices, wages, etc., as by government order. [n. use of v. phrase *roll back*]

roll′ book′, a book in which attendance records are kept, as of students, employees, etc.

roll′ call′, **1.** the calling of a list of names, as of soldiers or students, to identify any who may be absent. **2.** a military signal for this, as one given by a drum.

roll′ cloud′, **1.** arcus. **2.** See **rotor cloud.**

rolled′ glass′, a sheet of glass made by the extrusion of molten glass between two rollers.

rolled′ gold′. See **filled gold.**

rolled′ oats′, oats that are hulled and steamed, then flattened by rollers.

rolled′ roast′, meat which has had the bones removed and been rolled and tied for roasting.

roll·er[1] (rō′lər), *n.* **1.** one who or that which rolls. **2.** a cylinder, wheel, caster, or the like, upon which something is rolled along. **3.** a cylindrical body, revolving on a fixed axis, esp. one to facilitate the movement of something passed over or around it. **4.** a cylindrical body upon which cloth or other material is rolled up. **5.** a hollow, cylindrical body of plastic, stiff net, or the like, upon which hair is rolled up for setting in smooth waves. **6.** a cylindrical body for rolling over something to be spread out, leveled, crushed, smoothed, compacted, impressed, inked, etc. **7.** any of various other revolving cylindrical bodies, as the barrel of a music box. **8.** *Metalworking.* a person in charge of a rolling mill. **9.** *Horol.* (on a balance staff) a circular piece engaging with the fork of the pallet. Cf. **impulse roller, safety roller. 10.** a long, swelling wave advancing steadily. **11.** a rolled bandage. [ME; see ROLL, -ER[1]]
—**Syn. 10.** breaker, comber.

roll·er[2] (rō′lər), *n.* *Ornith.* **1.** one of a variety of tumbler pigeons. **2.** any of several Old World birds of the family *Coraciidae* that tumble or roll over in flight, esp. in the breeding season. **3.** one of a variety of canaries having a warbling or trilling song. [< G *Roller* ROLLER[1]]

roll′er bear′ing, *Mach.* a bearing consisting of cylindrical or tapered rollers running between races in two concentric rings, one of which is mounted on a rotating or oscillating part, as a shaft.

roll′er-blind shut′ter (rō′lər blīnd′), *Photog.* See **curtain shutter.**

roll′er chain′, a power chain consisting of parallel pairs of flat links joined by pins covered with rollers, and engaging with the teeth of sprockets.

roll′er chock′, *Naut.* **1.** a chock having one or more vertical rollers serving as a fairlead for a hawser. **2.** a horizontal roller serving as a fairlead for the lines of a fishing boat. Also called **roller fairlead.**

roll′er coast′er, **1.** a small gravity railroad, esp. in an amusement park, having a train with open cars that moves along a high, sharply winding trestle built with steep inclines that produce sudden, speedy plunges for thrill-seeking passengers. **2.** a car or train of cars for such a railroad.

roll′er dam′, a dam having roller gates. Also called **rolling crest dam.**

roll′er der′by, a contest between two teams on roller skates, held on a circular, usually banked board track, in which the teams race around the track in each unit of play, working to free a teammate or teammates for the opportunity to score by lapping one or more opponents.

roll′er fair′lead, *Naut.* See **roller chock.**

roll′er gate′, (on certain dams) a cylindrical gate that rises and falls by rotating against inclined racks.

roll′er gear′, *Naut.* any of various devices employing rolling booms or other rolling devices to roll or reef the fore-and-aft sails of small vessels.

roll′er jew′el, *Horol.* See **ruby pin.**

roll′er mill′, any mill that pulverizes, flattens, or otherwise changes material by passing it between rolls.

roll′er skate′, a form of skate with four wheels or rollers instead of a runner, for use on a sidewalk or other surface offering traction.

roll·er-skate (rō′lər skāt′), *v.i.,* **-skat·ed, -skat·ing.** to glide about by means of roller skates. [v. use of ROLLER SKATE] —**roll′er skat′er,** *n.*

roll′er tow′el, a long towel sewed together at the ends and hung on a roller.

Rolle's′ the′orem (rōlz), *Math.* the theorem that a differentiable function having equal values at the endpoints of an interval has a derivative equal to zero at some point in the interval.

roll′ film′, *Photog.* a strip of film with space for several exposures, packaged on a spool in roll form so as to permit daylight loading and unloading and ease of handling.

rol·lick (rol′ik), *v.i.* to move or act in a careless, frolicsome manner; behave in a free, hearty, gay, or jovial way. [b. RO(MP + FRO)LIC] —**rol′lick·er,** *n.*

rol·lick·ing (rol′i king), *adj.* swaggering and jolly: *a pair of rollicking drunken sailors.* [ROLLICK + -ING[2]] —**rol′lick·ing·ly,** *adv.* —**rol′lick·ing·ness,** *n.*

rol·lick·some (rol′ik səm), *adj.* rollicking; frolicsome. [ROLLICK + -SOME[1]] —**rol′lick·some·ness,** *n.*

roll·ing (rō′ling), *n.* **1.** the action, motion, or sound of anything that rolls. —*adj.* **2.** moving by revolving or turning over and over. **3.** rising and falling in gentle slopes, as land. **4.** moving in undulating billows, as clouds or waves. **5.** rocking or swaying from side to side. **6.** turning or folding over, as a collar. **7.** producing a deep, continuous sound. [late ME (n.); see ROLL, -ING[1], -ING[2]] —**roll′ing·ly,** *adv.*

roll′ing bunt′, *Naut.* See **low bunt.**

roll′ing chock′, *Naut.* See **bilge keel.**

roll′ing crest′ dam′. See **roller dam.**

roll′ing-el′e·ment bear′ing (rō′ling el′ə mənt), *Mach.* a roller bearing or ball bearing. Also called **antifriction bearing, roll′ing-con′tact bear′ing** (rō′-ling kon′takt). Cf. **plain bearing.**

roll′ing hitch′, a hitch on a spar or the like, composed of two round turns and a half hitch so disposed as to jam when a stress is applied parallel to the object on which the hitch is made.

roll′ing kitch′en, a mobile kitchen used for feeding troops outdoors.

roll′ing mill′, 1. a mill where ingots, slabs, sheets, etc., of metal are passed, usually hot, between rolls to give them a certain thickness or cross-sectional form. 2. a machine or set of rollers for rolling out or shaping metal.

roll′ing pin′, a cylinder of wood or other material, with a rounded handle a handbreadth in length at each end, for rolling out dough.

roll′ing stock′, the wheeled vehicles of a railroad, including locomotives, cars, etc.

roll′ joint′, (in sheet-metal work) a joint formed by rolling together and flattening the edges of adjoining sheets.

roll′ mold′ing, *Archit.* any molding of approximately cylindrical form.

roll·mop (rōl′mop′), *n.* a fillet of herring, rolled, usually around a pickle, marinated in brine, and served as an appetizer. [< G *Rollmops,* equiv. to *roll(en)* (to) ROLL + *Mops* pug (dog)]

Rol·lo (rol′ō), *n.* 1. Also called **Rolf, Roy, Hrolf, Rolf the Ganger.** A.D. c860–931?, Norse chieftain: 1st duke of Normandy 911?. 2. a boy's given name, form of **Rolf.**

rol·lock (rol′ək), *n.* rowlock.

roll-out (rōl′out′), *n.* 1. the first public showing of an aircraft. 2. *Football.* an offensive maneuver in which the quarterback, having the option to run or pass, takes the ball from center, moves back a distance toward his goal line, and then moves forward and toward a sideline. [n. use of v. phrase *roll out*]

roll·o·ver (rōl′ō′vər), *n.* 1. a rolling or turning over, esp. of an automobile. 2. an extension, renewal, or deferral of a financial obligation, as a loan, investment, or tax.

roll′ top′, a flexible, sliding cover for the working area of a desk, opening by rising upward and back in quadrantal grooves and rolling up beneath the top. —**roll′-top′, roll′top′,** *adj.*

roll·way (rōl′wā′), *n.* 1. a place on which things are rolled or moved on rollers. 2. an incline for rolling or sliding logs into a stream to begin them on their journey from lumber camp to mill. 3. a pile of logs in or at the side of a river or stream ready to go to the mill. [ROLL + WAY]

Röl·vaag (rōl′väg), *n.* **O·le Ed·vart** (ō′lə ed′värt), 1876–1931, U.S. novelist and educator, born in Norway.

ro·ly-po·ly (rō′lē pō′lē, -pō′lē), *adj., n., pl.* **-lies.** —*adj.* 1. short and plumply round, as a person, a young animal, etc. —*n.* 2. a roly-poly person or thing. 3. *Chiefly Brit.* a sheet of biscuit dough spread with jam, fruit, or the like, rolled up and steamed or baked. [earlier *rowle powle* ? var. of *roll ye, poll ye.* See ROLL (v.), POLL[1] (v.)]

Rom (rōm), *n.* a Gypsy man or boy. [< Romany: a married man < Skt *ḍomba, ḍoma*]

ROM (rom), *n.* a type of computer memory in which operating procedures are stored during manufacture and cannot be changed by the user. Cf. **RAM** [*r(ead)-o(nly) m(emory)*]

Rom., 1. Roman. 2. Romance. 3. Romanic. 4. Romans (New Testament). Also, **Rom** (for defs. 2, 3).

rom., roman type.

Ro·ma (rô′mä), *n.* 1. Italian name of **Rome.** 2. (in ancient Roman legend) according to some accounts, the daughter of Evander for whom Rome was named.

Ro·ma·gna (rō män′yə; *It.* rô mä′nyä), *n.* a former province of the Papal States, in NE Italy. *Cap.:* Ravenna.

Ro·ma·ic (rō mā′ik), *n.* 1. demotic (def. 4). —*adj.* 2. of or pertaining to modern Greece, its inhabitants, or their language. [< Gk *Rhōmaïk(ós)* Roman < *Rhṓm(ē)* Rome + *-a-* connective vowel + *-ikos* -IC]

ro·maine (rō mān′, rə-), *n.* 1. Also called **romaine′ let′tuce, cos, cos lettuce.** a variety of lettuce, *Lactuca sativa longifolia,* having a cylindrical head of long, relatively loose leaves. 2. Also called **romaine′ crepe′.** a sheer fabric made of silk or man-made fibers and constructed in a plain or basket weave. [< F, fem. of *romain* ROMAN]

Ro·mains (rô maN′), *n.* **Jules** (zhyl), (*Louis Farigoule*), 1885–1972, French novelist, poet, and dramatist.

Ro·ma·ji (rō′mə jē), *n., pl.* **-ji.** *Japanese.* 1. a Roman character used to represent a Japanese one. 2. a Japanese word represented by such characters.

ro·man (rô mäN′), *n., pl.* **-mans** (-mäN′). *French.* 1. a metrical narrative, esp. in medieval French literature. 2. a novel.

Ro·man (rō′mən), *adj.* 1. of or pertaining to the ancient or modern city of Rome, or to its inhabitants and their customs and culture: *Roman restaurants.* 2. of or pertaining to the ancient kingdom, republic, and empire whose capital was the city of Rome. 3. of a kind or character regarded as typical of the ancient Romans: *Roman virtues.* 4. (*usually l.c.*) designating or pertaining to the upright style of printing types most commonly used in modern books, periodicals, etc., of which the main text of this dictionary is an example. 5. of or pertaining to the Roman Catholic Church. 6. noting, pertaining to, or resembling the architecture of ancient Rome, esp. the public and religious architecture, characterized by the employment of massive brick and concrete construction, with such features as the semicircular arch, the dome, and groin and barrel vaults, by the use in interiors of marble and molded stucco revetments, by the elaboration of the Greek orders as purely decorative motifs for the adornment of façades and interiors, and by an over-all effect in which simplicity and grandeur of massing is often combined with excessive elaboration of detailing. 7. written in or pertaining to Roman numerals. —*n.* 8. a native, inhabitant, or citizen of ancient or modern Rome. 9. the dialect of Italian spoken in Rome. 10. (*usually l.c.*) roman type or lettering. 11. *Often offensive.* a member of the Roman Catholic Church. 12. *Rare.* the Latin language. 13. a boy's given name. [OE < L *Rōmān(us)* (see ROME, -AN); r. ME *Romain* < OF]

ro·man à clef (rô mä′ NA klā′), *pl.* **ro·mans à clef** (rô mäN′ ZA klā′). *French.* a novel that represents historical events and characters under the guise of fiction. [lit., novel with (a) key]

Ro′man al′phabet. See **Latin alphabet.**

Ro′man arch′, a semicircular arch.

Ro′man brick′, a long, thin face brick, usually yellow-brown and having a length about eight times its thickness.

Ro′man cal′endar, the calendar in use in ancient Rome until 46 B.C., when it was replaced with the Julian calendar. Cf. **Year of Confusion.**

Ro′man can′dle, a firework consisting of a tube which sends out a shower of sparks and a succession of balls of fire.

Ro′man Cath′olic, 1. of or pertaining to the Roman Catholic Church. 2. a member of the Roman Catholic Church. Cf. **Catholic.**

Ro′man Cath′olic Church′, the Christian church of which the pope, or bishop of Rome, is the supreme head. Cf. **Catholic Church.**

Ro′man Cathol′icism, the faith, practice, and system of government of the Roman Catholic Church.

ro·mance[1] (*n.* rō mans′, rō′mans; *v.* rō mans′; *adj.* rō′mans), *n., v.,* **-manced, -manc·ing,** *adj.* —*n.* 1. a narrative depicting heroic or marvelous achievements, colorful events or scenes, chivalrous devotion, unusual or even supernatural experiences, or other matters of a kind to appeal to the imagination. 2. the world, life, or conditions depicted in such tales: *She seemed a princess of romance.* 3. a medieval narrative, originally one in verse and in some Romance dialect, treating of heroic personages or events: *the Arthurian romances.* 4. a baseless, made-up story, usually full of exaggeration or fanciful invention. 5. a romantic spirit, sentiment, emotion, or desire. 6. romantic character or quality. 7. a romantic affair or experience; a love affair. 8. (*cap.*) Also, **Romanic.** Also called **Romance languages.** the group of Italic Indo-European languages descended since A.D. 800 from Latin, as French, Spanish, Italian, Portuguese, Rumanian, Provençal, Catalan, Rhaeto-Romanic, Sardinian, and Ladino. —*v.i.* 9. to invent or relate romances; indulge in fanciful or extravagant stories or daydreams. 10. to think or talk romantically. —*adj.* 11. (*cap.*) Also, **Romanic.** noting, of, or pertaining to Romance: *a Romance language.* [ME *romaunce* < OF < VL **Rōmānicē* (adv.) in a Romance language < L *Rōmānic(us)* ROMANIC] —**ro·manc′er,** *n.*
—**Syn.** 1. story, fiction. See **novel**[1]. 4. falsehood, fable.

ro·mance[2] (rō mans′), *n.* 1. *Music.* a short, simple melody, vocal or instrumental, of tender character. 2. *Sp. Lit.* a short epic poem, esp. a historical ballad. [< F < Sp: kind of poem, ballad < OF *romanz* ROMANCE[1]]

Ro·mance lan′guages, romance[1] (def. 8).

Ro·mances sans Pa·role (rô mäNs säN PA rôl′), a collection of poems (1874) by Verlaine.

Ro′man col′lar. See **clerical collar.**

Ro′man Cu′ria, 1. the judicial and executive organizations of the papal see comprising the government of the Catholic Church. 2. the court of the papal see.

Ro·ma·née-Con·ti (rō′mə nā′kon tē′; *Fr.* RÔ MA-nā′kôN tē′), *n.* a red wine from Burgundy.

Ro′man Em′pire, 1. the lands and peoples subject to the authority of ancient Rome. 2. the form of government established in ancient Rome in 27 B.C., comprising the Principate or Early Empire (27 B.C.–A.D. 284) and the Autocracy or Later Empire (A.D. 284–476). 3. a later empire, as that of Charlemagne or the Byzantine Empire, regarded as a restoration or continuation of the ancient Roman Empire or one of its branches. Cf. **Holy Roman Empire.**

Ro·man·esque (rō′mə nesk′), *adj.* 1. noting or pertaining to the style of architecture prevailing in western or southern Europe from the 9th through the 12th century, characterized by heavy masonry construction with narrow openings, features such as the round arch, the groin vault, and the barrel vault, and the introduction or development of the vaulting rib, the vaulting shaft, and central and western towers for churches. 2. pertaining to or designating the styles of sculpture, painting, or ornamentation of the corresponding period. 3. (*l.c.*) of or pertaining to fanciful or extravagant literature, as romance or fable; fanciful. —*n.* 4. the Romanesque style of art or architecture. [ROMAN + -ESQUE; cf. F *romanesque* romantic]

ro·man-fleuve (rô mäN′flœv′), *n., pl.* **ro·mans-fleuves** (rô mäN′flœv′). *French.* saga (def. 3). [lit.: stream-novel]

Ro′man hol′iday, 1. a public spectacle or controversy marked by barbarism, vindictiveness, or scandal. 2. pleasure or advantage gained from the discomfort or suffering of others.

Ro·ma·nia (rō mā′nē ə, -mān′yə), *n.* Rumania.

Ro·mâ·nia (RÔ mœ′nyä; *Eng.* rō mā′nē ə, -mān′yə), *n.* Rumanian name of **Rumania.**

Ro·man·ic (rō man′ik), *adj.* 1. derived from the Romans. 2. romance[1] (def. 11). —*n.* 3. romance[1] (def. 8). [< L *Rōmānic(us)* Roman < *Rōmān(us)* ROMAN + *-icus* -IC]

Ro·man·ise (rō′mə nīz′), *v.t., v.i.* **-ised, -is·ing.** *Chiefly Brit.* Romanize. —**Ro′man·i·sa′tion,** *n.*

Ro·man·ism (rō′mə niz′əm), *n.* *Usually Derogatory.* See **Roman Catholicism.** [ROMAN + -ISM]

Ro·man·ist (rō′mə nist), *n.* 1. *Usually Derogatory.* a member of the Roman Catholic Church. 2. one versed in Roman institutions, law, etc. 3. **Romanists,** *Fine Arts.* a group of Flemish and Dutch painters of the 16th century who traveled to Italy and returned to Flanders and Holland with the style and techniques of the High Renaissance and of Mannerism. [< NL *Romanist(a)* < L *Rōmān(us)* ROMAN *-ista* -IST] —**Ro′man·is′tic,** *adj.*

Ro·man·ize (rō′mə nīz′), *v.,* **-ized, -iz·ing.** —*v.t.* 1. to make Roman Catholic. 2. to make Roman in character. —*v.i.* 3. to conform to Roman Catholic doctrine and practices; to become Roman Catholic. 4. to follow Roman practices. Also, *esp. Brit.,* **Romanise.** [ROMAN + -IZE] —**Ro′man·i·za′tion,** *n.* —**Ro′man·iz′er,** *n.*

Ro′man law′, the system of jurisprudence elaborated by the ancient Romans, a strong and varied influence on the legal systems of many countries.

Ro′man lit′urgy. See **Latin rite** (def. 1).

Ro′man mile′, a unit of length used by the ancient Romans, equivalent to about 1620 yards.

Ro′man net′tle, an annual herb, *Urtica pilulifera,* of southern Europe, having oval or heart-shaped leaves.

Ro′man nose′, a nose having a prominent upper part or bridge. —**Ro′man-nosed′,** *adj.*

Ro′man nota′tion clock′, a tall-case clock having a Roman strike and a dial with Roman numerals.

Ro′man nu′merals, the numerals in the ancient Roman system of notation, still used for certain limited purposes, as in some pagination, dates on buildings, etc. The common basic symbols are **I**(=1), **V**(=5), **X**(=10), **L**(=50), **C**(=100), **D**(=500), and **M**(=1000). The Roman numerals for one to nine are: I, II, III, IV, V, VI, VII, VIII, IX. A bar over a letter multiplies it by 1000; thus, X̄ equals 10,000. Integers are written according to these two rules: If a letter is immediately followed by one of equal or lesser value, the two values are added; thus, XX equals 20, XV equals 15, VI equals 6. If a letter is immediately followed by one of greater value, however, the first is subtracted from the second; thus, IV equals 4, XL equals 40, CM equals 900. Examples: XLVII(=47), CXVI(=116), MCXX (=1120), MCMXIV(=1914). Roman numerals may be written in lower-case letters, though they appear more commonly in capitals.

Ro·ma·no (rō mä′nō), *n.* (*sometimes l.c.*) a hard, light-colored, sharp, Italian cheese, usually made of ewe's milk. Also called **Roma′no cheese′.** [< It: Roman]

Ro·ma·nov (rō′mə nôf′, -nof′; *Russ.* RO mä′nof), *n.* 1. a member of the imperial dynasty of Russia which ruled from 1613 to 1917. 2. **Mi·kha·il Fe·o·do·ro·vich** (mi KHI ēl′ fe ô′do RO vich), 1596–1645, emperor of Russia 1613–45: first ruler of the house of Romanov. Also, **Ro′ma·noff′.**

Ro′man pace′, an ancient Roman unit of measurement, equal to 5 Roman feet or about 58 U.S. inches.

Ro′man peace′, the establishment and maintenance of peace by armed force. [trans. of L *pax Rōmāna*]

Ro′man punch′, *Brit.* a lemon-water ice flavored with rum or other alcoholic beverage.

Ro′man ride′, a method of horseback riding in which a person stands astride a pair of horses.

Ro′man rite′. See **Latin rite** (def. 1).

Ro·mans (rō′mənz), *n.* (*construed as sing.*) an Epistle of the New Testament, written by Paul to the Christian community in Rome.

Ro·mansh (rō mansh′, -mänsh′), *n.* 1. a group of three Rhaeto-Romanic dialects spoken in the Swiss canton Grisons: its Engadine form has been recognized as a fourth national language of Switzerland since 1938. Cf. **Ladin** (def. 2). —*adj.* 2. of or pertaining to Romansh. [< Rhaetian: ROMANIC]

Ro′man strike′, *Horol.* a striking mechanism of c1700, intended to be used with a Roman notation clock and having two bells of different tones, one striking to indicate one o'clock, the other striking once for five o'clock and twice for ten o'clock.

ro·man·tic (rō man′tik), *adj.* 1. of, pertaining to, or of the nature of romance; characteristic or suggestive of the world of romance: *a romantic adventure.* 2. fanciful; unpractical; unrealistic: *romantic ideas.* 3. imbued with or dominated by idealism, a desire for adventure, chivalry, etc. 4. characterized by a preoccupation with love or by the idealizing of love or one's beloved. 5. displaying or expressing love or strong affection. 6. ardent; passionate; fervent. 7. (*usually cap.*) of, pertaining to, or characteristic of a style of literature and art which subordinates form to content, encourages freedom of treatment, emphasizes imagination, emotion, and introspection, and often celebrates nature, the common man, and freedom of the spirit (contrasted with *classical*). 8. of or pertaining to a musical style characteristic chiefly of the 19th century and marked by the free expression of imagination and emotion, virtuosic display, experimentation with form, and the adventurous development of orchestral and piano music and opera. 9. imaginary, fictitious, or fabulous. 10. noting, of, or pertaining to the role of a suitor or lover in a play about love: *the romantic lead.* —*n.* 11. a romantic person. 12. a romanticist. 13. **romantics,** romantic ideas, ways, etc. [< F *romantique,* deriv. of *romant* earlier form of *roman* novel. See ROMANCE[1]] —**ro·man′ti·cal·ly,** *adv.* —**ro·man′ti·cal·ness,** *n.*
—**Syn.** 2. extravagant, exaggerated, wild, imaginative, fantastic. 9. improbable, unreal. —**Ant.** 2. practical, realistic. 9. probable.

Roman′tic Clas′sicism, *Archit.* Neoclassicism, esp. that developed in France and Germany in the late 18th century in which scale, ornament, and overall composition are used to produce a dramatic effect.

ro·man·ti·cise (rō man′ti sīz′), *v.t., v.i.,* **-cised, -cis·ing.** *Chiefly Brit.* romanticize. —**ro·man′ti·ci·sa′tion,** *n.*

ro·man·ti·cism (rō man′ti siz′əm), *n.* 1. romantic spirit or tendency. 2. (*usually cap.*) the Romantic style or movement in literature and art, or adherence to its principles (contrasted with *classicism*). [ROMANTIC + -ISM]

ro·man·ti·cist (rō man′ti sist), *n.* an adherent of romanticism in literature or art (contrasted with *classicist*). [ROMANTIC + -IST] —**ro·man′ti·cis′tic,** *adj.*

ro·man·ti·cize (rō man′ti sīz′), *v.,* **-cized, -ciz·ing.** —*v.t.* 1. to make romantic; invest with a romantic character: *She romanticized her work as an editor.* —*v.i.* 2. to hold romantic notions, ideas, etc. Also, *esp. Brit.,* **romanticise.** [ROMANTIC + -IZE] —**ro·man′ti·ci·za′tion,** *n.*

Roman′tic Move′ment, the late 18th- and early 19th-century movement in France, Germany, England, and America to establish Romanticism in art and literature.

Ro·ma·nus (rō mā′nəs), *n.* died A.D. 897, Italian ecclesiastic: pope 897.

Ro′man worm′wood, 1. a European wormwood, *Artemesia pontica.* 2. the ragweed, *Ambrosia artemisiifolia.*

Rom·a·ny (rom′ə nē, rō′mə-), *n., pl.* **-nies,** *adj.* —*n.* 1. a Gypsy. 2. Gypsies collectively. 3. the Indic language of the Gypsies, its various forms differing greatly because of local influences. —*adj.* 4. pertaining to Gypsies, their language, or their customs. Also, **Rommany.** [< Gypsy *Romani*, fem. and pl. of *Romano* (adj.), deriv. of *Rom* Rom]

ro·maunt (rō mänt′, -mônt′), *n.* *Archaic.* a romantic tale or poem; romance. [< AF, var. of OF *romant* ROMANCE[1]]

Ro·mayne′ work′ (rō mān′), carved woodwork characteristic of the early Renaissance in England, consisting of portrait medallions, arabesques, scrollwork, etc. Also, **romayne′ work′.** [prob. < F *romaine* Roman (see ROMAINE)]

Rom·berg (rom′bûrg), *n.* **Sig·mund** (sig′mənd), 1887–1951, Hungarian composer of light opera, in the U.S. after 1913.

Rom. Cath., Roman Catholic.

Rom. Cath. Ch., Roman Catholic Church.

Rome (rōm), *n.* 1. **Harold (Jacob),** born 1908, U.S. lyricist and composer. 2. Italian, **Roma.** a city in and the capital of Italy, in the central part, on the Tiber: ancient capital of the Roman Empire; site of Vatican City, seat of authority of the Roman Catholic Church. 2,600,000. 3. a city in central New York, E of Oneida Lake. 51,646 (1960). 4. a city in NW Georgia. 32,226 (1960). 5. the ancient Italian kingdom, republic, and empire whose capital was the city of Rome. 6. the Roman Catholic Church. 7. See **Roman Catholicism.**

Ro·me·o (rō′mē ō′), *n.* 1. the romantic lover of Juliet in Shakespeare's *Romeo and Juliet.* 2. any man who is preoccupied with or has a reputation for amatory success with women. 3. a lover: *She found her Romeo at a charity ball.* 4. (used in communications to represent the letter R.) 5. a town in SE Michigan. 3327 (1960). 6. a boy's given name.

Ro′meo and Ju′liet, 1. a tragedy (produced between 1591 and 1596) by Shakespeare. 2. a ballet (1935) by Prokofiev.

Ro·me·o·ville (rō′mē ō vil), *n.* a town in NE Illinois. 3574 (1960).

Rö·mer (rō′mər), *n.* a crater in the first quadrant of the face of the moon: about 35 miles in diameter. Also, **Roe′mer.**

ro·me·ro (rō mâr′ō), *n., pl.* **-ros.** a shrubby herb, *Trichostema lanatum*, of California, having leaves which are hairy on the underside, and woolly, blue or purplish flowers. [< AmerSp: ROSEMARY]

Rome·ward (rōm′wərd), *adv.* to or toward Rome or the Roman Catholic Church. [ME; see ROME, -WARD]

Rom·ish (rō′mish), *adj.* *Often Derogatory.* of or pertaining to Rome as the center of the Roman Catholic Church; Roman Catholic. [ROME + -ISH[1]] —**Rom′ish·ly,** *adv.* —**Rom′ish·ness,** *n.*

Rom·ma·ny (rom′ə nē), *n., pl.* **-nies,** *adj.* Romany.

Rom·mel (rum′əl; *Ger.* rôm′əl), *n.* **Er·win** (ûr′win; *Ger.* er′vēn), ("*the Desert Fox*"), 1891–1944, German field marshal: commander of the German forces in North Africa in World War II.

Rom·ney (rom′nē, rum′-), *n.* 1. **George,** 1734–1802, English painter. 2. **George,** born 1907, U.S. businessman and politician. 3. a boy's given name.

Rom·ney (rom′nē, rum′-), *n.* one of an English breed of hardy sheep, having coarse, long wool. Also called **Rom′ney Marsh′.** [after the district in southwestern England]

Ro·mo·la (rə mō′lə), *n.* 1. (*italics.*) a novel (1863) by George Eliot. 2. a girl's given name.

romp (romp), *v.i.* 1. to play or frolic in a lively or boisterous manner. 2. to run or go rapidly and without effort, as in racing. —*n.* 3. a lively or boisterous frolic. 4. a person who romps, esp. a girl. 5. a quick or effortless pace: *The work was easy, and he went through it in a romp.* [var. of obs. *ramp* rough woman, lit., one who ramps; see RAMP (V.)] —**romp′er,** *n.* —**romp′ing·ly,** *adv.*
—**Syn. 1, 3.** gambol.

romp·ers (rom′pərz), *n.* (*construed as pl.*) 1. a loose outer garment combining a waist and short, bloused pants, worn by young children. 2. a similar garment, worn by women and girls for gymnastics. [ROMPER + -S[4]]

romp·ish (rom′pish), *adj.* given to romping; frolicsome. [ROMP + -ISH[1]] —**romp′ish·ly,** *adv.* —**romp′ish·ness,** *n.*

Ro·mu·lo (rom′yŏŏ lō′; *Sp.* rô′mōō lô′), *n.* **Car·los Pe·na** (kär′lôs pe′nä), born 1901, Philippine diplomat, journalist, and educator.

Rom·u·lus (rom′yə ləs), *n.* *Rom. Legend.* the founder of Rome, in 753 B.C., and its first king: a son of Mars and Rhea Silvia, he and his twin brother (**Remus**) were abandoned as babies, suckled by a she-wolf, and brought up by a shepherd; Remus was finally killed for mocking the fortifications of Rome, which Romulus had just founded.

Ro·mus (rō′məs), *n.* *Rom. Legend.* a son of either Aeneas or Ascanius sometimes believed to be the founder of Rome.

Ron·ald (ron′əld), *n.* a boy's given name.

Ro·nan (rō′nən), *n.* *Irish Legend.* a king who killed his son, Mael, after his wife had falsely accused the boy of attempting to seduce her, and who was himself killed by the children of Mael.

Ron·ces·valles (ron′sə valz′; *Sp.* rôn′thes vä′lyes), *n.* a village in N Spain, in the Pyrenees: defeat of part of Charlemagne's army and the death of Roland A.D. 788. French, **Ronce·vaux** (rôns vō′).

ron·co (roŋ′kō), *n., pl.* **-cos.** *Ichthyol.* any West Indian grunt of the genus *Haemulon*, esp. *H. parra*, the sailor's-choice. [< Sp, deriv. of *roncar* to grunt < Gk *rhonch(os)* a grunt, snore]

rond de jambe (*Fr.* rôN də zhäNb′), *n., pl.* **ronds de jambe** (*Fr.* rôN də zhäNb′). *Ballet.* a circular movement of the leg. [< F; see ROUND[1], JAMB[1]]

ronde (rond), *n.* *Print.* a type face imitative of upright, somewhat angular, handwriting. [< F, n. use of fem. of *rond* ROUND[1]]

ron·deau (ron′dō, ron dō′), *n., pl.* **-deaux** (-dōz, -dōz′). 1. *Pros.* a short poem of fixed form, consisting of 13 or 10 lines on two rhymes and having the opening words or phrase used in two places as an unrhymed refrain. 2. a 13th-century monophonic song form consisting of two phrases, each repeated several times, and occurring in the 14th and 15th centuries in polyphonic settings. 3. a 17th-century musical form consisting of a refrain alternating with contrasting couplets, developing in the 18th century into the sonata-rondo form. [< MF: little circle; see RONDEL]

ron·del (ron′dəl), *n.* 1. *Pros.* a short poem of fixed form, consisting usually of 14 lines on two rhymes, of which four are made up of the initial couplet repeated in the middle and at the end, with the second line of the couplet sometimes being omitted at the end. 2. *Theat.* roundel (def. 4). [ME < OF *rondel*, *rondeau*, dim. of *rond* ROUND[1]]

ron·de·let (ron′dəlet′, ron′dəlet′), *n.* a short poem of fixed form, consisting of five lines on two rhymes, and having the opening words or word used after the second and fifth lines as an unrhymed refrain. [< MF, dim. of *rondel* RONDEL]

ron·delle (ron del′), *n.* 1. a small disk of glass used as an ornament in a stained-glass window. 2. *Jewelry.* a flat bead, often of rock crystal or onyx, used in a necklace as a spacer between contrasting stones. [< F; see RONDEL]

ron·do (ron′dō, ron dō′), *n., pl.* **-dos.** *Music.* a work or movement, often the last movement of a sonata, having one principal subject which is stated at least three times in the same key and to which return is made after the introduction of each subordinate theme. [< It < F *rondeau*; see RONDEL]

Ron·dô·nia (rôN dô′nyə), *n.* a state in W Brazil. 70,783 (1960); 93,815 sq. mi. *Cap.:* Pôrto Velho. Formerly, **Guaporé.**

ron·dure (ron′jər), *n.* 1. a circle or sphere. 2. a graceful curving or roundness. [< F *rondeur*, deriv. of *rond* ROUND[1]]

ron·geur (rôn zhûr′; *Fr.* rôN zhœr′), *n., pl.* **-geurs** (-zhûrz′; *Fr.* -zhœr′). *Surg.* a strong forceps for use in gouging out bone tissue. [< F: lit., gnawer]

ron·ion (run′yən), *n.* *Obs.* ronyon.

Ron·kon·ko·ma (roŋ koŋ′kə mə, ron-), *n.* a town on central Long Island, in SE New York. 4220 (1960).

Rön·ne (*Dan.* rœn′ə), *n.* a seaport on W Bornholm island, in the S Baltic Sea: stone quarries. 13,195 (1960).

Ron·nie (ron′ē), *n.* a boy's or girl's given name, form of **Ronald** or **Veronica.** Also, **Ron′ni, Ron′ny.**

ron·quil (roŋ′kil), *n.* any of several percoid fishes of the family *Bathymasteridae*, found along the Pacific coast of North America. [< AmerSp *ronquillo*, dim. of *ronco* RONCO]

Ron·sard (rôN sar′), *n.* **Pierre de** (pyer də), 1524–85, French poet.

Rönt·gen (rent′gən, -jən, runt′-; *Ger.* rœnt′gən; *Du.* rōōnt′khen), *n.* 1. **Ju·li·us** (yōō′lē əs), 1855–1932, Dutch pianist, conductor, and composer; born in Germany. 2. **Wil·helm Kon·rad** (vil′helm kôn′rät). See **Roentgen, Wilhelm Konrad.**

rönt·gen·ize (rent′gə nīz′, -jə-, runt′-), *v.t.,* **-ized, -iz·ing.** roentgenize. —**rönt′gen·i·za′tion,** *n.*

röntgeno-, var. of **roentgeno-:** *röntgenoscope.*

rönt·gen·o·gram (rent′gə nə gram′, -jə-, runt′-), *n.* roentgenogram.

rönt·gen·o·graph (rent′gə nə graf′, -gräf′, -jə-, runt′-), *n.* roentgenograph. —**rönt·gen·o·graph·ic** (rent′gə nə graf′ik, -jə-, runt′-), *adj.* —**rönt′gen·o·graph′i·cal·ly,** *adv.* —**rönt·gen·og·ra·phy** (rent′gə nog′rə fē, -jə-, runt-′), *n.*

rönt·gen·ol·o·gy (rent′gə nol′ə jē, -jə-, runt′-), *n.* roentgenology. —**rönt·gen·o·log·ic** (rent′gə nəloj′ik, -jə-, runt-′), **rönt′gen·o·log′i·cal,** *adj.* —**rönt′gen·ol′o·gist,** *n.*

rönt·gen·o·scope (rent′gə nə skōp′, -jə-, runt′-), *n.* roentgenoscope. —**rönt·gen·o·scop·ic** (rent′gə nə-skop′ik, -jə-, runt′-), *adj.* —**rönt·gen·os·co·py** (rent′gə nos′kə pē, -jə-, runt′-), *n.*

ron·yon (run′yən), *n.* *Obs.* a mangy creature. Also, **ronion.** [? < F *rogne* mange]

roo (rōō), *v.t.,* **rooed, roo·ing.** *Brit.* to pluck (wool) from sheep by hand. [< Scand; cf. Norw (dial.) *rua*, Icel *rūinn* (prp.)]

'roo (rōō), *n., pl.* **'roos.** *Australian Informal.* kangaroo. [by shortening]

rood (rōōd), *n.* 1. a crucifix, esp. a large one at the entrance to the choir or chancel of a medieval church, often supported on a rood beam or rood screen. 2. a cross as used in crucifixion. 3. a unit of length varying locally from 5½ to 8 yards. 4. a unit of land measure equal to 40 square rods or ¼ acre. 5. a unit of 1 square rod or thereabout. 6. *Archaic.* the cross on which Christ died. [ME; OE *rōd*; c. G *Rute.* See ROD]

rood′ arch′, 1. an archway at the center of a rood screen. 2. the archway between a nave and a chancel.

rood′ beam′, a beam extending across the entrance to the choir or chancel of a church to support the rood, and usually forming the head of a rood screen.

Roo·de·poort-Ma·rais·burg (rōō′də pōōrt′mä rä′-bûrk), *n.* a city in S Transvaal, in the NE Republic of South Africa. 94,740 (1960).

rood′ loft′, a loft or gallery over a rood screen.

rood′ screen′, a screen, often of elaborate design and properly surmounted by a rood, separating the nave from the choir or chancel of a church.

rood′ spire′, a spire over the crossing of a church. Also called **rood′ stee′ple.**

rood′ stairs′, stairs leading to a rood loft.

roof (rōōf, rŏŏf), *n., pl.* **roofs,** *v.* —*n.* 1. the external upper covering of a house or other building. 2. the highest part or summit: *The Himalayas are the roof of the world.* 3. something that in form or position resembles the roof of a house, as the top of a car, the upper part of the mouth, etc. 4. a house. 5. *Mining.* the rock immediately above a horizontal mineral deposit. 6. **hit the roof,** *Slang.* to lose one's temper; become extremely angry. 7. **raise the roof,** *Slang.* **a.** to create a loud noise: *The applause raised the roof.* **b.** to complain or protest noisily: *He'll raise the roof when he sees that bill.* —*v.t.* 8. to provide or cover with a roof. [ME; OE *hrōf*; c. D *roef* cover, cabin, OIcel *hrōf*] —**roof′like′,** *adj.*

roof-deck (rōōf′dek′, rŏŏf′-), *n.* a part of a flat roof used for gardening, sunbathing, etc.

roof·er (rōō′fər, rŏŏf′-ər), *n.* one who makes or repairs roofs. [ROOF + -ER[1]]

roof′ gar′den, 1. a garden on the flat roof of a house or other building. 2. the top or top story of a building, having a garden, restaurant, or the like.

roof′ guard′. See **snow guard.**

roof·ing (rōō′fiŋ, rŏŏf′-iŋ), *n.* 1. the act of covering with a roof. 2. material for roofs. 3. a roof. [ME *rovyng.* See ROOF, -ING[1]]

Roofs
A, Lean-to; B, Gable; C, Hip; D, Gambrel; E, Mansard

roof′ing nail′, a short nail for nailing asphalt shingles or the like, having a broad head.

roof′ i′ris, an iris, *Iris tectorum*, of China and Japan.

roof·less (rōōf′lis, rŏŏf′-), *adj.* 1. having no roof. 2. without the shelter of a house: *roofless refugees.* [ROOF + -LESS]

roof′ prism′, *Optics.* See **Amici prism.**

roof′ rat′, a black rat, *Rattus rattus alexandrinus*, often found on the upper floors of buildings.

roof·top (rōōf′top′, rŏŏf′-), *n.* the roof of a building, esp. the outer surface. [ROOF + TOP[1]]

roof·tree (rōōf′trē′, rŏŏf′-), *n.* 1. the ridgepole of a roof. 2. the roof itself. [ME; see ROOF, TREE]

rook[1] (rŏŏk), *n.* 1. a black, European crow, *Corvus frugilegus*, noted for its gregarious habits. 2. a sharper at cards or dice; swindler. —*v.t.* 3. to cheat; fleece; swindle. [ME *rōk*, OE *hrōc*; c. OIcel *hrōk(r)*, OHG *hruoh*]

rook[2] (rŏŏk), *n.* *Chess.* one of two pieces of the same color, moved any unobstructed distance horizontally or vertically; castle. [ME *rok* < OF *roc* << Pers *rukhkh*]

rook·er·y (rŏŏk′ə rē), *n., pl.* **-er·ies.** 1. a colony of rooks. 2. a place where rooks congregate to breed. 3. a breeding place or colony of other gregarious birds or animals, as penguins, seals, etc. 4. *Informal.* a crowded tenement house. [ROOK[1] + -ERY]

rook·ie (rŏŏk′ē), *n.* 1. an athlete playing his first season as a member of a professional sports team: *The rookie replaced the injured regular at first base.* 2. a raw recruit, as in the army or on a police force. 3. a novice; tyro. [alter. of RECRUIT]

rook·y (rŏŏk′ē), *adj.,* **rook·i·er, rook·i·est.** full of or frequented by rooks. [ROOK[1] + -Y[1]]

room (rōōm, rŏŏm), *n.* 1. a portion of space within a building or other structure, separated by walls or partitions from other parts: *a dining room.* 2. **rooms,** lodgings or quarters, as in a house or building. 3. the persons present in a room: *The whole room laughed.* 4. space or extent of space occupied by or available for something: *The desk takes up too much room.* 5. opportunity or scope for or to do something: *room for improvement; room for doubt.* 6. status or a station in life considered as a place: *He fought for room at the top.* 7. capacity: *Her brain had no room for math.* 8. *Mining.* Also called **bord, stall.** a working area cut between pillars. 9. **no room to swing a cat,** very little space: *How can they live happily in an apartment where there is no room to swing a cat?* —*v.i.* 8. to occupy a room or rooms; lodge. [ME *roum*, OE *rūm*; c. D *ruim*, G *Raum*]

room′ and board′, lodging and meals.

room-and-pil·lar (rōōm′ən pil′ər, rŏŏm′-), *adj.* *Mining.* noting a means of extracting coal or other minerals from lagered underground deposits by first cutting out rooms, then robbing the pillars between them; pillar-and-breast. Cf. **longwall.**

room′ clerk′, a clerk at a hotel who assigns rooms to guests, keeps the guest register, sorts the incoming mail, etc.

room′ divid′er, an article of furniture, freestanding bookcase, or the like, that separates one part of a room from another.

room·er (rōō′mər, rŏŏm′ər), *n.* a lodger. [ROOM + -ER[1]]

room·ette (rōō met′, rŏŏ-), *n.* a small private compartment in the sleeping car of a train, usually for one person, containing its own washroom facilities and a bed that folds against the wall when not in use. [ROOM + -ETTE]

room·ful (rōōm′fŏŏl, rŏŏm′-), *n., pl.* **-fuls.** an amount or number sufficient to fill a room. [ROOM + -FUL]

room·ie (rōō′mē, rŏŏm′ē), *n.* *Informal.* roommate. Also, **roomy.** [by shortening and alter.]

room′ing house′. See **lodging house.**

room·mate (rōōm′māt′, rŏŏm′-), *n.* a person who is assigned to share or rents and shares a room or apartment with another or others. [ROOM + MATE[1]]

room′ serv′ice, 1. the serving of food, drinks, etc., to a guest in his room, as at a hotel. 2. the department or section, as at a hotel, responsible for rendering this service.

room·y[1] (rōō′mē, rŏŏm′ē), *adj.,* **room·i·er, room·i·est.** affording ample room; spacious; large. [ROOM + -Y[1]] —**room′i·ly,** *adv.* —**room′i·ness,** *n.*

room·y[2] (rōō′mē, rŏŏm′ē), *n., pl.* **room·ies.** *Informal.* roomie.

roor·back (rŏŏr′bak′), *n.* *U.S.* a false and more or less damaging report circulated for political effect. Also, **roor′bach.** [after Baron von *Roorback*, pretended traveler in whose alleged book of his experiences in the U.S. occurred an account of an incident damaging to the character of James K. Polk]

roose (ro͞oz; *Scot. also* RŒZ), *v.t., v.i.,* **roosed, roos·ing,** *n. Chiefly Scot.* praise. [< Scand; cf. OIcel *hrōsa* to praise]

Roo·se·velt (rō′zə velt′, -vəlt; *spelling pron.* ro͞o′zə-velt′), *n.* **1. (Anna) Eleanor,** 1884–1962, U.S. diplomat, author, and lecturer (wife of Franklin Delano Roosevelt). **2. Franklin Del·a·no** (del′ə nō′), ("*FDR*"), 1882–1945, 32nd president of the U.S. 1933–45. **3. Theodore** (*Teddy,* "*T.R.*"), 1858–1919, 26th president of the U.S. 1901–09: Nobel peace prize 1906. **4. Río.** Formerly, **Río da Duvida.** a river flowing N from W Brazil to the Madeira River. ab. 400 mi. long.

Roo′sevelt Cor′ollary, *U.S. Hist.* a corollary (1904) to the Monroe Doctrine, asserting that the U.S. might intervene in the affairs of an American republic threatened with seizure or intervention by a European country. [named after Theodore ROOSEVELT]

Roo′sevelt Dam′, a dam on the Salt River, in central Arizona. 284 ft. high; 1080 ft. long.

Roo·se·velt·i·an (rō′zə vel′tē ən; *spelling pron.* ro͞o′zə vel′tē ən), *adj.* of, pertaining to, advocating, or following the principles, views, or policies of Franklin Delano Roosevelt or of Theodore Roosevelt. [ROOSEVELT + -IAN]

Roo′sevelt Park′, a town in SW Michigan. 2578 (1960).

roost (ro͞ost), *n.* **1.** a perch upon which birds or fowls rest at night. **2.** a large cage, house, or place for fowls or birds to roost in. **3.** a place for sitting, resting, or staying: *The terrace made a pleasant roost.* **4. rule the roost,** to be in charge or control; dominate: *It was only too apparent that his mother ruled the roost.* —*v.i.* **5.** to sit or rest on a roost, perch, etc. **6.** to settle or stay, esp. for the night. **7. come home to roost,** (of an action) to revert or react unfavorably to the doer; boomerang: *an evil deed that came home to roost and ruined his life.* [ME *roost,* OE *hrōst;* c. MD, Flem *roest*]

roost·er (ro͞o′stər), *n.* **1.** the male of the domestic fowl; cock. **2.** a representation of this bird, used as an emblem of the Democratic party from 1842 to 1874. **3.** *Informal.* a cocky person. [ROOST + -ER¹]

Rooster (Domestic)

roost·er·fish (ro͞o′stər fish′), *n., pl.* **-fish·es,** (*esp. collectively*) **-fish.** a large, edible carangid fish, *Nematistius pectoralis,* found in the warmer waters of the Pacific Ocean, having the first dorsal fin composed of brightly colored filamentous rays. [ROOSTER + FISH]

root¹ (ro͞ot, ro͝ot), *n.* **1.** a part of the body of a plant which, typically, develops from the radicle and grows downward into the soil, fixing the plant and absorbing nutriment and moisture. **2.** a similar organ developed from some other part of a plant, as one of those by which ivy clings to its support. **3.** any underground part of a plant, as a rhizome. **4.** something resembling or suggesting the root of a plant in position or function: *roots of wires and cables.* **5.** the embedded or basal portion of a hair, tooth, nail, etc. **6.** the fundamental or essential part: *the root of a matter.* **7.** the source or origin of a thing: *The love of money is the root of all evil.* **8.** a person or family as the source of offspring or descendants. **9.** an offshoot or scion. **10.** *Math.* **a.** a quantity which, when multiplied by itself a certain number of times, produces a given quantity: *The number 2 is the square root of 4, the cube root of 8 and the fourth root of 16.* **b.** a quantity which, when substituted for the unknown quantity in an equation, satisfies the equation. **c.** a value of the argument of a function for which the function takes the value zero. **11.** *Gram.* **a.** a morpheme that underlies an inflectional or derivational paradigm, as *dance,* the root in *danced, dancer,* or *ten-,* the root of Latin *tendere* "to stretch." **b.** such a form reconstructed for a parent language, as *sed-,* the hypothetical proto-Indo-European root meaning "sit." **12. roots, a.** a person's original or true home, environment, and culture: *He's lived in New York for twenty years, but his roots are in France.* **b.** the personal relationships, affinity for a locale, habits, and the like, which make a country, region, city, or town one's true home: *He lived in Tulsa for a few years, but never established any roots there.* **c.** personal identification with a culture, religion, etc., seen as promoting the development of the character or the stability of society as a whole. **13.** *Music.* **a.** the fundamental tone of a compound tone or of a series of harmonies. **b.** the lowest tone of a chord when arranged as a series of thirds; the fundamental. **14.** *Mach.* **a.** (in a screw or other threaded object) the narrow inner surface between threads. Cf. **crest** (def. 16), **flank** (def. 7). **b.** (in a gear) the narrow inner surface between teeth. **15.** Also called **bosom.** *Shipbuilding.* the inner angle of an angle iron. **16. root and branch,** utterly; entirely: *to destroy something root and branch.* **17. take root, a.** to send out roots; begin to grow. **b.** to become fixed or established: *The prejudices of parents usually take root in their children.* —*v.i.* **18.** to become fixed or established. —*v.t.* **19.** to fix by or as by roots: *We were rooted to the spot by surprise.* **20.** to implant or establish deeply: *Good manners were rooted in him like a second nature.* **21.** to pull, tear, or dig up by the roots (often fol. by *up* or *out*). **22.** to extirpate; exterminate; remove completely (often fol. by *up* or *out*): *to root out crime.* [ME; OE *rōt* < Scand; cf. Icel *rōt;* akin to OE *wyrt* plant, WORT², G *Wurzel,* L *rādix*] —**root′like′,** *adj.* —**Syn. 6.** basis. **7.** beginning, derivation, rise, fountainhead. **8.** parent. **22.** eradicate.

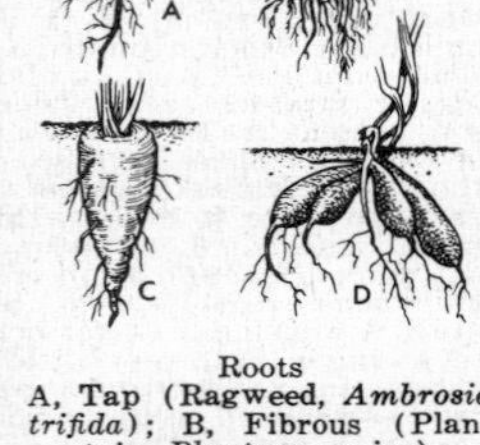

Roots
A, Tap (**Ragweed,** ***Ambrosia trifida***); B, Fibrous (Plantain, *Plantago major*); C, Fleshy (Carrot, *Daucus carota*); D, Tuberous (Rue-anemone, *Syndesmon thalictroides*)

root² (ro͞ot, ro͝ot), *v.i.* **1.** to turn up the soil with the snout, as swine. **2.** to poke, pry, or search, as if to find something: *to root around in a drawer for loose coins.* **3.** *Naut.* (of a vessel) to ship water at the bow in a heavy sea. —*v.t.* **4.** to turn over with the snout (often fol. by *up*). **5.** to unearth; bring to light (often fol. by *up*). [var. of obs. *wroot,* OE *wrōt(an),* akin to *wrōt* a snout]

root³ (ro͞ot, ro͝ot), *v.i.* **1.** to encourage a team or contestant by cheering or applauding enthusiastically. **2.** to lend moral support: *The whole group will be rooting for him.* [? var. of *rout* to make a loud noise < Scand; cf. Icel *rauta;* akin to L *rudere* to bellow]

Root (ro͞ot), *n.* **1. El·i·hu** (el′ə hyo͞o′), 1845–1937, U.S. lawyer and statesman: Nobel peace prize 1912. **2. John Well·born** (wel′bərn), 1851–91, U.S. architect.

root·age (ro͞o′tij, ro͝ot′ij), *n.* **1.** the act of taking root. **2.** a root system or firm fixture by means of roots. [ROOT¹ + -AGE]

root′ beer′, a carbonated beverage flavored with syrup made from the extracted juices of roots, barks, and herbs that have been fermented with sugar and yeast.

root′ canal′, *Dentistry.* the root portion of the pulp cavity. Also called **pulp canal.**

root′ canal′ ther′apy, endodontics. Also called **root′ canal′ treat′ment.**

root′ cel′lar, a cellar, partially or wholly underground and usually covered with dirt, where root crops and other vegetables are stored.

root′ chord′, *Aeron.* the most inboard chord of a wing or other lifting surface.

root′ crop′, a crop, as beets, turnips, sweet potatoes, etc., grown for its large and edible roots.

root′ divi′sion, the act or process of reproducing plants by a division of roots or crowns.

root·er¹ (ro͞o′tər), *n.* **1.** one who or that which roots, as with the snout. **2.** See **black buffalo.** [ROOT² + -ER¹]

root·er² (ro͞o′tər), *n.* **1.** a person who roots for, supports, or encourages a team or contestant. **2.** a loyal and enthusiastic helper, follower, or supporter. [ROOT³ + -ER¹]

root′ field′, *Math.* See **splitting field.**

root′ hair′, *Bot.* an elongated tubular extension of an epidermal cell of a root, serving to absorb water and minerals from the soil.

root·i (ro͞o′tē), *n. Anglo-Indian.* rooty².

root′ knot′, *Plant. Pathol.* a disease of plants, characterized by galls or knots on the roots and stunted growth, caused by any of several nematodes of the genus *Meloidogyne.*

root·less (ro͞ot′lis, ro͝ot′-), *adj.* **1.** having no roots. **2.** having no basis of stability; unsteady: *a rootless feeling resulting from economic and social change.* **3.** having no place or position in society; not in accord with the environment: *the homeless, rootless wanderer.* [ME *rooteles.* See ROOT¹, -LESS] —**root′less·ness,** *n.*

root·let (ro͞ot′lit, ro͝ot′-), *n. Bot.* **1.** a little root. **2.** a small or fine branch of a root. **3.** one of the adventitious roots by which ivy or the like clings to rocks or other supports. [ROOT¹ + -LET]

root′ mean′ square′, *Math.* the square root of the arithmetic mean of the squares of the numbers in a given set of numbers. *Abbr.:* rms

root′ of u′nity, *Math.* a complex number that when raised to some positive integral power results in 1.

root′ posi′tion, *Music.* the position of a triad in which the root is in the bass.

root′ rot′, *Plant Pathol.* **1.** a symptom or phase of many diseases of plants, characterized by discoloration and decay of the roots. **2.** any disease so characterized.

Roots′ blow′er (ro͞ots), a machine for compressing or evacuating air or gas by the rotation of a meshing pair of lobed wheels in a closely fitting case.

AIR

Roots blower

root·stalk (ro͞ot′stôk′, ro͝ot′-), *n. Bot.* a rhizome. [ROOT¹ + STALK¹]

root·stock (ro͞ot′stok′, ro͝ot′-), *n.* **1.** *Hort.* a root and its associated growth buds, used as a stock in plant propagation. **2.** *Bot.* a rhizome. [ROOT¹ + STOCK]

root′ test′, *Math.* the theorem that a given infinite series converges if the *n*th root of the absolute value of the *n*th term approaches a limit less than 1 as *n* increases without bound.

root·worm (ro͞ot′wûrm′, ro͝ot′-), *n.* **1.** the larva of any of several insects, as the cucumber beetle, that feeds on the roots of plants. **2.** any of several nematodes, esp. of the genus *Heterodera,* that puncture and feed in the roots of plants. [ROOT¹ + WORM]

root·y¹ (ro͞o′tē, ro͝ot′ē), *adj.,* **root·i·er, root·i·est.** abounding in or consisting of roots. [ROOT¹ + -Y¹] —**root′i·ness,** *n.*

root·y² (ro͞o′tē, ro͝ot′ē), *n. Anglo-Indian.* bread. Also, **rooti.** [< Urdu *rōṭī*]

roove (ro͞ov), *n., v.,* **rooved, roov·ing.** —*n.* **1.** *Shipbuilding.* Also, **rove.** Also called **bur, burr.** a washerlike piece of copper against which the point of a copper nail is clinched to make a snug and secure fit. —*v.t.* **2.** to secure (a nail) with a roove. [var. of ROVE⁴]

R.O.P., run-of-paper: a designation specifying that the position of a newspaper or magazine advertisement is to be determined by the publisher. Cf. **preferred position.**

rop·a·ble (rō′pə bəl), *adj.* **1.** capable of being roped. **2.** *Australian Informal.* angry. [ROPE + -ABLE]

rope (rōp), *n., v.,* **roped, rop·ing.** —*n.* **1.** a strong, thick line or cord, commonly one composed of twisted or braided strands of hemp, flax, or the like, or of wire or other material. **2.** a lasso. **3. ropes,** the cords used to enclose a prize ring or other space. **4.** a hangman's noose, halter, or cord. **5.** the sentence or punishment of death by hanging. **6.** a quantity of material or a number of things twisted or strung together in the form of a cord: *a rope of tobacco.* **7.** a stringy, viscid, or glutinous formation in a liquid: *ropes of slime.* **8. at the end of one's rope,** at the end of one's endurance or means; at the limit: *With all her savings gone and bills piling up, she was at the end of her rope.* **9. give someone enough rope,** to allow a person complete freedom to continue his misdeeds in hope that retribution will follow. **10. know the ropes,** *Informal.* to be completely familiar with the operations of a business or the details of any undertaking: *Because the new field was so technical, there were very few who knew the ropes.* **11. on the ropes, a.** *Boxing.* in a defenseless position, as leaning against the ropes to keep from falling. **b.** *Slang.* in a desperate or hopeless position; close to defeat or failure: *By repeatedly undercutting his prices, his competitors soon had him on the ropes.* —*v.t.* **12.** to tie, bind, or fasten with a rope. **13.** to enclose, partition, or mark off with a rope or ropes (often fol. by *off*). **14.** to catch with a lasso; lasso. **15.** *Naut.* to reinforce (a sail or awning) with a boltrope. —*v.i.* **16.** to be drawn out into a filament of thread; become ropy. **17. rope in,** *Slang.* to lure or entice, esp. by employing deception: *The swindler had roped in a number of gullible persons.* [ME; OE *rāp;* c. D *reep,* G *Reif*] —**rop′er,** *n.*

rope·a·ble (rō′pə bəl), *adj.* ropable.

rope·danc·er (rōp′dan′sər, -dän′-), *n.* one who walks across or performs acrobatics upon a rope stretched at some height above the floor or ground. [ROPE + DANCER] —**rope′dance′,** *n.* —**rope′danc′ing,** *n.*

rope·mak·ing (rōp′mā′king), *n.* the art, act, or process of making rope. [ROPE + MAKING] —**rope′-mak′er,** *n.*

rop·er·y (rō′pə rē), *n., pl.* **-er·ies. 1.** a place where ropes are made. **2.** *Archaic.* knavery; roguery. [ME *roperie.* See ROPE, -ERY]

rope′ sock′et, either of a pair of matching fittings soldered to the ends of lengths of wire rope to join them together. Also called **patent eye, socket eye.**

rope′ stitch′, (in embroidery) a stitch formed from the entwining of stitches.

rope·walk (rōp′wôk′), *n.* a long, narrow path or building where ropes are made. [ROPE + WALK]

rope·walk·er (rōp′wô′kər), *n.* a ropedancer. [ROPE + WALKER]

rope·way (rōp′wā′), *n.* tramway (def. 4). [ROPE + WAY]

rope′ yarn′. See under **yarn** (def. 3).

rop·ing (rō′ping), *n. Naut.* a reinforcement of boltrope for a sail or awning. [ROPE + -ING¹]

rop·y (rō′pē), *adj.,* **rop·i·er, rop·i·est. 1.** resembling a rope or ropes: *ropy muscles.* **2.** forming viscid or glutinous threads, as a liquid. [ROPE + -Y¹] —**rop′i·ly,** *adv.* —**rop′i·ness,** *n.*

roque (rōk), *n.* a form of croquet played on a clay or hard-surface court surrounded by a low wall off which the balls may be played. [back formation from ROQUET]

Roque·fort (rōk′fərt), *n.* a strongly flavored cheese, veined with mold, made wholly or in part of sheep's milk and ripened in caves at Roquefort, a town in S France. Also called **Roque′fort cheese′.**

roq·ue·laure (rok′ə lôr′, -lōr′, -lôr′, -lōr′, rok′ə-; *Fr.* rôkᵊ lōr′), *n., pl.* **-laures** (-lôrz′, -lōrz′, -lôrz′, -lōrz′; *Fr.* -lōr′). a cloak reaching to the knees, worn by men during the 18th century. [named after the Duc de *Roquelaure* (1656–1738), French marshal]

ro·quet (rō kā′), *v.,* **-queted** (-kād′), **-quet·ing** (-kā′-ing), *n. Croquet, Roque.* —*v.t.* **1.** to cause one's ball to strike (another player's ball). **2.** (of a ball) to strike (another player's ball). —*v.i.* **3.** to roquet a ball. —*n.* **4.** the act or an instance of roqueting. [var. of CROQUET]

Ro·ris (rôr′is), *n.* **Sinus.** See **Sinus Roris.**

ror·qual (rôr′kwəl), *n.* any of several whalebone whales of the genus *Balaenoptera;* finback. [< F < Norw *röyrkval* finner-whale]

Ror′schach test′ (rōr′shäk, rôr′-), *Psychol.* a test for revealing the underlying personality structure of an individual by the use of a standard series of 10 ink-blot designs to which the subject responds by telling what image or emotion each design evokes. [named after Hermann *Rorschach* (1884–1922), Swiss psychiatrist]

Ro·ry (rōr′ē, rôr′ē), *n.* a boy's given name.

Ro·sa (*It.* rô′zä; *Eng.* rō′zə), *n.* **1. Sal·va·tor** (säl′vä tôr′), 1615–73, Italian painter and poet. **2. Mon·te** (*It.* môn′te; *Eng.* mon′tē), a mountain between Switzerland and Italy, in the Pennine Alps: second highest peak of the Alps. 15,217 ft. **3.** a girl's given name.

Ro·sa·bel (rō′zə bel′), *n.* a girl's given name. Also, **Ro′sa·belle′.**

ro·sace (rō zās′, -zäs′), *n.* rosette (def. 3). [< F < L *rosāce(us)* ROSACEOUS]

ro·sa·ce·a (rō zā′shē ə), *n. Pathol.* a chronic form of acne affecting the nose, forehead, and cheeks, characterized by red pustular lesions. [< NL (*acne*) *rosācea* rose-colored (acne), L, fem. of *rosāceus* ROSACEOUS]

ro·sa·ceous (rō zā′shəs), *adj.* **1.** belonging to the *Rosaceae,* or rose family of plants, also comprising the blackberry, strawberry, agrimony, spiraea, etc. **2.** having a corolla of five broad petals, like that of a rose. **3.** like a rose; roselike: *rosaceous loveliness.* **4.** rose-colored; rosy. [< L *rosāceus* made of roses, equiv. to *ros(a)* ROSE¹ + *-āceus* -ACEOUS]

Ro·sa·lie (rō′zə lē, roz′ə-; *Fr.* RÔ ZA LĒ′), *n.* a girl's given name.

Ros·a·lind (roz′ə lind), *n.* a girl's given name.

Ro·sa·mund (rō′zə mənd, roz′ə-), *n.* a girl's given name. Also, **Ro′sa·mond.**

ros·an·i·line (rō zan′ᵊlin, -ᵊlēn′), *n. Chem.* **1.** a red dye, $C_{20}H_{20}N_3Cl$, derived from aniline and orthotoluidine, a constituent of fuchsin. **2.** the base, $C_{20}H_{21}N_3O$, which, with hydrochloric acid, forms this dye. [ROSE¹ + ANILINE]

Ros·anne (rō zan′), *n.* a girl's given name. Also, **Ros·an·na** (rō zan′ə).

ro·sar·i·an (rō zâr′ē ən), *n.* one who is fond of, develops, or cultivates roses. [ROSE¹ + -ARIAN]

Ro·sa·rio (rō zä′rē ō′, -sä′-; *Sp.* rô sä′ryô), *n.* a port in E Argentina, on the Paraná River. 671,852 (1960).

ro·sar·i·um (rō zâr′ē əm), *n., pl.* **-i·ums, -i·a** (-ē ə). a rose garden. [< L; see ROSARY]

ro·sa·ry (rō′zə rē), *n., pl.* **-ries. 1.** *Rom. Cath. Ch.* **a.** a series of prayers, usually consisting of 15 decades of aves, each decade being preceded by a paternoster and followed by a *Gloria Patri,* one of the mysteries or events in the life of Christ or the Virgin Mary being recalled at each decade. **b.** a string of beads used for counting these prayers during their recitation. **c.** a similar string of beads consisting of five decades. **2.** (among other religious bodies) a string of beads similarly used in praying. **3.** a rose garden or a bed of roses. [< ML *rosārī(um),* L: rose garden (n. use of neut. of *rosārius* of roses), equiv. to *ros(a)* ROSE¹ + *-ārium* -ARY]

ro′sary pea′. See **Indian licorice.**

ro·sa so·lis (rō′zə sō′lis), *pl.* **ro·sa so·lis·es.** sundew. [< NL, alter. (by influence of L *rosa* rose) of L *rōs sōlis* dew of the sun]

Ros·ci·an (rosh′ē ən), *adj.* **1.** of, pertaining to, or involving acting or actors: *a Roscian society.* **2.** highly skilled in acting: *He gave a Roscian performance.* —*n.* **3.** an actor, esp. one of outstanding skill. [Rosci(us) + -an]

Ros·ci·us (rosh′ē əs, rosh′əs), *n.* **Quin·tus** (kwin′təs), c126–c62 B.C., Roman actor.

ros·coe (ros′kō), *n. Slang.* a revolver or pistol. [? from the name *Roscoe*]

Ros·coe (ros′kō), *n.* a boy's given name.

ros·coe·lite (ros′kō līt′), *n. Mineral.* a brown variety of muscovite having the aluminum partly replaced by vanadium. [named after Sir Henry *Roscoe* (1833–1915), English chemist; see -lite]

Ros·com·mon (ros kom′ən), *n.* a county in Connacht, in the N Republic of Ireland. 59,217 (1961); 950 sq. mi. *Co. seat:* Roscommon.

rose[1] (rōz), *n., adj., v.,* **rosed, ros·ing.** —*n.* **1.** any of the wild or cultivated, usually prickly-stemmed, showy-flowered shrubs of the genus *Rosa.* **2.** any of various related or similar plants. **3.** the flower of any such shrub, of a red, pink, white, or yellow color. **4.** an ornament shaped like or suggesting this flower. **5.** the traditional reddish color of this flower, variously a purplish red, pinkish red, or light crimson. **6.** a pink or pinkish-red color in the cheek. **7.** See **rose window. 8.** *Heraldry.* a representation of a wild rose with five petals, usually seeded and barbed in a symmetrical design and used esp. as the cadency mark of a seventh son. **9.** any of various diagrams showing directions radiating from a common center, as a compass card, wind rose, etc. **10.** *Jewelry.* **a.** an obsolete gem style or cut, flat on the bottom and having an upper side with from 12, or fewer, to 32 triangular facets. **b.** a gem with this cut. **11.** a perforated cap or plate, as at the end of a pipe, the spout of a watering pot, etc., to break a flow of water into a spray. **12.** an ornamental plate or socket surrounding the shaft of a doorknob at the face of a door. **13.** *Math.* a plane polar curve consisting of three or more equal loops that meet at the origin. Equation: $r = a\sin n\theta$ or $r = a\cos n\theta$. **14. under the rose,** in secret; privately; stealthily: *The conspiracy was hatched under the rose.* Cf. **sub rosa.** —*adj.* **15.** of the color rose. **16.** for, containing, or growing roses: *a rose garden.* **17.** scented like a rose. —*v.t.* **18.** to make rose-colored. **19.** (of the cheeks, face, etc.) to flush a rose color. [ME, OE < L *rosa;* akin to Gk *rhódon*] —**rose′less,** *adj.* —**rose′like′,** *adj.*

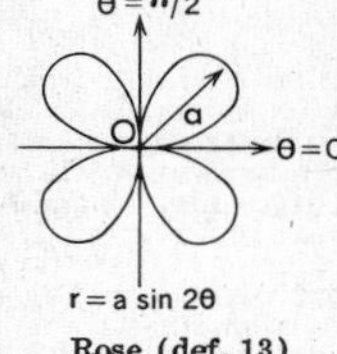

Rose (def. 13)

rose[2] (rōz), *v.* pt. of **rise.**

Rose (rōz), *n.* **1. Billy,** 1899–1966, U.S. theatrical producer. **2. (I·ain) Murray** (ē′ən), born 1939, Australian swimmer, born in England. **3.** a girl's given name.

ro·sé (rō zā′), *n.* a pink table wine in which the pale color is produced by removing the grape skins from the must before fermentation is completed. [< F: lit., pink]

rose′ aca′cia, a small tree, *Robina hispida,* of the southern Allegheny Mountains, having racemes of large, dark rose-colored flowers. Also called **pink locust.**

Rose·an·na (rō zan′ə), *n.* a girl's given name. Also, **Rosanna, Rosanne.**

rose′ ap′ple, 1. any of several tropical, myrtaceous trees of the genus *Eugenia,* esp. *E. Jambos,* of the East Indies, having showy, greenish-white flowers. **2.** the fragrant fruit of any of these trees, used in making jellies and confections.

ro·se·ate (rō′zē it, -āt′), *adj.* **1.** tinged with rose; rosy: *a roseate dawn.* **2.** bright or promising: *a roseate future.* **3.** optimistic. [< L *rose(us)* rose-colored + -ate[1]] —**ro′se·ate·ly,** *adv.*

ro′seate spoon′bill, a New World spoonbill, *Ajaia ajaja,* having rose-colored plumage and a bare head. See illus. under **spoonbill.**

rose·bay (rōz′bā′), *n.* **1.** an oleander. **2.** a rhododendron. **3.** *Brit.* the willow herb, *Epilobium angustifolium.* [rose[1] + bay[4]]

rose′ bee′tle, 1. See **rose chafer. 2.** See **Fuller rose beetle.**

Rose·ber·y (rōz′bə rē), *n.* **Archibald Philip Primrose** (prim′rōz′), **5th Earl of,** 1847–1929, British statesman and author: prime minister 1894–95.

rose′ box′, a perforated metal box used as a strainer; strum.

rose′-breast·ed gros′beak (rōz′bres′tid), an American grosbeak, *Pheucticus ludovicianus,* the male of which, in nuptial plumage, has a rose-pink triangular breast patch.

rose·bud (rōz′bud′), *n.* the bud of a rose. [rose[1] + bud[1]]

Rose·bud (rōz′bud′), *n.* a girl's given name.

Rose·burg (rōz′bûrg), *n.* a city in W Oregon. 11,467 (1960).

rose·bush (rōz′bo͝osh′), *n.* a shrub which bears roses. [rose[1] + bush[1]]

rose′ cam′pion, 1. Also called **dusty miller, mullein pink.** a campion, *Lychnis coronaria,* having crimson flowers. **2.** See **corn cockle.**

rose′ chaf′er, a tan scarabaeid beetle, *Macrodactylus subspinosis,* that feeds on the flowers and foliage of roses, grapes, peach trees, etc. Also called **rose beetle.**

rose′ cold′, *Pathol.* See **rose fever.**

rose-col·ored (rōz′kul′ərd), *adj.* **1.** of rose color; rosy. **2.** bright; promising; cheerful: *a rose-colored prospect of happiness.* **3.** optimistic; sanguine: *a rose-colored belief that things will be for the best.*

rose′-colored glass′es, a cheerful or optimistic view of things, usually without valid basis: *He had apparently turned his back on the squalid conditions and donned his rose-colored glasses.*

Rose·crans (rōz′krans), *n.* **William Starke** (stärk), 1819–98, U.S. general.

rose′ cut′ter, a hollow end mill having teeth formed on the end only. Also called **rose′ drill′.**

Rose·dale (rōz′dāl′), *n.* a town in central Ohio. 8204 (1960).

rose′ d'An·vers′ (*Fr.* rôz dän veʀ′), *Jewelry.* a gem having a rose cut of 12 or fewer facets. [< F: rose of Anvers]

Ros·el·len (rō zel′ən), *n.* a girl's given name.

rose′ en′gine, a lathe having an oscillating mandrel or tool rest, used in engine turning. Also called **geometrical lathe.**

rose′ fe′ver, *Pathol.* a form of hay fever caused by the inhalation of rose pollen, characterized by nasal discharge and lacrimation. Also called **rose cold.**

rose·fish (rōz′fish′), *n., pl.* (*esp. collectively*) **-fish,** (*esp. referring to two or more kinds or species*) **-fish·es. 1.** redfish (def. 1). **2.** See **blackbelly rosefish.** [rose[1] + fish]

rose′ gera′nium, any of a class of geraniums of the genus *Pelargonium,* esp. *Pigraveolens,* cultivated for their fragrant, lobed or narrowly subdivided leaves rather than for their small pink flowers.

rose′ hip′, hip[2].

Rose·land (rōz′lənd, -land′), *n.* **1.** a town in W California. 4510 (1960). **2.** a town in NE New Jersey. 2804 (1960).

ro·sel·la (rō zel′ə), *n.* any of several large, colorful parakeets of the genus *Platycercus,* of Australia and New Zealand. [alter. of *Rosehill,* district in southeast Australia]

ro·selle (rō zel′), *n.* a tropical, malvaceous plant, *Hibiscus sabdariffa,* grown for its thick, red calyx and bracts, used in making jellies and as a substitute for cranberries. [?]

Ro·selle (rō zel′), *n.* **1.** a city in NE New Jersey. 21,032 (1960). **2.** a town in NE Illinois. 3581 (1960).

rose′ mad′der, a pigment derived from anthraquinone and hydrated oxide of aluminum, characterized chiefly by its reddish color and permanence: used in painting. Cf. **madder lake** (def. 2).

rose′ mal′low, 1. any of several malvaceous plants of the genus *Hibiscus,* having rose-colored flowers. **2.** the hollyhock, *Althaea rosea.*

Rose·ma·rie (rōz′mə rē′), *n.* a girl's given name.

rose·mar·y (rōz′mâr′ē), *n., pl.* **-mar·ies.** an evergreen, menthaceous shrub, *Rosmarinus officinalis,* native to the Mediterranean region, used as a seasoning and in perfumery and medicine: a traditional symbol of remembrance. [ME *rose mary* (by folk etym., influenced by rose[1] and the name *Mary*) < L *rōs* dew + *marīnus* marine or *rōs maris* dew of the sea (in E the final *-s* mistaken for pl. sign)]

Rose·mar·y (rōz′mâr′ē, -mə rē′), *n.* a girl's given name.

Rose·mead (rōz′mēd′), *n.* a city in SW California, near Los Angeles. 15,476 (1960).

rose′ milk′weed. See **swamp milkweed.**

rose′ moss′, a trailing purslane, *Portulaca grandiflora,* having showy, pink, purple, red, white, or yellow flowers. Also called **garden portulaca.**

Ro·sen·berg (rō′zən bûrg′), *n.* a town in S Texas. 9698 (1960).

Ro·sen·berg·er (rō′zən bûr′gər), *n.* a crater in the fourth quadrant of the face of the moon: about 50 miles in diameter.

Ro·sen·kav·a·lier, Der (*Ger.* deʀ rō′zən kä vä lēʀ′), an opera (1911) by Richard Strauss.

rose′ no′ble, a former gold coin of England, first issued by Edward IV, being the existing noble with a figure of a rose added to the types on either side: much imitated on the Continent, esp. in the Netherlands. Also called **ryal.**

Ro·sen·stock (rō′zən stok′), *n.* **Joseph,** born 1895, U.S. conductor and composer, born in Poland.

Ro·sen·wald (rō′zən wôld′), *n.* **Julius,** 1862–1932, U.S. businessman and philanthropist.

rose′ of Chi′na. See **China rose** (def. 2).

rose′ of Heav′en, an annual herb, *Lychnis Coeli-rosa,* of the Mediterranean region, having solitary terminal, rose-pink flowers.

rose′ of Jer′icho, an Asian, cruciferous plant, *Anastatica hierochuntica,* which, after drying and curling up, expands when moistened. Also called **resurrection plant.**

rose′ of Shar′on, 1. the althea, *Hibiscus syriacus.* **2.** Also called **Aaron's-beard.** a St.-John's-wort, *Hypericum calycinum.* **3.** a plant mentioned in the Bible. Song of Solomon 2:1.

rose′ oil′, a pale yellow, green, or red, volatile, fragrant, sweet-tasting liquid, obtained by steam distillation from fresh roses, esp. damask roses: used in flavoring and perfume. Also called **attar of roses, otto of roses.**

ro·se·o·la (rō zē′ə lə), *n. Pathol.* **1.** a kind of rose-colored rash. **2.** measles; rubeola. [< NL, equiv. to L *rose(us)* rose-colored + *-ola* fem. dim. suffix] —**ro·se′o·lar,** *adj.*

rose-slug (rōz′slug′), *n.* the larva of any of several sawflies, esp. *Endelomyia aethiops* or *Cladius isomerus,* that skeletonize the foliage of roses.

ros·et (roz′it), *n. Scot.* resin; rosin. [var. of ME *rosine* rosin]

Ro·set·ta (rō zet′ə), *n.* **1.** a town in the N United Arab Republic, at a mouth of the Nile. 32,800 (est. 1957). **2.** a girl's given name.

Roset′ta stone′, a stone slab, found in 1799 near Rosetta, bearing parallel inscriptions in Greek, Egyptian hieroglyphic, and demotic characters, making possible the decipherment of ancient Egyptian hieroglyphics.

ro·sette (rō zet′), *n.* **1.** any arrangement, part, object, or formation more or less resembling a rose. **2.** a rose-shaped arrangement of ribbon or other material, used as an ornament or badge. **3.** Also, **rosace.** an architectural ornament resembling a rose or having a generally circular combination of parts. **4.** *Bot.* a circular cluster of leaves or other organs. **5.** a broad ornamental head for a screw or nail. **6.** one of the cams controlling the moving parts of a rose engine. **7.** *Metall.* **a.** any of a number of disks of refined copper formed when cold water is thrown onto the molten metal. **b.** a rounded microconstituent of certain alloys. **8.** *Plant Pathol.* any of several diseases of plants, characterized by the crowding of the foliage into circular clusters owing to a shortening of the internodes of stems or branches, caused by fungi, viruses, or nutritional deficiencies. **9.** one of the compound spots on a leopard. [< F: little rose, OF. See rose[1], -ette]

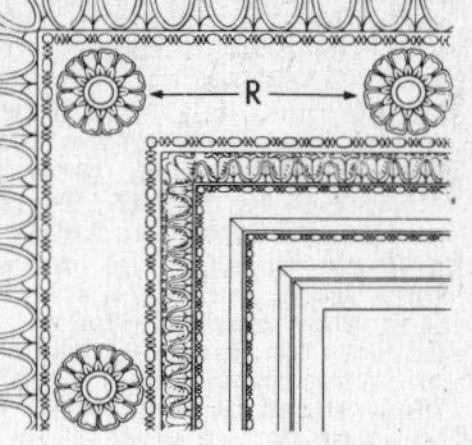

R, Rosette (def. 3)

Ro·sette (rō zet′), *n.* a girl's given name.

Rose·ville (rōz′vil), *n.* **1.** a city in SE Michigan, near Detroit. 50,195 (1960). **2.** a city in SE Minnesota, near St. Paul. 23,997 (1960).

Rose·wall (rōz′wôl′), *n.* **Ken(neth R.),** born 1934, Australian tennis player.

rose′ wa′ter, water tinctured with the essential oil of roses.

rose-wa·ter (rōz′wô′tər, wot′ər), *adj.* **1.** having the aroma or fragrance of rose water. **2.** affectedly delicate, nice, or fine; sentimental: *a Victorian novelist with a genteel, rose-water style.*

rose′ wee′vil. See **Fuller rose beetle.** Also called **rose beetle.**

rose′ win′dow, a circular window decorated with tracery symmetrical about the center.

rose·wood (rōz′wo͝od′), *n.* **1.** any of various reddish cabinet woods, sometimes with a roselike odor, yielded by certain tropical, fabaceous trees, esp. of the genus *Dalbergia.* **2.** a tree yielding such wood. [rose[1] + wood[1]]

Rose′wood Heights′, a town in SW Illinois. 4572 (1960).

Rosh Ha·sha·nah (rōsh′ hə shä′nə, -shō′-, hä-, rōsh′; *Heb.* rōsh′ hä shä nä′), a Jewish high holy day that marks the beginning of the Jewish New Year, celebrated on the first and second days of the month of Tishri by Orthodox and Conservative Jews outside of Israel and on the first day only by Reform Jews and Jews in Israel. Also, **Rosh′ Ha·sha′na, Rosh′ Ha·sho′noh, Rosh′ Ha·sho′no.** [< Heb *rōsh hashshānāh,* lit., beginning of the year]

Rosh Ho·desh (rōsh′ khō′desh), *Judaism.* the beginning of a new month in the Jewish calendar, celebrated in a specified manner during the morning service in the synagogue. Also, **Rosh′ Cho′desh.** [< Heb *rōsh ḥōdesh,* lit., beginning of the new moon]

Ro·si·cru·cian (rō′zə kro͞o′shən, roz′ə-), *n.* **1.** (in the 17th and 18th centuries) a person who belonged to an alleged secret society laying claim to various forms of occult knowledge and power and professing esoteric principles of religion. **2.** a member of any of several later or modern bodies or societies professing principles derived from or attributed to the earlier Rosicrucians, esp. of an organization (**Rosicru′cian Or′der** or **Ancient Mystic Order Rosae Crucis**) which is active in America. —*adj.* **3.** of, pertaining to, or characteristic of the Rosicrucians. [< L *Rosicruc-* (Latinized form of (Christian) *Rosenkreuz,* name of the supposed 15th-century founder of the society, equiv. to *ros(a)* rose + *-i-* + *cruc-* (s. of *crux*) cross) + -ian]

Ro·sie (rō′zē), *n.* a girl's given name, form of **Rose.** Also, **Rosy.**

ros·i·ly (rō′zə lē), *adv.* **1.** with a rosy color. **2.** in a rosy manner; brightly, cheerfully, or optimistically. [rosy + -ly]

ros·in (roz′in), *n.* **1.** *Chem.* the yellowish to amber, translucent, hard, brittle, fragmented resin left after distilling the oil of turpentine from the crude oleoresin of the pine: used chiefly in making varnish, varnish and paint driers, printing inks, and for rubbing on the bows of such string instruments as the violin. **2.** resin. —*v.t.* **3.** to cover or rub with rosin. Also called **colophony.** [ME < OF, var. of *resine* resin] —**ros′in·y,** *adj.*

Ro·si·na (rō zē′nə; *It.* rô zē′nä), *n.* a girl's given name, Italian form of **Rose.**

Ros·i·nan·te (roz′ə nan′tē, rō′zə nän′tē), *n.* **1.** the old, worn horse of Don Quixote. **2.** (*l.c.*) a broken-down old horse. Spanish, **Rocinante.**

ros′in jack′, sphalerite. Also, **resin jack.**

ros·in·weed (roz′in wēd′), *n.* **1.** any coarse, North American, composite plant of the genus *Silphium,* having a resinous juice. **2.** the compass plant, *S. laciniatum.* [rosin + weed[1]]

Ro·si·ta (rō zē′tə; *Sp.* rô sē′tä), *n.* a girl's given name, Spanish form of **Rose.**

Ros·lyn (roz′lin), *n.* a town on NW Long Island, in SE New York. 2681 (1960).

Ros′lyn rig′, *Naut.* a rig for a small sailing boat, including a jib, a mainsail on a sliding gunter having a short vertical club at the clew, and a leg-of-mutton mizzen.

Ros′lyn yawl′, *Naut.* a large sharpie having one or two jibs and a small jigger mast.

Ros·mers·holm (ros′mərs hōlm′, -holm′), *n.* a play (1886) by Henrik Ibsen.

ro·so·li·o (rō zō′lē ō′, rə-; *It.* rô zô′lyô), *n.* a cordial flavored with rose petals, cloves, cinnamon, or the like, popular in southern Europe. [< It, var. of *rosoli* < ML *rōs sōlis* dew of the sun]

ross (rôs, ros), *n.* **1.** the rough exterior of bark. —*v.t.* **2.** to remove the rough exterior of bark from (a log or the like). [?]

Ross (rôs, ros), *n.* **1. Betsy Gris·com** (gris′kəm), 1752–1836, maker of the first U.S. flag. **2. Harold Wallace,** 1892–1951, U.S. publisher and editor. **3. Sir James Clark,** 1800–62, English navigator: explorer of the Arctic and the Antarctic. **4.** his uncle, **Sir John,** 1777–1856, Scottish naval officer and arctic explorer. **5. Sir Ronald,** 1857–1932, English physician: Nobel prize 1902. **6.** a town in W California. 2551 (1960). **7.** a crater in the first quadrant of the face of the moon: about 18 miles in diameter. **8.** a boy's given name.

Ross′ and Crom′ar·ty (krom′ər tē, krum′-), a county in NW Scotland. 57,607 (1961); 3089 sq. mi. *Co. seat:* Dingwall.

Ross′ Depend′ency, a territory in Antarctica, including Ross Island, the coasts along the Ross Sea, and adjacent islands: a dependency of New Zealand. ab. 175,000 sq. mi.

Rosse (rôs, ros), *n.* a crater in the fourth quadrant of the face of the moon: about 10 miles in diameter.

Ros·sel·li·ni (rô′sə lē′nē, ros′ə-; *It.* rôs′sel lē′nē), *n.* **Ro·ber·to** (rə bâr′tō; *It.* rô ber′tô), born 1906, Italian motion-picture director.

ross·er (rô′sər, ros′ər), *n.* **1.** a logger who peels the bark from, and often smoothes one side of, a log so that it may be dragged easily. **2.** any of various machines or devices for removing bark from logs and pulpwood. **3.** an attachment on a circular saw for removing ross or bark ahead of the blade. [ROSS + -ER[1]]

Ros·set·ti (rō set′ē, -zet′ē, rə-), *n.* **1. Christina Georgina,** 1830–94, English poet. **2.** her brother, **Dante Gabriel** (*Gabriel Charles Dante Rossetti*), 1828–82, English poet and painter.

Ross·ford (rôs′fərd, ros′-), *n.* a town in NW Ohio. 4406 (1960).

Ross′ Ice′ Shelf′, an ice barrier filling the S part of the Ross Sea.

Ros·si·ni (rō sē′nē, rô-; *It.* rôs sē′nē), *n.* **Gio·ac·chi·no An·to·nio** (jô′äk kē′nô än tô′nyô), 1792–1868, Italian composer.

Ross′ Is′land, an island in the W Ross Sea, off the coast of Victoria Land: part of the Ross Dependency; location of Mt. Erebus.

Ros·si·ya (ro sē′yä), *n.* Russian name of **Russia.**

Ross′ Sea′, an arm of the Antarctic Ocean, S of New Zealand, extending into Antarctica.

Ross·ville (rôs′vil, ros′-), *n.* a town in NW Georgia. 4665 (1960).

Rost (rôst, rost), *n.* a crater in the third quadrant of the face of the moon: about 30 miles in diameter.

Ros·tand (rô stäN′), *n.* **Ed·mond** (ed môN′), 1868–1918, French dramatist and poet.

ros·tel·late (ros′tᵊlāt′, -tᵊlit), *adj. Bot.* having a rostellum. [< NL **rostellāt(us),* equiv. to L *rostell(um)* ROSTELLUM + *-ātus* -ATE[1]]

ros·tel·lum (ro stel′əm), *n., pl.* **ros·tel·la** (ro stel′ə). *Bot.* **1.** any small, beaklike process. **2.** a modification of the stigma in many orchids. [< L: little beak, snout, equiv. to *rōst(rum)* ROSTRUM + *-ellum* dim. suffix]

ros·ter (ros′tər), *n.* **1.** a list of persons or groups, as of military personnel or units with their turns or periods of duty. **2.** any list, roll, or register: *a roster of famous scientists; a roster of coming events.* [< D *rooster* list, orig., gridiron (deriv. of *roosten* to roast); from the ruled paper used]

Ros·tock (ros′tok; *Ger.* rôs′tôk), *n.* a seaport in N East Germany, on the Baltic. 179,352 (1964).

Ros·tov (rə stôf′; *Russ.* ro stôf′), *n.* a seaport in the SW RSFSR, in the S Soviet Union in Europe, on the Don River, near the Sea of Azov. 721,000 (1965). Also called **Ros·tov-on-Don** (rə stôf′on don′, -dôn′).

Ro·stov·tzeff (rə stôf′tsef), *n.* **Mi·chael I·va·no·vich** (mī′kəl i vä′nə vich), 1870–1952, U.S. historian, born in Russia.

ros·tra (ros′trə), *n.* a pl. of **rostrum.**

ros·tral (ros′trəl), *adj.* of or pertaining to a rostrum. [< LL *rōstrāl(is),* equiv. to L *rōstr(um)* ROSTRUM + *-ālis* -AL[1]] —**ros′tral·ly,** *adv.*

ros′tral col′umn, a memorial column having sculptures representing the rams of ancient ships.

ros·trate (ros′trāt), *adj.* furnished with a rostrum. Also, **ros′trat·ed.** [< L *rōstrāt(us)* having a beak, curved at the end, equiv. to *rōstr(um)* ROSTRUM + *-ātus* -ATE[1]]

ros·tro·car·i·nate (ros′trō kar′ə nāt′, -nit), *n.* a chipped flint cutting tool of the Lower Pleistocene in eastern England, having a beaklike shape and regarded by some specialists as having been formed by natural forces rather than by man. [*rostro* (comb. form of L *rōstrum* ROSTRUM) + CARINATE]

ros·trum (ros′trəm), *n., pl.* **-tra** (-trə), **-trums. 1.** any platform, stage, or the like, for public speaking. **2.** a pulpit. **3.** a beaklike projection from the prow of a ship, esp. one on an ancient warship for ramming an enemy ship; beak; ram. **4.** *Rom. Antiq.* (in the forum) the raised platform, adorned with the beaks of captured warships, from which orations, pleadings, etc., were delivered. **5.** *Biol.* a beaklike process or extension of some part. **6.** *Theat. Brit.* a raised platform or dais, esp. one with hinged sides that can be folded and stored within a relatively small space. [< L *rōstrum* bill, beak of a bird, ship's prow (in pl., speaker's platform), equiv. to *rōs(us)* gnawed, eaten away (ptp. of *rōdere*) + *-trum* instrumental suffix]

Ros·well (roz′wel), *n.* **1.** a city in SE New Mexico. 39,593 (1960). **2.** a town in central Georgia. 2983 (1960).

ros·y (rō′zē), *adj.,* **ros·i·er, ros·i·est. 1.** pink or pinkish-red; roseate. **2.** (of persons, the cheeks, lips, etc.) having a fresh, healthy redness. **3.** bright or promising: *a rosy future.* **4.** cheerful or optimistic: *rosy anticipations.* **5.** made or consisting of roses: *a rosy bower.* [ME; see ROSE[1], -Y[1]] —**ros′i·ness,** *n.*
—**Syn. 2.** flushed, blooming, healthy. —**Ant. 2.** pale. **3.** unpromising. **4.** cheerless.

Ro·sy (rō′zē), *n.* a girl's given name, form of **Rose.** Also, **Rosie.**

ros′y finch′, any of several finches of the genus *Leucosticte,* of Asia and western North America, having dark brown plumage with a pinkish wash on the wings and rump.

ros′y pas′tor. See under **pastor** (def. 3).

Ro·szak (rô′shäk, -shak), *n.* **Theodore,** born 1907, U.S. sculptor, born in Poland.

rot (rot), *v.,* **rot·ted, rot·ting,** *n., interj.* —*v.i.* **1.** to undergo decomposition; decay. **2.** to deteriorate, disintegrate, fall, or become weak due to decay (often fol. by *away, from, off,* etc.). **3.** to become morally corrupt or offensive. —*v.t.* **4.** to cause to rot: *Dampness rots wood.* **5.** to cause moral decay in; cause to become morally corrupt. **6.** to ret (flax, hemp, etc.). —*n.* **7.** the process of rotting. **8.** the state of being rotten; decay; putrefaction: *the rot of an old house.* **9.** rotting or rotten matter: *the rot and waste of a swamp.* **10.** moral or social decay or corruption. **11.** *Pathol.* any disease characterized by malodorous decay. **12.** *Plant Pathol.* **a.** any of various forms of decay produced by fungi or bacteria. **b.** any disease so characterized. **13.** *Vet. Pathol.* a disease, esp. of sheep, characterized by decay of the hoofs, caused by the organism *Distoma hepaticum.* **14.** *Informal.* nonsense. —*interj.* **15.** (a mild exclamation of distaste or disgust.) [ME < Scand; cf. OIcel *rot* (n.); akin to OE *rotian* to rot. See RET]
—**Syn. 1.** mold, molder, putrefy, spoil. See **decay. 8.** decomposition, mold. —**Ant. 3, 5.** purify.

ROT, rule of thumb.

rot., 1. rotating. **2.** rotation.

ro·ta[1] (rō′tə), *n.* **1.** *Chiefly Brit.* **a.** a round or rotation of duties; a period of work or duty taken in rotation with others. **b.** an agenda or circuit of sporting events, as a round of golf tournaments, played in different localities throughout the year. **2.** a roster. **3.** Official name, **Sacred Roman Rota.** the ecclesiastical tribunal in Rome, constituting the court of final appeal. [< L: wheel]

ro·ta[2] (rō′tə), *n.* rote[2].

Ro·ta (rô′tä), *n.* **Ni·no** (nē′nô), born 1911, Italian composer.

Ro·tan (rō tan′), *n.* a town in central Texas. 2788 (1960).

Ro·tar·i·an (rō târ′ē ən), *n.* **1.** a member of a Rotary Club. —*adj.* **2.** of or pertaining to Rotarians or Rotary Clubs. [ROTARY (CLUB) + -AN] —**Ro·tar′i·an·ism,** *n.*

ro·ta·ry (rō′tə rē), *adj., n., pl.* **-ries.** —*adj.* **1.** turning or capable of turning around on an axis, as a wheel. **2.** taking place around an axis, as motion. **3.** having a part or parts that turn on an axis, as a machine. **4.** noting or pertaining to an internal-combustion engine for an airplane, having radially arranged cylinders which move about a stationary crankshaft. —*n.* **5.** See **traffic circle. 6.** *Elect.* See **synchronous converter.** [< LL *rotāri(us),* equiv. to L *rot(a)* wheel + *-ārius* -ARY]

ro′tary beat′er, a culinary utensil or device, as an eggbeater, with one or more sets of rotary blades for beating, whipping, mixing, etc.

Ro′tary Club′, a local club of business and professional men belonging to an organization, founded in Chicago in 1905, that is a member of a world-wide organization of similar clubs (**Ro′tary Interna′tional**) devoted to serving the community and promoting world peace.

ro′tary en′gine, 1. an engine, as a turbine, in which the impelling fluid produces torque directly rather than by acting upon reciprocating parts. **2.** a revolving radial engine.

ro′tary hoe′, an implement consisting basically of a row of small wheels each with many fingerlike prongs, for pulling over the ground for early crop cultivation and destruction of weeds.

ro′tary plow′, a series of swinging blades mounted on a horizontal power-driven shaft, for pulverizing unplowed soil preparatory to planting. Also called **ro′tary till′er.**

ro′tary press′, *Print.* a printing press in which the type or plates to be printed are fastened upon a rotating cylinder and are impressed on a continuous roll of moving paper.

ro′tary pump′, a pump for transferring water or other fluids by the rotating action of its component parts, as by the meshing of vanes or screws.

ro′tary shut′ter, a camera shutter consisting of a rotating disk pierced with a slit that passes in front of the lens to expose the film or plate.

ro′tary wing′, *Aeron.* an airfoil that rotates about an approximately vertical axis, as that supporting a helicopter or autogiro in flight.

ro·tate[1] (rō′tāt, rō tāt′), *v.,* **-tat·ed, -tat·ing.** —*v.t.* **1.** to cause to turn around an axis or center point; revolve. **2.** to cause to go through a cycle of changes; cause to pass or follow in a fixed routine of succession: *to rotate crops.* **3.** to replace (a person, troops, etc.) by another or others, usually according to a schedule or plan. —*v.i.* **4.** to turn around on or as on an axis. **5.** to proceed in a fixed routine of succession: *The sentries rotated in keeping watch.* [< L *rotāt(us)* swung round, revolved (ptp. of *rotāre*), equiv. to *rot(a)* wheel + *-ātus* -ATE[1]] —**ro′tat·a·ble,** *adj.* —**ro′tat·a·bly,** *adv.*
—**Syn. 1.** wheel, whirl. See **turn.**

ro·tate[2] (rō′tāt), *adj.* wheel-shaped: applied esp. to a gamopetalous short-tubed corolla with a spreading limb. [< L *rot(a)* wheel + -ATE[1]]

ro′tating prism′, *Optics.* See **Dove prism.**

ro·ta·tion (rō tā′shən), *n.* **1.** the act of rotating; a turning around as on an axis. **2.** *Astron.* **a.** the movement or path of the earth or a heavenly body turning on its axis. **b.** one complete turn of such a body. **3.** regularly recurring succession, as of officials. **4.** *Agric.* the process or method of varying, in a definite order, the crops grown on the same ground. **5.** *Math.* curl (def. 16). **6.** *Pool.* a game in which the balls are played in order by number. [< L *rotātiōn-* (s. of *rotātiō*) a wheeling about, rolling, equiv. to *rotāt(us)* (see ROTATE[1]) + *-iōn-* -ION] —**ro·ta′tion·al,** *adj.*

rota′tion ax′is, *Crystall.* an imaginary line through a crystal about which the crystal may be rotated a specified number of degrees and be brought back to its original position. Also called **symmetry axis of rotation.** Cf. **symmetry element.**

ro·ta′tion-in·ver′sion ax′is (rō tā′shən in vûr′zhən, -shən), *Crystall.* an axis of a crystal such that rotating about the axis and then inverting the crystal brings the crystal back to its original position. Also called **symmetry axis of rotary inversion.** Cf. **symmetry element.**

rota′tion of ax′es (ak′sēz), *Math.* a process of replacing the axes in a Cartesian coordinate system with a new set of axes making a specified angle with and having the same origin as the original axes.

ro·ta·tive (rō′tā tiv), *adj.* **1.** rotating or pertaining to rotation. **2.** producing rotation. **3.** happening in regular succession. [< L *rotāt(us)* (see ROTATE[1]) + -IVE] —**ro·ta·tive·ly** (rō′tə tiv lē), *adv.*

ro·ta·tor (rō′tā tər, rō tā′-), *n., pl.* **ro·ta·tors** for 1, 3, **ro·ta·tor·es** (rō′tə tōr′ēz, -tôr′-) for 2. **1.** one who or that which rotates. **2.** *Anat.* a muscle serving to rotate a part of the body. **3.** *Naut.* a bladed device streamed to rotate in the water to actuate a patent log. [< L *rotātor,* equiv. to *rotāt(us)* (see ROTATE[1]) + *-or* -OR[2]]

ro·ta·to·ry (rō′tə tōr′ē, -tôr′ē), *adj.* **1.** pertaining to or of the nature of rotation: *rotatory motion.* **2.** rotating, as an object. **3.** passing or following in rotation or succession. **4.** causing rotation, as a muscle. [< NL *rotātōri(us),* equiv. to L *rotāt(us)* (see ROTATE[1]) + *-ōrius* -ORY[1]]

R.O.T.C. (är′ō tē sē′, rot′sē), Reserve Officers' Training Corps. Also, **ROTC**

rotche (roch), *n.* the dovekie (def. 1). [var. of earlier *rotge;* cf. D *rotje* petrel]

rote[1] (rōt), *n.* **1.** routine; a fixed, habitual, or mechanical course of procedure: *the rote of daily living.* **2. by rote,** from memory, without thought of the meaning; in a mechanical way: *Foreign languages are no longer taught by rote.* [ME < ?]

rote[2] (rōt), *n. Music.* crowd[2]. Also, **rota, rotta, rotte.** [ME < OF < Celt]

rote[3] (rōt), *n.* the sound of waves breaking on the shore. [? < Scand]

ro·te·none (rōt′ᵊnōn′), *n. Chem., Pharm.* a white, crystalline, water-insoluble, poisonous heterocyclic compound, $C_{23}H_{22}O_6$, obtained from derris root: used chiefly as the active ingredient of certain insecticides and in medicine in the treatment of chiggers and scabies. [< Jap *rōten* derris plant + -ONE]

rot·gut (rot′gut′), *n. Slang.* cheap and inferior liquor. [ROT + GUT]

Roth·er·ham (roth′ər əm), *n.* a city in S Yorkshire, in N England. 85,346 (1961).

Roth·er·mere (roth′ər mēr′), *n.* **1st Viscount.** See **Harmsworth, Harold Sidney.**

Rothe·say (roth′sē, -sā), *n.* a town in and the county seat of Bute, on Bute island, in SW Scotland: resort; ruins of 11th-century castle. 7656 (1961).

Roth·ko (roth′kō), *n.* **Mark,** born 1903, U.S. painter, born in Russia.

Roth·mann (rôth′mən, roth′-), *n.* a crater in the fourth quadrant of the face of the moon: about 27 miles in diameter.

Roth·schild (roth′chīld, roths′-, rôth-, rôths′-; *for 1, 2, also Ger.* rōt′shilt), *n.* **1. Lionel Nathan, Baron de** ("*Lord Natty*"), 1809–79, English banker: first Jewish member of Parliament. **2. May·er** (mī′ər, mā′ər; *Ger.* mī′ər) or **Mey·er** (mī′ər; *Ger.* mī′ər) **Am·schel** (am′shəl; *Ger.* äm′shəl) or **An·selm** (an′selm; *Ger.* än′zelm), 1743–1812, German banker: founder of the Rothschild family and international banking firm. **3.** his son, **Nathan Meyer, Baron de,** 1777–1836, English banker, born in Germany. **4.** a town in central Wisconsin. 2550 (1960).

Rotifer, *Philodina citrina*

rô·ti (rō tē′), *n. French.* roast.

ro·ti·fer (rō′tə fər), *n.* any microscopic animal of the class *Rotifera,* found in fresh and salt waters, having a ciliary apparatus on the anterior end; a wheel animalcule. [< NL *Rotifer(a),* equiv. to L *rot(a)* wheel + *-i-* -I- + *-fer* -FER] —**ro·tif·er·al** (rō tif′ər əl), **ro·tif′er·ous,** *adj.*

Ro·tif·er·a (rō tif′ər ə), *n.* the class comprising the rotifers. [< NL: ROTIFER]

ro·ti·form (rō′tə fôrm′), *adj.* shaped like a wheel. [< NL *rotiform(is),* equiv. to L *rot(a)* wheel + *-i-* -I- + *-formis* -FORM]

ro·tis·ser·ie (rō tis′ə rē), *n.* a small broiler with a motor-driven spit, for barbecuing fowl, beef, etc. [< F: roasting-place]

rot·l (rot′ᵊl), *n., pl.* **rotls, ar·tal** (är′täl). **1.** a unit of weight used in Islamic countries, varying widely in value, but of the order of the pound. **2.** a varying unit of dry measure, used in the same areas. [< Ar *raṭl* << Gk *lítra* or L *lībra* pound]

ro·to (rō′tō), *n., pl.* **ro·tos.** rotogravure. [by shortening]

roto-, a combining form meaning "rotary," used in the formation of compound words: *rotogravure.* [< L *rot(a)* wheel + -o-]

ro·to·gra·vure (rō′tə grə vyŏŏr′, -grā′vyər), *n.* **1.** a photomechanical process by which pictures, typeset matter, etc., are printed from an intaglio copper cylinder. **2.** a print made by this process. **3.** *U.S.* a roto section. [ROTO- + F *gravure* engraving]

ro·tor (rō′tər), *n.* **1.** *Elect.* a rotating member of a machine. Cf. **stator** (def. 1). **2.** *Aeron.* a system of rotating airfoils, as the horizontal ones of a helicopter or of the compressor of a jet engine. **3.** any of a number of tall, cylindrical devices mounted on a special ship (**ro′tor ship′**) and rotated in such a way that the Magnus effect on wind impinging on the cylinders is used to drive and maneuver the vessel. **4.** (in a self-winding watch) a weight eccentrically mounted on an arbor for keeping the mainspring wound. [short for ROTATOR]

ro′tor blade′, *Aeron.* one airfoil of the rotor of a rotary-wing aircraft.

ro′tor cloud′, a cloud within and around which the air is rotating about a horizontal axis, occurring in the lee of a large mountain barrier. Also called **roll cloud.**

ro·tor·craft (rō′tər kraft′, -kräft′), *n.* a rotary-wing aircraft. Also called **ro′tor plane′.** [ROTOR + CRAFT]

Ro·to·ru·a (rō′tə rōō′ə), *n.* a city on N central North Island, in New Zealand. 25,068 (1961).

ro′to sec′tion, 1. a section of a newspaper consisting of pages printed by the rotogravure process. **2.** a magazinelike section in the Sunday editions of many newspapers, containing articles rather than news items and often book reviews, short stories, puzzles, etc.

Ro·to·till·er (rō′tō til′ər), *n. Trademark.* an agricultural device with turning blades for breaking up soil.

rot·proof (rot′prōōf′), *adj.* resistant to rotting.

rotte (rot), *n. Music.* rote[2]. Also, **rot·ta** (rot′ə).

rot·ten (rot′ᵊn), *adj.* **1.** decomposing or decaying; putrid; tainted, foul, or bad-smelling. **2.** corrupt or morally offensive. **3.** *Informal.* wretchedly bad, unpleasant, or unsatisfactory; miserable: *a rotten piece of work; a rotten day at the office.* **4.** contemptible; despicable: *a rotten little liar; a rotten trick.* **5.** (of soil, rocks, etc.) soft, yielding, or friable as the result of decomposition. [ME *roten* < Scand; cf. Icel *rotinn* putrid] —**rot′ten·ly,** *adv.* —**rot′ten·ness,** *n.*
—**Syn. 1.** fetid, rank. **2.** immoral. **4.** disgusting, unwholesome; treacherous. —**Ant. 1.** sound. **2.** moral.

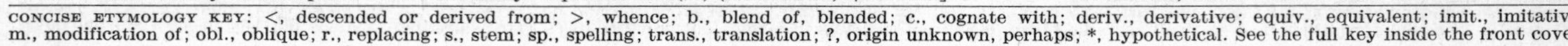

rot′ten bor′ough, **1.** (before the Reform Bill of 1832) any English borough that had very few voters yet was represented in Parliament. **2.** an election district that has more representatives in a legislative body than the number of its constituents would normally call for.

rot′ten ice′, *Naut.* ice pitted or honeycombed from melting.

rot·ten·stone (rot′ən stōn′), *n.* a friable stone resulting from the decomposition of a siliceous limestone, used as a powder for polishing metals. [ROTTEN + STONE]

rot′ten stop′, *Naut.* any of a number of frail pieces of thread, string, etc., used to wrap a sail being sent aloft to be set.

rot·ter (rot′ər), *n.* *Chiefly Brit. Slang.* a thoroughly bad, worthless, or objectionable person. [ROT + -ER[1]]

Rot·ter·dam (rot′ər dam′; *for 1, also Du.* RÔT′ƏR-däm′), *n.* **1.** a seaport in the SW Netherlands. 730,963 (1962). **2.** a town in E New York, on the Mohawk River. 16,871 (est. 1960).

Rott·wei·ler (rot′wī lər), *n.* one of a German breed of large, powerful dogs having a short, coarse, black coat with tan to brown markings. [< G, after *Rottweil* city in southwest Germany; see -ER[1]]

ro·tund (rō tund′), *adj.* **1.** round in shape; rounded: *ripe, rotund fruit.* **2.** plump; fat. **3.** full-toned or sonorous: *rotund speeches.* [< L *rotund(us)* round, circular, deriv. of *rota* wheel] —**ro·tund′ly,** *adv.*

ro·tun·da (rō tun′də), *n.* **1.** a round building, esp. one with a dome. **2.** a large and high circular hall or room in a building, esp. one surmounted by a dome. [alter. of It *rotonda* < L *rotunda,* fem. of *rotundus* ROTUND]

ro·tun·di·ty (rō tun′di tē), *n., pl.* **-ties. 1.** the condition or quality of roundness or plumpness, as of an object or person: *the rotundity of a globe; the rotundity of his midsection.* **2.** fullness, as in tone or speech: *Johnsonian rotundity.* **3.** a full or rounded tone, phrase, or the like: *oratorical rotundities.* Also, **ro·tund′ness.** [< L *rotunditās.* See ROTUND, -ITY]

ro·tu·rier (RÔ TY RYĀ′), *n., pl.* **-riers** (-RYĀ′). *French.* a person of low rank; plebeian.

Rou·ault (rōō ō′; *Fr.* RWŌ), *n.* **Georges** (zhôrzh), 1871–1958, French painter.

Rou·baix (rōō be′), *n.* a city in N France, NE of Lille. 113,163 (1962).

rou·ble (rōō′bəl), *n.* ruble.

rou·é (rōō ā′, rōō′ā), *n.* a debauchee or rake. [< F, n. use of ptp. of *rouer* to break on the wheel << L *rotāre* (see ROTATE[1]); name first applied to the profligate companions of the Duc d'Orléans (c1720)]
—**Syn.** profligate.

Rou·en (rōō äN′, -än′; *Fr.* RWäN), *n.* **1.** a city in and the capital of Seine-Maritime, in N France, on the Seine: famous cathedral; execution of Joan of Arc 1431. 123,474 (1962). **2.** one of a breed of domestic ducks resembling the wild mallard.

Rouen′ li′lac, a shrub, *Syringa chinensis,* of France, having clusters of fragrant, lilac-purple flowers.

rou·gail (rōō gī′), *n.* a combination of condiments and spices, as ginger, thyme, pimiento, and tomatoes, used esp. in Creole cookery. [< Creole F]

rouge (rōōzh), *n., v.,* **rouged, roug·ing.** —*n.* **1.** any of various red cosmetics for coloring the cheeks or lips. **2.** a reddish powder, chiefly ferric oxide, used for polishing metal, glass, etc. —*v.t.* **3.** to color with rouge. —*v.i.* **4.** to use rouge. [< F: red (adj.) < L *rube(us)*]

rouge (RŌŌZH), *adj. French.* red; noting the red numbers in roulette. [lit: red]

Rouge et le Noir, Le (*Fr.* lə RŌŌZH′ ā lə NWAR′). See **Red and the Black, The.**

rouge et noir (rōōzh′ ā nwär′; *Fr.* RŌŌZH ā NWAR′), a gambling game using cards, played at a table marked with two red and two black diamond-shaped spots on which the players place their stakes. [< F: red and black]

Rou·get de Lisle (RŌŌ ZHE′ də lēl′), **Claude Jo·seph** (klōd zhō zef′), 1760–1836, French army officer and composer of songs. Also, **Rou·get′ de l'Isle′.**

rough (ruf), *adj.* **1.** having a coarse or uneven surface, as from projections, irregularities, or breaks; not smooth: *rough, red hands; a rough road.* **2.** shaggy: *a dog with a rough coat.* **3.** (of an uninhabited region or large land area) steep or uneven and covered with high grass, brush, trees, stones, etc.: *to hunt over rough country.* **4.** acting with or characterized by violence: *Boxing is a rough sport.* **5.** characterized by unnecessary violence or infractions of the rules: *It was a rough prize fight.* **6.** violently disturbed or agitated; turbulent, as water, the air, etc.: *a rough sea.* **7.** having a violently irregular motion; uncomfortably or dangerously uneven: *The plane had a rough flight in the storm.* **8.** stormy or tempestuous, as wind, weather, etc. **9.** sharp or harsh: *a rough temper.* **10.** unmannerly or rude: *his rough and churlish manner; They exchanged rough words.* **11.** disorderly or riotous: *a rough mob.* **12.** difficult or unpleasant: *to have a rough time of it.* **13.** harsh to the ear; grating or jarring, as sounds. **14.** harsh to the taste; sharp or astringent. **15.** coarse, as food. **16.** lacking culture or refinement: *a rough, countrified manner.* **17.** without refinements, luxuries, or ordinary comforts or conveniences: *rough camping.* **18.** requiring exertion or strength rather than intelligence or skill: *rough manual labor.* **19.** not elaborated, perfected, or corrected; unpolished, as language, verse, style, etc.: *a rough draft.* **20.** made or done without any attempt at exactness, completeness, or thoroughness; approximate or tentative: *a rough guess.* **21.** crude, unwrought, nonprocessed, or unprepared: *rough rice.* **22.** *Phonet.* uttered with aspiration; having the sound of *h;* aspirated. —*n.* **23.** that which is rough, esp. rough ground. **24.** *Golf.* any part of the course bordering the fairway on which the grass, weeds, etc., are not trimmed. **25.** the unpleasant or difficult part of anything. **26.** anything in its crude or preliminary form, as a drawing. **27.** *Chiefly Brit.* a rowdy; ruffian. **28. in the rough,** in a rough, crude, or unfinished state: *The country has an exciting potential, but civilization there is still in the rough.* —*adv.* **29.** in a rough manner; roughly. —*v.t.* **30.** to make rough; roughen. **31.** to give a beating to, manhandle, or subject to physical violence (often fol. by *up*): *The mob roughed up the speaker.* **32.** to subject to some rough, preliminary process of working or preparation (often fol. by *down, off,* or *out*): *to rough off boards.* **33.** to sketch roughly or in outline (often fol. by *in* or *out*): *to rough out a diagram; to rough in the conversation of a novel.* **34.** *Sports.* to subject (a player on the opposing team) to unnecessary physical abuse, as in blocking or tackling: *The team was penalized 15 yards for roughing the kicker.* —*v.i.* **35.** to become rough, as a surface. **36.** to behave roughly. **37. rough it,** to live without the customary comforts or conveniences; endure rugged conditions: *We really roughed it on our fishing trip.* [ME; OE *rūh;* c. D *ruig,* G *rauh*] —**rough′ly,** *adv.* —**rough′ness,** *n.*
—**Syn. 1.** irregular, jagged, bumpy, craggy. **2.** hairy, bristly. **13.** noisy, cacophonous, raucous. **16.** impolite, uncivil, unpolished, rude. —**Ant. 1.** smooth, even, regular.

rough·age (ruf′ij), *n.* **1.** rough or coarse material. **2.** any coarse, rough food for livestock. **3.** food, as green vegetables, bran, and certain fruits, containing a high proportion of indigestible cellulose which stimulates peristalsis in the intestines. [ROUGH + -AGE]

rough-and-read·y (ruf′ən red′ē), *adj.* **1.** rough, rude, or crude, but good enough for the purpose: *a rough-and-ready estimate of future expenses.* **2.** exhibiting or showing rough vigor rather than refinement or delicacy: *a rough-and-ready person.* —**rough′-and-read′i·ness,** *n.*

rough-and-tum·ble (ruf′ən tum′bəl), *adj.* **1.** characterized by violent, random, disorderly action and struggles: *a rough-and-tumble fight; He led an adventuresome, rough-and-tumble life.* **2.** given to such action.

rough′ breath′ing, **1.** the symbol (ʽ) used in the writing of Greek to indicate aspiration of the initial vowel or of the ρ over which it is placed. **2.** the aspirated sound indicated by this mark. Cf. **smooth breathing.** [trans. of L *spiritus asper*]

rough′ cast′, trullisatio.

rough·cast (ruf′kast′, -käst′), *n., v.,* **-cast, -cast·ing.** —*n.* **1.** an exterior wall finish composed of mortar and fine pebbles mixed together and dashed against the wall. Cf. **depeter, pebble dash. 2.** a crudely formed pattern or model. —*v.t.* **3.** to cover or coat with roughcast. **4.** to make, shape, or prepare in a rough form: *to roughcast a story.* [ROUGH + CAST] —**rough′cast′er,** *n.*

rough-cut (ruf′kut′), *adj.* cut into small, irregular pieces (contrasted with *fine cut*).

rough-dry (ruf′drī′), *v.,* **-dried, -dry·ing,** *adj.* —*v.t.* **1.** to dry (laundry) after washing, without smoothing, ironing, etc. —*adj.* **2.** (of laundered clothes, sheets, etc.) dried but not ironed. Also, **rough′dry′.**

rough·en (ruf′ən), *v.t., v.i.* to make or become rough or rougher. [ROUGH + -EN] —**rough′en·er,** *n.*

rough·er (ruf′ər), *n.* one who or that which roughs or roughs out something, as certain crude cutting tools or a person who performs the first, rough parts of a process. [ROUGH + -ER[1]]

rough-hew (ruf′hyōō′), *v.t.,* **-hewed, -hewed** or **-hewn, -hew·ing. 1.** to hew (timber, stone, etc.) roughly or without smoothing or finishing. **2.** to shape roughly; give crude form to. Also, **rough′hew′.**

rough·house (ruf′hous′), *n., pl.* **-hous·es** (-hou′ziz), *v.,* **-housed** (-houst′, -houzd′), **-hous·ing** (-hou′-zing, -hous′-). —*n.* **1.** rough, disorderly playing, esp. indoors. —*v.i.* **2.** to engage in rough, disorderly play. —*v.t.* **3.** to handle or play with roughly. [ROUGH + HOUSE]

rough·ing-in (ruf′ing in′), *n.* *Building Trades.* **1.** the act or process of applying a base coat of plaster to a masonry surface. **2.** the act or process of installing plumbing that will later be concealed.

rough·ish (ruf′ish), *adj.* rather rough: *a roughish sea.* [ROUGH + -ISH[1]]

rough′-leg·ged hawk′ (ruf′leg′id, -legd′), a large hawk, *Buteo lagopus,* of the Northern Hemisphere, that feeds chiefly on small rodents.

rough′ log′, *Naut.* See **deck log.**

rough·neck (ruf′nek′), *n.* *Informal.* **1.** a rough, coarse person; a tough. **2.** *U.S.* any laborer working on an oil-drilling rig. Cf. **roustabout** (def. 4). [ROUGH + NECK]

rough·rid·er (ruf′rī′dər), *n.* **1.** one who breaks horses to the saddle. **2.** one accustomed to rough or hard riding. [ROUGH + RIDER]

Rough′ Rid′ers, the members of a volunteer regiment of cavalry, organized by Theodore Roosevelt and Leonard Wood for service in the Spanish-American War of 1898.

rough·shod (ruf′shod′), *adj.* **1.** shod with horseshoes having projecting nails or points. **2. ride roughshod over,** to treat harshly or domineeringly; override; crush: *He rode roughshod over his friends to advance himself in the business world.* [ROUGH + SHOD]

rough′ side′, *Shipbuilding.* the side of a bulkhead on which the stiffeners are located.

rough-spo·ken (ruf′spō′kən), *adj.* coarse or vulgar in speech: *a rough-spoken sort.*

rough′ spot′, *Plant Pathol.* a disease of Sudan grass, Johnson grass, and sorghums, characterized by hard, raised, black spots on the affected discolored parts, caused by a fungus, *Ascochyta sorghina.*

rough·string (ruf′string′), *n.* a concealed, inclined beam supporting the steps of a stair, esp. a string faced with a finish of woodwork. [ROUGH + STRING]

rough′ stuff′, *Slang.* **1.** violence, as physical assault, torture, shooting, etc. **2.** unnecessary violence or infractions of the rules, as in sports: *Fight fairly, no rough stuff is allowed.* **3.** blatant vulgarity or obscenity.

rough′-tree rail′ (ruf′trē′), *Naut. Obs.* the rail at the top of the bulwarks of a wooden vessel.

rough-voiced (ruf′voist′), *adj.* having a harsh or grating voice: *a rough-voiced barker.*

rough′-winged swal′low (ruf′wingd′), **1.** a New World swallow, *Stelgidopteryx serripennis,* having outer primary feathers with small, barblike hooks on the margins. **2.** any of several African swallows of the genus *Psalidoprocne,* having similar feathers.

rough′ wood′bine, a twining vine, *Lonicera hirsuta,* of eastern central North America, having downy leaves and bright yellow flowers in terminal clusters.

roul., *Philately.* roulette.

rou·lade (rōō läd′), *n.* **1.** a musical embellishment consisting of a rapid succession of tones sung to a single syllable. **2.** a slice of meat rolled about a filling of minced meat and cooked. [< F: a rolling, equiv. to *roul(er)* (to) roll + *-ade* -ADE[1]]

rou·leau (rōō lō′), *n., pl.* **-leaux, -leaus** (-lōz′). **1.** a roll or strip of something, as trimming on a hat brim. **2.** a stack or roll of coins put up in cylindrical form in a paper wrapping. [< F; MF *rolel,* dim. of *role* ROLL]

Rou·lers (rōō lârs′; *Fr.* RŌŌ LER′), *n.* a city in NW Belgium: battles 1914, 1918. 35,957 (est. 1964).

rou·lette (rōō let′), *n., v.,* **-let·ted, -let·ting.** —*n.* **1.** a wheel or revolving disk used in playing a game of chance. **2.** a game of chance played at a table marked off with numbers from 1 to 36, one or two zeros, and several other sections affording the players a variety of betting opportunities, and having in the center a revolving, dish-like device (**roulette′ wheel′**) into which a small ball is spun to come to rest finally in one of the 37 or 38 compartments, indicating the winning number and its characteristics, as odd or even, red or black, and between 1 and 18 or 19 and 36. **3.** a small wheel, esp. one with sharp teeth, mounted in a handle, for making lines of marks, dots, or perforations: *engravers' roulettes; a roulette for perforating sheets of postage stamps.* **4.** *Geom.* a curve generated by the locus of a point on a closed curve that rolls without slipping on a fixed curve; cycloid, epicycloid, or hypocycloid. **5.** *Philately.* a row of short cuts, in which no paper is removed, made between individual stamps to permit their ready separation. —*v.t.* **6.** to mark, impress, or perforate with a roulette. [< F, dim. of *rouelle* wheel. See ROWEL]

Roulettes (Engravers')

Roum., **1.** Roumania. **2.** Roumanian.

Rou·ma·ni·a (rōō mā′nē ə, -män′yə), *n.* Rumania. —**Rou·ma′ni·an,** *adj., n.*

Rou·me·li·a (rōō mē′lē ə, -mēl′yə), *n.* Rumelia.

rounce (rouns), *n.* *Print.* (in early presses) the handle for turning the roller that draws the bed from under the platen by means of a pair of leather straps. [< D *ronds(e), ronse*]

round[1] (round), *adj.* **1.** having a flat, circular surface, as a disk. **2.** ring-shaped, as a hoop. **3.** curved like part of a circle, as an outline. **4.** having a circular cross section, as a cylinder; cylindrical. **5.** spherical or globular, as a ball. **6.** shaped more or less like a part of a sphere; hemispherical. **7.** free from angularity; consisting of full, curved lines or shapes, as handwriting, parts of the body, etc. **8.** executed with or involving circular motion: *a round dance.* **9.** full, complete, or entire: *a round dozen.* **10.** noting, formed, or expressed by an integer or whole number with no fraction. **11.** expressed, given, or exact to the nearest multiple or power of ten; in tens, hundreds, thousands, or the like: *in round numbers.* **12.** roughly correct: *a round guess.* **13.** considerable in amount; ample: *a good, round sum of money.* **14.** brought to completeness or perfection. **15.** full and sonorous, as sound. **16.** vigorous or brisk: *a round trot.* **17.** plain, honest, or straightforward: *round dealing.* **18.** candid or outspoken. **19.** unmodified: *a round oath.* **20.** positive or unqualified: *You've certainly made a round assertion.*
—*n.* **21.** any round shape, as a circle, ring, sphere, etc. **22.** a circular, ring-shaped, curved, or spherical object; a rounded form. **23.** something circular in cross section, as a rung of a ladder. **24.** Sometimes, **rounds.** a completed course of time, series of events or operations, etc., ending at a point corresponding to that at the beginning: *We waited through the round of many years. The story has made the rounds of all the newspapers.* **25.** any complete course, series, or succession: *The strike was settled after a long round of talks.* **26.** Often, **rounds.** a going around from place to place, as in a habitual or definite circuit: *a round of all the parties; The doctor made his rounds.* **27.** a completed course or spell of activity, commonly one of a series, in some play or sport: *to play a round of bridge.* **28.** a recurring period of time, succession of events, duties, etc.: *the daily round.* **29.** a single outburst, as of applause or cheers. **30.** a single discharge of shot by each of a number of guns, rifles, etc. **31.** a single discharge by one firearm. **32.** a charge of ammunition for a single shot. **33.** a single serving, esp. of drink, made more or less simultaneously to everyone present, as at table or at a bar: *The next round is on me.* **34.** a dance with the dancers arranged or moving in a circle or ring. **35.** movement in a circle or around an axis. **36.** Also, **round of beef.** the portion of the thigh of beef below the rump and above the leg. **37.** *Brit.* a slice of bread. **38.** *Archery.* a specified number of arrows shot from a specified distance from the target in accordance with the rules. **39.** one of a series of three-minute periods making up a boxing match: *a 15-round bout.* **40.** *Music.* **a.** a short, rhythmical canon at the unison, in which the several voices enter at equally spaced intervals of time. **b. rounds,** the order followed in ringing a peal of bells in diatonic sequence from the highest to the lowest. **41.** *Golf.* a playing of the complete course. **42.** *Cards.* a division of play in a game, consisting of a turn each for every player to bid, bet, play a card, deal the cards, or be dealt cards. **43.** *Naut.* a convex curve given to the luff, head, or foot of a fore-and-aft sail. **44. go the rounds,** to be reported or told; circulate: *another rumor going the rounds.* **45. in the round, a.** (of a theater) having a stage completely surrounded by seats for the audience. **b.** with a broad or comprehensive understanding: *a character as seen in the round.* **c.** (of sculpture) not attached to a supporting background; freestanding. **46. make the rounds, a.** to go from one place to another, making a routine series of stops, visits, etc.: *The mailman makes the rounds before noon every day.* **b.** (of an actor, free-lance writer, etc.) to seek employment by contacting producers, editors, etc.
—*adv.* **47.** throughout or from the beginning to the end of a recurring period of time: *all year round.* **48.** Also, **'round.** around: *The music goes round and round.*
—*prep.* **49.** throughout (a period of time): *a resort visited all round the year.* **50.** around: *It happened round noon.*
—*v.t.* **51.** to make round. **52.** to free from angularity; fill out symmetrically; make plump. **53.** to bring to completeness or perfection; finish (often fol. by *off*): *to round off a lifetime of work with a masterpiece.* **54.** *Jewelry.* to form (a gem) roughly (sometimes fol. by *up*); girdle. **55.** to end (a sentence, paragraph, etc.) with

something specified: *He rounded his speech with a particularly apt quotation.* **56.** to encircle or surround. **57.** to make a complete circuit of; pass completely around. **58.** to make a turn or partial circuit around or to the other side of: *to round a corner; to round a cape.* **59.** to cause to move in a circle; turn around. **60.** *Phonet.* **a.** to make the opening at (the lips) relatively round or pursed during an utterance. **b.** to pronounce (a speech sound, esp. a vowel) with rounded lips; labialize. **c.** to contract (the lips) laterally. Cf. **spread** (def. 14), **unround. 61.** *Math.* to replace by the nearest multiple of 10, with 5 being increased to the next highest multiple: 15,837 can be rounded to 15,840; then to 15,800; then to 16,000.
—*v.i.* **62.** to become round. **63.** to become free from angularity; become plump. **64.** to develop to completeness or perfection. **65.** to take a circular course; make a circuit; go the round, as a guard. **66.** to make a turn or partial circuit around something. **67.** to turn around as on an axis: *to round on one's heels.* **68.** to reduce successively the number of digits to the right of the decimal point of a mixed number by dropping the final digit and adding 1 to the next preceding digit if the dropped digit was 5 or greater, or leaving the preceding digit unchanged if the dropped digit was 4 or less. **69. round down,** *Naut.* to separate the blocks of (a tackle) by pulling down on the lower one. **70. round in,** *Naut.* **a.** to haul in rope. **b.** to draw together the blocks of (a tackle). **71. round off, a.** to complete or perfect; finish. **b.** to express as a round number, usually to the nearest multiple of 10. **72. round out, a.** to complete or perfect: *The new coin rounded out his collection.* **b.** to fill out; become rounder: *She rounded out so nicely that they offered her a part as a chorus girl.* **73. round to,** *Naut.* to turn a sailing vessel in the direction from which the wind is blowing. **74. round up, a.** to drive or bring (cattle, sheep, etc.) together. **b.** to assemble; gather: *to round up all the suspects in an investigation.* **c.** *Naut.* to round in (a tackle). [ME < OF *rond* << L *rotund(us)* wheel-shaped; see ROTUND] —**round′ness,** *n.*
—**Syn. 9.** whole, unbroken. **22.** cylinder. **24.** cycle, revolution, period. —**Ant. 1.** angular.

round[2] (round), *v.t., v.i. Archaic.* to whisper. [ME *roun(en),* OE *rūnian,* cf. *rūn* a secret]

round·a·bout (round′ə bout′), *adj.* **1.** circuitous or indirect, as a road, journey, method, statement, person, etc. **2.** (of clothing) cut circularly at the bottom; having no tails, train, or the like. —*n.* **3.** a short, close-fitting coat or jacket, without skirts, for men or boys. **4.** *Chiefly Brit.* a merry-go-round. **5.** a circuitous or indirect road, method, etc. **6.** *Brit.* See **traffic circle.** [ROUND[1] + ABOUT]

round′about chair′. See **corner chair.**

round′ an′gle, perigon.

round′ arch′, an arch formed in a continuous curve, esp. in a semicircle.

round-built (round′bilt′), *adj. Naut.* (of a vessel) having a high ratio of beam to length.

round′ clam′, quahog.

round′ dance′, 1. a dance performed by couples and characterized by circular or revolving movement, as the waltz. **2.** a dance in which the dancers are arranged in or move about in a circle or ring.

round·ed (roun′did), *adj.* **1.** reduced to simple curves; made round. **2.** *Phonet.* pronounced with rounded lips; labialized: *"Boot" has a rounded vowel.* Cf. **spread** (def. 36), **unrounded. 3.** fully developed or characterized; presented as complete or having realized all potentialities, as a character in a play or a person living a well-balanced life. **4.** round (def. 11). [ME; see ROUND[1], -ED[2]] —**round′ed·ly,** *adv.* —**round′ed·ness,** *n.*

roun·del (roun′dəl), *n.* **1.** something round or circular. **2.** a small, round pane or window. **3.** a decorative plate, panel, tablet, or the like, round in form. **4.** Also, **rondel.** *Theat.* a round piece of colored gelatin or glass placed over stage lights as a color medium to obtain lighting effects. **5.** *Armor.* **a.** a metal disk that protects the armpit. **b.** a metal disk on a hafted weapon or a dagger to protect the hand. **6.** *Heraldry.* a small circular charge. **7.** *Pros.* **a.** a rondel or rondeau. **b.** a modification of the rondeau, consisting of nine lines with two refrains. **8.** a dance in a circle or ring; round dance. [ME *roundele* < OF *rondel,* deriv. of *rond* ROUND[1] (adj.)]

roun·de·lay (roun′də lā′), *n.* **1.** a song in which a phrase, line, or the like, is continually repeated. **2.** the music for such a song. **3.** a dance in a circle; round dance. [m. (influenced by LAY[4]) MF *rondelet,* dim. of *rondel* ROUNDEL]

round·er (roun′dər), *n.* **1.** one who or that which rounds something. **2.** one who makes a round. **3.** a habitual drunkard or wastrel. **4.** (*cap.*) *Brit.* a Methodist minister who travels a circuit among his congregations. **5. rounders,** (*construed as sing.*) a game somewhat resembling baseball, played in England. [ROUND[1] + -ER[1]]

round-faced (round′fāst′), *adj.* having a face that is round.

round′ hand′, a style of handwriting in which the letters are round, full, and clearly separated.

Round·head (round′hed′), *n. Eng. Hist.* a member or adherent of the Parliamentarians or Puritan party during the civil wars of the 17th century (so called in derision by the Cavaliers because they wore their hair cut short). [ROUND[1] + HEAD]

round·head·ed (round′hed′id), *adj.* **1.** (of a person) possessing a round head; brachycephalic. **2.** rounded or spherical at the head, as a screw. **3.** shaped like a semicircle at the top, as a window. **4.** (*usually cap.*) of or pertaining to the Roundheads. **5.** (*usually cap.*) puritanical (def. 2). [ROUND[1] + -HEADED] —**round′head′ed·ness,** *n.*

round′headed ap′ple tree′ bor′er. See **apple tree borer** (def. 2).

round′headed bor′er, the wood-boring larva of a long-horned beetle, having a small, round head.

round·heel (round′hēl′), *n. Slang.* one who is easily influenced or overcome, esp. a sexually compliant woman. [ROUND[1] + HEEL[1]]

round′ her′ring, any of several clupeoid fishes of the family *Dussumieriidae,* having a rounded abdomen, found chiefly in tropical, marine waters.

round·house (round′hous′), *n., pl.* **-hous·es** (-hou′ziz). **1.** a building for the servicing and repair of locomotives, built around a turntable in the form of some part of a circle. **2.** *Naut.* a cabin on the after part of a quarterdeck. **3.** *Slang.* a punch in which the arm is typically brought straight out to the side or rear of the body and in which the fist describes an exaggerated circular motion. **4.** Also called **round trip.** *Pinochle.* a meld of one king and queen of each suit. [ROUND[1] + HOUSE]

round·ing (roun′diṅg), *adj.* **1.** round or nearly round. **2.** of, pertaining to, or used for making something round. **3.** turning, curving, or circling around. —*n.* **4.** *Naut.* old cord or the like wrapped around a line to protect it against chafing. **5.** the act or process of making something round. [ROUND[1] + -ING[2], -ING[1]]

round′ing adz′, an adz used by coopers.

round·ish (roun′dish), *adj.* somewhat round: *He is rather roundish. Her furniture is roundish.* [ROUND[1] + -ISH[1]] —**round′ish·ness,** *n.*

round′ kum′quat, an evergreen shrub or small tree, *Fortunella japonica,* of Japan, having blunt, broad leaves and globe-shaped, edible fruit. Also called **marumi kumquat.**

Round′ Lake′ Beach′, a town in NE Illinois. 5011 (1960).

Round′ Lake′ Park′, a town in NE Illinois. 2565 (1960).

round·let (round′lit), *n.* a small circle or circular object. [ME *rondlet* < MF *rondelet;* see ROUNDELAY]

round·line (round′līn′), *n. Naut.* right-laid, three-stranded, tarred hemp cordage. [ROUND[1] + LINE[1]]

round′ lot′, *Stock Exchange.* **1.** the conventional unit or quantity in which commodities or securities are bought and sold. **2.** (in a transaction) a quantity of 100 shares of a stock that is active or 10 shares of a stock that is inactive. Cf. **odd lot.**

round·ly (round′lē), *adv.* **1.** in a round manner. **2.** vigorously or briskly. **3.** outspokenly, severely, or unsparingly. **4.** completely or fully. **5.** in round numbers or in a vague or general way. [ROUND[1] + -LY]

round′ of beef′, round (def. 36).

round′ rob′in, 1. a sequence or series. **2.** a petition, remonstrance, or the like, having the signatures arranged in circular form so as to disguise the order of signing. **3.** a letter, notice, or the like, circulated from person to person in a group, often with individual comments being added by each. **4.** *Sports.* a tournament in which all of the entrants play each other at least once, failure to win a contest not resulting in elimination.

round-shoul·dered (round′shōl′dərd, -shōl′-), *adj.* having the shoulders bent forward, giving a rounded form to the upper part of the back.

rounds·man (roundz′mən), *n., pl.* **-men. 1.** one who makes rounds, as of inspection. **2.** *Brit.* a deliveryman, as of milk, bread, etc. **3.** a police officer who inspects the policemen on duty in a particular district. [ROUND[1] + 's[1] + MAN[1]]

round′ steak′, a steak cut from directly above the hind leg of beef.

round′ ta′ble, 1. a number of persons gathered together for conference, discussion of some subject, etc., and often seated at a round table. **2.** the discussion, topic of discussion, or the conference itself. **3.** (*cap.*) *Arthurian Romance.* **a.** the famous table, made round to avoid quarrels as to precedence, about which King Arthur and his knights sat. **b.** King Arthur and his knights as a body.

round-ta·ble (round′tā′bəl), *adj.* noting or pertaining to a conference, discussion, or deliberation in which each participant has equal status, equal time to present his views, etc.: *round-table discussion.*

round-the-clock (round′thə klok′), *adj.* around-the-clock.

round′ trip′, 1. a trip to a given place and back again: *Fares for round trips often have a discount.* **2.** a transportation ticket for such a trip. **3.** *Pinochle.* roundhouse (def. 4). —**round′-trip′,** *adj.*

round-trip·per (round′trip′ər), *n. Baseball Slang.* a home run. [ROUND TRIP + -ER[1]]

round′ turn′, 1. a complete turn of a rope or the like around an object. **2. round turn in the hawse,** *Naut.* the state of a pair of anchor cables mooring a vessel which has rotated with the tides in one direction until the cables are completely wrapped around each other.

round·up (round′up′), *n.* **1.** the driving together of cattle, horses, etc., for inspection, branding, shipping to market, or the like, as in the western U.S. **2.** the men and horses who do this. **3.** the herd so collected. **4.** the gathering together of scattered items or groups of people: *a police roundup of suspects.* **5.** a summary, brief listing, or résumé of related facts, figures, or information: *Sunday's newspaper has a sports roundup giving the final score of every baseball game of the past week.* [n. use of v. phrase *round up*]

Round·up (round′up′), *n.* a town in central Montana. 2842 (1960).

round′ white′fish, a whitefish, *Prosopium cylindraceum,* found in northern North America and Siberia, having silvery sides and a dark bronze back. Also called **Menominee whitefish.**

round·worm (round′wûrm′), *n.* any nematode, esp. *Ascaris lumbricoides,* which infests the intestine of man and other mammals. [ROUND[1] + WORM]

roup[1] (ro͞op), *n. Vet. Pathol.* any catarrhal inflammation of the eyes and nasal passages of poultry. [?]

roup[2] (ro͞op), *n.* hoarseness or huskiness. [prob. imit.]

roup[3] (roup), *n., v.t. Scot. and North Eng.* auction (defs. 1, 3). [ME *roup(en)* (to) cry, shout < Scand cf. Icel *raupa* to boast]

roup·et (ro͞o′pit, ro͞o′-), *adj. Scot.* roupy[2]. [ROUP[2] + *-et,* var. of -ED[3]]

roup·y[1] (ro͞o′pē), *adj.* affected with the disease roup. [ROUP[1] + -Y[1]] —**roup′i·ly,** *adv.*

roup·y[2] (ro͞o′pē), *adj.,* **roup·i·er, roup·i·est.** hoarse or husky. [ROUP[2] + -Y[1]]

rous·ant (rou′zənt), *adj. Heraldry.* rising (def. 3). [ROUSE[1] + -ANT]

rouse[1] (rouz), *v.,* **roused, rous·ing,** *n.* —*v.t.* **1.** to bring out of a state of sleep, unconsciousness, inactivity, fancied security, apathy, depression, etc.: *He was roused to action by courageous words.* **2.** to stir or incite to strong indignation or anger. **3.** to cause (game) to start from a covert or lair. **4.** *Naut.* to pull by main strength; haul. —*v.i.* **5.** to come out of a state of sleep, unconsciousness, inactivity, apathy, depression, etc. **6.** to start up from a covert or lair, as game. **7. rouse and bitt!** *Naut.* wake up and turn out! **8. rouse out,** *Naut.* to awaken and turn (a seaman or group of seamen) out. —*n.* **9.** a rousing. **10.** a signal for rousing; reveille. [late ME] —**rous·ed·ness** (rou′zid nis), *n.* —**rous′er,** *n.*
—**Syn. 1.** arouse, stir, excite, animate, stimulate, awaken, kindle, inflame, fire. **2.** provoke, anger. —**Ant. 1, 2.** lull, calm, pacify.

rouse[2] (rouz), *n.* **1.** *Archaic.* a carouse. **2.** *Obs.* a bumper of liquor. [? var. of CAROUSE (*drink carouse* being wrongly analyzed as *drink a rouse*)]

rous·ing (rou′ziṅg), *adj.* **1.** exciting; stirring: *a rousing song.* **2.** active or vigorous: *a rousing campaign.* **3.** brisk; lively: *a rousing trade.* **4.** great of its kind; extraordinary: *a rousing lie.* [ROUSE[1] + -ING[2]] —**rous′ing·ly,** *adv.*

Rous·seau (ro͞o sō′; *Fr.* ro͞o sō′), *n.* **1. Hen·ri** (äN rē′), ("*Le Douanier*"), 1844–1910, French painter. **2. Jean Jacques** (zhäN zhäk), 1712–78, French philosopher, author, and social reformer; born in Switzerland. **3. (Pierre É·tienne) The·o·dore** (pyeR ā tyen′ te ô dôR′), 1812–67, French painter.

Rous·seau·ism (ro͞o sō′iz əm), *n.* the doctrines or principles of Jean Jacques Rousseau or his adherents. [ROUSSEAU + -ISM] —**Rous·seau′ist, Rous·seau′ite,** *n.* —**Rous′seau·is′tic,** *adj.*

Rous·sel (ro͞o sel′), *n.* **Al·bert (Charles Paul Ma·ri)** (al beR′ shaRl pôl mA Rē′), 1869–1937, French composer.

roust·a·bout (rous′tə bout′), *n.* **1.** a wharf laborer or deck hand, as on the Mississippi River. **2.** an unskilled laborer who lives by odd jobs. **3.** a circus laborer who helps in setting up and taking down the tents and in caring for the animals, equipment, and grounds. **4.** *Slang.* any unskilled laborer working in an oil field. Cf. **roughneck** (def. 2). [*roust* to rout out (? alter. of ROUSE[1]) + ABOUT]

rout[1] (rout), *n.* **1.** a defeat attended with disorderly flight; dispersal of a defeated force in complete disorder: *to put an army to rout; to put reason to rout.* **2.** a tumultuous or disorderly crowd of persons. **3.** the rabble or mob. **4.** *Law.* a disturbance of the public peace by three or more persons acting together in a manner that suggests an intention to riot although they do not actually carry out the intention. **5.** a large, formal evening party or social gathering. **6.** *Archaic.* a company or band of people. —*v.t.* **7.** to disperse in defeat and disorderly flight: *to rout an army.* **8.** to defeat decisively: *to rout an opponent in conversation.* [ME < AF *rute* << L *rupta* broken, fem. ptp. of *rumpere*]
—**Syn. 3.** swarm, horde. **8.** overwhelm, overcome, subdue.

rout[2] (rout), *v.i.* **1.** to root, as swine. **2.** to poke, search, or rummage. —*v.t.* **3.** to turn over or dig up (something) with the snout, as swine. **4.** to find or get by searching, rummaging, etc. (usually fol. by *out*). **5.** to cause to rise from bed (often fol. by *up* or *out*). **6.** to force or drive out. **7.** to hollow out or furrow, as with a scoop, gouge, or machine. [alter. of ROOT[2]; cf. MD *ruten* to root out]

rout[3] (rout), *v.i. Archaic.* to snore. [ME *rout(en),* OE *hrūtan;* c. OHG *hrūzan*]

rout[4] (rout, ro͞ot), *Chiefly Brit. Dial.* —*v.i., v.t.* **1.** to bellow; roar. —*n.* **2.** a bellow. Also **rowt, rowte.** [ME *rowt(en)* < Scand; see ROOT[3]]

route (ro͞ot, rout), *n., v.,* **rout·ed, rout·ing.** —*n.* **1.** a course, way, or road for passage or travel: *What's the shortest route to Boston?* **2.** a customary or regular line of passage or travel: *a ship on the North Atlantic route.* **3.** a specific territory, round, or number of stops regularly visited by a person in the performance of his work or duty, as by a vender, deliveryman, or the like. **4.** *Med.* the area of the body through which a curative is introduced: *the digestive route.* **5. go the route, a.** to see something through to completion: *It was a tough assignment, but he went the route.* **b.** *Baseball Slang.* to pitch the complete game: *The heat and the sun were intolerable, but the pitcher managed to go the route.* —*v.t.* **6.** to fix the route of: *to route a tour.* **7.** to send or forward by a particular route: *to route mail to its proper destination.* [ME < OF << L *rupta* (via) broken (road), fem. ptp. of *rumpere* to break] —**rout′er,** *n.*

route·man (ro͞ot′mən, rout′-), *n., pl.* **-men. 1.** a person who works in a specified area or covers a specific route, as a postman, truckdriver, etc. **2.** a supervisor who establishes a route, as for deliverymen, maintains office records, and handles customer relations for it. **3.** a person who routes work among a group of employees, as in a plant or shipyard. [ROUTE + MAN[1]]

rout·er (rou′tər), *n.* **1.** any of various tools or machines for routing, hollowing out, or furrowing. **2.** Also called **rout′er plane′.** *Carpentry.* a plane for cutting interior angles, as at the bottom of a groove. **3.** a machine or tool for cutting into or below a main surface, as of a die or engraving plate. —*v.t.* **4.** to cut with a router. [ROUT[2] + -ER[1]]

rout′er patch′, a plywood panel patch with parallel sides and rounded ends.

route′ sur′vey, a survey for determining the route, grades, etc., of a railroad, highway, power line, or the like.

routh (ro͞oth, routh), *n. Scot. and North Eng.* abundance; plenty. [?]

rou·tine (ro͞o tēn′), *n.* **1.** a customary or regular course of procedure. **2.** commonplace tasks, chores, or duties as must be done regularly or at specified intervals: *the routine of an office.* **3.** regular, unvarying, habitual, or unimaginative procedure. **4.** an unvarying and constantly repeated formula, as of speech or action: *Don't give me that brotherly-love routine!* **5.** *Computer Technol.* **a.** a complete set of coded instructions directing a computer to perform a series of operations. **b.** a series of operations performed by the computer. **6.** an individual act, performance, or part of a performance, as a song or dance, given regularly by an entertainer: *a comic routine; a dance routine.* —*adj.* **7.** of the nature of, proceeding by, or adhering to routine: *routine duties.* [< F, deriv. of *route* ROUTE] —**rou·tine′ly,** *adv.*

rout·ing (ro͞o′ting, rou′-), *n.* **1.** the scheduling of the route or itinerary of people, freight, etc. **2.** the arranging and scheduling of mail for delivery. **3.** delivery according to scheduled sequence. [ROUTE + -ING[1]]

rou·tin·ism (ro͞o tē′niz əm), *n.* adherence to routine. [ROUTINE + -ISM] —**rou·tin·ist** (ro͞o tē′nist), *n.*

rou·tin·ize (ro͞o tē′nīz), *v.t.*, **-ized, -iz·ing. 1.** to develop into a regular procedure. **2.** to reduce to a customary procedure: *He seems happier now that his life is thoroughly routinized.* [ROUTINE + -IZE]

roux (ro͞o), *n.* a mixture of fat and flour used to thicken sauces. [< F: browned, reddish << L *russ(us)*, akin to *ruber* RED]

Ro·va·ni·e·mi (rô′vä nē e mē), *n.* a city in N Finland, near the Arctic Circle. 25,743 (est. 1965).

rove[1] (rōv), *v.*, **roved, rov·ing,** *n.* —*v.i.* **1.** to wander about without definite destination; move hither and thither at random, esp. over a wide area. —*v.t.* **2.** to wander over or through; traverse: *to rove the woods.* —*n.* **3.** the act of roving. [ME *rove(n)* < Scand; cf. Icel *rāfa*] —**rov′ing·ly,** *adv.* —**rov′ing·ness,** *n.*
—**Syn. 1.** stroll, amble, stray. See **roam.**

rove[2] (rōv), *v.* a pt. and pp. of **reeve**[2].

rove[3] (rōv), *v.*, **roved, rov·ing,** *n.* —*v.t.* **1.** to form (slivers of wool, cotton, etc.) into slightly twisted strands in a preparatory process of spinning. **2.** to draw fibers or the like through an eye or other small opening. **3.** to attenuate, compress, and twist slightly in carding. —*n.* **4.** *Brit.* roving[1]. [?]

rove[4] (rōv), *n.* roove (def. 1).

rove′ bee′tle, any of numerous beetles of the family *Staphylinidae*, having a slender, elongated body and very short elytra, and capable of running swiftly.

rove-o·ver (rōv′ō′vər), *adj. Pros.* (in sprung rhythm) of or pertaining to the completion of a metrical foot, incomplete at the end of one line, with a syllable or syllables from the beginning of the next line.

rove′ punch′, *Shipbuilding.* a punch for clenching nails after they have been rooved. Also called **rove′ i′ron, roving iron.**

rov·er[1] (rō′vər), *n.* **1.** one who roves; wanderer. **2.** *Archery.* **a.** a mark selected at random. **b.** one of a group of fixed marks at a long distance. **c.** an archer who shoots from a distance. **3.** *Croquet.* a ball that has been driven through all the arches and needs only to strike the last peg to be out of the game. **4.** *Brit.* **a.** (at concerts or the like) a person who has a ticket for standing room only. **b.** a senior boy scout, 18 years of age or older. [ROVE[1] + -ER[1]]

rov·er[2] (rō′vər), *n.* **1.** a pirate. **2.** *Obs.* a pirate ship. [ME < MD or MLG: robber, equiv. to *rov(en)* (to) rob + *-er* -ER[1]]

rov·er[3] (rō′vər), *n.* **1.** a roving or routing machine. **2.** a roving-machine operator. [ROVE[3] + -ER[1]]

Ro·ver (rō′vər), *n. U.S.* a familiar name for a dog.

Rov′er Boy′, a courageous and principled person who is somewhat naïve and inexperienced: *Although now an old man, he was the perennial Rover Boy.* [after the heroes of the *Rover Boys* series, American children's books by Edward Stratemeyer (1862–1930)]

rov·ing[1] (rō′ving), *n.* **1.** a soft strand of fiber that has been twisted, attenuated, and freed of foreign matter preparatory to its conversion into yarn. **2.** the final phase of carding in which this is done. [ROVE[3] + -ING[1]]

rov·ing[2] (rō′ving), *n. Naut.* roband.

rov′ing i′ron. See **rove punch.**

row[1] (rō), *n.* **1.** a number of persons or things arranged in a line, esp. a straight line: *a row of apple trees.* **2.** a line of adjacent seats facing the same way, as in a theater: *seats in the third row of the balcony.* **3.** a street formed by two continuous lines of buildings. **4.** *Music.* See **tone row. 5.** *Checkers.* one of the horizontal lines of squares on a checkerboard; rank. **6. hard** or **long row to hoe,** a difficult task or set of circumstances: *At 32 and with a wife and two children, he found attending medical school a hard row to hoe.* —*v.t.* **7.** to put in a row (often fol. by *up*). [ME *row(e)*, OE *rāw;* akin to Lith *raiwe* stripe, L *rīma* cleft, fissure]

row[2] (rō), *v.i.* **1.** to propel a vessel by the leverage of an oar or the like. —*v.t.* **2.** to propel (a vessel) by the leverage of an oar or the like. **3.** to convey in a boat that is rowed. **4.** to convey or propel (something) in a manner suggestive of rowing. **5.** to employ, use, or be equipped with (a number of oars): *The captain's barge rowed twenty oars.* **6.** to use (oarsmen) for rowing. **7.** to perform or participate in by rowing: *to row a race.* **8.** to row against in a race: *Oxford rows Cambridge.* —*n.* **9.** the act or an instance or period of rowing: *It was a long row to the far bank.* **10.** an excursion in a rowboat: *to go for a row.* [ME *row(en)*, OE *rowan;* c. OIcel *rōa;* akin to L *rēmus* oar. See RUDDER] —**row′a·ble,** *adj.* —**row′er,** *n.*

row[3] (rou), *n.* **1.** a noisy dispute or quarrel; commotion. **2.** *Informal.* noise or clamor. —*v.i.* **3.** *Informal.* to quarrel noisily. —*v.t.* **4.** *Informal.* to upbraid severely; scold. [?]

row·an (rō′ən, rou′-), *n.* **1.** the European mountain ash, *Sorbus Aucuparia*, having red berries. **2.** either of two American mountain ashes, *Sorbus americana* or *S. sambucifolia.* **3.** the berry of any of these trees. [< Scand; cf Norw *raun*, OIcel *reynir*]

row·boat (rō′bōt′), *n.* a small boat designed for rowing. [ROW[2] + BOAT]

row·dy (rou′dē), *n., pl.* **-dies,** *adj.*, **-di·er, -di·est.** —*n.* **1.** a rough, disorderly person. —*adj.* **2.** rough and disorderly: *rowdy behavior at school.* [? irreg. from ROW[3]] —**row′di·ly,** *adv.* —**row′di·ness,** *n.*

row·dy·ish (rou′dē ish), *adj.* **1.** like or characteristic of a rowdy. **2.** disposed to or characterized by rowdyism. [ROWDY + -ISH[1]] —**row′dy·ish·ly,** *adv.* —**row′dy·ish·ness,** *n.*

row·dy·ism (rou′dē iz′əm), *n.* rough, disorderly behavior. [ROWDY + -ISM]

Rowe (rō), *n.* **Nicholas,** 1674–1718, British poet and dramatist, poet laureate 1715–18.

rowed′ of all′! (rōd), *Naut. Obs.* (to oarsmen) cease rowing!

row·el (rou′əl), *n., v.*, **-eled, -el·ing** or (*esp. Brit.*) **-elled, -el·ling.** —*n.* **1.** a small wheel with radiating points, forming the extremity of a horseman's spur. **2.** *Vet. Pathol.* a piece of leather or the like inserted beneath the skin of a horse or other animal to cause a discharge. —*v.t.* **3.** to prick or urge with a rowel. **4.** *Vet. Pathol.* to insert a rowel in. [ME *rowelle* < MF *ruelle*, OF *roel*, dim. of *roe, roue* wheel < L *rota*]

row·en (rou′ən), *n.* the second crop of grass or hay in a season; aftermath. [ME *reywayn* < ONF **rewain;* c. F *regain*]

Ro·we·na (rō wē′nə), *n.* a girl's given name.

row′ house′ (rō), **1.** one of a continuous row of houses having uniform, or nearly uniform, plans and fenestration, and usually having a uniform architectural treatment, as in certain housing developments. **2.** a house having at least one side wall in common with its neighbor; a house joined to another house by a common side wall.

row′ing boat′ (rō′ing), *Brit.* rowboat.

row′ing port′ (rō′ing), an opening in the side of a vessel for an oar to pass through.

Row·land·son (rō′lənd sən), *n.* **Thomas,** 1756–1827, English caricaturist.

row·lock (rol′ək, rul′- *for 1, 2;* rō′lok′ *for 3*), *n.* **1.** *Archit.* one of several concentric rings of masonry forming an arch. **2.** a brick laid on edge, esp. as a header. Cf. **soldier** (def. 6). **3.** *Chiefly Brit.* oarlock. Also, **rollock** (for defs. 1, 2). [var. of OARLOCK, by assoc. with ROW[2]]

rowte (rout), *v.i., v.t.*, **rowt·ed, rowt·ing,** *n. Brit. Dial.* rout[4]. Also, **rowt.**

row′ vec′tor (rō), *Math.* a collection of numbers, as the components of a vector, written horizontally. Cf. **column vector.**

Rox·an·a (rok san′ə), *n.* a girl's given name.

Rox·ane (rok san′), *n.* a girl's given name, French form of **Roxana.**

Rox·as (rō′häs; *Sp.* rô′häs), *n.* **Ma·nuel** (mä nwel′), 1892–1948, Philippine statesman: 1st president of the Philippines 1946–48.

Rox·bor·o (roks′bûr′ō, -bur′ō), *n.* a town in N North Carolina. 5147 (1960).

Rox·burgh (roks′bûr′ō, -bur′ō *or, esp. Brit.*, -brə), *n.* a county in SE Scotland. 43,171 (1961); 666 sq. mi. *Co. seat:* Jedburgh. Also called **Rox·burgh·shire** (roks′-bûr′ō shēr′, -shər, -bur′ō, -brə).

Rox·ie (rok′sē), *n.* a girl's given name, form of **Roxana.** Also, **Rox′i.**

Ro·y (rō′ē *for 1;* roi *for 2–4*), *n.* **1. Ram·mo·hun** (rä mō′hon), 1774–1833, Indian religious leader: founder of Brahmo Samaj. **2.** a town in N Utah. 9239 (1960). **3.** Rollo (def. 1). **4.** Also, **Ray.** a boy's given name.

roy·al (roi′əl), *adj.* **1.** of or pertaining to a king, queen, or other sovereign: *royal power; a royal palace.* **2.** descendent from or related to a king or line of kings: *a royal prince.* **3.** noting or having the rank of a king or queen. **4.** established or chartered by or existing under the patronage of a sovereign: *a royal society.* **5.** (*cap.*) serving or subject to a king, queen, or other sovereign. **6.** proceeding from or performed by a sovereign: *a royal warrant.* **7.** appropriate to or befitting a sovereign; kinglike or princely; magnificent; stately: *royal splendor.* **8.** (*usually cap.*) *Brit.* in the service of the monarch or of the Commonwealth: *Royal Marines; Royal Air Force.* **9.** *Informal.* fine; excellent: *in royal spirits.* **10.** beyond the common or ordinary in size, quality, etc. —*n.* **11.** *Naut.* a sail set on a royal mast. **12.** a size of printing paper, 19 × 28 to 20 × 25 inches. Cf. **double royal, super royal. 13.** *Chiefly Brit.* a size of drawing or writing paper, 19 × 24 inches. **14.** *Numis.* any of various former coins, as the real or ryal. **15. royal octavo,** a size of book, about 6¼ × 10 inches, untrimmed. *Abbr.:* royal 8vo **16. royal quarto,** *Chiefly Brit.* a size of book, about 10 × 12½ inches, untrimmed. *Abbr.:* royal 4to **17. super royal octavo,** a size of book: about 7 × 11 inches, untrimmed, in America; 6¾ × 10¼ inches, untrimmed, in England. *Abbr.:* super roy. 8vo **18. super royal quarto,** *Chiefly Brit.* a size of book, about 10¼ × 13½ inches, untrimmed. *Abbr.:* super roy. 4to [ME < MF < L *rēgāl(is)* kingly, equiv. to *rēg-* (s. of *rēx*) king + *-ālis* -AL[1]] —**roy′al·ly,** *adv.*
—**Syn. 7.** majestic. See **kingly.** —**Ant. 7.** servile.

Roy·al (roi′əl), *n.* a boy's given name.

Roy′al Acad′emy, a society founded in 1768 by George III of England for the establishment of a school of design and the holding of an annual exhibition of the works of living artists.

roy′al ant′ler, the third prong from the base of a stag's antler. Also called **tres-tine, trez-tine.** See diag. under **antler.**

roy′al blue′, a deep blue, often with a faint reddish tinge.

Roy′al Cana′dian, in the service of the Canadian federal government and the British monarch: *Royal Canadian Air Force; Royal Canadian Mounted Police.* Also, **roy′al Cana′dian.**

roy′al coach′man, *Angling.* a type of artificial fly, used chiefly for trout and salmon.

roy′al col′ony, 1. a colony ruled or administered by officials appointed by and responsible to the reigning sovereign of the parent state. **2.** *Amer. Hist.* a colony, as New York, administered by a royal governor and council appointed by the British crown, and having a representative assembly elected by the people. Cf. **charter colony.**

roy′al duke′, *Brit.* a hereditary title bestowed on male members of the royal family, esp. a son of the reigning monarch.

roy·ale (roi al′), *n.* custard cut into shapes and used as a garnish in soups. [< F, n. use of fem. of *royal* ROYAL]

roy′al fern′, a fern, *Osmunda regalis*, having tall, upright fronds.

roy′al fizz′, a beverage consisting of gin, lemon juice, sugar, and an egg.

roy′al flush′, *Poker.* the five highest cards of a suit.

Roy′al High′ness, 1. (*in England*) **a.** a title used prior to 1917 and designating a brother, sister, child, grandchild, aunt, or uncle belonging to the male line of the royal family. **b.** a title used since 1917 and designating a child or grandchild of the sovereign. **c.** any person given this title by the Crown. **2.** (*in other countries*) a person who is a member of a royal family.

Roy′al In′stitute of Brit′ish Ar′chitects, the principal association of architects in Great Britain, founded in 1834 and organized under its present title in 1866. *Abbr.:* R.I.B.A.

roy·al·ise (roi′ə līz′), *v.t., v.i.*, **-ised, -is·ing.** *Chiefly Brit. Archaic.* royalize. —**roy′al·i·sa′tion,** *n.*

roy·al·ist (roi′ə list), *n.* **1.** a supporter or adherent of a king or royal government, esp. in times of rebellion or civil war. **2.** (*cap.*) a Cavalier adherent of Charles I of England. **3.** a loyalist in the American Revolution; Tory. **4.** (*cap.*) an adherent of the house of Bourbon in France. —*adj.* **5.** of or pertaining to royalists: *royalist sympathies.* [ROYAL + -IST] —**roy′al·ism,** *n.* —**roy′al·is′tic,** *adj.*

roy·al·ize (roi′ə līz′), *v.*, **-ized, -iz·ing.** *Archaic.* —*v.t.* **1.** to render (someone) royal or give (something) royal status. —*v.i.* **2.** to become royal. [ROYAL + -IZE] —**roy′al·i·za′tion,** *n.*

roy′al jel′ly, a viscous aliment secreted from the pharyngeal glands of worker honeybees, fed to all larvae during their first few days and afterwards only to those larvae selected to be queens.

roy′al lil′y, a bulbous herb, *Lilium regale*, of western China, having fragrant flowers about six inches wide which are white inside, lilac-colored or purplish outside, and have a yellow base.

roy′al mar′riage, *Cards.* a meld of the king and queen of trumps, as in pinochle. Cf. **marriage** (def. 5).

roy′al mast′, *Naut.* a mast situated immediately above, and generally formed as a single spar with, a topgallant mast.

Roy′al Oak′, a city in SE Michigan, near Detroit. 80,195 (1960).

roy′al palm′, any of several tall, showy feather palms of the genus *Roystonea*, as *R. regia.*

roy′al pen′dulum. See **seconds pendulum.**

roy′al poincian′a, a showy, leguminous tree, *Delonix regia*, native to Madagascar, having racemes of brilliant scarlet or orange flowers and bearing a flat, woody pod which often grows to a length of two feet. Also called **flamboyant.**

roy′al pole′, *Naut.* a bare portion of a royal mast extending from the royal yard to the truck when no skysails exist.

roy′al pur′ple, a deep bluish purple.

roy′al road′, 1. an easy way or means to achieve something: *the royal road to success.* **2.** a highway in ancient Persia, 1677 miles long, extending from Susa in W Iran to W Asia Minor. Also, **Roy′al Road′.**

Roy′al Soci′ety, The Royal Society of London for the Advancement of Science, a society through which the British government has supported scientific investigation since 1662: it awards four annual medals for scientific achievement and merit.

roy′al ten′nis. See **court tennis.**

roy·al·ty (roi′əl tē), *n., pl.* **-ties. 1.** royal persons collectively. **2.** royal status, dignity, or power; sovereignty: *to be elevated to royalty.* **3.** a person of royal lineage; member of a royal family. **4.** a prerogative or right belonging to a king or other sovereign. **5.** a royal domain; kingdom; realm. **6.** character or quality proper to or befitting a sovereign; kingliness; nobility. **7.** a compensation or portion of the proceeds paid to the owner of a right, as a patent or oil or mineral right, for the use of it. **8.** an agreed portion of the income from a work paid to its author, composer, etc., usually a percentage of the retail price of each copy sold. **8.** a royal right, as over minerals, granted by a sovereign to a person or corporation. **9.** the payment made for such a right. [ME *roialte* < OF. See ROYAL, -TY[2]]

roy′al wa′ter lil′y, an aquatic plant, *Victoria regia*, of the Amazon River and British Guiana, having floating leaves from three to six feet wide, the upturned margins from two to four inches high, and dull crimson flowers. Also called **water platter.**

roy′al "we′", we (def. 5).

Roy′al Worces′ter. See **Worcester china.**

Royce (rois), *n.* **Josiah,** 1855–1916, U.S. philosopher and educator.

Roy·ers·ford (roi′ərz fərd), *n.* a town in SE Pennsylvania. 3969 (1960).

Roy·ette (roi et′), *n.* a girl's given name.

roze·ner (rōz′nər, rō′zə nər), *n. Australian Informal.* any strong alcoholic beverage. [?]

Ro·zi (rō′zē), *n.* a girl's given name, form of **Rosalind.**

Rp., rupiah.

R.P., 1. Reformed Presbyterian. **2.** Regius Professor.

rpm, revolutions per minute. Also, **r.p.m.**

R.P.O., Railway Post Office.

RPQ, request for price quotation.

rps, revolutions per second.

r.p.s., 1. revolutions per second. **2.** Royal Philatelic Society.

rpt., report.

R.Q., respiratory quotient.

r-qual·i·ty (är′kwol′i tē), *n. Phonet.* r-color.

R.R., 1. Railroad. **2.** Right Reverend.

RRB, Railroad Retirement Board.

RRC, Rubber Reserve Company.

-rrhagia, a learned borrowing from Greek meaning "bursting forth," used in the formation of compound words: *bronchorrhagia.* Also, **-rhagia, -rhage, -rrhage, -rhagy, -rrhagy.** [< Gk *-rrhagia*, comb. form akin to *rhēgnýnai* to break, burst, shatter]

-rrhaphy, a learned borrowing from Greek meaning "suture," used in the formation of compound words: *herniorrhaphy.* Also, **-rhaphy.** [< Gk *-rrhaphia* a sewing together]

-rrhea, a learned borrowing from Greek meaning "flow," "discharge," used in the formation of compound words: *gonorrhea.* Also, **-rhea.** Cf. **-rheo-.** [< NL *-rrhoea* < Gk *-rrhoia*, comb. form repr. *rhoîa* a flow]

-rrhexis, a learned borrowing from Greek meaning "rupture," used in the formation of compound words: *enterorrhexis.* [< NL < Gk *rhêxis* a breaking, bursting]

-rrhiza, var. of **rhizo-** as second element of compounds: *mycorrhiza.* Also, **-rhiza.** [< NL < Gk *rhíza* root]

-rrhoea, var. of **-rrhea.**

Rs., 1. reis. **2.** rupees.

R.S., 1. Recording Secretary. **2.** Reformed Spelling.

r.s., right side.

RSFSR, Russian Soviet Federated Socialist Republic. Also, **R.S.F.S.R.**

RSV, Revised Standard Version (of the Bible).

R.S.V.P., the favor of a reply is requested. [< F *r(épondez) s('il) v(ous) p(laît)* please reply] Also, **rsvp, r.s.v.p.**

rt., right.

r.t., *Football.* right tackle.

Rt. Hon., Right Honorable.

Rt. Rev., Right Reverend.

Rts., *Finance.* rights.

Ru, *Chem.* ruthenium.

ru·a·na (ro͞o ä′nə), *n.* a poncholike outer garment of heavy wool, worn esp. in the mountains of Colombia. [< AmerSp, Sp: woolen fabric]

Ru·an·da-U·run·di (ro͞o än′də o͝o ro͞on′dē), *n.* a former territory in central Africa, E of the Republic of the Congo: formerly part of German East Africa; administered by Belgium as a League of Nations mandate 1923–46 and as a United Nations trust territory 1946–62; now divided into the independent states of Rwanda and Burundi.

rub (rub), *v.,* **rubbed, rub·bing,** *n.* —*v.t.* **1.** to subject the surface of (something) to pressure and friction, as in cleaning, smoothing, polishing, etc.; to move one thing back and forth, or with a rotary motion along the surface of (something else): *to rub a table top with wax polish.* **2.** to move, spread, or apply (something) with pressure and friction over something else: *to rub wax polish over a table top.* **3.** to move (two things) with pressure and friction over or back and forth over each other (often fol. by *together*): *He rubbed his hands together.* **4.** to mark, polish, force, move, etc. (something) by pressure and friction (often fol. by *over, in,* or *into*). **5.** to remove by pressure and friction; erase: (often fol. by *off* or *out*). —*v.i.* **6.** to exert pressure and friction on something. **7.** to move with pressure against something. **8.** to admit of being rubbed in a specified manner: *Chalk rubs off easily.* **9.** *Informal.* to proceed, continue in a course, or keep going with effort or difficulty (usually fol. by *on, along,* or *through*): *He rubs along quite well.* **10. rub down, a.** to polish; finish; smooth: *to rub a chair down with sandpaper.* **b.** to give a massage to. **11. rub it in,** *Informal.* to emphasize or reiterate something unpleasant in order to tease or annoy: *The situation was embarrassing enough without having you rub it in.* **12. rub out, a.** to obliterate; erase. **b.** *Slang.* to murder: *They rubbed him out before he could get to the police.* **13. rub the wrong way,** to irritate; offend; annoy: *a manner that seemed to rub everyone the wrong way.* —*n.* **14.** the act or an instance of rubbing: *an alcohol rub.* **15.** something that annoys or irritates one's feelings, as a sharp criticism, a sarcastic remark, or the like: *to resent rubs concerning one's character.* **16.** an annoying experience or circumstance. **17.** an obstacle, impediment, or difficulty: *We'd like to travel, but the rub is that we have no money.* **18.** a rough or abraded area caused by rubbing. [ME *rubbe(n)*; c. Fris *rubben,* Dan *rubbe,* Sw *rubba*]

rub., (in prescriptions) red; ruddy. [< L *ruber*]

rub·a·boo (rub′ə bo͞o′), *n.* *Canadian Hist.* soup made from pemmican, flour, and water: a dish once common among fur trappers, hunters, etc. [?]

rub-a-dub (rub′ə dub′), *n.* the sound of a drum when beaten. [imit.]

Ru′bái·yát of O′mar Khay·yám′, The (ro͞o′bī-yät′, -bē-), *n.* a free translation (first published in 1859) by Edward FitzGerald of a group of quatrains by the Persian poet Omar Khayyám. [< Pers < Ar, fem. pl. of *rubā'iy* quatrain]

Rub′ al Kha·li (*Arab.* ro͝ob′ äl KHä′lē; *Eng.* ro͝ob′ al kä′lē), a desert in S Arabia, N of Hadhramaut and extending from Yemen to Oman. Also called **Ar Rimal, Dahna, Great Sandy Desert.**

ru·basse (ro͞o bas′, -bäs′), *n.* a variety of rock crystal containing minute flakes of iron ore which impart a bright-red color, used as a decorative stone, sometimes imitated with dyes in crackled quartz. [< F *rubace,* appar. deriv. of *rubis* RUBY]

ru·ba·to (ro͞o bä′tō; *It.* ro͞o bä′tô), *adj., n., pl.* **-tos,** *adv. Music.* —*adj.* **1.** having certain notes arbitrarily lengthened while others are correspondingly shortened, or vice versa. —*n.* **2.** a rubato phrase or passage. **3.** a rubato performance. —*adv.* **4.** in a rubato manner. [< It *(tempo) rubato* stolen (time), ptp. of *rubare* to steal < Gmc; see ROB]

rub·ber[1] (rub′ər), *n.* **1.** Also called **India rubber, natural rubber, gum elastic, caoutchouc.** a highly elastic, light cream or dark amber colored, solid substance polymerized by the drying and coagulation of the latex or milky juice of rubber trees and plants, esp. *Hevea* and *Ficus* species, containing the group, $[-CH_2C{=}(CH_3)CHCH_2-]_n$. **2.** a material made by chemically treating and toughening this substance, used in the manufacture of erasers, electrical insulation, elastic bands, crepe soles, toys, water hose, tires, and many other products. **3.** any of various similar substances and materials made synthetically. **4.** See **rubber band. 5.** an eraser of this material, for erasing pencil marks, ink marks, etc. **6.** a low overshoe of this material. **7.** an instrument or tool used for rubbing, polishing, scraping, etc. **8.** a person who rubs something, as to smooth or polish it. **9.** cutter (def. 6). **10.** *Brit.* a dishcloth. **11.** a person who gives massages; masseur or masseuse. **12.** swipe (def. 3). **13.** *Baseball.* an oblong piece of whitened material embedded in the mound at the point from which the pitcher delivers the ball. **14.** a coarse file. **15.** *Slang.* a condom. —*v.i.* **16.** *Informal.* to rubberneck. —*adj.* **17.** made of, containing, or coated with rubber: *a rubber bath mat.* **18.** pertaining to or producing rubber: *a rubber plantation.* [RUB + -ER[1]] —**rub′ber·less,** *adj.* —**rub′ber·like′,** *adj.*

rub·ber[2] (rub′ər) *n.* (in certain card games, as bridge and whist) **1.** a series or round played until one side reaches a specific score or wins a specific number of hands. **2.** a series consisting of an odd number of games won by the side winning the majority, usually two out of three. **3.** the deciding game in such a series. —*adj.* **4.** *Sports.* noting a deciding contest between two opponents who have previously won the same number of contests from each other. [?]

rub′ber band′, a narrow, circular or oblong band of rubber, used for holding things together, as papers, a box and its lid, etc.

rub′ber cement′, a thick, flammable liquid consisting of unvulcanized rubber dispersed in benzene, gasoline, or the like, used chiefly as an adhesive.

rub′ber check′, a check drawn on an account lacking the funds to pay it.

rub·ber-faced (rub′ər fāst′), *adj.* having a face with unusually mobile features: *a rubber-faced comedian.*

rub·ber·ise (rub′ə rīz′), *v.t.,* **-ised, -is·ing.** *Chiefly Brit.* rubberize.

rub·ber·ize (rub′ə rīz′), *v.t.,* **-ized, -iz·ing.** to coat or impregnate with rubber or some preparation of it. [RUBBER[1] + -IZE]

rub′ber la′tex, the milky sap of any of several trees of the genus *Hevea,* esp. *H. brasiliensis,* from which natural rubber is derived.

rub·ber·neck (rub′ər nek′), *Informal.* —*n.* **1.** a person who cranes his neck or turns his head to look at things, esp. in curiosity. **2.** a sightseer; tourist. —*adj.* **3.** pertaining to or for such people: *a rubberneck bus.* —*v.i.* **4.** to look about or stare with great curiosity, as by craning the neck or turning the head. [RUBBER[1] + NECK]

rub′ber plant′, 1. a moraceous plant, *Ficus elastica,* having oblong, shining, leathery leaves, growing native as a tall tree in India, the Malay Archipelago, etc., and cultivated in Europe and America as an ornamental house plant. **2.** any plant yielding caoutchouc or India rubber.

rub′ber stamp′, 1. a device with a rubber printing surface that is coated with ink by pressing it on an ink-saturated pad, used for imprinting dates, addresses, standard messages or notices, etc., by hand. **2.** *Informal.* one who gives approval automatically or without consideration.

rub·ber-stamp (rub′ər stamp′), *v.t.* **1.** to imprint with a rubber stamp. **2.** *Informal.* to give approval automatically or without consideration: *to rubber-stamp the president's proposals.* [v. use of RUBBER STAMP]

rub′ber tree′. See **rubber plant.**

rub·ber·y (rub′ə rē), *adj.* like rubber; elastic; tough. [RUBBER[1] + -Y[1]]

rub·bing (rub′ing), *n.* **1.** the act of one who or that which rubs. **2.** a reproduction of an incised or sculptured surface made by laying paper or the like upon it and rubbing with some marking substance. [ME; see RUB, -ING[1]]

rub′bing al′cohol, an aqueous solution of about 70-percent isopropyl alcohol or a solution of denatured ethyl alcohol, usually containing a perfume oil, used chiefly as a rubefacient and antiseptic.

rub′bing stone′, floatstone.

rub′bing strip′, *Naut.* any of various projecting strakes, strips, bars, etc., of timber or metal placed on a hull to defend it against the shock and friction of contact with piers, piling, etc.; fender.

rub·bish (rub′ish), *n.* **1.** worthless, unwanted material that is rejected or thrown out; debris; litter; trash. **2.** nonsense, as in writing, art, etc.: *sentimental rubbish.* [ME *rubbes, rob(b)ous* < ? Cf. RUBBLE]

rub·bish·y (rub′i shē), *adj.* **1.** full of rubbish: *a rubbishy cellar.* **2.** suggestive of rubbish; trashy: *a rubbishy book.* [RUBBISH + -Y[1]]

rub·ble (rub′əl *or, for 1, 2,* ro͞o′bəl), *n.* **1.** rough fragments of broken stone, formed by geological action, in quarrying, etc., and sometimes used in masonry. **2.** masonry built of rough fragments of broken stone. **3.** any solid substance, as ice, in irregularly broken pieces. **4.** broken bits and pieces of anything, as that which is demolished: *Bombing reduced the town to rubble.* [ME *rubel, robil* < ? Cf. RUBBISH]

rub·ble·work (rub′əl wûrk′, ro͞o′bəl-), *n.* masonry built of rubble or roughly dressed stones. [RUBBLE + WORK]

rub·bly (rub′lē), *adj.,* **-bli·er, -bli·est.** made or consisting of rubble. [RUBBLE + -Y[1]]

rub·down (rub′doun′), *n.* a massage, esp. after exercise or a steam bath. [n. use of v. phrase *rub down*]

rube (ro͞ob), *n.* *Slang.* an unsophisticated countryman; hick. [short for *Reuben,* man's name]

Rube (ro͞ob), *n.* a boy's given name, form of **Reuben.**

ru·be·ba (ro͞o bā′bə), *n.* a medieval fiddle similar to the rebec. [< ML < Ar *rabāb*]

ru·be·fa·cient (ro͞o′bə fā′shənt), *adj.* **1.** causing redness of the skin, as a medicinal application. —*n.* **2.** *Med.* a rubefacient application, as a mustard plaster. [< L *rubefacient-* (s. of *rubefaciēns,* prp. of *rubefacere*), equiv. to *rube(us)* RED + *-facient-* -FACIENT]

ru·be·fac·tion (ro͞o′bə fak′shən), *n.* **1.** the act or process of making red, esp. with a rubefacient. **2.** redness of the skin caused by a rubefacient. [< L *rubefact(us)* made red (ptp. of *rubefacere;* see RUBEFACIENT) + -ION]

Rube′ Gold′berg, 1. having a fantastically complicated, improvised appearance: *a Rube Goldberg arrangement of flasks and test tubes.* **2.** deviously complex and impractical: *a Rube Goldberg scheme for reducing taxes.* Also, **Goldbergian, Rube′ Goldberg′ian.** [named after *Rube (Reuben)* GOLDBERG]

ru·bel·la (ro͞o bel′ə), *n.* *Pathol.* See **German measles.** [< NL < L: reddish (neut. pl. of *rubellus*), equiv. to *rub(er)* red + *-ell-* dim. suffix + *-a* -A]

ru·bel·lite (ro͞o bel′īt, ro͞o′bə līt′), *n.* a deep-red variety of tourmaline, used as a gem. [< L *rubell(us)* reddish (see RUBELLA) + -ITE[1]]

Ru·ben (ro͞o′bən), *n.* **1.** *Douay Bible.* Reuben (defs. 1, 2). **2.** a boy's given name, form of **Reuben.**

Ru·ben·isme (RY be nēs′mᵊ), *n.* *French.* (in fine arts) the doctrine, advocated in the French Academy during the late 17th and early 18th centuries, that painting is primarily concerned with the imitation of nature and that color, as the chief instrument for effecting this imitation, should have status equal or superior to that of line. Also, **Ru·ben·ism** (ro͞o′bə-niz′əm). Cf. **Poussinisme.**

Ru·ben·iste (RY be nēst′), *n.* *French.* a follower and adherent of *Rubenisme.* Also, **Ru·ben·ist** (ro͞o′bə nist).

Ru·bens (ro͞o′bənz; *Flem.* RY′bəns), *n.* **Pe·ter Paul** (pē′tər pôl; *Flem.* pā′tər poul), 1577–1640, Flemish painter. —**Ru′ben·esque′, Ru·ben·si·an** (ro͞o ben′zē-ən), *adj.*

ru·be·o·la (ro͞o bē′ə lə, ro͞o′bē ō′lə), *n.* *Pathol.* **1.** measles. **2.** See **German measles.** [< NL, equiv. to L *rube(us)* reddish (deriv. of *ruber;* see RUBY) + *-ol-* dim. suffix + *-a* -A] —**ru·be′o·lar,** *adj.*

ru·bes·cent (ro͞o bes′ənt), *adj.* becoming red; blushing. [< L *rubescent-* (s. of *rubescēns,* prp. of *rubescere*), equiv. to *rub(ēre)* (to) be red (deriv. of *ruber* red; see RUBY) + *-esc-* inceptive suffix + *-ent-* -ENT] —**ru·bes′cence,** *n.*

ru·bi·a·ceous (ro͞o′bē ā′shəs), *adj.* belonging to the *Rubiaceae,* or madder family of plants, comprising the coffee, cinchona, and ipecac plants, the gardenia, partridgeberry, houstonia, bedstraw, etc. [< NL *Rubiace(ae)* name of family, equiv. to *Rubi(a)* name of genus (L *rubia* madder, deriv. of *rubeus* reddish) + *-aceae* -ACEAE + -OUS]

ru·bi·celle (ro͞o′bi sel′), *n.* *Mineral.* any of the yellow to orange-red varieties of spinel used as gems. [prob. < F *rubacelle,* dim. of *rubace* RUBASSE]

Ru·bi·con (ro͞o′bə kon′), *n.* **1.** a river in N Italy flowing E into the Adriatic. 15 mi. long: by crossing this ancient boundary between Cisalpine Gaul and Italy, to march against Pompey in 49 B.C., Julius Caeser committed himself to conquer or perish. **2. cross** or **pass the Rubicon,** to take a decisive, irrevocable step: *Our entry into the war made us cross the Rubicon and abandon isolationism forever.*

ru·bi·cund (ro͞o′bə kund′), *adj.* red or reddish; ruddy: *a rubicund complexion.* [< L *rubicund(us),* akin to *rubeus* RED] —**ru′bi·cun′di·ty,** *n.*

ru·bid·i·um (ro͞o bid′ē əm), *n.* *Chem.* a silver-white, metallic, active element resembling potassium, used in photoelectric cells and radio vacuum tubes. *Symbol:* Rb; *at. wt.:* 85.47; *at. no.:* 37; *sp. gr.:* 1.53 at 20°C. [< NL, equiv. to L *rubid(us)* red (in allusion to the two red lines in its spectrum) + *-ium* -IUM] —**ru·bid′ic,** *adj.*

ru·bied (ro͞o′bēd), *adj.* having a color like that of a ruby; deep red. [RUBY + -ED[3]]

ru·bi·fy (ro͞o′bə fī′), *v.t.,* **-fied, -fy·ing.** to make red; redden: *a distant fire that rubified the sky.* [ME *rubifi(en)* < OF *rubifi(er)* < L *rubefacere,* equiv. to *rube(us)* red + *facere* to make; see -IFY]

ru·big·i·nous (ro͞o bij′ə nəs), *adj.* *Bot., Zool.* rusty; rust-colored; brownish-red. Also, **ru·big·i·nose** (ro͞o-bij′ə nōs′). [< L *rūbīginōs(us)* (sp. var. of *rōbīginōsus*), equiv. to *rūbīgin-* (s. of *rubīgō* rust, deriv. of *ruber* red) + *-ōsus* -OUS]

Ru·bin·stein (ro͞o′bin stīn′; *Russ.* ro͞o bin shtīn′; *Pol.* ro͞o′ben stīn′), *n.* **1. An·ton** (än tôn′), 1829–94, Russian pianist and composer. **2. Ar·tur** (är′tər; *Pol.* är′to͞or), 1887–1982, U.S. pianist, born in Poland.

ru·bi·ous (ro͞o′bē əs), *adj.* ruby-colored. [RUBY + -OUS]

ru·ble (ro͞o′bəl), *n.* **a silver or copper-alloy coin and monetary unit of Russia, the Soviet Union, and its successor states, equal to 100 kopecks. Also, rouble.**

ru·bric (ro͞o′brik), *n.* **1.** a title, heading, direction, or the like, in a manuscript, book, statute, etc., written or printed in red or otherwise distinguished from the rest of the text. **2.** a direction for the conduct of divine service or the administration of the sacraments, inserted in liturgical books. **3.** *Archaic.* red ocher. **4.** any established mode of conduct or procedure. —*adj.* **5.** written, inscribed in, or marked with or as with red; rubrical. **6.** *Archaic.* red; ruddy. [< L *rubrīca* red earth (deriv. of *ruber* RED); r. ME *rubriche rubrike* < OF]

ru·bri·cal (ro͞o′bri kəl), *adj.* **1.** reddish; marked with red. **2.** of, pertaining to, contained in, or prescribed by rubrics, esp. liturgical rubrics. [RUBRIC + AL[1]] —**ru′bri·cal·ly,** *adv.*

ru·bri·cate (ro͞o′brə kāt′), *v.t.,* **-cat·ed, -cat·ing. 1.** to mark or color with red. **2.** to furnish with or regulate by rubrics. [< LL *rubrīcāt(us)* colored red (ptp. of *rubrīcāre,* equiv. to *rubric(a)* red earth (see RUBRIC) + *-ātus* -ATE[1]] —**ru′bri·ca′tion,** *n.* —**ru′bri·ca′tor,** *n.*

ru·bri·cat·ed (ro͞o′brə kā′tid), *adj.* (in ancient manuscripts, early printed books, etc.) having titles, catchwords, etc., distinctively colored. [RUBRICATE + -ED[2]]

ru·bri·cian (ro͞o brish′ən), *n.* an expert in or close adherent to liturgical rubrics. [RUBRIC + -IAN]

rub·stone (rub′stōn′), *n.* a stone, esp. a whetstone, used for polishing or sharpening. [ME; see RUB, STONE]

Rubt·sovsk (ro͞opt sôfsk′), *n.* a city in the SW RSFSR, in the W Soviet Union in Asia. 127,000 (est. 1962).

ru·by (ro͞o′bē), *n., pl.* **-bies,** *adj.* —*n.* **1.** a red variety of corundum, used as a gem. **2.** something made of this stone or one of its imitations, as a bearing in a watch. **3.** a deep-red port wine. **4.** deep red; carmine. **5.** *Brit. Print.* a 5½-point type nearly corresponding in size to American agate. —*adj.* **6.** ruby-colored: *ruby lips.* **7.** containing or set or adorned with a ruby or rubies: *a ruby necklace.* [ME *rubi* < MF, OF < L *rube(us)* RED, akin to *ruber*] —**ru′by·like′,** *adj.*

Ru·by (ro͞o′bē), *n.* a girl's given name. Also, **Ru′bye.**

ru′by-crowned king′let (ro͞o′bē kround′), an olive-gray, American kinglet, *Regulus calendula,* the male of which has an erectile, ruby crest.

ru′by pin′, *Horol.* (in a lever escapement) a pin on the impulse roller impelled by the fork of the lever. Also called **roller jewel.**

ru′by roll′er, *Horol.* the narrow, slotted, cylindrical part of the balance staff in a duplex escapement which locks and releases the teeth of the escape wheel.

ru′by sil′ver, 1. proustite. **2.** pyrargyrite.

ru′by spinel′, *Mineral.* a deep red, transparent variety of spinel, used as a gem. Also called **spinel ruby.**

ruche (ro͞osh), *n.* a strip of pleated lace, net, muslin, or other material for trimming or finishing a dress, as at the collar or sleeves. [< F: lit., beehive << LL *rūsca* bark < ? Celt]

ruch·ing (ro͞o′shing), *n.* **1.** material for making a ruche. **2.** ruches collectively. [RUCHE + -ING[1]]

ruck[1] (ruk), *n.* **1.** a large number or quantity; mass. **2.** the great mass of undistinguished or inferior persons or things. [ME *ruke* ? < Scand; cf. Norw *ruka,* in same senses; akin to RICK]

ruck[2] (ruk), *n.* **1.** a fold or wrinkle; crease. —*v.t., v.i.* **2.** to make or become creased or wrinkled. [< Scand; cf. OIcel *hrukka* to wrinkle]

ruck·sack (ruk′sak′, ro͝ok′-), *n.* a type of knapsack carried by hikers, bicyclists, etc. [< G: lit., back sack]

ruck·us (ruk′əs), *n.* **1.** *Informal.* a noisy commotion; fracas; rumpus: *The losers are sure to raise a ruckus.* **2.** a heated controversy: *Newspapers fostered the ruckus by printing the opponents' letters.* [prob. b. RUC(TION + RUMP)US]

ruc·tion (ruk′shən), *n.* *Informal.* a disturbance, quarrel, or row. [?]

Ru·da·kov (ro͞o dä kôf′), *n.* **A·le·xan·der P.** (ä le ksän′dər), born 1910, Russian government official: member of the Presidium since 1962.

rud·beck·i·a (rud bek′ē ə), *n.* any plant of the genus *Rudbeckia*, comprising the cornflowers. [< NL; named after Olaus *Rudbeck* (1630–1702), Swedish botanist; see -IA]

rudd (rud), *n.* a European, fresh-water fish, *Scardinius erythrophthalmus*, of the carp family. [appar. special use of *rud* (now dial.), ME *rude*, OE *rudu* redness; cf. RED, RUDDY]

rud·der (rud′ər), *n.* **1.** *Naut.* a vertical blade at the stern of a vessel for turning horizontally to change the vessel's direction when in motion. **2.** *Aeron.* a movable control surface attached to a vertical stabilizer, located at the rear of an airplane and used, along with the ailerons, to turn the airplane. **3.** any means of or device for governing, directing, or guiding a course: *Action without discipline lacks a rudder.* **4. ease the rudder!** *Naut.* lessen the angle at which the rudder is turned!; ease the helm! **5. full rudder!** *Naut.* turn the vessel as sharply as possible! **6. left rudder!** *Naut.* put the rudder to the port side! (thus turning the head of the vessel to port). **7. right rudder!** *Naut.* put the rudder to the starboard! (thus turning the head of the vessel to starboard). [ME *rodder, rōther, ruder*, OE *rōther*; c. G *Ruder* < Gmc **rō-*; see ROW²] —**rud′dered,** *adj.* —**rud′der·less,** *adj.* —**rud′der·like′,** *adj.*

rud′der chain′, *Naut.* either of a pair of chains formerly used to keep a rudder from swinging to more than a certain angle. Also called **rud′der pend′ant.**

rud′der coat′, *Naut.* (formerly) a piece of tarred canvas surrounding the rudderpost at the point at which it entered the hull of a wooden vessel.

rud·der·fish (rud′ər fish′), *n., pl.* (*esp. collectively*) **-fish,** (*esp. referring to two or more kinds or species*) **-fish·es.** **1.** any of various fishes having the habit of following behind ships, as a pilot fish. **2.** See **sea chub.** [RUDDER + FISH]

rud·der·head (rud′ər hed′), *n.* *Naut.* the upper end of a rudderpost, to which a tiller, quadrant, or yoke is attached. [RUDDER + HEAD]

rud′der horn′, *Naut.* (formerly) a metal crosspiece on a rudder to which chains from the quarters of a vessel were attached to control excessive movement of the rudder.

rud·der·post (rud′ər pōst′), *n.* *Naut.* **1.** Also called **rud·der·stock** (rud′ər stok′). the vertical member at the forward end of a rudder, hinged to the sternpost and attached to the helm or steering gear. **2.** the vertical member of a stern frame on which the rudder is hung. [RUDDER + POST¹]

rud′der snug′, *Naut.* any of several gudgeons by which a rudder is attached to the stern frame of a vessel. Also called **pintle boss.**

rud′der tack′le, *Naut.* See **relieving tackle.**

rud·de·va·tor (rud′ə vā′tər), *n.* *Aeron.* a control surface functioning both as a rudder and as an elevator. [RUDD(ER + EL)EVATOR]

rud·dle (rud′əl), *n., v.,* **-dled, -dling.** —*n.* **1.** a red variety of ocher, used for marking sheep, coloring, etc. —*v.t.* **2.** to mark or color with ruddle. Also, **raddle, reddle.** [dial. *rud* (see RUDD) + -LE]

rud·dle·man (rud′əl mən), *n., pl.* **-men.** one who deals in ruddle. Also, **raddleman, reddleman.** [RUDDLE + MAN¹]

rud·dock (rud′ək), *n.* *Brit. Dial.* the European robin, *Erithacus rubecula.* [ME *ruddok*, OE *rudduc.* See RUDD, -OCK]

rud·dy (rud′ē), *adj.,* **-di·er, -di·est,** *adv.* —*adj.* **1.** of or having a fresh, healthy red color: *a ruddy complexion.* **2.** red or reddish. **3.** *Brit. Slang.* bloody; damned: *a ruddy fool.* —*adv.* **4.** *Brit. Slang.* bloody; damned: *He'd ruddy well better be there.* [ME *rudi*, OE *rudig.* See RUDD, -Y¹] —**rud′di·ly,** *adv.* —**rud′di·ness,** *n.*

rud′dy duck′, a stiff-tailed, North American, fresh-water duck, *Oxyura jamaicensis rubida*, the adult male of which has a brownish-red body, black crown, and white cheeks.

rud′dy turn′stone, a North American subspecies of the turnstone, *Arenaria interpres morinella.*

rude (ro͞od), *adj.,* **rud·er, rud·est.** **1.** discourteous or impolite, usually deliberate: *a rude reply.* **2.** without culture, learning, or refinement: *rude, illiterate peasants.* **3.** rough in manners or behavior; unmannerly; uncouth. **4.** rough, harsh, or ungentle: *rude hands.* **5.** roughly wrought, built, or formed; of a crude make or kind: *a rude cottage.* **6.** unwrought, raw, or crude: *a rude, first stage of development.* **7.** harsh to the ear: *rude sounds.* **8.** without artistic elegance; of a primitive simplicity: *a rude design.* **9.** violent or tempestuous, as the waves. **10.** robust, sturdy, or vigorous: *rude strength.* [ME *rude, ruide* < OF *ru(i)de* or L *rudis*] —**rude′ly,** *adv.* —**rude′ness,** *n.*

—**Syn. 1.** uncivil, unmannerly, curt, brusque, impertinent, impudent, saucy, pert, fresh. **2.** unrefined, uncultured, uncivilized, uncouth, coarse, vulgar, rough. **6.** See **raw. 8.** rustic, artless. **9.** stormy, fierce, tumultuous, turbulent.

Rude (RYD), *n.* **Fran·çois** (FRÄN SWA′), 1784–1855, French sculptor.

ru·den·ture (ro͞o den′chər), *n.* *Arch.* a convex molding within one of the flutes of a classical column; reed. [< F < L *rudent-* (s. of *rudēns*) strong rope + F *-ure* -URE]

ru·der·al (ro͞o′dər əl), *Bot.* —*adj.* **1.** (of a plant) growing in waste places, along roadsides or among rubbish. —*n.* **2.** a ruderal plant. [< NL *rūderāl(is)*, equiv. to L *rūder(a)* (pl. of *rūdus* broken stone) + *-ālis* -AL¹]

rudes·by (ro͞odz′bē), *n.* *Archaic.* an ill-mannered, disorderly person. [RUDE + *-sby*, derisive or playful suffix, perh. in imit. of such surnames as *Ormsby*]

Rü·des·hei·mer (ro͞o′dis hī′mər; *Ger.* RY′dəs hī′mər), *n.* any of the Rheingau wines from the vineyards near Rüdesheim, a town on the Rhine River in West Germany.

ru·di·ment (ro͞o′də mənt), *n.* **1.** Usually, **rudiments. a.** the elements or first principles of a subject: *the rudiments of grammar.* **b.** a mere beginning, first slight appearance, or undeveloped or imperfect form of something: *the rudiments of a plan.* **2.** *Biol.* an organ or part incompletely developed in size or structure, as one in an embryonic stage, one arrested in growth, or one with no functional activity, as a vestige. [< L *rudīment(um)* beginning, equiv. to *rudi(s)* unformed, rough (see RUDE) + *-mentum* -MENT]

ru·di·men·ta·ry (ro͞o′də men′tə rē, -trē), *adj.* **1.** pertaining to rudiments or first principles; elementary: *a rudimentary knowledge of geometry.* **2.** of the nature of a rudiment; undeveloped. **3.** vestigial; abortive. Also, **ru′di·men′tal.** [RUDIMENT + -ARY] —**ru′di·men′ta·ri·ly,** *adv.* —**ru′di·men′ta·ri·ness,** *n.*

—**Syn. 1.** fundamental, initial. See **elementary. 2.** embryonic. —**Ant. 1.** advanced. **2.** mature.

Ru·dolf (ro͞o′dolf), *n.* **1. Max,** born 1902, U.S. orchestra conductor, born in Germany. **2. Lake,** a lake in E Africa, in N Kenya. 185 mi. long; 3500 sq. mi. **3.** Also, **Rudolph.** a boy's given name, form of **Rolf.**

Ru·dolf I (ro͞o′dolf; *Ger.* RŌŌ′dôlf), 1218–91, king of Germany and emperor of the Holy Roman Empire 1273–91: founder of the Hapsburg dynasty. Also, **Rudolph I.** Also called **Rudolph I of Hapsburg.**

Ru·dolph (ro͞o′dolf), *n.* **1. Wilma (Glo·de·an)** (glō′dē ən), born 1940, U.S. athlete. **2.** Also, **Rudolf.** a boy's given name, form of **Rolf.**

Ru·dy (ro͞o′dē), *n.* a boy's given name, form of **Rudolf.**

Rud·yard (rud′yərd), *n.* a boy's given name.

rue¹ (ro͞o), *v.,* **rued, ru·ing,** *n.* —*v.t.* **1.** to feel sorrow over; repent of; regret bitterly: *to rue the loss of opportunities.* **2.** to wish that (something) had never been done, taken place, etc.: *to rue the day one was born.* —*v.i.* **3.** to feel sorrow, repentance, or regret. —*n.* **4.** sorrow; repentance; regret. **5.** pity or compassion. [ME *rue(n), rewe(n)*, OE *hrēowan;* c. G *reuen*] —**ru′er,** *n.*

rue² (ro͞o), *n.* any strongly scented plant of the genus *Ruta*, esp. *R. graveolens*, having yellow flowers and leaves formerly used in medicine. [ME < MF < L *rūta* < Gk *rhytē*]

Rue (ro͞o), *n.* **Warren de la.** See **de la Rue, Warren.**

rue′ anem′one, a small, ranunculaceous plant, *Anemonella thalictroides*, of North America, having white or pinkish flowers.

rue·ful (ro͞o′fəl), *adj.* **1.** causing sorrow or pity; pitiable; deplorable: *a rueful plight.* **2.** feeling, showing, or expressing sorrow or pity; mournful; doleful: *the rueful look on her face.* [ME *reowful.* See RUE¹, -FUL] —**rue′ful·ly,** *adv.* —**rue′ful·ness,** *n.*

ru·fes·cent (ro͞o fes′ənt), *adj.* somewhat reddish; tinged with red; rufous. [< L *rūfescent-* (s. of *rūfescēns*, prp. of *rūfescere*), equiv. to *rūf(us)* RED + *-esc-* inceptive suffix + *-ent-* -ENT] —**ru·fes′cence,** *n.*

ruff¹ (ruf), *n.* **1.** a neckpiece or collar of lace, lawn, or the like, gathered or drawn into deep, full, regular folds, worn in the 16th and 17th centuries. **2.** something resembling such a piece in form or position. **3.** a collar, or set of lengthened or specially marked hairs or feathers, on the neck of an animal. —*v.t.* **4.** tease (def. 3). [? back formation from RUFFLE¹] —**ruff′like′,** *adj.*

Ruff (16th century)

ruff² (ruf), *Cards.* —*n.* **1.** the act or an instance of trumping when one cannot follow suit. **2.** an old game at cards, resembling whist. —*v.t., v.i.* **3.** to trump when unable to follow suit. [prob. < F *ro(u)fle;* c. It *ronfa* a card game]

ruff³ (ruf), *n.* a small, European, fresh-water fish, *Acerina cernua*, of the perch family. [ME *ruf, roffe;* ? special use of ROUGH]

ruffed (ruft), *adj.* displaying or wearing a ruff. [RUFF¹ + -ED²]

ruffed′ grouse′, a North American grouse, *Bonasa umbellus*, having a tuft of feathers on each side of the neck. See illus. under **grouse.**

ruf·fi·an (ruf′ē ən, ruf′yən), *n.* **1.** a tough, lawless person; a brutal bully. —*adj.* **2.** Also, **ruf′fi·an·ly.** tough; lawless; brutal. [earlier *rufian* < MF]

ruf·fi·an·ism (ruf′ē ə niz′əm, ruf′yə-), *n.* **1.** conduct befitting a ruffian. **2.** ruffian character. [RUFFIAN + -ISM]

ruf·fle¹ (ruf′əl), *v.,* **-fled, -fling,** *n.* —*v.t.* **1.** to destroy the smoothness or evenness of: *The wind ruffled the sand.* **2.** to erect (the feathers), as a bird in anger. **3.** to disturb, vex, or irritate: *to be ruffled by a slight.* **4.** to turn (the pages of a book) rapidly. **5.** to pass (cards) through the fingers rapidly in shuffling. **6.** to draw up (cloth, lace, etc.) into a ruffle by gathering along one edge. —*v.i.* **7.** to be or become ruffled; undulate; flutter: *Flags ruffle in the wind.* **8.** to be or become noisy and disturbing. **9.** to put on airs; swagger. —*n.* **10.** a break in the smoothness or evenness of some surface; undulation. **11.** a strip of cloth, lace, etc., drawn up by gathering along one edge, and used as a trimming on a dress, blouse, etc. **12.** some object resembling this, as the ruff of a bird. **13.** disturbance or vexation; annoyance; irritation: *It is impossible to live without some daily ruffles to our composure.* **14.** a disturbed state of mind; perturbation. [ME *ruffel(en)* (v.); c. LG *ruffelen* to crumple, rumple; cf. OIcel *hruffa*, to scratch] —**ruf′fly,** *adj.* —**ruf′fler,** *n.*

—**Syn. 1.** disarrange, disorder, wrinkle, rumple. **3.** upset, annoy, agitate. **10.** perturbation, flurry, agitation. **11.** frill, ruff. —**Ant. 1.** smooth, arrange, order. **3.** soothe, compose. **13.** tranquillity.

ruf·fle² (ruf′əl), *n., v.,* **-fled, -fling.** —*n.* **1.** a low, continuous beating of a drum. —*v.t.* **2.** to beat (a drum) in this manner. [archaic *ruff* in same sense (? imit.) + -LE]

ruf·fled (ruf′əld), *adj.* (of apparel) having ruffles. [RUFFLE¹ + -ED²]

Ru·fisque (*Fr.* RY fēsk′), *n.* a city in W Senegal, E of Dakar. 49,800 (1957).

Ru·ford (ro͞o′fərd), *n.* a boy's given name.

ru·fous (ro͞o′fəs), *adj.* reddish; tinged with red; brownish-red. [< L *rūf(us)* RED + -OUS]

ruf′ter hood′ (ruf′tər), *Falconry.* a temporary, loosely fitted hood used on newly captured hawks. [? deriv. of RUFF¹]

Ru·fus (ro͞o′fəs), *n.* a boy's given name.

rug (rug), *n.* **1.** a thick fabric for covering part of a floor, often woven of wool and often having an oblong shape with a border design. Cf. **carpet. 2.** *Chiefly Brit.* a piece of thick, warm cloth, used as a coverlet, lap robe, etc. **3. cut a rug,** *Slang.* to dance, esp. to jitterbug: *She could really cut a rug twenty years ago.* [< Scand; cf. dial. Norw *rugga* a coarse covering (for bed or body)] —**rug′like′,** *adj.*

ru·ga (ro͞o′gə), *n., pl.* **-gae** (-jē). Usually, **rugae.** *Biol., Anat.* a wrinkle, fold, or ridge. [< L]

ru·gate (ro͞o′gāt, -git), *adj.* wrinkle; rugose. [< L *rūgāt(us)*, ptp. of *rūgāre.* See RUGA, -ATE¹]

Rug·by (rug′bē), *n.* **1.** a city in E Warwickshire, in central England. 51,651 (1961). **2.** a famous boys' school located there: founded 1567. **3.** Also **rugger.** Also called **Rug′by foot′ball.** a form of football, played between two teams of 15 members each, that differs from soccer in freedom to carry the ball, block with the hands and arms, and tackle, and is characterized chiefly by continuous action and prohibition against the use of substitute players. **4.** a town in central North Dakota. 2972 (1960).

rug-cut·ter (rug′kut′ər), *n.* *Slang.* one who jitterbugs.

rug-cut·ting (rug′kut′ing), *n.* *Slang.* the act of dancing rhythmically to swing music, esp. jitterbugging.

rug·ged (rug′id), *adj.* **1.** having a roughly broken, rocky, hilly, or jagged surface: *rugged ground.* **2.** (of a face) wrinkled or furrowed, as by experience, the endurance of hardship, etc. **3.** roughly irregular, heavy, or hard in outline or form: *Lincoln's rugged features.* **4.** rough, harsh, or stern, as persons, nature, etc. **5.** full of hardship and trouble; severe; hard; trying: *a rugged life.* **6.** tempestuous; stormy: *rugged weather.* **7.** harsh to the ear: *rugged sounds.* **8.** rude, uncultivated, or unrefined. **9.** homely or plain: *rugged fare.* **10.** capable of enduring hardship, wear, etc.; strong and tough: *rugged floor covering; a rugged lumberjack.* [ME < Scand; cf. Sw *rugga* to roughen. See RUG] —**rug′ged·ly,** *adv.* —**rug′ged·ness,** *n.*

—**Syn. 1.** uneven, irregular, craggy. **4.** austere. **6.** rough. **7.** grating, cacophonous. **8.** unpolished, crude. —**Ant. 1.** smooth. **4.** mild. **10.** frail.

rug·ged·ize (rug′i dīz′), *v.t.,* **-ized, -iz·ing.** to construct (electronic equipment, cameras, and other delicate instruments) so as to be resistant to shock, vibration, etc. [RUGGED + -IZE]

rug·ger (rug′ər), *n.* *Brit.* Rugby (def. 3). [by alter.]

rug·ging (rug′ing), *n.* a bulky, coarse fabric with a full nap, used as a floor covering. [RUG + -ING¹]

ru·gose (ro͞o′gōs, ro͞o gōs′), *adj.* **1.** having wrinkles; wrinkled; ridged. **2.** *Bot.* rough and wrinkled: applied to leaves in which the reticulate venation is very prominent beneath, with corresponding creases on the upper side. [< L *rūgōs(us)* wrinkled. See RUGA, -OSE¹] —**ru′gose·ly,** *adv.* —**ru·gos·i·ty** (ro͞o gos′i tē), *n.*

ru·gu·lose (ro͞o′gyə lōs′), *adj.* finely rugose; having many small wrinkles. [< NL **rūgul(a)*, (dim. of L *rūga* RUGA) + -OSE¹]

Ruhm′korff coil′ (ro͞om′kôrf), *Elect.* See **induction coil.** [named after Heinrich Daniel *Ruhmkorff* (1803–77), German physicist, its inventor]

Ruhr (ro͝or), *n.* **1.** a river in W West Germany, flowing NW and W into the Rhine. 144 mi. long. **2.** a mining and industrial region centered in the valley of the Rhine River.

ru·in (ro͞o′in), *n.* **1. ruins,** the remains of a building, city, etc., that has been destroyed or that is decaying: *We visited the ruins of ancient Greece.* **2.** a destroyed or decayed building, town, etc. **3.** a fallen and wrecked or decayed condition: *The building fell to ruin.* **4.** the downfall, decay, or destruction of anything. **5.** the complete loss of health, means, position, hope, or the like. **6.** something that causes a downfall or destruction: *Alcohol was his ruin.* **7.** the downfall of a person: *the ruin of Oedipus.* **8.** a person as the wreck of his former self. **9.** the act of causing destruction or a downfall. —*v.t.* **10.** to reduce to ruin; devastate. **11.** to bring (a person, company, etc.) to financial ruin; bankrupt. **12.** to injure (a thing) irretrievably. **13.** to induce (a woman) to surrender her virginity. —*v.i.* **14.** to fall into ruins; fall to pieces. **15.** to come to ruin. [ME *ruine* < MF < L *ruīn(a)* overthrow, collapse, equiv. to *ru(ere)* (to) fall + *-īna* -INE²] —**ru′in·a·ble,** *adj.* —**ru′in·er,** *n.*

—**Syn. 3.** RUIN, DESTRUCTION, HAVOC imply irrevocable and often widespread damage. DESTRUCTION may be on a large or small scale (*destruction of tissue, of enemy vessels*); it emphasizes particularly the act of destroying, while RUIN and HAVOC emphasize the resultant state. RUIN, from the verb meaning to fall to pieces, suggests a state of decay or disintegration (or an object in that state) which is apt to be more the result of the natural processes of time and change, than of sudden violent activity from without: *The house has fallen to ruins;* only in its figurative application is it apt to suggest the result of destruction from without: *the ruin of her hopes.* HAVOC, originally a cry which served as the signal for pillaging, has changed its reference from that of spoliation to devastation, being used particularly of the destruction following in the wake of natural calamities: *the havoc wrought by flood and pestilence.* Today it is used figuratively to refer to the destruction of hopes and plans: *This sudden turn of events played havoc with her carefully laid designs.* **4.** fall, overthrow, defeat, wreck. **10.** demolish, destroy, damage. See **spoil.** —**Ant. 4.** construction, creation.

ru·in·ate (ro͞o′ə nāt′), *v.,* **-at·ed, -at·ing,** *adj. Dial.* —*v.t.* **1.** to ruin. —*adj.* **2.** ruined. [< ML *ruīnāt(us)*, ptp. of *ruīnāre.* See RUIN, -ATE¹]

ru·in·a·tion (ro͞o′ə nā′shən), *n.* **1.** the act or state of ruining or the state of being ruined. **2.** something that ruins. [RUINATE + -ION]

ru·in·ous (ro͞o′ə nəs), *adj.* **1.** bringing or tending to bring ruin; destructive; disastrous: *a ruinous war.* **2.** fallen into ruin; dilapidated: *a ruinous house.* **3.** consisting of ruins: *a ruinous city from antiquity.* [ME *ruynouse* < L *ruīnōs(us)*, equiv. to *ruīn(a)* RUIN + *-ōsus* -OUS] —**ru′in·ous·ly,** *adv.* —**ru′in·ous·ness,** *n.*

Ruis·dael (rois′däl, -dāl, rīz′-, rīs′-; *Du.* rœis′dāl), *n.* **1. Ja·cob van** (yä′kôp vän), 1628?–82, Dutch painter. **2.** his uncle, **Sa·lo·mon van** (sä′lô môn′ vän), 1601?–70, Dutch painter. Also, **Ruysdael.**

rule (ro͞ol), *n., v.,* **ruled, rul·ing.** —*n.* **1.** a principle or regulation governing conduct, action, procedure, arrangement, etc.: *the rules of chess.* **2.** the code of regulations observed by a religious order or congregation: *the Franciscan rule.* **3.** the customary or normal condition, occurrence, manner, practice, quality, etc.: *the rule rather than the exception.* **4.** control, government, or dominion: *under the rule of a dictator.* **5.** tenure or conduct of reign or office: *during the rule of George III.* **6.** a prescribed mathematical method for performing a calculation or solving a problem. **7.** ruler (def. 2). **8.** (*cap.*) *Astron.* the constellation Norma. **9.** *Print.* a thin, type-high strip of metal, for printing a solid or decorative line or lines. **10.** *Law.* **a.** a formal order or direction made by a court, as for governing the procedure of the court (**general rule**) or for sending the case before a referee (**special rule**). **b.** a legal principle. **c.** a court order in a particular case. **11. rules,** *Penol.* (formerly) **a.** a fixed area in the neighborhood of certain prisons within which certain prisoners were allowed to live on giving security not to escape. **b.** the freedom of such an area. **12.** *Obs.* behavior. **13. as a rule,** generally; usually: *He arrives at eleven o'clock, as a rule.* —*v.t.* **14.** to control or direct; exercise dominating power, authority, or influence over; govern: *to rule the people kindly.* **15.** to decide or declare judicially or authoritatively; decree: *The judge ruled that he should be exiled.* **16.** to mark with lines, esp. parallel straight lines, with the aid of a ruler or the like: *to rule paper.* **17.** to mark out or form (a line) by this method: *to rule lines on paper.* **18.** to be superior or preeminent in (a specific field or group); dominate by superiority: *For centuries, England ruled the seas.* —*v.i.* **19.** to exercise dominating power or influence; predominate. **20.** to exercise authority, dominion, or sovereignty. **21.** to make a formal decision or ruling, as on a point at law. **22.** to be prevalent or current: *Higher prices ruled throughout France.* **23. rule out,** to refuse to acknowledge or admit; eliminate; exclude: *to rule out the possibility of error.* [ME *riule, reule* < OF *riule* < L *rēgul(a)* straight stick, pattern]
—**Syn. 1.** standard, law, ruling, guide, precept, order. See **principle. 4.** command, domination, mastery, sway, authority, direction. **14.** RULE, ADMINISTER, COMMAND, GOVERN, MANAGE mean to exercise authoritative guidance or direction. RULE implies the exercise of authority as by a sovereign: *to rule a kingdom.* ADMINISTER places emphasis on the planned and orderly procedures used: *to administer the finances of an institution.* COMMAND suggests military authority and the power to exact obedience; to be in command of: *to command a ship.* To GOVERN is authoritatively to guide or direct persons or things, esp. in the affairs of a large administrative unit: *to govern a state.* To MANAGE is to conduct affairs, i.e., to guide them in a unified way toward a definite goal, or to direct or control people, often by tact, address, or artifice: *to manage a business.* **15.** deem, judge, settle, order.

ruled′ sur′face, *Geom.* a surface that can be generated by a straight line, as a cylinder or cone.

rule′ joint′, **1.** (in carpentry and joinery) a joint between two hinged pieces, as between the center and end leaves of a table, consisting of a quarter round and fillet fitting against a cove and fillet. **2.** a pivoted joint between two strips of wood placed end to end, as in a carpenter's folding rule.

rule′ of elev′en, *Bridge, Whist.* the rule that when a player leads his fourth highest card in any suit its numerical value subtracted from eleven gives the number of higher cards of that suit held by the other players.

rule′ of the road′, *Naut.* any of the regulations concerning the safe handling of vessels under way with respect to one another, imposed by a government on ships in its own waters, or upon its own ships on the high seas.

rule′ of three′, *Math.* the method of finding the fourth term in a proportion when three terms are given.

rule′ of thumb′, **1.** a general or approximate principle, procedure, or rule based on experience or practice rather than on scientific knowledge. **2.** a rough, practical method of procedure.

rul·er (ro͞o′lər), *n.* **1.** a person who rules or governs; sovereign. **2.** Also, **rule.** a strip of wood, metal, or other material, having a straight edge and often marked off in inches or centimeters, used for drawing lines, measuring, etc. **3.** one who or that which rules paper, wood, etc. [ME; see RULE, -ER[1]]

rules′ commit′tee, a special committee of a legislature, as of the House of Representatives, having the authority to establish rules or methods for expediting legislative action, and usually determining the date a bill is presented for consideration.

rul·ing (ro͞o′ling), *n.* **1.** an authoritative decision, as one by a judge on a debated point of law. **2.** the act of drawing straight lines with a ruler. **3.** ruled lines. —*adj.* **4.** governing or dominating: *the ruling party.* **5.** controlling; predominating: *the ruling factor in recovery from an illness.* **6.** widespread; prevalent: *ruling prices; ruling values.* [ME (n.); see RULE, -ING[1], -ING[2]]

rul′ing eld′er, an elder in a Presbyterian church.

rum[1] (rum), *n.* **1.** an alcoholic liquor or spirit distilled from molasses or some other fermented sugarcane product. **2.** alcoholic drink in general; intoxicating liquor: *He warned against demon rum.* [? short for obs. *rumbullion*; cf. F *rebouillir* to boil again] —**rum′less,** *adj.*

rum[2] (rum), *adj. Slang.* **1.** odd, strange, or queer: *a rum fellow.* **2.** *Archaic.* good or fine. [earlier *rome, room* great ? < Gypsy; see ROM]

rum[3] (rum), *n. Cards.* rummy[1].

Rum (ro͝om), *n.* Arabic name of Rome, once used to designate the Byzantine Empire.

Rum., **1.** Rumania. **2.** Also, **Rum** Rumanian.

ru·mal (ro͞o mäl′, ro͞o′mäl), *n.* a kerchief worn as a headdress by men in India. [< Urdu < Pers *rūmāl,* equiv. to *rū* face + *māl* wiping]

Ru·ma·ni·a (ro͞o mā′nē ə, -mān′yə), *n.* a republic in SE Europe, bordering on the Black Sea: one of the Balkan States. 18,927,081 (est. 1964); 91,654 sq. mi. *Cap.:* Bucharest. Also, **Romania, Roumania.** Rumanian, **România.**

Ru·ma·ni·an (ro͞o mā′nē ən, -mān′yən), *adj.* **1.** of or pertaining to Rumania, its inhabitants, or their language. —*n.* **2.** a native or inhabitant of Rumania. **3.** the language of Rumania, a Romance language. Also, **Romanian, Roumanian.** [RUMANI(A) + -AN]

ru·man·ite (ro͞o′mə nīt′), *n.* a fossil resin similar to amber, used for jewelry. Also called **Ruma′nian am′ber.** [named after RUMANIA; see -ITE[1]]

rum·ba (rum′bə, ro͝om′-; *Sp.* ro͞om′bä), *n., pl.* **-bas** (-bəz; *Sp.* -bäs), *v.,* **-baed** (-bəd), **-ba·ing** (-bə ing). —*n.* **1.** a dance, Cuban Negro in origin and complex in rhythm. **2.** an imitation or adaptation of this dance in the U.S. **3.** music for this dance or in its rhythm. —*v.i.* **4.** to dance the rumba. Also, **rhumba.** [< Sp, prob. of Afr orig.]

rum·ble (rum′bəl), *v.,* **-bled, -bling,** *n.* —*v.i.* **1.** to make a deep, heavy, somewhat muffled, continuous sound, as thunder. **2.** to move or travel with such a sound: *The train rumbled on.* **3.** *Slang.* to have or take part in a street fight between or among teen-age gangs: *Rival gangs rumbled on Saturday afternoon.* —*v.t.* **4.** to give forth or utter with a rumbling sound: *to rumble a command.* **5.** to cause to make or move with a rumbling sound: *to rumble a wagon over the ground.* **6.** to subject to the action of a rumble or tumbling box, as for the purpose of polishing. —*n.* **7.** a deep, heavy, somewhat muffled, continuous sound: *the rumble of tanks across a bridge.* **8.** See **rumble seat. 9.** a rear part of a carriage containing seating accommodations, as for servants, or space for baggage. **10.** See **tumbling box. 11.** *Slang.* a street fight between rival teenage gangs. [ME; cf. D *rommelen,* prob. of imit. orig.] —**rum′bler,** *n.* —**rum′bling·ly,** *adv.*

Rumble seat

rum′ble seat′, **1.** a seat recessed into the luggage area of a coupe or roadster, covered by a hinged lid which opens to form the back of the seat when in use. **2.** *Furniture.* See **wagon seat.**

rum·bly (rum′blē), *adj.* attended with, making, or causing a rumbling sound. [RUMBLE + -Y[1]]

Ru·me·li·a (ro͞o mē′lē ə, -mēl′yə), *n.* **1.** a division of the former Turkish Empire, in the Balkan Peninsula: included Albania, Macedonia, and Thrace. **2. Eastern,** a former autonomous province within this division: later became S Bulgaria. Also, **Roumelia.**

ru·men (ro͞o′min), *n., pl.* **-mi·na** (-mə nə). **1.** the first stomach of ruminating animals, lying next to the reticulum. See diag. under **ruminant. 2.** the cud of a ruminant. [< L: throat, gullet (sp. var. of *rūma*)]

Rum·ford (rum′fərd), *n.* **1. Count.** See **Thompson, Benjamin. 2.** a town in W Maine. 7233 (1960).

Ru·mi (*Pers.* ro͞o′mē), *n.* **Ja·lal ud-din** (*Pers.* jä-läl′ o͞od dēn′, o͞od-, ja-). See **Jalal ud-din Rumi.**

Ru·mi·na (ro͞o′mə nə), *n.* an ancient Roman goddess protective of sucklings.

Ruminant stomach
A, Esophagus; B, Rumen; C, Reticulum; D, Omasum; E, Abomasum; F, Small intestine

ru·mi·nant (ro͞o′mə-nənt), *n.* **1.** any even-toed, hoofed mammal of the suborder *Ruminantia,* being comprised of cloven-hoofed, cud-chewing quadrupeds, and including the cattle, bison, buffalo, deer, antelopes, giraffes, camels, chevrotains, etc. —*adj.* **2.** ruminating; chewing the cud. **3.** given to or characterized by meditation; meditative: *a ruminant scholar.* [< L *rūminant-* (s. of *rūmināns,* prp. of *rūmināri, rūmināre*), equiv. to *rumin-* (s. of *rūmen*) RUMEN + *-ant-* -ANT] —**ru′mi·nant·ly,** *adv.*

ru·mi·nate (ro͞o′mə nāt′), *v.,* **-nat·ed, -nat·ing.** —*v.i.* **1.** to chew the cud, as a ruminant. **2.** to meditate or muse; ponder. —*v.t.* **3.** to chew again or over and over. **4.** to meditate on; ponder. [< L *rūmindruminrūmin-* (s. of *rūmen* RUMEN) + *-ātus* -ATE[1]] —**ru′mi·nat′ing·ly,** *adv.* —**ru′mi·na′tion,** *n.* —**ru′mi·na′tive,** *adj.* —**ru′mi·na′tive·ly,** *adv.* —**ru′mi·na′tor,** *n.*
—**Syn. 2.** think, reflect.

Ruml (rum′əl), *n.* **Beards·ley** (bērdz′lē), 1894–1960, U.S. economist and businessman.

rum·mage (rum′ij), *v.,* **-maged, -mag·ing,** *n.* —*v.t.* **1.** to search thoroughly or actively through (a place, receptacle, etc.), esp. by moving around, turning over, or looking through contents. **2.** to find, bring, or fetch by searching (often fol. by *out* or *up*). —*v.i.* **3.** to search actively, as in a place or receptacle, or among contents, goods, etc.: *She rummaged in her mind for the forgotten name.* —*n.* **4.** miscellaneous articles; odds and ends. **5.** a rummaging search. [aph. m. MF *arrumage,* equiv. to *arrum(er)* (to) stow goods in the hold of a ship (< ?) + *-age* -AGE] —**rum′mag·er,** *n.*

rum′mage sale′, a sale of miscellaneous articles, old or new, as items contributed to raise money for charity, of unclaimed goods at a wharf or warehouse, or of odds and ends of merchandise at a shop.

rum·mer (rum′ər), *n.* a large drinking glass or cup. [< D *roemer;* see ROEMER]

rum·my[1] (rum′ē), *n.* any of various card games for two, three, or four players, each usually being dealt seven, nine, or ten cards, in which the object is to match cards into sets and sequences. Also called **rum.** [? special use of RUMMY[3]]

rum·my[2] (rum′ē), *n., pl.* **-mies,** *adj.* —*n.* **1.** *Slang.* a drunkard. —*adj.* **2.** of or like rum. [RUM[1] + -Y[1]]

rum·my[3] (rum′ē), *adj.,* **-mi·er, -mi·est.** *Slang, Chiefly Brit.* rum[2] (def. 1). [RUM[2] + -Y[1]]

ru·mor (ro͞o′mər), *n.* **1.** a story or statement in general circulation without confirmation or certainty as to facts: *a rumor of war.* **2.** gossip; hearsay: *Don't listen to rumor.* **3.** *Archaic.* a continuous, confused noise; clamor; din. —*v.t.* **4.** to circulate, report, or assert by a rumor: *It is rumored that the king is dead.* Also, *esp. Brit.,* **ru′mour.** [ME *rumour* < MF < L *rūmor;* akin to Skt *rāuti, ravati* he cries]
—**Syn. 1.** report.

Ru·mor (ro͞o′mər), *n. Class. Myth.* the messenger of Zeus.

ru·mor·mon·ger (ro͞o′mər mung′gər, -mong′-), *n.* a person given to spreading rumors, often maliciously. Also, *esp. Brit.,* **ru′mour·mon′ger.** [RUMOR + MONGER]

rump (rump), *n.* **1.** the hind part of the body of an animal, as the hindquarters of a quadruped or sacral of a bird. **2.** *Chiefly Brit.* a cut of beef from this part of the animal, behind the loin and above the round. **3.** the buttocks. **4.** the last, unimportant or inferior part: *a rump of territory.* **5.** the remnant of a legislature, council, etc., after a majority of the members have resigned or been expelled. **6. the Rump,** *Eng. Hist.* See **Rump Parliament.** [ME *rumpe* < Scand; cf. Dan *rumpe* rump; c. G *Rumpf* trunk] —**rump′less,** *adj.*

Rum·pel·stilts·kin (rum′pəl stilt′skin; *Ger.* ro͝om′-pəl shtilts′kin), *n.* a dwarf in a German folktale who spins flax into gold for a maiden to meet the demands of the prince she has married, on the condition that she give him her first child or else guess his name: she guesses his name and he vanishes or destroys himself in a rage.

rumpf (ro͝ompf), *n. Physical Chem.* kernel (def. 6). [< G; see RUMP]

rum·ple (rum′pəl), *v.,* **-pled, -pling,** *n.* —*v.t.* **1.** to crumple or crush into wrinkles: *to rumple a sheet of paper.* **2.** to ruffle; tousle (sometimes fol. by *up*): *The wind rumpled her hair.* —*v.i.* **3.** to become wrinkled or crumpled: *Tissue rumples easily.* —*n.* **4.** a wrinkle or irregular fold; crease. [< MD *rompel* (n.) or MLG *rumpel*]

Rump′ Par′liament, *Eng. Hist.* the remnant of the Long Parliament established by the expulsion of the Presbyterian members in 1648, dismissed by force in 1653, and restored briefly in 1659–60.

rum·pus (rum′pəs), *n., pl.* **-pus·es. 1.** a noisy or violent disturbance; commotion; uproar: *There was a terrible rumpus going on upstairs.* **2.** a heated controversy: *a rumpus over the school-bond issue.* [?]

rum′pus room′, a room in a home, for games, hobbies, parties, etc.

rum·run·ner (rum′run′ər), *n. U.S. Informal.* a person or ship engaged in smuggling liquor. [RUM[1] + RUNNER] —**rum′run′ning,** *n.*

Rum·sey (rum′zē), *n.* **James,** 1743–92, U.S. engineer and inventor.

Rum·son (rum′sən), *n.* a town in E New Jersey. 6405 (1960).

run (run), *v.,* **ran, run, run·ning,** *n., adj.* —*v.i.* **1.** to go quickly by moving the legs more rapidly than at a walk and in such a manner that for an instant in each step all feet are off the ground. **2.** to move with haste; act quickly: *Run upstairs and get the iodine.* **3.** to depart quickly; take to flight; flee or escape: *to run from danger.* **4.** to have recourse for aid, support, comfort, etc.: *He shouldn't run to his parents with every little problem.* **5.** to make a quick trip or informal visit for a short stay at a place: *to run up to New York; I will run over to see you after dinner.* **6.** to go around, rove, or ramble without restraint (often fol. by *about*): *to run about in the park.* **7.** to move, roll, or progress from momentum or from being hurled, kicked, or otherwise propelled: *The ball ran over the curb and into the street.* **8.** *Sports.* **a.** to take part in a race or contest. **b.** to finish in a race or contest in a certain numerical position: *The horse ran second.* **9.** to be or campaign as a candidate for election. **10.** to migrate, as fish: *to run huge shoals.* **11.** to migrate upstream or inshore from deep water to spawn. **12.** to move under continuing power or force, as of the wind, a motor, etc.: *The car ran along the highway.* **13.** (of a ship, automobile, etc.) to be sailed or driven from a safe, proper, or given route: *The ship ran aground.* **14.** to ply between places, as a vessel or conveyance: *This bus runs between New Haven and Hartford.* **15.** to move, glide, turn, rotate, or pass easily, freely, or smoothly: *A rope runs in a pulley.* **16.** to creep, trail, or climb, as growing vines: *The ivy ran up the side of the house.* **17.** to come undone or to unravel, as stitches or a fabric: *Silk stockings run more easily than nylons.* **18.** to flow, as a liquid: *The perfume ran down the side of the bottle.* **19.** to flow along, esp. strongly, as a stream, the sea, etc.: *The rapids ran over the rocks.* **20.** to empty or transfer contents: *The river ran into the sea.* **21.** to appear, occur, or exist within a certain limited range; include a specific range of variations (usually fol. by *from*): *Your work runs from fair to bad. New cars run from a ten-passenger limousine to a three-wheeled runabout with room for one.* **22.** to melt and flow: *Wax ran down the burning candle.* **23.** *Golf.* (of a golf ball) to bounce or roll along the ground just after landing from a stroke: *The ball struck the green and ran seven feet past the hole.* **24.** to spread on being applied to a surface, as a liquid: *Fresh paint ran over the window molding onto the pane.* **25.** to spread over a material when exposed to moisture: *The dyes in this fabric are guaranteed not to run in washing.* **26.** to undergo a spreading of colors: *materials which run when washed.* **27.** to flow forth as a discharge, as a liquid: *Let the water run before you drink it. Tears ran from her eyes.* **28.** to discharge or give passage to a liquid or fluid: *Her eyes ran with tears.* **29.** to overflow or leak, as a vessel: *The pot, brought too quickly to a boil, began to run over.* **30.** to operate or function: *How does your new watch run? Cars run on gasoline.* **31.** to be in operation: *the noise of a dishwasher running.* **32.** to continue in operation: *The furnace runs most of the day.* **33.** to elapse; pass or go by, as time: *Time is running out, and we must hurry.* **34.** to pass into or meet with a certain state or condition: *to run into debt; to run into trouble.* **35.** to get or become: *The well ran dry.* **36.** to amount; total: *The bill ran to $100.* **37.** to be stated or worded in a certain manner: *The minutes of the last meeting run as follows.* **38.** *Com.* **a.** to accumulate, follow, or become payable in due course, as interest on

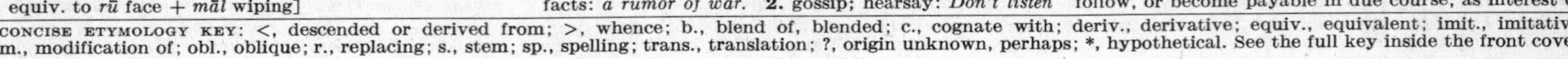

a debt: *Your interest runs from January 1st to December 31st.* **b.** to make many withdrawals in rapid succession, as from a bank. **39.** *Law.* **a.** to have legal force or effect, as a writ. **b.** to continue to operate. **c.** to go along with: *The easement runs with the land.* **40.** to proceed, continue, or go: *The story runs for eight pages.* **41.** to extend in a given direction: *This road runs north to Litchfield.* **42.** to extend for a certain length: *The unpaved section runs for eight miles.* **43.** to extend over a given surface: *Shelves ran from floor to ceiling.* **44.** to be printed, as on a printing press, a Mimeograph, etc.: *Two thousand copies ran before the typo was caught.* **45.** to appear in print or be published as a story, photograph, etc., in a newspaper, magazine, or the like: *The account ran in all the papers. The political cartoon always runs on the editorial page.* **46.** to be performed on a stage or be played continually, as a play: *The play ran for two years.* **47.** to occur or take place continuously, as a movie: *The picture runs for two hours.* **48.** to pass quickly: *A thought ran through his mind. Her eyes ran over the room.* **49.** to be disseminated, circulated, or spread rapidly: *The news of his promotion ran all over town.* **50.** to continue or return persistently; recur: *The old tune ran through his mind all day.* **51.** to have or tend to have or produce a specified character, quality, form, etc.: *This novel runs to long descriptions. Her sister is fat too, but the family runs to being overweight.* **52.** to be or continue to be of a certain or average size, number, etc.: *Potatoes are running large this year.* **53.** *Naut.* to sail before the wind.

—*v.t.* **54.** to move or run along (a surface, way, path, etc.): *Every morning he ran the dirt path around the reservoir to keep in condition. She ran her fingers over the keyboard.* **55.** to traverse (a distance) in running: *He ran the mile in just over four minutes.* **56.** to perform, compete in, or accomplish by or as by running: *to run a race; to run an errand.* **57.** to compete against in a race: *I ran him to the corner and beat him by three steps.* **58.** to go about freely on or in without supervision: *permitting children to run the streets.* **59.** to ride or cause to gallop: *to run a horse across a field.* **60.** to enter in a race: *He ran his best filly in the Florida Derby.* **61.** to bring into a certain state by running: *He ran himself out of breath trying to keep pace.* **62.** to trace, track, pursue or hunt, as game: *to run deer on foot.* **63.** to drive (an animal) or cause to go by pursuing: *to run a fox to cover; Run the stallion into the barn.* **64.** to leave, flee, or escape from: *He ran town before the robbery was discovered.* **65.** to cause to ply between places, as a vessel or conveyance: *to run a ferry between New York and New Jersey.* **66.** to convey or transport, as in a vessel or vehicle: *I'll run you home in my car.* **67.** to cause to pass quickly: *He ran his eyes over the letter. She ran a comb through her hair.* **68.** to get past or through: *to run a blockade.* **69.** to smuggle (contraband goods): *to run guns across the border.* **70.** to work, operate, or drive: *to run a sewing machine; Can you run a tractor?* **71.** to publish, print, or make copies of, as on a printing press, Mimeograph, etc. (sometimes fol. by *off*): *Run off 3000 of these posters. The newspapers ran the story on page one.* **72.** to process, refine, manufacture, or subject to an analysis or treatment: *The doctor wanted to run a blood test. The factory ran 50,000 gallons of paint a day.* **73.** to keep operating or going, as a machine: *They ran the presses 24 hours a day.* **74.** to keep (a motor) idling for an indefinite period: *On cold days he would run the car motor to prevent stalling.* **75.** to allow (a ship, automobile, etc.) to depart from a safe, proper, or given route, as by negligence or error: *He ran the ship aground. She ran the car up on the curb.* **76.** to sponsor, support, or nominate (a person) as a candidate for election. **77.** to manage or conduct: *to run a business; to run one's own life.* **78.** (in some games, as billiards) to continue or complete a series of successful strokes, shots, or the like. **79.** *Cards.* to lead a series (of one's assured tricks or winners in a given suit): *He ran the heart suit before leading spades.* **80.** to expose oneself to or be exposed to (a chance, risk, etc.): *Through his habitual lateness he ran the danger of being fired.* **81.** to cause (a liquid) to flow: *to run the water for a bath.* **82.** to fill (a tub or bath) with water: *She ran a hot tub for him.* **83.** to give forth or flow with (a liquid); pour forth or discharge: *The well ran 500 barrels of oil daily. Her eyes ran hot tears.* **84.** to charge (an item or items) as on a charge account or to accumulate (bills) to be paid all at one time: *He ran a large monthly tab at the club.* **85.** to cause to move easily, freely, or smoothly: *to run a rope in a pulley.* **86.** *Golf.* to cause (a golf ball) to move forward along the ground after landing from a stroke: *He ran his ball seven feet past the hole.* **87.** to sew or use a running stitch: *to run a seam.* **88.** to cause stitches in (a garment or fabric) to unravel or come undone: *to run a stocking on a nail.* **89.** to bring, lead, or force into a certain state or condition: *He ran his troops into an ambush. She ran her husband into debt.* **90.** to drive, force, or thrust: *to run a nail into a board; to run one's head against a wall; to run one's hand into one's pocket.* **91.** to graze; pasture: *They run sixty head of cattle on their ranch.* **92.** to extend (something) in a particular direction or to a given point or place: *to run a partition across a room; to run a telephone cable from Boston to Buffalo.* **93.** *Carpentry.* to make (millwork) from boards. **94.** to cause to fuse and flow, as metal for casting in a mold. **95.** to draw, trace, or mark out, as a line: *to run a line over a surface; to run a line through a word.* **96.** to cost (an amount or approximate amount): *This dress runs $30.* **97.** to cost (a person) an amount or approximate amount: *That dress will run you $30.* **98. run across,** to meet or find accidentally: *She ran across an old friend at the party. He ran across her name in the phone book.* **99. run afoul of, a.** *Naut.* to collide with so as to cause damage and entanglement. **b.** to incur or become subject to the wrath or ill will of: *to run afoul of the law; He argued with his father and has run afoul of him ever since.* **100. run after, a.** to follow; chase; pursue: *The dog ran after the burglar. She ran after him until he finally married her.* **b.** to attempt to become friendly with or part of the society of: *He runs after the country-club set.* **101. run around with,** *Informal.* **a.** to socialize; consort with: *She runs around with the strangest people.* **b.** to be unfaithful to one's wife or husband: *It was common knowledge that he was running around.* **102. run away, a.** to flee or escape; leave a place of confinement or control with the intention of never returning: *He ran away from home three times before he was ten.* **b.** *Naut.* to haul on a line by walking or running steadily. **103. run away with, a.** to go away with, esp. to elope with: *She deserted her family and ran away with a sailor.* **b.** to abscond with; steal: *to run away with some valuable jewelry.* **c.** to surpass others in; be outstanding in: *He surprised everyone by running away with academic honors.* **104. run down, a.** to strike and fell or overturn, esp. to drive a vehicle into (someone): *to run down an innocent pedestrian.* **b.** to pursue until captured; chase: *The detective swore that he would run down the criminal.* **c.** to peruse; review: *His eyes ran down the front row and stopped suddenly.* **d.** to cease operation; stop: *My watch has run down.* **e.** to speak disparagingly of; criticize severely: *She was always running down her husband at parties.* **f.** to search out; trace; find: *to run down information.* **g.** *Baseball.* to tag out (a base runner) between bases. **h.** *Naut.* to collide with and sink (another vessel). **i.** *Naut.* to sail closely parallel to (a coast). **105. run for it,** to hurry away or flee, esp. to evade something: *You had better run for it before anyone else arrives.* **106. run in, a.** to visit casually: *If I'm in the nighborhood, I may run in for a few minutes.* **b.** *Slang.* to arrest; take to jail: *They ran him in for burglary.* **c.** *Print.* to add (matter) to text without indenting. **d.** to break in (new machinery). **107. run into, a.** to crash into; collide with: *She was so sleepy that she ran into a lamppost.* **b.** to meet accidentally: *You never know whom you'll run into at a big party.* **c.** to amount to; total: *losses that ran into millions of dollars.* **d.** to succeed; follow: *One year ran into the next, and still there was no change.* **e.** to experience; encounter: *The project ran into difficulty.* **108. run in with,** *Naut.* to sail close to (a coast, vessel, etc.). **109. run off, a.** to leave quickly; depart. **b.** to create or perform rapidly or easily: *to run off a new song.* **c.** to determine the winner (of a contest, race, etc.) by a runoff. **d.** to drive away; expel: *to run someone off one's property.* **e.** to print, or otherwise duplicate: *Please run off 500 copies.* **110. run on, a.** to continue without interruption: *The account that he gave ran on at some length.* **b.** *Print.* to add (matter) to text without indenting. **c.** to add something, as at the end of a text: *to run on an adverb to a dictionary entry.* **111. run out, a.** to terminate; end: *My subscription ran out last month. Time ran out before we could score another touchdown.* **b.** to become used up: *His money soon ran out.* **c.** to drive out; expel: *They want to run him out of the country.* **112. run out of,** to exhaust a quantity or supply of: *She couldn't bake a cake because she had run out of sugar.* **113. run out on,** *Informal.* to withdraw one's support from; abandon: *No one could accuse him of running out on his friends.* **114. run over, a.** to hit and knock down, esp. with a vehicle: *She cried inconsolably when her cat was run over by a car.* **b.** to go beyond; exceed: *His speech ran over the time limit.* **c.** to repeat; review: *We'll run over that song again.* **115. run through, a.** to pierce or stab, as with a sword: *to run someone through.* **b.** to consume or use up recklessly; squander: *to run through a fortune.* **c.** to practice, review, or rehearse quickly or informally: *to run through a scene.* **116. run up, a.** to sew rapidly: *She ran up some curtains.* **b.** to amass; incur: *running up huge debts.* **c.** to cause to increase; raise: *to run up costs unnecessarily.* **d.** to build, esp. hurriedly: *They are tearing down old tenement blocks and running up skyscrapers.*

—*n.* **117.** the act, an instance, or period of running: *a five-minute run before breakfast.* **118.** a hurrying to or from some point, as on an errand: *a run to reach the store before it closes.* **119.** a fleeing, esp. in great haste; flight: *a run from the police who were hot on his trail.* **120.** a running pace: *The boys set out at a run.* **121.** the act, an instance, or a period of moving rapidly, as in a boat, automobile, or the like: *a run to shore before the storm.* **122.** distance covered, as by racing, running, during a trip, etc.: *a three-mile run.* **123.** the act, an instance, or a period of traveling or moving between two places; trip: *a truck on its daily run from farm to market; a nonstop run from Louisville to Memphis.* **124.** *Golf.* the distance that a golf ball moves along the ground after landing from a stroke: *He got a seven-foot run with his chip shot.* **125.** a quick trip for a short stay at a place: *to take a run up to New York.* **126.** *Mil.* **a.** See **bomb run. b.** any portion of a military flight during which the aircraft flies directly toward the target in order to begin its attack: *a strafing run.* **127.** *Aeron.* **a.** the rapid movement, under its own power, of an aircraft on a runway, water, or another surface. **b.** a routine flight from one place to another: *the evening run from New York to London.* **128.** beat (def. 50b). **129.** an interval or period during which something, as a machine, operates or continues operating: *They kept each press in the plant on a 14-hour run.* **130.** the amount of anything produced in such a period: *a daily run of 400,000 gallons of paint.* **131.** pressrun. **132.** a line or place in knitted work where a series of stitches have slipped out or come undone: *a run in a stocking.* **133.** onward movement, development, progress, course, etc.: *the run of our business from a small store to a large chain.* **134.** the direction of something or of its component elements: *the run of the grain of wood.* **135.** the particular course, order, or tendency of something: *in the normal run of events; the daily run of affairs.* **136.** freedom to move around in, pass through, or use something: *to allow one's guests the run of the house.* **137.** any rapid or easy course of progress: *Owing to his outstanding qualities, it was a simple run from trainee to supervisor.* **138.** a continual course of performances, as of a play: *a long run on Broadway.* **139.** an uninterrupted course of some state or condition; a spell: *a run of good luck; a run of good weather.* **140.** a continuous extent of something, as a vein of ore. **141.** an uninterrupted series or sequence of things, events, etc.: *a run of 30 scoreless innings.* **142.** a sequence of cards in a given suit: *a heart run.* **143.** any extensive continued demand, sale, or the like: *a run on umbrellas during the rainy season.* **144.** a series of sudden and urgent demands for payment, as on a bank. **145.** a period of being in demand or favor with the public: *Her last book had a briefer run than her first.* **146.** a period during which liquid flows: *They kept each oil well on an eight-hour run.* **147.** the amount that flows during such a period: *a run of 500 barrels a day.* **148.** a small stream; brook; rivulet. **149.** a flow or rush, as of water: *The snow melting on the mountains caused a run of water into the valley.* **150.** a kind or class, as of goods: *a superior run of blouses, of the finest fabric and in the latest style.* **151.** the typical, ordinary, or average kind: *The run of 19th-century novels tends to be of a sociological nature.* **152.** an inclined course, as on a slope, designed or used for a specific purpose: *a bobsled run; a run for training beginning skiers.* **153.** a fairly large enclosure within which domestic animals may move about freely; runway: *a chicken run.* **154.** *Australian.* a large sheep ranch or area of grazing land. **155.** the beaten track or usual trail used by deer or other wild animals; runway. **156.** a trough or pipe for water or the like. **157.** the movement of a number of fish upstream or inshore from deep water. **158.** large numbers of fish in motion, esp. inshore from deep water or up a river for spawning: *a run of salmon.* **159.** a number of animals moving together. **160.** *Music.* a rapid succession of tones; a roulade. **161.** *Building Trades.* **a.** the horizontal distance between the face of a wall and the ridge of a roof. **b.** the distance between the first and last risers of a flight of steps or staircase. **c.** the horizontal distance between successive risers on a flight of steps or a staircase. **162.** *Baseball.* the score unit made by safely running around all the bases and reaching home plate. **163.** a series of successful shots, strokes, or the like, in a game. **164.** *Naut.* the immersed portion of a hull abaft the middle body (opposed to *entrance*). **165.** *Horol.* slide (def. 19). **166. a run for one's money, a.** close or keen competition: *The out-of-town team gave us a run for our money.* **b.** enjoyment or profit in return for one's expense: *This may not be the best tool kit, but it will give you a run for your money.* **167. by the run,** *Naut.* without checking: *to let a rope go by the run.* **168. in the long run,** in the course of long experience; in the end: *Retribution will come, in the long run.* **169. on the run,** *Informal.* **a.** moving quickly; hurrying about: *He's so busy, he's always on the run.* **b.** while running or in a hurry: *He eats breakfast on the run.* **c.** escaping or hiding from the police: *He was on the run for two years.* **170. the runs,** *Slang.* diarrhea.

—*adj.* **171.** melted or liquefied: *run butter.* **172.** poured in a melted state; run into and cast in a mold: *run bronze.* [ME *rinne(n),* OE *rinnan;* c. G *rinnen,* Icel *rinna;* form *run* orig. ptp., later extended to present tense]

run·a·bout (run′ə bout′), *n.* **1.** a small, light automobile or other vehicle, usually with an open top; roadster. **2.** a small pleasure motorboat. **3.** one who roves around from place to place or group to group. [n. use of v. phrase *run about*]

run·a·gate (run′ə gāt′), *n. Archaic.* **1.** a fugitive or runaway. **2.** a vagabond or wanderer. [RUN (V.) + obs. *agate* away; sense influenced by contamination with obs. *renegate* (ME *renegat* < ML *renegāt(us)* RENEGADE)]

run-a·round (run′ə round′), *n.* **1.** *Informal.* indecisive or evasive treatment, esp. in response to a request: *Ask for a raise and he'll give you the run-around.* **2.** *Print.* an arrangement of type in which several lines are set in narrower measure than the others in a column to accommodate an illustration, initial, or the like. Also, **runround.** [n. use of v. phrase *run around*]

run·a·way (run′ə wā′), *n.* **1.** one who runs away; fugitive; deserter. **2.** a horse or team that has broken away from control. **3.** the act of running away. **4.** a film produced abroad by a U.S. company. —*adj.* **5.** having run away; escaped; fugitive. **6.** (of a horse or other animal) having escaped from the control of the rider or driver. **7.** pertaining to or accomplished by running away or eloping: *a runaway marriage.* **8.** easily won, as a contest: *a runaway victory at the polls.* **9.** of, pertaining to, or characteristic of a film produced abroad by a U.S. company. **10.** *Com.* characterized by a rapid, uncontrolled price rise: *runaway inflation.* [n., adj. use of v. phrase *run away*]

run′away ship′, *Naut. Slang.* a merchant vessel owned by a U.S. firm but given foreign registry; a vessel under a flag of convenience.

run′away shop′, *U.S.* a business establishment that has been relocated in order to avoid unionization of its employees or to escape local or State labor regulations.

run·back (run′bak′), *n.* **1.** *Football.* **a.** a run made by a player toward the goal line of the opponents after receiving a kick, intercepting a pass, or recovering an opponent's fumble. **b.** the distance covered in making such a run. **2.** *Tennis.* the space on a tennis court between the base line and the backstop. [n. use of v. phrase *run back*]

run′ci·ble spoon′ (run′sə bəl), a forklike utensil with two broad prongs and one sharp, curved prong, as used for serving hors d'oeuvres. [*runcible,* term coined in 1871 by Edward Lear]

run·ci·nate (run′sə nit, -nāt′), *adj. Bot.* pinnately incised, with the lobes or teeth curved backward, as of a leaf. [< L *runcināt(us)* planed off (ptp. of *runcināre*), equiv. to *runcin(a)* plane + *-ātus* -ATE[1]]

Runcinate leaf

run·dale (run′dāl′), *n.* (in Scotland and Ireland) a system of apportioning land by which detached sections or strips are occupied by tenants or landlords. [RUN + DALE]

Rund·bo·gen·stil (ro͝ont′bō′gən shtēl′), *n. German.* an eclectic architectural style of Germany in the early and middle part of the 19th century, largely Italian in derivation and combining Early Christian, Romanesque, and Quattrocento motifs and generally characterized by the use of the round arch. [lit., round-arch style]

run·dle (run′dᵊl), *n.* **1.** a rung of a ladder. **2.** a wheel or similar rotating object. **3.** *Dial.* a runnel. [var. of ROUNDEL]

rund·let (rund′lit), *n.* **1.** an old British measure of capacity, about 18 wine gallons. **2.** a small cask. Also, **runlet.** [ME *rondelet;* see ROUNDLET]

run-down (run′doun′), *adj.* **1.** fatigued; weary; exhausted. **2.** in a state of poor health: *He was in a run-down condition from months of overwork.* **3.** in neglected condition; fallen into disrepair: *It was a run-down house, but some paint and a new roof were all it needed.* **4.** (of a spring-operated device) not running because it is unwound. [adj. use of v. phrase *run down*]

run·down (run′doun′), *n.* **1.** a quick review or summary of main points of information, usually oral: *This brief rundown of past events will bring you up to date.* **2.** *Baseball.* a play in which a base runner is caught between bases by two or more players of the opposing team who toss the ball back and forth in an effort to tag the runner out. [n. use of v. phrase *run down*]

Rund·stedt (ro͝ont′stet, ro͝ond′-; *Ger.* ro͝ont′shtet), *n.* **Karl Ru·dolf Gerd von** (kärl ro͞o′dôlf gert fən), 1875–1953, German field marshal.

rune[1] (ro͞on), *n.* **1.** any of the characters of certain ancient alphabets, as of a script used for writing the Germanic languages, esp. of Scandinavia and Britain, from c200 to c1200, or a script used for inscriptions in a Turkic language of the 6th to 8th centuries from the area near the Orkhon River in Mongolia. **2.** something written or inscribed in such characters. **3.** an aphorism, poem, or saying with mystical meaning or for use in casting a spell. [< Icel *rūn* a secret, writing, runic character; r. ME *rune, roun* a writing, counsel, speech, OE *rūn,* akin to *rūnian* to whisper. See ROUND[2]] —**rune′like′,** *adj.*

rune[2] (ro͞on), *n.* *Poetic.* a poem, song, or verse. [< Finnish *rune* poem, canto < Scand. See RUNE[1]]

runed (ro͞ond), *adj.* having runes inscribed: *a runed ornament.* [RUNE[1] + -ED[3]]

rune·smith (ro͞on′smith′), *n.* a student, writer, transcriber, or decipherer of runes. [RUNE[1] + SMITH]

rune-stone (ro͞on′stōn′), *n.* a stone bearing one or more runic inscriptions.

rung[1] (rung), *v.* pt. and pp. of **ring**[2].

rung[2] (rung), *n.* **1.** one of the crosspieces, usually rounded, forming the steps of a ladder. **2.** a rounded or shaped piece fixed horizontally, for strengthening purposes, as between the legs of a chair. **3.** a stout stick, rod, or bar, esp. one of rounded section, forming a piece in something framed or constructed: *the rungs of a wheel.* [ME; OE *hrung;* c. Goth *hrunga* rod, G *Runge*] —**rung′less,** *adj.*

Rung′e-Kut′ta meth′od (ro͝ong′ə ko͝ot′ä), *Math.* a numerical method, involving successive approximations, used to solve differential equations. [named after Carl D. T. *Runge* (1856–1927) and W. *Kutta* (1867–1944), German mathematicians]

ru·nic[1] (ro͞o′nik), *adj.* **1.** consisting of or set down in runes: *runic inscriptions.* **2.** having some secret or mysterious meaning: *runic rhyme.* **3.** (of ornamental knots, figures, etc.) of an interlaced form seen on ancient monuments, metalwork, etc., of the northern European peoples. [RUNE[1] + -IC]

ru·nic[2] (ro͞o′nik), *adj.* of the ancient Scandinavian class or type, as literature, poetry, etc. [RUNE[2] + -IC]

run-in (run′in′), *n.* **1.** *Informal.* a quarrel; argument. **2.** *Print.* matter that is added to a text, esp. without indenting for a new paragraph. —*adj.* **3.** *Print.* added to a text without indenting. [n., adj. use of v. phrase *run in*]

Run·jeet Singh (run′jit sing′). See **Ranjit Singh.**

run·kle (rung′kəl, ro͝ong′-), *n.* *Scot. and North Eng.* a wrinkle or crease. [< Scand; cf. OIcel *hrukka* to wrinkle]

run·let[1] (run′lit), *n.* a runnel. [RUN (n.) + -LET]

run·let[2] (run′lit), *n.* rundlet.

run·nel (run′ᵊl), *n.* **1.** a small stream; brook; rivulet. **2.** a small channel, as for water. Also, **rundle, runlet.** [RUN (n.) + *-el* dim. suffix]

Run·ne·mede (run′i mēd′), *n.* a town in SW New Jersey. 8396 (1960).

run·ner (run′ər), *n.* **1.** one who or that which runs, esp. as a racer. **2.** a messenger. **3.** a messenger of a bank or brokerage house. **4.** *Baseball.* See **base runner. 5.** *Football.* the ball-carrier. **6.** one whose business it is to solicit patronage or trade. **7.** one acting as collector, agent, or the like for a bank, broker, etc. **8.** something in or on which something else runs or moves. **9.** either of the long, bladelike strips of metal or wood on which a sled or sleigh slides. **10.** the blade of an ice skate. **11.** a sharp, curved blade used to open a furrow for placing seed. **12.** the rotating system of blades driven by the fluid passing through a reaction turbine. **13.** the rotating member of a pair of millstones. Cf. **bed stone. 14.** a roller on which something moves along. **15.** *Furniture.* **a.** a sliding piece, as a loper. **b.** rocker (def. 1). **16.** an operator or manager, as of a machine. **17.** a long, narrow rug, suitable for a hall or passageway. **18.** a long, narrow strip of linen, embroidery, lace, or the like, placed across a table. **19.** *Bot.* **a.** a slender stolon that runs along the surface of the ground and sends out roots and leaves at the nodes, as in the strawberry. **b.** a plant that spreads by such stems. **20.** *Foundry.* any of the channels through which molten metal flows. **21.** a smuggler. **22.** a vessel engaged in smuggling. **23.** *Ichthyol.* a jurel, *Caranx crysos,* found from Cape Cod to Brazil. **24.** *Building Trades.* a horizontal longitudinal timber resting upon the uprights of a staging and supporting the footing pieces. **25.** *Theat.* a piece of carpet or matting placed in the wings for deadening offstage sounds. **26.** *Naut.* a seaman temporarily employed to move a vessel from one place to another. **27.** a tackle or part of a tackle consisting of a line rove through a single block and fixed at one end. See diag. under **tackle. 28.** any whip or fall used for hoisting. [ME; see RUN, -ER[1]]

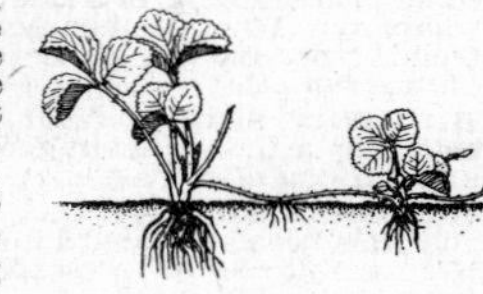
Runner of strawberry

run′ner and tack′le, any of various tackles, as a Spanish burton, employing a runner in addition to the fall.

run′ner bean′, *Brit.* See **string bean** (defs. 1, 2).

run′ner foot′, *Furniture.* a foot having the form of a bar connecting the corresponding front and rear legs of a piece. Also called **bar foot.**

run·ner-up (run′ər up′), *n., pl.* **run·ners-up. 1.** the competitor, player, or team finishing in second place, as in a race, contest, or tournament. **2. runners-up,** the competitors who do not win a contest but who place ahead of the majority of the contestants and share in prizes or honors, as those who place second, third, and fourth, or in the top ten.

run·ning (run′ing), *n.* **1.** the act of one who or that which runs. **2.** managing or directing: *the running of a business.* **3.** the act or an instance of racing: *the 93rd running of the Kentucky Derby.* **4.** the condition of a track or surface to be run or raced on; footing: *Our track team had muddy running today.* **5.** the amount, quality, or type of a liquid flow. **6. out of the running, a.** not competing in a contest or race. **b.** not among the winners or runners-up in a contest or race: *to finish out of the running.* —*adj.* **7.** galloping, racing, moving, or passing rapidly. **8.** (of a horse) **a.** going or proceeding rapidly at the gait of a gallop. **b.** taught to proceed at a gallop. **9.** creeping or climbing, as plants: *a running vine.* **10.** moving or proceeding easily or smoothly. **11.** moving when pulled or hauled, as a rope. **12.** slipping or sliding easily, as a knot or a noose. **13.** operating or functioning as a machine. **14.** (of measurement) linear; straight-line. **15.** cursive, as handwriting. **16.** flowing, as a stream. **17.** liquid or fluid. **18.** present; current: *the running month.* **19.** prevalent, as a condition, state, etc.: *running prices.* **20.** going or carried on continuously; sustained: *a running commentary.* **21.** extending or repeated continuously: *a running pattern.* **22.** performed with or during a run: *a running leap.* **23.** discharging pus or other matter: *a running sore.* **24.** *Naut.* noting any of various objects or assemblages of objects which may be moved in ordinary use: *running bowsprit; running gaff.* **25.** *Naut., Mach.* **a.** noting any block of a tackle that moves. **b.** noting the part of the fall of a tackle that moves through the blocks (opposed to *standing*). —*adv.* **26.** in succession; consecutively: *He slept badly for three nights running.* [ME; see RUN, -ING[1], -ING[2]]

run·ning-birch (run′ing bûrch′), *n.* See **creeping snowberry.**

run′ning board′, a small ledge, step, or footboard, formerly beneath the doors of an automobile, to assist passengers entering or leaving the car.

run′ning bond′, a brickwork bond having successive courses of overlapping stretchers. Also called **stretcher bond.**

run′ning bow′sprit, *Naut.* a bowsprit on a small sailing vessel, made to be hauled into the body of the vessel when the headsails are not set. Also called **reefing bowsprit.**

run′ning broad′ jump′. See under **broad jump** (def. 1).

run′ning dog′, *Archit.* See **Vitruvian scroll.**

run′ning Eng′lish, *Billiards U.S.* the giving of English or spin to the cue ball to enable it to bounce in the direction of a certain angle. Cf. **reverse English** (def. 1).

run′ning fix′, *Navig.* a fix made from a moving vessel or aircraft from observations made at different times, the course and distance run between the observations being considered.

run′ning gaff′, *Naut.* the hoisting gaff. See under **gaff**[1] (def. 4).

run′ning gear′, the working components of a motor-driven or steam-driven vehicle other than those used to develop or transmit power, as wheels, axles, springs, etc., as distinguished from the body.

run′ning head′, *Print.* a descriptive word, phrase, title, or the like, usually repeated at the top of each page of a book, periodical, etc. Also called **running title.**

run′ning knot′, a knot made around and so as to slide along a part of the same rope, thus forming a noose (**running noose**) that tightens as the rope is pulled.

run′ning light′, any of various lights required to be displayed by a vessel or aircraft operating between sunset and sunrise.

run′ning mar′tingale, martingale (def. 2).

run′ning mate′, 1. a horse entered in a race in which another, more important, horse from the same stable, or belonging to the same owner, is run. **2.** a candidate for an office linked with another and more important office, as for the vice-presidency. **3.** a close companion.

run′ning myr′tle, the periwinkle, *Vinca minor.*

run′ning noose′. See under **running knot.**

run′ning pine′, a ground pine, *Lycopodium clavatum.*

run′ning rhythm′, *Pros.* the usual English verse rhythm created by a succession of metrical feet each of which consists of a stressed syllable and one or two unstressed ones. Also called **common rhythm.** Cf. **sprung rhythm.**

run′ning rig′ging, *Naut.* **1.** rigging for handling sails, yards, etc. (opposed to *standing rigging*). **2.** rigging for handling cargo.

run′ning shed′, *Brit.* a railroad roundhouse.

run′ning start′, 1. *Sports.* a start, as in the hop, step, and jump or the running broad jump, in which a contestant begins moving before reaching the starting or take-off point. **2.** an initial advantage in undertaking something; a head start: *His background gave him a running start in business.*

run′ning stitch′, a sewing stitch made by passing the needle in and out repeatedly with short, even stitches.

run′ning sto′ry, *Journalism.* **1.** a story continued in subsequent issues of a newspaper or magazine; serial. **2.** a story sent to the compositor in takes.

run′ning text′, the body of text in a newspaper, magazine, or the like, rather than the heads, illustrations, etc.

run′ning ti′tle. See **running head.**

run·ny (run′ē), *adj.,* **-ni·er, -ni·est. 1.** tending to run or drip: *a runny paste.* **2.** (of the nose) discharging mucus. [RUN + -Y[1]]

Run·ny·mede (run′i mēd′), *n.* a meadow on the S bank of the Thames, W of London, England: supposed place of the signing of the Magna Charta by King John, 1215.

run·off (run′ôf′, -of′), *n.* **1.** something that drains or flows off, as rain which flows off from the land in streams. **2.** a final contest held to determine a victor after earlier contests have eliminated the weaker contestants. **3.** a deciding final contest held after one in which there has been no decisive victor, as between two contestants who have tied for first place. [n. use of v. phrase *run off*]

run′off pri′mary, *U.S.* (esp. in the Southern States) a second primary between the two leading candidates of the first primary to provide nomination by majority rather than by plurality.

run-of-pa·per (run′əv pā′pər), *adj.* See **R.O.P.**

run-of-the-mill (run′əv thə mil′), *adj.* merely average; commonplace; mediocre: *just a plain, run-of-the-mill house; a run-of-the-mill performance.*

run-of-the-mine (run′əv thə mīn′), *adj.* **1.** of or pertaining to ore or coal that is crude, ungraded, etc. **2.** common or ordinary; run-of-the-mill: *a run-of-the-mine performance.* Also, **run-of-mine** (run′əv mīn′).

run-on (run′on′, -ôn′), *adj.* **1.** of or designating something that is added or run on: *a run-on entry in a dictionary.* **2.** *Pros.* (of a line of verse) having a thought which carries over to the next line, esp. without a syntactical break. —*n.* **3.** run-on matter. [adj., n. use of v. phrase *run on*]

run-out (run′out′), *n.* *Manège.* the act of evading a jump or jumping outside of the limiting markers. [n. use of v. phrase *run out*]

run·out (run′out′), *n.* *Mach.* **1.** the gradual termination of a groove on the body of an object not ending there, as the upper termination of a flute in a twist drill. **2.** Also called **back clearance.** a space in a depressed area of an object into which a machine tool or grinding wheel may safely enter at the end of a pass or operation. **3.** the merging of a curved surface into another surface. **4.** an act or instance of running away so as to evade, abandon, or avoid something. [n. use of v. phrase *run out*]

run·o·ver (run′ō′vər), *n.* *Print.* the amount of type matter for a given article, story, etc., that is carried over to another page, column, or line. [n. use of v. phrase *run over*]

run·proof (run′pro͞of′), *adj.* made to resist unraveling, runs, or running, as stockings or dyes. [RUN + -PROOF]

run·round (run′round′), *n.* run-around.

runt (runt), *n.* **1.** an animal that is small or stunted as compared with others of its kind. **2.** the smallest or weakest of a litter, esp. of pigs or puppies. **3.** a person who is small and contemptible: *That runt causes most of the trouble at the meetings.* **4.** *Brit. Dial.* **a.** an old or decayed tree stump. **b.** an old cow or ox. **c.** an ugly old woman; hag. [< MD: ox, cow; akin to OHG *hrint,* G *Rind,* OE *hrīdher*] —**runt′ish,** *adj.* —**runt′ish·ly,** *adv.* —**runt′ish·ness,** *n.*

run-through (run′thro͞o′), *n.* **1.** the performing of a sequence of designated actions, esp. as a trial prior to actual performance; rehearsal; practice. **2.** a quick outline or review: *a run-through of his medical history.* [n. use of v. phrase *run through*]

runt·y (run′tē), *adj.,* **runt·i·er, runt·i·est.** stunted; dwarfish: *The runty puppy seems the most playful of the litter.* [RUNT + -Y[1]] —**runt′i·ness,** *n.*

run-up (run′up′), *n.* **1.** the testing of an airplane engine by accelerating the motor. **2.** an advance in prices, as in the stock market. **3.** *Sports.* **a.** the running up to the jump line by a broad jumper. **b.** the running up of the ball in soccer or polo toward the goal. **c.** the running up of a golf ball toward the putting green. [n. use of v. phrase *run up*]

run·way (run′wā′), *n.* **1.** a way along which something runs. **2.** Also called **airstrip.** a paved or cleared strip on which planes land and take off. **3.** a similar strip on which cars, trucks, etc., may park, load, or enter the stream of traffic. **4.** the beaten track or habitual path of deer or other wild animals. **5.** a fairly large enclosure in which domestic animals may range about: *a runway for dogs.* **6.** the bed of a stream. **7.** *Bowling.* approach (def. 16b). **8.** a narrow platform or ramp extending from a stage into the orchestra pit or into an aisle, as in a theater or nightclub: *The company was banned in Boston for staging the can-can number on the runway.* [RUN + WAY]

Run·yon (run′yən), *n.* **(Alfred) Da·mon** (dā′mən), 1884–1946, U.S. journalist and short-story writer.

ru·pee (ro͞o pē′, ro͞o′pē), *n.* **1.** a nickel coin and monetary unit of India, equal to 100 naye paise or 16 annas and equivalent to about .13 of a U.S. dollar. *Abbr.:* R, Re. **2.** a nickel coin and monetary unit of Pakistan, equal to 100 pice or 16 annas, and equivalent to about .21 of a U.S. dollar. **3.** a paper money and monetary unit of Ceylon, equal to 100 cents and equivalent to about .17 of a U.S. dollar. **4.** the monetary unit of Mauritius, equal to 100 cents and equivalent to about .18 of a U.S. dollar. **5.** Also called **gulf rupee.** the monetary unit of the Bahrein Islands and of Trucial Oman, equal to 100 naye paise and equivalent to about .21 of a U.S. dollar. **6.** the monetary unit of Oman, equal to 100 naye paise and equivalent to about .21 of a U.S. dollar. [< Hindi (Urdu) *rupiyā* < Skt *rūpya* wrought silver]

Ru·pert (ro͞o′pərt; *for 1 also Ger.* ro͞o′pərt), *n.* **1. Prince,** 1619–82, German Royalist general and admiral in the English Civil War (nephew of Charles I of England). **2.** a town in S Idaho. 4153 (1960). **3.** a boy's given name.

ru·pi·ah (ro͞o pē′ə), *n., pl.* **-ah, -ahs.** a paper money and monetary unit of Indonesia, equal to 100 sen and equivalent to about .022 of a U.S. dollar. *Abbr.:* Rp. [< Hindi *rupiyā* RUPEE]

rup·ture (rup′chər), *n., v.,* **-tured, -tur·ing.** —*n.* **1.** the act of breaking or bursting: *The flood led to the rupture of the dam.* **2.** the state of being broken or burst: *a rupture in the earth's surface.* **3.** a breach of harmonious, friendly, or peaceful relations. **4.** *Pathol.* hernia, esp. abdominal hernia. —*v.t.* **5.** to break or

burst: *He ruptured a blood vessel.* **6.** to cause a breach of: *to rupture friendly relations.* **7.** *Pathol.* to affect with hernia. **—***v.i.* **8.** to suffer a break or rupture. [late ME *ruptur* < L *ruptūra,* equiv. to *rupt(us)* (ptp. of *rumpere* to break) + *-ūra* -URE] **—rup/tur·a·ble,** *adj.*
—Syn. 2. fracture, break, split, burst. **5.** fracture, split, disrupt. **—Ant. 2.** seam, union. **5.** unite.

rup/tured duck/, *Slang.* the symbol of the eagle appearing in the honorable discharge emblem of the U.S. armed forces after World War II.

ru·ral (rŏŏr/əl), *adj.* **1.** of, pertaining to, or characteristic of the country, country life, or country people; rustic: *rural tranquility.* **2.** living in the country: *the rural population.* **3.** of or pertaining to agriculture: *rural economy.* [ME < MF < L *rūrāl(is),* equiv. to *rūr-* (s. of *rūs*) the country, as opposed to the city + *-ālis* -AL¹] **—ru/ral·ism,** *n.* **—ru/ral·ist, ru/ral·ite/,** *n.* **—ru/ral·ly,** *adv.* **—ru/ral·ness,** *n.*
—Syn. 1. unsophisticated, rough. RURAL and RUSTIC are terms which refer to the country. RURAL is the official term: *rural education.* It may be used subjectively, and usually in a favorable sense: *the charm of rural life.* RUSTIC, however, may have either favorable or unfavorable connotations. In a derogatory sense, it means rough, boorish, or crude; in a favorable sense, it may suggest a homelike unsophistication or ruggedness: *rustic simplicity.* **—Ant. 1.** urban.

ru/ral dean/, a cleric ranking just below an archdeacon, in charge of an archdeaconry.

Ru/ral Diony/sia. See **Lesser Dionysia.**

ru/ral free/ deliv/ery, free mail delivery in outlying country areas. *Abbr.:* R.F.D.

ru·ral·ise (rŏŏr/ə līz/), *v.t., v.i.,* **-ised, -is·ing.** *Chiefly Brit.* ruralize. **—ru/ral·i·sa/tion,** *n.*

ru·ral·i·ty (rŏŏ ral/i tē), *n., pl.* **-ties. 1.** rural character. **2.** a rural characteristic, matter, or scene. [RURAL + -ITY]

ru·ral·ize (rŏŏr/ə līz/), *v.,* **-ized, -iz·ing.** **—***v.t.* **1.** to make rural. **—***v.i.* **2.** to spend time in the country; rusticate. [RURAL + -IZE] **—ru/ral·i·za/tion,** *n.*

Ru·rik (rŏŏr/ik), *n.* died A.D. 879, Scandinavian prince: founder of the Russian monarchy. Russian, **Ryurik.**

Rus., 1. Russia. **2.** Russian.

ruse (rōōz), *n.* a trick, stratagem, or artifice. [ME (n. use of obs. *rusen* to detour) < MF, deriv. of *ruser* to retreat. See RUSH¹]
—Syn. See **trick.**

Ru·se (rōō/sä), *n.* a city in N Bulgaria, on the Danube. 117,500 (est. 1963).

rush¹ (rush), *v.i.* **1.** to move, act, or progress with speed, impetuosity, or violence. **2.** to dash, esp. to dash forward for an attack or onslaught. **3.** to appear, go, pass, etc., rapidly or suddenly: *Tears rushed to her eyes.* **—***v.t.* **4.** to perform, accomplish, or finish with speed, impetuosity, or violence: *He rushed the work.* **5.** to carry or convey with haste: *to rush an injured person to the hospital.* **6.** to cause to move, act, or progress quickly; hurry: *He rushed his wife to get to the party on time.* **7.** to send, push, force, impel, etc., with unusual speed or haste: *to rush a bill through Congress.* **8.** to attack suddenly and violently; charge. **9.** to overcome or take (a person, place, etc.). **10.** *Informal.* to heap attentions on; court intensively: *to rush a pretty girl.* **11.** to entertain (a prospective fraternity or sorority member) before making bids for membership. **12.** *Football.* **a.** to carry (the ball) forward across the line of scrimmage: *The home team rushed the ball a total of 145 yards.* **b.** to carry the ball (a distance) forward from the line of scrimmage: *The home team rushed 145 yards.* **c.** (of a defensive team member) to attempt to force a way quickly into the backfield in pursuit of (the back in possession of the ball). **—***n.* **13.** the act of rushing; a rapid, impetuous, or violent onward movement. **14.** a hostile attack. **15.** an eager rushing of numbers of persons to some region to be occupied or exploited, esp. to a new mine: *the gold rush to California.* **16.** a sudden appearance or access: *a rush of blood to his face.* **17.** hurried activity; busy haste: *the rush of city life.* **18.** a hurried state, as from pressure of affairs: *to be in a rush.* **19.** press of work, business, traffic, etc., requiring extraordinary effort or haste. **20.** *Football.* **a.** an attempt to carry or instance of carrying the ball across the line of scrimmage. **b.** the act or an instance of rushing the offensive back in possession of the ball. **21.** *U.S.* a scrimmage held as a form of sport between classes or bodies of students in colleges. **22.** Often, **rushes.** *Motion Pictures.* the first prints made after shooting a scene or scenes. **23.** *Informal.* a series of lavish attentions paid a girl by a suitor: *He gave her a big rush.* **24.** the rushing by a fraternity or sorority. **—***adj.* **25.** requiring or done in haste: *a rush order; rush work.* **26.** characterized by business, a press of work or traffic, etc.: *The cafeteria's rush period was from noon to two in the afternoon.* [ME *rusche(n)* < AF *russh(er), russ(er),* c. OF *re(h)usser, re(h)user, ruser* << LL *recūsāre,* to push back < L: to refuse. See RECUSE] **—rush/ing·ly,** *adv.*
—Syn. 1. hasten, run. RUSH, HURRY, DASH, SPEED imply swiftness of movement. RUSH implies haste and sometimes violence in motion through some distance: *to rush to the store.* HURRY suggests a sense of strain or agitation, a breathless rushing to get to a definite place by a certain time: *to hurry to an appointment.* DASH implies impetuosity or spirited, swift movement for a short distance: *to dash to the neighbor's.* SPEED means to go fast, usually by means of some type of transportation, and with some smoothness of motion: *to speed to a nearby city.* **—Ant. 17.** sloth, lethargy.

rush² (rush), *n.* **1.** any grasslike herb of the genus *Juncus,* having pithy or hollow stems, found in wet or marshy places. **2.** any plant of the family *Juncaceae.* **3.** any of various similar plants. **4.** a stem of such a plant, used for making chair bottoms, mats, baskets, etc. **5.** something of little or no value: *not worth a rush.* [ME *rusch, risch,* OE *rysc, risc;* c. D, obs. G *Rusch*] **—rush/like/,** *adj.*

Rush (rush), *n.* **1. Benjamin,** 1745–1813, U.S. physician and political leader: author of medical treatises. **2.** his son, **Richard,** 1780–1859, U.S. lawyer, politician, and diplomat.

rush/ can/dle, a candle having a wick of a dried and partly peeled, pithy-stemmed rush. Also called **rush/ light/.**

rush·ee (ru shē/), *n.* a college student who is rushed by a fraternity or sorority. [RUSH¹ + -EE]

rush·er (rush/ər), *n.* **1.** one who or that which rushes. **2.** *Football.* a player whose assignment is to rush or whose special skill is rushing. [RUSH¹ + -ER¹]

rush/ hour/, a time of day in which large numbers of people are in transit, as going to or returning from work, and which is characterized by particularly heavy traffic: *He left work at four to avoid the five o'clock rush hour.* **—rush/-hour/,** *adj.*

rush·ing (rush/ing), *n.* a sequence of social events sponsored by a fraternity or sorority for prospective members prior to bidding and pledging. [RUSH¹ + -ING¹]

Rush·ville (rush/vil), *n.* **1.** a town in E Indiana. 7264 (1960). **2.** a town in W Illinois. 2819 (1960).

rush·work (rush/wûrk/), *n.* **1.** the handicraft of making objects woven of rushes. **2.** an object so made. [RUSH² + WORK]

rush·y (rush/ē), *adj.,* **rush·i·er, rush·i·est. 1.** abounding with rushes or their stems. **2.** covered or strewn with rushes. **3.** consisting or made of rushes. **4.** rushlike. [ME; see RUSH², -Y¹] **—rush/i·ness,** *n.*

ru/sine ant/ler (rōō/sīn, -sin), an antler resembling that of the sambar. [< NL *Rus(a)* name of genus (< Hindi *rūsā*) + -INE¹]

rusk (rusk), *n.* **1.** a slice of sweet raised bread dried and cooked again in the oven; zwieback. **2.** light, soft, sweetened biscuit. [< Sp or Pg *rusca* twist of bread, lit., screw]

Rusk (rusk), *n.* **1. (David) Dean,** born 1909, U.S. statesman: Secretary of State 1961–69. **2.** a town in E Texas. 4900 (1960).

Rus·kin (rus/kin), *n.* **John,** 1819–1900, English author, art critic, and social reformer. **—Rus·kin/i·an,** *adj.*

Rus/kin Goth/ic, a mid-Victorian architectural style adapted from Italian Gothic work as a popular response to the writings of John Ruskin, characterized by the presence of mainly flat surfaces with horizontal banding and sharply contrasting voussoirs formed by alternating stonework and brickwork or by stonework in two colors.

Russ (rus), *n., pl.* **Russ, Russ·es,** *adj.* **—***n.* **1.** a Russian. **2.** *Archaic.* the Russian language. **—***adj.* **3.** Russian. [< Russ *Rus';* cf. F, G *russe,* D *rus*]

Russ (rōōs), *n.* Nieman.

Russ., 1. Russia. **2.** Russian.

Rus·sell (rus/əl), *n.* **1. Bertrand (Arthur William), 3rd Earl,** born 1872, English philosopher, mathematician, and author: Nobel prize for literature 1950. **2. Charles Edward,** 1860–1941, U.S. journalist, sociologist, biographer, and political leader. **3. Elizabeth Mary, Countess** (*Mary Annette Beauchamp*) ("*Elizabeth*"), 1866–1941, Australian novelist. **4. George William** ("*AE*"), 1867–1935, Irish poet and painter. **5. Henry Norris,** 1877–1957, U.S. astronomer. **6. John Russell, 1st Earl,** (*Lord John Russell*), 1792–1878, British statesman: prime minister 1846–52, 1865–66. **7. Lillian** (*Helen Louise Leonard*), 1861–1922, U.S. singer and actress. **8.** a town in central Kansas. 6113 (1960). **9.** a boy's given name.

Rus·sell·ite (rus/ə līt/), *n.* *Disparaging.* a member of the Jehovah's Witnesses. [after Charles T. *Russell* (1852–1916), American religious leader; see -ITE¹]

Rus·sell·ville (rus/əl vil), *n.* **1.** a town in central Arkansas. 8921 (1960). **2.** a town in NW Alabama. 6628 (1960). **3.** a town in S Kentucky. 5861 (1960).

Rus·se·lyn (rus/ə lin/, rus/ə lin), *n.* a girl's given name.

rus·set (rus/it), *n.* **1.** yellowish brown, light brown, or reddish brown. **2.** a coarse reddish-brown or brownish homespun cloth formerly used for clothing. **3.** any of various apples which have a rough brownish skin and ripen in the autumn. **4.** a brownish, roughened area on fruit, resulting from diseases, insects, or spraying. **—***adj.* **5.** yellowish-brown, light-brown, or reddish-brown. [ME < OF *rousset,* dim. of *rous* red << L *russ(us).* See RED] **—rus/set·ish, rus/set·y,** *adj.* **—rus/set·like/,** *adj.*

Rus·sia (rush/ə), *n.* **1.** Also called **Russian Empire.** Russian, **Rossiya.** a former empire in E Europe and N and W Asia: overthrown by the Russian Revolution 1917. *Cap.:* St. Petersburg (1703–1917). **2.** See **Union of Soviet Socialist Republics. 3.** See **Russian Federation.**

Rus/sia leath/er, a fine, smooth leather produced by careful tanning and dyeing, esp. in dark red: originally prepared in Russia, but imitated elsewhere. Also called **russia.**

Rus·sian (rush/ən), *adj.* **1.** of or pertaining to Russia, its people, or their language. **—***n.* **2.** a native or inhabitant of Russia. **3.** a member of the dominant Slavic race of Russia. **4.** the principal Slavic language, the predominant language of Russia, written in a Cyrillic script. Cf. **Byelorussian** (def. 3), **Great Russian** (def. 2), **Ukrainian** (def. 3).

Rus/sian Church/. See **Russian Orthodox Church.**

Rus/sian dan/delion, kok-saghyz.

Rus/sian dress/ing, a sharp mayonnaise dressing containing chopped pickles, chili sauce, pimientos, etc., and sometimes black or red caviar.

Rus/sian Em/pire, Russia (def. 1).

Rus/sian Federa/tion, a republic extending from E Europe to N and W Asia. 147,386,000; 6,593,000 sq. mi. *Cap.:* Moscow. Also called **Russia, Rus/sian Re·pub/lic.** Formerly (1918–91), **Russian Soviet Federated Socialist Republic.**

Rus·sian·ize (rush/ə nīz/), *v.t.,* **-ized, -iz·ing. 1.** to make Russian; impart Russian characteristics to. **2.** to subordinate and force to adhere to Russian culture, ideology, etc. **3.** (*sometimes l.c.*) to treat (leather) by a process similar to that used on Russia leather or by any process that will produce such leather. [RUSSIAN + -IZE] **—Rus/sian·i·za/tion,** *n.*

Rus/sian ol/ive, oleaster.

Rus/sian Or/thodox Church/, the autocephalous Eastern Church in Russia: the branch of the Orthodox Church that constituted the established church in Russia until 1917. Also called **Russian Church.**

Rus/sian Revolu/tion, 1. Also called **February Revolution.** the uprising in Russia in March, 1917 (February Old Style) in which the Czarist government collapsed and a provisional government was established. **2.** Also called **October Revolution.** the overthrow of this provisional government by a coup d'état on November 7, 1917 (October 25 Old Style), establishing the Soviet government.

Rus/sian roulette/, a game of chance in which each player in turn, using a revolver containing one bullet, spins the cylinder of the revolver, points the muzzle at his head, and pulls the trigger.

Rus/sian So/viet Fed/erated So/cialist Re·pub/lic, former name (1918–91) of the **Russian Federation.** *Abbr.:* RSFSR, R.S.F.S.R.

Rus/sian this/tle, a tumbleweed, *Salsola tragus,* growing from two to three feet in diameter and having small-leafed, spiny branches.

Rus/sian Tur/kestan. See under **Turkestan.**

Rus/sian wolf/hound, borzoi.

Rus/sian worm/wood, a tall, stiff herb, *Artemisia sacrorum,* of Siberia, having whitish leaves and greenish-white flower heads.

Rus/sian Zone/, a zone in Germany controlled by the Soviet Union 1945–89. Cf. **East Germany.**

Russo-, a combining form of **Russia** or **Russian:** *Russophobe.*

Rus/so-Jap/an·ese War/ (rus/ō jap/ə nēz/, -nēs/), the war (1904–1905) between Russia and Japan.

Rus·so·phile (rus/ə fīl/), *n.* one who is friendly to, admires, or prefers Russia or Russian customs, institutions, etc. [RUSSO- + -PHILE]

Rus·so·phobe (rus/ə fōb/), *n.* one who hates or fears Russia or the Russians. [RUSSO- + -PHOBE] **—Rus/so·pho/bi·a,** *n.*

rust (rust), *n.* **1.** Also called **iron rust.** the red or orange coating which forms on the surface of iron when exposed to air and moisture, consisting chiefly of ferric hydroxide and ferric oxide formed by oxidation. **2.** any film or coating on metal caused by oxidation. **3.** a stain resembling this coating. **4.** any growth, habit, influence, or agency tending to injure, deteriorate, or impair the mind, character, abilities, usefulness, etc. **5.** *Plant Pathol.* **a.** any of several diseases of plants, characterized by reddish, brownish, or black pustules on the leaves, stems, etc., caused by fungi of the order *Uredinales.* **b.** Also called **rust/ fun/gus.** a fungus causing this disease. **c.** any of several other diseases of unknown cause, characterized by reddish-brown spots or discolorations on the affected parts. **6.** reddish yellow, reddish brown, or yellowish red. **—***v.i.* **7.** to become or grow rusty, as iron. **8.** to contract rust. **9.** to deteriorate or become impaired, as through inaction or disuse. **10.** to become rust-colored. **—***v.t.* **11.** to affect with rust. **12.** to impair as if with rust. **13.** to make rust-colored. **14. rust together,** to join two metal pieces, as iron pipes, by causing the joint to rust. **—***adj.* **15.** having the color rust. [ME; OE *rūst;* c. G *Rost;* akin to RED]
—Syn. 2. corrosion. **9.** decay, decline.

rust-col·ored (rust/kul/ərd), *adj.* of the color rust.

rus·tic (rus/tik), *adj.* **1.** of, pertaining to, or living in the country, as distinguished from towns or cities; rural. **2.** simple, artless, or unsophisticated. **3.** uncouth, rude, or boorish. **4.** made of roughly dressed limbs or roots of trees, as garden seats. **5.** (of stonework) having the surfaces rough or irregular and the joints sunken or chamfered. **—***n.* **6.** a country person. **7.** an unsophisticated country person. [late ME < L *rūstic(us),* equiv. to *rūs* the country + *-t-* connective cons. + *-icus* -IC] **rus/ti·cal,** *adj.* **—rus/ti·cal·ly, rus/tic·ly,** *adv.* **—rus/ti·cal·ness, rus/tic·ness,** *n.*
—Syn. 1. See **rural. —Ant. 1.** urban.

rus·ti·cate (rus/tə kāt/), *v.,* **-cat·ed, -cat·ing.** **—***v.i.* **1.** to go to the country. **2.** to stay or sojourn in the country. **—***v.t.* **3.** to send to or domicile in the country. **4.** to make rustic, as persons, manners, etc. **5.** to finish (a wall surface) so as to produce or suggest rustication. **6.** *Brit.* to suspend (a student) from a university as punishment. [< L *rūsticāt(us)* (ptp. of *rūsticārī* to live in the country), equiv. to *rūstic(us)* RUSTIC + *-ātus* -ATE¹] **—rus/ti·ca/tor,** *n.*

rus·ti·ca·tion (rus/tə kā/shən), *n.* **1.** Also called **rus/tic work/.** *Archit.* any of various forms of ashlar so dressed and tooled that the visible faces are raised above or otherwise contrasted with the horizontal and usually the vertical joints. **2.** the act of one who or that which rusticates. [< L *rūsticātiōn-* (s. of *rūsticātiō*). See RUSTICATE, -ION]

rus·tic·i·ty (ru stis/i tē), *n., pl.* **-ties. 1.** state or quality of being rustic. **2.** rural character or life. [< MF *rusticite* < L *rustic(us)* RUSTIC + MF *-ite* -ITY]

rus/tic joint/, a joint between stones recessed from the faces between sunken drafts or bevels.

Rus·tin (rus/tin), *n.* **Bay·ard** (bā/ərd), born 1910, U.S. civil rights leader.

rust/ joint/, (in plumbing and metalwork) a watertight joint made between two pieces by rusting them together.

rus·tle (rus/əl), *v.,* **-tled, -tling,** *n.* **—***v.i.* **1.** to make a succession of slight, soft sounds, as of parts rubbing gently one on another, as leaves, silks, papers, etc. **2.** to cause such sounds by moving or stirring something. **3.** *U.S. Informal.* to move, proceed, or work energetically: *Rustle around and see what you can find.* **—***v.t.* **4.** to move or stir so as to cause a rustling sound: *The wind rustled the leaves.* **5.** *U.S. Informal.* to move, bring, or get by energetic action: *I'll go rustle some supper.* **6.** *U.S. Informal.* to steal (livestock, esp. cattle). **7. rustle up,** *Informal.* to find, gather, or assemble by effort or search: *to rustle up some supper.* **—***n.* **8.** the sound made by anything that rustles: *the rustle of leaves.* [ME; OE *hrūxl(ian)* (to) make a noise; c. RUSH¹] **—rus/tling·ly,** *adv.*

rus·tler (rus/lər), *n.* **1.** one who or that which rustles. **2.** *U.S. Informal.* an active, energetic person. **3.** *U.S. Informal.* a cattle thief. [RUSTLE + -ER¹]

rust·less (rust/lis), *adj.* **1.** free from rust. **2.** rustproof. [RUST + -LESS]

rust·proof (rust/prōōf/), *adj.* not subject to rusting. [RUST + -PROOF]

rus·tre (rus/tər), *n.* *Heraldry.* a lozenge having at the center a circular opening of the tincture of the field. [< F < ?]

rus·tred (rus/tərd), *adj.* *Armor.* noting armor formed of imbricated oval rings sewn to a flexible backing. [RUSTRE + -ED³]

rust·y¹ (rus/tē), *adj.,* **rust·i·er, rust·i·est. 1.** covered with or affected by rust. **2.** consisting of or produced by rust. **3.** of or tending toward the color rust; rust-colored. **4.** faded or shabby; impaired by time or wear, as clothes, drapery, etc. **5.** impaired through disuse or neglect: *My Latin is rusty.* **6.** having lost agility or alertness; out of practice: *I am a bit rusty at tennis.* **7.** (of plants) affected with the rust disease. [ME *rusti,* OE *rūstig.* See RUST, -Y[1]] —**rust′i·ly,** *adv.* —**rust′i·ness,** *n.*

rust·y[2] (rus′tē), *adj.,* **rust·i·er, rust·i·est. 1.** restive; stubborn: *a rusty horse.* **2.** *Chiefly Dial.* ill-tempered; cross. [appar. special use of RUSTY[1] in the sense of rough, churlish; but cf. obs. *resty* RESTIVE]

Rus·ty (rus′tē), *n.* a boy's or girl's given name.

rust′y black′bird, a North American blackbird, *Euphagus carolinus,* the male of which has plumage that is uniformly bluish-black in the spring and rusty-edged in the fall. Also called **rust′y grack′le.**

rust′y dab′. See **yellowtail flounder.**

rust′y gum′, gum-myrtle.

Rust′y Nail′, a cocktail made from Scotch and Drambuie, usually in equal portions, served over ice in an Old-Fashioned glass.

rut[1] (rut), *n., v.,* **rut·ted, rut·ting.** —*n.* **1.** a furrow or track in the ground, esp. one made by the passage of a vehicle or vehicles. **2.** any furrow, groove, etc. **3.** a fixed or established mode of procedure or course of life, usually dull or unpromising: *to fall into a rut.* —*v.t.* **4.** to make a rut or ruts in; furrow. [? var. of ROUTE]

rut[2] (rut), *n., v.,* **rut·ted, rut·ting.** —*n.* **1.** the periodically recurring sexual excitement of the deer, goat, sheep, etc. —*v.i.* **2.** to be in the condition of rut. [ME *rutte* < MF *rut, ruit* < LL *rugitus* a roaring, n. use of L ptp. of *rugīre* to roar]

ru·ta·ba·ga (ro͞o′tə bā′gə), *n.* **1.** a brassicaceous plant, *Brassica Napobrassica,* having a yellow- or white-fleshed, edible tuber. **2.** the edible tuber, a variety of turnip. Also called **Swedish turnip.** [< Sw (dial.) *rotabagge*]

ru·ta·ceous (ro͞o tā′shəs), *adj. Bot.* **1.** of or like rue. **2.** belonging to the *Rutaceae,* a family of plants comprising the rue, dittany, angostura bark tree, orange, lemon, shaddock, kumquat, etc. [< NL *Rutace(ae)* name of the family (L *rūt(a)* RUE[2] + *-aceae* -ACEAE) + -OUS]

ruth (ro͞oth), *n.* **1.** pity or compassion. **2.** sorrow or grief. [ME *ruthe, reuthe.* See RUE[1], -TH[1]]
—**Syn. 1.** mercy, sympathy. —**Ant. 1.** cruelty.

Ruth (ro͞oth), *n.* **1.** the wife of Boaz, the daughter-in-law of Naomi, and an ancestress of David. **2.** a book of the Bible bearing her name. **3.** a girl's given name.

Ruth (ro͞oth), *n.* **George Herman** ("*Babe*"), 1895–1948, U.S. baseball player.

Ru·the·ni·a (ro͞o thē′nē ə, -thēn′yə), *n.* a former province in E Slovakia. Cf. **Carpatho-Ukraine.**

Ru·the·ni·an (ro͞o thē′nē ən), *adj.* **1.** of or pertaining to the Little Russians, esp. a division of them dwelling in Galicia, Ruthenia, and neighboring regions. —*n.* **2.** one of the Ruthenian people. **3.** the dialect of Ukrainian spoken in Ruthenia. **4.** a member of a former Orthodox religious group which entered into communion with the Roman Catholic Church in 1596 and became the "Uniate Church of the Little Russians." [RUTHENI(A) + -AN]

ru·then·ic (ro͞o then′ik, -thē′nik), *adj. Chem.* containing ruthenium in a higher valence state than the corresponding ruthenious compound. [RUTHEN(IUM) + -IC]

ru·the·ni·ous (ro͞o thē′nē əs), *adj. Chem.* containing bivalent ruthenium. [RUTHEN(IUM) + -OUS]

ru·the·ni·um (ro͞o thē′nē əm), *n. Chem.* a difficultly fusible, steel-gray, rare metallic element, belonging to the platinum group of metals, and only slightly reactive with aqua regia. *Symbol:* Ru; *at. wt.:* 101.07; *at. no.:* 44; *sp. gr.:* 12.2 at 20°C. [< NL, named after RUTHENIA (from the fact it was first found in ore from the region); see -IUM]

Ruth·er·ford (ruth′ər fərd), *n.* **1. Ernest Rutherford, 1st Baron,** 1871–1937, English physicist, born in New Zealand: Nobel prize for chemistry 1908. **2. Joseph Franklin,** 1869–1942, U.S. leader of Jehovah's Witnesses. **3.** a city in NE New Jersey. 20,473 (1960). **4.** a boy's given name.

Ruth′erford scat′tering, *Physics.* the scattering of an alpha particle through a large angle with respect to the original direction of motion of the particle, caused by an atom (**Ruth′erford at′om**) with most of the mass and all of the positive electric charge concentrated at a center or nucleus. Also called **alpha-particle scattering, Ruth′erford al′pha-particle scat′tering.** [named after Baron Ernest RUTHERFORD]

Ruth·er·ford·ton (ruth′ər fərd tən), *n.* a town in W North Carolina. 3392 (1960).

Ruth·er·furd (ruth′ər fərd), *n.* a crater in the third quadrant of the face of the moon: about 25 miles in diameter.

ruth·ful (ro͞oth′fəl), *adj.* **1.** compassionate or sorrowful. **2.** causing or apt to cause sorrow or pity. [ME; see RUTH, -FUL] —**ruth′ful·ly,** *adv.* —**ruth′ful·ness,** *n.*

ruth·less (ro͞oth′lis), *adj.* without pity or compassion; cruel; merciless: *a ruthless tyrant.* [ME; see RUTH, -LESS] —**ruth′less·ly,** *adv.* —**ruth′less·ness,** *n.*
—**Syn.** hard, harsh, unrelenting, adamant, relentless, fell, inhuman, ferocious, barbarous. See **cruel.**

ru·ti·lant (ro͞ot′ᵊlənt), *adj.* glowing or glittering with ruddy or golden light. [ME < L *rutilant-* (s. of *rutilāns,* prp. of *rutilāre*), equiv. to *rutil(us)* red, reddish + *-ant-* -ANT]

ru·ti·lat·ed (ro͞ot′ᵊlā′tid), *adj. Mineral.* containing fine, embedded needles of rutile. [< L *rutilāt(us)* (ptp. of *rutilāre;* see RUTILANT) + -ED[2]]

ru·tile (ro͞o′tēl, -tīl), *n.* a common mineral, titanium dioxide, TiO_2, usually reddish-brown in color with a brilliant metallic or adamantine luster, occurring in crystals: used to coat welding rods. [< F < G *Rutil* < L *rutil(is)* red]

ru·tin (ro͞ot′ᵊn), *n. Pharm.* a bright yellow or greenish-yellow substance, $C_{27}H_{30}O_{16}$, obtained chiefly from buckwheat, and used in the treatment of capillary fragility. [*rut-* (< NL *Ruta*) + -IN[2]]

Rut·land (rut′lənd), *n.* **1.** a city in W Vermont. 18,325 (1960). **2.** Rutlandshire.

Rut·land·shire (rut′lənd shēr′, -shər), *n.* a county in central England. 23,959 (1961); 152 sq. mi. *Co. seat:* Oakham. Also called **Rutland.**

Rut·ledge (rut′lij), *n.* **1. Ann,** 1816–35, fiancée of Abraham Lincoln. **2. Edward,** 1749–1800, U.S. lawyer and statesman. **3.** his brother, **John,** 1739–1800, U.S. jurist and statesman: associate justice of the U.S. Supreme Court 1789–91. **4. Wi·ley Blount** (wī′lē blunt), 1894–1949, U.S. jurist: associate justice of the U.S. Supreme Court 1943–49.

rut·ter (rut′ər), *n.* portolano. [obs. form of *ruttier* < MF *routier,* equiv. to *route* ROUTE + *-ier* -ER[1]]

rut·tish (rut′ish), *adj.* salacious; lustful. [RUT[2] + -ISH[1]] —**rut′tish·ly,** *adv.* —**rut′tish·ness,** *n.*

rut·ty (rut′ē), *adj.,* **-ti·er, -ti·est.** full of or abounding in ruts, as a road. [RUT[1] + -Y[1]] —**rut′ti·ly,** *adv.* —**rut′ti·ness,** *n.*

Ru·wen·zo·ri (ro͞o′wen zōr′ē, -zôr′ē), *n.* a mountain group in central Africa between Lake Albert and Lake Edward: sometimes identified with Ptolemy's "Mountains of the Moon." Highest peak, Mt. Stanley, 16,790 ft.

Ruys·dael (rois′dāl, -däl, rīz′-, rīs′-; *Du.* rœis′däl), *n.* Ruisdael.

Ruy·ter (roi′tər; *Du.* rœi′tər), *n.* **Mi·chel A·dri·aans·soon de** (*Du.* mi′ᴋʜəl ä′drē än′so͞on də), 1607–76, Dutch admiral.

Ru·žič·ka (*Serbo-Croatian* ro͞o′zhēch kä; *Eng.* ro͞o′ zich kə, ro͞o zich′-), *n.* **Le·o·pold** (lā′ō pôlt′), 1887–1976, Swiss chemist, born in Yugoslavia: Nobel prize 1939.

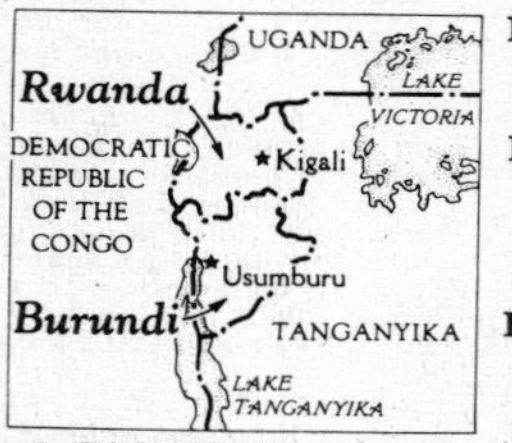

RV, 1. recreational vehicle: a van or other utility vehicle, usually used for camping and equipped with living facilities. **2.** Revised Version (of the Bible).

R.V.S.V.P., a prompt reply is requested. [< F *r(épondez) v(ite) s('il) v(ous) p(lait)* please reply quickly]

R.W., 1. Right Worshipful. **2.** Right Worthy.

Rwan·da (ro͝o än′də), *n.* a republic in central Africa, E of the Republic of the Congo: formerly comprising the northern part of the Belgian trust territory of Ruanda-Urundi; became independent July 1, 1962. 2,634,451 (1962); 10,169 sq. mi. *Cap.:* Kigali.

Rwy., Railway.

Rx, 1. prescription. **2.** (in prescriptions) take. [< L *recipe*] **3.** tens of rupees.

-ry, var. of **-ery:** *heraldry; husbandry; dentistry; tenantry; jewelry.* [ME *-rie* < OF; short form of -ERY]

Ry., Railway.

ry·al (rī′əl), *n.* **1.** See **rose noble. 2.** a former gold coin of Scotland, equal to 60 shillings. **3.** a former silver coin of Scotland, equal to 30 shillings. Also, **rial.** [ME: ROYAL]

Ry′ans Slough′, a town in NW California. 3634 (1960).

Rya·zan (ʀyä zän′yᵊ), *n.* a city in the W RSFSR, in the central Soviet Union in Europe, SE of Moscow. 275,000 (est. 1964).

Ry·binsk (*Russ.* ʀwē′binsk), *n.* former name of **Shcherbakov.**

Rych·ard (rich′ərd), *n.* a boy's given name. Also, **Richard.**

Ry·der (rī′dər), *n.* **1. Albert Pink·ham** (ping′kəm), 1847–1917, U.S. painter. **2.** Also, **Rider.** a boy's given name.

rye[1] (rī), *n.* **1.** a widely cultivated cereal grass, *Secale cereale,* having one-nerved glumes and two- or three-flowered spikelets. **2.** the seeds or grain of this plant, used for making flour and whiskey, and as a livestock feed. **3.** See **rye bread. 4.** a straight whiskey distilled from a mash containing 51 percent or more rye grain. **5.** *Eastern U.S. and Canada.* a blended whiskey. —*adj.* **6.** made with rye grain or flour: *rye rolls.* Also called **rye whiskey** (for defs. 4, 5). [ME; OE *ryge;* c. OIcel *rug(r);* akin to D *rogge,* G *Roggen*]

rye[2] (rī), *n.* a gentleman: *Romany rye.* [< Gypsy *rai* < Skt *rājan* king]

Rye (rī), *n.* a city in SE New York, on Long Island Sound. 14,225 (1960).

rye′ bread′, bread that is made either entirely or partly from rye flour, often with caraway seeds.

rye·grass (rī′gras′, -gräs′), *n.* any of several European grasses of the genus *Lolium,* as *L. perenne* (**perennial ryegrass**), grown for forage in the U.S. [RYE[1] + GRASS]

Rye′ House′ Plot′, *Eng. Hist.* a conspiracy (1683), plotted by radical Whigs, to assassinate Charles II and his brother James.

Rye·land (rī′lənd), *n.* one of an English breed of white-faced sheep, yielding wool of high quality. [after *Ryelands,* name of a district in Herefordshire, England]

rye′ whis′key, rye[1] (defs. 4, 5).

ryke (rīk, rēk), *Scot.* reach.

Ry·ley (rī′lē), *n.* a boy's given name. Also, **Riley.**

rynd (rīnd, rind), *n.* rind[2].

Ryo·jun·ko (ʀyô′jo͞on kô′), *n.* Japanese name of **Port Arthur.** Also called **Ryo·jun** (ʀyô′jo͞on′).

ry·ot (rī′ət), *n.* (in India) **1.** a peasant. **2.** one who holds land as a cultivator of the soil. [< Urdu *raiyat* < Pers < Ar *ra'īyah* flock or herd, peasantry]

Ry·sa·nek (rē′zə nek′), *n.* **Le·o·nie** (le′ō nē′), born 1926, Austrian soprano.

Rys·wick (riz′wik), *n.* a village in the SW Netherlands, near The Hague: Treaty of Ryswick 1697. Dutch, **Rijswijk.**

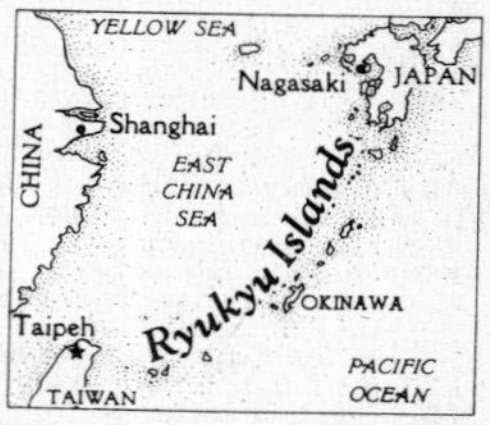

Ryu·kyu (*Jap.* ʀyo͞o′kyo͞o; *Eng.* rē o͞o′kyo͞o′), *n.* a chain of 55 islands in the W Pacific between Japan and Formosa. Islands S of 28° N latitude under U.S. administration; islands N of 28° returned to Japan. 913,000 (1960); 2046 sq. mi.

Ryu·rik (ʀyo͞o′ʀik), *n.* Rurik.

S

S, s (es), *n., pl.* **S's** or **Ss, s's** or **ss.** **1.** the 19th letter of the English alphabet, a consonant. **2.** any spoken sound represented by the letter *S* or *s*, as in *saw, sense, goose,* etc. **3.** something having the shape of an S. **4.** a written or printed representation of the letter *S* or *s*. **5.** a device, as a printer's type, for reproducing the letter *S* or *s*.

S, 1. satisfactory. **2.** Saxon. **3.** *Elect.* siemens. **4.** signature. **5.** small. **6.** soft. **7.** South. **8.** Southern.

S, 1. the 19th in order or in a series, or, when *I* is omitted, the 18th. **2.** (*sometimes l.c.*) the medieval Roman numeral for 7 or 70. Cf. **Roman numerals. 3.** *Physics.* S-state.

s, 1. satisfactory. **2.** signature. **3.** small. **4.** soft. **5.** south.

's[1], an ending used in writing to represent the possessive morpheme after most singular and some plural nouns, noun phrases, and noun substitutes, esp. after those not ending in a letter or combination of letters representing an *s* or *z* sound, as in *man's, men's, baby's, James's, witness's,* (or *witness'*), *king of England's, anyone else's,* etc. [ME, OE *-es*]

's[2], **1.** contraction of *is: He's here.* **2.** contraction of *does: What's he do for a living now?* **3.** contraction of *has: He's just gone.*

's[3], *Archaic.* a contraction of *God's*, as in *'swounds; 'sdeath; 'sblood.*

's[4], a contraction of *us*, as in *Let's go.*

's[5], a contraction of *as*, as in *so's to get there on time.*

-s[1], a native English suffix used in the formation of adverbs: *always; betimes; needs; unawares.* Cf. **-ways.** [ME, OE *-es*, orig. gen. ending]

-s[2], an ending marking the third person sing. indicative active of verbs: *walks.* [ME (north), OE (north) *-(e)s* (orig. ending of 2nd pers. sing., as in L and Gk); r. ME, OE *-eth* -ETH[1]]

-s[3], an ending marking the regular plural of nouns: *boys.* Also, **-es.** [ME *-(e)s*, OE *-as*, pl. ending (nom. and acc.) of some masculine nouns]

-s[4], a quasi-plural ending, occurring in words for which there is no proper singular: *trousers; pants; shorts; scissors; shears.* [prob. abstracted from *trousers* and *scissors*]

S., 1. Sabbath. **2.** Saint. **3.** Saturday. **4.** Saxon. **5.** schilling. **6.** School. **7.** Sea. **8.** Senate. **9.** September. **10.** shilling. **11.** (in prescriptions) **a.** mark; write; label. [< L *signā*] **b.** let it be written. [< L *signētur*] **12.** Signor. **13.** Small. **14.** Socialist. **15.** Society. **16.** Fellow. [< L *socius*] **17.** sol[2]. **18.** South. **19.** Southern. **20.** sucre. **21.** Sunday.

s., 1. saint. **2.** school. **3.** second. **4.** section. **5.** see. **6.** series. **7.** shilling; shillings. **8.** sign. **9.** signed. **10.** silver. **11.** singular. **12.** sire. **13.** small. **14.** society. **15.** son. **16.** south. **17.** southern. **18.** steamer. **19.** stem. **20.** stem of. **21.** substantive.

Sa, *Chem. Obs.* samarium.

S/A, *Com.* See **société anonyme.**

S.A., 1. Salvation Army. **2.** (in prescriptions) according to art. [< L *secundum artem*] **3.** South Africa. **4.** South America. **5.** South Australia. **6.** *Com.* See **société anonyme.**

s.a., 1. semiannual. **2.** sex appeal. **3.** without year or date. [< L *sine annō*] **4.** subject to approval.

S.A.A., Speech Association of America.

Saa·di (sä dē′), *n.* (*Muslih ud-Din*) 1184?–1291?, Persian poet. Also, **Sadi.**

Saar (zär, sär), *n.* **1.** Also called **Saar′ Ba′sin, Saarland.** a territory in W West Germany, in the Saar River valley: governed by the League of Nations 1919–35; returned to Germany 1935 as a result of a plebiscite; under French economic control following World War II until 1956. 1,102,000 (1963); 991 sq. mi. **2.** a river in W Europe, flowing N from the Vosges Mountains in NE France to the Moselle River in W West Germany. 150 mi. long. French, **Sarre.**

Saar·brück·en (zär bro͝ok′ən, sär-; *Ger.* zäʀ bʀʏk′ən), *n.* a city in W West Germany: the chief city of the Saar. 133,100 (1963).

Saa·re·maa (sär′ə mä′), *n.* an island in the Baltic, at the mouth of the Gulf of Riga, forming part of Estonia in the Soviet Union in Europe. ab. 60,000; 1144 sq. mi. Also, **Saa·re** (sär′ä). German, **Oesel, Ösel.**

Saa·ri·nen (sär′ə nen′, -nən), *n.* **Ee·ro** (ā′rō), 1910–61, U.S. architect born in Finland.

Saar·land (zär′land′, sär′-; *Ger.* zär′länt′), *n.* Saar (def. 1). —**Saar′land′er,** *n.*

Sa·a·ve·dra La·mas (sä′ä ve′thrä lä′mäs), **Car·los** (käʀ′lôs), 1878?–1959, Argentine statesman and diplomat: Nobel peace prize 1936.

Sab., Sabbath.

Sa·ba (sä′bə), *n.* **1.** an island in the Netherlands Antilles, in the N Leeward Islands. 1094 (est. 1960); 5 sq. mi. **2.** Biblical name, **Sheba.** an ancient kingdom in southwestern Arabia noted for its extensive trade, esp. in spices and gems.

Sa·ba·dell (sä′bä del′), *n.* a city in NE Spain, N of Barcelona. 105,152 (1960).

sab·a·dil·la (sab′ə dil′ə), *n.* **1.** a liliaceous plant, *Schoenocaulon officinale*, of Mexico, having long, grasslike leaves and bitter seeds. **2.** the seeds of this plant, used medicinally and as a source of veratrine and veratridine. [< Sp *cebadilla* Indian caustic barley, dim. of *cebada* barley < L *cibāta*, fem. ptp. of *cibāre* to feed, equiv. to *cib-* feed + *-āta* -ATE[1]]

Sa·bae·an (sə bē′ən), *adj., n.* Sabean.

Sa·bah (sä′bä), *n.* a part of the federation of Malaysia, on NE Borneo: formerly a British crown colony. 454,421 (est. 1960); 29,347 sq. mi. *Cap.:* Jesselton. Formerly, **North Borneo, British North Borneo.**

sa·ba·lo (sab′ə lō′), *n., pl.* **-los.** the tarpon. [< Sp *sábalo* shad < ?]

Sab·a·oth (sab′ē oth′, -ōth′, sab′ā-, sə bā′ōth), *n.* (*construed as pl.*) armies; hosts. Rom. 9:29; James 5:4. [< Heb *ç'bhāōth*, pl. of *çābā* army]

Sa·ba·ta (sä bä′tä), *n.* **Vic·tor de** (vēk tôʀ′ de), born 1892, Italian composer and conductor.

Sa·ba·tier (sᴀ bᴀ tyā′), *n.* **Paul** (pôl), 1854–1941, French chemist: Nobel prize 1912.

Sab·a·ti·ni (sab′ə tē′nē; *It.* sä′bä tē′nē), *n.* **Raf·a·el** (raf′ē əl), 1875–1950, English novelist and short-story writer, born in Italy.

sab·a·ton (sab′ə ton′), *n.* *Armor.* a foot defense of mail or of a number of lames with solid toe and heel pieces. Also called **solleret.** [ME < OPr, equiv. to *sabat(a)* shoe + *-on* aug. suffix. See SABOT]

sa·ba·yon (sᴀ bᴀ yôɴ′), *n.* zabaglione. [< F < It *zabaion(e)*]

Sab·bat (sab′ət), *n.* (*sometimes l.c.*) *Demonology.* (in the 14th–16th centuries) a secret rendezvous of witches and sorcerers for worshiping the Devil, characterized by orgiastic rites, dances, feasting, etc. Also, **sabbath.** Also called **witches' sabbath.** [< L *sabbat(um)* SABBATH]

Sab·ba·tar·i·an (sab′ə târ′ē ən), *n.* **1.** one who observes the seventh day of the week, Saturday, as the Sabbath. **2.** one who adheres to or favors a strict observance of Sunday. —*adj.* **3.** of or pertaining to the Sabbath and its observance. [< L *sabbatāri(us)* (*sabbat(um)* SABBATH + *-ārius* -ARY) + -AN] —**Sab′ba·tar′i·an·ism,** *n.*

Sab·bath (sab′əth), *n.* **1.** the seventh day of the week (Saturday) as the day of rest and religious observance among the Jews and some Christian churches. Ex. 20:8–11; Deut. 5:13–15. **2.** the first day of the week (Sunday), similarly observed by most Christians in commemoration of the Resurrection of Christ. **3.** (*sometimes l.c.*) *Demonology.* sabbat. [ME, var. of ME, OE *sabbat* < L *sabbat(um)* < Gk *sábbaton* < Heb *shabbat* rest] —**Sab′bath·less,** *adj.* —**Sab′bath·like′,** *adj.* —**Syn. 2.** See **Sunday.**

Sab′bath School′, 1. See **Sunday School. 2.** (among Seventh-Day Adventists) such a school held on Saturday, their holy day.

Sab·bat·i·cal (sə bat′i kəl), *adj.* **1.** of or pertaining or appropriate to the Sabbath. **2.** (*l.c.*) bringing a period of rest: *a sabbatical leave.* —*n.* **3.** (*l.c.*) See **sabbatical year.** Also, **Sab·bat′ic.** [< Gk *sabbatik(ós)* (*sábbat(on)* SABBATH + *-ikos* -IC) + -AL[1]] —**Sab·bat′i·cal·ly,** *adv.* —**Sab·bat′i·cal·ness,** *n.*

sabbat′ical year′, 1. (in a school, college, university, etc.) a year, usually every seventh, of release from normal teaching duties granted to a professor, as for study or travel. **2.** *Chiefly Biblical.* a yearlong period to be observed by Jews once every seven years, during which the fields were to be left untilled and all agricultural labors were to be suspended. Lev. 25. Cf. **jubilee** (def. 6).

Sab·ba·tise (sab′ə tīz′), *v.i., v.t.,* **-tised, -tis·ing.** (*often l.c.*) *Chiefly Brit.* sabbatize. —**Sab′ba·ti·sa′tion,** *n.*

Sab·ba·tize (sab′ə tīz′), *v.,* **-tized, -tiz·ing.** (*often l.c.*) —*v.i.* **1.** to keep the Sabbath. —*v.t.* **2.** to keep as the Sabbath. [ME *sabbatise(n)* < LL *sabbatiz(āre)* < Gk *sabbatíz(ein)*, equiv. to *sábbat(on)* SABBATH + *-izein* -IZE] —**Sab′ba·ti·za′tion,** *n.*

Sa·be·an (sə bē′ən), *adj.* **1.** of or pertaining to Saba. —*n.* **2.** an inhabitant of Saba. Also, **Sabaean.** [< L *sabae(us)* (< Gk *sabaîos* of Saba or Sheba) + -AN]

Sa·bel·li·an (sə bel′ē ən), *n.* a member of a group of early Italian peoples including the Samnites and Sabines. [< L *Sabell(ī)* group of Italian tribes + -IAN]

sa·ber (sā′bər), *n.* **1.** a heavy, one-edged sword, usually slightly curved, used esp. by cavalry. **2.** a soldier armed with such a sword. **3.** *Fencing.* **a.** a sword having two cutting edges and a blunt point. **b.** the art or sport of fencing with the saber, with the target being limited to the head, trunk, and arms, and hits being made with the front edge and the upper part of the back edge of the sword and by thrusts. —*v.t.* **4.** to strike, wound, or kill with a saber. Also, *Brit.,* **sabre.** [< F *sabre* < G *Sabel* (now *Säbel*) < Magyar *szablya* < Russ < ?] —**sa′ber·like′,** *adj.*

sa′ber bean′. See **sword bean.**

sa′ber rat′tling, an openly threatening display of military power or a verbal threat to use retaliatory military force.

sa′ber saw′, a portable electric jigsaw.

sa·ber-toothed (sā′bər to͞otht′), *adj.* having long, saberlike upper canine teeth, sometimes extending below the margin of the lower jaw.

Saber-toothed tiger, *Smilodon californicus* (Length 6 ft.; teeth to 8 in.)

sa′ber-toothed ti′ger, any of several extinct catlike mammals from the Oligocene to Pleistocene epochs, having greatly elongated, saberlike upper canine teeth.

sa·bin (sā′bin), *n.* *Physics.* a unit of sound absorption, equal to one square foot of a perfectly absorptive surface. [named after W. C. *Sabine* (1868–1919), American physicist]

Sa·bin (sā′bin), *n.* **Albert Bruce,** born 1906, U.S. physician, born in Russia: developed Sabin vaccine.

Sa·bi·na (sə bī′nə, -bē′-), *n.* a girl's given name.

Sa·bine (sā′bīn), *adj.* **1.** of or belonging to an ancient people of central Italy who lived chiefly in the Apennines NE of Rome and were subjugated by the Romans about 290 B.C. —*n.* **2.** one of the Sabine people. **3.** the Italic language of the Sabines. **4.** the smaller of two adjoining craters in the first quadrant of the face of the moon, the larger being Ritter: about 18 miles in diameter. [< L *Sabīn(us)*]

Sa·bine (sə bēn′), *n.* a river flowing SE and S from NE Texas, forming the boundary between Texas and Louisiana and then through Sabine Lake to the Gulf of Mexico. ab. 500 mi. long.

Sabine′ Lake′, a shallow lake on the boundary between Texas and Louisiana: formed by a widening of the Sabine River. ab. 17 mi. long, 7 mi. wide.

Sa·bin·i·a·nus (sə bin′ē ā′nəs), *n.* died A.D. 606, pope 604–606.

Sa′bin vaccine′, an orally administered vaccine of live viruses for immunization against poliomyelitis. [named after A. B. SABIN]

sa·ble (sā′bəl), *n., pl.* **-bles,** (*esp. collectively for 1, 2*) **-ble,** *adj.* —*n.* **1.** an Old World weasellike mammal, *Mustela zibellina,* of cold regions, valued for its dark brown fur. **2.** a marten, esp. *Mustela americana.* **3.** the fur of the sable. **4.** the color black, often being one of the heraldic colors. **5. sables,** mourning garments. —*adj.* **6.** of the heraldic color sable. **7.** made of the fur or hair of the sable. **8.** very dark; black. [ME < OF < MLG *sabel,* OHG *zobel* < Slav (cf. Pol *sobol*); meaning "black" is unexplained (sable fur is brown)]

Sable, *Mustela zibellina* (Total length 28 in.; tail 9½ in.)

Sa·ble (sā′bəl), *n.* **Cape, 1.** a cape on a small island at the SW tip of Nova Scotia, Canada: lighthouse. **2.** a cape at the S tip of Florida.

sa′ble an′telope, a large antelope, *Hippotragus niger,* of Africa, with long, saberlike horns.

Sable antelope (5 ft. high at shoulder; horns 2½ ft.; length 6½ ft.)

sa·ble·fish (sā′bəl fish′), *n., pl.* **-fish·es,** (*esp. collectively*) **-fish.** a large, blackish, food fish, *Anoplopoma fimbria,* found in the North Pacific. Also called **blackcod.** [SABLE + FISH]

sa·bo·ra (sə bôr′ə, -bôr′ə), *n., pl.* **sa·bo·ra·im** (sä′bō-rä′im, -bō-). (*often cap.*) *Judaism.* one of a group of Jewish scholars, active in the rabbinical academies of Babylonia during the 6th century A.D., whose editing of the work of the Babylonian amoraim constituted the final stage in the preparation of the Babylonian Gemara. Cf. **amora, tanna.** [< Aram *sābhōrā* scholar, thinker, deriv. of *sebhar* to think]

sab·ot (sab′ō; *Fr.* SA bō′), *n., pl.* **sab·ots** (sab′ōz; *Fr.* SA bō′). **1.** a shoe made of a single block of wood hollowed out, worn by peasants in France, Belgium, etc., and as part of the Dutch peasant costume. **2.** a shoe with a thick wooden sole and sides and a top of coarse leather. **3.** *Mil.* **a.** a wooden or metal disk formerly attached to a projectile in a muzzleloading cannon. **b.** a soft metal ring at the base of a projectile that makes the projectile conform to the rifling grooves of a gun. [< F, perh. MF, b. *savate* old shoe (c. OPr *sabata,* It *ciabatta,* Sp *zapato*) and *bot* BOOT] —**sa·boted** (sa bōd′, sab′ōd), *adj.*

sab·o·tage (sab′ə täzh′, sab′ə täzh′), *n., v.,* **-taged, -tag·ing.** —*n.* **1.** any underhand interference with production, work, etc., in a plant, factory, etc., as by enemy agents during wartime or by employees during a trade dispute. **2.** any undermining of a cause. —*v.t.* **3.** to injure or attack by sabotage. [< F, equiv. to *sabot-* (deriv. of *saboter* to botch) + *-age* -AGE]

sab·o·teur (sab′ə tûr′), *n.* one who commits or practices sabotage. [< F, equiv. to *sabot(er)* (to) botch + *-eur* -OR²]

sa·bra (sä′brə, -brä), *n.* a person born in Israel. [< NHeb *ṣābrāh*]

sa·bre (sā′bər), *n., v.,* **-bred, -bring.** *Brit.* saber.

sa·bre·tache (sā′bər tash′, sab′ər-), *n.* a case, usually of leather, hanging from long straps beside the saber of a cavalryman. [< F < G *Säbeltasche,* equiv. to *Säbel* SABER + *Tasche* pocket]

Sa·bri·na (sə brē′nə), *n.* a girl's given name.

sab·u·lous (sab′yə ləs), *adj.* sandy; gritty. [< L *sabul(um)* sand + -OUS] —**sab·u·los·i·ty** (sab′yə los′i tē), *n.*

sac (sak), *n.* a baglike structure in an animal or plant, as one containing fluid. [< L *sacc(us)* SACK¹] —**sac′like′,** *adj.*

Sac (sak, sôk), *n., pl.* **Sacs,** (*esp. collectively*) **Sac. 1.** a member of a tribe of Algonquian-speaking Indians, formerly of northern Wisconsin and Iowa, now in Iowa and Oklahoma. **2.** a member of this tribe. Also, **Sauk.**

S.A.C., Strategic Air Command. Also, **SAC**

sac-a-lait (sak′ə lā′, sak′ə lā′), *n.* the white crappie. See under **crappie.** [< LaF < Choctaw *sakli* trout, taken as *sac* SACK¹ + *à* for + *lait* milk]

sac·a·ton (sak′ə tōn′), *n.* a grass, *Sporobolus Wrightii,* used in the semiarid southwestern U.S. for pasture or hay. [< AmerSp *zacatón,* equiv. to *zacat(e)* coarse grass (< Nahuatl *zacatl*) + *-on* aug. suffix]

sac·but (sak′but′), *n.* sackbut (def. 1).

sac·cad·ic (sa kä′dik, sə-), *adj.* characterized by discontinuous or sporadic movement; jerky. [< F *saccade* jerk + -IC]

sac·cate (sak′it, -āt), *adj.* having a sac or the form of a sac. [< NL *saccāt(us),* equiv. to *sacc(us)* SACK¹ + *-ātus* -ATE¹]

sacchar-, a learned borrowing from Greek meaning "sugar," used in the formation of technical terms: *saccharoid.* Also, *esp. before a consonant,* **saccharo-.** [< Gk *sákchar*]

sac·cha·rate (sak′ə rāt′), *n.* *Chem.* **1.** a salt of saccharic acid. **2.** a compound formed by interaction of sucrose with a metallic oxide, usually lime, and useful in the purification of sugar. [SACCHAR- + -ATE²]

sac·char·ic (sə kar′ik), *adj.* *Chem.* **1.** of or derived from saccharin or a saccharine substance. **2.** of or derived from saccharic acid. [SACCHAR- + -IC]

sacchar′ic ac′id, *Chem.* a white, needlelike, crystalline, water-soluble solid or syrup, COOH(CHOH)$_4$COOH, usually made by the oxidation of cane sugar, glucose, or starch by nitric acid. Also called **glucaric acid.**

sac·cha·ride (sak′ə rīd′, -rid), *n.* *Chem.* **1.** an organic compound containing a sugar or sugars. **2.** a simple sugar; monosaccharide. **3.** an ester of sucrose. [SACCHAR- + -IDE]

sac·cha·rif·er·ous (sak′ə rif′ər əs), *adj.* *Chem.* containing or yielding sugar. [SACCHAR- + -I- + -FEROUS]

sac·char·i·fy (sə kar′ə fī′, sak′ər ə fī′), *v.t.,* **-fied, -fy·ing.** to convert (starch) into sugar. [SACCHAR- + -IFY] —**sac·char·i·fi·ca·tion** (sə kar′ə fə kā′shən), *n.* —**sac·char′i·fi′er,** *n.*

sac·cha·rim·e·ter (sak′ə rim′i tər), *n.* an optical instrument for determining the strength of sugar solutions by measuring the rotation of the plane of polarized light they produce. [SACCHAR- + -I- + -METER]

sac·cha·rim·e·try (sak′ə rim′i trē), *n.* *Biochem.* the process of measuring the amount of sugar in a sample, as with a saccharimeter or by polarimetry. [SACCHAR- + -I- + -METRY]

sac·cha·rin (sak′ə rin), *n.* *Chem.* a white, crystalline, slightly water-soluble powder, $C_6H_4COSO_2NH$, produced synthetically, which in dilute solution is 500 times as sweet as sugar: used chiefly as a noncaloric sugar substitute in the manufacture of syrups, foods, and beverages. Also called **benzosulfimide, gluside, sac′charin insol′uble.** Cf. **saccharin sodium.** [SACCHAR- + -IN²]

sac·cha·rine (sak′ə rin, -rīn′), *adj.* **1.** of a sugary sweetness: *a saccharine smile.* **2.** pertaining to, of the nature of, or containing sugar. [SACCHAR- + -INE¹] —**sac′cha·rine·ly,** *adv.* —**sac·cha·rin·i·ty** (sak′ə rin′i tē), *n.*

sac′charin so′dium, *Chem.* a white, crystalline, intensely sweet, water-soluble powder, $C_6H_4COSO_2NNa \cdot 2H_2O$, the sodium salt of saccharin, and used similarly. Also called **sac′charin sol′uble.**

sac·cha·rise (sak′ə rīz′), *v.t.,* **-rised, -ris·ing.** *Chiefly Brit.* saccharize. —**sac′cha·ri·sa′tion,** *n.*

sac·cha·rize (sak′ə rīz′), *v.t.,* **-rized, -riz·ing. 1.** to convert into sugar; saccharify. **2.** to convert (the starches in grain) to fermentable sugars during mashing. [SACCHAR- + -IZE] —**sac′cha·ri·za′tion,** *n.*

saccharo-, var. of **sacchar-** before a consonant: *saccharometer.*

sac·cha·ro·far·i·na·ceous (sak′ə rō far′ə nā′shəs), *adj.* pertaining to or consisting of sugar and meal. [SACCHARO- + FARINACEOUS]

sac·cha·roid (sak′ə roid′), *adj.* *Geol.* having a granular texture like that of loaf sugar. Also, **sac′cha·roi′dal.** [SACCHAR- + -OID]

sac′cha·ro·lac′tic ac′id (sak′ə rō lak′tik, sak′-), *Chem.* See **mucic acid.** [SACCHARO- + LACTIC ACID]

sac·cha·ro·lyt·ic (sak′ə rō lit′ik), *adj.* *Chem.* of or causing the hydrolysis of sugars. [SACCHARO- + -LYTIC]

sac·cha·rom·e·ter (sak′ə rom′i tər), *n.* *Chem.* an instrument for measuring the amount of sugar in a solution. [SACCHARO- + -METER] —**sac·cha·ro·met·ric** (sak′ə rō me′trik), **sac′cha·ro·met′ri·cal,** *adj.* —**sac′cha·rom′e·try,** *n.*

sac·cha·rose (sak′ə rōs′), *n.* *Chem.* sucrose. [SACCHAR- + -OSE²]

Sac·cid·a·nan·da (such′chid′ä nun′də), *n.* Satcitananda.

Sac′ Cit′y (sôk), a town in W Iowa. 3354 (1960).

Sac·co (sak′ō; *It.* säk′kō), *n.* **Ni·co·la** (nē kō′lä), 1891–1927, Italian anarchist, in the U.S. after 1908: together with Bartolomeo Vanzetti, was found guilty of robbery and murder, 1921; executed 1927.

sac·cu·lar (sak′yə lər), *adj.* having the form of a sac. [SACCUL(US) + -AR¹]

sac·cu·late (sak′yə lāt′), *adj.* formed into or having a saccule, sac, or saclike dilation. Also, **sac′cu·lat′ed.** [SACCUL(US) + -ATE¹] —**sac′cu·la′tion,** *n.*

sac·cule (sak′yōōl), *n.* **1.** *Anat.* the smaller of two sacs in the membranous labyrinth of the internal ear. Cf. **utricle** (def. 3). **2.** a little sac. [< L *saccul(us)* SACK¹ + -ULE]

sac·cu·lus (sak′yə ləs), *n., pl.* **-li** (-lī′). a saccule. [< L, equiv. to *sacc(us)* SACK¹ + *-ulus* -ULE]

sa·cel·lum (sə kel′əm, -sel′-), *n., pl.* **-la** (-lə). **1.** a small chapel, as a monument within a church. **2.** (in ancient Rome) a shrine open to the sky. [< L; dim. of SACRUM]

sac·er·do·tal (sas′ər dōt′əl), *adj.* of priests; priestly. [late ME < L *sacerdōtāl(is),* equiv. to *sacerdōt-* (s. of *sacerdōs*) priest + *-ālis* -AL¹] —**sac′er·do′tal·ly,** *adv.*

sac·er·do·tal·ism (sas′ər dōt′əliz′əm), *n.* **1.** the system, spirit, or methods of the priesthood. **2.** *Usually Disparaging.* priestcraft. [SACERDOTAL + -ISM] —**sac′er·do′tal·ist,** *n.*

SACEUR, Supreme Allied Commander, Europe. Also, **SACEur**

sa·chem (sā′chəm), *n.* **1.** (among some tribes of American Indians) **a.** the chief of a tribe. **b.** the chief of a confederation. **2.** a member of the governing body of the League of the Iroquois. **3.** one of the high officials in the Tammany Society. [< Narragansett *sachima*] —**sa′chem·dom,** *n.* —**sa·chem·ic** (sā chem′ik, sā′chə-mik), *adj.* —**sa′chem·ship′,** *n.*

Sa·cher-Ma·soch (zä′KHər mä′zōKH), **Le·o·pold von** (lā′ō pōlt′ fən), 1836–95, Austrian novelist.

Sa·cher tor·te (sä′kər tôr′tə; *Ger.* zä′KHər tôr′tə), *pl.* **Sa·cher tor·tes,** *Ger.* **Sa·cher tor·ten** (zä′KHər tôr′tən). a chocolate cake covered with apricot jam and chocolate icing, usually served with whipped cream. [after the *Sacher* Hotel, near Vienna, Austria]

sa·chet (sa shā′ *or, esp. Brit.,* sash′ā), *n.* **1.** a small bag, case, or pad containing perfuming powder or the like, placed among handkerchiefs, lingerie, etc., to impart a pleasant scent. **2.** Also, **sachet′ pow′der.** the powder contained in such a case. [late ME < MF, equiv. to *sach-* (var. of *sac* SACK¹) + *-et* -ET]

Sachs (zäks), *n.* **Hans** (häns), 1494–1576, German Meistersinger: author of stories, songs, poems and dramatic works.

Sach·sen (zäk′sən), *n.* German name of **Saxony.**

sack¹ (sak), *n.* **1.** a large bag of strong, coarsely woven material, as for grain, potatoes, coal, etc. **2.** the amount a sack holds. **3.** *U.S.* any bag: *a sack of candy.* **4.** Also, **sacque. a.** a loose-fitting dress, as a gown with a Watteau back, esp. one fashionable in the late 17th century and much of the 18th century. **b.** a loose-fitting coat, jacket, or cape. **5.** *U.S. Slang.* bed: *I bet he's still in the sack.* **6.** *Slang.* dismissal or discharge, as from a job. **7.** *Baseball Slang.* a base. **8. hit the sack,** *Slang.* to go to bed; go to sleep: *He never hits the sack before midnight.* **9. hold the sack.** See **bag** (def. 15). —*v.t.* **10.** to put into a sack or sacks. **11.** *Slang.* to dismiss or discharge, as from a job. **12. sack out,** *Slang.* to go to bed; fall asleep: *even too tired to sack out.* [ME *sak,* OE *sacc* < L *sacc(us)* bag, sackcloth < Gk *sákkos* < Sem (Heb *saq*); cf. Goth *sakkus* < Gk] —**sack′like′,** *adj.* —**Syn. 1.** See **bag.**

sack² (sak), *v.t.* **1.** to pillage or loot after capture; plunder: *to sack a city.* —*n.* **2.** the plundering of a captured place; pillage: *the sack of Troy.* [< MF phrase *mettre à sac* to put to pillage, lit., to put (the loot) in the bag; *sac,* in this sense < It *sacc(o)* looting, loot, special use of *sacco* SACK¹, bag] —**sack′er,** *n.* —**Syn. 1.** spoil, despoil. See **rob. 2.** looting; destruction, ruin.

sack³ (sak), *n.* any of various strong light-colored wines formerly brought from Spain, the Canary Islands, etc. [< F (*vin*) *sec* dry (wine) < L *sicc(us)* dry]

sack·but (sak′but′), *n.* **1.** Also, **sacbut, sagbut.** a medieval form of the trombone. **2.** *Bible.* an ancient stringed musical instrument. Dan. 3. [< MF *saquebute,* var. of *saqueboute,* equiv. to *saque(r)* (to) pull + *boute(r)* (to) push]

sack·cloth (sak′klôth′, -kloth′), *n.* **1.** sacking. **2.** coarse cloth worn as a sign of mourning or penitence. **3. in sackcloth and ashes,** in a state of repentance or sorrow; contrite: *She would be in sackcloth and ashes for days over every trifling error she made.* [ME; see SACK¹, CLOTH] —**sack′clothed′,** *adj.*

sack′ coat′, a short coat or jacket with a straight back and no seam at the waist. —**sack′-coat′ed,** *adj.*

sack′ dress′, a loose, unbelted dress that hangs straight from the shoulder to the hemline.

sack·er (sak′ər), *n.* *Baseball Slang.* a baseman: *a slick-fielding third sacker.* [SACK¹ + -ER¹]

sack·ful (sak′fŏŏl), *n., pl.* **-fuls.** the amount a sack holds. [late ME; see SACK¹, -FUL]

sack·ing (sak′ing), *n.* stout, coarse woven material of hemp, jute, or the like, chiefly for sacks. Also called **sackcloth.** [SACK¹ + -ING¹]

sack·less (sak′lis), *adj.* *Scot.* **1.** lacking energy; dispirited. **2.** feeble-minded. **3.** *Archaic.* guiltless. [ME *sakles,* OE *saclēas.* See SAKE¹, -LESS]

sack′ race′, a race in which each contestant jumps ahead while his legs are confined in a sack. —**sack′ rac′er.** —**sack′ rac′ing.**

sack′ suit′, a man's suit that has a loose-fitting jacket.

Sack·ville (sak′vil), *n.* **Thomas, 1st Earl of Dorset,** 1536–1608, British statesman and poet.

Sack·ville-West (sak′vil west′), *n.* **Dame Victoria Mary** ("*V. Sackville-West*"), 1892–1962, English poet and novelist, wife of Harold Nicolson.

sacque (sak), *n.* sack¹ (def. 4).

sa·cral¹ (sā′krəl), *adj.* of or pertaining to sacred rites or observances. [< L *sacr(um)* sacred thing + -AL¹]

sa·cral² (sā′krəl), *adj.* of or pertaining to the sacrum. [< NL *sacrāl(is)* pertaining to the SACRUM]

sac·ra·ment (sak′rə mənt), *n.* **1.** *Eccles.* **a.** a visible sign of an inward grace. **b.** a visible sign instituted by Jesus Christ to symbolize or confer grace: the sacraments of the Protestant churches are baptism and the Lord's Supper; the sacraments of the Roman Catholic and Greek Orthodox churches are baptism, confirmation, the Eucharist, matrimony, penance, holy orders, and extreme unction. **2.** (*often cap.*) Also called **Holy Sacrament.** the Eucharist or Lord's Supper. **3.** the consecrated elements of the Eucharist, esp. the bread. **4.** something regarded as possessing a sacred character or mysterious significance. **5.** a sign, token, or symbol. **6.** an oath; solemn pledge. [ME < eccl. L *sacrāment(um)* obligation, oath, equiv. to L *sacrā(re)* (to) devote + *-mentum* -MENT]

sac·ra·men·tal (sak′rə men′təl), *adj.* **1.** of, pertaining to, or of the nature of a sacrament, esp. the sacrament of the Eucharist. **2.** peculiarly sacred: *a sacramental obligation.* —*n.* **3.** *Rom. Cath. Ch.* an action (as the sign of the cross), a ceremony resembling a sacrament, or a sacred object, regarded as being instituted by the church and serving as a means of receiving sanctifying grace. [< LL *sacrāmentāl(is).* See SACRAMENT, -AL¹] —**sac′ra·men′tal·ly,** *adv.* —**sac′ra·men′tal·ness, sac′ra·men·tal′i·ty,** *n.*

sac·ra·men·tal·ist (sak′rə men′təlist), *n.* one who holds strong convictions about the importance and efficacy of the sacrament. [SACRAMENTAL + -IST]

sac′ramen′tal wine′, wine for use in a Eucharistic service. Also called **altar wine.**

Sac·ra·men·tar·i·an (sak′rə men târ′ē ən), *n.* **1.** one who maintains that the Eucharistic elements have only symbolic significance and are not corporeal manifestations of Christ. **2.** (*l.c.*) a sacramentalist. —*adj.* **3.** of or pertaining to the Sacramentarians. **4.** (*l.c.*) of or pertaining to the sacraments. [< NL *sacrāmentāri(us)* (see SACRAMENT, -ARY) + -AN] —**sac′ra·men·tar′i·an·ism,** *n.*

Sac·ra·men·to (sak′rə men′tō), *n.* **1.** a port in and the capital of California, in the central part, on the Sacramento River. 191,667 (1960). **2.** a river flowing S from N California to San Francisco Bay. 382 mi. long.

Sac′ramen′to Moun′tains, a mountain range in S New Mexico and SW Texas: highest peak, Sierra Blanco, 12,003 ft.

Sac′ramen′to stur′geon. See **white sturgeon.**

sa·crar·i·um (sə krâr′ē əm), *n., pl.* **-crar·i·a** (-krâr′ē-ə). **1.** *Rom. Cath. Ch.* a piscina. **2.** *Eccles.* the sanctuary or chancel. **3.** *Rom. Hist.* a shrine; a sanctuary. [< L, equiv. to *sacr(er)* holy + *-ārium* -ARY] —**sa·crar′i·al,** *adj.*

Sa·cra Ro·ma·na Ro·ta (sä′krə rō mä′nə rō′tə), *Rom. Cath. Ch.* the official name of the Rota.

sa·cred (sā′krid), *adj.* **1.** devoted or dedicated to a deity or to some religious purpose; consecrated. **2.** entitled to veneration or religious respect by association with divinity or divine things; holy. **3.** pertaining to or connected with religion, as literature, music, etc. (opposed to *profane* and *secular*). **4.** reverently dedicated

to some person or object: *a monument sacred to St. Peter.* **5.** regarded with reverence: *the sacred memory of a dead hero.* **6.** secured against violation, infringement, etc., by reverence, sense of right, etc.: *sacred oaths; sacred rights.* **7.** properly immune from violence, interference, etc., as a person or his office. [ME, deriv. of *sacr-* (s. of *sacren* to consecrate) < L *sacr(āre)* (to) devote, equiv. to *sacer* holy + *-āre* inf. suffix; see -ED²] —**sa′cred·ly,** *adv.* —**sa′cred·ness,** *n.*
—**Syn. 2.** venerable, divine. See **holy. 4.** consecrated. **5.** revered. **6.** sacrosanct. **7.** inviolate, inviolable. —**Ant. 2.** blasphemous.

sa′cred baboon′. See **hamadryas baboon.**

sa′cred bamboo′, nandin.

Sa′cred Col′lege of Car′dinals, the official name of the **College of Cardinals.**

sa′cred cow′, 1. any individual, group, or organization held in such high popular esteem as to appear exempt from all, even justified, criticism. **2.** *Journalism.* a person, institution, etc., invariably receiving favorable or discreet mention, esp. in or on a particular newspaper, radio station, or the like, as by fiat or implied fiat of the publisher or owner: *As the publisher's old college roommate he was a sacred cow, and his political errors were never exposed.*

Sa′cred Heart′, *Rom. Cath. Ch.* the physical heart of Jesus, to which special devotion is offered as a symbol of His love and redemptive sacrifice.

sa′cred i′bis, an African ibis, *Threskionis aethiopica,* having a black, naked head and neck and white and black plumage, venerated by the ancient Egyptians. See illus. under **ibis.**

sa′cred lo′tus. See **Indian lotus.**

Sa′cred Nine′, *Class. Myth.* the Muses.

sa′cred or′ders. See **major order.**

Sa′cred Ro′man Ro′ta, rota¹ (def. 3).

sa′cred thread′, *Hinduism.* a cord worn by Hindus of the three upper castes as a symbol of spiritual rebirth.

Sa·cre du Prin·temps, Le (lə sa′krᵊ dy praN-täN′). See **Rite of Spring, The.**

Sa′cred Writ′, Scripture.

sac·ri·fice (sak′rə fīs′), *n., v.,* **-ficed, -fic·ing.** —*n.* **1.** the offering of animal, plant, or human life or of some material possession to a deity, as in propitiation or homage. **2.** something that is so offered. **3.** the surrender or destruction of something prized or desirable for the sake of something considered as having a higher or more pressing claim. **4.** the thing so surrendered or devoted. **5.** a loss incurred in selling something below its value. **6.** Also called **sac′rifice bunt′, sac′rifice hit′.** *Baseball.* a bunt made when there are fewer than two players out, not resulting in a double play, that advances the base runner nearest home without an error being committed if there is an attempt to put him out, and that results in either the batter's being put out at first base, reaching first on an error made in the attempt for the put-out, or being safe because of an attempt to put out another runner. —*v.t.* **7.** to make a sacrifice or offering of. **8.** to surrender or give up, or permit injury or disadvantage to, for the sake of something else. **9.** to dispose of (goods, property, etc.) regardless of profit. **10.** *Baseball.* to cause the advance of (a base runner) by a sacrifice. —*v.i.* **11.** *Baseball.* to make a sacrifice: *He sacrificed with two on and none out.* **12.** to offer or make a sacrifice. [ME < OF < L *sacrific(ium),* equiv. to *sacri-* (comb. form of *sacer* holy) + *-fic-* -FIC + *-ium* n. suffix] —**sac′ri·fice′a·ble,** *adj.* —**sac′ri·fic′er,** *n.*

sac′rifice fly′, *Baseball.* a fly ball that enables a base runner, usually at third base, to score after the ball is caught.

sac·ri·fi·cial (sak′rə fish′əl), *adj.* pertaining to or concerned with sacrifice. [< L *sacrifici(um)* SACRIFICE + -AL¹] —**sac′ri·fi′cial·ly,** *adv.*

sac′rifi′cial an′ode, an anode that is attached to a metal object subject to electrolysis and is decomposed instead of the object.

sac·ri·lege (sac′rə lij), *n.* **1.** the violation or profanation of anything sacred or held sacred. **2.** an instance of this. **3.** the stealing of anything consecrated to the service of God. [ME < OF < L *sacrileg(ium),* equiv. to *sacri-* (comb. form of *sacrum* holy place) + *leg(ere)* (to) steal, gather + *-ium* n. suffix]

sac·ri·le·gious (sak′rə lij′əs, -lē′jəs), *adj.* **1.** guilty of sacrilege: *a sacrilegious person.* **2.** involving sacrilege: *sacrilegious practices.* [< L *sacrilegi(um)* SACRILEGE + -OUS] —**sac′ri·le′gious·ly,** *adv.* —**sac′ri·le′gious·ness,** *n.*

sa·cring (sā′kring), *n.* *Archaic.* the act or ceremony of consecrating, esp. the consecrating of the Eucharistic elements in the Mass. [ME, equiv. to *sacren* to consecrate (see SACRED) + *-ing* -ING¹]

sa′cring bell′, *Rom. Cath. Ch.* **1.** a small bell rung during Mass upon the Elevation. **2.** the occasion of tolling the church bell to signify the Elevation. [ME]

sac·ris·tan (sak′ri stən), *n.* **1.** Also called **sac·rist** (sak′rist, sā′krist). an official in charge of the sacred vessels, vestments, etc., of a church or a religious house. **2.** *Obs. or Archaic.* a sexton. [ME < ML *sacristān(us),* equiv. to *sacrist(a)* custodian of sacred objects + *-ānus* -AN]

sac·ris·ty (sak′ri stē), *n., pl.* **-ties.** an apartment in or a building connected with a church or a religious house, in which the sacred vessels, vestments, etc., are kept. [< ML *sacristia* vestry, equiv. to *sacrist(a)* SACRISTAN + *-ia* -Y³]

sacro-, a combining form of **sacrum:** *sacroiliac.*

Sac·ro·bos·co (sak′rō bos′kō), *n.* a walled plain in the fourth quadrant of the face of the moon: about 52 miles in diameter.

sac·ro·il·i·ac (sak′rō il′ē ak′, sā′krō-), *Anat.* —*n.* **1.** the joint where the sacrum and ilium meet. —*adj.* **2.** of, pertaining to, or affecting this joint. [SACRO- + ILIAC]

sac·ro·sanct (sak′rō saŋkt′), *adj.* especially or superlatively sacred or inviolable. [< L *sacrō sānctus* made holy by sacred rite. See SACRED, SAINT] —**sac′ro·sanc′ti·ty, sac′ro·sanct′ness,** *n.*

sac·ro·sci·at·ic (sak′rō sī at′ik, sā′krō-), *adj.* *Anat.* pertaining to the sacrum and the ischium: *the sacrosciatic ligament.* [SACRO- + SCIATIC]

sac·rum (sak′rəm, sā′krəm), *n., pl.* **sac·ra** (sak′rə, sā′krə). *Anat.* a bone resulting from the ankylosis of two or more vertebrae between the lumbar and the coccygeal regions, in man being composed usually of five fused vertebrae and forming the posterior wall of the pelvis. See diag. under **pelvis.** [< L *(os) sacrum* holy (bone); so called because used in sacrifices]

sad (sad), *adj.,* **sad·der, sad·dest. 1.** depressed by unhappiness or grief; sorrowful or mournful: *to feel sad because of a close friend's death.* **2.** expressive of or characterized by sorrow: *sad looks; a sad song.* **3.** causing sorrow: *a sad disappointment; sad news.* **4.** (of color) somber, dark, or dull; drab. **5.** deplorably bad; sorry: *a sad attempt.* **6.** *Dial.* soggy or doughy: *sad bread.* **7.** *Obs.* firm or steadfast. [ME; OE *sæd;* c. G *satt,* Goth *saths* full, satisfied, L *satis* enough, *satur* sated. See SATIATE, SATURATE] —**sad′ly,** *adv.*
—**Syn. 1.** unhappy, despondent, disconsolate, discouraged, gloomy, downcast, downhearted. SAD, DEPRESSED, DEJECTED, MELANCHOLY describe states of low spirits. SAD, the general term, varies in its suggestion from a slight, momentary unhappiness to deep-felt grief or to a continuous state of combined pensiveness, wistfulness, and resignation: *sorrowful and sad; sad and lonely.* DEPRESSED refers to a temporary lapse in natural buoyancy because of fatigue, unhappiness, a sense of being unable to change unsatisfactory conditions, or the like: *depressed by a visit to the slums.* DEJECTED, though also referring to a temporary state of discouragement caused by some definite event or circumstance, implies lower spirits, being cast down by disappointment, frustration, or the like: *dejected over losing one's position.* MELANCHOLY describes a state caused rather by temperament and a chronically gloomy outlook than by any external reason: *habitually melancholy.* —**Ant. 1.** happy.

sād (säd), *n.* the 14th letter of the Arabic alphabet. [< Ar]

sa·da·qat (sä′dä kät), *n.* *Islam.* voluntary almsgiving as one of the obligatory duties of a Muslim. Also, **zakat.** [< Ar]

Sa·dat (sə dät′), *n.* **An·war el-** (än wär′ el), 1918–81; Egyptian political leader: president 1970–81; Nobel peace prize 1978.

sad·den (sad′ᵊn), *v.t., v.i.* to make or become sad. [SAD + -EN¹] —**sad′den·ing·ly,** *adv.*

Sad·dhar·ma-Pun·da·ri·ka (sud dur′mə po͝on-dur′ē kə), *n.* *Buddhism.* a Mahayana sutra, forming with its references to Amida and the Bodhisattvas the basis for the doctrine that there is something of Buddha in everyone, so that salvation is universally available. Also called **Lotus of the Good Law, Lotus of the True Law, Lotus Sutra.**

sad·dle (sad′ᵊl), *n., v.,* **-dled, -dling.** —*n.* **1.** a seat for a rider on the back of a horse or other animal. **2.** a similar seat on a bicycle, tractor, etc. **3.** a part of a harness laid across the back of an animal and girded under the belly, to which the terrets and checkhook are attached. **4.** something resembling a saddle in shape or position. **5. a.** (of mutton, venison, lamb, etc.) a cut comprising both loins. **b.** this cut, trimmed and prepared for roasting. **6.** (of poultry) the posterior part of the back. **7.** a ridge connecting two higher elevations. **8.** the covering of a roof ridge. **9.** bolster (def. 7). **10.** a raised piece of flooring between the jambs of a doorway. **11.** an inverted bracket bearing on the axle of a railroad car wheel as a support for the car body. **12.** *Ordn.* the support for the trunnion on some gun carriages. **13.** *Mach.* a sliding part for spanning a space or other parts to support something else, as the cross slide and toolholder of a lathe. **14.** a strip of leather sewn on the vamp or instep of a shoe and extending to each side of the shank. **15.** *Ceram.* a bar of refractory clay, triangular in section, for supporting one side of an object being fired. **16.** (in a suspension bridge) a member at the top of a tower for supporting a cable. **17. in the saddle,** in a position of authority; in command: *After years of being in the saddle he found his retirement tedious.* —*v.t.* **18.** to put a saddle on: *to saddle a horse.* **19.** to load or charge, as with a burden: *He has saddled himself with a jealous wife.* **20.** to impose as a burden or responsibility. —*v.i.* **21.** to put a saddle on a horse (often fol. by *up*): *They saddled quickly. The groom saddled up for me.* [ME *sadel,* OE *sadol;* c. G *Sattel,* Icel *söthull;* akin to SIT] —**sad′dle·less,** *adj.* —**sad′dle·like′,** *adj.*

English saddle
A, Pommel; B, Seat; C, Cantle; D, Panel; E, Skirt; F, Flap; G, Girth; H, Stirrup leather; I, Stirrup

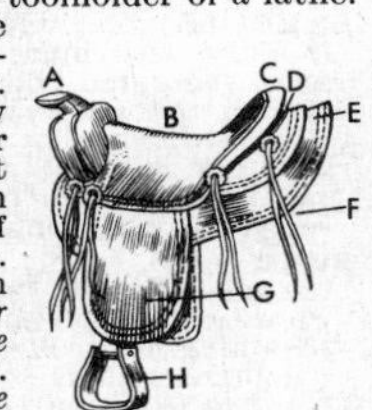

Western saddle
A, Pommel; B, Seat; C, Cantle; D, Back jockey; E, Skirt; F, Saddle strings; G, Flap; H, Stirrup

sad·dle·back (sad′ᵊl bak′), *n.* any of various animals having markings on the back that resemble a saddle, as a male harp seal. [SADDLE + BACK¹]

sad·dle-backed (sad′ᵊl bakt′), *adj.* **1.** having the back or upper surface curved like a saddle. **2.** having a saddlelike marking on the back, as certain birds.

sad′dleback roof′. See **saddle roof.**

sad·dle·bag (sad′ᵊl bag′), *n.* a large bag, usually one of a pair, hung from or laid over a saddle. [SADDLE + BAG]

sad′dle blan′ket, a saddle-shaped pad, as of felt, sheepskin, etc., placed beneath the saddle to prevent it from irritating the horse's skin.

sad·dle·bow (sad′ᵊl bō′), *n.* the arched front part of a saddle or saddletree. [SADDLE + BOW²]

sad·dle·cloth (sad′ᵊl klôth′, -kloth′), *n., pl.* **-cloths** (-klôthz′, -klothz′, -klôths′, -kloths′). **1.** *Horse Racing.* a cloth placed over the saddle of a race horse bearing the horse's number. **2.** See **saddle blanket.** [SADDLE + CLOTH]

sad′dle horse′. See **American saddle horse.**

sad′dle joint′, *Masonry.* (on a sill, coping, or the like) a vertical joint raised above the level of the washes on each side.

sad′dle leath′er, 1. hide, as from a cow or bull, that undergoes vegetable tanning and is used for saddlery. **2.** leather that simulates the vegetable-tanned product and is used for a variety of goods, as handbags, jackets, etc.

sad′dle ox′ford. See **saddle shoe.**

sad′dle point′, *Math.* a point at which a function of two variables has partial derivatives equal to zero but at which the function has neither a maximum or minimum value.

sad·dler (sad′lər), *n.* one who makes or deals in saddlery. [late ME *sadelere.* See SADDLE, -ER²]

sad′dle roof′, a gable roof, esp. one in an unusual position, as at the top of a tower. Also called **saddleback roof.**

sad·dler·y (sad′lə rē), *n., pl.* **-dler·ies. 1.** saddles and other articles pertaining to the equipment of horses. **2.** the work, business, or shop of a saddler. [late ME *sadelerie.* See SADDLER, -Y³]

sad′dle seat′, a chair seat having a double slope downward from a central ridge highest at the front.

sad′dle shoe′, an oxford with a saddle of contrasting color. Also called **saddle oxford.**

sad′dle soap′, a soap, usually consisting chiefly of Castile, used for cleaning and preserving saddles and other leather articles.

sad′dle sore′, 1. an irritation or sore on a horse caused by the rubbing of a poorly adjusted saddle. **2.** an irritation or sore on a rider caused by a saddle.

sad·dle·sore (sad′ᵊl sōr′, -sôr′), *adj.* **1.** feeling sore or stiff from horseback riding. **2.** irritated or having sores produced by a saddle. [SADDLE + SORE]

sad′dle stitch′, 1. *Sewing.* an overcasting stitch, esp. one made with a strip of leather or a thick leatherlike cord. **2.** *Bookbinding.* a binding stitch made by inserting a staple through the center of folded sheets from the back and clinching in the fold.

sad·dle·tree (sad′ᵊl trē′), *n.* the frame of a saddle. [ME *sadeltre.* See SADDLE, TREE]

Sad·du·cee (saj′ə sē′, sad′yə-), *n.* *Judaism.* a member of a Palestinian sect, consisting mainly of priests and aristocrats, that flourished from the 1st century B.C. to the 1st century A.D. and differed from the Pharisees chiefly in its literal interpretation of the Bible, rejection of oral laws and traditions, and denial of an afterlife and the coming of the Messiah. [back formation from ME *sadducees,* OE *saddūcēas* (pl.) < LL *saddūcaeī* < Gk *saddoukaioi* < Heb *tsaddūqīm* offspring of Zadok] —**Sad′du·ce′an,** *adj.* —**Sad′du·cee′ism,** *n.*

Sade (säd, sad; *Fr.* sad), *n.* **Comte Do·na·tien Al·phonse Fran·çois de** (dô na syaN′ al fôns′ fräN-swa′ də), *(Marquis de Sade),* 1740–1814, French soldier and novelist, notorious for his perverted sexual activities.

sad-faced (sad′fāst′), *adj.* having a face characterized by or expressing sorrow.

sa·dha·ka (sä′də kə), *n.* *Hinduism.* a student of the Tantras. Also, *referring to a woman,* **sa·dhi·ka** (sä′di-kə). [< Skt; see SADHU]

sa·dhe (sä′de, -dē), *n.* **1.** the 18th letter of the Hebrew alphabet. **2.** the consonant sound represented by this letter. Also, **sadi, tsadi.** [< Heb]

sa·dhu (sä′do͞o), *n.* *Hinduism.* a holy man, esp. a monk. [< Skt, n. use of *sādhu* straight]

sa·di (sä′dē), *n.* sadhe.

Sa·di (sä dē′), *n.* Saadi.

Sa·die (sā′dē), *n.* a girl's given name, form of **Sara** or **Sarah.** Also, **Sa′dye.**

sad·i·ron (sad′ī′ərn), *n.* a solid flatiron. [SAD + IRON]

sad·ism (sad′iz əm, sā′diz əm), *n.* *Psychiatry.* **1.** sexual gratification gained through causing physical pain and humiliation. **2.** any enjoyment in being cruel. Cf. **masochism.** [*sad-* (after Count D. A. F. de SADE) + -ISM. Cf. F *sadisme,* G *Sadismus,* etc.] —**sad′ist,** *n., adj.* —**sa·dis·tic** (sə dis′tik, sa-, sā-), *adj.* —**sa·dis′ti·cal·ly,** *adv.*

sad·ness (sad′nis), *n.* **1.** the quality of being sad; unhappiness. **2.** the state of being sad; grief. [ME *sadnesse.* See SAD, -NESS]
—**Syn. 2.** sorrow, depression, dejection, gloom. —**Ant. 1, 2.** joy, happiness.

Sa·doc (sā′dok), *n.* *Douay Bible.* Zadok (def. 1).

sad·o·mas·o·chism (sad′ō mas′ə kiz′əm, -maz′-, sā′-dō-), *n.* a disturbed personality condition marked by the presence of both sadistic and masochistic traits. [*sad-* (see SADISM) + -O- + MASOCHISM] —**sad′o·mas′ochis′tic,** *adj.*

Sa·do·vá (sä′dô vä′), *n.* a village in NE Bohemia, in the N Czech Republic: Prussian victory over Austrians 1866. German, **Sa·do·wa** (zä dō′vä).

sad′ sack′, *U.S. Informal.* a pathetically inept person, esp. a soldier, who continually blunders in spite of good intentions.

sad′ tree′. See **night jasmine** (def. 1). [trans. of NL *arbor tristis*]

sad·ware (sad′wâr′), *n.* heavy hammered pewter ware, as dishes. [SAD + WARE¹]

S.A.E., Society of Automotive Engineers.

Sae·hrim·nir (sâ rim′nir, sâr′im′-), *n.* *Scand. Myth.* a boar that is roasted and served up every night in Valhalla and grows whole by morning.

Sa·far (sə fär′), *n.* the second month of the Islamic calendar. [< Ar]

sa·fa·ri (sə fär′ē), *n., pl.* **-ris.** (in Eastern Africa) **1.** a journey or expedition, esp. for hunting. **2.** the hunters, guides, vehicles, equipment, etc., forming such an expedition. [< Swahili < Ar *safarī* pertaining to a journey, akin to *safara* to travel]

Sa·fa·vi (sä fä′wē), *n., pl.* **-vis.** Safavid.

Sa·fa·vid (sä fä′wēd), *n.* a member of a dynasty that ruled in Persia from c1500 to 1736. Also, **Safavi, Sa·fa·wid** (sä fä′wēd). [< Ar *safawī* (adj.) sprung from *Safī* ancestor of royal house + -ID²]

safe (sāf), *adj.,* **saf·er, saf·est,** *n.* —*adj.* **1.** secure from liability to harm, injury, danger, or risk: *a safe place.* **2.** free from hurt, injury, danger, or risk: *to arrive safe and sound.* **3.** involving little or no risk of mishap, error, etc.: *a safe estimate.* **4.** dependable or trustworthy: *a safe guide.* **5.** careful to avoid danger or controversy: *a safe player; a safe play.* **6.** denied the chance to do harm; in secure custody: *a criminal safe in jail.* **7.** *Baseball.* **a.** reaching base without being put out: *safe on the throw to first base.* **b.** making it possible to reach a base: *a safe slide.* —*n.* **8.** a steel or iron box or

repository for money, jewels, papers, etc. 9. any receptacle or structure for the storage or preservation of articles: *a meat safe.* 10. (in plumbing) a. a pan for catching leakage. b. template (def. 2). 11. *Slang.* a condom. [ME *sauf* < OF < L *salv(us)* intact, whole; see SAVE, SALVATION] —**safe′ly,** *adv.* —**safe′ness,** *n.*
—**Syn.** 1. protected, sound, guarded. SAFE, SECURE may both imply that something can be regarded as free from danger. These words are frequently interchangeable. SAFE, however, is applied rather to a person or thing that is out of or has passed beyond the reach of danger: *The ship is safe in port.* SECURE is applied to that about which there is no need to fear or worry: *to feel secure about the future; The foundation of the house does not seem very secure.* 4. sure, reliable. 5. wary, careful. 8. strongbox, coffer, chest, safe-deposit box. —**Ant.** 1. unsafe.

safe-con·duct (sāf′kon′dukt), *n.* 1. a document authorizing safe passage through a region, esp. in time of war. 2. this privilege. 3. the act of conducting in safety. [ME *sauf condut* < MF *sauf-conduit*]

safe-crack·er (sāf′krak′ər), *n.* one who breaks open safes to rob them. —**safe′crack′ing,** *n.*

safe-de·pos·it (sāf′di poz′it), *adj.* providing safekeeping for valuables: *a safe-deposit vault or box.* Also called **safety-deposit.**

safe·guard (sāf′gärd′), *n.* 1. something that serves as a protection or defense or that ensures safety. 2. a permit for safe passage. 3. a guard or convoy. 4. a mechanical device for ensuring safety. —*v.t.* 5. to guard; protect; secure. [late ME *savegarde* < MF *salvegarde, sauvegarde.* See SAFE, GUARD]

safe·keep·ing (sāf′kē′piŋ), *n.* protection; care. [ME *safe kepyng.* See SAFE, KEEPING]

safe·light (sāf′līt′), *n.* *Photog.* a darkroom light with a filter that transmits only those rays of the spectrum to which films, printing paper, etc., are not sensitive. [SAFE + LIGHT[1]]

safe′ pe′riod, an interval of the menstrual cycle when fertilization is considered to be least likely, usually a number of days prior and subsequent to menstruation.

safe-time (sāf′tīm′), *n.* *Rocketry.* the time during the flight of an armed rocket or missile when the warhead cannot be detonated by the fuze.

safe·ty (sāf′tē), *n., pl.* **-ties.** 1. the state of being safe; freedom from the occurrence or risk of injury, danger, or loss. 2. the quality of averting or not causing injury, danger, or loss. 3. a contrivance or device to prevent injury or avert danger. 4. Also called **lock, safety catch, safety lock.** a locking or cutoff device that prevents a gun from being fired accidentally. 5. the action of keeping safe. 6. *Football.* a. an act or play in which a player on the offensive team is tackled in his own end zone or downs the ball there, or in which the ball goes out of bounds on a fumble, having last been in bounds in or over the end zone and having last been in the possession of an offensive player. Cf. **touchback.** b. an award of two points to the opposing team on this play. c. See **safety man.** 7. *Baseball.* a base hit, esp. a one-base hit. 8. *Slang.* a condom. 9. *Obs.* close confinement or custody. [late ME *sauvete* < MF. See SAFE, -TY[2]]

safe′ty belt′, 1. See **seat belt.** 2. a belt or strap worn as a safety precaution by persons working at great heights: *The safety belt worn by a window washer is usually secured to each side of the window frame.* 3. See **life belt.**

safe′ty bi′cycle, bicycle (def. 2).

safe′ty car′, *Naut.* See **life car.**

safe′ty catch′, 1. a device used in mechanisms, as for elevators, to prevent falling in the event of mechanical failure. 2. safety (def. 4).

safe·ty-de·pos·it (sāf′tē di poz′it), *adj.* safe-deposit.

safe′ty fac′tor. See **factor of safety.**

safe′ty fuze′, a long tube attached to a detonator or percussion cap and filled with a powder that burns slowly when ignited.

safe′ty glass′, a pane made by joining two plates or panes of glass with a layer of usually transparent plastic or artificial resin between them which retains the fragments if the glass is broken.

safe′ty hook′, a hook that can be transformed into an eye by locking a hinged piece in place.

safe′ty is′land, an area provided for the safety of pedestrians from vehicular traffic, as between lanes on a busy street, highway, etc. Also called **safe′ty isle′, safety zone.**

Safe′ty Is′lands, a group of three islands in the Caribbean, off the coast of French Guiana, belonging to France. French, **Îles du Salut.**

safe′ty lamp′, a miner's lamp in which the flame is protected by wire gauze, thus preventing immediate ignition of explosive gases.

safe′ty lin′tel, an auxiliary lintel concealed behind a visible lintel, arch, etc.

safe′ty lock′, 1. a lock designed to prevent picking. 2. safety (def. 4).

safe′ty man′, *Football.* a player on defense who lines up farthest behind the line of scrimmage.

safe′ty match′, a match designed to ignite only when rubbed on a specially prepared surface.

safe′ty pin′, a pin bent back on itself to form a spring, with a guard to cover the point.

safe′ty ra′zor, a razor with a guard to prevent the blade from cutting the skin deeply.

safe′ty roll′er, *Horol.* (in a lever escapement) a roller on the balance staff meeting the guard pin of the lever in such a way as to prevent the lever from overbanking.

safe′ty spring′, *Horol.* See **brake spring.**

safe′ty squeeze′. See **squeeze play** (def. 1b). Also called **safe′ty squeeze′ play′.**

safe′ty valve′, 1. a device that, when actuated by a gas or vapor pressure above a predetermined level, opens and allows the gas or vapor to escape until its pressure is reduced to a pressure equal to or below that of the predetermined level. Cf. **relief valve.** 2. a harmless outlet for emotion, nervousness, etc.

safe′ty zone′. See **safety island.**

saf·flor·ite (saf′lə rīt′), *n.* a mineral, essentially cobalt diarsenide, $CoAs_2$. [< G *Safflorit.* See SAFFLOWER, -ITE[1]]

saf·flow·er (saf′lou′ər), *n.* 1. a thistlelike, composite herb, *Carthamus tinctorius,* native to the Old World, having large, orange-red flower heads. 2. its dried florets, used medicinally or as a red dyestuff. [< D *saffloer* < MF *saffleur* < It *saffiore,* equiv. to *saf-* (< Ar *asf(ar)* yellow) + *fiore* FLOWER]

saf′flower oil′, an oil expressed or extracted from safflower seeds, used in cooking, as a salad oil, and as a vehicle for medicines, paints, varnishes, etc.

Saf·ford (saf′ərd), *n.* a town in SE Arizona. 4648 (1960).

saf·fron (saf′rən), *n.* 1. Also called **vegetable gold.** a crocus, *Crocus sativus,* having showy purple flowers. 2. an orange-colored condiment consisting of its dried stigmas, used to color confectionery and to color and flavor rolls, rice dishes, etc. 3. Also, **saf′fron yel′low.** yellow-orange. [ME *saffran, saffron* < ML *safrān(um)* (medical term) < Ar *za'farān,* akin to *asfar* yellow]

Sa·fid Rud (sa fēd′ ro͞od′), *n.* a river flowing from NW Iran into the Caspian Sea. 450 mi. long.

S. Afr., 1. South Africa. 2. South African.

saf·ra·nine (saf′rə nēn′, -nin), *n.* *Chem.* 1. any of a class of chiefly red organic dyes, phenazine derivatives, used for dyeing wool, silk, etc. 2. Also called **phenosafranine.** a purplish-red, water-soluble dye, $C_{18}H_{14}N_4$, for textiles and used as a stain in microscopy. Also, **saf·ra·nin** (saf′rə nin). [< F or G *safran* SAFFRON + *-ine* -INE[2]]

S. Afr. D., South African Dutch. Also, **SAfrD**

saf·role (saf′rōl), *n.* *Chem.* a colorless or faintly yellow liquid, $C_3H_5C_6H_3O_2CH_2$, obtained from sassafras oil or the like: used chiefly in perfumery, for flavoring, and in the manufacture of soaps. Also, **saf·rol** (saf′rōl, -rōl, -rol). [(SAS)SAFR(AS) + -OLE]

sag (sag), *v.,* **sagged, sag·ging,** *n.* —*v.i.* 1. to sink or bend downward by weight or pressure, esp. in the middle: *The roof sags.* 2. to hang down unevenly; droop: *Her skirt was sagging.* 3. to droop; hang loosely: *His shoulders sagged.* 4. to yield through weakness, lack of effort, or the like: *Our spirits began to sag.* 5. to decline, as in price: *The stock market sagged today.* 6. *Naut.* a. (of a hull) to droop at the center or have excessive sheer because of structural weakness. Cf. **hog** (def. 16). b. to be driven to leeward; to make too much leeway. —*v.t.* 7. to cause to sag. —*n.* 8. an act or instance of sagging. 9. the degree of sagging. 10. a place where anything sags; depression. 11. moderate decline in prices. 12. *Naut.* a. deflection downward of a hull amidships, due to structural weakness. b. leeway (def. 1). [late ME *saggen,* prob. < Scand. Cf. D *zakken,* MLG *sacken,* Sw *sacka*]

sa·ga (sä′gə), *n.* 1. a medieval Icelandic or Norse prose narrative of achievements and events in the history of a personage, family, etc. 2. any narrative or legend of heroic exploits. 3. Also called **sa′ga nov′el, roman-fleuve.** a form of the novel in which the members or generations of a family or social group are chronicled in a long and leisurely narrative. [< Icel; c. SAW[3]] —**Syn.** 2. edda, epic, tale, history.

sa·ga·cious (sə gā′shəs), *adj.* 1. having or showing acute mental discernment and keen practical sense; shrewd: *a sagacious patriarch of the tribe.* 2. *Obs.* keen of scent. [SAGACI(TY) + -OUS] —**sa·ga′cious·ly,** *adv.* —**sa·ga′cious·ness,** *n.*
—**Syn.** 1. wise, sage, discerning, clever, intelligent, judicious, acute, sharp, keen, perspicacious. —**Ant.** 1. unwise.

sa·gac·i·ty (sə gas′i tē), *n.* acuteness of mental discernment and soundness of judgment. [< L *sagācitāt-* (s. of *sagācitās*) wisdom, equiv. to *sagāci-* (s. of *sagax*) wise + *-tāt-* -TY[2]]

sag·a·more (sag′ə mōr′, -môr′), *n.* (among the American Indians of New England) a chief or great man. [< Abnaki *sāgimo* one who overcomes]

sag·but (sag′but′), *n.* sackbut (def. 1).

sage[1] (sāj), *n., adj.,* **sag·er, sag·est.** —*n.* 1. a profoundly wise man; a man famed for wisdom. 2. a man venerated for his wisdom, judgment, and experience: *the seven sages of ancient Greece.* —*adj.* 3. wise, judicious, or prudent: *sage advice.* 4. *Archaic.* grave or solemn. [ME < OF < L *-sapius* wise; see SAPIENT] —**sage′ly,** *adv.* —**sage′ness,** *n.*
—**Syn.** 1. philosopher. 3. sagacious. —**Ant.** 1. fool.

sage[2] (sāj), *n.* 1. any menthaceous herb or shrub of the genus *Salvia.* 2. a perennial herb, *Salvia officinalis,* whose grayish-green leaves are used in medicine and for seasoning in cookery. 3. the leaves themselves. 4. sagebrush. [ME *sa(u)ge,* MF *sauge, saulge* a plant < L *salvia* (so named from its supposed healing powers). See SAFE]

Sage (sāj), *n.* **Russell,** 1816–1906, U.S. financier.

SAGE (sāj), *n.* *Rocketry.* an air-defense system that correlates information received from ground stations tracking enemy aircraft to determine optimum flight courses for interceptors. [*s(emi) a(utomatic) g(round) e(nvironment)*]

sage·brush (sāj′brush′), *n.* any of several sagelike, bushy, composite plants of the genus *Artemisia,* common on the dry plains of the western U.S. [SAGE[2] + BRUSH[2]]

sage′ cock′, the male sage grouse.

sage′ grouse′, a large grouse, *Centrocercus urophasianus,* of the sagebrush regions of western North America.

sage′ hen′, the sage grouse, esp. the female.

sage′ spar′row, a small gray finch, *Amphispiza nevadensis,* of western North America.

sage′ thrash′er, a grayish-brown thrasher, *Oreoscoptes montanus,* of sagebrush regions of the western U.S.

sag·ger (sag′ər), *n.* 1. a box or case made of refractory baked clay in which the finer ceramic wares are enclosed and protected while baking. 2. a hard unlayered clay underlying many coal beds. —*v.t.* 3. to place in or on a sagger. Also, **sag′gar, seggar.** [? var. of SAFEGUARD]

Sa·ghal·ien (sä′gäl yen′), *n.* Sakhalin.

Sag·i·naw (sag′ə nô′), *n.* a port in E Michigan, on the Saginaw River. 98,265 (1960).

Sag′inaw Bay′, *n.* an arm of Lake Huron, off the E coast of Michigan. 60 mi. long.

Sa·git·ta (sə jit′ə), *n., gen.* **-git·tae** (-jit′ē). *Astron.* the Arrow, a northern constellation between Aquila and Cygnus. [< L: arrow]

sag·it·tal (saj′i tᵊl), *adj.* 1. *Anat.* a. of or pertaining to the suture between the parietal bones of the skull or to a venous canal within the skull and parallel to this suture. b. (in direction or location) from front to back in the median plane or in a plane parallel to the median. 2. pertaining to or resembling an arrow or arrowhead. [< NL *sagittāl(is).* See SAGITTA, -AL[1]] —**sag′it·tal·ly,** *adv.*

Sag·it·ta·ri·us (saj′i târ′ē əs), *n., gen.* **-ta·ri·i** (-târ′ē ī′) for 1. 1. *Astron.* the Archer, a zodiacal constellation between Scorpius and Capricorn. 2. the ninth sign of the zodiac. See illus. under **zodiac.** [< L: archer]

sag·it·tar·y (saj′i ter′ē), *n., pl.* **-tar·ies.** a centaur with a bow, as Chiron. [< L *sagittāri(us)* archer. See SAGITTA, -ARY]

sag·it·tate (saj′i tāt′), *adj.* shaped like an arrowhead. Also, **sa·git·ti·form** (sə-jit′ə fôrm′, saj′i tə-). [< NL *sagittāt(us).* See SAGITTA, -ATE[1]]

Sagittate leaf

sa·go (sā′gō), *n.* 1. a starchy foodstuff derived from the soft interior of the trunk of various palms and cycads, used in making puddings. 2. See **sago palm.** [< Malay *sāgū*]

sa′go palm′, 1. any of several Malayan feather palms of the genus *Metroxylon,* as *M. laeve* or *M. Rumphii,* that yield sago. 2. any of various other palms that yield sago. 3. a cycad, *Cycas revoluta,* of China and the East Indies, grown as an ornamental.

sag′ rod′, (in a roof) a rod for preventing the sagging of an open-web steel joist that is used as a purlin with its depth at right angles to a roof slope.

Sa·guache (sə wach′), *n.* Sawatch.

sa·gua·ro (sə gwä′rō, -wä′rō), *n., pl.* **-ros.** a tall cactus, *Carnegiea* (or *Cereus*) *gigantea,* of Arizona and neighboring regions, yielding a useful wood and bearing an edible fruit. [< MexSp, var. of *sahuaro* < Opata]

Sag·ue·nay (sag′ə nā′), *n.* a river in SE Canada, in Quebec, flowing SE from Lake St. John to the St. Lawrence. 125 mi. long.

Sa·gui·a el Ham·ra (sä′gē ə el ham′rə; *Sp.* sä′gyä el äm′rä), the N part of Spanish Sahara.

Sa·gun·to (sə go͞on′tō; *Sp.* sä go͞on′tô), *n.* a city in E Spain, N of Valencia: besieged by Hannibal 219–218 B.C. 26,978 (est. 1959). Ancient, **Sa·gun·tum** (sə gun′təm).

Sa·hap·tin (sä hap′tən), *n., pl.* **-tins,** (*esp. collectively*) **-tin,** *adj.* —*n.* 1. a member of an American Indian people of Oregon, Washington, and Idaho. 2. a language used by several American Indian tribes, including the Nez Percés, of the Columbia River basin. —*adj.* 3. of or pertaining to the Sahaptins or to their languages. Also, **Shahaptian.** [< Salish (NAmer) *Sahaptin(i)* (pl. of *Sáptini*)]

Sa·har·a (sə hâr′ə, -här′ə), *n.* 1. a desert in N Africa, extending from the Atlantic to the Nile valley. ab. 3,500,000 sq. mi. 2. any arid waste. [< Ar *çahra* desert] —**Sa·har′an, Sa·har′i·an,** *adj.*

Sa·ha·ran·pur (sə här′ən po͝or′), *n.* a city in NW Uttar Pradesh, in N India. 185,200 (1961).

sa·hib (sä′ib, -ēb), *n.* 1. (in India) sir; master: a term of respect used by natives, esp. during the colonial period, when addressing or referring to a European. 2. (*cap.*) sing. of **Ashab.** [< Urdu < Ar *çāḥib* master, lit., friend]

saice (sīs), *n.* syce.

said[1] (sed), *v.* 1. pt. and pp. of **say.** 2. *Chiefly Law.* named or mentioned before; aforesaid; aforementioned: *said witness; said sum.*

sa·id[2] (sä′id), *n.* *Islam.* sayyid.

Saiga (2½ ft. high at shoulder; horns 9 in.; length 4½ ft.)

Sa·i·da (sä′ē dä′), *n.* a seaport in SW Lebanon: the site of ancient Sidon. 45,000.

sai·ga (sī′gə), *n.* a goat antelope, *Saiga tartarica,* of western Asia and eastern Russia, having a greatly enlarged muzzle. [< Russ]

Sai·gon (sī gon′), *n.* a seaport in Vietnam, in the S part: capital of former South Vietnam 1954–76. 1,750,000 (est. 1970). Official name, **Ho Chi Minh City.**

Sai′gon cin′namon. See under **cinnamon** (def. 1).

sail (sāl), *n.* 1. an area of canvas or other fabric extended to the wind in such a way as to transmit the force of the wind to an assemblage of spars and rigging mounted firmly on a hull, raft, iceboat, etc., so as to drive it along. Cf. **fore-and-aft sail, square sail.** 2. some similar piece or apparatus, as the part of an arm that catches the wind on a windmill. 3. a voyage or excursion, esp. in a sailing vessel: *They went for a sail around the island.* 4. a sailing vessel or ship. 5. sailing vessels collectively: *The fleet numbered 30 sail.* 6. sails for a vessel or vessels collectively. 7. (*cap.*) *Astron.* the constellation Vela. 8. **in sail,** with the sails set. 9. **make sail,** *Naut.* a. to set the sail or sails of a boat or increase the amount of sail already set. b. to set out on

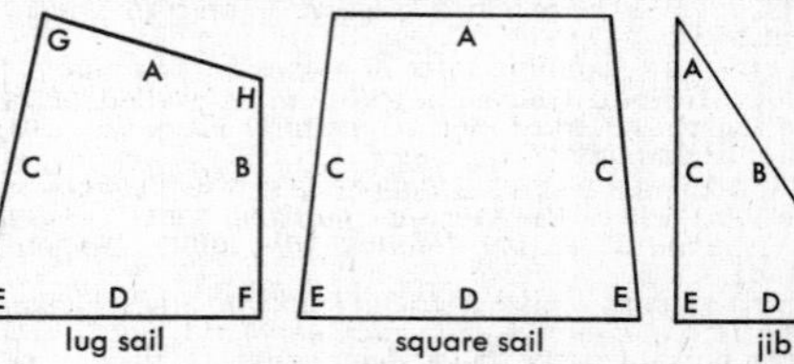

Parts of a sail
A, Head; B, Luff; C, Leech; D, Foot; E, Clew; F, Tack; G, Peak; H, Throat

a voyage: *Make sail for the Leeward Islands.* 10. **set sail,** to start a sea voyage: *We set sail at midnight for*

Nantucket. **11. under sail,** with sails set; in motion; sailing: *It was good to be under sail in the brisk wind and under the warm sun.* —*v.i.* **12.** to travel in a vessel conveyed by the action of wind, steam, etc. **13.** to move along or be conveyed by wind, steam, etc.: *steamships sailing to Lisbon.* **14.** to manage a sailboat, esp. for sport. **15.** to begin a journey by water: *We are sailing at dawn.* **16.** to move along in a manner suggestive of a sailing vessel: *caravans sailing along.* **17.** to travel through the air, as an airship. **18.** to move along in a stately, effortless way: *to sail into a room.* —*v.t.* **19.** to sail upon, over, or through: *to sail the seven seas.* **20.** to navigate (a vessel). **21. sail in** or **into,** *Informal.* **a.** to go vigorously into action; begin to act; attack. **b.** to attack verbally: *He would sail into his wife when work was going badly.* [ME; OE *segl;* c. G *Segel,* Icel *segl;* ? equiv. to *seg-* cut (c. L *secāre,* etc.) + *-l* suffix; if so, basic meaning is piece, something cut off] —**sail′a·ble,** *adj.* —**sail′less,** *adj.*

sail·boat (sāl′bōt′), *n.* a boat having sails as its principal means of propulsion. [SAIL + BOAT]

sail·cloth (sāl′klôth′, -kloth′), *n.* any of various fabrics, as of cotton, nylon, or Dacron, for boat sails or tents. **2.** a lightweight canvas or canvaslike fabric used esp. for clothing and curtains. [SAIL + CLOTH]

sail·er (sā′lər), *n.* **1.** a vessel propelled by a sail or sails. **2.** a vessel with reference to its powers or manner of sailing: *The schooner was judged a good sailer.* [late ME; see SAIL, -ER[1]]

sail′fin scul′pin (sāl′fin), a sculpin, *Nautichthys oculofasciatus,* found along the Pacific coast of North America, having the first five rays of the dorsal fin elongated into a saillike structure. Also called **sailorfish.** [SAIL + FIN]

Pacific Sailfish, *Istiophorus orientalis* (Length to 11 ft.)

sail·fish (sāl′fish′), *n., pl.* (*esp. collectively*) **-fish,** (*esp. referring to two or more kinds or species*) **-fish·es.** any of several large, marine fishes of the genus *Istiophorus,* related to the swordfishes and having a very large, saillike dorsal fin, as *I. americanus,* found in the warmer parts of the Atlantic Ocean. [SAIL + FISH]

sail·ing (sā′ling), *n.* **1.** the activity of one who or that which sails. **2.** *Navig.* any of various methods for determining courses and distances by means of charts or with reference to longitudes and latitudes, rhumb lines, great circles, etc. [ME *seiling,* OE *seglung.* See SAIL, -ING[1]]

sail′ing boat′, *Brit.* sailboat.

sail′ing length′, a measurement of a yacht, comprising its length on the water line as well as certain measurements taken from the overhangs at bow and stern.

sail′ing ship′, a large ship equipped with sails.

Sail′ing to Byzan′tium, a poem (1928) by W. B. Yeats.

sail·mak·er (sāl′mā′kər), *n.* **1.** a person who makes or repairs sails. **2.** a former rank of warrant officer in the U.S. Navy. [SAIL + MAKER]

sail′maker's palm′, palm[1] (def. 4).

sail·or (sā′lər), *n.* **1.** one whose occupation is sailing or navigation; mariner; seaman. **2.** a seaman below the rank of officer. **3.** a person, with reference to freedom from seasickness: *He was such a bad sailor that he always traveled to Europe by plane.* **4.** a flat-brimmed straw hat with a low, flat crown. [SAIL + -OR[2] (r. -ER[1])] —**sail′or·like′,** *adj.*

—**Syn. 1.** seafarer. SAILOR, MARINER, SALT, SEAMAN, TAR are terms for one who leads a seafaring life. A SAILOR or SEAMAN is one whose occupation is on board a ship at sea, one of a ship's crew below the rank of petty officer: *a sailor before the mast; an able-bodied seaman.* MARINER is a term now found only in certain technical expressions: *master mariner* (captain in merchant service); *mariner's compass* (ordinary compass as used on ships); formerly used much as "sailor" or "seafaring man," now the word seems elevated or quaint: *Rime of the Ancient Mariner.* SALT and TAR are familiar and colloquial terms for old and experienced sailors: *an old salt; a jolly tar.* —**Ant. 1.** landlubber.

sail′or cap′. See **mosquito bill.**

sail·or·fish (sā′lər fish′), *n., pl.* (*esp. collectively*) **-fish,** (*esp. referring to two or more kinds or species*) **-fish·es.** See **sailfin sculpin.** [SAILOR + FISH]

sail·or·ing (sā′lər ing), *n.* the occupation or duties of a sailor. [SAILOR + -ING[1]]

sail·or·ly (sā′lər lē), *adj.* like or befitting a sailor. [SAILOR + -LY]

sail′or's breast′plate. See **prolonge knot.**

sail·or's-choice (sā′lərz chois′), *n., pl.* **-choice.** any of several fishes found along the Atlantic coast of the U.S., esp. a pinfish, *Lagodon rhomboides,* ranging from Massachusetts to Texas, and a grunt, *Haemulon parra,* ranging from Florida to Brazil.

sail′or's knot′, any of various knots commonly used by sailors.

sail·o·ver (sāl′ō′vər), *n.* a repetition of an indecisive or interrupted run of a racing yacht.

sail′ plan′, *Naval Archit.* a side elevation of a sailing vessel showing all sails and spars and some or all of the standing rigging, as if set directly fore-and-aft so that the true proportions are visible: sometimes combined with the rigging plan of the vessel.

sail·plane (sāl′plān′), *n., v.,* **-planed, -plan·ing.** —*n.* **1.** a very light glider that can be lifted by an upward current of air. —*v.i.* **2.** to soar in a sailplane. [SAIL + PLANE[1]]

sail′ track′, *Naut.* a railway for guiding the hanks of a sail being raised, lowered, etc.

sail·yard (sāl′yärd′), *n.* a yard for a sail. [ME *seylyarde,* OE *seglyerd.* See SAIL, YARD[1]]

sain (sān), *v.t. Archaic.* **1.** to make the sign of the cross on, as for protection against evil influences. **2.** to safeguard by prayer. **3.** to bless. [ME; OE *segn(ian)* (c. G *segnen* to bless) < eccl. L *sign(āre)* (to) sign with the cross]

sain·foin (sān′foin), *n.* a European, fabaceous herb, *Onobrychis sativa viciae folia,* used for forage. [< F, equiv. to MF *sain* (< L *sān(us)* healthy) + *foin* (< L *fēn(um), faen(um)* hay)]

saint (sānt), *n.* **1.** any of certain persons of exceptional holiness of life, formally recognized by the Christian Church as having attained an exalted position in heaven and as being entitled to veneration on earth; a canonized person. **2.** (in certain religious groups) a designation applied by the members to themselves. **3.** a person of great holiness, virtue, or benevolence. **4.** a founder, sponsor, or patron, as of a movement or organization. —*v.t.* **5.** to enroll formally among the saints recognized by the Church. **6.** to give the name of saint to; reckon as a saint. [ME < OF < L *sanct(us)* sacred adj. use of ptp. of *sancīre* to consecrate, equiv. to *sanc-* + *-tus* ptp. suffix; r. OE *sanct* < L *sanct(us)*] —**saint′less,** *adj.*

Saint. For entries beginning with this word, see also **St., Ste.**

Saint′ Ag′nes's Eve′ (ag′nis siz), the night of January 20, superstitiously regarded as a time when a girl who performs certain rites might see the image of her future husband.

Saint′ An′drew's Cross′, an X-shaped cross. See illus. under **cross.**

Saint′ An′thony's Cross′, a T-shaped cross. See illus. under **cross.**

Saint′ An′thony's Fire′, *Pathol.* any of certain skin conditions that are of an inflammatory or gangrenous nature, as erysipelas, hospital gangrene, or ergotism.

Saint′ Barthol′o·mew's Day′ Mas′sacre, *Fr. Hist.* a massacre of over 3000 Huguenots, instigated by Catherine de Médicis and begun in Paris on St. Bartholomew's Day, August 24, 1572.

Saint Bernard (28 in. high at shoulder)

Saint′ Bernard′, one of a breed of very large dogs having a massive head and long or medium-length hair, noted for their use in the Swiss Alps in rescuing travelers from the snow. [named after the hospice of *Saint Bernard,* Saint Bernard Pass, Swiss Alps, where they were first bred]

saint·dom (sānt′dəm), *n.* sainthood. [SAINT + -DOM]

Sainte-Beuve (saNt bœv′), *n.* **Charles Au·gu·stin** (sharl ō gy staN′), 1804–69, French literary critic.

saint·ed (sān′tid), *adj.* **1.** enrolled among the saints. **2.** being a saint in heaven. **3.** sacred or hallowed. **4.** like a saint; saintly. [SAINT + -ED[3]]

Saint-Ex·u·pé·ry (saN teg zy pā rē′), *n.* **An·toine de** (äN twan′ də), 1900–45, French author and aviator.

saint·foin (sānt′foin), *n.* sainfoin.

Saint-Gau·dens (sānt gôd′ənz), *n.* **Augustus,** 1848–1907, U.S. sculptor, born in Ireland.

Saint′ George′'s Cross′, the Greek cross as used in the flag of Great Britain.

Saint′ George′'s Day′, April 23, celebrated in parts of the British Commonwealth in honor of the patron saint of Britain and esp. in New Zealand as a bank holiday.

saint·hood (sānt′ho͝od), *n.* **1.** the character or status of a saint. **2.** saints collectively. [SAINT + -HOOD]

Saint′ Joan′, a play (1923) by G. B. Shaw.

Saint-Just (saN zhyst′), *n.* **Louis An·toine Lé·on de** (lwē äN twan′ lā ôN′ də), 1767–94, French revolutionist.

saint·ly (sānt′lē), *adj.,* **-li·er, -li·est.** like, proper to, or befitting a saint: *saintly lives.* [SAINT + -LY] —**saint′li·ly,** *adv.* —**saint′li·ness,** *n.*

Saint′ Pat′rick's Day′, March 17 observed by the Irish in honor of St. Patrick, the patron saint of Ireland.

Saint-Pierre (*Fr.* saN pyer′), *n.* **Jacques Hen·ri Ber·nar·din de** (zhäk äN rē′ ber nar daN′ də). See **Bernardin de Saint-Pierre, Jacques Henri.**

Saint-Saëns (saN säns′, -säN′), *n.* **Charles Ca·mille** (sharl ka mē′yə), 1835–1921, French composer and pianist.

Saints·bur·y (sānts′bə rē), *n.* **George Edward Bate·man** (bāt′mən), 1845–1933, English literary critic and historian.

saint·ship (sānt′ship), *n.* the qualities or status of a saint. [SAINT + -SHIP]

Saint-Si·mon (saN sē môN′), *n.* **1. Count de,** 1760–1825, French philosopher and social scientist. **2. Louis de Rou·vroy** (lwē də ro͞o vrwa′), 1675–1755, French soldier, diplomat, and author.

Saint′ Val′en·tine's Day′ (val′ən tīnz′), February 14, observed in honor of St. Valentine as a day for the exchange of valentines and other tokens of affection.

Sai·on·ji (sī′ôn jē′), *n.* **Kim·mo·chi** (kēm′mô chē′), 1849–1940, Japanese statesman.

Sai·pan (sī pan′), *n.* one of the Mariana Islands in the N Pacific, about 1350 mi. S of Japan: taken by U.S. forces June–July 1944. 8138 (1960); 71 sq. mi.

Sa·ïs (sā′is), *n.* an ancient city in N Egypt, on the Nile delta: an ancient capital of Lower Egypt. —**Sa·ït·ic** (sā it′ik), *n., adj.*

Sai·shu·to (sī′sho͞o tô′), *n.* Japanese name of **Cheju.** Also called **Sai′shu.**

Sai·son en En·fer, Une (*Fr.* yn se zôN näN näN-fer′). See **Season in Hell, A.**

Sa·ite (sā′īt), *n.* **1.** a native or citizen of Saïs. —*adj.* **2.** Also, **Sa·it·ic** (sā it′ik). of or pertaining to Saïs or its inhabitants. **3.** of or pertaining to the period 663–525 B.C., when the Pharaohs ruled at Saïs. [< L *Saïtē(s)* < Gk *Saḯtēs.* See SAÏS, -ITE[1]]

saith (seth), *v. Archaic.* third pers. sing. pres. of **say.**

Sa·i·tis (sā ī′tis), *n. Class. Myth.* Athena: so called because of her identification with the Egyptian goddess Neith, of Saïs.

Sai·va (sī′və), *n. Hinduism.* a Bhakti sect devoted to Siva. [< Skt]

Sa·kai (sä′kī′), *n.* a seaport on S Honshu, in S Japan, near Osaka. 432,029 (1964).

Sa·kai (sä′kī), *n., pl.* **-kais,** (*esp. collectively*) **-kai.** a member of a tribal people of Malaya.

sake[1] (sāk), *n.* **1.** cause, account, interest, or benefit: *for the sake of all students.* **2.** purpose or end: *for the sake of appearances.* [ME; OE *sacu* lawsuit, cause; c. G *Sache* thing, Icel *sōk* lawsuit; akin to Goth *sakjo* quarrel]

sa·ke[2] (sä′kē), *n.* a Japanese fermented alcoholic beverage made from rice. Also, **sa′ké, saki.** [< Jap]

sa·ker[1] (sā′kər), *n.* an Old World falcon, *Falco sacer cherrug,* used in falconry. Also called **sa′ker fal′con.** [ME *sagre, sacre* < MF *sacre* << Ar *ṣaqr*]

sa·ker[2] (sā′kər), *n.* a light field gun that is smaller than a demi-culverin and fires a shot weighing six pounds or less. [special use of SAKER[1]]

SOVIET UNION
Sakhalin
SEA OF OKHOTSK
CHINA
SEA OF JAPAN
KURILE ISLANDS
Vladivostok
JAPAN

Sa·kha·lin (sak′ə lēn′; *Russ.* sä′khä lēn′), *n.* an island off the SE coast of the Soviet Union in Asia, N of Japan: divided between the Soviet Union and Japan 1905–45; Yalta agreement placed the southern, Japanese part **(Karafuto)** under Soviet administration. ab. 350,000; 28,957 sq. mi. Also, **Saghalien.**

Sa·kha·rov (sä′kə rôf′), *n.* **An·drei** (än′drā), born 1921, Soviet nuclear physicist and human-rights activist: Nobel peace prize 1975.

sa·ki[1] (sak′ē, sä′kē), *n.* any of several monkeys of the genus *Pithecia,* of tropical South America, having a golden-brown to black, thick, shaggy coat and a long, bushy, nonprehensile tail. [< F < Tupi *sagui*]

sa·ki[2] (sä′kē), *n.* sake[2].

Sa·ki (sä′kē), *n.* pen name of H. H. Munro.

Sak·ka·ra (sə kär′ə), *n.* Saqqara.

sak·kos (*Gk.* sä′kôs; *Eng.* sak′os), *n., pl.* **sak·koi** (*Gk.* sä′kē; *Eng.* sak′oi). *Eastern Ch.* an embroidered vestment worn by a bishop and corresponding to the dalmatic. [< eccl. Gk, special use of Gk *sákkos* SACK[1]]

Sak·ta (shäk′tə), *n. Hinduism.* Shakta.

Sak·ti (shuk′tē), *n. Hinduism.* Shakti.

Sak·tism (shuk′tiz əm), *n. Hinduism.* Shaktism.

Sa·kun·ta·la (sə ko͝on′tə lä, shə-), *n.* a Sanskrit drama written in the 6th century or earlier by Kalidasa. Also, **Shakuntala.**

Sa·kya·mu·ni (sä′kyə mo͝on′ē), *n.* one of the names of Buddha. [< Skt: lit., hermit of the *Sākya* tribe or family]

sal (sal), *n. Chiefly Pharm.* salt. [< L]

Sal (sal), *n.* a boy's given name, form of **Salvatore.**

sa·laam (sə läm′), *n.* **1.** (in the Orient) a salutation meaning "peace." **2.** a very low bow or obeisance, esp. with the palm of the right hand placed on the forehead. —*v.i.* **3.** to salute with a salaam. **4.** to perform a salaam. —*v.t.* **5.** to salute (someone) with a salaam. [< Ar: peace] —**sa·laam′like′,** *adj.*

sal·a·ble (sā′lə bəl), *adj.* subject to or suitable for sale; readily sold: *The books were sent back by the store in salable condition.* Also, **saleable.** [SALE + -ABLE] —**sal′a·bil′i·ty,** *n.* —**sal′a·bly,** *adv.*

Sa·la·cia (sə lā′shə), *n. Rom. Religion.* a partner of Neptune, sometimes identified with the ancient Greek goddess Amphitrite.

sa·la·cious (sə lā′shəs), *adj.* **1.** lustful or lecherous. **2.** (of writings, pictures, etc.) obscene; grossly indecent. [< L *salāci-* (s. of *salāx*) lustful + -OUS] —**sa·la′cious·ly,** *adv.* —**sa·la′cious·ness, sa·lac·i·ty** (sə las′i tē), *n.*

sal·ad (sal′əd), *n.* **1.** any of various cooked foods or foods that are edible raw, prepared singly or combined, usually cut up, mixed with a piquant or sweet dressing, and served cold as an appetizer, main course, or side dish. **2.** any herb or plant used for such a dish or eaten raw. **3.** *Dial.* lettuce; greens. [late ME *salad(e)* < MF *salade* < OPr *salad(a)* < VL **salāta* salted (fem. ptp. of **salāre* to salt), equiv. to *sal* salt + *-āta* -ATE[1]]

sal′ad bowl′, **1.** a large bowl in which a salad, esp. a tossed salad, is served. **2.** a small bowl for individual servings of salad.

sal′ad bur′net, a hardy, Eurasian, perennial herb, *Sanguisorba minor,* naturalized in North America, having greenish flowers in short spikes and edible leaves. Also called **toper's-plant.**

sal′ad days′, a period of youthful inexperience: *a man who never lost the immature attitudes of his salad days.*

sal′ad dress′ing, a sauce for a salad, usually with a base of oil and vinegar or of mayonnaise.

sa·lade (sə läd′, sal′əd), *n. Armor.* sallet.

sal′ad fork′, a small and broad fork, usually one of a set, for eating salad or dessert.

Sal·a·din (sal′ə din), *n.* (*Salāh-ed-Dīn Yūsuf ibn Ayyūb*) 1137–93, sultan of Egypt and Syria 1175–93.

Sa·la·do (sə lä′dō; *Sp.* sä lä′ᵺō), *n.* **Rí·o** (rē′ō; *Sp.* rē′ō), a river in N Argentina, flowing SE to the Paraná River. ab. 1200 mi. long.

sal′ad oil′, an oil used in salad dressing, esp. olive oil or a vegetable oil, as from sesame, corn, or safflower.

sal′ad plate′, **1.** a small plate used chiefly for serving an individual portion of salad. **2.** a selection of salad ingredients served cold on a bed of lettuce, esp. at luncheon in restaurants.

Sa·lah (sə lä′), *n. Islam.* prayer, considered as one of the five obligations, or Din, of a Muslim. [< Ar *salāt*]

sa·lal (sə lal′, sa-), *n.* an evergreen shrub, *Gaultheria Shallon,* of the western coast of North America, having clusters of pink or white flowers and purplish-black fruit. [< Chinook Jargon *sallal*]

Sal·a·man·ca (sal′ə mang′kə; *for 1 also Sp.* sä′lä-mäng′kä), *n.* **1.** a city in W Spain: Wellington's defeat of the French, 1812. 93,130 (est. 1963). **2.** a town in W New York. 8480 (1960).

sal·a·man·der (sal′ə man′dər), *n.* **1.** any tailed amphibian of the order *Urodeles,* having a soft, moist, scaleless skin and typically an aquatic larval state, and living in a moist or aquatic habitat as an adult. **2.** a mythical being, esp. a lizard or other reptile, thought to be able to live in fire. **3.** any of various portable stoves or burners. **4.** *Metall.* a mass of iron which accumulates at the bottom of a blast furnace as a result

of the escape of molten metal through the hearth. **5.** a metal plate or disk with a handle, heated and held over pastry, casserole crusts, etc., to brown or glaze it. **6.** an oven usually heated from the top and bottom by gas, for cooking, browning, and glazing food. [ME *salamandre* < L *salamandra* < Gk] —**sal′a·man′der·like′,** *adj.* —**sal·a·man·drine** (sal′ə man′drin), *adj.* —**sal′a·man′droid,** *adj.*
—**Syn. 2.** See **sylph.**

Tiger salamander, ***Ambystoma tigrinum*** **(Length 8 in.)**

Sa·lam·bri·a (sə lam′brē ə, sä′läm brē′ä), *n.* a river in N Greece, in Thessaly, flowing E into the Gulf of Salonika. 125 mi. long. Ancient, **Peneus.** Modern Greek, **Peneios.**

sa·la·mi (sə lä′mē), *n.* a kind of sausage, originally Italian, often flavored with garlic. [< It, pl. of *salame* < VL *salāmen, equiv. to *salā(re) (to) salt + -men n. suffix; see SAL]

Sal·a·mis (sal′ə mis; *Gk.* sä′lä mēs′), *n.* **1.** an island off the SE coast of Greece, W of Athens, in the Gulf of Aegina: Greeks defeated Persians in a naval battle 480 B.C. 17,738 (1951); 39 sq. mi. **2.** an ancient city on Cyprus, in the E Mediterranean: the apostle Paul made his first missionary journey to Salamis. Acts 13:5. **3.** *Class. Myth.* a daughter of Asopus and Metope who bore a son, Cychreus, by Poseidon. —**Sal·a·min·i·an** (sal′ə min′ē ən), *adj.*

sal′ ammo′niac, *Chem.* See **ammonium chloride.**

sal·a·ried (sal′ə rēd), *adj.* **1.** receiving a salary: *a salaried employee.* **2.** having a salary attached: *a salaried job.* [SALARY + -ED[3]]

sal·a·ry (sal′ə rē), *n., pl.* **-ries.** a fixed compensation periodically paid to a person for regular work or services, esp. work other than that of a manual, mechanical, or menial kind. [ME *salarie* < AF < L *salāri(um)* salt money. See SAL, -ARY] —**sal′a·ry·less,** *adj.*
—**Syn.** See **pay.**

sal′ary sav′ings insur′ance, life insurance in which the policyholder's employer deducts the premium from the wages or salary of the insured and pays it directly to the insurer. Also called **payroll deduction insurance.**

Sa·la·zar (sal′ə zär′, säl′-; *Port.* sə lä zäʀ′), *n.* **An·to·nio de O·li·vei·ra** (än tô′nyô də ô′lē vā′ʀə), born 1889, premier of Portugal 1933–68.

sale (sāl), *n.* **1.** the act of selling. **2.** a quantity sold. **3.** opportunity to sell; demand: *slow sale.* **4.** a special disposal of goods, as at reduced prices. **5.** transfer of property for money or credit. **6. for sale,** offered to be sold; made available to purchasers. [ME late OE *sala*; c. Icel, OHG *sala.* Cf. SELL[1]]

sale·a·ble (sā′lə bəl), *adj.* salable. —**sale′a·bil′i·ty,** *n.* —**sale′a·bly,** *adv.*

sale′ and lease′back, leaseback.

sal·e·brous (sal′ə brəs), *adj.* *Obs.* rough; rugged. [< LL *salebrōs(us)* rough, equiv. to *salebr(a)* roughness + *-ōsus* -OUS]

Sa·lem (sā′ləm), *n.* **1.** a seaport in NE Massachusetts: founded 1626; execution of persons accused of being witches 1692; home of Nathaniel Hawthorne. 39,211 (1960). **2.** a city in and the capital of Oregon, in the NW part, on the Willamette River. 49,142 (1960). **3.** a town in SW Virginia, near Roanoke. 16,058 (1960). **4.** a town in SW New Jersey. 8941 (1960). **5.** a town in central Illinois. 6165 (1960). **6.** a town in S Indiana. 4546 (1960). **7.** a town in NW Missouri. 3870 (1960). **8.** a city in central Madras, in S India. 249,100 (1961). **9.** an ancient city of Canaan, later identified with Jerusalem. Gen. 14:18; Psalms 76:2.

sa·le·ma (sə lē′mə), *n.* *Ichthyol.* **1.** a grunt, *Xenistius californiensis.* **2.** See **spottail pinfish.** [< Sp]

Sa′lem De′pot, a town in SE New Hampshire. 2523 (1960).

Sa′lem sec′retary, *U.S. Furniture.* a tall cabinet having a recessed upper part fitted with drawers and shelves and a lower part with doors and a section falling or pulling out to serve as a writing surface. Also called **Sa′lem desk′.**

sal·ep (sal′ep), *n.* a starchy, demulcent drug or foodstuff consisting of the dried tubers of certain orchids. [< Turk *sālep* < dial. Ar *sa'leb,* Ar *tha'leb,* short for *khasyu'th-tha'lab* fox's testicles]

sal·e·ra·tus (sal′ə rā′təs), *n.* sodium bicarbonate used in cookery; baking soda. [var. of L *sal aerātus.* See SAL, AERATE]

Sa·ler·no (sə lûr′nō; *It.* sä leʀ′nô), *n.* a seaport in SW Italy: taken by U.S. forces September 1943. 118,171 (1961).

sales (sālz), *n.* **1.** pl. of **sale.** —*adj.* **2.** of or pertaining to sales: *a sales department; sales records for the month of January.*

sales·clerk (sālz′klûrk′), *n.* a salesman or saleswoman in a store. [SALES + CLERK]

sales·girl (sālz′gûrl′), *n.* a girl who sells goods, esp. in a store. [SALES + GIRL]

Sa·le·sian (sə lē′zhən, -shən), *Rom. Cath. Ch.* —*n.* **1.** a member of the Society of St. Francis de Sales, a congregation founded in Turin in 1845 and engaged chiefly in missionary and educational work. —*adj.* **2.** of or pertaining to St. Francis de Sales or the Salesians. [St. Francis de *Sales* + -IAN]

sales·la·dy (sālz′lā′dē), *n., pl.* **-dies.** a saleswoman. [SALES + LADY]

sales·man (sālz′mən), *n., pl.* **-men.** a man who sells goods, services, etc. [SALES + MAN[1]]

sales·man·ship (sālz′mən ship′), *n.* **1.** the technique of selling a product: *They used a promotional gimmick that was the last word in salesmanship.* **2.** adeptness at creating interest in new ideas, products, methods, etc.: *The only ingredient lacking in the system was salesmanship.* [SALESMAN + -SHIP]

sales·peo·ple (sālz′pē′pəl), *n.pl.* people engaged in selling. [SALES + PEOPLE]

sales·per·son (sālz′pûr′sən), *n.* one who sells goods, esp. in a store. [SALES + PERSON]

sales′ promo′tion, the methods or techniques for creating public acceptance of or interest in a product, usually in addition to standard merchandising techniques, as advertising or personal selling, and generally consisting of the offer of free samples, gifts made to a purchaser, or the like.

sales′ resis′tance, the ability or inclination to refuse to buy a product, service, etc., offered.

sales·room (sālz′ro͞om′, -ro͝om′), *n.* **1.** a room in which goods are sold or displayed. **2.** an auction room. [SALES + ROOM]

sales′ talk′, **1.** a line of reasoning or argument intended to persuade someone to buy, accept, or do something. **2.** any persuasive argument.

sales′ tax′, a tax on sales or on receipts from sales, usually added to the selling price by the seller.

sales·wom·an (sālz′wo͝om′ən), *n., pl.* **-wom·en.** a woman who sells goods, esp. in a store. [SALES + WOMAN]

Sal·ford (sôl′fərd, sô′-, sal′-), *n.* a city in SE Lancashire, in N England, near Manchester. 154,693 (1961).

Sa·li·an (sā′lē ən, sāl′yən), *adj.* **1.** of, pertaining to, or designating a Frankish people who lived in the region of the Rhine near the North Sea. —*n.* **2.** a Salian Frank. [< L *Sali(ī)* tribal name + -AN]

Sal·ic (sal′ik, sā′lik), *adj.* of or pertaining to the Salian Franks. Also, **Salique.** [< ML *Salic(us),* equiv. to *Sal(iī)* tribal name + *-icus* -IC]

sal·i·ca·ceous (sal′ə kā′shəs), *adj.* belonging to the *Salicaceae,* a family of trees and shrubs comprising the willows and poplars. [< NL *Salicace(ae)* willow family (L *salic-,* s. of *salix* willow + *-aceae* -ACEAE) + -OUS]

sal·i·cin (sal′i sin), *n.* *Pharm.* a colorless, crystalline, water-soluble glucoside, $CH_2OHC_6H_4OC_6H_{11}O_5$, obtained from the bark of the American aspen: used in medicine chiefly as an antipyretic and analgesic. Also called **salicyl alcohol glucoside.** [< F *salicine* < L *salic-* (s. of *salix*) willow + F *-ine* -INE[2]]

Sal′ic law′, **1.** a code of laws of the Salian Franks and other Germanic tribes, esp. a provision in this code excluding females from the inheritance of land. **2.** the alleged fundamental law of the French monarchy by which females were excluded from succession to the crown. **3.** any law to the same effect.

sal′i·cyl al′cohol glu′coside (sal′i sil), *Pharm.* salicin. [SALIC(IN) + -YL]

sal·i·cyl·al·de·hyde (sal′i sil al′də hīd′), *n.* *Chem.* an oily, slightly water-soluble liquid, HOC_6H_4CHO, having an almondlike odor: used chiefly in perfumery and in the synthesis of coumarin. Also, **salicylic aldehyde.** [SALICYL + ALDEHYDE]

sa·lic·y·late (sə lis′ə lāt′, -lit, sal′i sil′āt, sal′i-sil′-), *n.* *Chem.* a salt or ester of salicylic acid. [SALICYL + -ATE[2]]

sal·i·cyl·ic (sal′i sil′ik), *adj.* *Chem.* of or derived from salicylic acid. [SALICYL(ATE) + -IC]

sal′icyl′ic ac′id, *Chem., Pharm.* a white, crystalline, very slightly water-soluble powder, $C_6H_4(OH)(COOH)$, prepared from salicin or phenol: used as a food preservative, in the manufacture of aspirin, and in medicine chiefly in the form of a salicylate as a remedy for rheumatic and gouty conditions.

sal′icyl′ic al′dehyde, *Chem.* salicylaldehyde.

Sa·li·da (sə lī′də), *n.* a town in central Colorado. 4560 (1960).

sa·li·ence (sā′lē əns, sāl′yəns), *n.* **1.** the state or condition of being salient. **2.** a salient or projecting object, part, or feature. [< L *sali-* (s. of *salīre* to spring) + -ENCE]

sa·li·en·cy (sā′lē ən sē, sāl′yən-), *n., pl.* **-cies.** salience. [< L *sali-* (s. of *salīre* to spring) + -ENCY]

sa·li·ent (sā′lē ənt, sāl′yənt), *adj.* **1.** prominent or conspicuous: *salient traits.* **2.** projecting or pointing outward: *a salient angle.* **3.** leaping or jumping: *a salient animal.* **4.** *Heraldry.* (of a beast) represented as leaping: *a lion salient.* —*n.* **5.** a salient angle or part, as the central outward-projecting angle of a bastion or an outward projection in a battle line. See diag. under **bastion.** [< L *salient-* (s. of *saliēns,* prp. of *salīre* to spring), equiv. to *sali-* + *-ent-* -ENT] —**sa′li·ent·ly,** *adv.*
—**Syn. 1.** important, striking, remarkable. —**Ant. 1.** inconspicuous, unimportant.

S, Salient angle
R, Reentering angle

sa·li·en·ti·an (sā′lē en′shē ən), *adj.* **1.** belonging or pertaining to the superorder *Salientia,* comprising the frogs and toads (order *Anura*) and extinct species. —*n.* **2.** a salientian amphibian. [< NL *Salienti(a)* leaping ones + -AN]

Sa·lie·ri (sä lye′ʀē), *n.* **An·to·nio** (än tô′nyô), 1750–1825, Italian composer and conductor.

sa·lif·er·ous (sə lif′ər əs), *adj.* containing or producing salt: *saliferous strata.* [SAL + -I- + -FEROUS]

sal·i·fy (sal′ə fī′), *v.t.,* **-fied, -fy·ing.** **1.** to form into a salt, as by chemical combination. **2.** to mix or combine with a salt. [SAL + -IFY] —**sal′i·fi′a·ble,** *adj.* —**sal·i·fi·ca·tion** (sal′ə fə kā′shən), *n.*

Sal·i·i (sal′ē ī′), *n.pl.* (in ancient Rome) a college of priests of Mars and Quirinus who guarded the ancilia and led the festivities in their honor. Cf. **ancile.**

sal·im·e·ter (sa lim′i tər), *n.* *Chem.* a salinometer. [SAL + -I- + -METER]

sa·li·na (sə lī′nə), *n.* **1.** a saline marsh, spring, or the like. **2.** a saltworks. [< Sp < L *salīnae* saltworks]

Sa·li·na (sə lī′nə), *n.* a city in central Kansas. 43,202 (1960).

Sa·li·nas (sə lē′nəs), *n.* a city in W California. 28,957 (1960).

sa·line (sā′līn, -lēn), *adj.* **1.** of, containing, or resembling common table salt; salty or saltlike: *a saline solution; a liquid with a saline taste.* **2.** of or pertaining to a chemical salt, esp. of sodium, potassium, magnesium, etc., as used as a cathartic. —*n.* **3.** a saline medicine. [< L *salīn(us)* salty, equiv. to *sal* salt + *-īnus* -INE[1]] —**sa·lin·i·ty** (sə lin′i tē), *n.*

Sal·in·ger (sal′ən jər), *n.* **J(erome) D(avid),** born 1919, U.S. novelist and short-story writer.

sal·i·nom·e·ter (sal′ə nom′i tər), *n.* *Chem.* an instrument for measuring the amount of salt in a solution; salimeter. [*salino-* (comb. form of SALINE) + -METER] —**sal′i·nom′e·try,** *n.*

Sa·lique (sə lēk′, sal′ik, sā′lik), *adj.* Salic.

Salis·bur·y (sôlz′ber′ē, -bə rē), *n.* **1. Robert Arthur Tal·bot Gas·coyne Cecil** (tôl′bət gas′koin, tal′-), **3rd Marquis of,** 1830–1903, British statesman. **2.** a city in and the county seat of Wiltshire, in S England: cathedral. 35,471 (1961). **3.** a city in and the capital of Rhodesia, in the NE part: capital of the former Federation of Rhodesia and Nyasaland. 313,600 (est. 1964). **4.** a city in central North Carolina. 21,297 (1960). **5.** a city in E Maryland. 16,302 (1960). **6.** a town in NW Connecticut. 3309 (1960). **7.** a town in NE Massachusetts. 3154 (1960).

Salis′bury Plain′, a plateau in S England, N of Salisbury: the site of Stonehenge.

Salis′bury steak′, ground beef, sometimes mixed with other foods, shaped like a hamburger patty and broiled or fried, often garnished or served with a sauce. [named after J. H. *Salisbury,* 19th-century English dietitian]

Sa·lish (sā′lish), *n.* a member of any of various American Indian peoples speaking a Salishan language. [< Salishan *sälst*]

Sa·lish·an (sā′lish ən, sal′ish-), *n.* **1.** a language family including Coeur d'Alêne and Kalispel and other languages of British Columbia and the northwestern U.S. —*adj.* **2.** of, pertaining to, or characteristic of this language family. [SALISH + -AN]

sa·li·va (sə lī′və), *n.* a viscid, colorless, watery fluid, secreted into the mouth by the salivary glands, that functions in the tasting, chewing, and swallowing of food, keeps the mouth moist, and starts the digestion of starches. [< L: spittle] —**sal·i·var·y** (sal′ə ver′ē), *adj.*

sal′ivary gland′, *Anat.* any of several glands, as the submaxillary glands, that secrete saliva.

sal·i·vate (sal′ə vāt′), *v.,* **-vat·ed, -vat·ing.** —*v.i.* **1.** to produce saliva. —*v.t.* **2.** to produce an excessive secretion of saliva in, as by the use of mercury. [< L *salīvāt(us)* (ptp. of *salīvāre* to spit), equiv. to *salīv-* (see SALIVA) + *-ātus* -ATE[1]]

sal·i·va·tion (sal′ə vā′shən), *n.* **1.** the act or process of salivating. **2.** an abnormally abundant flow of saliva. **3.** mercurial poisoning. [< L *salīvātiōn-* (s. of *salīvātiō*), equiv. to *salīvāt(us)* (see SALIVATE) + *-iōn-* -ION]

sal·i·va·tor (sal′ə vā′tər), *n.* *Med.* any agent that causes salivation. [< L: spitter, equiv. to *salīvāt(us)* (see SALIVATE) + *-or* -OR[2]]

Salk (sôlk, sôk), *n.* **Jonas E(dward),** born 1914, U.S. bacteriologist: developed Salk vaccine.

Salk′ vaccine′, a vaccine that contains three types of poliomyelitis viruses and induces immunity against the disease: produced by cultivation of the organisms on monkey kidney tissue followed by inactivation of the viruses with formaldehyde. [named after J. E. SALK]

Sal·lal (säl läl′), *n.* **Ab·dul·lah** (äb do͞ol′lä), born 1917, Yemeni army officer and statesman: president of the Revolutionary Council and Commander-in-Chief of the Republican forces since 1962.

salle à man·ger (SAL A mäN zhā′), *pl.* **salles à manger** (SAL A mäN zhā′). *French.* a dining room. [lit., hall for eating]

sal·len·ders (sal′ən dərz), *n.* (*construed as sing.*) *Vet. Pathol.* an eruption on the hind leg of a horse, on the inside of a hock. Cf. **malanders.** [?]

sal·let (sal′it), *n.* *Armor.* a light medieval helmet, usually with a vision slit or a movable visor. Also, **salade.** [ME, var. of *salade* < MF < Sp *celada* (or It *celata*) < L *caelāta* (*cassis*) engraved (helmet), fem. of *caelātus* (ptp. of *caelāre* to engrave); see -ATE[1]]

Sallet (15th century)

Sal·li·saw (sal′i sô′), *n.* a town in E Oklahoma. 3351 (1960).

sal·low[1] (sal′ō), *adj.* **1.** of a pale, sickly, yellowish color: *sallow cheeks; a sallow complexion.* —*v.t.* **2.** to make sallow. [ME *sal(o)we,* OE *salo;* c. Icel *sölr* yellow, F *sale* dirty (< Gmc)] —**sal′low·ish,** *adj.* —**sal′low·ness,** *n.*

sal·low[2] (sal′ō), *n.* a willow, esp. *Salix caprea* (**great sallow**), an Old World shrub or bushy tree used in making charcoal for gunpowder. [ME; OE *sealh;* c. OHG *salaha,* L *salix*]

sal·low·y (sal′ō ē), *adj.* full of sallows: *a sallowy glade.* [SALLOW[2] + -Y[1]]

Sal·lust (sal′əst), *n.* (*Caius Sallustius Crispus*) 86–34 B.C., Roman historian.

sal·ly (sal′ē), *n., pl.* **-lies,** *v.,* **-lied, -ly·ing.** —*n.* **1.** a sortie of troops from a besieged place upon an enemy. **2.** a sudden rushing forth or activity. **3.** an excursion or trip, usually off the main course. **4.** an outburst or flight of passion, fancy, etc.: *a sally of anger.* **5.** a clever, witty, or fanciful remark: *The first act is brightened by highly diverting sallies.* **6.** *Carpentry.* a projection, as of the end of a rafter beyond the notch by which the rafter is fitted over the wall plate. —*v.i.* **7.** to make a sally, as a body of troops from a besieged place. **8.** to set out on a side trip or excursion. **9.** to set out briskly or energetically. **10.** (of things) to issue forth. [< MF *saillie* attack, n. use of fem. ptp. of *saillir* to rush forward < L *salīre* to leap] —**sal′li·er,** *n.*

Sal·ly (sal′ē), *n.* a girl's given name, form of **Sara** or **Sarah.** Also, **Sal′lie, Sal′lye.**

sal′ly lunn′ (lun), a slightly sweetened teacake served hot with butter. Also, **Sal′ly Lunn′.** [named after a woman who sold them in Bath, England, at the end of the 18th century]

sal′ly port′, (in a fort or the like) **1.** a gateway permitting the passage of a large number of troops at a time. **2.** a postern.

Sal·ma·cis (sal′mə sis), *n.* *Class. Myth.* See under **Hermaphroditus.**

sal·ma·gun·di (sal′mə gun′dē), *n.* **1.** a mixed dish consisting of chopped meat, anchovies, eggs, onions, oil, etc., often served as a salad. **2.** any mixture or miscellany. [< F *salmigondis,* perh. < It *salami conditi* pickled SALAMI; see CONDIMENT]

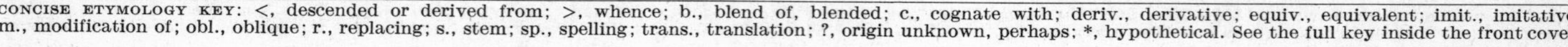

Sal·ma·gun·di (sal′mə gun′dē), *n.* a humorous periodical, 1807–8, issued by Washington Irving and others.

Sal·ma·na·zar (sal′mə naz′ər), *n.* a wine bottle holding from 10 to 12 quarts. [var. of *Shalmaneser,* name of biblical king; see 2 Kings 18:9]

sal·mi (sal′mē), *n.* a ragout of partially cooked game, as pheasant or woodcock, stewed in wine and butter. Also, **salmis.** [< F, short for *salmigondis* SALAMAGUNDI]

sal·mis (sal′mē; *Fr.* SAL mē′), *n., pl.* **-mis** (-mē; *Fr.* -mē′). salmi.

salm·on (sam′ən), *n., pl.* **-ons,** (*esp. collectively*) **-on,** *adj.* —*n.* **1.** a marine and fresh-water food fish, *Salmo salar,* of the family *Salmonidae,* having pink flesh, found off the North Atlantic coasts of Europe and North America near the mouths of large rivers, where it ascends to spawn. **2.** See **landlocked salmon. 3.** any of several salmonoid food fishes of the genus *Oncorhynchus,* found in the North Pacific. **4.** light yellowish-pink. —*adj.* **5.** of the color salmon. [ME *salmoun, samoun* < AF (c. OF *saumon*) < L *salmōn-,* s. of *salmō*] —**salm′on·like′,** *adj.*

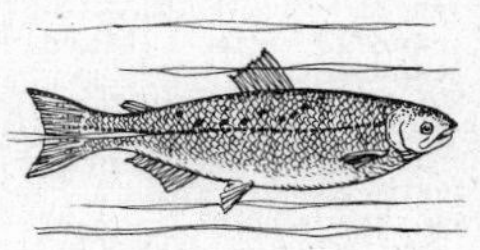
Chinook salmon, *Oncorhynchus tshawytscha* (Length to 6 ft.)

Salm·on (sam′ən), *n.* a town in E Idaho. 2944 (1960).

salm·on·ber·ry (sam′ən ber′ē), *n., pl.* **-ries. 1.** the salmon-colored, edible fruit of a raspberry, *Rubus spectabilis,* of the Pacific coast of North America. **2.** the plant itself. [SALMON + BERRY]

salm′on brick′, a soft, imperfectly fired brick having a reddish-orange color.

sal·mo·nel·la (sal′mə nel′ə), *n., pl.* **-nel·lae** (-nel′ē). *Bacteriol.* any of several rod-shaped, facultatively anaerobic bacteria of the genus *Salmonella,* as *S. typhosa,* that are pathogenic for man and warm-blooded animals. [< NL; named after Daniel E. *Salmon* (d. 1914), American veterinarian]

Sal·mo·ne·us (sal mō′nē əs), *n. Class. Myth.* a son of Aeolus and Enarete who was struck by lightning as a punishment for imitating Zeus, the thunderer.

sal·mo·nid (sal′mə nid), *adj.* **1.** belonging or pertaining to the family *Salmonidae,* including the salmons, trouts, chars, whitefishes, etc. —*n.* **2.** a salmonid fish. [< NL *Salmonid(ae)* name of the family. See SALMON, -ID[2]]

sal·mo·noid (sal′mə noid′), *adj.* **1.** resembling a salmon. **2.** belonging or pertaining to the suborder *Salmonoidea,* to which the salmon family belongs. —*n.* **3.** a salmonoid fish. [< NL *Salmōnoid(ea)* suborder of fishes. See SALMON, -OID]

salm′on pink′, salmon (defs. 4, 5).

Sal′mon Riv′er Moun′tains, a range in central Idaho. Highest peak, 10,340 ft.

salm′on tail′, *Naut.* a supplementary part fastened to the after edge of a rudder to increase its effective surface in restricted waters. Also called **Danube rudder, Suez Canal rudder.**

salm′on trout′, 1. a European trout, *Salmo trutta.* **2.** the lake trout, *Cristivomer namaycush.* **3.** the steelhead. **4.** any large trout.

sal·ol (sal′ōl, -ôl, -ol), *n. Pharm.* a white, crystalline, sparingly water-soluble powder, $HOC_6H_4COOC_6H_5$, having a pleasant aromatic odor and taste, produced by the interaction of salicylic acid and phenol: used as a preservative, a light absorber in suntan preparations, and in medicine chiefly as an antipyretic, antiseptic, and coating for pills in which the medicament is intended for enteric release. Also called **phenyl salicylate.** [formerly trademark]

Sa·lo·me (sə lō′mē *for 1, 3;* sal′ə mā′ *for 2*), *n.* **1.** the daughter of Herodias, who danced for Herod Antipas and so pleased him that he granted her request for the head of John the Baptist. Matt. 14:6–10. **2.** (*italics.*) a one-act opera (1905) by Richard Strauss based on a drama by Oscar Wilde. **3.** a girl's given name.

Sal·o·mon (sal′ə mən), *n.* **Haym** (hīm), 1740?–85, American financier and patriot, born in Poland.

sa·lon (sə lon′; *Fr.* SA LÔN′), *n., pl.* **-lons** (-lonz′; *Fr.* -lôN′). **1.** a drawing room or reception room in a large house. **2.** an assembly of guests in such a room, esp. an assembly, common during the 17th and 18th centuries, consisting of the leaders in society, art, politics, etc. **3.** a hall or place used for the exhibition of works of art. **4.** (*cap.*) (in France) **a. the Salon,** an annual exhibition of works of art by living artists, originally held at the Salon d'Apollon: it became, during the 19th century, the focal point of artistic controversy and was identified with academicism and official hostility to progress in art. **b.** a national exhibition of works of art by living artists: *Salon des Refusés; Salon des Indépendents; Salon d'Automne.* [< F < It *salone,* equiv. to *sal(a)* hall (< Gmc; cf. G *Saal,* OE *sæl,* etc.) + *-one* aug. suffix]

Sa·lo·ni·ka (sal′ə nē′kə, sə lon′ə kə), *n.* **1.** Also, **Sa·lo·ni·ca** (sə lon′ə kə), **Sa·lo·ni·ki** (sä′lô nē′kē). Official name, **Thessalonike.** Ancient, **Thessalonica, Therma.** a seaport in south-central Macedonia, in NE Greece, on the Gulf of Salonika. 250,920 (1961). **2. Gulf of,** an arm of the Aegean, in NE Greece. 70 mi. long.

salon′ mu′sic, music of a simple, agreeable, frequently sentimental character, played usually by a small orchestra.

sa·loon (sə lo͞on′), *n.* **1.** *U.S.* a place for the sale and consumption of alcoholic drinks. **2.** a room or place for general use for a specific purpose: *a dining saloon on a ship.* **3.** a large cabin for the common use of passengers on a passenger vessel. **4.** *Brit.* **a.** (in a tavern or pub) a section of a bar or barroom separated from the public bar and often having more comfortable furnishings and a quieter atmosphere. **b.** See **saloon car. 5.** a drawing room or reception room. [var. of SALON]

saloon′ car′, *Brit.* **1.** Also, **saloon′ car′riage.** a railway sleeping, dining, or parlor car similar to a U.S. Pullman. **2.** sedan (def. 1).

saloon′ keep′er, a person who owns or operates a saloon.

sa·loop (sə lo͞op′), *n.* a hot drink prepared originally from salep but later from sassafras, together with milk and sugar. [var. of SALEP]

Sal·op (sal′əp), *n.* Shropshire (def. 1). —**Sa·lo·pi·an** (sə lō′pē ən), *adj., n.*

sal·pa (sal′pə), *n., pl.* **-pas, -pae** (-pē). any free-swimming, oceanic tunicate of the genus *Salpa,* having a transparent, more or less fusiform body. [< NL, special use of L *salpa* < Gk *sálpē* kind of fish] —**sal·pi·form** (sal′pə fôrm′), *adj.*

sal·pi·glos·sis (sal′pə glos′is, -glô′sis), *n.* any Chilean solanaceous herb of the genus *Salpiglossis,* having showy, funnel-shaped flowers. [< NL < Gk *sálpi(nx)* + *glôssis* (var. of *glôttis* GLOTTIS)]

sal·pin·gec·to·my (sal′pin jek′tə mē), *n., pl.* **-mies.** *Surg.* excision of the Fallopian tube. [SALPING- + -ECTOMY]

sal·pin·gi·tis (sal′pin jī′tis), *n. Pathol.* inflammation of a Fallopian tube or of a Eustachian tube. [SALPING- + -ITIS] —**sal·pin·git·ic** (sal′pin jit′ik), *adj.*

salpingo-, a combining form of **salpinx:** *salpingotomy.* Also, *esp. before a vowel,* **salping-.** [< NL < Gk *salping-* (s. of *sálpinx*) + *-o-* -O-]

sal·pin·gos·to·my (sal′ping gos′tə mē), *n., pl.* **-mies.** *Surg.* the formation of an artificial opening into a Fallopian tube. Also, **sal·pin·go·sto·mat·o·my** (sal ping′gō stə mat′ə mē). [SALPINGO- + -STOMY]

sal·pin·got·o·my (sal′ping got′ə mē), *n., pl.* **-mies.** *Surg.* incision of a Fallopian tube. [SALPINGO- + -TOMY]

sal·pinx (sal′pingks), *n., pl.* **sal·pin·ges** (sal pin′jēz). *Anat.* a trumpet-shaped tube, as a Fallopian or Eustachian tube. [< Gk: trumpet] —**sal·pin·gi·an** (sal pin′jē ən), *adj.*

Sal·pinx (sal′pingks), *n. Class. Myth.* Athena: so called because she was believed to have invented the trumpet.

sal·sa (säl′sə, sal′-; *Sp.* säl′sä), *n., pl.* **-sas** (-səz; *Sp.* -säs). **1.** a vigorous, Latin American popular music, blending predominantly Cuban rhythms with elements of jazz and rock. **2.** a dance, similar to the mambo, performed to this music. [< Sp: lit., sauce, gravy]

sal·si·fy (sal′sə fē), *n., pl.* **-fies.** a purple-flowered plant, *Tragopogon porrifolius,* whose root has an oysterlike flavor and is used as a culinary vegetable. Also called **oyster plant, vegetable oyster.** [< F *salsifi(s),* var. of *sassefy, sassef(r)ique* < It *sassef(r)ic(a)* < ?]

sal′ so′da. See **sodium carbonate** (def. 2).

salt[1] (sôlt), *n.* **1.** a crystalline compound, sodium chloride, NaCl, occurring as a mineral, a constituent of sea water, etc., and used for seasoning food, as a preservative, etc. **2.** *Chem.* any of a class of compounds formed by the replacement of one or more hydrogen atoms of an acid with elements or groups, which are composed of anions and cations, and which usually ionize in solution; a product formed by the neutralization of an acid by a base. **3. salts,** any of various salts used as purgatives, as Epsom salts. **4.** an element that gives liveliness, piquancy, or pungency: *Anecdotes are the salt of his narrative.* **5.** wit; pungency. **6.** a small, usually open dish, as of silver or glass, used on the table for holding salt. **7.** *Informal.* a sailor, esp. an old or experienced one. **8. with a grain of salt,** with reserve or allowance; with an attitude of skepticism: *Diplomats took the reports of an impending crisis with a grain of salt.* **9. worth one's salt,** deserving of one's wages or salary: *She couldn't find a maid worth her salt.* —*v.t.* **10.** to season with salt. **11.** to cure, preserve, or treat with salt. **12.** to furnish with salt: *to salt cattle.* **13.** to treat with common salt or with any chemical salt. **14.** to introduce rich ore or other valuable matter fraudulently into (a mine, the ground, a mineral sample, etc.) to create a false impression of value. **15. salt away** or **down, a.** to preserve by adding quantities of salt to, as meat. **b.** *Informal.* to keep in reserve; store away; save: *to salt away most of one's earnings.* **16. salt out,** to separate (a dissolved substance) from a solution by the addition of a salt, esp. common salt. —*adj.* **17.** containing salt; having the taste of salt: *salt water.* **18.** cured or preserved with salt: *salt cod.* **19.** inundated by or growing in salt water: *salt marsh.* **20.** pungent or sharp: *salt speech.* [ME; OE *sealt;* c. G *Salz,* Icel, Goth *salt,* L *sal*] —**salt′like′,** *adj.* —**Syn. 7.** See **sailor.**

salt[2] (sôlt), *adj. Obs.* lustful; lecherous. [aph. var. of *assaut,* ME *a sawt* < MF (*a*) *saut* (on the) jump < L *salt(us)* leap, n. use of ptp. of *salīre*]

SALT (sôlt), Strategic Arms Limitation Talks.

Sal·ta (säl′tä), *n.* a city in NW Argentina. 121,491 (est. 1965).

sal·tan·do (säl tän′dō), *Music.* —*adj.* **1.** (of a performance with a stringed instrument) playing each note staccato by bouncing the bow on the strings. —*adv.* **2.** in a saltando manner. Also, **saltato.** [< It: lit., jumping, equiv. to *salt(are)* (see SALTANT) + *-ando* prp. suffix (< L *-and(um)* ger. suffix)]

salt-and-pep·per (sôlt′ᵊn pep′ər), *adj.* pepper-and-salt.

sal·tant (sal′tᵊnt), *adj.* dancing; leaping; jumping. [< L *saltant-* (s. of *saltāns,* prp. of *saltāre* to jump about, dance, freq. of *salīre* to leap), equiv. to *sal-* jump + *-t-* freq. suffix + *-ant-* -ANT]

sal·ta·rel·lo (sal′tə rel′ō, sôl′-; *It.* säl′tä REL′lô), *n., pl.* **-los,** *It.* **-li** (-lē). **1.** a lively Italian dance for one person or a couple. **2.** the music for it. [< It, equiv. to *saltar(e)* (see SALTANT) + *-ello* dim. suffix]

sal·ta·tion (sal tā′shən), *n.* **1.** dancing; leaping. **2.** an abrupt movement or transition. **3.** *Geol.* intermittent, leaping movement of particles of sand or gravel, as from the force of wind or running water. **4.** *Biol.* a mutation. [< L *saltātiōn-* (s. of *saltātiō*) a dancing, equiv. to *saltāt(us)* (ptp. of *saltāre;* see SALTANT) + *-iōn-* -ION]

sal·ta·to (säl tä′tō), *adj., adv. Music.* saltando. [< It: lit., jumped, equiv. to *salt(are)* (see SALTANT) + *-ato* (< L *-ātus*) -ATE[1]]

sal·ta·to·ri·al (sal′tə tôr′ē əl, -tōr′-), *adj.* **1.** pertaining to saltation. **2.** *Zool.* characterized by or adapted for leaping. [SALTATORY + -AL[1]]

sal·ta·to·ry (sal′tə tôr′ē, -tōr′ē), *adj.* **1.** pertaining to or adapted for saltation. **2.** proceeding by abrupt movements. [< L *saltātōri(us),* equiv. to *saltātor* dancer (*saltāt(us)*, ptp. of *saltāre* to dance + *-or* -OR[2]; see SALTATION) + *-ius* adj. suffix]

salt-box (sôlt′boks′), *n.* **1.** a box in which salt is kept. **2.** a type of house found in New England and dating from the 17th to the early 19th centuries, generally two full stories high in front and one story high in back, the roof having about the same pitch in both directions so that the ridge is well toward the front of the house. Also, **salt′box′.**

salt′ cake′, *Chem.* an impure form of sodium sulfate, esp. as obtained by the interaction of sulfuric acid and common salt in the synthesis of hydrochloric acid: used chiefly in the manufacture of glass, ceramic glazes, soaps, and sodium salts.

salt′ ce′dar, a shrub or small tree, *Tamarix gallica,* of the Mediterranean region, having bluish foliage and white or pinkish flowers. Also called **French tamarisk.**

salt·cel·lar (sôlt′sel′ər), *n.* a shaker or dish for salt. [SALT[1] + CELLAR; r. ME *saler* < OF *saliere* salt-holder < L *salāria,* n. use of fem. of *salārius* (adj.) pertaining to salt, equiv. to *sal* salt + *-ārius* -ARY]

salt′ dome′, *Geol.* a domelike rock structure that is formed beneath the earth's surface by the upward movement of a mass of salt, may reach thousands of feet in height, and is more or less circular in plan: often associated with oil and gas pools.

salt·ed (sôl′tid), *adj.* **1.** seasoned, cured, or otherwise treated with salt. **2.** *Informal.* experienced, as in some occupation. [ME; see SALT[1], -ED[3]]

Sal·ten (sôl′tᵊn; *Ger.* zäl′tən), *n.* **Fe·lix** (fē′liks; *Ger.* fā′liks), (*Siegmund Salzman*), 1869–1945, Austrian novelist, in Switzerland after 1938.

salt·er (sôl′tər), *n.* **1.** one who makes or sells salt. **2.** one who salts meat, fish, etc. [ME; OE *sealtere* salt-maker. See SALT[1], -ER[1]]

salt·ern (sôl′tərn), *n.* **1.** a saltworks. **2.** a plot of land laid out in pools for the evaporation of sea water to produce salt. [OE *sealtærn* saltworks, equiv. to *sealt* SALT[1] + *ærn* house]

salt′ glaze′, a ceramic glaze on stoneware produced by the chemical reaction that occurs when salt is thrown into a kiln during firing. —**salt′ glaz′ing.**

salt·glaze (sôlt′glāz′), *adj. Ceram.* having a salt glaze. Also, **salt′-glazed′, salt′glazed′.** [SALT[1] + GLAZE]

salt′ grass′, any of several grasses, as *Distichlis spicata,* that grow in salt marshes or meadows or in alkali soil.

salt′ hay′, hay made up of salt grass, often used as fodder.

salt′ horse′, *Naut. Slang.* salted beef; salt junk.

sal·ti·cid (sal′ti sid, sôl′-), *n.* **1.** a spider of the family *Salticidae,* comprising the jumping spiders. —*adj.* **2.** belonging or pertaining to the family *Salticidae.* [< NL *Salticid(ae)* name of the family, equiv. to LL *saltic(us)* jumping (L *salt(us)* leap (see SALT[2]) + *-icus* -IC) + *-idae* -ID[2]]

salt·i·er[1] (sôl′tē ər), *adj.* comparative of **salty.**

sal·tier[2] (sal′tēr, -tīᵊr), *n.* saltire.

sal·ti·grade (sal′tə grād′), *adj.* **1.** moving by leaping. **2.** belonging or pertaining to the family *Salticidae,* comprising the jumping spiders. [*salti-* comb. form of L *saltus* leap + -GRADE]

Sal·til·lo (säl tē′yô), *n.* a city in and the capital of Coahuila, in northern Mexico. 95,066 (est. 1960).

sal·tine (sôl tēn′), *n.* a crisp, salted cracker. [SALT[1] + -INE[2]]

sal·tire (sal′tir, -tīᵊr, sôl′-), *n. Heraldry.* **1.** an ordinary in the form of a cross with arms running diagonally from the dexter chief to the sinister base and from the sinister chief to the dexter base; St. Andrew's cross. **2. in saltire,** (of charges) arranged in the form of a saltire. **3. per saltire,** diagonally in both directions: *party per saltire.* Also, **saltier.** [late ME *sawtire* < MF *sautoir* crossed jumping bar << L *saltātōr(ium)* something pertaining to jumping; see SALTATORY]

sal·tire·wise (sal′tir wīz′, -tīᵊr, sôl′-), *adv. Heraldry.* in the direction or manner of a saltire. Also, **sal·tire·ways** (sal′tir wāz′, -tīᵊr-, sôl′-). [SALTIRE + -WISE]

salt·ish (sôl′tish), *adj.* somewhat salty. [SALT[1] + -ISH[1]] —**salt′ish·ly,** *adv.* —**salt′ish·ness,** *n.*

salt′ junk′, *Naut. Slang.* salted beef or pork.

salt′ lake′, a body of water having no outlet to the sea and containing in solution a high concentration of salts, esp. sodium chloride.

Salt′ Lake′ Cit′y, a city in and the capital of Utah, in the N part, near the Great Salt Lake. 184,454 (1960).

salt·less (sôlt′lis), *adj.* **1.** lacking salt. **2.** lacking vitality; dull; insipid: *a saltless person.* [ME; see SALT[1], -LESS]

salt′ lick′, a place to which wild animals go to lick naturally occurring salt deposits.

salt′ marsh′, a marshy tract that is wet with salt water or flooded by the sea. [ME *saltmerche,* OE *sealtne mersc*]

salt′-marsh cat′erpillar (sôlt′märsh′), the caterpillar of the Acrea moth, which infests various grasses, esp. salt grasses.

salt′ mine′, 1. a mine from which salt is excavated. **2.** Usually, **salt mines.** a place of habitual confinement and drudgery: *After two weeks of vacation it will be back to the salt mines for the staff.*

salt·ness (sôlt′nis), *n.* the state or quality of being salt or salty. [ME *saltnesse;* OE *sealtnes.* See SALT[1], -NESS]

Sal·to (säl′tô), *n.* a city in NW Uruguay, on the Uruguay River. 44,900 (est. 1954).

salt′ of phos′phorus. See **sodium ammonium phosphate.**

salt′ of sor′rel, *Chem.* See **potassium binoxalate.**

salt′ of the earth′, an individual or group considered as representative of the best or noblest elements of society.

Sal′ton Sea′ (sôl′tən, -tᵊn), a shallow saline lake in S California, in the Imperial Valley, formed by the diversion of water from the Colorado River into Salton Sink. 236 ft. below sea level.

Sal′ton Sink′, a former salt-covered depression in S California, at the N end of Imperial Valley: now Salton Sea. 283 ft. below sea level.

salt·pe·ter (sôlt′pē′tər), *n.* **1.** the form of potassium nitrate, KNO_3, that occurs naturally: used in the manufacture of fireworks, fluxes, gunpowder, etc.; niter. **2.** See **Chile saltpeter.** Also, **salt′pe′tre.** [earlier *salt peter;* r. ME *sal peter, salpetre* < ML *salpetrē,* L *sal petrae* salt of rock]

salt′ pit′, a pit where salt is obtained. [ME]

salt′ pork′, pork cured with salt, esp. the fat pork taken from the back, sides, and belly.

salt′ rheum′, *Pathol.* eczema.

salt′-ris·ing bread′ (sôlt′rī′zing), a kind of bread leavened with a fermented mixture of salted milk, corn meal, flour, sugar, and soda.

Salt′ Riv′er, a river flowing W from E Arizona to the Gila River near Phoenix: Roosevelt Dam. 200 mi. long.

salt′ shak′er, a container for salt with a perforated top to allow the salt to be shaken out.

salt′ spoon′, a small spoon with which to take salt at the table.

salt′ stick′, a crusty bread roll sprinkled with salt crystals, made in the shape of a cylinder tapered at the ends by rolling up a triangular piece of dough.

salt′ tree′. See **athel tree.**

sal·tus (sal′təs, sôl′-), *n., pl.* **-tus·es.** *Math.* oscillation (def. 5b). [< NL, L: a leap. See SALT[2]]

Salt·ville (sôlt′vil), *n.* a town in SW Virginia. 2844 (1960).

salt′ wa′ter, 1. water containing a large amount of salt. **2.** sea water. [ME *saltwater,* OE *sealter wæter*]

salt-wa·ter (sôlt′wô′tər, -wot′ər), *adj.* **1.** of or pertaining to salt water. **2.** inhabiting salt water: *a salt-water fish.*

salt′ well′, a well from which brine is obtained.

salt·works (sôlt′wûrks′), *n., pl.* **-works.** (*often construed as pl.*) a building or plant where salt is made. [SALT[1] + WORKS]

salt·wort (sôlt′wûrt), *n.* any of various plants of sea beaches, salt marshes, and alkaline regions, esp. of the genus *Salsola,* as *S. Kali,* a bushy plant having prickly leaves, or of the genus *Salicornia.* [trans. of D *zoutkruid.* See SALT[1], WORT[2]]

salt·y (sôl′tē), *adj.,* **salt·i·er, salt·i·est. 1.** tasting of or containing salt; saline. **2.** piquant; sharp; witty; racy: *some salty remarks about snobs.* **3.** of the sea, sailing, or life at sea. [late ME; see SALT[1], -Y[1]] —**salt′i·ly,** *adv.* —**salt′i·ness,** *n.*

sa·lu·bri·ous (sə lo͞o′brē əs), *adj.* favorable to or promoting health; healthful: *salubrious climate.* [< L *salūbr(is)* + -IOUS] —**sa·lu′bri·ous·ly,** *adv.* —**sa·lu′bri·ous·ness, sa·lu·bri·ty** (sə lo͞o′bri tē), *n.*

sa·lu·gi (sə lo͞o′jē), *n.* **1.** a gamelike prank in which one youth grabs something, as a hat, belonging to another and throws it to a third, the object being to prevent the owner from retrieving it as it is tossed back and forth. —*interj.* **2.** (used to signal the beginning of this prank.) [?]

Saluki (2 ft. high at shoulder)

Sa·lu·ki (sə lo͞o′kē), *n.* (*sometimes l.c.*) one of a breed of black and tan, white, gold, or tricolor dogs resembling the greyhound and having fringes of long hair on the ears, legs, and thighs, raised originally in Egypt and southwestern Asia. Also called **gazelle hound.** [< Ar *salūqī,* lit., of *Salūq* old city in Arabia]

Sa·lus (sā′ləs), *n.* the ancient Roman goddess of health and prosperity: identified with the Greek goddess Hygeia. [< L: health]

sa·lus po·pu·li su·pre·ma lex es·to (sä′lo͝os pō′po͝o lē′ so͞o prā′mä leks es′tō; *Eng.* sā′ləs pop′yə lī′ so͞o prē′mə leks es′tō), *Latin.* Let the welfare of the people be the supreme law: a motto of Missouri.

sal·u·tar·y (sal′yə ter′ē), *adj.* **1.** favorable to or promoting health; healthful. **2.** promoting or conducive to some beneficial purpose; wholesome. [< L *salūtāri(s),* equiv. to *salūt-* (s. of *salūs*) health + *-āris* -ARY] —**sal·u·tar·i·ly** (sal′yə ter′ə lē, sal′yə târ′-), *adv.* —**sal′u·tar′i·ness,** *n.* —**Syn. 1.** salubrious. See **healthy.**

sal·u·ta·tion (sal′yə tā′shən), *n.* **1.** the act of saluting. **2.** something uttered, written, or done by way of saluting. **3.** a word or phrase serving as the prefatory greeting in a letter or speech, as *Dear Sir* in a letter or *Mr. President, Distinguished Guests* in a speech. [< L *salūtātiōn-* (s. of *salūtātiō*) greeting, equiv. to *salūtāt(us)* (ptp. of *salūtāre* to greet; see SALUTE, -ATE[1]) + *-iōn-* -ION] —**sal′u·ta′tion·al,** *adj.* —**sal′u·ta′tion·less,** *adj.*

sa·lu·ta·to·ri·an (sə lo͞o′tə tôr′ē ən, -tōr′-), *n.* (in some U.S. schools and colleges) a student who delivers the salutatory at a commencement. [SALUTATORY + -AN]

sa·lu·ta·to·ri·um (sə lo͞o′tə tôr′ē əm, -tōr′-), *n., pl.* **-to·ri·a** (-tôr′ē ə, -tōr′-). a porch or room in a monastery or church serving as a meeting or almsgiving place for monks or priests and the laity. [< ML, neut. of *salūtātōrius* SALUTATORY]

sa·lu·ta·to·ry (sə lo͞o′tə tôr′ē, -tōr′ē), *adj., n., pl.* **-ries.** —*adj.* **1.** pertaining to or of the nature of a salutation. —*n.* **2.** a welcoming address, esp. one given at commencement in some U.S. schools and colleges by the second highest-ranking student in the graduating class. [< ML *salūtātōri(us),* equiv to L *salūtāt(us)* (ptp. of *salūtāre* to SALUTE) + *-ōrius* -ORY[1]] —**sa·lu′ta·to′ri·ly,** *adv.*

sa·lute (sə lo͞ot′), *v.* **-lut·ed, -lut·ing,** *n.* —*v.t.* **1.** to address with expressions of good will, respect, etc.; greet. **2.** to make a bow or other gesture to, as in greeting, farewell, or respect. **3.** *Mil., Navy.* to pay respect to or honor by some formal act, as by raising the right hand to the side of the headgear, presenting arms, firing cannon, dipping colors, etc. —*v.i.* **4.** to perform a salutation. **5.** *Mil., Navy.* to give a salute. —*n.* **6.** an act of saluting; salutation; greeting. **7.** *Mil., Navy.* **a.** the special act of respect paid in saluting. **b.** the position of the hand or rifle in saluting: *at the salute.* **8.** a French and Anglo-Gallic gold coin, bearing the image of the Virgin Mary receiving Gabriel's salutation, issued by Charles VI of France and by Henry V and Henry VI of England. [ME < L *salūt(āre)* (to) greet (lit., to hail), deriv. of *salūt-* (s. of *salūs*) health; r. *salue* < F *salue(r)* < L *salūtāre*] —**sa·lut′er,** *n.*

sa·lu·te (sä lo͞o′te), *interj. Italian.* (used after a person has sneezed or as a toast) Health! Your good health!

sal·u·tif·er·ous (sal′yə tif′ər əs), *adj.* salutary. [< L *salūtifer* health-bearing + -OUS; see SALUTE, -FER]

Salv., Salvador.

salv·a·ble (sal′və bəl), *adj.* fit for or capable of being saved or salvaged. [< LL *salv(āre)* (to) save + -ABLE] —**sal′va·bil′i·ty, sal′va·ble·ness,** *n.* —**sal′va·bly,** *adv.*

Sal·va·dor (sal′və dôr′; *for 1, 3 also Sp.* säl′vä ᴛʜôʀ′; *for 2, also Port.* säl′və dôr′), *n.* **1.** See **El Salvador. 2.** official name of **São Salvador. 3.** a boy's given name.

sal·vage (sal′vij), *n., v.,* **-vaged, -vag·ing.** —*n.* **1.** the act of saving a ship or its cargo from perils of the seas. **2.** the property so saved. **3.** compensation given to those who voluntarily save a ship or its cargo. **4.** the act of saving anything from fire, danger, etc. **5.** the property saved from danger. **6.** the value or proceeds upon sale of goods recovered from a fire. —*v.t.* **7.** to save from shipwreck, fire, etc. [< ML *salvāg(ium),* equiv. to *salv(āre)* (to) save + *-āgium* -AGE] —**sal′vage·a·ble,** *adj.* —**sal′vag·er,** *n.*

Sal·var·san (sal′vər san′), *n. Pharm., Trademark.* arsphenamine.

sal·va·tion (sal vā′shən), *n.* **1.** the act of saving or protecting from harm, risk, loss, destruction, etc. **2.** the state of being saved or protected from harm, risk, etc. **3.** a source, cause, or means of being saved or protected from harm, risk, etc. **4.** *Theol.* deliverance from the power and penalty of sin; redemption. [ME *salvatio(u)n* < LL *salvātiōn-* (s. of *salvātiō*), equiv. to *salvāt(us)* (ptp. of *salvāre* to save; see -ATE[1]) + *-iōn-* -ION; r. ME *sa(u)vaciun,* etc. < OF < L, as above] —**sal·va′tion·al,** *adj.*

Salva′tion Ar′my, an international Christian organization founded in England in 1865 by William Booth, organized along quasi-military lines and devoted chiefly to evangelism and to providing social services, esp. to the poor.

Sal·va·tion·ist (sal vā′shə nist), *n.* **1.** a member of the Salvation Army. **2.** (*l.c.*) a person who preaches salvation, deliverance from sin, etc., and the means of obtaining it; evangelist. [SALVATION + -IST] —**sal·va′tion·ism,** *n.*

Sal·va·tore (sal′və tôr′, -tōr′; *It.* säl′vä tô′ʀe), *n.* a boy's given name.

salve[1] (sav, säv), *n., v.,* **salved, salv·ing.** —*n.* **1.** a medicinal ointment for healing or relieving wounds and sores. **2.** anything that soothes, mollifies, or relieves. —*v.t.* **3.** to soothe with or as if with salve; assuage: *to salve one's conscience.* **4.** *Archaic.* to apply salve to. [ME; OE *sealf;* c. G *Salbe* salve, Skt *sarpis* melted butter, etc.]

salve[2] (salv), *v.i., v.t.,* **salved, salv·ing.** to save from loss or destruction; to salvage. [back formation from SALVAGE]

sal·ve[3] (sal′vē; *Lat.* säl′wā), *interj.* hail! [< L: be in good health; cf. SALUTE]

Sal·ve·mi·ni (säl′ve mē′nē), *n.* **Ga·e·ta·no** (gä′e-tä′nô), 1873–1957, Italian historian in the U.S.

sal·ver (sal′vər), *n.* a tray, esp. one used for serving food, beverages, etc. [< Sp *salv(a)* kind of tray (orig. protective foretasting, deriv. of *salvar* to save < L *salvāre*) + -ER[1]]

Sal·ve Re·gi·na (säl′vā ri jē′nə), *Rom. Cath. Ch.* a prayer in the form of a hymn to the Virgin Mary.

sal·ver·form (sal′vər fôrm′), *adj. Bot.* tubular with a flat, expanded limb, as certain gamopetalous corollas. [SALVER + -FORM]

sal·vi·a (sal′vē ə), *n.* any plant of the genus *Salvia,* comprising the sages. [< NL, L: sage]

Sal·vi·ni (säl vē′nē), *n.* **Tom·ma·so** (tôm mä′zô), 1829–1916, Italian actor, esp. of tragedy.

sal·vo[1] (sal′vō), *n., pl.* **-vos, -voes. 1.** a discharge of artillery or other firearms in regular succession, often performed as a salute. **2.** a round of cheers or applause. [earlier *salva* < It < L *salve* hail, greetings; see SALVE[3]]

sal·vo[2] (sal′vō), *n., pl.* **-vos.** *Archaic.* **1.** an excuse or quibbling evasion. **2.** something to save a person's reputation or soothe his feelings. [< L *salvō,* abl. of *salvus* safe, found in legal phrases]

sal vo·la·ti·le (sal vō lat′ᵊlē′), **1.** See **ammonium carbonate. 2.** an aromatic alcoholic solution of this salt. [< NL: volatile salt]

sal·vor (sal′vər), *n.* one who salvages or helps to salvage a ship, cargo, etc. [SALV(AGE) + -OR[2]]

Sal·ween (sal′wēn′), *n.* a river in SE Asia, flowing S from SW China through E Burma to the Bay of Bengal. 1750 mi. long.

Salz·burg (sôlz′bûrg; *Ger.* zälts′bo͝orᴋʜ), *n.* a city in W Austria: the birthplace of Mozart. 106,892 (1961).

Sam (sam), *n.* a boy's given name, form of **Samuel.**

SAM, surface-to-air missile.

Sam., *Bible.* Samuel.

S. Am., 1. South America. **2.** South American.

sa·ma·dhi (sə mä′dē), *n. Hinduism, Buddhism.* contemplation of an object of meditation, seen as one stage in which the distinction between subject and object is preserved, and another stage in which all distinctions are completely absorbed. [< Skt *samādhi* a drawing together (of mind), deep contemplation]

Sa·main (sä′win), *n.* Samhain.

sa·maj (sə mäj′), *n.* a Hindu religious society or movement. [< Hindi *samāj* meeting]

Sa·man (sä′män), *n.* a Persian noble who lived in the eighth century A.D., progenitor of the Samanid dynasty.

Sa·ma·nid (sə mä′nid, sam′ə-nid), *n.* a member of the rulers of Persia in the 9th and 10th centuries.

Sa·man·tha (sə man′thə), *n.* a girl's given name.

Sa·mar (sä′mär), *n.* an island in the E Philippines. 945,300 (est. 1960); 5309 sq. mi.

sam·a·ra (sam′ər ə, sə mâr′ə), *n. Bot.* an indehiscent, usually one-seeded, winged fruit, as of the elm or maple. [< NL, special use of L *samara* elm seed]

Samara A, White ash, *Fraxinus americana* B, Ashleaf maple, *Acer negundo* C, Hoptree, *Ptelea trifoliata*

Sa·ma·ra (sə mär′ə); *Russ.* sä-mä′nə), *n.* former name of **Kuibyshev.**

Sa·ma·rang (sə mä′räng), *n.* Semarang.

Sa·mar·i·a (sə mâr′ē ə), *n.* **1.** a district in ancient Palestine: later part of the Roman province of Syria; now in Jordan. See map under **Tyre. 2.** the northern kingdom of the ancient Hebrews; Israel. **3.** the ancient capital of this kingdom.

sam·a·ri·form (sam′ər ə fôrm′), *adj. Bot.* having the form of a samara. [SAMAR(A) + -I- + -FORM]

Sa·mar·i·tan (sə mar′i tᵊn), *n.* **1.** an inhabitant of Samaria. **2.** See **good Samaritan. 3.** (*often l.c.*) one who is compassionate and helpful to a person in distress. —*adj.* **4.** pertaining to Samaria or to Samaritans. [OE < LL *samarītān(us)* < Gk *samareít(ēs)* dweller in SAMARIA; see -AN] —**Sa·mar′i·tan·ism,** *n.*

sa·mar·i·um (sə mâr′ē əm), *n. Chem.* a rare-earth metallic element discovered in samarskite. *Symbol:* Sm; *at. wt.:* 150.35; *at. no.:* 62; *sp. gr.:* 7.49. [< NL; see SAMARSKITE, -IUM]

Sam·ar·kand (sam′ər kand′; *Russ.* sä′mär känt′), *n.* a city in E Uzbekistan in the SW Soviet Union in Asia, N of Afghanistan: taken by Alexander the Great 329 B.C.; Tamerlane's capital in the 14th century. 226,000 (est. 1964). Also, **Sam′ar·cand′.** Ancient, **Maracanda.**

SOVIET UNION
Tashkent
CHINA
Samarkand
IRAN
Kabul
AFGHANISTAN
PAKISTAN (WEST)
KASHMIR

Sa·mar·ra (sə mär′ə), *n.* a town in central Iraq, on the Tigris: seat of the early Abassid caliphs.

sa·mar·skite (sə mär′skīt), *n.* a velvet-black mineral, a complex columbate-tantalate of uranium, cerium, etc., occurring in masses: a minor source of uranium, thorium, and rare earth oxides. [named after Col. von *Samarski,* 19th-century Russian army officer and inspector of mines; see -ITE[1]]

Sa·ma-Ve·da (sä′mə vā′də, -vē′də), *n. Hinduism.* one of the Samhitas, a collection of mantras and tunes used in connection with the Rig-Veda. Cf. **Veda.**

sam·ba (sam′bə, säm′-), *n., pl.* **-bas,** *v.,* **-baed, -ba·ing.** —*n.* **1.** a rhythmic, Brazilian ballroom dance of African origin. —*v.i.* **2.** to dance the samba. [< Pg *samba* < Afr]

sam·bar (sam′bər, säm′-), *n.* a deer, *Rusa unicolor,* of India, Ceylon, southeastern Asia, the East Indies, and the Philippines, having three-pointed antlers. Also, **sam′bur, sam′bhar, sam′bhur.** [< Hindi < Skt *śambara*]

sam·bo (sam′bō), *n., pl.* **-bos. 1.** a Latin American of Negro and Indian or mulatto ancestry. **2.** *Disparaging and Offensive.* Negro. [< AmerSp *zambo* Negro, mulatto, perh. special use of Sp *zambo* bowlegged, supposedly < L *scamb(us)* < Gk *skambós* crooked]

Sam·bre (*Fr.* säɴ′bʀᵊ), *n.* a river in W Europe, flowing NE through N France and S Belgium into the Meuse at Namur: battle 1918. 120 mi. long.

Sam′ Browne′ belt′ (sam′ broun′), a sword belt having a supporting strap over the right shoulder, formerly worn by officers in the U.S. Army, now sometimes worn as part of the uniform by policemen, guards, and army officers in other nations. [named after its inventor, General Sir *Samuel Browne* (1824–1901)]

sam·bu·ca (sam byo͞o′kə), *n.* **1.** an ancient stringed musical instrument used in Greece and the Near East. **2.** a medieval hurdy-gurdy. [< L < Gk *sambýkē* < Sem]

sam·buk (sam bo͝ok′), *n.* a sailing vessel, used on the Red Sea, having lugsails or lateen sails on two masts raked forward and a greatly overhanging stem. [< Ar *sanbūq*]

same (sām), *adj.* **1.** identical with what is about to be or has just been mentioned: *This street is the same one we were on yesterday.* **2.** being one or identical though having different names, aspects, etc.: *These are the same rules though differently worded.* **3.** agreeing in kind, amount, etc.; corresponding: *two boxes of the same dimensions.* **4.** unchanged in character, condition, etc.: *It's the same town after all these years.* —*pron.* **5.** the same person or thing. **6.** the very person, thing, or set just mentioned: *Sighted sub sank same.* **7. all the same, a.** notwithstanding; nevertheless: *You don't have to go but we wish you would, all the same.* **b.** of no difference; immaterial: *It's all the same to me whether our team loses or wins.* **8. just the same, a.** in the same manner. **b.** nevertheless: *It was a success, but it could easily have failed, just the same.* **9. the same,** in the same manner; in an identical or similar way: *I see the same through your glasses as I do through mine.* [ME; OE *same* (adv.); c. Icel *samr,* Gk *homós,* Skt *samá*]

—**Syn. 1.** similar, like, corresponding, interchangeable, equal. SAME, SIMILAR agree in indicating a correspondence between two or more things. SAME means or pretends to mean alike in kind, degree, quality; that is, identical (with): *to eat the same food every day; at the same price.* SIMILAR means like, resembling, having certain qualities in common, somewhat the same as, of nearly the same kind as: *similar in appearance; Don't treat them as if they were the same when they are only similar.* —**Ant. 1.** different, unlike.

sa·mekh (sä′məᴋʜ), *n.* **1.** the 15th letter of the Hebrew alphabet. **2.** the consonant sound represented by this letter. Also, **sa′mech.** [< Heb: lit., a support]

same·ness (sām′nis), *n.* **1.** the state or quality of being the same; identity; uniformity. **2.** lack of variety; monotony. [SAME + -NESS]

S.Amer., 1. South America. **2.** South American.

Sa·mhain (sä′win), *n.* a festival of the ancient Celts, held around November 1 to celebrate the beginning of winter. Also, **Samain, sa·mh′in** (sä′win). [< IrGael]

Sam′ Hill′, *Slang.* hell: *Who in Sam Hill are you? What the Sam Hill is that for?* [*Sam* (orig. *salmon,* var. of *Sal(o)mon* an oath) + *hill,* euphemism for HELL]

Sam·hi·ta (sum′hi tä′), *n. Hinduism.* Veda (def. 2). [< Skt: a putting together]

Sa·mi·a (sā′mē ə), *n.* a comedy (c320 B.C.) by Menander, extant as a fragment.

Sa·mi·an (sā′mē ən), *adj.* **1.** of or pertaining to the Greek island of Samos. —*n.* **2.** a native or inhabitant of Samos. [< L *Sami(us)* (< Gk *Sámios* of Samos) + -AN]

sam·iel (sam yel′), *n.* simoom. [< Turk, equiv. to *sam* poisonous + *yel* wind]

Samisen

sam·i·sen (sam′i sen′), *n.* a guitarlike Japanese musical instrument having an extremely long neck and three strings, played with a plectrum. [< Jap < Chin *san-hsien* three-stringed (instrument)]

sam·ite (sam′īt, sā′mīt), *n.* a heavy silk fabric, sometimes interwoven with gold, worn in the Middle Ages. [ME *samit* < OF < ML *(e)xamit(ium), samit(ium)* < Gk *hexámiton,* neut. of *hexamítos* having six threads. See HEXA-, MITOSIS]

Sam·khya (sāng′kyə), *n. Hinduism.* Sankhya.

Saml., Samuel.

sam·let (sam′lit), *n.* a young salmon. [SALM(ON) + -LET]

Sam·mar·ti·ni (säm′mär tē′nē), *n.* **Gio·van·ni Bat·ti·sta** (jō vän′nē bät tē′stä), 1698–1775, Italian composer and organist.

Sam·my (sam′ē), *n., pl.* **-mies.** **1.** *Slang.* an American soldier in World War I. [(UNCLE) SAM + -Y²] **2.** a boy's given name, form of **Samuel. 3.** a girl's given name, form of **Samantha.** Also, **Sam′mie.**

Sam·ni·um (sam′nē əm), *n.* an ancient country in central Italy. —**Sam·nite** (sam′nīt), *adj., n.*

Sam·o (sam′ō), *n.* died A.D. 658, first ruler of the Slavs 623–658.

Sa·mo·a (sə mō′ə), *n.* a group of islands in the S Pacific, the islands W of 170° W longitude comprising an independent state and the rest belonging to the U.S. Formerly, **Navigators Islands.** Cf. **American Samoa, Western Samoa.**

Sa·mo·an (sə mō′ən), *adj.* **1.** pertaining to Samoa or its Polynesian people. —*n.* **2.** a native or inhabitant of Samoa. **3.** the Polynesian language of Samoa. [SAMO(A) + -AN]

Sa·mos (sā′mos, sam′ōs; *Gk.* sä′mōs), *n.* a Greek island in the E Aegean. 52,022 (1961); 194 sq. mi.

SAMOS (sam′ōs), *n. U.S.* one of a series of reconnaissance satellites. [*s(atellite) a(nti)m(issile) o(bservation) s(ystem)*]

Sam·o·set (sam′ə set′), *n.* a town in SW Florida. 4824 (1960).

Sam·o·thrace (sam′ə thrās′), *n.* a Greek island in the NE Aegean. Greek, **Sa·mo·thra·ke** (sä′mō thrä′kē). —**Sam·o·thra·cian** (sam′ə thrā′shən), *adj., n.*

sam·o·var (sam′ə vär′, sam′ə vär′), *n.* a metal urn, commonly of copper, used in the Soviet Union and elsewhere for heating water for making tea. [< Russ, equiv. to *samo-* self (see SAME) + *var* boiling, boiler]

Sam·o·yed (sam′ə yed′), *n.* **1.** a member of a Ural-Altaic people dwelling in NW Siberia and along the NE coast of the Soviet Union in Europe. **2.** Also, **Sam′o·yede′, Samoyedic.** a subfamily of Uralic languages spoken by the Samoyed people. **3.** one of a Russian breed of medium-sized dogs that have long, dense, white or cream hair and are used by the Samoyed people for herding reindeer and pulling sleds. [< Russ]

Sam·o·yed·ic (sam′ə yed′ik), *adj.* **1.** of or pertaining to the Samoyed people. —*n.* **2.** Samoyed (def. 2). [SAMOYED + -IC]

samp (samp), *n. U.S.* **1.** coarsely ground corn. **2.** a porridge made of it. [< Narragansett *(na)saump* mush]

sam·pan (sam′pan), *n.* any of various small boats of the Far East, as one propelled by a single scull over the stern and provided with a roofing of mats. [< Chin *san pan* kind of boat (lit., three boards)]

Sampan

sam·phire (sam′fīər′), *n.* **1.** a succulent, apiaceous herb, *Crithmum maritimum,* of Europe, growing in clefts of rock near the sea. **2.** the glasswort. [earlier *samp(i)ere* < MF *(herbe de) Saint Pierre* (herb of) Saint Peter]

sam·ple (sam′pəl, säm′-), *n., adj., v.,* **-pled, -pling.** —*n.* **1.** a small part of anything or one of a number, intended to show the quality, style, or nature of the whole; specimen. —*adj.* **2.** serving as a specimen: *a sample piece of cloth.* —*v.t.* **3.** to take a sample or samples of; test or judge by a sample. [ME < OF *essample.* See EXAMPLE]
—**Syn. 1.** pattern, model. See **example.**

sam′ple point′, *Math.* a possible result of an experiment, represented as a point. Cf. **sample space.**

sam·pler (sam′plər, säm′-), *n.* **1.** one who samples. **2.** a piece of cloth embroidered with various devices, serving to show a beginner's skill in needlework. **3.** a collection of samples, selections, or the like: *a sampler of French poetry.* [ME *samplere* < OF *(es)samplere, (e)xemplaire* < L *exemplār(ium)* EXEMPLAR]

sam′ple room′, a room, as in a hotel suite, in which merchandise is displayed for sale to the trade.

sam′ple space′, *Math.* the collection of all possible results of an experiment, represented as points. Cf. **sample point.**

sam·pling (sam′pling, säm′-), *n.* **1.** the act or process of selecting a sample for testing, analyzing, etc. **2.** the sample so selected. [SAMPLE + -ING¹]

sam′pling inspec′tion. See **acceptance sampling.**

Sam·po (säm′pō), *n. Finnish Legend.* an object of a form now unknown stolen by Ilmarinen, Vainamoinen, and Lemminkainen from Louhi because of its magical properties.

Samp·son (samp′sən), *n.* **1. William Thomas,** 1840–1902, U.S. admiral. **2.** Also, **Samson.** a boy's given name.

sam·sa·ra (səm sär′ə), *n.* **1.** *Buddhism.* the process of coming into existence as a differentiated, mortal creature. Cf. **nirvana** (def. 1). **2.** *Hinduism.* the endless series of births, deaths, and rebirths to which all beings are subject. Cf. **nirvana** (def. 2). [< Skt *samsāra,* lit., running together]

sam·shu (sam′shōō, -syōō), *n.* a Chinese liqueur distilled from millet or rice. [< pidginE, equiv. to *sam* (< ?) + *shu* (< Chin *chiu* spirits)]

Sam·son (sam′sən), *n.* **1.** a judge of Israel famous for his great strength. Judges 13–16. **2.** any man of extraordinary physical strength. **3.** Also, **Sampson.** a boy's given name.

Sam′son Ag·o·nis′tes (ag′ə nis′tēz), a poem (1671) by John Milton modeled on Greek tragedy.

Sam′son post′, *Naut.* **1.** a strong bitt or post at the bow or stern of a vessel. **2.** a king post for supporting cargo-handling booms on the deck of a ship. Also, **Samp′son post′.** [? named in allusion to the pillars that Samson dislodged]

Sam·sun (säm sōōn′), *n.* a city in N Turkey, in Asia. 106,921 (1965).

Sam·u·el (sam′yōō əl), *n.* **1.** a judge and prophet of Israel. I Sam. 1-3; 8-15. **2.** Also called *Douay Bible,* **I, II Kings.** either of two books of the Bible bearing his name. **3.** a boy's given name.

Sam·u·rai (sam′ōō rī′), *n., pl.* **-rai.** *Japanese Hist.* **1.** a member of the hereditary warrior class in feudal Japan. **2.** a retainer of a daimyo. [< Jap]

San (sän), *n.* a river in central Europe, flowing from the Carpathian Mountains in the W Soviet Union through SE Poland into the Vistula: battles 1914–15. ab. 280 mi. long.

Sa·n'a (sä nä′), *n.* a city in and the capital of Yemen, in the SW Arabian Peninsula. 100,000 (est. 1965). Also, **Sa·naa′.**

San An·ge·lo (san an′jə lō′), a city in W Texas. 58,815 (1960).

San An·to·ni·o (san′ an tō′nē ō′), a city in S Texas: site of the Alamo. 587,718 (1960). —**San′ Anto′nian.**

san·a·tive (san′ə tiv), *adj.* having the power to heal; curative. [< ML *sānātīv(us)* (see SANATORY, -IVE); r. ME *sanatif* < MF < ML, as above]

san·a·to·ri·um (san′ə tôr′ē əm, -tōr′-), *n., pl.* **-ri·ums, -ri·a** (-rē ə). **1.** a hospital for the treatment of chronic diseases, as tuberculosis or various nervous or mental disorders. **2.** sanitarium. [< NL, neut. of *sānātōrius* SANATORY]
—**Syn.** See **hospital.**

san·a·to·ry (san′ə tôr′ē, -tōr′ē,) *adj.* favorable for health; curative; healing. [< LL *sānātōri(us)* healthful, equiv. to L *sānāt(us)* (ptp. of *sānāre* to heal, deriv. of *sānus* SANE) + *-ōrius* -ORY¹]

San Au·gus·tine (san ô′gə stēn′), a town in E Texas. 2584 (1960).

san·be·ni·to (san′bə nē′tō), *n., pl.* **-tos.** (under the Spanish Inquisition) **1.** a yellow garment ornamented with flames, devils, etc., worn by a condemned heretic at an auto-da-fé. **2.** a penitential garment worn by a confessed heretic. [< Sp, named after *San Benito* Saint Benedict, from its resemblance to the scapular believed to have been introduced by him]

San Be·ni·to (san′ bə nē′tō), a city in S Texas. 16,422 (1960).

San Ber·nar·di·no (san′ bûr′nər dē′nō), **1.** a city in S California. 91,922 (1960). **2. Mount,** a mountain in S California, a peak of the San Bernardino Mountains. 10,630 ft. **3.** a mountain pass in the Alps, in SE Switzerland. 6766 ft. high.

San′ Bernardi′no Moun′tains, a mountain range in S California. Highest peak, San Gorgonio, 11,485 ft.

San Ber·nar·do (san′ bər när′dō; *Sp.* sän′ ber-när′thō), a city in central Chile, S of Santiago. 47,229 (est. 1959).

San Blas (sän bläs′), **1. Gulf of,** a gulf of the Caribbean on the N coast of Panama. **2. Isthmus of,** the narrowest part of the Isthmus of Panama. 31 mi. wide.

San·born (san′bôrn), *n.* a boy's given name.

San Bru·no (san brōō′nō), a city in W California, S of San Francisco. 29,063 (1960).

San Bue·na·ven·tu·ra (san bwā′nə ven tŏŏr′ə), a city in SW California. 29,114 (1960).

San Car·los (san kär′ləs), a city in W California, S of San Francisco. 21,370 (1960).

San Car·los de Ba·ri·lo·che (sän kär′lōs the bä′rē lō′che), a city in W Argentina, in Patagonia. 6562 (1947).

San·cho Pan·za (san′chō pan′zə; *Sp.* sän′chō pän′thä), the credulous and amusing squire of Don Quixote.

San Cle·men·te (san′ klə men′tē), a town in S California. 8527 (1960).

San Cris·tó·bal (sän′ krē stō′väl), a city in SW Venezuela. 116,176 (est. 1964).

sanc·ti·fied (sangk′tə fīd′), *adj.* **1.** made holy; consecrated: *sanctified wine.* **2.** sanctimonious: *a sickening, sanctified smile.* [SANCTIFY + -ED²] —**sanc·ti·fi·ed·ly** (sangk′tə fī′id lē), *adj.*

sanc·ti·fy (sangk′tə fī′), *v.t.,* **-fied, -fy·ing. 1.** to make holy; set apart as sacred; consecrate. **2.** to purify or free from sin: *Sanctify your hearts.* **3.** to impart religious sanction to; render legitimate or binding: *to sanctify a vow.* **4.** to entitle to reverence or respect. **5.** to make productive of or conducive to spiritual blessing. [< eccl. L *sanctificāre* (see SANCTUS, -IFY); r. ME *seintefie(n)* < OF *saintifie(r)* < L] —**sanc′ti·fi′a·ble,** *adj.* —**sanc′ti·fi′a·ble·ness,** *n.* —**sanc′ti·fi′a·bly,** *adv.* —**sanc′ti·fi·ca′tion,** *n.* —**sanc′ti·fi′er,** *n.* —**sanc′ti·fy′ing·ly,** *adv.*

sanc·ti·mo·ni·ous (sangk′tə mō′nē əs), *adj.* **1.** making a hypocritical show of religious devotion, piety, righteousness, etc.: *They resented his sanctimonious comments on immorality in America.* **2.** *Obs.* holy; sacred. [SANCTIMONY + -OUS] —**sanc′ti·mo′ni·ous·ly,** *adv.* —**sanc′ti·mo′ni·ous·ness,** *n.*

sanc·ti·mo·ny (sangk′tə mō′nē), *n.* **1.** pretended, affected, or hypocritical religious devotion, righteousness, etc. **2.** *Obs.* sanctity; sacredness. [< L *sanctimōnia* holiness. See SANCTUS, -MONY]

sanc·tion (sangk′shən), *n.* **1.** authoritative permission; countenance or support given, as to an action; solemn ratification. **2.** something that serves to support an action, condition, etc. **3.** something that gives binding force, as to an oath, rule of conduct, etc. **4.** *Law.* **a.** a provision of a law enacting a penalty for disobedience or a reward for obedience. **b.** the penalty or reward. **5.** *Internat. Law.* action by one or more states toward another state calculated to force it to comply with legal obligations. —*v.t.* **6.** to authorize, approve, or allow: *an expression now sanctioned by educated usage.* **7.** to ratify or confirm: *to sanction a law.* [< L *sanctiōn-* (s. of *sanctiō*), equiv. to *sanct(us)* (ptp. of *sancīre* to forbid) + *-iōn-* -ION] —**sanc′tion·a·ble,** *adj.* —**sanc′tion·er,** *n.* —**sanc′tion·less,** *adj.*
—**Syn. 1.** authority. **6.** permit. **7.** support; bind. —**Ant. 1.** disapproval. **6.** disapprove.

sanc·tion·a·tive (sangk′shə nā′tiv, -nə tiv), *adj.* pertaining to or tending toward sanction: *He discovered that his duties were more sanctionative than administrative.* [SANCTION + -ATIVE]

sanc·ti·tude (sangk′ti tōōd′, -tyōōd′), *n.* holiness; saintliness; sanctity: *an inspiring story of faith and sanctitude.* [< L *sanctitūd(ō), sanct-* (see SANCTUS) + *-itūdō* -I-, -TUDE]

sanc·ti·ty (sangk′ti tē), *n., pl.* **-ties. 1.** holiness, saintliness, or godliness. **2.** sacred or hallowed character: *inviolable sanctity of the temple.* **3.** a sacred thing. [< L *sanctitāt-* (s. of *sanctitās*) holiness, equiv. to *sanct-* (see SANCTUS) + *-itāt* -ITY; r. ME *sauntite* < AF]

sanc·tu·ar·y (sangk′chōō er′ē), *n., pl.* **-ar·ies. 1.** a sacred or holy place. **2.** *Judaism.* **a.** the Biblical tabernacle or the Temple in Jerusalem. **b.** the holy of holies of these places of worship. **3.** an especially holy place in a temple or church. **4.** the part of a church around the altar; the chancel. **5.** a church or other sacred place where fugitives were formerly entitled to immunity from arrest; asylum. **6.** immunity afforded by refuge in such a place. **7.** a tract of land where wild animals, esp. those hunted for sport, can breed and take refuge in safety from hunters. [ME < LL *sanctuāri(um),* equiv. to *sanctu-* (r. L *sanct-*) SANCTUS + *-ārium* -ARY] —**sanc′tu·ar′ied,** *adj.*
—**Syn. 1.** church, temple, altar, shrine, sanctum, adytum.

sanc·tum (sangk′təm), *n., pl.* **-tums, -ta** (-tə). **1.** a sacred or holy place. **2.** an inviolably private place or retreat. [< L; neut. of SANCTUS]

sanc′tum sanc·to′rum (sangk tôr′əm, -tōr′-), **1.** sanctum (def. 2). **2.** the holy of holies of the Biblical tabernacle and the Temple in Jerusalem. [< L, trans. of Heb *qōdesh haqqodāshīm* holy of holies]

Sanc·tus (sangk′təs), *n.* **1.** *(italics)* Also called **Tersanctus.** the hymn beginning "Holy, holy, holy, Lord God of hosts," with which the Eucharistic preface culminates. **2.** a musical setting for this hymn. [< L: holy, n. use of *sanctus* hallowed (ptp. of *sancīre* to hallow)]

Sanc′tus bell′, a bell rung during the celebration of Mass to call attention to the more solemn parts.

sanc′tus tur′ret, a bell cote holding a Sanctus bell.

San·cus (sang′kəs), *n.* an ancient Roman god of oaths, hospitality, international affairs, and the safety of roads: sometimes identified with Dius Fidius or with Hercules. Also called **Semo Sancus.**

sand (sand), *n.* **1.** the more or less fine debris of rocks, consisting of small, loose grains, often of quartz. **2.** Usually, **sands.** a tract or region composed principally of sand. **3.** the sand or a grain of sand in an hourglass. **4. sands,** moments of time or of one's life: *At this stage of his career the sands are running out.* **5.** *U.S. Informal.* courage; pluck. **6.** a dull reddish-yellow color. **7.** sleeper (def. 10). —*v.t.* **8.** to smooth or polish with sand, sandpaper, or some other abrasive: *to sand the ends of a board.* **9.** to sprinkle with or as if with sand: *to sand an icy road.* **10.** to fill up with sand, as a harbor. **11.** to add sand to: *The mischievous child sanded the sugar.* [ME, OE; c. G *Sand,* Icel *sandr*] —**sand′less,** *adj.* —**sand′like′,** *adj.*

Sand (sand; *Fr.* sänd), *n.* **George** (jôrj; *Fr.* zhôrzh) *(Lucile Aurore Dupin Dudevant),* 1804–76, French novelist.

San·da·kan (sän dä′kän), *n.* a city in E Sabah, in E Malaysia. 19,000 (est. 1957).

san·dal¹ (san′dəl), *n., v.,* **-daled, -dal·ing** or (*esp. Brit.*) **-dalled, -dal·ling.** —*n.* **1.** a shoe consisting of a sole of leather or other material fastened to the foot by thongs or straps. **2.** any of various low shoes or slippers. **3.** a light, low, rubber overshoe covering only the front part of a woman's shoe, for wear over high-heeled shoes. **4.** a band or strap that fastens a low shoe or slipper on the foot by passing over the instep or around the ankle. —*v.t.* **5.** to furnish with sandals. [< F *sandale;* r. ME *sandalie* < L *sandali(um)* < Gk *sandálion,* equiv. to *sándal(on)* + *-ion* dim. suffix]

san·dal² (san′dəl), *n.* sandalwood. [ME *sandell* < ML *sandal(um)* < LGk *sándalon,* dissimilated var. of *sándanon* < Skt *čandana*]

san·dal·wood (san′dəl wŏŏd′), *n.* **1.** the fragrant heartwood of any of certain Asian trees of the genus *Santalum,* used for ornamental carving and burned as incense. **2.** any of these trees, esp. *S. album* **(white sandalwood),** an evergreen of India. **3.** any of various related or similar trees or their woods, esp. an East Indian, fabaceous tree, *Pterocarpus santalinus* **(red sandalwood),** or its heavy dark-red wood that yields a dye. [SANDAL² + WOOD¹]

San′dalwood Is′land, Sumba.

san·da·rac (san′də rak′), *n.* **1.** a brittle, usually pale-yellow, more or less transparent, faintly aromatic resin exuding from the bark of the sandarac tree; used chiefly as incense and in making varnish. **2.** See **sandarac tree.** [< L *sandarac(a)* < Gk *sandarákē* realgar, beebread]

san′darac tree′, a pinaceous tree, *Tetraclinis articulata (Callitris quadrivalvis),* native to northwestern Africa, yielding the resin sandarac and a fragrant, hard, dark-colored wood much used in building.

sand·bag (sand′bag′), *n., v.,* **-bagged, -bag·ging.** —*n.* **1.** a bag filled with sand, used in fortification, as ballast, etc. **2.** such a bag used as a weapon. —*v.t.* **3.** to furnish with sandbags. **4.** to hit or stun with a sandbag. **5.** *Informal.* to set upon violently; coerce: *to sandbag the public with propaganda.* **6.** *Poker Slang.* to deceive (one or more opponents) into remaining in the pot by refraining from betting on a strong hand, then raising the bet in a later round. —*v.i.* **7.** *Poker Slang.* to sandbag one or more opponents. [SAND + BAG] —**sand′bag′ger,** *n.*

sand·bank (sand′bangk′), *n.* a large mass of sand, as on a shoal or hillside. [SAND + BANK¹]

sand′ bar′, a bar of sand formed in a river or sea by the action of tides or currents.

sand·blast (sand′blast′, -bläst′), *n.* **1.** a blast of air or steam laden with sand, used to clean, grind, cut, or decorate hard surfaces, as of glass, stone, or metal. **2.** the apparatus used to apply such a blast. —*v.t., v.i.* **3.** to clean, smooth, etc., with a sandblast. [SAND + BLAST] —**sand′blast′er,** *n.*

sand-blind (sand′blīnd′), *adj. Archaic.* partially blind; dim-sighted. [ME; OE **samblind* half-blind, equiv. to *sām-* SEMI- + blind BLIND] —**sand′-blind·ness,** *n.*

sand·box (sand′boks′), *n.* a box or receptacle for holding sand, esp. one large enough for children to play in. [SAND + BOX¹]

sand′box tree′, a euphorbiaceous tree, *Hura crepitans*, of tropical America, bearing a furrowed, roundish fruit about the size of an orange which when ripe and dry bursts with a sharp report and scatters the seeds.

sand·bug (sand′bug′), *n.* See **mole crab.** [SAND + BUG[1]]

sand·bur (sand′bûr′), *n.* **1.** any of several bur-bearing weeds growing in sandy places, as a nightshade, *Solanum rostratum*, of the western U.S. **2.** a weed, *Franseria acanthicarpa*, related to the bristly ragweeds. **3.** any of several grasses of the genus *Cenchrus*, bearing prickly burs. Also, **sand′burr′.** [SAND + BUR[1]]

Sand·burg (sand′bûrg, san′-), *n.* **Carl,** 1878–1967, U.S. poet and biographer.

sand-cast (sand′kast′, -käst′), *v.t.*, **-cast, -cast·ing.** to produce (a casting) by pouring molten metal into sand molds. —**sand′ cast′ing.**

sand′ cher′ry, 1. any of several low, North American cherries that grow on dry or sandy soil, esp. *Prunus pumila*, of the Great Lakes region. **2.** the fruit of any of these shrubs.

sand′ crab′, any of several crabs that live on sandy beaches, as the ghost crab or mole crab.

sand′ crack′, *Vet. Pathol.* a crack or fissure in the hoof of a horse, extending from the coronet downward toward the sole, occurring on any part of the wall of the hoof, caused by a dryness of horn and liable to cause lameness. Also called **quarter crack.**

sand·cul·ture (sand′kul′chər), *n.* the cultivation of plants in sand. [SAND + CULTURE]

sand′ dab′, any of several flatfishes used for food, esp. of the genus *Citharichthys*, found along the Pacific coast of North America.

sand′ div′er, any of several tropical, marine, and fresh-water fishes of the family *Trichonotidae*, found in shallow waters over coral sands into which they burrow when disturbed.

sand′ dol′lar, any of various flat, disklike sea urchins, esp. *Echinarachnius parma*, that live on sandy bottoms off the coasts of the U.S.

Sand dollar, *Mellita testudinata* (Width 3 in.)

sand·ed (san′did), *adj.* covered or filled with sand. [SAND + -ED[3]]

sand′ eel′, 1. See **sand lance. 2.** *New Zealand.* sandfish (def. 2).

san·dek (sän′dek), *n.* *Yiddish.* the man who holds the child during the Jewish rite of circumcision.

sand·er (san′dər), *n.* **1.** one who sands or sandpapers. **2.** an apparatus for sanding or sandpapering. [SAND + -ER[1]]

San·der (san′dər), *n.* a boy's given name. Also, **Sandor.**

sand·er·ling (san′dər liṅg), *n.* a small sandpiper, *Crocethia alba*, found on sandy beaches. [SAND + ME *urthling* plowman; see EARTH, -LING[1]]

San·ders·ville (san′dərz vil′), *n.* a town in central Georgia. 5425 (1960).

sand·fish (sand′fish′), *n., pl.* (*esp. collectively*) **-fish,** (*esp. referring to two or more kinds or species*) **-fish·es. 1.** either of two scaleless fishes of the family *Trichodontidae*, found in the North Pacific, which live in sand or mud. **2.** Also called **beaked salmon.** a fish, *Gonorhynchus gonorhynchus*, found in the sandy areas of the western Pacific and Indian oceans, having an angular snout with which it burrows into the sand. **3.** See **belted sandfish.** [SAND + FISH]

sand′ flea′, 1. See **beach flea. 2.** chigoe.

sand-float·ed (sand′flō′tid), *adj.* *Building Trades.* noting an exterior wall finish composed of mortar rubbed with sand and floated when it has partly set.

sand·fly (sand′flī′), *n., pl.* **-flies. 1.** any of several small, bloodsucking, dipterous insects of the genus *Phlebotomus* that are vectors of several diseases of man. **2.** any of several other small, bloodsucking, dipterous insects, as one of the genus *Culicoides*. [SAND + FLY[2]]

sand·glass (sand′glas′, -gläs′), *n.* an hourglass. [SAND + GLASS]

sand-grop·er (sand′grō′pər), *n.* *Australian Slang.* a native of the arid region of Western Australia.

sand′ grouse′, any of several birds of the genus *Pteroclidae*, found in sandy areas of the Old World, resembling the pigeons in shape and coloration.

san·dhi (san′dē, sän′-), *n., pl.* **-dhis.** *Ling.* morphophonemic alternation, esp. as determined by phonemic environment: *dontcha* for *don't you.* [< Skt, equiv. to *sam* together + *-dhi* a putting; see DO[1]]

sand′hill crane′ (sand′hil′), a North American crane, *Grus canadensis*, having bluish-gray plumage and a red forehead. [late ME *sond hille*, OE *sondhyll*. See SAND, HILL]

sand·hog (sand′hog′, -hôg′), *n.* **1.** a laborer who digs or works in sand. **2.** one who works, usually in a caisson, in digging underwater tunnels. Also, **sand′ hog′.** [SAND + HOG]

sand′ hop′per. See **beach flea.**

Sand·hurst (sand′hûrst), *n.* a village in SE Berkshire, in S England, near Reading: military college.

sandh·ya (sund′yä), *n.* *Hinduism.* a ritual of worship and meditation performed three times a day by Hindus of the higher castes. [< Skt; see SANDHI]

San·die (san′dē), *n.* **1.** a boy's given name, form of **Sandro. 2.** a girl's given name, form of **Sandra, Saundra,** or **Sondra.** Also, **Sandy.**

San Di·e·go (san′ dē ā′gō), **1.** a seaport in SW California: naval and marine base. 573,224 (1960). **2.** a town in S Texas. 4351 (1960).

sand·i·ness (san′dē nis), *n.* the state or quality of being sandy. [SANDY + -NESS]

San·di·nis·ta (san′də nē′stə), *n.* a member of the revolutionary movement in power in Nicaragua since 1979. [< AmerSp]

san·di·ver (san′də vər), *n.* a whitish, saline scum formed on the surface of molten glass. Also called **glass gall.** [ME *saundyver* < MF *suin de verre* grease of glass. See SWEAT, VITRI-]

sand′ jack′, *Shipbuilding.* any of a number of containers of sand driven beneath a hull about to be launched as a temporary support and then drained of sand so as to let the hull down onto the launching cradle.

sand′ lance′, any slender, sand-inhabiting, marine fish of the family *Ammodytidae*. Also, **sand′ launce′.**

sand′ lil′y, a small, stemless plant, *Leucocrinum montanum*, of the western U.S., having lilylike flowers.

sand′-lime brick′ (sand′līm′), a hard brick composed of silica sand and a lime of high calcium content, molded under high pressure and baked.

sand′ liz′ard, 1. a common lizard, *Lacerta agilis*, of Europe and central Asia. **2.** any of several lizards, as the fringe-toed lizard, that live in sandy areas.

sand·lot (sand′lot′), *U.S.* —*n.* **1.** a vacant lot used by city boys for games or sports. —*adj.* **2.** Also, **sand′-lot′.** of, pertaining to, or played in such a lot: *sandlot baseball.* [SAND + LOT]

sand·lot·ter (sand′lot′ər), *n.* a youngster who plays baseball in a sandlot. [SANDLOT + -ER[1]]

sand·man (sand′man′), *n., pl.* **-men.** the man who, in fairy tales or folklore, puts sand in the eyes of children to make them sleepy. [SAND + MAN[1]]

sand′ mar′tin, *Brit.* the bank swallow.

sand′ mist′, bai.

San·dor (san′dər), *n.* a boy's given name. Also, **Sander.**

Sán·dor (shän′dôr, shan′-), *n.* **Györ·gy** (jôr′jē), born 1912, U.S. pianist, born in Hungary.

sand′ paint′ing, 1. the ceremonial practice among Navaho, Hopi, and Pueblo Indians of creating symbolic designs on a flat surface with varicolored sand. **2.** the designs so made.

sand·pa·per (sand′pā′pər), *n.* **1.** strong paper coated with a layer of sand or other abrasive, used for smoothing or polishing. —*v.t.* **2.** to smooth or polish with or as if with sandpaper. [SAND + PAPER]

sand·pa·per·y (sand′pā′pə rē), *adj.* of or suggesting the grating sound of sandpaper rubbing against wood or the rough texure of sandpaper: *the sandpapery sound of claws scratching the wall; hands that were sandpapery from harsh detergents.* [SANDPAPER + -Y[1]]

sand′ pear′. See **Japanese pear.**

sand′ phlox′, an evergreen, creeping, perennial herb, *Phlox bifida*, found in sandy or rocky areas of the central U.S., having dense clusters of deeply notched, bright purple, pink, or white flowers.

sand′ pike′, sauger.

sand′ pile′, *Building Trades.* a base for a footing in soft soil, made by compacting sand in a cavity left by a wooden pile.

sand·pi·per (sand′pī′pər), *n.* any of numerous shore-inhabiting birds of the family *Scolopacidae*, related to the plovers, typically having a slender bill and a piping call. [SAND + PIPER]

Spotted sandpiper, *Actitis macularia* (Length 7 in.)

sand·pit (sand′pit′), *n.* a deep pit in sandy soil from which sand is excavated. [SAND + PIT[1]]

Sand·point (sand′point′), *n.* a town in N Idaho. 4355 (1960).

San·dra (san′drə, sän′-), *n.* a girl's given name, form of **Alexandra.** Also, **Saundra, Sondra.**

San·dro (san′drō; *It.* sän′drô), *n.* a boy's given name, Italian form of **Alexander.**

San·dro·cot·tus (san′drō kot′əs), *n.* Greek name of **Chandragupta.** Greek, **San·dra·kot·tos** (sän′drä-kôt′tôs).

sand·roll·er (sand′rō′lər), *n.* a North American, fresh-water fish, *Percopsis transmontana*, related to the troutperch but having a deeper, more compressed body. [SAND + ROLLER[1]]

San·dron (san′drən), *n.* a boy's given name, form of **Sandro.**

S. & S.C., (of paper) sized and supercalendered.

sand′ shark′, any of several sharks of the family *Carchariidae*, esp. *Odontaspis* (or *Carcharius*) *taurus*, found in shallow waters on both sides of the Atlantic Ocean, having sharp, jagged teeth. Also called **sand tiger.**

sand′ shoe′, *Brit.* a light tennis shoe; sneaker.

sand-sprayed (sand′sprād′), *adj.* *Building Trades.* noting an exterior wall finish composed of mortar to which is added a mixture of sand and cement in equal parts while the mortar is still wet.

Sand′ Springs′, a town in NE Oklahoma. 7754 (1960).

sand′ star′gazer, a fish of the family *Dactyloscopidae*, esp. *Dactyloscopus tridigitatus*, found in the Atlantic Ocean from Bermuda to Brazil, having tiny, tubular eyes on top of the head.

sand·stone (sand′stōn′), *n.* a rock formed of sand, usually quartz, cemented together by silica, calcium carbonate, iron oxide, and clay. [SAND + STONE]

sand·storm (sand′stôrm′), *n.* a windstorm, esp. in a desert, that blows along great clouds of sand. [SAND + STORM]

sand′ strake′, *Naut.* See **garboard strake.**

sand-struck (sand′struk′), *adj.* (of bricks) made with a mold lined with sand to permit freeing.

sand′ ta′ble, 1. a table with raised edges holding sand for children to play with. **2.** *Mil.* a table holding a scale model of a tract of land, including trees, streams, buildings, etc., made of hardened sand, used for training in gunnery or tactics.

sand′ ti′ger. See **sand shark.**

sand′ trap′, (on a golf course) a shallow pit partly filled with sand, usually located near a green, and designed to serve as a hazard.

San·dus·ky (sən dus′kē), *n.* a port in N Ohio, on Lake Erie. 31,989 (1960).

Sandus′ky South′, a town in N Ohio. 4724 (1960).

sand′ ver·be′na, any of several low, mostly trailing herbs of the genus *Abronia*, of the western U.S., having showy, verbenalike flowers.

sand′ vi′per, 1. See **hognose snake. 2.** See **horned viper.**

sand′ wasp′, any of certain sphecid wasps of the subfamily *Bembicinae* that nest in the ground and are commonly found along the seashore.

sand·wich (sand′wich, san′-), *n.* **1.** two or more slices of bread or the like with a layer of meat, fish, cheese, etc., between each pair. **2.** something resembling or suggesting a sandwich. —*v.t.* **3.** to put into a sandwich. **4.** to insert between two other things: *to sandwich an appointment in between two board meetings.* [named after the fourth Earl of *Sandwich* (1718–92)]

Sand·wich (sand′wich), *n.* **1.** a town in E Kent, in SE England: one of the Cinque Ports. 4234 (1961). **2.** a town in N Illinois. 3842 (1960).

sand′wich bat′ten, *Theat.* See **double batten.**

sand′wich beam′. See **flitch beam.** Also called **sand′wich gird′er.**

sand′wich board′, two connected posters or signboards that hang in front of and behind a person and usually bear some advertisement, notice, exhortation, or the like.

sand′wich coin′, *U.S.* a coin having a layer of one metal between outside layers of another, as a quarter with a layer of copper between layers of silver.

Sand′wich glass′, any of various forms of glassware manufactured at Sandwich, Mass., from 1825 to c1890.

Sand′wich Is′lands, former name of **Hawaii.**

sand′wich man′, a man with advertising boards hung from his shoulders.

sand·worm (sand′wûrm′), *n.* **1.** any of several polychaetes that live in sand. **2.** clamworm. [SAND + WORM]

sand·wort (sand′wûrt′), *n.* any caryophyllaceous plant of the genus *Arenaria*, many of which grow in sandy soil. [SAND + WORT[2]]

sand·y (san′dē), *adj.*, **sand·i·er, sand·i·est. 1.** of the nature of or consisting of sand. **2.** containing or covered with sand. **3.** of a yellowish-red color: *sandy hair.* **4.** having hair of a sandy color. **5.** shifting or unstable, like sand. [ME; OE *sandig.* See SAND, -Y[1]]

San·dy (san′dē), *n.* **1.** a boy's given name, form of **Sandro. 2.** a girl's given name, form of **Sandra, Saundra, Sondra.** Also, **Sandie.**

sand′y blight′, *Australian.* any minor inflammation of the eyelid, as pinkeye or trachoma. [so called from the fact that the eyelid feels full of sand]

Sand′y Cit′y, a town in central Utah. 3322 (1960).

Sand′y Hook′, a peninsula in E New Jersey, at the entrance to lower New York Bay. 6 mi. long.

sane (sān), *adj.*, **san·er, san·est. 1.** free from mental derangement; having a sound, healthy mind: *a sane person.* **2.** having or showing reason, sound judgment, or good sense: *sane advice.* **3.** sound; healthy. [< L *sān(us)* healthy] —**sane′ly,** *adv.* —**sane′ness,** *n.*

San Fe·li·pe (sän′ fe lē′pe), a city in NE Venezuela, on the Orinoco River. 20,000 (1950).

San Fer·nan·do (san′ fər nan′dō *for 1;* sän fer-nän′dō *for 2*), **1.** a city in SW California, near Los Angeles. 16,093 (1960). **2.** a city in E Argentina, near Buenos Aires. 61,600 (est. 1956).

San·ford (san′fərd), *n.* **1. Mount,** a mountain in SE Alaska. 16,208 ft. **2.** a city in E Florida. 19,175 (1960). **3.** a boy's given name.

San·for·ized (san′fə rīzd′), *adj.* *Trademark.* (of a fabric) treated to resist shrinking.

San Fran·cis·co (san′ fran sis′kō), a seaport in W California, on San Francisco Bay: earthquake and fire 1906; United Nations Conference 1945. 742,855 (1960). —**San′ Fran·cis′can.**

San′ Francis′co Bay′, a bay in W California: the harbor of San Francisco; connected with the Pacific by the Golden Gate strait. 50 mi. long; 3–12 mi. wide.

San′ Francis′co Peaks′, a mountain mass in N Arizona: highest point in the State, Humphrey's Peak, 12,611 ft. Also called **San′ Francis′co Moun′tain.**

sang (saṅg), *v.* pt. of **sing.**

San Ga·bri·el (san gā′brē əl), a city in SW California, near Los Angeles. 22,561 (1960).

San·gall·en·sis (saṅg′gô len′sis), *n.* the uncial codex, dating from the 9th or 10th century, that contains the text of the Gospels in Greek with an interlinear Latin translation. Cf. **codex** (def. 2). [< NL: lit., of St. Gall. See ST. GALLEN, -ESE]

San·gal·lo (säṅg gäl′lô), *n.* **1. An·to·nio Pic·co·ni da** (än tô′nyô pēk kô′nē dä), (*Antonio Cordiani*), 1484?–1546, Italian architect and engineer. **2.** his uncle **Giu·lia·no da** (jo͞o lyä′nô dä), (*Giuliano Giamberti*), 1445–1516, Italian architect, sculptor, and engineer.

san·ga·ree (saṅg′gə rē′), *n.* sangría.

San Gen·na·ro (sän′ jen nä′rô), Italian name of **Januarius.**

Sang·er (saṅg′ər), *n.* **1. Frederick,** born 1918, English biochemist: Nobel prize 1958. **2. Margaret Hig·gins** (hig′inz), 1883–1966, U.S. nurse and author: leader of birth-control movement. **3.** a town in central California. 8072 (1960).

sang-froid (*Fr.* säN frwa′), *n.* coolness of mind; calmness; composure: *They committed the robbery with complete sang-froid.* [< F: cold-bloodedness] —**Syn.** self-possession, poise, equanimity, self-control, nerve, courage, steadiness.

San·gha (suṅg′gə), *n.* the entire group of Buddhist monks. [< Skt *saṅgha*]

sang·li·er (saṅg′lē ər), *n.* a closely woven fabric made of mohair or worsted, constructed in plain weave, and finished to simulate the coat of a boar. [< MF < LL *singulār(is)* (*porcus*) solitary pig (boar); r. ME *singlere* < OF *sengler* < L, as above]

San·graal (saṅg grāl′), *n.* the Holy Grail. Also, **San·gre·al** (saṅg′grē əl). [prob. < OF *Saint Graal*]

San·gre de Cris·to (saṅg′grē də kris′tō; *Sp.* säṅg′gre the krēs′tô), a mountain range in S Colorado and N New Mexico: a part of the Rocky Mountains. Highest peak, Blanca Peak, 14,390 ft.

san·gri·a (saṅg grē′ə; *Sp.* säṅg grē′ä), *n.* an iced drink, usually of red wine that has been diluted, sweetened, and spiced. [< Sp: drink bloodlike in color, equiv. to *sangr(e)* blood (see SANGUINE) + *-ia* n. suffix]

sangui-, a learned borrowing from Latin meaning "blood," used in the formation of technical terms: *sanguiferous.* [< NL, var. of L *sanguin-*, s. of *sanguis*]

san·guic·o·lous (saṅg gwik′ə ləs), *adj.* living in the blood, as a parasite. [SANGUI- + -COLOUS]

san·guif·er·ous (saŋ gwif′ər əs), *adj.* conveying blood, as a blood vessel. [SANGUI- + -FEROUS]

san·gui·fi·ca·tion (saŋ′gwə fə kā′shən), *n.* hematopoiesis. [< NL *sanguificātiōn-* (s. of *sanguificātiō*). See SANGUI-, -FICATION]

san·gui·nar·i·a (saŋ′gwə nâr′ē ə), *n.* **1.** the bloodroot, *Sanguinaria canadensis.* **2.** its medicinal rhizome. [< NL (*herba*) *sanguināria* bloody (herb)]

san·gui·nar·y (saŋ′gwə ner′ē), *adj.* **1.** full of or characterized by bloodshed; bloody: *a sanguinary struggle.* **2.** ready or eager to shed blood; bloodthirsty: *a sanguinary villain.* **3.** composed of or marked with blood. [< L *sanguināri(us)* bloody. See SANGUINE, -ARY] —**san′gui·nar′i·ly,** *adv.* —**san′gui·nar′i·ness,** *n.*
—**Syn. 2.** murderous, cruel, savage, fell. —**Ant. 2.** kind.

san·guine (saŋ′gwin), *adj.* **1.** cheerful, hopeful, or confident: *a sanguine disposition; sanguine expectations.* **2.** reddish; ruddy: *a sanguine complexion.* **3.** (in old physiology) having blood as the predominating humor and consequently being ruddy-faced, cheerful, etc. **4.** bloody; sanguinary. **5.** blood-red; red. **6.** *Heraldry.* a reddish-purple tincture. —*n.* **7.** a red iron-oxide crayon used in making drawings. [ME < L *sanguine(us)* bloody, equiv. to *sanguin-* SANGUI- + *-eus* -EOUS] —**san′guine·ly,** *adv.* —**san′guine·ness,** *n.*
—**Syn. 1.** enthusiastic, buoyant, animated, lively, spirited. —**Ant. 1.** morose.

san·guin·e·ous (saŋ gwin′ē əs), *adj.* **1.** Also, **sanguinous.** of, pertaining to, or containing blood. **2.** of the color of blood. **3.** involving much bloodshed. **4.** sanguine; confident. [< L *sanguineus* bloody. See SANGUINE] —**san·guin′e·ous·ness,** *n.*

san·guin·o·lent (saŋ gwin′ᵊ lənt), *adj.* **1.** of or pertaining to blood. **2.** containing or tinged with blood; bloody. [< L *sanguinolent(us),* equiv. to *sanguin-* SANGUI- + *-olentus* -OLENT] —**san·guin′o·len·cy,** *n.*

san·guiv·or·ous (saŋ gwiv′ər əs), *adj.* feeding on blood, as a bat, insect, etc. [SANGUI- + -VOROUS]

San·hed·rin (san hed′rin, -hē′drin, san′hi drin, san′i-), *n.* *Jewish Hist.* **1.** Also called **Great Sanhedrin.** the supreme legislative council and highest ecclesiastical and secular tribunal of the Jews, consisting of 71 members and exercising its greatest authority from the 5th century B.C. to A.D. 70. **2.** Also called **Lesser Sanhedrin.** a lower tribunal of this period, consisting of 23 members. Also, **San·he·drim** (san′hi drim, san′i-). [< LHeb < Gk *synédrion,* equiv. to *syn-* SYN- + *hédr(a)* seat + *-ion* -IUM]

san·i·cle (san′i kəl), *n.* any umbelliferous herb of the genus *Sanicula,* as *S. marilandica,* of America, used in medicine. [ME < MF < ML *sānicul(a).* See SANE, -I-, -CLE]

san·i·dine (san′i dēn′, -din), *n.* *Mineral.* a glossy, often transparent variety of orthoclase occurring in eruptive rocks in the form of phenocrysts. [< G *Sanidin,* equiv. to *sanid-* (s. of Gk *sanís* plank) + *-in* -INE²] —**san·i·din·ic** (san′i din′ik), *adj.*

sa·ni·es (sā′nē ēz′), *n.* *Pathol.* a thin, often greenish, serous fluid that is discharged from ulcers, wounds, etc. [< L: bloody matter]

San Il·de·fon·so (sän ēl′the fôn′sō), a town in central Spain, near Segovia: termed the "Spanish Versailles" for its 18th-century palace **(La Granja)**: treaty 1800. 3245 (1950).

sa·ni·ous (sā′nē əs), *adj.* *Pathol.* characterized by the discharge of a thin fluid, as from an ulcer. [SANI(ES) + -OUS]

san·i·tar·i·an (san′i târ′ē ən), *adj.* **1.** sanitary; clean and wholesome. —*n.* **2.** a specialist in public sanitation and health. [SANITARY + -AN]

san·i·tar·i·um (san′i târ′ē əm), *n., pl.* **-tar·i·ums, -tar·i·a** (-târ′ē ə). an institution for the promotion of health; health resort. Also, **sanatorium.** [< L *sanit(ās)* health + *-arium*]
—**Syn. 1.** See **hospital.**

san·i·tar·y (san′i ter′ē), *adj., n., pl.* **-tar·ies.** —*adj.* **1.** of or pertaining to health or the conditions affecting health, esp. with reference to cleanliness, precautions against disease, etc. **2.** favorable to health; free from dirt, bacteria, etc.: *a sanitary washroom.* **3.** providing healthy cleanliness: *a sanitary wrapper on all sandwiches.* —*n.* **4.** a public washroom or toilet. [< L *sānit(ās)* health + -ARY] —**san′i·tar′i·ly,** *adv.* —**san′i·tar′i·ness,** *n.*
—**Syn. 1, 2.** clean, germ-free, unpolluted, antiseptic. SANITARY, HYGIENIC agree in being concerned with health. SANITARY refers more especially to conditions affecting health or measures for guarding against infection or disease: *to insure sanitary conditions in preparing food.* HYGIENIC is applied to whatever concerns the care of the body and the promotion of health: *to live in hygienic surroundings with plenty of fresh air.* **2.** healthy, salutary. —**Ant. 1, 2.** unclean, unwholesome; unhealthy, polluted, septic.

san′itary belt′, a narrow belt, usually of elastic, for holding a sanitary napkin in place.

san′itary cor′don. See **cordon sanitaire.**

san′itary engineer′ing, a branch of civil engineering dealing with matters affecting public health, as water supply or sewage disposal. —**san′itary engineer′.**

san′itary nap′kin, an absorbent pad of cotton worn by women during menstruation to absorb the uterine flow.

san′itary tow′el, *Brit.* See **sanitary napkin.**

san·i·tate (san′i tāt′), *v.t.,* **-tat·ed, -tat·ing.** to make sanitary; equip with sanitary appliances: *to sanitate a new town; a settlement newly sanitated.* [back formation from SANITATION]

san·i·ta·tion (san′i tā′shən), *n.* the development and practical application of sanitary measures for the sake of cleanliness, protecting health, etc. [SANIT(ARY) + -ATION]

san·i·tise (san′i tīz′), *v.t.,* **-tised, -tis·ing.** *Chiefly Brit.* sanitize. —**san′i·ti·sa′tion,** *n.*

san·i·tize (san′i tīz′), *v.t.,* **-tized, -tiz·ing.** to free from dirt, germs, etc., as by cleaning or sterilizing. [SANIT(ARY) + -IZE] —**san′i·ti·za′tion,** *n.*

san·i·tiz·er (san′i tī′zər), *n.* a substance or preparation for killing germs, designed for use esp. on food-processing equipment. Also, *esp. Brit.,* **san′i·tis′er.** [SANITIZE + -ER¹]

san·i·ty (san′i tē), *n.* **1.** the state of being sane; soundness of mind; mental normality. **2.** soundness of judgment. [ME *sanite* < L *sānitās.* See SANE, -ITY]

San Ja·cin·to (san′ jə sin′tō), **1.** a river in E Texas, flowing SE to Galveston Bay: Texans defeated Mexicans near the mouth of this river 1836. **2.** a town in S California. 2553 (1960).

San′ Jacin′to Day′, a legal holiday observed in Texas on April 21.

san·jak (san′jak′), *n.* (in Turkey) one of the administrative districts into which a vilayet is divided. [< Turk *sancak* district (lit., flag, standard)]

San Joa·quin (san′ wô kēn′), a river in California, flowing NW from the Sierra Nevada Mountains to the Sacramento River. 350 mi. long.

San Jo·se (san′ hō zā′), a city in W California. 204,196 (1960).

San Jo·sé (sän′ hô se′), a city in and the capital of Costa Rica, in the central part. 250,000 (est. 1963).

San′ Jo·se′ scale′ (san′ hō zā′), a scale insect, *Aspidiotus perniciosus,* that is highly destructive to fruit trees and shrubs throughout the U.S. [named after SAN JOSE, California, where first found]

San Juan (san′ wän′, hwän′; *for 1, 2 also Sp.* sän hwän′), **1.** a seaport in and the capital of Puerto Rico, in the N part. 432,377 (1960). **2.** a city in W Argentina. 107,000 (1965). **3.** a town in S Texas. 4371 (1960).

San Juan de la Cruz (*Sp.* sän′ hwän′ de lä krōōth). See **John of the Cross.**

San′ Juan′ Hill′, a hill in SE Cuba, near Santiago de Cuba: captured by U.S. forces in battle during the Spanish-American War in 1898.

San′ Juan′ Is′lands, a group of islands between NW Washington and SE Vancouver Island, Canada: a part of Washington.

San′ Juan′ Moun′tains, a mountain range in SW Colorado and N New Mexico: a part of the Rocky Mountains. Highest peak, Uncompahgre Peak, 14,306 ft.

sank (saŋk), *v.* a pt. of **sink.**

San·ka·ra (suŋ′kər ə), *n.* Shankara.

San·khya (säŋ′kyə), *n.* one of the six leading systems of Hindu philosophy, stressing the reality and duality of spirit and matter. Also, **Samkhya.** [< Skt *sāmkhya* reckoning, number]

Sankt Mo·ritz (zäŋkt mō′rits), German name of **St. Moritz.**

San Le·an·dro (san′ lē an′drō), a city in W California. 65,962 (1960).

San Lo·ren·zo (san′ lə ren′zō), a town in W California, near San Francisco Bay. 23,773 (1960).

San Lu·is O·bis·po (san lōō′is ə bis′pō), a city in W California. 20,437 (1960).

San Lu·is Po·to·sí (sän′ lōō ēs′ pô′tô sē′), **1.** a state in central Mexico. 1,048,297 (1960); 24,415 sq. mi. **2.** the capital of this state. 173,886 (est. 1960).

San Man·uel (san′ man wel′), a town in S Arizona. 4524 (1960).

San Ma·ri·no (san′ mə rē′nō; *It.* sän′ mä rē′nô), a small republic in E Italy: the oldest independent country in Europe. 17,000 (est. 1964); 38 sq. mi. *Cap.:* San Marino.

San Mar·tín (san′ mär tēn′; *Sp.* sän′ mär tēn′), **Jo·sé de** (hô se′ the), 1778–1850, South American general and statesman, born in Argentina: leader in winning independence for Argentina, Peru, and Chile; protector of Peru 1821–22.

San Ma·te·o (san′ mə tā′ō), a city in W California. 69,870 (1960).

San·mi·che·li (sän′mē ke′lē), *n.* **Mi·che·le** (mē ke′le), 1484–1559, Italian architect and military engineer.

San Mi·guel (sän′ mē gel′), a city in E El Salvador. 33,063 (est. 1958).

san·nup (san′up), *n.* a married American Indian man. [< Narragansett *sannop*]

sann·ya·si (sun yä′sē), *n.* a Hindu monk. Also, **sann·ya·sin** (sun yä′sin); *referring to a woman,* **sann·ya·si·ni** (sun yä′sē nē). [< Hindi: casting away]

San Pa·blo (san pä′blō), a city in W California, near San Pablo Bay. 19,687 (1960).

San Pa′blo Bay′, the N part of San Francisco Bay, in W California.

San Pe·dro (san pā′drō), a town in S Texas. 7634 (1960).

San Pe·dro Su·la (sän pe′thrô sōō′lä), a city in NW Honduras. 58,632 (1961).

San Ra·fael (san′ rə fel′; *for 2 also Sp.* sän rä′fä-el′), **1.** a city in W California, N of San Francisco. 20,460 (1960). **2.** a city in W Argentina. 55,443 (1961).

San Re·mo (san rē′mō, rā′-; *It.* sän re′mô), a seaport in NW Italy, on the Riviera: resort. 55,443 (1961).

sans (sanz; *Fr.* säN), *prep.* without. [ME < OF *sans,* earlier *sens* < VL **sene(s),* var. of L *sine* without]

Sans., Sanskrit.

San Sa·ba (san sä′bə, sab′ə), a town in central Texas. 2728 (1960).

San Sal·va·dor (san sal′və dôr′; *Sp.* sän säl′vä-thôr′), *n.* **1.** Also called **Watling Island.** an island in the E Bahamas: first land in the New World seen by Christopher Columbus 1492. 906 (est. 1955); 60 sq. mi. **2.** a city in and the capital of El Salvador. 281,122 (est. 1963).

San·scrit (san′skrit), *n., adj.* Sanskrit. —**San′scrit·ist,** *n.*

San·scrit·ic (san skrit′ik), *adj.* Sanskrit (def. 2).

sans-cu·lotte (sanz′kyŏŏ lot′; *Fr.* säN ky lôt′), *n., pl.* **sans-cu·lottes** (sanz′kyŏŏ lots′; *Fr.* säN ky lôt′). **1.** (in the French Revolution) a revolutionary of the poorer class: originally a term of contempt applied by the aristocrats but later adopted as a popular name by the revolutionaries. **2.** any extreme republican or revolutionary. [< F: lit., without knee-breeches] —**sans-cu·lot·tic** (sanz′kyŏŏ lot′ik), *adj.* —**sans′-cu·lot′tish,** *adj.* —**sans′-cu·lot′tism,** *n.* —**sans′-cu·lot′tist,** *n.*

sans-cu·lot·tide (sanz′kyŏŏ lot′id; *Fr.* säN ky lô-tēd′), *n., pl.* **sans-cu·lot·tides** (sanz′kyŏŏ lot′idz; *Fr.* säN ky lô tēd′). **1.** (in the French Revolutionary calendar) any of the five intercalary days (six in every fourth year) added at the end of the month of Fructidor. **2. sans-culottides,** the festivities held during these days. [< F; see SANS-CULOTTE; *-ide* (? < L *Idūs* IDES)]

sans doute (säN dōōt′), *French.* without doubt; certainly.

San Se·bas·tián (san′ si bas′chən; *Sp.* sän′ se-väs tyän′), **1.** a seaport in N Spain: resort. 123,935 (est. 1960). **2.** a tropical American plant, *Cattleya skinneri,* having cylindrical leaves and yellow-throated, rose-purple flowers.

San·sei (sän′sā′), *n.* a grandchild of Japanese immigrants to the U.S. Also, **san′sei′.** Cf. **Issei, Kibei, Nisei.** [< Jap: third generation]

san·se·vi·e·ri·a (san′sə vē ēr′ē ə, -sə vēr′ē ə), *n.* any plant of the genus *Sansevieria,* grown as a house plant for its stiff, sword-shaped leaves. [< NL; named after *San Seviero,* principality of Raimondo di Sangro (1710–71), learned Neapolitan; see -IA]

sans gêne (säN zhen′), *French.* without constraint or embarrassment; free and easy.

Sansk., Sanskrit.

San·skrit (san′skrit), *n.* **1.** an Indo-European, Indic language, in use since c1200 B.C. as the most important religious and literary language of India. *Abbr.:* Skt —*adj.* **2.** Also, **San·skrit′ic, Sanscritic.** of or pertaining to Sanskrit. Also, **Sanscrit.** [< Skt *saṁskṛta* well-made, perfected (lit., put together)] —**San′skrit·ist,** *n.*

San·som (san′səm), *n.* a boy's given name, form of **Samson.**

San′som Park′ Vil′lage, a town in N Texas. 4175 (1960).

San·so·vi·no (san′sō vē′nō; *It.* sän′sô vē′nô), *n.* **1. An·dre·a** (än dre′ä), (*Andrea Contucci*), 1460–1529, Italian sculptor and architect. **2.** his pupil **Ja·co·po** (yä′kô pô), (*Jacopo Tatti*), 1486–1570, Italian sculptor and architect.

sans pa·reil (säN pa re′yᵊ), *French.* without equal.

sans peur et sans re·proche (säN pœr ā säN rə prôsh), *French.* without fear and without reproach: said originally of the French knight, the Seigneur de Bayard.

sans′ ser′if (sanz), *Print.* a style of monotonal type without serifs. —**sans-ser·if** (sanz′ser′if), *adj.*

sans sou·ci (säN sōō sē′), *French.* carefree.

San Ste·fa·no (sän ste′fä nô′), the former name of Yesilkoy, a town in Turkey, near Istanbul: treaty between Russia and Turkey 1878.

sant (shunt), *n.* a Sikh religious leader.

San·ta (san′tə), *n.* See **Santa Claus.**

San·ta An·a (san′tə an′ə *or, for 2, 4, Sp.* sän′tä ä′nä), **1.** a city in SW California. 100,350 (1960). **2.** a city in NW El Salvador. 70,769 (est. 1958). **3.** *Meteorol.* (in southern California) a weather condition in which strong, hot, dust-bearing winds descend to the Pacific coast around Los Angeles from inland desert regions. **4.** See **Santa Anna.**

San·ta An·na (sän′tä ä′nä; *Eng.* san′tə an′ə), **An·to·nio Lo·pez de** (än tô′nyô lô′pes the), 1795?–1876, Mexican general and revolutionist: dictator 1844–45; president 1833–35, 1853–55. Also, **Santa Ana.**

San·ta Bar·ba·ra (san′tə bär′bər ə, -brə), a city on the SW coast of California: Spanish mission. 58,768 (1960).

San′ta Bar′bara Is′lands, a group of islands off the SW coast of California.

San·ta Cat·a·li·na (san′tə kat′ᵊlē′nə), an island off the SW coast of California, opposite Long Beach: resort. 1630 (1950); 132 sq. mi. Also called **Catalina Island.**

San·ta Cat·a·ri·na (san′tə kat′ə rē′nə; *Port.* säNN′-tə kä tə rē′nə), a state in S Brazil. 2,146,909 (1960); 36,856 sq. mi. *Cap.:* Florianópolis.

San·ta Cla·ra (san′tə klar′ə; *for 1 also Sp.* sän′tä klä′rä), **1.** a city in central Cuba. 105,600 (est. 1962). **2.** a city in central California, S of San Francisco. 58,880 (1960).

San·ta Claus (san′tə klôz′), the patron saint of children, dispenser of gifts on Christmas Eve; Saint Nicholas. Also, **Santa Klaus.** [< dial. D *Sante Klaas*]

San·ta Cruz (san′tə krōōz′; *Sp.* sän′tä krōōs′), **1.** a city in W California. 25,596 (1960). **2.** an island in NW Santa Barbara Islands. **3.** a city in central Bolivia. 49,305 (est. 1959). **4.** See **St. Croix** (def. 1).

San′ta Cruz′ de Te·ne·rife′ (də ten′ə rif′; *Sp.* de te′ne rē′fe), a seaport on NE Tenerife island, in the W Canary Islands. 145,273 (est. 1960).

San′ta Cruz′ wa′ter lil′y, an aquatic plant, *Victoria cruziana,* of Paraguay, having floating leaves from two to five feet wide and deep pink or red flowers. Also called **water platter.**

San·ta Fe (san′tə fā′), a city in and the capital of New Mexico, in the N part: founded c1605. 34,676 (1960). —**San′ta Fe′an.**

San·ta Fé (san′tə fā′; *Sp.* sän′tä fe′), a city in E Argentina. 259,560(1965).

San′te Fe′ Springs′, a city in SW California, near Los Angeles: oil wells. 16,342 (1960).

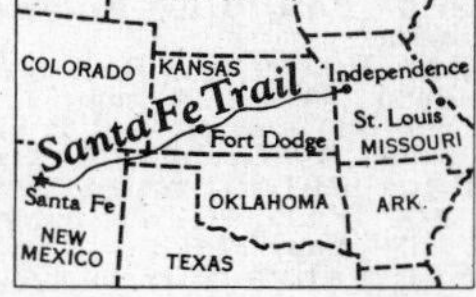

San′te Fe′ Trail′, an important trade route going between Independence, Missouri, and Santa Fe, New Mexico, used from about 1821 to 1880.

San·ta Ger·tru·dis (san′tə gər trōō′dis), one of an American breed of beef cattle, developed from Shorthorn and Brahman stock and resistant to torrid temperatures. [named after a division of a ranch in Texas]

San·ta Is·a·bel (san′tə iz′ə bel′; *Sp.* sän′tä ē′sä-bel′), a town in and the capital of Equatorial Guinea, on N Fernando Po island. 19,869 (1960).

San·ta Klaus (san′tə klôz′). See **Santa Claus.**

san·tal (san′tᵊl), *n.* sandalwood. [< F < ML *santa-l(um)* < LGk *sántalon* sandalwood, var. of *sándalon;* see SANDAL²]

san·ta·la·ceous (san′tᵊlā′shəs), *adj.* belonging to the *Santalaceae*, or sandalwood family of plants. [< NL *santalace(ae)* (see SANTAL, -ACEAE) + -OUS]

San·ta Ma·ri·a (san′tə mə rē′ə; *for 1, 2 also Sp.* sän′tä mä rē′ä), **1.** the flagship used by Columbus when he made his first voyage of discovery to America in 1492. **2.** an active volcano in W Guatemala. 12,300 ft. **3.** a city in W California. 20,027 (1960).

San′ta Mari′a tree′. See **calaba tree.**

San·ta Mar·ta (san′tə mär′tə; *Sp.* sän′tä mär′tä), **1.** a seaport in NW Colombia. 62,650 (est. 1961). **2.** a cactus, *Heliocereus speciosus*, of Mexico and Central America, having scarlet flowers six to seven inches long.

San·ta Mau·ra (sän′tä mou′rä), Italian name of **Levkas.**

San·ta Mon·i·ca (san′tə mon′ə kə), a city in SW California, near Los Angeles, on Santa Monica Bay: resort. 83,249 (1960).

San·tan·der (san′tän der′), *n.* **1. Fran·cis·co de Pau·la** (frän sēs′kô the pou′lä), 1792–1840, South American soldier and statesman: president of New Granada 1832–37. **2.** a seaport in N Spain: Altamira prehistoric cave drawings nearby. 103,108 (est. 1960).

San·ta·rém (san′tə rem′; *Port.* säɴ′tə reɴm′), *n.* a city in N Brazil, on the Amazon River. 32,615 (1960).

San·ta Ro·sa (san′tə rō′zə; *for 2 also Sp.* sän′tä rô′sä), **1.** a city in W California, N of San Francisco. 31,027 (1960). **2.** a city in central Argentina. 27,561 (est. 1965).

San·ta Ro·sa de Co·pán (sän′tä rô′sä the kô-pän′), a town in W Honduras: site of extensive Mayan ruins. 7946 (1961). Also called **Copán.**

San·ta·ya·na (san′tē an′ə; *Sp.* sän′tä yä′nä), *n.* **George,** 1863–1952, U.S. philosopher, novelist, and poet; born in Spain.

Sant·bech (sant′bek), *n.* a crater in the fourth quadrant of the face of the moon: about 44 miles in diameter.

San·tee (san tē′), *n.* a river flowing SE from central South Carolina to the Atlantic. 143 mi. long.

San·ti·a·go (san′tē ä′gō; *Sp.* sän′tyä′gô), *n.* **1.** a city in and the capital of Chile, in the central part. 646,731 (1960). **2.** Also called **Santia′go de Com·po·ste′la** (the kôm′pô ste′lä). a city in NW Spain: pilgrimage center; cathedral. 31,140 (est. 1960).

Santia′go de Cu′ba (də kyo͞o′bə; *Sp.* de ko͞o′vä), a seaport in SE Cuba: naval battle 1898. 219,800 (est. 1964).

San·tia·go del Es·te·ro (sän tyä′gô del e ste′rô), a city in N Argentina. 103,115 (est. 1965).

san·tims (sän′timz), *n., pl.* **-ti·mi** (-tə mē). a former coin of Latvia, the 100th part of a lat. [< Latvian < F *centime* CENTIME]

san·tir (sän′tēr), *n.* a Persian musical instrument resembling a dulcimer. [< Ar < Gk *psaltērion* PSALTERY]

San·to An·dré (säɴ′to͞o äɴ dre′), a city in E Brazil, near São Paulo. 231,705 (1960).

San·to Do·min·go (san′tō də ming′gō; *Sp.* sän′tô dô mēng′gô), **1.** Formerly, **Ciudad Trujillo.** a city in and the capital of the Dominican Republic, on the S coast: first European settlement in America 1496. 350,847 (1960). **2.** See **Dominican Republic.**

san·ton·i·ca (san ton′ə kə), *n.* **1.** a wormwood, *Artemisia Cina.* **2.** the dried flower heads of this plant, used as a vermifuge. [< NL *(herba) santonica* herb of the Santones, an Aquitanian tribe]

san·to·nin (san′tə nin), *n.* *Chem.* a crystalline compound, $C_{15}H_{18}O_3$, the active principle of santonica. [SANTON(ICA) + -IN²]

San·to·rin (san′tə rēn′), *n.* former name of **Thera.** Also, **San·to·ri·ni** (*Gr.* sän′dô rē′nē).

San·tos (san′təs; *Port.* säɴ′to͞os), *n.* a seaport in S Brazil: world's greatest coffee port. 263,054 (1960).

San·tos-Du·mont (san′təs do͞o mont′, -dyo͞o-; *Port.* säɴ′to͞oz do͞o mōɴt′), *n.* **Al·ber·to** (äl ber′tô), 1873–1932, Brazilian aeronaut in France: designer and builder of dirigibles and airships.

Sa·nu·si (sə no͞o′sē), *n., pl.* **-sis,** *(esp. collectively)* **-si.** a member of a fanatical, belligerent Muslim sect of North Africa. Also, **Senusi, Senussi.** [named after Muhammad ibn Ali as-*Sanūsi* (d. 1859), Algerian founder of the sect]

São Fran·cis·co (souɴ′ fräɴn sēs′ko͞o), a river flowing NE and E through E Brazil into the Atlantic. 1800 mi. long.

São Luiz do Ma·ra·nhão (souɴ′ lwēs′ do͞o mä′rə nyouɴ′), a seaport on an island off the NE coast of Brazil: capital of Maranhão. 139,075 (1960). Also called **São′ Luiz′.**

São Mi·guel (souɴ′ mē gel′), the largest island of the Azores. 177,057 (1950). 288 sq. mi.

Sa·on (sā′ən), *n.* *Class. Myth.* a Boeotian who sought advice from the shrine of Apollo at Delphi on how to end a drought: he eventually initiated the worship of Trophonius.

Saône (sōn), *n.* a river flowing S from NE France to the Rhone. 270 mi. long.

Saône-et-Loire (sōn′ā lwar′), *n.* a department in E France. 535,772 (1962); 3331 sq. mi. *Cap.:* Maçon.

São Pau·lo (souɴ′ pou′lo͞o), a city in S Brazil: second largest city in South America. 3,300,218 (1960).

São′ Pau′lo de Lu·an′da (də lô äɴn′də), Luanda.

São Pe·dro do Ri·o Gran·de do Sul (souɴ pe′-drō͞o do͞o rē′o͞o gräɴn′de do͞o so͞ol′), a seaport in SE Rio Grande do Sul, in SE Brazil. 87,528 (1960). Also called **Rio Grande, Rio Grande do Sul.**

Saor·stat Eir·eann (sâr′stät âr′ən; *Gaelic* sär′-stôt ā′rôn), Gaelic name of **Irish Free State.** Also called **Saor′stat′.**

São Sal·va·dor (souɴ′ säl′və dôr′), a seaport in E Brazil. 638,592 (1960). Also called **Bahia.** Official name, **Salvador.**

São To·mé (souɴ′ tô me′), Portuguese name of **St. Thomas.** Also, **São′ Tho·mé′.**

sap¹ (sap), *n.* **1.** the juice or vital circulating fluid, esp. of a woody plant. **2.** sapwood. **3.** *Slang.* a fool; dupe. **4.** *Metall.* soft metal at the core of a bar of blister steel. [ME; OE *sæp*; c. D *sap;* akin to G *Saft* juice, Icel *safi*]

sap² (sap), *n., v.,* **sapped, sap·ping.** —*n.* **1.** *Fort.* a deep, narrow trench constructed so as to form an approach to a besieged place or an enemy's position. —*v.t.* **2.** *Fort.* **a.** to approach (a besieged place, or enemy position) with deep, narrow trenches protected by gabions or parapets. **b.** to dig such trenches in (ground). **3.** to undermine; weaken or destroy insidiously. —*v.i.* **4.** *Fort.* to dig a sap. [earlier *zappe* < It *zapp(a)* sap, hoe; cf. ML *zapa* horseshoe]
—**Syn. 3.** impair, enfeeble, deplete, exhaust, enervate, invalidate.

s.ap., scruple (apothecary's weight).

sap·a·jou (sap′ə jo͞o′), *n.* a capuchin monkey. [< F < Tupi]

sa·pan·wood (sə pan′wo͝od′), *n.* sappanwood.

sa·pe·le (sə pē′lē), *n.* **1.** the mahoganylike wood of any of several African trees of the genus *Entandrophragma*, used for making furniture. **2.** a tree, esp. *Entandrophragma cylindricum*, yielding this wood. Also called **sape′le mahog′any.** [< WAfr]

sap′ green′, a green pigment obtained from the juice of buckthorn berries, used chiefly in dyes for wood, paper, and textiles.

sap·head (sap′hed′), *n.* *Slang.* a simpleton; a fool. [SAP¹ + HEAD]

sap·head·ed (sap′hed′id), *adj.* *Slang.* silly; foolish. [SAPHEAD + -ED³] —**sap′head′ed·ness,** *n.*

sa·phe·na (sə fē′nə), *n.* See **saphenous vein.** [ME < ML < Ar *ṣāfin*]

sa·phe·nous (sə fē′nəs), *adj.* **1.** of, pertaining to, or situated near the saphenous vein. —*n.* **2.** See **saphenous vein.** [SAPHEN(A) + -OUS]

saphe′nous vein′, *Anat.* either of two large, superficial veins of the foot, leg, and thigh, one on the inner side and the other on the outer and posterior sides.

sap·id (sap′id), *adj.* **1.** having taste or flavor. **2.** agreeable to the taste; palatable. **3.** agreeable, as to the mind; to one's liking. [< L *sapid(us)* flavored] —**sa·pid′i·ty, sap′id·ness,** *n.*

sa·pi·ent (sā′pē ənt), *adj.* (often used ironically) wise or sage. [< L *sapient-* (s. of *sapiēns*, prp. of *sapere* to be wise), equiv. to *sapi-* taste, think + *-ent-* -ENT] —**sa′pi·ence, sa′pi·en·cy,** *n.* —**sa′pi·ent·ly,** *adv.*
—**Syn.** sagacious. —**Ant.** stupid.

sa·pi·en·tial (sā′pē en′shəl), *adj.* containing, exhibiting, or affording wisdom; characterized by wisdom. [< eccl. L *sapientiāl(is).* See SAPIENT, -AL¹] —**sa′pi·en′tial·ly,** *adv.*

sap·in·da·ceous (sap′in dā′shəs), *adj.* belonging to the *Sapindaceae* or soapberry family of plants. [< NL *sapindace(ae)* soapberry family (*Sapind(us)* (L *sāp(ō)* soap + *Indus* Indian) + *-aceae* -ACEAE) + -OUS]

Sa·pir (sə pēr′), *n.* **Edward,** 1884–1939, U.S. anthropologist and linguist, born in Germany.

sap·less (sap′lis), *adj.* **1.** without sap; withered; dry: *sapless plants.* **2.** lacking vitality or spirit; insipid. [SAP¹ + -LESS] —**sap′less·ness,** *n.*

sap·ling (sap′ling), *n.* **1.** a young tree. **2.** a young person. [SAP¹ + -LING¹]

sap·o·dil·la (sap′ə dil′ə), *n.* **1.** a large evergreen tree, *Achras Zapota*, of tropical America, bearing an edible fruit and yielding chicle. **2.** Also called **sap′odil′la plum′.** the fruit itself. [< Sp *zapotillo*, equiv. to *zapot(e)* SAPOTA + *-illo* dim. suffix]

sap·o·na·ceous (sap′ə nā′shəs), *adj.* soaplike; soapy. [< NL *sāpōnāceus*, equiv. to L *sāpōn-* (s. of *sāpō*) SOAP + *-āceus* -ACEOUS] —**sap′o·na′ceous·ness,** *n.*

saponifica′tion num′ber, *Chem.* the number of milligrams of potassium hydroxide required to saponify one gram of a given ester, esp. a glyceride. Also called **saponifica′tion val′ue.** [SAPONI(FY) + -FICATION]

sa·pon·i·fy (sə pon′ə fī′), *v.,* **-fied, -fy·ing.** *Chem.* —*v.t.* **1.** to convert (a fat) into soap by treating with an alkali. **2.** to decompose (any ester), forming the corresponding alcohol and acid or salt. —*v.i.* **3.** to become converted into soap. [< L *sāpōn-* (s. of *sāpō*) SOAP + -IFY] —**sa·pon′i·fi·ca′tion,** *n.* —**sa·pon′i·fi′er,** *n.*

sap·o·nin (sap′ə nin), *n.* any of a group of amorphous glucosidal compounds of steroid structure, occurring in many plants, characterized by an ability to form emulsions and to foam in aqueous solutions, and used as detergents. [< F *saponine* < L *sāpōn-* (s. of *sāpō*) SOAP + F *-ine* -IN²]

sap·o·nite (sap′ə nīt′), *n.* a clay mineral, hydrous magnesium aluminum silicate, belonging to the montmorillonite group: found as a soft filling in rock cavities. [< Sw *saponit* < L *sāpōn-* (s. of *sāpō*) SOAP + Sw *-it* -ITE¹]

sa·por (sā′pər, -pôr), *n.* the quality in a substance that affects the sense of taste; savor; flavor. Also, *Brit.,* **sa′pour.** [ME *sapo(u)r* < L *sapor* SAVOR]

sap·o·rif·ic (sap′ə rif′ik), *adj.* producing or imparting flavor or taste. [< NL *saporific(us)*, equiv. to L *sapor* SAVOR + *-i-* -I- + *-ficus* -FIC]

sap·o·rous (sap′ər əs), *adj.* full of flavor or taste; flavorful. [< LL *saporōs(us)*, equiv. to L *sapor* SAVOR + *-ōsus* -OUS] —**sap·o·ros·i·ty** (sap′ə ros′i tē), *n.*

sa·po·ta (sə pō′tə), *n.* **1.** any of various tropical American fruits. **2.** a tree, *Calocarpum Sapota*, or its fruit. **3.** the sapodilla. [< NL < Sp *sapote, zapote* < Arahuacan *tsapotl*]

sap·o·ta·ceous (sap′ə tā′shəs), *adj.* belonging to the *Sapotaceae*, or sapodilla family of plants. [< NL *sapotāce(ae)* + -OUS; see SAPOTA, -ACEAE]

sap·pan·wood (sə pan′wo͝od′), *n.* **1.** a dyewood yielding a red color, produced by a small, East Indian, caesalpiniaceous tree, *Caesalpinia Sappan.* **2.** the tree itself. Also, **sapanwood.** [< Malay *sapan(g)* + WOOD¹]

sap·per (sap′ər), *n.* *Brit.* a soldier in a military unit of engineers, usually employed in the construction of trenches, fortifications, etc. [SAP² + -ER¹]

Sap·phic (saf′ik), *adj.* **1.** pertaining to Sappho or to certain meters or a form of strophe or stanza used by or named after her. —*n.* **2.** a Sapphic verse. [< L *sapphic(us)* < Gk *sapphikós*, equiv. to *Sapph(ṓ)* SAPPHO + *-ikos* -IC]

Sap′phic ode′, *Pros.* See **Horatian ode.**

Sap·phi·ra (sə fī′rə), *n.* **1.** a woman who, with her husband, Ananias, was struck dead for lying. Acts 5. **2.** Also, **Sap·phire** (saf′īᵊr). a girl's given name.

sap·phire (saf′īᵊr), *n.* **1.** any gem variety of corundum other than the ruby, esp. one of the blue varieties. **2.** a gem of this kind. **3.** the color of the gem, a deep blue. —*adj.* **4.** resembling sapphire; deep blue: *a sapphire sky.* [< L *sapphīr(us)* < Gk *sáppheiros*; r. ME *safir* < OF]

sap·phir·ine (saf′ər in, -ə rēn′, -ə rīn′), *adj.* **1.** consisting of sapphire; like sapphire, esp. in color. —*n.* **2.** a pale-blue or greenish, usually granular mineral, a silicate of magnesium and aluminum. **3.** a blue variety of spinel. [< G *Saphirin*, equiv. to *Saphir* SAPPHIRE + *-in* -INE²]

sap·phism (saf′iz əm), *n.* lesbianism. [SAPPH(O) + -ISM] —**sap′phist,** *n.*

Sap·pho (saf′ō), *n.* **1.** c620–c565 B.C., Greek poetess, born in Lesbos. **2.** a girl's given name.

Sap·po·ro (sä′pô rô′), *n.* a city on W Hokkaido, in N Japan. 704,182 (1964).

sap·py (sap′ē), *adj.,* **-pi·er, -pi·est. 1.** abounding in sap, as a plant. **2.** full of vitality and energy. **3.** *Slang.* silly or foolish. [SAP¹ + -Y¹] —**sap′pi·ness,** *n.*

sa·pre·mi·a (sə prē′mē ə), *n.* *Pathol.* a form of blood poisoning, esp. that caused by the toxins produced by certain microorganisms. [SAPR- + -EMIA] —**sa·pre′·mic,** *adj.*

sapro-, a learned borrowing from Greek meaning "rotten," used in the formation of technical terms: *saprogenic.* Also, *esp. before a vowel,* **sapr-.** [< Gk, comb. form of *saprós*]

sap·ro·gen·ic (sap′rō jen′ik), *adj.* **1.** producing putrefaction or decay, as certain bacteria. **2.** formed by putrefaction. Also, **sa·prog·e·nous** (sə proj′ə nəs). [SAPRO- + -GENIC]

sap·ro·leg·ni·a (sap′rə leg′nē ə), *n.* any aquatic fungus of the genus *Saprolegnia* that forms a white, furry coating on decaying organic matter or on fish and fish eggs. [SAPRO- + Gk *légn(on)* edging + -IA]

sap·ro·lite (sap′rə līt′), *n.* *Petrog.* soft, disintegrated, usually more or less decomposed rock remaining in its original place. [SAPRO- + -LITE] —**sap·ro·lit·ic** (sap′rə lit′ik), *adj.*

sap·ro·pel (sap′rə pel′), *n.* mud consisting chiefly of decomposed organic matter formed at the bottom of a stagnant sea or lake. [SAPRO- + Gk *pēl(ós)* mud] —**sap′ro·pel′ic,** *adj.*

sa·proph·a·gous (sa prof′ə gəs), *adj.* *Biol.* (of a plant or animal) feeding on dead or decaying animal matter. [SAPRO- + -PHAGOUS]

sap·ro·phyte (sap′rə fīt′), *n.* any organism that lives on dead organic matter, as certain fungi, bacteria, etc. [SAPRO- + -PHYTE] —**sap·ro·phyt·ic** (sap′rə fit′ik), *adj.* —**sap′ro·phyt′i·cal·ly,** *adv.*

sap·sa·go (sap′sə gō′), *n.* a strong, hard, usually green cheese of Swiss origin, made with sour skim milk and sweet clover. [alter. of G *Schabziger, Schabzieger*, equiv. to *schab(en)* (to) grate + *Zi(e)ger* a kind of cheese]

sap·suck·er (sap′suk′ər), *n.* either of two American woodpeckers of the genus *Sphyrapicus* that drill holes in maple, apple, hemlock, etc., drinking the sap and eating the insects that gather there. Cf. **yellow-bellied sapsucker.** [SAP¹ + SUCKER]

sap·wood (sap′wo͝od′), *n.* *Bot.* the softer part of the wood between the inner bark and the heartwood. Also called **alburnum.** [SAP¹ + WOOD¹]

Saq·qa·ra (sə kär′ə), *n.* a village in the S United Arab Republic, S of Cairo: site of the necropolis of ancient Memphis; step pyramids; mastabas. Also, **Sakkara.**

Sar., Sardinia.

S.A.R., Sons of the American Revolution.

Sa·ra (sär′ə), *n., pl.* **-ras,** *(esp. collectively)* **-ra.** a member of a Negro people of the Central African Republic.

Sar·a (sâr′ə), *n.* **1.** *Douay Bible.* Sarah. **2.** a girl's given name, form of **Sarah.**

sar·a·band (sar′ə band′), *n.* **1.** a popular and vigorous Spanish castanet dance. **2.** a slow, stately Spanish dance in triple meter derived from this. **3.** a piece of music for or using the rhythm of this dance, usually forming one of the movements in the classical suite and following the courante. [< F *sarabande* < Sp *zaraband(a)* < Ar, Pers *serbend* kind of dance]

Sar·a·cen (sar′ə sən), *n.* **1.** *Hist.* a member of any of the nomadic tribes on the Syrian borders of the Roman Empire. **2.** (in later use) an Arab. **3.** a Muslim, esp. one mentioned in connection with any of the Crusades. —*adj.* **4.** Also, **Sar·a·cen·ic** (sar′ə sen′ik), **Sar′a·cen′i·cal.** of or pertaining to the Saracens. [OE < LL *Saracēn(us)* < LGk *Sarakēnós*] —**Sar′a·cen·ism,** *n.* —**Sar′a·cen·like′,** *adj.*

Sa·ra·gat (sä′rä gät′), *n.* **Giu·sep·pe** (jo͞o zep′pe), born 1898, Italian statesman: president since 1964.

Sar·a·gos·sa (sar′ə gos′ə), *n.* a city in NE Spain, on the Ebro River. 291,181 (est. 1960). Spanish, **Zaragoza.**

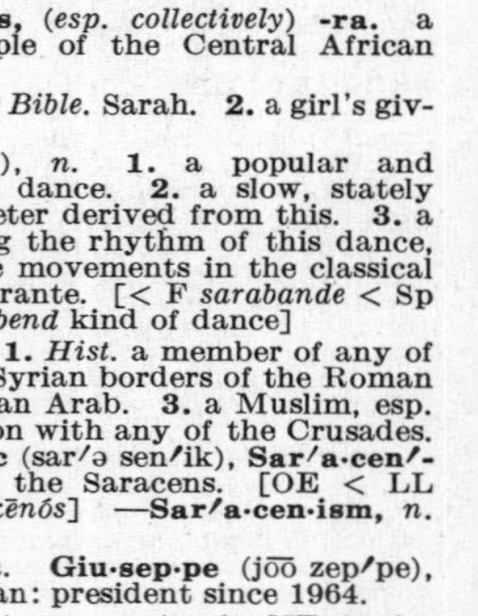

Sar·ah (sâr′ə), *n.* **1.** the wife of Abraham and mother of Isaac. Gen. 17:15–22. Also, **Sa·rai** (sâr′ī, -ā ī′); *Douay Bible,* **Sara. 2.** a girl's given name. [<< Heb *sārāh* princess]

Sa·ra·je·vo (sar′ə yā′vō; *Serbo-Croatian.* sä′rä ye-vô), *n.* a city in and the capital of Bosnia and Herzegovina, in the central part: assassination of the Austrian Archduke Francis Ferdinand here June 28, 1914, was the final event that precipitated World War I. 448,519. Also, **Serajevo.**

sa·ran (sə ran′), *n.* a thermoplastic copolymer of vinylidene chloride and usually small amounts of vinyl chloride or acrylonitrile: used as a fiber, for packaging, and for making acid-resistant pipe. [formerly trademark]

Sar′a·nac Lake′ (sar′ə nak′), a village in NE New York, near the Saranac Lakes: health resort. 6421 (1960).

Sar′anac Lakes′, a group of three lakes in NE New York, in the Adirondack Mountains: includes the Upper Saranac, the Middle Saranac, and the Lower Saranac.

Sar·a·nap (sar′ə nap′), *n.* a town in W California. 6450 (1960).

sa·ran·gi (sär′ung gē), *n.* (in India) a violinlike instrument used to accompany classical dancing. [Skt *sāraṅgī* a sort of violin]

Sa·ransk (sä ʀänsk′), *n.* a city in the W RSFSR, in the central Soviet Union in Europe. 132,000 (est. 1964).

sa·ra·pe (sə rä′pē; *Sp.* sä ʀä′pe), *n., pl.* **-pes** (-pēz; *Sp.* -pes). serape.

Sar·a·so·ta (sar′ə sō′tə), *n.* a city in W Florida. 34,083 (1960).

Sa·ras·va·ti (sə rus′və tē, sur′əs və-), *n.* the Hindu goddess of learning and the arts.

Sar·a·to·ga (sar′ə tō′gə), *n.* former name of **Schuylerville.**

Sar′ato′ga chip′. See **potato chip.** Also called **Sarato′ga pota′to.**

Sar′ato′ga Springs′, a city in E New York: health resort; horse races. 16,630 (1960).

Sar′ato′ga trunk′, a type of large traveling trunk used mainly by women during the 19th century. [named after SARATOGA (SPRINGS)]

Sa·ra·tov (sä ʀä′tof), *n.* a city in the SW RSFSR, in the E Soviet Union in Europe, on the Volga. 684,000 (1965).

Sa·ra·wak (sə rä′wäk, -wä), *n.* a region in Malaysia, on NW Borneo: formerly a British crown colony (1946–63) and British protectorate (1888–1946). 790,607 (est. 1962); ab. 50,000 sq. mi. *Cap.:* Kuching.

sarc-, var. of **sarco-,** esp. before a vowel: *sarcous.*

sar·casm (sär′kaz əm), *n.* **1.** harsh or bitter derision or irony. **2.** a sharply ironical taunt or gibe; a sneering or cutting remark. [< LL *sarcasm(us)* < Gk *sarkasmós,* deriv. of *sarkázein* to rend (flesh), sneer; see SARCO-] —**Syn. 1.** bitterness, ridicule. See **irony**[1]. **2.** jeer.

sar·cas·tic (sär kas′tik), *adj.* **1.** characterized by, of the nature of, or pertaining to sarcasm: *a sarcastic reply.* **2.** using or given to the use of sarcasm: *He is always sarcastic about her appearance.* Also, **sar·cas′ti·cal.** [SARC(ASM) + -ASTIC] —**sar·cas′ti·cal·ly,** *adv.* —**sar·cas′tic·ness, sar·cas′ti·cal·ness,** *n.* —**Syn. 2.** biting, cutting, mordant, bitter, derisive, ironic, sardonic. See **cynical.**

sarcas′tic fringe′head. See under **fringehead.**

sarce·net (särs′nit), *n.* a very fine, soft, silk fabric, used esp. for linings. Also, **sarsenet.** [ME *sarsenet* < AF *sarzinet,* prob. equiv. to *sarzin-* SARACEN + *-et* -ET]

sar·ci·na (sär′sə nə), *n., pl.* **-nas, -nae** (-nē′). *Bacteriol.* any of several spherical, saprophytic bacteria of the genus *Sarcina,* having a cuboidal cell arrangement. [< NL, L: bundle]

sarco-, a learned borrowing from Greek meaning "flesh," used in the formation of compound words: *sarcocarp.* Also, *esp. before a vowel,* **sarc-.** [< Gk *sark-* (s. of *sárx*) + -o-]

sar·co·ad·e·no·ma (sär′kō ad′ənō′mə), *n., pl.* **-mas, -ma·ta** (-mə tə). *Pathol.* adenosarcoma. [SARCO- + ADENOMA]

sar·co·car·ci·no·ma (sär′kō kär′sə nō′mə), *n., pl.* **-mas, -ma·ta** (-mə tə). *Pathol.* carcinosarcoma. [SARCO- + CARCINOMA]

sar·co·carp (sär′kō kärp′), *n. Bot.* **1.** the fleshy mesocarp of certain fruits, as the peach. **2.** any fruit of fleshy consistency. [SARCO- + -CARP]

sar·code (sär′kōd), *n. Obs.* protoplasm, esp. that of a unicellular animal. [< F, alter. of Gk *sarkṓd(ēs)* fleshly]

sar·co·din·i·an (sär′kə din′ē ən), *adj.* **1.** belonging or pertaining to the class *Sarcodina,* comprising protozoans that move and capture food by forming pseudopodia. —*n.* **2.** a sarcodinian protozoan. [< Gk *sarkṓd(ēs)* fleshly + NL *-in(a)* neut. pl. suffix + -IAN]

sar·co·en·chon·dro·ma (sär′kō en′kən drō′mə), *n., pl.* **-mas, -ma·ta** (-mə tə). *Pathol.* chondrosarcoma. [SARCO- + ENCHONDROMA]

sar·coid (sär′koid), *Pathol.* —*n.* **1.** a growth resembling a sarcoma. **2.** a lesion of sarcoidosis. **3.** sarcoidosis. —*adj.* **4.** resembling flesh; fleshy. **5.** resembling a sarcoma. [SARC- + -OID]

sar·coid·o·sis (sär′koi dō′sis), *n. Pathol.* a disease of unknown cause, characterized by granulomatous tuberculate lesions of the skin, lymph nodes, lungs, eyes, and other structures. [< NL; see SARCOID, -OSIS]

sar·co·lem·ma (sär′kō lem′ə), *n., pl.* **-mas, -ma·ta** (-mə tə). *Anat.* the membranous sheath of a muscle fiber. [SARCO- + LEMMA[1]] —**sar′co·lem′mic, sar′co·lem′mous,** *adj.*

sar·col·o·gy (sär kol′ə jē), *n. Archaic.* the branch of anatomy dealing with the soft or fleshy parts of the body. [SARCO- + -LOGY] —**sar·co·log·i·cal** (sär′kə loj′i kəl), **sar′co·log′ic,** *adj.* —**sar·col′o·gist,** *n.*

sar·co·ma (sär kō′mə), *n., pl.* **-mas, -ma·ta** (-mə tə). *Pathol.* any of various malignant tumors originating in the connective tissue and attacking esp. the bones. [< NL < Gk *sárkōma* fleshy growth. See SARC-, -OMA] —**sar·co·ma·toid** (sär kō′mə toid′), **sar·co·ma·tous** (sär kō′mə təs, -kom′ə-), *adj.*

sar·co·ma·to·sis (sär kō′mə tō′sis), *n. Pathol.* **1.** a condition marked by the production of an overwhelming number of sarcomas throughout the body. **2.** the condition in which a sarcoma has become disseminated throughout the body. [*sarcomat-* (comb. form of SARCOMA) + -OSIS]

sar·coph·a·gous (sär kof′ə gəs), *adj.* subsisting on flesh; carnivorous. Also, **sar·co·phag·ic** (sär′kə faj′ik). [< L *sarcophagus* < Gk *sarkophágos* flesh-eating]

sar·coph·a·gus (sär kof′ə gəs), *n., pl.* **-gi** (-jī′), **-gus·es.** **1.** a stone coffin, esp. one bearing sculpture, inscriptions, etc., often displayed as a monument. **2.** *Gk. Antiq.* a kind of stone thought to consume the flesh of corpses, used for coffins. [< L < Gk *sarkophágos,* equiv. to *sarko-* SARCO + *-phagos* -PHAGOUS]

sar·co·phile (sär′kə fil′), *n.* a flesh-eating animal, esp. the Tasmanian devil. [SARCO- + -PHILE]

sar·cous (sär′kəs), *adj.* consisting of or pertaining to flesh or skeletal muscle. [SARC- + -OUS]

sard (särd), *n.* a reddish-brown chalcedony, used as a gem. Also, **sardius, sardine.** [< L *sard(a)* < Gk *sárdios* SARDIUS]

sar·da·na (sär dä′nə; *Sp.* säʀ thä′nä), *n., pl.* **-nas** (-nəz; *Sp.* -näs). **1.** a dance of the region of Catalonia, Spain, in which the dancers form a moving circle. **2.** the music for this dance. [< Sp < Catalan]

Sar·da·na·pa·lus (sär′dənə pā′ləs, -dənap′ə ləs), *n.* a Greek name for **Ashurbanipal** or **Ashurnasirpal II** or, in certain literary works, a fictionalized representation of either with characteristics common to both. Also, **Sar·da·na·pal·los, Sar·da·na·pa·los** (sär′dənə pal′os, -ōs; *Gk.* sär′thä nä′pä lôs).

sar·dine[1] (sär dēn′), *n., pl.* (*esp. collectively*) **-dine,** (*esp. referring to two or more kinds or species*) **-dines. 1.** the pilchard, *Sardina pilchardus,* often preserved in oil and used for food. **2.** any of various similar, closely related fishes. [ME *sardeine* < MF *sardine* < L *sardīn(a),* equiv. to *sard(a)* sardine + *-īna* dim. suffix]

sar·dine[2] (sär′dīn, -dən), *n.* sard. [late ME < LL *sardin(us)* < Gk *sárdinos* SARDIUS]

Sar·din·i·a (sär din′ē ə, -din′yə), *n.* **1.** a large island in the Mediterranean, W of Italy: with small nearby islands it comprises a department of Italy. 1,413,289 (1961); 9301 sq. mi. **2.** a former kingdom 1720–1860, including this island and Savoy, Piedmont, and Genoa (after 1815) in NW Italy: ruled by the House of Savoy. *Cap.:* Turin.

Sar·din·i·an (sär din′ē ən, -din′yən), *adj.* **1.** of or pertaining to Sardinia, its inhabitants, or their language. —*n.* **2.** a native or inhabitant of Sardinia. **3.** a Romance language spoken on Sardinia. [SARDINI(A) + -AN]

Sar·dis (sär′dis), *n.* an ancient city in W Asia Minor: the capital of ancient Lydia. Also, **Sar·des** (sär′dēz), **Tarne.** —**Sar·di·an** (sär′dē ən), *n., adj.*

sar·di·us (sär′dē əs), *n.* **1.** sard. **2.** the precious stone, thought to have been a ruby, in the breastplate of the Jewish high priest. Ex. 28:17. [< L < Gk *sárdios* (stone) of SARDIS]

sar·don·ic (sär don′ik), *adj.* characterized by bitter or scornful derision; expressing disdain; cynical; sneering: *a sardonic grin.* [alter. of earlier *sardonian* (influenced by F *sardonique*) < L *sardoni(us)* (< Gk *sardónios* of Sardinia) + -AN; alluding to a Sardinian plant which when eaten was supposed to produce convulsive laughter ending in death] —**sar·don′i·cal·ly,** *adv.* —**sar·don′i·cism,** *n.* —**Syn.** biting, mordant contemptuous.

sar·don·yx (sär don′iks, sär′dəniks), *n.* a chalcedony that is used for cameos and has sard and chalcedony of another color, usually white, arranged in straight parallel bands. [ME < L < Gk; see SARD, ONYX]

Sar·dou (säʀ do͞o′), *n.* **Vic·to·rien** (vēk tô ʀyeɴ′) 1831–1908, French dramatist.

Sarg (särg), *n.* **Tony** (*Anthony Frederic Sarg*), 1882–1942, U.S. illustrator and marionette maker, born in Guatemala.

sar·gas·so (sär gas′ō), *n., pl.* **-sos.** a gulfweed. [< Pg, perh. special use of *sargaço* rockrose < L **salicaster,* equiv. to *salic-* (s. of *salix*) willow + *-aster* -ASTER[1]]

Sargas′so Sea′, a relatively calm area of water in the N Atlantic, NE of the West Indies.

sar·gas·sum (sär gas′əm), *n.* any seaweed of the genus *Sargassum,* widely distributed in the warmer waters of the globe, as *S. bacciferum,* the common gulfweed. [< NL; see SARGASSO]

sar·gas·sum·fish (sär gas′əm fish′), *n., pl.* **-fish·es,** (*esp. collectively*) **-fish.** an olive-brown and black frogfish, *Histrio histrio,* found in the tropical Atlantic and western Pacific oceans among floating sargassum weed. Also called **mousefish.** [SARGASSUM + FISH]

Sar·gent (sär′jənt), *n.* **1. Sir (Harold) Malcolm (Watts),** 1895–1967, English conductor. **2. John Singer,** 1856–1925, U.S. painter.

sar·go (sär′gō), *n., pl.* **-gos.** *Ichthyol.* a silvery grunt, *Anisotremus davidsonii,* found off the coasts of California and Mexico, having blackish markings and yellowish fins. [< Sp < L *sarg(us)* a sea fish < Gk *sárgos*]

Sar·gon II (sär′gon), died 705 B.C., king of Assyria 722–705.

sa·ri (sär′ē), *n., pl.* **-ris.** a long piece of cotton or silk, the principal outer garment of Hindu women, worn round the body with one end draped over the head or over one shoulder. [< Hindi]

Sa·rit Tha·na·rat (sä ʀēt′ tä nä ʀät′), 1908–63, Thai statesman: premier 1952–63.

sark (säʀk), *n. Scot. and North Eng.* any long, shirtlike garment worn next to the skin, as a chemise, nightshirt, or the like. [ME; OE *serc;* c. Icel *serkr*] —**sark′less,** *adj.*

sar·ky (sär′kē), *adj. Brit. Slang.* sarcastic. [by shortening and alter.]

Sar·ma·ti·a (sär mā′shē ə, -shə), *n.* the ancient name of a region now in Poland and the W Soviet Union in Europe, between the Vistula and the Volga. —**Sar·ma′ti·an,** *adj., n.*

sar·men·tose (sär men′tōs), *adj. Bot.* having runners. Also, **sar·men·tous** (sär men′təs), **sar·men·ta·ceous** (sär′mən tā′shəs). [< L *sarmentōs(us),* equiv. to *sarment(um)* twig + *-ōsus* -OSE[1]]

sar·men·tum (sär men′təm), *n., pl.* **-ta** (-tə). *Bot.* a slender running stem; runner. Also, **sar′ment.** [< L: twig]

Sar·nath (sär′nät), *n.* an ancient Buddhist pilgrimage center in N India, near Benares: Buddha's first sermon preached here; many ancient Buddhist monuments.

Sar·nen (*Ger.* zäʀ′nən), *n.* a town in and the capital of Obwalden, in central Switzerland, E of Bern.

Sar·noff (sär′nôf, -nof), *n.* **David,** 1891–1971, U.S. businessman and broadcasting executive, born in Russia.

sa·rod (sə rōd′), *n.* a lute of northern India, played with a bow. [< Hindi < Pers]

Sa·ron (sär′ən), *n. Class. Myth.* a king of Troezen who pursued a doe into the sea and was drowned.

sa·rong (sə rông′, -rong′), *n.* **1.** a loose-fitting skirtlike garment formed by wrapping a strip of cloth around the lower part of the body, the principal garment worn by both men and women in the Malay Archipelago and certain islands of the Pacific Ocean. **2.** a cloth for such garments. [< D < Malay]

Sa·ron′ic Gulf′ (sə ron′ik), an inlet of the Aegean, on the SE coast of Greece, between Attica and the Peloponnesus. 50 mi. long; 30 mi. wide.

sa·ros (sâr′os), *n. Astron.* the period of 223 synodic months, equaling 6585.32 days or 18 years, 11.32 days (or 10.32 days if 5 leap years occur in the interval), after which eclipses repeat, but are shifted 120° west. [< Gk *sáros* < Babylonian *shār(u)*] —**sa·ron·ic** (sə ron′ik), *adj.*

Sa·ros (sär′ōs, -ōs), *n.* **Gulf of,** an inlet of the Aegean, N of the Gallipoli Peninsula. 37 mi. long; 22 mi. wide.

Sa·rouk (sə ro͞ok′), *n.* a tightly woven oriental rug with soft colors and, usually, a center design. Also, **Saruk.** [after *Sarouk,* village in western Iran]

Sa·roy·an (sə roi′ən), *n.* **William,** 1908–81, U.S. dramatist, short-story writer, and novelist.

Sar·pe·don (sär pēd′ən, -pē′don), *n. Class. Myth.* a Lycian prince, son of Zeus, killed by Patroclus in the Trojan War.

sar·plar (sär′plär, -plər), *n.* **1.** a bale of wool weighing 2240 pounds or 80 tods. **2.** the weight of such a bale. **3.** a coarse cloth bagging. Also, **sar·pler** (sär′plər), **sar·pli·er** (sär′plē ər). [< AF (OF *sarpillere*)]

sar·ra·ce·ni·a (sar′ə sē′nē ə), *n.* any American marsh plant of the genus *Sarracenia,* having hollow leaves with a pitcherlike shape in which insects are trapped and digested, as *S. purpurea,* a common pitcher plant. [< NL, equiv. to *Sarracen* (alter. of surname *Sarrazin*) + *-ia* -IA; named after a 17th-century physician and botanist of Quebec, the first to send specimens to Europe]

sar·ra·ce·ni·a·ceous (sar′ə sē′nē ā′shəs), *adj.* belonging to the *Sarraceniaceae,* the American pitcher-plant family. [< NL; see SARRACENIA, -ACEOUS]

Sar·raute (sa ʀōt′), *n.* **Na·tha·lie** (na ta lē′), born 1902, French novelist.

sar·ra·zin (sar′ə zin), *n.* buckwheat (defs. 1–3). [< F (*blé*) *sarrasin* SARACEN (wheat)]

Sarre (saʀ), *n.* French name of **Saar.**

sar·ru·so·phone (sə ro͞o′zə fōn′, -rus′ə-), *n.* a metal double-reed wind instrument with a conical bore, related to the oboe and used esp. in military bands. [named after *Sarrus* (19th-century French bandmaster); see -O-, -PHONE] —**sar·ru′so·phon′ist,** *n.*

sar·sa·pa·ril·la (sar′sə pə ril′ə, sär′spə-, sas′pə-), *n.* **1.** any of various climbing or trailing tropical American plants of the genus *Smilax,* having a root which has been used in medicine as an alterative. **2.** the root. **3.** an extract or other preparation made of this root. **4.** a soft drink flavored with an extract of this root, as root beer. [< Sp *zarzaparrilla,* equiv. to *zarza* bush + *parrilla* (*parr(a)* vine + *-illa* dim. suffix)]

sar·sen (sär′sən), *n.* any of numerous large sandstone blocks or fragments found in south central England, probably remnants of eroded Tertiary beds. Also called **Druid stone, graywether.** [syncopated var. of SARACEN, short for *Saracen boulder* Druid stone]

sarse·net (särs′nit), *n.* sarcenet.

Sarthe (saʀt), *n.* a department in NW France. 443,019 (1962); 2411 sq. mi. *Cap.:* Le Mans.

Sar·to (sär′tō; *It.* säʀ′tô), *n.* **An·dre·a del** (än drā′ə del; *It.* än dʀe′ä del). See **Andrea del Sarto.**

sar·to·ri·al (sär tôr′ē əl, -tōr′-), *adj.* **1.** of or pertaining to a tailor or his work: *the finest sartorial workmanship.* **2.** of or pertaining to clothing or style or manner of dress: *He arrived in sartorial splendor.* **3.** *Anat.* pertaining to the sartorius. [< L *sartor* tailor + -IAL] —**sar·to′ri·al·ly,** *adv.*

sar·to·ri·us (sär tôr′ē əs, -tōr′-), *n., pl.* **-to·ri·i** (-tôr′ē ī′, -tōr′-). *Anat.* a long, flat, narrow muscle extending obliquely from the front of the hip to the inner side of the tibia, the action of which assists in bending the hip or knee joint and in rotating the thigh outward: the longest muscle in man. [< NL, equiv. to L *sartor* tailor + *-ius* -IOUS]

Sar·tor Re·sar·tus (sär′tər ri sär′təs), a satirical work (1833–34) by Carlyle.

Sar·tre (sär′trə, särt; *Fr.* saʀ′tʀə), *n.* **Jean Paul** (zhäɴ pôl), 1905–80, French philosopher, novelist, and dramatist: declined 1964 Nobel prize for literature.

Sa·ruk (sə ro͞ok′), *n.* Sarouk.

Sar′um use′ (sâr′əm), the liturgy or modified form of the Roman rite used in Salisbury (Sarum) before the Reformation and lately revived in part by some English churches.

sa′rus crane′ (sär′əs), a large, gray crane, *Grus antigone,* of Asia, having a naked, red head. [< Hindi *sāras* < Skt *sāras(a)* pertaining to lakes]

Sa·sa·me-yu·ki (*Jap.* sä′sä me′yo͝o kē′), *n.* See **Thin Snow, The.**

Sa·se·bo (sä′sə bō′), *n.* a seaport on NW Kyushu, in SW Japan. 253,585 (1964).

Sa·se·no (sä′sə nō′), *n.* an island off the W coast of Albania, at the entrance to Valona Bay: belongs to Albania. 2 sq. mi.

sash[1] (sash), *n.* a long band or scarf of silk or other material worn over one shoulder or around the waist, as by military officers as a part of the uniform or by women and children for ornament. [dissimilated var. of *shash* (turban of) muslin < Ar] —**sash′less,** *adj.*

sash[2] (sash), *n.* **1.** a fixed or movable framework, as in a window or door, in which panes of glass are set. **2.** such frameworks collectively. —*v.t.* **3.** to furnish with sashes or with windows having sashes. [back formation from *sashes* (pl.), dissimilated var. of *shashes* CHASSIS]

Sa·sha (sä′shə), *n.* a girl's given name, form of **Sandra.**

sa·shay (sa shā′), *v.i. U.S. Informal.* **1.** to glide, move, or proceed easily or nonchalantly: *She just sashayed in as if she owned the place.* **2.** to chassé in dancing. [metathetic var. of CHASSÉ]

sash′ bar′, muntin (def. 1).

sash′ chain′, a chain for connecting a vertically sliding window sash with a counterweight.

sash′ cord′, a cord for connecting a vertically sliding window sash with a counterweight. Also called **sash′ line′.**

sash′ rib′bon, a strip of steel or aluminum alloy for connecting a vertically sliding window sash with a counterweight.

sash′ weight′, a counterweight to a vertically sliding window sash.

sa·sin (sā′sin), *n.* See **black buck.** [< Nepalese]

Sask., Saskatchewan.

Sas·katch·e·wan (sas kach′ə won′), *n.* **1.** a province in W Canada. 925,181 (1961); 251,700 sq. mi. *Cap.:* Regina. **2.** a river in SW Canada, flowing E to Lake Winnipeg: formed by the junction of the North Saskatchewan and South Saskatchewan rivers. 1205 mi. long.

sas·ka·toon (sas′kə to͞on′), *n.* **1.** any of several shad bushes, esp. the serviceberry, *Amelanchier canadensis.* **2.** the berry of these bushes. [after SASKATOON]

Sas·ka·toon (sas′kə to͞on′), *n.* a city in S Saskatchewan, in SW Canada. 95,526 (1961).

sass[1] (sas), *n. Chiefly Midland U.S.* **1.** sauce. **2.** fresh vegetables. [var. of SAUCE]

sass[2] (sas), *Informal.* **—n. 1.** impudent or disrespectful back talk: *She refused to take any sass from her kids.* **—v.t. 2.** to answer back in an impudent manner: *Don't sass your mother.* [back formation from SASSY[1]]

sas·sa·by (sas′ə bē), *n., pl.* **-bies.** a large, blackish-red South African antelope, *Damaliscus lunatus.* [< Sechwana *tsêssábi*]

sas·sa·fras (sas′ə fras′), *n.* **1.** an American, lauraceous tree, *Sassafras albidum.* **2.** the aromatic bark of its root, used medicinally and esp. for flavoring beverages, confectionery, etc. [< Sp *sasafrás*]

sas′safras oil′, a yellowish or reddish-yellow, aromatic volatile oil distilled from the root of the sassafras tree, used in flavoring, perfumery, and medicine.

sas′safras tea′, a tea made from the aromatic dried bark of the root of the sassafras tree, often used medicinally as a stimulant, diaphoretic, and diuretic.

Sas·sa·nid (sə sä′nid, -san′id), *n., pl.* **-sa·nids, -san·i·dae** (-sä′ni dē′, -san′i-), *adj.* **—n. 1.** a member of a dynasty that ruled in Persia A.D. 226–651. **—adj. 2.** of or pertaining to the Sassanids or their dynasty. Also, **Sas·sa·ni·an** (sə sā′nē ən), **Sas·sa·nide** (sas′ə nīd). [< NL, equiv. to *Sassan* grandfather of first king of dynasty + *-idae* -ID[2]]

Sas·sa·ri (*It.* sas′sä rē), *n.* a city in NW Sardinia. 90,246 (1961).

Sas·se·nach (sas′ə naᴋʜ, -nak), *n.* Englishman: used, often disparagingly, by the Gaelic inhabitants of the British Isles. [< Ir *sasanach* English, equiv. to *sasan(a)* England (OE *seaxan* Saxons) + *-ach* adj. suffix]

Sas·ser·i·des (sa ser′i dēz′), *n.* a walled plain in the third quadrant of the face of the moon: about 60 miles in diameter.

Sas·set·ta (säs set′tä), *n.* **Ste·fa·no di Gio·van·ni** (ste′fä nô dē jô vän′nē), 1392?–1450, Italian painter.

Sas·soon (sa so͞on′), *n.* **Sieg·fried (Lo·raine)** (sēg′frēd lō rān′, lô-), 1886–1967, English poet and novelist.

sas·sy[1] (sas′ē), *adj.,* **-si·er, -si·est.** *Informal.* saucy.

sas·sy[2] (sas′ē), *n.* See **sassy bark.** [< WAfr]

sas′sy bark′, 1. the bark of a large, African, caesalpiniaceous tree, *Erythrophloeum guineense,* used by the natives as a poison in ordeals. **2.** Also called **sassy·wood** (sas′ē wo͝od′). the tree itself.

sas·tru·ga (sas′trə gə, sä′strə-, sa stro͞o′-, sä-), *n., pl.* **-gi** (-gē). Usually, **sastrugi.** ridges of snow formed on the surface of a snowfield by the action of the wind. Also, **zastruga.** [< Russ *zastruga* wind-made furrow]

sat[1] (sat), *v.* a pt. and pp. of **sit.**

sat[2] (sut), *n. Hinduism.* **1.** (in Vedic mythology) the realm of existence, populated by men and gods. Cf. **Asat. 2.** reality. Cf. **Sat-cit-ananda.** [< Skt: lit., being]

SAT, Scholastic Aptitude Test.

Sat., 1. Saturday. **2.** Saturn.

Sa·tan (sāt′ən), *n.* the chief evil spirit; the great adversary of man; the devil. [OE < L < Gk < Heb: adversary]

sa·tang (sä tang′), *n., pl.* **-tang.** a money of account of Thailand, the 100th part of a baht, equivalent to .0005 of a U.S. dollar: formerly, the hundredth part of a tical. [< Siamese *satāŋ*]

sa·tan·ic (sā tan′ik, sə-), *adj.* **1.** of Satan. **2.** characteristic of or befitting Satan; extremely wicked; devillike, diabolical. Also, **sa·tan′i·cal.** [< eccl. Gk *satanikós.* See SATAN, -IC] **—sa·tan′i·cal·ly,** *adv.* **—sa·tan′i·cal·ness,** *n.*

—Syn. 2. evil, devilish, hellish, fiendish, infernal. **—Ant. 2.** angelic, heavenly.

Sa·tan·ism (sāt′əniz′əm), *n.* **1.** the worship of Satan or the powers of evil. **2.** a travesty of Christian rites in which Satan is worshiped. **3.** diabolical or satanic disposition, behavior, or action. [SATAN + -ISM] **—Sa′tan·ist,** *n.*

satch·el (sach′əl), *n.* a small bag, sometimes with a shoulder strap. [ME *sachel* < OF < L *saccell(us),* equiv. to *sacc(us)* SAC + *-ellus* dim. suffix] **—satch′eled,** *adj.*

Sat-cit-a·nan·da (sut′chit′ä nun′də), *n. Hinduism.* reality, seen through the discovery of Brahman as *sat* or ultimate being, *cit* or pure consciousness, and *ananda* or perfect bliss. Also, **Saccidananda, Sat′-chit′-a·nan′da.**

sate[1] (sāt), *v.t.,* **sat·ed, sat·ing. 1.** to satisfy (any appetite or desire) fully. **2.** to surfeit; glut. [var. of obs. *sade* to satiate, OE *sad(ian),* perh. by contamination with L *sat* enough; see SAD]

—Syn. 1. satiate, fill. **2.** gorge, stuff.

sate[2] (sat, sāt), *v. Archaic.* pt. and pp. of **sit.**

sa·teen (sa tēn′), *n.* a cotton or linen fabric simulating satin in weave and gloss. [var. of SATIN, by assoc. with *velveteen*]

sat·el·lite (sat′əlīt′), *n.* **1.** *Astron.* a body that revolves around a planet; a moon. **2.** an attendant or follower of another person, often subservient or obsequious in manner. **3.** anything that depends on, accompanies, or serves something else. **4.** a country under the domination or influence of another. **5.** a man-made device designed to be launched from the earth into orbit around a planet or the sun. **—adj.** Also, **sat·el·lit·ic** (sat′əlit′ik). **6.** of, pertaining to, or constituting a satellite: *the nation's new satellite program.* **7.** subordinate to another authority, outside power, or the like: *summoned to a conference of satellite nations.* [< L *satellit-* (s. of *satelles*) attendant, member of bodyguard or retinue < Etr] **—sat′el·lit′ed,** *adj.*

—Syn. 2. lackey, parasite, sycophant, toady, flunky. **3.** follower, supporter, companion, associate.

sat·el·loid (sat′əloid′), *n. Rocketry.* a low-altitude, artificial satellite using engines with small thrust to maintain its orbit. [SATELL(ITE) + -OID]

sa·tem (sä′təm), *adj.* belonging to or consisting of those branches of the Indo-European family in which alveolar or palatal fricatives, as the sounds (s) or (sh), developed in ancient times from Proto-Indo-European palatal stops: the satem branches are Indo-Iranian, Armenian, Slavic, Baltic, and Albanian. Cf. **centum**[2]. [< Av *satem* hundred]

sa·ti·a·ble (sā′shē ə bəl), *adj.* capable of being satiated. [SATI(ATE) + -ABLE] **—sa′ti·a·bil′i·ty, sa′ti·a·ble·ness,** *n.* **—sa′ti·a·bly,** *adv.*

sa·ti·ate (*v.* sā′shē āt′; *adj.* sā′shē it, -āt′), *v.,* **-at·ed, -at·ing,** *adj.* **—v.t. 1.** to supply with anything to excess, so as to disgust or weary; surfeit. **2.** to satisfy to the full; sate. **—adj. 3.** *Archaic.* satiated. [< L *satiāt(us)* (ptp. of *satiāre* to satisfy), equiv. to *sati-* (see SAD) + *-ātus* -ATE[1]] **—sa′ti·a′tion,** *n.*

—Syn. 1. glut, stuff, gorge.

sa·ti·at·ed (sā′shē ā′tid), *adj.* satisfied, as one's appetite or desire, to the point of boredom. [SATIATE + -ED[2]]

Sa·tie (sä tē′), *n.* **E·rik Al·fred Les·lie** (e rēk′ al fred′ les lē′), 1866–1925, French composer.

sa·ti·e·ty (sə tī′i tē), *n.* the state of being satiated; surfeit. [< L *satie(tās)* sufficiency + -ITY; r. *sacietie* < F *sacieté*]

sat·in (sat′ən), *n.* **1.** See **satin weave. 2.** a fabric in a warp-effect or filling-effect satin weave, as acetate, rayon, nylon, or silk. **3.** a dress or other garment of satin: *She wore her green satin.* **—adj. 4.** of or like satin; smooth; glossy. **5.** made of or covered or decorated with satin: *a satin pillow; She wore her satin dress.* [ME *satyn,* etc. < MF *satin,* prob. < Ar *zaitūnī* of *Zaitun* a city in China where the cloth was made, prob. Tsinkiang] **—sat′in·like′,** *adj.*

sat·i·net (sat′ənet′), *n.* **1.** a low-quality, satin-weave fabric containing cotton. **2.** *Obs.* a thin, light satin. Also, **sat′i·nette′.** [< F; see SATIN, -ET]

sat·in·flow·er (sat′ən flou′ər), *n.* an herb, *Godetia grandiflora,* of California, having short spikes of red flowers with deep red-blotched centers.

sat′in glass′, an American art glassware having colored glass set into indentations in a thickness of opaque glass, the whole covered with clear glass and etched slightly with acid. Also called **mother-of-pearl glass.**

sat·in·leaf (sat′ən lēf′), *n., pl.* **-leaves.** a small, round-headed tree, *Chrysophyllum oliviforme,* of Florida, the Bahamas, and the West Indies, having showy leaves with a coppery underside and small, oval, deep purple fruit. [SATIN + LEAF]

sat·in·pod (sat′ən pod′), *n.* either of two European, cruciferous plants of the genus *Lunaria, L. annua* or *L. rediviva,* cultivated for their shiny flowers and large, round, flat, satiny pods. [SATIN + POD[1]]

sat′in pop′py, a perennial herb, *Meconopsis napaulensis,* of central Asia, having rusty-haired, ornamental foliage and crinkled, satiny, pale-blue flowers.

Sat′in Slip′per, The, a play (1925–28) by Paul Claudel. French, **Le Soulier de Satin.**

sat′in spar′, *Mineral.* a fibrous variety of gypsum having a silky luster, used as a gem.

sat′in stitch′, a stitch used in making an embroidered pattern of closely placed, parallel stitches that resembles satin.

sat′in weave′, one of the basic weave structures in which the filling threads are interlaced with the warp at widely separated intervals, producing the effect of an unbroken surface. Also called **satin.** Cf. **plain weave, twill weave.**

Satin weave

sat·in·wood (sat′ən wo͝od′), *n.* **1.** the satiny wood of an East Indian, meliaceous tree, *Chloroxylon Swietenia,* used esp. for making furniture. **2.** the tree itself. [SATIN + WOOD[1]]

sat·in·y (sat′ənē), *adj.* satinlike; smooth; glossy. [SATIN + -Y[1]]

sat·ire (sat′īər), *n.* **1.** the use of irony, sarcasm, ridicule, or the like, in exposing, denouncing, or deriding vice, folly, etc. **2.** a literary composition, in verse or prose, in which human folly and vice are held up to scorn, derision, or ridicule. **3.** a literary genre comprising such compositions. [< L *satir(a),* var. of *satura* medley, deriv. of *satur* sated, var. of *satis* enough; see SAD]

—Syn. 1. See **irony**[1]. **2, 3.** burlesque, caricature, parody, travesty. SATIRE, LAMPOON refer to literary forms in which vices or follies are ridiculed. SATIRE, the general term, often emphasizes the weakness more than the weak person, and usually implies moral judgment and corrective purpose: *Swift's satire of human pettiness and bestiality.* LAMPOON refers to a form of satire, often political or personal, characterized by the malice or virulence of its attack: *lampoons of the leading political figures.*

sa·tir·i·cal (sə tir′i kəl), *adj.* **1.** of, pertaining to, containing, or characterized by satire; of the nature of satire: *satirical novels.* **2.** indulging in or given to satire: *a satirical poet.* Also, **sa·tir′ic.** [< LL *satiric(us)* (*satir(a)* SATIRE + *-icus* -IC) + -AL[1]] **—sa·tir′i·cal·ly,** *adv.* **—sa·tir′i·cal·ness,** *n.*

—Syn. 1. sardonic, ironical, taunting, bitter, cutting, mordant, biting, acid. See **cynical.**

sat·i·rise (sat′ə rīz′), *v.t.,* **-rised, -ris·ing.** *Chiefly Brit.* satirize. **—sat′i·ris′a·ble,** *adj.* **—sat′i·ri·sa′tion,** *n.* **—sat′i·ris′er,** *n.*

sat·i·rist (sat′ər ist), *n.* **1.** a writer of satires. **2.** one who indulges in satire. [SATIRE + -IST]

sat·i·rize (sat′ə rīz′), *v.t.,* **-rized, -riz·ing.** to attack or ridicule with satire; subject to satire. Also, *esp. Brit.,* **satirise.** [SATIRE + -IZE] **—sat′i·riz′a·ble,** *adj.* **—sat′i·ri·za′tion,** *n.* **—sat′i·riz′er,** *n.*

sat·is·fac·tion (sat′is fak′shən), *n.* **1.** the act of satisfying; fulfillment; gratification. **2.** the state of being satisfied; contentment. **3.** the cause or means of being satisfied. **4.** confident acceptance of something as satisfactory, dependable, true, etc.; assurance. **5.** reparation or compensation, as for a wrong or injury. **6.** the opportunity of repairing a supposed wrong, as by a duel. **7.** payment or discharge, as of a debt or obligation. **8.** *Eccles.* **a.** the act of doing penance or making reparation for venial sin. **b.** the penance or reparation made. [< L *satisfactiōn-* (s. of *satisfactiō*) a doing enough, equiv. to *satisfact(us)* (ptp. of *satisfacere,* equiv. to *satis* enough + *facere* to do) + *-iōn-* -ION; r. ME *satisfaccioun* < AF] **—sat′is·fac′tion·al,** *adj.* **—sat′is·fac′tion·less,** *adj.*

—Syn. 2. gratification, enjoyment, pleasure, comfort. **5.** amends, expiation, atonement, indemnity, indemnification, requital, recompense. **7.** repayment, remuneration. **—Ant. 2.** displeasure, discontent.

sat·is·fac·to·ry (sat′is fak′tə rē), *adj.* **1.** giving or affording satisfaction; fulfilling all demands or requirements: *a satisfactory answer; a satisfactory substitute for meat.* **2.** *Theol.* atoning or expiating. [< ML *satisfactōri(us),* equiv. to L *satisfact(us)* (ptp. of *satisfacere* to do enough) + *-ōrius* -ORY[1]] **—sat′is·fac′to·ri·ly,** *adv.* **—sat′is·fac′to·ri·ness,** *n.*

sat·is·fied (sat′is fīd′), *adj.* **1.** content: *a satisfied look.* **2.** completely paid, as a bill. **3.** convinced, as in an argument: *Their opponents were finally satisfied.* [SATISFY + -ED[2]]

sat·is·fy (sat′is fī′), *v.,* **-fied, -fy·ing. —v.t. 1.** to fulfill the desires, expectations, needs, or demands of (a person, the mind, etc.); to give full contentment to: *The hearty meal satisfied him.* **2.** to put an end to (a desire, want, need, etc.) by sufficient or ample provision: *The hearty meal satisfied his hunger.* **3.** to give assurance to; convince: *to satisfy oneself by investigation.* **4.** to answer sufficiently, as an objection. **5.** to solve or dispel, as a doubt. **6.** to discharge fully (a debt, obligation, etc.). **7.** to make reparation to or for: *to satisfy an offended person; to satisfy a wrong.* **8.** to pay (a creditor). **9.** *Math.* **a.** to fulfill the requirements or conditions of: *to satisfy a theorem.* **b.** (of a value of an unknown) to change (an equation) into an identity when substituted for the unknown: $x = 2$ *satisfies* $3x = 6$. **—v.i. 10.** to give satisfaction. [ME *satisfi(en)* < MF *satisfie(r)* < VL **satisficāre* (r. L *satisfacere* to do enough); see -FY] **—sat′is·fi′a·ble,** *adj.* **—sat′is·fi′er,** *n.* **—sat′is·fy′ing·ly,** *adv.* **—sat′is·fy′ing·ness,** *n.*

—Syn. 1. gratify, appease, pacify, please. SATISFY, CONTENT refer to meeting one's desires or wishes. To SATISFY is to meet to the full one's wants, expectations, etc.: *to satisfy a desire to travel.* To CONTENT is to give enough to keep one from being disposed to find fault or complain: *to content oneself with a moderate meal.* **3.** persuade.

sa·to·ri (sə tôr′ē, -tōr′ē), *n. Zen.* sudden enlightenment. [< Jap]

sa·trap (sā′trap, sa′-), *n.* **1.** a governor of a province under the ancient Persian monarchy. **2.** a subordinate ruler, often a despotic one. [ME < L *satrap(a)* < Gk *satrápēs* < OPers *xshathra-pāvan-* country-protector]

sa·trap·y (sā′trə pē, sa′-), *n., pl.* **-trap·ies.** the province or jurisdiction of a satrap. [< L *satrapia* < Gk *satrapeía,* equiv. to *satrápē(s)* SATRAP + *-ia* -Y[3]]

Sa·tsu·ma (sä′tso͞o mä′), *n.* a former province on S Kyushu, in SW Japan: famous for its porcelain ware.

satt·va (sut′və), *n. Hinduism.* See under **guna.** [< Skt: state of being, deriv. of *sat* SAT[2]]

satt·vic (sät′vik), *adj.* characterized by sattva: having a serene, harmonious, balanced mind or attitude. [SATTV(A) + -IC]

Sa·tu-Ma·re (sä′to͞o mä′re), *n.* a city in NW Rumania. 64,060 (est. 1964).

sat·u·ra·ble (sach′ər ə bəl), *adj.* capable of being saturated. [< L *saturābil(is),* equiv. to *saturā(re)* to SATURATE + *-bilis* -BLE] **—sat′u·ra·bil′i·ty,** *n.*

sat·u·rant (sach′ər ənt), *n.* **1.** that which causes saturation. **—adj. 2.** that saturates; saturating. [< L *saturant-* (s. of *saturāns,* prp. of *saturāre* to SATURATE), equiv. to *satur-* (see SAD) + *-ant-* -ANT]

sat·u·rate (*v.* sach′ə rāt′; *adj.* sach′ər it, -ə rāt′), *v.,* **-rat·ed, -rat·ing,** *adj.* **—v.t. 1.** to cause (a substance) to unite with the greatest possible amount of another substance, through solution, chemical combination, or the like. **2.** to charge to the utmost, as with magnetism. **3.** to soak, impregnate, or imbue thoroughly or completely: *to saturate a sponge with water; a town saturated with charm.* **4.** to destroy (a target) completely with bombs and missiles. **5.** to send so many planes over (a target area) that the defensive electronic tracking equipment becomes ineffective. **—adj. 6.** saturated. [< L *saturāt(us)* (ptp. of *saturāre* to fill), equiv. to *satur-* (see SAD) + *-ātus* -ATE[1]] **—sat′u·rat′er, sat′u·ra′tor,** *n.*

—Syn. 3. See **wet.**

sat·u·rat·ed (sach′ə rā′tid), *adj.* **1.** soaked, impregnated, or imbued thoroughly; charged thoroughly or completely; brought to a state of saturation. **2.** (of colors) of maximum chroma or purity; of the highest intensity of hue; free from admixture of white. **3.** *Chem.* **a.** (of a solution) containing the maximum amount of solute capable of being dissolved under given conditions. **b.** (of an organic compound) containing no double or triple bonds; having each single bond attached to an atom or group. **c.** (of an inorganic compound) having no free valence electrons. [SATURATE + -ED[2]]

sat′urated liq′uid, *Thermodynamics.* a liquid at a temperature and pressure such that any decrease in pressure without change in temperature causes the liquid to boil. Cf. **saturated vapor.**

sat′urated va′por, *Thermodynamics.* a vapor confined at a temperature and pressure such that any compression of its volume at constant temperature causes the vapor to condense to liquid at a rate sufficient to maintain a constant pressure. Cf. **saturated liquid.**

sat·u·ra·tion (sach′ə rā′shən), *n.* **1.** the act or process of saturating. **2.** the state of being saturated. **3.** *Meteorol.* a condition in the atmosphere corresponding to 100 percent relative humidity. **4.** the degree of chroma or purity of a color; the degree of freedom from admixture with white. [< L *saturātiōn-* (s. of *saturātiō*) a filling, equiv. to *saturāt(us)* (see SATURATE) + *-iōn* -ION]

satura′tion bomb′ing, intense area bombing intended to destroy everything in the target area.

satura′tion lev′el. See **carrying capacity.**

sat·ura′tion point′, the point at which a substance will receive no more of another substance in solution, chemical combination, etc.

sat·u·ra·tor (sach′ə rā′tər), *n.* *Chem.* a device for saturating an inert gas with the vapor of a volatile liquid by slowly bubbling the gas through it. [SATUR-ATE + -OR[2]]

Sat·ur·day (sat′ər dē, -dā′), *n.* the seventh day of the week, following Friday. [OE *Sæter(nes)dæg*, trans. of L *Sāturnī diēs* Saturn's day; c. D *zaterdag*, LG *saterdag*]

Sat′urday-night′ spe′cial, *Slang.* a cheap, small-caliber handgun that is easily obtainable and concealable.

Sat·ur·days (sat′ər dēz, -dāz′), *adv.* on Saturdays: *Saturdays we go to the movies.*

Sat·urn (sat′ərn), *n.* **1.** an ancient Roman god of agriculture, the consort of Ops, believed to have ruled the earth during an age of happiness and virtue, identified with the Greek god Cronus. **2.** *Astron.* the planet sixth in order from the sun, having a diameter of 72,000 miles, a mean distance from the sun of 886,000,000 miles, a period of revolution of 29.5 years, and 10 satellites. It is the second largest planet in the solar system, encompassed by a series of thin, flat rings composed of small particles of matter, possibly ice. **3.** *Alchemy.* the metal lead. **4.** *U.S.* a space-vehicle booster developing from 2,000,000 to 9,000,000 pounds of thrust for launching satellites, probes, and spaceships.

Sat·ur·na·li·a (sat′ər nā′lē ə, -nāl′yə), *n., pl.* **-li·a, -li·as. 1.** (*sometimes construed as pl.*) the festival of Saturn, celebrated in December in ancient Rome and observed as a time of general feasting and unrestrained merrymaking. **2.** (*l.c.*) any period of unrestrained revelry. [< L, equiv. to *Sāturn(us)* SATURN + *-ālia*, neut. pl. of *-ālis* -AL[1]] —**Sat′ur·na′li·an,** *adj.*

Sa·tur·ni·an (sə tûr′nē ən), *adj.* **1.** of or pertaining to the planet Saturn. **2.** of or pertaining to the god Saturn, whose reign is referred to as the "golden age." **3.** prosperous, happy, or peaceful: *Saturnian days.* [< L *sāturni(us)* of Saturn + -AN]

sa·tur·ni·id (sə tûr′nē id), *n.* **1.** any of several large, brightly colored moths of the family *Saturniidae*, comprising the giant silkworm moths. —*adj.* **2.** belonging or pertaining to the family *Saturniidae*. [< NL *Sāturniid(ae)* name of the family. See SATURNIAN, -ID[2]]

sat·ur·nine (sat′ər nīn′), *adj.* **1.** having or showing a sluggish, gloomy temperament; gloomy; taciturn. **2.** suffering from lead poisoning, as a person. **3.** due to absorption of lead, as bodily disorders. [ME; see SATURN, -INE[1]] —**sat′ur·nine′ly,** *adv.* —**sat′ur·nine′ness, sat·ur·nin·i·ty** (sat′ər nin′i tē), *n.*

sat·ur·nism (sat′ər niz′əm), *n.* *Pathol.* See **lead poisoning** (def. 1b). [< ML *Sāturn(us)* lead + -ISM; in alchemy the planet was thought to have leadlike properties]

Sat·ya·gra·ha (sut′yə gru′hə, sət yä′grə-), *n.* (in India) the policy of passive resistance inaugurated by Mohandas Gandhi in 1919 as a method of gaining political and social reforms. [< Hindi < Skt, equiv. to *satyā* truth + *graha* grasping]

sat·ya·lo·ka (sut′yə lō′kə), *n.* *Hindu Myth.* the highest heaven, where Brahma and Sarasvati live with Brahmins. [< Skt, equiv. to *satyā* truth + *loka* shining]

Sat′ya Yu′ga (sut′yə yŏŏg′ə), *Hinduism.* the first and best of the four Yugas. Also called **Krita Yuga.**

sa·tyr (sā′tər, sat′ər), *n.* **1.** *Class. Myth.* one of a class of woodland deities, attendant on Bacchus, represented as part human and part goat and noted for riotousness and lasciviousness. **2.** a lascivious man; lecher. **3.** a man who has satyriasis. **4.** Also, **sa′tyr but′terfly.** any of several butterflies of the family *Satyridae*, having gray or brown wings marked with eyespots. [ME < L *satyr(us)* < Gk *sátyros*] —**sa·tyr·ic** (sə tir′ik), **sa·tyr′i·cal,** *adj.* —**sa′tyr·like′,** *adj.*

sa·ty·ri·a·sis (sā′tə rī′ə sis, sat′ə-), *n.* *Pathol.* abnormal, uncontrollable sexual desire in men. Also called **sa·tyr·o·ma·ni·a** (sā′tə rō mā′nē ə, sat′ə-). [< NL < Gk. See SATYR, -IASIS]

Sa·tyr·i·con (sa tir′i kon′), *n.* a satirical novel, interspersed with verse, written in the 1st century A.D. by Petronius, extant in fragments.

sa·tyr·o·ma·ni·ac (sā′tə rō mā′nē ak′, sat′ə-), *n.* a lascivious man; lecher. [< Gk *sátyro(s)* SATYR + MANIAC]

sa′tyr play′, (in ancient Greek drama) a burlesque or ribald drama having a chorus of satyrs, usually written by a poet to follow and form a group with the trilogy of his tragedies presented at the Dionysian festival.

Sau (sou), *n.* German name of **Sava.**

sauce (sôs), *n., v.,* **sauced, sauc·ing.** —*n.* **1.** any preparation, usually liquid or semiliquid, eaten as a gravy or as a relish accompanying food. **2.** something that adds special piquance or zest. **3.** *U.S.* stewed fruit: *cranberry sauce.* **4.** *Informal.* sauciness. **5.** *Dial.* garden vegetables eaten with meat. **6.** *Slang.* hard liquor (usually prec. by *the*): *His health has improved since he's been off the sauce.* —*v.t.* **7.** to dress or prepare with sauce; season: *meat well sauced.* **8.** to give special piquance or zest to. **9.** to make agreeable or less harsh. **10.** *Informal.* to speak impertinently or saucily to. [ME < MF < LL *salsa*, n. use of fem. of L *salsus* salted, ptp. of *sallere* to salt] —**sauce′less,** *adj.*

sauce·boat (sôs′bōt′), *n.* a low, boat-shaped container for serving sauce or gravy, typically having a handle at one end and a long, wide lip at the other end. [SAUCE + BOAT]

sauce·box (sôs′boks′), *n.* *Informal.* a saucy person. [SAUCE + BOX[1]]

sauce es·pagn·ole (sôs′ es′pən yōl′, -pan-; *Fr.* sō ses PA nyôl′). See **brown sauce.** [< F: Spanish sauce]

sauce financière (sôs′ fē näN syer′), financière (def. 2).

sauce·pan (sôs′pan′), *n.* a metal container of moderate depth, usually having a long handle and sometimes a cover, for stewing, boiling, etc. [SAUCE + PAN[1]]

sau·cer (sô′sər), *n.* **1.** a small, round, shallow dish to hold a cup. **2.** any similar dish, plate, or the like. [ME < OF *saussier.* See SAUCE, -ER[2]]

sau′cer dome′, a dome having the form of a sphere, with the center well below the springing line; a shallow dome, as in Roman or Byzantine architecture.

sau′cer lake′, a saucerlike lake formed between two adjacent rivers from the overflow of one or both.

sauce su·prême (sôs′ sə prēm′, -prām′, sōō-; *Fr.* sōs SY PREM′), suprême (def. 1).

sauch (soukн, sôкн, säкн), *n.* *Scot. and North Eng.* saugh.

sau·cy (sô′sē), *adj.,* **-ci·er, -ci·est. 1.** impertinent; insolent: *a saucy remark; a saucy child.* **2.** pert; boldly smart: *a saucy little hat for Easter.* [SAUCE + -Y[1]] —**sau′ci·ly,** *adv.* —**sau′ci·ness,** *n.*
—**Syn. 1.** rude, impudent, fresh, brazen. **2.** jaunty.

Sa·ud (sä ōōd′), *n.* (*Saud ibn Abdul-Aziz*), 1901?–69, king of Saudi Arabia 1953–64 (son of ibn-Saud and brother of Faisal).

Sa·u′di Ara′bia (sä-ōō′dē, sou′dē, sô′-), a kingdom in N and central Arabia, including Hejaz, Nejd, and dependencies. 6,600,000 (est. 1963); ab. 600,000 sq. mi. *Capitals:* Mecca and Riyadh.

sau·er·bra·ten (sour′brät′ən, sou′ər-; *Ger.* zou′əʀ bʀät′ən), *n.* a pot roast of beef, marinated before cooking in a mixture of vinegar, sugar, and seasonings. [< G, equiv. to *sauer* sour + *Braten* roast]

sauer·kraut (sour′krout′, sou′ər-), *n.* cabbage cut fine, salted, and allowed to ferment until sour. [< G, equiv. to *sauer* sour + *Kraut* greens]

sau·ger (sô′gər), *n.* a fresh-water, North American pikeperch, *Stizostedion canadense.* Also called **sand pike.** [?]

Sau·ger·ties (sô′gər tēz), *n.* a town in SE New York. 4286 (1960).

saugh (soukн, sôкн, säкн), *n.* *Scot. and North Eng.* sallow[2]. Also, **sauch.** [ME; OE *salh* SALLOW[2]]

Sau·gus (sô′gəs), *n.* a town in E Massachusetts, near Boston. 20,666 (1960).

Sauk (sôk), *n., pl.* **Sauks,** (*esp. collectively*) **Sauk.** Sac.

Sauk′ Cen′tre, a town in central Minnesota. 3573 (1960).

Sauk′ Rap′ids, a town in central Minnesota. 4038 (1960).

Saul (sôl), *n.* **1.** the first king of Israel. I Sam. 9. **2.** Also called **Saul′ of Tar′sus.** the original name of the apostle Paul. Acts 9:1–30; 22:3. **3.** a boy's given name.

sault (sōō), *n.* a waterfall or rapid. [ME *saut* < OF < L *salt(us)* leap. See SALT[2]]

Sault Ste. Ma·rie (sōō′ sānt′ mə rē′), **1.** the rapids of the St. Marys River, between NE Michigan and Ontario, Canada. **2.** a city in S Ontario, in S Canada, near these rapids. 43,088 (1961). **3.** a city opposite it, in NE Michigan. 18,722 (1960). Also, **Sault′ Sainte′ Ma·rie′.**

Sault Ste. Marie Ca·nals, two ship canals, one in Canada and the other in Michigan, N and S of Sault Ste. Marie rapids and connecting Lakes Superior and Huron. 1½ mi. long. Also, **Sault′ Sainte′ Marie′ Canals′, Soo Canals.**

sau·na (sou′nä, -nə, sô′-), *n.* **1.** a Finnish bath in which the bather is subjected to steam, usually produced by water thrown on red-hot stones, and to light strokings with switches made of cedar or birch leaves. **2.** a bathhouse equipped for such a bath. [< Finn]

saun·cy (son′sē, sôn′sē), *adj.,* **-ci·er, -ci·est.** *Scot. and North Eng., Irish Eng.* sonsy.

Saun·der (sôn′dər), *n.* a walled plain in the fourth quadrant of the face of the moon: about 25 miles in diameter.

Saun·dra (sôn′drə, sän′-), *n.* a girl's given name. Also, **Sandra, Sondra.**

saun·ter (sôn′tər, sän′-), *v.i.* **1.** to walk with a leisurely gait; stroll: *sauntering through the woods.* —*n.* **2.** a leisurely walk or ramble; stroll. **3.** a leisurely gait. [late ME *santre* to muse] —**saun′ter·er,** *n.*
—**Syn. 1–3.** amble, ramble.

-saur, var. of **sauro-,** occurring as final element in compound words: *dinosaur.*

Sau·rash·tra (sou räsh′trə), *n.* a former state in W India, comprising most of Kathiawar peninsula: now part of Gujarat state. 21,062 sq. mi.

sau·rel (sôr′əl), *n.* any of several marine carangid fishes of the genus *Trachurus.* [< F, equiv. to *saur-* (< LL *saur(us)* horse mackerel < Gk *saûros* sea fish) + *-el* n. suffix]

sau·ri·an (sôr′ē ən), *adj.* **1.** belonging or pertaining to the *Sauria*, a group of reptiles originally including the lizards, crocodiles, and several extinct forms but now technically restricted to the lizards. **2.** resembling a lizard. —*n.* **3.** a saurian animal, as a dinosaur or lizard. [< NL *Sauri(a)* an order of reptiles + -AN; see SAURO-]

-saurian, a combination of **-saur** and **-ian,** used in the formation of adjectives from nouns in **-saur:** *brontosaurian.*

-sauridae, a combination of **-saur** and **-idae,** used to indicate the family in zoological classification.

saur·is·chi·an (sô ris′kē ən), *n.* **1.** any herbivorous or carnivorous dinosaur of the order *Saurischia*, having a three-pronged pelvis resembling that of a crocodile. Cf. **ornithischian.** —*adj.* **2.** belonging or pertaining to the *Saurischia.* [< NL *Saurischi(a)* name of the order (*Saur(ia)* (see SAURO-) + L *-ischi(um)* ISCHIUM) + -AN]

sauro-, a learned borrowing from Greek meaning "lizard," used in the formation of technical terms (*sauropod*); specialized in zoological terminology to mean a group of extinct reptiles. Also, **-saur, -saurus;** *esp. before a vowel,* **saur-.** Cf. **-saurian, -sauridae.** [comb. form of Gk *saûros*]

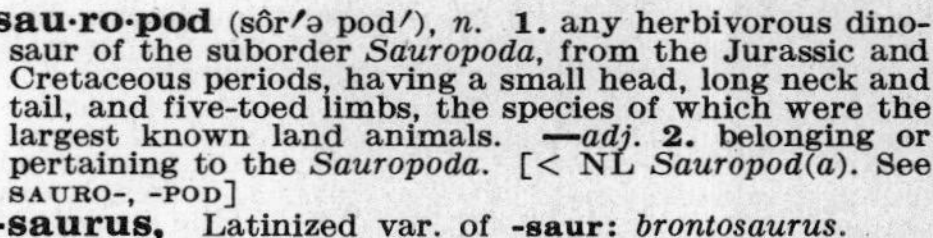

sau·ro·pod (sôr′ə pod′), *n.* **1.** any herbivorous dinosaur of the suborder *Sauropoda*, from the Jurassic and Cretaceous periods, having a small head, long neck and tail, and five-toed limbs, the species of which were the largest known land animals. —*adj.* **2.** belonging or pertaining to the *Sauropoda.* [< NL *Sauropod(a).* See SAURO-, -POD]

-saurus, Latinized var. of **-saur:** *brontosaurus.*

sau·ry (sô′rē), *n., pl.* **-ries. 1.** a sharp-snouted fish, *Scomberesox saurus*, found in the Atlantic Ocean. **2.** any of various related fishes. [< NL *saur(us)* + -Y[2]. See SAUREL]

sau·sage (sô′sij), *n.* **1.** minced pork, beef, or other meats, often combined, together with various added ingredients and seasonings, usually stuffed into a prepared intestine or other casing and often made in links. **2.** *Aeron.* a sausage-shaped observation balloon, formerly used in warfare. [ME *sausige* < dial. OF *saussiche* < LL *salsīcia*, neut. pl. of L *salsīcius* seasoned with salt. See SAUCE, -ITIOUS] —**sau′sage·like′,** *adj.*

sau′sage curl′, a lock of hair formed into a curl resembling a sausage in shape.

sau′sage turn′ing, *Furniture.* turning of members to resemble a continuous row of balls or sausages flatted at the ends.

Sau·sa·li·to (sô′sə lē′tō), *n.* a town in W California. 5331 (1960).

Saus·sure (*Fr.* sō syʀ′ *for 1;* sô sŏŏr′, sō- *for 2*), *n.* **1. Fer·di·nand de** (*Fr.* feʀ dē näN′ də), 1857–1913, Swiss linguist and Sanskrit scholar. **2.** a walled plain in the third quadrant of the face of the moon: about 30 miles in diameter.

saus·su·rite (sô′sə rīt′), *n.* a mineral aggregate of albite, zoisite, and other calcium aluminum silicates, formed by alteration of plagioclase feldspars in igneous rocks. [named after H. B. de *Saussure* (1740–99), Swiss geologist and physicist; see -ITE[1]] —**saus·su·rit·ic** (sô′sə rit′ik), *adj.*

saut de basque (*Fr.* sō də bask′), *pl.* **sauts de basque** (*Fr.* sō də bask′), *Ballet.* a jump in which the dancer turns in the air while keeping the foot of one leg drawn up to the knee of the other. [< F: lit., Basque jump]

sau·té (sō tā′, sô-), *adj., v.,* **-téed** (-tād′), **-té·ing** (-tā′ing), *n.* —*adj.* **1.** cooked or browned in a pan containing a small quantity of butter, oil, or other fat. —*v.t.* **2.** to cook in a small amount of fat; pan-fry. —*n.* **3.** a dish of sautéed food. [< F, ptp. of *sauter* < L *saltāre*, freq. of *salīre* to jump]

Sau·ternes (sō tûrn′, sô-; *Fr.* sō teʀn′), *n.* **1.** Also, **sau·terne′.** a rich, sweet white table wine of France. **2.** the district near Bordeaux producing this wine.

sau·til·lé (*Fr.* sō tē yā′), *adj., adv.* *Music.* saltando. [< F, ptp. of *sautiller* to jump about, freq. of *sauter* to jump. See SAUTÉ]

sau·toir (sō twär′, sô-; *Fr.* sō twaʀ′), *n., pl.* **-toirs** (-twärz′; *Fr.* -twaʀ′). **1.** a ribbon, chain, scarf, or the like, tied around the neck in such a manner that the ends cross over each other. **2.** a chain to which a pendant is attached, worn around the neck. [< F; see SALTIRE]

sauve qui peut (sōv kē pœ′), *French.* a complete and overwhelming disorderly rout; stampede. [lit: let him save (himself) who can]

Sa·va (sä′vä), *n.* a river flowing E from W Slovenia, through Croatia to the Danube at Belgrade, Yugoslavia. 450 mi. long. Also, **Save.** German, **Sau.**

sav·age (sav′ij), *adj.* **1.** fierce, ferocious, or cruel; untamed: *savage beasts.* **2.** uncivilized; barbarous: *savage tribes.* **3.** enraged or furiously angry, as a person. **4.** unpolished; rude: *savage manners.* **5.** wild or rugged, as country or scenery: *savage wilderness.* **6.** *Archaic.* uncultivated; growing wild. —*n.* **7.** an uncivilized human being. **8.** a fierce, brutal, or cruel person. **9.** a rude, boorish person. [ME *savage, sauvage* < MF *sauvage, salvage* < ML *salvatic(us)*, r. L *silvāticus*, equiv. to *silv(a)* woods + *-āticus* adj. suffix] —**sav′age·ly,** *adv.* —**sav′age·ness,** *n.*
—**Syn. 1.** wild, feral, fell; bloodthirsty. See **cruel. 2.** wild. **3.** infuriated. **5.** rough, uncultivated. **9.** churl, oaf. —**Ant. 1.** mild. **2, 4.** cultured. **5.** cultivated.

Sav·age (sav′ij), *n.* **1. Michael Joseph,** 1872–1940, New Zealand statesman and labor leader: prime minister 1935–40. **2. Richard,** 1697?–1743, English poet.

Sav′age Is′land, Niue.

sav·age·ry (sav′ij rē), *n., pl.* **-ries. 1.** an uncivilized or barbaric state or condition; barbarity. **2.** savage nature, disposition, conduct, or act. [SAVAGE + -RY]

Sav′age's Sta′tion, a locality in E Virginia, near Richmond: Civil War battle in 1862.

sav·ag·ism (sav′ə jiz′əm), *n.* barbarism; savagery. [SAVAGE + -ISM]

Sa·vai·i (sä vī′ē), *n.* an island in Western Samoa: largest of the Samoa group. 31,642 (1961); 703 sq. mi.

sa·van·na (sə van′ə), *n.* **1.** a plain characterized by coarse grasses and scattered tree growth, esp. on the margins of the tropics where the rainfall is seasonal, as in the Sudan of Africa. **2.** grassland region with scattered trees, grading into either open plain or woodland, usually in subtropical or tropical regions. Also, **sa·van′nah.** [earlier *zavana* < Sp < Taino *zabana*]

Sa·van·na (sə van′ə), *n.* a town in NW Illinois. 4950 (1960).

Sa·van·nah (sə van′ə), *n.* **1.** a seaport in E Georgia, near the mouth of the Savannah River. 149,245 (1960). **2.** a river flowing SE from E Georgia along most of the boundary between Georgia and South Carolina and into the Atlantic. 314 mi. long. **3.** a town in SW Tennessee. 4315 (1960).

Savan′nah spar′row, a North American sparrow, *Passerculus sandwichensis*, having brown and white plumage with a yellow stripe over each eye.

Sa·van·na·khet (sä wän nä ket′), *n.* a city in S Laos. 15,000 (est. 1957).

sa·vant (sa vänt′, sav′ənt; *Fr.* sa väN′), *n., pl.* **sa·vants** (sa vänts′, sav′ənts; *Fr.* sa väN′). a man of profound or extensive learning. [< F: man of learning, scholar, old prp. of *savoir* to know < L *sapere* to be wise; see SAPIENT]

sav·a·rin (sav′ə rin), *n.* a spongelike cake leavened with yeast, baked in a ring mold, and often soaked with a rum syrup. [< F, named after Anthelme Brillat-*Savarin* (d. 1826), French politician and gourmet]

sa·vate (sə vat′), *n.* a sport resembling boxing but permitting blows to be delivered with the feet as well as the hands. [< F: lit., old shoe. See SABOT]

save[1] (sāv), *v.,* **saved, sav·ing,** *n.* —*v.t.* **1.** to rescue from danger or possible harm, injury, or loss: *to save someone from drowning.* **2.** to keep safe, intact, or unhurt; safeguard: *God save the king.* **3.** to keep from being lost: *to save the game.* **4.** to avoid the spending, consumption, or waste of: *to save fuel with this new stove.* **5.** to set apart, reserve, or lay by: *to save money.* **6.** to treat carefully in order to reduce wear, fatigue, etc.: *to save one's eyes by reading under proper light.* **7.** to prevent the occurrence, use, or necessity of; obviate: *A stitch in time saves nine.* **8.** *Theol.* to deliver from the power and consequences of sin. **9.** *Sports.* to stop (a ball or puck) from entering one's goal. —*v.i.* **10.** to lay up money as the result of economy or thrift. **11.** to be economical in expenditure. **12.** to preserve something from harm, injury, loss, etc. **13.** to admit of being kept without spoiling, as food. **14.** *Sports.* to stop a ball or puck from entering one's goal. —*n.* **15.** an act or instance of saving, esp. in sports. [ME *sa(u)ve(n)* < OF *sauve(r)* < LL (esp. eccl.) *salvāre* to save; see SAFE] —**sav′a·ble, save′a·ble,** *adj.* —**sav′a·ble·ness, save′a·ble·ness,** *n.* —**sav′er,** *n.*
—**Syn. 1.** salvage. **5.** store up, husband. **5, 10.** economize, hoard.

save[2] (sāv), *prep.* **1.** except; but: *All the guests had left save one or two.* —*conj.* **2.** except; but: *He would have gone, save that he had no means.* [ME; var. of SAFE]
—**Syn. 1.** See **except**[1].

Save (*Fr.* sav), *n.* Sava.

save-all (sāv′ôl′), *n.* **1.** a means, contrivance, or receptacle for preventing loss or waste. **2.** *Chiefly Dial.* overalls. **3.** *Naut.* **a.** a net secured between a pier and a ship, beneath cargo being transferred from one to the other. **b.** a sail for utilizing wind spilled from the regular sails of a vessel, as the water sail of a schooner: used in very light winds. [n. use of v. phrase *save all*]

sav·e·loy (sav′ə loi′), *n.* *Chiefly Brit.* a highly seasoned, dried sausage. [prob. < F *cervelas,* MF *cervelat* < It *cervellat(o)* Milanese sausage, orig. containing pig's brains, equiv. to *cervell(o)* brain (see CEREBELLUM) + *-ato* -ATE[1]]

sav·in (sav′in), *n.* **1.** a juniper, *Juniperus Sabina,* of Europe and Asia. **2.** the drug derived from the dried tops of this plant, formerly used in treating amenorrhea. **3.** See **red cedar** (def. 1). Also, **sav′ine.** [ME; OE *safine, savene* << L *(herba) Sabina* Sabine (herb)]

sav·ing (sā′ving), *adj.* **1.** tending or serving to save; rescuing; preserving. **2.** compensating; redeeming: *a saving sense of humor; a dull person with no saving characteristics.* **3.** thrifty; economical: *a saving housekeeper.* **4.** making a reservation: *a saving clause.* —*n.* **5.** economy in expenditure, outlay, use, etc. **6.** a reduction or lessening of expenditure or outlay: *a saving of 10 percent.* **7.** something that is saved. **8. savings,** sums of money saved by economy and laid away. **9.** *Law.* a reservation or exception. —*prep.* **10.** except: *Nothing remains saving these ruins.* **11.** with all due respect to or for: *saving your presence.* —*conj.* **12.** except; save. [ME; see SAVE[1], -ING[2], -ING[1]] —**sav′ing·ly,** *adv.*

sav′ing grace′, a quality that makes up for other generally negative characteristics: *He was born a misfit whose saving grace was his boundless generosity.*

sav′ings account′, a bank account on which interest is paid and for which a bankbook is used to record deposits, withdrawals, and interest payments. Cf. **checking account.**

sav′ings and loan′ associa′tion, *U.S.* a cooperative savings institution, chartered and regulated by a State or the federal government, that receives deposits in exchange for shares of ownership and invests its funds chiefly in loans secured by first mortgages on homes. Also called **building and loan association, cooperative bank.**

sav′ings bank′, a bank that receives time deposits only and pays interest to its depositors.

sav′ings bond′, a U.S. government bond with principal amounts up to $10,000.

sav·ior (sāv′yər), *n.* Also, *esp. Brit.,* **sav′iour. 1.** one who saves, rescues, or delivers: *the savior of the country.* **2.** (*cap.*) a title of God, esp. of Christ. **3.** (*cap.*) *Class. Myth.* an epithet of Artemis. [ME *saveour,* etc. < OF < eccl. L *Salvātor* Redeemer. See SALVATION, -OR[2]] —**sav′ior·hood′;** *esp. Brit.,* **sav′iour·hood′, sav′ior·ship′;** *esp. Brit.,* **sav′iour·ship′,** *n.*

Sa·voie (SA VWA′), *n.* **1.** a department in E France. 266,678 (1962); 2389 sq. mi. *Cap.:* Chambéry. **2.** French name of **Savoy.**

sa·voir-faire (sav′wär fâr′; *Fr.* SA VWAR FER′), *n.* knowledge of just what to do in any situation; tact. [< F: lit., knowing how to do]
—**Syn.** adaptability, adroitness, diplomacy, discernment, skill, ability.

sa·voir-vi·vre (sav′wär vē′vrə, -vēv′; *Fr.* SA VWAR-VĒ′VR[ə]), *n.* knowledge of the world and the ways or usages of polite society. [< F: lit., knowing how to live]

Sa·vo·na (sä vô′nä), *n.* a city in N Italy on the Mediterranean. 72,047 (1961).

Sav·o·na·ro·la (sav′ə nə rō′lə; *It.* sä′vô nä RÔ′lä), *n.* **Gi·ro·la·mo** (ji rol′ə mō′; *It.* jē RÔ′lä mô), 1452–98, Italian monk, reformer, and martyr.

Savonaro′la chair′, *Italian Furniture.* a chair of the Renaissance having a number of transverse pairs of curved legs, crossing beneath the seat and rising to support the arms and back. Cf. **Dante chair.** [after Girolamo SAVONAROLA]

Savonarola chair

sa·vor (sā′vər), *n.* **1.** the quality in a substance that affects the sense of taste or of smell. **2.** a particular taste or smell. **3.** distinctive quality or property. **4.** power to excite or interest. **5.** *Archaic.* repute. —*v.i.* **6.** to have savor, taste, or odor. **7.** to exhibit the peculiar characteristics; smack (often fol. by *of*): *His business practices savor of greed.* —*v.t.* **8.** to give a savor to; season; flavor. **9.** to perceive by taste or smell, esp. with relish: *to savor the garden's odors.* **10.** to give oneself to the enjoyment of: *to savor the best in life.* Also, *esp. Brit.,* **savour.** [ME *savo(u)r* < OF *savour* (n.), *savourer* (v.) < L *sapor* taste, deriv. of *sapere* to taste] —**sa′vor·er,** *n.* —**sa′vor·ing·ly,** *adv.* —**sa′vor·less,** *adj.* —**sa′vor·ous,** *adj.*
—**Syn. 1.** relish, smack; odor, scent, fragrance. See **taste.**

sa·vor·y[1] (sā′və rē), *adj.,* **-vor·i·er, -vor·i·est,** *n.* —*adj.* **1.** pleasant or agreeable in taste or smell: *a savory aroma.* **2.** piquant: *a savory jelly.* **3.** pleasing, attractive, or agreeable. —*n.* **4.** *Brit.* an aromatic, often spicy course or dish served either as an appetizer or as a dessert, as pickled fish or brandied fruit. Also, *esp. Brit.,* **savoury.** [ME *savori* (see SAVOR, -Y[1]); r. ME *savure* < OF *savoure,* ptp. of *savourer* to savor] —**sa′vor·i·ly,** *adv.* —**sa′vor·i·ness,** *n.*

sa·vor·y[2] (sā′və rē), *n., pl.* **-vor·ies.** any aromatic, menthaceous herb of the genus *Satureia,* esp. *S. hortensis* **(summer savory)** and *S. montana* **(winter savory),** used in cookery. [ME *savery,* OE *sætherie, saturēge* < L *saturēia*]

sa·vour (sā′vər), *n., v.i., v.t.* *Chiefly Brit.* savor. —**sa′vour·er,** *n.* —**sa′vour·ing·ly,** *adv.* —**sa′vour·less,** *adj.* —**sa′vour·ous,** *adj.*

sa·vour·y (sā′və rē), *adj.,* **-vour·i·er, -vour·i·est,** *n.* *Chiefly Brit.* savory[1]. —**sa′vour·i·ly,** *adv.* —**sa′vour·i·ness,** *n.*

sa·voy (sə voi′), *n.* a variety of cabbage having a compact head of wrinkled, blistered leaves. [after SAVOY]

Sa·voy (sə voi′), *n.* **1.** a member of the royal house of Italy that ruled from 1861 to 1946. **2.** French, **Savoie.** a region in SE France, adjacent to the Swiss-Italian border: formerly a duchy; later a part of the kingdom of Sardinia; ceded to France, 1860.

Savoy′ Alps′, a mountain range in SE France: a part of the Alps. Highest peak, Mont Blanc, 15,781 ft.

Sa·voy·ard (sə voi′ərd, sav′oi ärd′; *Fr.* SA VWA-YAR′), *n., pl.* **Sa·voy·ards** (sə voi′ərdz, sav′oi ärdz′; *Fr.* SA VWA YAR′), *adj.* —*n.* **1.** a native or inhabitant of Savoy. **2.** one enthusiastic about or connected with Gilbert and Sullivan operas: so called from the Savoy Theater in London, where the operas were first given. —*adj.* **3.** of or pertaining to Savoy. [< F; see SAVOY, -ARD]

sav·vy (sav′ē), *v.,* **-vied, -vy·ing,** *n., adj.,* **-vi·er, -vi·est.** *Slang.* —*v.t., v.i.* **1.** to know; understand. —*n.* **2.** understanding; intelligence; sense. —*adj.* **3.** shrewdly informed; experienced and well-informed: *a trouble-shooting committee of savvy businessmen.* [< Sp *sabe,* pres. 3rd sing. of *saber* to know < L *sapere* to be wise; see SAPIENT]

saw[1] (sô), *n., v.,* **sawed, sawed** or **sawn, saw·ing.** —*n.* **1.** a tool or device for cutting, typically a thin blade of metal with a series of sharp teeth. **2.** any similar tool or device, as a rotating disk, in which a sharp continuous edge replaces the teeth. —*v.t.* **3.** to cut or divide with a saw. **4.** to form by cutting with a saw. **5.** to cut as if using a saw: *to saw the air with one's hands.* **6.** to work (something) from side to side like a saw. —*v.i.* **7.** to use a saw. **8.** to cut with or as with a saw. **9.** to cut as a saw does. [ME *sawe,* OE *saga, sagu;* c. D *zaag,* Icel *sög;* akin to G *Säge* saw, L *secāre* to cut] —**saw′er,** *n.* —**saw′like′,** *adj.*

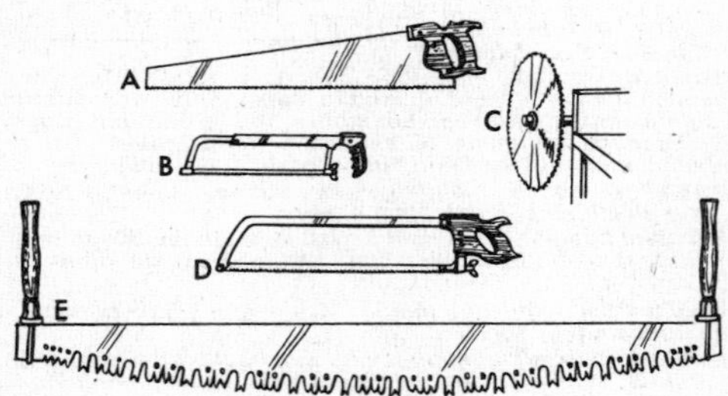

Saws
A, Handsaw; B, Hacksaw; C, Circular saw; D, Butcher's saw; E, Lumberman's saw

saw[2] (sô), *v.* a pt. of **see**[1].

saw[3] (sô), *n.* a sententious saying; maxim; proverb: *He could muster an old saw for almost every occasion.* [ME; OE *sagu;* c. G *Sage,* Icel *saga* SAGA; akin to SAY[1]]

Sa·watch (sə wach′), *n.* a mountain range in central Colorado: part of the Rocky Mountains. Highest peak, Mount Elbert, 14,431 ft. Also, **Saguache.**

saw·bones (sô′bōnz′), *n., pl.* **-bones, -bones·es.** (*construed as sing.*) *Slang.* a surgeon or physician. [SAW[1] + BONE[1] + -S[3]]

saw·buck[1] (sô′buk′), *n.* a sawhorse. [cf. D *zaagbok*]

saw·buck[2] (sô′buk′), *n.* *Slang.* a ten-dollar bill. [so called from Roman numeral X and the crossbars of SAWBUCK[1]]

saw′buck ta′ble, a table that has X-shaped legs.

saw′ cab′bage palm′. See **everglade palm.**

saw·dust (sô′dust′), *n.* small particles of wood produced in sawing. [SAW[1] + DUST] —**saw′dust′ish,** *adj.*

saw′dust trail′, **1.** the road to conversion or rehabilitation, as for a sinner, criminal, etc. **2.** the itinerary of revival meetings. [so called from the sawdust-covered aisles in the temporary constructions put up for the meetings]

saw·dust·y (sô′dus′tē), *adj.* **1.** filled with or suggesting sawdust. **2.** without profound meaning or interest; tiresome. [SAWDUST + -Y[1]]

sawed-off (sôd′ôf′, -of′), *adj.* **1.** sawed off at the end, as a shotgun or broomstick. **2.** *Slang.* smallish; of less than average size or stature.

saw′ fern′, a tropical fern, *Blechnum serrulatum,* having minutely toothed fronds.

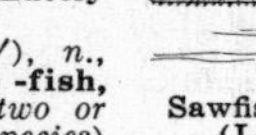

Sawfish, *Pristis pectinatus* (Length 10 to 20 ft.)

saw·fish (sô′fish′), *n., pl.* (*esp. collectively*) **-fish,** (*esp. referring to two or more kinds or species*) **-fish·es.** a large, elongated ray of the genus *Pristis,* found along tropical coasts and lowland rivers, with a bladelike snout bearing strong teeth on each side. [SAW[1] + FISH]

saw·fly (sô′flī′), *n., pl.* **-flies.** any of numerous hymenopterous insects of the family *Tenthredinidae,* the female of which has a sawlike ovipositor for inserting the eggs in the tissues of a host plant. [SAW[1] + FLY[2]]

saw′ grass′, any of various cyperaceous plants, esp. of the genus *Cladium,* having the margins of the leaves toothed like a saw.

saw·horse (sô′hôrs′), *n.* a movable frame or trestle for holding wood being sawed. [SAW[1] + HORSE]

saw′ log′, a log large enough to saw into boards.

saw·mill (sô′mil′), *n.* a place or building in which timber is sawed into planks, boards, etc., by machinery. [SAW[1] + MILL[1]]

sawn (sôn), *v.* a pp. of **saw**[1].

saw′ palmet′to, 1. a shrublike palmetto, *Serenoa repens,* of the southern U.S., having the leafstalks set with spiny teeth. **2.** a shrublike palmetto, *Paurotis Wrightii,* of Florida and the West Indies.

saw′ pit′, a place for pit sawing. Also, **saw′pit′.** [ME *sawpytt.* See SAW[1], PIT[1]]

saw′ set′, an instrument used to bend out slightly the point of each alternate tooth of a saw so that the kerf made by the saw will be wider than its blade.

saw·tim·ber (sô′tim′bər), *n.* trees suitable for sawing into planks, boards, etc. [SAW[1] + TIMBER]

saw·tooth (sô′to͞oth′), *n., pl.* **-teeth** (-tēth′), *adj.* —*n.* **1.** one of the cutting teeth of a saw. **2.** any of the small parallel roof structures forming a sawtooth roof. —*adj.* **3.** having a zigzag profile, similar to that of the cutting edge of a saw; sawtoothed; serrate: *a sawtooth mountain range.* [SAW[1] + TOOTH]

saw-toothed (sô′to͞otht′), *adj.* serrate.

saw′tooth roof′, a roof composed of a series of small parallel roofs of triangular cross section, usually asymmetrical with the shorter slope glazed.

saw′-whet owl′ (sô′hwet′, -wet′), a very small, North American owl, *Aegolius acadicus,* having streaked, brown plumage. [imit.]

saw·yer (sô′yər, soi′ər), *n.* **1.** one who saws, esp. as an occupation. **2.** Also called **saw′yer bee′tle.** any of several long-horned beetles, esp. one of the genus *Monochamus,* the larvae of which bore in the wood of coniferous trees. [ME *sawier,* equiv. to *sawe* SAW[1] + *-ier,* var. of -ER[1]]

sax[1] (saks), *n.* *Informal.* saxophone. [by shortening]

sax[2] (saks), *n.* a short, single-edged sword of ancient Scandinavia. [ME *sexe,* OE *seax, sæx;* c. ON *sax* (Sw, Dan *sax* scissors). See SAW[1]]

Sax., 1. Saxon. **2.** Saxony.

sax·a·tile (sak′sə til), *adj.* living or growing on or among rocks. [< L *saxātile,* neut. of *saxātilis* frequenting rocks, equiv. to *sax(um)* rock + *-āt-* formative suffix + *-ilis* -ILE]

Saxe (saks), *n.* **1. Comte Her·mann Mau·rice de** (ER MAN′ mô RĒS′ də), 1696–1750, French military leader: marshal of France 1744. **2.** French name of **Saxony.**

Saxe-Al·ten·burg (saks′äl′tən bûrg′), *n.* a former duchy in Thuringia in central Germany.

Saxe-Co·burg-Go·tha (saks′kō′bûrg gō′thə), *n.* **1.** a member of a British royal family which ruled from 1901 to 1917. **2. Albert Francis Charles Augustus Emanuel, Prince of.** See **Albert, Prince. 3.** a former duchy in central Germany.

Saxe-Mei·ning·en (saks′mī′ning ən), *n.* a former duchy in Thuringia in central Germany.

Saxe-Wei·mar-Ei·sen·ach (saks′vī′mär ī′zən äKH′), *n.* a former grand duchy in Thuringia in central Germany.

sax·horn (saks′hôrn′), *n.* any of a family of brass instruments close to the cornets and tubas. [named after A. *Sax* (1814–94), a Belgian who invented such instruments]

Saxhorn

sax·ic·o·line (sak sik′ə lin, -līn′), *adj.* *Bot., Zool.* living or growing among rocks. Also, **sax·ic·o·lous** (sak sik′ə ləs). [< NL *Saxicol(a)* (L *saxi-* rock + *-cola* dweller) + -INE[1]]

sax·i·fra·ga·ceous (sak′sə frə gā′shəs), *adj.* belonging to the *Saxifragaceae,* or saxifrage family of plants. [SAXIFRAGE + -ACEOUS]

sax·i·frage (sak′sə frij), *n.* any herb of the genus *Saxifraga,* certain species of which grow wild in the clefts of rocks, other species of which are cultivated for their flowers. [ME < L *saxifrag(a) (herba)* stone-breaking (herb), equiv. to *saxi-* stone + *-fraga,* fem. of *-fragus* brittle; see FRAGILE]

sax′ifrage pink′, a hardy, perennial herb, *Tunica Saxifraga,* of Europe, having thin, wiry stems and pink or lilac-colored flowers. Also called **coat flower, tunic flower.**

Sax·o Gram·mat·i·cus (sak′sō grə mat′ə kəs), c1150–1206?, Danish historian and poet.

Sax·on (sak′sən), *n.* **1.** an Englishman; Britisher. **2.** an Anglo-Saxon. **3.** (not in scholarly use) the Old English language. **4.** the Old English dialects of the regions settled by the Saxons. **5.** a native or inhabitant of Saxony in modern Germany. **6.** a member of a Germanic people in ancient times dwelling near the mouth of the Elbe, a portion of whom invaded and occupied parts of Britain in the 5th and 6th centuries. —*adj.* **7.** English (defs. 1, 2). **8.** of or pertaining to the early

Saxons or their language. **9.** of or pertaining to Saxony in modern Germany. [ME, prob. < L *Saxo, Saxonēs* (pl.) < Gmc; r. OE *Seaxan* (pl.)]

Sax·on (sak′sən), *n.* a town in NW South Carolina. 3917 (1960).

Sax·on·ism (sak′sə niz′əm), *n.* a word or idiom supposedly of English rather than of foreign, as Latin or French, origin. [SAXON + -ISM]

Sax·on·ite (sak′sə nīt′), *n.* a dark, coarse-grained, peridotite rock composed of olivine and orthorhombic pyroxene. [named after SAXONY, where first described; see -ITE[1]]

sax·o·ny (sak′sə nē), *n.* **1.** a fine, three-ply woolen yarn. **2.** a soft-finish, compact fabric, originally of high-grade merino wool from Saxony, for topcoats and overcoats.

Sax·o·ny (sak′sə nē), *n.* **1.** a former state in S East Germany 1947–52. 6561 sq. mi. *Cap.:* Dresden. **2.** a former state of the Weimar Republic in E central Germany. 5788 sq. mi. *Cap.:* Dresden. **3.** a former province in N Germany. 9857 sq. mi. *Cap.:* Magdeburg. **4.** a medieval division of N Germany with varying boundaries: extended at its height from the Rhine to E of the Elbe. German, **Sachsen;** French, **Saxe.** —**Sax·o·ni·an** (sak sō′nē ən), *n., adj.* —**Sax·on·ic** (sak son′ik), **Sax·on′i·cal,** *adj.* —**Sax·on′i·cal·ly,** *adv.*

sax·o·phone (sak′sə fōn′), *n.* a musical wind instrument consisting of a conical, usually brass tube with keys or valves and a mouthpiece with one reed. [*sax* (see SAXHORN) + -O- + -PHONE] —**sax·o·phon·ic** (sak′sə fon′ik), *adj.* —**sax′o·phon′ist,** *n.*

Saxophone

sax·tu·ba (saks′to͞o′bə, -tyo͞o′-), *n.* a large bass saxhorn. [*sax* (see SAXHORN) + TUBA]

say[1] (sā), *v.,* **said, say·ing,** *n.* —*v.t.* **1.** to utter or pronounce; speak: *What did he say? He said "Hello!"* **2.** to express in words; state; declare: *Say what you mean clearly and simply.* **3.** to state as an opinion or judgment: *It is hard to say what is wrong.* **4.** to recite or repeat: *to say one's prayers.* **5.** to assume as a hypothesis or an estimate: *I will probably get there in, say, 10 minutes.* **6.** to report or allege; maintain: *People say he will resign.* **7.** to express (a message, viewpoint, etc.), as through a literary or other artistic medium: *a writer with something to say.* —*v.i.* **8.** to speak; declare; express an opinion. **9. that is to say,** that is what is meant; in other words: *I believe his account of the story, that is to say, I have no reason to doubt it.* —*n.* **10.** what a person says or has to say. **11.** the right or opportunity to speak, decide, or exercise influence: *to have one's say in choosing the candidate.* **12.** a turn to say something: *It is now my say.* **13. have the say,** to have final authority: *The treasurer has the say on a budget of this size.* [ME *sey(en), segg(en),* OE *secgan;* c. D *zeggen,* G *sagen,* Icel *segja;* akin to SAW[3]] —**say′er,** *n.*
—**Syn. 1.** remark, affirm. **4.** iterate, utter. **6.** hold.

say[2] (sā), *v.t., n. Brit. Dial.* assay. [ME *say(en),* aph. var. of *assayen* to ASSAY]

say[3] (sā), *n.* a thin silk or woolen fabric similar to serge, much used in the 16th century. [ME < OF *saie* < L *saga,* pl. of *sagum* woolen cloak < Celt]

Say (sā), *n.* **1. Jean Bap·tiste** (zhäN bȧ tēst′), 1767–1832, French economist. Cf. **Say's law. 2. Thomas,** 1787–1834, U.S. entomologist.

say·a·ble (sā′ə bəl), *adj.* **1.** of the sort that can be said or spoken: *He felt a great deal that was not sayable. Certain of the sounds are sayable only by native speakers.* **2.** capable of being said or stated clearly, effectively, eloquently, etc.: *The speech is as sayable today as when Demosthenes first composed it.* [SAY[1] + -ABLE]

Sa·yan′ Moun′tains (sä yän′), a mountain range in the S Soviet Union in Asia. Highest peak, Munku Sardik, 11,447 ft.

Sa·yão (sä you′, -yä′o͞o; *Port.* sä youN′), *n.* **Bi·dú** (bē′do͞o; *Port.* bi do͞o′), (*Balduina de Oliveira Sayão*), born 1906?, Brazilian soprano.

say′ cast′, coarse wool from the tail of a sheep.

Say·ers (sā′ərz, sârz), *n.* **Dorothy L(eigh),** 1893–1957, English novelist, essayist, and dramatist.

say·est (sā′ist), *v. Archaic.* 2nd pers. sing. of **say.** Also, **sayst** (sāst).

say·ing (sā′ing), *n.* **1.** something said, esp. a proverb or apothegm. **2. go without saying,** to be completely self-evident; be understood: *It goes without saying that you are welcome to visit us at any time.* [ME; see SAY[1], -ING[1]]
—**Syn. 1.** maxim, adage, saw, aphorism.

sa·yo·na·ra (sī′ə när′ə; *Jap.* sä′yô nä′Rä), *interj., n.* farewell; good-by. [< Jap]

Sayre (sâr), *n.* **1.** a town in NE Pennsylvania. 7917 (1960). **2.** a town in W Oklahoma. 2913 (1960).

Sayre·ville (sâr′vil), *n.* a city in central New Jersey. 22,553 (1960).

says (sez), *v.* 3rd. pers. sing. pres. ind. of **say.**

Say's′ law′ (sāz), the principle, propounded by Jean Baptiste Say, that the supply of goods is always matched by the demand for them.

say-so (sā′sō′), *n., pl.* **say-sos. 1.** one's personal statement or assertion. **2.** final authority; directing influence. **3.** an authoritative statement.

say·yid (sā′yid, sä′id), *n.* (in Islamic countries) a supposed descendant of Muhammad through his grandson Husayn, the second son of his daughter Fatima. Also, **said, sa′yid.** [< Ar: lord]

Saz·e·rac (saz′ə rak′), *n.* a cocktail made with bourbon, bitters, absinthe or a substitute, and sugar, stirred or shaken with ice, strained and served with a twist of lemon rind. [?]

Sb, *Chem.* antimony. [< L *stibium*]

sb., substantive.

S.B., 1. Bachelor of Science. [< L *Scientia Baccalaureus*] **2.** South Britain (England and Wales).

s.b., *Baseball.* stolen base; stolen bases.

SBA, See **Small Business Administration.** Also, **S.B.A.**

SbE, See **south by east.**

SBIC, Small Business Investment Corporation.

SBLI, Savings Bank Life Insurance.

SbW, See **south by west.**

Sc, *Chem.* scandium.

Sc., 1. Scotch. **2.** Scotland. **3.** Scots. **4.** Scottish.

sc., 1. scale. **2.** scene. **3.** science. **4.** scientific. **5.** namely. [< L *scilicet,* contr. of *scire licet,* it is permitted to know] **6.** screw. **7.** scruple.

S.C., 1. Sanitary Corps. **2.** Security Council (of the U.N.). **3.** Signal Corps. **4.** South Carolina. **5.** Staff Corps. **6.** Supreme Court.

s.c., 1. small capitals. **2.** supercalendered.

scab (skab), *n., v.,* **scabbed, scab·bing.** —*n.* **1.** the incrustation that forms over a sore or wound during healing. **2.** *Vet. Pathol.* a mangy disease in animals, esp. sheep; scabies. Cf. **itch** (def. 8). **3.** *Plant Pathol.* **a.** a disease of plants characterized by crustlike lesions on the affected parts and caused by a fungus or bacterium. **b.** one of these crustlike lesions. **4.** a workman who refuses to join or act with a labor union, who takes a striker's place on the job, or the like. **5.** *Slang.* a rascal or scoundrel. **6.** *Foundry.* **a.** a projection or roughness on an ingot or casting from a defective mold. **b.** a surface defect on the sand in a mold. **7.** *Metall.* a surface defect on an iron or steel piece resulting from the rolling in of scale. **8.** *Carpentry.* a short, flat piece of wood used for various purposes, as binding two timbers butted together, strengthening a timber at a weak spot, etc. —*v.i.* **9.** to become covered with a scab. **10.** to act or work as a scab. [ME < Scand; cf. Sw *skabb,* c. dial. E *shab,* OE *sceabb;* cf. SHABBY, SHAVE] —**scab′like′,** *adj.*

scab·bard (skab′ərd), *n.* **1.** a sheath for a sword or the like. See illus. under **scimitar.** —*v.t.* **2.** to put into a scabbard; sheathe. [ME *scalburde, scauberge,* etc. (cf. AF *escauberz, escauberge,* ML *escauberca*) << dissimilated var. of OHG **skārberga* sword-protection. See SHEARS, HARBOR] —**scab′bard·less,** *adj.*

scab·bard·fish (skab′ərd fish′), *n., pl.* (*esp. collectively*) **-fish,** (*esp. referring to two or more kinds or species*) **-fish·es.** any compressed, ribbonlike fish of the genus *Trichiurus,* having daggerlike teeth. Also called **frostfish.** [SCABBARD + FISH]

scab·bed (skab′id, skabd), *adj.* **1.** covered with or affected by scabs. **2.** *Obs.* mean or petty. [ME; see SCAB, -ED[3]] —**scab′bed·ness,** *n.*

scab·ble (skab′əl), *v.t.,* **-bled, -bling.** to shape or dress (stone) roughly. [var. of *scapple* < MF *escapel(er)* (to) dress (timber)]

scab·by (skab′ē), *adj.,* **-bi·er, -bi·est. 1.** covered with scabs; having many scabs. **2.** consisting of scabs. **3.** (of an animal or plant) having scab. **4.** *Slang.* mean or contemptible: *a scabby trick.* [SCAB + -Y[1]] —**scab′bi·ly,** *adv.* —**scab′bi·ness,** *n.*

scab′by mouth′, *Vet. Pathol.* ecthyma.

scab·i·cide (skab′i sīd′), *adj.* **1.** Also, **scab′i·ci′dal.** destructive to the organisms causing scabies. —*n.* **2.** a scabicide agent. [SCABI(ES) + -CIDE]

sca·bies (skā′bēz, -bē ēz′), *n.* (*construed as sing.*) *Pathol.* a contagious skin disease occurring especially in sheep and cattle and also in man, caused by parasitic mites which burrow under the skin. Cf. **itch** (def. 8), **mange.** [< L: roughness, the itch, deriv. of *scabere* to scratch, scrape; c. SHAVE] —**sca·bi·et·ic** (skā′bē et′ik), *adj.*

sca·bi·ous[1] (skā′bē əs), *adj.* **1.** covered with or consisting of scabs; scabby. **2.** pertaining to or of the nature of scabies. [SCABI(ES) + -OUS]

sca·bi·ous[2] (skā′bē əs), *n.* **1.** any composite herb of the genus *Scabiosa,* having terminal heads of showy flowers, as *S. arvensis* **(field scabious),** having purple flowers, or *S. atropurpurea* **(sweet scabious),** having purple, pink, or white flowers. **2.** the shepherd's-scabious. Also, **sca·bi·o·sa** (skā′bē ō′sə). [ME *scabiose* < ML *scabiōsa (herba)* scabies-curing (herb)]

scab·land (skab′land′), *n.* rough, barren, volcanic topography with thin soils and little vegetation. [SCAB + LAND]

scab·rous (skab′rəs), *adj.* **1.** having a rough surface because of minute points or projections. **2.** full of difficulties. **3.** indecent; risqué; obscene: *scabrous books.* [< L *scab(e)r* rough + -OUS] —**scab′rous·ly,** *adv.* —**scab′rous·ness,** *n.*
—**Syn. 3.** lewd, wanton, improper.

scad[1] (skad), *n., pl.* (*esp. collectively*) **scad,** (*esp. referring to two or more kinds or species*) **scads. 1.** any carangid fish of the genus *Decapterus,* found in tropical and subtropical shore waters. **2.** any of several related carangid fishes, as of the genera *Trachurus* or *Selar.* [?]

scad[2] (skad), *n.* Often, **scads.** *Slang.* **1.** a great number or quantity: *a scad of jokes; scads of money.* **2.** a piece of money; coin. [dial. var. of *scalding* quantity, amount to be scalded. See SCALD[1]]

Scae·vo·la (sē′və lə, sev′ə-), *n.* **Ga·ius** (gā′əs) (or **Ca·ius**) (kā′əs) **Mu·ci·us** (myo͞o′ shē əs, -shəs), fl. 6th century B.C., Roman hero.

Sca′fell Pike′ (skô′fel′), a mountain in NW England, in Cumberland: highest peak in England. 3210 ft.

scaf·fold (skaf′əld, -ōld), *n.* **1.** a temporary structure for holding workmen and materials during the erection, repair, or decoration of a building. **2.** an elevated platform on which a criminal is executed, usually by hanging. **3.** a raised platform or stage for exhibiting spectacles, seating spectators, etc. **4.** any raised framework. **5.** a suspended platform that is used by painters, window-washers, and others for working on a tall structure, as a skyscraper. **6.** *Metall.* any piling or fusion of materials in a blast furnace, obstructing the flow of gases and preventing the uniform descent of the charge. **7.** a system of raised frameworks; scaffolding. —*v.t.* **8.** to furnish with a scaffold or scaffolding. **9.** to support by or place on a scaffold. [ME < OF *escadafaut, es-* E- + *cadafaut* CATAFALQUE]

scaf·fold·ing (skaf′əl ding, -ōl-), *n.* **1.** a scaffold or system of scaffolds. **2.** materials for scaffolds. [SCAFFOLD + -ING[1]]

scaf′fold nail′, a nail used in building temporary structures, having a stop on its shank to prevent its being driven in all the way and to leave the head free for pulling. Also called **staging nail.**

scagl·io·la (skal yō′lə), *n.* plasterwork imitating marble, granite, or the like. [< It, equiv. to *scagli(a)* a chip (< Goth *skalja* tile) + *-ola* dim. suffix] —**scagl·io′list,** *n.*

scaife (skāf), *n.* a wheel for grinding or polishing gems and industrial diamonds, consisting of a cast-iron disk treated with a mixture of olive oil and diamond dust. Also, **skeif.** [? < D *schijf* (c. G *Scheibe*) disk, wheel]

scal·a·ble (skā′lə bəl), *adj.* capable of being scaled: *the scalable slope of a mountain.* [SCALE[3] + -ABLE] —**scal′a·ble·ness,** *n.* —**scal′a·bly,** *adv.*

sca·la cor·do·na·ta (*It.* skä′lä kôR′dô nä′tä), *pl.* **sca·le cor·do·na·te** (*It.* skä′le kôR′dô nä′te). a ramp having the form of broad, slightly inclined steps. [< It; see SCALE[3], CORDON, -ATE[1]]

sca·lade (skə lād′), *n. Archaic.* escalade. [< OIt *scalado* a scaling, equiv to *scal(are)* (to) SCALE[3] + *-ada* -ADE[1]]

scal·age (skā′lij), *n.* **1.** a percentage deduction granted in dealings with goods that are likely to shrink, leak, or otherwise vary in the amount or weight originally stated. **2.** the amount of lumber estimated to be contained in a log being scaled. [SCALE[3] + -AGE]

sca·lar (skā′lər), *adj.* **1.** representable by position on a line; having only magnitude: *a scalar variable.* **2.** of, pertaining to, or utilizing a scalar. —*n.* **3.** *Math.* a quantity possessing only magnitude. Cf. **vector** (def. 1a). [< L *scālār(is)* of a ladder. See SCALE[3], -AR[1]]

sca·lar·e (skə lâr′ē, -lär′ē), *n.* any of three deep-bodied, bizarre, cichlid fishes, *Pterophyllum scalare, P. altum,* and *P. eimekei,* found in northern South American rivers, often kept in aquariums. [< L *scālāre,* neut. of *scālāris* (see SCALAR); from its ladderlike markings]

sca′lar field′, *Math., Physics.* a region with a number assigned at each point. Cf. **vector field.**

sca·lar·i·form (skə lar′ə fôrm′), *adj. Biol.* ladder-like. [< NL *scālāriform(is).* See SCALAR, -FORM]

sca′lar prod′uct, *Math.* See **inner product** (def. 1).

sca′lar tri′ple prod′uct, *Math.* the volume of the parallelepiped defined by three given vectors, *u, v,* and *w,* usually represented as *u·v·w.* Also, **triple scalar product.** Cf. **cross product, inner product** (def. 1).

scal·a·wag (skal′ə wag′), *n.* **1.** *Informal.* scamp; rascal. **2.** *U.S. Hist.* a native white Southerner who supported Republican policy during the Reconstruction period following the Civil War. Also, *esp. Brit.,* **scallawag.** [?] —**scal′a·wag′ger·y,** *n.* —**scal′a·wag′gy,** *adj.*

scald[1] (skôld), *v.t.* **1.** to burn or affect painfully with or as if with hot liquid or steam. **2.** to subject to the action of boiling or hot liquid. **3.** to heat to a temperature just short of the boiling point: *to scald milk.* **4.** to parboil or blanch (fruit, vegetables, etc.). —*v.i.* **5.** to be or become scalded. —*n.* **6.** a burn caused by the action of hot liquid or steam. **7.** any similar condition, esp. as the result of too much heat or sunlight. **8.** *Plant Pathol.* a blanching of the epidermis and adjacent tissues which turn pale or dark brown, caused by improper conditions of growth or storage, as in apples, or by fungi, as in cranberries. [ME *scald(en)* < dial. OF *escalde(r)* < LL *excaldāre* to wash in hot water. See EX-, CALDARIUM]

scald[2] (skôld, skäld), *n.* skald. —**scald′ic,** *adj.*

scald[3] (skôld), *adj.* **1.** Also, **scalled.** scabby; scurvy. —*n.* **2.** *Obs.* a scab. [SCALL + -ED[3]]

scale[1] (skāl), *n., v.,* **scaled, scal·ing.** —*n.* **1.** *Zool.* **a.** one of the thin, flat, horny plates forming the covering of certain animals, as snakes, lizards, and pangolins. **b.** one of the hard, bony or dentinal plates, either flat or denticulate, forming the covering of certain other animals, as fishes. **2.** any thin, platelike piece, lamina, or flake that peels off from a surface. **3.** *Bot.* **a.** Also called **bud scale.** a rudimentary body, usually a specialized leaf and often covered with hair, wax, or resin, enclosing an immature leaf bud. **b.** a thin, scarious or membranous part of a plant, as a bract of a catkin. **4.** See **scale insect. 5.** a coating or incrustation, as on the inside of a boiler, formed by the precipitation of salts from the water. **6.** Often, **scales.** *Metall.* an oxide, esp. an iron oxide, occurring in a scaly form on the surface of metal brought to a high temperature. **7. scales, a.** an imaginary cause of blindness to the true nature of a person, situation, etc.: *You're infatuated with her now, but the scales will soon fall from your eyes.* **b.** an unspecified affliction that caused Paul to become temporarily blind. Acts 9:18. —*v.t.* **8.** to remove the scales or scale from: *to scale a fish.* **9.** to remove in scales or thin layers. **10.** to cover with an incrustation or scale. **11.** to skip, as a stone over water. —*v.i.* **12.** to come off in scales. **13.** to shed scales. **14.** to become coated with scale, as the inside of a boiler. [ME < MF *escale* < WGmc **skāla* SCALE[2]] —**scale′less,** *adj.* —**scale′like′,** *adj.*

scale[2] (skāl), *n., v.,* **scaled, scal·ing.** —*n.* **1.** either of the pans or dishes of a balance. **2.** Often, **scales.** a balance or any of various other instruments or devices for weighing: *We gave the parents a baby scale. The butcher placed the meat on the scales.* **3. Scales,** *Astron., Astrol.* the constellation or sign of Libra. **4. tip the scale** or **scales, a.** to weigh: *He tips the scales at 190 lbs.* **b.** to turn the trend of favor, control, etc.: *The present crisis should tip the scales for our candidate.* **5. turn the scale** or **scales,** to decide in favor of one side or faction; determine the outcome: *It would take a miracle to turn the scales for us now.* —*v.t.* **6.** to weigh in or as if in scales. **7.** to have a weight of. [ME < Scand; cf. Icel *skālar* (pl.), c. OE *scealu* scale (of a balance)]

scale[3] (skāl), *n., v.,* **scaled, scal·ing.** —*n.* **1.** a succession or progression of steps or degrees; a graduated series: *the scale of taxation; the social scale.* **2.** a point on such a scale. **3.** a series of marks laid down at determinate distances, as along a line, for purposes of measurement or computation: *the scale of a thermometer.* **4.** a graduated line, as on a map, representing proportionate size. **5.** a table of graduated rates, as of prices, wages, etc.: *These unions use different scales.* **6.** a wage that conforms to such rates: *How much is scale? We cannot hire union labor for less than scale.* **7.** an instrument with graduated spaces, as for measuring. **8.** the proportion that a representation of an object bears to the object itself: *a model on a scale of one inch to one foot.* **9.**

the ratio of distances or sometimes of areas on a map to the corresponding values on the earth. **10.** a certain relative or proportionate size or extent: *They built a residence on a yet more magnificent scale.* **11.** a standard of measurement or estimation: *We have no scale by which to judge his achievements.* **12.** *Arith.* a system of numerical notation: *the decimal scale.* **13.** *Music.* a succession of tones ascending or descending according to fixed intervals, esp. such a series beginning on a particular note: *the major scale of C.* **14.** *Educ., Psychol.* a graded series of tests or tasks for measuring intelligence, achievement, adjustment, etc. **15.** anything by which one may ascend. **16.** *Obs.* **a.** a ladder. **b.** a flight of stairs. —*v.t.* **17.** to climb by or as by a ladder; climb up or over. **18.** to make according to scale. **19.** to reduce in amount according to a fixed scale or proportion (often fol. by *down*): *to scale down wages.* **20.** to measure by or as if by a scale. **21.** *Lumbering.* **a.** to measure (logs). **b.** to estimate the amount of (standing timber). —*v.i.* **22.** to climb; ascend; mount. **23.** to progress in a graduated series. [ME < L *scāl(ae)* ladder, stairs] —**Syn. 17.** See **climb.**

scale·board (skāl′bōrd′, -bôrd′, skab′ərd), *n.* **1.** a very thin board, as for the back of a picture. **2.** *Print.* a thin strip of wood used in justifying. **3.** a thin sheet of wood used as veneer. [SCALE[1] + BOARD]

scaled (skāld), *adj.* *Armor.* noting armor having imbricated metal plates sewn to a flexible backing. [late ME *scalid.* See SCALE[1], -ED[3]]

scale′ in′sect, any of numerous small, plant-sucking, homopterous insects of the superfamily *Coccoidea,* the males of which are winged and the females wingless and often attached to the food plant and covered by a waxy secretion or tough scale.

scale′ leaf′, a scalelike leaf, as a bud scale or certain bracts.

scale′ moss′, any thalloid liverwort.

sca·lene (skā lēn′), *adj.* **1.** *Geom.* **a.** (of a cone or the like) having the axis inclined to the base. **b.** (of a triangle) having three unequal sides. **2.** *Anat.* of or pertaining to a scalenus muscle. [< LL *scalēn(us)* < Gk *skalēnós* unequal]

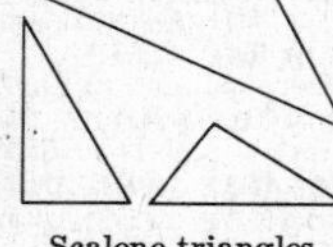
Scalene triangles

sca·le·no·he·dron (skā lē′nə hē′drən), *n., pl.* **-drons, -dra** (-drə). *Crystall.* a hemihedral crystal form of 8 or 12 faces, each face being a scalene triangle. [< Gk *skalēnó(s)* unequal + -HEDRON] —**sca·le′no·he′dral,** *adj.*

sca·le·nus (skā lē′nəs), *n., pl.* **-ni** (-nī). *Anat.* any of three muscles on each side of the neck, the action of which raise the first and second ribs in respiration and assist in bending the neck to one side. [< NL, LL. See SCALENE]

scal·er (skā′lər), *n.* **1.** one who or that which scales. **2.** Also called **counter, scal′ing cir′cuit.** *Electronics.* an electronic circuit devised to give a single pulse as output after a certain number of input pulses. [SCALE[1] + -ER[1]]

Sca·li·a (skə lē′ə), *n.* **An·to·nin** (an′tə nin), born 1936, U.S. jurist: associate justice of the U.S. Supreme Court since 1986.

Scal·i·ger (skal′i jər), *n.* **1. Joseph Jus·tus** (jus′təs), 1540–1609, French scholar and critic. **2.** (his father) **Julius Caesar,** 1484–1558, Italian scholar, philosopher, and critic in France.

scal′ing lad′der, a ladder for climbing high walls.

scall (skôl), *n.* a scurf. [< Icel *skalli* bald head. Cf. SKULL]

scal·la·wag (skal′ə wag′), *n.* *Chiefly Brit.* scalawag.

scalled (skôld), *adj.* scald[3] (def. 1).

scal·lion (skal′yən), *n.* **1.** any onion that does not form a large bulb. **2.** a shallot. **3.** a leek. [ME < OF **escaloigne* < VL **escalonia,* var. of L *Ascalōnia (caepa)* onion of Ascalon, a seaport of Palestine; r. ME *scalone,* etc. < AF *scaloun* < VL, as above]

scal·lop (skol′əp, skal′-), *n.* **1.** any bivalve mollusk of the genus *Pecten* and related genera, that swim by rapidly clapping the fluted shell valves together. **2.** the adductor muscle of certain species of such mollusks, esteemed as food. **3.** one of the shells of such a mollusk, usually having radial ribs and a wavy outer edge. **4.** a scallop shell or a dish in which flaked fish or the like is baked and served. **5.** *Cookery.* a thin slice of meat, usually further flattened by pounding with a mallet or other implement. **6.** one of a series of rounded projections along the edge of a garment, cloth, etc. —*v.t.* **7.** to finish (an edge) with scallops. **8.** *Cookery.* to escallop. Also, **scollop.** [ME *scalop* < MF *escalope* shell < Gmc; cf. SKALP] —**scal′lop·er,** *n.*

Scallop, *Pecten irradians* (Width 2 to 3 in.)

scal·lop·ing (skal′ə ping), *n.* **1.** the act or occupation of collecting scallops. **2.** a pattern or contour in the form of scallops, as along the edge of a garment. **3.** the act or occupation of finishing an edge with scallops. [SCALLOP + -ING[1]]

scal·ly·wag (skal′ē wag′), *n.* scalawag.

sca·lop·pi·ne (skä′lə pē′nē, skal′ə-), *n.* *Italian Cookery.* scallops, esp. of veal, flattened by pounding and dredged in flour or bread crumbs before being broiled or sautéed, usually in a wine sauce. Also, **scal′lo·pi′ni.** [< It *scaloppine,* pl. of *scaloppina,* equiv. to *scalopp(a)* thin slice of (perh. < MF *escalope* shell) + *-ina* dim. suffix]

scalp (skalp), *n.* **1.** the integument of the upper part of the head, usually including the associated subcutaneous structures. **2.** a part of this integument with the accompanying hair, taken by some North American Indians as a trophy of victory. **3.** any token of victory. **4.** the integument on the top of the head of an animal. **5.** *Informal.* a small profit made in quick buying and selling. —*v.t.* **6.** to cut or tear the scalp from. **7.** *Informal.* **a.** to buy and sell (stocks) so as to make small, quick profits. **b.** to sell (tickets) at higher than the official rates. **8.** to plane down the surfaces of (an ingot, billet, or slab). —*v.i.* **9.** *Informal.* to scalp tickets, stocks, or the like. [ME (north) < Scand; cf. Icel *skālpr* leather sheath] —**scalp′er,** *n.* —**scalp′less,** *adj.*

scal·pel (skal′pəl), *n.* a small, light, usually straight knife used in surgical and anatomical operations and dissections. [< L *scalpell(um),* equiv. to *scalp-* (cf. *scalpere* to carve) + *-ellum* dim. suffix] —**scal·pel·lic** (skal pel′ik), *adj.*

scalp′ lock′, a long lock or tuft of hair left on the scalp by members of some North American Indian tribes as an implied challenge to their enemies.

scal·pri·form (skal′prə fôrm′), *adj.* chisel-shaped, as the incisors of certain rodents. [< L *scalpri-* (comb. form of *scalprum* chisel) + -FORM]

scal·y (skā′lē), *adj.,* **scal·i·er, scal·i·est. 1.** covered with or abounding in scales or scale. **2.** characterized by or consisting of scales; scalelike. **3.** peeling or flaking off in scales. **4.** *Slang.* shabby; despicable. [SCALE[1] + -Y[1]] —**scal′i·ness,** *n.*

scal′y ant′eater, pangolin.

scam (skam), *n.* *Slang.* a fraudulent scheme, esp. for making a quick profit. [orig. uncert.]

Sca·man·der (skə man′dər), *n.* **1.** ancient name of the river **Menderes. 2.** *Class. Myth.* Also called **Xanthus.** the god of the river Scamander, a son of Oceanus and Tethys.

Sca·man·dri·us (skə man′drē əs), *n.* *Class. Myth.* **1.** Astyanax. **2.** (in the *Iliad*) the son of Strophius who was skilled in archery but was slain by Menelaus.

sca·mil·lus (skə mil′əs), *n.* *Archit.* **1.** a slight bevel at an arris of a stone, as in the necking of a Grecian Doric column. **2.** a plain stone beneath the plinth of a column. [< L, equiv. to *scam(num)* stool + *-illus* dim. suffix]

scam·mo·ny (skam′ə nē), *n., pl.* **-nies.** a twining, Asian convolvulus, *Convolvulus Scammonia.* [ME, OE *scamonie* < L *scammōnia* < Gk] —**scam·mo·ni·ate** (skə mō′nē it), *adj.*

scamp (skamp), *n.* **1.** a worthless and often mischievous person; rascal; rogue. **2.** a grouper, *Mycteroperca phenax,* of Florida: so called from its habit of stealing bait. —*v.t.* **3.** to do or perform in a hasty or careless manner: *to scamp work.* [obs. *scamp* to go (on highway) idly or for mischief, perh. < obs. D *schamp(en)* (to) be gone < OF *(e)scampe(r)* (to) DECAMP] —**scamp′er,** *n.* —**scamp′ing·ly,** *adv.* —**scamp′ish,** *adj.* —**scamp′ish·ly,** *adv.* —**scamp′ish·ness,** *n.*

scamp·er (skam′pər), *v.i.* **1.** to run or go hastily or quickly. **2.** to run playfully about, as a child. —*n.* **3.** a scampering; a quick run. [obs. *scamp* to go (see SCAMP) + -ER[6]]

scan (skan), *v.,* **scanned, scan·ning,** *n.* —*v.t.* **1.** to examine minutely; scrutinize carefully. **2.** to glance at or read hastily: *to scan a page.* **3.** to analyze (verse) as to its prosodic or metrical structure; read or recite (verse) so as to indicate or test the metrical form. **4.** *Television.* to traverse (a surface) with a beam of light or electrons in order to reproduce or transmit a picture. **5.** *Radar.* to traverse (a region) with a beam from a radar transmitter. —*v.i.* **6.** to examine the meter of verse. **7.** (of verse) to conform to the rules of meter. **8.** *Television.* to scan a surface or the like. —*n.* **9.** an act or instance of scanning; close examination or scrutiny. [ME *scanne,* var. of **scanden* < LL *scand(ere)* (to) scan verse, L: to climb] —**scan′na·ble,** *adj.* —**scan′ner,** *n.*
—**Syn. 1.** study, investigate, inspect, search. **2.** skim.

Scan., Scandinavia.

Scand, Scandinavian (def. 3).

Scand., **1.** Scandinavia. **2.** Scandinavian.

scan·dal (skan′dəl), *n., v.,* **-daled, -dal·ing** or (*esp. Brit.*) **-dalled, -dal·ling.** —*n.* **1.** a disgraceful or discreditable action, circumstance, etc. **2.** an offense caused by a fault or misdeed. **3.** damage to reputation; public disgrace. **4.** defamatory talk; malicious gossip. **5.** a person whose conduct brings disgrace or offense. —*v.t.* **6.** *Archaic.* to defame (someone) by spreading scandal. **7.** *Obs.* to disgrace. **8.** *Obs.* to scandalize. [< LL *scandal(um)* < eccl. Gk *skándalon* snare, cause of moral stumbling; r. ME *scandle* < OF (north) *(e)scandle* < LL, as above]
—**Syn. 3.** discredit, dishonor, shame, disrepute, opprobrium, odium, ignominy. **4.** slander, calumny, aspersion, detraction, obloquy. See **gossip.** —**Ant. 4.** honor, praise.

scan·dal·ise (skan′dəlīz′), *v.t.,* **-ised, -is·ing.** *Chiefly Brit.* scandalize. —**scan′dal·i·sa′tion,** *n.* —**scan′dal·is′er,** *n.*

scan·dal·ize (skan′dəlīz′), *v.t.,* **-ized, -iz·ing. 1.** to shock or horrify by something considered immoral or improper. **2.** *Naut.* to spill the wind from or reduce the exposed area of (a sail) in an unusual manner. [< eccl. L *scandaliz(āre)* < Gk *skandalízein.* See SCANDAL, -IZE] —**scan′dal·i·za′tion,** *n.* —**scan′dal·iz′er,** *n.*

scan·dal·mon·ger (skan′dəl mung′gər, -mong′-), *n.* one who spreads scandal or gossip. [SCANDAL + MONGER]

scan·dal·ous (skan′dələs), *adj.* **1.** disgraceful; shameful or shocking; improper: *scandalous behavior in public.* **2.** defamatory or libelous, as a speech or writing. **3.** addicted to scandal, as a person: *a scandalous, vicious gossip.* [< ML *scandalōs(us).* See SCANDAL, -OUS] —**scan′dal·ous·ly,** *adv.* —**scan′dal·ous·ness,** *n.*

scan′dal sheet′, a newspaper or magazine that emphasizes scandal or gossip

scan·dent (skan′dənt), *adj.* climbing, as a plant [< L *scandent-* (s. of *scandēns,* prp. of *scandere* to climb); see -ENT]

Scan·der·beg (skan′dər beg′), *n.* (*George Castriota*) 1403?–68, Albanian chief and revolutionary leader. Turkish, **Iskander Bey.**

scan·di·a (skan′dē ə), *n.* *Chem.* oxide of scandium, Sc_2O_3, a white infusible powder. [special use of SCANDIA]

Scan·di·a (skan′dē ə), *n.* ancient name of the S Scandinavian Peninsula. [< L]

Scan·di·an (skan′dē ən), *adj.* **1.** of or pertaining to Scandia. —*n.* **2.** a Scandinavian. [SCANDI(A) + -AN]

scan·dic (skan′dik), *adj.* *Chem.* of or pertaining to scandium: *scandic oxide.* [SCAND(IUM) + -IC]

Scan·di·na·vi·a (skan′də nā′vē ə), *n.* **1.** Norway, Sweden, Denmark, and sometimes Iceland and the Faroe Islands: the former lands of the Norsemen. **2.** Also, **Scandinavian Peninsula.** the peninsula consisting of Norway and Sweden.

Scan·di·na·vi·an (skan′də nā′vē ən), *adj.* **1.** of or pertaining to Scandinavia, its inhabitants, or their languages. —*n.* **2.** a native or inhabitant of Scandinavia. **3.** the group of languages composed of Danish, Icelandic, Norwegian, Old Norse, Swedish, and the language of the Faeroe Islands; North Germanic. [SCANDINAVI(A) + -AN]

Scandina′vian Penin′sula, Scandinavia (def. 2).

scan·di·um (skan′dē əm), *n.* *Chem.* a rare, trivalent, metallic element obtained from thortveitite. *Symbol:* Sc; *at. wt.:* 44.956; *at. no.:* 21; *sp. gr.:* 3.0. [< NL; see SCANDIA, -IUM]

scan·ner (skan′ər), *n.* **1.** one who or that which scans. **2.** *Photog.* any device for exposing an image on film, a sensitized plate, etc., by tracing light along a series of many closely spaced parallel lines. **3.** (in aerial photography) a device for estimating the ratio of aircraft speed to aircraft altitude. **4.** *Photoengraving.* a photoelectric device for scanning a picture to determine automatically the density of the hue or value in each area for transmission by wire or radio or for preparation of color process printing plates. [SCAN + -ER[1]]

scan′ning disk′, *Television.* (in mechanical scanning) a disk with a line of holes spiraling in from its edge, rotated in front of a surface so as to expose a small segment as each hole passes before it for transmitting or reproducing a picture.

scan′ning line′, (in a cathode ray or television tube) a single horizontal trace made by the electron beam in one traversal of the fluorescent screen. Cf. **frame** (def. 18).

scan·sion (skan′shən), *n.* *Pros.* the metrical analysis of verse. The usual marks for scansion are ˘ for a short or unaccented syllable, ¯ or ′ for a long or accented syllable, ˆ for a rest, | for a foot division, and ‖ for a caesura or pause. [< L *scānsiōn-* (s. of *scānsiō*), equiv. to *scāns(us)* (ptp. of *scandere* to climb) + *-iōn-* -ION]

scan·so·ri·al (skan sōr′ē əl, -sôr′-), *adj.* *Zool.* **1.** capable of or adapted for climbing, as the feet of certain birds, lizards, etc. **2.** habitually climbing, as a woodpecker. [< L *scānsōri(us)* for climbing + -AL[1]; see SCANSION, -ORY[1]]

scant (skant), *adj.* **1.** barely sufficient in amount or quantity; not abundant; almost inadequate: *to do scant justice.* **2.** limited; meager; not large: *a scant amount.* **3.** barely amounting to as much as indicated: *a scant two hours.* **4.** having an inadequate or limited supply (usually fol. by *of*): *scant of breath.* —*v.t.* **5.** to make scant; diminish. **6.** to stint the supply of; withhold. **7.** to treat slightly or inadequately. —*adv.* **8.** *Dial.* scarcely; barely; hardly. [ME < Scand; cf. Icel *skamt,* neut. of *skammr* short] —**scant′ly,** *adv.* —**scant′ness,** *n.*
—**Syn. 2.** scanty, small, restricted. **3.** bare, mere. **4.** short, lacking, wanting, deficient. **5.** lessen, reduce, decrease, curtail. **6.** limit, restrict, skimp, scrimp. **7.** slight, neglect.

scan·ties (skan′tēz), *n. pl.* extremely short panties. [SCANT + *-ies,* modeled on *panties*]

scant·ling (skant′ling), *n.* **1.** a timber of relatively slight width and thickness, as a stud or rafter in a house frame. **2.** such timbers collectively. **3.** the width and thickness of a timber. **4.** the dimensions of a building stone. **5.** *Naut.* **a.** a dressed timber or rolled metal member used as a framing member in a vessel. **b.** the dimension, in cross section, of a framing member. **6.** a small quantity or amount. [SCANT + -LING[1]; r. ME *scantilon* < OF *(e)scantillon* gauge]

scant′ling-draft ves′sel (skant′ling draft′, -dräft′), *Naut.* a cargo vessel not considered sufficiently strong in all cargo spaces to have the legal maximum draft. Cf. **full-scantling vessel.**

scant·y (skan′tē), *adj.,* **scant·i·er, scant·i·est. 1.** scant in amount, quantity, etc.; barely sufficient. **2.** meager; not adequate. **3.** lacking amplitude in extent or compass. [SCANT + -Y[1]] —**scant′i·ly,** *adv.* —**scant′i·ness,** *n.*
—**Syn. 1, 2.** SCANTY, MEAGER, SPARSE refer to insufficiency or deficiency in quantity, number, etc. SCANTY denotes smallness or insufficiency of quantity, number, supply, etc.: *a scanty supply of food.* MEAGER indicates that a person is gaunt and lean or that something is poor, stinted, inadequate: *meager in appearance; meager fare; a meager income.* SPARSE applies particularly to that which grows thinly or is thinly strewn or sown, often over a wide area: *sparse vegetation; a sparse population.* —**Ant. 1.** plentiful, ample.

Sca′pa Flow′ (skä′pə, skap′ə), an area of water off the N coast of Scotland, in the Orkney Islands: British naval base; German warships scuttled 1919.

scape[1] (skāp), *n.* **1.** *Bot.* a leafless peduncle rising from the ground. **2.** *Zool.* a stemlike part, as the shaft of a feather. **3.** *Archit.* th shaft of a column. **4.** *Entomol.* the stemlike basal segment of the antenna of certain insects. [< L *scāp(us)* stalk < Doric Gk *skâpos,* c. Attic *sképtron* staff, SCEPTER]

S, Scape

scape[2] (skāp), *n., v.t., v.i.,* **scaped, scap·ing.** *Archaic.* escape. Also, **'scape.**

scape·goat (skāp′gōt′), *n.* **1.** one who is made to bear the blame for others or to suffer in their place. **2.** *Chiefly Biblical.* a goat led into and let loose in the wilderness on Yom Kippur after the high priest symbolically laid the sins of the people on its head. Lev. 16:8–22. [SCAPE[2] + GOAT]

scape·goat·ism (skāp′gō tiz′əm), *n.* the act or practice of assigning blame or failure to someone or something. [SCAPEGOAT + -ISM]

scape·grace (skāp′grās′), *n.* a complete rogue or rascal; a habitually unscrupulous person; scamp. [SCAPE[2] + GRACE]

scape′ wheel′, *Horol.* See **escape wheel.**

scapho-, a learned borrowing from Greek meaning "boat," used in the formation of compound words: *scaphocephaly.* Also, *esp. before a vowel,* **scaph-.** [comb. form of Gk *skáphē*]

scaph·o·ceph·a·ly (skaf′ə sef′ə lē), *n.* *Pathol.* a deformed skull having an elongated, keellike shape, caused by premature closure of the sagittal suture.

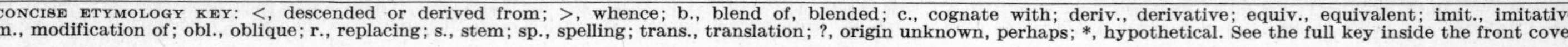
CONCISE ETYMOLOGY KEY: <, descended or derived from; >, whence; b., blend of, blended; c., cognate with; deriv., derivative; equiv., equivalent; imit., imitative; m., modification of; obl., oblique; r., replacing; s., stem; sp., spelling; trans., translation; ?, origin unknown, perhaps; *, hypothetical. See the full key inside the front cover.

Also, **scaph′o·ceph′a·lism.** [SCAPHO- + -CEPHALY] —**scaph·o·ce·phal·ic** (skaf′ō sə fal′ik), **scaph′o·ceph′a·lous,** *adj.*

scaph·oid (skaf′oid), *adj.* **1.** boat-shaped; navicular. —*n.* **2.** *Anat.* a navicular. [< NL *scaphoīd(ēs)* < Gk *skaphoeidēs* like a boat. See SCAPH-, -OID]

scaph·o·pod (skaf′ə pod′), *n.* **1.** any mollusk of the class *Scaphopoda,* comprising the tooth shells. —*adj.* **2.** Also, **sca·phop·o·dous** (skə fop′ə dəs). belonging or pertaining to the *Scaphopoda.* [< NL *Scaphopoda.* See SCAPHO-, -POD]

scapi-, a combining form of **scape**[1]: *scapiform.* [< L *scāp(us)* shaft, stem + -I-]

sca·pi·form (skā′pə fôrm′, skap′ə-), *adj.* *Chiefly Bot.* resembling a scape. [SCAPI- + -FORM]

scap·o·lite (skap′ə līt′), *n.* **1.** any of a group of minerals of variable composition, essentially silicates of aluminum, calcium, and sodium, occurring massive and in tetragonal crystals. **2.** Also called **wernerite.** the member of the scapolite group intermediate in composition between meionite and marialite. [< G *Skapolith.* See SCAP-, -LITE]

sca·pose (skā′pōs), *adj.* **1.** having scapes; consisting of a scape. **2.** resembling a scape. [SCAPE[1] + -OSE[1]]

s. caps., small capitals.

scapul-, var. of **scapulo-** before a vowel: *scapulalgia.*

scap·u·la (skap′yə lə), *n., pl.* **-lae** (-lē′), **-las.** **1.** *Anat.* either of two flat, triangular bones, each forming the back part of a shoulder in man; shoulder blade. See diags. under **shoulder, skeleton. 2.** *Zool.* a dorsal bone of the pectoral girdle. [< L: shoulder]

scap·u·lal·gi·a (skap′yə lal′jē ə), *n.* *Pathol.* pain in the region of the scapula. [SCAPUL- + -ALGIA]

scap·u·lar[1] (skap′yə lər), *adj.* **1.** of or pertaining to the shoulders or the scapula or scapulae. [< NL *scapulār(is).* See SCAPULA, -AR[1]]

scap·u·lar[2] (skap′yə lər), *n.* **1.** *Eccles.* a loose, sleeveless monastic garment, hanging from the shoulders. **2.** two small pieces of woolen cloth, joined by strings passing over the shoulders, worn under the ordinary clothing as a badge of affiliation with a religious order, a token of devotion, etc. **3.** *Surg.* scapulary. **4.** *Anat., Zool.* scapula. **5.** *Ornith.* one of the feathers of the scapular tract or pteryla. See diag. under **bird.** [< ML *scapulāre.* See SCAPULA, -AR[2]]

scap·u·lar·y (skap′yə ler′ē), *adj., n., pl.* **-lar·ies.** —*adj.* **1.** scapular. —*n.* **2.** Also, **scapular.** *Surg.* a shoulder dressing which keeps the shoulder or another bandage in place. [< ML *scapulāri(um).* See SCAPULA, -ARY]

scapulo-, a combining form of **scapula:** *scapulohumeral.* Also, *esp. before a vowel,* **scapul-.**

scap·u·lo·hum·er·al (skap′yə lō hyo͞o′mər əl), *adj.* *Anat.* of, pertaining to, or involving the scapula and humerus. [SCAPULO- + HUMERAL]

scar[1] (skär), *n., v.,* **scarred, scar·ring.** —*n.* **1.** the mark left by a healed wound, sore, or burn. **2.** any blemish remaining as a trace of or resulting from some injury: *scars upon one's good name.* **3.** *Bot.* a mark indicating a former point of attachment, as where a leaf has fallen from a stem. —*v.t.* **4.** to mark with a scar. —*v.i.* **5.** to heal with a resulting scar. [aph. var. of ESCHAR] —**scar′less,** *adj.*

scar[2] (skär), *n.* *Brit.* **1.** a precipitous, rocky place; cliff. **2.** a low or submerged rock in the sea. [ME *skerre* < Scand; cf. Icel *sker* SKERRY]

scar·ab (skar′əb), *n.* **1.** any scarabaeid beetle, esp. *Scarabaeus sacer,* regarded as sacred by the ancient Egyptians. **2.** a representation or image of a beetle, much used among the ancient Egyptians as a symbol, seal, amulet, or the like. **3.** a gem cut to resemble a beetle. Also, **scarabaeus** (for defs. 2, 3). [short for SCARABAEUS]

Scarab (def. 2)

scar·a·bae·id (skar′ə bē′id), *adj.* **1.** belonging or pertaining to the *Scarabaeidae,* a family of lamellicorn beetles, comprising the scarabs, dung beetles, June bugs, cockchafers, etc. —*n.* **2.** any scarabaeid beetle. Also, **scar′a·bae′an.** [< NL *scarabaeid(ae).* See SCARABAEUS, -ID[2]]

scar·a·bae·i·form (skar′ə bē′ə fôrm′), *adj.* resembling a scarabaeid or its larvae in form. [SCARABAE(US) + -I- + -FORM]

scar·a·bae·oid (skar′ə bē′oid), *adj.* Also, **scar·a·boid** (skar′ə boid′). **1.** resembling a scarab. **2.** of the nature of, or resembling, a scarabaeid. —*n.* **3.** an imitation or counterfeit scarab. [SCARABAE(US) + -OID]

scar·a·bae·us (skar′ə bē′əs), *n., pl.* **-bae·us·es, -bae·i** (-bē′ī). scarab (defs. 2, 3). [< L; cf. Gk *kárabos* kind of beetle]

Scar·a·mouch (skar′ə mouch′, -mo͞osh′), *n.* **1.** a stock character in commedia dell'arte and farce who is a cowardly braggart, easily beaten and frightened. **2.** (*l.c.*) a rascal or scamp. Also, **Scar′a·mouche′.** [< F *Scaramouche* < It *Scaramuccio,* deriv. of *scaramuccia* skirmish, applied in jest]

Scar·bor·ough (skär′bûr′ō, -bur′ō, -bər ə), *n.* a seaport in E Yorkshire, in NE England. 42,587 (1961).

Scar′borough lil′y, an amaryllidaceous herb, *Vallota speciosa,* of southern Africa, having funnel-shaped, scarlet flowers. [named after SCARBOROUGH]

scarce (skârs), *adj.,* **scarc·er, scarc·est,** *adv.* —*adj.* **1.** insufficient to satisfy the need or demand; not abundant: *Meat and butter were scarce during the war.* **2.** seldom met with; rare: *a scarce book.* **3. make oneself scarce,** *Informal.* **a.** to depart, esp. suddenly. **b.** to stay away; avoid: *He makes himself scarce at P.T.A. meetings.* —*adv.* **4.** scarcely. [ME *scars* < OF (north) *(e)scars* < VL **excarps(us)* plucked out, var. of L *excerptus;* see EXCERPT] —**scarce′ness,** *n.* —**Syn. 1.** deficient. **2.** uncommon, infrequent. —**Ant. 1.** abundant.

scarce·ly (skârs′lē), *adv.* **1.** barely; hardly; not quite: *The light is so dim we can scarcely see.* **2.** definitely not. **3.** probably not. [ME; see SCARCE, -LY] —**Syn. 1.** See **hardly.**

scarce·ment (skârs′mənt), *n.* a footing or ledge formed by a setoff in a wall. [obs. *scarce* to lessen (deriv. of SCARCE, adj.) + -MENT]

scar·ci·ty (skâr′si tē), *n., pl.* **-ties. 1.** insufficiency or smallness of supply; dearth. **2.** rarity; infrequency. [ME *scarsete* < OF (north) *escarsete.* See SCARCE, -ITY]

scare (skâr), *v.,* **scared, scar·ing,** *n.* —*v.t.* **1.** to fill suddenly with fear or terror; frighten; alarm. —*v.i.* **2.** to become frightened: *That horse scares easily.* **3. scare up,** *Informal.* to obtain with effort; find or gather: *to scare up money.* —*n.* **4.** a sudden fright or alarm, esp. with little or no reason. **5.** a time or condition of alarm or worry: *For three months there was a war scare.* [var. of ME *skerre* < Scand; cf. Icel *skirra,* deriv. of *skjarr* shy] —**scar′er,** *n.* —**scar′ing·ly,** *adv.* —**Syn. 1.** startle, intimidate. See **frighten.**

scare·crow (skâr′krō′), *n.* **1.** an object, usually a figure of a man in old clothes, set up to frighten crows or other birds away from crops. **2.** a person in ragged clothes. **3.** anything terrifying but not really dangerous. **4.** an extremely thin person. [SCARE + CROW[1]] —**scare′-crow′ish, scare′crow′y,** *adj.*

scared·y-cat (skâr′dē kat′), *n.* *Informal.* one who is easily frightened.

scare·head (skâr′hed′), *n.* *U.S. Informal.* a headline in exceptionally large type. Cf. **screamer** (def. 4a). [SCARE + HEAD]

scare·mon·ger (skâr′mung′gər, -mong′-), *n.* one who creates or spreads alarming news. [SCARE + MONGER] —**scare′mon′ger·ing,** *n.*

scarf[1] (skärf), *n., pl.* **scarfs,** (*esp. Brit.*) **scarves** (skärvz), *v.* —*n.* **1.** a long, broad strip of silk, lace, or other material worn by a woman about the neck, shoulders, or head, for ornament or protection against cold, drafts, etc. **2.** a muffler. **3.** a necktie or cravat with hanging ends. **4.** a long cover or ornamental cloth for a bureau, table, etc. —*v.t.* **5.** to cover or wrap with, or as with, a scarf. **6.** to use in the manner of a scarf. [? special use of SCARF[2]] —**scarf′less,** *adj.* —**scarf′like′,** *adj.*

scarf[2] (skärf), *n., pl.* **scarfs,** *v.* —*n.* **1.** a tapered or otherwise-formed end on each of the pieces to be assembled with a scarf joint. **2.** *Whaling.* a strip of skin along the body of the whale. —*v.t.* **3.** to assemble with a scarf joint. **4.** to form a scarf on (the end of a timber). **5.** to burn away the surface defects of (a bloom). **6.** *Whaling.* to make a groove in and remove (the blubber and skin). [< Scand; cf. Sw *skarf* piece (of wood or cloth) for piecing out or together] —**scarf′er,** *n.*

scar-faced (skär′fāst′), *adj.* with a face marked by a scar or scars.

scarf′ cloud′, pileus (def. 3).

scarf′ joint′, 1. a joint in which two timbers or other structural members are fitted together with long end laps of various forms and held in place with bolts, straps, keys, fishplates, etc., to resist tension or compression. **2.** (in welding) a butt joint between two pieces beveled on their meeting surfaces.

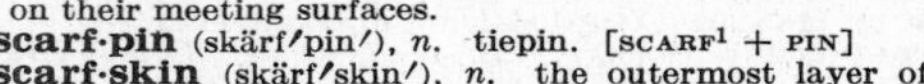

Scarf joints

scarf·pin (skärf′pin′), *n.* tiepin. [SCARF[1] + PIN]

scarf·skin (skärf′skin′), *n.* the outermost layer of the skin; epidermis. [SCARF[1] + SKIN]

scar·i·fi·ca·tion (skar′ə fə kā′shən), *n.* **1.** the act or an instance of scarifying. **2.** the result of scarifying; scratch or scratches. [< LL *scarificātiōn-* (s. of *scarificātiō*). See SCARIFY, -ATION]

scar·i·fi·ca·tor (skar′ə fə kā′tər), *n.* **1.** one who scarifies. **2.** a surgical instrument for scarifying. [< NL (coined by Ambrose Paré); see SCARIFY, -ATOR]

scar·i·fy (skar′ə fī′), *v.t.,* **-fied, -fy·ing. 1.** to make scratches or superficial incisions in (the skin, a wound, etc.), as in surgery. **2.** to lacerate by severe criticism. **3.** to loosen (the soil) with a type of cultivator. **4.** to hasten the sprouting of (hard-covered seeds) by making incisions in the seed coats. **5.** to break up (a road surface). [< MF *scarifi(er)* < LL *scarīficāre,* alter. of L *scarīfāre* to make scratches < Gk *skarīph(âsthai)* (to) sketch, deriv. of *skárīphos* stylus; see -IFY] —**scar′i·fi′er,** *n.*

scar·i·ous (skâr′ē əs), *adj.* *Bot.* thin, dry, and membranous, as certain bracts; chaffy. [alter. of *scariose* < NL *scariōs(us);* see -OUS]

scar·la·ti·na (skär′lə tē′nə), *n.* *Pathol.* **1.** See **scarlet fever. 2.** a mild form of scarlet fever. [< NL < It *scarlattina,* equiv. to *scarlatt(o)* SCARLET + *-ina* dim. suffix] —**scar′la·ti′nal, scar·la·ti·nous** (skär′lə-tē′nəs, skär lat′ənəs), *adj.*

scar·la·ti·noid (skär′lə tē′noid, skär lat′ənoid′), *adj.* *Pathol.* resembling scarlatina or its eruptions. [SCARLATIN(A) + -OID]

Scar·lat·ti (skär lät′ē; *It.* skäʀ lät′tē), *n.* **1. A·les·san·dro** (ä′les sän′dʀō), 1659–1725, Italian composer. **2.** his son **Do·me·ni·co** (dô me′nē kō′), 1685?–1757, Italian harpsichordist, organist, and composer.

scar·let (skär′lit), *n.* **1.** a bright-red color inclining toward orange. **2.** a cloth or garments of this color. —*adj.* **3.** of the color scarlet. [ME < ML *scarlett(um),* prob. < Pers *saqalāt* kind of cloth, usually bright red, rich and heavy]

scar′let bu′gler, a perennial herb, *Pentstemon centranthifolius,* of the western U.S., having bluish-green stems, thick leaves, and red flowers.

scar′let clem′atis, a slightly woody vine, *Clematis texensis,* of Texas, having bluish-green leaves, plumed fruit, and solitary, urn-shaped, scarlet-to-pink flowers.

scar′let egg′plant, a hairy, prickly, annual herb, *Solanum integrifolium,* of Africa, grown for its furrowed, nearly round, scarlet or yellow, ornamental fruit. Also called **tomato eggplant.**

scar′let fe′ver, *Pathol.* a contagious febrile disease caused by streptococci and characterized by a scarlet eruption.

scar′let hat′. See **red hat.**

scar′let lark′spur, a California larkspur, *Delphinium cardinale,* having showy, scarlet flowers.

scar′let let′ter, a scarlet letter "A," formerly worn by one convicted of adultery.

Scar′let Let′ter, The, a novel (1850) by Nathaniel Hawthorne.

scar′let light′ning, 1. See **scarlet lychnis. 2.** See **red valerian.**

scar′let lobel′ia. See **cardinal flower.**

scar′let lych′nis, a perennial lychnis, *Lychnis chalcedonica,* having scarlet or sometimes white flowers, the arrangement and shape of the petals resembling a Maltese cross. Also called **Maltese cross, Jerusalem cross, scarlet lightning.**

scar′let mon′key flow′er. See under **monkey flower.**

scar′let pim′pernel. See under **pimpernel.**

scar′let plume′, a small bush, *Euphorbia fulgens,* of Mexico, having showy flower clusters with bright scarlet bracts.

scar′let run′ner, a twining, South American bean plant, *Phaseolus coccineus,* having scarlet flowers.

scar′let sage′, a tender shrub, *Salvia splendens,* of Brazil, having scarlet flowers.

scar′let tan′ager, an American tanager, *Piranga olivacea,* the male of which is bright red with black wings and tail during the breeding season. See illus. under **tanager.**

scar′let Turk's′-cap lil′y, a bulbous herb, *Lilium chalcedonicum,* of Greece, having somewhat ill-scented, deep-scarlet flowers about three inches wide, with recurved petals.

scar′let wom′an, a symbol of pagan Rome or, opprobriously, of the church of Rome. Rev. 17:1–6.

scarp[1] (skärp), *n.* **1.** a line of cliffs formed by the faulting or fracturing of the earth's crust. **2.** *Fort.* an escarp. —*v.t.* **3.** to form or cut into a steep slope. [< It *scarp(a)* a slope. See ESCARP]

scarp[2] (skärp), *n.* *Heraldry.* scarpe.

scarpe (skärp), *n.* *Heraldry.* a diminutive of the bend sinister, one half the usual width; bendlet sinister. Also, **scarp.** [< ONF *(e)scarpe.* See SCARF[1]]

scarp·er (skär′pər), *v.i.* *Brit.* to flee or depart suddenly, esp. without having paid one's bills. [?]

scarph (skärf), *n., v.t.* *Shipbuilding.* scarf[2] (defs. 1, 3, and 4).

scarph′ joint′, *Shipbuilding.* See **scarf joint.**

Scar·ron (skȧ ʀôɴ′), *n.* **Paul** (pôl), 1610–60, French novelist, dramatist, and poet.

Scars·dale (skärz′dāl′), *n.* a town in SE New York, N of New York City. 17,968 (1960).

scart (skärt), *v.t., v.i.* *Scot.* to scratch, scrape, mark, or scar. [metathetic var. of *scrat* to SCRATCH]

scar′ tis′sue, connective tissue that has contracted and become dense and fibrous. Also called **cicatrical tissue.**

scarves (skärvz), *n.* *Chiefly Brit.* a pl. of **scarf**[1].

scar·y (skâr′ē), *adj.,* **scar·i·er, scar·i·est.** *Informal.* **1.** causing fright or alarm. **2.** easily frightened; timid. [SCARE + -Y[1]]

scat[1] (skat), *v.i.,* **scat·ted, scat·ting.** *Informal.* to go off hastily (often used in the imperative). [a hiss + CAT[1]]

scat[2] (skat), *n.* (in the Shetland and Orkney Islands) a crown tax, as for use of common lands. Also, **scatt.** [< Scand; cf. Dan *skat* tax, c. SCEAT]

scat[3] (skat), *n.* See **scat singing.** [? imit.]

scat-, var. of **scato-** before a vowel.

scathe (skāth), *v.,* **scathed, scath·ing,** *n.* —*v.t.* **1.** to attack with severe criticism. **2.** to hurt, harm, or injure, as by scorching. —*n.* **3.** hurt, harm, or injury. [ME < Scand; cf. Icel *skathi* damage, harm; c. OE *sc(e)atha* malefactor, injury, G *Schade* shame] —**scathe′-less,** *adj.* —**scathe′less·ly,** *adv.*

scath·ing (skā′thing), *adj.* **1.** bitterly severe, as a remark: *a scathing review of the play.* **2.** harmful, injurious, or searing. [SCATHE + -ING[2]] —**scath′ing·ly,** *adv.*

scato-, a learned borrowing from Greek meaning "excrement," used in the formation of compound words: *scatology.* Also, *esp. before a vowel,* **scat-.** [< Gk *skato-,* comb. form of *skôr* dung; akin to OE *scearn,* Icel *skarn* dung]

sca·tol·o·gy (skə tol′ə jē), *n.* **1.** the study of or preoccupation with excrement or obscenity. **2.** the study of fossil excrement. Also called **coprology.** [SCATO- + -LOGY] —**scat·o·log·ic** (skat′əloj′ik), **scat′o·log′i·cal,** *adj.*

sca·to·ma (skə tō′mə), *n., pl.* **-mas, -ma·ta** (-mə tə). *Med.* a tumorlike mass of feces in the colon or rectum. Also, **skatoma.** [SCAT- + -OMA]

sca·toph·a·gous (skə tof′ə gəs), *adj.* *Rare.* coprophagous. [SCATO- + -PHAGOUS]

sca·toph·a·gy (skə tof′ə jē), *n.* the religious or pathological practice of eating excrement. [SCATO- + -PHAGY]

sca·tos·co·py (skə tos′kə pē), *n.* *Med.* examination of the feces for diagnostic purposes. Also, **skatoscopy.** [SCATO- + -SCOPY]

scat′ sing′ing, *Jazz.* singing in which the singer substitutes improvised nonsense syllables for the words of a song, and tries to sound and phrase like a musical instrument.

scatt (skat), *n.* scat[2].

scat·ter (skat′ər), *v.t.* **1.** to throw loosely about; distribute at irregular intervals: *to scatter seeds.* **2.** to separate and drive off in various directions; disperse: *to scatter a crowd.* **3.** *Physics.* **a.** to refract or diffract (light or other electromagnetic radiation) irregularly so as to diffuse it in many directions. **b.** (of a medium) to diffuse or deflect (light or other wave phenomena) by collisions between the wave and particles of the medium. —*v.i.* **4.** to separate and disperse; go in different directions. —*n.* **5.** the act of scattering. **6.** that which is scattered. [ME *scatere;* cf. D *schateren* to burst out laughing] —**scat′ter·a·ble,** *adj.* —**scat′-tered·ly,** *adv.* —**scat′tered·ness,** *n.* —**scat′ter·er,** *n.* —**scat′ter·ing·ly,** *adv.*

—**Syn. 1.** broadcast. See **sprinkle. 2.** SCATTER, DISPEL, DISPERSE, DISSIPATE imply separating and driving something away so that its original form disappears. To SCATTER is to separate something tangible into parts at random, and drive these in different directions: *The wind scattered leaves all over the lawn.* To DISPEL is to drive away or scatter usually intangible things so that they vanish or cease to exist: *Photographs of the race dispelled all doubts as to which horse won.* To DISPERSE is to cause (usually) a compact or organized tangible body to separate or scatter in different directions, to be reassembled if desired: *Tear gas dispersed the mob.* To DISSIPATE is usually to scatter by dissolving or reducing to small atoms or parts which cannot be brought together again: *He dissipated his money and his energy in useless activities.*

scat·ter·brain (skat′ər brān′), *n.* one incapable of serious, connected thought. Also, **scat′ter·brains′.** [SCATTER + BRAIN] —**scat′ter·brained′,** *adj.*

scat′ter di′agram, *Statistics.* scattergram.

scat·ter·good (skat′ər go͝od′), *n.* a spendthrift. [SCATTER + GOOD]

scat·ter·gram (skat′ər gram′), *n.* *Statistics.* a graphic representation of the joint variation between two variables using pairs of corresponding sample values as pairs of Cartesian coordinates of points. Also called **scatter diagram.** [SCATTER + -GRAM[1]]

scat·ter·ing (skat′ər ing), *adj.* **1.** distributed or occurring here and there at irregular intervals. **2.** straggling, as an assemblage of parts. **3.** (of votes) cast in small numbers for various candidates. **4.** distributing, dispersing, or separating. —*n.* **5.** a small, scattered number or quantity. **6.** *Physics.* the process in which a wave or beam of particles is diffused or deflected by collisions with particles of the medium which it traverses. [ME; see SCATTER, -ING[2], -ING[1]]

scat′ter pin′, a woman's small ornamental pin, usually worn with other similar pins on a dress, suit jacket, etc.

scat′ter rug′, a small rug, placed on the floor in front of a chair, under a table, etc. Also called **throw rug.**

scat′ter shot′, shot prepared for a weapon having a rifled bore or barrel.

scat·ter·shot (skat′ər shot′), *adj.* delivered over a wide area and at random; generalized and indiscriminate: *a scattershot attack on his program.* [adj. use of SCATTER SHOT]

scaup′ duck′ (skôp), any of several diving ducks of the genus *Aythya*, esp *A. marila* **(greater scaup),** of the Northern Hemisphere, having a bluish-gray bill. Also called **scaup.** [var. of *scalp duck*]

scau·per (skô′pər), *n.* a graver with a flattened or hollowed blade, used in engraving. Also, **scorper.** [var. of *scalper* < L *scalpr(um)* knife. See SCALPEL]

scav·enge (skav′inj), *v.*, **-enged, -eng·ing.** —*v.t.* **1.** to cleanse from filth, as a street. **2.** to take or gather (something usable) from discarded material. **3.** to expel burnt gases from (the cylinder of an internal-combustion engine). **4.** *Metall.* to purify (molten metal) by introducing a substance which will combine chemically with its impurities. —*v.i.* **5.** to act as a scavenger. **6.** (of an engine or cylinder) to become scavenged of burnt gases. **7.** to search, esp. for food. [back formation from SCAVENGER]

scav·en·ger (skav′in jər), *n.* **1.** an organism, object, or person that scavenges, esp. any of various animals feeding on dead organic matter. **2.** a street cleaner. [nasalized var. of AF *scawager*, equiv. to *scawage* (north OF *escawage* inspection) + *-er* -ER[2]; *escawage*, equiv. to *escaw(er)* (to) inspect (< Flem *scauwen* to look at, c. SHOW) + *-age* -AGE]

scav′enger hunt′, a game in which individuals or teams are sent out to accumulate, without purchasing, a series of common, outlandish, or humorous objects, the winner being the person or team returning first with all the items.

scav′enger's daugh′ter, an instrument of torture that doubled over and squeezed the body so strongly and violently that blood was brought forth from the ears and nose: invented in 16th-century England.

Sc.B., Bachelor of Science. [< L *Scientia Baccalaureus*]

Sc.B.C., Bachelor of Science in Chemistry.

Sc.B.E., Bachelor of Science in Engineering.

Sc.D., Doctor of Science. [< L *Scientia Doctor*]

Sc.D.Hyg., Doctor of Science in Hygiene.

Sc.D.Med., Doctor of Medical Science.

sceat (shat), *n.* a silver Anglo-Saxon coin of the 7th and 8th centuries, sometimes including an amount of gold. Also, **sceat·ta** (shat′ə). [OE *sceat, scætt*; c. OS *skat*, OHG *scaz* (G *Schatz*) treasure, tribute. See SCAT[2]]

scelp (skelp), *n., v.t.* *Scot. and North Eng.* skelp[1].

sce·nar·i·o (si nâr′ē ō′, -när′-), *n., pl.* **-nar·i·os.** **1.** an outline of the plot of a dramatic work, giving particulars as to the scenes, characters, situations, etc. **2.** the outline or the manuscript of a motion-picture play, giving the action in the order in which it takes place, the description of scenes and characters, the printed matter to be shown on the screen, etc. [< It < L *scēnāri(um)*. See SCENE, -ARY]

sce·nar·ist (si nâr′ist, -när′-), *n.* a writer of motion-picture scenarios. [SCENAR(IO) + -IST]

scend (send), *Naut.* —*v.i.* (of a vessel) **1.** to heave in a swell. **2.** to lurch forward from the motion of a heavy sea. —*n.* **3.** the heaving motion of a vessel. **4.** the forward impulse imparted by the motion of a sea against a vessel. Also, **send.** [var. of SEND; cf. ASCEND]

scene (sēn), *n.* **1.** the place where some action or event occurs: *He returned to the scene of the murder.* **2.** any view or picture. **3.** an incident or situation in real life. **4.** an embarrassing outbreak or display of anger, strong feeling, or bad manners: *Please don't make a scene in such a public place.* **5.** a division of a play or of an act of a play, now commonly representing what passes between certain of the actors in one place. **6.** (within an act of a play, a motion picture, etc.) a unit of dramatic action in which a single point or effect is made. **7.** the place in which the action of a play or part of a play is supposed to occur. **8.** scenery (def. 2). **9.** *Literature.* **a.** an episode, situation, or the like, as in a narrative. **b.** the setting or locale of a story. **10.** the stage, esp. of an ancient Greek or Roman theater. **11. make the scene,** *U.S. Slang.* to appear in a particular place; engage in a particular activity: *Let's make the scene at the club tonight. Let's make the hipster's scene.* [< L *scēn(a)* background (of the stage) < Gk *skēnḗ* booth (where actors dressed)] —**Syn. 1.** arena, stage, location; center, focus. **2.** See **view. 3.** episode. **4.** demonstration, spectacle, show, display.

scene′ dock′, dock[1] (def. 7).

scene′ mas′ter, *Theat.* a master switch that controls several lighting circuits.

scene′ pack′, *Theat.* a group of flats used as a unit of scenery in a stage set.

scen·er·y (sē′nə rē), *n., pl.* **-er·ies. 1.** the general appearance of a place; the aggregate of features that give character to a landscape. **2.** hangings, draperies, structures, etc., used on a stage to represent a locale or furnish decorative background. **3. chew the scenery,** to act melodramatically; overact. [SCENE + -ERY]

scen′ery wag′on, *Theat.* a low platform on casters for supporting and moving heavy scenery so that sets may be changed rapidly during a play. Also called, *esp. Brit.*, **boat truck.**

sce·nic (sē′nik, sen′ik), *adj.* **1.** of or pertaining to natural scenery; having pleasing or beautiful scenery. **2.** of or pertaining to the stage or to stage scenery. **3.** representing a scene, action, or the like. Also, **sce′ni·cal.** [< L *scēnic(us)* < Gk *skēnikós* theatrical. See SCENE, -IC] —**sce′ni·cal·ly,** *adv.*

sce′nic rail′way, a miniature railroad that carries its passengers on a brief tour of an amusement park, resort, etc.

sce·nog·ra·phy (sē nog′rə fē), *n.* **1.** the art of representing objects in accordance with the rules of perspective. **2.** scene painting (used esp. with reference to ancient Greece). [< L *scēnographia* < Gk *skēnographía*. See SCENE, -O-, -GRAPHY] —**sce·nog′raph·er,** *n.* —**sce·no·graph·ic** (sē′nə graf′ik, sen′ə-), **sce′no·graph′i·cal,** *adj.* —**sce′no·graph′i·cal·ly,** *adv.*

scent (sent), *n.* **1.** a distinctive odor, esp. when agreeable: *the scent of roses.* **2.** an odor left in passing, by means of which an animal or person may be traced. **3.** a track or trail as or as if indicated by such an odor: *The dogs lost the scent and the prisoner escaped.* **4.** small pieces of paper dropped by the hares in the game of hare and hounds. **5.** *Chiefly Brit.* perfume. **6.** the sense of smell: *a remarkably keen scent.* —*v.t.* **7.** to perceive or recognize by the sense of smell: *to scent trouble.* **8.** to fill with an odor: perfume. —*v.i.* **9.** to hunt by the sense of smell, as a hound. [ME *sent* < MF *sent(ir)* (to) smell < L *sentīre* to feel. Cf. SENSE] —**scent′less,** *adj.* —**scent′less·ness,** *n.*

scent′less cam′omile, an annual plant, *Matricaria inodora*, of Eurasia, having yellow flowers with white rays, the foliage having very little scent. Also called **corn mayweed.**

Sceph·rus (skef′rəs), *n.* *Class. Myth.* a son of Tegeates who was murdered by his brother, Limon.

scep·ter (sep′tər), *n.* **1.** a rod or wand borne in the hand as an emblem of regal or imperial power. **2.** royal or imperial power or authority; sovereignty. —*v.t.* **3.** to give a scepter to; invest with authority. Also, *esp. Brit.*, **sceptre.** [ME *(s)ceptre* < OF < LL *sceptr(um)* < Gk *skēptron* staff] —**scep′ter·less,** *adj.* —**scep·tral** (sep′trəl), *adj.*

scep·tic (skep′tik), *n. adj.* skeptic

scep·ti·cal (skep′ti kəl), *adj.* skeptical. —**scep′ti·cal·ly,** *adv.*

scep·ti·cism (skep′ti siz′əm), *n.* skepticism.

scep·tre (sep′tər), *n., v.t.,* **-tred, -tring.** *Chiefly Brit.* scepter.

scf, standard cubic foot.

scfh, standard cubic feet per hour

scfm, standard cubic feet per minute.

Sch., schilling.

sch., **1.** school. **2.** schooner.

Schacht (shäkht), *n.* **(Horace Greeley) Hjal·mar** (yäl′mär), 1877–1970, German financier: acting minister of national economy 1934–37.

Schaer·beek (*Flemish.* skhär′bāk), *n.* a city in central Belgium, near Brussels. 120,768 (est. 1964).

Schaerf (sherf), *n.* **A·dolf** (ä′dôlf), 1890–1965, Austrian statesman: president 1957–65.

Scha′fer meth′od (shā′fər). See **prone pressure method.** Also, **Scha′fer's Meth′od.** [named after Sir Edward A. Sharpey-*Schafer* (1850–1935), English physiologist]

Schaff·hau·sen (shäf′hou′zən), *n.* **1.** a canton in N Switzerland. 65,981 (1960); 100 sq. mi. **2.** a city in and the capital of this canton, on the Rhine. 30,904 (1960).

schap·pe (shä′pə), *v.*, **schapped** (shäpt), **schap·ping,** *n.* —*v.t.* **1.** to remove sericin from (silk waste) by fermentation. —*n.* **2.** See **schappe silk.** [< Swiss G: raw silk leavings; cf. F *échappement* leakage]

schap′pe silk′, a yarn or fabric of or similar to spun silk. Also called **schappe, chappe.**

Scharn·horst (shärn′hôrst), *n.* **Ger·hard Jo·hann David von** ((gār′härt yō′hän dä′vēt fən), 1755–1813, Prussian general.

Schar·wen·ka (shär veng′kä), *n.* **1. (Lud·wig) Phi·lipp** (lo͞ot′vikh fē′lip, fil′ip; lo͞od′-), 1847–1917, German composer. **2.** his brother, **(Franz) Xa·ver** (fränts ksä′vər, ksä vär′), 1850–1924, German pianist and composer.

Schar·y (shâr′ē), *n.* **Do·re** (dôr′ē, dôr′ē), (*Isidore Schary*), 1905–80, U.S. motion-picture producer, writer, and playwright.

schat·chen (shät′khən), *n., pl.* **schat·cho·nim** (shät-khō′nim), **schat·chens.** *Yiddish.* shadchan.

Schaum·burg-Lip·pe (shoum′bo͝orkh lip′ə), *n.* a former state in NW Germany.

schav (shäv), *n.* *Jewish or Eastern European Cookery.* a cold soup of sorrel to which chopped egg, sour cream, lemon juice, and chopped scallions are sometimes added. [< Russ *shchavel* sorrel]

Schech·ter (shek′tər), *n.* **Solomon,** 1847–1915, U.S. Hebraist, born in Rumania.

Sche·di·us (skē′dē əs), *n.* (in the *Iliad*) a son of Iphitus and Hippolyte who was one of the suitors of Helen.

sched·ule (skej′o͞ol, -o͞ol, -o͞o əl; *Brit.* shed′yo͞ol, shej′o͞ol), *n., v.*, **-uled, -ul·ing.** —*n.* **1.** a plan of procedure, usually written, for a proposed objective, esp. with reference to the sequence of and time allotted for each item or operation necessary to its completion: *The schedule allows three weeks for this stage.* **2.** a series of items to be handled or of events to occur at or during a particular time or period: *He always has a full schedule.* **3.** a timetable. **4.** a written or printed statement of details, often in classified or tabular form, esp. one forming an appendix or explanatory addition to another document. **5.** *Obs.* a written paper. —*v.t.* **6.** to make a schedule of or enter in a schedule. **7.** to plan for a certain date: *to schedule publication for June.* [< LL *schedul(a)*, equiv. to L *sched(a)* leaf of paper + *-ula* -ULE; r. ME *cedule, sedule* < MF] —**sched′u·lar,** *adj.* —**Syn. 4.** table, register. See **list**[1]. **6.** register, list, enroll, tabulate.

Schee·le (shā′lə), *n.* **Karl Wil·helm** (kärl vil′helm), 1742–86, Swedish chemist.

Schee′le's green′, copper arsenite used as a pigment, esp. in paints. [named after K.W. SCHEELE]

scheel·ite (shā′līt, shē′-), *n.* *Mineral.* calcium tungstate, $CaWO_4$, usually occurring in tetragonal crystals: an important ore of tungsten. [< G *Scheelit*, named after K. W. SCHEELE, who first isolated tungstic acid; see -ITE[1]]

schef·fer·ite (shef′ə rīt′), *n.* *Mineral.* a member of the pyroxene group, containing manganese and sometimes iron, and occurring usually in the form of brown or black tabular crystals. [< Sw *schefferit*, named after H. T. *Scheffer* (1710–59), Swedish mineralogist; see -ITE[1]]

Sche·her·a·za·de (shə her′ə zä′də, -zäd′, -hēr′-), *n.* **1.** (in the *Arabian Nights' Entertainments*) the wife of the sultan of India, who relates such interesting tales nightly that the sultan spares her life. **2.** (*italics.*) a symphonic suite (1888) by Nikolai Rimski-Korsakov.

Scheidt (shīt), *n.* **Sa·mu·el** (zä′mo͞o el′), 1587–1654, German organist and composer.

Schein (shīn), *n.* **Jo·hann Her·mann** (yō′hän her′-män), 1586–1630, German composer.

Schei·ner (shī′nər), *n.* a crater in the third quadrant of the face of the moon: about 70 miles in diameter.

Scheldt (skelt), *n.* a river in W Europe, flowing from N France through W Belgium and SW Netherlands into the North Sea. 270 mi. long. Flemish, **Schel·de** (skhel′-də). French, **Escaut.**

Schel·ling (shel′ing), *n.* **Frie·drich Wil·helm Jo·seph von** (frē′drikh vil′helm yō′zef fən), 1775–1854, German philosopher. —**Schel′ling·ism, Schel·ling·i·an·ism** (she ling′ē ə niz′əm), *n.*

sche·ma (skē′mə), *n., pl.* **-ma·ta** (-mə tə). **1.** a diagram, plan, or scheme. **2.** (in Kantian epistemology) a concept, similar to a universal but limited to phenomenal knowledge, by which an object of knowledge or an idea of pure reason may be apprehended. [< Gk: form]

sche·mat·ic (skē mat′ik), *adj.* **1.** pertaining to or of the nature of a schema, diagram, or scheme; diagrammatic. —*n.* **2.** a diagram, plan, arrangement, drawing, or the like: *Read the schematic before attempting any repairs.* [< NL *schēmatic(us)* < Gk *schēmatikós*. See SCHEME, -IC] —**sche·mat′i·cal·ly,** *adv.*

sche·ma·tise (skē′mə tīz′), *v.t.,* **-tised, -tis·ing.** *Chiefly Brit.* schematize. —**sche′ma·ti·sa′tion,** *n.* —**sche′ma·tis′er,** *n.*

sche·ma·tism (skē′mə tiz′əm), *n.* **1.** the particular form or disposition of a thing. **2.** a schematic arrangement. [< Gk *schēmatism(ós)*. See SCHEMATIZE, -ISM]

sche·ma·tize (skē′mə tīz′), *v.t.,* **-tized, -tiz·ing.** to reduce to or arrange according to a scheme. [< Gk *schēmatíz(ein)* (to) form. See SCHEME, -IZE] —**sche′-ma·ti·za′tion,** *n.* —**sche′ma·tiz′er,** *n.*

scheme (skēm), *n., v.*, **schemed, schem·ing.** —*n.* **1.** a plan, design, or program of action to be followed; project. **2.** *Brit.* a plan, program, or policy officially adopted and followed, as by a government or business: *The company's pension scheme is very successful.* **3.** an underhand plot; intrigue. **4.** a visionary or impractical project. **5.** a body or system of related doctrines, theories, etc.: *a scheme of philosophy.* **6.** any system of correlated things, parts, etc., or the manner of its arrangement. **7.** an analytical or tabular statement. **8.** a diagram, map, or the like. **9.** an astrological diagram of the heavens. —*v.t.* **10.** to devise as a scheme; plan; plot; contrive. —*v.i.* **11.** to lay schemes; devise plans; plot. [< ML *schēma, schēmat-* < Gk: form, figure] —**scheme′-ful,** *adj.* —**scheme′less,** *adj.* —**schem′er,** *n.* —**Syn. 1–2.** See **plan. 3.** stratagem, cabal, conspiracy. **6.** pattern, schema, arrangement. **10.** project, design. See **plot**[1].

schem·ing (skē′ming), *adj.* given to making plans, esp. sly and underhand ones; crafty. [SCHEME + -ING[2]] —**schem′ing·ly,** *adv.*

Sche·nec·ta·dy (skə nek′tə dē), *n.* a city in E New York, on the Mohawk River. 81,682 (1960).

scherm (skerm, skûrm), *n.* a hut constructed by South African Bushmen from branches and scraped animal hides. [< D: SCREEN]

Scher·man (shûr′mən), *n.* **Thomas,** born 1917, U.S. orchestra conductor.

scher·zan·do (sker tsän′dō, -tsan′-), *adj.* (a musical direction) playful; sportive. [< It, prp. of *scherzare* to joke; see SCHERZO]

scher·zo (sker′tsō), *n., pl.* **-zos, -zi** (-tsē). *Music.* a movement or passage of light or playful character, esp. as the second or third division of a sonata or a symphony. [< It: joke < G *Scherz* joke]

Sche·ven·ing·en (skhā′vən ing′ən), *n.* a town in the W Netherlands, near The Hague: seaside resort.

Schia·pa·rel·li (skyä′pə rel′ē, *It.* skyä′pä rel′lē *for 1, 2;* skap′ə rel′ē, shap′- *for 3*), *n.* **1. El·sa** (el′sä), ?1900–73, French fashion designer, born in Italy. **2. Gio·van·ni Vir·gin·io** (jô vän′nē vēr jē′nyô), 1835–1910, Italian astronomer. **3.** a walled plain in the second quadrant of the face of the moon: about 16 miles in diameter.

schia·vo·ne (skyə vō′nē; *It.* skyä vô′ne), *n., pl.* **-nes,** *It.* **-ni** (-nē). an Italian double-edged sword having a basket hilt, used in the 17th and 18th centuries. Also, **schi·a·vo·na** (skī′ə vō′nə). [< It: lit., Slavonian, from its use by the Slavonian guards of the Doge]

Schick (shik), *n.* **1. Bé·la** (bā′lə; *Hung.* bā′lo), 1877–1967, U.S. pediatrician, born in Hungary. **2. George,** born 1908, U.S. orchestra conductor, born in Czechoslovakia. **3. Re·ne** (re ne′), (*Rene Schick Gutierez*), 1909–1966, Nicaraguan statesman: president 1963–65.

Schick·ard (shik′ərd), *n.* a walled plain in the third quadrant of the face of the moon: about 134 miles in diameter.

Schick′ test′, *Med.* a diphtheria-immunity test in which diphtheria toxoid is injected cutaneously, nonimmunity being characterized by an inflammation at the injection site. [named after Dr. Béla SCHICK]

Schie·dam (skhē däm′), *n.* a city in the SW Netherlands. 81,100 (1962).

schiff·li (shif′lē), *n.* **1.** a large, loomlike machine for embroidering textiles and working patterns in lace. **2.** the delicate work produced by such a machine, used on clothing, as lingerie and millinery, on furniture coverings, etc. [< SwissG: lit., little ship]

schil·ler (shil′ər), *n.* a bronzelike luster, sometimes with iridescence, occurring on certain minerals. [< G: play of colors, glitter]

Schil·ler (shil′ər), *n.* **1. Ferdinand Can·ning Scott** (kan′ing), 1864–1937, English philosopher in the U.S. **2. Jo·hann Chris·toph Frie·drich von** (yō′hän kris′tôf frē′driKH fən), 1759–1805, German poet, dramatist, and historian. **3.** an elliptical walled plain in the third quadrant of the face of the moon: about 112 miles in length and 60 miles in width.

schil·ler·ize (shil′ə rīz′), *v.t.*, **-ized, -iz·ing.** to give a schiller to (a crystal) by developing microscopic inclusions along certain planes. [SCHILLER + -IZE] —**schil′ler·i·za′tion,** *n.*

Schil′ler Park′, a town in NE Illinois. 5687 (1960).

schil′ler spar′, a mineral, a variety of serpentine produced by the alteration of enstatite, occurring in green or brown foliated masses exhibiting schiller. Also called **bastite.** [part. trans. of G *Schillerspat,* equiv. to *Schiller* SCHILLER + *Spat* spar]

schil·ling (shil′ing), *n.* **1.** a copper and aluminum coin and monetary unit of Austria, equal to 100 groschen. *Abbr.:* S., Sch. **2.** any of various former minor coins of Germany. [< G; c. SHILLING]

Schi·pa (skē′pä), *n.* **Ti·to** (tē′tō), 1890–1965, Italian operatic tenor.

schip·per·ke (skip′ər kē, -kə), *n.* one of a Belgian breed of small dogs having erect ears and a thick, black coat, originally used as a watchdog on boats in the Netherlands and Belgium. [< D: little boatman; see SKIPPER[1]]

Schip·pers (ship′ərz), *n.* **Thomas,** 1930–77, U.S. orchestra conductor.

schism (siz′əm), *n.* **1.** division or disunion, esp. into mutually opposed parties. **2.** the parties so formed. **3.** *Eccles.* **a.** a formal division within, or separation from, a church or religious body over some doctrinal difference. **b.** the state of a sect or body formed by such division. **c.** the offense of causing or seeking to cause such a division. [< eccl. L *schism(a), schismat-* < Gk, equiv. to *schiz(ein)* (to) split + *-ma, -mat-* n. suffix; r. ME *(s)cisme, sisme* < MF < L, as above] —**schism′less,** *adj.*

schis·mat·ic (siz mat′ik), *adj.* **1.** Also, **schis·mat′i·cal.** of, pertaining to, or of the nature of schism; guilty of schism. —*n.* **2.** one who promotes schism or is an adherent of a schismatic body. [< eccl. L *schismatic(us)* < Gk *schismatikós* (see SCHISM, -IC); r. ME *scismatik,* etc. < MF *scismatique* < L, as above] —**shis·mat′i·cal·ly,** *adv.* —**schis·mat′i·cal·ness,** *n.*

schist (shist), *n.* any of a class of crystalline rocks whose constituent minerals have a more or less parallel or foliated arrangement, due mostly to metamorphic action. [< NL *schist(us)* < L *(lapis) schistos* < Gk: splittable, equiv. to *schíz(ein)* (to) split + *-tos* adj. suffix]

schis·tose (shis′tōs), *adj.* of, resembling, or in the form of schist. Also, **schis·tous** (shis′təs). [SCHIST + -OSE[1]] —**schis·tos·i·ty** (shi stos′i tē), *n.*

schis·to·sis (shi stō′sis), *n.* *Pathol.* fibrosis of the lungs caused by inhaling dust from slate. [SCHIST + -OSIS]

schis·to·some (shis′tə sōm′), *n.* **1.** any elongated trematode of the genus *Schistosoma,* parasitic in the blood vessels of man and other mammals; a blood fluke. —*adj.* **2.** pertaining to or caused by schistosomes. [< NL *Schistosoma.* See SCHIST, -O-, -SOME[3]]

schis·to·so·mi·a·sis (shis′tə sō mī′ə sis), *n.* *Pathol.* infestation with schistosomes. [SCHISTOSOME + -IASIS]

schiz (skits, skiz), *n.* *Slang.* a schizophrenic person. Also, **schizo.** [by shortening]

schiz·o (skit′sō), *n., pl.* **-os.** schiz.

schizo-, a learned borrowing from Greek meaning "split," used in the formation of compound words: *schizogenetic.* Also, *esp. before a vowel,* **schiz-.** [< Gk, comb. form repr. *schízein* to part, split]

schiz·o·carp (skiz′ə kärp′), *n.* *Bot.* a dry fruit which at maturity splits into two or more one-seeded indehiscent carpels. [SCHIZO- + -CARP] —**schiz′o·car′pous, schiz′o·car′pic,** *adj.*

schi·zog·a·my (ski zog′ə mē), *n.* *Biol.* reproduction characterized by division of the organism into sexual and asexual parts, as in certain polychaetes. [SCHIZO- + -GAMY]

schiz·o·gen·e·sis (skiz′ə jen′i sis), *n.* *Biol.* reproduction by fission. [SCHIZO- + GENESIS]

schiz·o·ge·net·ic (skiz′ō jə net′ik), *adj.* *Biol.* reproducing or formed by fission. Also, **schiz·o·gen·ic** (skiz′ə jen′ik), **schizogenous.** [SCHIZO- + GENETIC] —**schiz′o·ge·net′i·cal·ly,** *adv.*

schi·zog·e·nous (ski zoj′ə nəs), *adj.* *Biol.* **1.** schizogenetic. **2.** schizogonous. [SCHIZO- + -GENOUS] —**schi·zog′e·nous·ly,** *adv.*

schi·zog·o·nous (ski zog′ə nəs), *adj.* *Biol.* pertaining to or reproducing by schizogony. Also, **schiz·o·gon·ic** (skiz′ə gon′ik), **schizogenous.** [SCHIZO- + -GONOUS]

schi·zog·o·ny (ski zog′ə nē), *n.* *Biol.* (in the asexual reproduction of certain sporozoans) the multiple fission of a trophozoite or schizont into merozoites. [< NL; see SCHIZO-, -GONY]

schiz·oid (skit′soid, skiz′oid), *adj.* *Psychol.* **1.** of or pertaining to a personality disorder marked by dissociation, passivity, withdrawal, depression, and autistic fantasies. **2.** of or pertaining to schizophrenia or multiple personality. —*n.* **3.** a schizoid person. [SCHIZ- + -OID]

schiz·o·my·cete (skiz′ō mī sēt′), *n.* any of numerous organisms of the class *Schizomycetes,* comprising the bacteria. [SCHIZO- + -MYCETE(S)] —**schiz′o·my·ce′tic, schiz′o·my·ce′tous,** *adj.*

schiz·o·my·co·sis (skiz′ō mī kō′sis), *n.* *Pathol.* any disease due to schizomycetes. [SCHIZO- + MYCOSIS]

schi·zont (skī′zont, skiz′ont), *n.* *Biol.* (in the asexual reproduction of certain sporozoans) a cell developed from a trophozoite, which undergoes multiple fission to form merozoites. [SCHIZ- + *-ont;* see ONTO-]

schiz·o·phre·ni·a (skit′sə frē′nē ə, -frēn′yə, skiz′ə-), *n.* a psychosis marked by withdrawn, bizarre, and sometimes delusional behavior and by intellectual and emotional deterioration. Also called **dementia praecox.** [SCHIZO- + -PHRENIA] —**schiz·o·phrene** (skit′sə frēn′, skiz′ə-), *n.* —**schiz·o·phren·ic** (skit′sə fren′ik, skiz′ə-), *adj.*

schiz·o·phy·ceous (skiz′ə fī′shəs, -fish′əs), *adj.* *Bot.* belonging to the *Schizophyceae,* a class or group of unicellular and multicellular green or bluish-green algae, occurring in both salt and fresh water and often causing pollution of drinking water. [SCHIZO- + -PHYCEOUS]

schiz·o·phyte (skiz′ə fīt′), *n.* any of the *Schizophyta,* a group of plants comprising the schizomycetes and the schizophyceous algae, characterized by a simple structure and reproduction by simple fission or spores. [SCHIZO- + -PHYTE] —**schiz·o·phyt·ic** (skiz′ə fit′ik), *adj.*

schiz·o·pod (skiz′ə pod′), *n.* **1.** any crustacean of the former order or division *Schizopoda,* now divided into the orders *Mysidacea,* comprising the opossum shrimps, and *Euphausiacea.* —*adj.* **2.** Also, **schi·zop·o·dous** (skizop′ə dəs, ski-). belonging or pertaining to the *Schizopoda.* [SCHIZO- + -POD]

schiz·o·thy·mi·a (skit′sə thī′mē ə, skiz′ə-), *n.* *Psychiatry.* an emotional state or temperament out of keeping with the ideational content. [SCHIZO- + NL *-thymia* < Gk *thym(ós)* soul, spirit, strength + *-ia* -IA] —**schiz′o·thy′mic,** *adj.*

Schle·gel (shlā′gəl), *n.* **1. Au·gust Wil·helm von** (ou′go͝ost vil′helm fən), 1767–1845, German poet, critic, and translator. **2.** his brother, **Frie·drich von** (frē′driKH fən), 1772–1829, German critic, philosopher, and poet.

Schlei·den (shlīd′ən), *n.* **Mat·thi·as Ja·kob** (mä tē′äs yä′kôp), 1804–81, German botanist.

Schlei·er·ma·cher (shlī′ər mä′KHər), *n.* **Frie·drich Ernst Da·ni·el** (frē′driKH ernst dä′nē el′), 1768–1834, German theologian and philosopher.

schle·miel (shlə mēl′), *n.* *Slang.* an awkward and unlucky person for whom things never turn out right. Also, **schle·mihl′, shlemiel.** [< Yiddish < G, after Peter *Schlemihl,* title character in a novel (1814) by Adelbert von Chamisso (1781–1838), German writer]

schlepp (shlep), *Slang.* —*v.t.* **1.** to carry; lug: *to schlepp an umbrella on a sunny day.* —*n.* **2.** Also, **schlepp′er.** a person of no importance; one who is unaccomplished: *a schlepp who sits around doing nothing.* [< Yiddish *shlep(en)* (to) drag < LG *schleppen;* c. HG *schleifen.* Cf. SLIP[1]]

Schle·si·en (shlā′zē ən), *n.* German name of **Silesia.**

Schles·in·ger (shles′ən jər, shlā′zing ər), *n.* **Arthur Mei·er** (mī′ər), 1888–1965, and his son, **Arthur Meier, Jr.,** born 1917, U.S. historians.

Schles·wig (shles′wig; *Ger.* shlās′viKH), *n.* **1.** a seaport in N West Germany, on the Baltic. 33,600 (1963). **2.** a former duchy of Denmark: annexed by Prussia 1864; the N part was returned to Denmark as the result of a plebiscite 1920. Also **Sleswick.** Danish, **Slesvig.**

Schles·wig-Hol·stein (shles′wig hōl′stīn; *Ger.* shlās′viKH hōl′shtīn), *n.* **1.** two contiguous duchies of Denmark that were a center of international tension in the 19th century: Prussia annexed Schleswig 1864 and Holstein 1866. **2.** a state of N West Germany, including the former duchies of Holstein and Lauenburg and part of Schleswig. 2,364,000 (1963); 6055 sq. mi. *Cap.:* Kiel.

Schley (slī), *n.* **Win·field Scott** (win′fēld′), 1839–1911, U.S. rear admiral.

Schlie·mann (shlē′män′), *n.* **Hein·rich** (hīn′riKH), 1822–90, German archaeologist and expert on Homer.

schlie·ren (shlēr′ən), *n.* (*construed as pl.*) **1.** *Petrog.* streaks or irregularly shaped masses in an igneous rock that differ in texture or composition from the main mass. **2.** *Physics.* the visible streaks in a turbulent, transparent fluid, each streak being a region that has a density and index of refraction differing from that of the greater part of the fluid. [< G, pl. of *Schliere* streak]

schlie′ren meth′od, *Physical Chem.* a method for detecting regions of differing densities in a clear fluid by photographing a beam of light passed obliquely through it.

schlie′ren photog′raphy, a high-speed photographic technique for photographing schlieren in turbulent fluids.

schli·ma·zel (shli mä′zəl), *n.* *Slang.* an inept, bungling person who suffers from unremitting bad luck. Also, **schli·mazl′, shlimazel, shlimazl.** [< Yiddish, equiv. to *shlim* bad (< MHG *slimp* wrong) + *mazel* luck < LHeb *mazāl*]

schlock (shlok), *Slang.* —*adj.* **1.** cheap; trashy: *a schlock store.* —*n.* **2.** something of cheap or inferior quality; junk. [< Yiddish]

Schloss (shlôs), *n., pl.* **Schlös·ser** (shlœ′sər). *German.* a castle or palace.

Schloss, Das (*Ger.* däs shlôs′). See **Castle, The.**

Schmal·kal·den (shmäl′käl′dən), *n.* a town in SW East Germany: a league to defend Protestantism formed here 1531. 12,663 (1946).

schmaltz (shmälts, shmôlts), *n.* *Informal.* **1.** exaggerated sentimentalism, as in music or soap operas. **2.** fat or grease, esp. of a chicken. Also, **schmalz.** [< G, Yiddish; c. SMELT[1]; orig. meaning was grease, butter]

Schmaltz′ pro′file mi′croscope (shmôlts, shmälts). See **profile microscope.** [named after its inventor]

schmaltz·y (shmält′sē, shmôlt′-), *adj.* **schmaltz·i·er, schmaltz·i·est.** *Slang.* of, pertaining to, or characterized by schmaltz. [SCHMALTZ + -Y[1]]

schmalz·y (shmält′sē, shmôlt′-), *adj.,* **schmalz·i·er, schmalz·i·est.** *Slang.* schmaltzy.

Schme·ling (shmel′ing; *Ger.* shmā′ling), *n.* **Max** (maks; *Ger,* mäks) born 1905, German boxer: world heavyweight champion 1930–32.

Schmidt (shmit), *n.* **1. Hel·mut** (hel′mo͝ot), born 1918, West German political leader: chancellor 1974–82. **2.** a crater in the fourth quadrant of the face of the moon: about 8 miles in diameter.

Schmidt′ tel′escope (shmit), a wide-angle reflecting telescope used primarily for astronomical photography, in which spherical aberration and coma are reduced to a minimum by means of a spherical mirror with a corrector plate near its focus. Also called **Schmidt′ cam′era.** [named after Bernard *Schmidt* (1879–1935), German inventor]

schmier·kase (shmēr′kāz′, -kā′zə), *n.* See **cottage cheese.** [< G: lit., smear-cheese]

Schmitt (shmit), *n.* **Ber·na·dotte Ev·er·ly** (bûr′nədot′ ev′ər lē), 1886–1969, U.S. historian.

schmo (shmō), *n., pl.* **schmoes.** *U.S. Slang.* a foolish, boring, or stupid person; a jerk. Also, **schmoe.** [< Yiddish; cf. SCHMUCK]

schmoose (shmo͞oz, shmo͞os), *v.i.,* **schmoosed, schmoos·ing.** schmooze. Also, **schmoos.**

schmooze (shmo͞oz), *v.i.,* **schmoozed, schmooz·ing,** *n.* *Slang.* —*v.i.* **1.** to chat idly; gossip. —*n.* **2.** idle conversation; chatter. Also, **schmoose, schmoos.** [< Yiddish, v. use of *schmues* < Heb *shemu'oth* reports, gossip (root *sm'* hear)]

schmuck (shmuk), *n.* *Slang.* fool; oaf; jerk. [< Yiddish: male member, lit., pendant; akin to OHG *smocko,* G *Schmuck* ornament, finery]

Sch.Mus.B., Bachelor of School Music.

Schna·bel (shnä′bəl), *n.* **Ar·tur** (är′to͝or), 1882–1951, Austrian pianist.

schnap·per (shnap′ər, snap′-), *n.* a food fish, *Pagrosomus auratus,* found in large numbers off the shores of Australia and New Zealand. [var. of SNAPPER; *sch* < G, cf. SCHNAPPS]

schnapps (shnäps, shnaps), *n.* spirituous liquor esp. Hollands or potato spirits. Also, **schnaps.** [< G, deriv. of *schnapper* to nip]

schnau·zer (shnou′zər; *Ger.* shnou′tsər), *n.* one of a German breed of dogs having a wiry, pepper-and-salt, black, or black-and-tan coat, occurring in three varieties differing only in size. [< G, equiv. to *Schnauze* SNOUT + *-er* -ER[1]]

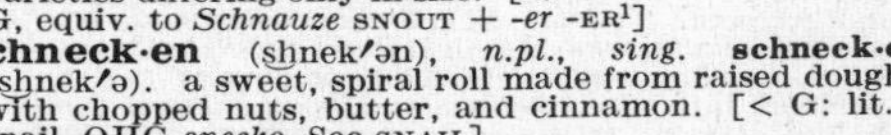

Schnauzer (19 in. high at shoulder)

schneck·en (shnek′ən), *n.pl., sing.* **schneck·e** (shnek′ə). a sweet, spiral roll made from raised dough with chopped nuts, butter, and cinnamon. [< G: lit., snail, OHG *snecko.* See SNAIL]

schnei·der (shnī′dər), (in gin rummy) —*v.t.* **1.** to prevent (an opponent) from scoring a point in a game or match. —*n.* **2.** an act of schneidering or fact of being schneidered. [< G: tailor]

Schnei·der·man (shnī′dər mən), *n.* **Rose,** 1884–1972, U.S. labor leader, born in Poland.

schnit·zel (shnit′səl), *n.* *German Cookery.* a veal cutlet. [< G: a shaving, deriv. of *schnitzeln* to whittle]

Schnitz·ler (shnits′lər; *Ger.* shnits′lər), *n.* **Ar·thur** (är′thər; *Ger.* är′to͝or), 1862–1931, Austrian dramatist and novelist.

schnook (shno͝ok), *n.* *Slang.* an unimportant or stupid person; dope. [< Yiddish, var. of *schmok* SCHMUCK]

schnor·kle (shnôr′kəl), *n.* snorkel (def. 1). Also, **schnor′kel.**

schnor·rer (shnōr′ər, shnôr′-), *n.* *Slang.* a beggar; one who seeks aid from another without justification; sponger. [< Yiddish < G *Schnurrer* beggar]

schnoz·zle (shnoz′əl), *n.* *Slang.* nose. [< Yiddish *schn(oitsl)* little snout + NOZZLE]

Schoen′flies sym′bol (shōn′flēz), *Crystall.* a notation that indicates a particular point group. [named after its inventor]

Schoe·ni·us (skē′nē əs), *n.* *Class. Myth.* a Boeotian sometimes described as the father of Atalanta.

Scho·field (skō′fēld′), *n.* **1. John Mc·Al·lis·ter** (məkal′i stər), 1831–1906, U.S. general. **2.** a town in central Wisconsin. 3038 (1960).

scho·la can·to·rum (skō′lə kan tōr′əm, -tôr′-), *pl.* **scho·lae can·to·rum** (skō′lē kan tōr′əm, -tôr′-). **1.** an ecclesiastical choir or choir school. **2.** a section of a church, cathedral, or the like, for use by the choir. [< ML: school of singers]

schol·ar (skol′ər), *n.* **1.** a learned or erudite person esp. one who has profound knowledge of a particular subject. **2.** a student; pupil. **3.** a student whose merit entitles him to money or other aid to pursue his studies. [< LL *scholār(is),* equiv. to L *schol(a)* SCHOOL[1] + *-āris* -AR[2]; r. ME *scoler(e),* OE *scolere* < LL, as above] —**schol′ar·less,** *adj.* —**Syn. 1.** savant. **2.** See **pupil**[1].

schol·arch (skol′ärk), *n.* **1.** the head of a school. **2.** the head of a school of philosophy in ancient Athens. [< Gk *scholárchēs.* See SCHOOL[1], -ARCH]

schol·ar·ly (skol′ər lē), *adj.* **1.** of, like, or befitting a scholar: *scholarly habits.* **2.** having the qualities of a scholar: *a scholarly person.* —*adv.* **3.** like a scholar. [SCHOLAR + -LY] —**schol′ar·li·ness,** *n.*

schol·ar·ship (skol′ər ship′), *n.* **1.** learning; knowledge acquired by study; the academic attainments of a scholar. **2.** the position of a student who, because of merit, need, etc., is granted money or other aid to pursue his studies. **3.** the sum of money or other aid granted to a scholar. **4.** a foundation to provide financial assistance to students. [SCHOLAR + -SHIP] —**Syn. 1.** See **learning.**

scho·las·tic (skə las′tik), *adj.* Also, **scho·las′ti·cal. 1.** of or pertaining to schools, scholars, or education: *scholastic attainments.* **2.** of or pertaining to secondary education or schools: *a scholastic meet.* **3.** of or pertaining to the medieval schoolmen. **4.** pedantic. —*n.* **5.** (*sometimes cap.*) a schoolman, a disciple of the schoolmen, or an adherent of scholasticism. **6.** a pedantic person. **7.** *Rom. Cath. Ch.* a student in a scholasticate. [< L *scholastic(us)* < Gk *scholastikós* studious, learned. See SCHOOL[1], -ISTIC] —**scho·las′ti·cal·ly,** *adv.*

scho·las·ti·cate (skə las′tə kāt′, -kit), *n.* *Rom. Cath. Ch.* **1.** a course of study for seminarians, taken prior to their theological studies. **2.** a school for this course of study. [< NL *scholasticāt(us).* See SCHOLASTIC, -ATE[1]]

scho·las·ti·cism (skə las′ti siz′əm), *n.* **1.** (*sometimes cap.*) the set of doctrines of the schoolmen; the system of theological and philosophical teaching predominant in the Middle Ages, based chiefly upon the authority of the church fathers and of Aristotle and his commentators. **2.** narrow adherence to traditional teachings, doctrines, or methods. [SCHOLASTIC + -ISM]

scho·li·ast (skō′lē ast′), *n.* **1.** an ancient commentator on the classics. **2.** one who writes scholia. [< LL *scholiast(a)* < Gk *scholiast(ḗs).* See SCHOLIUM, -IST] —**scho′li·as′tic,** *adj.*

scho·li·um (skō′lē əm), *n., pl.* **-li·a** (-lē ə). **1.** Often, **scholia. a.** an explanatory note or comment. **b.** an ancient annotation upon a passage in a Greek or Latin author. **2.** a note added to illustrate or amplify, as in a mathematical work. [< ML < Gk *schólion,* equiv. to *schol(ē)* SCHOOL[1] + *-ion* dim. suffix]

Schom·ber·ger (sho̲m′bər gər), *n.* a walled plain in the fourth quadrant of the face of the moon: about 50 miles in diameter. Also, **Schöm′ber·ger.**

Schön·bein (shœn′bīn), *n.* **Chris·ti·an Frie·drich** (kris′tē än′ frē′drikh), 1799–1868, Swiss chemist.

Schön·berg (shœn′bûrg; *Ger.* shœn′berkh), *n.* **Ar·nold** (är′nəld; *Ger.* är′nəlt), 1874–1951, Austrian composer in the U.S.

Schö·ne Mül·ler·in, Die (*Ger.* dē shœ′nə my′ler in), a song cycle (1823), by Franz Schubert, consisting of 20 songs set to poems by Wilhelm Müller.

Schon·gau·er (shōn′gou ər; *Ger.* shōn′gou ər), *n.* **Mar·tin** (mär′tᵊn; *Ger.* mär′tēn), c1430–91, German engraver and painter.

school[1] (sko͞ol), *n.* **1.** a place, institution, or building where instruction is given, esp. to children: *The children are at the school.* **2.** the body of students or pupils attending such an institution: *The entire school rose when the headmaster entered the auditorium.* **3.** a regular course of meetings of a teacher or teachers and students for instruction: *a school held during the summer months.* **4.** a session of such a course: *no school today; to be kept after school.* **5.** a building, room, etc., in a university, set apart for the use of one of the faculties or for some particular purpose: *the school of agriculture.* **6. schools,** *Archaic.* the faculties of a university. **7.** a high school (contrasted with *college*). **8.** a particular faculty or department of a modern university having the right to recommend candidates for degrees, and usually beginning its program of instruction after the student has completed general education: *medical school.* **9.** any place, situation, etc., tending to teach anything. **10.** the body of pupils or followers of a master, system, method, etc.: *the Platonic school of philosophy.* **11.** *Art.* **a.** a group of artists, as painters, writers, musicians, etc., whose works reflect a common conceptual, regional, or personal influence: *the modern school; Florentine school.* **b.** the art and artists of a geographical location considered independently of stylistic similarity: *the French school.* **12.** any body of persons who agree. **13.** *Obs.* the schoolmen. **14.** *Mil., Navy.* parts of close-order drill applying to the individual **(school of the soldier),** the squad **(school of the squad),** or the like. —*adj.* **15.** of or connected with a school or schools. **16.** *Obs.* of the schoolmen. —*v.t.* **17.** to educate in or as in a school; teach; train. **18.** *Archaic.* to reprimand. [ME *scole,* OE *scōl* < L *schol(a)* < Gk *scholē* leisure employed in learning] —**school′a·ble,** *adj.* —**school′less,** *adj.* —**school′like′,** *adj.*

school[2] (sko͞ol), *n.* **1.** a large number of fish, porpoises, whales, or the like, feeding or migrating together. —*v.i.* **2.** to form into, or go in, a school, as fish. [late ME *schol(e)* < D *school* troop, c. OE *scolu* SHOAL[2]]

school′ age′, 1. the age set by law for children to start school attendance. **2.** the period of school attendance required by law. —**school′-age′,** *adj.*

school·bag (sko͞ol′bag′), *n.* a bag used by students for carrying books, school supplies, etc., between home and school. [SCHOOL[1] + BAG]

school′ board′, a local board or committee in charge of public education.

school·book (sko͞ol′bo͝ok′), *n.* a book for study in schools. [SCHOOL[1] + BOOK]

school·boy (sko͞ol′boi′), *n.* a boy attending school. [SCHOOL[1] + BOY] —**school′boy′ish,** *adj.*

school′ bus′, a vehicle used to transport students to and from school or used for other related purposes.

school·child (sko͞ol′chīld′), *n., pl.* **-chil·dren.** a child attending a school.

School·craft (sko͞ol′kraft′, -kräft′), *n.* **Henry Rowe** (rō), 1793–1864, U.S. explorer, ethnologist, and author.

school′ day′, 1. any day on which school is conducted. **2.** the daily number of hours during which school is conducted: *The school day here is from nine to three.*

school·fel·low (sko͞ol′fel′ō), *n.* a schoolmate. [late ME; see SCHOOL[1], FELLOW]

School′ for Scan′dal, The, a comedy of manners (1777) by Richard Brinsley Sheridan.

school·girl (sko͞ol′gûrl′), *n.* a girl attending school. [SCHOOL[1] + GIRL] —**school′girl′ish,** *adj.*

school·house (sko͞ol′hous′), *n., pl.* **-hous·es** (-hou′ziz). a building in which a school is conducted. [late ME *scolehous.* See SCHOOL[1], HOUSE]

school·ing (sko͞o′ling), *n.* **1.** the process of being taught in a school. **2.** instruction, education, or training, esp. when received in a school. **3.** act of teaching. **4.** *Archaic.* reprimand. [late ME *scoling.* See SCHOOL[1], -ING[1]]

school·ma'am (sko͞ol′mam′, -mäm′), *n.* schoolmarm. [SCHOOL[1] + MA'AM]

school·man (sko͞ol′mən), *n., pl.* **-men. 1.** one versed in scholastic learning or engaged in scholastic pursuits. **2.** (*sometimes cap.*) a master in one of the schools or universities of the Middle Ages; one of the medieval writers who dealt with theology and philosophy after the methods of scholasticism. [SCHOOL[1] + MAN[1]]

school·marm (sko͞ol′märm′), *n.* a woman schoolteacher, esp. of the old-time country school type, popularly held to be strict and priggish. Also, **schoolma'am.** [var. of SCHOOLMA'AM] —**school′marm′ish,** *adj.*

school·mas·ter (sko͞ol′mas′tər, -mä′stər), *n.* **1.** a man who presides over or teaches in a school. **2.** anything that teaches or directs. **3.** a snapper, *Lutianus apodus,* a food fish found in Florida, the West Indies, etc. —*v.t., v.i.* **4.** to teach or direct in the capacity of schoolmaster. [ME *scolemaister.* See SCHOOL[1], MASTER] —**school′mas′ter·ship′,** *n.*

school·mate (sko͞ol′māt′), *n.* a companion or associate at school. [SCHOOL[1] + MATE[1]]

school·mis·tress (sko͞ol′mis′tris), *n.* a woman who presides over or teaches in a school. [SCHOOL[1] + MISTRESS]

School′ of Law′, (in Chinese philosophy) a Neo-Confucian school asserting the existence of transcendant universals, which form individual objects from a primal matter otherwise formless. Also called **Ch'eng-Chu school.**

School′ of Mind′, (in Chinese philosophy) a Neo-Confucian school asserting the original unity of all things, to be grasped through the perfect attainment of jen. Also, **Hsin Hsüeh, Lu-Wang school.**

school′ of the sol′dier. See under **school** (def. 14).

school′ of the squad′. See under **school** (def. 14).

school·room (sko͞ol′ro͞om′, -ro͝om′), *n.* a room in which a school is conducted or pupils are taught. [SCHOOL[1] + ROOM]

school′ ship′, a vessel used in training students for nautical careers.

school·teach·er (sko͞ol′tē′chər), *n.* a teacher in a school, esp. in one below the college level. [SCHOOL[1] + TEACHER]

school·teach·ing (sko͞ol′tē′ching), *n.* the profession of a schoolteacher. [SCHOOL[1] + TEACHING]

school′ tie′. See **old school tie.**

school·work (sko͞ol′wûrk′), *n.* the material studied in or for school, comprising homework and work done in class. [SCHOOL[1] + WORK]

school·yard (sko͞ol′yärd′), *n.* a playground or sports field near a school. [SCHOOL[1] + YARD[2]]

school′ year′, 1. the months of the year during which school is open and attendance at school is required. **2.** See **academic year.**

Fishing schooner

schoon·er (sko͞o′nər), *n.* **1.** *Naut.* any of various types of sailing vessel having a foremast and mainmast, with or without other masts, and having fore-and-aft sails on all lower masts. Cf. **fore-and-aft schooner, ketch, topsail schooner, yawl** (def. 2). **2.** *U.S. Informal.* a very tall glass, as for beer. **3.** See **prairie schooner.** [*scoon,* var. of dial. *scun* SCUD[1] (cf. dial. Sw *skunna,* OE *scyndan*) + -ER[1]]

schoon′er bark′, a jackass-rigged, five-masted sailing vessel, produced experimentally c1920, having square upper sails on the foremast and mizzenmast but otherwise rigged as a fore-and-aft schooner.

schoon′er ketch′, *Naut.* a three-masted schooner having a very small mizzenmast, usually without a mizzen gaff topsail.

schoon·er-rigged (sko͞o′nər rigd′), *adj.* **1.** rigged as a schooner, esp. one with gaff sails and staysails only. **2.** rigged with gaff sails, on two or more masts, and with staysails only.

Scho·pen·hau·er (shō′pən hou′ər), *n.* **Ar·thur** (är′to͝or), 1788–1860, German philosopher. —**Scho′pen·hau′er·i·an,** *adj.*

Scho·pen·hau·er·ism (shō′pən hou′ə riz′əm), *n.* the philosophy of Schopenhauer, who taught that only the cessation of desire can solve the problems arising from the universal impulse of the will to live. [SCHOPENHAUER + -ISM]

schorl (shôrl), *n.* a black tourmaline. [< G *Schörl*] —**schor·la·ceous** (shôr lā′shəs), *adj.*

schorl-rock (shôrl′rok′), *n.* a kind of rock composed of aggregates of black tourmaline and quartz. [SCHORL + ROCK[1]]

schot·tische (shot′ish), *n.* **1.** a round dance resembling the polka. **2.** the music for this dance. [< G: Scottish (dance)]

schrank (shrängk), *n.* (in Pennsylvania Dutch furniture) a two-door clothes cabinet one side of which has drawers and shelves and the other side an open space for hanging clothes. [< G *Schrank* cupboard]

Schreck·lich·keit (shrek′likh kīt′), *n. German.* frightfulness; horror. [< G, equiv. to *Schreck* fear + *-lich* -LY + *-keit* -HOOD]

schrei·ber·site (shrī′bər sīt′, -zīt′), *n.* a mineral, iron-nickel phosphide, $(Fe, Ni)_3P$, found only in meteorites. [< G *Schreibersit,* named after Carl von *Schreibers,* Viennese official; see -ITE[1]]

Schrei·ner (shrī′nər), *n.* **Olive** ("*Ralph Iron*"), c1862–1920, English author and feminist.

schrei′ner fin′ish, a lustrous surface imparted to a fabric by schreinerizing. [after the surname *Schreiner*]

schrei·ner·ize (shrī′nə rīz′), *v.t.,* **-ized, -iz·ing.** to produce a lustrous finish on (a fabric) by subjecting it to pressure exerted by rollers engraved with many fine lines. Also, **schrei′ner.** [surname *Schreiner* + -IZE]

schrik (skrik), *n.* (in southern Africa) a sudden fright or panic. [< D: fright; c. G *Schreck*]

Schrö′der-Bern′stein the′orem (shrō′dər bûrn′stēn, -stīn), *Math.* the theorem of set theory that if two sets are so related that each can be placed in one-to-one correspondence with a subset of the other, then the sets are equivalent.

Schrö·ding·er (shrœ′ding ər), *n.* **Er·win** (er′vin), 1887–1961, German physicist: Nobel prize 1933.

Schrö′ding·er wave′ equa′tion (shrō′ding ər; *Ger.* shrœ′ding ər), *Physics.* the fundamental equation of quantum theory, one form of which is $ih/2\pi \frac{\delta\psi}{\delta t} = -h^2/8\pi m^2\nabla^2\psi + V\psi$, where h is Planck's constant, $i = \sqrt{-1}$, m is the mass of a particle, ∇^2 is the Laplacian, V is the potential energy, t is the time, and ψ is the wave function. Also called **Schrö′dinger equa′tion, Schrö′dinger wave′ equa′tion contain′ing the time′, wave equation.** [named after E. SCHRÖDINGER]

Schrö·ter (shrō′tər), *n.* a walled plain in the second quadrant of the face of the moon: about 20 miles in diameter.

schry·a·ri (shrī′ə rī′), *n.* a musical woodwind instrument of the 16th and 17th centuries having a double reed concealed in a cylinder and producing a shrill tone. [< MLG *schrȳ(en)* (to) shriek + L *-ārium* -ARY]

Schu·bert (sho͞o′bərt; *Ger.* sho͞o′bert), *n.* **1. Franz** (fränts), 1797–1828, Austrian composer. **2.** a crater in the first quadrant of the face of the moon, in the libration area: about 46 miles in diameter.

schuit (skoit, skīt; *Du.* skhœit), *n.* a broad-beamed, flat-bottomed boat used on waterways in the Netherlands. Also, **schuyt.** [< D; c. MLG *schute*]

Schul (sho͞ol, shōōl), *n. Yiddish.* shul.

Schul·berg (sho͞ol′bərg), *n.* **Budd** (bud), born 1914, U.S. novelist, short-story writer, and scenarist.

Schu·ma·cher (sho͞o′mä kər), *n.* a walled plain in the first quadrant of the face of the moon: about 25 miles in diameter.

Schu·man (sho͞o′mən *or, for 1, Fr.* sho͞o män′), *n.* **1. Ro·bert** (rob′ərt; *Fr.* rô ber′), 1886–1963, French political leader: premier of France 1947–48. **2. William Howard,** born 1910, U.S. composer and teacher.

Schu·mann (sho͞o′män), *n.* **Ro·bert** (rob′ərt; *Ger.* rō′bert), 1810–56, German composer.

Schu·mann-Heink (sho͞o′män hīngk′), *n.* **Ernes·tine,** 1861–1936, U.S. contralto, born in Bohemia.

Schu′man Plan′, the plan for establishing the European Coal and Steel Community, proposed by Robert Schuman, French political leader, in 1950.

Schum·pe·ter (sho͝om′pā tər), *n.* **Joseph A·lois** (ə lois′), 1883–1950, U.S. economist, born in Austria.

Schurz (shûrz, sho͝orts), *n.* **Carl,** 1829–1906, U.S. general, statesman, and newspaperman; born in Germany.

Schusch·nigg (sho͝osh′nik), *n.* **Kurt von** (kûrt von; *Ger.* ko͝ort fən), born 1897, Austrian statesman in the U.S.: Chancellor of Austria 1934–38.

schuss (sho͝os, sho͞os), *Skiing.* —*n.* **1.** a straight run down a slope, in which a skier makes no attempt to decrease speed. —*v.i.* **2.** to execute a schuss. [< G; c. SHOT[1]]

Schütz (shyts), *n.* **Hein·rich** (hīn′rikh), 1585–1672, German composer.

Schutz·staf·fel (sho͝ots′shtä′fəl), *n. German.* an elite military unit of the Nazi party which served as Hitler's bodyguard and as a special police force. *Abbr.:* SS [lit., protection staff]

Schuy·ler (skī′lər), *n.* **1. Philip John,** 1733–1804, American statesman and general in the Revolutionary War. **2.** a town in E Nebraska. 3096 (1960).

Schuy·ler·ville (skī′lər vil′), *n.* a village in E New York, on the Hudson: scene of Burgoyne's defeat and surrender in the Battle of Saratoga 1777. 1361 (1960). Formerly, **Saratoga.**

Schuyl·kill (sko͞ol′kil), *n.* a river flowing SE from E Pennsylvania to the Delaware River at Philadelphia. 131 mi. long.

Schuyl′kill Ha′ven, a town in central Pennsylvania. 6470 (1960).

schuyt (skoit, skīt; *Du.* skhœit), *n.* schuit.

schwa (shwä; *Ger.* shvä), *n. Phonet.* **1.** the indeterminate vowel sound or sounds of most unstressed syllables of English, however represented; for example, the sound or sounds of *a* in *alone* and *sofa, e* in *system, i* in *easily, o* in *gallop, u* in *circus.* **2.** a mid-central, neutral vowel. **3.** the phonetic symbol ə. [< G < Heb *shewā,* name of a point marking want of a vowel sound]

Schwa·ben (shvä′bən), *n.* German name of **Swabia.**

Schwann (shvän), *n.* **The·o·dor** (tā′ō dôr′), 1810–82, German zoologist.

Schwartz (shwôrts), *n.* **Del·more** (del′mōr, -môr), 1913–1966, U.S. poet, short-story writer, and critic.

Schwarz (shwôrtz; *Ger.* shvärts), *n.* **Her·mann A·man·dus** (her′män ä män′do͝os), 1843–1921, German mathematician.

Schwarz′ inequal′ity, *Math.* **1.** the theorem that the inner product of two vectors is less than or equal to the product of the magnitudes of the vectors. **2.** the theorem that the square of the integral of the product of two functions is less than or equal to the product of the integrals of the square of each function. Also called **Cauchy-Schwarz inequality.** [named after H. A. SCHWARZ]

Schwarz·kopf (shwôrts′kôpf, -kopf, shwärts′-), *n.* **Elisabeth,** born 1915, German soprano, born in Poland.

Schwarz·wald (shvärts′vält′), *n.* German name of the **Black Forest.**

Schwed′ler's ma′ple (shwed′lərz), a variety of the Norway maple, *Acer platanoides Schwedleri,* producing red leaves that subsequently turn green. [from a surname *Schwedler*]

Schwein·furt (shvīn′fo͝ort), *n.* a city in N Bavaria, in West Germany, on the Main River. 57,800 (1963).

Schwein′furth green′ (shvīn′fo͝ort), *Chem.* See **Paris green** (def. 1). [named after SCHWEINFURT]

Schweit·zer (shwīt′sər, shvīt′-), *n.* **Albert,** 1875–1965, Alsatian writer, missionary, doctor, and musician in Africa: Nobel peace prize 1952.

Schweiz (shvīts), *n.* German name of **Switzerland.**

Schwenk·feld·er (shfengk′fel′dər, shvengk′-), *n.* a member of a Protestant group that emigrated in 1734 from Germany and settled in Pennsylvania, where they organized the Schwenkfelder Church. [< G, named after Kaspar von *Schwenkfeld* (1490–1561), German mystic; see -ER[1]]

Schwe·rin (shvā rēn′), *n.* a city in and the capital of Mecklenburg-Western Pomerania in N Germany. 130,685.

Schwin·ger (shwing′gər), *n.* **Julian Seymour,** born 1918, U.S. physicist: Nobel prize 1965.

Schwit·ters (shvit′ərs), *n.* **Kurt** (ko͝ort), 1887–1948, German artist.

Schwyz (shvēts), *n.* **1.** a canton in central Switzerland, bordering on the Lake of Lucerne. 78,048 (1960); 350 sq. mi. **2.** a city in and the capital of this canton, in the W part. 11,007 (1960).

schyn·bald (shin′bôld′), *n. Armor.* a plate for protecting the shin. [*schyn,* var. of SHIN[1] + *bald* protection (< ?)]

sci., 1. science. **2.** scientific.

sci·ae·noid (sī ē′noid), *adj.* **1.** belonging or pertaining to the *Sciaenidae,* a family of carnivorous acanthopterygian fishes including the drumfishes, certain kingfishes, etc. —*n.* **2.** a sciaenoid fish. Also, **sci·ae·nid** (sī ē′nid). [< L *sciaen(a)* kind of fish]

sci·am·a·chy (sī am′ə kē), *n., pl.* **-chies.** act or instance of fighting a shadow or an imaginary enemy. Also, **sciomachy.** [< Gk *skiamachía,* equiv. to *skiā* shadow + *-machia* -MACHY]

sci·at·ic (sī at′ik), *adj.* **1.** *Anat.* of, pertaining to, situated near, or affecting the ischium or back of the hip. **2.** affecting the hip or the sciatic nerves. —*n.* **3.** *Anat.*

CONCISE ETYMOLOGY KEY: <, descended or derived from; >, whence; b., blend of, blended; c., cognate with; deriv., derivative; equiv., equivalent; imit., imitative; m., modification of; obl., oblique; r., replacing; s., stem; sp., spelling; trans., translation; ?, origin unknown, perhaps; *, hypothetical. See the full key inside the front cover.

a sciatic part, as a nerve, vein, or artery. [< ML *sciatic(us)*, alter. of Gk *ischiadikós* ISCHIADIC] —**sci·at′i·cal·ly,** *adv.*

sci·at·i·ca (sī at′i kə), *n. Pathol.* **1.** pain and tenderness at some points of the sciatic nerve; sciatic neuralgia. **2.** any painful disorder extending from the hip down the back of the thigh and surrounding area. [< ML, n. use of fem. of *sciaticus* SCIATIC]

sci·ence (sī′əns), *n.* **1.** a branch of knowledge or study dealing with a body of facts or truths systematically arranged and showing the operation of general laws: *the mathematical sciences.* **2.** systematic knowledge of the physical or material world. **3.** systematized knowledge in general. **4.** knowledge, as of facts or principles; knowledge gained by systematic study. **5.** a particular branch of knowledge. **6.** skill; proficiency. [ME < MF < L *scienta* knowledge, equiv. to *sci-* (root of *scīre* to know) + *-entia* -ENCE]

sci′ence fic′tion, a form of fiction which draws imaginatively on scientific knowledge and speculation in its plot, setting, theme, etc.

sci·en·ti·a est po·ten·ti·a (skē en′tē ä′ est pō ten′tē ä′), *Latin.* knowledge is power.

sci·en·tial (sī en′shəl), *adj.* **1.** having knowledge. **2.** of or pertaining to science or knowledge. [< ML *scientiāl(is)*, equiv. to *scienti(a)* SCIENCE + *-ālis* -AL[1]]

sci·en·tif·ic (sī′ən tif′ik), *adj.* **1.** of or pertaining to science or the sciences: *scientific studies.* **2.** occupied or concerned with science: *scientific men.* **3.** regulated by or conforming to the principles of exact science: *scientific procedures.* **4.** systematic or accurate in the manner of an exact science. [< LL *scientific(us)*. See SCIENCE, -FIC] —**sci′en·tif′i·cal·ly,** *adv.*

sci′entific meth′od, a method of research in which a problem is identified, relevant data are gathered, a hypothesis is formulated from these data, and the hypothesis is empirically tested.

scientif′ic nota′tion, a method for expressing a given quantity as a number having significant digits necessary for a specified degree of accuracy, multiplied by 10 to the appropriate power, as 1385.62 written as 1.386×10^3.

sci·en·tism (sī′ən tiz′əm), *n.* **1.** *Often Disparaging.* the style, assumptions, techniques, practices, etc., typifying or regarded as typifying scientists. **2.** the belief that the assumptions, methods of research, etc., of the physical and biological sciences are equally appropriate and essential to all other disciplines, including the humanities and the social sciences. **3.** scientific or pseudoscientific language. [SCIENT(IST) + -ISM]

sci·en·tist (sī′ən tist), *n.* an expert in science, esp. one of the physical or natural sciences. [< L *scient(ia)* SCIENCE + -IST]

sci·en·tis·tic (sī′ən tis′tik), *adj.* **1.** characterized by or having an exaggerated belief in the principles and methods of science. **2.** of, pertaining to, or characterized by scientism. [SCIENTIST + -IC] —**sci′en·tis′ti·cal·ly,** *adv.*

scil·i·cet (sil′i set′), *adv.* to wit; namely. [< L: short for *scīre licet* to know is permitted]

scil·la (sil′ə), *n.* a liliaceous plant of the genus *Scilla*, having bell-shaped flowers. [< L < Gk *skílla* sea onion]

Scil·la (sil′ə; *It.* shēl′lä), *n.* modern name of **Scylla.**

scil·lism (sil′iz əm), *n. Pathol.* poisoning by squill, characterized by vomiting, slow pulse, cardiac arrhythmia, and ventricular fibrillation. [SCILL(A) + -ISM]

Scil′ly Isles′ (sil′ē), a group of about 140 small islands, SW of Land's End, England. 1732 (1951); 6½ sq. mi. *Cap.:* Hugh Town. Also, **Scil′ly Is′lands.** —**Scil·lo·ni·an** (si lō′nē ən), *adj., n.*

A
B

A, Scimitar; B, Scabbard

scim·i·tar (sim′i tər), *n.* a curved, single-edged sword of Oriental origin. Also, **scim′i·ter, simitar.** [< It *scimitar(ra)*] —**scim′i·tared,** *adj.*

scim′itar foot′, any short leg or foot, as to a pedestal table, having the form of an arc tangent to the floor plane.

Scimitar feet

scin·coid (siŋ′koid), *adj.* **1.** of, pertaining to, or resembling a skink. —*n.* **2.** a scincoid lizard. [< L *scinc(us)* SKINK + -OID]

scin·til·la (sin til′ə), *n.* a spark; a minute particle; trace: *not the slightest scintilla of remorse.* [< L: spark]

scin·til·lant (sin′tᵊlənt), *adj.* scintillating; sparkling. [< L *scintillant-* (s. of *scintillāns*, prp. of *scintillāre* to flash). See SCINTILLA, -ANT] —**scin′til·lant·ly,** *adv.*

scin·til·late (sin′tᵊlāt′), *v.,* **-lat·ed, -lat·ing.** —*v.i.* **1.** to emit sparks. **2.** to sparkle; flash: *a mind that scintillates with brilliance.* **3.** to twinkle, as the stars. **4.** (of a spot of light or image on a radar display) to shift rapidly around its mean position. **5.** (of the amplitude, phase, or polarization of an electromagnetic wave) to fluctuate in a random manner. **6.** (of an energetic photon or particle) to produce a flash of light in a phosphor by striking it. —*v.t.* **7.** to emit as sparks; flash forth. [< L *scintillāt(us)* (ptp. of *scintillāre* to flash). See SCINTILLA, -ATE[1]] —**scin′til·lat′ing·ly,** *adv.*

scin·til·la·tion (sin′tᵊlā′shən), *n.* **1.** the act of scintillating; a sparkling. **2.** a spark or flash. **3.** *Astron.* the twinkling or tremulous effect of the light of the stars. **4.** *Meteorol.* any small-scale twinkling or shimmering of objects that are viewed through the atmosphere, caused by an interception of the observer's line of view by inhomogeneities in the atmospheric refractive index. Cf. **laurence. 5.** *Physics.* a flash of light occurring as a result of the ionization of a phosphor, as when bombarded by an alpha particle. **6.** (on a radar display) a slight, rapid shifting of a spot of light or the image of an object about its mean position. **7.** *Radio.* random fluctuation of the amplitude, phase, or polarization of an electromagnetic wave. **8.** a flash of light produced in a phosphor by the impact of an energetic photon or particle. [< L *scintillātiōn-* (s. of *scintillātiō*). See SCINTILLATE, -ION]

scintilla′tion count′er, a device for detecting and measuring radioactivity, having a crystal scintillator, a photoelectric cell sensitive to the light from scintillations, and an amplifier.

scintilla′tion spectrom′eter, a scintillation counter adapted for measuring the energy distribution of particles emitted in radioactive processes.

scin·til·la·tor (sin′tᵊlā′tər), *n. Physics.* a phosphor capable of producing scintillations. [SCINTILLATE + -OR[2]]

sci·o·lism (sī′ə liz′əm), *n.* superficial knowledge. [< LL *sciol(us)* one who knows little + -ISM] —**sci′o·list,** *n.* —**sci′o·lis′tic,** *adj.*

sci·om·a·chy (sī om′ə kē), *n., pl.* **-chies.** sciamachy.

sci·on (sī′ən), *n.* **1.** a descendant. **2.** Also, **cion.** a shoot or twig, esp. one cut for grafting or planting; a cutting. [ME < OF *cion* < Frankish **kīth* offshoot (c. OE *cīth* seed) + OF *-on* dim. suffix]

sci·os·o·phy (sī os′ə fē), *n., pl.* **-phies.** supposed knowledge of natural or supernatural phenomena or forces, usually based on tradition, as astrology or phrenology. [< Gk *skio-* (comb. form of *skiá* shadow) + -SOPHY] —**sci·os′o·phist,** *n.*

Sci·o·to (sī ō′tə, -tō), *n.* a river in central Ohio, flowing S to the Ohio River. 237 mi. long.

Scip·i·o (sip′ē ō′), *n.* **1. Pub·li·us Cor·nel·ius Scip·i·o Af·ri·ca·nus Ma·jor** (pub′lē əs kôr nēl′yəs sip′ē ō′ af′ri kā′nəs mā′jər), (*"Scipio the Elder"*), 137–183 B.C., Roman general who defeated Hannibal. **2.** his adopted grandson **Publius Cornelius Scipio Ae·mil·i·a·nus Af·ri·ca·nus Mi·nor** (ē mil′ē ā′nəs af′ri kā′nəs mī′nər), (*"Scipio the Younger"*), c185–129 B.C., Roman general: besieger and destroyer of Carthage.

sci·re fa·ci·as (sī′rē fā′shē as′; *Lat.* skē′re fä′kē-äs′), *Law.* **1.** a writ requiring the party against whom it is brought to show cause why a judgment, letters patent, etc., should not be executed, vacated, or annulled. **2.** such a judicial proceeding. [< L: lit., make (him) know]

Sci·ron (sī′ron), *n. Class. Myth.* a robber, killed by Theseus, who ordered his victims to wash his feet and kicked them off a cliff when they knelt to do so.

Scir·o·pho·ri·a (skir′ə fôr′ē ə, -fōr′-), *n.* (*sometimes construed as pl.*) an ancient Greek festival in honor of Athena. Also, **Skirophoria.**

scir·rhoid (skir′oid, sir′-), *adj. Pathol.* resembling a scirrhus. [SCHIRRH(US) + -OID]

scir·rhous (skir′əs, sir′-), *adj. Pathol.* **1.** of a hard, fibrous consistency. **2.** of, relating to, or constituting a scirrhus. [SCHIRRH(US) + -OUS] —**scir·rhos·i·ty** (ski ros′i tē), *n.*

scir·rhus (skir′əs, sir′-), *n., pl.* **scir·rhi** (skir′ī, sir′ī), **scir·rhus·es.** *Pathol.* a hard, indolent tumor; a hard cancer. [< L < Gk *skírros*, var. of *skíros* hard covering, deriv. of *skirós* hard]

scis·sel (sis′əl, siz′-), *n.* the remains of a strip from which coin blanks have been cut; clippings. [< F *cisaille*, back formation from *cisailler* to clip. See CHISEL]

scis·sile (sis′il), *adj.* capable of being cut or divided; splitting easily. [< L *scissile*, neut. of *scissilis*, equiv. to *sciss(us)* (ptp. of *scindere* to cut) + *-ilis* -ILE]

scis·sion (sizh′ən, sish′-), *n.* **1.** a cutting, dividing, or splitting; division; separation. **2.** *Chem.* cleavage (def. 5). [< LL *scissiōn-* (s. of *scissiō*) a cutting, equiv. to *sciss(us)* (ptp. of *scindere* to cut) + *-iōn-* -ION]

scis·sor (siz′ər), *v.t.* to cut or clip out with scissors. [v. use of sing. of SCISSORS]

scis·sor·like (siz′ər līk′), *adj.* like scissors; moving, operating, or crossing in a manner suggesting the blades of scissors. [SCISSOR(S) + -LIKE]

scis·sors (siz′ərz), *n.* **1.** (*usually construed as pl.*) a cutting instrument for sheets of paper, pieces of cloth, or the like, consisting of two blades, each having a ring-shaped handle, that are so pivoted together that their sharp edges work one against the other (often used with *pair of*). **2.** (*construed as sing.*) *Gymnastics.* any of several feats in which the legs execute a scissorlike motion. **3.** (*construed as sing.*) *Wrestling.* a hold secured by clasping the legs around the body or head of the opponent. [ME *cisoures, sisoures* < MF *cisoires* < LL **cīsōria*, pl. of *cīsōrium* cutting tool. See CHISEL]

scis′sors chair′, a chair, as a Dante or Savonarola chair, having transverse pairs of crossed legs supporting the seat and arms.

scis′sors kick′, *Swimming.* a propelling motion of the legs in which they move somewhat like the blades of a pair of scissors, used in the sidestroke.

scis′sors truss′, a roof truss having tension members extending from the foot of each principal rafter to a point on the upper half of its opposite member.

scis·sor·tail (siz′ər tāl′), *n.* **1.** Also called **scis′sor-tailed fly′catcher** (siz′ər tāld′). a flycatcher, *Muscivora forficata*, of the southern U.S., Mexico, and Central America, having a long, deeply forked tail. **2.** any of various other birds having a long, forked tail. [SCISSOR(S) + TAIL[1]]

scis·sure (sizh′ər, sish′-), *n. Archaic.* a longitudinal cleft or opening. [< L *scissūr(a)*, equiv. to *sciss(us)* (ptp. of *scindere* to cut) + *-ūra* -URE]

Scit·u·ate (sich′o͞o āt′, -it), *n.* a town in E Massachusetts. 3229 (1960).

sci·u·rine (sī′yo͝o rīn′, -rin), *adj.* of or pertaining to the squirrels and allied rodents of the family *Sciuridae.* [< L *sciūr(us)* (< Gk *skíouros* squirrel) + -INE[1]]

sci·u·roid (sī yo͝or′oid), *adj.* **1.** sciurine. **2.** *Bot.* resembling a squirrel's tail, as the spikes of certain grasses. [*sciur-* (see SCIURINE) + -OID]

sciv·vy (skiv′ē), *n., pl.* **-vies.** skivvy.

sclaff (sklaf), *Golf.* —*v.t.* **1.** to scrape (the ground) with the head of the club just before impact with the ball. —*v.i.* **2.** to sclaff the ground with the club. —*n.* **3.** a sclaffing stroke. [special use of Scot *sclaf* to shuffle] —**sclaff′er,** *n.*

sclent (sklent), *n., v.i. Scot. and North Eng.* sklent.

scler-, var. of **sclero-** before a vowel: *sclerenchyma.*

scle·ra (sklēr′ə), *n. Anat.* a dense, white, fibrous membrane which, with the cornea, forms the external covering of the eyeball. See diag. under **eye.** [< Gk *sklērá* (fem.) hard]

scle·ral (sklēr′əl), *adj. Anat.* sclerotic (def. 1). [SCLER- + -AL[1]]

scle·rec·to·my (skli rek′tə mē), *n., pl.* **-mies.** *Surg.* **1.** excision of part of the sclera. **2.** removal of the adhesions formed in the middle ear during chronic otitis media. [SCLER- + -ECTOMY]

scle·re·ma (skli rē′mə), *n. Pathol.* sclerosis, or hardening, esp. of the skin. [SCLER- + (ED)EMA]

scle·ren·chy·ma (skli reŋ′kə mə), *n. Bot.* supporting or protective tissue composed of thickened and indurated cells from which the protoplasm has usually disappeared. [SCLER- + (PAR)ENCHYMA] —**scle·ren·chym·a·tous** (sklēr′eŋ kim′ə təs, skler′-), *adj.*

scle·ri·a·sis (skli rī′ə sis), *n. Pathol.* scleroderma. [SCLER- + -IASIS]

scle·rite (sklēr′īt, skler′-), *n. Zool.* any chitinous, calcareous, or similar hard part, plate, spicule, or the like. [SCLER- + -ITE[1]] —**scle·rit·ic** (skli rit′ik), *adj.*

scle·ri·tis (skli rī′tis), *n. Pathol.* inflammation of the sclera. Also, **sclerotitis.** [SCLER- + -ITIS]

scle·ri·ti·za·tion (sklēr′i ti zā′shən, skler′-), *n.* the formation of a sclerite or sclerites. [SCLERITE + -IZATION]

sclero-, a learned borrowing from Greek meaning "hard," used with this meaning, and as a combining form of **sclera,** in the formation of compound words: *sclerometer.* Also, *esp. before a vowel,* **scler-.** [< Gk *sklērō(s)* hard]

scle·ro·blast (sklēr′ə blast′, skler′-), *n.* **1.** *Zool.* one of the cells in a sponge that takes part in the formation of spicules. **2.** *Ichthyol.* a scale-forming cell in the corium of a fish. [SCLERO- + -BLAST] —**scle′ro·blas′tic,** *adj.*

scle·ro·cau·ly (sklēr′ə kô′lē), *n. Bot.* the normal development of much sclerenchyma in the stems of certain plants, as some desert plants, resulting in hardened, dry stems. [SCLERO- + CAUL- + -Y[3]]

scle·ro·der·ma (sklēr′ə dûr′mə, skler′-), *n. Pathol.* a disease in which all the layers of the skin become hardened and rigid. Also called **scleriasis.** [SCLERO- + DERMA]

scle·ro·der·ma·ti·tis (sklēr′ō dûr′mə tī′tis, skler′ō-), *n. Pathol.* inflammation and hardening of the skin. Also, **scle·ro·der·mi·tis** (sklēr′ō dər mī′tis, skler′-). [SCLERO- + DERMATITIS]

scle·ro·der·ma·tous (sklēr′ə dûr′mə təs, skler′-), *adj. Zool.* covered with a hardened tissue, as scales. [SCLERO- + DERMATOUS]

scle·rog·e·nous (skli roj′ə nəs), *adj. Pathol., Bot.* producing hard or sclerotic tissue. Also, **scle·ro·gen·ic** (sklēr′ə jen′ik, skler′-). [SCLERO- + -GENOUS]

scle·roid (sklēr′oid, skler′-), *adj. Biol.* hard or indurated. [SCLER- + -OID]

scle·ro·ma (skli rō′mə), *n., pl.* **-mas, -ma·ta** (-mə tə). *Pathol.* a tumorlike induration of tissue. [< Gk *sklērōma.* See SCLER-, -OMA]

scle·rom·e·ter (skli rom′i tər), *n.* any instrument for determining with precision the degree of hardness of a substance, esp. a mineral, as by measuring the pressure necessary to pierce or scratch it. [SCLERO- + -METER] —**scler·o·met·ric** (sklēr′ə me′trik, skler′-), *adj.*

scle·ro·phyll (sklēr′ə fil), *Bot.* —*adj.* **1.** Also, **scle·ro·phyl·lous** (sklēr′ə fil′əs). of, pertaining to, or exhibiting sclerophylly. —*n.* **2.** a plant exhibiting sclerophylly. [SCLERO- + -PHYLL]

scle·ro·phyl·ly (sklēr′ə fil′ē), *n. Bot.* the normal development of much sclerenchyma in the leaves of certain plants, as some desert plants, resulting in thickened, hardened foliage. [SCLERO- + PHYLL- + -Y[3]] —**scle′ro·phyl′lous,** *adj.*

scle·ro·pro·tein (sklēr′ō prō′tēn, -tē in), *n. Biochem.* protein that is fibrous and insoluble in water and serves a protective or supportive function in the body. Also called **albuminoid.** [SCLERO- + PROTEIN]

Scler·o·scope (sklēr′ə skōp′, skler′-), *n. Trademark.* a type of sclerometer that determines the hardness of a material by measuring the rebound of a standard ball dropped on the material from a fixed height.

scle·rosed (skli rōst′, sklēr′ōzd, skler′-), *adj. Pathol.* hardened or indurated, as by sclerosis. [SCLEROS(IS) + -ED[2]]

scle·ro·sis (skli rō′sis), *n., pl.* **-ses** (-sēz). **1.** *Pathol.* a hardening or induration of a tissue or part, or an increase of connective tissue or the like at the expense of more active tissue. **2.** *Bot.* a hardening of a tissue or cell wall by thickening or lignification. [< ML < Gk *sklērōsis* hardening. See SCLER-, -OSIS] —**scle·ro′sal,** *adj.*

scle·rot·ic (skli rot′ik), *adj.* **1.** Also, **scleral.** *Anat.* of or pertaining to the sclera. **2.** *Pathol., Bot.* pertaining to or affected with sclerosis. [< ML *sclērōtic(a)* < LGk *sklērōtikē* (fem. adj.) of hardening. See SCLEROTIN, -IC]

scle·ro·tin (sklēr′ə tin, skler′-), *n. Biochem.* an insoluble protein that serves to stiffen the chitin of the cuticle of arthropods. [< Gk *sklērót(ēs)* hardness + -IN[2]]

scle·ro·ti·tis (sklēr′ə tī′tis, skler′-), *n. Pathol.* scleritis. [SCLEROT(IC) + -ITIS] —**scle·ro·tit·ic** (sklēr′ə tit′ik, skler′ə-), *adj.*

scle·ro·ti·um (skli rō′shē əm), *n., pl.* **-ti·a** (-shē ə). *Bot.* a vegetative, resting, food-storage body in certain higher fungi, composed of a compact mass of indurated mycelia. [< NL; see SCLEROTIN, -IUM] —**scle·ro·tial** (skli rō′shəl), *adj.*

scle·ro·ti·za·tion (sklir′ə ti zā′shən, skler′-), *n.* the state of being sclerotized. [SCLEROTIZ(ED) + -ATION]

scle·ro·tized (sklēr′ə tīzd′, skler′-), *adj.* **1.** (esp. of the cuticle of an arthropod) hardened by the presence of substances other than chitin, as by scleroproteins, waxes, calcium salts, etc. **2.** *Pathol.* sclerosed. [SCLEROT(IC) + -IZE + -ED[2]]

scle·ro·tome (sklēr′ə tōm′, skler′-), *n.* **1.** *Embryol.* the part of a mesodermal somite contributing to the development of the vertebrae and ribs. **2.** *Surg.* an instrument for use in performing a sclerotomy. **3.** *Zool.* a fibrous partition separating successive myotomes. [SCLERO- + -TOME] —**scle·ro·tom·ic** (sklēr′ə tom′ik, skler′-), *adj.*

scle·rot·o·my (skli rot′ə mē), *n., pl.* **-mies.** *Surg.* incision into the sclera, as to extract foreign bodies. [SCLERO- + -TOMY]

scle·rous (sklēr′əs, skler′-), *adj.* hard; firm; bony. [SCLER- + -OUS]

Sc.M., Master of Science.

Sc.M.Hyg., Master of Science in Hygiene.

scoff[1] (skôf, skof), *n.* **1.** an expression of mockery, derision, doubt, or derisive scorn; jeer. **2.** an object of mockery or derision. —*v.i.* **3.** to speak derisively; mock; jeer (often fol. by *at*): *If you can't do any better, don't scoff. He scoffed at her attempt to drive a car.* —*v.t.* **4.** to mock at; deride. [ME *scof* < Scand; cf. obs. Dan *skof* mockery] —**scoff′er,** *n.* —**scoff′ing·ly,** *adv.*

—**Syn. 3.** gibe. SCOFF, JEER, SNEER imply behaving with scornful disapproval toward someone or about something. To SCOFF is to express insolent doubt or derision, openly and emphatically: *to scoff at a new invention.* To JEER is to shout in disapproval and scorn more coarsely and unintelligently than in scoffing: *The audience jeered at his singing.* To SNEER is to show by facial expression or tone of voice ill-natured contempt or disparagement: *He sneered unpleasantly in referring to his opponent's misfortunes.* —**Ant. 1.** praise.

scoff[2] (skôf, skof), *Chiefly Brit. Slang.* —*n.* **1.** food; grub. —*v.i., v.t.* **2.** to eat voraciously. [earlier *scaff* < ?]

scoff·law (skôf′lô′, skof′-), *n. Informal.* a person who flouts the law: *a scofflaw who failed to pay the fines for 12 traffic violations.* [SCOFF[1] + LAW]

scoin′son arch′ (skoin′sən). See **sconcheon arch.**

scoke (skōk), *n.* pokeweed. [< AmerInd (Massachusetts) *m'skok:* lit., that which is red]

scold (skōld), *v.t.* **1.** to find fault with angrily; chide; reprimand: *His mother scolded him for being naughty.* —*v.i.* **2.** to find fault; reprove. **3.** to use abusive language. —*n.* **4.** a person, esp. a woman, who is constantly scolding, often with loud and abusive speech. [ME, var. of *scald* < Scand (cf. Icel *skald-stöng* libelpole); akin to Ir *scéal* news] —**scold′a·ble,** *adj.* —**scold′er,** *n.* —**scold′ing·ly,** *adv.*

—**Syn. 1.** reprove; censure. See **reproach. 4.** nag, shrew, virago. —**Ant. 1.** praise.

scold′ing bri′dle, *Brit. Dial.* branks. Also called **scold's′ bri′dle** (skōldz).

scol·e·cite (skol′i sīt′, skō′li-), *n.* a zeolite mineral, a hydrous calcium aluminum silicate, $CaAl_2Si_3O_{10}·3H_2O$, occurring in masses and in needle-shaped, white crystals. [< Gk *skōlēk-* (s. of *skṓlēx*) SCOLEX + -ITE[1]]

sco·lex (skō′leks), *n., pl.* **sco·le·ces** (skō lē′sēz), **scol·i·ces** (skol′i sēz′, skō′li-). *Zool.* the anterior, headlike segment of a tapeworm, having suckers, hooks, or the like, for attachment. [< Gk *skṓlēx* worm]

sco·li·on (skō′lē on′), *n., pl.* **-li·a** (-lē ə). a song sung at banquets in ancient Greece. [< Gk, n. use of neut. of *skoliós* bent]

sco·li·o·sis (skō′lē ō′sis, skol′ē-), *n. Pathol.* lateral curvature of the spine. [< Gk: a bending] —**sco·li·ot·ic** (skō′lē ot′ik), *adj.*

scol·lop (skol′əp), *n., v.t.* scallop.

sco·lop·a·le (skə lop′ə lē), *n., pl.* **scol·o·pa·li·a** (skol′ə pā′lē ə, -pāl′yə). *Zool.* the peg-shaped, central, sensory element of a scolophore. Also called **scolops.** [< NL, equiv. to *scolop-* (comb. form of Gk *skólops* spike) + *-āle,* neut. sing. of *-ālis* -AL[1]]

scol·o·pen·drid (skol′ə pen′drid), *n.* any myriapod of the order *Scolopendrida,* including many large, poisonous centipedes. [< NL *Scolopendrid(ae),* equiv. to *scolopendr(a)* (< Gk *skolópendra* multipede) + *-idae* -ID[2]] —**scol·o·pen·drine** (skol′ə pen′drīn, -drin), *adj.*

scol·o·phore (skol′ə fōr′, -fôr′, skō′lə-), *n. Zool.* a sense organ in the body wall of insects that is sensitive to sound waves. Also, **sco·lop·o·phore** (skə lop′ə fōr′, -fôr′). [short for *scolopophore,* equiv. to *scolopo-* (s. of Gk *skólops* spike) + -PHORE]

scol·ops (skol′əps), *n., pl.* **-o·pes** (-ə pēz′). *Zool.* scolopale. [< Gk *skólops* spike]

scom·brid (skom′brid), *n.* **1.** any fish of the family *Scombridae,* comprising the mackerels and tunas. —*adj.* **2.** belonging or pertaining to the family *Scombridae.* [< NL *Scombrid(ae)* name of the family < L *scombr-* (s. of *scomber*) mackerel < Gk (see SCOMBROID) + *-idae* -ID[2]]

scom·broid (skom′broid), *adj.* **1.** resembling the mackerel. **2.** resembling or related to the mackerel family *Scombridae.* —*n.* **3.** a mackerel or related scombroid fish. [< Gk *skómbr(os)* mackerel + -OID]

sconce[1] (skons), *n.* **1.** a bracket for candles or other lights, placed on a wall, mirror, picture frame, etc. **2.** the hole or socket of a candlestick, for holding the candle. [ME *sconce, sconse* < monastic L *sconsa,* aph. var. of *absconsa,* n. use of fem. ptp. of *abscondere* to conceal; see ABSCOND]

sconce[2] (skons), *n., v.,* **sconced, sconc·ing.** —*n.* **1.** *Fort.* a small detached fort or defense work, as to defend a pass, bridge, etc. **2.** a protective screen or shelter. —*v.t.* **3.** *Fort.* to protect with a sconce. **4.** *Obs.* to protect; shelter. [< D *schans* < G *Schanze,* orig. bundle of wood]

sconce[3] (skons), *v.,* **sconced, sconc·ing,** *n.* —*v.t.* **1.** (at English universities) to fine (an undergraduate) for a breach of rules or etiquette. —*n.* **2.** a fine so imposed. [?]

sconce[4] (skons), *n.* **1.** the head or skull. **2.** sense or wit. [?]

scon·cheon (skon′chən), *n. Archit.* the reveal of a window or doorway from the frame to the inner face of the wall. Also, **scuncheon, esconson.** [ME < OF *(e)scoinson* corner, cut angle < L *ex-* from + *cuneus* wedge, corner]

scon′cheon arch′, an archway which includes the sconcheons of a door or window. Also, **scoinson arch.**

scone (skōn, skon), *n.* **1.** a flat, round, leavened cake made of oatmeal, wheat flour, barley meal, or the like. **2.** one of the four quadrant-shaped pieces into which such a cake is often cut. **3.** Also called **dropped scone.** biscuit (def. 1). [< MD *schoon (brod)* fine (bread); c. SHEEN]

Scone (sko͞on, skōn), *n.* **Stone of,** a stone, formerly at Scone, Scotland, upon which Scottish kings sat at coronation, now placed beneath the coronation chair in Westminster Abbey.

S. Con. Res., Senate concurrent resolution.

scoop (sko͞op), *n.* **1.** a ladle or ladlelike utensil, esp. a small, deep-sided shovel with a short, horizontal handle, for taking up flour, sugar, etc. **2.** a utensil composed of a palm-sized, hollow hemisphere attached to a horizontal handle, for dishing out ice cream or other soft foods. **3.** a hemispherical portion of food, esp. ice cream, as dished out by such a utensil: *two scoops of chocolate ice cream.* **4.** the bucket of a dredge, steam shovel, etc. **5.** *Surg.* a spoonlike apparatus for removing substances or foreign objects from the body. **6.** a hollow or hollowed-out place. **7.** the act of ladling, dipping, dredging, etc. **8.** the quantity held in a ladle, dipper, shovel, bucket, etc. **9.** a news item, report, or story first revealed in one paper, magazine, newscast, etc.; beat. **10.** *Informal.* news, information, or details, esp. as obtained from experience or an immediate source: *What's the scoop on working this machine?* **11.** a gathering to oneself or lifting with the arms or hands. **12.** *Informal.* a big haul, as of money. **13.** a unit containing several lights, used esp. in television and motion-picture production. —*v.t.* **14.** to take up or out with or as if with a scoop. **15.** to empty with a scoop. **16.** to form a hollow or hollows in. **17.** to form with or as if with a scoop. **18.** to get the better of (another or other publications, newscasters, etc.) by obtaining and publishing or broadcasting a news item, report, or story first: *They scooped all the other dailies with the story of the election fraud.* **19.** to gather up or to oneself or to put hastily by a sweeping motion of one's arms or hands: *He scooped the money into his pocket.* —*v.i.* **20.** to remove or gather something with or as if with a scoop: *to scoop with a ridiculously small shovel.* [ME *scope* < MD *schōpe*] —**scoop′er,** *n.* —**scoop′ing·ly,** *adv.*

scoop·ful (sko͞op′fo͝ol′), *n., pl.* **-fuls.** the amount that a scoop holds. [SCOOP + -FUL]

scoop′ neck′, a round, usually low, neckline on a dress, blouse, etc. Also called **scoop′ neck′line.**

scoop′ seat′, *Furniture.* See **dropped seat.**

scoot (sko͞ot), *v., n., pl.* **scoots,** (*esp. collectively for 4*) **scoot.** *Informal.* —*v.i.* **1.** to go swiftly or hastily; dart. —*v.t.* **2.** to send or impel at high speed. —*n.* **3.** a swift, darting movement or course. **4.** a scoter. [< Scand; cf. Icel *skjóta* to SHOOT]

scoot·er[1] (sko͞o′tər), *n.* **1.** a child's vehicle that typically has two wheels with a low footboard between them, is steered by a handlebar, and is propelled by pushing one foot against the ground while resting the other on the footboard. **2.** Also called **motor scooter.** a similar but larger and heavier vehicle for adults, having a saddlelike seat mounted on the footboard and being propelled by a motor. **3.** (in the U.S. and Canada) a sailboat equipped with runners for use on ice. **4.** See **Pacific barracuda.** —*v.i.* **5.** to sail or travel in or on a scooter. [SCOOT + -ER[1]]

scoot·er[2] (sko͞o′tər), *n., pl.* **-ers,** (*esp. collectively*) **-er.** scoter.

scop (skop), *n.* an Old English bard or poet. [OE; c. Icel *skop* mocking, OHG *skof* derision]

sco·pa (skō′pə), *n., pl.* **-pae** (-pē), **-pas.** See **pollen brush.** [< L *scōpae* twigs, shoots] —**sco·pate** (skō′pāt), *adj.*

Sco·pas (skō′pəs), *n.* fl. 4th century B.C., Greek sculptor and architect.

sco·pate (skō′pāt), *adj.* having a scopa, or pollen brush. [SCOP(A) + -ATE[1]]

scope (skōp), *n.* **1.** extent or range of view, outlook, application, operation, effectiveness, etc.: *an investigation of wide scope.* **2.** space for movement or activity; opportunity for operation: *to give one's fancy full scope.* **3.** extent in space; a tract or area. **4.** length: *a scope of cable.* **5.** aim or purpose. **6.** (used as a short form of *microscope, periscope, radarscope, telescopic sight,* etc.) [< It *scop(o)* < Gk *skopó(s)* aim, mark to shoot at] —**scope′less,** *adj.*

—**Syn. 1.** See **range. 2.** margin, room, liberty.

-scope, a learned borrowing from Greek used, with the meaning "instrument for viewing," in the formation of compound words: *telescope.* Cf. **-scopy.** [< NL *-scop(ium)* < Gk *-skópion, -skopeion,* equiv. to *skop(eîn)* (to) look at + *-ion, -eion* n. suffix]

Scopes (skōps), *n.* **John Thomas,** born 1901, U.S. high-school teacher whose teaching of the Darwinian theory of evolution became a cause célèbre **(Scopes** or **Monkey Trial)** in 1925.

scopol-, a combining form indicating any derivative of plants of the genus *scopolia: scopolamine.* [< NL *scopol(ia Japonica)* Japanese belladonna; genus *scopolia* named after G. K. *Scopoli* (1723–88), Italian naturalist]

sco·pol·a·mine (skə pol′ə mēn′, -min, skō′pə lam′in), *n. Pharm.* a colorless, syrupy, water-soluble alkaloid, $C_{17}H_{21}NO_4$, obtained from certain solanaceous plants: used chiefly in the form of its hydrobromide as a sedative, to augment the effect of narcotics in the production of twilight sleep, and as a mydriatic. Also called **hyoscine.** [SCOPOL- + AMINE]

sco·po·line (skō′pə lēn′, -lin), *n. Pharm.* a crystalline glucoside, $C_{18}H_{13}NO_2$, derived from scopolamine, used in medicine chiefly as a narcotic. [SCOPOL- + -INE[2]]

sco·po·phil·i·a (skō′pə fil′ē ə, -fēl′yə), *n. Psychiatry.* the obtaining of sexual pleasure by looking at nude bodies, erotic photographs, etc. Also, **scop·to·phil·i·a** (skop′tə fil′ē ə). [< NL; see -SCOPE, -O-, -PHILIA] —**sco·po·phil·i·ac** (skō′pə fil′ē ak′), **scop·to·phil·i·ac** (skop′tə fil′ē ak′), *n., adj.* —**sco′po·phil′ic, scop′to·phil′ic,** *adj.*

scop·u·la (skop′yə lə), *n., pl.* **-las, -lae** (-lē′). *Zool.* a dense tuft of hairs, as on the feet of certain spiders. [< LL, equiv. to *scōp(a)* broom + *-ula* -ULE]

scop·u·late (skop′yə lāt′, -lit), *adj. Zool.* broom-shaped; brushlike. [SCOPUL(A) + -ATE[1]]

-scopy, a suffix used to form abstract action nouns corresponding to nouns with stems ending in **-scope:** *telescopy.* [< Gk *skopía* watching. See -SCOPE, -Y[3]]

scor·bu·tic (skôr byo͞o′tik), *adj. Pathol.* pertaining to, of the nature of, or affected with scurvy. Also, **scor·bu′ti·cal.** [< NL *scorbūtic(us),* equiv. to ML *scorbūt(us)* scurvy (< MD **scorbūk*) + *-icus* -IC] —**scor·bu′ti·cal·ly,** *adv.*

scorch (skôrch), *v.t.* **1.** to affect the color, taste, etc., of by burning slightly: *The collar of the shirt was yellow where the iron had scorched it. She scorched the soup and ruined its flavor.* **2.** to parch or shrivel with heat: *The sun scorched the grass.* **3.** to criticize severely. **4.** *Mach.* burn[1] (def. 21). **5.** to destroy (crops, towns, etc.) by or as by fire in the path of an invading army's advance. —*v.i.* **6.** to become scorched: *Milk scorches easily.* **7.** *Informal.* to travel or drive at high speed: *The car scorched along the highway.* —*n.* **8.** a superficial burn. [ME *scorche(n),* b. *scorcnen* (< Scand; cf. Icel *skorpna* to shrivel) + TORCH]

—**Syn. 1.** char, blister. See **burn**[1]. **3.** excoriate, condemn. —**Ant. 3.** laud.

scorched′ earth′, a condition or policy in which all things useful to an invading army are destroyed, as by fire.

scorch·er (skôr′chər), *n.* **1.** one who or that which scorches. **2.** *Informal.* a very hot day: *We had a week of scorchers in August.* **3.** something caustic or severe: *He gave a scorcher of a critique.* **4.** *Informal.* one who drives extremely fast. **5.** *Print.* a device for drying and forming flong into a curve before casting. [SCORCH + -ER[1]]

scorch·ing (skôr′ching), *adj.* **1.** burning; very hot. **2.** caustic or scathing: *a scorching denunciation.* [SCORCH + -ING[2]] —**scorch′ing·ly,** *adv.*

scor·da·tu·ra (skôr′də to͝or′ə; *It.* skôr′dä to͞o′rä), *n., pl.* **-tu·re** (-to͝or′ā; *It.* -to͞o′re), **-tu·ras.** *Music.* the tuning of a stringed instrument in other than the usual way to facilitate the playing of certain compositions. [< It, equiv. to *scordat(o),* ptp. of *scordare* to be out of tune (< L *(di)scordāre;* see DISCORD) + *-ura* n. suffix]

score (skōr, skôr), *n., pl.* **scores, score** for 11, *v.,* **scored, scor·ing.** —*n.* **1.** the record of points or strokes made by the competitors in a game or match. **2.** the total points or strokes made by one side, individual, play, game, etc. **3.** the act or an instance of making or earning a point or points. **4.** *Educ., Psychol.* the performance of an individual or sometimes of a group on an examination or test, expressed by a letter, number, or other symbol. **5.** a notch, scratch, or incision; a stroke or line. **6.** a notch or mark for keeping an account or record. **7.** a reckoning or account so kept; tally. **8.** any account showing indebtedness. **9.** an amount recorded as due. **10.** a line drawn as a boundary, the starting point of a race, a goal line, etc. **11.** a group or set of 20: *about a score of years ago.* **12. scores,** a great many: *Scores of people were at the dance.* **13.** a reason, ground, or cause: *to complain on the score of low pay.* **14.** *Informal.* **a.** situation, point of progress, or basic facts: *What's the score on finding a cancer cure?* **b.** a successful move, remark, etc. **15.** *Music.* **a.** a written or printed piece of music with all the vocal and instrumental parts arranged on staves, one under the other. **b.** a written or printed copy of such a piece of music. **c.** the music itself. **d.** the music played as background to or part of a movie, play, or musical comedy. **16. pay off** or **settle a score,** to avenge a wrong; retaliate: *In the old West they paid off a score with bullets.* —*v.t.* **17.** to gain for addition to one's score in a game or match. **18.** to make a score of: *He scored 98 on the test.* **19.** to have as a specified value in points: *Four aces score 100.* **20.** *Educ., Psychol.* to evaluate the responses a person has made on (a test or an examination). **21.** *Music.* **a.** to orchestrate. **b.** to write out in score. **c.** to compose the music for (a movie, play, musical comedy, etc.) **22.** *Cookery.* to cut ridges or lines into (meat, fish, etc.) with shallow slashes, usually in a diamond pattern, before cooking. **23.** to make notches, cuts, marks, or lines in or on. **24.** to record or keep a record of (points, items, etc.), by or as by notches, marks, etc.; tally; reckon (often fol. by *up*). **25.** to write down as a debt. **26.** to record as a debtor. **27.** to gain, achieve, or win: *The play scored a great success.* **28.** to berate or censure: *The newspapers scored him severely for the announcement.* **29.** to crease (paper or cardboard) so that it can be folded easily and without damage. —*v.i.* **30.** to make a point or points in a game or contest. **31.** to keep score, as of a game. **32.** to achieve an advantage or a success: *The new product scored with the public.* **33.** to make notches, cuts, lines, etc. **34.** to run up a score or debt. [ME; late OE *scor(u)* < Scand; cf. Icel *skor* notch; akin to SHEAR] —**score′less,** *adj.* —**scor′er,** *n.*

score·board (skōr′bōrd′, skôr′bôrd′), *n.* a large, usually rectangular board in a ball park, sports arena, or the like, that shows the score of a contest and often other relevant facts and figures, as the count of balls and strikes on a baseball batter. [SCORE + BOARD]

score·card (skōr′kärd′, skôr′-), *n.* a card for keeping score of a sports contest and, esp. in team sports, for identifying the players by name, number, and position. [SCORE + CARD[1]]

score·keep·er (skōr′kē′pər, skôr′-), *n.* an official of a sports contest who keeps record of the score. [SCORE + KEEPER] —**score′keep′ing,** *n.*

score·pad (skōr′pad′, skôr′-), *n.* a pad whose sheets are printed with headings, vertical or horizontal lines, symbols, or the like, to facilitate the recording of scores in a game, as bowling or bridge. [SCORE + PAD[1]]

Scores·by (skōrz′bē, skôrz′-), *n.* a crater in the first quadrant of the face of the moon, in the libration area and near the North Pole: about 36 miles in diameter.

sco·ri·a (skōr′ē ə, skôr′-), *n., pl.* **sco·ri·ae** (skōr′ē ē′, skôr′-). **1.** the refuse, dross, or slag left after melting or smelting metal; scum. **2.** a cinderlike basic cellular lava. [< L < Gk *skōría,* deriv. of *skôr* dung] —**sco·ri·a·ceous** (skōr′ē ā′shəs, skôr′-), *adj.*

sco·ri·fy (skōr′ə fī′, skôr′-), *v.t.,* **-fied, -fy·ing.** to reduce to scoria. [SCORI(A) + -FY] —**sco′ri·fi·ca′tion,** *n.* —**sco′ri·fi′er,** *n.*

scorn (skôrn), *n.* **1.** open or unqualified contempt; disdain: *His face and attitude showed the scorn he felt.* **2.** an object of derision or contempt. **3.** *Archaic.* a derisive or contemptuous action or speech. **4. laugh to scorn,** to ridicule; deride: *Her good advice was laughed to scorn.* —*v.t.* **5.** to treat or regard with contempt or disdain: *He scorned the old beggar.* **6.** to reject, refuse, or ignore with contempt or disdain: *She scorned my help.* —*v.i.* **7.** to mock; jeer. [ME *scorn, scarn* < OF *(e)scarn* < Gmc; cf. obs. D *schern* mockery, trickery] —**scorn′er,** *n.* —**scorn′ing·ly,** *adv.*

—**Syn. 1.** contumely. See **contempt. 5.** disdain, contemn, despise, detest. **7.** disdain. —**Ant. 3.** praise.

scorn·ful (skôrn′fəl), *adj.* full of scorn; derisive; contemptuous: *He smiled in a scornful way.* [SCORN + -FUL] —**scorn′ful·ly,** *adv.* —**scorn′ful·ness,** *n.*

scor·pae·nid (skôr pē′nid), *n.* any of the *Scorpaenidae,* a family of marine fishes, including the rockfishes, scorpionfishes, lionfishes, etc. [< L *scorpaen(a)* (< Gk *skórpaina* kind of fish; see SCORPION) + -ID[2]]

scor·pae·noid (skôr pē′noid), *adj.* **1.** resembling or related to the family *Scorpaenidae.* —*n.* **2.** a scorpaenoid fish. [< L *scorpaen(a)* (see SCORPAENID) + -OID]

scor·per (skôr′pər), *n.* scauper.

Scor·pi·o (skôr′pē ō′), *n.* **1.** the eighth sign of the zodiac. See illus. under **zodiac. 2.** *Astron.* Scorpius. [< L: SCORPION]

scor·pi·oid (skôr′pē oid′), *adj.* **1.** resembling a scorpion. **2.** belonging or pertaining to the *Scorpionida,* the order of arachnids comprising the scorpions. **3.** curved at the end like the tail of a scorpion. [< L *scorpi(o)* SCORPION + -OID]

scor·pi·on (skôr′pē ən), *n.* **1.** any of numerous arachnids of the order *Scorpionida,* widely distributed in warmer parts of the world, having a long, narrow, segmented tail that terminates in a venomous sting. **2. the Scorpion,** *Astron.* Scorpius. **3.** any of various harmless lizards or skinks. **4.** *Bible.* a whip or scourge that has spikes attached. I Kings 12:11. [ME < L *scorpiōn-* (s. of *scorpiō*), equiv. to *scorp(ius)* scorpion (< Gk *skorpíos;* akin to SCARF^1) + *-iōn-* -ION] —**scor·pi·on·ic** (skôr′pē on′ik), *adj.*

Scorpion, ***Centruroides sculpturatus*** **(Length 2 to 3 in.)**

scor·pi·on·fish (skôr′pē ən fish′), *n., pl.* (*esp. collectively*) **-fish,** (*esp. referring to two or more kinds or species*) **-fish·es.** any of several marine scorpaenid fishes, esp. of the genus *Scorpaena,* having poisonous dorsal spines. [SCORPION + FISH]

scor·pi·on·fly (skôr′pē ən flī′), *n., pl.* **-flies.** any of several harmless insects of the order *Mecoptera,* the male of certain species having a structure at the rear of the abdomen that resembles the sting of a scorpion. [SCORPION + FLY^2]

scor′pion sen′na, a shrub, *Coronilla emerus,* of southern Europe, having green-striped twigs and yellow flowers.

scor′pion spi′der. See **whip scorpion.**

Scor·pi·us (skôr′pē əs), *n., gen.* **-pi·i** (-pē ī′). *Astron.* the Scorpion, a zodiacal constellation between Sagittarius and Libra, containing the bright star Antares. Also, **Scorpio.** [< L < Gk *skorpíos* SCORPION]

scot (skot), *n. Hist.* **1.** a payment or charge. **2.** one's share of a payment or charge. **3.** an assessment or tax. [ME < Scand; cf. Icel *skot,* c. OE *gescot* payment]

Scot (skot), *n.* **1.** a native or inhabitant of Scotland; Scotchman. **2.** one of an ancient Gaelic people who came from northern Ireland about the 6th century A.D. and settled in the northwestern part of Great Britain, and after whom Scotland was named. [ME; OE *Scott(as)* (pl.) < LL *Scott(ī)* the Irish <?]

Scot., 1. Scotch. **2.** Scotland. **3.** Also, **Scot** Scottish.

scot′ and lot′, 1. *Brit. Hist.* a municipal tax assessed proportionately upon the members of a community. **2. pay scot and lot,** to pay in full; settle finally. [rhyming phrase; see SCOT, LOT]

scotch^1 (skoch), *v.t.* **1.** to injure so as to make harmless. **2.** to cut, gash, or score. **3.** to put a definite end to; crush; stamp out: *The governor scotched all rumors about his interest in the presidency.* **4.** to block or prop with a wedge or chock. —*n.* **5.** a cut, gash, or score. **6.** a block or wedge put under a wheel, barrel, etc., to prevent slipping. [late ME *scocche,* prob. b. SC(ORE + N)OTCH (whence AF *escocher*)]

scotch^2 (skoch), *v.t., n. Masonry.* scutch (defs. 2, 4).

Scotch (skoch), *adj.* **1.** of or pertaining to Scotland, its inhabitants, or the dialect of English spoken in Scotland. **2.** (loosely) Scottish. —*n.* **3.** the people of Scotland collectively. **4.** See **Scotch whisky. 5.** (loosely) Scottish (def. 3). **6.** provident; frugal. [syncopated var. of SCOTTISH]
—**Syn. 1.** SCOTCH, SCOTS, SCOTTISH are proper adjectives corresponding to Scot and Scotland. SCOTCH is the form used originally in the dialect of the Midlands and southern England: *a Scotch accent.* In northern England and in Scotland, SCOTS and SCOTTISH (or *Scottis;* cf. *Inglis,* the N form of the word *English*) are preferred: *Scots language; Scottish Church.*

Scotch′ Black′face, one of a Scottish breed of mountain sheep having a black face and growing long, coarse wool.

Scotch′ broom′, the broom, *Cytisus scoparius.*

Scotch′ broth′, a thick soup prepared from mutton, vegetables, and barley.

Scotch′ cro′cus, a garden plant, *Crocus biflorus,* of southeastern Europe and Turkey, having purple-striped, yellow-throated flowers.

Scotch′ four′some, *Golf.* foursome (def. 1b).

Scotch′ fur′nace, *Metall.* See **ore hearth.** Also called **Scotch′ hearth′.**

Scotch′ Gael′ic, (not in technical use) See **Scots Gaelic.**

Scotch-I·rish (skoch′ī′rish), *adj.* **1.** of or pertaining to the descendants of Scotch immigrants in northern Ireland. **2.** of mixed Scotch and Irish blood. —*n.* **3.** a person of Scotch and Irish descent.

scotch·man (skoch′mən), *n., pl.* **-men.** *Naut.* See **rigging batten.** [special use of SCOTCHMAN]

Scotch·man (skoch′mən), *n., pl.* **-men. 1.** Scotsman. **2.** (*l.c.*) lingcod. [SCOTCH + MAN^1]

Scotch′ mist′, 1. a combination of mist or fog and drizzle, occurring frequently in Scotland and parts of England. **2.** a cocktail consisting of Scotch whisky poured over finely crushed ice.

Scotch′ pine′, a pine, *Pinus sylvestris,* of Eurasia.

Scotch′ Plains′, a town in NE New Jersey. 18,491 (1960).

Scotch′ rose′, a rose, *Rosa spinosissima,* of Eurasia, having pink, white, or yellow flowers. Also called **burnet rose.**

Scotch′ tape′, *Trademark.* any of various transparent or semi-transparent adhesive tapes made chiefly of cellulose acetate or cellophane, for sealing packages and the like.

scotch-tape (skoch′tāp′), *v.t.,* **-taped, -tap·ing.** to fasten or mend with Scotch tape. [after the trademark]

Scotch′ ter′rier. See **Scottish terrier.**

Scotch′ this′tle. See **cotton thistle.**

Scotch′ whis′ky, whiskey distilled in Scotland, esp. from malted barley in a patent still.

Scotch′ wood′cock, toast spread with anchovy paste and topped with loosely scrambled eggs.

sco·ter (skō′tər), *n., pl.* **-ters,** (*esp. collectively*) **-ter.** any of the large diving ducks of the genera *Melanitta* and *Oidemia,* found in northern parts of the Northern Hemisphere. Also, **scooter.** [?]

scot-free (skot′frē′), *adj.* **1.** free from harm or penalty: *He got off scot-free from the murder charge.* **2.** free from payment of scot. [ME; see SCOT, FREE]

ScotGael, Scots Gaelic.

sco·tia (skō′shə), *n. Archit.* a deep concave molding between two fillets, as in the Attic base. Also called **trochilus.** [< L < Gk *skotía* darkness (from its shadow)]

Sco·tia (skō′shə), *n.* **1.** *Literary.* Scotland. **2.** a town in E New York. 7625 (1960). [< L: Scotland. See SCOT, -IA]

Sco·tia (skō′shə), *n. Class. Myth.* an epithet of Aphrodite as goddess of death in life, meaning "dark one."

Sco·tism (skō′tiz əm), *n. Philos.* the set of doctrines of Duns Scotus. [(DUNS) SCOT(US) + -ISM] —**Sco′tist,** *n.* —**Sco·tis′tic, Sco·tis′ti·cal,** *adj.*

Scot·land (skot′lənd), *n.* **1.** a division of the United Kingdom in the N part of Great Britain. 5,178,490 (1961); 29,796 sq. mi. *Cap.:* Edinburgh. **2.** *Heraldry.* an escutcheon blazoned as follows: Or, a lion rampant gules armed and langued azure within a double tressure flory counter-flory gules.

Scot′land Neck′, a town in NE North Carolina. 2974 (1960).

Scot′land Yard′, 1. a short street in central London, England: formerly the site of the London police headquarters, which were removed 1890 to a Thames embankment **(New Scotland Yard). 2.** the London police, esp. the branch engaged in crime detection.

scoto-, a learned borrowing from Greek meaning "darkness," used in the formation of compound words: *scotoma.* [< L < Gk *skoto-* comb. form of *skótos* darkness]

Scoto-, a combining form of **Scotch:** *Scoto-Irish.* [comb. form of ML *Scōtus* SCOT]

sco·to·ma (skō tō′mə), *n., pl.* **-mas, -ma·ta** (-mə tə). *Pathol.* loss of vision in a part of the visual field; blind spot. [< LL < Gk *skótōma* dizziness. See SCOTO-, -OMA] —**sco·tom·a·tous** (skō tom′ə təs), *adj.*

sco·to·pi·a (skə tō′pē ə, skō-), *n. Ophthalm.* vision in dim light (opposed to *photopia*). Cf. **dark adaptation.** [SCOT(O)- + -OPIA] —**sco·top·ic** (skə top′ik, skō-), *adj.*

Scots (skots), *n.* **1.** Scottish (def. 3). —*adj.* **2.** Scottish or Scotch. [syncopated form of *Scottis,* var. (north) of SCOTTISH]
—**Syn. 2.** See **Scotch.**

Scots′ Gael′ic, the Gaelic of the Hebrides and the Highlands of Scotland, also spoken as a second language in Nova Scotia. *Abbr.:* ScotGael Also, **Scottish Gaelic.**

Scots·man (skots′mən), *n., pl.* **-men.** a Scot. Also, **Scotchman.** [SCOTS + MAN^1]

Scott (skot), *n.* **1. Cyril Meir,** born 1879, English pianist and composer. **2. Dred** (dred), 1795?–1858, a Negro slave whose suit for freedom was denied by the U.S. Supreme Court on the ground that a slave was not a citizen and therefore could not sue in a federal court. **3. Sir George Gilbert,** 1811–78, English architect. **4.** his grandson, **Sir Giles Gilbert,** born 1880, English architect. **5. Robert Fal·con** (fôl′kən, fal′-, fô′kən), 1868–1912, British naval officer and antarctic explorer. **6. Sir Walter,** 1771–1832, Scottish novelist and poet. **7. Win·field** (win′fēld′), 1786–1866, U.S. general. **8.** a walled plain in the fourth quadrant of the face of the moon, in the libration area and near the South Pole: about 66 miles in diameter. **9.** a boy's given name.

Scott′ City′, a town in W Kansas. 3555 (1960).

Scott·dale (skot′dāl′), *n.* a town in SW Pennsylvania. 6244 (1960).

Scot·ti (skôt′tē *for 1;* skot′ē *for 2, 3*), *n.* **1. An·to·nio** (än tô′nyô), 1866–1936, Italian baritone. **2.** a boy's given name, form of **Scott. 3.** a girl's given name. Also, **Scotty,** (for defs. 2, 3) **Scottie.**

Scot·ti·cism (skot′i siz′əm), *n.* a word or idiom peculiar to or characteristic of Scottish. [< LL *scōtic(us)* (*Scōt(us)* SCOT + *-icus* -IC) + -ISM]

Scot·tie (skot′ē), *n.* **1.** See **Scottish terrier. 2.** a boy's given name, form of **Scott. 3.** a girl's given name. Also, **Scotty,** (for defs. 2, 3) **Scotti.** [SCOT + -IE]

Scot·tish (skot′ish), *adj.* **1.** Also, **Scots.** of or pertaining to the Scots, their country, or the dialect of English spoken there. —*n.* **2.** the people of Scotland. **3.** Also, **Scots.** the dialect of English spoken in Scotland, marked by extensive differences in pronunciation, as a tongue-tip trill for the sound (r), a vowel ranging from (a) to (ä) for the sound (a), and the use of the sound (kh). *Abbr.:* Scot Cf. **Scots Gaelic.** [ME < LL *Scott(us)* SCOT + -ISH^1] —**Scot′tish·ly,** *adv.* —**Scot′tish·ness,** *n.*
—**Syn. 1.** See **Scotch.**

Scot′tish Gael′ic. See **Scots Gaelic.**

Scot′tish rite′, one of the two advanced divisions of Masonic membership, leading to the 33rd degree. Cf. **York rite.**

Scot′tish star′, mullet^2.

Scot′tish ter′rier, one of a Scottish breed of small terriers having short legs and a wiry, steel-gray, brindled, black, sandy, or wheaten coat. Also called **Scotch terrier.**

Scottish terrier (10 in. high at shoulder)

Scotts·bluff (skots′bluf′), *n.* a city in W Nebraska, on the North Platte River. 13,377 (1960).

Scotts·bor·o (skots′bûr ō, -bur ō), *n.* a town in NE Alabama. 6449 (1960).

Scotts·burg (skots′bûrg), *n.* a town in SE Indiana. 3810 (1960).

Scotts·dale (skots′dāl′), *n.* a city in central Arizona, near Phoenix. 10,026 (1960).

Scotts·ville (skots′vil), *n.* a town in S Kentucky. 3324 (1960).

Scot·ty (skot′ē), *n., pl.* **-ties. 1.** *Informal.* a Scot. **2.** See **Scottish terrier. 3.** a boy's given name, form of **Scott. 4.** a girl's given name. Also, **Scottie,** (for defs. 3, 4) **Scotti.** [SCOT + -Y^2]

Sco·tus (skō′təs), *n.* **John Duns.** See **Duns Scotus, John.**

scoun·drel (skoun′drəl), *n.* **1.** an unprincipled, dishonorable man; villain. —*adj.* **2.** mean or base in nature; villainous; unprincipled; dishonorable. [*scoun(d)* (< ?) + -REL]
—**Syn. 1.** cad, bounder, rapscallion, miscreant. See **knave.**

scoun·drel·ly (skoun′drə lē), *adj.* **1.** having the character of a scoundrel; unscrupulous; villainous. **2.** of or like a scoundrel. [SCOUNDREL + -LY]

scour^1 (skour, skou′ər), *v.t.* **1.** to remove dirt, grease, etc., from or to cleanse or polish by hard rubbing, as with a rough or abrasive material: *to scour pots and pans.* **2.** to remove (dirt, grease, etc.) from something by hard rubbing: *to scour grease from pots and pans.* **3.** to clear or dig out (a channel, drain, etc.), as by the force of water, by removing debris, etc. **4.** to purge thoroughly, as an animal. **5.** to clear or rid of what is undesirable: *to scour the nation of spies.* **6.** to remove by or as if by cleansing; get rid of. **7.** *Metall.* (of the contents of a blast furnace) to rub against and corrode (the refractory lining). —*v.i.* **8.** to rub a surface in order to cleanse or polish it. **9.** to remove dirt, grease, etc. **10.** to become clean and shiny. **11.** to be capable of being cleaned easily by a little rubbing: *The roasting pan scours better than the pot.* **12.** (of a plow, cultivator, etc.) to pass through the ground without soil clinging to the blade. **13.** (of a plow, shovel, etc.) to become polished from use. —*n.* **14.** the act of scouring. **15.** the place scoured. **16.** an apparatus or material used in scouring: *Sand is a good scour.* **17.** the erosive force of moving water, as in a river or sea. **18.** Usually, **scours.** *Vet. Pathol.* diarrhea in horses and cattle caused by intestinal infection. [ME *scour(en)* < Scand; cf. Dan *skure* to rub, scour, Icel *skora* to rub]

scour^2 (skour, skou′ər), *v.i.* **1.** to move rapidly or energetically. **2.** to range about, as in search of something. —*v.t.* **3.** to run or pass quickly over or along. **4.** to range over, as in search: *They scoured the countryside for the lost child.* [ME *scour(en)* < obs. *scour* speed, ? < Scand; cf. Icel *skūr* storm (of wind, rain, battle); c. SHOWER]

scour·er^1 (skour′ər, skou′ər ər), *n.* **1.** a person who scours or cleanses. **2.** an implement, device, or preparation for scouring. [SCOUR^1 + -ER^1]

scour·er^2 (skour′ər, skou′ər ər), *n.* **1.** a person who scours or ranges about. **2.** (in the 17th and 18th centuries) a prankster who roamed the streets at night. [SCOUR^2 + -ER^1]

scourge (skûrj), *n., v.,* **scourged, scourg·ing.** —*n.* **1.** a whip or lash, esp. for the infliction of punishment or torture. **2.** one who or that which applies or administers punishment or severe criticism. **3.** a cause of affliction or calamity: *Disease and famine are scourges of mankind.* —*v.t.* **4.** to whip with a scourge; lash. **5.** to punish, chastise, or criticize severely. [ME < AF *(e)scorge* << LL *excoriāre* to EXCORIATE] —**scourg′er,** *n.* —**scourg′ing·ly,** *adv.*
—**Syn. 3.** plague, bane. **5.** correct, castigate.

scour·ing (skour′ing, skou′ər-), *n.* **1.** *Vet. Pathol.* diarrhea in horses and cattle. **2. scourings,** (*construed as pl.*) **a.** dirt or refuse removed by scouring. **b.** refuse removed from grain. **3.** the act of one who or that which scours. [ME; see SCOUR^1, -ING^1]

scour′ing rush′, any of certain horsetails, esp. *Equisetum hyemale,* used for scouring and polishing. Also called **Dutch rush.**

scouse (skouz), *n. Brit. Naut.* a baked dish or stew made usually with meat and hardtack. [short for LOBSCOUSE]

scout^1 (skout), *n.* **1.** a soldier, warship, airplane, or the like, employed in reconnoitering. **2.** a person sent out to obtain information. **3.** *Sports.* **a.** a person who observes and reports on the techniques, players, etc., of opposing teams. **b.** a person sent out by a team to observe and recommend new talent for recruitment. **4.** the act or an instance of reconnoitering, inspecting, observing, etc. **5.** a Boy Scout or Girl Scout. **6.** *Informal.* a fellow: *He's a good scout.* **7.** a man acting as servant to a student at Oxford University. **8.** (*cap.*) *Rocketry.* a four-stage missile for launching small satellites. —*v.i.* **9.** to act as a scout; reconnoiter. —*v.t.* **10.** to examine, inspect, or observe for the purpose of obtaining information; reconnoiter: *to scout the enemy's defenses.* **11.** *Informal.* **a.** to seek; search for (usually fol. by *out* or *up*): *He's scouting up a date for Friday night.* **b.** to find by seeking, searching, or looking (usually fol. by *out* or *up*): *Scout out a good book for me to read.* [ME *scoute* < OF *(e)scoute,* back formation from *escolter, ascolter* (now *écouter* to listen) < LL *ascultāre,* var. of L *auscultāre* to AUSCULTATE]

scout^2 (skout), *v.t., v.i.* to reject with scorn; flout. [< Scand; cf. Icel *skūta* to scold]
—**Syn.** disdain, contemn, despise, scorn.

scout′ car′, a fast, lightly-armored military vehicle equipped with guns and used chiefly for reconnaissance.

scout·craft (skout′kraft′, -kräft′), *n.* **1.** practice of or skill at scouting. **2.** skill in the program of activities of the Boy Scouts or the Girl Scouts. [SCOUT^1 + CRAFT]

scout·er (skou′tər), *n.* **1.** one who scouts. **2.** a Boy Scout who is 18 years of age or over. [SCOUT^1 + -ER^1]

scouth (skōōth), *n. Scot.* **1.** abundance; plenty. **2.** opportunity; scope. Also, **skouth.** [?]

scout·hood (skout′hōōd), *n.* **1.** the state of being a scout, esp. a Boy Scout or a Girl Scout. **2.** the qualities or spirit of the Boy Scouts or the Girl Scouts. [SCOUT^1 + -HOOD]

scout·ing (skou′ting), *n.* **1.** the act or an instance of reconnoitering; reconnaissance. **2.** the activities of a scout or scouts. [SCOUT^1 + -ING^1] —**scout′ing·ly,** *adv.*

scout·mas·ter (skout′mas′tər, -mä′stər), *n.* **1.** the leader or officer in charge of a band of scouts. **2.** the adult leader of a troop of Boy Scouts. [SCOUT^1 + MASTER]

scow (skou), *n.* **1.** any of various vessels having a flat-bottomed rectangular hull with sloping ends, built in various sizes with or without means of propulsion, as barges, punts, rowboats, sailboats, etc. **2.** *Eastern U.S.* a barge carrying bulk material in an open hold. **3.** an old or clumsy boat; hulk; tub. —*v.t.* **4.** to transport by scow. [< D *schouw* ferryboat]

scowl (skoul), *v.i.* **1.** to draw down or contract the brows in a sullen, displeased, or angry manner. **2.** to have a gloomy or threatening look. —*v.t.* **3.** to affect or express with a scowl. —*n.* **4.** a scowling expression, look, or aspect. [ME *scoul* < Scand; cf. Dan *skule* to scowl] —**scowl′er,** *n.* —**scowl′ful,** *adj.* —**scowl′ing·ly,** *adv.*
—**Syn. 1.** frown. **2.** glower, gloom.

scr., scruple.

scrab·ble (skrab′əl), *v.*, **-bled, -bling,** *n.* —*v.t.* **1.** to scratch or scrape, as with the claws or hands. **2.** to grapple or struggle with or as with the claws or hands. **3.** to scrawl; scribble. —*v.i.* **4.** to jostle or struggle for possession of something; grab or collect something in a disorderly way; scramble. —*n.* **5.** a scratching or scraping, as with the claws or hands. **6.** a scrawled or scribbled writing. **7.** a disorderly struggle for possession of something; scramble: *After the fumble, there was a scrabble for the football.* [< D *schrabbel(en)*, freq. of *schrabben* to scratch, perh. var. of *schrapen* to SCRAPE] —**scrab′bler,** *n.*

Scrab·ble (skrab′əl), *n.* *Trademark.* a game combining anagrams and crosswords in which two to four players use counters of various point values to form words on a playing board.

scrag (skrag), *n.*, *v.*, **scragged, scrag·ging.** —*n.* **1.** a lean or scrawny person or animal. **2.** the lean end of a neck of veal or mutton. **3.** *Slang.* the neck of a human being. —*v.t.* **4.** *Slang.* to wring the neck of; hang; garrote. **5.** *Metall.* to test (spring steel) by bending. [var. of CRAG[2]]

scrag·gly (skrag′lē), *adj.*, **-gli·er, -gli·est.** **1.** irregular; uneven; jagged. **2.** shaggy; ragged; unkempt. [SCRAG + -LY]

scrag·gy (skrag′ē), *adj.*, **-gi·er, -gi·est.** **1.** lean or thin; scrawny. **2.** meager. **3.** irregular; craggy; jagged. [SCRAG + -Y[1]] —**scrag′gi·ly,** *adv.* —**scrag′gi·ness,** *n.*

scraich (skrāKH), *v.i.*, *n.* *Scot.* screech. Also, **scraigh** (skrāKH). [< Gael *scrèach, scrèiche* (gen. sing.)]

scram (skram), *v.i.*, **scrammed, scram·ming.** *Informal.* to go away; get out: *Let's scram before the teacher gets back.* [var. of SCRAMBLE (by apocope)]

scram·a·sax (skram′ə saks′), *n.* a single-edged knife or sword used by the Anglo-Saxons. Also, **scram′a·saxe′.** [< LL *scramasax(us)* < Gmc; cf. OHG *scrāma* big knife, OE *seax* short sword]

scram·ble (skram′bəl), *v.*, **-bled, -bling,** *n.* —*v.i.* **1.** to climb or move quickly using one's hands and feet, as down a rough incline. **2.** to compete or struggle with others for possession or gain: *The boys scrambled for the pennies we tossed.* **3.** to move in hasty urgency: *He scrambled into his coat and ran out the door.* **4.** *Mil.* (of pilots or aircraft) to take off quickly to intercept enemy planes. —*v.t.* **5.** to collect or organize (things) in a hurried or disorderly manner (often fol. by *together* or *up*): *He scrambled the papers up from the desk. He scrambled something together at the last minute.* **6.** to mix together confusedly: *She has hopelessly scrambled our names and faces.* **7.** to cause to move hastily, as if in panic: *He scrambled the boys out of the burning building.* **8.** to cook (eggs) in a pan, mixing whites and yolks together, usually with butter, milk, etc. **9.** to make (a radio or telephonic message) incomprehensible to interceptors by systematically changing the frequencies over which it is being transmitted. **10.** *Mil.* to cause (an intercepting aircraft or pilot) to take off in the shortest possible time, in response to an alert. —*n.* **11.** a quick climb or progression over rough, irregular ground, or the like. **12.** a struggle for possession or gain: *a scramble for choice seats in the stadium.* **13.** any disorderly or hasty struggle or proceeding. **14.** *Mil.* an emergency take-off of interceptors performed in the shortest possible time. [b. *scamble* to stumble along + SCRABBLE (in the same sense)]

scram·bler (skram′blər), *n.* **1.** one who or that which scrambles. **2.** an electronic device that mixes and confuses telecommunications signals in order to make them unintelligible through certain circuits. Cf. **unscrambler** (def. 2). [SCRAMBLE + -ER[1]]

scran·nel (skran′əl), *adj.* *Archaic.* **1.** thin or slight. **2.** squeaky or unmelodious. [? back formation from *scranly < Norw *skran* lean + -LY; see SCRAWNY]

Scran·ton (skran′tən), *n.* **1.** **William Warren,** born 1917, U.S. politician. **2.** a city in NE Pennsylvania. 111,443 (1960).

scrap[1] (skrap), *n.*, *adj.*, *v.*, **scrapped, scrap·ping.** —*n.* **1.** a small piece or portion; fragment: *scraps of paper.* **2.** **scraps, a.** bits or pieces of food, esp. of leftover or discarded food. **b.** the remains of animal fat after the oil has been tried out. **3.** a detached piece of something written or printed: *scraps of poetry.* **4.** an old, discarded, or rejected item or substance for use in reprocessing or as raw material, as old metal that can be melted and reworked. **5.** chips, cuttings, fragments, or other small pieces of raw material removed, cut away, flaked off, etc., in the process of making or manufacturing an item. —*adj.* **6.** consisting of scraps or fragments: *scrap heap.* **7.** existing in the form of fragments or remnants of use only for reworking, as metal. **8.** discarded or left over. —*v.t.* **9.** to make into scraps or scrap; break up: *to scrap old cars.* **10.** to discard as useless, worthless, or ineffective: *He urged that we scrap the old method of teaching mathematics.* [ME *scrappe* < Scand; cf. Icel *skrap*] —**scrap′ping·ly,** *adv.*
—**Syn. 1.** morsel, crumb, bit.

scrap[2] (skrap), *n.*, *v.i.*, **scrapped, scrap·ping.** *Informal.* —*n.* **1.** a fight or quarrel: *She got into a scrap with her in-laws.* —*v.i.* **2.** to engage in a fight or quarrel. [var. of SCRAPE]

scrap·book (skrap′bo͝ok′), *n.* an album in which pictures, newspaper clippings, etc., may be pasted or mounted. [SCRAP[1] + BOOK]

scrape (skrāp), *v.*, **scraped, scrap·ing,** *n.* —*v.t.* **1.** to deprive of or free from an outer layer, adhering matter, etc., or to smooth by drawing or rubbing something, esp. a sharp or rough instrument, over the surface: *to scrape a table to remove paint and varnish.* **2.** to remove (an outer layer, adhering matter, etc.) in this way: *to scrape the paint and varnish from a table.* **3.** to scratch, injure, or mar the surface of in this way: *to scrape one's arm on a rough wall.* **4.** to produce by scraping: *He scraped his initials on the rock.* **5.** to collect or do by or as if by scraping; do or gather laboriously or with difficulty (usually fol. by *up* or *together*): *She scraped together a meal from leftovers.* **6.** to rub harshly on or across (something): *Don't scrape the floor with your shoes!* **7.** to draw or rub (a thing) roughly across something: *Scrape your shoes on the door mat before you come in!* **8.** to level (an unpaved road) with a grader. —*v.i.* **9.** to scrape something. **10.** to rub against something gratingly. **11.** to produce a grating and unmusical tone from a string instrument. **12.** to draw one's foot back noisily along the ground in making a bow. **13.** to manage or get by with difficulty or with only the barest margin: *He barely scraped through on the test.* **14.** to economize or save by attention to even the slightest amounts: *By careful scraping they managed to survive.* —*n.* **15.** an act or instance of scraping. **16.** a drawing back of the foot noisily along the ground in making a bow. **17.** a harsh, shrill, or scratching sound made by scraping. **18.** a scraped place: *a scrape on one's elbow.* **19.** an embarrassing or distressing situation; predicament: *He is always in some kind of a scrape.* **20.** a difference of opinion, fight, or quarrel; scrap. [ME < Scand; cf. Icel *skrapa*] —**scrap′a·ble,** *adj.* —**scrape′age,** *n.*

scrap·er (skrā′pər), *n.* **1.** one who or that which scrapes. **2.** any of various tools or utensils for scraping. [SCRAPE + -ER[1]]

scrap·er·board (skrā′pər bōrd′, -bôrd′), *n.* scratchboard. [SCRAPER + BOARD]

scrap·ie (skrap′ē), *n.* *Vet. Pathol.* an infectious, usually fatal disease of adult sheep, caused by a filterable virus and characterized by a wild facial expression, nervousness, apprehensiveness, twitching of the neck and head, grinding of the teeth, and scraping of itching portions of skin against fixed objects with a subsequent loss of wool. [SCRAPE + -IE]

scrap·ing (skrā′ping), *n.* **1.** the act of one who or that which scrapes. **2.** the sound of something being scraped. **3.** Usually, **scrapings.** something that is scraped off, up, or together. [SCRAPE + -ING[1]] —**scrap′ing·ly,** *adv.*

scrap′ i′ron, old iron to be remelted or reworked.

scrap′ log′, *Naut.* See **deck log.**

scrap·per[1] (skrap′ər), *n.* one who removes or does away with scraps. [SCRAP[1] + -ER[1]]

scrap·per[2] (skrap′ər), *n.* *Informal.* a fighter, or aggressive competitor, esp. one always ready or eager for a fight, argument, or contest: *the best lightweight scrapper in boxing; a rugged political scrapper.* [SCRAP[2] + -ER[1]]

scrap·ple (skrap′əl), *n.* *U.S.* cornmeal mush made with the meat and broth of pork, seasoned with onions, spices, herbs, etc., and shaped into loaves and sliced for frying. [SCRAP[1] + -LE]

scrap·py[1] (skrap′ē), *adj.*, **-pi·er, -pi·est.** made up of scraps or of odds and ends; fragmentary; disconnected. [SCRAP[1] + -Y[1]] —**scrap′pi·ly,** *adv.* —**scrap′pi·ness,** *n.*

scrap·py[2] (skrap′ē), *adj.*, **-pi·er, -pi·est.** *Informal.* fond of fighting, arguing, or competing. [SCRAP[2] + -Y[1]]

scratch (skrach), *v.t.* **1.** to break or mar the surface of or to mark by rubbing, scraping, or tearing with something sharp or rough: *to scratch one's hand on a nail.* **2.** to dig, scrape, or tear (something) out or off with or as with the nails, claws, etc.: *to scratch the burs off one's coat.* **3.** to rub or scrape slightly, as with the fingernails, to relieve itching. **4.** to rub or draw along a rough, grating surface: *to scratch a match on the sidewalk.* **5.** to erase, cancel, strike out, or eliminate (a name, something written, etc.) by or as by drawing a line through it: *Scratch the third name on the list.* **6.** to withdraw (an entry) from a race or competition. **7.** *U.S.* **a.** to divide (one's vote) though predominantly supporting one political party or faction. **b.** to strike out or reject a particular name or names on (a party ticket) in voting. **8.** to write or draw by scraping or cutting the lines into a surface: *She scratched her initials on the glass.* —*v.i.* **9.** to use the nails, claws, etc., for tearing, digging, etc. **10.** to relieve itching by rubbing or scraping lightly, as with the fingernails. **11.** to make a slight grating noise, as a pen. **12.** to earn a living or to manage in any respect with great difficulty: *We scratched along that year on very little money.* **13.** to be withdrawn from a contest or competition. **14.** (in certain card games) to make no score; earn no points. **15.** *Billiards, Pool.* to make a shot which results in a penalty, esp. to pocket the cue ball without hitting the object ball. —*n.* **16.** a slight injury, mar, or mark, usually thin and shallow, caused by scratching: *three scratches on my leg; a noticeable scratch on the table.* **17.** a rough mark made by a pen, ballpoint, etc.; scrawl. **18.** an act of scratching. **19.** the slight grating sound caused by scratching. **20.** the starting place, starting time, or status of a competitor in a handicap who has no allowance and no penalty. **21.** *Billiards, Pool.* **a.** a shot resulting in a penalty, esp. a pocketing of the cue ball without hitting the object ball. **b.** a fluke or lucky shot. **22.** (in certain card games) a score of zero; nothing. **23.** *Baseball.* See **scratch hit.** **24.** See **scratch wig.** **25.** *Slang.* money; cash. **26.** **from scratch, a.** from the very beginning or starting point. **b.** from nothing; without resources: *After the depression he started another business from scratch.* **27.** **up to scratch,** in conformity with a certain standard; adequate; satisfactory: *The local symphony orchestra has improved this year, but it is still not up to scratch.* —*adj.* **28.** used for hasty writing, notes, etc.: *scratch paper; a scratch pad.* **29.** without any allowance, penalty, or handicap, as a competitor or contestant. **30.** *Informal.* done by or dependent on chance: *a scratch shot.* **31.** *Informal.* gathered hastily and indiscriminately: *a scratch crew.* [b. obs. *scr(at* to scratch (< ?) + obs. *cr)atch* (< MFlem *cratsen*; c. G *cratzen* to scratch)] —**scratch′a·ble,** *adj.* —**scratch′a·bly,** *adv.* —**scratch′er,** *n.* —**scratch′less,** *adj.* —**scratch′like′,** *adj.*

Scratch (skrach), *n.* Old Scratch; Satan. [alter. of *scrat* (OE *scratta hermaphrodite); c. Icel *skratti* the devil, OHG *skraz* wood-demon, etc.]

scratch′ awl′, *Carpentry.* an awllike device for scribing wood.

scratch·board (skrach′bōrd′, -bôrd′), *n.* a cardboard coated with impermeable white clay and covered by a layer of ink which is scratched or scraped in patterns revealing the white surface below. Also called **scratch′card′, scraperboard.** [SCRATCH + BOARD]

scratch′ coat′, **1.** (in plastering) a rough, deeply scored first coat upon which the brown coat is laid. **2.** trullisatio. —**scratch′-coat′ed,** *adj.*

scratch·es (skrach′iz), *n.* (*construed as sing.*) *Vet. Pathol.* a disease of horses marked by dry rifts or chaps that appear on the skin near the fetlock, behind the knee, or in front of the hock. [pl. of SCRATCH]

scratch′ hard′ness, resistance of a material, as a stone or metal, to scratching by one of several other materials, the known hardnesses of which are assembled into a standard scale, as the Mohs' scale of minerals.

scratch′ hit′, *Baseball.* a batted ball, usually poorly hit, barely enabling the batter to reach base safely: *a scratch hit off the end of the bat.*

scratch′ing post′, a block or post of wood, usually covered with carpeting, on which a cat can use its claws.

scratch′ pad′, a pad of paper used for jotting down ideas, informal notes, preliminary writing, etc.

scratch′ pa′per, paper used for an informal note, jotting down an idea, or the like.

scratch′ sheet′, a racing publication giving the betting odds and other information on the horses entered at a race track or tracks during a racing day.

scratch′ test′, a test for allergy in which the skin is scratched and an allergen applied to the area, an inflammatory reaction indicating an allergic condition.

scratch′ wig′, a short wig, esp. one that covers only part of the head. Also called **scratch.**

scratch·y (skrach′ē), *adj.*, **scratch·i·er, scratch·i·est.** **1.** causing or liable to cause a slight grating noise: *a scratchy record.* **2.** consisting of or marred by scratches: *a scratchy drawing.* **3.** uneven; haphazard: *He plays a scratchy game.* **4.** causing itching or other minor irritation of the skin: *a coarse, scratchy woolen sweater.* **5.** suffering from scratches. **6.** causing or liable to cause a scratch or scratches: *scratchy bushes.* [SCRATCH + -Y[1]] —**scratch′i·ly,** *adv.* —**scratch′i·ness,** *n.*

scrawl (skrôl), *v.t.* **1.** to write or draw in a sprawling, awkward manner: *He scrawled his name hastily across the blackboard.* —*n.* **2.** something scrawled, as a letter or a note. **3.** awkward or careless handwriting: *His letters are always written in careless scrawls.* [late ME *scraule*, b. SPR(AWL + CR)AWL; once said of movement of the limbs in general]

scrawl·er (skrô′lər), *n.* **1.** one who scrawls. **2.** an agricultural machine for laying out fields in which plants are to be placed in ridged rows. [SCRAWL + -ER[1]]

scrawl·y (skrô′lē), *adj.*, **scrawl·i·er, scrawl·i·est.** written or drawn awkwardly or carelessly. [SCRAWL + -Y[1]] —**scrawl′i·ness,** *n.*

scrawn·y (skrô′nē), *adj.*, **scrawn·i·er, scrawn·i·est.** excessively thin; lean; scraggy: *a long scrawny neck.* [var. of *scranny* < Norw *scran* lean + -Y[1]] —**scrawn′i·ly,** *adv.* —**scrawn′i·ness,** *n.*
—**Syn.** gaunt, emaciated. —**Ant.** fleshy, plump.

screak (skrēk), *v.i.* **1.** to screech. **2.** to creak. —*n.* **3.** a screech. **4.** a creak. [< Scand; cf. Icel *skrækja*] —**screak′y,** *adj.*

scream (skrēm), *v.i.* **1.** to utter a loud, sharp, piercing cry. **2.** to emit a shrill, piercing sound: *The sirens and whistles screamed.* **3.** to laugh immoderately or uncontrollably: *By the time the comic was through, he had the audience screaming.* **4.** to shout or speak shrilly, esp. with harsh or exaggerated words: *They screamed across the back fence.* **5.** to play or sing in a high, loud, harsh manner. **6.** to be conspicuous or startling: *That red dress really screams.* —*v.t.* **7.** to utter with or as with a scream or screams. **8.** to make by screaming: *to scream oneself hoarse.* —*n.* **9.** a loud, sharp, piercing cry: *Her scream frightened off the burglar.* **10.** a shrill, piercing sound: *the scream of the tires as the car rounded the curve.* **11.** someone or something that is hilariously funny: *The story of her experience with the garden club was a scream. He is a scream when he's in a good mood.* [ME *scream(en)*, OE *scrēaman; akin to Icel *skraumi* chatterbox, braggart, *skruma* to jabber; *sc-* (for *sh-*) from obs. *scritch* to SCREECH]
—**Syn. 1.** SCREAM, SHRIEK, SCREECH apply to crying out in a loud, piercing way. To SCREAM is to utter a loud, piercing cry, esp. of pain or fear: *to scream with terror.* The word is used also for a little, barely audible cry given by one who is startled. SHRIEK usually refers to a sharper and briefer cry than SCREAM; when caused by fear or pain, it is indicative of more terror or distress; SHRIEK is also used for the shrill half-suppressed cries of giddy women or girls: *to shriek with laughter.* SCREECH emphasizes the disagreeable shrillness and harshness of an outcry; the connotation is lack of dignity: *to screech like an old crone.* **9.** outcry, shriek, screech, screak.

scream·er (skrē′mər), *n.* **1.** one who or that which screams. **2.** *Informal.* something or someone causing screams of excitement, laughter, or the like. **3.** *Print. Slang.* an exclamation point. **4.** *Journalism.* **a.** a sensational headline. **b.** banner (def. 7). Cf. **scarehead.** **5.** *Baseball Slang.* an extremely hard-hit line drive. **6.** *Ornith.* any of several South American birds of the family *Anhimidae*, having a harsh, trumpeting call. Cf. **horned screamer.** [SCREAM + -ER[1]]

scream·ing (skrē′ming), *adj.* **1.** uttering screams. **2.** boldly striking or startling: *screaming colors; screaming headlines.* **3.** causing hilarious laughter; extremely funny: *a screaming farce.* —*n.* **4.** the act or sound of one who or that which screams. [SCREAM + -ING[2], -ING[1]] —**scream′ing·ly,** *adv.*

scream·ing-mee·mies (skrē′ming mē′mēz), *n.* (*construed as sing. or pl.*) *Informal.* extreme nervousness; hysteria (usually prec. by *the*). [after the name given to German shells in World War I; redupl. with alter. of SCREAMING]

scree (skrē), *n.* a steep mass of detritus on the side of a mountain. [< Scand; cf. Icel *skritha* landslide; akin to OE *scrīthan* to go, glide]

screech (skrēch), *v.i.* **1.** to utter or make a harsh, shrill cry or sound: *She was screeching hysterically. His brakes screeched.* —*v.t.* **2.** to utter with a screech: *She screeched her disapproval.* —*n.* **3.** a harsh, shrill cry or sound: *an owl's screech; the screech of brakes.* [var. of obs. *scritch* to scream] —**screech′er,** *n.*
—**Syn. 1.** See **scream.**

Screech owl, *Otus asio* (Length 9 in.)

screech·ing (skrē′ching), *adj.* **1.** causing or uttering screeches: *screeching women.* **2.** characteristic of screeches; harshly shrill: *a screeching tone.* —*n.* **3.** the act or sound of one who or that which screeches: *The usual screeching was heard.* [SCREECH + -ING[2], -ING[1]] —**screech′ing·ly,** *adv.*

screech′ owl′, **1.** any of numerous small, American owls of the genus *Otus*, having hornlike tufts of feathers, as *O. asio*, of North America. **2.** any owl having a harsh cry, esp. the barn owl.

screech·y (skrē′chē), *adj.*, **screech·i·er, screech·i·est.** **1.** like or suggesting screeching. **2.** producing screeches: *a screechy door.* [SCREECH + -Y[1]]

screed (skrēd), *n.* **1.** a long discourse or essay, esp. a diatribe. **2.** an informal letter, account, or other piece of writing. **3.** a strip of plaster or wood applied to a surface to be plastered to serve as a guide for making a true surface. **4.** a wooden strip serving as a guide for making a true level surface on a concrete pavement or the like. **5.** a board or metal strip dragged across a freshly poured concrete slab to give it its proper level. **6.** *Brit. Dial.* a fragment or shred, as of cloth. **7.** *Scot.* **a.** a tear or rip, esp. in cloth. **b.** a drinking bout. **—*v.t., v.i.*** **8.** *Scot.* to tear, rip, or shred, as cloth. [ME *screde* < Scand; cf. Icel *skrjōthr* shred, akin to OE *scrēade* SHRED]

screen (skrēn), *n.* **1.** a movable or fixed device, usually consisting of a covered frame, that provides shelter, serves as a partition, etc.: *a tall Oriental screen separating the living room from the dining room.* **2.** a permanent, usually ornamental partition, as around the choir of a church or across the hall of a medieval house. **3.** a specially prepared, light-reflecting surface on which motion pictures, slides, etc., may be projected. **4.** motion pictures collectively or the motion-picture industry. **5.** *Electronics, Television.* the external surface of the large end of a cathode ray tube of a television set, radar receiver, etc., on which an electronically created picture or image is formed. **6.** anything that shelters, protects, or conceals: *a screen of secrecy; A screen of fog prevented our seeing the ship.* **7.** a frame holding a mesh of cloth, wire, or plastic, for placing in a window or doorway, around a porch, etc., to admit air but exclude insects. **8.** a sieve, riddle, or other meshlike device used to separate smaller particles or objects from larger ones, as for grain, sand, etc. **9.** *Mil.* a body of troops sent out to protect the movement of an army. **10.** *Navy.* a protective formation of small vessels, as destroyers, around or in front of a larger ship or ships. **11.** *Physics.* a shield designed to prevent interference between various agencies: *electric screen.* **12.** *Electronics.* See **screen grid.** **13.** *Photog.* a plate of ground glass or the like on which the image is brought into focus in a camera before being photographed. **14.** *Photoengraving.* a transparent plate containing two sets of fine parallel lines, one crossing the other, used in the halftone process. **15.** *Sports.* **a.** any of various offensive plays in which teammates form a protective formation around the ball carrier, pass receiver, shooter, etc. **b.** any of various defensive plays in which teammates conceal or block an opposing ball carrier, pass receiver, shooter, or the goal, basket, net, etc., itself. **—*v.t.*** **16.** to shelter, protect, or conceal with or as if with a screen. **17.** to select, reject, consider, or group (people, objects, ideas, etc.) by a process of winnowing out: *His secretary screens his visitors so that salesmen never get to see him. The FBI screened possible traitors out of the organization.* **18.** to provide with a screen or screens to exclude insects: *He screened the porch so they could enjoy sitting out on summer evenings.* **19.** to sift or sort by passing through a screen. **20.** to project (a motion picture, slide, etc.) on a screen. **21.** *Motion Pictures.* **a.** to photograph with a motion-picture camera; film. **b.** to adapt (a story, play, etc.) for presentation as a motion picture. **22.** to lighten (type or areas of a line engraving) by etching a regular pattern of dots or lines into the printing surface. **—*v.i.*** **23.** to be projected on a motion-picture screen. [ME *screne* < AF; OF *escren* < MD *scherm*; c. G *Schirm* screen] **—screen′a·ble,** *adj.* **—screen′er,** *n.* **—screen′less,** *adj.* **—screen′like′,** *adj.*
—Syn. 6. guard, shield. See **cover. 16.** veil, defend, shield, hide, mask.

screen′ grid′, *Electronics.* a grid placed between the anode and the control electrode in a vacuum tube, usually maintained at a fixed positive potential.

screen·ing (skrē′ning), *n.* **1.** the act or work of one who screens, as in ascertaining the character and competence of applicants, employees, etc. **2.** the showing of a motion picture: *There will be screenings at 6 p.m. and 8 p.m.* **3. screenings,** (*construed as sing. or pl.*) undesirable material that has been separated from usable material by means of a screen or sieve: *screenings of imperfect grain.* **4.** the meshed material used in screens for windows and doors. [SCREEN + -ING[1]]

screen·o (skrē′nō), *n.* (*sometimes cap.*) bingo played at a motion-picture theater. [SCREEN + (BING)O]

screen′ pass′, *Football.* a pass thrown to a receiver with a wall of blockers directly in front of him, the receiver being behind or not far beyond the line of scrimmage.

screen·play (skrēn′plā′), *n.* **1.** a motion-picture scenario. **2.** See **motion picture.** [SCREEN + PLAY]

screen′ test′, a filmed audition to determine the suitability of an individual for appearing or acting in motion pictures.

screen-test (skrēn′test′), *v.t.* to give a screen test to: *The studio screen-tested 400 children before casting the part.* [v. use of n. phrase *screen test*]

screen-wip·er (skrēn′wī′pər), *n.* *Brit.* See **windshield wiper.**

screev·er (skrē′vər), *n.* *Chiefly Brit.* an artist who draws pictures on sidewalks, as with colored chalks, earning a living from the donations of spectators and passers-by. [*screeve* (v.) < It *scriv(ere)* (to) write (< L *scrībere*) + -ER[1]]

screw (skrōō), *n.* **1.** a metal fastener having a tapered shank with a helical thread, and topped with a slotted head, driven into wood or the like by rotating, esp. by means of a screwdriver. **2.** a threaded cylindrical pin or rod with a head at one end, engaging a threaded hole and used either as a fastener or as a device for applying power, as in a clamp, jack, etc. Cf. **bolt**[1] (def. 3). **3.** *Brit.* a tapped or threaded hole. **4.** something having a spiral form. **5.** See **screw propeller. 6.** Usually, **screws.** physical or mental coercion: *The terrified debtor soon felt the gangster's screws.* **7.** a single turn of a screw. **8.** a twist, turn, or twisting movement. **9.** *Chiefly Brit.* **a.** a little salt, sugar, tobacco, etc., carried in a twist of paper. **b.** *Slang.* a mean, old, or worn-out horse; a horse from which one can obtain no further service. **c.** *Slang.* a friend or employer from whom one can obtain no more money. **d.** *Slang.* a miser. **10.** *Brit. Informal.* salary; wages. **11.** *Slang.* a prison guard. **12.** *Slang* (*vulgar*). an act of coitus. **13. have a screw loose,** *Slang.* to be eccentric or neurotic; have crazy ideas: *The neighborhood kids thought the old lady must have a screw loose to keep so many cats.* **14. put on the screws,** to compel by exerting pressure on; use coercion or force: *to put the screws on a debtor.* **—*v.t.*** **15.** to fasten, tighten, force, press, stretch tight, etc., by or as by means of a screw or device operated by a screw or helical threads. **16.** to operate or adjust by a screw, as a press. **17.** to attach with a screw or screws: *to screw a bracket to a wall.* **18.** to insert, fasten, undo, or work (a screw, bolt, nut, bottle top with a helical thread, etc.) by turning. **19.** to contort as by twisting; distort: *Father screwed his face into a grimace of disgust.* **20.** to cause to become sufficiently strong or intense (usually fol. by *up*): *He screwed up his courage to ask her to dance.* **21.** to coerce or threaten. **22.** to extract or extort. **23.** to force (a seller) to lower a price (often fol. by *down*). **24.** *Slang.* to cheat or take advantage of (someone). **25.** *Slang* (*vulgar*). to have coitus with. **—*v.i.*** **26.** to turn as or like a screw. **27.** to be adapted for being connected, taken apart, opened, or closed by means of a screw or screws or parts with helical threads (usually fol. by *on, together,* or *off*): *Where is the top that screws on this bottle?* **28.** to turn or move with a twisting or rotating motion. **29.** to practice extortion. **30.** *Slang* (*vulgar*) to have coitus. **31. screw around,** *Slang.* to waste time in foolish or frivolous activity: *If you'd stop screwing around we could get this job done.* **32. screw up,** *Slang.* to ruin through bungling or stupidity: *Somehow the engineers screwed up the entire construction project.* [ME *scrwe, screw(e)*; cf. ME *escro(ue)* nut, MD *schrûve,* MHG *schrûbe* screw] **—screw′a·ble,** *adj.* **—screw′er,** *n.* **—screw′less,** *adj.* **—screw′like′,** *adj.*

A B C D E F G
Screws and heads (def. 1)
A, Round head; B, Flat head; C, Oval head; D, Fillister head; E, Metal screw; F, Phillips head screw; G, Lag screw

screw′ an′chor, *Naut.* See **mooring screw.**

screw′ au′ger, an auger having a helical outer surface suggesting a screw thread.

screw′ ax′is, *Crystall.* a symmetry element of a space group such that a rotation of the lattice about the axis and a translation of the lattice some fraction of the lattice's unit distance brings the lattice back to its original position.

screw·ball (skrōō′bôl′), *n.* **1.** *Slang.* an eccentric or whimsically eccentric person; a nut. **2.** *Baseball.* a pitched ball that curves toward the side of the plate from which it was thrown. **—*adj.*** **3.** *Slang.* eccentric or whimsically eccentric: *screwball ideas.* [SCREW + BALL[1]]

screw′ bean′, **1.** Also called **screw-pod mesquite.** a mimosaceous tree, *Strombocarpa odorata* (*Prosopis pubescens*), of the southwestern U.S., bearing twisted pods used as fodder. **2.** the pod itself. Also called **tornillo.**

screw′ cap′, a cap designed to screw onto the threaded mouth of a bottle, jar, or the like.

screw′ convey′or, a device for moving loose materials, consisting of a shaft with a broad, helically wound blade rotating in a tube or trough. Also called **worm.**

screw·driv·er (skrōō′drī′vər), *n.* **1.** a hand tool for turning a screw, consisting of a wooden handle attached to a long, narrow shank, usually of metal, which tapers and flattens out to a tip that fits into the slotted head of a screw. **2.** a mixed drink made with vodka and orange juice. Also, **screw′ driv′er.** [SCREW + DRIVER]

screwed (skrōōd), *adj.* **1.** fastened with a screw or screws. **2.** having grooves like a screw; threaded. **3.** twisted; awry. **4.** *Slang.* bilked; cheated. **5.** *Chiefly Brit. Slang.* drunk; intoxicated. [SCREW + -ED[2]]

screw′ eye′, a screw having a ring-shaped head.

screw·head (skrōō′hed′), *n.* the head or top of a screw having a slot for the end of a screwdriver. [SCREW + HEAD]

screw′ hook′, a hook having a shank in the form of a screw.

screw′ jack′, a jack the lifting force of which is given by a screw; jackscrew.

screw′ moor′ing, *Naut.* See **mooring screw.**

screw′ nail′. See **drive screw.**

screw′ nut′, a nut threaded to receive a screw.

screw′ pile′, a pile that is used for the foundations of bridges, lighthouses, etc., and has a screwlike lower end for drilling through and taking firm hold in compacted material. **—screw′ pil′ing.**

screw′ pine′, any tropical Asian tree or shrub of the genus *Pandanus,* having a palmlike or branched stem, long, narrow, rigid, spirally arranged leaves and aerial roots, and bearing an edible fruit. **—screw′-pine′,** *adj.*

screw·plate (skrōō′plāt′), *n.* a metal plate having threaded holes, used for cutting screw threads by hand. Also, **screw′ plate′.** [SCREW + PLATE[1]]

screw′-pod mesquite′ (skrōō′pod′). See **screw bean** (def. 1).

screw′ post′, *Naut.* See **propeller post.**

screw′ press′, a device for applying pressure by the turning of a threaded shaft.

screw′ propel′ler, a rotary propelling device, as for a ship or airplane, consisting of a number of blades that radiate from a central hub and are so inclined to the plane of rotation as to tend to drive a helical path through the substance in which they rotate. **—screw′-pro·pelled′,** *adj.*

screw′ stock′, diestock.

screw′ thread′, **1.** the helical ridge of a screw. **2.** a full turn of the helical ridge of a screw.

screw·worm (skrōō′wûrm′), *n.* the larva of any of certain flies of the genus *Callitroga,* which sometimes infests wounds and the nose and navel of domestic animals and man. [SCREW + WORM]

screw·y (skrōō′ē), *adj.,* **screw·i·er, screw·i·est.** *Slang.* **1.** crazy; nutty: *What a screwy guy, refusing an invitation to the governor's dinner!* **2.** disconcertingly strange: *There's something screwy about his story.* **3.** absurdly peculiar or impractical; ridiculous: *That's an awfully screwy getup to wear to the office.* [SCREW + -Y[1]]

Scria·bin (skrē ä′bin; *Russ.* skrya′bin), *n.* **A·le·ksan·dr Ni·ko·la·ie·vich** (ä′le ksän′dər ni ko lä′yə vich), 1872–1915, Russian composer and pianist.

scrib·anne (skri bän′, -ban′), *n.* *Furniture.* a writing desk or secretary made in Flanders and Holland in the 17th and 18th centuries, having a slant front with a two-door cabinet above and several wide drawers below. [? alter. of *scribent* scribbler]

scrib·ble[1] (skrib′əl), *v.,* **-bled, -bling,** *n.* **—*v.t.*** **1.** to write hastily or carelessly: *to scribble a letter.* **2.** to cover with meaningless writing or marks: *to scribble all over a blank page.* **—*v.i.*** **3.** to write or draw in a hasty or careless way. **4.** to make meaningless marks, scrolls, lines, etc., with a pencil or pen. **—*n.*** **5.** a note or other writing that has little or no meaning. **6.** a hasty or careless drawing or piece of writing. **7.** handwriting, esp. when illegible. [late ME < ML *scrībill(āre)* (to) scribble, dim. of *scrībere* to write; see SHRIVE] **—scrib′bling·ly,** *adv.*

scrib·ble[2] (skrib′əl), *v.t.,* **-bled, -bling.** to tear apart (wool fibers) in the first stages of carding. [< WFlem *schribbel(en)* < D *schrobbelen,* freq. of *schrobben* to SCRUB[1]]

scrib·bler[1] (skrib′lər), *n.* **1.** a writer whose work has little or no value. **2.** one who scribbles. [SCRIBBLE[1] + -ER[1]]

scrib·bler[2] (skrib′lər), *n.* a machine for scribbling wool fibers. [SCRIBBLE[2] + -ER[1]]

scrib′bling block′, *Brit.* See **scratch pad.**

scribe[1] (skrīb), *n.* **1.** a person who serves as a penman or copyist, esp. one who in former times made copies of manuscripts. **2.** a public clerk or writer, usually one having official status. **3.** Also called **sopher, sofer.** *Judaism.* one of the group of Palestinian scholars and teachers of Jewish law and tradition, active from the 5th century B.C. to the 1st century A.D., who transcribed, edited, and interpreted the Bible. **4.** a writer or author, esp. a newspaperman. [ME < L *scrīb(a)* clerk, deriv. of *scrībere* to write] **—scrib′al,** *adj.* **—scribe′ship,** *n.*

scribe[2] (skrīb), *v.t.,* **scribed, scrib·ing.** **1.** to mark or score (wood or the like) with a pointed instrument as a guide to cutting or assembling. **2.** *Rare.* to write or write down. [? aph. var. of INSCRIBE]

Scribe (skRēb), *n.* **Au·gus·tin Eu·gène** (ō gys taN′ œ zhen′), 1791–1861, French dramatist.

scrib·er (skrī′bər), *n.* a tool for scribing wood or the like. [SCRIBE[2] + -ER[1]]

scrieve′ board′ (skrēv), *Shipbuilding.* See **scrive board.**

scrim (skrim), *n.* **1.** a cotton or linen fabric of open weave used for bunting, curtains, etc. **2.** *Theat.* a piece of such fabric used as a drop, border, or the like, for creating the illusion of a solid wall or backdrop under certain lighting conditions or creating a semi-transparent curtain when lit from behind. [?]

scrim·mage (skrim′ij), *n., v.,* **-maged, -mag·ing.** **—*n.*** **1.** a rough or vigorous struggle. **2.** *Football.* **a.** the action that takes place between the teams from the moment the ball is snapped until it is declared dead. Cf. **line of scrimmage. b.** a practice session or informal games, as that played between two units of the same team. **—*v.t., v.i.*** **3.** to engage in a scrimmage. [var. of *scrimish,* metathetic form of SKIRMISH] **—scrim′mag·er,** *n.*

scrim′mage line′. See **line of scrimmage.**

scrimp (skrimp), *v.t.* **1.** to be sparing or restrictive of or in; limit severely: *to scrimp food.* **2.** to keep on short allowance; provide sparingly for: *to scrimp his elderly parents.* **—*v.i.*** **3.** to be sparing or frugal; economize (often fol. by *on*): *They scrimped and saved for everything they have. He spends most of his money on clothes, and scrimps on food.* [< Scand; cf. Sw *skrympa,* Norw, Dan *skrumpe* (orig. **skrimpa,* strong v.) to shrivel, c. MHG *schrimpfen* to contract; see SHRIMP]

scrimp·y (skrim′pē), *adj.,* **scrimp·i·er, scrimp·i·est.** scanty; meager; barely adequate. [SCRIMP + -Y[1]] **—scrimp′i·ly,** *adv.* **—scrimp′i·ness,** *n.*

scrim·shank (skrim′shangk′), *v.i.* *Brit. Slang.* to avoid one's obligations or share of work; shirk. [?] **—scrim′shank′er,** *n.*

scrim·shaw (skrim′shô′), *n.* **1.** a carved or engraved article, esp. of whale ivory, whalebone, walrus tusks, and the like, made by whalemen as a leisure occupation. **2.** such articles or work collectively. **3.** the art or technique of carving or engraving whale ivory, whalebone, walrus tusks, etc. **—*v.i.*** **4.** to produce scrimshaw. **—*v.t.*** **5.** to carve or engrave (whale ivory or whalebone) into scrimshaw. [?]

scrin·i·um (skrin′ē əm), *n., pl.* **scrin·i·a** (skrin′ē ə). a cylindrical container used by the early Romans for holding scrolls. [< L; see SHRINE]

scrip[1] (skrip), *n.* **1.** a receipt, certificate, list, or similar brief piece of writing. **2.** a scrap of paper. **3.** *Finance.* **a.** a certificate representing a fraction of a share of stock. **b.** a certificate to be exchanged for goods, as at a company store. **c.** a certificate indicating the right of the holder to receive payment later in the form of cash, goods, or land. **4.** paper currency in denominations of less than one dollar, formerly issued in the United States. **5.** such currency as a whole. [? b. ME *scri(t* SCRIPT and SCRA)P; in some senses, short for SUBSCRIPTION] **—scrip′less,** *adj.*

scrip[2] (skrip), *n.* *Archaic.* a bag or wallet carried by wayfarers. [ME *scrippe* < ML *scripp(um)* pilgrim's pack < ?]

scrip′ div′idend, a dividend issued in the form of a note entitling the holder to a cash payment at a specified later date.

Scripps (skrips), *n.* **Edward Wyl·lis** (wil′is), 1854–1926, U.S. newspaper publisher.

scrip·sit (skRēp′sit; *Eng.* skrip′sit), *v.* *Latin.* he wrote (it); she wrote (it).

script (skript), *n.* **1.** the letters or characters used in writing by hand; handwriting. **2.** a manuscript or document. **3.** the text of a manuscript or document. **4.** the manuscript or one of various copies of the written text of a play, motion picture, or radio or television broadcast. **5.** any system of writing. **6.** *Print.* a type imitating handwriting. Cf. **cursive.** [ME < L *script(um),* neut. ptp. of *scrībere* to write; r. ME *scrit* < OF *escrit* < L *script(um),* as above]

Script., **1.** Scriptural. **2.** Scripture.

script′ girl′, a secretarial assistant to the director of a motion picture.

scrip·to·ri·um (skrip tôr′ē əm, -tōr′-), *n., pl.* **-to·ri·ums, -to·ri·a** (-tôr′ē ə, -tōr′-). a room in a monastery set apart for the writing or copying of manuscripts. [< ML; see SCRIPT, -ORIUM]

script′ read′er, playreader.

scrip·tur·al (skrip′chər əl), *adj.* **1.** (*sometimes cap.*) of, pertaining to, or in accordance with sacred writings, esp. the Scriptures. **2.** rendered in or related to writing. [< NL *scriptūrāl(is).* See SCRIPTURE, -AL¹] —**scrip′tur·al·ly,** *adv.* —**scrip′tur·al·ness,** *n.*

Scrip·ture (skrip′chər), *n.* **1.** Often, **Scriptures.** Also called **Holy Scripture, Holy Scriptures.** the sacred writings of the Old or New Testaments or both together. **2.** a short passage of the Bible; text. **3.** any writing or book, esp. when of a sacred or religious nature. **4.** (*sometimes l.c.*) a particular passage from the Bible. [< L *scriptūr(a)* writing. See SCRIPT, -URE]

script·writ·er (skript′rī′tər), *n.* one who writes scripts, as for movies, radio, or television. [SCRIPT + WRITER] —**script′writ′ing,** *n.*

scrive′ board′ (skrīv, skrēv), *Shipbuilding.* a floorlike construction on which the lines of a vessel can be drawn or scribed at full size: often divided into portable sections so that it can be transferred from a mold loft and erected next to a bending slab. Also, **scrieve board.** [*scrive,* var. of SCRIBE²]

scrive·ner (skriv′nər), *n.* **1.** scribe¹ (defs. 1, 2). **2.** a notary. [ME *scriveyner,* equiv. to *scrivein* (< OF *(e)scrivein;* see scribe¹, -AN) + *-er* -ER¹]

scro·bic·u·late (skrō bik′yə lit, -lāt′), *adj. Bot., Zool.* furrowed or pitted. [< LL *scrobicul(us)* (*scrobi(s)* ditch + *-culus* -CULE) + -ATE¹]

scrod (skrod), *n. U.S.* young Atlantic codfish or haddock, esp. one split for cooking. [?]

scrod·dled (skrod′ᵊld), *adj. Ceram.* (of a glaze) mottled with different colors applied in such a way that they do not blend. [?; cf. LG *schrodel* scrap]

scrof·u·la (skrof′yə lə), *n. Pathol.* a constitutional disorder of a tuberculous nature, characterized chiefly by swelling and degeneration of the lymphatic glands, esp. of the neck, and by inflammation of the joints. [< ML, sing. of LL *scrofulae* (L *scrōf(a)* sow + *-ulae* -ULE); r. OE *scrofel* < LL]

scrof·u·lous (skrof′yə ləs), *adj.* **1.** pertaining to, resembling, of the nature of, or affected with scrofula. **2.** morally tainted. [SCROFUL(A) + -OUS] —**scrof′u·lous·ly,** *adv.* —**scrof′u·lous·ness,** *n.*

scrog (skrog), *n. Scot. and North Eng.* **1.** any naturally short or stunted tree or bush, as a crab-apple tree, blackthorn bush, etc. **2. scrogs,** underbrush; brushwood. [? var. of SCRAG] —**scrog′gy,** *adj.*

scroll (skrōl), *n.* **1.** a roll of parchment, paper, copper, or other material, esp. one with writing on it: *a scroll containing the entire Old Testament.* **2.** something, esp. an ornament, resembling a partly unrolled sheet of paper or having a spiral or coiled form. **3.** a note, message, or other piece of writing. **4.** a list, roll, roster, or schedule. **5.** (in Japanese and Chinese art) a painting or text on silk or paper that is either displayed on a wall (**hanging scroll**) or held by the viewer (**hand scroll**) and is rolled up when not in use. Cf. **kakemono, makimono. 6.** the curved head of a violin or other bowed instrument. —*v.t.* **7.** to cut into a curved form with a narrow-bladed saw. [ME *scrowle;* b. ESCROW and ROLL] —**scroll′-like′,** *adj.*

Scroll (def. 2)

scroll′ cas′ing. See **spiral casing.**

scroll′ foot′. See **French foot** (def. 1).

scroll·head (skrōl′hed′), *n. Naut.* billethead. [SCROLL + HEAD]

scroll′ saw′, 1. a narrow saw mounted vertically in a frame and operated with an up-and-down motion, used for cutting curved ornamental designs. **2.** such a saw mounted in a power-driven machine.

scroll·work (skrōl′wûrk′), *n.* **1.** decorative work in which scroll forms figure prominently. **2.** ornamental work cut out with a scroll saw. [SCROLL + WORK]

Scrooge (skro͞oj), *n.* **1. Eb·e·ne·zer** (eb′ə nē′zər), a miserly curmudgeon in Dickens' *Christmas Carol.* **2.** (*often l.c.*) any miserly person: *He's too much of a scrooge to contribute to the church fund.*

scroop (skro͞op), *v.i.* **1.** to emit a harsh, grating sound: *The gate scrooped as he swung it shut.* —*n.* **2.** a scrooping sound. **3.** ability to make a rustling sound added to silk or rayon fabrics during finishing by treating them with certain acids. [b. SCRAPE and WHOOP]

scroph·u·lar·i·a·ceous (skrof′yə lâr′ē ā′shəs), *adj.* belonging to the *Scrophulariaceae,* or figwort family of plants, comprising the snapdragon, foxglove, toadflax, mullein, eyebright, etc. [< NL *scrophulari(a)* genus name (see SCROFULA, -ARIA) + -ACEOUS]

scro·tum (skrō′təm), *n., pl.* **-ta** (-tə), **-tums.** *Anat.* the pouch of skin that contains the testes and their coverings. [< L] —**scro′tal,** *adj.*

scrouge (skrouj, skro͞oj), *v.t., v.i.,* **scrouged, scrouging.** *Chiefly Dial.* to squeeze; crowd. [b. obs. *scruze* (itself b. SCREW and BRUISE) and GOUGE]

scrounge (skrounj), *v.,* **scrounged, scroung·ing,** *n.* —*v.t.* **1.** to gather together by foraging; seek out: *We'll try to scrounge enough food for supper from the neighbors.* —*v.i.* **2.** to borrow, esp. a small item one is not expected to return or replace: *He scrounged a cigarette from his roommate.* **3. scrounge around,** to search or forage for something, esp. in a haphazard or disorganized fashion; hunt for: *We scrounged around for something to eat.* —*n.* **4.** Also, **scroung′er.** an habitual borrower; sponger. [alter. of dial. *scringe* to glean]

Scro·ve′gni Chap′el (skrō vān′yē; *It.* skrô ve′nyē). See **Arena Chapel.** [named after its patron, Enrico *Scrovegni,* a rich 14th-century Paduan]

scrub¹ (skrub), *v.,* **scrubbed, scrub·bing,** *n.* —*v.t.* **1.** to rub hard with a brush, cloth, etc., or against a rough surface in washing. **2.** to remove (dirt, grime, etc.) from something by hard rubbing while washing. **3.** to cleanse (a gas or vapor). **4.** *Rocketry.* to cancel or postpone (a missile flight). **5.** *Slang.* to do away with; cancel: *Scrub your vacation plans; there's work to do.* —*v.i.* **6.** to cleanse something by hard rubbing. —*n.* **7.** the act or an instance of scrubbing. **8.** *Rocketry.* a canceled or postponed missile flight. [ME *scrobbe* < MD *scrobbe(n)*] —**scrub′ba·ble,** *adj.*

scrub² (skrub), *n.* **1.** low trees or shrubs collectively. **2.** a large area covered with low trees and shrubs, as the Australian bush. **3.** a domestic animal of mixed or inferior breeding; mongrel. **4.** a small or insignificant person. **5.** anything undersized or inferior. **6.** *Sports.* a player not belonging to the varsity or regular team; a player who is not first-string. —*adj.* **7.** small, undersized, or stunted. **8.** inferior or insignificant. **9.** abounding in or covered with low trees and shrubs: *They rode through scrub country.* [< Scand; cf. dial. Dan *skrub* brushwood; see SHRUB¹]

scrub·bed (skrub′id), *adj. Archaic.* stunted; scrubby. [SCRUB² + -ED³]

scrub·ber¹ (skrub′ər), *n.* one who or that which scrubs. [SCRUB¹ + -ER¹]

scrub·ber² (skrub′ər), *n.* **1.** a mongrel, esp. a mongrel steer. **2.** a thin or stunted steer. **3.** *Australian.* **a.** an inhabitant of the bush. **b.** any domestic animal that has run off into the bush and become wild, esp. a steer. [SCRUB² + -ER¹]

scrub-bird (skrub′bûrd′), *n.* either of two Australian, passerine birds of the family *Atrichornithidae,* having a loud voice and reduced powers of flight. [SCRUB² + BIRD]

scrub·board (skrub′bōrd′, -bôrd′), *n.* washboard (defs. 1, 2). [SCRUB¹ + BOARD]

scrub·by (skrub′ē), *adj.,* **-bi·er, -bi·est. 1.** low or stunted, as trees. **2.** consisting of or covered with scrub, stunted trees, etc. **3.** undersized or inferior, as animals. **4.** wretched; shabby. [SCRUB² + -Y¹] —**scrub′bi·ly,** *adv.* —**scrub′bi·ness,** *n.*

scrub′ jay′, a jay, *Aphelocoma coerulescens,* of the western and southern U.S. and Mexico, having blue and grayish plumage.

scrub·land (skrub′land′), *n.* land on which the natural vegetation is chiefly scrub. [SCRUB² + LAND]

scrub′ nurse′, a nurse specially trained to assist surgeons in the operating room and serving as part of the surgically-clean medical team handling instruments during an operation.

scrub′ oak′, any of several oaks, as *Quercus ilicifolia* and *Q. prinoides,* characterized by a shrubby manner of growth, usually found on dry, rocky soil

scrub′ pine′, any of several pines, as the jack pine, characterized by a shrubby or irregular manner of growth, usually found in dry, sandy soil.

scrub′ ty′phus, *Pathol.* See **Japanese river fever.**

scrub-up (skrub′up′), *n.* the act of washing or bathing thoroughly, esp. the aseptic washing by doctors, nurses, etc., before a surgical operation.

scrub·wom·an (skrub′wo͝om′ən), *n., pl.* **-wom·en.** a woman hired to clean a place; charwoman. [SCRUB¹ + WOMAN]

scruff¹ (skruf), *n.* the nape or back of the neck. [var. of dial. *scuff, scuft* < D *schoft* horse's withers]

scruff² (skruf), *n. Metall.* (in tin-plating) dross formed in the bath. [metathetic var. of SCURF]

scruff·y (skruf′ē), *adj.,* **scruff·i·er, scruff·i·est.** untidy; shabby. [SCRUFF² + -Y¹]

scrum·mage (skrum′ij), *n., v.,* **-maged, -mag·ing.** *Rugby.* —*n.* **1.** Also called **scrum** (skrum). a play in which, typically, three members of each team line up opposite one another with a group of two and a group of three players behind them, making an eight-man, three-two-three formation on each side, the ball is then rolled between the opposing front lines, the players of which stand with arms around a teammate's waist, meeting the opponent shoulder to shoulder, and attempt to kick the ball backward to a teammate. —*v.i.* **2.** to engage in a scrummage. [var. of SCRIMMAGE] —**scrum′mag·er,** *n.*

scrump·tious (skrump′shəs), *adj. Informal.* very pleasing, esp. to the senses; delectable; splendid: *a scrumptious casserole; a scrumptious satin gown.* [dial. *scrumptious* stingy, equiv. to *scrumpt* stinted (see SCRIMP) + -IOUS] —**scrump′tious·ly,** *adv.* —**scrump′tious·ness,** *n.*

scrunch (skrunch, skro͝onch), *v.t., v.i.* **1.** to crunch, crush, or crumple. —*n.* **2.** the act or sound of scrunching. [var. of CRUNCH]

scru·ple (skro͞o′pəl), *n., v.,* **-pled, -pling.** —*n.* **1.** a moral or ethical consideration or standard that acts as a restraining force or inhibits certain actions. **2.** a very small portion or amount. **3.** a unit of weight equal to 20 grains or ⅓ of a dram, apothecaries' weight. **4.** an ancient Roman unit of weight equivalent to ¹/₂₄ of an ounce or ¹/₂₈₈ of an as or pound. —*v.i.* **5.** to have scruples. —*v.t.* **6.** to have scruples about; hesitate at. [< L *scrūpul(us),* equiv. to *scrūp(us)* rough pebble + *-ulus* -ULE] —**scru′ple·less,** *adj.*

—**Syn. 1.** qualm, compunction, restraint. **6.** waver, doubt.

scru·pu·lous (skro͞o′pyə ləs), *adj.* **1.** having scruples; having or showing a strict regard for what one considers right; principled. **2.** punctiliously or minutely careful, precise, or exact: *He conducted a scrupulous performance.* [< L *scrūpulōs(us).* See SCRUPLE, -OSE¹, -OUS] —**scru·pu·los·i·ty** (skro͞o′pyə los′i tē), **scru′pu·lous·ness,** *n.* —**scru′pu·lous·ly,** *adv.*

—**Syn. 1.** conscientious, cautious, careful, circumspect. **2.** exacting, rigorous. SCRUPULOUS, PUNCTILIOUS imply abiding exactly by rules. SCRUPULOUS implies conscientious carefulness in attending to details: *scrupulous attention to details.* PUNCTILIOUS suggests strictness, preciseness, and rigidity, esp. in observance of social conventions. —**Ant. 2.** careless.

scru·ta·ble (skro͞o′tə bəl), *adj.* capable of being understood by careful study or investigation. [< L *scrūt(ārī)* (see SCRUTINY) + -ABLE] —**scru′ta·bil′i·ty,** *n.*

scru·ta·tor (skro͞o tā′tər), *n.* one who investigates. [< L: searcher, examiner, equiv. to *scrūtāt(us)* (ptp. of *scrūtārī* to examine; see SCRUTINY, -ATE¹) + *-or* -OR²]

scru·ti·neer (skro͞ot′ᵊnēr′), *n. Chiefly Brit.* an official examiner, esp. of votes in an election. [SCRUTIN(Y) + -EER]

scru·ti·nise (skro͞ot′ᵊnīz′), *v.t., v.i.,* **-nised, -nis·ing.** *Chiefly Brit.* scrutinize. —**scru′ti·ni·sa′tion,** *n.* —**scru′ti·nis′er,** *n.* —**scru′ti·nis′ing·ly,** *adv.*

scru·ti·nize (skro͞ot′ᵊnīz′), *v.,* **-nized, -niz·ing.** —*v.t.* **1.** to examine in detail with careful or critical attention. —*v.i.* **2.** to conduct a scrutiny. [SCRUTIN(Y) + -IZE] —**scru′ti·ni·za′tion,** *n.* —**scru′ti·niz′er,** *n.* —**scru′ti·niz′ing·ly,** *adv.*

—**Syn. 1, 2.** investigate, study, search.

scru·ti·ny (skro͞ot′ᵊnē), *n., pl.* **-nies. 1.** a searching examination or investigation; minute inquiry. **2.** surveillance; close and continuous watching or guarding. **3.** a close and searching look. [< LL *scrūtini(um)* the action of searching, of scrutinizing, equiv. to L *scrūt(ārī)* (to) search + *-inium* n. suffix]

—**Syn. 1, 2, 3.** investigation, study, inquiry, search. See **examination.**

scru·toire (skro͞o twär′), *n.* escritoire.

SCS, Soil Conservation Service.

scu·ba (sko͞o′bə), *n.* **1.** a portable breathing device for free-swimming divers, consisting of a mouthpiece joined by hoses to one or two tanks of compressed air which are strapped on the back. —*adj.* **2.** done by a free-swimming diver equipped with scuba: *scuba diving.* **3.** of or pertaining to a scuba device. [*s(elf)-c(ontained) u(nderwater) b(reathing) a(pparatus)*]

scud¹ (skud), *v.,* **scud·ded, scud·ding,** *n.* —*v.i.* **1.** to run or move quickly or hurriedly. **2.** *Naut.* to run before a gale with little or no sail set. **3.** *Archery.* (of an arrow) to fly too high and wide of the mark. —*n.* **4.** the act of scudding. **5.** clouds, spray, or the like, driven by the wind; a driving shower or a gust of wind. **6.** low-drifting clouds appearing beneath a cloud from which precipitation is falling. [< Scand; cf. Norw *skudda* push]

scud² (skud), *v.,* **scud·ded, scud·ding,** *n.* —*v.t.* **1.** to cleanse (a trimmed and roughly depilated skin or hide) of remaining hairs or dirt. —*n.* **2.** the hairs or dirt removed by scudding. [obs. *scud* dirt < ?]

Scu·dé·ry (sky dā rē′), *n.* **Mag·de·leine de** (mag də len′ də), 1607–1701, French novelist.

scu·do (sko͞o′dō), *n., pl.* **-di** (-dē). any of various gold or silver coins, of various Italian states, issued from the late 16th through the early 19th centuries. [< It < L *scūtum* shield]

scuff (skuf), *v.i.* **1.** to walk without raising the feet from the ground; shuffle. **2.** to scrape or rub one's foot back and forth over something. **3.** to be or become marred or scratched by scraping or wear. **4.** (of machine parts, as gear teeth) to creep from pressure and friction so that ridges appear transversely to the direction of wear. —*v.t.* **5.** to scrape (something) with one's foot or feet. **6.** to rub or scrape (one's foot or feet) over something. **7.** to mar by scraping or hard use, as shoes, furniture, etc. **8.** *Chiefly Scot.* **a.** to brush against, as in passing. **b.** to brush off; wipe off. —*n.* **9.** the act or sound of scuffing. **10.** a flat-heeled slipper with a full-length sole and an upper part covering only the front of the foot. **11.** a marred or scratched place on an item, as from scraping or wear. [< Scand; cf. Sw *skuffa* to push]

scuf·fle (skuf′əl), *v.,* **-fled, -fling,** *n.* —*v.i.* **1.** to struggle or fight in a rough, confused manner. **2.** to go or move in hurried confusion. **3.** to move or go with a shuffle; scuff. —*n.* **4.** a rough, confused struggle or fight. **5.** a shuffling: *a scuffle of feet.* **6.** Also called **scuf′fle hoe′.** a spadelike hoe that is pushed instead of pulled. **7.** (in tap dancing) a forward and backward movement of the foot. [SCUFF + -LE] —**scuf′fling·ly,** *adv.*

scul·dud·der·y (skul dud′ə rē), *n., pl.* **-der·ies.** *Chiefly Brit.* obscene behavior; lewdness. [?]

scul·dug·ger·y (skul dug′ə rē), *n.* skulduggery. Also, **scull·dug′ger·y.**

sculk (skulk), *v.i., n.* skulk. —**sculk′er,** *n.*

scull (skul), *n.* **1.** an oar mounted on a fulcrum at the stern of a small boat and moved from side to side to propel the boat forward. **2.** either of a pair of oars rowed by one oarsman. **3.** a boat propelled by an oar or oars. **4.** a light, narrow racing boat for one, two, or sometimes four oarsmen, each equipped with a pair of oars. **5. sculls,** a race involving such boats. Cf. **double sculls, single sculls.** —*v.t.* **6.** to propel or convey by means of a scull or sculls. —*v.i.* **7.** to propel a boat with a scull or sculls. [ME *sculle* < ?] —**scull′er,** *n.*

S, Scull (def. 1)

scul·ler·y (skul′ə rē), *n., pl.* **-ler·ies.** *Chiefly Brit.* **1.** a small room or section of a pantry in which food is cleaned, trimmed, and cut into cooking portions before being sent to the kitchen. **2.** a small room or section of a pantry or kitchen in which cooking utensils are cleaned and stored. [ME *squillerye* < MF *(e)scuelerie,* equiv. to *escuele* dish (< L *scutella,* dim. of *scutra* pan) + *-rie* -RY]

Scul·lin (skul′in), *n.* **James Henry,** 1876–1953, Australian statesman: prime minister 1929–31.

scul·lion (skul′yən), *n.* **1.** a kitchen servant who does menial work. **2.** a low or contemptible person. [? < MF *(e)scou(v)illon* dishclout, equiv. to *escouve* broom (< L *scōpa*) + *-illon* dim. suffix]

sculp (skulp), *v.t.* to sculpture; carve or model. [< L *sculp(ere)* (to) carve]

—**Usage.** SCULP, like SCULPT, is often criticized as being a back formation from the verb SCULPTURE, but is actually from the Latin verb *sculpere.* SCULP is an older form than SCULPT, but less common in present-day writing. See note at **sculpt.**

sculp., **1.** sculptor. **2.** sculptural. **3.** sculpture. Also, **sculpt.**

scul·pin (skul′pin), *n., pl.* (*esp. collectively*) **-pin,** (*esp. referring to two or more kinds or species*) **-pins. 1.** any small, fresh-water fish of the genus *Cottus,* of the family *Cottidae,* having a large head with one or more spines on each side; bull-head. **2.** any of numerous marine fishes of the same family. **3.** (in California) a common scorpionfish, *Scorpaena guttata.* [?]

sculp·sit (sko͝olp′sit; *Eng.* skulp′sit), *v. Latin.* he engraved, carved, or sculptured (it); she engraved, carved, or sculptured (it).

sculpt (skulpt), *v.t., v.i.* **1.** *Fine Arts.* to carve, model, or make by using the techniques of sculpture. **2.** to form, shape, or manipulate, as in the manner of sculpture: *The ladies had their hair sculpted by the leading coiffeur of the day.* [< F *sculpt(er)* < L *sculpt-* (ptp. s. of *sculpere* to carve)]

—**Usage.** SCULPT is often criticized as being a nonstandard and irregular back formation from the verb SCULPTURE, but is actually from the French verb *sculpter.* SCULPT has been in use in serious writing for more than a century. See note at **sculp.**

sculp·tor (skulp′tər), *n., gen.* **Sculp·to·ris** (skulp-tôr′is, -tōr′-) for 2. **1.** a person who practices the art of sculpture. **2.** (*cap.*) *Astron.* a southern constellation between Phoenix and Cetus. [< L, equiv. to *sculpt-* (*us*) ptp. of *sculpere* to carve + *-or* -OR²]

Sculp′tor's Tool′, *Astron.* the constellation Caelum.

sculp·tress (skulp′tris), *n.* a female sculptor. [SCULP-T(O)R + -ESS]

sculp·ture (skulp′chər), *n., v.,* **-tured, -tur·ing.** —*n.* **1.** the art of carving, modeling, welding, or otherwise producing figurative or abstract works of art in three dimensions, as in relief, intaglio, or in the round. **2.** such works of art collectively. **3.** an individual piece of such work. —*v.t.* **4.** to carve, model, weld, or otherwise produce (a piece of sculpture). **5.** to produce a portrait or image of in this way; represent in sculpture. **6.** *Phys. Geog.* to change the form of (the land surface) by erosion. —*v.i.* **7.** to work as a sculptor. [< L *sculptūr(a)*, equiv. to *sculpt(us)* (ptp. of *sculpere* to carve) + *-ūra* -URE] —**sculp′tur·al,** *adj.* —**sculp′tur·al·ly,** *adv.*

sculp·tur·esque (skulp′chə resk′), *adj.* suggesting sculpture: *the sculpturesque beauty of her face.* [SCULP-TURE + -ESQUE] —**sculp′tur·esque′ly,** *adv.* —**sculp′-tur·esque′ness,** *n.*

scum (skum), *n., v.,* **scummed, scum·ming.** —*n.* **1.** a film or layer of foul or extraneous matter that forms on the surface of a liquid. **2.** refuse or offscourings. **3.** a low, worthless, or evil person. **4.** such persons collectively; riffraff; rabble. **5.** scoria (def. 1). —*v.t.* **6.** to remove the scum from. **7.** to remove as scum. —*v.i.* **8.** to form scum; become covered with scum. [ME *scume* < MD *schūme*; c. G *Schaum* foam] —**scum′-less,** *adj.* —**scum′like′,** *adj.*

scum·ble (skum′bəl), *v.,* **-bled, -bling,** *n. Painting.* —*v.t.* **1.** to modify (the color or tone of a painted area) by overlaying parts with opaque or semiopaque color applied thinly and lightly with an almost dry brush. —*n.* **2.** the effect produced by this technique. [SCUM (v.) + -LE]

scum·bling (skum′bling), *n.* the technique of producing a scumble. [SCUMBLE + -ING¹]

scum·board (skum′bōrd′, -bôrd′), *n.* a board or strip of material partly immersed in flowing water to hold back scum. [SCUM + BOARD]

scum·my (skum′ē), *adj.,* **-mi·er, -mi·est.** **1.** consisting of or having scum. **2.** *Informal.* despicable; contemptible: *That was a scummy trick.* [SCUM + -Y¹]

scun·cheon (skun′chən), *n. Archit.* sconcheon.

scun·ner (skun′ər), *n.* **1.** an irrational dislike; loathing: *She took a scunner to him.* —*v.i.* **2.** *Scot. and North Eng.* to feel or show violent disgust, esp. to flinch, blanch, or gag. —*v.t.* **3.** *Scot. and North Eng.* to disgust; nauseate. [ME (Scot) *skunner*, equiv. to *skurn* to flinch (akin to SCARE) + *-er* -ER², with loss of first *r* by dissimilation]

scup (skup), *n.* a sparid food fish, *Stenotomus versicolor*, found along the Atlantic coast of the U.S., having a compressed body and high back. [< Narragansett *mishcup*, equiv. to *mishe* big + *kuppe* close together, with reference to the scales]

scup·per (skup′ər), *n.* **1.** *Naut.* a drain at the edge of a deck exposed to the weather, for allowing accumulated water to drain away into the sea or into the bilges. Cf. **freeing port. 2.** a drain, closed by one or two flaps, for allowing water from the sprinkler system of a factory or the like to run off a floor of the building to the exterior. **3.** any opening in the side of a building, as in a parapet, for draining off rain water. —*v.t.* **4.** *Brit. Mil. Slang.* to overwhelm; surprise and massacre. [ME *skoper*. See SCOOP, -ER¹]

scup·per·nong (skup′ər nông′, -nong′), *n.* **1.** a silvery amber-green variety of muscadine grape. **2.** the vine bearing this fruit, grown in the southern U.S. [short for *scuppernong grape*, named after the North Carolina river]

scurf (skûrf), *n.* **1.** the scales or small shreds of epidermis that are continually exfoliated from the skin. **2.** any scaly matter or incrustation on a surface. [ME, OE < Scand; cf. Dan *skurv*, akin to OE *sceorf*] —**scurf′-like′,** *adj.*

scurf·y (skûr′fē), *adj.,* **scurf·i·er, scurf·i·est.** resembling, producing, or covered with or as if with scurf. [ME; see SCURF, -Y¹]

scur·rile (skûr′il), *adj. Archaic.* scurrilous. [< L *scurrīle*, neut. of *scurrīlis* jeering, equiv. to *scurr(a)* buffoon + *-īlis* -ILE]

scur·ril·i·ty (skə ril′i tē), *n., pl.* **-ties. 1.** a scurrilous quality or condition. **2.** a scurrilous remark or attack. [< L *scurrīlitas*. See SCURRILE, -ITY]
—**Syn. 2.** vituperation, abuse, vilification, invective; indecency, vulgarity.

scur·ril·ous (skûr′ə ləs), *adj.* **1.** grossly or obscenely abusive: *a scurrilous attack on the mayor.* **2.** characterized by or using low buffoonery; coarsely jocular or derisive: *a scurrilous jest.* [SCURRILE + -OUS] —**scur′-ril·ous·ly,** *adv.* —**scur′ril·ous·ness,** *n.*
—**Syn. 1.** vituperative, insulting, offensive, ribald. **2.** vulgar. —**Ant. 2.** decent.

scur·ry (skûr′ē, skur′ē), *v.,* **-ried, -ry·ing,** *n., pl.* **-ries.** —*v.i.* **1.** to go or move quickly or in haste. —*v.t.* **2.** to send hurrying along. —*n.* **3.** a scurrying rush: *We heard the scurry of little feet on the stairs.* **4.** a fairly short run or race. [abstracted from HURRY-SCURRY]

S-curve (es′kûrv′), *n.* a curve shaped like an S.

scur·vy (skûr′vē), *n., adj.,* **-vi·er, -vi·est.** —*n.* **1.** *Pathol.* a disease marked by swollen and bleeding gums, livid spots on the skin, prostration, etc., due to a diet lacking in vitamin C. —*adj.* **2.** contemptible; despicable; mean: *a scurvy trick.* [SCURF + -Y¹] —**scur′vi-ly,** *adv.* —**scur′vi·ness,** *n.*

scur′vy grass′, a brassicaceous plant, *Cochlearia officinalis*, supposed to be a remedy for scurvy.

scut (skut), *n.* a short tail, esp. that of a hare, rabbit, or deer. [< Scand; cf. Icel *skott* tail]

scu·ta (skyo͞o′tə), *n.* pl. of **scutum.**

scu·tage (skyo͞o′tij), *n.* (in the feudal system) a payment exacted by a lord in lieu of military service due to him by the holder of a fee. [< ML *scūtāg(ium)*. See SCUT(UM), -AGE]

Scu·ta·ri (sko͞o′tä rē′), *n.* **1.** Also, **Skutari.** Turkish, **Usküdar.** a section of Istanbul, Turkey, on the Asian shore of the Bosporus. 116,195 (1965). **2.** Albanian, **Shkodër, Shkodra.** a city in NW Albania, on Lake Scutari: a former capital of Albania. 47,040 (est. 1964). **3. Lake,** a lake between NW Albania and S Yugoslavia. ab. 135 sq. mi.

scu·tate (skyo͞o′tāt), *adj.* **1.** *Bot.* formed like a round buckler. **2.** *Zool.* having scutes, shields, or large scales. [< L *scūtāt(us)*. See SCUTUM, -ATE¹]

scutch (skuch), *v.t.* **1.** to dress (flax) by beating. **2.** to dress (brick or stone); scotch. —*n.* **3.** Also called **scutch′er.** a device for scutching flax fiber. **4.** Also, **scotch.** a small picklike tool with two cutting edges for trimming brick. [< MF *(*e*)*scoucher* (F *écoucher*) to beat flax < VL **excuticāre*, r. L *excutere* (*ex-* EX-¹ + *quatere* to shatter)]

scutch′ cane′, the small or switch cane. See under **cane** (def. 5).

scutch·eon (skuch′ən), *n.* **1.** escutcheon. **2.** *Zool.* a scute. —**scut′cheon·less,** *adj.* —**scut′cheon·like′,** *adj.*

scutch′ grass′, 1. See **couch grass. 2.** See **Bermuda grass.**

scute (skyo͞ot), *n. Zool.* **1.** a dermal bony plate, as on an armadillo, or a large horny plate, as on a turtle. **2.** a large scale. [< L *scūt(um)* shield]

scu·tel·late (skyo͞o tel′it, -āt, skyo͞ot′ᵊlāt′), *adj. Zool.* **1.** having scutes. **2.** formed into a scutellum. Also, **scu′tel·lat′ed.** [SCUTELL(UM) + -ATE¹]

scu·tel·la·tion (skyo͞ot′ᵊlā′shən), *n. Zool.* **1.** a scutellate state or formation; a scaly covering, as on a bird's leg. **2.** an arrangement of scutella or scales. [SCUTELL(UM) + -ATION]

scu·tel·li·form (skyo͞o tel′ə fôrm′), *adj. Zool., Bot.* shaped like a scutellum. [SCUTELL(UM) + -I- + -FORM]

scu·tel·lum (skyo͞o tel′əm), *n., pl.* **-tel·la** (-tel′ə). **1.** *Zool., Bot.* a small plate, scutum, or other shieldlike part. **2.** *Entomol.* the third dorsal sclerite of a thoracic segment, behind the scutum of an insect. [< NL, equiv. to L *scūt(um)* shield + *-ellum* dim. suffix]

scu·ti·form (skyo͞o′tə fôrm′), *adj.* shield-shaped. [< NL *scūtiform(is)*. See SCUTUM, -I-, -FORM]

scut·ter (skut′ər), *v.i., n. Brit. Dial.* scurry. [var. of SCUTTLE²]

scut·tle¹ (skut′ᵊl), *n.* **1.** a deep bucket for carrying coal. **2.** *Brit. Dial.* a broad, shallow basket. [ME, OE *scutel*, orig. a dish or platter < L *scutell(a)*, dim. of *scutra*]

scut·tle² (skut′ᵊl), *v.,* **-tled, -tling,** *n.* —*v.i.* **1.** to run with quick, hasty steps; hurry. —*n.* **2.** a quick pace. **3.** a short, hurried run. [? var. of *scuddle*, freq. of SCUD¹]

scut·tle³ (skut′ᵊl), *n., v.,* **-tled, -tling.** —*n.* **1.** *Naut.* **a.** a small hatch or port in the deck, side, or bottom of a vessel. **b.** a cover for this. **2.** a small hatchlike opening in a roof or ceiling. —*v.t.* **3.** to sink (a vessel) deliberately by opening seacocks or making openings in the bottom. **4.** to abandon, withdraw from, or cause to be abandoned or destroyed (as plans, hopes, rumors, etc.): *The lawyer scuttled his hopes of collecting the debt quickly.* [ME *skotel* < Sp (*e*)*scotill(a)* patchway, equiv. to *escot(e)* low neck (< Goth *skaut* seam) + *-illa* dim. suffix]

scut·tle·butt (skut′ᵊl but′), *n.* **1.** *Naut.* **a.** an open cask containing drinking water. **b.** a drinking fountain for use by the crew of a vessel. **2.** *Informal.* rumor; gossip. [SCUTTLE³ + BUTT¹]

scu·tum (skyo͞o′təm), *n., pl.* **-ta** (-tə) for 1–3, *gen.* **Scu·ti** (sko͞o′tī) for 4. **1.** *Zool.* scute (def. 1). **2.** a large, oblong shield used by the heavy legionaries of ancient Rome. **3.** *Entomol.* the second dorsal sclerite of a thoracic segment, behind the prescutum of an insect. **4.** (*Cap.*) *Astron.* the Shield, a southern constellation north of Sagittarius and east of Aquila, containing a small, very bright star cloud. [< L: shield]

scye·lite (sī′līt), *n.* a dark, coarse-grained amphibolic and biotitic peridotite. [named after Loch *Scye* in Caithness, Scotland + -LITE]

Scyl·a·ce·us (sil′ə sē′əs), *n. Class. Myth.* a Lycian ally of the Trojans who, on his return home from the Trojan War, was stoned to death by the Lycian women when he told them that their husbands and sons had been slain.

Scyl·la (sil′ə), *n.* **1.** Modern, **Scilla.** a rock in the Strait of Messina off the S coast of Italy. **2.** *Class. Myth.* a sea nymph who was transformed into a sea monster: later identified with the rock Scylla. Cf. **Charybdis** (def. 2). **3. between Scylla and Charybdis,** between two equally perilous alternatives, neither of which can be passed without encountering and probably falling victim to the other.

scy·phate (sī′fāt), *adj.* cup-shaped. [SCYPH(I)- + -ATE¹]

scyphi-, a combining form of **scyphus:** *scyphiform.* Also, **scyph-, scypho-.**

scy·phi·form (sī′fə fôrm′), *adj. Bot.* shaped like a cup or goblet. [SCYPHI- + -FORM]

Scyph·i·us (sif′ē əs), *n. Class. Myth.* the first horse created by Poseidon.

Scy·pho·zo·a (sī′fə zō′ə), *n.* the class comprising the marine jellyfishes. [< NL; see SCYPHO-, -ZOA]

scy·pho·zo·an (sī′fə zō′ən), *n.* **1.** any coelenterate of the class *Scyphozoa*, comprising the true marine jellyfishes. —*adj.* **2.** belonging or pertaining to the *Scyphozoa.* [SCYPHOZO(A) + -AN]

scy·phus (sī′fəs), *n., pl.* **-phi** (-fī). **1.** a cup-shaped part, as of a flower. **2.** skyphos. [< L < Gk *skýphos* drinking bowl]

Scy·ros (skī′ros, -rōs; *Gk.* skē′rôs), *n.* Skyros.

scythe (sīth), *n., v.,* **scythed, scyth·ing.** —*n.* **1.** an agricultural implement consisting of a long, curving blade fastened at an angle to a handle, for cutting grass, grain, etc., by hand. —*v.t.* **2.** to cut or mow with a scythe. [ME *sith*, OE *si(g)the*; c. Icel *sigth*; spelling *sc* by pseudo-etymological assoc. with L *scindere* to cut. Cf. SCISSORS] —**scythe′less,** *adj.* —**scythe′like′,** *adj.*

Scyth·i·a (sith′ē ə), *n.* the ancient name of a region in SE Europe and Asia, lying N and E of the Black and Caspian seas: now part of the Soviet Union.

Scyth·i·an (sith′ē ən), *adj.* **1.** pertaining to Scythia, its people, or their language. —*n.* **2.** a native or inhabitant of Scythia. **3.** an extinct Iranian language. [SCYTHI(A) + -AN]

Scyth′ian lamb′, a fern, *Cibotium Barometz*, of southeastern Asia, having shaggy, brownish stalks and large, feathery leaves, formerly believed to be a source of vegetable wool.

SD, *Statistics.* standard deviation.

sd., sound.

S/D, sight draft.

S.D., 1. doctor of science. [< L *Scientiae Doctor*] **2.** senior deacon. **3.** South Dakota. **4.** *Statistics.* standard deviation.

s.d., 1. without naming a date. [< L *sine die* without a day] **2.** *Statistics.* standard deviation.

S.D.A., Seventh Day Adventists.

S. Dak., South Dakota.

'sdeath (zdeth), *interj. Archaic.* (used as a mild oath). [(*God*)*'s death*]

SDI, Strategic Defense Initiative. See **Star Wars.**

S. Doc., Senate document.

se-, a formal element occurring in loan words from Latin, where it meant "apart": *seduce; select.* [< L *sē(d)-* without, apart]

SE, 1. southeast. **2.** southeastern. Also, **S.E.**

Se, *Chem.* selenium.

sea (sē), *n.* **1.** the salt waters that cover the greater part of the earth's surface. **2.** a division of these waters, of considerable extent, more or less definitely marked off by land boundaries: *the North Sea.* **3.** one of the seven seas; ocean. **4.** a large lake or landlocked body of water. **5.** the degree or amount of turbulence of the ocean or other body of water as caused by the wind. **6.** the waves. **7.** a large wave: *The heavy seas almost drowned us.* **8.** a widely extended, copious, or overwhelming quantity: *a sea of faces; a sea of troubles.* **9.** the work, travel, and shipboard life of a sailor: *The sea is a hard life for a man.* **10. at sea, a.** on the ocean. **b.** perplexed; uncertain: *completely at sea as to how to answer the question.* **11. follow the sea,** to pursue a nautical career: *Most boys at one time or another dream of following the sea.* **12. go to sea, a.** to set out on a voyage. **b.** to embark on a nautical career: *He went to sea and traveled around the world.* **13. half seas over,** *Slang.* partly or completely drunk: *They came home at dawn, looking half seas over.* Also, **half-seas over. 14. put to sea,** to embark on a sea voyage: *The expedition is nearly ready to put to sea.* Also, **put out to sea.** —*adj.* **15.** of, pertaining to, or adapted for use at sea. [ME *see*, OE *sǣ*; c. D *zee*, G *See*, Icel *sær* sea, Goth *saiws* marsh]

sea′ an′chor, *Naut.* any of various devices, as a drogue, that have great resistance to being pulled through the water and are dropped forward of a vessel at the end of a cable to hold the bow into the wind or sea during a storm.

Sea anemone, *Epiactis prolifera* (Width ¾ in.)

sea′ anem′one, any sedentary marine animal of the phylum *Coelenterata*, having a columnar body and one or more circles of tentacles surrounding the mouth.

sea′ bag′, a tubular canvas bag closed by a drawstring, used by a seaman or a sailor for his gear.

sea′ bass′ (bas), **1.** any of numerous marine fishes of the family *Serranidae.* Cf. **black sea bass. 2.** any of numerous related or similar marine food fishes.

Sea·bee (sē′bē′), *n.* a member of the construction battalions of the U.S. Navy, established in December, 1941, to build landing facilities, airfields, etc., in combat areas. [var. sp. of *CB C(onstruction) B(attalion)*]

sea′ bird′, a bird frequenting the sea or coast. Also called **seafowl.**

sea′ bis′cuit, ship biscuit; hardtack.

sea′ blite′ (blīt), any of several halophytic herbs of the genus *Suaeda*, having fleshy leaves.

sea·board (sē′bōrd′, -bôrd′), *n.* **1.** the line where land and sea meet. —*adj.* **2.** bordering on or adjoining the sea. [late ME *seebord.* See SEA, BOARD]

Sea·borg (sē′bôrg), *n.* **Glenn T(heodor),** born 1912, U.S. chemist: Nobel prize for chemistry 1951.

sea-born (sē′bôrn′), *adj.* **1.** born in or of the sea, as naiads. **2.** produced in or rising from the sea, as reefs.

sea·borne (sē′bōrn′, -bôrn′), *adj.* **1.** transported by ship over the sea. **2.** carried on or over the sea: *a seaborne fog; seaborne cargoes.* [SEA + BORNE]

sea′ bread′, ship biscuit; hardtack.

sea′ bream′, 1. any of numerous marine sparid fishes, as *Pagellus centrodontus*, found off the coasts of Europe. **2.** a porgy, *Archosargus rhomboidalis*, found in the Atlantic Ocean.

sea′ breeze′, a thermally produced wind blowing from a cool ocean surface onto adjoining warm land. Cf. **lake breeze, land breeze.**

sea′ cab′bage, a brown alga, *Hedophyllum sessile*, of the North Pacific, characterized by a compact mass of fronds resembling a cabbage.

sea′ calf′. See **harbor seal.**

sea′ cam′pion, a perennial herb, *Silene maritima*, of Europe, having grayish-green foliage and white flowers.

sea′ cap′tain, the master of a seagoing vessel.

sea′ change′, 1. a striking change, as in appearance, often for the better: *The dress shirt, once a boardlike torture device, has undergone a sea change.* **2.** a transformation brought about by the sea.

sea′ chest′, *Naut.* **1.** a fitting in a hull below the water line, for admitting or discharging water. **2.** a chest for the personal belongings of a sailor.

sea′ chub′, any of several marine fishes of the family *Kyphosidae*, as *Kyphosus sectatrix*, found in the tropical waters of the Atlantic Ocean. Also called **rudderfish.**

Sea′ Cliff′, a town on NW Long Island, in SE New York. 5669 (1960).

sea′ coal′, *Obs.* mineral coal, as distinguished from charcoal. [ME *see cole* coal brought by sea; OE *sǣcol* jet (this was washed up by the sea). See SEA, COAL]

sea·coast (sē′kōst′), *n.* the land immediately adjacent to the sea. [ME *see cost.* See SEA, COAST]

sea·cock (sē′kok′), *n. Naut.* a valve in the hull of a vessel for admitting outside water into some part of the hull, as a ballast tank. Also called **sea′ connec′tion, sea valve.** [SEA + COCK¹]

sea′ cow′, 1. any sirenian, as the manatee, dugong, etc. **2.** *Obs.* the hippopotamus.

sea′ cra′dle, chiton (def. 2).

sea′ cray′fish. See **spiny lobster.**

sea′ cu′cumber, any echinoderm of the class *Holothuroidea,* having a long, leathery body with tentacles around the anterior end.

sea′ dahl′ia, a perennial garden herb, *Coreopsis maritima,* of the southwestern coast of North America, having long-stalked, solitary, yellow flowerheads nearly three inches wide.

sea′ dev′il. See **manta ray.**

sea′ dog′, 1. a sailor, esp. an old or experienced one. 2. See **harbor seal.** 3. a dogfish. 4. a pirate or privateer.

sea·dog (sē′dôg′, -dog′), *n.* fogbow. [SEA + DOG]

sea·drome (sē′drōm′), *n.* *Aeron.* a floating airdrome serving as an intermediate or emergency landing place for aircraft flying over water. [SEA + -DROME]

sea′ duck′, any of various diving ducks, as the scaups, goldeneyes, scoters, and eiders, found principally on seas.

sea′ ea′gle, any of several large eagles of the genus *Haliaetus,* that usually feed on fish. Cf. **gray sea eagle.**

sea′ ear′, abalone.

sea′ el′ephant. See **elephant seal.**

sea′ fan′, any of certain anthozoans, esp. *Gorgonia flabellum,* of the West Indies, in which the colony assumes a fanlike form.

sea·far·er (sē′fâr′ər), *n.* 1. a sailor. 2. a traveler on the sea. [SEA + FARER]

sea·far·ing (sē′fâr′ing), *adj.* 1. traveling by sea. 2. following the sea as a trade, business, or calling. 3. of, pertaining to, or occurring during a voyage on the sea. —*n.* 4. the business or calling of a sailor. 5. traveling by sea. [SEA + FARE + -ING[2], -ING[1]]

sea′ feath′er, any of several anthozoans of the order *Gorgonacea,* having a branched skeleton resembling a feather.

sea′ fig′. See **ice plant.**

sea′ fight′, a fight between ships at sea. —**sea′-fight′er,** *n.*

sea′ foam′, 1. the foam of the sea. 2. meerschaum (def. 1). [ME *see fome*] —**sea′-foam′,** *adj.*

sea·food (sē′fōōd′), *n.* any salt-water fish or shellfish used for food.

Sea·ford (sē′fərd), *n.* a town in SW Delaware. 4430 (1960).

sea·fowl (sē′foul′), *n., pl.* **-fowls,** (*esp. collectively*) **-fowl.** See **sea bird.** [SEA + FOWL]

sea′ fox′, thresher (def. 3).

sea′ front′, an area, including buildings, along the edge of the sea; waterfront.

sea′ gate′, a navigable channel giving access to the sea.

sea′ gauge′, 1. an automatic sounding device registering the depth to which it is lowered. 2. the draft of a vessel.

sea·girt (sē′gûrt′), *n.* surrounded by the sea. [SEA + GIRT[1]]

sea·go·ing (sē′gō′ing), *adj.* 1. designed or fit for going to sea, as a vessel. 2. going to sea; seafaring. —*n.* 3. the activity of one who travels by sea. [SEA + GOING]

sea′ goose′berry, a ctenophore, esp. of the genus *Pleurobrachia.*

Sea·go·ville (sē′gō vil′), *n.* a town in N Texas. 3745 (1960).

sea′ grape′, 1. a polygonaceous tree, *Coccoloba uvifera,* of tropical America, bearing grapelike clusters of edible purple berries. 2. the fruit itself. 3. a gulfweed.

sea′ green′, clear, light, bluish green. —**sea′-green′,** *adj.*

sea′ gull′, a gull, esp. any of the marine species.

Sea′ Gull′, The, a play (1896) by Anton Chekhov.

sea′ heath′. See under **heath** (def. 4). —**sea′-heath′,** *adj.*

sea′ hog′, a porpoise.

sea′ hol′ly, the eryngo, *Eryngium maritimum.*

sea′ hol′lyhock, a rose mallow, *Hibiscus Moscheutos.*

sea′ horse′, 1. any fish of the genus *Hippocampus,* of the pipefish family, having a prehensile tail, an elongated snout, and a head bent at right angles to the body. 2. a fabled marine animal with the foreparts of a horse and the hind parts of a fish. 3. a walrus. [ME *sehors* walrus; cf. G *Seepferd*]

Sea horse, *Hippocampus hudsonius* (Length 3 to 4 in.)

sea-is·land (sē′ī′lənd), *adj.* of or pertaining to the Sea Islands.

sea′-island cot′ton, a long-staple cotton, *Gossypium barbadense,* raised originally in the Sea Islands, now grown chiefly in the West Indies.

Sea′ Is′lands, a group of islands in the Atlantic, along the coasts of South Carolina, Georgia, and N Florida.

sea′ kale′, a broad-leaved, maritime, cruciferous plant, *Crambe maritima,* of Europe, used as a potherb.

sea·kind·ly (sē′kīnd′lē), *adj.* *Naut.* (of a vessel) sailing easily in a rough sea. [SEA + KINDLY] —**sea′-kind′li·ness,** *n.*

sea′ king′, one of the piratical Scandinavian chiefs who ravaged the coasts of medieval Europe. [trans. of Icel *sækonungr;* c. OE *sǣcyning*]

seal[1] (sēl), *n.* 1. an embossed emblem, figure, symbol, word, letter, etc., used as attestation or evidence of authenticity: *He had his initials made into a seal.* 2. a stamp, medallion, ring, etc., engraved with such a device, for impressing paper, wax, lead, or the like: *The king took the seal from his finger and applied it to the document.* 3. the impression so obtained: *It was unmistakably the royal seal on the document.* 4. a mark or symbol attached to a legal document and imparting a formal character to it, originally wax with an impression. 5. a piece of wax or similar adhesive substance so attached to an envelope, folded document, etc., that it must be broken when the object is opened, insuring that the contents have not been tampered with or altered. 6. anything that tightly or completely closes or secures a thing, as closures or fastenings for doors and railroad cars, adhesive stamps and tapes used to secure the flap of an envelope, etc. 7. something that keeps a thing secret: *His vow was the seal that kept him silent.* 8. a decorative stamp, esp. as given to contributors to a charitable fund: *a Christmas seal.* 9. a mark, sign, symbol, or the like, serving as visible evidence of something. 10. that which serves as assurance, a confirmation, or bond: *His handshake was the only seal we needed to begin the work.* 11. *Plumbing.* a. a small amount of water held by a trap to exclude foul gases from a sewer or the like. b. the depth of the part of the water which actually excludes the gases. 12. **set one's seal to,** to give one's approval to; authorize; endorse: *Both families have set their seal to the marriage.* 13. **the seals,** *Brit.* the tokens or signs of public office. —*v.t.* 14. to affix a seal to in authorization, testimony, etc. 15. to assure, confirm, or bind with or as with a seal: *They sealed the bargain with a handshake.* 16. to impress a seal upon as evidence of legal or standard exactness, measure, quality, etc. 17. to close by any form of fastening that must be broken before access can be gained. 18. to fasten or close tightly by or as if by a seal: *She was sealing envelopes. They tried to seal his lips.* 19. to decide irrevocably: *to seal someone's fate.* 20. to grant under one's seal or authority, as a pardon. 21. *Mormon. Ch.* to make (a marriage or adoption) forever binding; solemnize. 22. *Elect.* to bring (a plug and jack or socket) into locked or fully aligned position. [ME *seel* < OF *seel* (> F *sceau*) < LL *sigill(um), L sigillum, dim. of *signum* SIGN; r. ME *seil,* OE (*in*)*segel* seal < LL, as above] —**seal′a·ble,** *adj.*

Great Seal of the United States

seal[2] (sēl), *n., pl.* **seals,** (*esp. collectively for 1*) **seal,** *v.* —*n.* 1. any of numerous marine carnivores of the suborder *Pinnipedia,* including the eared or fur seals, as the sea lion, and the earless or hair seals, as the harbor seal. 2. the skin of such an animal. 3. leather made from this skin. 4. the fur of the fur seal; sealskin. 5. a fur used as a substitute for sealskin. 6. a dark, gray brown. —*v.i.* 7. to hunt, kill, or capture seals. [ME *sele,* OE *seolh;* c. Icel *selr*] —**seal′like′,** *adj.*

seal[3] (sēl), *v.t.* *Falconry.* seel (def. 1).

sea′ lad′der, a set of rungs fixed to the side of a vessel, forming a ladder from the weather deck to the water line.

seal·ant (sē′lənt), *n.* 1. a substance used for sealing, as sealing wax, adhesives, etc. 2. any of various liquids, paints, chemicals, or soft substances which may be applied to a surface or circulated through a system of pipes or the like, drying to form a hard, watertight coating. [SEAL[1] + -ANT, prob. by analogy with COOLANT]

sea′ lav′ender, 1. an Old World, maritime, plumbaginaceous plant, *Limonium vulgare,* having one-sided spikes of small, lavender-colored flowers. 2. some similar plant of the same genus, as *Limonium carolinianum,* of the eastern coast of North America.

sea′ law′yer, *Naut. Slang.* a seaman inclined to question or complain about the orders given.

Seal′ Beach′, a town in S California. 6994 (1960).

seal′ brown′, a rich, dark brown suggestive of dressed and dyed sealskin. —**seal′-brown′,** *adj.*

sea′ leath′er, the skin of sharks, porpoises, dogfishes, etc., prepared and used for the same purposes as ordinary leather.

sealed′ book′, something beyond understanding and therefore unknown.

sealed′ or′ders, orders that are given in sealed form to a commander of a vessel and are to be opened after the vessel is out of contact with the shore.

sea′ legs′, 1. the ability to adjust one's sense of balance to the motion of a ship at sea: *He stumbled about the deck for three days before getting his sea legs.* 2. the ability to remain free of seasickness: *Breathing the fresh salt air helped her to gain her sea legs, and she could start eating normally.*

seal·er[1] (sē′lər), *n.* an officer appointed to examine and test weights and measures, and to set a stamp upon such as are true to the standard. [late ME *seler.* See SEAL[1], -ER[1]]

seal·er[2] (sē′lər), *n.* a person or vessel engaged in hunting seals. [SEAL[2] + -ER[1]]

seal·er·y (sē′lə rē), *n., pl.* **-er·ies.** 1. the occupation of hunting or taking seals. 2. a place where seals are caught. [SEAL[2] + -ERY]

sea′ let′tuce, any seaweed of the genus *Ulva,* having large leaflike blades.

sea′ lev′el, the horizontal plane or level corresponding to the surface of the sea at mean level between high and low tide.

sea′-lev·el pres′sure (sē′lev′əl), the atmospheric pressure, at any elevation, reduced by formula to a value approximating the pressure at sea level.

sea′ lil′y, a stalked, sessile crinoid.

seal′ing wax′, a resinous preparation, soft when heated, used for sealing letters, documents, etc. [ME *seling wax*]

sea′ li′on, 1. any of several large, eared seals, as *Eumetopias jubata* (**Steller's sea lion**), of the northern Pacific, and *Zalophus californicus* (**California sea lion**), of the Pacific coast of North America. 2. *Heraldry.* a monster having the forepart of a lion, webbed forepaws, and the dorsal fin and tail of a fish.

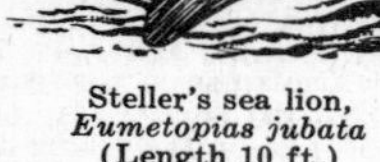

Steller's sea lion, *Eumetopias jubata* (Length 10 ft.)

seal′ point′, a Siamese cat having a fawn-colored body and dark-brown points.

seal′ ring′, a finger ring bearing an incised design for embossing a wax seal.

seal·skin (sēl′skin′), *n.* 1. the skin of a seal. 2. the skin or fur of the fur seal when prepared for making garments or leather items. 3. a garment or article made of this fur. —*adj.* 4. made of sealskin: *a sealskin purse.* [ME *seleskin.* See SEAL[2], SKIN]

sea′ lung′wort, a boraginaceous herb, *Mertensia maritima,* growing on northern seacoasts and having leaves with an oysterlike flavor.

Seal′y·ham ter′rier (sē′lē ham′, -lē əm), one of a Welsh breed of small terriers having short legs, a docked tail, and a wiry, mostly white coat. [named after *Sealyham,* Wales, where it was first bred]

Sealyham terrier (10½ in. high at shoulder)

sea′ lyme′ grass′, a stout, perennial grass, *Elymus arenarius,* of Eurasia, used as a binder for shifting sand. Also called **dune grass.** [SEA + *lyme* (obs.; see BIRDLIME) + GRASS]

seam (sēm), *n.* 1. the line formed by sewing together pieces of cloth, leather, or the like. 2. the stitches used to make such a line. 3. any line formed by abutting edges. 4. any linear indentation or mark, as a wrinkle or scar. 5. *Knitting.* a line of stitches formed by purling. 6. *Geol.* a comparatively thin stratum; a bed, as of coal. —*v.t.* 7. to join with or as with stitches; make the seam or seams of. 8. to furrow; mark with wrinkles, scars, etc. 9. *Knitting.* to knit with or in a seam. —*v.i.* 10. to become cracked, fissured, or furrowed. 11. *Knitting.* to make a line of stitches by purling. [ME *seme,* OE *sēam;* c. G *Saum* hem; akin to SEW] —**seam′er,** *n.* —**seam′less,** *adj.* —**seam′less·ly,** *adv.* —**seam′less·ness,** *n.*

sea·maid (sē′mād′), *n.* 1. a mermaid. 2. a goddess or nymph of the sea. Also, **sea-maid·en** (sē′mād′ən). [SEA + MAID]

sea·man (sē′mən), *n., pl.* **-men.** 1. a person skilled in seamanship. 2. a man whose trade or occupation is assisting in the handling, sailing, and navigating of a ship during a voyage, esp. one below the rank of officer; sailor. 3. *Navy.* an enlisted rating below petty officer. [ME *seeman,* OE *sǣmann.* See SEA, MAN[1]] —**Syn.** See **sailor.**

sea·man·like (sē′mən līk′), *adj.* like or befitting a seaman; showing good seamanship. [SEAMAN + LIKE]

sea·man·ship (sē′mən ship′), *n.* the knowledge of and skill in all things pertaining to the operation, navigation, management, safety, and maintenance of a ship. [SEAMAN + -SHIP]

sea′ mar′igold. See **ice plant.**

sea·mark (sē′märk′), *n.* a conspicuous object on land, visible from the sea, and serving to guide or warn mariners, as a beacon. [ME *see marke.* See SEA, MARK[1]]

sea′ mew′, a sea gull, esp. a common European species, *Larus canus.*

sea′ mile′, mile (def. 2).

sea′ milk′wort, a primulaceous, maritime plant, *Glaux maritima,* having small, pinkish-white flowers.

sea′ mist′, 1. a mist over or from the sea. 2. *Meteorol.* See **steam fog.**

sea′ moss′, a bryozoan.

sea·mount (sē′mount′), *n.* a submarine mountain rising several hundred fathoms above the floor of the sea but having its summit well below the surface of the water. [SEA + MOUNT[2]]

sea′ mouse′, any of several large, marine, annelids of the genus *Aphrodite* and related genera, having a covering of long, fine, hairlike setae.

seam·stress (sēm′stris *or, esp. Brit.,* sem′-), *n.* a woman whose occupation is sewing. Also, **sempstress.** [< ME *sem(e)ster* (OE *sēamestre,* equiv. to *sēam* SEAM + *-estre* -STER) + -ESS]

seam·y (sē′mē), *adj.,* **seam·i·er, seam·i·est.** 1. unpleasant; disagreeable: *He grew up in comfort, knowing little of the seamy side of life.* 2. morally low; sordid: *a seamy neighborhood near the docks.* 3. having, showing, or of the nature of a seam. [SEAM + -Y[1]] —**seam′i·ness,** *n.*

Sean (shôn), *n.* a boy's given name.

Sean·ad Eir·eann (san′äd âr′ən), the upper house of the parliament of the Republic of Ireland. Cf. **Oireachtas** (def. 1). [< Ir]

sé·ance (sā′äns), *n.* 1. a meeting in which a spiritualist attempts to communicate with the spirits of the dead. 2. a session or sitting, as of a class, organization, etc. [< F: session, equiv. to *sé-,* root of *seoir* to sit (< L *sedēre*) + *-ance* -ANCE]

sea′ on′ion, 1. Also called **sea squill.** a liliaceous plant, *Urginea maritima,* of Mediterranean regions, yielding medicinal squill. 2. a squill, *Scilla verna,* of the Isle of Wight.

sea′ ot′ter, a marine otter, *Enhydra lutris,* of the shores of the northern Pacific, with a very valuable fur.

Sea otter (Total length 4 ft.; tail 1 ft.)

sea′ palm′, a kelp, *Postelsia palmaeformis,* of the Pacific coast of North America, that resembles a miniature palm tree.

sea′ pen′, any of several colonial coelenterates of the genus *Pennatula* and related genera, having the shape of a fleshy feather.

sea·perch (sē′pûrch′), *n., pl.* (*esp. collectively*) **-perch,** (*esp. referring to two or more kinds or species*) **-perch·es.** surfperch. [SEA + PERCH[2]]

sea′ pink′, thrift (def. 2).

sea·plane (sē′plān′), *n.* a hydroplane for use over the sea, esp. one provided with floats rather than a boatlike underpart. [SEA + PLANE[1]]

sea-poach·er (sē′pō′chər), *n.* poacher[1] (def. 2).

sea′ pop′py. See **horn poppy.**

sea·port (sē′pôrt′, -pōrt′), *n.* 1. a port or harbor on or accessible to a seacoast and providing accommodation for seagoing vessels. 2. a town or city at such a place. [SEA + PORT[1]]

sea′ pow′er, 1. a nation that possesses formidable naval power. 2. naval strength.

sea′ purse′, the horny egg case of certain rays and sharks.

sea·quake (sē′kwāk′), *n.* an agitation of the sea caused by a submarine eruption or earthquake. [SEA + QUAKE]

sear[1] (sēr), *v.t.* 1. to burn or char the surface of: *She seared the steak to seal in the juices.* 2. to mark with a branding iron. 3. to burn or scorch injuriously or painfully: *He seared his hand with the boiling water.* 4. to make callous or unfeeling; harden: *The hardship of her youth has seared her emotionally.* 5. to dry up or wither; parch. —*v.i.* 6. to become dry or withered, as vegetation. —*n.* 7. a mark or scar made by searing. —*adj.* 8. sere[1]. [ME *sere* (v., adj.), OE *sēarian* (v.), deriv. of *sēar* (adj.); c. D *zoor*]
—**Syn. 1.** See **burn**[1].

sear[2] (sēr), *n.* a pivoted piece that holds the hammer at full cock or half cock in the firing mechanism of small arms. [< MF *serre* a grip, deriv. of *serre(r)* (to) lock up, close < VL **serrāre* < LL *serāre* to bar (a door), deriv. of L *ser(a)* door-bar; VL *-rr-* unexplained]

sea′ ra′ven, a large marine fish of the genus *Hemitripterus*, as *H. americanus*, common on the northern Atlantic coast of America.

search (sûrch), *v.t.* 1. to go or look through (a place, area, etc.) carefully in order to find something missing or lost: *They searched the woods for the missing child. He searched his desk for the letter.* 2. to look at or examine (a person, object, etc.) carefully in order to find something concealed: *He searched the vase for the slightest scratch. The police searched the suspect for the missing gems.* 3. to explore or examine in order to discover: *He searched the hills for gold.* 4. to look at, read, or examine (a record, writing, collection, repository, etc.) for information: *He searched the courthouse for a hint of his father's deed to the land.* 5. to look at or beneath the superficial aspects of to discover a motive, reaction, feeling, basic truth, etc.: *He searched her face for a clue to her true feelings.* 6. to look into, question, or scrutinize: *He searched his own motives.* 7. to probe (a wound, sinus, etc.) with a surgical instrument. 8. (*of natural elements*) to pierce or penetrate: *The sunlight searched the room's dark corners.* 9. to uncover or find by examination or exploration (often fol. by *out*): *to search out all the facts.* 10. *Mil.* to fire artillery over (an area) with successive changes in gun elevation. —*v.i.* 11. to inquire, investigate, examine, or seek; conduct an examination or investigation. 12. **search me,** *Slang.* (used as a negative response to a query): *Search me; I don't know who took your pen.* —*n.* 13. the act or an instance of searching; careful examination or investigation. 14. the practice, on the part of naval officers of a belligerent nation, of boarding and examining a suspected neutral vessel at sea in order to ascertain its true nationality and determine if it is carrying contraband: *the right of visit and search.* [late ME *serche(n)*, *cerche(n)* < MF *cerchie(r)* < LL *circāre* to go around, deriv. of *circ(us)* circle] —**search′a·ble,** *adj.* —**search′a·ble·ness,** *n.* —**search′er,** *n.*
—**Syn. 1.** investigate. **2.** examine. **13.** inspection, scrutiny.

search·ing (sûr′ching), *adj.* 1. examining carefully or thoroughly: *a searching inspection.* 2. acutely observant or penetrating: *a searching glance; a searching mind.* 3. piercing or sharp: *a searching wind.* [SEARCH + -ING[2]] —**search′ing·ly,** *adv.* —**search′ing·ness,** *n.*

search·light (sûrch′līt′), *n.* 1. a device, usually consisting of a light and reflector, for throwing a beam of light in any direction. 2. a beam of light so thrown. [SEARCH + LIGHT[1]]

search′ par′ty, a group of persons conducting an organized search for someone or something lost or hidden.

search′ war′rant, *Law.* a court order authorizing the examination of a dwelling or other private premise by police officials, as for stolen goods.

Sear·cy (sûr′sē), *n.* a town in central Arkansas. 7272 (1960).

sea′ reach′, a straight course at the mouth of a river, connecting with the sea.

sea′ return′, *Electronics.* radar signals that are reflected by a body of water and hamper target identification.

sea′ risk′, Often, **sea risks.** the hazard of traveling or transporting by sea.

sea′ rob′ber, a pirate.

sea′ rob′in, any of various gurnards, esp. certain American species of the genus *Prionotus*.

sea′ room′, unobstructed space at sea in which a vessel can be easily maneuvered or navigated.

sea′ rov′er, 1. a pirate. 2. a pirate ship. —**sea′-rov′ing,** *adj., n.*

sea·scape (sē′skāp′), *n.* a view, sketch, painting, or photograph of the sea. [SEA + *-scape*, modeled on *landscape*]

sea·scout·ing (sē′skou′ting), *n.* the branch of scouting that trains older boy scouts in boating and other water activities. [SEA + SCOUTING] —**sea′scout′,** *n.* —**sea′ scout′.**

sea′ ser′pent, 1. an enormous, imaginary, snakelike or dragonlike marine animal. 2. (*cap.*) *Astron.* the constellation Hydra.

sea′ shell′, the shell of any marine mollusk.

sea·shore (sē′shōr′, -shôr′), *n.* 1. land along the sea or ocean. 2. *Law.* the ground between the ordinary high-water and low-water marks. [SEA + SHORE[1]]

Sea′shore test′, *Psychol.* a test of musical ability in which items measuring tonal memory, rhythm sense, etc., are presented to the subject by means of phonograph records. [named after Carl *Seashore* (1866–1949), American psychologist]

sea·sick (sē′sik′), *adj.* afflicted with seasickness. [SEA + SICK]

sea·sick·ness (sē′sik′nis), *n.* nausea and dizziness, sometimes accompanied by vomiting, resulting from the rocking or swaying motion of a vessel in which one is traveling at sea. Cf. **motion sickness.** [SEA + SICKNESS]

sea·side (sē′sīd′), *n.* 1. the land along the sea; seacoast. —*adj.* 2. situated on or pertaining to the seaside. [ME *seeside.* See SEA, SIDE[1]]

Sea·side (sē′sīd′), *n.* 1. a city in W California, on Monterey Bay. 19,353 (1960). 2. a town in NW Oregon. 3877 (1960).

sea′side dai′sy. See **beach aster.**

sea′side gold′enrod. See **beach goldenrod.**

sea′side knot′weed. See under **knotweed.**

sea′side paint′ed-cup′, a perennial herb, *Castilleja latifolia*, of California, having thickish leaves and leafy, yellow or red flower bracts.

sea′side spar′row, a sparrow, *Ammospiza maritima*, found in salt marshes in eastern and southern North America.

sea′ slug′, a nudibranch.

sea′ smoke′. See **steam fog.**

sea·snail (sē′snāl′), *n., pl.* (*esp. collectively*) **-snail,** (*esp. referring to two or more kinds or species*) **-snails.** 1. any of several snailfishes of the genus *Liparis*, found on both sides of the North Atlantic. 2. any of several marine gastropods having a spirally coiled shell, as a whelk. [ME *seesnail*, OE *sǣsnægl.* See SEA, SNAIL]

sea′ snake′, any of several venomous, marine snakes of the family *Hydrophidae*, having a finlike tail.

sea·son (sē′zən), *n.* 1. one of the four periods of the year (spring, summer, autumn, and winter), beginning astronomically at an equinox or solstice, but geographically at different dates in different climates. 2. a period of the year characterized by particular conditions of weather, temperature, etc.: *the rainy season.* 3. a period of the year when something is best or available: *the oyster season.* 4. a period of the year marked by certain conditions, activities, etc.: *the baseball season; a dull season in trade.* 5. a period of the year immediately before and after a special holiday or occasion: *the Christmas season.* 6. *Sports.* **a.** a period with reference to the total number of games to be played by a team: *a 162-game season.* **b.** a period with reference to the won-lost record of a team after it has completed its schedule: *a .700 season.* 7. any period or time: *in the season of my youth.* 8. a suitable, proper, fitting, or right time: *It's not the season for frivolity.* 9. **for a season,** for a time, esp. a short time: *He lived in Paris for a season.* 10. **in good season,** in enough time; sufficiently early: *Applicants will be notified of our decision in good season.* 11. **in season, a.** in the time or state for use, eating, etc.: *Asparagus is now in season.* **b.** in the period regulated by law, as for hunting and fishing. **c.** at the right time; opportunely. **d.** in good season. 12. **in season and out of season,** regardless of time or season; at all times: *Misfortunes plague this family in season and out of season.* 13. **out of season,** not in season: *The price is so high because lilacs are out of season now.* —*v.t.* 14. to heighten or improve the flavor of (food) by adding condiments, spices, herbs, or the like. 15. to give relish or a certain character to: *conversation seasoned with wit.* 16. to mature, ripen, or condition by exposure to suitable conditions or treatment: *a writer seasoned by experience.* 17. to dry or otherwise treat (lumber) so as to harden it and render it immune to shrinkage, warpage, etc. 18. to accustom or harden: *troops seasoned by battle.* —*v.i.* 19. to become seasoned, matured, hardened, or the like. [ME *sesoun*, *seson* < OF *se(i)son* < L *satiōn-* (s. of *satiō*) a sowing (VL: sowing time), equiv. to *sa-* (root of *serere* to sow) + *-t-* ptp. suffix + *-iōn-* -ION] —**sea′soned·ly,** *adv.* —**sea′son·er,** *n.* —**sea′son·less,** *adj.*

sea·son·a·ble (sē′zə nə bəl), *adj.* 1. suitable to or characteristic of the season: *seasonable weather.* 2. timely; opportune: *The suggestion came at a seasonable time.* [late ME *sesounable.* See SEASON, -ABLE] —**sea′son·a·ble·ness,** *n.* —**sea′son·a·bly,** *adv.*
—**Syn. 1.** fit, appropriate. **2.** See **opportune.**

sea·son·al (sē′zə nəl), *adj.* pertaining to, dependent on, or accompanying the seasons of the year or some particular season; periodical: *seasonal work.* [SEASON + -AL[1]] —**sea′son·al·ly,** *adv.* —**sea′son·al·ness,** *n.*

sea·son·ing (sē′zə ning), *n.* salt or an herb, spice, or the like, for heightening or improving the flavor of food. [SEASON + -ING[1]] —**sea′son·ing·like′,** *adj.*

Sea′son in Hell′, A, a work in prose and verse (1873) by Rimbaud. French, **Une Saison en Enfer.**

Seasons, The, an oratorio (1801) by Franz Joseph Haydn.

sea′son tick′et, a ticket for a specified series or number of events or valid for use as many times as desired during a specified time, usually sold at a reduced rate, for athletic events, plays, concerts, transportation, etc.: *a season ticket for Philharmonic Hall.*

sea′ squill′. See **sea onion** (def. 1).

sea′ squirt′, any tunicate, esp. a sessile ascidian, so called from its habit of contracting its body and ejecting streams of water when disturbed.

sea′ stag′horn, any green seaweed of the genus *Codium*, as *C. fragile* or *C. dichotoma*, having spongy, forked branches that resemble antlers.

sea′ swal′low, 1. any of several terns, esp. *Sterna hirundo.* 2. *Brit. Dial.* any of several small petrels, esp. the storm petrel, *Hydrobates pelagicus.*

seat (sēt), *n.* 1. something designed to support a person in a sitting position, as a chair, bench or pew; a place on or in which one sits. 2. the part of a chair, sofa, or the like, on which one sits. 3. the part of the body on which one sits; the buttocks. 4. the part of the garment covering it: *the seat of one's pants.* 5. a manner or of posture used in sitting, as on a horse. 6. something on which the base of an object rests. 7. the base itself. 8. a place in which something belongs, occurs, or is established; site; location. 9. a place in which administrative power or the like is centered: *Washington is the seat of the U.S. government.* 10. a part of the body considered as the place in which an emotion or function is centered: *The heart is the seat of passion.* 11. the office or authority of a king, bishop, etc.: *the episcopal seat.* 12. a space in which a spectator or patron may sit; accommodation for sitting, as in a theater, stadium, etc. 13. right of admittance to such a space, esp. as indicated by a ticket. 14. a right to sit as a member in a legislative or similar body: *He was elected to a seat in the senate.* 15. a right to the privileges of membership in a stock exchange or the like. 16. *Carpentry.* an inwardly inclined surface on the bottom of a rafter providing a level resting place on the wall plate. —*v.t.* 17. to place on a seat or seats; cause to sit down. 18. to usher to a seat or find a seat for: *The usher seated us in the front row.* 19. to have seats for; accommodate with seats: *a theater that seats 1200 people.* 20. to put a seat on or into (a chair, garment, etc.). 21. to install in a position or office of authority, in a legislative body, etc. 22. (of a valve) to be closed. 23. to attach to or place firmly in or on something as a base: *Seat the telescope on the tripod and tighten the screws.* [ME *sete* < Scand; cf. Icel *sǣti*; c. D *gezeet*, G *Gesäss*; cf. OE *sǣt* house] —**seat′er,** *n.* —**seat′less,** *adj.*
—**Syn. 1.** throne, stool. **3.** bottom, fundament.

Sea·tack (sē′tak′), *n.* a town in SE Virginia. 3120 (1960).

sea′ tan′gle, any of various seaweeds, esp. of the genus *Laminaria.*

seat′ an′gle. See **angle cleat.**

seat′ belt′, a webbed belt or strap secured to the seat of an automobile, airplane, etc., and fastened around or sometimes diagonally across the midsection of the passenger to keep him safely secured to his seat, as during a sudden stop. Also called **safety belt.**

Seat′ed Scribe′, a statue in limestone (c2500 B.C.) from Egypt.

seat·ing (sē′ting), *n.* 1. the act or an instance of furnishing with, assigning, or escorting to a seat or seats. 2. the arrangement of seats in a theater, stadium, etc.: *The seating is divided by a center aisle.* 3. material for seats, esp. upholstery. —*adj.* 4. of or pertaining to seats or those who are sitting: *the seating plan of a theater.* [SEAT + -ING[1], -ING[2]]

SEATO (sē′tō), *n.* an organization formed in Manila (1954), comprising Australia, Great Britain, France, New Zealand, Pakistan, the Philippines, Thailand, and the United States, for collective defense against aggression in southeastern Asia and the southwestern Pacific. [*S(outh)e(ast) A(sia) T(reaty) O(rganization)*]

Seat′ Pleas′ant, a town in central Maryland. 5365 (1960).

sea·train (sē′trān′), *n.* a ship for the transportation of loaded railroad cars. [SEA + TRAIN]

sea′ trout′, 1. any of various species of trout found in salt water, as the salmon trout, *Salmo trutta.* 2. any of several fishes of the genus *Cynoscion.*

Se·at·tle (sē at′əl), *n.* a seaport in W Washington, on Puget Sound. 557,087 (1960).

sea′ tur′tle, any of several large turtles of the family *Cheloniidae*, cosmopolitan in tropical and subtropical seas, having the limbs modified into paddlelike flippers.

seat·work (sēt′wûrk′), *n. Educ.* work that can be done by a child at his seat in school without supervision. [SEAT + WORK]

sea′ ur′chin, 1. any echinoderm of the class *Echinoidea*, having a somewhat globular or discoid form, and a shell composed of many calcareous plates covered with projecting spines. 2. a tall, evergreen shrub or small tree, *Hakea laurina*, of Australia, having dense, globe-shaped clusters of crimson flowers.

A B

Sea urchin,
Arbacia punctulata
A, With spines
B, Without

sea′ valve′, *Naut.* seacock.

sea′ wall′, a strong wall or embankment to prevent the encroachments of the sea, serve as a breakwater, etc. —**sea′-walled′,** *adj.*

sea′ wal′nut, a ctenophore, as of the genus *Mnemiopsis*, shaped like a walnut.

sea·wan (sē′wən), *n.* wampum (def. 1). Also, **seawant** (sē′wänt′), **sewan.** [< Algonquian; cf. Natick *se(a)wan* scattered objects]

sea·ward (sē′wərd), *adv.* 1. Also, **sea′wards.** toward the sea: *a storm moving seaward.* —*adj.* 2. facing or tending toward the sea: *a seaward course.* 3. coming from the sea: *a seaward wind.* —*n.* 4. the direction toward the sea or away from the land. [SEA + -WARD]

sea·ware (sē′wâr′), *n.* seaweed, esp. coarse, large seaweed, used chiefly as a fertilizer. [OE *sǣwār*, equiv. to *sǣ* SEA + *wār* seaweed]

sea·way (sē′wā′), *n.* 1. a way over the sea. 2. the open sea. 3. the progress of a ship through the waves. 4. a more or less rough sea: *a hard vessel to steer in a seaway.* 5. a canal, enlarged river, etc., giving access to a landlocked port by ocean-going vessels. [ME *seewey*, OE *sǣweg.* See SEA, WAY]

sea·weed (sē′wēd′), *n.* 1. any plant or plants growing in the ocean. 2. a marine alga. [SEA + WEED[1]]

sea′weed mar′quetry, marquetry having the form of symmetrical, foliate scrolls, as on English cabinetwork of the late 17th and early 18th centuries.

sea′ whip′, a gorgonian coral that forms a flexible colony resembling shrubbery on the ocean floor.

sea′ wolf′, 1. any of several large, voracious, marine fishes, as the wolffish or sea bass. 2. a pirate. [ME *seewolf*]

Sea′ Wolf′, The, a novel (1904) by Jack London.

sea′ worm′wood, a perennial herb, *Artemisia canadensis*, of North America, usually grayish and hairless, having greenish flower heads in long, narrow clusters. Also called **wild wormwood.**

sea·wor·thy (sē′wûr′thē), *adj.* (of a vessel) 1. constructed, outfitted, manned, and in all respects fitted for a voyage at sea. 2. safe for a voyage at sea. [SEA + WORTHY] —**sea′wor′thi·ness,** *n.*

sea′ wrack′, seaweed or a growth of seaweed, esp. of the larger kinds cast up on the shore.

seb-, var. of **sebi-** before a vowel: *sebaceous.*

se·ba·ceous (si bā′shəs), *adj. Physiol.* 1. pertaining to, of the nature of, or resembling tallow or fat; fatty; greasy. 2. secreting a fatty substance. [< NL *sēbāceus.* See SEB-, -ACEOUS]

seba′ceous gland′, any of the cutaneous glands which secrete oily matter for lubricating hair and skin. See diag. under **hair.**

se·bac·ic (si bas′ik, -bā′sik), *adj. Chem.* of or derived from sebacic acid. [SEBAC(EOUS) + -IC]

sebac′ic ac′id, *Chem.* a crystalline, slightly water-soluble, dibasic acid, $HOOC(CH_2)_8COOH$, usually obtained from castor oil: used chiefly in the manufacture of plasticizers and resins.

Se·bas·tian (si bas′chən), *n.* 1. **Saint,** died A.D. 288?, Roman martyr. 2. a boy's given name.

Se·bas·to·pol (si bas′tə pōl′), *n.* 1. Sevastopol. 2. a town in W California. 2694 (1960).

SEbE, See **southeast by east.**

sebi-, a combining form of **sebum**: *sebiferous*. Also, **sebo-**. Also, *esp. before a vowel*, **seb-**.

se·bif·er·ous (si bif′ər əs), *adj. Biol.* secreting or producing fat or fatty matter; sebaceous. [SEBI- + -FEROUS]

Se·bo·im (si bō′im), *n. Douay Bible.* Zeboim.

seb·or·rhe·a (seb′ə rē′ə), *n. Pathol.* an excessive and abnormal discharge from the sebaceous glands. Also, **seb′or·rhoe′a.** [SEBO- + -RRHEA] —**seb′or·rhe′al, seb′or·rhe′ic,** *adj.*

seborrhe′ic dermati′tis, *Pathol.* a skin inflammation chiefly of the scalp and face, characterized by oiliness and scaling.

Se·bring (sē′briŋ), *n.* **1.** a town in central Florida. 6939 (1960). **2.** a town in E Ohio. 4439 (1960).

SEbS, See **southeast by south.**

se·bum (sē′bəm), *n. Physiol.* the fatty secretion of the sebaceous glands. [< L: tallow, grease]

sec[1] (sek), *adj.* (of wines) dry; not sweet. [< F]

sec[2] (sek), *n. Informal.* second[2] (def. 3). [by shortening]

SEC, *U.S. Govt.* Securities and Exchange Commission: a board, consisting of five members, charged with regulating the public offer and sale of securities. Also, **S.E.C.**

sec, secant.

sec., **1.** second. **2.** secondary. **3.** secretary. **4.** sector. **5.** secundum.

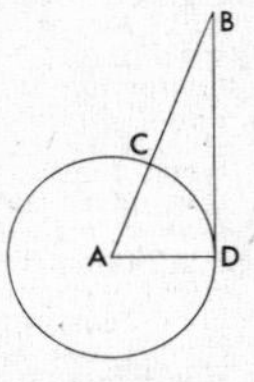

se·cant (sē′kant, -kənt), *n.* **1.** *Geom.* an intersecting line, esp. one intersecting a curve at two or more points. **2.** *Trig.* **a.** (in a right triangle) the ratio of the hypotenuse to the side adjacent to a given angle. **b.** (originally) a line from the center of a circle through one extremity of an arc to the tangent from the other extremity. **c.** the ratio of the length of this line to that of the radius of the circle; the reciprocal of the cosine of a given angle or arc. *Abbr.:* sec —*adj.* **3.** cutting or intersecting, as one line or surface in relation to another. [< L *secant-* (s. of *secāns*, prp. of *secāre* to cut), equiv. to *sec-* (see SAW[1]) + *-ant-* -ANT] —**se′cant·ly,** *adv.*

Secant
Ratio of AB to AD, secant of angle A; AB, secant of arc CD

sec·a·teurs (sek′ə tər, -tûr′), *n.* (*construed as pl. or sing.*) *Chiefly Brit.* scissors or shears, esp. pruning shears. [< F < L *sec(āre)* (to) cut (see SECANT) + *-ateurs* << L *-ātor* -ATOR]

Sec·chi (sek′ē), *n.* a crater in the first quadrant of the face of the moon: about 13 miles in diameter.

sec·co (sek′ō; *It.* sek′kô), *n.* **1.** See **fresco secco.** —*adj.* **2.** (of notes or passages in a musical score) played and released abruptly and without resonance. [< It: dry; see SACK[3]]

se·cede (si sēd′), *v.i.*, **-ced·ed, -ced·ing.** to withdraw formally from an alliance, federation, or association, as from a political union, a religious organization, etc. [< L *sēcēd(ere)* (to) withdraw. See SE-, CEDE] —**se·ced′er,** *n.*

se·cern (si sûrn′), *v.t.* **1.** to discriminate or distinguish in thought. —*v.i.* **2.** to become secerned. [< L *sēcern(ere)*, equiv. to *sē-* SE- + *cernere* to sift] —**se·cern′ment,** *n.*

se·cern·ent (si sûr′nənt), *adj. Physiol.* secreting. [< L *sēcernent-* (s. of *secernens*, prp. of *sēcernere* to SECERN); see -ENT]

se·ces·sion (si sesh′ən), *n.* **1.** the act or an instance of seceding. **2.** (*often cap.*) *U.S. Hist.* the withdrawal from the Union of 11 Southern States in the period 1860–61, which brought on the Civil War. **3.** (*usually cap.*) German, **sezession.** *Fine Arts.* a style of art in Germany and Austria concurrent with and related to Art Nouveau. [< L *sēcessiōn-* (s. of *sēcessiō*) withdrawal, equiv. to *sēcess(us)* (ptp. of *sēcēdere* to SECEDE) + *-iōn-* -ION] —**se·ces′sion·al,** *adj.*

se·ces·sion·ist (si sesh′ə nist), *n.* **1.** one who secedes, advocates secession, or claims secession as a constitutional right. —*adj.* **2.** of or pertaining to secession or secessionists. [SECESSION + -IST] —**se·ces′sion·ism,** *n.*

sech, hyperbolic secant. [SEC(ANT) + H(YPERBOLIC)]

Seck·el (sek′əl, sik′-), *n.* **1.** a small, yellowish-brown variety of pear. **2.** the tree bearing this fruit. [after surname of grower, Pennsylvania orchardist]

sec. leg., according to law. [< L *secundum lēgem*]

se·clude (si klōōd′), *v.t.*, **-clud·ed, -clud·ing.** **1.** to place in or withdraw into solitude; remove from social contact and activity, etc. **2.** to isolate; shut off; keep apart: *They secluded the garden from the rest of the property.* [< L *sēclūde(re)*, equiv. to *sē-* SE- + *claudere* to bolt, bar]

se·clud·ed (si klōō′did), *adj.* **1.** sheltered or screened from general activity, view, etc.: *a secluded cottage.* **2.** withdrawn from or involving little human or social activity: *a secluded life.* [SECLUDE + -ED[2]] —**se·clud′ed·ly,** *adv.* —**se·clud′ed·ness,** *n.*
—**Syn.** withdrawn, isolated, retired, sequestered, cloistered, private, secret.

se·clu·sion (si klōō′zhən), *n.* **1.** an act of secluding. **2.** the state of being secluded; retirement; solitude: *He sought seclusion in his study.* **3.** a secluded place. [< ML *sēclūsiōn-* (s. of *sēclūsiō*) < L *sēclūs(us)* (ptp. of *sēclūdere* to SECLUDE) + *-iōn-* -ION]

se·clu·sive (si klōō′siv), *adj.* **1.** tending to seclude, esp. oneself. **2.** causing or providing seclusion. [*secluse* (< L *sēclūs(us)* secluded) + -IVE] —**se·clu′sive·ly,** *adv.* —**se·clu′sive·ness,** *n.*

sec·o·bar·bi·tal (sek′ō bär′bi tal′, -tôl′), *n. Pharm.* a white, odorless, slightly bitter powder, $C_{12}H_{18}N_2O_3$, used chiefly in the form of its sodium salt as a sedative and hypnotic. [SECO(NAL) + BARBITAL]

Sec·o·nal (sek′ə nôl′, -nal′, -nᵊl), *n. Pharm., Trademark.* secobarbital.

sec·ond[1] (sek′ənd), *adj.* **1.** next after the first; being the ordinal number for two. **2.** being one of two equal parts. **3.** next after the first in place, time, or value: *the second house from the corner.* **4.** next after the first in rank, grade, degree, status, or importance: *He was promoted from the second team before the next game.* **5.** alternate: *I have my hair cut every second week.* **6.** inferior. **7.** *Gram.* noting or pertaining to the second person. **8.** *Music.* the lower of two parts for the same instrument or voice: *second alto; second trombone.* **9.** other or another: *a second Solomon; We had beans and then a second vegetable.* **10.** *Auto.* of, pertaining to, or operating at the gear transmission ratio at which drive shaft speed is greater than that of low gear but not so great as that of other gears for a given engine crankshaft speed: *second gear.* —*n.* **11.** a second part, esp. of one ($\frac{1}{2}$). **12.** the second member of a series. **13.** one who aids or supports another; assistant; backer. **14.** *Boxing.* a person who, between rounds of a prizefight, gives aid, advice, etc., to a boxer. **15.** one who serves as a representative or attendant of a duelist. **16.** *Auto.* second gear: *He shifted into second.* **17.** one who or that which is next after the first in place, time, or value. **18.** one who or that which is next after the first in rank, grade, degree, status, or importance. **19.** Often, **seconds.** an additional helping of food: *He had seconds on the meat and potatoes, but said he didn't want any more spinach.* **20.** (in parliamentary procedure) **a.** one who expresses formal support of a motion so that it may be discussed or put to a vote. **b.** the act or an instance of doing this. **21.** (in certain British universities) a type or grade of college degree granted according to a student's performance on specific written and oral examinations. **22.** *Music.* **a.** a tone on the next degree from a given tone. **b.** the interval between such tones. **c.** the harmonic combination of such tones. **d.** the lower of two parts in a piece of concerted music. **e.** a voice or instrument performing such a part. **f.** an alto. **23.** Usually, **seconds.** *Com.* a product or goods below the first or highest quality, esp. containing visible flaws. Cf. **first** (def. 21), **third** (def. 12). **24.** *Metall.* a piece of somewhat defective but salable tin plate. **25.** *Baseball.* See **second base.** —*v.t.* **26.** to assist or support. **27.** to further or advance, as aims. **28.** (in parliamentary procedure) to express formal support of (a motion, proposal, etc.), as a necessary preliminary to further discussion or to voting. **29.** to act as second to (a boxer, duelist, etc.). **30.** *Brit.* **a.** *Mil.* to retire (an officer) temporarily for the purpose of assigning him to a staff or other nonregimental post. **b.** to transfer (an officer, official, or the like) temporarily to another position. —*adv.* **31.** in the second place, group, etc.: *The catcher is batting second in today's lineup.* [ME < OF < L *secund(us)* following, next, second, equiv. to *sec-* (root of *sequī* to follow) + *-undus* adj. suffix] —**sec′ond·er,** *n.*

sec·ond[2] (sek′ənd), *n.* **1.** the sixtieth part of a minute of time. **2.** the sixtieth part of a minute of degree, often represented by the sign ″, as in 12° 10′ 30″, read as 12 degrees, 10 minutes, and 30 seconds. **3.** a moment or instant: *It takes only a second to phone.* [ME *seconde* < MF < ML *secund(a)* (*minūta*) second (minute); see SECOND[1]]

Sec′ond Ad′vent, advent (def. 4).

Sec′ond Ad′ventist, Adventist (def. 1).

sec·ond·ar·y (sek′ən der′ē), *adj., n., pl.* **-ar·ies.** —*adj.* **1.** next after the first in order, place, time, importance, etc. **2.** belonging or pertaining to a second order, division, stage, period, rank, grade, etc. **3.** derived or derivative; not primary or original: *secondary sources of historical research.* **4.** of minor importance; subordinate; auxiliary. **5.** of or pertaining to secondary schools. **6.** *Chem.* **a.** involving or obtained by the replacement of two atoms or groups. **b.** noting or containing a carbon atom united to two other carbon atoms in a chain or ring molecule. **7.** *Elect.* noting or pertaining to the current induced by a primary winding or to the winding in which the current is induced in an induction coil, transformer, or the like. **8.** *Geol.* noting or pertaining to a mineral produced from another mineral by decay, alteration, or the like. **9.** *Gram.* **a.** derived. **b.** derived from a word which is itself a derived word: *a secondary derivative.* **c.** having reference to past time; noting or pertaining to a past tense: *the Latin, Greek, or Sanskrit secondary tenses.* Cf. **primary** (def. 13). **10.** *Ornith.* pertaining to any of a set of flight feathers on the second segment of a bird's wing. **11.** *Ling.* of, pertaining to, or characteristic of a secondary accent: *secondary stress.* —*n.* **12.** one who or that which is secondary. **13.** a subordinate, assistant, deputy, or agent. **14.** *Elect.* a winding in a transformer or the like in which a current is induced by a primary winding. **15.** *Ornith.* a secondary feather. **16.** *Football.* the defensive unit that lines up behind the linemen. **17.** *Ling.* See **secondary accent.** [< L *secundāri(us).* See SECOND[1], -ARY] —**sec·ond·ar·i·ly** (sek′ən der′ə lē, sek′ən-dâr′-), *adv.* —**sec′ond·ar′i·ness,** *n.*

sec′ondary ac′cent, a stress accent weaker than primary accent but stronger than lack of stress.

sec′ondary articula′tion, *Phonet.* coarticulation (def. 2).

sec′ondary boy′cott, a boycott by union members against their employer in order to induce him to bring pressure on another company involved in a labor dispute with the union.

sec′ondary cell′, *Elect.* See **storage cell.**

sec′ondary col′or, a color, as orange, green, or violet, produced by mixing two primary colors.

sec′ondary con′tact, *Sociol.* communication or relationship between people characterized by impersonal and detached interest on the part of those involved. Cf. **primary contact.**

sec′ondary diag′onal. See under **diagonal** (def. 9).

sec′ondary emis′sion, the emission of electrons (**sec′ondary elec′trons**) from a material which is bombarded with electrons or ions.

sec′ondary group′, *Sociol.* a group of people with whom one's contacts are detached and impersonal. Cf. **primary group.**

sec′ondary o′ocyte. See under **oocyte.**

sec′ondary or′dinary, *Heraldry.* subordinary.

sec′ondary phlo′em, phloem derived from the cambium.

sec′ondary pro′pyl al′cohol, *Chem.* See **isopropyl alcohol.**

sec′ondary qual′ity, *Epistemology.* one of the qualities attributed by the mind to an object perceived, such as color, temperature, or taste. Cf. **primary quality.**

sec′ondary school′, a high school or a school of corresponding grade, ranking between a primary school and a college or university. —**sec′ond·ar′y-school′,** *adj.*

sec′ondary sev′enth chord′, *Music.* a chord formed by superposition of three thirds upon any degree of the scale except the dominant.

sec′ondary sex′ characteris′tic, *Med.* any of a number of manifestations specific to each sex and incipient at puberty, as development of breasts or beard, muscularity, distribution of fat tissue, and change of pitch in voice, but not essential to reproduction. Also called **sec′ondary sex′ char′acter.**

sec′ondary spermat′ocyte. See under **spermatocyte.**

sec′ondary stress′, **1.** *Engineering.* a stress induced by the elastic deformation of a structure under a temporary load. **2.** See **secondary accent.**

sec′ondary syph′ilis, *Pathol.* the second stage of syphilis, characterized by eruptions of the skin and mucous membrane.

sec′ondary wave′. See **S wave.**

sec′ondary xy′lem, xylem derived from the cambium.

sec′ond ax′iom of countabil′ity, *Math.* See under **axiom of countability.**

Sec′ond Bal′kan War′. See **Balkan War** (def. 2).

sec′ond base′, *Baseball.* **1.** the second in order of the bases from home plate. **2.** the position of the player covering the area of the infield between second and first bases.

sec′ond base′man, *Baseball.* the player whose position is second base.

sec·ond-best (sek′ənd best′), *adj.* next to the best in performance, achievement, craftsmanship, etc. —**sec′ond best′.**

Sec′ond Birth′, *Theol.* spiritual rebirth.

sec′ond cat′egory, *Math.* the property of a set that cannot be expressed as the union of a countable number of nowhere-dense sets. Cf. **Baire category theorem, first category.**

Sec′ond Cham′ber. See under **States-General** (def. 1).

sec′ond child′hood, senility; dotage.

sec′ond class′, **1.** the class of accommodations, as on a train, that are less costly and luxurious than first class but are more costly and luxurious than third class. Cf. **cabin class.** **2.** (in the U.S. postal system) the class of mail consisting of newspapers and periodicals not sealed against postal inspection. **3.** (in certain British universities) the group receiving next to highest distinction in an honors course.

sec·ond-class (sek′ənd klas′, -kläs′), *adj.* **1.** of a secondary class or quality. **2.** second-rate; inferior.

Sec′ond Com′ing, advent (def. 4).

sec′ond cous′in, a child of a first cousin. Cf. **cousin** (def. 1).

sec′ond-cut′ file′ (sek′ənd kut′), a metal file having the commercial grade of coarseness between bastard and smooth.

sec′ond-de·gree′ burn′ (sek′ənd di grē′), *Pathol.* See under **burn**[1] (def. 39).

sec′ond deriv′ative, *Math.* the derivative of the derivative of a function: *Acceleration is the second derivative of distance with respect to time.* Cf. **first derivative.**

sec′ond divi′sion, *Sports.* the half of a league comprising the teams having the poorest records at a particular time, esp. the five teams having the poorest records in either of the two major baseball leagues (opposed to *first division*).

se·conde (si kond′; *Fr.* sə gônd′), *n., pl.* **-condes** (-kondz′; *Fr.* -gônd′). *Fencing.* the second of the eight defensive positions. [< F, fem. of *second* SECOND[1]]

Sec′ond Em′pire, the empire established in France (1852–70) by Louis Napoleon: the successor to the Second Republic.

sec′ond estate′, the second of the three estates: the nobles in France; the lords temporal in England. Cf. **estate** (def. 5).

sec′ond fid′dle, **1.** a secondary role: *to play second fiddle to another person.* **2.** a person serving in a subsidiary capacity, esp. to one immediately superior.

sec′ond floor′, **1.** the floor or story above the ground floor. **2.** (in Britain and elsewhere outside the U.S.) the second story completely above ground level. Cf. **first floor.** Also called **second story.**

sec′ond growth′, the plant growth that follows the destruction of virgin forest.

sec·ond-guess (sek′ənd ges′), *v.t.* **1.** to use hindsight in criticizing or correcting. **2.** to predict (something) or outguess (someone): *We must try to second-guess what he'll do next.* —**sec′ond-guess′er,** *n.*

sec′ond hand (sek′ənd hand′ *for 1;* sek′ənd hand′ *for 2*), **1.** the hand that indicates the seconds on a clock or watch. **2.** an assistant or helper, as to a worker or foreman. **3.** **at second hand,** from or through an intermediate source or means: *She had it at second hand that a scandal was about to break.*

sec·ond·hand (sek′ənd hand′), *adj.* **1.** not directly known or experienced; obtained from others or from books: *Most of our knowledge is secondhand.* **2.** previously used or owned: *secondhand clothes; secondhand books.* **3.** dealing in previously used goods: *a secondhand bookseller.* —*adv.* **4.** when used or after being used or owned by another: *He bought the guitar secondhand.* **5.** indirectly; by way of an intermediate source: *He heard the news secondhand.* —**sec′ond-hand′ed·ness,** *n.*

sec′ond inten′tion, *Logic.* See under **intention** (def. 5).

Sec′ond Interna′tional, an international association formed in 1889 in Paris, uniting socialistic groups or parties of various countries and holding international congresses from time to time: in 1923 it joined with the Vienna International to form the Labor and Socialist International. Cf. **international** (def. 4).

sec′ond law′ of mo′tion, *Physics.* See under **law of motion.**

sec′ond law′ of thermodynam′ics. See under **law of thermodynamics** (def. 1).

sec′ond lieuten′ant, *U.S. Mil.* an Army, Air Force, or Marine officer of the lowest commissioned rank. Cf. **ensign** (def. 4).

sec·ond·ly (sek′ənd lē), *adv.* in the second place: *In the first place, I don't like fried eggs; secondly, these eggs are fried too hard.* [SECOND[1] + -LY]

sec′ond mate′, the officer of a merchant vessel next in command beneath the first mate. Also called **second officer.**

sec′ond mort′gage, a mortgage the lien of which is next in priority to a first mortgage.

sec′ond na′ture, an acquired habit or tendency in one's character which is so deeply ingrained that it appears automatic: *A love of the outdoor life is second nature to him.*

se·con·do (si kon′dō, -kōn′-; *It.* se kôn′dô), *n., pl.* **-di** (-dē). *Music.* **1.** the second or lower part in a duet, esp. in a piano duet. **2.** the performer playing this part. [< It; see SECOND[1]]

sec′ond of′ficer, *Naut.* See **second mate.**

sec′ond pa′pers, *U.S.* the second and final documents of record in the naturalization of an alien. Cf. **first papers, citizenship papers.**

sec′ond per′son, *Gram.* the person used by a speaker in referring to the one or ones to whom he is speaking: in English *you* is a second person pronoun.

sec′ond posi′tion, *Ballet.* a position in which the feet are spread apart and are at right angles to the direction of the body, the toes pointing out. See illus. under **first position.**

sec·ond-rate (sek′ənd rāt′), *adj.* **1.** of lesser or minor quality, importance, worth, or the like: *a second-rate poet.* **2.** inferior; mediocre: *a second-rate performance of the symphony.* **—sec′ond-rate′ness,** *n.* **—sec′ond-rat′er,** *n.*

Sec′ond Read′er, *Christian Science.* the elected official of a church or society who conducts services and reads from the Scriptures. Cf. **First Reader.**

Sec′ond Reich′, the German Empire 1871–1919. Cf. **Reich.**

Sec′ond Repub′lic, the republic established in France in 1848 and replaced by the Second Empire in 1852.

sec′ond self′, one who associates so closely with a given person as to assume that person's mode of behavior, personality, beliefs, etc.

sec′ond serv′ice, *Ch. of Eng.* the communion service: so called because it follows Morning Prayer.

sec′ond sheet′, **1.** a sheet of blank stationery, used in a letter as the second and following pages to a sheet having a letterhead. **2.** a sheet of lightweight paper, usually of inferior quality, used behind a carbon to make a duplicate.

sec′ond sight′, a supposed faculty of seeing future events; clairvoyance: *Her second sight warned her to refuse this offer, attractive though it seemed.* **—sec′ond-sight′ed,** *adj.* **—sec′ond-sight′ed·ness,** *n.*

sec′onds pen′dulum, a clock pendulum requiring exactly one second for an oscillation. Also called **royal pendulum.**

sec′ond sto′ry. See **second floor.**

sec·ond-sto·ry (sek′ənd stôr′ē, -stōr′ē), *adj.* **1.** of or located on the second story or floor. **2.** *Informal.* breaking in or carried out by breaking in through an upper-story window in order to burglarize an apartment or house: *The police said the theft was a second-story job.*

sec′ond-sto′ry man′, *Informal.* a burglar who enters through upstairs windows.

sec′ond thought′, Often, **second thoughts.** reservation about a previous action, position, decision, judgment, or the like: *He had second thoughts about the matter and was unwilling to commit himself further.*

sec′ond wind′ (wind), **1.** the return of ease in breathing, due to restored normal operation of the heart, after exhaustion caused by continued physical exertion, as in running. **2.** the energy for a renewed effort to continue an undertaking.

Sec′ond World′ War′. See **World War II.**

se·cos (sē′kos, -kôs), *n.* sekos.

se·cre·cy (sē′kri sē), *n., pl.* **-cies.** **1.** the state or condition of being secret, hidden, or concealed: *Complete secrecy enveloped their meeting.* **2.** privacy; retirement; seclusion. **3.** ability to keep a secret. **4.** the habit or characteristic of being secretive; reticence. [obs. *secre* (< MF *secré* SECRET) + -CY; r. ME *secretee,* equiv. to *secre* + *-tee* -TY[2]]

se·cret (sē′krit), *adj.* **1.** done, made, or conducted without the knowledge of others: *secret negotiations between Germany and Italy.* **2.** kept from the knowledge of any but the initiated or privileged: *a secret password.* **3.** faithful or cautious in keeping confidential matters confidential; close-mouthed; reticent. **4.** designed or working to escape notice, knowledge, or observation: *a secret drawer; the secret police.* **5.** secluded, sheltered, or withdrawn: *a secret hiding place.* **6.** beyond ordinary human understanding; esoteric. **7.** *U.S. Govt., Mil.* (of information, a document, etc.) **a.** bearing the classification *secret.* **b.** limited to persons authorized to use information documents, etc., so classified. **—***n.* **8.** something which is or is kept secret, hidden, or concealed. **9.** a mystery: *the secrets of nature.* **10.** a reason or explanation not immediately or generally apparent. **11.** a method, formula, plan, etc., known only to the initiated or the few: *a long search for the secret of happiness; a trade secret.* **12.** *U.S. Govt., Mil.* a classification assigned to information, a document, etc., considered less vital to national security than top secret but more vital than confidential, and limiting its use to persons who have been cleared by various government agencies as trustworthy to handle such material. Cf. **classification** (def. 5). **13.** (*cap.*) *Liturgy.* a variable prayer in the Roman and other Latin liturgies, said inaudibly by the celebrant after the offertory and immediately before the preface. **14. in secret,** unknown to others; in private; secretly: *A resistance movement was already being organized in secret.* [ME *secrette* < OF *secret* < L *sēcrēt(us)* hidden, orig. ptp. of *sēcernere* to SECERN] **—se′cret·ly,** *adv.* **—se′cret·ness,** *n.*
—Syn. 1. clandestine, hidden, concealed, covert. **1, 2.** private, confidential. **3.** secretive. **6.** occult, obscure, mysterious. **—Ant. 1.** open, manifest.

se′cret a′gent, **1.** an agent of a secret service. **2.** (loosely) a person employed to collect the military secrets of one country and relay them to another, esp. a person living in a foreign country while so working for his own nation; spy.

se·cre·taire (sek′ri târ′), *n. Fr. Furniture.* any writing desk resembling a secretary. [< F *secrétaire* SECRETARY]

sec·re·tar·i·al (sek′ri târ′ē əl), *adj.* noting, of, or pertaining to a secretary or a secretary's skills and work: *She learned shorthand and typing at a secretarial school.* [SECRETARY + -AL[1]]

sec·re·tar·i·at (sek′ri târ′ē ət), *n.* **1.** the officials or office entrusted with administrative duties, maintaining records, and overseeing or performing secretarial duties, esp. for an international organization: *the secretariat of the United Nations.* **2.** a group or department of secretaries. **3.** the place where a secretary transacts business, preserves records, etc. Also, **sec′re·tar′i·ate.** [< F *secrétariat* < ML *sēcrētāriāt(us).* See SECRETARY, -ATE[1]]

sec·re·tar·y (sek′ri ter′ē), *n., pl.* **-tar·ies.** **1.** a person, usually an official, who is in charge of the records, correspondence, minutes of meetings, and related affairs of an organization, company, association, etc.: *the secretary of the Linguistic Society of America.* **2.** a person employed to handle correspondence and do routine work in a business office, usually involving taking dictation, typing, filing, and the like. **3.** See **private secretary.** **4.** (*cap.*) an officer of state charged with the superintendence and management of a particular department of government, as a member of the president's cabinet in the U.S.: *Secretary of the Treasury.* **5.** a piece of furniture for use as a writing desk. **6.** Also called **sec′retary book′case.** a desk with bookshelves on top of it. [< ML *sēcrētāri(us)* < L *sēcrēt(um)* SECRET (n.) + *-ārius* -ARY] **—sec′re·tar′y·ship′,** *n.*

sec′retary bird′, a large, long-legged, raptorial bird, *Sagittarius serpentarius,* of Africa, which feeds on reptiles: so called from its crest, which resembles quill pens stuck over the ear.

Secretary bird (Height 4 ft.)

sec·re·tar·y-gen·er·al (sek′ri ter′ē jen′ər əl), *n., pl.* **sec·re·tar·ies-gen·er·al.** the head or chief administrative officer of a secretariat.

sec′retary of state′, **1.** *U.S.* the head and chief administrator of the Department of State. Cf. **foreign minister.** **2.** *Brit.* any of several ministers in the British government: *A new secretary of state for the Home Department has been appointed.* **3.** *U.S.* the appointed or elected official in a State government whose chief function is to distribute statutes, administer elections, keep archives, etc. Also, **Sec′retary of State′.**

se′cret block′, *Mach.* a block having a completely enclosed sheave to prevent fouling of nearby rigging.

se·crete[1] (si krēt′), *v.t.,* **-cret·ed, -cret·ing.** to dis charge, generate, or release by the process of secretion. [back formation from SECRETION]

se·crete[2] (si krēt′), *v.t.,* **-cret·ed, -cret·ing.** to place out of sight; hide; conceal: *squirrels secreting nuts in a hollow tree trunk.* [alter. of obs. *secret* (v. use of SECRET)]
—Syn. cover, shroud, disguise. See **hide**[1].

se·crète (sə kret′), *n. Armor.* a steel skullcap of the 17th century, worn under a soft hat. [< F; see SECRET]

se·cre·tin (si krē′tin), *n. Biochem.* a hormone, produced in the small intestine, that activates the pancreas to secrete pancreatic juice. [SECRETE[1] + -IN[2]]

se·cre·tion (si krē′shən), *n.* **1.** (in a cell or gland) the act or process of separating, elaborating, and releasing a substance that fulfills some function within the organism or undergoes excretion. **2.** the product of this act or process. [< L *sēcrētiōn-* (s. of *sēcrētiō*), equiv. to *sēcrēt(us)* (ptp. of *sēcernere* to SECERN) + *-iōn-* -ION] **—se·cre·tion·ar·y** (si krē′shə ner′ē), *adj.*

se·cre·tive[1] (sē′kri tiv, si krē′-), *adj.* having or showing a disposition to secrecy; reticent: *He seemed strangely secretive about his new job.* [SECRETE[1] + -IVE; r. *secretive* (stress on first syll.). See SECRET (n.), -IVE] **—se′cre·tive·ly,** *adv.* **—se′cre·tive·ness,** *n.*
—Syn. secret, close.

se·cre·tive[2] (si krē′tiv), *adj.* secretory. [SECRETE[2] + -IVE]

se′cret nail′ing. See **blind nailing.**

se·cre·to·ry (si krē′tə rē), *adj., n., pl.* **-ries.** **—***adj.* **1.** pertaining to secretion. **2.** performing the process of secretion. **—***n.* **3.** a secretory organ, vessel, or the like. [SECRETE[2] + -ORY[1]]

se′cret part′ner, a partner whose name as a member of a firm is not revealed to the public. Cf. **silent partner.**

se′cret serv′ice, **1.** the branch of governmental service that conducts secret investigations, esp. investigations into the military strength of other nations. **2.** (*caps.*) the branch of the U.S. Department of the Treasury charged chiefly with the discovery and apprehension of counterfeiters and of providing protection for the president and his immediate family. **3.** secret work for a government, esp. espionage. **—se′cret-serv′ice,** *adj.*

se′cret soci′ety, an organization, as a fraternal society, the members of which are bound to assist each other, take secret initiation oaths, share secret passwords and rites, etc.

Secs., **1.** seconds. **2.** sections.

sect (sekt), *n.* **1.** a body of persons adhering to a particular religious faith; a religious denomination. **2.** a group regarded as heretical or as deviating from a generally accepted religious tradition. **3.** (in the sociology of religion) a Christian denomination characterized by insistence on strict qualifications for membership, as distinguished from the more inclusive groups called churches. **4.** any group, party, or faction united by a specific doctrine or under a doctrinal leader. [ME *secte* < L *sect(a)* something to follow, pathway, course of conduct, school of thought, etc.; akin to *sequī* to follow]

-sect, a word element occurring in loan words from Latin, where it meant "cut": *intersect.* [< L *sect(us)* (ptp. of *secāre* to cut), equiv. to *sec-* (see SAW[1]) + *-tus* ptp. suffix]

sect., section.

sec·tar·i·an (sek târ′ē ən), *adj.* **1.** of or pertaining to sectaries or sects. **2.** narrowly confined or devoted to a particular sect. **3.** narrowly confined or limited in interest, purpose, scope, etc. **—***n.* **4.** a member of a sect. **5.** a bigoted adherent of a sect. [SECTARY + -AN] **—sec·tar′i·an·ly,** *adv.*

sec·tar·i·an·ise (sek târ′ē ə nīz′), *v.t.,* **-ised, -is·ing.** *Chiefly Brit.* sectarianize.

sec·tar·i·an·ism (sek târ′ē ə niz′əm), *n.* the spirit or tendencies of sectarians; adherence or excessive devotion to a particular sect, esp. in religion. [SECTARIAN + -ISM]

sec·tar·i·an·ize (sek târ′ē ə nīz′), *v.t.,* **-ized, -iz·ing.** to make sectarian. [SECTARIAN + -IZE]

sec·ta·ry (sek′tə rē), *n., pl.* **-ries.** **1.** a member of a particular sect, esp. an adherent of a religious body regarded as heretical or schismatic. **2.** a Protestant of nonconformist denomination, esp. a minor one. **3.** one zealously devoted to a particular sect. [< ML *sectāri(us),* equiv. to *sect(a)* SECT + *-ārius* -ARY]

sec·tile (sek′til), *adj.* capable of being cut smoothly with a knife. [< L *sectile,* neut. of *sectilis* cuttable, equiv. to *sect(us)* (ptp. of *secāre* to cut) + *-ilis* -ILE] **—sec·til′i·ty,** *n.*

sec·tion (sek′shən), *n.* **1.** a part that is cut off or separated. **2.** a distinct part or subdivision of anything, as an object, country, community, class, or the like: *the poor section of town; the left section of a drawer.* **3.** a distinct part or subdivision of a writing, as of a newspaper, legal code, chapter, etc.: *the financial section of a daily paper; section 2 of the by-laws.* **4.** one of a number of parts that can be fitted together to make a whole: *sections of a fishing rod.* **5.** (in most of the U.S. west of Ohio) one of the 36 numbered subdivisions, each one mile square, of a township. **6.** the act or an instance of cutting; separation by cutting. **7.** *Surg.* **a.** the making of an incision. **b.** an incision. **8.** a thin slice of a tissue, mineral, or the like, as for microscopic examination. **9.** a representation of an object as it would appear if cut by a plane, showing its internal structure. **10.** *Mil.* **a.** a small unit consisting of two or more squads. **b.** Also called **staff section.** any of the subdivisions of a staff. **c.** a small tactical division in naval and air units. **11.** *Railroads.* **a.** a division of a sleeping car containing both an upper and a lower berth. **b.** a length of trackage, roadbed, signal equipment, etc., maintained by one crew. **12.** any of two or more trains, buses, or the like, running on the same route and schedule at the same time, one right behind the other, and considered as one unit, as when a second is necessary to accommodate more passengers than the first can carry: *On holidays the New York to Boston train runs in three sections.* **13.** a segment of a naturally segmented fruit, as of an orange, grapefruit, etc. **14.** a division of an orchestra or of a band containing all the instruments of one class: *He loved the old records featuring Duke Ellington's rhythm section.* **15.** *Bookbinding.* signature (def. 6). **16.** Also called **section mark.** a mark used to indicate a subdivision of a book, chapter, or the like, or as a mark of reference to a footnote. **17.** *Theat.* one of a series of circuits for controlling certain lights, as footlights. **18.** shape (def. 12). **—***v.t.* **19.** to cut or divide into sections. **20.** to cut through so as to present a section. **21.** *Surg.* to make an incision. **22.** to cut out part of (a weld) as a sample. [< L *sectiōn-* (s. of *sectiō*) a cutting, equiv. to *sect(us)* (ptp. of *secāre* to cut) + *-iōn-* -ION]
—Syn. 1. See **part.**

sec·tion·al (sek′shə nəl), *adj.* **1.** pertaining or limited to a particular section; local or regional: *sectional pride; sectional politics.* **2.** composed of several independent sections: *a sectional sofa; a sectional bookcase.* **3.** of or pertaining to a section. **—***n.* **4.** a sofa composed of several independent sections that can be arranged individually or in various combinations. [SECTION + -AL[1]] **—sec′tion·al·ly,** *adv.*

sec·tion·al·ise (sek′shə nəlīz′), *v.t.,* **-ised, -is·ing.** *Chiefly Brit.* sectionalize. **—sec′tion·al·i·sa′tion,** *n.*

sec·tion·al·ism (sek′shə nəliz′əm), *n.* excessive regard for sectional or local interests; regional or local spirit, prejudice, etc. [SECTIONAL + -ISM] **—sec′tion·al·ist,** *n.*

sec·tion·al·ize (sek′shə nəlīz′), *v.t.,* **-ized, -iz·ing.** **1.** to render sectional. **2.** to divide into sections, esp. geographical sections. Also, *esp. Brit.,* **sectionalise.** [SECTIONAL + -IZE] **—sec′tion·al·i·za′tion,** *n.*

sec′tion boss′, *Railroads U.S.* the boss of a section gang.

sec′tion eight′, **1.** a military discharge for physical or mental unfitness as determined by an Army Regulation in effect from 1922 to 1944. **2.** a soldier receiving such a discharge.

sec′tion gang′, *Railroads U.S.* a group of workmen who take care of a section of railroad track. Cf. **floating gang.**

sec′tion hand′, *Railroads U.S.* one who works on a section gang. Also called **tracklayer.**

sec′tion mark′, section (def. 16).

sec′tion mill′, *Metalworking.* a mill for rolling structural shapes. Also called **structural mill.**

sec·tor (sek′tər), *n.* **1.** *Geom.* a plane figure bounded by two radii and the included arc of a circle. **2.** a mathematical instrument consisting of two flat rulers hinged together at one end and bearing various scales. **3.** *Mach.* a device used in connection with an index plate, consisting of two arms rotating about the center of the plate and set to indicate the angle through which the work is indexed. **4.** *Mil.* a designated defense area, usually in a combat zone, within which a particular military unit operates and for which it is responsible. **5.** *Astron.* an instrument shaped like a sector of a circle, having a variable central angle and sights along the two straight sides, for measuring the angular distance between two celestial bodies. **—***v.t.* **6.** to divide into sectors. [< L: cutter; in geometry, part cut out, equiv. to *sect(us)* (ptp. of *secāre* to cut) + *-or* -OR[2]] **—sec′tor·al,** *adj.*

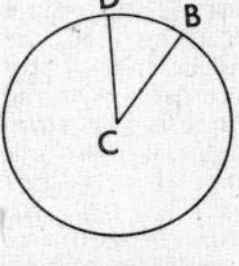

DCB, Sector of a circle

sec·to·ri·al (sek tôr′ē əl, -tōr′-), *adj.* **1.** of or pertaining to a sector. **2.** *Zool.* (of teeth) adapted for cutting; carnassial. [< NL *sectōri(us)* (see SECTOR, -ORY[1]) + -AL[1]]

sec·u·lar (sek′yə lər), *adj.* **1.** of or pertaining to worldly things or to things that are not regarded as religious, spiritual, or sacred; temporal: *secular interests.* **2.** not pertaining to or connected with religion (opposed to *sacred*): *secular music.* **3.** (of education, a school, etc.) concerned with nonreligious subjects: *The school had a curriculum providing a secular background only.* **4.** (of members of the clergy) not belonging to a religious order; not bound by monastic vows (opposed to *regular*). **5.** occurring or celebrated once in an age or century: *the secular games of Rome.* **6.** going on from age to age; continuing through long ages. —*n.* **7.** a layman. **8.** one of the secular clergy. [< ML *sēculār(is)* < LL *saeculāris* worldly, temporal (opposed to eternal), equiv. to L *saecul(um)* long period of time + *-āris* -AR¹; r. ME *seculer* < OF < L, as above] —**sec′u·lar·ly,** *adv.*

sec′ular hu′manism, any ethical system that promotes human values without specific allusion to religious doctrines. —**sec′ular hu′manist.**

sec·u·lar·ise (sek′yə lə rīz′), *v.t.*, **-ised, -is·ing.** *Chiefly Brit.* secularize. —**sec′u·lar·i·sa′tion,** *n.* —**sec′u·lar·is′er,** *n.*

sec·u·lar·ism (sek′yə lə riz′əm), *n.* **1.** secular spirit or tendency, esp. a system of political or social philosophy that rejects all forms of religious faith and worship. **2.** the view that public education and other matters of civil policy should be conducted without the introduction of a religious element. [SECULAR + -ISM] —**sec′u·lar·ist,** *n.* —**sec′u·lar·is′tic,** *adj.*

sec·u·lar·i·ty (sek′yə lar′i tē), *n., pl.* **-ties. 1.** secular views or beliefs; secularism. **2.** devoted to the affairs of the world; worldly. **3.** a secular matter. [SECULAR + -ITY]

sec·u·lar·ize (sek′yə lə rīz′), *v.t.*, **-ized, -iz·ing. 1.** to make secular; separate from religious or spiritual connection or influences; make worldly or unspiritual; imbue with secularism. **2.** to change (clergy) from regular to secular. **3.** to transfer (property) from ecclesiastical to civil possession or use. Also, *esp. Brit.*, **secularise.** [SECULAR + -IZE] —**sec′u·lar·i·za′tion,** *n.* —**sec′u·lar·iz′er,** *n.*

sec′ular ter′tiaries. See under **tertiary** (def. 5).

sec′ular vic′ar. See **lay vicar.**

se·cund (sē′kund, sek′und), *adj. Bot., Zool.* arranged on one side only; unilateral. [< L *secund(us)* following. See SECOND¹] —**se′cund·ly,** *adv.*

Se·cun·da (sə kun′də), *n.* a girl's given name.

Se·cun·der·a·bad (sə kun′dər ə bad′), *n.* a city in N Andhra Pradesh, in central India, part of Hyderabad.

sec·un·dine (sek′ən dīn′, -din), *n. Bot.* the inner integument of an ovule. Cf. **primine.** [< L *secundīn(ae)* (pl.) afterbirth]

se·cun·dum (se kōōn′dōōm; *Eng.* sə kun′dəm), *prep. Latin.* according to.

se·cun·dus (sə kun′dəs), *adj.* (in prescriptions) second. [< L]

se·cure (si kyŏŏr′), *adj., v.*, **-cured, -cur·ing.** —*adj.* **1.** free from or not exposed to danger; safe. **2.** dependable; firm; not liable to fail, yield, become displaced, etc., as a support or a fastening: *The building was secure, even in an earthquake.* **3.** affording safety, as a place: *He needed a secure hideout.* **4.** in safe custody or keeping: *Here in the vault the necklace was secure.* **5.** free from care; without anxiety: *emotionally secure.* **6.** firmly established, as a relationship or reputation: *He earned a secure place among the baseball immortals.* **7.** sure; certain; assured: *to be secure of victory; He was secure of his religious belief.* **8.** *Archaic.* overconfident. —*v.t.* **9.** to get hold or possession of; procure; obtain: *to secure materials; to secure a high government position.* **10.** to free from danger or harm; make safe: *The sandbags secured the town during the flood.* **11.** to effect; make certain of; ensure: *The novel secured his reputation.* **12.** to make firm or fast, as by attaching: *to secure a rope.* **13.** to assure a creditor of payment by the pledge or mortgaging of property. **14.** to lock or fasten against intruders: *Did you secure the doors and windows?* **15.** to protect from attack by taking cover, by building fortifications, etc.: *The regiment secured its position while awaiting the enemy attack.* **16.** to capture (a person or animal): *No one is safe until the murderer is secured.* **17.** to tie up (a person), esp. by binding his arms or hands; pinion: *Secure the prisoner so that he won't escape again.* —*v.i.* **18.** to be or become safe; have or obtain security. **19.** *Naut.* to cover openings and make movable objects fast: *The crew was ordered to secure for sea.* [< L *sēcūr(us)* carefree, equiv. to *sē-* SE- + *cūr(a)* care (see CURE) + *-us* adj. suffix] —**se·cur′a·ble,** *adj.* —**se·cure′ly,** *adv.* —**se·cure′ness,** *n.* —**se·cur′er,** *n.*
—**Syn. 1.** protected. See **safe. 2.** stable, fast, fixed. **7.** confident. **9.** gain. See **get. 10.** protect, guard.

se·cur·i·form (si kyŏŏr′ə fôrm′), *adj. Bot., Zool.* shaped like an ax. [< L *secūri-* (comb. form of *secūris* ax, deriv. of *sec(āre)* (to) cut) + -FORM]

Secu′rities and Exchange′ Commis′sion. See **SEC.**

se·cu·ri·ty (si kyŏŏr′i tē), *n., pl.* **-ties,** *adj.* —*n.* **1.** freedom from danger, risk, etc.; safety. **2.** freedom from care, apprehension, or doubt; well-founded confidence. **3.** something that secures or makes safe; protection; defense. **4.** freedom from financial cares or from want: *The insurance policy gave the widow security.* **5.** precautions taken to guard against theft, sabotage, the stealing of military secrets, etc.: *The senator claimed security was lax and potential enemies know our plans.* **6.** an assurance; guarantee. **7.** *Law.* **a.** something given or deposited as surety for the fulfillment of a promise or an obligation, the payment of a debt, etc. **b.** one who becomes surety for another. **c.** an evidence of debt or of property, as a bond or a certificate of stock. **8.** Usually, **securities.** stocks and bonds. **9.** *Archaic.* overconfidence; cockiness. —*adj.* **10.** of, pertaining to, or serving as security: *The security guard stopped visitors at the gate.*

secu′rity an′alyst, a person who specializes in evaluating information regarding stocks and bonds, as by measuring the ratio of their prices to their dividends and earnings. —**secu′rity anal′ysis.**

Secu′rity Coun′cil, the division of the United Nations charged with maintaining international peace, composed of five permanent members (U.S., Russian Federation, France, United Kingdom, and the People's Republic of China) and ten temporary members, each serving for two years.

sec'y., secretary. Also, **secy.**

Se·da·li·a (si dā′lē ə, -dāl′yə), *n.* a city in central Missouri. 23,874 (1960).

se·dan (si dan′), *n.* **1.** an enclosed automobile body having two or four doors and seating four or more persons on two full-width seats. **2.** See **sedan chair.** [cf. It *sede* seat (< L *sēdēs*)]

Se·dan (si dan′; *Fr.* sə däN′), *n.* a city in NE France, on the Meuse River: defeat and capture of Napoleon III 1870. 21,766 (1962).

sedan′ chair′, an enclosed vehicle for one person, borne on poles by two bearers and common during the 17th and 18th centuries.

Sedan chair

sedan′ clock′, an antique watch hung in a vehicle or sedan chair, having a dial several inches in diameter.

sedan′ cruis′er, a motorboat having a cabin resembling the body of an automobile.

se·date (si dāt′), *adj., v.*, **-dat·ed, -dat·ing.** —*adj.* **1.** calm, quiet, or composed; undisturbed by passion or excitement: *a sedate social gathering; a sedate, well-mannered young lady.* —*v.t.* **2.** to put (a person) under sedation. [< L *sēdāt(us)* (ptp. of *sēdāre* to allay, quieten), equiv. to *sēd-* + *-ātus* -ATE¹] —**se·date′ly,** *adv.* —**se·date′ness,** *n.*
—**Syn. 1.** collected, serene, unruffled, unperturbed. See **staid.**

se·da·tion (si dā′shən), *n. Med.* **1.** the calming of mental excitement or abatement of physiological function, esp. by the administration of a drug. **2.** such an induced state. [< L *sēdātiōn-* (s. of *sēdātiō*), equiv. to *sēdāt(us)* (see SEDATE) + *-iōn-* -ION]

sed·a·tive (sed′ə tiv), *adj.* **1.** tending to calm or soothe. **2.** *Med.* allaying irritability or excitement; assuaging pain; lowering functional activity. —*n.* **3.** a sedative agent or remedy. [< ML *sēdātīv(us)*, equiv. to L *sēdāt-* (see SEDATION) + *-īvus* -IVE]

Sed·don (sed′ən), *n.* **Richard John,** 1845–1906, New Zealand statesman, born in England: prime minister 1893–1906.

Sed·e·ci·as (sed′ə kī′əs), *n. Douay Bible.* Zedekiah.

se de·fen·den·do (sē def′en den′dō), *Law.* defending himself; in self-defense: *homicide committed se defendendo.* [< L]

sed·en·tar·y (sed′ən ter′ē), *adj.* **1.** characterized by or requiring a sitting posture: *a sedentary occupation.* **2.** accustomed to sit or rest a great deal or to take little exercise. **3.** *Chiefly Zool.* **a.** abiding in one place; not migratory. **b.** pertaining to animals that move about little or are permanently attached to something, as a barnacle. [< L *sedentāri(us)* sitting, equiv. to *sedent-* (*sed-* (see SIT) + *-ent-* -ENT) + *-ārius* -ARY] —**sed·en·tar·i·ly** (sed′ən târ′ə lē, sed′ən ter′-), *adv.* —**sed′en·tar′i·ness,** *n.*

Se·der (sā′dər), *n. Judaism.* a ceremonial dinner, held on the first night of Passover by Reform Jews and Jews in Israel or on both the first and second nights by Orthodox and Conservative Jews outside of Israel, that includes the reading of the Haggadah, the eating of specified foods symbolic of the Israelites' bondage in Egypt and of the Exodus, and singing of traditional songs. [< Heb: order, division]

sed-fes·ti·val (sed′fes′tə vəl), *n.* heb-sed.

sedge (sej), *n.* **1.** any rushlike or grasslike cyperaceous plant of the genus *Carex*, growing in wet places. **2.** any cyperaceous plant. **3.** siege (def. 5). [ME *segge*, OE *secg*; akin to *saw*¹; presumably so named from its sawlike edges]

sedged (sejd), *adj.* **1.** made of sedge. **2.** abounding or bordered with sedge: *sedged brooks.* [SEDGE + -ED³]

Sedge·moor (sej′mŏŏr′), *n.* a plain in SW England, in central Somerset: final defeat of Monmouth 1685.

Sedg·wick (sej′wik), *n.* **Ellery,** 1872–1960, U.S. journalist and editor.

sedg·y (sej′ē), *adj.*, **sedg·i·er, sedg·i·est. 1.** abounding, covered, or bordered with sedge. **2.** of or like sedge. [SEDGE + -Y¹]

se·di·le (se dī′lē), *n., pl.* **-dil·i·a** (-dil′ē ə). *Eccles.* one of the seats (usually three) on the south side of the chancel, often recessed, for the use of the officiating clergy. [< L *sedīle* sitting-place, equiv. to *sed(ēre)* (to) sit + *-īle* n. suffix]

sed·i·ment (sed′ə mənt), *n.* **1.** matter that settles to the bottom of a liquid; lees; dregs. **2.** *Geol.* mineral or organic matter deposited by water, air, or ice. [< L *sediment(um)*, equiv. to *sedi-* (comb. form of *sedēre* to sit, settle) + *-mentum* -MENT] —**sed′i·men′tous,** *adj.*

sed·i·men·ta·ry (sed′ə men′tə rē), *adj.* **1.** of, pertaining to, or of the nature of sediment. **2.** *Geol.* formed by the deposition of sediment, as certain rocks. Also, **sed′i·men′tal.** [SEDIMENT + -ARY] —**sed·i·men·tar·i·ly** (sed′ə mən târ′ə lē, sed′ə mən ter′ə lē), *adv.*

sed·i·men·ta·tion (sed′ə mən tā′shən), *n.* the deposition or accumulation of sediment. [SEDIMENT + -ATION]

sed·i·men·tol·o·gy (sed′ə mən tol′ə jē), *n.* the study of sedimentary rocks. [SEDIMENT + -O- + -LOGY] —**sed·i·men·to·log·ic** (sed′ə men′təloj′ik), **sed′i·men′to·log′i·cal,** *adj.* —**sed′i·men·tol′o·gist,** *n.*

sed′iment yeast′. See **bottom yeast.**

se·di·tion (si dish′ən), *n.* **1.** incitement of discontent or rebellion against a government. **2.** any action, esp. in speech or writing, promoting such discontent or rebellion. **3.** *Archaic.* rebellious disorder. [< L *sēditiōn-* (s. of *sēditio*), equiv. to *sēd-* SE- + *-itiōn-* a going (*it(us)*, ptp. of *īre* to go + *-iōn-* -ION); r. ME *sedicioun* < AF < L]
—**Syn. 1.** insurrection, mutiny. See **treason.**

se·di·tion·ar·y (si dish′ə ner′ē), *adj., n., pl.* **-ar·ies.** —*adj.* **1.** of or pertaining to sedition; seditious. —*n.* **2.** one guilty of sedition. [SEDITION + -ARY]

se·di·tious (si dish′əs), *adj.* **1.** of, pertaining to, or of the nature of sedition. **2.** given to or guilty of sedition. [ME *sedicious*, equiv. to *sedici(oun)* SEDITION + *-ous* -OUS; cf. L *sēditiōsus*] —**se·di′tious·ly,** *adv.* —**se·di′tious·ness,** *n.*

Sed·rah (sē drä′; *Eng.* sed′rə), *n., pl.* **Sed·roth** (sē drōt′), *Eng.* **Sed·rahs.** *Hebrew.* Sidrah.

Se·dro-Wool·ley (sē′drō wŏŏl′ē), *n.* a town in NW Washington. 3705 (1960).

se·duce (si dōōs′, -dyōōs′), *v.t.*, **-duced, -duc·ing. 1.** to lead astray, as from duty, rectitude, or the like; corrupt. **2.** to persuade or induce to have sexual intercourse. **3.** to lead or draw away, as from principles, faith, or allegiance: *He was seduced by the prospect of gain.* **4.** to win over; attract; entice: *a supermarket seducing customers with special sales.* [< L *sēdūce(re)* (to) lead aside, equiv. to *sē-* SE- + *dūcere* to lead; r. ME *seduise* < MF < L, as above] —**se·duc′er,** *n.* —**se·duc′i·ble, se·duce′a·ble,** *adj.* —**se·duc′ing·ly,** *adv.* —**se·duc′ive,** *adj.*
—**Syn. 1.** beguile, inveigle, decoy, allure, lure, deceive. See **tempt.** —**Ant. 1.** repel.

se·duc·tion (si duk′shən), *n.* **1.** the act or an instance of seducing, esp. sexually. **2.** the condition of being seduced. **3.** a means of seducing; enticement. Also, **se·duce·ment** (si dōōs′mənt, -dyōōs′-). [< L *sēductiōn-* (s. of *sēductiō*) a leading aside, equiv. to *sēduct(us)* (ptp. of *sēdūcere* to SEDUCE) + *-iōn-* -ION]

se·duc·tive (si duk′tiv), *adj.* enticing; beguiling; captivating: *a seductive smile.* [SEDUCT(ION) + -IVE] —**se·duc′tive·ly,** *adv.* —**se·duc′tive·ness,** *n.*
—**Syn.** tempting, alluring, attractive. —**Ant.** repellent.

se·duc·tress (si duk′tris), *n.* a woman who seduces. [obs. *seduct(o)r* + -ESS]

se·du·li·ty (si dōō′li tē, -dyōō′-), *n.* sedulous quality. [< L *sēdulitās*, equiv. to *sēdul(us)* SEDULOUS + *-itās* -ITY]

sed·u·lous (sej′ə ləs), *adj.* **1.** diligent in application or attention; persevering. **2.** persistently or carefully maintained: *sedulous flattery.* [< L *sēdulus* careful (OL *sē dolō* without guile); r. *sedulious.* See SEDULI(TY), -OUS] —**sed′u·lous·ly,** *adv.* —**sed′u·lous·ness,** *n.*
—**Syn. 1.** assiduous, constant, untiring, tireless.

se·dum (sē′dəm), *n.* any fleshy, crassulaceous plant of the genus *Sedum*, usually having yellow, white, or pink flowers. [< NL < L: houseleek]

see¹ (sē), *v.*, **saw, seen, see·ing.** —*v.t.* **1.** to perceive with the eyes; look at. **2.** to view; visit or attend as a spectator: *to see a play.* **3.** to perceive (things) mentally; discern; understand: *He could see the point of the argument.* **4.** to construct a mental image of: *He still saw his father as he was 25 years ago.* **5.** to accept or imagine or suppose as acceptable: *I can't see him as president.* **6.** to be cognizant of; recognize: *He was able to see charming traits in not-so-charming people. Can you see where the mistake is?* **7.** to foresee: *He could see war ahead.* **8.** to ascertain, learn, or find out: *See who is at the door. Look over my work and see what I'm doing wrong.* **9.** to have knowledge or experience of: *to see service in the foreign corps.* **10.** to make sure: *See that the work is done.* **11.** to meet and converse with: *Are you seeing him at lunch today?* **12.** to receive as a visitor: *The ambassador finally saw him.* **13.** to visit: *He finally saw the ambassador. I'll see you at your house tonight.* **14.** to court, keep company with, or date frequently: *She's seeing too much of the same boy.* **15.** to provide aid or assistance to; provide money, sympathy, encouragement, etc., to: *He's seeing his brother through college.* **16.** to attend or escort: *to see someone home.* **17.** *Cards.* to match (a bet) or match the bet of (a bettor) by staking an equal sum: *I'll see your five and raise you five more.* **18.** to prefer (someone or something) to be as indicated (usually used as a mild oath): *I'll see you in hell before I sell you this house. He'll see the business fail before he admits he's wrong about advertising.* **19.** to read. —*v.i.* **20.** to have the power of sight. **21.** to understand intellectually or spiritually; have insight: *The philosopher probes the meaning of life and teaches mankind to see.* **22.** to give attention or care: *See to it that the work is done.* **23.** to find out; make inquiry: *Go and see for yourself.* **24.** to consider; think; deliberate: *Let me see—how does that song go?* **25.** to look about; observe: *See—the sun is out!* **26. see about, a.** to investigate; inquire about. **b.** to turn one's attention to; take care of: *He said he would see about getting the license plates.* **27. see after,** to attend to; take care of: *Will you please see after my plants while I'm away?* **28. see off,** to take leave of someone setting out on a journey; accompany to the place of departure: *I went to the airport to see him off.* **29. see out,** to remain with (a task, project, etc.) until its completion: *We decided to see it out, even if it meant another year.* **30. see through, a.** to penetrate to the true nature of; comprehend; detect: *He could see through her fine ways.* **b.** to stay with to the end or until completion; persevere: *It is a mark of maturity to be able to see a difficult situation through.* [ME < OE *sēon*; c. G *sehen*, Goth *saihwan*, D *zien*, Icel *sjá*] —**see′a·ble,** *adj.* —**see′a·ble·ness,** *n.*
—**Syn. 1.** observe, notice, distinguish, discern, behold, regard. See **watch. 3.** comprehend, penetrate. **8.** determine. **9.** know, undergo. **16.** accompany.

see² (sē), *n. Eccles.* the seat, center of authority, office, or jurisdiction of a bishop. [ME *se(e)* < OF *se* (var. of *sie*) < L *sēd(ēs)* seat]

See′beck effect′ (sē′bek; *Ger.* zā′bek), *Physics.* See **thermoelectric effect.** [named after Thomas J. Seebeck (1770–1831), German physicist]

see·catch (sē′kach′), *n.* the adult male of the fur seal, *Callorhinus alascanus*, of Alaska. [< Russ *sekach*]

seed (sēd), *n., pl.* **seeds,** (*esp. collectively*) **seed,** *v.* —*n.* **1.** the fertilized, matured ovule of a flowering plant, containing an embryo or rudimentary plant. **2.** any propagative part of a plant, including tubers, bulbs, etc., esp. as preserved for growing a new crop. See diag. under **cotyledon, plumule. 3.** such parts collectively. **4.** any similar small part or fruit. **5.** the germ or propagative source of anything: *the seeds of discord.* **6.** offspring; progeny. **7.** birth: *not of mortal seed.* **8.** sperm; semen. **9.** the ovum or ova of certain animals, as the lobster and the silkworm moth. **10.** See **seed oyster. 11.** a small air bubble in a glass piece, caused by defective firing. **12. go** or **run to seed, a.** (of the flower of a plant) to pass to the stage of yielding seed. **b.** to lose vigor, power, or prosperity; deteriorate: *It is shocking how he has gone to seed in the last few years.* **13. in seed, a.** (of certain plants) in the state of bearing ripened seeds. **b.** (of a field, a lawn, etc.) sewn with seed. —*v.t.* **14.** to sow (a field, lawn, etc.) with seed. **15.** to sow or scatter (seed). **16.** to sow or scatter (clouds) with crystals or particles of silver iodide, solid carbon dioxide, etc., to induce precipitation. **17.** to remove the seeds from (fruit). **18.** *Sports.* **a.** to arrange (the drawings for positions in a tournament) so that ranking players or teams will not meet in the early rounds of play. **b.** to distribute (ranking players or teams) in this manner. **—***v.i.* **19.** to sow seed. **20.** to produce or shed seed. [ME; OE *sēd, sǣd;* c. G *Saat,* Icel *sāth,* Goth *-seths;* akin to sow[1]] **—seed′less,** *adj.* **—seed′less·ness,** *n.* **—seed′like′,** *adj.*

seed·bed (sēd′bed′), *n.* **1.** land prepared for seeding. **2.** a plot of ground where young plants are grown before transplanting. [SEED + BED]

seed′ bee′tle, any of several beetles of the family *Bruchidae* that infest the seeds of legumes. Also called **seed weevil.**

seed·cake (sēd′kāk′), *n.* a sweet cake containing aromatic seeds, usually caraway. [SEED + CAKE]

seed′ cap′sule, *Bot.* the ripened walls of the ovary.

seed·case (sēd′kās′), *n.* a seed capsule; pericarp. [SEED + CASE[2]]

seed′ coat′, *Bot.* the outer integument of a seed.

seed′ corn′, ears or kernels of corn set apart as seed.

seed·er (sē′dər), *n.* **1.** one who or that which seeds. **2.** any of various apparatus for sowing seeds in the ground, ranging from simple devices that deposit seed evenly over a plot of land to complex machines that prepare a hole in the earth, insert a seed or seeds at the proper depth, and cover the hole again. **3.** a plant that produces many seeds, esp. one grown mainly to produce seeds for growing other plants. **4.** a device or utensil for removing seeds, as from grapefruit. **5.** a device used to scatter particles of silver iodide, carbon dioxide, etc., in clouds to induce precipitation. [ME *sedere,* OE *sǣdere.* See SEED, -ER[1]]

seed′ leaf′, *Bot.* a cotyledon.

seed·ling (sēd′ling), *n.* **1.** a plant or tree grown from a seed. **2.** a tree not yet three feet high. **3.** any young plant, esp. one grown in a nursery for transplanting. [SEED + -LING[1]]

seed·man (sēd′mən), *n., pl.* **-men.** seedsman. [SEED + MAN[1]]

seed′ oil′ cake′. See **cotton cake.**

seed′ oy′ster, a very young oyster, esp. one used in cultivation and transplantation.

seed′ pearl′, a pearl weighing less than ¼ grain.

seed′ plant′, a seed-bearing plant; spermatophyte.

seeds·man (sēdz′mən), *n., pl.* **-men. 1.** a sower of seed. **2.** a dealer in seed. Also, **seedman.** [SEED + 'S[1] + MAN[1]]

seed-snipe (sēd′snīp′), *n.* any of several South American birds of the family *Thinocoridae,* related to the shore birds but superficially resembling the quail.

seed·time (sēd′tīm′), *n.* the season for sowing seed. [ME; OE *sǣdtīma.* See SEED, TIME]

seed′ ves′sel, *Bot.* a pericarp.

seed′ wee′vil. See **seed beetle.**

seed·y (sē′dē), *adj.,* **seed·i·er, seed·i·est. 1.** abounding in seed. **2.** containing many seeds, as a piece of fruit. **3.** gone to seed; bearing seeds. **4.** poorly kept; run-down; shabby. **5.** shabbily dressed; unkempt: *a seedy old tramp.* **6.** physically run-down; under the weather: *He has felt a bit seedy since his operation.* **7.** somewhat disreputable; degraded: *a seedy hotel.* [SEED + -Y[1]] **—seed′i·ly,** *adv.* **—seed′i·ness,** *n.*

See·ger (sē′gər), *n.* **1. Alan,** 1888–1916, U.S. poet. **2. Peter** (*Pete*), born 1919, U.S. folk singer and folklorist.

see·ing (sē′ing), *conj.* in view of the fact that; considering; inasmuch as. [SEE[1] + -ING[2]] **—see′ing·ly,** *adv.* **—see′ing·ness,** *n.*

See′ing Eye′ dog′, a dog that has been especially trained to lead or guide a blind person in walking about. [named after the *Seeing Eye* organization in Morristown, New Jersey]

see′ing glass′, *Brit. Dial.* a looking glass; mirror.

seek (sēk), *v.,* **sought, seek·ing.** **—***v.t.* **1.** to go in search or quest of: *to seek the truth.* **2.** to try to find or discover by searching or questioning: *to seek the solution to a problem.* **3.** to try to obtain: *to seek fame.* **4.** to try or attempt (usually fol. by an infinitive): *to seek to convince a person.* **5.** to go to: *to seek a place to rest.* **6.** to ask for; request: *to seek advice.* **7.** *Archaic.* to search or explore. **—***v.i.* **8.** to make inquiry. **9. be sought after,** to be desired or in demand: *Graduates in the physical sciences are most sought after by employers these days.* [ME *seke,* OE *sēca(n);* c. Icel *sækja,* G *suchen,* Goth *sōkjan,* L *sāgīre*]
—Syn. 3. pursue, follow.

seek·er (sē′kər), *n.* **1.** one who or that which seeks. **2.** *Rocketry.* **a.** a device in a missile which locates a target by sensing some characteristic of the target, as heat emission. **b.** a missile equipped with such a device. [ME; see SEEK, -ER[1]]

seel (sēl), *v.t.* **1.** *Falconry.* to sew shut (the eyes of a falcon) during parts of its training. **2.** *Archaic.* **a.** to close (the eyes). **b.** to blind. [ME *sile(n)* < MF *siller(r), cille(r),* deriv. of *cil* eyelash < L *cil(ium)* eyelid, eyelash; see CILIA]

See·land (sē′lənd), *n.* Zealand.

See·li·ger (sā′lə gər), *n.* a crater in the fourth quadrant of the face of the moon: about 6 miles in diameter.

see·ly (sē′lē), *adj. Archaic.* insignificant or feeble; poor. [ME *sely,* OE *sælig* happy, equiv. to *sæl* happiness + *-ig* -Y[1]; c. D *zalig,* G *selig;* akin to Icel *sæll,* Goth *sēls* good, OE *sēl* better; see SILLY] **—see′li·ly,** *adv.*

seem (sēm), *v.i.* **1.** to appear to be, feel, do, etc.: *She seems better this morning.* **2.** to appear to one's own senses, mind, observation, judgment, etc.: *I seem to hear someone calling.* **3.** to appear to exist: *There seems no need to go now.* **4.** to appear to be true, probable, or evident: *It seems likely to rain.* **5.** to give the outward appearance of being or to pretend to be: *He only seems friendly because he wants you to like him.* [ME *seme* < Scand; cf. Icel *sæma* (impersonal) befit]
—Syn. 4. SEEM, APPEAR, LOOK refer to an outward aspect which may or may not be contrary to reality. SEEM is applied to that which has an aspect of truth and probability: *It seems warmer today.* APPEAR suggests the giving of an impression which may be superficial or illusory: *The house appears to be deserted.* LOOK more vividly suggests the use of the eye (literally or figuratively) or the aspect as perceived by the eye: *She looked very much frightened.*

seem·er (sē′mər), *n.* a person who constantly pretends: *The party was filled with seemers.* [SEEM + -ER[1]]

seem·ing (sē′ming), *adj.* **1.** apparent; appearing, whether truly or falsely, to be as specified: *a seeming advantage.* **—***n.* **2.** appearance, esp. outward or deceptive appearance. [SEEM + -ING[2], -ING[1]] **—seem′ing·ly,** *adv.* **—seem′ing·ness,** *n.*
—Syn. 1. ostensible, external, superficial. **2.** semblance, face, pretense.

seem·ly (sēm′lē), *adj.,* **-li·er, -li·est,** *adv.* **—***adj.* **1.** fitting or becoming with respect to propriety or good taste; decent; decorous: *Her outburst of rage was hardly seemly.* **2.** suitable or appropriate; fitting: *Sending flowers would be a seemly gesture.* **3.** of pleasing appearance; handsome. **—***adv.* **4.** in a seemly manner; fittingly; becomingly. [ME *semeli* < Scand; cf. Icel *sæmilegr* becoming] **—seem′li·ness,** *n.*
—Syn. 1, 2. right, proper, appropriate, meet.

seen (sēn), *v.* pp. of **see**[1].

seep[1] (sēp), *v.i.* **1.** to pass, flow, or ooze gradually through a porous substance: *Water seeps through cracks in the wall.* **2.** (of ideas, methods, etc.) to enter or be introduced at a slow pace: *The new ideas finally seeped down to the lower echelons.* **3.** to become diffused; permeate: *Fog seeped through the trees, obliterating everything.* **—***n.* **4.** moisture that seeps out; seepage. **5.** a small spring, pool, or other place where liquid from the ground has oozed to the surface of the earth. [? var. of dial. *sipe* < OE *sīp(ian);* c. MLG *sīpen*]

seep[2] (sēp), *n.* a jeep equipped for amphibious service. [b. SEA + JEEP]

seep·age (sē′pij), *n.* **1.** the act or process of seeping; leakage. **2.** something that seeps or leaks out. **3.** a quantity that has seeped out. [SEEP[1] + -AGE]

seep·y (sē′pē), *adj.,* **seep·i·er, seep·i·est.** (esp. of ground, a plot of land, or the like) soaked or oozing with water; not drained. [SEEP[1] + -Y[1]]

se·er[1] (sē′ər *for 1;* sēr *for 2-4*), *n.* **1.** a person who sees; observer. **2.** a person who prophesies future events; prophet: *The industry seers predicted doom for the merger.* **3.** a person who is endowed with profound moral and spiritual insight or knowledge; a wise man or sage who possesses intuitive powers. **4.** a person who is reputed to have special powers of divination, as a crystal-gazer, palmist, etc. [SEE[1] + -ER[1]]

seer[2] (sēr, sâr), *n.* ser.

seer·ess (sēr′is), *n.* a female seer. [SEER[1] + -ESS]

seer·suck·er (sēr′suk′ər), *n.* a plainwoven cotton, rayon, or linen fabric, traditionally striped cotton with alternate stripes crinkled in the weaving. [< Hindi *sīrsakar* < Pers *shīr o shakkar* milk and sugar]

see·saw (sē′sô′), *n.* **1.** a recreation in which two children alternately ride up and down when seated at opposite ends of a plank balanced at the middle. **2.** a plank or apparatus for this recreation. **3.** an up-and-down or a back-and-forth movement or procedure. **4.** *Whist.* a crossruff. **—***adj.* **5.** moving up and down, back and forth, or alternately ahead and behind: *It was a seesaw game with the lead changing hands many times.* **—***v.t., v.i.* **6.** to move or cause to move in a seesaw manner: *The boat seesawed in the heavy sea.* [gradational compound based on SAW[1]]

seethe (sēth), *v.,* **seethed** or (*Obs.*) **sod; seethed** or (*Obs.*) **sod·den** or **sod; seeth·ing,** *n.* **—***v.t.* **1.** to soak or steep. **2.** to cook by boiling or stewing; boil. **—***v.i.* **3.** to boil. **4.** to surge or foam as if boiling. **5.** to be in a state of agitation or excitement. **—***n.* **6.** the act of seething. **7.** the state of being agitated or excited. [ME; OE *sēopan;* c. G *sieden,* Sw *sjuda,* etc.] **—seeth′ing·ly,** *adv.*
—Syn. 1. saturate. **4.** froth. **5.** See **boil**[1].

Seeth′ing Bay′. See **Sinus Aestuum.**

see-through (sē′thro͞o′), *n.* look-through. [n. use of v. phrase *see through*]

Se·fe·ri·a·des (se fe′rē ä′thes), *n.* **Gior·gos Sty·lia·nou** (yôr′gôs stē′lyä no͞o′), (*Giorgos Seferis*), born 1900, Greek poet and former diplomat: Nobel prize for literature 1963.

Se·fer To·rah (sā fer′ tō rä′; *Eng.* sā′fər tôr′ə, tôr′ə), *pl.* **Si·frei To·rah** (sē frā′ tō rä′), *Eng.* **Sefer Torahs.** *Hebrew.* See **Sepher Torah.**

se·gar (si gär′), *n.* cigar.

Se′ger cone′ (zā′gər, sā′-), a pyrometric cone composed of clay and salt. [named after Hermann A. *Segar* (d. 1893), German ceramist]

Se·ges·ta (si jes′tə), *n. Class. Myth.* Egesta.

seg·gar (seg′ər), *n., v.t.* sagger.

Se·ghers (zā′gərz), *n.* **An·na** (ä′nä), (*Netty Radvanyi*), born 1900, German novelist.

seg·ment (*n.* seg′mənt; *v.* seg ment′), *n.* **1.** one of the parts into which something naturally separates or is divided; a division, portion, or section: *a segment of an orange.* **2.** *Geom.* **a.** a part cut off from a figure, esp. a circular or spherical one, by a line or plane, as a part of a circular area contained by an arc and its chord or by two parallel lines or planes. **b.** a finite section of a line. **3.** *Zool.* **a.** any of the rings that compose the body of an annelid or arthropod. **b.** one of the sections of an arthropod appendage between the joints. **4.** an object, as a machine part, having the form of a segment or sector of a circle. **5.** an arclike support on which the typebars of a typewriter rest when not in use. **—***v.t., v.i.* **6.** to separate or divide into segments. [< L *segment(um),* equiv. to *seg-* (var. of *sec-,* root of *secāre* to cut) + *-mentum* -MENT] **—seg·men·tar·y** (seg′mən ter′ē), *adj.* **—seg′men·tate′,** *adj.*
—Syn. 1. See **part.**

seg·men·tal (seg men′tᵊl), *adj.* **1.** of, pertaining to, or characterized by segments or segmentation. **2.** *Linguistics.* noting or pertaining to sequential speech: *segmental phonemes.* [SEGMENT + -AL[1]] **—seg·men′tal·ly,** *adv.*

seg·men·tal·ize (seg men′tᵊlīz′), *v.t.,* **-ized, -iz·ing.** to make segmentalized. [SEGMENTAL + -IZE] **—seg·men′tal·i·za′tion,** *n.*

seg·men·tal·ized (seg men′tᵊlīzd′), *adj.* separated into parts, sections, elements, classes, etc.; compartmentalized: *a segmentalized society.* [SEGMENTALIZE + -ED[2]]

segmen′tal saw′, a circular saw having teeth set in detachable and replaceable units.

seg·men·ta·tion (seg′mən tā′shən), *n.* **1.** division into segments. **2.** *Biol.* **a.** the subdivision of an organism or of an organ into more or less equivalent parts. **b.** cell division. [SEGMENT + -ATION]

segmenta′tion cav′ity, *Embryol.* blastocoele.

Seg·ner (seg′nər), *n.* a crater in the third quadrant of the face of the moon: about 45 miles in diameter.

Se·gni (se′nyē), *n.* **An·to·nio** (än tô′nyô), born 1891, Italian teacher, lawyer, and statesman: president, 1962–64.

se·gno (sān′yō, sen′yō; *It.* se′nyô), *n., pl.* **se·gni** (sān′yē, sen′yē; *It.* se′nyē). *Music.* **1.** a sign. **2.** a sign or mark at the beginning or end of a section to be repeated. [< It < L *sign(um)* a sign]

se·go (sē′gō), *n., pl.* **-gos.** See **sego lily.** [< Paiute *(pa)sigo*]

se′go lil′y, **1.** a liliaceous plant, *Calochortus Nuttallii,* of the western U.S., having showy, bell-shaped flowers: the State flower of Utah. **2.** its edible root.

Se·gor (sē′gər), *n. Douay Bible.* Zoar.

Se·go·vi·a (sə gō′vē ə; *Sp.* se gô′vyä), *n.* **1. An·drés** (än drės′), 1893–1987, Spanish guitarist. **2.** a city in central Spain: well-preserved Roman aqueduct. 30,875 (1950).

Se·grè (sə grā′; *It.* se gre′), *n.* **E·mi·li·o** (ə mē′lē ō′, ə mēl′yō; *It.* e mē′lyô), born 1905, U.S. chemist, born in Italy: Nobel prize 1959.

seg·re·ant (seg′rē ənt), *adj. Heraldry.* (of a griffin) rampant. [?]

seg·re·gate (*v.* seg′rə gāt′; *n.* seg′rə git, -gāt′), *v.,* **-gat·ed, -gat·ing,** *n.* **—***v.t.* **1.** to separate or set apart from others or from the main body or group; isolate: *to segregate exceptional children; to segregate hardened criminals.* **2.** to require, often with force, the separation of (a specific racial, religious, or other group) from the general body of society. **—***v.i.* **3.** to separate, withdraw, go apart; separate from the main body and collect in one place; become segregated. **4.** to practice, require, or enforce segregation, esp. racial segregation. **5.** *Genetics.* (of allelic genes) to separate during meiosis. **—***n.* **6.** a segregated thing, person, or group. [ME *segregat* < L *sēgregāt(us)* (ptp. of *sēgregāre* to part from the flock), equiv. to *sē-* SE- + *greg-* (base of *grex* flock) + *-ātus* -ATE[1]; see GREGARIOUS] **—seg·re·ga·ble** (seg′rə gə bəl), *adj.* **—seg′re·ga′tive,** *adj.*
—Ant. 1. integrate

seg·re·gat·ed (seg′rə gā′tid), *adj.* **1.** characterized by or practicing racial segregation: *a segregated school system.* **2.** restricted to one group, esp. exclusively on the basis of racial or ethnic membership: *segregated clubs; segregated neighborhoods.* **3.** maintaining separate facilities for members of different, esp. racially different, groups: *segregated education; segregated buses.* **4.** discriminating against a group, esp. on the basis of race: *segregated economy; segregated zoning laws.* [SEGREGATE + -ED[2]] **—seg′re·gat′ed·ly,** *adv.* **—seg′re·gat′ed·ness,** *n.*

seg·re·ga·tion (seg′rə gā′shən), *n.* **1.** the act or practice of segregating. **2.** the state or condition of being segregated: *Segregation was most evident in the wealthier parts of the town.* **3.** something segregated. **4.** *Genetics.* the separation of allelic genes in different gametes during meiosis, resulting in the separation of their characters in the progeny. [< LL *sēgregātiōn-* (s. of *sēgregātiō*), equiv. to *sēgregāt(us)* (see SEGREGATE) + *-iōn-* -ION] **—seg′re·ga′tion·al,** *adj.*

seg·re·ga·tion·ist (seg′rə gā′shə nist), *n.* one who favors, encourages, or practices segregation, esp. racial segregation. [SEGREGATION + -IST]

seg·re·ga·tor (seg′rə gā′tər), *n. Med.* an instrument for collecting the urine excreted by one kidney only. [SEGREGATE + -OR[2]]

se·gue (sā′gwā, seg′wā), *v.,* **-gued, -gue·ing,** *n., adj., adv. Music.* **—***v.i.* **1.** to continue at once with the next section or composition. **—***n.* **2.** an uninterrupted transition made between one musical section or composition and another. **—***adj., adv.* (of a musical section or composition) **3.** performed at once without a break. **4.** performed in the manner or style of the preceding section. [< It: (there) follows, 3rd pers. sing. pres. ind. of *seguire* < L *sequī* to follow. See SUE]

se·gui·dil·la (sā′gə dēl′yə, -dē′yə, seg′ə-; *Sp.* se′gē-dē′lyä), *n., pl.* **-dil·las** (-dēl′yəz, -dē′yəz; *Sp.* -dē′lyäs). **1.** *Pros.* a stanza of four to seven lines with a distinctive rhythmic pattern. **2.** a Spanish dance in triple meter for two persons. **3.** the music for this dance. [< Sp, equiv. to *seguid(a)* sequence + *-illa* dim. suffix; *seguida,* equiv. to *segui-* (s. of *seguir* < L *sequī* to follow) + *-da* < L *-ta* fem. ptp. suffix]

Se·gu·ra (se go͞o′rä), *n.* **Fran·cis·co** (frän sēs′kô), ("*Pancho*"), born 1921, Ecuadorian tennis player.

Seh′na knot′ (sen′ə), a hand-tied knot, used in rug weaving, in which the ends of yarn looped around a warp thread appear at each of the interstices between adjacent threads and produce a compact and relatively even pile effect. Also, **Senna knot.** Also called **Persian knot.** Cf. **Ghiordes knot.** [var. of *Sinneh,* name of Persian town]

sei (sā), *n.* See **sei whale.**

sei·cen·to (sā chen′tō; *It.* se chen′tô), *n.* (*often cap.*) the 17th century, with reference to the Italian art or literature of that period. [< It: short for *mille seicento,* lit., a thousand six hundred]

seiche (sāsh), *n.* an occasional and sudden oscillation of the water of a lake, bay, estuary, etc., causing fluctuations in the water level and caused by wind, earthquakes, changes in barometric pressure, etc. [< SwissF]

sei·del (sīd′ᵊl, zīd′-), *n.* a large beer mug, often having a hinged lid. [< G < MHG *sīdel* < L *situl(a)* bucket]

Seid′litz pow′ders (sed′lits), a mild laxative consisting of two powders, tartaric acid and a mixture of sodium bicarbonate and Rochelle salt, which are dissolved separately, mixed, and drunk after effervescence. [arbitrarily named after Bohemian village]

seif (sāf, sīf), *n.* a long narrow sand dune parallel to the prevailing wind direction. [< Ar *saif* sword]

Seif′-al-Is′lam Moham′med al Badr′ (sīf′äl-is′läm, sīf′-; äl bä′dər), born 1926, imam of Yemen since 1962.

sei·gneur (sēn yûr′; *Fr.* se nyœr′), *n., pl.* **sei·gneurs** (sēn yûrz′; *Fr.* se nyœr′). (*sometimes cap.*) **1.** a feudal lord. **2.** (in Canada) a member of the landed gentry. [< F < VL *senior* lord. See SENIOR]

seign·ior (sēn′yər), *n.* (*sometimes cap.*) **1.** a lord; ruler. **2.** the lord of a manor; gentleman: formerly used as a title of respect. [ME *segnour* < AF; see SEIGNEUR]

seign·ior·age (sēn′yər ij), *n.* **1.** something claimed by a sovereign or superior as a prerogative. **2.** a charge on bullion brought to the mint to be coined. **3.** the difference between the cost of the bullion plus minting expenses and the value as money of the pieces coined, constituting a source of government revenue. Also, **seign′or·age.** [ME *seigneurage* < MF; see SEIGNEUR, -AGE]

seign·ior·y (sēn′yə rē), *n.*, *pl.* **-ior·ies. 1.** the power or authority of a seignior. **2.** *Hist.* a lord's domain. Also, **signory.** [ME *seignorie* < OF; see SEIGNEUR, -Y[3]]

sei·gno·ri·al (sēn yōr′ē əl, -yôr′-), *adj.* of or pertaining to a seignior. Also, **seign·ior·al** (sēn′yər əl), **sei·gnio·ri·al** (sēn yōr′ē əl, -yôr′-), **seign·or·al** (sēn′yər əl). [*seignor* (var. of SEIGNIOR) + -IAL]

seine (sān), *n.*, *v.*, **seined, sein·ing.** —*n.* **1.** a fishing net that hangs vertically in the water, having floats at the upper edge and sinkers at the lower. —*v.t.* **2.** to fish for or catch with a seine. **3.** to use a seine in (water). —*v.i.* **4.** to fish with a seine. [ME *seyne*, OE *segne*, deriv. of pre-E **sagīna* < L *sagēna* < Gk *sagḗnē* fishing net]

Seine (sān; *Fr.* sen), *n.* **1.** a river in France, flowing NW through Paris to the English Channel. 480 mi. long. **2.** a department in N France. 5,646,446 (1962); 185 sq. mi. *Cap.:* Paris.

Seine-et-Marne (sān′ā märn′; *Fr.* sen ā MARN′), *n.* a department in N France. 524,486 (1962); 2290 sq. mi. *Cap.:* Melun.

Seine-et-Oise (sen ā WAZ′), *n.* a department in N France. 2,298,931 (1962); 2185 sq. mi. *Cap.:* Versailles.

Seine-In·fé·rieure (sen AN fā RYŒR′), *n.* former name of **Seine-Maritime.**

Seine-Ma·ri·time (sen mä RE tēm′), *n.* a department in NW France. 1,035,844 (1962); 2449 sq. mi. *Cap.:* Rouen. Formerly, **Seine-Inférieure.**

sein·er (sā′nər), *n.* **1.** a fisherman who uses a seine. **2.** a boat used in fishing with a seine. [SEINE + -ER[1]]

sei·ren (sī′rin), *n.* *Heraldry.* a mermaid. Also, **siren.** [var. of SIREN]

seise (sēz), *v.*, **seised, seis·ing.** —*v.t.* **1.** *Chiefly Brit.* seize. **2.** *Law.* seize (def. 6). —*v.i.* **3.** *Chiefly Brit.* seize. —**seis′a·ble,** *adj.* —**seis′er,** *n.*

Sei·shin (sā shēn′), *n.* Japanese name of **Chongjin.**

sei·sin (sē′zin), *n.* *Law.* seizin.

seis·ing (sē′zing), *n.* *Chiefly Brit.* seizing.

seism (sī′zəm, -səm), *n.* an earthquake. [< Gk *seismó(s)*, equiv. to *seí(ein)* (to) shake, quake + *-(i)smos* -ISM]

seis·mic (sīz′mik, sīs′-), *adj.* pertaining to, of the nature of, or caused by an earthquake. Also, **seis′mal, seis′mi·cal.** [SEISM + -IC] —**seis′mi·cal·ly,** *adv.*

seis·mic·i·ty (sīz mis′i tē, sīs-), *n.*, *pl.* **-ties.** the frequency, intensity, and distribution of earthquakes in a given area. [SEISMIC + -ITY]

seis·mism (sīz′miz əm, sīs′-), *n.* the natural activity or group of phenomena associated with earthquakes. [SEISM + -ISM]

seismo-, a combining form of **seism:** *seismograph.*

seis·mo·gram (sīz′mə gram′, sīs′-), *n.* a record made by a seismograph. [SEISMO- + -GRAM[1]]

seis·mo·graph (sīz′mə graf′, -gräf′, sīs′-), *n.* any of various instruments for measuring and recording the vibrations of earthquakes. [SEISMO- + -GRAPH] —**seis·mo·graph·ic** (sīz′mə graf′ik, sīs′-), **seis′mo·graph′i·cal,** *adj.*

seis·mog·ra·phy (sīz mog′rə fē, sīs-), *n.* **1.** the scientific measuring and recording of the shock and vibrations of earthquakes. **2.** seismology. [SEISMO- + -GRAPHY] —**seis·mog′ra·pher,** *n.*

seismol., 1. seismological. **2.** seismology.

seis·mol·o·gy (sīz mol′ə jē, sīs-), *n.* the science or study of earthquakes and their phenomena. Also called **seismography.** [SEISMO- + -LOGY] —**seis·mo·log·ic** (sīz′mə loj′ik, sīs′-), **seis′mo·log′i·cal,** *adj.* —**seis′-mo·log′i·cal·ly,** *adv.* —**seis·mol′o·gist,** *n.*

seis·mom·e·ter (sīz mom′i tər, sīs-), *n.* a seismograph equipped for measuring the direction, intensity, and duration of earthquakes by measuring the actual movement of the ground. [SEISMO- + -METER] —**seis·mo·met·ric** (sīz′mə me′trik, sīs′-), **seis′mo·met′ri·cal,** *adj.* —**seis·mom′et·ry,** *n.*

seis·mo·scope (sīz′mə skōp′, sīs′-), *n.* an instrument for recording the occurrence of an earthquake. [SEISMO- + -SCOPE] —**seis·mo·scop·ic** (sīz′mə skop′ik, sīs′-), *adj.*

Seis·tan (sās tän′), *n.* (in eastern Iran or Afghanistan) a strong wind blowing from the north or north, west during the summer months, sometimes attaining gale force. Also called **bad-i-sad-o-bistroz, wind of 120 days.** [after *Seistan*, the region where it blows]

sei·sure (sē′zhər), *n.* *Chiefly Brit.* seizure.

sei′ whale′ (sā), a rorqual, *Balaenoptera borealis*, found in all seas. [< Norw *seihval*, equiv. to *sei* (Icel *seithr*) coalfish + *hval* WHALE]

seize (sēz), *v.*, **seized, seiz·ing.** —*v.t.* **1.** to take hold of suddenly or forcibly; grasp: *to seize a weapon.* **2.** to grasp mentally; understand clearly and completely: *to seize an idea.* **3.** to take possession of by force or at will: *to seize enemy ships.* **4.** to take possession or control of as if by suddenly laying hold: *Panic seized the crowd.* **5.** to take possession of by legal authority; confiscate: *to seize smuggled goods.* **6.** Also, **seise.** *Law.* to put in seizin or legal possession of. **7.** to capture; take into custody. **8.** to take advantage of promptly: *to seize an opportunity.* **9.** *Naut.* to bind or fasten together with a seizing. —*v.i.* **10.** to grab or take hold suddenly or forcibly (usually fol. by *on* or *upon*): *to seize on a rope.* **11.** to resort to a method, plan, etc., in desperation (usually fol. by *on* or *upon*): *He must seize on a solution, however risky.* Also, *esp. Brit.*, **seise.** [ME *saise(n)*, *seise(n)* < OF *saisi(r)* < ML *sacire* to place < Frankish cognate of Goth *satjan* to SET, put, place] —**seiz′a·ble,** *adj.* —**seiz′er;** *Law.* **sei·zor** (sē′zər, -zôr), *n.*
—**Syn. 1.** clutch, grab. **7.** arrest, apprehend, take. See **catch.** —**Ant. 7.** release.

seize quar·tiers (sez′ kär tyā′), *Heraldry.* the status of one whose great-great-grandparents were all armigerous. [< F: sixteen quarters]

sei·zin (sē′zin), *n.* *Law.* **1.** (originally) possession of either land or chattel. **2.** the kind of possession or right to possession characteristic of estates of freehold. Also, **seisin.** [ME < OF *saisine*, equiv. to *sais(ir)* (to) SEIZE + *-ine* -INE[2]]

seiz·ing (sē′zing), *n.* **1.** the act of one who or that which seizes. **2.** *Naut.* a means of binding or fastening together two objects, as two ropes or parts of the same rope, by a number of longitudinal and transverse turns of marline, wire, or other small stuff. Also, *esp. Brit.*, **seising.** [SEIZE + -ING[1]]

Seizing (def. 2)

seiz′ing stuff′, *Naut.* **1.** tarred hemp small stuff, ordinarily right-laid from three strands of from two to four threads each. **2.** any tarred or waxed small stuff suitable for various seizings. **3.** wire small stuff of from $\frac{1}{16}$ to $\frac{1}{4}$ of an inch in diameter.

sei·zure (sē′zhər), *n.* **1.** the act or an instance of seizing. **2.** a taking possession of an item, property, or person legally or by force. **3.** a sudden attack, as of epilepsy or some other disease. Also, *esp. Brit.*, **seisure.** [SEIZE + -URE]

se·jant (sē′jənt), *adj.* *Heraldry.* (of an animal) represented in a sitting posture: *a lion sejant.* Also, **se′jeant.** [var. of *seiante* < AF < MF *seant*, equiv. to *se-* (root of *seoir* < L *sedēre* to sit) + *-ant* -ANT]

se·jant-e·rect (sē′jənt i rekt′), *adj.* *Heraldry.* (of an animal) represented as seated upright with forelegs raised: *a lion sejant-erect.* Also, **se′jeant-e·rect′.**

Se·ja·nus (si jā′nəs), *n.* **1. Lucius Ae·li·us** (ē′lē əs), d. A.D. 31, Roman politician, commander of praetorian guard, and conspirator in the reign of Emperor Tiberius. **2.** (*italics*) a tragedy (1603) by Ben Jonson.

Sejm (sām), *n.* the unicameral parliament of Poland. [< Pol: assembly]

Sekh·met (sek′met), *n.* *Egyptian Myth.* a bloodthirsty goddess, sometimes identified with Hathor, who attempted to destroy mankind. [< Egypt]

se·kos (sē′kos), *n.* **1.** (in ancient Greece) **a.** a sanctuary. **b.** the cella of a temple. **2.** any of various other shrines or sanctuaries. Also, **secos.** [< Gk *sēkós* enclosed area]

sel (sel), *n.*, *adj.*, *pron.* *Scot.* self.

sel., 1. selected. **2.** selection; selections.

se·la·chi·an (si lā′kē ən), *adj.* **1.** belonging to the *Selachii*, a group of fishes comprising the sharks, skates, and rays. —*n.* **2.** a selachian fish. [< NL *selachi(ī)* (< Gk *selachē* shark) + -AN]

se·la·dang (si lä′däng), *n.* the gaur. [< Malay]

sel·a·gi·nel·la (sel′ə ji nel′ə), *n.* any terrestrial, mosslike cryptogamic plant of the genus *Selaginella.* [< NL, equiv. to *selāgin-* (s. of L *selāgō* a plant name) + *-ella* dim. suffix]

se·lah (sē′lə, sel′ə), *n.* an expression occurring frequently in the Psalms, thought to be a liturgical or musical direction, probably a direction by the leader to raise the voice or perhaps an indication of a pause. [< Heb]

Se·lah (sē′lə), *n.* a town in S Washington. 2824 (1960).

se·lam·lik (si läm′lik), *n.* the portion of a Turkish palace or house reserved for men. [< Turk]

Se·lan·gor (sə läng′gōr, -gôr), *n.* a state in Malaysia, on the SW Malay Peninsula. 1,159,914 (est. 1961); 3160 sq. mi. *Cap.:* Kuala Lumpur.

Sel·den (sel′dən), *n.* **John,** 1584–1654, English historian, Orientalist, and politician.

sel·dom (sel′dəm), *adv.* **1.** on only a few occasions; rarely; infrequently; not often: *We seldom see our old neighbors anymore.* —*adj.* **2.** rare; infrequent. [ME; OE *seldum*, var. of *seldan*; c. G *selten*, Goth *silda-*] —**sel′dom·ness,** *n.*

se·lect (si lekt′), *v.t.* **1.** to choose in preference to another or others; pick out. —*adj.* **2.** chosen in preference to another or others; selected. **3.** choice; of special value or excellence. **4.** careful or fastidious in selecting; discriminating. **5.** carefully or fastidiously chosen; exclusive: *a select group of friends.* [< L *sēlect(us)* (ptp. of *sēligere* to gather apart), equiv. to *sē-* SE- + *lec-* (deriv. of *leg-* gather) + *-tus* ptp. suffix] —**se·lect′a·ble,** *adj.* —**se·lect′ly,** *adv.* —**se·lect′ness,** *n.* —**se·lec′tor,** *n.*
—**Syn. 1.** See **choose. 2.** preferred.

se·lect·ance (si lek′təns), *n.* a measure of the drop in response of a radio receiving set or the like to a given frequency differing from the resonant frequency of the device, expressed as the ratio of the amplitude of the response at the resonant frequency to the amplitude of the response at the given frequency. [SELECT + -ANCE]

select′ commit′tee, a committee, as of a legislative body, that is formed to examine and report on a specific bill or issue. Also called **special committee.**

se·lect·ee (si lek tē′), *n.* one selected by draft for service in one of the armed forces. [SELECT + -EE]

se·lec·tion (si lek′shən), *n.* **1.** the act or an instance of selecting or the state of being selected; choice. **2.** a thing or a number of things selected. **3.** an aggregate of things displayed for choice, purchase, use, etc.; a group from which a choice may be made: *The store had a wide selection of bracelets.* **4.** *Biol.* a biological process resulting in the survival and perpetuation of only those forms of animal and plant life that are best adapted to the environment or have desirable inheritable characteristics. Cf. **artificial selection, natural selection. 5.** *Ling.* **a.** the choice of one form instead of another in a position where either can occur, as of *ask* instead of *tell* or *with* in the phrase *ask John.* **b.** the choice of one form class in a construction, to the exclusion of others which do not occur there, as of a noun like *John* as direct object of *ask*, to the exclusion of adjectives and adverbs. **c.** the feature of a construction resulting from such a choice. The phrases *ask John, tell John,* and *with John* differ in selection; no adjective or adverb occurs as direct object of a verb in English. [< L *sēlectiōn-* (s. of *sēlectiō*), equiv. to *sēlect(us)* (see SELECT) + *-iōn-* -ION]
—**Syn. 2.** collection, gathering, pick. —**Ant. 1.** rejection.

selec′tion rule′, *Physics.* any of several rules designating allowed transitions between quantum states in terms of the quantum numbers associated with the states.

se·lec·tive (si lek′tiv), *adj.* **1.** having the function or power of selecting; making a selection. **2.** characterized by selection, esp. fastidious selection. **3.** of or pertaining to selection. **4.** *Elect., Radio.* having good selectivity. [SELECT + -IVE] —**se·lec′tive·ly,** *adv.* —**se·lec′tive·ness,** *n.*

selec′tive assem′bly, *Mach.* assembly of pairs of mating parts which have been machined to a certain tolerance and then sorted into several degrees of variation within the tolerance, so that parts are matched with corresponding parts of the same classification of size.

selec′tive serv′ice, compulsory military service.

Selec′tive Serv′ice Sys′tem, *U.S.* the federal agency that administers all activities dealing with compulsory military service. *Abbr.:* SSS

selec′tive transmis′sion, *Auto.* a transmission in which the available forward and reverse speeds may be engaged in any order, without passing progressively through the different changes of gear.

se·lec·tiv·i·ty (si lek tiv′i tē), *n.* **1.** the state or quality of being selective. **2.** *Elect.* the property of a circuit, instrument, or the like, by virtue of which it can distinguish oscillations of a particular frequency. **3.** *Radio.* the ability of a receiving set to receive any one of a band of frequencies or waves to the exclusion of others. [SELECTIVE + -ITY]

se·lect·man (si lekt′mən), *n.*, *pl.* **-men.** (in most New England States) one of a board of town officers chosen to manage certain public affairs. [SELECT (adj.) + MAN[1]]

Se·lem·nus (sə lem′nəs), *n.* *Class. Myth.* **1.** a shepherd who died of unrequited love for the sea nymph Argyra and was turned into a river by Aphrodite. **2.** a river which enabled those who bathed in it to forget hopeless passions.

sel·e·nate (sel′ə nāt′), *n.* *Chem.* a salt or ester of selenic acid. [SELEN(IC) + -ATE[2]]

Se·le·ne (si lē′nē), *n.* **1.** *Class. Myth.* the goddess of the moon, a daughter of Hyperion and Theia, who loved Endymion: later identified with Artemis. Cf. **Thyone. 2.** Also, **Se·le′na.** a girl's given name. [< Gk: the moon]

Sel·en·ga (sel′eng gä′), *n.* a river in N central Asia, flowing E and N through the NW Mongolian People's Republic through the Buryat Republic in the SE Soviet Union to Lake Baikal. ab. 700 mi. long.

se·le·nic (si lē′nik, -len′ik), *adj.* *Chem.* of or containing selenium, esp. in the hexavalent state. [SELEN(IUM) + -IC]

sele′nic ac′id, *Chem.* a crystalline, water-soluble, strong, corrosive, dibasic acid, H_2SeO_4, resembling sulfuric acid.

sel·e·nide (sel′ə nīd′, -nid), *n.* *Chem.* any compound in which bivalent selenium is combined with a positive element, as potassium selenide, K_2Se, or with a group. [SELEN(IUM) + -IDE]

se·le·ni·ous (si lē′nē əs), *adj.* *Chem.* containing tetravalent or bivalent selenium. Also, **selenous.** [SELENI(UM) + -OUS]

sele′nious ac′id, *Chem.* a colorless, crystalline, water-soluble, poisonous powder, H_2SeO_3, used chiefly as a reagent.

sel·e·nite (sel′ə nīt′, si lē′nīt), *n.* **1.** a variety of gypsum, found in transparent crystals and foliated masses. **2.** *Chem.* a salt of selenious acid. [< L *selēnītē(s)* < Gk *selēnítēs líthos* moonstone] —**sel·e·nit·ic** (sel′ə-nit′ik), **sel′e·nit′i·cal,** *adj.*

se·le·ni·um (si lē′nē əm), *n.* *Chem.* a nonmetallic element chemically resembling sulfur and tellurium, occurring in several allotropic forms, as crystalline, amorphous, etc., and having an electrical resistance which varies under the influence of light. *Symbol:* Se; *at. wt.:* 78.96; *at. no.:* 34; *sp. gr.:* (gray) 4.80 at 25°C, (red) 4.50 at 25°C. [< Gk *selēn(ē)* moon + -IUM]

sele′nium cell′, *Elect.* a photovoltaic cell consisting of a thin strip of selenium placed between two metal electrodes.

sele′nium rec′tifier, a rectifier consisting of laminated plates of metal, usually iron, that have been coated with selenium on one side, with rectification taking place because the flow of electrons from the conductive metal to the selenium occurs more readily than the flow in the opposite direction.

seleno-[1], a learned borrowing from Greek meaning "moon," used in the formation of compound words: *selenography.* [comb. form repr. Gk *selḗnē*]

seleno-[2], a combining form of **selenium.**

sel·e·nod·e·sy (sel′ə nod′i sē), *n.* the branch of astronomy that deals with the measurement of the moon's surface and its gravitational field. [SELENO-[1] + Gk *daíes(thai)* (to) distribute + -Y[3]]

se·le·no·dont (si lē′nə dont′, -len′ə-), *adj.* having molar teeth with crowns formed of crescent-shaped cusps. [SELEN(O)-[1] + -ODONT] —**se·le′no·don′ty,** *n.*

sel·e·nog·ra·phy (sel′ə nog′rə fē), *n.* the branch of astronomy that deals with the charting of the moon's surface and with the study of the irregularities of the moon's limb. [SELENO-[1] + -GRAPHY] —**se·le·no·graph** (sə lē′nə graf′, -gräf′), *n.* —**sel′e·nog′ra·pher, sel′e·nog′ra·phist,** *n.* —**se·le·no·graph·ic** (si lē′nə graf′ik), **se·le′no·graph′i·cal,** *adj.* —**se·le′no·graph′i·cal·ly,** *adv.*

sel·e·nol·o·gy (sel′ə nol′ə jē), *n.* the branch of astronomy that deals with the physical characteristics of the moon, especially with the nature and origin of its surface features. [SELENO-[1] + -LOGY] —**se·le·no·log·i·cal** (sə lēn′əloj′i kəl), *adj.* —**sel′e·nol′o·gist,** *n.*

se·le·no·tro·pism (si lē′nə trō′piz əm, sel′ə nō-), *n.* *Biol.* movement or growth in response to moonlight. [SELENO-[1] + -TROPISM] —**se·le·no·trop·ic** (sə lē′nə-trop′ik, sel′ə nō-), *adj.*

se·le·nous (sə lē′nəs, sel′ə-), *adj.* *Chem.* selenious.

Se·ler (zā′lər), *n.* **E·du·ard** (ā′dŏŏ ärt′), 1859–1922, German archaeologist: first to decipher Mayan calendar and inscriptions.

Se·leu·cia (si lo͞o′shə), *n.* **1.** an ancient city in Iraq, on the Tigris River: capital of the Seleucid empire. **2.** an ancient city in Asia Minor, near the mouth of the Orontes River: the port of Antioch.

Se·leu·cid (si lo͞o′sid), *n., pl.* **-ci·dae** (-si dē′), *adj.* —*n.* **1.** a member of a Greek dynasty, 312–64 B.C., that ruled an empire which included much of Asia Minor, Syria, Persia, Bactria, and Babylonia. —*adj.* **2.** of or pertaining to the Seleucids or their dynasty. [< L *Seleucid(ēs)* < Gk *Seleukid(ēs)* offspring of Seleucus]

Se·leu·ci·dan (si lo͞o′si dən), *adj.* Seleucid. [SELEUCID + -AN]

Se·leu·cus (si lo͞o′kəs), *n.* a crater in the second quadrant of the face of the moon: about 32 miles in diameter.

Seleucus I, (*Seleucus Nicator*) 358?–281? B.C., Macedonian general under Alexander the Great: founder of the Seleucid dynasty.

self (self), *n., pl.* **selves,** *adj., pron., pl.* **selves.** —*n.* **1.** a person or thing referred to with respect to complete individuality: *one's own self.* **2.** a person's nature, character, etc.: *his better self.* **3.** personal interest; selfishness. **4.** *Philos.* **a.** the ego; that which knows, remembers, desires, suffers, etc., as contrasted with that known, remembered, etc. **b.** the uniting principle, as a soul, underlying all subjective experience. —*adj.* **5.** being the same throughout, as a color; uniform. **6.** being of one piece or material with the rest. **7.** *Obs.* same. —*pron.* **8.** myself, himself, etc.: *to make a check payable to self.* [ME, OE; c. D *zelf,* G *selb-,* Icel *sjalfr,* Goth *silba*]

self-, a combining form of **self:** *self-control; self-conscious; self-evident.*

self-a·base·ment (self′ə bās′mənt, self′-), *n.* humiliation of oneself, esp. as a result of guilt, shame, or the like.

self-ab·ne·ga·tion (self′ab nə gā′shən), *n.* self-denial or self-sacrifice.

self-ab·sorbed (self′ab sôrbd′, -zôrbd′, self′-), *adj.* preoccupied with one's thoughts, interests, etc.

self-ab·sorp·tion (self′ab sôrp′shən, -zôrp′-, self′-), *n.* preoccupation with oneself or one's own affairs.

self-a·buse (self′ə byo͞os′, self′-), *n.* **1.** reproach or blame of oneself. **2.** abuse of one's health. **3.** masturbation.

self-act·ing (self′ak′ting), *adj.* acting by itself; automatic. —**self′-ac′tion,** *n.*

self-ad·dressed (self′ə drest′), *adj.* addressed for return to the sender.

self-ag·gran·dize·ment (self′ə gran′diz mənt, self′-), *n.* increase of one's own power, wealth, etc., usually aggressively. —**self-ag·gran·diz·ing** (self′ə-gran′di zing), *adj.*

self-a·nal·y·sis (self′ə nal′i sis, self′-), *n.* the application of psychoanalytic techniques and theories to an analysis of one's own personality and behavior, esp. without the aid of a psychiatrist or other trained person. —**self-an·a·lyt·i·cal** (self′an′əlit′i kəl, self′-), *adj.*

self-an·a·lyzed (self′an′əlīzd′), *adj.* having undergone self-analysis.

self-an·ni·hi·la·tion (self′ə nī′ə lā′shən, self′-), *n.* **1.** self-destruction; suicide. **2.** surrender, abnegation, or immolation of the self in mystic contemplation of or union with God.

self-ap·point·ed (self′ə poin′tid), *adj.* chosen by oneself to act in a certain capacity or to fulfill a certain function, esp. pompously or self-righteously: *a self-appointed guardian of the public's morals.* —**self′-ap·point′ment,** *n.*

self-as·ser·tion (self′ə sûr′shən, self′-), *n.* insistence on or an expression of one's own importance, wishes, opinions, etc. —**self′as·sert′ing,** *adj.* —**self′-as·sert′ing·ly,** *adv.* —**self′-as·ser′tive,** *adj.* —**self′-as·ser′tive·ly,** *adv.* —**self′-as·ser′tive·ness,** *n.*
—**Syn.** assertiveness, aggressiveness, belligerence.

self-as·sur·ance (self′ə sho͝or′əns, self′-), *n.* self-confidence.

self-as·sured (self′ə sho͝ord′), *adj.* self-confident. —**self-as·sur·ed·ness** (self′ə sho͝or′id nis), *n.*

self-bi·as (self′bī′əs), *n.* *Electronics.* voltage developed on an electrode in a vacuum tube circuit as a result of current flowing through a resistor in a lead to the cathode or to a grid.

self-cen·tered (self′sen′tərd), *adj.* **1.** engrossed in self; selfish; egotistical. **2.** centered in oneself or itself. **3.** being fixed as a center. Also, *esp. Brit.,* **self′-cen·tred.** —**self′-cen′tered·ly;** *esp. Brit.,* **self′-cen′tred·ly,** *adv.* —**self′-cen′tered·ness;** *esp. Brit.,* **self′-cen′tred·ness,** *n.*

self-col·lect·ed (self′kə lek′tid, self′-), *adj.* having or showing self-control; composed; self-possessed. —**self′-col·lect′ed·ness,** *n.*

self-col·ored (self′kul′ərd, self′-), *adj.* **1.** of one color. **2.** of the natural color. Also, *esp. Brit.,* **self′-col′oured.**

self-com·mand (self′kə mand′, -mänd′, self′-), *n.* self-control.

self-com·pla·cent (self′kəm plā′sənt, self′-), *adj.* pleased with oneself; self-satisfied; smug. —**self′-com·pla′cence, self′-com·pla′cen·cy,** *n.* —**self′-com·pla′cent·ly,** *adv.*

self-com·posed (self′kəm pōzd′, self′-), *adj.* being or appearing to be composed; calm. —**self-com·pos·ed·ly** (self′kəm pō′zid lē, self′-), *adv.* —**self′-com·pos′ed·ness,** *n.*

self-con·ceit (self′kən sēt′, self′-), *n.* an excessively favorable opinion of oneself, one's abilities, etc. —**self′-con·ceit′ed,** *adj.* —**self′-con·ceit′ed·ly,** *adv.* —**self′-con·ceit′ed·ness,** *n.*

self-con·fessed (self′kən fest′, self′-), *adj.* openly admitting to being a type of person with a particular quality, habit, character, etc.: *He's a self-confessed gambler.*

self-con·fi·dence (self′kon′fi dəns, self′-), *n.* **1.** a realistic and objective confidence in one's own judgment, ability, power, etc. **2.** an excessive or inflated confidence in one's own judgment, ability, etc. —**self′-con′fi·dent,** *adj.* —**self′-con′fi·dent·ly,** *adv.*
—**Syn. 1.** assurance, self-possession. **2.** conceit, self-esteem.

self-con·grat·u·la·tion (self′kən grach′ə lā′shən, self′-), *n.* the expression or feeling of uncritical satisfaction with oneself or one's own accomplishment, good fortune, etc.; complacency. —**self-con·grat·u·la·to·ry** (self′kən grach′ə lə tôr′ē, -tōr′ē, self′-), *adj.* —**self′-con·grat′u·lat′ing,** *adj.*

self-con·scious (self′kon′shəs, self′-), *adj.* **1.** excessively conscious of oneself as an object of observation to others. **2.** conscious of oneself or one's own thoughts, well-being, etc. —**self′-con′scious·ly,** *adv.* —**self′-con′scious·ness,** *n.*

self-con·se·quence (self′kon′sə kwəns, self′-), *n.* **1.** self-important character or quality. **2.** an act reflecting or displaying a feeling of self-importance.

self-con·sist·ent (self′kən sis′tənt, self′-), *n.* consistent with oneself or itself. —**self′-con·sis′ten·cy,** *n.* —**self′-con·sis′tent·ly,** *adv.*

self-con·tained (self′kən tānd′, self′-), *adj.* **1.** containing in oneself or itself all that is necessary; independent. **2.** reserved or uncommunicative. **3.** self-controlled or self-possessed. **4.** (of a machine or mechanism) complete in itself. —**self-con·tain·ed·ly** (self′kən tā′nid lē, self′-), *adv.* —**self′-con·tain′ed·ness,** *n.*

self-con·tent (self′kən tent′, self′-), *n.* **1.** satisfaction with oneself; self-complacency. —*adj.* **2.** content with oneself; self-satisfied. Also, **self′-con·tent′ment.** —**self′-con·tent′ed·ly,** *adv.* —**self′-con·tent′ed·ness,** *n.*

self-con·tra·dic·tion (self′kon′trə dik′shən, self′-), *n.* **1.** the act or an instance of contradicting oneself or itself. **2.** a statement containing contradictory elements. —**self′-con′tra·dict′ing,** *adj.* —**self′-con′tra·dic′to·ry,** *adj.*

self-con·trol (self′kən trōl′, self′-), *n.* control or restraint of oneself or one's actions, feelings, etc. —**self′-con·trolled′,** *adj.* —**self′-con·trol′ling,** *adj.*

self-cor·rect·ing (self′kə rek′ting, self′-), *adj.* automatically adjusting to or correcting mistakes, malfunctions, etc.: *a self-correcting mechanism.* Also, **self′-cor·rec′tive.** —**self′-cor·rec′tion,** *n.*

self-crit·i·cal (self′krit′i kəl, self′-), *adj.* **1.** capable of criticizing oneself objectively. **2.** tending to find fault with one's own actions, motives, etc. —**self′-crit′i·cal·ly,** *adv.*

self-crit·i·cism (self′krit′i siz′əm, self′-) *n.* the act or fact of being self-critical.

self-de·ceit (self′di sēt′, self′-), *n.* self-deception.

self-de·ceived (self′di sēvd′, self′-), *adj.* **1.** holding an erroneous opinion of oneself, one's own effort, or the like: *If she thinks she's beautiful, she's self-deceived.* **2.** being mistaken, forming an erroneous judgment, etc., in one's own mind, as from hasty or illogical thinking: *If you thought my friendship was love, you were self-deceived.*

self-de·ceiv·ing (self′di sē′ving, self′-), *adj.* **1.** subject to self-deception; tending to deceive or fool oneself: *a self-deceiving person.* **2.** used in deceiving oneself, esp. in justifying a false belief, a morally reprehensible act, or the like: *a self-deceiving argument.*

self-de·cep·tion (self′di sep′shən, self′-), *n.* the act or fact of deceiving oneself. Also called **self-deceit.** —**self′-de·cep′tive,** *adj.*

self-de·feat·ing (self′di fē′ting, self′-), *adj.* serving to frustrate, thwart, etc., one's own intention: *His behavior was certainly self-defeating.*

self-de·fense (self′di fens′, self′-), *n.* **1.** the act of defending one's person when physically attacked, as by countering blows or overcoming an assailant: *the manly art of self-defense.* **2.** a claim or plea that the use of force or injuring or killing another was necessary in defending one's own person from physical attack: *He shot the man who was trying to stab him and pleaded self-defense at the murder trial.* **3.** the act or an instance of defending one's own effort, opinion, idea, plan, etc., as by argument. Also, *esp. Brit.,* **self′-de·fence′.** —**self′-de·fen′sive;** *esp. Brit.,* **self′-de·fen′cive,** *adj.*

self-de·lu·sion (self′di lo͞o′zhən, self′-), *n.* the act or fact of deluding oneself.

self-de·ni·al (self′di nī′əl, self′-), *n.* **1.** the sacrifice of one's own desires; unselfishness. **2.** the act or an instance of restraining or curbing one's desires: *To reduce, one has to practice self-denial at the dinner table.* —**self′-de·ny′ing,** *adj.* —**self′-de·ny′ing·ly,** *adv.*

self-dep·re·cat·ing (self′dep′rə kā′ting, self′-), *adj.* representing oneself as having little or no value; excessively modest. —**self′-dep′re·cat′ing·ly,** *adv.* —**self′-dep′re·ca′tion,** *n.*

self-de·struc·tive (self′di struk′tiv, self′-), *adj.* **1.** harmful, injurious, or destructive to oneself: *His constant arguing with the boss shows he's a self-destructive person.* **2.** reflecting or exhibiting suicidal desires or drives: *Careless driving may be a self-destructive tendency.* —**self′-de·struc′tive·ly,** *adv.*

self-de·ter·mi·na·tion (self′di tûr′mə nā′shən, self′-), *n.* **1.** determination by oneself or itself, without outside influence. **2.** freedom to live as one chooses, or to act or decide without consulting another or others. **3.** the determining by the people of the form their government shall have, without reference to the wishes of any other nation, esp. by people of a territory or former colony. —**self′-de·ter′mined,** *adj.* —**self′-de·ter′min·ing,** *adj., n.*

self-de·ter·min·ism (self′di tûr′mə niz′əm, self′-), *n.* *Philos.* a theory that every present state or condition of the self is a result of previous states or conditions of the self.

self-de·vo·tion (self′di vō′shən, self′-), *n.* **1.** intense devotion of oneself to an activity or to a field or profession, as art or science. **2.** devotion of oneself to the care or service of another or others; self-sacrifice: *Her self-devotion to her sick mother prevented her from marrying.* —**self′-de·vot′ed,** *adj.* —**self′-de·vot′ed·ly,** *adv.* —**self′-de·vot′ed·ness,** *n.*

self-dis·ci·pline (self′dis′ə plin, self′-), *n.* discipline and training of oneself, usually for improvement: *Acquiring the habit of promptness requires self-discipline.* —**self′-dis′ciplined,** *adj.*

self-dis·trust (self′dis trust′, self′-), *n.* lack of confidence in oneself, in one's abilities, etc. —**self′-dis·trust′ful,** *adj.* —**self′-dis·trust′ing,** *adj.*

self′-a·ban′don, *n.*
self′-a·ban′don·ment, *n.*
self′-ab·hor′rence, *n.*
self′-a·bom′i·nat′ing, *adj.*
self′-a·bom′i·na′tion, *n.*
self′-ac′cu·sa′tion, *n.*
self′-ac·cu′sa·tive, *adj.*
self′-ac·cu′sa·to′ry, *adj.*
self′-ac·cused′, *adj.*
self′-ac·cus′er, *n.*
self′-ac·cus′ing, *adj.*
self′-ac′tu·al·iz′ing, *adj.*
self′-ac′tu·at′ing, *adj.*
self′-ad·just′ing, *adj.*
self′-ad·min′is·tered, *adj.*
self′-ad·min′is·ter·ing, *adj.*
self′-ad′mi·ra′tion, *n.*
self′-ad·mir′ing, *adj.*
self′-a·dorn′ing, *adj.*
self′-a·dorn′ment, *n.*
self′-ad′u·la′tion, *n.*
self′-ad·vance′ment, *n.*
self′-ad′ver·tise′ment, *n.*
self′-ad′ver·tis′ing, *adj., n.*
self′-af·flict′ing, *adj.*
self′-af·fright′ed, *adj.*
self′-a·lign′ing, *adj.*
self′-a·lign′ment, *n.*
self′-a·line′ment, *n.*
self′-a·lin′ing, *adj.*
self′-a·mend′ment, *n.*
self′-a·muse′ment, *n.*
self′-an·nul′ling, *adj.*
self′-an·tith′e·sis, *n.*
self′-ap·par′ent, *adj.*
self′-ap·plaud′ing, *adj.*
self′-ap·plause′, *n.*
self′-ap·pre′ci·at′ing, *adj.*
self′-ap·pre′ci·a′tion, *n.*
self′-ap′pro·ba′tion, *n.*
self′-ap·prov′al, *n.*
self′-ap·proved′, *adj.*
self′-ap·prov′ing, *adj.*
self′-as·signed′, *adj.*
self′-as·sumed′, *adj.*
self′-as·sum′ing, *adj.*
self′-as·sump′tion, *n.*
self′-at·tach′ment, *n.*
self′-au′thor·ized′, *adj.*
self′-au′thor·iz′ing, *adj.*
self′-a·ware′, *adj.*
 -ness, *n.*
self′-bal′anced, *adj.*
self′-ban′ished, *adj.*
self′-ban′ish·ment, *n.*
self′-bap′tiz·er, *n.*
self′-be·got′ten, *adj.*
self′-ben′e·fit, *n.*
self′-ben′e·fit′ing, *adj.*
self′-be·tray′al, *n.*
self′-be·tray′ing, *adj.*
self′-blame′, *n.*
self′-blind′ed, *adj.*
self′-born′, *adj.*
self′-can′celed, *adj.*
self′-can′celled, *adj.*
self′-care′, *n.*
self′-cas′ti·gat′ing, *adj.*
self′-cas′ti·ga′tion, *n.*
self′-ca·tal′y·sis, *n.*
self′-cat′a·lyst, *n.*
self′-caused′, *adj.*
self′-chang′ing, *adj., n.*
self′-chas′tise, *v.t.,* **-tised, -tis·ing.**
self′-chas′tise·ment, *n.*
self′-clean′ing, *adj.*
self′-clear′ance, *n.*
self′-clos′ing, *adj.*
self′-cock′er, *n.*
self′-cock′ing, *adj.*
self′-cog·ni′tion, *n.*
self′-cog′ni·zance, *n.*
self′-com′bat·ing, *adj.*
self′-com·bus′tion, *n.*
self′-com·men·da′tion, *n.*
self′-com·mit′ment, *n.*
self′-com·mit′tal, *adj.*
self′-com·mit′ting, *adj.*
self′-com·mu′ni·ca′tion, *n.*
self′-com′pre·hend′ing, *adj.*
self′-con·cern′, *n.*
self′-con·dem·na′tion, *n.*
self′-con·dem′na·to′ry, *adj.*
self′-con·demned′, *adj.*
self′-con·demn′ing, *adj.*
self′-con·di′tioned, *adj.*
self′-con·di′tion·ing, *adj.*
self′-con·fine′ment, *n.*
self′-con·fin′ing, *adj.*
self′-con′flict, *n.*
self′-con′quest, *n.*
self′-con′ser·va′tion, *n.*
self′-con·serv′ing, *adj.*
self′-con·sol′ing, *adj.*
self′-con′sti·tut′ed, *adj.*
self′-con′sti·tut′ing, *adj.*
self′-con·sum′ing, *adj.*
self′-con·sump′tion, *n.*
self′-con·tam′i·nat′ing, *adj.*
self′-con·tam′i·na′tion, *n.*
self′-con·tempt′, *n.*
self′-con·vict′ed, *adj.*
self′-cook′ing, *adj.*
self′-cre·at′ed, *adj.*
self′-cre·at′ing, *adj.*
self′-cre·a′tion, *n.*
self′-cru′el·ty, *n.*
self′-cure′, *n.*
self′-cut′ting, *adj.*
self′-dam·na′tion, *n.*
self′-de·base′ment, *n.*
self′-ded′i·cat′ed, *adj.*
self′-ded′i·ca′tion, *n.*
self′-de·fin′ing, *adj.*
self′-def′i·ni′tion, *n.*
self′-de·flat′ed, *adj.*
self′-de·fla′tion, *n.*
self′-deg′ra·da′tion, *n.*
self′-de′i·fy′ing, *adj.*
self′-de·jec′tion, *n.*
self′-de·light′, *n.*
self′-de·mag′net·iz′ing, *adj.*
self′-de·pend′ence, *n.*
self′-de·pend′en·cy, *n.*
self′-de·pend′ent, *adj.;* **-ly,** *adv.*
self′-de·pend′ing, *adj.*
self′-de·praved′, *adj.*
self′-de·pre′ci·a′tion, *n.*
self′-de·pre′ci·a′tive, *adj.*
self′-dep′ri·va′tion, *n.*
self′-de·prived′, *adj.*
self′-de·priv′ing, *adj.*
self′-de·rived′, *adj.*
self′-de·ser′tion, *n.*
self′-de·serv′ing, *adj.*
self′-de·sign′, *n.*
self′-de·sign′er, *n.*
self′-de·sire′, *n.*
self′-de·spair′, *n.*
self′-de·stroyed′, *adj.*
self′-de·stroy′er, *n.*
self′-de·stroy′ing, *adj.*
self′-de·tach′ing, *adj.*
self′-de·vel′op·ing, *adj.*
self′-de·vel′op·ment, *n.*
self′-de·vised′, *adj.*
self′-de·vour′ing, *adj.*
self′-di′a·log′, *n.*
self′-di′a·logue′, *n.*
self′-dif′fer·en′ti·at′ing, *adj.*
self′-dif′fer·en′ti·a′tion, *n.*
self′-dif·fu′sion, *n.*
self′-dif·fu′sive, *adj.;* **-ly,** *adv.;* **-ness,** *n.*
self′-di·ges′tion, *n.*
self′-di·lat′ed, *adj.*
self′-di·la′tion, *n.*
self′-di·rect′ed, *adj.*
self′-di·rect′ing, *adj.*
self′-di·rec′tion, *n.*
self′-di·rec′tive, *adj.*
self′-di·rec′tor, *n.*
self′-dis′ap·pro·ba′tion, *n.*
self′-dis′ap·prov′al, *n.*
self′-dis·cern′ment, *n.*
self′-dis·closed′, *adj.*
self′-dis·clo′sure, *n.*
self′-dis·col′or·a′tion, *n.*
self′-dis′con·tent′ed, *adj.*
self′-dis·cov′er·y, *n.*
self′-dis·crep′ant, *adj.;* **-ly,** *adv.*
self′-dis·crim′i·na′tion, *n.*
self′-dis·dain′, *n.*
self′-dis′en·gag′ing, *adj.*
self′-dis·grace′, *n.*
self′-dis·graced′, *adj.*
self′-dis·grac′ing, *adj.*
self′-dis·gust′, *n.*
self′-dis·like′, *n.*
self′-dis·liked′, *adj.*
self′-dis·par′age·ment, *n.*
self′-dis·par′ag·ing, *adj.*
self′-dis·patch′, *n.*
self′-dis·play′, *n.*
self′-dis·pleased′, *adj.*
self′-dis·pos′al, *n.*
self′-dis·praise′, *n.*
self′-dis·qui′et·ing, *adj.*
self′-dis·sat′is·fac′tion, *n.*
self′-dis·sat′is·fied′, *adj.*
self′-dis·sect′ing, *adj.*
self′-dis·sec′tion, *n.*
self′-dis·ser′vice, *n.*
self′-dis·serv′ing, *adj.*
self′-dis·so′ci·a′tion, *n.*
self′-dis′so·lu′tion, *n.*
self′-dis·solved′, *adj.*
self′-dis·tin′guish·ing, *adj.*

self-doubt (self′dout′), *n.* lack of confidence in the reliability of one's own motives, personality, thought, etc.; absence of self-assurance. —**self′-doubt′ing,** *adj.*

self-dram·a·tiz·ing (self′dram′ə tī′zing, self′-), *adj.* exaggerating one's own qualities, characteristics, attributes, etc., for dramatic effect or as an attention-getting device; presenting oneself dramatically. —**self′-dram′a·ti·za′tion,** *n.*

self-driv·en (self′driv′ən, self′-), *adj.* (of a machine) containing its own power source, as an engine or motor.

self-ed·u·cat·ed (self′ej′o͝o kā′tid, self′-), *adj.* educated by one's own efforts, esp. without formal instruction. —**self′-ed′u·ca′tion,** *n.*

self-ef·face·ment (self′i fās′mənt, self′-), *n.* the act or fact of keeping oneself in the background, as in humility. —**self′-ef·fac′ing,** *adj.* —**self′-ef·fac′ing·ly,** *adv.* —**self′-ef·fac′ing·ness,** *n.*

self-em·ployed (self′em ploid′, self′-), *adj.* earning one's living directly from one's own profession or business, as a free-lance writer or artist, rather than as an employee earning salary or commission from another.

self-em·ploy·ment (self′em ploi′mənt, self′-), *n.* the act or fact of being self-employed.

self-es·teem (self′e stēm′, self′-), *n.* **1.** an objective respect for or favorable impression of oneself. **2.** an inordinately or exaggeratedly favorable impression of oneself.
—**Syn.** See **pride.** —**Ant.** diffidence.

self-ev·i·dent (self′ev′i dənt, self′-), *adj.* evident in itself without proof or demonstration; axiomatic. —**self′-ev′i·dence,** *n.* —**self′-ev′i·dent·ly,** *adv.*
—**Syn.** obvious, self-explanatory.

self-ex·am·i·na·tion (self′ig zam′ə nā′shən, self′-), *n.* examination into one's own state, conduct, motives, etc. —**self′-ex·am′in·ing,** *adj.*

self-ex·cit·ed (self′ik sī′tid), *adj. Elect.* noting a generator that has magnets which are excited by the current it produces. —**self-ex·ci·ta·tion** (self′ek′sī-tā′shən, -si-), *n.* —**self′-ex·cit′er,** *n.*

self-ex·e·cut·ing (self′ek′sə kyo͞o′ting, self′-), *adj.* going into effect immediately without the need of supplementary legislation: *a self-executing treaty.*

self-ex·ist·ent (self′ig zis′tənt, self′-), *adj.* **1.** existing independently of any cause, as God. **2.** having an independent existence. —**self′-ex·ist′ence,** *n.*

self-ex·plan·a·to·ry (self′ik splan′ə tôr′ē, -tōr′ē, self′-), *adj.* needing no explanation; obvious. Also, **self-ex·plain·ing** (self′ik splā′ning, self′-).

self-ex·pres·sion (self′ik spresh′ən, self′-), *n.* the expression or assertion of one's own personality, as in conversation, behavior, poetry, painting, etc. —**self′-ex·press′ive,** *adj.*

self-feed (self′fēd′, self′-), *v.t.*, **-fed, -feed·ing.** *Agric.* to provide a supply of food to (animals) so as to allow them to eat as much and as often as they want. Cf. **hand-feed.**

self-feed·er (self′fē′dər, self′-), *n.* an apparatus or machine that automatically discharges a supply of some material, esp. one consisting of a hopper and a trough for feeding livestock.

self-fer·ti·li·za·tion (self′fûr′tᵊli zā′shən, self′-), *n. Bot.* fertilization of the flower of one plant by a gamete from the same flower (opposed to *cross-fertilization*). —**self′-fer′ti·lized′,** *adj.*

self-flat·ter·y (self′flat′ə rē, self′-), *n.* praise and exaggeration of one's own achievements coupled with a denial or glossing over of one's faults or failings; self-congratulation. —**self′-flat′ter·ing,** *adj.*

self-for·get·ful (self′fər get′fəl, self′-), *adj.* forgetful or not thinking of one's own advantage, interest, etc. —**self′-for·get′ful·ly,** *adv.* —**self′-for·get′ful·ness,** *n.*

self-for·get·ting (self′fər get′ing, self′-), *adj.* self-forgetful. —**self′-for·get′ting·ly,** *adv.*

self-ful·fill·ment (self′fo͝ol fil′mənt, self′-), *n.* the act or fact of fulfilling one's ambitions, desires, etc., through one's own efforts. Also, *esp. Brit.,* **self′-ful·fil′ment.** —**self′-ful·fill′ing,** *adj.*

self-gen·er·at·ed (self′jen′ə rā′tid, self′-), *adj.* made without the aid of an external agent; produced spontaneously.

self-gen·er·at·ing (self′jen′ə rā′ting, self′-), *adj.* producing from within itself. Also, **self-gen·er·a·tive** (self′jen′ə rā′tiv, -ər ə tiv, self′-).

self-gen·er·a·tion (self′jen′ə rā′shən), *n.* production or reproduction of something without the aid of an external agent; spontaneous generation.

self-gov·erned (self′guv′ərnd, self′-), *adj.* **1.** governed by itself or having self-government, as a state or community; independent. **2.** self-regulating; self-determining. **3.** exercising self-restraint or self-control. —**self′-gov′ern·ing,** *adj.*
—**Syn. 1.** autonomous. —**Ant. 1.** dependent.

self-gov·ern·ment (self′guv′ərn mənt, -ər-, self′-), *n.* **1.** government of a state, community, or other body of persons by its members jointly; democratic government. **2.** the condition of being self-governed. **3.** self-control.

self-grat·i·fi·ca·tion (self′grat′ə fə kā′shən, self′-), *n.* the act of pleasing or satisfying oneself, esp. the gratifying of one's own impulses, needs, or desires.

self-hard·en·ing (self′här′dᵊning, self′-), *adj.* noting or pertaining to any of various steels which harden after heating without quenching or other treatment. —**self′-hard′ened,** *adj.*

self·heal (self′hēl′), *n.* **1.** a menthaceous plant, *Prunella vulgaris,* formerly believed to have healing properties. **2.** any of various other plants believed to have similar properties. [late ME *selfhele.* See SELF, HEAL]

self-help (self′help′, self′-), *n.* the act of providing for or helping or the ability to provide for or help oneself without assistance from others, esp. in education. —**self′-help′er,** *n.* —**self′-help′ful, self′-help′ing,** *adj.* —**self′-help′ful·ness,** *n.*

self·hood (self′ho͝od), *n.* **1.** the state of being an individual person. **2.** one's personality. **3.** selfishness. [SELF + -HOOD]

self-hyp·no·sis (self′hip nō′sis, self′-), *n.* autohypnosis. —**self-hyp·not·ic** (self′hip not′ik, self′-), *adj.* —**self-hyp·no·tism** (self′hip′nə tiz′əm), *n.*

self-hyp·no·tized (self′hip′nə tīzd′, self′-), *adj.* hypnotized by oneself. —**self′hyp′no·ti·za′tion,** *n.*

self-i·den·ti·fi·ca·tion (self′ī den′tə fə kā′shən, self′-), *n.* identification of oneself with some other person or thing.

self-i·den·ti·ty (self′ī den′ti tē, self′-), *n.* the identity or consciousness of identity of a thing with itself.

self-ig·nite (self′ig nīt′, self′-), *v.i.*, **-nit·ed, -nit·ing.** to ignite without spark or flame. —**self′-ig·ni′tion,** *n.*

self-im·age (self′im′ij), *n.* the idea, conception, or mental image one has of oneself.

self-im·mo·lat·ing (self′im′ə lā′ting, self′-), *adj.* of, pertaining to, or tending toward self-immolation.

self-im·mo·la·tion (self′im′ə lā′shən), *n.* voluntary sacrifice or denial of oneself, as for an ideal, another person, etc.

self-im·por·tant (self′im pôr′tᵊnt, self′-), *adj.* having or showing an exaggerated opinion of one's own importance; pompously conceited or haughty. —**self′-im·por′tance,** *n.* —**self′-im·por′tant·ly,** *adv.*

self-im·posed (self′im pōzd′, self′-), *adj.* imposed on one by oneself: *a self-imposed task.*

self-im·prove·ment (self′im pro͞ov′mənt, self′-), *n.* improvement of one's mind, character, etc., through one's own efforts. —**self′-im·prov′a·ble,** *adj.* —**self′-im·prov′er,** *n.* —**self′-im·prov′ing,** *adj.*

self-in·clu·sive (self′in klo͞o′siv, self′-), *adj.* including oneself or itself.

self-in·crim·i·nat·ing (self′in krim′ə nā′ting, self′-), *adj.* serving to incriminate oneself or to expose oneself to prosecution: *self-incriminating testimony.*

self-in·crim·i·na·tion (self′in krim′ə nā′shən, self′-), *n.* the act of incriminating oneself or exposing oneself to prosecution, esp. by giving evidence or testimony.

self-in·duced (self′in do͞ost′, -dyo͞ost′, self′-), *adj.* **1.** induced by oneself or itself. **2.** *Elect.* produced by self-induction.

self-in·duct·ance (self′in duk′təns), *n. Elect.* inductance inducing an electromotive force in the same circuit in which the motivating change of current occurs, equal to the number of flux linkages per unit of current.

self-in·duc·tion (self′in duk′shən), *n. Elect.* the process by which an electromotive force is induced in a circuit by a varying current in that circuit.

self-in·dul·gent (self′in dul′jənt, self′-), *adj.* **1.** indulging one's own desires, passions, whims, etc. **2.** characterized by such indulgence. —**self′-in·dul′gence,** *n.* —**self′-in·dul′gent·ly,** *adv.* —**self′-in·dulg′er,** *n.*

self-in·flict·ed (self′in flik′tid, self′-), *adj.* inflicted by oneself: *a self-inflicted wound.* —**self′-in·flic′tion,** *n.*

self-in·i·ti·at·ed (self′i nish′ē ā′tid, self′-), *adj.* initiated or begun by oneself.

self-in·sur·ance (self′in sho͝or′əns, self′-), *n.* insurance of one's property or interests against possible loss by the establishing of a special fund for the purpose instead of seeking coverage with an underwriter.

self-in·sur·er (self′in sho͝or′ər, self′-), *n.* one insured under self-insurance. —**self′-in·sured′,** *adj.*

self-in·ter·est (self′in′tər ist, -trist, self′-), *n.* **1.** regard for one's own interest or advantage, esp. with disregard for others. **2.** personal interest or advantage. —**self′-in′ter·est·ed,** *adj.* —**self′-in′ter·est·ed·ness,** *n.*

self·ish (sel′fish), *adj.* **1.** devoted to or caring only for oneself; concerned primarily with one's own interests, benefits, welfare, etc., regardless of others. **2.** characterized by or manifesting concern or care only for oneself: *selfish motives.* [SELF + -ISH[1]] —**self′ish·ly,** *adv.* —**self′ish·ness,** *n.*
—**Syn. 1.** self-interested, self-seeking, egoistic, illiberal, parsimonious, stingy.

self-judg·ment (self′juj′mənt, self′-), *n.* the act or fact of judging oneself.

self-jus·ti·fi·ca·tion (self′jus′tə fə kā′shən, self′-), *n.* the act or fact of justifying oneself, esp. of offering excessive reasons, explanations, excuses, etc., for an act, thought, or the like.

self-jus·ti·fy·ing (self′jus′tə fī′ing, self′-), *adj.* **1.** offering excuses for oneself, esp. in excess of normal demands. **2.** automatically adjusting printed or typed lines to fill a given space, esp. to conform to a rigid margin.

self-know·ledge (self′nol′ij, self′-), *n.* knowledge or understanding of oneself, one's character, abilities, motives, etc.

self·less (self′lis), *adj.* having little or no concern for oneself, esp. as regards fame, position, money, etc.; unselfish. [SELF + -LESS] —**self′less·ly,** *adv.* —**self′less·ness,** *n.*

self-lim·it·ed (self′lim′i tid, self′-), *adj.* (of a disease) running a definite and limited course.

self-liq·ui·dat·ing (self′lik′wi dā′ting, self′-), *adj.* **1.** capable of being sold and converted into cash within a short period of time or before the date on which the supplier must be paid. **2.** (of a property, loan, project, investment, etc.) used or operating in such a way as to repay the money needed to acquire it: *He rented half of the house to someone else so that his home loan became self-liquidating.*

self-load·ing (self′lō′ding, self′-), *adj.* noting or pertaining to an automatic or semiautomatic firearm.

self-love (self′luv′), *n.* the instinct by which man's actions are directed to the promotion of his own welfare or well-being, esp. an excessive regard for one's own advantage: *His self-love was intolerable.* —**self′-lov′ing,** *adj.*

self-made (self′mād′), *adj.* **1.** having succeeded in life unaided: *He is a self-made man.* **2.** made by oneself.

self-mail·er (self′mā′lər), *n.* an advertisement, booklet, or the like, that has space for a name, address, and postage and can be mailed without a wrapper or envelope.

self-mas·ter·y (self′mas′tə rē, -mä′stə-, self′-), *n.* self-control. —**self′-mas′tered,** *adj.* —**self′-mas′ter·ing,** *adj.*

---

self′-di·vid′ed, *adj.*
self′-di·vi′sion, *n.*
self′-doc′trine, *n.*
self′-dom′i·nance, *n.*
self′-do·min′ion, *n.*
self′-do·na′tion, *n.*
self′-doomed′, *adj.*
self′-drawing, *n., adj.*
self′-du′pli·cat′ing, *adj.*
self′-du′pli·ca′tion, *n.*
self′-eas′ing, *adj.*
self′-e·lab′o·rat′ed, *adj.*
self′-e·lab′o·ra′tion, *n.*
self′-e·la′tion, *n.*
self′-e·lect′ed, *adj.*
self′-e·lec′tion, *n.*
self′-e·mit′ted, *adj.*
self′-emp′ti·ness, *n.*
self′-emp′ty·ing, *adj.*
self′-en·am′ored, *adj.*
self′-en·am′oured, *adj.*
self′-en·closed′, *adj.*
self′-en·dear′ing, *adj.*
self′-en′er·gy, *n.*
self′-en·grossed′, *adj.*
self′-en·gross′ment, *n.*
self′-en·joy′ment, *n.*
self′-en·rich′ing, *adj.*
self′-en·rich′ment, *n.*
self′-en′ter·tain′ing, *adj.*
self′-en′ter·tain′ment, *n.*
self′-e·rect′ed, *adj.*
self′-es·cape′, *n.*
self′-es′sence, *n.*
self′-es′ti·mate, *n.*
self′-es′ti·ma′tion, *n.*
self′-es·trange′ment, *n.*
self′-e·val′u·a′tion, *n.*
self′-e·volved′, *adj.*
self′-e·volv′ing, *adj.*
self′-ex·ag′ger·at′ed, *adj.*
self′-ex·ag′ger·a′tion, *n.*
self′-ex′al·ta′tion, *n.*
self′-ex·alt′ed, *adj.*
self′-ex·alt′ing, *adj.*
self′-ex·clu′sion, *n.*
self′-ex′cul·pa′tion, *n.*
self′-ex·cuse′, *n.*
self′-ex·cused′, *adj.*
self′-ex·cus′ing, *adj.*
self′-ex·er′tion, *n.*
self′-ex·hib′it·ed, *adj.*
self′-ex′hi·bi′tion, *n.*
self′-ex′ile, *n.*
self′-ex′iled, *adj.*
self′-ex·pand′ed, *adj.*
self′-ex·pand′ing, *adj.*
self′-ex·pan′sion, *n.*
self′-ex·pa′tri·a′tion, *n.*
self′-ex′pli·ca′tion, *n.*
self′-ex·ploit′ed, *adj.*
self′-ex·ploit′ing, *adj.*
self′-ex·posed′, *adj.*
self′-ex·pos′ing, *adj.*
self′-ex·po′sure, *n.*
self′-ex·ter′mi·na′tion, *n.*
self′-ex·tolled′, *adj.*
self′-ex′ul·ta′tion, *n.*
self′-ex·ult′ing, *adj.*
self′-fame′, *n.*
self′-farm′ing, *n.*
self′-fear′ing, *adj.*
self′-fe·lic′i·ta′tion, *n.*
self′-fer′men·ta′tion, *n.*
self′-fig′ured, *adj.*
self′-fill′ing, *adj.*
self′-fit′ting, *adj.*
self′-flag′el·la′tion, *n.*
self′-flow′ing, *adj.*
self′-fo′cused, *adj.*
self′-fo′cus·ing, *adj.*
self′-fo′cussed, *adj.*
self′-fo′cus·sing, *adj.*
self′-fold′ing, *adj.*
self′-fond′ness, *n.*
self′-for·bid′den, *adj.*
self′-for·ma′tion, *n.*
self′-formed′, *adj.*
self′-for·sak′en, *adj.*
self′-fric′tion, *n.*
self′-fright′ed, *adj.*
self′-fru·i′tion, *n.*
self′-fur′nished, *adj.*
self′-gain′, *n.*
self′-gaug′ing, *adj.*
self′-giv′en, *adj.*
self′-giv′ing, *adj.*
self′-glazed′, *adj.*
self′-glaz′ing, *adj.*
self′-glo′ri·fi·ca′tion, *n.*
self′-glo′ri·fied′, *adj.*
self′-glo′ri·fy′ing, *adj.*
self′-glo′ry, *n.*
self′-glo′ry·ing, *adj.*
self′-got′ten, *adj.*
self′-grat′u·la′tion, *n.*
self′-grat′u·la·to′ry, *adj.*
self′-guard′, *n.*
self′-guard′ed, *adj.*
self′-guid′ance, *n.*
self′-harm′ing, *adj.*
self′-hate′, *n.*
self′-ha′tred, *n.*
self′-heal′ing, *adj.*
self′-heat′ing, *adj.*
self′-hit′ting, *adj.*
self′-ho′li·ness, *n.*
self′-hom′i·cide′, *n.*
self′-hon′ored, *adj.*
self′-hon′oured, *adj.*
self′-hope′, *n.*
self′-hum′bling, *adj.*
self′-hu·mil′i·at′ing, *adj.*
self′-hu·mil′i·a′tion, *n.*
self′-i·dol′a·ter, *n.*
self′-i·dol′a·try, *n.*
self′-i′dol·ized′, *adj.*
self′-i′dol·iz′ing, *adj.*
self′-ig′no·rance, *n.*
self′-ig′no·rant, *adj.*
self′-il·lu′mined, *adj.*
self′-il·lus′tra·tive, *adj.*
self′-im′i·ta′tion, *n.*
self′-im·mu′ni·ty, *n.*
self′-im·mure′ment, *n.*
self′-im·mur′ing, *adj.*
self′-im·pair′a·ble, *adj.*
self′-im·pair′ing, *adj.*
self′-im·part′ing, *adj.*
self′-im·ped′ance, *n.*
self′-im·preg′nat·ed, *adj.*
self′-im·preg′nat·ing, *adj.*
self′-im′preg·na′tion, *n.*
self′-im·preg′na·tor, *n.*
self′-im·pul′sion, *n.*
self′-in·closed′, *adj.*
self′-in·curred′, *adj.*
self′-in′dig·na′tion, *n.*
self′-in·fla′tion, *n.*
self′-in·i′ti·a·tive, *adj.*
self′-in·ju′ri·ous, *adj.*
self′-in′ju·ry, *n., pl.* **-ries.**
self′-in·oc′u·lat′ed, *adj.*
self′-in·oc′u·la′tion, *n.*
self′-in′sig·nif′i·cance, *n.*
self′-in·spect′ed, *adj.*
self′-in·spec′tion, *n.*
self′-in·struct′ed, *adj.*
self′-in·struct′ing, *adj.*
self′-in·struc′tion, *n.*
self′-in·struc′tor, *n.*
self′-in′suf·fi′cien·cy, *n.*
self′-in′te·grat′ing, *adj.*
self′-in′te·gra′tion, *n.*
self′-in·tel′li·gi·ble, *adj.*
self′-in·ten′si·fied′, *adj.*
self′-in·ten′si·fy′ing, *adj.*
self′-in·ter′pret·ed, *adj.*
self′-in·ter′pret·ing, *adj.*
self′-in·ter′pre·tive, *adj.*
self′-in·ter′ro·ga′tion, *n.*
self′-in′ter·rupt′ing, *adj.*
self′-in′ter·sect′ing, *adj.*
self′-in·tox′i·ca′tion, *n.*
self′-in′tro·duc′tion, *n.*
self′-in·trud′er, *n.*
self′-in·vent′ed, *adj.*
self′-in·ven′tion, *n.*
self′-in·vit′ed, *adj.*
self′-i′on·i·za′tion, *n.*
self′-i′ro·ny, *n., pl.* **-nies.**
self′-is′sued, *adj.*
self′-is′su·ing, *adj.*
self′-killed′, *adj.*
self′-kill′er, *n.*
self′-kill′ing, *adj.*
self′-kin′dled, *adj.*
self′-kind′ness, *n.*
self′-lac′er·at′ing, *adj.*
self′-lac′er·a′tion, *n.*
self′-lash′ing, *adj.*
self′-lau·da′tion, *n.*
self′-laud′a·to′ry, *adj.*
self′-lev′el·er, *n.*
self′-lev′el·ing, *adj.*
self′-lev′el·ler, *n.*
self′-lev′el·ling, *adj.*
self′-lev′ied, *adj.*
self′-lev′i·ta′tion, *n.*
self′-light′ing, *adj.*
self′-lik′ing, *adj.*
self′-loath′ing, *adj.*
self′-lo′cat·ing, *adj.*
self′-lock′ing, *adj.*
self′-lu′bri·cat′ed, *adj.*
self′-lu′bri·cat′ing, *adj.*
self′-lu′bri·ca′tion, *n.*
self′-lu′mi·nos′i·ty, *n.*
self′-lu′mi·nous, *adj.*
self′-mac′er·a′tion, *n.*

---

self-mate (self′māt′), *n. Chess.* a move that will cause a player's king to be mated within a certain number of subsequent moves. Also called **suimate.**

self-mor·ti·fi·ca·tion (self′môr′tə fə kā′shən), *n.* the inflicting of pain or privation on oneself: *He was certain that self-mortification was the only road to salvation.* —**self-mor·ti·fied** (self′môr′tə fīd′, self′-), *adj.*

self-mov·ing (self′mo͞o′ving, self′-), *adj.* capable of moving by itself without an external agency. —**self′-move′ment,** *n.* —**self′-mov′er,** *n.*

self-naught·ing (self′nô′ting, self′-), *n.* self-effacement.

self·ness (self′nis), *n.* selfhood. [SELF + -NESS]

self-op·er·at·ing (self′op′ə rā′ting, self′-), *adj.* automatic. Also, **self-op·er·a·tive** (self′op′ə rā′tiv, -ər ə tiv, self′-).

self-o·pin·ion (self′ə pin′yən, self′-), *n.* opinion of oneself, esp. when unduly high.

self-o·pin·ion·at·ed (self′ə pin′yə nā′tid, self′-), *adj.* **1.** conceited; having an inordinately high regard for oneself, one's own opinions, views, etc. **2.** stubborn or obstinate in holding to one's own opinions, views, etc. Also, **self-o·pin·ioned** (self′ə pin′yənd).

self-per·pet·u·at·ing (self′pər pech′o͞o ā′ting, self′-), *adj.* **1.** continuing oneself in office, rank, etc., beyond the normal limit, esp. arranging or producing conditions enabling oneself to continue in a position indefinitely. **2.** capable of indefinite continuation.

self-per·pet·u·a·tion (self′pər pech′o͞o ā′shən, self′-), *n.* the act or process of perpetuating oneself, as in office.

self-pit·y (self′pit′ē, self′-), *n.* pity for oneself, esp. a self-indulgent attitude concerning one's own difficulties, hardships, etc.: *Her self-pity was becoming mawkish.* —**self′-pit′y·ing,** *adj.* —**self′-pit′y·ing·ly,** *adv.*

self-pol·li·nat·ed (self′pol′ə nā′tid, self′-), *adj. Bot.* subjected to self-pollination.

self-pol·li·na·tion (self′pol′ə nā′shən, self′-), *n. Bot.* the transfer of pollen from the anther to the stigma of the same flower, another flower on the same plant, or the flower of a plant of the same clone. Cf. **cross-pollination.**

self-por·trait (self′pôr′trit, -trāt, -pôr′-, self′-), *n.* a portrait of and by oneself.

self-pos·sessed (self′pə zest′, self′-), *adj.* having or showing control of one's feelings, behavior, etc.; composed; poised. —**self-pos·sess·ed·ly** (self′pə zes′id lē, -zest′lē, self′-), *adv.*
—**Syn.** calm, collected, serene, cool, sedate.

self-pos·ses·sion (self′pə zesh′ən, self′-), *n.* the quality of being self-possessed; control of one's feelings, behavior, etc.; composure; poise.

self-pres·er·va·tion (self′prez′ər vā′shən, self′-), *n.* preservation of oneself from harm or destruction.

self-pride (self′prīd′, self′-), *n.* pride in one's abilities, status, possessions, etc.; self-esteem.

self-pro·duced (self′prə do͞ost′, -dyo͞ost′, self′-), *adj.* produced by oneself or itself. —**self-pro·duc·tion** (self′prə duk′shən, self′-), *n.*

self-pro·nounc·ing (self′prə noun′sing), *adj.* having the pronunciation indicated: *a self-pronouncing dictionary.*

self-pro·pelled (self′prə peld′, self′-), *adj.* **1.** propelled by itself. **2.** (of a vehicle) propelled by its own engine, motor, or the like, rather than drawn or pushed by a horse, locomotive, etc. **3.** (of a gun or a rocket launcher) having a vehicle as a base. Also, **self′-pro·pel′ling.**

self-pro·pul·sion (self′ prə pul′shən, self′-), *n.* propulsion by a vehicle's own engine, motor, or the like.

self-pro·tec·tion (self′prə tek′shən, self′-), *n.* protection of oneself or itself. —**self′-pro·tect′ing,** *adj.* —**self′-pro·tec′tive,** *adj.*

self-ques·tion·ing (self′kwes′chə ning, self′-), *n.* review or scrutiny of one's own motives or behavior.

self-re·al·i·za·tion (self′rē′ə li zā′shən, self′-), *n.* the fulfillment of one's potential capacities.

self-re·cord·ing (self′ri kôr′ding, self′-), *adj.* recording automatically, as an instrument.

self-ref·er·ence (self′ref′ər əns), *n. Logic.* the property of a statement that is a statement about itself, as "This statement is grammatical."

self-re·gard (self′ri gärd′, self′-), *n.* **1.** consideration for oneself or one's own interests. **2.** self-respect. —**self′-re·gard′ing,** *adj.*

self-reg·is·ter·ing (self′rej′i stər ing, -string, self′-), *adj.* registering automatically, as an instrument; self-recording. —**self′-reg′is·tra′tion,** *n.*

self-reg·u·lat·ed (self′reg′yə lā′tid, self′-), *adj.* governed or controlled from within; self-regulating.

self-reg·u·lat·ing (self′reg′yə lā′ting, self′-), *adj.* **1.** adjusting, ruling, or governing itself without outside interference; operating or functioning without externally imposed controls or regulations: *a self-regulating economy; the self-regulating market.* **2.** functioning automatically: *a self-regulating machine.*

self-reg·u·la·tion (self′reg′yə lā′shən, self′-), *n.* control by oneself or itself, as in an economy, business organization, etc., esp. such control as exercised independently of governmental supervision, laws, or the like.

self-reg·u·la·tive (self′reg′yə lā′tiv, self′-), *adj.* used for or capable of controlling or adjusting oneself or itself: *a self-regulative device.* Also, **self-reg·u·la·to·ry** (self′reg′yə lə tôr′ē, -tōr′ē, self′-).

self-re·la·tion (self′ri lā′shən, self′-), *n.* the relation of a thing to itself; self-identity.

self-re·li·ance (self′ri lī′əns, self′-), *n.* **1.** reliance on oneself or one's own powers. **2.** (*cap., italics*) a poem (1832) and essay (1841) by Ralph Waldo Emerson.

self-re·li·ant (self′ri lī′ənt, self′-), *adj.* relying on oneself or on one's own powers. —**self′-re·li′ant·ly,** *adv.*

self-re·nun·ci·a·tion (self′ri nun′sē ā′shən, self′-), *n.* renunciation of one's own will, interests, etc. —**self-re·nun·ci·a·to·ry** (self′ri nun′sē ə tôr′ē, -tōr′ē, -shē ə-, self′-), *adj.*

self-re·pres·sion (self′ri presh′ən, self′-), *n.* inhibition of one's feelings, instincts, etc., by oneself; extreme self-restraint. **self′-re·pressed′,** *adj.* —**self′-re·press′ing,** *adj.*

self-re·proach (self′ri prōch′), *n.* blame or censure by one's own conscience. —**self′-re·proach′ful, self′-re·proach′ing,** *adj.* —**self′-re·proach′ing·ly,** *adv.* —**self′-re·proach′ing·ness,** *n.*

self-re·proof (self′ri pro͞of′, self′-), *n.* an act or instance of censuring or reproving oneself.

self-re·spect (self′ri spekt′, self′-), *n.* proper esteem or regard for the dignity of one's character. —**self′-re·spect′ful, self′-re·spect′ing,** *adj.*

self-re·straint (self′ri strānt′, self′-), *n.* restraint imposed on one by oneself; self-control. —**self′-re·strained′,** *adj.* —**self′-re·strain′ing,** *adj.*

self-re·veal·ing (self′ri vē′ling, self′-), *adj.* displaying, exhibiting, or disclosing one's most private feelings, thoughts, etc.: *an embarrassingly self-revealing autobiography.* Also, **self-re·vel·a·to·ry** (self′ri vel′ə tôr′ē, -tōr′ē, -rev′ə lə-, self′-), **self-re·vel·a·tive** (self′ri-vel′ə tiv, -rev′ə lā′-, self′-).

self-rev·e·la·tion (self′rev′ə lā′shən, self′-), *n.* disclosure of one's private feelings, thoughts, etc., esp. when unintentional.

self-right·eous (self′rī′chəs, self′-), *adj.* confident of one's own righteousness, esp. when smugly moralistic and intolerant of the opinions and behavior of others. —**self′-right′eous·ly,** *adv.* —**self′-right′eous·ness,** *n.*

self-ris·ing (self′rī′zing), *adj. Cookery.* rising without the addition of leaven: *self-rising pancake flour.*

self-sac·ri·fice (self′sak′rə fīs′, self′-), *n.* sacrifice of one's interests, desires, etc., as for duty or the good of another. —**self′-sac′ri·fic′er,** *n.* —**self-sac·ri·fi·cial** (self′sak′rə fish′əl, self′-), *adj.* —**self′-sac′ri·fic′ing,** *adj.* —**self′-sac′ri·fic′ing·ly,** *adv.* —**self′-sac′ri·fic′ing·ness,** *n.*

self·same (self′sām′), *adj.* being the very same; identical. [late ME *selve same;* see SELF, SAME; c. Dan *selvsamme,* OHG *selbsama*] —**self′same′ness,** *n.*
—**Syn.** exact, very, same.

self-sat·is·fac·tion (self′sat′is fak′shən), *n.* satisfaction, usually smug, with oneself, one's achievements, etc.

self-sat·is·fied (self′sat′is fīd′, self′-), *adj.* feeling or showing satisfaction with oneself.

self-sat·is·fy·ing (self′sat′is fī′ing, self′-), *adj.* effecting satisfaction to oneself.

self-seal·ing (self′sē′ling, self′-), *adj.* capable of sealing itself automatically: *a self-sealing automobile tire.* —**self′-seal′er,** *n.*

self-seek·er (self′sē′kər), *n.* one who seeks his own interest or selfish ends.

self-seek·ing (self′sē′king), *n.* **1.** the seeking of one's own interest or selfish ends. —*adj.* **2.** given to or characterized by self-seeking; selfish. —**self′-seek′ing·ness,** *n.*

self-serv·ice (self′sûr′vis), *n.* **1.** the serving of oneself in a restaurant, shop, or the like, without the aid of a waiter, clerk, etc. —*adj.* **2.** noting or pertaining to a cafeteria, grocery, store, etc., designed for the patron or customer to gather food or merchandise from a display or display shelves without the aid of attendants and pay at a cashier's desk upon leaving.

self-serv·ing (self′sûr′ving), *adj.* **1.** preoccupied with one's own interests, often disregarding the truth or the interests, well-being, etc., of others. **2.** serving to further one's own selfish interests.

self-sown (self′sōn′), *adj.* **1.** sown by itself, or without human or animal agency, as of a plant grown from seeds dropped from another plant. **2.** sown by any agency other than man, as of a plant grown from seeds scattered by birds or the wind.

self-start·er (self′stär′tər), *n.* **1.** a device that starts an internal-combustion engine without cranking by hand, as an electric motor, a spring, etc. **2.** *Informal.* a person who begins work or undertakes a project on his own initiative, without needing to be told or encouraged to do so. —**self′-start′ing,** *adj.*

self-styled (self′stīld′), *adj.* styled, called, or considered by oneself as specified: *a self-styled leader.*

self-suf·fi·cient (self′sə fish′ənt, self′-), *adj.* **1.** able to supply one's own or its own needs without external assistance: *The nation grows enough grain to be self-sufficient.* **2.** having extreme confidence in one's own resources, powers, etc.: *He was self-sufficient, and always reminded you of it.* Also, **self-suf·fic·ing** (self′sə fī′sing). —**self′suf·fi′cien·cy,** *n.* —**self′-suf·fi′cient·ly,** *adv.*

self-sup·port (self′sə pōrt′, -pôrt′, self′-), *n.* the supporting or maintaining of oneself without relying on any outside aid. —**self′-sup·port′ed,** *adj.* —**self′-sup·port′ed·ness,** *n.* —**self′-sup·port′ing,** *adj.* —**self′-sup·port′ing·ly,** *adv.*

self-sur·ren·der (self′sə ren′dər, self′-), *n.* the surrender or yielding up of oneself, one's will, affections, etc., as to another person, an influence, cause, etc.

---

self′-maimed′, *adj.*
self′-main·tained′, *adj.*
self′-main·tain′ing, *adj.*
self′-main′te·nance, *n.*
self′-mak′ing, *adj.*
self′-man′i·fest′, *adj.*
self′-man′i·fes·ta′tion, *n.*
self′-mapped′, *adj.*
self′-ma·tured′, *adj.*
self′-meas′ure·ment, *n.*
self′-me′di·at′ing, *adj.*
self′-mer′it, *n.*
self′-mind′ed, *adj.*
self′-mis·trust′, *n.*
self′-mul′ti·plied′, *adj.*
self′-mul′ti·ply′ing, *adj.*
self′-mur′der, *n.*
self′-mur′dered, *adj.*
self′-mur′der·er, *n.*
self′-mu′ti·la′tion, *n.*
self′-named′, *adj.*
self′-neg·lect′, *adj.*
self′-neg·lect′ful, *adj.*
self′-neg·lect′ing, *adj.*
self′-nour′ished, *adj.*
self′-nour′ish·ing, *adj.*
self′-nour′ish·ment, *n.*
self′-ob·jec′ti·fi·ca′tion, *n.*
self′-ob·liv′i·on, *n.*
self′-ob·liv′i·ous, *adj.*
self′-ob′ser·va′tion, *n.*
self′-ob·served′, *adj.*
self′-ob·sessed′, *adj.*
self′-ob·ses′sion, *n.*
self′-oc′cu·pa′tion, *n.*
self′-oc′cu·pied′, *adj.*
self′-of·fence′, *n.*
self′-of·fense′, *n.*
self′-of′fered, *adj.*
self′-oil′ing, *adj.*
self′-o′pened, *adj.*
self′-o′pen·er, *n.*
self′-o′pen·ing, *adj.*
self′-op′er·a′tor, *n.*
self′-op·pres′sion, *n.*
self′-op·pres′sive, *adj.*
self′-op·pres′sor, *n.*
self′-or·dained′, *adj.*
self′-or·dain′er, *n.*
self′-o·rig′i·nat′ed, *adj.*
self′-o·rig′i·nat′ing, *adj.*
self′-o·rig′i·na′tion, *n.*
self′-out′law′, *n.*
self′-out′lawed′, *adj.*
self′-own′er·ship, *n.*
self′-ox′i·da′tion, *n.*
self′-paid′, *adj.*
self′-paint′er, *n.*
self′-pam′pered, *adj.*
self′-pam′per·ing, *adj.*
self′-pan′e·gyr′ic, *adj.*
self′-pay′ing, *adj.*
self′-peace′, *n.*
self′-pen′e·tra·bil′i·ty, *n.*
self′-pen′e·tra′tion, *n.*
self′-per·ceiv′ing, *adj.*
self′-per·cep′tion, *n.*
self′-per·cep′tive, *adj.*
self′-per·fect′i·bil′i·ty, *n.*
self′-per·fect′ing, *adj.*
self′-per·formed′, *adj.*
self′-per·mis′sion, *n.*
self′-per·plexed′, *adj.*
self′-per·sua′sion, *n.*
self′-pic′tured, *adj.*
self′-pit′i·ful, *adj.*
self′-pit′i·ful·ness, *n.*
self′-plant′ed, *adj.*
self′-play′er, *n.*
self′-play′ing, *adj.*
self′-pleased′, *adj.*
self′-pleas′er, *n.*
self′-pleas′ing, *adj.*
self′-point′ed, *adj.*
self′-poi′son·er, *n.*
self′-po·lic′ing, *adj.*
self′-pol′i·cy, *n.*
self′-pol′i·ti′cian, *n.*
self′-pol·lu′tion, *n.*
self′-posed′, *adj.*
self′-post′ing, *adj.*
self′-post·pone′ment, *n.*
self′-pow′ered, *adj.*
self′-praise′, *n.*
self′-prais′ing, *adj.*
self′-pre·cip′i·ta′tion, *n.*
self′-pref′er·ence, *n.*
self′-pre·oc′cu·pa′tion, *n.*
self′-prep′a·ra′tion, *n.*
self′-pre·pared′, *adj.*
self′-pre·scribed′, *adj.*
self′-pres′en·ta′tion, *n.*
self′-pre·sent′ed, *adj.*
self′-pre·tend′ed, *adj.*
self′-primed′, *adj.*
self′-prim′er, *n.*
self′-prim′ing, *adj.*
self′-priz′ing, *adj.*
self′-pro·claimed′, *adj.*
self′-pro·claim′ing, *adj.*
self′-pro·cured′, *adj.*
self′-pro·cure′ment, *n.*
self′-pro·cur′ing, *adj.*
self′-pro·fessed′, *adj.*
self′-prof′it, *n.*
self′-pro·jec′tion, *n.*
self′-prop′a·gat′ed, *adj.*
self′-prop′a·gat′ing, *adj.*
self′-prop′a·ga′tion, *n.*
self′-pro·pul′sion, *n.*
self′-prov′ing, *adj.*
self′-pro·vi′sion, *n.*
self′-pun′ished, *adj.*
self′-pun′ish·er, *n.*
self′-pun′ish·ing, *adj.*
self′-pun′ish·ment, *n.*
self′-pu′ni·tive, *adj.*
self′-pu′ri·fy′ing, *adj.*
self′-quo·ta′tion, *n.*
self′-raised′, *adj.*
self′-rais′ing, *adj.*
self′-rat′ing, *adj.*
self′-re·act′ing, *adj.*
self′-read′ing, *adj.*
self′-reck′on·ing, *adj.*
self′-rec′ol·lec′tion, *n.*
self′-rec′ol·lec′tive, *adj.*
self′-re′con·struc′tion, *n.*
self′-re·crim′i·na′tion, *n.*
self′-rec′ti·fy′ing, *adj.*
self′-re·duc′tion, *n.*
self′-re·du′pli·ca′tion, *n.*
self′-re·fine′ment, *n.*
self′-re·fin′ing, *adj.*
self′-re·flec′tion, *n.*
self′-re·flec′tive, *adj.*
self′-re·form′, *n.*
self′-ref′or·ma′tion, *n.*
self′-re·fut′ed, *adj.*
self′-re·fut′ing, *adj.*
self′-rel′ish, *n.*
self′-re·nounced′, *adj.*
self′-re·nounce′ment, *n.*
self′-re·nounc′ing, *adj.*
self′-re·peat′ing, *adj.*
self′-re·pel′len·cy, *n.*
self′-re·pel′lent, *adj.*
self′-re·pose′, *n.*
self′-rep′re·sen·ta′tion, *n.*
self′-re′pro·duc′ing, *adj.*
self′-re′pro·duc′tion, *n.*
self′-re·pul′sive, *adj.*
self′-rep′u·ta′tion, *n.*
self′-re·sent′ment, *n.*
self′-re·signed′, *adj.*
self′-re·source′ful, *adj.*
self′-re·source′ful·ness, *n.*
self′-re·splend′ent, *adj.*
self′-re·spon′si·bil′i·ty, *n.*
self′-re·stor′ing, *adj.*
self′-re·strict′ed, *adj.*
self′-re·stric′tion, *n.*
self′-re·tired′, *adj.*
self′-re·vealed′, *adj.*
self′-rev′er·ence, *n.*
self′-rev′er·ent, *adj.*
self′-rig′or·ous, *adj.*
self′-roofed′, *adj.*
self′-ru′in, *n.*
self′-ru′ined, *adj.*
self′-rule′, *n.*
self′-safe′ty, *n.*
self′-sanc′ti·fi·ca′tion, *n.*
self′-sat′i·rist, *n.*
self′-scanned′, *adj.*
self′-schooled′, *adj.*
self′-school′ing, *adj.*
self′-scorn′, *n.*
self′-scourg′ing, *adj.*
self′-scru′ti·nized′, *adj.*
self′-scru′ti·niz′ing, *adj.*
self′-scru′ti·ny, *n.*
self′-search′ing, *adj.*
self′-se·cu′ri·ty, *n.*
self′-sed′i·men·ta′tion, *n.*
self′-sed′i·ment′ed, *adj.*
self′-sent′, *adj.*
self′-se·ques′tered, *adj.*
self′-set′, *adj.*
self′-shad′owed, *adj.*
self′-shad′ow·ing, *adj.*
self′-shel′ter, *n.*
self′-shel′tered, *adj.*
self′-shine′, *n.*
self′-shin′ing, *adj.*
self′-sig·nif′i·cance, *n.*
self′-sim′i·lar, *adj.*
self′-sink′ing, *adj.*
self′-slain′, *adj.*
self′-sold′, *adj.*
self′-so·lic′i·tude′, *n.*
self′-soothed′, *adj.*
self′-sooth′ing, *adj.*
self′-so·phis′ti·ca′tion, *n.*
self′-sought′, *adj.*
self′-sound′ing, *adj.*
self′-sov′er·eign·ty, *n.*
self′-spaced′, *adj.*
self′-spac′ing, *adj.*
self′-speech′, *n.*
self′-spit′ted, *adj.*
self′-sprung′, *adj.*
self′-sta·bil′i·ty, *n.*
self′-sta′bi·lized′, *adj.*
self′-sta′bi·liz′ing, *adj.*
self′-starved′, *adj.*
self′-steered′, *adj.*
self′-stim′u·lat′ed, *adj.*
self′-stim′u·lat′ing, *adj.*
self′-stim′u·la′tion, *n.*
self′-strength′, *n.*
self′-strip′per, *n.*
self′-strong′, *adj.*
self′-stuck′, *adj.*
self′-sub·du′al, *n.*
self′-sub·dued′, *adj.*
self′-sub·jec′tion, *n.*
self′-sub′ju·gat′ing, *adj.*
self′-sub′ju·ga′tion, *n.*
self′-sub′or·dained′, *adj.*
self′-sub·or′di·nat′ing, *adj.*
self′-sub·or′di·na′tion, *n.*
self′-sub′si·da′tion, *n.*
self′-sub·sist′ence, *n.*
self′-sub·sist′ent, *adj.*
self′-sub·sist′ing, *adj.*
self′-sub·ver′sive, *adj.*
self′-sup·press′ing, *adj.*
self′-sup·pres′sion, *n.*
self′-sup·pres′sive, *adj.*

---

self-sus·tain·ing (self′sə stā′niṉg, self′-), *adj.* self-supporting. —**self′-sus·tained′,** *adj.* —**self′-sus·tain′ing·ly,** *adv.* —**self′-sus·tain′ment,** *n.*

self′-tap′ping screw′ (self′tap′iṉg), a screw designed to tap its corresponding female thread as it is driven. Also called **tapping screw.**

self-taught (self′tôt′), *adj.* **1.** taught to oneself or by oneself to be (as indicated) without the aid of a formal education: *self-taught typing; a self-taught typist.* **2.** learned by oneself: *a self-taught mastery of the guitar.*

self-tor·ment (self′tôr′ment, self′-), *n.* the act or an instance of tormenting oneself, as with worry, guilt, etc. —**self′-tor·ment′ed,** *adj.* —**self′-tor·ment′ing,** *adj.* —**self′-tor·ment′ing·ly,** *adv.* —**self′-tor·men′tor,** *n.*

self-un·load·er (self′un lō′dər, self′-), *n.* a bulk cargo vessel, as on the Great Lakes, having a system of machinery by which it can be unloaded without any assistance from the shore.

self-val·i·dat·ing (self′val′i dā′tiṉg, self′-), *adj.* requiring no external confirmation, sanction, or validation.

self·ward (self′wərd), *adv.* Also, **self′wards. 1.** in the direction of or toward oneself: *a selfward-moving gesture.* **2.** within oneself; inward: *She turned her thoughts selfward.* —*adj.* **3.** tending toward or directed at oneself. [SELF + -WARD] —**self′ward·ness,** *n.*

self-will (self′wil′, self′-), *n.* stubborn or obstinate willfulness, as in pursuing one's own wishes, aims, etc. [ME, OE; see SELF, WILL[2]] —**self′-willed′,** *adj.* —**self′-willed′ly,** *adv.* —**self′-willed′ness,** *n.*

self-wind·ing (self′wīn′diṉg), *adj.* (of a timepiece) kept wound or wound periodically by a mechanism, as an electric motor, a system of weighted levers, etc., so that winding by hand is not necessary.

self-wrong (self′rôṉg′, -roṉg′), *n.* wrong done to oneself.

Se·lig (sē′lig; *Ger.* zā′liḵʜ), *n.* a boy's given name. Also, **Zelig.**

Se·li·hoth (sə lē ḵʜōt′, slē-), *n. Hebrew.* **1.** (*construed as pl.*) liturgical prayers serving as expressions of repentance and pleas for God's forgiveness, recited by Jews during the period, usually beginning the preceding week, before Rosh Hashanah, during the period between Rosh Hashanah and Yom Kippur, and on fast days. **2.** (*construed as sing.*) a religious service at which such prayers are recited. Also, **Se·li·choth′.** [lit., pardons]

Se·lins·grove (sē′linz grōv′), *n.* a town in central Pennsylvania. 3948 (1960).

Sel·juk (sel jo͞ok′), *adj.* **1.** noting or pertaining to certain Turkish dynasties which ruled over large parts of Asia from the 11th to the 13th centuries. —*n.* **2.** a member of a Seljuk dynasty or of a tribe ruled by them. Also, **Sel·juk·i·an** (sel jo͞o′kē ən).

Sel·kirk (sel′kûrk), *n.* **1. Alexander** (originally *Alexander Selcraig*), 1676–1721, Scottish sailor marooned on a Pacific island: supposed prototype of Robinson Crusoe. **2.** Also called **Sel·kirk·shire** (sel′kûrk shēr′, -shər). a county in SE Scotland. 21,055 (est. 1961); 268 sq. mi. *Co. seat:* Selkirk.

Sel′kirk Moun′tains, a mountain range in SW Canada, in SE British Columbia. Highest peak, Mt. Sir Donald, 11,123 ft.

sell[1] (sel), *v.,* **sold, sell·ing,** *n.* —*v.t.* **1.** to give up or make over to another for a consideration; dispose of to a purchaser for a price: *He sold the car to me for $500.* **2.** to deal in; keep or offer for sale: *He sells insurance. This store sells my favorite brand.* **3.** to make a sale or offer for sale to: *He'll sell me the car for $500.* **4.** to persuade or induce (someone) to buy something: *The clerk sold her three pairs of shoes by being charming.* **5.** to persuade or induce someone to buy (something): *The clerk really sold the shoes to her by flattery.* **6.** to cause to be accepted: *to sell an idea to the public.* **7.** to cause or persuade to accept; convince: *to sell the voters on a candidate.* **8.** to accept a price for or make a profit of (something not a proper object for such action): *to sell one's soul for political power.* **9.** to force or exact a price for: *The defenders of the fort sold their lives dearly.* **10.** *Informal.* to cheat, betray, or hoax. —*v.i.* **11.** to make a sale of something. **12.** to be on sale. **13.** to offer something for sale: *I like his house—will he sell?* **14.** to be employed to persuade or induce others to buy, as a salesman or a clerk in a store: *One brother is a cashier and the other sells.* **15.** to have a specific price; be offered for sale at the price indicated (fol. by *at* or *for*): *Eggs sell at sixty cents a dozen. This shirt sells for five dollars.* **16.** to be in demand as a purchase: *On a rainy day, umbrellas really sell.* **17.** to win acceptance, approval, or adoption: *Here's an idea that'll sell.* **18. sell off,** to sell, esp. at reduced prices, in order to get rid of: *The city is selling off a large number of small lots at public auction.* **19. sell out, a.** to dispose of entirely by selling. **b.** *Informal.* to betray (an associate, one's country, a cause, etc.); turn traitor: *He committed suicide rather than sell out to the enemy.* **20. sell up,** *Brit.* to sell out: *She was forced to sell up her entire stock of crystal.* —*n.* **21.** *Slang.* a cheat; hoax. [ME *selle(n),* OE *sellan;* c. Icel *selja,* LG *sellen,* Goth *saljan,* orig. to cause to take; gradational var. of Gk *helein* to take]
—**Syn. 1.** exchange, vend. See **trade.** —**Ant. 1.** buy.

sell[2] (sel), *n., adj., pron. Scot.* self. [var. of SEL]

Sel·la (sel′ə), *n. Douay Bible.* Zillah.

sell·er (sel′ər), *n.* **1.** one who sells; salesman or vender. **2.** an article, as a hat, considered with reference to its sales: *one of the poorest sellers.* [SELL[1] + -ER[1]]

Sel·lers·burg (sel′ərz bûrg′), *n.* a town in S Indiana. 2679 (1960).

sell′ers′ mar′ket, a market in which goods and services are scarce and prices relatively high. Cf. **buyers' market.**

sell′er's op′tion, (on the New York Stock Exchange) a special transaction that gives the seller the right to make late delivery of a security within a specified period, ranging from 5 to not more than 60 business days for stocks.

Sel·li (sel′ī), *n.pl. Class. Myth.* the priests of Zeus at the sacred grove at Dodonna.

sell·ing (sel′iṉg), *adj.* **1.** of or pertaining to a sale or sales: *the selling price of oranges.* **2.** engaged in selling: *two selling offices in New York.* **3.** readily salable; in strong demand (often used in combination): *This is our fastest-selling model.* [ME; see SELL[1], -ING[1]]

sell·ing-plat·er (sel′iṉg plā′tər), *n. Rare.* a horse that competes in a selling race.

sell′ing race′, *Rare.* a claiming race at the end of which the winning horse is offered for sale.

sell·out (sel′out′), *n.* **1.** the act or an instance of selling out. **2.** an entertainment, as a show or athletic event, for which all the seats are sold. [n. use of v. phrase *sell out*]

Sel·ma (sel′mə), *n.* **1.** a city in central Alabama, on the Alabama River. 28,385 (1960). **2.** a town in central California. 6934 (1960). **3.** a town in central North Carolina. 3102 (1960). **4.** a girl's given name.

Selt·zer (selt′sər), *n.* **1.** a naturally effervescent mineral water containing common salt and small quantities of sodium, calcium, and magnesium carbonates. **2.** (*often l.c.*) a prepared water of similar composition. Also called **Selt′zer wa′ter.** [< G *Selterser* named after *Selters,* a village near Wiesbaden; see -ER[1]]

sel·vage (sel′vij), *n.* **1.** the edge of woven fabric finished to prevent raveling, often in a narrow tape effect, different from the body of the fabric. **2.** any similar strip or part of surplus material, as at the side of wallpaper. **3.** a plate or surface through which a bolt of a lock passes. Also, **sel′vedge.** [SELF + EDGE, modeled on D *zelfegge*] —**sel′vaged,** *adj.*

selves (selvz), *n.* pl. of **self.**

Sel·wyn (sel′win), *n.* a boy's given name.

Selz·nick (selz′nik), *n.* **David O(liver),** 1902–65, U.S. motion-picture producer.

Sem (sem), *n. Douay Bible.* Shem.

Sem., 1. Seminary. **2.** Semitic. Also, **Sem**

sem., semicolon.

se·mai·nier (sə men′yā; *Fr.* sə me nyā′), *n., pl.* **-mai·niers** (-men′yāz; *Fr.* -me nyā′). *Fr. Furniture.* a chest of the 18th century having seven long drawers. [< F, equiv. to *semaine* week < LL *septimān(a)* < L *septimān(us)* of seven < *sept(em)* SEVEN + F *-ier* < L *-ārius* -ARY]

se·maise (si mez′), *n.* cymaise.

Se·ma·le·us (si mā′lē əs), *n. Class. Myth.* an epithet of Zeus meaning "sign-giving."

Se·mang (si mäṉg′), *n., pl.* **-mangs,** (*esp. collectively*) **-mang.** a member of a Negrito people of the Malay Peninsula.

se·man·teme (si man′tēm), *n. Ling.* one of the minimum elements of lexical meaning in a language. [< F *sémantème,* equiv. to *sémant(ique)* SEMANTIC + *-ème* -EME]

se·man·tic (si man′tik), *adj.* **1.** of, pertaining to, or arising from the different meanings of words or other symbols: *semantic change; semantic confusion.* **2.** of or pertaining to semantics. [< Gk *sēmantik(ós)* having meaning, equiv. to *sēmant(ós)* (*sēman-,* base of *sēmaínein* to show, mark + *-tos* verbid adj. suffix) + *-ikos* -IC] —**se·man′ti·cal·ly,** *adv.*

se·man·tics (si man′tiks), *n.* (*construed as sing.*) **1.** *Ling.* **a.** the study of meaning. **b.** the study of linguistic development by classifying and examining changes in meaning and form. **2.** Also called **significs.** the branch of semiotic dealing with the relations between signs and what they denote. **3.** See **general semantics.** [see SEMANTIC, -ICS] —**se·man·ti·cist** (si man′tisist), **se·man·ti·cian** (sē′man tish′ən), *n.*

sem·a·phore (sem′ə fōr′, -fôr′), *n., v.,* **-phored, -phor·ing.** —*n.* **1.** an apparatus for conveying information by means of visual signals, as a light the position of which may be changed. **2.** any of various devices for signaling by changing the position of a light, flag, etc. **3.** a system of signaling, esp. a system by which a special flag is held in each hand and various positions of the arms indicate specific letters, numbers, etc. —*v.t., v.i.* **4.** to signal by semaphore or by some system of flags. [*sema-* (< Gk *sêma* sign) + -PHORE] —**sem·a·phor·ic** (sem′ə fôr′ik, -for′-), *adj.* —**sem′a·phor′i·cal,** *adj.* —**sem′a·phor′i·cal·ly,** *adv.*

Semaphore (railroad)

Se·ma·rang (sə mär′äṉg), *n.* a seaport on N Java, in S Indonesia. 487,006 (est. 1961). Also, **Samarang.**

se·ma·si·ol·o·gy (si mā′sē ol′ə jē, -zē-), *n.* semantics, esp. the study of semantic change. [< Gk *sēmasí(a)* meaning + -o- + -LOGY] —**se·ma·si·o·log·i·cal** (si mā′sē ə loj′i kəl, -zē-), *adj.* —**se·ma′si·o·log′i·cal·ly,** *adv.* —**se·ma′si·ol′o·gist,** *n.*

se·mat·ic (si mat′ik), *adj. Biol.* serving as a sign or warning of danger, as the conspicuous colors or markings of certain poisonous animals. [< Gk *sēmat-* (s. of *sêma*) sign + -IC]

sem·bla·ble (sem′blə bəl), *Archaic.* —*adj.* **1.** like or similar. **2.** seeming or apparent. —*n.* **3.** likeness; resemblance. [late ME < MF, equiv. to *sembl(er)* (to) seem + *-able* -ABLE. See SEMBLANCE] —**sem′bla·bly,** *adv.*

sem·blance (sem′bləns), *n.* **1.** outward aspect or appearance. **2.** an assumed or unreal appearance; show. **3.** a likeness, image, or copy. **4.** a spectral appearance; apparition. [late ME < MF, equiv. to *sembl(er)* (to) seem (see RESEMBLE) + *-ance* -ANCE]
—**Syn. 1.** aspect, exterior, mien, air. **2.** seeming.

Sem·brich (zem′brikʜ), *n.* **Mar·cel·la** (mär tsel′ä), (*Prazede Marcelline Kochanska*), 1858–1935, Austrian soprano.

se·mé (sə mā′), *adj. Heraldry.* covered with many small, identical figures: *an escutcheon gules semé of crosses or.* [< F: lit., sown, ptp. of *semer* < L *sēmināre* to sow, equiv. to *sēmin-* (s. of *sēmen*) seed + *-āre* inf. suffix]

se·mé-de-lys (sə mād′ᵊlē′), *adj. Heraldry.* semé of fleurs-de-lis.

se·mei·ol·o·gy (sē′mī ol′ə jē), *n.* **1.** the science of signs. **2.** sign language. Also, **semiology.** [< Gk *sēmeîo(n)* sign + -LOGY] —**se·mei·o·log·ic** (sē′mī ə-loj′ik), **se′mei·o·log′i·cal,** *adj.* —**se′mei·ol′o·gist,** *n.*

se·mei·ot·ic (sē′mī ot′ik, sē′mē-, sem′ī-, sem′ē-), *adj.* semiotic. Also, **se′mei·ot′i·cal.**

sem·el (sem′el), *adv.* (in prescriptions) once. [< L]

Sem·e·le (sem′ə lē′), *n. Class. Myth.* a daughter of Cadmus and mother, by Zeus, of Dionysus: she was destroyed when Zeus fulfilled her wish to see him in all his glory as god of lightning. Cf. **Thyone.**

sem·eme (sem′ēm), *n. Ling.* **1.** the meaning of a morpheme. **2.** a basic unit of meaning or content. [< Gk *sêm(a)* sign + -EME; coined by L. Bloomfield in 1933; cf. SEMANTEME]

se·men (sē′mən), *n.* the viscid, whitish fluid produced in the male reproductive organs, containing spermatozoa. [< L: seed]

Se·më·nov (sə myô′nof), *n.* **Ni·co·lai N.** (nē ko lī′), born 1896, Russian chemist: Nobel prize 1956.

se·mes·ter (si mes′tər), *n.* **1.** (in many educational institutions) a division constituting half of the regular academic year, lasting typically from 15 to 18 weeks. **2.** (in German universities) a session, lasting about six months and including periods of recess. [< G < L *sēme(n)stris,* equiv. to *sē* (comb. form of *sex* SIX) + *menstris* monthly] —**se·mes′tral, se·mes·tri·al** (si-mes′trē əl), *adj.*

sem·i (sem′ī), *n. Informal.* semitrailer. [by shortening]

semi-, an element borrowed from Latin, meaning "half," freely prefixed to English words of any origin: *semiautomatic; semidetached; semimonthly.* [ME < L; c. OE *sōm-, sām-* half (mod. dial. *sam-*), OHG *sāmi-,* Skt *sāmi-,* Gk *hēmi-*]

semi-ab·stract (sem′ē ab′strakt, -ab strakt′, sem′-ī-), *adj.* pertaining to or designating a style of painting or sculpture in which the subject remains recognizable although the forms are highly stylized in a manner derived from abstract art. —**sem·i-abstrac·tion** (sem′-ē ab strak′shən, sem′ī-), *n.*

sem·i·an·nu·al (sem′ē an′yo͞o əl, sem′ī-), *adj.* **1.** occurring, done, or published every half year or twice a

self′-sur′vey, *n.*
self′-sur·veyed′, *adj.*
self′-sur·viv′ing, *adj.*
self′-sur·vi′vor, *n.*
self′-sus·pend′ed, *adj.*
self′-sus·pi′cion, *n.*
self′-sus·pi′cious, *adj.*
self′-sus′te·nance, *n.*
self′-sus′ten·ta′tion, *n.*
self′-sway′, *n.*
self′-tap′ping, *adj.*
self′-tax·a′tion, *n.*
self′-taxed′, *adj.*
self′-teach′er, *n.*
self′-teach′ing, *adj.*
self′-tempt′ed, *adj.*
self′-ten′der·ness, *n.*
self′-ter′mi·nat′ing, *adj.*
self′-ter′mi·na′tive, *adj.*
self′-test′ing, *adj.*
self′-thin′ning, *adj.*
self′-thought′, *n.*
self′-thread′ing, *adj.*
self′-tight′en·ing, *adj.*
self′-tip′ping, *adj.*
self′-tire′, *v.i.,* **-tired, -tir·ing**
self′-tol′er·ant, *adj.;* **-ly,** *adv.*
self′-tor′ture, *n.*
self′-tor′tured, *adj.*
self′-tor′tur·ing, *adj.*
self′-trained′, *adj.*
self′-train′ing, *n.*
self′-trans′for·ma′tion, *n.*
self′-trans·formed′, *adj.*
self′-treat′ed, *adj.*
self′-treat′ment, *n.*
self′-tri′al, *n.*
self′-trit′u·rat′ing, *adj.*
self′-trou′bled, *adj.*
self′-trou′bling, *adj.*
self′-trust′, *n.*
self′-trust′ing, *adj.*
self′-tu·i′tion, *n.*
self′-un·con′scious, *adj.*
self′-un′der·stand′ing, *n.*
self′-un′der·stood′, *adj.*
self′-un·do′ing, *adj.*
self′-u′ni·form′, *adj.*
self′-un′ion, *n.*
self′-u′ni·ty, *n.*
self′-un·load′ing, *adj.*
self′-un·veil′ing, *adj.*
self′-un·wor′thi·ness, *n.*
self′-up·braid′ing, *n.*
self′-u·surp′, *v.i.*
self′-val′u·a′tion, *n.*
self′-val′ued, *adj.*
self′-val′u·ing, *adj.*
self′-var′i·ance, *n.*
self′-var′i·a′tion, *n.*
self′-var′y·ing, *adj.*
self′-vaunt′ed, *adj.*
self′-vaunt′ing, *adj.*
self′-ven·di′tion, *n.*
self′-ven′ti·lat′ed, *adj.*
self′-vex·a′tion, *n.*
self′-vin′di·cat′ed, *adj.*
self′-vin′di·cat′ing, *adj.*
self′-vin′di·ca′tion, *n.*
self′-vi′o·lence, *n.*
self′-vi′o·lent, *adj.*
self′-viv′i·sec′tor, *n.*
self′-vul′can·iz′ing, *adj.*
self′-want′, *n.*
self′-war′rant·ing, *adj.*
self′-watch′ful·ness, *n.*
self′-wea′ri·ness, *n.*
self′-wea′ry, *adj.*
self′-weight′, *n.*
self′-weight′ed, *adj.*
self′-whip′per, *n.*
self′-whip′ping, *adj.*
self′-whole′, *adj.*
self′-wise′, *adj.*
self′-wit′ness, *n.*
self′-wit′nessed, *adj.*
self′-work′ing, *adj.*
self′-worn′, *adj.*
self′-wor′ship, *n.*
self′-wor′ship·er, *n.*
self′-wor′ship·ing, *adj.*
self′-wor′ship·per, *n.*
self′-wor′ship·ping, *adj.*
self′-worth′, *n.*
self′-wor′thi·ness, *n.*
self′-wound′ed, *adj.*
self′-wound′ing, *adj.*
self′-writ′ing, *adj.*
self′-writ′ten, *adj.*
self′-wrought′, *adj.*

sem′i·ab·sorb′ent, *adj.*
sem′i·ac′a·dem′ic, *adj.*
sem′i·ac′a·dem′i·cal, *adj.;* **-ly,** *adv.*
sem′i·a·ce′tic, *adj.*
sem′i·ac′id, *adj.*
sem′i·a·cid′ic, *adj.*
sem′i·a·cid′i·fied′, *adj.*
sem′i·a·cid′u·lat′ed, *adj.*
sem′i·ac′ro·bat′ic, *adj.*
sem′i·ac′tive, *adj.;* **-ly,** *adv;* **-ness,** *n.*
sem′i·ad·he′sive, *adj.;* **-ly,** *adv.;* **-ness,** *n.*
sem′i·ag′ri·cul′tur·al, *adj.*
sem′i·al′co·hol′ic, *adj.*
sem′i·al′le·gor′ic, *adj.*
sem′i·al′le·gor′i·cal, *adj.;* **-ly,** *adv.*
sem′i·a·lu′mi·nous, *adj.*
sem′i·an′aes·thet′ic, *adj.*
sem′i·an′a·lyt′ic, *adj.*
sem′i·an′a·lyt′i·cal, *adj.;* **-ly,** *adv.*
sem′i·an′ar·chism, *n.*
sem′i·an′ar·chist, *n.*
sem′i·an′ar·chis′tic, *adj.*
sem′i·an′a·tom′ic, *adj.*
sem′i·an′a·tom′i·cal, *adj.;* **-ly,** *adv.*
sem′i·an·drog′e·nous, *adj.*
sem′i·an′es·thet′ic, *adj.*
sem′i·an′gle, *n.*
sem′i·an′gu·lar, *adj.*
sem′i·an′i·mal, *n., adj.*
sem′i·an′i·mate, *adj.*
sem′i·an′i·mat′ed, *adj.*
sem′i·an′thro·po·log′ic, *adj.*
sem′i·an′thro·po·log′i·cal, *adj.;* **-ly,** *adv.*

year. **2.** lasting for half a year: *a semiannual plant.* [SEMI- + ANNUAL] —**sem′i·an′nu·al·ly,** *adv.*

sem·i·a·quat·ic (sem′ē ə kwat′ik, -kwot′-, sem′ī-), *adj. Bot., Zool.* partly aquatic; growing or living close to water and sometimes found in water. [SEMI- + AQUATIC]

sem·i·arch (sem′ē ärch′), *n.* a half arch. [SEMI- + ARCH[1]]

sem·i·ar·id (sem′ē ar′id, sem′ī-), *adj.* (of a region, land, etc.) characterized by very little annual rainfall, usually from 10 to 20 inches: *the struggle to raise vegetables in semiarid regions.* [SEMI- + ARID] —**sem·i·a·rid·ity,** (sem′ē ə rid′i tē, sem′ī-), *n.*

sem·i·au·to·mat·ic (sem′ē ô′tə mat′ik, sem′ī-), *adj.* **1.** partly automatic. **2.** (of a firearm) automatically ejecting the cartridge case of a fired shot and loading the next cartridge from the magazine but requiring a squeeze of the trigger to fire each individual shot. —*n.* **3.** a self-loading rifle or other firearm. [SEMI- + AUTOMATIC] —**sem′i·au′to·mat′i·cal·ly,** *adv.*

sem·i·au·ton·o·mous (sem′ē ô ton′ə məs, sem′ī-), *adj.* partially self-governing, esp. with reference to internal affairs. [SEMI- + AUTONOMOUS]

sem·i·breve (sem′ē brēv′, sem′ī-), *n. Music Chiefly Brit.* a note half the length of a breve; whole note. See illus. under **note.** [SEMI- + BREVE]

sem·i·cen·te·nar·y (sem′ē sen′tᵊner′ē, sem′ī- *or, esp. Brit.,* -sen ten′ə rē, -tē′nə-), *adj., n., pl.* **-nar·ies.** semicentennial. [SEMI- + CENTENARY]

sem·i·cen·ten·ni·al (sem′ē sen ten′ē əl, sem′ī-), *adj.* **1.** of or pertaining to a 50th anniversary. —*n.* **2.** a 50th anniversary. **3.** the celebration of this anniversary. [SEMI- + CENTENNIAL]

Se·mi·chast·ny (se mi khäst′ni), *n.* **Vla·di·mir** (vlä dē′mir), born 1920, Russian government official.

sem·i·cir·cle (sem′i sûr′kəl), *n.* **1.** Also called **sem·i·cir·cum·fer·ence** (sem′ē sər kum′fər əns, -frəns, sem′ī-). half of a circle; the arc from one end of a diameter to the other. **2.** anything having or arranged in the form of a half of a circle. [< L *sēmicircul(us).* See SEMI-, CIRCLE] —**sem·i·cir·cu·lar** (sem′i sûr′kyə lər), *adj.* —**sem′i·cir′cu·lar·ly,** *adv.* —**sem′i·cir′cu·lar·ness,** *n.*

semicir′cular canal′, *Anat.* any of the three curved tubular canals in the labyrinth of the ear, associated with the sense of equilibrium. See diag. under **ear.**

sem·i·civ·i·lized (sem′ē siv′ə līzd′, sem′ī-), *adj.* half or partly civilized. [SEMI- + CIVILIZED] —**sem′i·civ′i·li·za′tion,** *n.*

sem·i·co·lon (sem′i kō′lən), *n.* the punctuation mark (;) used to indicate a major division in a sentence where a more distinct separation is felt between clauses or items on a list than is indicated by a comma, as between the two clauses of a compound sentence. [SEMI- + COLON[1]]

sem·i·co·ma (sem′ē kō′mə, sem′ī-), *n., pl.* **-mas.** a light coma from which a person can be roused. [SEMI- + COMA] —**sem·i·com·a·tose** (sem′i kom′ə tōs′, -kō′mə-), *adj.*

sem·i·con·duct·ing (sem′ē kən duk′ting, sem′ī-), *adj.* of, pertaining to, or having the characteristics of a semiconductor. Also, **sem′i·con·duc′tive.** [SEMI- + CONDUCT + -ING[2]]

sem·i·con·duc·tor (sem′ē kən duk′tər, sem′ī-), *n.* a substance whose electric conductivity at normal temperature is intermediate between that of a metal and an insulator, esp. germanium and silicon. [SEMI- + CONDUCTOR] —**sem′i·con·duc′tion,** *n.*

sem·i·con·scious (sem′ē kon′shəs, sem′ī-), *adj.* half-conscious; not fully conscious. [SEMI- + CONSCIOUS] —**sem′i·con′scious·ly,** *adv.* —**sem′i·con′scious·ness,** *n.*

sem·i·con·ver·gent (sem′ē kən vûr′jənt), *adj.* asymptotic (def. 7). —**sem′i·con·ver′gence,** *adj.*

sem·i·crys·tal·line (sem′ē kris′tᵊlin, -tᵊlīn′, sem′ī-), *adj.* partly or imperfectly crystalline. [SEMI- + CRYSTALLINE]

sem·i·cyl·in·der (sem′ē sil′in dər, sem′ī-), *n.* half of a cylinder divided lengthwise. [SEMI- + CYLINDER] —**sem·i·cy·lin·dri·cal** (sem′ē si lin′dri kəl, sem′ī-), **sem′i·cy·lin′dric,** *adj.*

sem·i·dai·ly (sem′ē dā′lē, sem′ī-), *adj.* twice daily. [SEMI- + DAILY]

sem·i·des·ert (sem′ē dez′ərt, sem′ī-), *n.* an extremely dry area characterized by sparse vegetation. [SEMI- + DESERT[1]]

sem·i·de·tached (sem′ē di tacht′, sem′ī-), *adj.* **1.** partly detached. **2.** (esp. in England) noting or pertaining to a house joined by a party wall to another house or row of houses. [SEMI- + DETACHED] —**sem′i·de·tach′ment,** *n.*

sem·i·di·am·e·ter (sem′ē dī am′i tər, sem′ī-), *n.* half of a diameter; radius. [SEMI- + DIAMETER]

sem·i·di·ur·nal (sem′ē dī ûr′nᵊl, sem′ī-), *adj.* **1.** pertaining to, consisting of, or accomplished in half a day. **2.** occurring every 12 hours or twice each day. [SEMI- + DIURNAL]

sem·i·di·vine (sem′ē di vīn′, sem′ī-), *adj.* somewhat more than mortal but less than divine: *a semidivine king.* [SEMI- + DIVINE]

sem·i·dome (sem′ē dōm′, sem′ī-), *n.* half a dome, esp. as formed by a vertical section, as over a semicircular apse. [SEMI- + DOME] —**sem′i·domed′,** *adj.*

sem·i·do·mes·ti·cat·ed (sem′ē də mes′tə kā′tid, sem′ī-), *adj.* living in a state of partial domestication. [SEMI- + DOMESTICATED] —**sem′i·do·mes′ti·ca′tion,** *n.*

sem·i·dry (sem′ē drī′, sem′ī-), *adj.* partially or nearly dry. [SEMI- + DRY] —**sem′i·dry′ing,** *n.*

sem·i·du·ra·bles (sem′ē dŏŏr′ə bəlz, -dyŏŏr′-, sem′ī-), *n.pl.* goods, as clothing or furniture, that are neither perishable nor truly durable. Also called **sem′i·du′ra·ble goods′.** [SEMI- + *durables* (pl. of DURABLE)]

sem·i·el·lipse (sem′ē i lips′, sem′ī-), *n. Geom.* a half ellipse, usually one containing both ends of the major axis. [SEMI- + ELLIPSE] —**sem·i·el·lip·tic** (sem′ē i lip′tik, sem′ī-), **sem′i·el·lip′ti·cal,** *adj.*

sem·i·fi·nal (sem′ē fīn′ᵊl, sem′ī-), *Sports.* —*adj.* **1.** of or pertaining to the round preceding the final one in a tournament from which losers are eliminated. **2.** (in boxing) of or pertaining to the second most important bout on a card, usually immediately preceeding the main bout. —*n.* **3.** a semifinal contest or round. **4.** (in boxing) the second most important bout on a card. [SEMI- + FINAL]

sem·i·fi·nal·ist (sem′ē fīn′ᵊlist, sem′ī-), *n. Sports.* a participant or one qualified to participate in a semifinal contest in a tournament. [SEMI- + FINALIST]

sem·i·fin·ished (sem′ē fin′isht, sem′ī-), *adj.* **1.** partially or almost finished. **2.** (of a manufactured object) being in a form suitable for working easily into a finished product. [SEMI- + FINISHED]

sem·i·fit·ted (sem′ē fit′id, sem′ī-), *adj.* designed to fit closely but not snugly: *a semifitted jacket.* [SEMI- + FIT[1] + -ED[2]]

sem·i·float·ing (sem′ē flō′ting, sem′ī-), *adj.* noting or pertaining to a driving axle of an automobile or the like, the inner end of which is carried by the differential gear and the outer end of which is keyed to a wheel supported by the axle housing. [SEMI- + FLOATING]

sem·i·flu·id (sem′ē flōō′id, sem′ī-), *adj.* **1.** imperfectly fluid; having both fluid and solid characteristics; semiliquid. —*n.* **2.** Also called **semiliquid.** a semifluid substance. [SEMI- + FLUID] —**sem′i·flu·id′i·ty,** *n.*

sem·i·for·mal (sem′ē fôr′məl, sem′ī-), *adj.* partly formal; containing some formal elements: *a semiformal occasion; semiformal attire.* [SEMI- + FORMAL]

sem·i·glob·u·lar (sem′ē glob′yə lər, sem′ī-), *adj.* possessing the form of half a globe; hemispheric. [SEMI- + GLOBULAR] —**sem′i·glob′u·lar·ly,** *adv.*

sem·i·group (sem′ē grōōp′), *n. Math.* an algebraic system closed under an associative binary operation. [SEMI- + GROUP]

semih., (in prescriptions) half an hour. [< L *sēmihōra*]

sem·i·liq·uid (sem′ē lik′wid, sem′ī-), *adj., n.* semifluid. [SEMI- + LIQUID] —**sem′i·li·quid′i·ty,** *n.*

sem·i·lit·er·ate (sem′ē lit′ər it, sem′ī-), *adj.* **1.** barely able to read and write. **2.** capable of reading but not writing. [SEMI- + LITERATE]

sem·i·lu·nar (sem′ē lōō′nər, sem′ī-), *adj.* shaped like a half-moon; crescent. [SEMI- + LUNAR]

sem′ilu′nar bone′, lunate (def. 2).

sem′ilu′nar valve′, *Anat.* either of two valves consisting of a set of three crescent-shaped flaps of tissue in the aorta and in the pulmonary artery that prevents blood from flowing back into the heart after contraction. Cf. **aortic valve, pulmonary value.**

sem′i·ma′jor ax′is (sem′ē mā′jər, sem′ī-, sem′ē-, sem′ī-), *Astron.* one half the major axis of the ellipse which one celestial body describes around another, as a planet around the sun or a satellite around a planet, equivalent to the mean distance between the two bodies. [SEMI- + MAJOR]

sem·i·mat (sem′ē mat′, sem′ī-), *adj.* midway between mat and glossy, as certain paper or paint. Also, **sem′i·matt′, sem′i·matte′.** [SEMI- + MAT[3]]

sem′i·mi′nor ax′is (sem′ē mī′nər, sem′ī-, sem′ē-, sem′ī-), *Astron.* one half the minor axis of the ellipse which one celestial body describes around another, as a planet around the sun. [SEMI- + MINOR]

sem·i·month·ly (sem′ē munth′lē, sem′ī-), *adj., n., pl.* **-lies,** *adv.* —*adj.* **1.** made, occurring, done, or published twice a month. —*n.* **2.** something occurring every half month or twice a month. **3.** a semimonthly publication. —*adv.* **4.** twice a month: *We went semimonthly to see her.* Cf. **bimonthly.** [SEMI- + MONTHLY]
—**Usage.** See usage note at BIMONTHLY.

sem·i·nal (sem′ə nᵊl), *adj.* **1.** pertaining to, containing, or consisting of semen. **2.** *Bot.* of or pertaining to seed. **3.** having possibilities of future development. **4.** highly original and influencing the development of future events: *a seminal artist; seminal ideas.* [late ME < L *sēminal(is),* equiv. to *sēmin-* (s. of *sēmen*) seed + *-ālis* -AL[1]] —**sem′i·nal′i·ty,** *n.* —**sem′i·nal·ly,** *adv.*

sem′inal prin′ciple, *Philos.* a potential, latent within an imperfect object, for attaining full development.

sem·i·nar (sem′ə när′), *n.* **1.** a small group of students, as in a university, engaged in advanced study and original research under a member of the faculty and meeting regularly to exchange information and hold discussions. **2.** the gathering place of such a group. **3.** a meeting of

sem′i·ar′chi·tec′tur·al, *adj.*; **-ly,** *adv.*
sem′i·ar·tic′u·late, *adj.*; **-ly,** *adv.*
sem′i·bald′, *adj.*; **-ly,** *adv.*; **-ness,** *n.*
sem′i·belt′ed, *adj.*
sem′i·bi′o·graph′ic, *adj.*
sem′i·bi′o·graph′i·cal, *adj*; **-ly,** *adv.*
sem′i·bi′o·log′ic, *adj.*
sem′i·bi′o·log′i·cal, *adj.*; **-ly,** *adv.*
sem′i·blas′phe·mous, *adj.*; **-ly,** *adv.*; **-ness,** *n.*
sem′i·bleached′, *adj.*
sem′i·boiled′, *adj.*
sem′i·bouf·fant′, *adj.*
sem′i·bour·geois′, *adj.*
sem′i·bu′reau·crat′ic, *adj.*
sem′i·bu′reau·crat′i·cal·ly, *adv.*
sem′i·cab′a·lis′tic, *adj.*
sem′i·cab′a·lis′ti·cal, *adj.*; **-ly,** *adv.*
sem′i·cal′cined, *adj.*
sem′i·cap′i·tal·is′tic, *adj.*
sem′i·cap′i·tal·is′ti·cal·ly, *adv.*
sem′i·car′bon·ate, *adj.*
sem′i·car′i·ca·tur′al, *adj.*
sem′i·carved′, *adj.*
sem′i·cat′a·lyst, *n.*
sem′i·cat′a·lyt′ic, *adj.*
sem′i·ca·thar′tic, *adj.*
sem′i·cel′lu·lose′, *n.*
sem′i·cel′lu·lous, *adj.*
sem′i·cha·ot′ic, *adj.*
sem′i·cha·ot′i·cal·ly, *adv.*
sem′i·chem′i·cal, *adj.*; **-ly,** *adv.*
sem′i·clas′si·cal, *adj.*; **-ly,** *adv.*
sem′i·cler′i·cal, *adj.*; **-ly,** *adv.*
sem′i·clin′i·cal, *adj.*; **-ly,** *adv.*
sem′i·closed′, *adj.*
sem′i·col′loid, *n.*
sem′i·col·loi′dal, *adj.*
sem′i·col·lo′qui·al, *adj.*; **-ly,** *adv.*
sem′i·co·lo′ni·al, *adj.*; **-ly,** *adv.*
sem′i·com·bined′, *adj.*
sem′i·com′ic, *adj.*
sem′i·com′i·cal, *adj.*; **-ly,** *adv.*
sem′i·com·mer′cial, *adj.*; **-ly,** *adv.*
sem′i·com·mu′ni·ca′tive, *adj.*
sem′i·con·cealed′, *adj.*
sem′i·con·di′tioned, *adj.*
sem′i·con·fine′ment, *n.*
sem′i·con·form′ist, *n.*
sem′i·con·form′i·ty, *n.*
sem′i·con′i·cal, *adj.*; **-ly,** *adv.*
sem′i·con·serv′a·tive, *adj.*
sem′i·con·tin′u·ous, *adj.*; **-ly,** *adv.*
sem′i·con·ven′tion·al, *adj.*; **-ly,** *adv.*
sem′i·con·ven′tion·al′i·ty, *n.*
sem′i·con·ver′sion, *n.*
sem′i·cor′date, *adj.*
sem′i·cot′ton, *n.*
sem′i·cre′tin, *n.*
sem′i·cul′ti·vat′ed, *adj.*
sem′i·cul′tured, *adj.*
sem′i·cured′, *adj.*
sem′i·cyn′i·cal, *adj.*; **-ly,** *adv.*
sem′i·dan′ger·ous, *adj.*; **-ly,** *adv.*; **-ness,** *n.*
sem′i·deaf′, *adj.*; **-ness,** *n.*
sem′i·de·ca′dent, *adj.*; **-ly,** *adv.*
sem′i·de·cay′, *n.*
sem′i·de·cayed′, *adj.*
sem′i·de·fen′sive, *adj.*; **-ly,** *adv.*; **-ness,** *n.*
sem′i·de·fined′, *adj.*
sem′i·def′i·nite, *adj.*; **-ly,** *adv.*; **-ness,** *n.*
sem′i·de′i·fi·ca′tion, *n.*
sem′i·de·lir′i·um, *n.*
sem′i·de·ment′ed, *adj.*
sem′i·de·pend′ence, *n.*
sem′i·de·pend′ent, *adj.*; **-ly,** *adv.*
sem′i·de·struc′tion, *n.*
sem′i·de·struc′tive, *adj.*
sem′i·de·ter′min·is′tic, *adj.*
sem′i·di·aph′a·nous, *adj.*; **-ly,** *adv.*; **-ness,** *n.*
sem′i·dic′ta·to′ri·al, *adj.*; **-ly,** *adv.*; **-ness,** *n.*
sem′i·di·gest′ed, *adj.*
sem′i·di·rect′, *adj.*; **-ness,** *n.*
sem′i·dis·a′bled, *adj.*
sem′i·di·vid′ed, *adj.*
sem′i·di·vi′sion, *n.*
sem′i·di·vi′sive, *adj.*; **-ly,** *adv.*; **-ness,** *n.*
sem′i·do·mes′tic, *adj.*
sem′i·do·mes′ti·cal·ly, *adv.*
sem′i·dor′mant, *adj.*
sem′i·dra·mat′ic, *adj.*
sem′i·dra·mat′i·cal, *adj.*; **-ly,** *adv.*
sem′i·duc′tile, *adj.*
sem′i·e·las′tic, *adj.*
sem′i·e·las′ti·cal·ly, *adv.*
sem′i·el′e·vat′ed, *adj.*
sem′i·e·mo′tion·al, *adj.*; **-ly,** *adv.*
sem′i·em·pir′i·cal, *adj.*; **-ly,** *adv.*
sem′i·en·clo′sure, *n.*
sem′i·ep′ic, *adj.*
sem′i·ep′i·cal, *adj.*; **-ly,** *adv.*
sem′i·e·rect′, *adj.*; **-ly,** *adv.*; **-ness,** *n.*
sem′i·ex·clu′sive, *adj.*; **-ly,** *adv.*; **-ness,** *n.*
sem′i·ex·ec′u·tive, *adj.*
sem′i·ex′hi·bi′tion·ist, *n.*
sem′i·ex·pand′ed, *adj.*
sem′i·ex·pan′si·ble, *adj.*
sem′i·ex·per′i·men′tal, *adj.*; **-ly,** *adv.*
sem′i·ex·posed′, *adj.*
sem′i·ex·pos′i·tive, *adj.*
sem′i·ex·pos′i·to′ry, *adj.*
sem′i·ex·po′sure, *n.*
sem′i·ex·pres′sion·is′tic, *adj.*
sem′i·ex·ter′nal, *adj.*; **-ly,** *adv.*
sem′i·ex·ter′nal·ized′, *adj.*
sem′i·fic′tion, *n.*
sem′i·fic′tion·al, *adj.*; **-ly,** *adv.*
sem′i·fic′tion·al·ized′, *adj.*
sem′i·fig′ur·a·tive, *adj.*; **-ly,** *adv.*; **-ness,** *n.*
sem′i·fine′, *adj.*
sem′i·fixed′, *adj.*
sem′i·formed′, *adj.*
sem′i·fos′sil·ized′, *adj.*
sem′i·fron·tier′, *n.*
sem′i·func′tion·al, *adj.*; **-ly,** *adv.*
sem′i·func′tion·al·ism, *n.*
sem′i·fur′nished, *adj.*
sem′i·fused′, *adj.*
sem′i·fu′tur·is′tic, *adj.*
sem′i·ge′o·met′ric, *adj.*
sem′i·ge′o·met′ri·cal, *adj.*; **-ly,** *adv.*
sem′i·glaze′, *n.*
sem′i·glazed′, *adj.*
sem′i·god′, *n.*
sem′i·gov′ern·men′tal, *adj.*; **-ly,** *adv.*
sem′i·hard′, *adj.*; **-ness,** *n.*
sem′i·hard′ened, *adj.*
sem′i·her·ba′ceous, *adj.*
sem′i·her′e·tic, *adj., n.*
sem′i·he·ret′i·cal, *adj.*
sem′i·hi′ber·na′tion, *n.*
sem′i·his·tor′ic, *adj.*
sem′i·his·tor′i·cal, *adj.*; **-ly,** *adv.*
sem′i·hos′tile, *adj.*; **-ly,** *adv.*
sem′i·hos·til′i·ty, *n.*
sem′i·hu′man·ism, *n.*
sem′i·hu′man·is′tic, *adj.*
sem′i·hu·man′i·tar′i·an, *adj., n.*
sem′i·hu′man·ized′, *adj.*
sem′i·hy′per·bol′ic, *adj.*
sem′i·hys·ter′i·cal, *adj.*; **-ly,** *adv.*
sem′i·il·lit′er·a·cy, *n.*
sem′i·il·lit′er·ate, *adj.*; **-ly,** *adv.*; **-ness,** *n.*
sem′i·il·lu′mi·nat′ed, *adj.*
sem′i·im·pres′sion·is′tic, *adj.*
sem′i·in′de·pend′ent, *adj.*; **-ly,** *adv.*
sem′i·in′di·rect′, *adj.*; **-ly,** *adv.*; **-ness,** *n.*
sem′i·in·duc′tive, *adj.*
sem′i·in′du·rate, *adj.*
sem′i·in′du·rat′ed, *adj.*
sem′i·in·dus′tri·al, *adj.*; **-ly,** *adv.*
sem′i·in·dus′tri·al·ized′, *adj.*
sem′i·in·hib′it·ed, *adj.*
sem′i·in·sol′u·ble, *adj.*
sem′i·in·stinc′tive, *adj.*; **-ly,** *adv.*; **-ness,** *n.*
sem′i·in′tel·lec′tu·al, *adj., n.*; **-ly,** *adv.*
sem′i·in′tel·lec′tu·al·ized′, *adj.*
sem′i·in·tel′li·gent, *adj.*; **-ly,** *adv.*
sem′i·in·ter′nal, *adj.*; **-ly,** *adv.*
sem′i·in·ter′nal·ized′, *adj.*
sem′i·in·tox′i·ca·ted, *adj.*
sem′i·in·tox′i·ca′tion, *n.*
sem′i·i·ron′ic, *adj.*
sem′i·i·ron′i·cal, *adj.*; **-ly,** *adv.*
sem′i·i′so·lat′ed, *adj.*
sem′i·joc′u·lar, *adj.*; **-ly,** *adv.*
sem′i·ju·di′cial, *adj.*; **-ly,** *adv.*
sem′i·ju·rid′ic, *adj.*
sem′i·ju·rid′i·cal, *adj.*; **-ly,** *adv.*
sem′i·leg′end·ar′y, *adj.*
sem′i·leg′is·la′tive, *adj.*; **-ly,** *adv.*
sem′i·lib′er·al, *adj., n.*; **-ly,** *adv.*
sem′i·lib′er·al·ism, *n.*
sem′i·lu′cent, *adj.*
sem′i·lu′mi·nous, *adj.*; **-ly,** *adv.*; **-ness,** *n.*
sem′i·lu′nate, *adj.*
sem′i·lu′nat·ed, *adj.*
sem′i·lux′u·ry, *n.*
sem′i·lyr′ic, *adj.*
sem′i·lyr′i·cal, *adj.*; **-ly,** *adv.*
sem′i·mag′i·cal, *adj.*; **-ly,** *adv.*
sem′i·mag·net′ic, *adj.*
sem′i·mag·net′i·cal, *adj.*; **-ly,** *adv.*
sem′i·ma·li′cious, *adj.*; **-ly,** *adv.*; **-ness,** *n.*
sem′i·ma·lig′nant, *adj.*; **-ly,** *adv.*
sem′i·man′a·ge′ri·al, *adj.*; **-ly,** *adv.*
sem′i·man′ner·is′tic, *adj.*
sem′i·man′u·fac′tured, *adj.*
sem′i·ma·rine′, *adj., n.*
sem′i·ma·te′ri·al·is′tic, *adj.*
sem′i·math′e·mat′i·cal, *adj.*; **-ly,** *adv.*
sem′i·ma·ture′, *adj.*; **-ly,** *adv.*; **-ness,** *n.*
sem′i·ma·tur′i·ty, *n.*
sem′i·me·chan′i·cal, *adj.*
sem′i·mech′a·nis′tic, *adj.*
sem′i·me·dic′i·nal, *adj.*
sem′i·mem′bra·nous, *adj.*
sem′i·me·tal′lic, *adj.*
sem′i·met′a·phor′ic, *adj.*
sem′i·met′a·phor′i·cal, *adj.*; **-ly,** *adv.*
sem′i·mild′, *adj.*; **-ness,** *n.*
sem′i·min′er·al, *adj.*
sem′i·min′er·al·ized′, *adj.*
sem′i·min′is·te′ri·al, *adj.*
sem′i·mo′bile, *adj.*
sem′i·mod′er·ate, *adj.*; **-ly,** *adv.*
sem′i·mo·nar′chic, *adj.*
sem′i·mo·nar′chi·cal, *adj.*; **-ly,** *adv.*
sem′i·mo·nop′o·lis′tic, *adj.*
sem′i·mor′al·is′tic, *adj.*
sem′i·moun′tain·ous, *adj.*; **-ly,** *adv.*
sem′i·mys′tic, *adj.*
sem′i·mys′ti·cal, *adj.*; **-ly,** *adv.*; **-ness,** *n.*
sem′i·myth′ic, *adj.*
sem′i·myth′i·cal, *adj.*; **-ly,** *adv.*
sem′i·na′ked, *adj.*

such a group. **4.** a course or subject of study for advanced graduate students. **5.** any meeting for exchanging information and holding discussions. [< G < L *sēminār(ium)* SEMINARY]

sem·i·nar·i·an (sem′ə nâr′ē ən), *n.* a student in a theological seminary. [SEMINARY + -AN]

sem·i·nar·y (sem′ə ner′ē), *n., pl.* **-nar·ies. 1.** a school for the education of men for the priesthood, ministry, or rabbinate. **2.** a school, esp. one of higher grade. **3.** a school of secondary or higher level for young women. **4.** seminar (def. 1). **5.** a place of origin and propagation: *a seminary of discontent.* [late ME < L *sēmināri(um)* seed plot, nursery. See SEMEN, -ARY] **—sem′i·nar′i·al,** *adj.*

sem·i·na·tion (sem′ə nā′shən), *n.* a sowing or impregnating; dissemination. [< L *sēminātiōn-* (s. of *sēminātiō*), equiv. to *sēmināt(us)* (ptp. of *sēmināre* to sow; see SEMEN) + *-iōn-* -ION]

sem·i·nif·er·ous (sem′ə nif′ər əs), *adj.* **1.** *Anat.* conveying or containing semen. **2.** *Bot.* bearing or producing seed. [< L *semini-* seed (see SEMEN) + -FEROUS]

sem·i·niv·or·ous (sem′ə niv′ər əs), *adj.* feeding on seeds: *seminivorous birds.* [< L *semini-* seed (see SEMEN) + -VOROUS]

Sem·i·nole (sem′ə nōl′), *n., pl.* **-noles,** (*esp. collectively*) **-nole,** *adj.* —*n.* **1.** a member of a Muskogean tribe of American Indians, an offshoot of the Creeks, resident in Florida and now also in Oklahoma. **2.** the Creek language as used by the Seminoles. —*adj.* **3.** of or pertaining to the Seminoles or their language. [< AmerInd (Creek) *Sim-a-nō-le* or *Iste siminōla* separatist, runaway]

Sem·i·nole (sem′ə nōl′), *n.* a town in NW Texas. 5737 (1960).

sem·i·no·ma (sem′ə nō′mə), *n., pl.* **-mas, -ma·ta** (-mə tə). *Pathol.* a tumor of the testis. [< L *semin-* seed (see SEMEN) + -OMA]

sem·i·of·fi·cial (sem′ē ə fish′əl, sem′ī-), *adj.* having some degree of official authority. [SEMI- + OFFICIAL] **—sem′i·of·fi′cial·ly,** *adv.*

se·mi·ol·o·gy (sē′mē ol′ə jē, sē′mī-, sem′ē-, sem′ī-), *n.* semeiology. **—se·mi·o·log·ic** (sē′mē ə loj′ik, sē′mi-, sem′ē-, sem′ī-), **se′mi·o·log′i·cal,** *adj.* **—se′mi·ol′o·gist,** *n.*

sem·i·o·paque (sem′ē ō pāk′, sem′ī-), *adj.* partly or nearly opaque. [SEMI- + OPAQUE] **—sem·i·o·pac·i·ty** (sem′ē ō pas′i tē, sem′ī-), *n.*

se·mi·ot·ic (sē′mē ot′ik, sē′mī-, sem′ē-, sem′ī-), *adj.* Also, **se′mi·ot′i·cal, semeiotic, semeiotical. 1.** pertaining to signs. **2.** *Med.* of or pertaining to symptoms; symptomatic. —*n.* **3.** Often, **semiotics.** *Logic, Philos.* a general theory of signs and symbolism, usually divided into the branches of pragmatics, semantics, and syntactics. [< Gk *sēmei(on)* sign + -OTIC]

sem·i·o·vip·a·rous (sem′ē ō vip′ər əs, sem′ī-), *adj.* bearing young in an incomplete state of development, as a marsupial. [SEMI- + OVIPAROUS]

Se·mi·pa·la·tinsk (se′mi pä lä′tinsk), *n.* a city in NE Kazakstan, in the S Soviet Union in Asia, on the Irtish River. 191,000 (est. 1964).

Semipalmate foot

sem·i·pal·mate (sem′ē pal′māt, -mit, sem′ī-), *adj.* partially or imperfectly palmate, as a bird's foot; half-webbed. Also, **sem′i·pal′mat·ed.** [SEMI- + PALMATE]

semipal′mated plov′er, a New World plover, *Charadrius hiaticula,* having a black ring around the chest and semipalmate feet.

semipal′mated sand′piper, a North American sandpiper, *Ereunetes pusillus,* having semipalmate feet.

sem·i·par·a·sit·ic (sem′ē par′ə sit′ik, sem′ī-), *adj.* **1.** *Biol.* commonly parasitic but capable of living on dead or decaying animal matter. **2.** *Bot.* partly parasitic and partly photosynthetic. [SEMI- + PARASITIC] **—sem·i·par·a·site** (sem′ē par′ə sīt′, sem′ī-), *n.* **—sem·i·par·a·sit·ism** (sem′ē par′ə sī′tiz əm, sem′ī-), *n.*

sem·i·per·ma·nent (sem′ē pûr′mə nənt, sem′ī-), *adj.* not quite permanent. [SEMI- + PERMANENT]

sem·i·per·me·a·ble (sem′ē pûr′mē ə bəl, sem′ī-), *adj.* permeable to certain substances only: *a semipermeable membrane.* [SEMI- + PERMEABLE] **—sem·i·per′me·a·bil′i·ty,** *n.*

sem·i·plas·tic (sem′ē plas′tik, sem′ī-), *adj.* imperfectly plastic; in a state between rigidity and plasticity. [SEMI- + PLASTIC]

sem·i·po·lit·i·cal (sem′ē pə lit′i kəl, sem′ī-), *adj.* of a partially political nature; having some political features. [SEMI- + POLITICAL] **—sem·i·pol·i·ti·cian** (sem′ē pol′i tish′ən, sem′ī-), *n.*

sem·i·por·ce·lain (sem′ē pōr′sə lin, -pôr′-, -pōrs′lin, -pôrs′-, sem′ī-), *n.* any of several vitrified ceramic wares lacking the translucency or hardness of true porcelain but otherwise similar to it. [SEMI- + PORCELAIN]

sem·i·post·al (sem′ē pōs′təl, sem′ī-), *Philately.* —*n.* **1.** a postage stamp sold by a government at a premium above its face value, the excess being used for a nonpostal purpose, as a charity. —*adj.* **2.** noting or pertaining to such a stamp. [SEMI- + POSTAL]

sem·i·pre·cious (sem′ē presh′əs, sem′ī-), *adj.* (of a stone) having commercial value as a gem but not classified as precious, as the amethyst, garnet, etc. [SEMI- + PRECIOUS]

sem·i·pri·vate (sem′ē prī′vit, sem′ī-), *adj.* having some degree of privacy but not fully private, as a hospital room with fewer beds than a ward. [SEMI- + PRIVATE] **—sem·i·pri·va·cy** (sem′ē prī′və sē, sem′ī-), *n.*

sem·i·pro (sem′ē prō′, sem′ī-), *adj., n., pl.* **-pros.** *Informal.* semiprofessional. [SEMI- + PRO[2]]

sem·i·pro·fes·sion·al (sem′ē prə fesh′ə nəl, sem′ī-), *adj.* **1.** actively engaged in some field or sport for pay but on a part-time basis: *semiprofessional baseball players.* **2.** engaged in by paid, part-time people: *semiprofessional football.* **3.** having some features of professional work but requiring less knowledge, skill, and judgment: *a semiprofessional field; a semiprofessional job.* —*n.* **4.** a person who is active in some field or sport for pay on a part-time basis. [SEMI- + PROFESSIONAL] **—sem·i·pro·fes′sion·al·ly,** *adv.*

sem·i·pub·lic (sem′ē pub′lik, sem′ī-), *adj.* partly or to some degree public. [SEMI- + PUBLIC]

sem·i·qua·ver (sem′ē kwā′vər), *Music Chiefly Brit.* a sixteenth note. See illus. under **note.** [SEMI- + QUAVER]

sem·i·qui·none (sem′ē kwi nōn′, -kwin′ōn, sem′ī-), *n.* *Chem.* any of the class of free radicals formed as intermediates in the oxidation of a hydroquinone to a quinone. [SEMI- + QUINONE]

Se·mir·a·mis (si mir′ə mis), *n.* a legendary Assyrian queen, the wife of Ninus and founder of Babylon, noted for her wisdom and beauty.

sem·i·re·li·gious (sem′ē ri lij′əs, sem′ī-), *adj.* having a somewhat religious character. [SEMI- + RELIGIOUS]

sem·i·rig·id (sem′ē rij′id, sem′ī-), *adj.* **1.** not fully rigid; partly rigid. **2.** *Aeron.* noting or pertaining to a type of airship whose shape is maintained by means of a rigid keellike structure and by internal gas pressure. [SEMI- + RIGID]

sem·i·round (sem′ē round′, sem′ī-), *adj.* having one surface that is round and another that is flat. [SEMI- + ROUND[1]]

se·mis (sā′mis, sē′-), *n.* a copper coin of ancient Rome, the half part of an as. [< L; see SEMI-, AS[2]]

sem·i·se·ri·ous (sem′ē sēr′ē əs, sem′ī-), *adj.* having serious undertones; partly serious. [SEMI- + SERIOUS] **—sem′i·se′ri·ous·ly,** *adv.* **—sem′i·se′ri·ous·ness,** *n.*

sem·i·skilled (sem′ē skild′, sem′ī-), *adj.* having or requiring more training and skill than unskilled labor but less than skilled labor. [SEMI- + SKILLED]

sem·i·soft (sem′ē sôft′, -soft′, sem′ī-), *adj.* having a somewhat soft consistency. [SEMI- + SOFT]

sem·i·sol·id (sem′ē sol′id, sem′ī-), *adj.* **1.** having a somewhat firm consistency; more or less solid. —*n.* **2.** a semisolid substance. [SEMI- + SOLID]

sem·i·spher·ic (sem′ē sfer′ik, sem′ī-), *adj.* shaped like half a sphere; hemispheric. Also, **sem′i·spher′i·cal.** [SEMI- + SPHERIC] **—sem·i·sphere** (sem′i sfēr′), *n.*

sem·i·sub·ter·ra·ne·an (sem′ē sub′tə rā′nē ən, sem′ī-), *adj.* half below the surface of the ground: *the semisubterranean houses of some Indian tribes.* [SEMI- + SUBTERRANEAN]

sem·i·sweet (sem′ē swēt′, sem′ī-), *adj.* somewhat sweet; containing a small amount of sweetening: *a semisweet cookie; semisweet chocolate.* [SEMI- + SWEET]

sem·i·syn·thet·ic (sem′ē sin thet′ik, sem′ī-), *adj.* *Chem.* derived synthetically from one or more substances of natural origin. [SEMI- + SYNTHETIC]

Sem·ite (sem′īt *or, esp. Brit.,* sē′mīt), *n.* **1.** a member of any of the peoples supposedly descended from Shem, the eldest son of Noah. **2.** a Jew. **3.** a member of any of various ancient and modern peoples originating in SW Asia, including the Sumerians, Akkadians, Canaanites, Phoenicians, Hebrews, and Arabs. [< NL *sēmīt(a)* < L, Gk *Sēm* (< Heb *Shēm*) SHEM + *-ita* -ITE[1]]

Se·mit·ic (sə mit′ik), *n.* **1.** an important subfamily of Afro-Asiatic languages, including Akkadian, Arabic, Aramaic, and Hebrew. —*adj.* **2.** of or pertaining to the Semites or their languages, esp. of or pertaining to the Jews. [< NL *sēmītic(us),* equiv. to *sēmīt(a)* SEMITE + *-icus* -IC]

Se·mit·ics (sə mit′iks), *n.* (*construed as sing.*) the study of the Semitic languages, literature, etc. [see SEMITIC, -ICS]

Sem·i·tism (sem′i tiz′əm *or, esp. Brit.,* sē′mi-), *n.* **1.** Semitic characteristics, esp. the ways, ideas, influence, etc., of the Jewish people. **2.** a word or idiom peculiar to, derived from, or characteristic of a Semitic language, esp. of Hebrew. [SEMITE + -ISM]

Sem·i·tist (sem′i tist *or, esp. Brit.,* sē′mi-), *n.* an authority on the Semitic languages, literature, etc. [SEMITE + -IST]

sem·i·tone (sem′ē tōn′), *n.* *Music.* a pitch interval halfway between two whole tones. Also called **half step, half tone.** [SEMI- + TONE] **—sem·i·ton·ic** (sem′i ton′ik), **sem·i·ton·al** (sem′i tōn′əl), *adj.* **—sem′i·ton′al·ly,** *adv.*

sem·i·trail·er (sem′i trā′lər), *n.* a detachable trailer for hauling freight, having its forward end supported by the rear of its truck tractor when attached. Cf. **full trailer.** [SEMI- + TRAILER]

sem·i·trans·lu·cent (sem′ē trans lo͞o′sənt, -tranz-, sem′ī-), *adj.* imperfectly or almost translucent. [SEMI- + TRANSLUCENT]

sem·i·trans·par·ent (sem′ē trans pâr′ənt, -par′-, sem′ī-), *adj.* imperfectly or almost transparent. [SEMI- + TRANSPARENT] **—sem′i·trans·par′en·cy, sem′i·trans·par′ent·ness,** *n.* **—sem′i·trans·par′ent·ly,** *adv.*

sem·i·trop·i·cal (sem′ē trop′i kəl, sem′ī-), *adj.* subtropical. Also, **sem·i·trop′ic.** [SEMI- + TROPICAL] **—sem′i·trop′ics,** *n.pl.* **—sem′i·trop′i·cal·ly,** *adv.*

sem·i·vit·re·ous (sem′ē vi′trē əs, sem′ī-), *adj.* partially vitreous, as mineral constituents of volcanic rocks. [SEMI- + VITREOUS]

sem·i·vow·el (sem′ē vou′əl), *n.* **1.** *Phonet.* a speech sound of vowel quality used as a consonant, as (w) in *wet* or (y) in *yet.* **2.** a speech sound of consonantal quality used as a vowel, as (m, n, ng, r, l). [SEMI- + VOWEL; r. *semivocal* < L *sēmivocāl(is)* half vowel]

sem·i·week·ly (sem′ē wēk′lē, sem′ī-), *adj., n., pl.* **-lies,** *adv.* —*adj.* **1.** occurring, done, appearing, or published twice a week: *semiweekly visits.* —*n.* **2.** a semiweekly publication. —*adv.* **3.** twice a week: *He traveled semiweekly to Detroit.* [SEMI- + WEEKLY]

sem·i·year·ly (sem′ē yēr′lē, sem′ī-), *adj.* **1.** semiannual (def. 1). —*adv.* **2.** twice a year; semiannually: *He seeded the lawn semiyearly.* [SEMI- + YEARLY]

sem′i·nar·cot′ic, *adj.*
sem′i·nar′ra·tive, *adj.*
sem′i·na′sal, *adj.;* **-ly,** *adv.*
sem′i·na·sal′i·ty, *n.*
sem′i·na′tion·al·ism, *n.*
sem′i·na′tion·al·is′tic, *adj.*
sem′i·na′tion·al·ized′, *adj.*
sem′i·ner′vous, *adj.;* **-ly,** *adv.;* **-ness,** *n.*
sem′i·neu·rot′ic, *adj.*
sem′i·neu·rot′i·cal·ly, *adv.*
sem′i·neu′tral, *adj.*
sem′i·neu·tral′i·ty, *n.*
sem′i·noc·tur′nal, *adj.*
sem′i·no′mad, *n.*
sem′i·no·mad′ic, *adj.*
sem′i·no·mad′i·cal·ly, *adv.*
sem′i·no′mad·ism, *n.*
sem′i·nor′mal, *adj.;* **-ly,** *adv.;* **-ness,** *n.*
sem′i·nor·mal′i·ty, *n.*
sem′i·nude′, *adj.*
sem′i·nu′di·ty, *n.*
sem′i·ob·jec′tive, *adj.;* **-ly,** *adv.;* **-ness,** *n.*
sem′i·ob·liv′i·ous, *adj.;* **-ly,** *adv.;* **-ness,** *n.*
sem′i·o′pen, *adj.;* **-ly,** *adv.;* **-ness,** *n.*
sem′i·op′ti·mis′tic, *adj.*
sem′i·op′ti·mis′ti·cal·ly, *adv.*
sem′i·or′a·tor′i·cal, *adj.;* **-ly,** *adv.*
sem′i·or·gan′ic, *adj.*
sem′i·or·gan′i·cal·ly, *adv.*
sem′i·o′ri·en′tal, *adj.;* **-ly,** *adv.*
sem′i·or′tho·dox′, *adj.*
sem′i·or′tho·dox′ly, *adv.*
sem′i·o′val, *adj.;* **-ly,** *adv.;* **-ness,** *n.*
sem′i·o′vate, *adj.*
sem′i·ox′y·gen·ized′, *adj.*
sem′i·pac′i·fist, *adj., n.*
sem′i·pac′i·fis′tic, *adj.*
sem′i·pa′gan, *n., adj.*
sem′i·pa′gan·ish, *adj.*
sem′i·pa·ral′y·sis, *adj.*
sem′i·par′a·lyt′ic, *n., adj.*
sem′i·par′a·lyzed′, *adj.*
sem′i·pa·ro′chi·al, *adj.*
sem′i·pas′sive, *adj.;* **-ly,** *adv.;* **-ness,** *n.*
sem′i·paste′, *n.*
sem′i·pas′to·ral, *adj.;* **-ly,** *adv.*
sem′i·path′o·log′ic, *adj.*
sem′i·path′o·log′i·cal, *adj.;* **-ly,** *adv.*
sem′i·pa′tri·ot, *n.*
sem′i·pa′tri·ot′ic, *adj.*
sem′i·pa′tri·ot′i·cal·ly, *adv.*
sem′i·pat′terned, *adj.*
sem′i·peace′, *n.*
sem′i·peace′ful, *adj.;* **-ly,** *adv.*
sem′i·pe·dan′tic, *adj.*
sem′i·pe·dan′ti·cal, *adj.;* **-ly,** *adv.*
sem′i·pend′ent, *adj.*
sem′i·pen′du·lous, *adj.;* **-ly,** *adv.;* **-ness,** *n.*
sem′i·per·cep′tive, *adj.*
sem′i·per′vi·ous, *adj.;* **-ness,** *n.*
sem′i·pet′ri·fied′, *adj.*
sem′i·phe·nom′e·nal, *adj.;* **-ly,** *adv.*
sem′i·phil′o·soph′ic, *adj.*
sem′i·phil′o·soph′i·cal, *adj.;* **-ly,** *adv.*
sem′i·phos′pho·res′cence, *n.*
sem′i·phos′pho·res′cent, *adj.*
sem′i·phre·net′ic, *adj.*
sem′i·pic·to′ri·al, *adj.;* **-ly,** *adv.*
sem′i·pi′ous, *adj.;* **-ly,** *adv.;* **-ness,** *n.*
sem′i·pneu·mat′ic, *adj.*
sem′i·pneu·mat′i·cal, *adj.;* **-ly,** *adv.*
sem′i·poi′son·ous, *adj.;* **-ly,** *adv.*
sem′i·pop′u·lar, *adj.;* **-ly,** *adv.*
sem′i·pop′u·lar′i·ty, *n.*
sem′i·pop′u·lar·ized′, *adj.*
sem′i·prac′ti·cal, *adj.*
sem′i·pre·served′, *adj.*
sem′i·prim′i·tive, *adj.*
sem′i·pro·duc′tive, *adj.;* **-ly,** *adv.;* **-ness,** *n.*
sem′i·pro′duc·tiv′i·ty, *n.*
sem′i·pro·fane′, *adj.;* **-ly,** *adv.;* **-ness,** *n.*
sem′i·pro·fan′i·ty, *n.*
sem′i·pro·gres′sive, *adj., n.;* **-ly,** *adv.;* **-ness,** *n.*
sem′i·prone′, *adj.;* **-ly,** *adv.;* **-ness,** *n.*
sem′i·prop′a·gan′dist, *adj.*
sem′i·pro·tect′ed, *adj.*
sem′i·pro·tec′tive, *adj.;* **-ly,** *adv.*
sem′i·prov′en, *adj.*
sem′i·pro·vin′cial, *adj.;* **-ly,** *adv.*
sem′i·psy·cho·log′ic, *adj.*
sem′i·psy′cho·log′i·cal, *adj.;* **-ly,** *adv.*
sem′i·psy′chot′ic, *adj.*
sem′i·pu′ni·tive, *adj.*
sem′i·pu′ni·to′ry, *adj.*
sem′i·pur′pos·ive, *adj.;* **-ly,** *adv.;* **-ness,** *n.*
sem′i·rad′i·cal, *adj.;* **-ly,** *adv.;* **-ness,** *n.*
sem′i·rare′, *adj.;* **-ly,** *adv.;* **-ness,** *n.*
sem′i·ra′tion·al·ized′, *adj.*
sem′i·raw′, *adj.;* **-ly,** *adv.;* **-ness,** *n.*
sem′i·re·ac′tion·ar′y, *adj.*
sem′i·re′al·is′tic, *adj.*
sem′i·re′al·is′ti·cal·ly, *adv.*
sem′i·reb′el, *n.*
sem′i·re·bel′lion, *n.*
sem′i·re·bel′lious, *adj.;* **-ly,** *adv.;* **-ness,** *n.*
sem′i·re·fined′, *adj.*
sem′i·re′flex, *n.*
sem′i·re·flex′ive, *adj.;* **-ly,** *adv.;* **-ness,** *n.*
sem′i·re·lief′, *n.*
sem′i·re·pub′lic, *n.*
sem′i·re·pub′li·can, *adj., n.*
sem′i·res′in·ous, *adj.*
sem′i·res′in·y, *adj.*
sem′i·res′o·lute′, *adj.;* **-ly,** *adv.;* **-ness,** *n.*
sem′i·re·spect′a·bil′i·ty, *n.*
sem′i·re·spect′a·ble, *adj.*
sem′i·re·tired′, *adj.*
sem′i·re·tire′ment, *n.*
sem′i·re·ver′ber·a·to′ry, *adj.*
sem′i·rev′o·lu′tion, *n.*
sem′i·rev′o·lu′tion·ar′y, *adj., n.*
sem′i·rev′o·lu′tion·ist, *n.*
sem′i·rhyth′mic, *adj.*
sem′i·rhyth′mi·cal, *adj.;* **-ly,** *adv.*
sem′i·rig′or·ous, *adj.;* **-ly,** *adv.;* **-ness,** *n.*
sem′i·ro·man′tic, *adj.*
sem′i·ro·man′ti·cal·ly, *adv.*
sem′i·ru′ral, *adj.;* **-ly,** *adv.*
sem′i·ru′ral·ism, *n.*
sem′i-Rus′sian, *adj., n.*
sem′i·sa′cred, *adj.*
sem′i·sa′line, *adj.*
sem′i·sa·tir′ic, *adj.*
sem′i·sa·tir′i·cal, *adj.;* **-ly,** *adv.*
sem′i·sav′age, *adj.*
sem′i·sav′age, *n.*
sem′i·scho·las′tic, *adj.*
sem′i·scho·las′ti·cal·ly, *adv.*
sem′i·se′cre·cy, *n.*
sem′i·se′cret, *adj.;* **-ly,** *adv.*
sem′i·sen′ti·men′tal, *adj.;* **-ly,** *adv.*
sem′i·sen′ti·men′tal·ized′, *adj.*
sem′i·shade′, *n.*
sem′i·slave′, *n.*
sem′i·so′cial·ism, *n.*
sem′i·so′cial·ist, *n.*
sem′i·so′cial·is′tic, *adj.*
sem′i·so′cial·is′ti·cal·ly, *adv.*
sem′i·sol′emn, *adj.;* **-ly,** *adv.;* **-ness,** *n.*
sem′i·so·lem′ni·ty, *n.*
sem′i·som·nam′bu·lis′tic, *adj.*
sem′i·som′no·lence, *n.*
sem′i·som′no·lent, *adj.;* **-ly,** *adv.*
sem′i·spec′u·la′tion, *n.*
sem′i·spec′u·la′tive, *adj.;* **-ly,** *adv.;* **-ness,** *n.*
sem′i·spon·ta′ne·ous, *adj.;* **-ly,** *adv.;* **-ness,** *n.*
sem′i·stiff′, *adj.;* **-ly,** *adv.;* **-ness,** *n.*
sem′i·stim′u·lat′ing, *adj.*
sem′i·strat′i·fied′, *adj.*
sem′i·su·bur′ban, *adj.*
sem′i·suc·cess′, *n.*
sem′i·suc·cess′ful, *adj.;* **-ly,** *adv.*
sem′i·su′per·nat′ur·al, *adj.;* **-ly,** *adv.;* **-ness,** *n.*
sem′i·tai′lored, *adj.*
sem′i·tex′tur·al, *adj.;* **-ly,** *adv.*
sem′i·the·at′ric, *adj.*
sem′i·the·at′ri·cal, *adj.;* **-ly,** *adv.*
sem′i·the·at′ri·cal·ism, *n.*
sem′i·the′o·log′i·cal, *adj.;* **-ly,** *adv.*
sem′i·tra·di′tion·al, *adj.;* **-ly,** *adv.*
sem′i·trained′, *adj.*
sem′i·truth′ful, *adj.;* **-ly,** *adv.;* **-ness,** *n.*
sem′i·tu′ber·ous, *adj.*
sem′i·un·dressed′, *adj.*
sem′i·ur′ban, *adj.*
sem′i·vol′a·tile, *adj.*
sem′i·vol·can′ic, *adj.*
sem′i·vol·can′i·cal·ly, *adv.*
sem′i·vol′un·tar′y, *adj.*
sem′i·vul′can·ized′, *adj.*
sem′i·war′fare, *n.*
sem′i·wild′, *adj.;* **-ly,** *adv.;* **-ness,** *n.*

Sem·mel·weis (zem′əl vīs′), *n.* **Ig·naz Phi·lipp** (ig′näts fē′lip), 1818–65, Hungarian physician and obstetrician.

Semmes (semz), *n.* **Raphael,** 1809–77, Confederate admiral in the American Civil War.

sem·o·li·na (sem′ə lē′nə), *n.* a granular, milled product of durum wheat, consisting almost entirely of endosperm particles, used chiefly in the making of macaroni. [< It *semolino,* equiv. to *semol(a)* bran (< L *simila* flour) + *-ino* dim. suffix]

Sem·pach (*Ger.* zem′päkh), *n.* a village in central Switzerland: Austrians defeated by Swiss 1386. 1345 (1960).

sem·per fi·de·lis (sem′per fi dā′lis; *Eng.* sem′pər fi dā′lis, -dē′-), *Latin.* always faithful: motto of the U.S. Marine Corps.

sem·per i·dem (sem′per ē′dem; *Eng.* sem′pər ī′dem, id′em), *Latin.* always the same.

sem·per pa·ra·tus (sem′per pä rä′to͞os; *Eng.* sem′pər pə rā′təs), *Latin.* always ready: motto of the U.S. Coast Guard.

sem·pi·ter·nal (sem′pi tûr′nəl), *adj. Literary.* everlasting; eternal. [late ME < LL *sempiternāl(is),* equiv. to L *sempitern(us)* everlasting (*semper,* always + *eternus* (see ETERNAL), + *-ālis* -AL¹] —**sem′pi·ter′nal·ly,** *adv.*

sem·pli·ce (sem′pli chā′; *It.* sem′plē che), *adj.* (used as a musical direction) simple; straightforward. [It: simple; see SIMPLICITY]

sem·pre (sem′prā; *It.* sem′pre), *adv.* (used in musical directions) throughout. [< It: always < L *semper*]

semp·stress (semp′stris, sem′tris), *n.* seamstress.

sen¹ (sen), *n., pl.* **sen.** a money of account of Japan, the 100th part of a yen, equal to 10 rin and equivalent to about .000028 of a U.S. dollar. [< Jap]

sen² (sen), *n., pl.* **sen.** a money of account of Cambodia, the 100th part of a riel, equivalent to about .0003 of a U.S. dollar. [< native name in Cambodia]

sen³ (sen), *n., pl.* **sen.** an aluminum coin of Indonesia, the 100th part of a rupiah, equivalent to about .0002 of a U.S. dollar; cent. [< native name in Indonesia]

sen., 1. senate. 2. senator. 3. senior. Also, **sen**

sen·ar·mon·tite (sen′ər mon′tīt), *n.* a mineral, antimony trioxide, Sb_2O_3, occurring in pearl-colored isometric octahedrons: a dimorph of valentinite. [named after Henri de *Sénarmont* (d. 1862), French mineralogist; see -ITE¹]

sen·a·ry (sen′ə rē), *adj.* of or pertaining to the number six. [< L *sēnāri(us),* equiv. to *sēn(ī)* six each (*se(x)* SIX + *nī* distributive suffix) + *-ārius* -ARY]

sen·ate (sen′it), *n.* **1.** an assembly or council of citizens having the highest deliberative functions in a government, esp. a legislative assembly of a state or nation. **2.** (*cap.*) the upper house of the legislature of certain countries, as the United States, France, Italy, Canada, Ireland, Republic of South Africa, Australia, and some Latin American countries. **3.** the room or building in which such a group meets. **4.** *Rom. Hist.* the supreme council of state the membership and functions of which varied at different periods. **5.** a governing, advisory, or disciplinary body, as in certain universities. [ME *senat* < L *senāt(us)* council of elders, equiv. to *sen(ex)* old + *-ātus* -ATE¹]

Sen·a·to·bi·a (sen′ə tō′bē ə), *n.* a town in NW Mississippi. 3259 (1960).

sen·a·tor (sen′ə tər), *n.* **1.** a member of a senate. **2.** (*cap.*) *U.S.* a title of respect accorded a person who is or has been a member of the Senate. [ME *senatour* < AF < L *senātor,* equiv. to *senāt(us)* SENATE + *-or* -OR²] —**sen′a·tor·ship′,** *n.*

sen·a·to·ri·al (sen′ə tōr′ē əl, -tôr′-), *adj.* **1.** of, pertaining to, characteristic of, or befitting a senator or senate: *senatorial oratory.* **2.** consisting of senators. [< L *senātōri(us)* (see SENATOR, -IOUS) + -AL¹] —**sen′a·to′ri·al·ly,** *adv.*

senato′rial cour′tesy, *U.S.* the practice in the Senate of confirming only those presidential appointees approved by both senators from the State of the appointee, or by one senator of the President's party.

senato′rial dis′trict, *U.S.* one of a fixed number of districts into which a State is divided, each electing one member to the State senate. Cf. **assembly district, Congressional district.**

se·na·tus con·sul·tum (sə nä′to͞os kōn so͞ol′to͞om; *Eng.* sə nā′təs kən sul′təm), *pl.* **se·na·tus con·sul·ta** (sə nä′to͞os kōn so͞ol′tä; *Eng.* sə nā′təs kən sul′tə). *Latin.* a decree of the senate of ancient Rome.

send¹ (send), *v.,* **sent, send·ing.** —*v.t.* **1.** to cause, permit, or enable to go: *to send a messenger; They sent their son to college.* **2.** to cause to be conveyed or transmitted to a destination: *to send a letter.* **3.** to order, direct, compel, or force to go: *to send someone away; The president sent troops to Asia.* **4.** to direct, propel, or deliver to a particular point, position, condition, or direction: *to send a punch to the jaw; The punch sent the fighter reeling.* **5.** to emit, discharge, or utter (usually fol. by *forth, off, out,* or *through*): *The lion sent a roar through the jungle. The flowers sent forth a sweet odor.* **6.** *Elect.* **a.** to transmit (a signal). **b.** to transmit (an electromagnetic wave or the like) in the form of pulses. **7.** *Slang.* to delight or excite: *Frank Sinatra's records used to send her.* —*v.i.* **8.** to dispatch a messenger, agent, message, etc. **9.** *Elect.* to transmit a signal: *The ship's radio sends on a special band of frequencies.* **10. send down,** *Brit.* to expel, esp. from Oxford or Cambridge. **11. send for,** to request the coming or delivery of; summon: *If her temperature goes up, send for the doctor.* **12. send forth, a.** to produce; bear; yield. **b.** to dispatch out of a country as an export. **c.** to issue, as a publication: *They have sent forth a report to the stockholders.* **13. send in,** to cause to be dispatched or delivered (to a destination): *Send in your contest entries to this station.* **14. send off,** to cause to depart or to be conveyed from oneself; dispatch; dismiss: *His teacher sent him off to the principal's office.* **15. send out, a.** to distribute; issue. **b.** to send on the way; dispatch: *They sent out their final shipment last week.* **16. send packing,** to dismiss curtly; send away in disgrace: *The cashier was stealing, so we sent him packing.* **17. send up, a.** to release or cause to go upward; let out. **b.** *Slang.* to sentence or send to prison: *He was convicted and sent up for life.* [ME *sende(n),* OE *sendan;* c. G *senden,* Goth *sandjan* (causative) < Gmc base **sinth-,* **santh-* go, whence OE *sīth* journey] —**send′a·ble,** *adj.*

—**Syn. 2.** transmit, dispatch, forward. **4.** cast, hurl, fling, project. —**Ant. 1.** receive.

send² (send), *v.i.,* **sent, send·ing,** *n. Naut.* scend.

Sen·dai (sen′dī′), *n.* a city on NE Honshu, in central Japan. 472,954 (1964).

sen·dal (sen′dəl), *n.* a silk fabric in use during the Middle Ages or a piece or garment of it. [ME *cendal* < OF, prob. < dissimilated var. of Gk *sindṓn* fine linen]

send·ee (sen dē′), *n.* the person to whom something is sent. [SEND¹ + -EE]

send·er (sen′dər), *n.* **1.** one who or that which sends. **2.** a transmitter of electric pulses, as in telegraphy. [SEND¹ + -ER¹]

send-off (send′ôf′, -of′), *n. Informal.* **1.** a demonstration of good wishes for a person setting out on a trip, career, or other venture: *They gave him a rousing send-off at the pier.* **2.** a start given to a person or thing. [n. use of v. phrase *send off*]

Sen·e·ca (sen′ə kə), *n., pl.* **-cas,** (*esp. collectively*) **-ca** for 1. **1.** a member of the largest tribe of the Iroquois Confederacy of North American Indians, formerly inhabiting western New York and being conspicuous in the wars south and west of Lake Erie. **2.** an Iroquoian language of the Seneca, Onondaga, and Cayuga tribes. [< D *Sennecaas* (pl.) < Mohegan *A'sinnika,* trans. of Iroquoian *Oneniute'* (people of the) outstanding stone; see ONEIDA]

Sen·e·ca (sen′ə kə), *n.* **1. Lucius An·nae·us** (ə nē′əs), c4 B.C.–A.D. 65, Roman philosopher and writer of tragedies. **2.** a town in NW South Carolina. 5227 (1960). **3.** a walled plain in the first quadrant of the face of the moon: about 34 miles in diameter.

Sen′eca Falls′, a town in central New York. 7439 (1960).

Sen′eca grass′. See **vanilla grass.**

Sen′eca Lake′, a lake in W New York: one of the Finger Lakes. 35 mi. long.

Sen·e·can (sen′ə kən), *adj.* of, pertaining to, or characteristic of the writings of Seneca.

Sen′eca snake′root. See under **snakeroot** (def. 1).

Se·ne·fel·der (zā′nə fel′dər), *n.* **A·lo·ys** (ä′lō ys, ä′lois), 1771–1834, German inventor of lithography.

sen·e·ga (sen′ə gə), *n.* **1.** the dried root of a milkwort, *Polygala Senega,* of the eastern U.S., used as an expectorant and diuretic. **2.** the plant itself. [var. of SENECA, from its use by this tribe]

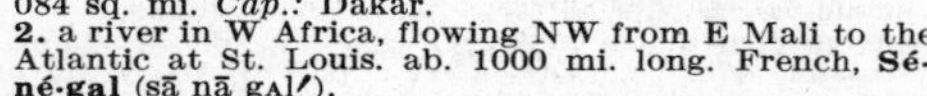

Sen·e·gal (sen′ə gôl′), *n.* **1.** a republic in W Africa: independent member of the French Community; formerly part of French West Africa. 3,400,000 (est. 1964); 76,084 sq. mi. *Cap.:* Dakar. **2.** a river in W Africa, flowing NW from E Mali to the Atlantic at St. Louis. ab. 1000 mi. long. French, **Sé·né·gal** (sā nā gal′).

Sen·e·ga·lese (sen′ə gô lēz′, -lēs′, -gə-), *adj., n., pl.* **-lese.** —*adj.* **1.** of or pertaining to the republic of Senegal. —*n.* **2.** a native or inhabitant of Senegal. [SENEGAL + -ESE]

Sen·e·gam·bi·a (sen′ə gam′bē ə), *n.* a region in W Africa between the Senegal and Gambia rivers; now mostly in Senegal. —**Sen′e·gam′bi·an,** *adj.*

se·nes·cent (sə nes′ənt), *adj.* growing old; aging. [< L *senēscent-* (s. of *senēscēns,* prp. of *senēscere* to grow old), equiv. to *sen-* old + *-ēscent-* -ESCENT] —**se·nes′cence,** *n.*

sen·e·schal (sen′ə shəl), *n.* an officer having full charge of domestic arrangements, ceremonies, the administration of justice, etc., in the household of a medieval prince or dignitary; steward. [ME < MF < (Latinized) Frankish *seniscalc(us)* senior servant; c. OHG *senescalh* (*sene-* old + *scalh* servant)]

Seng·hor (*Fr.* saN gôr′), *n.* **Lé·o·pold Sé·dar** (*Fr.* lā ô pôld′ sā dăr′), born 1906, African poet, teacher, and statesman: president of the Republic of Senegal since 1960.

se·nhor (sin yōr′, -yôr′; *Port.* si nyôr′), *n., pl.* **se·nhors,** *Port.* **se·nho·res** (si nyô′rish). a Portuguese title equivalent to *mister* or *Mr.,* used alone or capitalized and prefixed to the name of a man. *Abbr.:* Sr. [< Pg < L *senior;* see SENIOR]

se·nho·ra (sin yōr′ə, -yôr′ə; *Port.* si nyô′rə), *n., pl.* **se·nho·ras** (sin yōr′əz, -yôr′əz; *Port.* si nyô′rəsh). a Portuguese term of address equivalent to *Mrs.,* used alone or capitalized and prefixed to the name of a married woman. *Abbr.:* Sra. [< Pg, fem. of SENHOR]

se·nho·ri·ta (sēn′yə rē′tə, sän′-; *Port.* se′nyô rē′tə), *n., pl.* **-tas** (-təz; *Port.* -təsh). a Portuguese term of address equivalent to *miss,* used alone or capitalized and prefixed to the name of a girl or unmarried woman. *Abbr.:* Srta. [< Pg, dim. of SENHORA]

se·nile (sē′nīl, -nil, sen′īl), *adj.* **1.** of, pertaining to, or characteristic of old age, esp. referring to a decline of the mental faculties. **2.** *Phys. Geog.* (of topographical features) having advanced in reduction by erosion to a featureless plain that stands everywhere at base level. —*n.* **3.** a senile person. [< L *senīle,* neut. of *senīlis* old, equiv. to *sen(ex)* old man + *-īlis* -ILE]

se·nil·i·ty (si nil′i tē), *n.* the state of being senile, esp. the weakness or mental infirmity of old age. [SENILE + -ITY]

sen·ior (sēn′yər), *adj.* **1.** older or elder (usually designating the older of two men bearing the same name, as a father whose son is named after him: often written as *Sr.* or *sr.* following the name): *I would like to see the senior Mr. Hansen—Mr. Edward Andrew Hansen, Sr.* Cf. **junior** (def. 1). **2.** of earlier appointment or admission, as to an office, status, or rank: *a senior partner.* **3.** of higher or the highest rank or standing. **4.** (in American schools, colleges, and universities) of or pertaining to students in their final year or to their class. **5.** (in certain American colleges and universities) of or pertaining to the final two years of education, during which a student specializes in a certain field of study. **6.** of earlier date; prior to: *His appointment is senior to mine by a year.* —*n.* **7.** a person who is older than another. **8.** a person of higher rank or standing, than another, esp. by virtue of longer service. **9.** *U.S.* a student in his final year at a high school, preparatory school, college, or university. **10.** a fellow holding senior rank in a college at an English university. [< L *sen(ex)* old + *-ior* -ER⁴]

sen′ior cit′izen, *U.S.* an elderly or aged person, esp. one over 65 years of age who is retired or living on a pension.

sen′ior high′ school′. See under **high school** (def. 2).

sen·ior·i·ty (sēn yôr′i tē, -yor′-), *n., pl.* **-ties. 1.** the state of being senior; priority of birth; superior age. **2.** priority, precedence, or status obtained as the result of a person's length of service, as in a profession, trade, company, or union: *First choice of vacation time will be given to employees with seniority.* [< ML *seniōritās,* equiv. to *senior* SENIOR + *-itās* -ITY]

senior′ity rule′, *U.S.* the rule in Congress providing for the assignment of a committee chairmanship to that member of the majority party who has served on the committee the longest.

Sen·lac (sen′lak), *n.* a hill in SE England: site of the Battle of Hastings, 1066.

sen·na (sen′ə), *n.* **1.** any caesalpiniaceous herb, shrub, or tree of the genus *Cassia.* **2.** any of various cathartic drugs consisting of the dried leaflets of certain of these plants, as one drug **(Alexandria senna)** derived from *C. acutifolia,* or another **(Tinnevelly senna)** derived from *C. angustifolia.* **3.** See **wild senna.** [< NL < Ar *sanā*]

Sen·nach·er·ib (sə nak′ər ib), *n.* died 681 B.C., king of Assyria 705–681.

Sen′na knot′. See **Sehna knot.**

Sen·nar (sen när′), *n.* a region in the E Sudan between the White and Blue Nile rivers, S of Khartoum: a former kingdom.

sen·net¹ (sen′it), *n.* any of several small barracudas, as *Sphyraena borealis* **(northern sennet),** found along the eastern coast of North and Central America. [?]

sen·net² (sen′it), *n.* (in Elizabethan drama) a set of notes played on the trumpet or cornet to mark the entrance or exit of a group of actors. [? var. of SIGNET]

sen·net³ (sen′it), *n. Naut.* sennit.

Sen·nett (sen′it), *n.* **Mack** (*Michael Sinnott*), 1884–1960, U.S. motion-picture director and producer, born in Canada.

sen·night (sen′īt, -it), *n. Archaic.* a week. Also, **se'n′night.** [ME *sevenyht,* etc., OE *seofon nihta.* See SEVEN, NIGHT]

sen·nit (sen′it), *n.* a flat, braided cordage, formed by plaiting strands of rope yarn or other fiber, used as small stuff aboard ships. Also, **sennet, sinnet.** [?]

se·ñor (sän yôr′, -yōr′, sēn-; *Sp.* se nyôr′), *n., pl.* **se·ñors,** *Sp.* **se·ño·res** (se nyô′res). a Spanish term of address equivalent to *mister,* used alone or capitalized and prefixed to the name of a man. *Abbr.:* Sr. [< Sp < L *senior.* See SENIOR]

se·ño·ra (sän yōr′ə, -yôr′ə, sēn-; *Sp.* se nyô′rä), *n., pl.* **se·ño·ras** (sän yōr′əz, -yôr′-; *Sp.* se nyô′räs). **1.** a Spanish term of address equivalent to *Mrs.,* used alone or capitalized and prefixed to the name of a married or older woman. *Abbr.:* Sra. **2.** (in Spanish-speaking countries) a married woman or a spinster. [< Sp, fem. of SEÑOR]

se·ño·ri·ta (sän′yə rē′tə, sēn′-; *Sp.* se nyô rē′tä), *n., pl.* **-tas** (-təz; *Sp.* -täs). **1.** a Spanish term of address equivalent to *miss,* used alone or capitalized and prefixed to the name of a girl or unmarried woman. *Abbr.:* Srta. **2.** (in Spanish-speaking countries) a girl or young unmarried woman. **3.** a cigar-shaped wrasse, *Oxyjulis californica,* found off the coast of California, olive brown above shading to creamy white below. [< Sp, dim. of SEÑORA]

sen·sate (sen′sāt), *adj.* perceived by the senses. [< LL *sensāt(us).* See SENSE, -ATE¹]

sen·sa·tion (sen sā′shən), *n.* **1.** the operation or function of the senses; perception or awareness of stimuli through the senses. **2.** a mental condition resulting from stimulation of a sense organ; a physical feeling, as of cold, pain, etc. **3.** *Physiol.* the faculty of perception of stimuli. **4.** *Psychol.* an experience arising directly from stimulation of sense organs. **5.** a mental feeling, esp. a state of excited feeling. **6.** a state of excited feeling or interest caused among a number of persons or throughout a community, as by some rumor, occurrence, etc. **7.** a cause of such feeling or interest: *Her bright red dress was a sensation at the party.* [< ML *sensātiōn-* (s. of *sensātiō*), equiv. to LL *sensāt(us)* SENSATE + *-iōn-* -ION] —**sen·sa′tion·less,** *adj.*

—**Syn. 2.** See **sense. 6.** excitement, stimulation, animation; agitation, commotion, perturbation.

sen·sa·tion·al (sen sā′shə nəl), *adj.* **1.** of or pertaining to the senses or sensation. **2.** intended to produce or producing a startling effect, strong reaction, intense interest, etc., esp. by exaggerated, superficial, or lurid elements: *a sensational novel.* **3.** extraordinarily good; conspicuously excellent; phenomenal: *a sensational quarterback.* [SENSATION + -AL¹] —**sen·sa′tion·al·ly,** *adv.*

—**Syn. 1.** exciting, stimulating. —**Ant. 1.** prosaic, dull.

sen·sa·tion·al·ise (sen sā′shə nəlīz′), *v.t.,* **-ised, -is·ing.** *Chiefly Brit.* sensationalize.

sen·sa·tion·al·ism (sen sā′shə nəliz′əm), *n.* **1.** subject matter, language, or style producing or designed to produce startling or thrilling impressions or to excite and please vulgar taste. **2.** the use of or interest in this subject matter, language, or style: *The cheap tabloids relied on sensationalism to increase their circulation.* **3.** *Ethics.* the doctrine that the good is to be judged only by the gratification of the senses. **4.** *Philos.* the doctrine that all ideas are derived from and are essentially reducible to sensations. **5.** *Psychol.* sensationism. Also called **sensualism** (for defs. 3, 4). [SENSATIONAL + -ISM] —**sen·sa′tion·al·ist,** *n.* —**sen·sa′tion·al·is′tic,** *adj.*

sen·sa·tion·al·ize (sen sā′shə nəlīz′), *v.t.,* **-ized, -iz·ing.** to make sensational. [SENSATIONAL + -IZE]

sen·sa·tion·ism (sen sā′shə niz′əm), *n.* a theory of psychology maintaining that experience consists solely of sensations. Also, **sensationalism.** [SENSATION + -ISM] —**sen·sa′tion·ist,** *n., adj.* —**sen·sa′tion·is′tic,** *adj.*

sense (sens), *n., v.,* **sensed, sens·ing.** —*n.* **1.** any of the faculties, as sight, hearing, smell, taste, or touch, by which man and animals perceive stimuli originating from outside or inside the body. **2.** these faculties collectively. **3.** their operation or function;

sensation. **4.** a feeling or perception produced through the organs of touch, taste, etc., or resulting from a particular condition of some part of the body: *to have a sense of cold.* **5.** a faculty or function of the mind analogous to sensation: *the moral sense.* **6.** any special capacity for perception, estimation, appreciation, etc.: *a sense of humor.* **7.** Usually, **senses.** clear and sound mental faculties; sanity: *He has taken leave of his senses. Come to your senses.* **8.** a more or less vague perception or impression: *a sense of security.* **9.** a mental discernment, realization, or recognition; acuteness: *a just sense of the worth of a thing.* **10.** the recognition of something as incumbent or fitting: *a sense of duty.* **11.** sound practical intelligence: *He has no sense.* **12.** something that is sensible or reasonable: *to talk sense.* **13.** the meaning, reason, or value of something: *You missed the sense of his statement. There's no sense in worrying about the past.* **14.** the meaning of a word or phrase in a specific context, esp. as isolated in a dictionary or glossary; the semantic element in a word or group of words. **15.** an opinion or judgment formed or held, esp. by an assemblage or body of persons: *the sense of a meeting.* **16.** *Math.* one of two opposite directions in which a vector may point. **17.** **in a sense,** according to one explanation or view; to a certain extent: *In a sense it may have been the only possible solution.* **18.** **make sense,** to be reasonable or comprehensible: *His attitude doesn't make sense.* —*v.t.* **19.** to perceive (something) by the senses; become aware of. **20.** *Computer Technol.* **a.** to read (punched holes, tape, data, etc.) mechanically, electrically, or photoelectrically. **b.** to determine or locate the position or arrangement of (a computer part or parts). **21.** to grasp the meaning of; understand. [< L *sēnsus* sensation, feeling, understanding, equiv. to *sēns-* (ptp. stem of *sentīre* to feel) + *-us* n. suffix (4th decl.)]

—Syn. 4. SENSE, SENSATION refer to consciousness of stimulus or of a perception with an interpretation as pleasant or unpleasant. A SENSE is an awareness or recognition of something; the stimulus may be subjective and the entire process may be mental or intellectual; *a sense of failure.* A SENSATION is an impression derived from an objective (external) stimulus through any of the sense organs: *a sensation of heat.* The feeling is also applied to a general, indefinite bodily feeling: *a sensation of weariness.* **5.** awareness, apprehension. **7.** consciousness. **9.** estimation, appreciation. **13.** signification, import, denotation, connotation, interpretation. See **meaning.** **15.** feeling, sentiment. **19.** discern, appreciate, recognize.

Sense′ and Sensibil′ity, a novel (1811) by Jane Austen.

sense′ da′tum, **1.** *Psychol.* the basic unit of an experience resulting from the stimulation of a sense organ; a stimulus or an object of perception or sensation. **2.** *Epistemology.* datum (def. 5).

sense·less (sens′lis), *adj.* **1.** destitute or deprived of sensation; unconscious. **2.** lacking mental perception, appreciation, or comprehension. **3.** stupid or foolish, as persons or actions. **4.** nonsensical or meaningless, as words: *This letter is either cryptic or senseless.* [SENSE + -LESS] **—sense′less·ly,** *adv.* **—sense′less·ness,** *n.*
—Syn. 1. insensate, insensible. **2.** unperceiving, undiscerning. **3.** silly, idiotic, inane, witless, asinine.
—Ant. 2. sensitive. **3.** intelligent.

sense′ or′gan, a specialized bodily structure that receives or is sensitive to internal or external stimuli; receptor.

sense′ percep′tion, perception by the senses rather than by the intellect.

sense′ stress′. See **sentence stress.**

sen·si·bil·i·ty (sen′sə bil′i tē), *n., pl.* **-ties.** **1.** capacity for sensation or feeling; responsiveness or susceptibility to sensory stimuli. **2.** mental susceptibility or responsiveness; quickness and acuteness of apprehension or feeling. **3.** keen consciousness or appreciation. **4.** **sensibilities,** emotional capacities. **5.** Sometimes, **sensibilities.** liability to feel hurt or offended; sensitive feelings. **6.** Often, **sensibilities.** capacity for intellectual and aesthetic distinctions, feelings, tastes, etc.: *a man of refined sensibilities; vulgar sensibilities.* **7.** the property, as in plants or instruments, of being readily affected by external influences. [late ME *sensibilite* < MF < LL *sēnsibilitāt-* (s. of *sēnsibilitās*). See SENSIBLE, -ITY]
—Syn. 1. SENSIBILITY, SUSCEPTIBILITY, SENSITIVENESS, SENSITIVITY mean capacity to respond to or be affected by something. SUSCEPTIBILITY is the state or quality of being impressionable and responsive, esp. to emotional stimuli; in the plural much the same as SENSIBILITY: *a person of keen susceptibilities.* SENSIBILITY is, particularly, capacity to respond to aesthetic and emotional stimuli; delicacy of emotional or intellectual perception: *the sensibility of the artist.* SENSITIVENESS is the state or quality of being sensitive, having a capacity of sensation and of responding to external stimuli: *sensitiveness to light.* SENSITIVITY is a special capability of being sensitive to physiological, chemical action: *the sensitivity of a nerve.* **2.** alertness, awareness. **6.** sensitivity, perceptivity.

sen·si·ble (sen′sə bəl), *adj.* **1.** having, using, or showing good sense or sound judgment: *a sensible young man.* **2.** cognizant; keenly aware (usually fol. by *of*): *sensible of his fault.* **3.** significant in quantity, magnitude, etc.; considerable; appreciable: *a sensible reduction in price.* **4.** capable of being perceived by the senses; material: *the sensible universe.* **5.** capable of feeling or perceiving, as organs or parts of the body. **6.** perceptible to the mind. **7.** conscious: *The patient was speechless but still sensible.* **8.** *Archaic.* sensitive. [late ME < OF < L *sēnsibil(is),* equiv. to *sēns(us)* SENSE + *-ibilis* -IBLE] **—sen′si·ble·ness,** *n.* **—sen′si·bly,** *adv.*
—Syn. 1. intelligent, sagacious, rational, reasonable. See **practical.** **2.** conscious, understanding, observant. **4.** perceptible, discernible, palpable. **—Ant. 1.** stupid.

sen′sible hori′zon, *Astron.* See under **horizon** (def. 2a).

sen·sil·lum (sen sil′əm), *n., pl.* **-la** (-lə). **1.** *Zool.* a simple sense organ usually consisting of one or a few cells at the peripheral end of a sensory nerve fiber. **2.** one of the structural units composing a compound sense organ. [< NL, equiv. to L *sēnsil(is)* having sensation (*sēns(us)* SENSE + *-ilis* -ILE) + *-lum* dim. suffix]

sen·si·tise (sen′si tīz′), *v.t., v.i.,* **-tised, -tis·ing.** *Chiefly Brit.* sensitize. **—sen′si·ti·sa′tion,** *n.* **—sen′si·tis′er,** *n.*

sen·si·tive (sen′si tiv), *adj.* **1.** endowed with sensation; having perception through the senses. **2.** readily or excessively affected by external agencies or influences. **3.** having acute mental or emotional sensibility; easily affected, pained, annoyed, etc. **4.** pertaining to or connected with the senses or sensation. **5.** *Physiol.* having a low threshold of sensation or feeling. **6.** responding to stimuli, as leaves that move when touched. **7.** highly responsive to certain agents, as photographic plates, films, or paper. **8.** involving work, duties, or information of a highly secret or delicate nature, esp. in government: *a sensitive position in the State Department.* **9.** constructed to indicate, measure, or be affected by small amounts or changes, as a balance or thermometer. **10.** *Radio.* easily affected by external influences, esp. by radio waves. [< ML *sēnsitīv(us),* equiv. to L *sēnsi-* (see SENSIBLE) + *-tīvus* (irreg. for *-īvus* -IVE); r. ME *sensitif(e)* < MF < ML, as above] **—sen′si·tive·ly,** *adv.* **—sen′si·tive·ness,** *n.*
—Syn. 2, 3. impressionable, susceptible. **4.** sensate.

sen′sitive plant′, **1.** Also called **humble plant.** a tropical American plant, *Mimosa pudica,* cultivated in greenhouses, having bipinnate leaves whose leaflets fold together when touched. **2.** any of various other plants that are sensitive to touch.

sen·si·tiv·i·ty (sen′si tiv′i tē), *n., pl.* **-ties.** **1.** the state or quality of being sensitive. **2.** *Physiol.* **a.** the ability of an organism or part of an organism to react to stimuli; irritability. **b.** degree of susceptibility to stimulation. **3.** *Elect.* **a.** the ability of a radio device to react to incoming signals, expressed as the minimum input signal required to produce a specified output signal with a given noise level. **b.** the input, as voltage, current, or the like, required to produce full deflection in an electric measuring device, expressed as the ratio of the response to the magnitude of the input quantity. [SENSITIVE + -ITY]
—Syn. 1. See **sensibility.**

sen·si·tize (sen′si tīz′), *v.,* **-tized, -tiz·ing.** —*v.t.* **1.** to render sensitive. **2.** *Photog.* to render (a film or the like) sensitive to light or other forms of radiant energy. **3.** *Immunol.* to render sensitive to a serum by a series of injections. —*v.i.* **4.** to become sensitized. Also, *esp. Brit.,* **sensitise.** [SENSIT(IVE) + -IZE] **—sen′si·ti·za′tion,** *n.* **—sen′si·tiz′er,** *n.*

sen·si·tom·e·ter (sen′si tom′i tər), *n.* *Photog.* an instrument for testing the sensitivity of various types of film, consisting of an apparatus for exposing successive parts of the film to a light of standard intensity at successively increasing lengths of exposure. [SENSIT(IVE) + -O- + -METER] **—sen·si·to·met·ric** (sen′sə tō me′trik), *adj.* **—sen′si·to·met′ri·cal·ly,** *adv.* **—sen′si·tom′e·try,** *n.*

sen·so·ri·mo·tor (sen′sə rē mō′tər), *adj.* **1.** *Psychol.* of or pertaining to motor activity caused by sensory stimuli. Cf. **ideomotor.** **2.** *Physiol.* both sensory and motor, as parts of the cerebral cortex. Also, **sen·so·mo·tor** (sen′sə mō′tər). [SENSORY + MOTOR]

sen·so·ri·um (sen sōr′ē əm, -sôr′-), *n., pl.* **-so·ri·ums, -so·ri·a** (-sōr′ē ə, -sôr′-). **1.** a part of the brain or the brain itself regarded as the seat of sensation. **2.** *Anat., Biol.* the sensory apparatus of the body. [< LL, equiv. to L *sēns(us)* (ptp. of *sentīre* to feel) + *-ōrium* -ORIUM]

sen·so·ry (sen′sə rē), *adj.* **1.** of or pertaining to the senses or sensation. **2.** *Physiol.* noting a structure for conveying an impulse that results or tends to result in sensation, as a nerve. Also, **sen·so·ri·al** (sen sōr′ē əl, -sôr′-). [SENSE + -ORY[1]]

sen·su·al (sen′sho͞o əl), *adj.* **1.** pertaining to, inclined to, or preoccupied with the gratification of the senses or appetites; carnal; voluptuous. **2.** lacking in moral restraints; lewd or unchaste. **3.** arousing or exciting the senses or appetites. **4.** worldly; materialistic; irreligious. **5.** of or pertaining to the senses or physical sensation; sensory. **6.** pertaining to the philosophical doctrine of sensationalism. [late ME < L *sēnsuāl(is),* equiv. to *sēnsu(s)* SENSE + *-ālis* -AL[1]] **—sen′su·al·ly,** *adv.*
—Syn. 1. SENSUAL, SENSUOUS, VOLUPTUOUS refer to experience through the senses. SENSUAL refers, usually unfavorably, to the enjoyments derived from the senses, generally implying grossness or lewdness: *a sensual delight in eating; sensual excesses.* SENSUOUS refers, favorably or literally, to what is experienced through the senses: *sensuous impressions; sensuous poetry.* VOLUPTUOUS implies the luxurious gratification of sensuous or sensual desires: *voluptuous joys; voluptuous beauty.* **2.** lascivious. **4.** gross, licentious, dissolute.

sen·su·al·ise (sen′sho͞o ə līz′), *v.t.,* **-ised, -is·ing.** *Chiefly Brit.* sensualize. **—sen′su·al·i·sa′tion,** *n.*

sen·su·al·ism (sen′sho͞o ə liz′əm), *n.* **1.** subjection to sensual appetites; sensuality. **2.** *Ethics.* sensationalism (def. 3). **3.** *Philos.* sensationalism (def. 4). **4.** *Aesthetics.* emphasis on objective sensuality or on the quality of the sensual as the most important in the beautiful. [SENSUAL + -ISM]

sen·su·al·ist (sen′sho͞o ə list), *n.* **1.** one given to the indulgence of the senses or appetites. **2.** one who holds the doctrine of sensationalism. [SENSUAL + -IST] **—sen′su·al·is′tic,** *adj.*

sen·su·al·i·ty (sen′sho͞o al′i tē), *n., pl.* **-ties.** **1.** sensual nature: *the sensuality of Keats's poetry.* **2.** unrestrained indulgence in sensual pleasures. **3.** lewdness; unchastity. Also called **sen′su·al·ness.** [ME *sensualite* < OF < LL *sēnsuālitāt-* (s. of *sēnsuālitās*). See SENSUAL, -ITY]

sen·su·al·ize (sen′sho͞o ə līz′), *v.t.,* **-ized, -iz·ing.** to render sensual. Also, *esp. Brit.,* **sensualise.** [SENSUAL + -IZE] **—sen′su·al·i·za′tion,** *n.*

sen·su·ous (sen′sho͞o əs), *adj.* **1.** of or pertaining to sensible objects or to the senses. **2.** perceived by or affecting the senses: *the sensuous qualities of music.* **3.** readily affected through the senses: *a sensuous temperament.* [< L *sensu-* (see SENSUAL) + -OUS] **—sen′su·ous·ly,** *adv.* **—sen′su·ous·ness, sen·su·os·i·ty** (sen′sho͞o os′i tē), *n.*
—Syn. 1. See **sensual.** **2.** sentient. **3.** feeling, sensible.

sent[1] (sent), *v.* pt. and pp. of **send.**

sent[2] (sent), *n., pl.* **sent·i** (sen′tē), **sents.** a former coin of Estonia, the 100th part of a kroon: replaced the mark in 1928. [< Estonian *senti* (cf. Finn *sentti*) < L *centum* 100]

sen·tence (sen′təns), *n., v.,* **-tenced, -tenc·ing.** —*n.* **1.** *Gram.* a grammatical unit of one or more words, bearing minimal syntactic relation to the words that precede or follow it, often preceded and followed in speech by pauses, having one of a small number of characteristic intonation patterns, and typically expressing an independent statement, question, request, command, etc., as *Fire!* or *Summer is here.* or *Who is it?* **2.** *Law.* **a.** an authoritative decision; a judicial judgment or decree, esp. the judicial determination of the punishment to be inflicted on a convicted criminal. **b.** the punishment itself. **3.** *Music.* a period. **4.** *Archaic.* a saying, apothegm, or maxim. **5.** *Obs.* an opinion given on a particular question. —*v.t.* **6.** to pronounce sentence upon; condemn to punishment. [ME < OF < L *sententia* opinion, decision, equiv. to *sent-* (root of *sentīre* to feel) + *-entia* -ENCE] **—sen′tenc·er,** *n.*

sen′tence stress′, the stress pattern or patterns associated with words as arranged in sentences in a particular language. Also called **sense stress, sen′tence ac′cent.** Cf. **word stress.**

sen·ten·tial (sen ten′shəl), *adj.* pertaining to or of the nature of a judicial sentence. [< L *sententi(a)* SENTENCE + -AL[1]] **—sen·ten′tial·ly,** *adv.*

senten′tial cal′culus, the branch of symbolic logic dealing with the logical relationships between statements insofar as they can be analyzed into conjunctions, disjunctions, and negations of more elementary statements. Also called **propositional calculus.**

senten′tial connec′tive, *Logic.* any of several words or their equivalent symbols used in logical formulas to connect propositions, as "or," "not," "and," "if and only if," etc.

senten′tial func′tion, *Logic.* an expression that contains one or more variables and becomes meaningful when suitable constant terms are substituted for them. Also called **propositional function.**

sen·ten·tious (sen ten′shəs), *adj.* **1.** abounding in pithy aphorisms or maxims: *a sententious book.* **2.** given to excessive moralizing; self-righteous. **3.** given to or using pithy sayings or maxims: *a sententious poet.* **4.** of the nature of a maxim; pithy. [late ME < L *sententiōs(us)* meaningful. See SENTENCE, -OUS] **—sen·ten′tious·ly,** *adv.* **—sen·ten′tious·ness, sen·ten·ti·os·i·ty** (sen ten′shē os′i tē), *n.*

sen·tience (sen′shəns), *n.* sentient condition or character; capacity for sensation or feeling. Also, **sen′tien·cy.** [SENTI(ENT) + -ENCE]

sen·tient (sen′shənt), *adj.* **1.** having the power of perception by the senses. **2.** characterized by sensation. —*n.* **3.** one who or that which is sentient. **4.** the conscious mind. [< L *sentient-* (s. of *sentiēns,* prp. of *sentīre* to feel), equiv. to *senti-* feel + *-ent-* -ENT] **—sen′tient·ly,** *adv.*

sen·ti·ment (sen′tə mənt), *n.* **1.** an attitude toward something; regard; opinion. **2.** a mental feeling; emotion: *a sentiment of pity.* **3.** refined or tender emotion; manifestation of the higher or more refined feelings. **4.** exhibition or manifestation of feeling or sensibility, or appeal to the tender emotions, in literature, art, or music. **5.** a thought influenced by or proceeding from feeling or emotion. **6.** the thought or feeling intended to be conveyed by words, acts, or gestures as distinguished from the words, acts, or gestures themselves. [< ML *sentīment(um),* equiv. to L *senti(re)* (to) feel + *-mentum* -MENT; r. ME *sentement* < OF < ML, as above] **—sen′ti·ment·less,** *adj.*
—Syn. 1. See **opinion.** **2.** See **feeling.** **3.** SENTIMENT, SENTIMENTALITY are terms for sensitiveness to emotional feelings. SENTIMENT is a sincere and refined sensibility, a tendency to be influenced by emotion rather than reason or fact: *to appeal to sentiment.* SENTIMENTALITY implies affected, excessive, sometimes mawkish sentiment: *weak sentimentality.* **—Ant. 2.** realism, logic.

sen·ti·men·tal (sen′tə men′tᵊl), *adj.* **1.** expressive of or appealing to sentiment, esp. the tender emotions and feelings, as love, pity, nostalgia, etc.: *a sentimental song.* **2.** pertaining to or dependent on sentiment: *We kept the old photograph for purely sentimental reasons.* **3.** weakly emotional; mawkishly susceptible or tender: *a sentimental schoolgirl.* **4.** characterized by or showing sentiment or refined feeling. [SENTIMENT + -AL[1]] **—sen′ti·men′tal·ly,** *adv.*
—Syn. 1. warm, sympathetic, affectionate; loving.
—Ant. 1, 4. dispassionate.

sen·ti·men·tal·ise (sen′tə men′tᵊlīz′), *v.i., v.t.,* **-ised, -is·ing.** *Chiefly Brit.* sentimentalize. **—sen′ti·men′ta·li·sa′tion,** *n.* **—sen′ti·men′tal·is′er,** *n.*

sen·ti·men·tal·ism (sen′tə men′tᵊliz′əm), *n.* **1.** sentimental tendency or character; predominance of sentiment over reason. **2.** weak emotionalism; excessive indulgence in sentiment. **3.** a display of sentimentality. [SENTIMENTAL + -ISM]

sen·ti·men·tal·ist (sen′tə men′tᵊlist), *n.* one given to sentiment or sentimentality. [SENTIMENTAL + -IST]

sen·ti·men·tal·i·ty (sen′tə men tal′i tē), *n., pl.* **-ties.** **1.** the quality or state of being sentimental or excessively sentimental. **2.** an instance of being sentimental. **3.** a sentimental act, gesture, expression, etc. [SENTIMENTAL + -ITY]
—Syn. See **sentiment.**

sen·ti·men·tal·ize (sen′tə men′tᵊlīz′), *v.,* **-ized, -iz·ing.** —*v.i.* **1.** to indulge in sentiment. —*v.t.* **2.** to view (someone or something) sentimentally: *He sentimentalized the relationship until all real meaning was lost.* Also, *esp. Brit.,* **sentimentalise.** [SENTIMENTAL + -IZE] **—sen′ti·men′ta·li·za′tion,** *n.* **—sen′ti·men′tal·iz′er,** *n.*

sen·ti·nel (sen′tᵊnᵊl), *n., v.,* **-neled, -nel·ing** or (*esp. Brit.*) **-nelled, -nel·ling.** —*n.* **1.** one who or that which watches or stands as if watching. **2.** a soldier stationed as a guard to challenge all comers and prevent a surprise attack: *to stand sentinel.* **3.** *Naut.* kellet. **4.** Also called **tag.** (in computer programming) a symbol, mark, or other labeling device indicating the beginning or end of a unit of information. —*v.t.* **5.** to watch over or guard as a sentinel. [MF *sentinelle* < It *sentinell(a),* deriv. of OIt *sentin(a)* vigilance (L *sent(īre)* (to) observe) + *-īna* -INE[2])] **—sen′ti·nel·like′,** *adj.* **—sen′ti·nel·ship′,** *n.*

sen·try (sen′trē), *n., pl.* **-tries.** **1.** a soldier stationed at a place to stand guard and prevent the passage of unauthorized persons, watch for fires, etc., esp. a sentinel stationed at a pass, gate, opening in a defense work, or the like. 2. a member of a guard or watch. [short for *sentinel*, var. of SENTINEL]

sen′try box′, a small structure for sheltering a sentry from bad weather.

Se·nu·si (se no͞o′sē), *n., pl.* **-sis.** *Islam.* Sanusi. Also, **Se·nus′si.** —**Se·nu′si·an, Se·nus′si·an,** *adj.* —**Se·nu·sism, Se·nus·sism** (sə no͞o′siz əm), *n.*

Se·o de Ur·gel (*Sp.* se′ô de o͞or hel′), Urgel.

Se·oul (sā′o͞ol, sōl; *Kor.* syœ′o͞ol′), *n.* a city in and the capital of South Korea, in the W part. 3,470,880 with suburbs (est. 1965).

Sep., 1. September. 2. Septuagint.

sep., 1. sepal. 2. separate.

se·pal (sē′pəl), *n. Bot.* one of the individual leaves or parts of the calyx of a flower. [< NL *sepal(um),* equiv. to *scep-* (< Gk *sképē* covering) + *(pet)alum* PETAL] —**se′-paled, se′palled,** *adj.*

S, Sepal

se·pal·oid (sē′pə loid′, sep′ə-), *adj.* resembling a sepal. Also, **sep·al·ine** (sep′ə līn′, -lin, sē′pə-). [< NL *sepaloid(eus).* See SEPAL, -OID]

-sepalous, a combining form of **sepal** and **-ous:** *polysepalous.*

sep·a·ra·ble (sep′ər ə bəl, sep′rə-), *adj.* 1. capable of being separated, parted, or dissociated. 2. *Math.* containing a countable dense subset. [< L *sēparābil(is),* equiv. to *sēpar(āre)* (to) SEPARATE + *-ābilis* -ABLE] —**sep′a·ra·bil′i·ty, sep′a·ra·ble·ness,** *n.* —**sep′a·ra·bly,** *adv.*

sep·a·rate (*v.* sep′ə rāt′; *adj., n.* sep′ər it), *v.,* **-rat·ed, -rat·ing,** *adj., n.* —*v.t.* 1. to keep apart or divide, as by an intervening barrier, space, etc.: *to separate two fields by a fence.* 2. to put, bring, or force apart; part: *to separate two fighting boys.* 3. to set apart; disconnect; dissociate: *to separate church and state.* 4. to remove or sever from association, service, etc.: *separated from his wife; separated from the army.* 5. to sort, part, divide, or disperse (an assemblage, mass, compound, etc.), as into individual units, components, elements, etc. 6. to take by parting or dividing; extract (usually fol. by *from* or *out*): *to separate metal from ore.* —*v.i.* 7. to part company; withdraw from personal association (often fol. by *from*): *to separate from a church.* 8. (of a married pair) to stop living together but without getting a divorce. 9. to draw or come apart; become divided, disconnected, or detached. 10. to become parted from a mass or compound: *Cream separates from milk.* 11. to take or go in different directions: *We have to separate at the crossroad.* —*adj.* 12. detached, disconnected, or disjoined. 13. unconnected; distinct; unique: *two separate questions.* 14. being or standing apart; dispersed: *two separate houses; The desert has widely separated oases.* 15. existing or maintained independently: *separate organizations.* 16. individual or particular: *each separate item.* 17. not shared; private: *Waiter, we'll have separate checks. My brother and I have separate rooms.* 18. (*sometimes cap.*) noting or pertaining to a church or other organization no longer associated with the original or parent organization. —*n.* 19. Usually, **separates.** women's outer garments that may be worn in combination with a variety of others to make various ensembles, as matching and contrasting blouses, skirts, and sweaters, etc. Cf. **coordinate** (def. 6). 20. offprint (def. 1). 21. a bibliographical unit, as an article, chapter, or other portion of a larger work, printed from the same type but issued separately, sometimes with additional pages. [late ME < L *sēparāt(us)* (ptp. of *sēparāre*), equiv. to *sē-* SE- + *par-* put + *-ātus* -ATE[1]] —**sep′a·rate·ly,** *adv.* —**sep′a·rate·ness,** *n.*
—**Syn. 1, 2.** sever, sunder, split. SEPARATE, DIVIDE imply a putting apart or keeping apart of things from each other. To SEPARATE is to remove from each other things previously associated: *to separate a mother from her children.* To DIVIDE is to split or break up carefully according to measurement, rule, or plan: *to divide a cake into equal parts.* 3. disjoin, disengage. 9. unattached, severed. 12. discrete. 13. withdrawn, secluded, isolated. 15. independent. —**Ant. 1–3.** unite, connect.

sep′arate but e′qual, pertaining to a racial policy by which Negroes are segregated but granted equal opportunities and facilities, as for education, transportation, jobs, etc.

sep′arated broth′er, *Rom. Cath. Ch.* a non-Catholic, esp. a Protestant.

sep′arate school′, (in Canada) any school that is not part of the public-school system, esp. a Roman Catholic parochial school.

sep·a·ra·tion (sep′ə rā′shən), *n.* 1. the act, state, or an instance of separating or the state of being separated. 2. a place, line, or point of parting. 3. a gap, hole, rent, or the like. 4. *Law.* **a.** cessation of conjugal cohabitation, as by mutual consent. **b.** See **judicial separation.** 5. *Rocketry.* the time or act of releasing a burned-out stage of a missile from the remainder. [late ME < L *sēparātiōn-* (s. of *sēparātiō*), equiv. to *sēparāt(us)* SEPARATE + *-iōn-* -ION]

separa′tion cen′ter, a place at which military personnel are processed for release from service into civilian life.

separa′tion en′ergy, *Physics.* See **binding energy** (def. 1).

separa′tion neg′ative, (in color photography) a negative bearing one of the component colors of the final print, used in conjunction with other negatives.

separa′tion of pow′ers, *Govt.* the principle or system of vesting in separate branches the executive, legislative, and judicial powers of a government.

separa′tion of var′iables, *Math.* a grouping of the terms of a differential equation so that associated with each differential is a factor consisting entirely of functions of the independent variable appearing in the differential.

sep·a·ra·tist (sep′ə rā′tist, -ər ə tist), *n.* 1. one who separates, withdraws, or secedes, as from an established church. 2. an advocate of separation, esp. ecclesiastical or political separation. [SEPARATE (adj.) + -IST] —**sep′a·ra·tism,** *n.*

sep·a·ra·tive (sep′ə rā′tiv, -ər ə tiv), *adj.* 1. tending to separate. 2. causing separation. [< LL *sēparātīv(us)* < L *sēparāt(us)* SEPARATE + *-īvus* -IVE] —**sep′a·ra′tive·ly,** *adv.* —**sep′a·ra′tive·ness,** *n.*

sep·a·ra·tor (sep′ə rā′tər), *n.* 1. one who or that which separates. 2. any of various apparatus for separating one thing from another, as cream from milk, steam from water, or wheat from chaff. 3. *Elect.* a device that prevents metal contact between plates of opposite charge in a storage battery. 4. *Mach.* retainer[1] (def. 3). [<LL *sēparātor,* equiv. to *sēparāt(us)* SEPARATE + *-or* -OR[2]]

sep·a·ra·to·ry (sep′ər ə tôr′ē, -tōr′ē), *adj.* serving to separate. [< NL *sēparātōri(us),* equiv. to L *sēparāt(us)* SEPARATE + *-ōrius* -ORY[1]]

sep·a·ra·trix (sep′ə rā′triks, sep′ə rā′-), *n., pl.* **sep·a·ra·tri·ces** (sep′ə rā′tri sēz′, -ər ə trī′sēz), **sep·a·ra·trix·es.** 1. something that divides or separates, as the line between light and dark areas on a partially illuminated surface. 2. virgule. 3. *Math.* one of several symbols for separating components of a number, as a decimal point, comma, etc. [< NL < LL. See SEPARAT(OR), -TRIX]

Se·phar·dim (sə fär′dim, -fär dēm′), *n.pl., sing.* **-di** (-dē, -dē′). Jews of Spain and Portugal or their descendants, distinguished from the Ashkenazim chiefly by their liturgy, religious customs, and pronunciation of Hebrew. [pl. of ModHeb *sephardī* < Heb *sephārād* (region mentioned in Bible (Obadiah 20) and wrongly thought to be Spain) + *-ī* suffix of appurtenance] —**Se·phar′dic,** *adj.*

Se·phar·vites (sef′är vīts′, si fär′-), *n.pl.* people believed to be of the ancient Babylonian city of Sippar, some of whom later settled in Samaria.

Se·pher To·rah (sā fâr′ tō rä′; *Eng.* sā′fər tōr′ə, tôr′ə), *pl.* **Si·phrei To·rah** (sē frā′tō rä′), *Eng.* **Sepher Torahs.** *Hebrew.* a scroll of the Torah, typically of parchment, from which the designated Parashah is chanted or read on the prescribed days. Also, **Sefer Torah.** [lit., book of law]

Se·phor·a (si fōr′ə, -fôr′ə), *n. Douay Bible.* Zipporah.

se·pi·a (sē′pē ə), *n.* 1. a brown pigment obtained from the inklike secretion of various cuttlefish and used with brush or pen in drawing. 2. a drawing made with this pigment. 3. a dark brown. 4. *Photog.* a print or photograph made in this color. 5. a cuttlefish of the genus *Sepia* or related genera. —*adj.* 6. of a brown, grayish brown, or olive brown similar to that of sepia ink. [< L < Gk *sēpía* cuttlefish. See SEPSIS] —**se′pi·a·like′,** *adj.* —**se·pic** (sē′pik, sep′ik), *adj.*

se·pi·o·lite (sē′pē ə līt′), *n.* meerschaum (def. 1). [< G *Sepiolit* < Gk *sēpío(n)* cuttlefish + G *-lit* -LITE]

se·poy (sē′poi), *n.* (formerly, in India) a native soldier, usually an infantryman, in the service of Europeans, esp. of the British. [var. of *sipahi* < Urdu < Pers *siphāhī* horseman, soldier, deriv. of *sipāh* army]

Se′poy Rebel′lion, a revolt of the sepoy troops in British India (1857–59), resulting in the transfer of the administration of India from the East India Company to the crown. Also called **Se′poy Mu′tiny, Indian Mutiny.**

sep·pa (sā pä′; *Jap.* se pä′), *n., pl.* **-pa.** either of two washerlike fittings reinforcing a tsuba on both sides. [< Jap]

seppa′ dai′ (dī), *pl.* **seppa dai.** (on a tsuba) a plain oval space around the hole for the tang of the blade, sometimes containing the maker's signature. [< Jap]

sep·pu·ku (se po͞o′ko͞o), *n.* (in Japan) suicide by ripping open the abdomen; hara-kiri. [< Jap]

sep·sis (sep′sis), *n. Pathol.* local or generalized bacterial invasion of the body, esp. by pyogenic organisms: *dental sepsis; wound sepsis.* [< Gk *sēpsis* decay; cf. *sēpein* to make rotten]

sept (sept), *n.* 1. a clan, esp. with reference to tribes or families in Ireland. 2. *Anthropol.* a group believing itself derived from a common ancestor. [? < L *sēpt(um)* fold (in fig. use, e.g., *Sept of Christ*)]

sept (set), *n. French.* the number 7.

sept-, a learned borrowing from Latin meaning "seven," used in the formation of compound words: *septet; septillion.* Also, *esp. before a consonant,* **septi-**[1]. [< L *septem*]

Sept., 1. September. 2. Septuagint.

sep·ta (sep′tə), *n.* pl. of **septum.**

sep·tal (sep′tᵊl), *adj. Biol.* of or pertaining to a septum. [SEPT(UM) + -AL[1]]

sep·tar·i·um (sep târ′ē əm), *n., pl.* **-tar·i·a** (-târ′ē ə). *Geol.* a concretionary nodule or mass, usually of calcium carbonate or of argillaceous carbonate of iron, traversed within by a network of cracks filled with calcite and other minerals. [< NL; see SEPT(UM), -ARIUM] —**sep·tar′i·an,** *adj.* —**sep·tar·i·ate** (sep târ′ē it), *adj.*

sep·tate (sep′tāt), *adj. Biol.* divided by a septum or septa. [SEPT(UM) + -ATE[1]]

sep·ta·va·lent (sep′tə vā′lənt), *adj. Chem.* septivalent. [b. SEPT(IVALENT) and (HEPT)AVALENT]

sep·tec·to·my (sep tek′tə mē), *n., pl.* **-mies.** *Surg.* excision of part or all of a septum, esp. the nasal septum. [SEPT(UM) + -ECTOMY]

Sep·tem·ber (sep tem′bər), *n.* the ninth month of the year, containing 30 days. [OE < L: seventh (month) in the early Roman calendar; the *-re* of ME *Septembre* < OF *setembre*] —**Sep·tem·bral** (sep tem′brəl), *adj.*

Septem′ber Mas′sacre, (in the French Revolution) the massacre of royalists and other inmates of the prisons of Paris September 2–6, 1792.

Sep·tem·brist (sep tem′brist), *n.* a person who instigated or took part in the September Massacre. [SEPTEMBER + -IST, modeled on Pg *setembrista*]

sep·tem·par·tite (sep′tem pär′tīt), *adj.* separated into seven sections. [< L *septem* seven + PARTITE]

sep·tem·vir (sep tem′vər), *n., pl.* **-virs, -vi·ri** (-və-rī′). a member of a seven-man ruling body in ancient Rome. [sing. of L *septemvirī,* equiv. to *septem* seven + *virī* men]

sep·tem·vi·ral (sep tem′vər əl), *adj.* of or pertaining to septemvirs or a septemvirate. [< L *septemvirāl(is).* See SEPTEMVIR, -AL[1]]

sep·tem·vi·rate (sep tem′vər it, -və rāt′), *n.* (in ancient Rome) 1. the ruling body of septemvirs. 2. the office or rule of this body. [< L *septemvirāt(us).* See SEPTEMVIR, -ATE[1]]

sep·te·nar·y (sep′tə ner′ē), *adj., n., pl.* **-nar·ies.** —*adj.* 1. of or pertaining to the number seven or forming a group of seven. 2. septennial. —*n.* 3. a group or set of seven. 4. a period of seven years. 5. the number seven. 6. *Pros.* a line of seven feet. [< L *septēnāri(us),* equiv. to *septēn(ī)* seven apiece (*septe(m)* seven + *nī* distributive suffix) + *-ārius* -ARY]

sep·ten·de·cil·lion (sep′ten di sil′yən), *n., pl.* **-lions,** (*as after a numeral*) **-lion,** *adj.* —*n.* 1. a cardinal number represented in the U.S. and France by one followed by 54 zeros and, in Great Britain and Germany, by one followed by 102 zeros. —*adj.* 2. amounting to one septendecillion in number. [< L *septendec(im)* seventeen + *-illion,* as in *million*] —**sep′ten·de·cil′lionth,** *adj., n.*

sep·ten·ni·al (sep ten′ē əl), *adj.* 1. occurring every seven years. 2. of or for seven years. —*n.* 3. something that occurs every seven years. [< L *septenni(s)* lasting seven years (*sept(em)* seven + *-ennis* lasting a year, deriv. of *annus* year) + -AL[1]] —**sep·ten′ni·al·ly,** *adv.*

sep·ten·tri·o·nal (sep ten′trē ə nᵊl), *adj.* northern. [late ME < L *septentriōnāl(is),* equiv. to *septem triōn(ēs)* seven oxen (Great Bear constellation) + *-ālis* -AL[1]]

sep·tet (sep tet′), *n.* 1. any group of seven persons or things. 2. a company of seven singers or musicians. 3. a musical composition for seven voices or instruments. Also, *esp. Brit.,* **sep·tette′.** [< G; see SEPT-, -ET]

sept·foil (sept′foil′, sep′-), *n. Archit.* an ornament or decorative feature having seven foils or lobes. [< LL *septifol(ium).* See SEPTI-[1], FOIL[2]]

septi-[1], var. of **sept-,** before a consonant: *septilateral.*

septi-[2], a combining form of **septum:** *septicidal.*

sep·tic (sep′tik), *Pathol.* —*adj.* 1. infective, usually with a pus-forming microbe. 2. pertaining to or of the nature of sepsis; infected. —*n.* 3. an organism causing sepsis. [< L *sēptic(us)* < Gk *sēptikós,* equiv. to *sēpt(ós)* rotted + *-ikos* -IC] —**sep′ti·cal·ly,** *adv.* —**sep·tic·i·ty** (sep tis′i tē), *n.*

sep·ti·ce·mi·a (sep′ti sē′mē ə), *n. Pathol.* the invasion and persistence of pathogenic bacteria in the blood stream. Also, **sep′ti·cae′mi·a.** [< NL; see SEPTIC, -EMIA] —**sep′ti·ce′mic, sep′ti·cae′mic,** *adj.*

sep′tice′mic plague′, *Pathol.* an especially dangerous form of plague in which the infecting organisms invade the blood stream. Cf. **plague** (def. 2). [SEPTICEM(IA) + -IC]

sep·ti·cid·al (sep′ti sīd′ᵊl), *adj. Bot.* characterized by splitting through the septa or dissepiments, in dehiscence. [SEPTI-[2] + -CIDAL] —**sep′ti·ci′·dal·ly,** *adv.*

A, Septicidal dehiscence in capsule of a species of *Yucca*
B, Transverse section

sep′tic sore′ throat′, *Pathol.* an acute, toxic, streptococcus infection of the throat producing fever, tonsillitis, and other serious effects.

sep′tic tank′, a tank in which solid organic sewage is decomposed and purified by anaerobic bacteria.

sep·tif·ra·gal (sep tif′rə gəl), *adj. Bot.* characterized by the breaking away of the valves from the septa or dissepiments, in dehiscence. [SEPTI-[2] + L *frag-* (see FRAGILE) + -AL[1]] —**sep·tif′ra·gal·ly,** *adv.*

sep·ti·lat·er·al (sep′tə lat′ər əl), *adj.* having seven sides. [SEPTI-[1] + LATERAL]

sep·til·lion (sep til′yən), *n., pl.* **-lions,** (*as after a numeral*) **-lion,** *adj.* —*n.* 1. a cardinal number represented in the U.S. and France by one followed by 24 zeros and, in Great Britain and Germany, by one followed by 42 zeros. —*adj.* 2. amounting to one septillion in number. [< F, equiv. to *sept* seven + *-illion,* as in *million*] —**sep·til′lionth,** *n., adj.*

sep·ti·mal (sep′tə məl), *adj.* of or based on the number seven. [< L *septim(us)* seventh + -AL[1]]

sep·ti·ma·na (sep′ti mā′nə), *n., pl.* **-nae** (-nē). (in prescriptions) a week. [<L]

sep·time (sep′tēm), *n. Fencing.* the seventh of eight defensive positions. [< L *septima (positiō)* seventh (position)]

Sep·ti·mus (sep′tə məs), *n.* a boy's given name.

sep·ti·syl·la·ble (sep′ti sil′ə bəl), *n.* a word made up of seven syllables. [SEPTI-[1] + SYLLABLE] —**sep·ti·syl·lab·ic** (sep′ti si lab′ik), *adj.*

sep·ti·va·lent (sep′tə vā′lənt), *adj. Chem.* having a valence of seven; heptavalent. Also, **septavalent.** [SEPTI-[1] + -VALENT]

sep·to·let (sep′tə let′, sep′tə let′), *n.* septuplet (def. 4). [by alter.]

sep·tu·a·ge·nar·i·an (sep′cho͞o ə jə nâr′ē ən), *adj.* 1. of the age of 70 years or between 70 and 80 years old. —*n.* 2. a septuagenarian person. [< L *septuāgēnāri(us)* (see SEPTUAGENARY) + -AN]

sep·tu·ag·e·nar·y (sep′cho͞o aj′ə ner′ē *or, esp. Brit.,* -ə jē′nə rē), *adj., n., pl.* **-nar·ies.** septuagenarian. [< L *septuāgēnāri(us),* equiv. to *septuāgēn(ī)* seventy each (distributive of *septuāgintā* seventy; see SEPTUAGENT) + *-ārius* -ARY]

Sep·tu·a·ges·i·ma (sep′to͞o ə jes′ə mə, -tyo͞o-, sep′-cho͞o-), the third Sunday before Lent. Also called **Septuages′ima Sun′day.** [< eccl. L *septuāgēsima (diēs)* the seventieth (day); r. ME *septuages(i)me* < OF]

Sep·tu·a·gint (sep′to͞o ə jint′, -tyo͞o-, sep′cho͞o-), *n.* the oldest Greek version of the Old Testament, traditionally said to have been translated by 70 or 72 Jewish scholars at the request of Ptolemy II. Most modern scholars believe that only the Pentateuch was completed in the early part of the 3rd century A.D. and that the remaining books were translated in the next two centuries. [< L *septuāgint(ā)* seventy, equiv. to var. of *septem* seven + *-gintā* decade] —**Sep′tu·a·gint′al,** *adj.*

sep·tum (sep′təm), *n., pl.* **-ta** (-tə). *Biol.* a dividing wall, membrane, or the like, in a plant or animal structure; dissepiment. [var. of L *saeptum* enclosure, deriv. of neut. of *saeptus* (ptp. of *saepīre* to fence), equiv. to *saep-* fence + *-tus* ptp. suffix; akin to L *saepēs* hedge, fence]

sep·tu·or (sep′cho͞o ôr′), *n. Music.* septet. [b. L *sep(tem)* seven and *(quat)tuor* four]

sep·tu·ple (sep′to͞o pəl, -tyo͞o-, sep to͞o′pəl, -tyo͞o′-, -tup′əl), *adj., v.,* **-pled, -pling.** —*adj.* 1. sevenfold; seven times as great. —*v.t.* 2. to make seven times as great. [< LL *septupl(us);* see -PLE]

sep·tu·plet (sep tup′lit, -to͞o′plit, -tyo͞o′-), *n.* 1. any group or combination of seven. 2. one of seven offspring born at one birth. **3. septuplets,** seven offspring born at one birth. **4.** Also, **septolet.** *Music.* a group of seven notes of equal value performed in the same amount of time normally taken to perform four or six. [SEPTUPLE + -ET]

sep·tu·pli·cate (*adj., n.* sep to͞o′plə kit, -tyo͞o′-; *v.* sep to͞o′plə kāt′, -tyo͞o′-), *adj., n., v.,* **-cat·ed, -cat·ing.** —*adj.* **1.** existing or produced in seven identical copies. —*n.* **2.** any one or all of seven identical things. **3.** seven identical copies (usually prec. by *in*): *Type the letter in septuplicate.* —*v.t.* **4.** to make seven times as great, as by multiplying. [< ML *septuplicāt(us)* (ptp. of *septuplicāre* to multiply by seven), equiv. to LL *septupl(us)* SEPTUPLE + *-plicātus,* as in *quadruplicātus;* see QUADRUPLICATE]

sep·ul·cher (sep′əl kər), *n.* **1.** a tomb, grave, or burial place. **2.** Also called **Easter sepulcher.** *Eccles.* a structure or a recess in some old churches in which the sacred elements, the cross, etc., were deposited with due ceremonies on Good Friday and taken out at Easter in commemoration of Christ's entombment and Resurrection. —*v.t.* **3.** to place in a sepulcher; bury. Also, *esp. Brit.,* **sepulchre.** [ME *sepulcre* < OF < L *sepulcr(um),* equiv. to *sepul-* (ptp. stem of *sepelīre* to bury) + *-crum* n. suffix of place]

se·pul·chral (sə pul′krəl), *adj.* **1.** of, pertaining to, or serving as a tomb. **2.** of or pertaining to burial. **3.** proper to or suggestive of a tomb; funereal or dismal. **4.** hollow and deep: *sepulchral tone.* [< L *sepulcrāl(is).* See SEPULCHER, -AL¹] —**se·pul′chral·ly,** *adv.*

sep·ul·chre (sep′əl kər), *n., v.t.,* **-chred, -chring.** *Chiefly Brit.* sepulcher.

sep·ul·ture (sep′əl chər), *n.* **1.** the act of placing in a sepulcher or tomb; burial. **2.** *Archaic.* sepulcher; tomb. [ME < OF < L *sepultūr(a),* equiv. to *sepult(us)* (ptp. of *sepelīre* to bury) + *-ūra* -URE] —**se·pul·tur·al** (sə-pul′chər əl), *adj.*

seq., **1.** sequel. **2.** the following (one). [< L *sequens*]

seq. luce, (in prescriptions) the following day. [< L *sequentī lūce*]

seqq., the following (ones). [< L *sequentia*]

se·qua·cious (si kwā′shəs), *adj.* **1.** *Archaic.* following, imitating, or serving another person, esp. unreasoningly. **2.** following with smooth or logical regularity. [< L *sequāci-* (s. of *sequax*) following (akin to *sequī* to follow) + -OUS] —**se·qua′cious·ly,** *adv.* —**se·quac·i·ty** (si-kwas′i tē), **se·qua′cious·ness,** *n.*

se·quel (sē′kwəl), *n.* **1.** a literary work that is complete in itself but continues the narrative of a preceding work. **2.** an event or circumstance following something; subsequent course of affairs. **3.** a result, consequence, or inference. [late ME *sequel(e)* < L *sequēl(a)* what follows, equiv. to *seq(uī)* to follow + *-ēla* n. suffix]

se·que·la (si kwē′lə), *n., pl.* **-lae** (-lē). *Pathol.* an abnormal condition resulting from a previous disease. [< L: SEQUEL]

se·quence (sē′kwəns), *n.* **1.** the following of one thing after another; succession. **2.** order of succession: *a list of books in alphabetical sequence.* **3.** a continuous or connected series: *a sonnet sequence.* **4.** something that follows; a subsequent event; result; consequence. **5.** *Music.* a melodic or harmonic pattern repeated three or more times at different pitches with or without modulation. **6.** *Liturgy.* a hymn sometimes sung after the gradual and before the gospel; prose. **7.** *Motion Pictures.* a portion of a film story set in one place and time and without interruptions or breaks of any sort; episode. **8.** *Cards.* a series of three or more cards following one another in order of value, esp. of the same suit. **9.** *Math.* a set whose elements have an order similar to that of the positive integers; a map from the positive integers to a given set. [late ME < LL *sequentia,* equiv. to *sequ-* (root of *sequī* to follow) + *-entia* -ENCE]
—**Syn. 1.** See **series. 2.** arrangement. **4.** outcome, sequel.

se·quent (sē′kwənt), *adj.* **1.** following; successive. **2.** following logically or naturally; consequent. **3.** characterized by continuous succession; consecutive. —*n.* **4.** that which follows in order or as a result. [< L *sequent-* (s. of *sequēns,* prp. of *sequī* to follow), equiv. to *sequ-* follow + *-ent-* -ENT] —**se′quent·ly,** *adv.*

se·quen·tial (si kwen′shəl), *adj.* **1.** characterized by regular sequence of parts. **2.** following; subsequent; consequent. [SEQUENT + -IAL] —**se·quen·ti·al·i·ty** (si kwen′shē al′i tē), *n.* —**se·quen′tial·ly,** *adv.*

sequen′tially compact′ set′, *Math.* a set in which every sequence has a subsequence that converges to a point of the set.

se·ques·ter (si kwes′tər), *v.t.* **1.** to remove or withdraw into solitude or retirement; seclude. **2.** to remove or separate. **3.** *Law.* to remove (property) temporarily from the possession of the owner; seize and hold, as the property and income of a debtor, until legal claims are satisfied. **4.** *Internat. Law.* to requisition, hold, and control (enemy property). [late ME *sequestre* < legal L *sequestr(āre)* (to) put in hands of a trustee, deriv. of *sequester* trustee, depositary] —**se·ques′tra·ble,** *adj.*

se·ques·tered (si kwes′tərd), *adj.* secluded; isolated: *a sequestered village.* [SEQUESTER + -ED²]

se·ques·trate (si kwes′trāt), *v.t.,* **-trat·ed, -trat·ing. 1.** *Law.* **a.** to sequester (property). **b.** to confiscate. **2.** *Archaic.* to separate; seclude. [< L *sequestrāt(us)* (ptp. of *sequestrāre*) equiv. to *sequestr-* (see SEQUESTER) + *-ātus* -ATE¹] —**se·ques·tra·tor** (sē′kwes trā′tər, si kwes′-trā-), *n.*

se·ques·tra·tion (sē′kwes trā′shən, si kwes-), *n.* **1.** removal or separation; banishment or exile. **2.** a withdrawal into seclusion; retirement. **3.** *Law.* **a.** the sequestering of property. **b.** confiscation or seizure. **4.** *Chem.* the combining of metallic ions with a suitable reagent into a stable, soluble complex in order to prevent the ions from combining with a substance with which they would otherwise have formed an insoluble precipitate, from causing interference in a particular reaction, or from acting as undesirable catalysts. [late ME *sequestracion* < LL *sequestrātiōn-* (s. of *sequestrātiō*), equiv. to *sequestrāt(us)* (ptp. of *sequestrāre* to SEQUESTER) + *-iōn-* -ION]

se·ques·trec·to·my (sē′kwes trek′tə mē), *n., pl.* **-mies.** *Surg.* the removal of dead spicules or portions, esp. of bone. [SEQUESTR(UM) + -ECTOMY]

se·ques·trum (si kwes′trəm), *n., pl.* **-tra** (-trə). *Pathol.* a fragment of bone that has become necrotic as a result of disease or injury and has separated from the normal bone structure. [< L: something set aside; see SEQUESTER] —**se·ques′tral,** *adj.*

se·quin (sē′kwin), *n.* **1.** a small shining disk or spangle used to ornament a dress, a woman's sweater, etc. **2.** a former gold coin of Venice, introduced in 1284; ducat. **3.** a former gold coin of Malta, introduced c1535. **4.** a former gold coin of Turkey, introduced in 1478. Also, **zecchino, zechin** (for defs. 2–4). [< F *sequin* < It *zecchin(o),* equiv. to *zecc(a)* mint (< Ar *sikkah* die, coin) + *-ino* -INE²] —**se′quined,** *adj.*

se·quoi·a (si kwoi′ə), *n.* either of two large coniferous trees of California, the big tree or the redwood, formerly included in the genus *Sequoia:* the big tree is now classified in the genus *Sequoiadendron.* [named after SEQUOYA, inventor of a syllabary for writing Cherokee]

Sequoi′a Na′tional Park′, a national park in central California: giant sequoia trees. 604 sq. mi.

Se·quoy·a (si kwoi′ə), *n.* 1770?–1843, Cherokee Indian scholar. Also, **Se·quoy′ah.**

ser (sēr, sâr), *n.* a unit of weight in India, varying in value but usually $^1/_{40}$ of a maund: the government ser is divided into 80 tolas of 180 English grains and equals nearly 2 pounds 1 ounce avoirdupois. Also, **seer.** [< Hindi]

ser-, var. of **sero-** before a vowel: *serous.*

ser., **1.** series. **2.** sermon.

se·ra (sēr′ə), *n.* a pl. of **serum.**

sé·rac (si rak′; *Fr.* sā RAK′), *n., pl.* **-racs** (-raks′; *Fr.* -RAK′). a large block or pinnaclelike mass of ice on a glacier, formed by melting or movement of the ice. [< F *sérac* kind of white cheese; cf. ML *serācium,* der. of L *serum* whey]

Se·ra·fin (ser′ə fin; *It.* se′Rä fēn′), *n.* **Tul·lio** (to͞ol′-lyô), 1878–1968, Italian orchestra conductor.

se·rag·lio (si ral′yō, -räl′-), *n., pl.* **-rag·lios. 1.** the part of a Muslim house or palace in which the wives and concubines are secluded; harem. **2.** a Turkish palace, esp. of the sultan. Also called **se·rail** (sə rī′, -rīl′, -räl′). [< It *serraglio* cage for wild beasts; cf. ML *serācula* little lock (< L *sera* bar, bolt), and cf. SEAR²; by assoc. with Turk *seray* palace; *serraglio* also came to mean harem]

se·ra·i (sə rä′ē, sə rī′), *n., pl.* **-ra·is.** (in Eastern countries) a caravansary. [< Turk *seray* < Pers *serāī* abode, palace; see CARAVANSARY]

Sa·ra·je·vo (*Serbo-Croatian.* se′Rä′ye vô; *Eng.* ser′ə-yə vō′), *n.* Sarajevo.

ser·al (sēr′əl), *adj.* *Ecol.* of or pertaining to a sere. [SERE² + -AL¹]

Se·rang (se räng′), *n.* Ceram.

se·ra·pe (sə rä′pē; *Sp.* se Rä′pe), *n., pl.* **-pes** (-pēz; *Sp.* -pes). a blanketlike shawl or wrap, often of brightly-colored wool, as worn in Latin America. Also, **sarape.** [< MexSp *sarape*]

Ser·a·pe·um (ser′ə pē′əm), *n., pl.* **-pe·ums, -pe·a** (-pē′ə). a place, as a burial site, building, or group of buildings, dedicated to Serapis. [< L < Gk *Serapeion*]

ser·aph (ser′əf), *n., pl.* **-aphs, -a·phim** (-ə fim). **1.** one of the celestial beings hovering above God's throne in Isaiah's vision. Isa. 6. **2.** a member of the highest order of angels, often represented as a child's head with wings above, below, and on each side. [back formation from SERAPHIM] —**ser′aph·like′,** *adj.*

se·raph·ic (si raf′ik), *adj.* of, like, or befitting a seraph. Also, **se·raph′i·cal.** [< eccl. L *seraphicus.* See SERAPHIM, -IC] —**se·raph′i·cal·ly,** *adv.* —**se·raph′i·cal·ness,** *n.*

ser·a·phim (ser′ə fim), *n.* a pl. of **seraph.** [< LL (Vulgate) < Heb *serāphīm*]

Se·ra·pis (si rā′pis), *n.* **1.** a Greco-Egyptian deity, combining the attributes of Osiris and Apis, identified in Egypt with the Ptolemies: later worshiped throughout the Greek and Roman empires. **2.** (*italics*) the British man-of-war captured by John Paul Jones in 1779.

Serb (sûrb), *n., adj.,* **1.** Serbian. **2.** Serbo-Croatian. [< Serbian *Srb*]

Serb., **1.** Serbia. **2.** Serbian.

Ser·bi·a (sûr′bē ə), *n.* **a former kingdom in S Europe: now, with revised boundaries, a constituent republic of Yugoslavia, in the N part. 9,660,000; 34,116 sq. mi.** *Cap.:* **Belgrade. Formerly, Servia.**

Ser·bi·an (sûr′bē ən), *adj.* **1.** of or pertaining to Serbia, its inhabitants, or their language. —*n.* **2.** a native or inhabitant of Serbia, esp. one of the Slavic peoples inhabiting it. **3.** Serbo-Croatian, esp. as spoken and written in Serbia. Also, **Serb.** [SERB + -IAN]

Serbo-, a combining form of **Serb:** *Serbo-Croatian.*

Ser·bo-Cro·a·tian (sûr′bō krō ā′shən, -shē ən), *n.* **1.** the principal Slavic language of Yugoslavia, usually written with Cyrillic letters in Serbia but with Roman letters in Croatia. —*adj.* **2.** of or pertaining to Serbo-Croatian. Also, **Serb.**

Ser·bo·ni·an (sər bō′nē ən), *adj.* of, pertaining to, or designating the large marshy tract of land in the northern part of ancient Egypt in which entire armies are said to have been swallowed up. [< Gk *Serbōnī(s)* + -AN]

Serbs′, Cro′ats, and Slo′venes, Kingdom of, former name (1918–29) of **Yugoslavia.**

ser·dab (sər däb′), *n.* a chamber inside a mastaba containing a statue of the deceased. [< Ar *sirdāb* underground chamber < Pers *sardāb* cellar for ice, equiv. to *sard* cold + *āb* water]

sere¹ (sēr), *adj.* dry; withered. Also, **sear.** [var. of SEAR¹]

sere² (sēr), *n.* the series of stages in an ecological succession. [back formation from SERIES]

se·rein (sə ran′; *Fr.* sə RAN′), *n.* a very fine rain falling after sunset from a sky in which no clouds are visible. [< F; MF *serain* evening, nightfall < VL **serān(um),* equiv. to L *sēr(um)* a late hour (neut. of *sērus* late) + *-ānum,* neut. of *-ānus* -AN]

se·re·na (sə rā′nə), *n.* a Provençal song or poem concerned with the evening. [< Pr; see SEREIN]

Se·re·na (sə rē′nə), *n.* a girl's given name.

ser·e·nade (ser′ə nād′), *n., v.,* **-nad·ed, -nad·ing.** —*n.* **1.** a complimentary performance of vocal or instrumental music in the open air at night, as by a lover under the window of his lady. **2.** a piece of music suitable for such performance. **3.** serenata (def. 2). —*v.t., v.i.* **4.** to entertain with or perform a serenade. [< F *sérénade* < It *serenat(a);* see SERENATA] —**ser′e·nad′er,** *n.*

ser·e·na·ta (ser′ə nä′tə), *n., pl.* **-tas, -te** (-tā). *Music.* **1.** a form of secular cantata, often of a dramatic or imaginative character. **2.** an instrumental composition in several movements, intermediate between the suite and the symphony. [< It *serenata* evening song, equiv. to *seren(o)* open air (n. use of adj. *sereno* SERENE) + *-ata* n. suffix]

Ser·en·dip (ser′ən dip′), *n.* former name of **Ceylon.** Also, **Ser·en·dib** (ser′ən dēb′).

ser·en·dip·i·ty (ser′ən dip′i tē), *n.* the faculty for making desirable discoveries by accident. [SERENDIP + -ITY; Horace Walpole so named a faculty possessed by the heroes of a tale called *The Three Princes of Serendip*]

se·rene (sə rēn′), *adj.* **1.** calm, peaceful, or tranquil; unruffled: *a serene landscape; serene old age.* **2.** clear; fair: *serene weather.* **3.** (*usually cap.*) most high or august, used as a royal epithet (usually prec. by *his, your,* etc.): *his Serene Highness.* —*n.* **4.** *Archaic.* a clear or tranquil expanse of sea or sky. **5.** serenity; tranquility. [< L *serēn(us)*] —**se·rene′ly,** *adv.* —**se·rene′ness,** *n.*
—**Syn. 1.** undisturbed, imperturbable, unperturbed, composed, collected. See **peaceful. 2.** unclouded. —**Ant. 1.** disturbed. **2.** clouded.

Se·ren·i·ta·tis (sə ren′i tä′tis), *n.* **Mare.** See **Mare Serenitatis.**

se·ren·i·ty (sə ren′i tē), *n., pl.* **-ties. 1.** the state or quality of being serene, calm, or tranquil. **2.** (*usually cap.*) a title of honor, respect, or reverence, used in speaking of or to certain members of royalty (usually prec. by *his, your,* etc.). [late ME *serenite* < L *serēnitās.* See SERENE, -ITY]
—**Syn. 1.** composure, calm, peacefulness, peace. —**Ant. 1.** agitation.

Se·ren·i·ty (sə ren′i tē), *n.* **Sea of.** See **Mare Serenitatis.**

Se·reth (zā′Rət), *n.* German name of **Siret.**

serf (sûrf), *n.* **1.** a person in a condition of servitude, required to render services to his lord, commonly attached to the lord's land and transferred with it from one owner to another. **2.** a slave. [late ME < MF < L *serv(us)* slave] —**serf·dom** (sûrf′dəm), **serf′hood, serf·age** (sûr′fij), *n.* —**serf′ish, serf′like′,** *adj.* —**serf′ish·ly,** *adv.* —**serf′ish·ness,** *n.*

Serg., Sergeant. Also, **Sergt.**

serge (sûrj), *n.* **1.** a twilled worsted or woolen fabric used esp. for clothing. **2.** cotton, rayon, or silk in a twill weave. [< F; r. ME *sarge* < MF < VL **sārica* for L *sērica* (*lāna*) Chinese (wool), i.e., silk; see SERIC-]

Serge (sûrj), *n.* a boy's given name.

ser·geant (sär′jənt), *n.* **1.** a noncommissioned army officer of a rank above that of corporal. **2.** *U.S. Air Force.* any noncommissioned officer above the rank of airman first class. **3.** a police officer ranking immediately below a captain or a lieutenant in the U.S. and immediately below an inspector in Britain. **4.** a title of a particular office or function at the court of a monarch (often used in combination): *sergeant of the larder; sergeant-caterer.* **5.** See **sergeant at arms. 6.** Also called **ser′geant at law′.** *Brit.* (formerly) a member of a superior order of barristers. **7.** a damselfish of the genus *Abudefduf.* **8.** (*cap.*) *U.S.* a surface-to-surface, single-stage, ballistic missile. **9.** *Obs.* a tenant by military service, below the rank of knight. Also, *esp. Brit.,* **serjeant** (for defs. 1–7, 9). [ME *sergant, serjant, serjaunt* < OF *sergent* << L *servient-* (s. of *serviēns*), prp. of *servīre.* See SERVE, -ENT] —**ser·gean·cy** (sär′jən sē), **ser′geant·ship′,** *n.*

ser′geant at arms′, an executive officer of a legislative or other body, whose duty it is to enforce its commands, preserve order, etc.

ser′geant first′ class′, *U.S. Army.* a noncommissioned officer ranking next above a staff sergeant and below a first or master sergeant.

ser·geant·fish (sär′jənt fish′), *n., pl.* **-fish·es,** (*esp. collectively*) **-fish. 1.** the cobia. **2.** any of several other marine fishes, as a snook, *Centropomus undecimalis.* [SERGEANT + FISH; so called from the stripes on its fins]

ser′geant ma′jor, 1. *Mil.* **a.** (in the U.S. Army and Marine Corps) a noncommissioned officer of the highest enlisted rank. **b.** (in the U.S. Army, Air Force, and Marine Corps) a noncommissioned officer who is the chief enlisted assistant to the commander of a headquarters. **2.** a small damselfish, *Abudefduf saxatilis,* found in warm Atlantic waters, having vertical black stripes on each side.

ser·geant·y (sär′jən tē), *n.* *Medieval Eng. Law.* serjeanty.

Ser·ges·tus (sər jes′təs), *n.* (in the *Aeneid*) a Trojan companion of Aeneas on his flight from Troy.

Ser·gi·pe (səR zhē′pə), *n.* a state in E Brazil. 760,273 (1960); 8490 sq. mi. *Cap.:* Aracaju.

Ser·gi·us I (sûr′jē əs), died A.D. 701, Italian ecclesiastic: pope 687–701.

Sergius II, died A.D. 847, pope 844–847.

Sergius III, died A.D. 911, pope 904–911.

Sergius IV, died 1012, pope 1009–12.

se·ri·al (sēr′ē əl), *n.* **1.** anything published, broadcast, etc., in short installments at regular intervals, as a novel appearing in successive issues of a magazine. **2.** *Library Science.* a publication that is issued at regular intervals and is consecutively numbered. —*adj.* **3.** published in installments or successive parts: *a serial story.* **4.** pertaining to such publication. **5.** of, pertaining to, or arranged in a series. [< NL *seriāl(is).* See SERIES, -AL¹] —**se′ri·al·ly,** *adv.*

se·ri·al·ise (sēr′ē ə līz′), *v.t.,* **-ised, -is·ing.** *Chiefly Brit.* serialize. —**se′ri·al·i·sa′tion,** *n.*

se·ri·al·ize (sēr′ē ə līz′), *v.t.,* **-ized, -iz·ing. 1.** to publish in serial form. **2.** to broadcast, televise, or film in serial form. [SERIAL + -IZE] —**se′ri·al·ist,** *n.* —**se′ri·al·i·za′tion,** *n.*

se′rial num′ber, a number, usually one of a series, assigned for identification: *the serial number of an automobile engine; a soldier's name, rank, and serial number.*

se′rial opera′tion, *Computer Technol.* the use of one data channel or path at a time for the sequential transfer of information in a computer. Cf. **parallel operation.**

se′rial technique′, systematic musical composition based on a preestablished order of tones, as a tone row.

se·ri·ate (sēr′ē it, -āt′), *adj.* arranged or occurring in one or more series. [< L *seri(ēs)* SERIES + -ATE[1]] —**se′ri·ate·ly,** *adv.* —**se′ri·a′tion,** *n.*

se·ri·a·tim (sēr′ē ā′tim, ser′-), *adv.* in a series; one after another. [< ML, equiv. to L *seri(ēs)* SERIES + *-ātim* adv. suffix]

seric-, a learned borrowing from Latin meaning "silk," used in the formation of compound words: *sericin.* [comb. form of L *sēricum* < Gk *sērikón* silk, neut. of *sērikós* Chinese, silken, equiv. to *sēr* silkworm + *-ikos* -IC]

ser·i·cate (ser′ə kit, -kāt′), *adj.* sericeous; silky. [< L *sēricāt(us)* dressed in silk. See SERIC-, -ATE[1]]

se·ri·ceous (si rish′əs), *adj.* **1.** silky. **2.** covered with silky down, as a leaf. [< L *sēriceus.* See SERIC-, -EOUS]

ser·i·cin (ser′i sin), *n. Chem.* a gelatinous organic compound obtained from silk. [SERIC- + -IN[2]]

ser·i·cite (ser′i sīt′), *n. Mineral.* a fine-grained variety of muscovite produced by the alteration of feldspar. [< G *Sericit.* See SERIC-, -ITE[1]] —**ser·i·cit·ic** (ser′i-sit′ik), *adj.*

ser·ic·te·ri·um (ser′ik tēr′ē əm), *n., pl.* **-te·ri·a** (-tēr′ē ə). *Obs.* serictery. [< NL, equiv. to *seric-* SERIC- + *(sialis)tērium* salivary gland of insects, special use of Gk *sialistḗrion* bridle bit, akin to *sîalon* saliva]

se·ric·te·ry (si rik′tə rē), *n., pl.* **-ries.** *Obs.* a silk gland. [< NL *sericteri(um)*]

ser·i·cul·ture (ser′ə kul′chər), *n.* the raising of silk worms for the production of raw silk. [< Gk *sēr* silkworm + -I- + CULTURE] —**ser′i·cul′tur·al,** *adj.* —**ser′i·cul′tur·ist,** *n.*

ser·i·e·ma (ser′ē ē′mə, -ā′mə), *n.* either of two birds of the family *Cariamidae, Cariama cristata,* of southern Brazil, or *Chunga burmeisteri,* of Argentina, having long legs, an erectile crest, and a short, broad bill. Also, **cariama.** [< NL < Tupi: crested]

se·ries (sēr′ēz), *n., pl.* **-ries,** *adj.* —*n.* **1.** a group or a number of related or similar things, events, etc., arranged, ranged, or occurring in temporal, spatial, or other order or succession; sequence. **2.** a number of games, contests, or sporting events, with the same participants, considered as a unit: *The two baseball clubs played a five-game series last week.* **3.** a set, as of coins, stamps, etc. **4.** a set of successive volumes or issues of a periodical published in like form with similarity of subject or purpose. **5.** *Math.* **a.** a sequence of terms combined by addition, as $1 + \frac{1}{2} + \frac{1}{4} + \frac{1}{8} + \frac{1}{2^n}$. **b.** See **infinite series. 6.** *Rhet.* a succession of coordinate sentence elements. **7.** *Geol.* a division of stratified rocks that is of next higher rank to a stage and next lower rank to a system, comprising deposits formed during part of a geological epoch. **8.** *Elect.* an end-to-end arrangement of the components, as resistances, of a circuit so that the same current flows through each component. Cf. **parallel** (def. 12). —*adj.* **9.** *Elect.* consisting of or having component parts connected in series: *a series circuit; a series generator.* [< L *seriēs;* akin to *serere* to connect]
—**Syn. 1.** SERIES, SEQUENCE, SUCCESSION are terms for an orderly following of things one after another. SERIES is applied to a number of things of the same kind, usually related to each other, arranged or happening in order: *a series of baseball games.* SEQUENCE stresses the continuity in time, thought, cause and effect, etc.: *The scenes came in a definite sequence.* SUCCESSION implies that one thing is followed by another or others in turn, usually though not necessarily with a relation or connection between them: *succession to a throne; a succession of calamities.*

se·ries-wound (sēr′ēz wound′), *adj. Elect.* noting a commutator motor in which the field circuit and armature circuit are connected in series.

ser·if (ser′if), *n. Print.* a smaller line used to finish off a main stroke of a letter, as at the top and bottom of *M.* See diag. under **type.** [? < D *schreef* stroke < MD *shriv(en)* (to) write]

ser·i·graph (ser′ə graf′, -gräf′), *n.* a print made by the silk-screen process. [*seri-* (as in SERICULTURE) + -GRAPH] —**se·rig·ra·pher** (si rig′rə fər), *n.* —**se·rig′ra·phy,** *n.*

ser·in (ser′in), *n.* a small finch, *Serinus serinus,* of Europe and northern Africa, closely related to the canary. [< MF *sere(i)n;* cf. OPr *serena, sirena* bee-eater (a green bird) < LL *sīrēna* < L *sīrēn* SIREN]

ser·ine (ser′ēn, -in, sēr′-), *n. Biochem.* a crystalline, nonessential amino acid, $HOCH_2CH(NH_2)COOH$, obtained by the hydrolysis of sericin, the protein constituting silk gum. [SER(UM) + -INE[2]]

ser·i·nette (ser′ə net′), *n.* a small hand organ with a revolving barrel whose pins operate the pipes, used in training birds to sing. [< F, equiv. to *serin* canary (see SERIN) + *-ette* -ETTE]

se·rin·ga (sə ring′gə), *n.* any of several Brazilian trees of the genus *Hevea,* yielding rubber. [< Pg, var. of SYRINGA]

Se·rin·ga·pa·tam (sə ring′gə pə tam′), *n.* a town in S Mysore, in S India, former capital of Mysore: taken by the British 1799.

se·ri·o·com·ic (sēr′ē ō kom′ik), *adj.* partly serious and partly comic: *a seriocomic play.* Also, **se′ri·o·com′i·cal.** [*serio-* (comb. form of SERIOUS) + COMIC] —**se′ri·o·com′i·cal·ly,** *adv.*

se·ri·ous (sēr′ē əs), *adj.* **1.** of, showing, or characterized by deep thought. **2.** of grave or somber disposition, character, or manner: *a serious occasion; a serious man.* **3.** being in earnest; sincere; not trifling: *His interest was serious.* **4.** requiring thought, concentration, or application: *serious reading; a serious task.* **5.** weighty or important: *a serious book; Marriage is a serious matter.* **6.** giving cause for apprehension; critical: *a serious illness; The plan has one serious flaw.* —*n.* **7.** that which is of importance, grave, critical, or somber: *You have to learn to separate the serious from the frivolous.* [< L *sērius* or LL *sēriōs(us);* see -OUS, -OSE[1]] —**se′ri·ous·ly,** *adv.* —**se′ri·ous·ness,** *n.*
—**Syn. 1.** sober, sedate, staid. See **earnest**[1]. **5.** momentous, grave. —**Ant. 3, 5.** trivial.

se·ri·ous-mind·ed (sēr′ē əs mīn′did), *adj.* characterized by seriousness of intention, purpose, thought, etc.; earnest. —**se′ri·ous-mind′ed·ly,** *adv.* —**se′ri·ous-mind′ed·ness,** *n.*

ser·i·plane (ser′ə plān′), *n.* a test for evaluating the quality of raw silk by inspecting it under controlled conditions for variations in the diameter of the yarn and for imperfections and content. [SERI(ES) + PLANE[1]]

ser·jeant (sär′jənt), *n. Chiefly Brit.* sergeant (defs. 1–7, 9).

ser·jeant·y (sär′jən tē), *n. Medieval Eng. Law.* a form of land tenure in which a tenant holding of the king rendered services only to him. Also, **sergeanty.** Cf. **grand serjeanty, petit serjeanty.** [< OF *serjantie.* See SERGEANT, -Y[3]]

Ser·kin (sûr′kin; *Ger.* zer′kin), *n.* **Ru·dolf** (rōō′dolf; *Ger.* rōō′dôlf), born 1903, U.S. pianist, born in Bohemia.

Ser·lio (ser′lyô), *n.* **Se·bas·tia·no** (se′bäs tyä′nô), 1474?–1554, Italian architect and painter.

ser·mon (sûr′mən), *n.* **1.** a discourse for the purpose of religious instruction or exhortation, esp. one based on a text of Scripture and delivered from a pulpit by a clergyman as part of a church service. **2.** any serious speech, discourse, or exhortation, esp. on a moral issue, as in personal conduct, patriotic duty, etc. **3.** a long, tedious speech. [ME < ML, L *sermōn-* (s. of *sermō;* ML: speech from pulpit; L: discourse), equiv. to *ser-* (root of *serere* to link up, organize) + *-mōn-* n. suffix] —**ser′mon·less,** *adj.*
—**Syn. 1–3.** homily, preachment. **2, 3.** lecture.

ser·mon·ic (sər mon′ik), *adj.* of, pertaining to, or resembling a sermon. Also, **ser·mon′i·cal.** [SERMON + -IC] —**ser·mon′i·cal·ly,** *adv.*

ser·mon·ise (sûr′mə nīz′), *v.t., v.i.,* **-ised, -is·ing.** *Chiefly Brit.* sermonize. —**ser′mon·is′er,** *n.*

ser·mon·ize (sûr′mə nīz′), *v.,* **-ized, -iz·ing.** —*v.i.* **1.** to deliver or compose a sermon; preach. —*v.t.* **2.** to give exhortation to; lecture. [SERMON + -IZE] —**ser′mon·iz′er,** *n.*

Ser′mon on the Mount′, a discourse delivered by Jesus to the disciples and others, containing the Beatitudes and important fundamentals of Christian teaching. Matt. 5–7; Luke 6:20–49.

sero-, a combining form of **serum:** *serology.* Also, *esp. before a vowel,* **ser-.**

se·rol·o·gy (si rol′ə jē), *n.* the science dealing with the properties and actions of the serum of the blood. [SERO- + -LOGY] —**se·ro·log·ic** (sēr′ə loj′ik), **se′ro·log′i·cal,** *adj.* —**se′ro·log′i·cal·ly,** *adv.* —**se·rol′o·gist,** *n.*

se·ro·mu·cous (sēr′ō myōō′kəs), *adj. Med.* pertaining to or composed of serum and mucus. [SERO- + MUCOUS]

se·ro·re·ac·tion (sēr′ō rē ak′shən), *n. Med., Immunol.* any reaction occurring in serum. [SERO- + REACTION]

se·ro·re·sist·ance (sēr′ō ri zis′təns), *n. Med., Immunol.* a persistent, positive reaction in serological tests of a syphilitic person despite treatment. [SERO- + RESISTANCE] —**se·ro·re·sist·ant** (sēr′ō ri zis′tənt), *adj.*

se·ro·sa (si rō′sə, -zə), *n., pl.* **-sas, -sae** (-sē, -zē). **1.** *Embryol., Zool.* **a.** the chorion. **b.** a similar membrane in insects and other lower invertebrates. **2.** See **serous membrane.** [< NL, fem. of *serōsus,* equiv. to L *ser(um)* SERUM + *-ōsus* -OSE[1]]

se·ro·si·tis (sir′ō sī′tis, -zī′-, ser′-), *n. Pathol.* inflammation of a serous membrane. [< NL; see SEROSA, -ITIS]

se·ro·ther·a·py (sēr′ō ther′ə pē), *n. Med.* therapy by means of injections of a serum obtained esp. from an immune animal or person; serum therapy. [SERO- + THERAPY] —**se′ro·ther′a·pist,** *n.*

se·rot·i·nal (si rot′ənəl, ser′ə tīn′əl), *adj.* pertaining to, or occurring in late summer. [SEROTINE[1] + -AL[1]]

ser·o·tine[1] (ser′ə tin, -tīn′), *adj.* late in occurring, developing, or flowering. Also, **se·rot·i·nous** (si rot′ənəs). [< L *sērōtin(us),* equiv. to *sērō* (adv.) late + *-tinus* adj. suffix of time; cf. SEREIN]

ser·o·tine[2] (ser′ə tin, -tīn′), *n.* a small, brown, European bat, *Eptesicus serotinus.* [< F *sérotine* a serotine (bat), deriv. of fem. of L *sērōtinus* SEROTINE[1]]

ser·o·to·nin (ser′ə tō′nin), *n. Biochem.* a crystalline compound, $HOC_8H_5NCH_2CH_2NH_2$, occurring in the brain, intestines, and platelets, that induces vasoconstriction and muscular contraction. [SERO- + TONE + -IN[2]]

se·rous (sēr′əs), *adj.* **1.** resembling serum; of a watery nature. **2.** containing or secreting serum. **3.** pertaining to or characterized by serum. [< L *serōs(us),* equiv. to *ser(um)* whey + *-ōsus* -OUS] —**se·ros·i·ty** (si ros′i tē), **se′rous·ness,** *n.*

se′rous flu′id, any of various fluids in the body resembling the serum of the blood.

se′rous mem′brane, *Anat., Zool.* any of various thin membranes, as the peritoneum, that line certain cavities of the body and exude a serous fluid. Also called **serosa.**

Se·rov (se′rof), *n.* a city in the RSFSR, in the W Soviet Union in Asia, near the Ural Mountains. 102,000 (est. 1962).

ser·ow (ser′ō), *n.* a goat antelope of the genus *Capricornis,* of eastern Asia, related to the goral. [< Sikkimese *saro* king of goats]

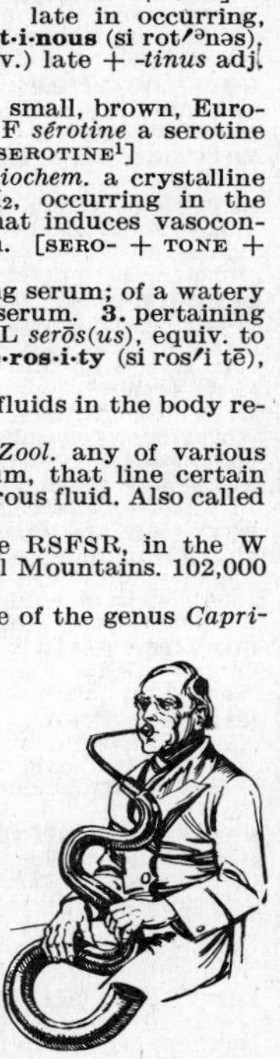

Ser·pa·sil (sûr′pə sil), *n. Pharm., Trademark.* reserpine.

Ser·pens (sûr′pənz, -penz), *n., gen.* **Ser·pen·tis** (sər pen′tis). *Astron.* the Serpent, a constellation consisting of two separate parts, the head (**Ser′pens Ca′put**) and the tail (**Ser′pens Cau′da**), with Ophiuchus in between. [< L, prp. of *serpere* to creep, crawl; c. Gk *hérpein*]

ser·pent (sûr′pənt), *n.* **1.** a snake. **2.** a wily, treacherous, or malicious person. **3.** the Devil; Satan. Gen. 3:1–5. **4.** a firework that burns with serpentine motion or flame. **5.** an obsolete wooden wind instrument with a serpentine shape and a deep, coarse tone. **6.** *(cap.) Astron.* the constellation Serpens. [ME (< MF) < L *serpent-,* s. of *serpēns;* see SERPENS]

Serpent (def. 5)

Ser′pent Bear′er, *Astron.* the constellation Ophiuchus.

ser·pen·ti·form (ser pen′tə fôrm′), *adj.* shaped like a snake. [SERPENT + -I- + -FORM]

ser·pen·tine[1] (sûr′pən tēn′, -tīn′), *adj.* **1.** of, characteristic of, or resembling a serpent, as in form or movement. **2.** having a winding course, as a road; sinuous. **3.** shrewd, wily, or cunning. —*n.* **4.** a device on a harquebus lock for holding the match. **5.** a cannon having any of various bore sizes, used from the 15th to the 17th century. [late ME < L *serpentīn(us)* snakelike, equiv. to *serpent-* SERPENT + *-īnus* -INE[1]]

ser·pen·tine[2] (sûr′pən tēn, -tīn′), *n.* a common mineral, hydrous magnesium silicate, $H_4Mg_3Si_2O_9$, usually oily green and sometimes spotted, occurring in many varieties: used for architectural and decorative purposes. [late ME *serpentyn* < ML *serpentīn(um),* deriv. of neut. of *serpentinus* SERPENTINE[1]]

Serpentine front (18th century)

ser′pentine front′, *Furniture.* a front, as of a chest of drawers, having a horizontal compound curve with a convex section between two concave ones. Cf. **oxbow front.**

ser′pentine jade′, *Jewelry.* a green variety of serpentine used as a gem: not a true jade.

ser′pentine stretch′er, *Furniture.* an X-stretcher having curved lines.

ser·pen·tin·ize (sûr′pən tē nīz′), *v.t.,* **-ized, -iz·ing.** *Mineral.* to convert (a mineral or rock) into serpentine. [SERPENTINE[2] + -IZE] —**ser·pen·tin·i·za·tion** (sûr′-pən tin′i zā′shən), *n.*

Ser′pent Sea′. See **Mare Angius.**

Ser′pent star′. See **brittle star.**

ser·pi·go (sər pī′gō), *n. Pathol.* a creeping or spreading skin disease, as ringworm. [< ML < L *serp-* (deriv. of *serpere* to creep) + *-īgō* as in *vertigo*] —**ser·pig·i·nous** (sər pij′ə nəs), *adj.*

Ser·pu·khov (ser pōō′kof), *n.* a city in the W RSFSR, in the central Soviet Union in Europe, S of Moscow. 113,000 (est. 1962).

Ser·ra Ju·ní·pe·ro (ser′rä hōō nē′pe rō′), **Mi·guel Jo·sé** (mē gel′ hō se′), 1713–84, Spanish Roman Catholic missionary to the Indians in California and Mexico.

ser·ra·nid (sə rā′nid, -rä′-, -ran′id), *n.* **1.** any of numerous percoid fishes of the family *Serranidae,* found chiefly in warm seas, including the sea basses and groupers. —*adj.* **2.** belonging or pertaining to the family *Serranidae.* [< NL *Serranid(ae).* See SERRANOID]

ser·ra·noid (ser′ə noid′), *adj.* **1.** resembling or related to the sea bass family *Serranidae.* —*n.* **2.** a serranoid fish. [< NL *serrān(us)* genus of fishes (L *serr(a)* sawfish + *-ānus* -AN) + -OID]

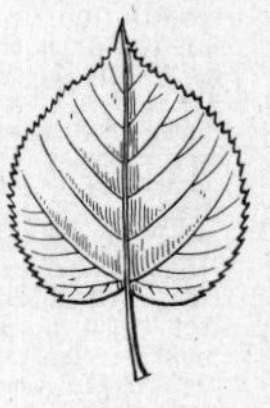

ser·rate (*adj.* ser′it, -āt; *v.* ser′āt), *adj., v.,* **-rat·ed, -rat·ing.** —*adj.* **1.** *Chiefly Biol.* notched on the edge like a saw: *a serrate leaf.* **2.** *Numis.* (of a coin) having a grooved edge. **3.** having notches or teeth at the edge, esp. for cutting: *a serrate blade.* —*v.t.* **4.** to make serrate or serrated: *He serrated the knives so they would cut meat easily.* [< L *serrāt(us),* equiv. to *serr(a)* saw + *-ātus* -ATE[1]]

Serrate leaf

ser·rat·ed (ser′ā tid), *adj.* **1.** having a notched edge or sawlike teeth: *the serrated blade of a bread knife.* **2.** serrate. [SERRATE + -ED[2]]

Ser·ra·tia (sə rā′shə, -shē ə, -rä′tē ə), *n. Bacteriol.* a genus of rod-shaped, aerobic bacteria that are saprophytic on decaying plant or animal materials. [< NL, named after Serafino *Serrat(i),* 19th-century Italian industrialist; see -IA]

ser·ra·tion (se rā′shən), *n.* **1.** serrated condition or form. **2.** a serrated edge or formation. **3.** one of the notches or teeth of such an edge or formation. Also, **ser·ra·ture** (ser′ə chər). [< NL *serrātiōn-* (s. of *serrātiō*). See SERRATE, -ION]

serre-pa·pier (sâr′pap yā′; *Fr.* ser pa pyā′), *n., pl.* **serre-pa·piers** (sâr pap yāz′; *Fr.* ser pa pyā′). cartonnier. [< F, equiv. to *serr(er)* (to) clasp, grip, squeeze (see SEAR[2]) + *papier* PAPER]

ser·ri·form (ser′ə fôrm′), *adj.* resembling the notched edge of a saw; serrated. [*serri-* (comb. form of L *serra* saw) + -FORM]

ser·ru·late (ser′yə lit, -lāt′, ser′ə-), *adj.* finely or minutely serrate, as a leaf. Also, **ser′ru·lat′ed.** [< NL *serrulāt(us),* equiv. to *serrul(a)* (dim. of *serra* saw) + *-ātus* -ATE[1]]

ser·ru·la·tion (ser′yə lā′shən, ser′ə-), *n.* **1.** serrulate condition or form. **2.** a fine or minute serration. [SERRULATE + -ION]

ser·ru·re·rie (se ryrə rē′), *n. French.* ornamental wrought-iron work. [lit., locksmith's work]

ser·ry (ser′ē), *v.i., v.t.,* **-ried, -ry·ing.** to crowd closely together. [< MF *serré,* ptp. of *serrer* to press tightly together; see SEAR[2]] —**ser′ried·ly,** *adv.* —**ser′ried·ness,** *n.*

Sert (sert), *n.* **Jo·sé Ma·rí·a** (hō se′ mä rē′ä), 1876–1945, Spanish painter.

Ser·to·ri·us (sər tôr′ē əs, -tōr′-), *n.* **Quin·tus** (kwin′-təs), died 72 B.C., Roman general and statesman.

ser·tu·lar·i·an (sûr′chŏŏ lâr′ē ən), *n. Zool.* a type of hydroid that forms stiff, feathery colonies in which the cups holding the zooids are sessile. [< NL *Sertulāri(a)* genus name (L *sertul(a),* dim. of *serta* wreath + *-āria* -ARIA) + -AN]

se·rum (sēr′əm) *n., pl.* **se·rums, se·ra** (sēr′ə). **1.** the clear, pale-yellow liquid which separates from the clot in the coagulation of blood; blood serum. **2.** a fluid of this kind obtained from the blood of an animal that has been rendered immune to some disease by inoculation, used as an antitoxic or therapeutic agent. **3.** any watery animal fluid. **4.** the thin clear fluid medium in which plant substances are held. **5.** (of milk) **a.** the portion left after butterfat, casein, and albumin have been removed. **b.** the portion left after the manufacture of cheese. [< L: whey] —**se′rum·al,** *adj.*

se′rum albu′min, 1. *Biochem.* the principal protein of the blood plasma. 2. the commercial form of this substance, obtained from ox blood, used in textile-printing dye preparations, foodstuffs, and in medicine esp. in the treatment of shock.

se′rum prothrom′bin accel′erator, *Biochem.* a globulin factor, found in plasma and serum, that serves to accelerate the conversion of prothrombin to thrombin, used chiefly as an agent to restore normal blood coagulation in the treatment of vitamin K deficiency.

Serval (About 2 ft. high at shoulder; total length 5 ft.; tail 1 ft.)

ser·val (sûr′vəl), *n.* a long-limbed African cat, *Felis serval,* having a tawny coat spotted with black, and about the size of a bobcat. [< NL < Pg (*lago*) *cerval* lynx (lit., staglike wolf) < L *cervāl(is)* deerlike, equiv. to *cerv(us)* stag + *-ālis* -AL[1]]

serv·ant (sûr′vənt), *n.* 1. a person employed by another, esp. one employed to perform domestic duties. 2. a person in the service of another. 3. a person employed by the government: *a public servant.* [ME < OF, deriv. of *servant* serving, equiv. to *serv-* (root of *servir* to SERVE) + *-ant* -ANT] —**serv′ant·less,** *adj.* —**serv′ant·like′,** *adj.*
—**Syn. 1.** domestic, maid, menial, retainer, houseman.
—**Ant. 1.** master.

Ser·va Pa·dro·na, La (*It.* lä ser′vä pä drô′nä), an opera (1733) by Giovanni Pergolesi.

serve (sûrv), *v.,* **served, serv·ing,** *n.* —*v.i.* 1. to act as a servant. 2. to wait on table, as a waiter. 3. to offer or have a meal or refreshments available, as for patrons or guests: *Come early, we're serving at six.* 4. to offer or distribute a portion or portions of food or a beverage, as a host or hostess: *It was her turn to serve at the faculty tea.* 5. to render assistance; be of use; help. 6. to go through a term of service; do duty as a soldier, sailor, congressman, juror, etc. 7. to have definite use. 8. to answer the purpose: *That will serve to explain my actions.* 9. to be favorable, suitable, or convenient, as weather, time, etc. 10. (in tennis, badminton, handball, etc.) to put the ball or shuttlecock in play with a stroke, swing, or hit. 11. *Eccles.* to act as a server. —*v.t.* 12. to be in the service of; work for. 13. to render service to; help. 14. to go through (a term of service, imprisonment, etc.). 15. to render active service to (a king, commander, etc.). 16. to render obedience or homage to (God, a sovereign, etc.). 17. to perform the duties of (a position, an office, etc.): *to serve his mayoralty.* 18. to be useful or of service to. 19. to answer the requirements of; suffice: *This will serve our needs for the moment.* 20. to contribute to; promote: *to serve a cause.* 21. to wait upon at table; act as a waiter or waitress to. 22. to carry and distribute (portions of food or drink) to a patron or a specific table, as a waiter or waitress. 23. to act as a host or hostess in offering (a person) a portion of food or drink: *May I serve you some tea and cake?* 24. to act as a host or hostess in offering or distributing (a portion or portions of food or drink) to another: *She served tea and cake to her guests.* 25. to provide with a regular or continuous supply of something. 26. to treat in a specified manner: *That served him ill.* 27. to gratify (desire, wants, needs, etc.). 28. (of a male animal) to mate with; service. 29. (in tennis, badminton, handball, etc.) to put (the ball or shuttlecock) in play. 30. *Law.* **a.** to make legal delivery of (a process or writ). **b.** to present (a person) with a writ. 31. to operate or keep in action (a gun, artillery, etc.). 32. *Naut.* to wrap (a rope) tightly with small stuff, keeping the turns as close together as possible, esp. after worming and parceling. 33. **serve one right,** to treat one as he deserves, esp. to punish justly: *It will serve you right if she never speaks to you again.* —*n.* 34. the act, manner, or right of serving, as in tennis. [ME *serve(n)* < OF *serv(ir)* < L *servīre,* equiv. to *serv(us)* slave + *-īre* inf. suffix] —**serv′a·ble, serve′a·ble,** *adj.*
—**Syn. 1, 2.** attend. 5. aid, succor.

serv·er (sûr′vər), *n.* 1. one who serves. 2. that which serves or is used in serving, as a salver. 3. a broad fork, spoon, or spatula for dishing out and serving individual portions of food, as vegetables, cake, pie, etc. 4. *Eccles.* an attendant on the priest at Mass, who arranges the altar, makes the responses, etc. 5. (in tennis, badminton, handball, etc.) the player who puts the ball or shuttlecock in play. [SERVE + -ER[1]]

Ser·ve·tus (sər vē′təs), *n.* **Michael,** 1511–53, Spanish physician and theologian, accused of heresy and burned at the stake. Spanish, **Mi·guel Ser·ve·to** (mē gel′ ser·ve′tō). —**Ser·ve·tian** (sər vē′shən), *n.* —**Ser·ve′tian·ism,** *n.*

Ser·vi·a (sûr′vē ə), *n.* former name of **Serbia.** —**Ser′vi·an,** *adj., n.*

serv·ice[1] (sûr′vis), *n., adj., v.,* **-iced, -ic·ing.** —*n.* 1. an act of helpful activity; help; aid: *to do someone a service.* 2. the supplying or supplier of utilities or commodities, as water, electricity, gas, required or demanded by the public. 3. the providing or a provider of accomodation and activities required by the public, as maintenance, repair, etc.: *The manufacturer guarantees service and parts.* 4. the organized system of apparatus, appliances, employees, etc., for supplying some accommodation required by the public: *a television repair service.* 5. the supplying or a supplier of public communication and transportation: *telephone service; bus service.* 6. the performance of duties or the duties performed as or by a waiter or servant; occupation or employment as a waiter or servant. 7. employment in any duties or work for a person, organization, government, etc. 8. a department of public employment, an administrative division of a government, or the body of public servants in it: *the diplomatic service.* 9. the duty or work of public servants. 10. the serving of a sovereign, state, or government in some official capacity. 11. *Mil.* **a.** the armed forces: *in the service.* **b.** a branch of the armed forces, as the army or navy: *Which service were you in during the war?* 12. *Ordn.* the actions required in loading and firing a cannon: *service of the piece.* 13. Often, **services.** the performance of any duties or work for another; helpful or professional activity: *medical services.* 14. something made or done by a commercial organization for the public benefit and without regard to direct profit: *Certain books are published at a loss as a public service.* 15. Also called **divine service.** public religious worship according to prescribed form and order. 16. a ritual or form prescribed for public worship or for some particular occasion: *the marriage service.* 17. the serving of God by obedience, piety, etc.: *voluntary service.* 18. a musical setting of the sung portions of a liturgy. 19. a set of dishes, utensils, etc., for general table use or for particular use: *a tea service; She bought a service for eight.* 20. *Law.* the serving of a process or writ upon a person. 21. *Naut.* tarred spun yarn or other small stuff for covering the exterior of a rope. 22. (in tennis, badminton, handball, etc.) **a.** act or manner of putting the ball or shuttlecock into play. **b.** the ball or shuttlecock as put into play. 23. the mating of a female animal with the male. 24. **at someone's service,** ready to be of help or use to someone; at one's disposal: *You will have an English-speaking guide at your service at all times.* 25. **be of service,** to be helpful or useful: *If we can be of service, do not hesitate to call on us.* —*adj.* 26. of service; useful. 27. of, pertaining to, or used by servants, delivery men, etc., or in serving food: *service stairs; the service pieces in a set of dishes.* 28. supplying aids or services rather than products or goods: *Medicine is one of the service professions.* 29. supplying maintenance and repair: *He operates a service center for electrical appliances.* 30. of or pertaining to the armed forces of a country or to a noncombatant unit or group supplying aid or maintenance to combat units. —*v.t.* 31. to make fit for use; repair; restore to condition for service: *to service an automobile.* 32. to supply with aid, information, or other incidental services. 33. (of a male animal) to mate with (a female animal). [ME < OF < L *servit(ium)* servitude, equiv. to *serv(us)* slave + *-itium* -ICE; r. ME *servise,* OE *serfise* < OF *servise* < L]

serv·ice[2] (sûr′vis), *n.* 1. a service tree, esp. *Sorbus domestica.* 2. the shadbush. [ME *serves,* pl. of *serve,* OE *syrfe* < VL **sorbea* < L *sorb(us)* SORB]

Ser·vice (sûr′vis), *n.* **Robert W(illiam),** 1874–1958, Canadian writer, born in England.

serv·ice·a·ble (sûr′vi sə bəl), *adj.* 1. capable of or being of service; useful. 2. wearing well; durable: *serviceable cloth.* 3. capable of being used, worn, cleaned, repaired, etc., easily. 4. *Archaic.* diligent or attentive in serving. [SERVICE[1] + -ABLE; r. ME *servisable* < MF] —**serv′ice·a·bil′i·ty, serv′ice·a·ble·ness,** *n.* —**serv′ice·a·bly,** *adv.*

serv′ice ace′, ace (def. 2a).

serv·ice·ber·ry (sûr′vis ber′ē), *n., pl.* **-ries.** 1. the fruit of any service tree. 2. a North American, rosaceous shrub or small tree, *Amelanchier canadensis,* bearing a berrylike fruit. 3. any of various other plants of the genus *Amelanchier.* [SERVICE[2] + BERRY]

serv′ice book′, a book containing the forms of worship used in divine services.

serv′ice cap′, *Mil.* a saucer-shaped uniform cap with a visor, standard in the U.S. Army and Air Force.

serv′ice ceil′ing, *Aeron.* the altitude, under standard conditions, above which a given airplane is unable to climb faster than at a specified rate (100 feet per minute in the U.S. and Britain). Cf. **combat ceiling.**

serv′ice clasp′, clasp (def. 3).

serv′ice club′, 1. any of several organizations maintained to contribute to the growth and general welfare of its members and the community. 2. a recreational center for members of the armed forces.

serv′ice el′evator, an elevator for the use of servants and delivery men and for carrying baggage, furniture, etc.

serv′ice en′trance, an entrance for the use of servants, delivery men, or the like.

serv′ice flat′, *Brit.* an apartment with daily cleaning or maid service provided by the landlord and, sometimes, meals when requested by the occupant; an apartment with complete hotel services.

serv·ice·man (sûr′vis man′, -mən), *n., pl.* **-men** (-men′, -mən). 1. a member of the armed forces of a country. 2. one whose occupation is to maintain or repair equipment: *Call the television serviceman.* [SERVICE[1] + MAN[1]]

serv′ice med′al, *Mil.* a medal awarded for performance of specified service, usually in time of war or national emergency. Also called **campaign medal.**

serv′ice pipe′, a pipe connecting a building with a water or gas main.

serv′ice sta′tion, 1. a place equipped for servicing automobiles, as by selling gasoline and oil, making repairs, etc. 2. a place that provides some service, as the repair of equipment, or where parts and supplies are sold, provided, dispensed, etc.

serv′ice stripe′, *Mil.* a stripe worn on the left sleeve by an enlisted man to indicate a specific period of time served on active duty.

serv′ice tree′, 1. either of two European trees, *Sorbus domestica,* bearing a small, acid fruit that is edible when overripe, or *S. torminalis* (**wild service tree**), bearing a similar fruit. 2. serviceberry (defs. 2, 3).

serv′ice u′niform, *Mil.* a uniform for routine duties and service, as distinguished from work, dress, or full-dress uniforms.

ser′vi·ent ten′ement (sûr′vē ənt), *Law.* land subject to an easement or servitude. Cf. **dominant tenement.** [< L *servient-* (s. of *serviēns,* prp. of *servīre*), equiv. to *servi-* (see SERVE) + *-ent-* -ENT]

ser·vi·ette (sûr′vē et′), *n.* a napkin. [late ME < MF, equiv. to *servi(r)* (to) SERVE + *-ette* -ETTE; for the formation, cf. OUBLIETTE]

ser·vile (sûr′vil, -vīl), *adj.* 1. slavishly submissive or obsequious; fawning: *servile flatterers.* 2. characteristic of, proper to, or customary for slaves; abject: *servile obedience.* 3. yielding slavishly; truckling (usually fol. by *to*). 4. extremely imitative, esp. in the arts; lacking in originality. 5. being in slavery; oppressed. 6. of, pertaining to, or involving slaves: *servile rebellions.* 7. of, pertaining to, or characteristic of a servant. 8. of or pertaining to a condition of servitude or property ownership in which a person is held as a slave or as partially enslaved: *medieval rebellions against servile laws.* [late ME < L *servīle,* neut. of *servīlis,* equiv. to *serv-* (root of *servīre* to be a slave) + *-īlis* -ILE] —**ser′vile·ly,** *adv.* —**ser·vil′i·ty, ser′vile·ness,** *n.*
—**Syn. 1, 2.** cringing, sycophantic. SERVILE, MENIAL, OBSEQUIOUS, SLAVISH characterize one who behaves like a slave or an inferior. SERVILE means cringing, fawning, abjectly submissive: *servile behavior.* MENIAL applies to that which is considered undesirable drudgery: *the most menial tasks.* OBSEQUIOUS implies the ostentatious subordination of oneself to the wishes of another, either from fear or from hope of gain: *an obsequious waiter.* SLAVISH stresses the dependence and laborious toil of one who follows or obeys with abject submission: *slavish attentiveness to orders.* 2. mean, base, low. —**Ant. 1.** aggressive. 2. exalted.

serv·ing (sûr′ving), *n.* 1. the act of one who or that which serves. 2. a single portion of food or drink; helping. 3. *Elect.* a layer of material, as jute yarn or tape, that is applied to the core or the exterior of a lead covered cable and acts as a protective covering. —*adj.* 4. for use in dishing out and distributing food at the table, esp. for separating and transferring a portion of food from a large bowl, plate, or pan and placing it on an individual plate: *Bring me a serving spoon so I can serve the stew.* 5. for use in carrying food to the table and passing it from person to person: *She needed a large serving tray for the roast.* [ME; see SERVE, -ING[1]]

Ser·vite (sûr′vīt), *n. Rom. Cath. Ch.* a member of an order of mendicant friars, founded in Florence in 1233, engaged in fostering devotion to the Virgin Mary. [< ML *Servītēs.* See SERVE, -ITE[1]]

ser·vi·tor (sûr′vi tər), *n.* 1. one who is in or at the service of another; attendant. 2. a glass worker who blocks the gather and does the preliminary blowing of glass for the gaffer. [ME *servitour* < AF < ML *servītor,* equiv. to L *servīt(us)* (ptp. of *servīre* to SERVE) + *-or* -OR[2]]

ser·vi·tude (sûr′vi to͞od′, -tyo͞od′), *n.* 1. slavery or bondage of any kind: *political or intellectual servitude.* 2. compulsory service or labor as a punishment for criminals: *penal servitude.* 3. *Law.* a right possessed by one person with respect to another's property, consisting either of a right to use the other's property or of a power to prevent certain uses of it. [late ME < L *servitūdō.* See SERVICE, -TUDE]
—**Syn. 1.** serfdom, thralldom. See **slavery.** —**Ant. 1.** liberty.

Ser·vi·us Tul·li·us (sûr′vē əs tul′ē əs), the legendary sixth king of ancient Rome who built the city walls and whose accession to the throne was prophesied by and secured with the help of Tanaquil, the widow of the previous king: assassinated by his daughter Tullia and her husband Tarquin.

ser·vo (sûr′vō), *adj., n., pl.* **-vos,** *v.,* **-voed, -vo·ing.** —*adj.* 1. acting as part of a servomechanism: *servo amplifier.* 2. pertaining to or having to do with servomechanisms: *servo engineer.* 3. noting the action of certain mechanisms, as brakes, which are set in operation by other mechanisms but which themselves augment the force of that action by the way in which they operate. —*n.* 4. *Informal.* servomechanism. —*v.t.* 5. to connect (a mechanism) to another as a servomechanism. [short form of SERVOMECHANISM]

servo-, a learned borrowing from Latin, where it meant "slave" or "servant," used in the formation of compound words: *servomechanism.* [< L *serv(us)* + -o-]

Servo-, var. of **Serbo-:** *Servo-Croatian.*

ser·vo·con·trol (*n.* sûr′vō kən trōl′; *v.* sûr′vō kən·trōl′), *n., v.,* **-trolled, -trol·ling.** —*n.* 1. control by means of a servomechanism. 2. a servomechanism used as a control. 3. Also called **Flettner control, servo tab.** *Aeron.* a tab that is directly activated by the control stick and that exerts an aerodynamic force to move a control surface to which it is attached. —*v.t.* 4. to operate (a mechanism) with such a device. [SERVO- + CONTROL]

Ser·vo-Cro·a·tian (sûr′vō krō ā′shən, -shē ən), *n., adj.* (formerly) Serbo-Croatian.

ser·vo·me·chan·i·cal (sûr′vō mə kan′i kəl), *adj.* employing a servomechanism or servomechanisms. [SERVO- + MECHANICAL] —**ser′vo·me·chan′i·cal·ly,** *adv.*

ser·vo·mech·an·ism (sûr′vō mek′ə niz′əm, sûr′vō·mek′-), *n.* an electronic control system in which a hydraulic, pneumatic, or other type of controlling mechanism is actuated and controlled by a low-energy signal. [SERVO- + MECHANISM]

ser·vo·mo·tor (sûr′vō mō′tər), *n.* a motor or the like forming part of a servomechanism. [SERVO- + MOTOR, modeled on F *servo-moteur*]

ser′vo sys′tem, a system using a servomechanism.

ser′vo tab′, servocontrol.

ses·a·me (ses′ə mē), *n.* 1. a tropical, herbaceous plant, *Sesamum indicum,* whose small oval seeds are edible and yield an oil. 2. the seeds themselves, used to add flavor to bread, crackers, etc. 3. See **open sesame.** Also called **benne** (for defs. 1, 2). [< Gk *sēsámē* < Sem; r. *sesame* < L *sēsam(um)* < Gk *sēsamon*]

ses′ame oil′, a yellow oil expressed from the seeds of the sesame, used in cooking, as a vehicle for medicines, and in the manufacture of margarine, soap, and cosmetics.

ses·a·moid (ses′ə moid′), *adj. Anat.* shaped like a sesame seed, as certain small nodular bones and cartilages. [< L *sēsamoīd(ēs)* < Gk *sēsamoeidḗs* like sesame seed. See SESAME, -OID]

ses·cun·ci·a (ses kun′shē ə), *n.* (in prescriptions) an ounce and a half. [< L]

Se·sos·tris (si sos′tris), *n.* (in Greek legend) a king of ancient Egypt believed to have conquered areas in Asia and Africa.

sesqui-, a learned borrowing from Latin meaning "one and a half," used in the formation of compound words: *sesquicentennial.* [< L, equiv. to *sē(mi)s* half-unit (*sēmi-* SEMI- + *as* AS[2]) + *-que* and (c. Gk *té,* Skt *ca,* Goth *-(u)h*]

ses·qui·car·bon·ate (ses′kwi kär′bə nāt′, -nit), *n. Chem.* a salt intermediate in composition between a

CONCISE ETYMOLOGY KEY: <, descended or derived from; >, whence; b., blend of, blended; c., cognate with; deriv., derivative; equiv., equivalent; imit., imitative; m., modification of; obl., oblique; r., replacing; s., stem; sp., spelling; trans., translation; ?, origin unknown, perhaps; *, hypothetical. See the full key inside the front cover.

carbonate and a bicarbonate or consisting of the two combined. [SESQUI- + CARBONATE]

ses·qui·cen·ten·ni·al (ses′kwi sen ten′ē əl), *adj.* **1.** pertaining to or marking the completion of a period of 150 years. —*n.* **2.** a 150th anniversary or its celebration. [SESQUI- + CENTENNIAL] —**ses′qui·cen·ten′ni·al·ly,** *adv.*

sesquih., (in prescriptions) an hour and a half. [< L *sesquihōra*]

ses·qui·ox·ide (ses′kwē ok′sīd, -sid), *n.* *Chem.* an oxide containing three atoms of oxygen and two of another element, as aluminum oxide, Al_2O_3. [SESQUI- + OXIDE]

ses·qui·pe·da·li·an (ses′kwi pi dā′lē ən, -dāl′yən), *adj.* Also, **ses·quip·e·dal** (ses kwip′i dəl). **1.** given to using long words. **2.** (of words or expressions) very long. —*n.* **3.** a sesquipedalian word. [< L *sesquipedāli(s)* of a foot and a half (see SESQUI-, PEDAL) + -AN] —**ses·qui·pe·dal·i·ty** (ses′kwi pi dal′i tē), **ses′qui·pe·da′le·an·ism, ses·quip·e·dal·ism** (ses kwip′i dəliz′əm, -kwi pēd′əliz′-), *n.*

ses·qui·plane (ses′kwi plān′), *n.* *Aeron.* a biplane having one wing with not more than half the surface area of the other wing. [SESQUI- + PLANE[1]]

ses·qui·ter·pene (ses′kwi tûr′pēn), *n.* *Chem.* See under **terpene.** [SESQUI- + TERPENE]

Ses·shu (ses shōō′), *n.* 1420?–1506, Japanese Zen Buddhist monk and painter.

ses·sile (ses′il, -īl), *adj.* *Biol.* **1.** attached by the base, or without any distinct projecting support, as a leaf issuing directly from the stem. **2.** permanently attached. [< L *sessile*, neut. of *sessilis* fit for sitting on, low enough to sit on, dwarfish (said of plants), equiv. to *sess(us)* (ptp. of *sedēre* to SIT) + *-ilis* -ILE] —**ses·sil·i·ty** (se sil′i tē), *n.*

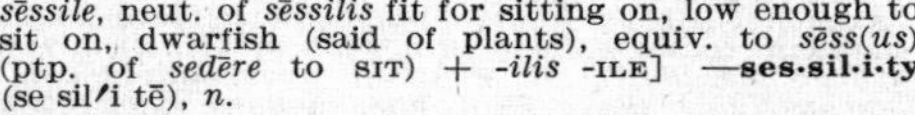

Sessile
A, Flower; B, Leaves

ses·sion (sesh′ən), *n.* **1.** the sitting together of a court, council, legislature, or the like, for conference or the transaction of business: *Congress is now in session.* **2.** a single continuous sitting, or period of sitting, of persons so assembled. **3.** a continuous series of sittings or meetings of a court, legislature, or the like. **4.** the period or term during which such a series is held. **5.** **sessions,** (in English law) the sittings or a sitting of justices in court, usually to deal with minor offenses, grant licenses, etc. **6.** a single continuous course or period of lessons, study, etc., in the work of a day at school: *two afternoon sessions a week.* **7.** a portion of the year into which instruction is organized at a college or other educational institution. **8.** the governing body of a local Presbyterian church, composed of the pastor who moderates and the elders. **9.** a period of time during which a group of persons meets to pursue a particular activity: *A few of the kids got together for a study session.* [late ME < ML, L *sessiōn-* (s. of *sessiō*, ML: law-court sitting, L: sitting), equiv. to *sess(us)* (ptp. of *sedēre* to sit) + *-iōn-* -ION] —**ses′sion·al,** *adj.*

ses′sional indem′nity, the remuneration paid to a member of the Canadian parliament.

Ses·sions (sesh′ənz), *n.* **Roger Huntington,** born 1896, U.S. composer.

ses·terce (ses′tûrs), *n.* a silver coin of ancient Rome, the quarter of a denarius, equal to 2½ asses: introduced in the 3rd century B.C. [< L *sēstertius*, equiv. to *sēs-* half-unit (see SESQUI-) + *tertius* THIRD (i.e., 2 units and half a 3rd one equal 2½ asses)]

ses·ter·ti·um (se stûr′shē əm, -shəm), *n., pl.* **-ti·a** (-shē ə, -shə). a money of account of ancient Rome, equal to 1000 sesterces. [< L, gen. pl. of *sēstertius* SESTERCE, taken as neut. sing.]

ses·ter·tius (se stûr′shəs, -shē əs), *n., pl.* **-ti·i** (-shē ī′). sesterce. [<L]

ses·tet (se stet′, ses′tet), *n.* **1.** *Pros.* the last six lines of a sonnet in the Italian form, considered as a unit. Cf. **octave** (def. 4a). **2.** sextet (def. 2). [< It *sestett(o)* sextet, equiv. to *sest(o)* (< L *sextus* SIXTH) + *-etto* -ET]

ses·ti·na (se stē′nə), *n., pl.* **-nas, -ne** (-nā). *Pros.* a poem of six six-line stanzas and a three-line envoy, originally without rhyme, in which each stanza repeats the end words of the lines of the first stanza, but in different order, the envoy using the six words again, three in the middle of the lines and three at the end. Also called **sextain.** [< It, equiv. to *sest(o)* (< L *sextus* SIXTH) + *-ina* -INE[2]]

Ses·tos (ses′tos), *n.* an ancient Thracian town on the Hellespont opposite Abydos: Xerxes crossed the Hellespont here when he began his invasion of Greece.

set (set), *v.,* **set, set·ting,** *n., adj., interj.* —*v.t.* **1.** to put (something or someone) in a particular place: *to set a vase on a table; The plane set us down in Miami at midnight.* **2.** to place in a particular position or posture: *to set a vase upside down on a table; Set the baby on his feet.* **3.** to place in some relation to something or someone: *to set a table beside a chair; We set a supervisor over the new workers.* **4.** to put into some condition: *to set a house on fire.* **5.** to put or apply: *to set fire to a house.* **6.** to put in the proper position: *to set a chair back on its feet.* **7.** to put in the proper or desired order or condition for use: *to set men up on a chess board; to set a trap.* **8.** to distribute or arrange china, silver, etc., for use on (a table): *to set the table for dinner.* **9.** to place (the hair, esp. when wet) on rollers, in clips, or the like, so that on removing the shaping implements the hair, after being combed out, will assume a particular style. **10.** to put (a price or value) upon something: *He set $500 as the right amount for the car. The teacher sets a high value on neatness.* **11.** to fix the value of at a certain amount or rate; value: *He set the car at $500. She sets neatness at a high value.* **12.** to post, station, or appoint for the purpose of performing some duty: *to set spies on a person.* **13.** to determine or fix definitely: *to set a time limit.* **14.** to resolve or decide upon: *to set a wedding date.* **15.** to cause to pass into a given state or condition: *to set one's mind at rest; to set a prisoner free.* **16.** to direct or settle resolutely or wishfully: *to set one's mind to a task; to set one's heart on a new dress.* **17.** to present as a model; place before others as a standard: *to set a good example.* **18.** to establish for others to follow: *to set a fast pace.* **19.** to prescribe or assign, as a task. **20.** to adjust (a mechanism) so as to control its performance. **21.** to adjust the hands of (a clock or watch) according to a certain standard: *I always set my watch by the clock in the library.* **22.** to adjust (a timer, alarm of a clock, etc.) so as to sound when desired: *He set the alarm for seven o'clock.* **23.** to fix or mount (a gem or the like) in a frame or setting. **24.** to ornament or stud with gems or the like: *a bracelet set with pearls.* **25.** to cause to sit; seat: *to set a child in a highchair.* **26.** to put (a hen) on eggs to hatch them. **27.** to place (eggs) under a hen or in an incubator for hatching. **28.** to place or plant firmly: *to set a flagpole in concrete.* **29.** to put into a fixed, rigid, or settled state, as the face, muscles, etc. **30.** to fix at a given point or calibration: *to set the dial on an oven; to set a micrometer.* **31.** to tighten (often fol. by *up*): *to set nuts well up.* **32.** to cause to take a particular direction: *to set one's course to the south.* **33.** *Surg.* to put (a broken or dislocated bone) back in position. **34.** (of a hunting dog) to indicate the position of (game) by standing stiffly and pointing with the muzzle. **35.** *Music.* **a.** to fit, as words to music. **b.** to arrange for musical performance. **c.** to arrange (music) for certain voices or instruments. **36.** *Theat.* **a.** to arrange the scenery, properties, lights, etc., on a stage) for an act or scene. **b.** to prepare (a scene) for dramatic performance. **37.** *Naut.* to spread and secure (a sail) so as to catch the wind. **38.** *Print.* **a.** to arrange (type) in the order required for printing. **b.** to put together types corresponding to (copy); compose in type: *to set an article.* **39.** *Baking.* to put aside (a substance to which yeast has been added) in order that it may rise. **40.** to change into curd: *to set milk with rennet.* **41.** to cause (glue, mortar, or the like) to become fixed or hard. **42.** to urge, goad, or encourage to attack: *to set the hounds on a trespasser.* **43.** *Bridge.* to cause (the opposing partnership or their contract) to fall short: *We set them two tricks at four spades. Only perfect defense could set four spades.* **44.** to affix or apply, as by stamping: *The king set his seal to the decree.* **45.** to fix or engage (a fishhook) firmly into the jaws of a fish by pulling hard on the line once the fish has taken the bait. **46.** to sharpen or put a keen edge on (a blade, knife, razor, etc.) by honing or grinding. **47.** to fix the length, width, and shape of (yarn, fabric, etc.). **48.** *Carpentry.* to sink (a nail head) with a nail set. **49.** to bend or form to the proper shape, as a saw tooth or a spring. **50.** to bend the teeth of (a saw) outward from the blade alternately on both sides in order to make a cut wider than the blade itself. —*v.i.* **51.** to pass below the horizon; sink: *The sun sets early in winter.* **52.** to decline; wane. **53.** to assume a fixed or rigid state, as the countenance, the muscles, etc. **54.** (of the hair) to be placed temporarily on rollers, in clips, or the like, in order to assume a particular style: *Long hair sets more easily than short hair.* **55.** to become firm, solid, or permanent, as mortar, glue, cement, or a dye, due to drying or physical or chemical change. **56.** to sit on eggs to hatch them, as a hen. **57.** to hang or fit, as clothes. **58.** to begin to move; start (usually fol. by *forth, out, off,* etc.). **59.** (of a flower's ovary) to develop into a fruit. **60.** (of a hunting dog) to indicate the position of game. **61.** to have a certain direction or course, as a wind, current, or the like. **62.** *Naut.* (of a sail) to be spread so as to catch the wind. **63.** *Print.* (of type) to occupy a certain width: *This copy sets to forty picas.* **64.** **set about, a.** to begin on; start. **b.** to undertake; attempt. **c.** to assault; attack. **65.** **set against, a.** to cause to be hostile or antagonistic. **b.** to compare or contrast: *The advantages must be set against the disadvantages.* **66.** **set apart, a.** to reserve for a particular purpose. **b.** to cause to be noticed; distinguish: *Her bright red hair sets her apart from her sisters.* **67.** **set aside, a.** to put to one side; reserve: *The clerk set aside the silver brooch for me.* **b.** to dismiss from the mind; reject. **c.** to prevail over; discard; annul: *to set aside a verdict.* **68.** **set back, a.** to hinder; impede. **b.** to turn the hands of (a watch or clock) to show an earlier time: *When your plane gets to California, set back your watch two hours.* **69.** **set down, a.** to write or to copy or record in writing or printing. **b.** to consider; estimate: *to set someone down as a fool.* **c.** to attribute; ascribe: *to set a failure down to bad planning.* **d.** to put in a position of rest on a level surface. **e.** to humble or humiliate. **f.** to land an airplane: *We set down in a heavy fog.* **70.** **set forth, a.** to give an account of; state; describe: *He set forth his theory in a scholarly report.* **b.** to begin a journey; start: *Columbus set forth with three small ships.* **71.** **set forward,** to turn the hands of (a watch or clock) to show a later time: *When your plane lands in New York, set your watch forward two hours.* **72.** **set in, a.** to begin to prevail; arrive: *Darkness set in.* **b.** (of winds or currents) to blow or flow toward the shore. **73.** **set off, a.** to cause to become ignited or to explode. **b.** to begin; start. **c.** to intensify or improve by contrast. **d.** to begin a journey or trip; depart. **74.** **set on, a.** Also, **set upon.** to attack or cause to attack: *to set one's dog on a stranger.* **b.** to instigate; incite: *to set a crew to mutiny.* **75.** **set one's face against.** See **face** (def. 32). **76.** **set out, a.** to begin a journey or course: *to set out for home.* **b.** to undertake; attempt: *He set out to prove his point.* **c.** to design; plan: *to set out a pattern.* **d.** to define; describe: *to set out one's arguments.* **e.** to plant: *debating whether to set out petunias or pansies.* **f.** to lay out (the plan of a building) in actual size at the site. **g.** to lay out (a building member or the like) in actual size. **77.** **set store by.** See **store** (def. 8). **78.** **set to, a.** to make a vigorous effort; apply oneself to work; begin. **b.** to begin to fight; contend. **79.** **set up, a.** to put upright; raise. **b.** to put into a high or powerful position. **c.** to construct; assemble; erect. **d.** to inaugurate; establish. **e.** to enable to begin in business; provide with means. **f.** *Slang.* to make a gift of; treat, as to drinks. **g.** *Slang.* to stimulate; elate. **h.** to propound; plan; advance. **i.** to bring about; cause. **j.** *Bridge.* to establish (a suit): *to set up spades.* —*n.* **80.** the act or state of setting or the state of being set. **81.** a collection of articles designed for use together: *a set of china; a chess set.* **82.** a collection, each member of which is adapted for a special use in a particular operation: *a set of golf clubs; a set of carving knives.* **83.** a number, group, or combination of things of similar nature, design, or function: *a set of ideas.* **84.** a series of volumes by one author, about one subject, etc. **85.** a number, company, or group of persons associated by common interests, occupations, conventions, or status: *a set of murderous thieves; the smart set.* **86.** the fit, as of an article of clothing: *the set of his coat.* **87.** fixed direction, bent, or inclination: *The set of his mind was obvious.* **88.** bearing or carriage: *the set of one's shoulders.* **89.** the assumption of a fixed, rigid, or hard state, as by mortar, glue, etc. **90.** a plate for holding a tool or die. **91.** an apparatus for receiving radio or television programs; receiver. **92.** *Philately.* a group of stamps which form a complete series. **93.** *Tennis.* a unit of a match, consisting of a group of not fewer than six games with a margin of at least two games between the winner and loser: *He won the match in straight sets of 6–3, 6–4, 8–6.* **94.** a construction representing a place or scene in which the action takes place in a stage, motion-picture, or television production. **95.** *Mach.* **a.** the bending out of the points of alternate teeth of a saw in opposite directions. **b.** a permanent deformation or displacement of an object or part. **c.** a tool for giving a certain form to something, as a saw tooth. **96.** a chisel having a wide blade for dividing bricks. **97.** *Hort.* a young plant, or a slip, tuber, or the like, suitable for planting. **98.** *Dancing.* **a.** the number of couples required to execute a quadrille or the like. **b.** a series of movements or figures that make up a quadrille or the like. **99.** *Music.* **a.** a group of pieces played by a band, as in a night club, and followed by an intermission. **b.** the period during which these pieces are played. **100.** *Bridge.* a failure to take the number of tricks specified by one's contract: *Our being vulnerable made the set even more costly.* **101.** *Naut.* **a.** the direction of a wind, current, etc. **b.** the form or arrangement of the sails, spars, etc., of a vessel. **c.** suit (def. 10). **102.** *Psychol.* a temporary state of an organism characterized by a readiness to respond to certain stimuli in a specific way. **103.** *Mining.* a timber frame bracing or supporting the walls or roof of a shaft or stope. **104.** *Carpentry.* See **nail set.** **105.** *Math.* a collection of objects or elements classed together. **106.** *Print.* the width of a body of type. —*adj.* **107.** fixed or prescribed beforehand: *a set time; set rules.* **108.** specified; fixed: *The hall holds a set number of people.* **109.** deliberately composed; customary: *set phrases.* **110.** fixed; rigid: *a set smile.* **111.** resolved or determined; habitually or stubbornly fixed: *to be set in one's opinions.* **112.** completely prepared; ready: *Is everyone set?* **113.** **all set,** *Informal.* in readiness; prepared: *They were at the starting line and all set to begin.* **114.** **get set!** (in calling the start of a race) get ready to start: *On your mark! Get set! Go!* Also, **set!** —*interj.* **115.** (in calling the start of a race) get ready to start: *Ready! Set! Go!* [ME *sette(n)*, OE *settan*; c. Icel *setja*, G *setzen*, Goth *satjan*, causative of *sitjan* to sit]

—**Syn. 1.** position, locate, situate, plant. See **put. 11.** estimate, appraise, evaluate, price, rate. **13.** establish. **55.** solidify, congeal, harden. **85.** clique. See **circle. 87.** attitude. **88.** posture. **107.** predetermined. **111.** stubborn, obstinate.

Set (set), *n.* *Egyptian Religion.* the brother and murderer of Osiris, represented as having the form of a donkey or other mammal and regarded as personifying the desert. Also, **Seth.**

se·ta (sē′tə), *n., pl.* **-tae** (-tē). *Zool., Bot.* a stiff hair; bristle or bristlelike part. [< L, var. of *saeta* bristle] —**se′tal,** *adj.*

se·ta·ceous (si tā′shəs), *adj.* **1.** bristlelike; bristle-shaped. **2.** having bristles. [< NL *sētāceus.* See SETA, -ACEOUS] —**se·ta′ceous·ly,** *adv.*

se·tar·i·a (si târ′ē ə), *n.* any grass of the genus *Setaria*, having a dense panicle, grown for forage. [< NL; see SETA, -ARIA]

set-back (set′bak′), *n.* *Survey.* the interval by which a chain or tape exceeds the length being measured. [special use of SETBACK]

set·back (set′bak′), *n.* **1.** a check to progress; a reverse or defeat: *The new law was a setback.* **2.** *Archit.* a recession of the upper part of a building from the building line, as to lighten the structure or to permit a desired amount of light and air to reach ground level at the foot of the building. [n. use of v. phrase *set back*]

set′ func′tion, *Math.* a function having a collection of sets as domain.

Seth (seth), *n.* **1.** the third son of Adam. Gen. 4:25 **2.** a boy's given name.

Seth (sāt), *n.* *Egyptian Religion.* Set.

seti-, a learned borrowing from Latin meaning "bristle"; used in the formation of compound words: *setiform.* [< L, var. of *saeti-*; see SETA]

se·ti·form (sē′tə fôrm′), *adj.* bristle-shaped; setaceous. [SETI- + -FORM]

se·tig·er·ous (si tij′ər əs), *adj.* having setae or bristles. Also, **se·tif·er·ous** (si tif′ər əs). [< L *sētiger* bristle-bearing + -OUS; see SETI-, -GEROUS]

set-in (set′in′), *adj.* made separately and placed within another unit. [adj. use of v. phrase *set in*]

set′-in sleeve′, a sleeve joined to the body of a garment at the shoulder and having a seam at that juncture. Cf. **raglan sleeve.**

se·ti·reme (sē′tə rēm′), *n.* the setose, oarlike leg of an aquatic insect. [SETI- + *-reme* < L *rēm(us)* oar]

set·off (set′ôf′, -of′), *n.* **1.** something that counterbalances or makes up for something else, as compensation for a loss. **2.** *Accounting.* a counterbalancing debt or claim, esp. one that cancels an amount a debtor owes. **3.** Also called **offset.** *Archit.* **a.** a reduction in the thickness of a wall. **b.** a flat or sloping projection on a wall, buttress, or the like, below a thinner part. **4.** something used to enhance the effect of another thing by contrasting it, as an ornament. **5.** *Print.* offset (def. 15). [n. use of v. phrase *set off*]

se·ton (sēt′ᵊn), *n. Surg.* **1.** a thread or the like inserted beneath the skin in order to maintain an artificial passage or issue. **2.** the issue itself. [< ML *sētōn-* (s. of *sētō*), equiv. to *sēt(a)* SETA + *-ōn-* aug. suffix]

Se·ton (sēt′ᵊn), *n.* **Ernest Thompson,** 1860–1946, English writer and illustrator in the U.S.

se·tose (sē′tōs, si tōs′), *adj.* covered with setae or bristles; bristly. [< L *sētōs(us).* See SETA, -OSE[1]]

set′ piece′, **1.** an arrangement of slow-burning fireworks forming a design or composition when lighted. **2.** *Theat.* a piece of scenery used as part of a stage set, as a profile or three-dimensional construction built to stand independently on the stage floor: *A few set pieces simulating rocks and a fence constituted the scenery for the first act.* **3.** a work of art, literature, music, etc., having a prescribed thematic and formal structure: *the set pieces of Restoration comedy.* **4.** a scene, action, or the like, having a conventional form and functioning as part of the structure of a work of art, literature, etc. **5.** a military operation carried out according to a rigid plan. **6.** (in a novel, narrative poem, or the like) a passage more or less extraneous to the sequence of events, introduced to supply background, color, or the like.

set′ point′, *Tennis.* the point that if won would enable the scorer or his side to win the set.

set·screw (set′skrōō′), *n.* a screw passing through a threaded hole in a part to tighten the contact of that part with another, as of a collar with the shaft on which it fits. [SET + SCREW]

set′ shot′, *Basketball.* a shot with two hands from a point relatively distant from the basket, in which a player stands still and shoots the ball usually from chest level.

sett (set), *n.* **1.** Also called **pitcher.** a small, rectangular paving stone. **2.** Also called **stake.** a hand-held tool which is struck by a hammer to shape or deform a metal object. [var. of SET]

set·tee (se tē′), *n.* a seat for two or more persons, having a back and usually arms, and often upholstered. [? var. of SETTLE[2]]

settee′ rig′, *Naut. Obs.* a lateen rig on two masts.

set·ter (set′ər), *n.* **1.** one who or that which sets. **2.** one of any of several breeds of hunting dogs which originally had the habit of crouching when game was scented but which are now trained to stand stiffly and point the muzzle toward the scented game. Cf. **English setter, Gordon setter, Irish setter.** [late ME; see SET, -ER[1]]

set′ the′ory, the branch of mathematics that deals with relations between sets.

set·ting (set′ing), *n.* **1.** the act of one who or that which sets. **2.** the surroundings or environment of anything: *The garden was a perfect setting for the house.* **3.** that in which something, as a jewel, is set or mounted. **4.** a group of all the articles, as of china, silver, glass, etc., required for setting a table or a single place at a table. **5.** the locale or period in which the action of a novel, play, film, etc., takes place: *The setting of this story is Verona in the 15th century.* **6.** the scenery and other properties used in a dramatic performance. **7.** *Music.* **a.** a piece of music composed for certain words. **b.** a piece of music composed for a particular medium, or arranged for other than the original medium. [ME; see SET, -ING[1]]

set′ting-up′ ex′ercises (set′ing up′), any of various exercises, as deep knee bends and push-ups, for improving one's posture, muscle tone, or limberness, or for reducing one's weight.

set·tle[1] (set′ᵊl), *v.*, **-tled, -tling.** —*v.t.* **1.** to appoint, fix, or resolve definitely and conclusively; agree upon (as time, price, conditions, result, etc.). **2.** to place in a desired state or in order: *to settle one's affairs.* **3.** to pay, as a bill. **4.** to close (an account) by payment. **5.** to migrate to and organize (an area, territory, etc.); colonize: *The pilgrims settled Plymouth.* **6.** to cause to take up residence: *They settled immigrants in urban areas.* **7.** to furnish (a place) with inhabitants or settlers: *The French settled this colony with army veterans.* **8.** to establish in a way of life, a business, etc. **9.** to quiet, calm, or bring to rest (the nerves, stomach, etc.). **10.** to stop from annoying or opposing: *A sharp word will settle that youngster.* **11.** to make stable; place in a permanent position or on a permanent basis. **12.** to cause (a liquid) to become clear by depositing dregs. **13.** to cause (dregs, sediment, etc.) to sink or be deposited. **14.** to cause to sink down gradually; make firm or compact. **15.** to dispose of finally; close up: *to settle an estate.* **16.** *Law.* **a.** to secure (property, title, etc.) on or to a person by formal or legal process. **b.** to terminate (legal proceedings) by mutual consent of the parties. —*v.i.* **17.** to decide, arrange, or agree (often fol. by *on* or *upon*): *to settle on a plan of action.* **18.** to arrange matters in dispute; come to an agreement: *to settle with a person.* **19.** to pay a bill; make a financial arrangement (often fol. by *up*). **20.** to take up residence in a new country or place: *Many Frenchmen settled along the Mississippi River following La Salle's explorations.* **21.** to come to rest, as from flight: *A bird settled on a bough.* **22.** to gather, collect, or become fixed in a particular place, direction, etc.: *A cold settles in one's head.* **23.** to become calm or composed (often fol. by *down*): *I'll wait until the class settles before starting the lesson.* **24.** to come to rest (often fol. by *down*): *We settled down for the night at an old country inn.* **25.** to sink down gradually; subside. **26.** to become clear by the sinking of suspended particles, as a liquid. **27.** to sink to the bottom, as sediment. **28.** to become firm or compact, as the ground. **29.** (of a female animal) to become pregnant; conceive. **30. settle down, a.** to become established in some routine, esp. upon marrying, after a period of independence or indecision. **b.** to become calm or quiet. **c.** to apply oneself to serious work: *There were so many distractions that we weren't able to settle down to studying.* [ME; OE *setl(an),* deriv. of *setl* SETTLE[2]; c. D *zetelen*] —**set′tle·a·bil′i·ty,** *n.* —**set′tle·a·ble,** *adj.* —**set′tled·ly,** *adv.* —**set′tled·ness,** *n.*

—**Syn. 1.** set, establish. **4.** liquidate. **6.** relocate. **7.** people, colonize. **9.** tranquilize, compose, still, pacify. **11.** stabilize, establish, confirm. **20.** locate, relocate. **25.** decline, fall, abate.

set·tle[2] (set′ᵊl), *n.* a long seat or bench, usually wooden, with arms and a high back. [ME; OE *setle;* c. G *Sessel* armchair, Goth *sitls* seat, L *sella* saddle]

Settle[2]

set·tle·ment (set′ᵊl mənt), *n.* **1.** the act or state of settling or the state of being settled. **2.** the act of making stable or putting on a permanent basis. **3.** a state of stability or permanence. **4.** an arrangement or adjustment, as of business affairs, a disagreement, etc. **5.** the establishment of a person in an employment, office, or charge. **6.** the settling of persons in a new country or place. **7.** a colony, esp. in its early stages. **8.** a small community, village, or group of houses in a thinly populated area. **9.** a community formed and populated by members of a particular religious or ideological group: *a Shaker settlement.* **10.** the satisfying of a claim or demand; a coming to terms. **11.** *Laws.* **a.** final disposition of an estate or the like. **b.** the settling of property, title, etc., upon a person. **c.** the property so settled. **12.** *Brit.* **a.** legal residence in a specific place. **b.** (of a pauper) the right to claim food and shelter from an official agency or specific town or district. **13.** *Social Work.* a welfare establishment in an underprivileged area providing facilities for the people in the area, including personnel to assist them. **14.** a subsidence or sinking of all or part of a structure. [SETTLE[1] + -MENT]

set′tlement op′tion, *Insurance.* any of the options, other than immediate payment in a lump sum, by which the policyholder or beneficiary may choose to have the benefits of a policy paid.

set′tlement work′er, a person who works with underprivileged people in a settlement.

set·tler (set′lər), *n.* **1.** one who or that which settles. **2.** a person who settles in a new country or area. [SETTLE[1] + -ER[1]]

set·tling (set′ling), *n.* **1.** the act of one who or that which settles. **2.** Usually, **settlings.** sediment. [SETTLE[1] + -ING[1]]

set·tlor (set′lər), *n. Law.* one who makes a settlement of property. [SETTLE[1] + -OR[2]]

set-to (set′tōō′), *n., pl.* **-tos.** *Informal.* a usually brief, sharp fight or argument. [n. use of v. phrase *set to*]

Se·tú·bal (si tōō′bäl), *n.* **1. Bay of,** an inlet of the Atlantic, in W Portugal. 20 mi. long; 35 mi. wide. **2.** a seaport on this bay, near Lisbon. 50,966 (1960).

set·u·la (sech′ə lə), *n., pl.* **-lae** (-lē′). *Bot. Zool.* a short blunt seta. Also, **set·ule** (sech′ōōl). [< NL, dim. of *sēta* SETA]

set·u·lose (sech′ə lōs′), *adj. Bot., Zool.* having or covered with setulae. Also, **set·u·lous** (sech′ə ləs). [SETUL(A) + -OSE[1]]

set-up (set′up′), *n. Survey.* **1.** station (def. 14a). **2.** a surveying instrument precisely positioned for observations from a station. **3.** a gap between the end of a chain or tape being used for a measurement and the point toward which it is laid. [special use of SETUP]

set·up (set′up′), *n.* **1.** organization; arrangement. **2.** the carriage of the body; bearing. **3.** everything required for an alcoholic drink except the liquor, as a glass, ice, soda water, etc., as served to patrons who provide their own liquor. **4.** *Informal.* **a.** an undertaking or contest deliberately made easy. **b.** a match or game arranged with an opponent who can be defeated without risk or effort. **c.** an opponent easy to defeat. **5.** *Sports.* **a.** a shot or play that results in a puck, shuttlecock, ball, or balls being so positioned as to provide a player with an easy opportunity for a winning shot: *a playmaker who excels in setups.* **b.** the position of such a puck, ball, etc.: *a setup close to and to the left of the goalkeeper.* **c.** the puck, ball, etc., itself: *The wing banged the setup into the goal.* **6.** an arrangement of all the tools, parts, apparatus, etc., necessary for any of various specific jobs or purposes. **7.** a plan or projected course of action. [n. use of v. phrase *set up*]

set′ width′, *Print.* (in automatic typesetting) the width which the lower-case alphabet of a particular size and font of type measures.

Seu·rat (sœ ʀA′), *n.* **Georges** (zhôʀzh), 1859–91, French painter.

Seuss (sōōs), *n.* **Dr.** See **Geisel, Theodore Seuss.**

Se·vas·to·pol (sə vas′tə pōl′; *Russ.* se′väs tô′pol′yᵊ), *n.* a fortified seaport in the S Ukraine, in the SW Soviet Union in Europe: famous for its heroic resistance during sieges of 349 days in 1854–1855, and 245 days in 1941–1942. 169,000 (est. 1962). Also, **Sebastopol.**

sève (sev), *n. French.* the characteristic flavor and body of a wine. [lit., sap]

sev·en (sev′ən), *n.* **1.** a cardinal number, 6 plus 1. **2.** a symbol for this number, as 7 or VII. **3.** a set of this many persons or things. **4.** a playing card with seven pips. **5. sevens,** (*construed as sing.*) fan-tan (def. 1). —*adj.* **6.** amounting to seven in number. [ME; OE *seofon;* c. G *sieben,* Goth *sibun,* L *septem,* Gk *heptá,* Skt *saptá*]

Sev′en against′ Thebes′, **1.** *Class. Myth.* seven heroes, Adrastus, Amphiaraus, Capaneus, Hippomedon, Parthenopaeus, Polynices, and Tydeus, who led an expedition against Thebes to depose Eteocles in favor of his brother Polynices: the expedition failed, but the Epigoni, the sons of the Seven against Thebes, conquered the city ten years later. **2.** (*italics*) a tragedy (468? B.C.) by Aeschylus.

sev·en·bark (sev′ən bärk′), *n.* See **wild hydrangea.** [SEVEN + BARK[2]; so called from its many layers]

sev′en-card stud′ (sev′ən kärd′), *Cards.* a variety of poker in which each player is dealt one card face down in each of the first two rounds, one card face up in each of the next four rounds, and one card face down in the last round, each of the last five rounds being followed by a betting interval. Cf. **stud poker** (def. 1).

sev′en dead′ly sins′. See **deadly sins.**

sev·en-e·lev·en (sev′ən i lev′ən), *n.* See **shiner perch.**

Sev·en·er (sev′ə nər), *n. Islam.* Ismailian. [SEVEN + -ER[1]]

sev·en·fold (sev′ən fōld′), *adj.* **1.** comprising seven parts or members. **2.** seven times as great or as much. —*adv.* **3.** until seven times as many or as great: *multiplied sevenfold.* [ME; OE *seofonfeald.* See SEVEN, -FOLD]

Sev′en Hills′, a town in N Ohio. 5708 (1960).

Sev′en Hills′ of Rome′, the seven hills (the Aventine, Caelian, Capitoline, Esquiline, Palatine, Quirinal, and Viminal) on and about which the ancient city of Rome was built.

sev·en·pen·ny (sev′ən pen′ē), *adj.* noting a nail 7¼ inches long. *Abbr.:* 7d [SEVEN + -PENNY]

Sev′en Pines′. See **Fair Oaks** (def. 1).

Sev′en Sag′es, seven wise men of ancient Greece, Bias, Chilon, Cleobulus, Periander, Pittacus, Solon, and Thales, who served their country as rulers, lawgivers, and advisers and who were reputed to have written many popular maxims.

sev′en seas′, the navigable waters of the world. Also, **Seven Seas.**

sev·en-sis·ters (sev′ən sis′tərz), *n., pl.* **sev·en-sis·ters.** a flat-topped cactus, *Ariocarpus retusus,* of Mexico, having whitish-pink or rose-colored flowers.

sev·en-spot (sev′ən spot′), *n. Slang.* a playing card the face of which bears seven pips.

sev·en·teen (sev′ən tēn′), *n.* **1.** a cardinal number, 10 plus 7. **2.** a symbol for this number, as 17 or XVII. **3.** a set of this many persons or things. —*adj.* **4.** amounting to 17 in number. **5.** (*cap., italics*) a novel (1916) by Booth Tarkington. [ME *seventene,* OE *seofontēne* (c. D *zeventien,* G *siebzehn*). See SEVEN, TEN]

sev·en·teenth (sev′ən tēnth′), *adj.* **1.** next after the sixteenth; being the ordinal number for 17. **2.** being one of 17 equal parts. —*n.* **3.** a seventeenth part, esp. of one (1/17). **4.** the seventeenth member of a series. [SEVENTEEN + -TH[2]; r. ME *seventethe,* OE *seofontēotha.* See SEVEN, TITHE]

sev′en·teen′-year lo′cust (sev′ən tēn′yēr′). See **periodical cicada.**

sev·enth (sev′ənth), *adj.* **1.** next after the sixth; being the ordinal number for seven. **2.** being one of seven equal parts. —*n.* **3.** a seventh part, esp. of one (1/7). **4.** the seventh member of a series. **5.** *Music.* **a.** a tone on the seventh degree from a given tone (counted as the first). **b.** the interval between such tones. **c.** the harmonic combination of such tones. [ME; see SEVEN, -TH[2]; r. ME *sevethe,* OE *seofotha*] —**sev′enth·ly,** *adv.*

Sev′en That Were Hanged′, a short story (1908) by Andreyev.

Sev′enth Av′enue, **1.** an avenue in the borough of Manhattan, in New York City. **2.** the women's fashion industry of New York City, esp. with respect to mass production: *A Paris designer no sooner gets a dress off the drawing board than Seventh Avenue is shipping copies at a tenth of the price.* **3.** See **Garment Center.**

sev′enth chord′, *Music.* a chord formed by the superposition of three thirds.

sev·enth-day (sev′ənth dā′), *adj.* designating certain Christian denominations that make Saturday their chief day of rest and religious observance: *Seventh-Day Adventists.* Also, **Sev′enth-Day′.**

sev′enth heav′en, **1.** (esp. in Islam and the cabala) the highest heaven, where God and the most exalted angels dwell. **2.** a state of intense happiness; bliss: *She was in seventh heaven in her new home.*

sev·en·ti·eth (sev′ən tē ith), *adj.* **1.** next after the sixty-ninth; being the ordinal number for 70. **2.** being one of 70 equal parts. —*n.* **3.** a seventieth part, esp. of one (1/70). **4.** the seventieth member of a series. [ME *seventithe.* See SEVENTY, -ETH[2]]

sev·en·ty (sev′ən tē), *n., pl.* **-ties,** *adj.* —*n.* **1.** a cardinal number, 10 times 7. **2.** a symbol for this number, as 70 or LXX. **3.** a set of this many persons or things. **4. seventies,** the numbers 70 through 79, esp. the 70th through the 79th years of a lifetime or of a century. **5. the Seventy,** the body of scholars who produced the Septuagint. —*adj.* **6.** amounting to 70 in number. [ME; OE *seofontig.* See SEVEN, -TY[1]]

sev·en·ty-eight (sev′ən tē āt′), *n.* **1.** a cardinal number, 70 plus 8. **2.** a symbol for this number, as 78 or LXXVIII. **3.** a set of this many persons or things. —*adj.* **4.** amounting to 78 in number.

sev·en·ty-eighth (sev′ən tē ātth′), *adj.* **1.** next after the seventy-seventh; being the ordinal number for 78. **2.** being one of 78 equal parts. —*n.* **3.** a seventy-eighth part, esp. of one (1/78). **4.** the seventy-eighth member of a series.

sev·en·ty-fifth (sev′ən tē fifth′), *adj.* **1.** next after the seventy-fourth; being the ordinal number for 75. **2.** being one of 75 equal parts. —*n.* **3.** a seventy-fifth part, esp. of one (1/75). **4.** the seventy-fifth member of a series.

sev·en·ty-first (sev′ən tē fûrst′), *adj.* **1.** next after the seventieth; being the ordinal number for 71. **2.** being one of 71 equal parts. —*n.* **3.** a seventy-first part, esp. of one (1/71). **4.** the seventy-first member of a series.

sev·en·ty-five (sev′ən tē fīv′), *n.* **1.** a cardinal number, 70 plus 5. **2.** a symbol for this number, as 75 or LXXV. **3.** a set of this many persons or things. **4.** *Mil.* **a.** a gun with a 75-mm. caliber. **b.** the field gun of that caliber used in the French and U.S. armies in World War I. —*adj.* **5.** amounting to 75 in number.

sev·en·ty-four (sev′ən tē fōr′, -fôr′), *n.* **1.** a cardinal number, 70 plus 4. **2.** a symbol for this number, as 74 or LXXIV. **3.** a set of this many persons or things. —*adj.* **4.** amounting to 74 in number.

sev·en·ty-fourth (sev′ən tē fōrth′, -fôrth′), *adj.* **1.** next after the seventy-third; being the ordinal number for 74. **2.** being one of 74 equal parts. —*n.* **3.** a seventy-fourth part, esp. of one (1/74). **4.** the seventy-fourth member of a series.

sev·en·ty-nine (sev′ən tē nīn′), *n.* **1.** a cardinal number, 70 plus 9. **2.** a symbol for this number, as 79 or LXXIX. **3.** a set of this many persons or things. —*adj.* **4.** amounting to 79 in number.

sev·en·ty-ninth (sev′ən tē nīnth′), *adj.* **1.** next after the seventy-eighth; being the ordinal number for 79. **2.** being one of 79 equal parts. —*n.* **3.** a seventy-ninth part, esp. of one (1/79). **4.** the seventy-ninth member of a series.

sev·en·ty-one (sev′ən tē wun′), *n.* **1.** a cardinal number, 70 plus 1. **2.** a symbol for this number, as 71 or LXXI. **3.** a set of this many persons or things. —*adj.* **4.** amounting to 71 in number.

sev·en·ty-sec·ond (sev′ən tē sek′ənd), *adj.* **1.** next after the seventy-first; being the ordinal number for 72. **2.**

being one of 72 equal parts. —*n.* **3.** a seventy-second part, esp. of one (1/72). **4.** the seventy-second member of a series.

sev·en·ty-sev·en (sev′ən tē sev′ən), *n.* **1.** a cardinal number, 70 plus 7. **2.** a symbol for this number, as 77 or LXXVII. **3.** a set of this many persons or things. —*adj.* **4.** amounting to 77 in number.

sev·en·ty-sev·enth (sev′ən tē sev′ənth), *adj.* **1.** next after the seventy-sixth; being the ordinal number for 77. **2.** being one of 77 equal parts. —*n.* **3.** a seventy-seventh part, esp. of one (1/77). **4.** the seventy-seventh member of a series.

sev·en·ty-six (sev′ən tē siks′), *n.* **1.** a cardinal number, 70 plus 6. **2.** a symbol for this number, as 76 or LXXVI. **3.** a set of this many persons or things. —*adj.* **4.** amounting to 76 in number.

sev·en·ty-sixth (sev′ən tē siksth′), *adj.* **1.** next after the seventy-fifth; being the ordinal number for 76. **2.** being one of 76 equal parts. —*n.* **3.** a seventy-sixth part, esp. of one (1/76). **4.** the seventy-sixth member of a series.

sev·en·ty-third (sev′ən tē thûrd′), *adj.* **1.** next after the seventy-second; being the ordinal number for 73. **2.** being one of 73 equal parts. —*n.* **3.** a seventy-third part, esp. of one (1/73). **4.** the seventy-third member of a series.

sev·en·ty-three (sev′ən tē thrē′), *n.* **1.** a cardinal number, 70 plus 3. **2.** a symbol for this number, as 73 or LXXIII. **3.** a set of this many persons or things. —*adj.* **4.** amounting to 73 in number.

sev·en·ty-two (sev′ən tē to͞o′), *n.* **1.** a cardinal number, 70 plus 2. **2.** a symbol for this number, as 72 or LXXII. **3.** a set of this many persons or things. —*adj.* **4.** amounting to 72 in number.

sev·en-up (sev′ən up′), *n.* See **all fours** (def. 2).

Sev′en Weeks′ War′. See **Austro-Prussian War.**

Sev′en Won′ders of the World′, the seven most remarkable structures of ancient times: the Egyptian pyramids, the Mausoleum at Halicarnassus, the Temple of Artemis at Ephesus, the Hanging Gardens of Babylon, the Colossus of Rhodes, the statue of Zeus by Phidias at Olympia, and the Pharos or lighthouse at Alexandria.

sev′en-year itch′ (sev′ən yēr′), **1.** scabies. **2.** *Facetious.* boredom or discontent considered as developing or liable to develop after about seven years of marriage.

Sev′en Years′ War′, the war (1756–63) in which England and Prussia defeated France, Austria, Russia, Sweden, and Saxony.

sev·er (sev′ər), *v.t.* **1.** to separate (a part) from the whole, as by cutting or the like. **2.** to divide into parts, esp. forcibly; cleave. **3.** to break off or dissolve (ties, relations, etc.). **4.** *Law.* to divide into parts; disunite (as an estate, titles of a statute, etc.). **5.** to distinguish; discriminate between. —*v.i.* **6.** to become separated, from each other or one from another; become divided into parts. [ME *sever(en)* < MF *sev(e)re(r)* (to) SEPARATE] —**sev′ered·ly,** *adv.* —**sev′er·ing·ly,** *adv.*
—**Syn. 1.** sunder, disunite, disjoin. —**Ant. 1.** unite.

sev·er·a·ble (sev′ər ə bəl, sev′rə-), *adj.* **1.** capable of being severed. **2.** *Law.* separable or capable of being treated as separate from a whole legal right or obligation: *a severable contract obligation.* [SEVER + -ABLE]

sev·er·al (sev′ər əl, sev′rəl), *adj.* **1.** being more than two but fewer than many in number or kind: *several people; several ways of doing it.* **2.** respective; individual: *They went their several ways.* **3.** separate; different: *several occasions.* **4.** single; particular. **5.** *Law.* binding two or more persons who may be sued separately on a common obligation. —*n.* **6.** several persons or things; a few; some. [ME < AF < ML *sēparāl(is),* equiv. to L *sēpar* SEPARATE + *-ālis* -AL[1]]

sev·er·al·ly (sev′ər ə lē, sev′rə-), *adv.* **1.** separately; singly. **2.** respectively. [ME; see SEVERAL, -LY]

sev·er·al·ty (sev′ər əl tē, sev′rəl-), *n., pl.* **-ties.** **1.** the state of being separate. **2.** *Law.* **a.** (of an estate, esp. land) the condition of being held or owned by separate and individual right. **b.** an estate held or owned by individual right. [< AF *severalte.* See SEVERAL, -TY[2]]

sev·er·ance (sev′ər əns, sev′rəns), *n.* **1.** the act of severing or the state of being severed. **2.** a breaking off, as of a friendship. **3.** *Law.* a division into parts; removal of a part from the whole. [< AF; see SEVER, -ANCE]

sev′erance pay′, money, exclusive of wages, back pay, etc., paid to an employee who has tenure and who is dismissed because of lack of work or other reasons beyond his control.

se·vere (si vēr′), *adj.,* **-ver·er, -ver·est.** **1.** harsh; unnecessarily extreme: *severe criticism; severe laws.* **2.** serious or stern in manner or appearance: *a severe face.* **3.** grave; critical: *a severe illness.* **4.** rigidly restrained in style, taste, manner, etc.; simple, plain, or austere. **5.** causing discomfort or distress by extreme character or conditions, as weather, cold, heat, etc.; unpleasantly violent, as rain or wind, a blow or shock, etc. **6.** difficult to endure, perform, fulfill, etc.: *a severe test of his powers.* **7.** rigidly exact, accurate, or methodical: *severe standards.* [< L *sevēr(us),* or back formation from SEVERITY] —**se·vere′ly,** *adv.* —**se·vere′ness,** *n.*
—**Syn. 2.** rigorous, strict, hard. See **stern**[1]. **4.** unadorned. **7.** demanding, exacting. —**Ant. 1.** lenient. **2.** gentle.

Se·ve·ri·ni (sev′ə rē′nē; *It.* se′ve Rē′nē), *n.* **Gi·no** (jē′nô), 1883–1966, Italian painter.

Sev·er·i·nus (sev′ə rī′nəs), *n.* died A.D. 640, pope 640.

se·ver·i·ty (si ver′i tē), *n., pl.* **-ties.** **1.** harshness, sternness, or rigor: *Their lives were marked by severity.* **2.** austere simplicity, as of style, manner, taste, etc.: *The severity of his decor was striking.* **3.** violence or sharpness, as of cold, pain, etc. **4.** grievousness; hard or trying character or effect: *The severity of his loss was finally becoming apparent.* **5.** rigid exactness or accuracy. **6.** an instance of strict or severe behavior, punishment, etc. [late ME < L *sevēritāt-* (s. of *sevēritās*), equiv. to *sevēr-* SEVERE + *-itāt* -ITY]

Sev·ern (sev′ərn), *n.* a river in Great Britain, flowing from central Wales through W England into the Bristol Channel. 210 mi. long.

Se·ver·sky (sə ver′skē), *n.* **Alexander Pro·co·fi·eff de** (prə kō′fē ef′ də),1894–1974, U.S. airplane designer, manufacturer, and writer; born in Russia.

Se·ve·rus (sə vēr′əs), *n.* **Lucius Sep·tim·i·us** (sep-tim′ē əs), A.D. 146–211, Roman emperor 193–211.

sev·er·y (sev′ə rē), *n., pl.* **-er·ies.** (in a vaulted structure) one bay between two principal transverse arches. [ME < OF **civorie, civoire* < L *cibōr(ium)* CIBORIUM]

Sé·vi·gné (sā vē nyā′), *n.* **Ma·rie de Ra·bu·tin-Chan·tal** (MA Rē′ də RA BY TAN shän TAL′), **Marquise de,** 1626–96, French writer, esp. of letters.

Se·ville (sə vil′, sev′il), *n.* a port in SW Spain, on the Guadalquivir River: site of the Alcazar; cathedral. 450,213 (est. 1960). Spanish, **Se·vil·la** (se vē′lyä). —**Se·vil·lian** (sə vil′yən), *adj., n.*

Seville′ or′ange. See under **orange** (def. 2).

Sè·vres (se′vRᵊ; *Eng.* sev′rə, sev), *n.* **1.** a suburb of Paris in N France. 20,292 (1962). **2.** Also, **Sè′vres ware′.** the porcelain made in this suburb since 1756.

sew[1] (sō), *v.,* **sewed, sewn** or **sewed, sew·ing.** —*v.t.* **1.** to join or attach by stitches. **2.** to make, repair, etc., (a garment) by such means. **3.** to enclose or secure with stitches: *to sew flour in a bag.* **4.** to close (a hole, wound, etc.) by means of stitches (usually fol. by *up*). —*v.i.* **5.** to work with a needle and thread or with a sewing machine. **6. sew up, a.** *Informal.* to get or have a monopoly of; control exclusively. **b.** *Slang.* to complete or conclude (arrangements, negotiations, etc.) successfully: *They were about to sew up the deal and call it a night.* **c.** to gain or be assured of: *He tried to sew up as many votes as possible before the convention.* [ME *sewe(n),* OE *siw(i)an;* c. OHG *siuwan,* Goth *siujan,* L *suere*] —**sew′a·ble,** *adj.*

sew[2] (so͞o), *v.,* **sewed, sew·ing,** *n. Naut.* —*v.t.* **1.** to ground (a vessel) at low tide (sometimes fol by *up*). —*v.i.* **2.** (of a vessel) to be grounded at low tide. —*n.* **3.** the amount of additional water necessary to float a grounded vessel. [< MF *sew(er)*, aph. var. of *essewer* < VL *exaquāre,* equiv. to L *ex-* EX-[1] + *aqu(a)* water + *-āre* inf. suffix]

sew·age (so͞o′ij), *n.* the waste matter which passes through sewers. Also, **sewerage.** [SEWER[1], with -AGE for *-er*]

Sew·all (so͞o′əl), *n.* **Samuel,** 1652–1730, American jurist, born in England.

se·wan (sē′wən), *n.* seawan.

Sew·ard (so͞o′ərd), *n.* **1. William Henry,** 1801–72, U.S. statesman: Secretary of State 1861–69. **2.** a town in SE Nebraska. 4208 (1960).

Sew′ard Penin′sula, a peninsula in W Alaska, on Bering Strait.

se·wel·lel (sə wel′əl), *n.* See **mountain beaver.** [< Chinook *š′ulal* robes of mountain beaver, understood as the animal itself]

sew·er[1] (so͞o′ər), *n.* an artificial conduit, usually underground, for carrying off waste water and refuse, as in a town or city. [ME *suer(e)* < OF *se(u)wiere* overflow channel (cf. OF *ess(e)ouer(e)* ditch) < L **exaquāria* drain for carrying water off. See EX-[1], AQUARIUM] —**sew′er·less,** *adj.* —**sew′er·like′,** *adj.*

sew·er[2] (sō′ər), *n.* one who or that which sews. [ME; see SEW[1], -ER[1]]

sew·er[3] (so͞o′ər), *n.* a former household officer or head servant in charge of the service of the table. [ME, by aphesis < AF *asseour* seater, equiv. to OF *asse(oir)* to seat (< L *adsidēre* to attend upon; see ASSIDUOUS) + *-our* -OR[2]]

sew·er·age (so͞o′ər ij), *n.* **1.** the removal of waste water and refuse by means of sewers. **2.** a system of sewers. **3.** sewage. [SEWER[1] + -AGE]

sew′er pill′ (so͞o′ər), a ribbed wooden ball for scraping the walls of a sewer through which it floats.

Se·wick·ley (sə wik′lē), *n.* a town in W Pennsylvania. 6157 (1960).

sew·ing (sō′ing), *n.* **1.** the act or work of one who sews. **2.** something sewn or to be sewn. [ME; see SEW[1], -ING[1]]

sew′ing cir′cle, a group of women who meet regularly to sew, esp. for charitable purposes.

sew′ing cot′ton, cotton thread used for sewing, embroidery, etc.

sew′ing machine′, any of various foot-operated or electric machines for sewing or making stitches, ranging from machines with a shuttle for a spool of thread and a needle for sewing garments to industrial machines for sewing leather, book pages together, etc.

sew′ing silk′, finely twisted silk thread used for sewing, embroidery, etc.

sew′ing ta′ble, a worktable for holding sewing materials and the like, often supplied with a bag or pouch for needlework. Cf. **bag table.**

sewn (sōn), *v.* a pp. of **sew.**

sex (seks), *n.* **1.** the fact or character of being either male or female: *persons of different sex.* **2.** either of the two groups of persons exhibiting this character: *the stronger sex; the gentle sex.* **3.** the sum of the structural and functional differences by which the male and female are distinguished, or the phenomena or behavior dependent on these differences. **4.** the instinct or attraction drawing one sex toward another, or its manifestation in life and conduct. **5.** coitus. **6. to have sex,** *Informal.* to engage in sexual intercourse. —*v.t.* **7.** to ascertain the sex of, esp. of newly-hatched chicks. **8. sex it up,** *Slang.* to neck passionately: *They were really sexing it up last night.* **9. sex up,** *Informal.* **a.** to arouse sexually: *She certainly knows how to sex up the men.* **b.** to increase the appeal of; to make more interesting, attractive, or exciting: *We've decided to sex up the movie with some battle scenes.* [ME < L *sex(us),* akin to *secus,* deriv. of *secāre* to cut, divide; see SECTION]

sex (seks), *adj. Latin.* six.

sex-, an element, occurring in loan words from Latin, meaning "six" (*sexagenary*); on this model used in the formation of compound words: *sexpartite.* Also, **sexi-.** [< L, comb. form of *sex* SIX]

sex′ act′, sexual intercourse; copulation.

sex·a·ge·nar·i·an (sek′sə jə nâr′ē ən), *adj.* **1.** of the age of 60 years or between 60 and 70 years old. —*n.* **2.** a sexagenarian person. [< L *sexāgēnāri(us)* SEXAGENARY + -AN]

sex·ag·e·nar·y (sek saj′ə ner′ē), *adj., n., pl.* **-nar·ies.** —*adj.* **1.** of or pertaining to the number 60. **2.** composed of or proceeding by sixties. **3.** sexagenarian. —*n.* **4.** a sexagenarian. [< L *sexāgēnāri(us),* equiv to *sexāgēn(ī),* distributive of *sexāgintā* sixty + *-ārius* -ARY]

Sex·a·ges·i·ma (sek′sə jes′ə mə, -jā′zə-), *n.* the second Sunday before Lent. Also called **Sexages′ima Sun′day.** [< L *sexāgēsima* (*diēs*) sixtieth (day), deriv. of *sexāgintā* sixty, equiv. to *sexā-* SIX + *-gintā* decade]

sex·a·ges·i·mal (sek′sə jes′ə məl), *adj.* **1.** pertaining to or based upon the number 60. —*n.* **2.** a fraction whose denominator is 60 or a power of 60. [< ML *sexāgēsimāl(is).* See SEXAGESIMA, -AL[1]]

sex′ appeal′, the quality of attracting members of the opposite sex.

sex·a·va·lent (sek′sə vā′lənt), *adj. Chem.* sexivalent.

sex·cen·te·nar·y (seks sen′t̸ner′ē, seks′sen ten′ə-rē), *adj., n., pl.* **-nar·ies.** —*adj.* **1.** pertaining to 600 or a period of 600 years; marking the completion of 600 years. —*n.* **2.** a 600th anniversary or its celebration. [SEX- + CENTENARY]

sex′ chro′mosome, *Genetics.* a chromosome, differing in shape or function from other chromosomes, that affects the determination of sex.

sex·de·cil·lion (seks′di sil′yən), *n., pl.* **-lions,** (*as after a numeral*) **-lion,** *adj.* —*n.* **1.** a cardinal number represented in the U.S. and France by one followed by 51 zeros and, in Great Britain and Germany, by one followed by 96 zeros. —*adj.* **2.** amounting to one sexdecillion in number. [SEX- + DECILLION]

sexed (sekst), *adj.* **1.** being of a particular sex or having sexual characteristics. **2.** characterized by sexuality; having sex appeal. [SEX + -ED[3]]

sexed-up (sekst′up′), *adj. Informal.* **1.** sexually aroused. **2.** made sexually attractive or more titillating: *The movie was a sexed-up version of the book.* **3.** made more attractive or interesting, esp. by adding decorative elements: *a sexed-up car.*

sex·e·nar·y (sek′sə ner′ē), *adj.* **1.** senary. **2.** sextuple (def. 1). **3.** (of a numerical system) with a base of six. [irreg. < L *sex* SIX + *-enary,* as in *septenary*]

sex·en·ni·al (sek sen′ē əl), *adj.* **1.** of or for six years. **2.** occurring every six years. [< L *sexenni(s)* six-year (*sex* SIX + *-ennis* yearly) + -AL[1]] —**sex·en′ni·al·ly,** *adv.*

sex·foil (seks′foil′), *n.* a round ornament consisting of six lobes divided by cusps. [SEX- + *-foil,* as in *trefoil*]

sex′ hor′mone, *Biochem.* any of a class of hormones that regulate the growth and function of the reproductive organs or stimulate the development of the secondary sexual characteristics.

sex′ hy′giene, a branch of hygiene which concerns itself with sex and sexual behavior as it relates to the well-being of the individual and the community.

sexi-, var. of **sex-:** *sexivalent.*

sex·ism (sek′siz əm), *n.* discrimination against women, as in restricted career choices, job opportunities, etc.

sex·ist (sek′sist), *n.* a person who discriminates against women, as by thinking they are fit only for housework and child rearing, should be subservient to men, etc.

sex·i·va·lent (sek′sə vā′lənt), *adj. Chem.* having a valence of six; hexavalent. Also, **sexavalent.** [SEXI- + -VALENT]

sex·less (seks′lis), *adj.* **1.** having or seeming to have no sex; neuter. **2.** having or seeming to have no sexual desires. **3.** having no sex appeal; sexually uninteresting. [SEX + -LESS] —**sex′less·ly,** *adv.* —**sex′less·ness,** *n.*

sex-lim·it·ed (seks′lim′i tid), *adj. Genetics.* (of a gene character) expressed in one sex only.

sex-link·age (seks′ling′kij), *n. Genetics.* an association between genes in sex chromosomes that causes the characters determined by these genes to appear more frequently in one sex than in the other.

sex-linked (seks′lingkt′), *adj. Genetics.* **1.** (of a gene) located in a sex chromosome. **2.** (of a character) determined by a gene located in a sex chromosome.

sex·ol·o·gy (sek sol′ə jē), *n.* the study of normal and abnormal sexual behavior. [SEX + -O- + -LOGY] —**sex·o·log·i·cal** (sek′sə loj′i kəl), *adj.* —**sex·ol′o·gist,** *n.*

sex·par·tite (seks pär′tīt), *adj.* **1.** divided into or consisting of six parts. **2.** *Archit.* (of a vault) divided into six compartments by two ogives and three transverse arches, one of which crosses the ogives at the point at which they cross each other. See illus. under **vault**[1]. [SEX- + PARTITE]

sex·pot (seks′pot′), *n. Slang.* a girl or woman of obvious physical attractiveness. [SEX + POT[1]]

sex′ ra′tio, *Sociol.* the proportional distribution of the sexes in a population aggregate, expressed as the number of males per 100 females.

sext (sekst), *n. Eccles.* the fourth of the seven canonical hours, or the service for it, originally fixed for the sixth hour of the day taken as noon. [ME *sext(a)* < eccl. L *sexta* (*hōra*) sixth (hour)]

sex·tain (seks′tān), *n. Pros.* **1.** a stanza of six lines. **2.** sestina. [b. two obs. F words: *sixain* six-line stanza and *sestine* SESTINA]

sex·tan (seks′tən), *adj.* **1.** (of a fever, ague, etc.) characterized by paroxysms which recur every sixth day. —*n.* **2.** a sextan fever or ague. [< NL *sextān(a)* (*febris*) sixth day (fever), equiv. to L *sext(us)* sixth + *-āna* -AN]

Sex·tans (seks′tənz), *n., gen.* **Sex·tan·tis** (sek-stan′tis) for 1. **1.** *Astron.* the Sextant, an equatorial constellation between Hydra and Leo. **2.** (*l.c.*) a bronze coin of ancient Rome, the sixth part of an as, issued during the period of the Republic. [< L: see SEXTANT]

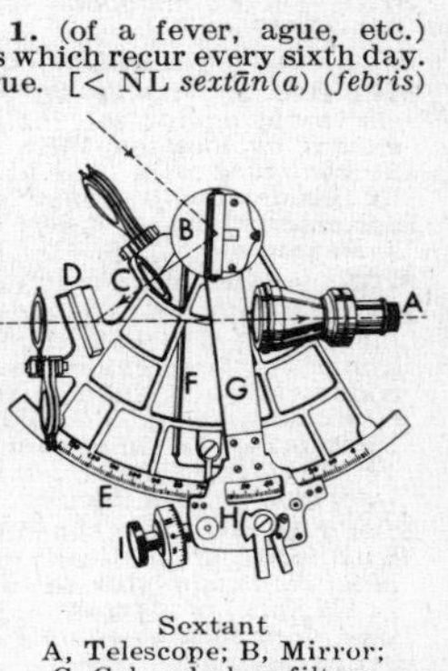

sex·tant (seks′tənt), *n.* **1.** an astronomical instrument used in measuring angular distances, esp. the altitudes of sun, moon, and stars at sea in determining latitude and longitude. **2.** (*cap.*) *Astron.* the constellation Sextans. [< L *sextānt-* (s. of *sextāns*) sixth part of a unit. See SEXT, -ANT]

Sextant
A, Telescope; B, Mirror; C, Colored glass filter; D, Half mirror, half glass; E, Graduated arc; F, Handle; G, Movable index arm; H, Index; I, Vernier

sex·tern (seks′tərn), *n. Bookbinding.* six gathered sheets folded in two for binding together. [< ML *sextern(um),* equiv. to L *sex* SIX + *-ternum,* as in VL **quaternum;* see QUIRE[1]]

sex·tet (seks tet′), *n.* **1.** any group or set of six. **2.** Also, **sestet.** *Music.* **a.** a company of six singers or players. **b.** a musical composition for six voices or instruments. Also, **sex·tette′.** [half-Latinized var. of SESTET; see SEX-]

sex·tic (seks′tik), *Math.* —*adj.* **1.** of the sixth degree. —*n.* **2.** a quantity of the sixth degree. [< L *sext(us)* sixth + -IC]

sex·tile (seks′til), —*adj.* **1.** *Astron.* noting or pertaining to the aspect or position of two heavenly bodies when 60° distant from each other. —*n.* **2.** *Astron.* a sextile position or aspect. **3.** *Statistics.* a quantile for the special case of six equal proportions. [< L *sextīle*, neut. of *sextīlis*, equiv. to *sext(us)* sixth + *-īlis* -ILE]

sex·til·lion (seks til′yən), *n., pl.* **-lions,** (*as after a numeral*) **-lion,** *adj.* —*n.* **1.** a cardinal number represented in the U.S. and France by one followed by 21 zeros and, in Great Britain and Germany, by one followed by 36 zeros. —*adj.* **2.** amounting to one sextillion in number. [< F < L *sext(us)* sixth (power of) + *-illion*, as in *million*] —**sex·til′lionth,** *adj., n.*

sex·to·dec·i·mo (seks′tō des′ə mō′), *n., pl.* **-mos,** *adj.* sixteenmo. [< L, abl. sing. of *sextusdecimus* sixteenth]

sex·to·let (seks′tə let′), *n.* *Music.* sextuplet (def. 3). [< G *Sextole* < L *sext(us)* sixth + G *-ole*, arbitrary suffix + -ET]

sex·ton (seks′tən), *n.* an official of a church charged with taking care of the edifice and its contents, ringing the bell, etc., and sometimes with burying the dead. [ME *sexteyn*, etc., syncopated var. of *segerstane*, etc. < AF *segerstaine* SACRISTAN] —**sex′ton·ship′,** *n.*

sex·tu·ple (seks to͞o′pəl, -tyo͞o′-, -tup′əl, seks′to͝o pəl, -tyo͝o-), *adj., v.,* **-pled, -pling.** —*adj.* **1.** consisting of six parts; sexpartite. **2.** six times as great or as many. **3.** *Music.* characterized by six beats or pulses to the measure: *sextuple rhythm.* —*v.t., v.i.* **4.** to make or become six times as great. [< L *sext(us)* sixth + *-uple*, as in *quadruple, quintuple, septuple*]

sex·tu·plet (seks tup′lit, -to͞o′plit, -tyo͞o′-, seks′to͝o plit, -tyo͝o-), *n.* **1.** one of six offspring born at one birth. **2.** a group or combination of six things. **3.** Also, **sextolet.** *Music.* a group of six notes of equal value performed in the same time normally taken to perform four. [SEXTUPLE + -ET; cf. TRIPLET]

sextu′ple time′, musical meter having six beats to the measure.

sex·tus (seks′təs), *adj.* (in prescriptions) sixth. [< L]

sex·u·al (sek′sho͞o əl), *adj.* **1.** of or pertaining to sex: *sexual matters.* **2.** occurring between or involving the two sexes: *sexual relations.* **3.** having sexual organs or reproducing by processes involving both sexes. [< LL *sexuāl(is)*. See SEX, -AL[1]] —**sex′u·al·ly,** *adv.*

sex′ual in′tercourse, genital contact, usually between humans, esp. the insertion of the penis into the vagina followed by ejaculation; coitus; copulation.

sex·u·al·ise (sek′sho͞o ə līz′), *v.t.,* **-ised, -is·ing.** *Chiefly Brit.* sexualize. —**sex′u·al·i·sa′tion,** *n.*

sex·u·al·i·ty (sek′sho͞o al′i tē), *n.* **1.** sexual character; possession of the structural and functional differentia of sex. **2.** recognition of or emphasis upon sexual matters. **3.** involvement in sexual activity. **4.** an organism's preparedness for engagement in sexual activity. [SEXUAL + -ITY]

sex·u·al·ize (sek′sho͞o ə līz′), *v.t.,* **-ized, -iz·ing.** to render sexual; endow with sexual characteristics. [SEXUAL + -IZE] —**sex′u·al·i·za′tion,** *n.*

sex′ual reproduc′tion, *Biol.* reproduction involving the union of gametes.

sex′ual selec′tion, the Darwinian theory that mate selection is based on certain attractive characteristics, as coloration, behavior, song, etc.

sex·y (sek′sē), *adj.,* **sex·i·er, sex·i·est.** *Informal.* **1.** concerned predominantly or excessively with sex; risqué: *a sexy novel.* **2.** sexually interesting or exciting; radiating sexuality: *the sexiest girl on campus.* **3.** exciting or interesting as a result of ornamentation: *a sexy abstract painting.* [SEX + -Y[1]]

Sey·chelles (sā shel′, -shelz′), *n.* (*construed as pl.*) a group of 92 islands in the Indian Ocean, NE of Madagascar: a British colony. 45,089 (est. 1963); 100 sq. mi. *Cap.:* Victoria.

Sey·han (sā hän′), *n.* Adana.

Sey·mour (sē′mōr, -môr), *n.* **1. Jane,** c1510–37, third wife of Henry VIII of England and mother of Edward VI. **2.** a town in N Texas. 3789 (1960). **3.** a boy's given name.

Se·zes·sion (zā tse syōn′), *n.* *German.* secession (def. 3).

sf, science fiction.

sf., *Music.* sforzando. Also, **sfz.**

Sfax (sfäks), *n.* a seaport in E Tunisia, in N Africa. 65,635 (1956).

Sfc, *Mil.* sergeant first class.

sfer·ics (sfēr′iks, sfer′-), *n.* **1.** (*construed as sing.*) electronic equipment for determining the position of storms by locating their accompanying atmospherics. **2.** (*construed as pl.*) the atmospheric discharges located by this device. **3.** (*construed as pl.*) atmospherics. Also, **spherics.** [var. of *spherics*, short for *atmospherics.* See ATMOSPHERIC, -ICS]

sfm, surface feet per minute.

Sfor·za (sfôrt′sə; *It.* sfôr′tsä), *n.* **1. Count Car·lo** (kär′lô), 1873–1952, Italian statesman: anti-Fascist leader. **2. Fran·ces·co** (frän ches′kô), 1401–66, Italian condottiere and duke of Milan 1450–66. **3.** his father, **Gia·co·muz·zo** (jä′kô mo͞ot′tsô) or **Mu·zio** (mo͞o′tsyô), 1369–1424, Italian condottiere. **4. Lo·do·vi·co** (lô′dô-vē′kô), ("*the Moor*"), 1451–1508, duke of Milan 1494–1500 (son of Francesco Sforza).

sfor·zan·do (sfôrt sän′dō; *It.* sfôr tsän′dô), *adj., adv.* with force; emphatically (used as a musical direction). Also, **forzando, sfor·za·to** (sfôrt sä′tō; *It.* sfôr tsä′tô). [< It, prp. of *sforzare;* cf. ML *exforciāre*, equiv. to *ex-* EX-[1] + *forciāre* to FORCE]

sfu·ma·to (sfo͞o mä′tō), *n.* *Fine Arts.* the subtle and minute gradation of tone and color used to blur or veil the contours of a form in painting: *Leonardo was expert in the use of sfumato.* [< It, ptp. of *sfumare* to gradate tone or color, equiv. to *s-* < L *ex-* EX-[1] + *fumare* to smoke < L; see FUME]

s.g., specific gravity.

sga·bel·lo (skä bel′ō; *It.* zgä bel′lô), *n., pl.* **-los,** *It.* **-li** (-lē). *Ital. Furniture.* a side chair of the Renaissance, consisting of a small seat, usually octagonal, often resting on a cubical part and supported either on two carved planks set transversely on edge or on three legs, with a back formed from a carved plank. [< It < L *scabellum* footstool, equiv. to *scab-* (var. of *scam-* in *scamnum* stool) + *-ellum* dim. suffix]

S gauge, a model railroad gauge of 7/8 inch.

sgd., signed.

sgraf·fi·to (skrä fē′tō; *It.* zgräf fē′tô), *n., pl.* **-ti** (-tē). **1.** a technique of ornamentation in which a surface layer of paint, plaster, slip, etc., is incised to reveal a ground of contrasting color. **2.** an object, esp. pottery, decorated by this technique. Cf. **graffito.** [< It; see EX-[1], GRAFFITO]

's Gra·ven·ha·ge (skhrä′vən hä′khə), Dutch name of **The Hague.**

Sgt., Sergeant.

Sgt. Maj., Sergeant Major.

sh., **1.** sheep. **2.** *Bookbinding.* sheet. **3.** shilling; shillings.

SHA, *Navig.* sidereal hour angle.

Sha·ban (shə bän′, shä-, shô-), *n.* the eighth month of the Islamic calendar. [< Ar *sha'bān*]

Shab·bas (shä′bəs), *n.* *Yiddish.* Sabbath (def. 1).

Shab·bas goy (shä′bəs goi′), *Yiddish.* a gentile who performs tasks for Jews in the home or synagogue on the Sabbath or on a holy day that are forbidden Jews on such occasions, as putting on the lights or firing the furnace.

shab·by (shab′ē), *adj.,* **-bi·er, -bi·est.** **1.** impaired by wear, use, etc.; worn: *shabby clothes.* **2.** showing conspicuous signs of wear or neglect: *The rooms on the upper floors of the mansion had a rather shabby appearance, as if they had not been much in use of late.* **3.** wearing worn clothes or having a slovenly or unkempt appearance: *a shabby person.* **4.** run-down, seedy, or dilapidated: *a shabby hotel.* **5.** meanly ungenerous or unfair; contemptible, as persons, actions, etc.: *shabby behavior.* **6.** inferior; not up to par in quality, performance, etc.: *a shabby rendition of the sonata.* [*shab* (ME; OE *sceabb* SCAB) + -Y[1]; c. G *schäbig*] —**shab′bi·ly,** *adv.* —**shab′bi·ness,** *n.*

shab·by-gen·teel (shab′ē jen tēl′), *adj.* trying to maintain dignity and self-respect despite shabbiness. —**shab·by-gen·til·i·ty** (shab′ē jen til′i tē), *n.*

Sha·bu·oth (shə vo͞o′ōs, -əs; *Heb.* shä bo͞o ôt′), *n.* a Jewish festival, immediately following the seven weeks of the Omer, that is celebrated on the sixth and seventh days of the month of Sivan by Orthodox and Conservative Jews outside Israel but on the sixth day only by Reform Jews and Jews in Israel, and that commemorates the giving of the Ten Commandments by God to Moses on Mt. Sinai. Also, **Shavuoth.** Also called **Feast of Weeks, Pentecost.** [lit., weeks]

Sha·cha·rith (shä khä rēt′; *Eng.* shä′khris), *n.* *Hebrew.* Shaharith.

shack[1] (shak), *n.* **1.** a rough cabin; shanty. **2.** *Railroads Slang.* a brakeman. **3.** *Informal.* See **radio shack.** —*v.i.* **4. shack up,** *Slang.* **a.** to live together as husband and wife without being legally married. **b.** to have illicit sexual relations. **c.** to live at a place; reside. [short for *shackle* (shaky) hovel; see RAMSHACKLE]
—**Syn. 1.** See **cottage.** —**Ant. 1.** palace.

shack[2] (shak), *v.t.* *Informal.* to chase and throw back; to retrieve: *to shack a ground ball.* [appar. special use of dial. *shack* to SHAKE]

shack·le (shak′əl), *n., v.,* **-led, -ling.** —*n.* **1.** a ring or other fastening, as of iron, for securing the wrist, ankle, etc.; fetter. **2.** a hobble or fetter for a horse or other animal. **3.** the U-shaped bar of a padlock, one end of which is pivoted or sliding, the other end of which can be released, as for passing through a staple, and then fastened, as for securing a hasp. **4.** any of various fastening or coupling devices. **5.** Often, **shackles.** anything that serves to prevent freedom of procedure, thought, etc. —*v.t.* **6.** to put a shackle or shackles on; confine or restrain by a shackle or shackles. **7.** to fasten or couple with a shackle. **8.** to restrain in action, thought, etc., as by restrictions; restrict the freedom of. [ME *shackle*, OE *sceacel* fetter; c. LG *schakel* hobble, Icel *skökull* wagon pole] —**shack′ler,** *n.*
—**Syn. 1.** chain, manacle, handcuff, gyve, bilboes. **5.** obstacle, obstruction, impediment, encumbrance. **6.** restrict, fetter, chain, handcuff, hobble. **8.** restrict, trammel, impede, slow, stultify, dull. —**Ant. 6, 8.** liberate, free.

Shack·le·ton (shak′əl tən), *n.* **Sir Ernest Henry,** 1874–1922, English explorer of the Antarctic.

shad (shad), *n., pl.* (*esp. collectively*) **shad,** (*esp. referring to two or more kinds or species*) **shads.** **1.** a deep-bodied herring, *Alosa sapidissima*, that migrates up streams to spawn, used for food. **2.** any other fish of the genus *Alosa* or related genera. **3.** any of several unrelated fishes. [OE *sceadd;* c. LG *schade*]

shad·ber·ry (shad′ber′ē, -bə rē), *n., pl.* **-ries.** **1.** the fruit of a shadbush. **2.** the plant itself. [*shad* (? dial. *shad* cool spot, OE *scead* SHADE, shelter) + BERRY]

shad·bush (shad′bo͝osh′), *n.* **1.** the serviceberry, *Amelanchier canadensis.* **2.** any of various other species of *Amelanchier.* Also called **shad·blow** (shad′blō′). [*shad* (see SHADBERRY) + BUSH[1]]

Shad·chan (shät′khən), *n., pl.* **shad·cha·nim** (shät-khô′nim), **shad·chans.** *Yiddish.* a person whose business is arranging meetings between Jewish men and women for the purpose of bringing about marriage; matchmaker. Also, **schatchen.**

Shad·dai (shä dī′), *n.* *Hebrew.* the Almighty; God. Also, **Sha·dai′.**

shad·dock (shad′ək), *n.* **1.** Also called **forbidden fruit, pomelo.** the large, roundish or pear-shaped, usually pale-yellow, orangelike, edible fruit of the rutaceous tree, *Citrus grandis*, grown in the Orient. **2.** the tree itself. [named after Captain *Shaddock*, 17th-century Englishman who brought the seed to the West Indies from the East Indies]

shade (shād), *n., v.,* **shad·ed, shad·ing.** —*n.* **1.** the comparative darkness caused by the interception or screening of rays of light from an object, place, or area. **2.** a place or an area of comparative darkness, as one sheltered from the sun. **3.** See **window shade.** **4.** a lampshade. **5. shades,** darkness gathering at the close of day: *Shades of night are falling.* **6.** Usually, **shades.** a secluded or obscure place: *He was living in the shades.* **7.** comparative obscurity. **8.** a specter or ghost. **9.** *Gk. and Rom. Religion.* one of the spirits of the dead inhabiting Hades. **10.** a shadow. **11.** the degree of darkness of a color, determined by the quantity of black or by the lack of illumination. **12.** comparative darkness, as the effect of shadow or dark and light, in pictorial representation; the dark part, or a dark part, of a picture or drawing. **13.** a slight variation or degree: *There is not a shade of difference between them.* **14.** a little bit; touch, esp. of something that may change the color of or lighten or darken something else: *coffee with a little sugar and a shade of cream.* **15.** anything used for protection against excessive light, heat, etc. **16.** (in architectural shades and shadows) a shadow upon those parts of a solid which are tangent to or turned away from the parallel rays from the theoretical light source. Cf. **shadow** (def. 11). **17. shades,** *Slang.* sunglasses. **18. cast** or **put someone in** or **into the shade,** to make another person's efforts seem insignificant by comparison; surpass: *Her playing puts mine in the shade.* **19. the shades,** Hades, as the abode of the spirits of the dead. —*v.t.* **20.** to produce shade in or on. **21.** to obscure, dim, or darken. **22.** to screen or hide from view. **23.** to protect (something) from light, heat, etc., by or as by a screen: *to shade the eyes from a bright light.* **24.** to cover or screen (a candle, light, etc.): *to shade a light to protect the eyes.* **25.** to introduce degrees of darkness into (a drawing or painting) in order to render light and shadow or give the effect of color. **26.** to render the values of light and dark in (a painting or drawing). **27.** to change by imperceptible degrees into something else. **28.** to reduce (the price of something) by way of a concession. —*v.i.* **29.** to pass or change by slight graduations, as one color, quality, or thing into another. [ME; OE *sceadu;* see SHADOW; c. G *Schatten*, Goth *skadus*, Gk *skótos*] —**shade′ful,** *adj.* —**shade′less,** *adj.* —**shade′less·ness,** *n.*
—**Syn. 1.** obscurity, gloom, dusk. SHADE, SHADOW imply partial darkness or something less bright than the surroundings. SHADE indicates the lesser brightness and heat of an area where the direct rays of light do not fall: *the shade of a tree.* It differs from SHADOW in that it implies no particular form or definite limit, while a SHADOW often represents in form or outline the object which intercepts the light: *the shadow of a dog.* **8.** apparition, phantom, spirit. **13.** hair. **14.** trace, hint, suggestion. **15.** veil, screen. See **curtain.** **21.** cloud, blur, obfuscate. **22.** conceal, shelter. —**Ant. 1.** light, glare.

shad·ed (shā′did), *adj.* *Print.* noting or pertaining to an ornamented type in which a thin white line appears along one edge of each of the main strokes of a character. [SHADE + -ED[2]] —**shad′ed·ness,** *n.*

shade′ deck′, *Naut.* **1.** a light deck supported by stanchions. **2.** the space below this, open at the sides.

shades′ and shad′ows, the science of defining the three-dimensional features shown on an architectural elevation by means of illuminated and shaded surfaces, the light source being assumed to cast parallel rays usually from the left at 45° to the picture plane and at 45° to the horizon.

shade′ tree′, a tree planted or valued for its shade.

shad·ing (shā′ding), *n.* **1.** a slight variation or difference of color, character, etc. **2.** the act of one who or that which shades. **3.** the representation of the different values of color or light and dark in a painting or drawing. [SHADE + -ING[1]]

sha·doof (shä do͞of′), *n.* a contrivance used in Egypt and other Eastern countries for raising water, esp. for irrigation, consisting of a long suspended rod with a bucket at one end and a weight at the other. Also, **shaduf.** [Anglicized spelling of SHADUF]

Shadoof

shad·ow (shad′ō), *n.* **1.** a dark figure or image cast on the ground or some surface by a body intercepting light. **2.** shade or comparative darkness, as in an area. **3. shadows,** darkness, esp. that coming after sunset: *The place was now in shadows.* **4.** shelter; protection: *sanctuary in the shadow of the church.* **5.** a slight suggestion; trace: *beyond the shadow of a doubt.* **6.** a specter or ghost: *pursued by shadows.* **7.** a hint or faint, indistinct image or idea; intimation: *shadows of things to come.* **8.** a mere semblance: *the shadow of power.* **9.** a reflected image. **10.** (in painting, drawing, graphics, etc.) **a.** the representation of the absence of light on a form. **b.** the dark part of a picture, esp. as representing the absence of illumination: *Rembrandt's figures often emerge gradually from the shadows.* **11.** (in architectural shades and shadows) a dark figure or image cast by an object or part of an object upon a surface which would otherwise be illuminated by the theoretical light source. Cf. **shade** (def. 16). **12.** a period or instance of gloom, unhappiness, mistrust, doubt, dissension, or the like, as in friendship or one's life: *Their relationship was not without shadows.* **13.** a dominant or pervasive threat, influence, or atmosphere, esp. one causing gloom, fear, doubt, or the like: *They lived under the shadow of war.* **14.** an inseparable companion: *The dog was his shadow.* **15.** one who follows a person in order to keep watch upon him, as a spy or detective. **16.** *Naut.* Also called **quadrilateral spinnaker.** a four-sided spinnaker having a short gaff. —*v.t.* **17.** to overspread with shadow; shade. **18.** to cast a gloom over; cloud: *The incident shadowed their meeting.* **19.** to screen or protect from light, heat, etc.; shade. **20.** to follow (a person) about secretly, in order to keep watch over his movements: *He felt he was being shadowed.* **21.** to represent faintly, prophetically, etc. (often fol. by *forth*). **22.** *Archaic.* to shelter or protect. **23.** *Archaic.* to shade in painting, drawing, etc. [ME; OE *scead(u)we*, obl. case of *sceadu* SHADE; c. D *schaduw*] —**shad′ow·er,** *n.* —**shad′ow·less,** *adj.* —**shad′ow·like′,** *adj.*
—**Syn. 1.** See **shade.**

shad′ow box′, a shallow, rectangular frame fronted with a glass panel, used to show and at the same time protect items on display, as paintings, coins, jewelry, etc. Also called **shad′ow box′ frame′.**

shad·ow·box (shad′ō boks′), *v.i.* **1.** to make the motions of attack and defense, as in boxing, in the absence of an opponent, esp. as a training or conditioning procedure. **2.** to evade or avoid positive, direct, or decisive action. [SHADOW + BOX[2]]

shad′ow cab′inet, (in the Brit. Parliament) a group of prominent members of the opposition who are expected to hold positions in the cabinet when their party assumes power.

shad·owed (shad′ōd), *adj. Print.* noting or pertaining to an ornamented type in which the embellishment is outside the character, esp. one in which a black line at one side and at the top or bottom gives the effect of a cast shadow. [late ME; see SHADOW, -ED[2]]

shad·ow·graph (shad′ō graf′, -gräf′), *n.* **1.** a picture produced by throwing a shadow, as of the hands, on a lighted screen, wall, or the like. **2.** See **shadow play. 3.** a radiograph. [SHADOW + -GRAPH] —**shad′ow·graph′ic,** *adj.* —**shad′ow·graph′ist,** *n.* —**shad′ow·graph′y,** *n.*

shad·ow·land (shad′ō land′), *n.* a land or region of shadows, phantoms, unrealities, or uncertainties: *He was living in a shadowland of his own making.* [SHADOW + LAND]

shad′ow pin′, *Navig.* a vertical pin set in an azimuth instrument or at the center of a compass card, indicating by the direction of its shadow the azimuth of the sun.

shad′ow play′, theatrical entertainment consisting of shadows of puppets, flat figures, or live actors projected onto a lighted screen and often performed in pantomime. Also called **shadowgraph, shad′ow pan′tomime, shad′ow show′, shad′ow the′ater.**

shad′ow roll′, sheepskin that is placed just below the eyes of a pacing horse in order to prevent him from seeing moving shadows cast by his body.

shad·ow·y (shad′ō ē), *adj.* **1.** resembling a shadow in faintness, slightness, etc.: *shadowy outlines.* **2.** unsubstantial, unreal, or illusory: *shadowy preoccupations.* **3.** abounding in shadow; shady: *a shadowy path.* **4.** enveloped in shadow. **5.** casting a shadow. [ME *shadewy.* See SHADOW, -Y[1]] —**shad′ow·i·ness,** *n.*

Shad·rach (shad′rak, shā′drak), *n.* a companion of Daniel who, with Meshach and Abednego, was thrown into the fiery furnace of Nebuchadnezzar and came out unharmed. Dan. 3:12–30.

sha·duf (shä do͞of′), *n.* shadoof. [< EgyptAr]

Shad·well (shad′wel′, -wəl), *n.* **Thomas,** 1642?–92, English dramatist: poet laureate 1688–92.

shad·y (shā′dē), *adj.,* **shad·i·er, shad·i·est. 1.** abounding in shade; shaded: *shady paths.* **2.** giving shade: *a shady tree.* **3.** shadowy; indistinct; spectral. **4.** *Informal.* of dubious character; rather disreputable: *shady dealings.* **5. keep shady,** *Slang.* to keep out of sight; stay in hiding: *They were warned to keep shady if they valued their lives.* **6. on the shady side of,** *Informal.* beyond (the specified age); more than: *on the shady side of 40.* [SHADE + -Y[1]] —**shad′i·ly,** *adv.* —**shad′i·ness,** *n.*

Sha·dy·side (shā′dē sīd′), *n.* a town in E Ohio. 5028 (1960).

SHAEF (shāf), Supreme Headquarters Allied Expeditionary Forces. Also, **Shaef** (shāf).

shaft (shaft, shäft), *n.* **1.** a long pole forming the body of various weapons, for handling or propelling, as lances, halberds, arrows, etc. **2.** something directed or barbed as in sharp attack: *shafts of sarcasm.* **3.** a ray or beam: *a shaft of sunlight.* **4.** a long, comparatively straight handle serving as an important or balancing part of an implement or device, as of a hammer, ax, golf club, or other implement. **5.** *Mach.* a rotating or oscillating round, straight bar for transmitting motion and torque, usually supported on bearings and carrying gears, wheels, or the like, as a propeller shaft on a ship, a drive shaft of an engine, etc. **6.** a flagpole. **7.** *Archit.* **a.** that part of a column or pier between the base and capital. **b.** any distinct, slender, vertical masonry feature engaged in a wall or pier and usually supporting or feigning to support an arch or vault. **8.** a monument in the form of a column, obelisk, or the like. **9.** either of the parallel bars of wood between which the animal drawing a vehicle is hitched. **10.** any well-like passage or vertical enclosed space, as in a building: *an elevator shaft.* **11.** *Mining.* a vertical or sloping passageway leading to the surface. **12.** *Bot.* the trunk of a tree. **13.** *Zool.* the main stem or midrib of a feather. **14.** Also called **leaf.** *Textiles.* the harness or warp with reference to the pattern of interlacing threads in weave constructions (usually used in combination): *an eight-shaft satin.* **15.** that part of a candelabrum which supports the branches. —*v.t.* **16.** to push or propel with a pole: *to shaft a boat through a tunnel.* [ME; OE *sceaft;* c. G *Schaft;* cf. L *scāpus* shaft, Gk *skêptron* SCEPTER] —**shaft′less,** *adj.* —**shaft′like′,** *adj.*

shaft′ al′ley, *Naut.* an enclosure on a ship for housing a propeller shaft and a walk for oilers. Also called **shaft′ tun′nel.**

Shaf·ter (shaf′tər), *n.* a town in central California. 4576 (1960).

Shaftes·bur·y (shafts′bə rē, shäfts′-), *n.* **1. Anthony Ash·ley Cooper** (ash′lē), **1st Earl of,** 1621–83, British statesman. **2. Anthony Ashley Cooper, 7th Earl of,** 1801–85, English philanthropist.

shaft′ grave′, *Archaeol.* a grave consisting of a deep, rectangular pit with vertical sides, roofed over with a stone slab.

shaft′ horse′power, the horsepower delivered to the driving shaft of an engine, as measured by a torsion meter. *Abbr.:* shp, SHP, S.H.P., s.hp., s.h.p.

shaft′ house′, a structure housing machinery and other equipment at the top of a mine shaft.

shaft·ing (shaf′ting, shäf′-), *n.* **1.** a number of shafts. **2.** *Mach.* a system of shafts, as the overhead shafts formerly used for driving the machinery of a mill. **3.** steel bar stock used for shafts. **4.** *Archit.* a system of shafts, as those around a pier or in the reveals of an archway. [SHAFT + -ING[1]]

shaft·way (shaft′wā′, shäft′-), *n. Chiefly Brit.* hoistway. [SHAFT + WAY]

shag[1] (shag), *n., v.,* **shagged, shag·ging.** —*n.* **1.** rough, matted hair, wool, or the like. **2.** a mass of this. **3.** a cloth with a nap, specifically one of silk but commonly a heavy or rough woolen fabric. **4.** a coarse tobacco cut into fine shreds. —*v.t.* **5.** to make rough or shaggy, esp. with vegetation. **6.** to make rough or sharp. [OE *sceacga* (wooly) hair; c. Icel *skegg* beard; akin to SHAW] —**shag′like′,** *adj.*

shag[2] (shag), *n.* any of several small cormorants, esp. *Phalacrocorax aristotelis,* of Europe and northern Africa. [special use of SHAG[1], applied first to bird's crest]

shag[3] (shag), *v.,* **shagged, shag·ging,** *n.* —*v.i.* **1.** to dance a step consisting of a vigorous hopping on each foot in succession. —*n.* **2.** this dance step. [? var. of SHOG]

shag[4] (shag), *v.t.,* **shagged, shag·ging. 1.** to chase or follow after; pursue. **2.** to go after and bring back; fetch. **3.** *Baseball Slang.* to retrieve and throw back (fly balls) in batting practice. [?]

shag·a·nap·pi (shag′ə nap′ē, shag′ə nap′ē), *n. Chiefly Canadian.* thongs, straps, or lacings made of rawhide. Cf. **babiche.** [< Cree *pishaganâbii,* equiv. to *pishagan* hide + *âbii* cord]

shag·bark (shag′bärk′), *n.* **1.** a hickory, *Carya ovata,* having rough bark and yielding a valuable wood. **2.** the wood. **3.** the ellipsoidal, slightly angular nut of this tree. Also called **shag′bark hick′ory** (for defs. 1, 2). [SHAG(GY) + BARK[2]]

shag·gy (shag′ē), *adj.,* **-gi·er, -gi·est. 1.** covered with or having long, rough hair. **2.** untidy; unkempt: *a shaggy person.* **3.** rough and matted; forming a bushy mass, as the hair, mane, etc. **4.** having a rough nap, as cloth. [SHAG[1] + -Y[1]] —**shag′gi·ly,** *adv.* —**shag′gi·ness,** *n.*

shag′gy dog′ sto′ry, 1. a funny story which, after an often long and involved narration of unimportant incidents, has an absurd or irrelevant punch line. **2.** a joke or story in which a talking animal, as a dog, plays a major part.

shag·gy-mane (shag′ē mān′), *n.* an edible, inky-cap mushroom, *Coprinus comatus,* having an elongated, shaggy pileus.

sha·green (shə grēn′), *n.* **1.** an untanned leather with a granular surface, prepared from the hide of a horse, shark, seal, etc. **2.** the rough skin of certain sharks, used as an abrasive. —*adj.* **3.** Also, **shagreened.** resembling, covered with, or made of shagreen. [< F *chagrin,* var. of *sagrin* < Turk *sâgri* rump; F *-in* attempt to imitate Turkish final vowel]

shah (shä), *n.* (*often cap.*) (formerly, in Iran) king; sovereign. [< Pers: king] —**shah′dom,** *n.*

Sha·ha·da (shä hä′dä), *n.* the Islamic profession of the uniqueness of Allah and of the prophecy of Muhammad. [< Ar: witness]

Sha·hap·ti·an (shä hap′tē ən), *n., pl.* **-ti·ans,** (*esp. collectively*) **-ti·an,** *adj.* Sahaptin.

Sha·ha·rith (shä′ḵнä rēt′; *Eng.* shäḵн′ris), *n. Hebrew.* the religious service celebrated by Jews every morning. Also, **Shacharith.** Cf. **Maarib, Minhah.** [lit., morning]

Shah Ja·han (shä′ jə hän′), 1592?–1666, Mogul emperor in India 1628?–58: built the Taj Mahal. Also, **Shah′ Je·han′.**

Shah·ja·han·pur (shä′jə hän′po͝or′), *n.* a city in Uttar Pradesh, in N India. 110,400 (1961).

Shahn (shän), *n.* **Ben,** 1898–1969, U.S. painter, born in Lithuania.

sha·'ir (shä ēr′), *n. Islam.* a prophet or seer expressing in rhymed prose the revelations of a jinn. [< Ar]

Shairp (shärp, shärp), *n.* **John Campbell** ("*Principal Shairp*"), 1819–85, English critic, poet, and educator.

Shai·tan (shī tän′), *n.* **1.** (in Muslim usage) Satan; the devil. **2.** (*l.c.*) a person or animal of evil or vicious disposition. Also, **Sheitan.** [< Ar; see SATAN]

Shak., Shakespeare.

shake (shāk), *v.,* **shook, shak·en, shak·ing,** *n.* —*v.i.* **1.** to move or sway with short, quick, irregular vibratory movements. **2.** to tremble with emotion, cold, etc. **3.** to become dislodged and fall (usually fol. by *off* or *down*): *Sand shakes off easily.* **4.** to move something, or its support or container, briskly to and fro or up and down, as in mixing: *Shake before using.* **5.** to totter; become unsteady. **6.** to clasp another's hand in greeting, agreement, congratulations, etc.: *Let's shake and be friends again.* **7.** *Music.* to execute a trill.
—*v.t.* **8.** to move (something or its support or container) to and fro or up and down with short, quick, forcible movements: *to shake a bottle of milk.* **9.** to brandish or flourish: *to shake a stick at someone.* **10.** to grasp (someone or something) firmly in an attempt to move or rouse by, or as by, vigorous movement to and fro: *We shook the tree. She grabbed the boy by the shoulders and shook him.* **11.** to dislodge or dispense (something) by short, quick, forcible movements of its support or container: *We shook nuts from the tree. He took the bottle and shook two aspirins into his hand.* **12.** to cause to sway, rock, totter, etc.: *to shake the very foundations of society; Don't shake the swing.* **13.** to agitate or disturb profoundly in feeling: *The experience shook him badly.* **14.** to cause to doubt or waver; weaken: *to shake one's faith; to shake one's self-esteem.* **15.** *Music.* to trill (a note). **16.** to mix (dice) by rolling in the palm of the hand before they are cast. **17.** to get rid of; elude: *It seemed that they would never shake their pursuers.* **18. shake down, a.** to cause to descend by shaking; bring down. **b.** to cause to settle. **c.** to condition; test: *to shake down a ship.* **d.** *Slang.* to extort money from. **e.** *Slang.* to search (someone), esp. to detect concealed weapons. **19. shake hands.** See **hand** (def. 63). **20. shake off, a.** to rid oneself of; reject. **b.** to get away from; leave behind. **c.** *Baseball, Softball.* (of a pitcher) to indicate rejection of (a sign by the catcher for a certain pitch) by shaking the head or motioning with the glove. **21. shake one's head, a.** to indicate disapproval, disagreement, negation, or uncertainty by turning one's head from one side to the other and back: *I asked him if he knew the answer, but he just shook his head.* **b.** to indicate approval, agreement, affirmation or acceptance by nodding one's head up and down. **22. shake the dust from one's feet.** See **dust** (def. 16). **23. shake up, a.** to shake in order to mix or loosen. **b.** to upset; jar. **c.** to agitate mentally or physically: *The threat of attack has shaken up the entire country.*
—*n.* **24.** the act or an instance of shaking, rocking, swaying, etc. **25.** tremulous motion. **26.** a tremor. **27. shakes,** (*construed as sing.*) a state or spell of trembling, as caused by fear, fever, cold, etc. (usually prec. by *the*): *We knew he'd get the shakes when he saw the enemy.* **28.** a disturbing blow; shock. **29.** See **milk shake. 30.** the act or a manner of clasping another's hand in greeting, agreement, etc.: *He has a strong shake.* **31.** *Informal.* chance or fate; deal: *a fair shake.* **32.** *Informal.* a cast of the dice: *He threw an eight on his last shake.* **33.** something resulting from shaking. **34.** an earthquake. **35.** a fissure in the earth. **36.** an internal crack or fissure in timber, produced by stress or pressure during growth, as by wind, sudden change of temperature, feeding of birds, etc. **37.** *Music.* trill. **38.** an instant: *I'll be with you in a shake.* **39.** *Carpentry.* a shingle or clapboard formed by splitting a short log into a number of tapered radial sections with a hatchet. **40.** *Horol.* (in an escapement) the distance between the nearer corner of one pallet and the nearest tooth of the escape wheel when the other pallet arrests an escape tooth. **41.** a dance deriving from the twist. **42. a brace of shakes,** a very short time; a moment: *We'll be ready in a brace of shakes.* **43. no great shakes,** *Informal.* of no particular ability; unimportant; common: *As opera companies go, this one is no great shakes.* **44. two shakes** or **two shakes of a lamb's tail,** a very short time; a moment. [ME; OE *sceac(an);* c. LG *schacken,* Icel *skaka*] —**shak′a·ble, shake′a·ble,** *adj.*

—**Syn. 1.** oscillate, waver. SHAKE, QUIVER, TREMBLE, VIBRATE refer to an agitated movement which, in living things, is often involuntary. To SHAKE is to agitate more or less quickly, abruptly, and often unevenly so as to disturb the poise, stability, or equilibrium of a person or thing: *a pole shaking under his weight.* To QUIVER is to exhibit a slight vibratory motion such as that resulting from disturbed or irregular (surface) tension: *The surface of the pool quivered in the breeze.* To TREMBLE (used more often of a person) is to be agitated by intermittent, involuntary movements of the muscles, much like shivering and caused by fear, cold, weakness, great emotion, etc.: *Even stout hearts tremble with dismay.* To VIBRATE is to exhibit a rapid, rhythmical motion: *A violin string vibrates when a bow is drawn across it.* **2.** shudder, shiver. **14.** daunt.

shake·down (shāk′doun′), *n.* **1.** extortion, as by blackmail or threats of violence. **2.** a thorough search: *a shakedown of prison cells to uncover hidden weapons.* **3.** a bed, as of straw or blankets, spread on the floor. **4.** any makeshift bed. **5.** the act or process of shaking down. —*adj.* **6.** (of a cruise or flight) intended to prepare a new vessel or aircraft for regular service by accustoming the crew to its features and peculiarities, breaking in and adjusting machinery, etc. Also, **shake′-down′.** [n. and adj. use of v. phrase *shake down*]

shake·fork (shāk′fôrk′), *n.* **1.** *Chiefly Dial.* a pitchfork, esp. for shaking off the grains from hay or straw. **2.** *Heraldry.* a charge resembling a pall couped. [ME *schakforke.* See SHAKE, FORK]

shake·out (shāk′out′), *n.* **1.** an elimination of business concerns, products, etc., as a result of intense competition in a market of declining sales or rising standards of quality. **2.** a rapid decline in the values of certain securities sold in stock exchanges or the like. [n. use of v. phrase *shake out*]

shak·er (shā′kər), *n.* **1.** one who or that which shakes. **2.** a container with a perforated top from which a seasoning, condiment, sugar, flour, or the like is shaken onto food. **3.** any of various containers, utensils, or kitchen or bar appliances for shaking beverages in order to mix the ingredients: *a cocktail shaker.* **4.** a dredger or caster. **5.** that with which something is shaken. **6.** (*cap.*) a member of the Millennial Church, originating in England in the middle of the 18th century and brought to the U.S. in 1774, advocating celibacy, common ownership of property, and a strict and simple way of life: so called popularly from the former practice of performing a dance with shaking movements of the body as part of their ritual. [late ME; see SHAKE, -ER[1]]

Shak′er Heights′, a city in NE Ohio, near Cleveland. 36,460 (1960).

Shak·er·ism (shā′kə riz′əm), *n.* the beliefs and practices of the Shakers. [SHAKER + -ISM]

Shake·speare (shāk′spēr), *n.* **William,** 1564–1616, English poet and dramatist. Also, **Shakspere, Shake′spear.**

Shake·spear·e·an (shāk spēr′ē ən), *adj.* **1.** of, pertaining to, or suggestive of Shakespeare or his works. —*n.* **2.** a Shakespearean scholar; a specialist in the study of the works of Shakespeare. Also, **Shake·spear′i·an.** [SHAKESPEARE + -AN] —**Shake·spear′e·an·ism, Shake·spear′i·an·ism,** *n.*

Shakespear′ean son′net, a sonnet form used by Shakespeare and having the rhyme scheme *abab, cdcd, efef, gg.* Also called **English sonnet.**

Shake′speare-Ba′con con′troversy (shāk′spēr bā′kən), a dispute provoked by the theory of Delia Bacon (1811–59) attributing authorship of Shakespeare's plays to Francis Bacon.

shake-up (shāk′up′), *n.* a thorough change in a business, department, or the like, as by dismissals, demotions, etc. [n. use of v. phrase *shake up*]

Shakh·ty (shäḵн′tē), *n.* a city in the SW RSFSR, in the S Soviet Union in Europe, in the Donets Basin. 201,000 (est. 1962).

shak·ing (shā′king), *n.* **1.** the act of one who or that which shakes. **2.** ague, with or without chill and fever. **3. shackings,** *Naut.* waste rope, canvas, etc. [ME; see SHAKE, -ING[1]] —**shak′ing·ly,** *adv.*

Shako

shak′ing pal′sy, *Pathol.* See **Parkinson's disease.**

shak·o (shak′ō, shā′kō), *n., pl.* **shak·os, shak·oes.** a military cap in the form of a cylinder or truncated cone, with a visor and a plume or pompon. [< F *schako* < Hung *csákó* < MHG *zacke* peak, point; see TACK[1]]

Shak·o·pee (shak′ō pē), *n.* a town in central Minnesota. 5201 (1960).

Shaks., Shakespeare.

Shak·spere (shäk′spēr), *n.* **William.** See **Shakespeare.** —**Shak·sper′i·an,** *adj., n.* —**Shak·sper′i·an·ism,** *n.*

Shak·ta (shäk′tə), *n. Hinduism.* one who worships Shakti as the wife of Shiva. Also, **Sakta.** [< Skt *śākta* pertaining to Shakti]

Shak·ti (shuk′tē), *n. Hinduism.* **1.** the female principle or organ of generative power. **2.** the wife of a deity, esp. of Shiva. Cf. **Divine Mother.** Also, **Sakti.** [< Skt *śakti*]

Shak·tism (shäk′tiz əm), *n. Hinduism.* the worship of Shakti as the wife of Shiva. Also, **Saktism.** [SHAKT(I) + -ISM]

sha·ku·do (shä′ko͞o dō′; *Jap.* shä′ko͞o dô′), *n.* an alloy of 97 percent copper and 3 percent gold, used esp. for Japanese sword mounts and treated so as to have a lustrous, black patina. [< Jap < Chin *ch'ih t'ung* red copper]

Sha·kun·ta·la (shə ko͝on′tə lä′), *n.* Sakuntala.

shak·y (shā′kē), *adj.,* **shak·i·er, shak·i·est.** **1.** shaking. **2.** trembling; tremulous. **3.** liable to break down or give way; insecure; not to be depended upon: *a shaky bridge.* **4.** wavering, as in allegiance: *His loyalty, always shaky, was now nonexistent.* [SHAKE + -Y[1]] —**shak′i·ly,** *adv.* —**shak′i·ness,** *n.*

sha·lach mo·noth (shä′läкн mō′nōs, -nəs, shläкн′), *Yiddish.* **1.** the Jewish social custom of giving gifts to one another or to the needy, esp. as one of the main events of the Purim celebration. **2.** any such gift, esp. of dainties, or of money for charity. Also, **sha′lach ma′nosh.** [lit., giving out parts]

shale (shāl), *n.* a rock of fissile or laminated structure formed by the consolidation of clay or argillaceous material. [obs. *shale* to split (said of stone), to shell, ME *shale* SCALE[1], shell, husk, OE *sceal(u)* shell, husk, SCALE[2]] —**shale′like′,** *adj.*

shale′ oil′, petroleum distilled from bituminous shale.

shall (shal; *unstressed* shəl), *auxiliary v., pres. sing. 1st pers.* **shall,** *2nd* **shall** or (*Archaic*) **shalt,** *3rd* **shall,** *pres. pl.* **shall;** *past sing. 1st pers.* **should,** *2nd* **should** or (*Archaic*) **shouldst** or **should·est,** *3rd* **should,** *past pl.* **should;** *imperative, infinitive, and participles lacking.* **1.** (generally used in the first person to denote simple future time) plan to, intend to, or expect to: *I shall go today.* **2.** (generally used in the second and third persons to denote authority or determination) will have to, is determined to, promises to, or definitely will: *You shall do it. He shall do it.* **3.** (used interrogatively in questions that admit of *shall* in the answer): *Shall he be told? He shall.* **4.** (used conditionally in all persons to indicate future time): *if he shall come.* [ME *shal,* OE *sceal;* c. OS *skal,* OHG *scal,* Icel *skal;* cf. G *soll,* D *zal*]

—**Usage.** In formal speech and writing, as well as in the informal speech of some educated speakers, SHALL is restricted to use with the first person, singular and plural: *I shall go. We shall be there.* WILL, in these contexts, is used with the second and third persons: *you, he, she, it,* and *they.* Within this style, SHALL used with pronouns other than *I* and *we* denotes determination or command (*You shall go, even if you don't want to*); it sometimes carries the same force when used with *I* or *we: I shall return.* Although there are some who feel that the meaning "to decide, bring about, or attempt to effect by act of will" is inherent in WILL, it is actually a sense of another word (cf. **will**[1], **will**[2]). Generally, in ordinary speech, SHALL has fallen into disuse, perhaps because its contraction (*'ll*) is indistinguishable from that of WILL.

shal·loon (sha lo͞on′), *n.* a light, twilled woolen fabric used chiefly for linings. [< F *chalon,* after *Châlons-sur-Marne,* where made]

shal·lop (shal′əp), *n.* any of various vessels formerly used for sailing or rowing in shallow waters, esp. a two-masted, gaff-rigged vessel of the 17th and 18th centuries. [< F *chaloupe* < G *Schlupe* SLOOP]

shal·lot (shə lot′), *n.* **1.** a liliaceous plant, *Allium ascalonicum,* whose bulb forms bulblets which are used for flavoring in cookery and as a vegetable. **2.** the bulb or bulblet itself. [< F (*é*)*chalote,* dim. of *eschaloigne* SCALLION]

shal·low (shal′ō), *adj.* **1.** of little depth; not deep: *shallow water; a shallow dish.* **2.** lacking depth; superficial: *a mind that is not narrow but shallow.* **3.** taking in a relatively small amount of air in each inhalation: *shallow breathing.* **4.** *Baseball.* relatively close to home plate: *The shortstop made the catch of the pop fly in shallow left field.* —*n.* **5.** Usually, **shallows.** (*construed as sing. or pl.*) a shallow part of a body of water; shoal. —*adv.* **6.** *Baseball.* at a shallow position: *With the pitcher up, the outfielders played shallow.* —*v.t., v.i.* **7.** to make or become shallow. [ME *schalowe;* akin to OE *sceald* shallow] —**shal′low·ly,** *adv.* —**shal′low·ness,** *n.*

Shal·ma·ne·ser III (shal′mə nē′zər), died 824? B.C., Assyrian ruler 859–824?.

sha·lom (shä lōm′; *Eng.* shə lōm′), *interj. Hebrew.* peace: a conventional Jewish greeting or farewell.

sha·lom a·lei·chem (shä lōm′ ä lā′кнəm, ä lā-кнem′; *Eng.* shə lōm′ ə lā′кнəm, shō′ləm), *Hebrew.* peace to you: a conventional Jewish greeting, the conventional reply being *aleichem shalom.*

sha·losh seu·doth (shä′lōsh so͞o′dōs, -dəs, -ləsh), *Yiddish.* the last of the three prescribed meals taken after *Minhah,* followed by the reassembly in the synagogue to sing psalms before the service in the evening. Also, **sha′losh seu′dos.** [lit., three meals]

shalt (shalt), *v. Archaic.* 2nd pers. sing. of **shall.**

shal·war (shul′wär), *n.* (*construed as pl.*) loose, pajamalike trousers worn by both men and women in India and southeast Asia. Also, **shulwar.** [< Hindi, Urdu < Pers *shalwār*]

shal·y (shā′lē), *adj.* of, like, or containing shale. [SHALE + -Y[1]]

sham (sham), *n., adj., v.,* **shammed, sham·ming.** —*n.* **1.** something that is not what it purports to be; a spurious imitation; fraud. **2.** a cover or the like for giving a thing a different outward appearance: *a pillow sham.* **3.** *Obs.* hoax. —*adj.* **4.** pretended; counterfeit; feigned: *sham attacks; a sham Gothic façade.* **5.** designed, made, or used as a sham. —*v.t.* **6.** to produce an imitation of. **7.** to assume the appearance of; pretend to be: *to sham illness.* —*v.i.* **8.** to make a false show of something; pretend. [?]

—**Syn. 1.** pretense. **4.** spurious, make-believe, simulated, mock. See **false. 6.** imitate. **7.** feign, fake. —**Ant. 4.** genuine.

sha·mal (shə mäl′), *n.* (in Iraq and the Persian Gulf) a hot, dry, and dust-laden wind that blows from the northwest. Also, **shemaal, shimal, shumal.** Also called **barih.** [< Ar: left (hand), north]

sha·man (shä′mən, shā′-, sham′ən), *n.* a medicine man; one, acting as both priest and doctor, who works with the supernatural. [< Turkic, perh. < Chin *shamēn* < Pali *samana* Buddhist monk] —**sha·man·ic** (shə man′ik), *adj.*

sha·man·ism (shä′mə niz′əm, shā′-, sham′ə-), *n.* **1.** the primitive religion of northern Asia, embracing a belief in powerful spirits who can be influenced only by shamans. **2.** any similar religion. [SHAMAN + -ISM] —**sha′man·ist,** *n., adj.* —**sha′man·is′tic,** *adj.*

sha·mash (shä mäsh′), *n., pl.* **sha·ma·shim** (shä′mä-shēm′). *Yiddish.* shammash.

Sha·mash (shä′mäsh), *n.* the Akkadian sun god: the counterpart of the Sumerian Utu.

sham·ble[1] (sham′bəl), *n.* **1.** **shambles,** (*construed as sing. or pl.*) **a.** a slaughterhouse. **b.** any place of carnage. **c.** any scene of destruction: *to turn cities into shambles.* **d.** any scene, place, or thing in disorder: *Her desk is a shambles.* **2.** *Brit. Dial.* a butcher's shop or stall. [ME *shamel,* OE *sc(e)amel* stool, table << LL *scamell(um),* dim. of L *scamnum* bench; cf. G *Schemel*]

sham·ble[2] (sham′bəl), *v.,* **-bled, -bling,** *n.* —*v.i.* **1.** to walk or go awkwardly; shuffle. —*n.* **2.** a shambling gait. [? *shamble-(legs)* one that walks wide (i.e., as if straddling), reminiscent of the legs of a SHAMBLE[1]]

shame (shām), *n., v.,* **shamed, sham·ing.** —*n.* **1.** the painful feeling arising from the consciousness of something dishonorable, improper, ridiculous, etc., done by oneself or another: *He was overcome with shame.* **2.** susceptibility to this feeling: *to be without shame.* **3.** disgrace; ignominy: *His actions brought shame upon his parents.* **4.** a fact or circumstance bringing disgrace or regret: *The bankruptcy of his business was a shame.* **5.** **for shame!** you should feel ashamed!: *What a thing to say to your mother! For shame!* **6.** **put to shame, a.** to cause to suffer shame or disgrace. **b.** to outdo; surpass: *He played so well he put all the other tennis players to shame.* —*v.t.* **7.** to cause to feel shame; make ashamed: *His cowardice shamed him.* **8.** to drive, force, etc., through shame: *He shamed her into going.* **9.** to cover with ignominy or reproach; disgrace. [ME; OE *sc(e)amu;* c. G *Scham,* Icel *skömm*] —**sham′a·ble, shame′a·ble,** *adj.* —**sham′a·ble·ness, shame′a·ble·ness,** *n.* —**sham′a·bly, shame′a·bly,** *adv.*

—**Syn. 1.** SHAME, EMBARRASSMENT, MORTIFICATION, HUMILIATION, CHAGRIN designate different kinds or degrees of painful feeling caused by lowering one's pride or self-respect. SHAME is a painful feeling caused by the consciousness or exposure of unworthy or indecent conduct or circumstances: *One feels shame at being caught in a lie.* It is similar to guilt in the nature and origin of the feeling. EMBARRASSMENT usually refers to a feeling less painful than that of SHAME, one associated with less serious situations, often of a social nature: *embarrassment over breaking a teacup at a party.* MORTIFICATION is a more painful feeling, akin to SHAME but also more likely to arise from specifically social circumstances: *his mortification at being singled out for rebuke.* HUMILIATION is mortification at being humbled in the estimation of others: *Being ignored gives one a sense of humiliation.* CHAGRIN is humiliation mingled with vexation or anger: *He felt chagrin at his failure to remember his promise.* **7.** humiliate, mortify, humble, abash, embarrass. —**Ant. 1.** pride, self-esteem, self-respect.

shame·faced (shām′fāst′), *adj.* **1.** modest or bashful. **2.** showing shame: *shamefaced apologies.* [SHAME + FACE + -ED[3]] —**shame·fac·ed·ly** (shām′fā′sid lē, shām′fāst′lē), *adv.* —**shame′fac′ed·ness,** *n.*

shame·ful (shām′fəl), *adj.* **1.** causing or characterized by causing shame: *shameful behavior.* **2.** disgraceful or scandalous: *shameful treatment.* [ME; OE *scamful.* See SHAME, -FUL] —**shame′ful·ly,** *adv.* —**shame′ful·ness,** *n.*

—**Syn. 1.** mortifying, humiliating. **2.** dishonorable, ignominious, infamous, vile, base, low. —**Ant. 2.** honorable.

shame·less (shām′lis), *adj.* **1.** lacking any sense of shame: immodest; audacious. **2.** insensible to disgrace. **3.** showing no shame. [ME; OE *sceamlēas.* See SHAME, -LESS] —**shame′less·ly,** *adv.* —**shame′less·ness,** *n.*

—**Syn. 1.** unblushing, brazen, indecent, impudent, bold, unabashed, unashamed. **2.** hardened, unprincipled, corrupt. —**Ant. 1.** modest.

Sham·mai (shä′mī), fl. 1st century B.C., Hebrew rabbi: founder of Beth Shammai, school of hermeneutics.

sham·mash (shä mäsh′; *Eng.* shä′məs), *n., pl.* **sham·ma·shim** (shä mä shēm′; *Eng.* shä mō′sim). *Yiddish.* **1.** a synagogue official responsible for keeping the building and religious equipment in proper condition for use, his other duties usually being chiefly to chant on the prescribed days the designated portion of the Torah and assist the cantor in conducting services on festivals; sexton. **2.** the candle used on the Jewish festival of Hanukkah to kindle the other candle or candles in the menorah and set afterwards in a specially reserved branch. Also, **shamash.**

sham·mer (sham′ər), *n.* one who shams. [SHAM + -ER[1]]

sham·my (sham′ē), *n., pl.* **-mies,** *v.,* **-mied, -my·ing.** chamois (defs. 2-4, 6, 7).

Sha·mo (shä′mō′), *n.* Chinese name of the **Gobi.**

Sha·mo·kin (shə mō′kin), *n.* a borough in E Pennsylvania. 13,674 (1960).

sham·oy (sham′ē), *n., pl.* **-oys,** *v.,* **-oyed, -oy·ing.** chamois (defs. 2-4, 6, 7).

sham·poo (sham po͞o′), *v.,* **-pooed, -poo·ing,** *n.* —*v.t.* **1.** to wash (the head or hair), esp. with a cleaning preparation that does not leave a soap film. **2.** to clean (rugs, upholstery, or the like) with a special preparation. **3.** *Archaic.* to massage. —*n.* **4.** the act of shampooing. **5.** a preparation used for shampooing, esp. one that does not leave a soap film. [earlier *champo* < Hindi, deriv. of *cāmpnā* to press] —**sham·poo′er,** *n.*

Shamrock, *Trifolium pratense*

sham·rock (sham′rok), *n.* any of several trifoliate plants, usually a yellow-flowered trefoil, *Trifolium dubium:* the national emblem of Ireland. [< Ir *seamróg* shamrock, trefoil, clover, bunch of green grass, equiv. to *seamar* trefoil, clover + *-óg* dim. suffix]

Sham·rock (sham′rok), *n.* a town in N Texas. 3113 (1960).

sham·rock-pea (sham′rok pē′), *n.* a trailing, herbaceous perennial, *Parochetus communis,* of Asia and east Africa, having shamrocklike leaves with a brown crescent at the base and pea-shaped, pink and blue flowers.

sham·shir (sham shēr′), *n.* a curved Persian saber having one edge on the convex side. [< Pers *shamshīr.* See SCIMITAR]

sha·mus (shä′məs, shā′-), *n., pl.* **-mus·es.** *Slang.* **1.** a detective. **2.** a policeman. [b. *shāmus,* var. of SHAMMASH and *shāmus* Anglicized sp. of Ir *Séamas* James]

Shan (shän, shan), *n., pl.* **Shans,** (*esp. collectively*) **Shan. 1.** a group of Mongoloid tribes in the hills of Burma. **2.** a language spoken in the Shan States and belonging to the Thai group of languages.

shan·dry·dan (shan′drē dan′), *n.* **1.** an old-fashioned hooded chaise. **2.** a rickety, old-fashioned conveyance. [?]

shan·dy (shan′dē), *n.* a mixture of beer and lemonade. [short for SHANDYGAFF]

shan·dy·gaff (shan′dē gaf′), *n. Chiefly Brit.* a mixed drink of beer with ginger beer. [?]

Shang (shäng), *n.* a Chinese dynasty whose dates are usually given as 1766–1122 B.C. and sometimes as 1523–1027 B.C. Also called **Yin.**

shang·hai (shang′hī, shang hī′), *v.t.,* **-haied, -hai·ing.** *Naut.* to enroll or obtain (a sailor) for the crew of a ship by unscrupulous means, as by force or the use of liquor or drugs. [special use of SHANGHAI]

Shang·hai (shang hī′; *Chin.* shäng′hī′), *n.* **1.** a seaport in E China, near the mouth of the Yangtze. 6,900,000 (est. 1957). **2.** a type of long-legged chicken believed to be of Asian origin.

Shan·gri-la (shang′grə lä′, shang′grə lä′), *n.* **1.** a paradise on earth. **2.** an area whose name or location is unknown or not mentioned. [after a hidden paradise in a novel by James Hilton, *Lost Horizon* (1933)]

Shang Ti (shäng′ tē′), the chief of the ancient Chinese gods.

Shan·hai·kwan (shän′hī′gwän′), *n.* former name of **Linyu.**

shank (shangk), *n.* **1.** *Anat.* the part of the lower limb in man between the knee and the ankle; leg. **2.** a corresponding or analogous part in certain animals. See diag. under **horse. 3.** the lower limb in man, including both the leg and the thigh. **4.** a cut of meat from the top part of the front (**fore shank**) or back (**hind shank**) leg of an animal. **5.** a narrow part of various devices, as a tool, bolt, etc., connecting the end by which the object is held or moved with the end which acts upon another object. **6.** a straight, usually narrow, shaftlike part of various objects connecting two more important or complex parts, as the stem of a pipe. **7.** a knob, small projection, or end of a device for attaching to another object, as a small knob on the back of a solid button, the end of a drill for gripping in a shaft, etc. **8.** the long, straight part of an anchor connecting the crown and the ring. **9.** the straight part of a fishhook away from the bent part or prong. See illus. under **fishhook. 10.** *Music.* crook[1] (def. 9). **11.** *Informal.* **a.** the early part of a period of time: *It was just the shank of the evening when the party began.* **b.** the latter part of a period of time: *They didn't get started until the shank of the morning.* **12.** the narrow part of the sole of a shoe, lying beneath the instep. **13.** shankpiece. **14.** *Print.* the body of a type, between the shoulder and the foot. See diag. under **type. 15.** *Golf.* a shot veering sharply to the right after being hit with the base of a club shaft. **16.** the part of a phonograph needle clamped into a phonograph pickup. **17. shank of the evening,** the main or best part of the evening: *Don't leave yet, it's just the shank of the evening.* —*v.t.* **18.** *Golf.* to hit (a golf ball) with the base of the shaft of a club just above the club head, causing the ball to go off sharply to the right. —*v.i.* **19.** (of a leaf, flower, etc.) to fall off because of decay resulting from a disease. **20.** *Chiefly Scot.* to travel on foot. Cf. **shanks' mare.** [ME; OE *sc(e)anca;* c. LG *schanke* leg, thigh; akin to G *Schenkel* thigh, *Schinken* ham]

Shan·kar (shän′kär), *n.* **Ra·vi** (rä′vē), born 1920?, Indian sitarist.

Shan·ka·ra (shung′kər ə), *n.* A.D. 789?–821?, Hindu Vedantist philosopher and teacher. Also, **Sankara.** Also called **Shan·ka·ra·char·ya** (shung′kər ə chär′yə).

shank·piece (shangk′pēs′), *n.* a piece of metal or fiber for giving form to the shank of a shoe. Also called **shank.** [SHANK + PIECE]

shanks′′ mare′, 1. one's own legs, esp. as a means of moving from one place to another: *The only way we can get there is by shanks' mare.* **2. ride shanks' mare,** to go on foot rather than ride; walk: *It was such a delightful day that we decided to ride shanks' mare to the fair.* Also, **shank's′ mare′.** Also called **shanks′′ po′ny, shank's′ po′ny.**

Shan·non (shan′ən), *n.* **1.** a river flowing SW from N Ireland to the Atlantic: the principal river of Ireland. 240 mi. long. **2.** international airport in W Ireland, near Limerick.

Shan·non·town (shan′ən toun′), *n.* a town in central South Carolina. 7064 (1960).

shan·ny (shan′ē), *n., pl.* **-nies. 1.** a scaleless blenny, *Blennius pholis,* found along the coast of Europe, having an olive-green body marked with dark spots. **2.** any of several pricklebacks, esp. *Lumpenus maculatus.* [?]

Shan·si (shän′sē′), *n.* a province in N China. 15,960,000 (est. 1957); 60,656 sq. mi. *Cap.:* Taiyüan.

Shan′ States′ (shän, shan), two groups of native states (**North′ern Shan′ State′** and **South′ern Shan′ State′**), in E Burma, along the Salween River. 1,987,000 (est. 1956); ab. 56,000 sq. mi. Cf. **Burma.**

shan't (shant, shänt), contraction of *shall not.*

shan·ti (shän′tē), *n. Hinduism.* peace. Also, **shan′tih.** [< Skt *shānti*h]

shan·tey (shan′tē), *n., pl.* **-teys.** chantey.

Shan·tung (shan′tung′ *or, for 3,* shan′tung′; *for 1, 2, also Chin.* shän′-dōōng′), *n.* **1.** a maritime province in NE China. 54,030,000 (est. 1957); 59,189 sq. mi. *Cap.:* Tsinan. **2.** a peninsula in the E part of this province, extending into the Yellow Sea. **3.** (*often l.c.*) *Textiles.* **a.** a heavy pongee. Cf. **tussah. b.** a fabric imitating this, of rayon or cotton.

shan·ty[1] (shan′tē), *n., pl.* **-ties,** *adj., v.,* **-tied, -ty·ing.** —*n.* **1.** a crudely built hut, cabin, or house. —*adj.* **2.** of, pertaining to, or constituting a shanty or shanties: *a shanty quarter outside the town walls.* **3.** of a low economic or social class, esp. when living in a shanty: *shanty people.* —*v.i.* **4.** to inhabit a shanty. [prob. < CanF *chantier* shed, workshop, log hut < L *canthēr(ius)* framework < Gk *kanthḗlios* pack ass] —**shan′ty·like′,** *adj.*
—**Syn. 1.** See **cottage.**

shan·ty[2] (shan′tē), *n., pl.* **-ties.** chantey.

shan·ty·town (shan′tē toun′), *n.* **1.** a section, as of a city or town, characterized by shanties and crudely built houses. **2.** a whole town or city that is chiefly made up of shantylike houses. [SHANTY[1] + TOWN]

Shao·hing·fu (shou′shing′fōō′), *n.* a city in NE Chekiang, in E China. 93,000 (est. 1950).

shape (shāp), *n., v.,* **shaped, shap·ing.** —*n.* **1.** the quality of a distinct object or body in having an external surface or outline of specific form or figure. **2.** this quality as found in some individual object or body form: *This lake has a peculiar shape.* **3.** something seen in outline, as in silhouette: *A vague shape appeared through the mist.* **4.** an imaginary form; phantom. **5.** an assumed appearance; guise: *an angel in the shape of a woman.* **6.** a particular or definite organized form or expression: *He could give no shape to his ideas.* **7.** proper form; orderly arrangement. **8.** condition or state of repair: *The old house was in bad shape. He was sick last year, but is in good shape now.* **9.** the collective conditions forming a way of life or mode of existence: *What will the shape of the future be?* **10.** the figure, physique, or body of a person, esp. of a woman considered as an object of sexual attraction: *She's ugly, but she's got a great shape.* **11.** something used to give form, as a mold or a pattern. **12.** Also called **section.** *Building Trades, Metalworking.* a flanged metal beam or bar of uniform section, as a channel iron, I-beam, etc. **13.** *Naut.* a ball, cone, drum, etc., used as a day signal, singly or in combinations, to designate a vessel at anchor or engaged in some particular operation. **14. take shape,** to assume a fixed form; become definite: *The house is beginning to take shape.* [ME; OE *gesceapu* (pl.); r. ME *shap,* OE *(ge)sceap* (sing.); c. Icel *skap* state, mood]
—*v.t.* **15.** to give definite form, shape, organization, or character to; fashion or form. **16.** to couch or express in words: *to shape a statement.* **17.** to adjust; adapt: *He shaped everything to suit his taste.* **18.** to direct (one's course, future, etc.). **19.** to file the teeth of (a saw) to uniform width after jointing. **20.** *Obs.* to appoint; decree. —*v.i.* **21.** to come to a desired conclusion or take place in a specified way: *If discussions shape properly, the companies will merge.* **22. shape up,** *Informal.* **a.** to assume a specific form: *The plan is beginning to shape up.* **b.** to evolve or develop, esp. favorably: *The football team is shaping up.* **c.** (of longshoremen) to get into a line or formation in order to be assigned the day's work. [ME; OE *sceape(n)* (ptp.); r. ME *sheppe, shippe,* OE *sceppa(n), scyppan;* c. Icel *skepja,* Goth *-skapjan,* G *schaffen* to make] —**shap′a·ble, shape′a·ble,** *adj.*
—**Syn. 1.** silhouette, appearance. See **form. 4.** specter, illusion. **7.** order, pattern. **8.** order, situation. **15.** mold, model.

Shapes (def. 12) A, Angle iron; B, Channel iron; C, Z-bar; D, T-bar; E, H-beam; F, I-beam

SHAPE (shāp), *n.* Supreme Headquarters Allied Powers, Europe. Also, **Shape** (shāp).

shaped (shāpt), *adj. Furniture.* having other than a plane surface. [SHAPE + -ED[2]]

shaped′ charge′, *Mil.* a warhead having a concave, hollow end and operating on the Munroe effect.

shape·less (shāp′lis), *adj.* **1.** having no definite or regular shape or form: *a shapeless mass of clay.* **2.** lacking beauty or elegance of form. [SHAPE + -LESS; r. ME *scapeles*] —**shape′less·ly,** *adv.* —**shape′less·ness,** *n.*

shape·ly (shāp′lē), *adj.,* **-li·er, -li·est.** having a pleasing shape, esp. with reference to a woman's figure. [SHAPE + -LY; r. ME *shaply, schaply;* cf. OE *gesceaplīce* (adv.) fitly] —**shape′li·ness,** *n.*

shap·er (shā′pər), *n.* **1.** one who or that which shapes. **2.** a machine tool for forming flat surfaces, consisting of a frame, usually horizontal, on which the work is held while a cutting tool moves along it with a reciprocating motion. Cf. **planer** (def. 2). [SHAPE + -ER[1]]

shape-up (shāp′up′), *n.* a former method of hiring longshoremen in which the applicants appeared daily at the docks and a union hiring boss chose those who would be given work. [n. use of v. phrase *shape up*]

Sha·pi·ro (shə pēr′ō), *n.* **Karl (Jay),** born 1913, U.S. poet and editor.

shap·ka (shäp′kə), *n.* a round, slightly tapered, brimless fur hat worn esp. in the Soviet Union. [< Russ]

Shap·ley (shap′lē), *n.* **Har·low** (här′lō), born 1885, U.S. astronomer.

Sha·ra (shär′ə), *n., pl.* **-ras,** (*esp. collectively*) **-ra.** Sharra.

Sha·ra·ku (shä rä′kōō), *n.* **Ta·shu·sai** (tô′shōō sī′), fl. 18th century, Japanese printmaker.

shard (shärd), *n.* **1.** a fragment, esp. of broken earthenware. **2.** *Zool.* **a.** a scale. **b.** a shell, as of an egg or snail. **3.** *Entomol.* an elytron of a beetle. Also, **sherd.** [ME; OE *sceard;* c. LG, D *schaard;* akin to SHEAR]

Shar·da·na (shär dä′nə), *n., pl.* **-na.** a member of an ancient people of the eastern Mediterranean who served as mercenaries in the Egyptian army and may have settled in Sardinia and Sicily.

share[1] (shâr), *n., v.,* **shared, shar·ing.** —*n.* **1.** the full or proper portion or part allotted or belonging to or contributed or owed by an individual or group. **2.** one of the equal fractional parts into which the capital stock of a joint-stock company or a corporation is divided. **3. on** or **upon shares,** on the principal of sharing the profits or losses of an undertaking: *They agreed to work on shares.* —*v.t.* **4.** to divide and distribute in shares; apportion. **5.** to use, participate in, enjoy, receive, etc., jointly: *The two chemists shared the Nobel prize.* —*v.i.* **6.** to have a share or part; take part (often fol. by *in*). **7.** to divide, apportion, or receive equally. [ME; OE *scear(u)* cutting, division; c. D *schaar,* G *Schar* troop. See SHEAR] —**shar′a·ble, share′a·ble,** *adj.* —**shar′er,** *n.*
—**Syn. 1.** allotment, allocation; contribution, assessment; quota, lot. **4.** allot, parcel out, deal out, dole, mete. **6.** SHARE, PARTAKE, PARTICIPATE mean to join with others or to receive in common with others. To SHARE is to give or receive a part of something, or to enjoy or assume something in common: *to share in another's experiences.* To PARTAKE is to take for one's own personal use a portion of something: *to partake of food.* To PARTICIPATE is esp. to join with others in some thought, feeling, or, particularly, some action: *to participate in a race, in a conversation.*

share[2] (shâr), *n.* a plow share. [ME; OE *scear;* c. G *Schar.* See SHEAR]

share·crop (shâr′krop′), *v.t., v.i.,* **-cropped, -crop·ping.** to farm as a sharecropper. [back formation from SHARECROPPER]

share·crop·per (shâr′krop′ər), *n.* a tenant farmer who pays as rent a share of the crop. [SHARE[1] + CROPPER]

share·hold·er (shâr′hōl′dər), *n.* a holder or owner of shares, esp. in a company or corporation. [SHARE[1] + HOLDER]

Sha·rett (shə ret′), *n.* **Mo·she** (mō′shə), (*Moshe Shertok*), 1894–1965, Israeli statesman, born in Russia: prime minister 1953–55. Also, **Sha·ret′.**

Sha·ri (shä′rē), *n.* a river in N central Africa, flowing NW from the Central African Republic into Lake Chad. 1400 mi. long. Also, **Chari.**

sha·ri·'ah (shä rē′ä), *n. Islam.* law, seen as deriving from the Koran, from the Sunna, and from human opinions and traditions. [< Ar]

sha·rif (shə rēf′), *n.* a descendant of Muhammad through his daughter Fatima. [var. of SHERIF]

shark[1] (shärk), *n.* any of a group of elongate elasmobranch, mostly marine, fishes, certain species of which are large and ferocious, and destructive to other fishes and sometimes dangerous to man. [?] —**shark′like′,** *adj.*

shark[2] (shärk), *n.* **1.** a person who preys greedily on others, as by cheating or usury. **2.** *Slang.* a person who has unusual ability in a particular field. —*v.t.* **3.** to obtain by trickery or fraud; steal. —*v.i.* **4.** to live by shifts and stratagems. [< G dial. *Schork,* var. of *Schurke* rascal]

shark′ pi′lot. See **banded rudderfish.**

shark·skin (shärk′skin′), *n.* **1.** a smooth fabric of acetate or rayon with a dull or chalklike appearance, for apparel. **2.** a fine worsted fabric in twill weave, compact in texture and light to medium in weight, for suits. [SHARK[1] + SKIN]

shark·suck·er (shärk′suk′ər), *n.* any of several remoras, as *Echeneis naucrates,* usually found attached to sharks. [SHARK[1] + SUCKER]

Shar·leen (shär lēn′), *n.* a girl's given name. Also, **Charleen.**

Shar·on (shar′ən), *n.* **1.** a fertile coastal plain in ancient Palestine. **2.** a city in W Pennsylvania. 25,267 (1960). **3.** a town in E Massachusetts. 5888 (1960). **4.** Also, **Shar′en, Shar′yn.** a girl's given name.

Shar′on Hill′, a town in SE Pennsylvania. 7123 (1960).

Shar·on·ville (shar′ən vil), *n.* a town in SW Ohio. 3890 (1960).

Shar′on West′, a town in NE Ohio. 3365 (1960).

sharp (shärp), *adj.* **1.** having a thin cutting edge or a fine point; well-adapted for cutting or piercing: *a sharp knife.* **2.** terminating in an edge or point; not blunt or rounded: *The table had sharp corners.* **3.** involving a sudden or abrupt change in direction or course: *a sharp curve in the road; The car made a sharp turn.* **4.** abrupt, as an ascent: *a sharp drop.* **5.** consisting of angular lines and pointed forms or of thin, long features: *He had a sharp face.* **6.** clearly defined; distinct: *a sharp photographic image.* **7.** distinct or marked, as a contrast: *sharp differences of opinion.* **8.** pungent or biting in taste: *a sharp cheese.* **9.** piercing or shrill in sound: *a sharp cry.* **10.** keenly cold, as weather: *a sharp, biting wind.* **11.** intensely painful; distressing: *sharp pain.* **12.** merciless, caustic, or harsh: *sharp words.* **13.** fierce or violent: *a sharp struggle.* **14.** keen or eager: *sharp desire.* **15.** quick, brisk or spirited. **16.** alert or vigilant: *They kept a sharp watch for the enemy.* **17.** mentally acute: *a sharp lad who will be an asset to the firm.* **18.** shrewd or astute: *sharp at making a bargain.* **19.** shrewd to the point of dishonesty: *sharp practice.* **20.** *Music.* **a.** (of a tone) raised a half step in pitch: *F sharp.* **b.** above an intended pitch, as a note; too high. **21.** *Slang.* ostentatiously stylish: *a sharp dresser; a sharp jacket.* **22.** *Radio, Electronics.* of, relating to, or responsive to a very narrow range of frequencies. Cf. **broadband. 23.** *Phonet.* fortis; voiceless. **24.** composed of hard, angular grains, as sand. —*v.t.* **25.** *Music.* to raise in pitch, esp. by one chromatic half step. —*v.i.* **26.** to sound above the true pitch. —*adv.* **27.** keenly or acutely. **28.** abruptly or suddenly: *to pull a horse up sharp.* **29.** punctually: *Meet me at one o'clock sharp.* **30.** vigilantly. **31.** briskly; quickly. **32.** *Music.* above the true pitch: *You're singing a little sharp.* —*n.* **33.** something sharp. **34.** a needle with a very sharp point: *a packet of cast-steel sharps.* **35.** a sharper. **36.** *Informal.* an expert. **37.** *Music.* **a.** a tone one chromatic half step above a given tone. **b.** (in musical notation) the symbol ♯ indicating this. [ME; OE *scearp;* c. G *scharf;* akin to Ir *cearb* a cut (n.), keen (adj.)] —**sharp′ly,** *adv.* —**sharp′ness,** *n.*
—**Syn. 1.** SHARP, KEEN refer to the edge or point of an instrument, tool, and the like. SHARP applies, in general, to a cutting edge or a point capable of piercing: *a sharp knife, razor.* KEEN is esp. applied to long edges, as of a saber: *a keen sword blade.* **6.** clear. **8.** acrid, bitter, piquant, sour. **10.** piercing, nipping, biting. **11.** severe, excruciating. **12.** unmerciful, cutting, acid, acrimonious, pointed, biting. **16.** attentive. **17.** clever, discriminating, discerning, perspicacious. SHARP, KEEN, QUICK may be applied figuratively to mental qualities. SHARP implies an acute, sensitive, alert, penetrating quality: *a sharp mind.* KEEN implies observant, incisive, and vigorous: *a keen intellect.* INTELLIGENT means not only acute, alert, and active, but also able to reason and understand: *an intelligent reader.* QUICK suggests lively and rapid comprehension, prompt response to instruction, and the like: *quick at figures.* **19.** shady, deceitful. —**Ant. 1.** dull.

Sharp (shärp), *n.* **William** ("*Fiona Macleod*"), 1855?–1905, Scottish poet and critic.

Sharp (shärp), *n.* a crater in the second quadrant of the face of the moon: about 22 miles in diameter.

sharp·bill (shärp′bil′), *n.* a passerine bird, *Oxyruncus cristatus,* of New World tropical forests, having greenish plumage and a pointed bill, related to the tyrant flycatchers. [SHARP + BILL[2]]

sharp-cut (shärp′kut′), *adj.* **1.** cut so as to have a sharp edge: *a tool with a sharp-cut blade.* **2.** distinctly outlined; clearly defined.

sharp-eared (shärp′ērd′), *adj.* **1.** having pointed ears. **2.** having keen or sensitive hearing.

sharp-edged (shärp′ejd′), *adj.* **1.** having a fine edge or edges. **2.** acute and caustic: *a sharp-edged wit.* [OE *scearpecgedne*]

sharp·en (shär′pən), *v.t., v.i.* to make or become sharp or sharper. [SHARP + -EN[1]] —**sharp′en·er,** *n.*

sharp·er (shär′pər), *n.* **1.** a shrewd swindler. **2.** a professional gambler. Also, **sharpie.** [SHARP + -ER[1]]

sharp-eyed (shärp′īd′), *adj.* having keen sight or perception.

sharp-fanged (shärp′fangd′), *adj.* **1.** having sharp fangs or teeth. **2.** cutting or sarcastic; biting: *sharp-fanged remarks.*

sharp-freeze (shärp′frēz′), *v.t.,* **-froze, -fro·zen, -freez·ing.** quick-freeze.

sharp·ie (shär′pē), *n.* **1.** a long, flat-bottomed boat having a triangular sail on one or two masts, formerly used along the northern Atlantic coast of the U.S. **2.** sharper. **3.** a very alert person. **4.** *Slang.* an ostentatiously stylish person. Also, **sharpy.** [SHARP + -IE]

sharp-nosed (shärp′nōzd′), *adj.* **1.** having a thin, pointed nose. **2.** having a sharp or projecting front: *a sharp-nosed airplane.* **3.** having a keen or sensitive sense of smell. —**sharp-nosed·ly** (shärp′nōzd′lē, -nō′zid-), *adv.* —**sharp′-nosed′ness,** *n.*

Sharps·burg (shärps′bûrg), *n.* **1.** a town in NW Maryland: nearby is the site of the battle of Antietam 1862. **2.** a town in SW Pennsylvania. 6096 (1960).

sharp-set (shärp′set′), *adj.* **1.** eager to satisfy the appetite, esp. for food. **2.** keen or eager. **3.** set to present a sharply angled edge. —**sharp′-set′ness,** *n.*

sharp′-shinned hawk′ (shärp′shind′), a North American hawk, *Accipiter striatus,* having extremely slender legs, a bluish-gray back, and a white, rusty barred breast.

sharp·shoot·er (shärp′shōō′tər), *n.* **1.** one skilled in shooting, esp. with a rifle. **2.** *Mil.* **a.** a rating below expert and above marksman, assigned to one who has qualified with a specific score in rifle marksmanship. **b.** a person who has achieved such a rating. **3.** an athlete noted for the accuracy of his aim in a sport, as basketball, hockey, archery, golf, etc. **4.** *Slang.* one who engages in short-term business dealings with the purpose of making a large, quick profit without regard to scruple. **5.** *Naut.* **a.** a fast schooner built in the area around Essex, Mass., in the middle of the 19th century, used by New England fishermen for illegal fishing in Canadian waters. **b.** a catboat or dinghy having a jib-headed sail with a loose foot. [SHARP (i.e., sharp-eyed) + SHOOTER; cf. G *Scharfschütz(e)* expert marksman] —**sharp′shoot′ing,** *n.*

sharp-sight·ed (shärp′sī′tid), *adj.* **1.** having keen sight. **2.** having or showing mental acuteness. —**sharp′-sight′ed·ly,** *adv.* —**sharp′-sight′ed·ness,** *n.*

Sharps·ville (shärps′vil), *n.* a town in W Pennsylvania. 6061 (1960).

sharp′-tailed grouse′ (shärp′tāld′), a grouse, *Pedioecetes phasianellus,* of prairies and open forests of western North America, similar in size to the prairie chicken but with a more pointed tail.

sharp′-tailed spar′row, a sparrow, *Ammospiza caudacuta,* found in salt marshes in North America, having narrow, sharply pointed tail feathers.

sharp′tail mo′la (shärp′tāl′), a fish, *Masturus lanceolatus,* related to the ocean sunfish but having a pointed tail. Also called **headfish.** [SHARP + TAIL[1]]

sharp-tongued (shärp′tungd′), *adj.* characterized by or given to harshness, bitterness, or sarcasm in speech.

sharp-wit·ted (shärp′wit′id), *adj.* having or showing mental acuity; intellectually discerning; acute. **—sharp′-wit′ted·ly,** *adv.* **—sharp′-wit′ted·ness,** *n.*

sharp·y (shär′pē), *n, pl.* **sharp·ies.** sharpie.

Shar·ra (shär′ə), *n., pl.* **-ras,** (*esp. collectively*) **-ra.** **1.** a member of a Mongol people inhabiting Outer Mongolia. **2.** the language of the Sharras.

Shar·rie (shar′ē), *n.* a girl's given name, form of **Sharon.**

shash·lik (shäsh lik′, shäsh′lik), *n.* See **shish kebab.** Also, **shash·lick′, shas·lik′.** [< Russ < some Turkic dial.; see SHISH KEBAB]

Shas·ta (shas′tə), *n.* **Mount,** a volcanic peak in N California, in the Cascade Range. 14,161 ft.

Shas′ta cy′press. See **macnab cypress.**

Shas′ta dai′sy, any of several horticultural varieties of *Chrysanthemum maximum,* having large, daisylike flowers. [named after Mt. SHASTA]

shas·tra (shäs′trə), *n.* any of the sacred books of Hinduism. [< Skt: lore] **—shas′trik, shas·tra·ik** (shä strä′ik), *adj.*

shas·tra·ca·ra (shäs′trä kä′rə), *n.* *Hinduism.* an action in accordance with the principles of the shastras. [< Skt]

Shas·tri (shäs′trē), *n.* **Lal Ba·ha·dur** (läl bä-hä′dŏŏr), 1904–66, Indian statesman: prime minister 1964–66.

Shatt-al-A·rab (shat′-al är′äb), *n.* a river in SE Iraq, formed by the junction of the Tigris and Euphrates rivers, flowing SE to the Persian Gulf. 123 mi. long.

shat·ter (shat′ər), *v.t.* **1.** to break (something) into pieces, as by a blow. **2.** to damage, as by breaking or crushing: *ships shattered by storms.* **3.** to impair or destroy (health, nerves, etc.): *The incident shattered his composure.* **4.** to weaken, destroy, or refute (ideas, opinions, etc.): *He wanted to shatter her illusions.* **—*v.i.*** **5.** to be broken into fragments or become weak or insubstantial. **—*n.*** **6.** Usually, **shatters.** *Chiefly Dial.* fragments made by shattering. [ME *schater(en)* < ?; cf. SCATTER] **—shat′ter·er,** *n.* **—shat′ter·ing·ly,** *adv.*
—Syn. 1. shiver, split, crack. See **break.**

shat·ter·proof (shat′ər prŏŏf′), *adj.* designed or made to resist shattering: *shatterproof glass in automobile windows.* [SHATTER + -PROOF]

Shaun (shôn), *n.* a boy's given name, form of **John.**

shave (shāv), *v.,* **shaved, shaved** or **shav·en, shav·ing,** *n.* **—*v.i.*** **1.** to remove a growth of beard with a razor. **—*v.t.*** **2.** to remove hair from (the face, legs, etc.) by cutting it off close to the skin with a razor. **3.** to cut off (hair, esp. the beard) close to the skin with a razor (often fol. by *off* or *away*). **4.** to cut or scrape away the surface of with a sharp-edged tool: *to shave hides in preparing leather.* **5.** to reduce to shavings or thin slices: *to shave wood.* **6.** to cut or trim closely: *to shave a lawn.* **7.** to scrape, graze, or come very near to: *The car just shaved the garage door.* **8.** to purchase (a note) at a rate of discount greater than is legal or customary. **9.** to reduce or deduct from: *The store shaved the price of winter suits in the spring.* **—*n.*** **10.** the act, process, or an instance of shaving or being shaved. **11.** a thin slice; shaving. **12.** any of various tools for shaving, scraping, removing thin slices, etc. [ME; OE *sceafan;* c. D *schaven* to plane (a plank), abrade (the skin), LG *schaven,* G *schaben,* Icel *skafa* to scrape, Goth *skaban* to shear, shave] **—shav′a·ble, shave′a·ble,** *adj.*

shave·ling (shāv′ling), *n.* **1.** *Often Disparaging.* a head-shaven clergyman. **2.** young fellow; youngster. [SHAVE + -LING[1]]

shav·en (shā′vən), *v.* **1.** a pt. of **shave.** **—*adj.*** **2.** closely trimmed.

shav·er (shā′vər), *n.* **1.** one who or that which shaves. **2.** an electric razor. **3.** *Informal.* a small boy; youngster. **4.** a fellow. **5.** one who makes close bargains or is extortionate. [late ME; see SHAVE, -ER[1]; cf. *chip off the old block*]

shave·tail (shāv′tāl′), *n.* *Slang.* **1.** *U.S. Army.* a second lieutenant. **2.** a young, newly-broken mule. [SHAVE + TAIL[1]; first said of unbroken army mules, whose tails were shaved to mark them as raw recruits]

Sha·vi·an (shā′vē ən), *adj.* **1.** of, pertaining to, or characteristic of George Bernard Shaw or his works: *Shavian humor.* **—*n.*** **2.** a specialist in the study of the works of George Bernard Shaw. [*Shav-* (Latinization of SHAW) + -IAN] **—Sha′vi·an·ism,** *n.*

Sha·vi·an·a (shā′vē an′ə, -ä′nə), *n.pl.* collected items pertaining to George Bernard Shaw. [SHAVIAN + L *-a* neut. pl. n. suffix; see -IANA]

shav·ie (shā′vē), *n.* *Scot.* a trick or prank. [special use of SHAVE swindle + -IE]

shav·ing (shā′ving), *n.* **1.** Often, **shavings.** a very thin piece or slice, esp. of wood. **2.** the act of one who or that which shaves. [ME; see SHAVE, -ING[1]]

shav′ing brush′, a short, cylindrical brush with long, soft, bristles, used in lathering the face before shaving.

shav′ing cream′, a preparation, as of soap and free fatty acid, that is lathered and applied to the face to soften and condition the beard for shaving.

shav′ing horse′, *Carpentry.* a trestle for supporting and steadying a piece of work being shaved.

shav′ing soap′, a special soap for lathering the face to soften and condition the beard for shaving, capable of producing a thick lather due to its high fat content and low alkalinity.

Sha·vu·oth (shə vōō′ōs, -əs), *n.* *Judaism.* Shabuoth.

shaw (shô), *n.* **1.** *Dial.* a small wood or thicket. **2.** *Scot.* the stalks and leaves of potatoes, turnips, and other cultivated root plants. [ME *shawe,* OE *sceaga, scaga;* akin to SHAG[1]]

Shaw (shô), *n.* **1. George Bernard,** 1856–1950, Irish dramatist, critic, and novelist: Nobel prize 1925. **2. Henry Wheeler** ("*Josh Billings*"), 1818–85, U.S. humorist. **3. Irwin,** born 1913, U.S. dramatist and author. **4. Richard Norman,** 1831–1912, English architect, born in Scotland. **5. Thomas Edward.** See **Lawrence, Thomas Edward.**

sha·wab·ti (shə wab′tē), *n.* a figurine placed in an ancient Egyptian tomb to serve as a slave for the soul or as a substitute for the soul in performing forced labor. Also, **ushabti.** [< Egypt *swbty,* var. of *wšbty*]

Sha·wa·no (shô′wə nō′, shô′nō), *n.* **1.** a town in NE Wisconsin. 6103 (1960).

shawl (shôl), *n.* a square, triangular, or oblong piece of wool or other material worn, esp. by women, about the shoulders, or the head and shoulders, in place of a coat or hat outdoors, and indoors as protection against chill or dampness. [< Pers *shāl*] **—shawl′less,** *adj.* **—shawl′like′,** *adj.*

shawl′ col′lar, a collar, attached to and reversed upon the garment, having a more or less rounded open edge and reaching usually to the waist or just below, where the two ends either meet, as on some single-breasted dinner jackets, or cross, as on a bathrobe, smoking jacket, or the like.

shawm (shôm), *n.* an early musical woodwind instrument with a double reed: the forerunner of the modern oboe. [late ME *schalme* < MF *chaume* < L *calam(us)* stalk, reed < Gk *kálamos* reed; r. ME *schallemele* < MF *chalemel;* c. ML *calamella* flageolet, dim. of L *calamus* stalk, reed-pipe]

Shawn (shôn), *n.* **1. Ted** (*Edwin M.*), born 1891, U.S. dancer and choreographer (husband of Ruth St. Denis). **2.** a boy's or girl's given name.

Shaw·nee (shô nē′), *n., pl.* **-nees,** (*esp. collectively*) **-nee.** **1.** a member of an Algonquian-speaking tribe formerly in the east-central U.S., now in Oklahoma. **2.** the Algonquian language of the Shawnee tribe. **3.** a city in central Oklahoma. 24,326 (1960). **4.** a town in E Kansas. 9072 (1960). [back formation from *Shawanese* < Algonquian *shawun* south + -ESE]

Shaw′nee sal′ad, waterleaf (def. 2).

Shaw·wal (shə wäl′), *n.* the tenth month of the Islamic calendar. [< Ar]

shay (shā), *n.* *Chiefly Dial.* a chaise. [back formation from CHAISE taken for plural]

Shays (shāz), *n.* **Daniel,** 1747–1825, American Revolutionary War soldier: leader of Shays' Rebellion.

Shays′ Rebel′lion, a popular insurrection (1786–87) in Massachusetts, led principally by Daniel Shays.

Sha·zar (shä zär′, sha-), *n.* **Zal·man** (zäl′män), (*Shneor Zalman Rubashev*), born 1889, Israeli statesman, born in Russia: president since 1963.

Shcher·ba·kov (shcher′bə kôf′), *n.* a city in the W RSFSR in the central Soviet Union in Europe, NNE of Moscow, on the Volga. 195,000 (est. 1962). Formerly, **Rybinsk.**

she (shē), *pron., sing. nom.* **she,** *poss.* **her** or **hers,** *obj.* **her;** *pl. nom.* **they,** *poss.* **their** or **theirs,** *obj.* **them;** *n., pl.* **shes.** **—*pron.*** **1.** the female in question or last mentioned. **2.** the woman: *She who listens learns.* **3.** anything considered, as by personification, to be feminine: *spring, with all the memories she conjures up.* **—*n.*** **4.** a woman or female. **5.** an object or device considered as female or feminine. [ME, sandhi var. of *ghe,* OE *hēo.* See HE[1]]

she-, a combining form of **she:** *she-wolf.*

shea (shē), *n.* See **shea tree.** [< Mandingo *sye*]

shea′ but′ter, a solid, greenish, yellowish, or whitish fat derived from the seeds of the shea tree, used for food and in the manufacture of soaps and candles.

sheaf (shēf), *n., pl.* **sheaves,** *v.* **—*n.*** **1.** one of the bundles in which cereal plants, as wheat, rye, etc., are bound after reaping. **2.** any bundle, cluster, or collection: *a sheaf of papers.* **—*v.t.*** **3.** to bind (something) into a sheaf or sheaves. [ME *shefe,* OE *scēaf;* c. D *schoof* sheaf, G *Schaub* wisp of straw, Icel *skauf* tail of a fox] **—sheaf′-like′,** *adj.*

sheal·ing (shē′ling), *n.* *Scot.* shieling.

shear (shēr), *v.,* **sheared** or (*esp. Dial.*) **shore; sheared** or **shorn; shear·ing,** *n.* **—*v.t.*** **1.** to cut (something). **2.** to remove by or as if by cutting or clipping with a sharp instrument: *to shear wool from sheep.* **3.** to cut or clip the hair, fleece, wool, etc., from: *to shear sheep.* **4.** to strip or deprive (usually fol. by *of*): *to shear someone of his power.* **5.** *Chiefly Scot.* to reap with a sickle. **6.** to travel through by or as by cutting: *Chimney swifts sheared the air.* **—*v.i.*** **7.** to cut or cut through something with a sharp instrument. **8.** to progress by or as by cutting: *The cruiser sheared through the water.* **9.** *Mech.* to become fractured under a load due to sliding action. **10.** *Chiefly Scot.* to reap crops with a sickle. **—*n.*** **11.** Usually, **shears.** (*sometimes construed as sing.*) **a.** Also called scissors of large size (usually used with *pair of*). **b.** any of various other cutting implements or machines having two blades that resemble or suggest those of scissors. **12.** the act or process of shearing or being sheared. **13.** a shearing of sheep (used in stating the age of sheep): *a sheep of one shear.* **14.** the quantity, esp. of wool or fleece, cut off at one shearing. **15.** one blade of a pair of large scissors. **16.** Usually, **shears.** (*sometimes construed as sing.*) Also, **sheers.** Also called **shear legs.** a framework for hoisting heavy weights, consisting of two or more spars with their legs separated, fastened together near the top and steadied by guys, which support a tackle. **17.** a machine for cutting rigid material, as metal in sheet or plate form, by moving the edge of a blade through it. **18.** *Mech.* the tendency produced by loads to deform or fracture a member by sliding one section against another. **19.** *Physics.* the lateral deformation produced in a body by an external force, expressed as the ratio of the lateral displacement between two points lying in parallel planes to the vertical distance between the planes. [ME *shere(n),* OE *sceran;* c. D, G *scheren,* Icel *skera*] **—shear′er,** *n.* **—shear′less,** *adj.*

sheared (shērd), *adj.* **1.** shaped or completed by or as by shearing. **2.** trimmed to an even, symmetrical, or uniform length, as fur, shrubbery, etc.: *a sheared muskrat coat.* [SHEAR + -ED[2]]

shear·hog (shēr′og), *n.* *Brit. Dial.* a sheep after its first shearing. [SHEAR + HOG]

shear′ legs′, shear (def. 16). Also, **sheerlegs.**

shear·ling (shēr′ling), *n.* **1.** *Chiefly Brit.* a yearling sheep that has been shorn once. **2.** short wool pulled from such a sheep. **3.** the skin from a recently shorn sheep or lamb, tanned with the wool still on it. [ME *scherling.* See SHEAR, -LING[1]]

shear′ mod′ulus, *Physics.* a coefficient of elasticity of a substance, expressing the ratio between the force per unit area **(shear′ing stress′)** that laterally deforms the substance and the shear **(shear′ing strain′)** that is produced by this force. Also called **modulus of rigidity.**

shear′ transforma′tion, *Math.* a map of a coordinate space in which one coordinate is held fixed and the other coordinate or coordinates are shifted.

shear·wa·ter (shēr′wô′tər, -wot′ər), *n.* any of several long-winged sea birds, esp. of the genus *Puffinus,* allied to the petrels, that appear to shear the water with their wings when flying low. [SHEAR + WATER]

sheat·fish (shēt′fish′), *n., pl.* **-fish·es,** (*esp. collectively*) **-fish.** a large, fresh-water catfish, *Silurus glanis,* found in central and eastern Europe, sometimes reaching a weight of 400 pounds. [dissimilated var. of *sheath-fish;* see SHEATH (false trans. of G *Scheide* sheatfish), FISH]

sheath (shēth), *n., pl.* **sheaths** (shēthz), *v.* **—*n.*** **1.** a case or covering for the blade of a sword, dagger, or the like. **2.** any similar close-fitting covering or case. **3.** *Biol.* a closely enveloping part or structure, as in an animal or plant organism. **4.** *Bot.* the leaf base when it forms a vertical coating surrounding the stem. **5.** a close-fitting dress, skirt, or coat, esp. an unbelted dress with a straight drape. **6.** *Elect.* the metal covering of a cable. **7.** *Electronics.* **a.** the metal wall of a wave guide. **b.** a space charge formed by ions near an electrode in a tube containing low-pressure gas. **c.** the region of a space charge in a cathode-ray tube. **—*v.t.*** **8.** to sheathe. [ME *sheth(e),* OE *scēath;* c. G *Scheide;* see SHED[2]] **—sheath′less,** *adj.* **—sheath′like′,** *adj.*

sheath·bill (shēth′bil′), *n.* either of two white sea birds, *Chionis alba* or *C. minor,* of the colder parts of the Southern Hemisphere: so called from the horny sheath covering the base of the upper bill. [SHEATH + BILL[2]]

sheathe (shēth), *v.t.,* **sheathed, sheath·ing.** **1.** to put (a sword, dagger, etc.) into a sheath. **2.** to plunge (a sword, dagger, etc.) in something as if in a sheath. **3.** to enclose in or as if in a casing or covering. **4.** to cover or provide with a protective layer or sheathing: *to sheathe a roof with copper.* **5.** to cover (a cable, electrical connector, etc.) with a metal sheath for grounding. [ME *shethe.* See SHEATH] **—sheath′er,** *n.*

sheath·ing (shē′thing), *n.* **1.** the act of one who sheathes. **2.** that which sheathes; a covering or outer layer of metal, wood, or other material, as one of metal plates on a ship's bottom, the first covering of boards on a house, etc. **3.** material for forming any such covering. [SHEATHE + ING[1]]

sheath′ knife′, a knife carried in a sheath.

sheath′ pile′. See **sheet pile.**

sheath·y (shē′thē, -thē), *adj.,* **sheath·i·er, sheath·i·est.** (esp. of women's clothes) like a sheath, as in shape, fit, or the like. [SHEATH + -Y[1]]

shea′ tree′, an African, sapotaceous tree, *Butyrospermum Parkii,* bearing a round, smooth-skinned fruit that contains one or more seeds yielding shea butter.

sheave[1] (shēv), *v.t.,* **sheaved, sheav·ing.** to gather, collect, or bind into a sheaf or sheaves. [from SHEAF]

sheave[2] (shiv, shēv), *n.* **1.** a pulley for hoisting or hauling, having a grooved rim for retaining a wire rope. **2.** a wheel with a grooved rim, for transmitting force to a cable or belt. [ME *sheeve;* akin to D *schijf* sheave, G *Scheibe* disk]

sheaves[1] (shēvz), *n.* **1.** pl. of **sheaf.** **2.** pl. of **sheave[1].**

sheaves[2] (shivz, shēvz), pl. of **sheave[2].**

She·ba (shē′bə), *n.* *Bible.* **1. Queen of,** the queen who visited Solomon to test his wisdom. I Kings 10:1–13. **2.** Saba (def. 2).

she·bang (shə bang′), *n.* *Informal.* **1.** the structure of something, as of an organization, contrivance, or affair: *The whole shebang fell apart when the chairman quit.* **2.** a primitive dwelling; shack; shanty. [?]

She·bat (shə bät′), *n.* a month of the Jewish calendar. Also, **Shevat.** Cf. **Jewish calendar.** [< Heb]

she·been (shə bēn′), *n.* *Scot., Irish Eng.* **1.** a tavern or house where liquor is sold illegally. **2.** any cheap or disreputable tavern. Also, **she·bean′, shibbeen.** [< Ir *sībīn,* cf. *séibín* small mug, hence (drink of) ale, very weak beer]

she·been·ing (shə bē′ning), *n.* *Scot., Irish Eng.* **1.** the act of visiting a tavern or taverns on a drinking bout. **2.** the consumption of liquor, esp. illegal liquor. [SHEBEEN + -ING[1]] **—she·been′er,** *n.*

She·be·li (shi bā′lē), *n.* **Webi.** See **Webi Shebeli.** Also, **Shibeli.**

She·boy·gan (shi boi′gən), *n.* a port in E Wisconsin, on Lake Michigan. 45,747 (1960).

Sheboy′gan Falls′, a town in E Wisconsin. 4061 (1960).

She·chem (shē′kəm, -kem, shek′əm, -em), *n.* a town of ancient Palestine, near the city of Samaria; now in NW Jordan: first capital of the northern kingdom of Israel. Modern name, **Nablus.**

She Chi (shu′ jē′), (in popular Chinese religion) the gods of the earth and the harvest.

She·chi·nah (shə kē′nə, -kī′-; *Heb.* shə кнē nä′), *n.* *Theol.* Shekinah.

she·chi·tah (shə кнē tä′), *n.* *Hebrew.* shehitah.

shed[1] (shed), *n.* **1.** a slight or rude structure built for shelter, storage, etc. **2.** a large, strongly built structure, often open at the sides or end. [OE *sced,* var. of *scead* SHADE, shelter] **—shed′like′,** *adj.*

shed[2] (shed), *v.,* **shed, shed·ding,** *n.* **—*v.t.*** **1.** to pour forth (water or other liquid), as a fountain. **2.** to emit and let fall, as tears. **3.** to impart or release; give or send forth (light, sound, fragrance, influence, etc.). **4.** to resist being penetrated or affected by: *cloth that sheds water.* **5.** to cast off or let fall by natural process (leaves, hair, feathers, skin, shell, etc.). **6.** *Textiles.* to separate (the warp) in forming a shed. **—*v.i.*** **7.** to fall off, as leaves. **8.** to drop out, as hair, seed, grain, etc. **9.** to cast off hair, feathers, skin, or other covering or parts by natural process. **—*n.*** **10.** *Textiles.* (on a loom) a triangular, transverse opening created between raised and lowered warp threads through which the shuttle passes in depositing the loose pick. **11. shed blood, a.** to cause

CONCISE ETYMOLOGY KEY: <, descended or derived from; >, whence; b., blend of, blended; c., cognate with; deriv., derivative; equiv., equivalent; imit., imitative; m., modification of; obl., oblique; r., replacing; s., stem; sp., spelling; trans., translation; ?, origin unknown, perhaps; *, hypothetical. See the full key inside the front cover.

blood to flow. **b.** to kill by violence; slaughter. [ME; OE *scēadan;* var. of *scēadan;* c. G *scheiden* to divide] —**shed′a·ble, shed′da·ble,** *adj.*
—**Syn. 3.** emit, radiate, effuse, spread. **4.** repel. **9.** molt.

she'd (shēd), **1.** contraction of *she had.* **2.** contraction of *she would.*

shed·der (shed′ər), *n.* **1.** one who or that which sheds. **2.** a lobster, crab, etc., just before it molts. [ME; see SHED[2], -ER[1]]

she-dev·il (shē′dev′il, -dev′-), *n.* a woman who resembles a devil, as in extreme wickedness, cruelty, or bad temper.

shed′ roof′, a roof having a single slope. Also called **penthouse.**

shee·fish (shē′fish), *n., pl.* **-fish·es,** (*esp. collectively*) **-fish.** inconnu (def. 2). [*shee* (prob. native name in Alaska or northwest Canada) + FISH]

Shee·lah (shē′lə), *n.* a girl's given name. Also, **Sheila, Sheilah, Shelagh.**

Shee·ler (shē′lər), *n.* **Charles,** 1883–1965, U.S. painter and photographer.

sheen (shēn), *n.* **1.** luster; brightness; radiance. **2.** gleaming attire. —*adj. Archaic.* **3.** shining. **4.** beautiful. —*v.i.* **5.** *Scot. and North Eng.* to shine. [ME *sheene,* OE *scēne* beautiful; c. G *schön*] —**sheen′ful,** *adj.* —**sheen′less,** *adj.* —**sheen′ly,** *adv.*
—**Syn. 1.** See **polish.**

Sheen (shēn), *n.* **Fulton (John),** born 1895, U.S. Roman Catholic clergyman, writer, and teacher.

shee·ney (shē′nē), *n., pl.* **-neys.** *Offensive.* sheeny[2].

sheen·y[1] (shē′nē), *adj.,* **sheen·i·er, sheen·i·est.** shining; lustrous. [SHEEN + -Y[1]]

sheen·y[2] (shē′nē), *n., pl.* **sheen·ies.** *Offensive.* a Jew. Also, **sheeney, shee′nie.** [?]

sheep (shēp), *n., pl.* **sheep. 1.** any of numerous ruminant mammals of the genus *Ovis,* of the family *Bovidae,* closely related to the goats, esp. *O. aries,* bred in a number of domesticated varieties. **2.** leather made from the skin of these animals. **3.** a meek, unimaginative, or easily led person. **4. separate the sheep from the goats,** to separate good people from bad or those intended for a specific end from unqualified people. [ME; OE (north) *scēp;* c. D *schaap,* G *Schaf*] —**sheep′-less,** *adj.* —**sheep′like′,** *adj.*

Domestic sheep

sheep·ber·ry (shēp′ber′ē, -bə rē), *n., pl.* **-ries. 1.** a caprifoliaceous shrub or small tree, *Viburnum Lentago,* of North America, having cymes of small white flowers and edible, berrylike black drupes. **2.** the fruit itself. **3.** the black haw, *Viburnum prunifolium.* [SHEEP + BERRY]

sheep·cote (shēp′kōt′), *n.* *Chiefly Brit.* a pen or covered enclosure for sheep. [SHEEP + COTE[1]]

sheep-dip (shēp′dip′), *n.* *Vet. Pathol.* a lotion or wash applied to the fleece or skin of sheep to kill vermin, usually applied by immersing the animals in vats.

sheep·dog (shēp′dôg′, -dog′), *n.* a dog trained to herd and guard sheep. Also, **sheep′ dog′.**

sheep·fold (shēp′fōld′), *n.* *Chiefly Brit.* an enclosure for sheep. [ME; OE *sceapa falda.* See SHEEP, FOLD[2]]

sheep·head (shēp′hed′), *n.* a large, California food fish, *Pimelometopon pulchrum,* of the wrasse family. Also called **fathead, redfish.** [so called from the resemblance of its teeth to those of a sheep]

sheep·herd·er (shēp′hûr′dər), *n.* shepherd (def. 1). [SHEEP + HERDER] —**sheep′herd′ing,** *n., adj.*

sheep·ish (shē′pish), *adj.* **1.** embarrassed or bashful, as by having done something wrong or foolish. **2.** like sheep, as in meekness, docility, etc. [ME *shepisshe.* See SHEEP, -ISH[1]] —**sheep′ish·ly,** *adv.* —**sheep′ish·ness,** *n.*

sheep′ ked′. See **sheep tick.**

sheep′ lau′rel, a low, North American, ericaceous shrub, *Kalmia angustifolia,* reputed to be poisonous to sheep and other animals. Also called **dwarf laurel, lambkill.**

sheep·man (shēp′mən, -man′), *n., pl.* **-men** (-mən, -men′). **1.** a man engaged in the tending or breeding of sheep, esp. the owner of a sheep ranch. **2.** a shepherd. [SHEEP + MAN[1]]

sheep's-bit (shēps′bit′), *n.* shepherd's-scabious.

sheep's′ eyes′, shy, amorous, lovesick glances (usually prec. by *make* or *cast*): *making sheep's eyes at the new girl in class.*

sheep's′ fes′cue, a low grass, *Festuca ovina,* of the North Temperate Zone.

sheep·shank (shēp′shangk′), *n.* a kind of knot, hitch, or bend made on a rope to shorten it temporarily. [short for *sheepshank knot*]

Sheep·shanks (shēp′shangks′), *n.* an elliptical crater in the first quadrant of the face of the moon: about 20 miles long and 15 miles wide.

sheeps·head (shēps′hed′), *n.* **1.** a deep-bodied, black-banded food fish, *Archosargus probatocephalus,* found along the Atlantic coast of the U.S. **2.** a freshwater drum, *Aplodinotus grunniens,* found in eastern North America. **3.** sheephead. **4.** *Obs.* a foolish or stupid person. [SHEEP + 'S[1] + HEAD]

sheep′shear·ing (shēp′shēr′ing), *n.* **1.** the act or an instance of shearing sheep. **2.** the time or season of shearing sheep. **3.** a festival held at this time. [SHEEP + SHEARING] —**sheep′-shear′er,** *n.*

sheep·skin (shēp′skin′), *n.* **1.** the skin of a sheep, esp. such a skin dressed with the wool on, as for a garment. **2.** leather, parchment, or the like, made from the skin of sheep. **3.** *Informal.* a diploma. —*adj.* **4.** made from the skin of a sheep. **5.** (of a garment) lined with the skin of a sheep dressed with the wool on. [ME *shepskinn.* See SHEEP, SKIN]

Sheep tick (Length ¼ in.)

sheep′ sor′rel, a slender, polygonaceous weed, *Rumex Acetosella,* found in poor, dry soils, having hastate leaves with an acid taste. Also called **sleeping beauty.**

sheeps′wool sponge′ (shēps′wŏŏl′). See **wool sponge.**

sheep′ tick′, a wingless, bloodsucking dipterous insect, *Melophagus ovinus,* that is parasitic on sheep. Also called **ked, sheep ked.** [late ME *scheptyke*]

sheep·walk (shēp′wôk′), *n.* *Brit.* a tract of land on which sheep are pastured. [SHEEP + WALK]

sheep·weed (shēp′wēd′), *n.* See **bog violet.** [SHEEP + WEED[1]]

sheer[1] (shēr), *adj.* **1.** transparently thin; diaphanous, as some fabrics: *sheer stockings.* **2.** unmixed with anything else: *We drilled a hundred feet through sheer rock.* **3.** unqualified; utter: *sheer nonsense.* **4.** extending down or up very steeply; almost completely vertical: *a sheer descent of rock.* **5.** *Brit. Obs.* bright; shining. —*adv.* **6.** clear; completely; quite: *ran sheer into the thick of battle.* **7.** perpendicularly; vertically; down or up very steeply. —*n.* **8.** a thin, diaphanous material, as chiffon or voile. [ME *scere;* OE *scēr* clear, undisputed (in legal context); c. Icel *skǣrr;* akin to OE *scīr,* Icel *skīrr,* G *schier,* Goth *skeirs* clear] —**sheer′ly,** *adv.* —**sheer′ness,** *n.*
—**Syn. 2.** mere, simple, pure, unadulterated. **3.** absolute, downright. **4.** abrupt, precipitous. **6.** totally, entirely. —**Ant. 1.** opaque.

sheer[2] (shēr), *v.i.* **1.** to deviate from a course, as a ship; swerve. —*v.t.* **2.** to cause to sheer. **3.** *Shipbuilding.* to give sheer to (a hull). —*n.* **4.** a deviation or divergence, as of a ship from her course; swerve. **5.** the fore-and-aft upward curve of the hull of a vessel at the main deck or bulwarks. **6.** the position in which a ship at anchor is placed to keep her clear of the anchor. [from SHEER[1]; cf. sense development of CLEAR]

sheer·legs (shēr′legz′), *n.* (*usually construed as pl.*) See **shear legs.** [SHEAR + LEG + -S[3]]

Sheer·ness (shēr′nis), *n.* a seaport in N Kent, in SE England, at the mouth of the Thames: government dockyards. 14,123 (1961).

sheer′ plan′, *Naval Archit.* a diagrammatic fore-and-aft elevation of the hull of a vessel, showing bow and buttock lines, stations, water lines, diagonals, decks, bulwarks, etc. Also called **profile plan.** Cf. **body plan, half-breadth plan.**

sheers (shērs), *n.* shear (def. 16).

sheer′ strake′, *Naut.* a strake of planking or plating at the level of the main or upper deck of a vessel.

sheet[1] (shēt), *n.* **1.** a large rectangular piece of linen, cotton, or other material used as an article of bedding, commonly spread in pairs so that one is immediately above and the other immediately below the sleeper. **2.** a broad, relatively thin, surface, layer, or covering. **3.** a relatively thin, usually rectangular form, piece, plate, or slab, as of photographic film, glass, metal, etc. **4.** material, as metal or glass, in the form of broad, relatively thin pieces. **5.** a sail, as on a ship or boat. **6.** a rectangular piece of paper or parchment, esp. one on which to write. **7.** a newspaper or periodical. **8.** *Printing and Bookbinding.* a large, rectangular piece of printing paper, esp. one for printing a complete signature. **9.** *Philately.* the impression from a plate or the like on a single sheet of paper before any division of the paper into individual stamps. **10.** an extent, stretch, or expanse, as of fire, water, etc.: *sheets of flame.* **11.** a thin, flat piece of metal or a very shallow pan on which to place food while baking. **12.** *Geol.* a more or less horizontal mass of rock, esp. eruptive rock intruded between strata or spread over a surface. **13.** *Math.* **a.** one of the separate pieces making up a geometrical surface: *a hyperboloid of two sheets.* **b.** one of the planes or pieces of planes making up a Riemann surface. **14.** a type of crystal structure in which certain atoms unite strongly in two dimensions to form a layer that is weakly joined to others. —*v.t.* **15.** to furnish with a sheet or sheets. **16.** to wrap in a sheet. **17.** to cover with a sheet or layer of something. [ME *shete,* OE *scēte* (north), *sciete,* deriv. of *scēat* corner, lap, sheet, etc.; c. D *schoot,* G *Schoss,* Icel *skaut*] —**sheet′less,** *adj.* —**sheet′like′,** *adj.*

sheet[2] (shēt), *n.* **1.** *Naut.* **a.** a rope or chain for extending the clews of a square sail along a yard. **b.** a rope for trimming a fore-and-aft sail. **c.** a rope or chain for extending the lee clew of a course. **2. three sheets in or to the wind,** *Slang.* intoxicated: *He was three sheets to the wind and had to be carried home.* —*v.t.* **3.** *Naut.* to trim, extend, or secure by means of a sheet or sheets. [ME *shete,* OE *scēatline,* equiv. to *scēat(a)* lower corner of a sail (see SHEET[1]) + *line* line, rope; c. LG *schote*]

sheet′ an′chor, 1. *Naut.* a large anchor used only in cases of emergency. **2.** a final reliance or resource, as when in danger.

sheet′ bend′, a knot made between two ropes by forming a bight in one and passing the end of the other through the bight, around it, and under itself. Also called **mesh knot, netting knot, weaver's hitch, weaver's knot.**

sheet-fed (shēt′fed′), *adj.* (of a printing press) fed by and designed to print individual flat sheets of paper. Cf. **web-fed.**

sheet′ film′, *Photog.* a flat piece of film cut to a required size before being placed in a camera.

sheet′ glass′, glass in sheet form produced by drawing or by the cylinder glass process.

sheet·ing (shē′ting), *n.* **1.** the act of covering with or forming into a sheet or sheets. **2.** wide muslin, chiefly for sheets. **3.** *Engineering, Building Trades.* a quantity of sheet piles. [SHEET[1] + -ING[1]]

sheet′ light′ning, lightning appearing merely as a general illumination over a broad surface, usually due to the reflection of the lightning of a distant thunderstorm.

sheet′ met′al, metal in sheets or thin plates.

sheet′ mu′sic, music, usually a single composition, printed on unbound sheets of paper.

sheet′ pile′, one of a number of piles, usually flat, driven side by side to retain earth, etc., or to prevent seepage into an excavation. Also called **sheath pile.** —**sheet′ pil′ing.**

Sheet·rock (shēt′rok′), *n.* *Trademark.* a plasterboard of gypsum between paper.

sheet′-web spi′der (shēt′web′), any of numerous spiders of the family *Linyphiidae,* that construct a closely-woven, horizontal, sheetlike web for snaring prey.

Shef·field (shef′ēld), *n.* **1.** a city in S Yorkshire, in N England. 493,954 (1961). **2.** a city in NW Alabama, on the Tennessee River. 13,491 (1960).

Shef′field Lake′, a town in N Ohio. 6884 (1960).

Shef′field plate′, sheet copper with a cladding of silver. [after SHEFFIELD, England + PLATE[1]]

she·getz (shā′gits), *n., pl.* **shkotz·im** (shkôt′sim). *Yiddish.* **1.** a boy or man who is not Jewish. **2.** a Jewish boy or man whose attitudes and behavior are felt to resemble those of a gentile. Cf. **shiksa.**

She·hab (she häb′), *n.* **Fu·ad** (fōō äd′). See **Chehab, Fuad.**

she·hi·tah (shə кнē tä′), *n.* *Hebrew.* the slaughtering of animals for food by a duly certified person in the manner prescribed by Jewish law. Also, **shechitah.** Cf. **shohet.**

sheik (shēk), *n.* **1.** (in Arab and other Muslim use) **a.** chief or head; the head man of a village or tribe. **b.** the head of a religious body. **2.** *Slang.* a man held to be masterful and irresistibly charming to women. Also, **sheikh.** [< Ar *shaikh* old man] —**sheik′like′,** *adj.*

sheik·dom (shēk′dəm), *n.* the land or territory under the control of a sheik. Also, **sheikh′dom.** [SHEIK + -DOM]

shei·la (shē′lə), *n.* *Australian Slang.* a girl or young woman. [special use of proper name]

Shei·la (shē′lə), *n.* a girl's given name. Also, **Sheelah, Shei′lah, Shelagh.**

Shei·tan (shī tän′), *n.* Shaitan.

shei·tel (shāt′əl), *n., pl.* **sheit·len** (shāt′lən). *Yiddish.* a wig worn by certain Orthodox Jewish married women in keeping with an old rabbinical precept that forbids a woman to leave her hair uncovered in the sight of a man other than her husband.

Shekel (Hebrew)

shek·el (shek′əl), *n.* **1.** an ancient, orig. Babylonian, unit of weight, of varying value, taken as equal to the fiftieth or the sixtieth part of a mina or to about a quarter to half an ounce. **2.** a coin of this weight, esp. the chief silver coin of the Hebrews. **3. shekels,** *Slang.* money; cash. [< Heb *sheqel*]

She·ki·nah (shi kē′nə, -kī′-; *Heb.* shə кнē nä′), *n.* *Theol.* the presence of God on earth or a symbol or manifestation of His presence: *May the Shekinah ever dwell in your midst.* Also, **Shechinah.** [< Heb]

She·lagh (shē′lə), *n.* a girl's given name. Also, **Sheelah, Sheila, Sheilah.**

Shel·by (shel′bē), *n.* **1.** a city in S North Carolina. 17,698 (1960). **2.** a town in central Ohio. 9106 (1960). **3.** a town in N Montana. 4017 (1960).

Shel·by·ville (shel′bē vil), *n.* **1.** a city in central Tennessee. 10,466 (1960). **2.** a town in central Illinois. 4821 (1960). **3.** a town in N Kentucky. 4525 (1960).

Shel·don (shel′dən, -dᵊn), *n.* **1.** a town in NW Iowa. 4251 (1960). **2.** a boy's given name.

Sheldrake, *Tadorna tadorna* (Length 26 in.)

shel·drake (shel′drāk′), *n., pl.* **-drakes,** (*esp. collectively*) **-drake. 1.** any of several Old World ducks of the genera *Tadorna* or *Casarca,* certain species of which have highly variegated plumage. **2.** any of various other ducks, esp. the goosander or merganser. [ME *sheldedrake,* equiv. to *sheld* particolored (now obs.) + *drake* DRAKE[1]]

shel·duck (shel′duk′), *n., pl.* **-ducks,** (*esp. collectively*) **-duck. 1.** a sheldrake. **2.** a female sheldrake. [*shel* (see SHELDRAKE) + DUCK[1]]

She·le·pin (she le′pin), *n.* **A·le·xan·dr Ni·ko·la·ye·vich** (ä′le ksän′dər ni ko lä′yə vich), born 1918, Russian government official: member of the Presidium since 1961.

She·lest (she′lest), *n.* **Pyotr Ye·fi·mo·vich** (pyô′tər ye fē′mo vich), born 1908, Russian government official: alternate member of the Presidium.

shelf (shelf), *n., pl.* **shelves** (shelvz). **1.** a thin slab of wood, metal, etc., fixed horizontally to a wall or in a frame, for supporting objects. **2.** the contents of this: *a shelf of books.* **3.** a surface or projection resembling this; ledge. **4.** a sand bank or submerged extent of rock in the sea or river. **5.** the bedrock underlying an alluvial deposit or the like. **6.** *Archery.* the upper part of the bow hand, on which the arrow rests. **7. off the shelf,** readily available from merchandise in stock: *Any of those parts can be purchased off the shelf.* **8. on the shelf,** *Slang.* **a.** put aside temporarily; postponed. **b.** inactive; useless. **c.** (of a woman) without prospects of marriage, as after having broken an engagement: *She was unhappy on the shelf but would have been even more unhappy married to that good-for-nothing.* [ME; OE *scylfe;* akin to LG *schelf* shelf, Icel *-skjalf* bench] —**shelf′like′,** *adj.*

shelf′ an′gle, an angle iron attached to or suspended from a girder to carry masonry or the ends of a number of joists.

shelf·ful (shelf′fŏŏl′), *n., pl.* **-fuls. 1.** an amount adequate to fill a shelf: *She buys canned goods by the shelfful.* **2.** the amount contained on a shelf: *We gave away a shelfful of books.* [SHELF + -FUL]

shelf′ ice′, ice forming part of or broken from an ice shelf.

shelf′ life′, the term or period during which a stored commodity remains effective, useful, or suitable for consumption: *Many medicines have a very short shelf life.* Also called **storage life.**

shelf′ mark′, *Library Science.* a symbol attached to or written on the lower spine of a book, indicating the shelf on which the book belongs.

shell (shel), *n.* **1.** a hard outer covering of an animal, as the hard case of a mollusk, or either half of the case of a bivalve mollusk. **2.** any of various objects resembling such a covering, as in shape or in being more or less concave or hollow. 3. the material constituting any of various coverings of this kind. 4. the hard exterior of an egg. 5. the usually hard, outer covering of a seed, fruit, or the like, as the hard outside portion of a nut, the pod of peas, etc. 6. a hard, protecting or enclosing case or cover. 7. an attitude or manner of reserve that usually conceals one's emotions, thoughts, etc.: *One could not penetrate his shell.* 8. a hollow projectile for a cannon, mortar, etc., filled with an explosive charge designed to explode during flight, upon impact, or after penetration. 9. a metallic cartridge used in small arms and small artillery pieces. 10. a metal or paper cartridge, as for use in a shotgun. 11. a cartridgelike pyrotechnic device that explodes in the air. 12. *Cookery.* the lower pastry crust of a pie, tart, or the like, baked before the filling is added. 13. *Physics.* **a.** any of several energy levels on which an electron may exist within an atom, the energies of the electrons on the same level being equal and on different levels being unequal. **b.** a group of nucleons of approximately the same energy. 14. a light, long, narrow racing boat, for rowing by one or more persons. 15. *Naut.* the plating, planking, or the like, covering the ribs and forming the exterior hull of a vessel. 16. See **tortoise shell.** 17. a mollusk. 18. *Engineering.* the curved solid forming a dome or vault. 19. an arena or stadium covered by a domed or arched roof. 20. a saucer-shaped arena or stadium. 21. the framework, external structure, or walls and roof of a building: *After the fire, only the shell of the school was left.* 22. a small glass for beer. 23. the metal, pressure-resistant outer casing of a fire-tube boiler. 24. *Metall.* **a.** scab on the surface of an ingot. **b.** a length of unfinished tubing. **c.** a pierced forging. **d.** a hollow object made by deep drawing. —*v.t.* 25. to take out of the shell, pod, etc.; remove the shell of. 26. to separate (Indian corn, grain, etc.) from the ear, cob, or husk. 27. to fire shells or explosive projectiles into, upon, or among; bombard. 28. *Baseball Slang.* to get many hits and runs off (an opposing pitcher): *He pitched one inning and was shelled.* —*v.i.* 29. to fall or come out of the shell, husk, etc. 30. to come away or fall off, as a shell or outer coat. 31. **shell out,** *Slang.* to hand over (money); contribute; pay: *The people are being asked to shell out ten dollars for front-row seats.* [ME; OE *scell* (north), *sciell;* c. D *schil* peel, skin, rink, Icel *skel* shell, Goth *skalja* tile] —**shell′-less,** *adj.* —**shell′-like′,** *adj.*

Shell (def. 14)

she'll (shēl), 1. contraction of *she will.* 2. contraction of *she shall.*

Shel·la·bar·ger (shel′ə bär′gər), *n.* **Samuel,** 1888–1954, U.S. novelist.

shel·lac (shə lak′), *n., v.,* **-lacked, -lack·ing.** —*n.* 1. lac which has been purified and formed into thin sheets, used for making varnish. 2. a varnish (**shellac′ var′nish**) made by dissolving this material in alcohol or a similar solvent. 3. a phonograph record made of a breakable material containing shellac, esp. one to be played at 78 r.p.m.: *an LP that can hold nearly 10 times as much as the old shellac.* —*v.t.* 4. to coat or treat with shellac. 5. *Slang.* **a.** to defeat; trounce **b.** to thrash soundly. Also, **shel·lack′.** [SHELL + LAC[1], trans. of F *laque en écailles* lac in thin plates]

shel·lack·ing (shə lak′ing), *n.* *Slang.* 1. an utter defeat: *a shellacking their team will remember.* 2. a sound thrashing: *His father gave him a shellacking for stealing the book.* [SHELLAC + -ING[1]]

shell′ back′, an underside of a spoon bowl ornamented with a shell motif.

shell·back (shel′bak′), *n.* 1. an old sailor. 2. one who has crossed the equator by boat. [SHELL + BACK[1]]

shell·bark (shel′bärk′), *n.* the shagbark tree. [SHELL + BARK[2]]

shell′ bean′, 1. any of various kinds of bean of which the unripe seeds are removed from the pods before cooking. 2. the seed itself.

shell′ cast′, *Print.* a thin stereotype mounted on a block to make it type-high.

shell′ construc′tion, construction, esp. in reinforced concrete, formed of very thin, curved surfaces subject only to compressive or tensile stresses in the directions of the curves, the loads carried being uniform at all points on the curves: most frequently encountered in the form of vaults or symmetrical cantilevered constructions about columns, but applicable also to vertical cylindrical structures, as tanks.

shell·crack·er (shel′krak′ər), *n.* See **redear sunfish.** [SHELL + CRACKER]

shell′ cut′, *Print.* a thin printing plate mounted on a wooden block.

shelled (sheld), *adj.* 1. having the shell removed: *shelled pecans.* 2. (esp. of field corn, grain, etc.) removed from the ear or husk: *shelled peas.* 3. having or enclosed in a shell: *tiny, shelled marine animals.* [SHELL + -ED[2]]

-shelled, a combining form of **shelled:** *hardshelled.*

shell′ expan′sion, *Naval Archit.* a plan or model of a hull to be built, showing each of its plates with pertinent information.

Shel·ley (shel′ē), *n.* 1. **Mary Woll·stone·craft (Godwin)** (wo͝ol′stən kraft′, -kräft′), 1797–1851, English author (wife of Percy Bysshe Shelley). 2. **Percy Bysshe** (bish), 1792–1822, English poet. 3. a town in SE Idaho. 2612 (1960). 4. Also, **Shel′lie, Shelly.** a boy's or girl's given name.

Shel·ley·an (shel′ē ən), *adj.* 1. Also, **Shel′li·an.** of, pertaining to, or characteristic of Percy Bysshe Shelley or his works. —*n.* 2. one who studies the works of Percy Bysshe Shelley. [SHELLEY + -AN]

shell·fire (shel′fīər′), *n.* *Mil.* the firing of explosive shells or projectiles. [SHELL + FIRE]

shell·fish (shel′fish′), *n., pl.* (*esp. collectively*) **-fish,** (*esp. referring to two or more kinds or species*) **-fish·es.** 1. an aquatic animal having a shell, as the oyster and other mollusks and the lobster and other crustaceans. 2. a trunkfish. [ME; OE *scilfisc.* See SHELL, FISH]

shell·flow·er (shel′flou′ər), *n.* 1. See **Bells of Ireland.** 2. a leafy-stemmed herb, *Alpinia speciosa,* of eastern Asia, having very showy, orchidlike flowers, the lip yellow with brownish-red markings, the corolla white and tinged with purple. 3. a turtlehead, *Chelone glabra,* having white flowers. [SHELL + FLOWER]

shell′ game′, 1. a sleight-of-hand swindling game resembling thimblerig but employing walnut shells or the like instead of thimblelike cups. 2. any deceit, swindle, fraud, or the like.

shell′ ice′. See **cat ice.**

shell′ jack′et, a close-fitting, semiformal jacket, with a short back, worn in the tropics in place of a tuxedo.

shell′ par′akeet, budgerigar.

shell·proof (shel′pro͞of′), *adj.* protected against the explosive effect of shells or bombs. [SHELL + -PROOF]

shell′ shock′, *Psychiatry.* nervous or mental disorder in various forms, characterized variously by loss of self-command, memory, speech, sight, or other powers, formerly believed to have been brought on by the shock of exploding shells in battle, but now explained as the result of the cumulative emotional and psychological strain of warfare. —**shell′-shocked′, shell′shocked′,** *adj.*

shell·y (shel′ē), *adj.,* **shell·i·er, shell·i·est.** 1. abounding in shells: *a shelly surf.* 2. consisting of a shell or shells. 3. like a shell or shells. [SHELL + -Y[1]]

Shel·ly (shel′ē), *n.* a boy's or girl's given name. Also, **Shelley, Shel′lie.**

Shel·ta (shel′tə), *n.* systematically disguised Gaelic used as a tinkers' jargon in Britain and Ireland. [?]

shel·ter (shel′tər), *n.* 1. something beneath, behind, or within which a person, animal, or thing is protected from storms, missiles, adverse conditions, etc.; refuge. 2. the protection or refuge afforded by such a thing: *He took shelter in a nearby barn.* 3. protection from blame, incrimination, etc. 4. a dwelling place or home considered as a refuge from the elements: *A man must provide food, clothing, and shelter for his family.* —*v.t.* 5. to be a shelter for; afford shelter to: *The old barn sheltered him from the rain.* 6. to provide with a shelter; place under cover. 7. to protect, as by shelter; take under one's protection: *He tried to shelter her from the harsh world.* —*v.i.* 8. to take shelter; find a refuge: *He sheltered in a barn.* [? var. of obs. *sheltron* testudo, OE *scieldtruma,* equiv. to *scield* SHIELD + *truma* body of fighting-men; see TRIM] —**shel′ter·er,** *n.* —**shel′ter·ing·ly,** *adv.* —**shel′ter·less,** *adj.* —**shel′ter·less·ness,** *n.*
—**Syn.** 1. retreat, asylum, sanctuary, shield, haven, harbor. See **cover.** 5. harbor, house. 7. guard, safeguard, shield, defend.

shel′ter deck′, *Naut.* 1. a weather deck covering a space not considered fully watertight. 2. the 'tween deck beneath this.

shel′ter-deck′ ves′sel (shel′tər dek′). See **open-shelter-deck vessel.**

shel·tered (shel′tərd), *adj.* 1. protected or shielded from storms, missiles, etc., by a wall, roof, barrier, or the like. 2. protected from the troubles, annoyances, sordidness, etc., encountered in competitive situations: *a sheltered life.* 3. providing an environment that is noncompetitive, as for the training of the physically disabled, the aged, retarded children, etc. 4. (of a business or industry) enjoying noncompetitive conditions, as because of a protective tariff. [SHELTER + -ED[2]]

shel′tering trust′. See **spendthrift trust.**

shel′ter tent′, a small, two-man, military tent consisting of two halves (**shel′ter halves′**) buttoned or tied together, held up by accessory ropes and poles. Also called **pup tent.**

Shel·ton (shel′tᵊn), *n.* 1. a city in SW Connecticut. 18,190 (1960). 2. a town in W Washington. 5651 (1960). 3. a boy's given name.

shel·ty (shel′tē), *n., pl.* **-ties.** 1. See **Shetland pony.** 2. See **Shetland sheepdog.** Also, **shel′tie.** [*shelt* (< Scand; cf. Icel *hjaltr* native of SHETLAND) + -Y[2]]

shelve[1] (shelv), *v.t.,* **shelved, shelv·ing.** 1. to place (an object or objects) on a shelf or shelves. 2. to put off or aside from consideration: *to shelve the question.* 3. to remove from active use or service; dismiss. 4. to furnish with shelves. [v. use of SHELVE(S)] —**shelv′er,** *n.*

shelve[2] (shelv), *v.i.,* **shelved, shelv·ing.** to slope gradually. [cf. WFris *skelf* not quite level]

shelves (shelvz), *n.* pl. of **shelf.**

shelv·ing (shel′ving), *n.* 1. material for shelves. 2. shelves collectively. [SHELVE[1] + -ING[1]]

Shem (shem), *n.* the eldest of the three sons of Noah. Gen 10:21. Also, *Douay Bible,* **Sem.**

She·ma (shə mä′), *n.* *Judaism.* a liturgical prayer, prominent in Jewish history and tradition, that is recited daily at the morning and evening services and consists of three paragraphs expressing Israel's ardent faith in and love of God. [< Heb: hear]

she·maal (shə mäl′), *n.* shamal.

She·mi·ni A·tze·reth (shə mē′nē at ser′es, -min′ē; *Heb.* shə mē nē′ ä tse′ret, shə mē′nē ä tse′res), a Jewish festival that is celebrated on the 22nd day of the month of Tishri, being the 8th day of Sukkoth. It is celebrated chiefly by a memorial service for the dead and prayers for rain in Israel. Also, **Shemi′ni Atze′ret.** [< Heb: eighth meeting]

Shem·ite (shem′īt), *n.* a Semite. —**Shem·it·ic** (shemit′ik), **Shem·it·ish** (shem′ī tish), *adj.*

She·mo·neh Es·reh (shə mō′nē es′rā; *Heb.* shə mōne′ es rā′), *Judaism.* the *Amidah,* consisting of 19 blessings, recited on days other than the Sabbath and holy days. [< Heb]

Shen·an·do·ah (shen′ən dō′ə), *n.* 1. a river flowing NE from N Virginia to the Potomac at Harpers Ferry, West Virginia. ab. 200 mi. long. 2. a valley in N Virginia, between the Blue Ridge and Allegheny mountains: Civil War campaigns 1862–64. 3. a borough in E Pennsylvania. 11,073 (1960). 4. a town in SW Iowa. 6567 (1960).

Shen′ando′ah Na′tional Park′, a national park in N Virginia, including part of the Blue Ridge mountain range. 302 sq. mi.

she·nan·i·gan (shə nan′ə gən), *n.* *Informal.* 1. nonsense; deceit; trickery. 2. Usually, **shenanigans.** mischievous nonsense; prankishness: *Cut out the shenanigans and start studying.* [?]

shend (shend), *v.t.,* **shent, shend·ing.** *Archaic.* 1. to put to shame. 2. to reproach or scold. 3. to destroy or injure; damage. [ME; OE (*ge*)*scendan* (c. D *schenden,* G *schänden*), deriv. of *scand* shame, infamy]

Shen·si (shen′sē′; *Chin.* shun′shē′), *n.* a province in N China. 18,130,000 (est. 1957); 75,598 sq. mi. *Cap.:* Sian.

Shen·stone (shen′stən), *n.* **William,** 1714–63, English poet.

Shen·yang (shun′yäng′), *n.* Mukden.

She·ol (shē′ōl), *n.* (in Hebrew theology) 1. the abode of the dead or of departed spirits. 2. (*l.c.*) hell. [< Heb]

Shep·ard (shep′ərd), *n.* **Alan Bartlett, Jr.,** born 1923, U.S. astronaut.

shep·herd (shep′ərd), *n.* 1. a man who herds, tends, and guards sheep. 2. one who protects, guides, or watches over a person or group of people. 3. a clergyman. 4. **the Shepherd,** Jesus Christ. 5. See **sheep dog.** —*v.t.* 6. to tend or guard as a shepherd: *to shepherd the flock.* 7. to watch over carefully. [ME *shepherde,* OE *scēphyrde.* See SHEEP, HERD[2]] —**shep′herd·less,** *adj.* —**shep′herd·like′,** *adj.*

Shep·herd (shep′ərd), *n.* a boy's given name.

shep′herd dog′. See **sheep dog.**

shep·herd·ess (shep′ər dis), *n.* 1. a girl or woman who herds sheep. 2. a rural girl. [ME *shepherdesse.* See SHEPHERD, -ESS]

Shep′herd King′, any of the Hyksos kings.

shep′herd's check′, 1. a pattern of even checks, used in a variety of fabrics. 2. a fabric having this pattern. Also called **shepherd's plaid′.**

shep′herd's di′al, a cylindrical sundial that can be suspended so that the gnomon at its upper end casts its shadow on that part of the barrel marked off with the time of year. Also called **chilindre.**

shep′herd's pie′, a baked dish of ground or diced meat with a crust of mashed potatoes.

shep·herd's-purse (shep′ərdz pûrs′), *n.* a cruciferous weed, *Capsella Bursa-pastoris,* having white flowers and purselike pods.

shep·herd's-sca·bi·ous (shep′ərdz skā′bē əs), *n.* a campanulaceous herb, *Jasione perennis,* of Europe, having heads of blue flowers. Also called **sheep's-bit.**

Shep′pard's adjust′ment (shep′ərdz), *Statistics.* a method of correcting the bias in standard deviations and higher moments of distributions due to grouping values of the variable. [named after William F. *Sheppard,* 20th-century English statistician]

Sher·ard (sher′ərd, -ärd), *n.* a boy's given name.

sher·ard·ize (sher′ər dīz′), *v.t.,* **-ized, -iz·ing.** *Metall.* to coat (steel) with a thin cladding of zinc by heating it in a mixture of sand and powdered zinc. [named after *Sherard* Cowper Coles (d. 1936), English inventor; see -IZE]

Sher·a·ton (sher′ə tᵊn, -tən), *n.* 1. **Thomas,** 1751–1806, English cabinetmaker and furniture designer. —*adj.* 2. of the style of furniture designed by Sheraton.

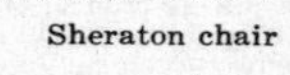

Sheraton chair

sher·bet (shûr′bit), *n.* 1. a frozen fruit-flavored mixture, similar to an ice, but with milk, egg white, or gelatin added. 2. *Brit.* a drink made of sweetened fruit juice diluted with water and ice. [< Turk < Pers *sharbat* < Ar *sharbah* a drink]

Sher·brooke (shûr′bro͝ok), *n.* a city in S Quebec, in SE Canada. 66,554 (1961).

sherd (shûrd), *n.* shard.

Sher·i·dan (sher′i dᵊn, -dən), *n.* 1. **Philip Henry,** 1831–88, Union general in the Civil War. 2. **Richard Brins·ley** (brinz′lē), 1751–1816, Irish dramatist and political leader. 3. a city in N Wyoming. 11,651 (1960). 4. a town in central Colorado. 3559 (1960). 5. a boy's given name.

she·rif (she rēf′), *n.* 1. a governor of Mecca descended from Muhammad. 2. an Arab chief, prince, or ruler. 3. amir (def. 3). Also, **she·reef′.** [< Ar *sharīf* exalted (person)]

sher·iff (sher′if), *n.* 1. the law-enforcement officer of a county or other civil subdivision of a state. 2. (formerly) an important civil officer in an English shire. [ME *sher(r)ef,* OE *scīrgerēfa.* See SHIRE, REEVE[1]] —**sher·iff·dom** (sher′if dəm), *n.*

sher·iff·al·ty (sher′i fəl tē), *n., pl.* **-ties.** shrievalty. [alter. by influence of SHERIFF]

sher·iff·wick (sher′if wik′), *n.* shrievalty. [SHERIFF + WICK[3]]

Sher·ley (shûr′lē), *n.* a boy's or girl's given name. Also, **Shirlee, Shirley, Shirlie.**

sher·lock (shûr′lok), *n.* *Informal.* 1. a private detective. 2. a person remarkably adept at solving mysteries, esp. by using insight and logical deduction: *Who's the sherlock who can tell me where my pen is?* Also, **Sher′-lock.** [after *Sherlock* Holmes, fictitious detective in writings of Sir Arthur Conan Doyle]

Sher·lock (shûr′lok), *n.* a boy's given name.

Sher·man (shûr′mən), *n.* 1. **Forrest Percival,** 1896–1951, U.S. naval officer. 2. **James School·craft** (sko͞ol′kraft′, -kräft′), 1855–1912, vice president of the U.S. 1909–12. 3. **John,** 1823–1900, U.S. statesman (brother of William T.). 4. **Roger,** 1721–93, American statesman. 5. **Stuart Pratt,** 1881–1926, U.S. critic and educator. 6. **William Tecumseh,** 1820–91, Union general in the Civil War. 7. a city in NE Texas. 24,988 (1960). 8. a boy's given name.

Sher′man Antitrust′ Act′, an act of Congress (1890) prohibiting any contract, conspiracy, or combination of business interests in restraint of foreign or interstate trade. Cf. **Clayton Antitrust Act.** [named after John SHERMAN, its author]

Sher·od (sher′əd, -od), *n.* a boy's given name, form of **Sherard.**

Sher·pa (sher′pə, shûr′-), *n., pl.* **-pas,** (*esp. collectively*) **-pa.** a member of a people of Tibetan stock living in the Nepalese Himalayas, who often serve as porters on mountain-climbing expeditions.

Sher·riff (sher′if), *n.* **Robert Cedric,** born 1896, British playwright and novelist.

Sher·rill (sher′il), *n.* **1.** a town in central New York. 2922 (1960). **2.** Also, **Cheryl, Sheryl.** a girl's given name, form of **Shirley.**

Sher·ring·ton (sher′ing tən), *n.* **Sir Charles Scott,** 1861–1952, English physiologist: Nobel prize for medicine 1932.

sher·ris (sher′is), *n. Archaic.* sherry. [< Sp (*vino de*) *Xeres* (wine of) Xeres (now JEREZ)]

sher·ry (sher′ē), *n., pl.* **-ries.** a fortified, amber-colored wine of southern Spain or any of various similar wines made elsewhere. [back formation from SHERRIS (the *-s* was mistaken for the plural sign)]

Sher·ry (sher′ē), *n.* a girl's given name. Also, **Sher′i, Sher′rie.**

sher′ry cob′bler, a cobbler drink made with sherry, sliced fruits, and ice.

's Her·to·gen·bosch (ser′tō KHən bôs′), a city in the S Netherlands. 71,286 (est. 1960). French, **Bois-le-Duc.**

Sher·tok (shər tōk′), *n.* **Mo·she** (mō′shə). See **Sharett, Moshe.**

Sher·wood (shûr′wo͝od′), *n.* **1. Robert Em·met** (em′it), 1896–1955, U.S. dramatist. **2.** a boy's given name.

Sher′wood For′est, an ancient royal forest in central England, chiefly in Nottinghamshire: the traditional haunt of Robin Hood.

Sher·yl (sher′əl), *n.* a girl's given name, form of **Shirley.** Also, **Cheryl, Sherrill.**

she's (shēz), **1.** contraction of *she is.* **2.** contraction of *she has.*

She′ Stoops′ to Con′quer, a comedy (1773) by Oliver Goldsmith.

Shet′land Is′lands (shet′lənd), an island group NE of the Orkney Islands, comprising a county of Scotland. 17,809 (1961); 550 sq. mi. *Co. seat:* Lerwick. Also called **Shetland, Zetland. —Shet′land Is′land·er.**

Shet′land po′ny, one of a breed of small but sturdy, rough-coated ponies, raised originally in the Shetland Islands.

Shetland pony (About 3 ft. high at shoulder)

Shet′land sheep′dog (shēp′dôg′, -dog′), one of a breed of small sheep dogs resembling a miniature collie, raised originally in the Shetland Islands.

Shet′land wool′, 1. the fine wool undercoat pulled by hand from Shetland sheep. **2.** thin, loosely twisted wool yarn for knitting or weaving.

sheugh (sho͞oKH), *Scot. and North Eng.* **—n. 1.** a furrow, ditch, or trench. **—v.t. 2.** to plow or dig (a furrow, ditch, etc.). Also, **sheuch** (sho͞oKH). [north var. of SOUGH[2]]

She·vat (shə vôt′), *n.* **Shebat.**

shev·e·ret (shev ə ret′, she vret′), *n.* cheveret.

shew (shō), *v.i., v.t.,* **shewed, shewn, shew·ing,** *n. Archaic.* show.

shew·bread (shō′bred′), *n. Judaism.* the 12 loaves of bread placed every Sabbath on the table in the holy of holies of the Biblical tabernacle and the Temple in Jerusalem as an offering by the priests to God and eaten by them at the end of the week. Ex. 25:30; Lev. 24:5–9. Also, **show-bread.** [SHEW + BREAD, modeled on G *Schaubrot,* which renders Gk *ártoi enṓpioi,* trans. of Heb *leḥem pānīm*]

SHF, See **superhigh frequency.**

shh (sh), *interj.* hush! be still!

Shi·ah (shē′ə), *n. Islam.* **1.** (*construed as pl.*) the Shiites. **2.** (*construed as sing.*) Shiite. [< Ar: sect]

shi·bah (shiv′ə), *n. Hebrew.* the mourning period, beginning on the day of the funeral and lasting traditionally for seven days, observed by Jews for a deceased parent, brother, or other close relative. Also, **shivah.** [lit., seven (days)]

Shi·bah A·sar Be·tam·muz (shē bä′ ä sär′ bə-tä′mo͞oz), a Jewish fast day observed on the 17th day of the month of Tammuz in memory of the breach of the walls of Jerusalem in A.D. 70 by the Romans under Titus. Also, **Shivah Asar Betammuz.**

shib·been (shə bēn′), *n. Scot., Irish Eng.* shebeen.

shib·bo·leth (shib′ə lith, -leth′), *n.* **1.** a peculiarity of pronunciation, behavior, mode of dress, etc., which distinguishes a particular class or set of persons. **2.** a test word or pet phrase of a party, sect, etc. **3.** a word used by the Gileadites to distinguish the fleeing Ephraimites, who could not pronounce the sound *sh.* Judges 12:4–6. [< Heb: freshet]

shi·bu·i·chi (shē′bo͞o ē′chē; *Jap.* shē′bo͞o ē′chē), *n.* an alloy of 75 percent copper and 25 percent silver, used esp. for Japanese decorative sword mounts and treated so as to have a lustrous, gray patina. [< Jap, equiv. to *shi* four + *bu* part + *ichi* one]

shi·bu·i·chi-do·shi (shē′bo͞o ē′chē dō′shē; *Jap.* shē′bo͞o ē′chē dô′shē), *n.* a Japanese decorative metalworking technique in which three compositions of shibuichi are melted and combined to give a clouded, slightly transparent effect, used esp. for sword mounts.

shi·cer (shī′sər), *n. Australian.* **1.** *Slang.* **a.** a swindler. **b.** any unscrupulous person. **c.** a shyster. **2.** *Archaic.* an unproductive gold mine. [< LG *scheisser,* equiv. to *scheiss(en)* (to) defecate + *-er* -ER[1]]

shied (shīd), *v.* pt. and pp. of **shy.**

shiel (shēl), *n. Scot.* shieling. [ME *schele,* OE (north) **scēla;* c. Icel *skāli* hut, shed; akin to OE *scȳr* hut, Icel *skūrr,* OHG *scūr* penthouse]

shield (shēld), *n.* **1.** a broad piece of armor, varying widely in form and size, carried apart from the body, usually on the left arm, as a defense against swords, lances, arrows, etc. **2.** something shaped like such a piece of armor, variously round, octagonal, triangular, or somewhat heart-shaped. **3.** something that or someone who protects. **4.** a policeman's, detective's, or sheriff's badge. **5.** *Ordn.* a steel screen attached to a gun to protect its crew, mechanism, etc. **6.** a movable framework for protecting a miner at the place at which he is working. **7.** *Elect.* a covering, usually made of metal, placed around an electric device or circuit in order to reduce the effects of external electric and magnetic fields. **8.** *Zool.* a protective plate or the like on the body of an animal, as a scute, enlarged scale, etc. **9.** See **dress shield. 10.** *Heraldry.* an escutcheon, esp. one broad at the top and pointed at the bottom, for displaying armorial bearings. See diag. under **coat of arms. 11.** (*cap.*) *Astron.* the constellation Scutum. **12.** *Shipbuilding.* mask (def. 13). **13.** *Geol.* a vast area of the earth's crust composed chiefly of Precambrian rocks. **—v.t. 14.** to protect (someone or something) with or as with a shield. **15.** to serve as a protection for. **16.** to hide or conceal; protect by hiding. **17.** *Obs.* to avert; forbid. **—v.i. 18.** to act or serve as a shield. [ME *shelde,* equiv. to OE *sceld;* c. D, G *Schild,* Goth *skildus*] **—shield′er,** *n.* **—shield′less,** *adj.* **—shield′less·ly,** *adv.* **—shield′less·ness,** *n.* **—shield′like′,** *adj.*

shield′ back′, a chair back having a form resembling that of a somewhat heart-shaped medieval shield. Also called **heart back.**

shield′ bear′er, an attendant who carries the shield or arms of a warrior.

shield′ bug′, 1. any of several stink bugs of the subfamily *Scutellerinae,* having a shieldlike scutellum extending over the abdomen. **2.** (loosely) any stink bug.

shield′ fern′, any of numerous ferns of the genera *Dryopteris* and *Polystichium,* having shield-shaped indusia.

Shield′ of Da′vid. See **Star of David.**

shield′-tailed snake′ (shēld′tāld′), any of several burrowing snakes of the family *Uropeltidae,* of the Indian peninsula and Ceylon, having a tail that ends in a flat disk. Also called **shield-tail** (shēld′tāl′).

shiel·ing (shē′ling), *n. Scot.* **1.** a pasture or grazing ground. **2.** a shepherd's or herdsman's hut or rough shelter on or near a grazing ground. Also, **shealing, shiel.** [SHIEL + -ING[1]]

shi·er[1] (shī′ər), *adj.* a compar. of **shy**[1].

shi·er[2] (shī′ər), *n.* a horse having a tendency to shy. Also, **shyer.** [SHY[2] + -ER[1]]

shi·est (shī′ist), *adj.* a superlative of **shy**[1].

shift (shift), *v.i.* **1.** to move from one place, position, direction, etc., to another. **2.** to manage to get along or succeed by oneself. **3.** to get along by indirect methods; use any expediency, trick or evasion to get along or succeed: *He shifted through life.* **4.** to change gears in driving an automobile. **5.** *Ling.* to undergo a systematic phonetic change. **6.** *Archaic.* to change one's clothes. **—v.t. 7.** to put (something) aside and replace it by another or others; change or exchange: *to shift friends; to shift ideas.* **8.** to transfer from one place, position, person, etc., to another: *to shift the blame onto someone else.* **9.** *Auto.* to change (gears) from one ratio or arrangement to another. **10.** *Ling.* to change phonetically and in a systematic way. **—n. 11.** a change or transfer from one place, position, direction, person, etc., to another: *a shift in the wind.* **12.** a person's scheduled period of work, esp. the portion of the day scheduled as a day's work when a shop, service, office, or industry operates continuously during both the day and night: *night shift.* **13.** a group of workmen scheduled to work during such a period: *The night shift reported.* **14.** *Auto.* a gearshift. **15.** *Clothing.* **a.** a straight, loose-fitting dress worn with or without a belt. **b.** a woman's chemise or slip. **16.** *Football.* a lateral or backward movement from one position to another, usually by two or more offensive players just before the ball is put into play. **17.** *Mining.* a dislocation of a seam or stratum; fault. **18.** *Music.* a change in the position of the left hand on the fingerboard in playing a stringed instrument. **19.** *Ling.* a change or system of parallel changes that affects the sound structure of a language, as the series of related changes in the English vowel system from Middle English to Modern English. **20.** an expedient; ingenious device. **21.** an evasion, artifice, or trick: *He was resorting to shifts and ruses again.* **22.** change or substitution. **23.** *Bridge.* See **shift bid. 24.** *Agric.* (in crop rotation) **a.** any of successive crops. **b.** the tract of land used. [ME *shift(en),* OE *sciftan;* c. G *schichten* to arrange in order, Icel *skipta* to divide; akin to SHED[2]] **—shift′ing·ly,** *adv.* **—shift′ing·ness,** *n.*
—Syn. 7. put, pass. **8.** change, move. **20.** contrivance, resource, resort. **21.** wile, ruse, subterfuge, stratagem.

shift·a·ble (shif′tə bəl), *adj.* **1.** able or designed to be shifted, changed, or removed: *shiftable furniture.* **2.** able to be transferred from one owner to another: *shiftable stocks, bonds, and other holdings.* [SHIFT + -ABLE]

shift′ bid′, *Bridge.* a bid in a suit different from the suit just bid by one's partner.

shift′ key′, a typewriter key which raises the carriage or lowers the typebar segment, causing the character on the top half of the type face to print: *To make a capital letter you must first depress the shift key.*

shift·less (shift′lis), *adj.* **1.** lacking in resourcefulness; inefficient; lazy. **2.** lacking in incentive, ambition, or aspiration. [SHIFT + -LESS] **—shift′less·ly,** *adv.* **—shift′less·ness,** *n.*

shift′ lock′, a typewriter key which locks the shift key in depressed position.

shift·y (shif′tē), *adj.,* **shift·i·er, shift·i·est. 1.** resourceful; fertile in expedients. **2.** given to or full of evasions; tricky. **3.** suggesting a deceptive or evasive character: *a shifty look.* [SHIFT + -Y[1]] **—shift′i·ly,** *adv.* **—shift′i·ness,** *n.*

Shi′ga bacil′lus (shē′gə, -gä), the bacterium *Shigella dysenteriae,* causing dysentery in man and monkeys. [named after Kiyoshi *Shiga;* see SHIGELLA]

shi·gel·la (shi gel′ə), *n., pl.* **-gel·lae** (-gel′ē), **-gel·las.** *Bacteriol.* any of several rod-shaped, aerobic bacteria of the genus *Shigella,* certain species of which, as *Shigella dysenteriae,* are pathogenic for man and warm-blooded animals. [named after Kiyoshi *Shiga* (b. 1870), Japanese scientist + L *-ella* n. suffix]

Shih Ching (shœ′ jing′). See **Book of Odes.** Also, **Shih′ King′** (ging′).

Shi·ite (shē′īt), *n. Islam.* a member of one of the two great religious divisions of Islam, regarding Ali, the son-in-law of Muhammad, as the legitimate successor of Muhammad, and disregarding the three caliphs who actually did succeed him. Also, **Shiah, Shi·i** (shē ē′, shē′ē). Cf. **Sunnite.** [SHIAH + -ITE[1]] **—Shi·ism** (shē′iz əm), *n.* **—Shi·it·ic** (shē it′ik), *adj.*

shi·kar (shi kär′), *n., v.,* **-karred, -kar·ring.** (in India) **—n. 1.** the hunting of game for sport. **—v.t., v.i. 2.** to hunt. [< Urdu < Pers]

shi·ka·ri (shi kär′ē), *n., pl.* **-ris.** (in India) one who hunts big game, esp. a professional guide or hunter. Also, **shi·ka′ree.** [< Urdu < Pers]

Shi·ki·bu (shē′kē bo͞o′), *n.* Murasaki.

Shi·ko·ku (shē′kô ko͞o′), *n.* an island in SW Japan, S of Honshu: the smallest of the main islands of Japan. 4,121,081 (1960); 7249 sq. mi.

shik·sa (shik′sə), *n. Yiddish.* **1.** a girl or woman who is not Jewish. **2.** a Jewish girl or woman whose attitudes and behavior are felt to resemble those of a gentile. Cf. **shegetz.**

Shilh (shilKH), *n., pl.* **Shluh** (shlo͞o). **1.** a member of a mountain people of Morocco. **2.** Shilha.

Shil·ha (shil hä′, -KHä′), *n.* a Berber language, the language of the Shluh. Also, **Shilh.**

shill[1] (shil), *n. Slang.* a person who poses as a customer in order to decoy others into participating, as at a gambling house, auction, confidence game, etc. [?]

shill[2] (shil), *adj. Archaic.* shrill. [ME; OE *scyl* resonant; c. D *schel* shrill, Icel *skjallr* loud]

shil·le·lagh (shə lā′lē, -lə), *n. Chiefly Irish Eng.* a cudgel, traditionally of blackthorn or oak. Also, **shil·la′la, shil·la′lah, shil·le′lah.** [after Irish town so named]

shil·ling (shil′ing), *n.* **1.** a cupronickel coin of the United Kingdom, the 20th part of a pound, equal to 12 pennies and equivalent to about .14 of a U.S. dollar. *Abbr.:* s. **2.** a fractional currency of various other nations and territories, as Australia, Ghana, Ireland, Jamaica, New Guinea, New Zealand, and Nigeria, equal to one tenth of a pound or 12 pennies. **3.** the monetary unit of Aden, Kenya, Somalia, Uganda, etc., equal to 100 cents and equivalent to about .14 of a U.S. dollar. **4.** any of various coins and moneys of account used in various parts of the U.S. in the 18th and 19th centuries. **5.** See **shilling mark.** [ME; OE *scilling;* c. D *schelling,* G *Schilling,* Goth *skillings;* akin to SHILL[2]]

shil′ling mark′, a virgule, as used as a divider between shillings and pence: *One reads 2/6 as "two shillings and sixpence" or "two and six."* Also called **shilling.**

Shil·ling·ton (shil′ing tən), *n.* a town in central Pennsylvania. 5639 (1960).

Shil·long (shil lông′), *n.* a city in and the capital of Assam, in NE India: resort. 72,400 (1961).

shil·ly-shal·ly (shil′ē shal′ē), *v.,* **-lied, -ly·ing,** *n., pl.* **-shal·lies,** *adj., adv.* **—v.i. 1.** to be irresolute; vacillate. **—n. 2.** irresolution; indecision; vacillation: *It was sheer shilly-shally on his part.* **—adj. 3.** irresolute; undecided; vacillating. **—adv. 4.** irresolutely. [orig. repeated question, *shall I? shall I?* later altered on the model of its synonym *dilly-dally*]

Shi·loh (shī′lō), *n.* **1.** a national park in SW Tennessee: Civil War battle 1862. **2.** an ancient town in central Palestine, in what is now Jordan.

shil·pit (shil′pit), *adj. Scot.* **1.** (of a person) sickly; puny; feeble. **2.** (of liquor) weak; watery. [?]

shim (shim), *n., v.,* **shimmed, shim·ming. —n. 1.** a thin slip or wedge of metal, wood, etc., for driving into crevices, as between machine parts to compensate for wear, or beneath bedplates, large stones, etc., to level them. **—v.t. 2.** to fill out or bring to a level by inserting a shim or shims. [?]

shi·mal (shə mäl′), *n.* shamal.

Shi·ma·za·ki (shē′mä zä′kē), *n.* **Tō·son** (tô′sôn), (*Haruki Shimazaki*), 1872–1943, Japanese author.

shim·mer (shim′ər), *v.i.* **1.** to shine with or reflect a subdued, tremulous light; gleam faintly. **2.** to appear to quiver or vibrate in faint light or while reflecting heat waves. **—n. 3.** a subdued, tremulous light or gleam. **4.** a quivering or vibrating motion or image as produced by reflecting faint light or heat waves. [ME *schimere,* OE *scimeri(an);* c. D *schemeren,* G *schimmern* to glisten] **—shim′mer·ing·ly,** *adv.*
—Syn. 1. glimmer. See **glisten.**

shim·mer·y (shim′ə rē), *adj.* shimmering; shining softly. [SHIMMER + -Y[1]]

shim·my (shim′ē), *n., pl.* **-mies,** *v.,* **-mied, -my·ing. —n. 1.** an American ragtime dance marked by shaking of the hips and shoulders. **2.** excessive wobbling in the front wheels of a motor vehicle. **3.** a chemise. **—v.i. 4.** to dance the shimmy. **5.** to shake, wobble, or vibrate. [back formation from *shimmies* (var. of CHEMISE), mistaken for a plural]

Shi·mo·no·se·ki (shim′ə nə sā′kē; *Jap.* shē′mô nô-se′kē), *n.* a seaport on SW Honshu, in SW Japan: treaty ending Chino-Japanese War signed 1895. 252,527 (1964).

shin[1] (shin), *n., v.,* **shinned, shin·ning. —n. 1.** the front part of the leg from the knee to the ankle. **2.** the lower part of the foreleg in cattle; the metacarpal bone. **3.** the shinbone or tibia, esp. its sharp edge or front portion. **4.** *Chiefly Brit.* a cut of beef similar to the U.S. shank, usually cut into small pieces for stewing. **—v.t., v.i. 5.** to climb by holding fast with the hands or arms and legs and drawing oneself up. [ME *shine,* OE *scin(u);* c. D *scheen,* G *Schien(bein)*]

shin[2] (shēn), *n.* **1.** the 22nd letter of the Hebrew alphabet. **2.** the consonant sound represented by this letter. [< Heb]

shīn (shēn), *n.* the 13th letter of the Arabic alphabet. [< Ar]

Shin (shin, shēn), *n. Buddhism.* a Japanese offshoot of the Pure Land Sect, requiring only faith in Amida for salvation through his accumulated merit. [< Jap: lit., faith]

Shi·nar (shī′när), *n.* a land mentioned in the Bible, often identified with Sumer.

shin·bone (shin′bōn′), *n.* the tibia. [ME; OE *scinban.* See SHIN¹, BONE¹]

shin·dig (shin′dig′), *n. Informal.* an elaborate or large dance, party, or other celebration. [? SHIN¹ + DIG; cf. slang *shinscraper* dance]

shin′dig danc′er, an attractive girl, often scantily clad, who dances the twist solo in a discotheque or similar establishment. Also called **go-go dancer.**

shin·dy (shin′dē), *n., pl.* **-dies.** *Informal.* **1.** a row; rumpus. **2.** a shindig. [var. of SHINDIG]

shine (shīn), *v.,* **shone** or, esp. for 9, 10, **shined; shin·ing;** *n.* —*v.i.* **1.** to give forth or glow with light; shed or cast light. **2.** to be bright with reflected light; glisten; sparkle. **3.** (of light) to appear brightly or strongly, esp. uncomfortably so: *Wear dark glasses so the sun won't shine in your eyes.* **4.** to be or appear unusually animated or bright, as the eyes or face. **5.** to appear with brightness or clearness, as feelings. **6.** to excel or be conspicuous: *to shine in society.* —*v.t.* **7.** to cause to shine. **8.** to direct the light of (a lamp, mirror, etc.): *Shine the flashlight on the steps so I can see.* **9.** to put a gloss or polish on; polish (as shoes, silverware, etc.). **10. shine up to,** *Slang.* **a.** to attempt to impress (a person), esp. in order to gain benefits for oneself. **b.** to become especially attentive to one of the opposite sex: *Men shine up to her like moths to a light.* —*n.* **11.** radiance or brightness caused by emitted or reflected light. **12.** luster; polish. **13.** sunshine; fair weather. **14.** a polish or gloss given to shoes. **15.** the act or an instance of polishing shoes. **16.** *Informal.* a foolish prank; caper. **17.** *Offensive.* a Negro. **18. come rain or shine, a.** regardless of the weather. **b.** no matter what the circumstances may be: *Come rain or shine, he is always on the job.* Also, **rain or shine. 19. take a shine to,** *U.S. Informal.* to take a liking or fancy to: *That little girl has really taken a shine to you.* [ME; OE *scīn(an)*; c. D *schijnen,* G *scheinen,* Icel *skīna,* Goth *skeinan*]
—**Syn. 1.** glimmer, shimmer. SHINE, BEAM, GLARE refer to the emitting or reflecting of light. SHINE refers to a steady glowing or reflecting of light: *to shine in the sun.* That which BEAMS gives forth a radiant or bright light: *to beam like a star.* GLARE refers to the shining of a light which is not only bright but so strong as to be unpleasant and dazzling: *to glare like a headlight.* **9.** buff, burnish, brighten. **12.** gloss, gleam, glow, sheen.

shin·er (shī′nər), *n.* **1.** one who or that which shines. **2.** *Slang.* See **black eye** (def. 1). **3.** any of various small, American, fresh-water fishes having glistening scales, esp. a minnow. **4.** any of various silvery, marine fishes, as the menhaden or butterfish. **5.** a defect in silk or man-made filament or fabric, produced either in the process of winding or as a result of shuttle friction and appearing on fabric as a shiny streak. [SHINE + -ER¹]

shin′er perch′, a small, silvery, viviparous perch, *Cymatogaster aggregata,* found along the Pacific coast of North America. Also called **seven-eleven, shin′er sea′perch.**

Shin·gen′ tsu′ba (shēn gen′), a tsuba of iron or brass wrapped with silver or copper wires. [so called from the fact that Takada *Shingen,* a daimyo, favored it]

Shin·gi·shu (shēn′gē shōō′), *n.* Japanese name of **Sinuiju.**

shin·gle¹ (shing′gəl), *n., v.,* **-gled, -gling.** —*n.* **1.** a thin piece of wood, slate, metal, asbestos, or the like, usually oblong, laid in overlapping rows to cover the roofs and walls of buildings. **2.** a woman's close-cropped haircut. **3.** *Informal.* a small signboard, esp. as hung before a doctor's or lawyer's office. **4. hang out one's shingle,** *Informal.* to establish a professional practice, esp. in law or medicine; open an office: *When he came out of the service, he hung out his shingle in his home town.* —*v.t.* **5.** to cover with shingles, as a roof. **6.** to cut (hair) close to the head. [ME, var. of *shindle* < L *scindula,* equiv. to *scind(ere)* (to) cut, cleave + *-ula* -ULE (cf. L *scandula* shingle)] —**shin′gler,** *n.*

shin·gle² (shing′gəl), *n. Chiefly Brit.* **1.** small, water-worn stones or pebbles such as lie in loose sheets or beds on the seashore. **2.** a beach, riverbank, or other area covered with such small pebbles or stones. [sandhi var. of earlier *chingle;* cf. Norw *singel* small stones]

shin·gle³ (shing′gəl), *v.t.,* **-gled, -gling.** *Metalworking.* to hammer or squeeze (puddled iron) into a bloom or billet, eliminating as much slag as possible; knobble. [< F *cingle(r)* (to) whip, beat < G *zängeln,* deriv. of *Zange* tongs]

shin′gle oak′, an oak, *Quercus imbricaria,* yielding a wood used for shingles, clapboards, etc.

shin·gles (shing′gəlz), *n.* (*construed as sing. or pl.*) *Pathol.* a disease of the skin affecting the posterior roots of the peripheral nerves, caused by a virus, and characterized by clusters of blisters. Also called **herpes zoster, zoster.** [< medical L *cingul(um)* (lit., girdle) trans. of Gk *zōnē* ZONE in its medical sense; English form expresses plurality of eruptions (cf. MEASLES)]

shin·gly (shing′glē), *adj. Chiefly Brit.* consisting of or covered with shingle. [SHINGLE² + -Y¹]

shin′ guard′, *Sports.* a protective covering, usually of leather or plastic and often padded, for the shins and sometimes the knees, worn chiefly by catchers in baseball and goalkeepers in ice hockey.

shin·ing (shī′ning), *adj.* **1.** radiant; gleaming; bright. **2.** resplendent; brilliant: *shining talents.* **3.** conspicuously fine: *a shining example.* [SHINE + -ING²] —**shin′ing·ly,** *adv.*
—**Syn. 1.** glistening, effulgent. See **bright. 2.** lustrous. **3.** outstanding, distinguished, eminent, prime, splendid.

shin·leaf (shin′lēf′), *n., pl.* **-leaves. 1.** a North American herb, *Pyrola elliptica,* having leaves used formerly for shinplasters. **2.** any plant of the genus *Pyrola.* [SHIN¹ + LEAF]

shin·ner·y (shin′ə rē), *n. Southern and Southwestern U.S.* a dense growth of small trees, esp. scrub oaks. [< LaF *chênière* CHENIER]

Shinn·ston (shin′stən), *n.* a town in N West Virginia. 2724 (1960).

shin·ny¹ (shin′ē), *n., pl.* **-nies,** *v.,* **-nied, -ny·ing.** —*n.* **1.** a simple variety of hockey, played with a ball, block of wood, or the like, and clubs curved at one end. **2.** the club used. —*v.i.* **3.** to play shinny. **4.** to drive the ball at shinny. [? var. of *shin ye,* cry used in the game]

shin·ny² (shin′ē), *v.i.,* **-nied, -ny·ing.** to shin: *He shinnied up the tree.* [SHIN¹ + -y of HURRY]

shin·plas·ter (shin′plas′tər, -plä′stər), *n.* a hardy orchid, *Orchis rotundifolia,* of central North America, having a solitary leaf and magenta flowers.

shin·plas·ter (shin′plas′tər, -plä′stər), *n.* **1.** a plaster for the shin or leg. **2.** *U.S.* (formerly) **a.** a piece of paper money of a denomination lower than one dollar. **b.** money of little value, as that issued on insufficient security. [SHIN¹ + PLASTER]

Shin·to (shin′tō), *n.* **1.** Also, **Shin′to·ism.** the native religion of Japan, primarily a system of nature and ancestor worship. —*adj.* **2.** Also, **Shin′to·is′tic.** of, pertaining to, or characteristic of Shinto. [< Jap < Chin *shin tao* way of the gods] —**Shin′to·ist,** *n., adj.*

shin·y (shī′nē), *adj.,* **shin·i·er, shin·i·est. 1.** bright or glossy in appearance. **2.** filled with light, as by sunshine. **3.** rubbed or worn to a glossy smoothness, as clothes. [SHINE + -Y¹] —**shin′i·ly,** *adv.* —**shin′i·ness,** *n.*

ship (ship), *n., v.,* **shipped, ship·ping.** —*n.* **1.** a vessel, esp. a large ocean-going one propelled by sails or engines. **2.** *Naut.* **a.** a sailing vessel square-rigged on all of three or more masts, having jibs, staysails, and a spanker on the aftermost mast. **b.** *Obs. Brit.* a bark having more than three masts. Cf. **shipentine. 3.** the crew of a vessel: *The captain gave the ship shore leave.* **4.** an airship or airplane. **5. when one's ship comes in** or **home,** when one's fortune is assured: *He gave her a fur coat when his ship came in.* —*v.t.* **6.** to put or take on board a ship or other means of transportation; to send or transport by ship, rail, truck, plane, etc. **7.** *Naut.* to take in (water) over the side, as a vessel does when waves break over it. **8.** to bring (an object) into a ship or boat. **9.** to engage (someone) for service on a ship. **10.** to fix in a ship or boat in the proper place for use. **11.** to place (an oar) in proper position for rowing. Cf. **boat** (def. 11). **12.** *Informal.* to send away: *They shipped the kids off to camp for the summer.* —*v.i.* **13.** to go on board or travel by ship; embark. **14.** to engage to serve on a ship. **15. ship out, a.** to leave a country, esp. one's native country, by or as by ship: *He said goodby to his family and shipped out for the West Indies.* **b.** to send (someone) to another country, esp. from his native country, by or as by ship: *As soon as we finish basic training, the army will ship us out.* **c.** *Informal.* to quit, resign, or be fired from a job: *Shape up or ship out!* [ME, OE *scip;* c. D *schip,* G *Schiff,* Icel, Goth *skip*] —**ship′less,** *adj.* —**ship′less·ly,** *adv.*

Ship (Full-rigged)
1, Foresail or forecourse; 2, Mainsail or main course; 3, Crossjack or mizzen course; 4, Fore lower topsail; 5, Main lower topsail; 6, Mizzen lower topsail; 7, Fore upper topsail; 8, Main upper topsail; 9, Mizzen upper topsail; 10, Fore lower topgallant; 11, Main lower topgallant; 12, Mizzen lower topgallant; 13, Fore upper topgallant; 14, Main upper topgallant; 15, Mizzen upper topgallant; 16, Fore royal; 17, Main royal; 18, Mizzen royal; 19, Skysail; 20, Spanker; 21, Fore staysail; 22, Jib; 23, Inner jib; 24, Outer jib; 25, Flying jib; 26, Main staysail; 27, Main topmast staysail; 28, Main topgallant staysail; 29, Main royal staysail; 30, Mizzen staysail; 31, Mizzen topgallant staysail

-ship, a native English suffix of nouns denoting condition, character, office, skill, etc.: *clerkship; friendship; statesmanship.* [ME, OE *-scipe;* akin to SHAPE; c. WFris, WFlem *schip*]

ship′ bis′cuit, hardtack.

ship·board (ship′bōrd′, -bôrd′), *n.* **1.** *Archaic.* **a.** the deck or side of a ship. **b.** the situation of being on a ship. **2. on shipboard,** aboard a seagoing vessel. —*adj.* **3.** done, conducted, or designed for use aboard ship, esp. during an ocean voyage: *a shipboard romance; a shipboard telephone.* [late ME *shipbord* (see SHIP, BOARD); r. ME *shipesbord*]

ship·boy (ship′boi′), *n.* See **ship's boy.** [SHIP + BOY]

ship′ bread′, hardtack.

ship·build·er (ship′bil′dər), *n.* **1.** one whose occupation is the designing or constructing of ships. **2.** a commercial firm for building ships. [SHIP + BUILDER] —**ship′build′ing,** *n.*

ship′ canal′, a canal navigable by ships.

ship′ chan′dler, one who deals in cordage, canvas, and other supplies for ships. —**ship′ chan′dlery.**

ship′ decant′er, a glass decanter with a very wide base.

ship·en·tine (ship′ən tēn′, -tīn′), *n. U.S. Naut. Obs.* a four-masted bark. [SHIP + *-entine* (as in BARKENTINE)]

ship·fit·ter (ship′fit′ər), *n. Shipbuilding.* one who forms plates, shapes, etc., of ships according to plans, patterns, or molds. [SHIP + FITTER]

Ship′ka Pass′ (ship′kä), a mountain pass in central Bulgaria, in the Balkan Mountains. 4375 ft. high.

ship·lap (ship′lap′), *n. Carpentry.* **1.** an overlapping joint, as a rabbet, between two boards joined edge to edge. **2.** boarding joined with such overlapping joints. See illus. under **siding.** [SHIP + LAP²]

ship·load (ship′lōd′), *n.* **1.** a full load for a ship. **2.** the cargo or load carried by a ship. [SHIP + LOAD]

ship·man (ship′mən), *n., pl.* **-men.** *Archaic.* **1.** a sailor. **2.** the master of a ship. [ME, OE *scipman;* c. MD *schipman,* G *Schiff(s)mann.* See SHIP, MAN¹]

ship·mas·ter (ship′mas′tər, -mä′stər), *n.* one who commands a ship; master; captain. [ME *schipmaster;* c. G *Schiffmeister*]

ship·mate (ship′māt′), *n.* one who serves with another on the same vessel. [SHIP + MATE¹]

ship·ment (ship′mənt), *n.* **1.** the act or an instance of shipping freight or cargo. **2.** a quantity of freight or cargo shipped at one time. **3.** that which is shipped. [SHIP + -MENT]
—**Syn. 3.** consignment. See **freight.**

ship′ mon′ey, *Early Eng. Law.* a tax levied on ports, maritime towns, etc., to provide support for the royal navy.

ship′ of state′, a nation or its affairs likened to a ship under sail.

ship′ of the line′, (formerly) a sailing warship armed powerfully enough to serve in the line of battle, usually having cannons ranged along two or more decks; battleship.

ship′ of war′, warship.

ship·own·er (ship′ō′nər), *n.* one who owns a ship or ships. [SHIP + OWNER]

ship·pa·ble (ship′ə bəl), *adj.* being in a suitable form or condition for shipping. [SHIP + -ABLE]

ship·pen (ship′ən), *n. Brit. Dial.* shippon.

Ship·pens·burg (ship′ənz bûrg′), *n.* a town in S Pennsylvania. 6138 (1960).

ship·per (ship′ər), *n.* one who ships goods or makes shipments. [SHIP + -ER¹]

ship·ping (ship′ing), *n.* **1.** the act or business of one who or that which ships. **2.** a number of ships, esp. merchant ships, taken as a whole; tonnage. **3.** *Obs.* a voyage. [SHIP + -ING¹]

ship′ping clerk′, a clerk who attends to the packing, unpacking, receiving, sending out, and recording of shipments.

ship′ping fe′ver, *Vet. Med.* a respiratory disease of cattle often occurring during the shipment of livestock, characterized by tiredness, fever, lack of appetite, and slight coughing. Also called **ship′ping pneumo′nia.** Cf. **hemorrhagic septicemia.**

ship′ping room′, a place in a business concern where goods are packed and shipped.

ship′ping ton′, See under **ton¹** (def. 5).

ship·pon (ship′ən), *n. Brit. Dial.* a cow barn or cattle shed. Also, **shippen.** [ME *schepon,* OE *scypen,* equiv. to *scyp-* SHOP + *-en* fem. suffix; c. G *Schuppen*]

ship-rigged (ship′rigd′), *adj. Naut.* (of a sailing vessel) rigged as a ship; full-rigged.

ship's′ boat′, a boat carried as a lifeboat or work boat by a larger vessel.

ship's′ boy′, a male attendant, as a cabin boy, steward, etc., employed to wait on a ship's passengers or officers.

ship's′ com′pany, company (def. 10).

ship·shape (ship′shāp′), *adj.* **1.** in good order; well-arranged; trim or tidy. —*adv.* **2.** in a shipshape manner. [SHIP + SHAPE]

ship's′ hus′band, one who accompanies a merchant vessel as the business agent of the owners.

ship·side (ship′sīd′), *n.* the area alongside a ship, as on a pier. [ME; see SHIP, SIDE¹]

ship's′ iner′tial naviga′tion sys′tem. See **SINS**

ship's′ pa′pers, necessary papers presented at all legal inspections of a ship, and containing the owner's name, description of cargo, destination, etc.

ship-to-shore (ship′tə shōr′, -shôr′), *adj.* **1.** operating between a ship and the shore: *a ship-to-shore radio.* —*adv.* **2.** from a ship to the shore: *The message was sent ship-to-shore.* —*n.* **3.** a ship-to-shore radio.

ship·way (ship′wā′), *n.* **1.** the structure that supports a ship being built. **2.** ship canal. [SHIP + WAY]

ship·worm (ship′wûrm′), *n.* any of various marine bivalve mollusks which burrow into the timbers of ships, wharves, etc. [SHIP + WORM]

ship·wreck (ship′rek′), *n.* **1.** the destruction or loss of a ship, as by sinking. **2.** the remains of a wrecked ship. **3.** destruction or ruin: *the shipwreck of one's hopes.* —*v.t.* **4.** to cause to suffer shipwreck. **5.** to destroy; ruin. —*v.i.* **6.** to suffer shipwreck. [SHIP + WRECK; r. ME *shipwrech,* OE **scipwræc*]

ship·wright (ship′rīt′), *n. Shipbuilding.* one who builds and launches wooden vessels or does carpentry work in connection with the building and launching of steel or iron vessels. [ME, OE *scipwyrhta.* See SHIP, WRIGHT]

ship·yard (ship′yärd′), *n.* a yard or enclosure in which ships are built or repaired. [SHIP + YARD²]

shir·a·lee (shir′ə lē), *n. Australian.* swag² (def. 2). [?]

Shi·raz (shē räz′), *n.* a city in SW Iran. 229,761 (est. 1963).

shire (shīᵊr), *n.* **1.** one of the counties of Great Britain. **2. the Shires,** the counties in the Midlands in which hunting is especially popular. [ME; OE *scīr* office of administration, jurisdiction of such an office, county]

Shi·ré (shē′rā), *n.* a river in SE Africa, flowing S from Lake Nyasa to the Zambezi River. 370 mi. long.

shire′ horse′, one of an English breed of large, strong draft horses having a usually brown or bay coat with white markings.

shirk (shûrk), *v.t.* **1.** to evade (work, duty, responsibility, etc.). —*v.i.* **2.** to evade work, duty, etc. —*n.* **3.** a shirker. [var. of SHARK²]

shirk·er (shûr′kər), *n.* one who evades work, duty, responsibility, etc. [SHIRK + -ER¹]

Shir·leen (shûr lēn′), *n.* a girl's given name, form of **Shirley.** Also, **Shir·lene′.**

Shir·ley (shûr′lē), *n.* **1. James,** 1596–1666, English dramatist. **2.** Also, **Sherley, Shir′lee, Shir′lie.** a boy's or girl's given name.

shirr (shûr), *v.t.* **1.** to draw up or gather (cloth or the like) on three or more parallel threads. **2.** to bake (eggs removed from the shell) in a shallow dish or in individual dishes. —*n.* **3.** Also, **shirr′ing.** a shirred arrangement, as of cloth. [?]

shirt (shûrt), *n.* **1.** a long- or short-sleeved garment for the upper part of the body, usually lightweight and having a collar and a front opening, worn chiefly by men. **2.** an undergarment of cotton, or other material, for the upper part of the body. **3.** a shirtwaist. **4.** a nightshirt. **5. in one's shirt sleeves,** without a coat:

It was so hot that they worked in their shirt sleeves. Also, **in one's shirt-sleeves. 6. keep one's shirt on,** *Slang.* to refrain from becoming angry or impatient; remain calm: *Tell him to keep his shirt on until we're ready.* **7. lose one's shirt,** *Slang.* to lose all that one possesses; suffer a severe financial reverse: *He lost his shirt in the stock market.* [ME *schirte,* OE *scyrte;* c. G *Schürze,* D *schort* apron, Icel *skyrta* SKIRT] **—shirt′less,** *adj.*

shirt·band (shûrt′band′), *n.* a band of material sewn into a shirt, as for stiffening or finishing, esp. a neckband to which the collar is sewn or buttoned. [SHIRT + BAND²]

shirt-dress (shûrt′dres′), *n.* shirtwaist (def. 2).

shirt′ front′, 1. the front of a shirt, esp. the part that is exposed when a jacket or vest is worn. **2.** dickey (def. 2).

shirt·ing (shûr′ting), *n.* any shirt fabric, as broadcloth or oxford. [SHIRT + -ING¹]

shirt·mak·er (shûrt′mā′kər), *n.* **1.** one who makes shirts. **2.** a woman's tailored blouse. [SHIRT + MAKER] **—shirt′mak′ing,** *n.*

shirt-sleeve (shûrt′slēv′), *adj.* **1.** not wearing a jacket; informally dressed: *a shirt-sleeve mob.* **2.** being simple, plain, and informal; direct and straightforward in approach, manner, etc.: *shirt-sleeve diplomacy.* Also, **shirt′-sleeved′.**

shirt·tail (shûrt′tāl′), *n.* **1.** the part of a shirt below the waistline. **2.** *Journalism.* a brief item added at the end of a related newspaper story. Cf. **follow-up** (def. 3b). [SHIRT + TAIL¹]

shirt·waist (shûrt′wāst′), *n.* **1.** a tailored blouse or shirt worn by women. **2.** Also called **shirt-dress, shirt′waist′ dress′.** a dress with a bodice and a front opening tailored like those of a dress shirt. [SHIRT + WAIST]

shirt·y (shûr′tē), *adj. Brit., Australian.* annoyed, angry. [SHIRT, in the phrase *to get a person's shirt out* + -Y¹]

shish ke·bab (shish′ kə bob′), a dish consisting of kabobs broiled or roasted on a skewer. Also called **shashlik, shashlick, shaslick.** [< Turk; cf. SHASHLIK, KABOB]

shish·ya (shish′yə), *n. Hinduism.* a pupil of a guru. [< Hindi]

shit (shit), *n., v.,* **shit, shit·ting,** *interj. Slang* (*vulgar*). —*n.* **1.** feces. **2.** an act of defecation. **3.** pretense, exaggeration, lies, or nonsense. —*v.i.* **4.** to defecate. —*interj.* **5.** (used to express disgust, contempt, disappointment, or the like.) [alter. of earlier shite (v.), ME *shiten,* OE **scītan;* n., deriv. of OE *scite* dung, *scitte* diarrhea]

shi·to′gi tsu′ba (shē tō′gē; *Jap.* shē tô′gē), a tsuba used with a tachi, oblong and narrow with the long sides concave. [< Jap: lit., rice-cake tsuba]

shit·tah (shit′ə), *n., pl.* **shit·tim** (shit′im), **shit·tahs.** a tree, said to be acacia, probably *Acacia Seyal* or *A. tortilis,* that yielded the shittim wood of the Old Testament. [< Heb *shiṭṭāh*]

shit′tim wood′, 1. the wood, probably acacia, of which the ark of the covenant and various parts of the tabernacle were made. Ex. 25, 26. **2.** the cascara, *Rhamnus Purshiana.* **3.** See **false buckthorn.** Also called **shittim.** [< Heb *shiṭṭīm,* pl. of *shiṭṭāh* (see SHITTAH)]

shit·ty (shit′ē), *adj.,* **-ti·er, -ti·est.** *Slang* (*vulgar*). **1.** inferior or contemptible. **2.** inept or insignificant. [SHIT + -Y¹]

shiv (shiv), *n. Slang.* a knife, esp. a switchblade. [? alter. of *chiv* blade < Gypsy]

Shi·va (shē′və), *n. Hinduism.* "the Destroyer," the third member of the Trimurti, along with Brahma the Creator and Vishnu the Preserver. Also, **Siva.** [< Skt: lit., the auspicious] **—Shi′va·ism,** *n.* **—Shi′va·ist,** *n.* **—Shi′va·is′tic,** *adj.*

shi·vah (shiv′ə), *n. Hebrew.* shibah.

Shi·vah A·sar Be·tam·muz (shē′vô ô′sôr bə tä′mo͞oz), *Judaism.* See **Shibah Asar Betammuz.**

shiv·a·ree (shiv′ə rē′), *n., v.,* **-reed, -ree·ing.** —*n.* **1.** a mock serenade with kettles, pans, horns, and other noisemakers given for a newly married couple; charivari. **2.** *Informal.* an elaborate, noisy celebration. —*v.t.* **3.** to serenade with a shivaree. [alter. of CHARIVARI]

Shi·va-Shak·ti (shē′və shuk′tē), *n. Hinduism.* the Godhead, of which the masculine, passive, transcendent, eternal principle is Shiva, and the feminine, active, immanent, temporal principle is Shakti, the Divine Mother. Cf. **Tantra.**

shive¹ (shīv), *n.* **1.** a sliver or fragment; splinter. **2.** a thin plug, as of wood or cork, for stopping the bunghole of a cask or the mouth of a bottle. [ME; c. G *Scheibe,* Icel *skīfa*]

shive² (shiv, shīv), *n.* **1.** a splinter or fragment of the husk of flax, hemp, etc. **2.** boon³. **3.** *Papermaking.* a small, partially cooked lump of wood fiber in the pulp, usually removed by bleaching. [late ME *scyfe;* c. Flem *schif,* MD *scheve,* G *Schebe*]

Shive·ly (shīv′lē), *n.* a city in N Kentucky, near Louisville. 15,155 (1960).

shiv·er¹ (shiv′ər), *v.i.* **1.** to shake or tremble with cold, fear, excitement, etc. **2.** *Naut.* **a.** (of a fore-and-aft sail) to shake when too close to the wind. **b.** (of a sailing vessel) to be headed so close to the wind that the sails shake. —*n.* **3.** a tremulous motion; a tremble or quiver: *The thought sent a shiver down her spine.* **4. shivers,** an attack of shivering or chills (usually preceded by *the*). [ME *chivere* (n.); later *sh-* for sake of alliteration in phrase *chiver and shake*] **—shiv′er·er,** *n.* **—shiv′er·ing·ly,** *adv.*

—Syn. 1. SHIVER, QUAKE, SHUDDER refer to a vibratory muscular movement, a trembling, usually involuntary. We SHIVER with cold, or a sensation such as that of cold: *to shiver in thin clothing on a frosty day; to shiver with pleasant anticipation.* We QUAKE esp. with fear: *to quake with fright.* We SHUDDER with horror or abhorrence; the agitation is more powerful and deep-seated than shivering or trembling: *to shudder at pictures of a concentration camp.*

shiv·er² (shiv′ər), *v.t., v.i.* **1.** to break or split into fragments. —*n.* **2.** a fragment; splinter. [ME *schivere* fragment; c. G *Schiefer* schist]

shiv·er·y¹ (shiv′ə rē), *adj.* **1.** inclined to or characterized by shivers, quivers, or tremors. **2.** causing shivering. [SHIVER¹ + -Y¹]

shiv·er·y² (shiv′ə rē), *adj.* readily breaking into shivers or fragments; brittle. [SHIVER² + -Y¹]

shive′ wheel′ (shīv), *Mining.* a sheave supporting a hoist rope.

shi·voo (shi vo͞o′), *n., pl.* **-voos.** *Australian.* a boisterous party or celebration. [?]

Shi·zu·o·ka (shē′zo͝o ô′kä), *n.* a seaport on S Honshu, in central Japan. 361,502 (1964).

Shko·dër (shkô′dər), *n.* Albanian name of **Scutari.** Also, **Shko·dra** (shkô′drä).

shkot·zim (shkô′tsim), *n. Yiddish.* pl. of **shegetz.**

shle·miel (shlə mēl′), *n.* schlemiel.

shli·ma·zel (shli mä′zəl), *n.* schlimazel. Also, **shli·ma′zl.**

Shluh (shlo͞o, shlo͞okh), *n.* pl. of **Shilh.**

S.H.M., See **simple harmonic motion.**

shmo (shmō), *n., pl.* **shmoes.** schmo.

shnaps (shnäps, shnaps), *n.* schnapps.

shnook (shno͝ok), *n. Slang.* schnook.

Sho·a (shō′ä), *n.* a former kingdom in E Africa: now a province of Ethiopia. 1,800,000 (est. 1939); 25,290 sq. mi. *Cap.:* Addis Ababa.

shoad (shōd), *n.* **1.** *Brit. Mining.* float (def. 30). —*v.i.* **2.** *Mining.* to examine the bed of a stream for ore. [akin to OE *scādan* to divide, scatter; c. G *schneiden*]

shoal¹ (shōl), *n.* **1.** a place where a sea, river, or other body of water is shallow. **2.** a sand bank or sand bar in the bed of a body of water, esp. one which is exposed above the surface of the water at low tide. —*adj.* **3.** of little depth, as water; shallow. **4.** *Naut.* **a.** (of a hull) drawing a relatively small amount of water. **b.** (of the draft of a hull) relatively shallow. —*v.i.* **5.** to become shallow or more shallow. —*v.t.* **6.** to cause to become shallow. **7.** *Naut.* to sail so as to lessen the depth of (the water under a vessel). [ME (Scot) *shald,* OE *sceald* shallow]

—Syn. 1. shallow, rapid, riffle. **2.** reef. **5.** shelve.

shoal² (shōl), *n.* **1.** any large number of persons or things. **2.** a school of fish. —*v.i.* **3.** to collect in a shoal; throng. [OE *scolu* shoal (of fish), multitude, troop; c. D *school;* see SCHOOL²]

shoal·y (shō′lē), *adj.,* **shoal·i·er, shoal·i·est.** full of shoals or shallows. [SHOAL¹ + -Y¹]

shoat (shōt), *n.* a young, weaned pig. Also, **shote.** [late ME *shote;* c. WFlem *schote*]

sho·chet (shō′khāt; *Eng.* shō′khit), *n., pl.* **sho·che·tim** (shō khə tēm′, shōkh-), *Eng.* **sho·chets.** *Hebrew.* shohet.

shock¹ (shok), *n.* **1.** a sudden and violent blow or impact; collision. **2.** a sudden or violent disturbance or commotion: *the shock of battle.* **3.** a sudden or violent disturbance of the mind, emotions, or sensibilities: *The burglary was a shock to her sense of security. The book provided a shock, nothing more.* **4.** the cause of such a disturbance: *The rebuke came as a shock.* **5.** *Pathol.* a collapse of circulatory function, caused by severe injury, blood loss, or disease, and characterized by pallor, sweating, weak pulse, and very low blood pressure. **6.** the physiological effect produced by the passage of an electric current through the body. **7.** (in a piece of metal) strong internal stresses, as from uneven heating. **8.** *Mach.* See **shock absorber.** —*v.t.* **9.** to strike or jar with intense surprise, horror, disgust, etc.: *He enjoyed shocking people.* **10.** to strike against violently. **11.** to give an electric shock to. **12.** to create strong internal stresses in (a piece of metal), as by uneven heating. —*v.i.* **13.** to undergo a shock. [< MF *choc,* back formation from *choquer* to clash (in battle) < Gmc; cf. D *schokken* to shake, jolt, jerk] **—shock′a·bil′i·ty,** *n.* **—shock′a·ble,** *adj.* **—shock′ed·ness,** *n.* **—shock′like′,** *adj.*

—Syn. 9. stagger, astound, stupefy. SHOCK, STARTLE, PARALYZE, STUN suggest a sudden, sharp surprise which affects one somewhat like a blow. SHOCK suggests a strong blow, as it were, to one's nerves, sentiments, sense of decency, etc.: *The onlookers were shocked by the accident.* STARTLE implies the sharp surprise of sudden fright: *to be startled by a loud noise.* PARALYZE implies such a complete shock as to render one temporarily helpless: *paralyzed with fear.* STUN implies such a shock as bewilders or stupefies: *stunned by the realization of an unpleasant truth.*

shock² (shok), *n.* **1.** a group of sheaves of grain placed on end and supporting one another in the field. —*v.t.* **2.** to make into shocks. [ME; c. LG *schok* shock of grain, group of sixty, G *Schock* sixty] **—shock′er,** *n.*

shock³ (shok), *n.* **1.** a thick, bushy mass, as of hair. **2.** Also, **shock′ dog′.** a dog with long, shaggy hair. —*adj.* **3.** shaggy, as hair. [special use of SHOCK², the hair being compared to a shock of wheat]

shock′ absorb′er, *Mach.* a device for damping sudden and rapid motion, as the recoil of a spring-mounted object from shock.

shock′ ac′tion, *Mil.* a method of attack by mobile units in which the suddenness, violence, and massed weight of the first impact produce the main effect.

shock′ cord′, an elastic cord used to absorb sudden pulls.

shock·er (shok′ər), *n.* **1.** one who or that which shocks. **2.** *Chiefly Brit. Informal.* a sensational work of fiction. [SHOCK¹ + -ER¹]

shock·head·ed (shok′hed′id), *adj.* having a shock or thick mass of hair on the head. [SHOCK³ + -HEADED]

shock·ing (shok′ing), *adj.* **1.** causing intense surprise, disgust, horror, etc. **2.** very bad: *shocking manners.* [SHOCK¹ + -ING²] **—shock′ing·ly,** *adv.* **—shock′ing·ness,** *n.*

Shock·ley (shok′lē), *n.* **William Bradford,** born 1910, U.S. physicist: Nobel prize 1956.

shock·proof (shok′pro͞of′), *adj.* **1.** Also, **shock′-proof′.** (of clockwork, machinery, etc.) protected against damage resulting from anticipated shocks. —*v.t.* **2.** to protect (clockwork, machinery, etc.) against damage resulting from anticipated shocks. [SHOCK¹ + -PROOF]

shock′ ther′apy, *Psychiatry.* a form or method of treating certain psychotic disorders, as schizophrenia, by the use of chemicals, as metrazol, insulin, etc., or by electrical means: the drugs are injected subcutaneously; electrical shocks are administered by electrodes; both are followed by coma and often convulsions. Also, **shock′ treat′ment.**

shock′ troops′, *Mil.* troops especially selected, trained, and equipped for engaging in assault.

shock′ wave′, a region of abrupt change of pressure and density moving as a wave front at or above the velocity of sound, caused by an intense explosion or supersonic flow over a body.

shod (shod), *v.* a pt. and pp. of **shoe.**

shod·dy (shod′ē), *n., pl.* **-dies,** *adj.,* **-di·er, -di·est.** —*n.* **1.** a fibrous material obtained by shredding unfelted rags or waste. Cf. **mungo. 2.** anything inferior made to resemble what is of superior quality; anything inferior but pretentious. **3.** pretense, as in art, manufacture, etc. —*adj.* **4.** pretending to a superiority not possessed; sham. **5.** made of or containing shoddy. [?] **—shod′di·ly,** *adv.* **—shod′di·ness,** *n.*

shoe (sho͞o), *n., pl.* **shoes,** (*esp. Dial.*) **shoon;** *v.,* **shod** or **shoed, shod** or **shoed** or **shod·den, shoe·ing.** —*n.* **1.** an external covering for the human foot, usually of leather and consisting of a more or less stiff or heavy sole and a lighter upper part ending a short distance above, at, or below the ankle. **2.** an object or part resembling a shoe in form, position, or use. **3.** a horseshoe or a similar plate for the hoof of some other animal. **4.** a ferrule or the like, as of iron, for protecting the end of a staff, pole, etc. **5.** the part of a brake mechanism fitting into the drum and extended outwardly to apply the friction lining to the drum rim for stopping or slowing a car, truck, etc. **6.** the outer casing of a pneumatic automobile tire. **7.** a drag or skid for a wheel of a vehicle. **8.** a part having a larger area than the end of an object on which it fits, serving to disperse or apply its weight or thrust. **9.** the sliding contact by which an electric car or locomotive takes its current from the third rail. **10.** *Civ. Eng.* **a.** a member supporting one end of a truss or girder in a bridge. **b.** a hard and sharp foot of a pile or caisson for piercing underlying soil. **11.** a small molding, as a quarter round, closing the angle between a baseboard and a floor. **12.** the outwardly curved portion at the base of a downspout. **13.** a piece of iron or stone, sunk into the ground, against which the leaves of a gateway are shut. **14.** subrail. **15.** a band of iron on the bottom of the runner of a sleigh. **16.** *Furniture.* **a.** a cuplike metal piece for protecting the bottom of a leg. **b.** a fillet beneath an ornamental foot, as a pad or scroll foot. **17.** *Print.* a box into which unusable type is thrown. **18.** a chute conveying grain to be ground into flour. **19.** *Carpentry.* soleplate. **20.** *Naut.* **a.** Also called **false keel.** a thickness of planking covering the bottom of the keel of a wooden vessel to protect it against rubbing. **b.** Also called **shoe′ piece′, solepiece.** a horizontal member connecting the bottom of a propeller post with that of a sternpost; skeg. **c.** a wooden slab fitted to a fluke of an anchor to increase its area when anchoring over a soft bottom or to prevent it from injuring deck planking. **21. fill someone's shoes,** to take the place and assume the obligations of another person: *She felt that no stepmother could ever hope to fill her late mother's shoes.* **22. in someone's shoes,** in a position or situation similar to that of another: *I wouldn't like to be in his shoes.* **23. the shoe is on the other foot,** the circumstances are reversed; a change of places has occurred: *Now that we are rich and they are poor the shoe is on the other foot.* **24. where the shoe pinches,** the true cause of the trouble or worry: *They have enough money to send their children to the best colleges, but where the shoe pinches is that the children are not intelligent enough to do the work.* —*v.t.* **25.** to provide or fit with a shoe or shoes. **26.** to protect or arm at the point, edge, or face with a ferrule, metal plate, or the like. [ME *scho(o),* OE *sceō(h);* c. G *Schuh,* Icel *skōr,* Goth *skōhs*] **—shoe′less,** *adj.*

Shoebill (Height 5 ft.; length 3½ ft.)

shoe·bill (sho͞o′bil′), *n.* a large, African, storklike bird, *Balaeniceps rex,* having a broad, flattened bill shaped somewhat like a shoe. [SHOE + BILL²]

shoe·black (sho͞o′blak′), *n.* bootblack. [SHOE + BLACK]

shoe′black plant′. See **China rose** (def. 2).

shoe′ boil′, *Vet. Pathol.* a swelling of the elbow of a horse due to irritation caused by the hoof striking the elbow when lying down. Also called **capped elbow.**

shoe·brush (sho͞o′brush′), *n.* a brush used in polishing shoes. [SHOE + BRUSH¹]

shoe·horn (sho͞o′hôrn′), *n.* a shaped piece of horn, metal, or the like, inserted in the heel of a shoe to make it slip on more easily. [SHOE + HORN]

shoe·lace (sho͞o′lās′), *n.* a string or lace for fastening a shoe. [SHOE + LACE]

shoe·mak·er (sho͞o′mā′kər), *n.* one who makes or mends shoes. [ME; see SHOE, MAKER] **—shoe′mak′ing,** *n.*

Shoe′maker's Hol′iday, The, (or *A Pleasant Comedy of the Gentle Craft*) a comedy (1600) by Thomas Dekker.

shoe′ piece′, *Naut.* shoe (def. 20b).

sho·er (sho͞o′ər), *n.* one who shoes horses or other animals. [ME; see SHOE, -ER¹]

shoe·shine (sho͞o′shīn′), *n.* **1.** the act or an instance of cleaning and polishing a pair of shoes. **2.** the surface of a polished shoe or shoes. [SHOE + SHINE]

shoe·shop (sho͞o′shop′), *n.* a shop or store where shoes are sold. [SHOE + SHOP]

shoe·string (sho͞o′string′), *n.* **1.** a shoelace. **2.** a very small amount of money. [SHOE + STRING]

shoe′string pota′to, a long, sticklike slice of raw potato which is fried until crisp.

shoe′string tack′le, *Football Slang.* a tackle made around the ankles of the ball carrier.

shoe·tree (sho͞o′trē′), *n.* one of a pair of foot-shaped devices, usually of metal or wood, for placing in a shoe to maintain its shape when it is not being worn. [SHOE + TREE]

sho·far (shō′fər; *Heb.* shō fär′), *n., pl.* **-fars,** *Heb.* **-froth** (-frōt′). *Judaism.* a ram's horn blown as a wind instrument, sounded in Biblical times chiefly to communicate signals in battle and announce certain religious occasions and in modern times chiefly at synagogue services on Rosh Hashanah and Yom Kippur. Also, **shophar.** [< Heb *shōphār*]

Shofar

CONCISE PRONUNCIATION KEY: *act, āble, dâre, ärt; ebb, ēqual; if, īce; hot, ōver, ôrder, oil, bo͝ok, o͞oze, out; up, ûrge; chief; sing; shoe; thin, that; zh* as in *measure.* ə = *a* as in *alone, e* as in *system, i* as in *easily, o* as in *gallop, u* as in *circus;* ᵊ as in *button* (but′ᵊn), *fire* (fīᵊr), *cradle* (krād′ᵊl). See the full key inside the front cover.

shog (shog, shôg), *v.*, **shogged, shog·ging,** *n. Dial.* —*v.t.* **1.** to shake; jolt. —*v.i.* **2.** to jog along. —*n.* **3.** a shake; jolt. [ME *shogge(n)*; perh. akin to SHOCK¹]

sho·gun (shō′gun′, -go͞on′), *n. Japanese Hist.* the title applied to the chief military commanders from about the 8th century A.D. to the end of the 12th century, then applied to a member of a quasi-dynasty holding virtual rule, with the emperor as nominal ruler, until 1868, when the shogunate was terminated and the ruling power was returned to the emperor. [< Jap < Chin *chiang chün* lead army] —**sho′gun′al,** *adj.*

sho·gun·ate (shō′gun′it, -āt, -go͞o′nit, -nāt), *n.* the office or rule of a shogun. [SHOGUN + -ATE¹]

sho·het (shō′ᴋʜāt; *Eng.* shō′ᴋʜit), *n., pl.* **sho·he·tim** (shō ᴋʜə tēm′, shōᴋʜ-), *Eng.* **sho·hets.** *Hebrew.* a person certified by a rabbi or Jewish court of law to slaughter animals for food in the manner prescribed by Jewish law. Also, **shochet.** Cf. **shehitah.**

sho·ji (shō′zhē, -jē), *n., pl.* **-ji, -jis.** a light screen consisting of a framework of wood covered with paper or other translucent material, used originally in Japanese homes as one of a series of sliding panels between the interior and exterior or between two interior spaces. [< Jap]

Sho·la·pur (shō′lə po͝or′), *n.* a city in S Maharashtra in SW India. 337,600 (1961).

shole (shōl), *n. Naut.* a wooden block providing a footing for a shoring. [?]

Sho·lo·khov (shō′lo ᴋʜof), *n.* **Mi·kha·il** (mi ᴋʜä ēl′), born 1905, Russian author: Nobel Prize 1965.

Sho·lom (shô′ləm, shō′-), *n.* a boy's given name.

Sho′lom A·lei′chem (ä lā′ᴋʜəm, ə lā′-). See **Rabinowitz, Solomon.**

shone (shōn; *esp. Brit.* shon), *v.* a pt. and pp. of **shine.**

shoo (sho͞o), *interj., v.,* **shooed, shoo·ing.** —*interj.* **1.** (used to scare or drive away a cat, dog, poultry, birds, etc.) —*v.t.* **2.** to drive away by saying or shouting "shoo." **3.** to request or force (a person) to leave: *I'll have to shoo you out of here now.* —*v.i.* **4.** to call out "shoo." [late ME *ssou* (interjection), imit.; cf. G *schu*]

shoo·fly (sho͞o′flī′), *n., pl.* **-flies. 1.** *U.S.* a child's rocker having a seat supported between two boards cut and painted to resemble animals. **2.** See **clover broom. 3.** *Print.* (in cylinder printing presses) **a.** one of a set of long arms for transferring the printed sheet from the cylinder to the delivery table or folder. **b.** Also called **shoo′fly fin′ger.** the mechanism for removing the printed sheet from the cylinder. **4.** *Railroads.* a temporary track. [SHOO + FLY²]

shoo′-fly pie′ (sho͞o′flī′), an open pie filled with a sweet crumb and molasses mixture and baked. [so called from the fact that flies, attracted by the molasses, have to be shooed away]

shoo-in (sho͞o′in′), *n. Informal.* a candidate, competitor, etc., regarded as certain to win. [n. use of v. phrase *shoo in*]

shook¹ (sho͝ok), *n.* **1.** a set of staves and headings sufficient for one hogshead, barrel, or the like. **2.** a set of the parts of a box, piece of furniture, or the like, ready to be put together. **3.** a shock of sheaves or the like. [short for *shook cask,* var. of *shaken cask* one dismounted for shipment]

shook² (sho͝ok), *v.* **1.** pt. of **shake.** —*adj.* **2.** Also, **shook′ up′.** *Slang.* strongly affected by an event, circumstance, etc.; emotionally unsettled: *She was so shook she couldn't say a word.*

shool (sho͞ol), *n., v.t., v.i. Dial.* shovel. [ME *schole,* etc., OE *scofl*]

shoon (sho͞on), *n. Chiefly Dial.* pl. of **shoe.**

shoot (sho͞ot), *v.,* **shot, shooting,** *n.* —*v.t.* **1.** to hit, wound, damage, kill, or destroy with a missile discharged from a weapon. **2.** to execute or put to death with a bullet: *to be shot at sunrise.* **3.** to send forth or discharge (a missile) from a weapon: *to shoot a bullet.* **4.** to discharge (a weapon): *to shoot a gun.* **5.** to send forth (words, ideas, etc.) rapidly: *to shoot questions at someone.* **6.** to fling; propel: *The volcano shot lava high into the air.* **7.** to direct suddenly or swiftly: *Shoot the spotlight on the doorway. He shot a smile at his wife.* **8.** to move suddenly; send swiftly along. **9.** to go over (country) in hunting game. **10.** to pass rapidly through, over, down, etc.: *to shoot a rapid.* **11.** to emit (a ray or rays, as of light) suddenly, briefly, or intermittently. **12.** to variegate by threads, streaks, etc., of another color. **13.** to cause to extend or project: *He shot out his arm and grabbed the ball.* **14.** to discharge or empty, as down a chute: *Do not shoot rubbish here!* **15.** *Sports.* **a.** to throw, kick, or otherwise propel (a ball, puck, etc.), as at a goal or teammate. **b.** to score (a goal, points, etc.) by propelling the ball, puck, etc.: *to shoot a goal.* **16.** *Games.* to propel (a marble) from the crook or first knuckle of the forefinger by flicking with the thumb **17.** (in dice games) **a.** to throw (the dice or a specific number). **b.** to wager or offer to bet (a sum of money): *I'll shoot ten bucks.* **18.** *Photog.* to photograph or film. **19.** to put forth (buds, branches, etc.), as a plant. **20.** to slide (a bolt or the like) into or out of its fastening. **21.** to pull (one's cuffs) abruptly toward one's hands. **22.** *Golf.* to make a final score of (so many strokes): *He shot a 73 on the first 18 holes of the tournament.* **23.** to take the altitude of (a heavenly body): *to shoot the sun.* **24.** *Carpentry.* **a.** to plane or trim (an edge of a board or the like). **b.** to plane or trim (adjoining edges of two boards or the like) in order to make a close joint be tween them. **25.** to detonate; cause to explode, as a charge of explosives. **26.** *Aeron.* to practice (a maneuver) by repetition: *to shoot landings.* —*v.i.* **27.** to send forth missiles, from a bow, firearm, or the like. **28.** to be discharged, as a firearm. **29.** to hunt with a gun for sport: *He fishes, but he doesn't shoot.* **30.** to move or pass suddenly or swiftly; spurt: *The car shot ahead and was soon out of sight.* **31.** *Naut.* to acquire momentum and coast into the wind, as a sailboat in a confined area. **32.** to grow forth from the ground, as a stem. **33.** to put forth buds or shoots, as a plant; germinate. **34.** *Photog.* to photograph. **35.** *Motion Pictures.* to film or begin to film a scene or movie. **36.** to extend; jut: *a cape shooting out into the sea.* **37.** *Sports, Games.* **a.** to propel a ball, puck, etc., at a goal, basket, pocket, etc., or in a specific direction: *He shot for the green with a five iron.* **b.** to propel a ball in a specific way: *The center shoots left-handed.* **38.** to be felt by or flow through or permeate the body: *Pain shot through his injured arm. Chills shot up and down her spine.* **39.** to carry by force of discharge or momentum: *The missile left its pad and shot thousands of miles into space.* **40.** *Informal.* to begin, esp. to begin to talk: *I want to hear your complaint, so go ahead and shoot.* **41. shoot for** or **at,** *Informal.* to attempt to obtain or accomplish; strive toward: *He is shooting for a higher production level.* **42. shoot down,** to cause to fall by hitting with a shot: *They shot down several ducks.* **43. shoot off one's mouth** or **face,** *Slang.* **a.** to talk indiscreetly, esp. to reveal confidences, make thoughtless remarks, etc. **b.** to exaggerate: *He likes to shoot off his mouth about what a great guy he is.* **44. shoot the breeze.** See **breeze¹** (def. 9). **45. shoot the bull.** See **bull¹** (def. 11). **46. shoot the works.** See **work** (def. 19). **47. shoot up, a.** to grow rapidly or suddenly. **b.** *Informal.* to damage or harass by reckless shooting: *It was a rip-roaring western with everyone shooting up the town.* **c.** *Informal.* to wound by shooting: *He shot up the lion, but his guide killed it.* —*n.* **48.** the act of shooting with a bow, firearm, etc. **49.** *Chiefly Brit.* a hunting trip or expedition. **50.** a match or contest at shooting. **51.** a growing or sprouting, as of a plant. **52.** a new or young growth which shoots off from some portion of a plant. **53.** the amount of such growth. **54.** a young branch, stem, twig, or the like. **55.** a sprout which is not three feet high. **56.** a chute. **57.** *Rocketry.* the launching of a missile. **58.** *Rowing.* the interval between strokes. **59.** *Mining.* **a.** a small tunnel branching off from a larger tunnel. **b.** a narrow vein of ore. **c.** a hole or passage through which ore falls or slides to a lower level. [ME *shote(n),* OE *scēotan,* var. of *scēotan;* c. D *schieten,* G *schiessen,* Icel *skjōta*] —**Syn. 3, 5.** project, impel, hurl, cast, throw. **17a.** roll. **29.** hunt. **30.** spring, start, dash, bolt, rush, fly. **36.** project, protrude.

shoot·er (sho͞o′tər), *n.* **1.** one who or that which shoots. **2.** *Games.* a marble used to shoot at other marbles. [ME; see SHOOT, -ER¹]

shoot′ing board′, *Carpentry.* a flat board having a stop at one end, for holding a piece being planed or shaped.

shoot′ing box′, *Chiefly Brit.* a small house or lodge for use during the shooting season. Also called **shooting lodge.**

shoot′ing brake′, *Brit.* See **station wagon.**

shoot′ing gal′lery, a place equipped with targets and used for practice in shooting.

shoot′ing i′ron, *Slang.* a firearm, esp. a pistol or revolver.

shoot′ing lodge′, *Chiefly Brit.* See **shooting box.**

shoot′ing match′ (sho͞o′ting *for 1;* sho͞ot′ⁿn, sho͞o′ting *for 2*), **1.** a contest in marksmanship. **2.** *Slang.* **a.** a number of persons or things collectively. **b.** everything involved with a particular matter: *He decided to sell the whole shooting match—his house, furniture, and car.*

shoot′ing script′, a motion-picture scenario having the scenes arranged in the order in which they are to be photographed.

shoot′ing star′, **1.** a meteor as seen streaking across the sky at night. **2.** Also called **American cowslip, prairie pointer.** a North American herb, *Dodecatheon meadia,* having bright, nodding flowers.

shoot′ing stick′, **1.** a device resembling a cane or walking stick, with a spike on one end and a small, folding seat on the other, often used by spectators at outdoor sporting events. **2.** *Print.* a wooden stick struck with a mallet to secure furniture in a chase by adjusting quoins.

shoot′ing war′, open conflict between hostile nations involving direct military engagements.

shoot′ the chutes′. See **chute the chute.**

shop (shop), *n., v.,* **shopped, shop·ping,** *interj.* —*n.* **1.** a retail store, esp. a small one. **2.** a small store or department in a large store selling a specific or select type of goods: *the ski shop at Smith's.* **3.** the workshop of a craftsman or artisan. **4.** the workshop of one who works in a manual trade; place for doing specific, skilled manual work: *a carpenter's shop.* **5.** any factory, office, or business: *General Motors is a well-run shop.* **6.** *Educ.* **a.** a course of instruction in a trade, as carpentry, printing, etc., consisting chiefly of training in the use of its tools and materials. **b.** a classroom in which such a course is given. **7.** one's trade, profession, or business as a subject of conversation or preoccupation: *Stop thinking of shop all the time!* **8. set up shop,** to go into business; begin business operations: *She saved her money and set up shop as a milliner.* **9. shut up shop, a.** to close a business temporarily, as at the end of the day. **b.** to suspend business operations permanently: *They couldn't make a go of it and had to shut up shop.* **10. talk shop,** to discuss one's trade, profession, or business: *The women gathered in the kitchen while their husbands talked shop in the den.* —*v.i.* **11.** to visit shops and stores for purchasing or examining goods. **12.** to seek or examine goods, property, etc., offered for sale: *Retail merchants often stock their stores by shopping in New York.* **13.** to seek a bargain, investment, service, etc. (usually fol. by *for*): *I'm shopping for a safe investment that pays six percent.* —*v.t.* **14.** to seek or examine goods, property, etc., offered for sale in or by: *She's shopping the shoe stores this afternoon.* **15.** *Chiefly Brit. Informal.* **a.** to put into prison; jail. **b.** to behave treacherously toward; inform on; betray. —*interj.* **16.** (used in a store, shop, etc., in calling an employee to wait on a customer.) [ME *shoppe,* OE *sceoppa* booth; akin to *scypen* stall (mod. dial. *shippon*), G *Schopf* lean-to, *Schuppen* shed]

shop′ assist′ant, *Brit.* a store clerk; clerk.

shop′ chair′man. See **shop steward.**

shop·ful (shop′fo͝ol′), *n., pl.* **-fuls. 1.** the contents of a shop. **2.** a quantity sufficient to fill a shop. [SHOP + -FUL]

shop·girl (shop′gûrl′), *n.* a salesgirl; female store clerk. [SHOP + GIRL]

sho·phar (shō′fər; *Heb.* shō fär′), *n., pl.* **-phars,** *Heb.* **-phroth** (-frōt′). *Judaism.* shofar.

shop·keep·er (shop′kē′pər), *n.* a retail merchant or tradesman; one who owns or operates a small store or shop. [SHOP + KEEPER] —**shop′keep′ing,** *n.*

shop·lift·er (shop′lif′tər), *n.* one who steals goods from the shelves or displays of a retail store while posing as a customer. [obs. *shoplift* shoplifter (SHOP + LIFT) + -ER¹] —**shop′lift′ing,** *n.*

shop·man (shop′mən), *n., pl.* **-men. 1.** a salesman in a shop. **2.** *Chiefly Brit.* a shopkeeper. [SHOP + MAN¹]

shop·per (shop′ər), *n.* **1.** one who shops. **2.** See **comparison shopper. 3.** a retail buyer for another person or a business concern. [SHOP + -ER¹]

shop·ping (shop′ing), *n.* **1.** the act of one who shops. **2.** the facilities or merchandise available to those who shop: *Chicago has good shopping.* —*adj.* **3.** of, for, or pertaining to examining and buying merchandise: *a shopping trip.* [SHOP + -ING¹, -ING²]

shop′ping cen′ter, a group of stores within a single architectural plan, supplying most of the basic shopping needs, esp. in suburban areas.

shop′ right′, *Patent Law.* the right of an employer to use an invention of his employee without compensating him for the use, in cases where the invention was made at the place of and during the hours of employment.

shop′ stew′ard, a unionized employee elected to represent a shop, department, or the like, in dealings with his employer. Also called **committeeman, shop chairman.**

shop·talk (shop′tôk′), *n.* **1.** conversation or vocabulary having to do with work or a field of work: *I don't understand electronics shoptalk.* **2.** talk about one's work or occupation, esp. after the workday is over. [SHOP + TALK]

shop·walk·er (shop′wô′kər), *n. Brit.* a floorwalker. [SHOP + WALKER]

shop·win·dow (shop′win′dō), *n.* a window used for display of merchandise. [SHOP + WINDOW]

shop·wom·an (shop′wo͝om′ən), *n., pl.* **-wom·en.** a saleswoman in a shop. [SHOP + WOMAN]

shop·worn (shop′wōrn′, -wôrn′), *adj.* worn or marred, as goods handled and exposed in a store. [SHOP + WORN]

shor·an (shōr′an, shôr′-), *n.* a system for aircraft navigation in which two signals sent from an aircraft are received and answered by two fixed transponders, the round-trip times of the signals enabling the navigator to determine his position. [*sho(rt) ra(nge) n(avigation)*]

shore¹ (shōr, shôr), *n.* **1.** the land along the edge of a sea, lake, broad river, etc. **2.** some particular country: *my native shore.* **3.** land, as opposed to sea or water: *a marine serving on shore.* **4.** *Law.* the space between the ordinary high-water and low-water mark. —*adj.* **5.** of, pertaining to, or located on land, esp. land along the edge of a body of water: *a marine on shore duty.* [ME *schore,* OE *scora;* c. MD, MLG *schore;* see SHEAR] —**Syn. 1.** strand, margin. SHORE, BANK, BEACH, COAST refer to an edge of land abutting on an ocean, lake, or other large body of water. SHORE is the general word: *The ship reached shore.* BANK denotes the land along a river or other watercourse, sometimes steep but often not: *The river flows between its banks.* BEACH refers to sandy or pebbly margins along a shore, esp. those made wider at ebb tide: *a private beach for bathers.* COAST applies only to land along an ocean: *the Pacific coast.*

S, Shore²
P, Post supporting footing of wall

shore² (shōr, shôr), *n., v.,* **shored, shor·ing.** *n.* **1.** a supporting post or beam with auxiliary members, esp. one placed obliquely against the side of a building, a ship in dock, or the like; prop; strut. —*v.t.* **2.** to support by a shore or shores; prop (usually fol. by *up*). [ME; c. MLG, MD *schore* prop] —**Syn. 1.** brace, buttress, stay.

shore³ (shōr, shôr), *v.* a pt. of **shear.**

shore⁴ (shōr, shôr), *v.t.,* **shored, shor·ing.** *Scot. and North Eng.* **1.** to threaten (someone). **2.** to offer or proffer (something). [ME (Scot) *schore* < ?]

Shore (shōr, shôr), *n.* **Jane,** 1445?–1527, mistress of Edward IV of England.

shore′ bird′, a bird that frequents seashores, estuaries etc., as the snipe, sandpiper, plover, turnstone, etc.; a limicoline bird.

shore′ crab′, any of numerous crabs that live along the shoreline between the tidemarks, as *Hemigrapsus nudus* (**pur′ple shore′ crab′**), of the Pacific coast of North America.

shore′ din′ner, a meal consisting almost entirely of sea food.

shore′ leave′, *Navy.* **1.** permission to spend time ashore, usually 48 hours or more, granted a member of a ship's company. **2.** the time spent ashore during such leave.

shore·less (shōr′lis, shôr′-), *adj.* **1.** limitless; boundless. **2.** without a shore or beach suitable for landing: *a shoreless island.* [SHORE¹ + -LESS]

shore·line (shōr′līn′, shôr′-), *n.* the line where shore and water meet. [SHORE¹ + LINE¹]

shore′ par′ty, *Mil.* a group organized to go ashore before an invasion force and to establish communications, supply lines, or the like.

shore′ patrol′, (*often cap.*) members of an organization in the U.S. Navy having police duties similar to those performed by military police. *Abbr.:* SP

Shore·view (shōr′vyo͞o′, shôr′-), *n.* a town in E Minnesota. 7157 (1960).

shore·ward (shōr′wərd, shôr′-), *adv.* **1.** Also, **shore′-wards.** toward the shore or land. —*adj.* **2.** facing, moving, or tending toward the shore or land: *a shoreward course.* **3.** coming from the shore, as a wind. —*n.* **4.** the direction toward the shore or away from the sea. [SHORE¹ + -WARD]

Shore·wood (shōr′wo͝od′, shôr′-), *n.* a city in SE Wisconsin, near Milwaukee. 15,990 (1960).

shor·ing (shōr′ing, shôr′-), *n.* **1.** a number or system of shores for steadying or supporting a wall, a ship in drydock, etc. **2.** the act of setting up shores. [SHORE² + -ING¹]

shorn (shôrn, shōrn), *v.* a pp. of **shear.**

short (shôrt), *adj.* **1.** having little length; not long. **2.** having little height; not tall: *a short man.* **3.** extending or reaching only a little way: *a short path.* **4.** brief in duration; not extensive in time: *a short wait.* **5.** brief or concise, as writing. **6.** rudely brief; abrupt; hurting: *short behavior.* **7.** low in amount; scanty: *short rations.* **8.** not reaching a point, mark, target, or the like; not long enough or far enough. **9.** below the standard in extent, quantity, duration, etc.: *short measure.* **10.** having a scanty or insufficient amount of (often fol. by *in* or *on*): *He was short in experience.* **11.** *Cookery.* **a.** (of pastry and the like) crisp and flaky; breaking or crumbling readily from being made with a large proportion of butter or other shortening. **b.** (of dough) containing a relatively large amount of shortening. **12.** (of metals) deficient in tenacity; friable; brittle. **13.** (of the head or skull) of less than ordinary length from front to back. **14.** *Finance.* **a.** not possessing at the time of sale commodities or stocks that one sells. **b.** noting or pertaining to a sale of commodities or stocks that the seller does not possess, depending for profit on a decline in prices. **15.** *Phonet.* **a.** lasting a relatively short time: *"Bit" has a shorter sound than "bid" or "bead."* **b.** belonging to a class of sounds considered as usually shorter in duration than another class, as the vowel of *but* as compared to that of *bought.* **c.** having the sound of the vowels in, conventionally, *bet, bit, put,* and *but,* and, popularly, in *hot* and *bat.* **d.** (in many languages) serving as a distinctive feature of phonemes, as the *a* in German *Bann* in contrast with the *ah* in *Bahn,* or the *t* in Italian *fato* in contrast with the *tt* in *fatto* (opposed to *long*). Cf. **distinctive feature. 16.** *Pros.* **a.** (of a syllable in quantitative verse) lasting a relatively shorter time than a long syllable. **b.** unstressed. **17.** (of an alcoholic drink) small: *a short drink.* **18.** *Chiefly Brit.* (of whiskey) undiluted; straight. **19.** *Ceram.* (of clay) not plastic enough to be modeled. **20.** *Ropemaking.* hard (def. 23). **21. short and sweet, a.** pleasantly brief. **b.** pertinent: *We're in a hurry, so make it short and sweet.* **22. short for,** being a shorter form of; abbreviated to: *"Phone" is short for "telephone."* **23. short of, a.** less than; inferior to. **b.** inadequately supplied with (money, food, etc.). **c.** without going to the length of; failing of; excluding: *Short of murder, there is nothing he wouldn't have tried to get what he wanted.* **24. make short work of.** See **work** (def. 17). —*adv.* **25.** abruptly or suddenly: *to stop short.* **26.** briefly; curtly. **27.** on the near side of an intended or particular point: *The arrow landed short.* **28.** *Baseball.* **a.** with the hands higher on the handle of the bat than usual: *He held the bat short and flied out.* **b.** in a fielding position closer to home plate than usual. **29. come** or **fall short, a.** to fail to reach a particular standard. **b.** to prove insufficient; be lacking: *Her funds fell short, and she had to wire home for help.* **30. cut short,** to end abruptly; terminate: *Her nap was cut short by a loud noise from outside.* **31. run short,** to be in insufficient supply: *My patience is running short.* **32. sell short, a.** *Stock Exchange.* to sell stocks or the like without having them in one's actual possession at the time of the sale. **b.** *Informal.* to disparage or underestimate: *Don't sell Tom short; he's really an excellent engineer.* —*n.* **33.** something that is short. **34.** that which is deficient or lacking. **35.** the sum and substance of a matter; gist (usually prec. by *the*). **36. shorts, a.** loose trousers, knee-length or shorter, worn by children and, for sports or as leisure apparel, by adults. **b.** short pants worn by men as an undergarment. **c.** knee breeches, formerly worn by men. **d.** *Finance.* short-term bonds. **e.** *Mining.* crushed ore failing to pass through a given screen, thus being of a larger given size than a specific grade. **f.** remnants, discards, or refuse of various cutting and manufacturing processes. **37.** a size of garment for men who are shorter than average: *He wears a 42 short.* **38.** a garment, as a suit or overcoat, in such a size. **39.** *Mil.* a shot that strikes or bursts short of the target. **40.** *Elect.* See **short circuit. 41.** *Pros.* a short sound or syllable. **42.** *Baseball.* shortstop (def. 1). **43.** *Motion Pictures.* See **short subject. 44.** *Finance.* one who has sold short; a short seller. **45.** a deficiency or the amount of a deficiency. **46.** *Chiefly Brit.* a small drink of straight whiskey; shot. **47. for short,** by way of abbreviation: *Her name is Patricia, and she's called Pat for short.* **48. in short, a.** in summary. **b.** in few words; in brief: *In short, this has been rather a disappointing day.* —*v.t., v.i.* **49.** *Elect.* short-circuit (often fol. by *out*). [ME; OE *sceort;* c. OHG *scurz* short, Icel *skortr* shortness, scarcity] —**short′ness,** *n.*

—**Syn. 4.** SHORT, BRIEF are opposed to long, and indicate slight extent or duration. SHORT may imply duration but is also applied to physical distance and certain purely spatial relations: *a short journey.* BRIEF refers esp. to duration of time: *brief intervals.* **5.** brief, terse, succinct, laconic, condensed. **6.** curt, sharp, testy. **7.** poor, deficient, inadequate, wanting, lacking. **11.** crumbly. **13.** brachycephalic. —**Ant. 3, 4.** long.

Short (shôrt), *n.* a walled plain in the third quadrant of the face of the moon: about 35 miles in diameter.

short′ account′, *Finance.* **1.** the account of a short seller. **2.** See **short interest.**

short·age (shôr′tij), *n.* **1.** a deficiency in quantity: *a shortage of cash.* **2.** the amount of such deficiency. [SHORT + -AGE]

short·bread (shôrt′bred′), *n.* a kind of butter cooky, commonly made in thick, pie-shaped wheels or rolled and cut in fancy shapes. [SHORT + BREAD]

short·cake (shôrt′kāk′), *n.* **1.** a cake made with a relatively large amount of butter or other shortening. **2.** a dessert made of short, sometimes sweetened, biscuit dough baked or split in layers, with a filling or topping of strawberries or other fruit. [SHORT + CAKE]

short-change (shôrt′chānj′), *v.t.,* **-changed, -chang·ing. 1.** to give less than the correct change to. **2.** to deal with unfairly or dishonestly, esp. to cheat. —**short′-chang′er,** *n.*

short′ cir′cuit, *Elect.* an abnormal, usually unintentional, condition of relatively low resistance between two points of different potential in a circuit, usually resulting in a flow of excess current.

short-cir·cuit (shôrt′sûr′kit), *Elect.* —*v.t.* **1.** to make inoperable by establishing a short circuit in. **2.** to carry (a current) as a short circuit. **3.** *Informal.* to bypass, impede, hinder, or frustrate: *Bad weather short-circuited my vacation plans.* —*v.i.* **4.** to form a short circuit or become inoperable due to a short circuit.

short·com·ing (shôrt′kum′ing), *n.* a failure, defect, or deficiency in conduct, condition, thought, ability, etc.: *a social shortcoming; a shortcoming of his philosophy.* [SHORT + COMING]

short·com·mons (shôrt′kom′ənz), *n.* (*construed as sing.*) *Chiefly Brit.* scanty allowance of food.

short′ cov′ering, *Finance.* purchases which close out short sales on stocks or commodities.

short-cut (shôrt′kut′), *v.,* **-cut, -cut·ting.** —*v.t.* **1.** to cause to be shortened by the use of a shortcut. —*v.i.* **2.** to use or take a shorter or quicker way.

short·cut (shôrt′kut′), *n.* **1.** a shorter or quicker way. —*adj.* **2.** comprising or providing a shorter or quicker way: *shortcut methods.* [SHORT + CUT]

short′ divi′sion, *Math.* division in which the steps of the process are performed mentally and are not written down.

short′-eared owl′ (shôrt′ērd′), a streaked, buffy brown, cosmopolitan owl, *Asio flammeus,* having very short tufts of feathers on each side of the head. Also called **prairie owl.**

short·en (shôr′tən), *v.t.* **1.** to make short or shorter. **2.** to reduce, decrease, take in, etc.: *to shorten sail.* **3.** to make (pastry, bread, etc.) short, as with butter or other fat. **4.** *Sports.* choke (def. 8). —*v.i.* **5.** to become short or shorter. **6.** (of odds) to decrease. [SHORT + -EN[1]] —**short′en·er,** *n.*

—**Syn. 1.** condense, lessen, limit, restrict. SHORTEN, ABBREVIATE, ABRIDGE, CURTAIL mean to make shorter or briefer. SHORTEN is a general word meaning to make less in extend or duration: *to shorten a dress, a prisoner's sentence.* The other three words suggest methods of shortening. To ABBREVIATE is to make shorter by omission or contraction: *to abbreviate a word.* To ABRIDGE is to reduce in length or size by condensing, summarizing, and the like: *to abridge a document.* CURTAIL suggests deprivation and lack of completeness because of cutting off some part: *to curtail an explanation.* **5.** contract, lessen. —**Ant. 1.** lengthen.

short·en·ing (shôr′tə ning, shôrt′ning), *n.* **1.** butter, lard, or other fat, used to make pastry, bread, etc., short. **2.** *Phonet.* the act, process, or an instance of making or becoming short. **3.** *Ling.* **a.** a word formed by dropping the latter part of a longer word or phrase, as *piano* from *pianoforte* or *hobby* from *hobby horse.* **b.** a word formed by clipping the initial part from a longer word, as *lone* from *alone.* [SHORTEN + -ING[1]]

Short′er Cat′echism, one of the two catechisms established by the Westminster Assembly in 1647, used chiefly in Presbyterian churches.

short·fall (shôrt′fôl′), *n.* **1.** the quantity or extent by which something falls short; deficiency; shortage. **2.** the act or fact of falling short. [SHORT + FALL; from v. phrase *fall short*]

short′ field′, *Baseball.* the area of the infield between third base and second, covered by the shortstop.

short′fin corvi′na (shôrt′fin′). See under **corvina.**

short′ game′, 1. the aspect of golf considered in relation to the ability of a player to hit medium or short shots, as chip shots, pitch shots, and putts, with accuracy. Cf. **long game** (def. 1). **2.** a card game in which not all cards in the pack are dealt before play. Cf. **long game** (def. 2).

A

B

Shorthand
"This is an example of shorthand"
A, Gregg system
B, Pitman system

short·hand (shôrt′hand′), *n.* **1.** a method of rapid handwriting using simple strokes, abbreviations, or symbols that designate letters, words, or phrases (distinguished from *longhand*). —*adj.* **2.** using or able to use shorthand. **3.** written in shorthand. **4.** of or pertaining to shorthand. [SHORT + HAND]

short-hand·ed (shôrt′han′did), *adj.* not having the usual or necessary number of workmen, helpers, etc. —**short′-hand′ed·ness,** *n.*

Short′ Hap′py Life′ of Fran′cis Ma·com′ber, The (mə kom′bər), a short story (1936) by Ernest Hemingway.

short·head (shôrt′hed′), *n.* **1.** a brachycephalic person. **2.** a head with a cephalic index of 81 or over. [SHORT + HEAD] —**short′head′ed,** *adj.*

Short·horn (shôrt′hôrn′), *n.* one of an English breed of red, white, or roan beef cattle having short horns. Also called **Durham.** [SHORT + HORN]

short′-horned grass′hopper (shôrt′hôrnd′), locust (def. 1).

shor·ti·a (shôr′tē ə), *n.* any plant of the genus *Shortia,* esp. *S. uniflora,* of Japan, and *S. galacifolia,* of the mountains of North and South Carolina, having evergreen, radical leaves and white, nodding flowers. [named after C. W. *Short* (1794–1863), American botanist; see -IA]

short·ie (shôr′tē), *n.* shorty.

short′ in′terest, *Finance.* the total amount by which a single seller or all sellers are short in a particular stock or commodity or in the market as a whole. Also called **short account, short position.**

short′ i′ron, *Golf.* a club, as a pitcher, pitching niblick, or niblick, with a short shaft and an iron head the face of which has great slope, for hitting approach shots. Cf. **long iron.**

short·ish (shôr′tish), *adj.* rather short. [SHORT + -ISH[1]]

short-laid (shôrt′lād′), *adj. Ropemaking.* hard-laid.

short′leaf pine′ (shôrt′lēf′), **1.** a pine, *Pinus echinata,* of the southern U.S., having short, flexible leaves. **2.** the hard, brownish-yellow wood of this tree, used in the construction of houses, for making furniture, and for pulp.

short′ leet′, *Chiefly Scot.* See **short list** (def. 1).

short′ line′, *Railroads.* the shortest route between two points.

short′ list′, *Chiefly Brit.* **1.** Also, *esp. Scot.,* **short leet.** a list of candidates who are especially favored for appointment, promotion, acceptance, or the like. **2.** *Slang.* a personal, mental list of people or things singled out as noteworthy: *He is on my short list as one of the greatest fools I know.*

short-list (shôrt′list′), *v.t. Chiefly Brit.* to put (someone) on a short list.

short-lived (shôrt′līvd′, -livd′), *adj.* living or lasting only a little while. —**short′-lived′ness,** *n.*

short·ly (shôrt′lē), *adv.* **1.** in a short time; soon. **2.** briefly; concisely. **3.** curtly; rudely. [SHORT + -LY]

short′ or′der, a dish or serving of food that is quickly prepared upon request at a lunch counter, restaurant, diner, or the like.

short-or·der (shôrt′ôr′dər), *adj.* **1.** of, pertaining to, or specializing in short orders: *a short-order cook; short-order diner.* **2.** performed or supplied quickly: *They obtained a short-order divorce decree.*

short′ posi′tion, *Finance.* See **short interest.**

short-range (shôrt′rānj′), *adj.* having a limited extent, as in distance or time: *a short-range shot; a short-range plan.*

short′ rate′, *Insurance.* a charge, proportionately higher than the annual rate, made for insurance issued or continued in force by the insured for less than one year.

short-sheet (shôrt′shēt′), *v.t.* **1.** to fold and tuck in the top sheet of (a bed) so that it simulates both the top and bottom sheets: when the victim of this joke enters the bed, his legs are obstructed by the fold. **2.** to short-sheet the bed of (someone). Cf. **apple-pie bed.**

short′ short′ sto′ry, a very short piece of prose fiction, much more condensed than the average short story.

short′ shrift′, 1. a brief time for confession or absolution given to a condemned prisoner before his execution. **2.** little attention or consideration in dealing with a person or matter: *to give short shrift to an opponent's arguments.*

short-sight·ed (shôrt′sī′tid), *adj.* **1.** unable to see far; near-sighted; myopic. **2.** lacking in foresight: *a short-sighted plan.* —**short′-sight′ed·ly,** *adv.* —**short′-sight′ed·ness,** *n.*

—**Syn. 2.** unthinking, improvident, heedless, careless. —**Ant. 2.** prudent.

short′ snort′er, *Aeron.* **1.** a member of an informal club of pilots, crewmen, and passengers who have made a transoceanic flight. **2.** a dollar bill bearing the signatures of two other members of this club, carried by a short snorter as his certificate of membership.

short′ splice′, a splice made in instances where an increased thickness of the united rope is not objectionable, made by unlaying the ends of both ropes a certain distance, uniting them so that their strands overlap, then tucking each alternately over and under others several times. Cf. **long splice.** See illus. under **splice.**

short-spo·ken (shôrt′spō′kən), *adj.* speaking in a short, brief, or curt manner.

short·stop (shôrt′stop′), *n.* **1.** *Baseball.* **a.** the position of the player covering the area of the infield between second and third base. **b.** a fielder who covers this position. **2.** Also called **short′stop bath′.** *Photog.* See **stop bath.** [SHORT + STOP]

short′ sto′ry, a piece of prose fiction, usually under 10,000 words. —**short′-sto′ry,** *adj.*

short′ sub′ject, *Motion Pictures.* a short film, as a documentary or travelogue, shown as part of a program with a feature-length film. Also called **short.**

short′ sweet′ening, *Chiefly Southern and Midland U.S.* sugar. Cf. **long sweetening.**

short′-tailed shrew′ (shôrt′tāld′), a grayish-black shrew, *Blarina brevicauda,* common in eastern North America, that has a tail less than half the length of the body. See illus. under **shrew.**

short-tem·pered (shôrt′tem′pərd), *adj.* having a quick, hasty temper; irascible.

short-term (shôrt′tûrm′), *adj.* **1.** covering or applying to a relatively short period of time. **2.** maturing over a relatively short period of time: *a short-term loan.*

short′ ti′tle, an abridged listing in a book catalog, giving only such essential information as the author's name and the book's title, publisher, and date and place of publication.

short′ ton′. See under **ton**[1] (def. 1). Also called **net ton.**

short-waist·ed (shôrt′wā′stid), *adj.* of less than average length between the shoulders and waistline; having a high waistline. Cf. **long-waisted.**

short·wave (shôrt′wāv′), *n., adj., v.,* **-waved, -wav·ing.** —*n.* **1.** *Elect.* an electromagnetic wave of 60 meters or less. **2.** See **shortwave radio.** —*adj.* **3.** of, pertaining to, or using shortwaves. —*v.i., v.t.* **4.** to transmit by shortwaves. [SHORT + WAVE]

short′wave ra′dio, a radio transmitter that transmits shortwaves.

short-wind·ed (shôrt′win′did), *adj.* **1.** short of breath; liable to difficulty in breathing. **2.** brief or concise; to the point, as in speech, writing, etc. (opposed to *long-winded*): *a short-winded treatise.*

short·y (shôr′tē), *n., pl.* **short·ies.** *Informal.* **1.** a person, esp. a man, of less than average stature. **2.** a garment designed to be of short length, as a hospital bed jacket. —*adj.* **3.** noting a garment designed to be of short length: *a shorty nightgown.* Also, **shortie.** [SHORT + -Y[2]]

Sho·sho·ne (shō shō′nē), *n., pl.* **-nes,** (*esp. collectively*) **-ne** for **3. 1.** a river in NW Wyoming, flowing NE into the Big Horn River. 120 mi. long. **2.** an American Indian language of the Shoshonean family. **3.** Shoshoni.

Sho·sho·ne·an (shō shō′nē ən, shō′shə nē′ən), *adj.* **1.** of or pertaining to a family of American Indian languages spoken in the western U.S. and including Shoshone, Comanche, Hopi, Paiute, and Ute. —*n.* **2.** the Shoshonean languages taken collectively. [SHOSHONE + -AN]

Shosho′ne Cav′ern, a large cave in NW Wyoming: a national monument.

Shosho′ne Dam′, a dam on the Shoshone River. 328 ft. high.

Sho·sho′ne Falls′, falls of the Snake River, in S Idaho. 210 ft. high.

Sho·sho·ni (shō shō′nē), *n., pl.* **-nis,** (*esp. collectively*) **-ni.** a member of any of several American Indian peoples, ranging from Wyoming to California, who speak a Shoshonean language. Also, **Shoshone.**

Sho·sta·ko·vich (shos′tə kō′vich; *Russ.* sho stä-kō′vich), *n.* **Di·mi·tri Di·mi·tri·e·vich** (di mē′trē di mē′trē ə vich; *Russ.* di mē′tʀi di mē′tʀi yə vich), 1906–75, Russian composer.

shot[1] (shot), *n., pl.* **shots** or, for 6, 8, **shot;** *v.,* **shot·ted, shot·ting.** —*n.* **1.** a discharge of a firearm, bow, etc. **2.** the range of or the distance traveled by a missile in its flight. **3.** an aimed discharge of a missile. **4.** an attempt to hit a target with a missile. **5.** the act or an instance of shooting a firearm, bow, etc. **6.** a small ball or pellet of lead, a number of which are loaded in a cartridge and used for one charge of a shotgun. **7.** such pellets collectively: *a charge of shot.* **8.** a projectile for discharge from a firearm or cannon. **9.** such projectiles collectively: *shot and shell.* **10.** a person who shoots; marksman: *He was a good shot.* **11.** anything like a shot, esp. in being sudden and forceful. **12.** a heavy metal ball which competitors cast as far as possible in shot-putting contests. **13.** an aimed stroke, throw, or the like, as in certain games, esp. in an attempt to score. **14.** an attempt or try: *I'll take a shot at solving the puzzle.* **15.** a remark aimed at some person or thing. **16.** a guess at something. **17.** a hypodermic injection, as of a serum, vaccine, narcotic, or anaesthetic: *The patient received a spinal shot. He took a series of immunizing shots for hay fever.* **18.** a small quantity, esp. an ounce, of undiluted liquor. **19.** an amount due, esp. at a tavern. **20.** *Photog.* **a.** a photograph, esp. a snapshot: *Here's a nice shot of my kids.* **b.** the act of making a photograph, esp. a snapshot. **21.** *Motion Pictures, Television.* a unit of action photographed without interruption and constituting a single camera view. **22.** an explosive charge in place for detonation, as in mining or quarrying. **23.** *Foundry.* comparatively hard globules of metal in the body of a casting. **24.** *Naut.* a 90-foot length of anchor cable or chain. **25.** *Checkers.* a compulsory series of exchanges, especially when it proves favorable to the aggressor. **26.** *Textiles.* **a.** a pick sent through the shed in a single throw of the shuttle. **b.** (in carpet weaving) filling yarn used to bind the pile to the fabric, usually expressed with a preceding number representing the quantity of picks used: *three-shot carpet.* **c.** a defect in a fabric caused by an unusual color or size in the yarn. **27.** a chance with odds for and against; a bet: *a 20 to 1 shot that his horse will come in first.* **28. by a long shot.** See **long shot** (def. 3). **29. call one's shots,** to indicate beforehand what one intends to do and how one intends to do it. **30. call the shots,** *Slang.* to exercise control over; direct the operation of: *He wanted a job where he would be calling the shots himself.* **31. like a shot,** instantly; quickly: *He bolted out of here like a shot.* **32. shot in the arm,** *Slang.* something that results in renewed vigor, confidence, etc.; stimulus: *Her recent promotion has given her a shot in the arm. The new members gave the club a shot in the arm.* **33. shot in the dark,** *Slang.* a wild guess; a random conjecture. **34. shot in the locker,** *Informal.* supplies in reserve; resources.
—*v.t.* **35.** to load or supply with shot. **36.** to weight with shot.
—*v.i.* **37.** to manufacture shot, as in a shot tower. [ME; OE *sc(e)ot, (ge)sceot;* c. G *schoss, geschoss;* akin to SHOOT] —**shot′less,** *adj.* —**shot′like′,** *adj.*

shot[2] (shot), *v.* **1.** pt. and pp. of **shoot.** —*adj.* **2.** woven so as to present a play of colors; having a changeable color; variegated, as silk. **3.** (of a board or the like) having straight and true edges. **4.** spread or streaked with color: *the dawn sky shot with gold.* **5.** in hopelessly bad condition; ruined: *Those sneakers are really shot. His morale is shot.* **6.** *Slang.* intoxicated.

shot′ bort′, ballas.

shote (shōt), *n.* shoat.

shot′ effect′, *Electronics.* random fluctuations in the emission of electrons from a hot cathode, causing a hissing or sputtering sound (**shot′ noise′**) in an audio amplifier and causing snow on a television screen.

shot′ glass′, a small, heavy glass for serving a shot of whiskey or liquor.

shot·gun (shot′gun′), *n., adj., v.,* **-gunned, -gun·ning.** —*n.* **1.** a smoothbore gun for firing small shot to kill birds and small quadrupeds, though often used with buckshot to kill larger animals. —*adj.* **2.** of, pertaining to, used in, or carried out with a shotgun: *a shotgun murder; shotgun pellets.* **3.** covering a wide area in an irregularly effective manner without concern for details or particulars; tending to be all-inclusive, nonselective, and haphazard; indiscriminate in choice and indifferent to specific results: *He favored the shotgun approach in his political attacks.* **4.** seeking a desired result through the use or inclusion of a wide variety of elements. **5.** gained or characterized by coercive methods. —*v.t.* **6.** to fire a shotgun at. **7.** to use coercive methods. [SHOT[1] + GUN[1]]

shot′gun wed′ding, **1.** *Slang.* a wedding occasioned or precipitated by pregnancy. **2.** a compromise, merger, accord, etc., occasioned by necessity: *The coalition government was obviously a shotgun wedding.* Also, **shot′gun mar′riage.**

shot′ hole′, a condition in plants in which small, rounded spots drop out of the leaves, appearing as if the leaves were riddled by shot, resulting from infection or injury.

shot-peen (shot′pēn′), *v.t. Metalworking.* to bombard (a steel object) with hard steel shot to improve its endurance.

shot′ put′, **1.** a field event in which a heavy ball or shot is thrown or put for distance. **2.** a single throw or put of the shot.

shot-put·ter (shot′po͝ot′ər), *n.* a participant in the shot put. [SHOT PUT + -ER[1]]

shot·ten (shot′ən), *adj.* **1.** (of fish, esp. herring) having recently ejected the spawn. **2.** *Obs.* (of a bone) dislocated. [old ptp. of SHOOT]

shot·ting (shot′ing), *n.* the act or process of making lead shot in a shot tower. [SHOT[1] + -ING[1]]

shot′ tow′er, a tower from the top of which finely divided streams of molten lead are dropped down a central well, breaking up into spherical drops during their fall to be quenched and hardened by a tank of water at the bottom.

Shot·well (shot′wel′, -wəl), *n.* **James Thomson,** 1874–1965, U.S. diplomat, historian, and educator.

should (sho͝od), *auxiliary v.* **1.** pt. of **shall.** **2.** (used with infinitive of a verb to form its subjunctive): *Were he to arrive, I should be pleased.* **3.** must; ought (used to indicate duty, propriety, or expediency): *You should not do that.* **4.** would (used to make a statement less direct or blunt): *I should hardly say that.* [ME *sholde,* OE *sc(e)olde;* see SHALL]
—**Syn. 3.** See **must**[1].
—**Usage.** See **would, shall.**

shoul·der (shōl′dər), *n.* **1.** the part of each side of the body in man, at the top of the trunk, extending from each side of the base of the neck to the region where the arm articulates with the trunk. **2.** Usually, **shoulders.** these two parts together with the part of the back joining them. **3.** a corresponding part in animals. See diag. under **horse.** **4.** the upper foreleg and adjoining parts of a sheep, goat, etc. **5.** the joint connecting the arm or the foreleg with the trunk. **6.** a shoulderlike part or projection. **7.** a cut of meat which includes the upper joint of the foreleg. **8.** Often, **shoulders.** *Informal.* capacity for bearing responsibility or blame or sympathizing with other people: *If you want to tell me your troubles, I have broad shoulders.* **9.** a steplike change in the contour of an object, as for opposing or limiting motion along it, for an abutment, etc. **10.** *Carpentry.* **a.** the end surface or surfaces of a piece from which a tenon or tenons project. **b.** an inclined and raised surface, as on a joggle post, for receiving and supporting the foot of a strut or the like. **11.** *Fort.* the angle of a bastion between the face and the flank. **12.** *Print.* the flat surface on a type body extending beyond the base of the letter or character. See diag. under **type.** **13.** that part of a garment which covers, or fits over, the shoulder. **14.** (in leather manufacturing) that part of the hide anterior to the butt. **15.** either of the two edges or borders along a road, esp. that portion on which vehicles can be parked in emergencies. Cf. **soft shoulder.** **16.** *Furniture.* knee (def. 6). **17.** *Naut.* the junction of the entrance of a ship's hull with the middle body. **18. cry on someone's shoulder,** to reveal one's problems to another person in order to obtain sympathy: *Don't cry on my shoulder—this mess is your own fault.* **19. put one's shoulder to the wheel,** to work energetically toward a goal; strive: *If we put our shoulders to the wheel, we'll be able to finish the job soon.* **20. rub shoulders with,** to come into association with; mingle with: *As a social worker in one of the worst slum areas, she rubs shoulders with the poor and the helpless.* **21. shoulder to shoulder,** with united effort; side by side: *The volunteers worked shoulder to shoulder with the natives in harvesting the crops.* **22. straight from the shoulder,** without evasion; directly; candidly: *The lawyer told him straight from the shoulder that his case was weak.* —*v.t.* **23.** to push with or as with the shoulder, esp. roughly: *to shoulder someone aside.* **24.** to take upon, support, or carry on or as on the shoulder or shoulders: *He shouldered his knapsack and walked on.* **25.** to assume as a responsibility: *to shoulder the expense.* —*v.i.* **26.** to push with or as with the shoulder: *to shoulder through a crowd.* **27. shoulder arms,** *Mil.* **a.** to place a rifle muzzle upward on the right or left shoulder, with the buttstock in the corresponding hand. **b.** the command to shoulder arms. [ME *sholder,* OE *sculdor;* c. D *schouder,* G *Schulter*]

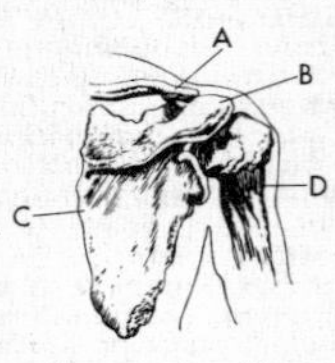

Human shoulder (front view)
A, Clavicle
B, Acromion
C, Scapula
D, Humerus

shoul′der bag′, a woman's handbag with shoulder strap attached.

shoul′der blade′, the scapula.

shoul′der board′, *U.S. Navy.* one of a pair of narrow, stiff, cloth patches bearing an insignia of rank and worn on the shoulders by a commissioned officer. Also called **shoul′der mark′.**

shoul′der knot′, **1.** a knot of ribbon or lace worn on the shoulder, as by men of fashion in the 17th and 18th centuries, by servants in livery, or by women or children. **2.** one of a pair of detachable ceremonial ornaments consisting of braided cord, worn on the shoulders by a commissioned officer.

shoul′der loop′, *U.S.* a flap on each shoulder of a service uniform on which metallic insignia of rank are worn by commissioned and warrant officers in the Army, Air Force, and Marines. Also called **shoul′der strap′.**

shoul′der sleeve′ insig′nia, *U.S. Mil.* **1.** a cloth patch worn on the left sleeve of a uniform one-half inch below the shoulder seam by a member of a specifically authorized unit of the Army or Air Force. **2.** a similarly distinctive patch worn on the right sleeve by a member of the military to indicate service overseas with a unit during a period of military operations. Also called **shoul′der patch′.**

shoul′der strap′, **1.** a strap worn over the shoulder, as to support a garment. **2.** a strip on the shoulder of a uniform to distinguish the rank of an officer.

shoul′der weap′on, a firearm that is fired while being held in the hands with the butt of the weapon braced against the shoulder. Also, **shoul′der gun′, shoul′der arm′.**

should·na (sho͝od′nə), *Scot.* contraction of *should not.* Also, **shudna.**

should·n't (sho͝od′ənt), contraction of *should not.*

shouldst (sho͝odst), *v. Archaic.* past 2nd pers. sing. of **shall.** Also, **should·est** (sho͝od′ist).

Shoul·tes (sho͞ol′tēz), *n.* a town in NW Washington. 3159 (1960).

shout (shout), *v.i.* **1.** to call or cry out loudly and vigorously. **2.** to speak or laugh noisily or unrestrainedly. —*v.t.* **3.** to utter or yell (something) loudly. **4.** *Australian.* to treat (another) to a drink, meal, amusement, or the like. —*n.* **5.** a loud call or cry: *He gave a shout for help.* **6.** a sudden loud outburst, as of laughter. **7. all over but the shouting,** having completed the major part of (a project, attempt, etc.) with the results becoming apparent, esp. assured of success: *The campaign is all over but the shouting.* [ME *shoute;* c. Icel *skūta* to scold, chide, *skūti, skúti* a taunt; akin to SHOOT] —**shout′er,** *n.* —**shout′ing·ly,** *adv.*
—**Syn. 1.** yell, vociferate, exclaim. See **cry.** —**Ant. 1.** whisper.

shove[1] (shuv), *v.,* **shoved, shov·ing,** *n.* —*v.t.* **1.** to move along by force from behind; push. **2.** to push roughly or rudely; jostle. **3.** *Masonry.* to thrust (a brick) obliquely into a bed of fresh mortar, and against the last brick laid, so as to bed it firmly and then force mortar up into the vertical joint. —*v.i.* **4.** to push. **5. shove off, a.** to push a boat from the shore. **b.** *Slang.* to go away; depart: *I think I'll be shoving off now.* —*n.* **6.** an act or instance of shoving. [ME *schouve(n),* OE *scūfan;* c. D *schuiven,* obs. G *schauben,* Icel *skūfa;* akin to Goth *-skiuban*] —**shov′er,** *n.*

shove[2] (shōv), *n.* boon[3]. [appar. var. of SHIVE[2]]

shoved′ joint′, *Masonry.* a joint in brickwork made by shoving the bricks into fresh mortar.

shove-ha′pen·ny (shuv′hā′pə nē, -hāp′nē), *n. Brit.* a shuffleboard game played with coins or brass disks which are pushed by the hand and thumb down a board toward a scoring pit. Also, **shove-half·pen·ny** (shuv′hā′pə nē, -hāp′nē).

shov·el (shuv′əl), *n., v.,* **-eled, -el·ing** or (*esp. Brit.*) **-elled, -el·ling.** —*n.* **1.** an implement consisting of a broad blade or scoop attached to a long handle, used for taking up, removing, or throwing loose matter, as earth, snow, coal, etc. **2.** any fairly large contrivance or machine with a broad blade or scoop for taking up or removing loose matter: *a steam shovel.* **3.** a shovelful. **4.** a device for polishing fine pivots, as of watch arbors, consisting of a semicylindrical shank covered with an abrasive powder. **5.** *Informal.* See **shovel hat.** —*v.t.* **6.** to take up and cast or remove with a shovel: *to shovel coal.* **7.** to gather up in large quantity roughly or carelessly with or as with a shovel: *He shoveled food into his mouth.* **8.** to dig or clear with or as with a shovel: *to shovel a path through the snow.* —*v.i.* **9.** to work with a shovel. [ME *schovel,* OE *scofl;* c. D *schoffel* hoe; akin to G *Schaufel* shovel]

shov·el·board (shuv′əl bōrd′, -bôrd′), *n.* the game of shuffleboard.

shov·el·er (shuv′ə lər, shuv′lər), *n.* **1.** one who or that which shovels. **2.** *Ornith.* **a.** a cosmopolitan, freshwater duck, *Anas clypeata,* having a broad, flat bill. **b.** any of several related, similar ducks. Also, *esp. Brit.,* **shov′el·ler.** [SHOVEL + -ER[1]]

shov·el·ful (shuv′əl fo͝ol′), *n., pl.* **-fuls.** the amount held by a shovel. [SHOVEL + -FUL]

shov′el hat′, a hat with a broad brim turned up at the sides and projecting with a shovellike curve in front and behind; worn by some ecclesiastics, chiefly in England. —**shov′el-hat′ted,** *adj.*

shov·el·head (shuv′əl hed′), *n.* **1.** bonnethead. **2.** See **shovelnose sturgeon.** [SHOVEL + HEAD]

shov·el·nose (shuv′əl nōz′), *n.* **1.** any of various animals with a shovellike snout or head, as a shark, *Hexanchus corinus,* of the Pacific, or a guitarfish, *Rhinobatos productus,* of California. **2.** See **shovelnose sturgeon.** [SHOVEL + NOSE]

shov·el-nosed (shuv′əl nōzd′), *adj.* having the head, snout, or beak broad and flat like the blade of a shovel.

shov′elnose stur′geon, a small sturgeon, *Scaphirhynchus platorhynchus,* of the Mississippi River, having a broad, flat snout. Also called **hackleback.**

show (shō), *v.,* **showed, shown** or **showed, show·ing,** *n.* —*v.t.* **1.** to cause or allow to be seen; exhibit; display. **2.** to present or perform as a public entertainment or spectacle: *to show a movie.* **3.** to indicate; point out: *to show the way.* **4.** to guide, escort, or usher: *He showed me to my room. Show him in.* **5.** to explain or make clear; make known: *He showed what he meant* **6.** to make known to; to inform, instruct, or prove to: *I'll show you what I mean.* **7.** to prove; demonstrate: *His experiment showed the falsity of the theory.* **8.** to indicate, register, or mark: *The thermometer showed 10 below zero.* **9.** to exhibit or offer for sale: *to show a house.* **10.** to allege, as in a legal document; plead, as a reason or cause. **11.** to produce, as facts in an affidavit or at a hearing. **12.** to express or make evident by appearance, behavior, speech, etc.: *to show one's feelings.* **13.** to accord or grant (favor, kindness, etc.): *He showed mercy in his decision.*
—*v.i.* **14.** to be seen; be or become visible: *Did her slip show?* **15.** to be seen in a certain way: *to show to advantage.* **16.** *Informal.* **a.** to put on an exhibition or performance; display one's goods or products: *Several dress designers are showing in New York now.* **b.** to be present or keep an appointment; show up: *He said he would be there, but he didn't show.* **17.** to finish third in a horse race, harness race, etc. **18. show off, a.** to display ostentatiously: *The parade was designed to show off all the latest weapons of war.* **b.** to seek to gain attention by displaying prominently one's abilities or accomplishments. **19. show up, a.** to make known, as faults; expose; reveal. **b.** to exhibit in a certain way; appear: *White shows up well against a blue background.* **c.** *Informal.* to come to or arrive at a place: *We waited for two hours, but he didn't show up.* **d.** *Informal.* to make another seem inferior; outdo.
—*n.* **20.** a display, exhibition, or demonstration: *a true show of freedom.* **21.** ostentatious display: *nothing but mere show.* **22.** any kind of public exhibition or exposition: *a show of Renoirs.* **23.** a radio or television program. **24.** a motion picture. **25.** a motion-picture theater. **26.** the act or an instance of showing. **27.** appearance; impression: *to make a sorry show.* **28.** an unreal or deceptive appearance: *He had the show of genius but not the genuine gift.* **29.** an indication; trace: *He frowned on the slightest show of emotion.* **30.** a theatrical production, performance, or company. **31.** *Informal.* a chance: *to get a fair show.* **32.** a sight or spectacle. **33.** the position of the competitor who comes in third in a horse race, harness race, etc. Cf. **place** (def. 29b), **win** (def. 16). **34.** *Med.* **a.** the first appearance of blood at the onset of menstruation. **b.** a blood-tinged mucous discharge from the vagina that indicates

the onset of labor. **35.** *Chiefly Brit. Informal.* any undertaking, group of persons, event, etc.; affair; thing. **36. give away the (whole) show,** *Informal.* to reveal the private or secret details of a plan, business venture, etc. **37. run the show,** to control a business, situation, etc.; manage: *My father runs the show in our house.* **38. steal the show, a.** to usurp the credit for; get the applause for: *That woman can act, but the child stole the show. He did all the work, but his wife stole the show.* **b.** to be the most pleasing or spectacular item or person in a group. **39. stop the show,** to win such enthusiastic applause that a theatrical performance is temporarily interrupted. [ME *showe(n)* (to) look at, show, OE *scēawian,* var. of *scēawian* to look at; c. G *schauen,* D *schowen*] —**show′a·ble,** *adj.* —**show′less,** *adj.*

—**Syn. 4.** lead, conduct. **5.** interpret, clarify, elucidate, reveal, disclose, divulge. **10.** asseverate, assert, affirm. **13.** bestow, confer. **20, 21.** SHOW, DISPLAY, OSTENTATION, POMP suggest the presentation of a more or less elaborate, often pretentious, appearance for the public to see. SHOW often indicates an external appearance which may or may not accord with actual facts: *a show of modesty.* DISPLAY applies to an intentionally conspicuous show: *a great display of wealth.* OSTENTATION is vain, ambitious, pretentious, or offensive display: *tasteless and vulgar ostentation.* POMP suggests such a show of dignity and authority as characterizes a ceremony of state: *The coronation was carried out with pomp and ceremonial.* **22.** spectacle. **28.** deception, pretense, simulation, illusion.

Sho·wa (shō′wä), *n.* the designation of the period of the reign Emperor Hirohito, begun in 1926.

show′ bill′, an advertising poster.

show′ biz′, *Informal.* See **show business.**

show·boat (shō′bōt′), *n.* a boat, esp. a paddle-wheel steamer, used as a traveling theater. [SHOW + BOAT]

show·bread (shō′bred′), *n.* *Judaism.* shewbread.

show′ busi′ness, the entertainment industry, comprising theater, motion pictures, television, radio, burlesque, etc.

show′ card′, an advertising placard or card.

show·case (shō′kās′), *n., v.,* **-cased, -cas·ing.** —*n.* **1.** a glass case for the display and protection of articles in shops, museums, etc. **2.** an exhibit or display, usually of an ideal or representative model of something. **3.** the setting, place, or vehicle for displaying something on a trial basis: *The club is a showcase for new comics.* —*v.t.* **4.** to exhibit or display. [SHOW + CASE[2]]

show·down (shō′doun′), *n.* **1.** the laying down of one's cards, face upward, in a card game, esp. poker. **2.** a conclusive settlement of an issue, difference, etc., in which all resources, power, or the like, are used; decisive confrontation: *An international showdown was inevitable.* [SHOW + DOWN[1]]

show·er[1] (shou′ər), *n.* **1.** a brief fall of rain or, sometimes, of hail or snow. **2.** a fall of many objects, as tears, sparks, missiles, etc. **3.** a large supply or quantity: *a shower of wealth.* **4.** a party given for a bestowal of presents of a specific kind, esp. such a party for a prospective bride or prospective mother: *a linen shower; a baby shower.* **5.** See **shower bath.** —*v.t.* **6.** to wet, as with a shower. **7.** to pour down in a shower. **8.** to bestow liberally or lavishly. **9.** to bathe (oneself) in a shower bath. —*v.i.* **10.** to rain in a shower. **11.** to take a shower bath. [ME *shour,* OE *scūr;* c. G *Schauer,* Icel *skūr,* Goth *skūra*] —**show′er·less,** *adj.* —**show′er·like′,** *adj.* —**show′er·i·ness,** *n.*

show·er[2] (shō′ər), *n.* one who or that which shows. [ME; see SHOW, -ER[1]]

show′er bath′ (shou′ər), **1.** a bath in which water is showered upon the body from above. **2.** the apparatus for such a bath.

show′er gate′ (shou′ər), *Foundry.* a gate dividing into a number of small channels so as to fill all parts of the mold cavity from the top at a uniform rate.

show·er·proof (shou′ər prōōf′), *adj.* (of clothing, fabric, etc.) treated so as to resist rain; rainproof. [SHOWER[1] + -PROOF]

Show·ers (shou′ərz), *n.* **Sea of.** See **Mare Imbrium.**

show·er·y (shou′ə rē), *adj.* **1.** characterized by or abounding with showers: *the showery season in the tropics.* **2.** falling in showers: *showery petals.* **3.** causing or bringing showers: *a bank of showery clouds.* **4.** of, pertaining to, or resembling showers: *showery spray from the ocean.* [SHOWER[2] + -Y[1]]

show·folk (shō′fōk′), *n. pl.* persons, esp. performers, whose vocation is within the field of entertainment. [SHOW + FOLK]

show′ gera′nium, a geranium, *Pelargonium domesticum,* of South Africa, having roundish clusters of large white, pink, or red flowers. Also called **fancy geranium, Lady Washington geranium.**

show′ girl′, a girl or woman who appears in the chorus of a show, nightclub act, etc., mainly for decorative purposes.

show·i·ly (shō′ə lē), *adv.* in a showy manner.

show·i·ness (shō′ē nis), *n.* the property or characteristic of being showy.

show·ing (shō′ing), *n.* **1.** a show, display, or exhibition. **2.** the act of putting something on display. **3.** a performance or record considered for the impression it makes: *She made a bad showing in high school but did better in college.* **4.** a setting forth or presentation, as of facts or conditions. **5.** Also called **show′ piece′.** a rock specimen revealing the presence of a certain mineral. [SHOW + -ING[1]]

show·man (shō′mən), *n., pl.* **-men. 1.** one who presents or produces a show, esp. of a theatrical nature. **2.** one who is gifted in doing or presenting things theatrically or dramatically: *He didn't have much voice but was a great showman.* [SHOW + MAN[1]] —**show′man·ly,** *adv.*

show·man·ship (shō′mən ship′), *n.* the skill or ability of a showman. [SHOWMAN + -SHIP]

shown (shōn), *v.* a pp. of **show.**

show-off (shō′ôf′, -of′), *n.* **1.** a person given to pretentious display. **2.** the act of showing off. [n. use of v. phrase *show off*] —**show′-off′ish,** *adj.* —**show′-off′ish·ness,** *n.*

show′ of hands′, an indication of approval, disapproval, volunteering, etc., on the part of a group of persons, usually made by each assenting person raising his or her hand.

show·piece (shō′pēs′), *n.* **1.** something that is displayed or exhibited. **2.** something exhibited or worthy of exhibiting as a fine example of its kind. [SHOW + PIECE]

show·place (shō′plās′), *n.* **1.** an estate, mansion, or the like, usually open to the public, renowned for its beauty, excellent design and workmanship, historical interest, etc. **2.** any home, building, office, etc., that is beautifully furnished and is considered of flawless taste: *His house was a showplace.* [SHOW + PLACE]

show·room (shō′rōōm′, -rŏŏm′), *n.* a room used for the display of goods or merchandise. [SHOW + ROOM]

show-stop·per (shō′stop′ər), *n.* *Theat.* a line, act, performance, etc., that gains such enthusiastic applause that it temporarily interrupts a theatrical performance. Also, **show′ stop′per, show′stop′per.**

show-through (shō′thrōō′), *n.* **1.** the visibility through paper of what is printed on the other side. **2.** a measure of the opacity of a paper.

show′ win′dow, a display window in a store.

show·y (shō′ē), *adj.,* **show·i·er, show·i·est. 1.** making an imposing display: *showy flowers.* **2.** pompous; ostentatious; gaudy. [SHOW + -Y[1]]

—**Syn. 2.** loud. See **gaudy**[1]. —**Ant. 2.** humble.

show′y crab′ ap′ple, a large bush or tree, *Malus floribunda,* of Japan or China, having red fruit and rose-colored flowers that fade to white.

show′y or′chis, a wild orchid, *Orchis spectabilis,* of eastern North America, having a spike of showy flowers, each with purple, pink, or white sepals and petals united into a galea and a white lip. Also called **gray orchis.**

shp, See **shaft horsepower.** Also, **SHP, S.H.P., s.hp., s.h.p.**

shpt., shipment.

shr., share; shares.

shrad·dha (shrä′də), *n.* *Hinduism.* one of several funeral rites performed at intervals after a death. [< Skt *śrāddha* < *śraddhā* belief]

shrank (shrangk), *v.* a pt. of **shrink.**

shrap·nel (shrap′nəl), *n.* **1.** *Mil.* **a.** a hollow projectile containing bullets or the like and a bursting charge, designed to explode before reaching the target, and to set free a shower of missiles. **b.** such projectiles collectively. **2.** shell fragments. [named after H. *Shrapnel* (1761–1842), English army officer, its inventor]

shread·head (shred′hed′), *n.* jerkinhead. [perh. obs. *shread* SHRED + HEAD]

shred (shred), *n., v.,* **shred·ded** or **shred, shred·ding.** —*n.* **1.** a piece cut or torn off, esp. in a narrow strip. **2.** a bit; scrap: *We haven't got a shred of evidence.* —*v.t.* **3.** to cut or tear into small pieces, esp. small strips; reduce to shreds. —*v.i.* **4.** to be cut up, torn, etc.: *The blouse had shredded.* [ME *schrede,* OE *scrēade;* c. Icel *skrjōthr* worn-out book, G *Schrot* chips] —**shred′der,** *n.* —**shred′less,** *adj.* —**shred′like′,** *adj.*

shred·ding (shred′ing), *n.* furring attached to the undersides of rafters. Also, **shread′ing.** [?]

Shreve·port (shrēv′pōrt′, -pôrt′), *n.* a city in NW Louisiana, on the Red River. 164,372 (1960).

shrew[1] (shrōō), *n.* a woman of violent temper and speech; termagant. [ME; special use of SHREW[2]] —**shrew′like′,** *adj.*

—**Syn.** virago, nag, scold.

shrew[2] (shrōō), *n.* any of several small, mouselike insectivores of the genus *Sorex* and related genera, having a long, sharp snout. [ME; OE *scrēawa* < ?]

Short-tailed shrew, *Blarina brevicauda* (Total length 5 in.; tail 1 in.)

shrewd (shrōōd), *adj.* **1.** astute or sharp in practical matters: *a shrewd politician.* **2.** *Archaic.* keen; piercing. **3.** *Archaic.* malicious. **4.** *Obs.* bad. **5.** *Obs.* shrewish. **6.** *Obs.* artful. [ME *shrewed,* ptp. of *shrew* to curse (now obs.), v. use of SHREW[1]] —**shrewd′ly,** *adv.* —**shrewd′ness,** *n.*

—**Syn. 1.** quick, discerning, perceptive, perspicacious, sagacious, keen; discriminating, intelligent. See **acute.** —**Ant. 1.** dull, stupid.

shrew·ish (shrōō′ish), *adj.* having the disposition of a shrew. [SHREW[1] + -ISH[1]] —**shrew′ish·ly,** *adv.* —**shrew′ish·ness,** *n.*

shrew′ mole′, a grayish-black mole, *Neurotrichus gibbsii,* of the western coast of the U.S. and Canada, that grows to a length of about three inches.

shrew·mouse (shrōō′mous′), *n., pl.* **-mice.** a shrew, esp. *Sorex vulgaris,* of Europe. [SHREW[2] + MOUSE]

Shrews·bur·y (shrōōz′ber′ē, -bə rē *or, for 1,* shrōz′-), *n.* **1.** a city in and the county seat of Shropshire, in W England. 49,726 (1961). **2.** a town in E Missouri. 4730 (1960). **3.** a town in E New Jersey. 3222 (1960).

shriek (shrēk), *n.* **1.** a loud, sharp, shrill cry. **2.** a loud, high sound of laughter. **3.** any loud, shrill sound, as of a whistle. —*v.i.* **4.** to utter a loud, sharp, shrill cry, as birds. **5.** to cry out sharply in a high voice: *to shriek with pain.* **6.** to utter loud, high-pitched sounds in laughing. **7.** (of a musical instrument, a whistle, the wind, etc.) to give forth a loud, shrill sound. —*v.t.* **8.** to utter in a shriek or shrieks: *to shriek defiance.* [earlier *shrick,* north var. of *shritch* (now dial.), ME *schriche(n),* back formation from OE *scriccettan;* akin to SHRIKE] —**shriek′er,** *n.* —**shriek′ing·ly,** *adv.* —**shriek′y,** *adj.*

—**Syn. 1, 5.** scream, screech. **5.** See **scream.**

shriev·al (shrē′vəl), *adj.* of, belonging to, or relating to a sheriff. [SHRIEVE[1] + -AL[1]]

shriev·al·ty (shrē′vəl tē), *n., pl.* **-ties.** the office, term, or jurisdiction of a sheriff. Also called **sheriffalty.** [SHRIEVE[1] + *-alty,* as in *mayoralty*]

shrieve[1] (shrēv), *n.* *Archaic.* sheriff.

shrieve[2] (shrēv), *v.t., v.i.,* **shrieved, shriev·ing.** *Archaic.* shrive.

shrift (shrift), *n.* *Archaic.* **1.** the imposition of penance by a priest on a penitent after confession. **2.** absolution or remission of sins granted after confession and penance. **3.** confession to a priest. **4.** the act of shriving. Cf. **short shrift.** [ME; OE *scrift* penance; c. G, D *schrift* writing; see SHRIVE, SCRIPT]

shrike (shrīk), *n.* any of numerous predaceous, oscine birds of the family *Laniidae,* having a strong, hooked, and toothed bill, feeding on insects and sometimes on small birds and other animals: the members of certain species impale thier prey on thorns or suspend it from the branches of trees to tear it apart more easily, and are said to kill more than is necessary for them to eat. [OE *scrīc;* imit.; akin to Icel *skrīkja* to twitter; see SHRIEK]

shrill (shril), *adj.* **1.** high-pitched and piercing: *a shrill cry.* **2.** producing such a sound. **3.** full of or characterized by such a sound: *shrill music.* **4.** betraying some strong emotion or attitude in an exaggerated amount, as antagonism or defensiveness. **5.** marked by great intensity; keen: *the shrill, incandescent light of the exploding bomb.* —*v.t., v.i.* **6.** to cry shrilly. —*n.* **7.** a shrill sound. —*adv.* **8.** in a shrill manner; shrilly. [ME *shrille* (adj., v.); akin to OE *scrallettan* to sound loudly; c. G *schrill* (adj.) *schrillen* (v.); cf. Icel *skrīll* rabble] —**shrill′ness,** *n.* —**shril′ly,** *adv.*

Shrimp, *Crangon vulgaris* (2 in. long)

shrimp (shrimp), *n., pl.* **shrimps,** (*esp. collectively for 1*) **shrimp,** *v., adj.* —*n.* **1.** any of several small, long-tailed, chiefly marine, decapod crustaceans of the genera *Crangon, Penaeus,* etc., certain species of which are used as food. **2.** a diminutive or insignificant person. —*v.i.* **3.** to catch or try to catch shrimps. —*adj.* **4.** (of food) made of or containing shrimp: *shrimp salad.* **5.** of or pertaining to shrimp or their catching, processing, and marketing: *a shrimp boat.* [ME *shrimpe;* akin to MHG *schrimpfen* to contract, OE *scrimman* to shrink] —**shrimp′like′,** *adj.*

shrimp·er (shrim′pər), *n.* **1.** a shrimp fisherman. **2.** a boat used for shrimping. **3.** *Informal.* a shrimp. [SHRIMP + -ER[1]]

shrimp·fish (shrimp′fish′), *n., pl.* (*esp. collectively*) **-fish,** (*esp. referring to two or more kinds or species*) **-fish·es.** any of several fishes of the family *Centriscidae,* found in shallow waters from eastern Africa to Hawaii, having a compressed body covered with transparent plates. [SHRIMP + FISH]

shrine (shrīn), *n., v.,* **shrined, shrin·ing.** —*n.* **1.** a receptacle for sacred relics; a reliquary. **2.** a building or other shelter, often of a stately or sumptuous character, enclosing the remains or relics of a saint or other holy person and forming an object of religious veneration and pilgrimage. **3.** any structure or place consecrated or devoted to some saint, holy person, or deity, as an altar, chapel, church, or temple. **4.** any place or object hallowed by its history or associations: *a historic shrine.* —*v.t.* **5.** to enshrine. [ME *schrine,* OE *scrīn;* c. G *Schrein,* D *schrijn* << L *scrīn(ium)* case for books and papers] —**shrine′less,** *adj.* —**shrine′like′,** *adj.*

Shrin·er (shrī′nər), *n.* a member of a fraternal order **(Ancient Arabic Order of Nobles of the Mystic Shrine)** which is an auxiliary of the Masonic order and is dedicated to good fellowship, health programs, charitable works, etc. [SHRINE + -ER[1]]

shrink (shringk), *v.,* **shrank** or, often, **shrunk; shrunk** or **shrunk·en; shrink·ing;** *n.* —*v.i.* **1.** to draw back, as in retreat or avoidance: *to shrink from danger; to shrink from contact.* **2.** to contract or lessen in size, as from exposure to conditions of temperature or moisture: *This cloth will not shrink if washed in lukewarm water.* **3.** to become reduced in extent or compass. —*v.t.* **4.** to cause to shrink or contract; reduce. **5.** *Textiles.* to cause (a fabric) to contract during finishing, thus preventing shrinkage, during laundering, of the garments made from it. **6.** *Metalworking.* to fit (an outer metal part) tightly onto an inner one by heating it so that it expands, placing it around the inner part, and letting it cool so that it contracts. —*n.* **7.** the act or an instance of shrinking. **8.** a shrinking movement. **9.** shrinkage. [ME *schrinke(n),* OE *scrincan;* c. MD *schrinken,* Sw *skrynka* to shrink, Norw *skrukka* old shrunken woman] —**shrink′a·ble,** *adj.* —**shrink′er,** *n.* —**shrink′ing·ly,** *adv.*

—**Syn. 1.** withdraw, recoil, flinch, retire, quail, blench. **3.** See **decrease.** —**Ant. 3.** increase.

shrink·age (shring′kij), *n.* **1.** the act or fact of shrinking. **2.** the amount or degree of shrinking. **3.** reduction or depreciation in quantity, value, etc. **4.** contraction of a fabric in finishing or washing. **5.** the difference between the original weight of livestock and that after it has been prepared for marketing. [SHRINK + -AGE]

shrink′ing vi′olet, a shy, modest, or self-effacing person.

shrive (shrīv), *v.,* **shrove** or **shrived, shriv·en** or **shrived, shriv·ing.** —*v.t.* **1.** to impose penance on (a sinner). **2.** to grant absolution to (a penitent). **3.** to hear the confession of (a person). —*v.i.* **4.** to hear confessions. **5.** to go to or make confession; confess one's sins, as to a priest. [ME; OE *scrīfa(n)* (to) prescribe; c. G *schreiben* to write << L *scrībere;* see SCRIBE[1]]

shriv·el (shriv′əl), *v.t., v.i.,* **-eled, -el·ing** or (*esp. Brit.*) **-elled, -el·ling. 1.** to contract and wrinkle, as from great heat, cold, dryness, etc. **2.** to wither; make or become helpless or useless. [akin to Sw *skrofliq* uneven, rough (? orig. wrinkled, shrunken), dial. Sw *skryvla* to wrinkle, OE *sceorfan* to roughen; see SCURF]

—**Syn. 1.** shrink. See **wither.**

shriv·en (shriv′ən), *v.* a pp. of **shrive.**

Shri·ver (shrī′vər), *n.* **(Robert) Sar·gent, Jr.** (sär′jənt), born 1915, U.S. businessman and government official: first director of the U.S. Peace Corps, 1961–66.

shroff (shrof), *n.* **1.** (in India) a banker or money-changer. **2.** (in the Far East, esp. China) a native expert employed to test coins and separate the base from the genuine. —*v.t.* **3.** to test (coins) in order to separate the base from the genuine. [earlier *sharoffe* < Pg *xarrafo* < Hindi *çairāf* money-changer]

Shrop·shire (shrop′shēr, -shər), *n.* **1.** Also called **Salop.** a county in W England. 297,313 (1961); 134 sq. mi. *Co. seat:* Shrewsbury. **2.** one of an English breed of dark-faced sheep, yielding good mutton and white wool.

Shrop′shire Lad′, A, a volume of poetry (1896) by A. E. Housman.

shroud (shroud), *n.* **1.** a cloth or sheet in which a corpse is wrapped for burial. **2.** something which covers or conceals like a garment: *a shroud of rain.* **3.** *Naut.* any of a number of taut ropes or wires converging from both sides on the head of a lower or upper mast of the outer end of a bowsprit to steady it against lateral sway: a part of the standing rigging. **4.** Also called **shroud/ing.** *Mach.* **a.** (on a nonmetallic gear) an extended metal rim enclosing the ends of the teeth on either side. **b.** (on a water wheel) one of two rings of boards or plates enclosing the buckets at their ends. —*v.t.* **5.** to wrap or clothe for burial. **6.** to cover; hide from view. **7.** to veil, as in obscurity or mystery: *They shrouded their past lives in an effort to forget.* **8.** to provide (a water wheel) with a shroud. **9.** *Obs.* to shelter. —*v.i.* **10.** *Archaic.* to take shelter. [ME; OE *scrūd;* c. Icel *skrūth;* akin to SHRED] **—shroud/less,** *adj.* **—shroud/like/,** *adj.*
—Syn. 1. winding-sheet. **6.** conceal, screen. **—Ant. 6.** reveal.

shroud/ knot/, *Naut.* any of several knots for uniting large ropes of the same size or for repairing broken shrouds.

shroud-laid (shroud/lād/), *adj.* *Cordage.* noting a fiber rope of four strands laid right-handed with or without a heart.

shrove (shrōv), *v.* a pt. of **shrive.** [ME *shroof,* OE *scrāf*]

Shrove/ Mon/day, the Monday before Ash Wednesday. [ME *shrovemonday.* See SHROVE, MONDAY]

Shrove/ Sun/day, the Sunday before Ash Wednesday. [ME *shrofsunday.* See SHROVE, SUNDAY]

Shrove·tide (shrōv/tīd/), *n.* the three days before Ash Wednesday, once a time of confession and absolution. [ME *shroftyde.* See SHROVE, TIDE[1]]

Shrove/ Tues/day, the last day of Shrovetide, long observed as a season of merrymaking before Lent. [ME *chroftetewesday.* See SHROVE, TUESDAY]

shrub[1] (shrub), *n.* a woody, perennial plant smaller than a tree, usually having permanent stems branching from or near the ground. [ME *shrubbe,* OE *scrybb* brushwood; c. Dan (dial.) *skrub*] **—shrub/less,** *adj.* **—shrub/like/,** *adj.*

shrub[2] (shrub), *n.* any of various acidulated beverages made from the juice of fruit, sugar, and other ingredients, often including alcohol. [< Ar, metathetic var. of *shurb* drink; see SHERBET]

shrub·ber·y (shrub/ə rē), *n., pl.* **-ber·ies.** shrubs collectively. [SHRUB[1] + -ERY]

shrub·by (shrub/ē), *adj.,* **-bi·er, -bi·est. 1.** consisting of or abounding in shrubs. **2.** resembling a shrub; shrublike. [SHRUB[1] + -Y[1]] **—shrub/bi·ness,** *n.*

shrub/by cinque/foil, a small shrub, *Potentilla fruticosa,* of Europe, Asia, and North America, having numerous, showy, bright-yellow flowers. Also called **hardhack.**

shrug (shrug), *v.,* **shrugged, shrug·ging,** *n.* —*v.t.* **1.** to raise and contract (the shoulders), expressing indifference, disdain, etc. —*v.i.* **2.** to raise and contract the shoulders. **3. shrug off, a.** to disregard; minimize: *to shrug off an insult.* **b.** to rid oneself of: *to shrug off the effects of a drug.* —*n.* **4.** the movement of raising and contracting the shoulders. **5.** a short sweater or jacket that ends above or at the waistline. [late ME *schrugge* to shudder, shrug]

shrunk (shrungk), *v.* a pp. and pt. of **shrink.**

shrunk·en (shrung/kən), *v.* a pp. of **shrink.**

shtg., shortage.

shtrei·mel (shtrī/məl), *n.* a round close-fitting cap trimmed on the outside with a band of fur. [< Yiddish *schtreimel,* dim. of MHG *streime* stripe, band]

shu (sho͞o), *n.* the Confucian principle of refraining from actions toward others which would be disagreeable if done to oneself. [< Chin (Peking)]

Shu (sho͞o), *n.* *Egyptian Religion.* the god of the air, sometimes represented with arms upraised, supporting the vault of heaven. Cf. **Nut.**

shuck (shuk), *n.* **1.** a husk or pod, as the outer covering of corn, hickory nuts, chestnuts, etc. **2.** Usually, **shucks.** *Informal.* something useless or worthless: *They don't care shucks about the project.* **3.** the shell of an oyster or clam. —*v.t.* **4.** to remove the shucks from: *to shuck corn.* **5.** to remove or discard as or like shucks; peel off: *to shuck one's clothes.* —*interj.* **6. shucks,** *Informal.* (used as a mild exclamation of disgust or regret.) [?] **—shuck/er,** *n.*

shud·der (shud/ər), *v.i.* **1.** to tremble with a sudden convulsive movement, as from horror, fear, or cold. —*n.* **2.** a convulsive movement of the body, as from horror, fear, or cold. [ME *shodder* (c. G *schaudern* < LG), freq. of OE *scūdan* to tremble; see -ER[6]]
—Syn. 1. quiver. See **shiver**[1].

shud·der·ing (shud/ər ing), *adj.* **1.** trembling or quivering with fear, dread, cold, etc. **2.** Also, **shud/der·y.** characterized by or causing a shudder: *a shuddering plunge of the ship.* [SHUDDER + -ING[2]] **—shud/der·ing·ly,** *adv.*

shud·na (sho͝od/nə), *Scot.* shouldna.

shuf·fle (shuf/əl), *v.,* **-fled, -fling,** *n.* —*v.i.* **1.** to walk without lifting the feet or with clumsy steps and a shambling gait. **2.** to scrape the feet over the floor in dancing. **3.** to move clumsily (usually fol. by *into*): *to shuffle into one's clothes.* **4.** to act underhandedly or evasively with respect to a stated situation (often fol. by *in, into,* or *out of*): *to shuffle out of one's responsibilities.* **5.** to intermix so as to change the relative positions of cards in a pack. —*v.t.* **6.** to move (one's feet) along the ground or floor without lifting them. **7.** to perform (a dance) with such movements. **8.** to move (an object or objects) this way and that. **9.** to put, thrust, or bring trickily, evasively, or haphazardly (usually fol. by *in, into, out,* etc.): *to shuffle one's way into favor.* **10.** to mix (cards in a pack) so as to change their relative position. **11.** to jumble together, mix, or interchange the positions of (objects). **12. shuffle off, a.** to thrust aside; get rid of. **b.** to move away by, or as if by, shuffling: *They shuffled off to school with little enthusiasm.* —*n.* **13.** a scraping movement; dragging gait. **14.** an evasive trick; evasion. **15.** an act or instance of shuffling. **16.** *Cards.* **a.** a shuffling of cards in a pack. **b.** the right or turn to shuffle preparatory to dealing: *You win the shuffle.* **17.** a dance in which the feet are shuffled along the floor. [< LG *schuffeln* to walk clumsily or with dragging feet, mix (cards); akin to SHOVEL]

shuf·fle·board (shuf/əl bōrd/, -bôrd/), *n.* **1.** a game in which standing players shove or push wooden or plastic disks with a long cue toward numbered scoring sections marked on a floor or deck. **2.** the board or marked surface, as on a floor or deck, on which this game is played. [alter. of earlier *shove board*]

Shuffleboard (def. 2)

shuf·fler (shuf/lər), *n.* **1.** one who shuffles. **2.** one who mixes the cards, as before the deal in a card game. **3.** *Dial.* a scaup duck. [SHUFFLE + -ER[1]]

shuf·fling (shuf/ling), *adj.* **1.** moving in a dragging or clumsy manner. **2.** prevaricating; evasive. [SHUFFLE + -ING[2]] **—shuf/fling·ly,** *adv.*

Shu·fu (sho͞o/fo͞o/), *n.* Kashgar.

Shu·ha (sho͞o/hä), *adj.* of or pertaining to any Shinto sect other than the Kokka.

shul (sho͝ol, sho͞ol), *n., pl.* **shuln** (sho͝oln, sho͞oln), *Yiddish.* a synagogue. Also, **schul.**

Shu·lam·ite (sho͞o/lə mīt/), *n.* an epithet meaning "princess," applied to the bride in the Song of Solomon 6:13.

Shul·han A·ruk (sho͞ol KHän/ ä ro͞oKH/), an authoritative, Sephardic-oriented code of Jewish law and custom compiled by the Talmudic scholar Joseph Caro (1488–1575) and published in Vienna in 1565. Also, **Shulchan/ Aruch/.** Cf. **Mappah.**

shul·war (shul/wär), *n.* (*construed as pl.*) shalwar.

shu·mal (shə mäl/), *n.* shamal.

shun (shun), *v.t.,* **shunned, shun·ning.** to keep away from (a place, person, object, etc.), from motives of dislike, caution, etc.; take pains to avoid. [ME *shun(en),* OE *scunian* to avoid, fear] **—shun/na·ble,** *adj.* **—shun/ner,** *n.*
—Syn. evade, eschew. **—Ant.** seek.

Shun (sho͞on), *n.* See under **Yao.**

shunt (shunt), *v.t.* **1.** to shove or turn (someone or something) aside or out of the way. **2.** to sidetrack; get rid of. **3.** *Elect.* **a.** to divert (a part of a current) by connecting a circuit element in parallel with another. **b.** to place or furnish with a shunt. **4.** *Railroads.* to shift (rolling stock) from one track to another; switch. **5.** *Surg.* to divert blood by means of a shunt. **6.** to move or turn aside or out of the way. **7.** (of a locomotive with rolling stock) to move from track to track or from point to point, as in a railroad yard; switch. —*n.* **8.** the act of shunting; shift. **9.** *Elect.* a conducting element bridged across a circuit or a portion of a circuit, establishing a current path auxiliary to the main circuit, as a resistor placed across the terminals of an ammeter for increasing the range of the device. **10.** a railroad switch. **11.** *Anat., Surg.* a vascular channel through which blood is diverted from its normal path, esp. such a channel formed surgically. **12.** *Anat.* an anastomosis. —*adj.* **13.** *Elect.* being, having, or operating by means of a shunt: *a shunt circuit; a shunt generator.* [ME *schunt* to shy (said of horses); akin to SHUN] **—shunt/er,** *n.*

shunt/ing en/gine, *Chiefly Brit.* See **switch engine.**

shunt-wound (shunt/wound/), *adj.* *Elect.* noting a motor or a generator that has the field circuit connected in parallel with the armature winding. **—shunt/ wind/ing.**

shush (shush), *interj.* **1.** hush (used as a command to be quiet or silent). —*v.t.* **2.** to make (someone or something) silent; hush. [imit.] **—shush/er,** *n.*

Shu·shan (sho͞o/shan), *n.* Biblical name of **Susa.**

shut (shut), *v.,* **shut, shut·ting,** *adj., n.* —*v.t.* **1.** to put (a door, cover, etc.) in position to close or obstruct. **2.** to close the doors of (often fol. by *up*): *to shut up a shop for the night.* **3.** to close (something) by bringing together or folding its parts: *Shut your book. Shut the window!* **4.** to confine; enclose: *to shut a bird into a cage.* **5.** to bar; exclude: *They shut him from their circle.* **6.** to cause (a business, factory, store, etc.) to end or suspend operations: *He shut his store, sold his house, and moved away. We're shutting the office for two weeks in June.* **7.** *Obs.* to bolt; bar. —*v.i.* **8.** to become shut or closed; close. **9. shut down, a.** to settle over so as to envelop or darken: *The fog shut down rapidly.* **b.** *Informal.* to close, esp. temporarily, as a factory; cease manufacturing or business operations. **c.** Also, **shut down on** or **upon.** *Informal.* to hinder; check; stop. **10. shut in, a.** to enclose. **b.** to confine, as from illness: *She broke her leg in a fall and has been shut in for several weeks.* **11. shut off, a.** to stop the passage of (water, traffic, electricity, etc.); close off. **b.** to isolate; separate: *an outpost almost completely shut off from civilization.* **12. shut out, a.** to keep from entering; exclude. **b.** to hide from view. **c.** to prevent the opposite side from scoring, as in a game of baseball. **13. shut up, a.** to imprison; confine. **b.** to close entirely. **c.** *Informal.* to stop talking; become silent: *one of those women who couldn't shut up even if she wanted to.* **d.** *Informal.* to stop (someone) from talking; silence. —*adj.* **14.** closed; fastened up: *a shut door.* **15.** *Phonet.* checked. **16. shut of,** *Dial.* or *Informal.* free of; rid of: *He wished he were shut of all his debts.* —*n.* **17.** the act or time of shutting or closing. **18.** the line where two pieces of welded metal are united. [ME *schutte,* OE *scytta(n)* (to) bolt (a door); akin to SHOOT]
—Syn. 1. See **close. 4.** jail, imprison, cage. **5.** prohibit. **—Ant. 1.** open.

shut·down (shut/doun/), *n.* a shutting down; a closing of a factory or the like for a time. [n. use of v. phrase *shut down*]

Shute (sho͞ot), *n.* **Nevil** (*Nevil Shute Norway*), 1899–1960, British novelist and aeronautical engineer.

shut-eye (shut/ī/), *n.* *Slang.* sleep.

shut-in (shut/in/), *adj.* **1.** confined to one's home, a hospital, etc., as from illness. **2.** *Psychiatry.* disposed to desire solitude. —*n.* **3.** a person confined by infirmity or disease to the house, a hospital, etc. [adj., n. use of v. phrase *shut in*]

shut·off (shut/ôf/, -of/), *n.* an object or device that shuts (something) off: *the automatic shutoff on a heater.* [n. use of v. phrase *shut off*]

shut·out (shut/out/), *n.* **1.** the act or an instance of shutting out. **2.** the state of being shut out. **3.** *Sports.* **a.** a preventing of the opposite side from scoring, as in baseball. **b.** any game in which one side does not score. [n. use of v. phrase *shut out*]

shut·ter (shut/ər), *n.* **1.** a solid or louvered movable cover for a window. **2.** a movable cover, slide, etc., for an opening. **3.** one who or that which shuts. **4.** *Photog.* a mechanical device for opening and closing the aperture of a camera lens to expose film or the like. —*v.t.* **5.** to close or provide with shutters: *She shuttered the windows.* [SHUT + -ER[1]] **—shut/ter·less,** *adj.*
—Syn 1. See **curtain.**

shut·ter·bug (shut/ər bug/), *n.* *Photog. Slang.* an amateur photographer, esp. one who is greatly devoted to the hobby. [SHUTTER + BUG[1]]

shut·ter·ing (shut/ər ing), *n.* *Brit.* formwork, as for poured concrete or rammed earth. [SHUTTER + -ING[1]]

shut/ting stile/, the stile of a door or shutter that closes against the frame of the opening. Cf. **hanging stile.**

shut·tle (shut/əl), *n., v.,* **-tled, -tling.** —*n.* **1.** a device in a loom for passing or shooting the weft thread through the shed from one side of the web to the other, usually consisting of a boat-shaped piece of wood containing a bobbin on which the weft thread is wound. **2.** the sliding container that carries the lower thread in a sewing machine. **3.** a public conveyance, as a train, airplane, or bus, which travels back and forth at regular intervals over a particular route, esp. a short route or one connecting two transportation systems. **4.** shuttlecock (def. 1). —*v.t.* **5.** to cause (someone or something) to move to and fro or back and forth by or as if by a shuttle: *They shuttled the salesman back and forth.* —*v.i.* **6.** to move to and fro: *constantly shuttling between city and suburb.* [ME *shotil,* OE *scyttel* dart, arrow; c. Icel *skutill* harpoon; akin to SHUT, SHOOT] **—shut/tle·like/,** *adj.*

shut·tle·cock (shut/əl kok/), *n.* **1.** Also called **shuttle.** the object which is struck back and forth in badminton and battledore, consisting of a feathered cork head and a plastic crown. **2.** the game of battledore. —*v.t.* **3.** to send or bandy to and fro like a shuttlecock. —*v.i.* **4.** to move or be bandied to and fro. —*adj.* **5.** of such a state or condition: *a shuttlecock existence.* [SHUTTLE + COCK[1]]

Shuttlecock (length 3½ in.)

Shver·nik (shver/nik), *n.* **Ni·ko·lai** (ni ko lī/), born 1888, Russian government official: president of the Soviet Union 1946–53.

shwa (shwä; *Ger.* shvä), *n.* schwa.

shy[1] (shī), *adj.,* **shy·er** or **shi·er, shy·est** or **shi·est,** *v.,* **shied, shy·ing,** *n., pl.* **shies.** —*adj.* **1.** bashful; retiring. **2.** easily frightened away; timid. **3.** suspicious; distrustful: *I am a bit shy of that sort of person.* **4.** reluctant; wary. **5.** deficient: *shy of funds.* **6.** scant; short of a full amount or number: *still a few dollars shy of our goal; an inch shy of being six feet.* **7.** (in poker) indebted to the pot. **8.** not bearing or breeding freely, as plants or animals. **9. fight shy of,** to keep away from; avoid: *She fought shy of making the final decision.* —*v.i.* **10.** (esp. of a horse) to start back or aside, as in fear. **11.** to draw back; recoil. —*n.* **12.** a sudden start aside, as in fear. [late ME *schey,* early ME *scheowe,* OE *scēoh;* c. MHG *schiech;* akin to D *schuw,* G *scheu*] **—shy/er,** *n.* **—shy/ly,** *adv.* **—shy/ness,** *n.*
—Syn. 1. SHY, BASHFUL, DIFFIDENT imply a manner which shows discomfort or lack of confidence in association with others. SHY implies a constitutional shrinking from contact or close association with others, together with a wish to escape notice: *shy and retiring.* BASHFUL suggests timidity about meeting others, and trepidation and awkward behavior when brought into prominence or notice: *a bashful child.* DIFFIDENT emphasizes self-distrust, fear of censure, failure, etc., and a hesitant, tentative manner as a consequence: *a diffident approach to a subject.* **4.** heedful, cautious, careful, chary. **11.** shrink. **—Ant. 1.** forward. **2.** trusting. **4.** careless. **11.** advance.

shy[2] (shī), *v.,* **shied, shy·ing,** *n., pl.* **shies.** —*v.t., v.i.* **1.** to throw with a swift, sudden movement: *to shy a stone.* —*n.* **2.** a quick, sudden throw. **3.** *Informal.* **a.** a gibe or sneer. **b.** a try. [? orig. causative use of SHY[1] (v.)] **—shy/er,** *n.*
—Syn. 1. toss, pitch, fling, cast, flip.

Shy·lock (shī/lok), *n.* **1.** a relentless and revengeful moneylender in Shakespeare's *Merchant of Venice.* **2.** any usurer.

shy·ster (shī/stər), *n.* *Informal.* **1.** a lawyer who uses unprofessional or questionable methods. **2.** one who gets along by petty, sharp practices. [appar. SHY[1], in slang sense of shady, disreputable + -STER]

si[1] (sē), *n.* *Music.* the syllable used for the seventh tone of a scale and sometimes for the tone B. [see GAMUT]

si[2] (sī), *conj.* (in prescriptions) if. [< L]

Si (sē; *Chin.* shē), *n.* a river in S China, flowing E from Yünnan province to the South China Sea near Canton. 1250 mi. long. Also called **Si-kiang.**

Si, *Chem.* silicon.

S.I., 1. Sandwich Islands. **2.** Staten Island.

si·al (sī/al), *n.* *Geol.* a layer of rocks, rich in silica and alumina, believed to occur beneath the surface rocks of continents. [SI + -AL[1]] **—si·al/ic,** *adj.*

si·a·lad·e·ni·tis (sī/ə lad/ə nī/tis), *n.* *Pathol.* inflammation of one or more of the salivary glands. [< Gk *sial(on)* saliva + ADENITIS]

si·al·a·gog·ic (sī/ə lə goj/ik), *Med.* —*adj.* **1.** encouraging salivary flow. —*n.* **2.** sialagogue (def. 2). Also, **si/a·lo·gog/ic.** [SIALAGOGUE + -IC]

si·al·a·gogue (sī al/ə gôg/, -gog/), *Med.* —*adj.* **1.** sialagogic (def. 1). —*n.* **2.** a sialagogic agent or medicine. Also, **si·al/o·gogue/.** [< NL *sialagōg(us)* < Gk *sial(on)* saliva + *agōgós* -AGOGUE]

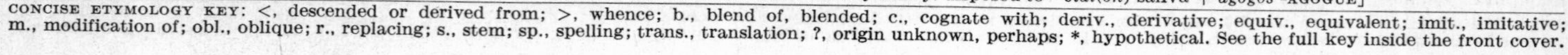

si·a·lid (sī′ə lid), *n.* **1.** any neuropterous insect of the family *Sialidae*, comprising the alderflies. —*adj.* **2.** belonging or pertaining to the family *Sialidae*. [< NL *Sialid(ae)* name of the family < Gk *sialídai*, pl. of *sialís* kind of bird; see -ID²]

Si·al·kot (sē äl′kōt′), *n.* a city in NE W Punjab, in W Pakistan: military station. 168,000 (est. 1961).

si·a·loid (sī′ə loid′), *adj.* resembling saliva. [< Gk *sial(on)* saliva, spittle + -OID]

Si·am (sī am′, sī′am), *n.* **1.** former name of **Thailand.** **2. Gulf of,** an arm of the South China Sea, S of Thailand.

si·a·mang (sē′ə mang′), *n.* a large, black gibbon, *Hylobates syndactylus*, of Sumatra and the Malay Peninsula, having very long arms and the second and third digits partially united by a web of skin. [< Malay]

Si·a·mese (sī′ə mēz′, -mēs′), *adj., n., pl.* **-mese.** —*adj.* **1.** of or pertaining to Siam, its people, or their language. **2.** Thai. **3.** twin; closely connected; similar. —*n.* **4.** a native of Siam. **5.** Thai. **6.** See **Siamese cat.** **7.** (*usually l.c.*) an inlet placed outside a building close to ground level, having two or more openings so that fire engines can pump water to the standpipes and sprinkler system of the building. [SIAM + -ESE]

Siamese (def. 7)

Si′amese cat′, one of a breed of slender, short-haired cats, raised originally in Siam, having a fawn or grayish body with extremities of a darker shade of the same color.

Si′amese fight′ing fish′, a labyrinth fish, *Betta splendens*, that has been bred for centuries to develop brilliant coloration, very long fins, and pugnacity.

Si′amese twins′, **1.** congenitally united twins, Chang and Eng (1811–74), born in Siam, who were joined to each other by a short tubular cartilaginous band. **2.** any twins who are born joined together in any manner.

Siamese cat

si·am·oise (sē′am woz′), *n.* tête-à-tête (def. 3). [< F, short for *couche siamoise* Siamese birth, in allusion to the birth (then recent) of the Siamese twins]

Si·an (sē′än′, shē′-), *n.* a city in and the capital of Shensi province, in central China: capital of the ancient Chinese Empire. 1,310,000 (est. 1957). Also called **Singan.**

Siang·tan (syäng′tän′, shyäng′-), *n.* a city in NE Hunan, in S China. 183,600 (est. 1957).

sib¹ (sib), *adj.* **1.** related by blood; akin. —*n.* **2.** a kinsman; relative. **3.** one's kin or kindred. [ME *(i)sib*, OE *(ge)sibb* related (as n.: a relation); c. Icel *sifjar* relatives; see GOSSIP]

sib² (sib), *n.* *Anthropol.* a unilateral descent group. [ME, OE; c. Goth *sibja*, G *Sippe*]

Si·be·li·us (si bā′lē əs, -bāl′yəs; *Fin.* si bā′lyōōs), *n.* **Jean Ju·li·us Chris·tian** (zhän yōō′lyōōs kris′tyän), 1865–1957, Finnish composer.

Si·be·ri·a (sī bēr′ē ə), *n.* **1.** Russian **Si·ber** (si bēr′yə). a part of the Soviet Union in N Asia, extending from the Ural Mountains to the Pacific. **2.** any undesirable or isolated locale, job, etc. to which one is assigned as punishment, a mark of disfavor, or the like. —**Si·be′ri·an,** *adj., n.*

Sibe′rian crab′ ap′ple, a round-headed tree, *Malus baccata*, of northern Asia, having white flowers and yellow or red fruit.

Sibe′rian high′, *Meteorol.* the prevailing high over Asia in winter.

Sibe′rian Husk′y, one of a Siberian breed of medium-sized dogs having a thick, soft coat, raised originally as sled dogs.

Sibe′rian lark′spur, a perennial herb, *Delphinium grandiflorum*, of eastern Asia, having blue or whitish flowers and hairy fruit. Also called **bouquet larkspur.**

Sibe′rian ru′by, a red tourmaline used as a gem: not a true ruby.

Sibe′rian squill′, a bulbous herb, *Scilla sibirica*, of Eurasia, having nodding, deep blue flowers.

Sibe′rian tea′, a perennial herb, *Bergenia crassifolia*, of eastern Asia, having clusters of rose-pink or lilac-colored flowers which stand above the foliage.

Sibe′rian wall′flower, a perennial herb, *Erysimum asperum*, of North America, having orange-yellow flowers.

si·be·rite (sī bēr′īt, sī′bə rīt′), *n.* a violet or violet-red tourmaline, used as a gem. [< F *sibérite*, after *Sibérie* SIBERIA; see -ITE¹]

sib·i·lant (sib′ə lənt), *adj.* **1.** hissing. **2.** *Phonet.* characterized by a hissing sound; noting sounds like those spelled with *s* in *this* (this), *rose* (rōz), *pressure* (presh′ər), *pleasure* (plezh′ər), and certain similar uses of *ch, sh, z, zh,* etc. —*n.* **3.** *Phonet.* a sibilant consonant. [< L *sibilant-* (s. of *sibilāns* hissing, whistling, prp. of *sibilāre*), equiv. to *sibil(us)* a hissing, whistling + *-ant-* -ANT] —**sib′i·lance, sib′i·lan·cy,** *n.* —**sib′i·lant·ly,** *adv.*

sib·i·late (sib′ə lāt′), *v.,* **-lat·ed, -lat·ing.** —*v.i.* **1.** to hiss. —*v.t.* **2.** to utter or pronounce with a hissing sound. [< L *sibilāt(us)* (ptp. of *sibil(āre)*; see SIBILANT) + *-ātus* -ATE¹] —**sib′i·la′tion,** *n.* —**sib′i·la′tor,** *n.*

Si·biu (sē byōō′), *n.* a city in central Rumania. 102,959 (est. 1964).

Sib·ley (sib′lē), *n.* a town in NW Iowa. 2852 (1960).

sib·ling (sib′ling), *n.* **1.** a brother or sister. **2.** *Anthropol.* a comember of a sib. —*adj.* **3.** of or pertaining to a brother or sister: *sibling rivalry.* [OE; see SIB¹, -LING¹]

sib·ship (sib′ship), *n.* *Anthropol.* the condition of being a member of a sib. [SIB¹ + -SHIP]

sib·yl (sib′il), *n.* **1.** any of certain women of antiquity reputed to possess powers of prophecy or divination. **2.** a prophetess or witch. [< Gk *Sibyll(a)* prophetess, the sybil; r. ME *Sibil* < ML *Sibill(a)*] —**si·byl·ic, si·byl·lic** (si bil′ik), **sib·yl·line** (sib′ə lēn′, -līn′, -lin), *adj.*

Sib·yl (sib′əl), *n.* a girl's given name. Also, **Sib′ylle, Sybil, Sy′ble.**

Sib′ylline Books′, a collection of oracular utterances from the Roman period written in Greek hexameters and concerning religious worship and Roman policy: they were reputedly bought by Tarquinius Superbus from the Cumaean sibyl. [< L *Sibyllīn(us)* of, belonging to the sibyl. See SIBYL, -INE¹]

sic¹ (sik), *v.t.,* **sicked, sick·ing.** **1.** to attack (used esp. as an imperative to a dog): *Sic 'em!* **2.** to incite to attack (usually fol. by *on*). Also, **sick.** [var. of SEEK]

sic² (sik), *adj.* *Chiefly Scot.* such.

sic (sēk; *Eng.* sik), *adv.* *Latin.* so; thus: usually written parenthetically to denote that a word, phrase, passage, etc., which may appear strange or incorrect has been written intentionally or has been quoted verbatim: *He signed his name as e. e. cummings* (sic).

Sic., 1. Sicilian. **2.** Sicily.

sic., (in prescriptions) dry; dried. Also, **sicc.** [< L *siccus*]

Si·ca·ni·an (si kā′nē ən), *adj.* Sicilian. [< L *Sīcani(us)* (*Sīcani(a)* Sicily + *-us* -OUS) + -AN]

sic·ca·tive (sik′ə tiv), *adj.* **1.** causing or promoting absorption of moisture; drying. —*n.* **2.** a siccative substance, esp. in paint. [< LL *siccātīv(us)* < L *siccāt(us)* made dry, dried (ptp. of *siccāre*; see SACK³, -ATE¹) + *-īvus* -IVE]

sice (sīs), *n.* syce.

Si·ci·lia (sē chē′lyä *for 1;* si sil′yə, -sil′ē ə *for 2*), *n.* **1.** Italian name of **Sicily.** **2.** an ancient name of **Sicily.**

si·cil·i·a·no (si sil′ē ä′nō), *n., pl.* **-nos.** **1.** a graceful folk dance of Sicily. **2.** the music for this dance. Also, **si·cil·i·a·na** (si sil′ē ä′nä). [< It: lit., Sicilian]

Sicil′ian Ves′pers, a general massacre of the French in Sicily by the natives, begun at the sound of the vesper bell on Easter Monday, 1282.

Sic·i·lies, Two (sis′ə lēz). See **Two Sicilies.**

Sic·i·ly (sis′ə lē), *n.* an island in the Mediterranean, comprising a region of Italy, and separated from the SW tip of the mainland by the Strait of Messina: largest island in the Mediterranean. 4,711,783 (1961); 9924 sq. mi. *Cap.:* Palermo. Italian, **Sicilia.** Ancient, **Sicilia, Trinacria.** —**Si·cil·ian** (si sil′yən, -sil′ē ən), *adj., n.*

sick¹ (sik), *adj.* **1.** afflicted with ill health or disease; ailing. **2.** affected with nausea; inclined to vomit. **3.** deeply affected with some unpleasant feeling, as of sorrow, disgust, boredom, longing, weariness, etc.: *sick at heart; to be sick of parties.* **4.** mentally, morally, or emotionally deranged, corrupt, or unsound: *a sick mind; wild statements that made him seem sick.* **5.** characteristic of a sick mind: *sick fancies.* **6.** dwelling on or obsessed with that which is gruesome, sadistic, ghoulish, or the like; morbid: *a sick comedian; sick jokes.* **7.** of, pertaining to, or for use during sickness: *He applied for sick benefits.* **8.** attended with or suggestive of sickness; sickly: *a sick pallor; the sick smell of disinfectant in the corridors.* **9.** *Informal.* disgusted; chagrined. **10.** not in proper condition; impaired. **11.** menstruating. **12.** *Agric.* **a.** failing to sustain adequate harvests of some crop, usually specified: *a wheat-sick soil.* **b.** containing harmful microorganisms: *a sick field.* —*n.* **13.** (*construed as pl.*) sick persons collectively (usually prec. by *the*). [ME *sik, sek,* OE *sēoc;* c. D *ziek,* G *siech,* Icel *sjūkr,* Goth *siuks*]

—**Syn. 1.** infirm. SICK, AILING, INDISPOSED refer to any departure from a state of health. SICK refers to a condition presumably temporary, however severe. AILING implies a somewhat unhealthy condition, usually extending over some time. INDISPOSED applies to a slight, temporary illness. See also **ill.** **2.** nauseous, nauseated. —**Ant. 1.** well, hale, healthy.

sick² (sik), *v.t.* sic¹.

sick′ bay′, a hospital or dispensary, esp. aboard ship.

sick·bed (sik′bed′), *n.* the bed used by a sick person. [ME; see SICK¹, BED]

sick′ call′, *Mil.* **1.** a daily formation for those requiring medical attention. **2.** the period during which this formation is held.

sick·en (sik′ən), *v.t., v.i.* to make or become sick. [ME *seknen, sicnen;* c. Icel *sjūkna.* See SICK¹, -EN¹]

sick·en·er (sik′ə nər), *n.* something that sickens or disgusts. [SICKEN + -ER¹]

sick·en·ing (sik′ə ning), *adj.* causing or capable of causing sickness, esp. nausea, disgust, or loathing: *sickening arrogance.* [SICKEN + -ING²] —**sick′en·ing·ly,** *adv.*

sick·er¹ (sik′ər), *adj.* *compar. of* **sick** *with* **sickest** *as superl.*

sick·er² (sik′ər), *Scot. and North Eng.* —*adj.* **1.** safe from danger; secure. **2.** dependable; trustworthy. —*adv.* **3.** certainly; without doubt. Also, **siker.** [ME *siker,* OE *sicor;* c. D *zeker,* G *sicher,* all < L *sēcūr(us);* see SECURE]

Sick·ert (sik′ərt), *n.* **Walter Richard,** 1860–1942, English painter.

sick′ head′ache, migraine.

sick·ish (sik′ish), *adj.* **1.** somewhat sickening or nauseating. **2.** somewhat sick or ill. [SICK¹ + -ISH¹] —**sick′ish·ly,** *adv.* —**sick′ish·ness,** *n.*

Sickle

sick·le (sik′əl), *n.* **1.** an implement for cutting grain, grass, etc., consisting of a curved, hooklike blade mounted in a short handle. **2.** (*cap.*) *Astron.* a group of stars in the constellation Leo, likened to this implement in formation. [ME *sikel,* OE *sicol;* c. D *zikkel,* G *Sichel,* all < L *secul(a);* akin to *secāre* to cut; see -ULE]

sick′ leave′, leave from duty, work, or the like, granted because of illness.

sick·le·bill (sik′əl bil′), *n.* any of various birds having a long, curved bill. [SICKLE + BILL²]

sick′le cell′, *Pathol.* an erythrocyte having an abnormal shape due to the presence of an abnormal hemoglobin. [so called from the fact that the cells are often sickle-shaped] —**sick′le-cell′,** *adj.*

sick′le cell′ ane′mia, *Pathol.* a form of anemia caused by excessive fragility of the deformed red cells in sicklemia, and characterized by ulcerations on the legs. Also called **sick′le cell′ disease′, meniscocytosis.**

sick′le feath′er, one of the paired, elongated, sickle-shaped, middle feathers of the tail of the rooster.

sick·le-hocked (sik′əl hokt′), *adj.* *Vet. Pathol.* noting or pertaining to a condition of horses in which the hock, due to strained tendons and ligaments, is flexed so that the foot is abnormally bowed far under the body. Also called **sick·le-hammed** (sik′əl hamd′).

sick·le·mi·a (sik′ə lē′mē ə, sik lē′-), *n.* *Pathol.* a hereditary trait occurring chiefly among Negroes, caused by a defective form of hemoglobin and characterized by cell deformities, which may occur in an entire family, but with only some members showing the anemia. Cf. **sickle cell anemia.** [SICKLE + -EMIA] —**sick·le·mic** (sik lē′mik, sik′ə-), *adj.*

sick′le thorn′, a leafless, spiny vine, *Asparagus falcatus,* of South Africa, having sickle-shaped, leathery branches, white, fragrant flowers, and brown berries, grown as an ornamental.

sick·le·weed (sik′əl wēd′), *n.* a weedy, umbelliferous herb, *Falcaria vulgaris,* introduced into the U.S. from Europe. [SICKLE + WEED¹]

sick′ list′, **1.** a list of persons who are sick. **2. on the sick list,** in poor health; not well; ill: *Mrs. Jones has been on the sick list for weeks.*

sick·ly (sik′lē), *adj.,* **-li·er, -li·est,** *adv., v.,* **-lied, -ly·ing.** —*adj.* **1.** not strong; unhealthy; ailing. **2.** of, connected with, or arising from ill heath: *a sickly complexion.* **3.** marked by the prevalence of ill health, as a region: *the epidemic left the town sickly.* **4.** causing sickness. **5.** nauseating. **6.** maudlin and insipid; mawkish: *sickly sentimentality.* **7.** faint or feeble, as light, color, etc. —*adv.* **8.** in a sick or sickly manner. —*v.t.* **9.** to cover with a sickly hue. [ME *siklich, sekly.* See SICK¹, -LY] —**sick′li·ness,** *n.*

—**Syn. 1.** frail, weak, puny, sick, feeble, infirm.

sick·ness (sik′nis), *n.* **1.** a particular disease or malady. **2.** the state or an instance of being sick; illness. **3.** nausea; queasiness. [ME *siknesse, seknesse,* OE *sēocnesse.* See SICK¹, -NESS]

sick′ pay′, wages or other compensation received from an employer during an illness.

sick·room (sik′rōōm′, -rŏŏm′), *n.* a room in which a sick person is confined. [SICK¹ + ROOM]

sic pas·sim (sēk päs′sim; *Eng.* sik pas′im), *Latin.* so throughout: used esp. as a footnote to indicate that a word, phrase, or idea recurs throughout the book being cited.

sic sem·per ty·ran·nis (sēk sem′per ty rän′nis; *Eng.* sik sem′pər ti ran′is), *Latin.* thus always to tyrants (motto of the State of Virginia).

sic tran·sit glo·ri·a mun·di (sēk trän′sit glō′rē ä′ mōōn′dē; *Eng.* sik tran′sit glôr′ē ə mōōn′dī, glôr′-), *Latin.* thus passes away the glory of this world.

sic·ut pat·ri·bus, sit De·us no·bis (sē′kōōt pä′tri bōōs′, sit dē′ōōs nō′bis; *Eng.* sik′ut pa′tri bus, sit dē′əs nō′bis), *Latin.* as with our fathers, may God be with us.

Si·cy·on (sish′ē on′, sis′-), *n.* an ancient city in S Greece, near Corinth. —**Sic·y·o·ni·an** (sis′ē ō′nē ən), *adj., n.*

Sid (sid), *n.* a boy's or girl's given name, form of **Sidney** or **Sydney.** Also, **Syd.**

Sid·dhar·tha (si där′tə, -thə), *n.* **1.** an epithet of Buddha meaning "he who has attained his goal." **2.** (*italics*) a novel (1922) by Hermann Hesse.

sid·dhi (sid′dē), *n.* *Buddhism.* any occult power acquired through discipline. Pali, **iddhi.** [< Skt]

Sid·dons (sid′ənz), *n.* **Sarah (Kemble),** 1755–1831, English actress.

sid·dur (sē dōōr′; *Eng.* sid′ər), *n., pl.* **-du·rim** (-dōō rēm′), *Eng.* **-durs.** *Hebrew.* a Jewish prayer book designed for use chiefly on days other than festivals and holy days; a daily prayer book. Cf. **mahzor.** [lit., order]

side¹ (sīd), *n., adj., v.,* **sid·ed, sid·ing.** —*n.* **1.** one of the surfaces forming the outside of or bounding a thing, or one of the lines bounding a geometric figure. **2.** either of the two broad surfaces of a thin, flat object, as a door, a piece of paper, etc. **3.** one of the lateral surfaces of an object, as opposed to the front, back, top, and bottom. **4.** either of the two lateral parts or areas of a thing: *the right side and the left side.* **5.** either lateral half of the body, esp. of the trunk, of a man or animal. **6.** an aspect or phase, esp. as contrasted with another aspect or phase: *to consider all sides of a problem.* **7.** region, direction, or position with reference to a central line, space, or point: *the east side of a city.* **8.** a slope, as of a hill. **9.** one of two or more contesting teams, groups, parties, etc.: *Our side won the baseball game.* **10.** the position, course, or part of a person or group opposing another: *I am on your side in this issue.* **11.** line of descent through either the father or the mother: *grandparents on one's maternal side.* **12.** the space immediately adjacent to something or someone indicated: *Stand at my side.* **13.** Usually, **sides.** *Theat.* **a.** pages of a script containing only the lines and cues of a specific role to be learned by a performer. **b.** the lines of the role. **14.** *Brit. Slang.* **a.** affected manner; pretension; assumed haughtiness: *to put on side.* **b.** impudence; gall: *He has a lot of side.* **15.** *Naut.* the hull portion that is normally out of the water, located between the stem and stern to port or starboard. **16.** *Billiards.* English (def. 5). **17. on the side,** *Informal.* **a.** separate from the main issue or point of interest. **b.** in addition to one's regular, or known work, interest, relationships, etc.: *She tried selling cosmetics on the side. He dates another girl on the side.* **c.** as a side dish: *a hamburger with French fries on the side.* **18. on the** (specified) **side,** rather more than less; tending toward (the quality or condition specified): *This cake is a little on the sweet side.* **19. side by side, a.** next to one another; together. **b.** closely associated or related; in proximity: *A divided city in which democracy and communism must live side by side.* **20. take sides,** to give one's support to one person or group in a dispute; be partial to one side: *We were careful not to take sides for* *fear of getting personally involved.* —*adj.* **21.** being at or on one side: *the side aisles of a theater.* **22.** coming from one side. **23.** directed toward one side: *a side blow.* **24.** subordinate or incidental: *a side issue.* —*v.i.* **25. side with** or **against,** to favor or support or refuse to support one group, opinion, etc., against opposition; take sides, as in a dispute: *He always sides with the underdog.* [ME, OE; c. D *zijde,* G *Seite,* Icel *sītha*] —**side′less,** *adj.*

side[2] (sīd), *adj. Scot. and North Eng.* (esp. of a woman's dress or a man's beard) long and loose-flowing. [ME; OE *sīd;* c. Icel *sīthr* long, LG *sied* low]

side (shē), *n.pl.* the fairies of Ireland, believed to belong to the Tuatha De Danaan. [< Ir *sīdh*]

side′ arm′, *Mil.* a weapon, as a pistol, sword, etc., carried at the side or in the belt.

side·arm (sīd′ärm′), *adv.* **1.** with a swinging motion of the arm moving to the side of the body at shoulder level or below and nearly parallel to the ground: *to pitch sidearm.* —*adj.* **2.** thrown or performed sidearm: *a sidearm curve ball; sidearm stroke.* [SIDE[1] + ARM[1]]

side′ ax′, an ax for trimming timbers, having its edge off center on the blade.

side′ band′, *Radio.* the band of frequencies at the sides of the carrier frequency of a modulated signal. Also, **side′band′.**

side·bar (sīd′bär′), *n.* follow-up (def. 3b). [SIDE[1] + BAR[1]]

side′ bet′, a bet made, as with another player, in addition to one's principal bet: *a side bet as to which of us would draw the highest card during the game.*

side·board (sīd′bōrd′, -bôrd′), *n.* **1.** a piece of furniture, as in a dining room, often with shelves, drawers, etc., for holding articles of table service. **2.** a board forming a side or a part of a side; sidepiece. **3. sideboards,** *Slang.* See **side whiskers.** [ME; see SIDE[1], BOARD]

side·bone (sīd′bōn′), *n. Vet. Pathol.* ossification of the cartilages in the lateral portion of the foot of a horse, resulting in lameness. Also, **side′bones′.** [SIDE[1] + BONE[1]]

side′ boy′, one of several crew members of a ship who line up at the gangway as a mark of respect to a high-ranking officer or distinguished visitor embarking or disembarking.

side·burns (sīd′bûrnz′), *n.pl.* **1.** short whiskers extending from the hairline to below the ears and worn with an unbearded chin. **2.** the projections of the hairline forming a border on the face in front of each ear. [alter. of BURNSIDES]

side·car (sīd′kär′), *n.* **1.** a small car attached on one side to a motorcycle and supported on the other side by a wheel of its own, used for a passenger, parcels, etc. **2.** a cocktail made with brandy, orange liqueur, and lemon juice. [SIDE[1] + CAR[1]]

side′ card′, *Cards.* **1.** *Poker.* the highest card in a hand that is not part of a scoring combination, as not being one of a pair, three of a kind, etc., and that serves to determine by its denomination the higher ranking of two otherwise equal hands. **2.** a card other than a trump; plain card.

side′ chain′, *Chem.* an open chain of atoms attached to an atom of a larger chain, or to a ring. Also called **lateral chain.**

side′ chair′, a straight-backed chair without arms. Also, **side′chair′.**

side′check′, a checkrein passing from the bit through the dee and back to the saddle of the harness. See illus. under **harness.** [SIDE[1] + CHECK]

side′ cir′cuit, *Elect.* See under **phantom circuit.**

side′ cut′, *Carpentry.* See **cheek cut.**

side′ dish′, **1.** a serving of a portion of food in addition to the principal food, usually on a separate dish. **2.** the small additional dish used for such food.

side-dress (sīd′dres′), *v.t.,* **-dressed, -dress·ing.** to fertilize (growing plants) by mixing fertilizer into the soil along each row.

side′ dress′ing, the fertilizer used to side-dress plants.

side′ effect′, any effect of a drug, chemical, or other medicine that is in addition to its intended effect, esp. an effect that is harmful or unpleasant. Also, **side′ef·fect′.**

side-glance (sīd′glans′, -gläns′), *n.* a glance directed to the side; an oblique or sideways look: *a side-glance of displeasure at her interrupter.*

side·head (sīd′hed′), *n. Print.* a heading or subhead run in the margin of a book or magazine. [SIDE[1] + HEAD]

side·hill (sīd′hil′), *n.* a hillside. [SIDE[1] + HILL]

side′ horse′, *Gymnastics.* a cylindrical, leather-covered block that has two curved handles or pommels on the top surface and is mounted in horizontal position on two vertical, adjustable posts set in a steel frame, often used in vaulting. Cf. **long horse.**

side·kick (sīd′kik′), *n.* **1.** a close friend. **2.** a confederate or assistant. [SIDE[1] + KICK]

side′-lev·er en′gine (sīd′lev′ər, -lē′vər), a steam engine having the motion of the piston transmitted in the direction opposite to that of the crankshaft by means of a pivoted lever **(side′ lev′er)** underneath both.

side·light (sīd′līt′), *n.* **1.** light coming from the side. **2.** an item of incidental information. **3.** either of two lights carried by a vessel under way at night, a red one on the port side and a green on the starboard. **4.** a window or other aperture for light in the side of a building, ship, etc. **5.** a window at the side of a door or another window. [SIDE[1] + LIGHT[1]]

side′light cas′tle, *Naut.* lighthouse (def. 2). Also called **side′light tow′er.**

side·line (sīd′līn′), *n., v.,* **-lined, -lin·ing.** —*n.* **1.** a line at the side of something. **2.** a business or activity pursued in addition to one's primary business; a second occupation. **3.** an additional or auxiliary line of goods: *a grocery store with a sideline of household furnishings.* **4.** *Sports.* **a.** either of the two lines defining the side boundaries of a field or court. **b. sidelines,** the area immediately beyond either sideline, where the substitute players sit. —*v.t.* **5.** *Informal.* to render incapable of participation, esp. in anything involving vigorous, physical action, as a sport: *An injury to his throwing arm sidelined the quarterback for two weeks.* [SIDE[1] + LINE[1]]

side·ling (sīd′ling), *adv.* **1.** sidelong or sideways; obliquely. —*adj.* **2.** having an oblique position; inclined or sloping. [ME; see SIDE[1], -LING[2]]

side·long (sīd′lông′, -long′), *adj.* **1.** directed to one side: *a sidelong glance.* **2.** inclined or slanting to one side. **3.** indirect; roundabout: *sidelong comments about his appearance.* —*adv.* **4.** toward the side; obliquely. [SIDE[1] + LONG[1]]

side·man (sīd′man′, -mən), *n., pl.* **-men** (-men′, -mən). **1.** an instrumentalist in a band or orchestra. **2.** an instrumentalist supporting a soloist or a principal performer. [SIDE[1] + MAN[1]]

side′ meat′, *Chiefly Southern and Midland U.S.* salt pork and bacon taken from the sides of a hog.

side·piece (sīd′pēs′), *n.* a piece forming a side or a part of a side, or fixed by the side, of something. [SIDE[1] + PIECE]

side′ pond′, (in a canal) a reservoir beside a lock for holding part of the water drained from the upper reach of the canal at each use.

sider-, var. of **sidero-**[1] before a vowel: *siderite.*

si·de·re·al (sī dēr′ē əl), *adj.* **1.** determined by or from the stars: *sidereal time.* **2.** of or pertaining to the stars. [< L *sīdere(us)* of, belonging to the stars (*sīder-,* s. of *sīdus* constellation + *-eus* adj. suffix) + -AL[1]] —**si·de′re·al·ly,** *adv.*

side′real day′, the interval between two successive passages of the vernal equinox over the meridian, being about four minutes shorter than a mean solar day.

side′real hour′, one 24th part of a sidereal day.

side′real hour′ an′gle, *Astron.* the angle, measured westward through 360°, between the hour circle passing through the vernal equinox and the hour circle of a celestial body. Cf. **hour angle.**

side′real min′ute, *Astron.* the sixtieth part of a sidereal hour.

side′real month′. See under **month** (def. 5).

side′real sec′ond, *Astron.* the sixtieth part of a sidereal minute.

side′real year′, year (def. 4c).

sid·er·ite (sid′ə rīt′), *n.* **1.** Also called **chalybite.** a common mineral, iron carbonate, $FeCO_3$, usually occurring in yellowish to deep-brown cleavable masses: a minor ore of iron. **2.** a meteorite consisting almost entirely of metallic minerals. [SIDER- + -ITE[1]; in earlier (obs.) senses, var. of *siderites* < L < Gk *siderī́tēs* loadstone] —**sid·er·it·ic** (sid′ə rit′ik), *adj.*

Si·de·ro (sī dēr′ō), *n. Class. Myth.* the second wife of Salmoneus: she was killed by the sons of her stepdaughter, Tyro, in revenge for her poor treatment of their mother.

sidero-[1], a learned borrowing from Greek meaning "iron," used in the formation of compound words: *siderolite.* Also, *esp. before a vowel,* **sider-.** [< Gk *sidēro(s)* iron]

sidero-[2], a learned borrowing from Latin meaning "star," "constellation," used in the formation of compound words: *siderostat.* [< L *sīder-* (s. of *sīdus*) star-group + -o-]

sid·er·o·cyte (sid′ər ə sīt′), *n. Anat.* an erythrocyte that contains iron in forms other than hematin. [SIDERO-[1] + -CYTE]

sid·er·og·ra·phy (sid′ə rog′rə fē), *n.* **1.** the art or technique of engraving on steel. **2.** a method of increasing the number of reproductions obtained from a steel engraving by first rolling a soft-steel cylinder over a hardened steel plate and then rolling the hardened cylinder over a soft-steel plate. [SIDERO-[1] + -GRAPHY] —**sid′er·og′ra·pher,** *n.* —**sid·er·o·graph·ic** (sid′ər ə graf′ik), *adj.*

sid·er·o·lite (sid′ər ə līt′), *n.* a meteorite of roughly equal proportions of metallic iron and stony matter. [SIDERO-[1] + -LITE]

sid·er·o·phile (sid′ər ə fīl′), *adj.* **1.** (of a cell or tissue) having an affinity for iron. **2.** *Geol.* (of a chemical element in the earth) having an affinity for metallic iron. —*n.* **3.** a siderophile element, tissue, or cell. [SIDERO-[1] + -PHILE]

sid·er·o·scope (sid′ər ə skōp′), *n. Ophthalm. Rare.* an apparatus for detecting splinters of iron or steel in the eye. [SIDERO-[1] + -SCOPE]

sid·er·o·sis (sid′ə rō′sis), *n. Pathol.* a disease of the lungs caused by inhaling iron or other metallic particles. [< NL < Gk *sidḗrōsis* ironwork. See SIDER-, -OSIS] —**sid·er·ot·ic** (sid′ə rot′ik), *adj.*

sid·er·o·stat (sid′ər ə stat′), *n.* a telescopic device for reflecting the light of a star in a constant direction, the chief component of which is a plane mirror turned by a clock mechanism to correct for the rotation of the earth. [SIDERO-[2] + -STAT] —**sid′er·o·stat′ic,** *adj.*

side·sad·dle (sīd′sad′əl), *n.* **1.** a saddle for women on which the rider sits, facing forward, usually with both feet on the left side of the horse. —*adv.* **2.** seated on a sidesaddle: *The girl hunted sidesaddle.* [late ME *syd saddyl.* See SIDE[1], SADDLE]

side′saddle flow′er. See **common pitcher plant.**

side·shake (sīd′shāk′), *n. Horol.* free, nonrotative movement, other than endshake, of arbors or the like within bearings. [SIDE[1] + SHAKE]

side′ show′, **1.** a minor show or exhibition in connection with a principal one, as at a circus. **2.** any subordinate event or matter.

side·slip (sīd′slip′), *v.,* **-slipped, -slip·ping,** *n.* —*v.i.* **1.** to slip to one side. **2.** (of an airplane when banked excessively) to slide sideways in a downward direction, toward the center of the curve described in turning. —*n.* **3.** the act or an instance of sideslipping. [SIDE[1] + SLIP[1]]

side·spin (sīd′spin′), *n.* a spinning motion imparted to a ball that causes it to rotate in course about its vertical axis. [SIDE[1] + SPIN]

side·split·ting (sīd′split′ing), *adj.* **1.** convulsively uproarious: *sidesplitting laughter.* **2.** producing uproarious laughter; extremely funny: *sidesplitting farce.* [SIDE[1] + SPLITTING] —**side′split′ting·ly,** *adv.*

side′ step′, a step to one side, as in dancing, skiing, boxing, etc.

side-step (sīd′step′), *v.,* **-stepped, -step·ping.** —*v.i.* **1.** to step to one side. **2.** to evade or avoid a decision, problem, or the like. —*v.t.* **3.** to avoid or dodge by stepping aside. **4.** to evade or avoid (a decision, problem, or the like). —**side′-step′per,** *n.*

side·stick (sīd′stik′), *n. Print.* a tapered strip of wood or metal, laid at the side of a form or type in a galley or chase, against which the quoins are tightened. [SIDE[1] + STICK[1]]

side′ street′, a street leading away from a main street; an unimportant street or one carrying but little traffic: *a narrow, deserted side street.* Cf. **back street.**

side·stroke (sīd′strōk′), *n. Swimming.* a stroke in which the body is turned sideways in the water, the hands pull alternately, and the legs perform a scissors kick. [SIDE[1] + STROKE[1]]

side′ suit′, *Cards.* See **plain suit.**

side·swipe (sīd′swīp′), *v.,* **-swiped, -swip·ing,** *n.* —*v.t.* **1.** to strike with a sweeping stroke or blow along the side; strike a glancing blow obliquely. —*n.* **2.** such a strike or blow. [SIDE[1] + SWIPE] —**side′swip′er,** *n.*

side′ ta′ble, a table intended to be placed against a wall.

side·track (sīd′trak′), *v.t., v.i.* **1.** to move from the main track to a siding, as a train. **2.** to move or distract from the main subject or course. —*n.* **3.** a short railroad track for loading, unloading, or storing cars. Cf. **siding.** [SIDE[1] + TRACK]

side·walk (sīd′wôk′), *n.* a walk, esp. a paved one, at the side of a street or road. [SIDE[1] + WALK]

side′walk art′ist, **1.** an artist who draws pictures on the sidewalk, esp. with colored chalk, as a means of soliciting money from passers-by. **2.** an artist who draws portraits in the streets, esp. of passing individuals who sit for quick sketches executed in charcoal or pastel.

side′walk el′evator, an elevator rising from a shaft or frame to an open area, as a sidewalk.

side′walk superintend′ent, *Informal.* a bystander who watches the building, demolition, repair, or other work being done at a construction site.

side·wall (sīd′wôl′), *n.* the part of a pneumatic tire between the edge of the tread and the rim of the wheel. See diag. under **tire**[2]. [ME; see SIDE[1], WALL]

side·ward (sīd′wərd), *adj.* **1.** directed or moving toward one side. —*adv.* **2.** Also, **side′wards.** toward one side. [ME; see SIDE[1], -WARD]

side·way (sīd′wā′), *n.* **1.** a byway. —*adj., adv.* **2.** sideways. [SIDE[1] + WAY]

side·ways (sīd′wāz′), *adv.* **1.** with a side foremost. **2.** facing to the side. **3.** toward or from one side. **4.** with a deceitful, scornful, disparaging, or amorous glance. —*adj.* **5.** moving, facing, or directed toward one side. **6.** indirect or evasive. Also, **sideway, side·wise** (sīd′wīz′). [SIDE[1] + -WAYS]

side-wheel (sīd′hwēl′, -wēl′), *adj.* having a paddle wheel on each side, as a steamboat. —**side′-wheel′er,** *n.*

side·wheel (sīd′hwēl′, -wēl′), *n. Naut.* either of a pair of paddle wheels on the sides of a vessel. [SIDE[1] + WHEEL]

side′ whisk′ers, whiskers worn long and with the chin clean-shaven. —**side′-whisk′ered,** *adj.*

side·wind·er (sīd′wīn′dər), *n.* **1.** a severe swinging blow from the side. **2.** a rattlesnake, *Crotalus cerastes,* of the southwestern U.S. and northern Mexico, that has a hornlike process over each eye and that moves in loose sand by throwing loops of the body forward. **3.** (*cap.*) *U.S.* an air-to-air, supersonic weapon that intercepts and destroys enemy aircraft, using an infrared homing-guidance system. [SIDE[1] + WINDER]

Si·di-bel-Ab·bès (sē′dē bel ə bes′), *n.* a city in NW Algeria. 105,357 with suburbs (1960).

Si·di If·ni (sē′dē ēf′nē), a seaport in and the capital of Ifni, on the NW coast of Africa. 12,751 (1960).

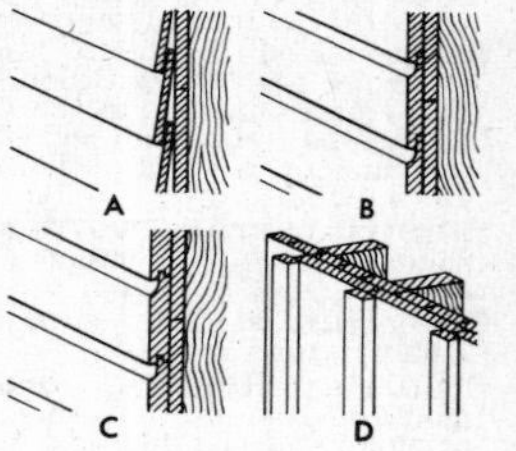

sid·ing (sī′ding), *n.* **1.** a short railroad track, usually opening onto a main track at both ends, on which one of two meeting trains is switched until the other has passed. **2.** *U.S.* any of several varieties of weatherproof facing for frame buildings, composed of pieces attached separately as shingles, plain or shaped boards, or of various units of sheet metal or various types of composition materials. **3.** *Shipbuilding.* the fore-and-aft thickness of a frame. [SIDE[1] + -ING[1]]

A B C D

Wood sidings
A, Clapboard siding; B, Shiplap siding; C, Drop siding; D, Board and batten siding

si·dle (sīd′əl), *v.,* **-dled, -dling,** *n.* —*v.i.* **1.** to move sideways or obliquely. **2.** to edge along furtively. —*n.* **3.** a sidling movement. [back formation from *sid(e)ling* (ME, OE *sīdling*) SIDELONG] —**si′dling·ly,** *adv.*

Sid·ney (sid′nē), *n.* **1. Sir Philip,** 1554–86, English poet, writer, statesman, and soldier. **2.** a town in W Nebraska. 8004 (1960). **3.** a town in S New York. 5157 (1960). **4.** a town in NE Montana. 4564 (1960). **5.** a boy's or girl's given name. Also, **Sydney** (for defs. 1, 5).

Si·don (sīd′ən), *n.* a city of ancient Phoenicia: site of modern Saida. —**Si·do·ni·an** (sī dō′nē ən), *adj., n.*

Si·do·nie (sē dō nē′), *n.* a girl's given name, French form of **Sidonia** or **Sidony.**

Si·do·ny (sīd′ənē), *n.* a girl's given name. Also, **Si·do·nia** (si dō′nyə), **Sidonie.**

Sid·ra (sid′rä), *n.* **Gulf of,** an inlet of the Mediterranean, on the N coast of Libya.

Sid·rah (sē drä′; *Eng.* sid′rə), *n., pl.* **Sid·roth** (sē-drōt′), *Eng.* **Sid·rahs.** *Hebrew.* a Parashah chanted or read on the Sabbath. Also, **Sedrah.** [lit., order]

siè·cle (sye′klə), *n., pl.* **-cles** (-klə). *French.* an age, century, or generation.

siè·cle d'or (sye′klə dôr′), *French.* the period of the reign of Louis XIV of France. [lit., century of gold]

Sieg (zēkh), *n. German.* victory.

Sieg·bahn (sēg′bän), *n.* **Karl Man·ne Ge·org** (kärl män′nə yā′ôr yə), born 1886, Swedish physicist: Nobel prize 1924.

siege (sēj), *n., v.,* **sieged, sieg·ing.** —*n.* **1.** the act or process of surrounding and attacking a fortified place in such a way as to isolate it from help and supplies, for the purpose of lessening the resistance of the defenders and thereby making capture possible. **2.** any prolonged or persistent effort to overcome resistance. **3.** a series of illnesses, troubles, or annoyances besetting a person or group: *a siege of head colds.* **4.** a prolonged period of trouble or annoyance. **5.** Also, **sedge.** *Ornith.* **a.** a flock of herons. **b.** the station of a heron at prey. **6.** the shelf or floor of a glassmaking furnace on which the glass pots are set. **7.** *Obs.* **a.** a seat, esp. one used by a person of distinction, as a throne. **b.** station as to rank or class. **8. lay siege to,** to besiege: *The invaders laid siege to the city for over a month.* —*v.t.* **9.** to lay siege to; besiege. [ME *sege* < OF: seat, back formation from *siegier* < VL *sedicāre to set, deriv. of L *sedēre* to sit] —**siege′a·ble,** *adj.*

—**Syn. 1.** SIEGE, BLOCKADE are terms for prevention of free movement to or from a place during wartime. SIEGE implies surrounding a city and cutting off its communications, and usually includes direct assaults on its defenses. BLOCKADE is applied more often to naval operations which block all commerce, especially to cut off food and other supplies from defenders.

Siege′ Per′ilous, *Arthurian Romance.* a vacant seat at the Round Table which could be filled only by the predestined finder of the Holy Grail and was fatal to pretenders.

siege′ piece′, a piece of gold or silver stamped as provisional legal tender in a besieged area. Also called **obsidional coin.**

Sieg·fried (sēg′frēd; *Ger.* zēKH′frēt), *n.* **1.** (in the *Nibelungenlied*) the son of Sigmund and Sieglinde and the husband of Kriemhild. He kills the dragon Fafnir, acquires the treasure of the Nibelungs, wins Brünnhilde for Gunther, and is finally killed by Hagen at the behest of Brünnhilde, whom he had once promised to marry: corresponds to the Sigurd of the *Volsunga Saga.* Cf. **Brünnhilde. 2.** See **Ring of the Nibelung. 3.** a boy's given name.

Sieg′fried Line′, a zone of fortifications in W Germany facing the Maginot Line, constructed in the years preceding the 1940 invasion of France. [named after SIEGFRIED]

Sieg heil (zēKH hīl′), *German.* hail to victory: a salute used by the Nazis.

Sieg·lin·de (sēg lin′də; *Ger.* zēKH lin′də), *n.* (in the *Nibelungenlied*) the wife of Sigmund and mother of Siegfried. Cf. **Signy.**

sie·mens (sē′mənz), *n.* (*construed as sing.*) a unit of conductance equal to one mho. *Abbr.:* S

Sie·mens (sē′mənz; *Ger.* zē′məns), *n.* **Sir William** (*Karl Wilhelm Siemens*), 1823–83, English inventor, born in Germany.

Si·em Re·ap (sē′əm rē′əp, syem′ ryap′), a city in NW Cambodia, near Angkor. ab. 10,000. Also, **Si′em-re′ap, Si′em-ré′ap.**

Sie·na (sē en′ə; *It.* sye′nä), *n.* a city in Tuscany, in central Italy, S of Florence: cathedral. 62,215 (1961).

Si·en·ese (sē′ə nēz′, -nēs′), *adj., n., pl.* **-ese.** —*adj.* **1.** of or pertaining to Siena or its people. **2.** pertaining to or designating the style of painting developed in Siena during the late 13th and 14th centuries, characterized by a use of Byzantine forms and iconography modified by an increased three-dimensional quality, decorative linear rhythms, and harmonious, although sometimes ornamental, color. —*n.* **3.** an inhabitant of Siena. [< It; see SIENA, -ESE]

Sien·kie·wicz (shen kye′vich; *Eng.* shen kyā′vich), *n.* **Hen·ryk** (hen′rik), 1846–1916, Polish novelist: Nobel prize 1905.

si·en·na (sē en′ə), *n.* **1.** a ferruginous earth used as a yellowish-brown pigment, as raw sienna or, after roasting in a furnace, as a reddish-brown pigment, burnt sienna. **2.** the color of such a pigment. [< It (*terra di*) *Sien(n)a* (earth of) SIENA]

Se·pi (sē ep′ē; *It.* sye′pē), *n.* **Ce·sa·re** (che′zä re), born 1923, Italian singer.

si·er·ra (sē er′ə), *n.* **1.** a chain of hills or mountains, the peaks of which suggest the teeth of a saw. **2.** any of several Spanish mackerels of the genus *Scomberomorus,* esp. *S. sierra,* found in western North America. **3.** a word used in communications to represent the letter S. [< Sp: lit., saw < L *serra*]

Si·er·ra Le·o·ne (sē er′ə lē ō′nē, lē ōn′), an independent country in W Africa: member of the British Commonwealth of Nations; formerly a British colony and protectorate. 2,180,355 (1963); 27,925 sq. mi. *Cap.:* Freetown.

Sier′ra lil′y, a bulbous herb, *Lilium parvum,* of the northwestern U.S., having purple-spotted, orange-red flowers with a yellow base.

Si·er·ra Ma·dre (sē er′ə mä′drā; *for 2 also Sp.* syer′rä mä′thre), **1.** a mountain range extending from S Wyoming into N Colorado. **2.** two parallel mountain chains in Mexico, bordering the central plateau on the E and W, and extending SE into N Guatemala. **3.** a town in S California. 9732 (1960).

Si·er·ra Ne·vad·a (sē er′ə nə vad′ə, -vä′də *for 1; Sp.* syer′rä ne vä′thä *for 2*). **1.** a mountain range in E California. Highest peak, Mt. Whitney, 14,495 ft. **2.** a mountain range in S Spain. Highest peak, Mulhacén, 11,420 ft.

Sier′ra shoot′ing star′, a perennial herb, *Dodecatheon jeffreyi,* of western North America, having deep-reddish-purple flowers, growing well in rocky soil.

Sier′ra Vis′ta, a town in S Arizona. 3121 (1960).

si·es·ta (sē es′tə), *n.* a midday or afternoon rest or nap, esp. as taken in Spain and Latin American countries. [< Sp << L *sexta* (*hōra*) the sixth (hour), midday]

sieur (syœr), *n. French.* an old title of rank or respect for a man, now chiefly in legal use.

sieve (siv), *n., v.,* **sieved, siev·ing.** —*n.* **1.** an instrument with a meshed or perforated bottom, used for separating coarse from fine parts of loose matter, for straining liquids, etc., esp. one with a circular frame and fine meshes or perforations. **2.** a person who cannot keep a secret. —*v.t., v.i.* **3.** to put or force through a sieve; sift. [ME *sive,* OE *sife;* c. D *zeef,* G *Sieb;* akin to SIFT] —**sieve′like′,** *adj.*

sieve′ cell′, *Bot.* an elongated cell whose walls contain perforations (**sieve′ pores′**) which are arranged in circumscribed areas (**sieve′ plates′**) and which afford communication with similar adjacent cells.

Sie·vers (zē′fərs), *n.* **E·du·ard** (ā′do͞o ärt), 1850–1932, German philologist.

sieve′ tube′, *Bot.* **1.** a vertical series of sieve cells in the phloem, specialized for the conduction of food materials. **2.** a single sieve cell.

Sie·yès (sye yes′), *n.* **Em·ma·nu·el Jo·seph** (e ma ny el′ zhō zef′), ("*Abbé Sieyès*"), 1748–1836, French priest and revolutionist.

Sif·nos (sif′nos), *n.* Siphnos.

Si·frei To·rah (sē frā′ tō rä′), *Hebrew.* a pl. of **Sefer Torah.**

sift (sift), *v.t.* **1.** to separate and retain the coarse parts of (flour, ashes, etc.) with a sieve. **2.** to scatter or sprinkle through or by means of a sieve: *to sift sugar onto cake.* **3.** to separate by or as by a sieve. **4.** to examine closely: *The detectives are still sifting the evidence.* **5.** to question closely. —*v.i.* **6.** to sift something. **7.** to pass or fall through or as through a sieve. [ME *sift(en),* OE *siftan;* c. D, MLG *siften;* see SIEVE] —**sift′er,** *n.*

sift·ings (sif′tingz), *n.* (*construed as pl.*) **1.** something sifted: *siftings of flour.* **2.** that which is separated by sifting: *to discard the siftings.* [SIFT + -ING[1] + -S[3]]

Sig., (in prescriptions) **1.** write; mark; label. [< L *signā*] **2.** let it be written. [< L *signētur*] **3.** signor. **4.** signore; signori.

sig., 1. signal. **2.** signature. **3.** signor. **4.** signore; signori.

si·gan·id (sə gan′id, -gā′nid), *n.* **1.** any fish of the family *Siganidae,* comprising the rabbitfishes. —*adj.* **2.** belonging or pertaining to the family *Siganidae.* [< NL *Siganid(ae),* equiv. to *Sigan(us)* genus name (< Ar *sijān* rabbitfish) + *-idae* -ID[2]]

Sig·a·to·ka (sig′ə tō′kə), *n. Plant Pathol.* a disease of bananas, characterized by discolored spots on the leaves, caused by a fungus, *Mycosphaerella musicola.* [named after *Sigatoka,* river and district in the Fiji Islands]

Sig·geir (sig′gâr), *n.* See under **Signy.**

sigh (sī), *v.i.* **1.** to let out one's breath audibly, as from sorrow, weariness, relief, etc. **2.** to yearn or long; pine. **3.** to make a sound suggesting a sigh: *sighing wind.* —*v.t.* **4.** to express or utter with a sigh. **5.** to lament with sighing. —*n.* **6.** the act or sound of sighing. [ME *sighe(n),* back formation from *sihte* sighed, past tense of ME *siken, sichen,* OE *sīcan*] —**sigh′er,** *n.* —**sigh′less,** *adj.* —**sigh′like′,** *adj.*

sigh·ful (sī′fəl), *adj.* mournful; sorrowful: *a sighful ballad.* [SIGH + -FUL] —**sigh′ful·ly,** *adv.*

sight (sīt), *n.* **1.** the power or faculty of seeing; perception of objects by use of the eyes; vision. **2.** the act, fact, or an instance of seeing. **3.** one's range of vision on some specific occasion: *Land is in sight. We are within sight of land.* **4.** a view; glimpse. **5.** mental perception or regard; judgment. **6.** something seen or worth seeing; spectacle: *the sights of London and Paris.* **7.** something unusual, surprising, shocking, or distressing: *Their clothes were a sight after the fight.* **8.** *Chiefly Dial.* a multitude; great deal: *It's a sight better to work than to starve.* **9.** an observation taken with a surveying, navigating, or other instrument, to ascertain an exact position or direction. **10.** any of various mechanical or optical viewing devices, as on a firearm or surveying instrument, for aiding the eye in aiming. **11.** *Obs.* skill; insight. **12. at first sight,** at the first glimpse; at once: *It was love at first sight.* **13. at sight, a.** immediately upon seeing, esp. without referring elsewhere for information: *to translate something at sight.* **b.** *Com.* on presentation: *a draft payable at sight.* **14. catch sight of,** to get a glimpse of; see: *We caught sight of the lake below as we drove through the pass.* **15. know by sight,** to recognize (a person or thing) seen previously: *I know him by sight, but I know nothing about him.* **16. not by a long sight,** *Informal.* **a.** probably not. **b.** definitely not: *Is that all? Not by a long sight.* **17. on** or **upon sight,** immediately upon seeing: *Shoot him on sight. I don't know her name, but I'd recognize her on sight.* **18. out of sight, a.** beyond one's range of vision. **b.** beyond reason; exceedingly high: *The price that he asks is out of sight.* **c.** at a distance; remote: *out of sight, out of mind.* **19. sight unseen,** without previous examination: *to buy something sight unseen.* —*v.t.* **20.** to see, glimpse, notice, or observe: *to sight a ship to the north.* **21.** to take a sight or observation of, esp. with surveying or navigating instruments. **22.** to direct or aim by a sight or sights, as a firearm. **23.** to provide with sights, or adjust the sights of, as a gun. —*v.i.* **24.** to aim or observe through a sight. **25.** to look carefully in a certain direction. [ME; OE (*ge*)*siht,* var. of (*ge*)*sihth* (c. G *gesicht* face), deriv. of *sēon* to SEE[1]; see -TH[1]] —**sight′a·ble,** *adj.* —**sight′er,** *n.*

sight′ draft′, a draft payable upon presentation.

sight′ edge′, *Shipbuilding.* an edge of a plate or plank that overlaps an adjoining plate or plank as seen from outside the hull of a vessel, above the deck, or on the side of a bulkhead opposite to that on which the stiffeners are placed. Cf. **landing edge.**

sight′ gag′, a comic effect produced by visual means rather than by spoken lines, as in a play or motion picture.

sight·hole (sīt′hōl′), *n.* a hole, as on a quadrant, through which to see or to sight. [SIGHT + HOLE]

sight·less (sīt′lis), *adj.* **1.** unable to see; blind. **2.** incapable of being seen; invisible. [ME. See SIGHT, -LESS] —**sight′less·ly,** *adv.* —**sight′less·ness,** *n.*

sight·ly (sīt′lē), *adj.,* **-li·er, -li·est. 1.** pleasing to the sight; attractive; comely. **2.** affording a fine view. [SIGHT + -LY] —**sight′li·ness,** *n.*

sight-read (sīt′rēd′), *v.t., v.i.,* **-read, -read·ing.** to read, play, or sing without previous practice, rehearsal, or study of the material to be treated: *to sight-read music from a score; ability to sight-read in four languages.* —**sight′-read′er,** *n.*

sight′ rhyme′, *Pros.* agreement in spelling, but not in sound, of the ends of words or of lines of verse, as in *have, grave.* Also called **eye rhyme.**

sight′ rule′, alidade (def. 1). Also called **sight′ vane′.**

sight′ screen′, *Cricket.* a white screen set in line with the wicket as an aid to the batsman in sighting the ball.

sight·see·ing (sīt′sē′ing), *n.* **1.** the act of visiting and seeing places and objects of interest. —*adj.* **2.** seeing, showing, or used for visiting sights: *a sightseeing bus.* Also, **sight′-see′ing.** [SIGHT + SEEING] —**sight′-se′er, sight′-se′er,** *n.*

sig·il (sij′il), *n.* a seal or signet. [< LL *sigill(um),* dim. of *signum* SIGN; see SEAL[1]] —**sig·il·lar·y** (sij′ə ler′ē), *adj.* —**sig′il·is′tic,** *adj.*

sig·il·late (sij′ə lāt′, -lit), *adj.* **1.** (of a ceramic object) having stamped decorations. **2.** *Bot.* having markings that resemble the impressions of a seal. [< LL *sigillāt(us).* See SIGIL, -ATE[1]] —**sig·il·la·tion** (sij′ə lā′shən), *n.*

Sig·is·mund (sij′is mənd, sig′is-; *Ger.* zē′gis mo͝ont′), *n.* 1368–1437, Holy Roman emperor 1411–37.

sig·los (sig′los), *n., pl.* **-loi** (-loi). a silver coin of ancient Persia, the 20th part of a daric. [< Gk < Sem]

sig·ma (sig′mə), *n.* **1.** the 18th letter of the Greek alphabet Σ, σ, ς. **2.** the consonant sound represented by this letter. [< L < Gk]

sig′ma fi′nite set′, *Math.* a set on which a measure is defined and in which there exist disjoint subsets, each having measure less than infinity, whose union contains the set.

sig·ma-ring (sig′mə ring′), *n. Math.* a nonempty collection of sets having the property that the relative complement of each set with respect to every other set of the collection is in the collection and that the union of a countable number of sets of the collection is a set in the collection. Cf. **algebra of sets, Boolean ring.**

sig·mate (sig′mit, -māt), *adj.* having the form of the Greek sigma or the letter *S.* [SIGM(A) + -ATE[1]] —**sig·ma·tion** (sig mā′shən), *n.*

sig·ma·tism (sig′mə tiz′əm), *n.* defective pronunciation of sibilant sounds. [SIGMATE + -ISM]

sig·moid (sig′moid), *adj.* **1.** shaped like the letter C. **2.** shaped like the letter S. **3.** of, pertaining to, or situated near the sigmoid flexure of the large intestine. Also, **sig·moi′dal.** [< Gk *sigmoeid(ḗs)* shaped like a sigma. See SIGMA, -OID] —**sig·moi′dal·ly,** *adv.*

sig′moid flex′ure, 1. *Zool.* an S-shaped curve consisting of several parts. **2.** an S-shaped curve of the large intestine between the descending colon and the rectum.

Sig·mund (sig′mənd, sēg′mo͝ond; *Ger* zēKH′mo͝ont), *n.* **1.** (in the *Volsunga Saga*) the son of Volsung and Liod; the father, through his sister, Signy, of Sinfiotli; the husband first of Borghild, then of Hiordis; and the father of Sigurd. **2.** (in the *Nibelungenlied*) the king of the Netherlands and father of Siegfried. **3.** a boy's given name.

sign (sīn), *n.* **1.** a token; indication. **2.** a conventional or arbitrary mark, figure, or symbol used technically as an abbreviation for the word or words it represents. **3.** an arbitrary or conventional symbol used in musical notation to indicate tonality, tempo, etc. **4.** a motion or gesture used to express or convey an idea, command, decision, etc.: *Her nod was a sign that it was time to leave.* **5.** a means of conveying information, as a name, direction, warning, or advertisement, that is prominently displayed for public view and that consists of letters or symbols inscribed or mounted on wood, metal, paper, or other material: *a traffic sign; a store sign; a danger sign.* **6.** *Med.* the objective indications of a disease. **7.** a trace; vestige: *There wasn't a sign of them.* **8.** Usually, **signs.** traces, as footprints, of a wild animal. **9.** an omen; portent: *a sign of approaching decadence.* **10.** zodiac (def. 1). —*v.t.* **11.** to affix a signature to: *to sign a letter.* **12.** to write as a signature: *to sign one's name.* **13.** to engage by written agreement: *to sign a new player.* **14.** to indicate; betoken: *to sign a new era in international relations.* **15.** to mark with a sign, esp. the sign of the cross. **16.** to communicate by means of a sign; signal: *He signed his wish to leave.* **17.** *Obs.* to direct or appoint by a sign. —*v.i.* **18.** to write one's signature, as a token of agreement, obligation, receipt, etc.: *to sign for a package.* **19.** to make a sign or signal: *He signed to her to go away.* **20.** to obligate oneself by signature: *He signed with another team for the next season.* **21. sign away** or **over,** to assign or dispose of by affixing one's signature to a document: *She signed over her mansion to the church for use as a school.* **22. sign off, a.** to withdraw, from some responsibility or connection. **b.** to cease radio or television broadcasting, esp. at the end of the day. **c.** *Slang.* to become silent: *He had exhausted conversation topics and signed off.* **23. sign on, a.** to employ; hire. **b.** to bind oneself to work, as by signing a contract: *He signed on as a pitcher with a major-league team.* **24. sign up, a.** to join an organization or group, esp. to enlist in the armed forces. **b.** to persuade to join an organization or to sign a contract: *The recruiting officer signed up my brother for a four-year hitch.* [ME *signe* < OF < L *sign(um)* mark, sign, token, ensign, signal, image] —**sign′a·ble,** *adj.* —**sign′less,** *adj.* —**sign′like′,** *adj.*

—**Syn. 1.** trace, hint, suggestion. **1, 4.** signal. **9.** indication, hint, augury. SIGN, OMEN, PORTENT name that which gives evidence of a future event. SIGN is a general word for whatever gives evidence of an event, past, present, or future: *Dark clouds are a sign of rain or snow.* An OMEN is an augury or warning of things to come; formerly depending upon religious practices or beliefs, it is used only of the future, in general, as good or bad: *birds of evil omen.* PORTENT, limited, like OMEN, to prophecy of the future, may be used of a specific event, usually a misfortune: *portents of war.* **14.** signify, mean, signal.

sig·na (sig′nə), *v.* (used imperatively, in prescriptions) mark; write; label. [< L]

Si·gnac (sē nyak′), *n.* **Paul** (pôl), 1863–1935, French painter.

sig·nal (sig′nəl), *n., adj., v.,* **-naled, -nal·ing** or (*esp. Brit.*) **-nalled, -nal·ling.** —*n.* **1.** anything that serves to warn, direct, command, or the like, as a light, a gesture, an act, etc.: *a traffic signal; a signal to leave.* **2.** anything agreed upon or understood as the occasion for concerted action. **3.** an act, event, or the like, that causes or incites

some action: *The unjust execution was the signal for revolt.* **4.** a token; indication. **5.** *Elect., Radio.* an impulse, sound wave, etc., transmitted or received. **6.** *Cards.* a play which reveals to one's partner a wish that he continue or discontinue the suit led. **—*adj.* 7.** serving as a signal; used in signaling: *a signal flag.* **8.** unusual; notable; outstanding: *a signal exploit.* **—*v.t.* 9.** to make a signal to. **10.** to communicate or make known by a signal. **—*v.i.* 11.** to make communication by a signal or signals. [ME < ML, LL *signāle,* n. use of neut. of *signālis* of a sign. See SIGN, -AL[1]] **—sig′nal·er;** *esp. Brit.* **sig′nal·ler,** *n.*
—Syn. 1, 4. sign.

sig′nal board′, a board for recording electrical signals and indicating their source, often installed in kitchens, elevators, etc.

sig′nal box′, *Brit.* a railway signal tower.

sig′nal corps′, *U.S. Army.* a branch of the army responsible for military communications, meteorological studies, and related work.

Sig′nal Hill′, a town in S California. 4627 (1960).

sig·nal·ise (sig′nəlīz′), *v.t.,* **-ised, -is·ing.** *Chiefly Brit.* signalize.

sig·nal·ize (sig′nəlīz′), *v.t.,* **-ized, -iz·ing. 1.** to make notable or conspicuous. **2.** to point out or indicate particularly. [SIGNAL + -IZE]

sig·nal·ly (sig′nəlē), *adv.* conspicuously; notably. [SIGNAL + -LY]

sig·nal·man (sig′nəl mən), *n., pl.* **-men.** one whose occupation or duty is signaling, as on a railroad or in the army. [SIGNAL + MAN[1]]

sig·nal·ment (sig′nəl mənt), *n.* a detailed description, esp. of distinctive features, of a person for identification, usually for police purposes. [< F *signalement,* deriv. of *signaler* to signalize. See SIGNAL, -MENT]

Sig′nal Moun′tain, a town in SE Tennessee. 3413 (1960).

sig′nal red′, pimento (def. 4).

sig·na·to·ry (sig′nə tōr′ē, -tôr′ē), *adj., n., pl.* **-ries.** **—*adj.* 1.** having signed or joined in signing, a document: *the signatory powers to a treaty.* **—*n.* 2.** a signer, or one of the signers, of a document: *France and Holland were among the signatories of the treaty.* [< L *signātōri(us)* of, belonging to sealing, equiv. to *signāt(us)* marked, sealed (ptp. of *signāre;* see SIGN, -ATE[1]) + *-ōrius* -ORY[1]]

sig·na·ture (sig′nə chər), *n.* **1.** a person's name, or a mark representing it, as signed or written by himself or by deputy, as in subscribing a letter or other document. **2.** the act of signing a document. **3.** *Music.* a sign or set of signs at the beginning of a staff to indicate the key or the time of a piece. **4.** *Radio.* a song, musical arrangement, sound effect, etc., used as a theme identifying a program. **5.** *Med.* that part of a prescription which gives the directions to be marked on the container of the medicine. *Abbr.:* S, Sig. **6.** *Bookbinding.* a printed sheet folded to page size for binding together, with other such sheets, to form a book, magazine, etc. **7.** *Print.* **a.** a letter or other symbol generally placed by the printer at the foot of the first page of every section to guide the binder in arranging the sections in sequence. **b.** a sheet so marked. [< ML *signātūra* a signing, equiv. to L *signāt(us)* marked, sealed (see SIGNATORY) + *-ūra* -URE] **—sig′na·ture·less,** *adj.*

sig′nature loan′, a loan requiring no collateral.

sig′nature tune′. See **theme song** (def. 2).

sign·board (sīn′bōrd′, -bôrd′), *n.* a board bearing a sign. [SIGN + BOARD]

sign·er (sī′nər), *n.* **1.** one who signs. **2.** one who writes his name, as in token of agreement. [SIGN + -ER[1]]

sig·net (sig′nit), *n.* **1.** a small seal, as in a finger ring. **2.** a small official seal for legal documents, contracts, etc. **3.** an impression made by or as if by a signet. **—*v.t.* 4.** to stamp or mark with a signet. [ME < ML *signēt(um).* See SIGN, -ET]

sig′net ring′, a finger ring containing a small seal, one's initial, or the like.

sig·ne·tur (sig′ne to͞or′), *v. Latin.* let it be written.

sig·nif·i·cance (sig nif′ə kəns), *n.* **1.** importance; consequence: *the historical significance of an international blunder.* **2.** meaning; import: *The familiar place had a new significance for her.* **3.** the quality of being significant or having a meaning: *to give significance to the dullest of chores.* [late ME < L *significantia* force, meaning. See SIGNIFY, -ANCE]
—Syn. 1. moment, weight. See **importance. 2.** See **meaning. —Ant. 1.** triviality.

sig·nif·i·can·cy (sig nif′ə kən sē), *n., pl.* **-cies.** significance. [< L *significantia.* See SIGNIFICANCE, -Y[3]]

sig·nif·i·cant (sig nif′ə kənt), *adj.* **1.** important; of consequence. **2.** having or expressing a meaning; indicative; suggestive. **3.** having a special, secret, or disguised meaning: *a significant wink.* **4.** *Archaic.* something significant; a sign. [< L *significant-* (s. of *significāns*), prp. of *significāre* to SIGNIFY; see -ANT] **—sig·nif′i·cant·ly,** *adv.*
—Syn. 1. consequential, momentous, weighty. **2.** See **expressive.**

signif′icant dig′its, *Math.* all the nonzero digits of a number and the zeros that are included between them or that are final zeros and signify accuracy: *The significant digits of 0.01230 are 1, 2, 3, and the final 0, which signifies accuracy to five places.* Also called **signif′icant fig′ures.**

sig·ni·fi·ca·tion (sig′nə fə kā′shən), *n.* **1.** meaning; import; sense. **2.** the act or fact of signifying; indication. [ME *significacion* < L *significātiōn-* (s. of *significātiō*) signal, emphasis, meaning. See SIGNIFY, -ATION]

sig·nif·i·ca·tive (sig nif′ə kā′tiv), *adj.* **1.** serving to signify. **2.** significant; suggestive. [< LL *significātīv(us)* denoting, equiv. to L *significāt(us)* meant (ptp. of *significāre;* see SIGNIFY, -ATE[1]) + *-īvus* -IVE] **—sig·nif′i·ca′tive·ly,** *adv.* **—sig·nif′i·ca′tive·ness,** *n.*

sig·nif·ics (sig nif′iks), *n.* (*construed as sing.*) semantics (def. 2). [SIGNIF(Y) + -ICS]

sig·ni·fy (sig′nə fī′), *v.,* **-fied, -fy·ing. —*v.t.* 1.** to make known by signs, speech, or action. **2.** to be a sign of; mean; portend. **—*v.i.* 3.** to be of importance or consequence. [ME *signifi(en)* < OF *signifie(r)* < L *significāre.* See SIGN, -IFY] **—sig′ni·fi′a·ble,** *adj.* **—sig′ni·fi′er,** *n.*
—Syn. 1. signal, express, indicate. **2.** represent, indicate, denote, betoken, imply.

si·gnior (sēn′yōr, -yôr, sin yōr′, -yôr′; *It.* sē nyôr′), *n., pl.* **-gniors,** *It.* **-gnio·ri** (-nyô′rē). signor.

sign′ lan′guage, a means of communication in which gestures, usually manual, substitute for spoken words, used by deaf-mutes, between speakers of different languages, etc.

sign′ man′ual, *pl.* **signs manual.** a personal signature, esp. that of a sovereign or official on a public document.

sign-off (sīn′ôf′, -of′), *n.* the act or fact of signing off. [n. use of v. phrase *sign off*]

sign′ of the cross′, (esp. in the Roman Catholic Church) a movement of the hand to indicate a cross, as from forehead to breast and left shoulder to right, or, in the Eastern Orthodox Church, from right shoulder to left.

sign′ of the zo′diac, sign (def. 10).

si·gnor (sēn′yōr, -yôr, sin yōr′, -yôr′; *It.* sē nyôr′) *n., pl.* **-gnors,** *It.* **-gno·ri** (-nyô′rē). a conventional Italian term of address or title of respect for a man, either used separately or prefixed to the name. *Abbr.:* Sig., sig. Also, **signior.** [< It; see SIGNORE[1]]

si·gno·ra (sin yōr′ə, -yôr′ə; *It.* sē nyô′rä), *n., pl.* **-ras,** *It.* **-re** (-re). a conventional Italian term of address or title of respect for a married woman, either used separately or prefixed to the name. [< It; fem. of SIGNORE[1]]

si·gno·re[1] (sin yōr′ā, -yôr′ā; *It.* sē nyô′re), *n., pl.* **si·gno·ri** (sin yōr′ē, -yôr′ē; *It.* sē nyô′rē). a conventional Italian title of respect for a man, usually used separately; signor. [< It << L *senior;* see SENIOR]

si·gno·re[2] (sin yōr′ā, -yôr′ā; *It.* sē nyô′re), *n.* a pl. of **signora.**

Si·gno·rel·li (sē nyô rel′lē), *n.* **Lu·ca** (lo͞o′kä), c1445–1523, Italian painter.

si·gno·ri·na (sēn′yô rē′nə; *It.* sē′nyô rē′nä), *n., pl.* **-nas,** *It.* **-ne** (-ne). a conventional Italian term of address or title of respect for a girl or unmarried woman, either used separately or prefixed to the name. [< It; dim. of SIGNORA; see -INE[1]]

si·gno·ri·no (sēn′yô rē′nō; *It.* sē′nyô rē′nô), *n., pl.* **-nos,** *It.* **-ni** (-nē). a conventional Italian title of respect for a young man. [< It; dim. of SIGNORE[1]; see -INE[1]]

si·gno·ry (sē′nyə rē), *n., pl.* **-ries.** seigniory.

sign·post (sīn′pōst′), *n.* **1.** a post bearing a sign that gives information or guidance. **2.** any immediately perceptible indication, obvious clue, etc. [SIGN + POST[1]]

Sig·ny (sig′nē, -nY), *n.* (in the *Volsunga Saga*) the daughter of Volsung and mother, by her brother, Sigmund, of Sinfiotli, with whose help she kills her husband (**Siggeir**) to avenge his murder of Volsung. Cf. **Sieglinde.**

Sigr·dri·fa (sig′ər drē′vä), *n.* (in the *Elder Edda*) a Valkyrie who, for disobedience to Odin, sleeps within a circle of fire until awakened by Sigurd. Also called **Brynhildr Sigrdrifa.** Cf. **Brynhild.**

Si·grid (sē′grid, sig′rid; *Ger.* zē′grit, -grēt; *Nor.* si′-grē; *Swed.* sē′grid), *n.* a girl's given name.

Sigs·bee (sigz′bē), *n.* **Charles Dwight,** 1845–1923, U.S. naval officer: captain of the *Maine* in 1898.

Sig·urd (sig′ərd; *Ger.* zē′go͝ort), *n.* (in the *Volsunga Saga*) the son of Sigmund and Hiordis and the husband of Gudrun. He kills the dragon Fafnir, acquires the treasure of Andvari, wins Brynhild for Gunnar, and is finally killed at the behest of Brynhild, whom he had once promised to marry: corresponds to Siegfried of the *Nibelungenlied.*

Sig·yn (seg′in, -yn, sē′gin, -gyn), *n. Scand. Myth.* the last wife of Loki.

Si·kan·dar·a·bad (si kun′drä bäd′), *n.* Secunderabad.

Si·kang (shē′käng′), *n.* a former province in W China; now a part of Szechwan.

sike (sīk, sik), *n. Scot. and North Eng.* **1.** a small stream. **2.** a gully or ditch, esp. one that fills with water after a heavy rain. Also, **syke.** [ME < Scand; cf. Icel *sīk* ditch, c. OE *sīc* (now *sitch*) rill, MLG *sīk* puddle; akin to OHG *seih* urine, OE *sicerian* to ooze]

sik·er (sik′ər), *adj., adv. Scot. and North Eng.* sicker[2].

Sikh (sēk), *n.* **1.** a member of a Hindu religious sect, founded in the Punjab c1500 by the guru Nanak as a reformed offshoot of Hinduism, refusing to recognize the caste system or the supremacy of the Brahmanical priests and forbidding magic, idolatry, and pilgrimages. **—*adj.* 2.** of or pertaining to the Sikhs or to Sikhism. [< Hindi: lit., disciple < Skt *śikṣati*]

si·kha·ra (shik′ər ə), *n.* (in Indian architecture) a convexly tapering tower, capped by an amalaka. Also, **sikra.** [< Skt]

Sikh·ism (sē′kiz əm), *n.* the religion and practices of the Sikhs. [SIKH + -ISM]

Si·kiang (shē′kyäng′), *n.* Si.

Sik·kim (sik′im), *n.* a state in NE India, in the Himalayas between Nepal and Bhutan. 162,189 (1961); 2745 sq. mi. *Cap.:* Gangtok.

Si·kor·sky (si kôr′skē), *n.* **I·gor** (ē′gôr), born 1889, U.S. aeronautical engineer, born in Russia.

si·kra (sik′rə), *n.* sikhara.

si·lage (sī′lij), *n.* fodder preserved in a silo; ensilage. [SIL(O) + -AGE]

Si·las (sī′ləs), *n.* a boy's given name.

Si·las Mar·ner (sī′ləs mär′nər), a novel (1861) by George Eliot.

Si·las·tic (si las′tik), *n. Trademark.* any of a group of substances containing polymeric silicones, having the properties of rubber but more capable of withstanding extremely high and low temperatures and other causes of deterioration, used in jet-plane engines, medical prosthetic devices, gaskets, electrical insulation, etc.

Sil·ber·schlag (sil′bər shläg′), *n.* a crater in the first quadrant of the face of the moon: about 8 miles in diameter.

si·le·na·ceous (sī′lə nā′shəs), *adj. Bot.* caryophyllaceous. [< NL *Silen(e)* name of the genus (named after SILENUS) + -ACEOUS]

si·lence (sī′ləns), *n., v.,* **-lenced, -lenc·ing,** *interj.* **—*n.* 1.** absence of any sound or noise; stillness. **2.** the state or fact of being silent; muteness. **3.** absence or omission of mention: *the conspicuous silence of our newspaper on local graft.* **4.** the state of being forgotten; oblivion: *in the news again after years of silence.* **5.** concealment; secrecy. **—*v.t.* 6.** to put or bring to silence; still. **7.** to put (doubts, fears, etc.) to rest; quiet. **8.** *Mil.* to still (enemy guns), as by a more effective fire. **—*interj.* 9.** be silent! *"Silence!" the teacher shouted.* [ME < OF < L *silent(ium).* See SILENT, -ENCE]

si·lenc·er (sī′lən sər), *n.* **1.** one who or that which silences. **2.** a device for deadening the report of a firearm. **3.** *Chiefly Brit.* the muffler on an internal-combustion engine. [SILENCE + -ER[1]]

si·lent (sī′lənt), *adj.* **1.** making no sound; quiet; still: *a silent motor.* **2.** refraining from speech. **3.** speechless; mute. **4.** not inclined to speak; taciturn; reticent. **5.** characterized by absence of speech or sound: *a silent prayer.* **6.** unspoken; tacit: *a silent assent.* **7.** omitting mention of something, as in a narrative: *The records are silent about this crime.* **8.** inactive or quiescent, as a volcano. **9.** not sounded or pronounced: *The "b" in doubt is a silent letter.* **10.** *Motion Pictures.* not having spoken dialogue or a sound track. **—*n.* 11.** Usually, **silents.** silent films. [< L *silent-* (s. of *silēns*), prp. of *silēre* to be quiet; see -ENT] **—si′lent·ly,** *adv.* **—si′lent·ness,** *n.*
—Syn. 1. soundless. See **still**[1]. **8.** dormant. **—Ant. 1.** noisy. **4.** talkative.

si′lent bar′ter. See **dumb barter.**

si′lent but′ler, a small receptacle having a handle and a hinged lid, used for collecting the contents of ashtrays, crumbs from a dinner table, etc., for disposal.

si′lent chain′, a power chain consisting of a number of thin parallel links, joined by pins and bearing teeth inverted with respect to teeth on the sprockets with which they engage.

si′lent dis′charge, *Elect.* the gradual discharge into the atmosphere of electricity from a conductor, without the noise characteristic of a corona.

Si′lent Don′, The, a novel (1928–40) by Mikhail Sholokhov.

si′lent part′ner, a partner taking no active part in the conduct of a business. Cf. **secret partner.**

si′lent serv′ice, (*sometimes cap.*) the submarine service (usually prec. by *the*).

si′lent trade′. See **dumb barter.**

si′lent treat′ment, the act or an instance of maintaining silence or aloofness toward another person, esp. as a means of indicating disapproval, disgust, etc.

si′lent vote′, the vote of persons or groups that have not previously expressed a preference, as between candidates, platforms, etc.

Si·le·nus (sī lē′nəs), *n., pl.* **-ni** (-nī) for 2. *Class. Myth.* **1.** a god of the forest, the oldest of the satyrs and the foster father, teacher, and companion of Dionysus: often represented as a hairy old man with the ears and legs of a horse, drunk, and seated astride a cask or a donkey. **2.** (*l.c.*) any of a group of forest spirits similar to satyrs but having the legs of horses.

Si′ler Cit′y (sī′lər), a town in central North Carolina. 4455 (1960).

si·le·sia (si lē′zhə, -shə, sī-), *n.* a lightweight, smoothly finished, twilled fabric of acetate, rayon, or cotton, for garment linings. [after SILESIA]

Si·le·sia (si lē′zhə, -shə, sī-), *n.* a region in central Europe: formerly divided between Germany (which had the largest portion), Poland, and Czechoslovakia; by provision of the Potsdam agreement 1945 the greater part of German Silesia is now under Polish administration; rich deposits of coal, iron, and other minerals. German, **Schlesien.** Polish, **Slask.** Czech, **Slezsko. —Si·le′sian,** *adj., n.*

sil·hou·ette (sil′o͞o et′), *n., v.,* **-et·ted, -et·ting. —*n.* 1.** a two-dimensional representation of the outline of an object, as a cutout or outline drawing, uniformly filled in with black, esp. a black-paper, miniature cutout of the outlines of a famous person's face. **2.** the outline or general shape of something: *the slim silhouette of a skyscraper.* **3.** a dark image outlined against a lighter background. **—*v.t.* 4.** to show in or as in a silhouette. **5.** *Print.* to remove nonessential background details from (a halftone cut) so as to produce an outline effect. [named after Etienne de *Silhouette* (1709–67), French finance minister]

Silhouette

silic-, a learned borrowing from Latin used, with the meaning "flint," "silica," "silicon," in the formation of compound words: *silicide.* Also, **silici-, silico-.** [comb. form repr. L *silic-,* s. of *silex* flint]

sil·i·ca (sil′ə kə), *n.* the dioxide form of silicon, SiO_2, occurring esp. as quartz, sand flint, and agate: used usually in the form of its prepared white powder chiefly in the manufacture of glass, water glass, ceramics, and abrasives. Also called **silicon dioxide.** [< NL, equiv. to *silic-* SILIC- + *-a* n. suffix]

sil′ica gel′, *Chem.* a highly adsorbent gelatinous form of silica, used chiefly as a dehumidifying and dehydrating agent.

sil′ica glass′, glass made entirely from silica, having a very low rate of thermal expansion. Also called **fused silica.**

sil·i·cate (sil′ə kit, -kāt′), *n. Chem.* any salt derived from the silicic acids or from silica. [SILIC(A) + -ATE[2]] **—sil·i·ca·tion** (sil′ə kā′shən), *n.*

si·li·ceous (si lish′əs), *adj.* **1.** containing, consisting of, or resembling silica. **2.** growing in soil rich in silica. Also, **silicious.** [< L *siliceus* of flint or limestone. See SILIC-, -EOUS]

silici-, var. of **silic-:** *siliciferous.*

si·lic·ic (si lis′ik), *adj. Chem.* **1.** containing silicon. **2.** of or pertaining to silica or acids derived from it. [SILIC(A) + -IC]

sil·ic′ic ac′id, *Chem.* any of certain amorphous gelatinous masses, formed when alkaline silicates are treated with acids, which dissociate readily into silica and water.

sil·i·cide (sil′i sīd′, -sid), *n.* *Chem.* a compound of two elements, one of which is silicon. [SILIC- + -IDE]

sil·i·cif·er·ous (sil′i sif′ər əs), *adj.* containing, combined with, or producing silica. [SILICI- + -FEROUS]

silic′ified wood′, wood which has been changed into quartz by a replacement of the cellular structure of the wood by siliceous waters.

si·lic·i·fy (si lis′ə fī′), *v.t., v.i.,* **-fied, -fy·ing.** to convert or be converted into silica. [SILIC- + -IFY] **—si·lic′i·fi·ca′tion,** *n.*

sil·i·cle (sil′i kəl), *n.* *Bot.* a short silique. [< L *silicul(a)* little husk or pod. See SILIQUE, -ULE]

silico-, var. of **silic-:** *silicomanganese.*

sil·i·con (sil′ə kən, -kon′), *n.* *Chem.* a nonmetallic element, having amorphous and crystalline forms, occurring in a combined state in minerals and rocks and constituting more than one fourth of the earth's crust: used in steel-making, alloys, etc. *Symbol:* Si; *at. wt.:* 28.086; *at. no.:* 14; *sp. gr.:* 2.4 at 20°C. [SILIC- + *-on,* modeled on *boron*]

sil′icon car′bide, *Chem.* a very hard, insoluble, crystalline compound, SiC, used as an abrasive and as an electrical resistor in objects exposed to high temperatures.

sil′icon diox′ide, *Chem.* silica.

sil·i·cone (sil′ə kōn′), *n.* *Chem.* any of a number of polymers containing alternate silicon and oxygen atoms, as $(\text{–Si–O–Si–O–})_n$, whose properties are determined by the organic groups attached to the silicon atoms, and which are fluid, resinous, rubbery, extremely stable in high temperatures, and water-repellent: used as adhesives, lubricants, and hydraulic oils and in electrical insulation, cosmetics, etc. [SILIC- + -ONE]

sil′icon tetrachlo′ride, *Chem.* a colorless, fuming liquid, $SiCl_4$, used chiefly for making smokescreens and various derivatives of silicon.

sil′icon tetraflu′oride, *Chem.* a colorless, fuming gas, SiF_4, used chiefly in the manufacture of fluosilicic acid.

Sil′icon Val′ley, an area just south of San Francisco, in the Santa Clara Valley, where many computer firms are located. [from the silicon wafers used in semiconductors]

sil·i·co·sis (sil′ə kō′sis), *n.* *Pathol.* a disease of the lungs caused by the inhaling of siliceous particles, as by stonecutters. [SILIC- + -OSIS] **—sil·i·cot·ic** (sil′ə kot′ik), *adj.*

si·lic·u·lose (si lik′yə lōs′), *adj.* *Bot.* **1.** bearing silicles. **2.** having the form or appearance of a silicle. [< NL *siliculōs(us).* See SILICLE, -OSE[1]]

sil·i·qua (sil′ə kwə), *n., pl.* **-quae** (-kwē′). a silver coin of ancient Rome, the 24th part of a solidus, first issued by Constantine. [< L: lit., pod]

si·lique (si lēk′, sil′ik), *n.* *Bot.* the long two-valved seed vessel or pod of cruciferous plants. [var. (< F) of SILIQUA] **—sil·i·qua·ceous** (sil′ə kwā′shəs), *adj.*

sil·i·quose (sil′ə kwōs′), *adj.* **1.** bearing siliques. **2.** resembling a silique or silicle. Also, **sil·i·quous** (sil′ə kwəs). [< NL *siliquōs(us).* See SILIQUE, -OSE[1]]

Silique of plant, genus *Brassica*

silk (silk), *n.* **1.** the soft, lustrous fiber obtained as a filament from the cocoon of the silkworm. **2.** thread made from this fiber. **3.** cloth made from this fiber. **4.** a garment of this cloth. **5. silks,** the blouse and peaked cap, considered together, worn by a jockey or sulky driver in a race. **6.** a gown of such material worn distinctively by a King's or Queen's Counsel at the English bar. **7.** any fiber or filamentous matter resembling silk, as a filament produced by certain spiders, the thread of a mollusk, or the like. **8.** the hairlike styles on an ear of corn. **9.** *Brit. Informal.* **a.** a King's or Queen's Counsel. **b.** any barrister of high rank. **10. hit the silk,** *Slang.* to parachute from an aircraft; bail out: *It was a thrill to see hundreds of men hitting the silk.* **11. take silk,** *Brit.* to become a Queen's or King's Counsel. **—***adj.* **12.** made of silk. **13.** resembling silk; silky. **14.** of or pertaining to silk. **—***v.i.* **15.** (of corn) to be in the course of developing silk. [ME; OE *sioloc, seol(o)c* (c. Icel *silki*) < Baltic or Slav; cf. OPruss *silkas,* Russ *shëlk* << Gk *sērikón* silk, n. use of neut. of *sērikós* silken, lit., of Seres (i.e., China)]

silk·a·line (sil′kə lēn′), *n.* a soft, thin cotton fabric with a smooth finish, for curtains, bedspreads, garment linings, etc. Also, **silk′o·line′, silk′o·lene′.** [SILK + *-aline,* var. of *-oline,* as in *crinoline*]

silk′ cot′ton, the silky covering of the seeds of certain tropical trees of the family *Bombacaceae,* used for stuffing cushions, pillows, etc.

silk′-cot·ton tree′ (silk′kot′ən), any of several trees of the family *Bombacaceae,* having seeds surrounded by silk cotton, esp. *Ceiba pentandra,* from which kapok is obtained.

silk·en (sil′kən), *adj.* **1.** made of silk. **2.** like silk in smoothness, softness, glossiness, or delicateness. **3.** clad in silk. **4.** smoothly ingratiating or appealing: *the Senator's silken oratory.* **5.** elegant; luxurious. [ME; OE *seolcen.* See SILK, -EN[2]]

silk′ gland′, any of several glands, as in various insects and spiders, that secrete a viscid protein substance which hardens into silk on contact with air.

silk′ hat′, a tall, cylindrical, black hat covered with silk plush, worn by men for formal dress. Cf. **beaver**[1] (def. 4), **opera hat, top hat. —silk′-hat′ted,** *adj.*

silk′ oak′, any of several Australian trees of the genus *Grevillea,* esp. *G. robusta,* having feathery, fernlike leaves and showy orange, red, or white flowers. Also, **silky oak.**

silk·screen (silk′skrēn′), *n.* **1.** Also called **silk′-screen proc′ess.** a printmaking technique in which a mesh cloth is stretched over a heavy wooden frame and the design, painted on the screen by tusche or affixed by stencil, is printed by having a squeegee force color through the pores of the material in areas not blocked out by a glue sizing. **2.** a print made by this technique. **—***v.t.* **3.** to print by silkscreen. **—***adj.* **4.** of, made by, or printed with silkscreen. [SILK + SCREEN]

silk-stock·ing (silk′stok′ing), *adj.* **1.** rich or luxurious in dress. **2.** aristocratic or wealthy: *a silk-stocking neighborhood.* **—***n.* **3.** one who dresses richly or luxuriously. **4.** an aristocratic or wealthy person.

silk′ tree′, a tree, *Albizzia julibrissin,* ranging from Iran to central China, having light-pink flowers.

Silkworm and cocoon

silk·weed (silk′wēd′), *n.* any milkweed of the family *Asclepiadaceae,* the pods of which contain a silky down. [SILK + WEED[1]]

silk·worm (silk′wûrm′), *n.* **1.** the larva of the Chinese silkworm moth, *Bombyx mori,* which spins a cocoon of commercially valuable silk. **2.** the larva of any of several moths of the family *Saturniidae,* which spins a silken cocoon. [ME *sylkewyrme,* OE *seolcwyrm.* See SILK, WORM]

silk′worm moth′, any of several moths of the families *Bombycidae* and *Saturniidae,* the larvae of which are silkworms.

silk·y (sil′kē), *adj.,* **silk·i·er, silk·i·est. 1.** of or like silk; smooth, lustrous, soft, or delicate: *silky skin.* **2.** *Bot.* covered with fine, soft, closely set hairs, as a leaf. [SILK + -Y[1]] **—silk′i·ly,** *adv.* **—silk′i·ness,** *n.*

silk′y ant′eater an arboreal, tropical American anteater, *Cyclopes didactylus,* about the size of a rat, having a prehensile tail, glossy, golden fur, and two toes on each forelimb. Also called **two-toed anteater.**

silk′y camel′lia, a shrub, *Stewartia Malachodendron,* of the southeastern U.S., having hairy twigs and leaves and white flowers nearly four inches wide.

silk′y cor′nel, a cornel, *Cornus Amomum,* of the eastern U.S., having leaves covered with short, silky hairs on the underside.

silk′y fly′catcher, any of several passerine birds of the family *Ptilogonatidae,* of the southwestern U.S. to Panama, related to the waxwings.

silk′y oak′. See **silk oak.**

sill (sil), *n.* **1.** a horizontal timber, block, or the like, serving as a foundation of a wall, house, etc. **2.** the horizontal piece or member beneath a window, door, or other opening. See diag. under **double-hung. 3.** *Geol.* a tabular body of intrusive igneous rock, ordinarily between beds of sedimentary rocks or layers of volcanic ejecta. [ME *sille,* OE *syl, sylle;* c. LG *süll,* Icel *syll;* akin to Icel *svill,* G *Schwelle*] **—sill′-like′,** *adj.*

sil·la·bub (sil′ə bub′), *n.* a drink or dish made of milk or cream mixed with wine, cider, or the like, often sweetened and flavored. Also, **sil′li·bub′, syllabub.** [?]

Sil·lan·pää (sil′län pa′), *n.* **Frans Ee·mil** (fräns e′mil), 1888–1964, Finnish author: Nobel prize 1939.

sill·cock (sil′kok′), *n.* hosecock. [SILL + COCK[1]; so called from the fact that it is often attached to a house at about the height of a sill]

sil·ler (sil′ər), *n.* *Scot.* silver.

sil·li·man·ite (sil′ə mə nīt′), *n.* a mineral, aluminum silicate, Al_2SiO_5, occurring in the form of long, slender, and often fibrous crystals. Also called **fibrolite.** [named after Benjamin *Silliman* (d. 1864), American chemist and geologist; see -ITE[1]]

sil·ly (sil′ē), *adj.,* **-li·er, -li·est,** *n., pl.* **-lies. —***adj.* **1.** weak-minded; lacking good sense; stupid or foolish: *a silly writer.* **2.** absurd; ridiculous; irrational: *a silly idea.* **3.** *Informal.* stunned; dazed: *He knocked me silly.* **4.** *Cricket.* (of a fielder or his playing position) extremely close to the batsman's wicket: *silly mid off.* **5.** *Obs.* rustic; plain; homely. **6.** *Obs.* lowly in rank or state; humble. **7.** *Archaic.* weak; helpless. **—***n.* **8.** *Informal.* a silly or foolish person: *Don't be such a silly.* [ME *sely, silly* happy, innocent, weak, OE (Anglian) *sēlig,* equiv. to *sēl, sǣl* happiness + *-ig* -Y[1]; c. G *selig*] **—sil′li·ly,** *adv.* **—sil′li·ness,** *n.*

—Syn. 1. witless, senseless, dull-witted, dim-witted. See **foolish. 2.** inane, asinine, nonsensical, preposterous. **—Ant. 1.** sensible.

sil′ly bil′ly, a clownish person.

sil′ly sea′son, a time of year, usually in midsummer or during a holiday period, characterized by exaggerated news stories, frivolous entertainments, outlandish publicity stunts, etc.: *The new movie reminds us that the silly season is here.*

si·lo (sī′lō), *n., pl.* **-los,** *v.,* **-loed, -lo·ing. —***n.* **1.** a structure, typically cylindrical, in which fodder or forage is kept. **2.** a pit or underground space for storing grain, green feeds, etc. **3.** *Mil.* an underground installation constructed of concrete and steel, designed to house a ballistic missile and the equipment for firing it. **—***v.t.* **4.** to put into or preserve in a silo. [< Sp, perh. < Celt; akin to OE *sāwan* to sow[1]]

Si·lo·am (si lō′əm, sī-), *n.* a spring and pool near Jerusalem. John 9:7.

Si′loam Springs′ (sī′lōm), a town in NW Arkansas. 3953 (1960).

Si·lo·ne (si lō′nē; *It.* sē lô′ne), *n.* **I·gna·zio** (ē nyä′tsyô), 1900–78, Italian author.

si·lox·ane (si lok′sān), *n.* *Chem.* any of the class of compounds containing the structural unit, R_2SiO, where R is an organic group or hydrogen. [SIL(ICON) + OX(YGEN) + -ANE]

Sils·bee (silz′bē), *n.* a town in E Texas. 6277 (1960).

silt (silt), *n.* **1.** earthy matter, fine sand, or the like, carried by moving or running water and deposited as a sediment. **—***v.i.* **2.** to become filled or choked up with silt. **—***v.t.* **3.** to fill or choke up with silt. [late ME *cylte* gravel, ? orig. salty deposit; cf. OE *unsylt* unsalted, unseasoned, *sylting* seasoning, *syltan* to salt, season, Norw *sylt* salty swamp, *sylte,* G *Sülze* brine] **—sil·ta′tion,** *n.*

silt·stone (silt′stōn′), *n.* *Petrog.* a very fine-grained sandstone, mainly consolidated silt. [SILT + STONE]

silt·y (sil′tē), *adj.,* **silt·i·er, silt·i·est.** of, pertaining to, or containing silt. [SILT + -Y[1]]

si·lun·dum (si lun′dəm), *n.* See **silicon carbide.** [SIL(ICON + CARBOR)UNDUM]

Sil·u·res (sil′yə rēz′), *n.pl.* an ancient British people who lived chiefly in southeastern Wales at the time of the Roman conquest and were in active resistance to it about A.D. 48.

Si·lu·ri·an (si lo͝or′ē ən, sī-), *adj.* **1.** of or pertaining to the Silures or their country. **2.** *Geol.* noting or pertaining to a period of the Paleozoic era, occurring from 400,000,000 to 440,000,000 years ago and characterized by the advent of air-breathing animals. See table under **era. —***n.* **3.** *Geol.* the Silurian period or system of rocks. [SILUR(ES) + -IAN]

si·lu·rid (si lo͝or′id, sī-), *n.* **1.** any of numerous fishes of the family *Siluridae,* comprising the catfishes. **—***adj.* **2.** belonging or pertaining to the family *Siluridae.* [< NL *Silurid(ae)* name of the family, deriv. of *Silūr(us)* genus name, special use of L *silūrus* < Gk *silouros* a kind of fish; see -IDAE, -ID[2]]

sil·va (sil′və), *n.* **1.** the forest trees of a particular area. **2.** a descriptive flora of forest trees. Also, **sylva.** [< NL, special use of L *silva* woodland]

sil·van (sil′vən), *adj., n.* sylvan. **—sil·van·i·ty** (sil van′i tē), *n.*

Sil·van·a (sil van′ə), *n.* a girl's given name, form of **Silvia** or **Sylvia.** Also, **Sylvana.**

Sil·va·nus (sil vā′nəs), *n., pl.* **-ni** (-nī) for 2. *Rom. Religion.* **1.** a god of woods and uncultivated land, later worshiped under three aspects, as the protector of the house, of the herds, and of the boundaries of the farm. **2.** (*l.c.*) any of a number of forest spirits, identified with fauns. Also, **Sylvanus.** [< L; see SYLVAN]

sil·ver (sil′vər), *n.* **1.** *Chem.* a white, ductile metallic element, used for making mirrors, coins, ornaments, table utensils, etc. *Symbol:* Ag; *at. wt.:* 107.870; *at. no.:* 47; *sp. gr.:* 10.5 at 20°C. **2.** coin made of this metal; money: *a handful of silver.* **3.** this metal as a commodity or considered as a currency standard. **4.** table articles made of or plated with silver, including flatware and hollowware. **5.** any flatware: *The kitchen silver is of stainless steel.* **6.** something resembling this metal in color, luster, etc. **7.** a lustrous grayish white or whitish gray; the color of the metal: *the silver of the leaves.* **8.** *U.S. Photog.* any of the silver halides used for photographic purposes, as silver bromide, silver chloride, or silver iodide. **—***adj.* **9.** consisting of, made of, or plated with silver. **10.** of or pertaining to silver. **11.** producing or yielding silver. **12.** resembling silver; silvery: *the silver moon.* **13.** clear and soft: *silver sounds.* **14.** eloquent; persuasive: *a silver tongue.* **15.** urging the use of silver as a currency standard: *silver economists.* **16.** indicating the 25th event of a series, as a wedding anniversary. **17.** having the color silver: *a silver dress.* **—***v.t.* **18.** to coat with silver or some silverlike substance. **19.** to give a silvery color to. **—***v.i.* **20.** to become a silvery color. [ME, OE *siolfor;* c. G *Silber,* Icel *silfr,* Goth *silubr*] **—sil′ver·er,** *n.* **—sil′ver·ish,** *adj.* **—sil′ver·less,** *adj.* **—sil′ver·like′,** *adj.* **—sil′ver·ness,** *n.*

Sil·ver (sil′vər), *n.* **Ab·ba Hillel** (ab′ə), 1893–1963, U.S. rabbi, born in Lithuania.

sil′ver age′, 1. *Class. Myth.* the second of the four ages of man, inferior to the golden age but superior to the bronze age that followed: characterized by an increase of impiety and of human weakness. **2.** (*usually cap.*) a period in Latin literature, A.D. c14–138, following the Augustan Age: the second phase of classical Latin. Cf. **golden age** (def. 3).

sil′ver bass′ (bas). See **white bass.**

Sil′ver Bay′, a town in NE Minnesota. 3723 (1960).

sil′ver bell′, any North American shrub or small tree of the genus *Halesia,* having white, bell-shaped flowers. Also called **sil′ver-bell tree′.**

sil·ver·ber·ry (sil′vər ber′ē), *n., pl.* **-ries.** a shrub, *Elaeagnus argentea,* of north-central North America, having silvery leaves and flowers and silvery, drupelike edible fruit. Also called **wolfberry.** [SILVER + BERRY]

sil′ver birch′, 1. See **paper birch. 2.** See **yellow birch** (def. 2).

Sil′ver Bow′ Park′ (bō), a town in SW Montana. 4798 (1960).

sil′ver bro′mide, *Chem.* a yellowish, water-insoluble powder, AgBr, which darkens on exposure to light, produced by the reaction of silver nitrate with a bromide: used chiefly in the manufacture of photographic emulsions.

sil′ver certif′icate. See under **certificate** (def. 4a).

sil′ver chlo′ride, *Chem.* a white, granular, water-insoluble powder, AgCl, which darkens on exposure to light, produced by the reaction of silver nitrate with a chloride: used chiefly in the manufacture of photographic emulsions and in the making of antiseptic silver preparations.

Sil′ver Cit′y, a town in SW New Mexico. 6972 (1960).

Sil′ver Cord′, The, a play (1926) by Sidney Howard.

Sil′ver Creek′, a town in W New York. 3310 (1960).

sil′ver doc′tor, *Angling.* a type of artificial fly, used chiefly for trout and salmon

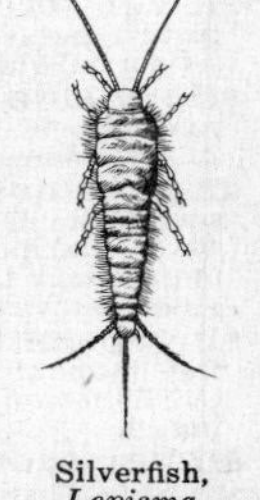

Silverfish, *Lepisma saccharina* (Length ⅓ in.)

sil·vered (sil′vərd), *adj.* **1.** coated or plated with silver. **2.** coated with a silverlike substance, as quicksilver, tinfoil, etc.: *a mirror of carefully silvered plate glass.* **3.** tinted a silver color, or having silver highlights: *newly waved and silvered hair.* [late ME *silverid.* See SILVER, -ED[3]]

sil·ver-eye (sil′vər ī′), *n., pl.* **-eyes.** white-eye.

sil·ver·fish (sil′vər fish′), *n., pl.* (*esp. collectively*) **-fish,** (*esp. referring to two or more kinds or species*) **-fish·es. 1.** a white or silvery goldfish, *Carassius auratus.* **2.** any of various other silvery fishes, as the tarpon, silversides, or shiner. **3.** a wingless, silvery-gray thysanuran insect, *Lepisma saccharina,* that feeds on starch, damaging books, wallpaper, etc. [SILVER + FISH]

sil′ver fizz′, an alcoholic drink made with gin, lemon juice, sugar, and egg white.

sil′ver flu′oride, *Chem.* a yellow or brownish, crystalline, water-soluble, hygroscopic solid, AgF, used chiefly as an antiseptic and disinfectant. Also called **tachiol.**

sil′ver foil′, silver or silver-colored metal in foil form. [ME *silverfoile*]

sil′ver fox′, a red fox in the color phase in which the fur is black with silver-gray ends on the longer hairs.
sil′ver frost′, glaze (def. 12).
sil′ver gilt′, an ornamental coating of silver, silver leaf, or a silver-colored substance. [late ME]
sil′ver gray′, a light brownish-gray to light olive-brown color. —**sil′ver-gray′,** *adj.*
sil′ver hal′oid, any of a group of chemicals, including silver chloride, bromide, or iodide, found in the upper part of a silver deposit.
sil·ver·ing (sil′vər ing), *n.* **1.** the act or process of coating with silver or a substance resembling silver. **2.** the coating thus applied: *the silvering of the mirror.* [SILVER + -ING[1]]
sil′ver i′odate, *Chem.* a white, crystalline, slightly water-soluble powder, $AgIO_3$, used in medicine chiefly as an antiseptic and as an astringent.
sil′ver i′odide, *Chem.* a pale-yellow, water-insoluble solid, AgI, which darkens on exposure to light: used chiefly in medicine, photography, and artificial rain-making.
sil·ver·ise (sil′və rīz′), *v.t.,* **-ised, -is·ing.** *Chiefly Brit.* silverize.
Sil·ve·ri·us (sil vēr′ē əs), *n.* **Saint,** died A.D. 537?, pope 536–537.
sil·ver·ize (sil′və rīz′), *v.t.,* **-ized, -iz·ing.** to cover, plate, or treat with silver. Also, *esp. Brit.,* **silverise.** —**sil′ver·iz′er,** *n.*
sil′ver jen′ny, a silvery mojarra, *Eucinostomus gula,* found in the warm waters of the western Atlantic Ocean, along sandy shores.
sil′ver ju′bilee. See under **jubilee** (def. 1).
sil′ver king′, *pl.* (*esp. collectively*) **silver king,** (*esp. referring to two or more kinds or species*) **silver kings. 1.** the tarpon. **2.** the louvar. [so called from its color and size]
sil′ver-lace vine′ (sil′vər lās′), a hardy, twining, woody perennial, *Polygonum auberti,* of western China and Tibet, having greenish-white, fragrant flowers in drooping clusters. Also called **Chinese fleece-vine, fleece-vine, lace-vine.**
Sil′ver Lake′, 1. a town in NE Massachusetts. 4654 (1960). **2.** a town in NE Ohio. 2655 (1960).
sil′ver leaf′, silver in the form of very thin foil.
sil·ver·leaf (sil′vər lēf′), *n., pl.* **-leaves.** the buffalo berry, *Shepherdia argentea.* [SILVER + LEAF]
sil′ver lin′ing, a sign of hope in an unfortunate situation; a bright prospect: *Every cloud has a silver lining.*
sil′ver·ly (sil′vər lē), *adv.* with a silvery appearance or sound. [SILVER + -LY]
sil′ver ma′ple, 1. a maple, *Acer saccharinum,* having leaves that are light green above and silvery white beneath. **2.** the hard, close-grained wood of this tree, used for making furniture.
sil′ver morn′ing-glory, a tall morning-glory, *Argyreia splendens,* of India, having solitary, rose-colored flowers and large leaves with silvery hair beneath, grown as an ornamental.
sil·vern (sil′vərn), *adj. Archaic.* made of or like silver. [ME *silver(e)n, selvern,* OE *seolfren, seolfern.* See SILVER, -EN[2]]
sil′ver ni′trate, *Chem., Pharm.* a white, crystalline, water-soluble, bitter, corrosive, poisonous powder, $AgNO_3$, produced by the reaction of silver and dilute nitric acid: used chiefly in the manufacture of photographic emulsions, mirrors, as a laboratory reagent, and in medicine as an antiseptic, astringent, and in the routine prophylaxis of ophthalmia neonotorum.
sil′ver perch′, 1. Also called **mademoiselle.** *Ichthyol.* a drum, *Bairdiella chrysura,* found in the southern U.S. **2.** any of various silvery, perchlike fishes, as the white perch.
sil′ver plate′, 1. silver tableware. **2.** a coating of silver, esp. one electroplated on base metal.
sil·ver-plate (sil′vər plāt′), *v.t.,* **-plat·ed, -plat·ing.** to coat (base metal) with silver, esp. by electroplating.
sil′ver point′, the melting point of silver, equal to 960.8°C, used as a fixed point on the international temperature scale.
sil·ver·point (sil′vər point′), *n.* **1.** a technique of drawing with a silver stylus on specially prepared paper. **2.** a drawing made by this technique. [SILVER + POINT]
sil′ver queen′, gold-dust.
sil·ver-rag (sil′vər rag′), *n.* a butterfish, *Cubiceps nigriargenteus,* found in the Atlantic Ocean.
sil·ver·rod (sil′vər rod′), *n.* a weedy herb, *Solidago bicolor,* of eastern North America, having hairy leaves and narrow, spikelike, clusters of white flowers. Also called **white goldenrod.** [SILVER + ROD]
sil′ver sage′, a biennial herb, *Salvia argentea,* of the Mediterranean region, covered with white-woolly hairs and having showy, whitish-yellow or purplish flowers.
sil′ver screen′, 1. motion pictures; the motion-picture industry: *a star of the silver screen.* **2.** a special screen on which motion pictures are projected.
sil·ver·side (sil′vər sīd′), *n.* **1.** *Chiefly Brit.* a rump roast of beef, esp. one taken from the crown of the rump. **2.** silversides. [SILVER + SIDE[1]]
sil·ver·sides (sil′vər sīdz′), *n., pl.* **-sides.** any of several small fishes of the family *Atherinidae,* having a silvery stripe along each side, as *Menidia menidia,* found along the Atlantic coast of the U.S. Also, **silverside.** [SILVER + SIDE[1] + -S[3]]
sil·ver·smith (sil′vər smith′), *n.* one whose occupation is making and repairing articles of silver. [ME, OE *seolforsmith.* See SILVER, SMITH] —**sil′ver·smith′ing,** *n.*
sil′ver spoon′, spoon (def. 6).
Sil′ver Spring′, a town in central Maryland, near Washington, D.C. 66,348 (1960).
sil′ver stand′ard, a monetary standard or system using silver of specified weight and fineness to define the basic unit of currency.
Sil′ver Star′, *U.S. Army.* a bronze star with a small silver star at the center, awarded to a soldier who has been cited in orders for gallantry in action, when the citation does not warrant the award of a Medal of Honor or the Distinguished Service Cross. Also called **Sil′ver Star′ Med′al.**
sil′ver storm′. See **ice storm.**
sil′ver thaw′, glaze (def. 12).
sil′ver tin′, tin plate composed of a heavy coating of tin with a dull luster on a mechanically roughened base plate.
Sil·ver·ton (sil′vər tən), *n.* **1.** a town in SW Ohio. 6682 (1960). **2.** a town in NW Oregon. 3081 (1960).
sil·ver-tongued (sil′vər tungd′), *adj.* persuasive; eloquent: *a silver-tongued orator.*
sil′ver trout′, 1. a variety of cutthroat trout, *Salmo clarki henshawi,* having silvery coloration. **2.** the kokanee.
sil′ver-trum′pet tree′ (sil′vər trum′pit), an evergreen tree, *Tabebuia argentea,* of Paraguay, having soft, corky, whitish bark, silvery leaflets, and yellow flowers.
sil′ver vine′, a polygamous vine, *Actinidia polygama,* of eastern Asia, having fragrant, white flowers, and yellow, edible fruit on the female plant only.
sil·ver·ware (sil′vər wâr′), *n.* articles, esp. eating and serving utensils, made of silver, silver-plated metals, stainless steel, etc. [SILVER + WARE[1]]
sil′ver wat′tle, a variety of the green wattle, *Acacia dealbata,* having silvery-gray foliage.
sil′ver wed′ding, the 25th anniversary of a wedding.
sil·ver·weed (sil′vər wēd′), *n.* **1.** a rosaceous plant, *Potentilla anserina,* the leaves of which have a silvery pubescence on the underside. **2.** a related short-stemmed plant, *P. argentea,* of Europe and North America, having similar leaves. **3.** See **meadow rue.** [SILVER + WEED[1]]
sil·ver·work (sil′vər wûrk′), *n.* fine or decorative work executed in silver. [SILVER + WORK]
sil·ver·y (sil′və rē), *adj.* **1.** resembling silver; of a lustrous grayish-white color: *the silvery moon.* **2.** having a clear, ringing sound like that of silver: *the silvery peal of bells.* **3.** containing or covered with silver: *silvery deposits.* [SILVER + -Y[1]] —**sil′ver·i·ness,** *n.*
sil′very cinque′foil. See under **cinquefoil** (def. 1).
sil′very spleen′wort, a fern, *Athyrium thelypteroides,* of eastern North America, having fronds from 20 to 30 inches long on yellowish-green stalks.
Sil·ves·ter (sil ves′tər), *n.* a boy's given name. Also, **Sylvester.**
Silvester I. See **Sylvester I.**
Silvester II. See **Sylvester II.**
Sil·vi·a (sil′vē ə), *n.* a girl's given name. Also, **Sylvia.**
sil·vic·o·lous (sil vik′ə ləs), *adj.* living or growing in woodlands. [< L *silvi-* (comb. form of *silva* woodland) + -COLOUS; modeled on L *silvicola* sylvan]
sil·vi·cul·ture (sil′və kul′chər), *n.* the cultivation of forest trees; forestry. Also, **sylviculture.** [< L *silvi-* (comb. form of *silva* woodland) + CULTURE] —**sil′vi·cul′tur·al,** *adj.* —**sil′vi·cul′tur·al·ly,** *adv.* —**sil′vi·cul′tur·ist,** *n.*
Sil·vis (sil′vis), *n.* a town in NW Illinois. 3973 (1960).
Sil·vi·us (sil′vē əs), *n.* (in the *Aeneid*) a son of Aeneas.
s'il vous plait (sēl vōō ple′), *French.* if you please; please.
Sim (sim), *n.* a boy's given name, form of **Simon** or **Simeon.**
sim., 1. similar. **2.** simile.
si·ma[1] (sī′mə), *n. Geol.* a layer of rocks, rich in silica and magnesium, found beneath the ocean floors and the sial of continents. [< G; see SILICIUM, MAGNESIUM] —**si·mat·ic** (sī mat′ik), *adj.*
si·ma[2] (sī′mə), *n. Archit.* the uppermost member of a full classical order, usually a cyma recta, representing a roof gutter; cymatium. [var. of CYMA]
si·mar (si mär′), *n.* **1.** Also, **cymar.** a loose, lightweight jacket or robe for women, fashionable in the 17th and 18th centuries. **2.** zimarra. [earlier *simarre* < F < It *zimarr(a)* gown < Sp *zamarra* sheepskin coat, *zamarro* sheepskin < Basque *zamar*]
sim·a·rou·ba (sim′ə rōō′bə), *n.* **1.** any tropical American, simaroubaceous tree of the genus *Simaruba,* having pinnate leaves, a drupaceous fruit, and a root whose bark contains an appetite stimulant. **2.** the bark of this family of trees and shrubs. Also, **sim′a·ru′ba.** [< Carib *simaruba*]
sim·a·rou·ba·ceous (sim′ə rōō bā′shəs), *adj.* belonging to the *Simarubaceae,* a family of trees and shrubs, comprising the mountain damson, paradise tree, ailanthus, quassia, etc. Also, **sim′a·ru·ba′ceous.** [< NL *Simarub(a)* (see SIMAROUBA) + -ACEOUS]
Sim·chath To·rah (sim′khäs tōr′ə, tôr′ə; *Heb.* sēm khät′ tō rä′, sim′khäs tō′rō). See **Simhath Torah.**
Sim·e·on (sim′ē ən), *n.* **1.** a son of Jacob and Leah. Gen. 29:33. **2.** one of the 12 tribes of Israel. **3.** a devout man of Jerusalem who praised God for letting him see the infant Jesus. Luke 2:25–35. Cf. **Nunc Dimittis** (def. 1). **4.** a boy's given name.
Sim·e·on ben Yo·hai (sim′ē ən ben yō′khī), fl. 2nd century A.D., Palestinian rabbi and cabalist.
Sim·e·on·ite (sim′ē ə nīt′), *n.* a member of the Israelite tribe of Simeon. [< LL *Simeonitae* (pl.). See SIMEON, -ITE[1]] —**Sim′e·on·ism,** *n.*
Sim′eon Sty·li′tes (stī lī′tēz), **Saint,** A.D. 390?–459, Syrian monk and stylite.
Sim·fe·ro·pol (sim fe rō′pol yə), *n.* a city in the S Ukraine, in the SW Soviet Union in Europe, on the S Crimean Peninsula. 208,000 (est. 1964).
Sim·hath To·rah (sim′khäs tōr′ə, tôr′ə; *Heb.* sēm khät′ tō rä′, sim′khäs tō′rō), a Jewish festival that is joyously celebrated on the 23rd day of the month of Tishri, being the 9th day of Sukkoth, and that marks both the annual completion of the reading of the Torah in the synagogue and the beginning of the annual repetition. Also, **Simchath Torah.** [< Heb: lit., celebration of the Torah]
sim·i·an (sim′ē ən), *adj.* **1.** of or pertaining to an ape or monkey. **2.** characteristic of apes or monkeys: *long, simian fingers.* —*n.* **3.** an ape or monkey. [< L *sīmi(a)* an ape (? deriv. of *sīmus* flat-nosed < Gk *sīmós*) + -AN] —**sim·i·an·i·ty** (sim′ē an′i tē), *n.*
sim′ian shelf′, a shelflike thickening along the inside of the mandible, characteristic of the anthropoid apes.
sim·i·lar (sim′ə lər), *adj.* **1.** having likeness or resemblance, esp. in a general way: *two similar houses.* **2.** *Geom.* (of figures) having the same shape; having corresponding sides proportional and corresponding angles equal: *similar triangles.* **3.** *Math.* (of two matrices) having the property that there exists a third matrix with an inverse such that one matrix can be written as the second matrix multiplied on one side by the third matrix and on the other side by the inverse of the third matrix. [earlier *similary,* alter. of late ME *similable* similar < L *simil(is)* like + late ME *-able* -ABLE; see -ARY, -AR[1]] —**sim′i·lar·ly,** *adv.*
—**Syn. 1.** like, resembling. See **same.** —**Ant. 1.** different.
sim·i·lar·i·ty (sim′ə lar′i tē), *n., pl.* **-ties. 1.** the state of being similar; likeness; resemblance. **2.** a point or feature like or resembling another or another's: *a similarity of diction.* [SIMILAR + -ITY]
—**Syn. 1.** similitude, correspondence, parallelism. See **resemblance.** —**Ant. 1.** difference.
similar′ity transforma′tion, *Math.* a mapping of a set by which each element in the set is mapped into a positive constant multiple of itself, the same constant being used for all elements. Also called **homothetic transformation.**
sim·i·le (sim′ə lē), *n.* **1.** a figure of speech in which two unlike things are explicitly compared, as in "she is like a rose." Cf. **metaphor. 2.** an instance of such a figure of speech or a use of words exemplifying it. [< L: likeness, comparison, n. use of neut. of *similis* like]
si·mi·li·a si·mi·li·bus cu·ran·tur (si mil′i ä′ si-mi′li bōōs′ kōō rän′tōōr; *Eng.* si mil′ē ə si mil′i bəs kyōō ran′tər), *Latin.* likes are cured by likes: the principle of homeopathy.
si·mil·i·tude (si mil′i tōōd′, -tyōōd′), *n.* **1.** likeness; resemblance: *a similitude of habits.* **2.** a person or thing that is like or the match or counterpart of another: *This expression is a similitude of the other.* **3.** semblance; image: *a similitude of the truth.* **4.** a likening or comparison; parable or allegory: *He spoke by similitudes.* [< L *similitūdō* likeness, equiv. to *simili(s)* like + *-tūdō* -TUDE]
Si·mio·na·to (sē′myō nä′tō), *n.* **Giu·liet·ta** (jōō lyet′-tä), born 1916, Italian mezzo-soprano.
sim·i·ous (sim′ē əs), *adj.* pertaining to or characteristic of apes or monkeys; simian. [< L *sīmi(a)* ape + -OUS] —**sim′i·ous·ness,** *n.*
sim·i·tar (sim′i tər), *n.* scimitar.
Sim·la (sim′lə), *n.* a city in and the capital of Himachal Pradesh, in N India: the summer capital of India. 42,600 (1961).
Sim·mel (zim′əl), *n.* **Ge·org** (gā ôrk′), 1858–1918, German sociologist and philosopher.
sim·mer (sim′ər), *v.i.* **1.** to cook or cook in a liquid at or just below the boiling point. **2.** to make a gentle murmuring sound, as liquids cooking just below the boiling point. **3.** to be in a state of subdued or restrained activity, development, excitement, anger, etc.: *The whole town was simmering with rumors.* —*v.t.* **4.** to keep (liquid) in a state approaching boiling. **5.** to cook in a liquid which is kept at or just below the boiling point. **6. simmer down, a.** to reduce in volume by simmering. **b.** *Slang.* to become calm or quiet: *We waited for the audience to simmer down.* —*n.* **7.** the state or process of simmering. [earlier *simber,* late ME *simper,* ? freq. of *sim, imit. of sound made in simmering; see -ER[6]] —**sim′mer·ing·ly,** *adv.*
—**Syn. 3.** See **boil**[1].
Simms (simz), *n.* **William Gilmore,** 1806–70, U.S. author.
sim′nel cake′ (sim′nəl), *Chiefly Brit.* any of several kinds of rich fruit cake covered with almond paste. [ME *simenel* < OF, unexplained alter. of L *simila* or Gk *semidālis* fine flour]
Sim·o·is (sim′ō is), *n.* (in the *Iliad*) a river god.
Sim·o·is·i·us (sim′ō is′ē əs), *n.* (in the *Iliad*) a Trojan youth killed by Telamonian Ajax in the Trojan War.
si·mo·le·on (sə mō′lē ən), *n. Slang.* a dollar. [?]
Si·mon (sī′mən), *n.* **1.** the original name of the apostle Peter. Cf. **Peter. 2.** a relative, perhaps a brother, of Jesus. Mark 6:3. **3.** a tanner of Joppa at whose house Peter resided. Acts 10:6. **4.** ("*Simon Magus*") the Samaritan sorcerer who was converted by the apostle Philip. Acts 8:9–24. **5. Sir John (Allse·brook)** (ôlz′-brŏŏk′), 1873–1954, British statesman and lawyer. **6.** a boy's given name, form of **Simeon.**
Si·mo·na (si mō′nə), *n.* a girl's given name.
Si·mon Boc·ca·ne·gra (sī′mən bō′kə nā′grə, -neg′rə), an opera (1857) by Giuseppe Verdi. Also, **Si·mo·ne Boc·ca·ne·gra** (*It.* sē mô′ne bôk′kä ne′grä).
si·mo·ni·ac (si mō′nē ak′), *n.* a person who practices simony. [ME < ML *simoniac(us)* (n., adj.). See SIMONY, -AC] —**si·mo·ni·a·cal** (sī′mə nī′ə kəl, sim′ə-), *adj.* —**si′mo·ni′a·cal·ly,** *adv.*
Si·mon·i·des (sī mon′i dēz′), *n.* 556?–468? B.C., Greek poet. Also called **Simon′ides of Ce′os** (sē′os).
si·mon·ize (sī′mə nīz′), *v.t.,* **-ized, -iz·ing.** to shine or polish to a high sheen, esp. with wax: *to simonize an automobile.* [formerly trademark]
Si′mon Le·gree′ (li grē′), **1.** the brutal slave dealer in *Uncle Tom's Cabin.* **2.** any harsh, merciless master: *Our math teacher was a Simon Legree if there ever was one.*
Si′mon Ma′gus, Simon (def. 4).
Si·mo·nov (sē′mo nof), *n.* **Kon·stan·tin M.** (kon-stän tēn′), born 1915, Russian journalist and playwright.
Si′mon Pe′ter, Peter (def. 1).
si·mon-pure (sī′mən pyŏŏr′), *adj.* real; genuine: *a simon-pure accent.* [short for *the real Simon Pure,* alluding to the victim of impersonation in Mrs. S. Centlivre's play *A Bold Stroke for a Wife* (1718)]
Si′mon says′, a children's game in which all players must imitate only those movements and commands of a leader that are preceded by the words "Simon says."
si·mo·ny (sī′mə nē, sim′ə-), *n.* **1.** the making of profit out of sacred things. **2.** the sin of buying or selling ecclesiastical preferments, benefices, etc. [ME *simonie* < eccl. L *simonia;* so called from SIMON MAGUS, who tried to purchase apostolic powers; see -Y[3]] —**si′mon·ist,** *n.*
si·moom (si mōōm′), *n.* a hot, suffocating, sand-laden wind of the deserts of Arabia, Syria, Africa, etc. Also, **si·moon** (si mōōn′). [< Ar *samūm,* akin to *samm* poisoning]

simp (simp), *n. Slang.* a fool; simpleton. [by shortening]

sim·pa·ti·co (sim pä′ti kō′, -pat′i-), *adj.* congenial; sympathetic as to personality, ideas, etc.: *I find our new neighbor simpatico in every respect.* [< It: lit., sympathetic, equiv. to *simpat(ia)* SYMPATHY + *-ico* -IC. Cf. Sp *simpático,* F *sympathique,* G *sympatisch*]

Sim·pel·i·us (sim pel′ē əs), *n.* an irregularly shaped, somewhat elliptical, walled plain in the fourth quadrant of the face of the moon: about 50 miles long and 42 miles wide.

sim·per (sim′pər), *v.i.* **1.** to smile in a silly, self-conscious way. —*v.t.* **2.** to say with a simper. —*n.* **3.** a silly, self-conscious smile. [akin to MD *zimperlijc,* dial. Dan *simper* affected, Dan *sippe* affected woman, orig. one who sips (see SIP), a way of drinking thought to be affected] —**sim′per·er,** *n.* —**sim′per·ing·ly,** *adv.*
—**Syn. 1, 3.** smirk.

sim·ple (sim′pəl), *adj.,* **-pler, -plest,** *n.* —*adj.* **1.** easy to understand, deal with, use, etc.: *a simple matter; simple tools.* **2.** plain; not elaborate or artificial: *a simple style.* **3.** unadorned; not ornate or luxurious: *a simple gown.* **4.** unaffected; unassuming; modest: *a simple manner.* **5.** not complicated: *a simple design.* **6.** single; not complex or compound. **7.** occurring or considered alone; mere; bare: *the simple truth; a simple fact.* **8.** free from deceit or guile; sincere; unconditional: *a frank, simple answer.* **9.** common or ordinary: *a simple soldier.* **10.** unpretentious; fundamental: *a simple way of life.* **11.** humble or lowly: *simple folk.* **12.** unimportant or insignificant. **13.** unlearned; ignorant. **14.** lacking mental acuteness or sense: *a dangerously simple way of thinking.* **15.** unsophisticated; naïve; credulous. **16.** *Chem.* **a.** composed of only one substance or element: *a simple substance.* **b.** not mixed. **17.** *Bot.* not divided into parts: *a simple leaf; a simple stem.* **18.** *Zool.* not compound: *a simple ascidian.* **19.** *Music.* single; uncompounded or without overtones: *simple tone.* **20.** *Math.* **a.** linear (def. 7). **b.** (of a group) having no normal subgroup except the group itself and the identity. **21.** *Optics.* (of a lens) having two optical surfaces only. **22.** *Engineering.* noting a complete truss opposing vertical loads directly, reacting to inclined loads in a manner capable of determination by fundamental static equations, and having the axes of all members converging on a single point at any panel point. —*n.* **23.** an ignorant, foolish, or gullible person. **24.** something simple, unmixed, or uncompounded. **25. simples,** *Textiles.* cords for controlling the warp threads in forming the shed on drawlooms. **26.** a person of humble origins; commoner. **27.** *Archaic.* an herb or other plant used for medicinal purposes: *country simples.* [ME < OF < L *simpl(us)* or *simplex.* See SIMPLEX] —**sim′ple·ness,** *n.*
—**Syn. 1.** clear, intelligible, understandable, unmistakable, lucid. **2.** plain, natural, unembellished, neat. **4.** unpretentious. **8.** artless, guileless, ingenuous. **10.** See **homely. 12.** trifling, trivial, nonessential, unnecessary. **13.** untutored, stupid.

sim′ple algebra′ic exten′sion, *Math.* a simple extension in which the specified element is a root of an algebraic equation in the given field. Cf. **simple transcendental extension.**

sim′ple arc′, *Math.* a curve that does not cross itself and has no points missing; a curve that can be put into one-to-one correspondence with the closed interval from 0 to 1. Also called **Jordan arc.**

sim′ple chan′cre, *Pathol.* chancroid.

sim′ple closed′ curve′, *Math.* a curve that is closed and that has no loops or points missing; a curve for which there exists a homeomorphism mapping it to a circle. Also called **Jordan curve.**

sim′ple enumera′tion, *Logic, Philos.* a procedure for arriving at empirical generalizations by haphazard accumulation of positive instances.

sim′ple exten′sion, *Math.* an extension field of a given field, obtained by forming all polynomials in a specified element with coefficients contained in the given field.

sim·ple-faced (sim′pəl fāst′), *adj.* **1.** having an ordinary or common face. **2.** having a face expressive of a simple or naïve mind.

sim′ple Fink′ truss′ (fingk). See **inverted king post truss.**

sim′ple frac′tion, a ratio of two integers.

sim′ple frac′ture, a fracture in which the bone does not pierce the skin. Also called **closed fracture.**

sim′ple fruit′, a fruit formed from one pistil.

sim′ple harmon′ic mo′tion, *Physics.* vibratory motion in a system in which the restoring force is proportional to the displacement from equilibrium. *Abbr.:* s.h.m.

sim·ple-heart·ed (sim′pəl här′tid), *adj.* free of deceit; artless; sincere. [late ME *symple herted*]

sim′ple hon′ors, *Auction Bridge.* three honors in the trump suit, or three aces in no-trump, held by a partnership.

sim′ple in′terest, interest payable only on the principal; interest that is not compounded.

sim′ple in′terval, *Music.* an interval of an octave or less.

sim′ple machine′, *Mech.* machine (def. 4b).

sim′ple major′ity, **1.** (of votes) less than half of the total cast but more than the minimum required to win, as when there are more than two candidates or choices. **2.** (of voters) less than half of the number registered. Cf. **absolute majority.**

sim′ple meas′ure. See **simple time.**

sim′ple mi′croscope, a microscope having a single lens.

sim·ple-mind·ed (sim′pəl mīn′did), *adj.* **1.** free of deceit or guile; artless or unsophisticated. **2.** lacking in mental acuteness or sense. **3.** mentally deficient. —**sim′ple-mind′ed·ly,** *adv.* —**sim′ple-mind′ed·ness,** *n.*

sim′ple pen′dulum, *Physics.* a hypothetical apparatus consisting of a point mass suspended from a weightless, frictionless thread whose length is constant, the motion of the body about the string being periodic and, if the angle of deviation from the original equilibrium position is small, representing simple harmonic motion (distinguished from *physical pendulum*).

sim′ple pole′, *Math.* a pole of order 1 of a function of a complex variable.

sim′ple sen′tence, a sentence having only one clause, as *I saw him the day before yesterday.* Cf. **complex sentence, compound-complex sentence, compound sentence.**

Sim′ple Si′mon, a simpleton: *He's a Simple Simon about politics.* [after the nursery rhyme character]

sim′ple syr′up, **1.** a thick, sweet liquid, usually prepared from sugar and water and used chiefly as a base for soda fountain flavors. **2.** *Pharm.* syrup (def. 36).

sim′ple time′, *Music.* rhythm characterized by two or three beats or pulses to a measure. Also called **simple measure.**

sim·ple·ton (sim′pəl tən), *n.* an ignorant, foolish, or silly person. [SIMPLE + -TON]

sim′ple transcenden′tal exten′sion, *Math.* a simple extension in which the specified element is not a root of any algebraic equation in the given field. Cf. **simple algebraic extension.**

sim′ple vow′, *Rom. Cath. Ch.* a temporary or perpetual public vow taken by a religious, under which property may be retained and marriage, though held to be illicit, is valid under canon law. Cf. **solemn vow.**

sim·plex (sim′pleks), *adj.* **1.** simple; consisting of or characterized by a single element, action, or the like: *a simplex movement.* **2.** pertaining to or noting a telegraphic or telephonic system in which communication between two stations takes place in only one direction at a time. **3.** *Math.* a basic geometric element in a Euclidean space, being a line segment in one dimension, a triangle in two dimensions, a tetrahedron in three dimensions, and so on: used in topology and linear programming. [< L: lit., one-fold, equiv. to *sim-* one + *plec-* PLY[2] + *-s* nom. sing. ending]

sim′plex meth′od, *Math.* a numerical method for solving problems in linear programming.

sim·pli·ci·den·tate (sim′pli si den′tāt), *adj.* belonging or pertaining to the *Simplicidentata,* formerly regarded as a suborder or division of rodents having only one pair of upper incisor teeth. [back formation from NL *Simplicidentāta* group-name, equiv. to L *simplici-* (s. of *simplex*) SIMPLEX + *dentata,* neut. pl. of *dentātus* DENTATE]

sim·plic·i·ty (sim plis′i tē), *n., pl.* **-ties. 1.** the state, quality, or an instance of being simple. **2.** freedom from complexity, intricacy, or division into parts: *an organism of great simplicity.* **3.** absence of luxury, pretentiousness, ornament, etc.; plainness: *Though wealthy, they lived a life of simplicity.* **4.** freedom from deceit or guile; sincerity; artlessness; naturalness: *a simplicity of manner.* **5.** lack of mental acuteness or shrewdness: *Politics is not a field for simplicity about human nature.* [ME *simplicite* < L *simplicitās* simpleness, equiv. to *simplici-* (s. of *simplex*) SIMPLEX + *-tās* -TY[2]]

Sim·pli·ci·us (sim plish′ē əs), *n.* **Saint,** died A.D. 483, pope 468–483.

sim·pli·fy (sim′plə fī′), *v.t.,* **-fied, -fy·ing.** to make less complex or complicated; make plainer or easier: *to simplify a problem.* [< F *simplifi(er)* < ML *simplificāre* to make simple, equiv. to L *simpli-* (comb. form of *simplus* SIMPLE) + *-ficāre* -FY] —**sim′pli·fi·ca′tion,** *n.* —**sim′pli·fi·ca′tive,** *adj.* —**sim′pli·fi′er, sim′pli·fi·ca′tor,** *n.*

sim·plism (sim′pliz əm), *n.* exaggerated simplicity, as in concentrating on a single aspect or factor of a problem or situation while disregarding all more complicated aspects or factors; oversimplification: *The senator revealed an astonishing simplism in dealing with international issues.* [SIMPLE + -ISM]

sim·plis·tic (sim plis′tik), *adj.* characterized by extreme simplification; oversimplified: *He tended to reduce political problems to a simplistic notion of good and bad.* [SIMPLE + -ISTIC] —**sim·plis′ti·cal·ly,** *adv.*

Sim·plon (sim′plon; *Fr.* SAN plôN′), *n.* **1.** a mountain pass in S Switzerland, in the Lepontine Alps: crossed by a road constructed by Napoleon. 6592 ft. high. **2.** a tunnel between Switzerland and Italy, NE of the Simplon Pass: longest tunnel in the world. 12¼ mi. long.

sim·ply (sim′plē), *adv.* **1.** in a simple manner; clearly and easily. **2.** plainly; unaffectedly. **3.** sincerely; artlessly: *to speak simply as a child.* **4.** merely; only: *It is simply a cold.* **5.** unwisely; foolishly: *If you behave simply toward him, you're bound to be betrayed.* **6.** wholly; absolutely: *simply irresistible.* [ME *simpleliche.* See SIMPLE, -LY]

sim·ply-con·nect·ed (sim′plē kə nek′tid), *adj. Math.* **1.** (of a set or domain) having a connected complement. **2.** (of a set or domain, usually in space) having the property that every simple closed curve in the set can be shrunk to a point without intersecting the boundary of the set.

sim′ply or′dered set′, *Math.* See **totally ordered set.**

Simp′son's rule′ (simp′sənz), *Math.* a method for approximating the value of a definite integral by approximating, with parabolic arcs, the area under the curve defined by the integrand. [named after Thomas *Simpson* (1710–61), English mathematician]

sim·pu·lum (sim′pyŏŏ ləm), *n., pl.* **-la** (-lə). an ancient dipper having the rim of the bowl at right angles to the handle. [< L: lit., small ladle]

Sims (simz), *n.* **William Sow·den** (soud′ən), 1858–1936, U.S. admiral, born in Canada.

Sims·bur·y (simz′ber′ē, -bə rē), *n.* a town in central Connecticut. 2745 (1960).

sim·ul (sim′əl), *adv.* (in prescriptions) together. [< L]

sim·u·la·cre (sim′yə lā′kər), *n. Archaic.* simulacrum. [ME < MF < L *simulācr(um)* SIMULACRUM] —**sim·u·la·cral** (sim′yə lā′krəl), *adj.*

sim·u·la·crum (sim′yə lā′krəm), *n., pl.* **-cra** (-krə). **1.** a slight, unreal, or superficial likeness or semblance. **2.** an effigy, image, or representation: *a simulacrum of Aphrodite.* [< L: likeness, image, equiv. to *simulā(re)* (to) SIMULATE + *-crum* instrumental suffix]

sim·u·lant (sim′yə lənt), *adj.* **1.** simulating; feigning; imitating. **2.** *Biol.* similar in form or position (usually fol. by *of*): *stamens simulant of petals.* —*n.* **3.** one who or that which simulates. [< L *simulant-* (s. of *simulāns*) imitating (prp. of *simulāre*). See SIMULATE, -ANT]

sim·u·lar (sim′yə lər), *Archaic.* —*n.* **1.** one who or that which simulates; pretender. —*adj.* **2.** simulated; false; counterfeit. **3.** imitative; simulative. [< L *simul(āre)* (to) SIMULATE + -AR[1]]

sim·u·late (*v.* sim′yə lāt′; *adj.* sim′yə lit, -lāt′), *v.,* **-lat·ed, -lat·ing,** *adj.* —*v.t.* **1.** to make a pretense of; feign: *to simulate knowledge.* **2.** to assume or have the appearance or characteristics of: *He simulated the manners of the rich.* —*adj.* **3.** *Archaic.* simulated. [< L *simulāt(us)* imitated (ptp. of *simulāre*), equiv. to *simul-* (var. of *simil-*; see SIMILAR) + *-ātus* -ATE[1]] —**sim′u·la′tive, sim·u·la·to·ry** (sim′yə lə tôr′ē, -tōr′ē), *adj.* —**sim′u·la′tive·ly,** *adv.*
—**Syn. 1.** pretend, counterfeit. **2.** affect.

sim·u·la·tion (sim′yə lā′shən), *n.* **1.** the act or process of pretending; feigning. **2.** an assumption or imitation of a particular appearance or form; counterfeit; sham. **3.** *Psychiatry.* a conscious attempt to feign some mental or physical disorder to escape punishment or to gain a desired objective. [ME *simulacion* < L *simulātiōn-* (s. of *simulātiō*) a pretense. See SIMULATE, -ION]

sim·u·la·tor (sim′yə lā′tər), *n.* **1.** one who or that which simulates. **2.** a machine for simulating certain environmental and other conditions for purposes of training or experimentation: *a flight simulator.* [< L: imitator, counterfeiter. See SIMULATE, -OR[2]]

si·mul·cast (sī′məl kast′, -käst′, sim′əl-), *n., v.,* **-cast, -cast·ing.** —*n.* **1.** a program broadcast simultaneously on radio and television. —*v.t.* **2.** to broadcast (a program) simultaneously on radio and television. [SIMUL(TANEOUS + BROAD)CAST]

si·mul·ta·ne·ous (sī′məl tā′nē əs, sim′əl-), *adj.* existing, occurring, or operating at the same time; concurrent: *simultaneous movements.* [< ML *simult(im)* at the same time (L *simul* together + *-tim* adv. suffix) + (CONTEMPOR)ANEOUS] —**si′mul·ta′ne·ous·ly,** *adv.* —**si′mul·ta′ne·ous·ness, si·mul·ta·ne·i·ty** (sī′məl tə nē′i tē, sim′əl-), *n.*
—**Syn.** synchronous, coincident.

simulta′neous equa′tions, *Algebra.* a set of two or more equations, each containing two or more variables whose values can simultaneously satisfy both or all the equations in the set, the number of variables being equal to or less than the number of equations in the set.

sin[1] (sin), *n., v.,* **sinned, sin·ning.** —*n.* **1.** transgression of divine law: *the sin of Adam.* **2.** any act regarded as such a transgression, esp. a willful or deliberate violation of some religious or moral principle. **3.** any serious transgression, offense, or fault: *It's a sin to waste time.* —*v.i.* **4.** to commit a sinful act. **5.** to offend against a principle, standard, etc. —*v.t.* **6.** to commit or perform sinfully: *He sinned his crimes without compunction.* **7.** to bring, drive, etc., by sinning: *He sinned his soul to perdition.* [ME; OE *syn(n)*; akin to G, D *sünde,* Icel *synd* sin, L *sons* guilty] —**sin′like′,** *adj.* —**sin′ning·ly,** *adv.* —**sin′ning·ness,** *n.*
—**Syn. 1.** trespass, violation. **2.** wrong, wickedness. **3.** See **crime. 4.** transgress, trespass.

sin[2] (sēn), *n.* **1.** the 21st letter of the Hebrew alphabet. **2.** the consonant sound represented by this letter. [< Heb]

sin[3] (sin), *adv., prep., conj. Scot. and North Eng.* since. [ME, var. of *sithen,* OE *siththan* SITH]

sin[4] (sin, sen), *n. Scot.* sun.

sīn (sēn), *n.* the 12th letter of the Arabic alphabet. [< Ar]

Sin (sēn), *n.* the Akkadian god of the moon: the counterpart of the Sumerian Nanna.

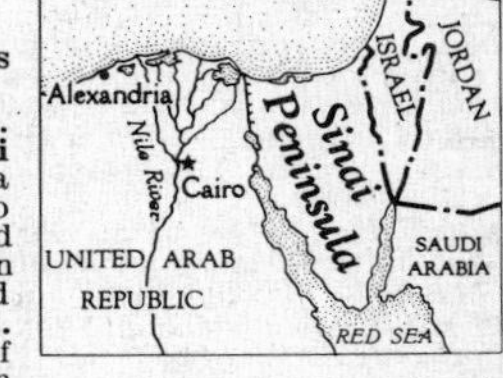

sin, *Math.* sine.

Si·na (sē′nə), *n.* a girl's given name.

Si·nai (sī′nī, sī′nē ī′), *n.* **1.** Also called **Si′nai Penin′sula.** a peninsula in the NE United Arab Republic, at the N end of the Red Sea between the Gulfs of Suez and Aqaba. 230 mi. long. **2. Mount,** the mountain, of uncertain identity, on which Moses received the law. Ex. 19. —**Si·na·it·ic** (sī′nē it′ik), **Si·na·ic** (si nā′ik), *adj.*

Si·nai·ti·cus (sī nī′tə kəs, sī′nē it′ə-), *n.* the Greek uncial codex, dating from the 4th century A.D., that contains the New Testament and much of the Old Testament. Cf. **codex.** [< L: of SINAI (see -ITE[1], -IC); so called from its first known owner, a monastery on the Sinai peninsula]

si·nal (sīn′əl), *adj.* of, pertaining to, or involving a sinus. [SIN(US) + -AL[1]]

sin·al·bin (si nal′bin), *n. Chem.* a white, crystalline, water-soluble glucoside, $C_{30}H_{42}N_2O_{15}S_2$, found in the seeds of the white mustard. [< L *sin(āpi)* mustard (< Gk) + *alb(um)* white (see ALB) + -IN[2]]

Si·na·lo·a (sēn′əlō′ə, sin′-; *Sp.* sē′nä lô′ä), *n.* a state in W Mexico, bordering on the Gulf of California. 838,404 (1960); 22,582 sq. mi. *Cap.:* Culiacán.

Si·nan (si nän′), *n.* 1489?–1587, Turkish architect, esp. of mosques.

sin·a·pine (sin′ə pīn′, -pin), *n. Chem.* an alkaloid, $C_{16}H_{25}NO_6$, found in the seeds of the black mustard. [< L *sināp(is)* mustard (< Gk) + -INE[2]]

sin·a·pism (sin′ə piz′əm), *n. Med.* See **mustard plaster.** [< medical L *sināpism(us)* < Gk *sināpismós* application of mustard, equiv. to *sināp(izein)* (to) apply mustard + *-ismos* -ISM]

Sin·ar·quist (sin′är kist, -kwist), *n.* a member or advocate of an ultrareactionary, semifascist movement organized in Mexico about 1937. [< AmerSp *sinarquist(a),* equiv. to *sin* (< L *sine* without) + *arquista;* see ANARCHIST] —**Sin′ar·quism,** *n.* —**Sin′ar·quis′tic,** *adj.*

Si·nar·quis·ta (sē′när kēs′tä; *Eng.* sin′är kēs′tə), *n., pl.* **-tas** (-täs; *Eng.* -təz). *Spanish.* Sinarquist.

Si·nas (sī′nəs), *n.* a crater in the first quadrant of the face of the moon: about 7 miles in diameter.

Si·na·tra (si nä′trə), *n.* **Frank,** born 1915, U.S. actor and singer.

Sin·bad (sin′bad), *n.* See **Sindbad the Sailor.**

since (sins), *adv.* **1.** from then till now (often prec. by *ever*): *He was elected in 1950 and has been chairman ever since.* **2.** between a particular past time and the present; subsequently: *He at first refused, but has since consented.* **3.** ago; before now: *long since.* **—***prep.* **4.** continuously from or counting from: *It has been warm since noon.* **5.** between a past time or event and the present: *There have been many changes since the war.* **—***conj.* **6.** in the period following the time when: *He has written once since he left.* **7.** continuously from or counting from the time when: *He has been busy since he came.* **8.** because; inasmuch as: *Since you're already here, you might as well stay.* [late ME *syn(ne)s,* ME *sithenes,* equiv. to *sithen* (OE *siththan* since, orig. *sīth thām* after that; see SITH, THE[2]) + *-es* -s[1]]
—Syn. 8. See **because.**

sin·cere (sin sēr′), *adj.*, **-cer·er, -cer·est. 1.** free from deceit, hypocrisy, or falseness; earnest: *a sincere letter of apology.* **2.** genuine; real: *a sincere effort to improve; a sincere friend.* **3.** *Archaic.* pure; unmixed; unadulterated. **4.** *Obs.* sound; unimpaired. [< L *sincēr(us)* pure, clean, untainted] **—sin·cere′ly,** *adv.* **—sin·cere′ness,** *n.*
—Syn. 1. frank, candid, honest, open, guileless; unaffected. See **earnest. —Ant.** false.

sin·cer·i·ty (sin ser′i tē), *n., pl.* **-ties.** freedom from deceit, hypocrisy, or duplicity; earnestness: *His sincerity was beyond question.* [< L *sincēritās.* See SINCERE, -ITY]
—Syn. truth, candor, frankness. See **honor. —Ant.** duplicity.

sin·ci·put (sin′sə put′), *n., pl.* **sin·ci·puts, sin·cip·i·ta** (sin sip′i tə). *Anat.* **1.** the forepart of the skull. **2.** the upper part of the skull. [< L: lit., half-head, equiv. to *sin-* (var. of *sēmi-* SEMI-) + *-ciput,* var. of *caput* head] **—sin·cip·i·tal** (sin sip′i tᵊl), *adj.*

Sin·clair (sin klâr′), *n.* **1. May,** 1865?–1946, British novelist. **2. Up·ton (Beall)** (up′tən bel), 1878–1968, U.S. novelist, socialist, and reformer. **3.** a boy's given name.

Sind (sind), *n.* a former province of Pakistan, in the lower Indus valley; now part of West Pakistan. 48,136 sq. mi. *Cap.:* Karachi.

Sind′bad the Sail′or (sind′bad, sin′-), (in the *Arabian Nights' Entertainments*) a wealthy citizen of Baghdad who relates the adventures of his seven wonderful voyages. Also called **Sinbad.**

Sin·dhi (sin′dē), *n.* a modern Indic language of the lower Indus valley. [< Ar *sindī* of SIND]

sin·don (sin′dən), *n.* *Archaic.* cloth of fine linen or silk, used esp. for shrouds. [late ME < L < Gk *sindṓn*]

sine (sīn), *n.* **1.** *Trig.* **a.** (in a right triangle) the ratio of the side opposite a given angle to the hypotenuse. **b.** (of an angle) a trigonometric function equal to the ratio of the ordinate of the end point of the arc to the radius vector of this end point, the origin being at the center of the circle on which the arc lies and the initial point of the arc being on the x-axis. *Abbr.:* sin **2.** (originally) a perpendicular line drawn from one extremity of an arc of a circle to the diameter which passes through its other extremity. [< L *sin(us)* a curve, fold, pocket; NL *sine* rendering the synonymous Ar *jaib* for *jiba* < Skt *jīva* chord of an arc, lit., bowstring]

BD, Sine of arc AB; ratio of BD to CB, sine of angle ACB

si·ne·cure (sī′nə kyŏŏr′, sin′ə-), *n.* **1.** an office or position requiring little or no work, esp. one yielding profitable returns: *The position of poet laureate is now a sinecure.* **2.** an ecclesiastical benefice without cure of souls. [< L phrase *(beneficium) sine cūrā* (distinction) without care; see CURE] **—si′ne·cure·ship′,** *n.* **—si′ne·cur·ism,** *n.* **—si′ne·cur′ist,** *n.*

sine′ curve′, *Math.* a curve described by the equation $y = \sin x$, the ordinate being equal to the sine of the abscissa.

si·ne di·e (sī′ne dē′e; *Eng.* sī′nē dī′ē), *Latin.* without fixing a day for future action or meeting: *The assembly adjourned* sine die.

si·ne pro·le (sī′nē prō′lē), *Law.* without offspring or progeny: *to die sine prole.* [< L]

si·ne qua non (si′ne kwä nōn′; *Eng.* sī′nē kwā non′), *Latin.* something essential; an indispensable condition: *Her presence was the* sine qua non *of every social event.* [lit., without which not]

sin·ew (sin′yo͞o), *n.* **1.** a tendon. **2.** Often, **sinews.** the source of strength, power, or vigor: *the sinews of the nation.* **3.** strength; power; resilience: *a man of great moral sinew.* **—***v.t.* **4.** to furnish with sinews; strengthen, as by sinews. [ME; OE *sinu* (nom.), *sinuwe* (gen.); c. D *zenuw,* G *Sehne,* Icel *sin;* akin to Skt *snāva*] **—sin′ew·less,** *adj.*

sine′ wave′, *Physics.* a periodic oscillation, as a sound wave, having the same geometric representation as a sine function.

sin·ew·y (sin′yo͞o ē), *adj.* **1.** having strong sinews: *a sinewy back.* **2.** of or like sinews; tough, firm, braided, or resilient: *a sinewy rope.* **3.** having conspicuous sinews; stringy: *tough, sinewy meat.* **4.** vigorous or forceful, as language, style, etc.: *a sinewy argument.* [ME; see SINEW, -Y[1]] **—sin′ew·i·ness,** *n.*

Sin·fiot·li (sin′fyôt′lē), *n.* (in the *Volsunga Saga*) the son of Signy by her brother Sigmund. Also, **Sin′fjot′li.**

sin·fo·ni·a (sin′fō nē′ə; *It.* sēn′fô nē′ä), *n., pl.* **-ni·e** (-nē′ā; *It.* -nē′e). *Music.* a symphony. [< It]

sin·fo·niet·ta (sin′fən yet′ə, -fōn-), *n.* **1.** a short symphony. **2.** a small symphony orchestra, often comprised solely of stringed instruments. **3.** a symphony for fewer than the usual number of instruments. [< It; dim. of SINFONIA]

sin·ful (sin′fəl), *adj.* characterized by or full of sin; wicked: *a sinful life.* [ME; OE *synfull.* See SIN[1], -FUL] **—sin′ful·ly,** *adv.* **—sin′ful·ness,** *n.*
—Syn. iniquitous, depraved, evil, immoral, corrupt.

sing (sing), *v.*, **sang** or, often, **sung; sung; sing·ing;** *n.* **—***v.i.* **1.** to utter words or sounds in succession with musical modulations of the voice. **2.** to perform a song or voice composition, as a professional singer: *She promised to sing for us.* **3.** to produce melodious sounds, as certain birds, insects, etc.: *The crickets sang in the bushes.* **4.** to compose poetry: *Keats sang briefly but gloriously.* **5.** to tell about or praise someone or something in verse or song: *He sang of the warrior's prowess in battle.* **6.** to admit of being sung, as verses: *This lyric sings well.* **7.** to give out a continuous ringing, whistling, murmuring, or other sound of musical quality, as a teakettle, a brook, etc. **8.** to make a short whistling, ringing, or whizzing sound: *The bullet sang past his ear.* **9.** (of an electrical amplifying system) to produce an undesired self-sustained oscillation. **10.** to have the sensation of a ringing or humming sound, as the ears. **11.** *Slang.* to confess or act as an informer; squeal. **—***v.t.* **12.** to utter with musical modulations of the voice, as a song. **13.** to escort or accompany with singing. **14.** to proclaim enthusiastically. **15.** to bring, send, put, etc., with or by singing: *She sang the baby to sleep.* **16.** to chant or intone: *to sing mass.* **17.** to tell or praise in verse or song. **18. sing out,** *Informal.* to call in a loud voice; shout: *They lost their way in the passages of the cavern and sang out for help.* **—***n.* **19.** the act or performance of singing. **20.** a gathering or meeting of persons for the purpose of singing: *a community sing.* **21.** a singing, ringing, or whistling sound, as of a bullet. [ME; OE *sing(an);* c. D *zingen,* G *singen,* Icel *syngva,* Goth *siggwan*] **—sing′a·bil′i·ty,** *n.* **—sing′a·ble·ness,** *n.* **—sing′a·ble,** *adj.* **—sing′ing·ly,** *adv.*

sing., singular.

Si·ngan (*Chin.* sē′ngän′), *n.* Sian.

Sin·ga·pore (sing′gə pōr′, -pôr′, sing′ə-), *n.* **1.** an island in the South China Sea, S of the Malay Peninsula: a British crown colony 1946–59; a member of the federation of Malaysia 1963–65; became a self-governing state within the British Commonwealth 1959. 1,820,000 (est. 1964); 220 sq. mi. **2.** a seaport on this island: naval base. 912,343 (1957).

singe (sinj), *v.*, **singed, singe·ing,** *n.* **—***v.t.* **1.** to burn superficially or slightly; scorch. **2.** to burn the ends, projections, nap, or the like, of (hair, cloth, etc.). **3.** to subject (the carcass of an animal or bird) to flame in order to remove hair, bristles, feathers, etc. **—***n.* **4.** a superficial burn. **5.** the act of singeing. [ME *senge,* OE *sencgan;* c. G *sengen,* D *zengen;* akin to Icel *sangr* singed, burnt] **—singe′ing·ly,** *adv.*
—Syn. 1. char. See **burn**[1].

sing·er[1] (sing′ər), *n.* **1.** one who sings, esp. a trained or professional vocalist. **2.** a poet. **3.** a singing bird. [ME; see SING, -ER[1]]

sing·er[2] (sin′jər), *n.* one who or that which singes. [SINGE + -ER[1]]

Sing·er (sing′ər), *n.* **Isaac Mer·rit** (mer′it), 1811–75, U.S. inventor.

Singh., Singhalese.

Sin·gha·lese (sing′gə lēz′, -lēs′), *adj., n., pl.* **-lese.** **—***adj.* **1.** pertaining to Ceylon, its native people, or their language. **—***n.* **2.** a member of the Singhalese people. **3.** an Indic language that is the language of most of Ceylon, including Colombo. Also, **Sinhalese.** [var. of *Sinhalese* < Skt *Sinhal(a)* Ceylon + -ESE]

sing·ing·fish (sing′ing fish′), *n., pl.* (*esp. collectively*) **-fish,** (*esp. referring to two or more kinds or species*) **-fish·es.** midshipman (def. 3). [SINGING + FISH; so called because of the humming sound it produces with its air bladder]

sin·gle (sing′gəl), *adj., v.*, **-gled, -gling,** *n., adv.* **—***adj.* **1.** one only; only one in number; unique; sole: *a single example.* **2.** of, pertaining to, or suitable for one person only: *a single room; a single bed.* **3.** lone; solitary: *He was the single survivor.* **4.** unmarried: *a single man.* **5.** pertaining to the unmarried state: *A single life has its advantages.* **6.** of one against one, as combat or fight. **7.** consisting of only one part, element, or member: *a single lens.* **8.** sincere; honest; undivided: *single devotion.* **9.** separate; individual: *Every single one of you must do your best.* **10.** uniform; applicable to all: *A single safety code is used by the electrical appliance manufacturers.* **11.** having only one set of petals, as a flower. **12.** *Brit.* of only moderate strength or body, as ale, beer, etc. **13.** (of the eye) seeing rightly. **—***v.t.* **14.** to pick or choose out from others (usually fol. by *out*): *to single out a fact for special mention.* **15.** *Baseball.* **a.** to cause the advance of (a base runner) by a one-base hit. **b.** to cause (a run) to be scored by a one-base hit (often fol. by *in*). **—***v.i.* **16.** *Baseball.* to make a one-base hit. **17.** *Obs.* (of a horse) to go at single-foot. **—***n.* **18.** one person or thing; a single one. **19.** an accommodation designed or suitable for one person only, as a hotel room, table at a restaurant, berth, cabin on a ship, etc.: *His parents checked into the double room and he took the single.* **20.** an unoccupied or unsold seat in a theater, the seats on each side of which are occupied or sold: *Only singles were left, so my brother and I couldn't sit next to each other.* **21.** a ticket for such a seat. **22.** *Railroads. Brit.* **a.** a one-way ticket. **b.** a steam locomotive having one driving wheel on each side. **23.** *Baseball.* See **one-base hit. 24. singles,** (*construed as sing.*) a match with one player on each side. **25.** *Golf.* twosome (def. 4). **26.** *Cricket.* a hit for which one run is scored. **27.** *Informal.* a one-dollar bill: *a five and five singles.* **28.** a phonograph record, esp. one revolving at 78 or 45 r.p.m., having only one musical piece on each side. **29.** Often, **singles.** *Textiles.* **a.** reeled or spun silk that may or may not be thrown. **b.** a one-ply yarn of any fiber that has been drawn and twisted. **—***adv.* **30.** alone; singly: *Most of the guests came single.* [late ME; ME *sengle* < MF < L *singul(us);* see SIMPLE]
—Syn. 1. distinct, particular. **3.** isolated. **4.** unwed. **14.** select. **18.** individual.

sin·gle-act·ing (sing′gəl ak′ting), *adj.* (of a reciprocating engine, pump, etc.) having pistons accomplishing work only in one direction. Cf. **double-acting** (def. 1).

sin·gle-ac·tion (sing′gəl ak′shən), *adj.* (of a firearm) requiring the cocking of the hammer before firing each shot: *a single-action revolver.*

sin·gle-bank (sing′gəl bangk′), *v.t.* *Naut.* to have one man pull (each of a number of oars).

sin·gle-bar·rel (sing′gəl bar′əl), *n.* a gun having one barrel, esp. a shotgun. **—sin′gle-bar′reled;** *esp. Brit.,* **sin′gle-bar′relled,** *adj.*

sin′gle block′, *Mach.* a block having one sheave or pulley.

sin′gle bond′, *Chem.* a chemical linkage consisting of one covalent bond between two atoms of a molecule, represented in chemical formulas by one line or two vertical dots, as *C–H* or *C:H.*

sin·gle-breast·ed (sing′gəl bres′tid), *adj.* (of a garment, esp. a coat or jacket) having a single button or row of buttons in front for the center closing. Cf. **double-breasted.**

sin′gle com′bat, combat between two persons.

sin·gle-cross (sing′gəl krôs′, -kros′), *n.* *Genetics.* a cross between two inbred lines.

sin′gle cut′, *Jewelry.* a simple form of brilliant cut, having eight facets above and eight facets below the girdle, as well as the table, and usually a culet. Also called **eight cut, half-brilliant cut, Old English cut.**

sin·gle-cut (sing′gəl kut′), *adj.* noting a file having a series of parallel cutting ridges in one direction only. Cf. **double-cut.**

sin·gle-end·ed (sing′gəl en′did), *adj.* **1.** (of a boiler) fired from one end only. **2.** *Elect.* (of a circuit or transmission line) unbalanced, as when one part of a circuit is grounded.

sin′gle en′try, *Bookkeeping.* **1.** an item noted only once. **2.** a simple accounting system noting only amounts owed by and due to a business. Cf. **double entry. —sin′gle-en′try,** *adj.*

sin′gle file′, a line of persons or things arranged one behind the other; Indian file.

sin·gle-foot (sing′gəl fo͝ot′), *n.* **1.** rack[3] (def. 1). **—***v.i.* **2.** (of a horse) to go at a rack.

sin·gle-hand·ed (sing′gəl han′did), *adj.* **1.** accomplished or done by one person alone; unaided: *a single-handed victory; single-handed sailing.* **2.** having, using, or requiring the use of only one hand or one person. **—***adv.* **3.** by oneself; alone; without aid: *He built the garage single-handed.* **—sin′gle-hand′ed·ness,** *n.*

sin·gle-hand·ed·ly (sing′gəl han′did lē), *adv.* in a single-handed manner; single-handed.

sin·gle-heart·ed (sing′gəl här′tid), *adj.* sincere and undivided in feeling or spirit; dedicated; not reflecting mixed emotions: *He was single-hearted in his patriotism.* **—sin′gle-heart′ed·ly,** *adv.* **—sin′gle-heart′ed·ness,** *n.*

sin·gle-hung (sing′gəl hung′), *adj.* (of a window) having two sashes only one of which is movable.

sin′gle-lens re′flex cam′era (sing′gəl lenz′). See under **reflex camera.**

sin′gle man′, *Checkers.* an individual checker restricted to forward moves, as contrasted with a king.

sin·gle-mind·ed (sing′gəl mīn′did), *adj.* **1.** having or showing a single aim or purpose: *a single-minded program.* **2.** dedicated; steadfast: *He was single-minded in his concern for truth.* **—sin′gle-mind′ed·ly,** *adv.* **—sin′gle-mind′ed·ness,** *n.*

sin′gle-name pa′per (sing′gəl nām′), *Banking.* commercial paper bearing only the signature of the maker.

sin·gle·ness (sing′gəl nis), *n.* the state or quality of being single. [SINGLE + -NESS]

sin·gle-phase (sing′gəl fāz′), *adj.* *Elect.* noting or pertaining to a circuit having an alternating current with one phase or with phases differing by 180°.

sin′gle pur′chase, *Mach., Naut.* any of various tackles employing one single running block.

sin′gle quotes′, (one pair of single quotation marks, written as (' ') and used esp. for a quotation within another quotation): *He said, "I told you to say 'Open, sesame' when you want to enter the mountain."*

sin′gle rhyme′, a rhyme of monosyllables, as in *heart, part.*

sin′gle sculls′, a race for sculls rowed by one oarsman using a pair of oars. Cf. **double sculls.**

sin′gle shell′. See **racing skiff.**

sin·gle-shot (sing′gəl shot′), *adj.* (of a firearm) requiring loading before each shot; not having or using a cartridge magazine.

sin·gle-space (sing′gəl spās′), *v.*, **-spaced, -spac·ing. —***v.t.* **1.** to type (copy) on each line space. **—***v.i.* **2.** to type copy leaving no blank spaces between lines.

sin′gle Span′ish bur′ton, a tackle having a runner as well as the fall supporting the load, the runner being rove through the standing block and supporting the block through which the fall is rove, giving a mechanical advantage of three, neglecting friction. See diag. under **tackle.**

sin′gle stand′ard, 1. a single set of principles or rules applying to everyone, as a single moral code applying to both men and women, esp. in sexual behavior. Cf. **double standard. 2.** monometallism.

sin·gle·stick (sing′gəl stik′), *n.* **1.** a short, heavy stick. **2.** (formerly) **a.** a wooden stick held in one hand, used instead of a sword in fencing. **b.** fencing with such a stick. [SINGLE + STICK[1]]

sin·gle·stick·er (sing′gəl stik′ər), *n.* *Informal.* a vessel, esp. a sloop or cutter, having one mast. [SINGLE + STICK[1] + -ER[1]]

sin·glet (sing′glit), *n.* *Chiefly Brit.* a man's undershirt or jersey. [SINGLE + -ET]

sin′gle tape′. See under **magnetic tape.**

sin′gle tax′, *Econ.* a tax, as on land, which constitutes the sole source of public revenue. **—sin′gle-tax′,** *adj.*

sin·gle·ton (sing′gəl tən), *n.* **1.** something occurring singly. **2.** *Cards.* a card that is the only one of a suit in a hand. **3.** *Math.* a set consisting of one given element. [SINGLE + -TON]

sin·gle-track (sing′gəl trak′), *adj.* **1.** (of a railroad or section of a railroad's route) having but one set of tracks, so that trains going in opposite directions must be scheduled to meet only at points where there are sidings. **2.** having a narrow scope; one-track: *He has a single-track mind.*

sin·gle·tree (sing′gəl trē′), *n.* whiffletree. [var. of SWINGLETREE]

sin·gle-val·ued (siŋg′gəl val′yo͞od), *adj. Math.* (of a function) having the property that each element in the domain has corresponding to it exactly one element in the range. Cf. **many-valued.**

sin′gle whip′. See under **whip** (def. 26).

sin′gle wick′et, a rare form of cricket in which only one wicket is used.

sin′gle wing′back forma′tion, *Football.* an offensive formation in which the wingback lines up outside of and about one yard behind an end, the quarterback lines up even with the wingback about midway between the same end and the center, the fullback is three or four yards behind the middle of the line, and the tailback lines up one yard behind the fullback on the other side of the line from the wingback and quarterback. Also called **sin′gle wing′.** Cf. **double wingback formation.**

sin·gly (siŋg′glē), *adv.* **1.** apart from others; separately. **2.** one at a time; as single units. **3.** single-handed; alone. [ME *senglely.* See SINGLE, -LY]

Sing Sing (siŋg′ siŋg′), **1.** the state prison at Ossining, New York. **2.** former name of **Ossining.**

sing·song (siŋg′sôŋg′, -soŋg′), *n.* **1.** verse, or a piece of verse, of a jingling or monotonous character. **2.** monotonous rhythmical cadence, tone, or sound. **3.** *Brit.* an unrehearsed singing of well-known songs by an audience or other informal, untrained group; a community sing. —*adj.* **4.** monotonous in rhythm. [SING + SONG]

sing·spiel (siŋg′spēl′; *Ger.* ziŋg′shpēl′), *n.* a German opera, esp. of the 18th century, using spoken dialogue and resembling ballad opera. [< G: lit., sing-speech]

sin·gu·lar (siŋg′gyə lər), *adj.* **1.** extraordinary; remarkable; exceptional: *a singular success.* **2.** unusual or strange; odd; different: *singular behavior.* **3.** being the only one of its kind; unique: *a singular example.* **4.** separate; individual. **5.** *Gram.* noting or pertaining to a member of the category of number found in many languages that indicates that a word form has one referent or denotes one person, place, thing, or instance, as English *man* and *thing,* which are singular nouns, or *goes,* a singular form of the verb *go.* Cf. **dual** (def. 3), **plural** (def. 4). **6.** *Logic.* **a.** of or pertaining to something individual, specific, or not general. **b.** (of a proposition) containing no quantifiers, as "Socrates was mortal." **7.** *Math.* **a.** of or pertaining to a linear transformation from a vector space to itself which is not one-to-one. **b.** of or pertaining to a matrix having a determinant equal to zero. **8.** *Obs.* personal; private. **9.** *Obs.* single. —*n. Gram.* **10.** the singular number. **11.** a form in the singular. [ME < L *singulār(is).* See SINGLE, -AR¹] —**sin′gu·lar·ly,** *adv.* —**sin′gu·lar·ness,** *n.*
—**Syn. 1–4.** peculiar. **2.** bizarre, queer, curious. **3.** uncommon, rare. **4.** single. —**Ant. 1.** usual. **5.** plural.

sin·gu·lar·ise (siŋg′gyə lə rīz′), *v.t.,* **-ised, -is·ing.** *Chiefly Brit.* singularize. —**sin′gu·lar·i·sa′tion,** *n.*

sin·gu·lar·i·ty (siŋg′gyə lar′i tē), *n., pl.* **-ties. 1.** the state, fact, or quality of being singular. **2.** a singular, unusual, or unique quality; peculiarity. **3.** *Math.* See **singular point.** [ME *singularite* < LL *singulāritās.* See SINGULAR, -ITY]

sin·gu·lar·ize (siŋg′gyə lə rīz′), *v.t.,* **-ized, -iz·ing.** to make singular. Also, *esp. Brit.,* **singularise.** [SINGULAR + -IZE] —**sin·gu·lar·i·za·tion** (siŋg′gyə lər i zā′shən), *n.*

sin′gular point′, *Math.* a point at which a given function of a complex variable has no derivative but of which every neighborhood contains points at which the function has derivatives. Also called **singularity.**

sin·gul·tus (siŋg gul′təs), *n., pl.* **-tus·es.** *Med.* a hiccup. Also, **sin·gul·ta·tion** (siŋg′gəl tā′shən). [< L] —**sin·gul′tous,** *adj.*

sinh, hyperbolic sine. [SIN(E) + H(YPERBOLIC)]

Sin·ha·lese (sin′hə lēz′, -lēs′), *adj., n., pl.* **-lese.** Singhalese.

sin·ha·lite (sin′hə līt′, sin′ə-), *n.* a rare mineral, magnesium aluminum borate, resembling peridot, sometimes used as a gem. [*sinhal-* (as in SINHALESE) + -ITE¹]

Sin·i·cise (sin′i sīz′), *v.t.,* **-cised, -cis·ing.** *Chiefly Brit.* Sinicize. —**Sin′i·ci·sa′tion,** *n.*

Sin·i·cism (sin′i siz′əm), *n.* something characteristic of or peculiar to the Chinese; a Chinese method, custom, or usage. [*Sinic* Chinese (< ML *Sīnic(us)* < MGk *Sinikós,* equiv. to LGk *Sín(ai)* the Chinese + *-ikos* -IC) + -ISM]

Sin·i·cize (sin′i sīz′), *v.t.,* **-cized, -ciz·ing.** to make Chinese in character; bring under Chinese influence. Also, *esp. Brit.,* **Sinicise.** [*Sinic* (see SINICISM) + -IZE] —**Sin·i·ci·za·tion** (sin′i si zā′shən), *n.*

Sin·i·fy (sin′ə fī′), *v.t.,* **-fied, -fy·ing.** to Sinicize. [< LL *Sīn(ae)* the Chinese (< LGk *Sínai*) + -IFY] —**Sin·i·fi·ca·tion** (sin′ə fə kā′shən), *n.*

sin·i·grin (sin′ə grin), *n. Chem.* a colorless, crystalline, water-soluble solid, $KC_{10}H_{16}NO_9S_2 \cdot H_2O$, found chiefly in the seeds of the black mustard, that yields mainly glucose on hydrolysis. Also called **potassium myronate.** [< NL *Sina(pis ni)gr(a)* genus yielding black mustard seed (lit., black mustard; see SINAPINE, NEGRO) + -IN²]

Si·ning (shē′niŋg′), *n.* a city in and the capital of Chinghai, in W China 300,000 (est. 1957). Also, **Hsining.**

Si·nis (sī′nis), *n. Class. Myth.* a robber, killed by Theseus, who killed his victims by catapulting them or tearing them apart with pine trees which he bent and then released. Also, **Sinnis.**

sin·is·ter (sin′i stər), *adj.* **1.** threatening or portending evil, harm, or trouble; ominous: *a sinister remark.* **2.** bad, evil, base, or wicked: *his sinister purposes.* **3.** unfortunate; disastrous; unfavorable: *He was incapacitated by a sinister accident.* **4.** of or on the left side; left. **5.** *Heraldry.* noting the side of an escutcheon or achievement of arms which is to the left of the bearer (opposed to *dexter*). [late ME < L: on the left hand or side, hence unfavorable, injurious] —**sin′is·ter·ly,** *adv.* —**sin′is·ter·ness,** *n.*
—**Syn. 1.** inauspicious, portentous. **3.** unlucky. —**Ant. 1.** benign. **3.** favorable.

sinistr-, a learned borrowing from Latin meaning "left," "on the left," used in the formation of compound words: *sinistrous.* Also, *esp. before a consonant,* **sinistro-.** [< L *sinistr-,* s. of *sinister*]

sin·is·trad (sin′i strad′, si nis′trad), *adv.* **1.** to or toward the left; sinistrally. —*adj.* **2.** moving, proceeding, reading, etc., from right to left: *sinistrad writing.* [SINISTR- + *-ad* toward < L *ad;* see AD-]

sin·is·tral (sin′i strəl), *adj.* **1.** of, pertaining to, or on the left side; left (opposed to *dextral*). **2.** left-handed. **3.** (of certain gastropod shells) coiling from left to right, as seen from the apex. [late ME < ML *sinistrāl(is).* See SINISTR-, -AL¹] —**sin′is·tral·ly,** *adv.*

sin·is·tral·i·ty (sin′i stral′i tē), *n.* preference for using the left hand or side (opposed to *dextrality*). [SINISTRAL + -ITY]

sin·is·tra·tion (sin′i strā′shən), *n.* the quality or state of being left-handed. [SINISTR- + -ATION]

sinistro-, var. of **sinistr-** before a consonant: *sinistrodextral.*

sin·is·troc·u·lar (sin′i strok′yə lər), *adj. Ophthalm.* favoring the left eye, rather than the right, by habit or for effective vision (opposed to *dextrocular*). [SINISTR- + OCULAR] —**sin′is·troc′u·lar′i·ty,** *n.*

sin·is·tro·dex·tral (sin′i strō deks′trəl, si nis′trō-), *adj.* moving or extending from the left to the right. [SINISTRO- + DEXTRAL]

sin·is·tro·gy·ra·tion (sin′i strō′jī rā′shən, si nis′-trō-), *n. Optics, Chem.* levorotation. [SINISTRO- + GYRATION] —**sin·is·tro·gy·ric** (sin′i strō jī′rik), *adj.*

sin·is·trorse (sin′i strôrs′, si nis′trôrs, sin′i strôrs′), *adj. Bot.* (from a point of view at the center of the spiral) rising spirally from right to left, as a stem. [< L *sinistrōrs(us),* lit., turned leftwards, contr. of **sinistrōvorsus,* var. of **sinistrōversus.* See SINISTRO-, VERSUS] —**sin·is·trorse·ly** (sin′i strôrs′lē, sin′i-strôrs′-), *adv.*

sin·is·trous (sin′i strəs), *adj.* **1.** ill-omened; unlucky; disastrous. **2.** sinistral; left. [SINISTR- + -OUS] —**sin′is·trous·ly,** *adv.*

Si·nit·ic (si nit′ik), *n.* **1.** a branch of Sino-Tibetan consisting of the various local languages and dialects whose speakers share literary Chinese as their standard language. —*adj.* **2.** of or pertaining to the Chinese, their language, or their culture. [< LL *Sīn(ae)* the Chinese (< LGk *Sínai*) + -ITIC]

sink (siŋgk), *v.,* **sank** or, often, **sunk; sunk; sink·ing;** *n.* —*v.i.* **1.** to fall, drop, or descend gradually to a lower level: *The river sank two feet during the dry spell.* **2.** to go down toward or below the horizon: *as the sun slowly sinks in the west.* **3.** to slope downward; dip: *The field sinks toward the highway.* **4.** to displace the volume of a supporting substance or object and become submerged or partially submerged; fall or descend into or below the surface or to the bottom (often fol. by *in* or *into*): *The battleship sank within two hours. His foot sank in the mud. She relaxed and let her head sink into the pillows.* **5.** to settle or fall gradually, as a heavy structure: *The tower is sinking on one side.* **6.** to fall or collapse slowly from weakness, fatigue, etc.: *He gave a gasp and sank to his knees.* **7.** to become engulfed or absorbed in or gradually to enter a state (usually fol. by *in* or *into*): *to sink into slumber; He sank easily into a new way of life.* **8.** to pass or fall into some lower state, as of fortune, estimation, etc.: *After losing his job he sank until he was almost a bum.* **9.** to degenerate; decline: *The level of service at the hotel had sunk.* **10.** to fail in physical strength or health. **11.** to decrease in amount, extent, intensity, etc.: *The temperature sank to 30° at noon. The price of eggs sank during the summer.* **12.** to become lower in volume, tone, or pitch: *Her voice sank to a whisper.* **13.** to enter or permeate the mind; become known or understood (usually fol. by *in* or *into*): *He said it four times before the words really sank in.* **14.** to become concave; become hollow, as the cheeks. **15.** to be or become deeply absorbed or involved in a mood or mental state (usually fol. by *in* or *into*): *He's sunk in thought. She sank into a state of depression.* **16.** to sit, recline, or lie (usually fol. by *down in, down on,* or *in, into, on,* or *on to*): *He sank down on the bench and waited for the next bus.*
—*v.t.* **17.** to cause to fall, drop, or descend gradually. **18.** to cause to become submerged; force into or below the surface; cause to plunge in or down: *The submarine sank the battleship. He sank his fist into the pillow.* **19.** to lower or depress the level of: *They sank the roadway by five feet.* **20.** to bury, plant, or lay (a pipe, conduit, etc.) into or as into the ground. **21.** to bring to a worse or lower state or status. **22.** to bring to ruin or perdition: *Drinking and gambling sank him completely.* **23.** to reduce in amount, extent, intensity, etc. **24.** to lower in volume, tone, or pitch. **25.** to suppress; ignore; omit. **26.** to invest in the hope of making a profit or gaining some other return: *He sank a large part of his capital in automotive stock.* **27.** to lose (money) in an unfortunate investment, enterprise, etc. **28.** to dig, bore, or excavate (a hole, shaft, well, etc.). **29.** *Metalworking.* to cold-draw (a tube) without using a mandrel. **30.** *Sports.* to throw, shoot, hit, or propel (a ball) so that it goes through or into the basket, hole, pocket, etc.: *to sink a putt; to sink a free throw; He sank the 10 ball into the side pocket.*
—*n.* **31.** a basin or receptacle, as in a kitchen or laundry, usually connected with a water supply and drainage system, for washing dishes, clothing, etc. **32.** a low-lying, poorly drained area where waters collect or disappear by sinking down into the ground or by evaporation. **33.** sinkhole. **34.** a place of vice or corruption. **35.** a drain or sewer. **36.** a device or place for disposing of energy within a system, as a power-consuming device in an electrical circuit or a condenser in a steam engine. **37.** any pond or pit for sewage or waste, as a cesspool or a pool for industrial wastes. [ME; OE *sinc(an);* c. D *zinken,* G *sinken,* Icel *sökkva,* Goth *singkwan*] —**sink′a·ble,** *adj.* —**sink′like′,** *adj.*

sink·age (siŋg′kij), *n.* **1.** the act, process, or an amount of sinking. **2.** a surface sunk for decorative effect. **3.** *Print.* **a.** the lowering of the first line of body text on a page from its usual position, as at the beginning of a chapter. **b.** the amount of such lowering. [SINK + -AGE]

sink·er (siŋg′kər), *n.* **1.** one who or that which sinks. **2.** one employed in sinking, as one who sinks shafts. **3.** a weight, as of lead, for sinking a fishing line or net below the surface of the water. **4.** *Slang.* a doughnut or, sometimes, a biscuit or muffin. **5.** *Baseball.* a pitched ball that curves downward sharply as it reaches the plate. [SINK + -ER¹] —**sink′er·less,** *adj.*

sink·hole (siŋgk′hōl′), *n.* **1.** a hole formed in soluble rock by the action of water, serving to conduct surface water to an underground passage. **2.** Also called **sink, swallow, swallow hole.** a depressed area in which waste or drainage collects. [ME; see SINK, HOLE]

Sin·kiang (sin′kyaŋg′; *Chin.* shin′kyäŋg′), *n.* the westernmost division of China, bordering Tibet, India, the Soviet Union, and Mongolia: formerly a province. 5,640,000 (est. 1957); 635,829 sq. mi. *Cap.:* Urumchi. Official name, **Sin′kiang-Ui′gur Auton′omous Re′gion** (sin′kyaŋg′wē′gər, -go͝or; *Chin.* shin′kyäŋg′wē′-go͝or′).

sink′ing bowl′, a timepiece consisting of a bowl pierced with a hole which fills at a known rate when floated on water.

sink′ing fund′, a fund to extinguish an indebtedness, usually a bond issue.

sink′ing spell′, a temporary decline, as in health or market values: *Wall Street is over its sinking spell.*

sink·less (siŋgk′lis), *adj.* unsinkable, as a ship. [SINK + -LESS]

sin·less (sin′lis), *adj.* free from or without sin. [ME *sinles,* OE *synlēas.* See SIN¹, -LESS] —**sin′less·ly,** *adv.* —**sin′less·ness,** *n.*

sin·ner (sin′ər), *n.* one who sins; transgressor. [ME; see SIN¹, -ER¹]

sin·net (sin′it), *n. Naut.* sennit.

Sinn Fein (shin′ fān′), **1.** a political organization in Ireland, founded about 1905, advocating the advancement of Ireland along national lines and its complete political separation from Great Britain. **2.** a member of this organization. [< Ir: we ourselves] —**Sinn′ Fein′er.** —**Sinn′ Fein′ism.**

sino-, a combining form of **sinus:** *sinorespiratory.*

Sino-, a combining form meaning "Chinese": *Sino-Tibetan; Sinology.* [< NL, comb. form repr. LL *Sīnae* the Chinese < LGk *Sínai* << Chin *Ch'in* CHIN]

si′no·a′tri·al node′ (sī′nō ā′trē əl, sī′-), *Anat.* a small mass of tissue in the right atrium functioning as pacemaker of the heart by giving rise to the electric impulses that initiate heart contractions. Also called **sinus node.** [SINO- + ATRIAL]

Si·nol·o·gist (si nol′ə jist, si-), *n.* a person who specializes in Sinology. Also, **Si·no·logue** (sīn′ᵊ lôg′, -log′, sin′-). [SINOLOG(UE) (see SINO-, -LOGUE) + -IST]

Si·nol·o·gy (si nol′ə jē, si-), *n.* the study of the language, literature, history, customs, etc., of China. [SINO- + -LOGY; cf. F, G *sinologie*] —**Si·no·log·i·cal** (sīn′ᵊloj′i kəl, sin′-), *adj.*

Si·non (sī′non), *n.* a Greek, posing as a deserter, who was left before Troy with the Trojan Horse and pretended to Priam that Troy would conquer the Greeks if it took the Horse within its walls.

sin·o·pis (sin′ə pəs, si nō′pəs), *n.* a red ochre, used from antiquity to the Middle Ages. Also, **si·no·pi·a** (si nō′pē ə), **sin·o·per** (sin′ə pər). [< NL, L]

si·no·res·pi·ra·to·ry (sī′nō res′pər ə tôr′ē, -tōr′ē, -ri spīᵊr′ə-), *adj. Anat.* of, pertaining to, or affecting the paranasal sinuses and the respiratory tract. [SINO- + RESPIRATORY]

Si·no-Ti·bet·an (sī′nō ti bet′ᵊn, sin′ō-), *n.* **1.** a family of languages including esp. Burmese, Tibetan, and the various local languages and dialects whose speakers share literary Chinese as their standard language. —*adj.* **2.** of, belonging to, or pertaining to Sino-Tibetan. [SINO- + TIBETAN]

SINS (sinz), *n.* a gyroscopic device indicating the exact speed and position of a vessel, as indicated by differences in positions over a given period on a given course, as well as the direction of true north. [*s(hip's) i(nertial) n(avigation) s(ystem)*]

sin·syne (sin′sīn), *adv. Scot. and North Eng.* from that time; since then. [SIN³ + SYNE; r. ME *sensyne,* equiv. to *sen,* var. of *sethen,* OE *seothan* SINCE) + *syne*]

sin·ter (sin′tər), *n.* **1.** siliceous or calcareous matter deposited by springs, as that formed around the vent of a geyser. **2.** *Metall.* the product of a sintering operation. —*v.t.* **3.** *Metall.* to bring about agglomeration in by heating. [< G: dross; see CINDER]

Sin·ton (sin′tən, -tᵊn), *n.* a town in S Texas. 6008 (1960).

sin·u·ate (*adj.* sin′yo͞o it, -āt′, *v.* sin′yo͞o-āt′), *adj., v.,* **-at·ed, -at·ing.** —*adj.* Also, **sin′u·at′ed. 1.** bent in and out; winding; sinuous. **2.** *Bot.* having the margin strongly or distinctly wavy, as a leaf. —*v.i.* **3.** to curve or wind in and out; creep in a winding path: *The snake sinuated along the ground.* [< L *sinuāt(us)* bent, curved (ptp. of *sinuāre*). See SINUS, -ATE¹] —**sin′u·ate·ly,** *adv.*

Sinuate leaf

sin·u·a·tion (sin′yo͞o ā′shən), *n.* a winding; sinuosity. [< LL *sinuātiōn-* (s. of *sinuātiō*). See SINUATE, -ION]

Si·nu·i·ju (sē′no͞o′ē′jo͞o′), *n.* a city in W North Korea, on the Yalu River. 118,414 (1944). Japanese, **Shingishu.**

sin·um′bra lamp′ (si num′brə), an unshaded sperm-oil lamp consisting of a translucent glass globe supported on a pedestal: a form of astral lamp. Also, **si·num′bral lamp′.** [< L *sin(e)* without + *umbra* shade, shadow]

sin·u·os·i·ty (sin′yo͞o os′i tē), *n., pl.* **-ties. 1.** Often, **sinuosities.** a curve, bend, or turn: *a sinuosity of the road.* **2.** a sinuous form or character: *The river was marked by sinuosity.* [< ML *sinuōsitās.* See SINUOUS, -ITY]

sin·u·ous (sin′yo͞o əs), *adj.* **1.** having many curves, bends, or turns; winding: *a sinuous path.* **2.** indirect; devious: *sinuous questions.* **3.** *Bot.* sinuate, as a leaf. [< L *sinuōs(us).* See SINUS, -OUS] —**sin′u·ous·ly,** *adv.* —**sin′u·ous·ness,** *n.*
—**Syn. 1.** curving, meandering, twining, twisting, coiled, curved, serpentine. **2.** roundabout. —**Ant. 1.** straight. **2.** direct.

si·nus (sī′nəs), *n., pl.* **-nus·es. 1.** a curve; bend. **2.** a curving part or recess. **3.** *Anat.* **a.** any of various cavities, recesses, or passages, as a hollow in a bone, or a reservoir or channel for venous blood. **b.** one of the hollow cavities in the skull connecting with the nasal cavities. **c.** an expanded area in a canal or tube. **4.** *Pathol.* a narrow, elongated abscess with a small orifice; a narrow passage leading to an abscess or the like. **5.** *Bot.* a small, rounded depression between two projecting lobes, as of a leaf. [< L: bent or curved surface, curve, fold, bay, hollow] —**si′nus·like′,** *adj.*

Si·nus Aes·tu·um (sē′nəs ā′sto͞o əm), a dark plain in the second quadrant and near the center of the face of the moon. Also called **Bay of Billows, Seething Bay.**

Si·nus As·tro·nau·ta·rum (sē′nəs as′trə nô tä′rəm, -nə-), a dark plain in the Mare Moscoviae in the averted hemisphere or far side of the moon. Also called **Gulf of the Astronauts.**

Si·nus Ir·i·dum (sē′nəs ir′i dəm), a somewhat semicircular dark plain in the second quadrant of the face of the moon, in the Mare Imbrium and bordered by the Jura Mountains. Also called **Bay of Rainbows.**

si·nus·i·tis (sī′nə sī′tis), *n.* *Pathol.* inflammation of a sinus or the sinuses. [< NL; see SINUS, -ITIS]

Si·nus Me·di·i (sē′nəs mā′dē ē′), a dark plain in the center of the face of the moon: about 13,000 square miles. Also called **Central Bay.**

Si·nus Me·rid·i·a·ni (sē′nəs mə rid′ē ä′nē ē), an area on the equator of Mars, appearing as a dark region when viewed telescopically from the earth.

si′nus node′, *Anat.* See **sinoatrial node.**

Si′nus of Val·sal′va (val sal′və), *Anat.* any of the pouches of the aorta and the pulmonary artery opposite the flaps of the semilunar valves, into which blood returning to the heart flows, closing the valves.

si·nus·oid (sī′nə soid′), *n.* *Math.* a curve described by the equation $y = a\sin x$, the ordinate being proportional to the sine of the abscissa. [SINUS + -OID]

si·nus·oi·dal (sī′nə soid′əl), *adj.* **1.** *Math.* of or pertaining to a sinusoid. **2.** having a magnitude that varies as the sine of an independent variable: *a sinusoidal current.* [SINUSOID + -AL[1]] —**si′nus·oi′dal·ly,** *adv.*

sinusoi′dal projec′tion, *Cartog.* an equal-area projection in which parallels are straight lines spaced at regular intervals, the central meridian is a straight line one-half the length of the equator, and the other meridians are curves symmetrical to the central meridian.

Si·nus Ro·ris (sē′nəs rōr′is, rôr′-), a dark plain in the second quadrant of the face of the moon, between Mare Frigoris and Oceanus Procellarum. Also called **Bay of Dew, Bay of Dews.**

Si·nus Sa·bae·us (sē′nəs sa bē′əs), an area in the southern hemisphere and near the equator of Mars, appearing dark when viewed telescopically from the earth.

Sion (*Fr.* syôɴ), *n.* a town in and the capital of Valais, in SW Switzerland. 16,051 (1960).

Si·on (sī′ən), *n.* Zion.

-sion, a noun suffix appearing in loan words from Latin: *compulsion.* Cf. **-tion.** [< L, equiv. to *-s(us)*, var. of *-tus* ptp. suffix + *-iōn-* -ION]

si op. sit, (in prescriptions) if necessary. [< L *si opus sit*]

Siou·an (so͞o′ən), *n.* **1.** a language family formerly widespread from Saskatchewan to the lower Mississippi, also found in the Virginia and Carolina piedmont, and including Catawba, Crow, Dakota, Hidatsa, Mandan, Osage, and Winnebago. **2.** Sioux (def. 1). —*adj.* **3.** of or pertaining to the Sioux or the Siouan languages. [SIOUX + -AN]

Sioux (so͞o), *n., pl.* **Sioux** (so͞o, so͞oz), *adj.* —*n.* **1.** a member of any of various American Indian peoples, esp. of the Dakota tribe, speaking a Siouan language. —*adj.* **2.** of or pertaining to this tribe. [< F, short for *Nadowessioux* < Ojibwa *Nadoweisiu* enemy, lit., little snake]

Sioux′ Cit′y, a port in W Iowa, on the Missouri River. 89,159 (1960).

Sioux′ Falls′, a city in SE South Dakota. 65,466 (1960).

Sioux′ State′, a nickname of the State of North Dakota.

Sioux′ War′, *U.S. Hist.* any of a series of skirmishes or wars between the Sioux Indians and settlers or the U.S. Army from 1854 to 1890.

sip (sip), *v.,* **sipped, sip·ping,** *n.* —*v.t.* **1.** to drink a little at a time; take small tastes of (a liquid): *He sipped the hot tea noisily.* **2.** to drink from a little at a time: *He sipped the hot cup.* **3.** to take in; absorb: *He sipped knowledge at its source.* —*v.i.* **4.** to drink by sips. —*n.* **5.** an instance of sipping; a small taste of a liquid: *A sip told him that the milk was sour.* **6.** a small quantity taken by sipping: *Take just a sip, not a gulp or a swallow.* [ME *sippe*, OE **syppan*, deriv. of *sopa* a sip] —**sip′ping·ly,** *adv.*
—**Syn. 1.** See **drink.**

sipe (sīp), *v.i.,* **siped, sip·ing.** *Scot. and North Eng.* (of liquid) to drip, trickle, ooze, or soak through. [OE *sīp(ian)*; c. D *zijpen*, MLG *sīpen.* See SEEP[1]] —**sip′er,** *n.*

Siph·nos (sif′nos), *n.* a Greek island in the SW Aegean Sea, in the Cyclades group: gold and silver mines. 28 sq. mi. Also, **Sifnos.**

si·phon (sī′fən), *n.* **1.** a tube or conduit bent into legs of unequal length, for use in drawing a liquid from one container into another on a lower level by placing the shorter leg into the container above and the longer leg into the one below, the liquid being forced up the shorter leg and into the longer one by the pressure of the atmosphere. **2.** See **siphon bottle. 3.** a projecting tubular part of some animals, through which liquid enters or leaves the body. —*v.t., v.i.* **4.** to convey or pass through a siphon. Also, **syphon.** [< L *sīphōn-* (s. of *sīphō*) < Gk *síphōn* pipe, tube] —**si′phon·al, si·phon·ic** (sī fon′ik), *adj.* —**si′phon·less,** *adj.* —**si′phon·like′,** *adj.*

Siphon

si·phon·age (sī′fə nij), *n.* the action of a siphon. [SIPHON + -AGE]

si′phon bot′tle, a bottle for aerated water, fitted with a bent tube through the neck, the water being forced out, when a valve is opened, by the pressure on its surface of the gas accumulating within the bottle.

siphono-, a learned borrowing from Greek meaning "tube," "siphon," used in the formation of compound words: *siphonostele.* [< Gk *siphōno-*, comb. form of *síphōn* SIPHON + *-o-* -O-]

si·pho·no·phore (sī′fə nə fōr′, -fôr′, sī fon′ə-), *n.* any pelagic hydrozoan of the order *Siphonophora*, being a floating or swimming colony composed of polyps. [< NL *Siphonophor(a)* name of the group < Gk *siphōnophóros* tube-carrying, equiv. to *siphōno-* SIPHONO- + *-phóros* -PHORE + L *-a* n. suffix] —**si·pho·noph·o·rous** (sī′fə nof′ər əs), *adj.*

si·phon·o·stele (sī fon′ə stēl′, sī′fə nō stēl′), *n.* *Bot.* a hollow tube of vascular tissue enclosing a pith and embedded in ground tissue. [SIPHONO- + STELE] —**si·pho·no·ste·lic** (sī′fə nə stē′lik), *adj.*

Si·phrei To·rah (sē frā′ tō rä′), *Hebrew.* a pl. of **Sepher Torah.**

sip·id (sip′id), *adj.* **1.** having a pleasing taste or flavor. **2.** of agreeably distinctive character. [back formation from INSIPID] —**si·pid·i·ty** (si pid′i tē), *n.*

Si·ple (sī′pəl), *n.* **Mount,** a mountain in Antarctica, on the E coast of Marie Byrd Land, S of Amundsen Sea. 15,000 ft.

Sip·par (si pär′), *n.* an ancient Babylonian city on the Euphrates, in SE Iraq.

sip·per (sip′ər), *n.* **1.** one who sips. **2.** a paper tube through which to sip; drinking straw. [SIP + -ER[1]]

sip·pet (sip′it), *n.* **1.** a small bit; fragment. **2.** a small piece of bread or the like for dipping in liquid food, as in gravy or milk; a small sop. **3.** a crouton. [SIP + -ET]

Sip′py di′et, a diet, usually lasting a month, for the treatment of gastric ulcer, initiated with milk, cereals, and eggs, and terminating with toast and sieved vegetables. Also called **Sip′py reg′imen.** [named after Benjamin W. Sippy (d. 1924), American physician]

si·pun·cu·lid (sī pun̄g′kyə lid), *n.* **1.** an invertebrate of the phylum *Sipunculoidea*, comprising the peanut worms. —*adj.* **2.** belonging or pertaining to the *Sipunculoidea.* [< NL *Sipunculid(a)*, equiv. to *Sipuncul(us)* name of a genus (L: little pipe) + *-ida* -ID[4]]

si quae·ris pen·in·su·lam a·moe·nam, cir·cum·spi·ce (sē kwī′ris pen in′so͝o läm′ ä moi′näm kēr ko͝om′spi ke′; *Eng.* sī kwē′ris pe nin′so͝o lam′ ə mē′nam sər kum′spi sē′), *Latin.* if you are seeking a pleasant peninsula, look around you: motto of Michigan.

Si·quei·ros (sē kā′rôs), *n.* **Da·vid Al·fa·ro** (dä vēth′ äl fä′rō), born 1896, Mexican painter.

sir (sûr), *n.* **1.** a respectful or formal term of address used to a man: *No, sir.* **2.** (*cap.*) the distinctive title of a knight or baronet: *Sir Walter Scott.* **3.** (*cap.*) a title of respect for some notable personage of ancient times: *Sir Pandarus of Troy.* **4.** a lord or gentleman: *noble sirs and ladies.* **5.** an ironic or humorous title of respect: *sir critic.* **6.** *Archaic.* a title of respect used before a noun to designate profession, rank, etc.: *sir priest; sir clerk.* [weak var. of SIRE]

Si·rach (sī′rak), *n.* **Son of,** Jesus (def. 2).

Si·ra·cu·sa (sē′rä ko͞o′zä), *n.* Italian name of **Syracuse.**

Si·raj-ud-dau·la (si räj′o͞od dou′lə), *n.* 1728?–57, Nawab of Bengal 1756–57. Also, **Su·ra·jah Dow·lah** (sə rä′jə dou′lə).

sir·dar (sər där′), *n.* **1.** (in India, Pakistan, and Afghanistan) a military chief or leader. **2.** (formerly) the British commander of the Egyptian army. [< Hindi *sardār* < Pers]

sire (sīᵊr), *n., v.,* **sired, sir·ing.** —*n.* **1.** the male parent of a quadruped. **2.** a respectful term of address, now used only to a male sovereign. **3.** *Archaic.* a father or forefather. **4.** *Archaic.* a person of importance or in a position of authority, as a lord. —*v.t.* **5.** to beget; procreate as the father. [ME < OF (nom. sing.) < VL **seior*, for L *senior* SENIOR] —**sire′less,** *adj.*

sir·ee (sə rē′), *n.* (*sometimes cap.*) sirree.

si·ren (sī′rən), *n.* **1.** *Class. Myth.* one of several sea nymphs, part woman and part bird, supposed to lure mariners to destruction by their seductive singing. **2.** a seductively beautiful or charming woman, esp. one who beguiles and deceives men: *a siren of the silver screen.* **3.** an acoustical instrument for producing musical tones, consisting essentially of a disk pierced with holes arranged equidistantly in a circle, rotated over a jet or stream of compressed air, steam, or the like, so that the stream is alternately interrupted and allowed to pass. **4.** an implement of this kind used as a whistle, fog signal, or warning device. **5.** any of several aquatic, eellike salamanders of the family *Sirenidae*, having permanent external gills, small forelimbs, and no posterior limbs. **6.** *Heraldry.* seiren. —*adj.* **7.** of or like a siren. **8.** seductive, alluring, or tempting, esp. dangerously or harmfully: *the siren call of adventure; a siren song.* —*v.i.* **9.** to go with the siren sounding, as a fire engine. —*v.t.* **10.** to allure in the manner of a siren. [ME *sereyn* < OF *sereine* < LL *Sīrēn(a)* for L *Sīrēn* < Gk *Seirḗn*] —**si′ren·like′,** *adj.*
—**Syn. 2.** seductress, temptress, vamp.

Si·re·na (sī rē′nə, sə-), *n.* a girl's given name.

Si·re·ni·a (sī rē′nē ə), *n.* the order comprising the sirenians. [< NL; see SIRENIAN]

si·re·ni·an (sī rē′nē ən), *n.* an aquatic, herbivorous mammal of the order *Sirenia*, including the manatee, dugong, etc. [< NL *Sireni(a)* (see SIREN, -IA) + -AN]

si·ren·ic (sī ren′ik), *adj.* of or characteristic of a siren; melodious, tempting, or alluring. Also, **si·ren′i·cal.** [SIREN + -IC] —**si·ren′i·cal·ly,** *adv.*

Si·re·num (si rē′nəm), *n.* **Mare.** See **Mare Sirenum.**

Si·ret (si ret′), *n.* a river in SE Europe, flowing SE from the Carpathian Mountains, in the SW Soviet Union in Europe, through E Rumania to the Danube. 270 mi. long. German, **Sereth.**

Sir′ Ga′wain and the Green′ Knight′, an alliterative poem of unknown authorship, dating from the 14th century.

si·ri·a·sis (si rī′ə sis), *n.* *Pathol.* sunstroke. [< L < Gk *seiríasis*, equiv. to *seir(ân)* (to) be hot, scorching + *-iasis* -IASIS]

Si·ri·ci·us (si rish′ē əs), *n.* **Saint,** died A.D. 399, pope 384–399.

si·ris (sə rēs′), *n.* lebbek (def. 1). [< Hindi *sirīs* < Skt *śirīṣa*]

Sir·i·us (sir′ē əs), *n.* *Astron.* the Dog Star, the brightest star in the heavens, located in the constellation Canis Major. [< L *Sīrius* < Gk *Seírios*]

sir·loin (sûr′loin), *n.* the portion of the loin of beef in front of the rump. [late ME *surloyn.* See SUR-[1], LOIN]

si·roc·co (sə rok′ō), *n., pl.* **-cos. 1.** a hot, dry, dust-laden wind blowing from northern Africa and affecting parts of southern Europe. **2.** a warm, sultry south or southeast wind accompanied by rain, occurring in the same regions. **3.** any hot, oppressive wind, esp. one in the warm sector of a cyclone. [< It, var. of *scirocco* < Ar *sharq* east]

si·rop (sē rō′), *n.* *French.* syrup.

sir·rah (sir′ə), *n.* *Archaic.* a term of address used to inferiors or children to express impatience, contempt, etc. [unexplained var. of SIR]

sir·ree (sə rē′), *n.* (*sometimes cap.*) (used as an intensive with *no* or *yes*): *Will I go there again? No, sirree!* Also, **siree.** [alter. of SIR]

sir-rev·er·ence (sûr′rev′ər əns), *n.* *Obs.* (used as an expression of apology, as before unseemly or indelicate words.) [alter. of *save your reverence*]

Sir Rog′er de Cov′erley, an English country dance performed by two rows of dancers facing each other.

Sir·sa·lis (sûr′sə lis), *n.* the smaller crater of two adjoining craters in the third quadrant of the face of the moon, the other crater being Bertaud: about 20 miles in diameter.

sir·up (sir′əp, sûr′-), *n., v.t.* syrup.

sir·up·y (sir′ə pē), *adj.* syrupy.

sir·vente (sər vent′; *Fr.* sēr väɴt′), *n., pl.* **-ventes** (-vents′; *Fr.* -väɴt′). a medieval poem or song of heroic or satirical character, as composed by a troubadour. Also, **sir·ventes′.** [back formation from Pr *sirventes*, lit., pertaining to a servant, i.e., lover (the *-s* being taken as pl. sign). See SERVANT, -ESE]

sis (sis), *n.* *Informal.* sister. [shortened form; cf. D *zus* for *zuster* SISTER]

Sis (sis), *n.* a girl's given name, form of **Cissy.**

-sis, a suffix appearing in loan words from Greek, where it was used to form abstract nouns of action, process, state, condition, etc.: *thesis; aphesis.* [< Gk, fem. n. suffix corresponding to adj. suffix *-tikos* -TIC]

si·sal (sī′səl, sis′əl), *n.* **1.** Also called **si′sal hemp′,** a fiber yielded by an agave, *Agave sisalana*, of Yucatán, used for making rope, rugs, etc. **2.** the plant itself. [short for *Sisal grass* or *hemp*, after *Sisal*, former seaport of Yucatán]

sis·co·wet (sis′kə wet′), *n.* a variety of lake trout, *Salvelinus namaycush siscowet*, found in the deeper waters of Lake Superior. [< CanF *ciscoette*, alter. of Ojibwa *pemitewiskawet*, lit., that which has oily flesh]

Sis·er·a (sis′ər ə), *n.* the commander of the Canaanite army of King Jabin. Judges 4:2.

Si·sin·ni·us (si sin′ē əs), *n.* pope A.D. 708.

sis·kin (sis′kin), *n.* any of several small, cardueline finches, esp. *Spinus spinus*, of Europe. Cf. **pine siskin.** [earlier *sysken* < MD *sijsken*, equiv. to *sijs* (? < MHG *zise*; cf. Pol *czyzik* siskin) + *-ken* -KIN]

Sis·ler (sis′lər), *n.* **George Harold,** born 1893, U.S. baseball player.

Sis·ley (sis′lē; *Fr.* sēs lā′), *n.* **Al·fred** (al fred′), 1839–99, French painter.

Sis·mon·di (sis mon′dē; *Fr.* sēs môɴ dē′), *n.* **Jean Charles Lé·o·nard Si·monde de** (zhäɴ sharl lā ô nar′ sē môɴd′ də), 1773–1842, Swiss historian and economist.

Sis·se·ton (sis′i tən, -tᵊn), *n.* a town in NE South Dakota. 3218 (1960).

Sis·sie (sis′ē), *n.* a girl's given name, form of **Cecilia.** Also, **Cissie, Cissy.**

sis·si·fied (sis′ə fīd′), *adj.* *Informal.* sissy. [SISSY + -FY + -ED[2]]

sis·sonne (si son′, -sōn′; *Fr.* sē sôn′), *n., pl.* **-sonnes** (-sonz′, -sōnz′; *Fr.* -sôn′). *Ballet.* a jump in which the dancer lands on one foot, with the other extended to the back, front, or side. [named after the Comte de *Sissonne*, 17th-century French noble, said to have invented it]

sis·sy[1] (sis′ē), *n., pl.* **-sies. 1.** an effeminate boy or man. **2.** a timid or cowardly person. **3.** a little girl. [SIS + -Y[2]] —**sis′sy·ish,** *adj.*

sis·sy[2] (sis′ē), *adj.* of, pertaining to, or characteristic of a sissy. [SIS + -Y[1]] —**sis′si·ness, sis′sy·ness,** *n.*

sis·ter (sis′tər), *n.* **1.** a female offspring of a specific set of parents with respect to any other offspring of those parents; a female sibling. **2.** Also called **half sister.** a female offspring of one specific parent with respect to any other offspring with whom she has that parent in common. **3.** a female friend or protector regarded as a sister. **4.** a thing regarded as feminine and associated as if by kinship with something else: *The ships are sisters.* **5.** a female fellow member, as of a church. **6.** a female member of a religious community that observes the simple vows of poverty, chastity, and obedience; nun. **7.** *Brit.* a nurse in charge of a hospital ward; head nurse. **8.** *Informal.* a form of address used to a woman or girl, esp. jocularly or in contempt: *Listen, sister, you've had enough.* —*adj.* **9.** being or considered a sister; related by, or as by, sisterhood: *sister ships.* —*v.t.* **10.** *Naut.* to strengthen (a broken or weakened member) by securing an auxiliary piece alongside it. [ME < Scand; cf. Icel *systir*; c. OE *sweoster*, D *zuster*, G *Schwester*, Goth *swistar*, Russ *sestra*, L *soror*, Skt *svasar*] —**sis′ter·less,** *adj.* —**sis′ter·like′,** *adj.*

sis′ter block′, *Naut.* a block having two sheaves, either side by side or in tandem.

Sis′ter Car′rie, a novel (1900) by Theodore Dreiser.

sis·ter·hood (sis′tər ho͝od′), *n.* **1.** the state of being a sister. **2.** a group of sisters, esp. of nuns or of female members of a church. **3.** an organization of women with a common interest or purpose, esp. a social or charitable one. [ME *sosterhode.* See SISTER, -HOOD]

sis·ter-in-law (sis′tər in lô′), *n., pl.* **sis·ters-in-law. 1.** the sister of one's husband or wife. **2.** the wife of one's brother. **3.** the wife of the brother of one's husband or wife. [ME *suster-in-lawe.* See SISTER, IN-LAW]

sis·ter·ly (sis′tər lē), *adj.* of, like, or befitting a sister: *sisterly affection.* [SISTER + -LY] —**sis′ter·li·ness,** *n.*

Sis′ter of Char′ity, *Rom. Cath. Ch.* a member of a congregation of sisters founded in 1634 by St. Vincent de Paul and devoted chiefly to hospital work.

Sis′ter of Lo·ret′to (lə ret′ō), *Rom. Cath. Ch.* a member of a congregation of sisters founded at Loretto, Kentucky, in 1812, and engaged in educational and missionary works.

Sis′ter of Mer′cy, *Rom. Cath. Ch.* a member of a congregation of sisters founded in Dublin in 1827 by Catherine McAuley (1787–1841) and engaged chiefly in works of spiritual and corporal mercy.

Sis·tine (sis′tēn, -tin, -tīn), *adj.* of or pertaining to any pope named Sixtus. Also, **Sixtine.** [< It *Sistin(o)*, pertaining to *Sisto* man's name (< L *Sextus*, special use of *sextus* sixth); see -INE¹]

Sis′tine Chap′el, the chapel of the pope in the Vatican at Rome, built for Pope Sixtus IV and decorated with frescoes by Michelangelo and others.

Sis′tine Madon′na, a Madonna painted by Raphael for the Church of St. Sixtus at Piacenza, Italy.

sis·troid (sis′troid), *adj.* *Geom. Rare.* included between the convex sides of two intersecting curves (opposed to *cissoid*): *a sistroid angle.* [?]

sis·trum (sis′trəm), *n., pl.* **-trums, -tra** (-trə). an ancient Egyptian percussion instrument consisting of a looped metal frame set in a handle and fitted with loose crossbars that rattled when shaken. [< L < Gk *seîstron*, deriv. of *seíein* to shake]

Sistrum

Sis·y·phe·an (sis′ə fē′ən), *adj.* **1.** of or pertaining to Sisyphus. **2.** endless and unavailing, as labor or a task. [< L *Sīsyphē(ius)* of SISYPHUS (< Gk *Sisýpheios*, equiv. to *Sísyph(os)* + *-eios* adj. suffix) + -AN]

Sis·y·phus (sis′ə fəs), *n.* *Class. Myth.* a son of Aeolus and ruler of Corinth, noted for his trickery: he was punished in Tartarus by being compelled to roll a stone to the top of a slope, the stone always escaping him near the top and rolling down again.

sit¹ (sit), *v.,* **sat** or (*Archaic*) **sate; sat** or (*Archaic*) **sit·ten; sit·ting.** —*v.i.* **1.** to rest with the body supported by the buttocks or thighs; be seated. **2.** to be located or situated: *The house sits well up on the slope.* **3.** to rest or lie (usually fol. by *on* or *upon*): *An aura of greatness sits easily upon him.* **4.** to place oneself in position for an artist, photographer, etc.; pose: *to sit for a portrait.* **5.** to remain quiet or inactive: *They let the matter sit.* **6.** (of a bird) to perch or roost. **7.** (of a hen) to cover eggs to hatch them; brood. **8.** to fit or be adjusted, as a garment: *The jacket sits well on your shoulders.* **9.** to occupy a place or have a seat in an official assembly or in an official capacity, as a legislator, judge, or bishop. **10.** to be convened or in session, as an assembly. **11.** to act as a baby-sitter. **12.** (of wind) to blow from the indicated direction: *The wind sits in the west tonight.* **13.** *Informal.* to be accepted or considered in the way indicated: *Something about his looks just didn't sit right with me.* **14.** *Informal.* to be acceptable to the stomach: *Something I ate for breakfast didn't sit too well.* —*v.t.* **15.** to cause to sit; seat (often fol. by *down*): *Sit yourself down right here.* **16.** to sit astride or keep one's seat on (a horse or other animal): *She sits her horse gracefully.* **17.** to provide seating accommodations or seating room for; seat: *The waiter couldn't sit us for half an hour. Our dining-room table only sits six people.* **18. sit down, a.** to take a seat. **b.** to descend to a sitting position; alight. **c.** to take up a position, as to encamp, besiege, etc.: *The military forces sat down at the approaches to the city.* **19. sit in on,** to be a spectator, observer, or visitor at; participate in: *The visitors to the school were allowed to sit in on classes.* **20. sit on** or **upon, a.** to inquire into or deliberate over: *A coroner's jury was called to sit on the case.* **b.** *Informal.* to suppress; silence: *They sat upon the bad news as long as they could.* **c.** *Informal.* to check or rebuke; squelch: *I'll sit on her if she tries to interrupt me.* **21. sit out, a.** to stay to the end of: *Though bored, we sat out the play.* **b.** to surpass in endurance: *He sat out his tormentors.* **c.** to keep one's seat during (a dance, competition, etc.); fail to participate in: *We sat out all the Latin-American numbers.* **22. sit pretty,** *Informal.* to be in a comfortable situation: *He's been sitting pretty ever since he got that new job.* **23. sit shibah,** *Judaism.* to observe *shibah* by sitting on hard seats during certain hours to receive visits of condolence and by following various duties and abstinences. **24. sit tight,** to bide one's time; take no action: *I'm going to sit tight till I hear what they're going to do next.* **25. sit up, a.** to rise from a supine to a sitting position. **b.** to delay the hour of retiring beyond the usual time. **c.** to sit upright; hold oneself erect. **d.** *Informal.* to become interested or astonished: *We all sat up when the holiday was announced.* [ME *sitte(n)*, OE *sittan*; c. D *zitten*, G *sitzen*, Icel *sitja*; akin to Goth *sitan*, L *sedēre*]

sit² (sit), *v.* (in prescriptions) may it be. [< L]

Si·ta (sē′tä), *n.* (in the Ramayana) the wife of Ramachandra, abducted by Ravana and later rescued.

si·tar (si tär′), *n.* a lute of India with a small pear-shaped body and a long, broad, fretted neck. [< Hindi *sitār*] —**si·tar′ist,** *n.*

sit·a·tun·ga (sit′ə to͝ong′gə), *n.* an antelope, *Limnotragus spekii*, found in marshy regions of central and eastern Africa. Also, **situtunga.** Also called **marsh buck.** [< EAfr]

sit·com (sit′kom′), *n.* a situation comedy: a comedy drama, esp. a television series involving discrete episodes about the same group of people, family members, etc. [SIT(UATION) + COM(EDY)]

sit-down (sit′doun′), *n.* **1.** *Brit. Informal.* a period or instance of sitting, as to relax, talk, or the like: *They had a pleasant sit-down together.* **2.** See **sit-down strike.** [n. use of v. phrase *sit down*]

sit′-down strike′, a strike during which workers occupy their place of employment and refuse to work or allow others to work until the strike is settled.

site (sīt), *n., v.,* **sit·ed, sit·ing.** —*n.* **1.** the position or location of a town, building, etc., esp. as to its environment: *the site of our summer cabin.* **2.** the area or exact plot of ground on which anything is, has been, or is to be located: *the site of ancient Troy.* —*v.t.* **3.** to place in or provide with a site; locate. **4.** to put in position for operation, as artillery: *to site a cannon.* [ME < L *sit(us)* site, akin to *situs* founded, built, ptp. of *sinere* to set down]

sith (sith), *adv., conj., prep.* *Archaic.* since. [ME; OE *siththa*, dial. var. of *siththan*, orig. *sīth thām* after that < *sīth* later (than), comp. adv. (akin to Goth *seithus*, Icel *sīth-* late, G *seit* since) + *thām*, dat. of demonstrative pronoun; see THE², THAT]

sit-in (sit′in′), *n.* **1.** an organized passive protest, esp. against racial segregation, in which the demonstrators occupy seats prohibited to them, as in restaurants and other public places. **2.** See **sit-down strike.** [n. use of v. phrase *sit in*]

Sit·ka (sit′kə), *n.* a town in SE Alaska, on an island in the Alexander Archipelago: the capital of former Russian America. 3237 (1960). —**Sit′kan,** *n.*

Sit′ka cy′press. See **Alaska cedar.**

Sit′ka spruce′, **1.** a spruce, *Picea sitchensis*, of western North America, grown as an ornamental. **2.** the soft, pale-brown wood of this tree, used for making furniture and in the construction of houses.

sito-, a learned borrowing from Greek meaning "grain," "food," used in the formation of compound words: *sitomania; sitosterol.* [< Gk, comb. form of *sîtos* grain]

si·tol·o·gy (sī tol′ə jē), *n.* the branch of medicine dealing with nutrition and dietetics. [SITO- + -LOGY]

si·to·ma·ni·a (sī′tə mā′nē ə, -mān′yə), *n.* *Pathol.* abnormal or insane craving for food. [SITO- + -MANIA]

si·to·pho·bi·a (sī′tə fō′bē ə), *n.* *Pathol.* abnormal or insane aversion to food. [SITO- + -PHOBIA]

si·tos·ter·ol (sī tos′tə rōl′, -rôl′, -rol′), *n.* *Chem.* any of five steroid alcohols having the formula $C_{22}H_{49}OH$, esp. the beta form, obtained from various plant sources: used in organic synthesis. [SITO- + STEROL]

Si·tsang (sē′tsäng′), *n.* Chinese name of **Tibet.**

sit·ten (sit′ən), *v.* *Archaic.* pp. of **sit¹.**

sit·ter (sit′ər), *n.* **1.** one who sits. **2.** a brooding hen. **3.** one who stays with young children while the parents go out, usually for the evening; baby-sitter. **4.** *Slang.* the buttocks; rump. [ME; see SIT, -ER¹]

Sit·ter (sit′ər), *n.* **Wil·lem de** (wil′əm də), 1872–1934, Dutch astronomer and mathematician.

sit·ting (sit′ing), *n.* **1.** the act of one who or that which sits. **2.** a period of remaining seated, as in posing for a portrait or reading a book. **3.** the space on or in which one sits, as in a church. **4.** a brooding, as of a hen upon eggs; incubation. **5.** the number of eggs on which a bird sits during a single hatching; clutch. **6.** a session, as of a court or legislature. **7.** the time or space allotted to the serving of a meal to a group, as aboard a ship. [ME; see SIT, -ING¹]

Sit′ting Bull′, 1834–90, American-Indian warrior and tribal leader.

sit′ting duck′, *Slang.* a helpless or open target or victim: *The wealthy widow is a sitting duck for a confidence man.*

sit′ting room′, a small living room, often one that forms part of a suite in a hotel, private house, etc.

si·tu (sē′to͞o), *n.* *Latin.* See **in situ.**

sit·u·ate (*v.* sich′o͞o āt′; *adj.* sich′o͞o it, -āt′), *v.,* **-at·ed, -at·ing,** *adj.* —*v.t.* **1.** to put in or on a particular site or place; locate. —*adj.* **2.** *Archaic.* located; placed; situated. [< LL *situāt(us)* sited. See SITE, -ATE¹]

sit·u·at·ed (sich′o͞o ā′tid), *adj.* **1.** located; placed. **2.** placed in a particular position or condition, esp. with reference to the possession of money: *The income on their investments leaves them well situated.* [SITUATE + -ED²]

sit·u·a·tion (sich′o͞o ā′shən), *n.* **1.** manner of being situated; location or position with reference to environment: *The situation of the house allowed for a beautiful view.* **2.** a place or locality. **3.** condition; case; plight: *He is in a desperate situation.* **4.** the state of affairs; combination of circumstances: *The present international situation is dangerous.* **5.** a position or post of employment; job. **6.** a state of affairs of special or critical significance in the course of a play, novel, etc. **7.** *Sociol.* the aggregate of biological, psychological, and sociocultural factors acting on an individual or group to condition behavioral patterns. [< ML *situātiōn-* (s. of *situātiō*). See SITUATE, -ION] —**sit′u·a′tion·al,** *adj.* —**sit′u·a′tion·al·ly,** *adv.*
—**Syn. 1.** site. **4.** See **state. 5.** See **position.**

sit·u·a·tion·ism (sich′o͞o ā′shə niz′əm), *n.* *Psychol.* the theory that behavior is chiefly in response to immediate situations. [SITUATION + -ISM] —**sit′u·a′tion·ist,** *n.*

sit·u·la (sich′ə lə, sit′ələ), *n., pl.* **-u·lae** (-ə lē′, -əlē′). a deep urn, vase, or bucket-shaped vessel, esp. one made in the ancient world. [< L: bucket]

sit-up (sit′up′), *n.* an exercise in which a person, lying flat on the back and with the legs straight, lifts the torso to a sitting position without bending the legs. [n. use of v. phrase *sit up*]

sit-up·on (sit′ə pon′, -pôn′), *n.* *Chiefly Brit. Informal.* the buttocks. [n. use of v. phrase *sit upon*]

si·tus (sī′təs), *n., pl.* **-tus. 1.** position; situation. **2.** the proper or original position, as of a part or organ. [< L; see SITE]

si′tus in·ver′sus (in vûr′səs), *Med.* a congenital defect in which an organ is on the side opposite from its normal position. [< NL: inverse situs; see INVERSE]

sit·u·tun·ga (sit′ə to͝ong′gə), *n.* sitatunga.

Sit·well (sit′wəl, -wel), *n.* **1. Dame Edith,** 1887–1964, English poet and critic. **2.** her brother, **Sir Osbert,** born 1892, English poet and novelist. **3.** her brother, **Sa·chev·er·ell** (sə shev′ər əl), born 1900, English poet and novelist.

sitz′ bath′ (sits, zits), **1.** a chairlike bathtub in which the thighs and hips are immersed in warm water, usually as part of a therapeutic treatment. **2.** the bath so taken. [half adoption, half trans. of G *Sitzbad*, lit., seat-bath]

sitz·krieg (sits′krēg′, zits′-), *n.* slow-moving warfare marked by repeated stalemate. [< G, equiv. to *Sitz* seat + *Krieg* war]

sitz·mark (sits′märk′), *n.* *Skiing.* a sunken area in the snow marking a backward fall of a skier. [< G, equiv. to *Sitz* seat + *Mark* mark]

Si·va (sē′və, shē′və), *n.* *Hinduism.* Shiva. —**Si′va·ism,** *n.* —**Si′va·ist,** *n.* —**Si′va·is′tic,** *adj.*

Si·van (siv′ən; *Heb.* sē vän′), *n.* a month of the Jewish calendar. Cf. **Jewish calendar.** [< Heb]

Si·vas (sē väs′), *n.* a city in central Turkey. 109,165 (1965).

si·ver (sī′vər), *v.i.* *Obs.* to simmer. [var. of SEWER¹]

si vir. perm., (in prescriptions) if the strength will permit. [< L *sī vīres permitant*]

Si·wash (sī′wosh, -wôsh), *n.* a conventional designation for any small, provincial college or for such colleges collectively (often prec. by *old*): *Students from old Siwash met their slick Ivy League cousins at the national convention.* [< Chinook Jargon < F *sauvage* wild, SAVAGE]

six (siks), *n.* **1.** a cardinal number, five plus one. **2.** a symbol for this number, as 6 or VI. **3.** a set of this many persons or things. **4.** a playing card, die face, or half of a domino face with six pips. **5.** *Cricket.* a hit in which the ball crosses the boundary line of the field without a bounce, counting six runs for the batsman. Cf. **boundary** (def. 3). **6. at sixes and sevens, a.** in disorder or confusion. **b.** in disagreement or dispute. —*adj.* **7.** amounting to six in number. [ME, OE; c. D *zes*, LG *ses*, G *sechs*, Icel *sex*, Goth *saihs*, L *sex*, Gk *héx*, Skt *ṣaṣ*]

Six′ Char′acters in Search′ of an Au′thor, a play (1921) by Luigi Pirandello.

six·fold (siks′fōld′), *adj.* **1.** having six elements or parts. **2.** six times as great or as much. —*adv.* **3.** in sixfold measure. [ME *sexfold*, OE *sixfeald.* See SIX, -FOLD]

six-foot·er (siks′fo͝ot′ər), *n.* *Informal.* a person who is roughly six feet tall: *He's the broad-shouldered six-footer with the close-set eyes.*

six-gun (siks′gun′), *n.* a six-shooter.

Six′ Na′tions, the Five Nations of the Iroquois confederacy and the Tuscaroras.

six-pack (siks′pak′), *n.* six bottles or cans of a beverage, esp. beer, packed in a cardboard container, usually equipped with a handle.

six·pence (siks′pəns), *n., pl.* **-pence, -penc·es** for 2. **1.** (*construed as sing. or pl.*) *Brit.* a sum of six pennies. **2.** (*construed as sing.*) a cupronickel coin of the United Kingdom, the half of a shilling, equal to six pennies and equivalent to .07 of a U.S. dollar. [ME *sexe pans.* See SIX, PENCE]

six·pen·ny (siks′pen′ē, -pə nē), *adj.* **1.** of the amount or value of sixpence; costing sixpence. **2.** of trifling value; cheap; paltry. **3.** noting a nail two inches long. *Abbr.:* 6d [ME; see SIX, -PENNY]

six-shoot·er (siks′sho͞o′tər, -sho͞o′-), *n.* a revolver from which six shots can be fired without reloading.

six-spot (siks′spot′), *n.* a playing card or the upward face of a die bearing six pips; a domino one half of which bears six pips.

sixte (sikst), *n.* *Fencing.* the sixth of eight defensive positions. [< F < L *sext(us)* sixth]

six·teen (siks′tēn′), *n.* **1.** a cardinal number, ten plus six. **2.** a symbol for this number, as 16 or XVI. **3.** a set of this many persons or things. —*adj.* **4.** amounting to 16 in number. [ME, OE *sixtēne*; c. D *zestien*, G *sechzehn*, Icel *sextān.* See SIX, TEN, -TEEN]

six·teen·mo (siks′tēn′mō), *n., pl.* **-mos,** *adj.* —*n.* **1.** Also called **sextodecimo.** a book size (about 4 × 6 inches) determined by printing on sheets folded to form 16 leaves or 32 pages. **2.** a book of this size. *Abbr.:* 16mo, 16° —*adj.* **3.** printed, folded, or bound in sixteenmo; sextodecimo. [SIXTEEN + -MO]

six·teen·pen·ny (siks′tēn′pen′ē), *adj.* noting a nail 3½ inches long. *Abbr.:* 16d [SIXTEEN + -PENNY]

six·teenth (siks′tēnth′), *adj.* **1.** next after the fifteenth; being the ordinal number for 16. **2.** being one of 16 equal parts. —*n.* **3.** a sixteenth part, esp. of one (1/16). **4.** the sixteenth member of a series. **5.** *Music.* See **sixteenth note.** [SIXTEEN + -TH²; r. ME *sixtenthe*, *sixtethe*, OE *sixtēotha.* See SIX, TITHE]

six′teenth′ note′, *Music.* a note having one sixteenth of the time value of a whole note; semiquaver. See illus. under **note.**

sixth (siksth), *adj.* **1.** next after the fifth; being the ordinal number for six. **2.** being one of six equal parts. —*n.* **3.** a sixth part, esp. of one (1/6). **4.** the sixth member of a series. **5.** *Music.* **a.** a tone on the sixth degree from a given tone (counted as a first). **b.** the interval between such tones. **c.** the harmonic combination of such tones. [SIX + -TH²; r. *sixt*, ME *sixte*, OE *sixta*] —**sixth′ly,** *adv.*

sixth′ chord′, *Music.* an inversion of a triad in which the second note (next above the root) is in the bass.

sixth′ col′umn, **1.** the persons residing in a country at war who are devoted to aiding the fifth column in its activities, esp. by lowering morale, spreading rumors, etc. **2.** the persons residing in a country at war who are devoted to blocking the efforts of the fifth column.

sixth′ sense′, a power of perception beyond the five senses; intuition: *Even though there were no physical signs, a sixth sense told her that someone had been in the house.*

six·ti·eth (siks′tē ith), *adj.* **1.** next after the fifty-ninth; being the ordinal number for 60. **2.** being one of 60 equal parts. —*n.* **3.** a sixtieth part, esp. of one (1/60). **4.** the sixtieth member of a series. [SIXTY + -ETH²; r. ME *sixtithe*, OE *sixtigetha.* See SIX, TITHE]

Six·tine (siks′tēn, -tin, -tīn), *adj.* Sistine.

Six·tus I (siks′təs), **Saint,** pope A.D. 116?–125?. Also, **Xystus I.**

Sixtus II, Saint, died A.D. 258, pope 257–258. Also, **Xystus II.**

Sixtus III, Saint, pope A.D. 432–440. Also, **Xystus III.**

Sixtus IV, (*Francesco della Rovere*) 1414–84, Italian ecclesiastic: pope 1471–84.

Sixtus V, (*Felice Peretti*) 1521–90, Italian ecclesiastic: pope 1585–90.

six·ty (siks′tē), *n., pl.* **-ties,** *adj.* —*n.* **1.** a cardinal number, 10 times 6. **2.** a symbol for this number, as 60 or LX. **3.** a set of this many persons or things. **4. sixties,** the numbers 60 through 69, esp. the 60th through the 69th years of a lifetime or of a given or implied century. **5. like sixty,** *Informal.* very easily or quickly: *She can prepare a meal like sixty.* —*adj.* **6.** amounting to 60 in number. [ME, OE *sixtig*; c. D *zestig*, G *sechzig*, Icel *sextigir.* See SIX, -TY¹]

six·ty-eight (sik′stē āt′), *n.* **1.** a cardinal number, 60 plus 8. **2.** a symbol for this number, as 68 or LXVIII. **3.** a set of this many persons or things. —*adj.* **4.** amounting to 68 in number.

six·ty-eighth (siks′tē ātth′), *adj.* **1.** next after the sixty-seventh; being the ordinal number for 68. **2.**

being one of 68 equal parts. —*n.* **3.** a sixty-eighth part, esp. of one (1/68). **4.** the sixty-eighth member of a series.

six·ty-fifth (siks′tē fifth′), *adj.* **1.** next after the sixty-fourth; being the ordinal number for 65. **2.** being one of 65 equal parts. —*n.* **3.** a sixty-fifth part, esp. of one (1/65). **4.** the sixty-fifth member of a series.

six·ty-first (siks′tē fûrst′), *adj.* **1.** next after the sixtieth; being the ordinal number for 61. **2.** being one of 61 equal parts. —*n.* **3.** a sixty-first part, esp. of one (1/61). **4.** the sixty-first member of a series.

six·ty-five (siks′tē fīv′), *n.* **1.** a cardinal number, 60 plus 5. **2.** a symbol for this number, as 65 or LXV. **3.** a set of this many persons or things. —*adj.* **4.** amounting to 65 in number.

six·ty-four (siks′tē fōr′, -fôr′), *n.* **1.** a cardinal number, 60 plus 4. **2.** a symbol for this number, as 64 or LXIV. **3.** a set of this many persons or things. —*adj.* **4.** amounting to 64 in number.

six′ty-four-dol′lar ques′tion (siks′tē fōr′dol′ər, -fôr′-), the critical or basic question or problem: *Whether the measure will get through Congress this session or not is the sixty-four-dollar question.* [from the fact that 64 dollars was the largest prize on a popular radio quiz show in the 1940's]

six·ty-four·mo (siks′tē fōr′mō, -fôr′-), *n., pl.* **-mos,** *adj.* —*n.* **1.** a book size (about 2 × 3 inches) determined by printing on sheets folded to form 64 leaves or 128 pages. **2.** a book of this size. *Abbr.:* 64mo, 64° —*adj.* **3.** printed, folded, or bound in sixty-fourmo.

six·ty-fourth (siks′tē fōrth′, -fôrth′), *adj.* **1.** next after the sixty-third; being the ordinal number for 64. **2.** being one of 64 equal parts. —*n.* **3.** a sixty-fourth part, esp. of one (1/64). **4.** the sixty-fourth member of a series.

six′ty-fourth′ note′, *Music.* a note having 1/64th of the time value of a whole note; hemidemisemiquaver. See illus. under **note.**

six·ty-nine (siks′tē nīn′), *n.* **1.** a cardinal number, 60 plus 9. **2.** a symbol for this number, as 69 or LXIX. **3.** a set of this many persons or things. —*adj.* **4.** amounting to 69 in number.

six·ty-ninth (siks′tē nīnth′), *adj.* **1.** next after the sixty-eighth; being the ordinal number for 69. **2.** being one of 69 equal parts. —*n.* **3.** a sixty-ninth part, esp. of one (1/69). **4.** the sixty-ninth member of a series.

six·ty-one (siks′tē wun′), *n.* **1.** a cardinal number, 60 plus 1. **2.** a symbol for this number, as 61 or LXI. **3.** a set of this many persons or things. —*adj.* **4.** amounting to 61 in number.

six·ty-pen·ny (siks′tē pen′ē), *adj.* noting a nail six inches long. *Abbr.:* 60d [SIXTY + -PENNY]

six·ty-sec·ond (siks′tē sek′ənd), *adj.* **1.** next after the sixty-first; being the ordinal number for 62. **2.** being one of 62 equal parts. —*n.* **3.** a sixty-second part, esp. of one (1/62). **4.** the sixty-second member of a series.

six·ty-sev·en (siks′tē sev′ən), *n.* **1.** a cardinal number, 60 plus 7. **2.** a symbol for this number, as 67 or LXVII. **3.** a set of this many persons or things. —*adj.* **4.** amounting to 67 in number.

six·ty-sev·enth (siks′tē sev′ənth), *adj.* **1.** next after the sixty-sixth; being the ordinal number for 67. **2.** being one of 67 equal parts. —*n.* **3.** a sixty-seventh part, esp. of one (1/67). **4.** the sixty-seventh member of a series.

six·ty-six (siks′tē siks′), *n.* **1.** a cardinal number, 60 plus 6. **2.** a symbol for this number, as 66 or LXVI. **3.** a set of this many persons or things. **4.** a card game that is played by two opponents with a 24-card pack made by removing all cards below the nines from a regular 52-card pack, the object being to score 66 points before one's opponent. —*adj.* **5.** amounting to 66 in number.

six·ty-sixth (siks′tē siksth′), *adj.* **1.** next after the sixty-fifth; being the ordinal number for 66. **2.** being one of 66 equal parts. —*n.* **3.** a sixty-sixth part, esp. of one (1/66). **4.** the sixty-sixth member of a series.

six·ty-third (siks′tē thûrd′), *adj.* **1.** next after the sixty-second; being the ordinal number for 63. **2.** being one of 63 equal parts. —*n.* **3.** a sixty-third part, esp. of one (1/63). **4.** the sixty-third member of a series.

six·ty-three (siks′tē thrē′), *n.* **1.** a cardinal number, 60 plus 3. **2.** a symbol for this number, as 63 or LXIII. **3.** a set of this many persons or things. —*adj.* **4.** amounting to 63 in number.

six·ty-two (siks′tē to͞o′), *n.* **1.** a cardinal number, 60 plus 2. **2.** a symbol for this number, as 62 or LXII. **3.** a set of this many persons or things. —*adj.* **4.** amounting to 62 in number.

siz·a·ble (sī′zə bəl), *adj.* **1.** of considerable size; fairly large: *He inherited a sizable fortune.* **2.** *Obs.* of convenient size. Also, **sizeable.** [SIZE[1] + -ABLE] —**siz′a·ble·ness,** *n.* —**siz′a·bly,** *adv.*

siz·ar (sī′zər), *n.* (at Cambridge University and at Trinity College, Dublin) an undergraduate who receives aid from the college for his maintenance. Also, **sizer.** [SIZE[1] + -AR[3]] —**siz′ar·ship′,** *n.*

size[1] (sīz), *n., v.,* **sized, siz·ing.** —*n.* **1.** the spatial dimensions, proportions, magnitude, or bulk of anything: *the size of a farm; What size was that fish you caught?* **2.** considerable or great magnitude: *to seek size rather than quality.* **3.** one of a series of graduated measures for articles of manufacture or trade: *children's sizes of shoes.* **4.** extent; amount; range: *a fortune of great size.* **5.** actual condition, circumstance, or state of affairs: *That's about the size of it.* **6.** a number of population or contents: *What size is Springfield, Illinois? The size of that last shipment was only a dozen.* **7.** *Metalworking.* the operation of sizing. **8.** *Obs.* a fixed standard of quality or quantity, as for food, drink, or the like. **9. of a size,** of the same or similar size: *The two poodles are of a size and of the same color.* —*v.t.* **10.** to separate or sort according to size. **11.** to make of a certain size. **12.** *Metalworking.* to coin (a forging) to close tolerances. **13.** *Metall.* to press (a sintered compact) to close tolerances. **14.** *Obs.* to regulate or control according to a fixed standard. **15. size up,** *Informal.* **a.** to form an estimate of (a situation, person, etc.); judge: *They sized him up with a look.* **b.** to meet a certain standard: *He doesn't size up to my expectations.* [ME *syse* < OF *sise,* aph. var. of *assise* ASSIZE; orig. control, regulation]

—**Syn. 1.** SIZE, VOLUME, MASS, BULK are terms referring to extent or dimensions of that which has magnitude and occupies space. SIZE is the general word: *of great size; small in size.* VOLUME often applies to something that has no fixed shape: *Smoke has volume.* MASS, also, does not suggest shape, but suggests a quantity of matter in a solid body: *a mass of concrete.* BULK suggests weight, and often a recognizable, though perhaps unwieldy, shape: *the huge bulk of an elephant.*

size[2] (sīz), *n., v.,* **sized, siz·ing.** —*n.* **1.** any of various gelatinous or glutinous preparations made from glue, starch, etc., used for filling the pores of cloth, paper, etc., or as an adhesive ground for gold leaf on books. —*v.t.* **2.** to coat or treat with size. [ME *sise, syse;* special use of SIZE[1]]

size·a·ble (sī′zə bəl), *adj.* sizable. —**size′a·ble·ness,** *n.* —**size′a·bly,** *adv.*

sized (sīzd), *adj.* having size as specified (often used in combination): *middle-sized.* [SIZE[1] + -ED[3]]

siz·er[1] (sī′zər), *n.* **1.** any device for measuring or sorting objects according to size. **2.** a worker who judges or sorts objects according to size. [SIZE[1] + -ER[1]]

siz·er[2] (sī′zər), *n.* sizar.

size-up (sīz′up′), *n.* **1.** an appraisal or estimation, esp. as the result of sizing up: *asking for a size-up of the new office equipment.* **2.** the act of sizing up a person, situation, etc.: *He made a rapid and skillful size-up as he viewed each sketch.* [n. use of v. phrase *size up*]

siz·ing (sī′zing), *n.* **1.** the act or process of applying size or preparing with size. **2.** size, as for glazing paper. [SIZE[2] + -ING[1]]

siz·y (sī′zē), *adj.,* **siz·i·er, siz·i·est.** *Archaic.* thick; viscous. [SIZE[2] + -Y[1]] —**siz′i·ness,** *n.*

siz·zle (siz′əl), *v.,* **-zled, -zling,** *n.* —*v.i.* **1.** to make a hissing sound, as in frying or burning. **2.** *Informal.* to be very hot: *It's sizzling out.* **3.** *Informal.* to be very angry; harbor deep resentment or anger: *She's still sizzling over that snub.* —*n.* **4.** a sizzling sound. [imit.] —**siz′zler,** *n.* —**siz′zling·ly,** *adv.*

S.J., Society of Jesus.

Sjael·land (shel′län), *n.* Danish name of **Zealand.**

sjam·bok (sham bok′, -buk′), *n.* **1.** (in Southern Africa) a heavy whip, usually of rhinoceros hide. —*v.t.* **2.** to whip with or as with such a whip. [< SAfrD *sambok* < Malay *cambok* big whip < Hindi *cābuk*]

S.J.D., Doctor of Juridical Science. [< L *Scientiae Juridicae Doctor*]

S.J. Res., Senate joint resolution.

sk., sack.

Ska·gen (skä′gən), *n.* See **Skaw, The.**

Skag·er·rak (skag′ə rak′, skä′gə räk′), *n.* an arm of the North Sea, between Denmark and Norway. 150 mi. long; 80–90 mi. wide.

Skag·way (skag′wā′), *n.* a town in SE Alaska, near the famous White and Chilkoot passes to the Klondike gold fields: railway terminus. 659 (1960).

skald (skôld, skäld), *n.* one of the ancient Scandinavian poets. Also, **scald.** [< Icel: poet] —**skald′ic,** *adj.* —**skald′ship,** *n.*

Skan·e·at·e·les (skan′ē at′lis, skin′-), *n.* a town in central New York. 2921 (1960).

Ska·ra Brae (skar′ə brā′), the site of an excavated Neolithic village on Pomona in the Orkney Islands, dating from c2000 B.C.

skat (skät), *n.* a card game for three players, using a pack of 32 playing cards, sevens through aces, the object being to fulfill any of various contracts, with scoring computed on strategy and on tricks won. [< It *scart(o)* a discard, back formation from *scartare* to discard, equiv. to *s-* EX-[1] + *cart-* CARD[1] + *-o* masc. n. ending]

skate[1] (skāt), *n., v.,* **skat·ed, skat·ing.** —*n.* **1.** See **ice skate** (def. 1). **2.** See **roller skate. 3.** the blade of an ice skate. **4.** a skid on a lifeboat to facilitate launching from a listing ship. —*v.i.* **5.** to glide or propel oneself over ice, the ground, etc., on skates. **6.** to glide or slide smoothly along. —*v.t.* **7.** to slide (a flat) across the floor of a stage. **8. skate on thin ice,** to be or place oneself in a risky or delicate situation: *To take a public stand on the question would be skating on thin ice.* [back formation from D *schaats* skate, MD *schaetse* stilt (ML *scatia*) < ?] —**skate′a·ble,** *adj.*

Skate[2], *Raja erinacea* (Length to 2 ft.)

skate[2] (skāt), *n., pl.* (*esp. collectively*) **skate,** (*esp. referring to two or more kinds or species*) **skates.** any of several rays of the genus *Raja,* usually having a pointed snout, as *R. binoculata* **(big skate),** found along the Pacific coast of the U.S., growing to a length of eight feet. [ME *scate* < Scand; cf. Icel *skata*]

skate[3] (skāt), *n. Slang.* **1.** a contemptible person. **2.** an inferior, decrepit horse; nag. **3.** a person; fellow: *He's a good skate.* [? special use of SKATE[2]]

skate·board (skāt′bōrd′, -bôrd′), *n.* a device for riding upon, usually while standing, consisting of an oblong piece of wood mounted on skate wheels, used on smooth surfaces and requiring better balance of the rider than the ordinary roller skate does. [SKATE[1] + BOARD]

skate·mo·bile (skāt′mō bēl′), *n.* a scooterlike vehicle built of boxes, boards, or the like, and mounted on skate wheels. [SKATE[1] + (AUTO)MOBILE]

skat·er (skā′tər), *n.* **1.** one who skates. **2.** See **water strider.** [SKATE[1] + -ER[1]]

skat·ole (skat′ōl, -ol), *n.* a white, crystalline, water-soluble solid, C_9H_9N, having a strong, fecal odor: used chiefly as a fixative in the manufacture of perfume. [< Gk *skat-* (s. of *skōr*) dung + -OLE]

ska·to·ma (skə tō′mə), *n., pl.* **-mas, -ma·ta** (-mə tə). *Med.* scatoma.

ska·tos·co·py (skə tos′kə pē), *n. Med.* scatoscopy.

Skaw (skô), *n.* **The,** a cape at the N tip of Denmark. Also called **Skagen.**

skean (shkēn, skēn), *n.* a knife or dagger formerly used in Ireland and in the Scottish Highlands. Also, **skene.** [< IrGael *sgian*]

skean dhu (shkēn′ tho͞o′, skēn′), a small knife tucked into or worn against the top of a stocking in the full dress of Highland Scottish males. Also, **skene dhu.** [< ScotGael: lit., black skean]

Skeat (skēt), *n.* **Walter William,** 1835–1912, English philologist and lexicographer.

ske·dad·dle (ski dad′əl), *v.,* **-dled, -dling,** *n. Informal.* —*v.i.* **1.** to run away hurriedly; flee. —*n.* **2.** a hasty flight. [?] —**ske·dad′dler,** *n.*

skee (skē), *n., pl.* **skees, skee,** *v.i., v.t.,* **skeed, skee·ing.** ski.

Skee-Ball (skē′bôl′), *n. Trademark.* a game in which players roll balls up a sloping, table-sized ramp, attempting to score points by making them drop into slots in a target.

skeech (skēkh), *adj., adv. Scot.* skeigh.

skeet[1] (skēt), *n.* a form of trapshooting in which two traps are used and targets are hurled singly or in pairs at varying elevations and speeds so as to simulate the angles of flight taken by game birds. Also called **skeet′ shoot′ing.** [? special use of dial. *skeet* to scatter, var. of SCOOT]

skeet[2] (skēt), *n. Poker.* a hand consisting of a nine, five, two, and two other cards of denominations below nine but not of the same denomination, being of special value in certain games. Also called **kilter, pelter.** [?]

skeg (skeg), *n. Naut.* **1.** a knee reinforcing the junction between a keel and sternpost. **2.** a projection supporting a rudder at its lower end, located abaft a sternpost or rudderpost; shoe. **3.** a piece projecting downward from the forefoot of a ship, as for holding lines for towing paravanes. **4.** an area of deadwood built as an extension of the keel under the stern of a small craft to improve steering qualities. **5.** a short keel, as on a rowboat, extending part of the way forward from the stern. [< D *scheg* cutwater < Scand; cf. Icel *skegg* cutwater, beard]

skeif (skīf, skāf), *n.* scaife.

skeigh (skēkh), *Scot.* —*adj.* **1.** (of horses) spirited; inclined to shy. **2.** (of women) proud; disdainful. —*adv.* **3.** proudly. Also, **skeech, skiech.** [earlier *skeich,* late ME *skey,* OE *scēoh* SHY[2]; *sk-* perh. < MD *schu* shy] —**skeigh′ish,** *adj.*

skein (skān), *n.* **1.** a length of yarn or thread wound on a reel or swift preparatory for use in manufacturing. **2.** anything wound in or resembling such a coil: *a skein of hair.* **3.** something suggestive of the twistings of a skein: *an incoherent skein of words.* **4.** a flock of geese, ducks, or the like, in flight. [late ME *skeyne, skayne* < MF *(e)scaigne*]

skel·e·tal (skel′i təl), *adj.* of, pertaining to, or like a skeleton. [SKELET(ON) + -AL[1]]

skel·e·ton (skel′i tən), *n.* **1.** *Anat., Zool.* **a.** the bones of a man or an animal considered as a whole, together forming the framework of the body. **b.** the bony or cartilaginous framework supporting and protecting the vertebrate body. **2.** any of various structures forming a rigid framework in an invertebrate. **3.** a very lean person or animal. **4.** a supporting framework, as of a leaf, building, or ship. **5.** mere lifeless, dry, or meager remains: *His humorless approach soon made a skeleton of the subject.* **6.** an outline, as of a literary work: *the skeleton of the plot.* **7.** something reduced to its essential parts: *Stripped of chrome and upholstery, the car was a skeleton.* **8.** an accurately triangulated network of survey lines upon which other surveys can be based. **9. skeleton at the feast,** a person or thing that casts gloom over a joyful occasion; a note or reminder of sorrow in the midst of joy. **10. skeleton in the closet** or **cupboard,** a family scandal that is kept concealed to avoid public disgrace; a shameful secret. —*adj.* **11.** of or pertaining to a skeleton. **12.** like a skeleton or mere framework; reduced to the essential parts or numbers: *skeleton staff.* [< NL < Gk: mummy, n. use of neut. of *skeletós* dried up, verbal of *skéllein* to dry] —**skel′e·ton·less,** *adj.* —**skel′e·ton·like′,** *adj.*

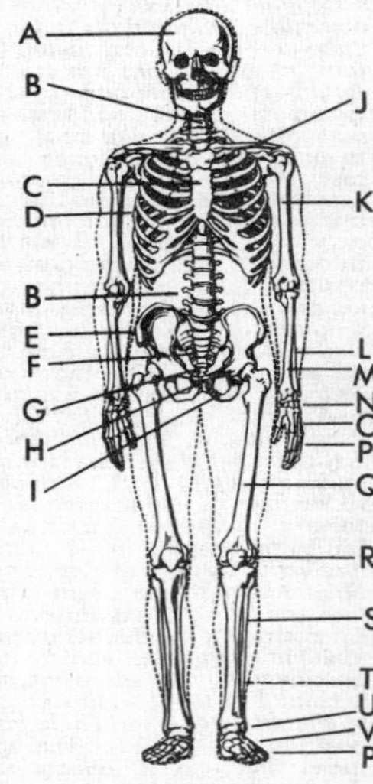

Skeleton (Human)
A, Cranium; B, Vertebrae; C, Sternum; D, Ribs; E, Ilium; F, Sacrum; G, Coccyx; H, Pubis; I, Ischium; J, Clavicle; K, Humerus; L, Ulna; M, Radius; N, Carpus; O, Metacarpus; P, Phalanx; Q, Femur; R, Patella; S, Tibia; T, Fibula; U, Tarsus; V, Metatarsus

skel′eton clock′, a clock the works of which are exposed. Also called **squelette clock.**

skel·e·ton·ise (skel′i tənīz′), *v.t.,* **-ised, -is·ing.** *Chiefly Brit.* skeletonize. —**skel′e·ton·i·sa′tion,** *n.* —**skel′e·ton·is′er,** *n.*

skel·e·ton·ize (skel′i tənīz′), *v.t.,* **-ized, -iz·ing.** **1.** to reduce to a skeleton, outline, or framework. **2.** to reduce in size or number, as a military unit. **3.** to construct in outline. [SKELETON + -IZE] —**skel′e·ton·i·za′tion,** *n.* —**skel′e·ton·iz′er,** *n.*

skel′eton key′, a key with nearly the whole substance of the bit filed away, so that it may open various locks. Also called **passkey.**

skel′ic in′dex (skel′ik), *Anthropometry.* the ratio of the length of a person's leg to the length of his trunk, multiplied by 100. [< Gk *skél(os)* leg + -IC]

skel·lum (skel′əm), *n. Chiefly Scot.* a rascal. [< D *schelm* rogue, knave < MLG; c. G *Schelm* rogue, OHG *skelmo, scalmo* plague, corpse]

skelp[1] (skelp), *Scot. and North Eng.* —*n.* **1.** a slap, smack, or blow, esp. one given with the open hand. **2.** the sound of such a slap or smack. —*v.t.* **3.** to slap, smack, or strike (someone), esp. on the buttocks; spank. **4.** to drive (animals) by slapping or goading them. Also, **scelp.** [late ME; prob. imit.]

skelp[2] (skelp), *n.* metal in strip form that is fed into various rolls and welded to form tubing. [? special use of SKELP[1]]

Skel·ton (skel′tᵊn), *n.* **John,** c1460–1529, English poet.

ske·ne[1] (skē′nē), *n., pl.* **-nai** (-nī). (in the ancient Greek theater) a structure facing the audience and forming the background before which performances were given. [< Gk; see SCENE]

skene[2] (s͟hkēn, skēn), *n.* skean.

skene dhu (s͟hkēn′ t͟hōō′, skēn′). See **skean dhu.**

skep (skep), *n.* **1.** a round farm basket of wicker or wood. **2.** Also, **skepful.** the amount contained in a skep. **3.** a beehive, esp. of straw. [ME *skeppe,* late OE *sceppe* < Scand; cf. Icel *skeppa* half-bushel; akin to G *Scheffel*]

skep·ful (skep′fŏŏl), *n., pl.* **-fuls.** skep (def. 2). [SKEP + -FUL]

skep·tic (skep′tik), *n.* **1.** a person who questions the validity or authenticity of something purporting to be factual. **2.** a person who maintains a doubting attitude, as toward values, plans, statements, or the character of others. **3.** a person who doubts the truth of a religion, esp. Christianity, or of important elements of it. **4.** (*cap.*) *Philos.* **a.** a member of a philosophical school of ancient Greece, the earliest group of which consisted of Pyrrho and his followers, who maintained that real knowledge of things is impossible. **b.** any later thinker who doubts or questions the possibility of real knowledge of any kind. —*adj.* **5.** pertaining to skeptics or skepticism; skeptical. **6.** (*cap.*) pertaining to the Skeptics. Also, **sceptic.** [< L *sceptic(us)* < Gk *skeptikós* thoughtful, inquiring, equiv. to *sképt(esthai)* (to) consider + *-ikos* -IC]
—**Syn. 3.** doubter. See **atheist.** —**Ant. 3.** believer.

skep·ti·cal (skep′ti kəl), *adj.* **1.** inclined to skepticism; having doubt: *a skeptical young man.* **2.** showing doubt: *a skeptical smile.* **3.** denying or questioning the tenets of a religion: *a skeptical approach to the nature of miracles.* **4.** (*cap.*) of or pertaining to Skeptics or Skepticism. Also, **sceptical.** [SKEPTIC + -AL[1]] —**skep′ti·cal·ly,** *adv.* —**skep′ti·cal·ness,** *n.*
—**Syn. 1.** skeptic. See **doubtful. 3.** unbelieving. —**Ant. 1.** confident.

skep·ti·cism (skep′ti siz′əm), *n.* **1.** skeptical attitude or temper; doubt. **2.** doubt or unbelief with regard to a religion, esp. Christianity. **3.** (*cap.*) the doctrines or opinions of philosophical Skeptics; universal doubt. Also, **scepticism.** [< NL *scepticism(us),* equiv. to L *sceptic(us)* SKEPTIC + *-ismus* -ISM]
—**Syn. 1.** questioning, probing, testing. **2.** disbelief, atheism, agnosticism. —**Ant. 2.** faith.

skep·to·phy·lax·is (skep′tō fi lak′sis), *n.* *Med.* tachyphylaxis. Also, **skep·to·phy·lax·i·a** (skep′tō fi lak′sē ə). [< NL < Gk *sképt(ein)* (to) prop, support + *-o-* -o- + *phýlaxis* a watching, guarding, equiv. to *phyláss(ein)* (to) watch + *-sis* -SIS]

sker·rick (sker′ik), *n.* *Australian.* a small piece or quantity; a bit: *Not even a skerrick of cake was left.* [perh. irreg. *scerre,* var. of SCAR[1] (rough cinder)]

sker·ry (sker′ē; *Scot.* skeʀ′ē), *n., pl.* **-ries.** *Chiefly Scot.* **1.** a small, rocky island. **2.** a coastline with a series of such islands offshore. [Shetland *skerri* a rock in the sea < Scand; cf. Icel *sker* (*skerja,* gen. pl.) rock or reef (in the sea). See SCAR[2]]

sketch (skech), *n.* **1.** a simply or hastily executed drawing or painting, esp. a preliminary one, giving the essential features without the details. **2.** a rough design, plan, or draft, as of a book. **3.** a brief or hasty outline of facts, occurrences, etc.: *a sketch of his life.* **4.** a short, usually descriptive, essay, history, or story. **5.** a short play or slight dramatic performance, as one forming part of a vaudeville program. —*v.t.* **6.** to make a sketch of. **7.** to set forth in a brief or general account: *He sketched his own part in the affair.* **8.** *metall.* (in a steel mill or the like) to mark (a piece) for cutting. —*v.i.* **9.** to make a sketch or sketches. [< D *schets* << It *schizzo* < L *schedium* extemporaneous poem < Gk *schédion,* neut. of *schédios* extempore] —**sketch′er,** *n.* —**sketch′ing·ly,** *adv.* —**sketch′like′,** *adj.*
—**Syn. 2.** outline. **5.** skit, act, routine. **6.** draw, outline, design, rough out, delineate, represent. See **depict.**

sketch·a·ble (skech′ə bəl), *adj.* suitable for being sketched. [SKETCH + -ABLE] —**sketch′a·bil′i·ty,** *n.*

sketch·book (skech′bŏŏk′), *n.* **1.** a book or pad of drawing paper for sketches. **2.** a book of literary sketches. Also, **sketch′ book′.** [SKETCH + BOOK]

Sketch′ Book′, The, a collection of essays and stories (1819–20) by Washington Irving.

Sketch′es of a Sports′man. See **Sportsman's Notebook, A.**

sketch′ map′, a rough, freehand map of the principal features of a locale, as one drawn from memory.

sketch′ plate′, *Metall.* a metal plate not rectangular in shape.

sketch·y (skech′ē), *adj.,* **sketch·i·er, sketch·i·est. 1.** like a sketch; giving only outlines or essentials. **2.** imperfect, incomplete, slight, or superficial: *a sketchy meal.* [SKETCH + -Y[1]] —**sketch′i·ly,** *adv.* —**sketch′i·ness,** *n.*

ske·te (skē′tē; *Eng.* skēt), *n.* *Gk. Orth. Ch.* a settlement of monks or ascetics. [< Gk *skḗtē,* after *Skē̂tis* a desert in Lower Egypt known for its hermits]

skew (skyōō), *v.i.* **1.** to turn aside or swerve; take an oblique course. **2.** to look obliquely; squint. —*v.t.* **3.** to give an oblique direction to; shape, form, or cut obliquely. **4.** to distort; depict unfairly. —*adj.* **5.** having an oblique direction or position; slanting. **6.** having a part that deviates from a straight line, right angle, etc.: *skew gearing.* **7.** *Math.* (of a dyad or dyadic) equal to the negative of its conjugate. **8.** (of an arch, bridge, etc.) having the centerline of its opening forming an oblique angle with the direction in which its spanning structure is built. **9.** *Statistics.* (of a distribution) having skewness not equal to zero; asymmetric. —*n.* **10.** an oblique movement, direction, or position. **11.** Also called **skew′ chis′el.** a wood chisel having a cutting edge set obliquely. [late ME *skewe* to slip away, swerve < MD *schuwe(n)* (to) get out of the way, shun, deriv. of *schu* to SHY[2]]

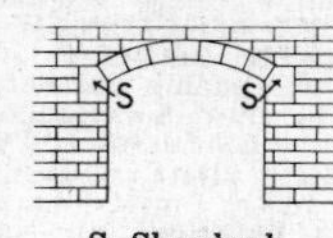

S, Skewback

skew·back (skyōō′bak′), *n.* *Archit.* **1.** a sloping surface against which the end of an arch rests. **2.** a stone, course of masonry, or the like, presenting such a surface. [SKEW + BACK[1]] —**skew′-backed′,** *adj.*

skew·bald (skyōō′bôld′), *adj.* **1.** (esp. of horses) having patches of brown and white. —*n.* **2.** a skewbald horse or pony. [SKEW+ (PIE)BALD]

skew′ cor′bel, *Masonry.* a kneeler at the foot of a gable or the like, esp. one projecting well beyond the surface of the wall; footstone. Also called **skew′ putt′.**

skew·er (skyōō′ər), *n.* **1.** a long pin of wood or metal for inserting through meat or other food to hold it together or in place while being cooked. **2.** any similar pin for fastening or holding an item in place. —*v.t.* **3.** to fasten with, or as with, a skewer. [earlier *skiver* < ?]

skew·er·wood (skyōō′ər wŏŏd′), *n.* *Brit. Dial.* **1.** the spindle tree, *Euonymus europaeus.* **2.** the red dogwood, *Cornus sanguinea.* [SKEWER + WOOD[1]]

skew′ field′, *Math.* a ring in which the equations $ax = b$ and $xa = b$ have solutions for x.

skew·ing (skyōō′ing), *n.* **1.** a process of removing excess gold leaf from a stamped surface. **2. skewings,** the gold leaf so removed. [?]

skew·ness (skyōō′nis), *n.* *Statistics.* **1.** asymmetry in a frequency distribution. **2.** a measure of such asymmetry. [SKEW + -NESS]

skew-sym·met·ric (skyōō′si me′trik), *adj.* *Math.* noting a square matrix that is equal to the negative of its transpose.

skew′ ta′ble, footstone (def. 2).

ski (skē *or, esp. Brit.,* s͟hē), *n., pl.* **skis, ski,** *v.,* **skied, ski·ing.** —*n.* **1.** one of a pair of long, slender runners made of wood, plastic, or metal that can be clamped to ski boots, for use in gliding over snow. **2.** See **water ski.** —*v.i.* **3.** to travel on skis, as for sport. —*v.t.* **4.** to use skis on; travel on skis over: *to ski the slopes of Switzerland.* Also, **skee.** [< Norw, var. of *skid;* c. Icel *skīth,* OE *scīd* thin slip of wood, G *Scheit* thin board] —**ski′a·ble,** *adj.*

ski·a·graph (skī′ə graf′, -gräf′), *n.* **1.** a radiograph made with x-rays. —*v.t.* **2.** to make a skiagraph of. Also, **skiograph.** [back formation from *skiagraphy* < Gk *skiāgraphía* painting in light and shade, equiv. to *skiá* shadow + *-graphia* -GRAPHY] —**ski·ag·ra·pher** (skī ag′rə fər), *n.* —**ski·a·graph·ic** (skī′ə graf′ik), **ski′a·graph′i·cal,** *adj.* —**ski′a·graph′i·cal·ly,** *adv.*

ski·a·scope (skī′ə skōp′), *n.* *Ophthalm.* an apparatus that determines the refractive power of the eye by observing the lights and shadows on the pupil when a mirror illumines the retina; retinoscope. [< Gk *skiá* shadow, shade + -SCOPE] —**ski·as·co·py** (skī as′kə pē), *n.*

Skia·took (skī tōōk′, -tŏŏk′), *n.* a town in NE Oklahoma. 2503 (1960).

ski·a·tron (skī′ə tron′), *n.* *Electronics.* See **dark-trace tube.** [< Gk *skiá* a shadow, shade + -TRON]

ski′ boot′, a heavy, thick-soled, ankle-high shoe for skiing, often having padding and extra supporting straps and laces around the ankle, with grooves at the back of the heel for binding to a ski.

skid (skid), *n., v.,* **skid·ded, skid·ding.** —*n.* **1.** a plank, bar, log, or the like, esp. one of a pair, on which something heavy may be slid or rolled along. **2.** one of a number of such logs or timbers forming a skidway. **3.** a low mobile platform on which goods are placed for ease in handling, moving, etc. Cf. **stillage. 4.** a plank, log, low platform, etc., on or by which a load is supported. **5.** *Naut.* **a.** any of a number of parallel beams or timbers fixed in place as a raised support for boats, spars, etc. **b.** any of a number of timbers on which a heavy object is placed to be shoved along on rollers or slid. **c.** an arrangement of planks serving as a runway for cargo. **d.** an arrangement of planks serving as a fender to protect the side of a vessel during transfer of cargo. **e.** sidewise motion of a vessel; leeway. **6.** a shoe or some other choke or drag for preventing the wheel of a vehicle from rotating, as when descending a hill. **7.** a runner on the under part of some airplanes, enabling the aircraft to slide along the ground when landing. **8.** the act or an instance of skidding: *The car went into a skid on the icy pavement.* **9. put the skids under,** *Slang.* to bring about the downfall of; cause to fail: *Lack of money put the skids under our plans.* **10. the skids,** the downward path to ruin, poverty, or depravity: *After losing his job he began to hit the skids.* —*v.t.* **11.** to place on or slide along a skid or skids. **12.** to check or prevent motion with a skid, as a wheel. —*v.i.* **13.** to slide along without rotating, as a wheel to which a brake has been applied. **14.** to slip or slide sideways relative to direction of wheel rotation, as an automobile in turning a corner rapidly. **15.** to slide forward under the force of momentum after forward motion has been braked, as a vehicle. **16.** (of an airplane when not banked sufficiently) to slide sideways, away from the center of the curve described in turning. Cf. **slip**[1] (def. 12). [appar. < Scand; cf. Icel *skīth,* c. OE *scīd* thin slip of wood; see SKI] —**skid′der,** *n.* —**skid′ding·ly,** *adv.*
—**Syn. 11, 13.** slip. **14.** slither.

Skid·blad·nir (skēd′bläd nir), *n.* *Scand. Myth.* the huge collapsible ship, made by two dwarfs for Frey, which always had a favoring wind.

skid′ chain′. See **tire chain.**

skid·doo (ski dōō′), *v.i.,* **-dooed, -doo·ing.** *Informal.* to go away; get out. [? alter. of SKEDADDLE]

skid′ fin′, *Aeron.* an upright projection or fin, positioned from leading edge to trailing edge in the center of the upper wing of some early airplanes and used to retard skidding.

skid·proof (skid′prōōf′), *adj.* preventing or resistant to skidding, as certain road surfaces, vehicle tires, etc. [SKID + -PROOF]

skid′ row′ (rō), a run-down area of cheap barrooms, luncheonettes, and shabby hotels, frequented by alcoholics and vagrants. Also called **Skid′ Road′.**

skid·way (skid′wā′), *n.* **1.** a road or path formed of logs, planks, etc., for sliding objects. **2.** a platform, usually inclined, for piling logs to be sawed or to be loaded onto a vehicle. [SKID + WAY]

skiech (skēᴋʜ), *adj., adv.* *Scot.* skeigh.

skied[1] (skēd), *v.* pt. of **ski.**

skied[2] (skīd), *v.* a pt. of **sky.**

ski·er (skē′ər), *n.* a person who skis. [SKI + -ER[1]]

skies (skīz), *n.* **1.** pl. of **sky.** —*v.* **2.** 3rd pers. sing. pres. of **sky.**

skiff (skif), *n.* **1.** any of various types of boats small enough for sailing or rowing by one person. **2.** Also called **St. Lawrence skiff.** a light boat having a centerboard, usually propelled by a spritsail but sometimes by oars. [< early It *schif(o)* < OHG *scif* SHIP] —**skiff′less,** *adj.*

skif·fle[1] (skif′əl), *v.t.,* **-fled, -fling.** knob (def. 5). [? alter. of SCABBLE]

skif·fle[2] (skif′əl), *n.* **1.** a jazz style of the 1920's deriving from blues, ragtime, and folk music, played by bands made up of both standard and improvised instruments. **2.** a style of popular music developing in England during the 1950's, deriving from hillbilly music and rock-'n'-roll, and played on a heterogeneous group of instruments, as guitar, washboard, ceramic jug, washtub, and kazoo. [?]

ski·ing (skē′ing), *n.* the act or sport of gliding on skis. [SKI + -ING[1]]

ski·jor·ing (skē jôr′ing, -jōr′-, skē′jôr-, -jōr-), *n.* a sport in which a skier is pulled over snow or ice, generally by a horse. [< Norw *skikjøring* (*kj-* pronounced somewhat like E *j*), lit., ski-driving] —**ski·jor′er,** *n.*

ski′ jump′, 1. a snow-covered chute or slide at the side of a hill or built up on top of the hill, the base of the chute having a horizontal ramp that enables a skier to speed down the chute, take off at the end of the ramp, and land further down the hill. **2.** a jump made by a skier from a ski jump. —**ski′ jump′er.**

skil·fish (skil′fish′), *n., pl.* **-fish·es,** (*esp. collectively*) **-fish.** a sablefish, *Erilepsis zonifer,* found in the North Pacific. [< Haida *sqil* + FISH]

skil·ful (skil′fəl), *adj.* skillful. —**skil′ful·ly,** *adv.* —**skil′ful·ness,** *n.*

ski′ lift′, an apparatus for conveying skiers up the side of a slope, consisting typically of a series of chairs suspended from an endless cable driven by motors.

skill[1] (skil), *n.* **1.** the ability, coming from one's knowledge, practice, aptitude, etc., to do something well: *Carpentry was one of his many skills.* **2.** competent excellence in performance; expertness; dexterity: *The dancers performed with skill.* **3.** a craft, trade, or job requiring manual dexterity or special training in which a person has competence and experience: *What skills do you have other than typing and shorthand?* **4.** *Obs.* understanding; discernment. **5.** *Obs.* reason; cause. [ME < Scand; cf. Icel *skil* distinction, difference; c. D *geschil* difference, quarrel. See SKILL[2]]
—**Syn. 1.** proficiency, facility. **2.** deftness, cleverness. —**Ant. 1.** inability.

skill[2] (skil), *v.i.* *Archaic.* **1.** to matter. **2.** to help; avail. [ME *skil(ien)* < Scand; cf. Icel *skilja* to distinguish, divide, akin to OE *scylian* to separate, Goth *skilja* butcher, Lith *skelti* to split]

skilled (skild), *adj.* **1.** having skill; trained or experienced in work that requires skill. **2.** showing, involving, or requiring skill, as certain work. [SKILL[1] + -ED[3]]
—**Syn. 1.** See **skillful.**

skilled′ la′bor, 1. labor that requires special training for its satisfactory performance. **2.** the workers employed in such labor.

skil·less (skil′lis), *adj.* skill-less. —**skil′less·ness,** *n.*

skil·let (skil′it), *n.* **1.** See **frying pan. 2.** *Chiefly Brit.* a long-handled saucepan. **3.** a cylindrical serving vessel of the late 17th and early 18th centuries, having a hinged lid, a handle, and, sometimes, feet. [late ME *skelet,* dim. of *skele* < Scand; cf. Icel *skjōla* pail, bucket; see -ET]

skil·let·fish (skil′it fish′), *n., pl.* **-fish·es,** (*esp. collectively*) **-fish.** a clingfish, *Gobiesox strumosis,* found in the eastern U.S. [SKILLET + FISH]

skill·ful (skil′fəl), *adj.* **1.** having or exercising skill: *a skillful juggler.* **2.** showing or involving skill: *a skillful display of fancy diving.* **3.** *Obs.* reasonable; rational. Also, **skilful.** [ME; see SKILL[1], -FUL] —**skill′ful·ly,** *adv.* —**skill′ful·ness,** *n.*
—**Syn. 1.** ready, adroit, deft, adept, apt, clever, ingenious. SKILLFUL, SKILLED, EXPERT refer to readiness and adroitness in an occupation, craft, or art. SKILLFUL suggests esp. adroitness and dexterity: *a skillful watchmaker.* SKILLED implies having had long experience and thus having acquired a high degree of proficiency: *not an amateur but a skilled workman.* EXPERT means having the highest degree of proficiency; it may mean much the same as SKILLFUL or SKILLED, or both: *expert workmanship.* —**Ant. 1.** awkward, clumsy, amateurish.

skil·ling[1] (skil′ing), *n.* **1.** a former silver coin of Denmark, Sweden, and the Danish West Indies. **2.** any of various former copper coins of Sweden and Norway. [< Scand; cf. SHILLING]

skil·ling[2] (skil′ing), *n.* *Brit., Australian.* a lean-to attached to a house or hut. Also, **skil·lion** (skil′yən). [ME *skelyng,* equiv. to *skel-* (< Scand) + *-yng* -ING[1]]

skill-less (skil′lis), *adj.* **1.** without skill; unskilled or unskillful. **2.** *Archaic.* **a.** without knowledge; ignorant. **b.** (of things) done or made in a clumsy or unskilled manner. Also, **skilless.** [ME; see SKILL[1], -LESS] —**skill′-less·ness,** *n.*

skim (skim), *v.,* **skimmed, skim·ming,** *n.* —*v.t.* **1.** to take up or remove (floating matter) from the surface of a liquid, as with a spoon, ladle, etc.: *to skim the cream from milk.* **2.** to clear (liquid) thus: *to skim milk.* **3.** *Metall.* to remove (slag, scum, or dross) from the surface of molten metal. **4.** to move or glide lightly over or along (a surface, as of the ground, water, etc.): *The sailboat skimmed the lake.* **5.** to throw in a smooth gliding path over or near a surface, or so as to bounce or ricochet along the surface: *to skim a stone across the lake.* **6.** to read, study, consider, treat, etc., in a superficial or cursory manner. **7.** to cover, as a liquid, with a thin layer: *Ice skimmed the lake at night.* —*v.i.* **8.** to pass or glide lightly along over or near a surface. **9.** to read, study, consider, etc., something in a superficial or cursory way (usually fol. by *over*). **10.** to become covered with a thin layer. —*n.* **11.** the act or an instance of skimming. **12.** that which is skimmed off. **13.** a thin layer or film formed on the surface of something, esp. a liquid, as the coagulated protein material formed on boiled milk. **14.** a thin layer, as of mortar. **15.** See **skim milk.** **16.** *Obs.* scum. [late ME *skym*, var. of obs. *scum* to skim; see SCUM]

skim·ble-scam·ble (skim′bəl skam′bəl, skim′əl, skam′əl), *adj.* rambling; confused; nonsensical: *a skimble-scamble explanation.* Also, **skim′ble-skam′ble.** [gradational redupl. of dial. *scamble* to struggle, trample]

skimmed′ milk′. See **skim milk.**

skim·mer (skim′ər), *n.* **1.** one who or that which skims. **2.** a shallow utensil, usually perforated, used in skimming liquids. **3.** any of several gull-like birds of the family *Rynchopidae*, that skim the water with the elongated lower mandible immersed while in search of food. **4.** a stiff, wide-brimmed hat with a shallow flat crown, usually made of straw. [SKIM + -ER[1]; r. ME *skemour, skymour*, var. of *schumour* < MF *(e)scumoir* ladle for skimming; see SCUM]

skim′mer gate′, *Foundry.* a sprue or screen for holding slag or scum from metal entering the mold cavity.

skim·mi·a (skim′ē ə), *n.* any Asian, evergreen, rutaceous shrub of the genus *Skimmia*, having a red, berrylike fruit, grown as an ornamental. [< NL]

skim′ milk′, milk from which the cream has been skimmed. Also called **skimmed milk.**

skim·ming (skim′ing), *n.* **1.** Usually, **skimmings.** that which is removed by skimming. **2. skimmings,** *Metall.* dross. [late ME *skemmyng.* See SKIM, -ING[1]]

Ski·mo (skē′mō), *n., pl.* **-mos.** *Canadian Slang.* an Eskimo. [by shortening]

skimp (skimp), *v.t., v.i.* **1.** to scrimp: *He skimped to save money for his children.* **2.** to scamp. —*adj.* **3.** scrimpy; scanty. [?] —**skimp′ing·ly,** *adv.*

skimp·y (skim′pē), *adj.,* **skimp·i·er, skimp·i·est.** **1.** lacking in size, fullness, etc.; scanty: *a skimpy hem; a skimpy dinner.* **2.** too thrifty; stingy: *a skimpy housewife.* [SKIMP + -Y[1]] —**skimp′i·ly,** *adv.* —**skimp′i·ness,** *n.*

skin (skin), *n., v.,* **skinned, skin·ning.** —*n.* **1.** the external covering or integument of an animal body, esp. when soft and flexible. **2.** such an integument stripped from the body of an animal, esp. a small animal; pelt: *a beaver skin.* **3.** any integumentary covering, casing, outer coating, or surface layer, as an investing membrane, the rind or peel of fruit, or a film on liquid: *a skin of thin ice; the aluminum skin of an airplane.* **4.** *Jewelry.* **a.** the outermost layer of a pearl. **b.** the outermost layer of a diamond as found: often different in color and refraction from the inner part of the stone. **5.** *Naut.* **a.** the shell or ceiling of a hull. **b.** the outer, exposed part of a furled sail. **6.** *Metall.* an outer layer of a metal piece having characteristics differing from those of the interior. **7.** *Foundry.* the surface of a wall of a sand mold, when drier or more compact than the remainder of the sand. **8.** a container made of animal skin, used for holding liquids, esp. wine. **9.** *Slang.* a swindler; cheat. **10.** *Slang.* a skinflint. **11.** *Slang.* a horse. **12.** *Slang.* a dollar bill. **13.** *Rocketry.* the outer surface of a missile or rocket. **14. by the skin of one's teeth,** *Informal.* by an extremely narrow margin; just barely; scarcely: *We made the last train by the skin of our teeth.* **15. get under one's skin,** *Slang.* **a.** to irritate; bother: *His laugh really gets under my skin.* **b.** to affect deeply; impress; penetrate: *That sort of music always gets under my skin.* **16. have a thick skin,** to be insensitive to criticism or rebuffs: *Working at the complaint desk of a store is a good job for someone who has a thick skin.* **17. have a thin skin,** to be extremely sensitive to criticism or rebuffs; be easily offended: *Be careful what you say to her, she has a thin skin.* **18. in** or **with a whole skin,** without harm; unscathed; safely: *He escaped from a burning building with a whole skin.* **19. no skin off one's back, nose,** or **teeth,** *Slang.* of no interest or concern or involving no risk to one: *That's no skin off your back.* **20. save one's skin,** *Informal.* to avoid harm, esp. to escape death: *They betrayed their country to save their skins.* —*v.t.* **21.** to strip or deprive of skin; flay; peel; husk. **22.** to remove or strip off (any covering, outer coating, surface layer, etc.). **23.** to scrape or rub a small piece of skin from (one's hand, leg, etc.), as in falling or scraping against something: *He skinned his knee playing basketball.* **24.** to urge on, drive, or whip a draft animal, as a mule or ox. **25.** to climb or jump (often fol. by *up* or *over*): *He skinned the rope to the top of the wall.* **26.** to cover with or as with skin. **27.** *Slang.* to strip of money or belongings; fleece, as in gambling. **28.** *Cards Slang.* to slide cards one at a time off the top of (the pack) in dealing. **29.** *Slang.* to defeat completely: *He was skinned at the polls.* **30.** *Slang.* to castigate; reprimand: *He was skinned for his disobedience.* —*v.i.* **31.** *Slang.* to slip off or depart hurriedly (often followed by *out*). **32. skin alive,** *Informal.* **a.** to reprimand; scold. **b.** to subdue completely, esp. in a cruel or ruthless manner: *The home team was skinned alive this afternoon.* [ME < Scand; cf. Icel *skinn*; c. G (dial.) *Schind(e)* skin of fruit] —**skin′like′,** *adj.*
—**Syn. 2.** fur. SKIN, HIDE, PELT are names for the outer covering of animals, including man. SKIN is the general word: *an abrasion of the skin; the skin of a muskrat.* HIDE applies to the skin of large animals, as cattle, horses, elephants: *a buffalo hide.* PELT applies to the untanned skin of smaller animals: *a mink pelt.* **3.** hull, shell, husk, crust.

skin′ and bones′, a person or constitution of extreme or abnormal thinness, usually the result of malnutrition; emaciation: *There was nothing left of the poor thing after her illness but skin and bones.*

skin-deep (skin′dēp′), *adj.* **1.** superficial or slight; not profound or substantial: *Her generosity is only skin-deep.* —*adv.* **2.** slightly; superficially: *He went into the subject only skin-deep.*

skin-dive (skin′dīv′), *v.i.,* **-dived** or **-dove** (-dōv′), **-div·ing.** to engage in skin diving. —**skin′-div′er,** *n.*

skin′ div′ing, an underwater sport in which the swimmer, equipped with a lightweight mask, foot fins, and either a snorkel or a portable air cylinder and breathing device, can move about quickly and easily underwater, as for exploring or spear fishing. Also called, *esp. Brit.,* **free diving.**

skin′ effect′, *Elect.* the phenomenon in which an alternating current tends to concentrate in the outer layer of a conductor, caused by the self-induction of the conductor and resulting in increased resistance.

skin·flint (skin′flint′), *n.* a mean, niggardly person; miser. [SKIN + FLINT] —**skin′flint′i·ly,** *adv.* —**skin′flint′i·ness,** *n.* —**skin′flint′y,** *adj.*

skin′ fric′tion drag′, *Aeron.* aerodynamic resistance or drag due to the contact of moving air with the surface of an airplane, a glider, etc.

skin·ful (skin′fo͝ol′), *n., pl.* **-fuls.** **1.** the amount that a skin container can hold. **2.** *Informal.* a large or satisfying amount of food and drink. **3.** *Informal.* an amount of liquor sufficient to make one drunk. [SKIN + -FUL]

skin′ game′, **1.** a dishonest or unscrupulous business operation, scheme, etc. **2.** any cheating or fraudulent trick.

skin′ graft′, *Surg.* skin used for transplanting in skin grafting.

skin′ graft′ing, *Surg.* the transplanting of healthy skin from the patient's or another's body to a wound or burn, to form new skin. Also called **dermatoplasty.**

skin·head (skin′hed′), *n. Slang.* **1.** a marine recruit; boot. **2.** a boy or young man with closely cropped hair or a shaved head. **3.** a baldheaded man. [SKIN + HEAD]

skink[1] (skingk), *n.* any of numerous lizards of the family *Scincidae*, common in many regions of the Old and New World, typically having flat, smooth, overlapping scales and comprising terrestrial, arboreal, and fossorial species. [< L *scinc(us)* < Gk *skínkos* lizard]

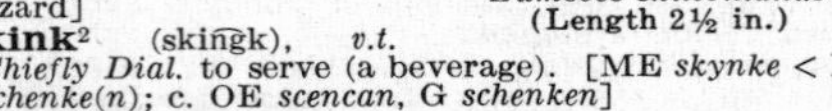

Skink,
Eumeces skiltonianus
(Length 2½ in.)

skink[2] (skingk), *v.t. Chiefly Dial.* to serve (a beverage). [ME *skynke* < MD *schenke(n)*; c. OE *scencan*, G *schenken*]

skink·ing (sking′king), *adj. Scot.* (of liquor, soup, etc.) watery; diluted or thin. [SKINK[2] + -ING[2]]

skin·less (skin′lis), *adj.* **1.** deprived of skin: *a skinless carcass.* **2.** (of frankfurters or sausages) having no casing. [ME *skinles.* See SKIN, -LESS]

skin·ner (skin′ər), *n.* **1.** one who skins. **2.** one who prepares or deals in skins or hides. **3.** one who drives draft animals, as mules or oxen. **4.** the operator of a piece of heavy equipment used in clearing land or in construction work, as a tractor or bulldozer. [ME; see SKIN, -ER[1]]

Skin·ner (skin′ər), *n.* **1. Cornelia Otis,** born 1901, U.S. actress and author. **2.** her father, **O·tis** (ō′tis), 1858–1942, U.S. actor.

Skin′ner box′, *Psychol.* a boxlike testing device used in experiments on animal learning, esp. in operant conditioning, equipped with a mechanism that, when operated properly, automatically gives it a reward, as food, or permits escape, as by opening a door. [named after B. F. *Skinner* (b. 1904), American psychologist who invented it]

skin·ner·y (skin′ə rē), *n., pl.* **-ner·ies.** a place where skins are prepared, as for the market. [ME; see SKIN, -ERY]

skin·ny (skin′ē), *adj.,* **-ni·er, -ni·est.** **1.** very lean or thin; emaciated: *a skinny little kitten.* **2.** of or like skin. [SKIN + -Y[1]] —**skin′ni·ness,** *n.*
—**Syn. 1.** lank, gaunt, scrawny.

skin·ny-dip (skin′ē dip′), *v.i.,* **-dipped** or **-dipt, -dip·ping.** *Informal.* to swim in the nude. Also, **skin′ny dip′.** —**skin′ny-dip′per,** *n.* —**skin′ny dip′per.**

Skin′ of Our Teeth′, The, a play (1942) by Thornton Wilder.

skin′ plan′ing, *Surg.* dermabrasion.

skin′ reac′tion, an irritation or inflammation of the skin due to an allergy or infection, brought about by natural means or by a specific skin test.

skin′ resist′ance, friction between the plating of a vessel or airplane and the medium through which it moves.

skin′ test′, a test in which a substance is introduced into the skin, as by application to a purposely abraded area or by injection, for the detection of allergic sensitivity to a specific pollen, protein, etc., or the presence of a disease.

skin·tight (skin′tīt′), *adj.* fitting almost as tightly as skin: *skintight trousers.* [SKIN + TIGHT]

skin·tle (skin′təl), *v.t., v.i.,* **-tled, -tling.** to lay bricks and apply mortar so as to produce an irregular, uneven surface for picturesque effect. [?]

ski·o·graph (skī′ə graf′, -gräf′), *n., v.t.* skiagraph.

skip[1] (skip), *v.,* **skipped, skip·ping,** *n.* —*v.i.* **1.** to spring, jump, or leap lightly; gambol; move by nimble leaps and bounds. **2.** to pass from one point, thing, subject, etc., to another, disregarding or omitting what intervenes: *He skipped through the book quickly.* **3.** *Informal.* to go away hastily and secretly; flee without notice. **4.** *Educ.* to be advanced two or more classes or grades at once. **5.** to ricochet or bounce along a surface: *The stone skipped over the lake.* —*v.t.* **6.** to jump lightly over: *The horse skipped the fence.* **7.** to pass over without reading, noting, acting, etc.: *He skipped the bad parts.* **8.** to miss or omit (one of a repeated series of rhythmic actions): *My heart skipped a beat.* **9.** to be absent from; avoid attendance at: *to skip a school class.* **10.** to send (a missile) ricocheting along a surface. **11.** *Informal.* to leave hastily and secretly or to flee from (a place): *He skipped town without a word to anyone.* —*n.* **12.** a skipping movement; a light jump or bounce. **13.** a gait marked by such jumps. **14.** a passing from one point or thing to another, with disregard of what intervenes: *a quick skip through Europe.* **15.** *Music.* a melodic interval greater than a second. **16.** a natural depression below the surface of a planed board. **17.** *Informal.* a person who has absconded in order to avoid paying his debts. [ME *skippe* < Scand; cf. MSw *skuppa* to skip, Icel *skoppa* to spin (like a top), spring, run] —**skip′ping·ly,** *adv.*
—**Syn. 1.** caper, hop. SKIP, BOUND refer to an elastic, springing movement. To SKIP is to give a series of light, quick leaps alternating the feet: *to skip about.* BOUND suggests a series of long, rather vigorous leaps; it is also applied to a springing or leaping type of walking or running rapidly and actively: *A dog came bounding up to meet him.* **2.** skim. **12.** leap, spring, caper, hop.

skip[2] (skip), *n., v.,* **skipped, skip·ping.** —*n.* **1.** the captain of a curling or bowling team. **2.** *Informal.* skipper[1]. —*v.t.* **3.** to serve as skip of (a curling or bowling team). **4.** *Informal.* skipper[1]. [short for SKIPPER[1]]

skip[3] (skip), *n.* **1.** *Mining.* a metal box for carrying ore, hauled vertically or on an incline. **2.** See **skip car.** [alter. of SKEP]

Skip (skip), *n.* a boy's given name, form of **Skipper.**

ski′ pants′, pants worn for skiing, having the legs tapered to fit snugly at the ankles and sometimes having a strap going under the arch, often made of a stretch fabric.

skip-bomb (skip′bom′), *v.t. Mil.* to attack (a target) by skip bombing.

skip′ bomb′ing, bombing, as by a low-flying plane, carried out so that each bomb, when released, skips along the surface below before striking the target.

skip′ bridge′, the incline on which a skip car travels. Also called **skipway.**

skip′ car′, an open car for charging a blast furnace. Also called **skip.**

skip·dent (skip′dent′), *n.* an open-weave effect in fabric, produced by purposely omitting specific warp ends in the drawing-in process. [SKIP[1] + DENT[1]]

skip′ dis′tance, *Radio.* the distance along the earth's surface between the position of a short-wave transmitter and the region where its signal is received after one reflection from the ionosphere.

skip·jack (skip′jak′), *n., pl.* (*esp. collectively*) **-jack,** (*esp. referring to two or more kinds or species*) **-jacks** for 1; **-jacks** for 2, 3. **1.** any of various fishes that leap above the surface of the water, as a tuna, *Katsuwonus pelamis*, or the bonito. **2.** *Entomol.* See **click beetle.** **3.** *Naut.* an American sailing vessel having a clipper stem, broad transom stern, V-shaped bottom with pronounced chines, and one mast with a sloop rig; bateau: used for oystering and as a yacht. [SKIP[1] + JACK[1]]

ski·plane (skē′plān′), *n. Aeron.* an airplane equipped with skis to enable it to land on and take off from snow. [SKI + PLANE[1]]

ski′ pole′, a slender pole or stick, usually with a metal point at one end, a loop for the hand at the other, and a disk near the lower end to prevent its sinking into snow, used to gain momentum and maintain balance in skiing.

Skipp (skip), *n.* a boy's given name.

skip·pa·ble (skip′ə bəl), *adj.* able to be skipped, omitted, or passed over without loss; unimportant. [SKIP[1] + -ABLE]

skip·per[1] (skip′ər), *n.* **1.** the master or captain of a vessel, esp. of a small trading or fishing vessel. **2.** a captain or leader, as of a team. —*v.t.* **3.** to act as skipper of. [ME < MD *schipper.* See SHIP, -ER[1]]

skip·per[2] (skip′ər), *n.* **1.** one who or that which skips. **2.** any of various insects that hop or fly with jerky motions. **3.** any of numerous quick-flying, lepidopterous insects of the family *Hesperiidae*, closely related to the true butterflies. **4.** saury (def. 1). [SKIP[1] + -ER[1]]

Skip·per (skip′ər), *n.* a boy's given name.

skip·pet (skip′it), *n.* a small, round box for protecting an official or personal seal, as on a document. [ME *skipet.* See SKIP[3], -ET]

Skip·py (skip′ē), *n.* **1.** a boy's given name, form of **Skip** or **Skipper.** **2.** a girl's given name. Also, **Skip′pie.**

skip′ rope′. See **jump rope.**

skip′ straight′, *Poker.* a hand consisting of five cards following one another by two in order of denomination, as a five, seven, nine, jack, and king, being of special value in certain games. Also called **alternate straight, Dutch straight.**

skip′ trac′er, *Informal.* an investigator whose job is to locate missing persons, esp. debtors.

skip·way (skip′wā′), *n.* See **skip bridge.** [SKIP[3] + WAY]

skip′ weld′ing, a technique of spacing welds on thin structural members in order to balance and minimize internal stresses due to heat.

skirl (skûrl), *v.i.* **1.** to play the bagpipe. **2.** *Scot. and North Eng.* to shriek. —*n.* **3.** the sound of a bagpipe. **4.** *Scot. and North Eng.* any shrill sound. [metathetic var. of late ME *scrille* < Scand; cf. Norw (dial.) *skrylla*]

skirl·ing (skûr′ling), *n. Scot. and North Eng.* the act of shrieking. [SKIRL + -ING[1]]

skir·mish (skûr′mish), *n.* **1.** *Mil.* a fight between small bodies of troops, esp. advanced or outlying detachments of opposing armies. **2.** any brisk conflict or encounter: *She had a skirmish with her landlord about the rent.* —*v.i.* **3.** to engage in a skirmish. [ME *skirmysshe* < OF *(e)skirmiss-*, long s. of *eskirmir* < OHG *skirm(an)*; r. ME *scarmouche* < OF *(e)scaramouche(r)*; see SCARAMOUCH] —**skir′mish·er,** *n.*
—**Syn. 1.** combat, brush. See **battle**[1].

Skír·nir (skēr′nir), *n. Scand. Myth.* the servant of Frey.

Skir·o·pho·ri·a (skir′ə fôr′ē ə, -fōr′-), *n.* (*sometimes construed as pl.*) Scirophoria.

skirr (skûr), *v.i.* **1.** to go rapidly; fly; scurry. —*v.t.* **2.** to go rapidly over. —*n.* **3.** a grating or whirring sound. [var. of SCOUR[2]]

skir·ret (skir′it), *n.* an umbelliferous plant, *Sium Sisarum*, cultivated in Europe for its edible tuberous root. [ME *skirwhite*, lit., pure white (*skir* < Scand; c. OE *scīr*), alter., by folk etymology, of MF *scherwitz*, unexplained var. of OF *carvi* CARAWAY]

skirt (skûrt), *n.* **1.** the part of a gown, dress, slip, or coat that extends downward from the waist. **2.** a one-piece garment extending downward from the waist and

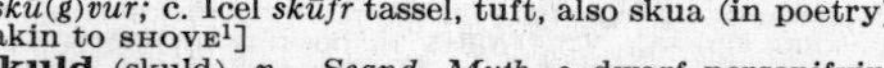

not joined between the legs, worn by women and girls. 3. some part resembling or suggesting the skirt of a garment in shape or use, as the flared lip of a bell or a protective and ornamental cloth strip covering the legs of furniture. 4. a small leather flap on each side of a saddle, covering the metal bar from which the stirrup hangs. See diag. under **saddle.** 5. *Building Trades.* **a.** baseboard (def. 1). **b.** apron (def. 12). 6. Also called **apron.** *Furniture.* **a.** a flat horizontal brace set immediately beneath the seat of a chair, chest of drawers, or the like, to strengthen the legs. **b.** Also called **bed, frieze.** a flat brace or support immediately beneath a table top. 7. Usually, **skirts.** the bordering, marginal, or outlying part of a place, group, etc.; the outskirts. 8. *Slang.* a woman or girl. 9. *Naut.* the leech of a square sail. —*v.t.* 10. to lie on or along the border of: *The highway skirts the town.* 11. to border or edge with something. 12. to pass along or around the border or edge of: *Traffic skirts the town.* 13. to avoid, go around the edge of, or keep distant from (something that is controversial, risky, etc.): *The senator skirted the issue of religion in the public schools.* 14. to remove low-grade wool and foreign matter from (the outer edge of fleece). —*v.i.* 15. to be, lie, live, etc., on or along the edge of something. 16. to pass or go along or around the border of something. [ME *skirte* < Scand; cf. Icel *skyrta* SHIRT] —**skirt′less,** *adj.* —**skirt′like′,** *adj.*

skirt·ing (skûr′ting), *n.* 1. fabric for making skirts. 2. Often, **skirtings.** low-grade wool and foreign matter removed from the outer edges of fleece. 3. baseboard (def. 1). [SKIRT + -ING[1]]

ski′ run′, a trail, slope, course, or the like, used for skiing.

ski′ suit′, a lightweight but warm costume for skiing and other outdoor winter activities, often of a synthetic fabric and usually consisting of a short, zippered jacket and close-fitting trousers.

skit (skit), *n.* 1. a short literary piece of a humorous or satirical character. 2. a short, usually comic, theatrical sketch or act. 3. a gibe or taunt. 4. *Brit. Dial.* a joke or prank. [ME: dirt, diarrhea; in 16th century, frivolous female < Scand; cf. Icel *skītr* filth, excrement, *skīta* diarrhea; akin to OE *scitte* purging]

skite[1] (skīt), *n.* *Scot. and North Eng.* 1. a quick, oblique blow or stroke; a chopping blow. 2. a joke or prank. 3. the butt of a joke or prank. 4. a person whose opinions are not taken seriously; one held in mild contempt. Also, **skyte.** [? < Scand; cf. Icel *skȳt,* 1st pers. sing. pres. indic. of *skjōta* to shoot]

skite[2] (skīt), *v.i.,* **skit·ed, skit·ing.** *Australian.* to boast; brag. [? dial. *skite* to defecate < Scand; cf. Icel *skīta,* SKIT]

ski′ tow′, a type of ski lift in which skiers are hauled up a slope while grasping a looped, endless rope driven by a motor.

ski′ troops′, a body of soldiers trained to fight on skis.

skit·ter (skit′ər), *v.i.* 1. to go, run, or glide lightly or rapidly. 2. to skim along a surface. 3. *Angling.* to draw a lure or a baited hook over the water with a skipping motion. —*v.t.* 4. to cause to skitter. [*skit,* var. of SKITE[1] + -ER[6]]

skit·tish (skit′ish), *adj.* 1. apt to start or shy: *a skittish horse.* 2. restlessly or excessively lively: *a skittish mood.* 3. fickle; uncertain. 4. shy; coy. [late ME, equiv. to *skit* (see SKITTER) + *-ish* -ISH[1]] —**skit′tish·ly,** *adv.* —**skit′tish·ness,** *n.*

skit·tle (skit′əl), *n.* *Chiefly Brit.* 1. **skittles,** (*construed as sing.*) ninepins in which a wooden ball or disk is used to knock down the pins. 2. one of the pins used in this game. [< Scand; cf. Dan *skyttel* SHUTTLE]

skive (skīv), *v.t.,* **skived, skiv·ing.** 1. to split or cut, as leather, into layers or slices. 2. to shave, as hides. 3. to finish the turning of (a metal object) by feeding a tool against it tangentially. [< Scand; cf. Icel *skīfa* slice, c. ME *schive* slice (of bread), G *Scheibe*]

skiv·er (skī′vər), *n.* 1. one who or that which skives. 2. a thin sheepskin used for bookbinding. [SKIVE + -ER[1]]

skiv·vy (skiv′ē), *n., pl.* **-vies.** *Slang.* 1. Also called **skiv′vy shirt′.** a man's cotton T-shirt. 2. **skivvies,** underwear consisting of cotton T-shirt and shorts. Cf. B.V.D. Also, **scivvy.** [?]

skiv·y (skiv′ē), *n., pl.* **skiv·ies.** *Brit. Disparaging.* a female servant, esp. a chambermaid. [?]

sklent (sklent), *Scot. and North Eng.* —*n.* 1. any slanting surface, as a slope. 2. a sideward motion; oblique movement. 3. a sideward look; a look out of the corners of one's eyes. —*v.i.* 4. to move, or lie obliquely or on a slant. 5. to deviate from a straight course; go the long way about. 6. to deviate from the truth; lie. Also, **sclent.** [late ME *sklente,* var. of ME *slente* SLANT]

skoal (skōl), *interj.* 1. (used as a toast in drinking someone's health.) —*n.* 2. a toast. —*v.i.* 3. to drink a toast. [< Scand; cf. Dan *skaal* bowl, toast; c. G *Schale* SCALE[2]]

Ško·da (skō′də; *Czech.* shkô′dä), *n.* **E·mil von** (e′mil fən), 1839–1900, Czech engineer and manufacturer of artillery.

Sko·kie (skō′kē), *n.* a city in NE Illinois, near Chicago. 59,364 (1960).

skoo·kum (sko͞o′kəm), *adj.* *Northwest U.S., Canada.* 1. large; powerful; impressive. 2. excellent; first-rate. [< Chinook Jargon]

Skop·je (skôp′ye), *n.* a city in and the capital of Macedonia, in the N part. 504,932. Serbo-Croatian, **Skop·lje** (skôp′lye). Turkish, **Usküb, Usküp.**

skouth (sko͞oth), *n.* *Scot.* scouth.

Skow·he·gan (skou hē′gən), *n.* a town in central Maine. 6667 (1960).

skreegh (skrēKH), *v.i., v.t., n.* *Scot.* screech. Also, **skreigh.**

Skry·mir (skrē′mir), *n.* *Scand. Myth.* a giant who took Thor, Thialfi, and Loki to Jotunheim. Also called **Utgard-Loki.**

Skt., Sanskrit. Also, **Skt, Skr., Skrt.**

sku·a (skyo͞o′ə), *n.* 1. Also called **great skua.** a large, brown, predatory bird, *Catharacta skua,* related to the jaegers, found in colder waters of both northern and southern seas. 2. *Brit.* jaeger (def. 1). [< Faeroese *skū(g)vur;* c. Icel *skūfr* tassel, tuft, also skua (in poetry), akin to SHOVE[1]]

Skua
Catharacta skua
(Length 2 ft.)

Skuld (skuld), *n.* *Scand. Myth.* a dwarf personifying the future: one of the three Norns that developed from Urdar. Cf. **Urd, Verdandi.**

skul·dug·ger·y (skul dug′ə rē), *n.* dishonorable proceedings; mean dishonesty or trickery: *bribery, graft, and other such skulduggery.* Also, **skullduggery, sculduggery, scullduggery.** [Amer var. of Scot *sculduddery* illicit sexual intercourse, obscenity, euphemistic alter. of ADULTERY]

skulk (skulk), *v.i.* 1. to lie or keep in hiding, as for some evil reason: *The thief skulked in the shadows.* 2. to move or go in a mean, stealthy manner; sneak; slink: *The panther skulked about in his cage.* 3. *Brit.* to shirk duty; malinger. —*n.* 4. one who skulks. 5. a pack or group of foxes. 6. *Rare.* the act or an instance of skulking. Also, **sculk.** [ME < Scand; cf. Dan *skulke*] —**skulk′er,** *n.* —**skulk′ing·ly,** *adv.* —**Syn.** 1. See **lurk.**

Human skull (Lateral view)
A, Frontal bone; B, Sphenoid bone; C, Eye socket; D, Nasal bone; E, Zygomatic bone; F, Maxilla; G, Mandible; H, Parietal bone; I, Occipital bone; J, Temporal bone; K, Mastoid process; L, Styloid process; M, Zygomatic arch

skull (skul), *n.* 1. the bony framework of the head, enclosing the brain and supporting the face; the skeleton of the head. 2. *Usually Disparaging.* the head as the seat of intelligence or knowledge: *I'd like to drive the idea into that thick skull of yours.* 3. *Armor.* the part of a helmet that covers the top of the head. 4. *Metall.* a solidified metal shell remaining on the sides and bottom of a furnace, ladle, or the like, after tapping, teeming, or pouring. [ME *scolle* < Scand; cf. Sw (dial.) *skulle* skull, Norw (dial.) *skol, skul* shell (of an egg or nut)] —**skull′-less,** *adj.* —**skull′-like′,** *adj.*

skull′ and cross′bones, a representation of a front view of a human skull above two crossed bones, originally used on pirates' flags and now used as a warning sign, as in designating substances as poisons.

skull·cap (skul′kap′), *n.* 1. a small, brimless close-fitting cap, often made of silk or velvet, worn on the crown of the head, as for religious functions. 2. the domelike roof of the skull. 3. *Bot.* any of various labiate herbs of the genus *Scutellaria,* having a calyx resembling a helmet. [SKULL + CAP[1]]

skull·dug·ger·y (skul dug′ə rē), *n.* skulduggery.

skull′ ses′sion, 1. a meeting, as of executives or administrators, in which ideas and information are exchanged, problems discussed, etc. 2. an informal gathering, esp. of scholars, for the purpose of intellectual discussion, development, or exercise. 3. a class held by an athletic coach, as of football, to instruct team members in new plays or special strategy. Also called **skull′ prac′tice** (for defs. 2, 3).

Skunk
Mephitis mephitis
(Total length 2 ft.; tail 8 in.)

skunk (skungk), *n., pl.* **skunks,** (*esp. collectively*) **skunk,** *v.* —*n.* 1. a small, black, North American mammal, *Mephitis mephitis,* of the weasel family, having a longitudinal, white, V-shaped stripe on the back, and ejecting a fetid odor when alarmed or attacked. 2. any of several related or similar animals. 3. *Informal.* a thoroughly contemptible person: *Keep away from that skunk.* 4. *U.S. Navy Slang.* an unidentified ship or target. —*v.t.* 5. *U.S. Slang.* to defeat thoroughly in a game, esp. while keeping an opponent from scoring: *The team skunked the favorites in the crucial game.* [< Algonquian; cf. Abnaki *segankw, segonkw*]

skunk′ cab′bage, 1. a low, fetid, broad-leaved, araceous plant, *Symplocarpus foetidus,* of North America, growing in moist ground. 2. a similar araceous plant, *Lysichitum americanum,* found on the western coast of North America and in Siberia, Japan, etc. Also called **skunkweed.**

skunk·weed (skungk′wēd′), *n.* 1. a rank-smelling, perennial herb, *Polemonium confertum,* of the western U.S., having bluish-violet or violet-colored flowers. 2. See **skunk cabbage.** [SKUNK + WEED[1]]

Sku·ta·ri (sko͞o′tä rē, -tə-), *n.* Scutari (def. 1).

skut·te·rud·ite (skut′ə rud′īt), *n.* a mineral, chiefly cobalt and nickel arsenide, (Co,Ni)As_3, with some iron, occurring in the form of gray cubic crystals, usually in masses: a source of cobalt and nickel. [< G *Skutterudit,* named after *Skutterud* in Norway; see -ITE[1]]

sky (skī), *n., pl.* **skies,** *v.* **skied** or **skyed, sky·ing.** —*n.* Often, **skies** (for defs. 1–4). 1. the region of the clouds or the upper air; the upper atmosphere of the earth: *high in the sky; rainy skies.* 2. the heavens or firmament, appearing as a great arch or vault. 3. the supernal or celestial heaven: *They prayed to the sky for help.* 4. the climate: *the sunny skies of Italy.* 5. *Obs.* a cloud. 6. **out of a clear sky,** without advance notice or warning; abruptly: *An old beau phoned her out of a clear sky.* Also, **out of a clear blue sky.** 7. **to the skies,** with lavishness or enthusiasm; extravagantly: *to praise someone to the skies.* Also, **to the sky.** —*v.t.* 8. *Informal.* to raise, throw, or hit aloft or into the air. 9. *Informal.* to hang (a painting) high on a wall, above the line of vision. 10. **sky up,** *Falconry.* (of prey, when flushed) to fly straight upward. [ME < Scand; cf. Icel *ský* cloud, c. OE *scēo* cloud; akin to Ir *cēo* fog, mist, smoke] —**sky′less,** *adj.* —**sky′like′,** *adj.*

sky′ blue′, the color of the unclouded sky in daytime; azure. —**sky′-blue′,** *adj.*

sky·borne (skī′bôrn′, -bōrn′), *adj.* airborne. [SKY + BORNE[1]]

sky·cap (skī′kap′), *n.* a porter or other employee who carries passenger baggage at an airport or airline terminal. [SKY + (RED)CAP]

sky′ com′pass, *Navig.* a device for taking a bearing by means of polarized sunlight when the sun is invisible.

sky′ cov′er, the amount of the sky that is covered by clouds, fog, haze, smoke, or the like, usually expressed in tenths of the total sky.

sky·dive (skī′dīv′), *v.i.,* **-dived** or (*U.S. Informal and Brit Dial.*) **-dove; -dived; -div·ing.** *Sports.* to make a parachute jump, delaying the opening of the parachute as long as possible. [SKY + DIVE] —**sky′div′er,** *n.*

Skye (skī), *n.* an island in the Hebrides, in NW Scotland. 7478 (1961). 670 sq. mi.

Skye terrier
(9 in. high at shoulder)

Skye′ ter′rier, one of a Scottish breed of small terriers having short legs and a dark or light blue-gray or fawn coat. [after SKYE]

sky·ey (skī′ē), *adj.* *Chiefly Literary.* 1. of or from the sky. 2. in the sky; lofty. 3. skylike; sky blue. [SKY + -EY[1]]

sky·flow·er (skī′flou′ər), *n.* a showy, evergreen, woody vine, *Thunbergia grandiflora,* of India, having blue flowers nearly three inches long in drooping clusters.

sky′ gaz′er, *Naut.* a light triangular skysail.

sky-high (skī′hī′), *adv., adj.* very high: *Costs have gone sky-high since the war.*

sky·jack (skī′jak′), *v.t.* to hijack (an airliner), esp. to force it to fly to a country where one's own government forbids travelers to go or in order to hold the passengers and plane for ransom or for political reasons. [SKY + (HI)JACK] —**sky′jack′er,** *n.*

sky·lark (skī′lärk′), *n.* 1. either of two Eurasian larks, *Alauda arvensis* or *A. gulgula,* noted for their song in flight. —*v.i.* 2. *Informal.* to frolic; sport: *The children were skylarking on the beach.* [SKY + LARK[1]] —**sky′lark′er,** *n.*

Skylark,
Alauda arvensis
(Length 7 in.)

sky·light (skī′līt′), *n.* 1. an opening in a roof or ceiling, fitted with glass, for admitting daylight. 2. the frame set with glass fitted to such an opening. 3. *Meteorol.* the diffuse light from the sky, scattered by air molecules, as distinguished from the direct radiation from the sun. [SKY + LIGHT[1]]

sky·line (skī′līn′), *n., v.,* **-lined, -lin·ing.** —*n.* Also, **sky′ line′.** 1. the boundary line between earth and sky; the apparent horizon: *A sail appeared against the skyline.* 2. the outline of something, as the buildings of a city, against the sky: *the New York skyline.* —*v.t.* 3. to outline (something) against the sky. [SKY + LINE[1]]

sky·man (skī′mən), *n., pl.* **-men.** *Informal.* aviator. [SKY + MAN[1]]

sky·phos (skī′fos), *n., pl.* **-phoi** (-foi). *Gk. and Rom. Antiq.* a cup characterized by a deep bowl, two handles projecting horizontally near the rim, and either a flat base or a foot. Also, **scyphus.** [< Gk: two-handled cup, beaker, flagon]

sky′ pi′lot, *Slang.* 1. a clergyman, esp. a chaplain of the armed forces. 2. an aviator.

sky·pipe (skī′pīp′), *n.* *Naut.* a pipe on a steamship leading from one or more safety valves to the open air above the top deck. [SKY + PIPE[1]]

sky·rock·et (skī′rok′it), *n.* 1. a rocket firework that ascends into the air and explodes at a height, usually in a brilliant array of sparks of one or more colors. 2. an herb, *Gilia aggregata,* of California, having fragrant, fiery red flowers. 3. an organized group cheer, usually led by a cheerleader, as at a football or basketball game, which begins with a hissing or whistling and ends with a shout. —*v.i.* 4. to rise, succeed, or become famous rapidly or suddenly: *Prices skyrocketed during the war.* —*v.t.* 5. to cause to rise, succeed, or become famous rapidly or suddenly: *His talent skyrocketed him to fame.* [SKY + ROCKET[1]]

Sky·ros (skī′ros, -rōs; *Gk.* skē′rôs′), *n.* a Greek island in the W Aegean: the largest island of the Northern Sporades. 3193 (1951); 81 sq. mi. Also, **Scyros.**

sky·sail (skī′sāl′; *Naut.* skī′səl), *n.* *Naut.* 1. (in a square-rigged vessel) a light square sail next above the royal. See diag. under **ship.** 2. a triangular sail set on a stay between the fore and main trucks of a racing schooner. [SKY + SAIL]

sky′sail pole′, *Naut.* a tall pole extension of a royal mast on which skysails and other light sails are set flying.

sky·scape (skī′skāp′), *n.* 1. a section or portion of the sky, usually extensive and often including part of the horizon, that may be seen from a single viewpoint. 2. a picture representing this. [SKY + *-scape* (as in *landscape*)]

sky·scrap·er (skī′skrā′pər), *n.* 1. a relatively tall building of many stories, esp. one for office or commercial use. 2. *Archit.* a building completely supported by a framework, as of girders, from which the walls are suspended, as opposed to a building supported by load-bearing walls. 3. *Naut.* **a.** a light triangular sail used in the racing rig of a staysail schooner. **b.** (in a square rig) a small square sail set above a royal. [SKY + SCRAPER]

sky·scrap·ing (skī′skrā′ping), *adj.* of or like a skyscraper; very high: *a skyscraping chimney.* [SKY-SCRAP(ER) + -ING[2], modeled on *scraper, scraping*]

sky′ screen′, *Rocketry.* an optical device for detecting lateral deviation in a missile trajectory.

sky·sweep·er (skī′swē′pər), *n.* *U.S. Mil.* a 75-millimeter antiaircraft gun that locates and aims at aircraft by means of radar and is capable of firing 45 shells per minute. [SKY + SWEEPER]

skyte (skīt), *n.* *Scot. and North Eng.* skite.

sky′ train′, an airplane towing one or more gliders. Also called **air train.**

sky·troop·er (skī′tro͞o′pər), *n.* a paratrooper. [SKY + (PARA)TROOPER]

sky·troops (skī′tro͞ops′), *n.pl.* paratroops. [SKY + (PARA)TROOPS]

sky·ward (skī′wərd), *adv.* 1. Also, **sky′wards.** toward the sky. —*adj.* 2. directed toward the sky. [SKY + -WARD]

sky′ wave′, *Radio.* a radio wave propagated upward from earth, whether reflected by the ionosphere or not.

sky·way (skī′wā′), *n.* **1.** *Informal.* See **air lane. 2.** an elevated highway, esp. one well above ground level and composed of a series of spans, passing over a swamp region, a heavily populated area, etc. [SKY + WAY]

sky·write (skī′rīt′), *v.,* **-wrote, -writ·ten, -writ·ing.** —*v.i.* **1.** to engage in skywriting. —*v.t.* **2.** to produce (a message, advertisement, etc.) by skywriting. [SKY + WRITE]

sky·writ·er (skī′rī′tər), *n.* an aviator skilled in skywriting. [SKY + WRITER]

sky·writ·ing (skī′rī′ting), *n.* **1.** the act or practice of writing against the sky with chemically produced smoke released from a maneuvering airplane. **2.** the words, letters, designs, etc., so traced. [SKY + WRITING]

s.l., without place. [< L *sine locō*]

slab[1] (slab), *n., v.,* **slabbed, slab·bing.** —*n.* **1.** a broad, flat, somewhat thick piece of stone, wood, or other solid material. **2.** a thick slice of anything: *a slab of bread.* **3.** a semifinished piece of iron or steel so rolled that its breadth is at least twice its thickness. **4.** a rough outside piece cut from a log, as when sawing one into boards. **5.** *Baseball Slang.* rubber (def. 10). **6.** a section of concrete pavement. **7.** *Print.* table (def. 14). —*v.t.* **8.** to make into a slab or slabs. **9.** to cover or lay with slabs. **10.** to cut the slabs or outside pieces from (a log). [ME *s(c)labbe*]

slab[2] (slab), *adj.* *Archaic.* thick; viscous. [appar. < Scand; cf. Dan *slab* slippery (adj.), mire (n.), Icel *slabb* slush]

slab·ber (slab′ər), *v.i., v.t., n.* slobber.

slab·ber·y (slab′ə rē), *adj.* slobbery.

slab′ dash′ing, the act or process of covering an exterior wall with roughcast. Also called **slap dashing.**

slab′ plas′tering, coarse plastering, as between the studs in a half-timbered wall. Also called **slap plastering.**

slab-sid·ed (slab′sī′did), *adj.* *Informal.* **1.** having the sides long and flat, like slabs. **2.** tall and lank.

slab′ top′, *Furniture.* a top, as to a table, formed from a slab of marble or the like.

slack[1] (slak), *adj.* **1.** not tight, taut, or tense; loose: *a slack rope.* **2.** negligent; careless; remiss: *slack proofreading.* **3.** slow, sluggish, or indolent: *He is slack in answering letters.* **4.** not active or busy; dull; not brisk: *the slack season in an industry.* **5.** moving very slowly, as the tide, wind, or water. **6.** *Naut.* easy (def. 12). —*adv.* **7.** in a slack manner. —*n.* **8.** a slack condition or part. **9.** the part of a rope, sail, or the like, that hangs loose, without strain upon it. **10.** a decrease in activity, as in business, work, etc.: *a sudden slack in output.* **11.** a period of decreased activity. **12.** *Geog.* a cessation in a strong flow, as of a current at its turn. **13.** a depression between hills, in a hillside, or in the land surface. **14.** *Scot. and North Eng.* a morass; marshy ground; a hollow or dell with soft, wet ground at the bottom. **15.** *Pros.* (in sprung rhythm) the unaccented syllable or syllables. —*v.t.* **16.** to be remiss in respect to (some matter, duty, right, etc.); shirk; leave undone: *He slacked the most important part.* **17.** to make or allow to become less active, vigorous, intense, etc.; relax (efforts, labor, speed, etc.); lessen; moderate (often fol. by *up*). **18.** to make loose, or less tense or taut, as a rope; loosen (often fol. by *off* or *out*). **19.** to slake (lime). —*v.i.* **20.** to be remiss; shirk one's duty or part. **21.** to become less active, vigorous, rapid, etc. (often fol. by *up*): *Business is slacking up.* **22.** to become less tense or taut, as a rope; to ease off. **23.** to become slaked, as lime. **24. slack back,** *Mach.* (of a jack) to yield partly beneath a load under continued pressure from the load. [ME *slac,* OE *sleac slæc;* c. Icel *slakr,* OHG *slach*] —**slack′ing·ly,** *adv.* —**slack′ly,** *adv.* —**slack′ness,** *n.*
—**Syn. 1.** relaxed. **2.** lazy, weak. **3.** dilatory, tardy, late. **4.** idle, quiet. **10.** slowing, relaxation. **16.** neglect. **17.** reduce, slacken. **20.** malinger.

slack[2] (slak), *n.* the fine screenings of coal; small or refuse coal. [late ME *sleck* < MFlem or MLG *slecke*]

slack-baked (slak′bākt′), *adj.* **1.** improperly baked. **2.** imperfectly made.

slack·en (slak′ən), *v.t., v.i.* **1.** to make or become less active, vigorous, intense, etc. **2.** to make or become looser or less taut. [SLACK[1] + -EN[1]]
—**Syn. 1, 2.** relax, loosen, slack, abate. —**Ant. 2.** tighten, tense.

slack·er (slak′ər), *n.* **1.** one who evades his duty or work; shirker. **2.** one who evades military service. [SLACK[1] + -ER[1]]

slack-jawed (slak′jôd′), *adj.* having the mouth open, esp. as an indication of astonishment, bewilderment, etc.

slacks (slaks), *n.* (*construed as pl.*) men's or women's trousers for informal wear. [SLACK[1] + -S[4]]

slack′ suit′, 1. a man's suit for casual wear consisting of slacks and a matching shirt or short or loose-fitting jacket. **2.** a woman's suit for casual wear consisting of slacks and a matching jacket.

slack′ wa′ter, 1. a period when a body of water is between tides. **2.** water that is free of currents.

Slade (slād), *n.* a boy's given name.

slag (slag), *n., v.,* **slagged, slag·ging.** —*n.* **1.** Also called **cinder.** the more or less completely fused and vitrified matter separated during the reduction of a metal from its ore. **2.** the scoria from a volcano. **3.** waste left over after the re-sorting of coal. —*v.t.* **4.** to convert into slag. **5.** *Metall.* to remove slag from (a steel bath). —*v.i.* **6.** to form slag; become a slaglike mass. [< MLG *slagge;* c. G *Schlacke* dross, slag; see SLACK[2]] —**slag′a·bil′i·ty,** *n.* —**slag′a·ble,** *adj.* —**slag′less,** *adj.* —**slag′less·ness,** *n.*

slag′ cement′, a cement composed of about 80 percent granulated slag and about 20 percent hydrated lime.

slag·gy (slag′ē), *adj.,* **-gi·er, -gi·est.** of, pertaining to, or like slag. [SLAG + -Y[1]]

slag′ wool′, mineral wool made by forcing steam through molten slag.

slain (slān), *v.* pp. of **slay.**

slake (slāk), *v.,* **slaked, slak·ing.** —*v.t.* **1.** to allay (thirst, desire, wrath, etc.) by satisfying. **2.** to cool or refresh: *He slaked his lips with ice.* **3.** to make less active, vigorous, intense, etc.: *His calm manner slaked their enthusiasm.* **4.** to cause disintegration of (lime) by treatment with water. Cf. **slaked lime. 5.** *Obs.* to make loose or less tense; slacken. —*v.i.* **6.** (of lime) to become slaked. **7.** *Archaic.* to become less active, intense, vigorous, etc.; abate. [ME; c. OE *slac(ian),* equiv. to *slæc* SLACK[1] + *-ian* v. suffix] —**slak′a·ble, slake′a·ble,** *adj.* —**slake′less,** *adj.*

slaked′ lime′, a soft, white, crystalline, very slightly water-soluble powder, $Ca(OH)_2$, obtained by the action of water on lime: used chiefly in mortars, plasters, and cements. Also called **calcium hydroxide, calcium hydrate, hydrated lime, lime hydrate.**

slak·er (slā′kər), *n.* **1.** one who or that which slakes. **2.** *Papermaking.* a machine for mixing various caustic chemicals by agitation. [SLAKE + -ER[1]]

sla·lom (slä′ləm, -lōm), *n.* *Skiing.* a downhill race over a winding and zigzag course marked by poles or gates. Cf. **giant slalom.** [< Norw: lit., slope-track]

slam[1] (slam), *v.,* **slammed, slam·ming,** *n.* —*v.t., v.i.* **1.** to shut with force and noise: *to slam the door.* **2.** to dash, strike, etc., with violent and noisy impact: *He slammed his books upon the table.* **3.** *Informal.* to criticize harshly; attack verbally: *She slammed his taste mercilessly.* —*n.* **4.** a violent and noisy closing, dashing, or impact. **5.** the noise so made. **6.** *Informal.* a harsh criticism; verbal attack: *He was sick of her slams.* [< Scand; cf. Icel *slambra,* Norw *slemma,* Sw (dial.) *slämma* to slam]

slam[2] (slam), *n.* *Cards.* **1.** the winning or bidding of all the tricks or all the tricks but one in a deal. Cf. **grand slam, little slam. 2.** an old type of card game associated with ruff. [perh. special use of SLAM[1]]

slam-bang (slam′bang′), *adv.* *Informal.* **1.** with noisy violence: *He drove slam-bang through the back of the garage.* **2.** quickly and carelessly; slapdash.

slam′ming stile′, doorstop (def. 2).

slan·der (slan′dər), *n.* **1.** defamation; calumny: *rumors full of slander.* **2.** a malicious, false, and defamatory statement or report: *a slander against his good name.* **3.** *Law.* defamation by oral utterance rather than by writing, pictures, etc. —*v.t.* **4.** to utter slander concerning; defame. —*v.i.* **5.** to utter or circulate slander. [ME *sclaundre* < AF *(e)sclaundre,* c. OF *esclandre* < LL *scandal(um)* cause of offense, snare; see SCANDAL] —**slan′der·er,** *n.* —**slan′der·ing·ly,** *adv.* —**slan′der·ous,** *adj.* —**slan′der·ous·ly,** *adv.* —**slan′der·ous·ness,** *n.*

slang[1] (slang), *n.* **1.** very informal usage in vocabulary and idiom that is characteristically more metaphorical, playful, elliptical, vivid, and ephemeral than ordinary language, as *Hit the road.* **2.** (in English and some other languages) speech and writing characterized by the use of vulgar and socially taboo vocabulary and idiomatic expressions. **3.** the jargon of a particular class, profession, etc. **4.** the special vocabulary of thieves, vagabonds, etc.; argot. —*v.i.* **5.** to use slang or abusive language. —*v.t.* **6.** to assail with abusive language. [?]
—**Syn. 4.** cant.

slang[2] (slang), *v.* *Chiefly Dial.* pt. of **sling**[1].

slang·y (slang′ē), *adj.,* **slang·i·er, slang·i·est. 1.** of, of the nature of, or containing slang: *a slangy expression.* **2.** using much slang: *slangy speech.* [SLANG[1] + -Y[1]] —**slang′i·ly,** *adv.* —**slang′i·ness,** *n.*

slank (slangk), *v.* *Archaic.* pt. of **slink.**

slant (slant, slänt), *v.i.* **1.** to slope. **2.** to have or be influenced by a subjective point of view, bias, personal feeling or inclination, etc. (usually fol. by *toward*). —*v.t.* **3.** to cause to slope. **4.** *Journalism.* **a.** (in writing) to distort (information) by rendering it unfaithfully or incompletely, esp. in order to reflect a particular viewpoint: *He slanted the story to discredit the Administration.* **b.** to write, edit, or publish for the interest or amusement of a specific group of readers: *Slant that story for women.* —*n.* **5.** slanting or oblique direction; slope: *the slant of a roof.* **6.** a slanting line, surface, etc. **7.** virgule. **8.** a mental leaning, bias, or distortion: *His mind shows a curious slant.* **9.** viewpoint; opinion; attitude: *Let him give you his slant.* **10.** *Informal.* a glance or look. **11.** Also called **angle.** *Journalism.* the particular mood or vein in which something is written, edited, or published: *His column always has a humorous slant.* —*adj.* **12.** sloping; oblique: *a slant roof; a slant approach.* [aph. var. of ASLANT] —**slant′ly,** *adv.*
—**Syn. 1.** lean, incline. See **slope. 5.** incline, inclination, pitch, obliquity, obliqueness.

slant-eyed (slant′īd′, slänt′-), *adj.* (of a person) **1.** having eyes with epicanthic folds. **2.** having eyes that appear to slant. **3.** *Offensive.* being of Far Eastern origin, as a Chinese or Japanese.

slant′ front′, *Furniture.* a flap of a desk, sloping upward and inward to close the desk, and opening forward and downward to a horizontal position as a writing surface: a form of fall front.

slant′ rhyme′, *Pros.* rhyme in which either the vowels or the consonants of stressed syllables are identical, as in *eyes, light; years, yours.* Also called **half rhyme, imperfect rhyme, near rhyme.**

slant-top (slant′top′, slänt′-), *adj.* (esp. of a desk) having a top or cover which folds over the front and rests at an angle when closed.

slant·wise (slant′wīz′, slänt′-), *adv.* **1.** aslant; obliquely. —*adj.* **2.** slanting; oblique. Also, **slant·ways** (slant′wāz′, slänt′-). [SLANT + -WISE]

slap[1] (slap), *n., v.,* **slapped, slap·ping,** *adv.* —*n.* **1.** a sharp blow or smack, esp. with the open hand or with something flat. **2.** a sound made by or as if by such a blow or smack: *He listened to the slap of the waves against the dock.* **3.** a sharply worded or sarcastic rebuke, censure, or comment. —*v.t.* **4.** to strike sharply, esp. with the open hand or with something flat. **5.** to bring (the hand, something flat, etc.) with a sharp blow against something. **6.** to dash or cast forcibly: *He slapped the package down.* **7.** *Informal.* to put or place promptly and sometimes haphazardly (often fol. by *on*): *The policeman slapped a ticket on the car. He slapped tons of mustard on that sandwich.* —*adv.* **8.** smartly; suddenly. **9.** *Informal.* directly; straight: *The tug rammed slap into the side of the freighter.* [< LG *slapp, slappe;* imit.] —**slap′per,** *n.*
—**Syn. 1.** See **blow**[1].

slap[2] (slap), *n., v.,* **slapped, slap·ping.** *Scot.* —*n.* **1.** a gap or opening, as in a fence, wall, cloud bank, or line of troops. **2.** a mountain pass. **3.** a wound or gash. —*v.t.* **4.** to make a gap or opening in; breach. [ME *slop* < MD or MLG; c. G *Schlupf* refuge, cover, lit., a slipping, sliding, OE *slype* SLIP[1]]

slap·dash (slap′dash′), *adv.* **1.** in a hasty, haphazard manner: *He assembled the motor slapdash.* —*adj.* **2.** hasty and careless; offhand: *a slapdash answer.* [SLAP[1] (adv.) + DASH[1]]

slap′ dash′ing. See **slab dashing.**

slap·hap·py (slap′hap′ē), *adj.,* **-pi·er, -pi·est.** *Informal.* **1.** severely befuddled; punch-drunk: *a slaphappy boxer.* **2.** agreeably giddy or foolish: *After a martini he was slaphappy.* **3.** cheerfully irresponsible: *a slaphappy crowd.* [SLAP[1] + HAPPY]

slap·jack (slap′jak′), *n.* **1.** a simple card game. **2.** *U.S.* a flapjack or griddlecake. [SLAP[1] + (FLAP)JACK]

slap′ plas′tering. See **slab plastering.**

slap·stick (slap′stik′), *n.* **1.** broad comedy characterized by violently boisterous action, as the throwing of pies in actors' faces, mugging, and obvious farcical situations and jokes; farce combined with horseplay in a comic form. **2.** a stick or lath used by harlequins, clowns, etc., as in pantomime, for striking other performers, esp. a combination of laths that make a loud, clapping noise without hurting the person struck. —*adj.* **3.** using, or marked by the use of, broad farce and horseplay: *a slapstick motion picture.* [SLAP[1] + STICK[1]]

slash[1] (slash), *v.t.* **1.** to cut with a violent sweeping stroke or by striking violently and at random, as with a knife or sword. **2.** to lash. **3.** to curtail, reduce, or alter: *The editors slashed the story to half its length.* **4.** to make slits in (a garment) to show an underlying fabric. —*v.i.* **5.** to lay about one with sharp, sweeping strokes; make one's way by cutting. **6.** to make a sweeping, cutting stroke. —*n.* **7.** a sweeping stroke, as with a knife, sword, or pen. **8.** a cut, wound, or mark made with such a stroke. **9.** a curtailment, reduction, or alteration: *a drastic slash of prices.* **10.** an ornamental slit in a garment showing an underlying fabric. **11.** *U.S.* virgule. **12.** (in forest land) **a.** an open area strewn with debris of trees from felling or from wind or fire. **b.** the debris itself. [ME *slasch(en)* < ?] —**slash′er,** *n.*
—**Syn. 3.** abridge, abbreviate.

slash[2] (slash), *n.* Often, **slashes.** *U.S.* a tract of wet or swampy ground overgrown with bushes or trees. [?]

slash·ing (slash′ing), *n.* **1.** a slash. —*adj.* **2.** sweeping; cutting. **3.** violent; severe: *a slashing wind.* **4.** dashing; impetuous. **5.** *Informal.* very large or fine; splendid: *a slashing fortune.* [SLASH[1] + -ING[1], -ING[2]] —**slash′ing·ly,** *adv.*

slash′ pine′, 1. a pine, *Pinus caribaea,* found in slashes and swamps in the southeastern U.S., yielding a hard, durable wood. **2.** the wood of this tree. **3.** the loblolly pine.

slash′ pock′et, a pocket set into a garment, esp. below the waistline, to which easy access is provided by an exterior, vertical or diagonal slit.

slash-saw (slash′sô′), *v.t.,* **-sawed, -sawed** or **-sawn, -saw·ing.** plain-saw.

Śląsk (shlônsk), *n.* Polish name of **Silesia.**

slat[1] (slat), *n., v.,* **slat·ted, slat·ting.** —*n.* **1.** a long thin, narrow strip of wood, metal, etc., used as a support for a bed, as one of the horizontal laths of a Venetian blind, etc. **2. slats,** *Slang.* **a.** the ribs. **b.** the buttocks. **c.** (*cap.*) a nickname for a tall, slender man. —*v.t.* **3.** to furnish or make with slats. [ME *sclat, slatt* < MF *(e)sclat* splinter, fragment; see ÉCLAT]

slat[2] (slat), *v.,* **slat·ted, slat·ting,** *n.* *Chiefly Brit. Dial.* —*v.t.* **1.** to throw or dash with force. —*v.i.* **2.** to flap violently, as sails. —*n.* **3.** a slap; a sharp blow. [ME *sleaten* < Scand; cf. Icel *sletta* to slap; akin to SLAY]

S. Lat., south latitude.

slatch (slach), *n.* *Naut.* a relatively smooth interval between heavy seas. [alter. of SLACK[1]]

slate[1] (slāt), *n., v.,* **slat·ed, slat·ing.** —*n.* **1.** a fine-grained rock formed by the compression of clay, shale, etc., that tends to split along parallel cleavage planes, usually at an angle to the planes of stratification. **2.** a thin piece or plate of this rock or a similar material, used esp. for roofing or as a writing surface. **3.** a dull, dark bluish gray. **4.** a list of candidates, officers, etc., to be considered for nomination, appointment, election, or the like. **5. clean slate,** a record marked by honorable or creditable conduct; a good record: *A security check gave him a clean slate.* —*v.t.* **6.** to cover with or as with slate. **7.** to write or set down for nomination or appointment: *The party regulars slated the Manhattan district leader for State chairman.* **8.** to plan or designate an appearance or occurrence in a particular place or at a particular time; schedule: *The première was slated for January.* **9.** to censure or criticize harshly or violently; scold. **10.** to punish severely. [ME *sclate* < MF *(e)sclate,* fem. of *esclat;* see SLAT[1]]

slate[2] (slāt), *v.t.,* **slat·ed, slat·ing.** *Brit.* to sic or set a dog on (a person or animal). [ME *slayt* < ON **sleita;* c. OE *slǣtan*]

slate′-col·ored jun′co (slāt′cul′ərd). See under **junco.**

slat·er[1] (slā′tər), *n.* one who lays slates, as for roofing. [ME *sclater.* See SLATE[1], -ER[1]]

slat·er[2] (slā′tər), *n.* any of various cursorial isopods. [SLATE[2] + -ER[1]]

Sla·ter (slā′tər), *n.* **1. Samuel,** 1768–1835, U.S. industrialist, born in England. **2.** a town in central Missouri. 2767 (1960).

slath·er (slath′ər), *Informal.* —*v.t.* **1.** to spread or apply thickly: *slather butter on toast.* **2.** to spend or use lavishly. —*n.* **3.** Often, **slathers.** a generous amount: *They have slathers of money.* [?]

slat·ing (slā′ting), *n.* **1.** the act or work of covering something with slates. **2.** materials for roofing with slates. [SLATE[1] + -ING[1]]

Slat·ing·ton (slā′ting tən), *n.* a town in E Pennsylvania. 4316 (1960).

Sla·ton (slat′ən), *n.* a town in NW Texas. 6568 (1960).

slat·tern (slat′ərn), *n.* **1.** a slovenly, untidy woman or girl. **2.** a slut; harlot. [? akin to late ME *slatter* to slash or slit (clothes), freq. of SLAT[2]]

slat·tern·ly (slat′ərn lē), *adj.* **1.** slovenly and untidy. **2.** characteristic or suggestive of a slattern. —*adv.* **3.** in the manner of a slattern. [SLATTERN + -LY] —**slat′tern·li·ness,** *n.*

slat·ting (slat′ing), *n.* **1.** the act of furnishing with or making from slats. **2.** a number of slats, taken as a whole. [SLAT[1] + -ING[1]]

slat·y (slā/tē), *adj.*, **slat·i·er, slat·i·est.** **1.** consisting of, resembling, or pertaining to slate. **2.** having the color of slate. [SLATE[1] + -Y[1]] —**slat/i·ness,** *n.*

slaugh·ter (slô/tər), *n.* **1.** the killing or butchering of cattle, sheep, etc., esp. for food. **2.** the brutal or violent killing of a person. **3.** the killing of great numbers of people or animals indiscriminately; carnage: *the slaughter of war.* —*v.t.* **4.** to kill or butcher (animals), esp for food. **5.** to kill in a brutal or violent manner. **6.** to slay in great numbers; massacre. **7.** to defeat thoroughly; trounce: *They slaughtered our team.* [ME *slaghter* < Scand; cf. Icel *slātr* butcher's meat (earlier **slahtr*), *slātra* to butcher; akin to SLAY] —**slaugh/ter·er,** *n.* —**slaugh/ter·ing·ly,** *adv.*
—**Syn. 2.** homicide, murder. **4–6.** SLAUGHTER, BUTCHER, MASSACRE all imply violent and bloody methods of killing. SLAUGHTER and BUTCHER, primarily referring to the killing of animals for food, are used also of the brutal or indiscriminate killing of human beings: *to slaughter cattle; to butcher a hog.* MASSACRE indicates a general slaughtering of helpless or unresisting victims: *to massacre the peasants of a region.*

slaugh·ter·house (slô/tər hous/), *n.*, *pl.* **-hous·es** (-hou/ziz). a building or place where animals are butchered for food; abattoir. [ME; see SLAUGHTER, HOUSE]

Slaugh/ter on Tenth/ Av/enue, a ballet (1936) by Richard Rodgers.

slaugh·ter·ous (slô/tər əs), *adj.* murderous; destructive. [SLAUGHTER + -OUS] —**slaugh/ter·ous·ly,** *adv.*

Slav (släv, slav), *n.* **1.** one of a race of peoples in eastern, southeastern, and central Europe, including the Russians and Ruthenians (**Eastern Slavs**), the Bulgars, Serbs, Croats, Slavonians, Slovenes, etc. (**Southern Slavs**), and the Poles, Czechs, Moravians, Slovaks, etc. (**Western Slavs**). —*adj.* **2.** of, pertaining to, or characteristic of the Slavs; Slavic. [< ML *Slāv-(us)*, var. of *Sclāvus* (see SLAVE); r. ME *Sclave* < ML *Sclāv(us)*, c. LGk *Sklábos*]

Slav., Slavic. Also, **Slav**

slave (slāv), *n.*, *v.*, **slaved, slav·ing.** —*n.* **1.** one who is the property of and wholly subject to another; a bond servant. **2.** one entirely under the domination of some influence or person: *a slave to a drug.* **3.** a drudge: *a housekeeping slave.* **4.** *Photog.* a subsidiary flash lamp activated through its photoelectric cell when the principal flash lamp is discharged. **5.** *Mach.* a mechanism under control of and repeating the actions of a similar mechanism. Cf. **master** (def. 19). —*v.i.* **6.** to work like a slave; drudge. —*v.t.* **7.** to enslave. **8.** to connect (a machine or machines) to a master as its slave or slaves. [ME *sclave* < ML *sclāv(us)* (masc.), *sclāv(a)* (fem.) slave, special use of *Sclāv(us)* Slav, so called because so many Slavs were enslaved in the early Middle Ages; see SLAV] —**slave/less,** *adj.* —**slave/like/,** *adj.*

slave/ ant/, an ant enslaved by ants of another species.

slave/ brace/let, a braceletlike, ornamental circlet or chain worn around the ankle.

Slave/ Coast/, the coast of W equatorial Africa, between the Benin and Volta rivers: a center of slavery traffic 16th–19th centuries.

slave/ driv/er, 1. an overseer of slaves. **2.** a hard taskmaster: *He couldn't keep a secretary because he was such a slave driver.*

slave·hold·er (slāv/hōl/dər), *n.* one who owns slaves. [SLAVE + HOLDER] —**slave/hold/ing,** *n.*

slave/ la/bor, 1. persons, esp. a large group, forced to perform labor under duress or threats, as political prisoners, prisoners in concentration camps, etc.; a labor force of slaves or slavelike prisoners. **2.** labor done by slaves. **3.** any forced, coerced, or poorly remunerated labor or work: *Typing at that salary is slave labor.* —**slave/-la/bor,** *adj.*

slave/ la/bor camp/. See **labor camp** (def. 1).

slave/-mak·ing ant/ (slāv/mā/king), an ant that raids the colonies of other ant species, carrying off larvae and pupae to be reared as slaves.

Sla·ven·ska (slä ven/skä), *n.* **Mi·a** (mē/ä), (*Mia Corak*), born 1917, U.S. dancer and choreographer, born in Yugoslavia.

slav·er[1] (slā/vər), *n.* **1.** a dealer in or an owner of slaves. **2.** See **slave ship.** [SLAVE + -ER[1]]

slav·er[2] (slav/ər, slā/vər, slä/-), *v.i.* **1.** to let saliva run from the mouth; slobber. **2.** to fawn. —*v.t.* **3.** to wet or smear with saliva. —*n.* **4.** saliva coming from the mouth. **5.** drivel; twaddle. [ME < Scand; cf. Icel *slafra.* See SLOBBER]

slav·er·y (slā/və rē, slāv/rē), *n.* **1.** the condition of a slave; bondage. **2.** the keeping of slaves as a practice or institution. **3.** a state of subjection like that of a slave: *He was kept in slavery by drugs.* **4.** severe toil; drudgery. [SLAVE + -ERY]
—**Syn. 1.** thralldom, enthrallment. SLAVERY, BONDAGE, SERVITUDE refer to involuntary subjection to another or others. SLAVERY emphasizes the idea of complete ownership and control by a master: *to be sold into slavery.* BONDAGE indicates a state of subjugation or captivity often involving burdensome and degrading labor: *in bondage to a cruel master.* SERVITUDE is compulsory service, often such as is required by a legal penalty: *penal servitude.* **4.** moil, labor.

slave/ ship/, a ship for transporting slaves from their native homes to places of bondage.

Slave/ Ship/, The, a painting (1839) by J. M. W. Turner.

Slave/ State/, *U.S. Hist.* any of the States where Negro slavery was legal before the Civil War.

slav·ey (slā/vē), *n.*, *pl.* **-eys.** *Brit. Informal.* a female servant, esp. a maid of all work in a boarding house. [SLAVE + -Y[2]]

Slav·ic (slav/ik, slä/vik), *n.* **1.** a branch of the Indo-European family of languages, usually divided into East Slavic (Russian, Ukrainian, Byelorussian), West Slavic (Polish, Czech, Slovak, Sorbian), and South Slavic (Old Church Slavonic, Bulgarian, Serbo-Croatian, Slovene). —*adj.* **2.** of or pertaining to the Slavs or their languages. Also, **Slavonic.** [SLAV + -IC]

Slav·i·cism (slä/vi siz/əm, slav/i-), *n.* Slavism. [SLAVIC + -ISM]

Slav·i·cist (slä/vi sist, slav/i-), *n.* a specialist in the study of the Slavic languages or literatures. Also, **Slavist** (slä/vist, slav/ist). [SLAVIC + -IST]

slav·ish (slā/vish), *adj.* **1.** of or befitting a slave: *slavish subjection.* **2.** being or resembling a slave; abjectly submissive: *He was slavish in his obedience.* **3.** base; mean; ignoble: *slavish fears.* **4.** deliberately imitative; lacking originality: *a slavish reproduction.* [SLAVE + -ISH[1]] —**slav/ish·ly,** *adv.* —**slav/ish·ness,** *n.*
—**Syn. 2.** groveling, fawning, cringing. See **servile.**

Slav·ism (slä/viz əm, slav/iz-), *n.* that which is native to, characteristic of, or associated with the Slavs or Slavic. Also, **Slavicism.** [SLAV + -ISM]

Slavo-, a combining form of **Slav**: *Slavophile.*

slav·oc·ra·cy (slā vok/rə sē), *n.*, *pl.* **-cies. 1.** the rule or domination of slaveholders: *the slavocracy of the old plantations.* **2.** a dominating body of slaveholders. [SLAVE + -O- + -CRACY] —**slav·o·crat** (slā/və krat/), *n.* —**slav·o·crat·ic** (slā/və krat/ik), *adj.*

Sla·vo·ni·a (slə vō/nē ə), *n.* a historic region in N Croatia.

Sla·vo·ni·an (slə vō/nē ən), *adj.* **1.** of or pertaining to Slavonia or its inhabitants. **2.** Slavic. —*n.* **3.** a native or inhabitant of Slavonia. **4.** a Slav. [SLAVONI(A) + -AN]

Sla·von·ic (slə von/ik), *adj.* **1.** Slavonian. **2.** Slavic. [< NL *slavonic(us)*, equiv. to ML *Slavon(ia)* SLAVONIA + *-icus* -IC] —**Sla·von/i·cal·ly,** *adv.*

Slav·o·phile (slä/və fīl/, -fil, slav/ə-), *n.* **1.** one who greatly admires the Slavs and Slavic ways. —*adj.* **2.** admiring or favoring the Slavs and Slavic interests, aims, customs, etc. Also, **Slav·o·phil** (slä/və fil, slav/ə-). [SLAVO- + -PHILE] —**Sla·voph·i·lism** (slə vof/ə liz/əm, slä/və fil iz/əm, slav/ə-), *n.*

Slav·o·phobe (slä/və fōb/, slav/ə-), *n.* one who fears or hates the Slavs, their influence, or things Slavic. [SLAVO- + -PHOBE] —**Slav/o·pho/bi·a,** *n.*

slaw (slô), *n.* coleslaw. [< D *sla*, short for *salade* SALAD]

slay (slā), *v.*, **slew, slain, slay·ing,** *n.* —*v.t.* **1.** to kill by violence. **2.** to destroy; extinguish. **3.** sley. **4.** *Informal.* to affect or impress very strongly; overwhelm, esp. by means of amusement: *Your jokes slay me.* **5.** *Obs.* to strike. —*n.* **6.** sley. [ME; OE *slēan;* c. D *slaan*, G *schlagen*, Icel *slā*, Goth *slahan* to strike, beat] —**slay/a·ble,** *adj.* —**slay/er,** *n.*
—**Syn. 1.** murder, slaughter, massacre, butcher.

SLBM, satellite-launched ballistic missile.

sld., 1. sailed. **2.** sealed.

sleave (slēv), *v.*, **sleaved, sleav·ing,** *n.* —*v.t.* **1.** to divide or separate into filaments, as silk. —*n.* **2.** anything matted or raveled. **3.** a filament of silk obtained by separating a thicker thread. **4.** a silk in the form of such filaments. [OE *slǣfan*, c. *slīfan* to split; see SLIVER]

sleaze (slēz), *n.* *Slang.* sleazy quality, behavior, character, etc. [back formation from SLEAZY]

slea·zy (slē/zē, slā/zē), *adj.*, **-zi·er, -zi·est. 1.** thin or poor in texture, as a fabric; flimsy: *a sleazy dress; a sleazy excuse.* **2.** contemptibly low, mean, or unimportant: *a sleazy little pickpocket.* [?] —**slea/zi·ly,** *adv.* —**slea/zi·ness,** *n.*

sled (sled), *n.*, *v.*, **sled·ded, sled·ding.** —*n.* **1.** a small vehicle consisting of a platform mounted on runners for use in coasting or being drawn over snow or ice. **2.** a sledge. —*v.i.* **3.** to coast, ride, or be carried on a sled. —*v.t.* **4.** to convey on a sled. [ME *sledde* < MFlem or MLG; akin to G *schlitten*, Icel *sleði.* See SLIDE] —**sled/like/,** *adj.*

sled/ cul/tivator, go-devil (def. 5).

sled·der (sled/ər), *n.* **1.** one who rides on or steers a sled. **2.** a horse or other animal for drawing a sled. [SLED + -ER[1]]

sled·ding (sled/ing), *n.* **1.** the state of the ground permitting use of a sled: *The snow made a good sledding.* **2.** the going, or kind of travel, for sleds, as determined by the state of the ground, weather conditions, etc.: *rough sledding.* **3.** a going, progress, or advance in any field: *It won't be easy sledding to get this bill through the assembly.* **4.** the act of conveying or riding on a sled. [SLED + -ING[1]]

sledge[1] (slej), *n.*, *v.*, **sledged, sledg·ing.** —*n.* **1.** a vehicle of various forms, mounted on runners and often drawn by draft animals, used for traveling or for conveying loads over snow, ice, rough ground, etc. **2.** a sled. **3.** *Brit.* a sleigh. —*v.t.*, *v.i.* **4.** to convey or travel by sledge. —*v.i.* **5.** *Brit.* to sleigh. [< D (dial.) *sleedse*, deriv. of *slede*, var. of *sledde* SLED]

sledge[2] (slej), *n.*, *v.*, **sledged, sledg·ing.** —*n.* **1.** See **sledge hammer.** —*v.t.*, *v.i.* **2.** to sledge-hammer. [ME *slegge*, OE *slecg;* c. D *slegge*, Icel *sleggja;* akin to SLAY]

sledge/ ham/mer, a large, heavy hammer wielded with both hands.

sledge-ham·mer (slej/ham/ər), *v.t.*, *v.i.* **1.** to strike, hammer, or beat with or as with a sledge hammer. —*adj.* **2.** like a sledge hammer; powerful; ruthless: *The troops made a sledge-hammer advance.*

sleek[1] (slēk), *adj.* **1.** smooth or glossy, as hair, an animal, etc. **2.** well-fed or well-groomed. **3.** smooth in manners, speech, etc.; suave. **4.** cleverly or deceitfully skillful; slick: *a sleek confidence man.* [var. of SLICK[1]] —**sleek/ly,** *adv.* —**sleek/ness,** *n.*

sleek[2] (slēk), *v.t.* to make sleek; smooth; slick: *to sleek leather.* Also, **sleek/en.** [var. of SLICK[2]] —**sleek/er,** *n.*

sleek·it (slē/kit), *adj.* *Scot.* sleeky. [ptp. of SLEEK[2]]

sleek·y (slē/kē), *adj.*, **sleek·i·er, sleek·i·est. 1.** sleek; smooth. **2.** *Chiefly Scot.* sly; sneaky. Also, *Scot.*, **sleeked** (slēkt), **sleekit.** [SLEEK[1] + -Y[1]]

sleep (slēp), *v.*, **slept, sleep·ing,** *n.* —*v.i.* **1.** to take the repose or rest afforded by a suspension of the voluntary exercise of the bodily functions and the natural suspension, complete or partial, of consciousness; cease being awake. **2.** *Bot.* to assume, esp. at night, a state similar to the sleep of animals, marked by closing of petals, leaves, etc. **3.** to be dormant, quiescent, or inactive, as faculties. **4.** to be careless or unalert; allow one's alertness, vigilance, or attentiveness to lie dormant: *While England slept, Germany prepared for war.* **5.** to lie in death: *They are sleeping in their tombs.* **6.** (of a Yo-Yo) to continue to spin at the extreme end of the string until tripped to make it roll back up to the operator's hand. —*v.t.* **7.** to take rest in (a specified kind of sleep): *He slept the sleep of the innocent.* **8.** to accommodate for sleeping; have sleeping accommodations for: *This trailer sleeps three people.* **9.** to spend or pass in sleep (usually fol. by *away* or *out*): *to sleep the day away.* **10.** to get rid of (a headache, hangover, etc.) by sleeping (usually fol. by *off* or *away*). **11.** to cause (a Yo-Yo) to sleep. **12. sleep in, a.** (of domestic help) to sleep at the place of one's employment. **b.** to sleep beyond one's usual time of arising: *After the dance they all slept in.* **13. sleep out, a.** (of domestic help) to sleep away from one's place of employment. **b.** to sleep away from one's home. [ME *slepe*, OE *slēpan*, *slǣpan*, *slāpan;* c. D *slapen*, G *schlafen*, Goth *slēpan*]
—*n.* **14.** the state of a person who or animal or plant that sleeps. **15.** a period of sleeping: *a brief sleep.* **16.** dormancy or inactivity. **17.** the repose of death. **18.** sleeper (def. 10). [ME; OE *slēp* (Anglian), *slǣp; slāp;* c. D *slaap*, G *Schlaf*, Goth *slēps*] —**sleep/ful,** *adj.* —**sleep/like/,** *adj.*
—**Syn. 1.** slumber, nap, drowse, doze. **14.** rest, repose. **15.** nap.

Sleep (slēp), *n.* **Marsh of.** See **Palus Somnii.**

sleep·coat (slēp/kōt/), *n.* a man's lightweight garment for sleep or informal wear at home, having a sash and often a collar like that of a pajama top and reaching to the knees or just above. [SLEEP + COAT]

sleep·er (slē/pər), *n.* **1.** one who or that which sleeps. **2.** a heavy horizontal timber for distributing loads. **3.** *Brit.* a timber or beam laid in a railway track, serving as a foundation or support for the rails; a cross tie, bridge tie, or switch tie in a railroad track. **4.** *Building Trades.* **a.** any long wooden, metal, or stone piece lying horizontally as a sill or footing. **b.** any of a number of wooden pieces, laid upon the ground or upon masonry or concrete, to which floorboards are nailed. **5.** a sleeping car. **6.** merchandise that is not quickly sold because its value is not immediately recognized. **7.** Often, **sleepers.** one-piece or two-piece pajamas with feet, worn by children. **8.** bunting[3]. **9.** *Informal.* something that or someone who becomes or may become unexpectedly successful or important after a period of being unnoticed, ignored or considered a failure: *The play was the sleeper of the season. I think he's a sleeper and will win the championship.* **10.** Also called **sleep, sand.** a globule which forms at the inner corner of the eye, esp. during sleep, from the accumulated secretion of the glands of the eyelid. **11.** any of several gobioid fishes of the family *Eleotridae*, found in tropical seas, most species of which have the habit of resting quietly on the sea bottom. **12.** *Bowling Slang.* a pin that is hidden from view by another pin. **13.** a Yo-Yo with a looped string, allowing it to sleep. [ME; see SLEEP, -ER[1]]

Sleep·ers (slē/pərz), *n.* **Lake of the.** See **Lacus Somniorum.**

sleep-in (slēp/in/), *adj.* **1.** (of domestic help) sleeping at the place of employment. —*n.* **2.** a servant, nurse, etc., who sleeps at the place of employment. [adj., n. use of v. phrase *sleep in*]

sleep·ing (slē/ping), *n.* **1.** the condition of being asleep. —*adj.* **2.** asleep. **3.** of, noting, or pertaining to a vehicle with sleeping accommodations: *a sleeping compartment.* **4.** used to sleep in or on: *sleeping jacket.* **5.** used to induce or aid sleep or while asleep: *sleeping mask.* [ME; see SLEEP, -ING[1], -ING[2]]

sleep/ing bag/, a large bag, usually of warmly padded canvas, or nylon and having a zipper in front, in which a person sleeps, as when camping out of doors.

sleep/ing beau/ty. See **sheep sorrel.**

Sleep/ing Beau/ty, 1. a beautiful princess who, as the heroine of a popular fairy tale, is put to sleep under an evil spell and can be awakened only by the kiss of the prince who is her true love. **2.** (*italics*) the fairy tale itself. **3.** (*italics*) a ballet (1889) by Tchaikovsky. **4.** *Facetious.* any person sleeping soundly.

sleep/ing car/, a railroad car fitted with berths, compartments, bedrooms, or drawing rooms, for travelers who wish to sleep during the journey.

sleep/ing chair/, a chair of the 17th century, having a high back, usually adjustable, with deep wings of the same height.

sleep/ing part/ner, *Brit.* See **silent partner.**

sleep/ing pill/, a pill or capsule, usually prescribed by a physician, for inducing sleep.

sleep/ing porch/, a porch enclosed with glass or screening or a room with open sides or a row of windows used for sleeping in the open air.

sleep/ing sick/ness, *Pathol.* **1.** Also called **African sleeping sickness, African trypanosomiasis.** a generally fatal disease, common in parts of Africa, characterized by fever, wasting, and progressive lethargy: caused by a parasitic protozoan, *Trypanosoma gambiense*, which is carried by a tsetse fly, *Glossina palpalis.* **2.** Also called **epidemic encephalitis, lethargic encephalitis, nona.** a virus disease affecting the brain, characterized by apathy, sleepiness, extreme muscular weakness, and impairment of vision. Also, *Brit.*, **sleepy sickness.**

sleep·less (slēp/lis), *adj.* **1.** without sleep: *a sleepless night.* **2.** watchful; alert: *sleepless devotion to duty.* **3.** always active: *the sleepless ocean.* [ME; see SLEEP, -LESS] —**sleep/less·ly,** *adv.* —**sleep/less·ness,** *n.*

sleep-out (slēp/out/), *adj.* **1.** (of domestic help) sleeping away from the place of employment. —*n.* **2.** a servant, nurse, etc., who lives elsewhere than at the place of employment. [adj., n. use of v. phrase *sleep out*]

sleep·walk·ing (slēp/wô/king), *n.* **1.** the act or state of walking while asleep; somnambulism. —*adj.* **2.** of or pertaining to the state of walking while asleep; somnambulistic. [SLEEP + WALKING] —**sleep/walk/er,** *n.*

sleep·wear (slēp/wâr/), *n.* garments, as robes, nightgowns, pajamas, etc., worn for sleeping or at bedtime, taken collectively. [SLEEP + WEAR]

sleep·y (slē/pē), *adj.*, **sleep·i·er, sleep·i·est. 1.** ready or inclined to sleep; drowsy. **2.** of or showing drowsiness. **3.** languid; languorous: *a sleepy gesture.* **4.** lethargic; sluggish: *a sleepy lagoon.* **5.** quiet: *a sleepy village.* **6.** inducing sleep; soporific: *sleepy warmth.* [ME; see SLEEP, -Y[1]] —**sleep/i·ly,** *adv.* —**sleep/i·ness,** *n.*
—**Syn. 1.** tired, somnolent, slumbrous.

sleep/y Dick/, Star-of-Bethlehem (def. 1).

Sleep/y Eye/, a town in S Minnesota. 3492 (1960).

sleep·y·head (slē/pē hed/), *n.* a sleepy person. [SLEEPY + HEAD]

Sleep/y Hol/low chair/, *U.S. Furniture.* an armchair of the mid-19th century, sometimes on rockers, having a single piece forming a high upholstered back and a concave upholstered seat. [after *Sleepy Hollow,* New York]

sleep′y sick′ness, *Brit. Pathol.* See **sleeping sickness.**

sleep·y-voiced (slē′pē voist′), *adj.* having a dull or lethargic voice.

sleet (slēt), *n.* **1.** the frozen coating that sometimes forms on trees, roads, wires, etc., when rain or partly frozen rain falls while the temperature is low. **2.** precipitation in the form of frozen raindrops; ice pellets. **3.** *Chiefly Brit.* the precipitation of snow and rain simultaneously. —*v.i.* **4.** to send down sleet. **5.** to fall as or like sleet. [ME *slete;* akin to LG *slote,* G *Schlossen* hail]

sleet·y (slē′tē), *adj.,* **sleet·i·er, sleet·i·est.** of or pertaining to sleet. [SLEET + -Y[1]] —**sleet′i·ness,** *n.*

sleeve (slēv), *n., v.,* **sleeved, sleev·ing.** —*n.* **1.** the part of a garment that covers the arm, varying in form and length but commonly tubular. **2.** an envelope, usually of paper, for holding a phonograph record: *Each record in the album has its own sleeve.* **3.** *Mach.* a tubular piece, as of metal, fitting over a rod or the like. **4. laugh up** or **in one's sleeve,** to be secretly amused or contemptuous; laugh inwardly: *to laugh up one's sleeve at someone's affectations.* **5. up one's sleeve,** kept secretly ready or close at hand: *I could tell by his sly look that he had something up his sleeve.* —*v.t.* **6.** to furnish with sleeves. **7.** *Mach.* to fit with a sleeve; join or fasten by means of a sleeve. [ME *sleve,* OE *slēfe* (Anglian); akin to D *sloof* apron] —**sleeve′like′,** *adj.*

sleeve·less (slēv′lis), *adj.* **1.** without a sleeve or sleeves. **2.** *Rare.* amounting to nothing; unprofitable; futile: *a sleeveless errand.* [ME, OE *slieflēas.* See SLEEVE, -LESS] —**sleeve′less·ness,** *n.*

sleeve·let (slēv′lit), *n.* a fitted sleeve or cover worn on the forearm for warmth or to protect a shirt sleeve. [SLEEVE + -LET]

sleeve′ link′, *Brit.* See **cuff link.**

sleeve′ valve′, an intake or exhaust valve for an engine, consisting of one or more sleeves reciprocating within a cylinder, so that ports in the cylinder and in the sleeves are opposed at regular intervals to open the valve.

sleigh[1] (slā), *n.* **1.** a light vehicle on runners, that is usually open and generally horse-drawn, and that is used esp. for transporting persons over snow or ice. —*v.i.* **2.** to travel or ride in a sleigh. [< D *slee,* short for *slede* SLED] —**sleigh′er,** *n.*

sleigh[2] (slā), *n., v.t.* sley.

sleigh′ bed′, a bed of the Empire period having raised ends terminating in outward scrolls. Also called **boat bed.**

sleigh′ bells′, any of several kinds of small bells attached to a sleigh or to the harness of the animal drawing the sleigh.

sleight (slīt), *n.* **1.** skill; dexterity. **2.** an artifice; stratagem. **3.** cunning; craft. [ME; early ME *slegth* < Scand; cf. Icel *slægth.* See SLY, -TH[1]]

sleight′ of hand′, **1.** skill in feats requiring quick and clever movements of the hands, esp. for entertainment or deception, as jugglery, palming, etc.; legerdemain. **2.** the performance of such feats. **3.** a feat of legerdemain.

Sleip·nir (slāp′nir), *n. Scand. Myth.* the eight-legged horse of Odin. Also, **Sleip·ner** (slāp′nər).

slen·der (slen′dər), *adj.* **1.** having a circumference that is small in proportion to the height or length: *a slender post.* **2.** attractively thin and well-formed: *the slender girls who work as models.* **3.** small in size, amount, extent, etc.; meager: *a slender income.* **4.** having little value, force, or justification: *slender prospects.* **5.** thin or weak, as sound. [ME *slendre, sclendre* < ?] —**slen′der·ly,** *adv.* —**slen′der·ness,** *n.*

—**Syn. 2.** spare, narrow. SLENDER, SLIGHT, SLIM imply a tendency toward thinness. As applied to the human body, SLENDER implies a generally attractive and pleasing thinness: *slender hands.* SLIGHT often adds the idea of frailness to that of thinness: *a slight figure almost fragile in appearance.* SLIM implies a lithe or delicate thinness: *a slim and athletic figure.* **4.** trivial, trifling. **5.** fragile, feeble, fine, delicate, flimsy. —**Ant. 2.** fat, stocky.

slen′der blind′ snake′, any of several wormlike, fossorial snakes of the family *Leptotyphlopidae,* of the New World, Africa, and southwestern Asia, having the eyes covered by scales.

slen′der blue′ flag′, an iris, *Iris prismatica,* of eastern North America, having grasslike leaves and bluish-violet flowers, growing in wet places.

slen·der·ize (slen′də rīz′), *v.,* **-ized, -iz·ing.** —*v.t.* **1.** to make slender or more slender. **2.** to cause to appear slender: *dresses that slenderize the figure.* —*v.i.* **3.** to become slender: *She's slenderizing so that the new styles will look well on her.* [SLENDER + -IZE] —**slen·der·i·za·tion** (slen′dər i zā′shən), *n.* —**slen′der·iz′er,** *n.*

slen′der lo′ris, loris (def. 1).

slen′derness ra′tio, *Rocketry.* See **aspect ratio** (def. 4a).

slept (slept), *v.* pt. and pp. of **sleep.**

Sles·vig (sles′vikh), *n.* Danish name of **Schleswig.**

Sles·wick (sles′wik), *n.* Schleswig.

sleuth (slōōth), *n.* **1.** *Informal.* a detective. **2.** a bloodhound. —*v.t., v.i.* **3.** to track or trail, as a detective. [short for SLEUTHHOUND] —**sleuth′like′,** *adj.*

sleuth·hound (slōōth′hound′), *n.* **1.** a bloodhound. **2.** *Informal.* a detective. [ME *slōth* track, trail (< Scand; cf. Icel *slōth*) + HOUND[1]]

slew[1] (slōō), *v.* pt. of **slay.**

slew[2] (slōō), *v.t., v.i., n.* slue[1]. [?]

slew[3] (slōō), *n. U.S., Canadian.* slough[1] (def. 3).

slew[4] (slōō), *n. Informal.* a great number; lot: *a whole slew of people.* Also, **slue.** [< Ir *sluagh* multitude, army]

sley (slā), *n., pl.* **sleys,** *v.* —*n.* **1.** the reed of a loom. **2.** the warp count in woven fabrics. **3.** *Brit.* the lay of a loom. —*v.t.* **4.** to draw (warp ends) through the heddle eyes of the harness or through the dents of the reed in accordance with a given plan for weaving a fabric. Also, **slay, sleigh.** [late ME *sleye,* OE *slege* weaver's reed; akin to D *slag,* Icel *slag,* G *Schlag,* Goth *slahs* a blow; see SLAY]

Slezs·ko (sles′kô), *n.* Czech name of **Silesia.**

SLIC, (Federal) Savings and Loan Insurance Corporation. Also, **S.L.I.C.**

slice (slīs), *n., v.,* **sliced, slic·ing.** —*n.* **1.** a thin, broad, flat piece cut from something: *a slice of bread.* **2.** a part; portion: *a slice of land.* **3.** any of various implements with a thin, broad blade or part, as for turning food in a frying pan, serving fish at the table, taking up printing ink, etc.; spatula. **4.** *Sports.* **a.** the path described by a ball, as in baseball or golf, that curves in a direction corresponding to the side from which it was struck. **b.** a ball describing such a path. —*v.t.* **5.** to cut into slices; divide into parts. **6.** to cut through or cleave with or as with a knife: *The ship sliced the sea.* **7.** to cut or cut as a slice or slices (sometimes fol. by *off, away, from,* etc.). **8.** to remove by means of a slice, slice bar, or similar implement. **9.** *Sports.* to hit (a ball) so as to result in a slice. —*v.i. Sports.* **10.** (of a player) to slice the ball. **11.** (of a ball) to describe a slice in flight. [ME *s(c)lice* < OF *(e)sclice,* back formation from *esclicier* to split up < OHG *slīzan;* c. OE *slītan,* Icel *slīta,* D *slijten;* see SLIT] —**slice′a·ble,** *adj.* —**slic′er,** *n.* —**slic′ing·ly,** *adv.*

slice′ bar′, a long-handled instrument with a blade at the end, for clearing away or breaking up clinkers, coal, etc., in a furnace.

slick[1] (slik), *adj.* **1.** smooth and glossy; sleek. **2.** smooth in manners, speech, etc.; suave. **3.** sly; shrewdly adroit: *He's a slick customer, all right.* **4.** ingenious; cleverly devised: *a slick plan to get out of work.* **5.** slippery, esp. from being covered with or as with ice, water, or oil. **6.** pertaining to, resembling, or adapted to the style of a popular, nonliterary magazine; glib: *a writer who has mastered every formula of slick fiction.* **7.** *Slang.* wonderful; remarkable; first-rate. —*n.* **8.** a smooth or slippery place or spot or the substance causing it: *oil slick.* **9.** *Informal.* **a.** a magazine printed on paper having a more or less glossy finish. **b.** such a magazine regarded as possessing qualities, as expensiveness, chic, and sophistication, which hold appeal for a particular readership, as one whose members enjoy or are seeking affluence. **c.** such a magazine regarded as having a sophisticated, deftly executed, but shallow or glib literary content. Cf. **pulp** (def. 6). **10.** any of various paddlelike tools for smoothing a surface. —*adv.* **11.** smoothly; cleverly. [ME *slike;* c. Flem *sleek* even, smooth; akin to SLICK[2]] —**slick′ly,** *adv.* —**slick′ness,** *n.*

slick[2] (slik), *v.t.* **1.** to make sleek or smooth. **2.** to use a slicker on (skins or hides). **3.** *Informal.* to make smart or fine; spruce up (usually fol. by *up*). —*n.* **4.** Also, **slicker.** *Foundry.* a small trowel used for smoothing the surface of the mold. **5.** any woodworking chisel having a blade more than two inches wide. [ME *slicke(n),* OE *slician;* akin to Icel *slīkja* to give a gloss to]

slick·en·side (slik′ən sīd′), *n. Geol.* a rock surface which has become more or less polished and striated from the sliding or grinding motion of an adjacent mass of rock. [SLICK[2] + -EN[3] + SIDE[1]]

slick·er[1] (slik′ər), *n.* **1.** *U.S.* **a.** a long, loose, oilskin raincoat. **b.** any raincoat. **2.** *Informal.* a swindler; a sly cheat. **3.** a sophisticated person from a large city: *Watch out for those New York slickers.* [SLICK[1] + -ER[1]] —**slick′ered,** *adj.*

slick·er[2] (slik′ər), *n.* **1.** a tool, usually of stone or glass, for scraping, smoothing, and working tanning agents into a skin or hide. **2.** *Foundry.* slick[2] (def. 4). [SLICK[2] + -ER[1]]

slick·pa·per (slik′pā′pər), *adj.* slick[1] (def. 6). [SLICK[1] + PAPER]

slide (slīd), *v.,* **slid, slid** or **slid·den, slid·ing,** *n.* —*v.i.* **1.** to move along in continuous contact with a smooth or slippery surface: *to slide down a snow-covered hill.* **2.** to slip or skid. **3.** to glide or pass smoothly onward. **4.** to slip easily, quietly, or unobtrusively on or as if on a track, channel, or guide rail (usually fol. by *in, out, away,* etc.). **5.** to pass or fall gradually into a specified state, character, practice, etc. **6.** *Baseball.* (of a base runner) to cast oneself, usually feet first, forward along the ground in the direction of the base being approached, to present less of a target for a baseman attempting to make a tag. **7. let slide,** to fail to give proper attention to; be negligent: *He let his studies slide to go to football practice.* —*v.t.* **8.** to cause to slide, slip, or coast, as over a surface or with a smooth, gliding motion. **9.** to hand, pass along, or slip (something) easily or quietly (usually fol. by *in, into,* etc.): *to slide a letter into someone's hand.* —*n.* **10.** the act or an instance of sliding. **11.** a smooth surface for sliding on, esp. a type of chute in a playground. **12.** an object intended to slide. **13.** *Geol.* **a.** a landslide or the like. **b.** the mass of matter sliding down. **14.** a single transparency, object, or image for projection in a projector, as a lantern slide. **15.** a usually rectangular plate of glass on which objects are placed for microscopic examination. **16.** *Furniture.* a shelf sliding into the body of a piece when not in use. **17.** *Music.* **a.** an embellishment or grace consisting of an upward or downward series of three or more tones, the last of which is the principal tone. **b.** a portamento. **c.** a U-shaped section of the tube of an instrument of the trumpet class, as the trombone, which can be pushed in or out to alter the length of the air column and change the pitch. **18.** a vehicle mounted on runners, for conveying loads, as of grain or wood, esp. over a level surface. **19.** Also called **run.** *Horol.* the movement of a pallet to a banking pin under the influence of draw. **20.** (of a machine or mechanism) **a.** a moving part working on a track, channel, or guide rails. **b.** the surface, track, channel, or guide rails on which the part moves. **21.** any of various chutes used in logging, mining, or materials handling. [ME; OE *slīdan;* c. MLG *slīden,* MHG *slīten;* akin to SLED] —**slid′a·ble,** *adj.* —**slid′a·ble·ness,** *n.*

—**Syn. 1.** slither. SLIDE, GLIDE, SLIP suggest movement over a smooth surface. SLIDE suggests a rather brief movement of one surface over another in contact with it: *to slide downhill.* GLIDE suggests a continuous, smooth, easy, and (usually) noiseless motion: *A skater glides over the ice.* To SLIP is to slide smoothly, often in a sudden or accidental way: *to slip on the ice and fall.*

slide-ac·tion (slīd′ak′shən), *adj.* (of a rifle or shotgun) having a lever that when slid back and forth ejects the empty case and cocks and reloads the piece.

slide′ fas′tener, zipper.

slide·film (slīd′film′), *n.* filmstrip. [SLIDE + FILM]

slide′ knot′, a knot formed by making two half hitches on the standing part of the rope, the second hitch being next to the loop, which can be tightened.

Sli·dell (slī del′), *n.* a town in SE Louisiana. 6356 (1960).

Slide′ Moun′tain, a mountain in SE New York: highest peak of the Catskill Mountains. 4204 ft.

slid·er (slī′dər), *n.* **1.** one who or that which slides. **2.** *Baseball.* a fast pitch that curves slightly and sharply in front of a batter, away from the side from which it was thrown. **3.** any of several fresh-water turtles of the genus *Pseudemys,* of North America, having a smooth shell usually olive brown above and yellowish below. [SLIDE + -ER[1]]

slide′ rule′, a device for rapid calculation, consisting essentially of a rule having a sliding piece moving along it, both marked with graduated, usually logarithmic, scales.

slide′ trombone′. See under **trombone.**

slide′ valve′, *Mach.* a valve that slides without lifting to open or close an aperture, as the valves of the ports in the cylinders of certain steam engines.

slide·way (slīd′wā′), *n.* an inclined surface along which something can slide. [SLIDE + WAY]

slid·ing (slī′ding), *adj.* **1.** rising or falling, increasing or decreasing, according to a standard or to a set of conditions. **2.** operated, adjusted, or moved by sliding: *a sliding door.* [ME; OE *slīdende.* See SLIDE, -ING[2]] —**slid′ing·ly,** *adv.* —**slid′ing·ness,** *n.*

slid′ing keel′, *Naut.* centerboard.

slid′ing rule′, *Archaic.* See **slide rule.**

slid′ing scale′, **1.** a variable scale, esp. of industrial costs, as wages, raw materials, etc., which may be adapted to demand. **2.** a wage scale varying with the selling price of goods produced, the cost of living, or profits.

slid′ing vec′tor, *Math.* a vector having specified magnitude and lying on a given line. Also called **line vector.**

slid′ing way′, *Shipbuilding.* a timber that slides upon a groundway, forming a runner for the cradle on which a hull is launched.

sli·er (slī′ər), *adj.* a comparative of **sly.**

sli·est (slī′ist), *adj.* a superlative of **sly.**

slight (slīt), *adj.* **1.** small in amount, degree, etc.: *a slight increase; a slight odor.* **2.** of little importance, influence, etc.; trivial: *a slight cut.* **3.** slender or slim; not heavily built. **4.** frail; flimsy; delicate: *a slight fabric.* **5.** of little substance or strength. —*v.t.* **6.** to treat as of little importance. **7.** to treat (someone) with indifference; ignore, esp. pointedly or contemptuously; snub: *She was slighted by society.* **8.** to do negligently; scamp: *Students with spring fever slight their studies.* —*n.* **9.** slighting indifference or treatment. **10.** an instance of slighting treatment: *Slights and oversights marred his work.* **11.** a pointed and contemptuous discourtesy; affront: *She considered not being invited an unforgivable slight.* [ME; OE *sliht* (in *eorth-slihtes* close to ground); c. Icel *slēttr,* G *schlicht,* Goth *slaihts* smooth] —**slight′er,** *n.* —**slight′ly,** *adv.* —**slight′ness,** *n.*

—**Syn. 2.** insignificant, trifling, paltry. **3.** See **slender. 4.** weak, feeble, fragile. **5.** unsubstantial, inconsiderable. **6.** disdain, scorn. SLIGHT, DISREGARD, NEGLECT, OVERLOOK mean to pay no attention or too little attention to someone or something. To SLIGHT is irresponsibly to give only superficial attention to something important: *to slight one's work.* To DISREGARD is to pay no attention to a person or thing: *to disregard the rules;* in some circumstances, to DISREGARD may be admirable: *to disregard a handicap.* To NEGLECT is to shirk paying sufficient attention to a person or thing: *to neglect one's correspondence.* To OVERLOOK is to fail to see someone or something (possibly because of carelessness): *to overlook a bill which is due.* **9.** neglect, disregard, inattention; disdain, scorn. **11.** See **insult.** —**Ant. 1.** considerable.

slight·ing (slī′ting), *adj.* derogatory and disparaging; belittling. [SLIGHT + -ING[2]] —**slight′ing·ly,** *adv.*

Sli·go (slī′gō), *n.* **1.** a county in Connaught province, in the NW Republic of Ireland. 53,561 (1961); 694 sq. mi. **2.** its county seat: a seaport. 13,145 (1961).

sli·ly (slī′lē), *adv.* slyly.

slim (slim), *adj.,* **slim·mer, slim·mest,** *v.,* **slimmed, slim·ming.** —*adj.* **1.** slender, as in girth or form; slight in build or structure. **2.** poor or inferior: *a slim chance; a slim excuse.* **3.** small or inconsiderable; meager; scanty: *a slim income.* —*v.t., v.i.* **4.** to make or become slim. [special use of obs. *slimme* lanky, despicable person < MD *slimme* crafty person, n. use of *slim* crafty; the dominant element in English usage came to be lankiness, whence thinness] —**slim′ly,** *adv.* —**slim′ness,** *n.*

—**Syn. 1.** thin. See **slender. 3.** insignificant, trifling, trivial, paltry. —**Ant. 1.** fat. **3.** considerable; abundant.

slime (slīm), *n., v.,* **slimed, slim·ing.** —*n.* **1.** thin, glutinous mud. **2.** any ropy or viscous liquid matter, esp. of a foul or offensive kind. **3.** a viscous secretion of animal or vegetable origin. —*v.t.* **4.** to cover or smear with or as with slime. **5.** to remove slime from, as fish for canning. [ME *slyme,* OE *slīm;* c. D *slijm,* Icel *slīm,* G *Schleim*]

slime′ mold′, **1.** an organism usually considered to be a plant belonging to the class *Myxomycetes* or sometimes considered to be an animal belonging to the order *Mycetozoa,* characterized by a noncellular, multinucleate, creeping somatic phase and a propagative phase in which fruiting bodies are produced bearing spores that are covered by cell walls. **2.** an organism of the class *Acrasieae,* differing from the true slime molds in being cellular and uninucleate during both somatic and propagative phases.

slim·line (slim′līn′), *adj.* of, pertaining to, or noting a long, slender fluorescent lamp. [SLIM + LINE[1]]

slim·mer (slim′ər), *n. Brit.* a person who is on a reducing diet or takes special exercises to reduce weight. [SLIM + -ER[1]]

slim·sy (slim′zē), *adj.* flimsy; frail. Also, **slimp·sy** (slimp′sē). [b. SLIM and FLIMSY]

slim·y (slī′mē), *adj.,* **slim·i·er, slim·i·est.** **1.** of or like slime. **2.** abounding in or covered with slime. **3.** offensively foul or vile: *a slimy speech against the Congress.* [ME; see SLIME, -Y[1]] —**slim′i·ly,** *adv.* —**slim′i·ness,** *n.*

sling[1] (sling), *n., v.,* **slung, sling·ing.** —*n.* **1.** an instrument for hurling stones or other missiles that consists, typically, of a short strap with a long string at each end and that is operated by placing the missile in the strap, and, holding the ends of the strings in one hand, whirling the instrument around in a circle, and releasing one of

the strings to discharge the missile. **2.** a slingshot. **3.** a bandage used to suspend or support an injured part of the body, commonly a bandage suspended from the neck to support an injured arm or hand. **4.** a strap, band, or the like, forming a loop by which something is suspended or carried, as a strap attached to a rifle and passed over the shoulder. **5.** the act or an instance of slinging. **6.** a rope, chain, net, etc., for hoisting freight or for holding it while being hoisted. **7.** *Naut.* **a.** a chain for supporting a hoisting yard. **b. slings,** the area of a hoisting yard to which such chains are attached; the middle of a hoisting yard. —*v.t.* **8.** to throw, cast, or hurl; fling, as from the hand. **9.** to place in or secure with a sling to raise or lower. **10.** to raise, lower, etc., by such means. **11.** to hang by a sling or place so as to swing loosely: *to sling a rifle over one's shoulder.* **12.** to suspend: *to sling a hammock between two trees.* **13. sling hash,** *Slang.* to work as a waiter or waitress, esp. in a lunch counter or cheap restaurant. [ME *slynge(n)* < Scand; cf. Icel *slyngva* to hurl, akin to OE *slingan* to wind, twist, c. G *schlingen*]
—**Syn. 8.** pitch, toss.

sling[2] (sliŋ), *n.* *U.S.* an iced alcoholic drink, containing gin or the like, water, sugar, and lemon or lime juice. [special use of *sling* a drinking, draught, lit., a flinging (into the throat); see SLING[1]]

sling′ chair′, any of several varieties of chairs having a seat and back formed from a single sheet of canvas, leather, or the like, hanging loosely in a frame.

sling·er (sliŋ′ər), *n.* **1.** one who or that which slings. **2.** *Mach.* flinger (def. 2). [SLING[1] + -ER[1]]

sling′er ring′, *Aeron.* a tube around the hub of an airplane propeller for delivering an anti-icer to the propeller blades.

sling′ psychrom′eter, a psychrometer so designed that the wet-bulb thermometer can be ventilated, to expedite evaporation, by whirling in the air.

sling·shot (sliŋ′shot′), *n.* a Y-shaped stick with an elastic strip between the prongs for shooting stones and other small missiles. [SLING[1] + SHOT[1]]

slink (sliŋk), *v.,* **slunk** or (*Archaic*) **slank; slunk; slink·ing;** *n.; adj.* —*v.i.* **1.** to move or go in a furtive, abject manner, as from fear, cowardice, or shame. **2.** *Informal.* (of a woman) to walk or move in a slow, sinuous, provocative way. —*v.t.* **3.** (esp. of cows) to bring forth (young) prematurely. —*n.* **4.** a prematurely born calf or other animal. —*adj.* **5.** born prematurely: *a slink calf.* [ME *slynke,* OE *slinca(n)* (to) creep, crawl; c. LG *slinken,* G *schlinken*] —**slink′ing·ly,** *adv.*
—**Syn. 1.** skulk, sneak; lurk.

slink·y (sliŋ′kē), *adj.,* **slink·i·er, slink·i·est. 1.** characterized by or proceeding with slinking or stealthy movements. **2.** (esp. of women's clothing) made of soft, often clinging material and fitting the figure closely so as to enhance or flatter one's appearance and movements: *She invested a week's pay in a slinky little black dress.* [SLINK + -Y[1]] —**slink′i·ly,** *adv.* —**slink′i·ness,** *n.*

slip[1] (slip), *v.,* **slipped** or (*Archaic*) **slipt; slipped; slip·ping;** *n.* —*v.i.* **1.** to move, flow, pass, or go smoothly or easily; glide; slide: *Water slips off a smooth surface.* **2.** to slide suddenly or involuntarily; to lose one's foothold, as on a smooth surface: *She slipped on the icy ground.* **3.** to move, slide, or start gradually from a place or position: *His hat had slipped over his eyes.* **4.** to slide out of or become disengaged from a fastening, the grasp, etc.: *The plate slipped from her hand and crashed to the floor.* **5.** to pass without having been acted upon or used; be lost; get away: *to let an opportunity slip.* **6.** to pass from the mind, memory, or consciousness. **7.** to elapse or pass quickly or imperceptibly (often fol. by *away* or *by*): *The years slipped by. Money slips through his fingers.* **8.** to become involved or absorbed easily: *to slip into a new way of life.* **9.** to move or go quietly, cautiously, or unobtrusively: *to slip out of a room.* **10.** to read, study, consider, etc., without attention: *He slipped over the most important part.* **11.** to make a mistake or error: *As far as I know, he has never slipped once.* **12.** *Aeron.* (of an aircraft when excessively banked) to slide sideways, toward the center of the curve described in turning. Cf. **skid** (def. 16). **13.** to fall below a standard or accustomed level, or to decrease in quantity or quality; decline; deteriorate: *His work slipped last year.* **14.** to be said or revealed inadvertently (usually fol. by *out*): *The words slipped out before he could stop himself.*
—*v.t.* **15.** to cause to move, pass, go, etc., with a smooth, easy, or sliding motion. **16.** to put, place, pass, insert, or withdraw quickly or stealthily: *to slip a letter into a person's hand.* **17.** to put on or take off (a garment) easily or quickly: *He slipped the shirt over his head.* **18.** to let or make (something) slide out of a fastening, the hold, etc.: *He slipped the lock, and the door creaked open.* **19.** to release from a leash, harness, etc., as a hound or a hawk. **20.** to get away or free oneself from; escape (a pursuer, restraint, leash, etc.): *The cow slipped its halter and ran out of the barn.* **21.** to untie or undo (a knot). **22.** *Naut.* to let go entirely, as an anchor cable or an anchor. **23.** to let pass unheeded; neglect or miss. **24.** to ignore, pass over, or omit, as in speaking or writing. **25.** to pass from or escape (one's memory, attention, knowledge, etc.). **26.** to dislocate; put out of joint or position: *I slipped a disk in my back and couldn't move for a month.* **27.** to shed or cast: *The rattlesnake slipped its skin.* **28.** *Boxing.* to evade or avoid (a blow) by moving or turning the body quickly: *Clay slipped a right and countered with a hard left.* **29.** (of animals) to bring forth (offspring) prematurely. **30.** *Brit.* to detach (a railway car) from a moving train as it passes through a station. **31. let slip,** to reveal unintentionally: *to let slip the truth.* **32. slip a cog.** See **cog**[1] (def. 4). **33. slip into,** to put on (a garment) easily or quickly. **34. slip off,** to take off (a garment): *She slipped off her blouse.* **35. slip on,** to put on (a garment): *She slipped on the new sweater.* **36. slip out of,** to take off (a garment) easily or quickly. **37. slip someone's mind,** to be forgotten: *He was supposed to have brought home a loaf of bread, but it slipped his mind.* **38. slip something over on,** *Informal.* to deceive; defraud; trick: *He tried to slip something over on his customers by substituting inferior merchandise for that ordered.* **39. slip up,** to make an error; fail: *She slipped up and put the letters in the wrong envelopes again.* —*n.* **40.** the act or an instance of slipping. **41.** a sudden losing of one's foothold, as on slippery ground. **42.** a mistake in judgment; blunder. **43.** a mistake or oversight, as in speaking or writing, esp. a small one due to carelessness: *a minor slip in addition; a slip of the tongue.* **44.** an error in conduct; indiscretion. **45.** something easily slipped on or off. **46.** a decline or fall in quantity, quality, extent, etc., or from a standard or accustomed level: *A slip in prices is expected toward the end of the year.* **47.** *Clothing.* **a.** a woman's underdress, sleeveless and usually having shoulder straps, extending from above the bust down to the hemline of the outer dress. **b.** an underskirt, as a half-slip or petticoat. **48.** a pillowcase. **49.** an inclined plane, sloping to the water, on which vessels are built or repaired. **50.** *Naut.* the difference between the speed at which a screw propeller or paddle wheel would move if it were working against a solid and the actual speed at which it advances through the water. **51.** *U.S.* a space between two wharves or in a dock for vessels to lie in. **52.** *Elect.* the difference between the synchronous and the operating speeds of a motor. **53.** *Mach.* **a.** the difference between output speed and input or theoretical speed in certain fluid or electromagnetic devices, as couplings or motors. **b.** (in pumps) the difference between the actual volume of water or other liquid delivered by a pump during one complete stroke and the theoretical volume as determined by calculation of the displacement. **54.** unintended movement or play between mechanical parts or the like. **55.** *Cricket.* **a.** the position of a fielder who stands behind and to the offside of the wicketkeeper. **b.** the fielder playing this position. **56.** *Geol.* **a.** the relative displacement of formerly adjacent points on opposite sides of a fault, measured along the fault plane. **b.** a small fault. **57.** Also called **glide.** *Metall.* plastic deformation of one part of a metallic crystal relative to the other part due to shearing action. **58. give someone the slip,** to elude a pursuer; escape: *The police thought they had the murderer at last, but he gave them the slip.* [ME *slipp(e)* < MD *slippe(n)*; c. OHG *slipfan*; akin to SLIPPER[2]] —**slip′less,** *adj.* —**slip′ping·ly,** *adv.*
—**Syn. 2.** slither. See **slide. 11.** err, blunder. **43.** error, fault.

slip[2] (slip), *n., v.,* **slipped, slip·ping.** —*n.* **1.** a piece suitable for propagation cut from a plant; scion or cutting. **2.** any long, narrow piece or strip, as of wood, paper, land, etc. **3.** a young person, esp. one of slender form: *a mere slip of a girl.* **4.** a small paper form on which information is noted: *a withdrawal slip.* **5.** a small whetstone with a wedge-shaped cross section and one or two rounded sides. **6.** a long seat or narrow pew in a church. **7.** *Bookbinding.* one of the ends of a band, extending at the sides of a book after sewing. —*v.t.* **8.** to take slips or cuttings from (a plant). **9.** to take (a part), as a slip from a plant. [late ME < MFlem *slippe* a cut, slip, strip]

slip[3] (slip), *n.* **1.** *Ceram.* a clay solution of creamy consistency for coating or decorating biscuit. **2.** a glass-bearing liquid fired onto steel as a cladding, as in making enamel ware. [ME, OE *slype;* see SLOP[1]]

slip[4] (slip), *n.* *Archit.* slype.

slip′ car′riage, *Brit.* a railway car detached from a moving train as it passes through a station. Also called **slip′ coach′.**

slip·case (slip′kās′), *n.* a box for a book or set of books, open on one side so that the spine is visible. [SLIP[1] + CASE[2]]

slip′ clutch′, *Mach.* a friction clutch arranged to slip when excessive torque is applied.

slip·cov·er (slip′kuv′ər), *n.* Also, **slip′ cov′er. 1.** a cloth cover for a piece of furniture, made so as to be easily removable. **2.** a book jacket. —*v.t.* **3.** to cover (a piece of furniture) with a slipcover. [SLIP[1] + COVER]

slipe (slīp), *n., v.,* **sliped, slip·ing.** *Scot.* —*n.* **1.** a sledge, drag, or sleigh. —*v.t.* **2.** to peel or strip the outer coating from, esp. to peel bark from (a tree or twig). **3.** to slice. [ME *slype(n)* < ?]

slip′ hook′. See **pelican hook.**

slip′ in′dicator. See **bank indicator.**

slip′ joint′, a joint made between an older and a newer masonry wall to form a continuous surface, masonry at the end of the newer wall fitting into a vertical groove cut in the end of the older wall.

slip·knot (slip′not′), *n.* a knot that slips easily along the cord or line around which it is made. Also, **slip′ knot′.** See illus. under **knot.** [SLIP[1] + KNOT[1]]

slip′ mor′tise, *Carpentry.* **1.** Also called **slot mortise.** a mortise in the end of a timber. **2.** a slotlike mortise into which a tenon is fitted by swinging it into place from one side.

slip·noose (slip′no͞os′), *n.* a noose with a knot that slides along the rope, thus forming a noose that tightens as the rope is pulled. Also, **slip′ noose′.** [SLIP[1] + NOOSE]

slip-on (slip′on′, -ôn′), *adj.* **1.** designed to be slipped on easily, as a loose sweater. —*n.* **2.** a slip-on garment or article of dress. [adj., n. use of v. phrase *slip on*]

slip·o·ver (slip′ō′vər), *n., adj.* pull-over. [n., adj. use of v. phrase *slip over*]

slip·page (slip′ij), *n.* **1.** the act or an instance of slipping. **2.** an amount or extent of slipping. **3.** *Mach.* the amount of work dissipated by slipping of parts, excess play, etc. [SLIP[1] + -AGE]

slipped (slipt), *adj.* *Heraldry.* (of a flower, leaf, or plant) showing a part of the stem as if cut: *a lily slipped.* [SLIP[2] + -ED[3]]

slipped′ ten′don, *Vet. Pathol.* perosis.

slip·per[1] (slip′ər), *n.* **1.** any light, low-cut shoe into which the foot may be easily slipped, for casual wear in the home, for dancing, etc. Cf. **bedroom slipper, house slipper.** —*v.t.* **2.** to strike or beat with a slipper. [SLIP[1] + -ER[1]] —**slip′per·like′,** *adj.*

slip·per[2] (slip′ər), *adj.* *Chiefly Dial.* slippery. [ME *sliper,* OE *slipor;* see SLIPPERY]

slip′per chair′, a small bedroom chair with a low seat.

slip′per foot′, *Furniture.* an elongated pad foot.

slip′per sock′, a sock with a soft leather sole sewn onto it, used as indoor footwear.

slip·per·wort (slip′ər wûrt′), *n.* any of several scrophulariaceous plants of the genus *Calceolaria,* of tropical America, having slipper-shaped flowers. [SLIPPER[1] + WORT[2]]

Slipperwort, *Calceolaria crenatiflora*

slip·per·y (slip′ə rē, slip′rē), *adj.,* **-per·i·er, -per·i·est. 1.** tending or liable to cause slipping or sliding, as ice, oil, a wet surface, etc.: *a slippery road.* **2.** tending to slip from the hold or grasp or from position: *a slippery rope.* **3.** likely to slip away or escape: *slippery prospects.* **4.** not to be depended on; fickle; shifty, tricky, or deceitful. **5.** unstable or insecure, as conditions: *a slippery situation.* [alter. of SLIPPER[2]; cf. LG *slipperig;* see -Y[1]] —**slip′per·i·ness,** *n.*

slip′pery dick′, *Ichthyol.* a wrasse, *Halichoeres bivittatus,* found in the tropical Atlantic Ocean.

slip′pery elm′, 1. an elm, *Ulmus fulva,* of eastern North America, having a mucilaginous inner bark. **2.** the bark, used as a demulcent.

Slip′pery Rock′, a town in W Pennsylvania. 2563 (1960).

slip·py (slip′ē), *adj.,* **-pi·er, -pi·est. 1.** *Informal.* slippery. **2.** *Chiefly Brit.* quick; alert; sharp. [SLIP[1] + -Y[1]] —**slip′pi·ness,** *n.*

slip-rail (slip′rāl′), *n.* *Australian.* one of a vertical set of fence rails that can be removed easily to leave a gateway.

slip′ ring′, *Elect.* a metal ring, usually of copper or cast iron, mounted so that current may be conducted through stationary brushes into or out of a rotating member. —**slip′-ring′,** *adj.*

slip′ seat′, *Furniture.* an upholstered seat having its own frame which fits loosely into the frame of a chair.

slip·sheet (slip′shēt′), *Print.* —*v.t., v.i.* **1.** to insert (blank sheets) between printed sheets as they come off the press to prevent offset. —*n.* **2.** a sheet so inserted. [SLIP[1] + SHEET[1]]

slip·shod (slip′shod′), *adj.* **1.** careless, untidy, or slovenly: *slipshod work.* **2.** wearing slippers or loose shoes, esp. ones worn at the heel. [SLIP[1] + SHOD] —**slip′shod′di·ness, slip′shod′ness,** *n.*
—**Syn. 1.** loose, sloppy.

slip′ sill′, *Masonry.* a sill having no lugs. Cf. **lug sill.**

slip·slop (slip′slop′), *n.* **1.** sloppy or weak food or drink. **2.** meaningless or trifling talk or writing. [gradational compound based on SLOP[1]]

slip·sole (slip′sōl′), *n.* an insole placed in a shoe for warmth or to adjust the size. [SLIP[1] + SOLE[2]]

slip′ spring′, *Horol.* See **brake spring.**

slip′ stem′, a spoon handle cut obliquely at the end from top to bottom.

slip·stick (slip′stik′), *n.* *Slang.* See **slide rule.** [SLIP[1] + STICK[1]]

slip′ stitch′, *Sewing.* a loose stitch taken between two layers of fabric, as on a facing or hem, so as to be invisible on the right side or outside surface, used in stoating.

slip-stitch (slip′stich′), *v.t., v.i.* *Sewing.* to sew with slip stitches.

slip·stone (slip′stōn′), *n.* a specially shaped oilstone for sharpening gouges and molding plane irons. [SLIP[1] + STONE]

slip·stream (slip′strēm′), *n.* *Aeron.* the stream of air pushed back by a revolving aircraft propeller. Also, **slip′ stream′.** Cf. **backwash** (def. 2), **wash** (def. 30). [SLIP[1] + STREAM]

slipt (slipt), *v.* *Archaic.* pt. of **slip**[1].

slip′ top′, the end of a slip stem on a spoon.

slip′ trail′ing, *Ceram.* the act of decorating an object with a poured stream of slip. Also called **slip′ trac′ing.**

slip-up (slip′up′), *n.* *Informal.* a mistake, blunder, or oversight: *Several slip-ups caused a delay in the delivery of books.* [n. use of v. phrase *slip up*]

slip·ware (slip′wâr′), *n.* pottery decorated with slip. [SLIP[3] + WARE[1]]

slip·way (slip′wā′), *n.* *Naut.* **1.** (in a shipyard) the area sloping toward the water, on which the ways are located. **2.** way (def. 19). **3.** See **marine railway. 4.** a ramp on a factory ship for hauling aboard carcasses of whales for processing. [SLIP[1] + WAY]

slit (slit), *v.,* **slit, slit·ting,** *n.* —*v.t.* **1.** to cut apart or open along a line; make a long cut, fissure, or opening in. **2.** to cut or rend into strips; split. —*n.* **3.** a straight, narrow cut, opening, or aperture. [ME *slitte* (n., v.), OE (north) *slitta* (v.); c. G *schlitzen* to split, slit; akin to OE *slite* a slit, *geslit* a bite, *slītan* to split; see SLICE] —**slit′less,** *adj.* —**slit′like′,** *adj.*

slit-drum (slit′drum′), *n.* a hollowed-out log with a long, narrow slit, beaten with a stick or stamped upon to produce a drumming sound for keeping rhythm, sending signals, etc., common to primitive cultures.

slith·er (sli*th*′ər), *v.i.* **1.** to slide down or along a surface, esp. unsteadily, from side to side, or with some friction or noise: *The box slithered down the hill.* **2.** to go or walk with a sliding motion: *The snake slithered across the path.* —*v.t.* **3.** to cause to slither or slide. —*n.* **4.** a slithering movement; slide. [ME; var. of *sliddren,* OE *slid(e)rian,* freq. of *slīdan* to SLIDE; see -ER[6]] —**slith′er·y,** *adj.*

slit′ trench′, 1. a narrow trench for one or more persons for protection against enemy fire and fragmentation bombs. **2.** a foxhole.

sliv·er (sliv′ər), *n.* **1.** a small, slender piece, as of wood, split, broken, or cut off, usually lengthwise or with the grain; splinter. **2.** a strand of loose, untwisted fibers produced in carding. —*v.t.* **3.** to split or cut off (a sliver) or to split or cut into slivers: *to sliver a log into kindling.* **4.** to form (textile fibers) into slivers. —*v.i.* **5.** to split. [ME *slivere,* deriv. of *slive* to split, OE *-slīfan* (in *tōslīfan* to split up] —**sliv′er-like′,** *adj.*

sliv·o·vitz (sliv′ə vits, -wits, shliv′-), *n.* a dry usually colorless slightly bitter plum brandy from E Europe.

Also, **sliv·o·vic, sliv·o·witz** (sliv′ə vits). [< Serbo-Croatian *šljivovic(a)*, deriv. of *šljiva* plum]

Sloan (slōn), *n.* **1. John,** 1871–1951, U.S. painter. **2.** a town in W New York. 5803 (1960). **3.** a boy's given name.

Sloane (slōn), *n.* **Sir Hans,** 1660–1753, English physician and naturalist.

sloat (slōt), *n. Brit. Theat.* an apparatus for raising or lowering actors or scenery above or below the level of the stage. Also, **slote.** [late ME *sloot* bar < MD, var. of *slot*; c. G *Schloss* door bolt, lock, castle]

Sloats·burg (slōts′bûrg′), *n.* a town in SE New York. 2565 (1960).

slob (slob), *n.* **1.** *Slang.* a clumsy, slovenly, or boorish person: *He's an awful slob when it comes to eating.* **2.** *Irish Eng.* mud or ooze, esp. a stretch of mud along a shore. **3.** sludge (def. 5). [< Ir *slab* mud << E, n. use of SLAB[2]]

slob·ber (slob′ər), *v.i.* **1.** to let saliva or liquid run from the mouth; slaver; drivel. **2.** to indulge in mawkish sentimentality: *His aunts slobbered all over him when he fell ill.* —*v.t.* **3.** to wet or make foul by slobbering: *Baby has slobbered his bib.* **4.** to utter with slobbering: *She sobbed and slobbered the bad news.* —*n.* **5.** saliva or liquid dribbling from the mouth; slaver. **6.** mawkishly sentimental speech or actions. Also, **slabber.** [var. of *slabber.* See SLAB[2], -ER[6]] —**slob′ber·er,** *n.*

slob·ber·y (slob′ə rē), *adj.* **1.** characterized by slobbering. **2.** disagreeably wet; sloppy. Also, **slabbery.** [ME; see SLOBBER, -Y[1]]

slob′ ice′, *Chiefly Canadian.* sludge (def. 5).

Slo·cum (slō′kəm), *n.* **Joshua,** 1844–c1910, U.S. mariner, author, and lecturer; born in Nova Scotia.

sloe (slō), *n.* **1.** the small, sour, blackish fruit of the blackthorn, *Prunus spinosa.* **2.** the shrub itself. **3.** any of various other plants of the genus *Prunus,* as a shrub or small tree, *P. alleghaniensis,* bearing dark-purple fruit. [ME *slo,* OE *slā(h)*; c. G *Schlehe,* D *slee*]

sloe-eyed (slō′īd′), *adj.* **1.** having very dark eyes; dark-eyed. **2.** having slanted eyes.

sloe′ gin′, a cordial or liqueur flavored with sloe.

slog (slog), *v.,* **slogged, slog·ging.** —*v.t.* **1.** to hit hard, as in boxing, cricket, etc. **2.** to drive with blows. —*v.i.* **3.** to deal heavy blows. **4.** to walk or plod heavily. **5.** to toil. [var. of SLUG[2]] —**slog′ger,** *n.*

slo·gan (slō′gən), *n.* **1.** a distinctive cry, phrase, or motto of any party, group, product, manufacturer, or person; catchword or catch phrase. **2.** a war cry or gathering cry, as formerly used among the Scottish clans. [< Gael *sluagh-ghairm* army cry]

slo·gan·eer (slō′gə nēr′), *n.* a person who creates and uses slogans frequently. [SLOGAN + -EER]

sloid (sloid), *n.* sloyd. Also, **slojd.**

sloke (slōk), *v.,* **sloked, slok·ing,** *n. Scot.* —*v.t.* **1.** slake. —*n.* **2.** scum or slime, esp. on a body of water. [< Ir *sleabhac,* lit., horn]

sloop (sloop), *n.* a single-masted, fore-and-aft-rigged sailing vessel, with or without a bowsprit, having a jib-headed or gaff mainsail, the latter sometimes with a gaff topsail, and one or more headsails. Cf. **cutter** (def. 2), **knockabout.** [< D *sloep*; c. G *Schlup*; akin to OE *slūpan* to glide]

sloop′ of war′, (formerly) a sailing or steam naval vessel having cannons on only one deck.

sloop′ rig′. See **gaff-topsail catfish.**

sloop-rigged (sloop′rigd′), *adj.* (of a sailboat) fore-and-aft rigged with a mainsail and a jib.

slop[1] (slop), *v.,* **slopped, slop·ping,** *n.* —*v.t.* **1.** to spill or splash (liquid). **2.** to spill liquid upon. **3.** to feed slop to (pigs or other livestock): *to take turns slopping the hogs.* —*v.i.* **4.** to spill or splash liquid (sometimes fol. by *about*): *She slopped about with her mop and bucket.* **5.** (of liquid) to run in spilling (usually fol. by *over*): *The milk slopped over the rim of the glass.* **6.** to walk or go through mud, slush, or water. **7.** *Informal.* to be unduly effusive or sentimental; gush: *She slopped over the wedding arrangements.* —*n.* **8.** a quantity of liquid carelessly spilled or splashed about. **9.** *Slang.* badly cooked or unappetizing food or drink. **10.** bran from bolted cornmeal mixed with an equal part of water and used as a feed for swine and other livestock. **11.** any similar, watery feed; swill. **12.** Often, **slops. a.** the dirty water, liquid refuse, etc., of a household or the like. **b.** *Chiefly Brit.* weak or unappetizing soup, stew, tea, or semiliquid food. **13.** kitchen refuse, often used as food for swine; swill. **14.** liquid mud. **15. slops,** *Distilling.* the mash remaining after distilling. [ME *sloppe,* OE *-sloppe* (in *cūsloppe* cowslip, lit., cow slime); akin to SLIP[3]]

slop[2] (slop), *n.* **1.** clothing, bedding, etc., supplied to seamen from the ship's stores. **2.** a loose outer garment, as a jacket, tunic, or smock. **3.** cheap ready-made clothing in general. [ME *sloppe,* OE *-slop* (in *overslop* overgarment); c. Icel *sloppr* gown]

slop′ ba′sin, *Brit.* a basin or bowl into which the dregs, leaves, and grounds of teacups and coffee cups are emptied at the table. Also called **slop′ bowl′.**

slop′ chest′, 1. a supply of clothing, boots, tobacco, and other personal goods for sale to seamen during a voyage. **2.** (formerly) a chest containing this supply.

slope (slōp), *v.,* **sloped, slop·ing,** *n.* —*v.i.* **1.** to have or take an inclined or oblique direction or angle considered with reference to a vertical or horizontal plane; slant. **2.** to move at an inclination or obliquely: *They sloped downhill. They sloped gradually westward.* —*v.t.* **3.** to direct at a slant or inclination; incline from the horizontal or vertical: *The sun sloped its beams.* **4.** to form with a slope or slant: *to slope an embankment.* —*n.* **5.** ground which has a natural incline, as the side of a hill. **6.** inclination or slant, esp. downward or upward. **7.** deviation from the horizontal or vertical. **8.** an inclined surface. **9.** Usually, **slopes.** hills, esp. foothills or bluffs: *They camped on the slopes of Mt. Kilimanjaro.* **10.** *Math.* **a.** the tangent of the angle between a given straight line and the *x*-axis of a system of Cartesian coordinates. **b.** the derivative of the function whose graph is a given curve evaluated at a designated point. [abstracted from ASLOPE] —**slop′ing·ly,** *adv.* —**slop′ing·ness,** *n.*

—**Syn. 1.** SLOPE, SLANT mean to incline away from a relatively straight surface or line used as a reference. To SLOPE is to incline vertically in an oblique direction: *The ground slopes (upward* or *downward) sharply here.* To SLANT is to fall to one side, is to lie obliquely to some line whether horizontal or perpendicular: *The road slants off to the right.*

slop·er (slō′pər), *n.* **1.** one who or that which slopes. **2.** *Tailoring.* a garment made of linen or muslin, fitted to a mannequin and used as a basic pattern for the subsequent sizing of garments. [SLOPE + -ER[1]]

slop′ pail′, a pail for collecting or conveying slop, often used in feeding livestock, esp. pigs.

slop·py (slop′ē), *adj.,* **-pi·er, -pi·est. 1.** muddy, slushy, or very wet or made muddy or wet, as ground, walking, weather, etc. **2.** splashed or soiled with liquid. **3.** (of food or drink) prepared or served in an unappetizing way. **4.** overly emotional; gushy: *sloppy sentiment.* **5.** careless; loose: *sloppy grammar.* **6.** untidy; slovenly: *sloppy clothes; a sloppy eater.* **7.** (of the surface of a race track) wet from a recent or continuing heavy rain and containing puddles and mud still too thin and watery to be sticky. [SLOP[1] + -Y[1]] —**slop′pi·ly,** *adv.* —**slop′pi·ness,** *n.*

—**Syn. 2, 3.** messy. **5.** slipshod. **6.** slatternly.

Slop′py Joe′, 1. *Slang.* a man or youth whose appearance is habitually slovenly. **2.** (*sometimes l.c.*) a baggy, overlarge sweater worn by girls. **3.** (*usually l.c.*) a sandwich of barbecued beef or the like, usually served on a bun.

Slop′py Joe's′, *Slang.* See **greasy spoon.**

slop·shop (slop′shop′), *n.* a store at which cheap, ready-made clothing may be purchased. [SLOP[2] + SHOP]

slop′ sink′, a deep sink for emptying scrub buckets and the like.

slop·work (slop′wûrk′), *n.* **1.** the manufacture of cheap clothing. **2.** clothing of this kind. **3.** work that is carelessly or poorly done. [SLOP[2] + WORK] —**slop′work′er,** *n.*

slosh (slosh), *n.* **1.** watery mire or partly melted snow; slush. **2.** the lap or splash of liquid: *the slosh of waves against the shore.* **3.** a small quantity of liquid: *There is a slosh of milk left in the pail.* **4.** *Informal.* a watery or weak drink. —*v.i.* **5.** to splash in slush, mud, or water. **6.** (of a liquid) to move about actively within a container. —*v.t.* **7.** to stir or splash (something) around in a fluid: *to slosh the mop in the pail.* **8.** to splash (liquid) clumsily or haphazardly: *She sloshed tea all over his new suit. They sloshed the first coat of paint on the wall in one afternoon.* [SLO(P[1] + SLU)SH]

slosh·y (slosh′ē), *adj.,* **slosh·i·er, slosh·i·est.** of or pertaining to slosh. [SLOSH + -Y[1]] —**slosh′i·ly,** *adv.* —**slosh′i·ness,** *n.*

slot[1] (slot), *n., v.,* **slot·ted, slot·ting.** —*n.* **1.** a narrow, elongated depression, groove, notch, slit, or aperture, esp. a narrow opening for receiving or admitting something, as a coin or a letter. **2.** a place or position, as in a sequence or series: *The program received a new time slot on the broadcasting schedule.* **3.** *Journalism.* **a.** the interior opening in a copy desk, occupied by the slot man. **b.** the job or position of slot man: *He had the slot at the Gazette for 20 years.* Cf. **rim** (def. 7). **4.** *Ornith.* a narrow notch or other similar opening between the tips of the primaries of certain birds, which during flight helps to maintain a smooth flow of air over the wings. —*v.t.* **5.** to provide with a slot or slots; make a slot in. [ME < MF *(e)sclot* the hollow between the breasts < ?]

slot[2] (slot), *n.* **1.** the track or trail of a deer or other animal, as shown by the marks of the feet. **2.** a track, trace, or trail of something. [< AF, MF *(e)sclot* the hoofprint of a horse, prob. < Scand; cf. Icel *slōth* track, trail; see SLEUTHHOUND]

slot·back (slot′bak′), *n. Football.* **1.** an offensive back who lines up about one yard behind the gap in the line between a tackle and an end stationed a distance outside of the tackle. **2.** the position played by this back. [SLOT[1] + BACK[1]]

Two-toed sloth, *Choloepus hoffmanni* (Length 2 ft.)

slote (slōt), *n. Theat. Brit.* sloat.

sloth (slôth *or, esp. for 3,* slōth), *n.* **1.** habitual disinclination to exertion; indolence; laziness. **2.** a pack or group of bears. **3.** any of several sluggish, arboreal, tropical American edentates of the family *Bradypodidae,* having long, coarse hair and long, hooklike claws used by the animal to hang and move along upside down on the branches of trees. [ME *slowth* (see SLOW, -TH[1]); r. OE *slǣwth,* deriv. of *slǣw,* var. of *slāw* slow]

sloth′ bear′, a coarse-haired, long-snouted bear, *Melursus ursinus,* of India and Indochina.

sloth·ful (slôth′fəl, slōth′-), *adj.* sluggardly; indolent; lazy. [ME; see SLOTH, -FUL] —**sloth′ful·ly,** *adv.* —**sloth′ful·ness,** *n.*

—**Syn.** sluggish; inactive, torpid, slack. See **idle.**

Sloth bear (2½ ft. high at shoulder; length 5½ ft.)

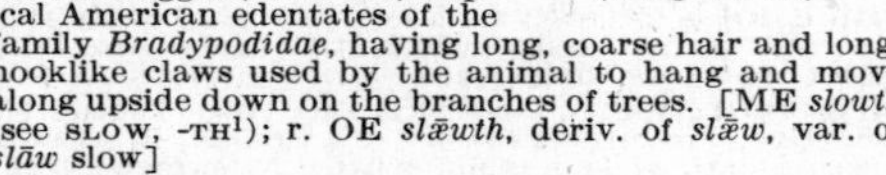

slot′ machine′, a machine for vending small articles, weighing, gambling, etc., actuated by dropping a coin in a slot.

slot′ man′, the head copyreader on a newspaper. Also called **copy editor.** Cf. **rim man.**

slot·man (slot′man′), *n., pl.* **-men.** See **slot man.** [SLOT[1] + MAN[1]]

slot′ mor′tise. See **slip mortise** (def. 1).

slot·ter (slot′ər), *n.* **1.** one who or that which slots. **2.** a machine tool for shaping vertical surfaces with a cutting tool held in a vertically reciprocating ram. [SLOT[1] + -ER[1]]

slouch (slouch), *v.i.* **1.** to sit or stand with an awkward, drooping posture. **2.** to move or walk with loosely drooping body and careless gait. **3.** to have a droop or downward bend, as a hat. —*v.t.* **4.** to cause to droop or bend down, as the shoulders or a hat. —*n.* **5.** a drooping or bending forward of the head and shoulders; an awkward, drooping posture or carriage. **6.** an awkward, clumsy, or slovenly person. **7.** See **slouch hat. 8.** *Informal.* a lazy or inefficient person: *He's no slouch when it comes to practicing law.* [?] —**slouch′er,** *n.* —**slouch′ing·ly,** *adv.*

slouch′ hat′, a soft hat, esp. one with a broad, flexible brim.

slouch·y (slou′chē), *adj.,* **slouch·i·er, slouch·i·est.** of or pertaining to a slouch, or to a slouching manner, posture, etc. [SLOUCH + -Y[1]] —**slouch′i·ly,** *adv.* —**slouch′i·ness,** *n.*

slough[1] (slou *for 1, 2, 4;* sloo *for 3*), *n.* **1.** an area of soft, muddy ground; swamp or swamplike region. **2.** a hole full of mire, as in a road. **3.** Also, **slew, slue.** *U.S., Canadian.* a marshy or reedy pool, pond, inlet, backwater, or the like. **4.** a condition of degradation, embarrassment, or helplessness, as that described in Bunyan's *Pilgrim's Progress: He was sinking into a slough of despair.* [ME; OE *slōh*; c. MLG *slōch,* MHG *sluoche* ditch]

slough[2] (sluf), *n.* **1.** the outer layer of the skin of a snake, which is cast off periodically. **2.** *Pathol.* a mass or layer of dead tissue separated from the surrounding or underlying tissue. **3.** *Cards.* a discard. —*v.i.* **4.** to be or become shed or cast off, as the slough of a snake. **5.** to cast off a slough. **6.** *Pathol.* to separate from the sound flesh, as a slough. **7.** *Cards.* to discard a card or cards. —*v.t.* **8.** to dispose or get rid of; cast (often fol. by *off*): *He managed to slough off his smoking habit.* **9.** to shed as or like a slough. **10.** *Cards.* to discard (a card or cards). Also, **sluff** (for defs. 3, 7, 10). [ME *slughe, slouh*; c. G *Schlauch* skin, bag] —**slough′i·ness,** *n.* —**slough′y,** *adj.*

—**Syn. 5.** molt.

Slo·vak (slō′vak, -väk, slō vak′, -väk′), *n.* **1.** one of a Slavic people dwelling in Slovakia. **2.** the language of Slovakia, a Slavic language very similar to Czech. —*adj.* **3.** of or pertaining to the Slovaks or Slovak. [< Slovak *Slovák* Slav]

Slo·va·ki·a (slō vä′kē ə, -vak′ē ə), *n.* a republic in central Europe: formerly a part of Czechoslovakia; under German protection 1939–45. 5,177,441; 18,921 sq. mi. *Cap.:* Bratislava. Czech and Slovak, **Slo·ven·sko** (slô′ven skô). —**Slo·va′ki·an,** *adj., n.*

slov·en (sluv′ən), *n.* **1.** one who is habitually negligent of neatness or cleanliness in dress, appearance, etc. **2.** one who works, acts, speaks, etc., in a negligent, slipshod manner. [late ME < MFlem *sloovin* slattern; akin to SHUFFLE]

Slo·vene (slō vēn′, slō′vēn), *n.* **1.** one of a Slavic people dwelling in Slovenia. **2.** a South Slavic language spoken in Slovenia. —*adj.* **3.** of or pertaining to the Slovenes or Slovene. [< G < Slovenian << OSlav *Slovēne*; cf. SLAV, SLOVAK]

Slo·ve·ni·a (slō vē′nē ə, -vēn′yə), *n.* a republic in SE Europe: formerly part of Yugoslavia. 1,930,000; 7819 sq. mi. *Cap.:* Ljubljana.

slov·en·ly (sluv′ən lē), *adj.,* **-li·er, li·est,** *adv.* —*adj.* **1.** habitually untidy or unclean; not neat in appearance: *a slovenly old woman.* **2.** characteristic of a sloven; slipshod: *slovenly work.* —*adv.* **3.** in an untidy, careless, or slipshod manner. [SLOVEN + -LY] —**slov′en·li·ness,** *n.*

—**Syn. 1.** sluttish, slatternly. **2.** careless, loose, disorderly.

—**Ant. 1.** neat. **2.** careful.

slow (slō), *adj.* **1.** taking or requiring a comparatively long time for moving, going, acting, etc.; not fast, rapid, or swift: *a slow gait; a slow trip.* **2.** requiring or taking a long time for growing, changing, or occurring; gradual. **3.** sluggish in nature, disposition, or function. **4.** dull of perception or understanding, as a person, the mind, etc.; mentally dull: *a slow child.* **5.** not prompt, readily disposed, or in haste (usually fol. by *to* or an infinitive): *slow to anger; slow to take offense.* **6.** burning or heating with little speed or intensity, as a fire or an oven. **7.** slack; not busy: *The market was slow today.* **8.** having some quality that retards speed or causes movement, progress, work, etc., to be accomplished at less than the usual or expected rate of speed: *He's a good worker, but a slow one.* **9.** running at less than the proper rate of speed or registering less than the proper time, as a clock. **10.** passing heavily or dragging, as time: *It's been a slow afternoon.* **11.** not progressive; behind the times: *slow, underdeveloped nations.* **12.** dull, humdrum, uninteresting, or tedious: *What a slow party!* **13.** *Photog.* requiring long exposure, as by having a narrow shutter opening or low film sensitivity: *a slow lens or film.* **14.** (of the surface of a race track) sticky from a fairly recent rain and in the process of drying out. —*adv.* **15.** in a slow manner; slowly: *Drive slow.* —*v.t.* **16.** to make slow or slower (often fol. by *up* or *down*). **17.** to retard; reduce the speed of: *His illness slowed him at school.* —*v.i.* **18.** to become slow or slower; slacken in speed (often fol. by *up* or *down*). [ME; OE *slāw* sluggish, dull; c. D *sleeuw*; see SLOTH] —**slow′ly,** *adv.* —**slow′ness,** *n.*

—**Syn. 1.** unhurried. SLOW, DELIBERATE, GRADUAL, LEISURELY mean unhurried and not happening rapidly. That which is SLOW acts or moves without haste or rapidity: *a slow procession of cars.* DELIBERATE implies the slowness which marks careful consideration before and while acting: *a deliberate and calculating manner.* GRADUAL suggests the slowness of that which advances one step at a time: *a gradual improvement in service.* That which is LEISURELY moves with the slowness allowed by ample time or the absence of pressure: *an unhurried and leisurely stroll.* **3.** sluggardly, dilatory, indolent, lazy, slothful. **4.** dense. See **dull. 12.** boring. **17.** hinder, impede, obstruct. —**Ant. 1.** fast. **17.** advance.

slow′ burn′, *Slang.* a gradual building up of anger, as opposed to an immediate outburst: *He did a slow burn as the conversation progressed.*

slow′-burn·ing construc′tion (slō′bûr′ning). See **mill construction.**

slow′ coach′, *Chiefly Brit. Informal.* a slowpoke.

slow·down (slō′doun′), *n.* a slowing down or delay in progress, action, etc., esp. a deliberate slowing of pace by workers to win demands from their employers. [n. use of v. phrase *slow down*]

CONCISE ETYMOLOGY KEY: <, descended or derived from; >, whence; b., blend of, blended; c., cognate with; deriv., derivative; equiv., equivalent; imit., imitative; m., modification of; obl., oblique; r., replacing; s., stem; sp., spelling; trans., translation; ?, origin unknown, perhaps; *, hypothetical. See the full key inside the front cover.

slow′ lo′ris, loris (def. 2).

slow′ match′, a slow-burning match or fuse, often consisting of a rope or cord soaked in a solution of saltpeter.

slow-mo·tion (slō′mō′shən), *adj.* noting or pertaining to motion pictures in which the images on the screen appear to move more slowly than in nature, either by operating the camera at a higher rate of speed than is usual or by causing the projector to project a relatively smaller number of frames per second.

slow-mov·ing (slō′mo͞o′ving), *adj.* proceeding with or characterized by slow, sluggish, or leisurely movement or activity.

slow·poke (slō′pōk′), *n.* *Informal.* one who makes slow progress. [SLOW + POKE[1]]

slow-up (slō′up′), *n.* a delay or retardation in progress or activity, as of an action, process, etc. [n. use of v. phrase *slow up*]

slow-wit·ted (slō′wit′id), *adj.* mentally slow or dull; below average in intelligence, understanding, or brightness.

slow·worm (slō′wûrm′), *n.* a blindworm. [SLOW + WORM; r. ME *slowerm, slowurme,* OE *slāwerm, slāwyrm,* equiv. to *slā-* (cf. dial. Sw *slo,* Norw *slō* slowworm) + *wyrm* worm]

sloyd (sloid), *n.* a system of manual training based on experience gained in woodworking, originally developed in Sweden. Also, **sloid, slojd.** [< Sw *slöjd* craft, industrial art, woodworking; c. SLEIGHT]

S.L.P., Socialist Labor Party.

slub (slub), *v.,* **slubbed, slub·bing,** *n.* —*v.t.* **1.** to extend (slivers) and twist slightly in carding. —*n.* **2.** the fibers produced by slubbing. **3.** a slight irregularity in yarn produced either accidentally or purposely by knotting or twisting or by including uneven lengths of fiber in spinning. [?]

slub·ber (slub′ər), *v.t.* to perform hastily or carelessly. [prob. < MD or LG; cf. MD *overslubberen* to wade through mud, LG *slubbern* to do work carelessly] —**slub′ber·ing·ly,** *adv.*

sludge (sluj), *n.* **1.** mud, mire, or ooze; slush. **2.** a deposit of ooze at the bottom of a body of water. **3.** any of various more or less mudlike deposits or mixtures. **4.** the sediment in a steam boiler or water tank. **5.** broken ice, as on the sea. **6.** a mixture of some finely powdered substance and water. **7.** sediment deposited during the treatment of sewage. **8.** Also called **activated sludge.** *Bacteriol.* sewage sediment that contains a heavy growth of microorganisms, resulting from vigorous aeration. **9.** a fine, mudlike powder produced by a mining drill. **10.** swarf. [var. of dial. *slutch, slitch,* ME *slich* slime, wet mud, whence *slucched* muddy]

sludg·y (sluj′ē), *adj.,* **sludg·i·er, sludg·i·est.** **1.** of or pertaining to sludge. **2.** covered or lined with or containing sludge. [SLUDGE + -Y[1]]

slue[1] (slo͞o), *v.,* **slued, slu·ing,** *n.* —*v.t.* **1.** to turn (a mast or other spar) around on its own axis, or without removing it from its place. **2.** to swing around. —*v.i.* **3.** to turn about; swing around. —*n.* **4.** the act of sluing. **5.** a position slued to. Also, **slew.** [?]

slue[2] (slo͞o), *n.* *Informal.* slew[4].

slue[3] (slo͞o), *n.* slough[1] (def. 3).

sluff (sluf), *n., v.t., v.i.* *Cards.* slough[2].

slug[1] (slug), *n., v.,* **slugged, slug·ging.** —*n.* **1.** any of various slimy, elongated, terrestrial gastropods related to the terrestrial snails, but having no shell or only a rudimentary one. **2.** a nudibranch. **3.** a slow-moving animal, vehicle, or the like. **4.** any heavy piece of crude metal. **5.** a piece of lead or other metal for firing from a gun. **6.** a metal disk used as a coin, generally counterfeit. **7.** *Print.* **a.** a thick strip of type metal less than type-high. **b.** such a strip containing a type-high number or other character for temporary use. **c.** a line of type in one piece, as produced by a Linotype. **8.** a gold coin of California, privately issued in 1849 and for some time after, worth 50 dollars. **9.** *Journalism.* **a.** Also called **catchline.** a short phrase or title used to indicate the story content of newspaper or magazine copy. **b.** the line of type carrying this information. **10.** *Physics.* a unit of mass, equivalent to approximately 32.2 pounds and having the property that a force of one pound acting upon a mass of this unit produces an acceleration of one foot per second per second. **11.** an irregular projection or knob on the surface of yarn, usually produced by lint or by defects in weaving. **12.** *Slang.* a shot of liquor taken neat; belt. —*v.t.* **13.** *Print. Informal.* **a.** to make (corrections) by replacing entire lines of type, esp. as set by a Linotype. **b.** to check only the first word of each line of (typeset copy) in galley to ensure that no line has been omitted, esp. before printing or plating. **14.** *Journalism.* to furnish (copy) with a slug. **15.** to interpolate pieces of metal into (a joint being welded). [ME *slugge* sluggard < Scand; cf. Norw (dial.) *sluggje* heavy, slow person] —**slug′like′,** *adj.*

Slug,
Limax maximus
(Length 4 in.)

slug[2] (slug), *v.,* **slugged, slug·ging.** *Informal.* —*v.t.* **1.** to strike heavily; hit hard, esp. with the fist. **2.** to hit or drive (a baseball) very hard or a great distance. —*v.i.* **3.** to hit or be capable of hitting hard: *Don't fight with him, he really slugs.* **4.** to trudge, fight, or push onward, as against obstacles or through mud or snow: *The infantry slugged up the hill and dug in.* [orig. from phrase *hit with a slug;* see SLUG[1]]

slug·a·bed (slug′ə bed′), *n.* a lazy person who stays in bed long after the usual time for arising. [SLUG[1] + ABED]

slug·fest (slug′fest′), *n.* *Informal.* **1.** a baseball game in which both teams make many runs and extra-base hits. **2.** a boxing bout in which the boxers exchange powerful blows vigorously and aggressively with little care for defense. [SLUG[2] + -FEST]

slug·gard (slug′ərd), *n.* **1.** a person who is habitually inactive or lazy. —*adj.* **2.** lazy; sluggardly. [ME *slogarde.* See SLUG[1], -ARD]

slug·gard·ly (slug′ərd lē), *adj.* like or befitting a sluggard; slothful; lazy. [SLUGGARD + -LY] —**slug′gard·li·ness,** *n.*

slug·ger (slug′ər), *n.* **1.** a person who strikes hard, esp. a boxer noted chiefly for his ability to deliver hard punches. **2.** *Baseball.* a player who frequently gets extra-base hits; a strong hitter. [SLUG[2] + -ER[1]]

slug′ging av′erage, *Baseball.* a measure of the effectiveness of a batter in making base hits, obtained by dividing the total bases reached by hitting by the number of official times at bat and carrying out the result to three decimal places. A batter making 275 total bases in 500 times at bat has a slugging average of .550. Also called **slug′ging percent′age.** Cf. **batting average.**

slug·gish (slug′ish), *adj.* **1.** indisposed to action or exertion; lacking in energy; lazy; indolent: *a sluggish disposition.* **2.** not acting or working with full vigor, as bodily organs: *a sluggish liver.* **3.** moving slowly, or having little motion, as a stream. **4.** slow, as motion. **5.** slack, as trade, business, sales, etc. [ME *slugissh.* See SLUG[1], -ISH[1]] —**slug′gish·ly,** *adv.* —**slug′gish·ness,** *n.*
—**Syn. 1.** slow, slothful. See **inactive.** —**Ant. 1.** quick, active.

sluice (slo͞os), *n., v.,* **sluiced, sluic·ing.** —*n.* **1.** an artificial channel for conducting water, fitted with a gate **(sluice′ gate′)** at the upper end for regulating the flow. **2.** the body of water held back or controlled by a sluice gate. **3.** any contrivance for regulating a flow from or into a receptacle. **4.** a channel, esp. one carrying off surplus water; drain. **5.** a stream of surplus water. **6.** an artificial stream or channel of water for moving solid matter: *a lumbering sluice.* **7.** *Mining.* **a.** a long, sloping trough or the like, with grooves in its bottom, into which water is directed to separate gold from gravel or sand. **b.** a long, inclined trough to wash ores. —*v.t.* **8.** to let out (water) by or as by opening a sluice. **9.** to drain (a pond, lake, etc.) by or as by opening a sluice. **10.** to open a sluice upon. **11.** to flush or cleanse with a rush of water: *to sluice the decks of a boat.* **12.** *Mining.* to wash in a sluice. **13.** to send (logs) down a sluiceway. —*v.i.* **14.** to flow or pour through or as through a sluice. [ME *scluse* < OF *(e)scluse* < LL *exclūsa,* fem. of L *exclūsus,* ptp. of *exclūdere* to EXCLUDE] —**sluice′like′,** *adj.*

sluice·way (slo͞os′wā′), *n.* **1.** a channel controlled by a sluice gate. **2.** any artificial channel for water. [SLUICE + WAY]

sluit (slo͞ot), *n.* (in South Africa) a deep, dry gulch or channel formed by erosion due to heavy rains. [< SAfrD *sloot* ditch]

slum (slum), *n., v.,* **slummed, slum·ming.** —*n.* **1.** Often, **slums.** a thickly populated, squalid part of a city, inhabited by the poorest people. —*v.i.* **2.** to visit slums, esp. from curiosity: *They went slumming for the evening.* **3.** to visit or frequent a place, group, or amusement spot considered to be low in social status. [first occurs as slang word for room; <?] —**slum′mer,** *n.*

slum·ber (slum′bər), *v.i.* **1.** to sleep, esp. lightly; doze; drowse. **2.** to be in a state of inactivity, negligence, quiescence, or calm: *Vesuvius is slumbering.* —*v.t.* **3.** to spend or pass (time) in slumbering (often fol. by *away, out,* or *through*): *to slumber the afternoon away.* **4.** to dispel or forget by slumbering (often fol. by *away*): *to slumber cares away.* —*n.* **5.** Sometimes, **slumbers.** sleep, esp. light sleep. **6.** a period of sleep, esp. light sleep. **7.** a state of inactivity, quiescence, etc. [ME *slumer(en)* (with epenthetic *b*), freq. of *slumen* to doze, deriv. of OE *slūma* sleep; cf. G *schlummern*] —**slum′ber·er,** *n.* —**slum′ber·less,** *adj.*

slum·ber·land (slum′bər land′), *n.* an imaginary land described to children as the place they enter during sleep. [SLUMBER + LAND]

slum·ber·ous (slum′bər əs), *adj.* **1.** sleepy; heavy with drowsiness, as the eyelids. **2.** causing or inducing sleep. **3.** pertaining to, characterized by, or suggestive of slumber. **4.** inactive or sluggish; calm or quiet. Also, **slum′ber·y, slum′brous.** [ME; see SLUMBER, -OUS] —**slum′ber·ous·ly,** *adv.* —**slum′ber·ous·ness,** *n.*

slum′ber par′ty. See **pajama party.**

slum·gul·lion (slum gul′yən, slum′gul′-), *n.* **1.** a stew of meat, vegetables, potatoes, etc. **2.** a beverage made weak or thin, as watery tea, coffee, or the like. **3.** the refuse from processing whale carcasses. **4.** a reddish, muddy deposit in mining sluices. [SLUM + *gullion,* prob. alter. of CULLION]

slum·lord (slum′lôrd′), *n.* a landlord who refuses to make improvements in the slum buildings he owns and who charges his tenants exorbitant rents. [SLUM + LORD]

slum·my (slum′ē), *adj.,* **-mi·er, -mi·est.** of, pertaining to, or designating slums: *We're passing through the slummy part of town.* [SLUM + -Y[1]] —**slum′mi·ness,** *n.*

slump (slump), *v.i.* **1.** to drop heavily. **2.** to sink into a bog, muddy place, etc., or through ice or snow. **3.** to decrease or fall suddenly and markedly, as prices, the market, etc. **4.** to decline or deteriorate, as health, business, quality, efficiency, etc. **5.** to assume a slouching, bowed, or bent position or posture: *The older she became, the more her shoulders slumped.* **6.** to sink heavily, as the spirits. —*n.* **7.** the act or an instance of slumping. **8.** a decrease, decline, or deterioration. **9.** a period of decline or deterioration. **10.** a period in which the prices of stocks fall or are low, esp. a minor or short depression. **11.** a period during which a person performs slowly, inefficiently, or ineffectively, esp. a period during which an athlete fails to play or score as well as usual. **12.** a slouching, bowed, or bent position or posture, esp. of the shoulders. [special use of *slump* bog; c. LG *schlump*]

slung (slung), *v.* pt. and pp. of **sling.**

slung′ shot′, a weight, as a stone or a piece of metal, fastened to a short strap, chain, or the like, and used as a weapon.

slunk (slungk), *v.* a pt. and the pp. of **slink.**

slur (slûr), *v.,* **slurred, slur·ring,** *n.* —*v.t.* **1.** to pass over lightly or without due mention or consideration (often fol. by *over*): *The report slurred over his contribution to the enterprise.* **2.** to pronounce (a syllable, word, etc.) indistinctly, as in hurried or careless utterance. **3.** to cast aspersions on; calumniate; disparage; depreciate: *The candidate was viciously slurred by his opponent.* **4.** *Music.* **a.** to sing to a single syllable or play without a break (two or more tones of different pitch). **b.** to mark with a slur. **5.** *Chiefly Brit. Dial.* to smirch, sully, or stain. —*v.i.* **6.** to read, speak, or sing hurriedly and carelessly. —*n.* **7.** a slurred utterance or sound. **8.** a disparaging remark or a slight: *He was quick to take offense at a slur.* **9.** a blot or stain, as upon reputation: *a slur on his good name.* **10.** *Music.* **a.** the combination of two or more tones of different pitch, sung to a single syllable or played without a break. **b.** a curved mark indicating this. **11.** *Print.* a spot which is blurred or unclear. [? dial. *slur* mud; akin to Icel *slor* offal (of fish)]
—**Syn. 1.** slight, disregard, gloss. **3.** slander, asperse. **8.** innuendo, insult, affront. **9.** stigma, disgrace. —**Ant. 8.** compliment.

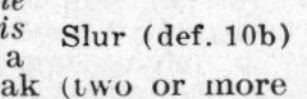

Slur (def. 10b)

slurp (slûrp), *v.t.* **1.** to make a loud sucking noise in consuming (food or drink): *He slurped his coffee.* —*v.i.* **2.** to eat or drink with loud sucking noises: *Don't slurp when you eat your soup!* —*n.* **3.** a noisy intake of food or drink: *He finished his milk in about three slurps.* [< D *slurp(en),* MD *slorpen*]

slur·ry (slûr′ē), *n., pl.* **-ries,** *v.,* **-ried, -ry·ing,** *adj.* —*n.* **1.** a suspension of a solid in a liquid. **2.** *Ceram.* a thin slip. —*v.t.* **3.** to prepare a suspension of (a solid in a liquid). —*adj.* **4.** of or pertaining to such a suspension. [late ME *slory;* akin to SLUR]

slur·vi·an (slûr′vē ən), *Derogatory.* —*adj.* **1.** of, pertaining to, or characteristic of slurred speech. —*n.* **2.** the speech of those who talk this way. [irreg. coinage based on SLUR]

slur·vi·an·ism (slûr′vē ə niz′əm), *n.* an instance or an example of slurred speech. [SLURVIAN + -ISM]

slush (slush), *n.* **1.** partly melted snow. **2.** liquid mud; watery mire. **3.** waste, as fat, grease, or other refuse, from the galley of a ship. **4.** a mixture of grease and other materials for lubricating. **5.** silly, sentimental, or weakly emotional talk or writing: *romantic slush.* —*v.t.* **6.** to splash with slush. **7.** to grease, polish, or cover with slush. **8.** to fill or cover with mortar or cement. **9.** to wash with a large quantity of water, as by dashing it on. [appar. c. Norw *slusk* slops, Sw *slask* mud, slops]

slush′ cast′ing, *Foundry.* casting of a shell by pouring off the center metal before it is hard and after the outer metal has hardened.

slush′ fund′, **1.** a sum of money used for illicit or corrupt political purposes, as for buying influence or votes, bribing public officials, or the like. **2.** a fund from the sale of slush, refuse fat, etc., aboard ship, spent for any small luxuries.

slush·y (slush′ē), *adj.,* **slush·i·er, slush·i·est.** **1.** of or pertaining to slush. **2.** *Informal.* tritely sentimental; mushy. [SLUSH + -Y[1]] —**slush′i·ly,** *adv.* —**slush′i·ness,** *n.*

slut (slut), *n.* **1.** a dirty, slovenly woman. **2.** an immoral or dissolute woman; prostitute. **3.** a female dog. [ME *slutte;* cf. dial. *slut* mud, Norw (dial.) *slutr* sleet, impure liquid] —**slut′tish, slut′ty,** *adj.* —**slut′tish·ly,** *adv.* —**slut′tish·ness,** *n.*

sly (slī), *adj.,* **sly·er** or **sli·er, sly·est** or **sli·est,** *n.* —*adj.* **1.** cunning or wily, as persons or animals, or their actions, ways, etc.: *sly as a fox.* **2.** stealthy, insidious, or secret. **3.** playfully artful, mischievous, or roguish: *sly humor.* —*n.* **4.** **on the sly,** secretly; furtively: *He wore his brother's cuff links on the sly.* [ME *sly, sley* < Scand; cf. Icel *slægur,* Sw *slög* dexterous] —**sly′ly, sli′ly,** *adv.* —**sly′ness,** *n.*
—**Syn. 1.** artful, subtle, foxy, crafty, shrewd, astute. **2.** surreptitious, furtive, underhand, clandestine. —**Ant. 1.** direct, obvious.

sly-grog (slī′grog′), *n.* *Australian Slang.* bootleg liquor.

slype (slīp), *n.* *Archit.* a covered passage, esp. one from the transept of a cathedral to the chapter house. Also, **slip.** [cf. WFlem *slijpe* secret path]

Sm, *Chem.* samarium.

S.M., **1.** Master of Science. [< L *Scientiae Magister*] **2.** sergeant major. **3.** State Militia.

SMA, Surplus Marketing Administration.

smack[1] (smak), *n.* **1.** a taste or flavor, esp. a slight flavor distinctive or suggestive of something: *The chicken had just a smack of garlic.* **2.** a trace, touch, or suggestion of something. **3.** a taste, mouthful, or small quantity. —*v.i.* **4.** to have a taste, flavor, trace, or suggestion (often fol. by *of*): *Your politeness smacks of condescension.* [ME *smacke,* OE *smæc;* c. MLG *smak,* G *(Ge)schmack* taste]
—**Syn. 1.** savor. **2.** hint. **4.** taste, suggest.

smack[2] (smak), *v.t.* **1.** to strike sharply, esp. with the open hand or a flat object. **2.** to drive or send with a sharp, resounding blow or stroke: *to smack a ball over a fence.* **3.** to close and open (the lips) smartly so as to produce a sharp sound, often as a sign of relish, as in eating. **4.** *Informal.* to kiss with or as with a loud sound. —*v.i.* **5.** to smack the lips. **6.** to collide, come together, or strike something forcibly. **7.** to make a sharp sound as of striking against something. —*n.* **8.** a sharp, resounding blow, esp. with something flat. **9.** a smacking of the lips, as in relish or anticipation. **10.** *Informal.* a resounding or loud kiss: *He gave his grandmother a smack on the cheek.* —*adv.* *Informal.* **11.** suddenly and violently: *He rode smack up against the side of the house.* **12.** directly; straight: *The street runs smack along the river.* [cf. D, LG *smakken,* G (dial.) *schmacken;* imit.]

smack[3] (smak), *n.* **1.** *Eastern U.S.* a fishing vessel, esp. one having a well for keeping the catch alive. **2.** *Brit.* any of various small, fully decked, fore-and-aft-rigged vessels used for trawling or coastal trading. [prob. < D *smak;* c. MLG *smacke*]

smack-dab (smak′dab′), *adv.* *Informal.* directly; squarely: *He landed smack-dab in the middle of the corn field.*

smack·er (smak′ər), *n.* *Slang.* a dollar. [SMACK[2] + -ER[1]]

smack·er·oo (smak′ə ro͞o′), *n., pl.* **-er·oos.** *Slang.* **1.** a hard slap or swat: *He gave the ball a smackeroo.* **2.** smacker. [alter. of SMACKER]

smack·ing (smak′ing), *adj.* **1.** smart, brisk, or strong, as a breeze. **2.** *Chiefly Brit. Slang.* smashing. [SMACK[2] + -ING[2]] —**smack′ing·ly,** *adv.*

small (smôl), *adj.* **1.** of limited size; of comparatively restricted dimensions; not big; little: *a small box.* **2.** slender, thin, or narrow: *a small waist.* **3.** not large as compared with others of the same kind: *a small elephant.* **4.** (of letters) lower-case (def. 1). **5.** not great in amount, degree, extent, duration, value, etc.: *a small salary.* **6.**

not great numerically: *a small army; a small dinner party.* **7.** of low numerical value; denoted by a low number. **8.** having but little land, capital, power, influence, etc., or carrying on business or some activity on a limited scale: *a small enterprise; a small businessman.* **9.** of minor importance, moment, weight, or consequence: *a small problem.* **10.** humble, modest, or unpretentious: *small circumstances.* **11.** characterized by or indicative of littleness of mind or character; mean-spirited; petty: *a small, miserly man.* **12.** of little strength or force: *A small effort to improve is often worse than none.* **13.** (of sound or the voice) gentle; with little volume. **14.** young, esp. very young: *when I was a small boy.* **15.** diluted; weak. **16.** (of the scale of a map, model, or the like) such that large areas or volumes are reproduced in a relatively little size, showing comparatively few details. **17. feel small,** to be ashamed or mortified: *Such unselfishness made us feel small.* —*adv.* **18.** in a small manner: *They talked big but lived small.* **19.** into small pieces: *Slice the cake small.* **20.** in low tones; softly. **21. sing small,** to become meek or apologetic; humble oneself: *He was so brilliant in his rebuttal that he made all of his colleagues sing small.* —*n.* **22.** that which is small: *Do you prefer the small or the large?* **23.** a small or narrow part, as of the back. **24.** those who are small: *Death comes alike to the great and the small.* **25. smalls,** goods or products of relatively small size. **26. smalls,** *Brit.* **a.** underclothes. **b.** household linen, as napkins, pillowcases, etc. **27. smalls,** *Brit. Informal.* the responsions at Oxford University. [ME *smale,* OE *smæl;* c. D *smal,* G *schmal*] —**small′ness,** *n.*

—**Syn. 1.** tiny. See **little. 2.** slight. **3.** SMALLER, LESS indicate a diminution, or not so large a size or quantity in some respect. SMALLER, as applied to concrete objects, is used with reference to size: *smaller apples.* LESS is used of material in bulk, with reference to amount, and in cases where attributes such as value and degree are in question: *A nickel is less than a dime* (in value). *A sergeant is less than a lieutenant* (in rank). As an abstraction, amount may be either SMALLER or LESS, though SMALLER is usually used when the idea of size is suggested: *a smaller opportunity.* LESS is used when the idea of quantity is present: *less courage.* **9.** trifling, petty, unimportant, minor, secondary, nugatory, inconsequential, paltry, insignificant. **11.** stingy, mean, parsimonious, niggardly, selfish, tight, narrow. **12.** feeble. —**Ant. 1.** large **3.** larger, more.

small·age (smô′lij), *n.* the celery, *Apium graveolens,* esp. in its wild state. [ME *smalege, smalache,* equiv. to *smal* small + *ache* parsley < OF < L *apium*]

small′ arm′, Usually, **small arms.** a firearm designed to be held in one or both hands while being fired: in the U.S. the term is applied to weapons of a caliber of up to one inch. —**small′-armed′,** *adj.*

small′ beer′, 1. weak beer. **2.** *Chiefly Brit. Slang.* matters or persons of little or no importance.

small-bore (smôl′bōr′, -bôr′), *adj.* **1.** of, noting, or relating to a .22-caliber firearm. **2.** insular or parochial in scope, attitude, etc.: *small-bore jobs; small-bore officials.*

small′ bow′er (bou′ər), *Naut.* the lighter of two bower anchors carried by a vessel. Cf. **best bower.**

Small′ Busi′ness Administra′tion, *U.S. Govt.* a federal agency, created in 1953, that grants or guarantees long-term loans to small businesses. *Abbr.:* SBA, S.B.A.

small′ cal′orie, calorie (def. 1b).

small′ cane′. See under **cane** (def. 5).

small′ cap′ital, a capital letter of a particular font, the same height as the x-high letters. Also called **small′ cap′.**

small′ change′, 1. coins of small denomination. **2.** someone or something insignificant or trifling: *Those people are small change as far as I'm concerned.*

small′ cir′cle, a circle on a sphere, the plane of which does not pass through the center of the sphere. Cf. **great circle** (def. 1).

small·clothes (smôl′klōz′, -klōthz′), *n.pl.* **1.** *Brit.* small, personal items of clothing, as underwear, handkerchiefs, etc. **2.** knee breeches, esp. the close fitting ones worn in the 17th, 18th, and early 19th centuries. [SMALL + CLOTHES]

small′ cran′berry. See under **cranberry** (def. 1).

small′ end′, *Mach.* that end of a connecting rod attached to a piston or piston rod.

Smal·lens (smä′linz), *n.* **Alexander,** born 1889, U.S. orchestra conductor, born in Russia.

small′ fry′, 1. small or young fish. **2.** children: *a special dinner for the small fry.* **3.** unimportant persons or objects: *Her parties were closed to the small fry.*

small′ game′, wild animals and birds hunted for sport, as rabbits or doves, that are smaller than animals, as deer, bears, and the like, classified as big game.

small′ hold′er, *Brit.* the tenant or owner of a small holding.

small′ hold′ing, *Brit.* a piece of land, usually from one to fifty acres, rented or sold to a farmer by county authorities for purposes of cultivation.

small′ hon′eysuckle, a shrub, *Lonicera dioica,* of eastern North America, having spreading or twining branches, sometimes purple-tinged yellow flowers, and red fruit. Also called **small woodbine.**

small′ hours′, the hours after midnight; early morning hours: *The party went on into the small hours.*

small′ intes′tine, intestine (def. 2).

small·ish (smô′lish), *adj.* rather small. [ME; see SMALL, -ISH¹]

small-mind·ed (smôl′mīn′did), *adj.* selfish, petty, or narrow-minded. —**small′-mind′ed·ly,** *adv.* —**small′-mind′ed·ness,** *n.*

small·mouth bass (smôl′mouth′ bas′), a North American, fresh-water game fish, *Micropterus dolomieu,* yellowish-green above and lighter below, having the lower jaw extending up to the eye. Cf. **largemouth bass.**

small′ pas′tern bone′. See under **pastern.**

small′ pi′ca, *Print.* an 11-point type.

small′ pota′toes, *Informal.* a person or thing of little significance, importance, or value: *His salary was small potatoes for an executive of his ability.*

small·pox (smôl′poks′), *n. Pathol.* an acute, highly contagious, febrile disease, caused by a virus, and characterized by a pustular eruption that often leaves permanent pits or scars. [SMALL + POX]

small′ print′. See **fine print.**

small-scale (smôl′skāl′), *adj.* **1.** of limited extent; of small scope: *a small-scale enterprise.* **2.** being a relatively small map, model, etc., of the original.

small′ slam′, *Bridge.* See **little slam.**

small′ stores′, *Navy.* personal articles of regulation issue sold to sailors by a supply officer and charged to their pay, as extra clothing.

small′ stuff′, *Naut.* small cordage, as marlines, yarns, etc.

small·sword (smôl′sōrd′, -sôrd′), *n.* a light, tapering sword for thrusting, formerly used in fencing or dueling. [SMALL + SWORD]

small′ talk′, light, unimportant conversation; chitchat: *She is a beautiful girl, but incapable of anything weightier than small talk.*

small-talk (smôl′tôk′), *v.i.* to engage in or have a propensity for small talk.

small′ time′, *Theat.* (in vaudeville) a circuit of minor theaters that give three or more performances daily.

small-time (smôl′tīm′), *adj.* of modest or insignificant size, importance, or influence: *a small-time politician.* —**small′-tim′er,** *n.*

small-town (smôl′toun′), *adj.* **1.** of, pertaining to, or characteristic of a town or village: *a typical, small-town general store.* **2.** provincial or unsophisticated: *small-town manners.* —**small′town′er,** *n.*

Small′ White′, *Brit.* one of a strain of small Yorkshire hogs.

small′ wood′bine. See **small honeysuckle.**

smalt (smôlt), *n.* a coloring agent made of blue glass produced by fusing silica, potassium carbonate, and cobalt oxide, used in powdered form to add color to vitreous materials. [< MF < It *smalt(o)* SMALTO]

smalt·ite (smôl′tīt), *n.* a mineral, originally thought to have been a diarsenide of cobalt, $CoAs_2$, but which is actually a skutterudite rich in cobalt. Also, **smalt·ine** (smôl′tin, -tēn). [SMALT + -ITE¹]

smal·to (smäl′tō; *It.* zmäl′tô), *n., pl.* **-tos. 1.** colored glass or similar vitreous material used in mosaic. **2.** a piece of this. [< It < Gmc; akin to SMELT¹]

smar·agd (smar′agd), *n. Rare.* emerald. [ME *smaragde* < OF *smaragde, esmaragde;* see EMERALD]

sma·rag·dine (smə rag′din), *adj.* **1.** of or pertaining to emeralds. **2.** emerald-green in color. —*n.* **3.** *Rare.* smaragd. [< L *smaragdīn(us)* < Gk *smarágdinos,* equiv. to *smáragd(os)* (akin to Skt *marakata*) + *-inos* -INE¹]

sma·rag·dite (smə rag′dīt), *n. Mineral.* a green, foliated member of the amphibole group. [< F < Gk *smáragd(os)* EMERALD + F *-ite* -ITE¹]

smarm (smärm), *n.* trite and cloying sentimentality. [?]

smarm·y (smär′mē), *adj.,* **smarm·i·er, smarm·i·est.** excessively or unctuously flattering, ingratiating, servile, affectionate, etc.: *the emcee with the smarmy welcome.* [SMARM + -Y¹]

smart (smärt), *v.i.* **1.** to be a source of sharp, local, and usually superficial pain, as a wound. **2.** to be the cause of a sharp, stinging pain, as an irritating application, a blow, etc. **3.** to wound the feelings, as with words. **4.** to feel a sharp, stinging pain, as in a wound. **5.** to suffer keenly from wounded feelings: *She smarted under their criticism.* **6.** to feel shame or remorse or to suffer in punishment or in return for something. —*v.t.* **7.** to cause a sharp pain to or in. [ME *smert(en),* OE *smeortan;* c. G *schmerzen* to smart, L *mordēre* to bite] —*adj.* **8.** sharp or keen: *a smart pain.* **9.** sharply severe, as a blow, stroke, etc. **10.** sharply brisk, vigorous, or active: *to walk with smart steps.* **11.** quick or prompt in action, as persons. **12.** having or showing quick intelligence or ready mental capability: *a smart student.* **13.** shrewd or sharp, as a person in dealing with others or as in business dealings: *a smart businessman.* **14.** clever, witty, or readily effective, as a speaker, speech, rejoinder, etc. **15.** dashingly or impressively neat or trim in appearance, as persons, dress, etc. **16.** socially elegant; sophisticated or fashionable: *the smart crowd.* **17.** saucy; pert: *Let's not have any of your smart remarks.* **18.** *Chiefly Dial.* considerable; fairly large. [ME; OE *smeart*] —*adv.* **19.** in a smart manner; smartly. [ME *smerte*] —*n.* **20.** a sharp local pain, usually superficial, as from a wound, blow, or sting. **21.** keen mental suffering, as from wounded feelings, affliction, grievous loss, etc. [ME *smerte;* c. G *Schmerz*] —**smart′ing·ly,** *adv.* —**smart′ly,** *adv.* —**smart′ness,** *n.*

—**Syn. 1.** pain, hurt, sting. **8.** stinging, poignant, penetrating. **10.** energetic. **11.** lively, nimble, agile, alert, active. **12.** bright, sharp, expert, adroit. **13.** cunning, adept. **15.** spruce; pretentious, showy. **16.** chic. —**Ant. 12.** stupid.

smart-al·ec (smärt′al′ik), *n.* **1.** See **smart aleck.** —*adj.* **2.** smart-alecky.

smart′ al′eck (al′ik), **1.** an obnoxiously conceited person. **2.** a wiseguy. [special use of *Aleck,* nickname for *Alexander*] —**smart′-al′eck·y, smart′-al′eck,** *adj.*

smart·en (smär′tᵊn), *v.t.* **1.** to make more trim or spruce; improve in appearance (usually fol. by *up*): *Try to smarten up your suit.* **2.** to make brisker, as a pace. **3.** to sharpen the judgment or broaden the experience of; educate (usually fol. by *up*): *Someone has to smarten him up about dealing with people.* [SMART + -EN¹]

smart·ish (smär′tish), *adj.* **1.** rather smart; fairly intelligent or quick-witted: *smartish answers on a quiz.* **2.** rather fashionable; fairly chic or exclusive: *a smartish new restaurant.* **3.** fairly impressive or significant: *a smartish number of supporters at the rally.* **4.** rather saucy or pert. [SMART + -ISH¹]

smart′ mon′ey, 1. *Law.* punitive or exemplary damages. **2.** money invested or wagered by experienced investors or betters: *The smart money was on the other horse.* **3.** knowledgeable investors or betters: *The smart money predicted the show would be a hit.*

smart′ set′, sophisticated, fashionable people as a group: *a new shop catering exclusively to the smart set.*

smart·weed (smärt′wēd′), *n.* any of several weeds of the genus *Polygonum,* having a smarting, acrid juice. [SMART + WEED¹]

smart·y¹ (smär′tē), *n., pl.* **smart·ies.** a person, esp. an adolescent, who is impertinent, cocky, and show-offish; smart aleck. [SMART + -Y²]

smart·y² (smär′tē), *adj.* being or characteristic of a smarty; smart-alecky: *several smarty answers to our questions; accompanied by her smarty son.* [SMART + -Y¹]

smart·y-pants (smär′tē pants′), *n.* (*construed as sing.*) smarty¹.

smash¹ (smash), *v.t.* **1.** to break to pieces with violence and often with a crashing sound, as by striking, letting fall, or dashing against something; shatter: *He smashed the vase against the wall.* **2.** to defeat, disappoint, or disillusion utterly. **3.** to hit or strike (someone or something) with force. **4.** to overthrow or destroy something considered as harmful: *They smashed the drug racket.* **5.** to ruin financially: *The depression smashed him.* **6.** *Tennis, Badminton, Table Tennis.* to hit (a ball or shuttlecock) overhead with a hard downward motion, causing the shot to move very swiftly and to strike the ground or table usually at a sharp angle. —*v.i.* **7.** to break to pieces from a violent blow or collision. **8.** to dash with a shattering or crushing force or with great violence; crash (usually fol. by *against, into, through,* etc.). **9.** to become financially ruined or bankrupt (often fol. by *up*). **10.** to flatten and compress the signatures of a book in a press before binding. —*n.* **11.** the act or an instance of smashing or shattering. **12.** the sound of such a smash. **13.** a blow, hit, or slap. **14.** a destructive collision, as between automobiles. **15.** a smashed or shattered condition. **16.** a process or state of collapse, ruin, or destruction: *the total smash that another war would surely bring.* **17.** financial failure or ruin. **18.** *Informal.* something achieving great success; hit: *Her dance was an absolute smash.* **19.** a drink made of brandy, or other liquor, with sugar, water, mint, and ice. **20.** *Tennis, Badminton, Table Tennis.* **a.** an overhead stroke in which the ball or shuttlecock is hit with a hard, downward motion causing it to move very swiftly and to strike the ground or table usually at a sharp angle. **b.** a ball hit with such a stroke. —*adj.* **21.** *Informal.* of, relating to, or constituting a great success: *That composer has written many smash tunes.* [? b. SMACK² and MASH] —**smash′a·ble,** *adj.*

—**Syn. 1.** See **break. 5.** bankrupt. **11.** crash.

smash² (smash), *n. Slang.* coins; change. [b. SMALL and CASH¹]

smash-and-grab (smash′ən grab′), *adj.* (of a robbery) done by smashing a store window and grabbing valuable articles displayed there: *It was his third smash-and-grab offense.*

smashed (smasht), *adj. Slang.* drunk. [SMASH¹ + -ED²]

smash·er (smash′ər), *n.* **1.** one who or that which smashes. **2.** someone or something that is excellent, impressive, extraordinary, or the like: *That new off-Broadway show is a real smasher.* **3.** a heavy blow, fall, etc.: *He took a smasher off his horse.* **4.** one who plays a hard, fast, driving game of tennis, badminton, or handball. **5.** a severely cutting remark or squelching reply: *His letter to the Times was a smasher.* **6.** a machine for smashing or compressing books. **7.** the operator of such a machine. [SMASH¹ + -ER¹]

smash′ hit′, an extremely successful box-office hit.

smash·ing (smash′ing), *adj. Informal.* terribly good; marvelous: *We had a smashing time on our vacation.* [SMASH¹ + -ING²] —**smash′ing·ly,** *adv.*

smash-up (smash′up′), *n.* a complete smash, esp. a wreck of one or more vehicles. [n. use of v. phrase *smash up*]

smat·ter (smat′ər), *v.t.* **1.** to speak (a language, words, etc.) with superficial knowledge or understanding. **2.** to dabble in. —*n.* **3.** slight or superficial knowledge; smattering. [ME < Scand; cf. Sw *smattra* to patter, rattle] —**smat′ter·er,** *n.*

smat·ter·ing (smat′ər ing), *n.* **1.** a slight, superficial, or introductory knowledge of something: *a smattering of Latin.* —*adj.* **2.** slight or superficial. [SMATTER + -ING¹, -ING²] —**smat′ter·ing·ly,** *adv.*

smaze (smāz), *n.* a mixture of haze and smoke. [SM(OKE + H)AZE¹]

S.M.B., Bachelor of Sacred Music.

sm. c., small capital; small capitals. Also, **sm. cap.** or **sm. caps**

S.M.D., Doctor of Sacred Music.

smear (smēr), *v.t.* **1.** to spread or daub (an oily, greasy, viscous, or wet substance) on or over something: *to smear butter on bread.* **2.** to spread or daub an oily, greasy, viscous, or wet substance on: *to smear bread with butter.* **3.** to stain, spot, or make dirty with something oily, greasy, viscous, or wet. **4.** to sully, vilify, or soil (a reputation, good name, etc.). **5.** *Slang.* to defeat decisively; overwhelm: *They smeared the home team.* **6.** *Cards Slang.* to play a card of scoring value on (a trick taken by one's partner). **7.** *Slang.* to bribe. —*n.* **8.** an oily, greasy, viscous, or wet substance, esp. a dab of such a substance. **9.** a stain, spot, or mark made by such a substance. **10.** a smudge. **11.** something smeared or to be smeared on a thing, as a glaze for pottery. **12.** a small quantity of something smeared on a slide for microscopic examination. **13.** vilification: *The smear by the cheap gossip columnists was part of a campaign to ruin her career.* **14.** *Cards Slang.* the play of a card of scoring value on a trick taken by one's partner. [ME *smere,* OE *smeoru;* c. D *smear,* G *Schmer* grease] —**smear′er,** *n.*

smear·case (smēr′kās′), *n. Dial.* any soft cheese suitable for spreading, esp. cream cheese. Also, **smier·case.** [half trans., half adoption of G *Schmierkäse,* lit., smear-cheese]

smear-sheet (smēr′shēt′), *n.* a newspaper, magazine, or other periodical specializing in gossip, scandal, malicious innuendo, etc.

smear′ word′, a slanderous, vilifying, or denigrating epithet.

smear·y (smēr′ē), *adj.,* **smear·i·er, smear·i·est. 1.** showing smears; smeared; bedaubed. **2.** tending to smear or soil. [SMEAR + -Y¹] —**smear′i·ness,** *n.*

Smea·ton (smēt′ᵊn), *n.* **John,** 1724–92, English engineer.

smec·tic (smek′tik), *adj. Crystall.* noting a mesomorphic state in which the arrangement of the molecules is in layers or planes. Cf. **nematic.** [< L *smēctic(us)* < Gk *smēktikós,* equiv. to *smēch(ein)* (to) wash out, clean + *-tikos* -TIC]

smed·dum (smed′əm), *n. Chiefly Scot.* **1.** finely ground flour or powder. **2.** vigor; energy; alertness. [OE *smeodoma, smed(e)ma* < ?]

Smed·ley (smed′lē), *n.* a boy's given name.

smeek (smēk), *Scot. and North Eng.* —*n.* **1.** smoke, steam, or vapor. —*v.i.* **2.** to give off smoke, steam, or vapor. [ME *smeke,* OE *smēoc(an)*; c. D *smook,* G *Schmauch*] —**smeek′y,** *adj.*

smeg·ma (smeg′mə), *n.* a thick, foul-smelling, cheeselike, sebaceous secretion, consisting chiefly of desquamated epithelial cells, that collects beneath the foreskin or around the clitoris. [< L < Gk *smêgma* detergent, cleansing medicine]

smell (smel), *v.,* **smelled** or **smelt, smell·ing,** *n.* —*v.t.* **1.** to perceive the odor or scent of through the nose by means of the olfactory nerves; inhale the odor of: *I smell something burning.* **2.** to test by the sense of smell: *She smelled the meat to see if it was fresh.* **3.** to perceive, detect, or discover by shrewdness or sagacity: *The detective smelled foul play.* —*v.i.* **4.** to perceive or receive an odor or scent through the nose by means of the olfactory nerves; inhale the odor of a thing (usually fol. by *at* or *of*). **5.** to search or investigate (usually fol. by *about*). **6.** to give off or have an odor or scent: *to smell delicious.* **7.** to give out an offensive odor; reek; stink. **8.** to be ineffectual in character or appearance: *His design for the stage set smells.* **9.** to have a particular odor (usually fol. by *of*): *My hands smell of fish.* **10.** to have a trace or suggestion (usually fol. by *of*). **11. smell a rat.** See **rat** (def. 7). **12. smell out,** to look for or detect as if by smelling; search out: *to smell out enemy spies.* **13. smell up,** to fill with an offensive odor; stink up: *The burnt toast smelled up the whole apartment.* —*n.* **14.** the sense of smell; faculty of smelling. **15.** that quality of a thing which is or may be smelled; odor; scent. **16.** a trace or suggestion. **17.** the act or an instance of smelling. **18.** a pervading appearance, character, quality, or influence: *the smell of money.* [early ME *smell(en), smull(en)* < ?] —**smell′a·ble,** *adj.* —**smell′-less,** *adj.*

smell·er (smel′ər), *n.* **1.** one who smells. **2.** one who tests by smelling. **3.** *Slang.* the nose. **4.** a tactile hair or process, as one of the whiskers of a cat; a feeler. [SMELL + -ER[1]]

smell′ing bot′tle, a small bottle or vial for holding smelling salts or perfume.

smell′ing salts′, a preparation for smelling, consisting essentially of ammonium carbonate with some agreeable scent, used as a stimulant and restorative in cases of faintness, headache, and nausea.

smell·y (smel′ē), *adj.,* **smell·i·er, smell·i·est.** emitting a strong or unpleasant odor; reeking. [SMELL + -Y[1]] —**smell′i·ness,** *n.*

smelt[1] (smelt), *v.t.* **1.** to fuse or melt (ore) in order to separate the metal contained. **2.** to obtain or refine (metal) in this way. [prob. < MD or MLG *smelt(en)*; c. G *schmelzen* to MELT, smelt]

smelt[2] (smelt), *n., pl.* (*esp. collectively*) **smelt,** (*esp. referring to two or more kinds or species*) **smelts. 1.** a small, silvery food fish, *Osmerus eperlanus,* found in Europe. **2.** any other fish of the family *Osmeridae,* as the American smelt, *Osmerus mordax.* **3.** any of several superficially similar but unrelated fishes, esp. certain silversides, found in California. [ME, OE; cf. Norw *smelta* whiting]

smelt[3] (smelt), *v.* a pt. and pp. of **smell.**

smelt·er (smel′tər), *n.* **1.** one who or that which smelts. **2.** one who owns or works in a place where ores are smelted. **3.** a place where ores are smelted. [SMELT[1] + -ER[1]]

smelt·er·y (smel′tə rē), *n., pl.* **-er·ies.** smelter (def. 3). [SMELT[1] + -ERY]

Sme·ta·na (sme′tä nä; *Eng.* smet′ənə), *n.* **Be·dřich** (*Czech.* be′dʀzhiᴋʜ) or **Frederick,** 1824–84, Czech composer.

Smeth·wick (smeth′ik), *n.* a city in S Staffordshire, in central England, near Birmingham. 68,372 (1961).

smew (smyo͞o), *n.* a merganser, *Mergus albellus,* of the northern parts of the Eastern Hemisphere, the male of which is white marked with black and gray. [?]

smid·gen (smij′ən), *n.* *Informal.* a very small amount: *a smidgen of jam for your toast.* Also, **smid′gin.** [?]

smier·case (smēr′kās′), *n.* smearcase.

smi·la·ca·ceous (smī′lə kā′shəs), *adj.* belonging to the *Smilacaceae,* the smilax or greenbrier family of plants. [< NL *Smīlace(ae)* name of the family (L *smīlac-,* s. of *smīlax* bindweed (see SMILAX) + *-aceae* -ACEAE + -OUS]

smi·lax (smī′laks), *n.* **1.** any plant of the genus *Smilax,* of the tropical and temperate zones, consisting mostly of vines having woody stems. **2.** a delicate, twining, liliaceous plant, *Asparagus medeoloides,* having glossy, bright-green leaves, cultivated by florists. [< L *smīlax* bindweed < Gk *smīlax* bindweed, yew]

smile (smīl), *v.,* **smiled, smil·ing,** *n.* —*v.i.* **1.** to assume a facial expression indicating usually pleasure, favor, or amusement, but sometimes derision or scorn, characterized by an upturning of the corners of the mouth and usually accompanied, esp. in indicating pleasure, by a brightening of the face and eyes. **2.** to have a pleasant or agreeable appearance or aspect, as natural scenes, objects, etc.: *The landscape smiled in the sunlight.* **3.** to regard with favor (often fol. by *on* or *upon*): *Luck smiled on us that night.* —*v.t.* **4.** to assume or give (a smile, esp. of a given kind): *She smiled a warm and friendly smile.* **5.** to express by a smile: *to smile approval.* **6.** to bring, put, drive, etc., by or as by smiling: *to smile one's tears away.* **7. smile at, a.** to regard with pleasure or amusement, as with a smile. **b.** to regard with mild derision: *to smile at someone's affectations.* **c.** to endure patiently: *to smile at one's troubles.* —*n.* **8.** the act or an instance of smiling; a smiling expression of the face. **9.** favor or kindly regard: *fortune's smile.* **10.** a pleasant or agreeable appearance, look, or aspect. [ME *smylle;* c. OHG *smīlan,* Dan *smile*] —**smile′less,** *adj.* —**smile′less·ly,** *adv.* —**smile′less·ness,** *n.* —**smil′er,** *n.* —**smil′ing·ly,** *adv.*
—**Syn. 8.** See **laugh.** —**Ant. 8.** frown.

smil′ing wake′robin. See **painted trillium.**

smi·lo·grass (smī′lə gras′, -gräs′), *n.* a European grass, *Oryzopsis miliacea.* [?]

Smin·the·us (smin′thē əs, -tho͞os), *n.* *Class. Myth.* an epithet of Apollo as protector against pestilence and plagues of mice.

smirch (smûrch), *v.t.* **1.** to discolor or soil; spot or smudge with or as with soot, dust, dirt, etc. **2.** to sully or tarnish (a person, reputation, character, etc.); disgrace; discredit. —*n.* **3.** a dirty mark or smear, as of soot, dust, dirt, etc. **4.** a stain or blot, as on reputation. [ME *smorche;* b. SMEAR and SMUTCH] —**smirch′less,** *adj.*
—**Syn. 1.** smear, smut, dirty. **2.** taint, blot. **3.** smudge, smut, smutch. **4.** taint. —**Ant. 1.** clean. **2.** honor.

smirk (smûrk), *v.i.* **1.** to smile in an affected or offensively familiar way. —*v.t.* **2.** to express with a smirk: *He smirked his lewd delight at the scene.* —*n.* **3.** the smile or the facial expression of one who smirks. [ME; OE *smearc(ian)*] —**smirk′er,** *n.* —**smirk′ing·ly,** *adv.*
—**Syn. 1, 3.** simper.

smitch (smich), *n.* *Informal.* smidgen. [?]

smite (smīt), *v.,* **smote** or (*Obs.*) **smit; smit·ten** or **smit; smit·ing.** —*v.t.* **1.** to strike or hit hard, with or as with the hand, a stick or other weapon, etc.: *She smote him on the back with her broom.* **2.** to deliver or deal (a blow, hit, etc.) by striking hard. **3.** to render by, or as by, a blow: *to smite someone unconscious.* **4.** to strike down, injure, or slay: *His sword had smitten thousands.* **5.** to afflict, chasten, or punish in a grievous manner. **6.** to fall upon or attack with deadly or disastrous effect, as lightning, blight, pestilence, etc. **7.** to affect mentally or morally with a sudden pang: *His conscience smote him.* **8.** to affect suddenly and strongly with a specified feeling: *They were smitten with terror.* **9.** to impress favorably; charm; enamor: *He was smitten by her charms.* —*v.i.* **10.** to strike; deal a blow or blows. **11.** to appear, fall, etc., with or as with the force of a blow. **12. smite hip and thigh.** See **hip**[1] (def. 6). [ME; OE *smīt(an)*; c. G *schmeissen* to throw, D *smijten*] —**smit′er,** *n.*
—**Syn. 1.** knock, cuff, buffet, slap. **5.** chastise.

smith (smith), *n.* **1.** a worker in metal. **2.** a blacksmith. [ME, OE; c. G *Schmied,* OIcel *smidhr,* Goth *-smitha*]

Smith (smith), *n.* **1. Adam,** 1723–90, Scottish economist. **2. Alfred E(manuel),** 1873–1944, U.S. political leader. **3. Bessie,** 1894?–1937, U.S. singer. **4. Charles Henry** ("*Bill Arp*"), 1826–1903, U.S. humorist. **5. David,** 1906–65, U.S. sculptor. **6. Edmond Kir·by** (kûr′bē), 1824–93, Confederate general in the Civil War. **7. Francis Hopkinson,** 1838–1915, U.S. novelist, painter, and engineer. **8. George,** 1840–76, English archaeologist and Assyriologist. **9. Ian Douglas,** born 1919, Rhodesian political leader: prime minister 1964–79. **10. John,** 1580–1631, English adventurer and colonist in Virginia. **11. Joseph,** 1805–44, U.S. religious leader: founded the Mormon Church. **12. Lo·gan Pear·sall** (lō′gən pēr′sôl), 1865–1946, U.S. essayist in England. **13. Margaret Chase,** born 1897, U.S. politician. **14. Oliver,** 1918–77, U.S. set designer and theatrical producer. **15. Sydney,** 1771–1845, English clergyman, writer, and wit. **16. William,** 1769–1839, English geologist. **17.** a boy's given name.

smith·er·eens (smith′ə rēnz′), *n.pl.* *Informal.* small pieces; bits: *The vase broke into smithereens.* Also, **smith·ers** (smith′ərz). [*smithers* (< ?) + Ir dim. suffix *-een*]

smith·er·y (smith′ə rē), *n., pl.* **-er·ies. 1.** the work or craft of a smith. **2.** a smithy. [SMITH + -ERY]

Smith·field (smith′fēld′), *n.* a town in central North Carolina. 6117.

Smith′field ham′, *Trademark.* See **Virginia ham.**

Smith·son (smith′sən), *n.* **James,** 1765–1829, English chemist and mineralogist: his bequest was used to found the Smithsonian Institution.

Smith·so′ni·an Institu′tion (smith sō′nē ən), an institution in Washington, D.C., founded 1846 with a grant left by James Smithson, for the increase and diffusion of knowledge: U.S. national museum and repository.

smith·son·ite (smith′sə nīt′), *n.* **1.** a native carbonate of zinc, $ZnCO_3$, that is an important ore of the metal. Cf. **calamine** (defs. 2, 3). **2.** *Obs.* zinc silicate calamine. [named after J. SMITHSON (who distinguished it from calamine); see -ITE[1]]

Smith·ville (smith′vil), *n.* a town in central Texas. 2933 (1960).

smith·y (smith′ē, smith′ē), *n., pl.* **smith·ies. 1.** the workshop of a smith, esp. a blacksmith. **2.** a blacksmith. [ME *smithi* < OIcel *smithja;* akin to OE *smiththe.* See SMITH, -Y[2]]

smit′ing line′, *Naut.* a line for breaking out a light sail which has been raised furled.

smit·ten (smit′ən), *adj.* **1.** struck, as with a hard blow. **2.** grievously or disastrously stricken or afflicted. **3.** very much in love. —*v.* **4.** a pp. of **smite.**

Smit·ty (smit′ē), *n.* a boy's given name, form of **Smith.**

S.M.M., Master of Sacred Music.

smock (smok), *n.* **1.** a loose, lightweight overgarment worn to protect the clothing while working, as by artists, salesgirls, etc. —*v.t.* **2.** to clothe in a smock. **3.** to draw (a fabric) by needlework into a honeycomb pattern with diamond-shaped recesses. [ME; OE *smocc;* orig. name for a garment with a hole for the head; cf. OIcel *smjūga* to put on (a garment) over the head] —**smock′-like′,** *adj.*

smock′ frock′, a loose overgarment of linen or cotton, as that worn by European farm laborers. Cf. **blouse** (def. 3).

smock·ing (smok′ing), *n.* **1.** smocked needlework. **2.** embroidery stitches used to hold gathered cloth in even folds. [SMOCK + -ING[1]]

smock′ mill′, a windmill having the sails and their shaft carried by a cap rotating on an octagonal timber tower.

smog (smog, smôg), *n.* a mixture of fog and smoke. [SM(OKE + F)OG[1]]
—**Syn.** haze.

smog·gy (smog′ē, smô′gē), *adj.,* **-gi·er, -gi·est.** full of or characterized by smog. [SMOG + -Y[1]]

smok·a·ble (smō′kə bəl), *adj.* **1.** suitable for being smoked. —*n.* **2.** Usually, **smokables.** things for smoking, as cigars, cigarettes, or the like. Also, **smoke′a·ble.** [SMOKE + -ABLE]

smoke (smōk), *n., v.,* **smoked, smok·ing.** —*n.* **1.** the visible vapor and gases given off by a burning or smoldering substance, esp. the gray, brown, or blackish mixture of gases and suspended carbon particles resulting from the combustion of wood, peat, coal, or other organic matter. **2.** something resembling this, as vapor or mist, flying particles, etc. **3.** something unsubstantial, evanescent, or without result: *Their hopes and dreams proved to be smoke.* **4.** an obscuring condition: *When the smoke of controversy has cleared, you will recognize him as the great man he is.* **5.** an act or spell of smoking something, esp. tobacco: *They had a smoke during the intermission.* **6.** something for smoking, as a cigar or cigarette: *This is the best smoke on the market.* **7.** *Slang.* a homemade drink consisting of denatured alcohol and water. **8.** *Physics, Chem.* a system of solid particles suspended in a gaseous medium. **9. go up** or **end in smoke,** to terminate without producing a result; be unsuccessful: *All our dreams went up in smoke.* —*v.i.* **10.** to give off or emit smoke, as in burning. **11.** to give out smoke offensively or improperly, as a stove. **12.** to send forth steam or vapor, dust, or the like. **13.** to draw into the mouth and puff out the smoke of tobacco or the like, as from a pipe, cigar, or cigarette: *The students were not allowed to smoke in class.* **14.** *Slang.* to ride or travel with great speed. **15.** *Australian.* **a.** to flee. **b.** to abscond. —*v.t.* **16.** to draw into the mouth and puff out the smoke of: *to smoke tobacco.* **17.** to use (a pipe, cigarette, etc.) in this process. **18.** to expose to smoke. **19.** to fumigate (rooms, furniture, etc.). **20.** to cure (meat, fish, etc.) by exposure to smoke. **21.** to color or darken by smoke. **22. smoke out, a.** to drive from a refuge by means of smoke. **b.** to force into public view or knowledge; reveal: *The agent swore he would smoke out the leaders of the spy ring.* [ME; OE *smoca;* c. SMEEK] —**smoke′like′,** *adj.*

smoke′ bomb′, a bomb that upon detonation produces a continuous discharge of smoke rather than an explosion, used to mark an enemy target for aerial attack, indicate wind direction, produce a smoke screen, etc.

smoke′ cham′ber, an enlarged area between the throat of a fireplace and the chimney flue.

smoke·chas·er (smōk′chā′sər), *n.* one who fights forest fires, esp. a fire fighter whose lightweight equipment permits him to reach a fire quickly. [SMOKE + CHASER[1]]

smoke′ dome′, the smoke chamber covering of a prefabricated metal fireplace unit.

smoke-dry (smōk′drī′), *v.,* **-dried, -dry·ing.** —*v.t.* **1.** to dry or cure (meat or other food) using smoke. —*v.i.* **2.** to become dried by smoke: *to be eaten as soon as it smoke-dries.*

smoke′-eat·er (smōk′ē′tər), *n.* *Slang.* a fireman.

smoke′-filled room′ (smōk′fild′, -fild′), a place, as a hotel room, for conducting secret negotiations, effecting compromises, devising strategy, etc., as by party chiefs during a political convention.

smoke·house (smōk′hous′), *n., pl.* **-hous·es** (-hou′ziz). a building or place in which meat, fish, etc., are treated with smoke. [SMOKE + HOUSE]

smoke·jack (smōk′jak′), *n.* an apparatus for turning a roasting spit, set in motion by the current of ascending gases in a chimney. [SMOKE + JACK[1]]

smoke·jump·er (smōk′jum′pər), *n.* a fire fighter who parachutes to forest fires inaccessible to ground crews. [SMOKE + JUMPER[1]]

smoke·less (smōk′lis), *adj.* emitting, producing, or having little or no smoke. [SMOKE + -LESS] —**smoke′less·ly,** *adv.* —**smoke′less·ness,** *n.*

smoke′less pow′der, any of various substitutes for ordinary gunpowder that give off little or no smoke, esp. one composed wholly or mostly of guncotton.

smoke′ pot′, a can containing a chemical mixture that on being ignited produces a great quantity of smoke.

smoke·proof (smōk′pro͞of′), *adj.* that cannot be penetrated by smoke, as a door, room, etc.: *The paintings were transported in a fireproof and smokeproof compartment.* [SMOKE + -PROOF]

smok·er (smō′kər), *n.* **1.** one who or that which smokes. **2.** *Railroads.* **a.** Also called **smoking car.** a passenger car for those who wish to smoke. **b.** a compartment for those who wish to smoke. **3.** an informal gathering of men, for smoking and informal entertainment. **4.** *Brit.* smoking-concert. [SMOKE + -ER[1]]

smoke′ screen′, 1. a mass of dense smoke produced to conceal an area, vessel, or plane from the enemy. **2.** something intended to disguise, conceal, or deceive; camouflage.

smoke′ shelf′, a ledge at the bottom of a smoke chamber, so made as to deflect or break downdrafts from the chimney. Also called **wind shelf.**

smoke·stack (smōk′stak′), *n.* a pipe for the escape of the smoke or gases of combustion, as on a steamboat, locomotive, or building. Also called **stack.** [SMOKE + STACK]

smoke′ tree′, 1. Also called **Venetian sumac.** a treelike, anacardiaceous shrub, *Cotinus Coggygria,* of Europe and Asia Minor, having small flowers in large panicles that have a light, feathery appearance resembling smoke. **2.** a related American species, *Cotinus americanus.*

smo·king (smô kēng′), *n., pl.* **-kings** (-kēng′). *French.* dinner jacket; tuxedo.

smok′ing car′, smoker (def. 2a).

smok·ing-con·cert (smō′king kon′sərt), *n.* *Brit.* a concert at which the audience is allowed to smoke.

smok′ing gun′, *Slang.* conclusively incriminating evidence.

smok′ing jack′et, a loose-fitting jacket for men, often of a heavy fabric and trimmed with braid, worn indoors, esp. as a lounging jacket.

smok′ing room′, a room set apart for smoking, as in a hotel, clubhouse, or the like.

smok′ing stand′, an ashtray mounted on a low pedestal, often placed next to an armchair, sofa, etc.

smok·o (smō′kō), *n., pl.* **smok·os.** *Australian Slang.* a brief rest period from work, as for smoking a cigarette. Also, **smoke′-oh.** [SMOKE + *-o* associative suffix]

smok·y (smō′kē), *adj.,* **smok·i·er, smok·i·est. 1.** emitting smoke, as a fire, torch, etc., esp. in large amounts. **2.** hazy; darkened or begrimed with smoke. **3.** having the character or appearance of smoke: *smoky colors.* **4.** pertaining to or suggestive of smoke: *a smoky haze.* **5.** of a dull or brownish gray; cloudy. [ME; see SMOKE, -Y[1]] —**smok′i·ly,** *adv.* —**smok′i·ness,** *n.*

Smok′y Hill′, a river flowing E from E Colorado to the Republican River in central Kansas. 540 mi. long.

Smok′y Moun′tains. See **Great Smoky Mountains.**

smok′y quartz′, a crystallized variety of quartz, smoky-yellow to dark brown or black, used as a gem. Also called **cairngorm, Cairngorm stone.**

smok′y to′paz, *Jewelry.* smoky quartz used as a gemstone: not a true topaz.

smol·der (smōl′dər), *v.i.* **1.** to burn or smoke without flame; undergo slow or suppressed combustion. **2.** to exist or continue in a suppressed state or without outward demonstration: *Hatred smoldered beneath the surface of polite manners.* **3.** to display repressed feelings, as of indignation, anger, or the like: *His eyes smoldered with rage.* —*n.* **4.** dense smoke resulting from slow or suppressed combustion. **5.** a smoldering fire. Also, **smoulder.** [ME *smoulder(en),* deriv. of *smolder* smoky vapor, dissimilated var. of *smorther* SMOTHER]

Smo·lensk (smo lensk′), *n.* a city in the W RSFSR, in the W Soviet Union in Europe, SW of Moscow: Russians defeated by Napoleon 1812. 171,000 (est. 1964).

Smol·let (smol′it), *n.* **Tobias George,** 1721–71, English novelist.

smolt (smōlt), *n.* a young, silvery salmon migrating to the sea. [late ME; ? akin to SMELT[2]]

S.M.O.M., Sovereign and Military Order of Malta.

smooch[1] (smo͞och), *v.t., n.* smutch.

smooch[2] (smo͞och), *Informal.* —*v.i.* **1.** to kiss. **2.** to pet. —*n.* **3.** a kiss; smack. [?]

smoodge (smo͞oj), *v.i.,* **smoodged, smoodg·ing.** *Australian.* to curry favor; seek unwarranted recognition. [perh. alter. of SMOOCH[2]] —**smoodg′er,** *n.*

smooth (smo͞oth), *adj.* **1.** free from projections or graininess of surface; not rough to the touch: *a smooth piece of wood.* **2.** free from inequalities or unevenness of surface, ridges or hollows, obstructions, etc.: *a smooth road.* **3.** generally flat or unruffled, as a calm sea. **4.** free from hairs or a hairy growth: *a smooth cheek.* **5.** of uniform consistency; free from lumps, as a batter, sauce, etc. **6.** free from or proceeding without abrupt curves, bends, etc.: *You will have smooth traveling once you reach the highway.* **7.** allowing or having an even, uninterrupted movement or flow: *smooth driving.* **8.** easy and uniform, as motion, a curve, the working of a machine, etc. **9.** having projections worn away: *a smooth tire casing.* **10.** noting a metal file having the minimum commercial grade of coarseness for a single-cut file. Cf. **dead-smooth.** **11.** free from hindrances or difficulties: *a smooth day at the office.* **12.** undisturbed, tranquil, or equable, as the feelings, temper, etc.; serene: *a smooth disposition.* **13.** elegant, easy, or polished, as a speech, speaker, etc. **14.** pleasant, agreeable, or ingratiatingly polite, as manner, persons, etc.; suave; soigné: *a smooth operator.* **15.** free from harshness, sharpness, or bite; bland or mellow, as cheese or wine. **16.** not harsh to the ear, as sound: *the smooth music of a ballroom dance band.* **17.** *Phonet.* without aspiration. —*adv.* **18.** in a smooth manner; smoothly. —*v.t.* **19.** to make smooth of surface, as by scraping, planing, pressing, stroking, etc. **20.** to remove (projections, ridges, etc.) in making something smooth (often fol. by *away* or *out*). **21.** to make free from hindrances, difficulties, etc. **22.** to make something free from (hindrances, difficulties, etc.). **23.** to make more polished, elegant, agreeable, or plausible, as wording, verse, manners, the person, etc. **24.** to tranquilize, calm, or soothe (a person, the feelings, etc.). **25.** to gloss over or palliate, as something unpleasant or wrong (usually fol. by *over, out,* or *away*). **26.** *Math.* to simplify (an expression) by substituting approximate or certain known values for the variables. —*n.* **27.** act of smoothing: *She adjusted the folds with a smooth of her hand.* **28.** that which is smooth; a smooth part or place: *through the rough and the smooth.* [ME *smothe,* OE *smōth;* cf. OE *smēthe* smooth; c. OS *smōthi*] —**smooth′a·ble,** *adj.* —**smooth′er,** *n.* —**smooth′ly,** *adv.* —**smooth′ness,** *n.*
—**Syn. 1.** glossy, polished. **2, 3.** even, flat. See **level. 4.** bald, hairless. **8.** regular, even. **12.** unruffled, calm, peaceful, pacific, peaceable. **13.** fluent, glib, voluble. **14.** courtly, courteous. **19.** level, flatten, roll. **23.** refine. **24.** assuage, mollify. **25.** soften. —**Ant. 1.** rough.

smooth·bore (smo͞oth′bōr′, -bôr′), *adj.* **1.** (of firearms) having a smooth bore; not rifled. —*n.* **2.** a smoothbore gun. [SMOOTH + BORE[1]]

smooth′ breath′ing, a symbol (ʼ) used in the writing of Greek to indicate that the initial vowel over which it is placed is unaspirated. Cf. **rough breathing.**

smooth′ dog′fish, any of several requiem sharks having no spines in front of the dorsal fin, esp. *Mustela canis,* found along the American coast of the Atlantic Ocean.

smooth·en (smo͞o′thən), *v.t., v.i.* to make or become smooth. [SMOOTH + -EN[1]]

smooth-faced (smo͞oth′fāst′), *adj.* **1.** beardless; clean-shaven; smooth-shaven. **2.** having a smooth, satinlike, or polished surface: *smooth-faced stone.* **3.** deceitfully ingratiating.

smooth′ floun′der, a small right-eyed flounder, *Liopsetta putnami,* found along the coast of northeastern North America. Also called **eelback.**

smooth·hound (smo͞oth′hound′), *n.* a smooth dogfish, esp. *Mustelus mustelus,* found along the coast of Europe. Also called **smooth′hound shark′.** [SMOOTH + HOUND[1]]

smooth·ie (smo͞o′thē), *n.* *Informal.* a man who has a winningly polished manner, esp. in dealing with women: *He's such a smoothie he could charm the stripes off a tiger.* Also, **smoothy.** [SMOOTH + -IE]

smooth′ mus′cle, involuntary muscle in the walls of viscera and blood vessels, consisting of nonstriated, spindle-shaped fibers, each with a central nucleus.

smooth′ plane′, *Carpentry.* a small plane for finish work.

smooth-shav·en (smo͞oth′shā′vən), *adj.* having the beard and mustache shaved off; clean-shaven.

smooth-spo·ken (smo͞oth′spō′kən), *adj.* speaking or spoken easily and softly; gentle and persuasive.

smooth′ su′mac, a shrub or small tree, *Rhus glabra,* of North America, having green flowers in a dense terminal cluster.

smooth-tongue (smo͞oth′tung′), *n.* a deep-sea smelt, *Leuroglossus stilbius,* found in the North Pacific. [SMOOTH + TONGUE]

smooth-tongued (smo͞oth′tungd′), *adj.* fluent or convincing in speech; glib.

smooth′ win′terberry, a shrub, *Ilex laevigata,* of the northeastern U.S., having showy, orange-red fruit. Also called **hoopwood.**

smooth·y (smo͞o′thē), *n., pl.* **smooth·ies.** smoothie.

smor·gas·bord (smôr′gəs bōrd′, -bôrd′), *n.* **1.** a buffet meal of various hot and cold hors d'oeuvres, salads, casserole dishes, meats, cheeses, etc. **2.** any conglomeration or medley. Also, **smör·gås·bord** (*Swed.* smœr′gōs bo͞ord′). [< Sw *smörgåsbord,* equiv. to *smörgås* sandwich + *bord* table]

smor·zan·do (smôrt sän′dō; *It.* zmôr tsän′dō), *adj.* *Music.* fading away; dying out (a musical direction). [< It, prp. of *smorzare* to extinguish]

smote (smōt), *v.* a pt. of **smite.**

smoth·er (smuth′ər), *v.t.* **1.** to stifle or suffocate, as by smoke or other means of preventing free breathing. **2.** to kill by depriving of air. **3.** to extinguish or deaden (fire, coals, etc.) by covering so as to exclude air. **4.** to cover closely or thickly; envelop: *to smother a steak with mushrooms.* **5.** to suppress: *to smother a scandal.* **6.** to repress, as feelings, impulses, etc.: *She smothered her grief with ceaseless work.* **7.** *Cookery.* to cook in a closed vessel: *smothered chicken.* —*v.i.* **8.** to become stifled or suffocated; be prevented from breathing freely, as by smoke. **9.** to be stifled; be suppressed or concealed. —*n.* **10.** dense, stifling smoke. **11.** a smoking or smoldering state, as of burning matter; a smoldering fire. **12.** dust, fog, spray, etc., in a dense or enveloping cloud. **13.** an overspreading profusion of anything: *a smother of papers.* [ME *smorther,* OE *smor(ian)* (to) suffocate + *-ther* agent suffix] —**smoth′er·a·ble,** *adj.* —**smoth′er·y,** *adj.*

smoth′ered mate′, *Chess.* checkmate delivered by a knight when the king's mobility is restricted by his own pieces.

smoth·er·y (smuth′ə rē), *adj.* stifling; close: *a smothery atmosphere.* [SMOTHER + -Y[1]]

smoul·der (smōl′dər), *v.i., n.* smolder.

Smrit·i (smrit′ē), *n.* *Hinduism.* writings containing traditions concerning law, rituals, and the teachings of sages. [< Skt: lit., what is remembered]

smudge (smuj), *n., v.,* **smudged, smudg·ing.** —*n.* **1.** a dirty mark or smear. **2.** a smeary state. **3.** a stifling smoke. **4.** a smoky fire, esp. one made for driving away mosquitoes or safeguarding fruit trees from frost. —*v.t.* **5.** to mark with dirty streaks or smears. **6.** to fill with smudge, as to drive away insects or protect fruit trees from frost. —*v.i.* **7.** to form a smudge on something. **8.** to become smudged: *White shoes smudge easily.* **9.** to smolder or smoke; emit smoke, as a smudge pot. [ME *smoge* < ?] —**smudg′ed·ly,** *adv.* —**smudge′less,** *adj.*

smudge′ pot′, a container for burning oil or other fuels to produce smudge, as for protecting fruit trees from frost.

smudg·y (smuj′ē), *adj.,* **smudg·i·er, smudg·i·est. 1.** marked with smudges; smeared; smeary. **2.** emitting a stifling smoke; smoky. **3.** *Brit. Dial.* humid; sweltering; sultry. [SMUDGE + -Y[1]] —**smudg′i·ly,** *adv.* —**smudg′i·ness,** *n.*

smug (smug), *adj.,* **smug·ger, smug·gest. 1.** contentedly confident of one's own respectability, ability, superiority, or correctness; self-righteous and self-satisfied; complacent. **2.** trim; spruce; smooth; sleek. [perh. < D *smuk* neat; c. G *schmuck*] —**smug′ly,** *adv.* —**smug′ness,** *n.*
—**Syn. 1.** conceited, self-important. **2.** neat.

smug·gle (smug′əl), *v.,* **-gled, -gling.** —*v.t.* **1.** to import or export (goods) secretly, in violation of the law, esp. without payment of legal duty. **2.** to bring, take, put, etc., surreptitiously: *She smuggled the gun into the jail inside a cake.* —*v.i.* **3.** to import, export, or convey goods surreptitiously or in violation of the law. [< LG *smuggel(n);* c. G *schmuggeln*] —**smug′gler,** *n.*

smut (smut), *n., v.,* **smut·ted, smut·ting.** —*n.* **1.** a particle of soot; sooty matter. **2.** a black or dirty mark; smudge. **3.** indecent language or publications; obscenity. **4.** *Plant Pathol.* **a.** a disease of plants, esp. cereal grasses, characterized by the conversion of affected parts into black, powdery masses of spores, caused by fungi of the order *Ustilaginales.* **b.** a fungus causing this disease. —*v.t.* **5.** to soil or smudge. —*v.i.* **6.** to become affected with smut, as a plant. [alter. of earlier *smit* (OE *smitte*), by assoc. with SMUDGE, SMUTCH]

smutch (smuch), *v.t.* **1.** to smudge or soil. —*n.* **2.** a smudge or stain. **3.** dirt, grime, or smut. Also, **smooch.** [? < MHG *smutz(en)* (to) smear; c. G *Schmutz,* SMUT] —**smutch′less,** *adj.*

smutch·y (smuch′ē), *adj.,* **smutch·i·er, smutch·i·est.** of or pertaining to smutch; dirty; grimy; soiled; smudged. [SMUTCH + -Y[1]]

Smuts (*Du.* smœts; *Eng.* smuts), *n.* **Jan Chris·ti·aan** (*Du.* yän kris′tē än′), 1870–1950, South African statesman and general: prime minister 1919–24, 1939–48.

smut·ty (smut′ē), *adj.,* **-ti·er, -ti·est. 1.** soiled with smut, soot, or the like; grimy; dirty. **2.** indecent or obscene, as talk, writing, etc.: *a smutty novel.* **3.** given to indecent or obscene talk, writing, etc., as a person. **4.** (of plants) affected with the disease smut. [SMUT + -Y[1]] —**smut′ti·ly,** *adv.* —**smut′ti·ness,** *n.*

Smyr·na (smûr′nə), *n.* **1.** former name of **Izmir. 2.** a town in central Tennessee. 3612 (1960). **3.** a town in central Delaware. 3241 (1960). **4. Gulf of,** former name of the Gulf of Izmir. **5.** *Class. Myth.* Myrrha.

Smyr′na fig′, a fig, *Ficus Carica smyrniaca,* that requires caprification in order to produce fruit.

Smyr·ne·an (smûr′nē ən), *adj.* of or pertaining to Smyrna, Turkey. [< L *Smyrnae(us)* of SMYRNA + -AN]

Smyth (smith), *n.* **1st Baron.** See **Baden-Powell, Robert Stephenson Smythe.**

Smyth·i·i (smith′ē ī′), *n.* **Mare.** See **Mare Smythii.**

Smyth's′ Sea′ (smiths). See **Mare Smythii.**

smy·trie (smī′trē, smi′-), *n.* *Scot.* a miscellaneous collection or heap of small items; litter. [?]

Sn, *Chem.* tin. [< L *stannum*]

S.N., (in prescriptions) according to nature. Also, **s.n.** [< L *secundum nātūram*]

snack (snak), *n.* **1.** a small portion of food or drink or a light meal, esp. one eaten between regular meals. **2.** a share or portion. **3. go snack** or **snacks,** to share (profits or returns). —*v.i.* **4.** to have a snack or light meal, esp. between regular meals: *They snacked on tea and cake.* [orig. n. use of *snack* to snap; cf. MD *snacken* to snap]

snack′ bar′, a lunchroom or restaurant where light meals are sold.

snack′ ta′ble, a small, portable folding table used for an individual serving of food or drink. Also called **TV table.**

A, Snaffle; B, Cheek snaffle; C, Cheekpiece

snaf·fle[1] (snaf′əl), *n., v.,* **-fled, -fling.** —*n.* **1.** Also called **snaf′fle bit′.** a bit having a large ring at each end to which a rein and cheekpiece are attached. —*v.t.* **2.** to put a snaffle on (a horse). **3.** to control with or as with a snaffle. [cf. D *snavel,* G *Schnabel* beak, mouth]

snaf·fle[2] (snaf′əl), *v.t.,* **-fled, -fling.** *Brit. Slang.* to steal; purloin. [?]

sna·fu (sna fo͞o′, snaf′o͞o), *adj., v.,* **-fued, -fu·ing,** *n.* —*adj.* **1.** in disorder; out of control; chaotic. —*v.t.* **2.** to throw into disorder; muddle. —*n.* **3.** a badly confused or ridiculously muddled situation. [*s(ituation) n(ormal): a(ll) f(ouled) u(p)*]

snag (snag), *n., v.,* **snagged, snag·ging.** —*n.* **1.** a tree or part of a tree held fast in the bottom of a river or other body of water and forming an impediment or danger to navigation. **2.** a short, projecting stump, as of a branch broken or cut off. **3.** any sharp or rough projection. **4.** a stump of a tooth or a projecting tooth; snaggletooth. **5.** a small, jagged hole or run as made from catching or tearing on a sharp projection. **6.** any obstacle or impediment: *to strike a snag in carrying out plans.* —*v.t.* **7.** to run or catch up on a snag. **8.** to damage by so doing. **9.** to obstruct or impede, as a snag does: *His hostility snagged all my efforts.* —*v.i.* **10.** to become entangled with some obstacle or hindrance: *This line snags every time I cast.* **11.** (of a boat) to strike a snag. [< Scand; cf. Norw (dial.) *snag* stump, OIcel *snagi* clothespin] —**snag′like′,** *adj.*

snag·gle·tooth (snag′əl to͞oth′), *n., pl.* **-teeth.** a tooth growing out beyond or apart from others. [appar. SNAG + -LE + TOOTH] —**snag·gle-toothed** (snag′əl to͞otht′, -to͞othd′), *adj.*

snag·gy (snag′ē), *adj.,* **-gi·er, -gi·est. 1.** having snags or sharp projections, as a tree. **2.** abounding in snags or obstructions, as a river. **3.** snaglike; projecting sharply or roughly. [SNAG + -Y[1]]

Snail, *Liguus fasciatus* (Shell length to 3 in.)

snail (snāl), *n.* **1.** any mollusk of the class *Gastropoda,* having a spirally coiled shell of a single valve and a ventral muscular foot on which it slowly glides about. **2.** a slow or lazy person; sluggard. **3.** a cam having the form of a spiral. **4.** *Midwestern and Western U.S.* a sweet roll in spiral form, esp. a cinnamon roll or piece of Danish pastry. [ME; OE *snegel;* c. LG *snagel,* G (dial.) *Schnegel*] —**snail′like′,** *adj.*

snail·fish (snāl′fish′), *n., pl.* (*esp. collectively*) **-fish,** (*esp. referring to two or more kinds or species*) **-fish·es.** any of several elongated, flabby-skinned fishes of the family *Liparididae,* found in cold seas, having the ventral fins modified to form a sucking disk. [SNAIL + FISH]

snail·flow·er (snāl′flou′ər), *n.* a tropical perennial vine, *Phaseolus Caracalla,* having fragrant, yellowish or purplish flowers, a segment of which is shaped like a snail's shell. Also called **corkscrew flower.** [SNAIL + FLOWER]

snail·ing (snā′ling), *n.* *Horol.* ornamental patterning of watch or clock parts by means of abrasive disks. Also called **damaskeening.** [SNAIL + -ING[1]]

snail-paced (snāl′pāst′), *adj.* slow of pace or motion, like a snail; sluggish.

snail's′ pace′, an extremely slow rate of progress: *His health is improving at a snail's pace.*

snake (snāk), *n., v.,* **snaked, snak·ing.** —*n.* **1.** any of numerous limbless, scaly, elongated reptiles of the suborder *Ophidia (Serpentes),* comprising venomous and nonvenomous species found in tropical and temperate areas. **2.** a treacherous person; an insidious enemy. Cf. **snake in the grass** (def. 2). **3.** *Building Trades.* **a.** (in plumbing) a device for dislodging obstructions in curved pipes, having a head fed into the pipe at the end of a flexible metal band. **b.** a length of resilient steel wire, for threading through an electrical conduit so that wire can be pulled through after it. —*v.i.* **4.** to move, twist, or wind in the manner of a snake: *The road snakes among the mountains.* —*v.t.* **5.** to wind or make (one's course, way, etc.) in the manner of a snake; progress in a serpentine course: *to snake one's way through a crowd.* **6.** to drag or haul, esp. by a chain or rope, as a log. **7.** to drag or pull forcibly; yank. [ME; OE *snaca;* c. G *Schnake* adder, OIcel *snākr*] —**snake′like′,** *adj.*

snake·bird (snāk′bûrd′), *n.* any of various totipalmate swimming birds of the family *Anhingidae,* having a long, snaky neck. Also called **anhinga.** [SNAKE + BIRD]

snake·bite (snāk′bīt′), *n.* **1.** the bite of a snake, esp. of one that is venomous. **2.** the resulting painful, toxic condition. [SNAKE + BITE]

snake′bite rem′edy, *Slang.* hard liquor.

snake·blen·ny (snāk′blen′ē), *n., pl.* (*esp. collectively*) **-ny,** (*esp. referring to two or more kinds or species*) **-nies.** any of several pricklebacks of the genus *Lumpenus.* [SNAKE + BLENNY]

snake′ charm′er, an entertainer who seems to charm venomous snakes, usually by music.

snake′ dance′, 1. a ceremonial dance of the American Indian in which snakes or representations of snakes are handled or imitated by the dancers. **2.** a parade or procession, esp. in celebration of a victory, in which the participants weave in single file in a serpentine course.

snake-dance (snāk′dans′, -däns′), *v.i.*, **-danced, -danc·ing.** to perform a snake dance.

snake′ doc′tor, **1.** a dragonfly. **2.** a hellgrammite.

snake′ eyes′, *Craps.* a cast of two; two aces.

snake′ feed′er, *Midland U.S.* a dragonfly.

snake′ fence′, a fence, zigzag in plan, made of rails resting across one another at an angle. Also called **Virginia fence, Virginia rail fence, worm fence.**

snake·fish (snāk′fish′), *n., pl.* **-fish·es,** (*esp. collectively*) **-fish.** a lizardfish, *Trachinocephalus myops,* found in the eastern Pacific and western Atlantic oceans. [SNAKE + FISH]

snake·fly (snāk′flī′), *n., pl.* **-flies.** any neuropterous insect of the family *Raphidiidae,* of western North America, having an elongated prothorax resembling a neck. [SNAKE + FLY²]

snake′ foot′, *Furniture.* an elongated foot or short leg, as to a pedestal table, having the form of an ogee tangent to the floor surface.

Snake feet

snake·head (snāk′hed′), *n.* **1.** a turtlehead plant. **2.** any elongated labyrinth fish of the family *Channidae* (or *Ophicephalidae*), having a large head with a deeply cleft mouth. [SNAKE + HEAD]

snake-hipped (snāk′hipt′), *adj.* having thin, sinuous hips.

snake′ in the grass′, **1.** a concealed danger: *The scheme seemed foolproof, but there was a snake in the grass that hadn't been reckoned with.* **2.** a treacherous person, esp. one who feigns friendship.

snake′ lil′y, an herb, *Brodiaea volubilis,* of California, having a twining stem and rose-red or pink flowers.

snake′ mack′erel, any of several elongated, carnivorous fishes of the family *Gempylidae,* found in tropical and temperate seas, having jutting jaws and strong teeth.

snake·mouth (snāk′mouth′), *n., pl.* **-mouths** (-mouthz′). a swamp orchid, *Pogonia ophioglossoides,* of eastern North America, having rose-colored, nodding flowers on a slender stem. [SNAKE + MOUTH; so called because of the resemblance of the flower to a snake's open mouth]

snake′ oil′, *Slang.* any of various liquid concoctions of questionable medical value sold as an all-purpose curative, esp. by traveling hucksters.

snake′ palm′, devil's-tongue.

snake′ pit′, *Informal.* **1.** a mental hospital marked by squalor and inhumane or indifferent care for the patients. **2.** an intensely chaotic or disagreeable place or situation.

Snake′ Riv′er, a river flowing from NW Wyoming through S Idaho into the Columbia River in SE Washington: Shoshone Falls. 1038 mi. long.

snake·root (snāk′ro͞ot′, -ro͝ot′), *n.* **1.** any of various plants whose roots have been regarded as a remedy for snakebites, as an herb, *Aristolochia Serpentaria* **(Virginia snakeroot),** having a medicinal rhizome and rootlets, and a white-flowered plant, *Polygala Senega* **(Seneca snakeroot),** having a medicinal root. **2.** the root or rhizome of such a plant. **3.** the North American bugbane. **4.** a white eupatorium, *Eupatorium rugosum.* **5.** the dogbane, *Rauwolfia serpentina,* having roots that yield drugs. [SNAKE + ROOT¹]

snake's-head (snāks′hed′), *n.* See **toad lily** (def. 2).

snake·skin (snāk′skin′), *n.* **1.** the skin of a snake. **2.** leather made from the skin of a snake. [SNAKE + SKIN]

snake·stone (snāk′stōn′), *n.* **1.** a piece of porous material popularly supposed to neutralize the toxic effect of a snakebite. **2.** See **ayr stone.** [SNAKE + STONE]

snake·weed (snāk′wēd′), *n.* bistort (def. 1). [SNAKE + WEED¹]

snak·y (snā′kē), *adj.*, **snak·i·er, snak·i·est.** **1.** of or pertaining to snakes. **2.** abounding in snakes, as a place. **3.** snakelike; twisting, winding, or sinuous. **4.** venomous; treacherous or insidious: *a snaky look; a snaky remark.* **5.** consisting of, entwined with, or bearing a representation of snakes or serpents, as a ring. [SNAKE + -Y¹] —**snak′i·ly,** *adv.* —**snak′i·ness,** *n.*

snap (snap), *v.,* **snapped, snap·ping,** *n., adj., adv.* —*v.i.* **1.** to make a sudden, sharp, distinct sound; crack, as a whip; crackle. **2.** to click, as a mechanism or the jaws or teeth coming together. **3.** to move, strike, shut, catch, etc., with a sharp sound, as a door, lid, or lock. **4.** to break suddenly, esp. with a sharp, cracking sound, as something slender and brittle: *The branch snapped, and I fell to the ground.* **5.** to be radiant; sparkle; flash, as the eyes. **6.** to act or move with quick or abrupt motions of the body: *to snap to attention.* **7.** *Photog.* to take a photograph, esp. without formal posing of the subject. **8.** to make a quick or sudden bite or grab (often fol. by *at*). **9.** to utter a quick, sharp sentence or speech, esp. a command, reproof, retort, etc. (often fol. by *at*). —*v.t.* **10.** to seize with or take, buy, or obtain as with a quick bite or grab (usually fol. by *up* or *off*): *The bargains were snapped up almost immediately.* **11.** to secure, judge, vote, etc., hastily, as a decision, legislation, etc., not subjected to due deliberation: *They snapped the bill through Congress.* **12.** to cause to make a sudden, sharp sound: *to snap one's fingers.* **13.** to crack (a whip). **14.** to bring, strike, shut, open, operate, etc., with a sharp sound or movement: *to snap a lid down.* **15.** to address or interrupt (a person) quickly and sharply (usually fol. by *up*). **16.** to say or utter (words, a command, a retort, etc.) in a quick, sharp manner (sometimes fol. by *out*): *The irate customer snapped out his complaints.* **17.** to break suddenly, esp. with a cracking sound: *to snap a stick in half.* **18.** *Photog.* to take a photograph of, esp. quickly. **19.** *Building Trades.* to transfer (a line) to a surface by means of a chalk line. **20.** *Football.* to put (the ball) into play by tossing it back to the quarterback or other member of the offensive backfield, esp. from between the legs when bent over double and facing the line of scrimmage; center. **21.** *Hunting.* to fire (a shot) quickly, esp. without raising the gun to aim from the eye. **22. snap one's fingers at,** to be indifferent to or contemptuous of; flout: *It's no use telling them the dangers of smoking, because they'll just snap their fingers at well-meant advice.* **23. snap out of it,** *Informal.* to regain one's composure, energy, or good spirits; recover: *Her husband's death came as a great shock, and so far she hasn't been able to snap out of it.* **24. snap someone's head off,** *Informal.* to speak angrily or curtly to someone: *I must have said the wrong thing to make him to snap my head off like that.* —*n.* **25.** a quick, sudden action or movement, as the flick of a whip or the breaking of a twig. **26.** a short, sharp sound, as that caused by breaking a twig or closing a latch. **27.** a catch or fastener that closes by pressure and clicks together. **28.** *Informal.* briskness, vigor, or energy: *That song has a lot of snap. He has plenty of snap.* **29.** a quick, sharp speech or manner of speaking: *He uttered his commands with a snap.* **30.** a quick or sudden bite or grab, as at something: *The fish ate with little snaps.* **31.** something obtained by or as by biting or grabbing: *a snap of food.* **32.** a short spell or period, as of cold weather: *an unexpected cold snap.* **33.** *Photog.* a snapshot. **34.** *Informal.* an easy, profitable, or agreeable position, piece of work, or the like: *This job is a snap.* **35.** *Football.* the act or an instance of snapping the ball. **36.** *Brit.* a packed lunch, as that carried by a workman or traveler. **37. not give** or **care a snap of one's fingers for,** to regard with indifference; treat lightly. Also, **not give** or **care a snap.** —*adj.* **38.** noting devices closing by pressure on a spring catch, or articles using such devices. Cf. **snap fastener.** **39.** made, done, taken, etc., suddenly or offhand: *a snap judgment.* **40.** easy: *a snap course at college.* —*adv.* **41.** in a brisk, sudden manner. [< D or LG *snapp(en)*] —**snap′less,** *adj.* —**snap′pa·ble,** *adj.* —**snap′ping·ly,** *adv.*

snap·back (snap′bak′), *n.* **1.** a sudden rebound or recovery. **2.** *Football.* snap (def. 35). [n. use of v. phrase *snap back*]

snap′ bean′, *Bot.* See **string bean.**

snap′ brim′, **1.** a hat brim that can be turned up or down. **2.** Also called **snap′-brim hat′.** a man's fedora, usually of felt and often worn with the brim turned up in back and down in front. —**snap′-brim′, snap′-brimmed′,** *adj.*

snap·drag·on (snap′drag′ən), *n.* **1.** any scrophulariaceous plant of the genus *Antirrhinum,* esp. *A. majus,* cultivated for its spikes of showy flowers, each having a corolla supposed to resemble the mouth of a dragon. **2.** flapdragon. [SNAP + DRAGON]

snap′ fas′tener, a fastening device in two pieces having a projection on one piece that fits into a hole in the other, used esp. for holding pieces of fabric or parts of clothing together.

snap·head (snap′hed′), *n.* a hemispherical rivet head. Also called **button head.** [SNAP + HEAD]

snap·line (snap′līn′), *n.* See **chalk line** (def. 1). [SNAP + LINE¹]

snap′ link′, a link having a latchlike opening at one side through which another link or catch can be fitted.

snap-on (snap′on′, -ôn′), *adj.* attached or fitting into place by means of a snap or snaps: *a winter coat with a snap-on hood.* [adj. use of v. phrase *snap on*]

snap·out (snap′out′), *n.* **1.** an order form, receipt, sheet of ruled or writing paper, or the like, bound into a pad with others and perforated near the binding for easy separation, often interleaved with carbon paper so that copies are made automatically. **2.** a set of sheets of paper so perforated. Also, **snap′ out′.** [n. use of v. phrase *snap out*]

snap·per (snap′ər), *n., pl.* (*esp. collectively*) **-per,** (*esp. referring to two or more kinds or species*) **-pers** for 1, 2; **-pers** for 3, 4. **1.** any of several large, marine fishes of the family *Lutjanidae.* **2.** any of various other fishes, as the bluefish, *Pomatomus saltatrix.* **3.** See **snapping turtle.** **4.** *Informal.* one in charge of a group of workers; foreman. [SNAP + -ER¹]

snap·per·back (snap′ər bak′), *n. Football Rare.* the center on the offensive team. [SNAPPER + BACK¹]

snap′ping bee′tle. See **click beetle.**

snap′ping tur′tle, any of several large, predaceous turtles of the family *Chelydridae* of fresh waters of North and South America, esp. the edible *Chelydra serpentina,* having powerful jaws with which it bites viciously.

Snapping turtle, *Chelydra serpentina* (Length of carapace to 1 ft.; tail to 11 in.)

snap·pish (snap′ish), *adj.* **1.** apt to snap or bite, as a dog. **2.** disposed to speak or reply in an impatient or irritable manner. **3.** impatiently or irritably sharp; curt: *a snappish reply.* [SNAP + -ISH¹] —**snap′pish·ly,** *adv.* —**snap′pish·ness,** *n.*

snap·py (snap′ē), *adj.*, **-pi·er, -pi·est.** **1.** apt to snap or bite; snappish, as a dog. **2.** impatient or irritable, as a person or a reply. **3.** snapping or crackling in sound, as a fire. **4.** quick or sudden in action or performance. **5.** *Informal.* crisp, smart, lively, brisk, etc.: *Only snappy people get ahead in this world.* **6. make it snappy,** *Slang.* to speed up; hurry: *Father told me to make it snappy or else he would leave without me.* [SNAP + -Y¹] —**snap′pi·ly,** *adv.* —**snap′pi·ness,** *n.*

snap′ ring′, *Mach.* any of various kinds of metal rings that must be forced open to be used and snap back into place to make a snug fit.

snap′ roll′, *Aeron.* a maneuver in which an airplane makes a rapid and complete revolution about its longitudinal axis while maintaining approximately level flight.

snap-roll (snap′rōl′), *Aeron.* —*v.t.* **1.** to put (an airplane) through the maneuver of a snap roll. —*v.i.* **2.** to execute a snap roll.

snap′ shack′le, a shackle with a hinged jaw and a fastening pin on a spring to allow for rapid attachment and removal.

snap·shoot (snap′sho͞ot′), *v.t.*, **-shot, -shoot·ing.** to take a snapshot of (a subject). [back formation from SNAPSHOT]

snap·shot (snap′shot′), *n., v.,* **-shot·ted, -shot·ting.** —*n.* **1.** an informal photograph, esp. one taken quickly by a hand-held camera. **2.** *Hunting.* a quick shot taken without deliberate aim. —*v.t., v.i.* **3.** to photograph informally and quickly. [SNAP + SHOT¹]

snap′ the whip′. See **crack the whip** (def. 1).

snare¹ (snâr), *n., v.,* **snared, snar·ing.** —*n.* **1.** a device, usually consisting of a noose, for capturing birds or small animals. **2.** anything serving to entrap, entangle, or catch unawares; trap: *His candid manner was only a snare for my confidence.* **3.** *Surg.* a wire noose for removing tumors or the like by the roots or at the base. —*v.t.* **4.** to catch with a snare; entrap; entangle. **5.** to catch or involve by trickery or wile: *She snared me into going by using flattery.* [ME < Scand; cf. OIcel *snara;* r. OE *snearu;* c. OHG *snarahha*] —**snare′less,** *adj.* —**snar′er,** *n.* —**snar′ing·ly,** *adv.* —**Syn. 1.** See **trap¹.** **2.** net, seine.

snare² (snâr), *n.* one of the strings of gut or of tightly spiraled metal stretched across the skin of a snare drum. [< MLG *snare* or MD *snaer* string; r. OE *snēr* string of a musical instrument]

snare′ drum′, a small double-headed drum, carried at the side, having snares across the lower head to produce a rattling or reverberating effect.

Snare drum

snark (snärk), *n.* a mysterious, imaginary animal. [SN(AIL + SH)ARK; coined by Lewis Carroll]

snarl¹ (snärl), *v.i.* **1.** to growl angrily or viciously, as a dog. **2.** to speak in a savagely sharp, angry, or quarrelsome manner. —*v.t.* **3.** to say by snarling: *to snarl a threat.* —*n.* **4.** the act of snarling. **5.** a snarling sound or utterance. [obs. *snar* to snarl (c. D, LG *snarren,* G *schnarren*) + -LE] —**snarl′er,** *n.* —**snarl′ing·ly,** *adv.* —**snarl′y,** *adj.*

snarl² (snärl), *n.* **1.** a tangle, as of thread or hair. **2.** a complicated or confused condition or matter: *a traffic snarl.* **3.** a knot in wood. **4.** a kink remaining in a length of wire pulled tight. —*v.t.* **5.** to bring into a tangled condition, as thread, hair, etc.; tangle. **6.** to render complicated or confused (often fol. by *up*): *Your stupid questions snarl me up.* **7.** to raise or emboss, as parts of a thin metal vessel, by hammering on a tool **(snarl′ing i′ron)** held against the inner surface of the vessel. —*v.i.* **8.** to become tangled; get into a tangle. [ME < Scand; cf. OSw *snarel* noose, equiv. to *snar(a)* SNARE¹ + *-el* -LE]

snash (snash, snäsh), *Scot.* —*n.* **1.** insolence; impertinence. —*v.i.* **2.** to use abusive language; speak disrespectfully. [?]

snatch (snach), *v.i.* **1.** to make a sudden effort to seize something, as with the hand; grab (usually fol. by *at*). —*v.t.* **2.** to seize by a sudden or hasty grasp (often fol. by *up, from, out of, away,* etc.): *He snatched the old lady's purse and ran.* **3.** to take, get, secure, etc., suddenly or hastily. **4.** to rescue or save by prompt action: *He snatched the baby from the fire.* **5.** *Slang.* to kidnap. —*n.* **6.** the act or an instance of snatching. **7.** a sudden motion to seize something; grab: *He made a snatch as if to stop her.* **8.** a bit, scrap, or fragment of something: *snatches of conversation.* **9.** a brief spell of effort, activity, or any experience: *to work in snatches.* **10.** *Naut.* a sheave or projecting member serving as a fairlead. **11.** a brief period of time. **12.** *Slang.* an act of kidnaping. [ME *snacche(n)* < ?; c. MD *snacken*] —**snatch′a·ble,** *adj.* —**snatch′er,** *n.* —**snatch′ing·ly,** *adv.*

snatch′ block′, *n. Naut.* a fairlead having the form of a block that can be opened to receive the bight of a rope at any point along its length.

snatch·y (snach′ē), *adj.*, **snatch·i·er, snatch·i·est.** consisting of, occurring in, or characterized by snatches; spasmodic; irregular. [SNATCH + -Y¹] —**snatch′i·ly,** *adv.*

snath (snath), *n.* the shaft or handle of a scythe. Also, **snathe** (snāth). [unexplained var. of *snead* (ME *snede,* OE *snǣd* < ?)]

snaz·zy (snaz′ē), *adj.*, **-zi·er, -zi·est.** *Slang.* extremely attractive or stylish; flashy; fancy: *a snazzy dresser.* [?] —**snaz′zi·ness,** *n.*

SNCC (snik), *n.* a U.S. civil-rights organization, established in 1960 to achieve political and economic power for Negroes through local and regional action groups. [*S(tudent) N(onviolent) C(oordinating) C(ommittee)*]

Snead (snēd), *n.* **Samuel Jackson** ("*Slamming Sammy*"), born 1912, U.S. golfer.

sneak (snēk), *v.,* **sneaked** or (*esp. Dial.*) **snuck; sneak·ing;** *n.* —*v.i.* **1.** to go in a stealthy or furtive manner; slink; skulk (usually fol. by *about, along, in, off, out,* etc.). **2.** to act in a furtive, underhand, or mean way. **3.** *Brit. Slang.* to tattle; inform. —*v.t.* **4.** to move, put, pass, etc., in a stealthy or furtive manner: *He sneaked the gun into his pocket.* **5.** *Informal.* to take surreptitiously; steal: *to sneak a smoke.* —*n.* **6.** one who sneaks; a sneaking, underhand, or contemptible person. **7.** *Informal.* a stealthy or furtive departure. **8.** *Brit. Slang.* tattletale; informer. **9. sneaks,** *Informal.* a pair of sneakers. **10.** *Informal.* a sneak preview. **11.** *Cards Slang.* the lead of a singleton in a suit other than the trump suit, as in whist. [var. of ME *snik(an),* OE *snīcan* to creep; c. OIcel *snīkja* to hanker after] —**Syn. 1.** steal. See **lurk.**

sneak·box (snēk′boks′), *n.* a light, fast, low skiff of the 19th century, used in New Jersey, esp. by duck hunters. [SNEAK + BOX¹]

sneak·er (snē′kər), *n.* **1.** a high or low shoe, usually of canvas, with a rubber or similar synthetic sole. **2.** one who sneaks; a sneak. [SNEAK + -ER¹]

sneak·ing (snē′king), *adj.* **1.** acting in a furtive or underhand way. **2.** deceitfully underhand, as actions; contemptible. **3.** secret; not generally avowed, as a feeling, notion, suspicion, etc.: *I have a sneaking suspicion that we are not welcome here.* [SNEAK + -ING²] —**sneak′ing·ly,** *adv.* —**sneak′ing·ness,** *n.*

sneak′ pre′view, a preview of a motion picture, usually shown in addition to an announced film, in order to observe the reactions of the audience.

sneak′ thief′, a burglar who steals by sneaking into houses through open doors, windows, etc.

sneak·y (snē′kē), *adj.*, **sneak·i·er, sneak·i·est.** like or suggestive of a sneak; furtive; deceitful; sneaking. [SNEAK + -Y¹] —**sneak′i·ly,** *adv.* —**sneak′i·ness,** *n.*

sneak′y pete′, *Slang.* a homemade or an inferior, commercially produced liquor or wine.

sneck[1] (snek), *Scot. and North Eng.* —*n.* **1.** a door latch or its lever. —*v.t.* **2.** to latch (a door, gate, or the like). [ME *snek(k)*; c. SNATCH]

sneck[2] (snek), *Masonry.* —*n.* **1.** a small stone, as a spall, inserted into the spaces between larger pieces of rubble in a wall. —*v.t.* **2.** to fill (spaces between larger stones) with snecks. [?] —**sneck′er,** *n.*

snecked (snekt), *adj. Masonry.* built of uncoursed, roughly squared rubble. [SNECK[2] + -ED[2]]

sneck′ harl′ing, *Chiefly Brit.* harling of rubble masonry so as to leave the larger stones exposed.

sned (sned), *v.t.,* **sned·ded, sned·ding.** *Scot. and North Eng.* to prune (a tree or bush); cut off (a branch). [ME *-snæd(en)*, OE *snǣdan* to cut; c. G *schneiden*, OIcel *sneitha*]

sneer (snēr), *v.i.* **1.** to smile or curl the lip in a manner that shows scorn, contempt, etc.: *They sneered at him when he started telling off-color jokes in mixed company.* **2.** to speak or write in a manner expressive of derision, scorn, or contempt. —*v.t.* **3.** to utter or say in a sneering manner. **4.** to bring, put, force, etc., by sneering: *to sneer someone to silence.* —*n.* **5.** a look or expression suggestive of derision, scorn, or contempt. **6.** a derisive or scornful utterance or remark, esp. one more or less covert or insinuative. **7.** an act of sneering. [ME *snere*; c. NFris *sneere* scorn, perh. also SNARL[1]] —**sneer′er,** *n.* —**sneer′ful,** *adj.* —**sneer′ful·ness,** *n.* —**sneer′ing·ly,** *adv.* —**sneer′less,** *adj.*
—**Syn. 2.** gibe. See **scoff. 6.** scoff, gibe, jeer.

sneesh (snēsh), *n. Scot. and North Eng.* snuff. [perh. < Scand; cf. Dan *snus* snuff]

sneeze (snēz), *v.,* **sneezed, sneez·ing,** *n.* —*v.i.* **1.** to emit air or breath suddenly, forcibly, and audibly through the nose and mouth by involuntary, spasmodic action. **2. sneeze at,** *Informal.* to treat with contempt; scorn: *That sum of money is nothing to sneeze at.* —*n.* **3.** an act or sound of sneezing. [late ME *snese*; r. earlier *fnese*, OE *fnēosan*; c. D *fniezen*, OIcel *fnȳsa*] —**sneeze′less,** *adj.* —**sneez′er,** *n.* —**sneez′y,** *adj.*

sneeze·weed (snēz′wēd′), *n.* any of several coarse, composite herbs of the genus *Helenium*, the flowers of which resemble sunflowers and cause sneezing. [SNEEZE + WEED[1]]

sneeze·wort (snēz′wûrt′), *n.* an asteraceous plant, *Achillea Ptarmica*, of Europe, the powdered leaves of which cause sneezing. [SNEEZE + WORT[2]]

Snef·ru (snef′ro͞o), *n.* fl. c2920 B.C., Egyptian ruler of the 4th dynasty.

snell (snel), *n.* a short piece of nylon, gut, or the like, by which a fishhook is attached to a line. [?]

Snell·i·us (snel′ē əs), *n.* a crater in the fourth quadrant of the face of the moon: about 50 miles in diameter.

Snell's′ law′ (snelz), *Optics.* the law that, for a ray incident on the interface of two media, the sine of the angle of incidence times the index of refraction of the first medium is equal to the sine of the angle of refraction times the index of refraction of the second medium. [named after Willebrod *Snell* van Royen (d. 1626), Dutch mathematician]

snick (snik), *v.t.* **1.** to cut, snip, or nick. **2.** to strike sharply: *He snicked the ball with his cue.* **3.** to snap or click (a gun, trigger, etc.). —*v.i.* **4.** to click. —*n.* **5.** a small cut; nick. **6.** a click. **7.** *Cricket.* **a.** a glancing blow given to the ball. **b.** the ball so hit. [? cf. Scot *sneck* to cut (off), OIcel *snikka* to whittle]

snick·er (snik′ər), *v.i.* **1.** to laugh in a half-suppressed, often indecorous or disrespectful manner. —*v.t.* **2.** to utter with a snicker. —*n.* **3.** a snickering laugh: *His slip of speech provoked snickers among the audience.* Also, **snigger.** [imit.] —**snick′er·ing·ly,** *adv.*

snick·er·snee (snik′ər snē′), *n.* a knife, esp. one used as a weapon. [var. (by alliterative assimilation) of earlier *stick or snee* thrust or cut < D *steken* to STICK[2] + *snijen* to cut]

snide (snīd), *adj.,* **snid·er, snid·est.** derogatory in a nasty, insinuating manner: *snide remarks about his wife.* [?] —**snide′ness,** *n.*

sniff (snif), *v.i.* **1.** to draw air through the nose in short, audible inhalations. **2.** to clear the nose by so doing; sniffle, as with emotion. **3.** to smell by short inhalations. **4.** to show disdain, contempt, etc., by or as by drawing air through the nose in short, audible inhalations (usually fol. by *at*). —*v.t.* **5.** to draw in or up through the nose by sniffing, as air, odor, liquid, powder, etc.; inhale through the nose. **6.** to perceive by or as by smelling: *They were quick to sniff a scandal.* —*n.* **7.** an act of sniffing; a single, short, audible inhalation. **8.** the sound made by such an act. **9.** a scent or odor perceived: *A sniff of perfume was in the air.* [ME; back formation from SNIVEL] —**sniff′ing·ly,** *adv.*

sniff·er (snif′ər), *n.* **1.** one who or that which sniffs. **2.** a device or mechanism for detecting something. [SNIFF + -ER[1]]

sniff·ish (snif′ish), *adj.* haughtily disdainful; contemptuous: *a sniffish dowager accustomed to having her own way.* [SNIFF + -ISH[1]]

snif·fle (snif′əl), *v.,* **-fled, -fling,** *n.* —*v.i.* **1.** to sniff repeatedly, as from a head cold or in repressing tearful emotion: *She sniffled woefully.* —*n.* **2.** an act or sound of sniffling. **3. sniffles,** a condition, as a cold, marked by sniffling (usually prec. by *the*): *This draft is giving me the sniffles.* [SNIFF + -LE] —**snif′fler,** *n.*

snif·fy (snif′ē), *adj.,* **-fi·er, -fi·est.** *Informal.* inclined to sniff, as in scorn; disdainful; supercilious: *He was very sniffy about breaches of etiquette.* [SNIFF + -Y[1]] —**sniff′i·ly,** *adv.* —**sniff′i·ness,** *n.*

snif·ter (snif′tər), *n.* **1.** a pear-shaped glass, narrowing at the top to intensify the aroma of brandy, liqueur, etc. **2.** *U.S. Slang.* a very small drink of liquor. [ME *snyfter* to sniff; imit.]

snift′ing valve′, a valve for releasing small quantities of steam, compressed air, or condensate, as from the cylinder of a steam engine.

snig (snig), *v.t.,* **snigged, snig·ging.** to drag a heavy load, esp. logs, by means of ropes or chains. [?]

snig·ger (snig′ər), *v.i., v.t., n.* snicker. —**snig′ger·er,** *n.* —**snig′ger·ing·ly,** *adv.*

snig·gle (snig′əl), *v.,* **-gled, -gling.** —*v.i.* **1.** to fish for eels by thrusting a baited hook into their lurking places. —*v.t.* **2.** to catch by sniggling. [*snig* eel (late ME *snigge*) + -LE] —**snig·gler** (snig′lər), *n.*

snip (snip), *v.,* **snipped, snip·ping,** *n.* —*v.t.* **1.** to cut with a small, quick stroke, or a succession of such strokes, with scissors or the like. **2.** to remove or cut off (something) by or as by cutting in this manner: *to snip a rose.* —*v.i.* **3.** to cut with small, quick strokes. —*n.* **4.** the act of snipping, as with scissors. **5.** a small cut made by snipping. **6.** a small piece snipped off. **7.** a small piece, bit, or amount of anything: *a snip of food.* **8.** *Informal.* a small or insignificant person. **9. snips,** small, strong hand shears for the use of sheet metal workers. **10.** *Brit. Slang.* a bargain. [?; cf. D, LG *snippen* to snip, catch, clip]

snipe (snīp), *n., pl.* **snipes,** (*esp. collectively*) **snipe** for 1, 2; *v.* **sniped, snip·ing.** —*n.* **1.** any of several long-billed, limicoline game birds of the genera *Gallinago* or *Limnocryptes*, found in marshy areas, as *G. gallinago* **(common snipe),** of Eurasia and America, having brownish, black, or white plumage. **2.** any of several related or unrelated, long-billed birds. **3.** a shot, usually from a hidden position. —*v.i.* **4.** to shoot or hunt snipe. **5.** to shoot at individuals as opportunity offers from a concealed or distant position: *The enemy was sniping from the roofs.* **6.** to attack a person or his work with petulant or snide criticism, esp. anonymously or from a safe distance. [ME *snype* < Scand; cf. OIcel *snīpa*] —**snipe′like′,** *adj.* —**snip′er,** *n.*

Wilson's snipe,
Capella delicata
(Length 11 in.)

snipe·bill (snīp′bil′), *n. Carpentry.* a plane for forming quirks in moldings. Also, **snipes′bill′, snipe's′ bill′.**

snipe·fish (snīp′fish′), *n., pl.* (*esp. collectively*) **-fish,** (*esp. referring to two or more kinds or species*) **-fish·es.** any of several fishes of the genus *Macroramphosus*, found in tropical and temperate seas, having a long, tubular snout and a compressed body. Also called **bellows fish.** [SNIPE + FISH]

snip·er·scope (snī′pər skōp′), *n.* a snooperscope designed for attaching to a rifle or carbine. [SNIPER + -SCOPE]

snip·pet (snip′it), *n.* **1.** a small piece snipped off; a small bit, scrap, or fragment: *an anthology of snippets.* **2.** *Informal.* a small or insignificant person. [SNIP + -ET]

snip·py (snip′ē), *adj.,* **-pi·er, -pi·est. 1.** *Informal.* sharp or curt, esp. in a supercilious or haughty way. **2.** scrappy or fragmentary. Also, **snip·pe·ty** (snip′i tē). [SNIP + -Y[1]] —**snip′pi·ly,** *adv.* —**snip′pi·ness, snip′pet·i·ness,** *n.*

snit (snit), *n.* an agitated or irritated state: *She got herself into a snit because the train was so late.* [?]

snitch[1] (snich), *v.t. Informal.* to snatch or steal; pilfer. [? var. of SNATCH]

snitch[2] (snich), *Informal.* —*v.i.* **1.** to inform; tattle. —*n.* **2.** Also called **snitch′er.** an informer. [?]

snitch·y (snich′ē), *adj.,* **snitch·i·er, snitch·i·est.** *Brit., Australian.* cross; ill-tempered. [SNITCH[2] + -Y[1]]

sniv·el (sniv′əl), *v.,* **-eled, -el·ing** or (*esp. Brit.*) **-elled, -el·ling,** *n.* —*v.i.* **1.** to weep or cry with sniffling. **2.** to affect a tearful state; whine. **3.** to run at the nose; have a runny nose: *She sniveled from the cold all winter.* **4.** to draw up mucus audibly through the nose: *Stop sniveling and use your handkerchief.* —*v.t.* **5.** to utter with sniveling or sniffling. —*n.* **6.** weak, whining, or pretended weeping. **7.** a light sniff or sniffle, as in weeping. **8.** a hypocritical show of feeling: *a sentimental snivel.* **9.** mucus running from the nose. **10. snivels,** a sniveling condition; a slight head cold (usually prec. by *the*). [ME *snyvele*; cf. OE *snyflung*, deriv. of *snofl* mucus; c. LG *snüfeln*] —**sniv′el·er,** *esp. Brit.,* **sniv′el·ler,** *n.*

sniv·el·y (sniv′ə lē), *adj.* characterized by or given to sniveling. Also, *esp. Brit.,* **sniv′el·ly.** [SNIVEL + -Y[1]]

snob (snob), *n.* **1.** one who imitates, cultivates, or slavishly admires those with social rank, wealth, etc., and is condescending or overbearing to others. **2.** one who pretends to have social importance, intellectual superiority, etc. **3.** one who believes himself an expert or connoisseur in a given field and is condescending toward or disdainful of those who hold other opinions or have different tastes regarding this field: *a musical snob.* [orig. nickname for cobbler or cobbler's apprentice < ?]

snob·ber·y (snob′ə rē), *n., pl.* **-ber·ies.** snobbish character, conduct, trait, or act. [SNOB + -ERY]

snob·bish (snob′ish), *adj.* **1.** of, pertaining to, or characteristic of a snob: *snobbish ideas about rank.* **2.** having the character of a snob. [SNOB + -ISH[1]] —**snob′bish·ly,** *adv.* —**snob′bish·ness,** *n.*

snob·by (snob′ē), *adj.,* **-bi·er, -bi·est.** condescending, patronizing, or socially exclusive; snobbish. [SNOB + -Y[1]] —**snob′bi·ly,** *adv.* —**snob′bi·ness, snob′bism,** *n.*

snod (snod), *adj. Scot. and North Eng.* **1.** smooth; sleek. **2.** neat; tidy. [< Scand; cf. OIcel *snodhinn* bald] —**snod′ly,** *adv.*

Sno·ho·mish (snō hō′mish), *n.* a town in NW Washington. 3894 (1960).

snol·ly·gos·ter (snol′ē gos′tər), *n. Slang.* a clever, unscrupulous person. [?]

snood (sno͞od), *n.* **1.** the distinctive headband formerly worn by young unmarried women in Scotland and northern England. **2.** a fillet for the hair. **3.** a netlike hat or part of a hat or fabric that holds or covers the back of a woman's hair. —*v.t.* **4.** to bind or confine (the hair) with a snood. [ME, OE *snōd*; c. NEEDLE]

snook[1] (sno͝ok, sno͞ok), *v.i. Dial.* to sniff or smell the air, as if searching for or trying to identify an odor. Also, **snowk.** [ME *snoke* < Scand; cf. Norw (dial.) *snoka* to snuff, smell]

snook[2] (sno͝ok, sno͞ok), *n., pl.* (*esp. collectively*) **snook,** (*esp. referring to two or more kinds or species*) **snooks. 1.** any basslike fish of the genus *Centropomus*, esp. *C. unidecimalis*, found in the waters off Florida and the West Indies and south to Brazil, valued as food and game. **2.** any of several related marine fishes. [< D *snoek*]

snook[3] (sno͝ok, sno͞ok), *n.* **1.** a gesture of defiance, disrespect, or derision. **2. cock a snook** or **cock one's snook,** to thumb the nose (usually fol. by *at*): *a painter who cocks a snook at traditional techniques.* Also, **cock a snoot.** [?]

snook·er (sno͝ok′ər), *n.* a variety of pool played with 15 red balls and 6 balls of colors other than red, in which a player must shoot one of the red balls, each with a point value of 1, into a pocket before shooting at one of the other balls, with point values of from 2 to 7. [?]

snool (sno͞ol), *Scot. and North Eng.* —*n.* **1.** a meek, submissive person. —*v.t.* **2.** to dominate (someone); keep in submission. —*v.i.* **3.** to submit meekly; obey humbly. [?]

snoop (sno͞op), *Informal.* —*v.i.* **1.** to prowl or pry; go about in a sneaking, prying way; pry in a mean, sly manner. —*n.* **2.** an act or instance of snooping. **3.** one who snoops: *the neighborhood snoops and gossips.* [< D *snoep(en)* (to) take and eat (food) on the sly] —**snoop′er,** *n.*

snoop·er·scope (sno͞o′pər skōp′), *n.* a device that transmits infrared radiations and receives those reflected back from solid objects, producing an image on a fluorescent screen, enabling the user effectively to see objects obscured by darkness. [SNOOPER + -SCOPE]

snoop·y (sno͞o′pē), *adj.,* **snoop·i·er, snoop·i·est.** *Informal.* characterized by meddlesome curiosity; prying. [SNOOP + -Y[1]]

snoose (sno͞os, sno͞oz), *n. Dial.* finely powdered tobacco; snuff. [< Sw *snusa*, Dan, Norw *snuse*, short for Sw, Dan *snustobak*, Norw *snustobakk* snuff (sniff) tobacco]

snoot (sno͞ot), *n.* **1.** *Slang.* the nose. **2.** *Informal.* a snob. —*v.t.* **3.** *Informal.* to behave disdainfully toward; condescend to: *New arrivals in the town were snooted by older residents.* [var. of SNOUT]

snoot·ful (sno͞ot′fo͝ol′), *n., pl.* **-fuls.** *Informal.* a sufficient amount of liquor to cause intoxication. [SNOOT + -FUL]

snoot·y (sno͞o′tē), *adj.,* **snoot·i·er, snoot·i·est.** *Informal.* snobbish. [SNOOT + -Y[1]] —**snoot′i·ly,** *adv.* —**snoot′i·ness,** *n.*

snooze (sno͞oz), *v.,* **snoozed, snooz·ing,** *n. Informal.* —*v.i.* **1.** to sleep; slumber; doze; nap. —*n.* **2.** a short sleep; nap. [?] —**snooz′er,** *n.* —**snooz′y,** *adj.*

Sno·qual′mie Falls′ (snō kwol′mē), falls of the Snoqualmie River, in W Washington. 270 ft. high.

snore (snōr, snôr), *v.,* **snored, snor·ing,** *n.* —*v.i.* **1.** to breathe during sleep with hoarse or harsh sounds as caused by the vibrating of the soft palate. —*v.t.* **2.** to pass or spend (time) in snoring (usually fol. by *away* or *out*): *to snore the day away.* —*n.* **3.** the act, instance, or sound of snoring. **4.** Also called **snore′ piece′.** the intake of a suction pump, as of a sump pump. [ME *snore(n)*; c. MLG, MD *snorren*] —**snor′er,** *n.*

snor·kel (snôr′kəl), *n.* **1.** Also, **schnorkle, schnorkel.** Also called, *Brit.,* **snort.** a device permitting a submarine to remain submerged for prolonged periods, consisting of tubes extended above the surface of the water to take in air for the diesel engine and for general ventilation and to discharge exhaust gases and foul air. **2.** a tube, usually of plastic, through which a person may breathe while swimming face down in the water on or close to the surface by inserting one end in the mouth and letting the other end project above the surface. —*v.i.* **3.** to swim face down in the water on or close to the surface, breathing by means of such a tube. [< G *Schnorkel* air-intake]

Snor·ri Stur·lu·son (snoʀ′ʀē stœʀ′lə son; *Eng.* snôr′ē stûr′lə sən), 1179–1241, Icelandic historian and poet.

snort (snôrt), *v.i.* **1.** (of animals) to force the breath violently through the nostrils with a loud, harsh sound: *The spirited horse snorted and shied at the train.* **2.** (of persons) to express contempt, indignation, etc., by a similar sound. —*v.t.* **3.** to utter with a snort. **4.** to expel (air, sound, etc.) by or as by snorting. —*n.* **5.** the act or sound of snorting. **6.** *Slang.* a quick drink of liquor; shot. **7.** *Brit.* snorkel. [ME *snort(en)*; prob. akin to SNORE] —**snort′ing·ly,** *adv.*

snort·er (snôr′tər), *n.* **1.** one who or that which snorts. **2.** *Informal.* something extraordinary of its kind: *a real snorter of a storm.* [SNORT + -ER[1]]

snot (snot), *n.* **1.** *Vulgar.* mucus from the nose. **2.** *Informal.* a disrespectful or supercilious person. [ME; E *(ge)snot*; c. Dan *snot*]

snot-rag (snot′rag′), *n. Vulgar.* a handkerchief.

snot·ty (snot′ē), *adj.,* **-ti·er, -ti·est. 1.** *Vulgar.* of or pertaining to snot. **2.** *Informal.* snobbish; arrogant; supercilious: *a snotty kid.* [SNOT + -Y[1]] —**snot′ti·ly,** *adv.* —**snot′ti·ness,** *n.*

snout (snout), *n.* **1.** the part of an animal's head projecting forward and containing the nose and jaws; muzzle. **2.** *Entomol.* an anterior prolongation of the head bearing the mouth parts, as in snout beetles. **3.** anything that resembles or suggests an animal's snout in shape, function, etc. **4.** a nozzle or spout. **5.** *Usually Disparaging.* a person's nose, esp. when large or prominent. [ME *snute*; c. D *snuite*, G *Schnauze*] —**snout′less,** *adj.* —**snout′like′,** *adj.*

snout′ bee′tle, a weevil of the family *Curculionidae*, having the head prolonged into a snout.

snow[1] (snō), *n.* **1.** *Meteorol.* a precipitation in the form of ice crystals, mainly of intricately branched, hexagonal form and often agglomerated into snowflakes, formed directly from the freezing of the water vapor in the air. Cf. **ice crystals, snow grains, snow pellets. 2.** these flakes as forming a layer on the ground or other surface. **3.** the fall of these flakes or a storm during which these flakes fall. **4.** something resembling a layer of these flakes in whiteness, softness, or the like: *the snow of fresh linen.* **5.** Also, **snows.** *Poetic.* the white hairs of age. **6.** *Poetic.* white blossoms. **7.** *Poetic.* the white color of snow. **8.** *Chem.* See **dry ice** (def. 1). **9.** *Slang.* cocaine or heroin. **10.** white spots on a television screen caused by a weak signal. —*v.i.* **11.** to send down snow; fall as snow. **12.** to descend like snow. —*v.t.* **13.** to let fall as or like snow. **14.** to cover, obstruct, etc., with snow (usually fol. by *over, under,* etc.). **15.** *Slang.* **a.** to make an overwhelming impression on: *The view from the skyscraper really snowed them.* **b.** to persuade or deceive: *She was snowed into believing everything he told her.* **16. snow under,** *Slang.* to overwhelm with a larger amount (of work, correspondence, etc.) than can be conveniently dealt with: *Upon returning from vacation he found himself completely snowed under.* [ME; OE *snāw*; c. D *sneeuw*, G *Schnee*, OIcel *snǣr*, Goth *snaiws*, L *nix* (gen. *nivis*), Gk *nípha* (acc.), OCS *sněgŭ*] —**snow′less,** *adj.* —**snow′like′,** *adj.*

snow[2] (snō), *n.* a sailing vessel rigged in a manner similar to a brig but with a trysail mast just abaft the mainmast. [< D *snaauw*]

Snow (snō), *n.* **Sir Charles Percy** (*C. P. Snow*), 1905–80, English novelist and scientist.

snow′ ap′ple, a Fameuse.

snow·ball (snō′bôl′), *n.* **1.** a ball of snow pressed or rolled together, as for throwing. **2.** any of several shrubs of the genus *Viburnum*, having large clusters of white, sterile flowers. **3.** a confection of crushed ice, usually in the shape of a ball, which is flavored with fruit or other syrup and served in a paper cup. —*v.t.* **4.** to throw snowballs at. **5.** to cause to grow or become larger, greater, more intense, etc., at an accelerating rate: *to snowball a small business into a great enterprise.* —*v.i.* **6.** to grow or become larger, greater, more intense, etc., at an accelerating rate. [ME; see SNOW[1], BALL[1]]

snow·bank (snō′baŋgk′), *n.* a mound or heap of snow, as a snowdrift, a mass of snow shoveled from a road or sidewalk, or the like. [SNOW[1] + BANK[1]]

snow′ ban′ner, snow being blown off a mountain top. Also called **snow plume, snow smoke.**

snow·bell (snō′bel′), *n.* a small, styracaceous tree of the genus *Styrax*, having white flowers. [SNOW[1] + BELL[1]]

snow·ber·ry (snō′ber′ē, -bə rē), *n., pl.* **-ries. 1.** a caprifoliaceous shrub, *Symphoricarpos albus*, of North America, cultivated for its ornamental white berries. **2.** any of certain other white-berried plants. [SNOW[1] + BERRY]

snow·bird (snō′bûrd′), *n.* **1.** a junco. **2.** See **snow bunting. 3.** *Slang.* a cocaine or heroin addict. [SNOW[1] + BIRD]

snow-blind (snō′blīnd′), *adj.* affected with snow blindness.

snow′ blind′ness, the usually temporary dimming of the sight caused by the glare of reflected sunlight on snow.

snow·blink (snō′bliŋgk′), *n.* a white luminosity on the underside of clouds, caused by the reflection of light from a snow surface. Cf. **iceblink.** [SNOW[1] + BLINK]

snow′ board′, a board serving as a snow guard.

snow·bound (snō′bound′), *adj.* shut in or immobilized by snow: *The farm was snowbound for two months last winter.* [SNOW[1] + -BOUND[1]]

Snow-Bound (snō′bound′), *n.* a poem (1866) by John Greenleaf Whittier.

snow-broth (snō′brôth′, -broth′), *n.* **1.** melted snow. **2.** a mixture of snow and water. **3.** ice-cold liquid.

snow′ bun′ny, *Slang.* **1.** a beginner in skiing, esp. a girl. **2.** a girl or woman who frequents ski resorts mainly for the purpose of meeting men.

snow′ bunt′ing, a bunting, *Plectrophenax nivalis*, of the northern parts of the Northern Hemisphere. Also called **snowbird, snowflake.**

snow·bush (snō′bŏŏsh′), *n.* **1.** any of several ornamental shrubs having a profusion of white flowers, as *Ceanothus velutinus*, of western North America. **2.** a shrub, *Breynia nivosa*, of the South Sea Islands, having leaves speckled or mottled with white, inconspicuous, greenish flowers, and red fruit. [SNOW[1] + BUSH[1]]

snow·cap (snō′kap′), *n.* a layer of snow forming a cap on or covering the top of something, as a mountain peak or ridge. [SNOW[1] + CAP]

snow-capped (snō′kapt′), *adj.* topped with snow: *the snow-capped Alps.*

snow-clad (snō′klad′), *adj.* covered with snow.

snow′ cov′er, 1. a layer of snow on the ground. **2.** the amount of an area that is covered by snow, usually given as a percentage of the total area. **3.** the depth of snow on the ground.

snow·creep (snō′krēp′), *n.* a continuous, slow, downhill movement of snow. [SNOW[1] + CREEP]

snow′ crust′, a relatively hard, upper layer or film of ice or compacted snow on a snow surface.

snow′ crys′tal, a crystal of ice sufficiently heavy to fall from the atmosphere. Cf. **snowflake.**

Snow·den (snōd′ᵊn), *n.* a boy's given name.

Snow·don (snōd′ᵊn), *n.* a mountain in NW Wales: highest peak in Wales. 3560 ft.

snow·drift (snō′drift′), *n.* **1.** a mound or bank of snow driven together by the wind. **2.** snow driven before the wind. [SNOW[1] + DRIFT]

snow·drop (snō′drop′), *n.* **1.** a low, spring-blooming herb, *Galanthus nivalis*, having drooping, white flowers. **2.** its bulbous root or flower. **3.** the woodland anemone. [SNOW[1] + DROP]

snow′drop wind′flower, a perennial herb, *Anemone sylvestris*, of Eurasia, having one or two fragrant, white flowers.

snow·fall (snō′fôl′), *n.* **1.** a fall of snow. **2.** the amount of snow at a particular place or in a given time. [SNOW[1] + FALL]

snow′ fence′, a barrier erected on the windward side of a road, house, barn, etc., serving as a protection from drifting snow.

snow·field (snō′fēld′), *n.* *Geol.* a large and relatively permanent expanse of snow. [SNOW[1] + FIELD]

snow·flake (snō′flāk′), *n.* **1.** one of the small, feathery masses or flakes in which snow falls. **2.** *Meteorol.* **a.** an agglomeration of snow crystals falling as a unit. **b.** any snow particle. **3.** any of certain European, amaryllidaceous plants of the genus *Leucojum*, resembling the snowdrop. **4.** See **snow bunting.** [SNOW[1] + FLAKE[2]]

snow′ gauge′, an instrument for measuring the depth of snow.

snow′ goose′, a white, wild goose, *Chen hyperborea*, of North America.

snow′ grains′, precipitation consisting of white, opaque ice particles usually less than one millimeter in diameter.

snow′ guard′, any device for preventing snow from sliding off a sloping roof. Also called **roof guard.**

snow′ ice′, opaque ice formed from partly melted snow or ice; frozen slush.

snow-in-sum·mer (snō′in sum′ər), *n.* a prostrate garden plant, *Cerastium tomentosum*, of Europe, having white flowers and numerous, white, woolly leaves in large patches, growing in sand.

snow′ job′, *Slang.* an attempt to deceive or persuade as to the merits of something or someone, esp. one that involves flattery or exaggeration: *He gave her a snow job on his army career.*

snowk (snouk, snōk, snŏŏk), *v.i.* *Dial.* snook[1].

snow′ leop′ard, ounce[2].

snow′ lil′y. See **glacier lily.**

snow′ line′, 1. the line, as on mountains, above which there is perpetual snow. **2.** the latitudinal line marking the limit of the fall of snow at sea level.

snow·man (snō′man′), *n., pl.* **-men.** a figure, resembling that of a man, made out of packed snow. [SNOW[1] + MAN[1]]

snow·mast (snō′mast′, -mäst′; *Naut.* snō′məst), *n.* *Naut.* See **trysail mast.** [SNOW[1] + MAST[1]]

snow′ mist′. See **ice crystals.**

snow·mo·bile (snō′mə bēl′), *n.* a vehicle adapted for traveling on or through snow. [SNOW[1] + (AUTO)MOBILE]

snow′ mold′, *Plant. Pathol.* a disease of cereals and other grasses, characterized by a dense, cottony growth that covers the affected parts as the snow melts in the spring, caused by any of several fungi of the genera *Calonectria, Fusarium, Pythium*, and *Typhula*. **2.** any fungus causing this disease.

snow-on-the-moun·tain (snō′on thə moun′tᵊn, -ôn-), *n.* a spurge, *Euphorbia marginata*, of the western U.S., having leaves with white margins and white flower bracts. Also called **ghost-weed.**

snow·pack (snō′pak′), *n.* an extensive upland field of packed snow that melts slowly. [SNOW[1] + PACK[1]]

snow′ pear′, a small tree, *Pyrus nivalis*, of eastern Europe and Asia Minor, having showy flowers and nearly globe-shaped fruit.

snow′ pel′lets, precipitation, usually of brief duration, consisting of crisp, white, opaque ice particles, round or conical in shape and about two to five millimeters in diameter. Also called **graupel, soft hail, tapioca snow.**

snow′ plant′, a leafless, parasitic plant, *Sarcodes sanguinea*, of the pine forests of the Sierra Nevada in California, having numerous erect flowers, a thickly scaled stem, and a corallike mass of roots.

snow·plow (snō′plou′), *n.* **1.** an implement or machine for clearing away snow from highways, railroad tracks, etc. **2.** *Skiing.* a maneuver in which a skier pushes the heels of both skis outward so that they are far apart, as for turning, decreasing speed, or stopping. [SNOW[1] + PLOW]

snow′ plume′. See **snow banner.**

snow′ pud′ding, a light pudding, prepared by folding whipped egg whites into a lemon gelatin mixture.

snow-rigged (snō′rigd′), *adj.* (of a sailing vessel) rigged in the manner of a snow.

snow′ scale′. See **snow stake.**

snow·shed (snō′shed′), *n.* a structure, as over an extent of railroad track on a mountainside, for protection against snow. [SNOW[1] + SHED[1]]

snow·shoe (snō′shōō′), *n., v.,* **-shoed, -shoe·ing.** —*n.* **1.** a contrivance that may be attached to the foot to enable the wearer to walk on deep snow without sinking, esp. a light, racket-shaped frame across which is stretched a network of rawhide. **2.** See **Indian yellow** (def. 1). —*v.i.* **3.** to walk or travel on snowshoes. [SNOW[1] + SHOE] —**snow′sho′er,** *n.*

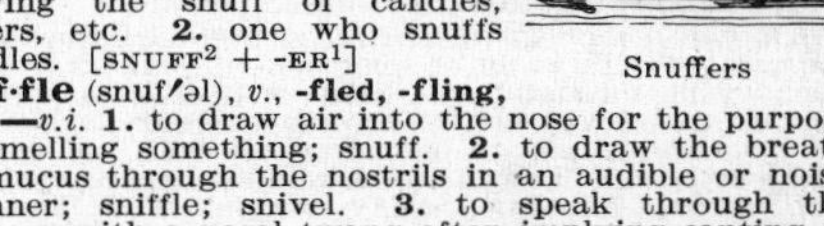
Snowshoes

snow·slide (snō′slīd′), *n.* an avalanche consisting largely or entirely of snow. Also, *esp. Brit.,* **snow-slip** (snō′slip′). [SNOW[1] + SLIDE]

snow′ smoke′. See **snow banner.**

Snows′ of Kilimanja′ro, The, a short story (1936) by Ernest Hemingway.

snow′ stake′, a calibrated wooden stake for measuring the depth of snow. Also called **snow scale.**

snow·storm (snō′stôrm′), *n.* a storm accompanied by a heavy fall of snow. [SNOW[1] + STORM]

snow·suit (snō′sōōt′), *n.* a child's one- or two-piece outer garment for cold weather, often consisting of heavily lined pants and jacket fitting snugly at the ankles, wrists, and neck, often with a hood. [SNOW[1] + SUIT]

snow′ tire′, an automobile tire with a deep tread to give increased traction on snow or ice.

snow′ train′, a train that takes passengers to and from a winter resort area.

snow′ tril′lium, a hardy, perennial herb, *Trillium nivale*, of the northeastern U.S., having small, white flowers.

snow-white (snō′hwīt′, -wīt′), *adj.* white as snow.

snow·y (snō′ē), *adj.,* **snow·i·er, snow·i·est. 1.** abounding in or covered with snow: *snowy fields.* **2.** characterized by snow, as the weather: *a snowy day.* **3.** pertaining to, consisting of, or resembling snow. **4.** of the color of snow; snow-white: *snowy skin.* **5.** immaculate; unsullied; stainless. [ME *snawy*, OE *snāwig*. See SNOW[1], -Y[1]] —**snow′i·ly,** *adv.* —**snow′i·ness,** *n.*

snow′y e′gret, a white egret, *Egretta thula*, of the warmer parts of the Western Hemisphere, formerly hunted in great numbers for its plumes or aigrettes.

snow′y owl′, a diurnal, arctic and subarctic owl, *Nyctea scandiaca*, having white plumage with dark brown markings.

snub (snub), *v.,* **snubbed, snub·bing,** *n., adj.* —*v.t.* **1.** to treat with disdain or contempt, esp. by ignoring. **2.** to put, force, etc., by doing this: *to snub one into silence.* **3.** to check (another's talk) or rebuke sharply. **4.** to check or stop suddenly (a rope or cable that is running out). **5.** to check (a boat, an unbroken horse, etc.) by means of a rope or line made fast to a post or other fixed object. **6.** to pull up or stop abruptly in such a manner. **7.** *Naut.* **a.** to slow (a vessel) by dragging an anchor through the water. **b.** to slow (a moving line) by the friction of a turn around a cleat or bollard. **c.** to attach a snub to (a mooring line). **8.** *Shipbuilding.* to gather in (the waterlines of a hull) abruptly at either end. —*n.* **9.** the act or an instance of snubbing. **10.** a disdainful affront, slight, or rebuff. **11.** a sudden check given to a rope or cable running out, a moving boat, or the like. **12.** *Naut.* a short length of strong elastic material, used esp. as a shock absorber on a mooring line. —*adj.* **13.** (of the nose) short and turned up at the tip. **14.** blunt. [ME < Scand; cf. OIcel *snubba* a rebuke] —**snub′ber,** *n.* —**snub′bing·ly,** *adv.*
—**Syn. 1.** slight. **3.** stop, reprove, reprimand. **10.** insult.

snub·by (snub′ē), *adj.,* **-bi·er, -bi·est. 1.** somewhat snub, as the nose. **2.** short and thick or wide; stubby; stumpy: *snubby fingers.* **3.** tending to snub people. [SNUB + -Y[1]] —**snub′bi·ness,** *n.*

snub-nosed (snub′nōzd′), *adj.* having a snub nose: *snub-nosed pliers.*

snuck (snuk), *Chiefly Dial.* pp. and pt. of **sneak.**

snuff[1] (snuf), *v.t.* **1.** to draw in through the nose by inhaling. **2.** to perceive by or as by smelling; sniff. **3.** to examine by smelling, as an animal does. —*v.i.* **4.** to draw air into the nostrils by inhaling, as in order to smell something; snuffle: *After snuffing around, he detected the source of the gas leak.* **5.** to draw powdered tobacco into the nostrils; take snuff. **6.** *Obs.* to express disdain, contempt, displeasure, etc., by sniffing (often fol. by *at*). —*n.* **7.** an act of snuffing; an inhalation through the nose; a sniff. **8.** smell, scent, or odor. **9.** a preparation of powdered tobacco, usually taken into the nostrils by inhalation. **10.** a pinch of such tobacco. **11. up to snuff,** *Informal.* **a.** *Brit.* not easily imposed upon; shrewd; sharp. **b.** up to a certain standard, as of health, performance, etc.; satisfactory: *This was once a fine restaurant, but the food now isn't nearly up to snuff.* [< MD *snuff(en)* (to) snuffle] —**snuff′ing·ly,** *adv.*

snuff[2] (snuf), *n.* **1.** the charred or partly consumed portion of a candlewick. **2.** a thing of little or no value, esp. if left over. —*v.t.* **3.** to cut off or remove the snuff of (candles, tapers, etc.). **4.** to extinguish (often fol. by *out*). **5. snuff out, a.** to extinguish: *to snuff out a candle.* **b.** to suppress; crush: *to snuff out opposition.* **c.** *Informal.* to die: *Greedy heirs waited for the old man to snuff out.* [ME *snoffe* < ?]

snuff·box (snuf′boks′), *n.* a box for holding snuff, esp. one small enough to be carried in the pocket. [SNUFF[1] + BOX[1]]

snuf·fer[1] (snuf′ər), *n.* **1.** one who snuffs or sniffs. **2.** one who takes snuff. [SNUFF[1] + -ER[1]]

snuf·fer[2] (snuf′ər), *n.* **1.** Usually, **snuffers.** an instrument for removing the snuff of candles, tapers, etc. **2.** one who snuffs candles. [SNUFF[2] + -ER[1]]

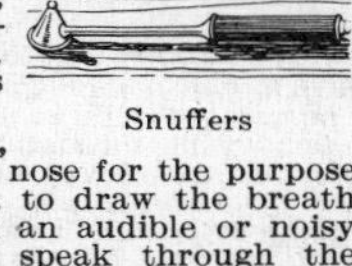
Snuffers

snuf·fle (snuf′əl), *v.,* **-fled, -fling,** *n.* —*v.i.* **1.** to draw air into the nose for the purpose of smelling something; snuff. **2.** to draw the breath or mucus through the nostrils in an audible or noisy manner; sniffle; snivel. **3.** to speak through the nose or with a nasal twang often implying canting or hypocritical speech. **4.** to whine; snivel. **5.** *Archaic.* to speak in a canting or hypocritical manner. —*v.t.* **6.** to utter in a snuffling or nasal tone. —*n.* **7.** an act of snuffling. **8. snuffles,** a condition of the nose, as from a cold, causing snuffling (usually prec. by *the*). **9.** a nasal tone of voice. [< Flem *snuffel(en)*, equiv. to *snuff(en)* (to) SNUFF[1] + *-el-* -LE] —**snuf′fler,** *n.* —**snuf′fling·ly,** *adv.* —**snuf′fly,** *adj.*

snuff′ stick′, *Dial.* a twig, stick, or brush used to apply snuff on the teeth or gums. Also called **snuff′ brush′.**

snuff·y (snuf′ē), *adj.,* **snuff·i·er, snuff·i·est. 1.** resembling snuff. **2.** soiled with snuff. **3.** given to the use of snuff. **4.** having an unpleasant appearance. **5.** having hurt feelings. **6.** easily displeased. [SNUFF[1] + -Y[1]] —**snuff′i·ness,** *n.*

snug (snug), *adj.,* **snug·ger, snug·gest,** *v.,* **snugged, snug·ging,** *adv., n.* —*adj.* **1.** warmly comfortable or cozy, as a place, accommodations, etc.: *a snug little house.* **2.** trim, neat, or compactly arranged, as a ship or its parts. **3.** fitting closely, as a garment: *a snug jacket.* **4.** more or less compact or limited in size, and sheltered or warm: *a snug harbor.* **5.** comfortably circumstanced, as persons. **6.** pleasant or agreeable, esp. in a small, exclusive way: *a snug coterie of writers.* **7.** enabling one to live in comfort: *a snug fortune.* **8.** allowing privacy; private. **9.** secret; concealed; well-hidden: *a snug hide-out.* —*v.i.* **10.** to lie closely or comfortably; nestle. —*v.t.* **11.** to make snug. **12.** *Naut.* to prepare for a storm by taking in sail, lashing deck gear, etc. (usually fol. by *down*). —*adv.* **13.** in a snug manner: *The shirt fit snug around the neck.* —*n.* **14.** *Brit.* a small, secluded room in a tavern, as for private parties. [< Scand; cf. OIcel *snöggr* short-haired, etc.] —**snug′ly,** *adv.* —**snug′ness,** *n.*
—**Syn. 2.** tidy, ordered, orderly. **6.** intimate, cozy. **10.** cuddle, snuggle. **11.** settle, arrange. **12.** secure.

snug·ger·y (snug′ə rē), *n., pl.* **-ger·ies.** *Brit.* **1.** a snug place or position. **2.** a comfortable or cozy room. Also, **snug′ger·ie.** [SNUG + -ERY]

snug·gies (snug′ēz), *n.* (*construed as pl.*) *Informal.* warm knitted underwear, esp. long underpants, for women or children. [SNUG + -IE + -S[4]]

snug·gle (snug′əl), *v.,* **-gled, -gling,** *n.* —*v.i.* **1.** to lie or press closely, as for comfort or from affection; nestle; cuddle. —*v.t.* **2.** to draw or press closely against, as for comfort or from affection. —*n.* **3.** the act of snuggling. [SNUG + -LE]

sny (snī), *v.,* **snyed, sny·ing,** *n., pl.* **snies.** *Shipbuilding.* —*v.t.* **1.** to give a warped form to (a shell plate) by forcing it onto a mold while hot. **2.** to form (shell planking) into an upward curve. —*n.* **3.** the upward curve of a timber or plank, esp. in a strake of shell planking toward the ends of a hull. [?]

sny·ing (snī′iŋg), *n.* *Shipbuilding.* an area of a wooden hull where the shell planking is snyed. [SNY + -ING[1]]

so[1] (sō), *adv.* **1.** in the way or manner indicated, described, or implied: *Do it so.* **2.** in that or this manner or fashion; thus: *So it turned out.* **3.** in the aforesaid state or condition: *It is broken and has long been so.* **4.** to the extent or degree indicated or suggested: *Do not walk so fast.* **5.** very or extremely: *I'm so sad. You are so kind.* **6.** very greatly: *My head aches so!* **7.** (used before an adverb or an adverbial clause and fol. by *as*) to such a degree or extent: *so far as I know.* **8.** having the purpose of: *a speech so commemorating the victory.* **9.** for this or that reason; hence; therefore: *She is ill, and so cannot come to the party. So what?* **10.** (used as

an affirmative to emphasize or confirm a previous statement) most certainly: *I said I would come, and so I will.* **11.** (used as an emphatic affirmative to contradict a previous statement) indeed; truly; too: *I was so at the party!* **12.** likewise or correspondingly; also; too: *If he is going, then so am I. I did it, and so did he.* **13.** in such manner as to follow or result from: *As he learned, so did he teach.* **14.** in the way that follows; in this way: *The audience was seated, and so the famous speech began.* **15.** in the way that precedes; in that way: *So ended the speech, and the listeners arose and cheered.* **16.** in such way as to end in: *So live your life that old age will bring you no regrets.* **17.** then; subsequently: *and so to bed.* **18. so as, a.** with the result or purpose (usually fol. by an infinitive): *to turn up the volume of the radio so as to drown out the noise from the next apartment.* **b.** *Dial.* provided that: *I like any flower, just so as it's real.* **19. so that, a.** with the effect or result. **b.** in order that: *He wrote so that they might expect him.* **20. so to speak.** See **speak** (def. 18). **21. so what?** See **what** (def. 2). —*conj.* **22.** in order that (often fol. by *that*): *Check carefully, so any mistakes will be caught.* **23.** with the result that (often fol. by *that*): *He checked carefully, so that the mistakes were caught.* **24.** on the condition that; if. —*pron.* **25.** such as has been stated: *to be good and stay so.* **26.** something that is about or near the persons or things in question, as in number or amount: *Of the original twelve, five or so remain.* —*interj.* **27.** (used as an exclamation of surprise, shock, discovery, inquiry, indifference, etc., according to the manner of utterance.) **28.** that will do! stop! —*adj.* **29.** true as stated or reported; conforming with reality or the fact: *Say it isn't so.* [ME; OE *swā*; c. D *zoo*, G *so*, Goth *swa*]
—**Syn. 9.** See **therefore.**
—**Usage. 5.** Although many object to the use of so to mean "very," it is inoffensive enough to be so used in all but the most formal context.
22. In ordinary speech and writing, THAT is frequently dropped after so, even though careful stylists usually include it.
23. The use of so in place of a SINCE . . . clause is widely regarded as poor, if not childish style: *Since we couldn't go anyway, he sold our tickets to someone else.* (Not, *We couldn't go anyway, so he sold our tickets to someone else.*)

so[2] (sō), *n.* *Music.* sol[1].

So., **1.** South. **2.** southern.

S.O., **1.** Signal Officer. **2.** Special Order. **3.** Standing Order.

s.o., **1.** seller's option. **2.** shipping order.

soak (sōk), *v.i.* **1.** to lie in and become saturated or permeated with water or some other liquid. **2.** to pass, as a liquid, through pores, holes, or the like (usually fol. by *in, through, out,* etc.): *The rain soaked through the tear in the umbrella.* **3.** to be thoroughly wet. **4.** to penetrate or become known to the mind or feelings (usually fol. by *in*): *The lesson didn't soak in.* **5.** *Informal.* to drink immoderately, esp. alcoholic beverages: *They were soaking at the bar.* —*v.t.* **6.** to place or keep in liquid in order to saturate thoroughly; steep. **7.** to wet thoroughly; saturate or drench. **8.** to permeate thoroughly, as liquid or moisture does. **9.** *Metall.* to heat (a piece) for reworking. **10.** *Informal.* to intoxicate oneself by drinking an excess of liquor. **11.** *Slang.* to beat hard; punish severely: *I was soaked for that mistake.* **12.** to absorb or take in or up by absorption (often fol. by *up*): *Blotting paper soaks up ink. He needs to soak up more facts.* **13.** to extract or remove by or as by soaking (often fol. by *out*): *to soak a stain out of a napkin.* **14.** *Slang.* to overcharge; tax exorbitantly: *He was soaked by the waiter.* **15.** *Slang.* to pawn. —*n.* **16.** the act or state of soaking or the state of being soaked. **17.** the liquid in which anything is soaked. **18.** *Slang.* a heavy drinker. **19.** *Australian.* any small area of land, as near a spring or at the foot of a hill, that becomes swamplike or holds water after a period of heavy rain. [ME *soke,* OE *sōcia(n)*; c. SUCK] —**soak′er,** *n.* —**soak′ing·ly,** *adv.*
—**Syn. 2, 4.** seep. **7.** steep. See **wet. 8.** infuse, penetrate. —**Ant. 7.** dry.

soak·age (sō′kij), *n.* **1.** the act of soaking. **2.** liquid which has seeped out or been absorbed. [SOAK + -AGE]

soak·ers (sō′kərz), *n.* (*construed as pl.*) absorbent, knitted briefs or shorts, often of wool, used as a diaper cover on infants. [SOAKER + -S[3]]

soak′ing pit′, *Metall.* (in a steel mill) a sunken furnace in which ingots are heated to a uniform temperature before rolling.

so-and-so (sō′ən sō′), *n., pl.* **so-and-sos. 1.** someone or something not definitely named: *Mr. So-and-so.* **2.** a vicious or disliked person (used as a euphemism): *Tell the old so-and-so to mind his own business.*

Soane (sōn), *n.* **Sir John,** 1753–1837, English architect.

soap (sōp), *n.* **1.** a substance used for washing and cleansing purposes, usually made by treating a fat with an alkali, as sodium or potassium hydroxide, and consisting chiefly of the sodium or potassium salts of the acids contained in the fat. **2.** any metallic salt of an acid derived from a fat. **3.** *Slang.* money, esp. as used for bribery in politics. **4. no soap,** *Slang.* the proposal, plan, etc., is rejected; to no effect: *He wanted me to vote for him, but I told him no soap.* —*v.t.* **5.** to rub, cover, lather, or treat with soap. [ME *sope,* OE *sāpe*; c. G *Seife,* D *zeep*] —**soap′less,** *adj.* —**soap′like′,** *adj.*

soap·bark (sōp′bärk′), *n.* **1.** a Chilean, rosaceous tree, *Quillaja Saponaria,* having evergreen leaves and small, white flowers. **2.** the inner bark of this tree, used as a substitute for soap. **3.** any of various other saponaceous barks, as of several tropical American, mimosaceous shrubs of the genus *Pithecolobium.* **4.** a plant yielding such bark. [SOAP + BARK[2]]

soap·ber·ry (sōp′ber′ē, -bə rē), *n., pl.* **-ries. 1.** the fruit of any of certain tropical and subtropical trees of the genus *Sapindus,* esp. *S. Saponaria,* used as a substitute for soap. **2.** a tree bearing such fruit. [SOAP + BERRY]

soap·box (sōp′boks′), *n.* **1.** Also, **soap′ box′.** a wooden box, as one in which soap had been packed, used as a temporary platform by an emotional speaker haranguing people on the streets. **2.** any place, platform, discussion, publication, etc., used by a person to make an impassioned speech, appeal, or harangue. —*v.i.* **3.** to address an audience from or as from a soapbox; make an impassioned speech or appeal. —*adj.* **4.** of or characteristic of an impassioned speech, appeal, or harangue. **5.** of or characteristic of one who speaks from or as from a soapbox; impassioned. [SOAP + BOX[1]]

soap′box der′by, a race for children driving motorless, wooden vehicles down a ramplike course, the vehicles being built by the drivers to resemble midget racing cars.

soap′ brick′, a brick of less than normal breadth, used to fill out a wall to the proper dimensions.

soap′ bub′ble, 1. a bubble of soapsuds. **2.** something that lacks substance or permanence.

soap′ dish′, a metal, glass, or plastic dish designed to hold a bar of soap, esp. as a bathroom or kitchen fixture attached to a sink, lavatory, or bathtub.

soap′ earth′, soapstone.

soap·fish (sōp′fish′), *n., pl.* (*esp. collectively*) **-fish,** (*esp. referring to two or more kinds or species*) **-fish·es.** any of several serranid fishes of the genus *Rypticus,* producing a body mucus that gives the skin a soapy quality, as *R. saponaceus,* found in the shallow waters of the Atlantic Ocean. [SOAP + FISH]

soap′ flakes′, small flakes or chips of soap commercially produced and packaged for washing laundry, dishes, etc. Also called **soap′ chips′.**

soap′ op′era (op′ər ə, op′rə), *Informal.* a serialized program presented on radio or television dramatizing the personal and domestic problems, successes, and failures of a fictional character, family, or group in a sentimental, melodramatic way. [so called from the fact that many such programs were sponsored by soap companies]

soap′ plant′, 1. a liliaceous herb, *Chlorogalum pomeridianum,* of California, the bulb of which was used by the Indians as a soap. **2.** any of various other plants having parts which can be used as a soap.

soap′ pow′der, soap produced and packaged in powdered form.

soap·stone (sōp′stōn′), *n.* a massive variety of talc with a soapy or greasy feel, used for hearths, washtubs, table tops, carved ornaments, etc. Also called **soap earth, steatite.** [SOAP + STONE]

soap·suds (sōp′sudz′), *n.* (*construed as pl.*) suds made with water and soap. [SOAP + SUDS] —**soap′suds′y,** *adj.*

soap·wort (sōp′wûrt′), *n.* an herb, *Saponaria officinalis,* whose leaves are used for cleansing. [SOAP + WORT[2]]

soap·y (sō′pē), *adj.,* **soap·i·er, soap·i·est. 1.** containing or impregnated with soap: *soapy water.* **2.** covered with soap or lather: *soapy dishes.* **3.** of the nature of soap; resembling soap: *a soft, soapy fiber.* **4.** pertaining to or characteristic of soap: *a clean, soapy smell.* [SOAP + -Y[1]] —**soap′i·ly,** *adv.* —**soap′i·ness,** *n.*

soar (sōr, sôr), *v.i.* **1.** to fly upward, as a bird. **2.** to fly at a great height, without visible movements of the pinions, as a bird. **3.** to glide along at a height, as an airplane. **4.** to rise or ascend to a height, as a mountain. **5.** to rise or aspire to a higher or more exalted level: *His hopes soared.* —*n.* **6.** the act or an instance of soaring. **7.** the height attained in soaring. [ME *sore* < MF *(e)ssor(er)* < VL **exaurāre,* equiv. to *ex-* EX-[1] + *aur(a)* air + *-āre* inf. suffix] —**soar′a·bil′i·ty,** *n.* —**soar′a·ble,** *adj.* —**soar′er,** *n.* —**soar′ing·ly,** *adv.*
—**Syn. 1.** See **fly**[1]. **4.** tower; mount.

soar·ing (sōr′ing, sôr′-), *adj.* *Heraldry.* (of a bird) represented as flying upward: *an eagle soaring.* Cf. **rising** (def. 3). [SOAR + -ING[2]]

so·a·ve (sō ä′vā; *It.* sô ä′ve), *n.* a dry, white wine from Verona, Italy. [< It < L *suavis* sweet]

sob (sob), *v.,* **sobbed, sob·bing,** *n.* —*v.i.* **1.** to weep with a sound caused by a convulsive catching of the breath. **2.** to make a sound resembling this. —*v.t.* **3.** to utter with sobs. **4.** to put, send, etc., by sobbing or with sobs: *to sob oneself to sleep.* —*n.* **5.** the act of sobbing; a convulsive catching of the breath in weeping. **6.** any sound suggesting this. [ME *sobb(en),* appar. imit.] —**sob′ber,** *n.* —**sob′bing·ly,** *adv.* —**sob′ful,** *adj.*
—**Syn. 1.** cry; blubber.

S.O.B., (*sometimes l.c.*) *Slang.* See **son of a bitch.** Also, **SOB**

so·be·it (sō bē′it), *conj.* *Archaic.* if it be so that; provided that. [SO[1] + BE + IT]

so·ber (sō′bər), *adj.* **1.** not intoxicated or drunk: *He insisted he was sober at the time.* **2.** habitually temperate, esp. in the use of liquor. **3.** quiet or sedate in demeanor, as persons. **4.** marked by seriousness, gravity, solemnity, etc., as of demeanor, speech, etc.: *a sober occasion.* **5.** subdued in tone, as color; not gay or showy, as clothes. **6.** free from excess, extravagance, or exaggeration: *sober facts.* **7.** showing self-control: *sober restraint.* **8.** sane or rational: *a sober solution to the problem.* —*v.t., v.i.* **9.** to make or become sober. [ME *sobre* < OF < L *sōbr(ius)*] —**so′ber·er,** *n.* —**so′ber·ing·ly,** *adv.* —**so′ber·ly,** *adv.* —**so′ber·ness,** *n.*
—**Syn. 2.** abstinent, abstemious. **4.** serious, quiet, sedate, subdued, staid. See **grave**[2]. **5.** somber, dull. **7.** composed, collected. **8.** reasonable, sound. —**Ant. 4.** gay.

so·ber-head·ed (sō′bər hed′id), *adj.* characterized by clear, logical thinking; not fanciful or capricious.

so·ber-mind·ed (sō′bər mīn′did), *adj.* self-controlled; sensible. —**so′ber-mind′ed·ness,** *n.*

so·ber·sid·ed (sō′bər sī′did), *adj.* solemn or grave in disposition, attitude, character, etc.; not given to humor, levity, or the like; serious-minded. [SOBER + SIDE[1] + -ED[3]]

so·ber·sides (sō′bər sīdz′), *n., pl.* **-sides.** (*construed as sing.*) *Slang.* a humorless or habitually serious person. [SOBER + SIDE[1] + -S[3]]

So·bies·ki (sô byes′kē), *n.* **John.** See **John III** (def. 2).

So·bor (sə bôr′), *n.* (*sometimes l.c.*) *Eastern Ch.* a council, synod, or convention. [< Russ; ORuss *sŭborŭ*]

So·bran·je (sô bʀän′yə), *n.* the national assembly of Bulgaria, consisting of a single chamber of elected deputies. [< Bulgarian: assembly]

so·bri·e·ty (sə brī′i tē, sō-), *n.* **1.** the state or quality of being sober. **2.** temperance or moderation, esp. in the use of alcoholic beverages. **3.** seriousness, gravity, or solemnity: *The parliament convened with traditional sobriety.* [ME *sobrietie* < L *sōbrietās,* equiv. to *sōbri(us)* SOBER + *-etās,* var. of *-itās* -ITY]

so·bri·quet (sō′brə kā′, -ket′, sō′brə kā′, -ket′; *Fr.* sô bʀē ke′), *n., pl.* **-quets** (-kāz′, -kets′, -kāz′, -kets′; *Fr.* -ke′). a nickname. Also, **soubriquet.** [< F < ?] —**so′bri·quet′i·cal,** *adj.*

sob′ sis′ter, 1. a journalist who writes a newspaper or magazine column devoted chiefly to human-interest stories described with sentimental pathos. **2.** a persistently sentimental do-gooder.

sob′ sto′ry, 1. an excessively sentimental human-interest story. **2.** an alibi or excuse, esp. one designed to arouse sympathy: *Instead of a new paint job, the landlord gave us another sob story about higher taxes.*

Soc., 1. socialist. **2.** (*often l.c.*) society. **3.** sociology.

soc·age (sok′ij), *n.* *Medieval Eng. Law.* a tenure of land held by the tenant in performance of specified services or by payment of rent, and not requiring military service. Also, **soc′cage.** [ME *sokage* < AF *socage,* equiv. to *soc* SOKE + *-age* -AGE]

soc·ag·er (sok′ə jər), *n.* a tenant holding land by socage; sokeman. [SOCAGE + -ER[1]]

so-called (sō′kôld′), *adj.* **1.** called or designated thus: *the so-called Southern bloc.* **2.** incorrectly called or styled thus: *our so-called intellectual leaders.*

soc·cer (sok′ər), *n.* a form of football played between two teams of 11 players, in which the ball may be advanced by kicking or by bouncing it off any part of the body but the arms and hands, except in the case of the goalkeepers who may use their hands to catch, carry, throw, or stop the ball. [(AS)SOC(IATION) + -ER[1]]

So·che (sō′chu′), *n.* a city in W Sinkiang, in W China, in a large oasis of the Tarim Basin. 80,000 (est. 1957). Also called **Yarkand.**

So·chi (sô′chi), *n.* a seaport in the SW RSFSR, in the S Soviet Union in Europe, on the Black Sea: resort. 174,000 (est. 1962).

so·cia·bil·i·ty (sō′shə bil′i tē), *n.* **1.** the act or an instance of being sociable. **2.** the quality, state, disposition, or inclination of being sociable. [SOCIABLE + -ITY]

so·cia·ble (sō′shə bəl), *adj.* **1.** inclined to associate with or be in the company of others. **2.** friendly or agreeable in company; companionable. **3.** characterized by or pertaining to companionship with others: *a sociable evening at the home of friends.* —*n.* **4.** *Chiefly Northern and Midland U.S.* an informal social gathering, esp. of members of a church. [< L *sociābil(is),* equiv. to *soci(āre)* (to) unite (deriv. of *socius* comrade) + *-ābilis* -ABLE] —**so′cia·ble·ness,** *n.* —**so′cia·bly,** *adv.*
—**Syn. 1.** See **social.**

so·cial (sō′shəl), *adj.* **1.** pertaining to, devoted to, or characterized by friendly companionship or relations: *a social club.* **2.** friendly or sociable, as persons or the disposition, spirit, etc. **3.** of, pertaining to, connected with, or suited to polite or fashionable society: *a social event.* **4.** living or disposed to live in companionship with others or in a community, rather than in isolation: *Man is a social being.* **5.** of or pertaining to human society, esp. as a body divided into classes according to worldly status: *social rank.* **6.** of or pertaining to the life, welfare, and relations of human beings in a community: *social problems.* **7.** noting or pertaining to activities designed to remedy or alleviate certain unfavorable conditions of life in a community, esp. among the poor. **8.** pertaining to or advocating socialism. **9.** *Zool.* living habitually together in communities, as bees, ants, etc. Cf. **solitary** (def. 8). **10.** *Bot.* growing in patches or clumps. **11.** *Rare.* occurring or taking place between allies or confederates. —*n.* **12.** a social gathering or party, esp. of or as given by an organized group: *a church social.* [< L *sociāl(is),* equiv. to *soci(us)* comrade + *-ālis* -AL[2]] —**so′cial·ly,** *adv.* —**so′cial·ness,** *n.*
—**Syn. 1.** amiable, companionable, genial, affable. SOCIAL, SOCIABLE agree in being concerned with the mutual relations of mankind living in an organized society. SOCIAL is a general word: *social laws, equals, advancement.* SOCIABLE means fond of company and society, companionable, genial, and affable, good at "mixing": *a friendly and sociable sort of person.* A SOCIAL evening is one spent enjoyably in company with others at a more or less formal event; a SOCIABLE evening is one spent companionably with perhaps only one person or a few. —**Ant. 4.** introverted, withdrawn.

so′cial anthropol′ogy. See **cultural anthropology.** —**so′cial anthropol′ogist.**

so′cial bee′, any of several bees, as the honeybees or bumblebees, that live together in communities. Cf. **solitary bee.**

so′cial class′, *Sociol.* a broad group in society having common economic, cultural, or political status.

so′cial climb′er, one who attempts to gain admission into a group with a higher social standing. —**so′cial climb′ing.**

so′cial con′tract, the voluntary agreement among individuals by which, according to any of various theories, as of Hobbes, Locke, or Rousseau, organized society is brought into being and invested with the right to secure mutual protection and welfare or to regulate the relations among its members. Also called **so′cial com′pact.**

so′cial control′, 1. *Sociol.* the enforcement of conformity by society upon its members, either by law or by social pressure. **2.** the influence of any element in social life working to maintain the pattern of such life.

So′cial Cred′it, *Econ.* the doctrine that under capitalism there is an inadequate distribution of purchasing power, for which the remedy lies in governmental control of retail prices and the distribution of national dividends to consumers.

so′cial danc′ing, dancing performed by couples or by groups, usually as a form of recreation.

So′cial Democ′racy, the principles and policies of a Social Democratic party.

So′cial Dem′ocrat, (esp. in Europe) a member of any of certain Social Democratic parties.

So′cial Democrat′ic par′ty, 1. *Hist.* a political party in Germany advocating a form of social organization based on the economic and political ideology of Karl Marx. **2.** any of several European political parties advocating a gradual transition to socialism or a modified form of socialism by and under democratic processes.

So′cial-Dem·o·crat′ic par′ty (sō′shəl dem′ə krat′ik), *U.S.* a political party, organized about 1897, that joined former members of the Socialist Labor party to form the Socialist party.

So′cial Democrat′ic Work′ingmen's par′ty, the name of the Socialist Labor party from 1874 to 1877.

so′cial differentia′tion, *Sociol.* the distinction made between social groups and persons on the basis of biological, physiological, and sociocultural factors, as sex, age, race, nationality, etc.

so′cial disease′, a disease ordinarily spread by social contact, esp. a venereal disease.

so′cial disorganiza′tion, *Sociol.* disruption or breakdown of the structure of social relations and values resulting in the loss of social controls over individual and group behavior, the development of social isolation and conflict, and a sense of estrangement or alienation from the mainstream of one's culture; the condition or state of anomie.

so′cial dis′tance, *Sociol.* the extent to which individuals or groups are removed from or excluded from participating in each other's lives.

so′cial envi′ronment, *Sociol.* the environment developed by man as contrasted with the natural environment; society as a whole, esp. in its relation to the individual.

so′cial e′vil, 1. anything detrimental to a society or its citizens, as alcoholism, organized crime, etc. **2.** (euphemistically) prostitution.

so′cial evolu′tion, *Sociol.* the gradual development of society and social forms, institutions, etc., usually through a series of peaceful stages. Cf. **revolution** (def. 2).

so′cial gos′pel, *Protestantism.* a movement in America, chiefly in the early part of the 20th century, stressing the social teachings of Jesus and their applicability to public life.

so′cial her′itage, *Sociol.* the entire inherited pattern of cultural activity present in a society.

so′cial insur′ance, any of various forms of insurance in which a government is an insurer, esp. such insurance that provides assistance to disabled or unemployed workers and to aged persons.

so′cial interac′tion, *Sociol.* the interstimulation and response taking place between individuals and between groups, with particular reference to cultural activity.

so·cial·ise (sō′shə līz′), *v.t., v.i.,* **-ised, -is·ing.** *Chiefly Brit.* socialize. —**so′cial·i·sa′tion,** *n.*

so·cial·ism (sō′shə liz′əm), *n.* **1.** a theory or system of social organization which advocates the vesting of the ownership and control of the means of production, capital, land, etc., in the community as a whole. **2.** procedure or practice in accordance with this theory. **3.** (in Marxist theory) the stage following capitalism in the transition of a society to communism, characterized by the imperfect implementation of collectivist principles. Cf. **utopian socialism.** [SOCIAL + -ISM]

so′cial isola′tion, *Sociol.* a state or process in which persons, groups, or cultures lose or do not have communication or cooperation with one another, often resulting in open conflict.

so·cial·ist (sō′shə list), *n.* **1.** an advocate or supporter of socialism. **2.** (*cap.*) *U.S.* a member of the Socialist party. —*adj.* **3.** socialistic. [SOCIAL(ISM) + -IST]

so·cial·is·tic (sō′shə lis′tik), *adj.* **1.** of or pertaining to socialists or socialism. **2.** in accordance with socialism. **3.** advocating or supporting socialism: *The Senator accused the school of socialistic teachings.* [SOCIAL(ISM) + -ISTIC] —**so′cial·is′ti·cal·ly,** *adv.*

So′cialist La′bor par′ty, *U.S.* a political party, organized in 1874, advocating the peaceful introduction of socialism.

So′cialist par′ty, 1. *U.S.* a political party advocating socialism, formed about 1900 chiefly by former members of the Socialist-Democratic party and the Socialist Labor party. **2.** any political party advocating socialism.

so·cial·ite (sō′shə līt′), *n.* a socially prominent person. [SOCIAL + -ITE[1]]

so·ci·al·i·ty (sō′shē al′i tē), *n.* **1.** social nature or tendencies as shown in the assembling of individuals in communities. **2.** the action on the part of individuals of associating together in communities. **3.** the state or quality of being social. [< L *socialitāt-* (s. of *socialitās*). See SOCIAL, -ITY]

so·cial·ize (sō′shə līz′), *v.,* **-ized, -iz·ing.** —*v.t.* **1.** to make social; make fit for life in companionship with others. **2.** to make socialistic; establish or regulate according to the theories of socialism. **3.** *Educ.* to treat as a group activity: *to socialize spelling quizzes.* —*v.i.* **4.** to associate or mingle sociably with others: *to socialize with one's fellow workers.* [SOCIAL + -IZE] —**so′cial·iz′a·ble,** *adj.* —**so′cial·i·za′tion,** *n.* —**so′cial·iz′er,** *n.*

so′cialized med′icine, any of various systems to provide the entire population with complete medical care through government subsidization of medical and health services, general regulation of these services, etc.

so·cial-mind·ed (sō′shəl mīn′did), *adj.* interested in or concerned with social conditions or the welfare of society. —**so′cial-mind′ed·ly,** *adv.* —**so′cial-mind′ed·ness,** *n.*

so′cial organiza′tion, *Sociol.* the structure of social relations within a group, usually the relations between its subgroups and institutions.

so′cial pathol′ogy, 1. a social factor, as poverty, old age, or crime, that tends to increase social disorganization and inhibit personal adjustment. **2.** the study of such factors and the social problems they produce.

so′cial proc′ess, *Sociol.* the means by which culture and social organization change or are preserved.

so′cial psychol′ogy, the psychological study of social behavior, esp. of the reciprocal influence of the individual and the group with which he interacts.

So′cial Reg′ister, *Trademark.* the book listing the names, addresses, clubs, etc., of the principal members of fashionable society in a given city or area.

so′cial sci′ence, 1. the study of society and social behavior. **2.** a science or field of study, as history, economics, etc., dealing with an aspect of society or forms of social activity. —**so′cial sci′entist.**

so′cial sec′retary, a personal secretary employed to make the social appointments and handle the personal correspondence of a person with an active social life.

so′cial secu′rity, 1. (*usually cap.*) *U.S.* a life-insurance and old-age pension plan maintained by the federal government through compulsory payments by specific employer and employee groups. **2.** the theory or practice of providing economic security and social welfare for the individual through government programs maintained by moneys from public taxation.

so′cial serv′ice, organized welfare efforts carried on under professional auspices by trained personnel. —**so′cial-serv′ice,** *adj.*

so′cial set′tlement, settlement (def. 13).

so′cial stud′ies, a course of instruction in an elementary or secondary school comprising such subjects as history, geography, civics, etc.

So′cial War′, 1. *Gk. Hist.* the war between Athens and its confederates, 357–355 B.C. **2.** *Rom. Hist.* the war in Italy between Rome and its allies, 90–88 B.C.

so′cial wasp′, any of several wasps, as the hornets or yellowjackets, that live together in a community. Cf. **solitary wasp.**

so′cial wel′fare, the various services provided by a government or its agencies for the benefit of the citizens.

so′cial work′, organized work directed toward the betterment of social conditions in the community, as by seeking to improve the condition of the poor, to promote the welfare of children, etc.

so′cial work′er, a person who is trained for professional social work.

so·ci·e·tal (sə sī′i tᵊl), *adj.* noting or pertaining to large social groups, or to their activities, customs, etc. [SOCIET(Y) + -AL[1]] —**so·ci′e·tal·ly,** *adv.*

soci′etal devel′opment, *Sociol.* the formation and transformation of social life, customs, institutions, etc.

so·cié·té a·no·nyme (sô syā tā′ A nô nēm′), *French.* a firm or corporation whose partners or stockholders have liability limited to their total investment. *Abbr.:* S.A., S/A [lit., anonymous society]

so·ci·e·ty (sə sī′i tē), *n., pl.* **-ties,** *adj.* —*n.* **1.** an organized group of persons associated together for religious, benevolent, cultural, scientific, political, patriotic, or other purposes. **2.** a body of individuals living as members of a community: *a society pledging equal rights for all.* **3.** the body of human beings generally, associated or viewed as members of a community: *the evolution of human society.* **4.** a highly structured system of human organization for large-scale community living that normally furnishes protection, continuity, security, and a national identity for its members: *our American society.* **5.** such a system characterized by its dominant economic class or form: *a middle-class society; an industrial society.* **6.** those with whom one has companionship. **7.** companionship; company: *to enjoy one's society.* **8.** the social life of wealthy, prominent, or fashionable persons. **9.** the social class that comprises such persons. **10.** the condition of those living in companionship with others, or in a community, rather than in isolation. **11.** a community. **12.** *Ecol.* a closely integrated group of social organisms of the same species held together by mutual dependence and exhibiting division of labor. **13.** *Eccles.* an ecclesiastical society. —*adj.* **14.** of, pertaining to, or characteristic of elegant society: *society column; society photographer.* [< MF *societe* < L *societāt-* (s. of *societās*), equiv. to *soci(us)* a companion + *-itāt-* -ITY] —**so·ci′e·ty·less,** *adj.* —**Syn. 1.** association, fellowship, fraternity, brotherhood, company. See **circle. 7.** fellowship.

Soci′ety Is′lands, a group of islands in the S Pacific: a part of French Polynesia; largest island, Tahiti. (Excluding minor islands) 51,092 (1956); 453 sq. mi. *Cap.:* Papeete.

Soci′ety of Friends′. See **Religious Society of Friends.**

Soci′ety of Je′sus. See under **Jesuit** (def. 1).

soci′ety verse′, light, graceful, entertaining poetry considered as appealing to polite society. [trans. of F *vers de société*]

So·cin·i·an (sō sin′ē ən), *n.* **1.** a follower of Faustus and Laelius Socinus who rejected a number of traditional Christian doctrines, as the Trinity, the divinity of Christ, and original sin, and who held that Christ was miraculously begotten and that salvation will be granted to those who adopt Christ's virtues. —*adj.* **2.** of or pertaining to the Socinians or their doctrines. [< NL *Sociniān(us)* of, pertaining to SOCINUS; see -IAN] —**So·cin′i·an·ism,** *n.*

So·ci·nus (sō sī′nəs), *n.* **Faus·tus** (fô′stəs), (*Fausto Sozzini*), 1539–1604, and his uncle, **Lae·li·us** (lē′lē əs), (*Lelio Sozzini*), 1525–62, Italian Protestant theologians and reformers.

socio-, a word element used, with the meaning "social," "sociological," or "society," in the formation of compound words: *sociometry; sociopath; socioeconomic.* [comb. form of L *socius* a fellow, companion, comrade; see -O-]

so·ci·o·cul·tur·al (sō′sē ō kul′chər əl, sō′shē ō-), *adj.* of, pertaining to, or signifying the combination or interaction of social and cultural elements. [SOCIO- + CULTURAL] —**so′ci·o·cul′tur·al·ly,** *adv.*

so·ci·o·ec·o·nom·ic (sō′sē ō ek′ə nom′ik, sō′shē-), *adj.* of, pertaining to, or signifying the combination or interaction of social and economic factors: *socioeconomic study; socioeconomic status.* [SOCIO- + ECONOMIC] —**so′ci·o·ec′o·nom′i·cal·ly,** *adv.*

so·ci·o·ge·net·ic (sō′sē ō jə net′ik, sō′shē ō-), *adj.* contributing to or affecting the course of social development: *a study of sociogenetic factors leading to dictatorship.* [SOCIO- + GENETIC] —**so·ci·o·gen·e·sis** (sō′sē ō jen′i sis, sō′shē-), *n.*

so·ci·o·gen·ic (sō′sē ō jen′ik, sō′shē-), *adj.* caused or influenced by society or social factors: *sociogenic problems.* [SOCIO- + GENIC]

so·ci·o·gram (sō′sē ə gram′, sō′shē-), *n.* *Sociol.* a sociometric diagram representing the pattern of relationships between individuals in a group, usually expressed in terms of which persons they prefer to associate with. [SOCIO- + -GRAM[1]]

sociol., 1. sociological. **2.** sociology.

so·ci·o·log·i·cal (sō′sē ə loj′i kəl, sō′shē-), *adj.* **1.** of, pertaining to, or characteristic of sociology and its methodology. **2.** dealing with social questions or problems, esp. focusing on cultural and environmental factors rather than on psychological or personal characteristics: *The sociological approach to art and literature has lost considerable favor since the 1930's.* **3.** organized and structured into a society; social. Also, **so′ci·o·log′ic.** [SOCIOLOG(Y) + -IC + -AL[1]] —**so′ci·o·log′i·cal·ly,** *adv.*

so·ci·ol·o·gism (sō′sē ol′ə jiz′əm, sō′shē-), *n.* an explanation, expression, concept, etc., characteristic of sociology, esp. when lacking reference to other disciplines concerned with human development. [SOCIOLOG(Y) + -ISM]

so·ci·ol·o·gis·tic (sō′sē ol′ə jis′tik, sō′shē-), *adj.* making reference only to the concepts of sociology, esp. emphasizing social factors to the exclusion of others. [SOCIOLOGIST + -IC] —**so′ci·ol′o·gis′ti·cal·ly,** *adv.*

so·ci·ol·o·gize (sō′sē ol′ə jīz′, sō′shē-), *v.t., v.i.,* **-gized, -giz·ing.** to explain, study, or interpret in sociological or social terms. [SOCIOLOG(Y) + -IZE]

so·ci·ol·o·gy (sō′sē ol′ə jē, sō′shē-), *n.* the science or study of the origin, development, organization, and functioning of human society; the science of the fundamental laws of social relations, institutions, etc. [< F *sociologie.* See SOCIO-, -LOGY] —**so′ci·ol′o·gist,** *n.*

so·ci·om·e·try (sō′sē om′i trē, sō′shē-), *n.* the measurement of attitudes of social acceptance or rejection through expressed preferences among members of a social grouping. [SOCIO- + -METRY] —**so·ci·o·met·ric** (sō′sē ə me′trik, sō′shē-), *adj.* —**so′ci·om′e·trist,** *n.*

so·ci·o·path (sō′sē ə path′, sō′shē-), *n.* a person who is hostile to society. [SOCIO- + -PATH] —**so′ci·o·path′ic,** *adj.* —**so·ci·op·a·thy** (sō′sē op′ə thē, sō′shē-), *n.*

so·ci·o·psy·cho·log·i·cal (sō′sē ō sī′kə loj′i kəl, sō′shē-), *adj.* of, pertaining to, or characterized by interrelated social and psychological factors. [SOCIO- + PSYCHOLOGICAL]

sock[1] (sok), *n., pl.* **socks** or, for 1, also **sox. 1.** a short stocking usually reaching to the calf or just above the ankle. **2.** a lightweight shoe worn by ancient Greek and Roman comic actors. **3.** comedy; comic drama. **4.** the art of the stage comedian; comic acting. Cf. **buskin** (def. 4). **5.** *Furniture.* a raised vertical area of a club or pad foot. [ME *socke,* OE *socc* << L *socc(us)*] —**sock′less,** *adj.* —**sock′less·ness,** *n.*

sock[2] (sok), *Slang.* —*v.t.* **1.** to strike or hit hard. **2. sock away,** to put into savings or reserve. **3. sock in,** to be unable to fly because of adverse weather conditions. —*n.* **4.** a hard blow. **5.** a very successful show, performance, actor, etc.; wow: *The show was a sock.* —*adj.* **6.** extremely successful: *a sock performance.* [?]

sock·dol·a·ger (sok dol′ə jər), *n.* *Slang.* **1.** something unusually large, heavy, etc. **2.** a decisive reply, argument, etc. **3.** a heavy, finishing blow: *His right jab is a real sockdolager.* [coinage based on SOCK[2] + DOXOLOGY (in slang sense of finish) + -ER[1]]

sock·er·oo (sok′ə rōō′), *n., pl.* **-oos.** *Slang.* a notable success: *Her performance was a sockeroo.* [SOCK[2] + -EROO]

sock·et (sok′it), *n.* **1.** a hollow part or piece for receiving and holding some part or thing. **2.** *Elect.* **a.** a device intended to hold an electric light bulb mechanically and connect it electrically to circuit wires. **b.** Also called **wall socket.** a socket placed in a wall to receive a plug that makes an electrical connection with supply wiring. **3.** *Anat.* **a.** a hollow in one part which receives another part: *the socket of the eye.* **b.** the concavity of a joint: *the socket of the hip.* **4.** *Carpentry.* a mortise in a dovetail joint. —*v.t.* **5.** to place in or fit with a socket. [ME *soket* < AF; OF *soc* plowshare < Celt; see -ET] —**sock′et·less,** *adj.*

sock′et eye′. See **rope socket.**

sock′et wrench′, a box wrench with a socket that is an extension of the shank. See illus. under **wrench.**

sock′eye salm′on (sok′ī′), an important food fish, *Oncorhynchus nerka,* found in the North Pacific. Also called **blueback salmon, red salmon, sock′eye′.** [< AmerInd (Salishan) *sukkegh* (by folk etymology)]

sock·o (sok′ō), *adj.* *Slang.* extremely impressive or successful: *a socko performance; a show with socko box office sales.* [SOCK[2] + *-o-* suffix of association]

sock′ set′, *Slang.* See **high-hat cymbals.**

sock′ suspend′er, *Brit.* garter (def. 1).

so·cle (sok′əl, sō′kəl), *n.* *Archit.* a low, plain part forming a base for a column, pedestal, or the like; plinth. [< F < It *zoccul(o)* wooden shoe, base of a pedestal < L *soccul(us),* equiv. to *socc(us)* SOCK[1] + *-ulus;* see -CLE]

soc·man (sok′mən, sōk′-), *n., pl.* **-men.** sokeman. [< AL *socmann(us),* var. of *sokemannus* SOKEMAN]

So·cor·ro (sə kôr′ō), *n.* a town in central New Mexico. 5271 (1960).

So·co·tra (sō kō′trə, sok′ə trə), *n.* an island in the Indian Ocean, S of Arabia: a part of the Protectorate of South Arabia. ab. 12,000; 1382 sq. mi. *Cap.:* Tamarida. Also, **Sokotra.** —**So·co′tran,** *n., adj.*

Soc·ra·tes (sok′rə tēz′), *n.* 469?–399 B.C., Athenian philosopher.

So·crat·ic (sə krat′ik, sō-), *adj.* **1.** of or pertaining to Socrates or his philosophy, followers, etc. —*n.* **2.** a follower of Socrates. **3.** any of the Greek philosophers influenced by Socrates. [< L *Socratic(us)* < Gk *Sōkratikós* of, pertaining to SOCRATES; see -IC] —**So·crat′i·cal·ly,** *adv.*

Socrat′ic i′rony, pretended ignorance in discussion.

Socrat′ic meth′od, the use of questions, as employed by Socrates, to develop a latent idea, as in the mind of a pupil, or to elicit admissions, as from an opponent, tending to establish a proposition.

sod[1] (sod), *n., v.,* **sod·ded, sod·ding.** —*n.* **1.** a section cut or torn from the surface of grassland, containing the matted roots of grass. **2.** the surface of the ground, esp. when covered with grass; turf; sward. —*v.t.* **3.** to cover with sods or sod. [ME < MD or MLG *sode* turf] —**sod′less,** *adj.*

sod[2] (sod), *v.* *Archaic.* pt. of **seethe.**

sod[3] (sod), *n.* *Chiefly Brit. Slang.* (*usually contemptuous*) **1.** sodomite; homosexual. **2.** chap; fellow; guy. **3.** child; kid; brat. Cf. **bugger.** [by shortening]

so·da (sō′də), *n.* **1.** See **sodium hydroxide. 2.** See **sodium monoxide. 3.** See **sodium carbonate** (def. 2). **4.** sodium, as in carbonate of soda. **5.** See **soda water. 6.** a drink made with soda water, flavoring, such as fruit or other syrups, and often ice cream, milk, etc. **7.** (in faro) the card turned up in the dealing box before one begins to play. [perh. < It < ML < Ar *suwwād* kind of plant; cf. MF *soulde, soude*] —**so′da·less,** *adj.*

so′da ash′, *Chem.* See **sodium carbonate** (def. 1).

so′da bis′cuit, 1. a biscuit having soda and sour milk or buttermilk as leavening agents. 2. See **soda cracker.**

so′da crack′er, a thin, crisp cracker or wafer prepared from a yeast dough which has been neutralized by baking soda.

so′da foun′tain, 1. a counter, as in a restaurant or drug store, at which sodas, ice cream, light meals, etc., are served. 2. a container from which soda water is dispensed, usually through faucets.

so′da jerk′, *Informal.* a person who prepares and serves sodas and ice cream at a soda fountain. Also, **so′da jerk′er.** [shortened form of *soda jerker*]

so′da lime′, a mixture of sodium hydroxide and calcium hydroxide. —**so′da-lime′,** *adj.*

so′da-lime feld′spar, plagioclase.

so·da·lite (sō′dᵊlīt′), *n.* a mineral, sodium aluminum silicate with sodium chloride, $3NaAlSiO_4 \cdot NaCl$, occurring massive and in crystals, usually blue in color and found in certain alkali-rich igneous rocks. [SODA + -LITE]

so·dal·i·ty (sō dal′i tē, sə-), *n., pl.* **-ties.** 1. fellowship; comradeship. 2. an association or society. 3. *Rom. Cath. Ch.* a lay society for religious and charitable purposes. [< L *sodalitāt-* (s. of *sodalitās*) companionship, equiv. to *sodāl(is)* companion + *-itāt-* -ITY]

so·da·mide (sō′də mīd′), *n.* *Chem.* See **sodium amide.** [SOD(IUM) + AMIDE]

so′da pop′, a carbonated and artificially flavored soft drink.

so′da wa′ter, 1. an effervescent beverage consisting of water charged with carbon dioxide and often flavored. 2. See **soda pop.** 3. a weak solution of sodium bicarbonate, taken as a stomachic.

sod·bust·er (sod′bus′tər), *n.* a farmer who works the soil. [SOD[1] + BUSTER]

sod·den (sod′ᵊn), *adj.* 1. soaked with liquid or moisture; saturated. 2. heavy, lumpy, or soggy, as food that is poorly cooked. 3. having a soaked appearance. 4. bloated, as the face. 5. expressionless, dull, or stupid. 6. lacking spirit or alertness; inert; torpid; listless. 7. *Archaic.* boiled. —*v.t., v.i.* 8. to make or become sodden. 9. *Archaic.* pp. of **seethe.** [ME *soden,* ptp. of to SEETHE] —**sod′den·ly,** *adv.* —**sod′den·ness,** *n.*

Sod·dy (sod′ē), *n.* **Frederick,** 1877–1956, English chemist: Nobel prize 1921.

Sö·der·blom (sœ′dər blŏŏm′), *n.* **Nathan,** 1866–1931, Swedish theologian: Nobel peace prize 1930.

sodio-, (in organic chemistry) a combining form of **sodium:** *sodio-cupric chloride.*

so·di·um (sō′dē əm), *n.* *Chem.* a soft, silver-white, metallic element which oxidizes rapidly in moist air, occurring in nature only in the combined state: used in the synthesis of sodium peroxide, sodium cyanide, and tetraethyllead. *Symbol:* Na; *at. wt.:* 22.9898; *at. no.:* 11; *sp. gr.:* 0.97 at 20°C. [< NL; see SOD(A), -IUM]

so′dium ac′id car′bonate, *Chem.* See **sodium bicarbonate.**

so′dium am′ide, *Chem.* a white, crystalline, water-insoluble, flammable powder, $NaNH_2$, used chiefly in the manufacture of sodium cyanide. Also, **sodamide.**

so′dium ammo′nium phos′phate, *Chem.* a colorless, odorless, crystalline, water-soluble solid, $NaNH_4HPO_4 \cdot 4H_2O$, originally obtained from human urine: used as a blowpipe flux in testing metallic oxides. Also called **microcosmic salt, salt of phosphorus.**

so′dium ar′senite, *Chem.* a white or grayish-white, water-soluble, poisonous powder, $NaAsO_2$, used chiefly in arsenical soaps for hides, as an insecticide, and as a weed-killer. Also called **sodium metaarsenite.**

so′dium ben′zoate, *Chem., Pharm.* a white, crystalline or granular, water-soluble powder, C_6H_5COONa, used chiefly as a food preservative and as an antiseptic. Also called **benzoate of soda.**

so′dium bicar′bonate, *Chem., Pharm.* a white, crystalline, water-soluble powder or granules, $NaHCO_3$, usually prepared by the reaction of soda ash with carbon dioxide or obtained from the intermediate product of the Solvay process by purification: used chiefly in the manufacture of sodium salts, baking powder, and beverages, as a laboratory reagent, as a fire extinguisher, and in medicine as an antacid. Also called **bicarbonate of soda, baking soda, sodium acid carbonate.**

so′dium bichro′mate, *Chem.* See **sodium dichromate.**

so′dium bo′rate, *Chem.* borax[1].

so′dium bro′mide, *Chem.* a white, crystalline, hygroscopic, water-soluble solid, NaBr, used chiefly in photography as a developer, and in medicine as a diuretic.

so′dium car′bonate, *Chem.* 1. Also called **soda ash.** an anhydrous, grayish-white, odorless, water-soluble powder, Na_2CO_3, usually obtained by the Solvay process and containing about 1 percent of impurities consisting of sulfates, chlorides, and bicarbonates of sodium: used in the manufacture of glass, ceramics, soaps, paper, petroleum, sodium salts, as a cleanser, for bleaching, and in water treatment. 2. Also called **sal soda, washing soda.** the decahydrated form of this salt, $Na_2CO_3 \cdot 10H_2O$, used similarly. 3. the monohydrated form of this salt, $Na_2CO_3 \cdot H_2O$, used similarly, esp. in photography.

so′dium chlo′rate, *Chem.* a colorless, water-soluble solid, $NaClO_3$, cool and salty to the taste, used chiefly in the manufacture of explosives and matches, as a textile mordant, an oxidizing and bleaching agent, and as a weak antiseptic for skin and mucous membranes.

so′dium chlo′ride, *Chem.* salt (def. 1).

so′dium ci′trate, *Chem.* a white, crystalline or granular, water-soluble, odorless solid, $Na_3C_6H_5O_7 \cdot 2H_2O$, having a cool, saline taste: used in photography, in soft drinks, and in medicine chiefly to prevent the coagulation of blood.

so′dium cy′anide, *Chem.* a white, crystalline, deliquescent, water-soluble, poisonous powder, NaCN, prepared by heating sodium amide with charcoal: used chiefly in casehardening alloys, in the leaching and flotation of ore, and in electroplating.

so′dium cyc′la·mate (sik′lə māt′, sī′klə-), *Chem.* a white, crystalline, water-soluble powder, $C_6H_{11}NHSO_3Na$, used chiefly as a sweetening agent, as in soft drinks, for low-calorie or diabetic diets. Also called **sodium cyclohexylsulfamate.** Cf. **calcium cyclamate.** [CYCL- + AM(IDE) + -ATE[2]]

so′dium cy·clo·hex·yl·sul′fa·mate (sī′klə hek′səl sul′fə māt′, sik′lə-), *Chem.* See **sodium cyclamate.** [CYCLO- + HEXYL + SULF(O)- + AM(IDE) + -ATE[2]]

so′dium dichro′mate, *Chem.* a red or orange crystalline, water-soluble solid, $Na_2Cr_2O_7 \cdot 2H_2O$, used as an oxidizing agent in the manufacture of dyes and inks, as a corrosion inhibitor, a mordant, a laboratory reagent, in the tanning of leather, and in electroplating. Also, **sodium bichromate.**

so′dium dithi′onite, *Chem.* See **sodium hydrosulfite.** [DI[1] + THIONITE]

so′dium eth·ox′ide (e thok′sīd, -sid), *Chem.* See **sodium ethylate.** [ETH(YL) + OXIDE]

so′dium eth′ylate, *Chem.* a white, hygroscopic powder, C_2H_5ONa, which is decomposed by water into sodium hydroxide and alcohol: used chiefly in organic synthesis. Also called **caustic alcohol, sodium ethoxide.**

so′dium eth·yl·mer·cu·ri·thi·o·sa·lic′y·late (eth′əl mər kyŏŏr′ə thī′ō sə lis′ə lāt′), *Pharm.* thimerosal. [ETHYL + MERCUR(Y) + -I- + THIO- + SALICYLATE]

so′dium flu′oride, a colorless, crystalline, water-soluble, poisonous solid, NaF, used chiefly in the fluoridation of water, as an insecticide, and as a rodenticide.

so′dium flu·o·ro·ac′e·tate (flōō′ə rō as′i tāt′, flŏŏr′ō-, flōr′ō-, flôr′ō-), *Chem.* a white amorphous, water-soluble, poisonous powder, FCH_2COONa, used for killing rodents. Also called **1080.**

so′dium glu′tamate, *Chem.* See **monosodium glutamate.**

so′dium hydrosul′fite, *Chem.* a white, crystalline, water-soluble powder, $Na_2S_2O_4$, used as a reducing agent, esp. in dyeing, and as a bleach. Also called **hydrosulfite, sodium dithionate, sodium hyposulfite.**

so′dium hydrox′ide, *Chem.* a white, deliquescent, water-soluble solid, NaOH, usually in the form of lumps, sticks, chips, or pellets, which upon solution in water generates heat: used chiefly in the manufacture of other chemicals, rayon, film, soap, as a laboratory reagent, and in medicine as a caustic. Also called **caustic soda.**

so′dium hyposul′fite, *Chem.* 1. See **sodium thiosulfate.** 2. See **sodium hydrosulfite.**

so′dium i′odide, *Chem.* a colorless or white, crystalline, deliquescent, water-soluble solid, NaI, used chiefly in the manufacture of photographic emulsions, in organic synthesis, and as a disinfectant in veterinary medicine.

so′dium lamp′, *Elect.* See **sodium-vapor lamp.**

so′dium met·a·ar′se·nite (met′ə är′sə nīt′), *Chem.* See **sodium arsenite.**

so′dium meth′ylate, *Chem.* a white, free-flowing, flammable powder, CH_3ONa, decomposed by water to sodium hydroxide and methyl alcohol: used chiefly in organic synthesis. Also called **so′dium methox′ide.**

so′dium monox′ide, *Chem.* a white powder, Na_2O, that reacts violently with water to produce sodium hydroxide. Also called **sodium oxide.**

so′dium ni′trate, *Chem.* a crystalline, water-soluble compound, $NaNO_3$, which occurs naturally as Chile saltpeter: used in fertilizers, explosives, and glass.

so′dium ox′ide, *Chem.* See **sodium monoxide.**

So′dium Pen′tothal, *Pharm., Trademark.* the sodium salt of Pentothal; sodium thiopental. Cf. **thiopental.**

so′dium perbo′rate, *Chem.* a white, crystalline, water-soluble solid, $NaBO_2 \cdot H_2O_2 \cdot 3H_2O$ or $NaBO_3 \cdot 4H_2O$, used chiefly as a bleaching agent and disinfectant. Also called **perborax.**

so′dium perox′ide, *Chem.* a yellowish-white, hygroscopic, water-soluble powder, Na_2O_2, used chiefly as a bleaching agent and as an oxidizing agent.

so′dium phos′phate, *Chem.* 1. Also called **monobasic sodium phosphate.** a white, crystalline, slightly hygroscopic, water-soluble powder, NaH_2PO_4, used chiefly in dyeing and in electroplating. 2. Also called **dibasic sodium phosphate.** a water-soluble compound which in its anhydrous form, Na_2HPO_4, occurring as a white, crystalline, hygroscopic powder, is used chiefly in the manufacture of ceramic glazes, enamels, baking powder, and cheeses, and which in its hydrated form, $Na_2HPO_4 \cdot xH_2O$, occurring as clear colorless crystals, is used chiefly in the manufacture of dyes, fertilizers, detergents, and pharmaceuticals. 3. Also called **tribasic sodium phosphate.** a water-soluble compound, $Na_3PO_4 \cdot 12H_2O$, occurring as colorless crystals: used chiefly in the manufacture of water-softening agents, detergents, paper, and textiles.

so′dium polysul′fide, *Chem.* a yellow-brown, water-soluble, granular powder, Na_2S_n, used chiefly in the manufacture of sulfur dyes, insecticides, and synthetic rubber.

so′dium pro′pionate, *Chem.* a transparent, crystalline, water-soluble powder, CH_3CH_2COONa, used in foodstuffs to prevent mold growth, and in medicine as a fungicide.

so′dium pyrobo′rate, *Chem.* borax. [PYRO- + BORATE]

so′dium sil′icate, *Chem.* any of several water-soluble compounds of formulas varying in ratio from $Na_2O \cdot 3.75SiO_2$ to $2Na_2O \cdot SiO_2$, and occurring as white powders, as cloudy or clear, viscous-to-fluid liquids, or as lumps: used chiefly in dyeing, printing, and fireproofing textiles and in the manufacture of paper products and cement.

so′dium sul′fate, *Chem.* a white, crystalline, water-soluble solid, Na_2SO_4, used chiefly in the manufacture of dyes, soaps, detergents, glass, and ceramic glazes.

so′dium sul′fide, *Chem.* a yellow or brick-red, crystalline, deliquescent, water-soluble solid, Na_2S, used chiefly in the manufacture of dyes, soaps, and rubber, as a depilatory for leather, and in the flotation of lead and copper ores.

so′dium sul′fite, *Chem.* a white, crystalline, water-soluble solid, Na_2SO_3, used chiefly as a food preservative, as a bleaching agent and as a developer in photography.

so′dium tetrabo′rate, *Chem.* borax. [TETRA- + BORATE]

so′dium thiocy′anate, *Chem., Pharm.* a white powder or colorless deliquescent crystals, NaSCN, used chiefly in organic synthesis and in medicine in the treatment of hypertension.

so′dium thiosul′fate, *Chem.* a white, crystalline, water-soluble powder, $Na_2S_2O_3 \cdot 5H_2O$, used as a bleach and in photography as a fixing agent. Also called **antichlor, hypo, hyposulfite, sodium hyposulfite.**

so′dium-va·por lamp′ (sō′dē əm vā′pər), *Elect.* an electric lamp in which sodium vapor is activated by current passing between two electrodes, producing a yellow, glareless light: used on streets and highways. Also called **sodium lamp.**

Sod·om (sod′əm), *n.* 1. an ancient city destroyed, with Gomorrah, because of its wickedness. Gen. 18–19. 2. any very sinful, corrupt, vice-ridden place.

So·do·ma, Il, (ēl sô′dô mä), **Gio·van·ni An·to·nio de Baz·zi** (jô vän′nē än tô′nyô de bät′tsē), 1477–1549, Italian painter.

Sod·om·ite (sod′ə mīt′), *n.* 1. an inhabitant of Sodom. 2. (*l.c.*) one who practices sodomy. [ME < MF < LL *Sodomīt(a)* < Gk *Sodomī́tēs.* See SODOM, -ITE[1]]

sod·om·y (sod′ə mē), *n.* 1. unnatural, esp. anal, copulation with a human or an animal. 2. copulation of a human with an animal; bestiality. [ME *sodomie* < OF. See SODOM, -Y[3]] —**sod·o·mit·i·cal** (sod′ə mit′i kəl), **sod′o·mit′ic,** *adj.* —**sod′o·mit′i·cal·ly,** *adv.*

Soe·kar·no (sōō kär′nō), *n.* Sukarno.

Soem·ba (sōōm′bä), *n.* Dutch name of **Sumba.**

Soem·ba·wa (sōōm bä′wä), *n.* Dutch name of **Sumbawa.**

Soen′da Is′lands (sōōn′dä). See **Sunda Islands.**

Soe·ra·ba·ja (sōō′rä bä′yä), *n.* Dutch name of **Surabaya.**

so·ev·er (sō ev′ər), *adv.* at all; in any case; of any kind; in any way (used with generalizing force after *who, what, when, where, how, any, all,* etc., sometimes separated by intervening words): *Choose what thing soever you please.* [SO[1] + EVER]

-soever, a combining form of **soever:** *whatsoever.*

so·fa (sō′fə), *n.* a long, upholstered couch with a back and two arms or raised ends. [< Ar *ṣuffah* platform used as a seat or Turk *sofa*]

so′fa bed′, a sofa having a back that can be lowered flush with the seat so as to form a bed. Also, **so′fa-bed′.**

so·far (sō′fär), *n.* a system for determining a position at sea by exploding a charge under water and measuring the time the shock waves take to reach three widely separated shore stations at known distances from each other. [*so(und) f(ixing) a(nd) r(anging)*]

so′fa ta′ble. See **davenport table.**

so·fer (sō′fər), *n., pl.* **-fer·im** (-fər im). (*often cap.*) *Judaism.* scribe[1] (def. 3). [< Heb]

sof·fit (sof′it), *n.* *Archit.* the underside of an architectural feature, as a beam, arch, ceiling, vault, or cornice. [< F *soffite* < It *soffitt(o)* < LL **suffict(us)* < L *suffixus,* equiv. to *suf-* SUF- + *fig-* fasten + *-t-* ptp. suffix]

sof′fit brick′, a brick used with metal reinforcement to form a soffit, having one of the lengthwise edges rabbeted.

sof·frit·to (sō frē′tō; *It.* sôf frēt′tô), *n.* *Italian Cookery.* a base for stews and soups, consisting of hot oil, butter, or fat in which a chopped onion or crushed garlic clove has been browned, often with the addition of chopped parsley, celery, and carrot. Also called **battuto.** [< It, ptp. of *soffrigere,* var. of *suffrigere,* equiv. to *suf-* SUF- + *frigere* to fry]

So·fi·a (sō′fē ə, sō fē′ə *or, for 2,* sō fī′ə), *n.* 1. Also **So·fi·ya** (*Bulg.* sô′fē yä′). a city in and the capital of Bulgaria, in the W part. 724,600 (est. 1963). 2. Also, **Sophia, Sophie.** a girl's given name.

S. of Sol., Song of Solomon.

soft (sôft, soft), *adj.* 1. yielding readily to touch or pressure; easily penetrated, divided, or changed in shape; not hard or stiff: *a soft pillow.* 2. relatively deficient in hardness, as metal, wood, etc. 3. smooth and agreeable to the touch; not rough or coarse: *a soft fabric; soft skin.* 4. producing agreeable sensations; pleasant or comfortable: *soft slumber.* 5. low or subdued in sound; gentle and melodious: *soft music; a soft voice.* 6. not harsh or unpleasant to the eye; not glaring: *soft light; a soft color.* 7. not hard or sharp: *soft outlines.* 8. gentle or mild, as wind, rain, etc.: *soft breezes.* 9. genial or balmy, as climate, air, etc. 10. gentle, mild, warm-hearted, or compassionate: *a soft, grandmotherly woman.* 11. smooth, soothing, or ingratiating: *soft words.* 12. not harsh or severe, as a penalty or demand. 13. responsive or sympathetic to the feelings, emotions, needs, etc., of others; tender-hearted. 14. sentimental or flowery, as language: *soft, meaningless talk.* 15. not strong or robust; delicate; incapable of great endurance or exertion: *He was too soft for the Marines.* 16. *Informal.* easy; involving little effort; not difficult, laborious, trying, or severe: *a soft job.* 17. *Informal.* easily influenced or swayed; easily imposed upon; impressionable. 18. (of water) relatively free from mineral salts that interfere with the action of soap. 19. (of money) paper as distinguished from metal. 20. (of a currency) subject to sharp or unusual fluctuations in value. 21. (of a market) subject to a steady decline in prices. 22. *Metall.* (of solder) fusing readily. 23. *Photog.* **a.** (of a photographic image) having delicate gradations of tone. **b.** (of a focus) lacking in sharpness. **c.** (of a lens) unable to be focused sharply. 24. *Phonet.* **a.** (of consonants) lenis, esp. lenis and voiced. **b.** (of *c* and *g*) pronounced as in *cent* and *gem.* **c.** (of consonants in Slavic languages) palatalized. Cf. **hard** (def. 34). 25. *Mil.* (of a missile-launching base) aboveground and relatively unprotected from enemy attack. 26. *Rocketry.* (of a landing of a space vehicle) gentle; not harmful to the vehicle or its contents, usually made at a velocity of not more than 20 miles per hour: *a soft landing on the moon.* 27. foolish or stupid: *to be soft in the head.* 28. **be soft on someone,** *Informal.* to be amorously inclined toward a person; have an affection for: *He's been soft on her for years.* —*n.* 29. that which is soft or yielding; the soft part. 30. softness. —*adv.* 31. in a soft manner. —*interj.* *Archaic.* 32. be quiet! hush! 33. not so fast! stop! [ME *softe,* OE *sōfte;* c. G *sanft*] —**soft′ly,** *adv.* —**soft′ness,** *n.*

—**Syn. 1.** pliable, plastic, malleable. **5.** mellifluous, dulcet, sweet. **10.** tender, sympathetic. **11.** mollifying. **15.** weak, feeble. **17.** compliant, irresolute, submissive. —**Ant. 1.** hard.

sof·ta (sôf′tə, sof′-), *n.* a Turkish Muslim theological student. [< Turk < Pers *sōkhta*, lit., fired (by love of learning)]

soft′ ar′mor, quilted fabric used as armor.

soft·ball (sôft′bôl′, soft′-), *n.* **1.** a form of baseball played on a smaller diamond with a larger and softer ball. **2.** the ball itself. [SOFT + BALL[1]]

soft·board (sôft′bōrd′, -bôrd′, soft′-), *n.* a soft, porous-particle board. [SOFT + BOARD]

soft-boiled (sôft′boild′, soft′-), *adj. Cookery.* (of an egg) boiled in the shell not long enough to cause the yolk or white to solidify, usually less than five minutes.

soft′ chan′cre, *Pathol.* chancroid.

soft′ clam′. See **soft-shell clam.**

soft′ coal′. See **bituminous coal.**

soft-cov·er (sôft′kuv′ər, soft′-), *n., adj.* paperback.

soft′ drink′, a beverage that is not alcoholic or intoxicating and is usually carbonated, as root beer, ginger ale, etc.

sof·ten (sô′fən, sof′ən), *v.t.* **1.** to make soft or softer. —*v.i.* **2.** to become soft or softer. [ME; see SOFT, -EN[1]] —**Syn. 1.** melt; mollify, mitigate, soothe, alleviate, calm, quiet, ease, allay, abate, temper, dull. —**Ant. 1, 2.** harden.

sof·ten·er (sô′fə nər, sof′ə-), *n.* **1.** one who or that which softens. **2.** *Chem.* **a.** any admixture to a substance for promoting or increasing its softness, smoothness, or plasticity. **b.** See **water softener.** [SOFTEN + -ER[1]]

sof′tening of the brain′, *Pathol.* **1.** a softening of the cerebrum, caused by impairment of the blood supply; encephalomacia. **2.** *Obs.* dementia associated with general paresis.

soft-finned (sôft′find′, soft′-), *adj. Ichthyol.* having fins supported by articulated rays rather than by spines, as a malacopterygian.

soft′ fo′cus, *Photog.* a focus, often created by a specifically ground lens, which results in an image that is recognizable but somewhat blurred or diffused.

soft-fo·cus (sôft′fō′kəs, soft′-), *adj. Photog.* formed with or characterized by a soft focus or focuses.

soft′ goods′, merchandise of limited durability, as textiles, carpets, clothing, etc. Cf. **hard goods.**

soft′ ground′, **1.** an etching ground usually mixed with tallow. Cf. **hard ground. 2.** a technique of etching in which a design is drawn on paper placed on a plate covered with a soft ground, resulting in a granular effect resembling pencil, chalk, or crayon.

soft′ hail′. See **snow pellets.**

soft-head·ed (sôft′hed′id, soft′-), *adj.* foolish; stupid. —**soft′head′,** *n.* —**soft′-head′ed·ness,** *n.*

soft-heart·ed (sôft′här′tid, soft′-), *adj.* very sympathetic or responsive; generous in spirit: *a soft-hearted judge.* —**soft′-heart′ed·ly,** *adv.* —**soft′-heart′ed·ness,** *n.*

soft·ie (sôf′tē, sof′-), *n.* softy.

soft·ish (sôf′tish, sof′-), *adj.* somewhat or relatively soft. [SOFT + -ISH[1]]

soft′ nose′ stem′, *Shipbuilding.* See **fashion plate stem.**

soft′ pal′ate. See under **palate** (def. 1).

soft′ paste′, any of a variety of artificial porcelains, usually incorporating glass or glass ingredients. French, **pâte tendre.** Cf. **hard paste.**

soft′ patch′, a temporary patch on a vessel that has been hulled.

soft′ ped′al, **1.** Also called **una corda pedal.** a pedal, as in a piano, for reducing tonal volume. **2.** *Informal.* something that restrains or dampens: *to put a soft pedal on one's enthusiasm.*

soft-ped·al (sôft′ped′əl, soft′-), *v.,* **-aled, -al·ing** or (*esp. Brit.*) **-alled, -al·ling.** —*v.i.* **1.** to use the soft pedal. —*v.t.* **2.** to soften the sound of by using the soft pedal. **3.** *Informal.* to tone or play down; to make less strong, as an idea, fact, or the like: *The dean soft-pedaled the reports of cheating.* [v. use of n. phrase *soft pedal*]

soft′-rock geol′ogy (sôft′rok′, soft′-), geology dealing with sedimentary rocks. Cf. **hard-rock geology.**

soft′ rot′, *Plant Pathol.* a disease of fruits and vegetables, characterized by a soft, watery decay of affected parts, caused by any of several bacteria or fungi.

soft′ sell′, a method of advertising or selling which is quietly persuasive, subtle, and indirect (opposed to *hard sell*).

soft-shell (sôft′shel′, soft′-), *adj.* **1.** Also, **soft′-shelled′.** having a soft, flexible, or fragile shell, as a crab having recently molted. —*n.* **2.** a soft-shell animal, esp. a soft-shell crab.

soft′-shell clam′, an edible clam, *Mya arenaria,* found on both coasts of North America, having an oval, relatively thin, whitish shell. Also called **long clam, soft clam, steamer, steamer clam.**

soft′-shell crab′, a crab, esp. the blue crab, that has recently molted, therefore having a soft, edible shell.

soft′-shelled tur′tle, any of numerous aquatic turtles of the family *Trionychidae,* found in North America, Asia, and Africa, having the shell covered with flexible, leathery skin instead of horny plates.

soft-shoe (sôft′shōō′, soft′-), *adj.* of, pertaining to, or characteristic of tap dancing done in soft-soled shoes, without taps.

soft′ shoul′der, the unpaved edge of a road.

soft′ sign′, **1.** the Cyrillic letter (Ь) as used in Russian to indicate that the preceding consonant is palatalized. **2.** the same symbol used for the front vowel of Old Slavic from which this Russian usage and phenomenon are historically derived.

soft′ soap′, **1.** the semifluid soap produced when potassium hydroxide is used in the saponification of a fat or an oil. **2.** *Informal.* persuasive talk; flattery: *It's obvious that he uses soft soap to get his own way.*

soft-soap (sôft′sōp′, soft′-), *v.t.* **1.** to apply soft soap to. **2.** *Informal.* to cajole; flatter. —*v.i.* **3.** to use soft soap in washing. [v. use of n. phrase *soft soap*]

soft-soap·er (sôft′sō′pər, soft′-), *n. Informal.* one who flatters or cajoles, esp. for reasons of self-interest or personal advantage: *He's a soft-soaper who specializes in rich, elderly women.* [SOFT-SOAP + -ER[2]]

soft′ sol′der, a solder fusible at temperatures below 700°F, generally an alloy of lead and tin. Cf. **hard solder.**

soft-spo·ken (sôft′spō′kən, soft′-), *adj.* **1.** (of persons) speaking with a soft or gentle voice; mild: *a soft-spoken person who never showed his anger.* **2.** (of words) softly or mildly spoken; persuasive.

soft′ spot′, **1.** a weak or vulnerable position, place, condition, etc.: *a soft spot in their fortifications; a soft spot in the economy.* **2.** emotional susceptibility: *a soft spot for dogs and babies.*

soft′ tick′, any of numerous ticks of the family *Argasidae,* lacking a dorsal shield and having the mouthparts on the ventral side of the head. Cf. **hard tick.**

soft′ touch′, *Slang.* **1.** a person who is easily convinced, esp. to give or lend money: *He's a pathetically soft touch for charities.* **2.** a person who is easily influenced, duped, or imposed upon: *She's a soft touch for anybody with a sob story.* **3.** a person, team, etc., that is easily defeated: *The Mets are a soft touch for almost any ball team.* **4.** a task or activity that is easily or quickly done, esp. a job that pays well and requires little work.

soft′ tube′, *Electronics.* a vacuum tube not highly evacuated, with the residual gas significantly affecting the performance of the tube. Cf. **hard tube.**

soft·ware (sôft′wâr′, soft′-), *n. Computer Technol.* any of the written programs, flow charts, etc., including general subroutines, that may be inserted in computer programs. Cf. **hardware** (def. 4). [SOFT + WARE[1]]

soft′ wheat′, a wheat characterized by soft, starchy kernels that yield a flour used in making pastry, breakfast cereals, etc.

soft·wood (sôft′wŏŏd′, soft′-), *n.* **1.** any wood which is relatively soft or easily cut. **2.** a tree yielding such a wood. **3.** *Forestry.* a coniferous tree or its wood. —*adj.* **4.** of, pertaining to, or made of softwood. [SOFT + WOOD[1]]

soft·y (sôf′tē, sof′-), *n., pl.* **-ties.** *Informal.* **1.** a person easily stirred to sentiment or tender emotion. **2.** a man who is effeminate or lacks virility. **3.** a weak, silly, or foolish person. Also, **softie.** [SOFT + -Y[2]]

Sog·di·an (sog′dē ən), *n.* **1.** a native or inhabitant of Sogdiana. **2.** the extinct Iranian language of Sogdiana. [< L *Sogdiān(us).* See SOGDIANA, -IAN]

Sog·di·a·na (sog′dē ā′nə, -an′ə), *n.* a province of the ancient Persian empire between the Oxus and Jaxartes rivers: now in the SW Soviet Union in Asia. *Cap.:* Samarkand.

sog·gy (sog′ē), *adj.,* **-gi·er, -gi·est. 1.** soaked; thoroughly wet; sodden. **2.** damp and heavy, as poorly baked bread. **3.** spiritless, heavy, dull, or stupid: *a soggy novel.* [dial. *sog* bog + -Y[1]; cf. Norw (dial.) *soggjast* to get soaked] —**sog′gi·ly,** *adv.* —**sog′gi·ness,** *n.*

So·ho (sō′hō, sō hō′), *n.* a district in London, England, including Soho Square: a predominantly foreign section since 1685; noted for its restaurants.

So′ho Square′, a formerly fashionable residential district of London, England.

Soh·rab and Rus·tum (sō′räb; rōō′stəm), a narrative poem (1853) by Matthew Arnold.

soi-di·sant (swa dē zäɴ′), *adj. French.* **1.** calling oneself thus; self-styled. **2.** so-called or pretended.

soi·gné (swän yā′; *Fr.* swa nyā′), *adj.* **1.** carefully or elegantly done, operated, or designed. **2.** well-groomed. Also, **soi·gnée′.** [< F, adj. use of ptp. of *soigner* to take care of < ML *soniāre*]

soil[1] (soil), *n.* **1.** the portion of the earth's surface consisting of disintegrated rock and humus. **2.** a particular kind of earth: *sandy soil.* **3.** the ground as producing vegetation or as cultivated for its crops: *fertile soil.* **4.** a country, land, or region: *an act committed on American soil.* **5.** the ground or earth: *tilling the soil.* **6.** any place or condition providing the opportunity for growth or development: *Poverty provides the soil for crime.* [ME *soile* < AF *soyl* < L *sol(ium)* seat, confused with *solum* ground] —**soil′less,** *adj.*

soil[2] (soil), *v.t.* **1.** to make unclean, dirty, or filthy, esp. on the surface: *to soil one's clothes while gardening.* **2.** to smirch, smudge, or stain: *The ink soiled his hands.* **3.** to sully or tarnish, as with disgrace; defile morally, as with sin. —*v.i.* **4.** to become soiled: *White soils too easily.* —*n.* **5.** the act or fact of soiling. **6.** the state of being soiled. **7.** a spot, mark, or stain caused by soiling. **8.** dirty or foul matter; filth; sewage. **9.** ordure; manure. [ME *soil(en)* < OF *souill(er), soill(ier)* (to) dirty < LL **suculāre,* equiv. to *sus* pig + *-culus* -CLE + *-āre* inf. ending]

soil[3] (soil), *v.t.* **1.** to feed (cattle, horses, etc.) freshly cut green fodder in order to fatten them. **2.** to purge (horses, cattle, etc.) by feeding them green food. [?]

soil·age (soi′lij), *n.* grass or leafy plants raised as feed for fenced-in livestock. [SOIL[3] + -AGE]

soil′ bank′, a plan providing cash payments to farmers who cut production of certain surplus crops in favor of soil-enriching ones. —**soil′-bank′,** *adj.*

soil′ condi′tioner, any of various organic or inorganic materials added to soil to improve its structure.

soil′ conserva′tion, any of various methods, sponsored chiefly by a government agency, to achieve the maximum utilization of the land and preservation of its resources through such controls as crop rotation, prevention of soil erosion, etc.

soil′ pipe′, a pipe carrying wastes from water closets and sometimes from waste pipes. Cf. **waste pipe** (def. 2).

soil′ rot′, *Plant Pathol.* pox (def. 3).

soil′ sci′ence, pedology[1]. —**soil′ sci′entist.**

soil·ure (soil′yər), *n. Archaic.* a stain. [ME *soylure* < OF *soilleure,* equiv. to *soill(ier)* (see SOIL[2]) + *-eure* -URE]

soi·ree (swä rā′), *n.* an evening party or social gathering, esp. one held for a particular purpose: *a musical soiree.* [< F < OF *soir* evening (< L *sērō* late) + *-ée* ptp. suffix (as if < L *-āta*)]

soi·rée (swä rā′; *Fr.* swa rā′), *n., pl.* **-rées** (-rāz′; *Fr.* -rā′). soiree.

Soi·rée a·vec Mon·sieur Teste, La (*Fr.* la swa rā′ a vek mə syœ test′). See **Evening With Mr. Teste, An.**

Sois·sons (swa sôɴ′), *n.* a city in N France, on the Aisne River: battles A.D. 486, 1918, 1944. 24,359 (1962).

so·ja (sō′jə, -yə, soi′ə), *n.* soybean. [< NL < D: soybean; see SOY]

so·journ (*v.* sō′jûrn, sō jûrn′; *n.* sō′jûrn), *v.i.* **1.** to stay for a time in a place; live temporarily: *to sojourn on the Riviera for two months.* —*n.* **2.** a temporary stay: *during his sojourn in Paris.* [ME *sojurne* < OF *sojorn,* deriv. of *sojorn(er)* (to) rest, stay < LL **subdiurnāre,* equiv. to L *sub-* SUB- + *diurn(us)* of a day; see JOURNEY] —**so′journ·er,** *n.*

soke (sōk), *n. Early Eng. Law.* **1.** the privilege of holding court, usually connected with the feudal rights of lordship. **2.** a district over which local jurisdiction was exercised. [late ME < ML *soc(a)* << OE *sōcn* seeking, inquiry, jurisdiction; c. SEEK]

soke·man (sōk′mən), *n., pl.* **-men.** a tenant holding land in socage. Also, **socman.** [ME < ML *sokemann(us)* < OE *sōcn* SOKE + *man* MAN[1]]

soke·man·ry (sōk′mən rē), *n., pl.* **-ries. 1.** tenure of land subject to the soke of someone else. **2.** sokemen. [< AF *sokemanerie* < ML *sokemman(us)* SOKEMAN + AF *-erie* -RY]

so·ken (sō′kən), *n.* a district held by socage. [ME *socne, soken.* See SOKE]

So·ko·to (sō′kō tō′, sō′kō tō′, sə kō′tō), *n.* a sultanate and province in NW Nigeria: center of a Fulah empire in the 19th century. 2,680,558 (1953); 36,477 sq. mi.

So·ko·tra (sō kō′trə, sok′ə trə), *n.* Socotra.

sol[1] (sōl, sol), *n. Music.* **1.** the syllable used for the fifth tone of a diatonic scale. **2.** (in the fixed system of solmization) the tone G. Also, **so.** Cf. **sol-fa** (def. 1). [ME < L *sol(ve);* see GAMUT]

sol[2] (sōl, sol), *n.* a former coin and money of account of France, the 20th part of a livre and equal to 12 deniers: originally gold, later silver, finally copper, it was discontinued in 1794. Also, **sou.** Cf. **solidus**[1] (def. 2). [< OF *sol* < LL *sol(idus)* SOLIDUS; cf. It *soldo,* Sp *sueldo*]

sol[3] (sōl, sol; *Sp.* sôl), *n., pl.* **sols,** *Sp.* **so·les** (sô′les). **1.** a bronze coin and monetary unit of Peru, equal to 100 centavos and equivalent to about .037 of a U.S. dollar. *Abbr.:* S. **2.** Also called **libra.** a former gold coin of Peru. [< AmerSp, Sp: sun < L *sōl*]

sol[4] (sol, sōl), *n. Physical Chem.* a colloidal suspension of a solid in a liquid. [shortened form of HYDROSOL]

Sol (sol), *n.* **1.** an ancient Roman god personifying the sun, variously identified with the Greek Helios or the Indo-Iranian god Mithras. **2.** the sun, personified by the Romans as a god. **3.** a boy's given name, form of **Solomon.**

Sol., 1. Solicitor. **2.** Solomon.

sol., 1. soluble. **2.** solution.

S.O.L., *Slang.* strictly out (of) luck.

so·la (sō′lä), *n.* a leguminous shrub, *Aeschynomene aspera,* of India, the pith of which is used for making helmets. Cf. **topee.** [< Hindi *solā*]

so·la (sō′lä; *Eng.* sō′lə), *adj. Latin.* (referring to a woman) alone; by oneself (used formerly in stage directions). Cf. **solus.**

sol·ace (sol′is), *n., v.,* **-aced, -ac·ing.** —*n.* Also called **sol′ace·ment. 1.** comfort in sorrow, misfortune, or trouble; alleviation of distress or discomfort. **2.** something that gives comfort, consolation, or relief: *The minister's visit was the dying man's only solace.* —*v.t.* **3.** to comfort, console, or cheer (a person, oneself, the heart, etc.). **4.** to alleviate or relieve (sorrow, distress, etc.): *to solace the distress of flood victims.* [ME *solas* < OF < L *sōlāc(ium), sōlāt(ium),* equiv. to *sōlāt(us)* (ptp. of *sōlārī* to comfort; see -ATE[1]) + *-ium* n. suffix] —**sol′ac·er,** *n.* —**Syn. 1.** consolation, relief, cheer. **4.** soothe, mitigate, assuage, allay, soften.

so·lan (sō′lən), *n.* a gannet. Also called **so′lan goose′.** [ME *soland* < Scand; cf. OIcel *sūla* gannet, Dan *and* goose]

sol·a·na·ceous (sol′ə nā′shəs), *adj.* belonging to the *Solanaceae,* or nightshade family of plants, comprising the solanums, belladonna, henbane, mandrake, stramonium, tobacco, capsicum pepper, tomato, petunia, etc. [< NL *Sōlānāce(ae)* name of the family, equiv. to L *sōlān(um)* nightshade + *-āceae;* see -ACEOUS]

so·lan·der (sə lan′dər), *n.* a case for maps, plates, etc., made to resemble a book and having the front cover and fore edge hinged. [named after Daniel Charles *Solander* (1736–82), Swedish naturalist who invented it]

so·la·no (sō lä′nō; *Sp.* sô lä′nô), *n.* a hot, easterly wind blowing during the summer on the southeast coast of Spain. [< Sp < L *sōlān(us),* equiv. to *sōl* sun + *-ānus* -AN]

so·la·num (sō lā′nəm), *n.* any gametopetalous herb, shrub, or small tree of the genus *Solanum,* comprising the nightshade, eggplant, potato, etc. [< L: nightshade]

so·lar[1] (sō′lər), *adj.* **1.** of or pertaining to the sun: *solar phenomena.* **2.** determined by the sun: *solar hour.* **3.** proceeding from the sun, as light or heat. **4.** operating by the light or heat of the sun, as a mechanism: *a solar stove.* **5.** indicating time by means of or with reference to the sun: *a solar chronometer.* **6.** *Astrol.* subject to the influence of the sun. [< L *sōlār(is),* equiv. to *sōl-* (s. of *sōl*) the sun + *-āris* -AR[1]]

so·lar[2] (sō′lər, sol′ər), *n.* a private or upper chamber in a medieval English house. Also, **sollar, soller.** [ME, OE; akin to MD *solre* loft << L *sōlār(ium)* SOLARIUM]

so′lar a′pex, *Astron.* the point on the celestial sphere, near Vega, toward which the solar system is moving relative to the visible stars. Also called **apex of the sun's way.** Cf. **antapex.**

so′lar bat′tery, a device for converting solar energy into electricity by means of photovoltaic cells.

so′lar char′iot, (in ancient Egypt) a chariot placed in the tomb of a king to transport him to the sun.

so′lar con′stant, the average rate at which radiant energy is received from the sun by the earth, equal to 1.94 small calories per minute per square centimeter of area perpendicular to the sun's rays, measured at a point outside the earth's atmosphere when the earth is at its mean distance from the sun.

so′lar day′, **1.** *Astron.* the time interval between two successive transits by the sun of the meridian directly opposite that of the observer; the 24-hour interval from one midnight to the following midnight. **2.** *Law.* the period of time from sunrise to sunset.

so′lar eclipse′. See under **eclipse** (def. 1a). —**so′lar eclip′tic.**

so′lar fur′nace, a furnace using sunlight concentrated by concave mirrors as the direct source of heat.

so′lar house′, a house designed to absorb and store solar heat.

so·lar·ise (sō′lə rīz′), *v.t., v.i.,* **-ised, -is·ing.** *Chiefly Brit.* solarize. —**so′lar·i·sa′tion,** *n.*

so·lar·ism (sō′lə riz′əm), *n.* the interpretation of myths by reference to the sun, esp. such interpretation carried to an extreme. [SOLAR[1] + -ISM] —**so′lar·ist,** *n.*

so·lar·i·um (sō lâr′ē əm, sə-), *n., pl.* **-lar·i·ums, -lar·i·a** (-lâr′ē ə). a glass-enclosed room, porch, or the like, exposed to the sun's rays, as at a seaside hotel or for convalescents in a hospital. [< L: sundial, balcony, terrace, equiv. to *sōl* the sun + *-ārium* -ARY]

so·lar·ize (sō′lə rīz′), *v.,* **-ized, -iz·ing.** —*v.t.* **1.** *Photog.* to reverse (an image) partially, as from negative to positive, by exposure to light during development. **2.** to affect by sunlight. —*v.i.* **3.** *Photog.* (of material) to become injured by overexposure. Also, *esp. Brit.,* **solarise.** [SOLAR[1] + -IZE] —**so′lar·i·za′tion,** *n.*

so′lar month′, month (def. 1).

so′lar plex′us, **1.** Also called **celiac plexus.** *Anat.* a network of nerves situated at the upper part of the abdomen, behind the stomach and in front of the aorta. **2.** *Informal.* a point on the stomach wall, just below the sternum, where a blow will affect this nerve center. [so called from the raylike pattern of the nerve fibers]

so′lar prom′inences, *Astron.* eruptions of luminous gas on the sun that rise above the chromosphere.

so′lar ship′, (in ancient Egypt) a boat placed in the tomb of a king to transport him to the sun.

so′lar sys′tem, the sun together with all the planets and other bodies that revolve around it.

so′lar wind′ (wind), a cloud of protons, produced by solar storms, moving outward from the sun and affecting the magnetic fields of the earth, moon, and other planetary bodies.

so′lar year′, year (def. 4b).

so·la·ti·um (sō lā′shē əm), *n., pl.* **-ti·a** (-shē ə). **1.** something given in compensation for inconvenience, loss, injury, or the like; recompense. **2.** *Law.* damages awarded to a plaintiff to compensate him for personal suffering or grief arising from an injury. [< L: comfort, relief. See SOLACE]

sold (sōld), *v.* pt. and pp. of **sell.**

Sol·dan (sol′dən, sōl′-, sōd′ən), *n.* **1.** the ruler of a Muslim country. **2.** *Archaic.* a sultan, esp. the sultan of Egypt. [ME < MF < Ar. See SULTAN]

sol·der (sod′ər), *n.* **1.** any of various alloys fused and applied to the joint between metal objects to unite them without heating the objects to the melting point. **2.** anything that joins or unites: *They were united by the solder of their common cause.* —*v.t.* **3.** to join with solder. **4.** to join closely and intimately: *two fates inseparably soldered by misfortune.* **5.** to mend; repair; patch up. —*v.i.* **6.** to unite things with solder. **7.** to become soldered or united; grow together. [ME *sondur* < OF *soldure,* deriv. of *sold(er)* (to) solder < L *solidāre* to make solid, equiv. to *solid(us)* SOLID + *-āre* inf. suffix] —**sol′der·a·ble,** *adj.* —**sol′der·er,** *n.* —**sol′der·less,** *adj.*

sol′dering i′ron, an instrument for melting and applying solder.

sol′dering paste′, a pastelike mixture consisting chiefly of rosin or inorganic salts, used in soldering to promote the fusion of metals.

sol·dier (sōl′jər), *n.* **1.** a person who serves in an army for pay; a person engaged in military service. **2.** a person of the rank and file in such service, sometimes including noncommissioned officers: *the soldiers' mess and the officers' mess.* **3.** a man of military skill or experience: *George Washington was a great soldier.* **4.** a person who contends or serves in any cause: *a soldier of the Lord.* **5.** *Entomol.* an ant or termite with powerful jaws or other device for protection. **6.** a brick laid vertically with the narrower long face out. Cf. **rowlock**[2] (def. 2). **7.** *Informal.* a person who avoids work or pretends to work; loafer; malingerer. —*v.i.* **8.** to act or serve as a soldier. **9.** *Informal.* to loaf while pretending to work; malinger: *He was soldiering on the job.* [ME *souldiour* < OF, equiv. to *soulde* pay (< L *solidus;* see SOL[2]) + *-ier* -IER] —**sol′dier·ship′,** *n.*

sol·dier·fish (sōl′jər fish′), *n., pl.* (*esp. collectively*) **-fish,** (*esp. referring to two or more kinds or species*) **-fish·es.** **1.** any of several squirrelfishes of the family *Holocentridae,* esp. of the genus *Myripristis.* **2.** any of various other brightly colored fishes. [so called from its sharp spines and rough scales]

sol′dier fly′, any of several dipterous insects of the family *Stratiomyidae,* characterized by brightly colored abdominal stripes, and having aquatic or terrestrial larvae.

sol·dier·ly (sōl′jər lē), *adj.* of, like, or befitting a soldier. [SOLDIER + -LY] —**sol′dier·li·ness,** *n.*

sol′dier of for′tune, **1.** a military adventurer, ready to serve anywhere for pay or for pleasure. **2.** a courageous or spirited person who independently seeks pleasure, wealth, etc., through adventurous exploits.

sol′dier's heart′, *Pathol.* See **cardiac neurosis.**

sol′diers' home′, an institution that provides care and shelter for retired soldiers.

Sol′dier's Med′al, a medal awarded to any member of the Army of the United States, or of any military organization serving with it, who distinguishes himself by heroism not involving conflict with an enemy.

sol·dier·y (sōl′jə rē), *n., pl.* **-dier·ies** for 2. **1.** soldiers collectively. **2.** a body of soldiers. **3.** military training or skill [SOLDIER + -RY]

sol·do (sol′dō; *It.* sôl′dô), *n., pl.* **-di** (-dē). a former copper coin of Italy, the twentieth part of a lira, equal to five centesimi. [< It < L *solid(um);* see SOL[2]]

sole[1] (sōl), *adj.* **1.** being the only one or ones; only: *the sole living relative.* **2.** being the only one of the kind; unique; unsurpassed; matchless: *the sole brilliance of the diamond.* **3.** belonging or pertaining to one individual or group to the exclusion of all others; exclusive: *He has the sole right to the estate.* **4.** functioning automatically or with independent power: *the sole authority in this matter.* **5.** *Chiefly Law.* unmarried. **6.** without company or companions; lonely: *the sole splendor of her life.* **7.** *Archaic.* alone. [< L *sōl(um),* acc. sing. of *sōlus* alone; r. ME *soule* alone < OF *sol* < L *sōl(um)*] —**sole′ness,** *n.*
—**Syn. 1.** solitary. **3.** individual.

sole[2] (sōl), *n., v.,* **soled, sol·ing.** —*n.* **1.** the bottom or under surface of the foot. **2.** the corresponding under part of a shoe, boot, or the like, or this part exclusive of the heel. **3.** the bottom, under surface, or lower part of anything. **4.** *Carpentry.* **a.** the underside of a plane. **b.** soleplate. **5.** *Golf.* the part of the head of the club which touches the ground. **6.** *Naut.* the bottom of the cabin or cockpit of a small pleasure vessel. **7.** the cylindrical surface of a water wheel, from which the paddles project. —*v.t.* **8.** to furnish with a sole, as a shoe. **9.** *Golf.* to place the sole of (a club) on the ground, as in preparation for a stroke. [ME < OE < LL **sol(a),* L *solea* sandal, sole; cf. Sp *suela*] —**sole′less,** *adj.*

sole[3] (sōl), *n., pl.* (*esp. collectively*) **sole,** (*esp. referring to two or more kinds or species*) **soles.** **1.** a European flatfish, *Solea solea,* used for food. **2.** any other flatfish of the families *Soleidae, Achiridae,* and *Cynoglossidae,* having a hooklike snout. [ME < MF < LL **sola* (see SOLE[2]), so called from the flat shape of the fish; cf. Sp *suela,* It *soglia,* Pg *solha*]

sol·e·cism (sol′i siz′əm), *n.* **1.** a substandard or ungrammatical usage, as *they was, unflammable.* **2.** a breach of good manners or etiquette. **3.** any error, impropriety, or inconsistency. [< L *soloecism(us)* < Gk *soloikismós,* equiv. to *sóloik(os)* (*Sól(i)* a city in Cilicia where incorrect Greek was spoken + *-ikos* -IC) + *-ismos* -ISM] —**sol′e·cist,** *n.* —**sol′e·cis′tic, sol′e·cis′ti·cal,** *adj.* —**sol′e·cis′ti·cal·ly,** *adv.*

Sol·e·dad (sol′i dad′), *n.* a town in W California. 2837 (1960).

sole·ly (sōl′lē), *adv.* **1.** as the only one or ones: *solely responsible.* **2.** exclusively or only: *plants found solely in the tropics.* **3.** merely: *She wanted solely to get out of the house for a while.* [SOLE[1] + -LY]

sol·emn (sol′əm), *adj.* **1.** grave, sober, or mirthless, as a person, the face, speech, tone, mood, etc.: *a solemn judge; solemn remarks.* **2.** gravely or somberly impressive; causing serious thoughts or a grave mood: *solemn music.* **3.** serious or earnest: *solemn assurances.* **4.** characterized by dignified or serious formality, as proceedings; of a formal or ceremonious character: *a solemn occasion.* **5.** made in due legal or other express form, as a declaration, agreement, etc.: *a solemn oath.* **6.** marked or observed with religious rites; having a religious character: *a solemn holy day.* **7.** uttered, prescribed, or made according to religious forms: *a solemn ban on intermarriage.* [ME *solempne* < LL *sōlennis, solempnis,* L *sōlemnis* consecrated, holy] —**sol′emn·ly,** *adv.* —**sol′emn·ness,** *n.*
—**Syn. 1.** unsmiling, serious. See **grave**[2]. **2.** awe-inspiring, august, imposing, stately. **4.** ritual, ceremonial. **6.** reverential, devotional, sacred. —**Ant. 1.** humorous. **2.** trivial.

sol·em·nise (sol′əm nīz′), *v.t., v.i.,* **-nised, -nis·ing.** *Chiefly Brit.* solemnize. —**sol′em·ni·sa′tion,** *n.* —**sol′em·nis′er,** *n.*

so·lem·ni·ty (sə lem′ni tē), *n., pl.* **-ties.** **1.** the state or character of being solemn; earnestness; gravity; impressiveness: *the solemnity of a state funeral.* **2.** Often, **solemnities.** a solemn observance, ceremonial proceeding, or special formality: *solemnities appropriate to the Christmas season.* **3.** observance of rites or ceremonies, esp. a formal, solemn, ecclesiastical observance, as of a feast day. **4.** *Law.* a formality which renders an act or document valid. [ME *solempnete* < OF < LL *sollemnitāt-* (s. of *sollemnitās*), equiv. to L *sōlemn(is)* SOLEMN + *-itāt-* -ITY]

sol·em·nize (sol′əm nīz′), *v.,* **-nized, -niz·ing.** —*v.t.* **1.** to observe or commemorate with rites or ceremonies: *to solemnize an occasion by speeches and prayers.* **2.** to hold or perform (ceremonies, rites, etc.) in due manner. **3.** to perform the ceremony of (marriage). **4.** to go through with ceremony or formality. **5.** to render solemn, serious, or grave; dignify. —*v.i.* **6.** to become solemn; conduct oneself with solemnity. Also, *esp. Brit.,* **solemnise.** [ME *solempnise* < ML *solemniz(āre),* equiv. to L *sōlemn(is)* + *-izāre* -IZE] —**sol′em·ni·za′tion,** *n.* —**sol′em·niz′er,** *n.*

Sol′emn League′ and Cov′enant, an agreement (1643) between the parliaments of Scotland and England permitting the promotion of Presbyterianism in Scotland, England, and Ireland. Cf. **National Covenant.**

Sol′emn Mass′. See **High Mass.**

sol′emn vow′, *Rom. Cath. Ch.* a perpetual, irrevocable public vow taken by a religious, in which property may not be owned by the individual, and marriage is held invalid under canon law. Cf. **simple vow.**

so·le·no·don (sō lē′nə don′, -len′ə-), *n.* an insectivore of the family *Solenodontidae,* resembling a large shrew and having an elongate snout and a hairless, scaly tail. [< NL, equiv. to *solen* (L: razor clam < Gk *sōlḗn* channel, pipe, syringe, etc.) + Gk *odṓn* tooth]

Solenodon, *Solenodon paradoxus* (Total length 2 ft.; tail 10 in.)

so·le·noid (sō′lə noid′), *n.* **1.** *Elect.* an electric conductor wound as a helix with small pitch, or as two or more coaxial helices, so that current through the conductor establishes a magnetic field within the conductor. **2.** *Meteorol.* a space formed by the intersection of isobaric and isosteric surfaces. [< F *solénoïde* < Gk *sōlḗn* pipe, channel; see -OID]

so·le·noi·dal (sō′lə noid′əl), *adj.* **1.** of or pertaining to a solenoid. **2.** *Math.* (of a vector or vector function) having divergence equal to zero. [SOLENOID + -AL[1]] —**so′le·noi′dal·ly,** *adv.*

So·lent (sō′lənt), *n.* **The,** a channel between the Isle of Wight and the mainland of S England. 2–5 mi. wide.

sole·piece (sōl′pēs′), *n.* **1.** *Naut.* shoe (def. 20b). **2.** *Carpentry.* soleplate. [SOLE[2] + PIECE]

sole·plate (sōl′plāt′), *n.* *Carpentry.* a plate upon which studding is erected. Also called **shoe, sole, solepiece.** [SOLE[2] + PLATE[1]]

sole·print (sōl′print′), *n.* a print of the sole of a foot: often used in hospitals for identifying infants. [SOLE[2] + PRINT]

So·ler (sō lâr′; *Sp.* sô leR′), *n.* **Padre An·to·nio** (än tô′nyô), 1729–83, Spanish organist and composer.

So·lesmes (sō lem′), *n.* a Benedictine monastery in Solesmes, France, known esp. for the work of its monks in editing and performing Gregorian chant.

sole′ trad′er, *Law.* See **feme-sole trader.**

So·leure (sô lœR′), *n.* French name of **Solothurn.**

sol-fa (sōl′fä′, sōl′-; sōl′fä′, sōl′-), *n., v.,* **-faed, -fa·ing.** —*n.* **1.** *Music.* the set of syllables, *do, re, mi, fa, sol, la,* and *ti,* sung to the respective tones of the scale. All but *do* and *ti* are attributed to Guido d'Arezzo. **2.** the system of singing tones to these syllables. —*v.i.* **3.** to use the sol-fa syllables in singing, or to sing these syllables. —*v.t.* **4.** to sing to the sol-fa syllables, as a tune. [see GAMUT] —**sol′-fa′ist,** *n.*

sol·fa·ta·ra (sōl′fə tär′ə, sol′-), *n.* a volcanic vent or area which gives off only sulfurous gases, steam, and the like. [< It (Neapolitan) *solfatara,* deriv. of *solf(o)* < L *sulfur;* see SULFUR] —**sol′fa·ta′ric,** *adj.*

sol·fège (sol fezh′), *n.* *Music.* solfeggio. [< F < It]

sol·feg·gio (sol fej′ō, -fej′ē ō′), *n., pl.* **-feg·gi** (-fej′ē), **-feg·gios.** *Music.* **1.** a vocal exercise in which the sol-fa syllables are used. **2.** the use of the sol-fa syllables to name or represent the tones of a melody or voice part, or the tones of the scale, or of a particular series, as the scale of C; solmization. [< It, deriv. of *solfeggi(are),* equiv. to *solf(a)* GAMUT + *-eggiare* v. suffix]

Sol·fe·ri·no (sôl′fe Rē′nô *for 1;* sol′fə rē′nō *for 2, 3*). *n.* **1.** a village in SE Lombardy, in N Italy: battle 1859. 1810 (1961). **2.** (*l.c.*) a dye obtained from rosaniline. **3.** (*l.c.*) vivid purplish pink. [dye so named from its being discovered after the battle of Solferino]

soli-[1], a learned borrowing from Latin meaning "alone," "solitary," used in the formation of compound words: *solifidian.* [< L, comb. form of *sōlus.* See SOLE[1]]

soli-[2], a learned borrowing from Latin meaning "sun," used in the formation of compound words: *soliform.* [comb. form repr. L *sōl* sun + -I-]

so·lic·it (sə lis′it), *v.t.* **1.** to seek for by entreaty, earnest or respectful request, formal application, etc.: *He solicited aid from the minister.* **2.** to entreat or petition for something or for someone to do something; urge; importune: *to solicit the committee for funds; to solicit support for a housing bill.* **3.** to seek to influence or incite to action, esp. unlawful or wrong action. **4.** to accost or lure (someone) with immoral intentions, as by or on behalf of a prostitute. —*v.i.* **5.** to make a petition or request, as for something desired. **6.** to solicit orders or trade, as for a business house: *No soliciting allowed in this building.* **7.** to accost someone with immoral intentions, esp. as a prostitute. [ME *solicit(en)* < MF *solliciter* < L *sollicitāre* to excite, agitate, deriv. of *sollicitus* troubled (*soll(us)* whole + *citus,* ptp. of *ciēre* to arouse)]
—**Syn. 2.** beseech, beg, sue. **3.** excite, arouse, provoke.

so·lic·i·ta·tion (sə lis′i tā′shən), *n.* **1.** act of soliciting. **2.** entreaty, urging, or importunity; a petition or request. **3.** enticement or allurement. **4.** *Law.* the crime of asking another to commit or to aid in a crime. [< L *sollicitātiōn-* (s. of *sollicitātiō*), equiv. to *sollicitāt(us)* (ptp. of *sollicitāre;* see SOLICIT, -ATE[1]) + *-iōn-* -ION]

so·lic·i·tor (sə lis′i tər), *n.* **1.** a person who solicits. **2.** a person whose business it is to solicit business, trade, etc. **3.** *U.S.* an officer having charge of the legal business of a city, town, etc. **4.** *Brit.* a member of that branch of the legal profession whose services consist of advising clients, representing them before the lower courts, and preparing cases for barristers to try in the higher courts. Cf. **barrister** (def. 1). [ME *solicitour* < MF *soliciteur.* See SOLICIT, -OR[2]] —**so·lic′i·tor·ship′,** *n.*
—**Syn. 4.** lawyer, attorney, counselor.

solic′itor gen′eral, *pl.* **solicitors general.** **1.** a law officer who maintains the rights of the state in suits affecting the public interest, next in rank to the attorney general. **2.** *U.S.* **a.** (*caps.*) the law officer of the U.S. government next below the Attorney General, having charge of appeals, as to the Supreme Court. **b.** the chief legal officer in some States.

so·lic·i·tous (sə lis′i təs), *adj.* **1.** anxious or concerned (usually fol. by *about, for,* etc., or a clause): *solicitous about a person's health.* **2.** anxiously desirous: *solicitous of the esteem of others.* **3.** eager (usually fol. by an infinitive): *He was always solicitous to please.* **4.** careful or particular: *a solicitous housekeeper.* [< L *sollicitus* agitated. See SOLICIT, -OUS] —**so·lic′i·tous·ly,** *adv.* —**so·lic′i·tous·ness,** *n.*
—**Ant. 1.** unconcerned, careless.

so·lic·i·tude (sə lis′i to͞od′, -tyo͞od′), *n.* **1.** the state of being solicitous; anxiety or concern; anxious desire or care. **2.** **solicitudes,** causes of anxiety or care. **3.** excessive anxiety or assistance: *His solicitude about my health is tiresome indeed.* [< L *sollicitūdō* uneasiness of mind, deriv. of *sollicitus* agitated. See SOLICIT, -TUDE]

sol·id (sol′id), *adj.* **1.** having three dimensions (length, breadth, and thickness), as a geometrical body or figure. **2.** of or pertaining to bodies or figures of three dimensions. **3.** having the interior completely filled up, free from cavities, or not hollow: *a solid piece of chocolate.* **4.** without openings or breaks: *a solid wall.* **5.** firm, hard, or compact in substance: *solid ground.* **6.** having relative firmness, coherence of particles, or persistence of form, as matter that is not liquid or gaseous: *solid particles suspended in a liquid.* **7.** pertaining to such matter: *Water in a solid state is ice.* **8.** dense, thick, or heavy in nature or appearance: *solid masses of cloud.* **9.** not flimsy, slight, or light, as buildings, furniture, fabrics, food, etc.; substantial. **10.** of a substantial character; not superficial, trifling, or frivolous: *a solid work of scientific scholarship.* **11.** without separation or division; continuous: *a solid row of buildings.* **12.** whole or entire: *one solid hour.* **13.** forming the whole; consisting entirely of one substance or material: *solid gold.* **14.** uniform in tone or shades as a color: *a solid blue dress.* **15.** real or genuine: *solid comfort.* **16.** sound or good, as reasons, arguments, etc.: *a solid basis.* **17.** sober-minded; fully reliable or sensible: *a solid citizen.* **18.** financially sound or strong: *Our company is solid.* **19.** cubic: *A solid foot contains 1728 solid inches.* **20.** written without a hyphen, as a compound word. **21.** having the lines not separated by leads, or having few open spaces, as

type or printing. **22.** thorough, vigorous, great, big, etc. (with emphatic force, often after *good*): *a good solid blow.* **23.** firmly united or consolidated: *a solid combination.* **24.** united or unanimous in opinion, policy, etc.: *the Solid South.* **25.** *Informal.* on a friendly, favorable, or advantageous footing (often prec. by *in*): *He was in solid with her parents.* **26.** *Slang.* excellent, esp. musically. —*n.* **27.** a body or object having three dimensions (length, breadth, and thickness). **28.** a solid substance or body; a substance exhibiting rigidity. **29.** *Mining.* a virgin mineral deposit: *to drive a shaft into the solid.* [ME < L *solidus*] —**sol′id·ly,** *adv.* —**sol′id·ness,** *n.*
—**Syn. 1.** cubic. **5.** dense. See **firm**[1]. **6.** cohesive, firm. **9.** sound, stable, stout. **11.** unbroken. **18.** solvent, safe, trustworthy. **22.** strong, stout. —**Ant. 1.** flat. **6.** loose. **11, 24.** divided.

sol·i·da·go (sol′i dā′gō), *n., pl.* **-gos.** any plant of the genus *Solidago,* comprising the goldenrods. [< NL *Solidago* name of genus < ML *solidago* comfrey < L *solidāre* to heal, make whole, deriv. of *solidus* SOLID]

sol′id an′gle, *Geom.* an angle formed by three or more planes intersecting in a common point or formed at the vertex of a cone.

sol·i·dar·i·ty (sol′i dar′i tē), *n., pl.* **-ties. 1.** union or fellowship arising from common responsibilities and interests, as between members of a group or between classes, peoples, etc.: *to promote solidarity among union members.* **2.** community of interests, feelings, purposes, etc. **3.** community of responsibilities and interests. [< F *solidarité,* equiv. to *solidaire* SOLIDARY + *-ité* -ITY]
—**Syn. 1.** stability, soundness, reliability. **2.** unanimity.

sol·i·da·rize (sol′i də rīz′), *v.i.,* **-rized, -riz·ing.** to unite or come together; to become solidified. [< F *solidaris(er).* See SOLIDARY, -IZE]

sol·i·dar·y (sol′i der′ē), *adj.* characterized by or involving community of responsibilities and interests. [< F *solidaire* < MF; see SOLID, -ARY[1]] —**sol′i·dar′i·ly,** *adv.*

sol′id geom′etry, the geometry of solid figures; geometry of three dimensions.

so·lid·i·fy (sə lid′ə fī′), *v.,* **-fied, -fy·ing.** —*v.t.* **1.** to make solid; make into a hard or compact mass; change from a liquid or gaseous to a solid form. **2.** to unite firmly or consolidate. **3.** to form into crystals; make crystallized. —*v.i.* **4.** to become solid. **5.** to form into crystals; become crystallized. [< F *solidifier.* See SOLID, -IFY] —**so·lid′i·fi′a·bil′i·ty, so·lid′i·fi′a·ble·ness,** *n.* —**so·lid′i·fi′a·ble,** *adj.* —**so·lid′i·fi·ca′tion,** *n.* —**so·lid′i·fi′er,** *n.*

sol′id injec′tion, injection of fuel into an internal-combustion engine without an air blast. Cf. **air injection.**

so·lid·i·ty (sə lid′i tē), *n., pl.* **-ties. 1.** the state, property, or quality of being solid. **2.** firmness and strength; substantialness: *an argument with little solidity.* **3.** strength of mind, character, finances, etc. **4.** *Obs.* the amount of space occupied by a solid body; volume. [< L *soliditāt-* (s. of *soliditās*), equiv. to *solid(us)* SOLID + *-itāt-* -ITY]

sol·id-look·ing (sol′id lo͝ok′ing), *adj.* reassuringly substantial or stable in appearance: *They're a very solid-looking, intelligent couple.*

sol′id of revolu′tion, a three-dimensional figure formed by revolving a plane area about a given axis.

sol′id solu′tion, 1. a solid, homogeneous mixture of substances, as glass, certain alloys, etc. **2.** (in a crystal structure) the more or less complete substitution of one kind of atom, ion, or molecule for another that is chemically different but similar in size and shape; isomorphism.

Sol′id South′, *U.S.* those Southern States that traditionally support the programs and candidates of the Democratic party.

sol·id-state (sol′id stāt′), *adj. Electronics.* designating or pertaining to electronic devices, as transistors, crystals, etc., that can control current without the use of moving parts, heated filaments, or vacuum gaps.

sol·id·un·gu·late (sol′i dung′gyə lit, -lāt′), *adj.* **1.** having a single, undivided hoof on each foot, as a horse. —*n.* **2.** Also called **soliped.** a solidungulate animal. [SOLID + UNGULATE]

sol·i·dus[1] (sol′i dəs), *n., pl.* **-di** (-dī′). **1.** a gold coin of Rome, introduced by Constantine and continued in the Byzantine Empire; bezant. **2.** (in medieval Europe) a money of account equal to 12 denarii. Cf. **sol**[2]. **3.** virgule. [< LL *solidus (nummus)* a solid (coin), a gold (coin), later, shilling, represented by a long s, whence the shilling mark (virgule)]

sol·i·dus[2] (sol′i dəs), *n. Physical Chem.* the portion of a temperature composition diagram which consists of the curve connecting the temperatures at which a solid solution is in equilibrium with its vapor and with the liquid solution, and therefore connecting melting temperatures of solid solutions. Cf. **liquidus.** [< L]

sol·i·fid·i·an (sol′ə fid′ē ən), *n. Theol.* one who maintains that faith alone, without the performance of good works, is all that is necessary for salvation. [SOLI-[1] + L *fīd(ēs)* faith, belief, trust + -IAN] —**so′li·fid′i·an·ism,** *n.*

so·li·fluc·tion (sō′lə fluk′shən, sol′ə-), *n. Geol.* creep (def. 17). [< L *sol(um)* soil + *-i-* -I- + *fluctiōn-* a flowing (s. of *fluctiō*), equiv. to *fluct(us)* flowed (see FLUCTUATE) + *-iōn-* -ION]

so·lil·o·quise (sə lil′ə kwīz′), *v.i., v.t.,* **-quised, -quis·ing.** *Chiefly Brit.* soliloquize. —**so·lil′o·quis′er,** *n.* —**so·lil′o·quis′ing·ly,** *adv.*

so·lil·o·quize (sə lil′ə kwīz′), *v.,* **-quized, -quiz·ing.** —*v.i.* **1.** to utter a soliloquy; talk to oneself. —*v.t.* **2.** to utter in a soliloquy; say to oneself. [SOLILOQU(Y) + -IZE] —**so·lil·o·quist** (sə lil′ə kwist), **so·lil′o·quiz′er,** *n.* —**so·lil′o·quiz′ing·ly,** *adv.*

so·lil·o·quy (sə lil′ə kwē), *n., pl.* **-quies. 1.** the act of talking while or as if alone. **2.** an utterance or discourse by a person who is talking to himself or is disregardful of or oblivious to any hearers present (often used as a device in drama to disclose a character's innermost thoughts): *Hamlet's soliloquy begins with "To be or not to be."* [< LL *sōliloquium* a talking to oneself, soliloquy, equiv. to *soli-* SOLI-[1] + *loqu(ī)* (to) speak + *-ium;* see -Y[3]]

Sol·i·man I (sol′ə mən), *n.* See **Suleiman I.**

So·li·me·na (sô′lē me′nä), *n.* **Fran·ces·co** (frän-ches′kô), 1657–1747, Italian painter.

So·li·mões (sô′li moins′), *n.* Brazilian name of the Amazon from its junction with the Rio Negro to the border of Peru.

sol·ing (sō′ling), *n.* pitching. [SOLE[2] + -ING[1]]

So·ling·en (zō′ling ən), *n.* a city in W West Germany, in the Ruhr region. 172,200 (1963).

sol·i·ped (sol′ə ped′), *n.* solidungulate. [< NL *soliped-* (s. of *solipes*), equiv. to L *soli(dus)* SOLID + *ped-* -PED]

sol·ip·sism (sol′ip siz′əm), *n. Philos.* the theory that only the self exists, or can be proven to exist. [SOLI-[1] + L *ips(e)* self + -ISM] —**sol′ip·sis′mal,** *adj.* —**sol′ip·sist,** *n., adj.* —**sol·ip·sis·tic** (sol′ip sis′tik), *adj.*

So·lis Lac·us (sō′lis lak′əs). See **Lacus Solis.**

So·li·ta (sə lē′tə, sō lē′tä), *n.* a girl's given name.

sol·i·taire (sol′i târ′), *n.* **1.** a game played by one person alone, as a game played with marbles or pegs on a board having hollows or holes. **2.** Also called **patience.** any of various games played by one person with one or more regular 52-card packs, part or all of which are usually dealt out according to a given pattern, the object being to arrange the cards in a predetermined manner. **3.** a precious stone, esp. a diamond, set by itself, as in a ring. [< F < L *sōlitārius* SOLITARY]

sol·i·tar·y (sol′i ter′ē), *adj., n., pl.* **-tar·ies.** —*adj.* **1.** alone; without companions; unattended: *a solitary passer-by.* **2.** living alone; avoiding the society of others: *a solitary existence.* **3.** by itself; alone: *one solitary house.* **4.** characterized by the absence of companions: *a solitary journey.* **5.** done without assistance or accompaniment; done in solitude: *solitary chores.* **6.** being the only one or ones: *a solitary exception.* **7.** characterized by solitude, as a place; unfrequented, secluded, or lonely: *a solitary cabin in the woods.* **8.** *Zool.* living habitually alone or in pairs, as certain wasps. Cf. **social** (def. 9). —*n.* **9.** a person who lives alone or in solitude, or avoids the society of others. **10.** a person who lives in solitude from religious motives. **11.** See **solitary confinement.** [ME < L *sōlitārius* alone, by itself, solitary, equiv. to *sōlit(ās)* soleness (*sōlus* SOLE[1]; see -ITY) + *-ārius* -ARY] —**sol′i·tar′i·ly,** *adv.* —**sol′i·tar′i·ness,** *n.*
—**Syn. 1.** lone. **7.** isolated, retired, sequestered, remote. **9, 10.** hermit, recluse. **10.** eremite.

sol′itary bee′, any of numerous bees, as the leaf-cutting bees, that do not live in a community. Cf. **social bee.**

sol′itary confine′ment, the confinement of a prisoner in a cell or other place in which he is completely isolated from others.

sol′itary sand′piper, a North American sandpiper, *Tringa solitaria,* having a brownish-gray, white-spotted back and whitish underparts.

sol′itary vir′eo. See **blue-headed vireo.**

sol′itary wasp′, any of numerous wasps, as the sand wasps or mud wasps, that do not live in a community. Cf. **social wasp.**

sol·i·tude (sol′i to͞od′, -tyo͞od′), *n.* **1.** the state of being or living alone; seclusion: *The misanthrope enjoys his solitude.* **2.** remoteness from habitations, as of a place; absence of human life or activity: *the solitude of the mountains.* **3.** a lonely, unfrequented place: *solitudes that were unfit for habitation.* [ME < MF < L *sōlitūdō.* See SOLI-[1], -TUDE] —**sol·i·tu·di·nous** (sol′i to͞od′ᵊnəs, -tyo͞od′-), *adj.*
—**Syn. 1.** retirement, privacy. SOLITUDE, ISOLATION refer to a state of being or living alone. SOLITUDE emphasizes the quality of being or feeling lonely and deserted: *to live in solitude.* ISOLATION may mean merely a detachment and separation from others: *to be put in isolation with an infectious disease.* **2.** loneliness. **3.** desert, waste, wilderness.

sol·lar (sol′ər), *n.* solar[2].

sol·ler (sol′ər), *n.* solar[2].

sol·ler·et (sol′ə ret′, sol′ə ret′), *n. Armor.* sabaton. [< F, dim. of OF *soller* shoe << LL *subtēl* hollow under the sole of a shoe, equiv. to *sub-* SUB- + *-tēl* (deriv. of *talus* ankle)]

sol·lick·er (sol′ə kər), *Brit., Australian Informal.* —*n.* **1.** force; momentum. —*adj.* Also **sol′lick·ing. 2.** very large. **3.** remarkable; wonderful. [?]

Sol·ly (sol′ē), *n.* a boy's given name, form of **Solomon.** Also, **Sol′lie.**

sol·mi·za·tion (sol′mi zā′shən), *n. Music.* act, process, or system of using certain syllables, esp. the sol-fa syllables, to represent the tones of the scale. [< F *solmisation,* equiv. to *solmis(er)* (< *sol* SOL[1] + *mi* MI + *-iser* -IZE) + *-ation* -ATION]

so·lo (sō′lō), *n., pl.* **-los, -li** (-lē), *adj., adv., v.* —*n.* **1.** a musical composition or a passage or section in a musical composition written for performance by one singer or instrumentalist, with or without accompaniment: *She sang a solo at the concert.* **2.** any performance, as a dance, by one person. **3.** a flight in an airplane during which the pilot is unaccompanied by an instructor or other person: *I'll be ready for my first solo next week.* **4.** *Cards.* any of certain games in which one person plays alone against others. —*adj.* **5.** *Music.* performing alone, as an instrument or its player: *a part for solo bassoon.* **6.** performed alone; not combined with other parts of equal importance; not concerted. **7.** alone; without a companion or partner: *a solo flight in an airplane.* —*adv.* **8.** on one's own; alone or unaccompanied: *After six lessons he was flying solo.* —*v.i.* **9.** to perform or do a solo: *He's going to solo on the trumpet.* [< It <L *sōlus* alone]

So·lo (sō′lō), *n.* former name of **Surakarta.**

so·lo·ist (sō′lō ist), *n.* a person who performs a solo or solos. [SOLO + -IST] —**so′lo·is′tic,** *adj.*

So′lo man′, an early man of the Upper Pleistocene, known from skull fragments found in Java. [named after the *Solo* River, central Java, near which remains were found]

Sol·o·mon (sol′ə mən), *n.* **1.** fl. 10th century B.C., king of Israel (son of David). **2.** an extraordinarily wise man; a sage. **3.** a boy's given name.

Sol·o·mon·ic (sol′ə mon′ik), *adj.* **1.** of or pertaining to the Hebrew King Solomon. **2.** wise or reasonable in character: *a Solomonic decision.* Also, **Sol·o·mo·ni·an** (sol′ə mō′nē ən, -mōn′yən). [SOLOMON + -IC]

Sol′omon Is′lands, 1. an archipelago in the W Pacific Ocean, E of New Guinea; important World War II battles; NW islands of Bougainville and Buka (formerly a German colony) now part of Papua New Guinea. **2.** an independent country comprising the larger, SE part of the archipelago; independence from Great Britain in 1978. 152,000; 11,458 sq. mi. *Cap.:* Honiara (on Guadalcanal). —**Sol′omon Is′lander.**

Sol′omon's lil′y. See **black calla.**

Sol′omon's seal′, a mystic or talismanic symbol in the form of an interlaced outline of either a five-pointed or six-pointed star.

Solomon's seal

Sol·o·mon's-seal (sol′ə mənz sēl′), *n.* any of several liliaceous plants of the genus *Polygonatum,* having a thick rootstock bearing seallike scars. [trans. of ML *sigillum Solomōnis*]

So·lon (sō′lən), *n.* **1.** c638–c558 B.C., Athenian statesman. **2.** (*often l.c.*) a wise lawgiver. —**So·lo·ni·an** (sō-lō′nē ən), **So·lon·ic** (sō lon′ik), *adj.*

So·lon (sō′lən), *n.* **1.** a town in N Ohio. 6333 (1960). **2.** a boy's given name.

so′ long′, *Informal.* good-by: *I said so long and left.*

So·lo·thurn (*Ger.* zō′lō to͝orn′), *n.* **1.** a city in NW Switzerland, on the Aar River: capital of canton of Solothurn. 18,394 (1960). **2.** a canton in NW Switzerland. 200,816 (1960). French, **Soleure.**

so′lo whist′, *Cards.* a variety of whist in which each player can offer to play any of seven specified bids.

sol·stice (sol′stis, sōl′-), *n.* **1.** *Astron.* either of the two times a year when the sun is at its greatest distance from the celestial equator: about June 21, when the sun reaches its northernmost point on the celestial sphere, or about December 22, when it reaches its southernmost point. Cf. **summer solstice, winter solstice. 2.** either of the two points in the ecliptic farthest from the equator. **3.** a furthest or culminating point; a turning point. [< ME < OF < L *sōlstitium,* equiv. to *sōl-* sun + *-stitium* (*stat(us)* ptp. of *sistere* to stand still + *-ium;* see -ICE)]

sol·sti·tial (sol stish′əl, sōl′-), *adj.* **1.** of or pertaining to a solstice or the solstices: *a solstitial point.* **2.** occurring at or about the time of a solstice. **3.** characteristic of the summer solstice. [< L *sōlstitiālis,* equiv. to *sōlstiti(um)* SOLSTICE + *-ālis* -AL[1]] —**sol·sti′tial·ly,** *adv.*

Sol·ti (sōl′tē), *n.* **Ge·org** (ge′ôrg), born 1912, Hungarian orchestra conductor.

sol·u·bil·i·ty (sol′yə bil′i tē), *n.* the quality or property of being capable of being dissolved; relative capability of being dissolved. [SOLUBLE + -ITY]

solubil′ity prod′uct, *Physical Chem.* the maximum number of undissociated ions, of an electrolyte in a saturated solution, capable at a given temperature of remaining in equilibrium with the undissolved phase of the solution.

sol·u·ble (sol′yə bəl), *adj.* **1.** capable of being dissolved or liquefied: *a soluble powder.* **2.** capable of being solved or explained: *a soluble problem.* —*n.* **3.** something soluble. [ME < LL *solūbilis,* equiv. to L *solū(ere)* (to) dissolve + *-bilis* -BLE] —**sol′u·ble·ness,** *n.* —**sol′u·bly,** *adv.*

sol′uble glass′. See **sodium silicate.**

so·lus (sō′ləs), *adj. Latin.* (referring to a man) alone; by oneself (used formerly in stage directions). Cf. **sola.**

sol·ute (sol′yo͞ot, sō′lo͞ot), *n.* **1.** the substance dissolved in a given solution. —*adj.* **2.** *Bot.* not adhering; free. [< L *solūt(us)* loosened, freed (ptp. of *solvere*). See SOLVE]

so·lu·tion (sə lo͞o′shən), *n.* **1.** the act of solving a problem, question, etc.: *The situation is approaching solution.* **2.** state of being solved: *a problem capable of solution.* **3.** a particular instance or method of solving; an explanation or answer: *The solution is as good as any other.* **4.** *Math.* **a.** the process of determining the answer to a problem. **b.** the answer. **5.** *Chem.* **a.** the act by which a gas, liquid, or solid is dispersed homogeneously in a gas, liquid, or solid without chemical change. **b.** such a substance, as dissolved sugar or salt in solution. **c.** a homogeneous, molecular mixture of two or more substances. **6.** *Pharm.* a liquid, usually water, in which a medication is dissolved. **7.** *Med.* **a.** the termination of a disease. **b.** a breach or break in anything, esp. one in parts of the body normally continuous, as from fracture or laceration: *solution of continuity.* [ME < L *solūtiōn-* (s. of *solūtiō*), deriv. of *solūt(us);* see SOLUTE, -ION] —**so·lu′tion·al,** *adj.*

sol·u·tiz·er (sol′yə tī′zər), *n. Chem.* any admixture to a substance for promoting or increasing its solubility or that of one or more of its components. [SOLUT(ION) + -IZE + -ER[1]]

So·lu·tre·an (sə lo͞o′trē ən), *adj.* of, pertaining to, or characteristic of an Upper Paleolithic culture of Europe, characterized by the manufacture of bifacial blades. [named after *Solutré,* village in central France where the archeological relics were found; see -AN]

so·lu·tus (sō lo͞o′təs), *adj.* (in prescriptions) dissolved. [< L]

solv., (in prescriptions) dissolve. [< L *solve*]

solv·a·ble (sol′və bəl), *adj.* **1.** capable of being solved, as a problem. **2.** *Math.* (of a group) having a normal series of subgroups in which successive quotient groups are Abelian. **3.** *Archaic.* soluble (def. 1). [SOLVE + -ABLE] —**solv′a·bil′i·ty, solv′a·ble·ness,** *n.*

solv·ate (sol′vāt), *n., v.,* **-at·ed, -at·ing.** *Chem.* —*n.* **1.** a compound formed by the interaction of a solvent and a solute. —*v.t.* **2.** to convert into a solvate. [SOLV(ENT) + -ATE[2]] —**solv·a′tion,** *n.*

Sol·vay (sol′vā *or, Fr.* sôl vā′ *for 1;* sōl′vā *for 2*), *n.* **1.** **Er·nest** (ûr′nist; *Fr.* er nest′), 1838–1922, Belgian chemist. **2.** a town in central New York. 8732 (1960).

Sol′vay proc′ess, a process for manufacturing sodium carbonate from sodium chloride and calcium carbonate consisting of saturating a concentrated solution of sodium chloride with ammonia, passing carbon dioxide through it, and calcining the product, sodium bicarbonate. [named after Ernest SOLVAY]

solve (solv), *v.t.,* **solved, solv·ing. 1.** to find the answer or explanation for; clear up; explain: *to solve the mystery of the missing books.* **2.** to work out the answer or solution to (a mathematical problem). [ME < L *solvere* to loosen, free, release, dissolve] —**solv′er,** *n.*

sol·ven·cy (sol′vən sē), *n.* solvent condition; ability to pay all just debts. [SOLVEN(T) + -CY]

sol·vent (sol′vənt), *adj.* **1.** able to pay all just debts. **2.** having the power of dissolving; causing solution. —*n.* **3.** a substance that dissolves another to form a solution: *Water is a solvent for sugar.* **4.** something that solves or explains. [< L *solvent-* (s. of *solvens*), prp. of *solv(ere)*. See SOLVE, -ENT] —**sol′vent·ly,** *adv.*

sol·ve·re (sol vēr′ē), *v.t.* (in prescriptions) to dissolve. [< L]

sol·vol·y·sis (sol vol′i sis), *n. Chem.* a chemical reaction in which the solvent and a dissolved substance interact; lyolysis. [< NL < L *solv(ere)* (see SOLVE) + -o- -o- + -LYSIS] —**sol·vo·lyt·ic** (sol′və lit′ik), *adj.*

Sol′way Firth′ (sol′wā), an arm of the Irish Sea between SW Scotland and NW England. 38 mi. long.

Sol·y·man (sol′ə mən), *n.* See **Suleiman I.**

Sol·y·mi (sol′ə mī′), *n.pl. Class. Myth.* warriors of Asia Minor.

so·ma[1] (sō′mə), *n., pl.* **-ma·ta** (-mə tə), **-mas.** *Biol.* the body of an organism as contrasted with its germ cells. [< NL < Gk *sôma* the body; body as opposed to soul]

so·ma[2] (sō′mə), *n.* haoma (def. 1). [< Skt]

So·ma (sō′mə), *n. Pharm., Trademark.* carisoprodol.

-soma, a learned borrowing from Greek meaning "body," used esp. in the formation of names of zoological genera: *Schistosoma.* Also, **-some**[3]. [< NL < Gk *sôma*]

So·ma·li (sō mä′lē, sə-), *n., pl.* **-lis,** (*esp. collectively*) **-li.** **1.** a member of a Hamitic race showing an admixture of Arab, Negro, and other ancestry, and dwelling in Somaliland and adjacent regions. **2.** the Cushitic language of the Somali.

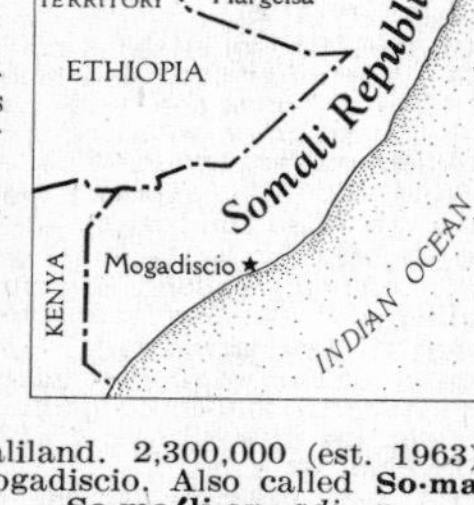

Soma′li cur′rent, an ocean current along the coast of Somaliland, flowing northward in summer and southwestward the rest of the year.

So·ma·li·land (sō mä′lē land′, sə-), *n.* a coastal region in E Africa, including the Afars and Issas Territory, Somali Republic, and part of Ethiopia.

Soma′liland Protec′torate, official name of the former **British Somaliland.**

Soma′li Repub′lic, an independent republic on the E coast of Africa, formed from the former British Somaliland and the former Italian Somaliland. 2,300,000 (est. 1963); 246,198 sq. mi. *Cap.:* Mogadiscio. Also called **Soma·li·a** (sō mä′lē ə, -mäl′yə). —**So·ma′li·an,** *adj., n.*

somat-, var. of **somato-** before a vowel: *somatist.*

so·mat·ic (sō mat′ik, sə-), *adj.* **1.** *Anat., Zool.* pertaining to the cavity of the body of an animal or, more especially, to its walls. **2.** *Biol.* pertaining to or affecting the somatic cells, as distinguished from the germ cells. **3.** of the body; bodily; physical. [< Gk *sōmatikós* of, pertaining to the body, equiv. to *sômat-* SOMAT- + *-ikos* -IC] —**so·mat′i·cal·ly,** *adv.*
—**Syn. 3.** corporal. —**Ant. 3.** psychic.

somat′ic cell′, *Biol.* **1.** one of the cells whch take part in the formation of the body, becoming differentiated into the various tissues, organs, etc. **2.** any cell other than a germ cell.

so·ma·tist (sō′mə tist), *n. Psychiatry.* a psychiatrist who considers all mental illnesses to have physical origins. [SOMAT- + -IST] —**so′ma·tism,** *n.*

somato-, a learned borrowing from Greek meaning "body," used in the formation of compound words: *somatotonia.* Also, *esp. before a vowel,* **somat-.** [< Gk *sômato-*, comb. form equiv. to *sômat-* (s. of *sôma* body) + *-o-* -o-]

so·ma·to·gen·ic (sō′mə tə jen′ik, sə mat′ə-), *adj. Biol.* developing from somatic cells. Also, **so·ma·to·ge·net·ic** (sō′mə tə jə net′ik). [SOMATO- + -GENIC]

so·ma·tol·o·gy (sō′mə tol′ə jē), *n.* the branch of anthropology which deals with man's physical characteristics. [SOMATO- + -LOGY] —**so·ma·to·log·ic** (sō′mə təloj′ik, sə mat′əloj′-), **so′ma·to·log′i·cal,** *adj.* —**so′ma·to·log′i·cal·ly,** *adv.* —**so′ma·tol′o·gist,** *n.*

so·ma·to·plasm (sō′mə tə plaz′əm, sə mat′ə-), *n. Biol.* the protoplasm of a somatic cell, esp. as distinguished from germ plasm. [SOMATO- + -PLASM] —**so′ma·to·plas′tic,** *adj.*

so·ma·to·pleure (sō′mə tə plŏŏr′, sə mat′ə-), *n. Embryol.* the double layer formed by the association of the upper layer of the lateral plate of mesoderm with the overlying ectoderm, functioning in the formation of the body wall and amnion. Cf. **splanchnopleure.** [alter. of NL *somatopleura.* See SOMATO-, PLEURA] —**so′ma·to·pleu′ral, so′ma·to·pleu′ric,** *adj.*

so·ma·to·to·ni·a (sō′mə tə tō′nē ə, sə mat′ə-), *n. Psychol.* a personality pattern accompanying the mesomorphic body type and characterized by aggressiveness, vigor, and preference for physical activity. Cf. **cerebrotonia, viscerotonia.** [< NL; see SOMATO-, TONUS, -IA] —**so·ma·to·ton·ic** (sō′mə tə ton′ik, sə mat′ə-), *adj., n.*

som·ber (som′bər), *adj.* **1.** gloomily dark; shadowy; dimly lighted: *a somber passageway.* **2.** dark and dull, as color, or as things in respect to color: *a somber dress.* **3.** gloomy, depressing, or dismal: *a somber mood.* **4.** extremely serious; grave: *a somber expression on his face.* Also, *esp. Brit.,* **som′bre.** [< F *sombre* perh. << L *umbra* shade] —**som′ber·ly;** *esp. Brit.,* **som′bre·ly,** *adv.* —**som′ber·ness;** *esp. Brit.,* **som′bre·ness,** *n.*
—**Syn. 1.** dusky, murky, cloudy, dull, sunless, dismal. **3.** lugubrious, mournful, doleful, melancholy. —**Ant. 1.** bright. **3.** cheerful.

Sombrero

som·bre·ro (som brâr′ō; *Sp.* sôm bre′rô), *n., pl.* **-bre·ros** (-brâr′ōz; *Sp.* -bre′rôs). a broad-brimmed hat of straw or felt, usually tall-crowned, worn in Spain, Mexico, the southwestern U.S., etc., esp. by Spanish-Americans. Cf. **cowboy hat, ten-gallon hat.** [< SP, deriv. of *sombra* shade] —**som·bre′roed,** *adj.*

Som·bre·ro de Tres Pi·cos, El (*Sp.* el sôm bre′rô the tres′ pē′kôs). See **Three-cornered Hat, The.**

som·brous (som′brəs), *adj. Archaic.* somber. [< F *sombre* shade + -OUS]

some (sum; *unstressed* səm), *adj.* **1.** being an undetermined or unspecified one: *Some person may object.* **2.** (used with plural nouns) certain: *Some days I stay home.* **3.** of a certain unspecified number, amount, degree, etc.: *to some extent.* **4.** unspecified but considerable in number, amount, degree, etc.: *We talked for some time. He was here some weeks.* **5.** (used with numerals and with words expressing degree, extent, etc.) approximately; about: *Some 300 were present.* **6.** *Informal.* of considerable worth or consequence; striking for its kind: *That was some storm.* —*pron.* **7.** certain persons, individuals, instances, etc., not specified: *Some think he is dead.* **8.** an unspecified number, amount, etc., as distinguished from the rest or in addition: *He paid a thousand dollars and then some.* —*adv.* **9.** *Informal.* to some degree or extent; somewhat: *I like baseball some.* **10.** *Informal.* to a great degree or extent; considerably: *That's going some.* [ME; OE *sum,* c. MLG, MHG *sum,* Icel *sumr,* Goth *sums*]
—**Syn. 1.** SOME, ANY refer to an appreciable amount or number, and often to a portion of a larger amount. SOME suggests that no specified quantity is meant. ANY suggests that no particular amount is being distinguished from any other or from the remainder; it is any at all (or none). Both SOME and ANY may be used in affirmative or negative questions: *Will you (won't you) have some? Do you (don't you) have any?* But SOME must be used in affirmative statements and answers: *You may have some. Yes, I'd like some.* And ANY may be used only in negative statements and answers: *I don't care for any. No, I can't take any.* —**Ant. 1.** none.

-some[1], a native English suffix formerly used in the formation of adjectives: *quarrelsome; burdensome.* [ME, OE *-sum;* akin to Goth *-sama,* G *-sam;* see SAME]

-some[2], a collective suffix used with numerals: *twosome; threesome.* [ME *-sum,* OE *sum;* special use of SOME (pronoun)]

-some[3], a learned borrowing from Greek meaning "body," used in the formation of compound words: *chromosome.* Also, **-soma.** [< Gk; see SOMA]

some·bod·y (sum′bod′ē, -bud′ē, -bə dē), *pron., n., pl.* **-bod·ies.** —*pron.* **1.** some person. —*n.* **2.** a person of some note or importance. [ME; see SOME, BODY]

some·day (sum′dā′), *adv.* at an indefinite future time. [ME; see SOME, DAY]

some·deal (sum′dēl′), *adv. Archaic.* somewhat. [ME *somdel,* OE *sume dǣle,* dat. of *sum dǣl* some portion. See SOME, DEAL[1]]

some·how (sum′hou′), *adv.* **1.** in some way not specified, apparent, or known. **2. somehow or other,** in an undetermined way; by any means possible: *She was determined to finish college somehow or other.* [SOME + HOW]

some·one (sum′wun′, -wən), *pron.* some person; somebody. [ME; see SOME, ONE]
—**Usage.** See **anyone.**

some·place (sum′plās′), *adv.* somewhere. [SOME + PLACE]
—**Usage.** See **anywhere.**

som·er (sum′ər), *n. Obs.* summer[2] (def. 1).

Som·er·dale (sum′ər dāl′), *n.* a town in SW New Jersey. 4839 (1960).

som·er·sault (sum′ər sôlt′), *n.* **1.** an acrobatic movement, either forward or backward, in which the body rolls end over end, making a complete revolution. **2.** such a movement performed in the air as part of a dive, tumbling routine, etc. **3.** a complete overturn or reversal, as of opinion. —*v.i.* **4.** to perform a somersault. Also, **som·er·set** (sum′ər set′), **summersault, summerset.** [< OF *sombresaut,* alter. of *sobresault;* cf. OPr *sobre* over (< L *super*), *saut* a leap (< L *saltus*)]

Som·er·set (sum′ər set′, -sit), *n.* **1.** a town in S Kentucky. 7112 (1960). **2.** a town in SW Pennsylvania. 6347 (1960). **3.** Somersetshire. **4.** a boy's given name.

Som·er·set·shire (sum′ər set shēr′, -shər, -sit-), *n.* a county in SW England. 598,556 (1961); 1616 sq. mi. *Co. seat:* Taunton. Also called **Somerset.**

Som′ers Point′ (sum′ərz), a town in SE New Jersey. 4504 (1960).

Som·ers·worth (sum′ərz wûrth′), *n.* a town in SE New Hampshire. 8529 (1960).

Som·er·ville (sum′ər vil′), *n.* **1.** a city in E Massachusetts, near Boston. 94,697 (1960). **2.** a town in central New Jersey. 12,458 (1960).

some·thing (sum′thing), *pron.* **1.** some thing; a certain undetermined or unspecified thing: *Something is wrong there. Something's happening.* **2.** an additional amount, as of cents, minutes, etc., that is unknown, unspecified, or forgotten: *He charged me ten something for the hat. Our train gets in at two something.* —*n.* **3.** *Informal.* a thing or person of some value or consequence: *He is really something! This writer has something to say and he says it well.* —*adv.* **4.** in some degree; to some extent; somewhat. **5.** *Informal.* to a high or extreme degree; quite: *He took on something fierce about my tardiness.* [ME, OE *sum thing.* See SOME, THING[1]]

some·time (sum′tīm′), *adv.* **1.** at some indefinite or indeterminate point of time: *He will arrive sometime next week.* **2.** at an indefinite future time: *Come to see me sometime.* **3.** *Rare.* sometimes; on some occasions. **4.** *Archaic.* at one time; formerly. **5.** *Obs.* on a certain occasion in the past. —*adj.* **6.** having been formerly; former: *sometime professor of history at Oxford.* [ME; see SOME, TIME]

some·times (sum′tīmz′), *adv.* **1.** on some occasions; at times; now and then. **2.** *Obs.* once; formerly. [SOMETIME + -S[3]]

some·way (sum′wā′), *adv.* in some way; somehow. Also, **some′ way′, some′ways′.** [ME; see SOME, WAY]

some·what (sum′hwut′, -hwot′, -hwət, -wut′, -wot′, -wət), *adv.* **1.** in some measure or degree; to some extent: *not angry, just somewhat disturbed.* —*n.* **2.** some part, portion, amount, etc. [ME; see SOME, WHAT]

some·when (sum′hwen′, -wen′), *adv.* at some future indefinite time; sometime. [ME *sumwhanne;* see SOME, WHEN]

some·where (sum′hwâr′, -wâr′), *adv.* **1.** in or at some place not specified, determined, or known: *They live somewhere in Michigan.* **2.** to some place not specified or known: *They went out somewhere.* **3.** at or to some point in amount, degree, etc. (usually fol. by *about, near,* etc.): *He is somewhere about 60 years old.* **4.** at some point of time (usually fol. by *about, between, in,* etc.): *somewhere about 1930; somewhere between 1930 and 1940; somewhere in the 1930's.* —*n.* **5.** an unspecified or uncertain place. [ME; see SOME, WHERE]
—**Usage.** See **anyplace.**

some·wheres (sum′hwârz′, -wârz′), *adv. Chiefly Dial.* somewhere. [SOMEWHERE + -S[1]]

some·while (sum′hwīl′, -wīl′), *adv. Archaic.* **1.** at some former time. **2.** at one time or another; sometime. **3.** at times; sometimes. **4.** for some time. [ME; see SOME, WHILE]

some·whith·er (sum′hwith′ər, -with′-), *adv.* **1.** to some unspecified place; somewhere. **2.** in some direction. [ME; see SOME, WHITHER]

some·why (sum′hwī′, -wī′), *adv. Rare.* for some reason. [SOME + WHY]

some·wise (sum′wīz′), *adv. Archaic.* by some means; somehow. [ME; see SOME, WISE[2]]

so·mite (sō′mīt), *n.* **1.** any of the longitudinal series of segments or parts into which the body of certain animals is divided; a metamere. **2.** *Embryol.* one member of a series of paired segments into which the thickened dorsal zone of mesoderm is divided. [SOM(A) + -ITE[1]] —**so·mi·tal** (sō′mi təl), **so·mit·ic** (sō mit′ik), *adj.*

Somme (sôm), *n.* **1.** a river in N France, flowing NW to the English Channel: battles, World War I, 1916, 1918; World War II, 1944. 150 mi. long. **2.** a department in N France. 488,225 (1962); 2424 sq. mi. *Cap.:* Amiens.

som·me·lier (sum′əl yā′; *Fr.* sô mə lyā′), *n., pl.* **som·me·liers** (sum′əl yāz′; *Fr.* sô mə lyā′). a waiter, as in a club or restaurant, who is in charge of wines. [< F, MF, m. *sommier* one charged with arranging transportation, equiv. to *somme* burden (<< LL *sagma* horse load < Gk: covering, pack saddle) + *-ier* -IER]

Söm·mer·ing (sum′ər ing), *n.* a walled plain in the second quadrant of the face of the moon: about 17 miles in diameter.

som·nam·bu·late (som nam′byə lāt′, səm-), *v.,* **-lat·ed, -lat·ing.** —*v.i.* **1.** to walk during sleep, as a somnambulist does. —*v.t.* **2.** to traverse during sleep. [< L *somn(us)* sleep + *ambulātus;* see AMBULATE] —**som·nam·bu·lance** (som nam′byə ləns, səm-), *n.* —**som·nam′bu·lant,** *adj., n.* —**som·nam′bu·la′tor,** *n.*

som·nam·bu·la·tion (som nam′byə lā′shən, səm-), *n.* the act of walking in one's sleep. [< NL *somnambulātiōn-* (s. of *somnambulātiō*). See SOMNAMBULATE, -ION]

som·nam·bu·lism (som nam′byə liz′əm, səm-), *n.* the fact or habit of walking about, and often performing various other acts, while asleep; sleepwalking. [< NL *somnambulismus.* See SOMNAMBULATE, -ISM] —**som·nam′bu·list,** *n.* —**som·nam′bu·lis′tic,** *adj.*

Som·ni (som′nē), *n.* **Palus.** See **Palus Somni.**

som·ni·fa·cient (som′nə fā′shənt), *adj.* **1.** causing or inducing sleep. —*n.* **2.** a drug or other agent that induces or tends to induce sleep. [< L *somn(us)* sleep + *-i-* -I- + -FACIENT]

som·nif·er·ous (som nif′ər əs, səm-), *adj.* bringing or inducing sleep, as drugs, influences, etc. [< L *somnifer* sleep-bringing (*somni-* sleep (comb. form of *somnus*) + *-fer*); see -FEROUS] —**som·nif′er·ous·ly,** *adv.*

som·nif·ic (som nif′ik, səm-), *adj.* causing sleep; soporific; somniferous. [< L *somnificus* causing sleep, equiv. to *somni-* sleep (comb. form of *somnus*) + *-ficus* -FIC]

som·nil·o·quy (som nil′ə kwē, səm-), *n.* the act or habit of talking while asleep. [< L *somni-* (comb. form of *somnus*) sleep + *-loquy;* cf. COLLOQUY, SOLILOQUY] —**som·nil′o·quist,** *n.* —**som·nil′o·quous,** *adj.*

Som·ni·o·rum (som′nē ôr′əm, -ōr′əm), *n.* **Lacus.** See **Lacus Somniorum.**

som·noe (som′nō), *n. Obs.* a night table or the like.

som·no·lent (som′nə lənt), *adj.* **1.** sleepy; drowsy. **2.** tending to cause sleep. [ME *sompnolent* < OF < L *somnolentus,* deriv. of *somn(us)* sleep] —**som′no·lence, som′no·len·cy,** *n.* —**som′no·lent·ly,** *adv.*
—**Syn. 1.** slumberous. **2.** somniferous, soporific.

Som·nus (som′nəs), *n.* the ancient Roman god of sleep, a son of Nyx and brother of Mors: identified with the Greek god Hypnos.

So·mo·za (sô mô′sä), *n.* **Luis** (lwēs), 1922–1967, Nicaraguan statesman: president 1956–63.

son (sun), *n.* **1.** a male child or person in relation to his parents. **2.** a male child or person adopted as a son; a person in the legal position of a son. **3.** any male descendant: *a son of the Aztecs.* **4.** a son-in-law. **5.** a person related as if by ties of sonship. **6.** a male person looked upon as the product or result of particular agencies, forces, influences, etc.: *a true son of the soil.* **7.** a familiar term of address to a man or boy from an older person, an ecclesiastic, etc. **8. the Son,** the second person of the Trinity; Jesus Christ. [ME *sone,* OE *sunu;* c. D *zoon,* G *Sohn,* Icel *sunr, sonr,* Goth *sunus,* Lith *sūnùs,* Skt *sūnús*] —**son′less,** *adj.* —**son′like′,** *adj.*

son-, var. of **soni-** before a vowel: *sonance.*

so·na·gram (sō′nə gram′), *n.* See **sound spectrogram.** [? < L *sonā(re)* (to) sound + -GRAM[1]]

so·nal (sōn′əl), *adj.* pertaining to sound; sonic. [SON- + -AL[1]]

so·nance (sō′nəns), *n.* **1.** the condition or quality of being sonant. **2.** *Obs.* a sound; a tune. [SON- + -ANCE]
—**Syn. 1.** voice, sound, noise.

so·nant (sō′nənt), *adj.* **1.** sounding; having sound. **2.** *Phonet.* voiced (opposed to *surd*). —*n. Phonet.* **3.** a speech sound which by itself makes a syllable or subordinates to itself the other sounds in the syllable; a syllabic sound (opposed to *consonant*). **4.** a voiced sound (opposed to *surd*). **5.** (in Indo-European) a sonorant. [< L *sonant-* (s. of *sonāns,* prp. of *sonāre*) sounding. See SON-, -ANT] —**so·nan·tal** (sō nan′təl), **so·nan·tic** (sō nan′tik), *adj.*

so·nar (sō′när), *n.* **1.** a method for detecting and locating objects submerged in water by means of the sound waves they reflect or produce. **2.** the apparatus used in sonar. Also called, *Brit.,* **asdic.** [*so(und) na(vigation) r(anging)*]

so·nar·man (sō′när mən), *n., pl.* **-men.** *U.S. Navy.* a petty officer who operates and maintains sonar.

so·na·ta (sə nä′tə), *n. Music.* an extended instrumental composition usually in several (commonly three or four) movements in contrasted moods and keys, each movement being developed with a balanced form in mind. [< It < L *sonāta*, fem. of *sonātus* (ptp. of *sonāre*). See SONANT, -ATE[1]]

so·na′ta form′, a musical form comprising an exposition, in which the main themes are stated, a development section, a recapitulation of the material in the exposition, and, usually, a coda.

so·na·ta-ron·do (sə nä′tə ron′dō, -ron dō′), *n., pl.* **-dos.** a musical form combining characteristics of both the sonata form and the rondo.

son·a·ti·na (son′ə tē′nə; *It.* sô′nä tē′nä), *n., pl.* **-nas,** *It.* **-ne** (-ne). *Music.* a short or simplified sonata. [< It, dim. of SONATA]

sonde (sond), *n. Rocketry.* a rocket, balloon, or rockoon used as a probe for observing phenomena in the atmosphere. [< F: plumb line; see SOUND[3]]

son·der·class (zon′dər klas′, -kläs′), *n.* a special class of small racing yachts, restricted as to size, sail area, cost, etc. [part trans. of G *Sonderklasse*]

Son·dra (son′drə), *n.* a girl's given name. Also, **Sandra, Saundra.**

sone (sōn), *n.* a unit for measuring the loudness of sound, equal to the loudness of a sound which, in the judgment of a group of listeners, is equal to that of a 1000-cycle-per-second reference sound having an intensity of 40 decibels. [< L *son(us)* sound]

So·net·te an Or·phe·us (*Ger.* zō net′ə än ôʀ′fā-ōōs′). See **Sonnets to Orpheus.**

song (sông, song), *n.* **1.** a short metrical composition intended or adapted for singing, esp. one in rhymed stanzas; a lyric; a ballad. **2.** a musical piece adapted for singing or simulating a piece to be sung: *Mendelssohn's "Songs without Words."* **3.** poetical composition; poetry. **4.** the art or act of singing; vocal music. **5.** that which is sung. **6.** the musical or tuneful sounds produced by certain birds, insects, etc. **7. for a song,** at a very low price; as a bargain: *Because the company was moving to another State, many employees had to sell their homes for a song.* [ME, OE; c. G *Sang*, OIcel *söngr*, Goth *saggws*] —**song′like′,** *adj.*

song′ and dance′, *Informal.* a story or statement, esp. an untrue or misleading one designed to evade the matter at hand: *Every time she's late, she gives me a song and dance about oversleeping.*

song·bird (sông′bûrd′, song′-), *n.* **1.** a bird that sings. **2.** any passerine bird of the suborder *Oscines* or *Passeres*. **3.** a woman who sings. [SONG + BIRD]

song′ cy′cle, a group of art songs that are usually all by the same poet and composer and have a unifying subject or idea.

song·fest (sông′fest′, song′-), *n.* **1.** an informal, often spontaneous gathering at which people sing folk songs, popular ballads, etc. **2.** an informal gathering at a studio, concert hall, or the like, in which people participate by singing along with the performers. [SONG + -FEST]

song·ful (sông′fəl, song′-), *adj.* abounding in song; melodious. [SONG + -FUL] —**song′ful·ly,** *adv.* —**song′ful·ness,** *n.*

Song·ka (song′kä′), *n.* a river in SE Asia, flowing SE from SW China through Indochina to the Gulf of Tonkin. 500 mi. long. Also called **Red River.**

song·less (sông′lis, song′-), *adj.* devoid of song; lacking the power of song, as a bird. [SONG + -LESS] —**song′less·ly,** *adv.* —**song′less·ness,** *n.*

Song′ of Ber·na·dette′, The (bûr′nə det′), a novel (1942) by Franz Werfel.

Song′ of Ro′land, The. See **Chanson de Roland.**

Song′ of Sol′omon, The, a book of the Bible. Also called **Song′ of Songs′, Canticles;** *Douay Bible,* **Canticle of Canticles.**

Song′ of the Three′ Chil′dren, a book of the Apocrypha, included as part of the third chapter of Daniel in the Douay Bible.

Songs′ of Expe′rience, a collection of poems (1794) by William Blake.

Songs′ of In′nocence, a collection of poems (1789) by William Blake.

song′ spar′row, a small fringilline songbird, *Melospiza melodia*, of North America.

song·ster (sông′stər, song′-), *n.* **1.** a person who sings; a singer. **2.** a writer of songs or poems; a poet. **3.** a songbird. [ME; OE *sangestre* woman singer. See SONG, -STER]

song·stress (sông′stris, song′-), *n.* a female singer, esp. one who specializes in popular songs. [SONG + -STRESS]

song′ thrush′, a common, European songbird, *Turdus philomelos.*

song·writ·er (sông′rī′tər, song′-), *n.* a person who writes the words or music, or both, for popular songs. [SONG + WRITER]

soni-, a learned borrowing from Latin meaning "sound," used in the formation of compound words: *soniferous.* Also, **son-, sono-.** [< L *soni-*, comb. form of *sonus* sound]

So·nia (sō′nyə; *Russ.* sô′nyä), *n.* a girl's given name, Russian form of **Sophia.** Also, **So′nja, Sonya.**

son·ic (son′ik), *adj.* **1.** of or pertaining to sound. **2.** noting or pertaining to a speed equal to that of sound in air at the same height above sea level. [SON- + -IC]

son′ic bar′rier. See **sound barrier.**

son′ic boom′, a loud noise caused by the shock wave generated by an aircraft moving at supersonic speed.

son′ic depth′ find′er, a sonar instrument used to measure depths under water. Also called **fathometer.**

son′ic mine′. See **acoustic mine.**

son·ics (son′iks), *n.* (*construed as sing.*) the branch of science that deals with the practical applications of sound. [see SONIC, -ICS]

so·nif·er·ous (sə nif′ər əs, sō-), *adj.* conveying or producing sound. [SONI- + -FEROUS]

son-in-law (sun′in lô′), *n., pl.* **sons-in-law.** the husband of one's daughter. [ME]

son·net (son′it), *n.* **1.** *Pros.* a poem, properly expressive of a single, complete thought, idea, or sentiment, of 14 lines, usually in iambic pentameter, with rhymes arranged according to one of certain definite schemes, being in the strict or Italian form divided into a major group of 8 lines (the octave) followed by a minor group of 6 lines (the sestet), and in a common English form into 3 quatrains followed by a couplet. —*v.i.* **2.** to compose sonnets. —*v.t.* **3.** to celebrate in a sonnet or sonnets. [< It *sonett(o)* < OPr *sonet*, equiv. to *son* poem (< L *sonus* sound) + *-et* -ET] —**son′net·like′,** *adj.*

son·net·eer (son′i tēr′), *n.* **1.** a composer of sonnets. —*v.i.* **2.** to compose sonnets; sonnetize. [SONNET + -EER; r. earlier *sonnetier* < It *sonnettiere*]

son·net·ise (son′i tīz′), *v.i., v.t.,* **-ised, -is·ing.** *Chiefly Brit.* sonnetize. —**son′net·i·sa′tion,** *n.*

son·net·ize (son′i tīz′), *v.,* **-ized, -iz·ing.** —*v.i.* **1.** to write or compose sonnets. —*v.t.* **2.** to write sonnets on or to. [SONNET + -IZE] —**son′net·i·za′tion,** *n.*

son′net se′quence, a group of sonnets composed by one poet and having a unifying theme or subject.

Son′nets from the Por′tuguese, a sonnet sequence (1850) by Elizabeth Barrett Browning.

Son′nets to Or′pheus, a collection of 55 sonnets (1923) by Rainer Maria Rilke. German, **Sonette an Orpheus.**

son·ny (sun′ē), *n.* **1.** little son (often used as a familiar term of address to a boy). **2.** (used as a term of direct address to express contempt, derision, etc.): *No, sonny, you can't park there!* [SON + -Y[2]]

Son·ny (sun′ē), *n.* a boy's given name.

sono-, var. of **soni-:** *sonometer.*

son·o·buoy (son′ə boi′, -bōō′ē), *n. Navig.* a buoy that emits a radio signal on receiving an underwater signal from a vessel. [SONO- + BUOY]

son′ of a bitch′, *pl.* **sons of bitches.** *Slang.* **1.** a contemptible or thoroughly disagreeable person; scoundrel. **2.** a disagreeable matter; a chore. **3.** (used as an exclamation of impatience, irritation, astonishment, etc.)

son′ of Ad′am, a man: *He had all the weaknesses to which a son of Adam is heir.*

son′ of a gun′, *pl.* **sons of guns.** *Slang.* **1.** rogue; rascal; scoundrel: *That son of a gun still owes me $20.* **2.** a tiresome or disagreeable matter, chore, etc. **3.** (used as an affectionate greeting, term of address, etc.): *Charlie Humpelmeyer, you old son of a gun, how are you?* **4.** (used as an exclamation of irritation, surprise, dismay, etc.)

Son′ of God′, **1.** Jesus Christ, esp. as the Messiah. **2.** any person responding to God or acknowledging God as Father. Rom. 8:14. [ME]

Son′ of Man′, Jesus Christ, esp. as at the Last Judgment. [ME]

So·no·ma (sə nō′mə), *n.* a town in W California. 3023 (1960).

so·nom·e·ter (sə nom′i tər), *n. Med.* audiometer. [SONO- + -METER]

So·no·ra (sô nô′rä *for 1;* sə nōr′ə, -nôr′ə *for 2, 3*), *n.* **1.** a state in NW Mexico. 783,378 (1960); 70,484 sq. mi. *Cap.:* Hermosillo. **2.** a town in central California. 2725 (1960). **3.** a town in W Texas. 2619 (1960). —**So·no·ran** (sə nōr′ən, -nôr′ən), *adj.*

so·no·rant (sə nōr′ənt, -nôr′-, sō-), *Phonet.* —*n.* **1.** a voiced sound less sonorous than a vowel but more sonorous than a stop or fricative, as *l, r, m, n, y, w:* such a sound may be a sonant at one time and a consonant at another, as English *y*, which is a sonant in *any* and a consonant in *yet.* —*adj.* **2.** having the properties of a sonorant. [< L *sonōr-* (s. of *sonor*) sound, noise + -ANT; see SONOROUS]

so·nor·i·ty (sə nôr′i tē, -nor′-), *n., pl.* **-ties.** the condition or quality of being resonant or sonorous. [< ML *sonōritāt-* (s. of *sonōritās*) < LL: melody, equiv. to L *sonōr(us)* (see SONOROUS) + *-itāt-* -ITY]

so·no·rous (sə nōr′əs, -nôr′-, son′ər əs), *adj.* **1.** giving out or capable of giving out a sound, esp. a deep, resonant sound, as a thing or place: *a sonorous cavern.* **2.** loud, deep, or resonant, as a sound. **3.** rich and full in sound, as language, verse, etc. **4.** high-flown; grandiloquent: *a sonorous address.* [< L *sonōrus* noisy, sounding, equiv. to *sonōr-* (s. of *sonor*) sound + *-us* -OUS] —**so·no′rous·ly,** *adv.* —**so·no′rous·ness,** *n.*

-sonous, a combination of **soni-** and **-ous,** as final element of compound words: *dissonous.*

Sons′ and Lov′ers, a novel (1913) by D. H. Lawrence.

son·ship (sun′ship), *n.* the state, fact, or relation of being a son. [SON + -SHIP]

Sons′ of Lib′erty, *Amer. Hist.* **1.** any of several patriotic societies, originally secret, that opposed the Stamp Act and thereafter supported moves for American independence. **2.** (during the Civil War) a secret society of Copperheads.

son·sy (son′sē), *adj.,* **-si·er, -si·est.** *Scot. and North Eng., Irish Eng.* **1.** lucky; fortunate. **2.** strong and healthy; robust. **3.** agreeable; good-natured. **4.** comfortable. Also, **saucy, son′sie.** [see UNSONSY]

Son·ya (sō′nyə; *Russ.* sô′nyä), *n.* a girl's given name, Russian form of **Sophia.** Also, **Sonia, Sonja.**

Soo′ Canals′ (sōō). See **Sault Ste. Marie Canals.**

Soo·chow (sōō′chou′; *Chin.* sōō′jō′), *n.* former name of **Wuhsien.**

soo·ey (sōō′ē), *interj.* (a shout used in calling pigs.) [? alter. of SOW[2]]

soo·gee (sōō′jē), *n., v.,* **-geed, -gee·ing.** *Naut.* —*n.* **1.** Also, **soo·gee-moo·gee** (sōō′jē mōō′jē), **suegee, sujee-mujee, suji-muji.** a solution of soap or detergent for cleaning decks or painted surfaces. —*v.t.* **2.** to clean decks or painted surfaces with soogee. [perh. < Jap *sōji* cleaning]

sool (sōōl), *v.t.* **1.** *Australian.* **a.** to incite to violence; sic. **b.** *Archaic.* to seize or capture an animal. **2.** *Brit. Archaic.* to seize an animal by the ears. Also, **sowl.** [?]

soom (sōōm), *n. Scot. and North Eng.* swim.

soon (sōōn), *adv.* **1.** within a short period after this or that time, event, etc.: *We shall know soon after he calls.* **2.** before long; in the near future; at an early date: *Let's leave soon.* **3.** promptly or quickly: *He came as soon as he could.* **4.** readily or willingly: *I would as soon walk as ride.* **5.** *Dial.* early in a period of time; before the time specified is much advanced: *soon at night; soon in the evening.* **6.** *Obs.* immediately; at once; forthwith. **7. had sooner.** See **have** (def. 22). **8. sooner or later,** in the future; eventually: *Sooner or later his luck will run out.* [ME; OE *sōna* at once; c. OHG *sān*, Goth *suns*]

soon·er (sōō′nər), *n.* **1.** a person who settles on government land before it is legally opened to settlers in order to gain the choice of location. **2.** a person who gains an unfair advantage by getting ahead of others.

Soon·er (sōō′nər), *n.* a native or inhabitant of Oklahoma (the **Sooner State**) (used as a nickname).

Soon′er State′, Oklahoma (used as a nickname).

Soong (sōōng), *n.* **1. Charles Jones,** died 1927, Chinese merchant (father of Ai-ling, Chin-ling, Mei-ling, and Tse-ven Soong). **2. Ai-ling** (ī′ling′), born 1888, wife of H. H. Kung. **3. Ching-ling** (ching′ling′), born 1890, widow of Sun Yat-sen. **4. Mei-ling** (mā′ling′), born 1898, wife of Chiang Kai-shek. **5. Tse-ven** or **Tsŭ-vên** (tsōō′wun′), (*T.V.*), born 1891, Chinese financier.

soo·ny (sōō′nē), *adj. Australian.* sentimental; emotional. [dial. var. of SWOUND + -Y[1]]

soot (sŏŏt, sōōt), *n.* **1.** a black, carbonaceous substance produced during the imperfect combustion of coal, wood, oil, etc., rising in fine particles and adhering to the sides of the chimney or pipe conveying the smoke: also conveyed in the atmosphere to other locations. —*v.t.* **2.** to mark, cover, or treat with soot. [ME; OE *sōt*; c. OIcel *sōt*] —**soot′less,** *adj.* —**soot′like′,** *adj.*

sooth (sōōth), *n.* **1.** *Archaic.* truth, reality, or fact. [ME; OE *sōth*; c. OS *sōth*; see below] —*adj. Archaic.* **2.** soothing, soft, or sweet. **3.** true or real. [ME; OE *sōth*; c. OS *sōth*, OIcel *sannr*, Goth *sunjis* true, Skt *sat, sant*, based on a root meaning *be*, as in IS] —**sooth′ly,** *adv.*

soothe (sōōth), *v.,* **soothed, sooth·ing.** —*v.t.* **1.** to tranquilize or calm, as a person, the feelings, etc.; relieve, comfort, or refresh: *soothing someone's anger; to soothe someone with a hot drink.* **2.** to mitigate, assuage, or allay, as pain, sorrow, doubt, etc.: *to soothe sunburned skin.* —*v.i.* **3.** to exert a soothing influence; bring tranquillity, calm, ease, or comfort. [ME *sothe*, OE *sōth(ian)*, equiv. to *sōth* SOOTH + *-ian* inf. suffix] —**sooth′er,** *n.* —**sooth′ing·ly,** *adv.* —**sooth′ing·ness,** *n.*
—**Syn. 1.** See **comfort. 2.** alleviate, appease, mollify, soften, lull. —**Ant. 1.** upset.

sooth·fast (sōōth′fast′, -fäst′), *adj. Archaic.* **1.** based on the truth; true. **2.** truthful; veracious. [ME *sothfast*, OE *sōthfæst*. See SOOTH, FAST[1]] —**sooth′fast′ly,** *adv.* —**sooth′fast′ness,** *n.*

sooth·say (sōōth′sā′), *v.i.,* **-said, -say·ing.** to foretell events; predict. [back formation from SOOTHSAYER]

sooth·say·er (sōōth′sā′ər), *n.* a person who professes to foretell events. [ME *sothseyere, sothseyer*. See SOOTH, SAY, -ER[1]]

sooth·say·ing (sōōth′sā′ing), *n.* **1.** the practice or art of foretelling events. **2.** a prediction or prophecy. [SOOTH + SAYING]

soot·y (sŏŏt′ē, sōō′tē), *adj.,* **soot·i·er, soot·i·est.** **1.** covered, blackened, or smirched with soot. **2.** consisting of or resembling soot. **3.** of a black, blackish, or dusky color. [ME; see SOOT, -Y[1]] —**soot′i·ly,** *adv.* —**soot′i·ness,** *n.*

soot′y blotch′, *Plant Pathol.* **1.** a disease, esp. of apples and pears, characterized by sootlike spots or blotches on the fruit, caused by a fungus, *Gloeodes pomigena.* **2.** a disease of clover, characterized by black, crusty blotches on the underside of the leaves, caused by a fungus, *Cymadothea trifolii.*

soot′y mold′, **1.** *Plant Pathol.* a disease of plants, characterized by a black, sooty growth covering the affected parts, caused by any of several fungi. **2.** any fungus, esp. of the family *Capnodiaceae*, causing this disease.

soot′y tern′, a tern, *Sterna fuscata*, of southern seas, that is blackish above and white below.

sop (sop), *n., v.,* **sopped, sop·ping.** —*n.* **1.** a piece of solid food, as bread, for dipping in liquid food. **2.** anything thoroughly soaked. **3.** something given to pacify or quiet, or as a bribe: *The political boss gave him some cash as a sop.* **4.** a weak-willed or spineless person; milksop. —*v.t.* **5.** to dip or soak in liquid food: *to sop bread in gravy.* **6.** to drench. **7.** to take up (liquid) by absorption (usually fol. by *up*): *He used bread to sop up the gravy.* —*v.i.* **8.** to become or be soaking wet. **9.** (of a liquid) to soak (usually fol. by *in*). [ME; OE *sopp*; c. OIcel *soppa*]

SOP, Standard Operating Procedure. Also, **S.O.P.**

sop., soprano.

soph (sof), *n.* a sophomore. [by shortening]

So·phar (sō′fər), *n. Douay Bible.* Zophar.

so·pher (sō′fər), *n., pl.* **-pher·im** (-fər im). (*often cap.*) *Judaism.* scribe[1] (def. 3). [< Heb *sōphēr*]

So·phi (sō′fē), *n.* (*sometimes l.c.*) Sophy.

So·phi·a (sō fī′ə, -fē′ə, sō′fē ə), *n.* a girl's given name. Also, **Sofia, So·phie** (sō′fē; *Fr.* sô fē′).

soph·ism (sof′iz əm), *n.* **1.** a specious argument for displaying ingenuity in reasoning or for deceiving someone. **2.** any false argument; fallacy. [< L *sophism(a)* < Gk, deriv. of *sophíz(esthai)* (to) act the sophist, become wise; r. *sophim* < ME < MF *sophime* < L, as above]

soph·ist (sof′ist), *n.* **1.** (*often cap.*) *Gk. Hist.* **a.** any of a class of professional teachers in ancient Greece who gave instruction in various fields, as in general culture, rhetoric, politics, or disputation. **b.** a person belonging to this class at a later period who, while professing to teach skill in reasoning, concerned himself with ingenuity and specious effectiveness rather than soundness of argument. **2.** one who reasons adroitly and speciously rather than soundly. **3.** a man of learning. [< L *sophist(a)* < Gk *sophistḗs* sage, equiv. to *sophíz(esthai)* (see SOPHISM) + *-istēs* -IST]

soph·ist·er (sof′i stər), *n.* **1.** a second or third year student at a university, esp. a British university. **2.** a specious, unsound, or fallacious reasoner. **3.** *Obs.* an ancient Greek sophist. [ME < MF < L *sophista.* See SOPHIST]

so·phis·tic (sə fis′tik), *adj.* **1.** of the nature of sophistry; fallacious. **2.** characteristic or suggestive of sophistry. **3.** given to the use of sophistry. **4.** of or pertaining to sophists or sophistry. Also, **so·phis′ti·cal.** [< L *sophistic(us)* < Gk *sophistikós*, equiv. to *sophist(ḗs)* (see SOPHIST) + *-ikos* -IC] —**so·phis′ti·cal·ly,** *adv.* —**so·phis′ti·cal·ness,** *n.*

so·phis·ti·cate (*n., adj.* sə fis′tə kit, -kāt′; *v.* sə fis′tə kāt′), *n., adj., v.,* **-cat·ed, -cat·ing.** —*n.* **1.** a sophisticated person. —*adj.* **2.** sophisticated. —*v.t.* **3.** to make less natural, simple, or ingenuous; to make worldly-wise. **4.** to mislead or pervert: *to sophisticate a meaning beyond* *recognition.* —*v.i.* **5.** to use sophistry; quibble. [< ML *sophisticāt(us)* (ptp. of *sophisticāre*), equiv. to L *sophistic(us)* (see SOPHISTIC) + *-ātus* -ATE[1]]

so·phis·ti·cat·ed (sə fis′tə kā′tid), *adj.* **1.** (of a person, ideas, tastes, manners, etc.) altered by education, experience, etc., so as to be worldly-wise; not naïve: *a sophisticated young socialite; the sophisticated eye of a newspaperman.* **2.** pleasing or satisfactory to the tastes of sophisticates: *sophisticated music.* **3.** deceptive; misleading. **4.** complex or intricate, as a system, process, piece of machinery, or the like: *a sophisticated electronic control system.* Also, **sophisticate.** [< ML *sophisticāt(us)* SOPHISTICATE + -ED[2]] —**so·phis′ti·cat′ed·ly,** *adv.*
—**Syn. 1.** worldly. —**Ant. 1.** naïve.

so·phis·ti·ca·tion (sə fis′tə kā′shən), *n.* **1.** sophisticated character, ideas, tastes, or ways as the result of education, worldly experience, etc.: *the sophistication of the wealthy.* **2.** change from the natural character or simplicity, or the resulting condition. **3.** impairment or debasement, as of purity or genuineness. **4.** the use of sophistry; a sophism, quibble, or fallacious argument. [< ML *sophisticātiōn-* (s. of *sophisticātiō*) < *sophisticāt(us)* (see SOPHISTICATE) + *-iōn-* -ION]

soph·ist·ry (sof′i strē), *n., pl.* **-ries. 1.** a subtle, tricky, superficially plausible, but generally fallacious method of reasoning. **2.** a false argument; sophism. [ME *sophistrie* < MF, equiv. to *sophistre* SOPHISTER + *-ie* -Y[3]]

Soph·o·cles (sof′ə klēz′), *n.* 495?–406? B.C., Greek dramatist. —**Soph·o·cle·an** (sof′ə klē′ən), *adj.*

soph·o·more (sof′ə mōr′, -môr′; sof′mōr, -môr), *n.* a student in his second year at a high school, college, or university. [< Gk *soph(ós)* wise, clever + *-o-* -O- + *mōr(ós)* foolish, silly]

soph·o·mor·ic (sof′ə môr′ik, -mor′-), *adj.* **1.** of or pertaining to a sophomore or sophomores. **2.** suggestive of or resembling the traditional sophomore, esp. in intellectual pretension, conceit, overconfidence, assumed knowledge, or the like: *a lot of sophomoric questions.* Also, **soph′o·mor′i·cal.** [SOPHOMORE + -IC] —**soph′o·mor′i·cal·ly,** *adv.*

Soph·o·ni·as (sof′ə nī′əs), *n. Douay Bible.* Zephaniah.

so·phros·y·ne (sə fros′ə nē), *n.* moderation; discretion; prudence. Cf. **hubris.** [< Gk *sōphrosýnē*, deriv. of *sṓphrō(n)* prudent]

So·phy (sō′fē, sof′ē), *n., pl.* **-phies.** *(sometimes l.c.)* any of the Safavid rulers of Persia: used as a title. Also, **Sophi.** [< Pers, m. *Çafī* surname of a dynasty]

-sophy, an element occurring in loan words from Greek (*philosophy; theosophy*); on this model used, with the meaning "science of," in the formation of compound words (*anthroposophy*). [< Gk *-sophia*, comb. form of *sophía* skill, wisdom; see -Y[3]]

so·por (sō′pər), *n. Pathol.* a deep, unnatural sleep; lethargy. [< L]

sop·o·rif·er·ous (sop′ə rif′ər əs, sō′pə-), *adj.* bringing sleep; soporific. [< L *sopōrifer*, equiv. to *sopōr-* SOPOR + *-i-* -I- + *-fer;* see -FEROUS] —**sop′o·rif′er·ous·ly,** *adv.* —**sop′o·rif′er·ous·ness,** *n.*

sop·o·rif·ic (sop′ə rif′ik, sō′pə-), *adj.* **1.** causing or tending to cause sleep. **2.** pertaining to or characterized by sleep or sleepiness; sleepy; drowsy. —*n.* **3.** something that causes sleep, as a medicine or drug. [< L *sopor* SOPOR + *-i-* -I- + -FIC; cf. F *soporifique*] —**sop′o·rif′i·cal·ly,** *adv.*

sop·o·rose (sop′ə rōs′, sō′pə-), *adj. Med.* sleepy; comatose; characterized by abnormal slumber. Also, **sop·o·rous** (sop′ər əs, sō′pər-). [SOPOR + -OSE[1]]

sop·ping (sop′ing), *adj.* soaked; drenched: *Her clothes were sopping from the rain.* [SOP + -ING[2]]

sop·py (sop′ē), *adj.,* **-pi·er, -pi·est. 1.** soaked, drenched, or very wet, as ground. **2.** rainy, as weather. **3.** *Brit. Slang.* excessively sentimental; mawkish. [SOP + -Y[1]] —**sop′pi·ness,** *n.*

so·pran·o (sə pran′ō, -prä′nō), *n., pl.* **-pran·os,** *adj. Music.* —*n.* **1.** the uppermost part or voice. **2.** the highest singing voice in women and boys. **3.** a part for such a voice. **4.** a singer with such a voice. —*adj.* **5.** of or pertaining to soprano; having the compass of a soprano. [< It: lit., what is above, high, equiv. to *sopra* (< L *suprā* above) + *-ano* adj. suffix]

sopran′o clef′, *Music.* a sign locating middle C on the bottom line of the staff. See illus. under **C clef.**

so·ra (sōr′ə, sôr′ə), *n.* a small, short-billed rail, *Porzana carolina*, of North America. Also called **so′ra rail′, Carolina rail.** [?]

so·ra·li·um (sə rā′lē əm), *n., pl.* **-li·a** (-lē ə). (in a lichen) a group of soredia. [SOR(US) + -AL[1] + -IUM]

So·ra·ta (sô rä′tə), *n.* **Mount,** a mountain in W Bolivia, in the Andes, near Lake Titicaca: two peaks, Ancohuma, 21,490 ft., and Illampu, 21,276 ft.

sorb (sôrb), *n.* **1.** a European tree, *Sorbus domestica.* **2.** Also called **sorb′ ap′ple.** the fruit of this tree. [< L *sorb(um)* serviceberry, or *sorb(us)* service tree] —**sorb′ic,** *adj.*

Sorb (sôrb), *n.* a Wend. [< G *Sorbe* SERBE]

Sor·bi·an (sôr′bē ən), *adj.* **1.** of or pertaining to the Wends or their language. —*n.* **2.** Also called **Lusatian, Wendish.** a Slavic language spoken by an isolated group in SE East Germany. **3.** a Wend. [SORB + -IAN]

sor·bi·tol (sôr′bi tōl′, -tôl′, -tol′), *n. Biochem.* a white, crystalline, sweet, water-soluble powder, $HOCH_2(HCOH)_4CH_2OH$, occurring in cherries, plums, pears, seaweed, and many berries, obtained by the breakdown of dextrose and used as a sugar substitute for diabetics and in the manufacture of vitamin C, synthetic resins, candy, varnishes, etc.; d-glucitol; d-sorbitol; sorbol. [SORB + -ITOL]

sor·bol (sôr′bōl, -bôl, -bol), *n. Chem.* sorbitol. [by shortening]

Sor·bon·ist (sôr bun′ist, sôr′bə nist), *n.* a student or graduate of the Sorbonne. [< NL *Sorbonist(a).* See SORBONNE, -IST]

Sor·bonne (sôr bon′, -bun′; *Fr.* sôʀ bôn′), *n.* **1.** the seat of the faculties of arts and letters of the University of Paris. **2.** a theological college founded in Paris in 1257 by Robert de Sorbon, suppressed in 1792, and ceasing to exist about 1850.

sor·bose (sôr′bōs), *n. Biochem.* a ketohexose, $C_6H_{12}O_6$, occurring in mountain ash and obtained industrially from sorbitol by bacterial oxidation: used in the synthesis of vitamin C. [SORB(ITOL) + -OSE[2]]

sor·cer·er (sôr′sər ər), *n.* a person who is supposed to exercise supernatural powers through the aid of evil spirits; black magician; wizard. Also, *referring to a woman,* **sor·cer·ess** (sôr′sər is). [< MF *sorcier*, perh. < VL **sortiār(ius)* one who casts lots, eqviv. to L *sort-* (s. of *sors*) lot, fate + *-i-* -I- + *-ārius* -AR[2]]

sor·cer·ous (sôr′sər əs), *adj.* **1.** of the nature of or involving sorcery. **2.** using sorcery. [SORCER(Y) + -OUS] —**sor′cer·ous·ly,** *adv.*

sor·cer·y (sôr′sə rē), *n., pl.* **-cer·ies.** the art, practices, or spells of a person who is supposed to exercise supernatural powers through the aid of evil spirits; black magic; witchery. [ME *sorcerie* < ML *sorceria.* See SORCERER, -Y[3]]
—**Syn.** enchantment. See **magic.**

Sor·del·lo (sôr del′ō; *It.* sôʀ del′lô), *n.* **1.** 13th-century Italian troubadour. **2.** *(italics.)* a narrative poem (1840) by Robert Browning.

sor·did (sôr′did), *adj.* **1.** dirty or filthy. **2.** squalid; wretchedly poor and run-down: *sordid housing.* **3.** morally ignoble or base; vile: *sordid methods.* **4.** meanly selfish, self-seeking, or mercenary. [< L *sordid(us)*, equiv. to *sord(es)* dirt + *-idus* -ID[4]] —**sor′did·ly,** *adv.* —**sor′did·ness,** *n.*
—**Syn. 1.** soiled, unclean, foul. **3.** degraded, depraved. See **mean**[2]. **4.** avaricious, tight, close, stingy. —**Ant. 1.** clean. **3.** honorable. **4.** generous.

sor·di·no (sôr dē′nō; *It.* sôʀ dē′nô), *n., pl.* **-ni** (-nē). *Music.* mute (def. 10). [< It: a mute < L *surd(us)* deaf + *-īnus* -INE[1]]

sore (sōr, sôr), *adj.,* **sor·er, sor·est,** *n., adv.* —*adj.* **1.** physically painful or sensitive, as a wound, hurt, diseased part, etc.: *a sore arm.* **2.** suffering bodily pain from wounds, bruises, etc., as a person: *He is sore because of all that exercise.* **3.** suffering mental pain; grieved, distressed, or sorrowful: *to be sore at heart.* **4.** causing great mental pain, distress, or sorrow: *a sore bereavement.* **5.** causing very great suffering, misery, hardship, etc.: *sore need.* **6.** *Informal.* annoyed; irritated; offended; angered: *He was sore because he had to wait.* **7.** causing annoyance or irritation: *a sore subject.* —*n.* **8.** a sore spot or place on the body. **9.** a source or cause of grief, distress, irritation, etc. —*adv.* **10.** *Archaic.* sorely. [ME; OE *sār;* c. D *zeer*, OIcel *sārr*, G *sehr*] —**sore′ly,** *adv.* —**sore′ness,** *n.*
—**Syn. 1.** tender. **3.** aggrieved, hurt, pained, vexed. **4.** grievous, distressing, painful, depressing. **8.** infection, abscess, ulcer, wound. —**Ant. 1.** tough.

so·re·di·al (sə rē′dē əl), *adj.* pertaining to or resembling a soredium. [SOREDI(UM) + -AL[1]]

so·re·di·um (sə rē′dē əm), *n., pl.* **-di·a** (-dē ə). (in a lichen) a group of algal cells surrounded by hyphal tissue, occurring on the surface of the thallus and functioning in vegetative reproduction. Also called **brood bud, hologonidium.** [< NL, dim. of Gk *sōrós* a heap] —**so·re·di·ate** (sə rē′dē it, -āt′), *adj.*

sore′ head′, *Vet. Pathol.* See **fowl pox.**

sore·head (sōr′hed′, sôr′-), *n. Informal.* a disgruntled or vindictive person, esp. an unsportsmanlike loser: *He was a real sorehead over his defeat.* [prob. < Scot *sorehead* a headache] —**sore′head′ed·ly,** *adv.* —**sore′head′ed·ness,** *n.*

So·rel (sô ʀel′), *n.* **Georges** (zhôʀzh), 1847–1922, French engineer and social philosopher.

sore′ mouth′, *Vet. Pathol.* ecthyma.

sore′ shin′, *Plant Pathol.* a disease of plant seedlings, characterized by stem cankers which girdle the stem near the soil line, caused by any of several fungi, esp. *Rhizoctonia solani.*

sore′ throat′, *Pathol.* a painful or sensitive condition of the throat exaggerated by swallowing or talking, usually caused by bacteria or viruses; laryngitis; pharyngitis; tonsillitis.

sor·gho (sôr′gō), *n., pl.* **-ghos.** sorgo.

sor·ghum (sôr′gəm), *n.* **1.** a cereal grass, *Sorghum vulgare*, having broad, cornlike leaves and a tall, pithy stem bearing the grain in a dense terminal cluster. **2.** the syrup made from sorgo. [< NL < It *sorgo* (see SORGO)]

sor·go (sôr′gō), *n., pl.* **-gos.** any of several varieties of sorghum grown chiefly for the sweet juice yielded by the stems, used in making sugar and syrup and also for fodder. Also, **sorgho.** Also called **sweet sorghum, sugar sorghum.** [< It perh. < VL **Syricum* (*grano*) Syrian (grain), neut. of L *Syricus* (masc.) of Syria]

so·ri (sōr′ī, sôr′ī), *n.* pl. of **sorus.**

sor·i·cine (sôr′i sīn′, -sin, sor′i-), *adj. Zool.* of or resembling the shrews. [< L *sōricīn(us)*, equiv. to *sōric-* (s. of *sōrex*) + *-īnus* -INE[1]]

so·ri·tes (sō rī′tēz, sō-), *n. Logic.* a form of argument having several premises and one conclusion, capable of being resolved into a chain of syllogisms, the conclusion of each of which is a premise of the next. [< L < Gk *sōreitēs*, lit., heaped, piled up, deriv. of *sōr(ós)* a heap] —**so·rit·i·cal** (sō rit′i kəl, sō-), **so·rit′ic,** *adj.*

sorn (sôʀn), *v.i. Scot.* **1.** to impose on another's hospitality; obtain free food, drink, or lodging by making demands on the friendship or generosity of others. **2.** to beg. [?] —**sorn′er,** *n.*

sor·o·ban (sôr′ə bän′), *n.* a Japanese abacus of Chinese derivation. [< Jap < Chin *suan p'an*]

so·ro·i·mo·no (sə rō′ē mō′nō; *Jap.* sō ʀō′ē mô′nô), *n., pl.* **-no.** a matching set of Japanese sword mounts, excluding those forming a mitokoromono. [< Jap, equiv. to *soroi* matched, suited + *mono* objects, items]

So·ro·kin (sə rō′kin, sō-; *Russ.* sô′ʀo kin), *n.* **Pi·ti·rim A·le·xan·dro·vitch** (pi ti rēm′ äl′ig zan′drə vich; *Russ.* pi ti ʀēm′ ä′le ksän′dʀo vich), born 1889, U.S. sociologist, born in Russia.

So·rol·la y Bas·ti·da (sô ʀô′lyä ē bäs tē′thä), **Joa·quín** (hwä kēn′), 1863–1923, Spanish painter.

so·rop·ti·mist (sə rop′tə mist), *n.* a member of an international association of professional or executive businesswomen **(Sorop′timist Club′),** devoted primarily to welfare work. [< L *sorōr-* (s. of *soror*) sister + OPTIMIST]

so·ror·ate (sôr′ə rāt′, sôr′-), *n.* subsequent or concurrent marriage with a wife's sister. [< L *sorōr-* (s. of *soror*) sister + -ATE[1]]

so·ror·i·cide (sə rôr′i sīd′, -ror′-), *n.* **1.** a person who kills his or her sister. **2.** the act of killing one's own sister. [< L *sorōricīd(a)* one who kills his sister, *-cīd(um)* the act of killing one's sister, equiv. to *sorōr-* (s. of *soror*) sister + *-cīda, -cīdum* -CIDE] —**so·ror′i·cid′al,** *adj.*

so·ror·i·ty (sə rôr′i tē, -ror′-), *n., pl.* **-ties.** a society or club of women or girls, esp. in a college. [< ML *sorōritās*, equiv. to L *sorōri-* (s. of *soror*) sister + *-itās* -ITY]

so·ro·sil·i·cate (sôr′ō sil′ə kit, -kāt′, sôr′-), *n. Mineral.* any of the silicates each of whose tetrahedral silicate groups shares one of its four oxygen atoms with a neighboring silicate group, the ratio of silicon to oxygen being two to seven. Cf. **cyclosilicate, inosilicate, nesosilicate, tektosilicate.** [< Gk *sōrós* heap + SILICATE]

so·ro·sis[1] (sə rō′sis), *n., pl.* **-ses** (-sēz). *Bot.* a fleshy multiple fruit composed of many flowers, seed vessels, and receptacles consolidated, as in the pineapple and mulberry. [< NL < Gk *sōrós* heap + NL *-ōsis* -OSIS]

so·ro·sis[2] (sə rō′sis), *n., pl.* **-ses** (-sēz), **-sis·es.** a women's society or club. [after the name of a club established in 1869; based on L *soror* sister]

sorp·tion (sôrp′shən), *n. Physical Chem.* the binding of one substance by another by any mechanism, such as absorption, adsorption, or persorption. [back formation from ABSORPTION, ADSORPTION, etc.]

sor·rel[1] (sôr′əl, sor′-), *n.* **1.** light reddish-brown. **2.** a horse of this color, often with a light-colored mane and tail. —*adj.* **3.** having the color sorrel. [ME *sorrelle* < OF *sorel*, equiv. to *sor* brown (< Gmc) + *-el* dim. suffix]

sor·rel[2] (sôr′əl, sor′-), *n.* **1.** any of various plants of the genus *Rumex*, having succulent acid leaves used in salads, sauces, etc. **2.** Also called **wood sorrel.** any of various sour-juiced plants of the genus *Oxalis.* **3.** any of various similar plants. [ME *sorell* < OF *surele*, equiv. to *sur* sour (+ *-el* dim. suffix) < Gmc; akin to OHG *sūr* sour]

sor′rel salt′. See **potassium binoxalate.**

sor′rel tree′, a North American, ericaceous tree, *Oxydendrum arboreum*, having leaves with an acid flavor and racemes of white flowers. Also called **sourwood.**

Sor·ren·to (sə ren′tō; *It.* sôʀ ʀen′tô), *n.* a seaport in SW Italy, on the Bay of Naples: resort; cathedral; ancient ruins. 11,837 (1961). —**Sor·ren·tine** (sôr′ən-tēn′, sə ren′tēn), *adj.*

sor·row (sor′ō, sôr′ō), *n.* **1.** distress caused by loss, affliction, disappointment, etc.; grief, sadness, or regret. **2.** a cause or occasion of grief or regret, as an affliction, a misfortune, or trouble: *His first sorrow was the bank failure.* **3.** the expression of grief, sadness, disappointment, or the like: *muffled sorrow.* —*v.i.* **4.** to feel sorrow; grieve. [ME; OE *sorg;* c. G *Sorge*, D *zorg*, OIcel *sorg*, Goth *saurga*] —**sor′row·er,** *n.* —**sor′row·less,** *adj.*
—**Syn. 1.** SORROW, DISTRESS, GRIEF, MISERY, WOE imply bitter suffering, especially as caused by loss or misfortune. SORROW is the most general term. GRIEF is keen suffering, esp. for a particular reason. DISTRESS implies anxiety, anguish, or acute suffering caused by the pressure of trouble or adversity. MISERY suggests such great and unremitting pain or wretchedness of body or mind as crushes the spirit. WOE is deep or inconsolable grief or misery. **2.** adversity. **4.** mourn, lament. —**Ant. 1.** joy.

sor·row·ful (sor′ə fəl, sôr′-), *adj.* **1.** full of or feeling sorrow; grieved; sad. **2.** showing or expressing sorrow; mournful; plaintive: *a sorrowful song.* **3.** involving or causing sorrow; distressing: *a sorrowful event.* [ME *sorowful*, OE *sorgful.* See SORROW, -FUL] —**sor′row·ful·ly,** *adv.* —**sor′row·ful·ness,** *n.*
—**Syn. 1.** unhappy, dejected, grieving, depressed. **2.** melancholy. **3.** dismal, dreary, doleful, piteous. —**Ant. 1.** happy.

Sor′rows of Wer′ther, The, a romantic novel (1774) in epistolary form by Goethe. German, **Die Leiden des Jungen Werther.** Also called **The Sor′rows of Young′ Wer′ther, The Sufferings of Young Werther.**

sor·ry (sor′ē, sôr′ē), *adj.,* **-ri·er, -ri·est. 1.** feeling regret, compunction, sympathy, pity, etc.: *to be sorry to leave one's friends; to be sorry for a remark; to be sorry for someone in trouble.* **2.** of a deplorable, pitiable, or miserable kind: *to come to a sorry end.* **3.** sorrowful, grieved, or sad: *Was she sorry when her brother died?* **4.** associated with sorrow; suggestive of grief or suffering; melancholy; dismal. **5.** wretched, poor, useless, or pitiful: *a sorry horse.* **6.** (used interjectionally as a conventional apology or expression of regret): *Sorry, you're misinformed. Did I bump you? Sorry.* [ME; OE *sārig;* c. LG *sērig*, OHG *sērag.* See SORE, -Y[1]] —**sor′ri·ly,** *adv.* —**sor′ri·ness,** *n.*
—**Syn. 1.** regretful, sympathetic, pitying. **3.** unhappy, depressed, sorrowing, melancholy. **4.** grievous, mournful, painful. **5.** abject, contemptible, paltry, worthless, shabby. See **wretched.** —**Ant. 1.** happy.

sort (sôrt), *n.* **1.** a particular kind, species, variety, class, or group, distinguished by a common character or nature: *to develop a new sort of painting; nice people, of course, but not really our sort.* **2.** character, quality, or nature: *girls of a nice sort.* **3.** an example of something that is undistinguished or barely adequate: *He is a sort of poet.* **4.** manner, fashion, or way: *We spoke in this sort for several minutes.* **5.** *Print.* **a.** any of the individual characters making up a font of type. **b.** characters of a particular font that are rarely used. **6. of sorts, a.** of a mediocre or poor kind: *a tennis player of sorts.* **b.** of one sort or another; of an indefinite kind. Also, **of a sort. 7. out of sorts, a.** in low spirits; depressed. **b.** in poor health; indisposed; ill. **c.** in a bad temper; irritable: *Everyone has been feeling out of sorts because of the terrible weather.* **d.** *Print.* short of certain characters of a font of type. **8. sort of,** *Informal.* in a way; quite; rather: *Their conversation was sort of tiresome.* —*v.t.* **9.** to arrange according to sort, kind, or class; separate into sorts; classify: *to sort socks; to sort eggs by grade.* **10.** to separate or take from other sorts or from others (often fol. by *out*): *to sort the good from the bad; to sort out the children's socks.* **11.** to assign to a particular class, group, or place (often fol. by *with, together,* etc.): *to sort people together indiscriminately.* **12.** *Scot.* to provide with food and shelter. —*v.i.* **13.** *Archaic.* to suit; agree; fit. **14.** *Brit. Dial.* to associate, mingle, or be friendly. [ME < MF < ML *sort-* (s. of *sors*) kind, in L: chance, lot] —**sort′a·ble,** *adj.* —**sort′a·bly,** *adv.* —**sort′er,** *n.*
—**Syn. 1.** family, order, race, rank, character, nature, type. **4.** method, means, style. **9.** order, class, divide, assort, distribute.

sor·tie (sôr′tē), *n., v.,* **-tied, -tie·ing.** —*n.* **1.** a rapid movement of troops from a besieged place to attack the besiegers. **2.** a body of troops involved in such a movement. **3.** the flying of an airplane on a combat mission. —*v.i.* **4.** to go on a sortie; sally forth. [< F, n. use of fem. ptp. of *sortir* to go out]

sor·ti·lege (sôr′t^{ə}lij), *n.* **1.** the drawing of lots for divination; divination by lot. **2.** sorcery; magic. [ME < ML *sortileg(ium),* L *sortileg(us),* equiv. to *sort-* (s. of *sors*) lot, chance + *-i-* -I- + *legus* (deriv. of *legere* to read, choose out)] —**sor·ti·leg·ic** (sôr′t^{ə}lej′ik), **sor·ti·le·gious** (sôr′t^{ə}lē′jəs), *adj.*

sort′ing tracks′, the part of a railroad yard used for the final sorting of cars from a classification yard. Also called **sort′ing yard′.**

so·rus (sōr′əs, sôr′-), *n., pl.* **so·ri** (sōr′ī, sôr′ī). *Bot.* one of the clusters of sporangia on the back of the fronds of ferns. See diag. under **fern.** [< NL < Gk *sōrós* heap]

SOS, 1. the letters represented by the radio telegraphic signal (··· — — — ···) used, esp. by ships in distress, as an internationally recognized call for help. **2.** any call for help.

S.O.S., (in prescriptions) if necessary. [< L *sī opus sit*]

So·sig·e·nes (so sij′ə nēz′), *n.* a crater in the first quadrant of the face of the moon: about 14 miles in diameter.

Sos·no·wiec (sôs nô′vyets), *n.* a city in S Poland. 137,000 (est. 1963).

so-so (sō′sō′), *adj.* **1.** Also, **so′so′.** indifferent; neither very good nor very bad. —*adv.* **2.** in an indifferent or passable manner; indifferently; tolerably. Also, **so′ so′.**

Sos·pi·ta (sos′pi tə), *n.* an ancient Roman epithet of Juno as goddess of healing. [< L, fem. of *sospes* saving, delivering]

sos·te·nu·to (sos′tə no͞o′tō, sō′stə-; *It.* sôs′te no͞o′tô), *adj., n., pl.* **-tos,** *It.* **-ti** (-tē). *Music.* —*adj.* **1.** sustained or prolonged in the time value of the tones. —*n.* **2.** a movement or passage played in this manner. [< It, ptp. of *sostenere* to SUSTAIN]

sostenu′to ped′al, *Music.* a pedal on a grand piano that raises the dampers, allowing the tone to be sustained for those strings struck at the time the pedal is depressed.

sot (sot), *n.* a person who is habitually drunk; a chronic drunkard. [ME < ?]

So·ter (sō′tər), *n.* **1. Saint,** pope A.D. 166?–175?. **2.** *Class. Myth.* an epithet of Zeus, meaning "savior."

so·te·ri·ol·o·gy (sə tēr′ē ol′ə jē), *n. Theol.* the doctrine of salvation through Jesus Christ. [< Gk *sōtērí(a)* salvation, deliverance (*sōtēr-* (s. of *sōtḗr*) deliverer + *-ia* n. suffix) + -o- + -LOGY] —**so·te·re·o·log·ic** (sə-tēr′ē ə loj′ik), **so·te′re·o·log′i·cal,** *adj.*

Soth·ern (suŧħ′ərn), *n.* **E(dward) H(ugh),** 1859–1933, U.S. actor, born in England: husband of Julia Marlowe.

So·thic (sō′thik, soth′ik), *adj.* of Sirius, the Dog Star. [< Gk *Sôth(is)* Egyptian name for Sirius + -IC]

So′thic cy′cle, (in the ancient Egyptian calendar) a period of 1460 Sothic years. Also called **So′thic pe′riod.**

So′thic year′, the fixed year of the ancient Egyptians, determined by the heliacal rising of Sirius, and equivalent to 365¼ days.

so·tie (sō tē′), *n.* a satirical and topical comedy employing actors dressed in traditional fool's costume, popular in France during the late Middle Ages, and often used as a curtain raiser to mystery and morality plays. Also, **sot·tie′.** [< F < MF, lit., foolishness, equiv. to *sot* fool + *-ie* -Y[3]]

So·ti·ris (sō tī′ris), *n.* a boy's given name.

so·tol (sō′tōl, sō tōl′), *n.* any liliaceous plant of the genus *Dasylirion,* of the southwestern U.S. and northern Mexico, resembling the yucca. [< MexSp < Nahuatl *tzotolli*]

sot·ted (sot′id), *adj.* drunken; besotted. [ME; see SOT, -ED[2]]

sot·tish (sot′ish), *adj.* **1.** stupefied with or as with drink; drunken. **2.** given to excessive drinking. **3.** pertaining to or befitting a sot. [SOT + -ISH[1]] —**sot′-tish·ly,** *adv.* —**sot′tish·ness,** *n.*

sot·to vo·ce (sot′ō vō′chē; *It.* sôt′tô vô′che), in a low, soft voice so as not to be overheard. [< It: lit., under (the) voice]

sou (so͞o), *n.* **1.** (formerly) either of two bronze coins of France, equal to 5 centimes and 10 centimes. **2.** sol[2]. [< F < MF < OF *sol* SOL[2]]

sou., 1. south. **2.** southern.

sou·a′ri nut′ (so͞o är′ē), the large, edible, oily nut of a tall tree, *Caryocar nuciferum,* of tropical South America. Also called **butternut.** [< F *saouari* < Galibi *sawarra*]

sou·bise (so͞o bēz′), *n.* a brown or white sauce containing onions, strained or puréed, and served with meat. Also called **soubise′ sauce′.** [< F, named after Prince Charles *Soubise* (1715–87), marshal of France]

sou·bre·saut (so͞o′brə sō′; *Fr.* so͞o brə sō′), *n., pl.* **-sauts** (-sōz′; *Fr.* -sō′). *Ballet.* a jump performed with the legs held together and the body erect but slightly curved to the side. [< F; see SOMERSAULT]

sou·brette (so͞o bret′), *n.* **1.** a maidservant or lady's maid in a play, opera, or the like, esp. one displaying coquetry, pertness, and a tendency to engage in intrigue. **2.** an actress playing such a role. **3.** any lively or pert young woman. [< F; lady's maid < Pr *soubret(o),* deriv. of *soubret* affected < OPr *sobrar* < L *superāre* to be above] —**sou·bret′tish,** *adj.*

sou·bri·quet (so͞o′brə kā′, -ket′, so͞o′brə kā′, -ket′), *n.* sobriquet.

sou·car (sou kär′), *n.* a Hindu banker. Also, **sowcar.** [< Urdu *sāhūkār* great merchant]

Sou·chong (so͞o′shông′, -chông′), *n.* a variety of black tea grown in India and Ceylon. [< Chin (Cantonese) *sin-chung* small sort]

Sou·dan (so͞o dän′), *n.* French name of **Sudan.**

Sou·da·nese (so͞od′ənēz′, -ənēs′), *n., pl.* **-nese,** *adj.* Sudanese.

Sou·der·ton (sou′dər tən, -tən), *n.* a town in SE Pennsylvania. 5381 (1960).

souf·fle (so͞o′fəl), *n. Pathol.* a murmuring or blowing sound. [< F; see SOUFFLÉ]

souf·flé (so͞o flā′, so͞o′flā), *adj., n., v.,* **-fléed, -flé·ing.** —*adj.* **1.** Also, **souf·fléed′.** puffed up; made light, as by beating and cooking. —*n.* **2.** a light baked dish made fluffy with beaten egg whites combined with egg yolks, white sauce, and fish, cheese, or other ingredients. **3.** a similar dish made with fruit juices, chocolate, vanilla, or the like, and served as dessert. —*v.t.* **4.** to make (food) puffed up and light, as by beating and cooking, adding stiffly beaten egg whites, etc.; make resemble a soufflé: *to soufflé leftover mashed potatoes.* [< F, n. use of ptp. of *souffler* to blow, puff < L *sufflāre* to breathe on, blow on]

Souf·flot (so͞o flō′), *n.* **Jacques Ger·main** (zhäk zher maN′), 1713–80, French architect.

Sou·frière (so͞o fryer′), *n.* **1.** a volcano in the British West Indies, on St. Vincent island. 4048 ft. **2.** a volcano in the French West Indies, on Guadeloupe. 4869 ft.

sough[1] (sou, suf), *v.i.* **1.** to make a rushing, rustling, or murmuring sound: *the wind soughing in the meadow.* **2.** *Scot. and North Eng.* to speak, esp. to preach, in a whining, singsong voice. —*n.* **3.** a sighing, rustling, or murmuring sound. **4.** *Scot. and North Eng.* **a.** a sigh or deep breath. **b.** a whining, singsong manner of speaking. **c.** a rumor; unconfirmed report. [ME *swoghe,* OE *swōg(an)* (to) make a noise; c. OS *swōgan,* OE *swēgan,* Goth *-swōgjan*] —**sough′ful·ly,** *adv.* —**sough′less,** *adj.*

sough[2] (suf, sou), *Brit.* —*n.* **1.** drain; drainage ditch, gutter, or sewer. **2.** a swampy or marshy area. —*v.t.* **3.** to drain (land or a mine) by building drainage ditches or the like. Also, *esp. Scot.,* **sugh.** [ME *sogh, sohn* < ?; cf. D (dial.) *zoeg* little ditch]

sought (sôt), *v.* pt. and pp. of **seek.**

sought-af·ter (sôt′af′tər, -äf′-), *adj.* that is in demand; desirable: *a sought-after advertising account; a sought-after speaker.*

souk (so͞ok), *n.* sug.

soul (sōl), *n.* **1.** the principle of life, feeling, thought, and action in man, regarded as a distinct entity separate from the body, and commonly held to be separable in existence from the body; the spiritual part of man as distinct from the physical part. **2.** the spiritual part of man regarded in its moral aspect, or as believed to survive death and be subject to happiness or misery in a life to come: *arguing the immortality of the soul.* **3.** a disembodied spirit of a deceased person: *He feared the soul of the deceased would haunt him.* **4.** the emotional part of man's nature; the seat of the feelings or sentiments. **5.** a human being; person. **6.** high-mindedness; noble warmth of feeling, spirit or courage, etc. **7.** the animating principle; the essential element or part of something. **8.** the inspirer or moving spirit of some action, movement, etc. **9.** the embodiment of some quality: *He was the very soul of tact.* **10.** *(cap.) Christian Science.* God, or the attributes of God in man. [ME; OE *sāwl;* c. D *ziel,* G *Seele,* OIcel *sāl,* Goth *saiwala,* ult. related to SEA, fancied habitation of the soul] —**soul′-like′,** *adj.*
—**Syn. 1.** spirit. **4.** heart. **7.** essence, core, heart.

soul′ cake′, *Brit.* a round, sweet bun or small oval cake traditionally made to celebrate All Souls' Day.

soul·ful (sōl′fəl), *adj.* of or expressive of deep feeling or emotion: *soulful eyes.* [SOUL + -FUL] —**soul′ful·ly,** *adv.* —**soul′ful·ness,** *n.*

Sou·lier de Sa·tin, Le (*Fr.* lə so͞o lyā′ də sa taN′). See **Satin Slipper, The.**

soul′ kiss′, an open-mouthed kiss in which the tongue of one partner is manipulated in the mouth of the other. Also called **deep kiss, French kiss.**

soul-kiss (sōl′kis′), *v.t.* **1.** to give (someone) a soul kiss. —*v.i.* **2.** to be engaged or involved in a soul kiss.

soul·less (sōl′lis), *adj.* **1.** without a soul. **2.** lacking in nobility of soul, as persons; without spirit or courage. —**soul′less·ly,** *adv.* —**soul′less·ness,** *n.*

soul′ mate′, 1. a person with whom one has a strong affinity, esp. a person of the opposite sex. **2.** a sexual partner in an illicit relationship; one's lover or mistress.

soul-search·ing (sōl′sûr′ching), *n.* the act or process of close and penetrating analysis of oneself, to determine one's true motives and sentiments.

Soult (so͞olt), *n.* **Ni·co·las Jean de Dieu** (nē kô lä′ zhäN də dyœ), *(Duke of Dalmatia),* 1769–1851, French marshal.

Sou·mak′ rug′ (so͞o mäk′), a hand-woven Kashmir rug.

sou mar·qué (so͞o′ mär kā′ *or, for 2,* -kē′; *Fr.* so͞o mar kā′), *n., pl.* **sous mar·qués** (so͞o′ mär kā′ *or, for 2,* -kē′; *Fr.* so͞o mar kā′). **1.** a billon coin of France, issued in the 18th century for circulation in the colonies. **2.** that which has little or no value. Also, **sou mar·kee** (so͞o′ mär′kē). [< F: marked sou]

sound[1] (sound), *n.* **1.** the sensation produced by stimulation of the organs of hearing by vibrations transmitted through the air or other medium. **2.** mechanical vibrations transmitted through an elastic medium, traveling in air at a speed of approximately 1100 feet per second at sea level. **3.** the particular auditory effect produced by a given cause: *the sound of music.* **4.** any auditory effect; any audible vibrational disturbance: *all kinds of sounds.* **5.** a noise, vocal utterance, musical tone, or the like: *the sounds from the next room.* **6.** *Phonet.* **a.** See **speech sound. b.** the audible result of an utterance or portion of an utterance: *the s-sound in "slight"; the sound of* m *in "mere."* **7.** the auditory effect of sound waves as transmitted or recorded by a particular system of sound reproduction: *the sound of a stereophonic recording.* **8.** the quality of an event, letter, etc., as it affects a person: *This report has a bad sound.* **9.** the distance within which the noise of something may be heard. **10.** mere noise, without meaning: *all sound and fury.* **11.** *Archaic.* a report or rumor; news; tidings. [ME *soun* < AF (OF *son*) < L *son(us)*] —*v.i.* **12.** to make or emit a sound. **13.** to give forth a sound as a call or summons: *The bugle sounded as the troops advanced.* **14.** to be heard, as a sound. **15.** to convey a certain impression when heard or read: *to sound strange.* **16.** to give a specific sound: *to sound loud.* **17.** to give the appearance of being: *The report sounds true.* **18.** *Law.* to have as its basis or foundation (usually fol. by *in*): *His action sounds in contract.* —*v.t.* **19.** to cause to make or emit a sound: *to sound a bell.* **20.** to give forth (a sound): *The oboe sounded an A.* **21.** to announce, order, or direct by or as by a sound: *The bugle sounded retreat. His speech sounded a warning to aggressor nations.* **22.** to utter audibly, pronounce, or express: *to sound each letter.* **23.** to examine by percussion or auscultation: *to sound a patient's chest.* **24. sound off,** *Slang.* **a.** to call out one's name, sequence number, etc. **b.** to speak freely or frankly, esp. to complain in such a manner. **c.** to exaggerate; boast: *Has he been sounding off about his golf game again?* [ME *soun(en)* < OF *sun(er)* < L *sonāre,* deriv. of *son(us)* sound] —**sound′a·ble,** *adj.*
—**Syn. 1.** SOUND, NOISE, TONE refer to something heard. SOUND and NOISE are often used interchangeably for anything perceived by means of hearing. SOUND, however, is more general in application, being used for anything within earshot: *the sound of running water.* NOISE, caused by irregular vibrations, is more properly applied to a loud, discordant, or unpleasant sound: *the noise of shouting.* TONE is applied to a musical sound having a certain quality, resonance, and pitch.

sound[2] (sound), *adj.* **1.** free from injury, damage, defect, disease, etc.; in good condition; healthy; robust: *a sound heart; a sound mind.* **2.** financially strong, secure, or reliable: *a sound business; sound investments.* **3.** competent, sensible, or valid: *sound judgment.* **4.** having no defect as to truth, justice, wisdom, or reason: *sound advice.* **5.** of substantial or enduring character: *sound moral values.* **6.** following in a systematic pattern without any apparent defect in logic: *sound reasoning.* **7.** having no legal defect: *a sound title to property.* **8.** theologically correct or orthodox, as doctrines or a theologian. **9.** free from moral defect or weakness; upright, honest, or good; honorable; loyal. **10.** uninterrupted and untroubled; deep: *sound sleep.* **11.** vigorous, thorough, or severe: *a sound thrashing.* [ME *sund,* OE *(ge)sund;* c. D *gezond,* G *gesund*] —**sound′ly,** *adv.* —**sound′ness,** *n.*
—**Syn. 1.** unharmed, whole, hale, unbroken, hardy. **2.** solvent. **4, 6.** valid, rational, logical.

sound[3] (sound), *v.t.* **1.** to measure or try the depth of (water, a deep hole, etc.) by letting down a lead or plummet at the end of a line, or by some equivalent means. **2.** to measure (depth) in such a manner, as at sea. **3.** to examine or test (the bottom, as of the sea or a deep hole) with a lead that brings up adhering bits of matter. **4.** to examine or investigate; seek to fathom or ascertain: *to sound a person's views.* **5.** to seek to elicit the views or sentiments of (a person) by indirect inquiries, suggestive allusions, etc. (often fol. by *out*): *We sounded out his receptiveness to the plan.* **6.** *Surg.* to examine, as the urinary bladder, with a sound. —*v.i.* **7.** to use the lead and line or some other device for measuring depth, as at sea. **8.** to go down or touch bottom, as a lead. **9.** to plunge downward or dive, as a whale. **10.** to make investigation; seek information, esp. by indirect inquiries. —*n.* **11.** *Surg.* a long, solid, slender instrument for sounding or exploring body cavities or canals. [ME; OE *sund-* channel (in *sundgyrd* sounding pole, lit., channel pole) < Scand; cf. OIcel *sund* channel; c. OE *sund* sea (ult. related to SWIM)] —**sound′a·ble,** *adj.*

sound[4] (sound), *n.* **1.** a relatively narrow passage of water between larger bodies of water or between the mainland and an island: *Long Island Sound.* **2.** an inlet, arm, or recessed portion of the sea: *Puget Sound.* **3.** the air bladder of a fish. [ME; OE *sund* swimming, channel, sea; see SOUND[3]]

Sound (sound), *n.* **The,** a strait between SW Sweden and Zealand, connecting the Kattegat and the Baltic. 87 mi. long; 3–30 mi. wide. Swedish and Danish, **Øresund.**

sound′ bar′rier, (not in technical use) a hypothetical barrier to flight beyond the speed of sound, so postulated because aircraft undergo an abruptly increasing drag force induced by compression of the surrounding air when traveling near the speed of sound. Also called **sonic barrier, transonic barrier.**

sound′ bite′, a brief, striking remark or statement excerpted from an audiotape or videotape for insertion in a broadcast news story.

sound′ block′, a small block of wood for rapping with a gavel. Also, **sound′ing block′.**

sound·board (sound′bōrd′, -bôrd′), *n.* See **sounding board.** [SOUND[1] + BOARD]

sound′ bow′ (bō), that part of a bell against which the tongue strikes.

sound·box (sound′boks′), *n.* **1.** a chamber in a musical instrument, as the body of a violin, for increasing the sonority of its tone. **2.** the part of a phonograph pickup in which the mechanical movements of the needle are converted into acoustic impulses, usually by a diaphragm vibrated by the needle. [SOUND[1] + BOX[1]]

sound′ effect′, any sound, other than music or speech, artificially reproduced to create an effect in a dramatic presentation, as the sound of a storm, a creaking door, etc.

sound·er[1] (soun′dər), *n.* **1.** one who or that which makes a sound or noise, or sounds something. **2.** *Telegraphy.* an instrument for receiving telegraphic impulses that emits the sounds from which the message is read. [SOUND[1] + -ER[1]]

sound·er[2] (soun′dər), *n.* one who or that which sounds depth, as of water. [SOUND[3] + -ER[1]]

sound′ film′, 1. a film on which sound has been or is to be recorded, as for the sound track of a motion picture. **2.** See **sound motion picture.**

sound′ head′, *Motion Pictures.* a mechanism through which film passes in a projector for conversion of the sound track into audio-frequency signals which can be amplified and reproduced. Also called **sound′ gate′.**

sound′ hole′, an opening in the soundboard of a musical stringed instrument, as a violin or lute, for increasing the soundboard's capacity for vibration.

sound·ing[1] (soun′ding), *adj.* **1.** emitting or producing a sound or sounds. **2.** resounding or sonorous. **3.** having an imposing sound; high-sounding; pompous. [SOUND[1] + -ING[2]] —**sound′ing·ly,** *adv.* —**sound′ing·ness,** *n.*

sound·ing[2] (soun′ding), *n.* **1.** Often, **soundings.** the act of sounding an area of water or examining the bottom with or as with a lead and line. **2. soundings, a.** an area of water able to be sounded with an ordinary lead and line, the depth being 100 fathoms or less. **b.** the results or measurement obtained by sounding with a lead and line. **3.** *Meteorol.* any vertical penetration of the atmosphere for scientific measurement, esp. a radiosonde or rocketsonde observation. **4. off soundings,** *Naut.* in waters beyond the 100-fathom depth. **5. on soundings,** *Naut.* in waters less than 100 fathoms deep, so that the lead can be used. [SOUND[3] + -ING[1]] —**sound′ing·ly,** *adv.* —**sound′ing·ness,** *n.*

sound′ing board′, 1. a thin, resonant plate of wood forming part of a musical instrument, and so placed as to enhance the power and quality of the tone. 2. a structure over or behind and above a speaker, orchestra, etc., to reflect the sound toward the audience. 3. a board used in floors, partitions, etc., for deadening sound. 4. a person or persons whose reactions serve as a measure of the effectiveness, acceptability, popularity, etc., of the methods, ideas, etc., put forth. 5. a person or group that propagates ideas, opinions, etc.: *He was more of a sounding board than a novelist.* Also called **soundboard.**

sound′ing lead′ (led). See under **sounding line.**

sound′ing line′, a line weighted with a lead or plummet (**sounding lead**) and bearing marks to show the length paid out, used for sounding, as at sea.

sound′ing machine′, *Navig.* any of various machines for taking and recording soundings.

sound′ing rock′et, a rocket equipped with instruments for making meteorological observations in the upper atmosphere.

sound·less[1] (sound′lis), *adj.* without sound; silent; quiet. [SOUND[1] + -LESS] —**sound′less·ly,** *adv.* —**sound′less·ness,** *n.*

sound·less[2] (sound′lis), *adj.* unfathomable; very deep. [SOUND[3] + -LESS] —**sound′less·ly,** *adv.* —**sound′less·ness,** *n.*

sound′ man′, a technician who produces sound effects.

sound′ mo′tion pic′ture, a motion picture with a sound track.

sound′ pres′sure, *Physics.* 1. Also called **instantaneous sound pressure, excess sound pressure.** the difference between the pressure at a point in a medium through which a sound wave is passing and the static pressure of the medium at that point. 2. See **effective sound pressure.**

sound·proof[1] (sound′pro͞of′), *adj.* impervious to sound. [SOUND[1] + PROOF] —**sound′proof′ing,** *n.*

sound·proof[2] (sound′pro͞of′), *v.t.* to cause to be soundproof. [back formation from *soundproofing*]

sound′ rang′ing, a method for determining the distance between a point and the position of a sound source by measuring the time lapse between the origin of the sound and its arrival at the point.

sound′ slide′film, a filmstrip having a synchronized sound track.

sound′ spec′trogram, a graphic representation, produced by a sound spectrograph, of the frequency, intensity, duration, and variation with time of the resonance of a sound or series of sounds. Also called **sonagram.**

sound′ spec′trograph, an electronic device for recording a sound spectrogram.

sound′ track′, a sound record on a motion-picture film.

sound′ truck′, a truck carrying a loudspeaker from which speeches, music, etc., are broadcast, as for advertising, campaigning, or the like.

sound′ wave′, *Physics.* a longitudinal wave in an elastic medium, esp. a wave producing an audible sensation.

soup (so͞op), *n.* 1. a liquid food made by boiling or simmering meat, fish, or vegetables with various added ingredients. 2. *Informal.* a thick fog. 3. *Slang.* added power, esp. horsepower. 4. *Slang.* nitroglycerine. 5. **in the soup,** *Slang.* in trouble: *He'll be in the soup when the truth comes out.* —*v.t.* 6. **soup up,** *U.S. Slang.* a. to improve the capacity for speed or increase the efficiency of (a motor or engine) by increasing the richness of the fuel mixture or the efficiency of the fuel, or by adjusting the engine. b. to give spirit or vivacity to; enliven: *a political rally souped up by the appearance of the candidates.* [< F *soupe* < OF < Gmc; cf. D *sopen* to dunk. See SOP] —**soup′less,** *adj.* —**soup′like′,** *adj.*
—**Syn. 1.** broth, stock, potage.

soup-and-fish (so͞op′ən fish′), *n.* *Informal.* a man's formal evening clothes. [alluding to the early courses of a formal dinner]

soup·bone (so͞op′bōn′), *n.* 1. a bone used for making soup or broth. 2. *Baseball Slang.* a pitcher's throwing arm. [SOUP + BONE]

soup·çon (so͞op sôN′, so͞op′sôN), *n.* 1. a slight trace or flavor; suspicion. 2. a very small amount. [< F: a suspicion < MF *sospecon* < LL *suspectiōn-* (s. of *suspectiō*), r. *suspiciō* SUSPICION]

soup′fin shark′ (so͞op′fin′), a requiem shark, *Galeorhinus zyopterus,* found in the Pacific Ocean, valued for its fins which are used by the Chinese in the preparation of a soup and for its liver which is rich in vitamin A. Also called **soup′fin′.**

sou·pière (*Fr.* so͞o pyer′), *n., pl.* **-pières** (*Fr.* -pyer′). a covered classical urn used as an ornamental motif. [< F: soup tureen, equiv. to *soupe* SOUP + *-ière* instrumental n. suffix]

soup′ kitch′en, 1. a place where food, usually soup, is served at little or no charge to the needy. 2. *Mil. Slang.* (in World War I) a mobile kitchen.

sou·ple (sup′əl), *n.* silk from which only a portion of the sericin has been removed. Also called **sou′ple silk′.** [short for F *soie souple* supple silk]

soup·meat (so͞op′mēt′), *n.* beef used for making soup stock. [SOUP + MEAT]

soup′ plate′, a deep, concave plate used esp. for serving soup.

soup·spoon (so͞op′spo͞on′), *n.* a large spoon, commonly having a rounded bowl, with which to eat soup. [SOUP + SPOON[1]]

soup·y (so͞o′pē), *adj.,* **soup·i·er, soup·i·est.** 1. resembling soup in consistency: *soupy oatmeal.* 2. very thick; dense: *a soupy fog.* 3. overly sentimental; mawkish: *soupy love scenes.* [SOUP + -Y[1]]

sour (sour, sou′ər), *adj.* 1. having an acid taste, resembling that of vinegar, lemon juice, etc.; tart. 2. rendered acid or affected by fermentation; fermented. 3. characteristic of something fermented: *a sour smell.* 4. distasteful or disagreeable; unpleasant. 5. below standard; poor. 6. harsh in spirit or temper; austere; morose; peevish. 7. *Agric.* (of soil) having excessive acidity. 8. (of gasoline or the like) contaminated by sulfur compounds. 9. *Music Informal.* off-pitch; badly produced: *a sour note.* —*n.* 10. that which is sour; something sour. 11. any of various cocktails consisting typically of whiskey or gin with lemon or lime juice and sugar and sometimes soda water, often garnished with a slice of orange, a maraschino cherry, or both. 12. an acid or an acidic substance used in laundering and bleaching to neutralize alkalis and to decompose residual soap or bleach. —*v.i.* 13. to become sour, rancid, mildewed, etc.; spoil: *Milk sours quickly in warm weather. The laundry soured before it was ironed.* 14. to become bitter, disillusioned, or disinterested: *I guess I soured when I learned he was married. My loyalty soured after his last book.* 15. *Agric.* (of soil) to develop excessive acidity. —*v.t.* 16. to make sour; cause sourness in: *What do they use to sour the mash?* 17. to cause spoilage in; rot: *Defective cartons soured the apples.* 18. to make bitter, disillusioned, or disagreeable: *One misadventure needn't have soured him. That swindle soured a great many potential investors.* [ME; OE *sūr;* c. G *sauer,* D *zuur,* OIcel *sūrr*] —**sour′ish,** *adj.* —**sour′ly,** *adv.* —**sour′ness,** *n.*
—**Syn. 4.** bitter. **6.** severe, testy, touchy, acrimonious, cross, petulant, crabbed. —**Ant. 1.** sweet.

sour·ball (sour′bôl′, sou′ər-), *n.* 1. a round piece of hard candy with a tart or acid fruit flavoring. 2. *Informal.* a chronic grouch; grumbler. [SOUR + BALL[1]]

sour·ber·ry (sour′ber′ē, sou′ər-), *n., pl.* **-ries.** an evergreen shrub or small tree, *Rhus integrifolia,* of southern California, having pinkish-white flowers in hairy clusters, and deep-red, hairy fruits. [SOUR + BERRY]

source (sōrs, sôrs), *n.* 1. any thing or place from which something comes, arises, or is obtained; origin: *Which foods are sources of calcium?* 2. the beginning or place of origin of a stream or river. 3. a book, statement, person, etc., supplying information. 4. the person or business making interest or dividend payments. 5. *Archaic.* a natural spring or fountain. [ME *sours* < OF *sors,* ptp. of *sourdre* < L *surgere* to spring up, forth] —**source′ful,** *adj.* —**source′ful·ness,** *n.* —**source′less,** *adj.*
—**Syn. 1.** supplier, originator. **3.** authority, reference.

source′ book′, 1. an original writing, as a document, record, diary, or the like, that supplies an authoritative basis for future writing, study, evaluation, etc. 2. a volume containing a small collection of such writings, usually on a specific subject, used in research.

source′ mate′rial, original, authoritative, or basic materials utilized in research, as diaries, manuscripts, records, etc.

sour′ cher′ry, 1. a cherry, *Prunus Cerasus,* characterized by gray bark and the spreading habit of its branches. 2. the red, tart fruit of this tree, used in making pies and preserves.

sour′ cream′, cream soured by the lactic acid produced by a ferment.

sour·dine (so͞or dēn′), *n.* *Music.* 1. sordino. 2. kit[2]. 3. an obsolete member of the oboe family. [< F: *damper,* muted < It *sordina* (fem.); see SORDINO]

sour′ dock′. See under **dock**[4] (def. 1).

sour·dough (sour′dō′, sou′ər-), *n.* 1. *Western U.S. and Canada, Alaska, Brit. Dial.* leaven, esp. fermented dough kept from one baking to start the next instead of beginning each time with fresh yeast. 2. a prospector or pioneer, esp. in Alaska or Canada. —*adj.* 3. *Western U.S. and Canada, Alaska.* leavened with sourdough: *sourdough bread.* [ME; see SOUR, DOUGH]

sour′ gourd′, 1. the acid fruit of a bombaceous tree, *Adansonia Gregorii,* of northern Australia. 2. the tree. 3. the fruit of the baobab, *Adansonia digitata,* of Africa.

sour′ grapes′, pretended disdain for something one does not or cannot have: *She said that she and her husband didn't want to join the club anyway, but it was clearly sour grapes.* [in allusion to Aesop's fable concerning the fox who, in an effort to save face, described as sour those grapes he could not reach]

sour′ gum′, the tupelo, *Nyssa sylvatica.* Also called **cotton gum.**

sour′ mash′, a blended grain mash used in the distilling of some whiskeys, consisting of new mash and a portion of mash from a preceding run and yielding a high rate of lactic acid.

sour′ or′ange. See under **orange** (def. 2).

sour·puss (sour′po͝os′, sou′ər-), *n.* *Informal.* a person having a grouchy disposition that is often accompanied by a scowling facial expression. [SOUR + PUSS[2]]

sour′ salt′, crystals of citric acid used as a flavoring in foods, carbonated beverages, and pharmaceuticals.

sour·sop (sour′sop′, sou′ər-), *n.* 1. the large, slightly acid, pulpy fruit of a small tree, *Annona muricata,* of the West Indies. 2. the tree. Also called **guanabana.** [SOUR + SOP]

sour·wood (sour′wo͝od′, sou′ər-), *n.* See **sorrel tree.** [SOUR + WOOD[1]]

Sou·sa (so͞o′zə), *n.* **John Philip,** 1854–1932, U.S. band conductor and composer.

sou·sa·phone (so͞o′zə fōn′, -sə-), *n.* a form of bass tuba, similar to the helicon, used in brass bands. [named after J. P. SOUSA + -PHONE] —**sou′sa·phon′ist,** *n.*

souse[1] (sous), *v.,* **soused, sous·ing,** *n.* —*v.t.* 1. to plunge into water or other liquid; immerse. 2. to drench, as with water. 3. to dash or pour, as water. 4. to steep in pickling brine; pickle. 5. *Slang.* to intoxicate; make drunk. —*v.i.* 6. to plunge into water or other liquid; fall with a splash. 7. to be soaked or drenched. 8. to be steeping or soaking in something. 9. *Slang.* to drink to intoxication; get drunk. —*n.* 10. an act of sousing. 11. something kept or steeped in pickle, esp. the head, ears, and feet of a pig. 12. a liquid used as a pickle. 13. *Slang.* a drunkard. [ME *sows* < MF *souce* pickled < Gmc]

souse[2] (sous), *v.,* **soused, sous·ing,** *n.* *Archaic.* —*v.i.* 1. to swoop down. —*v.t.* 2. to swoop or pounce upon. —*n. Falconry.* 3. a rising while in flight. 4. a swooping or pouncing. [see SOURCE in obs. sense of rise]

sous·lik (so͞os′lik), *n.* suslik.

sous-sous (so͞o′so͞o′), *n.* *Ballet.* a small jump beginning and ending in the fifth position, usually performed in series moving forward, backward, or to the side. [< F *sous-sus,* equiv. to *(des)sous* (< L *subtus* under) + *(des)sus* (< L *sursum* over)]

Sous·telle (so͞o stel′), *n.* **Jacques** (zhäk), born 1912, French government official.

sou·tache (so͞o tash′; *Fr.* so͞o TASH′), *n.* a narrow braid, commonly of mohair, silk, or rayon, used for trimming. [< F: braid of a hussar's shako < Hung *sujtas* flat braid for trimming]

sou·tane (so͞o tän′), *n.* *Eccles.* a cassock. [< F < It *sottan(a),* equiv. to *sott(o)* under (< L *subtus*) + *-ana* dim. suffix]

sou·te·nu (so͞ot′ᵊno͞o′; *Fr.* so͞otᵊ NY′), *adj.* *Ballet.* performed in a carefully sustained manner. [< F: lit., SUSTAINED]

sou·ter (so͞o′tər), *n.* *Scot. and North Eng.* a person who makes or repairs shoes; cobbler; shoemaker. Also, **soutter.** [ME *sutor,* OE *sūtere* < L *sūtor,* equiv. to *su(ere)* (to) SEW + *-t-* ptp. suffix + *-or* -OR[2]]

sou·ter·rain (so͞o′tə rān′, so͞o′tə rān′), *n.* *Chiefly Archaeol.* a subterranean passage or structure; grotto. [< F: lit., underground]

south (*n., adj., adv.* south; *v.* south, south), *n.* 1. a cardinal point of the compass directly opposite to the north. 2. the direction in which this point lies. 3. (*often cap.*) a quarter or territory situated in this direction. 4. (*cap.*) the general area south of Pennsylvania and the Ohio River and east of the Mississippi, consisting mainly of those States which formed the Confederacy. —*adj.* 5. lying toward or situated in the south; directed or proceeding toward the south. 6. coming from the south, as a wind. —*adv.* 7. toward, in, or from the south. —*v.i.* 8. to turn or move in a southerly direction. 9. *Astron.* to cross the meridian. [ME; OE *sūth;* c. OHG *sund-,* G *süd*]

South′ Af′rica, Repub′lic of, a country in S Africa; member of the British Commonwealth until 1961. 15,982,664 (1960); 472,000 sq. mi. *Capitals:* Pretoria and Cape Town. Formerly, **Union of South Africa.**

South′ Af′rican, 1. of southern Africa. 2. of the Republic of South Africa. 3. a native or inhabitant of the Republic of South Africa, esp. one of European descent.

South′ Af′rican Dutch′, 1. Afrikaans. *Abbr.:* SAfrD 2. the Boers.

South′ Af′rican jade′. See **Transvaal jade.**

South′ Af′rican Repub′lic, former name of **Transvaal.**

South′ Am′boy (am′boi), a town in E New Jersey. 8422 (1960).

South′ Amer′ica, a continent in the S part of the Western Hemisphere. 158,000,000 (est. 1963); ab. 6,900,000 sq. mi. —**South′ Amer′ican.**

South·amp·ton (south amp′tən, -hamp′-), *n.* 1. an administrative county in S England: a part of Hampshire. 1,197,170 (1951); 1503 sq. mi. *Co. seat:* Winchester. 2. a seaport in this county. 204,707 (1961). 3. a town on SE Long Island, in SE New York. 4582 (1960).

Southamp′ton Is′land, an island in N Canada, in the Northwest Territories at the entrance to Hudson Bay. 19,100 sq. mi.

South′ Ara′bia, 1. **Protectorate of,** a protectorate of Great Britain in S Arabia, comprised of 20 states and tribal units and the island of Socotra. 1,000,000 (est. 1964); ab. 112,000 sq. mi. Formerly, until 1962, **Protectorate of Aden.** 2. **Federation of,** a federation in S Arabia, formed 1959; now includes 16 states of the Protectorate of South Arabia, joined by the Colony of Aden in 1963. *Cap.:* Al Ittihad.

South′ Austral′ia, a state in S Australia. 969,340 (1961); 380,070 sq. mi. *Cap.:* Adelaide. —**South′ Austral′ian.**

South′ Beloit′, a town in N Illinois. 3781 (1960).

South′ Bend′, a city in N Indiana. 132,445 (1960).

South′ Bos′ton, a town in S Virginia. 5974 (1960).

south·bound (south′bound′), *adj.* 1. traveling southward. 2. pertaining to southward travel. [SOUTH + -BOUND[2]]

South′ Bound′ Brook′, a town in central New Jersey. 3626 (1960).

South·bridge (south′brij′), *n.* a town in S Massachusetts. 15,889 (1960).

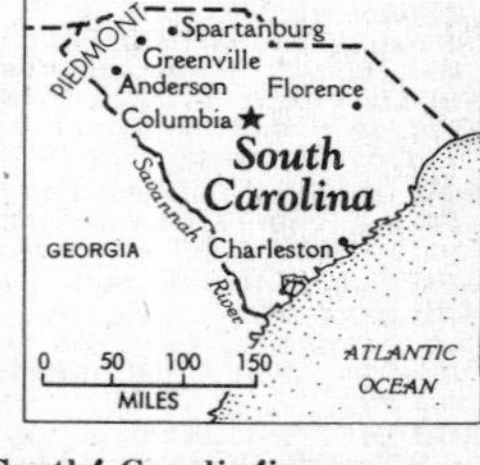

South′ Broad′way, a town in S Washington. 3661 (1960).

south′ by east′, *Navig., Survey.* a point on the compass 11°15′ east of south. *Abbr.:* SbE

south′ by west′, *Navig., Survey.* a point on the compass 11°15′ west of south. *Abbr.:* SbW

South′ Caroli′na, a State in the SE United States, on the Atlantic coast. 2,382,594 (1960); 31,055 sq. mi. *Cap.:* Columbia. *Abbr.:* S.C. —**South′ Carolin′ian.**

South′ Cauca′sian, 1. a family of languages including Georgian, Mingrelian, and others that are spoken on the south slopes of the Caucasus. 2. of or pertaining to South Caucasian.

South′ Charles′ton, a city in W West Virginia. 19,180 (1960).

South′ Chica′go Heights′, a town in NE Illinois. 4043 (1960).

South′ Chi′na Sea′, a part of the W Pacific, bounded by SE China, Vietnam, the Malay Peninsula, Borneo, and the Philippines.

South′ Cov′entry, a town in central Connecticut. 3568 (1960).

South′ Dako′ta, a State in the N central United States: a part of the Midwest. 680,514 (1960); 77,047 sq. mi. *Cap.:* Pierre. *Abbr.:* S. Dak. —**South′ Dako′tan.**

South·down (south′doun′), *n.* one of an English breed of sheep, yielding mutton of high quality. [after SOUTH DOWN(s) where the breed was developed]

South′ Downs′, a range of low hills in S England.

south·east (south′ēst′; *Naut.* sou′ēst′), *n.* 1. the point or direction midway between south and east. 2. a region in this direction.

3. (*cap.*) the southeast region of the United States. —*adj.* 4. lying toward, situated in, or directed toward the southeast. 5. coming from the southeast, as a wind. —*adv.* 6. in the direction midway between south and east. 7. from this direction. [ME *southest*, OE *sūthēast*. See SOUTH, EAST] —**south/east/ern,** *adj.* —**south·east·ern·most** (south/ē/stərn mōst/ *or, esp. Brit.,* -məst), *adj.*

South/east A/sia Trea/ty Organiza/tion. See **SEATO.**

southeast/ by east/, *Navig., Survey.* a point on the compass 11°15′ east of southeast. *Abbr.:* SEbE

southeast/ by south/, *Navig., Survey.* a point on the compass 11°15′ south of southeast. *Abbr.:* SEbS

south·east·er (south/ē/stər; *Naut.* sou/ē/stər), *n.* a wind, or storm from the southeast. [SOUTHEAST + -ER[1]]

south·east·er·ly (south/ē/stər lē; *Naut.* sou/ē/stər lē), *adj., adv.* toward or from the southeast. [SOUTH + EASTERLY]

south·east·ern·er (south/ē/stər nər), *n.* 1. a native or inhabitant of the southeast. 2. (*cap.*) a native or inhabitant of the southeastern U.S. [SOUTHEASTERN + -ER[1]]

south·east·ward (south/ēst/wərd; *Naut.* sou/ēst/-wərd), *adv.* 1. Also, **south/east/wards.** toward the southeast. —*adj.* 2. facing or tending toward the southeast. 3. coming from the southeast, as a wind. —*n.* 4. the southeast. [SOUTHEAST + -WARD]

south·east·ward·ly (south/ēst/wərd lē; *Naut.* sou/-ēst/wərd lē), *adj., adv.* toward or from the southeast. [SOUTHEASTWARD + -LY]

South/ El/gin, a town in NE Illinois. 2624 (1960).

South/ El Mon/te, a town in SW California. 4850 (1960).

South·end-on-Sea (south/end/on sē/, -ôn-), *n.* a seaport in SE Essex, in SE England, on Thames estuary. 164,976 (1961).

south/ equato/rial cur/rent, an ocean current, flowing westward, found near the equator in the Atlantic, Pacific, and Indian oceans.

south·er (sou/thər), *n.* a wind or storm from the south. [SOUTH + -ER[1]]

south·er·ly (suth/ər lē), *adj., adv., n., pl.* **-lies.** —*adj., adv.* 1. toward the south: *a southerly course.* 2. (esp. of a wind) coming from the south: *a gentle southerly breeze.* —*n.* 3. a wind that blows from the south. [SOUTH + *-erly*, modeled on *easterly*] —**south/er·li·ness,** *n.*

south/erly burst/er, buster (def. 6). Also, **south/erly bust/er.**

south·ern (suth/ərn), *adj.* 1. lying toward, situated in, or directed toward the south. 2. coming from the south, as a wind. 3. of or pertaining to the south. 4. (*cap.*) of or pertaining to the South of the United States. 5. *Astron.* being or located south of the celestial equator or of the zodiac: *a southern constellation.* —*n.* 6. *Chiefly Dial.* southerner (def. 2). 7. (*cap.*) the dialect of English spoken in the eastern parts of Maryland, Virginia, and the Carolinas, in Florida, in the southern parts of Georgia, Alabama, Mississippi, and Louisiana, and in southeastern Texas. [ME; OE *sūtherne.* See SOUTH, -ERN]

South/ern Alps/, a mountain range in New Zealand, on South Island. Highest peak, Mt. Cook, 12,349 ft.

South/ern Bap/tist, a member of the Southern Baptist Convention, founded in Augusta, Georgia, in 1845, that is strictly Calvinistic and active in religious publishing and education.

south/ern blight/, *Plant Pathol.* a disease of plants, characterized by stem rot, wilting, and small, white or brown sclerotia on the affected parts, caused by a fungus, *Sclerotium rolfsii.*

South/ern Cameroons/. See under **Cameroons** (def. 2).

south/ern cane/. See under **cane** (def. 5).

South/ern Coal/sack, *Astron.* See under **Coalsack.**

south/ern crab/ ap/ple, a tree, *Malus angustifolia*, of the eastern U.S., having fragrant, pink or rose-colored flowers and small, round, yellow-green fruit.

South/ern Cross/, *Astron.* a southern constellation between Centaurus and Musca. Also called **Cross.**

South/ern Crown/, *Astron.* the constellation Corona Australis.

south/ern cy/press. See **bald cypress.**

South/ern Dem/ocrat, *U.S.* a member of the Democratic party in one of the southern States who has political views traditionally more conservative than those of the members of the same party in the western and northern States, esp. on racial issues.

south/ern dew/berry, a creeping or trailing blackberry, *Rubus trivialis*, of the southeastern U.S., having prickly stems with sticky bristles, white or pinkish flowers, and oblong, black fruit.

south·ern·er (suth/ər nər), *n.* 1. a native or inhabitant of the south. 2. (*cap.*) a native or inhabitant of the southern U.S. [SOUTHERN + -ER[1]]

South/ern Fish/, *Astron.* the constellation Piscis Austrinus.

South/ern Hem/isphere, the half of the earth between the South Pole and the equator.

south·ern·ism (suth/ər niz/əm), *n.* a pronunciation, figure of speech, or behavioral trait characteristic of the U.S. South. [SOUTHERN + -ISM]

South/ern Lights/, *Astron.* See **aurora australis.**

south·ern·ly (suth/ərn lē), *adj.* southerly. [SOUTHERN + -LY] —**south/ern·li·ness,** *n.*

south/ern magno/lia. See **evergreen magnolia.**

south·ern·most (suth/ərn mōst/ *or, esp. Brit.,* -məst), *adj.* farthest south. [SOUTHERN + -MOST]

South/ern Pai/ute. See under **Paiute** (def. 2).

South/ern Pines/, a town in central North Carolina. 5198 (1960).

South/ern Rhode/sia, former name of **Rhodesia** (def. 1). —**South/ern Rhode/sian.**

south/ern right/ whale/, a blackish right whale, *Eubalaena australis*, of the South Atlantic and adjacent waters.

South/ern Sea/. See **Mare Australe** (def. 1).

South/ern Slavs/. See under **Slav.**

South/ern Spor/ades. See under **Sporades.**

south/ern stud/fish. See under **studfish.**

south/ern toad/, a common toad, *Bufo terrestris terrestris*, of the southeastern U.S., having prominent knoblike crests on its head.

South/ern Tri/angle, *Astron.* the constellation Triangulum Australe.

south·ern·wood (suth/ərn wo͝od/), *n.* a woody-stemmed wormwood, *Artemisia Abrotanum*, of southern Europe, having aromatic, finely dissected leaves. Also called **old man.** [ME *southernewode*, OE *sūtherne wudu.* See SOUTHERN, WOOD[1]]

South/ Eu/clid, a city in NE Ohio, near Cleveland. 27,569 (1960).

Sou·they (sou/thē, suth/ē), *n.* **Robert,** 1774–1843, English poet and prose writer: poet laureate 1813–43.

South/ Farm/ingdale, a town on central Long Island, in SE New York. 16,318 (1960).

South/ Fay/etteville, a town in central North Carolina. 3411 (1960).

South·field (south/fēld/), *n.* a city in SE Michigan, W of Detroit. 31,501 (1960).

South/ Fort/ Mitch/ell, a town in N Kentucky. 4086 (1960).

South/ Frig/id Zone/, the part of the earth's surface between the Antarctic Circle and the South Pole.

South/ Ful/ton, a town in NW Tennessee. 2512 (1960).

South/ Gasto/nia, a town in S North Carolina. 3762 (1960).

South·gate (south/git, -gāt/), *n.* a city in SE Michigan, near Detroit. 29,404 (1960).

South/ Gate/, a city in SW California, near Los Angeles. 53,831 (1960).

South/ Geor/gia, a British island in the S Atlantic, about 800 mi. SE of the Falkland Islands. 1271 (1959); ab. 1000 sq. mi. —**South/ Geor/gian.**

South/ Glens/ Falls/, a town in E New York. 4129 (1960).

South/ Greens/burg, a town in central Pennsylvania. 3058 (1960).

South/ Ha/ven, a town in SW Michigan. 6149 (1960).

South/ Hol/land, a province in the SW Netherlands. 2,697,894 (est. 1960); 1086 sq. mi. *Cap.:* The Hague.

South/ Hous/ton, a town in S Texas. 7523 (1960).

South/ Hun/tington, a town on central Long Island, in SE New York. 7084 (1960).

south·ing (sou/thing), *n.* 1. *Astron.* a. the transit of a heavenly body across the celestial meridian. b. *Obs.* south declination. 2. movement or deviation toward the south. 3. distance due south made by a vessel. [SOUTH + -ING[1]]

South·ing·ton (suth/ing tən), *n.* a town in central Connecticut. 9952 (1960).

South/ Is/land, the largest island of New Zealand. 729,925 (est. 1961); 58,093 sq. mi.

South/ Kore/a, a country in E Asia: formed 1948 after the division of the former country of Korea at 38° N. 28,647,176 (est. 1965); 36,600 sq. mi. *Cap.:* Seoul. Cf. **Korea.** Official name, **Republic of Korea.**

south·land (south/lənd, -land/), *n.* 1. a southern area. 2. the southern part of a country. [SOUTH + LAND] —**south/land/er,** *n.*

South/ Miam/i, a town in S Florida. 9846 (1960).

South/ Milwau/kee, a city in SE Wisconsin. 20,307 (1960).

South/ Modes/to, a town in central California. 5465 (1960).

South/ Monroe/, a town in SE Michigan. 2919 (1960).

South·mont (south/mont), *n.* a town in central Pennsylvania. 2857 (1960).

south·most (south/mōst/ *or, esp. Brit.,* -məst), *adj.* southernmost. [SOUTH + -MOST]

South/ Nor/folk, a city in SE Virginia. 22,035 (1960).

South/ Ny/ack, a town in SE New York. 3113 (1960).

South/ Og/den, a town in N Utah. 7405 (1960).

South/ Or/ange, a city in NE New Jersey. 16,175 (1960).

South/ Ork/ney Is/lands, a group of islands in the British Antarctic Territory, N of the Antarctic Peninsula: formerly a dependency of the Falkland Islands; claimed by Argentina.

South/ O/roville, a town in N California. 3704 (1960).

South/ Osse/tian Auton/omous Re/gion, an autonomous region of the Georgian Republic, in the N part. 99,000; 1428 sq. mi. *Cap.:* Tskhinvali.

South/ Park/, a town in W California. 3261 (1960).

South/ Pasade/na, a city in SW California, near Los Angeles. 19,706 (1960).

south·paw (south/pô/), *Informal.* —*n.* 1. a person who is left-handed. 2. *Sports.* a. a player who throws with his left hand, esp. a pitcher. b. *Boxing.* a boxer who leads with his right hand and stands with his right foot forward. —*adj.* 3. left-handed. [SOUTH + PAW]

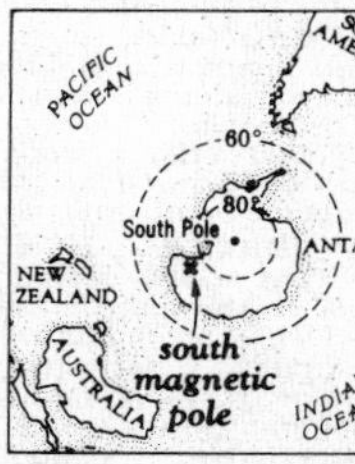

South/ Pitts/burg, a town in S Tennessee. 4130 (1960).

South/ Plain/field, a city in N New Jersey. 17,879 (1960).

South/ Platte/, a river flowing NE from central Colorado to the Platte River in W Nebraska. 424 mi. long.

South/ Pole/, 1. *Geog.* the end of the earth's axis of rotation marking the southernmost point of the earth. 2. *Astron.* the point at which the axis of the earth extended cuts the southern half of the celestial sphere; the south celestial pole. 3. (*l.c.*) the pole of a magnet that seeks the earth's south magnetic pole. 4. (*l.c.*) See under **magnetic pole.**

South·port (south/pôrt/, -pōrt/), *n.* a seaport in W Lancashire, in NW England: resort. 81,976 (1961).

South/ Port/land, a city in SW Maine. 22,788 (1960).

south·ron (suth/rən), *n.* 1. *Chiefly Dial.* southerner (def. 2). 2. (*usually cap.*) *Scot.* an Englishman. [ME; earlier *southren* (var. of SOUTHERN), modeled on *Saxon*, etc.]

South/ Salis/bury, a town in central North Carolina. 3065 (1960).

South/ Salt/ Lake/, a town in N Utah. 9520 (1960).

South/ San/ Francis/co, a city in central California. 39,418 (1960).

South/ San/ Ga/briel, a town in SW California, near Los Angeles. 26,213 (1960).

South/ Sea/ Is/lands, the islands in the S Pacific Ocean. Cf. **Oceania.** —**South/ Sea/ Is/lander.**

South/ Seas/, the seas south of the equator.

South/ Shet/land Is/lands, a group of islands in the British Antarctic Territory, N of the Antarctic Peninsula: formerly a dependency of the Falkland Islands; claimed by Argentina and Chile.

South/ Shields/, a seaport in NE Durham, in NE England, at the mouth of the Tyne River. 109,533 (1961).

South/ Sioux/ Cit/y, a town in NE Nebraska. 7200 (1960).

south-south·east (south/south/ēst/; *Naut.* sou/-sou/ēst/), *Navig., Survey.* —*n.* 1. the point on the compass midway between south and southeast. —*adj.* 2. coming from this point: *a south-southeast wind.* 3. directed toward this point: *a south-southeast course.* —*adv.* 4. from this point: *The wind is blowing south-southeast.* 5. toward this point: *sailing south-southeast.* *Abbr.:* SSE [ME *south south est.* See SOUTH, EAST]

south-south·east·ward (south/south/ēst/wərd; *Naut.* sou/sou/ēst/wərd), *adv., adj.* toward the south-southeast. Also, **south/-south/east/ward·ly.**

south-south·west (south/south/west/; *Naut.* sou/-sou/west/), *Navig., Survey.* —*n.* 1. the point on the compass midway between south and southwest. —*adj.* 2. coming from this point: *a south-southwest wind.* 3. directed toward this point: *a south-southwest course.* —*adv.* 4. from this point: *The wind is blowing south-southwest.* 5. toward this point: *sailing south-southwest.* *Abbr.:* SSW [SOUTH + SOUTHWEST]

south-south·west·ward (south/south/west/wərd; *Naut.* sou/sou/west/wərd), *adv., adj.* toward the south-southwest. Also, **south/-south/west/ward·ly.**

South St. Paul, a city in SE Minnesota. 22,032 (1960).

South/ Tem/perate Zone/, the part of the earth's surface between the tropic of Capricorn and the Antarctic Circle.

South/ Tuc/son, a town in SE Arizona. 7004 (1960)

South/ Un/iontown, a town in SW Pennsylvania. 3603 (1960).

South/ Vietnam/, a former country in SE Asia that comprised Vietnam S of about 17° N latitude: now part of reunified Vietnam. Cf. **North Vietnam, Vietnam.**

south·ward (south/wərd; *Naut.* suth/ərd), *adj.* 1. moving, bearing, facing, or situated toward the south. 2. coming from the south, as a wind. —*adv.* 3. Also, **south/wards.** toward the south; south. —*n.* 4. the southward part, direction, or point. [ME; OE *sūth weard.* See SOUTH, -WARD]

south·ward·ly (south/wərd lē; *Naut.* suth/ərd lē), *adj., adv.* toward or from the south. [SOUTHWARD + -LY]

South·wark (suth/ərk), *n.* a borough of central London, England, S of the Thames. 86,175 (1961).

south·west (south/west/; *Naut.* sou/west/), *n.* 1. the point or direction midway between south and west. 2. a region in this direction. 3. (*cap.*) the southwest region of the United States. —*adj.* 4. lying toward, situated in, or directed toward the southwest. 5. coming from the southwest, as a wind. —*adv.* 6. in the direction which is midway between south and west. 7. from this direction. [ME; OE *sūthwest.* See SOUTH, WEST] —**south/west/ern,** *adj.*

South/-West A/frica (south/west/), a territory in SW Africa: a former German protectorate; a mandate of the Republic of South Africa 1919–66; status now in dispute. 525,064 (1960); 317,725 sq. mi. *Cap.:* Windhoek. Formerly, **German Southwest Africa.** Official (UN) name, **Namibia.** —**South/-West Af/rican.**

southwest/ by south/, *Navig., Survey.* a point on the compass 11°15′ south of southwest. *Abbr.:* SWbS

southwest/ by west/, *Navig., Survey.* a point on the compass 11°15′ west of southwest. *Abbr.:* SWbW

south·west·er (south/wes/tər; *Naut.* sou/wes/tər), *n.* 1. a wind, gale, or storm from the southwest. 2. a waterproof hat, usually of oilskin, having the brim very broad behind, worn esp. by seamen. 3. Also called **nor'wester.** a slicker, fastening with buckles, worn esp. by seamen in rough weather. Also, **sou'·west·er** (sou/wes/tər). [SOUTHWEST + -ER[1]]

south·west·er·ly (south/wes/tər lē; *Naut.* sou/wes/-tər lē), *adj., adv.* toward or from the southwest. [SOUTHWEST + *-erly*, modeled on *westerly*]

south·west·ern·er (south/wes/tər nər), *n.* 1. a native or inhabitant of the southwest. 2. (*cap.*) a native or inhabitant of the southwestern U.S. [SOUTHWESTERN + -ER[1]]

South/ West/ Far/go, a town in E North Dakota. 3328 (1960).

South/west Greens/burg, a town in central Pennsylvania. 3264 (1960).

south·west·ward (south/west/wərd; *Naut.* sou/-west/wərd), *adv.* 1. Also, **south/west/wards.** toward the southwest. —*adj.* 2. facing or tending toward the southwest. 3. coming from the southwest, as a wind. —*n.* 4. the southwest. [SOUTHWEST + -WARD]

south·west·ward·ly (south/west/wərd lē; *Naut.* sou/west/wərd lē), *adj., adv.* toward or from the southwest. [SOUTHWESTWARD + LY]

South/west Wau/sau, a town in central Wisconsin. 4105 (1960).

South/ Wil/liamsport, a town in central Pennsylvania. 6972 (1960).

South/ Yem/en, a republic in S Arabia, formed in 1967 from the Federation of South Arabia and the Eastern Aden Protectorate. 1,000,000 (est. 1964); ab. 112,000 sq. mi. *Cap.:* Medina as-Shaab. Official name, **South/ Yem/en Peo/ple's Repub/lic.**

South′ Yu′ba, a town in central California. 3200 (1960).

Sou·tine (so͞o tēn′), *n.* **Cha·im** (ᴋʜī im′, ᴋʜī′im), 1894–1943, Lithuanian painter in France.

sout·ter (so͞o′tər), *n. Scot. and North Eng.* souter.

Sou·van·na Phou·ma (so͞o vän′nä po͞o′mä), **Prince,** born 1901, Laotian statesman: premier 1962–75.

sou·ve·nir (so͞o′və nēr′, so͞o′və nēr′), *n.* **1.** something given or kept as a reminder of a place visited, an incident, etc.; memento: *The pennant was the only souvenir he brought back from Niagara Falls.* **2.** a memory. [< F, n. use of (*se*) *souvenir* to remember < L *subvenīre,* equiv. to *sub-* sub- + *venīre* to come (to one's mind)]

sov·er·eign (sov′rin, sov′ər in, suv′-), *n.* **1.** a monarch; a king, queen, or other supreme ruler. **2.** a person who has sovereign power or authority. **3.** a group or body of persons or a state having sovereign authority. **4.** a gold coin of the United Kingdom, equal to one pound sterling: went out of circulation after 1914. —*adj.* **5.** belonging to or characteristic of a sovereign or sovereignty; royal. **6.** having supreme rank, power, or authority. **7.** supreme, as power, authority, etc. **8.** greatest in degree; utmost or extreme. **9.** being above all others in character, importance, excellence, etc. **10.** efficacious; potent: *a sovereign remedy.* [ME *soverain* (alter. by influence of reign) < OF *soverain* < VL **superān(us)* < L *super-* super- + *-ānus* -an] —**sov′er·eign·ly,** *adv.*
—**Syn. 1.** emperor, empress, potentate. **3.** government. **5.** regal, majestic, imperial, princely, monarchical, kingly. **7.** chief, paramount, principal, predominant. **10.** effective, effectual.

sov·er·eign·ty (sov′rin tē, suv′-), *n., pl.* **-ties. 1.** the quality or state of being sovereign. **2.** the status, dominion, power, or authority of a sovereign; royalty. **3.** supreme and independent power or authority in government as possessed or claimed by a state or community. **4.** a sovereign state, community, or political unit. [ME *soveraynte* < AF *sovereynete* (OF *soverainete*), equiv. to *soverain* sovereign + *-ete* -ty[2]]

So·vetsk (so vyetsk′), *n.* a city in the W RSFSR, in the W Soviet Union in Europe, NE of Kaliningrad on the Memel River: formerly in East Prussia; peace treaty (1807) between France, Prussia, and Russia. 85,900 (1959). Formerly (until 1945), **Tilsit.**

so·vi·et (sō′vē et′, -it, sō′vē et′), *n.* **1.** (in the Soviet Union) **a.** (before the revolution) a council of any kind, presumably elected by all. **b.** (after the revolution) a local council, originally elected only by manual workers, with certain powers of local administration. **c.** (after the revolution) a higher council elected by a local council, being part of a hierarchy of soviets culminating in the Supreme Soviet. **2.** any similar council or assembly connected with a socialistic governmental system elsewhere. **3. Soviets,** the governing officials or the people of the Soviet Union: *The Soviets have denied our charge.* —*adj.* **4.** of or pertaining to a soviet. **5.** (*cap.*) of the Soviet Union: *a Soviet statesman.* [< Russ *sovyet* council < ORuss *sŭvĕtŭ*] —**so·vi·et·dom** (sō′vē et′dəm, -it-, sō′vē et′-), *n.*

So·vi·et·ise (sō′vē i tīz′), *v.t.,* **-ised, -is·ing.** *Chiefly Brit.* Sovietize. —**So′vi·et·i·sa′tion,** *n.*

So·vi·et·ism (sō′vē i tiz′əm), *n.* **1.** (*sometimes l.c.*) a soviet system of government. **2.** (*often l.c.*) the practices and principles of a soviet government, esp. as it implies communism. **3.** a characteristic, mannerism, phrase, etc., expressive of or identifiable with the ideology of the Soviet Union. [soviet + -ism] —**So′vi·et·ist,** *n., adj.*

So·vi·et·ize (sō′vē i tīz′), *v.t.,* **-ized, -iz·ing. 1.** (*sometimes l.c.*) to bring under the influence or domination of the Soviet Union. **2.** (*often l.c.*) to impose or institute a soviet system of government similar to that of the Soviet Union. [soviet + -ize] —**So′vi·et·i·za′tion,** *n.*

So′viet Moun′tains, a mountain range in the averted hemisphere or far side of the moon: about 1250 miles long. Also called **So′viet Range′, So′viet Ridge′.**

So′viet of National′ities. See under **Supreme Soviet.**

So′viet of the Un′ion. See under **Supreme Soviet.**

So′viet Rus′sia, 1. a conventional name of the Soviet Union. **2.** See **Russian Soviet Federated Socialist Republic.**

So′viet Un′ion, a federal union of fifteen constituent republics, in E Europe and W and N Asia, comprising the larger part of the former Russian Empire. 260,040,000; 8,650,069 sq. mi. *Cap.:* Moscow. Also called **Russia.** Official name, **Union of Soviet Socialist Republics.**

sov·ran (sov′rən, suv′-), *n., adj. Poetic.* sovereign. [17th-century alter., modeled on It *sovrano*]

Sov. Un., Soviet Union.

sow[1] (sō), *v.,* **sowed, sown** or **sowed, sow·ing.** —*v.t.* **1.** to scatter (seed) over land, earth, etc., for growth; plant. **2.** to plant seed for: *to sow a crop.* **3.** to scatter seed over (land, earth, etc.) for the purpose of growth. **4.** to introduce for development; seek to propagate or extend; disseminate: *to sow distrust or dissension.* **5.** to strew or sprinkle with anything. —*v.i.* **6.** to sow seed, as for the production of a crop. [ME *sow(en),* OE *sāwan;* c. G *säen,* D *zaaien,* OIcel *sā,* Goth *saian,* L *serere*] —**sow′a·ble,** *adj.* —**sow′er,** *n.*

sow[2] (sou), *n.* **1.** an adult female swine. **2.** the adult female of various other animals, as the bear. **3.** *Metall.* **a.** a large oblong mass of iron which has solidified in the common channel through which the molten metal flows to the smaller channels in which the pigs solidify. **b.** the common channel itself. **c.** a basin holding any of certain molten nonferrous metals to be cast. [ME *sowe,* OE *sugu;* c. G *Sau,* OIcel *sȳr,* L *sūs,* Gk *hûs,* Tocharian *suwo*] —**sow′like′,** *adj.*

sow·ans (sō′ənz, so͞o′ənz), *n.* (*construed as sing.*) *Scot., Irish Eng.* sowens.

so·war (sō wär′, -wôr′), *n.* (in India) a mounted native soldier. [< Urdu < Pers *suwār* horseman, MPers *asbār,* OPers *asabāra,* equiv. to *asa-* horse + *-bara* borne by]

sow·bel·ly (sou′bel′ē), *n.* See **side meat.**

sow′ block′ (sou), (on a drop hammer or steam hammer) a steel block standing on the anvil and supporting the die.

sow′ bug′ (sou), any of several small, terrestrial isopods, esp. of the genus *Oniscus;* wood louse.

sow·car (sou kär′), *n.* soucar.

sow·ens (sō′ənz, so͞o′-), *n.* (*construed as sing.*) *Scot., Irish Eng.* porridge made from oat bran or husks that have been soaked in water, slightly fermented, and then boiled. Also, **sowans.** [< ScotGael *sūghan,* deriv. of *sūgh* sap]

So·we·to (sə wē′tō, -wā′-), *n.* a black township in South Africa, SW of Johannesburg: largest black urban settlement in southern Africa; racial riots 1976. 550,000.

sowl (so͞ol), *v.t.* sool.

sown (sōn), *v.* a pp. of **sow**[1].

sow′ this′tle (sou), any cichoriaceous plant of the genus *Sonchus,* esp. *S. oleraceus,* a weed having thistlelike leaves, yellow flowers, and a milky juice. [ME *sowethistel,* var. of *sugethistel* < OE. See sow[2], thistle]

sox (soks), *n.* a pl. of **sock**[1].

soy (soi), *n.* **1.** Also called **soy′ sauce′, soy′a sauce′** (soi′ə). a salty, fermented sauce much used on fish and other dishes in the Orient, prepared from soybeans. **2.** the soybean. [< Jap *shoy,* deriv. of *shōyū* < Chin (Peking) *shi-yu,* equiv. to *shi* salted food, sauce + *yu* oil]

soy·bean (soi′bēn′), *n.* **1.** a bushy, leguminous plant, *Glycine Soja,* of the Old World, grown in the U.S. chiefly for forage and soil improvement. **2.** the seed of this plant, used for food, as a livestock feed, and for a variety of other commercial uses. Also called **soja, soy·a** (soi′ə). [soy + bean]

soy′bean oil′, a pale-yellow oil derived from soybeans by expression or solvent extraction: used as a food and in the manufacture of soap, candles, inks, paints, varnishes, etc.

so·zin (sō′zin), *n. Biochem.* any protein normally present in the animal body and serving as a defense against disease. Cf. **mycosozin, toxosozin.** [< Gk *sōz(ein)* (to) save, keep, preserve + -in[2]]

Soz·zi·ni (sôt tsē′nē), *n.* Italian name of **Socinus.**

soz·zled (soz′əld), *adj. Slang.* drunk; inebriated. [*sozzle* confused state, sloppy person (earlier *sossle;* akin to souse) + -ed[3]]

SP, 1. Shore Patrol. **2.** Submarine Patrol.

Sp., 1. Spain. **2.** Spaniard. **3.** Also, **Sp** Spanish (def. 3).

sp., 1. special. **2.** species. **3.** specific. **4.** specimen. **5.** spelling. **6.** spirit.

S.P., 1. Shore Patrol. **2.** Socialist party. **3.** Submarine Patrol.

s.p., without issue. [< L *sine prole*]

spa (spä), *n.* **1.** a mineral spring, or a locality in which such springs exist. **2.** a resort hotel, esp. one situated near mineral springs. **3.** *New. Eng.* See **soda fountain.** [generalized use of Spa]

Spa (spä), *n.* a resort town in E Belgium, SE of Liège: famous mineral springs. 9391 (1964).

Spaak (späk; *Fr.* spᴀk), *n.* **Paul Hen·ri** (pôl hen′rē; *Fr.* pôl äɴ rē′), 1899–1972, Belgian statesman: prime minister of Belgium 1938–39, 1946–49; first president of the General Assembly of the United Nations 1946–47; secretary-general of NATO 1957–61.

Spaatz (späts), *n.* **Carl,** 1891–1974, U.S. general.

space (spās), *n., v.,* **spaced, spac·ing.** —*n.* **1.** the unlimited or indefinitely great three-dimensional expanse in which all material objects are located and all events occur. **2.** the portion or extent of this in a given instance; extent or room in three dimensions: *the space occupied by a body.* **3.** extent or area in two dimensions; a particular extent of surface: *to fill out blank spaces in a document.* **4.** *Fine Arts.* **a.** the designed and structured surface of a picture: *In Mondrian's later work he organized space in highly complex rhythms.* **b.** the illusion of depth on a two-dimensional surface. **5.** the region beyond the earth's atmosphere that contains the rest of the cosmos: *man's determination to travel through space.* **6.** a seat, berth, or room on a train, airplane, etc. **7.** linear distance; a particular distance: *trees set at equal spaces apart.* **8.** *Math.* a system of objects with relations between the objects defined. **9.** extent, or a particular extent, of time: *a space of two hours.* **10.** an interval of time; a while: *After a space he continued his story.* **11.** an area or interval allowed for or taken by advertising, as in a periodical, on the radio, etc. **12.** *Music.* the interval between two adjacent lines of the staff. **13.** *Print.* one of the blank pieces of metal, less than type-high, used to separate words, sentences, etc. **14.** *Telegraphy.* an interval during the transmitting of a message when the key is not in contact. **15.** radio or television broadcast time allowed or available for a program, advertisement, etc. —*v.t.* **16.** to fix the space or spaces of; divide into spaces. **17.** to set some distance apart. **18.** *Print., Writing.* **a.** to separate (words, letters, or lines) by spaces. **b.** to extend by inserting more space or spaces (usually fol. by *out*). [ME < OF (*e*)*space* < L *spatium*] —**spac′er,** *n.*

space′ bar′, a horizontal bar on a typewriter keyboard that is depressed in order to move the carriage one space to the left.

space′ cap′sule, a container or vehicle for launching into space and designed to be recovered on its return, containing experimental animals and instruments or people.

space′ car′rier, *Rocketry.* a vehicle designed to put payloads in orbit about the earth or to boost payloads for extraterrestrial exploration.

space′ charge′, *Elect.* a distribution of an excess of electrons or ions over a three-dimensional region, in contrast to the distribution of an electric charge over the surface of a conductor.

space·craft (spās′kraft′, -kräft′), *n.* any vehicle capable of traveling through space outside the earth's atmosphere. [space + craft]

space′ flight′, flight of manned or unmanned vehicles outside the earth's atmosphere.

space′ frame′, a building frame, as of a floor or roof, having its members arranged as trusses in three dimensions.

space′ group′, *Crystall.* a set of symmetry elements which brings a periodic arrangement of points on a Bravais space lattice to its original position.

space′ heat′er, a small furnace for heating the air of the room in which it is situated.

space′ lat′tice, lattice (def. 4).

space·less (spās′lis), *adj.* **1.** having no limits or dimensions in space; limitless; unbounded. **2.** occupying no space. [space + -less]

space′ link′age, *Mach.* a linkage for transmitting motion in three dimensions.

space′ man′. See **space writer.**

space·man (spās′man′, -mən), *n., pl.* **-men** (-men′, -mən). an astronaut. [space + man[1]]

space′ med′icine, the branch of aviation medicine dealing with the effects on man of flying outside the earth's atmosphere.

space′ op′era, a television or radio drama or motion picture, usually mediocre in quality, having a plot based on science-fiction adventures that take place in outer space.

space·port (spās′pōrt′, -pôrt′), *n.* a site at which spacecraft are tested, launched, sheltered, maintained, etc. [space + port[1]]

space′ rate′, a unit of compensation for written work, based on the amount of space which the submitted material occupies in print, and usually computed in column inches. Cf. **piece rate.**

space-sav·ing (spās′sā′ving), *adj.* **1.** that saves space. —*n.* **2.** act of saving space. [space + saving]

space·ship (spās′ship′), *n.* a rocket-propelled vehicle designed to carry man and cargo from the earth to the moon or planets. [space + ship]

space′ shut′tle, a large, rocket-powered space vehicle designed for transporting passengers, material, and equipment repeatedly between earth and an orbiting space station.

space′ stage′, a stage set, often limited to an arrangement of ramps and platforms, in which actors and set pieces are spotlighted against the bare background of a dark or black cyclorama.

space′ sta′tion, a manned artificial satellite in orbit around the earth: proposed esp. for the construction and launching of spaceships.

space·suit (spās′so͞ot′), *n.* a sealed and pressurized suit designed to allow the wearer to leave a pressurized cabin in outer space or at extremely high altitudes within the atmosphere. [space + suit]

space-time (spās′tīm′), *n.* **1.** Also called **space′-time′ contin′uum.** the four-dimensional continuum, having three spatial coordinates and one temporal coordinate, in which all physical quantities may be located. **2.** the physical reality that exists within this four-dimensional continuum. —*adj.* **3.** of, pertaining to, or noting a system with three spatial coordinates and one temporal coordinate. **4.** noting, pertaining to, or involving both space and time: *a space-time problem.*

space′ trav′el, space flight of manned vehicles.

space′ writ′er, a journalist or copywriter paid according to a space rate. Also called **space man.** Cf. **stringer** (def. 6).

spa·cial (spā′shəl), *adj.* spatial. —**spa·ci·al·i·ty** (spā′shē al′i tē), *n.* —**spa′cial·ly,** *adv.*

spac·ing (spā′sing), *n.* **1.** act of one who or that which spaces. **2.** the fixing or arranging of spaces. [space + -ing[1]]

spa·cious (spā′shəs), *adj.* **1.** containing much space, as a house, room, court, street, etc.; amply large: *a spacious yard.* **2.** occupying much space; vast. **3.** of a great extent or area; broad; large; great: *the spacious prairies.* **4.** broad in scope, range, inclusiveness, etc.: *a spacious approach to a problem.* [ME < L *spatiōsus.* See space, -ous] —**spa′cious·ly,** *adv.* —**spa′cious·ness,** *n.*
—**Syn. 1.** roomy, capacious, wide. **2.** extensive, huge, tremendous. —**Ant. 1.** small, cramped.

spack·le (spak′əl), *n., v.,* **-led, -ling.** —*n.* **1.** (*cap.*) *Trademark.* a quick-drying, plasterlike material for patching plasterwork. —*v.t., v.i.* **2.** to patch with Spackle. Also, **sparkle.**

spad (spad), *n.* a nail from which a plummet is hung. Also, **spud.** [alter. of spud]

spade[1] (spād), *n., v.,* **spad·ed, spad·ing.** —*n.* **1.** a tool for digging, having an iron blade adapted for pressing into the ground with the foot and a long handle commonly with a grip or crosspiece at the top. **2.** some implement, piece, or part resembling this. **3.** a sharp projection on the bottom of a gun trail, designed to dig into the earth to restrict backward movement of the carriage during recoil. **4.** a cutting tool used to strip the blubber or skin, as from a whale. **5. call a spade a spade,** to call something by its real name; speak plainly or bluntly: *To call a spade a spade, he's a crook.* **6. in spades,** *Slang.* **a.** in the extreme; positively: *He's a hypocrite, in spades.* **b.** without restraint; outspokenly: *I told him what I thought, in spades.* —*v.t.* **7.** to dig, cut, or remove with a spade (sometimes fol. by *up*): *Let's spade up the garden and plant some flowers.* [ME; OE *spadu;* c. G *Spaten,* Icel *spathi* spade, D *spade,* Gk *spáthē* broad, flat piece of wood] —**spade′like′,** *adj.* —**spad′er,** *n.*

spade[2] (spād), *n.* **1.** a black figure shaped like an inverted heart with a short stem at the cusp opposite the point, used on playing cards. **2.** a card of the suit bearing such figures. **3. spades, a.** (*construed as sing. or pl.*) the suit so marked: *Spades is trump. Spades count double.* **b.** (*construed as pl.*) *Casino.* the winning of seven spades or more. **4.** *Offensive.* a Negro. [< It, pl. of *spada,* orig. sword, later mark on cards < L *spatha* < Gk *spáthē;* see spade[1]]

spade·fish (spād′fish′), *n., pl.* (*esp. collectively*) **-fish,** (*esp. referring to two or more kinds or species*) **-fish·es.** a deep-bodied, marine fish of the genus *Chaetodipterus,* esp. *C. faber,* found along the Atlantic coast of North America. [prob. spade[2] + fish, in allusion to its shape]

spade′ foot′, *Furniture.* a square foot, tapering toward its bottom.

spade·foot (spād′fo͝ot′), *n., pl.* **-foots.** See **spadefoot toad.** [spade[1] + foot]

spade′foot toad′, any of several nocturnal toads of the family *Pelobatidae,* common in the Northern Hemisphere, characterized by a horny, spadelike projection on each hind foot for burrowing under the soil.

spade·ful (spād′fo͝ol), *n., pl.* **-fuls.** the amount that can be dug out with or carried on a spade. [spade[1] + -ful]

spade′ han′dle, *Mach.* a forked end on a rod or shaft between which another moving part swivels freely; yoke.

spade′ rud′der, *Naut.* a rudder supported and steadied only in its upper part, the lower part being free of the stern frame. Also called **underhung rudder.**

spade·work (spād′wûrk′), *n.* preliminary or initial work, such as the gathering of data, on which further activity is to be based. [SPADE[1] + WORK]

spa·di·ceous (spā dish′əs), *adj.* **1.** *Bot.* **a.** of the nature of a spadix. **b.** bearing a spadix. **2.** of a bright brown color. [< NL *spādīceus* < L *spādīc-* (s. of *spadix*). See SPADIX, -EOUS]

spa·dix (spā′diks), *n., pl.* **spa·di·ces** (spā dī′sēz). *Bot.* an inflorescence consisting of a spike with a fleshy or thickened axis, usually enclosed in a spathe. [< L: a broken palm branch and its fruit < Gk: a (torn-off) palm bough, akin to *spân* to tear off]

spa·do (spā′dō), *n., pl.* **spa·do·nes** (spā dō′nāz, spə-). **1.** *Civil Law.* an impotent person; one unable to procreate. **2.** a castrated man or animal. [late ME < L < Gk *spádōn* eunuch; see SPADIX]

spae (spā), *v.t.,* **spaed, spae·ing.** *Scot. and North Eng.* to prophesy; foretell; predict. [ME *spa(n)* < ON *spā*] —**spa′er,** *n.*

spae·ing (spā′ing), *n. Scot. and North Eng.* the act of prophesying; predicting. [SPAE + -ING[1]]

spaetz·le (shpet′slə, -slē), *n.* a dish consisting of lumps or threads made from a batter of flour, milk, eggs, and salt, usually poured through a coarse colander into boiling water, and then either drained and mixed in butter, lightly pan-fried, or added to sauces, stews, etc. [< G (dial.) *Spätzle*, dim. of *Spatz* dumpling, sparrow < MHG, deriv. of *spar* SPARROW]

spa·ghet·ti (spə get′ē), *n.* **1.** a white, starchy food paste of Italian origin, made in the form of long strings, boiled, and served with any of a variety of meat, tomato, or other sauces. **2.** *Elect.* an insulating tubing of small diameter into which bare wire can be slipped. [< It, pl. of *spaghetto*, dim. of *spago* cord]

spa·gyr·ic (spə jēr′ik), *Archaic.* —*adj.* **1.** pertaining to alchemy. —*n.* **2.** an alchemist. [< NL *spagyric(us)*, prob. coined by Paracelsus] —**spa·gyr′i·cal·ly,** *adv.*

spa·hi (spä′hē), *n., pl.* **-his.** **1.** one of a body of native Algerian cavalry in the French service. **2.** (formerly) a cavalryman in the Turkish army. Also, **spa′hee.** [< MF < Turk *sipahi* < Pers *sipāhī*. See SEPOY]

spail (spāl), *n. Scot. and North Eng.* spale.

Spain (spān), *n.* a nominal kingdom in SE Europe. Including the Balearic and Canary islands, 31,077,104 (est. 1963); 194,988 sq. mi. *Cap.:* Madrid. Spanish, **España.**

spake (spāk), *v.* a pt. of **speak.**

Spa·la·to (spä′lä tō), *n.* Italian name of **Split.**

Spal·ding (spôl′ding), *n.* **1. Albert,** 1888–1953, U.S. violinist. **2.** a boy's given name.

spale (spāl), *n. Brit. Dial.* a splinter; chip. [perh. < Scand; cf. OIcel *spölr* short piece]

spall (spôl), *n.* **1.** a chip or splinter, as of stone or ore. —*v.t.* **2.** to break into smaller pieces, as ore; split or chip. —*v.i.* **3.** to break or split off in chips or bits. [ME *spalle* chip; cf. SPALE, *spald* (dial.) to split; c. G *spalten*] —**spall′er,** *n.*

Spal·lan·za·ni (spä′lən zä′nē; *for 1 also It.* späl′län-tsä′nē), *n.* **1. Laz·za·ro** (läd′dzä rô), 1729–99, Italian biologist. **2.** a crater in the fourth quadrant of the moon: about 20 miles in diameter.

spall·a·tion (spô lā′shən), *n. Physics.* a nuclear reaction in which several nucleons are released from the nucleus of an atom. [SPALL + -ATION]

spal·peen (spal pēn′, spal′pēn), *n. Irish Eng.* **1.** a lad or boy. **2.** a rascal; scamp. [< Ir *spailpín*, equiv. to *spailp-* (< ?) + *-ín* dim. suffix]

Spam (spam), *n. Trademark.* a type of canned loaf meat, esp. of pork.

Sp. Am., **1.** Spanish America. **2.** Spanish American.

span[1] (span), *n., v.,* **spanned, span·ning.** —*n.* **1.** the distance between the tip of the thumb and the tip of the little finger when the hand is fully extended. **2.** a unit of length corresponding to this distance, commonly taken as nine inches. **3.** a distance, amount, piece, etc., of this length or of some small extent: *a span of lace.* **4.** the distance or space between two supports of a bridge. **5.** the full extent, stretch, or reach of anything: *a long span of memory.* **6.** *Aeron.* the distance between the wing tips of an airplane. **7.** a short space of time, as the term or period of living: *Man's span is short.* **8.** *Math.* the smallest subspace of a vector space which contains a given element or set of elements. —*v.t.* **9.** to measure by or as by the hand with the thumb and little finger extended. **10.** to encircle with the hand or hands, as the waist. **11.** to extend over or across (a section of land, a river, etc.). **12.** to provide with something that extends over: *to span a river with a bridge.* **13.** to extend, reach, or pass over (space or time): *a memory that spans 90 years.* **14.** *Math.* to function (in a subspace of a vector space) as a span. **15.** to bend the bow of (a crossbow) in preparation for shooting. [ME, OE; c. G *Spanne*, D *span*, OIcel *spönn*]

span[2] (span), *n.* a pair of horses or other animals harnessed and driven together. [< Flem, D or LG *spann(en)* (to) fasten, unite]
—**Syn.** team. See **pair.**

span[3] (span), *v.* a pt. of **spin.**

Span., **1.** Spaniard. **2.** Spanish.

span′ beam′, a beam for holding upright or spacing a part or parts of a machine.

span·cel (span′səl), *n., v.,* **-celed, -cel·ing** or (*esp. Brit.*) **-celled, -cel·ling.** —*n.* **1.** a noosed rope with which to hobble an animal, esp. a horse or cow. —*v.t.* **2.** to fetter with or as with a spancel. [< LG *spansel*, deriv. of *spann(en)* (to) stretch; see SPAN[2]]

Span·dau (shpän′dou), *n.* a city in Germany: incorporated into Berlin 1920. 165,509 (1950).

span·dex (span′deks), *n. Chem.* a synthetic fiber, composed of a long-chain synthetic polymer of at least 85 percent of a segmented polyurethane, used chiefly in the manufacture of garments to add elasticity. [anagram of *expands*]

span·drel (span′drəl), *n.* **1.** *Archit.* an area between the extradoses of two adjoining arches, or between the extrados of an arch and a perpendicular through the extrados at the springing line. **2.** (in a steel-framed building) a panellike area between the head of a window on one level and the sill of a window immediately above. **3.** *Philately.* the decoration occupying the space at the corner of a stamp between the border and an oval or circular central design. **4.** *Horol.* **a.** (in a square clock dial) any of the four spaces outside the chapter ring at the corners. **b.** an ornament for filling such a space. [ME *spaundrell*, prob. < AF *spaundre*, perh. c. OF *espandre* to EXPAND]

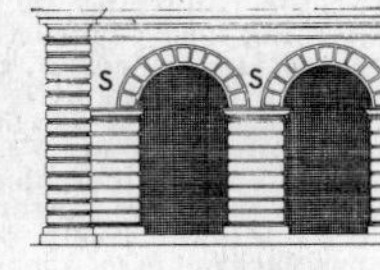

S, Spandrel

span′drel beam′, (in an iron-framed or steel-framed building) a beam forming the outer edge of the framing at each floor.

span′drel step′, a solid step having an underside forming part of an inclined stair soffit.

spa·ne·mi·a (spə nē′mē ə), *n. Pathol.* anemia. Also, **spa·nae′mi·a.** [< NL, equiv. to Gk *span(ós)* scarce + NL *-emia* -EMIA] —**spa·ne′mic, spa·nae′mic,** *adj.*

spang (spang), *adv. Informal.* directly, exactly: *The bullet landed spang on target.* [?]

span·gle (spang′gəl), *n., v.,* **-gled, -gling.** —*n.* **1.** a small, thin, often circular piece of glittering metal or other material, used esp. for decorating garments. **2.** any small, bright drop, object, spot, or the like. **3.** the appearance given to galvanized metal by the crystallization of zinc. —*v.t.* **4.** to decorate with spangles. **5.** to sprinkle or stud with small, bright pieces, objects, spots, etc. —*v.i.* **6.** to glitter with or like spangles. [ME *spangele*, equiv. to *spange* spangle (< MD) + *-le* -LE] —**span′gly,** *adj.*

span′gled glass′, an American art glass having flakes of mica in a layer of clear glass flashed with colored glass.

Spang·ler (spang′glər), *n.* **1.** a town in central Pennsylvania. 2658 (1960). **2.** a boy's given name.

Span·iard (span′yərd), *n.* a native or inhabitant of Spain. [ME *Spaignarde* < OF *(e)spaignart*, equiv. to *Espaigne* SPAIN + *-art* -ARD]

span·iel (span′yəl), *n.* **1.** one of any of several breeds of small or medium-sized dogs, usually having a long, silky coat and long, drooping ears. **2.** a submissive, fawning, or cringing person. [ME *spaynel* < OF *espaignol* Spanish dog < L *Hispāniol(us)* of Spain, equiv. to *Hispāni(a)* SPAIN + *-olus* dim. suffix] —**span′iel·like′,** *adj.*

Span·ish (span′ish), *adj.* **1.** of or pertaining to Spain, its people, or their language. —*n.* **2.** the Spanish people collectively. **3.** a Romance language, the language of Spain, standard also in most of Latin America except Brazil. *Abbr.:* Sp [ME; see SPAIN, -ISH[1]]

Span′ish A·mer′ica, the Spanish-speaking countries south of the U.S.: Mexico, Central America (with the exception of British Honduras), South America (with the exceptions of Brazil and the Guianas), and most of the West Indies.

Span·ish-A·mer·i·can (span′ish ə mer′i kən), *adj.* **1.** noting or pertaining to the parts of America where Spanish is the prevailing language. **2.** pertaining to Spain and America, sometimes to Spain and the United States: *an example of Spanish-American cooperation.* —*n.* **3.** a native or inhabitant of a Spanish-American country, esp. a person of Spanish descent.

Span′ish-Amer′ican War′, the war between the U.S. and Spain in 1898.

Span′ish Arma′da, Armada (def. 1).

Span′ish bayonet′, any of certain liliaceous plants of the genus *Yucca*, having narrow, spine-tipped leaves. [in allusion to its tropical American origin]

Span′ish blue′bell, a low, bulbous herb, *Scilla hispanica*, of Spain and Portugal, having blue flowers. Also called **Spanish jacinth.**

Span′ish broom′, a spiny, often leafless shrub, *Genista hispanica*, of southern Europe, having clustered, golden-yellow flowers and hairy pods.

Span′ish bur′ton, *Naut.* any of several tackles employing a runner in addition to the fall. Cf. **single Spanish burton, double Spanish burton.**

Span′ish but′ton, knapweed.

Span′ish ce′dar, **1.** a tropical American meliaceous tree, *Cedrela odorata*. **2.** the hard, fragrant, mahogany-like brown wood of this tree, used for making furniture and esp. cigar boxes. Also called **West Indian cedar.**

Spanish fly, *Lytta vesicatoria* (Length ¾ in.)

Span′ish Civ′il War′, the civil war in Spain 1936–39.

Span′ish dag′ger, a stemless or short-trunked plant, *Yucca gloriosa*, of the southeastern U.S., having leaves nearly 2½ feet long, with a stiff, sharp point, and greenish-white or reddish flowers nearly four inches wide.

Span′ish fly′, **1.** Also called **cantharides.** a preparation of powdered blister beetles, esp. the Spanish fly, used medicinally as a skin irritant, diuretic, and aphrodisiac. **2.** Also called **cantharis.** a blister beetle, *Lytta vesicatoria*, which yields this preparation. [so called from the fact that the beetles are found in abundance in Spain]

Span′ish foot′, *Furniture.* a carved pyramidal foot having concave fluted sides usually ending in a scroll at the bottom.

Span′ish Fork′ Cit′y, a town in central Utah. 6472 (1960).

Span′ish grippe′, *Pathol.* influenza.

Span′ish Guin′ea, a former Spanish colony in W equatorial Africa; now Equatorial Guinea, comprising the provinces of Río Muni and Fernando Po.

Spanish foot

Span′ish heel′, a high, curved heel with a straight heel breast, used on women's shoes. Cf. **French heel.**

Span′ish influen′za, *Pathol.* **1.** an acute, highly infectious respiratory disease, caused by a virus, characterized by fever, cough, and generalized body aches. **2.** the pandemic respiratory infection that spread throughout the world during 1917–1918.

Span′ish Inquisi′tion, the Inquisition in Spain, under state control from 1480 to 1834, marked by the extreme severity and cruelty of its proceedings in the 16th century.

Span′ish i′ris, an iris, *Iris Xyphium*, of the Mediterranean region, having blue-purple flowers with a yellow or orange patch.

Span′ish ja′cinth. See **Spanish bluebell.**

Span′ish jas′mine, a shrub, *Jasminum grandiflorum*, of India, having crimson-tinged, fragrant white flowers, grown as an ornamental and for perfume. Also called **Catalonian jasmine.**

Span′ish lime′, the genip *Melicocca bijuga.*

Span′ish mack′erel, **1.** an American game fish, *Scomberomorus maculatus*, found in the Atlantic Ocean. **2.** any of various other similar scombroid fishes. **3.** (in California) the jack mackerel.

Span′ish Main′, **1.** (formerly) the mainland of America adjacent to the Caribbean Sea, esp. the area between the mouth of the Orinoco River and the Isthmus of Panama. **2.** the Caribbean Sea: the route of the Spanish treasure galleons and a former haunt of pirates.

Span′ish Moroc′co. See under **Morocco** (def. 1).

Span′ish moss′, an epiphytic, bromeliaceous plant, *Tillandsia usneoides*, of the southern U.S., growing in long festoons which drape the branches of trees.

Span′ish nee′dles, **1.** a composite plant, *Bidens bipinnata*, having achenes with downwardly barbed awns. **2.** the achenes of this plant. [in allusion to its tropical American origin]

Span′ish om′elet, an omelet served with a sauce of tomatoes, onions, green peppers, and seasonings.

Span′ish on′ion, a large-sized, mild, succulent onion, often eaten raw.

Span′ish oys′ter plant′, a biennial herb, *Scolymus hispanicus*, of southern Europe, having spiny, thistlelike, leaf margins and small, yellow flowers. Also called **golden thistle.**

Span′ish papri′ka, **1.** a cultivated pepper, *Capsicum frutescens*, grown originally in Spain. **2.** a spice or condiment made from the ground-up pod of this plant.

Span′ish plum′. See **purple mombin.**

Span′ish rice′, rice prepared with chopped onions, tomatoes, green peppers, and sometimes diced ham, seasoned with cayenne pepper and mixed with butter.

Span′ish Sahar′a, a Spanish province in NW Africa, comprising Río de Oro and Saguia el Hamra. 23,793 (1960); 102,703 sq. mi. *Cap.:* Aaiún.

Span′ish to′paz, citrine (def. 2).

Span′ish Trag′edy, The, a tragedy (1592) by Thomas Kyd.

Span′ish tre′foil, alfalfa.

spank[1] (spangk), *v.t.* **1.** to strike (a person, usually a child) with the open hand, a slipper, etc., esp. on the buttocks, as in punishment. —*n.* **2.** a blow given in spanking; a smart or resounding slap. [imit.]

spank[2] (spangk), *v.i.* to move rapidly, smartly, or briskly. [back formation from SPANKING]

spank·er (spang′kər), *n.* **1.** *Naut.* **a.** a fore-and-aft sail on the aftermost lower mast of a sailing vessel having three or more masts. **b.** a designation given to the mast abaft the mizzenmast, usually the aftermost mast in any vessel: if not aftermost, such a mast would be called a jiggermast, driver, or pusher. **2.** *Informal.* a smartly moving person or animal, esp. a fast horse. **3.** *Dial.* something remarkably fine. —*adj. Naut.* **4.** of or pertaining to a spanker mast. **5.** noting or pertaining to a sail, yard, boom, etc., or to any rigging belonging to a spanker lower mast or to some upper mast of a spanker mast. **6.** noting any stay running aft and upward to the head of a spanker lower mast or to some specified upper mast of a spanker mast: *spanker topmast stay.* [?]

spank·ing (spang′king), *adj.* **1.** moving rapidly and smartly. **2.** quick and vigorous: *a spanking pace.* **3.** blowing briskly: *a spanking breeze.* **4.** *Informal.* unusually fine, great, large, etc.; remarkable; distinctive: *a spanking monogram in gold embroidery.* —*adv.* **5.** *Informal.* extremely, unusually, or remarkably; very: *three little girls in spanking new dresses.* [? < Scand; cf. Dan *spanke* to strut] —**spank′ing·ly,** *adv.*

span′ load′ing, *Aeron.* See under **loading** (def. 4).

span·ner (span′ər), *n.* **1.** one who or that which spans. **2.** Also called **span′ner wrench′.** a wrench having a curved head with a hook or pin at one end for engaging notches or holes in collars, certain kinds of nuts, etc. Cf. **pin wrench.** **3.** *Chiefly Brit.* a wrench, esp. one with fixed jaws. [SPAN[1] + -ER[1]]

span-new (span′nōō′, -nyōō′), *adj.* brand-new. [ME < Scand; cf. Icel *spān-nȳr*, lit., chip-new]

span′ of atten′tion, *Psychol.* the ability to concentrate, as measured by the number of objects that can be perceived in a momentary presentation and reported immediately afterwards.

span·piece (span′pēs′), *n.* See **collar beam.** [SPAN[1] + PIECE]

span·rail (span′rāl′), *n.* a rail connecting two legs of furniture; a stretcher. [SPAN[1] + RAIL[1]]

span′ roof′, a roof having two slopes of equal breadth and pitch meeting at a common ridge.

span·worm (span′wûrm′), *n.* measuringworm. [SPAN[1] + WORM]

spar[1] (spär), *n., v.,* **sparred, spar·ring.** —*n.* **1.** *Naut.* a stout pole such as those used for masts, etc.; a mast, yard, boom, gaff, or the like. **2.** *Aeron.* a principal lateral member of the framework of a wing of an airplane. —*v.t.* **3.** to provide or make with spars. [ME *sparre*; c. G *Sparren*, D *spar*, OIcel *sparri*] —**spar′like′,** *adj.*

spar[2] (spär), *v.,* **sparred, spar·ring,** *n.* —*v.i.* **1.** (of boxers) to make the motions of attack and defense with the arms and fists, esp. as a part of training. **2.** to box, esp. with light blows. **3.** to strike or fight with the feet or spurs, as cocks do. **4.** to bandy words; dispute. —*n.* **5.** a motion of sparring. **6.** a boxing match. **7.** a dispute. [ME: orig., thrust (n. and v.); perh. c. SPUR]

spar[3] (spär), *n.* any of various more or less lustrous crystalline minerals: *fluor spar.* [back formation from *sparstone* spar, OE *spærstān* gypsum; cf. MLG *spar*] —**spar′like′,** *adj.*

Spar (spär), *n.* a woman enlisted in the women's reserve of the U.S. Coast Guard. Also, **SPAR.** [S(EMPER) PAR(ATUS)]

spar·a·ble (spar′ə bəl), *n.* a small headless nail used by shoemakers. [var. of *sparrow bill*]

spar′ buoy′, *Naut.* a buoy shaped like a log or spar, anchored vertically.

spar′ deck′, *Naut.* **1.** the upper deck of a vessel, extending from stem to stern. **2.** a weather deck supported on scantlings somewhat heavier than those of an awning deck. **3.** the weather deck of a Great Lakes ore vessel. Cf. **main deck** (def. 2).

spare (spâr), *v.,* **spared, spar·ing,** *adj.,* **spar·er, spar·est,** *n.* —*v.t.* **1.** to refrain from harming or destroying; leave uninjured; forbear to punish, hurt, or destroy: *to spare one's enemy.* **2.** to deal gently or leniently with; show consideration for: *We wanted to spare him embarrassment.* **3.** to save from strain, discomfort, annoyance, or the like, or from a particular cause of it: *to spare him the bother.* **4.** to refrain from, forbear, omit, or withhold, as action or speech: *Spare us the gory details.* **5.** to refrain from employing, as some instrument, means, aid, etc.: *to spare the rod.* **6.** to set aside for a particular purpose: *to spare land for a garden.* **7.** to give or lend, as from a supply, esp. without inconvenience or loss: *Can you spare a cup of sugar? Can you spare me a dollar till payday?* **8.** to dispense with or do without: *We can't spare a single worker during the rush hour.* **9.** to use economically or frugally; refrain from using up or wasting: *A walnut sundae and don't spare the whipped cream!* **10.** to have remaining as excess or surplus: *We can make the curtains and have a yard to spare.* —*v.i.* **11.** to use economy; be frugal. **12.** to refrain from inflicting injury or punishment; exercise lenience or mercy. **13.** *Obs.* to refrain from action; forbear. —*adj.* **14.** kept in reserve, as for possible use: *a spare tire.* **15.** being in excess of present need; free for other use: *spare time.* **16.** frugally restricted; meager, as living, diet, etc.: *a spare regime.* **17.** lean or thin, as a person. **18.** scanty or scant, as in amount, fullness, etc. **19.** sparing, economical, or temperate, as persons. —*n.* **20.** a spare thing, part, etc., as an extra tire for emergency use. **21.** *Ceram.* an area at the top of a plaster mold for holding excess slip. **22.** *Bowling.* **a.** the knocking down of all the pins with two bowls. **b.** a score so made. Cf. **strike** (def. 63). [ME; OE *spar(ian)*; c. D, G *sparen,* OIcel *spara*] —**spare′a·ble,** *adj.* —**spare′ly,** *adv.* —**spare′ness,** *n.* —**spar′er,** *n.*
—**Syn. 6.** reserve. **14, 15.** extra. **17.** See **thin.**

spare·rib (spâr′rib′), *n.* a cut of pork containing ribs from the upper or fore end of the row, where there is little meat adhering. [transposed var. of earlier *ribspare* < MLG *ribbespēr* rib cut; cf. *spare* (obs.) a cut, slice]

sparge (spärj), *v.,* **sparged, sparg·ing,** *n.* —*v.t., v.i.* **1.** to scatter or sprinkle. —*n.* **2.** a sprinkling. [< L *sparg(ere)* (to) sprinkle, scatter] —**sparg′er,** *n.*

spar·id (spar′id), *n.* **1.** any of numerous fishes of the family *Sparidae,* found chiefly in tropical and subtropical seas, comprising the porgies, the scups, etc. —*adj.* **2.** belonging or pertaining to the *Sparidae.* [< NL *Sparid(ae),* deriv. of *Spar(us)* name of the genus < L: gilthead < Gk *spáros*]

Spar·ine (spâr′ēn), *n. Pharm., Trademark.* promazine.

spar·ing (spâr′ing), *adj.* **1.** that spares. **2.** economical; chary (often fol. by *in* or *of*). **3.** lenient or merciful. **4.** frugally restricted. **5.** scanty; limited. [ME; see SPARE, -ING[2]] —**spar′ing·ly,** *adv.* —**spar′ing·ness,** *n.*
—**Syn. 2.** frugal, saving, penurious. **5.** meager, sparse.

spark[1] (spärk), *n.* **1.** an ignited or fiery particle such as is thrown off by burning wood, or produced by one hard body striking against another. **2.** *Elect.* **a.** the light produced by a sudden discontinuous discharge of electricity through air or another dielectric. **b.** the discharge itself. **c.** any electric arc of relatively small energy content. **d.** the electric discharge produced by a spark plug in an internal-combustion engine. **3.** a small amount or trace of something. **4.** a trace of life or vitality. **5. sparks,** (*construed as sing.*) *Slang.* a radio operator on a ship or aircraft. —*v.i.* **6.** to emit or produce sparks. **7.** to issue as or like sparks. **8.** to send forth gleams or flashes. **9.** (of the ignition of an internal-combustion engine) to function correctly in producing sparks. —*v.t.* **10.** *Informal.* to kindle, animate, or stimulate (interest, activity, spirit, etc.): *These bright students have sparked her enthusiasm for teaching. The arrival of the piano player really sparked the party.* [ME; OE *spearca;* c. MD, MLG *sparke*] —**spark′less,** *adj.* —**spark′less·ly,** *adv.* —**spark′like′,** *adj.*

spark[2] (spärk), *n.* **1.** a gay, elegant, or foppish young man. **2.** a beau, lover, or suitor. **3.** a woman of outstanding beauty, charm, or wit. —*v.t.* **4.** *Informal.* to woo; court. —*v.i.* **5.** *Informal.* to engage in courtship; woo. [fig. use of SPARK[1], or metathetic var. of *sprack* lively < Scand; cf. OIcel *sprækr* sprightly] —**spark′ish,** *adj.* —**spark′ish·ly,** *adv.* —**spark′ish·ness,** *n.* —**spark′like′,** *adj.*

spark′ arrest′er, **1.** a device consisting of wire netting or other material, used to stop or deflect sparks thrown from an open fireplace, a smokestack, or the like. **2.** *Elect.* a device to reduce sparking at contacts where a circuit is opened and closed.

spark′ coil′, *Elect.* a coil of many turns of insulated wire on an iron core, used for producing sparks.

spark·er[1] (spär′kər), *n.* **1.** something that produces sparks. **2.** an apparatus used to test insulation on wires. [SPARK[1] + -ER[1]]

spark·er[2] (spär′kər), *n.* a lover, swain, or beau. [SPARK[2] + -ER[1]]

spark′ gap′, *Elect.* **1.** a space between two electrodes, across which a discharge of electricity may take place. **2.** the electrodes and the space between, considered as a unit: used in ignition systems.

spark′ gen′erator, an alternating current power source with a condenser discharging across a spark gap.

spark′ing plug′, *Brit.* See **spark plug.**

spark′ing volt′age, *Elect.* the minimum voltage required to produce a spark across a given spark gap.

spark-kil·ler (spärk′kil′ər), *n. Elect.* a device for diminishing sparking, consisting of a capacitor and a resistor connected in series across two points where sparking may occur in a circuit. [SPARK[1] + KILLER]

spar·kle[1] (spär′kəl), *v.,* **-kled, -kling,** *n.* —*v.i.* **1.** to issue in or as in little sparks as fire, light, etc.: *The candlelight sparkled in the crystal.* **2.** to emit little sparks, as burning matter: *The flames leaped and sparkled.* **3.** to shine with little gleams of light, as a brilliant gem; glisten brightly; glitter. **4.** to effervesce, as wine. **5.** to be brilliant, lively, or vivacious. —*v.t.* **6.** to cause to sparkle: *moonlight sparkling the water; pleasure sparkling her eyes.* —*n.* **7.** a little spark or fiery particle. **8.** a sparkling appearance, luster, or play of light: *the sparkle of a diamond.* **9.** brilliance, liveliness, or vivacity. [SPARK[1] + -LE]
—**Syn. 3.** See **glisten. 8.** glitter.

spar·kle[2] (spär′kəl), *n., v.t., v.i.,* **-kled, -kling.** spackle.

spar·kler (spär′klər), *n.* **1.** one who or that which sparkles. **2.** a firework that emits little sparks. **3.** a sparkling gem, esp. a diamond. **4.** *Informal.* a bright eye. [SPARKLE[1] + -ER[1]]

spark·let (spärk′lit), *n.* **1.** a small spark. **2.** something small that glitters like a spark. [SPARK[1] + -LET]

spar′kling wa′ter. See **soda water** (def. 1).

spar′kling wine′, a wine that is naturally carbonated by a second fermentation.

spark·o·ver (spärk′ō′vər), *n. Elect.* a spark, esp. an undesired one between two or more electrodes or conductors that are normally insulated from one another. [SPARK[1] + OVER]

spark′ photog′raphy, **1.** photography of fast-moving objects, as bullets, by the light of an electric spark. **2.** photography of sparks by their own light.

spark′ plug′, **1.** a device inserted in the cylinder of an internal-combustion engine, containing the two terminals between which passes the electric spark for igniting the explosive gases. **2.** *Informal.* a person who leads, inspires, or animates a group.

spark·plug (spärk′plug′), *v.t.,* **-plugged, -plug·ging.** *Informal.* to lead, inspire, or animate something or someone. [v. use of SPARK PLUG]

Sparks (spärks), *n.* **1. Jar·ed** (jâr′id), 1789–1866, U.S. historian and editor. **2.** a city in W Nevada, E of Reno. 16,618 (1960).

spark′ spec′trum, *Physics.* a spectrum formed from the light produced by an electric spark, characteristic of the gas or vapor through which the spark passes.

spark′ transmit′ter, *Radio.* a transmitting set which generates electromagnetic waves by the oscillatory discharge from a capacitor through an inductor and a spark gap.

spar·ling (spär′ling), *n., pl.* **-lings,** (*esp. collectively*) **-ling.** the European smelt, *Osmerus eperlanus.* [ME *sperlynge* < OF *(e)sperlinge* < Gmc; cf. G *Spierling*]

spar·oid (spâr′oid, spar′-), *adj.* **1.** resembling or pertaining to the porgy family, *Sparidae.* —*n.* **2.** a sparoid fish. [< NL *Sparoīd(ēs),* equiv. to *Spar(us)* (see SPARID) + *-oīdes* -OID]

spar·piece (spär′pēs′), *n.* See **collar beam.** [SPAR[1] + PIECE]

spar′ring part′ner, a boxer who spars with and otherwise assists a boxer who is in training for a bout. Also called **spar′ring mate′.**

spar·row (spar′ō), *n.* **1.** any of numerous American finches of the family *Fringillidae.* Cf. **chipping sparrow, song sparrow. 2.** *Brit.* a house sparrow. **3.** any of several weaverbirds of the family *Ploceidae.* Cf. **Java sparrow. 4.** any of several other unrelated small birds. Cf. **hedge sparrow.** [ME *sparowe,* OE *spearwa;* c. Goth *sparwa,* OIcel *spörr*] —**spar′row·less,** *adj.* —**spar′row·like′,** *adj.*

spar·row·grass (spar′ō gras′, -gräs′), *n. Informal.* asparagus. [by folk etymology]

spar′row hawk′, **1.** a small, short-winged, European hawk, *Accipiter nisus,* which preys on smaller birds. **2.** a small, American falcon, *Falco sparverius,* which preys esp. on grasshoppers, small mammals, etc.

spar·ry (spär′ē), *adj.* of or pertaining to mineral spar. [SPAR[3] + -Y[1]]

sparse (spärs), *adj.,* **spars·er, spars·est. 1.** thinly scattered or distributed: *a sparse population.* **2.** thin; not thick or dense: *sparse hair.* **3.** scanty; meager. [< L *spars(us)* scattered, ptp. of *spargere* to SPARGE] —**sparse′ly,** *adv.* —**sparse′ness, spar·si·ty** (spär′si tē), *n.*
—**Syn. 1–3.** See **scanty.**
—**Ant. 1–3.** abundant.

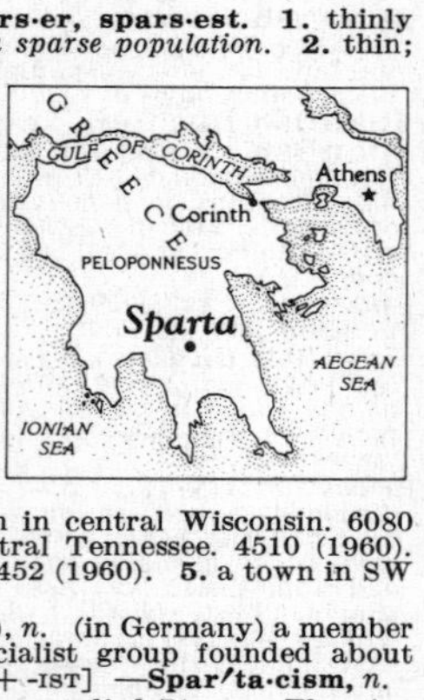

Spar·ta (spär′tə), *n.* **1.** Also called **Lacedaemon.** an ancient city in S Greece: the capital of Laconia and the chief city of the Peloponnesus, at one time the dominant city of Greece: famous for strict discipline and training of soldiers. **2.** a town in central Wisconsin. 6080 (1960). **3.** a town in central Tennessee. 4510 (1960). **4.** a town in SW Illinois. 3452 (1960). **5.** a town in SW Michigan. 2749 (1960).

Spar·ta·cist (spär′tə sist), *n.* (in Germany) a member of an extreme radical socialist group founded about 1918. [after SPARTAC(US) + -IST] —**Spar′ta·cism,** *n.*

Spar·ta·cus (spär′tə kəs), *n.* died 71 B.C., Thracian slave, gladiator, and insurrectionist.

Spar·tan (spär′tən), *adj.* Also, **Spar·tan·ic** (spär tan′ik). **1.** of or pertaining to Sparta or its people. **2.** suggestive of the ancient Spartans; sternly disciplined and rigorously simple, frugal, or austere. **3.** brave; undaunted. —*n.* **4.** a native or inhabitant of Sparta. **5.** a person of Spartan characteristics. [< L *Spartān(us),* equiv. to *Spart(a)* SPARTA + *-ānus* -AN] —**Spar′tan·ism,** *n.* —**Spar′tan·ly, Spar·tan′i·cal·ly,** *adv.*

Spar·tan·burg (spär′tən bûrg′), *n.* a city in NW South Carolina. 44,352 (1960).

spar·te·ine (spär′tē ēn′, -in), *n.* a bitter, poisonous, liquid alkaloid obtained from the common broom, *Cytisus scoparius,* used in medicine. [< NL *Sparti(um)* name of a genus (< Gk *spárt(os)* a kind of broom + L *-ium* n. suffix) + -INE[1]]

Spar·ti (spär′tī), *n.pl. Class. Myth.* a group of warriors who sprang fully armed from the dragon's teeth that Cadmus had planted in the ground. The warriors immediately fought among themselves until there were left only the five survivors who were to become the ancestors of the Theban nobility.

Spar·ti·ate (spär′tē āt′, -shē-), *n.* a member of the ruling class of ancient Laconia; a Spartan citizen. Cf. **Helot** (def. 1), **Perioeci.** [< L *Spartiatē(s)* < Gk, equiv. to *Spárt(a)* SPARTA + *-iātēs* agentive suffix]

spar′ var′nish, **1.** a durable, weather-resistant varnish applied to unpainted wooden areas, esp. on ships. **2.** a varnish made from sulfur, rosin, and linseed oil.

spar·ver (spär′vər), *n.* **1.** a tentlike bed curtain or canopy. **2.** a bed curtain suspended from a flat circular covering on the ceiling. **3.** a bed having a tentlike curtain or canopy. [ME *sperver* < MF *(e)sprevier* sparrow hawk, canopy bed < Gmc]

spasm (spaz′əm), *n.* **1.** *Med.* a sudden, abnormal, involuntary muscular contraction; an affection consisting of a continued muscular contraction **(tonic spasm),** or of a series of alternating muscular contractions and relaxations **(clonic spasm). 2.** any sudden, brief spell of great energy, activity, feeling, etc. [ME *spasme* < L *spasm(us)* < Gk *spasmós* convulsion, deriv. of *spâ(n)* (to) pull off]

spasm′ band′, an old-time jazz band, flourishing esp. in the late 19th century, the members of which used improvised instruments, as cigar boxes, barrels, kazoos, whistles, and jugs, and often marched in the street while performing.

spas·mod·ic (spaz mod′ik), *adj.* **1.** pertaining to or of the nature of a spasm; characterized by spasms. **2.** resembling a spasm or spasms; sudden but brief, often vigorous or violent; intermittent: *spasmodic efforts at reform.* **3.** given to or characterized by bursts of excitement. Also, **spas·mod′i·cal.** [< ML *spasmodic(us)* < Gk *spasmṓd(es),* deriv. of *spasmós* SPASM; see -IC] —**spas·mod′i·cal·ly,** *adv.*

spas·mo·dist (spaz′mə dist), *n.* a person who is spasmodic, esp. in style, as a writer, painter, etc. [SPASMOD(IC) + -IST] —**spas′mo·dism,** *n.*

spas·mol·y·sis (spaz mol′i sis), *n. Med.* the relaxation or relief of muscle spasm. [SPASM + -O- + -LYSIS]

spas·mo·lyt·ic (spaz′mə lit′ik), *Med.* —*adj.* **1.** of or noting spasmolysis. —*n.* **2.** a spasmolytic substance; antispasmodic. Also, **spas·mol·y·sant** (spaz mol′i zənt). [SPASM + -O- + -LYTIC]

spas·mo·phil·i·a (spaz′mə fil′ē ə), *n. Pathol.* a condition in which only moderate mechanical or electrical stimulation produces spasms, convulsions, or tetany. [< NL; see SPASM, -O-, -PHILIA]

spas·mo·phil·ic (spaz′mə fil′ik), *adj.* of or noting spasmophilia. Also, **spas·mo·phile** (spaz′mə fil′). [SPASM + -O- + -PHILE + -IC]

spas·tic (spas′tik), *Pathol.* —*adj.* **1.** pertaining to, of the nature of, or characterized by spasm, esp. tonic spasm. —*n.* **2.** a person exhibiting such spasms, esp. one who has cerebral palsy. [< L *spastic(us)* afflicted with spasms < Gk *spastikós* of a spasm. See SPASM, -TIC] —**spas′ti·cal·ly,** *adv.*

spas′tic paral′ysis, *Pathol.* a condition in which the muscles affected are marked by tonic spasm, increased tendon reflexes, and decreased superficial reflexes.

spat[1] (spat), *n., v.,* **spat·ted, spat·ting.** —*n.* **1.** a petty quarrel. **2.** a light blow; slap; smack. —*v.i.* **3.** to engage in a petty quarrel or dispute. **4.** to splash or spatter: *rain spatting against the window.* —*v.t.* **5.** to strike lightly; slap. [? imit.]

spat[2] (spat), *v.* a pt. and pp. of **spit.**

spat[3] (spat), *n.* a short gaiter worn over the instep and usually fastened under the foot with a strap, worn esp. in the late 19th and early 20th centuries. [short for SPATTERDASH]

spat[4] (spat), *n.* **1.** the spawn of an oyster or similar shellfish. **2.** young oysters collectively. **3.** a young oyster. [? c. SPIT[1]]

spate (spāt), *n.* **1.** a sudden, almost overwhelming, outpouring: *a spate of angry words.* **2.** *Brit.* **a.** a flood or inundation. **b.** a river flooding its banks. **c.** a sudden or heavy rainstorm. [?]

spa·tha·ceous (spə thā′shəs), *adj. Bot.* **1.** of the nature of or resembling a spathe. **2.** having a spathe. [< NL *spathāce(us),* equiv. to L *spath(a)* (see SPATHE) + *-āceus;* see -ACEOUS]

spathe (spāth), *n. Bot.* a bract or pair of bracts, often large and colored, subtending or enclosing a spadix or flower cluster. [< L *spath(a)* < Gk *spáthē* blade, sword, stem] —**spathed,** *adj.*

spath·ic (spath′ik), *adj. Mineral.* like spar. [< G *Spat* (earlier sp., *Spath*) spar + -IC]

spa·those[1] (spā′thōs, spath′ōs), *adj.* spathic. [*spath-,* as in SPATHIC + -OSE[1]]

spa·those[2] (spā′thōs, -thōs), *adj.* spathaceous. Also, **spa·thous** (spā′thəs, -thəs). [SPATHE + -OSE[1]]

spath·u·late (spath′yə lit, -lāt′), *adj.* Chiefly *Bot.* spatulate.

spa·tial (spā′shəl), *adj.* **1.** of or pertaining to space. **2.** existing or occurring in space; having extension in space. Also, **spacial.** [< L *spati(um)* space + -AL[1]] —**spa·ti·al·i·ty** (spā′shē al′i tē), *n.* —**spa′tial·ly,** *adv.*

spa·ti·og·ra·phy (spā′shē og′rə fē), *n.* the study of the characteristics of space beyond the atmosphere, including the mapping of the movements of celestial bodies and the recording of electrical, magnetic, and gravitational effects, esp. those likely to affect missiles and spacecraft. [< L *spati(um)* space + -O- + -GRAPHY]

spa·ti·o·tem·po·ral (spā′shē ō tem′pər əl), *adj.* **1.** pertaining to space-time. **2.** of or pertaining to both space and time. [< L *spati(um)* space + -O- + TEMPORAL[1]] —**spa′ti·o·tem′po·ral·ly,** *adv.*

spat·ter (spat′ər), *v.t.* **1.** to scatter or dash in small particles or drops: *The dog spattered mud on everyone when he shook himself.* **2.** to splash with something in small particles: *to spatter the ground with water.* **3.** to sprinkle or spot with something that soils or stains. —*v.i.* **4.** to send out small particles or drops, as falling water: *rain spattering on a tin roof.* **5.** to strike as in a shower, as bullets. —*n.* **6.** the act or the sound of spattering: *the spatter of rain on a roof.* **7.** a splash or spot of something spattered. [perh. < D *spatt(en)* (to) burst, spout + -ER[6]] —**spat′ter·ing·ly,** *adv.*

spat′ter dash′, roughcast (def. 1).

spat·ter·dash (spat′ər dash′), *n.* a long gaiter to protect the trousers or stockings, as from mud while riding. [SPATTER + DASH] —**spat′ter·dashed′,** *adj.*

spat·ter·dock (spat′ər dok′), *n.* **1.** a yellow-flowered pond lily, *Nuphar advena,* common in stagnant waters. **2.** any other water lily of the genera *Nuphar* and *Nymphaea,* esp. one having yellow flowers. [SPATTER + DOCK[4]]

spat·ter·ware (spat′ər wâr′), *n.* earthenware decorated with spattered colors. [SPATTER + WARE[1]]

spat·u·la (spach′ə lə), *n.* an implement with a broad, flat, usually flexible blade, used for blending foods or removing them from cooking utensils, mixing drugs, spreading plasters and paints, etc. [< L: a broad piece < *spath(a)* SPATHE + *-ula* -ULE] —**spat′u·lar,** *adj.*

spat·u·late (spach′ə lit, -lāt′), *adj.* **1.** shaped like a spatula; rounded more or less like a spoon. **2.** *Bot.* having a broad, rounded end and a narrow, attenuate base, as a leaf. [< NL *spatulāt(us).* See SPATULA, -ATE[1]]

Spatulate leaf

spätz·le (shpet′slə), *n. German.* spaetzle.

spaul·der (spôl′dər), *n. Armor.* a pauldron, esp. one for protecting only a shoulder. Also called **monnion.** [earlier *spauld* shoulder (ME *spald, spalde* < OF *(e)spalde, (e)spalle* < L *spatula* SPATULA) + -ER[1]]

spa·viet (spā′vit, spav′it), *adj. Chiefly Scot.* spavined. Also, **spa·vied** (spā′vid, spav′id).

spav·in (spav′in), *n. Vet. Pathol.* **1.** a disease of the hock joint of horses in which enlargement occurs due to collection of fluids **(bog spavin),** bony growth **(bone spavin),** or distention of the veins **(blood spavin).** **2.** an excrescence or enlargement so formed. [ME *spaveyne* < OF *(e)spavain, esparvain* swelling < ?]

spav·ined (spav′ind), *adj.* **1.** suffering from or affected with spavin. **2.** being of or marked by decrepit or broken-down condition: *a spavined old school bus abandoned in a field.* [late ME *spaveyned.* See SPAVIN, -ED[3]]

spawn (spôn), *n.* **1.** *Zool.* the mass of eggs deposited by fishes, amphibians, mollusks, crustaceans, etc. **2.** *Bot.* the mycelium of mushrooms, esp. of the species grown for the market. **3.** *Usually Disparaging.* **a.** a swarming brood; numerous progeny. **b.** (*construed as pl.*) any person or thing regarded as the offspring of some stock, idea, etc. —*v.i.* **4.** to deposit eggs or sperm directly into the water, as fishes. —*v.t.* **5.** to produce (spawn). **6.** to give birth to; give rise to: *His sudden disappearance spawned many rumors.* **7.** to produce in large number. **8.** to plant with mycelium. [ME *spaunn(en),* prob. < AF *(e)spaund(re)* (OF *espandre*) (to) EXPAND] —**spawn′er,** *n.*

spay[1] (spā), *v.t. Vet. Med.* to remove the ovaries of (an animal). [ME *spay(en)* < AF *(e)spei(er)* (to) cut with a sword (OF *espeer*), deriv. of *espee* sword; see ÉPÉE]

spay[2] (spā), *n.* a three-year-old male red deer. Also called **spay·ad** (spā′əd), **spay·ard** (spā′ərd). [?]

S.P.C.A., Society for the Prevention of Cruelty to Animals.

S.P.C.C., Society for the Prevention of Cruelty to Children.

speak (spēk), *v.,* **spoke** or (*Archaic*) **spake; spo·ken** or (*Archaic*) **spoke; speak·ing.** —*v.i.* **1.** to utter words or articulate sounds with the ordinary voice; talk: *He was too ill to speak.* **2.** to communicate vocally; mention: *to speak to a person of various matters.* **3.** to converse: *She spoke with him for an hour.* **4.** to deliver an address, discourse, etc.: *to speak at a meeting.* **5.** to make a statement in written or printed words. **6.** to communicate, signify, or disclose by any means; convey significance. **7.** *Phonet.* to produce sounds or audible sequences of individual or concatenated sounds of a language, esp. through phonation, amplification, and resonance, and through any of a variety of articulatory processes. **8.** to emit a sound, as a musical instrument; make a noise or report. **9.** *Chiefly Brit.* (of dogs) to bark when ordered. **10.** *Fox Hunting.* (of a hound or pack) to bay on finding a scent. —*v.t.* **11.** to utter vocally and articulately: *to speak words of praise.* **12.** to express or make known with the voice: *to speak the truth.* **13.** to declare in writing or printing, or by any means of communication. **14.** to make known, indicate, or reveal. **15.** to use, or be able to use, in oral utterance, as a language: *to speak French.* **16.** *Naut.* to communicate with (a passing vessel) at sea, as by voice or signal: *We spoke a whaler on the fourth day at sea.* **17.** *Archaic.* to speak to or with. **18. so to speak,** to use a manner of speaking; figuratively speaking: *We still don't have our heads above water, so to speak.* **19. speak by the book,** to say with great authority or precision: *I can't speak by the book, but I know this is wrong.* **20. speak for, a.** to intercede for or recommend; speak in behalf of. **b.** to choose or prefer; have reserved for oneself: *This item is already spoken for.* **21. speak out,** to express one's opinion openly and unreservedly: *He was not afraid to speak out when it was something he believed in strongly.* **22. speak well for,** to bear witness to something favorable; testify to: *Her manners speak well for her upbringing.* **23. to speak of,** worth mentioning: *The country has no mineral resources to speak of.* [ME *spek(en),* OE *specan,* var. of *sprecan;* c. G *sprechen;* cf. OHG *spehhan*] —**speak′a·ble,** *adj.* —**speak′a·ble·ness,** *n.* —**speak′a·bly,** *adv.*

—**Syn. 1.** SPEAK, CONVERSE, TALK mean to make vocal sounds, usually for purposes of communication. To SPEAK is to utter one or more words, not necessarily connected; it usually implies conveying information and may apply to anything from an informal remark to a formal address before an audience: *to speak sharply.* To CONVERSE is to exchange ideas with someone by speaking: *to converse with a friend.* To TALK is to utter intelligible sounds, sometimes without regard to content: *The child is learning to talk.* **11.** pronounce, articulate. **12.** say. **14.** disclose.

speak-eas·y (spēk′ē′zē), *n., pl.* **-eas·ies.** a place where alcoholic beverages are illegally sold. Also, **speak′eas′y.** [SPEAK + EASY]

speak·er (spē′kər), *n.* **1.** a person who speaks. **2.** a person who speaks formally before an audience; orator. **3.** (*usually cap.*) the presiding officer of the U.S. House of Representatives, the British House of Commons, or other such legislative assembly. **4.** a loudspeaker. **5.** a book of selections for practice in declamation. **6. be** or **not be on speakers,** *Brit.* See **speaking** (def. 8). [ME; see SPEAK, -ER[1]] —**speak′er·ship′,** *n.*

Speak·er (spē′kər), *n.* **Tris(tram E.)** 1888–1958 U.S. baseball player.

speak·ing (spē′king), *n.* **1.** the act, utterance, or discourse of a person who speaks. **2. speakings,** literary works composed for recitation, as ancient bardic poetry; oral literature. —*adj.* **3.** that speaks; giving information as if by speech: *a speaking proof of a thing.* **4.** highly expressive: *speaking eyes.* **5.** lifelike: *a speaking likeness.* **6.** used in, suited to, or involving speaking or talking: *the speaking voice.* **7.** of or pertaining to declamation. **8. be** or **not be on speaking terms, a.** to know (a person) only casually, as to greet or to converse with. **b.** (in negative sense) to refuse to speak with, as on account of a quarrel or misunderstanding: *They haven't been on speaking terms for ten years.* Also, *Brit.,* **be** or **not be on speakers.** [ME; see SPEAK, -ING[1], -ING[2]] —**speak′ing·ly,** *adv.* —**speak′ing·ness,** *n.*

speak′ing choir′, an ensemble or chorus that performs through choral speaking.

speak′ing in tongues′, a prayer characterized chiefly by incomprehensible speech, originating in primitive Christianity and now practiced by Pentecostal groups in ecstatic forms of worship. Also called **gift of tongues, glossolalia.**

speak′ing tube′, a tube for conveying the voice to a distance, as from one part of a building, ship, etc., to another.

speak′ing type′, *Numis.* a device on a medal or coin that has a punning reference to a person or thing.

spean (spēn), *Scot. and North Eng.* —*n.* **1.** a nipple or teat, esp. of a cow. —*v.t.* **2.** to wean. Also, **speen.** [var. of dial. *spane* (ME *spanen*); cf. OE *spanu* teat; c. LG, D *spenen,* G *Spänen*]

spear[1] (spēr), *n.* **1.** a weapon for thrusting or throwing, consisting of a long wooden staff to which a sharp head, as of iron or steel, is attached. **2.** a soldier or other person armed with such a weapon; spearman: *an army of 40,000 spears.* **3.** some similar weapon or instrument, as one for use in fishing. **4.** the act of spearing. **5.** a long connecting rod to a pump in a well or mine from an engine on the surface. —*adj.* **6.** See **spear side.** —*v.t.* **7.** to pierce with or as with a spear. —*v.i.* **8.** to go or penetrate like a spear: *The plane speared through the clouds.* [ME, OE *spere;* c. D, G *speer*] —**spear′er,** *n.*

spear[2] (spēr), *n.* **1.** a sprout or shoot of a plant, as a blade of grass, an acrospire of grain, etc. —*v.i.* **2.** to sprout; shoot; send up or rise in a spear or spears. [var. of SPIRE[1], ? influenced by SPEAR[1]]

spear·fish (spēr′fish′), *n., pl.* (*esp. collectively*) **-fish,** (*esp. referring to two or more kinds or species*) **-fish·es,** *v.* —*n.* **1.** any of several billfishes of the genus *Tetrapturus,* resembling the sailfish but having the first dorsal fin much less developed. **2.** any of several related fishes. —*v.i.* **3.** to fish underwater using a spearlike implement propelled manually or mechanically. [SPEAR[1] + FISH]

Spear·fish (spēr′fish′), *n.* a town in W South Dakota. 3682 (1960).

spear′ grass′, any of various grasses, as a meadow grass or a bent grass, having lanceolate leaves or floral spikes.

spear′ gun′, a device for shooting a barbed missile under water usually by means of gas under pressure, a strong rubber band, or a powerful spring.

spear·head (spēr′hed′), *n.* **1.** the sharp-pointed head which forms the piercing end of a spear. **2.** any person or thing that leads an attack, undertaking, etc. —*v.t.* **3.** to act as a spearhead for: *He spearheaded the drive for more members.* [ME; see SPEAR[1], HEAD]

spear′-head spoon′ (spēr′hed′). See **diamond-point spoon.**

spear·man (spēr′mən), *n., pl.* **-men.** a person who is armed with or uses a spear. [ME; see SPEAR[1], MAN[1]]

Spear·man (spēr′mən), *n.* a town in N Texas. 3555 (1960).

spear·mint (spēr′mint′), *n.* an aromatic herb, *Menta spicata,* used for flavoring. Also called **garden mint, green mint.** [SPEAR[1] + MINT[1]]

spear·point (spēr′point′), *n.* **1.** the point at the end of a spearhead. **2.** a spearhead. [ME; see SPEAR[1], POINT]

spear′ side′, the male side, or line of descent, of a family (opposed to *distaff side* or *spindle side*).

spear·wort (spēr′wûrt′), *n.* any of several buttercups, esp. *Ranunculus Flammula,* having lanceolate leaves. [ME *sperewort,* OE *sperewyrt.* See SPEAR[1], WORT[2]]

spec (spek), *n.* **1.** *Informal.* specification. **2.** speculation (usually prec. by *on*): *to buy something on spec.* **3.** a spectacle or spectacular. [by shortening]

spec., 1. special. **2.** specially. **3.** specification.

spe·cial (spesh′əl), *adj.* **1.** of a distinct or particular kind or character: *a special kind of key.* **2.** being a particular one; particular, individual, or certain: *You'd better call the special number.* **3.** pertaining or peculiar to a particular person, thing, instance, etc.: *the special features of a plan.* **4.** having a particular function, purpose, application, etc.: *a special messenger.* **5.** dealing with particulars; specific: *a special statement.* **6.** distinguished or different from what is ordinary or usual: *a special occasion; to fix something special.* **7.** extraordinary; exceptional, as in amount or degree; especial: *special importance.* **8.** great; being such in an exceptional degree: *a special friend.* —*n.* **9.** a special person or thing. **10.** a train used for a particular purpose, occasion, or the like. **11.** a special edition of a newspaper. **12.** *Theat.* a spotlight reserved for a particular area, property, actor, etc.: *Give me the coffin special.* **13.** a temporary, arbitrary reduction in the price of regularly stocked goods, esp. food; a special offer or price: *The special this week is on sirloin steaks.* **14.** *Television.* a single program not forming part of a regular series. [ME *(e)special* < L *speciāl(is)* of a given species, equiv. to *speci(es)* SPECIES + *-ālis* -AL[1]] —**spe′cial·ly,** *adv.*

—**Syn. 6.** singular. SPECIAL, PARTICULAR, SPECIFIC refer to something pointed out for attention and consideration. SPECIAL means given unusual treatment because of being uncommon: *a special sense of a word.* PARTICULAR implies something selected from the others of its kind and set off from them for attention: *a particular variety of orchid.* SPECIFIC implies plain and unambiguous indication of a particular instance, example, etc.: *a specific instance of cowardice.* —**Ant. 1.** general.

spe′cial ar′ea, *Brit.* See **distressed area.**

spe′cial check′ing account′, *U.S.* a checking account that requires no minimum balance but in which a small charge is made for each check issued or drawn and for monthly maintenance. Cf. **regular checking account.**

spe′cial commit′tee. See **select committee.**

spe′cial court′-martial, *U.S. Mil.* a court-martial established to try violations of military law less serious than those tried by a general court-martial but more serious than those tried by a summary court-martial.

spe′cial deliv′ery, delivery of mail outside the regularly scheduled hours, by a special messenger, upon the payment of an extra fee. —**spe′cial-de·liv′er·y,** *adj.*

spe′cial div′idend, a dividend paid to stockholders in addition to the regular dividend. Also called **extra dividend.**

spe′cial educa′tion, education geared for those with unusual needs or disabilities, as handicapped or maladjusted people, slow learners, or gifted children.

spe′cial effect′, an imitation of some natural phenomenon, as thunder or lightning, effected by mechanical or other artificial means, used in theatrical, radio, television, or motion-picture productions.

spe′cial han′dling, (in the U.S. postal system) the handling of fourth-class mail as first-class upon the payment of a fee.

spe′cial in′terest, a body of persons, corporation, or industry which by reason of its alleged importance to the public good, seeks or receives benefits or privileged treatment, esp. through legislation.

spe·cial·ism (spesh′ə liz′əm), *n.* devotion or restriction to a particular pursuit, branch of study, etc.

spe·cial·ist (spesh′ə list), *n.* **1.** a person who devotes himself to one subject or to one particular branch of a subject or pursuit. **2.** a medical practitioner who devotes his attention to a particular class of diseases, patients, etc. **3.** *U.S. Army.* a soldier with special technical or other qualifications, entitled to the pay of a noncommissioned officer but ranking below a corporal. [SPECIAL + -IST]

spe·cial·is·tic (spesh′ə lis′tik), *adj.* pertaining to or characteristic of specialists or specialism. [SPECIALIST + -IC]

spé·cia·li·té de la mai·son′ (spe syä lē tā′ də lȧ mā zôN′), *French.* the specialty of the house (used in referring to the most important dish served by a restaurant).

spe·ci·al·i·ty (spesh′ē al′i tē), *n., pl.* **-ties.** *Chiefly Brit.* specialty. [ME *specialite* < LL *speciālitāt-;* see SPECIALTY]

spe·cial·ize (spesh′ə līz′), *v.,* **-ized, -iz·ing.** —*v.i.* **1.** to pursue some special line of study, work, etc.; have a specialty: *The doctor specializes in gastroenterology.* **2.** *Biol.* (of an organism or one of its organs) to modify or differentiate in order to adapt to a special function or environment. —*v.t.* **3.** to render special or specific; invest with a special character, function, etc. **4.** to adapt to special conditions; restrict to specific limits. **5.** to restrict payment of (a negotiable instrument) by endorsing over to a specific payee. **6.** to specify; particularize. Also, *esp. Brit.,* **spe′cial·ise′.** [< F *spécialis(er).* See SPECIAL, -IZE] —**spe′cial·i·za′tion,** *n.*

spe′cial ju′ry, *Law.* **1.** See **struck jury. 2.** See **blue-ribbon jury.**

spe′cial li′brary, a library maintained by an organization, as a corporation or government agency, for collecting reference materials of special relevance to the work of the organization.

spe′cial or′ders, *Mil.* a set of instructions from a headquarters affecting the activity or status of an individual or group of individuals. Cf. **general order.**

spe′cial part′ner, a partner whose liability for his firm's debts is limited to the amount of his investment. Also called **limited partner.** Cf. **general partner.**

spe′cial part′nership. See **limited partnership.**

spe′cial plea′, *Law.* a plea that alleges special or new matter as an answer to the allegations made by the opposite side and not as a denial of them.

spe′cial plead′ing, 1. *Law.* pleading that alleges special or new matter in avoidance of the allegations made by the opposite side. **2.** pleading or arguing that ignores unfavorable features of a case.

spe′cial priv′ilege, privilege enjoyed by a specifically designated individual or group: *Students maintaining honors grades would be accorded special privilege.*

spe′cial rule′, *Law.* See under **rule** (def. 9).

spe′cial ses′sion, a session, as of a legislature or council, called to meet in addition to those held regularly.

spe′cial staff′, *Mil.* all staff officers assigned to headquarters of a division or higher unit who are not members of the general staff or personal staff. Cf. **general staff, personal staff.**

spe′cial term′, *Law.* **1.** the sitting of a court for the trial of a special case. **2.** the sitting of a court at an extraordinary time.

spe′cial the′ory of relativ′ity, *Physics.* See under **relativity** (def. 2). Also called **restricted theory of relativity.**

spe·cial·ty (spesh′əl tē), *n., pl.* **-ties,** *adj.* —*n.* **1.** the state or condition of being special. **2.** a special subject of study, line of work, area of interest, or the like: *His specialty is art criticism.* **3.** an article particularly dealt in, manufactured, etc., or one to which the dealer or manufacturer claims to devote special care: *The manufacturer's specialty is fine hats.* **4.** an article of unusual or superior design or quality. **5.** a novelty; a new article. **6.** an article with such strong consumer demand that it is at least partially removed from price competition. **7.** a special or particular point, item, matter, characteristic, or peculiarity. **8.** *Law.* **a.** a special agreement, contract, etc., expressed in an instrument under seal. **b.** a negotiable instrument not under seal. —*adj.* **9.** *Theat.* (in vaudeville) **a.** performing or performed in a manner that is unusual or not customary for a type of act, esp. a performance involving dexterity or ingenuity, as a patter song: *specialty actor; specialty act.* **b.** (of a song or dance) isolated from the rest of the show: *specialty number.* [ME *specialte* < MF *(e)specialte* < L *speciālitāt-* (s. of *speciālitās*). See SPECIAL, -ITY]

spe·ci·a·tion (spē′shē ā′shən), *n. Biol.* the process by which new species are formed. [SPECI(ES) + -ATION]

spe·cie (spē′shē, -sē), *n.* **1.** coin; coined money. **2. in specie, a.** in the same kind. **b.** (of money) in coin. **c.** in a similar manner: *Such treachery should be repaid in specie.* **d.** *Law.* in the identical shape, form, etc., as specified. [< L *(in) speciē* (in) kind; see SPECIES]

spe·cies (spē′shēz, -sēz), *n., pl.* **-cies. 1.** a class of individuals having some common characteristics or qualities; distinct sort or kind. **2.** *Biol.* the major subdivision of a genus or subgenus, regarded as the basic category of biological classification, composed of related individuals that resemble one another, are able to breed among themselves, but are not able to breed with members of another species. **3.** *Logic.* **a.** one of the classes of things included with other classes in a genus. **b.** the set of things within one of these classes. **4.** *Eccles.* **a.** the external form or appearance of the bread or the wine in the Eucharist. **b.** either of the Eucharistic elements. **5.** *Obs.* specie; coin. **6. the species,** the human race; mankind: *a study of the species.* [< L: appearance, sort, form, equiv. to *spec-* look, behold + *-i-* thematic vowel + *-ēs* n. suffix]

specif., **1.** specific. **2.** specifically.

spec·i·fi·a·ble (spes′ə fī′ə bəl), *adj.* that can be specified. [SPECIFY + -ABLE]

spe·cif·ic (spi sif′ik), *adj.* **1.** having a special application, bearing, or reference; specifying, explicit, or definite: *to state one's specific purpose.* **2.** specified, precise, or particular: *a specific sum of money.* **3.** peculiar or proper to something, as qualities, characteristics, effects, etc.: *His specific problems got him into trouble.* **4.** of a special or particular kind. **5.** *Biol.* of or pertaining to a species: *specific characters.* **6.** *Med.* **a.** (of a disease) produced by a special cause or infection. **b.** (of a remedy) having special effect in the prevention or cure of a certain disease. **7.** *Immunol.* (of an antigen or antibody) having a particular effect on only one antigen or antibody or affecting it in only one way. **8.** *Com.* noting customs or duties levied in fixed amounts per unit, as number, weight, or volume. **9.** *Physics.* **a.** designating a physical constant that, for a particular substance, is expressed as the ratio of the quantity in the substance to the quantity in an equal volume of a standard substance, as water or air. **b.** designating a physical constant that expresses a property or effect as a quantity per unit length, area, volume, or mass. —*n.* **10.** something specific, as a statement, quality, etc. **11.** *Med.* a specific remedy: *There is no specific for the common cold.* [< ML *specific(us)*, equiv. to L *speci(ēs)* SPECIES + *-ficus* -FIC] —**spe·cif′i·cal·ly,** *adv.*
—**Syn. 1.** See **special.** —**Ant. 2.** vague.

spec·i·fi·ca·tion (spes′ə fə kā′shən), *n.* **1.** the act of specifying. **2.** a detailed description of requirements, dimensions, materials, etc., as of a proposed building, machine, bridge, etc. **3.** something specified, as in a bill of particulars; a specified particular, item, or article. **4.** the act of making specific. **5.** the state of having a specific character. [< ML *specificātiōn-* (s. of *specificātiō*), equiv. to *specificāt(us)* mentioned, described (ptp. of *specificāre*; see SPECIFIC, -ATE[1]) + *-iōn-* -ION]

specif′ic charge′, *Physics.* the ratio of the charge on a particle to the mass of the particle.

specif′ic conduct′ance, *Elect.* conductivity (def. 2).

specif′ic grav′ity, *Physics.* the ratio of the density of any substance to the density of some other substance taken as standard, water being the standard for liquids and solids, and hydrogen or air being the standard for gases. Also called **relative density.** —**spe·cif′ic-grav′i·ty,** *adj.*

specif′ic heat′, *Physics.* **1.** the number of calories required to raise the temperature of 1 gram of a substance 1°C, or the number of BTU's per pound per degree F. **2.** (originally) the ratio of the thermal capacity of a substance to that of standard material.

specif′ic humid′ity, the ratio of the mass of water vapor in air to the total mass of the mixture of air and water vapor. Cf. **mixing ratio, absolute humidity, dew point, humidity.**

specif′ic im′pulse, *Rocketry.* **1.** a measure, usually in seconds, of the efficiency with which a rocket engine utilizes its propellants, equal to the number of pounds of thrust produced per pound of propellant burned per second. **2.** Also called **ideal specific impulse, theoretical specific impulse.** the specific impulse which a given combination of propellants would produce in an ideal rocket engine providing complete combustion, no friction losses, and no lateral expansion of the exhaust.

specif′ic induc′tive capac′ity, *Elect.* See **dielectric constant.**

specif′ic resist′ance, *Elect.* resistivity (def. 2).

specif′ic vol′ume, *Physics.* volume per unit mass; the reciprocal of density.

spec·i·fy (spes′ə fī′), *v.,* **-fied, -fy·ing.** —*v.t.* **1.** to mention or name specifically or definitely; state in detail: *He did not specify the amount needed.* **2.** to give a specific character to. **3.** to name or state as a condition: *He specified that he be given my power of attorney.* —*v.i.* **4.** to make a specific mention or statement. [ME *specyfy* < OF *specifi(er)* < ML *specificāre.* See SPECIFICATION, -FY] —**spec·i·fi·ca·tive** (spes′ə fə kā′tiv), *adj.* —**spec′i·fi·ca′tive·ly,** *adv.* —**spec′i·fi′er,** *n.*

spec·i·men (spes′ə mən), *n.* **1.** a part or an individual taken as exemplifying a whole mass or number; a typical animal, plant, mineral, part, etc. **2.** (in medicine, microbiology, etc.) a sample of a substance or material for examination or study: *a urine specimen; a tissue specimen.* **3.** *Informal.* a particular or peculiar kind of person: *a weird female specimen.* [< L: mark, example, indication, sign, equiv. to *spec-* look + *-i-* -I- + *-men* n. suffix denoting result or means]
—**Syn. 1.** type, model, pattern. See **example.**

spe·ci·os·i·ty (spē′shē os′i tē), *n., pl.* **-ties. 1.** the state of being specious or plausible. **2.** something pleasing to the eye but deceptive. **3.** *Obs.* the state or quality of being beautiful. [< LL *speciōsitās* good looks, beauty. See SPECIOUS, -ITY]

spe·cious (spē′shəs), *adj.* **1.** apparently good or right though lacking real merit; superficially pleasing; plausible: *specious arguments.* **2.** pleasing to the eye, but deceptive. **3.** *Obs.* pleasing to the eye; fair. [< L *speciōs(us)* fair, good-looking, beautiful, equiv. to *speci(ēs)* SPECIES + *-ōsus* -OUS] —**spe′cious·ly,** *adv.* —**spe′cious·ness,** *n.*
—**Syn. 1.** See **plausible. 2.** false, misleading. —**Ant. 1, 2.** genuine.

spe′cious pres′ent, *Philos.* a short time span in which change and duration are alleged to be directly experienced.

speck (spek), *n.* **1.** a small spot differing in color or substance from that of the surface or material upon which it appears or lies: *Specks of soot on the window sill.* **2.** a very little bit or particle: *We haven't a speck of sugar.* **3.** something appearing small by comparison or by reason of distance: *By then the town was just a speck.* —*v.t.* **4.** to mark with, or as with, a speck or specks. [ME *specke,* OE *specca;* c. D *spikkel*] —**speck·ed·ness** (spek′id nis), *n.* —**speck′less,** *adj.* —**speck′less·ly,** *adv.* —**speck′less·ness,** *n.*

speck·le (spek′əl), *n., v.,* **-led, -ling.** —*n.* **1.** a small speck, spot, or mark, as on skin. **2.** speckled coloring or marking. —*v.t.* **3.** to mark with or as with speckles. [late ME; see SPECK, -LE] —**speck′led·ness,** *n.*

speck′led trout′. See **brook trout** (def. 1).

specs (speks), *n.pl. Informal.* **1.** spectacles; eyeglasses. **2.** specifications. [by shortening]

spec·ta·cle (spek′tə kəl), *n.* **1.** anything presented to the sight or view, esp. something of a striking or impressive kind: *The stars make a fine spectacle tonight.* **2.** a public show or display, esp. on a large scale: *The coronation was a lavish spectacle.* **3. spectacles.** eyeglasses, esp. with pieces passing over or around the ears for holding in place (usually used with *pair of*). **4.** Often, **spectacles. a.** something resembling spectacles in shape or function. **b.** any of various devices suggesting spectacles as one attached to a semaphore to display lights or different colors by colored glass. **5.** *Obs.* a spyglass. **6. make a spectacle of oneself,** to call attention to one's unseemly behavior; behave badly in public: *We understand she got roaring drunk and made a spectacle of herself in the Place de la Concorde.* [ME < L *spectācul(um),* deriv. of *spectāre,* freq. of *specere.* See SPECIES, -CLE] —**spec′ta·cle·less,** *adj.* —**spec′ta·cle·like′,** *adj.*

spec′tacle clew′, *Naut.* a clew iron having the form of three joined rings.

spec·ta·cled (spek′tə kəld), *adj.* **1.** provided with or wearing spectacles. **2.** (of an animal) having a marking resembling a pair of spectacles. [SPECTACLE + -ED[3]]

spec′tacled co′bra. See **Indian cobra.**

spec′tacle flange′, (in plumbing) an oblong plate, for bolting between the flanges of two adjoining sections of pipe in either of two positions so as to allow or obstruct the passage of fluids.

spec′tacle frame′, *Naut.* **1.** a casting in the after body vessel containing bearings for propeller shafts on each side of the fore-and-aft center line. **2.** any of various frames specially formed to fit around propeller shafts projecting from the after body of a vessel on either side of the fore-and-aft center line.

spec·tac·u·lar (spek tak′yə lər), *adj.* **1.** of or like a spectacle; marked by or given to an impressive, large-scale display. **2.** dramatically daring or thrilling: *a spectacular dive from a cliff.* —*n.* **3.** a single television production featuring well-known performers and characterized by elaborate sets, costumes, staging, etc. Cf. **special** (def. 14). **4.** an impressive, large-scale display: *another Hollywood spectacular.* [< L *spectācul(um)* (see SPECTACLE) + -AR[1]] —**spec·tac·u·lar·i·ty** (spek tak′yə lar′i tē), **spec·tac′u·lar·ism,** *n.* —**spec·tac′u·lar·ly,** *adv.*

spec·ta·tor (spek′tā tər, spek tā′-), *n.* **1.** a person who looks on or watches; onlooker; observer. **2.** a person who is present at and views a spectacle, display, or the like. [< L, deriv. of *spectātus,* ptp. of *spectāre.* See SPECTACLE, -OR[2]] —**spec·ta·to·ri·al** (spek′tə tôr′ē əl, -tōr′-), *adj.*

Spectator, The, a weekly periodical (1711–12, 1714) conducted by Joseph Addison and Richard Steele.

spec·ta·tress (spek tā′tris, spek′tā-), *n.* a female spectator. [SPECTAT(O)R + -ESS]

spec·ta·trix (spek tā′triks, spek′tā-), *n., pl.* **-tri·ces** (-tri sēz′), **-trix·es.** spectatress. [< L, fem. of *spectātor* SPECTATOR; see -TRIX]

spec·ter (spek′tər), *n.* **1.** a visible incorporeal spirit, esp. one of a terrifying nature; ghost; phantom; apparition. **2.** some object or source of terror or dread: *the specter of disease or famine.* Also, *esp. Brit.,* **spec′tre.** [< L *spectr(um);* see SPECTRUM]
—**Syn. 1.** shade. See **ghost.**

spec·tra (spek′trə), *n.* a pl. of **spectrum.**

spec·tral (spek′trəl), *adj.* **1.** of or pertaining to a specter; ghostly; phantom. **2.** resembling or suggesting a specter. **3.** of, pertaining to, or produced by a spectrum or spectra. **4.** resembling or suggesting a spectrum or spectra. [< L *spectr(um)* (see SPECTRUM) + -AL[1]] —**spec·tral′i·ty, spec′tral·ness,** *n.* —**spec′tral·ly,** *adv.*

spec′tral classifica′tion, *Astron.* the classification of a star by classifying its spectrum into one of ten major classes each of which is further divided into ten subclasses.

spec′tral se′ries, *Physics.* a series of lines in the spectrum of light emitted by excited atoms of an element, each line being related to the others in the series by a simple numerical equation and identified with a particular energy level of an atom of the element.

spec′tra yel′low, a vivid yellow color. Also called **Hansa yellow.**

spectro-, a combining form of **spectrum:** *spectrometer.*

spec·tro·bo·lom·e·ter (spek′trō bō lom′i tər), *n. Physics.* an instrument consisting of a spectroscope and a bolometer, for determining the distribution of radiant energy in a spectrum. [SPECTRO- + BOLOMETER] —**spec·tro·bo·lo·met·ric** (spek′trō bō′lə me′trik), *adj.*

spec·tro·chem·i·cal (spek′trō kem′i kəl), *adj.* of, pertaining to, or utilizing the techniques of spectrochemistry. [SPECTRO- + CHEMICAL]

spec·tro·chem·is·try (spek′trō kem′i strē), *n.* the branch of chemistry that deals with the chemical analysis of substances by means of the spectra of light they absorb or emit. [SPECTRO- + CHEMISTRY]

spec·tro·col·o·rim·e·try (spek′trō kul′ə rim′i trē), *n.* the quantitative measure of colors by spectrophotometry. [SPECTRO- + COLORIMETRY]

spec·tro·gram (spek′trə gram′), *n.* a representation or photograph of a spectrum. [SPECTRO- + -GRAM[1]]

spec·tro·graph (spek′trə graf′, -gräf′), *n.* a spectroscope for photographing or producing a representation of a spectrum. [SPECTRO- + -GRAPH] —**spec·trog·ra·pher** (spek trog′rə fər), *n.* —**spec·tro·graph·ic** (spek′trə graf′ik), *adj.* —**spec′tro·graph′i·cal·ly,** *adv.* —**spec·trog′ra·phy,** *n.*

spec·tro·he·li·o·gram (spek′trō hē′lē ə gram′), *n.* a photograph of the sun made with a spectroheliograph. [SPECTRO- + HELIOGRAM]

spec·tro·he·li·o·graph (spek′trō hē′lē ə graf′, -gräf′), *n.* an apparatus for making photographs of the sun with a monochromatic light to show the details of the sun's surface and surroundings as they would appear if the sun emitted only that light. [SPECTRO- + HELIOGRAPH] —**spec·tro·he·li·o·graph·ic** (spek′trō hē′lē ə graf′ik), *adj.*

spec·tro·he·li·o·scope (spek′trō hē′lē ə skōp′), *n.* **1.** a spectroheliograph. **2.** a similar instrument, used for visual instead of photographic observations. [SPECTRO- + HELIO- + -SCOPE] —**spec·tro·he·li·o·scop·ic** (spek′trō hē′lē ə skop′ik), *adj.*

spec·trol·o·gy (spek trol′ə jē), *n.* the study of ghosts, phantoms, or apparitions. [< L *spectr(um)* SPECTER + -O- + -LOGY] —**spec·tro·log·i·cal** (spek′trə loj′i kəl), *adj.* —**spec′tro·log′i·cal·ly,** *adv.*

spec·trom·e·ter (spek trom′i tər), *n. Optics.* an optical device for measuring wavelengths, deviation of refracted rays, and angles between faces of a prism, esp. an instrument **(prism spectrometer)** consisting of a slit through which light passes, a collimator, a prism that deviates the light, and a telescope through which the deviated light is viewed and examined. [SPECTRO- + -METER] —**spec·tro·met·ric** (spek′trə me′trik), *adj.* —**spec·trom′e·try,** *n.*

spec·tro·mi·cro·scope (spek′trō mī′krə skōp′), *n.* a microscope with an attached spectroscope. [SPECTRO- + MICROSCOPE] —**spec·tro·mi·cro·scop·i·cal** (spek′trō mī′krə skop′i kəl), *adj.*

spec·tro·pho·to·e·lec·tric (spek′trō fō′tō i lek′trik), *adj. Physics.* pertaining to the relationship between the wave length of the incident radiation and the number of electrons released by a substance during a photoelectric effect. [SPECTRO- + PHOTOELECTRIC]

spec·tro·pho·tom·e·ter (spek′trō fō tom′i tər), *n.* an instrument for making photometric comparisons between parts of spectra. [SPECTRO- + PHOTOMETER] —**spec·tro·pho·to·met·ric** (spek′trō fō′tə me′trik), *adj.* —**spec′tro·pho′to·met′ri·cal·ly,** *adv.* —**spec′tro·pho·tom′e·try,** *n.*

spec·tro·po·lar·im·e·ter (spek′trō pō′lə rim′i tər), *n. Optics.* an instrument for determining the extent to which plane-polarized light of various wavelengths is rotated by certain solutions, consisting of a combination of a spectroscope and a polarimeter. [SPECTRO- + POLARIMETER]

spec·tro·po·lar·i·scope (spek′trō pō lar′i skōp′), *n. Optics.* an instrument combining the functions of a spectroscope with those of a polariscope. Cf. **spectropolarimeter.** [SPECTRO- + POLARISCOPE]

spec·tro·ra·di·om·e·ter (spek′trō rā′dē om′i tər), *n. Optics.* an instrument for determining the radiant-energy distribution in a spectrum, combining the functions of a spectroscope with those of a radiometer. [SPECTRO- + RADIOMETER] —**spec·tro·ra·di·o·met·ric** (spek′trō rā′dē ə me′trik), *adj.* —**spec′tro·ra′di·om′e·try,** *n.*

spec·tro·scope (spek′trə skōp′), *n. Optics.* an optical device for producing and observing a spectrum of light or radiation from any source, consisting essentially of a slit through which the radiation passes, a collimating lens, and an Amici prism. [SPECTRO- + -SCOPE] —**spec·tro·scop·ic** (spek′trə skop′ik), **spec′tro·scop′i·cal,** *adj.* —**spec′tro·scop′i·cal·ly,** *adv.*

spec′troscop′ic bi′nary, *Astron.* a binary star having components that are not sufficiently separated to be resolved by a telescope, known to be a binary only by the variations in wave length of emitted light that are detected by a spectroscope. Cf. **visual binary.**

spec·tros·co·py (spek tros′kə pē, spek′trə skō′pē), *n.* the science that deals with the use of the spectroscope and with spectrum analysis. [SPECTRO- + -SCOPY] —**spec·tros·co·pist** (spek tros′kə pist), *n.*

spec·trum (spek′trəm), *n., pl.* **-tra** (-trə), **-trums. 1.** *Physics.* **a.** an array of entities, as light waves or particles, ordered in accordance with the magnitudes of a common physical property, as wavelength or mass: often the band of colors produced when sunlight is passed through a prism, comprising red, orange, yellow, green, blue, indigo, and violet. **b.** this band or series of colors together with extensions at the ends which are not visible to the eye, but which can be studied by means of photography, heat effects, etc., and which are produced by the dispersion of radiant energy other than ordinary light rays. **2.** a broad range of varied but related ideas or objects, the individual features of which tend to overlap so as to form a continuous series or sequence: *the spectrum of political beliefs.* [< L: appearance, form, deriv. of *spectāre;* see SPECTACLE]

spec′trum anal′ysis, 1. the determination of the constitution or condition of bodies and substances by means of the spectra they produce. **2.** the ascertaining of the number and character of the constituents combining to produce a sound spectrogram.

spec·u·lar (spek′yə lər), *adj.* **1.** pertaining to or having the properties of a mirror. **2.** pertaining to a speculum. [< L *speculār(is)* (*specul(um)* a mirror, equiv. to *spec-* look (see SPECIES) + *-ul-* -ULE) + *-āris* -AR[1]] —**spec′u·lar·ly,** *adv.*

spec·u·late (spek′yə lāt′), *v.i.,* **-lat·ed, -lat·ing. 1.** to engage in thought or reflection; meditate (often fol. by *on, upon,* or a clause). **2.** to indulge in conjectural thought. **3.** to buy and sell commodities, stocks, etc., in the expectation of profit through a change in their market value; engage in any business transaction involving considerable risk or the chance of large gains. [< L *speculāt(us)* observed, watched, examined; see SPECULATOR]
—**Syn. 1.** think, reflect, cogitate. **2.** conjecture, guess, surmise, suppose, theorize.

spec·u·la·tion (spek′yə lā′shən), *n.* **1.** the contemplation or consideration of some subject: *to engage in speculation on man's ultimate destiny.* **2.** a single instance or process of consideration. **3.** a conclusion or opinion reached by such contemplation: *His speculation was impossible to verify.* **4.** conjectural consideration of a matter; conjecture or surmise: *a speculation that was on the level of guesswork.* **5.** trading in commodities, stocks, etc., in the hope of profit from changes in the market price; engagement in business transactions involving considerable risk but offering the chance of large gains. **6.** a speculative commercial venture or undertaking. [ME *speculacioun* < LL *speculātiōn-* (s. of *speculātiō*) exploration, observation. See SPECULATOR, -ION]
—Syn. 3. supposition, view, theory, hypothesis.

spec·u·la·tive (spek′yə lā′tiv, -lə tiv), *adj.* **1.** pertaining to, of the nature of, or characterized by speculation, contemplation, conjecture, or abstract reasoning: *We must approach the problem in a speculative way.* **2.** theoretical, rather than practical: *We are left with merely speculative conclusions.* **3.** given to speculation, as persons, the mind, etc. **4.** of the nature of or involving commercial or financial speculation: *He lost a fortune in speculative ventures.* **5.** engaging in or given to such speculation. [ME *speculatif* < LL *speculātīv(us).* See SPECULATOR, -IVE] **—spec′u·la′tive·ly,** *adv.* **—spec′u·la′tive·ness,** *n.*

spec′ulative philos′ophy, philosophy embodying beliefs insusceptible of proof and attempting to gain insight into the nature of the ultimate by intuitive or a priori means.

spec·u·la·tor (spek′yə lā′tər), *n.* **1.** a person who is engaged in commercial or financial speculation. **2.** a person who makes advance purchases of tickets, as to games, theatrical performances, etc., that are likely to be in demand, for resale later at a higher price. **3.** a person who is devoted to mental speculation. [< L: explorer, equiv. to *speculāt(us),* ptp. of *speculārī* (*specul(a)* lookout, equiv. to *spec(ere)* (to) look at + *-ula* fem. suffix, + *-ātus* -ATE¹) + *-or* -OR²]

spec·u·la·to·ry (spek′yə lə tōr′ē, -tôr′ē), *adj. Archaic.* speculative. [< L *speculāt(us)* (see SPECULATOR) + -ORY¹]

spec·u·lum (spek′yə ləm), *n., pl.* **-la** (-lə), **-lums. 1.** a mirror or reflector, esp. one of polished metal, as on a reflecting telescope. **2.** See **speculum metal. 3.** *Surg.* an instrument for rendering a part accessible to observation, as by enlarging an orifice. **4.** *Ornith.* a lustrous or specially colored area on the wing of certain birds. [< L: mirror, equiv. to *spec(ere)* (to) behold + *-ulum* -ULE]

spec′ulum met′al, any of several bronze alloys, often containing other materials, as silver, brass, lead, zinc, or arsenic, used for making mirrors and reflectors. Also called **speculum.**

sped (sped), *v.* a pt. and pp. of **speed.**

Sp.Ed., Specialist in Education.

Spee (shpā), *n.* **Ma·xi·mi·li·an von** (mäk′si mē′lē än′ fən), 1861–1941, German admiral.

speech (spēch), *n.* **1.** the faculty or power of speaking; oral communication; ability to express one's thoughts and emotions by speech sounds and gesture: *Losing his speech isolated him from humanity.* **2.** the act of speaking: *He expresses himself better in speech than in writing.* **3.** that which is spoken; an utterance, remark, or declaration: *We waited in vain for some speech that would indicate his true feelings.* **4.** a form of communication in spoken language, made by a speaker before an audience for a given purpose: *a fiery speech.* **5.** any single utterance of an actor in the course of a play, motion picture, etc. **6.** the form of utterance characteristic of a particular people or region; a language or dialect. **7.** manner of speaking, as of a person: *His slovenly speech is holding back his career.* **8.** a field of study devoted to the theory and practice of oral communication. **9.** *Archaic.* rumor. [ME *speche,* OE *spǣc,* var. of *sprǣc;* c. G *Sprache*]
—Syn. 1. parlance, parley, conversation, communication. SPEECH, LANGUAGE refer to the means of communication used by people. SPEECH is the expression of ideas and thoughts by means of articulate vocal sounds, or the faculty of thus expressing ideas and thoughts. LANGUAGE is a set of conventional signs, used conventionally and not necessarily articulate or even vocal (any set of signs, signals, or symbols, which convey meaning, including written words, may be called language): *a spoken language.* Thus, LANGUAGE is the set of conventions, and SPEECH is the action of putting these to use: *He couldn't understand the speech of the natives because it was in a foreign language.* **3.** observation, assertion, asseveration, averral, comment, mention, talk. **4.** talk, discourse. SPEECH, ADDRESS, ORATION, HARANGUE are terms for a communication to an audience. SPEECH is the general word, with no implication of kind or length, or whether planned or not. An ADDRESS is a rather formal, planned speech, appropriate to a particular subject or occasion. An ORATION is a polished, rhetorical address, given usually on a notable occasion, that employs eloquence and studied methods of delivery. A HARANGUE is a violent, informal speech, often addressed to a casual audience, and intended to arouse strong feeling (sometimes to lead to mob action). **6.** tongue, patois.

speech′ clin′ic, a place at which specialists in speech therapy reeducate those with a speech handicap.

speech′ commu′nity, *Ling.* **1.** the aggregate of all the people who use a given language or dialect. **2.** a group of people geographically distributed so that there is no break in intelligibility from place to place.

speech′ correc′tion, the reeducation of speech habits which deviate from accepted speech standards.

speech′ form′. See **linguistic form.**

speech·i·fy (spē′chə fī′), *v.i.,* **-fied, -fy·ing.** to make a speech or speeches; harangue. [SPEECH + -IFY] **—speech′i·fi·ca′tion,** *n.* **—speech′i·fi′er,** *n.*

speech′ is′land, *Ling.* a speech community that is completely surrounded by another, usually larger, speech community.

speech·less (spēch′lis), *adj.* **1.** temporarily deprived of speech by strong emotion, physical weakness, exhaustion, etc.: *speechless with alarm.* **2.** characterized by absence or loss of speech: *speechless joy.* **3.** lacking the faculty of speech; dumb. **4.** not expressed in speech or words: *speechless compliments.* **5.** refraining from speech. [ME *specheles,* OE *spǣclēas.* See SPEECH, -LESS] **—speech′less·ly,** *adv.* **—speech′less·ness,** *n.*
—Syn. 1. dumfounded, shocked, mute. See **dumb. 3.** silent, mute. **—Ant. 1–3.** loquacious, voluble, talkative.

speech·mak·er (spēch′mā′kər), *n.* a person who delivers speeches. [SPEECH + MAKER]

speech·mak·ing (spēch′mā′king), *n.* the act or practice of making speeches. [SPEECH + MAKING]

speech′ or′gan, any part of the body, as tongue, velum, diaphragm, lungs, etc., that participates, actively or passively, voluntarily or involuntarily, in the production of the sounds of speech.

speech′ pathol′ogy, the scientific study and treatment of defects, disorders, and malfunctions of speech and voice, as stuttering, lisping, lalling, etc., and of language disturbances, as aphasia, delayed language acquisition, etc.

speech′ read′ing, the act or process of determining the intended meaning of a speaker by utilizing all visual clues accompanying speech attempts, as lip movements, facial expressions, and bodily gestures, used esp. by people with impaired hearing. Cf. **lip reading.**

speech′ sound′, *Phonet.* **1.** any of the set of distinctive sounds of a given language. Cf. **phoneme. 2.** any audible, elemental, acoustic event occurring in speech: *"Go" contains the speech sound "o."* Cf. **phone².** **3.** any of the sounds of the entire phonetic system of a language. Cf. **allophone.**

speech·way (spēch′wā′), *n.* a pattern, style, or feature of spoken language shared by the people of a particular group or area. [SPEECH + WAY]

speed (spēd), *n., v.,* **sped** or **speed·ed, speed·ing.** **—n. 1.** rapidity in moving, going, traveling, proceeding, or performing; swiftness; celerity: *the speed of light; the speed of sound.* **2.** relative rapidity in moving, going, etc.; rate of motion or progress: *full speed ahead.* **3.** *Auto.* a transmission gear ratio. **4.** *Photog.* **a.** the sensitivity of a film or paper to light. **b.** the length of time a shutter is opened to expose film. **c.** the largest opening at which a lens can be used. **5.** *Slang.* a stimulating drug, as amphetamine or Methedrine. **6.** *Optics, Photog.* See **F number. 7.** *Archaic.* success or prosperity. **8. at full** or **top speed, a.** at the greatest speed possible: *We drove down the highway at full speed.* **b.** to the maximum of one's capabilities; with great rapidity: *He worked at full speed.* **—v.t. 9.** to promote the success of (an affair, undertaking, etc.); further, forward, or expedite. **10.** to direct (the steps, course, way, etc.) with speed. **11.** to increase the rate of speed of (usually fol. by *up*): *to speed up industrial production.* **12.** to bring to a particular speed, as a machine. **13.** to cause to move, go, or proceed with speed. **14.** to expedite the going of: *to speed the parting guest.* **15.** *Archaic.* to cause to succeed or prosper. **—v.i. 16.** to move, go, pass, or proceed with speed or rapidity. **17.** to drive a vehicle at a rate that exceeds the legally established maximum: *He was arrested for speeding.* **18.** to increase the rate of speed or progress (usually fol. by *up*). **19.** to get on or fare in a specified or particular manner. **20.** *Archaic.* to succeed or prosper. [ME *spede* good luck, OE *spēd;* c. D *spoed,* OHG *spōt;* akin to OE *spōwan* to prosper, succeed] **—speed′er,** *n.* **—speed′ful,** *adj.* **—speed′ful·ly,** *adv.* **—speed′ful·ness,** *n.* **—speed′ing·ly,** *adv.* **—speed′ing·ness,** *n.* **—speed′less,** *adj.*
—Syn. 1, 2. fleetness, alacrity, dispatch, expedition; hurry. SPEED, VELOCITY, QUICKNESS, RAPIDITY, CELERITY, HASTE refer to swift or energetic movement or operation. SPEED (originally prosperity or success) may apply to human or nonhuman activity and emphasizes the rate in time at which something travels or operates: *the speed of light, of a lens, of an automobile, of thought.* VELOCITY, a more learned or technical term, is sometimes interchangeable with SPEED: *the velocity of light;* it is commonly used to refer to high rates of speed, linear or circular: *velocity of a projectile.* QUICKNESS, a native word, and RAPIDITY, a synonym of Latin origin, suggest speed of movement or operation on a small or subordinate scale; QUICKNESS applies more to people (*quickness of mind, of perception, of bodily movement*), RAPIDITY more to things, often in a technical or mechanical context: *the rapidity of moving parts; a lens of great rapidity.* CELERITY, a somewhat literary synonym of Latin origin, refers usually to human movement or operation and emphasizes expedition, dispatch, or economy in an activity: *the celerity of his response.* HASTE refers to the energetic activity of human beings under stress; it often suggests lack of opportunity for care or thought: *to marry in haste; a report prepared in haste.* **9.** advance, favor. **11.** accelerate. **16.** See **rush¹.** **—Ant. 1.** slowness.

speed·ball (spēd′bôl′), *n.* a game similar to soccer with the chief difference that a player catching the ball on the fly can pass it with the hands. [SPEED + BALL¹]

speed·boat (spēd′bōt′), *n.* a motorboat designed for high speeds. [SPEED + BOAT]

speed·boat·ing (spēd′bō′ting), *n.* the act, practice, or sport of traveling in a speedboat. [SPEED + BOATING]

speed′ de′mon, *Informal.* one who travels or works at high speed.

speed′ gear′, an adjustable gear for driving a machine at various speeds.

speed′ in′dicator, a hand instrument for counting the number of revolutions of a gasoline engine, in contrast with a watch for determining engine speed. Also called **speed′ count′er.**

speed′ light′, *Photog.* an electronic flash lamp. Also called **speed′ lamp′.**

speed′ lim′it, the maximum speed at which a vehicle is legally permitted to travel, as within a specific area, on a certain road, under given conditions, etc.

speed·om·e·ter (spē dom′i tər, spi-), *n.* a device on an automobile or other vehicle for recording the rate of travel in miles per hour and often the distance covered. [SPEED + -O- + -METER]

speed′ skate′. See **racing skate.**

speed·ster (spēd′stər), *n. Informal.* a person who travels at high speed. [SPEED + -STER]

speed′ trap′, a section of a road where hidden policemen, radar, etc., carefully check the speed of motorists and strictly enforce traffic regulations: sometimes characterized by hard-to-see signals, hidden traffic signs, etc.

speed-up (spēd′up′), *n.* **1.** an increasing of speed. **2.** an imposed increase in the rate of production of a worker without a corresponding increase in the rate of pay. [n. use of v. phrase *speed up*]

speed·walk (spēd′wôk′), *n.* an endless conveyor belt, moving walk, or the like used to transport standing persons from place to place. [SPEED + WALK]

speed·way (spēd′wā′), *n.* **1.** a road or course for fast driving, motoring, or the like, or on which more than ordinary speed is allowed. **2.** a track on which automobile or motorcycle races are held. [SPEED + WAY]

Speed·way (spēd′wā′), *n.* a town in central Indiana. 9624 (1960).

speed·well (spēd′wel′), *n.* any of several herbs, shrubs or small trees of the genus *Veronica.* [SPEED + WELL¹; so called because its petals fade and fall early]

speed·y (spē′dē), *adj.,* **speed·i·er, speed·i·est. 1.** characterized by speed; rapid; swift; fast. **2.** coming, given, or arrived at quickly or soon; prompt; not delayed: *a speedy recovery.* [ME *spedy.* See SPEED, -Y¹] **—speed′i·ly,** *adv.* **—speed′i·ness,** *n.*
—Syn. 1. quick. **2.** expeditious.

speel (spēl), *v.t., v.i. Scot. and North Eng.* to climb; ascend; mount. Also, **speil.** [?]

speen (spēn), *n., v.t. Scot. and North Eng.* spean.

speer¹ (spēr), *Scot. and North Eng.* **—v.i. 1.** to ask; inquire. **—v.t. 2.** to ask (a question). **3.** to learn, know, or find by asking or seeking. Also, **speir** (spēr), **spier.** [ME *spere, spire,* OE *spyr(ian)* (to) make tracks, trace, ask about; c. G *spüren,* Icel *spyrja;* akin to SPOOR]

speer² (spēr), *n.* spier².

Spei·cher (spī′kər), *n.* **Eugene Edward,** born 1883, U.S. painter.

speil (spēl), *v.t., v.i. Scot. and North Eng.* speel.

speiss (spīs), *n. Metall.* a product obtained in smelting certain ores, consisting of one or more metallic arsenides, as of iron, nickel, etc. [< G *Speise,* lit., food]

spe·lae·an (spi lē′ən), *adj.* of, pertaining to, or inhabiting a cave or caves. Also, **spe·le′an.** [< NL *spelae(us)* (adj., for L *spēlaeum* < Gk *spḗlaion* cave) + -AN]

Spe·la·i·tes (spə lā′i tēz′), *n. Class. Myth.* an epithet of Hermes, meaning "of the cave," referring to his advising certain warring generals to hide their women and children in a cave for safety.

spe·le·ol·o·gy (spē′lē ol′ə jē), *n.* the exploration and study of caves. Also, **spe′lae·ol′o·gy.** [< L *spēlae(um)* (see SPELAEAN) + -O- + -LOGY] **—spe·le·o·log·i·cal, spe·lae·o·log·i·cal** (spē′lē ə loj′i kəl), *adj.* **—spe′le·ol′o·gist, spe′lae·ol′o·gist,** *n.*

spell¹ (spel), *v.,* **spelled** or **spelt, spell·ing.** **—v.t. 1.** to name, write, or otherwise give the letters, in order, of (a word, syllable, etc.): *Did I spell your name right?* **2.** (of letters) to form (a word, syllable, etc.): *The letters spelled a rather rude word.* **3.** to read letter by letter or with difficulty (often fol. by *out*): *He painfully spelled out the message.* **4.** to discern or find, as if by reading or study (often fol. by *out*). **5.** to signify; amount to: *This delay spells disaster for us.* **—v.i. 6.** to name, write, or give the letters of words, syllables, etc.: *He spells poorly.* **7.** to express words by letters, esp. correctly. **8. spell out, a.** *Informal.* to explain something explicitly, so that the meaning is unmistakable: *Must I spell it out for you?* **b.** to write out in full or enumerate the letters of which a word is composed: *The title "Mrs." is seldom spelled out.* [ME *spell(en)* < OF *(e)spell(er)* < some Gmc tongue; cf. OE *spellian* to talk, announce, deriv. of *spell* SPELL²] **—spell′a·ble,** *adj.*

spell² (spel), *n.* **1.** a word, phrase, or form of words supposed to have magic power; charm; incantation: *The wizard cast a spell.* **2.** state or period of enchantment: *She was under a spell.* **3.** any dominating or irresistible influence; fascination: *the spell of fine music.* [ME, OE *spell* discourse; c. OHG *spel,* Goth *spill,* Icel *spjall* tale; akin to OE *spellian,* Icel *spjalla,* Goth *spillon,* etc. (see SPELL¹)] **—spell′ful,** *adj.* **—spell′-like′,** *adj.*

spell³ (spel), *n.* **1.** a continuous course or period of work or other activity: *to take a spell at the wheel.* **2.** a turn of work so taken. **3.** a turn, bout, fit, or period of anything experienced or occurring: *a spell of coughing.* **4.** an indefinite interval or space of time. **5.** a period of weather of a specified kind: *a hot spell.* **6.** *Australian.* a rest period. **7.** *Rare.* a person or set of persons taking a turn of work to relieve another. **—v.t. 8.** to take the place of for a time; relieve: *Let me spell you at the wheel.* **9.** *Australian.* to declare or give a rest period to. **—v.i. 10.** *Australian.* to have or take a rest period. [ME *spel(en),* OE *spelian* to be a substitute for, OE *gespelia* substitute; akin to OE *spala* substitute]

spell·bind (spel′bīnd′), *v.t.,* **-bound, -bind·ing.** to hold or bind by, or as by, a spell; enchant; entrance; fascinate. [SPELL² + BIND, deduced from SPELLBOUND]

spell·bind·er (spel′bīn′dər), *n.* **1.** a speaker, esp. a politician, who holds his audience spellbound. **2.** a spellbinding work or production. [SPELLBIND + -ER¹]

spell·bound (spel′bound′), *adj.* bound by or as if by a spell; enchanted, entranced, or fascinated: *a spellbound audience.* [SPELL² + -BOUND¹]

spell·down (spel′doun′), *n.* a spelling competition which begins with all the contestants standing and which ends when all but one, the winner, have been required to sit down due to a specified number of misspellings. [from phrase *spell down* to outspell others in a spelling match]

spell·er (spel′ər), *n.* **1.** a person who spells words. **2.** Also called **spelling book.** an elementary textbook or manual to teach spelling. [late ME; see SPELL¹, -ER¹]

spell·ing (spel′ing), *n.* **1.** the manner in which words are spelled; orthography. **2.** a group of letters representing a word. **3.** the act of a speller. [late ME; see SPELL¹, -ING¹] **—spell′ing·ly,** *adv.*

spell′ing bee′, a spelling competition won by the individual or team spelling the greatest number of words correctly; spelldown.

spell′ing book′, speller (def. 2).

spell′ing pronuncia′tion, a pronunciation based on spelling, usually a variant of the traditional pronunciation. The spelling pronunciation of *waistcoat* is (wāst′kōt′) rather than (wes′kət).

spell′ing reform′, an attempt to change the spelling of English words to make it conform more closely to their pronunciation.

Spell·man (spel′mən), *n.* **Francis Joseph, Cardinal,** 1889–1967, U.S. Roman Catholic clergyman: archbishop of New York 1939–67.

spelt[1] (spelt), *v.* a pt. and pp. of **spell**[1].

spelt[2] (spelt), *n.* a wheat, *Triticum spelta*, native to southern Europe and western Asia, used chiefly for livestock feed. [ME, OE < LL *spelta;* cf. OHG *spelza*, G *Spelt*]

spel·ter (spel′tər), *n.* zinc, esp. in the form of ingots. [akin to MD *speauter* spelter and to PEWTER]

spe·lunk (spi lungk′), *v.i.* to explore caves. [< L *spēlunc(a)* a cave < Gk *spêlunx;* see SPELEAN]

spe·lun·ker (spi lung′kər), *n.* a person who explores caves. [SPELUNK + -ER[1]]

Spe·mann (shpā′män), *n.* **Hans** (häns), 1869–1941, German zoologist: Nobel prize for medicine 1935.

Spe·nard (spə närd′), *n.* a town in S Alaska, near Anchorage. 9074 (1960).

spence (spens), *n. Brit. Dial.* a pantry. [late ME *spense, spence*, by aphesis < MF *despense* pantry < L *dispensa*, n. use of fem. of *dispensus*, ptp. of *dispendere* to weigh out; see DISPENSE]

Spence (spens), *n.* a boy's given name, form of **Spencer.**

spen·cer[1] (spen′sər), *n.* **1.** a short, close-fitting jacket, frequently trimmed with fur, worn in the 19th century by women and children. **2.** a close-fitting jacket, having a collar and lapels and reaching just below the waist, worn as an outer garment by men in the late 18th and early 19th centuries. **3.** an English wig of the 18th century. [defs. 1, 2 named after G. J. *Spencer* (1758–1834), English earl; def. 3 after Charles SPENCER]

spen·cer[2] (spen′sər), *n. Naut.* a large gaff sail, usually loose-footed, hooped to a trysail mast or horse abaft a square-rigged foremast or abaft the mainmast of a ship or bark. [? after the surname]

spen·cer[3] (spen′sər), *n. Obs.* a steward or butler. [late ME, by aphesis < AF *espenser* (for OF *dispenser*). See SPENCE, -ER[2]]

Spen·cer (spen′sər), *n.* **1. Charles, 3rd Earl of Sunderland,** 1674–1722, British statesman: prime minister 1718–21. **2. Herbert,** 1820–1903, English philosopher. **3.** a town in NW Iowa. 8864 (1960). **4.** a town in central Massachusetts. 5593 (1960). **5.** a town in central North Carolina. 2904 (1960). **6.** a town in W West Virginia. 2660 (1960). **7.** a town in SW Indiana. 2557 (1960). **8.** a boy's given name.

Spen·ce·ri·an (spen sēr′ē ən), *adj.* **1.** of Herbert Spencer or his philosophy. —*n.* **2.** a follower of Herbert Spencer. [SPENCER + -IAN]

Spen·ce·ri·an (spen sēr′ē ən), *adj.* pertaining to or characteristic of a system of penmanship, characterized by clear, rounded letters slanting to the right. [named after P. R. *Spencer* (d. 1864), American handwriting expert]

Spen·ce·ri·an·ism (spen sēr′ē ə niz′əm), *n.* the philosophy of Herbert Spencer, consisting mainly of an attempted synthesis of the various sciences. [SPENCERIAN + -ISM]

spen′cer mast′, *Naut.* See **trysail mast.**

spend (spend), *v.*, **spent, spend·ing.** —*v.t.* **1.** to pay out, disburse, or expend; dispose of (money, wealth, resources, etc.): *resisting the temptation to spend one's money.* **2.** to employ (labor, thought, words, time, etc.) on some object, in some proceeding, etc.: *Don't spend much time on it.* **3.** to pass (time) in a particular manner, place, etc. **4.** to use up, consume, or exhaust: *The storm had spent its fury.* **5.** to give (one's blood, life, etc.) for some cause. —*v.i.* **6.** to spend money, energy, time, etc. **7.** *Obs.* to be consumed or exhausted. [ME *spend(en)*, OE *(a)spendan* < WGmc < L *expendere* to pay out, EXPEND; cf. G *spenden*]

—**Syn. 1.** SPEND, DISBURSE, EXPEND, SQUANDER refer to paying out money. SPEND is the general word: *We spend more for living expenses now.* DISBURSE implies expending from a specific source or sum to meet specific obligations, or paying in definite allotments: *The treasurer has authority to disburse funds.* EXPEND is more formal, and implies spending for some definite and (usually) sensible or worthy object: *to expend most of one's salary on necessities.* SQUANDER suggests lavish, wasteful, or foolish expenditure: *to squander a legacy.* **2.** use, apply, devote. —**Ant. 1.** earn, keep.

spend·a·ble (spen′də bəl), *adj.* available for spending. [SPEND + -ABLE]

spend·er (spen′dər), *n.* a person who spends, esp. one who habitually spends excessively or lavishly; spendthrift. [ME; see SPEND, -ER[1]]

Spen·der (spen′dər), *n.* **Stephen,** born 1909, English poet and critic.

spend′ing mon′ey, money for small personal expenses.

spend·thrift (spend′thrift′), *n.* **1.** a person who spends his possessions or money extravagantly or wastefully; prodigal. —*adj.* **2.** wastefully extravagant; prodigal. [SPEND + THRIFT]

spend′thrift trust′, *Law.* a trust that provides a fund for a beneficiary, as a minor, with the title vested so that the fund or its income cannot be claimed by others, as creditors of the beneficiary. Also called **sheltering trust.**

Spe·ner (shpā′nər), *n.* **Phi·lipp Ja·kob** (fē′lēp yä′kōp), 1635–1705, German theologian: founder of Pietism. —**Spe·ner·ism** (shpā′nə riz′əm, spā′-), *n.*

Speng·ler (speng′glər; *Ger.* shpeng′glər), *n.* **Os·wald** (oz′wôld; *Ger.* ôs′vält), 1880–1936, German philosopher. —**Speng·le·ri·an** (speng glēr′ē ən, shpeng-), *adj.*

Spen·ser (spen′sər), *n.* **Edmund,** c1552–99, English poet.

Spen·se·ri·an (spen sēr′ē ən), *adj.* **1.** of or characteristic of Spenser or his work. —*n.* **2.** an imitator of Spenser. **3.** See **Spenserian stanza. 4.** verse in Spenserian stanzas. [SPENSER + -IAN]

Spense′rian son′net, a sonnet following the rhyme scheme *abab, bcbc, cdcd, ee.*

Spense′rian stan′za, the stanza used by Spenser in his *Faerie Queene* and employed since by other poets, consisting of eight iambic pentameter lines and a final Alexandrine, with a rhyme scheme of *ababbcbcc.*

spent (spent), *v.* **1.** pt. and pp. of **spend.** —*adj.* **2.** used up, consumed, or exhausted.

Spen·ta A·me·sha (spen′tə ä′me shə), *Zoroastrianism.* See **Amesha Spenta.**

Spen′ta Main′yu (mīn′yo͞o), *Zoroastrianism.* the good and creative spirit which is the offspring of Ahura Mazda.

spe·os (spē′os), *n.* a cavelike temple, tomb, or the like, cut in living rock. [< Gk *spéos* a cave]

spere (spēr), *n.* spier[2].

sperm[1] (spûrm), *n.* **1.** See **spermatic fluid. 2.** a male reproductive cell; spermatozoon. [late ME *sperme* < LL *sperma* < Gk *spérma* seed, equiv. to *sper-* (root of *speírein* to sow) + *-ma* n. suffix]

sperm[2] (spûrm), *n.* **1.** spermaceti. **2.** See **sperm whale. 3.** See **sperm oil.** [by shortening]

sperm-, var. of **spermo-** before a vowel: *spermine.*

-sperm, var. of **spermo-,** as final element of a compound word: *gymnosperm.*

sper·ma·ce·ti (spûr′mə set′ē, -sē′tē), *n. Chem., Pharm.* a pearly white, waxy, almost colorless and tasteless water-insoluble solid, obtained from the oil in the head of the sperm whale: used chiefly in the manufacture of cosmetics, candles, for lustering linens, and in medicine as an emollient in ointments, emulsions, and cerates. Also called **cetaceum.** [< ML *sperma cētī* sperm of whale (see SPERM[1], CET-); r. ME *sperma cete* < ML *sperma cētē* sperm of whales (L *cētē* < Gk *kḗtē* whales)] —**sper′ma·cet′i·like′,** *adj.*

-spermal, a word element used to form adjectives corresponding to nouns with stems ending in **-sperm:** *gymnospermal.* [-SPERM + -AL[1]]

sper·ma·ry (spûr′mə rē), *n., pl.* **-ries.** an organ in which spermatozoa are generated; testis. [< NL *spermāri(um)*, equiv. to LL *sperm(a)* SPERM[1] + *-ārium* -ARY]

spermat-, var. of **spermato-** before a vowel: *spermatid.*

sper·mat·ic (spûr mat′ik), *adj.* **1.** of, pertaining to, or resembling sperm; seminal; generative. **2.** pertaining to a spermary. [< LL *spermatic(us)* < Gk *spermatikós* relating to seed, equiv. to *spermat-* (s. of *spérma*) SPERM[1] + *-ikos* -IC] —**sper·mat′i·cal·ly,** *adv.*

spermat′ic cord′, *Anat.* the cord by which a testis is suspended in the scrotum, containing the vas deferens, the blood vessels and nerves of the testis, etc.

spermat′ic flu′id, the male generative fluid; semen.

sper·ma·tid (spûr′mə tid), *n.* one of the cells that result from the meiotic divisions of a spermatocyte and mature into spermatozoa. [SPERMAT- + -ID[3]]

sper·ma·ti·um (spûr mā′shē əm), *n., pl.* **-ti·a** (-shē ə). *Bot.* **1.** the nonmotile male gamete of a red alga. **2.** a minute, colorless cell, believed to be a male reproductive body, developed within spermogonia. [< NL < Gk *spermátion*, equiv. to *spermat-* (s. of *spérma*) SPERM[1] + *-ion* dim. suffix]

spermato-, a learned borrowing from Greek, where it meant "seed"; used as a combining form of **sperm**[1] in the formation of compound words: *spermatogonium.* Cf. **sperm-, -sperm, -spermal, spermat-, -spermic, spermo-, -spermous.** [< Gk *spermat-* (s. of *spérma;* see SPERM[1]) + -o-]

sper·mat·o·cyte (spûr mat′ə sīt′, spûr′mə tə-), *n. Biol.* a male germ cell **(primary spermatocyte)** that gives rise by meiosis to a pair of haploid cells **(secondary spermatocytes)** which give rise in turn to spermatids. [SPERMATO- + -CYTE] —**sper′ma·to·cyt′al,** *adj.*

sper·mat·o·gen·e·sis (spûr mat′ə jen′i sis, spûr′mə tə-), *n. Biol.* the origin and development of spermatozoa. [< NL; see SPERMATO-, GENESIS] —**sper·ma·to·ge·net·ic** (spûr′mə tō jə net′ik, spər mat′ō-), *adj.*

sper·ma·tog·e·nous (spûr′mə toj′ə nəs), *adj.* producing spermatozoa. [SPERMATO- + -GENOUS]

sper·mat·o·go·ni·um (spûr mat′ə gō′nē əm, spûr′mə tə-), *n., pl.* **-ni·a** (-nē ə). *Biol.* one of the undifferentiated germ cells giving rise to spermatocytes. [< NL; see SPERMATO-, -GONIUM] —**sper·mat′o·go′ni·al,** *adj.*

sper·ma·toid (spûr′mə toid′), *adj.* resembling sperm. [SPERMAT- + -OID]

sper·mat·o·phore (spûr mat′ə fōr′, -fôr′, spûr′mə tə-), *n. Zool.* a special case or capsule containing a number of spermatozoa, produced by the male of certain insects, mollusks, annelids, etc., and some vertebrates. [SPERMATO- + -PHORE] —**sper·ma·toph·or·al** (spûr′mə tof′ər əl), **sper·ma·toph·o·rous** (spûr′mə tof′ər əs), *adj.*

sper·mat·o·phyte (spûr mat′ə fīt′, spûr′mə tə-), *n.* any of the *Spermatophyta*, a primary division or group of plants comprising those that bear seeds. [SPERMATO- + -PHYTE, modeled on NL *spermatophyta*] —**sper·ma·to·phyt·ic** (spûr′mə tə fit′ik, spər mat′ə-), *adj.*

sper·ma·tor·rhe·a (spûr′mə tə rē′ə, spûr mat′ə-), *n. Pathol.* abnormally frequent involuntary emission of semen. Also, **sper′ma·tor·rhoe′a.** [< NL; see SPERMATO-, -RRHEA]

sper·ma·to·zo·id (spûr′mə tə zō′id, spûr mat′ə-), *n. Bot.* a motile male gamete produced in an antheridium. [SPERMATOZO(ON) + -ID[3]]

sper·ma·to·zo·on (spûr′mə tə zō′ən, -on, spûr mat′ə-), *n., pl.* **-zo·a** (-zō′ə). *Biol.* one of the minute, usually actively motile, gametes in semen, which serve to fertilize the ovum; a mature male reproductive cell. Also, **sper′ma·to·zo′ön.** [< NL; see SPERMATO-, -ZOÖN] —**sper′ma·to·zo′al, sper′ma·to·zo′an, sper′ma·to·zo′ic,** *adj.*

Spermatozoon
A, Head
B, Neck
C, Tail

sper·mic (spûr′mik), *adj.* spermatic. [SPERM- + -IC]

-spermic, a word element used to form adjectives corresponding to nouns with stems ending in **-sperm:** *endospermic.* [< NL *-spermicus.* See -SPERM, -IC]

sperm·ine (spûr′mēn, -min), *n. Biochem., Pharm.* a colorless to white, crystalline, water-soluble base, $H_2N(CH_2)_3NH(CH_2)_4NH(CH_2)_3NH_2$, found esp. in semen, sputum, pancreatic tissue, and certain yeasts: used in medicine chiefly as a nerve stimulant. Also called **diaminopropyltetramethylenediamine, gerontine, musculamine, neuridine.** [SPERM- + -INE[2]]

sper·mi·o·gen·e·sis (spûr′mē ō jen′i sis), *n. Biol.* the development of a spermatozoon from a spermatid [< NL *spermio-* (comb. form of *spermium;* see SPERM[1]) + GENESIS] —**sper·mi·o·ge·net·ic** (spûr′mē ō jə net′ik), *adj.*

Sper·mo (spûr′mō), *n. Class. Myth.* a daughter of King Anius of Delos who had the power of changing whatever she wished into grain.

spermo-, a combining form of **sperm**[1]: *spermophyte.* Also, *esp. before a vowel,* **sperm-.**

sper·mo·go·ni·um (spûr′mə gō′nē əm), *n., pl.* **-ni·a** (-nē ə). *Bot.* one of the cup-shaped or flask-shaped receptacles in which the spermatia of certain thallophytic plants are produced. [SPERMO- + -GONIUM]

sperm′ oil′, *Chem.* a yellow, thin, water-insoluble liquid obtained from the sperm whale, used chiefly as a lubricant in light machinery, as watches, clocks, and scientific apparatus.

-spermous, a word element used to form adjectives corresponding to nouns with stems ending in **-sperm:** *gymnospermous.* [-SPERM + -OUS]

sper·mo·phile (spûr′mə fīl′, -fil), *n.* any of various burrowing rodents of the squirrel family, esp. of the genus *Citellus* (or *Spermophilus*), sometimes sufficiently numerous to do much damage to crops, as the ground squirrels, susliks, etc. [SPERMO- + -PHILE, modeled on NL *spermophilus*]

sper·mo·phyte (spûr′mə fīt′), *n. Bot.* spermatophyte. [SPERMO- + -PHYTE, modeled on NL *spermophyta*] —**sper·mo·phyt·ic** (spûr′mə fit′ik), *adj.*

Sperm whale (Length 60 ft.)

sper·mous (spûr′məs), *adj.* of the nature of or pertaining to sperm. [SPERM[1] + -OUS]

sperm′ whale′, a large, square-snouted whale, *Physeter catodon*, valued for its oil and spermaceti.

spe·ro·ne (spə rō′nē; *It.* spe rô′ne), *n.* a porous leucitite containing melanite crystals. [< It: lit., spur, buttress]

Sper·ry (sper′ē), *n.* **Elmer Ambrose,** 1860–1930, U.S. inventor and manufacturer.

sper·ry·lite (sper′ə līt′), *n.* a mineral, platinum arsenide, $PtAs_2$, occurring in minute tin-white crystals, usually cubes: a minor ore of platinum. [named after F. L. *Sperry*, 19th-century Canadian chemist, who found it; see -LITE]

spes·sart·ite (spes′ər tīt′), *n.* a mineral, manganese garnet, containing some iron and yellow or red in color, used as a semiprecious gem. Also called **spes·sar·tine** (spes′ər tēn′, -tin). [named after *Spessart*, a district in Bavaria, where it is found; see -ITE[1]]

spew (spyo͞o), *v.i.* **1.** to discharge the contents of the stomach through the mouth; vomit. —*v.t.* **2.** to eject from the stomach through the mouth; vomit. **3.** to cast forth, gush, or eject, as in disgust, anger, or the like: *The angry sergeant spewed his charges at us.* —*n.* **4.** that which is spewed; vomit. Also, **spue.** [ME; OE *spīw(an);* c. G *speien*, Goth *speiwan*, Icel *spýja*, L *spuere*] —**spew′er,** *n.*

Spey·er (shpī′ər), *n.* a city in SW West Germany, on the Rhine. 35,600 (est. 1955). Also called **Spires.**

Spe·zia (*It.* spe′tsyä), *n.* See **La Spezia.**

sp. gr., specific gravity.

sphac·e·late (sfas′ə lāt′), *v.t., v.i.,* **-lat·ed, -lat·ing.** *Pathol.* to affect or be affected with sphacelus; mortify. [SPHACEL(US) + -ATE[1]] —**sphac′e·la′tion,** *n.* —**sphac′e·lism,** *n.*

sphac·e·lus (sfas′ə ləs), *n. Pathol.* a gangrenous or mortified mass of tissue. [< NL < Gk *sphákelos* gangrene]

sphae·ris·te·ri·um (sfēr′i stēr′ē əm), *n., pl.* **sphae·ris·te·ri·a** (sfēr′i stēr′ē ə). an ancient Roman handball court. [< L < Gk *sphairistḗrion*, deriv. of *sphaîra* ball; see SPHERE]

sphaero-, var. of **sphero-:** *sphaerometer.*

sphag·nous (sfag′nəs), *adj.* pertaining to, abounding in, or consisting of sphagnum. [SPHAGN(UM) + -OUS]

sphag·num (sfag′nəm), *n.* any soft moss of the genus *Sphagnum*, found chiefly on the surface of bogs, used by gardeners in potting and packing plants, by surgeons for dressing wounds, etc. [< NL, alter. of Gk *sphágnos* a moss]

sphal·er·ite (sfal′ə rīt′, sfā′lə-), *n.* a very common mineral, zinc sulfide, ZnS, usually containing some iron and a little cadmium, occurring in yellow, brown, or black crystals or cleavable masses with resinous luster: the principal ore of zinc and cadmium; blackjack; rosin jack. [< Gk *spaler(ós)* slippery, deceptive + -ITE[1]]

sphe·cid (sfē′sid), *adj.* **1.** belonging or pertaining to the *Sphecidae*, a family of solitary wasps, including the mud daubers, sand wasps, etc. —*n.* **2.** a sphecid wasp. [< NL *Sphecid(ae)*, equiv. to *Sphec-* (s. of *Sphex*) name of a genus (< Gk: wasp) + *-idae* -ID[4]]

sphen-, var. of **spheno-** before a vowel: *sphenic.*

sphene (sfēn), *n.* a mineral, calcium titanium silicate, $CaTiSiO_5$, occurring in many rocks, usually in small, wedge-shaped crystals. Also called **titanite.** [< Gk *sphḗn* wedge]

sphe·nic (sfē′nik), *adj.* wedge-shaped. [SPHEN- + -IC]

spheno-, a learned borrowing from Greek meaning "wedge," used in the formation of compound words: *sphenography.* Also, *esp. before a vowel,* **sphen-.** [< NL < Gk *sphḗn* wedge + -o- -o-]

sphe·no·gram (sfē′nə gram′), *n.* a cuneiform character. [SPHENO- + -GRAM[1]]

sphe·nog·ra·phy (sfē nog′rə fē), *n. Rare.* **1.** the art of writing in cuneiform characters. **2.** the study of cuneiform writing. [SPHENO- + -GRAPHY] —**sphe·nog′ra·pher, sphe·nog′ra·phist,** *n.* —**sphe·no·graph·ic** (sfē′nə graf′ik), *adj.*

sphe·noid (sfē′noid), *adj.* Also, **sphe·noi′dal. 1.** wedge-shaped. **2.** *Anat.* of or pertaining to the compound bone of the base of the skull, at the roof of the pharynx. See diag. under **skull.** —*n.* **3.** *Anat.* the sphenoid bone. [< NL *sphēnoīd(ēs)* < Gk *sphēnoeidḗs.* See SPHEN-, -OID]

spher·al (sfēr′əl), *adj.* **1.** of or pertaining to a sphere. **2.** spherical. **3.** symmetrical; perfect in form. [< LL *sphaerāl(is).* See SPHERE, -AL[1]] —**sphe·ral·i·ty** (sfi ral′i tē), *n.*

sphere (sfēr), *n.*, *v.*, **sphered, spher·ing.** —*n.* **1.** a solid geometric figure generated by the revolution of a semicircle about its diameter; a round body whose surface is at all points equidistant from the center. Equation: $x^2 + y^2 + z^2 = r^2$. **2.** any rounded body approximately of this form; a globular mass, shell, etc. **3.** a planet or star; heavenly body. **4.** See **celestial sphere. 5.** *Astron.* any of the transparent, concentric, spherical shells, or layers, in which, according to ancient belief, the planets, stars, and other heavenly bodies were set. **6.** the place or environment within which a person or thing exists; a field of activity or operation: *to be out of one's professional sphere.* **7.** a particular social world, stratum of society, or walk of life: *His social sphere is small.* **8.** a field of something specified: *a sphere of knowledge.* —*v.t.* **9.** to enclose in or as in a sphere. **10.** to form into a sphere. **11.** to place among the heavenly spheres. [< LL *sphēr(a)*, var. of L *sphaera* globe < Gk *sphaîra* ball; r. ME *spere* < OF (*e*)*spere* < LL *spēra*, var. of *sphēra*] —**sphere′less,** *adj.* —**sphere′like′,** *adj.*
—**Syn. 2.** See **ball**[1]. **6.** orbit, area, province, compass, realm, domain. **7.** class, rank.

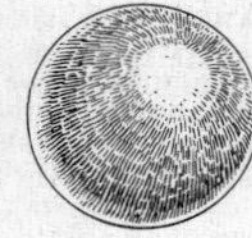
Sphere

-sphere, a combining form of **sphere** (*planisphere*); having a special use in the names of the layers of gases and the like, surrounding the earth and other celestial bodies (*ionosphere*).

sphere′ of in′fluence, 1. any area in which one nation wields dominant power over another or others. **2.** a region where underdeveloped countries or territories are subjected chiefly to economic or political exploitation and domination by a powerful and often imperialistic state.

spher·i·cal (sfer′i kəl), *adj.* **1.** having the form of a sphere; globular. **2.** formed in or on a sphere, as a figure. **3.** of or pertaining to a sphere or spheres. **4.** pertaining to the heavenly bodies, or to their supposed revolving spheres or shells. **5.** pertaining to the heavenly bodies regarded astrologically as exerting influence on mankind and events. Also, **spher′ic.** [< LL *sphēric(us)* (see SPHERICS[1]) + -AL[1]] —**spher′i·cal′i·ty,** *n.* —**spher′i·cal·ly,** *adv.*
—**Syn. 1.** rounded.

spher′ical aberra′tion, variation in focal length of a lens or mirror from center to edge, due to its spherical shape.

spher′ical an′gle, *Geom.* an angle formed by arcs of great circles of a sphere.

spher′ical coor′dinates, *Math.* a system of coordinates for locating a point in space by the length of its radius vector and the angles this vector makes with two perpendicular polar planes.

spher′ical geom′etry, the branch of geometry that deals with figures on spherical surfaces.

spher′ical pol′ygon, *Geom.* a closed figure formed by arcs of great circles of a sphere.

spher′ical sail′ing, a method of navigation in which the curvature of the earth is taken into consideration. Also called **circular sailing.**

spher′ical tri′angle, *Geom.* a triangle formed by arcs of great circles of a sphere.

spher′ical trigonom′etry, the branch of trigonometry that deals with spherical triangles.

sphe·ric·i·ty (sfi ris′i tē), *n.*, *pl.* **-ties.** a spherical state or form. [< NL *sphēricitāt-* (s. of *sphēricitās*), equiv. to LL *sphēric(us)* (see SPHERICS[1]) + *-itāt-* -ITY]

spher·ics[1] (sfer′iks), *n.* (*construed as sing.*) the geometry and trigonometry of figures formed on the surface of a sphere. [< LL *sphēric(us)* < Gk *sphairikós.* See SPHERE, -IC, -ICS]

spher·ics[2] (sfer′iks), *n.* (*construed as sing.*) a branch of meteorology in which weather forecasting and atmospheric conditions are studied by means of electronic devices. [short for ATMOSPHERICS]

sphero-, a combining form of **sphere:** *spherometer.* Also, **sphaero-, -sphere.**

sphe·roid (sfēr′oid), *Geom.* —*n.* **1.** a solid geometrical figure generated by rotating an ellipse about one of its axes. See diag. under **prolate.** —*adj.* **2.** spheroidal. [< L *sphaeroīd(ēs)* < Gk *sphairoeidḗs.* See SPHERE, -OID]

sphe·roi·dal (sfi roid′ᵊl), *adj.* **1.** pertaining to a spheroid or spheroids. **2.** shaped like a spheroid; approximately spherical. Also, **sphe·roi′dic.** [SPHEROID + -AL[1]] —**sphe·roi′dal·ly, sphe·roi′di·cal·ly,** *adv.*

sphe·roi·dic·i·ty (sfēr′oi dis′i tē), *n.* a spheroidal state or form. Also, **sphe·roi·di·ty** (sfi roi′di tē). [SPHEROID + -IC + -ITY]

sphe·rom·e·ter (sfi rom′i tər), *n.* an instrument for measuring the curvature of spheres and curved surfaces. [SPHERO- + -METER, modeled on F *sphéromètre*]

spher·ule (sfer′o͞ol, -yo͞ol, sfēr′-), *n.* a small sphere or spherical body. [< LL *sphaerul(a).* See SPHERE, -ULE] —**spher·u·lar** (sfer′yo͞o lər, sfēr′-), *adj.* —**spher·u·late** (sfer′yo͞o lāt′, -lit, sfēr′-), *adj.*

spher·u·lite (sfer′o͝o līt′, -yo͝o-, sfēr′-), *n.* a rounded aggregate of radiating crystals found in obsidian and other glassy igneous rocks. [SPHERULE + -ITE[1]] —**spher·u·lit·ic** (sfer′o͝o lit′ik, -yo͝o-, sfēr′-), *adj.*

spher·y (sfēr′ē), *adj.* **1.** having the form of a sphere; spherelike. **2.** pertaining to or resembling a heavenly body; starlike. [SPHERE + -Y[1]]

sphinc·ter (sfingk′tər), *n.* *Anat.* a circular band of voluntary or involuntary muscle which encircles an orifice of the body or one of its hollow organs. [< LL < Gk *sphinktḗr*, equiv. to *sphink-* (var. of *sphing-*, root of *sphíngein* to hold tight) + *-tēr* suffix denoting agent] —**sphinc′ter·al, sphinc·te·ri·al** (sfingk tēr′ē əl), **sphinc·ter·ic** (sfingk ter′ik), **sphinc·ter·ate** (sfingk′tər it, -tə rāt′), *adj.*

sphin·go·my·e·lin (sfing′gō mī′ə lin), *n.* *Biochem.* any of the class of phospholipids occurring in the brain, spinal cord, kidney, liver, and egg yolk, composed of phosphoric acid, choline, sphingosine, and a fatty acid. [*sphingo-* (< Gk *sphíng(ein)* (to) draw tight) + MYELIN]

sphin·go·sine (sfing′gə sēn′, -sin), *n.* *Biochem.* a basic unsaturated amino alcohol, $C_{18}H_{33}(OH)_2NH_2$, produced by the hydrolysis of sphingomyelin. [*sphingo-* (see SPINGOMYELIN) + connective *-s-* + -INE[2]]

sphinx (sfingks), *n.*, *pl.* **sphinx·es, sphin·ges** (sfin′jēz). **1.** (in ancient Egypt) **a.** a figure of an imaginary creature having the head of a man or an animal and the body of a lion. **b.** (*usually cap.*) the colossal recumbent stone figure of this kind near the pyramids of Gizeh. **2.** (*cap.*) *Class. Myth.* a monster, daughter of Echidna, usually represented as having the head and breast of a woman, the body of a lion, and the wings of an eagle. Seated on a rock outside of Thebes, she proposed a riddle to travelers, killing them when they answered incorrectly, as all did before Oedipus. When he answered her riddle correctly the Sphinx killed herself. **3.** any similar monster. **4.** a mysterious, inscrutable person or thing, esp. one given to enigmatic questions or answers. [late ME < L < Gk, equiv. to *sphink-* (see SPHINCTER) + *-s* nom. sing. ending; lit., she who holds (her victims) fast] —**sphin·gine** (sfin′jīn, -jin), **sphinx′i·an, sphinx′like′,** *adj.*

Sphinx (Egyptian)

sphinx′ moth′. See **hawk moth.**

sphra·gis·tic (sfrə jis′tik), *adj.* of or pertaining to seals or signet rings. [< LGk *sphrāgistik(ós)*, equiv. to Gk *sphrāgist(ós)* (ptp. of *sphrāgízein* to seal, deriv. of *sphrāgís* a seal) + *-ikos* -IC]

sphra·gis·tics (sfrə jis′tiks), *n.* (*construed as sing.*) the scientific study of seals or signet rings. [see SPHRAGISTIC, -ICS]

sp. ht., specific heat.

sphyg·mic (sfig′mik), *adj.* *Physiol.*, *Med.* of or pertaining to the pulse. [< Gk *sphygmik(ós)*, equiv. to *sphygm(ós)* SPHYGMUS + *-ikos* -IC]

sphygmo-, a combining form of **sphygmus:** *sphygmometer.*

sphyg·mo·gram (sfig′mə gram′), *n.* a tracing or diagram produced by a sphygmograph. [SPHYGMO- + -GRAM[1]]

sphyg·mo·graph (sfig′mə graf′, -gräf′), *n.* an instrument for recording the rapidity, strength, and uniformity of the arterial pulse. [SPHYGMO- + -GRAPH] —**sphyg·mo·graph·ic** (sfig′mə graf′ik), *adj.* —**sphyg·mog·ra·phy** (sfig mog′rə fē), *n.*

sphyg·moid (sfig′moid), *adj.* *Physiol.*, *Med.* resembling the pulse; pulselike. [SPHYGM(O)- + -OID]

sphyg·mo·ma·nom·e·ter (sfig′mō mə nom′i tər), *n.* *Physiol.* an instrument for measuring the pressure of the blood in an artery. [SPHYGMO- + MANOMETER] —**sphyg·mo·man·o·met·ric** (sfig′mō man′ə me′trik), *adj.* —**sphyg′mo·ma·nom′e·try,** *n.*

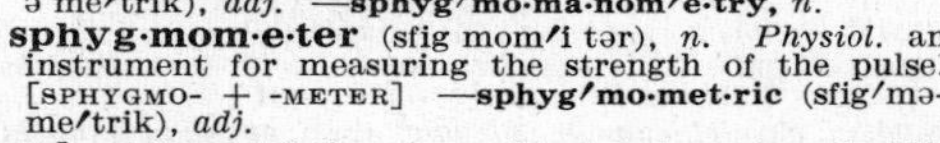
Sphygmomanometer

sphyg·mom·e·ter (sfig mom′i tər), *n.* *Physiol.* an instrument for measuring the strength of the pulse. [SPHYGMO- + -METER] —**sphyg′mo·met·ric** (sfig′mə me′trik), *adj.*

sphyg·mus (sfig′məs), *n.* *Physiol.* the pulse. [< NL < Gk *sphygmós* a throbbing, pulsation; cf. ASPHYXIA]

spic (spik), *n.* *Offensive.* a Spanish-American person. Also, **spik, spick.** [? from a mispronunciation of SPEAK]

spi·ca (spī′kə), *n.*, *pl.* **-cae** (-sē), **-cas** for 1, 2. **1.** spike[2]. **2.** a type of bandage extending from an extremity to the trunk by means of successive turns and crosses. **3.** (*cap.*) *Astron.* a first-magnitude star in the constellation Virgo. [< L: ear of grain]

spi·cate (spī′kāt), *adj.* *Bot.* **1.** having spikes, as a plant. **2.** arranged in spikes, as flowers. **3.** in the form of a spike, as in inflorescence. [< L *spīcāt(us)*, equiv. to *spīc(a)* SPICA + *-ātus* -ATE[1]]

spic·ca·to (spi kä′tō; *It.* spēk kä′tô), *adj.* (of violin music) performed with short, abrupt, rebounding motions of the bow. [< It, equiv. to *spicc-* (s. of *spiccare* to detach) + *-ato* < L *-ātus* -ATE[1]]

spice (spīs), *n.*, *v.*, **spiced, spic·ing.** —*n.* **1.** any of a class of pungent or aromatic substances of vegetable origin, as pepper, cinnamon, cloves, and the like, used as seasoning, preservatives, etc. **2.** such substances collectively or as material: *Cookies without spice can be tasteless.* **3.** *Poetic.* a spicy or aromatic odor or fragrance. **4.** something that gives zest: *a spice of humor in his solemnity.* **5.** a piquant, interesting element or quality; zest; piquancy: *The anecdotes lent spice to his talk.* **6.** *Archaic.* a small quantity of something; trace; bit. —*v.t.* **7.** to prepare or season with a spice or spices. **8.** to give zest, piquancy, or interest to by something added. [ME, OE < LL **spīcea* aromatic herb, n. use of fem. of L *spīceus* pertaining to plants with spiky tufts or heads, equiv. to *spīc(a)* SPIKE[2] + *-eus* -EOUS; confused with L *speciēs* shape, form, kind, sort, whence LL *speciēs* (pl.) spices] —**spice′a·ble,** *adj.* —**spice′less,** *adj.* —**spice′like′,** *adj.*

spice·ber·ry (spīs′ber′ē, -bə rē), *n.*, *pl.* **-ries. 1.** the checkerberry or American wintergreen, *Gaultheria procumbens.* **2.** a Caribbean, myrtaceous tree, *Eugenia rhombea*, cultivated in Florida for its black or orange fruit. [SPICE + BERRY]

spice′ box′, a box containing small drawers for holding individual spices.

spice·bush (spīs′bo͝osh′), *n.* **1.** Also called **spicewood.** a yellow-flowered, lauraceous shrub, *Lindera Benzoin*, of North America, whose bark and leaves have a spicy odor. **2.** a North American shrub, *Calycanthus occidentalis*, having fragrant, light-brown flowers. Also called **Benjamin-bush.** [SPICE + BUSH[1]]

spice′bush silk′ moth′. See **promethea moth.**

spice′bush swal′lowtail, a swallowtail butterfly, *Papilio troilus*, having a dark body with yellow spots on the forewings and greenish hind wings. Also called **troilus butterfly.**

Spice′ Is′lands, Moluccas.

spic·er·y (spī′sə rē), *n.*, *pl.* **-er·ies** for 3. **1.** spices. **2.** spicy flavor or fragrance. **3.** *Archaic.* a storeroom or place for spices. [ME *spicerie* < OF (*e*)*spicerie.* See SPICE, -ERY]

spice·wood (spīs′wo͝od′), *n.* spicebush (def. 1). [SPICE + WOOD[1]]

spic·y (spī′sē), *adj.*, **spic·i·er, spic·i·est.** spicy.

spick (spik), *n.* spic.

spick-and-span (spik′ən span′), *adj.* **1.** spotlessly clean and neat: *a spick-and-span kitchen.* **2.** perfectly new; fresh. —*adv.* **3.** in a spick-and-span manner. [short for *spick-and-span-new*, alliterative extension of SPAN-NEW]

spic·u·la (spik′yə lə), *n.*, *pl.* **-lae** (-lē′). a spicule. [< NL, ML, equiv. to L *spīc(a)* SPIKE[2] + *-ula* -ULE]

spic·u·late (spik′yə lāt′, -lit), *adj.* **1.** having the form of a spicule. **2.** covered with or having spicules; consisting of spicules. Also, **spic·u·lar** (spik′yə lər). [< L *spīculāt(us)*, equiv. to *spīcul(um)* (see SPICULE) + *-ātus* -ATE[1]]

spic·ule (spik′yo͞ol), *n.* **1.** a small or minute, slender, sharp-pointed body or part; a small, needlelike crystal, process, or the like. **2.** *Zool.* one of the small, hard, calcareous or siliceous bodies which serve as the skeletal elements of various animals. **3.** *Astron.* a jet of gas several hundred miles in diameter rising from the sun's surface to heights of 3,000 to 6,000 miles. [< L *spīcul(um)*, equiv. to *spīc(a)* SPIKE[2] + *-ulum* -ULE]

spic·u·lum (spik′yə ləm), *n.*, *pl.* **-la** (-lə). *Zool.* a small, needlelike body, part, process, or the like. [< L; see SPICULE]

spic·y (spī′sē), *adj.*, **spic·i·er, spic·i·est. 1.** seasoned with or containing spice: *a spicy salad dressing.* **2.** characteristic or suggestive of spice. **3.** of the nature of or resembling spice. **4.** abounding in or yielding spices. **5.** aromatic or fragrant. **6.** piquant or pungent: *spicy criticism.* **7.** of a slightly improper or risqué nature; somewhat sexy: *a spicy novel.* **8.** *Informal.* full of spirit; lively. Also, **spicey.** [SPICE + -Y[1]] —**spic′i·ly,** *adv.* —**spic′i·ness,** *n.*
—**Syn. 6.** hot, sharp, peppery.

spi·der (spī′dər), *n.* **1.** any of numerous predaceous arachnids of the order *Araneae* (*Araneida*), most of which spin webs that serve as nests and as traps for prey. **2.** (loosely) any of various other arachnids resembling or suggesting these. **3.** any of various things resembling or suggesting a spider. **4.** a frying pan, originally one with legs or feet. **5.** a trivet or tripod, as for supporting a pot or pan on a hearth. **6.** *Mach.* **a.** a part having a number of radiating spokes or arms, usually not connected at their outer ends. **b.** Also called **cross.** (in a universal joint) a crosslike part pivoted between the forked ends of two shafts to transmit motion between them. **7.** an evil person who entraps or lures others by his wiles. **8.** a device attached to a cultivator, for pulverizing the soil. [ME *spithre*, OE *spīthra*; c. Dan *spinder*, lit., spinner; see SPIN] —**spi′der·less,** *adj.* —**spi′der·like′,** *adj.*

Spider, *Argiope aurantia* (Length ¾ in.)

spi′der band′, *Naut.* See **futtock band.**

spi′der bug′. See **thread-legged bug.**

spi′der crab′, any of various crabs having long, slender legs and a comparatively small, triangular body.

spi′der fly′, *Angling.* an artificial fly having a hackle body, little or no tail, no wings, and unusually long legs, dressed to resemble a spider.

spi·der·hunt·er (spī′dər hun′tər), *n.* any of several sunbirds of the genus *Arachnothera*, of southwestern Asia, having dull-colored plumage and a long bill. [SPIDER + HUNTER]

spi′der-leg ta′ble (spī′dər leg′), a gate-leg table having extremely slender uprights.

spi′der lil′y, 1. any of several tropical American, amaryllidaceous herbs of the genus *Hymenocallis*, having fragrant, tubular flowers. **2.** a spiderwort of the genus *Tradescantia.*

spi·der·ling (spī′dər ling), *n.* the young of a spider. Also, **spi·der·let** (spī′dər lit). [SPIDER + -LING[1]]

spi′der mon′key, any of several tropical American monkeys of the genus *Ateles*, having a slender body, long, slender limbs, and a long, prehensile tail.

Spider monkey, genus *Ateles* (Total length 4½ ft.; tail 2½ ft.)

spi′der pha′eton, a lightly built carriage with a very high body and large, slender wheels, having a covered seat for the driver and an open seat for a footman on the back.

spi′der wasp′, any of certain wasps, esp. of the family *Pompilidae*, that provision their nests with paralyzed spiders.

spi′der web′, the web, usually characteristic in form of its family or genus and made of interlaced threads of viscous fluid that harden on exposure to air, that is spun by a spider to catch its prey. Also, **spi′der's web′.**

spi·der·web (spī′dər web′), *v.t.*, **-webbed, -web·bing.** to cover with a spider web or a network of fine lines resembling a spider web. [v. use of SPIDER WEB]

spi·der·wort (spī′dər wûrt′), *n.* **1.** any herb of the genus *Tradescantia*, having blue, purple, or rose-colored flowers. **2.** any of several related plants. [SPIDER + WORT[2]]

spi·der·y (spī′də rē), *adj.* **1.** like a spider or a spider's web. **2.** full of spiders. [SPIDER + -Y[1]]

spie·gel·ei·sen (spē′gəl ī′zən), *n.* a lustrous, crystalline pig iron containing a large amount of manganese, sometimes 15 percent or more, used in making steel. Also called **spie′gel, spie′gel i′ron.** [< G, equiv. to *Spiegel* mirror + *Eisen* iron]

spiel[1] (spēl, shpēl), *Informal.* —*n.* **1.** a usually high-flown talk or speech, esp. for the purpose of luring people to a movie, a sale, etc.; pitch. —*v.i.* **2.** to speak extravagantly. [< G (dial.): gossip, talk; cf. SPELL[2]]

spiel[2] (spēl), *n. Scot.* a curling match between persons belonging to the same club. [shortened form of BONSPIEL]

spiel·er (spē′lər), *n.* **1.** a barker, as at a circus sideshow. **2.** a person with an extravagant line of talk. **3.** *Austral.* a swindler. **4.** *U.S. Slang.* an announcer for radio or television, esp. one who gives commercials. **5.** *Brit. Slang.* a gambling den. [< G; see SPIEL[1], -ER[1]]

spi·er[1] (spī′ər), *n.* a person who spies, watches, or discovers. [ME; see SPY[1], -ER[1]]

spier[2] (spēr), *n.* (in medieval British architecture) an architectural screen, esp. one dividing the hall of a house from a passage. Also, **speer, spere.** [ME *spere;* akin to SPAR[1], SPEAR]

spier[3] (spēr), *v.i., v.t. Scot. and North Eng.* speer.

spiff·y (spif′ē), *adj.,* **spiff·i·er, spiff·i·est.** *Slang.* spruce; smart; fine. Also, **spif·fing** (spif′ing); *esp. Brit.,* **spivvy, spivving.** [dial. *spiff* well-dressed (< ?) + -Y[1]] —**spiff′i·ly,** *adv.* —**spiff′i·ness,** *n.*

spif·li·cat·ed (spif′lə kā′tid), *adj. Slang.* moderately intoxicated. [*spiflicate* to beat, overcome (< ?) + -ED[2]]

spig·ot (spig′ət), *n.* **1.** a small peg or plug for stopping the vent of a cask. **2.** a peg or plug for stopping the passage of liquid in a faucet or cock. **3.** a faucet or cock for controlling the flow of liquid from a pipe or the like. **4.** the end of a pipe which enters the enlarged end of another pipe to form a joint. [ME *spigot,* perh. < OF *(e)spigot < OPr *espig(a)* (< L *spīca* SPIKE[2]) + OF *-ot* dim. suffix]

spik (spik), *n.* spic.

spike[1] (spīk), *n., v.,* **spiked, spik·ing.** —*n.* **1.** a naillike fastener, 3 to 12 inches long and proportionately thicker than a common nail, for fastening together heavy timbers or railroad track. **2.** something resembling such a nail; a stiff, sharp-pointed piece or part: *to set spikes in the top of a cement wall.* **3.** a sharp-pointed piece of metal set with the point outward, as on a weapon. **4.** a rectangular or naillike metal projection on the heel and sole of a shoe, as of a baseball player or a runner for improving traction. **5.** **spikes,** a pair of shoes having such projections. **6.** the straight, unbranched antler of a young deer. **7.** a young mackerel about six inches long. —*v.t.* **8.** to fasten or secure with a spike or spikes. **9.** to provide or set with a spike or spikes. **10.** to pierce with or impale on a spike. **11.** to set or stud with something suggesting spikes. **12.** to injure (another player or a competitor) with the spikes of one's shoe, as in baseball. **13.** *Volleyball.* to hit (a ball in the air) with a powerful, overarm motion from a position close to the net so as to cause it to travel almost straight down into the court of the opponents. **14.** to render (a muzzle-loading gun) useless by driving a spike into the touchhole. **15.** to make ineffective; frustrate the action or purpose of: *to spike a rumor; to spike someone's chances for promotion.* **16.** *Informal.* to add alcoholic liquor to (a drink). **17.** *Journalism Slang.* to refuse (a story) by or as if by placing on a spindle. **18.** **spike someone's guns.** See **gun**[1] (def. 10). [ME *spik(e)* < Scand or D; cf. Icel *spīk* splinter, Sw *spik,* MD *spīke* nail; c. OE *spīc-* (in *spīcing* nail); all << L *spīca* (see SPIKE[2])] —**spike′like′,** *adj.*

A B C

Spikes
A, Barge spike; B, Large cut nail; C, Railroad spike

spike[2] (spīk), *n.* **1.** an ear, as of wheat or other grain. **2.** *Bot.* an inflorescence in which the flowers are sessile, or apparently so, along an elongated, unbranched axis. [< L *spīc(a)* spike, sharp point, ear of grain; akin to SPILE[1], SPINE, SPIRE[1]]

spike′ bow′sprit, *Naut.* a spar combining a bowsprit and jib boom in one piece. Also called **horn bowsprit.**

spike·dace (spīk′dās′), *n., pl.* **-dac·es** (*esp. collectively*) **-dace.** a scaleless cyprinid fish, *Meda fulgida,* of the Gila River system in New Mexico and Arizona, having two dorsal spines. [SPIKE[1] + DACE]

spiked′ al′der. See **sweet pepperbush.**

spike·fish (spīk′fish′), *n., pl.* (*esp. collectively*) **-fish,** (*esp. referring to two or more kinds or species*) **-fish·es.** **1.** any of several marine fishes of the family *Triacanthodidae.* **2.** a billfish. [SPIKE[1] + FISH]

spike′ heath′, an evergreen shrub, *Bruckenthalia spiculifolia,* of southeastern Europe and Asia Minor, having bell-shaped, pink flowers, growing in gritty soil.

spike′ heel′, a very high heel that tapers to a narrow base, used on women's shoes.

spike′ lav′ender, a lavender, *Lavandula latifolia,* having spikes of pale-purple flowers, and yielding an oil used in painting.

spike·let (spīk′lit), *n. Bot.* a small or secondary spike in grasses; one of the flower clusters, the unit of inflorescence, consisting of two or more flowers and subtended by one or more glumes variously disposed around a common axis. [SPIKE[2] + -LET]

spike·nard (spīk′nərd, -närd), *n.* **1.** an aromatic, East Indian, valerianaceous plant, *Nardostachys Jatamansi,* believed to be the nard of the ancients. **2.** an aromatic substance used by the ancients, supposed to be obtained from this plant. **3.** any of various other plants, esp. an American, araliaceous herb, *Aralia racemosa,* having an aromatic root. [ME < ML *spīca nardī.* See SPIKE[2], NARD]

spike-pitch (spīk′pich′), *v.t., v.i.* to pitch (hay, straw, or the like) with a pitchfork. —**spike′-pitch′er,** *n.*

spik·er (spī′kər), *n.* a pointed, perforated tube connected to a garden hose, pushed into the soil for deep watering. [SPIKE[1] + -ER[1]]

spik·y (spī′kē), *adj.,* **spik·i·er, spik·i·est.** **1.** having a spike or spikes. **2.** having the form of a spike; spikelike. [SPIKE[1] + -Y[1]] —**spik′i·ly,** *adv.* —**spik′i·ness,** *n.*

spile[1] (spīl), *n., v.,* **spiled, spil·ing.** —*n.* **1.** a peg or plug of wood, esp. one used as a spigot. **2.** a spout for conducting sap from the sugar maple. **3.** a heavy wooden stake or pile. **4.** *Mining.* forepole. —*v.t.* **5.** to stop up (a hole) with a spile or peg. **6.** to furnish with a spigot or spout, as for drawing off a liquid. **7.** to tap by means of a spile. **8.** to furnish, strengthen, or support with spiles or piles. [< MD or MLG *spile* splinter, peg; c. G *Speil;* akin to SPIKE[1], SPINE, SPIRE[1]]

spile[2] (spīl), *v.t., v.i.,* **spiled, spiling,** *n. Eye Dialect.* spoil.

spil·i·kin (spil′ə kin), *n.* spillikin.

spil·ing[1] (spī′ling), *n.* piles; spiles. [?]

spil·ing[2] (spī′ling), *n. Shipbuilding.* the curve of a tapered plate of strake. [?]

spill[1] (spil), *v.,* **spilled** or **spilt, spill·ing,** *n.* —*v.t.* **1.** to cause or allow to run or fall from a container, esp. accidentally or wastefully: *to spill a bag of marbles; to spill milk.* **2.** to shed (blood), as in killing or wounding. **3.** to scatter: *to spill papers all over everything.* **4.** *Naut.* **a.** to let the wind out of (a sail). **b.** to lose (wind) from a sail. **5.** *Informal.* to cause to fall from a horse, vehicle, or the like: *His horse spilled him.* **6.** *Slang.* to divulge, disclose, or tell: *Don't spill the secret.* —*v.i.* **7.** (of a liquid, loose particles, etc.) to run or escape from a container, esp. by accident or in careless handling. —*n.* **8.** a spilling, as of liquid. **9.** a quantity spilled. **10.** the mark made by something spilled. **11.** a spillway. **12.** Also called **spill′ light′.** superfluous or useless light rays, as from theatrical or photographic lighting units. **13.** *Theat.* an area of a stage illuminated by spill light. **14.** *Informal.* a throw or fall from a horse, vehicle, or the like: *He broke his arm in a spill.* [ME *spill(en),* OE *spillan* to destroy; c. MHG, MD *spillen;* akin to SPOIL]

spill[2] (spil), *n.* **1.** a splinter. **2.** a slender piece of wood or of twisted paper, for lighting candles, lamps, etc. **3.** a peg made of metal. **4.** a small pin for stopping a cask; spile. **5.** *Mining.* forepole. [ME *spille;* akin to SPILE[1]]

spill·age (spil′ij), *n.* **1.** the act, process, or an instance of spilling. **2.** an amount which spills or is spilled. [SPILL[1] + -AGE]

spil·li·kin (spil′ə kin), *n.* **1.** a jackstraw. **2.** **spillikins,** (*construed as sing.*) the game of jackstraws. Also, **spilikin.** [var. of *spellican* < obs. D *spelleken,* equiv. to *spelle* peg, pin + *-ken* -KIN]

spill′ing line′, *Naut.* a line for gathering in the foot of a sail in order to spill the wind prior to furling or reefing.

spill·o·ver (spil′ō′vər), *n.* **1.** the act of spilling over. **2.** that which is spilled over; overflow. [n. use of v. phrase *spill over*]

spill·pipe (spil′pīp′), *n. Naut.* a pipelike passage through which anchor chain passes in and out of a chain locker. Also called **deckpipe, naval pipe, spurling pipe.** [SPILL[1] + PIPE[1]]

spill·way (spil′wā′), *n.* a passageway through which surplus water escapes from a reservoir, lake, or the like. [SPILL[1] + WAY]

spi·lo·site (spī′lə sīt′), *n. Geol.* a schistose rock spotted with incipient metacrysts. [< Gk *spílos* spot, speck + -ITE[1]]

spilt (spilt), *v.* a pt. and pp. of **spill**[1].

spilth (spilth), *n.* **1.** spillage (def. 1). **2.** that which is spilled. **3.** refuse; trash. [SPILL[1] + -TH[1]]

spin (spin), *v.,* **spun** or (*Archaic*) **span; spun; spin·ning;** *n.* —*v.t.* **1.** to make (yarn) by drawing out, twisting, and winding fibers: *Pioneer women spun yarn on spinning wheels.* **2.** to form (the fibers of any material) into thread or yarn: *The machine spins nylon thread.* **3.** (of spiders, silkworms, etc.) to produce (a thread, cobweb, gossamer, silk, etc.) by extruding from the body a long, slender filament of a natural viscous matter that hardens in the air. **4.** to cause to turn around rapidly, as on an axis; twirl; whirl: *to spin a coin on a table.* **5.** *Metalworking.* to shape (sheet metal) into a hollow, rounded form by pressure from a tool while rotating the metal on a lathe or wheel. **6.** to produce, fabricate, or evolve in a manner suggestive of spinning thread: *to spin a tale of sailing ships and bygone days.* **7.** *Rocketry.* to cause intentionally (a rocket or guided missile) to undergo a roll. **8.** to draw out, protract, or prolong (often fol. by *out*): *He spun the project out for over three years.* **9.** *Brit.* to flunk a student in an examination or a term's work. —*v.i.* **10.** to revolve or rotate rapidly, as the earth, a top, etc. **11.** to produce a thread from the body, as spiders, silkworms, etc. **12.** to produce yarn or thread by spinning. **13.** to move, go, run, ride, or travel rapidly. **14.** to have a sensation of whirling; reel: *My head began to spin and I fainted.* **15.** to fish with a spinning or revolving bait. **16.** **spin off,** to create something new, as a company, assets, or the like, without detracting from or affecting the relative size or stability of the original: *After the acquisition, the company was required to spin off about a third of its assets.* —*n.* **17.** the act of causing a spinning or whirling motion. **18.** a spinning motion given to a ball or other object when thrown. **19.** a downward movement or trend, esp. one that is sudden, alarming, etc.: *Steel prices went into a spin.* **20.** a rapid run, ride, drive, or the like, as for exercise or enjoyment: *They went for a spin in the car.* **21.** Also called **tailspin, tail spin.** *Aeron.* a maneuver in which an airplane descends in a vertical direction along a helical path of large pitch and small radius at an angle of attack greater than the critical angle, dangerous when not done intentionally or under control. **22.** *Rocketry.* **a.** the act of intentionally causing a rocket or guided missile to undergo a roll. **b.** a roll so caused. **23.** *Physics.* the component of angular momentum of a particle or atom which the particle has when at rest. **24.** *Australian.* a run of luck; fate. [ME *spinne(n),* OE *spinnan;* c. D, G *spinnen,* Icel *spinna,* Goth *spinnan*] —**spin′na·bil′i·ty,** *n.* —**spin′na·ble,** *adj.*
—**Syn. 6.** develop, narrate, relate. **8.** extend, lengthen. **10.** gyrate. See **turn.**

spi·na (spī′nə), *n., pl.* **-nae** (-nē). *Anat., Zool.* a spine or spinelike projection. [< L: thorn, backbone; see SPINE]

spin·a·cene (spin′ə sēn′, spī′nə-), *n. Biochem.* squalene. [< NL *Spinac(ia)* + -ENE]

spi·na·ceous (spi nā′shəs), *adj.* pertaining to or of the nature of spinach; belonging to the *Chenopodiaceae,* the spinach or goosefoot family of plants. [< NL *Spin(acia)* + -ACEOUS]

spin·ach (spin′ich), *n.* **1.** an herbaceous annual, *Spinacia oleracea,* cultivated for its succulent leaves. **2.** the leaves. [< MF *(e)spinache, (e)spinage* < OSp *espinaca,* alter. of Ar *isfānākh* < Pers] —**spin′ach-like′,** *adj.*

spin′ach dock′. See **herb patience.**

spin·ach-rhu·barb (spin′ich rōō′bärb), *n.* a perennial herb, *Rumex abyssinicus,* of Abyssinia, having leaves that are sometimes used as spinach and leafstalks sometimes used as rhubarb.

spi·nal (spīn′əl), *adj.* **1.** of, pertaining to, or belonging to a spine or thornlike structure, esp. to the backbone. —*n.* **2.** *Med.* a spinal anesthetic. [< L *spīnāl(is),* equiv. to *spīn(a)* SPINA + *-ālis* -AL[1]] —**spi′nal·ly,** *adv.*

spi′nal acces′sory nerve′. See **accessory nerve.**

spi′nal anesthe′sia, *Med.* anesthesia produced by the injection of an anesthetic into the spinal canal which reduces sensitivity to pain without loss of consciousness.

spi′nal canal′, the tube formed by the vertebrae in which the spinal cord and its membranes are located. See diag. under **vertebra.**

spi′nal col′umn, the series of vertebrae in a vertebrate animal forming the axis of the skeleton and protecting the spinal cord; spine; backbone. Also called **vertebral column.**

spi′nal cord′, the cord of nerve tissue extending through the spinal canal of the spinal column.

spi′nal tap′, the withdrawal of spinal fluid, often for replacement by an anesthetic.

A B C D E side view
A B C D E front view

Spinal column (Human)
Vertebrae: A, Seven cervical; B, Twelve dorsal; C, Five lumbar; D, Five sacral; E, Four caudal or coccygeal, forming a coccyx

spin′ cast′ing, spinning (def. 2). —**spin′ cast′er.**

Spin·dale (spin′dāl′), *n.* a town in S North Carolina. 4082 (1960).

spin·dle (spin′dəl), *n., adj., v.,* **-dled, -dling.** —*n.* **1.** a rounded rod, usually of wood, tapering toward each end, used in hand-spinning to twist into thread the fibers drawn from the mass on the distaff, and on which the thread is wound as it is spun. **2.** the rod on a spinning wheel by which the thread is twisted and on which it is wound. **3.** one of the rods of a spinning machine that bear the bobbins on which the spun thread is wound. **4.** any rod or pin suggestive of a spindle used in spinning, as one which turns around or on which something turns; an axle, axis, or shaft. **5.** either of two shafts or arbors that support the work on a lathe, one **(live spindle)** on the headstock, rotating with and imparting motion to the work, the other **(dead spindle)** on the tailstock, motionless. **6.** a small axis, arbor, or mandrel. **7.** an iron rod or the like, usually with a ball or cage at the top, fixed to a rock, sunken reef, etc., to serve as a guide in navigation. **8.** a measure of yarn, containing, for cotton, 15,120 yards, and for linen, 14,400 yards. **9.** a hydrometer. **10.** *Biol.* the fine threads of achromatic material arranged within the cell, during mitosis, in a spindle-shaped manner. **11.** a short, turned or circular ornament, as in a baluster or stair rail. **12.** a narrow spike set upright on a desk, table, or the like and used to hold cards or papers kept together, as for sorting purposes. —*adj.* **13.** See **spindle side.** —*v.t.* **14.** to give the form of a spindle to. **15.** to provide or equip with a spindle or spindles. **16.** to impale (a card or paper) on a spindle, as for sorting purposes. —*v.i.* **17.** to shoot up, or grow, into a long, slender stalk or stem, as a plant. **18.** to grow tall and slender, often disproportionately so. [ME *spindel* (with intrusive *d*), OE *spin(e)l,* SPIN, -LE; c. G *Spindel*] —**spin′dle·like′,** *adj.*

Spindle

spin·dle·age (spin′dəlij), *n.* total number or capacity of spindles in a mill, area, etc. [SPINDLE + -AGE]

spin·dle·legs (spin′dəl legz′), *n., pl.* **-legs** for 2. **1.** (*construed as pl.*) long, thin legs. **2.** (*construed as sing.*) *Informal.* a tall, thin person with such legs. [SPINDLE + LEG + -S[3]] —**spin·dle-leg·ged** (spin′dəl leg′id, -legd′), *adj.*

spin·dle·shanks (spin′dəl shangks′), *n., pl.* **-shanks.** (*construed as sing. or pl.*) spindlelegs. [SPINDLE + SHANK + -S[3]] —**spin·dle-shanked** (spin′dəl shangkt′), *adj.*

spin′dle side′, the female side or line of descent of a family; distaff side (opposed to *spear side*).

spin′dle tree′, **1.** a European shrub, *Euonymus europaeus,* whose wood was formerly used for making spindles. **2.** any of various allied plants. Also called **prick-timber.**

spin·dling (spind′ling), *adj.* **1.** long or tall and slender, often disproportionately so. **2.** growing into a long, slender stalk or stem, often a too slender or weakly one. —*n.* **3.** a spindling person or thing. [SPINDLE + -ING[2], -ING[1]]

spin·dly (spind′lē), *adj.,* **-dli·er, -dli·est.** long or tall, thin, and usually frail: *The colt wobbled on its spindly legs.* [SPINDLE + -Y[1]]

spin·drift (spin′drift′), *n.* spray swept by a violent wind along the surface of the sea. Also, **spoondrift.** [var. of Scot *speendrift* SPOONDRIFT]

spin-dry (spin′drī′), *v.t.,* **-dried, -dry·ing.** to remove moisture from by centrifugal force, as in an automatic washing machine. —**spin′-dri′er, spin′-dry′er,** *n.*

spine (spīn), *n.* **1.** the spinal or vertebral column; backbone. **2.** any backbonelike part. **3.** a stiff, pointed process or appendage on an animal, as a quill of a porcupine, or a sharp, bony ray in the fin of a fish. **4.** something, as a quality or trait, which constitutes a principal strength; resolution; stamina; backbone: *a situation that would test a man's spine.* **5.** a ridge, as of ground, rock, etc. **6.** a sharp-pointed, hard or woody outgrowth on a plant; thorn. **7.** *Bookbinding.* the back of a book cover or binding, usually indicating the title and author. [late ME < L *spīn(a)* backbone; akin to SPIKE[1], SPILE[1], SPIRE[1]] —**spined,** *adj.* —**spine′like′,** *adj.*

spi·nel (spi nel′, spin′əl), *n.* **1.** any of a group of minerals composed principally of oxides of magnesium, aluminum, iron, manganese, chromium, etc., characterized by their hardness and octahedral crystals. **2.** a mineral of this group, essentially magnesium aluminate, $MgAl_2O_4$, some variables being used as gems. Also called **spi·nelle′.** [< F *spinelle* < It *spinell(a),* equiv. to *spin(a)* thorn (< L) + *-ella* dim. suffix (< L *-illa*)]

spine·less (spīn′lis), *adj.* **1.** having no spines or quills. **2.** having no spine or backbone. **3.** having a weak spine; limp. **4.** without moral force, resolution, or courage; feeble: *a spineless, lily-livered coward.* [SPINE + -LESS] —**spine′less·ly,** *adv.* —**spine′less·ness,** *n.* —**Syn. 4.** weak, irresolute, indecisive. —**Ant. 4.** strong, resolute.

spinel′ ru′by. See **ruby spinel.**

spi·nes·cent (spī nes′ənt), *adj.* **1.** *Bot.* **a.** becoming spinelike. **b.** ending in a spine. **c.** bearing spines. **2.** *Zool.* somewhat spinelike; coarse, as hair. [< LL *spīnēscent-* (s. of *spīnēscēns* growing thorny, prp. of *spīnēscere*). See SPINE, -ESCENT] —**spi·nes′cence,** *n.*

spin·et (spin′it), *n.* **1.** a small harpsichord. **2.** an early, small, square piano. **3.** a small upright piano. [aph. var. of obs. *espinette* < F < It *spinetta,* named after G. *Spinetti,* Venetian craftsman who invented (c1500) an oblong form of the instrument]

spin′ fish′ing, spinning (def. 2). —**spin′ fish′erman.**

Spin·garn (spin′gärn), *n.* **Joel Elias,** 1875–1939, U.S. literary critic, publisher, and editor.

spi·nif·er·ous (spī nif′ər əs), *adj.* abounding in or covered with spines; spiny. Also, **spi·nig·er·ous** (spī nij′ər əs). [< L *spīnifer* spine-bearing (see SPINE, -I-, -FER) + -OUS]

spin·i·fex (spin′ə feks′), *n.* any of the spiny grasses of the genus *Spinifex,* chiefly of Australia, used to bind sand on seashores. [< NL, equiv. to L *spīn(a)* SPINE + *-i-* -I- + *-fex* maker (*fec-,* var. of *fac-,* root of *facere* make, + *-s* nom. sing. ending)]

spink (spiŋk), *n.* See **maiden pink.** [?]

spin·na·ker (spin′ə kər), *n.* *Naut.* a large, triangular sail, sometimes with a light boom (**spin′naker boom′**) attached to its windward clew for control, carried by yachts as a headsail when running before the wind or when the wind is abaft the beam. [appar. SPIN + (*mo*)*naker,* var. of MONIKER; but said to be alter. of *Sphinx,* name of first yacht making regular use of this sail]

spin′naker stay′sail, *Naut.* a relatively small triangular sail, sometimes bent on a headstay abaft a spinnaker to catch the wind.

spin·ner (spin′ər), *n.* **1.** one who or that which spins. **2.** *Angling.* a lure, as a spoon bait, that revolves in the water in trolling and casting. **3.** Also called **spin′ner play′.** *Football.* a play in which the player carrying the ball twirls about, to deceive the other team as to where he intends to hit the line. **4.** *Brit. Informal.* nightjar. [ME *spinnere.* See SPIN, -ER[1]]

spin·ner·et (spin′ə ret′), *n.* **1.** an organ or part by means of which a spider, insect larva, or the like spins a silky thread for its web or cocoon. **2.** Also, **spin′nerette′.** *Textiles.* a thimblelike device with tiny holes through which chemicals are pumped in the spinning of synthetic filaments, as rayon. [SPINNER + -ET]

spin·ner·y (spin′ə rē), *n., pl.* **-ner·ies.** a spinning mill. [SPIN + -ERY]

spin·ney (spin′ē), *n., pl.* **-neys.** *Brit.* **1.** a small wood, thicket, or grove. **2.** a group of trees. [ME < MF (*e*)*spinei* (masc.), (*e*)*spinaie* (fem.); cf. L *spīnēt(um)* thorn-brake, equiv. to *spīn(a)* thorn (see SPINE) + *-ētum* collective suffix]

spin·ning (spin′iŋ), *n.* **1.** the act or process of converting fibrous substances into yarn or thread. Cf. **cap spinning, mule spinning, ring spinning. 2.** Also called **spin casting, spin fishing, thread-line fishing.** *Angling.* act or technique of casting a relatively light lure attached to a threadlike line wound on a stationary spool. [ME; see SPIN, -ING[1]] —**spin′ning·ly,** *adv.*

spin′ning box′. See **centrifugal box.** Also called **spin′ning pot′.**

spin′ning frame′, a machine for drawing, twisting, and winding yarn.

spin′ning jen′ny, an early spinning machine having more than one spindle, enabling a person to spin a number of yarns simultaneously.

spin′ning ring′, ring (def. 20).

spin′ning wheel′, a device formerly used for spinning wool, flax, etc., into yarn or thread, consisting essentially of a single spindle driven by a large wheel operated by hand or foot. [late ME]

Spinning wheel

spin·ny (spin′ē), *n., pl.* **-nies.** *Brit.* spinney.

spi·node (spī′nōd), *n.* cusp (def. 3). [irreg. < L *spīn(a)* spine + NODE]

spin-off (spin′ôf′, -of′), *n.* **1.** *Com.* a process of reorganizing a corporate structure whereby the capital stock of a division or subsidiary of a corporation or of a newly affiliated company is transferred to the stockholders of the parent corporation without an exchange of any part of the stock of the latter. Cf. **split-off** (def. 3), **split-up** (def. 2). **2.** *Television.* a series based upon characters or situations derived from a previous series. [n. use of v. phrase *spin off*]

spi·nose (spī′nōs, spī nōs′), *adj.* *Chiefly Biol.* full of spines; spiniferous; spinous. [< L *spīnōs(us).* See SPINE, -OSE[1]] —**spi′nose·ly,** *adv.* —**spi·nos·i·ty** (spī nos′i tē), *n.*

spi·nous (spī′nəs), *adj.* **1.** covered with or having spines; thorny, as a plant. **2.** armed with or bearing sharp-pointed processes, as an animal; spiniferous. **3.** spinelike. [< L *spīnōsus* (see SPINOSE), with -OUS r. -OSE[1]] —**spi′nous·ness,** *n.*

spi′nous proc′ess, *Anat., Zool.* a spinelike process of a bone, esp. the dorsal projection from the center of the arch of a vertebra.

Spi·no·za (spi nō′zə), *n.* **Ba·ruch** (bə ro͞ok′) or **Be·ne·dict de** (ben′ə dikt də), 1632–77, Dutch philosopher.

Spi·no·zism (spi nō′ziz əm), *n.* the philosophical system of Spinoza, which defines God as the unique substance, as an impersonal deity, and as possessing an infinite number of attributes, of which we know only thought and extension, and an infinite number of modes, each modifying all of the attributes, these attributes and modes being regarded both as proceeding necessarily from the nature of God and as constituents of God. [SPINOZ(A) + -ISM] —**Spi·no′zist,** *n.* —**Spi·no·zis·tic** (spi nō zis′tik, spin′ō-), *adj.*

spin·proof (spin′pro͞of′), *adj.* **1.** (of an airplane) designed so as to be highly resistant to a tailspin. [SPIN + -PROOF]

spin′ quan′tum num′ber, *Physics.* the quantum number that designates the total angular momentum associated with electron spin and has a value of ½ in units of $h/2\pi$.

spin·ster (spin′stər), *n.* **1.** a woman still unmarried beyond the usual age of marrying; an old maid. **2.** *Chiefly Law.* a woman who has never married. **3.** a woman whose occupation is spinning. [late ME *spinnestere.* See SPIN, -STER] —**spin′ster·hood′,** *n.* —**spin′ster·ish,** *adj.* —**spin′ster·ish·ly,** *adv.* —**spin′ster·like′,** *adj.*

spin·thar·i·scope (spin thar′i skōp′), *n.* *Physics.* an instrument for observing scintillations that are produced by alpha particles and that are visible as minute sparks on a phosphorescent screen. [< Gk *spintharí(s),* dim. of *spinthḗr* spark + -SCOPE] —**spin·thar·i·scop·ic** (spin thar′i skop′ik), *adj.*

spin′ the bot′tle, a parlor game in which a boy spins a bottle and receives a kiss from the girl to whom the bottle points on coming to rest.

spin′ the plat′ter, a parlor game in which one member of a group spins a platter on its edge and a designated member of the opposite sex must catch it before it falls or pay a forfeit of a kiss. Also called **spin′ the plate′.**

spi·nule (spī′nyo͞ol, spin′yo͞ol), *n.* *Zool., Bot.* a small spine. [< L *spīnul(a).* See SPINE, -ULE] —**spin·u·lose** (spin′yə lōs′, spīn′-), *adj.*

spin·y (spī′nē), *adj.,* **spin·i·er, spin·i·est. 1.** abounding in or having spines; thorny, as a plant. **2.** covered with or having sharp-pointed processes, as an animal. **3.** in the form of a spine; resembling a spine; spinelike. **4.** troublesome or difficult to handle; thorny: *a spiny problem.* [SPINE + -Y[1]] —**spin′i·ness,** *n.*

spin′y ant′eater, echidna (def. 1).

spin′y cock′lebur, a cocklebur, *Xanthium spinosum,* introduced into North America from Europe.

spin′y dog′fish, any of several dogfish sharks of the genus *Squalus,* having a spine in front of each of the two dorsal fins, esp. *S. acanthias,* found along the coasts of both Europe and America.

spin·y-finned (spī′nē find′), *adj.* *Ichthyol.* having fins with sharp bony rays, as an acanthopterygian.

spin′y liz′ard, any of numerous iguanid lizards of the genus *Sceloporus,* common in North and Central America, usually having keeled scales that may end in a sharp point.

spin′y lob′ster, any of several edible crustaceans of the family *Palinuridae,* differing from the true lobsters in having a spiny shell and lacking the large pincers.

spi·ra (spī′rə), *n., pl.* **-rae** (-rē). *Archit.* a series of moldings at the base of a classical column. [< L < Gk *speîra* anything coiled, wreathed, or twisted; see SPIRE[2]]

spi·ra·cle (spī′rə kəl, spir′ə-), *n.* **1.** a breathing hole; an opening by which a confined space has communication with the outer air; an air hole. **2.** *Zool.* **a.** an aperture or orifice through which air or water passes in the act of respiration, as the blowhole of a cetacean. **b.** an opening in the head of sharks and rays through which water is drawn and passed over gills. **c.** one of the external orifices of a tracheal respiratory system, usually on the sides of the body. See diag. under **insect.** [< L *spīrācul(um)* air-hole, equiv. to *spīrā(re)* (to) breathe + *-culum* -CLE] —**spi·rac·u·lar** (spī rak′yə lər, spi-), *adj.*

spi·rae·a (spī rē′ə), *n.* spirea.

spi·ral (spī′rəl), *n., adj., v.,* **-raled, -ral·ing** or (*esp. Brit.*) **-ralled, -ral·ling.** —*n.* **1.** *Geom.* a plane curve generated by a point moving round a fixed point while constantly receding from or approaching it. **2.** a helix. **3.** a single circle or ring of a spiral or helical curve or object. **4.** a spiral or helical object, formation, or form. **5.** *Aeron.* a maneuver in which an airplane descends in a helix of small pitch and large radius, with the angle of attack within that of the normal flight range. **6.** *Football.* a type of kick or pass in which the ball turns on its longer axis as it flies through the air. **7.** *Econ.* a continuous increase in costs, wages, prices, etc. (**inflationary spiral**), or a decrease in costs, wages, prices, etc. (**deflationary spiral**). —*adj.* **8.** running continuously around a fixed point or center while constantly receding from or approaching it; coiling in a single plane: *a spiral curve.* **9.** coiling around a fixed line or axis in a constantly changing series of planes; helical. **10.** of or of the nature of a spire or coil; spirelike. —*v.i.* **11.** to take a spiral form or course. **12.** *Aeron.* to move an airplane through a spiral course. —*v.t.* **13.** to cause to take a spiral form or course. [< ML *spīrāl(is),* equiv. to *spīr(a)* coil (see SPIRA) + *-ālis* -AL[1]] —**spi·ral·i·ty** (spī ral′i tē), *n.* —**spi′ral·ly,** *adv.*

Spiral (def. 1)

Spirals (def. 4)

spi′ral bev′el gear′, *Mach.* a bevel gear having curved teeth tending to converge on the axis of rotation. Also called **spiral gear.**

spi·ral-bound (spī′rəl bound′), *adj.* (of a set of individual prepunched leaves of a loose-leaf notebook, booklet, etc.) bound together by means of a spiral of wire or plastic that coils through each of several or many holes and around the back of the binding.

spi′ral cas′ing, a spiral passage for directing the water from a penstock around a water turbine and into its rotor at the proper positions and angles. Also called **scroll casing.**

spi′ral gear′, 1. (not in technical use) See **helical gear. 2.** See **spiral bevel gear.**

spi′ral neb′ula, *Astron.* a stellar system having a spiral structure.

spi′ral spring′, a form of spring consisting of a wire coiled in a helix. See illus. under **spring.**

spi·rant (spī′rənt), *Phonet.* —*n.* **1.** fricative. —*adj.* **2.** spirantal. [< L *spīrant-* (s. of *spīrāns,* prp. of *spīrāre* to breathe), equiv. to *spīr-* breathe + *-ant-* -ANT]

spi·ran·tal (spī ran′təl), *adj.* *Phonet.* fricative. Also, **spirant, spi·ran·tic** (spī ran′tik). [SPIRANT + -AL[1]] —**spi′rant·ism,** *n.*

spi·rant·ize (spī′rən tīz′), *v.t.,* **-ized, -iz·ing.** to change into or pronounce as a spirantal sound. [SPIRANT + -IZE] —**spi′rant·i·za′tion,** *n.*

spire[1] (spīər), *n., v.,* **spired, spir·ing.** —*n.* **1.** a tall, acutely pointed pyramidal roof or rooflike construction upon a tower, roof, etc.; steeple. **2.** a similar construction forming the upper part of a steeple. See illus. under **steeple. 3.** a tapering, pointed part of something; a tall, sharp-pointed summit, peak, or the like: *the distant spires of the mountains.* **4.** the highest point or summit of something: *the spire of a hill; the spire of one's profession.* **5.** a sprout or shoot of a plant, as an acrospire of grain, a blade or spear of grass, etc. —*v.i.* **6.** to shoot or rise into spirelike form; rise or extend to a height in the manner of a spire. [ME; OE *spīr* spike, blade; c. Icel *spíra* stalk, MD *spier,* MG *spīr* shoot, sprout, sprig; akin to SPIKE[1], SPILE[1], SPINE] —**spire′less,** *adj.*

spire[2] (spīər), *n.* **1.** a coil or spiral. **2.** one of the series of convolutions of a coil or spiral. **3.** *Zool.* the upper, convoluted part of a spiral shell, above the aperture. [< L *spīr(a);* see SPIRA] —**spire′less,** *adj.*

spi·re·a (spī rē′ə), *n.* any rosaceous herb or shrub of the genus *Spiraea,* having racemes, cymes, panicles, or corymbs of small, white or pink flowers, certain species of which are cultivated as ornamentals. Also, **spiraea.** [< L < Gk *speiraía* meadowsweet]

spired (spīərd), *adj.* having a spire. [SPIRE[1] + -ED[3]]

spire·let (spīər′lit), *n.* a small spire, as on a turret. [SPIRE[1] + -LET]

spire′ light′, a window or ventilator in a spire, having the form of an attenuated dormer.

spi·reme (spī′rēm), *n.* *Biol.* the chromatin of a cell nucleus, when in a continuous or segmented threadlike form, during mitosis. [< Gk *speírēm(a)* coil. See SPIRA, -EME]

Spires (spīərz), *n.* Speyer.

spi·rif·er·ous (spī rif′ər əs), *adj.* **1.** having a spire, or spiral upper part, as a univalve shell. **2.** having spiral appendages, as a brachiopod. [< NL *spirifer* (see SPIRA, -I-, -FER) + -OUS]

spi·ril·lum (spī ril′əm), *n., pl.* **-ril·la** (-ril′ə). *Bacteriol.* **1.** any of several spirally twisted, aerobic bacteria of the genus *Spirillum,* certain species of which are pathogenic for man. See diag. under **bacteria. 2.** any of various similar microorganisms. [< NL, equiv. to L *spīr(a)* (see SPIRA) + *-illum* dim. suffix] —**spi·ril′lar,** *adj.*

spir·it (spir′it), *n.* **1.** the principle of conscious life; the vital principle in man, animating the body or mediating between body and soul. **2.** the incorporeal part of man: *present in spirit though absent in body.* **3.** the soul regarded as separating from the body at death. **4.** conscious, incorporeal being, as opposed to matter: *the world of spirit.* **5.** a supernatural, incorporeal being, esp. one inhabiting a place, object, etc., or having a particular character: *evil spirits.* **6.** a fairy, sprite, or elf. **7.** an angel or demon. **8.** an attitude or principle that inspires, animates, or pervades thought, feeling, or action: *the spirit of reform.* **9.** (*cap.*) the divine influence as an agency working in the heart of man. **10.** a divine, inspiring, or animating being or influence. Num. 11:25; Is. 32:15. **11.** (*cap.*) the third person of the Trinity; Holy Spirit. **12.** the soul or heart as the seat of feelings or sentiments, or as prompting to action: *a man of broken spirit.* **13. spirits,** feelings or mood with regard to exaltation or depression: *low spirits; good spirits.* **14.** excellent disposition or attitude in terms of vigor, courage, firmness of intent, etc.; mettle: *That's the spirit!* **15.** temper or disposition: *meek in spirit.* **16.** an individual as characterized by a given attitude, disposition, character, action, etc.: *A few brave spirits remained to face the danger.* **17.** the dominant tendency or character of anything: *the spirit of the age.* **18.** vigorous sense of membership in a group: *college spirit.* **19.** the general meaning or intent of a statement, document, etc. (opposed to *letter*): *the spirit of the law.* **20.** *Chem.* the essence or active principle of a substance as extracted in liquid form, esp. by distillation. **21.** Often, **spirits.** a strong distilled alcoholic liquor. **22.** *Chiefly Brit.* alcohol. **23.** Also called **essence.** *Pharm.* a solution in alcohol of an essential or volatile principle. **24.** any of certain subtle fluids formerly supposed to permeate the body. **25. out of spirits,** in low spirits; depressed: *We were feeling out of spirits after so many days of rain.* **26. the Spirit,** God. —*adj.* **27.** pertaining to something which works by burning alcoholic spirits: *a spirit stove.* **28.** of or pertaining to spiritualist bodies or activities. —*v.t.* **29.** to animate with fresh ardor or courage; inspirit. **30.** to encourage; urge on or stir up, as to action. **31.** to carry off mysteriously or secretly (often fol. by *away* or *off*): *His captors spirited him away.* [ME < L *spīrit(us)* breathing, equiv. to *spīri-* (akin to *spīrā-,* s. of *spīrāre* to breathe) + *-tus* n. suffix] —**spir′it·like′,** *adj.*
—**Syn. 2.** life, mind, consciousness, essence. **5.** apparition, phantom, shade. See **ghost. 6.** goblin, hobgoblin. **7.** genius. **14.** enthusiasm, energy, zeal, ardor, fire, enterprise. **15.** attitude, mood, humor. **17.** nature, drift, tenor, gist, essence, sense, complexion. **19.** intention, significance, purport.

spir′it com′pass, *Navig.* a wet compass filled with a mixture of alcohol and water.

spir·it·ed (spir′i tid), *adj.* having or showing mettle, courage, vigor, liveliness, etc.: *a spirited defense of poetry.* [SPIRIT + -ED[3]] —**spir′it·ed·ly,** *adv.* —**spir′it·ed·ness,** *n.*
—**Syn.** animated, vivacious, ardent, active, energetic, lively, vigorous, courageous, mettlesome.

spir′it gum′, a special glue used in fastening false hair, as a beard or mustache, to an actor's skin.

spir·it·ing (spir′i ting), *n.* **1.** *Literary.* the action or work of a spirit. **2.** inspiration. [SPIRIT + -ING[1]]

spir·it·ism (spir′i tiz′əm), *n.* the doctrine or practices of spiritualism. [SPIRIT + -ISM] —**spir′it·ist,** *n.* —**spir′it·is′tic,** *adj.*

Spir′it Lake′, a town in NW Iowa. 2685 (1960).

spir·it·less (spir′it lis), *adj.* **1.** without spirit. **2.** without ardor, vigor, zeal, animation, etc.: *a spiritless reply to criticism.* [SPIRIT + -LESS] —**spir′it·less·ly,** *adv.* —**spir′it·less·ness,** *n.*

A B

Spirit level
A, Glass tube for determining level surfaces; B, Glass tube for determining perpendicular surfaces

spir′it lev′el, a device for determining true horizontal or vertical directions by the centering of a bubble in a slightly curved glass tube or tubes filled with alcohol or ether. Also called **level.**

spir′it lev′eling, *Survey.* leveling according to the indications of a spirit level.

spir′it of harts′horn, *Chem.* a colorless, pungent, suffocating, aqueous solution of about 28.5 percent ammonia gas: used chiefly as a detergent, for removing stains, extracting certain vegetable coloring agents, and in the manufacture of ammonium salts. Also, **spir′its of harts′horn.**

Spir′it of Laws′, The, a political tract (1748) by Montesquieu. French, **L'Esprit des Lois.**

spir′it of ni′trous e′ther, *Pharm.* See **ethyl nitrite spirit.**

spi·ri·to·so (spir′i tō′sō; *It.* spē′rē tô′sô), *adj.* spirited; lively (used as a musical direction). [< It; see SPIRIT, -OSE[1]]

spir·i·tous (spir′i təs), *adj.* *Archaic.* of the nature of spirit; immaterial, ethereal, or refined. [SPIRIT + -OUS]

spir′it rap′ping, *Spiritualism.* a form of communication between living persons and the spirits of deceased persons by tapping out messages on a table, board, or the like. —**spir′it rap′per.**

spir′its of tur′pentine, *Chem.* See **oil of turpentine.** Also, **spir′it of tur′pentine.**

spir′its of wine′, alcohol.

spir·it·u·al (spir′i chōō əl), *adj.* **1.** of, or pertaining to, or consisting of spirit; incorporeal. **2.** of or pertaining to the spirit or soul, as distinguished from the physical nature: *a spiritual approach to life.* **3.** closely akin in interests, attitude, outlook, etc.: *the professor's spiritual heir in linguistics.* **4.** of or pertaining to spirits or to spiritualists; supernatural or spiritualistic. **5.** characterized by or suggesting predominance of the spirit; ethereal or delicately refined: *She is more of a spiritual type than her rowdy brother.* **6.** of or pertaining to the spirit as the seat of the moral or religious nature. **7.** of or pertaining to sacred things or matters; religious; devotional; sacred. **8.** of or belonging to the church; ecclesiastical: *lords spiritual and temporal.* **9.** of or relating to the conscious thoughts and emotions. —*n.* **10.** a spiritual or religious song: *Negro spirituals.* **11. spirituals,** affairs of the church. **12.** a spiritual thing or matter. [ME < ML *spīrituāl(is),* equiv. to *spīritu-* (s. of L *spīritus* SPIRIT) + *-ālis* -AL[1]; r. ME *spirituel* < MF] —**spir′it·u·al·ly,** *adv.* —**spir′it·u·al·ness,** *n.*

spir′itual death′, death (def. 8).

spir′itual in′cest, *Eccles.* sexual intercourse between persons who have been baptized or confirmed together.

spir·it·u·al·ise (spir′i chōō ə līz′), *v.t.,* **-ised, -is·ing.** *Chiefly Brit.* spiritualize. —**spir′it·u·al·i·sa′tion,** *n.* —**spir′i·tu·al·is′er,** *n.*

spir·it·u·al·ism (spir′i chōō ə liz′əm), *n.* **1.** the belief or doctrine that the spirits of the dead, surviving after the mortal life, can and do communicate with the living, esp. through a person (a medium) particularly susceptible to their influence. **2.** the practices or the phenomena associated with this belief. **3.** the belief that all reality is spiritual. **4.** *Metaphys.* idealism. **5.** spiritual quality or tendency. **6.** insistence on the spiritual side of things, as in philosophy or religion. [SPIRITUAL + -ISM] —**spir′it·u·al·is′tic,** *adj.*

spir·it·u·al·ist (spir′i chōō ə list), *n.* **1.** an adherent of spiritualism. **2.** a person who concerns himself with or insists on the spiritual side of things. [SPIRITUAL + -IST] —**spir′it·u·al·is′ti·cal·ly,** *adv.*

spir·it·u·al·i·ty (spir′i chōō al′i tē), *n., pl.* **-ties.** **1.** the quality or fact of being spiritual. **2.** incorporeal or immaterial nature. **3.** predominantly spiritual character as shown in thought, life, etc.; spiritual tendency or tone. **4.** Often, **spiritualities.** property or revenue of the church or of an ecclesiastic in his official capacity. [late ME < ML *spīrituālitās.* See SPIRITUAL, -ITY]

spir·it·u·al·ize (spir′i chōō ə līz′), *v.t.,* **-ized, -iz·ing.** **1.** to make spiritual. **2.** to invest with a spiritual meaning. [SPIRITUAL + -IZE] —**spir′it·u·al·i·za′tion,** *n.* —**spir′i·tu·al·iz′er,** *n.*

spir·it·u·al·ty (spir′i chōō əl tē), *n., pl.* **-ties.** **1.** Often, **spiritualties.** ecclesiastical property or revenue. **2.** the body of ecclesiastics; the clergy. [late ME *spiritualte* < MF; see SPIRITUALITY]

spi·ri·tu·el (spir′i chōō el′; *Fr.* spē rē tʏel′), *adj.* **1.** showing or having a refined and graceful mind or wit. **2.** light and airy in movement; ethereal. Also, **spi′ri·tu·elle′.** [< F: lit., SPIRITUAL]

spir·it·u·ous (spir′i chōō əs), *adj.* **1.** containing, of the nature of, or pertaining to alcohol; alcoholic. **2.** (of alcoholic beverages) distilled, rather than fermented. [SPIRITU(AL) + -OUS] —**spir′it·u·ous·ly,** *adv.* —**spir′it·u·ous·ness,** *n.*

spir·i·tus as·per (spir′i təs as′pər; *Lat.* spē′ri tōōs′ äs′per). See **rough breathing.** [< LL]

spi·ri·tus fru·men·ti (spir′i təs frōō men′tī), whiskey. [< NL: lit., the spirit (or life) of grain]

spir·i·tus le·nis (spir′i təs lē′nis; *Lat.* spē′ri tōōs′ le′nis). See **smooth breathing.** [< LL]

spir·i·tus vi·no·sus (spir′i təs vī nō′səs), (in prescriptions) spirits of wine; alcohol. [< L]

spir′it var′nish. See under **varnish** (def. 1).

Spir′it Wres′tler, a Doukhobor.

spir′it writ′ing, writing allegedly produced by spirits or supernatural forces.

spir·ket (spûr′kit), *n.* *Shipbuilding Obs.* a space between adjacent floor timbers. [? akin to OE *spircing* a scattering; see BESPRENT]

spir·ket·ing (spûr′ki ting), *n.* *Naut.* **1.** the outermost planking of a deck. **2.** strakes of ceiling fitted between ports and a deck. Also, *esp. Brit.,* **spir′ket·ting.** [SPIRKET + -ING[1]]

spiro-[1], a learned borrowing from Latin used, with the meaning "respiration," in the formation of compound words: *spirograph.* [comb. form of L *spīrāre* to breathe]

spiro-[2], a learned borrowing from Latin and Greek meaning "coil," "spiral," used in the formation of compound words: *spirochete.* [comb. form of L *spīra* < Gk *speîra* coil]

spi·ro·chae·to·sis (spī′rə kē tō′sis), *n.* *Pathol.* spirochetosis. —**spi·ro·chae·tot·ic** (spī′rə kē tot′ik), *adj.*

spi·ro·chete (spī′rə kēt′), *n.* *Bacteriol.* any of several spiral-shaped bacteria of the order *Spirochaetales,* certain species of which are pathogenic for man and animals, other species being free-living, saprophytic, or parasitic. Also, **spi′ro·chaete′.** [< NL *spirochaet(a).* See SPIRO-[2], CHAETO-] —**spi′ro·chet′al, spi′ro·che′tic,** *adj.*

spi·ro·che·to·sis (spī′rə kē tō′sis), *n.* *Pathol.* a disease caused by infection with a spirochete. Also, **spirochaetosis.** [SPIROCHETE + -OSIS] —**spi·ro·che·tot·ic** (spī′rə kē tot′ik), *adj.*

spi·ro·graph (spī′rə graf′, -gräf′), *n.* an instrument for recording respiratory movements. [SPIRO-[1] + -GRAPH] —**spi·ro·graph·ic** (spī′rə graf′ik), *adj.*

spi·ro·gy·ra (spī′rə jī′rə), *n.* *Bot.* a widely distributed fresh-water green alga of the genus *Spirogyra.* [< NL, equiv. to *spīro-* SPIRO-[2] + *-gȳra,* alter. of Gk *gŷros* circle or *gȳrós* round]

spi·roid (spī′roid), *adj.* more or less spiral; resembling a spiral. [< NL *spīroīd(ēs)* < Gk *speiroeidḗs.* See SPIRO-[2], -OID]

spi·rom·e·ter (spī rom′i tər), *n.* an instrument for determining the capacity of the lungs. [SPIRO-[1] + -METER] —**spi·ro·met·ric** (spī′rə me′trik), **spi′ro·met′ri·cal,** *adj.* —**spi·rom′e·try,** *n.*

spirt (spûrt), *v.i., v.t., n.* spurt.

spir·u·la (spir′yə lə, -ōō lə), *n., pl.* **-lae** (-lē′). any cephalopod of the genus *Spirula,* having a flat, spiral shell that is partly inside and partly outside the posterior part of the body. [< LL; see SPIRA, -ULE]

spir·y[1] (spīər′ē), *adj.* **1.** having the form of a spire, slender shoot, or tapering pointed body; tapering up to a point like a spire. **2.** abounding in spires or steeples. [SPIRE[1] + -Y[1]]

spir·y[2] (spī′rē), *adj.* spiral; coiled; coiling; helical. [SPIRE[2] + -Y[1]]

spis·sa·tus (spi sā′təs), *adj.* *Meteorol.* (of a cloud) dense enough to obscure the sun. [< NL; see SPISSUS, -ATE[1]]

spis·sus (spis′əs), *adj.* (in prescriptions) dense; hard. [< L]

spit[1] (spit), *v.,* **spit or spat, spit·ting,** *n.* —*v.i.* **1.** to eject saliva from the mouth; expectorate. **2.** to express hatred, contempt, etc., by or as if by ejecting saliva from the mouth. **3.** to sputter: *grease spitting on the fire.* **4.** to fall in scattered drops or flakes, as rain or snow. —*v.t.* **5.** to eject from the mouth: *The children were spitting watermelon seeds over the fence.* **6.** to throw out or emit like saliva: *The kettle spits boiling water over the stove.* **7.** to set a flame to. —*n.* **8.** saliva, esp. when ejected. **9.** act of spitting. **10.** *Entomol.* spittle. **11.** a light fall of rain or snow. **12. spit and image,** *Informal.* exact likeness; counterpart: *Hunched over his desk, smoking, he was the spit and image of his father at work.* Also, **spitting image.** [ME *spitt(en),* OE *spittan;* c. G (dial.) *spitzen* to spit; akin to OE *spǣtan* to spit, *spātl* spittle] —**spit′like′,** *adj.*

spit[2] (spit), *n., v.,* **spit·ted, spit·ting.** —*n.* **1.** a pointed rod or bar for thrusting through and holding meat that is to be cooked before or over a fire. **2.** any of various rods, pins, or the like used for particular purposes. **3.** a narrow point of land projecting into the water. **4.** a long, narrow shoal extending from the shore. —*v.t.* **5.** to pierce, stab, or transfix, as with a spit; impale on something sharp. **6.** to thrust a spit into or through. [ME *spite,* OE *spit(u);* c. MD, MLG *spit, spet,* OHG *spiz* spit; akin to Icel *spīta* peg, and to SPIKE[1], SPILE[1], SPINE, SPIRE[1]]

spit·al (spit′əl), *n.* *Obs.* **1.** a hospital, esp. one for lazars. **2.** a shelter on a highway. [alter. of *spittle,* ME *spitel* < ML *hospitale;* see HOSPITAL]

spit′ and pol′ish, great care in maintaining smart appearance and crisp efficiency: *The commander was concerned more with spit and polish than with the company's morale.*

spit-and-pol·ish (spit′ən pol′ish), *adj.* concerned with or showing the results of spit and polish: *a spit-and-polish marching band.*

spit·ball (spit′bôl′), *n.* **1.** a small ball or lump of chewed paper used as a missile. **2.** Also called **spitter.** *Baseball.* a pitch, now illegal, made to curve by moistening one side of the ball with saliva or perspiration. [SPIT[1] + BALL[1]]

spit·ball·er (spit′bô′lər), *n.* *Baseball.* a pitcher who is known or believed to throw spitballs. [SPITBALL + -ER[1]]

spitch·cock (spich′kok′), *n.* **1.** an eel split, cut into pieces, and broiled or fried. —*v.t.* **2.** to split, cut up, and broil or fry (an eel). **3.** to treat severely. [? OE *spic* fat bacon + *cuc,* var. of *cwic* QUICK; from the way the eel moves about in cooking as if alive]

spit′ curl′, a tight curl of hair, usually pressed against the forehead or cheek.

spite (spīt), *n., v.,* **spit·ed, spit·ing.** —*n.* **1.** a malicious, usually petty, desire to harm, annoy, frustrate, or humiliate another person; bitter ill will; malice. **2.** a particular instance of such an attitude or action; grudge. **3.** *Obs.* something that causes vexation; annoyance. **4. in spite of,** in disregard or defiance of; notwithstanding; despite: *She arrived at school on time in spite of the snowstorm.* —*v.t.* **5.** to treat with spite or malice. **6.** to annoy or thwart, out of spite. **7.** to fill with spite; vex; offend. **8. cut off one's nose to spite one's face.** See **nose** (def. 15). [ME; aph. var. of DESPITE] —**spite′less,** *adj.*
—**Syn.** **1.** malevolence, maliciousness, rancor, venom, spleen. See **grudge.** **2.** hate, hatred, pique. **4.** See **notwithstanding.** **6.** injure, hurt, harm.

spite′ fence′, a wall or fence erected solely to annoy one's neighbor or injure the value of his property.

spite·ful (spīt′fəl), *adj.* full of spite or malice; showing spite; malicious; malevolent; venomous: *a spiteful child.* [ME; see SPITE, -FUL] —**spite′ful·ly,** *adv.* —**spite′ful·ness,** *n.*
—**Syn.** vengeful, mean, cruel, rancorous. SPITEFUL, REVENGEFUL, VINDICTIVE refer to a desire to inflict a wrong or injury on someone, usually in return for one received. SPITEFUL implies a mean or malicious desire for (often petty) revenge: *a spiteful attitude toward a former friend.* REVENGEFUL is a strong word, implying a deep, powerful, and continued intent to repay a wrong: *a fierce and revengeful spirit.* VINDICTIVE does not imply action necessarily, but stresses the unforgiving nature of the avenger: *a vindictive look.* —**Ant.** benevolent.

spit·fire (spit′fīər′), *n.* **1.** a person, esp. a girl or woman, who is of fiery temper and easily provoked to outbursts. **2.** (*cap.*) a British fighter plane with a single in-line engine used by the R.A.F. throughout World War II. [SPIT[1] + FIRE]

spit′fire jib′, *Naut.* See **storm jib.**

Spit·head (spit′hed′), *n.* a roadstead off the S coast of England between Portsmouth and the Isle of Wight.

spit′ in the o′cean, *Cards.* a variety of poker in which four cards are dealt face down to each player and one card, forming the fifth for all hands, is dealt face up in the center of the table, the exposed card and others of its denomination being wild cards.

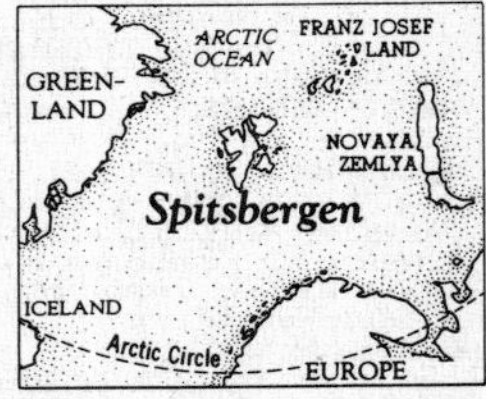

Spits·ber·gen (spits′bûr′gən), *n.* a group of islands in the Arctic Ocean, N of and belonging to Norway. 1200 (est. 1959); 24,293 sq. mi. Also, **Spitzbergen.** Norwegian, **Svalbard.**

Spit·te·ler (*Ger.* shpit′əl ər), *n.* **Carl** (*Ger.* kärl), ("*Felix Tandem*"), 1845–1924, Swiss poet, novelist, and essayist: Nobel prize 1919.

spit·ter[1] (spit′ər), *n.* one who or that which spits. [ME; see SPIT[1], -ER[1]]

spit·ter[2] (spit′ər), *n.* **1.** *Rare.* brocket (def. 2). **2.** *Baseball.* spitball (def. 2). [SPIT[2] + -ER[1]]

spit′ting im′age, *Informal.* See **spit[1]** (def. 12). [from the phrase *spit and image* (see SPIT[1]) by confusion of *spit and* with *spittin'* in utterance]

spit·tle (spit′əl), *n.* **1.** saliva; spit. **2.** *Entomol.* a frothy or spitlike secretion exuded by spittle insects. [b. ME *spit* (n.) (see SPIT[1]) and *spetil,* OE *spǣtl,* var. of *spātl* saliva]

spit′tle in′sect, froghopper. Also called **spit′tle bug′.**

spit·toon (spi tōōn′), *n.* a cuspidor. [SPIT[1] + *-oon,* abstracted from words of various origins, as *buffoon, lagoon, saloon*]

spitz (spits), *n.* any of several dogs having a stocky body, a thick coat, erect, pointed ears, and a tail curved over the back, as a chow chow, Pomeranian, or Samoyed. [< G *spitz* pointed]

Spitz·ber·gen (spits′bûr′gən), *n.* Spitsbergen.

spitz·en·burg (spit′sən bûrg′), *n.* any of several red or yellow varieties of apple which ripen in the autumn. Also, **spitz′en·berg′.** [short for *Esopus Spitzenberg,* after *Esopus,* N.Y., + D *spits* point (in reference to its shape) + *berg* mountain; so called from its being found on a hill near Esopus]

spiv (spiv), *n.* *Brit. Informal.* a petty criminal, esp. a black marketeer, racetrack tout, or petty thief. [back formation from dial. *spiving* smart; akin to SPIFFY]

spiv·vy (spiv′ē), *adj.,* **-vi·er, -vi·est.** *Chiefly Brit.* spiffy. Also, **spiv·ving** (spiv′ing).

splad (splad), *n.* splat[1] (def. 1).

splake (splāk), *n., pl.* **splakes,** (*esp. collectively*) **splake.** the hybrid offspring of a lake trout and a brook trout. [SP(ECKLED TROUT) + LAKE (TROUT)]

splanch·nic (splangk′nik), *adj.* of or pertaining to the viscera or entrails; visceral. [< NL *splanchnic(us)* < Gk *splanchnikós,* equiv. to *splánchn(a)* entrails (pl.) + *-ikos* -IC]

splanch·ni·cec·to·my (splangk′ni sek′tə mē), *n., pl.* **-mies.** *Surg.* excision of the splanchnic nerves and, usually, of the celiac ganglion. [SPLANCHNIC + -ECTOMY]

splanchno-, a learned borrowing from Greek meaning "viscera," used in the formation of compound words: *splanchnopleure.* [comb. form of Gk *splánchna* entrails (pl.)]

splanch·nol·o·gy (splangk nol′ə jē), *n.* the branch of medicine dealing with the viscera. [< NL. See SPLANCHNO-, -LOGY] —**splanch·no·log·ic** (splangk′nəloj′ik), *adj.*

splanch·no·pleure (splangk′nə plōōr′), *n.* *Embryol.* the double layer formed by the association of the lower layer of the lateral plate of mesoderm with the underlying entoderm, which functions in the formation of the embryonic viscera and of such extraembryonic structures as the allantois. Cf. **somatopleure.** [< NL *splanchnopleur(a).* See SPLANCHNO-, PLEURA] —**splanch′no·pleu′ral, splanch′no·pleu′ric,** *adj.*

splash (splash), *v.t.* **1.** to wet or soil by dashing masses or particles of water, mud, or the like; spatter: *Don't splash her dress!* **2.** to fall upon (something) in scattered masses or particles, as a liquid does. **3.** to cause to appear spattered. **4.** to dash (water, mud, etc.) about in scattered masses or particles. **5.** to make (one's way) with splashing: *He splashed his way across the pool.* **6.** *Logging.* to move (logs) by releasing a body of water from a splash dam. —*v.i.* **7.** to dash a liquid or semiliquid substance about. **8.** to fall, move, or go with a splash or splashes. **9.** (of liquid) to dash with force in scattered masses or particles. **10.** (of a space vehicle) to land in a body of water (usually fol. by *down*). —*n.* **11.** the act of splashing. **12.** the sound of splashing. **13.** a quantity of some liquid or semiliquid substance splashed upon or in a thing. **14.** a spot caused by something splashed. **15.** a patch, as of color or light. **16.** *Logging.* **a.** act of splashing logs. **b.** water released, as from a splash dam, for splashing logs. **17.** a striking show or an ostentatious display. [alter. of PLASH[1]] —**splash′ing·ly,** *adv.*

splash·board (splash′bōrd′, -bôrd′), *n.* **1.** a board, guard, or screen to protect from splashing, as a dashboard of a vehicle or a guard placed over a wheel to intercept water, dirt, etc. **2.** *Naut.* washboard (def. 3). [SPLASH + BOARD]

splash′ dam′, a flood dam built to contain water which is released for driving logs.

splash·down (splash′doun′), *n.* **1.** the landing of a space vehicle on a body of water. **2.** the exact place where such a landing is made. **3.** the time of such a landing.

splash·er (splash′ər), *n.* **1.** one who or that which splashes. **2.** something that protects from splashes. [SPLASH + -ER[1]]

splash′ ero′sion, erosion caused by the impact of falling raindrops.

splash′ guard′, a large flap behind a rear tire to prevent mud, water, etc., being splashed on the following car.

splash·y (splash′ē), *adj.,* **splash·i·er, splash·i·est. 1.** making a splash or splashes. **2.** making the sound of splashing. **3.** full of or marked by splashes, or irregular spots; spotty. **4.** making an ostentatious display; showy. [SPLASH + -Y[1]] —**splash′i·ness,** *n.*

splat[1] (splat), *n.* **1.** Also, **splad.** a broad, flat piece of wood, either pierced or solid, forming the center upright part of a chair back or the like. **2.** a batten for covering joints between sheets of wallboard; panel strip. [? akin to OE *splātan* to split]

splat[2] (splat), *n.* a sound made by splattering or slapping. [back formation from SPLATTER]

splat·ter (splat′ər), *v.t., v.i.* to spatter, as by splashing. [b. SPLASH and SPATTER]

S, Splay (def. 7)

splay (splā), *v.t.* **1.** to spread out, expand, or extend. **2.** to form with an oblique angle; make slanting; bevel. **3.** to make with a splay or splays. **4.** to disjoin; dislocate. —*v.i.* **5.** to have an oblique or slanting direction. **6.** to spread or flare. —*n.* **7.** *Archit.* a surface which makes an oblique angle with another, as where the opening through a wall for a window or door widens from the window or door proper toward the face of the wall. —*adj.* **8.** spread out; wide and flat; turned outward. **9.** clumsy or awkward. **10.** oblique or awry. [aph. var. of DISPLAY]

splay·foot (splā′fo͝ot′), *n., pl.* **-feet,** *adj.* —*n.* **1.** a broad, flat foot, esp. one turned outward. **2.** *Pathol.* this condition as a deformity; flatfoot. —*adj.* **3.** Also, **splay′foot′ed.** of or pertaining to splayfoot. [SPLAY + FOOT]

spleen (splēn), *n.* **1.** a highly vascular, glandular, ductless organ, situated in man at the cardiac end of the stomach, serving chiefly in the formation of lymphocytes, in the destruction of worn-out erythrocytes, and as a reservoir for blood. **2.** this organ conceived of as the seat of spirit and courage or of such emotions as mirth, ill humor, melancholy, etc. **3.** ill humor, peevish temper, or spite. **4.** *Archaic.* melancholy. **5.** *Obs.* caprice. [ME < L *splēn* < Gk *splḗn;* akin to Skt *plīhan,* L *liēn* spleen] —**spleen′ish,** *adj.*
—**Syn. 3.** petulance, rancor, acrimoniousness; wrath, ire, anger.

spleen·ful (splēn′fəl), *adj.* **1.** full of or displaying spleen. **2.** ill-humored; irritable or peevish; spiteful. [SPLEEN + -FUL] —**spleen′ful·ly,** *adv.*

spleen·wort (splēn′wûrt′), *n.* any of various temperate and tropical ferns of the genus *Asplenium,* certain species of which are grown as ornamentals. [SPLEEN + WORT[2]]

spleen·y (splē′nē), *adj.,* **spleen·i·er, spleen·i·est.** abundant in spleen. [SPLEEN + -Y[1]]

splen-, var. of **spleno-** before a vowel: *splenectomy.*

splen·dent (splen′dənt), *adj.* **1.** shining or radiant, as the sun. **2.** gleaming or lustrous, as metal, marble, etc. **3.** brilliant in appearance, color, etc.; gorgeous; magnificent; splendid. **4.** eminent; illustrious. [late ME < L *splendent-* (s. of *splendēns,* prp. of *splendēre* to shine), equiv. to *splend-* shine + *-ent-* -ENT] —**splen′dent·ly,** *adv.*

splen·did (splen′did), *adj.* **1.** gorgeous; magnificent; sumptuous. **2.** grand; superb, as beauty. **3.** distinguished or glorious, as a name, reputation, victory, etc. **4.** strikingly admirable or fine: *splendid talents.* **5.** excellent, fine, or very good: *to have a splendid time.* **6.** *Rare.* brilliant in appearance, color, etc. [< L *splendid(us)* brilliant, equiv. to *splend-* shine + *-idus* -ID[4]] —**splen′did·ly,** *adv.* —**splen′did·ness,** *n.*
—**Syn. 1.** luxurious, dazzling, imposing. See **magnificent. 3.** renowned, famed, famous, illustrious, eminent, conspicuous, celebrated, remarkable, brilliant; noble. —**Ant. 1.** sordid. **3.** ignoble.

splen·dif·er·ous (splen dif′ər əs), *adj. Informal.* splendid; magnificent; fine. [late ME < LL *splend(or)ifer* brightness-bearing (see SPLENDOR, -FER, -OUS); loss of *-or* prob. by shift of stress, syncope, and dissimilation] —**splen·dif′er·ous·ly,** *adv.* —**splen·dif′er·ous·ness,** *n.*

splen·dor (splen′dər), *n.* **1.** brilliant or gorgeous appearance, coloring, etc.; magnificence: *the splendor of the palace.* **2.** an instance or display of imposing pomp or grandeur: *the splendor of the coronation.* **3.** grandeur; glory; brilliant distinction: *the splendor of ancient Greek architecture.* **4.** great brightness; brilliant light or luster. —*v.t.* **5.** to make splendid by decorating lavishly; adorn. —*v.i.* **6.** to move or proceed with splendor, grandeur, or pomp. Also, *esp. Brit.,* **splen′dour.** [< L *splendor,* equiv. to *splend-* (root of *splendēre* to shine) + *-or* -OR[1]; r. ME *splendure* < AF] —**splen′dor·ous, splendrous** (splen′drəs), *adj.*
—**Syn. 1.** show, dash. **3.** fame, eminence, renown, celebrity. **4.** dazzle, refulgence. —**Ant. 1.** squalor.

sple·nec·to·mize (spli nek′tə mīz′), *v.t.,* **-mized, -miz·ing.** *Surg.* to perform a splenectomy on. [SPLENECTOM(Y) + -IZE]

sple·nec·to·my (spli nek′tə mē), *n., pl.* **-mies.** *Surg.* excision or removal of the spleen. Also called **lienectomy.** [SPLEN- + -ECTOMY]

sple·net·ic (spli net′ik), *adj.* Also, **sple·net′i·cal. 1.** of the spleen; splenic. **2.** irritable; peevish; spiteful. **3.** *Obs.* affected with, characterized by, or tending to produce melancholy. —*n.* **4.** a splenetic person. [< LL *splēnēticus.* See SPLEEN, -ETIC] —**sple·net′i·cal·ly,** *adv.*
—**Syn. 2.** vexatious, irascible, testy, fretful, touchy, petulant, choleric. —**Ant. 2.** moderate, temperate.

splen·ic (splē′nik, splen′ik), *adj.* of, pertaining to, connected with, or affecting the spleen: *splenic nerves.* [< L *splēnic(us)* < Gk *splēnikós.* See SPLEEN, -IC]

sple·ni·tis (spli nī′tis), *n. Pathol.* inflammation of the spleen. [< NL; see SPLEN-, -ITIS]

splen·i·tive (splen′i tiv), *adj. Obs.* **1.** impetuous; passionate. **2.** splenetic, ill-humored, or irritable. [SPLEN- + -ITIVE]

sple·ni·us (splē′nē əs), *n., pl.* **-ni·i** (-nē ī′). *Anat.* a broad muscle on each side of the back of the neck and the upper part of the thoracic region, the action of which draws the head backward and assists in turning it to one side. [< NL, alter. of L *splēnium* < Gk *splḗnion* plaster, patch] —**sple′ni·al,** *adj.*

spleno-, a learned borrowing from Greek, used as the combining form of **spleen** in compound words: *splenomegaly.* Also, *esp. before a vowel,* **splen-.** [comb. form repr. Gk *splḗn*]

sple·no·meg·a·ly (splē′nə meg′ə lē, splen′ə-), *n. Pathol.* enlargement of the spleen. Also, **sple·no·me·ga·li·a** (splē′nō mə gā′lē ə, -gal′yə, splen′ō-). [SPLENO- + MEGALY]

spleu·chan (splo͞o′KHən), *n. Scot., Irish Eng.* a small pouch, esp. for carrying tobacco or money. Also, **spleu·ghan** (splo͞o′KHən). [< Gael *spliuchan*]

splice (splīs), *v.,* **spliced, splic·ing,** *n.* —*v.t.* **1.** to join together or unite (two ropes or parts of a rope) by the interweaving of strands. **2.** to unite (timbers, spars, or the like) by overlapping the ends and fastening. **3.** to unite (film, electromagnetic tape, or the like) by butting and cementing. **4.** to join or unite. **5.** *Slang.* to unite in marriage: *They'll be spliced in June.* **6. splice the main brace,** *Naut.* **a.** to issue a ration of spirits, as grog, to all hands. **b.** to drink spirits. —*n.* **7.** a joining of two ropes or parts of a rope by splicing. **8.** the union or junction made by splicing. **9.** a joining or junction of two pieces of timber, spar, etc., by overlapping and fastening the ends. **10.** a joining of film, electromagnetic tape, or the like. [< MD *spliss(en);* akin to SPLIT] —**splice′a·ble,** *adj.*

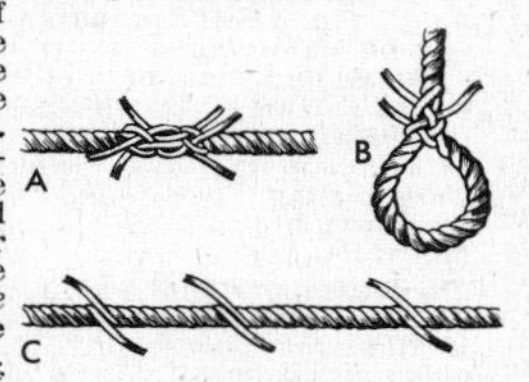

Rope splices
A, Short splice; B, Eye splice; C, Long splice

spline (splīn), *n., v.,* **splined, splin·ing.** —*n.* **1.** a long, narrow, thin strip of wood, metal, etc.; slat. **2.** a long, flexible strip of wood or the like, used in drawing curves. **3.** *Mach.* **a.** any of a series of uniformly spaced ridges on a shaft, parallel to its axis and fitting inside corresponding grooves in the hub of a gear, etc., to transmit torque. **b.** See **feather key. 4.** *Building Trades.* a thin strip of material inserted into the edges of two boards, acoustic tiles, etc., to make a butt joint between them; a feather. —*v.t. Mach.* **5.** to provide with a spline or key. **6.** to provide with a keyway. [EAnglian dial. word, perh. akin to SPLINT; cf. OE *splin* spindle]

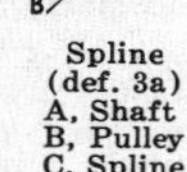

Spline (def. 3a)
A, Shaft
B, Pulley
C, Spline

spline′ joint′, *Carpentry.* a joint between two boards having grooved edges and united by a spline.

splint (splint), *n.* **1.** a thin piece of wood or other rigid material used to immobilize a fractured or dislocated bone, or to maintain any part of the body in a fixed position. **2.** one of a number of thin strips of wood woven together to make a chair seat, basket, etc. **3.** *Vet. Med.* an exostosis or bony enlargement of a splint bone of a horse or a related animal. **4.** *Armor.* **a.** any of a number of narrow plates or lames joined with rivets or a backing to form a piece of armor. **b.** a partial vambrace protecting only the outer part of the arm. **5.** *Brit. Dial.* a splinter. —*v.t.* **6.** to secure, hold in position, or support by means of a splint or splints, as a fractured bone. **7.** to support as if with splints. [ME < MD or MLG *splinte;* akin to Norw *splint* peg; see SPLINTER] —**splint′like′,** *adj.*

splint′ bone′, one of the rudimentary, splintlike metacarpal or metatarsal bones of the horse or some allied animal, closely applied one on each side of the back of each cannon bone.

splin·ter (splin′tər), *n.* **1.** a small, thin, sharp piece of wood, bone, or the like, split or broken off from the main body. **2.** See **splinter group. 3.** a splint. —*v.t.* **4.** to split or break into splinters. **5.** to break off (something) in splinters. **6.** to split or break (a larger group) into separate factions or independent groups. **7.** *Obs.* to secure or support by a splint or splints, as a broken limb. —*v.i.* **8.** to be split or broken into splinters. **9.** to break off in splinters. [ME < MD or MLG; see SPLINT] —**splin′ter·less,** *adj.* —**splin′ter·y,** *adj.*
—**Syn. 1.** sliver. **9.** separate, part, split.

splin′ter bar′, 1. a crossbar in a horse-drawn vehicle, for supporting the springs. **2.** a whiffletree.

splin′ter group′, a small organization that becomes separated from or acts apart from a larger group or a number of other small groups, with which it would normally be united, because of disagreement over isolated matters, because of the lack of a personality, force, etc., capable of bringing about unification, or because of some practical consideration that requires an independent group of limited size.

splint′ seat′, a seat for a chair or the like, made from thin, flat strips of wood woven together.

split (split), *v.,* **split, split·ting,** *n., adj.* —*v.t.* **1.** to divide or separate from end to end or into layers: *to split a log in two.* **2.** to separate by cutting, chopping, etc., usually lengthwise: *to split a piece from a block.* **3.** to tear or break apart; rend or burst: *The wind split the sail.* **4.** to divide into distinct parts or portions (often fol. by *up*): *We split up our rations.* **5.** to separate (a part) by such division. **6.** to divide (persons) into different groups, factions, parties, etc., as by discord: *to split a political party.* **7.** to separate (a group, family, etc.) by such division. **8.** to divide between two or more persons, groups, etc.; share: *We split a bottle of wine.* **9.** to separate into parts by interposing something: *to split an infinitive.* **10.** *Chem.* to divide (molecules or atoms) by cleavage into smaller parts. **11.** to issue additional shares of (stock) without charge to existing stockholders, thereby dividing their interest into a larger number of shares and reducing the price per share. —*v.i.* **12.** to divide, break, or part lengthwise: *The board split in half.* **13.** to part, divide, or separate in any way (often fol. by *up*). **14.** to break asunder, as a ship by striking on a rock. **15.** to become separated off by such division, as a piece or part from a whole. **16.** to part or separate, as through disagreement: *They split up after a year of marriage.* **17.** to divide or share something with another or others; apportion. **18.** *Slang.* to leave; depart: *Man, let's split.* **19. split hairs.** See **hair** (def. 8). **20. split the difference.** See **difference** (def. 12). —*n.* **21.** the act of splitting. **22.** a crack, tear, or fissure caused by splitting. **23.** a piece or part separated by or as by splitting. **24.** a strip split from an osier, used in basketmaking. **25.** a breach or rupture, as between persons, in a party or organization, etc. **26.** a faction, party, etc., formed by a rupture or schism. **27.** *Colloq.* an ice-cream dish made from sliced fruit, usually a banana, and ice cream, and covered with syrup and nuts. **28.** Also called, *esp. Brit.,* **nip.** a bottle for wine or, sometimes, another beverage, containing from 6 to 6½ ounces. **29.** *Informal.* a bottle, as of soda, liquor, etc., which is half the usual size. **30.** *Masonry.* a brick of normal length and breadth but of half normal thickness, used to give level support to a course of bricks laid over one not level. **31.** Often, **splits.** the feat of separating the legs while sinking to the floor, until they extend at right angles to the body, as in stage performances. **32.** *Bowling.* the arrangement of the remaining pins after the first bowl so that a spare is difficult. **33.** *Philately.* bisect (def. 4). **34.** one of the layers of leather into which a skin is cut. **35.** the act of splitting a stock. —*adj.* **36.** that has undergone splitting; parted lengthwise; cleft. **37.** disunited; divided: *a split opinion.* **38.** (of a stock quotation) given in sixteenths instead of eighths of a point. **39.** (of a stock) having undergone a split. **40.** *Football.* (of an end) lined up some distance outside of a tackle: *a T formation with both ends split.* [< MD *splitt(en);* akin to MLG *splīten,* G *spleissen* to split] —**split′ta·ble,** *adj.* —**split′ter,** *n.*
—**Syn. 2–6, 12, 13.** splinter.

Split (split), *n.* a seaport in S Croatia, on the Adriatic: Roman ruins. 180,571. Italian, **Spalato.**

split′ bal′ance, *Horol.* See **compensating balance.**

split′ deci′sion, *Boxing.* a decision of a bout on whose outcome the referee and judges did not unanimously agree.

split-face (split′fās′), *adj.* pertaining to building stone that is dressed and then split down the middle to produce stones with one rough face which is laid exposed.

split′ flap′, *Aeron.* **1.** a flap that is located on the under surface of the trailing edge of an aircraft wing and that splits away from the wing structure when rotated downward, producing an increase in lift or drag or both. Cf. **landing flap. 2.** a flap that is located on the upper surface of the trailing edge of an aircraft wing and that acts as a spoiler when rotated upward.

split′ infin′itive, *Gram.* an expression in which there is a word or group of words, esp. an adverb or adverbial phrase, between *to* and its accompanying verb form in an infinitive, as in *to readily understand.*
—**Usage.** The "rule" against splitting infinitives seems to have begun in the 17th century with John Dryden, who, in addition to being a famous dramatist, was a careful stylist and Latin scholar. In Latin, the infinitive is one word, hence cannot be split. Modeling English style on Latin style and grammar was then considered the epitome of good writing, so Dryden inveighed against the practice of using sentences like, *To really get to know someone you have to have lived with him.* But there is nothing inherent in English grammar or style to justify such an injunction, and, in a sentence like the preceding, placing *really* anywhere else makes for awkward phrasing. Traditionalists', purists', and other schoolmarmish stylists' objections notwithstanding, there is nothing wrong with a split infinitive in English.

split-lev·el (split′lev′əl), *adj.* **1.** noting a house having a room or rooms that are a partial story above or below adjacent rooms. —*n.* **2.** a split-level house.

split-off (split′ôf′, -of′), *n.* **1.** the act of separating or splitting away from something else. **2.** that which has split or has been split from something else. **3.** *Com.* a process of reorganizing a corporate structure whereby the capital stock of a division or subsidiary of a corporation or of a newly affiliated company, is transferred to the stockholders of the parent corporation in exchange for part of the stock of the latter. Cf. **spin-off** (def. 1), **split-up** (def. 3). [n. use of v. phrase *split off*]

split′ page′, 1. (in a newspaper) a page replacing one of an earlier edition and containing chiefly the same material in altered form. **2.** the first page of the second section of a newspaper.

split′ personal′ity. See **multiple personality.**

split-phase (split′fāz′), *adj. Elect.* **1.** pertaining to or noting a current in one of two parallel circuits that have a single-phase current source but unequal impedances and that produce currents of different phase. **2.** pertaining to or noting a motor or system utilizing a split-phase current.

split′ run′, a pressrun, as that of a newspaper or magazine, which is interrupted after the running of a specified number of copies to permit the substitution of type or of a cut, as in a keyed advertisement: a device for testing the relative effectiveness of different versions of an advertisement.

split′ screen′, *Motion Pictures, Television.* a type of process photography in which two or more shots are juxtaposed and projected simultaneously on the screen. Also called **composite shot.**

split′ sec′ond, 1. a fraction of a second. 2. an infinitesimal amount of time; instant. —**split′-sec′ond,** *adj.*

split′ spin′dle, *Furniture.* a turned piece halved lengthwise for use as applied ornament, as on a chest or cupboard, or as part of a chair back or the like; half-turning.

split′ sprit′, *Naut.* wishbone (def. 2).

split·tail (split′tāl′), *n.* a minnow, *Pogonichthys macrolepidota,* found in the Sacramento River, having the upper lobe of the tail much longer than the lower lobe. [SPLIT + TAIL[1]]

split′ tick′et, *U.S. Pol.* 1. a ballot on which not all votes have been cast for candidates of the same party. 2. a ticket on which not all the candidates nominated by a party are members of the party. Cf. **straight ticket.**

split-time (split′tīm′), *n.* a daylight-saving time based on a half-hour advance.

split·ting (split′ing), *adj.* 1. being split or causing something to split. 2. violent or severe, as a headache. 3. very fast or rapid. —*n.* 4. Usually, **splittings.** a part or fragment that has been split off from something: *Some cavemen made their smaller tools from the splittings of stone.* [SPLIT + -ING[2], -ING[1]]

split′ting field′, *Math.* a field containing a given field in which every polynomial can be written as the product of linear factors.

split-up (split′up′), *n.* 1. a splitting or separating into two or more parts. 2. a separation or dissociation of two groups or people. 3. *Com.* a process of reorganizing a corporate structure whereby all the capital stock and assets are exchanged for those of two or more newly established companies, resulting in the liquidation of the parent corporation. Cf. **spin-off** (def. 1), **split-off** (def. 3). [n. use of v. phrase *split up*]

splore (splōr, splôr), *n. Scot.* 1. a frolic; revel; carousal. 2. a commotion; disturbance. [? aph. var. of EXPLORE]

splosh (splosh), *v.t., v.i., n.* splash.

splotch (sploch), *n.* 1. a large, irregular spot; blot; stain. —*v.t.* 2. to mark with splotches. —*v.i.* 3. to be susceptible to stains or blots; show or retain stains, blots, or spots of dirt or liquid: *Don't buy that tablecloth, the material splotches easily.* 4. to cause or be liable to cause stains, blots, or spots: *Be careful of that paint—it splotches.* [? b. OE *splott* spot, blot, patch (of land) and PATCH]

splotch·y (sploch′ē), *adj.,* **splotch·i·er, splotch·i·est.** marked or covered with splotches. [SPLOTCH + -Y[1]]

splurge (splûrj), *v.,* **splurged, splurg·ing,** *n.* —*v.i.* 1. to indulge oneself in some luxury or pleasure, esp. a costly one: *She splurged on a new hat.* 2. to show off. —*v.t.* 3. to spend (money) lavishly or ostentatiously: *He splurged thousands on the party.* —*n.* 4. an ostentatious display, esp. an extravagantly expensive one. [? b. SPLASH and SURGE] —**splurg′i·ly,** *adv.* —**splurg′y,** *adj.*

splut·ter (splut′ər), *v.i.* 1. to talk rapidly and somewhat incoherently, as when confused, excited, or embarrassed: *When pushed for an explanation, he always spluttered.* 2. to make a sputtering sound, or emit particles of something explosively, as water dropped onto a hot griddle. 3. to fly or fall in particles or drops; spatter, as a liquid. —*v.t.* 4. to utter hastily and confusedly or incoherently; sputter: *Out of breath, she spluttered a poor excuse for her lateness.* 5. to spatter (a liquid, small particles, etc.). 6. to bespatter (someone or something). —*n.* 7. spluttering utterance or talk; noise or fuss. 8. a spluttering or spattering, as of liquid. [b. SPLASH and SPUTTER] —**splut′ter·er,** *n.*

Spock (spok), *n.* **Benjamin (Mc·Lane)** (mə klān′), born 1903, U.S. physician and educator.

Spode (spōd), *n.* 1. **Josiah,** 1733–97, and his son, **Josiah,** 1754–1827, English potters. 2. Also called **Spode′ chi′na.** *Trademark.* china or porcelain manufactured by the Spodes or the firm which they established.

Spo·di·us (spō′dē əs), *n. Class. Myth.* an epithet of Apollo, meaning "god of ashes."

spod·u·mene (spoj′o͝o mēn′), *n.* a mineral, lithium aluminum silicate, $LiAlSi_2O_6$, occurring in prismatic crystals, transparent varieties being used as gems. [< F *spodumène* < G *Spodumen* < Gk *spodoúmen(os)* being burnt to ashes, equiv. to *spodou-* (deriv. of *spodós* wood ash) + *-menos* verbid suffix]

Spohr (shpōr), *n.* **Lud·wig** (lo͞ot′viкн, lo͞od′-) or **Lou·is** (lo͞o′ē), 1784–1859, German violinist, composer, and conductor.

spoil (spoil), *v.,* **spoiled** or **spoilt, spoil·ing,** *n.* —*v.t.* 1. to damage or harm (something), esp. with reference to its excellence, value, usefulness, etc.: *to spoil a sheet of paper.* 2. to impair, damage, or harm the character or nature of (someone) by unwise treatment, excessive indulgence, etc.: *to spoil a child by pampering him.* 3. *Archaic.* to strip (persons, places, etc.) of goods, valuables, etc.; plunder; pillage; despoil. 4. *Archaic.* to take by force, or carry off as booty on a field of battle. —*v.i.* 5. to become bad, or unfit for use, as food or other perishable substances; become tainted or putrid: *Milk spoils if not refrigerated.* 6. to plunder, pillage, or rob. 7. **be spoiling for,** *Informal.* to be very eager for; be desirous of: *It was obvious that he was spoiling for a fight.* —*n.* 8. Often, **spoils.** booty, loot, or plunder taken in war or robbery. 9. Usually, **spoils.** *Chiefly U.S.* **a.** the emoluments and advantages of public office viewed as won by a victorious political party: *the spoils of office.* **b.** prizes won or treasures accumulated: *a child's spoils brought home from a party.* 10. waste material, as that which is cast up in mining, excavating, quarrying, etc. [ME *spoil(en)* < MF *(e)spoillie(r)* < L *spoliāre* to despoil, equiv. to *spoli(um)* booty + *-āre* inf. suffix] —**spoil′a·ble,** *adj.* —**spoil′less,** *adj.*

—**Syn.** 1. disfigure, destroy, demolish, mar. SPOIL, RUIN, WRECK agree in meaning to reduce the value, quality, usefulness, etc., of anything. SPOIL is the general term: *to spoil a delicate fabric.* RUIN implies doing completely destructive or irreparable injury: *to ruin one's health.* WRECK implies a violent breaking up or demolition: *to wreck oneself with drink; to wreck a building.*

spoil·age (spoi′lij), *n.* 1. act of spoiling; state of being spoiled. 2. material or the amount of material that is spoiled: *The spoilage in today's shipment is much too great.* 3. the decay of foodstuffs due to the action of bacteria; rotting: *He was concerned about the spoilage of fruit on the way to market.* [SPOIL + -AGE]

spoil′ bank′, a bank of excavated refuse or waste earth, as of shale from surface coal mining.

spoil·er (spoi′lər), *n.* 1. one who or that which spoils. 2. *Aeron.* a device used to break up the airflow around an aerodynamic surface, as an aircraft wing, in order to slow the movement through the air or to decrease the lift on the surface and, as a result, provide bank or descent control. 3. *Sports Slang.* a person or team gaining or able to gain victory against a higher ranked, usually favored opponent. [SPOIL + -ER[1]]

spoil·five (spoil′fīv′), *n. Cards.* a game played by two to ten persons having five cards each. [SPOIL + FIVE]

spoil′ ground′, an area within a body of water, esp. in the sea, where dredged material is deposited.

spoils·man (spoilz′mən), *n., pl.* **-men.** 1. a person who seeks or receives a share in political spoils. 2. an advocate of the spoils system in politics. [SPOILS + MAN[1]]

spoil·sport (spoil′spōrt′, -spôrt′), *n.* a person whose selfish or unsportsmanlike attitudes or actions spoil the pleasure of others, as in a game or social gathering. [from phrase *spoil the sport*]

spoils′ sys′tem, *Chiefly U.S.* the system or practice in which public offices with their emoluments and advantages are at the disposal of the victorious party for its own purposes.

spoilt (spoilt), *v.* a pt. and pp. of **spoil.**

Spo·kane (spō kan′), *n.* a city in E Washington. 181,608 (1960).

spoke[1] (spōk), *v.* 1. a pt. of **speak.** 2. *Archaic.* pp. of **speak.**

spoke[2] (spōk), *n., v.,* **spoked, spok·ing.** —*n.* 1. one of the bars, rods, or rungs radiating from the hub or nave of a wheel and supporting the rim or felloe. 2. one of a number of radiating parts projecting from a cylinder or wheel, or joining the hub and rim, as on a steering wheel. 3. a rung of a ladder. —*v.t.* 4. to fit or furnish with, or as with, spokes. [ME; OE *spāca;* c. D *speek,* G *Speiche*] —**spoke′less,** *adj.*

spoke-dog (spōk′dôg′, -dog′), *n.* a stick used by wheelwrights to force the outer ends of spokes into the rim or felloe.

spo·ken (spō′kən), *v.* 1. a pp. of **speak.** —*adj.* 2. uttered or expressed by speaking; oral (opposed to *written*): *the spoken word.* 3. speaking, or using speech, as specified (usually used in combination): *fair-spoken; plain-spoken.*

spoke·shave (spōk′shāv′), *n.* a cutting tool having a blade set between two handles, originally for shaping spokes, but now in general use for dressing curved edges of wood and forming round bars and shapes. [SPOKE[2] + SHAVE]

Spokeshave

spokes·man (spōks′mən), *n., pl.* **-men.** 1. a person who speaks for another or for a group. 2. a public speaker. [SPOKE[1] (used as n.) + 's[1] + MAN[1]]

spokes·wom·an (spōks′wo͝om′ən), *n., pl.* **-wom·en.** a woman who speaks for another person or for a group. [SPOKE[1] (used as n.) + 's[1] + WOMAN]

spoke·wise (spōk′wīz′), *adv.* 1. in relation to, away from, or toward a center, as the spokes on a wheel: *The projections were arranged spokewise around the core.* —*adj.* 2. having the parts placed as the spokes on a wheel; radiating from a center: *a spokewise structure.* [SPOKE[2] + -WISE]

spo·li·a o·pi·ma (spō′lē ə ō pī′mə; *Lat.* spō′lē ä′ ō-pē′mä), (in ancient Rome) the arms taken by a victorious general from the leader of a defeated army. [< L: rich spoils]

spo·li·ate (spō′lē āt′), *v.t., v.i.,* **-at·ed, -at·ing.** to plunder, rob, or ruin. [< L *spoliāt(us),* ptp. of *spoliāre* to spoil. See SPOIL, -ATE[1]]

spo·li·a·tion (spō′lē ā′shən), *n.* 1. the act or an instance of plundering or despoiling. 2. authorized plundering of neutrals at sea in time of war. 3. *Law.* the destruction or material alteration of a bill of exchange, will, or the like. 4. the act of spoiling or damaging something. [late ME < L *spoliātiōn-* (s. of *spoliātiō*), equiv. to *spoliāt(us)* (ptp. of *spoliāre* to SPOIL) + *-iōn-* -ION]

spon·da·ic (spon dā′ik), *adj. Pros.* 1. of or pertaining to a spondee. 2. noting or constituting a spondee. 3. consisting of spondees; characterized by a spondee or spondees. Also, **spon·da′i·cal.** [< L *spondaic(us),* metathetic var. of *spondīacus* < Gk *spondeiakós,* equiv. to *spondeî(os)* SPONDEE + *-akos,* var. of *-ikos* -IC]

spon·dee (spon′dē), *n. Pros.* a foot of two syllables, both of which are long in quantitative meter or stressed in accentual meter. [< L *spondē(us)* < Gk *spondeîos,* deriv. of *spondḗ* ceremonial]

spon·du·licks (spon do͞o′liks), *n. Slang.* money; cash. Also, **spon·du′lix.** [?]

spondyl-, a learned borrowing from Greek meaning "vertebra," used in the formation of compound words: *spondylitis.* Also, *esp. before a vowel,* **spondylo-.** [comb. form of L *spondylus* < Gk *spóndylos* vertebra, whorl, mussel]

spon·dy·li·tis (spon′dᵊlī′tis), *n. Pathol.* inflammation of the vertebrae. [< NL; see SPONDYL-, -ITIS] —**spon·dy·lit·ic** (spon′dᵊlit′ik), *adj.*

sponge (spunj), *n., v.,* **sponged, spong·ing.** —*n.* 1. any aquatic, chiefly marine animal of the phylum *Porifera,* having a porous structure and usually a horny, siliceous or calcareous skeleton or framework, occurring in large, complex, sessile, often plantlike colonies. 2. the light, yielding, porous, fibrous skeleton or framework of certain animals or colonies of this group, from which the living matter has been removed, characterized by readily absorbing water, and becoming soft when wet while retaining toughness: used in bathing, in wiping or cleaning surfaces, etc. 3. any of various other similar substances. 4. See **sponge bath.** 5. one who or that which absorbs something freely: *His mind is a sponge gathering historical data.* 6. *Informal.* one who persistently borrows from or lives at the expense of others; sponger; parasite. 7. *Informal.* a drunkard. 8. *Metall.* a porous mass of fine, loosely cohering, metallic particles, as of platinum, obtained by the reduction of an oxide or purified compound in a suitable atmosphere and at a temperature below the melting point. 9. *Surg.* a sterile surgical dressing of absorbent material, usually cotton gauze, for wiping or absorbing pus, blood, or other fluids during a surgical operation. 10. *Cookery.* **a.** dough raised with yeast, esp. before kneading, as for bread. **b.** a light, sweet pudding of a porous texture, made with gelatin, eggs, fruit juice or other flavoring material, etc. 11. *Brit.* See **sponge cake.** 12. **throw in the sponge,** *Slang.* to concede defeat; yield; give up: *The early election returns were heavily against him, but he wasn't ready to throw in the sponge.* —*v.t.* 13. to wipe or rub with or as with a wet sponge, as to moisten or clean. 14. to remove with or as with a wet sponge (usually fol. by *off, away,* etc.). 15. to wipe out or efface with or as with a sponge (often fol. by *out*). 16. to take up or absorb with or as with a sponge (often fol. by *up*): *to sponge up water.* 17. *Informal.* to borrow, use, or obtain by imposing on another's good nature, friendship, hospitality, or the like: *He sponged 40 bucks from his friend and went to the city.* 18. *Ceram.* to decorate (a ceramic object) by dabbing at it with a sponge soaked with color. —*v.i.* 19. to take in or soak up liquid by absorption. 20. to gather sponges. 21. *Informal.* to live at the expense of others (often fol. by *on* or *off*): *He came back home and sponged off his family for awhile.* [ME, OE < L *spong(ia), spong(ea)* < Gk *spongiá*] —**sponge′less,** *adj.* —**sponge′like′,** *adj.* —**spong′ing·ly,** *adv.*

—**Syn.** 6. leech. 13. wash. 17. beg, fawn, toady.

sponge′ bag′, *Brit.* a small, usually waterproof, case for carrying toilet articles.

sponge′ bath′, a bath in which the bather is cleaned by a wet sponge or washcloth dipped in water, without getting into a tub of water.

sponge′ cake′, a light, sweet cake made with a comparatively large proportion of eggs but no shortening.

sponge′ cloth′, 1. a cotton fabric loosely woven of coarse yarn in a variety of weaves, as honeycomb, used in the manufacture of summer dresses or sports clothes. 2. ratiné.

sponge′ fin′ger, *Brit.* a ladyfinger.

sponge·fly (spunj′flī′), *n., pl.* **-flies.** any of several neuropterous insects of the family *Sisyridae,* the aquatic larvae of which feed on fresh-water sponges. Also, **spongillafly.** [SPONGE + FLY[2]]

sponge′ i′ron, finely divided, porous iron, reduced from an oxide at a temperature below the melting point. Also called **iron sponge.**

spong·er (spun′jər), *n.* 1. one who or that which sponges. 2. *Informal.* a person who habitually borrows or lives at the expense of others; parasite. 3. a person or boat engaged in gathering sponges. [SPONGE + -ER[1]]

sponge′ rub′ber, a light, spongy rubber, usually prepared by bubbling carbon dioxide through, or whipping air into, latex, used for padding, insulation, etc.; foam rubber.

sponge′ tree′, huisache.

spon·gil·la·fly (spun jil′ə flī′, spon-), *n., pl.* **-flies.** spongefly. [< NL *spongilla,* equiv. to L *spong(ia)* SPONGE + *-illa* dim. suffix + FLY[2]]

spon·gin (spun′jin), *n.* a scleroprotein occurring in the form of fibers that form the skeleton of certain sponges. [SPONGE + -IN[2]]

spong′ing house′, *Eng. Law.* a house in which persons arrested for debt were kept for a day in order to give them an opportunity to settle the debt before imprisonment: so called from its high charges.

spong·i·o·blast (spun′jē ō blast′), *n. Embryol.* one of the primordial cells in the embryonic brain and spinal cord capable of developing into neuroglia. [*spongio-* (comb. form of Gk *spongiá* SPONGE) + -BLAST] —**spon′gi·o·blas′tic,** *adj.*

spon·go·coel (spong′gō sēl′), *n. Zool.* the central cavity in the body of a sponge. [< Gk *spongó(s),* var. of *spongiá* SPONGE + *-coel,* var. of -COELE]

spon·gy (spun′jē), *adj.,* **-gi·er, -gi·est.** 1. of the nature of or resembling a sponge; light and porous, without firmness, or readily compressible, as pith, bread, etc. 2. having the absorbent characteristics of a sponge; absorbing or holding liquid or yielding liquid when pressed. 3. of or pertaining to a sponge. 4. porous but hard, as bone. [SPONGE + -Y[1]] —**spon′gi·ly,** *adv.* —**spon′gi·ness,** *n.*

spon·sion (spon′shən), *n.* 1. an engagement or promise, esp. one made on behalf of another. 2. *Internat. Law.* an engagement made on behalf of a government by an agent acting beyond his authority or without the required authorization and not binding on the government unless ratified. 3. the act of becoming surety for another. [< L *spōnsiōn-* (s. of *spōnsiō*) guarantee, equiv. to *spōns(us)* (ptp. of *spondēre*) + *-iōn-* -ION]

spon·son (spon′sən), *n.* 1. a structure projecting from the side or main deck of a vessel to support a gun or the outer edge of a paddle box. 2. a buoyant appendage at the gunwale of a canoe to resist capsizing. 3. Also called **paddle wing.** a projecting structure supporting and protecting a paddle box and the outer paddle-wheel bearing on each side of a sidewheel steamer. 4. *Aeron.* a protuberance at the side of a flying-boat hull, designed to increase lateral stability in the water. [var. of EXPANSION]

spon·sor (spon′sər), *n.* 1. one who vouches or is responsible for a person or thing. 2. a person, firm, or other organization that finances and buys the time to broadcast a radio or television program in return for advertisement of a commercial product, a political party, etc. 3. one who makes an engagement or promise on behalf of another. 4. one who answers for an infant at baptism, making the required professions and assuming responsibility for the child's religious upbringing; godfather or godmother. —*v.t.* 5. to act as sponsor for; promise, vouch, or answer for. [< L: answerable person, equiv. to *spons(us)* (see SPONSION)

+ *-or* -OR²] —**spon·so·ri·al** (spon sôr′ē əl, -sōr′-), *adj.* —**spon′sor·ship′,** *n.*
—**Syn. 1.** patron, backer; guarantor. **2.** advertiser. **5.** guarantee, finance, back, underwrite.

spon·ta·ne·i·ty (spon′tə nē′i tē, -nā′-), *n., pl.* **-ties.** **1.** the state, quality, or fact or being spontaneous. **2.** spontaneous activity. **3. spontaneities,** spontaneous impulses, movements, or actions. [< LL *spontāne(us)* SPONTANEOUS + -ITY]

spon·ta·ne·ous (spon tā′nē əs), *adj.* **1.** coming or resulting from a natural impulse or tendency; without effort or premeditation; natural and unconstrained; unplanned: *a spontaneous burst of applause.* **2.** (of impulses, motion, natural processes, etc.) arising from internal forces or causes; independent of external agencies; self-acting. **3.** growing naturally or without cultivation, as plants, fruits, etc. **4.** produced by natural process. [< LL *spontāneus,* equiv. to L *spont(e)* willingly + *-āneus* (*-ān-* -AN + *-eus* -EOUS)] —**spon·ta′ne·ous·ly,** *adv.* —**spon·ta′ne·ous·ness,** *n.*
—**Syn. 1.** unpremeditated, free. See **voluntary.** —**Ant. 1.** premeditated.

sponta′neous combus′tion, the ignition of a substance or body from the rapid oxidation of its own constituents, without heat from any external source.

sponta′neous genera′tion, *Biol.* abiogenesis.

Spon·ti·ni (spôn tē′nē), *n.* **Ga·spa·ro Lu·i·gi Pa·ci·fi·co** (gä′spä rô lo͞o ē′jē pä chē′fē kô), 1774–1851, Italian composer and conductor.

spon·toon (spon to͞on′), *n.* a shafted weapon having a pointed blade at the head and a crossbar at the base, used by infantry officers in the 17th and 18th centuries. Also called **half-pike.** [< F *(e)sponton* < It *spuntone,* equiv. to *s-* EX-¹ + *puntone* kind of weapon (lit., pointed object) (*punt(o)* POINT + *-one* aug. suffix)]

spoof (spo͞of), *n.* **1.** a mocking imitation of someone or something, usually light and good-humored: *The show was a spoof of college life.* **2.** a hoax; prank. —*v.t.* **3.** to mock (something or someone) lightly and good humoredly; kid. **4.** to fool by a hoax; play a trick on, esp. one intended to deceive. —*v.i.* **5.** to scoff at something lightly and good-humoredly; kid: *The campus paper was always spoofing about the regulations.* [after a game invented and named by A. Roberts (1852–1933), British comedian; appar. b. SPORT and GOOF]

spoof·er·y (spo͞o′fə rē), *n.* good-humored mockery or teasing. [SPOOF + -ERY]

spook (spo͝ok), *n.* **1.** *Informal.* a ghost; specter. **2.** *Disparaging.* a Negro. —*v.t.* **3.** to haunt; inhabit or appear in or to as a ghost or specter. **4.** *Slang.* to frighten; scare. [< D; c. G *Spuk*]

spook·y (spo͞o′kē), *adj.,* **spook·i·er, spook·i·est.** *Informal.* **1.** like or befitting a spook or ghost; suggestive of spooks. **2.** eerie; scary. **3.** (esp. of horses) nervous; skittish. [SPOOK + -Y¹] —**spook′i·ly,** *adv.* —**spook′i·ness,** *n.*

spool (spo͞ol), *n.* **1.** any cylindrical piece or device on which something is wound. **2.** a small cylindrical piece of wood or other material on which yarn is wound in spinning, for use in weaving; a bobbin. **3.** a small cylinder of wood or other material on which thread, wire, or tape is wound, typically expanded or with a rim at each end and having a hole lengthwise through the center. **4.** the material or quantity of material wound on such a device. **5.** *Angling.* the cylindrical drum in a reel that bears the line. —*v.t.* **6.** to wind on a spool. **7.** to unwind from a spool (usually fol. by *off* or *out*). [ME *spole* < MD or MLG; c. G *Spule*] —**spool′like′,** *adj.*

spool′ turn′ing, *Furniture.* turning of members to resemble a continuous row of spools.

spoom¹ (spo͞om), *v.i. Obs.* to run or scud, as a ship before the wind. [? akin to FOAM; cf. SPUME]

spoom² (spo͞om), *n.* a kind of sherbet made from fruit juice or wine, mixed after freezing with uncooked meringue. [< It *spum(a)* foam, froth]

spoon (spo͞on), *n.* **1.** a utensil for eating, stirring, measuring, ladling, etc., consisting of a small, shallow bowl with a handle. **2.** any of various implements, objects, or parts resembling or suggesting this. **3.** Also called **spoon′ bait′.** *Angling.* a lure used in casting or trolling for fish, consisting of a bright spoon-shaped piece of metal or the like, swiveled above one or more fishhooks, and revolving as it is drawn through the water. **4.** Also called **number three wood.** *Golf.* a club with a wooden head, the face of which has a greater slope than the brassie or driver, for hitting long, high drives from the fairway. **5.** a curved piece projecting from the top of a torpedo tube to guide the torpedo horizontally and prevent it from striking the side of the ship from which it was fired. **6. born with a silver spoon in one's mouth,** born into a wealthy family; having an inherited fortune: *She was born with a silver spoon in her mouth and never worked a day in her life.* —*v.t.* **7.** to eat with, take up, or transfer in or as in a spoon. **8.** to hollow out or shape like a spoon. **9.** *Games.* **a.** to push or shove (a ball) with a lifting motion instead of striking it soundly, as in croquet or golf. **b.** to hit (a ball) up in the air, as in cricket. **10.** *Informal.* to show affection or love toward, esp. in an openly sentimental manner. —*v.i.* **11.** *Informal.* to show affection or love, esp. in an openly sentimental manner. **12.** *Games.* to spoon a ball. **13.** *Angling.* to fish with a spoon. [ME; OE *spōn;* c. LG *spon,* Icel *spónn,* G *Span* chip, Gk *sphēn* wedge; see SPHENE] —**spoon′less,** *adj.* —**spoon′like′,** *adj.*

Roseate spoonbill, *Ajaia ajaja* (Length about 3 ft.)

spoon′back′, a back of a chair, or the like, having a splat curved outward at the bottom.

spoon·bill (spo͞on′bil′), *n.* **1.** any of several wading birds of the genera *Platalea* or *Ajaia,* related to the ibises, having a long, flat bill with a spoonlike tip. **2.** any of various birds having a similar bill, as the shoveler duck. **3.** the paddlefish. [SPOON + BILL²]

spoon′ bow′ (bou), *Naut.* an overhanging bow having a convex, curved stem. —**spoon′-bowed′,** *adj.*

Spoon bow

spoon′ bread′, **1.** a baked dish made with corn meal, milk, eggs, and shortening, served as an accompaniment to meat. **2.** *Dial.* any of various types of biscuits shaped by dropping batter into a baking pan from a spoon.

spoon·drift (spo͞on′drift′), *n.* spindrift. [*spoon,* var. of SPOOM¹ + DRIFT]

spoon·er (spo͞o′nər), *n.* an article for holding spoons. [SPOON + -ER¹]

spoon·er·ism (spo͞o′nə riz′əm), *n.* the transposition of initial or other sounds of words, usually by accident, as in *our queer old dean* for *our dear old queen.* [after W. A. *Spooner* (1844–1930), English clergyman noted for such slips; see -ISM]

spoon·ey (spo͞o′nē), *adj.,* **spoon·i·er, spoon·i·est,** *n., pl.* **spoon·ies.** spoony.

spoon-fed (spo͞on′fed′), *adj.* **1.** fed with a spoon. **2.** treated with excessive solicitude; pampered. **3.** given no opportunity to act or think for oneself: *Having always been spoon-fed, she couldn't meet the challenge of college.*

spoon-feed (spo͞on′fēd′, -fēd′), *v.t.,* **-fed, -feed·ing.** to cause to be spoon-fed.

spoon·ful (spo͞on′fo͝ol), *n., pl.* **-fuls.** **1.** as much as a spoon can hold. **2.** a small quantity. [ME *sponeful.* See SPOON, -FUL]

spoon′ hook′, *Angling.* a fishhook equipped with a spoon lure.

spoon′ nail′, *Med.* an abnormal condition in which the outer surfaces of the nails are concave; koilonychia.

spoon·y¹ (spo͞o′nē), *adj.,* **spoon·i·er, spoon·i·est.** *Informal.* **1.** foolishly or sentimentally amorous. **2.** *Chiefly Brit.* foolish; silly. [SPOON + -Y¹] —**spoon′i·ly,** *adv.* —**spoon′i·ness,** *n.*

spoon·y² (spo͞o′nē), *n., pl.* **spoon·ies.** **1.** a person who is foolishly or sentimentally amorous. **2.** *Chiefly Brit.* a simple or foolish person. [SPOON + -Y²]

spoor (spo͝or, spōr, spôr), *n.* **1.** a track or trail, esp. that of a wild animal pursued as game. —*v.t., v.i.* **2.** to track by or follow a spoor. [< SAfrD; c. OE, Icel *spor,* G *Spur;* cf. SPEER¹] —**spoor′er,** *n.*

spor-, var. of **sporo-** before a vowel: *sporangium.*

Spor·a·des (spôr′ə dēz′; *Gk.* spô rä′thes), *n.pl.* two groups of Greek islands in the Aegean: the one **(Northern Sporades)** off the E coast of Greece; the other **(Southern Sporades),** including the Dodecanese, off the SW coast of Asia Minor.

spo·rad·ic (spō rad′ik, spô-, spə-), *adj.* **1.** (of similar things or occurrences) appearing or happening at irregular intervals in time; occasional: *sporadic renewals of enthusiasm.* **2.** appearing in scattered or isolated instances, as a disease. **3.** isolated, as a single instance of something; being or occurring apart from others. **4.** occurring singly or widely apart in locality: *the sporadic growth of plants.* Also, **spo·rad′i·cal.** [< ML *sporadic(us)* < Gk *sporadikós,* equiv. to *sporad-* (s. of *sporás* strewn, akin to *sporá* SPORE) + *-ikos* -IC] —**spo·rad′i·cal·ly,** *adv.* —**spo·rad′i·cal·ness,** *n.* —**spo·ra·dic·i·ty** (spôr′ə dis′i tē, spōr′-), **spo′ra·dism,** *n.*
—**Syn. 3.** separate, unconnected. —**Ant. 1.** continuous.

sporad′ic chol′era, *Pathol.* a form of gastroenteritis having characteristics similar to those of cholera, as diarrhea, cramps, vomiting, etc., but caused by a different organism, *Vibrio massuah.* Also called **cholera morbus, cholera nostras.** Cf. **cholera.**

spo·ra·do·sid·er·ite (spôr′ə dō sid′ə rīt′, spōr′-), *n.* a meteorite containing scattered grains of iron. [*sporad-* (see SPORADIC) + *-o-* + *sider-* (s. of Gk *sídēros*) iron + -ITE¹]

spo·ran·gi·um (spō ran′jē əm, spô-), *n., pl.* **-gi·a** (-jē ə). *Bot.* the case or sac in which the asexual spores are produced in cryptogams and phanerogams. Also called **spore′ case′.** [< NL, equiv. to *spor-* SPOR- + Gk *angeîon* vessel] —**spo·ran′gi·al,** *adj.*

spore (spōr, spôr), *n., v.,* **spored, spor·ing.** —*n.* **1.** *Biol.* a walled, single-to-many-celled, reproductive body of an organism, capable of giving rise to a new individual either directly or indirectly. **2.** a germ, germ cell, seed, or the like. —*v.i.* **3.** to bear or produce spores. [< NL *spor(a)* < Gk *sporá* sowing, seed, akin to *speírein* to sow; see SPERM¹] —**spo′ral,** *adj.* —**spo′roid,** *adj.*

-spore, var. of **sporo-,** as final element of compound words: *teliospore.*

spore′ fruit′, *Bot.* a spore-bearing structure, as an ascoscarp; sporocarp.

Spö·rer (spœr′ər, spôr′-), *n.* a walled plain in the third quadrant of the face of the moon: about 14 miles in diameter.

spori-, var. of **sporo-** before elements of Latin origin: *sporiferous.*

spo·ri·cide (spōr′i sīd′, spôr′-), *n.* a substance or preparation for killing spores. [SPOR- + -I- + -CIDE] —**spo′ri·ci′dal,** *adj.*

spo·rif·er·ous (spō rif′ər əs, spô-), *adj.* bearing spores. [SPOR- + -I- + -FEROUS]

sporo-, a combining form of **spore:** *sporophyte.* Also, **spor-, -spore, spori-.** Cf. **-sporous.**

spo·ro·carp (spōr′ə kärp′, spôr′-), *n. Bot.* (in higher fungi, lichens, and red algae) a pluricellular body developed for the formation of spores. [SPORO- + -CARP]

spo·ro·cyst (spōr′ə sist′, spôr′-), *n. Zool.* **1.** a walled body resulting from the multiple division of a sporozoan, which produces one or more sporozoites. **2.** a stage in development of trematodes which gives rise, asexually, to cercaria. [SPORO- + -CYST] —**spo·ro·cys·tic** (spōr′ə sis′tik, spôr′-), *adj.*

spo·ro·gen·e·sis (spōr′ə jen′i sis, spôr′-), *n. Biol.* **1.** the production of spores; sporogony. **2.** reproduction by means of spores. [SPORO- + GENESIS] —**spo·rog·e·nous** (spō roj′ə nəs, spô-), *adj.*

spo·ro·go·ni·um (spōr′ə gō′nē əm, spôr′-), *n., pl.* **-ni·a** (-nē ə). *Bot.* the sporangium of mosses and liverworts. [SPORO- + -GONIUM] —**spo′ro·go′ni·al,** *adj.*

spo·rog·o·ny (spō rog′ə nē, spô-), *n. Biol.* (in certain sporozoans) the multiple fission of an encysted zygote or oocyte, resulting in the formation of sporozoites. [SPORO- + -GONY]

spo·ront (spōr′ont, spôr′-), *n.* (in the sexual reproduction of certain sporozoans) an encysted spore developed from a zygote, which undergoes sporogony to form sporozoites. [SPOR- + Gk *ónt-* (s. of *ṓn*) prp. of *einai* to be]

spo·ro·phore (spōr′ə fōr′, spôr′ə fôr′), *n. Bot.* a simple or branched fungus hypha specialized to bear spores. [SPORO- + -PHORE] —**spo·ro·phor·ic** (spōr′ə-fôr′ik, -for′-, spôr′-), **spo·roph·o·rous** (spō rof′ər əs, spô-), *adj.*

spo·ro·phyll (spōr′ə fil, spôr′-), *n. Bot.* a modified leaf which bears sporangia. Also, **spo′ro·phyl.** [SPORO- + -PHYLL] —**spo·ro·phyl·la·ry** (spōr′ə fil′ə rē, spôr′-), *adj.*

spo·ro·phyte (spōr′ə fīt′, spôr′-), *n. Bot.* the asexual form of a plant in the alternation of generations (opposed to *gametophyte*). [SPORO- + -PHYTE] —**spo·ro·phyt·ic** (spōr′ə fit′ik, spôr′-), *adj.*

spo·ro·tri·cho·sis (spōr′ə tri kō′sis, spôr′-), *n. Pathol.* an infectious fungus disease of horses and man, marked by ulceration of superficial lymph vessels of the skin. [< NL *sporotrich-* (s. of *sporothrix* kind of fungus; see SPORO-, TRICH-) + -OSIS] —**spo·ro·tri·chot·ic** (spōr′ə tri kot′ik, spôr′-), *adj.*

-sporous, a word element used to form adjectives corresponding to nouns with stems ending in **-spore:** *teliosporous.* [-SPORE + -OUS]

Spo·ro·zo·a (spōr′ə zō′ə, spôr′-), *n.* the class comprising the sporozoans. [< NL; see SPORO-, -ZOA]

spo·ro·zo·an (spōr′ə zō′ən, spôr′-), *n.* **1.** any parasitic protozoan of the class *Sporozoa,* certain species of which cause malaria. —*adj.* **2.** belonging or pertaining to the *Sporozoa.* [SPOROZO(A) + -AN]

spo·ro·zo·ite (spōr′ə zō′īt, spôr′-), *n. Zool.* one of the minute, active bodies into which the spore of certain *Sporozoa* divides, each developing into an adult individual. [SPOROZO(A) + -ITE¹]

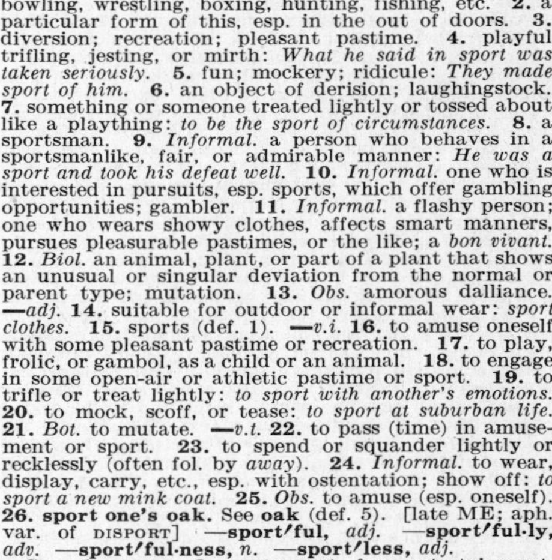

S, Sporran

spor·ran (spor′ən), *n.* (in Scottish Highland costume) a large purse for men, commonly of fur, worn, suspended from a belt, in front of the kilt. [< ScotGael *sporan;* c. Ir *sparán* purse]

sport (spōrt, spôrt), *n.* **1.** an athletic activity requiring skill or physical prowess and often of a competitive nature, as racing, baseball, tennis, golf, bowling, wrestling, boxing, hunting, fishing, etc. **2.** a particular form of this, esp. in the out of doors. **3.** diversion; recreation; pleasant pastime. **4.** playful trifling, jesting, or mirth: *What he said in sport was taken seriously.* **5.** fun; mockery; ridicule: *They made sport of him.* **6.** an object of derision; laughingstock. **7.** something or someone treated lightly or tossed about like a plaything: *to be the sport of circumstances.* **8.** a sportsman. **9.** *Informal.* a person who behaves in a sportsmanlike, fair, or admirable manner: *He was a sport and took his defeat well.* **10.** *Informal.* one who is interested in pursuits, esp. sports, which offer gambling opportunities; gambler. **11.** *Informal.* a flashy person; one who wears showy clothes, affects smart manners, pursues pleasurable pastimes, or the like; a *bon vivant.* **12.** *Biol.* an animal, plant, or part of a plant that shows an unusual or singular deviation from the normal or parent type; mutation. **13.** *Obs.* amorous dalliance. —*adj.* **14.** suitable for outdoor or informal wear: *sport clothes.* **15.** sports (def. 1). —*v.i.* **16.** to amuse oneself with some pleasant pastime or recreation. **17.** to play, frolic, or gambol, as a child or an animal. **18.** to engage in some open-air or athletic pastime or sport. **19.** to trifle or treat lightly: *to sport with another's emotions.* **20.** to mock, scoff, or tease: *to sport at suburban life.* **21.** *Bot.* to mutate. —*v.t.* **22.** to pass (time) in amusement or sport. **23.** to spend or squander lightly or recklessly (often fol. by *away*). **24.** *Informal.* to wear, display, carry, etc., esp. with ostentation; show off: *to sport a new mink coat.* **25.** *Obs.* to amuse (esp. oneself). **26. sport one's oak.** See **oak** (def. 5). [late ME; aph. var. of DISPORT] —**sport′ful,** *adj.* —**sport′ful·ly,** *adv.* —**sport′ful·ness,** *n.* —**sport′less,** *adj.*
—**Syn. 1.** game. **3.** amusement, fun, entertainment. See **play. 17.** romp, caper. **19.** toy.

sport·er (spōr′tər, spôr′-), *n.* **1.** one who or that which sports, as a participant in a sport. **2.** an animal or piece of equipment for use in a sport, as a hunting dog or rifle. [SPORT + -ER¹]

sport·ing (spōr′ting, spôr′-), *adj.* **1.** engaging in, disposed to, or interested in open-air or athletic sports: *a rugged, sporting man.* **2.** concerned with or suitable for such sports: *sporting equipment.* **3.** sportsmanlike. **4.** interested in or connected with sports or pursuits involving betting or gambling: *He enjoyed the sporting life of Las Vegas.* **5.** *Informal.* involving or inducing the taking of risk, as in a sport. [SPORT + -ING²] —**sport′ing·ly,** *adv.*

sport′ing chance′, an even or fair opportunity for a favorable outcome in an enterprise, as winning in a game of chance or in any kind of contest: *They gave the less experienced players a sporting chance by handicapping the experts.*

sport′ing house′, **1.** *Informal.* a brothel. **2.** *Archaic.* an establishment, as a tavern, inn, or the like, catering to gamblers or sportsmen.

sport′ing la′dy, *Informal.* a prostitute.

spor·tive (spōr′tiv, spôr′-), *adj.* **1.** playful or frolicsome; jesting, jocose, or merry: *a sportive puppy.* **2.** done in sport, rather than in earnest: *a sportive show of affection.* **3.** pertaining to or of the nature of a sport or sports. **4.** *Biol.* mutative. **5.** *Archaic.* ardent; wanton. [SPORT + -IVE] —**spor′tive·ly,** *adv.* —**spor′tive·ness;** *Archaic.* **sport′a·bil′i·ty,** *n.*
—**Syn. 1.** jocular, gay, sprightly, frisky.

sports (spōrts, spôrts), *adj.* **1.** of or pertaining to a sport or sports, esp. of the open-air or athletic kind: *a sports festival.* **2.** (of garments, equipment, etc.) suitable for use in open-air sports, or for outdoor or informal use. [see SPORT]

sports′ car′, a small, high-powered automobile with long, low lines, usually seating two persons. Also, **sport′ car′.**

sports·cast (spōrts′kast′, -käst′, spôrts′-), *n.* a radio or television program consisting of sports news or of a running description of a sports event. [SPORTS + CAST, modeled on *broadcast*] —**sports′cast′er,** *n.*

sports·dom (spōrts′dəm, spôrts′-), *n.* the world of professional and amateur competitive sports. [SPORTS + -DOM]

sport′ shirt′, a long- or short-sleeved soft shirt for men, having a squared-off shirttail that may be left outside the trousers, usually worn without a tie. Also, **sports′ shirt′.** Cf. **dress shirt.**

sports′ jack′et, a jacket, often of textured wool, with a collar, lapels, sleeves, and buttons in the front, cut somewhat fuller than the jacket of a business suit, worn with slacks for informal occasions.

sports·man (spōrts′mən, spôrts′-), *n., pl.* **-men. 1.** a man who engages in sports, esp. in some open-air sport, as hunting, fishing, racing, etc. **2.** one who exhibits qualities especially esteemed in those who engage in sports, as fairness, courtesy, good temper, etc. [SPORTS + MAN[1]] —**sports′man·like′, sports′man·ly,** *adj.* —**sports′man·li·ness,** *n.*

sports·man·ship (spōrts′mən ship′, spôrts′-), *n.* **1.** the character, practice, or skill of a sportsman. **2.** sportsmanlike conduct, as fairness, courtesy, being a cheerful loser, etc. [SPORTSMAN + -SHIP]

Sports′man's Note′book, A, a collection of sketches (1852) written by Turgenev. Also called **A Sports′man's Sketch′es, Sketches of a Sportsman.**

sports·wear (spōrts′wâr′, spôrts′-), *n.* informal clothing; originally, clothing for wear while playing golf or tennis, bicycling, etc. [SPORTS + WEAR]

sports·wom·an (spōrts′wo͝om′ən, spôrts′-), *n., pl.* **-wom·en.** a woman who engages in sports. [SPORTS + WOMAN]

sports·writ·er (spōrts′rī′tər, spôrts′-), *n.* a journalist who reports on or writes about sports and sporting events. [SPORTS + WRITER]

sport·y (spōr′tē, spôr′-), *adj.,* **sport·i·er, sport·i·est.** *Informal.* **1.** flashy; showy. **2.** smart in dress, behavior, etc. **3.** like or befitting a sportsman. [SPORT + -Y[1]] —**sport′i·ly,** *adv.* —**sport′i·ness,** *n.*

spor·u·late (spôr′yə lāt′, spor′-), *v.i.,* **-lat·ed, -lat·ing.** *Biol.* to undergo multiple division resulting in the production of spores. [SPORULE + -ATE[1]] —**spor′u·la′tion,** *n.*

spor·ule (spôr′yo͞ol, spor′-), *n. Biol.* a spore, esp. a small one. [< NL *sporul(a).* See SPORE, -ULE] —**spor·u·lar** (spôr′yə lər), *adj.*

spot (spot), *n., v.,* **spot·ted, spot·ting,** *adj.* —*n.* **1.** a mark made by foreign matter, as mud, blood, paint, ink, etc.; a stain, blot, or speck. **2.** a moral stain, as on character or reputation; blemish; flaw. **3.** a pimple. **4.** a comparatively small, usually roundish, part of a surface differing from the rest in color, texture, character, etc.: *a bald spot; a sun spot.* **5.** a place or locality: *A monument marks the spot where Washington slept.* **6.** Usually, **spots.** places of entertainment or sightseeing interest: *We went to a few night spots to dance and see the floor shows.* **7.** See **spot announcement. 8.** a specific position in a sequence or hierachy: *The choral group has the second spot on the program, right after the dancers. He moved up from second spot to become president of the firm.* **9.** *Cards.* **a.** one of various traditional, geometric drawings of a club, diamond, heart, or spade on a playing card for indicating suit and value. **b.** any playing card from a two through a ten: *He drew a jack, a queen, and a three spot.* **10.** *Informal.* a pip, as on dice or dominoes. **11.** *Slang.* a piece of paper money, almost always indicated as a five or ten dollar bill: *Can you loan me a five spot until payday?* **12.** Also called **spot′ illustra′tion.** a small drawing, usually black and white, appearing within or accompanying a text. **13.** *Chiefly Brit. Informal.* **a.** a small quantity of anything. **b.** a drink: *a spot of tea.* **14.** a small, sciaenoid food fish, *Leiostomus xanthurus,* of the eastern coast of the U.S. **15. spots,** commodities, as grain, wool, and soybeans, sold for immediate delivery. **16.** *Informal.* spotlight (def. 1). **17. hit the high spots,** *Informal.* to deal with or include only the major points of interest: *With but a limited amount of vacation time, he concentrated on hitting the high spots of Europe.* **18. hit the spot,** *Slang.* to satisfy a want or need, as to quench thirst: *Iced tea hits the spot during the hot summer months.* **19. in a (bad) spot,** *U.S. Slang.* in an uncomfortable or dangerous predicament: *Whenever she was in a spot she'd write to her father and he'd send a check.* **20. on the spot, a.** without delay; at once; instantly. **b.** at the very place in question. **c.** *U.S. Slang.* in a difficult or embarrassing position. **d.** *U.S. Slang.* in a position of being expected to act or to respond in some way.
—*v.t.* **21.** to stain with spots: *The grease spotted my dress.* **22.** to remove a spot or spots from (clothing), esp. before dry-cleaning. **23.** to sully; blemish. **24.** to mark or diversify with spots or dots, as of color: *We spotted the wall with blue paint.* **25.** to ornament (watch or clock parts) with spaced whirls by means of abrasive disks. **26.** *Informal.* to detect or recognize; locate or identify by seeing: *to spot a hiding child.* **27.** to place or position on a particular place: *to spot a billiard ball.* **28.** to scatter in various places: *to spot chairs here and there in the room.* **29.** *Informal.* to illuminate with a spotlight: *Spot the down-stage door when he enters.* **30.** *Mil.* **a.** to determine (a location) precisely on either the ground or a map. **b.** to observe (the results of gunfire at or near a target) for the purpose of correcting aim. **31.** *Photog.* to remove spots from (a negative or print) by covering them with opaque color. **32.** *Sports Slang.* to give or grant a certain margin or advantage to (an opponent): *He spotted the tyro 12 points a game. The champion won, although spotting the challenger twenty pounds.* **33.** (in gymnastics) to watch or assist (a performer) in order to prevent injury.
—*v.i.* **34.** to make a spot; cause a stain: *Ink spots badly.* **35.** to become spotted, as some fabrics when spattered with water.
—*adj.* **36.** *Radio, Television.* **a.** pertaining to the point of origin of a local broadcast. **b.** broadcast between announced programs. **37.** made, paid, delivered, etc., at once: *a spot sale.* [ME *spotte;* c. MD, LG *spot* speck, Icel *spotti* bit] —**spot′like′,** *adj.* —**spot′ta·ble,** *adj.*
—**Syn. 2.** taint, stigma. **5.** locale, site, situation. **23.** stain, taint, stigmatize, soil, tarnish. **24.** speckle.

spot′ announce′ment, a brief radio or television announcement, usually an advertisement, made by an individual station during or after a network program.

spot′ card′, *Cards.* spot (def. 9b).

spot′ check′, a random sampling or quick sample investigation: *They did a spot check on the number of people who cooperated in the civil defense alert.*

spot′ height′, 1. the elevation of a certain point. **2.** a figure on a map showing such an elevation.

spot·less (spot′lis), *adj.* **1.** free from any spot, stain, etc.; immaculately clean: *a spotless kitchen.* **2.** irreproachable; pure; undefiled: *a spotless reputation.* [late ME; see SPOT, -LESS] —**spot′less·ly,** *adv.* —**spot′less·ness,** *n.*

spot·light (spot′līt′), *n.* **1.** a strong, focused light thrown upon a particular spot, as on a small area of a stage or in a television studio, for making some object, person, or group especially conspicuous. **2.** a brilliant light with a focused beam, carried on an automobile for examining objects, street address numbers, and other things beside the road after dark. **3.** the area of immediate or conspicuous public attention: *Asia is in the spotlight now.* —*v.t.* **4.** to direct the beam of a spotlight upon; light with a spotlight. **5.** to make conspicuous; call attention to: *Newspapers spotlighted the story for a week.* [SPOT + LIGHT[1]]

spot′ line′, *Theat.* a rope or wire hung from a specific place on the gridiron for flying a piece of scenery that could not be flied by the existing battens.

spot′ news′, *Journalism.* **1.** the latest news, reported immediately. **2.** news that occurs unexpectedly.

spot′ pass′, *Basketball, Football.* a pass intentionally directed to a specific place in the court or field instead of a particular receiver, the receiver being expected to arrive at the place at the same time as the ball.

spot′ plate′, *Chem.* a flat ceramic slab containing scooped-out areas on which spot tests are made.

Spots·wood (spots′wo͝od′), *n.* a town in E New Jersey. 5788 (1960).

Spot·syl·va·ni·a (spot′sil vā′nē ə, -vān′yə), *n.* a village in NE Virginia: the scene of battles between the armies of Grant and Lee, May 8–21, 1864.

spot′tail pin′fish (spot′tāl′), a steel-blue sparid fish, *Diplodus holbrooki,* found along the south Atlantic and Gulf coasts of the U.S. Also called **salema.** [so called from the spot on its tail]

spot·ted (spot′id), *adj.* **1.** marked with or characterized by a spot or spots. **2.** sullied; blemished. [ME; see SPOT, -ED[3]] —**spot′ted·ly,** *adv.* —**spot′ted·ness,** *n.*

spot′ted ad′der. See **milk snake.**

spot′ted cal′la lil′y, an herb, *Zantedeschia albomaculata,* of the Cape of Good Hope, having white-spotted leaves and cream-white or yellowish flowers.

spot′ted ca′vy, paca.

spot′ted cow′bane, a North American water hemlock, *Cicuta maculata,* having a purple-mottled stem, white flowers, and deadly poisonous, tuberlike roots. Also called **musquash root, spotted hemlock.**

spot′ted crake′, a small, short-billed rail, *Porzana porzana,* of Europe.

spot′ted crane's′-bill, the American, wild geranium, *Geranium maculatum.*

spot′ted fe′ver, *Pathol.* **1.** any of several fevers characterized by spots on the skin, esp. as in cerebrospinal meningitis or typhus fever. **2.** See **tick fever.**

spot′ted hem′lock. See **spotted cowbane.**

spot′ted hye′na, an African hyena, *Crocuta crocuta,* having a yellowish-gray coat with brown or black spots, noted for its distinctive howl. Also called **laughing hyena.** See illus. under **hyena.**

spot′ted joe-pye′ weed′. See **joe-pye weed** (def. 2).

spot′ted sand′piper, a North American sandpiper, *Actitis macularia,* that has brownish-gray upper parts and white underparts, and is spotted with black in the summer. See illus. under **sandpiper.**

spot′ted sun′fish, a sunfish, *Lepomis punctatus,* found in streams from South Carolina to Florida, having the body marked with longitudinal rows of spots. Also called **stumpknocker.**

spot′ted wilt′, *Plant Pathol.* a disease of plants, characterized by brown, sunken spots and streaks on the stems and leaves and by wilting, caused by a virus, *Lethum australiense.*

spot′ted win′tergreen, an evergreen herb, *Chimaphila maculata,* of central North America, having leaves with mottled white veins and white or pinkish flowers. Also called **dragon's-tongue, rheumatism-root.**

spot·ter (spot′ər), *n.* **1.** (in civil defense) a civilian who watches for enemy airplanes. **2.** *Informal.* a person employed to watch the activity and behavior of others, esp. employees, as for evidence of dishonesty. **3.** *Mil.* **a.** the person who determines for the gunner the fall of shots in relation to the target. **b.** an observer at a forward position who singles out targets for gunners. **4.** (in small-arms practice firing) a small black disk attached to the target to make more prominent the places where a bullet has hit. **5.** a person employed to remove spots from clothing, esp. at a dry-cleaning establishment. **6.** an assistant to a sportscaster who provides the names of the players chiefly involved in each play of a game, esp. a football game. **7.** *Gymnastics, Tumbling.* a person who stations himself where he can serve most effectively to guard against an injury to a performer in the act of executing a maneuver. [SPOT + -ER[1]]

spot′ test′, 1. an informal test run without elaborate preparation in order to obtain an immediate sample response. **2.** *Chem.* a test for the identification of an element or compound in which, upon the addition of a specific reagent to a drop or more of a solution of the questionable sample, the presence of a suspected substance is indicated by a color change or precipitate. Cf. **spot plate.**

spot·ty (spot′ē), *adj.* **-ti·er, -ti·est. 1.** full of, having, or occurring in spots: *spotty coloring.* **2.** irregular or uneven in quality or character: *a spotty performance.* [ME; see SPOT, -Y[1]] —**spot′ti·ly,** *adv.* —**spot′ti·ness,** *n.*

spot-weld (spot′weld′), *v.t.* **1.** to weld (two pieces of metal) together in a small area or spot by the application of heat and pressure. —*n.* **2.** a welded joint made by this process.

spous·al (spou′zəl), *n.* **1.** Often, **spousals.** the ceremony of marriage; nuptials. —*adj.* **2.** nuptial; matrimonial. [ME *spousaile,* aph. var. of *espousaille* ESPOUSAL] —**spous′al·ly,** *adv.*

spouse (*n.* spous, spouz; *v.* spouz, spous), *n., v.,* **spoused, spous·ing.** —*n.* **1.** either member of a married pair in relation to the other; one's husband or wife. —*v.t.* **2.** *Obs.* to join, give, or take in marriage. [ME < OF *spus* (masc.), *spuse* (fem.) < L *spons(us), spons(a)* pledged (man, woman) (n. uses of ptp. of *spondere* to pledge), equiv. to *spond-* pledge + *-tus, -ta* ptp. suffix] —**spouse′hood,** *n.* —**spouse′less,** *adj.*

spout (spout), *v.t.* **1.** to emit or discharge forcibly (a liquid, granulated substance, etc.) in a stream or jet. **2.** *Informal.* to state or declaim volubly or in an oratorical manner: *He spouted his theories on foreign policy for the better part of the night.* —*v.i.* **3.** to discharge, as a liquid, in a jet or continuous stream. **4.** to issue forth with force, as liquid or other material through a narrow orifice. **5.** *Informal.* to talk or speak at some length or in an oratorical manner. —*n.* **6.** a pipe, tube, or liplike projection through or by which a liquid is discharged, poured, or conveyed. **7.** a trough or shoot for discharging or conveying grain, flour, etc. **8.** a waterspout. **9.** a continuous stream of liquid, granulated substance, etc., discharged from or as if from a pipe, tube, shoot, etc. **10.** a spring of water. **11.** a downpour or fall, esp. of water, from a high place; waterfall. **12.** a dumbwaiter or chute, formerly common in pawnbrokers' shops, by which articles pawned were sent to another floor for storage. **13.** *Brit. Slang.* pawnshop. **14. up the spout,** *Brit. Slang.* **a.** pawned. **b.** in a desperate situation; beyond help: *His financial affairs are up the spout.* [ME *spoute(n);* c. D *spuiten;* akin to Icel *spýta* to SPIT[1]] —**spout′er,** *n.* —**spout′less,** *adj.* —**spout′like′,** *adj.*
—**Syn. 3.** squirt, stream, pour. **5.** declaim, rant, harangue, speechify. **6.** nozzle, nose.

spout′ cup′, a deep vessel used in feeding babies and invalids, having a long, curved, rising spout. Also called **feeding cup.**

spout·ed (spou′tid), *adj.* fitted with a spout: *a spouted pitcher.* [SPOUT + -ED[3]]

spp., species (pl. of **specie**).

S.P.Q.R., the Senate and People of Rome. Also, **SPQR** [< L *Senātus Populusque Rōmānus*]

S.P.R., Society for Psychical Research.

Sprach·ge·fühl (shpräkh′gə fyl′), *n. German.* feeling for language, esp. for what is grammatically or idiomatically acceptable in a given language.

sprack·le (sprak′əl), *v.i.,* **-led, -ling.** *Scot.* sprauchle.

sprad·dle (sprad′əl), *v.,* **-dled, -dling.** —*v.t.* **1.** to straddle. —*v.i.* **2.** to sprawl. [< Scand; cf. Norw *spradla* to thrash about, c. OHG *spratalōn* in same sense]

sprad·dle-leg·ged (sprad′əl leg′id, -legd′), *adj.* **1.** moving with or having the legs wide apart: *a spraddle-legged walk.* —*adv.* **2.** with the legs sprawled, spread apart, etc.: *sitting spraddle-legged on the chair.*

sprag[1] (sprag), *n., v.,* **spragged, sprag·ging.** —*n.* **1.** a pole or bar hinged to the rear axle of a cart or the like in such a way that it can brace the vehicle against a road to prevent it from rolling downhill. **2.** *Mining.* a short timber for propping up loose walls or spacing two sets. —*v.t.* **3.** to prop, support, or immobilize (a vehicle) by means of a sprag. [special use of dial. *sprag* twig, OE *spræc(g)* shoot, slip; c. Sw (dial.) *spragg(e)* branch; akin to SPRIG]

sprag[2] (sprag), *n.* a young cod. [special use of dial. *sprag* twig, lively young man; see SPRAG[1] and for meaning cf. SPRIG]

Sprague (sprāg), *n.* a town in S West Virginia. 3073 (1960).

sprain (sprān), *v.t.* **1.** to overstrain or wrench (the ankle, wrist, or other part of the body at a joint) so as to injure without fracture or dislocation. —*n.* **2.** a violent straining or wrenching of the parts around a joint, without dislocation. **3.** condition of being sprained. [?]
—**Syn. 1.** twist. See **strain**[1].

sprang (sprang), *v.* a pt. of **spring.**

sprat (sprat), *n.* **1.** a small, herringlike, marine fish, *Clupea sprattus,* of Europe. **2.** a small or inconsequential person or thing. [var. of earlier *sprot,* ME, OE *sprott* sprat (c. G *Sprott*); appar. same word as OE *sprott* sprout, twig (for the two meanings cf. SPRAG[2]), whence OE *spryttan* to sprout; akin to SPROUT]

sprat·tle (sprat′əl), *n. Scot.* a struggle; fight. [metathetic var. of *spartle* to scatter, itself alter. of *sparple* (ME < OF *(e)sparpeill(er)* < ?)]

sprau·chle (sprä′khəl), *v.i.,* **-chled, -chling.** *Scot.* to clamber. Also, **sprackle.** [?]

sprawl (sprôl), *v.i.* **1.** to be stretched or spread out in an unnatural or ungraceful manner: *The puppy's legs sprawled in all directions.* **2.** to sit or lie in a relaxed position with the limbs spread out carelessly or ungracefully: *He sprawled across the bed.* **3.** to spread out in a straggling or irregular manner, as vines, buildings, handwriting, etc. **4.** to crawl awkwardly with the aid of all the limbs; scramble. —*v.t.* **5.** to stretch out (the limbs) as in sprawling. **6.** to spread out or distribute in a straggling manner. —*n.* **7.** the act or an instance of sprawling; a sprawling posture. **8.** a straggling array of something. [ME *spraule(n),* OE *spréawlian;* c. North Fris *spraweli*] —**sprawl′er,** *n.* —**sprawl′ing·ly,** *adv.*

sprawl·y (sprô′lē), *adj.,* **sprawl·i·er, sprawl·i·est.** tending to sprawl; straggly: *The colt's legs were long and sprawly.* [SPRAWL + -Y[1]]

spray[1] (sprā), *n.* **1.** water or other liquid broken up into small or fine particles and blown or falling through the air. **2.** a jet of fine particles of liquid, as medicine, insecticide, paint, perfume, etc., discharged from an atomizer or other device for direct application to a surface. **3.** a liquid to be discharged or applied in such a jet. **4.** an apparatus or device for discharging such a liquid. **5.** a quantity of small objects, flying or discharged through the air: *a spray of shattered glass.* —*v.t.* **6.** to scatter in the form of fine particles. **7.** to apply as a spray: *to spray an insecticide on plants.* **8.**

to sprinkle or treat with a spray: *to spray plants with insecticide.* **9.** to direct a spray of particles, missiles, etc., upon: *to spray the mob with tear gas.* **—*v.i.* 10.** to scatter spray; discharge a spray: *The hose sprayed over the flowers.* **11.** to issue as spray: *The water sprayed from the hose.* [< MD *spraeien;* c. MHG *spreien* to sprinkle] **—spray′er,** *n.* **—spray′ful,** *adj.* **—spray′ful·ly,** *adv.* **—spray′less,** *adj.* **—spray′like′,** *adj.*

spray[2] (sprā), *n.* **1.** a single, slender shoot, twig, or branch with its leaves, flowers, or berries. **2.** a group or bunch of cut flowers, leafy twigs, etc., arranged decoratively and for display, as in a vase. **3.** an ornament having a similar form. [ME; akin to SPRAG[1]] **—spray′like′,** *adj.*

Spray (sprā), *n.* a town in N North Carolina. 4565 (1960).

spray′ gun′, a device consisting of a container from which liquid is sprayed through a nozzle by air pressure from a pump.

spray′ tank′, a closed tank into which air is pumped to force out a liquid, esp. for a spray.

spread (spred), *v.,* **spread, spread·ing,** *n., adj.* **—*v.t.* 1.** to draw, stretch, or open out in extent, esp. over a flat surface, as a piece of cloth, a rolled or folded map, etc. (often fol. by *out*). **2.** to stretch out or unfurl in the air, as folded wings, a flag, etc. (often fol. by *out*). **3.** to distribute over a greater or a relatively great area of space or time (often fol. by *out*): *to spread out the papers on the table.* **4.** to display or exhibit the full extent of; set out in full: *He spread the pots on the ground and started hawking his wares.* **5.** to dispose or distribute in a sheet or layer: *to spread hay to dry.* **6.** to apply in a thin layer or coating: *to spread butter on a slice of bread.* **7.** to overlay or cover, with something: *She spread the blanket over her knees.* **8.** to set or prepare (a table), as for a meal. **9.** to extend or distribute over a region, place, etc. **10.** to send out, scatter, or shed in various directions, as sound, light, etc. **11.** to scatter abroad; diffuse or disseminate, as knowledge, news, disease, etc.: *to spread the word of the gospel.* **12** to move or force apart: *He spread his arms over his head in surrender.* **13.** to flatten out: *to spread the end of a rivet by hammering.* **14.** *Phonet.* **a.** to extend the aperture between the lips laterally, so as to reduce it vertically, during an utterance. **b.** to delabialize. Cf. **round** (def. 60c), **unround.**
—*v.i.* 15. to become stretched out or extended, as a flag in the wind; expand, as in growth. **16.** to extend over a greater or a considerable area or period: *The factory spread along the river front.* **17.** to be or lie outspread or fully extended or displayed, as a landscape or scene. **18.** to be capable of being spread or applied in a thin layer, as a soft substance: *Margarine spreads easily.* **19.** to become extended or distributed over a region, as population, animals, plants, etc. **20.** to become shed abroad, diffused, or disseminated, as light, influences, rumors, ideas, infection, etc. **21.** to be forced apart, as the rails of a railroad track; separate. **22. spread oneself thin,** to carry on so many projects simultaneously that none is done adequately, or that one's health suffers: *Many college students spread themselves thin by taking on too many activities during the semester.*
—*n.* 23. expansion, extension, or diffusion. **24.** the extent of spreading: *to measure the spread of branches.* **25.** *Finance.* **a.** the difference between the price paid for stock by an underwriter and the price of the stock when sold to the public: *a spread of three points.* **b.** the difference between the bid and asking price of a commodity or security. **c.** straddle (def. 10). **26.** capacity for spreading: *the spread of an elastic material.* **27.** a stretch, expanse, or extent of something: *a spread of timber.* **28.** a cloth covering for a bed, table, or the like, esp. a bedspread. **29.** *Informal.* an abundance of food set out on a table; feast. **30.** any food preparation for spreading on bread, crackers, etc., as jam or peanut butter. **31.** *Aeron.* wing span. **32.** Also called **layout.** *Journalism.* (in newspapers and magazines) an extensive, varied treatment of a subject, consisting primarily either of a number of cuts **(picture spread)** or of a major story and several supplementary stories, usually extending across three or more columns. Cf. **double truck. 33.** an advertisement, photograph, or the like, covering several columns, a full page, or two facing pages of a newspaper, magazine, etc.: *a full-page spread; a two-page spread.* **34.** *Informal.* landed property, as a farm or ranch.
—*adj.* 35. *Jewelry.* (of a gem) cut with the table too large and the crown too shallow for maximum brilliance; swindled. **36.** *Phonet.* (of the opening between the lips) extended laterally. Cf. **rounded** (def. 2), **unrounded.** [ME *sprede(n),* OE *sprǣdan;* c. MD *spreden,* G *spreiten*]
—Syn. 1. unfold, unroll, expand. **10.** emit, diffuse, radiate. **11.** disperse, scatter, publish, circulate, promulgate, propagate. **15.** stretch, dilate. **24.** reach, compass.

spread·a·ble (spred′ə bəl), *adj.* capable of being spread; easily spread: *a soft, spreadable cheese.* [SPREAD + -ABLE]

spread′ ea′gle, 1. a representation of an eagle with outspread wings: used as an emblem of the U.S. **2.** an acrobatic figure in skating.

spread-ea·gle (spred′ē′gəl), *adj., v.,* **-gled, -gling. —*adj.* 1.** having or suggesting the form of a spread eagle. **2.** lying prone with arms and legs outstretched. **3.** boastful or bombastic, esp. in the display of patriotic or nationalistic pride in the U.S. **—*v.t.* 4.** to stretch out (something) in the manner of a spread eagle. **—*v.i.* 5.** to assume the position, or perform the acrobatic figure of a spread eagle: *The skater spread-eagled across the rink.*

spread-ea·gle·ism (spred′ē′gə liz′əm), *n.* boastfulness or bombast, esp. in the display of patriotic or nationalistic pride in the U.S.; flag-waving. [SPREAD-EAGLE + -ISM] **—spread′-ea′gle·ist,** *n.*

spread·er (spred′ər), *n.* **1.** one who or that which spreads. **2.** a small, dull knife or spatula used for spreading butter, jelly, etc., on bread. **3.** a machine for dispersing bulk material: *manure spreader.* **4.** a device for spacing or keeping apart two objects, as electric wires. **5.** *Naut.* a strut for spreading shrouds on a mast. [SPREAD + -ER[1]]

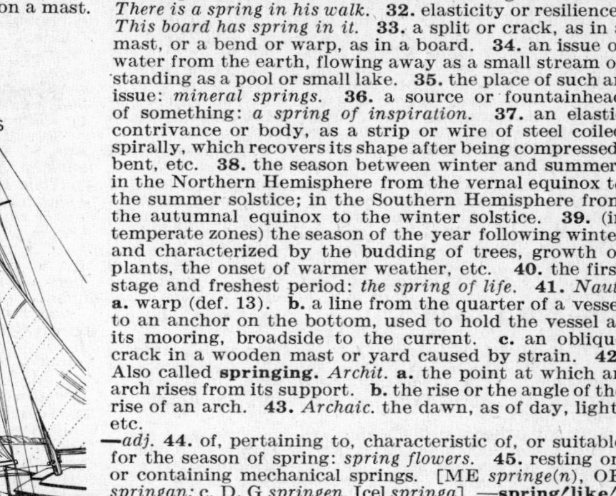

S, Spreader

spread′er beam′, a crosspiece for spacing the chains or cables hanging from the boom of a crane. Also called **yoke.**

spread·er-ditch·er (spred′ər-dich′ər), *n. Railroads.* a machine for shaping and cleaning roadbeds and ditches and for freeing tracks of ice and snow by plowing and digging.

spread′ing dog′bane, a stout, perennial herb *Apocynum androsaemifolium,* of North America, having pinkish flowers. Also called **honey-bloom, wild ipecac.**

spread·sheet (spred′shēt′), *n.* a work sheet used in accounting to show related entries, arranged side by side in parallel columns.

Sprech·ge·sang (shprekн′gə zäng′), *n. German.* (in music) a vocal style intermediate between speech and singing but without exact pitch intonation. [lit., sung speech]

spree (sprē), *n.* **1.** a lively frolic or outing. **2.** a bout or spell of drinking to intoxication; binge; carousal. **3.** a period, spell, or bout of indulgence, as of a particular wish, craving, or whim: *an eating spree; a spending spree.* **4.** a period or outburst of extreme activity: *Our basketball team went on a scoring spree.* [?]

Spree (shprā), *n.* a river in East Germany, flowing N through Berlin to the Havel River. 220 mi. long.

spri·er (sprī′ər), *adj.* a comparative of **spry.**

spri·est (sprī′ist), *adj.* a superlative of **spry.**

sprig (sprig), *n., v.,* **sprigged, sprig·ging. —*n.* 1.** a small spray of some plant with its leaves, flowers, etc. **2.** an ornament having the form of such a spray. **3.** a shoot, twig, or small branch. **4.** *Facetious.* a scion, offspring, or heir of a family, class, etc. **5.** a youth or young fellow. **6.** See **glazier's point. 7.** Also called **dowel pin.** a headless brad. **8.** *Foundry.* **a.** a small peg for reinforcing the walls of a mold. **b.** a metal insert, used to chill certain portions of cast metal, that becomes an integral part of the finished casting. **—*v.t.* 9.** to mark or decorate (fabrics, pottery, etc.) with a design of sprigs. **10.** to fasten with brads. **11.** *Foundry.* to reinforce the walls of (a mold) with sprigs. **12** to remove a sprig or sprigs from (a plant). [ME *sprigge;* akin to SPRAG[1], SPRAY[2]]

sprig·gy (sprig′ē), *adj.,* **-gi·er, -gi·est.** possessing sprigs or small branches. [SPRIG + -Y[1]]

spright·ful (sprīt′fəl), *adj.* sprightly. [*spright* (sp. var. of SPRITE) + -FUL]

spright·ly (sprīt′lē), *adj.,* **-li·er, -li·est,** *adv.* **—*adj.* 1.** animated, vivacious, or gay; lively. **—*adv.* 2.** in a sprightly manner. [*spright* (sp. var. of SPRITE) + -LY] **—spright′li·ness,** *n.*
—Syn. 1. spirited, blithe, buoyant, spry.

sprig·tail (sprig′tāl′), *n.* **1.** the pintail, *Anas acuta.* **2.** See **ruddy duck. 3.** See **sharp-tailed grouse.** [SPRIG + TAIL[1]]

spring (spring), *v.,* **sprang** or, often, **sprung; sprung; spring·ing;** *n.; adj.* **—*v.i.* 1.** to rise, leap, move, or act suddenly and swiftly, as by a sudden dart or thrust forward or outward, or being suddenly released from a coiled or constrained position: *to spring into the air; a tiger about to spring.* **2.** to appear or be aroused suddenly: *His anger springs to the surface easily.* **3.** to be released from a constrained position, as by resilient or elastic force or from the action of a spring: *A trap springs. The door sprang open and in he walked.* **4.** to issue forth suddenly, as water, blood, sparks, fire, etc. (often fol. by *forth, out,* or *up*): *Tears spring to her eyes.* **5.** to come into being, rise, or arise (usually fol. by *up*): *Industries sprang up in the suburbs.* **6.** to come into being by growth, as from a seed or germ, bulb, root, etc.; grow, as plants. **7.** to proceed or originate, as from a source or cause. **8.** to have as one's birth or lineage; be descended, as from a person, family, stock, etc.; come from: *to spring from ancient aristocracy.* **9.** to rise or extend upward, as a spire. **10.** to take an upward course or curve from a point of support, as an arch. **11.** to start or rise from cover, as a pheasant, woodcock, or the like. **12.** to become bent or warped, as boards. **13.** to shift or work loose, as parts of a mechanism, structure, etc.: *The board sprang from the fence during the storm.* **14.** to explode, as a mine. **15.** *Archaic.* to begin to appear, as day, light, etc.; dawn.
—*v.t.* 16. to cause to spring. **17.** to cause to fly back, move, or act, as by resiliency, elastic force, a spring, etc.: *to spring a lock.* **18.** to cause to shift out of place, work loose, warp, split, or crack: *Moisture sprang the board from the fence.* **19.** to split or crack: *The ship sprang its keel on a rock.* **20.** to develop by or as by splitting or cracking: *The boat sprang a leak.* **21.** to bend by force, or force in by bending, as a resilient slat or bar. **22.** to stretch or bend (a spring or other resilient device) beyond its elastic tolerance: *This clip has been sprung.* **23.** to bring out, disclose, produce, make, etc., suddenly: *to spring a joke.* **24.** to leap over. **25.** *Slang.* to secure the release of (someone) from confinement, as of jail, military service, or the like. **26.** *Naut.* to move (a vessel) into or out of its berth at a pier by pulling on the offshore end of a warp made fast to the pier. **27.** to explode (a mine).
—*n.* 28. a leap, jump, or bound. **29.** a springing or starting from place. **30.** a recoiling or flying back from a forced position. **31.** an elastic or bouncing movement: *There is a spring in his walk.* **32.** elasticity or resilience: *This board has spring in it.* **33.** a split or crack, as in a mast, or a bend or warp, as in a board. **34.** an issue of water from the earth, flowing away as a small stream or standing as a pool or small lake. **35.** the place of such an issue: *mineral springs.* **36.** a source or fountainhead of something: *a spring of inspiration.* **37.** an elastic contrivance or body, as a strip or wire of steel coiled spirally, which recovers its shape after being compressed, bent, etc. **38.** the season between winter and summer: in the Northern Hemisphere from the vernal equinox to the summer solstice; in the Southern Hemisphere from the autumnal equinox to the winter solstice. **39.** (in temperate zones) the season of the year following winter and characterized by the budding of trees, growth of plants, the onset of warmer weather, etc. **40.** the first stage and freshest period: *the spring of life.* **41.** *Naut.* **a.** warp (def. 13). **b.** a line from the quarter of a vessel to an anchor on the bottom, used to hold the vessel at its mooring, broadside to the current. **c.** an oblique crack in a wooden mast or yard caused by strain. **42.** Also called **springing.** *Archit.* **a.** the point at which an arch rises from its support. **b.** the rise or the angle of the rise of an arch. **43.** *Archaic.* the dawn, as of day, light, etc.
—*adj.* 44. of, pertaining to, characteristic of, or suitable for the season of spring: *spring flowers.* **45.** resting on or containing mechanical springs. [ME *springe(n),* OE *springan;* c. D, G *springen,* Icel *springa*] **—spring′like′,** *adj.*
—Syn. 1. jump, bound, hop, vault. **3.** recoil, rebound. **4.** shoot, dart, fly. **5.** start, originate. **7.** emerge, emanate, issue, flow. **12.** bend, warp. **32.** resiliency, buoyancy. **36.** origin, head. **46.** vernal.

Springs (def. 37) A, Spiral; B, Coil; C, Volute; D, Leaf

Spring (spring), *n.* a girl's given name.

spring·al[1] (spring′əl), *n. Archaic.* an ancient military engine for throwing stones or other missiles. Also, **springald.** [ME < OF *(e)springale* < Gmc (see SPRING- + *-l-* suffix)]

spring·al[2] (spring′əl), *n.* springald[1].

spring·ald[1] (spring′əld), *n. Archaic.* a youth; young fellow. [late ME, deriv. of **springard* leaper, jumper (by dissimilation). See SPRING, -ARD]

spring·ald[2] (spring′əld), *n. Archaic.* springal[1].

spring′ beau′ty, any American, portulacaceous spring herb of the genus *Claytonia,* esp. *C. virginica,* having a raceme of white or pink flowers.

spring′ bell′, a hardy perennial herb, *Sisyrinchium douglasi,* of western North America, having reddish-purple flowers.

spring′ bind′er, a loose-leaf binder in which a single, long, clamplike spring, forming the spine, holds the leaves.

spring·board (spring′bōrd′, -bôrd′), *n.* **1.** a flexible board, projecting over water, from which divers leap or spring. **2.** a flexible board used as a take-off in vaulting, tumbling, etc., to increase the height of leaps. **3.** *Informal.* something that supplies the impetus or conditions for a beginning, change, or progress; a point of departure: *a lecture to serve as a springboard for a series of seminars.* [SPRING + BOARD]

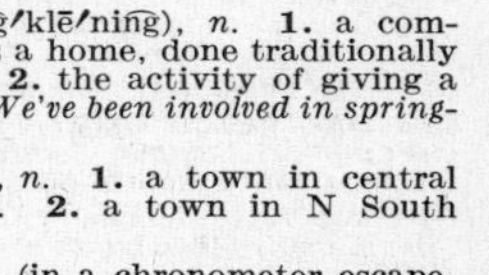

Springbok (2½ ft. high at shoulder; horns 15 in.; length 5 ft.)

spring·bok (spring′bok′), *n., pl.* **-boks,** (esp. *collectively*) **-bok.** a gazelle, *Antidorcas marsupialis,* of southern Africa, noted for its habit of springing into the air when alarmed. [< SAfrD. See SPRING, BUCK[1]]

spring·buck (spring′buk′), *n., pl.* **-bucks,** *(esp. collectively)* **-buck.** springbok.

spring′ can′kerworm. See under **cankerworm.**

spring′ chick′en, 1. a young chicken, esp. a broiler or fryer. **2.** *Slang.* a young person: *I don't know her age, but she's no spring chicken.*

Spring′ Cit′y, a town in SE Pennsylvania. 3162 (1960).

spring-clean (spring′klēn′), *v.t.* to subject (a place) to a spring-cleaning.

spring-clean·ing (spring′klē′ning), *n.* **1.** a complete cleaning of a place, as a home, done traditionally in the spring of the year. **2.** the activity of giving a place a complete cleaning: *We've been involved in spring-cleaning and are exhausted.*

Spring·dale (spring′dāl′), *n.* **1.** a town in central Pennsylvania. 5602 (1960). **2.** a town in N South Carolina. 2981 (1960).

spring′ detent′, *Horol.* (in a chronometer escapement) a detent having the form of a bar, mounted on the loose end of a flexible length of steel, which supports a pallet for locking the escape wheel as well as a passing spring.

springe (sprinj), *n., v.,* **springed, spring·ing. —*n.* 1.** a snare for catching small game. **—*v.t.* 2.** to catch in a springe. **—*v.i.* 3.** to set a springe or springes. [ME, var. of *sprenge,* lit., something that is made to spring, deriv. of *sprenge(n)* (to) make spring, OE *sprengean,* causative of *springan* to SPRING]

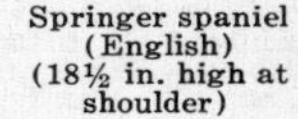

Springer spaniel (English) (18½ in. high at shoulder)

spring·er (spring′ər), *n.* **1.** one who or that which springs. **2.** *Archit.* the first voussoir above the impost of an arch. See diag. under **arch**[1]. [ME. see SPRING, -ER[1]]

spring′er span′iel, a dog of either of two breeds of medium-sized spaniels, used for flushing and retrieving game. Cf. **English springer spaniel, Welsh springer spaniel.**

spring′ fe′ver, a listless, lazy, or restless feeling commonly associated with the beginning of spring.

Spring·field (spring′fēld′), *n.* **1.** a city in S Massachusetts, on the Connecticut River. 174,463 (1960). **2.** a city in SW Missouri. 95,865 (1960). **3.** a city in and the capital of Illinois, in the central part. 83,271 (1960). **4.** a city in W Ohio. 82,723 (1960). **5.** a town in SE Pennsylvania, near Philadelphia. 26,733 (1960). **6.** a city in W Oregon. 19,616 (1960). **7.** a town in N Tennessee. 9221 (1960). **8.** a town in SE Vermont. 6600 (1960). **9.** a town in NW Florida. 4628 (1960). **10.** a town in SW Minnesota. 2701 (1960).

Spring′field Place′, a town in S Michigan. 5136 (1960).

Spring′field ri′fle, **1.** a single-shot, breech-loading .45-caliber rifle used by the U.S. Army from 1867 to 1893. **2.** Also called **Springfield 1903.** a bolt-operated, magazine-fed, .30-caliber rifle adopted by the U.S. Army in 1903 and used during World War I. **3.** a single-shot, muzzleloading rifle of .58-inch caliber, used by the U.S. Army during the Civil War. [named after SPRINGFIELD, Mass., from U.S. arsenal there]

spring·halt (spring′hôlt′), *n.* *Vet. Pathol.* stringhalt. [alter. by assoc. with SPRING]

spring·head (spring′hed′), *n.* **1.** a spring or fountainhead from which a stream flows. **2.** the source of something: *the springhead of desire.* [SPRING + HEAD]

Spring·hill (spring′hil′), *n.* a town in NW Louisiana. 6437 (1960).

spring·house (spring′hous′), *n., pl.* **-hous·es** (-hou′ziz). a small storehouse built over a spring or part of a brook, for keeping such foods as meat and dairy products cool and fresh. [SPRING + HOUSE]

spring·ing (spring′ing), *n.* **1.** the act or process of one who or that which springs. **2.** the mechanical springs or the type or arrangement of springs with which any of various devices are equipped, esp. a vehicle. **3.** *Archit.* spring (def. 42). [ME; see SPRING, -ING[1]] —**spring′ing·ly,** *adv.*

spring′ing line′, *Archit.* an imaginary line at the level of the spring of an arch.

Spring′ Lake′, a town in E New Jersey. 2922 (1960).

Spring′ Lake′ Heights′, a town in E New Jersey. 3309 (1960).

spring′ lamb′, a lamb born in the late winter or early spring and sold for slaughter prior to July 1.

spring·less (spring′lis), *adj.* **1.** having no springs: *a springless bed.* **2.** lacking liveliness or resilience; lifeless: *His shoulders drooped and his walk had become springless.* [SPRING + -LESS]

spring·let (spring′lit), *n.* a small spring of water. [SPRING + -LET]

spring′ line′, *Naut.* warp (def. 13).

spring-load·ed (spring′lō′did), *adj.* (of a machine part) kept normally in a certain position by a spring: *a spring-loaded safety valve.*

spring·lock (spring′lok′), *n.* a lock that fastens automatically by a spring. [SPRING + LOCK[1]]

spring′ mold′ing, *Carpentry.* See **sprung molding.**

spring′ peep′er, a tree frog, *Hyla crucifer,* having an X-shaped mark on the back and voicing a shrill call commonly heard near ponds and swamps of eastern North America in the early spring.

Springs (springz), *n.* a city in the E Republic of South Africa, ESE of Johannesburg. 135,231 (1960).

Spring′ Sea′. See **Mare Veris.**

spring′ star′flower, an herb, *Brodiaea uniflora,* of Argentina, having solitary, slightly onion-scented, blue-tinged, white flowers.

spring′ stay′, *Naut.* a horizontal stay connecting the lower topmasts of a vessel.

spring·tail (spring′tāl′), *n.* any of numerous small, wingless insects of the order *Collembola,* having a ventral, forked appendage on the abdomen, which is suddenly extended to spring the insect into the air. [SPRING + TAIL[1]]

spring′ tide′, **1.** the large rise and fall of the tide at or soon after the new or the full moon. **2.** any great flood or swelling rush: *a spring tide of compliments.*

spring·time (spring′tīm′), *n.* **1.** the season of spring. **2.** the first or earliest period: *the springtime of love.* Also called **spring·tide** (spring′tīd′). [SPRING + TIME]

spring′ train′ing, **1.** a program of physical exercise, practice, and exhibition games followed by a baseball team in the late winter and early spring, before the start of the regular season. **2.** the period during which such a program takes place, usually from the beginning of March until the middle of April.

Spring′ Val′ley, **1.** a town in SE New York. 6538 (1960). **2.** a town in N Illinois. 5371 (1960). **3.** a town in SE Minnesota. 2628 (1960).

spring′ vetch′, the vetch, *Vicia satira.*

spring′ vetch′ling, a perennial herb, *Lathyrus vernus,* of Europe, having clusters of bluish-violet flowers and smooth pods.

Spring·ville (spring′vil), *n.* **1.** a town in central Utah. 7913 (1960). **2.** a town in W New York. 3852 (1960).

spring·wood (spring′wŏŏd′), *n.* that part of an annual ring of wood, characterized by large, thin-walled cells, formed during the first part of the growing season. Also called **early wood.** Cf. **summerwood.** [SPRING + WOOD[1]]

spring·y (spring′ē), *adj.,* **spring·i·er, spring·i·est. 1.** characterized by spring or elasticity; flexible; resilient: *He walks with a springy step.* **2.** (of land) abounding in or having springs of water. [SPRING + -Y[1]] —**spring′i·ly,** *adv.* —**spring′i·ness,** *n.*
—**Syn. 1.** buoyant, bouyancy; youthful.

sprin·kle (spring′kəl), *v.,* **-kled, -kling,** *n.* —*v.t.* **1.** to scatter (a liquid, powder, etc.) in drops or particles: *She sprinkled powder on the baby.* **2.** to disperse or distribute here and there. **3.** to overspread with drops or particles of water, powder, or the like: *to sprinkle a lawn.* **4.** to diversify or intersperse with objects scattered here and there. —*v.i.* **5.** to scatter or disperse liquid, a powder, etc. in drops or particles. **6.** to be sprinkled. **7.** to rain slightly (often used impersonally with *it* as subject): *It may sprinkle this evening.* —*n.* **8.** the act or an instance of sprinkling. **9.** that which is sprinkled on something. **10.** Usually, **sprinkles.** small particles of chocolate, candy, sugar, etc., used as a decorative topping for cookies, cakes, ice-cream cones, and the like. **11.** a light rain. **12.** a small quantity or number. [ME *sprenkle;* c. D *sprenkelen,* G *sprenkeln;* akin to OE *sprengan* to sprinkle, make (things) spring, scatter, causative of *springan* to SPRING]
—**Syn. 1.** distribute, rain. SPRINKLE, SCATTER, STREW mean to fling, spread, or disperse. To SPRINKLE means to fling about small drops or particles: *to sprinkle water on clothes, powder on plants.* To SCATTER is to disperse or spread widely: *to scatter seeds.* To STREW is to scatter, esp. in such a way as to cover or partially cover a surface: *to strew flowers on a grave.*

sprink·ler (spring′klər), *n.* **1.** any of various devices for sprinkling, as a watering pot, a container of water with a perforated top used to sprinkle clothes before ironing, or esp. a perforated ring or small stand with a revolving nozzle to which a hose is attached for watering a lawn with a fine, even spray. **2.** a person who sprinkles. —*v.t.* **3.** to provide (a warehouse, school, office building, etc.) with a sprinkler system. [SPRINKLE + -ER[1]]

sprin′kler sys′tem, a device for extinguishing fires in a building, consisting of a system of water pipes in or below the ceilings, with valves or sprinklers usually made to open automatically at a certain temperature.

sprin·kling (spring′kling), *n.* **1.** a small quantity or number scattered here and there. **2.** a small quantity sprinkled or to be sprinkled. [late ME *sprenclyng.* See SPRINKLE, -ING[1]] —**sprin′kling·ly,** *adv.*

sprin′kling can′. See **watering pot.**

sprint (sprint), *v.i.* **1.** to race or move at full speed, esp. for a short distance, as in running, rowing, etc. —*v.t.* **2.** to traverse in sprinting: *to sprint a half mile.* —*n.* **3.** a short race at full speed. **4.** a burst of speed at any point during a long race, as near the finish line. **5.** a brief spell of great activity. [OE **sprintan* (cf. *gesprintan* to emit); c. OSw *sprenta,* Icel *spretta,* OHG *sprinzan* to jump up] —**sprint′er,** *n.*

sprint′ med′ley, *Track.* a medley relay in which the first member of a team runs 440 yards, the second and third members run 220 yards each, and the fourth member runs 880 yards. Cf. **distance medley.**

sprit (sprit), *n.* *Naut.* a small pole or spar crossing a fore-and-aft sail diagonally from the mast to the upper aftermost corner, serving to extend the sail. [ME *spret,* OE *sprēot;* c. D, G *Spriet;* akin to SPROUT]

S, Sprit

sprite (sprit), *n.* an elf, fairy, or goblin. [ME *sprit* < OF *(e)sprit* < L *spīrit(us)* SPIRIT] —**sprite′hood,** *n.* —**sprite′less,** *adj.* —**sprite′like′,** *adj.*
—**Syn.** See **fairy.**

sprite′ crab′. See **ghost crab.**

sprit·sail (sprit′sāl′; *Naut.* sprit′səl), *n.* *Naut.* a sail extended by a sprit. [late ME *sprete seyle* (see SPIRIT, SAIL); cf. D *sprietzeil*]

sprit′sail top′mast, *Naut.* a short, vertical mast on ships of the 17th and early 18th centuries, fitted at the end of the bowsprit, carrying a single square sail.

spritz (sprits, shprits), *Chiefly Dial.* —*v.t.* **1.** to spray briefly and quickly; squirt: *He spritzed a little soda in his drink.* —*n.* **2.** a quick, brief spray of liquid; squirt. [< PaG *schpritze* < MHG *sprütze(n)* (to) squirt]

spritz·er (sprit′sər, shprit′-), *n.* a tall drink made with chilled wine and soda. [< G, deriv. of *spritzen* to squirt]

sproat (sprōt), *n.* *Angling.* a fishhook having a circular bend. Also, **sproat′ hook′.** [named after W. H. *Sproat,* 19th-century English angler]

sprock·et (sprok′it), *n.* *Mach.* **1.** Also called **sprock′et wheel′.** a toothed wheel engaging with a conveyor or power chain. **2.** *Obs.* one tooth of such a wheel. **3.** *Carpentry.* a wedge-shaped piece of wood extending a sloping roof over the eaves with a flatter pitch. [*sprock-* (? metathetic var. of *spork-,* OE *spor(a)* SPUR[1] + *-k-* suffix) + -ET]

Sprockets

sprout (sprout), *v.i.* **1.** to begin to grow; shoot forth, as a plant from a seed. **2.** (of a seed or plant) to put forth buds or shoots. **3.** to develop or grow quickly: *a boy awkwardly sprouting into manhood.* —*v.t.* **4.** to cause to sprout. **5.** to remove sprouts from: *Sprout and boil the potatoes.* —*n.* **6.** a shoot of a plant. **7.** a new growth from a germinating seed, or from a rootstock, tuber, bud, or the like. **8.** something resembling or suggesting a sprout, as in growth. **9. sprouts.** See **Brussels sprout.** [ME *spr(o)uten,* OE *-sprūtan;* c. MD *sprūten,* G *spriessen* to sprout; akin to Gk *speírein* to scatter]

Spru·ance (sprōō′əns), *n.* **Raymond Ames** (āmz), born 1886, U.S. admiral.

spruce[1] (sprōōs), *n.* **1.** any evergreen, coniferous tree of the genus *Picea,* having short, angular, needle-shaped leaves attached singly around twigs. **2.** any of various allied trees, as the Douglas fir and the hemlock spruce. **3.** the wood of any such tree. —*adj.* **4.** made from the wood of a spruce tree or trees. **5.** containing or abounding in spruce trees. [late ME, special use of *Spruce* sandhi var. of *Pruce* < OF *Pruce* < ML *Prussia,* var. of *Borussia* Prussia, whence the timber came]

spruce[2] (sprōōs), *adj.,* **spruc·er, spruc·est,** *v.,* **spruced, spruc·ing.** —*adj.* **1.** trim in dress or appearance; neat; smart; dapper. —*v.t.* **2.** to make spruce or smart (often fol. by *up*): *Spruce up the children before the company comes.* —*v.i.* **3.** to make oneself spruce (usually fol. by *up*). [obs. *spruce jerkin,* orig. jerkin made of *spruce leather,* i.e., leather imported from Prussia (see SPRUCE[1]), hence fine, smart, etc.] —**spruce′ly,** *adv.* —**spruce′ness,** *n.*

spruce′ bark′ bee′tle, a bark beetle, *Polygraphus rufipennis,* that feeds on and nests in spruce, pine, and other evergreen trees.

spruce′ beer′, a fermented beverage made with spruce leaves and twigs, or an extract from them.

spruce′ bud′worm (bud′wûrm′), the larva of a tortricid moth, *Choristoneura fumiferana,* that feeds on the foliage of spruce, fir, balsam, etc.

spruce′ grouse′, a grouse, *Canachites canadensis,* of coniferous forests of northern North America.

Spruce′ Pine′, a town in W North Carolina. 2504 (1960).

spruce′ saw′fly, any of several sawflies of the family *Diprionidae,* esp. *Diprion hercyniae* **(European spruce sawfly),** the larvae of which feed on the foliage of spruce.

sprue[1] (sprōō), *n., v.,* **sprued, spru·ing.** —*n.* **1.** *Foundry.* **a.** an opening through which molten metal is poured into a mold. **b.** the waste metal left in this opening after casting. **2.** *Metalworking.* a channel in a forging die permitting the die to clear that part of the rough piece not being forged. —*v.t.* **3.** to cut the sprues from (a casting). [?]

sprue[2] (sprōō), *n.* *Pathol.* a chronic disease, occurring chiefly in the tropics, characterized by diarrhea, ulceration of the mucous membrane of the digestive tract, and a smooth, shining tongue; psilosis. [< D *spruw;* c. MLG *sprūwe* tumor < ?]

spruik (sprōōk), *v.i.* *Australian Slang.* to make or give a speech, esp. extensively or elaborately; spiel; orate. [?] —**spruik′er,** *n.*

spruit (sprōōt, sprāt), *n.* (in southern Africa) a small stream. [< SAfrD; MD *sprute* SPROUT]

sprung (sprung), *v.* a pt. and pp. of **spring.**

sprung′ mold′ing, *Carpentry.* a molded board, as one forming part of a cornice, placed diagonally and secured at the ends to two surfaces intersecting at a right angle. Also called **spring molding.**

sprung′ rhythm′, a system of prosody with the accent always on the first syllable of every foot followed by a varying number of unaccented syllables, all feet being given equal time length.

spry (sprī), *adj.,* **spry·er, spry·est** or **spri·er, spri·est.** active; nimble; agile; energetic; brisk. [?] —**spry′ly,** *adv.* —**spry′ness,** *n.*

spt., seaport.

spud (spud), *n., v.,* **spud·ded, spud·ding.** —*n.* **1.** *Informal.* a potato. **2.** a spadelike instrument, esp. one with a narrow blade, as for digging up or cutting the roots of weeds. **3.** a chisellike tool for removing bark. **4.** a pointed leg or stake for staying or supporting dredging or earth-boring machinery. **5.** *Survey.* spad. **6.** a short pipe, as for connecting a water pipe with a meter. **7.** *Surg.* an instrument having a dull flattened blade for removing substances or foreign bodies from certain parts of the body, as wax from the ear. —*v.t.* **8.** to remove with a spud. **9. spud in,** to set up earth-boring equipment, esp. for drilling an oil well. [ME *spuddle* a kind of knife < ?]

spud·der (spud′ər), *n.* **1.** one who prepares and operates a rig for drilling oil wells. **2.** a light drilling rig used chiefly in beginning a well. **3.** spud (def. 3). [SPUD + -ER[1]]

spue (spyōō), *v.i., v.t.,* **spued, spu·ing.** spew.

Spu·mans (spōō′mänz, -mənz), *n.* **Mare.** See **Mare Spumans.**

spu·man·te (*It.* spōō män′te; *Eng.* spə män′tē, spyə-), *n.* See **Asti′spumante.** [< It: lit., foaming; see SPUME]

spume (spyōōm), *v.,* **spumed, spum·ing,** *n.* —*v.t.* **1.** to eject or discharge as or like foam or froth; spew (often fol. by *forth*). —*v.i.* **2.** to foam; froth. —*n.* **3.** foam, froth, or scum. [ME < L *spūm(a)* foam, froth, equiv. to *spū-* (var. of *spu-* in *spuere* to spit out; see SPEW) + *-ma* n. suffix] —**spu′mous, spum′y,** *adj.*

spu·mes·cent (spyōō mes′ənt), *adj.* foamy; foamlike; frothy. [SPUME + -ESCENT] —**spu·mes′cence,** *n.*

spu·mo·ne (spə mō′nē, -nä; *It.* spōō mô′ne), *n.* an Italian style of ice cream of a very fine and smooth texture, usually containing layers of various colors and flavors and chopped fruit or nuts. Also, **spu·mo·ni** (spə mō′nē). [< It, equiv. to *spum(a)* SPUME + *-one* aug. suffix]

spun (spun), *v.* **1.** a pt. and pp. of **spin.** —*adj.* **2.** formed by or as by spinning.

spun′ glass′. See **fiber glass.**

spunk (spungk), *n.* **1.** *Informal.* pluck; spirit; mettle. **2.** touchwood, tinder, or punk. [b. SPARK[1] and obs. *funk* spark, touchwood (c. D *vonk,* G *Funke*)] —**spunk′less,** *adj.*

spunk·ie (spung′kē), *n.* *Scot.* **1.** a will-o'-the-wisp. **2.** *Informal.* a lively, courageous person. [SPUNK + -IE]

spunk·y[1] (spung′kē), *adj.,* **spunk·i·er, spunk·i·est.** *Informal.* plucky; spirited. [SPUNK + -Y[1]] —**spunk′i·ly,** *adv.* —**spunk′i·ness,** *n.*

spunk·y[2] (spung′kē), *n., pl.* **spunk·ies.** *Scot.* spunkie.

spun′ ray′on, **1.** yarn produced by spinning short, uniform lengths of rayon filaments into a continuous strand. **2.** a fabric woven from this yarn.

spun′ silk′, **1.** yarn produced by spinning silk waste and short, broken filaments from which the sericin has been removed. Cf. **reeled silk. 2.** a fabric woven from this yarn.

spun′ sug′ar, a confection resembling fluff or floss, made from hot boiled sugar that has threaded, used as a garnish, frosting, or in making cotton candy.

spun·ware (spun′wâr′), *n.* *Metalworking.* objects formed by spinning. [SPUN + WARE[1]]

spun′ yarn′, **1.** yarn produced by spinning fibers into a continuous strand. **2.** *Naut.* cord formed of rope yarns loosely twisted together, for serving ropes, bending sails, etc.

spur[1] (spûr), *n., v.,* **spurred, spur·ring.** —*n.* **1.** a U-shaped device which slips over and straps to the heel of a boot and has a blunt, pointed, or roweled projection at the back for use by a mounted rider to urge a horse forward. **2.** anything that goads, impels, or urges, to action, speed, or achievement. **3.** *Ornith.* a stiff, usually sharp, horny process on the leg of various birds, esp. the domestic rooster. **4.** a sharp, piercing, or cutting instrument fastened to the leg of a gamecock in cockfighting; gaff. **5.** *Phys. Geog.* a ridge or line of elevation projecting from or subordinate to the main

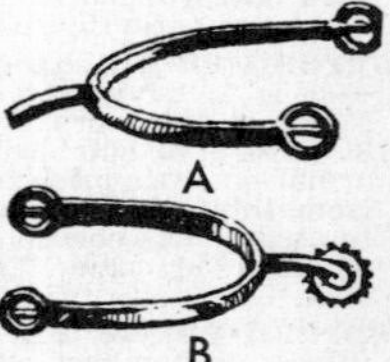

Spurs
A, Spur[1] (def. 1)
B, Rowel spur

body of a mountain or mountain range. **6.** something that projects and resembles or suggests a gaff; sharp projection. **7.** a short or stunted branch or shoot, as of a tree. **8.** *Archit.* griffe[2]. **9.** *Typography.* a short, seriflike projection from the bottom of the short vertical stroke in the capital G in some fonts. **10.** See **wing dam.** **11.** *Bot.* **a.** a slender, usually hollow, projection from some part of a flower, as from the calyx of the larkspur or the corolla of the violet. **b.** a short shoot bearing flowers, as in fruit trees. **12.** *Archit.* **a.** a short wooden brace, usually temporary, for strengthening a post or some other part. **b.** any offset from a wall, as a buttress. **13.** *Ceram.* a triangular support of refractory clay for an object being fired. **14.** *Railroads.* See **spur track.** **15. on the spur of the moment,** without deliberation; impulsively; suddenly: *We headed for the beach on the spur of the moment.* **16. win one's spurs,** to achieve distinction or success for the first time; prove one's ability or worth: *Our team hasn't won its spurs yet.* —*v.t.* **17.** to prick with or as with a spur or spurs; incite or urge on: *Appreciation spurs ambition.* **18.** to strike or wound with the spur, as a gamecock. **19.** to furnish with spurs or a spur. —*v.i.* **20.** to goad or urge one's horse with spurs or a spur; ride quickly. **21.** to proceed hurriedly; press forward: *We spurred onward through the night.* [ME *spure,* OE *spur(a)*; c. OHG *sporo,* Icel *spori* spur; akin to SPURN] —**spur′less,** *adj.* —**spur′like′,** *adj.* —**spur′rer,** *n.*
—**Syn. 1, 2.** goad. **2.** incitement, stimulus, incentive, inducement, provocation, instigation. **17.** goad, provoke, stimulate, impel, inspire, induce, instigate. —**Ant. 17.** discourage.

spur[2] (spûr), *n.* *Papermaking.* a batch of newly made rag-paper sheets. [?]

spur′ blight′, *Plant Pathol.* a disease of raspberries, characterized by reddish-brown spots on the stems, caused by a fungus, *Didymella applanata.*

spur′ gall′, a hairless and indurated area or gall on the side of a horse, caused by the irritation of a spur.

spurge (spûrj), *n.* any of numerous plants of the genus *Euphorbia,* having a milky juice and flowers with no petals or sepals. [late ME < MF *(e)spurge,* appar. back formation from *espurgier* < L *expurgāre* to cleanse. See EX-[1], PURGE]

spur′ gear′, *Mach.* a gear having straight teeth cut on the rim parallel to the axis of rotation.

Spur gear

spur′ gear′ing. 1. a system of spur gears. **2.** any system of gears with parallel axes of rotation.

spurge′ lau′rel, a laurellike shrub, *Daphne Laureola,* of southern and western Europe and western Asia, having evergreen leaves and green axillary flowers.

Spur·geon (spûr′jən), *n.* **Charles Had·don** (had′ᵊn), 1834–92, English Baptist preacher.

spu·ri·ous (spyŏŏr′ē əs), *adj.* **1.** not genuine, authentic, or true; not from the claimed, pretended, or proper source; counterfeit. **2.** of illegitimate birth; bastard. **3.** *Biol.* (of two or more parts, plants, etc.) having a similar appearance but a different structure. [< L *spurius;* see -OUS] —**spu′ri·ous·ly,** *adv.* —**spu′ri·ous·ness,** *n.*
—**Syn. 1.** false, sham, bogus, mock, feigned, phony; meretricious, deceitful. —**Ant. 1.** genuine.

spu′rious wing′, alula (def. 1).

spurl′ing pipe′ (spûr′ling), *Naut.* spillpipe. [*spurling* (< ?)]

spurn (spûrn), *v.t.* **1.** to reject with disdain; scorn. **2.** to treat with contempt; despise. **3.** *Obs.* to kick. —*v.i.* **4.** to show disdain or contempt; scorn something. —*n.* **5.** disdainful rejection. **6.** contemptuous treatment. **7.** a kick. [ME *spurn(en),* OE *spurnan;* c. Icel *sporna,* OS, OHG *spurnan* to kick; akin to L *spernere* to put away] —**spurn′er,** *n.*
—**Syn. 1.** See **refuse**[1]. **6.** contumely. —**Ant. 1.** accept.

spur-of-the-mo·ment (spûr′əv thə mō′mənt), *adj.* extemporaneous; unplanned: *The senator gave a spur-of-the-moment talk to the workers.*

spurred (spûrd), *adj.* **1.** having spurs or a spur. **2.** bearing spurs or spurlike spines. [late ME; see SPUR[1], -ED[3]]

spur·rey (spûr′ē, spur′ē), *n., pl.* **-reys.** spurry.

spur·ri·er (spûr′ē ər, spur′-), *n.* a maker of spurs. [ME *sporier.* See SPUR[1], -IER]

spurr·ite (spûr′īt, spur′-), *n.* a rare mineral, a silicate and carbonate of calcium, occurring in the metamorphic aureoles around igneous intrusions. [named after Josiah E. *Spurr* (1870–1950), American geologist]

spur-row·el (spûr′rou′əl), *n.* *Heraldry.* a mullet having a circular opening usually of the tincture of the field.

spur·ry (spûr′ē, spur′ē), *n., pl.* **-ries. 1.** any of several caryophyllaceous herbs of the genus *Spergula,* esp. *S. arvensis,* having white flowers and numerous whorled, linear leaves. **2.** any of various allied or similar plants. [SPUR[1] + -Y[1]]

spurt (spûrt), *v.i.* **1.** to gush or issue suddenly in a stream or jet, as a liquid; spout. **2.** to show marked, usually increased, activity or energy for a short period: *The runners spurted forward in the last lap of the race.* —*v.t.* **3.** to expel or force out suddenly in a stream or jet, as a liquid; spout. —*n.* **4.** a sudden, forceful gush or jet of or as of liquid. **5.** a marked increase of effort for a short period or distance, as in running, rowing, etc. **6.** a sudden outburst, as of activity, feeling, etc. Also, **spirt.** [var. of *spirt,* by metathesis from ME *sprutten,* OE *sprytten* to spring, come forth; akin to OE *sprytting* a shoot, sprout, increase; and to SPROUT] —**spurt′er,** *n.* —**spur′tive,** *adj.* —**spur′tive·ly,** *adv.*
—**Syn. 1.** well, spring. **4.** spout. —**Ant. 1.** drip, ooze.

spur·tle (spûr′tᵊl), *n.* *Scot. and North Eng.* **1.** a cooking spatula. **2.** a stirring stick, as used to stir porridge in a kettle. **3.** sword. [*spurt-* (by metathesis from SPRIT) + -LE]

spur′ track′, *Railroads.* a short branch track leading from the main track, and connected with it at one end only. Also called **stub track.**

spur′ wheel′. See **spur gear.**

sput·nik (spŏŏt′nik, sput′-; *Russ.* spōōt′nik), *n.* a man-made satellite launched by the Soviet Union. [< Russ: lit. fellow-wayfarer, equiv. to *s-* with + *-put-* path + *-nik* agent suffix]

sputter (sput′ər), *v.i.* **1.** to emit particles, sparks, etc., forcibly or explosively. **2.** to eject particles of saliva, food, etc., from the mouth in a light spray, as when speaking angrily or excitedly. **3.** to utter or spit out words or sounds explosively or incoherently, as when angry or flustered. —*v.t.* **4.** to emit (anything) forcibly and in small particles, as if by spitting: *The fire sputtered cinders.* **5.** to eject (saliva, food, etc.) in small particles explosively and involuntarily, as in excitement. **6.** to utter explosively and incoherently. —*n.* **7.** the act or sound of sputtering. **8.** explosive, incoherent utterance. **9.** matter ejected in sputtering. [*sput-* (var. of SPOUT) + -ER[6]; c. D *sputteren*] —**sput′ter·er,** *n.* —**sput′ter·ing·ly,** *adv.*

spu·tum (spyōō′təm), *n., pl.* **-ta** (-tə). **1.** matter, as saliva mixed with mucus or pus, expectorated from the mouth in diseases of the respiratory tract. **2.** that which is expectorated; spittle. [< L *spūtum,* n. use of neut. of *spūtus* (ptp. of *spuere* to spit), equiv. to *spū-* spit + *-tus* ptp. suffix]

Spuy′ten Duy′vil Creek′ (spīt′ᵊn dī′vəl), a channel in New York City at the north end of Manhattan Island, connecting the Hudson and Harlem rivers.

spy (spī), *n., pl.* **spies,** *v.,* **spied, spy·ing.** —*n.* **1.** one who keeps close and secret watch on the actions and words of another or others. **2.** one employed by a government to obtain secret information or intelligence about another country, esp. with reference to military or naval affairs. **3.** the act of spying. —*v.i.* **4.** to observe secretively or furtively with hostile intent (often fol. by *on* or *upon*). **5.** to be on the lookout; keep watch. **6.** to examine or search closely or carefully. —*v.t.* **7.** to observe (a person, place, enemy, etc.) secretively or furtively with hostile intent. **8.** to inspect or examine or to search or look for closely or carefully. **9.** to discover or find out by observation or scrutiny. **10.** to catch sight of suddenly; espy; descry: *to spy a rare bird overhead.* [ME *spi(en),* aph. var. of *espien* to ESPY] —**spy′-ship,** *n.*

spy·glass (spī′glas′, -gläs′), *n.* a small telescope. [SPY + GLASS]

Spy·ri (shpē′rē), *n.* **Jo·han·na** (*Ger.* yô hä′nä; *Eng.* jō han′ə, -an′ə), 1827–1901, Swiss author.

Sq., **1.** Squadron. **2.** Square (of a city or town).

sq., **1.** sequence. **2.** the following one. [< L *sequēns*] **3.** the following ones. [< L *sequentia*] **4.** squadron. **5.** square.

sq. cm., square centimeter or square centimeters.

sqd., squad.

sq. ft., square foot or square feet.

sq. in., square inch or square inches.

sq. km., square kilometer or square kilometers.

sq. mi., square mile or square miles.

sq. mm., square millimeter or square millimeters.

sqq., the following ones. [< L *sequentia*]

sq. r., square rod or square rods.

squab (skwob), *n. pl.* **squabs,** (*esp. collectively for 1*) **squab,** *adj.* —*n.* **1.** a nestling pigeon, marketed when fully grown but still unfledged. **2.** a short, stout person. **3.** a thickly stuffed, soft cushion. —*adj.* **4.** short and thick or broad. **5.** (of a bird) unfledged or newly hatched. [< Scand; cf. dial Sw *skvabb* loose fat flesh, dial. Norw *skvabb* soft wet mass]

squab·ble (skwob′əl), *v.,* **-bled, -bling,** *n.* —*v.i.* **1.** to engage in a petty quarrel. —*v.t.* **2.** *Print. Obs.* to disarrange and mix (composed type). —*n.* **3.** a petty quarrel. [< Scand; cf. dial. Sw *skvabbel* to quarrel, Norw *skvabbe* to gabble; perh. akin to SCUFFLE] —**squab′bler,** *n.* —**squab′bling·ly,** *adv.*
—**Syn. 1.** quarrel, wrangle, bicker, fight.

squab·by (skwob′ē), *adj.,* **-bi·er, -bi·est.** short and stout; squat. [SQUAB + -Y[1]]

squad (skwod), *n., v.,* **squad·ded, squad·ding.** —*n.* **1.** a small number of soldiers, commonly 10 men, a staff sergeant, and a corporal; the smallest military unit. **2.** any small group or party of persons engaged in a common enterprise: *A squad of children raided the kitchen for cookies.* —*v.t.* **3.** to form into squads. **4.** to assign to a squad. [< F *(e)squade,* alter. of *esquadre* < Sp *escuadra* SQUARE; so called from square shape of formation]

squad′ car′, an automobile used by policemen, equipped with a radiotelephone for communicating with police headquarters. Also called **cruise car, police car.**

squad·der (skwod′ər), *n.* a member of a squad: *riot squadder; fire squadder.* [SQUAD + -ER[1]]

squad′ lead′er, *Mil.* an enlisted man in charge of a squad, usually of sergeant's rank.

squad·ron (skwod′rən), *n.* **1.** a portion of a naval fleet or a detachment of warships; a subdivision of a fleet. **2.** an armored cavalry or cavalry unit consisting of two or more troops, a headquarters, and various supporting units. **3.** (in the U.S. Air Force) **a.** the basic administrative and tactical unit, smaller than a group and composed of two or more flights. **b.** a flight formation. **4.** a number of persons grouped or united together for some purpose; group. —*v.t.* **5.** to form into a squadron or squadrons; marshal or array in or as in squadrons. [< It *squadron(e),* equiv. to *squadr(a)* SQUARE + *-one* aug. suffix]

squad′ room′, **1.** *Mil.* (in a barracks) a room in which a number of men sleep. **2.** a room in a police station where policemen assemble, as for inspection, roll call, or duty assignments.

squa·lene (skwā′lēn), *n.* *Biochem.* an oil, $C_{30}H_{50}$, found in human fat secretions, obtained for commercial use chiefly from the liver oil of sharks, and used as an intermediate in the synthesis of cholesterol, and in the manufacture of vehicles for cosmetics and pharmaceuticals. Also called **spinacene.** [< NL *Squal(us)* name of a family, L: a kind of fish + -ENE]

squal·id (skwol′id, skwôl′-), *adj.* **1.** foul and repulsive, as from lack of care or cleanliness; neglected and filthy. **2.** wretched; miserable; degraded; sordid. [< L *squālid(us)* dirty, equiv. to *squāl-* (root of *squālēre* to be dirty from neglect) + *-idus* -ID[4]] —**squal′id·ly,** *adv.* —**squal′id·ness, squa·lid·i·ty** (skwo lid′i tē), *n.*
—**Syn. 1.** unclean. See **dirty.** —**Ant. 1, 2.** splendid.

squall[1] (skwôl), *n.* **1.** a sudden, violent gust of wind, often accompanied by rain, snow, or sleet. **2.** a sudden disturbance or commotion. —*v.i.* **3.** to blow as a squall. [? special use of SQUALL[2]] —**squall′ish,** *adj.*

squall[2] (skwôl), *v.i.* **1.** to cry or scream loudly and violently: *The hungry baby began to squall.* —*v.t.* **2.** to utter in a screaming tone: *The baby squalled "Mama!"* —*n.* **3.** the act or sound of squalling: *The baby's squall was heard next door.* [< Scand; cf. Icel *skvala* to shout] —**squall′er,** *n.*

squall′ line′, *Meteorol.* a line or extended narrow region along a cold front within which squalls or thunderstorms occur, often several hundred miles long.

squal·ly (skwô′lē), *adj.,* **-li·er, -li·est. 1.** characterized by squalls. **2.** *Informal.* threatening. [SQUALL[1] + -Y[1]]

squal·or (skwol′ər, skwô′lər), *n.* the condition of being squalid; filth and misery. [< L *squālor* dirtiness, equiv. to *squāl-* (see SQUALID) + *-or* -OR[1]]
—**Syn.** wretchedness. —**Ant.** splendor.

squam-, var. of **squamo-** before a vowel: *squamation.*

squa·ma (skwā′mə), *n., pl.* **-mae** (-mē). a scale or scalelike part, as of epidermis or bone. [< L: scale]

squa·mate (skwā′māt), *adj.* provided or covered with squamae or scales; scaly. [< LL *squāmāt(us).* See SQUAMA, -ATE[1]]

squa·ma·tion (skwā mā′shən), *n.* **1.** the state of being squamate. **2.** the arrangement of the squamae or scales of an animal. [SQUAM- + -ATION]

squa·mi·form (skwā′mə fôrm′), *adj.* shaped like a scale. [SQUAMA- + -I- + -FORM]

squamo-, a combining form of **squama:** *squamocellular.* Also, *esp. before a vowel,* **squam-.**

squa·mo·cel·lu·lar (skwā′mə sel′yə lər), *adj.* pertaining to or having a squamous epithelium. [SQUAMO- + CELLULAR]

squa·mo·sal (skwə mō′səl), *adj.* **1.** *Anat.* of or pertaining to the thin, scalelike portion of the temporal bone that is situated on the side of the skull above and behind the ear. **2.** *Zool.* pertaining to a corresponding bone in other vertebrates. **3.** squamous. —*n.* **4.** a squamosal bone. [SQUAMOSE + -AL[1]]

squa·mous (skwā′məs), *adj.* covered with or formed of squamae or scales; scalelike. Also, **squamosal, squa·mose** (skwā′mōs, skwə mōs′). [<L *squāmōsus.* See SQUAMA, -OUS, -OSE[1]] —**squa′mous·ly, squa′mose·ly,** *adv.* —**squa′mous·ness, squa′mose·ness,** *n.*

squa′mous epithe′lium, *Biol.* epithelium consisting of one or more layers of scalelike cells.

squam·u·lose (skwam′yə lōs′, skwā′myə-), *adj.* furnished or covered with small scales. [< L *squāmul(a)* (*squām(a)* scale + *-ula* -ULE) + -OSE[1]]

squan·der (skwon′dər), *v.t.* **1.** to spend or use (money, time, etc.) extravagantly or wastefully (often fol. by *away*). **2.** to scatter. —*n.* **3.** extravagant or wasteful expenditure. [?] —**squan′der·er,** *n.* —**squan′der·ing·ly,** *adv.*
—**Syn. 1.** waste, dissipate, lavish. See **spend.** —**Ant. 1.** save.

square (skwâr), *n., v.,* **squared, squar·ing,** *adj.,* **squar·er, squar·est,** *adv.* —*n.* **1.** a rectangle having all four sides of equal length. **2.** anything having this form or a form approximating it, as a city block, rectangular piece of candy, etc. **3.** an open area or plaza, in a city or town, formed by the meeting or intersecting of two or more streets and often planted with grass, trees, etc., in the center. **4.** a rectangularly shaped area on a game board, as in chess or checkers. **5.** a try square, T-square, or the like. **6.** *Math.* **a.** the second power of a quantity, expressed as $a^2 = a \times a$, where a is the quantity. **b.** a quantity that is the second power of another: *Four is the square of two.* **7.** *Slang.* a person who is ignorant of or uninterested in current fads, ideas, manners, tastes, etc.; conformer; conventionalist. **8.** *Mil.* (formerly) a body of troops drawn up in quadrilateral form. **9.** *Building Trades.* a unit of measure for roofing materials, equal to 100 square feet. **10.** *Naut.* the area at the bottom of a hatchway. **11.** *Obs.* a pattern, standard, or example. **12. on the square, a.** at right angles. **b.** *Informal.* straightforward; honest; just: *Their dealings with us have always been on the square.* **13. out of square, a.** not at right angles. **b.** *Informal.* not in agreement; incorrect; irregular: *The measurements are out of square.* —*v.t.* **14.** to reduce to square, rectangular, or cubical form (often fol. by *off*): *He squared off the log to make a timber for his house.* **15.** to mark out in one or more squares or rectangles. **16.** to test with measuring devices for deviation from a right angle, straight line, or plane surface. **17.** *Math.* **a.** to find the equivalent of in square measure. **b.** to multiply (a number or quantity) by itself; raise to the second power. **c.** to describe or find a square which is equivalent in area to: *to square a circle.* **18.** to bring to the form of a right angle or right angles; set at right angles to something else. **19.** to even the score of (a contest): *to square a game.* **20.** to set (the shoulders and back) in an erect posture so they form an angle similar to a right angle. **21.** to make straight, level, or even: *Square the cloth on the table.* **22.** to regulate, as by a standard; adapt; adjust. **23.** to adjust harmoniously or satisfactorily (often fol. by *with*): *How could he square such actions with his conscience?* **24.** to balance; pay off; settle: *to square a debt.* **25.** *Slang.* to secure a desired action or attitude by means of bribery; bribe. —*v.i.* **26.** to accord or agree (often fol. by *with*): *His theory does not square with the facts.* **27.** to settle, even, or balance a matter, as by paying a bill, returning a favor, tying a score, etc. **28. square away, a.** *Naut.* to arrange the yards so as to sail before the wind. **b.** *Informal.* to prepare; get ready: *Square away for dinner.* **c.** to assume a position of defense or offense: *The wrestlers squared away for the first fall.* **29. square off,** to assume a posture of defense or offense, as in boxing: *They squared off for a fight.* **30. square the circle,** to strive without chance of success; attempt the impossible: *He wants to be a doctor, but in his circumstances it would be squaring the circle.* **31. square up,** to pay or settle an account, bill, etc.: *He squared up with the cashier and checked out of the hotel.* —*adj.* **32.** formed by or as a right angle; having some part or parts rectangular: *a square corner.* **33.** having four sides and four right angles in two dimensions or three pairs of parallel sides meeting at right angles in three dimensions; having each dimension in the shape of a square or rectangle and all angles right angles: *a square box.* **34.** at right angles, or perpendicular. **35.** *Naut.* at right angles to the mast and the keel, as a

yard. **36.** noting a unit representing an area in the form of a square. **37.** pertaining to such units, or to surface measurement. **38.** having a specified length on each of four equal sides: *a farm a mile square.* **39.** having a square or rectangular section: *a square file.* **40.** having a solid, sturdy form, esp. when characterized by a rectilinear or angular outline. **41.** straight, level, or even, as a surface or surfaces. **42.** leaving no balance of debt on either side; having all accounts settled: *He was square with his landlord.* **43.** *Informal.* just, fair, or honest. **44.** *Informal.* straightforward, direct, or unequivocal. **45.** *Informal.* substantial or satisfying: *a square meal.* **46.** *Slang.* conventional or conservative in style or outlook; not hip: *Playing those old love songs in waltz time is as square as you can get.*
—*adv.* **47.** so as to be square; in square or rectangular form. **48.** at right angles. **49.** *Informal.* fairly, honestly, or straightforwardly. [ME < OF (*e*)*squarre* < VL _*exquadra_, deriv. of _*exquadrāre_ (L *ex-* EX-[1] + *quadrāre* to square; see QUADRATE)] —**squar′a·ble,** *adj.* —**square′like′,** *adj.* —**square′ness,** *n.* —**squar′er,** *n.*
—**Syn. 3.** place, park. **21.** straighten. **22.** rectify. **42.** balanced. **44.** downright, straight.

square′ and rab′bet, annulet (def. 2).

square′ bod′y. See **dead flat** (def. 1).

square′ brack′et, *Print.* either of two parenthetical marks, [or].

square′ cen′timeter, a unit of area measurement equal to a square measuring one centimeter on each side. *Abbr.:* cm^2, sq. cm.

square′ dance′, **1.** a dance, as a quadrille, by a set of couples arranged in a square or in some set form. **2.** hoedown (def. 1). —**square′ danc′er.**

square-dance (skwâr′dans′, -däns′), *v.i.,* **-danced, -danc·ing.** **1.** to perform or participate in a square dance. **2.** to participate in a hoedown.

square′ deal′, *Informal.* a fair and honest arrangement or transaction: *You can always count on him to give you a square deal.*

squared′ pa′per, graph paper with a pattern of squares formed by lines crossing at right angles.

squared′ ring′, *Informal.* See **boxing ring.** Also called **squared′ cir′cle.**

squared′ splice′. See **square splice.**

square·face (skwâr′fās′), *n. Brit. Slang.* gin[1]. [so called from the shape of the bottle, with *square* understood also in the sense of good]

square′ foot′, a unit of area measurement equal to a square measuring one foot on each side. *Abbr.:* ft^2, sq. ft.

square′ frame′, *Shipbuilding.* any of the frames of the parallel middle body of a hull.

square·head (skwâr′hed′), *n. Offensive.* **1.** a German or a Dutchman. **2.** a Scandinavian. [SQUARE + HEAD]

square′ inch′, a unit of area measurement equal to a square measuring one inch on each side. *Abbr.:* in^2, sq. in.

square′ joint′. See **straight joint** (def. 2). —**square′-joint′ed,** *adj.*

square′ kil′ometer, a unit of area measurement equal to a square measuring one kilometer on each side. *Abbr.:* km^2, sq. km.

square′ knot′, a common knot in which the ends come out alongside of the standing parts. See illus. under **knot.**

square-law (skwâr′lô′), *adj. Electronics.* of or pertaining to an electronic circuit or device that produces an output voltage proportional to the square of its input voltage over the range of input voltages for which it is designed to function: *square-law detector.*

square′ leg′, *Cricket.* **1.** the position of a fielder on the left of the batsman and almost on the opposite side of the wicket. **2.** the fielder occupying this position. Also, **square′-leg′.**

square·ly (skwâr′lē), *adv.* **1.** in a square shape, form, or manner. **2.** directly; without evasion; in a straight or straightforward manner: *He faced the problem squarely.* **3.** in an honest or open manner; straightforwardly; fairly. [SQUARE + -LY]

square′ ma′trix, *Math.* a matrix in which the number of rows is equal to the number of columns.

square′ meas′ure, a system of units for the measurement of surfaces or areas.

square′ me′ter, a unit of area measurement equal to a square measuring one meter on each side. *Abbr.:* m^2, sq. m.

square′ mile′, a unit of area measurement equal to a square measuring one mile on each side. *Abbr.:* mi^2, sq. mi.

square′ mil′limeter, a unit of area measurement equal to a square measuring one millimeter on each side. *Abbr.:* mm^2, sq. mm.

square′ num′ber, a number that is the square of another integer, as 1 of 1, 4 of 2, 9 of 3, etc.

square′ pian′o, a large, spinet-type piano with a rectangular, horizontal body. Cf. **spinet** (def. 2).

square-rigged (skwâr′rigd′), *adj. Naut.* having square sails as the principal sails. —**square′-rig′ger,** *n.*

square′ rod′, a unit of area measurement equal to a square measuring one rod on each side.

square′ root′, a quantity of which a given quantity is the square: *The square root of 36 is 6.*

square′ sail′, *Naut.* a sail set beneath a horizontal yard, the normal position of which, when not trimmed to the wind, is directly athwartships.

square′ ser′if, *Typography.* a font of type having serifs with a weight equal to or greater than that of the main strokes. Cf. **Egyptian** (def. 6).

square′ set′, *Mining.* a set having 12 timbers joined in a cube.

square′ shake′, *Informal.* See **square deal.**

square′ shoot′er, *Informal.* an honest, fair person. —**square′ shoot′ing.**

square-shoul·dered (skwâr′shōl′dərd), *adj.* having the shoulders held back, giving a straight form to the upper part of the back.

square′ splice′, *Carpentry.* a scarf joint between two pieces, having the form of a half-lap joint with a thicker and a thinner section for each piece, the thicker one being at the end: used to resist tension.

square·tail (skwâr′tāl′), *n.* any of several fishes of the genus *Tetragonurus,* found in the deep waters of tropical and temperate seas, having a squarish tail and an armor of tough, bony scales. [SQUARE + TAIL[1]]

square-toed (skwâr′tōd′), *adj.* **1.** having a broad, square toe, as a shoe. **2.** old-fashioned or conservative in habits, ideas, etc.; prim. [SQUARE + TOED] —**square′-toed′ness,** *n.*

square-toes (skwâr′tōz′), *n.* (*construed as sing.*) an old-fashioned or strait-laced person.

square′ yard′, a unit of area measurement equal to a square measuring one yard on each side. *Abbr.:* yd^2, sq. yd.

squar′ing the cir′cle. See **quadrature of the circle.**

squar·ish (skwâr′ish), *adj.* approximately square. [SQUARE + -ISH[1]] —**squar′ish·ly,** *adv.*

squar·rose (skwar′ōs, skwo rōs′), *adj. Biol.* denoting any rough or ragged surface. [< L *squarrōs*(*us*) scurfy, scabby] —**squar′rose·ly,** *adv.*

squash[1] (skwosh), *v.t.* **1.** to press into a flat mass or pulp; crush: *He squashed the flower under his heel.* **2.** to suppress or put down; quash. **3.** *Informal.* to silence or disconcert (someone), as with a crushing retort, emotional or psychological pressure, or the like. —*v.i.* **4.** to be pressed into a flat mass or pulp. **5.** (of a soft, heavy body) to fall heavily. **6.** to make a splashing sound; splash. **7.** to be capable of being or likely to be squashed: *Tomatoes squash easily.* —*n.* **8.** the act or sound of squashing. **9.** the fact of squashing or of being squashed. **10.** something squashed or crushed. **11.** something soft and easily crushed. **12.** Also called **squash′ rac′quets.** a game for two or four persons, similar to racquets but played on a smaller court and with a racket having a round head and a long handle. **13.** Also called **squash′ ten′nis.** a game for two persons, resembling squash racquets except that the ball is larger and livelier and the racket is shaped like a tennis racket. **14.** *Brit.* a beverage made from fruit juice and soda water: *lemon squash.* [< MF (*e*)*squasser* < VL _*exquassāre_. See EX[1], QUASH] —**squash′er,** *n.*

squash[2] (skwosh), *n., pl.* **squash·es,** (*esp. collectively*) **squash.** **1.** the fruit of any of various vinelike, tendril-bearing plants of the genus *Cucurbita,* used as a vegetable, esp. *C. moschata* and *C. maxima.* **2.** any of these plants. [< Narragansett *askútasquash,* lit., vegetables eaten green]

squash′ bug′, a dark brown hemipterous insect, *Anasa tristis,* that sucks the sap from the leaves of squash, pumpkin, and other cucurbitaceous plants.

squash′ vine′ bor′er, the larva of a clearwing moth, *Melittia cucurbitae,* that bores into the stems of squash and other cucurbitaceous plants.

squash·y (skwosh′ē), *adj.,* **squash·i·er, squash·i·est.** **1.** easily squashed; pulpy. **2.** soft and wet, as the ground after rain. **3.** having a squashed appearance. [SQUASH[1] + -Y[1]] —**squash′i·ly,** *adv.* —**squash′i·ness,** *n.*

squas·sa·tion (skwo sā′shən), *n.* a form of strappado in which the victim, with arms bound behind and feet heavily weighted, was jerked up and down at the end of a rope passed under his arms. [< It *squassa*(*re*) (to) shake severely + -TION]

squat (skwot), *v.,* **squat·ted** or **squat, squat·ting,** *adj., n.* —*v.i.* **1.** to sit in a low or crouching position with the legs drawn up closely beneath or in front of the body; sit on one's haunches or heels. **2.** to crouch or cower down, as an animal. **3.** to settle on land, esp. public or new land, without any title or right. **4.** to settle on public land under government regulation, in order to acquire title. **5.** *Naut.* (of a vessel, esp. a power vessel) to draw more water astern when in motion forward than when at rest. —*v.t.* **6.** to cause to squat. —*adj.* **7.** (of a person, animal, the body, etc.) short and thickset. **8.** low and thick or broad: *The building had a squat shape.* **9.** seated or being in a squatting position; crouching. —*n.* **10.** the act or fact of squatting. **11.** a squatting position or posture. **12.** *Naut.* the tendency of a vessel to draw more water astern when in motion than when stationary. [ME *squatt*(*en*) < OF (*e*)*squate*(*r*), (*e*)*squati*(*r*), equiv. to *es-* EX-[1] + *quatir* < VL _*coactīre_ to compress, equiv. to L *coact*(*us*), ptp. of *cōgere* to compress (*co-* CO- + *-ac-* drive (var. of *ag-*) + *-tus* ptp. suffix) + *-īre* inf. suffix]

squat·ly (skwot′lē), *adv.* so as to be or look short and wide; in a squat manner: *a squatly built house.* [SQUAT + -LY]

squat·ness (skwot′nis), *n.* the quality or appearance of being short and wide: *The squatness of the house made it ugly.* [SQUAT + -NESS]

squat·ter (skwot′ər), *n.* **1.** one who or that which squats. **2.** one who settles on land, esp. public or new land, without title or right. **3.** one who settles on land under government regulation, in order to acquire title. [SQUAT + -ER[1]] —**squat′ter·dom,** *n.*

squat′ter sov′ereignty, *U.S. Hist.* (used contemptuously by its opponents) See **popular sovereignty** (def. 2).

squat′ter's right′, *Law Informal.* a claim to real property, esp. public land, that may be granted to a person who has openly possessed and continuously occupied it without legal authority for a prescribed period of years.

squat·ty (skwot′ē), *adj.,* **-ti·er, -ti·est.** short and thick; low and broad. [SQUAT + -Y[1]] —**squat′ti·ly,** *adv.* —**squat′ti·ness,** *n.*

squaw (skwô), *n.* a North American Indian woman, esp. a wife. [< some Algonquian tongue; cf. Natick *squa* a female]

squaw·bush (skwô′bŏŏsh′), *n.* a rank-smelling, sprawling shrub, *Rhus trilobata,* found from Illinois and Texas to the Pacific Coast, having greenish flowers. Also called **lemonade sumac.** [SQUAW + BUSH[1], so called from its use by the Indians]

squaw·fish (skwô′fish′), *n., pl.* (*esp. collectively*) **-fish,** (*esp. referring to two or more kinds or species*) **-fish·es.** **1.** any of several large, voracious cyprinid fishes of the genus *Ptychocheilus,* found in the rivers of the western U.S. and Canada. **2.** a viviparous perch, *Taeniotoca lateralis,* found off the Pacific Coast of the U.S. [SQUAW + FISH]

squawk (skwôk), *v.i.* **1.** to utter a loud, harsh cry, as a duck or other fowl when frightened. **2.** *Slang.* to complain loudly and vehemently. —*v.t.* **3.** to utter or give forth with a squawk. —*n.* **4.** a loud, harsh cry or sound. **5.** *Slang.* a loud, vehement complaint. **6.** the black-crowned night heron. See under **night heron.** [b. SQUALL[2] and HAWK[3]] —**squawk′er,** *n.*

squawk′ box′, *Slang.* the speaker of a public address system or of an intercommunication system; loudspeaker.

squawk·y (skwô′kē), *adj.,* **squawk·i·er, squawk·i·est.** unpleasantly discordant or harsh in sound; cacophonous. [SQUAWK + -Y[1]]

squaw′ man′, a white or other non-Indian man married to a North American Indian woman.

squaw·root (skwô′rōōt′, -rŏŏt′), *n.* **1.** a fleshy, leafless, orobanchaceous plant, *Conopholis americana,* of eastern North America, found in clusters, esp. under oaks. **2.** the blue cohosh. See under **cohosh.** [SQUAW + ROOT[1], from its former use by Indians in treating female ailments]

squaw′ wa′terweed, kidneywort.

squeak (skwēk), *n.* **1.** a short, sharp, shrill cry; a sharp, high-pitched sound. **2.** *Informal.* opportunity; chance: *their last squeak to correct the manuscript.* **3.** *Informal.* an escape from defeat, danger, death, or destruction (usually qualified by *narrow* or *close*): *His getting out of the accident alive was a narrow squeak.* —*v.i.* **4.** to utter or emit a squeak or squeaky sound. **5.** *Slang.* to confess or turn informer; squeal. —*v.t.* **6.** to utter or sound with a squeak or squeaks. **7. squeak by** or **through,** to succeed, pass, win, etc. by a very narrow margin: *He squeaked by on the job. The team managed to squeak through.* [ME *squeke,* perh. < Scand; cf. Sw *skväka* to croak] —**squeak′er,** *n.* —**squeak′ing·ly,** *adv.*

squeak·y (skwē′kē), *adj.,* **squeak·i·er, squeak·i·est.** squeaking; tending to squeak: *His squeaky shoes could be heard across the lobby.* [SQUEAK + -Y[1]] —**squeak′i·ly,** *adv.* —**squeak′i·ness,** *n.*

squeal (skwēl), *n.* **1.** a somewhat prolonged, sharp, shrill cry, as of pain, fear, surprise, etc. **2.** *Slang.* **a.** an instance of informing against someone. **b.** a protest or complaint; beef. —*v.i.* **3.** to utter or emit a squeal or squealing sound. **4.** *Slang.* **a.** to turn informer; inform. **b.** to protest or complain; beef. —*v.t.* **5.** to utter or produce with a squeal. [ME *squel*(*en*); imit.] —**squeal′er,** *n.*

squeam·ish (skwē′mish), *adj.* **1.** easily shocked by anything slightly immodest; prudish. **2.** excessively particular or scrupulous as to the moral aspect of things. **3.** fastidious or dainty. **4.** easily nauseated or disgusted: *She's squeamish at the sight of blood.* [late ME *squeamish,* var. of *squemes, squaymes,* deriv. of *squaymour* < AF (*e*)*scoymo*(*u*)*s* < ?] —**squeam′ish·ly,** *adv.* —**squeam′-ish·ness,** *n.*
—**Syn. 1.** modest. **3.** finical, finicky, delicate. —**Ant. 1–3.** bold.

squee·gee (skwē′jē, skwē jē′), *n., v.,* **-geed, -gee·ing.** —*n.* **1.** an implement edged with rubber or the like, for removing water from windows after washing, sweeping water from wet decks, etc. **2.** a similar and smaller device for removing surplus water from photographic negatives or prints, forcing paint, ink, etc., through a porous surface, as in serigraphy, etc. —*v.t.* **3.** to sweep or scrape with or as with a squeegee. **4.** to force (paint, ink, etc.) through a screen in making a silk-screen print. Also, **squilgee, squillagee, squillgee.** [? rhyming compound based on SQUEEZE]

squeez·a·ble (skwē′zə bəl), *adj.* **1.** easily squeezed, compressed, or the like. **2.** (of a person) susceptible to intimidation or pressure, esp. by blackmail. [SQUEEZE + -ABLE] —**squeez′a·bil′i·ty, squeez′a·ble·ness,** *n.* —**squeez′a·bly,** *adv.*

squeeze (skwēz), *v.,* **squeezed, squeez·ing,** *n.* —*v.t.* **1.** to press forcibly together; compress. **2.** to apply pressure to in order to extract (juice, sap, or the like): *to squeeze an orange.* **3.** to force out, extract, or procure by pressure (sometimes fol. by *out*): *to squeeze juice from an orange.* **4.** to thrust forcibly; force by pressure; cram: *He squeezed three suits into the small suitcase.* **5.** to give (someone) a hug: *He squeezed her and kissed her goodby.* **6.** to enclose (another person's hand, arm, etc.) in one's hand and apply pressure as a token of affection, friendship, sympathy, or the like: *His father squeezed his hand and wished him luck.* **7.** *Informal.* to threaten, intimidate, harass, or oppress (a person or persons) in order to obtain a favor, money, or an advantageous attitude or action. **8.** to obtain a facsimile impression of. **9.** to cause to merge, as two or more lines of traffic into fewer lanes. **10.** *Baseball.* **a.** to enable (a runner on third base) to score on a squeeze play (often fol. by *in*): *He squeezed him in with a perfect bunt.* **b.** to score (a run) in this way (often fol. by *in*): *The Dodgers squeezed in a run in the eighth inning.* **11.** *Bridge.* to force (an opponent) to play a potentially winning card on a trick he cannot win. —*v.i.* **12.** to exert a compressing force. **13.** to force a way through some narrow or crowded place (usually fol. by *through, in, out,* etc.). **14.** to merge or come together. —*n.* **15.** the act or fact of squeezing or the fact of being squeezed. **16.** a clasping of one's hand around another's hand, arm, etc., as a token of affection, friendship, sympathy, or the like. **17.** a hug or close embrace. **18.** squeak (def. 3). **19.** a small quantity or amount of anything obtained by squeezing. **20.** a facsimile impression of an inscription or the like, obtained by pressing some plastic substance over or around it. **21.** See **squeeze play.** **22.** *Bridge.* a play or circumstance whereby an opponent is forced to waste or discard a potentially winning card. **23.** *Informal.* an act of threatening, intimidating, harassing, or oppressing a person or persons to obtain a favor, money, or an advantageous attitude or action. [? var. of obs. *squize,* OE *cwȳsan* to squeeze (initial *s* by false division of words in sandhi)] —**squeez′er,** *n.* —**squeez′ing·ly,** *adv.*

squeeze′ bot′tle, a flexible bottle, usually of plastic, the contents of which can be forced out by squeezing.

squeezed′ joint′, *Building Trades.* a joint between two members cemented or glued together under pressure. Also, **squeeze′ joint′.**

squeeze′ play′, **1.** *Baseball.* **a.** Also called **suicide squeeze, suicide squeeze play.** a play executed when there is a runner on third base and usually not more than one out, in which the runner starts for home as soon as the pitcher makes a motion to pitch, and the batter bunts. **b.** Also called **safety squeeze, safety squeeze play.** a similar play in which the runner on third base waits until the batter has successfully bunted before trying to score. 2. the application of pressure or influence on a person or group, as by promises, threats, etc., esp. from several sources, in order to force compliance or gain an advantage. Also called **squeeze.**

squeg (skweg), *v.i.*, **squegged, squeg·ging.** (of an electronic circuit or component) to produce an output that oscillates between a certain maximum and zero, esp. when due to the effect of a grid. [b. SQUEEZE and PEG]

squelch (skwelch), *v.t.* **1.** to strike or press with crushing force; crush down; squash. **2.** *Informal.* to put down, suppress, or silence as with a crushing argument or retort, emotional or psychological pressure, etc. **—*v.i.* 3.** to make a splashing sound. **4.** to tread heavily in water, mud, wet shoes, etc., with such a sound. **—*n.* 5.** a squelched or crushed mass of anything. **6.** a splashing sound. **7.** *Informal.* an act of squelching or suppressing, as by a crushing retort or argument. **8.** Also called **squelch′ cir′cuit, noise suppressor.** *Electronics.* a circuit in a receiver, as a radio receiver, that automatically reduces or eliminates noise when the receiver is tuned to a frequency at which virtually no carrier wave occurs. [var. of *quelch* in same sense (? QUELL + (QUA)SH); initial *s* perh. from SQUASH¹] **—squelch′er,** *n.* **—squelch′ing·ly,** *adv.* **—squelch′ing·ness,** *n.*

sque·lette′ clock′ (skə let′). See **skeleton clock.**

sque·teague (skwē tēg′), *n., pl.* **-teague. 1.** an Atlantic food fish, *Cynoscion regalis,* of the croaker family. **2.** any of several other Atlantic fishes of the same genus; sea trout. [< Narragansett *pesukwiteag,* lit., they give glue (i.e., serve as material for glue-making)]

squib (skwib), *n., v.,* **squibbed, squib·bing. —*n.* 1.** a short and witty or sarcastic saying or writing. **2.** *Journalism.* a short news story, often used as a filler. **3.** a firework consisting of a tube or ball filled with powder, which burns with a hissing noise terminated usually by a slight explosion. **4.** a firecracker broken in the middle so that it burns with a hissing noise but does not explode. **5.** *Brit.* any firecracker. **6.** *Australian.* a coward. **7.** an electric, pyrotechnic device for firing the igniter of a rocket engine, esp. of a solid-propellant engine. **8.** *Obs.* a mean or paltry fellow. **—*v.i.* 9.** to write squibs. **10.** to shoot a squib. **11.** to explode with a small, sharp sound. **12.** to move swiftly and irregularly. **13.** *Australian.* **a.** to be afraid. **b.** to flee; escape. **—*v.t.* 14.** to assail in squibs or lampoons. **15.** to toss, shoot, or utilize as a squib. [?] **—squib′bish,** *adj.*

Squid, *Loligo pealeii* (Total length 8 in.; mantle 5 in.)

squid (skwid), *n., pl.* (*esp. collectively*) **squid,** (*esp. referring to two or more kinds or species*) **squids.** any of several ten-armed cephalopods, as of the genera *Loligo* and *Ommastrephes,* having a slender body and a pair of rounded or triangular caudal fins and varying in length from 4-6 inches to 60-80 feet. [?]

squif·fer (skwif′ər), *n. Brit. Slang.* a concertina. [? alter. of SQUEEZER]

squif·fy (skwif′ē), *adj. Chiefly Brit. Slang.* slightly intoxicated. Also, **squiffed** (skwift). [? arbitrary alter. of TIPSY]

squig·gle (skwig′əl), *n., v.,* **-gled, -gling. —*n.* 1.** a short, irregular curve or twist, as in writing or drawing. **—*v.i.* 2.** to move in, or appear as squiggles: *His handwriting squiggled across the page.* **—*v.t.* 3.** to form in or cause to appear as squiggles; scribble. [b. SQUIRM and WRIGGLE] **—squig′gly,** *adj.*

squil·gee (skwil′jē, skwil jē′), *n., v.t.,* **-geed, -gee·ing.** squeegee. [unexplained var.]

squill (skwil), *n.* **1.** the bulb of the sea onion, *Urginea maritima,* cut into thin slices and dried, and used in medicine chiefly as an expectorant. **2.** the plant itself. **3.** any liliaceous plant of the genus *Scilla.* [< L *squill(a),* var. of *scilla* < Gk *skílla*] **—squill′-like′,** *adj.*

squil·la (skwil′ə), *n., pl.* **squil·las, squil·lae** (skwil′ē). See **mantis shrimp.** [see SQUILL]

squil·la·gee (skwil′ə jē′), *n., v.t.,* **-geed, -gee·ing.** squeegee.

squill·gee (skwil′jē, skwil jē′), *n., v.t.,* **-geed, -gee·ing.** squeegee.

squin·an·cy (skwin′ən sē, -ə sē), *n.* a prostrate, perennial herb, *Asperula cynanchica,* of Eurasia, having smooth, weak stems and sparse white or pink flowers, formerly believed to be a cure for quinsy. [ME *squynancy* quincy < ML *squinancia, -antia* < Gk *synánchē, kynánchē,* diseases of the throat]

squinch (skwinch), *n. Archit.* a small arch, corbeling, or the like, built across the interior angle between two walls, as in a square tower for supporting the side of a superimposed octagonal spire. [var. of *scunch,* short for *scuncheon,* ME *sconch(e)on* < MF *(e)scoinson, (e)sconchon,* equiv. to *es-* EX-¹ + *conch-* (< L *cune(us)* wedge) + *-on* n. suffix]

Squinch

squin·ny (skwin′ē), *v.,* **-nied, -ny·ing,** *n., pl.* **-nies.** *Obs.* **—*v.i.* 1.** to squint. **—*n.* 2.** a squint. [*squin-* (ME *skuin* asquint < MD; cf. D *schuin* oblique) + *-y* (ME *ye* EYE)]

squint (skwint), *v.i.* **1.** to look with the eyes partly closed. **2.** *Ophthalm.* to be affected with strabismus; be cross-eyed. **3.** to look or glance obliquely or sidewise; look askance. **4.** to make or have an indirect reference to or bearing on; tend or incline toward (usually fol. by *toward, at,* etc.). **—*v.t.* 5.** to close (the eyes) partly in looking: *The baby squinted his eyes at the bright lights.* **6.** to cause to squint; cause to look obliquely. **—*n.* 7.** *Ophthalm.* a condition of the eye consisting in noncoincidence of the optic axes; strabismus. **8.** *Informal.* a quick glance: *Let me have a squint at that paper.* **9.** a looking obliquely or askance. **10.** an indirect reference. **11.** inclination or tendency, esp. an oblique or perverse one. **12.** Also called **hagioscope.** (in a church) a small opening in a wall giving a view of the altar. **—*adj.* 13.** looking obliquely; looking with a side glance; looking askance. **14.** *Ophthalm.* (of the eyes) affected with strabismus. [aph. var. of ASQUINT] **—squint′er,** *n.* **—squint′ing·ly,** *adv.* **—squint′ing·ness,** *n.*

squint′ brick′, a brick molded or cut to a special form, esp. one having one or more oblique sides.

squint-eyed (skwint′īd′), *adj.* **1.** affected with or characterized by strabismus. **2.** looking obliquely or askance. **3.** manifesting a malicious, envious, or spiteful attitude or disposition: *squint-eyed with vengefulness and blind to reason.*

squint·y (skwin′tē), *adj.* characterized by or having a squint. [SQUINT + -Y¹]

squir·ar·chy (skwīər′är kē), *n., pl.* **-chies.** *Chiefly Brit.* squirearchy. **—squir·ar′chal, squir·ar′chi·cal,** *adj.*

squire (skwīər), *n., v.,* **squired, squir·ing. —*n.* 1.** (in England) a country gentleman, esp. the chief landed proprietor in a district. **2.** a young man of noble birth who, as an aspirant to knighthood, served a knight; an esquire. **3.** a personal attendant, as of a person of rank. **4.** a man who accompanies or escorts a woman. **5.** *U.S.* a title applied to a justice of the peace, local judge, or other local dignitary of a rural district or small town. **—*v.t.* 6.** to attend as, or in the manner of, a squire. **7.** to escort (a woman), as to a dance or social gathering. [ME *squier;* aph. var. of ESQUIRE] **—squire′less,** *adj.* **—squire′like′,** *adj.*

Squire (skwīər), *n.* a boy's given name.

squire·arch (skwīər′ärk), *n. Chiefly Brit.* a member of the squirearchy. Also, **squir′arch.** [back formation from SQUIREARCHY]

squire·ar·chy (skwīər′är kē), *n., pl.* **-chies.** *Chiefly Brit.* **1.** the collective body of squires or landed gentry of a country. **2.** the social, economic, and political class formed by the landed gentry. Also, **squirarchy.** [SQUIRE + -ARCHY] **—squire·ar′chal, squire·ar′chi·cal,** *adj.*

squire·dom (skwīər′dəm), *n.* **1.** the squirearchy. **2.** the position or status of a squire. [SQUIRE + -DOM]

squi·reen (skwī rēn′), *n. Chiefly Irish Eng.* the landowner of a small estate; a squire of a small domain. [SQUIRE + *-een,* dim. suffix of Ir orig.]

squire·ling (skwīər′ling), *n.* **1.** a landowner of a small estate. **2.** a petty squire. [SQUIRE + -LING¹]

squirm (skwûrm), *v.i.* **1.** to wriggle or writhe. **2.** to feel or display discomfort or distress, as from reproof, embarrassment, pain, etc.: *He squirmed under parental questioning.* **—*n.* 3.** the act of squirming; a squirming or wriggling movement. [? b. SQUID and WORM] **—squirm′ing·ly,** *adv.*

squirm·y (skwûr′mē), *adj.,* **squirm·i·er, squirm·i·est.** characterized by squirming. [SQUIRM + -Y¹]

squir·rel (skwûr′əl, skwur′- *or, esp. Brit.,* skwer′əl), *n., pl.* **-rels,** (*esp. collectively*) **-rel,** *adj., v.,* **-reled, -rel·ing** or (*esp. Brit.*) **-relled, -rel·ling. —*n.* 1.** any of numerous arboreal, bushy-tailed rodents of the genus *Sciurus,* of the family *Sciuridae.* **2.** any of various other members of the family *Sciuridae,* as the chipmunks, flying squirrels, woodchucks, etc. **3.** the meat of such an animal. **4.** the pelt or fur of such an animal: *Her coat was trimmed with squirrel.* **—*adj.* 5.** of, pertaining to, or characteristic of a squirrel or squirrels. **6.** containing the meat of a squirrel or squirrels. **7.** made from or ornamented with the fur of a squirrel or squirrels. **—*v.t.* 8. squirrel away,** to hoard (money, valuables, etc.). [ME *squirel* < AF *(e)scuirel* (cf. OF *escuireul*) << LL *sciūr(us)* (< Gk *skíouros,* equiv. to *ski(á)* shade + *ourá* tail) + *-ellus* dim. suffix] **—squir′rel·ish, squir′rel·like′,** *adj.*

Gray squirrel, *Sciurus carolinensis* (Total length 21 in.; tail 10 in.)

squir′rel cage′, 1. a cage containing a cylindrical framework that is rotated by a squirrel or other small animal running inside of it. **2.** any situation that seems to be endlessly without goal or achievement.

squir′rel corn′, an American, papaveraceous herb, *Dicentra canadensis,* having finely dissected leaves and cream-colored flowers. Also called **turkey corn.**

squir·rel·fish (skwûr′əl fish′, skwur′-), *n., pl.* (*esp. collectively*) **-fish,** (*esp. referring to two or more kinds or species*) **-fish·es. 1.** any of several brightly-colored, nocturnal fishes of the family *Holocentridae,* found in the shallow waters of tropical reefs, esp. the reddish *Holocentrus ascensionis* of the West Indies, armed with sharp spines and scales. **2.** any of several small, tropical sea basses of the genus *Diplectrum,* found in the Atlantic Ocean. [named from its cry, likened to a squirrel's bark]

squir·rel·ly (skwûr′ə lē, skwur′-), *adj. Slang.* eccentric; peculiar; nutty. Also, **squir′rel·y.** [SQUIRREL + -Y¹]

squir·rel's-ear (skwûr′əlz ēr′, skwur′-), *n.* a woodland orchid, *Goodyera repens,* having leaves mottled with white and greenish-white flowers.

squir′rel's-foot fern′ (skwûr′əlz fo͝ot′, skwur′-). See **ball fern.**

squir′rel-tail grass′ (skwûr′əl tāl′, skwur′-), a perennial grass, *Hordeum jubatum,* of the North Temperate Zone, often a troublesome weed.

squirt (skwûrt), *v.i.* **1.** to eject liquid in a jet from a narrow orifice: *The hose squirted all over us.* **2.** to eject a spurt of liquid: *The lemon squirted in my eye.* **—*v.t.* 3.** to cause (liquid or a viscous substance) to spurt or issue in a jet, as from a narrow orifice: *Squirt the water over that way!* **4.** to wet or bespatter with a liquid or viscous substance so ejected: *Don't squirt me with that hose!* **—*n.* 5.** the act of squirting. **6.** a spurt or jetlike stream, as of water. **7.** an instrument for squirting, as a syringe. **8.** a small quantity of liquid or viscous substance squirted: *Put a squirt of chocolate sauce on my ice cream.* **9.** *Informal.* **a.** a youngster, esp. a meddlesome one. **b.** a short person. **c.** an insignificant, self-assertive fellow, esp. one who is small or young. [late ME *squirt(en),* appar. var. of *swirten;* c. LG *swirtjen* in same sense; perh. akin to SWIRL] **—squirt′er,** *n.* **—squirt′ing·ly,** *adv.*

squirt′ can′, an oilcan with a flexible body which ejects oil when compressed.

squirt′ gun′, 1. See **spray gun. 2.** See **water pistol.**

squirt′ing cu′cumber, a cucurbitaceous plant, *Ecballium Elaterium,* of the Mediterranean region, whose ripened fruit forcibly ejects the seeds and juice.

squish (skwish), *v.t.* **1.** *Dial.* to squeeze or squash. **—*v.i.* 2.** (of water, soft mud, etc.) to make a gushing or splashing sound when walked in or on: *The soaking wet sneakers squished as he walked.* **—*n.* 3.** a squishing sound: *the squish of footsteps on wet leaves.* [alter. of SQUASH¹]

squish·y (skwish′ē), *adj.,* **squish·i·er, squish·i·est. 1.** soft and wet: *The ground was squishy from the rain.* **2.** softly gurgling or splashing: *The sponge made a squishing sound when it was squeezed.* [SQUISH + -Y¹]

sqush·y (skwush′ē, skwo͝osh′ē), *adj.,* **sqush·i·er, sqush·i·est.** squishy.

squush (skwush, skwo͝osh), *v.t.* **1.** to squash. **—*v.i.* 2.** to squish. Also, **sqush.**

squush·y (skwush′ē, skwo͝osh′ē), *adj.,* **squush·i·er, squush·i·est.** squishy.

sq. yd., square yard or square yards.

Sr, *Chem.* strontium.

Sr., 1. Senhor. **2.** Senior. **3.** Señor. **4.** Sir.

S.R., Sons of the Revolution.

Sra., 1. Senhora. **2.** Señora.

SRBM, short-range ballistic missile.

S. Rept., Senate report.

S. Res., Senate resolution.

sri (shrē), *n. Hindustani.* Mr.; Sir. [lit., majesty, holiness]

Sri Lan·ka (srē läng′kə), official name of **Ceylon.**

Sri·na·gar (srē nug′ər), *n.* a city in and the capital of Kashmir, on the Jhelum River. 285,300 (1961).

S.R.O., standing room only.

Srta., 1. Senhorita. **2.** Señorita.

sru·ti (shro͞ot′ē), *n. Hinduism.* the Vedas and some of the Upanishads, regarded as divinely revealed. [< Skt *śruti-* that which is heard; akin to LOUD]

SS, 1. Schutzstaffel. **2.** steamship. **3.** supersonic.

ss, (in prescriptions) a half. Also, **ss.** [< L *sēmis*]

SS., 1. Saints. [< L *sancti*] **2.** Schutzstaffel. **3.** namely. [< L *scilicet*]

ss., 1. sections. **2.** *Baseball.* shortstop.

S.S., 1. Schutzstaffel. **2.** (in prescriptions) in the strict sense. [< L *sensū strictō*] **3.** steamship. **4.** Sunday School.

SSA, 1. Social Security Act. **2.** Social Security Administration.

SSB, Social Security Board.

S.Sc.D., Doctor of Social Science.

S-scroll (es′skrōl′), *n.* an ornamental motif in the form of the letter S.

SS.D., Most Holy Lord: a title of the Pope. [< L *Sanctissimus Dominus*]

S.S.D., Doctor of Sacred Scripture. [< L *Sacrae Scripturae Doctor*]

SSE, south-southeast. Also, **S.S.E., s.s.e.**

SSM, surface-to-surface missile.

SSR, Soviet Socialist Republic. Also, **S.S.R.**

SSS, Selective Service System.

S-state (es′stāt′), *n. Physics.* the energy state of an electron in an atom having an orbital angular momentum of zero: so called because spectral lines from such states in alkali spectra are relatively sharp. *Symbol:* S

SST, supersonic transport.

SS Troops, Schutzstaffel.

SSW, south-southwest. Also, **S.S.W., s.s.w.**

-st¹, var. of **-est¹**: *first; least.*

-st², var. of **-est²**: *hadst; wouldst; dost.*

St., 1. Saint. **2.** statute; statutes. **3.** Strait. **4.** Street.

st., 1. stanza. **2.** statute; statutes. **3.** stet. **4.** stone (weight). **5.** strait. **6.** street.

s.t., short ton.

Sta., 1. Santa. **2.** Station.

sta., 1. station. **2.** stationary.

stab (stab), *v.,* **stabbed, stab·bing,** *n.* **—*v.t.* 1.** to pierce or wound with or as with a pointed weapon: *He stabbed the man in the chest.* **2.** to thrust, plunge, or jab (a knife, pointed weapon, or the like) into something: *He stabbed the knife into the man's chest.* **3.** to penetrate sharply or painfully: *Their misery stabbed his conscience.* **4.** to make a piercing, thrusting, or pointing motion at or in: *He stabbed me in the chest with his finger. The speaker stabbed the air in anger.* **5.** *Bookbinding.* to pierce holes through (the backs of collated signatures) before sewing. **6.** to prick the face of (brickwork) to provide a hold for plasterwork. **—*v.i.* 7.** to thrust with or as with a knife or other pointed weapon: *to stab at an attacker.* **8.** to deliver a wound, as with a pointed weapon. **9. stab (someone) in the back,** *Slang.* to do harm to (someone), esp. one who is unsuspecting or in a defenseless position: *She may be pleasant to your face, but wouldn't hesitate to stab you in the back.* **—*n.* 10.** the act of stabbing. **11.** a thrust or blow with, or as with, a pointed weapon. **12.** *Informal.* a brief attempt; try: *Make a stab at an answer before giving up.* **13.** a wound made by stabbing. **14.** a sudden, brief, and usually painful, sensation: *He felt a stab of pain in his foot. A stab of pity ran through her.* **15. stab in the back,** *Slang.* an act of treachery: *Such a vicious lie could be nothing but a stab in the back.* [ME, var. of *stob* in same sense; ? v. use of ME *stob* stich]
—Syn. 1. spear, penetrate, pin, transfix.

Sta·bat Ma·ter (stä′bät mä′tər, stā′bat mā′tər), **1.** (*italics*) a Latin hymn, composed in the 13th century, commemorating the sorrows of the Virgin Mary at the Cross. **2.** a musical setting for this. [lit., the mother was standing]

stab·bing (stab′ing), *adj.* **1.** penetrating; piercing: *a stabbing pain.* **2.** emotionally wounding: *a stabbing remark.* **3.** incisive or trenchant: *a stabbing, satirical phrase.* [STAB + -ING²] **—stab′bing·ly,** *adv.*

sta·bile (*adj.* stā′bil, -bəl *or, esp. Brit.,* -bīl; *n.* stā′bēl *or, esp. Brit.,* -bīl), *adj.* **1.** fixed in position; stable. **2.** *Med.* **a.** resistant to moderate degrees of heat, as certain constituents of plasma. **b.** noting or pertaining to the application of electricity in which the active electrode is kept stationary over the part of the body to be acted upon, as opposed to labile. **—*n.* 3.** a piece of sculpture having immobile units constructed of sheet metal or other material and attached to fixed supports. Cf. **mobile** (def. 7). [< L: *stabile*, neut. of *stabilis*, equiv. to *sta-* (s. of *stāre* to stand) + *-bilis* -BLE]

sta·bi·lise (stā′bə līz′), *v.t., v.i.*, **-lised, -lis·ing.** *Chiefly Brit.* stabilize. —**sta′bi·li·sa′tion,** *n.*

sta·bi·lis·er (stā′bə lī′zər), *n. Brit.* stabilizer.

sta·bil·i·ty (stə bil′i tē), *n., pl.* **-ties.** **1.** the state or quality of being stable. **2.** firmness in position. **3.** continuance without change; permanence. **4.** *Chem.* resistance or the degree of resistance to chemical change or disintegration. **5.** resistance to change, esp. sudden change or deterioration: *The stability of the economy encourages investment.* **6.** steadfastness; constancy, as of character or purpose: *The job calls for a man with a great deal of emotional stability.* **7.** *Aeron.* the ability of an aircraft to return to its original flying position when abruptly displaced. **8.** *Rom. Cath. Ch.* a vow taken by a Benedictine monk, binding him to residence for life in the same monastery in which he made the vow. [< L *stabilitāt-* (s. of *stabilitās*), equiv. to *stabili(s)* STABILE + *-tāt-* -TY; r. ME *stablete* < OF < L] —**Syn. 6.** steadiness, strength.

sta·bil·i·volt (stə bil′ə vōlt′), *n. Elect.* a gas-filled tube that maintains a constant voltage across its terminals, used in voltage regulators or as a voltage source for apparatus that draw little current. [< L *stabili(s)* (see STABLE) + VOLT]

stabiliza′tion fund′, a monetary reserve established by a country to provide funds for maintaining the official exchange rates of its currency by equalizing the buying and selling of foreign exchange. Also called **equalization fund, exchange equalization fund, exchange stabilization fund.**

sta·bi·lize (stā′bə līz′), *v.*, **-lized, -liz·ing.** —*v.t.* **1.** to make or hold stable, firm, or steadfast. **2.** to maintain at a given or unfluctuating level or quantity: *The government will try to stabilize the cost of living.* **3.** *Aeron.* to put or keep (an aircraft) in stable equilibrium, as by some special device. —*v.i.* **4.** to become stabilized. Also, *esp. Brit.*, **stabilise.** [STABILE + -IZE; cf. F *stabiliser*] —**sta′bi·li·za′tion,** *n.*

sta·bi·liz·er (stā′bə lī′zər), *n.* **1.** one who or that which stabilizes. **2.** *Aeron.* a device for stabilizing an aircraft, as the fixed, horizontal tail surface on an airplane. Cf. **horizontal stabilizer, vertical stabilizer. 3.** *Naut.* **a.** a mechanical device for counteracting the roll of a vessel, consisting of a pair of retractable fins so pivoted as to oppose a downward force with an upward one, and vice versa. **b.** a gyrostabilizer. **4.** any compound which, when included with an explosive, decreases the ability of the latter to decompose spontaneously. **5.** a substance, as beeswax or aluminum stearate, added to a fast-drying oil paint to improve the dispersion of pigment. **6.** any of various substances added to foods, chemical compounds, or the like, to prevent deterioration or the loss of desirable properties. **7.** a comparatively large shock absorber for motor vehicles. **8.** *Mil.* **a.** any of various devices or systems that keep a gun mounted on a moving ship, tank, or plane automatically aimed at its target. **b.** any of various mechanical devices, such as fins, or electronic systems that keep a shell, bomb, rocket, etc., aligned with its target. **9.** *Navy.* any of various devices or systems used to keep a submarine or a torpedo at the proper depth or in the proper position. Also, *esp. Brit.*, **stabiliser.** [STABILIZE + -ER[1]]

sta·ble[1] (stā′bəl), *n., v.*, **-bled, -bling.** —*n.* **1.** a building for the lodging and feeding of horses, cattle, etc. **2.** such a building with stalls. **3.** a collection of animals housed in such a building. **4.** *Horse Racing.* **a.** an establishment where race horses are kept and trained. **b.** the horses belonging to, or the persons connected with, such an establishment. **5.** *Informal.* a number of people, usually in the same profession, as certain employees, clients, etc., who work for or are represented by the same company or individual: *That comedian has a large stable of gag writers.* **6.** *Slang.* a group of boxers controlled by the same manager. —*v.t.* **7.** to put or lodge in or as in a stable. —*v.i.* **8.** to live in or as in a stable. [ME *stable* < OF *(e)stable* < L *stabul(um)* standing-room, equiv. to *sta-* stand + *-bulum* n. suffix] —**sta′ble·like′,** *adj.*
—**Syn. 1.** barn, mews.

sta·ble[2] (stā′bəl), *adj.* **1.** not likely to fall or give way, as a structure, support, foundation, etc.; firm; steady. **2.** able or likely to continue or last; firmly established; enduring or permanent: *a stable government.* **3.** resistant to sudden change or deterioration: *A stable economy is the aim of every government.* **4.** steadfast; not wavering or changeable, as a person, the mind, etc.: *A stable, perceptive man is needed to guide emotionally disturbed boys.* **5.** reliable; sane; mentally sound. **6.** *Physics.* having the ability to react to a disturbing force by maintaining or reestablishing position, form, etc. **7.** *Chem.* not readily decomposing, as a compound; resisting molecular or chemical change. [ME < OF *(e)stable* < L *stabil(is)* STABILE] —**sta′ble·ness,** *n.* —**sta′bly,** *adv.*
—**Syn. 1.** fixed, strong, sturdy. **4.** invariable, unvarying, stanch, constant, reliable, steady, solid.

sta·ble·boy (stā′bəl boi′), *n.* one who works in or performs various tasks around a stable. [STABLE[1] + BOY]

sta′ble equa′tion, *Math.* a differential equation each solution of which tends to zero as the independent variable increases to infinity. Cf. **transient** (def. 6).

sta′ble fly′, a muscid fly, *Stomoxys calcitrans*, having the mouthparts adapted for biting, and commonly found as a household and stable pest. Also called **biting housefly.**

sta·ble·man (stā′bəl mən, -man′), *n., pl.* **-men** (-mən, -men′). one who works in a stable. [STABLE[1] + MAN[1]]

sta·ble·mate (stā′bəl māt′), *n.* **1.** a horse sharing a stable with another. **2.** one of several horses owned by the same person. [STABLE[1] + MATE[1]]

sta·bling (stā′bling), *n.* **1.** accommodation for horses or other draft or farm animals in a stable or stables. **2.** stables collectively. [ME; see STABLE[1], -ING[1]]

stab·lish (stab′lish), *v.t. Archaic.* establish. [ME *stablisse(n)*, aph. var. of ESTABLISH]

stacc., *Music.* staccato.

stac·ca·to (stə kä′tō), *adj., adv., n., pl.* **-tos, -ti** (-tē). —*adj.* **1.** abruptly disconnected; discontinuous; disjointed; detached: *staccato notes.* **2.** *Music.* characterized by performance in which the notes are abruptly disconnected: *a staccato style of playing.* Cf. **legato.** —*adv.* **3.** in a staccato manner. —*n.* **4.** *Music.* **a.** performance in a staccato manner. **b.** a staccato passage. **5.** something that is abruptly discontinuous or disjointed in quality or character. [< It: disconnected (ptp. of *staccare*, equiv. to *distaccare* to DETACH) aph. var. of *stacc-* detach + *-ato* -ATE[1]]

Staccato phrase

Sta·cey (stā′sē), *n.* a boy's or girl's given name.

stach·er (stakh′ər), *v.i., v.t. Brit. Dial.* stacker.

stach·er·ing (stakh′ə ring), *n. Brit. Dial.* stackering.

Sta·cia (stā′shə), *n.* a girl's given name.

stack (stak), *n.* **1.** a large, usually conical, circular, or rectangular pile of hay, straw, or the like. **2.** a more or less orderly pile or heap: *a precariously balanced stack of books; a neat stack of papers.* **3.** Often, **stacks.** a set of bookshelves ranged compactly one above the other, as in a library. **4. stacks,** the area or part of a library in which the books are stored or kept. **5.** a number of chimneys or flues grouped together. **6.** smokestack. **7.** a vertical duct for conveying warm air from a leader to a register on an upper story of a building. **8.** a vertical waste pipe or vent pipe serving a number of floors. **9.** *Informal.* a great quantity or number. **10.** *Radio.* an antenna consisting of a number of components connected in a substantially vertical series. **11.** *Mil.* a conical, free-standing group of three rifles placed on their butts and hooked together with stacking swivels. **12.** Also called **air stack.** a group of airplanes circling over an airport awaiting their turns to land. **13.** *Theat. U.S.* See **scene pack. 14.** an English measure for coal and wood, equal to 108 cubic feet. **15.** *Geol.* a column of rock isolated from a shore by the action of waves. **16.** *Games* **a.** a given quantity of chips that can be bought at one time, as in poker or other gambling games. **b.** the quantity of chips held by a player at a given point in a gambling game. **17. blow one's stack,** *Slang.* to lose one's temper or become uncontrollably angry, esp. to display one's fury, as by shouting: *When he came in and saw the mess he blew his stack.* —*v.t.* **18.** to pile or arrange in a stack: *to stack hay.* **19.** to place (rifles) in a stack. **20.** to cover or load with something in stacks or piles. **21.** to arrange (a pack or cards in a pack) so as to cheat: *He stacked the deck and won.* **22.** *Informal.* to arrange or select unfairly in order to force a desired result, esp. to load (a jury) with members having a biased viewpoint: *The lawyer charged that the jury had been stacked against his client.* **23.** to keep (a number of incoming airplanes) flying nearly circular patterns at various altitudes over an airport where crowded runways, a low ceiling, or other temporary conditions prevent immediate landings. **24. stack up, a.** *Aeron.* to control the flight patterns of airplanes waiting to land at an airport so that each circles at a designated altitude. **b.** *Slang.* compare: *She doesn't stack up to you, honey.* **c.** *Slang.* appear plausible or in keeping with the known facts: *Your story just doesn't stack up.* [ME *stak* < Scand; cf. Icel *stakkr* haystack; akin to Russ *stog* haystack] —**stack′er,** *n.* —**stack′less,** *adj.*

stacked (stakt), *adj. Slang.* (of a woman) having a voluptuous figure. [STACK (V.) + -ED[2]]

stack·er (stak′ər), *v.i., v.t. Brit. Dial.* stagger. Also, **stacher.**

stack·er·ing (stak′ər ing), *n. Brit. Dial.* staggering. Also, **stachering.**

stack·freed (stak′frēd′), *n.* a device for maintaining a constant impulse to the mechanism of a spring-driven timepiece, consisting of a spring pressing against a snail, so geared to the mechanism that pressure upon it is least when the spring has run down, and greatest when it is fully wound. [?]

stack′ing swiv′el, a metal swivel attached to the stock of a military rifle for use in hooking three rifles together to form a stack.

stack·yard (stak′yärd′), *n. Chiefly Brit.* a farmyard or field in which stacked straw or grain is kept. [STACK + YARD[2]]

stac·te (stak′tē), *n.* one of the sweet spices used in the holy incense of the ancient Hebrews. Ex. 30:34. [ME < L *stactē* < Gk *staktḗ*, fem. of *staktós* (ptp. of *stázein* to fall in drops), equiv. to *stak-* (var. of *stag-* drop) + *-tos* adj. suffix]

stac·tom·e·ter (stak tom′i tər), *n.* stalagmometer. [*stacto-* (see STACTE) + -METER]

stad·dle (stad′əl), *n.* **1.** the lower part of a stack of hay or the like. **2.** a supporting frame for a stack, or a platform on which a stack is placed. **3.** any supporting framework or base. [ME *stathel*, OE *stathol* base, support, tree trunk; c. OHG *stadal* barn, Icel *stöthull* milking place; akin to STEAD]

stade (stād), *n. Geol.* a period of time represented by a glacial deposit. Also, **stadial.** [< MF, (earlier *estade*) < L *stad(ium)*; see STADIUM]

Sta′der splint′ (stā′dər), *Vet. Med.* a splint consisting of two steel pins inserted in the bone above and below a fracture or a break and joined and held together by a turnbuckle. [named after O. *Stader*, (b. 1894), American veterinary surgeon]

stad·hold·er (stad′hōl′dər), *n.* **1.** the chief magistrate of the former republic of the United Provinces of the Netherlands. **2.** (formerly, in the Netherlands) the viceroy or governor of a province. Also, **stadtholder.** [< D *stadhouder*, equiv. to *stad* city (see STEAD) + *houder* HOLDER] —**stad′hold′er·ate, stad′hold′er·ship′,** *n.*

sta·di·a[1] (stā′dē ə), *n.* **1.** a method of surveying in which distances are read by noting the interval on a graduated rod intercepted by two parallel cross hairs (**sta′dia hairs′** or **sta′dia wires′**) mounted in the telescope of a surveying instrument, the rod being placed at one end of the distance to be measured and the surveying instrument at the other. —*adj.* **2.** pertaining to such a method of surveying. [prob. special use of STADIA[2]]

sta·di·a[2] (stā′dē ə), *n.* a pl. of **stadium.**

sta·di·al (stā′dē əl), *Geol.* —*n.* **1.** stade. —*adj.* **2.** of or pertaining to a stade or stades. [STADE + -IAL]

sta′dia rod′, *Survey.* rod (def. 19).

sta·dim·e·ter (stə dim′i tər), *n.* an instrument for determining the distance between an observer and an object of known height by measurement of the angle subtended by the object. [STADI(A)[1] + -METER]

sta·di·om·e·ter (stā′dē om′i tər), *n.* **1.** an instrument for measuring the lengths of curves, dashed lines, etc., by running a toothed wheel over them. **2.** *Survey.* an obsolete form of tachymeter. [STADI(UM) + -O- + -METER]

sta·di·um (stā′dē əm), *n., pl.* **-di·ums, -di·a** (-dē ə). **1.** a sports arena, usually oval or horseshoe-shaped, with tiers of seats for spectators. **2.** an ancient Greek course for foot races, typically semicircular, with tiers of seats for spectators. **3.** an ancient Greek unit of length, equal at Athens to about 607 feet. **4.** *Entomol.* stage (def. 10b). [< L < Gk *stádion* stade, racecourse]

stad·le (stad′əl), *n. Agric.* staddle.

stadt·hold·er (stat′hōl′dər), *n.* stadholder. —**stadt′hold′er·ate, stadt′hold′er·ship′,** *n.*

Staël-Hol·stein (stäl′ôl sten′), *n.* **Anne Louise Ger·maine Neck·er** (AN lwēz zher men′ ne ker′), **Baronne de,** (*Madame de Staël*) 1766–1817, French writer.

staff[1] (staf, stäf), *n., pl.* **staves** (stāvz) or **staffs** for 1–3, 9, 10; **staffs** for 4–8; *adj., v.* —*n.* **1.** a stick, pole, or rod for aid in walking or climbing, for use as a weapon, etc. **2.** a rod or wand serving as an ensign of office or authority, as a crozier, baton, truncheon, or mace. **3.** a pole on which a flag is hung or displayed. **4.** something which serves to support or sustain: *Courage is the staff of my ambitions.* **5.** a group of assistants to a manager, superintendent, or executive. **6.** a group of persons, as employees, charged with carrying out the work of an establishment or executing some undertaking. **7.** *Mil., Navy.* **a.** a body of officers without command authority, appointed to assist a commanding officer. **b.** the parts of any army concerned with administrative matters, planning, etc., rather than with actual participation in combat. **8.** those members of an organization serving only in an auxiliary or advisory capacity on a given project. Cf. **line**[1] (def. 39). **9.** Also, **stave.** *Music.* a set of horizontal lines, now five in number, with the corresponding four spaces between them, on which music is written. **10.** *Archaic.* the shaft of a spear, lance, etc. —*adj.* **11.** noting, of, or pertaining to a member of a military or naval staff or unit or to such a staff or unit: *staff officer.* —*v.t.* **12.** to provide with a staff of assistants or workers: *He staffed his office with excellent secretaries.* [ME *staf*, OE *stæf*; c. D *staf*, Icel *stafr*, G *Stab* staff, Skt *stabh-* support] —**staff′less,** *adj.*

staff[2] (staf, stäf), *n.* a composition of plaster and fibrous material used for a temporary finish and in ornamental work, as on exposition buildings or the like. [? < G *Stoff* STUFF]

Staf·fa (staf′ə), *n.* an island in W Scotland, in the Hebrides: site of Fingal's Cave.

staff′ cap′tain, one who assists the master of a large ocean passenger vessel, being especially responsible for safety apparatus, fire and lifeboat drills, etc.

staff·er (staf′ər, stäf′fər), *n.* **1.** a member of a staff of employees or co-workers. **2.** *Journalism.* an editorial employee, esp. a writer. Cf. **stringer** (def. 6). [STAFF[1] + -ER[1]]

staff·man (staf′man′, stäf′-), *n., pl.* **-men.** staffer. [STAFF[1] + MAN[1]]

staff′ of′ficer, *Mil., Navy.* a commissioned officer who is a member of a staff.

staff′ of life′, bread, considered as the mainstay of the human diet.

Staf·ford (staf′ərd), *n.* **1.** a city in and the county seat of Staffordshire, in central England. 47,814 (1961). **2.** Staffordshire.

Staf·ford·shire (staf′ərd shēr′, -shər), *n.* a county in central England. 1,733,887 (1961); 1154 sq. mi. *Co. seat:* Stafford. Also called **Stafford, Staffs** (stafs).

Staf′fordshire ter′rier, one of an English breed of stocky dogs having a short, glossy coat of any of various colors.

Staf′ford Springs′, a town in NE Connecticut. 3322 (1960).

staff′ sec′tion, *Mil.* section (def. 10b).

staff′ ser′geant, *U.S.* **1.** *Air Force.* a noncommissioned officer ranking below a technical sergeant and above an airman first class. **2.** *Army.* a noncommissioned officer ranking above a sergeant and below a sergeant first class. **3.** *Marine Corps.* a noncommissioned officer ranking below a gunnery sergeant and above a sergeant.

stag (stag), *n., v.*, **stagged, stag·ging,** *adj., adv.* —*n.* **1.** an adult male deer. **2.** the male of various other animals. **3.** *Informal.* See **stag party. 4.** *Informal.* a man, esp. one unaccompanied by a woman at a social gathering. **5.** a swine castrated after maturation of the sex organs. **6.** *Brit.* a speculator who buys securities of a new issue in the hope of selling them quickly at a higher price. —*v.i.* **7.** *Informal.* (of a man) to attend a social function without a female companion. —*adj.* **8.** for or of men only: *a stag dinner.* —*adv.* **9.** without escorting a female companion or date: *He couldn't get a date for the dance, so he went stag.* [ME *stagge*, OE **stagga*; akin to Icel *steggr* male fox, tomcat] —**stag′like′,** *adj.*

Stag of red deer, *Cervus elaphus* (4 ft. high at shoulder; antlers to 3½ ft.; length 6½ ft.)

stag′ bee′tle, any of numerous lamellicorn beetles of the family *Lucanidae*, some of the males of which have mandibles resembling the antlers of a stag.

stag′ bush′. See **black haw** (def. 1).

stage (stāj), *n.*, *v.*, **staged, stag·ing.** —*n.* **1.** a single step or degree in a process; a particular phase, period, position, etc., in a process, development, or series. **2.** a raised platform or floor, as for speakers, performers, etc. **3.** *Theat.* **a.** the platform on which the actors perform in a theater. **b.** this platform with all the parts of the theater and all the apparatus back of the proscenium. **4.** **the stage,** the theater, drama, or dramatic profession: *He plans to make the stage his career.* **5.** the scene of any action. **6.** a stagecoach. **7.** a place of rest on a journey; a regular stopping place of a stagecoach or the like, for the change of horses, mules, etc. **8.** the distance between two places of rest on a journey; each of the portions of a journey. **9.** a portion or period of a course of action, of life, etc.: *the seven stages of man.* **10.** *Zool.* **a.** any one of the major time periods in the development of an insect, as the embryonic, larval, pupal, and imaginal stages. **b.** any one of the periods of larval growth between molts. **11.** *Econ., Sociol.* a major phase of the economic or sociological life of man or society: *the patriarchal stage.* **12.** *Geol.* any of the several divisions of stratified rocks forming a period, corresponding to a single age. **13.** the small platform of a microscope on which the object to be examined is placed. See illus. under **microscope.** **14.** *Radio.* an element in a complex mechanism, as a tube and its accessory structures in a multiple amplifier. **15.** *Rocketry.* a section of a rocket containing a rocket engine or cluster of rocket engines, usually separable from other such sections when its propellant is exhausted. **16.** **by easy stages,** working, traveling, etc., slowly, with frequent pauses; unhurriedly, with many stops; gradually: *All the neighbors pitched in, and the barn was rebuilt by easy stages.* **17.** **hold the stage, a.** to continue to be produced, as a play or other theatrical production. **b.** to be the center of attention. —*v.t.* **18.** to represent, produce, or exhibit on or as on a stage: *The drama class staged a play during Christmas vacation.* **19.** to furnish with a stage, staging, stage set, etc. **20.** to write, direct, or produce (a play) as if the action were taking place in a specific locale or time: *He staged the fantasy on Mars in the year 2500 A.D.* **21.** to plan, organize, or carry out (an activity) in which each participant has a specific role to perform: *The Dodgers staged a beautiful squeeze play in the eighth inning.* —*v.i.* **22.** to be suitable for presentation or performance on the stage: *The script didn't stage well.* **23.** to travel by stagecoach. [ME < OF (*e*)*stage* (F *étage*) < VL *static(um) standing-place, equiv. to *stat(us)* STATUS + *-icum,* neut. of *-icus* -IC] —**stage′a·bil′i·ty, stage′a·ble·ness,** *n.* —**stage′a·ble,** *adj.* —**stage′a·bly,** *adv.*

stage′ brace′, a brace for supporting upright pieces of theatrical scenery.

stage′ busi′ness, business (def. 10).

stage·coach (stāj′kōch′), *n.* (formerly) a horse-drawn coach traveling regularly over a fixed route with passengers, parcels, etc. [STAGE + COACH]

Stagecoach

stage·craft (stāj′kraft′, -kräft′), *n.* skill in or the art of writing, adapting, or staging plays. [STAGE + CRAFT]

staged (stājd), *adj.* **1.** adapted for or produced on the stage. **2.** contrived for a desired impression: *It was a staged, rather than spontaneous, demonstration of affection.* **3.** occurring or planned to occur in stages: *a staged increase in wages.* [STAGE + -ED[3]]

stage′ direc′tion, **1.** instruction written into the script of a play, indicating stage actions, movements of performers, or production requirements. **2.** the art and technique of a stage director.

stage′ direc′tor, **1.** one who directs a theatrical production. **2.** *Brit.* one who works as the producer and stage manager of a theatrical production.

stage′ door′, a door at the back or side of a theater, used by performers and theater personnel.

stage′-door John′ny (stāj′dōr′, -dôr′), *Informal.* a man who goes often to a theater to court an actress or show girl: so called from the past practice of waiting for girls at the stage door.

stage-driv·er (stāj′drī′vər), *n.* the driver of a stagecoach.

stage′ effect′, a highly spectacular or artificial device or means, esp. for attracting attention.

stage′ fright′, the nervousness felt by a performer or speaker when appearing before an audience.

stage·hand (stāj′hand′), *n.* a person who moves properties, regulates lighting, etc., in a theatrical production. [STAGE + HAND]

stage′ left′, *Theat.* the part of the stage that is left of center as one faces the audience. Also called **left stage.**

stage-man·age (stāj′man′ij), *v.*, **-aged, -ag·ing.** —*v.t.* **1.** to work as a stage manager for: *When he wasn't acting, he stage-managed a repertory theater.* **2.** to arrange or stage in order to produce a theatrical or spectacular effect: *She stage-managed the most gala garden party of the season.* **3.** to arrange or direct unobtrusively or in secret: *He stage-managed Mediterranean black-market operations from his secluded villa on the Riviera.* —*v.i.* **4.** to work as a stage manager: *He stage-managed in straw-hat theaters for three summers.* [back formation from STAGE MANAGER]

stage′ man′ager, a person responsible for the technical details of a theatrical production, assisting the director during rehearsal, supervising the lighting, costuming, setting, prompting, etc., and assuming full responsibility for the stage during a performance of a play. —**stage′ man′agership.**

stage′ pock′et, *Theat.* one of several metal boxes placed backstage in the floor or wall of a theater and containing jacks for electric cables used in lighting units.

stag·er (stā′jər), *n.* **1.** a person of experience in some profession, way of life, etc. **2.** *Archaic.* an actor. [STAGE + -ER[1]]

stage′ right′, *Theat.* the part of the stage that is right of center as one faces the audience. Also called **right stage.**

stage′ screw′, a large, tapered screw fitted with a handle, used to secure braces for scenery to the floor of a stage. Also called **stage′ peg′.**

stage-struck (stāj′struk′), *adj.* **1.** obsessed with the desire to become an actor or actress. **2.** overly impressed by the theater and the people, customs, traditions, etc., associated with it.

stage′ wait′, *Theat.* an unintentional pause during a performance, usually caused by a performer's or stagehand's missing a cue: *There was an embarrassing stage wait when the curtain failed at the end of Act I.*

stage′ whis′per, a loud whisper on a stage, meant to be heard by the audience.

stage·y (stā′jē), *adj.*, **stag·i·er, stag·i·est.** stagy.

stag·fla·tion (stag′flā′shən), *n.* a condition of simultaneously declining business activity, increasing unemployment, and rapid inflation. [STAG(NATION) + (IN)FLATION]

Stagg (stag), *n.* **Amos Alonzo,** 1862–1965, U.S. football coach.

stag·gard (stag′ərd), *n.* a four-year-old male red deer. Also, **stag·gart** (stag′ərt). [late ME; see STAG, -ARD]

stag·ger (stag′ər), *v.i.* **1.** to walk, move, or stand unsteadily. **2.** to falter or begin to give way, as in an argument, fight, or the like: *He staggered in his argument for a while, and then went on.* **3.** to waver or begin to doubt, as in purpose or opinion; hesitate: *After staggering momentarily, he recognized that he had to make a decision.* —*v.t.* **4.** to cause to reel, totter, or become unsteady: *This load would stagger an elephant.* **5.** to shock; render helpless with amazement or the like; astonish: *The vastness of outer space staggers the mind.* **6.** to cause to waver or falter: *The news staggered his belief in the triumph of justice.* **7.** to arrange in a zigzag order or manner on either side of a center: *The captain staggered his troops along the road.* **8.** *Aeron.* to arrange (the wings of a biplane or the like) so that the entering edge of an upper wing is either in advance of or behind that of a corresponding lower wing. **9.** to arrange otherwise than at the same time, esp. in a series of alternating or continually overlapping intervals: *They planned to stagger lunch hours so that the cafeteria would not be rushed.* —*n.* **10.** the act of staggering; a reeling or tottering movement or motion. **11.** a staggered order or arrangement. **12.** *Aeron.* **a.** a staggered arrangement of wings. **b.** the amount of staggering. **13.** **staggers.** Also called **blind staggers, mad staggers.** (*construed as sing.*) *Vet. Pathol.* any of various forms of cerebral and spinal disease in horses, cattle, etc., characterized by blindness, a staggering gait, sudden falling, etc. [earlier *stacker* to reel, ME *stakere* < Scand; cf. Icel *stakra,* equiv. to *stak(a)* to stagger + *-ra* freq. suffix; akin to STAKE[1]] —**stag′ger·er,** *n.* —**stag′ger·ing·ly,** *adv.*
—**Syn. 1.** STAGGER, REEL, TOTTER suggest an unsteady manner of walking. To STAGGER is successively to lose and regain one's equilibrium and the ability to maintain one's direction: *to stagger with exhaustion, a heavy load, or intoxication.* To REEL is to sway dizzily and be in imminent danger of falling: *to reel when faint with hunger.* TOTTER suggests the immediate likelihood of falling from weakness or feebleness, and is used particularly of infants, or the very aged, who walk with shaky, uncertain, faltering steps: *An old man tottered along with a cane.* **3.** vacillate. **5.** astound, dumfound. **7.** alternate.

stag·ger·bush (stag′ər bo͝osh′), *n.* an American, ericaceous shrub, *Lyonia mariana,* having a foliage poisonous to animals. [STAGGER + BUSH[1]]

stag′ger head′, dropline. Also, **stag′gered head′.**

stag′gering bob′, *Brit., Australian.* **1.** a newborn calf. **2.** any newborn or young animal.

stag·gy (stag′ē), *n., pl.* **-gies.** *Scot.* a colt. Also, **stag′gie.** [STAG + -Y[2]]

stag′horn cor′al (stag′hôrn′), any of several stony corals of the genus *Acropora,* having the skeleton branched like the antlers of a stag. Also, **stag's-horn coral.** [STAG + HORN]

stag′horn su′mac, a sumac, *Rhus typhina,* of eastern North America, having leaves that turn scarlet, orange, and purple in the autumn.

stag·hound (stag′hound′), *n.* a hound trained to hunt stags and other large animals. [STAG + HOUND[1]]

stag·ing (stā′jing), *n.* **1.** the act, process, or manner of presenting a play on the stage. **2.** a temporary platform or structure of posts and boards for support, as in building; scaffolding. **3.** the business of running stagecoaches. **4.** the act of traveling by stages or by stagecoach. [ME; see STAGE, -ING[1]]

stag′ing ar′ea, an area, as a port of embarkation, where troops are assembled and readied for transit to a new field of operations.

stag′ing nail′. See **scaffold nail.**

Sta·gi·ra (stə jī′rə), *n.* an ancient town in NE Greece, in Macedonia on the E Chalcidice peninsula: birthplace of Aristotle. Also, **Sta·gi·ros** (stə jī′ros), **Sta·gi·rus** (stə jī′rəs).

Stag·i·rite (staj′ə rīt′), *n.* **1.** a native or inhabitant of Stagira. **2.** **the Stagirite,** Aristotle. Also, **Stagyrite.** [< L *Stagīrītē(s)* < Gk. See STAGIRA, -ITE[1]] —**Stag·i·rit·ic** (staj′ə rit′ik), *adj.*

stag·nant (stag′nənt), *adj.* **1.** not flowing or running, as water, air, etc. **2.** stale or foul from standing, as a pool of water. **3.** characterized by lack of development, advancement, or progressive movement: *a stagnant economy.* **4.** inactive, sluggish, or dull. [< L *stagnant-* (s. of *stagnāns,* prp. of *stagnāre* to STAGNATE), equiv. to *stagn(um)* pool of standing water + *-ant-* -ANT] —**stag′nan·cy, stag′nance,** *n.* —**stag′nant·ly,** *adv.*

stag·nate (stag′nāt), *v.i.*, **-nat·ed, -nat·ing.** **1.** to cease to run or flow, as water, air, etc. **2.** to be or become stale or foul from standing, as a pool of water. **3.** to stop developing, growing, progressing, or advancing: *Her mind is stagnating from too much TV. His friends attained successful careers, but his stagnated.* **4.** to be or become sluggish and dull: *Because of disinterest, the show tended to stagnate.* [< L *stagnāt(us)* (ptp. of *stagnāre*). See STAGNANT, -ATE[1]] —**stag·na′tion,** *n.* —**stag·na·to·ry** (stag′nə tôr′ē, -tōr′ē), *adj.*

stagna′tion masti′tis, *Pathol.* See **caked breast.**

stag′ par′ty, **1.** a social gathering or outing for men only. **2.** a party given a bachelor by his male friends before his marriage, often on the night before the wedding, ranging from a formal gathering to a night of carousing. **3.** a gathering considered suitable for men only, esp. one for the purpose of watching sexually titillating movies or exhibitions.

stag's′-horn cor′al (stagz′hôrn′). See **staghorn coral.**

stag·y (stā′jē), *adj.*, **stag·i·er, stag·i·est.** **1.** of, pertaining to, or suggestive of the stage. **2.** theatrical; unnatural. Also, **stagey.** [STAGE + -Y[1]] —**stag′i·ly,** *adv.* —**stag′i·ness,** *n.*

Stag·y·rite (staj′ə rīt′), *n.* Stagirite.

Stahl·helm (shtäl′helm′), *n. German.* (formerly) an organization founded by ex-soldiers in Germany after World War I, having strong monarchist and nationalist aims. [lit., steel helmet]

staid (stād), *adj.* **1.** of settled or sedate character; not flighty or capricious. **2.** *Rare.* fixed, settled, or permanent. —*v.* **3.** a pt. and pp. of **stay**[1]. —**staid′ly,** *adv.* —**staid′ness,** *n.*
—**Syn. 1.** proper, serious, decorous, solemn. STAID, SEDATE, SETTLED indicate a sober and composed type of conduct. STAID indicates an ingrained seriousness and propriety which shows itself in complete decorum; a colorless kind of correctness is indicated: *a staid and uninteresting old maid.* SEDATE applies to one who is noticeably quiet, composed, and sober in conduct: *a sedate and dignified young man.* One who is SETTLED has become fixed, esp. in a sober or determined way, in his manner, judgments, or mode of life: *He is young to seem so settled in his ways.* —**Ant. 1.** wild, frivolous.

stain (stān), *n.* **1.** a discoloration produced by foreign matter having penetrated into or chemically reacted with a material; a spot not easily removed. **2.** a natural spot or patch of color different from that of the basic color, as on the body of an animal. **3.** a cause of reproach; stigma; blemish: *a stain on one's reputation.* **4.** coloration produced by a dye that penetrates a substance. **5.** a dye made into a solution for coloring woods, textiles, etc. **6.** a reagent or dye used in treating a specimen for microscopic examination. —*v.t.* **7.** to discolor with spots or streaks of foreign matter. **8.** to bring reproach or dishonor upon; blemish. **9.** to sully with guilt or infamy; corrupt. **10.** to color or dye (wood, cloth, etc.) by any of various processes that change or react with the substance chemically. **11.** to color with something that penetrates the substance. **12.** to treat (a microscopic specimen) with some reagent or dye in order to color the whole or parts and so give distinctness, contrast of tissues, etc. —*v.i.* **13.** to produce a stain. **14.** to become stained; take a stain: *This fabric stains easily.* [late ME *steyne(n)* < Scand; cf. Icel *steina* to paint; in some senses, aph. var. of DISTAIN] —**stain′a·bil′i·ty, stain′a·ble·ness,** *n.* —**stain′a·ble,** *adj.* —**stain′a·bly,** *adv.* —**stain′er,** *n.* —**stain′ful,** *adj.*
—**Syn. 2, 3.** mark, imperfection, blot. **3.** taint. **7.** spot, streak, soil, dirty. **8.** sully, taint, tarnish, disgrace, dishonor, debase, defile, contaminate, pollute.

stained′ glass′, glass that has been colored, enameled, painted, or stained, esp. by having pigments baked onto its surface or by having various metallic oxides fused into it, as used in church windows, decorative lampshades, etc. —**stained′-glass′,** *adj.*

stain·less (stān′lis), *adj.* **1.** having no stain; spotless. **2.** made of stainless steel. **3.** resistant to staining, rusting, the corrosive effect of chemicals, etc. —*n.* **4.** flatware made of stainless steel. [STAIN + -LESS] —**stain′less·ly,** *adv.* —**stain′less·ness,** *n.*

stain′less steel′, alloy steel containing four percent or more chromium so as to be resistant to rust and attack from various chemicals.

stair (stâr), *n.* **1.** one of a flight or series of steps for going from one level to another, as in a building. **2.** **stairs,** such steps collectively, esp. as forming a flight or a series of flights: *He felt so good he ran all the way up the stairs.* **3.** a series or flight of steps; stairway: *a winding stair.* [ME *stey(e)r,* OE *stǣger;* c. D, LG *steiger* landing; akin to STY[2]] —**stair′less,** *adj.* —**stair′like′,** *adj.*

stair·case (stâr′kās′), *n.* a flight of stairs with its framework, banisters, etc., or a series of such flights. [STAIR + CASE[2]]

stair·head (stâr′hed′), *n.* the top of a staircase. [STAIR + HEAD]

stair′ rod′, a rod for holding a stair carpet in place against the bottom of a riser.

stair·way (stâr′wā′), *n.* a passageway from one level (of a building) to another by a series of stairs; staircase. [STAIR + WAY]

stair·well (stâr′wel′), *n.* the vertical shaft or opening containing a stairway. Also, **stair′ well′.** [STAIR + WELL[2]]

stair′ wire′, a light stair rod.

staith (stāth, stāth), *n.* *Brit. Dial.* **1.** a riverbank, lakeshore, or seashore. **2.** an embankment. **3.** a dock or wharf, esp. for loading coal vessels. [ME *stath(e)* < Scand; cf. Icel *stöth* landing-place, c. OE *stæth* riverbank, shore, OS *stath* shore, G *Gestade* shore]

stake[1] (stāk), *n.*, *v.*, **staked, stak·ing.** —*n.* **1.** a stick or post pointed at one end for driving into the ground as a boundary mark, part of a fence, support for a plant, etc. **2.** a post to which one is bound for execution, usually by burning. **3.** one of a number of vertical posts fitting into sockets or staples on the edge of the platform of a truck or other vehicle, as to retain the load. **4.** any of a variety of small anvils used in the forming of sheet-metal objects. **5.** *Mormon Ch.* a division of ecclesiastical territory, consisting of a number of wards presided over by a president and two counselors. **6.** sett (def. 2). **7.** **pull up stakes,** *Informal.* to leave one's job, place of residence, etc.; move: *They pulled up stakes and went to California.* **8.** **the stake,** the punishment of death by burning: *Joan of Arc was sentenced to the stake.* —*v.t.* **9.** to mark with or as with stakes (often fol. by *off* or *out*): *He staked out the boundaries of the garden.* **10.** to possess, claim, or reserve a share of (land, profit, glory, etc.) as if by marking or bounding with stakes (usually fol. by *out* or *off*): *I'm staking out ten percent of the gross for myself, without even considering net profit.* **11.** to separate or close off by a barrier of stakes. **12.** to support with a stake or stakes, as a plant: *to stake tomato vines.* **13.** to tether or secure to a stake, as an animal: *They staked the goat in the back yard.* **14.** to fasten with a stake or stakes. **15.** **stake out,** *Slang.* **a.** to keep (a suspect) under police surveillance. **b.** to appoint (a policeman) to maintain constant watch over (a suspect or place): *The sheriff's men were staked out in the neighborhood.* [ME; OE *staca* pin; c. D *staak,* G *Stake,* Icel *-staki* (in *lȳsistaki* candlestick); akin to STICK[1]]
—**Syn. 1.** pale, picket, pike.

stake[2] (stāk), *n., v.,* **staked, stak·ing.** —*n.* **1.** that which is wagered in a game, race, or contest. **2.** a monetary or businesslike interest, investment, share or involvement in something as in hope of gain: *He has a big stake in the success of the firm.* **3.** a personal or emotional concern, interest, involvement, or share: *Parents have a big stake in their children's happiness.* **4.** the funds with which a gambler operates. **5.** Often, **stakes.** a prize, reward, increase in status, etc., in or as in a contest. **6. stakes.** *Poker.* the cash values assigned to the various colored chips, various bets, and raises: *Our stakes are 5, 10, and 25 cents: you can bet out 10 cents on a pair and reraise twice at 25 cents.* **7.** *Informal.* a grubstake. **8. at stake,** in danger of being lost, as something that has been wagered; critically involved. —*v.t.* **9.** to risk (something), as upon the result of a game or the occurrence or outcome of any uncertain event, venture, etc.: *He staked his reputation on the success of the invention.* **10.** *Informal.* to furnish (someone) with necessaries or resources, esp. money. *He staked me to a good meal and a train ticket.* [? < D *stake(n)* (to) fix, place, or special use of STAKE[1]]
—**Syn. 1.** wager, bet. **5.** winnings, purse. **9.** bet; jeopardize.

stake′ boat′, **1.** an anchored boat to which barges or other boats are temporarily moored. **2.** an anchored boat used as a turning point in yacht races.

stake′ bod′y, *Auto.* an open truck body having a platform with sockets at the edge into which upright stakes may be placed to form a fence around the load.

Staked′ Plain′. See **Llano Estacado.**

stake·hold·er (stāk′hōl′dər), *n.* the holder of the stakes of a wager. [STAKE[2] + HOLDER]

stake′ horse′, a horse that is regularly entered in stake races.

stake·out (stāk′out′), *n. Slang.* **1.** the surveillance of a location by the police, as in anticipation of a crime or the arrival of a wanted person. **2.** the place from which such surveillance is carried out. [n. use of v. phrase *stake out*]

stake′ race′, *Horse Racing.* a race in which part of the prize or purse is put up by the owners of the horses nominated to run in the race. Also, **stakes′ race′.**

Sta·kha·nov·ism (stə kä′nə viz′əm, stä hä′no-), *n.* a method for increasing production by rewarding individual initiative, developed in the Soviet Union in 1935. [named after A. G. *Stakhanov* (b. 1905) Russian efficiency expert; see -ISM]

Sta·kha·nov·ite (stə kä′nə vīt′, -kan′ə-), *n.* **1.** a worker in the Soviet Union who regularly surpasses his production quota and is specially honored and rewarded. —*adj.* **2.** of or pertaining to a Stakhanovite or to Stakhanovism. [STAKHANOV(ISM) + -ITE[1]]

sta·lac·ti·form (stə lak′tə fôrm′), *adj.* resembling or shaped like a stalactite. [STALACT(ITE) + -I- + -FORM]

sta·lac·tite (stə lak′tīt, stal′ək tīt′), *n.* a deposit, usually of calcium carbonate, shaped like an icicle, hanging from the roof of a cave or the like, and formed by the dripping of percolating calcareous water. [< NL *stalactites* < Gk *stalaktós* dripping (*stalak-*, var. of *stalag-*, s. of *stalássein* to drip + *-tos* verbid suffix) + *-ites* -ITE[1]] —**sta·lac·tit·ic** (stal′ək tit′ik), **stal′ac·tit′i·cal,** *adj.* —**stal′ac·tit′i·cal·ly,** *adv.*

A, Stalactite
B, Stalagmite

stalac′tite work′, (in Islamic architecture) intricate decorative corbeling in the form of brackets, squinches, and portions of pointed vaults. Also called **honeycomb work.**

sta·lag (stal′ag; *Ger.* shtä′läk), *n.* a German camp for prisoners of war. [< G, short for *Sta(mm)lag(er)*, group camp; akin to STEM[1], LAIR]

sta·lag·mite (stə lag′mīt, stal′əg mīt′), *n.* a deposit, usually of calcium carbonate, more or less resembling an inverted stalactite, formed on the floor of a cave or the like by the dripping of percolating calcareous water. See illus. under **stalactite.** [< NL *stalagmite(s)* < Gk *stálagm(a)*, (akin to *stalássein;* see STALACTITE) + *-ites* -ITE[1]] —**stal·ag·mit·ic** (stal′əg mit′ik), **stal′ag·mit′i·cal,** *adj.* —**stal′ag·mit′i·cal·ly,** *adv.*

stal·ag·mom·e·ter (stal′əg mom′i tər), *n. Chem., Physics.* an instrument for determining the number of drops, or the weight of each drop, in a given volume of liquid. Also called **stactometer.** [< Gk *stalagmó(s)* (see STALAGMITE) + -METER] —**stal·ag·mo·met·ric** (stə lag′mə me′trik), *adj.* —**stal′ag·mom′e·try,** *n.*

St. Al·bans (ôl′bənz), **1.** a city in W Hertfordshire, in SE England: Norman cathedral; battles of Wars of the Roses 1455, 1461. 50,276 (1961). **2.** a city in W West Virginia, near Charleston. 15,103 (1960). **3.** a town in NW Vermont. 8806 (1960).

stale[1] (stāl), *adj.,* **stal·er, stal·est,** *v.* —*adj.* **1.** not fresh; vapid or flat, as beverages; dry or hardened, as bread. **2.** having lost novelty or interest; hackneyed; trite: *a stale joke.* **3.** having lost freshness, vigor, quick intelligence, initiative, or the like, as from overstrain, boredom, surfeit, etc.: *He had grown stale on the job and needed a long vacation.* **4.** *Law.* having lost force or effectiveness through absence of action, as a claim. —*v.t., v.i.* **5.** to make or become stale. [ME; akin to MD *stel* in same sense; ? akin to STAND or to STALE[2]] —**stale′ly,** *adv.* —**stale′ness,** *n.*
—**Syn. 1.** hard, tasteless, sour, insipid. **2.** uninteresting, stereotyped, old, common. —**Ant. 1.** fresh.

stale[2] (stāl), *v.i.,* **staled, stal·ing.** (of livestock) to urinate. [late ME *stale(n)* (to) urinate; c. G *stallen*, Dan *stalle*, Norw, Sw *stalla*, F *estaller* (< OFrankish); akin to Gk *stalássein* to drip (see STALAGMITE), Breton *staot* urine]

stale·mate (stāl′māt′), *n., v.,* **-mat·ed, -mat·ing.** —*n.* **1.** *Chess.* a position of the pieces when no move can be made by either player without putting his own king in check, the result being a draw. **2.** any position or situation in which no action can be taken; deadlock: *Talks between union and management resulted in a stalemate.* —*v.t.* **3.** to subject to a stalemate. **4.** to bring to a standstill. [late ME *stale* stalemate (whence AF *estale*) (appar. special use of STALE[1]) + MATE[2]]
—**Syn. 2.** impasse.

Sta·lin (stä′lin, -lēn), *n.* **1. Joseph V.** (*Iosif Vissarionovich Dzhugashvili* or *Dzugashvili*), 1879–1953, Russian statesman, secretary general of the Communist party 1922–53; premier of the U.S.S.R. 1941–53. **2.** Also, **Stalino.** former name of **Donetsk.** **3.** former name of **Varna.** **4.** former name of **Brasov.**

Sta·lin·a·bad (*Russ.* stä′li nä bät′), *n.* former name of **Dyushambe.**

Sta·lin·grad (stä′lin grad′; *Russ.* stä′lin gRät′), *n.* former name of **Volgograd.**

Sta·lin·ism (stä′li niz′əm), *n.* the principles of communism associated with Joseph Stalin, characterized esp. by the extreme suppression of dissident political or ideological views, the concentration of power in one person, and an aggressive international policy. [STALIN + -ISM]

Sta·lin·ist (stä′li nist), *adj.* **1.** of or pertaining to Joseph Stalin or Stalinism. —*n.* **2.** an advocate or supporter of Stalin or Stalinism. [STALIN + -IST]

Sta·li·no (*Russ.* stä′li no), *n.* a former name of **Donetsk.**

Sta·linsk (*Russ.* stä′linsk), *n.* former name of **Novokuznetsk.**

stalk[1] (stôk), *n.* **1.** the stem or main axis of a plant. **2.** any slender supporting or connecting part of a plant, as the petiole of a leaf, the peduncle of a flower, or the funicle of an ovule. **3.** a similar structural part of an animal. **4.** a stem, shaft, or slender supporting part of anything. [ME *stalke*, OE *stæl(a)* + *-k* suffix] —**stalk′like′,** *adj.*

stalk[2] (stôk), *v.i.* **1.** to pursue or approach prey, quarry, etc., stealthily. **2.** to walk with measured, stiff, or haughty strides: *He was so angry he stalked away without saying goodby.* **3.** to proceed in a steady, deliberate, or sinister manner: *Famine stalked through the nation.* **4.** *Obs.* to walk or go stealthily along. —*v.t.* **5.** to pursue (game, a person, etc.) stealthily. —*n.* **6.** an act or course of stalking quarry, prey, or the like: *We shot the mountain goat after a five-hour stalk.* **7.** a slow, stiff stride or gait. [ME *stalke*, OE *(be)stealc(ian)* (to) move stealthily, STEAL, equiv. to *stal(u)* stealing + *-k* suffix] —**stalk′a·ble,** *adj.* —**stalk′er,** *n.* —**stalk′ing·ly,** *adv.*

stalked (stôkt), *adj.* having a stalk or stem. [STALK[1] + -ED[3]]

stalk·ing-horse (stô′king hôrs′), *n.* **1.** a horse, or a figure of a horse, behind which a hunter conceals himself in stalking game. **2.** anything put forward to mask plans or efforts; pretext. **3.** *Politics.* a candidate used to conceal the candidacy of a more important candidate or to draw votes from a rival and hence cause his defeat.

stalk·less (stôk′lis), *adj.* **1.** having no stalk. **2.** *Bot.* sessile. [STALK[1] + -LESS]

stalk·y (stô′kē), *adj.,* **stalk·i·er, stalk·i·est.** **1.** abounding in stalks. **2.** stalklike; long and slender. [STALK[1] + -Y[1]] —**stalk′i·ly,** *adv.* —**stalk′i·ness,** *n.*

stall[1] (stôl), *n.* **1.** a compartment in a stable or shed for the accommodation of one animal. **2.** a stable or shed for horses or cattle. **3.** a booth or stand in which merchandise is displayed for sale, or in which some business is carried on (often used in combination): *a butcher's stall; a bookstall.* **4.** carrel. **5.** one of a number of fixed enclosed seats in the choir or chancel of a church for the use of the clergy. **6.** any small compartment or booth for a specific activity or housing a specific thing: *a shower stall.* **7.** a rectangular space marked off or reserved for parking a car or other vehicle, as in a parking lot. **8.** an instance or the condition of causing an engine, or a vehicle powered by an engine, to stop by supplying it with a poor fuel mixture or by overloading it. **9.** *Aeron.* an instance or the condition of causing an airplane to fly at an angle of attack greater than the angle of maximum lift, causing loss of control and a downward spin. Cf. **critical angle** (def. 2). **10.** a protective covering for a finger or toe, as various guards and sheaths or one finger of a glove. **11.** *Brit.* a chairlike seat in a theater, separated from others by arms or rails, esp. one in the front section of the parquet. **12.** *Brit. Mining.* room (def. 6). —*v.t.* **13.** to assign to, put, or keep in a stall or stalls, as an animal, a car, etc. **14.** to confine in a stall for fattening, as cattle. **15.** to cause (a motor or the vehicle it powers) to stop by supplying it with a poor fuel mixture or overloading it. **16.** *Aeron.* **a.** to cause (an airplane) to fly at an angle of attack greater than the angle of maximum lift. **b.** to lose control of or crash (an airplane) from so doing. **17.** to bring to a standstill; check the progress or motion of, esp. unintentionally. **18.** to cause to stick fast, as in mire or snow. —*v.i.* **19.** (of an engine, car, airplane, etc.) to be stalled or go through the process of stalling. **20.** to come to a standstill; be brought to a stop. **21.** to stick fast, as in mire. **22.** to occupy a stall, as an animal. [ME; OE *steall;* c. G *Stall*, Icel *stallr;* akin to OE *stellan*, G *stellen* to put, place] —**stall′-like′,** *adj.*

stall[2] (stôl), *Informal.* —*n.* **1.** a pretext, as a ruse, trick, or the like, used to delay or deceive. —*v.i.* **2.** to delay, esp. by evasion or deception. **3.** *Sports.* to play below one's best in order to deceive for any reason. —*v.t.* **4.** to delay or put off, esp. by evasion or deception (often fol. by *off*): *He stalled the police for 15 minutes so his accomplice could get away.* [ME *stal(e)* decoy bird (whence AF *estale* decoy pigeon), OE *stælkdecoy* (in *stælhrān* decoy reindeer); akin to STALL[1]]

stall·age (stô′lij), *n. Old Eng. Law.* **1.** the right or liberty to set up a stall in a fair or market. **2.** rent paid for such a stall. [< AL *stalla(gium)*, AF *estalage.* See STALL[2], -AGE]

stall′ an′gle, *Aeron.* See **critical angle** (def. 2). Also called **stall′ an′gle of attack′.**

stall-fed (stôl′fed′), *adj.* (of animals) confined to and fed in a stall, esp. for fattening.

stall-feed (stôl′fēd′), *v.t.,* **-fed, -feed·ing.** **1.** to keep and feed (an animal) in a stall. **2.** to fatten (an animal) for slaughter by this process.

stall′ing an′gle, *Aeron.* See **critical angle** (def. 2). Also called **stall′ing an′gle of attack′.**

stal·lion (stal′yən), *n.* an uncastrated adult male horse, esp. one used for breeding. [late ME *stalon* < OF *(e)stalon*, equiv. to *stal-* (< Gmc; see STALL[1]) + *-on* n. suffix]

stall′ plate′, *Heraldry.* a plate bearing the arms of a member of an order, placed in his stall in the chapel of the order.

stal·wart (stôl′wərt), *adj.* **1.** strongly and stoutly built; sturdy and robust. **2.** strong and brave; valiant: *a stalwart knight.* **3.** firm, steadfast, or uncompromising: *a stalwart supporter of the U.N.* —*n.* **4.** a physically stalwart person. **5.** a steadfast or uncompromising partisan: *They counted on the party stalwarts for major support in the off-year campaigns.* [ME (Scot), var. of *stalward*, earlier *stalwurthe*, OE *stælwirthe* serviceable, equiv. to *stǣl* (contr. of *stathol* STADDLE) + *wierthe* WORTH] —**stal′wart·ly,** *adv.* —**stal′wart·ness,** *n.*
—**Syn. 1.** brawny, muscular, strapping, strong. **2.** intrepid, fearless, resolute, indomitable. —**Ant. 1.** weak. **2.** fearful.

stal·worth (stôl′wərth), *adj. Archaic.* stalwart.

stam·ba (stam′bä), *n.* (in India) a memorial pillar. [< Skt *stambha* pillar, column]

Stam·bul (stäm bo͞ol′), *n.* **1.** the oldest part and principal Turkish residential section of Istanbul, south of the Golden Horn. **2.** Istanbul. Also, **Stam·boul** (stäm bo͞ol′; *Fr.* stäN bo͞ol′).

sta·men (stā′mən), *n., pl.* **sta·mens, stam·i·na** (stam′ə nə). *Bot.* the pollen-bearing organ of a flower, consisting of the filament and the anther. See diag. under **flower.** [< L: warp in upright loom, thread, filament, equiv. to *stā(re)* (to) stand + *-men* n. suffix; akin to Gk *stēmōn* warp, Skt *sthāman* place, deriv. of *sthā-* STAND] —**sta′mened,** *adj.*

sta′men blight′, *Plant Pathol.* a disease of blackberries, characterized by a gray, powdery mass of spores covering the anthers, caused by a fungus, *Hapalosphaeria deformans.*

Stam·ford (stam′fərd), *n.* **1.** a city in SW Connecticut. 92,713 (1960). **2.** a town in central Texas. 5259 (1960). **3.** Also, **Stanford.** a boy's given name.

stam·in (stam′in), *n.* a coarse woolen fabric, used in the manufacture of garments. [ME < MF *(e)stamine* < L *stāmin(ea)*, fem. of *stāmineus* consisting of threads, equiv. to *stāmin-* (see STAMEN) + *-eus* -EOUS]

stamin-, var. of **stamini-** before a vowel: *staminate.*

stam·i·na[1] (stam′ə nə), *n.* strength of physical constitution; power to endure disease, fatigue, privation, etc. [< L, pl. of *stāmen* thread (see STAMEN); namely, the life-threads spun by the Fates]
—**Syn.** endurance, resistance, health. —**Ant.** weakness.

stam·i·na[2] (stam′ə nə), *n.* a pl. of **stamen.**

stam·i·nal[1] (stam′ə nᵊl), *adj. Bot.* of or pertaining to stamens. Also, **sta·min·e·al** (stə min′ē əl). [STAMIN- + -AL[1]]

stam·i·nal[2] (stam′ə nᵊl), *adj.* of or pertaining to stamina or endurance. [STAMIN(A)[1] + -AL[1]]

stam·i·nate (stam′ə nit, -nāt′), *adj. Bot.* **1.** having a stamen or stamens. **2.** having stamens but no pistils. See illus. under **monoecious.** [STAMIN- + -ATE[1]]

stamini-, a combining form of **stamen:** *staminiferous.* Also, *esp. before a vowel,* **stamin-.** [comb. form repr. L *stamin-* (s. of *stamen*); see -I-]

stam·i·nif·er·ous (stam′ə nif′ər əs), *adj. Bot.* bearing or having a stamen or stamens. Also, **stam·i·nig·er·ous** (stam′ə nij′ər əs). [STAMINI- + -FEROUS]

stam·i·no·di·um (stam′ə nō′dē əm), *n., pl.* **-di·a** (-dē ə). *Bot.* **1.** a sterile or abortive stamen. **2.** a part resembling such a stamen. Also, **stam·i·node** (stam′ə nōd′). [STAMIN- + -ODE[1] + -IUM]

stam·i·no·dy (stam′ə nō′dē), *n. Bot.* the metamorphosis of any of various flower organs, as a sepal or a petal, into a stamen. [STAMINODIUM, with -Y[3] r. -IUM]

stam·mel (stam′əl), *n. Obs.* **1.** a coarse woolen fabric often dyed red, formerly used in the manufacture of undergarments. **2.** a bright red color, as of such a cloth. [< MF *(e)stamel*, equiv. to *estame* (< L *stāmen* warp; see STAMEN) + *-el* n. suffix]

stam·mer (stam′ər), *v.i.* **1.** to speak with involuntary breaks and pauses, or with spasmodic repetitions of syllables or sounds. —*v.t.* **2.** to say with a stammer (often fol. by *out*). —*n.* **3.** a stammering mode of utterance. **4.** a stammered utterance. [ME; OE *stam(e)r(ian)* (c. G *stammern*), equiv. to *stam* stammering + *-erian* -ER[6]; akin to Icel *stamma* to stammer, Goth *stams* stammering] —**stam′mer·er,** *n.* —**stam′mer·ing·ly,** *adv.* —**stam′mer·ing·ness,** *n.*
—**Syn. 1.** pause, hesitate, falter. STAMMER, STUTTER mean to speak with some form of difficulty. STAMMER, the general term, suggests a speech difficulty which results in broken or inarticulate sounds and sometimes in complete stoppage of speech; it may be temporary, caused by sudden excitement, confusion, embarrassment, or other emotion, or it may be so deep-seated as to require special treatment for its correction. STUTTER, the parallel term preferred in technical usage, designates a broad range of defects that produce spasmodic interruptions of the speech rhythm, repetitions, or prolongations of sounds or syllables: *The child's stutter was no mere stammer of embarrassment.*

stamm·rel (stam′rəl), *n., adj. Scot.* staumrel.

stam·nos (stam′nos), *n., pl.* **-noi** (-noi). *Gk. and Rom. Antiq.* a storage jar having an oval body tapering at the base and two horizontal handles set on the shoulder. Cf. **amphora, pelike.** [< Gk, equiv. to *sta-* + *(h)istán(ai)* (to) cause (to) stand]

stamp (stamp), *v.t.* **1.** to strike or beat with a forcible, downward thrust of the foot. **2.** to bring (the foot) down forcibly or smartly on the ground, floor, etc. **3.** to extinguish, crush, etc., by striking with a forcible downward thrust of the foot (usually fol. by *out*): *to stamp out a fire; to stamp out a cigarette.* **4.** to suppress or quell (a rebellion, uprising, etc.) quickly through the use of overwhelming force (usually fol. by *out*). **5.** to crush or pound with or as with a pestle. **6.** to impress with a particular mark or device, as to indicate genuineness, approval, ownership, etc.: *to stamp a document with a seal.* **7.** to mark or impress with a design, word, mark, etc.: *to stamp a document with one's initials; Age stamped his face with lines.* **8.** to impress (a design, word, mark, etc.) on: *to stamp one's initials on a document.* **9.** to affix an adhesive paper stamp to (a letter, envelope, etc.). **10.** to characterize, distinguish, or reveal: *His ingenuity with words stamped him as a potential poet.* —*v.i.* **11.** to bring the foot down forcibly or smartly, as in crushing something, expressing rage, etc. **12.** to walk with forcible or heavy, resounding

steps: *He stamped out of the room in anger.* —*n.* **13.** See **postage stamp. 14.** the act or an instance of stamping. **15.** a die or block with raised or engraved letters, a design, seal or the like, for impressing or imprinting. **16.** an impression, design, characters, words, etc., made with or as with a die or block. **17.** an official mark indicating genuineness, validity, etc., or payment of a duty or charge. **18.** the impression of a public seal required for revenue purposes, to be obtained from a government office, for a fee, on the paper or parchment on which deeds, bills, receipts, etc., are written. **19.** a peculiar or distinctive impression or mark: *a great man who left his stamp on legal procedure.* **20.** character, kind, or type: *a man of serious stamp.* **21.** any device written, printed, or stuck on a document, envelope, etc., to indicate that a fee has been paid, or is to be paid, to the proper authority. **22.** Also called **local, local stamp.** such a device, often similar to a postage stamp, issued by a private organization to show that the charges for mail carrying have been paid. **23.** See **trading stamp. 24.** an instrument for stamping, crushing, or pounding. **25.** a heavy piece of iron or the like, as in a stamp mill, for crushing ore or other material. [early ME *stamp(en)* (to) pound (c. G *stampfen*); r. OE *stempan;* akin to Icel *stappa* to stamp, Gk *stémbein* to shake up] —**stamp′a·ble,** *adj.* —**stamp′less,** *adj.*
—**Syn. 4.** eliminate, squash, quash. See **abolish. 6.** label, brand, imprint. **15.** cut, engraving, brand. **16.** pattern, brand, mark, print, seal. **20.** sort, description, cut, mold, cast, form, make, fashion, style.

Stamp′ Act′, *Amer. Hist.* an act of the British Parliament for raising revenue in the American colonies by requiring the use of stamps and stamped paper for legal and official documents, commercial writings, and various articles: it was to go into effect on November 1, 1765, but met with intense opposition and was repealed in March, 1766.

stam·pede (stam pēd′), *n., v.,* **-ped·ed, -ped·ing.** —*n.* **1.** a sudden, frenzied rush or headlong flight of a herd of frightened animals, esp. cattle or horses. **2.** any headlong general flight or rush. **3.** *Western U.S., Canada.* a celebration, usually held annually, combining a rodeo, contests, exhibitions, dancing, etc. **4.** (in the Northwest) a rodeo. —*v.i.* **5.** to scatter or flee in a stampede: *People stampeded from the burning theater.* **6.** to make a general rush: *On hearing of the sale, they stampeded to the store.* —*v.t.* **7.** to cause to stampede. **8.** to rush or overrun (a place, exits, counters, etc.): *Customers stampeded the stores.* [< AmerSp *(e)stampid(a),* Sp, equiv. to *estamp(ar)* (to) stamp + *-ida* n. suffix] —**stam·ped′a·ble,** *adj.* —**stam·ped′er,** *n.* —**stam·ped′ing·ly,** *adv.*

stamp·er (stam′pər), *n.* **1.** one who or that which stamps. **2.** (in a post office) an employee who applies postmarks and cancels postage stamps. **3.** an instrument for stamping. **4.** a pestle, esp. one in a stamp mill. **5.** a mold, usually of metal, from which disk recordings are pressed. [ME *stampere.* See STAMP, -ER[1]]

stamp′ing ground′, *Informal.* a place habitually frequented by an animal or person; favorite haunt: *It felt strange to be in my old stamping ground again after so many years.*

stamp′ mill′, *Metall.* a mill or machine in which ore is crushed to powder by means of heavy stamps or pestles.

Stamps (stamps), *n.* a town in SW Arkansas. 2591 (1960).

Stan (stan), *n.* a boy's given name, form of **Stanley.**

stance (stans), *n.* **1.** the position or bearing of the body while standing: *legs spread in a wide stance; the threatening stance of the bull.* **2.** a mental or emotional position adopted with respect to something: *They assumed an increasingly hostile stance in their foreign policy.* **3.** *Sports.* the relative position of the feet, as in addressing a golf ball or in making a stroke. [< F < It *stanz(a)* station; see STANZA]
—**Syn. 1, 2.** posture. **2.** attitude. **3.** placement.

stanch[1] (stônch, stänch, stanch), *v.t.* **1.** to stop the flow of (a liquid, esp. blood). **2.** to stop the flow of blood or other liquid from (a wound, leak, etc.). **3.** *Archaic.* to check, allay, or extinguish. —*v.i.* **4.** to stop flowing, as blood; be stanched. —*n.* **5.** Also called **flash-lock, navigation weir.** a lock which, after being partially emptied, is opened suddenly to send a boat over a shallow place with a rush of water. Also, **staunch.** [ME *sta(u)nche(n)* < OF *(e)stanch(i)e(r)* (to) close, stop, slake (thirst) < VL **stanticāre,* equiv. to *stanti-* (s. of *stāns,* prp. of *stāre* to STAND) + *-cāre* causative suffix] —**stanch′a·ble,** *adj.* —**stanch′er,** *n.*

stanch[2] (stônch, stänch, stanch), *adj.* staunch[2]. —**stanch′ly,** *adv.* —**stanch′ness,** *n.*

stan·chion (stan′shən), *n.* **1.** an upright bar, beam, post, or support, as in a window, stall, ship, etc. —*v.t.* **2.** to furnish with stanchions. **3.** to secure by or to a stanchion or stanchions. [ME *stanchon* < OF *(e)stanchon,* equiv. to *estanche* (var. of *estance,* prob. < VL **stantia,* equiv. to L *stant-* (s. of *stāns* prp. of *stāre* to STAND) + *-ia* -Y[3]) + *-on* n. suffix]

S, Stanchion

stanch·less (stônch′lis, stänch′-, stanch′-), *adj.* **1.** not to be stanched. **2.** incessant: *a stanchless torrent of words.* [STANCH[1] + -LESS] —**stanch′less·ly,** *adv.*

stand (stand), *v.,* **stood, stand·ing,** *n., pl.* **stands** for 43–61, **stands, stand** for 62. —*v.i.* **1.** to assume or keep an upright position on the feet. **2.** to have a specified height when in this position: *a basketball player who stands six feet seven inches.* **3.** to remain motionless or steady on the feet. **4.** to cease moving; halt; stop: *Who goes there? Stand and be identified!* **5.** to take a position or place as indicated: *to stand aside.* **6.** to remain firm or steadfast, as in a cause. **7.** to take up or maintain a position or attitude with respect to a person, issue, or the like: *to stand as sponsor for a person.* **8.** to have or adopt a certain policy, course, or attitude, as of adherence, support, opposition, or resistance: *He stands for free trade.* **9.** (of things) to be in an upright or vertical position, be set on end, or rest on or as on a support. **10.** to be set, placed, fixed, located, or situated: *The building stands at 34th Street and 5th Avenue.* **11.** (of an account, score, etc.) to show, be, or remain as indicated; show the specified position of the parties concerned: *The score stood 18 to 14 at the half.* **12.** to remain erect or whole; resist change, decay, or destruction (often fol. by *up*): *The ruins still stand. The old building stood up well.* **13.** to continue in force or remain valid: *The agreement stands as signed.* **14.** to remain still, stationary, or unused: *The bicycle stood in the basement all winter.* **15.** to be or become stagnant, as water. **16.** (of persons or things) to be or remain in a specified state, condition, relation, relative position, etc.: *He stood in jeopardy of losing his license. I stand third in line for promotion.* **17.** *Chiefly Brit.* to become or be a candidate, as for public office (usually fol. by *for*). **18.** *Naut.* **a.** to take or hold a particular course at sea. **b.** to move in a certain direction: *to stand offshore.* **19.** (of a male domestic animal, esp. a stud) to be available as a sire, usually for a fee: *Three Derby winners are now standing in Kentucky.*
—*v.t.* **20.** to cause to stand; set upright; set: *Stand the chair by the lamp.* **21.** to face or encounter: *to stand a barrage of questions; to stand an assault.* **22.** to undergo or submit to: *to stand trial.* **23.** to endure or undergo without harm or damage or without giving way: *His eyes are strong enough to stand the glare.* **24.** to endure or tolerate: *He cannot stand criticism. She can't stand her father.* **25.** *Informal.* to treat or pay for: *I'll stand you to a drink when the manuscript is in. I'll stand a round of drinks.* **26.** to perform the duty of or participate in as part of one's job or duty: *to stand watch aboard ship; to stand roll call in the army.* **27.** **stand a chance** or **show,** to have a chance or possibility, esp. of winning or surviving: *He's a good shortstop but doesn't stand a chance of making the major leagues because he can't hit.* **28.** **stand by, a.** to uphold; support: *She stood by him whenever he was in trouble.* **b.** to adhere to (an agreement, promise, etc.); affirm: *She stood by her decision despite her sister's arguments.* **c.** to stand ready; wait: *Please stand by while I fix this antenna.* **d.** to get ready to speak, act, etc., as at the beginning of a radio or television program. **29.** **stand down,** *Law.* to leave the witness stand. **30.** **stand for, a.** to represent; symbolize: *P.S. stands for "postscript."* **b.** to advocate; favor: *He stands for both freedom and justice.* **c.** *Informal.* to tolerate; allow: *I won't stand for any nonsense!* **31.** **stand in with,** *Informal.* **a.** to be in association or conspiracy with. **b.** to enjoy the favor of; be on friendly terms with. **32.** **stand off, a.** to keep or stay at a distance. **b.** to put off; evade. **33.** **stand on, a.** to depend on; rest on: *The case stands on his testimony.* **b.** to be particular about; demand: *to stand on ceremony.* **c.** *Naut.* to continue on the same course or tack. **34.** **stand out, a.** to project; protrude: *The piers stand out from the harbor wall.* **b.** to be conspicuous or prominent: *She stands out in a crowd.* **c.** to persist in opposition or resistance; be inflexible. **d.** *Naut.* to maintain a course away from shore. **35.** **stand over, a.** to supervise very closely; watch constantly: *He won't work unless someone stands over him.* **b.** to put aside temporarily; postpone: *to let a project stand over until the following year.* **36.** **stand to, a.** to continue to hold; persist in: *to stand to one's statement.* **b.** to keep at steadily: *Stand to your rowing, men!* **c.** to wait in readiness; stand by: *Stand to for action.* **37.** **stand to reason.** See **reason** (def. 11). **38.** **stand up, a.** to come to or remain in a standing position: *to stand up when being introduced.* **b.** to remain strong, convincing, or durable: *The case will never stand up in court. Wool stands up better than silk.* **c.** *Slang.* to fail to keep an appointment with someone: *She stood him up again.* **39.** **stand up for, a.** to defend the cause of; support: *No one could understand why he stood up for an incorrigible criminal.* **b.** to serve a bridegroom as best man at a wedding. **40.** **stand up to,** to meet or deal with fearlessly; confront: *to stand up to a bully.*
—*n.* **41.** the act of standing; an assuming of or a remaining in an upright position. **42.** a cessation of motion; halt or stop. **43.** a determined effort for or against something, esp. a final defensive effort: *Custer's last stand. The Giants used a nine-man line in their goal-line stand.* **44.** a determined policy, position, attitude, etc., taken or maintained: *We must take a stand on political issues.* **45.** the place in which a person or thing stands; station. **46.** See **witness stand. 47.** a raised platform, as for a judge at an athletic contest, the officers reviewing a military parade, a speaker, a band, or the like. **48.** **stands,** a raised section of seats for spectators at a race course, playing field, arena, or the like; grandstand. **49.** a framework on or in which articles are placed for support, exhibition, etc.: *a hat stand.* **50.** a piece of furniture of various forms, on or in which to put articles (often used in combination): *a nightstand; a washstand.* **51.** a small, light table. **52.** a stall, booth, counter, or the like, where articles are displayed for sale or where some business is carried on: *a fruit stand.* **53.** a site or location for business: *After 20 years the ice cream vendor was still at the same stand.* **54.** a place or station occupied by vehicles available for hire: *a taxicab stand.* **55.** the vehicles occupying such a place. **56.** the growing trees, or those of a particular species or grade, in a given area. **57.** a standing growth, as of grass, wheat, etc. **58.** a halt of a theatrical company on tour, to give a performance or performances: *a series of one-night stands on the straw-hat trail.* **59.** the town at which a touring theatrical company gives a performance. **60.** hive (def. 2). **61.** *Metalworking.* a rolling unit in a rolling mill. **62.** *Archaic.* a complete set of arms or accoutrements for one soldier. [ME; OE *stand(an);* c. Icel *standa, standan;* akin to L *stā(re),* Skt *sthā* to stand]
—**Syn. 6.** continue, persist, stay, abide. **20.** place, put, fix. **21.** meet, resist, oppose. **24.** abide, stomach. See **bear. 57.** grove. **58.** crop.

stand·ard (stan′dərd), *n.* **1.** an object considered by an authority or by general consent as a basis of comparison; an approved model. **2.** anything, as a rule or principle, that is used as a basis for judgment: *They tried to establish standards for a new philosophical approach.* **3.** an average or normal requirement, quality, quantity, level, grade, etc.: *His work this week hasn't been up to his usual standard.* **4.** **standards,** those morals, ethics, habits, etc., established by authority, custom, or an individual as acceptable: *He tried to live up to his father's standards.* **5.** the authorized exemplar of a unit of weight or measure. **6.** a certain commodity in or by which a basic monetary unit is stated. Cf. **gold standard, silver standard, bimetallism, monometallism. 7.** the legally established content of full-weight coins. **8.** the prescribed degree of fineness for gold or silver. **9.** the prescribed degree of fineness for gold or silver coins. **10.** *Brit.* a class or grade in elementary schools. **11.** a musical piece of sufficiently enduring popularity to be made part of a permanent repertoire, esp. a popular song that is held in continuing esteem and is commonly used as the basis of jazz arrangements or improvisations. **12.** a flag indicating the presence of a sovereign or public official. **13.** a flag, emblematic figure, or other object raised on a pole to indicate the rallying point of an army, fleet, etc. **14.** *Mil.* **a.** any of various military or naval flags. **b.** the colors of a mounted unit. **15.** *Heraldry.* a long, tapering flag or ensign, as of a king or a nation. **16.** something which stands or is placed upright. **17.** a long candlestick or candelabrum used in a church. **18.** an upright support or supporting part. **19.** an upright timber, bar, or rod. **20.** *Armor.* a standing collar of mail. **21.** *Hort.* a plant trained or grafted to have a single, erect, treelike stem. **22.** *Bot.* a vexillum or banner. **23.** *Obs.* a large packing case or chest, esp. for carrying jewels, gold or silver plate, or similar articles of value. —*adj.* **24.** serving as a basis of weight, measure, value, comparison, or judgment. **25.** of recognized excellence or established authority: *a standard reference on medieval history.* **26.** usual, common, or customary: *Chairs are part of the standard furniture in American households. Corned beef and cabbage is his standard lunch.* **27.** conforming in pronunciation, grammar, vocabulary, etc., to the usage of those speakers whose language is generally considered to be correct or preferred: *standard American English; standard pronunciation.* **28.** fulfilling specific requirements as established by an authority, law, rule, custom, etc.: *The program was broadcast on the standard broadcast band. We'll need 200 bricks of standard size.* [ME < OF, prob. alter. of Frankish **standord* (cf. G *Standort* standing-point), conformed to *-ard* -ARD]
—**Syn. 1, 2.** gauge, basis, pattern, guide. STANDARD, CRITERION refer to the basis for making a judgment. A STANDARD is an authoritative principle or rule that usually implies a model or pattern for guidance, by comparison with which the quantity, excellence, correctness, etc., of other things may be determined: *She could serve as the standard of good breeding.* A CRITERION is a rule or principle used to judge the value, suitability, probability, etc., of something, without necessarily implying any comparison: *Wealth is no criterion of a man's worth.* **12.** ensign, banner, pennant, pennon, streamer. **24.** guiding.

stand′ard at′mosphere, 1. an arbitrarily determined vertical distribution of atmospheric pressure, temperature, and density, assumed to have physical constants and conforming to parametric equations, used for calculations in ballistics, the design of pressure altimeters, etc. **2.** a standard unit of atmospheric pressure, having a value of 1013.2 millibars, 29.9213 inches, or 760 millimeters of mercury.

stand·ard-bear·er (stan′dərd bâr′ər), *n.* **1.** an officer or soldier of an army or military unit who bears a standard. **2.** a conspicuous leader of a movement, political party, or the like. [late ME] —**stand′ard-bear′er·ship′,** *n.*

stand·ard-bred (stan′dərd bred′), *adj.* pertaining to a horse of the Standardbred breed.

Stan·dard·bred (stan′dərd bred′), *n.* one of an American breed of trotting and pacing horses used chiefly for harness racing. [STANDARD + BRED]

stand′ard can′dle, *Optics.* candle (def. 3c).

stan′dard coin′, a coin having value in bullion at least equal to its face value.

stand′ard coke′, a grade of hot-dipped tin plate having an average coating of 1.35 pounds per base box.

stand′ard com′pass, the compass of a vessel used as a reference to check all other compasses: kept as free as possible from magnetic influences, usually on the flying bridge.

stand′ard cost′, a predetermined cost of material, labor, etc., based on specifications prepared from time-and-motion studies, accounting records, and the like. Cf. **actual cost.**

stand′ard devia′tion, *Statistics.* a measure of dispersion in a frequency distribution, equal to the square root of the mean of the squares of the deviations from the arithmetic mean of the distribution.

stand′ard dol′lar, the basic monetary unit of the U.S., since January 31, 1934, containing $15^5/_{21}$ grains of gold, 0.900 fine: previously contained 25.8 grains of gold, 0.900 fine.

Stand′ard Eng′lish, the English language as written and spoken by literate people, in both formal and informal usage, and that is universally current while incorporating regional differences.

stand′ard gauge′. See under **gauge** (def. 10). —**stand′ard-gauge′,** **stand′ard-gage′,** *adj.* —**stand′ard-gauged′, stand′ard-gaged′,** *adj.*

stand·ard·ise (stan′dər dīz′), *v.t., v.i.,* **-ised, -is·ing.** *Chiefly Brit.* standardize. —**stand′ard·is′a·ble,** *adj.* —**stand′ard·i·sa′tion,** *n.* —**stand′ard·is′er,** *n.*

standardiza′tion tri′als. See **progressive trials.**

stand·ard·ize (stan′dər dīz′), *v.,* **-ized, -iz·ing.** —*v.t.* **1.** to bring to or make of an established standard size, weight, quality, strength, or the like: *to standardize manufactured parts.* **2.** to compare with or test by a standard. **3.** to choose or establish a standard for. —*v.i.* **4.** to become standardized. Also, *esp. Brit.,* **standardise.** [STANDARD + -IZE] —**stand′ard·iz′a·ble,** *adj.* —**stand′ard·i·za′tion,** *n.* —**stand′ard·iz′er,** *n.*

stand′ard lin′ing, *Print.* **1.** a system for aligning type so that all fonts of the same point size have a common baseline. **2.** a design of type that provides room on the body for accommodation of descenders of all standard type of the same point size. Cf. **art lining, title lining.**

stand′ard mon′ey, money made of a metal that has utility and value apart from its use as a unit of monetary exchange.

stand′ard of liv′ing, a grade or level of subsistence and comfort in everyday life enjoyed by a community, class, or individual: *Widespread unemployment will depress the nation's standard of living. The well-educated generally have a high standard of living.*

stand′ard refrac′tion, *Physics.* the refraction that would occur in the earth's atmosphere if the index of refraction of the atmosphere decreased uniformly with height at the rate of 39×10^{-6} per kilometer.

stand′ard time′, the civil time officially adopted for a country or region, usually the civil time of some specific meridian lying within the region. The standard time zones in the U.S. **(Eastern time, Central time, Mountain time, Pacific time, Yukon time, Alaska time,** and **Bering time)** use the civil times of the 75th, 90th, 105th, 120th, 135th, 150th, and 165th meridians respectively, the difference of time between one zone and the next being exactly one hour. See diag. under **time zone.**

stand-by (stand′bī′), *n., pl.* **-bys,** *adj.* —*n.* **1.** a staunch supporter or adherent; one who can be relied upon. **2.** something upon which one can rely and therefore choose or use regularly. **3.** something or someone held ready to serve as a substitute, esp. a radio or television program used as a filler in case of cancellation of a regularly scheduled program. **4.** the situation of being in readiness, as of a passenger to occupy canceled accommodations or of a soldier, machine, etc., to go on emergency service (sometimes prec. by *on*). —*adj.* **5.** kept readily available for use in an emergency, shortage, or the like: *a stand-by player; a stand-by amount of money.* **6.** of or pertaining to a waiting period. [n., adj. use of v. phrase *stand by*]

stand·ee (stan dē′), *n. Informal.* one who stands, as a spectator in a theater, a passenger in a train, etc., because no seats are available. [STAND + -EE]

stand·fast (stand′fast′, -fäst′), *n.* a rigid or unyielding position. [n. use of v. phrase *stand fast*]

stand-in (stand′in′), *n.* **1.** a substitute for a motion-picture star during the preparation of lighting, cameras, etc., or in dangerous scenes. **2.** any substitute. **3.** *Informal.* an influential or favorable position; good standing. [n. use of v. phrase *stand in*]

stand·ing (stan′ding), *n.* **1.** rank or status, esp. with respect to social, economic, or personal position, reputation, etc.: *He had little standing in the community.* **2.** good position, reputation, or credit: *He is a merchant of standing in the community.* **3.** length of existence, continuance, residence, membership, experience, etc.: *a friend of long standing.* **4. standings,** *Sports.* a list of teams or contestants arranged according to their past records, showing which is rated above or leading the others: *According to the standings, the White Sox are leading the league by three games.* **5.** the act of one who or that which stands. **6.** the period during which a person or thing stands. **7.** a place where a person or thing stands. —*adj.* **8.** having an erect or upright position: *a standing lamp.* **9.** performed in or from an erect position: *a standing jump.* **10.** still; not flowing or stagnant, as water; stationary. **11.** continuing without cessation or change; lasting or permanent. **12.** continuing in operation, force, use, etc.: *a standing rule.* **13.** customary or habitual; generally understood: *We have a standing bridge game every Friday night.* **14.** *Print.* kept for use in subsequent printings: *standing type.* **15.** out of use; idle: *a standing engine.* **16.** *Naut.* noting any of various objects or assemblages of objects fixed in place or position, unless moved for adjustment or repairs: *standing bowsprit.* **17.** *Naut., Mach.* **a.** noting any block of a tackle that is fixed in place. **b.** noting the part of the fall of a tackle that is fixed at the end to a standing block or other fixed point and is not rove through a block (opposed to *running*). **18.** *Knots.* noting the part of a rope that is in use and terminates in a knot or the like. [ME; see STAND, -ING[1], -ING[2]] —**Syn. 2.** See **credit. 10.** motionless. **11.** continuous, constant, steady.

stand′ing ar′my, a permanently organized military force maintained by a nation.

stand′ing broad′ jump′. See under **broad jump** (def. 1).

stand′ing commit′tee, a permanent committee, as of a legislature, society, etc., intended to consider all matters pertaining to a designated subject.

stand′ing cup′, a tall decorative cup of the Middle Ages and Renaissance, having a raised cover.

stand′ing cy′press, a North American herb, *Gilia rubra,* having clusters of flowers that are scarlet on the outside but yellow and red-dotted inside.

stand′ing gaff′, *Naut.* See under **gaff**[1] (def. 4).

stand′ing lug′, *Naut.* a lugsail the yard of which is simply rotated about the mast, without being dipped, in order to tack or jibe.

stand′ing mar′tingale, martingale (def. 1).

stand′ing or′der, **1.** *Mil.* (formerly) a general order always in force in a command and establishing uniform procedures for it; standard operating procedure. **2. standing orders,** *Parl. Proc.* the rules ensuring continuity of procedure during the meetings of an assembly.

stand′ing rig′ging, *Naut.* rigging remaining permanently in position as a means of steadying various spars, shrouds, stays, etc. (opposed to *running rigging*).

stand′ing room′, **1.** room or space in which to stand. **2.** accommodation only for standing, as in a theater, stadium, or the like.

stand′ing salt′, a tall, ornamental salt cellar of the 16th century and after, having a depression on top for holding the salt.

stand′ing wave′, *Physics.* a wave in a medium in which each point on the axis of the wave has an associated constant amplitude ranging from zero at the nodes to a maximum at the antinodes. Also called **stationary wave.**

stand′ing way′, *Shipbuilding.* groundway.

stand·ish (stan′dish), *n. Archaic.* a stand for ink, pens, and other writing materials. [perh. STAND + DISH]

Stan·dish (stan′dish), *n.* **Myles** or **Miles** (mīlz), c1584–1656, American settler, born in England: military leader in Plymouth Colony.

stand-off (stand′ôf′, -of′), *n.* **1.** a standing off or apart; aloofness. **2.** a tie or draw, as in a game. **3.** something that counterbalances. **4.** a prop for holding the top of a ladder away from the vertical surface against which it is leaning. —*adj.* **5.** standing off or apart; aloof; reserved: *an uncordial and stand-off manner.* Also, **stand′off′.** [n., adj. use of v. phrase *stand off*]

stand-off·ish (stand′ô′fish, -of′ish), *adj.* somewhat aloof or reserved; cold and unfriendly. Also, **stand′off′ish.** [STAND-OFF + -ISH[1]] —**stand′-off′ish·ly, stand′off′ish·ly,** *adv.* —**stand′-off′ish·ness, stand′off′ish·ness,** *n.*

stand′ oil′, a thick oil made by heating linseed oil to temperatures of 600°F and higher, used chiefly as a medium in paints.

stand′-on ves′sel (stand′on′, -ôn′), *Naut.* the privileged one of two meeting vessels.

stand·out (stand′out′), *n.* **1.** something or someone, as a person, performance, etc., remarkably superior to others: *Evans was a standout in the mixed doubles.* **2.** *Informal.* someone who is conspicuous in an area because of his refusal to conform with the actions, opinions, desires, etc., of the majority. —*adj.* **3.** outstanding; superior. Also, **stand′-out′.** [n., adj. use of v. phrase *stand out*]

stand·pat (stand′pat′), *Informal.* —*n.* **1.** standpatter. —*adj.* **2.** characterized by refusing to consider or accept change. [n., adj. use of v. phrase *stand pat*]

stand·pat·ter (stand′pat′ər, -pat′-), *n. Informal.* a person who refuses to consider or accept change. [STANDPAT + -ER[1]]

stand·pipe (stand′pīp′), *n.* **1.** a vertical pipe or tower into which water is pumped to obtain a required head. **2.** a water pipe for supplying the fire hoses of a building, connected with the water supply of the building and usually with a siamese outside the building. [STAND + PIPE[1]]

stand·point (stand′point′), *n.* **1.** the point or place at which one stands to view something. **2.** the mental position, attitude, etc., from which one views and judges things: *From the lawyer's standpoint, his client is right.* [STAND + POINT, modeled on G *Standpunkt*]

St. An·drews (an′drōōz), a seaport in E Fife, in E Scotland: resort; golf courses. 10,350 (est. 1964).

St. Andrew's cross, a cross composed of four diagonal arms of equal length; saltire. See illus. under **cross.**

St. An·drew's-cross (an′drōōz krôs′, -kros′), a shrubby, perennial herb, *Ascyrum hypericoides,* found from Massachusetts to tropical America, having flowers in clusters of three.

stand·still (stand′stil′), *n.* a state of cessation of movement or action; halt; stop: *The ball rolled to a standstill just short of the boundary.* [n. use of v. phrase *stand still*]

stand-up (stand′up′), *adj.* **1.** standing erect or upright, as a collar. **2.** performed, taken, etc., while one stands: *a stand-up meal; a stand-up lecture.* **3.** designed for or requiring a standing position: *a stand-up lunch counter.* **4.** (of a fight) characterized by the rapid exchange of many blows with little attention being given to defensive maneuvering. **5.** characterized by an erect or bold stance: *a stand-up batter who hits many doubles.* **6.** *Theat.* (of a comedian) delivering a comic monologue while completely alone on the stage. [adj. use of v. phrase *stand up*]

stane (stān), *n., adj., v.,* **staned, stan·ing.** *Scot. and North Eng.* stone.

Stan·ford (stan′fərd), *n.* a boy's given name. Also, **Stamford.**

Stan′ford-Bi·net′ test′ (stan′fərd bi nā′), *Psychol.* a revised version of the Binet-Simon scale, prepared at Stanford University for use in the U.S. [named after *Stanford* University, Palo Alto, California and A. BINET]

stang[1] (stang), *v.* **1.** *Obs.* pt. of **sting.** —*n.* **2.** *Scot. and North Eng.* a sting or the wound caused by a sting.

stang[2] (stang), *n. Brit. Dial.* **1.** a wooden beam, bar, pole, or stick. **2.** rood (def. 5). [ME < Scand; cf. Icel *stöng,* akin to OE *steng,* OS, OHG *stanga* pole; see STING]

stan·hope (stan′hōp′, stan′əp), *n.* a light, open, one-seated, horse-drawn carriage with two or four wheels, the body of which is hung on four springs. [named after Fitzroy *Stanhope* (1787–1864), British clergyman]

Stan·hope (stan′hōp′, stan′əp), *n.* **1. James, 1st Earl Stanhope,** 1673–1721, British soldier and statesman: prime minister 1717–18. **2. Philip Dor·mer** (dôr′mər). See **Chesterfield, 4th Earl of.**

Stan·is·laus (stan′is lôs′, -lous′; *Ger.* shtä′nis lous′, stä′-), *n.* a boy's given name.

Stanislaus I, (*Stanislaus Leszczynski*) 1677–1766, king of Poland 1704–09, 1733–35. Also, **Stan·is·las I** (stan′is ləs, -läs′).

Stan·i·slav·ski (stan′i släv′skē, -släf′-; *Russ.* stä-ni släf′ski), *n.* **Kon·stan·tin** (kon stän tēn′), 1863–1938, Russian actor, producer, and director. Also, **Stan′i·slav′sky.**

Stanislav′ski Meth′od, method (def. 5). Also called **Stanislav′ski Sys′tem.** [named after K. STANISLAVSKI]

Sta·ni·sla·wów (*Pol.* stä′nē slä′vōōf), *n.* a city in the SW Ukraine, in the SW Soviet Union in Europe: formerly in Poland. 66,000 (1959). German, **Stan·is·lau** (shtä′nis lou′). Russian, **Sta·ni·sla·vov** (stä′ni slä′-vof).

stank (stangk), *v.* a pt. of **stink.**

Stan·lee (stan′lē), *n.* a girl's given name.

Stan·leigh (stan′lē), *n.* a boy's given name. Also, **Stanley.**

Stan·ley (stan′lē), *n.* **1. Arthur Pen·rhyn** (pen′rin), (*Dean Stanley*) 1815–81, English clergyman and author. **2. Edward George Geoffrey Smith, 14th Earl of Derby,** 1799–1869, British statesman: prime minister 1852, 1858–59, 1866–68. **3. Sir Henry Morgan,** (originally *John Rowlands*) 1841–1904, English explorer in Africa. **4. Wendell M(eredith),** born 1904, U.S. biochemist: Nobel prize 1946. **5. Mount,** a mountain with two summits, in central Africa, between Uganda and the Congo: highest peak in the Ruwenzori group. 16,790 ft. **6.** Also, **Stanleigh.** a boy's given name.

Stan′ley Falls′, seven cataracts of the Congo River, in the NE Republic of the Congo, on the equator.

Stan′ley Pool′, a lake on the boundary between the W Republic of the Congo and the S Republic of Congo, formed by the widening of the Congo River about 330 miles from its mouth. ab. 20 mi. long; ab. 15 mi. wide.

Stan·ley·ville (stan′lē vil′), *n.* former name of **Kisangani.**

stann-, a combining form of **stannum:** *stannite.*

stan·na·ry (stan′ə rē), *n., pl.* **-ries. 1.** a tin-mining region or district. **2.** *Brit.* a place where tin is mined or smelted. [late ME < ML *stannāri(a)* tin mine, equiv. to LL *stann(um)* STANNUM + *-āria* -ARY]

stan·nate (stan′āt), *n. Chem.* a salt of a stannic acid. [STANN- + -ATE[2]]

stan·nic (stan′ik), *adj. Chem.* of or containing tin, esp. in the tetravalent state. [STANN- + -IC]

stan′nic ac′id, *Chem.* any of the series of acids usually occurring as amorphous powders and varying in composition from H_2SnO_3 **(alpha-stannic acid)** to H_4SnO_4.

stan′nic ox′ide, *Chem.* a white, amorphous, water-insoluble powder, SnO_2, used chiefly in the manufacture of ceramic glazes and glass, and of polishing powders for metal, glass, and marble. Also called **tin ash.**

stan′nic sul′fide, *Chem.* a yellowish or brownish, water-insoluble powder, SnS_2, usually used suspended in lacquer or varnish for gilding and bronzing metals, wood, paper, etc.; mosaic gold.

stan·nite (stan′īt), *n.* a mineral, iron-black to steel-gray in color, with a metallic luster, copper iron tin sulfide, Cu_2FeSnS_4: an ore of tin. [STANN- + -ITE[1]]

stan·nous (stan′əs), *adj. Chem.* containing bivalent tin. [STANN- + -OUS]

stan′nous chlo′ride, *Chem.* a white, crystalline, water-soluble solid, $SnCl_2 \cdot 2H_2O$, used chiefly as a reducing and tinning agent, and as a mordant in dyeing with cochineal.

stan·num (stan′əm), *n.* tin. [< LL: tin, L: alloy of silver and lead; perh. < Celt]

Sta·no·voi (stä′no voi′), *n.* a mountain range in the E Soviet Union in Asia: a watershed between the Pacific and Arctic oceans; highest peak, 8143 ft.

Stans (shtäns), *n.* a town in and the capital of Nidwalden, in central Switzerland.

St. Anthony, **1.** a town in E Minnesota. 5084 (1960). **2.** a town in E Idaho. 2700 (1960).

St. Anthony's cross. See **tau cross.**

Stan·ton (stan′tən), *n.* **1. Edwin Mc·Mas·ters** (mək mas′tərz, -mä′stərz), 1814–69, U.S. statesman: Secretary of War 1862–67. **2. Mrs. Elizabeth Ca·dy** (kā′dē), 1815–1902, U.S. social reformer. **3.** a boy's given name.

stan·za (stan′zə), *n. Pros.* an arrangement of a certain number of lines, usually four or more, sometimes having a fixed length, meter, or rhyme scheme, forming a division of a poem. [< It: room, station, stopping-place (pl. *stanze*) < VL **stantia,* equiv. to L *stant-* (s. of *stāns,* prp. of *stāre* to STAND) + *-ia* -Y[3]] —**stan′zaed,** *adj.* —**stan·za·ic** (stan zā′ik), **stan·za′i·cal,** *adj.* —**stan·za′i·cal·ly,** *adv.*
—**Syn.** See **verse.**

stan·za (stän′tsä), *n., pl.* **-ze** (-tse). *Italian.* a room or apartment: *the stanze of Raphael in the Vatican.*

sta·pe·li·a (stə pē′lē ə), *n.* any asclepiadaceous plant of the genus *Stapelia,* of southern Africa, having short, fleshy, leafless stems, and flowers that are oddly colored or mottled and in most species emit a fetid, carrionlike odor. [named after J. B. van *Stapel* (d. 1636), Dutch botanist; see -IA]

sta·pes (stā′pēz), *n., pl.* **sta·pes, sta·pe·dez** (stə pē′dēz). *Anat.* the outer, stirrup-shaped bone of a chain of three small bones in the middle ear of man and other mammals. Cf. **incus** (def. 1), **malleus.** See diag. under **ear.** [< NL, ML: stirrup] —**sta·pe·di·al** (stə pē′dē-əl), *adj.*

staph (staf), *n. Informal.* staphylococcus. [by shortening]

staphylo-, a learned borrowing from Greek, where it meant "bunch of grapes," "uvula", used with these meanings, and also with reference to the palate and to staphylococcus, in the formation of compound words: *staphyloplasty; staphylotomy.* [comb. form repr. Gk *staphylḗ*]

staph·y·lo·coc·cus (staf′ə lə kok′əs), *n., pl.* **-coc·ci** (-kok′sī). *Bacteriol.* any of several spherical bacteria of the genus *Staphylococcus,* occurring in pairs, tetrads, and irregular clusters, certain species of which, as *S. aureus,* can be pathogenic for man. [STAPHYLO- + COCCUS] —**staph·y·lo·coc·cal** (staf′ə lə kok′əl), **staph·y·lo·coc·cic** (staf′ə lə kok′sik), *adj.*

staph·y·lo·ma (staf′ə lō′mə), *n., pl.* **-mas, -ma·ta** (-mə tə). *Pathol.* any of various local bulgings of the eyeball. [< LL < Gk; see STAPHYLO-, -OMA] —**staph·y·lo·mat·ic** (staf′ə lō mat′ik), **staph′y·lom′a·tous** (staf′ə lom′ə təs), *adj.*

staph·y·lo·plas·ty (staf′ə lə plas′tē), *n.* the remedying of defects of the soft palate by plastic surgery. [STAPHYLO- + -PLASTY] —**staph′y·lo·plas′tic,** *adj.*

staph·y·lor·rha·phy (staf′ə lôr′ə fē, -lor′-), *n., pl.* **-phies.** the surgical operation of uniting a cleft palate. [STAPHYLO- + -RRHAPHY] —**staph·y·lor·rhaph·ic** (staf′ə lō raf′ik, -lo-, -lə-), *adj.*

staph·y·lot·o·my (staf′ə lot′ə mē), *n., pl.* **-mies.** *Surg.* **1.** uvulotomy. **2.** uvulectomy. **3.** the excision of a staphyloma. [< NL *staphylotomia.* See STAPHYLO-, -TOMY]

sta·ple[1] (stā′pəl), *n., v.,* **-pled, -pling.** —*n.* **1.** a short piece of wire bent so as to bind together papers, sections of a book, or the like, by driving the ends through the sheets and clinching them on the other side. **2.** a similar, often U-shaped piece of wire or metal with pointed ends for driving into a surface to hold a hasp, hook, pin, bolt, wire, or the like. —*v.t.* **3.** to secure or fasten by a staple or staples: *to staple three sheets together.* [ME *stapel,* OE *stapol* support, post; c. MD *stapel* foundation, Icel *stöpull* pillar, G *Stapel* stake]

sta·ple[2] (stā′pəl), *n., adj., v.,* **-pled, -pling.** —*n.* 1. a principal raw material or commodity grown or manufactured in a locality. 2. a principal commodity in a mercantile field; goods in steady demand or of known or recognized quality. 3. a basic or necessary item of food: *She bought flour, sugar, salt, and other staples. Beans are a staple of many foreign diets.* 4. a basic or principal item, thing, feature, element, or part: *Cowboy dramas are a staple on television. His blue suit was a staple in his wardrobe.* 5. the fiber of wool, cotton, flax, rayon, etc., considered with reference to length and fineness. 6. *Textiles.* a standard length of textile fibers, representing the average of such fibers taken collectively, as short-staple or long-staple cotton. 7. *Hist.* a town or place appointed by royal authority as the seat of a body of merchants having the exclusive right of purchase of certain classes of goods for export. —*adj.* 8. chief or prominent among the products exported or produced by a country or district; chiefly or largely dealt in or consumed. 9. basic, chief, or principal: *staple industries.* 10. principally used: *staple subjects of conversation.* —*v.t.* 11. to sort or classify according to the staple or fiber, as wool. [ME *stapel* < MD: warehouse, mart; see STAPLE[1]]

sta·pler[1] (stā′plər), *n.* 1. a machine for fastening together sheets of paper or the like, with wire staples. 2. a wire-stitching machine, esp. one used in bookbinding. [STAPLE[1] + -ER[1]]

sta·pler[2] (stā′plər), *n.* 1. one who staples, as of wool. 2. a merchant who deals in a staple or staples. [STAPLE[2] + -ER[1]]

Sta·ples (stā′pəlz), *n.* a town in central Minnesota. 2706 (1960).

sta·pling (stā′pling), *n. Shipbuilding.* a collar formed of angle iron surrounding a structural member passing through a deck or bulkhead to make a seal that is watertight, oiltight, etc. Also called **angle collar.** [STAPLE[1] + -ING[1]]

star (stär), *n., adj., v.,* **starred, star·ring.** —*n.* 1. any of the heavenly bodies, except the moon, appearing as fixed luminous points in the sky at night. 2. *Astron.* any of the large, self-luminous, heavenly bodies, as the sun. 3. any heavenly body. 4. *Astrol.* a heavenly body, esp. a planet, considered as influencing mankind and events. 5. a person's destiny, fortune, temperament, etc., regarded as influenced and determined by the stars. 6. a conventionalized figure usually having five or six points radiating from or disposed about a center. 7. this figure used as an ornament, award, badge, mark of excellence, etc. 8. *Jewelry.* a brilliant with six facets of equilateral triangles immediately beneath the table, instead of the normal eight. 9. *Print.* an asterisk. 10. a person who is celebrated or distinguished in some art, profession, or other field. 11. a prominent actor, singer, or the like, esp. one who plays the leading role in a performance. 12. *U.S. Mil., Navy.* See **battle star.** 13. *U.S. Navy.* **a.** a gold or bronze star worn on the ribbon of a decoration or medal to represent a second or subsequent award of the same decoration or medal. **b.** a silver star worn in place of five gold or bronze stars. 14. a white spot on the forehead of a horse. 15. (in English pool) an additional life or lives that may be bought by the player who is first put out, or by the next player out if the former forfeits the privilege. 16. *Mach.* See **star wheel.** 17. *Heraldry.* **a.** an estoile. **b.** a mullet. 18. **make someone see stars,** to deal someone a severe blow causing the illusion of brilliant streaks of light before the eyes: *The blow on the head made him see stars, and the next thing he knew he was in the hospital.* 19. **thank one's lucky stars,** to acknowledge one's good fortune; be grateful: *Instead of complaining about hospital bills she should thank her lucky stars she's still alive.* Also, **thank one's stars.** —*adj.* 20. celebrated, prominent, or distinguished; preeminent: *a star basketball player; a star reporter.* 21. of or pertaining to a star or stars. —*v.t.* 22. to set with or as with stars; spangle. 23. to present (a performer) as a star: *The studio starred her in her first movie.* 24. to feature as a star: *This movie stars Marlon Brando.* 25. to mark with a star or asterisk, as for special notice. —*v.i.* 26. to shine as a star; be brilliant or prominent. 27. (of a performer) to appear as a star: *He starred in several productions of Shaw's plays.* 28. (in English pool) to buy an additional life or lives. [ME *sterre,* OE *steorra;* c. OHG *sterra;* akin to OHG *sterno,* Icel *stjarna,* Goth *stairno,* L *stella,* Gk *astḗr,* Skt *star*] —**star′less,** *adj.* —**star′less·ly,** *adv.* —**star′less·ness,** *n.*

star′ aca′cia, a small tree or shrub, *Acacia verticillata,* having yellow flowers in numerous, finger-shaped spikes.

star′ an′ise, a shrub or small tree, *Illicium verum,* of China, having purplish-red flowers and anise-scented, star-shaped clusters of carminative fruit. Also called **Chinese anise.**

star′ ap′ple, 1. the edible fruit of a West Indian, sapotaceous tree, *Chrysophyllum Cainito,* which when cut across exhibits a star-shaped figure within. 2. the tree itself.

Sta·ra Za·go·ra (stä′rä zä gô′rä), a city in central Bulgaria. 55,322 (1956).

star·bloom (stär′blōōm′), *n.* the pinkroot, *Spigelia marilandica.* [STAR + BLOOM[1]]

star·board (stär′bərd, -bōrd′, -bôrd′), *n.* 1. the right-hand side on or direction from a vessel or aircraft, facing forward. —*adj.* 2. of or pertaining or located to the starboard. —*adv.* 3. toward the right side. —*v.t., v.i.* 4. to turn (the helm) to starboard. [ME *sterbord,* equiv. to OE *stēorbord,* equiv. to *stēor* steering (see STEER[1]) + *bord* side (see BOARD)]

starch (stärch), *n.* 1. a white, tasteless, solid carbohydrate, $(C_6H_{10}O_5)_n$, occurring in the form of minute granules in the seeds, tubers, and other parts of plants, and forming an important constituent of rice, corn, wheat, beans, potatoes, and many other vegetable foods. 2. a commercial preparation of this substance used to stiffen textile fabrics in laundering. 3. **starches,** foods rich in natural starch. 4. stiffness or formality, as of manner: *He is so full of starch he can't relax.* 5. *Informal.* vigor; energy; stamina; boldness. —*v.t.* 6. to stiffen or treat with starch. 7. to make stiff or rigidly formal (sometimes fol. by *up*). [ME *sterche(n),* OE *stercean* to make stiff, strengthen,

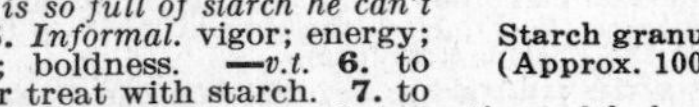

Starch granules (Approx. 100X)

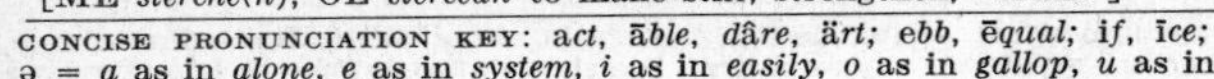

deriv. of *stearc* STARK[1]; c. G *stärken* to strengthen] —**starch′less,** *adj.* —**starch′like′,** *adj.*

Star′ Cham′ber, 1. a former court of inquisitorial and criminal jurisdiction in England that sat without a jury and that became noted for its arbitrary methods and severe punishments, abolished 1641. 2. any tribunal, committee, or the like, which proceeds by arbitrary or unfair methods.

star′ chart′, a chart showing the relative position of the stars in a particular area of the sky.

starch′ syr′up, glucose (def. 2).

starch·y (stär′chē), *adj.,* **starch·i·er, starch·i·est.** 1. of, pertaining to, or of the nature of starch. 2. containing starch. 3. stiffened with starch. 4. stiff and formal, as in manner. [STARCH + -Y[1]] —**starch′i·ly,** *adv.* —**starch′i·ness,** *n.*

star′ cloud′, *Astron.* a cloudlike patch of light on the celestial sphere, consisting of a multitude of stars.

star-crossed (stär′krôst′, -krost′), *adj.* thwarted or opposed by the stars; ill-fated: *star-crossed lovers.*

star′ cut′, a gem cut having a hexagonal table surrounded by six facets in the form of equilateral triangles.

star·dom (stär′dəm), *n.* 1. the world or class of professional stars, as of the stage. 2. the status of a star or preeminent performer. [STAR + -DOM]

star′ drift′, *Astron.* the apparently very slow motion of a group of stars with respect to another group in the same part of the heavens.

star′ drill′, a chisellike drill for masonry or plasterwork, having a pointed head faceted in alternately projecting and reentering angles.

star′ dust′, 1. a mass of distant stars appearing as tiny particles of dust. 2. *Informal.* an extremely and naïvely romantic quality: *There was star dust in her eyes.* Also, **star′dust′.**

stare (stâr), *v.,* **stared, star·ing,** *n.* —*v.i.* 1. to gaze fixedly and intently, esp. with the eyes wide open. 2. to be boldly or obtrusively conspicuous: *The bright modern painting stares out at you in the otherwise conservative gallery.* 3. (of hair, feathers, etc.) to stand on end; bristle. —*v.t.* 4. to stare at. 5. to effect or have a certain effect on by staring: *to stare one out of countenance.* 6. **stare down,** to cause to become uncomfortable by gazing steadily at one; overcome by staring: *An elderly woman at the next table tried to stare me down.* 7. **stare one in the face,** to be urgent or impending; confront: *The income-tax deadline is staring us in the face.* —*n.* 8. a staring gaze; a fixed look with the eyes wide open: *The banker greeted him with a glassy stare.* [ME; OE *star(ian);* c. D *staren,* Icel *stara,* G *starren*] —**star′ing·ly,** *adv.*
—**Syn.** 1. See **gaze.**

sta·re de·ci·sis (stâr′ē di sī′sis), *Law.* the doctrine that principles of law established by judicial decision be accepted as authoritative in cases similar to those from which such principles were derived. [< L: to stand by things (that have been) settled]

star′ fac′et, *Jewelry.* (in a brilliant) any of the eight small facets of the crown immediately below the table.

star·fish (stär′fish′), *n., pl.* (*esp. collectively*) **-fish,** (*esp. referring to two or more kinds or species*) **-fish·es.** any echinoderm of the class *Asteroidea,* having the body radially arranged, usually in the form of a star, with five or more rays or arms radiating from a central disk; asteroid. [STAR + FISH]

Starfish, *Asterias rubens* (Diameter 3½ in.)

star·flow·er (stär′flou′ər), *n.* any of several plants having starlike flowers, as the star-of-Bethlehem or a primulaceous plant of the genus *Trientalis.* [STAR + FLOWER]

star·gaze (stär′gāz′), *v.i.,* **-gazed, -gaz·ing.** 1. to gaze at or observe the stars. 2. to daydream. [back formation from STARGAZER]

star·gaz·er (stär′gā′zər), *n.* 1. one who stargazes, as an astronomer or astrologer. 2. a daydreamer. 3. an impractical idealist. 4. a horse that carries its head too high. 5. any of several marine fishes of the family *Uranoscopidae,* having the eyes at the top of the head. 6. See **sand stargazer.** 7. *Naut. Slang.* See **jolly jumper.** [STAR + GAZER]

star′ grass′, any of various grasslike plants having star-shaped flowers or a stellate arrangement of leaves, as an American, amaryllidaceous plant, *Hypoxis hirsuta.*

star′ hy′acinth, a low, bulbous herb, *Scilla amoena,* of central Europe, having small clusters of blue or whitish flowers.

star′ ipomoe′a, an annual vine, *Quamoclit coccinea,* of tropical America, having heart-shaped leaves and yellow-throated, scarlet flowers.

stark (stärk), *adj.* 1. sheer, utter, downright, or complete: *stark madness.* 2. harsh, grim, or desolate, as a view, place, etc.: *a stark landscape.* 3. extremely simple or severe: *a stark interior.* 4. stiff or rigid in substance, muscles, etc. 5. rigid in death. —*adv.* 6. utterly, absolutely, or quite: *stark mad.* 7. *Chiefly Scot. and North Eng.* in a stark manner; stoutly or vigorously. [ME; OE *stearc* stiff, firm; c. G *Stark* story; akin to Icel *sterkr* strong; see STARCH, STARE] —**stark′ly,** *adv.* —**stark′ness,** *n.*
—**Syn.** 1. mere, pure, absolute, entire. 2. dreary, drear. 6. completely.

Stark (stärk; *for 2 also Ger.* shtärk), *n.* 1. **Harold Rayns·ford** (rānz′fərd), born 1880, U.S. admiral. 2. **Jo·han·nes** (yō hä′nəs), 1874–1957, German physicist: Nobel prize 1919. 3. **John,** 1728–1822, American Revolutionary War general.

Starke (stärk), *n.* a town in N Florida. 4806 (1960).

stark-nak·ed (stärk′nā′kid), *adj.* absolutely naked. [STARK + NAKED; r. *start-naked; start,* ME; OE *steort* tail; c. D *staart,* Icel *stertr,* OHG *sterz*]

Stark·ville (stärk′vil), *n.* a town in E Mississippi. 9041 (1960).

star·let (stär′lit), *n.* 1. a young actress promoted and publicized as a future star, esp. in motion pictures. 2. a small star or other heavenly body. [STAR + -LET]

star·light (stär′līt′), *n.* 1. the light emanating from the stars. —*adj.* 2. of or pertaining to starlight. 3. Also, **star′light′ed.** starlit. [late ME; see STAR, LIGHT[1]]

star·like (stär′līk′), *adj.* 1. of the shape of or like a star. 2. shining like a star. 3. *Math.* (of a set with respect to a point) having the property that the line segment connecting a given point and any other point in a region lies completely within the region. [STAR + -LIKE]

star′ lil′y, a bulbous herb, *Lilium concolor,* of Japan, having erect, somewhat fragrant, bright-red flowers.

star·ling (stär′ling), *n.* 1. any of numerous Old World, passerine birds of the family *Sturnidae,* esp. *Sturnus vulgaris,* introduced into North America from Europe. 2. *Brit.* any of various American birds of the family *Icteridae.* [ME; OE *stærling,* equiv. to *stær* starling (c. OHG *stara,* Icel *stari*) + *-ling* -LING[1]; akin to OE *stearn* TERN, L *sturnus* starling]

Starling, *Sturnus vulgaris* (Length 8½ in.)

star·lit (stär′lit), *adj.* lighted by the stars: *a starlit night.* Also, **starlight.** [STAR + LIT[1]]

star′ net′work, *Elect.* a circuit with three or more branches all of which have one common terminal.

star′-nosed mole′ (stär′nōzd′), a North American mole, *Condylura cristata,* having a starlike ring of fleshy processes around the end of the snout. Also, **star′nose mole′.** Also called **star′nose′.**

star-of-Beth·le·hem (stär′əv beth′lē əm, -li hem′), *n., pl.* **stars-of-Beth·le·hem.** 1. an Old World, liliaceous plant, *Ornithogalum umbellatum,* having star-shaped flowers. 2. a related herb, *O. nutans,* of Asia Minor, having green flowers with white inside.

Star′ of Beth′lehem, the star that guided the Magi to the manger of the infant Jesus in Bethlehem. Matt. 2:1–10.

Star′ of Da′vid, a figure consisting of a six-pointed star formed of two equilateral triangles placed one upon the other such that the base of each triangle bisects two sides of the other, used as a symbol of Judaism. Also called **Magen David, Mogen David, Shield of David.**

Star of David

star-of-Je·ru·sa·lem (stär′əv jə rōō′sə ləm), *n., pl.* **stars-of-Je·ru·sa·lem.** See **meadow salsify.**

star′ plate′, (in an astronomical clock) a plate marked to represent the stars visible at a certain latitude.

Starr (stär), *n.* a boy's or girl's given name.

starred (stärd), *adj.* 1. set or studded with or as with stars. 2. (of a performer) presented as a star. 3. decorated with a star, as of an order. 4. marked with a starlike figure or spot, esp. an asterisk. 5. noting a number of angle irons placed with their exterior angles touching so as to make a composite member with a starlike or cruciform cross section. [ME; see STAR, -ED[3]]

star′ route′, a mail-delivery route between postal stations, given on contract to a private carrier and often requiring, in rural areas, delivery to home mailboxes.

star·ry (stär′ē), *adj.,* **-ri·er, -ri·est.** 1. abounding with or lighted by stars: *a starry night.* 2. of, pertaining to, or proceeding from the stars. 3. of the nature of or consisting of stars: *starry worlds.* 4. resembling a star; star-shaped or stellate. 5. shining like stars: *starry reflections on the dark water.* 6. studded with starlike figures or markings. [late ME; see STAR, -Y[1]] —**star′ri·ly,** *adv.* —**star′ri·ness,** *n.*

star′ry cam′pion, a perennial herb, *Silene stellata,* of the eastern U.S., having white, starlike flowers.

star·ry-eyed (stär′ē īd′), *adj.* overly romantic or idealistic: *He was a starry-eyed dreamer.*

star′ry grass′wort (gras′wûrt′), a weedy herb, *Cerastium arvense,* of the North Temperate Zone, having white flowers. Also called **field chickweed.** [GRASS + WORT[2]]

Star′ry Night′, The, a painting (1889) by Vincent van Gogh.

star′ry Sol′omon's-seal, a perennial herb, *Smilacina stellata,* of North America, having greenish-white flowers.

Stars′ and Bars′, the flag adopted by the Confederate States of America, consisting of two broad horizontal bars of red separated by one of white, with a blue union marked with as many white stars, arranged in a circle, as the number of Confederate States.

Stars′ and Stripes′, the national flag of the U.S., consisting of 13 horizontal stripes which are alternately red and white, representing the original States, and of a blue field containing 50 white stars, representing the present States. Also called **Old Glory, The Star-Spangled Banner.**

star′ sap′phire, a sapphire, cut cabochon, exhibiting asterism in the form of a colorless six-rayed star.

star′ shake′, (in a piece of timber) a radial shake caused by improper seasoning or decay at the center. Also called **heartshake.**

star-shaped (stär′shāpt′), *adj.* 1. of the shape of or like a star. 2. *Math.* starlike (def. 3).

star′ shell′, a shell that bursts in the air and produces a bright light to illuminate enemy positions.

star′ shift′er, *Naut. Slang.* See **jolly jumper.**

star-span·gled (stär′spang′gəld), *adj.* spangled with stars.

Star′-Spangled Ban′ner, The, 1. See **Stars and Stripes.** 2. (*italics*) the national anthem of the United States of America, based on a poem written by Francis Scott Key on September 14, 1814, and set by him to the melody of the English song *To Anacreon in Heaven:* officially adopted by the U.S. Congress in 1931.

star-stud·ded (stär′stud′id), *adj.* 1. lighted by or full of stars; bright: *a star-studded night.* 2. exhibiting or characterized by the presence of many preeminent performers: *a star-studded Hollywood party.*

star′ sys′tem, 1. the practice of casting star actors and actresses in plays, motion pictures, etc., often in leading roles that have been written or revised to emphasize or conform to the popularized image of the starring personality. **2.** the practice of emphasizing a preeminent performer rather than the script, direction, or general quality of a play, motion picture, etc. **3.** the system whereby a performer is made a star, as by publicity, personal appearances, etc. **4.** the practice or system of exploiting famous personalities without regard for their capabilities in a particular situation or role, as in the arts or in politics.

start (stärt), *v.i.* **1.** to begin or set out, as on a journey. **2.** to commence or begin any process, performance, course of action, or procedure, as one's career, life, etc. **3.** to appear or come suddenly into action, life, view, etc.; rise, or issue suddenly forth. **4.** to spring, move, or dart suddenly from a position or place: *The rabbit started from the bush.* **5.** to give a sudden, involuntary jerk, jump, or twitch, as from a shock of surprise, alarm, or pain: *The sudden clap of thunder caused everyone to start.* **6.** to protrude: *eyes seeming to start from their sockets.* **7.** to spring, slip, or work loose from place or fastenings, as timbers or other structural parts. **8.** to be among the entrants in a race or the initial participants in a game or contest. —*v.t.* **9.** to set moving, going, or acting; to set in operation: *to start an automobile; to start a fire.* **10.** to establish or found: *to start a new business.* **11.** to enter upon or begin: *to start a book.* **12.** to cause, enable, or help (someone) set out on a journey, a course of action, a career, or the like: *The record started the young singer on the road to stardom.* **13.** to cause or choose to be an entrant in a game or contest: *He started his ace pitcher in the crucial game.* **14.** to cause (timbers, structural parts, etc.) to slip, spring, or work loose from place or fastenings. **15.** to force (a nail or screw) partly into a substance to give it a hold before driving. **16.** to rouse (game) from its lair or covert; flush. **17.** to draw or discharge (liquid or other contents) from a vessel or container; empty (a container). **18.** *Archaic.* to cause to twitch, jump, or flinch involuntarily; startle. —*n.* **19.** a beginning of motion, an action, a journey, performance, contest, etc.; the beginning or outset of anything; a setting in motion. **20.** an impulse or signal to move, proceed, or begin, as on a course or in a race. **21.** a place from which something begins, as a line marking the beginning point of a race. **22.** the first part or beginning segment of anything: *The start of the book was good but the last half was dull.* **23.** an instance of being a participant in a race or an initial participant in a game, or contest: *The horse won his first two starts.* **24.** a sudden, springing movement from a position. **25.** a sudden, involuntary jerking movement of the body: *to awake with a start.* **26.** a lead or advance of specified amount, as over competitors or pursuers. **27.** the position or advantage of one who starts first: *The youngest child should have the start over the rest.* **28.** a chance, opportunity, aid, or encouragement given to one starting on a course or career: *The bride's parents gave the couple a start by buying them a house.* **29.** a spurt of activity. **30.** a starting of parts from their place or fastenings in a structure. **31.** the resulting break or opening. **32.** *Archaic.* an outburst or sally, as of emotion, wit, or fancy. [ME *sterten* (c. MHG *sterzen*); r. OE *styrtan*, c. G *stürzen*] —**start′ing·ly,** *adv.*
—**Syn. 10.** institute. **11.** See **begin. 19.** commencement, onset. **25.** twitch, jump. —**Ant. 11.** end, terminate.

start·er (stär′tər), *n.* **1.** one who or that which starts. **2.** a person who gives the signal to begin, as for a race, the running of a train, bus, elevator, etc. **3.** a self-starter. **4.** one who or that which starts in a race or contest: *Only five starters finished the race.* **5.** *Cribbage.* the card turned face up on the stack before the play. **6.** a culture of bacteria used to start a particular fermentation, as in the manufacture of cheese, buttermilk, sour cream, etc. **7.** *Cookery.* sourdough (def. 1). [START + -ER[1]]

star′ this′tle, **1.** a low, spreading, composite plant, *Centaurea Calcitrapa*, of Europe, having purple flowerheads and spiny involucres and leaves. **2.** a related but more erect plant, *C. solstitialis*, having yellow flowers.

start′ing block′, *Track.* a device used by runners, esp. sprinters, for increasing their speed off the mark, consisting of a metal or wooden frame, usually secured to the ground at both ends, with adjustable, triangular-shaped blocks on each side for bracing the feet.

start′ing gate′, any of various types of movable barriers, esp. one containing individual stall-like compartments or boxes with gates or doors that automatically and simultaneously spring open on signal, for lining up and giving an equal start to the entries in a horse race or dog race.

start′ing han′dle, *Brit.* a crank used to start the motor of an automobile.

start′ing step′, the lowermost step of a flight of stairs.

star·tle (stär′tᵊl), *v.,* **-tled, -tling,** *n.* —*v.t.* **1.** to disturb or agitate suddenly by a shock of surprise, alarm, or the like: *The horn blasting in the morning quiet startled me.* **2.** to cause to start involuntarily, by or as by a sudden shock. —*v.i.* **3.** to start involuntarily, as from a shock of surprise or alarm. —*n.* **4.** a sudden shock of surprise, alarm, or the like. **5.** something that startles. [ME *stertle* to rush, caper; akin to OE *steartlian* to kick, struggle] —**star′tler,** *n.* —**star′tling·ly,** *adv.*
—**Syn. 1.** scare, frighten, astonish. See **shock**[1]. —**Ant. 1.** calm.

start-up (stärt′up′), *n.* the act or fact of starting something; a setting in motion. [n. use of v. phrase *start up*]

star·va·tion (stär vā′shən), *n.* **1.** the act or state of starving; condition of being starved. —*adj.* **2.** liable or seeming to cause starving: *a starvation diet.* [STARVE + -ATION]

starva′tion wag′es, wages below the level necessary for subsistence.

starve (stärv), *v.,* **starved, starv·ing.** —*v.i.* **1.** to die or perish from lack of food or nourishment. **2.** to be in the process of perishing or suffering severely from hunger. **3.** to suffer from extreme poverty and need. **4.** to feel a strong need or desire (usually fol. by *for*): *The child was starving for affection.* **5.** *Chiefly Brit. Dial.* to perish or suffer extremely from cold. **6.** *Obs.* to die. —*v.t.* **7.** to cause to starve; kill, weaken, or reduce by lack of food. **8.** to subdue, or force to some condition or action, by hunger: *to starve a besieged garrison into a surrender.* **9.** to cause to suffer for lack of something needed or craved. **10.** *Chiefly Brit. Dial.* to cause to perish, or to suffer extremely, from cold. [ME *sterve(n)*, OE *steorfan* to die; c. G *sterben*; akin to STARE] —**starved·ly** (stärvd′lē, stär′vid-), *adv.* —**starv′er,** *n.*
—**Syn. 1, 2.** See **hungry.**

starve·ling (stärv′ling), *adj.* **1.** starving; suffering from lack of nourishment. **2.** pining with want. **3.** poverty-stricken. **4.** poor in condition or quality. **5.** such as to entail or suggest starvation. —*n.* **6.** a person, animal, or plant that is starving. [STARVE + -LING[1]]

star′ vi′olet, a perennial garden plant, *Houstonia serpyllifolia*, found in meadows and along stream banks in the eastern and southern U.S., having deep-blue flowers.

Star′ Wars′, a weapons research program, begun by the U.S. in 1984, to develop high-tech methods of attacking missiles launched from Earth or space: called **Strategic Defense Initiative (SDI).**

star′ wheel′, *Mach.* a wheel having prongs or pointed teeth engaging momentarily with levers, as in the striking mechanism of a clock.

star·wort (stär′wûrt′), *n.* **1.** any of several chickweeds of the genus *Stellaria*. **2.** any of several plants of the genera *Aster* and *Arenaria*. [ME; see STAR, WORT[2]]

stash (stash), *v.t., v.i.* *Informal.* to put by or away as for safekeeping or future use, usually in a secret place (usually fol. by *away*): *The squirrel stashes away nuts for winter.* [b. STOW and CACHE]

sta·sid·i·on (stə sid′ē ən), *n., pl.* **-sid·i·a** (-sid′ē ə). a choir stall in an Orthodox church. [< MGk: station, seat in a church, prob. equiv. to Gk *stási(s)* position, station, + *-idion* dim. suffix]

stas·i·met·ric (stas′ə me′trik), *adj.* *Obs.* of or pertaining to a surveying technique employing triangulation from one base line to locate a number of points. [*stasi-* (< Gk *stásis* STASIS) + METRIC[1]]

Stas·i·mon (stas′ə mon′), *n., pl.* **-ma** (-mə). *Greek.* (in ancient Greek drama) a choral ode, esp. in tragedy.

sta·sis (stā′sis, stas′is), *n.* **1.** the state of equilibrium or inactivity caused by opposing equal forces. **2.** *Pathol.* stagnation in the flow of any of the fluids of the body, as of the blood in an inflamed area, the intestinal contents proximal to an obstruction, etc. [< Gk: state of standing, equiv. to *sta-* (s. of *histánai* to stand; akin to L *stāre* to STAND) + *-sis* -SIS]

Stas·sen (stas′ən), *n.* **Harold Edward,** born 1907, U.S. politician.

stass·fur·tite (stas′fər tīt′, shtäs′-), *n.* *Mineral.* a variety of boracite, massive and having a subcolumnar structure, resembling a fine-grained marble in appearance. [after *Stassfurt*, Germany; see -ITE[1]]

-stat, a learned borrowing from Greek meaning "standing," "stationary," "set," used in the formation of compound words: *thermostat; rheostat.* [< Gk *-statēs*, equiv. to *sta-* (s. of *histánai* to make stand) + *-tēs* n. agent suffix]

stat., 1. (in prescriptions) immediately. [< L *statim*] **2.** statuary. **3.** statue. **4.** statute.

stat·am·pere (stat am′pēr, stat′am pēr′), *n.* *Elect.* the electrostatic unit of current, equivalent to 3.3356 $\times 10^{-10}$ ampere and equal to the current produced by an electromotive force of one statvolt acting through a resistance of one statohm. [*stat-* (comb. form representing ELECTROSTATIC; see -STAT) + AMPERE]

sta·tant (stāt′ᵊnt), *adj.* *Heraldry.* (of an animal) represented as standing with all feet on the ground: *a bear statant.* [< L *stat(us)* (ptp. of *stāre*; see STATUS) + -ANT]

stat·cou·lomb (stat ko͞o′lom, stat′ko͞o lom′), *n.* *Elect.* the electrostatic unit of a quantity of electricity, equivalent to 3.3356 $\times 10^{-10}$ coulomb and equal to the quantity of charge transferred in one second across a conductor in which there is a constant current of one statampere. [*stat-* (see STATAMPERE) + COULOMB]

state (stāt), *n., adj., v.,* **stat·ed, stat·ing.** —*n.* **1.** the condition of a person or thing, as with respect to circumstances or attributes: *a state of health.* **2.** condition with respect to structure, form, constitution, phase, or the like: *a gaseous state; the larval state.* **3.** a mode or condition of existence: *Some bachelors enjoy the single state.* **4.** status, rank, or position in life; station: *He dresses in a manner befitting his state.* **5.** the style of living befitting a person of wealth and high rank; a sumptuous, splendid, or formal display of dignity; pomp: *to travel in state.* **6.** an abnormally tense, nervous, or perturbed condition: *This last confrontation with his mother left him in a taut state.* **7.** a particular condition of mind or feeling: *to be in an excited state.* **8.** a body of people occupying a definite territory and organized under one government, esp. a sovereign government. **9.** the territory, or one of the territories, of a government. **10.** (*sometimes cap.*) any of the commonwealths or bodies politic, each more or less independent as regards internal affairs, which together make up a federal union, as in the United States of America or the Commonwealth of Australia. **11.** the domain or the authority of such a territory or commonwealth. **12.** the body politic as organized for civil rule and government (distinguished from *church*). **13.** the operations or activities of a central civil government, or the sphere of the highest civil authority and administration: *affairs of state.* **14.** (*cap.*) *U.S. Informal.* the Department of State. **15.** *Print.* a set of copies of an edition of a publication which differ from others of the same printing because of additions, corrections, or transpositions made during printing or at any time before publication. **16.** *Math.* the position of the system in a Markov process after some specified trial. **17. lie in state,** (of a corpse) to be exhibited publicly with honors before burial: *The president's body lay in state for two days.* **18. the States,** *Informal.* the United States (usually used outside its borders): *After a year's study in Spain, he returned to the States.* —*adj.* **19.** of or pertaining to the central civil government or authority. **20.** of, pertaining to, maintained by, or under the authority of one of the commonwealths which make up a federal union: *a Texas State highway.* **21.** characterized by, attended with, or involving ceremony: *a state dinner.* **22.** used on or reserved for occasions of ceremony. —*v.t.* **23.** to declare definitely or specifically: *He stated his position on the case.* **24.** to set forth formally in speech or writing: *to state a hypothesis.* **25.** to set forth in proper or definite form: *to state a problem.* **26.** to say. **27.** to fix or settle, as by authority. [ME *stat*, partly var. of *estat* (see ESTATE), partly < L *stat(us)* condition (see STATUS); in defs. 8–13 < L *status* (*rērum*) state of things or *status* (*reī publicae*) state of the republic] —**stat′a·ble, state′a·ble,** *adj.*
—**Syn. 1.** case, environment. STATE, CONDITION, SITUATION, STATUS are terms for existing circumstances or surroundings. STATE is the general word, often with no concrete implications or material relationships: *the present state of affairs.* CONDITION carries an implication of a relationship to causes and circumstances: *The conditions made flying impossible.* SITUATION suggests an arrangement of circumstances, related to one another and to the character of a person: *He was master of the situation.* STATUS carries official or legal implications; it suggests a complete picture of interrelated circumstances as having to do with rank, position, standing, a stage reached in progress, etc.: *the status of negotiations.* **4.** standing. **5.** grandeur, magnificence. **21.** stately, ceremonial, imposing, dignified. **23.** aver, assert, asseverate, affirm. **24.** specify. **27.** determine, authorize.

state′ aid′, financial support extended by a state government to a local institution serving the public, as a school or library.

State′ bank′, *U.S.* a bank chartered by a State and operated under the banking laws of that State.

state′ cap′italism, a form of capitalism in which the central government controls most of the capital, industry, natural resources, etc.

state′ cham′ber, a room for public ceremonies and celebrations.

state′ church′. See **established church.**

State′ Col′lege, a city in central Pennsylvania. 22,409 (1960).

state′ coor′dinate sys′tem, *Survey.* a system of right-angled planar coordinates established by the U.S. Coast and Geodetic Survey for each State in the United States.

state·craft (stāt′kraft′, -kräft′), *n.* **1.** the art of government and diplomacy. **2.** *Archaic.* crafty statesmanship. [STATE + CRAFT]

stat·ed (stā′tid), *adj.* **1.** fixed or settled: *a stated price.* **2.** explicitly set forth; declared as fact. **3.** recognized or official. [STATE + -ED[2]] —**stat′ed·ly,** *adv.*

State′ flow′er, the floral symbol of a State of the U.S., selected by the legislature or some other group within that State.

state·hood (stāt′ho͝od), *n.* the status or condition of being a state, esp. a State of the U.S. [STATE + -HOOD]

State·house (stāt′hous′), *n., pl.* **-hous·es** (-hou′ziz). *U.S.* the building in which the legislature of a State sits; the capitol of a State. [STATE + HOUSE]

state·less (stāt′lis), *adj.* lacking nationality. [STATE + -LESS] —**state′less·ness,** *n.*

state·ly (stāt′lē), *adj.,* **-li·er, -li·est,** *adv.* —*adj.* **1.** majestic; imposing in magnificence, elegance, etc.: *a stately home.* **2.** dignified. —*adv.* **3.** in a stately manner. [late ME *statly*. See STATE, -LY] —**state′li·ness,** *n.*
—**Syn. 1.** grand, magnificent.

state′ med′icine. See **socialized medicine.**

state·ment (stāt′mənt), *n.* **1.** something stated. **2.** a communication or declaration in speech or writing, setting forth facts, particulars, etc. **3.** a single sentence or assertion: *I agree with everything you said except for your last statement.* **4.** *Com.* an abstract of an account, as one rendered to show the balance due. **5.** an appearance of a theme, subject, or motif within a musical composition. **6.** the act or manner of stating something. [STATE (v.) + -MENT]
—**Syn. 2.** report, announcement, proclamation.

Stat′en Is′land (stat′ən), an island facing New York Bay, comprising Richmond borough of New York City. 221,991 (1960); 64½ sq. mi.

State′ of A′den, Aden (def. 1).

state′ of war′, **1.** a condition marked by armed conflict between or among states, existing whether or not war has been declared formally by any of the belligerents. **2.** a legal condition initiated and concluded by formal declaration, and not necessarily involving armed conflict. **3.** the duration of such a condition.

state′ police′, a police force under state authority rather than under the authority of a city or county in the state.

State′ pris′on, a prison maintained by a State for the confinement of felons. Also, **state′ pris′on.**

sta·ter (stā′tər), *n.* any of various gold or silver or electrum coin units or coins of the ancient Greek states or cities. [< LL < Gk *statḗr*, akin to *histánai* to place in the balance]

state′ reli′gion, the official religion of a state as established by law.

State′ rights′. See **States' rights.**

state·room (stāt′ro͞om′, -ro͝om′), *n.* a private room or compartment on a ship, train, etc. [STATE (adj.) + ROOM]

State's′ Attor′ney, *U.S.* (in judicial proceedings) the legal representative of the State.

States·bor·o (stāts′bûr ō, -bur ō), *n.* a town in E Georgia. 8356 (1960).

state's′ ev′idence, *U.S.* **1.** evidence given by an accomplice in a crime who becomes a voluntary witness against the other defendants: *The defendants' case was lost when one of them turned state's evidence.* **2.** evidence for the State, esp. in criminal trials.

States-Gen·er·al (stāts′jen′ər əl), *n.* **1.** the parliament of the Netherlands, consisting of an upper chamber **(First Chamber)** and a lower chamber **(Second Chamber). 2.** *Fr. Hist.* the legislative body in France before the French Revolution.

state·side (stāt′sīd′), *adj.* **1.** being in or toward the U.S. —*adv.* **2.** in or toward the U.S. Also, **State′side′.** [(the) STATES + SIDE[1]]

ates·man (stāts′mən), *n., pl.* **-men.** **1.** a man who experienced in the art of government or versed in the iministration of government affairs. **2.** a man who khibits great wisdom and ability in directing the af-irs of a government or in dealing with important ıblic issues. [STATE + 's[1] + MAN[1], modeled on *steersman;* . the phrase *ship of state*] **—states′man·like′,** **tates′man·ly,** *adj.*
-Syn. 1. See **politician.**

ates·man·ship (stāts′mən ship′), *n.* the ability, ualifications, or practice of a statesman; wisdom and cill in the management of public affairs. [STATESMAN -SHIP]

ate′ so′cialism, the theory, doctrine, and move-ıent advocating a planned economy controlled by the ate, with state ownership of all industries and natural sources. **—state′ so′cialist.**

ates′ of the Church′. See **Papal States.**

ates′ right′er, one who opposes U.S. federal ıtervention in affairs he considers to be solely the usiness of the separate States, as educational and labor onditions, interracial relations, etc., supporting his osition by a strict interpretation of the Constitution s it regards States' rights. [STATES' RIGHT(S) + -ER[1]]

ates′ rights′, *U.S.* the rights belonging to the arious States, esp. with reference to the strict interpre-ation of the Constitution, by which all rights not elegated by the Constitution to the federal govern-ıent belong to the States.

ates′ Rights′ Democrat′ic par′ty, a polit-al party formed by dissident Southern Democrats 'ho opposed the candidacy of Harry Truman in 1948 nd campaigned on a platform of States' rights.

ates·ville (stāts′vil), *n.* a city in central North 'arolina. 19,844 (1960).

ate′ troop′er, a member of a police force in the '.S. operated by a State government and having state-ide jurisdiction.

ate′ univer′sity, *U.S.* a university maintained y the government of a State as its highest public edu-ational institution.

ate·wide (stāt′wīd′), *adj.* **1.** (*sometimes cap.*) ex-ending throughout all parts of a state in the U.S.: *a tatewide search.* **—adv. 2.** (*sometimes cap.*) throughout state: *It was applauded statewide.* [STATE + WIDE]

at·far·ad (stat far′əd, -ad), *n.* *Elect.* the electro-tatic unit of capacitance, equivalent to 1.1126×10^{-12} arad and equal to the capacitance of a condenser in vhich one statcoulomb is transferred from one con-uctor of the condenser to the other per volt of potential ifference between the conductors. [*stat-* (see STATAM-ERE) + FARAD]

at·hen·ry (stat′hen′rē), *n., pl.* **-ries, -rys.** *Elect.* he electrostatic unit of inductance, equivalent to $.9876 \times 10^{11}$ henries and equal to the inductance of a ircuit in which an electromotive force of one statvolt s produced by a current in the circuit which varies at he rate of one ampere per second. [*stat-* (see STATAM-ERE) + HENRY]

at·ic (stat′ik), *adj.* Also, **stat′i·cal. 1.** pertaining to r characterized by a fixed or stationary condition. . showing little or no change: *a static concept; a static elationship.* **3.** lacking movement, development, or 'itality: *The novel was marred by static characteriza-ions, especially in its central figures.* **4.** *Sociol.* referring o a condition of social life bound by tradition. **5.** *Elect.* pertaining to or noting static electricity. **6.** oting or pertaining to atmospheric electricity interfer-ng with radar, radio, the sending and receiving of vireless messages, etc. **7.** *Physics.* acting by mere veight without producing motion: *static pressure.* **8.** *Econ.* pertaining to fixed relations, or different combina-ions of fixed quantities: *static population.* **—n. 9.** *Elect.* **a.** static or atmospheric electricity. **b.** inter-erence due to such electricity. **10.** *Slang.* difficulty; rouble: *Will your dad give you any static on using the car?* [< NL *static(us)* < G *statikós,* equiv. to *sta-* (s. of *histánai* to make stand) + *-tikos* -TIC] **—stat′i·cal·ly,** *idv.*

tat′ic electric′ity, *Elect.* the electricity contained r produced by charged bodies.

tat·ics (stat′iks), *n.* (*construed as sing.*) the branch of mechanics that deals with bodies at rest or forces in equilibrium. [see STATIC, -ICS]

tat′ic tube′, a tube for measuring the static pres-sure of a fluid in motion, placed in the fluid so as not to be affected by the pressure changes caused by the motion of the fluid.

tat′ic wa′ter, *Brit.* water collected and stored in reservoirs, tanks, etc., as for urban use.

ta·tion (stā′shən), *n.* **1.** a place or position in which a person or thing is assigned to stand or remain or is standing or remaining. **2.** the place at which something stops or is scheduled to stop; a regular stopping place, as on a railroad. **3.** the building or buildings at such a stopping place. **4.** the district or municipal head-quarters of certain public services: *police station; fire station; postal station.* **5.** a place equipped for some particular kind of work, service, research, or the like: *gasoline station; geophysical station.* **6.** the position, as of persons or things, in a scale of estimation, rank, or dignity; standing: *the responsibility of persons of high station.* **7.** a position, office, rank, calling, or the like. **8.** *Mil.* **a.** a military place of duty. **b.** a semi-permanent army post. **9.** *Navy.* a place or region to which a ship or fleet is assigned for duty. **10.** (formerly in India) the area in which the British officials of a district or the officers of a garrison resided. **11.** *Radio and Television.* **a.** a studio, room, or building from which broadcasts regularly originate. **b.** a person, as a ham-radio operator, organization, or business firm originating and broadcasting radio messages or programs or televi-sion programs. **c.** a specific broadcasting frequency or band of frequencies assigned to a broadcaster or to a special type of broadcasting equipment or program: *Tune to the Civil Defense station.* **d.** the complete equipment used in transmitting radio or television broadcasts or in receiving noncommercial broadcasts. **12.** *Biol.* a particular area or type of region where a given animal or plant is found. **13.** *Australian.* a ranch with its buildings, land, etc., esp. for raising sheep. **14.** *Survey.* **a.** Also called **set-up.** a point where an observation is taken. **b.** a precisely located reference point. **c.** a length of 100 feet along a survey line. **15.** Also called **cross section.** *Naval Archit.* any of a series of lines on the lines plan of a hull, corresponding to the location of a frame and representing the intersection of a series of vertical planes perpendicular to the fore-and-aft midship line with the surface of the shell, the inner surface being the one most commonly used: such a line appears as a vertical line on the sheer plan, as a transverse line on the half-breadth plan, and as a curved or angular form on the body plan. **16.** a section or area assigned to a waiter, soldier, etc., for servicing, guarding, or the like; post: *The waiter says this isn't his station.* **17.** *Archaic.* the fact or condition of standing still.
—v.t. 18. to assign a station to; place or post in a station or position. [< L *statiōn-* (s. of *statiō*) a standing still, standing-place, equiv. to *stat(us)* (ptp. of *stāre* to stand) + *-iōn-* -ION; r. ME *stacioun* < AF] **—sta′tion·al,** *adj.*
—Syn. 1. situation, location. **3.** STATION, DEPOT, and TERMINAL are not properly synonyms. A STATION is a stopping place where passengers may get on and off trains or other vehicles: *Union Station.* A DEPOT is a storehouse or warehouse: *a depot in the wing of the station building.* In the early days in America, the station wait-ing room and the freight depot were usually in the same building and, as a result, the names were confused. Since STATION seemed somewhat more dignified, DEPOT was the more commonly used term. STATION has now become the regular word in urban use, and is also widely used in smaller communities. Some people insist on distinguishing between a TERMINAL, which is, literally, at the end of a rail, bus, or other transportation line, and a STATION, which is one of the stopping points along the route traveled, but STATION has become the more common of the two and is applied generally to both, with TERMINAL, when used, being restricted to the end of a route: *a bus terminal.* **7.** metier, occupa-tion, trade, business, employment. See **appointment.** **18.** position, locate, establish, set, fix.

sta′tion a′gent, one who manages a small railroad station.

sta·tion·ar·y (stā′shə ner′ē), *adj., n., pl.* **-ar·ies.** **—adj. 1.** standing still; not moving. **2.** having a fixed position; not movable. **3.** established in one place; not itinerant or migratory. **4.** remaining in the same condi-tion or state; not changing: *The market price has re-mained stationary for a week.* **—n. 5.** one who or that which is stationary. [< L *stationāri(us).* See STATION, -ARY] **—sta·tion·ar·i·ly** (stā′shə ner′ə lē, stā′shə-nâr′-), *adv.* **—sta′tion·ar′i·ness,** *n.*

sta′tionary en′gine, an engine with a fixed foundation in a building, used for driving generators, compressors, etc.

sta′tionary engineer′, one who runs or is licensed to run a stationary engine. **—sta′tionary engineer′-ing.**

sta′tionary state′, *Physics.* any of several energy states an atom may occupy without emitting electro-magnetic radiation.

sta′tionary wave′. See **standing wave.**

sta′tion break′, *Radio and Television.* an interval between or during programs for identifying the station, making announcements, etc.

sta·tion·er (stā′shə nər), *n.* **1.** one who sells the ma-terials used in writing, as paper, pens, pencils, ink, etc. **2.** *Archaic.* **a.** a bookseller. **b.** a publisher. [ME *stacio(u)ner* < ML *statiōnār(ius)* (see STATIONARY) of dealers with permanent shops as distinguished from itinerant vendors]

Sta′tioners' Com′pany, a company or guild of the city of London comprised of booksellers, printers, bookbinders, and dealers in writing materials, or the like, incorporated in 1557.

sta·tion·er·y (stā′shə ner′ē), *n.* **1.** writing paper. **2.** writing materials, as pens, pencils, paper, etc. [STA-TIONER + -Y[3]]

sta′tion house′, a house or building at or serving as a station, esp. a police station.

sta′tion mark′, *Survey.* a point from which sights are taken.

sta·tion·mas·ter (stā′shən mas′tər, -mä′stər), *n.* a person in charge of a railroad station; station agent. [STATION + MASTER]

sta′tion point′er, *Survey.* See **three-arm pro-tractor.**

sta′tions of the cross′, *Eccles.* a series of 14 representations of successive incidents from the passion of Christ, each with a wooden cross, or a series of wooden crosses alone, set up in a church, or sometimes outdoors, and visited in sequence, for prayer and meditation. Also, **Sta′tions of the Cross′.**

sta·tion-to-sta·tion (stā′shən tə stā′shən), *adj.* **1.** (of a long-distance telephone call) chargeable upon speaking with anyone at the number called: *a station-to-station call to his home in Dallas.* **—adv. 2.** from one station to another. **3.** by telephone at station-to-station rates: *After nine o'clock we can call her station-to-station.* Cf. **person-to-person** (defs. 1, 3).

sta′tion wag′on, *U.S.* an automobile with one or more rows of folding or removable seats behind the driver and no luggage compartment but an area behind the seats into which suitcases, parcels, etc., can be loaded through a tail gate. Also called **beach wagon, ranch wagon;** *esp. Brit.,* **estate car, estate wagon.**

stat·ism (stā′tiz əm), *n.* **1.** the principle or policy of concentrating extensive economic, political, and related controls in the state at the cost of individual liberty. **2.** support of or belief in the sovereignty of a state, usually a republic. **3.** *Obs.* statecraft; politics. [STATE + -ISM]

stat·ist[1] (stā′tist), *n.* **1.** an advocate of statism. **—adj.** **2.** of, pertaining to, or characteristic of a statist or stat-ism. [STATE + -IST]

stat·ist[2] (stat′ist), *n.* statistician. [short form]

sta·tis·tic (stə tis′tik), *n.* a numerical fact or datum. [< NL *statistic(us).* See STATUS, -ISTIC]

sta·tis·ti·cal (stə tis′ti kəl), *adj.* of, pertaining to, consisting of, or based on statistics. [STATISTIC(S) + -AL[1]] **—sta·tis′ti·cal·ly,** *adv.*

statis′tical independ′ence, *Statistics.* a condi-tion in the two-way probability distribution of two variables such that the conditional probability distribu-tion of one variable for a given value of a second variable is identical with that for any other given value of the second variable.

stat·is·ti·cian (stat′i stish′ən), *n.* an expert in or compiler of statistics. Also, **statist.** [STATISTIC(S) + -IAN]

sta·tis·tics (stə tis′tiks), *n.* **1.** (*construed as sing.*) the science that deals with the collection, classification, analysis, and interpretation of numerical facts or data, and that, by use of mathematical theories of probability, imposes order and regularity on aggregates of more or less disparate elements. **2.** (*construed as pl.*) the nu-merical facts or data themselves. [see STATISTIC, -ICS]

Sta·ti·us (stā′shē əs), *n.* **Pub·li·us Pa·pin·i·us** (pub′-lē əs pə pin′ē əs), A.D. c45–c96, Roman poet.

sta·tive (stā′tiv), *adj.* (of a verb) expressing a state. [< NL *stativ(us),* L, equiv. to *stat(us)* (ptp. of *stāre* to stand) + *-īvus* -IVE]

stat·o·blast (stat′ə blast′), *n.* (in certain bryozoans) an asexually produced group of cells encased in a chitin-ous covering which can survive unfavorable conditions, as freezing or drought, and germinate to produce a new colony. [*stato-* (comb. form of Gk *statós* standing; akin to STATUS, STATIC) + -BLAST]

stat·o·cyst (stat′ə sist′), *n.* *Zool.* (in certain inverte-brates) a sense organ consisting of a sac enclosing sensory hairs and particles of sand, lime, etc., that has an equilibrating function serving to indicate position in space. [*stato-* (see STATOBLAST) + -CYST]

stat·ohm (stat′ōm′), *n.* *Elect.* the electrostatic unit of resistance, equivalent to 8.9876×10^{11} ohms and equal to the resistance in a conductor in which one statvolt of potential differences produces a current of one statampere. [*stat-* (see STATAMPERE) + -OHM]

stat·o·lith (stat′ᵊlith), *n.* **1.** *Zool.* any of the granules of lime, sand, etc., contained within a statocyst. **2.** *Bot.* an inclusion, as a starch grain, that by a change in position within the cells of an organ or part is assumed to cause a corresponding change in position of the organ or part. [*stato-* (see STATOBLAST) + -LITH] **—stat′-o·lith′ic,** *adj.*

sta·tor (stā′tər), *n.* **1.** *Elect.* a portion of a machine which remains fixed with respect to rotating parts, esp. the collection of stationary parts in the magnetic cir-cuits of a machine. **2.** *Aeron.* the system of stationary airfoils in the compressor of a jet engine. [< NL, L: one that stands. See STATUS, -OR[2]]

stat·o·scope (stat′ə skōp′), *n.* **1.** an aneroid barom-eter for registering minute variations of atmospheric pressure. **2.** *Aeron.* an instrument for detecting a small rate of rise or fall of an aircraft. [*stato-* (see STATO-BLAST) + -SCOPE]

stat·u·ar·y (stach′o͞o er′ē), *n., pl.* **-ar·ies,** *adj.* **—n. 1.** statues collectively. **2.** a group or collection of statues. **—adj. 3.** of, pertaining to, or suitable for statues. [< L *statuāri(us).* See STATUE, -ARY]

stat′uary bronze′, an alloy of 97 percent copper, 2 percent tin, and 1 percent zinc.

stat·ue (stach′o͞o), *n.* a three-dimensional work of art, as a representation of a person or animal or an abstract form, carved in stone or wood, molded in a plastic material, cast in bronze, or the like. [ME < MF < L *statu(a),* equiv. to *statu(s)* (see STATUS) + *-a* fem. ending] **—stat′ue·less,** *adj.* **—stat′ue·like′,** *adj.*

stat·ued (stach′o͞od), *adj.* having or ornamented with statues: *a statued building; a statued avenue.* [STATUE + -ED[3]]

Stat′ue of Lib′erty, **1.** a large copper statue, on Liberty Island, in New York harbor: presented to the U.S. by France, and designed by F. A. Bartholdi; unveiled 1886. **2.** Also called **Stat′ue of Lib′erty play′.** *Football.* a play in which a back, usually the quarterback, fakes a pass, and a back or end running behind him takes the ball from his upraised hand and runs with it.

stat·u·esque (stach′o͞o esk′), *adj.* like or suggesting a statue, as in massive or majestic dignity, grace, or beauty. [STATUE + -ESQUE] **—stat′u·esque′ly,** *adv.* **—stat′u·esque′ness,** *n.*

stat·u·ette (stach′o͞o et′), *n.* a small statue. [< F; see STATUE, -ETTE]

stat·ure (stach′ər), *n.* **1.** the height of an animal body, esp. of a person. **2.** the height of any object. **3.** degree of development attained; level of achievement: *a minister of great stature.* [ME < OF *(e)stature* < L *statūr(a).* See STATUS, -URE]
—Syn. 1. measurement. **2.** altitude. **3.** status; im-portance.

sta·tus (stā′təs, stat′əs), *n.* **1.** the position of an individual in relation to another or others of the same class, social standing, profession, etc.: *He tried to choose a doctor on the basis of his professional status.* **2.** the social position or rank of an individual or group in relation to another or others of a different class, social standing, profession, etc.: *The wealthy man enjoyed his status in the poor mining village.* **3.** state or condition of affairs: *Arbitration has failed to change the status of the disagreement.* **4.** *Law.* the standing of a person before the law. [< L, equiv. to *sta-* (var. s. of *stāre* to STAND) + *-tus* n. use of *-tus* ptp. suffix]
—Syn. 3. See **state.**

sta′tus quo′ (kwō), the existing state or condition. Also called **sta′tus in quo′.** [< L: lit., state in which]

sta′tus sym′bol, **1.** an object, habit, etc., by which the social or economic status of the possessor may be judged. **2.** an object, habit, etc., designed or acquired to display the possessor's status or a higher status he wishes others to believe he has attained: *He doesn't really enjoy his big hi-fi set—it's just a status symbol.*

stat·u·ta·ble (stach′o͞o tə bəl), *adj.* **1.** (of an offense) recognized by statute; legally punishable. **2.** prescribed, authorized, or permitted by statute: *the statutable age of a voter.* [STATUTE + -ABLE] **—stat′u·ta·ble·ness,** *n.* **—stat′u·ta·bly,** *adj.*

stat·ute (stach′o͞ot, -o͝ot), *n.* **1.** *Law.* **a.** an enactment made by a legislature and expressed in a formal docu-ment. **b.** the document in which such an enactment is expressed. **2.** *Internat. Law.* an instrument annexed or subsidiary to an international agreement, as a treaty. **3.** a permanent rule established by an organization, corporation, etc. to govern its internal affairs. [ME

statut < OF (e)statut < LL statūt(um), neut. of statūtus (ptp. of statuere to make stand, set up) equiv. to statū- (see STATUS) + -tus ptp. suffix]
—Syn. 1. act, law, ordinance.

stat′ute book′, a book containing the laws enacted by the legislature of a state or nation.

stat′ute law′. See **statutory law.**

stat′ute mile′, mile (def. 1).

stat′ute of limita′tions, *Law.* a statute defining the period within which legal action may be taken.

stat·u·to·ry (stach′ŏŏ tôr′ē, -tōr′ē), *adj.* **1.** of, pertaining to, or of the nature of a statute. **2.** prescribed or authorized by statute. **3.** conforming to statute. **4.** (of an offense) recognized by statute; legally punishable. [STATUTE + -ORY¹] —**stat′u·to′ri·ly,** *adv.*

stat′utory crime′. See **statutory offense.**

stat′utory deck′ line′, *Naut.* a line painted on a hull above the Plimsoll marks, showing the level of the freeboard deck.

stat′utory law′, the written law established by enactments expressing the will of the legislature, as distinguished from the unwritten law or common law. Also called **statute law.**

stat′utory offense′, *Law.* a wrong punishable under a statute, rather than at common law. Also called **statutory crime.**

stat′utory rape′, *U.S. Law.* sexual intercourse with a girl under the age of consent, which age varies in different States from 10 to 18 years.

stat·volt (stat′vōlt′), *n.* *Elect.* the electrostatic unit of electromotive force or potential difference, approximately equivalent to 300 volts and equal to the electromotive force or potential difference that will cause a current of one statampere to flow through a conductor with a resistance of one statohm. [*stat-* (see STATAMPERE) + VOLT¹]

Stau·ding·er (shtou′ding ər), *n.* **Her·mann** (her′män), 1881–1965, German chemist: Nobel prize 1953.

St. Au·gus·tine (ô′gə stēn′), a seacoast city in NE Florida: founded by the Spanish 1565; oldest city in the U.S.; resort. 14,734 (1960).

staum·rel (stam′rəl, stôm′-), *Scot.* —*adj.* **1.** stupid; half-witted. —*n.* **2.** a stupid person. Also, **stammrel, staume·ral** (stam′rəl, stam′ə rəl, stôm′rəl, stô′mərəl). [*staumer* to stumble (Scot var. of STAMMER) + -REL]

staunch¹ (stônch), *v.t., v.i.* stanch¹. —**staunch′er,** *n.* —**staunch′ly,** *adv.* —**staunch′ness,** *n.*

staunch² (stônch, stänch), *adj.* **1.** firm or steadfast in principle, adherence, loyalty, etc., as a person: *a staunch Republican; a staunch friend.* **2.** characterized by firmness, steadfastness, or loyalty: *He delivered a staunch defense of the government.* **3.** strong; substantial: *a staunch little hut in the woods.* **4.** impervious to water or other liquids; watertight: *a staunch vessel.* Also, **stanch.** [late ME *sta(u)nch* < MF *(e)stanche* (fem.), *estanc* (masc.), deriv. of *estancher* to STANCH¹]
—**Syn. 1.** constant, true, faithful. See **steadfast. 2.** resolute. **3.** stout, sound.

Staun·ton (stôn′tən *or, for 2,* stän′-), *n.* **1.** a city in N Virginia. 22,232 (1960). **2.** a town in SW Illinois. 4228 (1960).

stau·ro·lite (stôr′ə līt′), *n.* a mineral, basic iron aluminum silicate, $HFeAl_5Si_2O_{13}$, occurring in brown to black prismatic crystals, which are often twinned in the form of a cross. [< Gk *staurό(s)* cross + -LITE] —**stau·ro·lit·ic** (stôr′ə lit′ik), *adj.*

stau·ro·pe·gi·on (stäv′rō pē′ʏʜē ôn; *Eng.* stav′rō pē′jē on′), *n., pl.* **-gi·a** (-ʏʜē ä; *Eng.* -jē ə). *Gk. Orth. Ch.* (in an autocephalous church) a monastery subject directly to the primate. [< MGk *stauropḗgion,* equiv. to Gk *staurό(s)* cross + *pḗg(nynai)* (to) fix, fasten + *-ion* n. suffix] —**stau·ro·pe·gi·al** (stav′rō pē′jē əl), *adj.*

stau·ro·scope (stôr′ə skōp′), *n.* *Obs.* an optical instrument for determining the position of the planes of light vibration in sections of crystals. [< Gk *staurό(s)* cross + -SCOPE] —**stau·ro·scop·ic** (stôr′ə skop′ik), *adj.* —**stau′ro·scop′i·cal·ly,** *adv.*

Sta·vang·er (stä väng′ər), *n.* a seaport in SW Norway. 50,647 (est. 1959).

stave (stāv), *n., v.,* **staved** or **stove, stav·ing.** —*n.* **1.** one of the thin, narrow, shaped pieces of wood which form the sides of a cask, tub, or similar vessel. **2.** a stick, rod, pole, or the like. **3.** a rung of a ladder, chair, etc. **4.** *Pros.* **a.** a verse or stanza of a poem or song. **b.** the alliterating sound in a line of verse, as the *w*-sound in *wind in the willows.* **5.** *Music.* staff¹ (def. 9). —*v.t.* **6.** to break in a stave or staves of (a cask or barrel) so as to release the wine, liquor, or other contents. **7.** to release (wine, liquor, etc.) by breaking the cask or barrel. **8.** to break or crush (something) inward (often fol. by *in*). **9.** to break (a hole) in, esp. in the hull of a boat. **10.** to break to pieces; splinter; smash. **11.** to furnish with a stave or staves. **12.** to beat with a stave or staff. —*v.i.* **13.** to become staved in, as a boat; break in or up: *to stave in a wooden crate.* **14.** to move along rapidly. **15. stave off, a.** to put, ward, or keep off, as by force or evasion. **b.** to prevent in time; forestall: *He wasn't able to stave off the accident, but slowed down in time to avoid much damage.* [ME; back formation from STAVES] —**stav′a·ble, stave′a·ble,** *adj.* —**stave′less,** *adj.*
—**Syn. 4.** See **verse.**

staves (stāvz), *n.* **1.** a pl. of **staff¹. 2.** pl. of **stave.**

staves·a·cre (stāvz′ā′kər), *n.* **1.** a larkspur, *Delphinium staphisagria,* of Europe and Asia Minor, having violently emetic and cathartic poisonous seeds. **2.** the seeds themselves. [late ME *staphisagre* < L *staphis agria* < Gk *staphìs* raisin + *agría* wild (fem.)]

Stav·ro·pol (stäv′rə pol′), *n.* **1.** a territory of the RSFSR, in the S Soviet Union in Europe, in the Caucasus mountains. **2.** Formerly, **Voroshilovsk.** a city in and the capital of this territory, on the Volga River. 162,000 (est. 1964).

staw (stô), *n., v.t., v.i.* *Chiefly Scot.* stall¹.

stay¹ (stā), *v.,* **stayed** or **staid, stay·ing,** *n.* —*v.i.* **1.** to remain in a place situation, company, etc.; dwell or reside: *He stayed in the army for ten years. We stayed at a motel for the weekend.* **2.** to continue to be as specified, as to condition or state: *to stay clean.* **3.** to hold out or endure, as in a contest or task (usually fol. by *with*): *Please stay with the project as long as you can.* **4.** to keep up, as with a competitor (usually fol. by *with*). **5.** *Poker.* to continue in a hand by matching a bet, ante, or raise. **6.** to stop or halt. **7.** to pause or wait, as for a moment, before proceeding or continuing; linger or tarry. **8.** *Archaic.* to cease or desist. **9.** *Archaic.* to stand firm. —*v.t.* **10.** to stop or halt. **11.** to hold back, detain, or restrain, as from going further. **12.** to suspend or delay (actions, proceedings, etc.). **13.** to suppress or quell (an emotion, violence, strife, etc.): *stay your anger.* **14.** to appease or satisfy temporarily the cravings of (the stomach, appetite, etc.). **15.** to remain for (a meal, performance, etc.). **16.** to remain through or during (a period of time): *We stayed two days in San Francisco.* **17.** to remain to the end of; remain beyond (usually fol. by *out*). **18.** to endure (the demands of a contest, task, etc.): *The horse is a good sprinter but can't stay the distance.* **19.** *Archaic.* to await. —*n.* **20.** the act of stopping or being stopped. **21.** a stop, halt, or pause; a standstill. **22.** a sojourn or temporary residence: *a week's stay in Miami.* **23.** *Law.* a stoppage or arrest of action; suspension of a judicial proceeding: *The governor granted a stay of execution.* **24.** *Informal.* staying power; endurance. **25.** *Obs.* a cause of stoppage or restraint; obstacle. [late ME *staie(n)* < AF *(e)stai(er),* OF *estai-,* s. of *ester* < L *stāre* to STAND] —**stay′a·ble,** *adj.* —**stay′er,** *n.*
—**Syn. 1.** abide, sojourn, rest. **2.** remain. **7.** delay. **11.** obstruct, arrest, check, hinder, delay, hold, curb, prevent. **12.** adjourn, recess. **14.** curb, allay. **21.** interruption, break. —**Ant. 1.** leave.

stay² (stā), *n., v.,* **stayed, stay·ing.** —*n.* **1.** something used to support or steady a thing; prop; brace. **2.** a flat strip of steel, plastic, etc., used esp. for stiffening corsets, collars, etc. **3.** a long rod running between opposite walls, heads or sides of a furnace, boiler, tank, or the like, to strengthen them against internal pressures. **4. stays,** *Chiefly Brit.* a corset. —*v.t.* **5.** to support, prop, or hold up (sometimes fol. by *up*). **6.** to sustain or strengthen mentally or spiritually. **7.** to rest on (something, as a foundation or base) for support. **8.** to cause something to become fixed or to rest on (a support, foundation, base, etc.) [appar. same as STAY³; cf. OF *estayer* to hold in place, support, perh. deriv. of ME *steye* STAY³]

stay³ (stā), *n., v.,* **stayed, stay·ing.** *Chiefly Naut.* —*n.* **1.** any of various strong ropes or wires for steadying masts, funnels, etc. **2. in stays, a.** (of a fore-and-aft-rigged vessel) heading into the wind with sails shaking, as in coming about. **b.** (of a square-rigged vessel) with the fore yards aback, as in tacking. Cf. **iron** (def. 14a). **3. miss stays,** (of a sailing vessel) to fail to come about, as through loss of headway, so as to fall back eventually on the original tack. Also, **refuse stays.** —*v.t.* **4.** to support or secure with a stay or stays: *to stay a mast.* **5.** to put (a ship) on the other tack. —*v.i.* **6.** (of a ship) to change to the other tack. [ME *stey(e),* OE *stæg;* c. G *Stag*]

stay-at-home (stā′ət hōm′), *adj.* **1.** not inclined to travel or seek diversions or pastimes outside one's residence, area, or country. **2.** of or pertaining to time spent at home: *a stay-at-home evening.* —*n.* **3.** one who stays at home a good deal; one not inclined to travel; homebody.

stay·bolt (stā′bōlt′), *n.* a long rod with threaded ends, used as a stay for a boiler, tank, etc. [STAY² + BOLT¹]

stay′ fore′sail, *Naut.* **1.** a sail set on a forestay; forestaysail. **2.** (on a yawl or ketch) a jib-headed sail set on a stay to the head of the mainmast.

stay′ing pow′er, ability or strength to last or endure; endurance; stamina.

stay′-in strike′ (stā′in′), *Brit.* See **sit-down strike.** Also called **stay′-in′.**

stay·sail (stā′sāl′; *Naut.* stā′səl), *n.* *Naut.* any sail set on a stay, as a triangular sail between two masts. [STAY³ + SAIL]

S.T.B., 1. Bachelor of Sacred Theology. [< L *Sacrae Theologiae Baccalaureus*] **2.** Bachelor of Theology. [< L *Scientiae Theologicae Baccalaureus*]

St. Ber·nard (sānt′ bər närd′; *for 1, 2 also Fr.* san ber nar′), **1. Great,** a mountain pass between SW Switzerland and NW Italy, in the Pennine Alps: Napoleon led his army through it in 1800; location of a hospice. 8108 ft. high. See map under **Simplon** and **St. Gotthard. 2. Little,** a mountain pass between SE France and NW Italy, in the Alps, S of Mont Blanc. 7177 ft. high. **3.** a town in SW Ohio. 6778 (1960). **4.** one of a breed of very large dogs having a massive head and a dense red and white or brindle and white coat, originally bred in the Alps as guide dogs.

St. Bernard's lily, a perennial herb, *Anthericum Liliago,* of southern Europe and northern Africa, having small, flat flowers.

St. Bri·euc (san brē œ′), a city in and the capital of the Cote-du-Nord, in W France. 47,307 (1962).

St. Catharines, a city in SE Ontario, in SE Canada. 84,472 (1961).

St. Charles, 1. a city in E Missouri, on the Missouri River. 21,189 (1960). **2.** a town in NE Illinois. 9269 (1960).

St. Christopher. See **St. Kitts.**

St. Clair, 1. Arthur, 1736–1818, American Revolutionary War general, born in Scotland: 1st governor of the Northwest Territory, 1787–1802. **2.** a river in the N central U.S. and S Canada, flowing S from Lake Huron to Lake St. Clair, forming part of the boundary between Michigan and Ontario. 41 mi. long. **3. Lake,** a lake between SE Michigan and Ontario, Canada. 26 mi. long; 460 sq. mi. **4.** a town in central Pennsylvania. 5159 (1960). **5.** a town in E Michigan. 4538 (1960). **6.** a town in central Missouri. 2711 (1960).

St. Clair Shores, a city in SE Michigan, near Detroit. 76,657 (1960).

St. Clairs·ville (klârz′vil), a town in E Ohio. 3865 (1960).

St. Cloud (sānt′ kloud′ *for 1, 3;* san klōō′ *for 2*). **1.** a city in central Minnesota, on the Mississippi. 33,815 (1960). **2.** a suburb of Paris in N France, on the Seine: former royal palace. 26,746 (1962). **3.** a town in central Florida. 4353 (1960).

St. Croix (kroi), **1.** Also called **Santa Cruz.** a U.S. island in the N Lesser Antilles: the largest of the Virgin Islands. 14,973 (1960); 82 sq. mi. **2.** a river flowing from NW Wisconsin along the boundary between Wisconsin and Minnesota into the Mississippi. 164 mi. long. **3.** a river in the NE United States and SE Canada, forming a part of the boundary between Maine and New Brunswick, flowing into Passamaquoddy Bay. 75 mi. long.

St. Cyr-l'É·cole (san sēr lā kôl′), a town in N France, W of Versailles: military academy. 9610 (1962).

std., standard.

S.T.D., Doctor of Sacred Theology. [< L *Sacrae Theologiae Doctor*]

St. Den·is (sānt′ den′is; *for 2, 3 also Fr.* san də nē′), **1. Ruth,** 1880?–1968, U.S. dancer. **2.** a suburb of Paris in N France: famous abbey, the burial place of many French kings. 95,072 (1962). **3.** a seaport in and the capital of Réunion island, in the Indian Ocean. 41,863 (est. 1960).

Ste., (referring to a woman) Saint. [< F *Sainte*]

stead (sted), *n.* **1.** the place of a person or thing as occupied by a successor or substitute: *The nephew of the queen came in her stead.* **2.** *Obs.* a place or locality. **3. stand in good stead,** to be useful to, esp. in a critical situation: *Your experience will stand you in good stead.* —*v.t.* **4.** *Archaic.* to be of service, advantage, or avail to. [ME, OE *stede;* c. G *Stätte* place; akin to G *Stadt,* Icel *stathr,* Goth *staths;* see STATION, STASIS]

stead·fast (sted′fast′, -fäst′, -fəst), *adj.* **1.** fixed in direction; steadily directed: *a steadfast gaze.* **2.** firm in purpose, resolution, faith, attachment, etc., as a person: *a steadfast friend.* **3.** unwavering, as resolution, faith, adherence, etc. **4.** firmly established, as an institution or a state of affairs. **5.** firmly fixed in place or position. Also, **stedfast.** [ME *stedefast,* OE *stedefæst.* See STEAD, FAST¹] —**stead′fast′ly,** *adv.* —**stead′fast′ness,** *n.*
—**Syn. 2.** sure, dependable, reliable, constant, unwavering. STEADFAST, STAUNCH, STEADY imply a sureness and continuousness that may be depended upon. STEADFAST literally means fixed in place, but is chiefly used figuratively to indicate undeviating constancy or resolution: *steadfast in one's faith.* STAUNCH literally means watertight, as of a vessel, and therefore strong and firm; fig., it is used of loyal support that will endure strain: *a staunch advocate of free trade.* Literally, STEADY is applied to that which is relatively firm in position or continuous in movement or duration; fig., it implies sober regularity or persistence: *to run at a steady pace.* **4, 5.** stable. —**Ant. 2.** capricious, variable.

stead·ing (sted′ing), *n.* *Scot. and North Eng.* **1.** the farmhouse, barns, and all outbuildings on a farm. **2.** a building lot or site. [STEAD + -ING¹]

stead·y (sted′ē), *adj.,* **stead·i·er, stead·i·est,** *interj., n., pl.* **stead·ies,** *v.,* **stead·ied, stead·y·ing.** —*adj.* **1.** firmly placed or fixed; stable in position or equilibrium: *a steady ladder.* **2.** even or regular in movement: *the steady swing of the pendulum.* **3.** free from change, variation, or interruption; uniform; continuous: *a steady diet of meat and potatoes; a steady wind.* **4.** constant, regular, or habitual: *steady customers of a store; a steady job.* **5.** free from excitement or agitation; calm: *steady nerves.* **6.** firm; unfaltering: *a steady gaze; a steady hand.* **7.** steadfast or unwavering; resolute: *a steady purpose.* **8.** settled, staid, or sober, as a person, habits, etc. **9.** *Naut.* (of a vessel) keeping nearly upright, as in a heavy sea. **10. go steady,** *Informal.* to date exclusively one person of the opposite sex: *Her father didn't approve of her going steady at such an early age.* —*interj.* **11.** be calm; control yourself. **12.** *Naut.* (a helm order to keep a vessel steady on its present heading.) —*n.* **13.** *Informal.* a person of the opposite sex whom one dates exclusively; sweetheart; boyfriend or girlfriend. —*v.t.* **14.** to make or keep steady, as in position, movement, action, character, etc.: *His calm confidence steadied the nervous passengers.* —*v.i.* **15.** to become steady. —*adv.* **16.** in a firm or steady manner: *Hold the ladder steady.* [STEAD + -Y¹] —**stead′i·er,** *n.* —**stead′i·ly,** *adv.* —**stead′i·ness,** *n.* —**stead′y·ing·ly,** *adv.*
—**Syn. 1.** balanced. **3.** undeviating, invariable. **7.** See **steadfast.**

stead·y-go·ing (sted′ē gō′ing), *adj.* **1.** steadfast; faithful; unchanging: *steady-going service to the cause of justice.* **2.** regular and dependable, as in habits of living: *a steady-going family man.*

stead·y-hand·ed (sted′ē han′did), *adj.* having steady hands; having self-control; calm.

stead′y state′ the′ory, *Astron.* the theory that the universe does not go through a cycle of explosion and contraction but is unlimited and will constantly expand. Cf. **big bang theory.**

steak (stāk), *n.* **1.** a slice of meat or fish, esp. beef, cooked by broiling, frying, etc. **2.** chopped meat prepared in the same manner as a steak. [ME *steike* < Scand; cf. Icel *steik,* akin to *steikja* to roast on a spit, *stikna* to be roasted; see STICK¹]

steak·house (stāk′hous′), *n., pl.* **-hous·es** (-hou′ziz). a restaurant specializing in beefsteak. [STEAK + HOUSE]

steak′ knife′, a sharp dinner knife the blade of which is made of steel and usually serrated, used in cutting meat.

steak′ set′, a carving set for steaks.

steak′ tar′tare. See **tartare steak.**

steal (stēl), *v.,* **stole, sto·len, steal·ing,** *n.* —*v.t.* **1.** to take (the property of another or others) without permission or right, esp. secretly or by force: *A pickpocket stole his watch.* **2.** to appropriate (ideas, credit, words, etc.) without right or acknowledgment. **3.** to take, get, or win insidiously, surreptitiously, subtly, or by chance: *He stole my girl friend.* **4.** to move, bring, convey, or put secretly or quietly; smuggle (usually fol. by *away, from, in, into,* etc.): *They stole the bicycle into the bedroom to surprise the child.* **5.** *Baseball.* (of a base runner) to gain (a base) without the help of a walk or batted ball, as by running to it during the delivery of a pitch. **6.** *Games.* to gain (a point, advantage, etc.) by strategy, chance, or luck. **7.** to gain or seize more than one's share of attention, as by giving a superior performance: *The comedian stole the show.* —*v.i.* **8.** to commit or practice theft. **9.** to move, go, or come secretly, quietly, or unobserved: *She stole out of the house at midnight.* **10.** to pass, happen, etc., imperceptibly, gently, or gradually: *The years steal by.* **11.** *Baseball.* (of a base runner) to advance a base without the help of a walk or batted ball. **12. steal someone's thunder, a.** to appropriate or use another's idea, plan, words, etc. **b.** to gain an advantage over another by expressing the mood, idea, words, etc., that person had intended to use: *Before I could tell my wife she had spent too much for the dress, she stole my thunder by asking why I spent so much for my new fishing rod.* —*n.* **13.** *Informal.* an act of stealing; theft. **14.** *Informal.* the thing stolen; booty. **15.** *Informal.* something acquired at a cost far below its real value; bargain: *This dress is a steal at $20.* **16.** *Baseball.* the act of advancing a base by stealing: *The runner on first base attempted a steal but failed.* [ME *stele(n)* OE *stelan;* c. G *stehlen,* Icel *stela,* Goth *stilan*] —**steal′a·bil′i·ty,** *n.* —**steal′a·ble,** *adj.*

steal·age (stē′lij), *n.* **1.** the act of stealing. **2.** losses due to theft. [STEAL + -AGE]

steal·er (stē′lər), *n.* **1.** one who steals. **2.** *Naut.* a plate or plank at the bow or stern, made the height of two adjacent strakes that would diminish excessively if carried all the way forward or aft because of the diminishing sectional area of the hull. [STEAL + -ER[1]]

steal·ing (stē′ling), *n.* **1.** the act of one who steals. **2.** Usually, **stealings.** that which is stolen. —*adj.* **3.** given to or characterized by theft. [ME *steling* (*n.*). See STEAL, -ING[1], -ING[2]] —**steal′ing·ly,** *adv.*

stealth (stelth), *n.* **1.** secret, clandestine, or surreptitious procedure. **2.** *Obs.* a furtive departure or entrance. **3.** (*cap.*) a U.S. Air Force project for a range of technologies used to develop aircraft that are difficult to detect by sight, sound, radar, or infrared energy. **4.** *Obs.* **a.** an act of stealing; theft. **b.** the thing stolen; booty. [ME *stelthe;* cf. OE *stælthing* theft. See STEAL, -TH[1]] —**stealth′ful,** *adj.* —**stealth′ful·ly,** *adv.* —**stealth′less,** *adj.*

stealth·y (stel′thē), *adj.,* **stealth·i·er, stealth·i·est.** done, characterized, or acting by stealth; furtive: *stealthy footsteps.* [STEALTH + -Y[1]] —**stealth′i·ly,** *adv.* —**stealth′i·ness,** *n.*
—**Syn.** surreptitious, secret, clandestine, sly.

steam (stēm), *n.* **1.** water in the form of an invisible gas or vapor. **2.** water changed to this form by boiling, extensively used for the generation of mechanical power, for heating purposes, etc. **3.** the mist formed when the gas or vapor from boiling water condenses in the air. **4.** an exhalation of a vapor or mist. **5.** *Informal.* power or energy. **6.** **blow off** or **let off steam,** *Slang.* to give vent to one's repressed emotions, esp. by talking or behaving in an unrestrained manner: *Don't take her remarks too seriously—she was just blowing off steam.* —*v.i.* **7.** to emit or give off steam or vapor. **8.** to rise or pass off in the form of steam or vapor. **9.** to become covered with condensed steam, as a window or other surface (often fol. by *up*). **10.** to generate or produce steam, as in a boiler. **11.** to move or travel by the agency of steam. **12.** to move rapidly or evenly: *He steamed out of the room.* **13.** *Informal.* to be angry or show anger. —*v.t.* **14.** to expose to or treat with steam, as in order to heat, cook, soften, renovate, or the like. **15.** to emit or exhale (steam or vapor). **16.** to convey by the agency of steam: *to steam the ship safely into port.* —*adj.* **17.** heated by or heating with steam: *steam radiator.* **18.** propelled by or propelling with a steam engine. **19.** operated by steam. **20.** conducting steam: *a steam line.* **21.** bathed with or affected by steam. **22.** of or pertaining to steam. [ME *steme,* OE *stēam;* c. D *stoom*] —**steam′less,** *adj.*

steam′ bath′, **1.** a bath of steam, usually in a specially equipped room or enclosure, for cleansing or refreshing oneself. **2.** a special room or enclosure, or an establishment containing it, for such a bath. **3.** a bath of steam used in laboratories for sterilizing equipment.

steam·boat (stēm′bōt′), *n.* a steam-driven vessel, esp. a small one or one used on inland waters. [STEAM + BOAT]

steam′boat Goth′ic, *U.S.* a 19th-century style of architecture in which windows, doorways, beams, railings, etc., were elaborately ornamented in imitation of the gingerbread trimming on river steamboats.

steam′ boil′er, a receptacle in which water is boiled to generate steam.

steam′ cab′inet, a small, airtight cabinet designed to accommodate one person in a sitting position, with the head exposed, and equipped to give a steam bath to the occupant.

steam′ chest′, the chamber from which steam enters the cylinder of an engine. Also called **steam′ box′.**

steam′ en′gine, an engine worked by steam, typically one in which a sliding piston in a cylinder is moved by the expansive action of the steam generated in a boiler. —**steam′-en′gine,** *adj.*

steam·er (stē′mər), *n.* **1.** something propelled or operated by steam, as a steamship. **2.** one who or that which steams. **3.** a device or container in which something is steamed. **4.** See **soft-shell clam.** —*v.i.* **5.** to travel by steamship. [STEAM + -ER[1]] —**steam′er·less,** *adj.*

steam′er bas′ket, a basket, usually elaborately arranged and decorated, containing fruit, sweets, canned delicacies, and the like, often including brandy or champagne, sent to a person or persons departing on a trip, esp. by ship.

steam′er chair′. See **deck chair.**

steam′er clam′. See **soft-shell clam.**

steam′er rug′, **1.** a coarse, heavy laprobe used by ship passengers sitting in deck chairs. **2.** rug (def. 2).

steam′er trunk′, a rectangular traveling trunk low enough to slide under a bunk on a ship.

steam′ fit′ter, one who installs and repairs steam-pipes and their accessories. —**steam′ fit′ting.**

steam′ fog′, *Meteorol.* fog caused by cold air flowing over a body of comparatively warm water, the vapor condensing in small convective columns near the water surface and giving the appearance of smoke or steam. Also called **arctic sea smoke, arctic smoke, frost smoke, sea mist, sea smoke, steam′ mist′, water smoke.**

steam′ heat′, heat obtained by the circulation of steam in pipes, radiators, etc.

steam-heat·ed (stēm′hē′tid), *adj.* heated by steam.

steam′ heat′er, a device or system for heating by means of steam.

steam′ heat′ing, a heating system utilizing steam circulated through radiators and pipes.

steam′ i′ron, an electric iron with a water chamber that emits steam on the fabric or garment being ironed.

steam′ jack′et, a casing, as on the cylinder of a steam engine, filled with live steam to keep the interior hot. —**steam′-jack′et·ed,** *adj.*

steam′ lance′, *Mach.* a lance using steam. Also called **steam′ noz′zle.**

steam-lance (stēm′lans′, -läns′), *v.t.,* **-lanced, -lanc·ing.** to clean with a steam lance.

steam′ locomo′tive, a locomotive moved by steam power generated in its own boiler.

steam·pipe (stēm′pīp′), *n.* a pipe for conveying steam from a boiler. [STEAM + PIPE[1]]

steam′ point′, the temperature at which water vapor condenses at a pressure of one unit of atmosphere, represented by 100°C and 212°F. Cf. **ice point.**

steam′ ra′dio, *Brit. Informal.* radio as distinguished from television: *There was nothing good on the telly, so we listened to good old steam radio.*

steam′ roll′er, **1.** a heavy steam-powered vehicle having a roller for crushing, compacting, or leveling materials used for a road or the like. **2.** (not in technical use) any powered vehicle having a roller for this purpose. **3.** an overpowering force, esp. one that crushes all opposition with ruthless disregard for individual rights. Also, **steam′roll′er.**

steam-roll·er (stēm′rō′lər), *v.t.* **1.** to move, go over, crush, or defeat as with a steam roller or an overpowering force. —*adj.* **2.** suggestive of a steam roller; ruthlessly overpowering: *steam-roller tactics.* Also, **steam-roll, steam·roll** (stēm′rōl′), **steamroller.** [v. use of phrase *steam roller*]

steam′ room′, a steam-filled and heated room to induce sweating, as in a Turkish bath.

steam·ship (stēm′ship′), *n.* a large commercial power vessel, esp. one driven by steam. [STEAM + SHIP]

steam′ shov′el, a machine for digging or excavating operated by its own engine and boiler.

Steam shovel

steam′ ta′ble, a box-like table or counter, usually of stainless steel, with receptacles in the top into which containers of food may be fitted to be kept warm by steam or hot water in the compartment below.

steam·tight (stēm′tīt′), *adj.* impervious to steam. [STEAM + TIGHT] —**steam′tight′ness,** *n.*

steam′ tur′bine, a turbine driven by steam pressure. —**steam′-tur′bine,** *adj.*

steam·y (stē′mē), *adj.,* **steam·i·er, steam·i·est.** **1.** consisting of or resembling steam. **2.** full of or abounding in steam; emitting steam. **3.** covered with or as if with condensed steam: *a steamy bathroom mirror.* **4.** hot and humid. [STEAM + -Y[1]] —**steam′i·ly,** *adv.* —**steam′i·ness,** *n.*

Ste. Anne de Beau·pré (sānt an′ də bō prā′; *Fr.* saN tan də bō prā′), a village in S Quebec, in SE Canada, on the St. Lawrence, NE of Quebec: Roman Catholic shrine. 1878 (1961).

ste·ap·sin (stē ap′sin), *n.* *Biochem.* the lipase of the pancreatic juice. [STEA(R)- + (PE)PSIN]

stear-, var. of **stearo-** before a vowel: *stearate.*

ste·a·rate (stē′ə rāt′, stēr′āt), *n.* *Chem.* a salt or ester of stearic acid. [STEAR- + -ATE[2]]

ste·ar·ic (stē ar′ik, stēr′ik), *adj.* **1.** of or pertaining to suet or fat. **2.** of or derived from stearic acid. [STEAR- + -IC]

stear′ic ac′id, *Chem.* a colorless, waxlike, sparingly water-soluble, odorless solid, $CH_3(CH_2)_{16}COOH$, the most common fatty acid, occurring as the glyceride in tallow and other animal fats and in some animal oils: used chiefly in the manufacture of soaps, stearates, candles, cosmetics, and in medicine in suppositories and pill coatings. Also called **octadecanoic acid.**

ste·a·rin (stē′ərin, stēr′in), *n.* **1.** *Chem.* any of the three glyceryl esters of stearic acid, esp. $C_3H_5(C_{18}H_{35}O_2)_3$, a soft, white, odorless solid found in many natural fats. **2.** the crude commercial form of stearic acid, used chiefly in the manufacture of candles. Also, **ste·a·rine** (stē′ər-in, -ə rēn′, stēr′in). [< F *stéarine* < Gk *stéar* fat, grease + F *-ine* -INE[2], -IN[2]]

stearo-, a learned borrowing from Greek, where it meant "fat", used with this meaning, and with reference to stearic acid and its related compounds, in the formation of compound words: *stearoptene; stearoyl.* Also, *esp. before a vowel,* **stear-.** [comb. form repr. Gk *stéar* fat, grease. Cf. STEATO-]

ste·a·rop·tene (stē′ə rop′tēn), *n.* *Chem.* the oxygenated solid part of an essential oil (opposed to *eleoptene*). [< Gk *stéar* fat, grease + -o- + *ptēn(ós)* winged, volatile; cf. ELAEOPTENE]

ste·ar·o·yl (stē ar′ō il, stēr′ō-), *adj.* *Chem.* containing the stearoyl group. [STEARO- + -YL]

stear′oyl group′, *Chem.* the univalent group, $C_{22}H_{35}CO$-, derived from stearic acid. Also called **stear′oyl rad′ical.**

ste·ar·rhe·a (stē′ə rē′ə), *n.* *Pathol.* steatorrhea. Also, **ste′ar·rhoe′a.** [STEAR- + -RHEA]

ste·a·tite (stē′ə tīt′), *n.* soapstone. [< L *steatītē(s)* < Gk *steat-* (s. of *stéar*) fat, tallow + *-ītēs* -ITE[1]] —**ste·a·tit·ic** (stē′ə tit′ik), *adj.*

steato-, a learned borrowing from Greek meaning "fat," "tallow"; used in the formation of compound words: *steatopygia.* Also, *esp. before a vowel,* **steat-.** [< Gk *steat-* (s. of *stéar;* see STEARO-) + -o-]

ste·a·to·py·gi·a (stē′ə tō pī′jē ə, -pij′ē ə), *n.* extreme accumulation of fat on and about the buttocks, esp. of women, as among the Hottentots, Bushmen, and certain other South African peoples. [STEATO- + Gk *pyg(ḗ)* buttocks + *-ia* -IA] —**ste·a·to·pyg·ic** (stē′ə tō-pij′ik), **ste·a·to·py·gous** (stē′ə tō pī′gəs, -top′ə gəs), *adj.*

ste·a·tor·rhe·a (stē′ə tə rē′ə), *n.* *Pathol.* the presence of excess fat in the stools, usually caused by disease of the pancreas or intestine, and characterized by chronic diarrhea and weight loss. Also, **ste′a·tor·rhoe′a.** [STEATO- + -RRHEA]

stech (stekн), *Scot. and North Eng.* —*v.t.* **1.** to fill or gorge (one's stomach) with food. —*v.i.* **2.** to eat voraciously. Also, **stegh.** [appar. var. of STACK]

Stech·helm (stek′helm′), *n.* a heavy German jousting helm of the 15th and 16th centuries, having a bluntly pointed front with a V-shaped vision slit. [< G; see STEEK[2], HELM[2]]

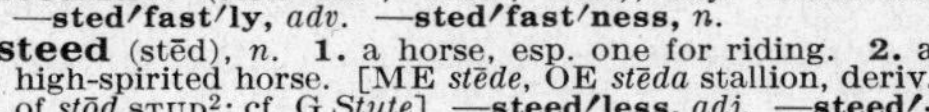

sted·fast (sted′fast′, -fäst′, -fəst), *adj.* steadfast. —**sted′fast′ly,** *adv.* —**sted′fast′ness,** *n.*

steed (stēd), *n.* **1.** a horse, esp. one for riding. **2.** a high-spirited horse. [ME *stede,* OE *stēda* stallion, deriv. of *stōd* STUD[2]; cf. G *Stute*] —**steed′less,** *adj.* —**steed′-like′,** *adj.*

steek[1] (stēk, stäk), *Scot.* —*n.* **1.** (in sewing) a stitch. —*v.t.* **2.** to stitch. **3.** to shut, close, fasten or lock (a window, door, or the like). **4.** to enclose, confine, or imprison. —*v.i.* **5.** to sew. [ME (north) *steke,* OE *stic(ian)* (to) prick, stab, whence STITCH[1]]

steek[2] (stēk), *v.t., v.i.* *Brit. Dial.* stick[2]. [ME *steke,* ?, deriv. of OE *stecan* < Gmc alter. of STICK[2]]

steel (stēl), *n.* **1.** any of various modified forms of iron, artificially produced, having a carbon content less than that of pig iron and more than that of wrought iron, and having qualities of hardness, elasticity, and strength varying according to composition and heat treatment: generally categorized as having a high, medium, or low-carbon content. **2.** a thing or things made of this metal. **3.** a flat strip of this metal used for stiffening, esp. in corsets; stay. **4.** a bar of this metal that has one end formed as a bit for driving through rock. **5.** **steels,** stocks or bonds of companies producing this metal. **6.** a sword. —*adj.* **7.** pertaining to or made of steel. **8.** like steel in color, hardness, or strength. —*v.t.* **9.** to fit with steel, as by pointing, edging, or overlaying. **10.** to cause to resemble steel in some way. **11.** to render insensible, inflexible, unyielding, determined, etc.: *He steeled himself to perform the dangerous task.* [ME, OE (north) *stēle;* c. D *staal,* G *Stahl,* Icel *stāl*] —**steel′less,** *adj.* —**steel′like′,** *adj.*

steel′ band′, *Music.* a band, native to Trinidad and common in other of the Caribbean Islands, using steel oil drums cut to various heights and tuned to specific pitches.

steel′ blue′, dark bluish gray.

Steele (stēl), *n.* **Sir Richard,** 1672–1729, English essayist, journalist, dramatist, and political leader; born in Ireland.

steel′ engrav′ing, *Print.* **1.** a method of incising letters, designs, etc., on steel. **2.** the imprint, as on paper, from a plate of engraved steel.

steel-faced (stēl′fāst′), *adj.* having the front or outer surfaces covered with or characterized by steel.

steel′ gray′, dark metallic gray with a bluish tinge.

steel·head (stēl′hed′), *n., pl.* **-heads,** (*esp. collectively*) **-head.** a silvery rainbow trout that migrates to the sea before returning to fresh water to spawn. [STEEL + HEAD]

Steel′ Hel′met, **1.** a member of the *Stahlhelm.* **2.** Stahlhelm.

steel′ lum′ber, metal lumber composed of sheet steel.

steel·mak·er (stēl′mā′kər), *n.* a manufacturer of steel. [STEEL + MAKER]

steel·mak·ing (stēl′mā′king), *n.* the manufacture of steel. [STEEL + MAKING]

steel·man (stēl′mən), *n., pl.* **-men.** one engaged in the steelmaking business. [STEEL + MAN[1]]

steel′ mill′, a steelworks.

steel′ square′, *Carpentry.* See **framing square.**

steel′ wool′, a tangled or matted mass of stringlike steel shavings, used for scouring, polishing, smoothing, etc.

steel·work (stēl′wûrk′), *n.* **1.** steel parts or articles. **2.** the steel frame or girders of a skyscraper. [STEEL + WORK]

steel·work·er (stēl′wûr′kər), *n.* one employed in the process of manufacturing steel. [STEEL + WORKER]

steel·works (stēl′wûrks′), *n., pl.* **-works.** (*construed as sing. or pl.*) an establishment where steel is made and often manufactured into girders, rails, etc. [STEEL + WORKS]

steel·y (stē′lē), *adj.,* **steel·i·er, steel·i·est.** **1.** consisting or made of steel. **2.** resembling or suggesting steel, as in color, strength, or hardness. [STEEL + -Y[1]] —**steel′i·ness,** *n.*

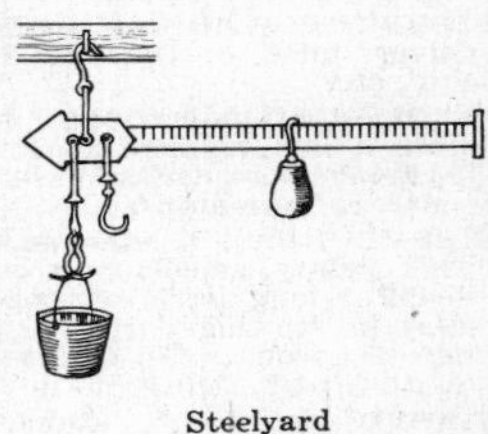

Steelyard

steel·yard (stēl′yärd′, stil′yərd), *n.* a portable balance with two unequal arms, the longer one having a movable counterpoise, and the shorter one bearing a hook or the like for holding the object to be weighed. [STEEL + YARD[1]]

Steen (stān), *n.* **Jan** (yän), 1626–79, Dutch painter.

steen·bok (stēn′bok′, stān′-), *n., pl.* **-boks,** (*esp. collectively*) **-bok.** a small antelope, *Raphicerus campestris,* of grassy areas of eastern and southern Africa. Also, **steinbok.** [< SAfrD: stone buck]

steen·ing (stē′ning, stā′-), *n.* a dry masonry lining for a well or the like. Also called **steen** (stēn). [*steen* to line with stone (ME *stene(n),* OE *stǣnan,* deriv. of *stān* STONE; c. Goth *stainjan*) + -ING[1]; see STAIN]

steep[1] (stēp), *adj.* **1.** having an almost vertical slope or pitch, or a relatively high gradient, as a hill, an ascent, stairs, etc. **2.** *Informal.* (of a price or amount) unduly high; exorbitant: *Those prices are too steep for me.* **3.** *Informal.* extreme or incredible, as a statement or story. **4.** *Obs.* high or lofty. —*n.* **5.** a steep place; declivity, as of a hill. [ME *stepe,* OE *stēap;* akin to STOOP[1]] —**steep′ly,** *adv.* —**steep′ness,** *n.*
—**Syn. 1.** precipitous, abrupt. —**Ant. 1.** flat.

steep[2] (stēp), *v.t.* **1.** to soak in water or other liquid, as to soften, cleanse, or extract some constituent: *to steep tea in boiling-hot water; to steep reeds for basket weaving.* **2.** to wet thoroughly in or with a liquid; drench; saturate; imbue. **3.** to immerse in or saturate or imbue with some pervading, absorbing, or stupefying influence or agency: *an incident steeped in mystery.* —*v.i.* **4.** to lie soaking in a liquid. —*n.* **5.** the act, process, or state of steeping or the state of being steeped. **6.** a liquid in which something is steeped. [ME *stepe;* c. Sw *stöpa*] —**steep′er,** *n.*
—**Syn. 1.** infuse. **2.** permeate.

steep·en (stē′pən), *v.t., v.i.* to make or become steeper. [STEEP[1] + -EN[1]]

stee·ple (stē′pəl), *n.* **1.** an ornamental construction, usually ending in a spire, erected on a roof or tower of a church, public building, etc., to hold a clock or bells, or to provide a compositional feature. **2.** a tower terminating in such a construction. **3.** a spire. [ME *stepel*, OE *stēpel* tower. See STEEP[1], -LE] **—stee′pled,** *adj.* **—stee′ple·less,** *adj.* **—stee′ple·like′,** *adj.*

A, Steeple
B, Spire

stee·ple·bush (stē′pəl bo͝osh′), *n.* the hardhack. [STEEPLE + BUSH[1]; so called because of its steeplelike blossom shoots]

stee·ple·chase (stē′pəl chās′), *n., v.,* **-chased, -chasing.** **—***n.* **1.** a horse race over a turf course furnished with artificial ditches, hedges, and other obstacles over which the horses must jump. **2.** a point-to-point race. **3.** a foot race run on a cross-country course or over a course having obstacles, as ditches, hurdles, or the like, which the runners must clear. **—***v.i.* **4.** to ride or run in a steeplechase. [STEEPLE + CHASE[1]; so called because the course was kept by sighting a church steeple] **—stee′ple·chas′er,** *n.*

stee·ple·chas·ing (stē′pəl chā′sing), *n.* the sport of riding or running in a steeplechase. [STEEPLECHASE + -ING[1]]

stee′ple cup′, a standing cup of the 17th century having a cover with a tall finial.

stee′ple en′gine, a steam engine having vertically guided crossheads above the cylinders and crankshaft.

stee′ple head′dress, hennin.

stee·ple·jack (stē′pəl jak′), *n.* a person who climbs steeples, towers, or the like, to build or repair them. [STEEPLE + JACK[1]]

steer[1] (stēr), *v.t.* **1.** to guide the course of (something in motion) by a rudder, helm, wheel, etc.: *to steer a bicycle.* **2.** to follow or pursue (a particular course). **3.** *Informal.* to direct the course of; guide: *I can steer you to the best restaurant in town.* **—***v.i.* **4.** to direct the course of a vessel, vehicle, airplane, or the like, by the use of a rudder or other means. **5.** to pursue a course of action. **6.** (of a vessel, vehicle, airplane, etc.) to admit of being steered or steered in a certain manner; be steered or guided in a particular direction or manner. **7. steer clear of,** to stay away from purposely; avoid: *She steered clear of any deep emotional involvements.* **—***n.* **8.** *Informal.* a suggestion about a course of action; tip: *He got a good steer about finding the right job.* [ME *stere*, OE *stēor(an)*, deriv. of *stēor* steering; c. G *steuern*, Icel *stȳra*, Goth *stiurjan*] **—steer′a·bil′i·ty,** *n.* **—steer′a·ble,** *adj.* **—steer′er,** *n.*
—Syn. 1. direct, pilot.

steer[2] (stēr), *n.* a castrated male bovine, esp. one raised for beef; ox. [ME; OE *stēor;* c. D, G *Stier*, Icel *stjōrr*, Goth *stiur*]

steer[3] (stēr), *v.t., v.i., n. Brit. Dial.* stir[1].

steer·age (stēr′ij), *n.* **1.** a part or division of a ship, formerly the part containing the steering apparatus. **2.** (in a passenger ship) the part or accommodations allotted to the passengers who travel at the cheapest rate. [late ME *sterage*. See STEER[1], -AGE]

steer·age·way (stēr′ij wā′), *n. Naut.* sufficient speed to permit a vessel to be maneuvered. [STEERAGE + WAY]

steer′ing commit′tee, a committee, esp. of a deliberative or legislative body, charged with preparing the agenda of a session.

steer′ing gear′, the apparatus or mechanism for steering a ship, automobile, bicycle, airplane, etc.

steer′ing wheel′, a wheel held and turned by the driver, pilot, or the like, in steering an automobile, ship, etc.

steers·man (stērz′mən), *n., pl.* **-men.** **1.** one who steers a ship; helmsman. **2.** one who drives a machine. [ME *steresman*, OE *stēoresmann*. See STEER[1], 's[1], MAN[1]] **—steers′man·ship′,** *n.*

steeve[1] (stēv), *v.,* **steeved, steev·ing,** *n.* **—***v.t.* **1.** to pack tightly, as cotton or other cargo in a ship's hold. **—***n.* **2.** a long derrick or spar, with a block at one end, used in stowing cargo in a ship's hold. [late ME *steve(n)*, prob. < Sp *(e)stiba(r)* (to) cram < L *stīpāre* to stuff, pack tightly; akin to OE *stīf* STIFF]

steeve[2] (stēv), *v.,* **steeved, steev·ing,** *n. Naut.* **—***v.i.* **1.** (of a bowsprit or the like) to incline upward at an angle instead of extending horizontally. **—***v.t.* **2.** to set (a spar) at an upward inclination. **—***n.* **3.** the angle that a bowsprit or the like makes with the horizontal. [cf. OE *stīfig* steep]

Stef·a·na (stef′ə nə; *It.* ste′fä nä), *n.* a girl's given name. Also, **Stefania, Stefanie, Stephana, Stephania, Stephanie, Stephany.**

Ste·fa·ni·a (ste fä′nē ə), *n.* a girl's given name. Also, **Stefana, Stefanie, Stephana, Stephania, Stephanie, Stephany.**

Stef·a·nie (stef′ə nē; *Fr.* ste fA nē′), *n.* a girl's given name. Also, **Stefana, Stefania, Stephana, Stephania, Stephanie, Stephany.**

Stef·ans·son (stef′ən sən), *n.* **Vil·hjal·mur** (vil′hyoul′mər), 1879–1962, U.S. arctic explorer and author, born in Canada.

Stef·fan (stef′ən), *n.* a boy's given name, form of **Stephen.**

Stef·fens (stef′ənz), *n.* **(Joseph) Lincoln,** 1866–1936, U.S. author, journalist, and editor.

Stef·fy (stef′ē), *n.* a girl's given name, form of **Stephana** or **Stephanie.**

Ste. Genevieve, a town in E Missouri. 4443 (1960).

Ste·ger (stā′gər), *n.* a town in NE Illinois. 6432 (1960).

stegh (stekH), *v.t., v.i. Scot. and North Eng.* stech.

stego-, a learned borrowing from Greek meaning "cover," used in the formation of compound words: *stegosaur.* [comb. form of Gk *stégos* roof]

steg·o·saur (steg′ə sôr′), *n.* any herbivorous dinosaur of the genus *Stegosaurus*, from the Jurassic and Cretaceous periods, having a heavy, bony armor, and growing to a length of about 40 feet. [STEGO- + -SAUR]

Stegosaur,
Stegosaurus stenops
(Length 18 ft.)

Stei·chen (stī′kən), *n.* **Edward,** born 1879, U.S. photographer.

Stei·er·mark (shtī′ər märk′), *n.* German name of **Styria.**

stein (stīn), *n.* **1.** a mug, usually earthenware, esp. for beer. **2.** the quantity of beer or other liquid contained in a stein. [< G: lit., stone]

Stein (stīn *for 1;* shtīn *for 2*), *n.* **1. Gertrude,** 1874–1946, U.S. author in France. **2. Hein·rich Frie·drich Karl** (hīn′rikH frē′drikH kärl), **Baron vom und zum** (fôm o͝ont tso͞om), 1757–1831, German statesman.

Stein·am·ang·er (shtīn′äm äng′ər), *n.* German name of **Szombathely.**

Stein·beck (stīn′bek), *n.* **John (Ernst)** (ûrnst), born 1902, U.S. novelist: Nobel prize 1962.

Stein·berg (stīn′bûrg), *n.* **1. Saul,** born 1914, U.S. painter, cartoonist, and illustrator; born in Rumania. **2. William,** born 1899, U.S. conductor, born in Germany.

stein·bok (stīn′bok), *n., pl.* **-boks,** *(esp. collectively)* **-bok.** **1.** steenbok. **2.** an ibex.

Stei·ner (stī′nər; *Ger.* shtī′nər), *n.* **Ja·kob** (yä′kôp), 1796–1863, Swiss mathematician.

Stein·heil (stīn′hīl′), *n.* one of two adjoining, elliptical walled plains in the fourth quadrant of the face of the moon, the other being Watt: about 41 miles long and 31 miles wide.

Stein′heim man′ (shtīn′hīm, stīn′-), a prehistoric man, probably of the second interglacial period, known from a skull found in West Germany. [named after *Steinheim* am Murr, Germany]

Stein·metz (stīn′mets), *n.* **Charles Pro·te·us** (prō′tē əs), 1865–1923, U.S. electrical engineer, born in Germany.

ste·la (stē′lə), *n., pl.* **ste·lae** (stē′lē). stele (defs. 1–3).

Stel·a·zine (stel′ə zēn′), *n. Pharm., Trademark.* trifluoperazine.

ste·le (stē′lē, stēl *for 1–3;* stēl, stē′lē *for 4*), *n., pl.* **ste·lai** (stē′lī), **ste·les** (stē′lēz, stēlz). **1.** an upright stone slab or pillar bearing an inscription or design and serving as a monument, marker, or the like. **2.** *Archit.* a prepared surface on the face of a building a rock, etc., bearing an inscription or the like. **3.** (in ancient Rome) a burial stone. **4.** *Bot.* the central cylinder or cylinders of vascular and related tissue in the stem, root, petiole, leaf, etc., of the higher plants. Also, **stela** (for defs. 1–3). [< Gk *stḗlē*, akin to *histánai*, L *stāre* to STAND] **—ste·lar** (stē′lər), *adj.*

St. Elias, Mount, a mountain on the boundary between Alaska and Canada, a peak of the St. Elias Mountains. 18,008 ft.

St. Elias Mountains, a mountain range between SE Alaska and the SW Yukon territory. Highest peak, Mount Logan, 19,850 ft.

Stel·la (stel′ə), *n.* a girl's given name.

Stel′la Polar′is, Polaris.

stel·lar (stel′ər), *adj.* **1.** of or pertaining to the stars; consisting of stars. **2.** like a star, as in brilliance, shape, etc. **3.** pertaining to a preeminent performer, athlete, etc. [< LL *stellār(is)*, equiv. to *stell(a)* star + *-āris* -AR[1]]

stel·late (stel′it, -āt), *adj.* being or arranged in the form of a conventionalized figure of a star; star-shaped. Also, **stel′lat·ed.** [< L *stellāt(us)* starry, equiv. to *stell(a)* STAR + *-ātus* -ATE[1]] **—stel′late·ly,** *adv.*

Stel′ler's jay′ (stel′ərz), a jay, *Cyanocitta stelleri*, of western North America, having blackish-brown and dusky-blue plumage. [named after George W. Steller (1709–46), German naturalist]

Stel′ler's sea′ li′on. See under **sea lion.** [see STELLER'S JAY]

stel·lif·er·ous (ste lif′ər əs), *adj.* having or abounding with stars. [< L *stellifer* star-bearing (*stell(a)* star + *-i-* -I- + *-fer* -FER) + -OUS; see -FEROUS]

stel·li·form (stel′ə fôrm′), *adj.* star-shaped. [*stelli-* (see STELLIFEROUS) + -FORM]

stel·lion·ate (stel′yə nit, -nāt′), *n. Civil Law, Scots Law.* any crime of unspecified class that involves fraud, esp. one that involves the selling of the same property to different people. [< LL *stelliōnāt(us)*, equiv. to *stelliōn-* (s. of *stelliō*) newt, crafty person + *-ātus* -ATE[1]]

stel·lu·lar (stel′yə lər), *adj.* **1.** having the form of a small star or small stars. **2.** spotted with star-shaped specks of color. [< LL *stellul(a)* (*stell(a)* star + *-ula* -ULE) + -AR[1]] **—stel′lu·lar·ly,** *adv.*

St. Elmo's fire (el′mōz). See **corona discharge.** Also called **St. Elmo's light, St. Ulmo's fire, St. Ulmo's light.** [named after *St. Elmo* (d. A.D. 303), patron saint of sailors]

stem[1] (stem), *n., v.,* **stemmed, stem·ming.** **—***n.* **1.** the ascending axis of a plant, whether above or below ground, which ordinarily grows in an opposite direction to the root or descending axis. **2.** the stalk which supports a leaf, flower, or fruit. **3.** the main body of that portion of a tree, shrub, or other plant which is above ground; trunk; stalk. **4.** a petiole; peduncle; pedicel. **5.** a stalk of bananas. **6.** something resembling or suggesting a leaf or flower stalk. **7.** a long, slender part: *the stem of a tobacco pipe.* **8.** the slender, vertical part of a goblet, wineglass, etc., between the bowl and the base. **9.** the handle of a spoon. **10.** a projection from the rim of a watch, having on its end a knob for winding the watch. **11.** the circular rod in some locks about which the key fits and rotates. **12.** the rod or spindle by which a valve is operated from outside. **13.** the stock or line of descent of a family; ancestry or pedigree. **14.** *Gram.* the underlying form, often consisting of a root plus an affix, to which the inflectional endings of a word are added, as *tend-*, the stem in Latin *tendere* "to stretch," the root of which is *ten-*. Cf. **base** (def. 17), **theme** (def. 4). **15.** *Music.* the vertical line forming part of a note. **16. stems,** *Slang.* the legs of a human being: *She's got gorgeous stems.* **17.** the main or relatively thick stroke of a letter in printing. See diag. under **type.** **—***v.t.* **18.** to remove the stem from (a leaf, fruit, etc.): *Stem the cherries before cooking.* **—***v.i.* **19.** to arise or originate: *This project stems from last week's lecture.* [ME; OE *stemn, stefn*, equiv. to *ste-* (mutated var. of *sta-;* see STAND) + *-mn-* suffix; akin to G *Stamm* stem, tribe, Icel *stamn, stafn* stem of a ship; see STAFF[1]] **—stem′less,** *adj.* **—stem′like′,** *adj.*
—Syn. 13. lineage, race. **19.** rise.

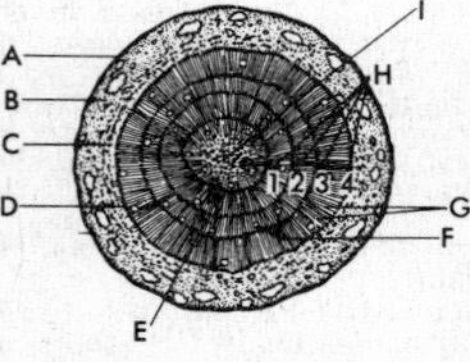

Stem of a dicotyledonous plant (Transverse section)
A, Epidermis; B, Cork; C, Cortex; D, Phloem; E, Xylem; F, Resin canals; G, Xylem rays; H, Annual rings; I, Pith

stem[2] (stem), *v.,* **stemmed, stem·ming,** *n.* **—***v.t.* **1.** to stop, check, or restrain. **2.** to dam up; stop the flow of (a stream, river, or the like). **3.** to tamp, plug, or make tight, as a hole or joint. **4.** *Scot.* to stanch (bleeding). **5.** *Skiing.* to maneuver (a ski or skis) in executing a stem. **—***v.i.* **6.** *Skiing.* to execute a stem. **—***n.* **7.** *Skiing.* the act or instance of a skier pushing the heel of one or both skis outward so that the heels are far apart, as in making certain turns or slowing down. [ME *stemme* < Scand; cf. Icel *stemma;* c. G *stemmen* to prop]
—Syn. 2. obstruct, hinder.

stem[3] (stem), *v.t.,* **stemmed, stem·ming.** **1.** to make headway against (a tide, current, gale, etc.). **2.** to make progress against (any opposition). [v. use of STEM[4]]
—Syn. 1. breast, withstand.

stem[4] (stem), *n. Naut.* **1.** (at the bow of a vessel) an upright into which the side timbers or plates are jointed. **2.** the forward part of a vessel (often opposed to *stern*). [OE *stefn, stemn* prow, stern; special use of STEM[1]]

stem[5] (stem), *v.t.,* **stemmed, stem·ming.** to arrange the loading of (a merchant vessel) within a specified time. [var. of *steven* to direct one's course < ON *stefna* to sail directly, aim, deriv. of *stefn* STEM[4]]

stem′ can′ker, *Plant Pathol.* a disease of plants characterized by cankers on the stems and twigs and caused by any of several fungi.

stem′ duch′y, (esp. in medieval Germany) any of the independent duchies that preserved the ancient tribal cultures from which they arose.

stem′-end rot′ (stem′end′), *Plant Pathol.* a disease of fruits characterized by discoloration, shriveling, and decay of the stem and adjacent parts of the fruit and caused by any of several fungi of the genera *Diplodia* and *Phomopsis.*

St.-É·mi·li·on (sānt′ə mē′lē ən, -ə mēl′yən; *Fr.* saN tā-mē lyôN′), *n.* a dry claret wine from the parish of St.-Émilion in the Bordeaux region of France.

stemmed (stemd), *adj.* **1.** having a stem or a specified kind of stem (often used in combination): *a long-stemmed rose.* **2.** having the stem or stems removed: *stemmed cherries.* [STEM[1] + -ED[2]]

stem·mer[1] (stem′ər), *n.* **1.** one who removes stems. **2.** a device for removing stems, as from tobacco, grapes, etc. [STEM[1] + -ER[1]]

stem·mer[2] (stem′ər), *n.* an implement for stemming or tamping. [STEM[2] + -ER[1]]

stem·mer·y (stem′ə rē), *n., pl.* **-mer·ies.** a factory or other place where tobacco leaves are stripped. [STEM[1] + -ERY]

stem′ rot′, *Plant Pathol.* **1.** a symptom or phase of many diseases of plants, characterized by decay of the stem tissues. **2.** any disease so characterized.

stem′ rust′, *Plant Pathol.* **1.** a disease of wheat and other grasses, characterized by pustules of red and then black spores on the stems, leaf sheaths, etc., caused by a rust fungus, *Puccinia graminis.* **2.** the fungus itself.

stem·son (stem′sən), *n. Naut.* a curved timber in a wooden bow, scarphed at its lower end to the keelson. [STEM[4] + (KEEL)SON]

stem′ turn′, *Skiing.* a turn in which a skier stems one ski in the direction to be turned and brings the other ski around so that both skis are parallel.

stem·ware (stem′wâr′), *n.* glass or crystal vessels, esp. for beverages and desserts, having rounded bowls mounted on footed stems. [STEM[1] + WARE[1]]

stem-wind·er (stem′wīn′dər), *n.* a stem-winding watch.

stem-wind·ing (stem′wīn′ding), *adj.* wound by turning a knob at the stem.

stench (stench), *n.* **1.** an offensive smell or odor; stink. **2.** a foul quality. [ME; OE *stenc* odor (good or bad); akin to G *Stank* and to STINK] **—stench′ful,** *adj.*

stench′ bomb′. See **stink bomb.**

sten·cil (sten′səl), *n., v.,* **-ciled, -cil·ing** or *(esp. Brit.)* **-cilled, -cil·ling.** **—***n.* **1.** a device for applying a pattern, design, words, etc. to a surface, consisting of a thin sheet of cardboard, metal, or other material from which figures or letters have been cut out, a coloring substance, ink, etc., being rubbed, brushed, or pressed over the sheet, passing through the perforations and onto the surface. **2.** the letters, designs, etc., produced on a surface by this method. **—***v.t.* **3.** to mark or paint (a surface) by means of a stencil. **4.** to produce (letters, figures, designs, etc.) by means of a stencil. [earlier *stanesile*, ME *stansele* to ornament with diverse colors or spangles < MF *(e)stanceler(r)*, deriv. of *estencele* a spark, ornamental spangle < VL **stincilla*, metathetic var. of L *scintilla* SCINTILLA] **—sten′cil·er;** *esp. Brit.,* **sten′cil·ler,** *n.*

Stencil

Sten·dhal (sten däl′, stan-; *Fr.* stän dAl′), *n.* (*Marie Henri Beyle*) 1783–1842, French novelist and critic. **—Sten·dhal′i·an,** *adj.*

Steng·el (steng′gəl), *n.* **Charles Dillon** (*"Casey"*), born 1891, U.S. baseball player and manager.

sten′ gun′, a British light submachine gun. [*S(hep-pard)* + *T(urpin)* + *En(gland)*, the designers and their country]

sten·o (sten′ō), *n., pl.* **sten·os** for 1. **1.** a stenographer. **2.** the art or practice of a stenographer; stenography. [by shortening; see STENO-]

steno-, a learned borrowing from Greek meaning "narrow," "close," used in the formation of compound words: *stenopetalous.* [< Gk *stenó(s)*]

sten·o·cho·ric (sten′ə kôr′ik, -kōr′-), *adj. Ecol.* (of a plant or animal) not widely distributed geographically. Cf. **eurychoric.** [STENO- + L *chor-* place (< Gk *chṓr(os)* place, country) + -IC]

sten·o·graph (sten′ə graf′, -gräf′), *n.* **1.** any of various keyboard instruments, somewhat resembling a typewriter, used for writing in shorthand, as by means of phonetic or arbitrary symbols. **2.** a character written in shorthand. —*v.t.* **3.** to write in shorthand. [STENO- + -GRAPH]

ste·nog·ra·pher (stə nog′rə fər), *n.* a person who specializes in taking dictation in shorthand. Also, **ste·nog′ra·phist.** [STENOGRAPH + -ER[1]]

ste·nog·ra·phy (stə nog′rə fē), *n.* the art of writing in shorthand. [STENO- + -GRAPHY] —**sten·o·graph·ic** (sten′ə graf′ik), **sten′o·graph′i·cal,** *adj.* —**sten′o·graph′i·cal·ly,** *adv.*

sten·o·ha·line (sten′ə hā′līn, -lin, -hal′īn, -in), *adj. Ecol.* (of a plant or animal) restricted to an environment of only slightly varying salinity. Cf. **euryhaline.** [STENO- + Gk *hálin(os)* of salt, equiv. to *hál(s)* salt + *-inos* -INE[1]]

sten·o·pe·ic (sten′ə pē′ik), *adj.* **1.** pertaining to or containing a narrow slit or minute opening: *a stenopeic device to aid vision after eye surgery.* —*n.* **2.** a device, as of wood, metal, cardboard, etc., with a narrow horizontal slit, worn over the eyes for protection against bright sunlight. Also, **sten′o·pae′ic, sten·o·pa·ic** (sten′ə pā′ik). [STEN(O)- + Gk *opaí(os)* having a hole + -IC]

sten·o·pet·al·ous (sten′ō pet′ᵊləs), *adj. Bot.* having narrow petals. [STENO- + PETALOUS]

ste·noph·a·gous (sti nof′ə gəs), *adj. Ecol.* (of an animal) able to subsist on a limited variety of foods. Cf. **euryphagous.** [STENO- + -PHAGOUS]

sten·o·phyl·lous (sten′ō fil′əs), *adj. Bot.* having narrow leaves. [STENO- + -PHYLLOUS]

ste·nosed (sti nōst′, -nōzd′), *adj. Med.* characterized by stenosis; abnormally narrowed. [*stenose* to produce STENOSIS + -ED[2]]

ste·no·sis (sti nō′sis), *n. Pathol.* narrowing of a passage or vessel. [< NL < Gk *sténōsis.* See STENO-, -OSIS] —**ste·not·ic** (sti not′ik), *adj.*

sten·o·ther·mal (sten′ə thûr′məl), *adj. Ecol.* (of a plant or animal) able to withstand only slight variations in temperature. Also, **sten′o·ther′mic.** Cf. **eurythermal.** [STENO- + THERMAL]

sten·o·ther·mo·phile (sten′ə thûr′mə fil′, -fil), *n.* a stenothermophilic bacterium. [STENO- + THERMO- + -PHILE]

sten·o·ther·mo·phil·ic (sten′ə thûr′mə fil′ik), *adj.* (of obligate bacteria) growing best at temperatures of 60°C or higher. [STENO- + THERMO- + -PHILIC]

sten·o·top·ic (sten′ə top′ik), *adj. Ecol.* (of a plant or animal) able to tolerate only limited variations in conditions of the environment, as in temperature, humidity, etc. Cf. **eurytopic.** [STENO- + Gk *tóp(os)* place + -IC; see TOPIC]

Sten·o·type (sten′ə tīp′), *n.* **1.** *Trademark.* a keyboard machine resembling a typewriter, used in a system of phonetic shorthand. **2.** the symbols typed in one stroke on this machine.

sten·o·typ·y (sten′ə tī′pē), *n.* shorthand in which alphabetic letters or types are used to produce shortened forms of words or groups of words. [STENOTYPE + -Y[3]] —**sten·o·typ·ic** (sten′ə tip′ik), *adj.* —**sten′o·typ′ist,** *n.*

Sten·tor (sten′tôr), *n.* **1.** (in the *Iliad*) a Greek herald with a loud voice. **2.** (*l.c.*) a person having a very loud or powerful voice. **3.** (*l.c.*) a trumpet-shaped, ciliate protozoan of the genus *Stentor.*

sten·to·ri·an (sten tōr′ē ən, -tôr′-), *adj.* very loud or powerful in sound: *a stentorian voice.* [STENTOR + -IAN] —**sten·to′ri·an·ly,** *adv.*

sten·to·ri·ous (sten tōr′ē əs, -tôr′-), *adj.* stentorian. [STENTOR + -I- + -OUS] —**sten·to′ri·ous·ly,** *adv.*

step (step), *n., v.,* **stepped, step·ping.** —*n.* **1.** a movement made by lifting the foot and setting it down again in a new position, accompanied by a shifting of the weight of the body in the direction of the new position, as in walking, running, or dancing. **2.** such a movement followed by a movement of equal distance of the other foot: *The soldier took one step forward and stood at attention.* **3.** the space passed over or the distance measured by one movement of the foot in such a movement. **4.** the sound made by the foot in making such a movement. **5.** a mark or impression made by the foot on the ground; footprint. **6.** the manner of walking; gait; stride. **7.** pace in marching: *double-quick step.* **8.** a pace uniform with that of another or others, or in time with music. **9. steps,** movements or course in walking or running: *to retrace one's steps.* **10.** a move, act, or proceeding, as toward some end or in the general course of some action; stage, measure, or period: *the five steps to success.* **11.** rank, degree, or grade, as on a vertical scale. **12.** a support for the foot in ascending or descending: *a step of a ladder; a stair of 14 steps.* **13.** a very short distance: *She was never more than a step away from her children.* **14.** a repeated pattern or unit of movement in a dance formed by a combination of foot and body motions. **15.** *Music.* **a.** a degree of the staff or of the scale. **b.** the interval between two adjacent scale degrees; second. Cf. **semitone, whole step. 16. steps,** *Brit.* a stepladder. **17.** an offset part of anything. **18.** *Naut.* a socket, frame, or platform for supporting the lower end of a mast. **19.** *Quarrying.* a flat-topped ledge on the face of a quarry. **20.** *Radio Obsolesc.* a stage. **21. break step,** to interrupt or cease walking or marching in step: *The marching units were allowed to break step after they had passed the reviewing stand.* **22. in step, a.** moving in time to a rhythm or with the corresponding step of others. **b.** in harmony or conformity with: *They are not in step with the times.* **23. keep step,** to keep pace with; stay in step: *The construction of classrooms and the training of teachers have not kept step with population growth.* **24. out of step, a.** not in time to a rhythm; not corresponding to the step of others. **b.** not in harmony or conformity with: *They are out of step with the others in their group.* **25. step by step, a.** from one stage to the next in sequence. **b.** gradually and steadily: *We were shown the steelmaking process step by step.* **26. take steps,** to set about putting something into operation; begin to act: *I will take steps to see that your application is processed.* **27. watch one's step,** *Informal.* to proceed with caution; behave prudently: *If she doesn't watch her step, she will be fired from her job.* —*v.i.* **28.** to move, go, etc., by lifting the foot and setting it down again in a new position, or by using the feet alternately in this manner: *to step forward.* **29.** to walk, or go on foot, esp. for a few strides or a short distance: *Step over to the bar.* **30.** to move with measured steps, as in a dance. **31.** to go briskly or fast, as a horse. **32.** to obtain, find, win, come upon, etc., something easily and naturally, as if by a mere step of the foot: *to step into a good business opportunity.* **33.** to put the foot down; tread by intention or accident: *to step on a cat's tail.* **34.** to press with the foot, as on a lever, spring, or the like, in order to operate some mechanism. —*v.t.* **35.** to take (a step, pace, stride, etc.). **36.** to go through or perform the steps of (a dance). **37.** to move or set (the foot) in taking a step. **38.** to measure (a distance, ground, etc.) by steps (sometimes fol. by *off* or *out*). **39.** to make or arrange in the manner of a series of steps. **40.** *Naut.* to fix (a mast) in its step. **41. step down, a.** to lower or decrease by degrees. **b.** to relinquish one's authority or control; resign: *Although he was past retirement age, he refused to step down and let his son take over the business.* **42. step in,** to become involved in; enter into: *The brawl was well under way by the time the police stepped in.* **43. step on it,** *Slang.* to hasten one's activity or steps; hurry up: *If we don't step on it, we'll miss the show.* **44. step out, a.** to leave a place, esp. for a brief period of time. **b.** to walk or march at a more rapid pace. **c.** to go out to a social gathering or on a date: *We're stepping out tonight.* **45. step up, a.** to raise or increase by degrees: *to step up production.* **b.** to be promoted; advance. **c.** to make progress; improve. [ME *stepp(en),* OE *steppan;* c. OHG *stepfan;* akin to STAMP] —**step′less,** *adj.* —**step′like′,** *adj.*

step-, a prefix indicating connection between members of a family by the remarriage of a parent and not by blood: *stepbrother.* [ME; OE *stēop-;* c. G *stief-,* Icel *stjūp-* step-; akin to OE *āstēpan* to bereave, *bestēpan* to deprive (of children)]

step-and-re·peat (step′ən ri pēt′), *adj.* noting or pertaining to a process by which successive photo-offset plates are produced automatically or semi-automatically with great precision: used esp. in making plates for multicolor printing.

step·broth·er (step′bruth′ər), *n.* one's stepfather's son or stepmother's son by a former marriage. [late ME; see STEP-, BROTHER]

step·chair (step′châr′), *n.* a set of steps folding into a chair. [STEP + CHAIR]

step·child (step′chīld′), *n., pl.* **-child·ren.** a child of one's husband or wife by a former marriage. [ME; OE *stēopcild.* See STEP-, CHILD]

step′ cut′, *Jewelry.* a cut consisting of a rectangular girdle, often faceted, with two or more tiers of narrow facets running parallel to the girdle on both the crown and the pavilion: used esp. in stones in which color is more important than brilliance. Also called **trap cut.** —**step′-cut′,** *adj.*

step·dame (step′dām′), *n. Archaic.* a stepmother. [late ME; see STEP-, DAME]

step·dance (step′dans′, -däns′), *n.* a dance in which the steps are the most important characteristic; specifically, a solo dance with intricate, vigorous steps, often performed with the hands kept in the pockets. [STEP + DANCE] —**step′danc′er,** *n.* —**step′danc′ing,** *n.*

step·daugh·ter (step′dô′tər), *n.* a daughter of one's husband or wife by a former marriage. [ME *stepdohter,* OE *stēopdohtor.* See STEP-, DAUGHTER]

step-down (step′doun′), *adj. Elect.* serving to reduce or decrease voltage: *a step-down transformer.* [adj. use of v. phrase *step down*]

step·fa·ther (step′fä′thər), *n.* a man who occupies one's father's place by marriage to one's mother. [ME *stepfader,* OE *stēopfæder.* See STEP-, FATHER] —**step′fa′ther·ly,** *adv.*

step′ func′tion, *Math.* a function that is constant on each of a finite set of subintervals of its domain, the union of the subintervals being the domain.

Steph·a·na (stef′ə nə, ste fä′nə), *n.* a girl's given name. Also, **Stefana, Stefania, Stefanie, Stephania, Stephanie, Stephany.**

steph·a·ne (stef′ə nē), *n.* a hair ornament resembling a coronet, represented in Greek sculpture as wide in the center and narrowing toward the sides, worn high and forward on the head. [< Gk *stephánē,* akin to *stéphanos* crown]

Steph·a·nie (stef′ə nē), *n.* a girl's given name. Also, **Stefania, Stefanie, Stephana, Ste·pha·ni·a** (ste fä′nē ə), **Steph′a·ny.**

steph·an·ite (stef′ə nīt′), *n.* a mineral, silver antimony sulfide, Ag_5SbS_4: an ore of silver. [named after *Stephan,* Archduke of Austria (d. 1867); see -ITE[1]]

steph·a·no·tis (stef′ə nō′tis), *n.* any asclepiadaceous vine of the genus *Stephanotis,* having fragrant, waxy, white flowers and leathery leaves. [< NL < Gk *stephanōtís* (fem. adj.) fit for a crown, deriv. of *stéphanos* crown]

step·head (step′hed′), *n.* dropline. [STEP + HEAD]

Ste·phen (stē′vən), *n.* **1. Saint,** died A.D. c35, first Christian martyr. **2. Saint,** c975–1038, first king of Hungary 997–1038. **3.** (*Stephen of Blois*) 1097?–1154, king of England 1135–54. **4. Sir Leslie,** 1832–1904, English critic, biographer, and philosopher. **5.** Also, **Steven.** a boy's given name.

Stephen I, Saint, died A.D. 257?, pope 254–257.

Stephen II, died A.D. 757, pope 752–757.

Stephen III, died A.D. 772, pope 768–772.

Stephen IV, died A.D. 817, pope 816–817.

Stephen V, died A.D. 891, pope 885–891.

Stephen VI, died A.D. 897, pope 896–897.

Stephen VII, died A.D. 931, pope 928–931.

Stephen VIII, died A.D. 942, pope 939–942.

Stephen IX, died 1058, pope 1057–58.

Ste·phens (stē′vənz), *n.* **1. Alexander Hamilton,** 1812–83, U.S. statesman: vice-president of the Confederacy 1861–65. **2. James,** 1882–1950, Irish poet and novelist.

Ste·phen·son (stē′vən sən), *n.* **1. George,** 1781–1848, English inventor and engineer. **2.** his son **Robert,** 1803–59, English engineer.

Ste·phen·ville (stē′vən vil′), *n.* a town in central Texas. 7359 (1960).

step-in (step′in′), *adj.* **1.** (of garments, shoes, etc.) put on by being stepped into. —*n. Clothing.* **2. step-ins,** panties. **3.** any step-in garment. [adj., n. use of v. phrase *step in*]

step·lad·der (step′lad′ər), *n.* **1.** a ladder having flat steps or treads in place of rungs. **2.** any ladder, esp. a tall one with a hinged frame opening up to form four supporting legs. [STEP + LADDER]

step·moth·er (step′muth′ər), *n.* a woman who occupies one's mother's place by marriage to one's father. [ME *stepmoder,* OE *stēopmōdor.* See STEP-, MOTHER] —**step′moth′er·ly,** *adv.* —**step′moth′er·li·ness,** *n.*

Step·ney (step′nē), *n.* a borough of E London, England. 91,940 (1961).

step-off (step′ôf′, -of′), *n.* an abrupt drop, as from a shoreline into deep water. [n. use of v. phrase *step off*]

step-on (step′on′, -ôn′), *adj.* made to open by the operation of a pedal, as a can for kitchen garbage. [adj. use of v. phrase *step on*]

step·par·ent (step′pâr′ənt, -par′-), *n.* a stepfather or stepmother. [STEP- + PARENT]

steppe (step), *n.* **1.** an extensive plain, esp. one without trees. **2. The Steppes, a.** the vast Russian grasslands, esp. those in the S and E European and W and SW Asian parts of the Soviet Union. **b.** See **Kirghiz Steppe.** [< Russ *step′*]

stepped′ line′, dropline.

stepped-up (stept′up′), *adj.* increased; augmented; expanded; heightened.

Step·pen·wolf (*Ger.* shtep′ən vôlf′; *Eng.* step′ən-wo͝olf′), *n.* a novel (1927) by Hermann Hesse.

step·per (step′ər), *n.* **1.** a person or animal that steps, esp. a horse that lifts its front feet high at the knee. **2.** *Informal.* a dancer. [STEP + -ER[1]]

step′ping line′, *Shipbuilding.* bearding (defs. 1, 2). Also called **step′ping point′.**

step′ping stone′, 1. a stone, or one of a line of stones, in shallow water, a marshy place, or the like, that are stepped on in crossing. **2.** a stone for use in mounting or ascending. **3.** any means or stage of advancement or improvement: *He looked on the governorship as a stepping stone to the presidency.* Also, **step′ping·stone′.** [ME]

step′ rock′et, *Rocketry.* a multistage rocket that discards burned-out stages.

step·sis·ter (step′sis′tər), *n.* one's stepfather's or stepmother's daughter by a previous marriage. [late ME; see STEP-, SISTER]

step·son (step′sun′), *n.* a son of one's husband or wife by a former marriage. [ME *stepsone,* OE *stēopsunu.* See STEP-, SON]

Step·te·ri·a (step tēr′ē ə), *n.* (*sometimes construed as pl.*) an ancient festival at Delphi commemorating the slaying of Python by Apollo.

step·stool (step′sto͞ol′), *n.* a low set of hinged steps, often folding into or under a stool, used typically in a kitchen for reaching high shelves. [STEP + STOOL]

step·toe (step′tō′), *n. Western U.S.* an isolated hill or mountain surrounded by lava. [STEP + TOE]

step′ turn′, *Skiing.* a turn in which a skier lifts one ski from the snow, faces the ski slightly outward in the direction to be turned, sets it down, and brings the other ski around so that both skis are parallel.

step-up (step′up′), *adj.* **1.** effecting an increase. **2.** *Elect.* serving to increase voltage: *a step-up transformer.* **3.** (of a lease) allowing for gradual rent increases to the highest amount permissible. —*n.* **4.** an increase or rise in the rate or quantity of something. [adj., n. use of v. phrase *step up*]

step·wise (step′wīz′), *adv.* **1.** in a steplike arrangement. **2.** *Music.* from one adjacent tone to another: *The melody ascends stepwise.* —*adj.* **3.** *Music.* moving from one adjacent tone to another: *stepwise melodic progression.* [STEP + -WISE]

-ster, a suffix used in forming nouns, often derogatory, referring especially to occupation or habit or association: *songster; gamester; trickster.* [ME, OE *-estre;* c. D *-ster,* MLG *-(e)ster*]

ster., sterling.

ste·ra·di·an (stə rā′dē ən), *n. Geom.* a solid angle at the center of a sphere subtending a section on the surface equal in area to the square of the radius of the sphere. *Abbr.:* sr [STERE(O)- + RADIAN]

ster·co·ra·ceous (stûr′kə rā′shəs), *adj. Physiol.* consisting of, resembling, or pertaining to dung or feces. Also, **ster·co·rous** (stûr′kər əs). [< L *stercor-* (s. of *stercus*) dung + -ACEOUS]

ster·co·ric·o·lous (stûr′kə rik′ə ləs), *adj.* living in dung. [*stercor-* (see STERCORACEOUS) + -I- + -COLOUS]

ster·cu·li·a·ceous (stûr kyo͞o′lē ā′shəs), *adj.* belonging to the *Sterculiaceae,* a family of trees and shrubs comprising the cacao and kola nut trees. [< NL *sterculi(a)* (special use of *Sterculius* Roman god of manuring) + -ACEOUS]

stere (stēr), *n. Metric System.* a cubic meter equivalent to 35.315 cubic feet or 1.3080 cubic yards, used to measure cordwood. *Abbr.:* s [< F *stère* < Gk *stere(ós)* solid]

ster·e·o (ster′ē ō′, stēr′-), *n., pl.* **ster·e·os,** *adj., v.* —*n.* **1.** stereoscopic photography. **2.** a stereoscopic photograph. **3.** stereophonic sound reproduction. **4.** a system or the equipment for reproducing stereophonic sound. **5.** *Print.* stereotype (defs. 1, 2). —*adj.* **6.** pertaining to stereophonic sound, stereoscopic photography, etc. —*v.t.* **7.** *Print.* stereotype (def. 5). [by shortening]

stereo-, a learned borrowing from Greek, where it meant "solid", used with reference to hardness, solidity, three-dimensionality in the formation of compound words: *stereochemistry; stereogram; stereoscope.* Also, *esp. before a vowel,* **stere-.** [< Gk *stereó(s)*]

stereo., stereotype.

ster·e·o·bate (ster′ē ə bāt′, stēr′-), *n. Archit.* **1.** the foundation or base upon which a building or the like is erected. **2.** the solid platform forming the floor and substructure of a classical temple; crepidoma; podium. Cf. **stylobate.** [< L *stereobat(a)* < Gk *stero-* STEREO- + *-batēs* walker; cf. STYLOBATE] —**ster·e·o·bat·ic** (ster′ē ə bat′ik, stēr′-), *adj.*

ster·e·o·cam·er·a (ster′ē ō kam′ər ə, -kam′rə, stēr′-), *n.* a stereoscopic camera. [STEREO- + CAMERA]

ster·e·o·chem·is·try (ster′ē ō kem′i strē, stēr′-), *n.* the branch of chemistry that deals with the determination of the relative positions in space of the atoms or groups of atoms in a compound and with the effects of these positions on the properties of the compound. [STEREO- + CHEMISTRY] —**ster·e·o·chem·ic** (ster′ē ō kem′ik, stēr′-), **ster′e·o·chem′i·cal,** *adj.* —**ster′e·o·chem′i·cal·ly,** *adv.*

ster·e·o·chrome (ster′ē ə krōm′, stēr′-), *n.* a picture produced by a process in which water glass is used as a vehicle or as a preservative coating. [back formation from STEREOCHROMY]

ster·e·o·chro·my (ster′ē ə krō′mē, stēr′-), *n.* the stereochrome process. Also called **waterglass painting.** [STEREO- + *-chromy* (see -CHROME, -Y[3])] —**ster′e·o·chro′mic, ster·e·o·chro·mat·ic** (ster′ē ō krə mat′ik, -krō-, stēr′-), *adj.* —**ster′e·o·chro′mi·cal·ly, ster′e·o·chro·mat′i·cal·ly,** *adv.*

ster·e·og·no·sis (ster′ē og nō′sis, stēr′-), *n.* the ability to determine the shape and weight of an object by touching or lifting it. [< NL; see STEREO-, -GNOSIS] —**ster·e·og·nos·tic** (ster′ē og nos′tik, stēr′-), *adj.*

ster·e·o·gram (ster′ē ə gram′, stēr′-), *n.* **1.** a diagram or picture representing objects in a way to give the impression of solidity. **2.** a stereograph. [STEREO- + -GRAM[1]]

ster·e·o·graph (ster′ē ə graf′, -gräf′, stēr′-), *n.* **1.** a single or double picture for a stereoscope. —*v.t.* **2.** to make a stereograph of. [STEREO- + -GRAPH]

ster·e·og·ra·pher (ster′ē og′rə fər, stēr′-), *n.* one who takes stereoscopic photographs. [STEREOGRAPH + -ER[1]]

ster′eograph′ic projec′tion, *Math.* a one-to-one correspondence between the points on a sphere and the extended complex plane where the north pole on the sphere corresponds to the point at infinity of the plane. Cf. **extended complex plane.**

ster·e·og·ra·phy (ster′ē og′rə fē, stēr′-), *n.* the art of delineating the forms of solid bodies on a plane; a branch of solid geometry dealing with the construction of regularly defined solids. [STEREO- + -GRAPHY] —**ster·e·o·graph·ic** (ster′ē ə graf′ik, stēr′-), **ster′e·o·graph′i·cal,** *adj.* —**ster′e·o·graph′i·cal·ly,** *adv.*

ster·e·o·i·so·mer (ster′ē ō ī′sə mər, stēr′-), *n. Chem.* any of two or more isomers exhibiting stereoisomerism. [STEREO- + ISOMER]

ster·e·o·i·so·mer·ic (ster′ē ō ī′sə mer′ik, stēr′-), *adj. Chem.* pertaining to or exhibiting stereoisomerism. [STEREOISOMER(ISM) + -IC]

ster·e·o·i·som·er·ism (ster′ē ō ī som′ə riz′əm, stēr′-), *n. Chem.* the isomerism ascribed to different relative positions of the atoms or groups of atoms in the molecules of optically active organic compounds. [STEREO- + ISOMERISM]

ster·e·om·e·try (ster′ē om′i trē, stēr′-), *n.* the measurement of volumes. [< NL *stereometria.* See STEREO-, -METRY] —**ster·e·o·met·ric** (ster′ē ə me′trik, stēr′-), **ster′e·o·met′ri·cal,** *adj.* —**ster′e·o·met′ri·cal·ly,** *adv.*

ster·e·o·mi·cro·scope (ster′ē ō mī′krə skōp′, stēr′-), *n.* See **stereoscopic microscope.** [STEREO- + MICROSCOPE] —**ster·e·o·mi·cros·co·py** (ster′ē ō mī kros′kə pē, -mī′krə skō′pē, stēr′-), *n.*

ster·e·o·pair (ster′ē ō pâr′, stēr′-), *n. Photogrammetry.* a pair of photographs of the same area taken from slightly different positions so as to give a stereoscopic effect when properly mounted and viewed. [STEREO + PAIR]

ster·e·o·phon·ic (ster′ē ə fon′ik, stēr′-), *adj.* of or noting a system of separately placed microphones or loudspeakers for imparting greater realism of sound, used esp. with wide-screen motion pictures, high-fidelity recordings, etc. (opposed to *monaural*). [STEREO- + PHONIC] —**ster′e·o·phon′i·cal·ly,** *adv.*

ster·e·oph·o·ny (ster′ē of′ə nē, stēr′-, ster′ē ə fō′nē, stēr′-), *n.* the state or condition of being stereophonic. [STEREO- + -PHONY]

ster·e·o·pho·tog·ra·phy (ster′ē ō fə tog′rə fē, stēr′-), *n.* photography producing stereoscopic images. [STEREO- + PHOTOGRAPHY] —**ster·e·o·pho·to·graph** (ster′ē ō fō′tə graf′, -gräf′, stēr′-), *n.* —**ster′e·o·pho′to·graph′ic** (ster′ē ō fō′tə graf′ik, stēr′-), *adj.*

ster·e·op·sis (ster′ē op′sis, stēr′-), *n.* stereoscopic vision. [STERE(O)- + -OPSIS]

ster·e·op·ter (ster′ē op′tər, stēr′-), *n. Ophthalm.* an apparatus for measuring depth perception. [STERE(O)- + Gk *optēr* looker, equiv. to *op-* (see -OPSIS) + *-tēr* agent suffix]

ster·e·op·ti·con (ster′ē op′tə kən, -kon′, stēr′-), *n. Optics.* a projector usually consisting of two complete lanterns arranged so that one picture appears to dissolve while the next is forming. [STERE(O)- + Gk *optikón* (neut.) OPTIC] —**ster′e·op′ti·can,** *adj.* —**ster·e·op·ti·cian** (ster′ē op tish′ən, stēr′-), *n.*

ster·e·o·scope (ster′ē ə skōp′, stēr′-), *n.* an optical instrument through which two pictures of the same object, taken from slightly different points of view, are viewed, one by each eye, producing the effect of a single picture of the object, with the appearance of depth or relief. [STEREO- + -SCOPE]

ster·e·o·scop·ic (ster′ē ə skop′ik, stēr′-), *adj.* **1.** noting or pertaining to three-dimensional vision or any of various processes and devices for giving the illusion of depth from two-dimensional images or reproductions, as of a photograph, motion picture, etc. **2.** of, relating to, or characterized by a stereoscope or stereoscopy. Also, **ster′e·o·scop′i·cal.** [STEREOSCOPE + -IC] —**ster′e·o·scop′i·cal·ly,** *adv.*

ster′eoscop′ic mi′croscope, a microscope that produces a three-dimensional image of an object by focusing on the object from slightly different positions in each of two lenses.

ster·e·os·co·py (ster′ē os′kə pē, stēr′-), *n.* **1.** the study of the stereoscope and its techniques. **2.** three-dimensional vision. [STEREO- + -SCOPY] —**ster′e·os′co·pist,** *n.*

ster·e·o·tax·is (ster′ē ə tak′sis, stēr′-), *n. Biol.* movement of an organism in response to contact with a solid. [STEREO- + -TAXIS] —**ster·e·o·tac·tic** (ster′ē ə tak′tik, stēr′-), *adj.* —**ster′e·o·tac′ti·cal·ly,** *adv.*

ster·e·ot·o·my (ster′ē ot′ə mē, stēr′-), *n.* the technique of cutting solids, as stones, to specified forms and dimensions. [STEREO- + -TOMY] —**ster·e·o·tom·ic** (ster′ē ə tom′ik, stēr′-), **ster′e·o·tom′i·cal,** *adj.* —**ster′e·ot′o·mist,** *n.*

ster·e·ot·ro·pism (ster′ē o′trə piz′əm, stēr′-), *n. Biol.* a tropism determined by contact with a solid. [STEREO- + TROPISM]

ster·e·o·type (ster′ē ə tīp′, stēr′-), *n., v.,* **-typed, -typ·ing.** —*n.* **1.** a process of making metal printing plates by taking a mold of composed type or the like in papier-mâché or other material and then taking from this mold a cast in type metal. **2.** a plate made by this process. **3.** a set form; convention. **4.** *Sociol.* a simplified and standardized conception or image invested with special meaning and held in common by members of a group: *The cowboy and Indian are American stereotypes.* —*v.t.* **5.** to make a stereotype of. **6.** to give a fixed form to. [STEREO- + -TYPE] —**ster′e·o·typ′er, ster′e·o·typ′ist,** *n.* —**ster·e·o·typ·ic** (ster′ē ə tip′ik, stēr′-), **ster′e·o·typ′i·cal,** *adj.*

ster·e·o·typed (ster′ē ə tīpt′, stēr′-), *adj.* **1.** reproduced in or by stereotype plates. **2.** fixed or settled in form; hackneyed; conventional. [STEREOTYPE + -ED[2]] —**Syn. 2.** lifeless, stale, worn, dull. See **commonplace.** —**Ant. 2.** rare, unusual.

ster·e·o·typ·y (ster′ē ə tī′pē, stēr′-), *n.* the stereotype process. [STEREOTYPE + -Y[3]]

ster·ic (ster′ik, stēr′-), *adj. Chem.* of or pertaining to the spatial relationships of atoms in a molecule. Also, **ster′i·cal.** [STER(EO)- + -IC] —**ster′i·cal·ly,** *adv.*

ste·rig·ma (sti rig′mə), *n., pl.* **-ma·ta** (-mə tə). *Bot.* a small stalk that bears a sporangium, a conidium, or esp. a basidiospore. [< NL < Gk: a support, equiv. to *stērίz(ein)* (to) support + *-ma* n. suffix] —**ster·ig·mat·ic** (ster′ig mat′ik), *adj.*

ster·i·lant (ster′ə lənt), *n. Chem.* a sterilizing agent. [STERILE + -ANT]

ster·ile (ster′il *or, esp. Brit.,* -īl), *adj.* **1.** free from living germs or microorganisms: *sterile surgical instruments.* **2.** incapable of producing offspring; not producing offspring. **3.** barren; not producing vegetation: *sterile soil.* **4.** *Bot.* **a.** noting a plant in which reproductive structures fail to develop. **b.** bearing no stamens or pistils. **5.** not productive of results, ideas, etc.; fruitless. [< L *steril(is)* unfruitful] —**ster′ile·ly,** *adv.* —**ste·ril·i·ty** (stə ril′i tē), **ster′ile·ness,** *n.*

—**Syn. 1.** uncontaminated, unpolluted, antiseptic. **2.** infecund, unfruitful. **3.** fruitless. —**Ant. 2, 3.** fertile.

ster·i·lise (ster′ə līz′), *v.t.,* **-lised, -lis·ing.** *Chiefly Brit.* sterilize. —**ster′i·lis′a·bil′i·ty,** *n.* —**ster′i·lis′a·ble,** *adj.* —**ster′i·lis′er,** *n.*

ster·i·li·za·tion (ster′ə li zā′shən), *n.* **1.** the act of sterilizing. **2.** the condition of being sterilized. **3.** the destruction of all living microorganisms, as pathogenic or saprophytic bacteria, vegetative forms, and spores. Also, *esp. Brit.,* **ster′i·li·sa′tion.** [STERILE + -IZATION]

ster·i·lize (ster′ə līz′), *v.t.,* **-lized, -liz·ing. 1.** to destroy microorganisms in or on, usually by bringing to a high temperature with steam, dry heat, or boiling liquid. **2.** to destroy the ability to reproduce by removing the sex organs or inhibiting their functions. **3.** to make (land) barren or unproductive. Also, *esp. Brit.,* **sterilise.** [STERILE + -IZE] —**ster′i·liz′abil′i·ty,** *n.* —**ster′i·liz′a·ble,** *adj.* —**ster′i·liz′er,** *n.*

ster·let (stûr′lit), *n.* a small sturgeon, *Acipenser ruthenus,* found in the areas of the Black and Caspian seas, valued as a source of caviar. [< Russ *sterlyad′*]

ster·ling (stûr′ling), *adj.* **1.** noting, of, or pertaining to British money: *The sterling equivalent is 6s. 8d.* **2.** (of silver) having the standard fineness of .925. **3.** made of silver of this fineness: *a sterling teapot.* **4.** thoroughly excellent: *a man of sterling worth.* —*n.* **5.** the standard of fineness for gold and silver coin in the United Kingdom: now 0.91666 for gold and 0.500 for silver; formerly 0.995 for gold and 0.925 for silver. **6.** silver having a fineness of .925, now used esp. in the manufacture of table utensils, jewelry, etc. **7.** manufactured articles of sterling silver. [ME: name of a silver coin; OE **steorling* (see STAR, -LING[1]) with reference to the little star on some of the mintages] —**ster′ling·ly,** *adv.* —**ster′ling·ness,** *n.*

Ster·ling (stûr′ling), *n.* **1.** a city in NW Illinois. 15,688 (1960). **2.** a boy's given name.

ster′ling bloc′, those countries having currencies whose values tend to vary directly with the rise and fall of the value of the pound sterling. Also called **ster′ling ar′ea.**

Ster·li·ta·mak (sterʟ′li tä mäk′), *n.* a city in the RSFSR, in the E Soviet Union in Europe, W of the Southern Urals. 131,000 (est. 1962).

stern[1] (stûrn), *adj.* **1.** firm, strict, or uncompromising: *stern discipline.* **2.** hard, harsh, or severe: *a stern reprimand.* **3.** rigorous or austere; of an unpleasantly serious character: *stern times.* **4.** grim or forbidding in aspect: *a stern face.* [ME; OE *styrne* < Gmc **star-* (see STARE, STARVE) + **-nio-* suffix] —**stern′ly,** *adv.* —**stern′ness,** *n.*

—**Syn. 1, 2.** adamant, unrelenting, unsympathetic, cruel, unfeeling. STERN, SEVERE, HARSH agree in referring to methods, aspects, manners, or facial expressions. STERN implies uncompromising, inflexible firmness, and sometimes a hard, forbidding, or withdrawn aspect or nature: *a stern parent.* SEVERE implies strictness, lack of sympathy, and a tendency to impose a hard discipline on others: *a severe judge.* HARSH suggests a great severity and roughness, and cruel, unfeeling treatment of others: *a harsh critic.* —**Ant. 1.** lenient.

stern[2] (stûrn), *n.* **1.** the after part of a vessel (often opposed to *stem*). **2.** the back or rear of anything. **3.** (*cap.*) *Astron.* the constellation Puppis. **4.** *Fox Hunting.* the tail of a hound. **5. by the stern,** *Naut.* drawing more water aft than forward. [ME *sterne* < Scand; cf. Icel *stjǫrn* steering (done aft; see STERNPOST)]

Stern (stûrn), *n.* **1. Isaac,** born 1920, U.S. violinist, born in Russia. **2. Otto,** born 1888, U.S. physicist, born in Germany: Nobel prize 1943.

stern-, var. of **sterno-** before a vowel: *sternite.*

ster·nal (stûr′nəl), *adj.* of or pertaining to the sternum. [< NL *sternāl(is).* See STERNUM, -AL[1]]

stern·ber·gi·a (stûrn bûr′gē ə, -jē ə), *n.* any of several bulbous herbs of the genus *Sternbergia,* of Europe and Asia, having yellow flowers that bloom in the autumn, grown as an ornamental. [< NL, named after Count Kasper *Sternberg* (d. 1838); see -IA]

stern′ chase′, *Naut.* a chase in which the pursuing vessel follows astern or in the wake of the other.

stern′ chas′er, a cannon mounted at or near the stern of a sailing ship, facing aft.

Sterne (stûrn), *n.* **Laurence,** 1713–68, English clergyman and novelist.

stern·fore·most (stûrn′fōr′mōst, -fôr′- *or, esp. Brit.,* -məst), *adv.* **1.** *Naut.* with the stern foremost. **2.** awkwardly; with difficulty. [STERN[2] + FOREMOST]

stern′ frame′, *Naut.* a framework used in place of a sternpost to accomodate a propeller placed amidships, consisting of a propeller post and rudder post, one or the other being regarded as the sternpost, connected at their bottoms by a shoe.

stern′ gal′lery, *Naut.* an open platform at the stern of a ship, below the level of the quarterdeck.

ster·nite (stûr′nīt), *n. Entomol.* a sclerite of the sternum of an insect, esp. a ventral sclerite of an abdominal segment. [STERN- + -ITE[1]] —**ster·nit·ic** (stər nit′ik), *adj.*

stern′ knee′, *Naut.* a knee in a wooden ship forming part of the deadwood of the stern and reinforcing the angle between the keel and the sternpost.

stern·most (stûrn′mōst *or, esp. Brit.,* -məst), *adj. Naut.* **1.** farthest aft. **2.** nearest the stern. [STERN[2] + -MOST]

sterno-, a combining form of **sternum:** *sternocostal.* Also, *esp. before a vowel,* **stern-.**

ster·no·clei·do·mas·toid (stûr′nō klī′də mas′toid), *Anat.* —*adj.* **1.** of, pertaining to, or involving the sternum, the clavicle, and the mastoid process. —*n.* **2.** a thick muscle on each side of the neck, the action of which assists in bending the head and neck forward and sideways. [< NL *sternocleidomastoid(es).* See STERNO-, CLEIDO-, MASTOID]

ster·no·cos·tal (stûr′nō kos′təl, -kô′stəl), *adj. Anat., Zool.* of, pertaining to, or situated between the sternum and ribs. [STERNO- + COSTAL]

stern·post (stûrn′pōst′), *n. Naut.* an upright member rising from the after end of a keel; a rudderpost or propeller post. Also called **body post.** Cf. **stern frame.** [STERN[2] + POST[1]]

stern′ sheets′, *Naut.* the after part of an open boat, occupied by the person in command or by passengers.

stern·son (stûrn′sən), *n.* a knee in a timber-framed vessel, reinforcing the angle between the keelson and the sternpost. [STERN[2] + (KEEL)SON]

ster·num (stûr′nəm), *n., pl.* **-na** (-nə), **-nums. 1.** *Anat., Zool.* a bone or series of bones extending along the middle line of the ventral portion of the body of most vertebrates, consisting in man of a flat, narrow bone connected with the clavicles and the true ribs; breastbone. See diag. under **skeleton. 2.** the ventral surface of a body segment of an arthropod. [< NL < Gk *stérnon* chest, breastbone]

ster·nu·ta·tion (stûr′nyə tā′shən), *n.* act of sneezing. [< L *sternūtātiōn-* (s. of *sternūtātiō*), equiv. to *sternūtāt(us)* (ptp. of *sternūtāre,* freq. of *sternuere* to sneeze) + *-iōn-* -ION]

ster·nu·ta·tor (stûr′nyə tā′tər), *n. Chemical Warfare.* a chemical agent causing nose irritation, coughing, etc. [back formation from STERNUTATORY]

ster·nu·ta·to·ry (stər nōō′tə tōr′ē, -tôr′ē, -nyōō′-), *adj., n., pl.* **-ries.** —*adj.* **1.** Also, **ster·nu′ta·tive.** causing or tending to cause sneezing. —*n.* **2.** a sternutatory substance. [< LL *sternūtātōri(us),* equiv. to *sternūtāt(us)* (see STERNUTATION) + *-ōrius* -ORY[1]]

stern·ward (stûrn′wərd), *adv.* toward the stern; astern. [STERN[2] + -WARD]

stern·way (stûrn′wā′), *n.* **1.** *Naut.* the movement of a vessel backward, or stern foremost. **2. have sternway on,** (of a vessel) to move or be moving backwards. [STERN[2] + WAY]

stern-wheel (stûrn′hwēl′, -wēl′), *adj.* (of a vessel) propelled by a paddle wheel at the stern.

stern·wheel (stûrn′hwēl′, -wēl′), *n. Naut.* a paddle wheel at the stern of a vessel. [STERN[2] + WHEEL]

stern·wheel·er (stûrn′hwē′lər, -wē′-), *n.* a boat propelled by a paddle wheel at the stern. [STERNWHEEL + -ER[1]]

Stern wheeler

ster·oid (ster′oid, stēr′-), *Biochem.* —*n.* **1.** any of a large group of fat-soluble organic compounds, as the sterols, bile acids, and sex hormones, most of which have specific physiological action. —*adj.* **2.** Also, **ste·roi·dal** (ste roid′əl, sti-). pertaining to or characteristic of a steroid. [STER(OL) + -OID]

ster·ol (ster′ōl, -ol, stēr′-), *n. Biochem.* any of a group of solid, mostly unsaturated, polycyclic alcohols, as cholesterol and ergosterol, derived from plants or animals. [STER(IC) + -OL[1]]

Ster·o·pe (ster′ə pē′), *n. Class. Myth.* one of the Pleiades and the mother of Oenomaus by Ares. Also called **Asterope.**

Ster·o·pes (stûr′ə pēz′), *n. Class. Myth.* one of the Cyclopes.

ster·tor (stûr′tər), *n. Pathol.* a heavy snoring sound accompanying respiration in certain diseases. [< L *stert-* (s. of *stertere* to snore) + -OR[1]]

ster·to·rous (stûr′tər əs), *adj.* **1.** characterized by stertor or heavy snoring. **2.** breathing in this manner. [STERTOR + -OUS] —**ster′to·rous·ly,** *adv.* —**ster′to·rous·ness,** *n.*

stet (stet), *v.,* **stet·ted, stet·ting.** —*v.i.* **1.** let it stand (used imperatively as a direction on a printer's proof, manuscript, or the like, to retain material previously cancelled, usually accompanied by a row of dots under or beside the material). —*v.t.* **2.** to mark (a manuscript, printer's proof, etc.) with the word "stet" or with dots as a direction to let cancelled material remain. [< L, pres. subj. 3rd pers. sing. of *stāre* to stand]

stetho-, a learned borrowing from Greek meaning "chest," used in the formation of compound words: *stethoscope.* [comb. form of Gk *stêthos*]

ste·thom·e·ter (ste thom′i tər), *n.* an instrument for measuring the respiratory movements of the walls of the chest and abdomen. [STETHO- + -METER] —**steth·o·met·ric** (steth′ə me′trik), *adj.* —**ste·thom′e·try,** *n.*

Stethoscope

steth·o·scope (steth′ə skōp′), *n.* *Med.* an instrument used in auscultation to convey sounds in the chest or other parts of the body to the ear of the examiner. [STETHO- + -SCOPE] —**steth′o·scoped′,** *adj.* —**ste·thos·co·pist** (ste thos′kə pist), *n.* —**ste·thos·co·py** (ste thos′kə pē, steth′ə skō′-), *n.*

steth·o·scop·ic (steth′ə skop′ik), *adj.* **1.** pertaining to the stethoscope or to stethoscopy. **2.** made or obtained by the stethoscope: *Stethoscopic study of his chest revealed a peculiar heartbeat.* Also, **steth′o·scop′i·cal.** [STETHOSCOPE + -IC] —**steth′o·scop′i·cal·ly,** *adv.*

St.-É·tienne (saN tā tyen′), *n.* a city in and the capital of Loire, in SE France. 203,633 (1962).

Stet·son (stet′sən), *n.* (*often l.c.*) *Slang.* a felt hat with a broad brim and high crown, esp. one worn as part of a cowboy's outfit. [after the trademark]

Stet·tin (shte tēn′), *n.* a seaport in NW Poland: formerly in Germany. 291,000 (est. 1963). Polish, **Szczecin.**

Stet·tin·i·us (stə tin′ē əs), *n.* **Edward Reil·ley** (rī′lē), 1900–49, U.S. industrialist: Secretary of State 1944–45.

Steu·ben (sto͞o′bən, styo͞o′-, sto͞o ben′, styo͞o-; *Ger.* shtoi′bən), *n.* **Frie·drich Wil·helm Lu·dolf Ger·hard Au·gus·tin von** (frē′drikн vil′helm lo͞o′dôlf gär′härt ou′go͞os tēn′ fən), 1730–94, Prussian major general in the American Revolutionary army.

Steu·ben·ville (sto͞o′bən vil, styo͞o′-), *n.* a city in E Ohio, on the Ohio River. 32,495 (1960).

St. Eu·sta·ti·us (yo͞o stā′shē əs, -shəs), an island in the Netherlands Antilles, in the E West Indies. 1026 (est. 1960); 7 sq. mi.

Steve (stēv), *n.* a boy's given name, form of **Steven** or **Stephen.**

ste·ve·dore (stē′vi dōr′, -dôr′), *n., v.,* **-dored, -dor·ing.** —*n.* **1.** a firm or individual engaged in the loading or unloading of a vessel. —*v.t.* **2.** to load or unload the cargo of (a ship). —*v.i.* **3.** to load or unload a vessel. [< Sp (*e*)*stibador,* equiv. to *estib(ar)* (to) pack, stow (see STEEVE¹) + *-ad-* -ATE¹ + *-or* -OR²]

ste′vedore's knot′, a knot that forms a lump in a line to prevent it from passing through a hole or grommet.

Ste·ven (stē′vən), *n.* a boy's given name. Also, **Stephen.**

Ste·ven·age (stē′və nij), *n.* a town in N Hertfordshire, in SE England. 42,422 (1961).

Ste·vens (stē′vənz), *n.* **1. Alfred,** 1817–75, English painter and sculptor. **2. George (Cooper),** 1904–75, U.S. motion-picture director. **3. John Cox** (koks), 1749–1838, and his son **Robert Livingston,** 1787–1856, U.S. engineers and inventors. **4. John Paul,** born 1920, U.S. jurist: associate justice of the U.S. Supreme Court since 1975. **5. Thaddeus,** 1792–1868, U.S. abolitionist and political leader. **6. Wallace,** 1879–1955, U.S. poet.

Ste·ven·son (stē′vən sən), *n.* **1. Ad·lai Ew·ing** (ad′lā yo͞o′ing), 1835–1914, vice-president of the U.S. 1893–97. **2.** his grandson, **Adlai E(wing),** 1900–65, U.S. statesman and diplomat: ambassador to the U.N. 1960–65. **3. Andrew,** 1784–1857, U.S. politician: Speaker of the House 1827–34. **4. Robert Louis** (*Robert Lewis Balfour*), 1850–94, Scottish novelist, essayist, and poet.

Ste′vens Point′, a city in central Wisconsin. 17,837 (1960).

Ste·vin (stə vīn′), *n.* **Si·mon** (sē′mōn), 1548–1620, Dutch mathematician and physicist.

Stev·i·nus (sti vē′nəs *or, for 2,* stev′ə nəs), *n.* **1.** See **Stevin, Simon. 2.** a crater in the fourth quadrant of the face of the moon: about 50 miles in diameter.

stew (sto͞o, styo͞o), *v.t.* **1.** to cook (food) by simmering or slow boiling. —*v.i.* **2.** to undergo cooking by simmering or slow boiling. **3.** *Informal.* to fret, worry, or fuss: *He stewed about his chaotic state of affairs all day.* **4.** to feel uncomfortable due to a hot, humid, stuffy atmosphere, as in a closed room; swelter. **5. stew in one's own juice,** to suffer the consequences of one's own actions. —*n.* **6.** a preparation of meat, fish, or other food cooked by stewing, esp. a mixture of meat and vegetables. **7.** *Informal.* a state of agitation, uneasiness, or worry. **8.** *Obs.* a vessel for boiling or stewing. [late ME *stue(n)* (to) take a vapor bath < MF (*e*)*stuve(r)* < VL **extūfāre,* equiv. to *ex-* EX-¹ + **tūf(us)* steam < Gk *tŷphos;* see TYPHUS] —**stew′a·ble,** *adj.* —**Syn. 1.** See **boil¹. 6.** ragout.

stew·ard (sto͞o′ərd, styo͞o′-), *n.* **1.** one who manages another's property or financial affairs; one who administers anything as the agent of another or others. **2.** one who has charge of the household of another, buying or obtaining food, directing the servants, etc. **3.** an employee who has charge of the table, wine, servants, etc., in a club, restaurant, or the like. **4.** one who attends to the domestic concerns of persons on board a vessel, as in overseeing maids and waiters. **5.** an employee on a ship, train, or airplane who waits on and is responsible for the comfort of passengers, takes orders for or distributes food, etc. **6.** a person appointed by an organization or group to supervise the affairs of that group at certain functions. **7.** *U.S. Navy.* a petty officer in charge of officer's quarters and mess. —*v.t.* **8.** to act as steward of; manage. —*v.i.* **9.** to act or serve as steward. [ME; OE *stīweard, stigweard,* equiv. to *stig* hall (see STY¹) + *weard* WARD²] —**stew′ard·ship′,** *n.*

stew·ard·ess (sto͞o′ər dis, styo͞o′-), *n.* a woman who works as a steward, esp. on an airplane, ship, or train. [STEWARD + -ESS]

stew′ard's depart′ment, *Naut.* the department of a merchant vessel concerned with the feeding, housing, and other personal requirements of the passengers and crew.

Stew·art (sto͞o′ərt, styo͞o′-), *n.* **1.** See **Darnley, Lord Henry. 2. Du·gald** (do͞o′gəld, dyo͞o′-), 1753–1828, Scottish philosopher. **3. Potter,** 1915–85, U.S. jurist: associate justice of the U.S. Supreme Court 1958–81. **4.** a boy's given name. Also, **Stuart** (for defs. 1, 4).

Stew′art Is′land, one of the islands of New Zealand, S of South Island. 542 (1961); 670 sq. mi.

stew·bum (sto͞o′bum′, styo͞o′-), *n.* *Slang.* a drunken bum. [STEW + BUM]

stewed (sto͞od, styo͞od), *adj.* **1.** cooked by simmering or slow boiling, as food. **2.** *Slang.* intoxicated; drunk. [late ME; see STEW, -ED²]

stew·pan (sto͞o′pan′, styo͞o′-), *n.* a pan for stewing; saucepan. [STEW + PAN¹]

stew·pot (sto͞o′pot′, styo͞o′-), *n.* a large, heavy, covered pot used for making stews. [STEW + POT¹]

St. Ex., Stock Exchange.

stey (stā), *adj.* *Scot.* steep. [ME *stay,* OE **stǣge* (cf. *stǣgel* steep); c. G *Steil*]

stg., sterling.

St. Gal·len (gä′lən), **1.** a canton in NE Switzerland. 339,489 (1960); 777 sq. mi. **2.** a city in and the capital of this canton. 76,279 (1960). French, **St. Gall** (saN-gal′).

stge., storage.

St. George, a town in SW Utah. 5130 (1960).

St. George's (jôr′jiz), a seaport in SW Grenada, in the SE West Indies. 26,894 (1960).

St. George's Channel, a channel between Wales and Ireland, connecting the Irish Sea and the Atlantic. 100 mi. long; 50–90 mi. wide.

St.-Ger·main (saN zher maN′), *n.* St.-Germain-en-Laye.

St.-Ger·main-des-Prés (saN zher maN′ dā prā′), *n.* an area in Paris, on the Left Bank.

St.-Ger·main-en-Laye (saN zher maN′-näN lā′), *n.* a city in N France, near Paris: royal chateau and forest; treaties 1570, 1632, 1679, 1919. 37,391 (1962). Also called **St.-Germain.**

St. Got·thard (sānt′ got′ərd; *Fr.* saN gô-tar′), **1.** a mountain range in S Switzerland; a part of the Alps; highest peak, 10,490 ft. **2.** a mountain pass over this range. 6935 ft. high. **3.** a railway tunnel under this pass. 9¼ mi. long.

St. Hel·e·na (hə lē′nə), **1.** a British island in the S Atlantic: Napoleon's place of exile 1815–21. 4613 (est. 1963); 47 sq. mi. **2.** a British colony comprising this island, Ascension Island, and the Tristan da Cunha group. 5091 (est. 1963); 126 sq. mi. *Cap.:* Jamestown.

St. Hel·ens (hel′inz), **1.** a city in SW Lancashire, in NW England, near Liverpool. 194,700. **2.** a town in NW Oregon. 6566. **3. Mount,** an active volcano in NW United States, S of Seattle, Washington: major eruptions 1980. ab. 8600 ft.

St. Hel·ier (sānt′ hel′yər; *Fr.* saN te lyā′), a seaport on the island of Jersey in the English Channel: resort. 28,135.

Sthen·e·boe·a (sthen′ə bē′ə), *n.* *Class. Myth.* Antia.

Sthen·e·la·us (sthen′ᵊlā′əs), *n.* (in the *Iliad*) a Trojan warrior killed by Patroclus.

Sthen·e·le (sthen′ᵊlē′), *n.* *Class. Myth.* a daughter of Acastus sometimes believed to have been the mother of Patroclus by Menoetius.

Sthen·e·lus (sthen′ᵊləs), *n.* *Class. Myth.* **1.** a son of Actor and a companion of Hercules in the war against the Amazons. **2.** one of the Epigoni. **3.** a son of Perseus and Andromeda who became king of Mycenae: he was the father, by Nicippe, of Eurystheus.

sthe·ni·a (sthə nī′ə, sthē′nē ə), *n.* *Pathol.* strength; excessive vital force. Cf. **asthenia.** [< NL, abstracted from ASTHENIA]

Sthen·i·as (sthen′ē əs), *n.* *Class. Myth.* an epithet of Athena, meaning "strong."

sthen·ic (sthen′ik), *adj.* sturdy; heavily and strongly built. [abstracted from ASTHENIC]

Sthen·i·us (sthen′ē əs), *n.* *Class. Myth.* an epithet of Zeus, meaning "strong."

Sthe·no (sthē′nō, sthen′ō), *n.* *Class. Myth.* one of the three Gorgons.

stibi-, a combining form of **stibium:** *stibial.* Also, *esp. before a vowel,* **stib-.**

stib·i·al (stib′ē əl), *adj.* of or resembling antimony. [STIBI- + -AL¹]

stib·ine (stib′ēn, -in), *n.* **1.** *Chem.* a colorless, slightly water-soluble, poisonous gas, SbH_3, usually produced by the reaction of dilute hydrochloric acid with an alloy of antimony and either zinc or magnesium. **2.** any derivative of this compound in which the hydrogen atoms are replaced by one or more organic groups. Also called **antimonous hydride.** [STIBI- + -INE²; cf. ARSINE, PHOSPHINE]

stib·i·um (stib′ē əm), *n.* *Chem.* antimony. [late ME < L < Gk *stíbi* (var. of *stímmi* < Egypt *stm*)]

stib·nite (stib′nīt), *n.* a soft mineral, antimony sulfide, Sb_2S_3, lead-gray in color with a metallic luster, occurring in crystals, often acicular, or in bladed masses: the most important ore of antimony. [STIB(I)NE (in obs. sense of stibnite) + -ITE¹]

stich¹ (stik), *n.* a verse or line of poetry. [< Gk *stích(os)* row, line, verse]

stich² (stik), *n.* *Cards.* the last trick, being of special scoring value in certain games, as pinochle or klaberjass. [< G: lit., sting; OHG *stih* prick; see STITCH¹]

sti·cha·ri·on (stē кнä′rē ôn; *Eng.* stik âr′ē on′), *n., pl.* **-cha·ri·a** (-кнä′rē ä; *Eng.* -kâr′ē ə). *Gk. Orth. Ch.* a white tunic of silk or linen, corresponding to the alb, worn by deacons, priests, and bishops. [< Gk, dim. of *stíchē* tunic, deriv. of *stích(os)* STICH¹]

stich·ic (stik′ik), *adj.* **1.** pertaining to or consisting of stichs or verses. **2.** composed of lines of the same metrical form throughout. [< Gk *stichikós.* See STICH¹, -IC] —**stich′i·cal·ly,** *adv.*

Stich·i·us (stik′ē əs), *n.* (in the *Iliad*) a captain of Athenian forces in the Trojan War, slain by Hector.

sti·chom·e·try (sti kom′i trē), *n.* the practice of writing a prose text in lines the length of which correspond to divisions in the sense and indicate phrasal rhythms. [< Gk *sticho(s)* (see STICH¹) + -METRY] —**stich·o·met·ric** (stik′ə me′trik), **stich′o·met′ri·cal,** *adj.* —**stich′o·met′ri·cal·ly,** *adv.*

sti·cho·myth·i·a (stik′ə mith′ē ə), *n.* dramatic dialogue, as in a Greek play, characterized by brief exchanges between two characters, each of whom usually speaks in one line of verse during a scene of intense emotion or strong argumentation. Also, **sti·chom·y·thy** (sti kom′ə thē). [< Gk, equiv. to *sticho(s)* (see STICH¹) + *mŷthia* (*mŷth(os)* speech, story + *-ia* -IA)] —**stich′o·myth′ic,** *adj.*

-stich·ous, *Bot., Zool.* a word element referring to rows: *distichous.* [< LL *-stichus* < Gk *-stichos,* as comb. form; see STICH¹]

stick¹ (stik), *n., v.,* **sticked, stick·ing.** —*n.* **1.** a branch or shoot of a tree or shrub which has been cut or broken off. **2.** a relatively long and slender piece of wood. **3.** a long piece of wood for use as fuel, in carpentry, etc. **4.** a rod or wand. **5.** a baton. **6.** *Chiefly Brit.* a walking stick or cane. **7.** a club or cudgel. **8.** a long, slender piece or part of anything: *a stick of candy; sticks of celery.* **9.** *Sports.* an implement used to drive or propel a ball or puck, as a crosse or a hockey stick. **10.** *Aeron.* a lever, usually with a handle, by which the longitudinal and lateral motions of an airplane are controlled. **11.** *Naut.* a mast or spar. **12.** *Print.* See **composing stick. 13.** *Mil.* **a.** a group of bombs so arranged as to be released in a row across a target. **b.** the bomb load. **14.** *Informal.* a portion of liquor, as brandy, added to a nonalcoholic drink. **15.** *Slang.* a marijuana cigarette. **16.** *Informal.* an unenthusiastic or uninteresting person. **17. on the stick,** *Slang.* alert; moving; active: *If you're going with us you'd better get on the stick.* **18. the sticks,** *U.S. Informal.* any region distant from cities or towns, as rural districts; the country: *Having lived in a large city all his life, he found it hard to adjust to the sticks.* —*v.t.* **19.** to furnish (a plant, vine, etc.) with a stick or sticks in order to prop or support. **20.** *Print.* to set (type) in a composing stick. [ME *stikke,* OE *sticca;* akin to OHG *stehho,* Icel *stik* stick; see STICK²] —**stick′less,** *adj.* —**stick′like′,** *adj.*

stick² (stik), *v.,* **stuck, stick·ing,** *n.* —*v.t.* **1.** to pierce or puncture with something pointed, as a pin, dagger, spear, etc.; stab: *to stick one's finger with a needle.* **2.** to kill by this means: *to stick a pig.* **3.** to thrust (something pointed) in, into, through, etc.: *to stick a needle into a blister.* **4.** to fasten in position by thrusting a point or end into something: *to stick a peg in a pegboard.* **5.** to fasten in position by or as by something thrust through: *to stick a painting on the wall.* **6.** to put or hold something pointed; impale: *to stick a marshmallow on a fork.* **7.** to decorate or furnish with things piercing the surface: *to stick a cushion full of pins.* **8.** to furnish or adorn with things attached or set here and there: *to stick shelves full of knickknacks.* **9.** to place upon a stick or pin for exhibit: *to stick butterflies.* **10.** to thrust or poke into a place or position indicated: *to stick one's head out of the window.* **11.** to place or set in a specified position; put: *Stick the chair in the corner.* **12.** to fasten or attach by causing to adhere: *to stick a stamp on a letter.* **13.** to bring to a standstill; render unable to proceed or go back (usually used in the passive): *The car was stuck in the mud.* **14.** *Carpentry.* to start (a nail). **15.** *Ceram.* to join (pieces of partially hardened clay) together, using slip as an adhesive. **16.** *Chiefly Brit.* to tolerate; endure: *He couldn't stick the job more than three days.* **17.** to confuse or puzzle; bewilder; perplex; nonplus: *He was stuck by the very first problem on the test.* **18.** *Informal.* to impose something disagreeable upon (a person or persons), as a large bill, a difficult task, etc.: *The committee persistently stuck him with fund collection.* **19.** *Slang.* to cheat.
—*v.i.* **20.** to have the point piercing or embedded in something: *The arrow stuck in the tree.* **21.** to remain attached by adhesion. **22.** to hold, cleave, or cling: *The young rider stuck to the back of his terrified horse.* **23.** to remain persistently or permanently: *a fact that sticks in the mind.* **24.** to remain firm, as in resolution, opinion, statement, attachment, etc.; hold faithfully, as to a promise or bargain. **25.** to keep or remain steadily or unremittingly, as to a task, undertaking, or the like: *to stick to a job until it is finished.* **26.** to become fastened, hindered, checked, or stationary by some obstruction: *Her zipper stuck halfway up.* **27.** to be at a standstill, as from difficulties: *I'm stuck on this problem.* **28.** to be embarrassed or puzzled; hesitate or scruple (usually fol. by *at*). **29.** to be thrust or placed so as to extend, project, or protrude (usually fol. by *through, from, out, up,* etc.). **30. stick around,** *Slang.* to wait in the vicinity; linger: *If you had stuck around, you'd have seen the fireworks.* **31. stick by** or **to,** to maintain one's attachment or loyalty to; remain faithful: *They vowed to stick by one another no matter what happened.* **32. stick one's neck out.** See **neck** (def. 20). **33. stick something out,** *Informal.* to stay with to the end; put up with; endure: *It was a long train trip, but we managed to stick it out by playing cards.* **34. stick to one's guns.** See **gun¹** (def. 11). **35. stick to the** or **one's ribs,** *Informal.* to be substantial and nourishing, as a hearty meal: *Hot cereal sticks to your ribs on those cold winter mornings.* **36. stick up,** *Slang.* to rob, esp. at gunpoint: *A lone gunman stuck up a gas*

station and killed the proprietor. **37. stick up for,** *Informal.* to speak in favor of; come to the defense of; support: *She always sticks up for him, even though he doesn't deserve it.*
—n. 38. a thrust with a pointed instrument; stab. **39.** a stoppage or standstill. **40.** something causing delay or difficulty. **41.** the quality of adhering or of causing things to adhere. **42.** something causing adhesion. [ME *stike(n),* OE *stician;* akin to G *stechen* to sting, L *-stig-* in *instigāre* (see INSTIGATE)] **—stick′a·bil′i·ty,** *n.* **—stick′a·ble,** *adj.*
—Syn. 1. penetrate, spear, transfix, pin. **12.** glue, cement, paste. **21.** STICK, ADHERE, COHERE mean to cling to or be tightly attached to something. ADHERE implies that one kind of material clings tenaciously to another; COHERE adds the idea that a thing is attracted to and held by something like itself: *Particles of sealing wax cohere and form a mass which will adhere to tin.* STICK, more colloquial, often used as the general term, is used particularly when a third kind of material is involved: *A gummed label will stick to a package.* **28.** stickle, waver, doubt.

stick-at-it·ive (stik′at′it iv, -i tiv), *adj. Informal.* stick-to-it-ive. **—stick′-at′-it·ive·ness,** *n.*

stick·ball (stik′bôl′), *n.* a form of baseball played in the streets, on playgrounds, etc., in which a rubber ball and a broomstick or the like are used in place of a baseball and bat. [(BROOM)STICK + BALL[1]]

stick·boat (stik′bōt′), *n. Naut.* a lighter having equipment for lifting cargo. [STICK[1] + BOAT]

stick·er[1] (stik′ər), *n.* **1.** one who or that which sticks. **2.** an adhesive label. **3.** a persistent, diligent person. **4.** *Informal.* something, as a problem or riddle, that puzzles or nonpluses one. **5.** *Slang.* a knife, esp. one used as a weapon by a criminal. **6.** a worker who kills animals in a slaughterhouse by piercing the jugular vein with a pointed instrument. **7.** a bur, thorn, or the like. **8.** *Metall.* **a.** an ingot not readily removable from its mold. **b.** either of a pair of sheets partly welded together by accidental contact while hot. **c.** a coke oven from which coke will not emerge readily. **9.** *Foundry.* a lump left on a casting by a flaw in the mold, part of the face of which has adhered to and been removed with the pattern. **10.** a machine for cutting moldings on millwork. [STICK[2] + -ER[1]]

stick·er[2] (stik′ər), *n.* any of a number of small pieces of wood for separating stacked boards in a lumberyard. [STICK[1] + -ER[1]]

stick·et (stik′it), *adj. Scot.* stickit.

stick′ fig′ure, a diagrammatic drawing representing a human or animal, usually made with one line each for the torso and appendages, and often a circle for the head. Also called **stick′ draw′ing.**

stick·ful (stik′fŏŏl′), *n., pl.* **-fuls.** *Print.* as much set type as a composing stick will hold, usually about two column inches. [STICK[1] + -FUL]

stick·ing (stik′ing), *n. Carpentry.* a molding cut on the edge of a stile, rail, or the like. [late ME; see STICK[2], -ING[1]]

stick′ing place′, 1. Also called **sticking point.** the place or point at which something stops and holds firm. **2.** the place in the lower part of an animal's neck where the knife is thrust in slaughtering.

stick′ing plas′ter, an adhesive cloth or other material for covering and closing superficial wounds, holding bandages in place, etc.

stick′ing point′, 1. a point, detail, or circumstance causing or likely to cause a stalemate or impasse: *The bill would have gone through the Senate quickly but for one sticking point.* **2.** See **sticking place** (def. 1).

stick′ in′sect. See **walking stick** (def. 2).

stick-in-the-mud (stik′in *th*ə mud′), *n. Informal.* someone who avoids new activities, ideas, or attitudes; old fogy.

stick·it (stik′it), *adj. Scot.* **1.** (of a task or product) imperfect; ruined. **2.** (of a person) unsuccessful, esp. in a chosen occupation. Also, **sticket.** [var. of *sticked.* See STICK[2], -ED[2]]

stick·jaw (stik′jô′), *n. Chiefly Brit.* gummy candy, cake, pudding, etc., that requires much chewing. [STICK[2] + JAW]

stick·le (stik′əl), *v.i.,* **-led, -ling. 1.** to argue or haggle insistently, esp. on trivial matters. **2.** to raise objections; scruple; demur. [ME *stightle* to set in order, freq. of obs. *stighte,* OE *stiht(an)* (to) arrange; c. G *stiften,* Icel *stētta* to set up]

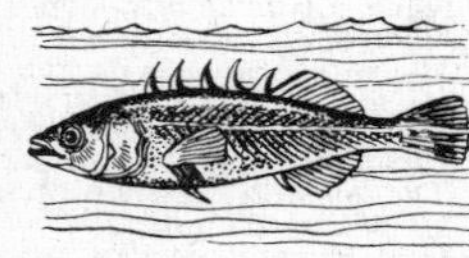

Stickleback,
Eucalia inconstans
(Length 2½ in.)

stick·le·back (stik′əl bak′), *n.* any of the small, pugnacious, spiny-backed fishes of the family *Gasterosteidae,* found in northern fresh waters and sea inlets. Also called **prickleback.** [late ME *stykylbak,* OE *sticol* scaly + *bæc* BACK[1]]

stick·ler (stik′lər), *n.* **1.** a person who insists on something unyieldingly (usually fol. by *for*): *a stickler for ceremony.* **2.** any puzzling or difficult problem. [STICKLE + -ER[1]]

Stick·ney (stik′nē), *n.* a town in NE Illinois. 6239 (1960).

stick·out (stik′out′), *Informal.* **—n. 1.** one who is outstanding or conspicuous, usually for superior endowments, talents, etc.: *Jimmy Brown is the stickout among running backs.* **—adj. 2.** outstanding; conspicuous: *a stickout actor.* [n., adj. use of v. phrase *stick out*]

stick·pin (stik′pin′), *n.* a decorative straight pin with a jeweled or ornamented head and a long shaft with a sheath for encasing the point, used for holding an ascot or necktie in place. [STICK[2] + PIN]

stick·seed (stik′sēd′), *n.* any of the boraginaceous herbs of the genus *Lappula,* having prickly seeds which adhere to clothing. [STICK[2] + SEED]

stick·tight (stik′tīt′), *n.* **1.** a composite herb, *Bidens frondosa,* having flat, barbed achenes which adhere to clothing. **2.** any of several other plants of this genus. **3.** the barbed achene of any of these plants. **4.** any of various other plants bearing burs that stick to clothing or fur. [n. use of v. phrase *stick tight*]

stick-to-it·ive (stik′tōō′it iv, -i tiv), *adj. Informal.* tenaciously resolute; persevering: *Stick-to-it-ive people get ahead.* [adj. use of v. phrase *stick to it;* see -IVE] **—stick′-to′-it·ive·ness,** *n.*

stick·um (stik′əm), *n. Informal.* an adhesive substance. [STICK[2] + *-um* (alter. of 'EM)]

stick·up (stik′up′), *n. Slang.* a holdup; robbery. Also, **stick′-up′.** [n. use of v. phrase *stick up*]

stick′up man′, *Slang.* a man who commits a stickup.

stick·weed (stik′wēd′), *n.* the ragweed. [STICK[2] + WEED[1]]

stick·work (stik′wûrk′), *n. Informal.* a player's degree of competence or proficiency as a baseball batter, hockey or lacrosse player, etc.: *Frequent practice improved his stickwork.* [STICK[1] + WORK]

stick·y (stik′ē), *adj.,* **stick·i·er, stick·i·est. 1.** having the property of adhering, as glue; adhesive. **2.** covered with adhesive or viscid matter: *sticky hands.* **3.** (of the weather or climate) hot and humid: *It was an unbearably sticky day.* **4.** requiring careful treatment; awkwardly difficult: *a rather sticky diplomatic problem; Breaking the news is going to be a bit sticky.* [STICK[2] + -Y[1]] **—stick′i·ly,** *adv.* **—stick′i·ness,** *n.*

stick·y·beak (stik′ē bēk′), *n. Australian Slang.* a busybody; meddler. [STICKY + BEAK[1]]

stick′y charge′, *Mil.* an explosive charge equipped with an adhesive material that makes it stick to the target until the charge explodes. Also called **stick′y bomb′, stick′y grenade′.**

stick·y-fin·gered (stik′ē fing′gərd), *adj.* prone to steal; thievish.

stick′y tape′, *Chiefly Brit.* See **Scotch tape.**

stick′y wick′et, 1. *Cricket.* the area of ground around a wicket when it is tacky because of recent rain and therefore does not allow the ball to bounce well. **2.** *Chiefly Brit.* a situation requiring delicate treatment; an awkward situation: *In telling his wife that he has to be away for a month in Cannes, he'll be batting on a sticky wicket.*

Stie·dry (stē′drē; *Ger.* shtē′drē), *n.* **Fritz** (frits), born 1883, Austrian orchestra conductor.

Stie·gel (stē′gəl; *Ger.* shtē′gəl), *n.* **Henry William,** 1729–85, German iron and glass manufacturer in America.

Stieg·litz (stēg′lits), *n.* **Alfred,** 1864–1946, U.S. photographer and editor.

stiff (stif), *adj.* **1.** rigid or firm; difficult or impossible to bend or flex: *a stiff collar.* **2.** not moving or working easily: *The motor was a little stiff from the cold weather.* **3.** (of a person or animal) not supple; moving with difficulty, as from cold, age, exhaustion, injury, etc. **4.** strong; forceful; powerful: *stiff winds; The fighter threw a stiff right to his opponent's jaw.* **5.** strong or potent to the taste or system, as a beverage or medicine: *He was cold and wanted a good stiff drink.* **6.** resolute; firm in purpose; unyielding; stubborn. **7.** stubbornly maintained: *a stiff battle.* **8.** firm against any tendency to decrease, as stock-market prices. **9.** rigidly formal; cold and unfriendly, as people, manners, or proceedings. **10.** lacking ease and grace; awkward: *a stiff style of writing.* **11.** excessively regular or formal, as a design; not graceful in form or arrangement. **12.** laborious or difficult, as a task. **13.** severe or harsh, as a penalty or demand. **14.** excessive; unusually high or great: *$50 is pretty stiff to pay for that.* **15.** firm from tension; taut: *to keep a stiff rein.* **16.** relatively firm in consistency, as semisolid matter; thick: *a stiff jelly; a stiff batter.* **17.** dense or compact; not friable: *stiff soil.* **18.** *Naut.* (of a vessel) having a high resistance to rolling; stable (opposed to *crank*). **19.** *Scot. and North Eng.* sturdy, stout, or strongly built. **—n. 20.** *Slang.* **a.** a dead body; corpse. **b.** a formal or priggish person. **c.** a poor tipper; tightwad. **d.** a drunk. **21.** *Slang.* **a.** a fellow: *lucky stiff; poor stiff.* **b.** a tramp; hobo. **c.** a laborer. **22.** *Slang.* **a.** a forged check. **b.** a promissory note or bill of exchange. **c.** a letter or note, esp. if secret or smuggled. **23.** *Slang.* a contestant, esp. a racehorse, sure to lose. **—adv. 24.** in or to a firm or rigid state: *The wet shirt was frozen stiff.* **25.** completely, intensely, or extremely: *I'm bored stiff by these lectures. She's scared stiff.* **—v.t. 26.** *Slang.* to fail or refuse to tip (a waiter, porter, etc.). [ME; OE *stīf;* c. G *steif;* akin to STIFLE[1], STEEVE[1]] **—stiff′ish,** *adj.* **—stiff′ly,** *adv.* **—stiff′ness,** *n.*
—Syn. 1. unbending, unyielding. See **firm**[1]. **6.** unrelenting, resolved, obstinate, pertinacious. **9.** reserved, constrained, starched, prim. **10.** graceless, clumsy, inelegant.

stiff-arm (stif′ärm′), *v.t., n.* straight-arm.

stiff·en (stif′ən), *v.t.* **1.** to make stiff. **—v.i. 2.** to become stiff. **3.** to become suddenly tense, rigid, or taut, as in bracing oneself for or drawing back from shock, fear, or displeasure: *He stiffened, expecting to hear the worst.* [STIFF + -EN[1]]

stif·fen·er (stif′ə nər, stif′nər), *n.* **1.** one who or that which stiffens. **2.** Also called **stif′fening bar′.** *Shipbuilding.* a studlike iron or steel shape for stiffening the plating of a bulkhead. [STIFFEN + -ER[1]]

stiff-necked (stif′nekt′), *adj.* **1.** having a stiff neck. **2.** haughty and obstinate; refractory. **—stiff-neck·ed·ly,** (stif′nek′id lē, -nekt′lē), *adv.* **—stiff′-neck′ed·ness,** *n.*

sti·fle[1] (stī′fəl), *v.,* **-fled, -fling. —v.t. 1.** to kill by impeding respiration; smother. **2.** to suppress, curb, or withhold: *to stifle a yawn.* **3.** to quell, crush, or end by force: *to stifle a revolt; to stifle free expression.* **—v.i. 4.** to become stifled or suffocated. **5.** to suffer from difficulty in breathing, as in a close atmosphere. [< Scand; cf. Icel *stīfla* to stop up; akin to STIFF] **—sti′fler,** *n.*
—Syn. 1. suffocate, strangle, choke. **2.** check. **3.** prevent, preclude, put down. **—Ant. 2, 3.** encourage.

sti·fle[2] (stī′fəl), *n.* the joint of a horse or other quadruped that is between the femur and the tibia and joins the hind leg and the body, corresponding anatomically to the human knee. Also called **sti′fle joint′.** See diag. under **horse.** [ME < ?]

sti·fling (stī′fling), *adj.* suffocating; oppressively close: *a stifling atmosphere.* [STIFLE[1] + -ING[2]] **—sti′fling·ly,** *adv.*

stig·ma (stig′mə), *n., pl.* **stig·ma·ta** (stig′mə tə, stig mä′tə, -mat′ə), **stig·mas. 1.** a mark of disgrace or infamy; a stain or reproach, as on one's reputation. **2.** a characteristic mark or sign of defect, degeneration, disease, etc.: *the stigmata of leprosy.* **3.** *Pathol.* a spot or mark on the skin, esp. a place or point on the skin that bleeds during certain mental states, as in hysteria. **4.** *Zool.* **a.** a small mark, spot, or pore on an animal or organ. **b.** the eyespot of a protozoan. **c.** an entrance into the respiratory system of insects. **5.** *Bot.* the part of a pistil which receives the pollen. See diag. under **flower. 6. stigmata,** marks resembling the wounds of the crucified body of Christ, said to be supernaturally impressed on the bodies of certain persons, esp. nuns, tertiaries, and monastics. **7.** *Archaic.* a mark made by a branding iron on the skin of a criminal or slave. [< L < Gk: tattoo mark, equiv. to *stig-* (s. of *stízein* to tattoo) + *-ma* n. suffix denoting result of action]

stig·mas·ter·ol (stig mas′tə rōl′, -rôl′), *n. Biochem.* a crystalline, water-insoluble steroid, $C_{29}H_{48}O$, found in soybeans or calabar beans, used chiefly as a raw material in the manufacture of progesterone. [< NL (*Phȳso*)*stigm(a)* (see PHYSOSTIGMINE) + STEROL]

stig·mat·ic (stig mat′ik), *adj.* Also, **stig·mat′i·cal. 1.** pertaining to a stigma, mark, spot, or the like. **2.** *Bot.* pertaining to or having the character of a stigma. **3.** *Optics.* converging to a point; anastigmatic. **—n. 4.** one marked with supernatural stigmata. [< ML *stigmatic(us),* equiv. to *stigmat-* (s. of Gk *stígma*) STIGMA + *-icus* -IC] **—stig·mat′i·cal·ly,** *adv.* **—stig·mat′i·cal·ness,** *n.*

stig·ma·tise (stig′mə tīz′), *v.t.,* **-tised, -tis·ing.** *Chiefly Brit.* stigmatize. **—stig′ma·ti·sa′tion,** *n.* **—stig′ma·tis′er,** *n.*

stig·ma·tism (stig′mə tiz′əm), *n.* **1.** *Optics.* the property of a lens that is stigmatic. **2.** *Pathol.* the condition in which stigmata are present. [*stigmat-* (see STIGMATIC) + -ISM]

stig·ma·tize (stig′mə tīz′), *v.t.,* **-tized, -tiz·ing. 1.** to mark with a stigma or brand. **2.** to set some mark of disgrace or infamy upon: *The crime of the father stigmatized the whole family.* **3.** to produce stigmata, marks, spots, or the like, on. [< ML *stigmatiz(āre),* equiv. to *stigmat-* (see STIGMATIC) + *-izāre* -IZE] **—stig′ma·ti·za′tion,** *n.* **—stig′ma·tiz′er,** *n.*

stig·ma·typ·y (stig′mə tī′pē), *n. Print.* the art or technique of making a design or portrait by combining small types of dots of various sizes. [STIGMA + -TYPE + -Y[3]]

St. Ig·nace (ig′nəs), a town in NW Michigan, in the Upper Peninsula. 3334 (1960).

Stijl, De (də stīl), *Dutch.* a group of Dutch artists of the early 20th century whose theories and works influenced the development of contemporary architecture and applied arts. Cf. **Neo-Plasticism.** [*The Style,* name of a Dutch art periodical]

stilb (stilb), *n. Optics.* a unit of luminance, equal to one candle per square centimeter. [< Gk *stilb(ē)* lamp]

stil·bene (stil′bēn), *n. Chem.* a colorless to slightly yellow, crystalline, water-insoluble solid, $C_6H_5CH{=}CHC_6H_5$, used chiefly in the manufacture of dyes (**stil′bene dyes′**). [< Gk *stilb-* (s. of *stílbein* to shine) + -ENE]

stil·bes·trol (stil bes′trōl, -trôl, -trol), *n. Pharm.* diethylstilbestrol. Also, **stil·boes′trol.** [STILB(ENE) + ESTR(US) + -OL[1]]

stil·bite (stil′bīt), *n.* a white-to-brown or red zeolite mineral, a hydrous silicate of calcium and aluminum, occurring in sheaflike aggregates of crystals and in radiated masses. [< Gk *stilb-* (s. of *stílbein* to shine) + -ITE[1]]

stile[1] (stīl), *n.* **1.** a series of steps or rungs by means of which a person may pass over a wall or fence which remains a barrier to sheep or cattle. **2.** a turnstile. [ME; OE *stigel,* deriv. of *stīgan* to climb, c. G *steigen*]

stile[2] (stīl), *n. Carpentry, Furniture.* any of various upright members framing panels or the like, as in a system of paneling, a paneled door, window sash, chest of drawers, etc. Cf. **rail**[1] (def. 7). [perh. < D *stijl* pillar, prop]

sti·let·to (sti let′ō), *n., pl.* **-tos, -toes,** *v.,* **-toed, -to·ing. —n. 1.** a short dagger with a blade that is thick in proportion to its width. **2.** a small pointed instrument for making eyelet holes in needlework. **—v.t. 3.** to stab or kill with a stiletto. [< It, equiv. to *stil(o)* dagger (< L *stilus* STYLUS) + *-etto* -ETTE] **—sti·let′to·like′,** *adj.*

Stil·i·cho (stil′ə kō′), *n.* **Fla·vi·us** (flā′vē əs), A.D. 359?–408, Roman general and statesman.

still[1] (stil), *adj.* **1.** remaining in place or at rest; motionless; stationary: *to stand still.* **2.** free from sound or noise, as a place, persons, etc.; silent: *to keep still about a matter.* **3.** subdued or low in sound; hushed: *a still, small voice.* **4.** free from turbulence or commotion; peaceful; tranquil; calm: *the still air.* **5.** without waves or perceptible current; not flowing, as water. **6.** not effervescent or sparkling, as wine. **7.** *Photog.* noting, pertaining to, or used for making a photograph of a stationary subject or one instantaneous photograph of a moving subject. **—n. 8.** stillness or silence: *the still of the night.* **9.** *Photog.* an instantaneous photograph of a moving subject, esp. a print of one of the frames of a motion-picture film. **—adv. 10.** at this or that time; as previously: *Are you still here?* **11.** up to this or that time; as yet: *A day before departure we were still lacking an itinerary.* **12.** in the future as in the past: *Objections will still be made.* **13.** even; in addition; yet (used to emphasize a comparative): *still more complaints; still greater riches.* **14.** even then; yet; nevertheless: *to be rich and still crave more.* **15.** without sound or movement: *Sit still!* **16.** at or to a greater distance or degree. **17.** *Archaic.* steadily; constantly; always. **—conj. 18.** and yet; but yet; nevertheless: *It was futile, still they fought.* **19. still and all,** *U.S.* nonetheless; even with everything considered: *Even though you dislike us, still and all you should be polite.* **—v.t. 20.** to silence or hush (sounds, voices, etc.). **21.** to calm, appease, or allay: *to still a craving.* **22.** to quiet, subdue, or cause to subside (waves, winds, commotion, tumult, passion, pain, etc.). **—v.i. 23.** to become still or quiet. [ME, OE *stille;* c. G *still;* akin to STALL[1]]
—Syn. 1. unmoving, inert, quiescent. **2.** soundless, mute. STILL, QUIET, HUSHED, NOISELESS, SILENT indicate the absence of noise and of excitement or activity accompanied by sound. STILL indicates the absence of sound or movement: *The house was still.* QUIET implies relative freedom from noise, activity, or excitement: *a quiet engine; a quiet vacation.* HUSHED implies the suppression of sound or noise: *a hushed whisper.* NOISELESS and SILENT characterize that

which does not reveal its presence or movement by any sound: *a noiseless footstep; a room silent and deserted.* **4.** peaceful, peaceable, pacific, placid, serene. **8.** quiet, hush, calm. **18.** See **but**[1]. **20.** quiet, mute, stifle, muffle, smother. **21.** soothe, compose, pacify, smooth, tranquilize. **—Ant. 1.** moving. **2.** noisy.

still[2] (stil), *n.* **1.** a distilling apparatus, consisting of a vessel in which a liquid is heated and vaporized and a cooling device or coil for condensing the vapor. **2.** a distillery. **—*v.t., v.i.* 3.** to distill. [aph. var. of DISTILL]

still[3] (stil), *v.i., v.t. Obs.* to fall or let fall in tiny drops. [ME *still(en)* < L *stillāre* (to) drip, drop; see INSTILL]

Still (stil), *n.* **1. Andrew Taylor,** 1828–1917, U.S. founder of osteopathy. **2. William Grant,** born 1895, U.S. composer.

stil·lage (stil′ij), *n.* a low platform on which goods are stored in a warehouse or factory to keep them off the floor, to aid in handling, etc. Cf. **skid** (def. 3). [appar. < D *stellagie, stellaadje, stellage* scaffold, stand, equiv. to *stell(en)* (to) place + *-age* -AGE]

still′ alarm′, a fire alarm given by telephone or means other than a regular fire-signal system.

stil·la·tim (sti lā′tim), *adv.* (in prescriptions) by drops; in small quantities. [< L]

still·birth (stil′bûrth′), *n.* **1.** the birth of a dead child or organism. **2.** a fetus dead at birth. [STILL[1] + BIRTH]

still·born (stil′bôrn′), *adj.* **1.** dead when born. **2.** ineffectual from the beginning; abortive; fruitless: *a stillborn plan of escape.* [STILL[1] + BORN]

still·er (stil′ər), *n. Archaic.* a distiller. [STILL[2] + -ER[1]]

still′ hunt′, 1. a hunt for game carried on stealthily, as by stalking, or under cover, as in ambush. **2.** *Informal.* a quiet or secret pursuit of any object.

still-hunt (stil′hunt′), *v.t.* **1.** to pursue or ambush by a still hunt. **—*v.i.* 2.** to carry on a still hunt. **—still′-hunt′er,** *n.*

stil·li·form (stil′ə fôrm′), *adj.* drop-shaped; globular. [*stilli-* (comb. form of L *stilla* drop) + -FORM]

still′ life′, *pl.* **still lifes. 1.** the category of subject matter in which inanimate objects are represented, as in painting or photography. **2.** a representation chiefly of inanimate objects, as a painting of a bowl of fruit. **—still′-life′,** *adj.*

still·ness (stil′nis), *n.* **1.** absence of motion. **2.** silence; quiet; hush. [ME *stilnesse,* OE *stilnes.* See STILL[1], -NESS]

still′ pack′, *Cards.* the pack not in play in a game in which two packs are used alternately.

still·room (stil′ro͞om′, -ro͝om′), *n.* **1.** (in a large house) a room for distilling or for the preparation of special foods and drinks. **2.** a room off a kitchen for making tea, coffee, etc., and for storing liquors, tea, preserves, jams, wine, etc. [STILL[2] + ROOM]

Still′son wrench′ (stil′sən), *Trademark.* a monkey wrench with a pivoted, adjustable jaw that grips pipes, bars, etc., more tightly when pressure is exerted on the handle.

Stillson wrench

still′ trail′er, any dog which follows the trail of its quarry silently. Cf. **open trailer.**

still′ wa′ter, a part of a stream where the level of inclination is so slight that no current is visible.

Still·wa·ter (stil′wô′tər, -wot′ər), *n.* **1.** a city in N Oklahoma. 23,965 (1960). **2.** a town in E Minnesota. 8310 (1960).

stil·ly (*adv.* stil′lē; *adj.* stil′ē), *adv.* **1.** quietly; silently. **—*adj.* 2.** *Chiefly Literary.* still; quiet. [ME; OE *stillīce.* See STILL[1], -LY]

stilt (stilt), *n.* **1.** one of two poles, each with a support for the foot at some distance above the bottom end, enabling the wearer to walk with his feet above the ground. **2.** one of several posts supporting a structure built above the surface of land or water. **3.** *Ceram.* a three-armed support for an object being fired. **4.** any of several limicoline birds, esp. of the genus *Himantopus,* found chiefly in marshes, having long legs, a long neck, and a slender bill. **5.** *Brit. Dial.* **a.** a plow handle. **b.** a crutch. **—*v.t.* 6.** to raise on or as on stilts. [ME *stilte;* c. LG *stilte* pole, G *Stelze*] **—stilt′like′,** *adj.*

stilt·ed (stil′tid), *adj.* **1.** stiffly dignified or formal, as speech, literary style, etc.; pompous. **2.** *Archit.* (of an arch) resting on imposts treated in part as downward continuations of the arch, which therefore seems to rise perpendicularly for some distance. **3.** *Bookbinding.* (of a cover) projecting more than usual from the edges of the leaves. [STILT + -ED[3]]

Stil·ton (stil′tᵊn), *n.* a rich, waxy, white cheese, veined with mold: made principally in England. Also called **Stil′ton cheese′.** [after *Stilton,* place in England where it was first sold]

Still·well (stil′wel, -wəl), *n.* **Joseph W.** ("*Vinegar Joe*"), 1883–1946, U.S. general.

sti·lya·ga (sti lyä′gä), *n., pl.* **-gi** (-gi). *Russian.* (in the Soviet Union and various countries that make up the Balkans) a person, usually young, who adopts the dress and manners of a beatnik, Mod, Rocker, etc., of Western Europe and America and who may be a delinquent: *The Soviet government was concerned with the* stilyagi, *who posed both practical and ideological problems.*

stime (stīm), *n. Scot., Irish Eng.* the smallest bit; a drop, taste, or glimpse. [ME, perh. var. (by mishearing) of **skime* < Scand; cf. Icel *skīma,* c. OE *scīma* ray, light; akin to SHINE]

Stim·son (stim′sən), *n.* **Henry L(ewis),** 1867–1950, U.S. statesman: Secretary of War 1911–13, 1940–45; Secretary of State 1929–33.

stim·u·lant (stim′yə lənt), *n.* **1.** *Physiol., Med.* something that temporarily quickens some vital process or the functional activity of some organ or part: *Adrenalin is a stimulant for the heart.* **2.** any food or beverage that stimulates, esp. coffee, tea, or, in its initial effect, alcoholic liquor. **3.** a stimulus or incentive. **—*adj.* 4.** *Physiol., Med.* temporarily quickening some vital process or functional activity. **5.** stimulating. Cf. **depressant.** [< L *stimulant-* (s. of *stimulāns,* prp. of *stimulāre* to goad). See STIMULUS, -ANT]

stim·u·late (stim′yə lāt′), *v.,* **-lat·ed, -lat·ing.** **—*v.t.* 1.** to rouse to action or effort, as by encouragement or pressure; spur on; incite: *to stimulate his interest in mathematics.* **2.** *Physiol., Med.* to excite (a nerve, gland, etc.) to its functional activity. **3.** to invigorate by a food or beverage containing a stimulant, as coffee, tea, or alcoholic liquor. **—*v.i.* 4.** to act as a stimulus or stimulant. [< L *stimulāt(us)* (ptp. of *stimulāre* to goad). See STIMULUS, -ATE[1]] **—stim·u·la·bil·i·ty** (stim′yə lə-bil′i tē), *n.* **—stim′u·la·ble,** *adj.* **—stim′u·lat′ing·ly,** *adv.* **—stim′u·la′tor, stim′u·lat′er,** *n.* **—stim′u·la′tion,** *n.*

—Syn. 1. arouse, activate, excite, urge, provoke, instigate, goad, spur, prod, prick, inflame, fire. See **animate.**

stim·u·la·tive (stim′yə lā′tiv), *adj.* **1.** serving to stimulate. **—*n.* 2.** a stimulating agency. [STIMULATE + -IVE]

stim·u·lus (stim′yə ləs), *n., pl.* **-li** (-lī′). **1.** something that incites to action or exertion or quickens action, feeling, thought, etc.: *The approval of others is a potent stimulus.* **2.** *Physiol., Med.* something that excites an organism or part to functionable activity. [< L: a goad] **—Syn. 1.** incitement, enticement, motive, provocation. **2.** stimulant. **—Ant. 1.** discouragement.

stim′ulus generaliza′tion, *Psychol.* generalization (def. 4a).

sti·my (stī′mē), *n., pl.* **-mies,** *v.t.,* **-mied, -my·ing.** stymie.

sting (sting), *v.,* **stung** or (*Archaic* or *Obs.*) **stang; stung; sting·ing;** *n.* **—*v.t.* 1.** to prick or wound with a sharp-pointed, often venom-bearing organ. **2.** to affect painfully or irritatingly as a result of contact, as certain plants do: *to be stung by nettles.* **3.** to cause to smart or to cause a sharp pain: *The flying sand stung his eyes.* **4.** to cause mental or moral anguish: *to be stung with remorse.* **5.** to goad or drive, as by sharp irritation. **6.** *Slang.* to cheat or take advantage of, esp. to overcharge; soak. **—*v.i.* 7.** to use, have, or wound with a sting, as bees. **8.** to cause a sharp, smarting pain, as some plants, an acrid liquid or gas, a slap or hit, etc. **9.** to cause acute mental pain or irritation, as annoying thoughts, conscience, etc.: *The memory of that insult still stings.* **10.** to feel acute mental pain or irritation: *He was stinging from the blow to his pride.* **11.** to feel a smarting pain, as from the sting of an insect or from a blow. **—*n.* 12.** the act or an instance of stinging. **13.** a wound, pain, or smart caused by stinging. **14.** any sharp physical or mental wound, hurt, or pain. **15.** anything or an element in anything that wounds, pains, or irritates: *to feel the sting of defeat; Death, where is thy sting?* **16.** capacity to wound or pain: *Satire has a sting.* **17.** a sharp stimulus or incitement: *driven by the sting of jealousy; the sting of ambition.* **18.** *Bot.* a glandular hair on certain plants, as nettles, which emits an irritating fluid. **19.** *Zool.* any of various sharp-pointed, often venom-bearing organs of insects and other animals capable of inflicting painful or dangerous wounds. [ME; OE *sting(an);* c. Icel *stinga* to pierce, Goth *-stangan* (in *usstangan* to pull out)] **—sting′ing·ly,** *adv.* **—sting′ing·ness,** *n.* **—sting′less,** *adj.*

sting·a·ree (sting′ə rē′, sting′ə rē′), *n.* a stingray.

sting·er (sting′ər), *n.* **1.** one who or that which stings. **2.** an animal or plant having a stinging organ. **3.** the sting or stinging organ of an insect or other animal. **4.** *Informal.* a stinging blow, remark, or the like. **5.** a cocktail made of brandy and crème de menthe. **6.** *Brit. Informal.* a highball of whiskey and soda. [STING + -ER[1]]

sting′ing cap′sule, *Zool.* a nematocyst. Also called **sting′ing cell′.**

sting′ing hair′, *Bot.* sting (def. 18).

sting′ing net′tle, a bristly, stinging, Eurasian herb, *Urtica dioica,* naturalized in North America, having forked clusters of greenish flowers, the young foliage sometimes cooked and eaten like spinach by the Scots. Also called **great nettle.**

sting′less bee′, any of certain social, honey-producing tropical bees of the family *Apidae,* as of the genus *Melipona,* having a nonfunctional sting.

stin·go (sting′gō), *n.* *Chiefly Brit. Slang.* **1.** strong beer or ale. **2.** vitality; kick. [STING + *-o;* cf. BLOTTO, STINKO]

sting·ray (sting′rā′), *n.* any of the rays, esp. of the family *Dasyatidae,* having a long, flexible tail armed near the base with a strong, serrated bony spine with which they can inflict severe and very painful wounds. [STING + RAY[1]]

Stingray, *Dasyatis centroura* (Width 5 ft.; total length 10 ft.; tail 7¼ ft.)

stin·gy[1] (stin′jē), *adj.,* **-gi·er, -gi·est. 1.** reluctant to give or spend; not generous; niggardly; penurious: *He's a stingy old miser.* **2.** scanty or meager: *a stingy little income.* [dial. *stingy* spiky, hence bad-tempered, equiv. to *stinge* (OE *steng* stake) + *-y*[1]; akin to STING] **—stin′gi·ly,** *adv.* **—stin′gi·ness,** *n.*

—Syn. 1. parsimonious, mean, miserly, close, tight, avaricious. **2.** sparse, paltry, poor. **—Ant. 1.** generous.

sting·y[2] (sting′ē), *adj.* having a sting. [STING + -Y[1]]

stink (stingk), *v.,* **stank** or, often, **stunk; stunk; stink·ing;** *n.* **—*v.i.* 1.** to emit a strong offensive smell. **2.** to be offensive to honesty or propriety; to be in extremely bad repute or disfavor. **3.** *Slang.* to be disgustingly inferior: *That book stinks.* **4.** *Slang.* to have a large quantity of something (usually fol. by *of* or *with*): *They stink of money. She stinks with jewelry.* **—*v.t.* 5.** to cause to stink (often fol. by *up*): *That dead bird stinks up the attic terribly.* **6. stink out,** to repel or drive out by means of a highly offensive smell. **—*n.* 7.** a strong offensive smell; stench. **8.** *Slang.* an unpleasant fuss; scandal: *There was a big stink about his accepting a bribe.* **9. stinks,** (*construed as sing.*) *Brit. Slang.* chemistry or natural science as a course of study. [ME *stink(en),* OE *stincan;* c. G *stinken.* Cf. STENCH]

stink·ard (sting′kərd), *n. Obs.* a despicable person; stinker. [STINK + -ARD] **—stink′ard·ly,** *adv.*

stink·a·roo (sting′kə ro͞o′, sting′kə ro͞o′), *n., pl.* **-roos.** *Slang.* something bad, as an inferior movie or play; a stinker: *a stinkaroo of a motion picture.* Also, **stinkeroo.** [STINKER + (KANGA)ROO (in bad sense, as in *kangaroo court*)]

stink′ bomb′, a small bomb made to emit a foul smell on exploding. Also called **stench bomb.**

stink′ bug′, 1. any of numerous broad, flat, hemipterous insects of the family *Pentatomidae* that emit a disagreeable odor. **2.** any of various malodorous bugs.

stink·er (sting′kər), *n.* **1.** one who or that which stinks. **2.** *Slang.* a mean or despicable person; louse. **3.** *Slang.* something, esp. some form of entertainment, of inferior quality. **4.** *Slang.* something difficult: *a real stinker of a crossword puzzle.* **5.** any device emitting an offensive odor, as a stink bomb, stinkpot, etc. **6.** *Dial.* any of several large petrels. [STINK + -ER[1]]

stink·er·oo (sting′kə ro͞o′, sting′kə ro͞o′), *n., pl.* **-oos.** stinkaroo.

stink·horn (stingk′hôrn′), *n.* any of various rank-smelling, basidiomycetous fungi of the genus *Phallus,* esp. *P. impudicus.* [STINK + HORN]

stink·ing (sting′king), *adj.* **1.** foul-smelling. **2.** *Slang.* very drunk; plastered. **3.** *Slang.* very rich: *His father left him so much money he's stinking.* **4.** contemptible; disgusting: *a stinking shame.* [ME *stinkinge,* OE *stincende.* See STINK, -ING[2]] **—stink′ing·ly,** *adv.* **—stink′ing·ness,** *n.*

—Syn. 1. smelly, putrid, rotten, putrescent, foul, miasmatic, rank.

stink′ing ce′dar, an evergreen tree, *Torreya taxifolia,* of Florida, having rank-smelling foliage and egg-shaped fruit.

stink′ing clo′ver. See **Rocky Mountain beeplant.**

stink′ing smut′, bunt[3].

stink·o (sting′kō), *adj. Slang.* drunk. [STINK + (BLOTT)O]

stink·pot (stingk′pot′), *n.* **1.** a jar containing combustibles or other materials that generate offensive and suffocating vapors, formerly used in warfare. **2.** *Slang.* a stinker; meany. **3.** a common musk turtle, *Sternotherus odoratus,* of the eastern and southern U.S. [STINK + POT[1]]

stink·stone (stingk′stōn′), *n.* any of various stones which emit a fetid odor on being struck or rubbed, as from embedded decomposed organic matter. [STINK + STONE, modeled on G *Stinkstein*]

stink·weed (stingk′wēd′), *n.* **1.** any of various rank-smelling plants, as the jimson weed. **2.** See **tree of heaven.** [STINK + WEED[1]]

stink·wood (stingk′wo͝od′), *n.* **1.** any of several trees yielding fetid wood. **2.** the wood of any of these trees. [STINK + WOOD[1]]

stink·y (sting′kē), *adj.,* **stink·i·er, stink·i·est.** foul smelling; stinking. [STINK + -Y[1]]

stink·y·foot (sting′kē fo͝ot′), *n. Vet. Pathol.* See **foot rot.** [STINKY + FOOT]

stink′y pink′y, an oral word game in which one player provides a definition to which the others are to supply a rhyming phrase, as "a mighty nightie" for "a powerful pair of pajamas." Also, **stink′y pink′ie.**

Stin·nes (shtin′əs), *n.* **Hu·go** (ho͞o′gō; *Eng.* hyo͞o′gō), 1870–1924, German industrialist.

Stin·nett (sti net′), *n.* a town in N Texas. 2695 (1960).

stint[1] (stint), *v.t.* **1.** to limit to a certain amount, number, share, or allowance, often unduly; set limits to; restrict. **2.** *Archaic.* to bring to an end; check. **—*v.i.* 3.** to be frugal; get along on a scanty allowance: *Don't stint on the food. They stinted for years in order to save money.* **4.** *Archaic.* to cease action; desist. **—*n.* 5.** limitation or restriction, esp. as to amount: *to give without stint.* **6.** a limited, prescribed, or expected quantity, share, rate, etc.: *to exceed one's stint.* **7.** an allotted amount or piece of work: *to do one's daily stint.* **8.** *Obs.* a pause; halt. [ME; OE *stynt(an)* (to) make blunt, dull; c. Icel *stytta* to shorten; cf. STUNT[1]] **—stint′ed·ly,** *adv.* **—stint′ed·ness,** *n.* **—stint′er,** *n.* **—stint′ing·ly,** *adv.* **—stint′less,** *adj.*

—Syn. 1. confine, restrain. **5.** restraint, constraint. **6.** allotment, portion. **—Ant. 1.** liberate, free.

stint[2] (stint), *n.* any of various small sandpipers, as the least sandpiper. [late ME *stynte,* appar. OE **stynte* or **stynta,* lit., the foolish one, deriv. of *stunt* foolish; see STUNT[1], STINT[1]]

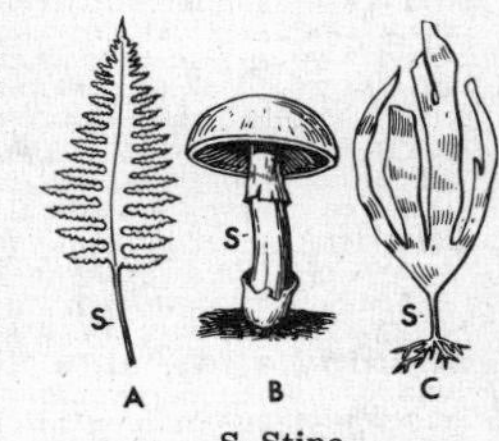

S, Stipe
A, Fern; B, Mushroom; C, Kelp

stipe (stīp), *n.* **1.** *Bot.* a stalk or slender support, as the petiole of a fern frond, the stem supporting the pileus of a mushroom, or a stalklike elongation of the receptacle of a flower. **2.** *Zool.* a stemlike part, as a footstalk; stalk. [< F: < L *stīp(es)* post, tree-trunk or branch, log; see STIFF]

sti·pel (stī′pəl), *n. Bot.* a secondary stipule situated at the base of a leaflet of a compound leaf. [< NL *stipell(a),* alter. of L *stipula* (see STIPULE), with *-ella* r. *-ula* -ULE] **—sti·pel·late** (stī-pel′it, -āt, stī′pə lit, -lāt′), *adj.*

sti·pend (stī′pend), *n.* **1.** fixed or regular pay; salary. **2.** any periodic payment, esp. a scholarship or fellowship allowance granted to a student. [late ME *stipend(i)e* < L *stīpendi(um)* soldier's pay, equiv. to *sti-* (for *stipi-,* s. of *stips* a coin) + *pend-* weigh out, pay (see PEND) + *-ium* n. suffix] **—sti′pend·less,** *adj.*

—Syn. 1, 2. See **pay.**

sti·pen·di·ar·y (stī pen′dē er′ē), *adj., n., pl.* **-ar·ies.** **—*adj.* 1.** receiving a stipend; performing services for regular pay. **2.** paid for by a stipend: *stipendiary services.* **3.** pertaining to or of the nature of a stipend. **—*n.* 4.** one who receives a stipend. [< L *stīpendiāri(us),* equiv. to *stīpendi(um)* STIPEND + *-ārius* -ARY]

sti·pes (stī′pēz), *n., pl.* **stip·i·tes** (stip′i tēz′). **1.** *Zool.* the second joint in a maxilla of crustaceans and insects. **2.** *Bot.* a stipe. [< L; see STIPE]

stip·i·tate (stip′i tāt′), *adj.* having or supported by a stipe: *a stipitate ovary.* [< NL *stipitāt(us),* equiv. to *stipit-* (s. of *stīpes*) STIPE + *-ātus* -ATE[1]]

stip·i·ti·form (stip′i tə fôrm′), *adj.* having the form of a stipe. [*stipit-* (see STIPITATE) + -I- + -FORM]

sti·po (stē′pō), *n., pl.* **-pos.** a tall, ornate, Italian desk with a drop lid. [< It]

stip·ple (stip′əl), *v.*, **-pled, -pling,** *n.* —*v.t.* **1.** to paint, engrave, or draw by means of dots or small touches. —*n.* Also, **stip′pling. 2.** the method of painting, engraving, etc., by stippling. **3.** stippled work; a painting, engraving, or the like, executed by means of dots or small spots. [< D *stippel(en)*, freq. of *stippen* to dot, speckle, deriv. of *stip* point, dot] —**stip′pler,** *n.*

stip·u·late[1] (stip′yə lāt′), *v.*, **-lat·ed, -lat·ing.** —*v.i.* **1.** to make an express demand or arrangement as a condition of agreement (often fol. by *for*). —*v.t.* **2.** to arrange expressly or specify in terms of agreement: *to stipulate a price.* **3.** to require as an essential condition in making an agreement: *Total disarmament was stipulated in the peace treaty.* **4.** to promise, in making an agreement. [< L *stipulāt(us)* (ptp. of *stipulārī* to demand a formal agreement), equiv. to *stipul-* firm (see STIPULE) + *-ātus* -ATE[1]] —**stip·u·la·ble** (stip′yə lə bəl), *adj.* —**stip′u·la′tor,** *n.* —**stip·u·la·to·ry** (stip′yə lə tôr′ē, -tōr′ē), *adj.*

stip·u·late[2] (stip′yə lit, -lāt′), *adj.* *Bot.* having stipules. [< NL *stipulāt(us)*. See STIPULE, -ATE[1]]

stip·u·la·tion (stip′yə lā′shən), *n.* **1.** the act of stipulating. **2.** a condition, demand, or promise in an agreement or contract. [< L *stipulātiōn-* (s. of *stipulātiō*). See STIPULATE, -ION]

stip·ule (stip′yōōl), *n.* *Bot.* one of a pair of lateral appendages, often leaflike, at the base of a leaf petiole in many plants. See illus. under **leaf.** [< L *stipul(a)* stalk, n. use of fem. of **stipulus* firm (recorded in LL); akin to STIPES; see STIFF] —**stip′u·lar,** *adj.*

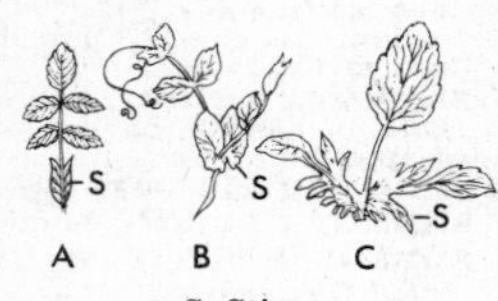

S, Stipule
A, Dog rose, *Rosa canina*
B, Pea, *Pisum satium*
C, Pansy, *Viola tricolor hortensis*

stip·u·li·form (stip′yə lə fôrm′), *adj.* *Bot.* shaped like a stipule. [STIPULE + -I- + -FORM]

stir[1] (stûr), *v.*, **stirred, stir·ring,** *n.* —*v.t.* **1.** to move one's hand or an implement continuously or repeatedly through (a liquid or other substance) in order to cool, mix, agitate, dissolve, etc., any or all of the component parts: *to stir one's coffee with a spoon.* **2.** to move, esp. in a slight way: *He would not stir a finger to help them.* **3.** to set in tremulous, fluttering, or irregular motion: *A soft breeze stirred the leaves.* **4.** to move briskly; bestir: *to stir oneself.* **5.** to rouse from inactivity, quiet, contentment, indifference, etc. (usually fol. by *up*): *to stir up his potential.* **6.** to incite, instigate, or prompt (usually fol. by *up*): *to stir up a people to rebellion.* **7.** to affect strongly; excite: *to stir pity; to stir one's heart.* **8.** *Archaic.* to bring up for notice or discussion. **9.** *Archaic.* to disturb; trouble. —*v.i.* **10.** to move, esp. slightly or lightly: *Not a leaf stirred.* **11.** to move around, esp. briskly; be active: *Everyone in the house was stirring.* **12.** to be in circulation, current, or afoot: *Is there any news stirring?* **13.** to become active, as from some rousing or quickening impulse. **14.** to be emotionally moved or strongly affected. —*n.* **15.** the act of stirring or moving. **16.** movement, esp. brisk and busy movement: *There was too much clamor and stir for her.* **17.** the sound made by stirring or moving slightly. **18.** a state or occasion of general excitement; commotion: *The news created a stir.* **19.** a mental impulse, sensation, or feeling: *a stir of hope.* **20.** a jog, poke, or thrust: *He gave the refuse a stir with his foot.* [ME *stir(en)*, OE *styrian*; c. G *stören*; akin to Icel *styrr* disturbance; see STORM] —**stir′ra·ble,** *adj.* —**stir′less,** *adj.* —**stir′less·ly,** *adv.* —**stir′less·ness,** *n.*
—**Syn. 1.** disturb. **6.** rouse, foment, arouse, provoke, stimulate, goad, spur. **16.** bustle, **18.** fuss, pother, agitation, disorder, uproar. See **ado.** —**Ant. 18.** quiet.

stir[2] (stûr), *n.* *Slang.* prison. [? var. of obs. *steer*, OE *stēor* discipline, correction, restraint, penalty, punishment]

stir-cra·zy (stûr′krā′zē), *adj.* *Slang.* mentally ill because of long imprisonment. [STIR[2] + CRAZY]

stir-fry (stûr′frī′), *v.*, **-fried, -fry·ing,** *n.* —*v.t.* **1.** to cook (food) quickly by stirring constantly in a lightly oiled wok or pan over high heat: a traditional method of Chinese cooking. —*n.* **2.** a dish of sliced or diced meat, vegetables, etc., prepared in this way.

stirk (stûrk), *n.* *Brit.* a young bull or cow, esp. one in its second year. [ME; OE *stirc* calf, equiv. to *stir-* (akin to STEER[2]) + suffixal *-c* (see -OCK)]

Stir·ling (stûr′ling), *n.* **1.** Also called **Stir·ling·shire** (stûr′ling shēr′, -shər). a county in central Scotland. 144,858 (1961); 451 sq. mi. **2.** its county seat, a port on the Forth River. 27,503 (est. 1964).

Stir′ling's for′mula (stûr′lingz), *Math.* a relation which approximates the value of *n* factorial, by $(2\pi)^{1/2}n^{n+1/2}e^{-n}$. [named after James *Stirling* (d. 1770), Scottish mathematician]

stir·pi·cul·ture (stûr′pə kul′chər), *n.* the production of special stocks or strains by careful breeding. [< L *stirpi-* (s. of *stirps*) stock, stem + CULTURE] —**stir′pi·cul′tur·al,** *adj.* —**stir′pi·cul′tur·ist,** *n.*

stirps (stûrps), *n., pl.* **stir·pes** (stûr′pēz). **1.** a stock; family or branch of a family; line of descent. **2.** *Law.* one from whom a family is descended. **3.** *Bot. Obs.* a race or permanent variety. [< L: root-stock, trunk]

stir·rer (stûr′ər), *n.* **1.** one who or that which stirs. **2.** an implement or device for stirring something. [ME; see STIR[1], -ER[2]]

stir·ring (stûr′ing), *adj.* **1.** rousing, exciting, or thrilling: *a stirring speech.* **2.** moving, active, bustling, or lively: *a stirring business.* [ME *stiringe*, OE *styriende.* See STIR[1], -ING[2]] —**stir′ring·ly,** *adv.*

stir·rup (stûr′əp, stir′-, stur′-), *n.* **1.** a loop, ring, or other contrivance of metal, wood, leather, etc., suspended from the saddle of a horse to support the rider's foot. **2.** any of various similar supports or clamps used for special purposes. **3.** *Naut.* a short rope with an eye at the end hung from a yard to support a footrope, the footrope being rove through the eye. **4.** Also called **bridle iron, hanger.** a heavy metal strap or casting hung from a beam, wall, or post to support one end of a timber. **5.** Also called **binder.** (in reinforced-concrete constructions) a U-shaped or W-shaped bent rod for supporting longitudinal reinforcing rods. **6.** *Anat.* the stapes. [ME; OE *stigrāp* (*stige* ascent + *rāp* ROPE); c. G *Stegreif*] —**stir′rup·less,** *adj.* —**stir′rup·like′,** *adj.*

A B
Stirrups
A, Metal; B, Leather

stir′rup cup′, 1. *Chiefly Brit.* a farewell drink, esp. one offered to a rider already mounted for departure. **2.** a cup of the late 17th and early 18th centuries for holding such a drink, having the form of the mask of a fox or greyhound and no handle or foot.

stir′rup jar′, pseudamphora. Also called **stir′rup vase′.**

stir′rup leath′er, the strap which holds the stirrup of a saddle. Also called **stir′rup strap′.**

stir′rup pump′, a small hand pump held steady by a stirruplike foot bracket, often used in firefighting.

stitch[1] (stich), *n.* **1.** one complete movement of a threaded needle through a fabric or material such as to leave behind it a single loop or portion of thread, as in sewing, embroidery, the surgical closing of wounds, etc. **2.** a loop or portion of thread disposed in place by one such movement in sewing: *to rip out stitches.* **3.** a particular mode of disposing the thread in sewing or the style of work produced by one such method. **4.** one complete movement of the needle or other implement used in knitting, crocheting, netting, tatting, etc. **5.** the portion of work produced. **6.** a thread, bit, or piece of any fabric or of clothing: *every stitch of clothes.* **7.** the least bit of anything: *He wouldn't do a stitch of work.* **8.** a sudden, sharp pain, esp. in the intercostal muscles: *a stitch in the side.* —*v.t.* **9.** to work upon, join, mend, or fasten with stitches; sew; ornament with stitches. **10.** to put staples through for fastening: *to stitch cartons.* —*v.i.* **11.** to make stitches, join together, or sew. [ME *stiche*, OE *stice*; c. G *Stich* prick; akin to STICK[2]] —**stitch′er,** *n.* —**stitch′like′,** *adj.*

stitch[2] (stich), *n.* *Brit. Dial.* a distance, as in walking. [ME *sticche*, OE *stycce* piece; c. G *Stück*]

stitch·ing (stich′ing), *n.* **1.** the act of one who or that which stitches. **2.** a series or line of stitches. **3.** mending by means of sewing. [STITCH[1] + -ING[1]]

stitch·work (stich′wûrk′), *n.* embroidery or needlework. [STITCH[1] + WORK]

stitch·wort (stich′wûrt′), *n.* any of certain herbs of the genus *Stellaria* (or *Alsine*), as *S. Holostea*, of the Old World, having white flowers. [ME *stichewort*, OE *sticwyrt* agrimony. See STITCH[1], WORT[2]]

stith·y (stith′ē, stith′ē), *n., pl.* **stith·ies,** *v.*, **stith·ied, stith·y·ing.** —*n.* **1.** an anvil. **2.** a forge or smithy. —*v.t.* **3.** *Obs.* to forge. [ME *stithie*, var. of *stethie* < Scand; cf. Icel *stethja* (acc. of *stethi*); akin to STAND]

sti·ver (stī′vər), *n.* **1.** Also, **stuiver.** a former nickel coin of the Netherlands, equal to five Dutch cents. **2.** the smallest possible amount: *not worth a stiver; not a stiver of work.* [< D *stuiver*]

St. James, 1. a town in S Minnesota. 4174 (1960). **2.** a town on N Long Island, in SE New York. 3524 (1960).

St.-James's-flow·er (sānt′jāmz′flou′ər, -jām′ziz-), *n.* a perennial herb, *Lotus Jacobaeus*, of the Cape Verde Islands, having black-purple or yellow flowers. Also called **St.-James's-pea.**

St. James's Palace (sānt′ jām′ziz, sənt), a palace in London, England: the royal residence from the time of Henry VIII until the accession of Victoria. Also called **St. James's.** Cf. **Court of St. James's.**

St.-James's-pea (sānt′jāmz′pē′, -jām′ziz-), *n.* See **St.-James's-flower.**

St. Joe, *Informal.* St. Joseph, Missouri.

St. John (sānt′ jon′; *for 1 also* sin′jən), **1. Henry, 1st Viscount Bolingbroke.** See **Bolingbroke, 1st Viscount. 2.** an island of the Virgin Islands of the United States, in the E West Indies. 925 (1960); ab. 20 sq. mi. **3. Lake,** a lake in SE Canada, in Quebec province, draining into the Saguenay River. 365 sq. mi. **4.** a river in the NE United States and SE Canada, flowing NE and E from Maine to New Brunswick province and then S to the Bay of Fundy. 450 mi. long. **5.** a town in E Missouri. 7342 (1960). **6.** See **St. John's.**

St.-John Perse (sin′jən′ pûrs′), (*Alexis Saint-Léger Léger*), born 1887, French diplomat and poet: Nobel prize 1960.

St. Johns, 1. a river flowing N and E through NE Florida into the Atlantic. 276 mi. long. **2.** a town in central Michigan. 5629 (1960).

St. John's, 1. a seaport in and the capital of Newfoundland, on the SE part of the island. 57,078 (1961). **2.** a seaport on and the capital of Antigua, in the E West Indies. 21,637 (1960). Also, **St. John.**

St. John's-bread (jonz′bred′), carob (def. 1).

St. Johns·bur·y (jonz′ber′ē, -bə rē), a town in NE Vermont. 6809 (1960).

St. John's Day. See **Midsummer Day.**

St. John's Eve. See **Midsummer Eve.** Also called **St. John's Night.**

St.-John's-wort (sānt′jonz′wûrt′), *n.* any of various herbs or shrubs of the genus *Hypericum*, having yellow flowers and pellucid-dotted leaves. [so named because gathered on eve of St. John the Baptist's day to ward off evil]

St. Joseph, a city in NW Missouri, on the Missouri River. 79,673 (1960).

St.-Jo·seph's-wand (sānt′jō′zəfs wond′, -səfs-), *n.* a perennial herb, *Pentstemon acuminatus*, of the northwestern U.S., having bluish-green stems and blue, bearded flowers.

St. Julian cross, *Heraldry.* a cross-crosslet saltirewise, or diagonally.

stk., stock.

St. Kitts (kits), one of the Leeward Islands, in the E West Indies: a member of the West Indies Associated States; formerly a British colony. 38,291 (1960); 68 sq. mi. Also called **St. Christopher.**

St. Kitts-Ne·vis-An·guil·la (kits′nē′vis ang gwil′ə, -nev′is), a former British colony in the Leeward Islands, in the E West Indies: comprising St. Kitts, Nevis, Anguilla, and adjacent small islands; a member of the West Indies Associated States. 56,591 (est. 1964); 155 sq. mi.

S.T.L., Licentiate in Sacred Theology.

St. Lau·rent (san lô räN′), **1. Louis Ste·phen** (lwē ste fen′), born 1882, prime minister of Canada 1948–57. **2. Yves Ma·thieu** (ēv ma tyœ′), born 1936, French fashion designer.

St. Lawrence, 1. a river in SE Canada, flowing NE from Lake Ontario, forming part of the boundary between New York and Ontario, and emptying into the Gulf of St. Lawrence. 760 mi. long. **2. Gulf of,** an arm of the Atlantic between SE Canada and Newfoundland.

St. Lawrence Seaway, a series of channels, locks, and canals between Montreal and the mouth of Lake Ontario, a distance of 182 miles, enabling most deep-draft vessels to travel from the Atlantic Ocean, up the St. Lawrence River, to all the Great Lakes ports: developed jointly by the U.S. and Canada.

St. Lawrence skiff, skiff (def. 2).

stlg., sterling.

St. Lô (san lō′), a city in and the capital of Manche, in NW France: World War II battle June–July 1944. 16,072 (1962).

St. Lou·is (sānt′ lōō′is, lōō′ē), **1.** a port in E Missouri, on the Mississippi. 750,026 (1960). **2.** a town in central Michigan. 3808 (1960).

St. Louis Park, a city in E Minnesota, near Minneapolis. 43,310 (1960).

St. Louis School, *Philos.* a group of philosophers, working mainly in St. Louis, Mo., c1860–80, advocating a Neo-Hegelianism influenced somewhat by American transcendentalism. Also called **St. Louis Movement.**

St. Lu·ci·a (lōō′shē ə, -sē ə), one of the Windward Islands, in the E West Indies: a member of the West Indies Associated States; formerly a British colony. 86,108 (est. 1964); 238 sq. mi. *Cap.:* Castries.

St. Lucie cherry, mahaleb.

S.T.M., Master of Sacred Theology.

St. Ma·lo (san ma lō′), **1.** a fortified seaport in NW France, on the Gulf of St. Malo: resort; surrendered by German forces August 1944. 17,800 (1962). **2. Gulf of,** an arm of the English Channel in NW France. 60 mi. wide.

St. Mar·tin (sānt′ mär′tən, -tin; *Fr.* san mar tan′), an island in the N Leeward Islands, in the E West Indies, divided in two parts: the N section is a dependency of Guadeloupe. 3366 (1955); 20 sq. mi.; the S section is an administrative part of the Netherlands Antilles. 1537 (1960); 17 sq. mi.

St. Mar·tin·ville (mär′tən vil′, -tin-), a town in S Louisiana. 6468 (1960).

St. Mar·ys (mâr′ēz), **1.** a river in the north-central U.S. and S Canada, forming the boundary between NE Michigan and Ontario, flowing SE from Lake Superior into Lake Huron. 63 mi. long. Cf. **Sault Ste. Marie. 2.** a town in central Pennsylvania. 8065 (1960). **3.** a town in W Ohio. 7737 (1960). **4.** a town in SE Georgia. 3272 (1960).

St. Matthews, a town in N Kentucky. 8738 (1960).

St.-Mi·hiel (san mē yel′), *n.* a town in NE France, on the Meuse River, NW of Nancy: captured by American forces 1918. 5366 (1962).

St. Mo·ritz (mō rits′, mō-, mə-; mōr′its, môr′-), a resort town in SE Switzerland: a popular center for winter sports. 3751 (1960); 6037 ft. high. German, **Sankt Moritz.**

St. Na·zaire (san na zar′), a seaport in W France, on the Loire estuary. 59,181 (1962).

sto·a (stō′ə), *n., pl.* **sto·as, sto·ai** (stō′ī), **sto·ae** (stō′ē). **1.** *Gk. Archit.* a portico, usually a detached portico of considerable length, that is used as a promenade or meeting place. **2.** *Philos.* (*often cap.*) any of the phases of Stoicism: early, middle, or late. [< Gk *stoá*]

stoat (stōt), *n.* the ermine, *Mustela erminea*, esp. when in brown summer pelage. [ME *stote* < ?]

stoa·ting (stō′ting), *n.* *Tailoring.* the process or technique of finishing a facing, collar, or the like, or of mending material with concealed stitching. Also, **stoting.** [?]

stob (stob), *n.* *Chiefly Dial.* a post. [ME; var. of STUB[1]]

stoc·ca·do (stə kä′dō), *n., pl.* **-dos.** *Archaic.* a thrust with a rapier or other pointed weapon. Also, **stoc·ca·ta** (stə kä′tə). [alter. of It *stoccata*, equiv. to *stocc(o)* swordpoint, dagger (< Gmc; cf. OE *stocc* stake) + *-ata* -ADE[1]; *-ado* < Sp, as in *renegado*]

sto·chas·tic (stə kas′tik), *adj.* *Statistics.* of or pertaining to a process involving a randomly determined sequence of observations each of which is considered as a sample of one element from a probability distribution. Stochastic variation implies randomness as opposed to a fixed rule or relation in passing from one observation to the next in order. [< Gk *stochastik(ós)*, equiv. to *stochas-* (var. s. of *stocházesthai* to aim at) + *-tikos* -TIC] —**sto·chas′ti·cal·ly,** *adv.*

stochas′tic independ′ence, *Math.* the property of two events so related that the probability of the occurrence of both is equal to the product of the probabilities of the occurrence of each.

stochas′tic ma′trix, *Math.* a square matrix with positive entries in which the entries in each row add to 1.

stock (stok), *n.* **1.** a supply of goods kept on hand for sale to customers by a merchant, distributor, manufacturer, etc.; inventory. **2.** a quantity of something accumulated, as for future use: *a stock of provisions.* **3.** livestock. **4.** *Theat.* a stock company: *He played in summer stock.* **5.** *Finance.* **a.** the outstanding capital of a company or corporation. **b.** the shares of a particular company or corporation. **c.** the certificate of ownership of such stock; stock certificate. **d.** (formerly) a tally or stick used in transactions between a debtor and a creditor. **6.** *Hort.* **a.** a stem in grafting in which the bud or scion is inserted. **b.** a stem, tree, or plant that furnishes slips or cuttings; stock plant. **7.** the trunk or main stem of a tree or other plant, as distinguished from roots and branches. **8.** the type from which a group of animals or plants has been derived. **9.** a race or other related group of animals or plants. **10.** the person from whom a given line of descent is derived; the original progenitor. **11.** a line of de-

scent; a tribe, race, or ethnic group. **12.** *Anthropol.* a major division of mankind: *Caucasoid stock; Mongoloid stock.* **13.** *Ling.* a category consisting of language families which, because of resemblances in grammatical structure or sometimes because of cognates in vocabulary, are considered likely to be related by common origin. Cf. **family** (def. 10), **phylum** (def. 2). **14.** any grouping of related languages. **15.** the center of a wheel; hub. **16.** the handle of a whip, fishing rod, etc. **17.** *Firearms.* **a.** the wooden or metal piece to which the barrel and mechanism of a rifle are attached. **b.** a part of an automatic weapon, as a machine gun, similar in position or function. **18.** the trunk or stump of a tree, left standing. **19.** *Archaic.* a log or block of wood. **20.** a dull or stupid person. **21.** something lifeless or senseless. **22.** the main upright part of anything, esp. a supporting structure. **23. stocks, a.** a former instrument of punishment consisting of a framework with holes for securing the ankles and, sometimes, the wrists, used to expose an offender to public derision. Cf. **pillory** (def. 1). **b.** a frame in which a horse or other animal is secured in a standing position for shoeing or for a veterinary operation. **c.** the frame on which a boat rests while under construction. **24.** *Naut.* a vertical shaft forming part of a rudder and controlling the rudder's movement. **25.** the metal or wooden body of a carpenter's plane. **26.** *Metall.* **a.** material being smelted in a blast furnace. **b.** a metal piece to be forged. **27.** *Printing, Publishing.* **a.** a specified quality or kind of paper: *glossy stock; card stock; offset stock.* **b.** the paper for printing a particular job: *We don't have enough stock for that large a run.* **28.** the raw material from which something is made. **29.** *Naut.* a transverse piece of wood or metal near the ring occurring on some anchors. See diag. under **anchor. 30.** *Papermaking.* stuff (def. 14). **31.** *Cookery.* the liquor or broth prepared by boiling meat, fish, chicken, etc., with or without vegetables or seasonings, and used esp. as a foundation for soups and sauces. **32.** any of several plants of the genus *Mathiola*, esp. *M. incana*, having fragrant white, blue, purple, reddish, or yellowish flowers. **33.** a rhizome or rootstock. **34.** *Zool.* a compound organism. **35.** a collar or a neckcloth fitting like a band around the neck. **36.** *Cards.* that portion of a pack of cards which, in certain games, is not dealt out to the players, but is left on the table, to be drawn from as occasion requires. **37.** an adjustable wrench for holding dies for cutting screws. **38.** *Railroads.* See **rolling stock. 39.** *Dominoes.* boneyard (def. 1). **40.** *Archaic.* a stocking. **41.** *Rom. Cath. Ch.* one of a set of three metal containers for holy oil. **42.** *Obs.* the frame of a plow to which the share, handles, etc., are attached. **43. in stock,** on hand for use or sale: *There are no more blue skirts in stock.* **44. lock, stock, and barrel.** See **lock**[1] (def. 11). **45. on the stocks, a.** under construction, as esp. a ship. **b.** in progress or preparation: *a new novel on the stocks.* **46. out of stock,** lacking a supply of, esp. temporarily: *We are out of stock in this item.* **47. take stock, a.** to make an inventory of stock on hand. **b.** to make an appraisal of resources or prospects: *She took stock of her decorating scheme and decided it was time for a change.* **48. take** or **put stock in,** *Informal.* to put confidence in or attach importance to; believe; trust; *Considering his general unreliability, I can't take stock in what he has told you.*
—*adj.* **49.** kept regularly on hand, as for use or sale; staple; standard: *stock articles.* **50.** having as one's job the care of a concern's goods: *a stock clerk.* **51.** of the common or ordinary type; in common use: *a stock argument.* **52.** banal; commonplace: *a stock remark.* **53.** pertaining to or designating the breeding and raising of livestock: *stock farming.* **54.** of or pertaining to the stock of a company or corporation: *a stock report.* **55.** *Theat.* **a.** pertaining to stock plays or pieces, or to a stock company. **b.** appearing together in a repertoire, as a company. **c.** forming part of a repertoire, as a play. **d.** being a character type fixed by convention, as in the commedia dell' arte, a harlequinade, minstrel show, or the like.
—*v.t.* **56.** to furnish with a stock or supply. **57.** to furnish with stock, as a farm with horses, cattle, etc. **58.** to lay up in store, as for future use. **59.** to fasten to or provide with a stock, as a rifle, plow, bell, anchor, etc. **60.** *Obs.* to put in the stocks as a punishment.
—*v.i.* **61.** to lay in a stock of something (often fol. by *up*). [ME; OE *stoc(c)* stump, stake, post, log; c. G *Stock*, Icel *stokkr* tree-trunk] —**stock′like′,** *adj.*
—**Syn. 1.** store, supply, provision, reserve. **11.** lineage, family. **16.** haft. **51.** ordinary, usual.

Stocks (def. 23a)

Stock (stok), *n.* **Frederick August,** 1872–1942, U.S. orchestra conductor, born in Germany.

stock·ade (sto kād′), *n., v.,* **-ad·ed, -ad·ing.** —*n.* **1.** *Fort.* a defensive barrier consisting of strong posts or timbers fixed upright in the ground. **2.** an enclosure or pen made with posts and stakes. **3.** *U.S. Mil.* a prison for military personnel. —*v.t.* **4.** to protect, fortify, or encompass with a stockade. [< MF (*e*)*stocade*, var. of *estacade* < Sp *estacad(a)*. See STAKE[1], -ADE[1]]

stock·a·teer (stok′ə tēr′), *n.* *Slang.* a person who deals in fraudulent securities, usually using high-pressure selling techniques. [STOCK + *-ateer*, as in *racketeer*]

stock′ book′, 1. See **stock ledger** (def. 1). **2.** See **stores ledger.**

stock·breed·er (stok′brē′dər), *n.* one who breeds and raises livestock for market or exhibition. [STOCK + BREEDER] —**stock′breed′ing,** *adj.*

stock·brok·er (stok′brō′kər), *n.* a broker, esp. one employed by a member firm of a stock exchange, who buys and sells stocks and other securities for his customers. [STOCK + BROKER] —**stock·brok·er·age** (stok′brō′kər ij), *n.*

stock′ car′, 1. a standard model of automobile changed in various ways for racing purposes. **2.** *Railroads.* a boxcar for carrying livestock. —**stock′-car′,** *adj.*

stock′ certif′icate, a certificate evidencing ownership of one or more shares of stock in a corporation.

stock′ clerk′, a worker in a stockroom who is in charge of the materials and goods stored there.

stock′ com′pany, 1. *Finance.* a company or corporation whose capital is divided into shares represented by stock. **2.** *Theat.* a company acting a repertoire of plays, more or less permanently together, usually at its own theater.

stock′ div′idend, *Finance.* **1.** a form of dividend collected by a stockholder in extra shares of the corporation's stock rather than in cash. **2.** the stock received in such dividend.

stock′ dove′, a wild pigeon, *Columba oenas*, of Europe. [ME *stokdove;* c. G *Stocktaube;* so called because it nests in hollow tree-trunks]

stock·er (stok′ər), *n.* **1.** one who or that which stocks. **2.** a young steer or heifer that is fed chiefly pasture or other roughage prior to more intensive feeding. Cf. **feeder** (def. 3). [STOCK + -ER[1]]

stock′ exchange′, 1. a building or place where stocks and other securities are bought and sold. **2.** an association of brokers and dealers in stocks and bonds who meet together and transact business according to fixed rules.

stock′ farm′, a farm devoted to breeding livestock. —**stock′ farm′er.** —**stock′ farm′ing.**

stock·fish (stok′fish′), *n., pl. (esp. collectively)* **-fish,** *(esp. referring to two or more kinds or species)* **-fish·es.** fish, as the cod or haddock, cured by splitting and drying in the air without salt. [ME *stokfish* < MD *stokvisch.* See STOCK, FISH]

stock′ foot′age, *Motion Pictures, Television.* film containing stock shots.

stock′ guard′, *Railroad.* a barrier for keeping cattle and other animals off the tracks or right of way.

stock·hold·er (stok′hōl′dər), *n.* **1.** a holder or owner of stock in a corporation. **2.** *Australian.* an owner of livestock, as a rancher. [STOCK + HOLDER]

stock′holder of rec′ord, a stockholder or his agent whose name is registered on the books of the issuing corporation at the close of a business day set for determining that stockholders shall receive dividends or vote on an issue.

Stock·holm (stok′hōm, -hōlm; *Swed.* stôk′hôlm′), *n.* the chief seaport in and the capital of Sweden, in the SE part. 791,500 (1965); with suburbs 1,245,748 (1965).

stock·horn (stok′hôrn′), *n.* pibgorn. [STOCK stem, reed + HORN]

stock′ horse′, *Western U.S.* a horse or pony used in herding cattle.

stock·i·net (stok′ə net′), *n.* **1.** *Chiefly Brit.* an elastic machine-knitted fabric used for making undergarments, infants' wear, etc. **2.** a stitch in knitting, all knit on the right side and all purl on the wrong side. [earlier *stocking-net*]

stock·ing (stok′ing), *n.* **1.** a close-fitting covering for the foot and part of the leg, usually knitted, of wool, cotton, nylon, silk, or similar material. **2.** something resembling such a covering. **3.** *Brit.* stockinet (def. 2). **4. in one's stocking feet,** wearing stockings, but without shoes: *Be careful of glass splinters if you walk through here in your stocking feet.* [STOCK + -ING[1]] —**stock′-inged,** *adj.* —**stock′ing·less,** *adj.*

stock′ing cap′, a long, conical, knitted cap, usually with a tassel or pompon at the tip.

stock′ing stuff′er, a small gift that is placed with others in a Christmas stocking, as a piece of fruit or a tiny picture book.

stock′ in trade′, 1. the requisites for carrying on a business, esp. goods kept on hand for sale in a store. **2.** resources or abilities peculiar to an individual or group or employed for a specific purpose: *A sense of style is part of the stock in trade of any writer.* Also, **stock′-in-trade′.**

stock·ish (stok′ish), *adj.* like a block of wood; stupid. [STOCK + -ISH[1]] —**stock′ish·ly,** *adv.* —**stock′ish·ness,** *n.*

stock·ist (stok′ist), *n.* *Brit.* a wholesale or retail establishment that stocks merchandise. [STOCK + -IST]

stock·job·ber (stok′job′ər), *n.* **1.** *Often Contemptuous.* a stock salesman, esp. one who sells or promotes worthless securities. **2.** *Brit.* a stock-exchange operator who acts as an intermediary between brokers but does not do business with the public. [STOCK + JOBBER] —**stock′-job′ber·y, stock′job′bing,** *n.*

stock′ ledg′er, 1. a permanent record of the capital stock of a corporation, listing the names and addresses of the stockholders, the number of the shares owned, the serial numbers of their stock certificates, etc. **2.** See **stores ledger.** Also, **stock book.**

stock·less (stok′lis), *adj.* having no stock, as an anchor. [STOCK + -LESS]

stock·man (stok′mən *or, for 3,* -man′), *n., pl.* **-men** (-mən *or, for 3,* -men′). **1.** *U.S. and Australia.* a man who raises livestock. **2.** a man employed on a stock farm. **3.** a man in charge of a stock of goods, as in a warehouse. [STOCK + MAN[1]]

stock′ mar′ket, 1. a particular market where stocks and bonds are traded; stock exchange. **2.** the market for securities, esp. stocks, throughout a nation: *The stock market reacted strongly to the President's speech.*

stock′ op′tion, an option giving the holder, usually an officer or employee, the right to buy stock of the issuing corporation at a specific price within a stated period.

stock·pile (stok′pīl′), *n., v.,* **-piled, -pil·ing.** —*n.* **1.** a supply of material, as a pile of gravel in road maintenance. **2.** a large supply of some metal, chemical, food, etc., gathered and held in reserve for use during a shortage or during a period of higher prices. **3.** a quantity, as of munitions or weapons, accumulated for possible future use. —*v.t.* **4.** to accumulate for future use; put or store in a stockpile. —*v.i.* **5.** to accumulate in a stockpile. [STOCK + PILE[1]] —**stock′pil′er,** *n.*

Stock·port (stok′pôrt′, -pōrt′), *n.* a city in NE Cheshire, in NW England, near Manchester. 142,469 (1961).

stock·pot (stok′pot′), *n.* a pot in which stock for soup, sauces, etc., is made and kept. [STOCK + POT[1]]

stock′ pow′er, a power of attorney permitting a person other than the owner of stock in a corporation to transfer the title of ownership to a third party.

stock′ rais′ing, the breeding and raising of livestock. —**stock′ rais′er.**

stock′ rec′ord. See **stores ledger.**

stock·rid·er (stok′rī′dər), *n.* *Australian.* a cowboy. [STOCK + RIDER]

stock·room (stok′ro͞om′, -ro͝om′), *n.* a room in which a stock of materials or goods is kept for use or sale. [STOCK + ROOM]

stock-route (stok′ro͞ot′, -rout′), *n.* *Australian.* a public trail having right of way across private properties and over which cattle and sheep may be herded to grazing grounds or to market.

stock′ sad′dle. See **Western saddle.**

stock′ shot′, *Motion Pictures, Television.* a film clip, as from a newsreel or travelogue, kept and used as an insert or background shot for other motion pictures.

stock′ solu′tion, *Photog.* a concentrated chemical solution, diluted before using.

stock-still (stok′stil′), *adj.* motionless. [ME *stok still.* See STOCK, STILL[1]]

stock·tak·ing (stok′tā′king), *n.* **1.** the examination or counting over of materials or goods on hand, as in a stockroom or store. **2.** the act of appraising a present situation, condition, degree of progress, etc., in terms of accomplishments and ultimate goals. [STOCK + TAKING]

stock′ tick′er, ticker (def. 2).

Stock·ton (stok′tən), *n.* **1. Frank R.** (*Francis Richard Stockton*), 1834–1902, U.S. novelist and short-story writer. **2.** a city in central California, on the San Joaquin River. 86,321 (1960).

Stock·ton-on-Tees (stok′tən on tēz′, -ôn-), *n.* a seaport in SE Durham, in NE England, near the mouth of the Tees River. 81,189 (1961).

stock·y (stok′ē), *adj.,* **stock·i·er, stock·i·est. 1.** of solid and sturdy form or build; thick-set and, usually, short. **2.** having a strong, stout stem, as a plant. [late ME *stokky.* See STOCK, -Y[1]] —**stock′i·ly,** *adv.* —**stock′i·ness,** *n.*

stock·yard (stok′yärd′), *n.* **1.** an enclosure with pens, sheds, etc., connected with a slaughterhouse, railroad, market, etc., for the temporary keeping of cattle, sheep, swine, or horses. **2.** a yard for livestock. [STOCK + YARD[2]]

stodge (stoj), *v.,* **stodged, stodg·ing,** *n.* —*v.t.* **1.** to stuff full, esp. with food or drink; gorge. —*v.i.* **2.** *Informal.* to trudge: *to stodge along through the mire.* —*n.* **3.** food that is particularly filling. [?; in some senses b. *stoff* (earlier form of STUFF) and GORGE]

stodg·y (stoj′ē), *adj.,* **stodg·i·er, stodg·i·est. 1.** heavy, dull, or uninteresting; tediously commonplace; boring: *a stodgy Victorian novel.* **2.** of a thick, semisolid consistency; heavy, as food. **3.** stocky; thick-set. **4.** old-fashioned; unduly formal and traditional: *a stodgy old gentleman.* **5.** dull; graceless; inelegant: *a stodgy business suit.* [STODGE + -Y[1]] —**stodg′i·ly,** *adv.* —**stodg′i·ness,** *n.*

stoe·chi·om·e·try (stē′kē om′i trē), *n.* stoichiometry. —**stoe·chi·o·met·ri·cal·ly** (stē′kē ə me′trik lē), *adv.*

Stöf·ler (stô′flər), *n.* an irregularly shaped, somewhat elliptical, walled plain in the fourth quadrant of the face of the moon: about 82 miles long and 62 miles wide.

sto·gey (stō′gē), *n., pl.* **-gies.** stogy.

sto·gy (stō′gē), *n., pl.* **-gies. 1.** a long, slender, roughly made, inexpensive cigar. **2.** a coarse, heavy boot or shoe. [*stog(a)* (short for *Conestoga,* town in Pennsylvania) + -Y[2]]

Sto·ic (stō′ik), *adj.* **1.** of or pertaining to the school of philosophy founded by Zeno, who taught that men should be free from passion, unmoved by joy or grief, and submit without complaint to unavoidable necessity. **2.** (*l.c.*) stoical. —*n.* **3.** a member or adherent of the Stoic school of philosophy. **4.** (*l.c.*) one who maintains or affects the mental attitude advocated by the Stoics. [< L *Stōic(us)* < Gk *Stōikós*, equiv. to *stō(i)-* (var. s. of *stoá* STOA) + *-ikos* -IC]

sto·i·cal (stō′i kəl), *adj.* **1.** impassive; characterized by a calm, austere fortitude befitting the Stoics: *a stoical sufferer.* **2.** (*cap.*) of or pertaining to the Stoics. [STOIC + -AL[1]] —**sto′i·cal·ly,** *adv.* —**sto′i·cal·ness,** *n.*
—**Syn. 1.** imperturbable, cool, indifferent. —**Ant. 1.** sympathetic, warm.

stoi·chei·om·e·try (stoi′kē om′i trē), *n.* stoichiometry. —**stoi·chei·o·met·ri·cal·ly** (stoi′kē ə me′trik lē), *adv.*

stoi·chi·o·met·ric (stoi′kē ə me′trik), *adj.* *Chem.* **1.** of or pertaining to stoichiometry. **2.** pertaining to or involving substances which are in the exact proportions required for a given reaction. Also, **stoi′chi·o·met′ri·cal.** [< Gk *stoicheío(n)* component (akin to *stíchos* STICH[1]) + METRIC[2]] —**stoi′chi·o·met′ri·cal·ly,** *adv.*

stoi·chi·om·e·try (stoi′kē om′i trē), *n.* **1.** the calculation of the quantities of chemical elements or compounds involved in chemical reactions. **2.** the branch of chemistry dealing with relationships of combining elements, esp. quantitatively. Also, **stoechiometry, stoicheiometry.** [< Gk *stoicheío(n)* (see STOICHIOMETRIC) + -METRY]

Sto·i·cism (stō′i siz′əm), *n.* **1.** the philosophy of the Stoics. **2.** (*l.c.*) conduct conforming to the precepts of the Stoics, as repression of emotion, indifference to pleasure or pain, etc. [STOIC + -ISM]
—**Syn. 2.** See **patience.**

stoit (stōt, stoit), *Brit. Dial.* —*v.i.* **1.** to move, esp. to walk, unsteadily; stagger; totter. —*n.* **2.** a lurch; stagger. [appar. < Scand; cf. Icel *stauta* to kick, thrust, c. G *stossen* to push (the *i* of *oi* serves simply to mark the *o* long); akin to Scot *stot* to lurch, bounce; cf. ME, OE *stot* kind of horse (orig. a frisky one)]

stoit·er (stō′tər, stoi′-), *v.i., n.* *Chiefly Scot.* stoit.

stoke[1] (stōk), *v.,* **stoked, stok·ing.** —*v.t.* **1.** to poke, stir up, and feed (a fire). **2.** to tend the fire of (a furnace, esp. one used with a boiler to generate steam for an engine); supply with fuel. —*v.i.* **3.** to shake up the coals of a fire. **4.** to tend a fire or furnace; act as a stoker: *to stoke for a living.* [< D *stoke(n)* (to) feed or stock a fire; see STOCK]

stoke[2] (stōk), *n.* *Physics.* a unit of kinematic viscosity, equal to the viscosity of a fluid in poises divided by the density of the fluid in grams per cubic centimeter. [after Sir George *Stokes* (1819–1903), British physicist]

stoke·hold (stōk′hōld′), *n.* See **fire room.** Also, **stokehole.** [STOKE[1] + HOLD[2]]

stoke·hole (stōk′hōl′), *n.* **1.** stokehold. **2.** a hole in a furnace through which the fire is stoked. [STOKE[1] + HOLE]

Stoke-on-Trent (stōk′on trent′, -ôn-), *n.* a city in N Staffordshire, in central England, on the Trent River: pottery and china. 265,506 (1961). Also, **Stoke′-up·on-Trent′.** Cf. **Potteries.**

Stoke Po·ges (stōk′ pō′jis), a village in S Buckinghamshire, in S England, W of London: the churchyard here is probably the setting of Gray's *Elegy.*

stok·er (stō′kər), *n.* **1.** one who or that which stokes. **2.** a laborer employed to tend and fuel a furnace, esp. a furnace used to generate steam, as on a steamship. **3.** *Chiefly Brit.* the fireman on a locomotive. **4.** a mechanical device for supplying coal or other solid fuel to a furnace. [< D, equiv. to *stok(en)* (to) STOKE[1] + *-er* -ER[1]] —**stok′er·less,** *adj.*

Stokes (stōks), *n.* **Sir Frederick Wilfrid Scott,** 1860–1927, British inventor and engineer.

Stokes′-Ad′ams syn′drome (stōks′ad′əmz), *Med.* a combination of symptoms characterizing a condition resembling epilepsy, as sudden attacks of unconsciousness, irregular pulse, and intermittent convulsive seizures, caused by blockage and consequent independence of beat between the auricle and ventricle. Also, **Stokes′-Ad′ams disease′, Adams-Stokes syndrome, Adams-Stokes disease.** [named after W. *Stokes* (1804–78), and R. *Adams* (1791–1875), Irish physicians]

Stokes′′ as′ter (stōks), a composite herb, *Stokesia laevis,* having lavender-blue, asterlike flowers. [named after J. *Stokes* (d. 1831), English botanist]

Sto·ke·si·a (stō kē′zhē ə, -zē ə, -zhə, stōk′sē ə), *n.* a plant of the genus *Stokesia.* Cf. **Stokes' aster.** [< NL; see STOKES' ASTER, -IA]

Stokes′′ Law′, *Physics.* **1.** the law that the force that retards a sphere moving through a viscous fluid is directly proportional to the velocity of the sphere, the radius of the sphere, and the viscosity of the fluid. **2.** the law that the frequency of luminescence induced by radiation is usually less than the frequency of the radiation. [see STOKE[2]]

Sto·kow·ski (stə kou′skē, -kôf′-, -kôv′-), *n.* **Le·o·pold An·to·ni Sta·ni·slaw** (lē′ə pōld′ än tō′nē stä nē′släf), 1882–1977, U.S. orchestra conductor, born in England.

STOL (es′tôl′), *n.* a convertiplane capable of becoming airborne after a short takeoff run, having forward speeds comparable to those of conventional aircraft. [*s(hort) t(ake)o(ff and) l(anding)*]

sto·la (stō′lə), *n., pl.* **-lae** (-lē), **-las.** a long, loose tunic or robe, with or without sleeves, worn by women of ancient Rome. [< L < Gk *stolḗ;* see STOLE[2]]

stole[1] (stōl), *v.* pt. of **steal.**

stole[2] (stōl), *n.* **1.** an ecclesiastical vestment consisting of a narrow strip of silk or other material worn over the shoulders or, by deacons, over the left shoulder only, and arranged to hang down in front to the knee or below. Cf. **tippet** (def. 2). **2.** a woman's shoulder scarf of fur, marabou, silk, or other material. Cf. **tippet** (def. 1). **3.** *Archaic.* a long robe, esp. one worn by Roman matrons. [ME, OE < L *stol(a)* < Gk *stolḗ* clothing, robe; akin to Gk *stéllein* to array, OE *stellan* to place, put]

stole′ fee′, *Rom. Cath. Ch.* a fee paid by a lay person to a priest for a sacrament or rite.

sto·len (stō′lən), *v.* pp. of **steal.**

stol·id (stol′id), *adj.* not easily stirred or moved mentally; unemotional; impassive. [< L *stolid(us)* immovable, dull, stupid; akin to STILL[1], STOLE[2]] —**sto·lid·i·ty** (stə lid′i tē), **stol′id·ness,** *n.* —**stol′id·ly,** *adv.*

sto·lon (stō′lən), *n.* **1.** *Bot.* a prostrate stem at or just below the surface of the ground, which produces new plants from buds at its tips or nodes. **2.** *Zool.* a rootlike extension in a compound organism, usually giving rise to new zooids by budding. [< L *stolōn-* (s. of *stolō*) branch, shoot, twig] —**sto·lon·ic** (stō lon′ik), *adj.*

sto·lon·ate (stō′lə nit, -nāt′), *adj.* having stolons; developing from a stolon. [< NL; see STOLON, -ATE[1]]

sto·lo·nif·er·ous (stō′lə nif′ər əs), *adj.* producing or bearing stolons. [STOLON + -I- + -FEROUS] —**sto′lon·if′er·ous·ly,** *adv.*

sto·lon·i·za·tion (stō′lə ni zā′shən), *n.* the production of stolons. [STOLON + -IZE + -ATION]

sto·ma (stō′mə), *n., pl.* **sto·ma·ta** (stō′mə tə, stom′ə-), **sto·mas.** **1.** *Bot.* any of various small apertures, esp. one of the minute orifices or slits in the epidermis of leaves, stems, etc. **2.** *Zool.* a mouth or ingestive opening, esp. when in the form of a small or simple aperture. [< NL < Gk: mouth]

stom·ach (stum′ək), *n.* **1.** *Anat. Zool.* **a.** a saclike enlargement of the alimentary canal, as in man and certain animals, forming an organ for storing, diluting, and digesting food. **b.** such an organ or an analogous portion of the alimentary canal when divided into two or more sections or parts. **c.** any one of these sections. **2.** any analogous digestive cavity or tract in invertebrates. **3.** the part of the body containing the stomach; belly or abdomen. **4.** appetite for food. **5.** desire, inclination, or liking: *I have no stomach for this trip.* **6.** *Obs.* **a.** spirit; courage. **b.** pride; haughtiness. **c.** resentment; anger. —*v.t.* **7.** to take into or retain in the stomach. **8.** to endure or tolerate (someone or something): *He couldn't stomach her constant nagging.* **9.** *Obs.* to be offended at or resent. [late ME *stomak* < L *stomach(us)* gullet, stomach < Gk *stómachos,* orig. opening; akin to STOMA]

A
B
E
C
D
F

Human stomach
A, Esophagus
B, Fundus
C, Cardiac portion
D, Pyloric portion
E, Pylorus
F, Duodenum

stom′ach ache′, pain in the stomach or abdomen; gastralgia; colic. —**stom′ach-ach′y,** *adj.*

stom·ach·er (stum′ə kər), *n.* a richly ornamented garment covering the stomach and chest, worn by both sexes in the 15th and 16th centuries, and later worn under a bodice by women. [late ME; see STOMACH, -ER[1]]

Stomacher

sto·mach·ic (stō mak′ik), *adj.* Also, **sto·mach′i·cal.** **1.** of or pertaining to the stomach; gastric. **2.** beneficial to the stomach; stimulating gastric digestion; sharpening the appetite. —*n.* **3.** a stomachic agent or drug. [< L *stomachic(us)* < Gk *stomachikós.* See STOMACH, -IC] —**sto·mach′i·cal·ly,** *adv.*

stom′ach pump′, *Med.* a suction pump for removing the contents of the stomach, used esp. in cases of poisoning.

stom′ach sweet′bread. See under **sweetbread** (def. 1).

stom′ach tooth′, a lower canine milk tooth of infants. [so called because there is often gastric disturbance at the time of its appearance]

stom′ach worm′, a nematode, *Haemonchus contortus,* parasitic in the stomach of sheep, cattle, and related animals. Also called **twisted stomach worm, wireworm.**

stom·ach·y (stum′ə kē), *adj.* **1.** *Brit. Dial.* irritable; quick to take offense. **2.** paunchy; having a prominent stomach. [STOMACH + -Y[1]]

sto·ma·ta (stō′mə tə, stom′ə-), *n.* pl. of **stoma.**

stom·a·tal (stom′ə t^{ə}l, stō′mə-), *adj.* **1.** of, pertaining to, or of the nature of a stoma. **2.** having stomata. [STOMAT- + -AL[1]]

sto·mat·ic (stō mat′ik), *adj.* **1.** pertaining to the mouth. **2.** stomatal. [< Gk *stomatikós.* See STOMAT-, -IC]

sto·ma·ti·tis (stō′mə tī′tis, stom′ə-), *n.* *Pathol.* inflammation of the mouth. [STOMAT- + -ITIS] —**sto·ma·tit·ic** (stō′mə tit′ik, stom′ə-), *adj.*

stomato-, a learned borrowing from Greek meaning "mouth," used in the formation of compound words: *stomatoplasty.* Also, *esp. before a vowel,* **stomat-.** Cf. **-stome, -stomous, -stomy.** [< Gk *stomat-,* s. of *stóma;* see STOMA]

sto·ma·tol·o·gy (stō′mə tol′ə jē, stom′ə-), *n.* the science dealing with the mouth and its diseases. [STOMATO- + -LOGY] —**sto·ma·to·log·ic** (stō′mə t^{ə}loj′ik), **sto′ma·to·log′i·cal,** *adj.* —**sto′ma·tol′o·gist,** *n.*

sto·mat·o·my (stō mat′ə mē), *n., pl.* **-mies.** *Surg.* stomatotomy.

sto·ma·to·plas·ty (stō′mə tə plas′tē, stom′ə-), *n.* plastic surgery of the mouth. [STOMATO- + -PLASTY] —**stom′a·to·plas′tic,** *adj.*

sto·ma·to·pod (stō′mə tə pod′, stom′ə), *n.* any crustacean of the order *Stomatopoda,* having a carapace that does not cover the posterior thorax and a broad abdomen bearing gills on the appendages. [STOMATO- + -POD]

sto·ma·tot·o·my (stō′mə tot′ə mē, stom′ə-), *n., pl.* **-mies.** *Surg.* incision of the cervix to facilitate labor. Also, **stomatomy.** [STOMATO- + -TOMY]

stom·a·tous (stom′ə təs, stō′mə-), *adj.* stomatal. [STOMAT- + -OUS]

-stome, var. of **stomato-** as second element of compound words: *cyclostome.* Cf. **-stomous, -stomy.** [comb. form repr. Gk *stóma* mouth, and *stómion* little mouth]

sto·mo·dae·um (stō′mə dē′əm, stom′ə-), *n., pl.* **-dae·a** (-dē′ə). stomodeum. —**sto′mo·dae′al,** *adj.*

sto·mo·de·um (stō′mə dē′əm, stom′ə-), *n., pl.* **-de·a** (-dē′ə). *Embryol.* a depression in the ectoderm of the oral region of a young embryo, which develops into the mouth and oral cavity. [< NL < Gk *stóm(a)* STOMA + *hodaîon* (neut. sing.) on the way; akin to -ODE[2]] —**sto′mo·de′al,** *adj.*

-stomous, a word element used to form adjectives corresponding to nouns with stems ending in **-stome.** *monostomous.* [-STOME + -OUS]

stomp (stomp), *v.t.* **1.** *Informal.* stamp. —*v.i.* **2.** *Informal.* stamp. **3.** to dance the stomp. —*n.* **4.** *Informal.* stamp. **5.** a jazz composition, esp. in early jazz, marked by a driving rhythm and a fast tempo. **6.** a dance to this music, usually marked by heavy stamping of the feet. [var. of STAMP] —**stomp′er,** *n.* —**stomp′ing·ly,** *adv.*

-stomy, a combining form used in names of surgical operations for making an artificial opening: *gastrostomy.* [< Gk *-stomia,* deriv. of *stóma* mouth. See -STOME, -Y[3]]

stone (stōn), *n., pl.* **stones** for 1–5, 7–19; **stone** for 6; *adj.; v.,* **stoned, ston·ing.** —*n.* **1.** the hard substance, formed from mineral and earth material, of which rocks consist. **2.** a rock or particular piece or kind of rock, as a boulder or piece of agate. **3.** a piece of rock quarried and worked into a specific size and shape for a particular purpose: *paving stone; building stone.* **4.** a piece of rock of small or moderate size, as a pebble. **5.** See **precious stone.** **6.** one of various units of weight, esp. the British unit equivalent to 14 pounds. **7.** something resembling a small piece of rock in size, shape, or hardness. **8.** any small, hard seed, as of a date; pit. **9.** *Bot.* the hard endocarp of a drupe, as of a peach. **10.** *Med.* **a.** a calculous concretion in the body, as in the kidney, gall bladder, or urinary bladder. **b.** a disease arising from such a concretion. **11.** a gravestone or tombstone. **12.** a grindstone. **13.** a millstone. **14.** a hailstone. **15.** *Building Trades.* any of various artificial materials imitating cut stone or rubble: *Coade stone.* **16.** *Print.* a table with a smooth surface, formerly made of stone, on which page forms are composed. **17.** (in lithography) any surface on which an artist draws or etches a picture or design from which a lithograph is made. **18.** a playing piece in the game of dominoes, checkers, or backgammon. **19.** Usually, **stones.** *Obs.* the testes. **20. cast the first stone,** to be the first to condemn or blame a wrongdoer; be hasty in one's judgment: *What right has she to cast the first stone?* **21. leave no stone unturned,** to exhaust every possibility in attempting to achieve one's goal; spare no effort: *We will leave no stone unturned in our efforts to find the culprit.* —*adj.* **22.** made of or pertaining to stone. **23.** made of stoneware: *a stone mug or bottle.* —*v.t.* **24.** to throw stones at; drive by pelting with stones. **25.** to put to death by pelting with stones. **26.** to provide, fit, pave, line, face or fortify with stones. **27.** to rub (something) with or on a stone, as to sharpen, polish, smooth, etc. **28.** to remove stones from, as fruit. **29.** *Obs.* to make insensitive or unfeeling. [ME; OE *stān;* c. D *steen,* G *Stein,* Icel *steinn,* Goth *stains;* akin to Gk *stía* pebble, L *stīria* icicle; basic sense, something hard] —**ston′a·ble, stone′a·ble,** *adj.* —**stone′less,** *adj.* —**stone′less·ness,** *n.* —**stone′like′,** *adj.* —**ston′er,** *n.*

Stone (stōn), *n.* **1. Edward Du·rell** (dŏŏ rel′, dyŏŏ-), 1902–78, U.S. architect. **2. Har·lan Fiske** (här′lən), 1872–1946, U.S. jurist: Chief Justice of the U.S. 1941–46. **3. Irving,** born 1903, U.S. author. **4. Lucy,** 1818–93, U.S. suffragist (wife of Henry Brown Blackwell).

Stone′ Age′, the period in the history of mankind, preceding the Bronze Age and the Iron Age, and marked by the use of stone implements and weapons: subdivided into the Paleolithic, Mesolithic, and Neolithic periods.

stone′ bass′ (bas), wreckfish.

stone-blind (stōn′blīnd′), *adj.* completely blind. [late ME (north) *staneblynde* blind as a stone] —**stone′-blind′ness,** *n.*
—**Syn.** See **blind.**

stone-broke (stōn′brōk′), *adj.* *Informal.* having no money whatsoever.

stone′ bruise′, a bruise on the sole of the foot, caused by walking on or striking against a small stone or other hard object. —**stone′-bruised′,** *adj.*

stone′ canal′, (in certain echinoderms) a tube lined with calcareous deposits, connecting the madreporite with a circular canal around the mouth.

stone·cat (stōn′kat′), *n.* a yellowish-brown, freshwater catfish, *Noturus flavus,* found in the Mississippi River valley and Great Lakes areas, having poisonous pectoral spines. Also called **beadeye.** [STONE + CAT[1]]

stone·chat (stōn′chat′), *n.* any of several small Old World thrushes, esp. of the genus *Saxicola,* as *S. torquata.* [STONE + CHAT[1], so called from its warning cry which sounds like a clash of stones]

stone′ chi′na, hard earthenware containing china stone.

stone′ crab′, an edible crab, *Menippe mercenaria,* of rocky shores from the southern U.S. to Mexico.

stone·crop (stōn′krop′), *n.* **1.** any plant of the genus *Sedum,* esp. a mosslike herb, *Sedum acre,* having small, fleshy leaves and yellow flowers, frequently growing on rocks and walls. **2.** any of various related plants. [ME *stooncrop,* OE *stāncrop.* See STONE, CROP]

stone′ cur′lew, thick-knee.

stone·cut·ter (stōn′kut′ər), *n.* **1.** one who cuts or carves stone. **2.** a machine for cutting or dressing stone. [STONE + CUTTER] —**stone′cut′ting,** *n.*

stoned (stōnd), *adj.* *Slang.* drunk. [STONE + -ED[2]]

stone-dead (stōn′ded′), *adj.* completely lifeless. [ME (north) *standed.* See STONE, DEAD]

stone-deaf (stōn′def′), *adj.* completely deaf.

stone·fish (stōn′fish′), *n., pl.* **-fish·es,** (*esp. collectively*) **-fish.** a tropical scorpaenid fish, *Synanceja verrucosa,* having dorsal-fin spines from which a deadly poison is discharged. [STONE + FISH]

stone·fly (stōn′flī′), *n., pl.* **-flies.** any of numerous drab-colored, membranous-winged insects of the order *Plecoptera,* having aquatic larvae often found under stones in streams. [ME *ston flie.* See STONE, FLY[2]]

stone′ fruit′, a fruit with a stone or hard endocarp, as a peach or plum; drupe.

Stone·ham (stō′nəm), *n.* a town in E Massachusetts, near Boston. 17,821 (1960).

stone-hand (stōn′hand′), *n.* *Print.* stoneman.

Stone·henge (stōn′henj), *n.* a prehistoric monument on Salisbury Plain, Wiltshire, England, consisting mainly of a large circle of megalithic posts and lintels.

stone′ lil′y, a fossil crinoid.

stone·man (stōn′mən), *n., pl.* **-men.** *Print.* the compositor who imposes type and secures it in the chase. Also called **imposer, stone-hand.** [STONE + MAN[1]]

stone′ mar′ten, a marten, *Mustela foina,* of Europe and Asia, having a white mark on the throat and breast. Also called **beech marten.**

stone·ma·son (stōn′mā′sən), *n.* one who builds with or dresses stone. [STONE + MASON] —**stone′ma′son·ry,** *n.*

Stone′ Moun′tain, a mountain in NW Georgia, near Atlanta: sculptures of Confederate heroes.

Stone′ Park′, a town in NE Illinois. 3038 (1960).

stone′ pars′ley, an umbelliferous herb, *Sison amomum,* of Eurasia, bearing aromatic seeds that are used as a condiment.

stone′ proof′, *Print.* a proof made from type while it is on the composing stone. Cf. **beaten proof.**

Stone′ Riv′er, a river in central Tennessee, flowing NW to the Cumberland River. Cf. **Murfreesboro** (def. 1).

stone·roll·er (stōn′rō′lər), *n.* **1.** an American minnow, *Campostoma anomalum,* named from its habit of moving stones in constructing its nest. **2.** any of several other minnows or suckers with similar habits, as *Hypentelium nigricans.* [STONE + ROLLER]

stone's′ throw′, a short distance: *The railroad station is only a stone's throw from our house.*

stone·wall (stōn′wôl′), *v.i.* **1.** *Cricket.* (of a batsman) to play a defensive game, as by persistently blocking the ball instead of batting it for distance and runs. **2.** *Brit.* filibuster (def. 4). —*v.t.* **3.** *Brit.* to obstruct (the passage of a legislative bill) in Parliament, esp. by excessive or prolonged debate. [from phrase *stone wall*] —**stone′wall′er,** *n.*

stone·wall·ing (stōn′wô′ling), *n.* *Brit.* the act of filibustering. [STONEWALL + -ING[1]]

Stone′wall Jack′son (stōn′wôl′), nickname of Thomas Jonathan Jackson.

stone·ware (stōn′wâr′), *n.* a hard, opaque, vitrified ceramic ware. [STONE + WARE[1]]

stone·work (stōn′wûrk′), *n.* **1.** any construction, as walls or the like, of stone; stone masonry. **2.** the techniques, processes, work, or art of dressing, setting, or designing in stone. **3.** Usually, **stoneworks.** a place where stone is dressed, as for building. [ME *stoonwerk*, OE *stānweorc*. See STONE, WORK] —**stone′work′er,** *n.*

stone·wort (stōn′wûrt′), *n.* a green alga of the class *Charophyceae*, having a jointed plant body frequently encrusted with lime and usually growing in fresh water. [STONE + WORT[2]]

ston·ey (stō′nē), *adj.*, **ston·i·er, ston·i·est.** stony.

stonk·er (stoŋ′kər), *v.t. Australian Informal.* **1.** to hit someone hard, esp. to knock someone unconscious. **2.** to defeat a person or team decisively. **3.** to baffle or confuse someone. [?]

ston·y (stō′nē), *adj.*, **ston·i·er, ston·i·est.** **1.** full of or abounding in stones or rock: *a stony beach.* **2.** pertaining to or characteristic of stone. **3.** resembling or suggesting stone, esp. in its hardness. **4.** unfeeling; merciless; obdurate: *a stony heart.* **5.** motionless or rigid; without expression, as the eyes or look: *a hard, stony stare.* **6.** petrifying; stupefying: *stony fear.* **7.** having a stone or stones, as fruit. **8.** *Slang.* stone-broke. Also, **stoney.** [ME; OE *stānig.* See STONE, -Y[1]] —**ston′i·ly,** *adv.* —**ston′i·ness,** *n.*
—**Syn. 1.** rocky, pebbly. **4.** adamant, hard, flinty, pitiless, inflexible, unbending.

ston·y-broke (stō′nē brōk′), *adj. Brit. Slang.* stone-broke.

Ston′y Brook′, a town in N Long Island, in SE New York. 3548 (1960).

ston′y cor′al, a true coral or madrepore consisting of numerous anthozoan polyps imbedded in the calcareous material that they secrete.

ston·y-faced (stō′nē fāst′), *adj.* having a rigid, expressionless face.

ston·y-heart·ed (stō′nē här′tid), *adj.* hard-hearted. —**ston′y-heart′ed·ly,** *adv.* —**ston′y-heart′ed·ness,** *n.*

ston′y pit′, *Plant Pathol.* a disease of pears, caused by a virus and characterized by deformed, pitted fruit.

Ston′y Point′, a village in SE New York, on the Hudson: site of a strategic fort in the Revolutionary War. 3330 (1960).

stood (stŏŏd), *v.* pt. and pp. of **stand.**

stooge (stōōj), *n., v.,* **stooged, stoog·ing.** —*n.* **1.** *Informal.* an entertainer who feeds lines to the main comedian and usually serves as the butt of his jokes. **2.** *Slang.* any underling, assistant, or accomplice. —*v.i.* **3.** *Slang.* to act as a stooge. [?]

stook (stŏŏk, stōōk), *Brit.* —*n.* **1.** shock[2] (def. 1). —*v.t.* **2.** shock[2] (def. 2). —*v.i.* **3.** to stack sheaves of grain; form a pile of straw. [ME *stouk*, OE *stūc* heap; c. MLG *stūke*, G *Stauche*; akin to STOCK] —**stook′er,** *n.*

stool (stōōl), *n.* **1.** a single seat on legs or a pedestal and without arms or a back. **2.** a short, low support on which to stand, step, kneel, rest the feet while sitting, etc. **3.** *Hort.* the stump, base, or root of a plant from which propagative organs are produced, as shoots for layering. **4.** the base of plants which annually produce new stems or shoots. **5.** a cluster of shoots or stems springing up from such a base or from any root, or a single shoot or layer. **6.** a bird fastened to a pole or perch and used as a decoy. **7.** an artificial duck or other bird, usually made from wood, used as a decoy by hunters. **8.** a privy. **9.** a mass of matter evacuated at each movement of the bowels. **10.** the sill of a window. See diag. under **double-hung.** **11.** a bishop's seat considered as symbolic of his authority; see. **12.** the sacred chair of certain African chiefs, symbolic of their kingship. **13. fall between two stools,** to fail, through hesitation or indecision, to select either of two alternatives. —*v.i.* **14.** to put forth shoots from the base or root, as a plant; form a stool. **15.** *Slang.* to turn informer; serve as a stool pigeon. [ME; OE *stōl*; c. G *Stuhl*, Icel *stōll*, Goth *stols* chair; all < *stō-* (< IE *root of* STAND) + *l-* suffix as in OSlav *stolu* seat] —**stool′like′,** *adj.*

stool′ pi′geon, 1. a pigeon used as a decoy. **2.** Also called **stool·ie** (stōō′lē). *Slang.* a person employed or acting as a decoy or informer, esp. for the police.

stoop[1] (stōōp), *v.i.* **1.** to bend the head and shoulders, or the body generally, forward and downward from an erect position: *to stoop over a desk.* **2.** to carry the head and shoulders habitually bowed forward: *to stoop from age.* **3.** (of trees, precipices, etc.) to bend, bow, or lean. **4.** to descend from one's level of dignity; condescend; deign: *Don't stoop to argue with him.* **5.** to swoop down, as a hawk at prey. **6.** *Rare.* to submit; yield. **7.** *Obs.* to come down from a height. —*v.t.* **8.** to bend (oneself, one's head, etc.) forward and downward. **9.** *Archaic.* to abase, humble, or subdue. —*n.* **10.** the act or an instance of stooping. **11.** a stooping position or carriage of body: *The elderly man walked with a stoop.* **12.** a descent from dignity or superiority; a condescension. **13.** a downward swoop, as of a hawk. [ME *stoup(en)*, OE *stūpian*; c. MD *stūpen* to bend, bow; akin to STEEP[1]] —**stoop′er,** *n.* —**stoop′ing·ly,** *adv.*
—**Syn. 1.** lean, crouch. See **bend**[1].

stoop[2] (stōōp), *n. U.S.* a small raised platform, approached by steps and sometimes having a roof and seats, at the entrance of a house; a small porch. [< D *stoep*; c. MLG *stope*, OHG *stuofa* step in a stair; akin to OE *stōpel* footprint, *stōp*, preterit of *steppan* to STEP]

stoop[3] (stōōp), *n. Brit. Dial.* a post or prop. [ME *stoupe*, deriv. of *stulpe* post; c. MLG *stolpe*, Icel *stolpi* post; akin to STELE[2]]

stoop[4] (stōōp), *n.* stoup.

stoop′ ball′, a game resembling baseball, played in a street, schoolyard, or other confined paved area, in which a ball is thrown forcibly against a stairway or wall so that it rebounds into the air, bases and runs being awarded depending on the number of bounces the ball takes before being caught by the opposing player or team.

stop (stop), *v.*, **stopped** or (*Archaic*) **stopt; stop·ping;** *n.* —*v.t.* **1.** to cease from, leave off, or discontinue: *to stop running.* **2.** to cause to cease; put an end to: *to stop noise in the street.* **3.** to interrupt, arrest, or check (a course, proceeding, process, etc.): *Stop your work just a minute.* **4.** to cut off, intercept, or withhold: *to stop supplies.* **5.** to restrain, hinder, or prevent (usually fol. by *from*): *I couldn't stop him from going.* **6.** to prevent from proceeding, acting, operating, continuing, etc.: *to stop a speaker; to stop a car.* **7.** to block, obstruct, or close (a passageway, channel, opening, duct, etc.) (usually fol. by *up*): *She stopped up the sink with a paper towel. He stopped the hole in the tire with a patch.* **8.** to fill the hole or holes in (a wall, a decayed tooth, etc.). **9.** to close (a container, tube, etc.) with a cork, plug, bung, or the like. **10.** to close the external orifice of (the ears, nose, mouth, etc.). **11.** *Sports.* **a.** to check (a stroke, blow, etc.); parry; ward off. **b.** to defeat (an opposing player or team): *The Browns stopped the Colts.* **c.** *Boxing.* to defeat by a knockout or technical knockout: *Louis stopped Conn in the 13th round.* **12.** *Banking.* to notify a bank to refuse payment of (a check) upon presentation. **13.** *Bridge.* to have an honor card and a sufficient number of protecting cards to keep an opponent from continuing to win in (a suit). **14.** *Music.* **a.** to close (a fingerhole) in order to produce a particular note from a wind instrument. **b.** to press down (a string of a violin, viola, etc.) in order to alter the pitch of the tone produced from it. **c.** to produce (a particular note) by so doing.
—*v.i.* **15.** to come to a stand, as in a course or journey; halt. **16.** to cease moving, proceeding, speaking, acting, operating, etc.; to pause; desist. **17.** to cease; come to an end. **18.** to halt for a brief visit (often fol. by *at*, *in*, or *by*): *He is stopping at the best hotel in town.* **19. stop by,** to make a brief visit on one's way elsewhere: *I'll stop by on my way home.* **20. stop down,** *Photog.* to reduce the diaphragm opening of (a camera). **21. stop in,** to make a brief, incidental visit: *If you're in town, be sure to stop in.* **22. stop off,** to halt for a brief stay at some point on the way elsewhere: *On the way to Rome we stopped off at Florence.* **23. stop out,** to mask (certain areas of an etching plate, photographic negative, etc.) with varnish, paper, or the like, to prevent their being etched, printed, etc. **24. stop over,** to stop briefly in the course of a journey: *Many motorists were forced to stop over in that town because of floods.*
—*n.* **25.** the act of stopping. **26.** a cessation or arrest of movement, action, operation, etc.; end: *The noise came to a stop. Put a stop to that behavior!* **27.** a stay or sojourn made at a place, as in the course of a journey: *Above all, he enjoyed his stop in Trieste.* **28.** a place where trains or other vehicles halt to take on and discharge passengers: *Is this a bus stop?* **29.** a closing or filling up, as of a hole. **30.** a blocking or obstructing, as of a passage or channel. **31.** a plug or other stopper for an opening. **32.** an obstacle, impediment, or hindrance. **33.** any piece or device that serves to check or control movement or action in a mechanism. **34.** *Archit.* a feature terminating a molding or chamfer. **35.** *Com.* **a.** an order to refuse payment of a check. **b.** See **stop order.** **36.** *Music.* **a.** the act of closing a fingerhole or pressing a string of an instrument in order to produce a particular note. **b.** a device or contrivance, as on an instrument, for accomplishing this. **c.** (in an organ) a graduated set of pipes of the same kind and giving tones of the same quality. **d.** Also called **stop knob.** a knob or handle which is drawn out or pushed back to permit or prevent the sounding of such a set of pipes or to control some other part of the organ. **e.** (in a reed organ) a group of reeds functioning like a pipe-organ stop. **37.** *Sports.* an individual defensive play or act preventing an opponent or opposing team from scoring, advancing, or gaining an advantage, as a catch in baseball, a tackle in football, deflecting a shot in hockey, etc. **38.** *Naut.* a piece of small line used to lash or fasten something, as a furled sail. **39.** *Phonet.* **a.** an articulation that interrupts the flow of air from the lungs. Cf. **continuant.** **b.** a consonant sound characterized by stop articulation, as *p*, *b*, *t*, *d*, *k*, and *g*. **40.** *Photog.* the diaphragm opening of a lens, esp. as indicated by an F number. **41.** *Building Trades.* **a.** See **stop bead.** **b.** doorstop (def. 2). **42.** any of various marks used as punctuation at the end of a sentence, esp. a period. **43.** the word "stop" printed in the body of a telegram or cablegram to indicate a period. **44. stops,** (*construed as sing.*) a family of games in which a player continues to play cards in a certain sequence until he is stopped and can no longer play. **45.** *Zool.* a depression in the face of certain animals, esp. dogs, marking the division between the forehead and the projecting part of the muzzle. See diag. under **dog.** [ME *stopp(en)*, OE *-stoppian*; c. D, LG *stoppen*, G *stopfen*; all < WGmc < VL **stuppāre* to plug with oakum, deriv. of L *stuppa* < Gk *styppē* oakum] —**stop′less,** *adj.* —**stop′less·ness,** *n.*
—**Syn. 3.** STOP, ARREST, CHECK, HALT imply causing a cessation of movement or progress (literal or figurative). STOP is the general term for the idea: *to stop a clock.* ARREST usually refers to stopping by imposing a sudden and complete restraint: *to arrest development.* CHECK implies bringing about an abrupt, partial, or temporary stop: *to check a trotting horse.* To HALT means to make a temporary stop, esp. one resulting from a command: *to halt a company of soldiers.* **5.** thwart, obstruct, impede. **16.** quit. **26.** halt; termination. **28.** terminal. **33.** governor. —**Ant. 1–3.** start.

stop-and-go (stop′ən gō′), *adj.* characterized by periodically enforced stops, as caused by heavy traffic or traffic signals: *stop-and-go traffic.*

stop′ bath′, *Photog.* an acid bath or rinse for stopping the action of a developer before fixing a negative or print. Also called **shortstop, shortstop bath.**

stop′ bead′, (in a window) a strip of molding along the inside of the frame for holding a sliding sash Also called **stop.**

stop′ clause′, a clause by which a contract or other agreement may be terminated, esp. between theatrical producers and theater owners in whose agreements it is often stipulated that when weekly receipts fall below a certain minimum usually for two consecutive weeks, the production must vacate the theater. Also called **eviction clause.**

stop·cock (stop′kok′), *n.* cock[1] (def. 7). [STOP + COCK[1]]

stope (stōp), *n., v.,* **stoped, stop·ing.** —*n.* **1.** any excavation made in a mine to remove the ore which has been rendered accessible by the shafts and drifts. —*v.i., v.t.* **2.** to mine or work by stopes. [appar. < LG *stope*; see STOOP[2]]

stop·er (stō′pər), *n.* a machine for drilling rock from below. [STOPE + -ER[1]]

stop·gap (stop′gap′), *n.* **1.** something that fills the place of something else that is lacking; temporary substitute; makeshift: *Candles are a stopgap when the electricity fails.* —*adj.* **2.** makeshift: *This is only a stopgap solution.* [n., adj. use of v. phrase *stop a gap*]

stop·ing (stō′piŋ), *n. Geol.* a process by which magmas move upward in the earth by breaking off and engulfing blocks of overlying rocks. [STOPE + -ING[1]]

stop′ knob′, stop (def. 36d).

stop·light (stop′līt′), *n.* **1.** a taillight that lights up as the driver of a vehicle steps on the brake pedal to slow down or stop. **2.** See **traffic light.** [STOP + LIGHT[1]]

stop-loss (stop′lôs′, -los′), *adj.* designed or planned to prevent continued loss, as a customer's order to his broker to sell a stock if its price declines to a specified amount.

stop′ num′ber, *Optics, Photog.* See **F number.**

stop-off (stop′ôf′, -of′), *n.* stopover. [n. use of v. phrase *stop off*]

stop′ or′der, an order from a customer to a broker to sell a security if the market price drops below a designated level.

stop·o·ver (stop′ō′vər), *n.* **1.** a brief stop in the course of a journey, as to eat, sleep, visit friends, etc. **2.** such a stop made with the privilege of proceeding later on the ticket originally issued. [n. use of v. phrase *stop over*]

stop·pa·ble (stop′ə bəl), *adj.* capable of being stopped. [STOP + -ABLE] —**stop′pa·bil′i·ty, stop′pa·ble·ness,** *n.* —**stop′pa·bly.** *adv.*

stop·page (stop′ij), *n.* **1.** the act or an instance of stopping; cessation of activity: *the stoppage of all work at the factory.* **2.** the state of being stopped: *During the stoppage of bus service he drove to work.* [late ME; see STOP, -AGE]

stop′ pay′ment, an order by the drawer of a check to his bank not to pay a specified check.

stopped (stopt), *adj.* **1.** halted or checked. **2.** closed or obstructed: *a stopped drain.* **3.** *Music.* **a.** having the upper end plugged or closed, as an organ pipe. **b.** acted upon by stopping, as a string. **c.** produced by the stopping of a string. **d.** having the bell closed by the inserted hand, as in a French horn, to lower the pitch or to muffle the sound. **4.** *Phonet.* involving stop articulation. [ME; see STOP, -ED[2]]

stopped′ diapa′son. See under **diapason** (def. 4).

stop·per (stop′ər), *n.* **1.** one who or that which stops. **2.** a plug, cork, bung, or other piece for closing a bottle, tube, drain, or the like. **3.** *Informal.* something or someone that commands attention, as an unusual window display, a glamorous woman, etc. **4.** *Cards.* a card in a suit that prevents the successive taking of all tricks in the suit by the opponents. **5.** *Baseball Slang.* **a.** a highly skilled pitcher who is used in crucial games or to stop his team's losing streak. **b.** a relief pitcher who enters a game at a crucial point. —*v.t.* **6.** to close, secure, or fit with a stopper. [late ME; see STOP, -ER[1]] —**stop′per·less,** *adj.*

stop·ping (stop′iŋ), *n. Mining.* a barrier erected to prevent the flow of air or gas. [late ME; see STOP, -ING[1]]

Stop′ping by Woods′ on a Snow′y Eve′ning, a poem (1923) by Robert Frost.

stop·ple (stop′əl), *n., v.,* **-pled, -pling.** —*n.* **1.** a stopper for a bottle or the like. —*v.t.* **2.** to close or fit with a stopple. [late ME *stoppel.* See STOP, -LE]

stop′ rib′, *Armor.* a flange on a breastplate or other plate piece, for deflecting the point of a weapon.

stop′ street′, a street at the intersections of which all traffic must stop before continuing. Cf. **through street.**

stopt (stopt), *v. Archaic.* a pt. and pp. of **stop.**

stop′ vol′ley, *Tennis.* a softly hit volley that barely falls over the net and cannot be reached for a return.

stop·watch (stop′woch′), *n.* a watch with a hand or hands that can be stopped or started at any instant, used for precise timing, as in races. [STOP + WATCH]

stop·wa·ter (stop′wô′tər, -wot′ər), *n. Naut.* an object or piece of material for rendering watertight areas of the hull difficult or impossible to calk. [STOP + WATER]

stop′ work′, *Horol.* a mechanism for halting the winding mechanism of a timepiece that is about to be overwound.

stor·a·ble (stôr′ə bəl, stōr′-), *adj.* **1.** capable of being stored for considerable time without loss of freshness or usability. —*n.* **2.** Usually, **storables.** articles which are storable. [STORE + -ABLE] —**stor′a·bil′i·ty,** *n.*

stor·age (stôr′ij, stōr′-), *n.* **1.** the act of storing; state or fact of being stored: *All my furniture is in storage.* **2.** capacity or space for storing. **3.** a place, as a room or building, for storing. **4.** *Computer Technol.* memory (def. 10). **5.** the price charged for storing goods. [STORE + -AGE]

stor′age bat′tery, *Elect.* **1.** a voltaic battery consisting of two or more storage cells. **2.** See **storage cell.**

stor′age cell′, *Elect.* a cell whose energy can be renewed by passing a current through it in the direction opposite to that of the flow of current generated by the cell. Also called **secondary cell, storage battery.**

stor′age disease′, *Pathol.* thesaurosis.

stor′age wall′, a set of shelves, cabinets, or the like, that covers or forms a wall.

sto·rax (stōr′aks, stôr′-), *n.* **1.** a solid resin with a vanillalike odor, obtained from a small styracaceous tree, *Styrax officinalis*: formerly used in medicine and perfumery. **2.** a liquid balsam (**liquid storax**) obtained from species of *Liquidambar*, esp. from the wood and inner bark of *Liquidambar orientalis* (**Levant storax**), a tree of Asia Minor: used chiefly in medicine and perfumery. **3.** any shrub or tree of the genus *Styrax*, having racemes of showy, white flowers. [late ME < LL; L *styrax* < Gk]

store (stōr, stôr), *n., v.,* **stored, stor·ing.** —*n.* **1.** an establishment where merchandise is sold, usually on a retail basis. **2.** a stall, room, floor, or building housing or suitable for housing a retail business. **3.** a supply or stock of something, esp. one for future use. **4. stores,** supplies of food, clothing, or other requisites, as for a household, inn, naval or military forces, etc. **5.** *Chiefly Brit.* a storehouse or warehouse. **6.** quantity, esp. great quantity; abundance, or plenty: *a rich store of grain.* **7. in store, a.** in readiness or reserve. **b.** about to happen; imminent: *There is a great deal of trouble in store for them if they persist in their ways.* **8. set** or **lay store by,** to have high regard for; value; esteem: *She sets great store by good character.* —*v.t.* **9.** to supply or stock with something, as for future use. **10.** to accumulate or put away, for future use (usually fol. by *up* or *away*). **11.** to deposit in a storehouse, warehouse, or other place for keeping. **12.** (in data processing) **a.** to put (data) into a memory unit. **b.** to retain (data) in a memory unit. —*v.i.* **13.** to take in or hold supplies, goods, or articles, as for future use. **14.** to remain fresh and usable for considerable time on being stored: *Flour stores well.* [ME *store(n),* aph. var. of *astoren* < OF *estore(r)* < L *instaurāre* to set up, renew, equiv. to *in-* IN-[2] + *staur-* (akin to Gk *stauros* cross and to STEER[1]) + *-āre* inf. suffix] —**stor′er,** *n.*

store-bought (stōr′bôt′ stôr′-), *adj.* commercially made rather than homemade.

store·front (stōr′frunt′, stôr′-), *n.* the side of a store facing a street, usually containing display windows. [STORE + FRONT]

store·house (stōr′hous′, stôr′-), *n., pl.* **-hous·es** (-hou′ziz). **1.** a building in which things are stored. **2.** any repository or source of abundant supplies, as of facts or knowledge. [ME *storhous.* See STORE, HOUSE]

store·keep·er (stōr′kē′pər, stôr′-), *n.* **1.** *Chiefly U.S.* a tradesman who owns a store. **2.** one who has charge of or operates a store or stores. **3.** *U.S. Navy.* one in charge of naval or military stores. [STORE + KEEPER] —**store′keep′ing,** *n.*

store·room (stōr′ro͞om′, -ro͝om′, stôr′-), *n.* **1.** a room in which stores are kept. **2.** room or space for storage. [STORE + ROOM]

stores′ ledg′er, a record kept of the amount, type, etc., of raw materials and supplies on hand, as in a manufacturing plant. Also called **stock book, stock ledger, stock record.**

sto·rey (stōr′ē, stôr′ē), *n., pl.* **-reys.** *Chiefly Brit.* story[2].

sto·ried[1] (stōr′ēd, stôr′-), *adj.* **1.** recorded or celebrated in history or story: *the storied cities of ancient Greece.* **2.** ornamented with designs representing historical, legendary, or similar subjects. [STORY[1] + -ED[3]]

sto·ried[2] (stōr′ēd, stôr′-), *adj.* having stories or floors (often used in combination): *a two-storied house.* Also, *esp. Brit.,* **sto′reyed.** [STORY[2] + -ED[3]]

sto·ri·ette (stōr′ē et′, stôr′-), *n.* a very short story. [STORY[1] + -ETTE]

stork (stôrk), *n., pl.* **storks,** (*esp. collectively*) **stork.** any of several wading birds of the family *Ciconiidae,* related to the ibises and herons, having long legs and a long neck and bill. Cf. **adjutant stork, jabiru, marabou** (def. 1), **white stork, wood ibis.** [ME; OE *storc;* c. Icel *storkr,* G *Storch;* akin to STARK; the bird presumably owes its name to the rigidity of its stiltlike legs] —**stork′like′,** *adj.*

White stork, *Ciconia ciconia* (Length 3½ ft.)

stork's-bill (stôrks′bil′), *n.* **1.** any geranium of the genus *Pelargonium.* **2.** a heron's-bill.

storm (stôrm), *n.* **1.** a disturbance of the normal condition of the atmosphere, manifesting itself by winds of unusual force or direction, often accompanied by rain, snow, hail, thunder, and lightning, or flying sand or dust. **2.** a heavy fall of rain, snow, or hail, or a violent outbreak of thunder and lightning, unaccompanied by strong winds. **3.** (on the Beaufort scale) a wind of 64–72 miles per hour. **4.** a violent military assault on a fortified place, strong position, or the like. **5.** a heavy or sudden volley or discharge: *a storm of criticism; a storm of bullets.* **6.** a violent disturbance of affairs, as a civil, political, social, or domestic commotion. **7.** a violent outburst or outbreak of expression: *a storm of applause.* **8. storm in a teacup,** a great to-do about trivia; much ado about nothing. —*v.i.* **9.** (of the wind or weather) to blow with unusual force, or to rain, snow, hail, etc., esp. with violence (usually used impersonally with *it* as subject): *It stormed all day.* **10.** to rage or complain with violence or fury: *He stormed angrily at me.* **11.** to deliver a violent attack or fire, as with artillery: *The troops stormed against the garrison.* **12.** to rush to an assault or attack: *The tanks stormed towards the city.* **13.** to rush angrily: *to storm out of a room.* —*v.t.* **14.** to subject to or as if to a storm: *The salesman stormed them with offers.* **15.** to utter or say with angry vehemence: *He stormed his contempt.* **16.** to attack or assault (persons, places, or things): *to storm a fortress.* [ME, OE; c. D *storm,* Icel *stormr,* G *Sturm;* akin to STIR[1]] —**storm′like′,** *adj.*
—**Syn. 1.** gale, hurricane, tempest, tornado, cyclone, squall, wind, blizzard.

Storm (shtôrm), *n.* **The·o·dore Wold·sen** (tā′ô dôr′ vôlt′sən), 1817–88, German poet and novelist.

storm′ boat′. See **assault boat.**

storm·bound (stôrm′bound′), *adj.* confined, detained, or isolated by storms: *a stormbound ship; a stormbound village.* [STORM + -BOUND[1]]

storm′ can′vas, *Naut.* the group of sails set during a gale.

storm′ cel′lar, a cellar or underground chamber for refuge during violent storms; cyclone cellar.

storm′ cen′ter, 1. the center of a cyclonic storm, the area of lowest pressure and of comparative calm. **2.** a center of disturbance, tumult, trouble, or the like: *South Africa has been a storm center of racial conflict.*

storm′ coat′, an overcoat, usually of a water-repellent fabric, lined with material serving as insulation against very cold weather, often having a fur collar.

storm′ door′, a supplementary outside door, usually glazed, for protecting the entrance door against drafts, driving rain, etc.

storm′ drain′. See **storm sewer.**

storm·er (stôr′mər), *n.* one who storms or assaults; a member of an assaulting party. [STORM + -ER[1]]

storm′ jib′, *Naut.* a small jib used in bad weather. Also called **spitfire jib.**

Storm′ Lake′, a town in NW Iowa. 7728 (1960).

storm·less (stôrm′lis), *adj.* without storms. [STORM + -LESS] —**storm′less·ly,** *adv.* —**storm′less·ness,** *n.*

storm′ pet′rel, any of several small sea birds of the family *Hydrobatidae,* usually having black or sooty-brown plumage with a white rump, esp. *Hydrobates pelagicus,* of the eastern North Atlantic and Mediterranean. Also called **stormy petrel.**

storm·proof (stôrm′pro͞of′), *adj.* protected from or not affected by storms. [STORM + -PROOF]

Storms (stôrmz), *n.* **Ocean of.** See **Oceanus Procellarum.**

storm′ sash′. See **storm window.**

storm′ sew′er, a sewer for carrying off rainfall drained from paved surfaces, roofs, etc.

storm′ sig′nal, 1. a visual signal, as a flag, giving advance notice of a heavy storm, used esp. along coastal areas. **2.** See **storm warning** (def. 3).

storm′ surge′, an abnormal rise in the level of the sea along a coast, caused by the onshore winds of a severe cyclone. Also called **storm′tide′, surge.**

storm′ track′, the path followed by the center of a cyclonic storm.

storm′ troop′er, 1. a member of the storm troops. **2.** a member of the uniformed organization, Sturmabteilung, of the former Nazi party; Brown Shirt.

storm′ troops′, *Mil.* (formerly) German troops specially chosen and equipped for carrying out assault operations.

storm′ warn′ing, 1. a showing of storm signals. **2.** an announcement, esp. by radio, of a heavy storm. **3.** any sign of approaching trouble: *The troops on the border were a storm warning, and we prepared for war. His angry look was a storm warning.*

storm′ win′dow, a supplementary window sash for protecting a window against drafts, driving rain, etc. Also called **storm sash.**

storm·y (stôr′mē), *adj.,* **storm·i·er, storm·i·est. 1.** affected, characterized by, or subject to storms; tempestuous: *a stormy sea.* **2.** characterized by violent commotion, actions, speech, passions, etc.: *a stormy debate.* [ME; OE *stormig.* See STORM, -Y[1]] —**storm′i·ly,** *adv.* —**storm′i·ness,** *n.*

storm′y pet′rel, 1. See **storm petrel. 2.** a person who causes or likes trouble or strife.

Stor·no·way (stôr′nə wā′), *n.* a city in NW Scotland, in the Hebrides. 5248 (est. 1964).

Storrs (stôrz), *n.* a town in NE Connecticut. 6054 (1960).

Stor·ting (stōr′ting′, stôr′-), *n.* the parliament of Norway, elected by popular vote, which divides into two bodies to vote on legislative proposals, the Lagting, comprising one quarter of the members, and the Odelsting, comprising the rest. Also, **Stor′thing.** [< Norw, equiv. to *stor* great + *ting* assembly, court; c. THING[2]]

sto·ry[1] (stōr′ē, stôr′ē), *n., pl.* **-ries,** *v.,* **-ried, -ry·ing.** —*n.* **1.** a narrative, either true or fictitious, in prose or verse, designed to interest, amuse, or instruct the hearer or reader; tale. **2.** a fictitious tale, shorter and less elaborate than a novel. **3.** such narratives or tales as a branch of literature: *song and story.* **4.** the plot or succession of incidents of a novel, poem, drama, etc.: *The characterizations were good, but the story was weak.* **5.** a narration of an incident or a series of events or an example of these that is or may be narrated, as an anecdote, joke, etc. **6.** a narration of the events in the life of a person or the existence of a thing, or such events as a subject for narration: *the story of medicine; The story of his life is amazing.* **7.** a report or account of a matter; statement or allegation: *The story goes that he rejected the offer.* **8.** See **news story. 9.** *Informal.* a lie: *What he said about himself turned out to be a story.* **10.** *Obs.* history. —*v.t.* **11.** to ornament with pictured scenes, as from history or legend. **12.** *Obs.* to tell the history or story of. [ME *storie* < AF *(e)storie* < L *historia* HISTORY] —**sto′ry·less,** *adj.*
—**Syn. 1.** legend, fable, romance; anecdote, record, history, chronicle. **5.** recital, rehearsal. **7.** description.

sto·ry[2] (stōr′ē, stôr′ē), *n., pl.* **-ries. 1.** a complete horizontal section of a building, having one continuous or practically continuous floor. **2.** the set of rooms on the same floor or level of a building. **3.** any major horizontal architectural division, as of a façade, the wall of a nave, etc. **4.** a layer. Also, *esp. Brit.,* **storey.** [late ME *storie* < AL *historia* picture decorating a building, a part of the building so decorated, hence floor, story < L *historia* HISTORY]

Sto·ry (stōr′ē, stôr′ē), *n.* **1. Joseph,** 1779–1845, U.S. jurist. **2. William Wet·more** (wet′mōr′, -môr′), 1819–95, U.S. sculptor and poet.

sto·ry·board (stōr′ē bōrd′, stôr′ē bôrd′), *n.* a panel or panels on which a sequence of sketches depict the significant changes of action and scene in a planned film, as for a movie, television show, or advertisement. [STORY[1] + BOARD]

sto·ry·book (stōr′ē bo͝ok′, stôr′-), *n.* a book that contains a story or stories, esp. for children. [STORY[1] + BOOK]

sto′ry line′, plot[1] (def. 2).

sto′ry post′, (in an open story, as a shop front) any of several posts supporting lintels upon which upper stories rest.

sto′ry rod′, *Building Trades.* a pole equal in height to one story of a building, with markings showing the heights of stair risers, doorframes, etc. Also called **sto′ry pole′.**

sto·ry·tell·er (stōr′ē tel′ər, stôr′-), *n.* **1.** one who tells or writes stories or anecdotes. **2.** *Informal.* one who tells more or less trivial falsehoods; fibber. [STORY[1] + TELLER[1]]

sto·ry·tell·ing (stōr′ē tel′ing, stôr′-), *n.* the telling or writing of stories. [STORY[1] + TELLING]

Sto·ry·ville (stōr′ē vil′, stôr′-), *n.* a red-light district of New Orleans known as a center of jazz development before World War I.

stoss (stōs; *Ger.* shtōs), *adj. Geol.* noting or pertaining to the side, as of a hill, dale, etc., that receives or has received the thrust of a glacier or other impulse. [< G: thrust, push. Cf. STOIT]

Stoss (shtōs), *n.* **Veit** (fīt), c1440–1533, German sculptor and painter.

sto·ting (stō′ting), *n.* stoating.

sto·tin·ka (stô ting′kä), *n., pl.* **-ki** (-kē). a minor coin of Bulgaria, the 100th part of a lev, equivalent to about .0085 of a U.S. dollar. [< Bulg]

St.-Ouen (san twän′), *n.* a suburb of Paris in N France. 52,103 (1962).

Stough·ton (stōt′ən), *n.* a town in S Wisconsin. 5555 (1960).

stound[1] (stound, sto͞ond), *Brit. Dial.* —*n.* **1.** a state of astonishment, amazement, or stupefaction. —*v.t.* **2.** to stupefy or bewilder; astound. **3.** to stun or benumb, as with a blow. [ME *stund,* ptp. of *stounen.* See STUN]

stound[2] (stound, sto͞ond), *Brit. Dial.* —*n.* **1.** a short time; short while. **2.** *Obs.* a period of pain, worry, or misfortune. —*v.t., v.i.* **3.** *Obs.* to pain; hurt. [ME *sto(u)nd,* OE *stund* space of time; c. Icel *stund,* G *Stunde* hour; akin to STAND]

stoup (sto͞op), *n.* **1.** a basin for holy water, as at the entrance of a church. **2.** *Scot.* a pail or bucket. **3.** *Scot. and North Eng.* **a.** a drinking vessel, as a cup or tankard, of various sizes. **b.** the amount it holds. [late ME *stowp* < Scand; cf. Icel *staup* cup; c. OE *stēap* flagon; see STEEP[1]]

Stoup (def. 1)

stour (sto͝or), *n.* **1.** *Brit. Dial.* **a.** tumult; confusion. **b.** a storm. **2.** *Brit. Dial.* blowing dust or a deposit of dust. **3.** *Archaic.* armed combat; battle. **4.** *Obs.* a time of tumult. [ME < OF *(e)stour* battle < Gmc; akin to STORM]

stoush (stoush), *Australian Informal.* —*v.t.* **1.** stonker (defs. 1, 2). —*n.* **2.** a fight or brawl. [? imit.]

stout (stout), *adj.* **1.** bulky in figure; heavily built; corpulent; thickset; fat: *She is getting too stout for her dresses.* **2.** bold, brave, or dauntless: *a stout heart; stout fellows.* **3.** firm; stubborn; resolute: *stout resistance.* **4.** forceful; harsh; vigorous: *a stout argument; a stout wind.* **5.** strong of body, hearty, or sturdy: *stout seamen.* **6.** having endurance or staying power, as a horse. **7.** strong in substance or body, as a beverage. **8.** strong and thick or heavy: *a stout cudgel.* —*n.* **9.** *Brewing.* a dark, sweet brew made of roasted malt and having a higher percentage of hops than porter. **10.** porter of extra strength. **11.** a stout person. **12.** a garment size designed for a stout man. **13.** a garment, as a suit or overcoat, in this size. [ME < OF *(e)stout* bold, proud < Gmc; cf. MD *stout* bold, MLG *stolt,* MHG *stolz* proud] —**stout′ly,** *adv.* —**stout′ness,** *n.*
—**Syn. 1.** portly, fleshy. STOUT, FAT, PLUMP imply corpulence of body. STOUT describes a heavily built but usually strong and healthy body: *a handsome stout lady.* FAT, an informal word with unpleasant connotations, suggests an unbecoming fleshy stoutness; it may, however, apply also to a hearty fun-loving type of stout person: *a fat old man; fat and jolly.* PLUMP connotes a pleasing roundness and is often used as a complimentary or euphemistic equivalent for stout, fleshy, etc.: *a plump figure attractively dressed.* **2.** valiant, gallant, intrepid, fearless, indomitable, courageous. **3.** resolute, obstinate. **5.** brawny, sinewy. —**Ant. 1.** thin, lean.

Stout (stout), *n.* **Robert,** 1844–1930, New Zealand jurist and statesman: prime minister 1884–87.

stout-heart·ed (stout′här′tid), *adj.* brave and resolute; dauntless. —**stout′-heart′ed·ly,** *adv.* —**stout′-heart′ed·ness,** *n.*

stout·ish (stou′tish), *adj.* rather stout. [STOUT + -ISH[1]]

stove[1] (stōv), *n., v.,* **stoved, stov·ing.** —*n.* **1.** a portable or fixed apparatus that furnishes heat for warmth, cooking, etc., commonly using coal, oil, gas, or electricity as a source of power. **2.** a heated chamber or box for some special purpose, as a drying room or a kiln for firing pottery. —*v.t.* **3.** to treat with or subject to heat, as in a stove. [late ME; OE *stofa* hot-air bathroom; c. D *stoof,* G *Stube* room (orig. heated room)] —**stove′less,** *adj.*

stove[2] (stōv), *v.* a pt. and pp. of **stave.**

stove′ bolt′, a small bolt, similar to a machine screw but with a coarser thread. See diag. under **bolt.**

stove·pipe (stōv′pīp′), *n.* **1.** a pipe, as of sheet metal, serving as a stove chimney or to connect a stove with a chimney flue. **2.** *U.S. Informal.* See **stovepipe hat.** [STOVE[1] + PIPE[1]]

stove′pipe hat′, *U.S. Informal.* a tall silk hat.

sto·ver (stō′vər), *n.* **1.** coarse roughage used as feed for livestock. **2.** *Chiefly U.S.* stalks and leaves, not including grain, of such forages as corn and sorghum. **3.** *Brit. Dial.* fodder minus the grain portion of the plant. [ME; aph. var. of ESTOVER]

stow[1] (stō), *v.t.* **1.** *Naut.* **a.** to put (cargo, provisions, etc.) in the places intended for them. **b.** to put (sails, spars, gear, etc.) in the proper place or condition when not in use. **2.** to put in a place or receptacle, as for storage or reserve; pack: *He stowed the potatoes in our cellar.* **3.** to fill (a place or receptacle) by packing: *to stow a carton with books.* **4.** (of a place or receptacle) to afford room for; hold. **5.** *Slang.* to stop; break off: *Stow it! Stow the talk!* **6.** to put away, as in a safe or convenient place (often fol. by *away*). **7.** *Obs.* to lodge or quarter. **8. stow away,** to conceal oneself aboard a ship or other conveyance in order to obtain free transportation or to elude pursuers. [ME *stow(en),* OE *stōwigan* to keep, hold back (lit., to place), deriv. of *stōw* place; akin to *-sto-* place in Icel *eldstō* fireplace, Goth *stojan* to judge (lit., to place)] —**stow′a·ble,** *adj.*

CONCISE ETYMOLOGY KEY: <, descended or derived from; >, whence; b., blend of, blended; c., cognate with; deriv., derivative; equiv., equivalent; imit., imitative; m., modification of; obl., oblique; r., replacing; s., stem; sp., spelling; trans., translation; ?, origin unknown, perhaps; *, hypothetical. See the full key inside the front cover.

stow[2] (stōō, stou), *v.t. Brit. Dial.* to cut close or trim, esp. to crop (a sheep's ears) or prune (a tree or shrub).

stow[3] (stō), *n. Brit.* See **tinning stack.** [see STOVE[1]]

stow·age (stō′ij), *n.* 1. the act or operation of stowing. 2. the state or manner of being stowed. 3. room or accommodation for stowing something. 4. a place in which something is or may be stowed. 5. that which is stowed or to be stowed. 6. a charge for stowing something. [STOW[1] + -AGE]

stow·a·way (stō′ə wā′), *n.* one who conceals himself aboard a ship or airplane in order to obtain free transportation or elude pursuers.

Stowe (stō), *n.* 1. **Harriet (Elizabeth) Beecher,** 1811–96, U.S. abolitionist and novelist. 2. a town in SE Pennsylvania. 2765 (1960). 3. a town in N Vermont: ski resort. 534 (1960).

stown·lins (stoun′linz), *adv. Scot.* secretly; stealthily.

stowp (stōp), *n. Scot.* stoup.

St. Pat′rick's cab′bage. See **London pride.**

St. Paul, a port in and the capital of Minnesota, in the SE part, on the Mississippi. 313,411 (1960).

St. Paul′ Park′, a town in E Minnesota. 3267 (1960).

St. Paul's, a cathedral in London, England: designed by Sir Christopher Wren.

St. Peter, a town in S Minnesota. 8484 (1960).

St. Peter's, a basilica in Vatican City: dome designed by Michelangelo.

St. Petersburg, 1. Formerly, **Leningrad** (1924–91); **Petrograd** (1914–24). a seaport in NW Russian Federation in Europe, in the Gulf of Finland, off the Baltic Sea: founded 1703 by Peter the Great; capital of the Russian Empire (1712–1917). 5,020,000. 2. a city in W Florida, on Tampa Bay: 238,629.

St. Pe′tersburg Beach′, a town in W Florida. 6268 (1960).

St. Pierre (sānt′ pyâr′; *Fr.* SAN PYER′), 1. a city on Réunion Island, in the Indian Ocean. 27,573 (1954). 2. a former city on Martinique, in the French West Indies: destroyed 1902, with the entire population of 26,000, by an eruption of the volcano Mt. Pelée.

St. Pierre and Miq·ue·lon (mik′ə lon′; *Fr.* mēklôN′), two small groups of islands off the S coast of Newfoundland: an overseas territory of France; important base for fishing. 5134 (1960); 93 sq. mi. *Cap.:* St. Pierre.

St. Quen·tin (sānt′ kwen′tᵊn; *Fr.* SAN KÄN TAN′), a city in N France, on the Somme: retaken from the Germans 1918. 62,579 (1962).

str., 1. steamer. 2. strait. 3. *Music.* string; strings.

Stra·bane (strə bān′), *n.* a town in SW Pennsylvania. 3036 (1960).

stra·bis·mus (strə biz′məs), *n. Ophthalm.* a disorder of vision due to the turning of one eye or both eyes from the normal position so that both cannot be directed at the same point or object at the same time; squint; cross-eye. [< NL < Gk *strabismós,* equiv. to *strab(ós)* squinting + *-ismos* -ISM] —**stra·bis′mal, stra·bis′mic, stra·bis′mi·cal,** *adj.* —**stra·bis′mal·ly,** *adv.*

Stra·bo (strā′bō), *n.* 1. 63? B.C.–A.D. 21?, Greek geographer and historian. 2. a crater in the first quadrant of the face of the moon: about 32 miles in diameter.

stra·bot·o·my (strə bot′ə mē), *n., pl.* **-mies.** *Surg.* the operation of dividing one or more of the muscles of the eye for the cure of strabismus. [< Gk *strabó(s)* (see STRABISMUS) + -TOMY]

Stra·chey (strā′chē), *n.* **(Giles) Lyt·ton** (jīlz lit′ᵊn), 1880–1932, English biographer and literary critic.

strad·dle (strad′ᵊl), *v.,* **-dled, -dling,** *n.* —*v.i.* 1. to walk, stand, or sit with the legs wide apart; stand or sit astride. 2. to stand wide apart, as the legs. 3. *Informal.* to favor or appear to favor both sides of an issue, political division, or the like, at once; maintain an equivocal position. —*v.t.* 4. to walk, stand, or sit with one leg on each side of; stand or sit astride of: *to straddle a horse.* 5. to spread (the legs) wide apart. 6. to favor or appear to favor both sides of (an issue, political division, etc.). —*n.* 7. the act or an instance of straddling. 8. the distance straddled over. 9. *Informal.* the taking of a noncommittal position. 10. *Finance.* a privilege consisting of a put and a call combined, giving the holder the right, at his option, either of delivering a certain amount of stock, shares, etc., at a specified price, or of buying a certain amount at another specified price, within a stipulated period. [OE *strād* (preterit of *strīdan* to STRIDE) + -LE] —**strad′dler,** *n.* —**strad′dling·ly,** *adv.*

strad′dle car′rier. See **straddle truck.**

strad′dle mill′, (on a milling machine) a pair of cutters spaced for milling parallel faces of a piece.

strad·dle-mill (strad′ᵊl mil′), *v.t.* to form with a straddle mill.

strad′dle truck′, a self-propelled vehicle, having a chassis far above the ground, for carrying loads of lumber or the like beneath the chassis and between the wheels. Also called **straddle carrier, unit carrier.**

Stra·del·la (strä del′lä), *n.* **A·les·san·dro** (ä′les sän′drô), 1645?–82?, Italian composer.

Stra·di·va·ri (strad′ə vâr′ē; *It.* strä′dē vä′rē), *n.* **An·to·nio** (än tô′nyô), 1644?–1737, Italian violinmaker of Cremona (pupil of Nicolò Amati). Latin, **Stradivarius.**

Strad·i·var·i·us (strad′ə vâr′ē əs), *n.* 1. a violin or other instrument made by Stradivari or his family. 2. See **Stradivari, Antonio.**

strafe (strāf, sträf), *v.,* **strafed, straf·ing,** *n.* —*v.t.* 1. to attack (ground troops or installations) by airplanes with machine-gun fire. 2. to bombard heavily. 3. *Slang.* a. to punish. b. to reprimand viciously. —*n.* 4. a strafing attack. [< G *strafe(n)* (to) punish] —**straf′er,** *n.*

Straf·ford (straf′ərd), *n.* **1st Earl of** (*Thomas Wentworth*), 1593–1641, English statesman: chief adviser of Charles I of England.

strag·gle (strag′əl), *v.i.,* **-gled, -gling.** 1. to stray from the road, course, or line of march. 2. to wander about in a scattered fashion; ramble. 3. to go, come, or spread in a scattered fashion or at irregular intervals: *The trees straggle over the countryside.* [b. STRAY and DRAGGLE] —**strag′gler,** *n.* —**strag′gling·ly,** *adv.*

strag·gly (strag′lē), *adj.,* **-gli·er, -gli·est.** straggling; rambling. [STRAGGLE + -Y[1]]

straight (strāt), *adj.* 1. without a bend, angle, or curve; not curved; direct: *a straight path.* 2. exactly vertical or horizontal; in a perfectly vertical or horizontal plane: *Don't we have a straight table that things won't slide off of?* 3. (of a line) generated by a point moving at a constant velocity with respect to another point. 4. evenly formed or set: *straight shoulders.* 5. without circumlocution; frank; candid: *straight speaking.* 6. honest, honorable, or upright, as conduct, dealings, methods, or persons. 7. *Informal.* reliable, as reports or information. 8. right or correct, as reasoning, thinking, or a thinker. 9. in the proper order or condition: *Things are straight now.* 10. continuous or unbroken: *in straight succession.* 11. *U.S.* thoroughgoing or unreserved: *a straight Republican.* 12. unmodified or unaltered: *a straight comedy.* 13. without change in the original melody or tempo: *She does straight songs, with just the piano backing her.* 14. *Slang.* heterosexual. 15. undiluted, as whiskey. 16. *Theat.* (of acting) straightforward; not striving for effect. 17. *Journalism.* written or to be written in a direct and objective manner, with no attempt at individual styling, comment, etc.: *a straight story; Treat it as straight news.* Cf. **featurish.** 18. *Cards.* containing cards in consecutive denomination, as a two, three, four, five, and six, in various suits. —*adv.* 19. in a straight line: *to walk straight.* 20. in an even form or position: *pictures hung straight.* 21. in an erect posture: *to stand up straight.* 22. directly: *to go straight to a place.* 23. without circumlocution; frankly; candidly (often fol. by *out*). 24. honestly, honorably, or virtuously: *to live straight.* 25. without intricate involvement; not in a roundabout way; directly to the point: *He can think straight.* 26. in a steady course (often fol. by *on*): *to keep straight on after the second traffic light.* 27. into the proper form or condition: *to put a room straight.* 28. in possession of the truth or of true ideas: *I want to set you straight before you make mistakes.* 29. sold without discount regardless of the quantity bought: *Candy bars are six cents straight.* 30. *Journalism.* directly and objectively: *Write the circus story straight.* 31. without personal embellishments, additions, etc.: *Tell the story straight. Sing the song straight.* 32. **straight off,** without delay; immediately: *I told him straight off what I thought about the matter.* Also, **straight away.** —*n.* 33. the condition of being straight. 34. a straight form or position. 35. a straight line. 36. a straight part, as of a racecourse. 37. *Chiefly Games.* a succession of strokes, plays, etc., which gives a perfect score. 38. *Poker.* a sequence of five consecutive cards of various suits. Cf. **sequence** (def. 8). [ME; orig. ptp. of STRETCH] —**straight′ly,** *adv.* —**straight′ness,** *n.*
—**Syn.** 5. open, direct. 6. virtuous, just, fair, equitable. —**Ant.** 1. crooked. 5. devious.

straight′ and nar′row, the way of virtuous or proper conduct: *After his release from prison he resolved to follow the straight and narrow.*

straight′ an′gle, the angle formed by two radii of a circle that are drawn to the extremities of an arc equal to one half of the circle; an angle of 180°.

straight-arm (strāt′ärm′), *Football.* —*v.t.* 1. to push (a potential tackler) away by holding the arm out straight; stiff-arm. —*n.* 2. Also called **stiff-arm.** the act or an instance of straight-arming.

straight·a·way (strāt′ə wā′), *adj.* 1. straight onward, without turn or curve, as a racecourse. 2. *Mach.* straight-flute. —*n.* 3. a straightaway course or part. —*adv.* 4. immediately; right away. [from phrase *straight away*]

straight′ bill′ of lad′ing, a bill of lading that is issued to a specified consignee for the delivery of the goods and that cannot be endorsed to another party. Cf. **order bill of lading.**

straight′ chain′, *Chem.* an open chain of atoms, usually carbon, with no side chains attached to it. Cf. **branched chain.**

straight′ chair′, a chair with a straight back, esp. one which is unupholstered and has straight legs and straight arms or no arms.

straight′ coil′, *Naut.* a fake having the form of a spiral.

straight′ deck′, *Shipbuilding.* a wooden deck having its planking laid fore-and-aft throughout. Cf. **laid deck.**

straight·edge (strāt′ej′), *n.* a bar or strip of wood or metal having at least one long edge of sufficiently reliable straightness for use in drawing or testing straight lines, plane surfaces, etc. [STRAIGHT + EDGE]

straight·en (strāt′ᵊn), *v.t., v.i.* to make or become straight in direction, form, position, character, conduct, condition, etc. [STRAIGHT + -EN[1]] —**straight′en·er,** *n.*

straight′ face′, a serious facial expression that conceals one's true feelings about something, esp. a suppression of the desire to laugh: *We tried to keep a straight face, but the scene was too ludicrous.* —**straight′-faced′,** *adj.*

straight′ flush′, *Poker.* a sequence of five consecutive cards of the same suit.

straight-flute (strāt′flōōt′), *adj. Mach.* noting a drill having several flutes parallel to the axis of rotation, used for soft metals; straightaway.

straight·for·ward (strāt′fôr′wərd), *adj.* 1. going or directed straight ahead: *a straightforward gaze.* 2. direct; not roundabout: *a straightforward approach to a problem.* 3. free from crookedness or deceit; honest: *straightforward in one's dealings.* —*adv.* 4. Also, **straight′for′wards.** straight ahead; directly or continuously forward. [STRAIGHT + FORWARD] —**straight′for′ward·ly,** *adv.* —**straight′for′ward·ness,** *n.*
—**Syn.** 1. undeviating, unswerving. —**Ant.** 1, 2. devious.

straight-from-the-shoul·der (strāt′frəm thə shōl′dər), *adj.* direct, honest, and forceful in expression; outspoken.

straight′ jack′et. See **strait jacket.**

straight′ joint′, 1. *Building Trades.* a continuous joint made by the termination of parallel members, as floorboards or bricks, at the same line. 2. *Carpentry.* Also called **square joint.** a joint between two timbers having no overlap and no dowels to bind them together.

straight-laced (strāt′lāst′), *adj.* strait-laced. —**straight-lac·ed·ly** (strāt′lā′sid lē, -lāst′lē), *adv.* —**straight′-lac′ed·ness,** *n.*

straight′ life′ insur′ance. See **ordinary life insurance.**

straight-line (strāt′līn′), *adj. Mach.* 1. noting a machine or mechanism the working parts of which act or are arranged in a straight line. 2. noting a mechanism for causing one part to move along a straight line.

straight′ man′, an entertainer who plays his part straight, usually as a foil for a comedian.

straight′ mat′ter, *Print.* 1. the body text of an article, story, etc., as distinguished from the title, subhead, and other display matter. 2. editorial text as distinguished from advertising.

straight-out (strāt′out′), *adj. U.S. Informal.* 1. thoroughgoing: *a straight-out Democrat.* 2. frank; aboveboard. [from phrase *straight out*]

Straight′ Range′, a mountain range in the second quadrant of the face of the moon in the Mare Imbrium: about 40 miles long with highest peaks about 6,000 feet.

straight′ ra′zor, a razor having a stiff blade made of steel that is hinged to a handle into which it folds.

straight′ shoot′er, one who is forthright and upstanding in behavior.

straight′ stall′, a narrow, oblong stall in which a horse or other animal cannot turn around. Cf. **box stall.**

straight′ tick′et, *U.S. Politics.* 1. a ballot on which all votes have been cast for candidates of the same party. 2. a ticket on which all the candidates nominated by a party are members of the party. Cf. **split ticket.**

straight′ time′, 1. the time or number of hours established as standard for a specific work period in a particular industry, usually computed on the basis of a workweek and fixed variously at from 35 to 40 hours. 2. the rate of pay established for the period (distinguished from *overtime*). —**straight′-time′,** *adj.*

Straight′ Wall′, an escarpment in the third quarter of the face of the moon in the Mare Nubium: about 60 miles long.

straight·way (strāt′wā′), *adv.* straightaway. [late ME; see STRAIGHT, WAY]

straight′ whis′key, *U.S.* pure, unblended whiskey of 80 to 110 proof.

strain[1] (strān), *v.t.* 1. to draw tight or taut; stretch esp. to the utmost tension: *to strain a rope.* 2. to exert to the utmost: *to strain one's ears to catch a sound.* 3. to impair, injure, or weaken (a muscle, tendon, etc.) by stretching or overexertion. 4. to cause mechanical deformation in (a body or structure) as the result of stress. 5. to stretch beyond the proper point or limit: *to strain the meaning of a word.* 6. to make excessive demands upon: *to strain one's luck; to strain one's resources.* 7. to pour (liquid containing solid matter) through a filter, sieve, or the like, in order to hold back the denser solid constituents: *to strain gravy.* 8. to draw off (clear or pure liquid) by means of a filter or sieve: *to strain the water from spinach; to strain broth.* 9. to hold back (solid particles) from liquid matter by means of a filter or sieve: *to strain seeds from orange juice; to strain rice.* 10. to clasp tightly in the arms, the hand, etc.: *The mother strained her child close to her breast.* 11. *Obs.* to constrain, as to a course of action. —*v.i.* 12. to pull forcibly: *a dog straining at a leash.* 13. to stretch one's muscles, nerves, etc., to the utmost. 14. to make violent physical efforts; strive hard. 15. to resist forcefully; balk: *to strain at accepting an unpleasant fact.* 16. to be subjected to tension or stress; suffer strain. 17. to filter, percolate, or ooze. 18. to trickle or flow: *Sap strained from the bark.* —*n.* 19. any force or pressure tending to alter shape, cause a fracture, etc. 20. strong muscular or physical effort. 21. great or excessive effort or striving after some goal, object, or effect. 22. an injury to a muscle, tendon, etc., due to excessive tension or use; sprain. 23. an injury to or deformation of any body or structure resulting from stress. 24. condition of being strained or stretched. 25. *Informal.* a task, goal, object, or effect accomplished or obtained only with great effort: *Housecleaning is a real strain.* 26. severe, trying, or fatiguing pressure or effect: *the strain of hard work.* 27. a severe demand on resources, feelings, a person, etc.: *a strain on one's hospitality.* 28. a flow or burst of language, eloquence, etc.: *the lofty strain of Cicero.* 29. Often, **strains.** a passage of music or songs as rendered or heard: *the strains of the nightingale.* 30. *Music.* a section of a piece of music, more or less complete in itself. 31. a passage or piece of poetry. 32. the tone, style, or spirit of an utterance, writing, etc.: *a humorous strain.* 33. a particular degree, height, or pitch attained: *a strain of courageous enthusiasm.* [ME *strein(en)* < OF *(e)strein-,* s. of *estreindre* to press tightly, grip < L *stringere* to bind, tie, draw tight. See STRINGENT, STRANGURY] —**strain′ing·ly,** *adv.* —**strain′less,** *adj.* —**strain′less·ly,** *adv.*
—**Syn.** 1. tighten. 3. STRAIN, SPRAIN imply a wrenching, twisting, and stretching of muscles and tendons. To STRAIN is to stretch tightly, make taut, wrench, tear, cause injury to, by long-continued or sudden and too violent effort or movement: *to strain one's heart by overexertion, one's eyes by reading small print.* To SPRAIN is to strain excessively (but without dislocation) by a sudden twist or wrench, the tendons and muscles connected with a joint, esp. those of the ankle or wrist: *to sprain an ankle.* 7. filter, sieve. 10. hug, embrace, press. 17. seep. 20. exertion. 22. wrench.

strain[2] (strān), *n.* 1. the body of descendants of a common ancestor, as a family or stock. 2. any of the different lines of ancestry united in a family or an individual. 3. a group of plants distinguished from other plants of the variety to which it belongs by some intrinsic quality, such as a tendency to yield heavily; race. 4. an artificial variety of a species of domestic animal or cultivated plant. 5. a variety, esp. of microorganisms. 6. ancestry or descent. 7. hereditary or natural character, tendency, or trait: *a strain of insanity in a family.* 8. a streak or trace. 9. a kind or sort. 10. *Obs.* procreation. [ME *streen,* OE **strend* (north), c. *striend* (West Saxon) lineage, race, stock, tribe (with early loss of *-d*); akin to *strienan* to beget]

strained (strānd), *adj.* affected or produced by effort; forced; not natural or spontaneous: *strained hospitality.* [late ME; see STRAIN[1], -ED[2]] —**strained·ly** (strānd′lē, strā′nid-), *adv.* —**strained′ness,** *n.*

strain·er (strā′nər), *n.* 1. one who or that which strains. 2. a filter, sieve, or the like, for straining liquids. 3. a stretcher or tightener. [ME; see STRAIN[1], -ER[1]]

strain′er gate′, *Foundry.* a perforated disk or core placed in a gate or sprue to divide the falling metal into a number of streams and to retain scum and slag. Also called **strain′er core′.**

strain′ hard′ening, *Metalworking.* an increase in the hardness and tensile strength of a cold-worked object, due to the permanent distortion of its crystalline structure.

strain′ing arch′, an arch for resisting thrusts, as in a flying buttress. Also, **strain′er arch′.**

strain′ing piece′, (in a queen-post roof) a horizontal beam uniting the tops of the two queen posts, and resisting the thrust of the roof. Also called **strain′ing beam′.**

strain′ing sill′, (in a roof with a queen post) a compression member lying along the tie beam and separating the feet of the struts.

strain′ rosette′, an arrangement of three or more strain gauges surrounding a point on an object under stress to determine the direction and magnitude of the surface stresses.

strait (strāt), *n.* **1.** Often, **straits.** (*construed as sing.*) a narrow passage of water connecting two large bodies of water. **2.** Often, **straits.** a position of difficulty, distress, or need: *Ill and penniless, he was in sad straits indeed.* **3.** *Archaic.* a narrow passage or area. **4.** *Rare.* an isthmus. —*adj. Archaic.* **5.** narrow: *Strait is the gate.* **6.** affording little space; confined in area. **7.** strict, as in requirements or principles. [ME *streit* < OF *(e)streit* < L *strict(us),* equiv. to *stric-* (var. of *strig-,* s. of *stringere;* see STRAIN[1]) + *-tus* ptp. suffix] —**strait′ly,** *adv.* —**strait′ness,** *n.*
—**Syn. 2.** exigency, pinch, dilemma, predicament, plight. See **emergency.** —**Ant. 2.** ease.

strait·en (strāt′ən), *v.t.* **1.** to put into difficulties, esp. financial ones: *His obligations had straitened him.* **2.** to restrict in range, extent, amount, pecuniary means, etc: *Poverty straitens one's way of living.* **3.** *Archaic.* **a.** to make narrow. **b.** to confine within narrow limits. [STRAIT + -EN[1]]

Strait′ is the Gate′, a novel (1909) by André Gide. French, **La Porte Étroite.**

strait′ jack′et, 1. a garment made of strong material and designed to bind the arms, as of a violently insane or delirious person. **2.** anything that severely confines, constricts, or hinders: *Conventional attitudes can be a strait jacket, preventing original thinking.* Also, **straight jacket.**

strait-jack·et (strāt′jak′it), *v.t.* to put in or as in a strait jacket: *Her ambition was strait-jacketed by her family.*

strait-lace (strāt′lās′), *v.t.,* **-laced, -lac·ing.** to bind, confine, or restrain with or as if with laces. [back formation from STRAIT-LACED]

strait-laced (strāt′lāst′), *adj.* **1.** excessively strict in conduct or morality; puritanical; prudish: *strait-laced censors.* **2.** *Archaic.* **a.** tightly laced, as a bodice. **b.** wearing tightly laced garments. Also, **straight-laced.** —**strait-lac′ed·ly** (strāt′lā′sid lē, -lāst′lē), *adv.* —**strait′-lac′ed·ness,** *n.*

Straits′ dol′lar (strāts), a former British silver coin and monetary unit of the Straits Settlements.

Straits′ Set′tlements, a former British crown colony in SE Asia: included the settlements of Singapore, Penang, Malacca, and Labuan. *Cap.:* Singapore.

strake[1] (strāk), *n.* **1.** *Naut.* a continuous course of planks or plates forming a hull shell, deck, the side of a deckhouse, etc. **2.** an iron band joining the felloe of a wheel. [ME; appar. akin to STRETCH] —**straked,** *adj.*

strake[2] (strāk), *n. Mining.* a trough for washing gold from fine pulp. [?]

Stral·sund (shträl′zŏŏnt), *n.* a seaport in N East Germany: a member of the medieval Hanseatic League; besieged by Wallenstein 1628. 65,275 (est. 1955).

stra·mash (strə mash′, stram′əsh), *n. Scot.* an uproar; disturbance. [?]

stra·min·e·ous (strə min′ē əs), *adj.* **1.** of or resembling straw. **2.** straw-colored; yellowish. [< L *strāmineus* of straw, equiv. to *strāmin-* (s. of *strāmen;* akin to STRATUM) + *-eus* -EOUS] —**stra·min′e·ous·ly,** *adv.*

stra·mo·ni·um (strə mō′nē əm), *n.* **1.** See **jimson weed. 2.** the dried leaves of this plant, used in medicine as an analgesic, antispasmodic, etc. [< NL < ?]

strand[1] (strand), *v.t.* **1.** to drive or leave (a ship, fish, etc.) aground or ashore: *The receding tide stranded the whale.* **2.** (usually used in the passive) to bring into or leave in a helpless position: *He was stranded in the middle of nowhere.* —*v.i.* **3.** to be driven or left ashore; run aground. **4.** to be halted or struck by a difficult situation: *He stranded in the middle of his speech.* —*n.* **5.** the land bordering the sea, a lake, or a river; shore. [ME, OE; c. G *Strand,* D *strand,* Icel *strönd;* akin to STREW]

strand[2] (strand), *n.* **1.** a number of fibers, threads, or yarns which are plaited or twisted together to form a rope, cord, or the like. **2.** a similar part of a wire rope. **3.** a rope made of such twisted or plaited fibers. **4.** a fiber or filament, as in animal or plant tissue. **5.** a thread or threadlike part of anything: *the strands of a plot.* **6.** a tress of hair. **7.** a string of pearls, beads, etc. —*v.t.* **8.** to form (a rope, cable, etc.) by twisting strands together. **9.** to break one or more strands of (a rope). [?] —**strand′less,** *adj.*

Strand (strand), *n.* a street parallel to the Thames, in W central London, England: famous for hotels and theaters.

strand′ line′, a shoreline, esp. one from which the sea or a lake has receded.

strand′ shoe′, (in a suspension bridge) a member or device connecting the end of a cable to an anchorage.

strand′ wolf′. See **brown hyena.**

strange (strānj), *adj.,* **strang·er, strang·est,** *adv.* —*adj.* **1.** unusual, extraordinary, or curious; odd; queer: *a strange remark to make.* **2.** estranged, alienated, etc., as a result of being out of one's natural environment: *In Bombay I felt strange.* **3.** situated, belonging, or coming from outside of one's own or a particular locality: *to move to a strange place; strange religions.* **4.** outside of one's previous experience; hitherto unknown; unfamiliar: *strange faces; strange customs.* **5.** unaccustomed to or inexperienced in; unacquainted (usually fol. by *to*): *I'm strange to this part of the job.* **6.** distant or reserved; shy. **7.** *Archaic.* foreign: *strange strands.* —*adv.* **8.** Also, **strange′ly.** in a strange manner. [ME < OF *(e)strange* < L *extrāne(us)* EXTRANEOUS] —**strange′ness,** *n.*
—**Syn. 1.** bizarre, singular, abnormal, anomalous. STRANGE, PECULIAR, ODD, QUEER refer to that which is out of the ordinary. STRANGE implies that the thing or its cause is unknown or unexplained; it is unfamiliar and unusual: *a strange expression.* That which is PECULIAR mystifies, or exhibits qualities not shared by others: *peculiar behavior.* That which is ODD is irregular or unconventional, and sometimes approaches the bizarre: *an odd custom.* QUEER sometimes adds to ODD the suggestion of something abnormal and eccentric: *queer in the head.* **6.** aloof. —**Ant. 1.** familiar.

Strange′ In′terlude, a play (1928) by Eugene O'Neill.

stran·ger (strān′jər), *n.* **1.** a person with whom one has or has had no personal acquaintance: *He is a perfect stranger to me.* **2.** a newcomer in a place or locality: *a stranger in town.* **3.** an outsider: *They want no strangers in on the club meetings.* **4.** one who is unacquainted with or unaccustomed to something (usually fol. by *to*): *He is no stranger to poverty.* **5.** one who is not a member of the family, group, community, or the like, as a visitor or guest: *Our town shows hospitality to strangers.* **6.** *Law.* one not privy or party to an act, proceeding, etc. **7.** *Archaic.* a foreigner or alien. [late ME < MF *(e)strangier,* equiv. to *estrange* STRANGE + *-ier* -ER[2]] —**stran′ger·like′,** *adj.*
—**Syn. 1.** STRANGER, ALIEN, FOREIGNER all refer to someone regarded as outside of or distinct from a particular group. STRANGER may apply to one who does not belong to some group—social, professional, national, etc.—or may apply to a person with whom one is not acquainted. ALIEN emphasizes a difference in political allegiance and citizenship from that of the country in which one is living. FOREIGNER emphasizes a difference in language, customs, and background. —**Ant. 1.** acquaintance.

Stranger, The, a novel (1942) by Albert Camus. French, **L'Étranger.**

stran·gle (straŋ′gəl), *v.,* **-gled, -gling.** —*v.t.* **1.** to kill by squeezing the throat in order to compress the windpipe and prevent the intake of air, as with the hands or a tightly drawn cord. **2.** to kill by stopping the breath in any manner; choke; stifle; suffocate. **3.** to prevent the continuance, growth, rise, or action of; suppress: *Suburbs strangled the city.* —*v.i.* **4.** to be choked, stifled, or suffocated. [ME *strangel(en)* < OF *(e)strangler* < L *strangulāre* < Gk *strangalân,* deriv. of *strangálē* halter, akin to *strangós* twisted] —**stran′gler,** *n.* —**stran′gling·ly,** *adv.*
—**Syn. 1.** garrote, throttle, choke. **2.** smother.

stran′gle hold′, 1. *Wrestling.* an illegal hold by which an opponent's breath is choked off. **2.** any force or influence which restricts the free actions or development of a person or group: *the strangle hold of superstition.*

stran·gles (straŋ′gəlz), *n.* (*construed as sing.*) *Vet. Pathol.* distemper[1] (def. 1b). [pl. of obs. *strangle* act of strangling]

stran·gu·late (straŋ′gyə lāt′), *v.t.,* **-lat·ed, -lat·ing. 1.** *Pathol., Surg.* to compress or constrict (a duct, intestine, vessel, etc.) so as to prevent circulation or suppress function. **2.** to strangle. [< L *strangulāt(us)* strangled, equiv. to *strangul-* (s. of *strangulāre* to strangle) + *-ātus* -ATE[1]] —**stran·gu·la·ble** (straŋ′gyə lə bəl), *adj.* —**stran′gu·la′tion,** *n.* —**stran′gu·la′tive,** *adj.* —**stran·gu·la·to·ry** (straŋ′gyə lə tōr′ē, -tôr′ē), *adj.*

stran·gu·ry (straŋ′gyə rē), *n. Pathol.* a condition of the urinary organs in which the urine is emitted painfully and drop by drop. [< L *strangūria* < Gk *strangouría,* equiv. to *strang(ós)* flowing drop by drop + *oûr(on)* urine + *-ia* -Y[3]]

strap (strap), *n., v.,* **strapped, strap·ping.** —*n.* **1.** a narrow strip of flexible material, esp. leather, as for fastening or holding things together. **2.** a looped band by which an item may be held, pulled, lifted, etc., as a bootstrap or a ring which standing passengers may hold on to in a bus, subway, or the like. **3.** a strop for a razor. **4.** a long, narrow object or piece of something; strip; band. **5.** an ornamental strip or band. **6.** See **shoulder strap. 7.** *Mach.* a shallow metal fitting surrounding and retaining other parts, as on the end of a rod. **8.** *Shipbuilding.* a narrow plate, overlapping and riveted or welded to other plates butted together. **9.** *Naut., Mach.* strop (def. 2). **10.** watchband. —*v.t.* **11.** to fasten or secure with a strap or straps. **12.** to fasten (a thing) around something in the manner of a strap. **13.** to sharpen on a strap or strop: *to strap a razor.* **14.** to beat or flog with a strap. [var. of STROP] —**strap′pa·ble,** *adj.* —**strap′like′,** *adj.*

strap·hang·er (strap′haŋ′ər), *n. Informal.* a passenger who stands in a crowded bus or subway train and holds onto a strap or other support suspended from above. [STRAP + HANGER]

strap·hang·ing (strap′haŋ′iŋ), *n.* standing in a public conveyance because of a lack of empty seats. [STRAP + HANGING]

strap-hinge (strap′hinj′), *n.* a hinge having a flap, esp. a long one, attached to one face of a door or the like. See illus. under **hinge.**

strap-laid (strap′lād′), *adj. Ropemaking.* noting a type of flat cordage made by stitching strands together side by side.

strap·less (strap′lis), *adj.* **1.** without a strap or straps. **2.** designed and made without shoulder straps: *a strapless evening gown; a strapless bra.* [STRAP + -LESS]

strap·pa·do (strə pā′dō, -pä′-), *n., pl.* **-does. 1.** (formerly) a type of punishment or torture in which the victim, with arms bound behind him, was raised from the ground by a rope fastened to his wrists, abruptly released, then arrested with a painful jerk just before reaching the ground. **2.** the instrument used for this purpose. [alter. of MF *strapade* or its source, It *strappata* a sharp pull or tug, equiv. to *strapp-* (s. of *strappare* to snatch < Gmc; cf. dial. G *strapfen* to stretch tight) + *-ata* -ADE[1]]

strapped (strapt), *adj.* needy; wanting: *The company is rather strapped for funds.* [STRAP + -ED[3]]

strap·per (strap′ər), *n.* **1.** one who or that which straps. **2.** *Informal.* a large, robust person. [STRAP + -ER[1]]

strap·ping[1] (strap′iŋ), *adj.* **1.** powerfully built; robust. **2.** *Informal.* large; whopping. [STRAP + -ING[2]]

strap·ping[2] (strap′iŋ), *n.* straps collectively. [STRAP + -ING[1]]

Stras·berg (sträs′bərg, stras′-), *n.* **Lee,** born 1901, U.S. theatrical director, teacher, and actor, born in Austria.

Stras·bourg (stras′bûrg, sträz′bŏŏrg; *Fr.* straz-bōōr′), *n.* a fortress city in and the capital of Bas-Rhin, in NE France, near the Rhine: cathedral; taken by Allied forces November 1944. 233,549 (1962). German, **Strass·burg** (shträs′bŏŏrkh).

strass[1] (stras), *n.* a flint glass with a high lead content, used to imitate gemstones. [< G, named after J. *Strass(er),* 18th-century German jeweler who invented it]

strass[2] (stras), *n.* silk waste produced in making skeins. [< F *strasse* < It *straccio*]

stra·ta (strā′tə, strat′ə, strä′tə), *n.* **1.** a pl. of **stratum. 2.** (*usually considered nonstandard*) stratum.

strat·a·gem (strat′ə jəm), *n.* **1.** a plan, scheme, or trick for surprising or deceiving an enemy. **2.** any artifice, ruse, or trick devised or used to attain a goal or to gain an advantage over an adversary: *business stratagems.* [< MF *stratageme* or its source, It *stratagemma* war ruse < L *stratēgēma* < Gk *stratḗgēma* instance of generalship, deriv. of *stratēgein* to be in command; see STRATEGOS] —**strat·a·gem·i·cal** (strat′ə jem′i kəl), *adj.* —**strat′a·gem′i·cal·ly,** *adv.*
—**Syn. 1, 2.** See **trick. 2.** deception, intrigue, device, maneuver, contrivance.

stra·tal (strāt′əl), *adj.* of a stratum or strata. [STRAT(UM) + -AL[1]]

stra·te·gic (strə tē′jik), *adj.* **1.** pertaining to, characterized by, or of the nature of strategy: *strategic movements.* **2.** important in or essential to strategy. **3.** (of an action, as a military operation or a move in a game) forming an integral part of a stratagem: *a strategic move in a game of chess.* **4.** *Mil.* **a.** intended to render the enemy incapable of making war, as by the destruction of materials, factories, etc.: *a strategic bombing mission.* **b.** essential to the conduct of a war: *Copper is a strategic material.* Also, **stra·te′gi·cal.** [< Gk *stratēgik(ós),* equiv. to *stratēg(ós)* STRATEGOS + *-ikos* -IC] —**stra·te′gi·cal·ly,** *adv.*

stra·te·gics (strə tē′jiks), *n.* (*construed as sing.*) strategy (def. 1). [see STRATEGIC, -ICS]

strat·e·gist (strat′i jist), *n.* an expert in strategy, esp. in warfare: *Julius Caesar was a great military strategist.* [STRATEG(Y) + -IST]

stra·te·gos (strə tē′gos), *n., pl.* **-goi** (-goi). strategus. [< Gk *stratēgós,* equiv. to *strat(ós)* army + *-ēgos* leader (*-ēg-,* var. s. of *ágein* to lead + *-os* n. suffix)]

stra·te·gus (strə tē′gəs), *n., pl.* **-gi** (-jī). a military leader, esp. in an army in ancient Greece. [Latinized form of STRATEGOS]

strat·e·gy (strat′i jē), *n., pl.* **-gies. 1.** Also, **stra·te·gics** (strə tē′jiks). generalship; the science or art of combining and employing the means of war in planning and directing large military movements and operations. **2.** the use or an instance of using this science or art. **3.** skillful use of a stratagem: *Her strategy was to seem always to agree with her husband.* **4.** a plan, method, or series of maneuvers or stratagems for obtaining a specific goal or result: *a strategy for getting ahead in the world.* [< Gk *stratēgía* generalship, equiv. to *stratēg-* (see STRATEGOS) + *-ia* -Y[3]]
—**Syn. 1.** In military usage, a distinction is made between STRATEGY and TACTICS. STRATEGY is the utilization, during both peace and war, of all of a nation's forces, through large-scale, long-range planning and development, to ensure security or victory. TACTICS deals with the use and deployment of troops in actual combat.

Strat·ford (strat′fərd), *n.* **1.** a town in SW Connecticut, near Bridgeport: Shakespeare theater. 45,012 (1960). **2.** a city in SE Ontario, in S Canada: Shakespeare theater. 20,467 (1961). **3.** a town in SW New Jersey. 4308 (1960). **4.** a boy's given name.

Strat′ford de Red′cliffe (də red′klif), **1st Viscount** (*Stratford Canning*), 1786–1880, English diplomat.

Strat·ford-on-A·von (strat′fərd on ā′vən, -ôn-), *n.* a town in SW Warwickshire, in central England, on the Avon River: birthplace and burial place of Shakespeare. 16,847 (1961). Also, **Strat′ford-up·on-A′von.**

strath (strath; *Scot.* sträth), *n. Scot.* a wide valley. [< Gael *srath;* akin to STRATUM]

strath·spey (strath′spā′, strath′spā′), *n.* **1.** a slow Scottish dance in quadruple meter. **2.** the music for this dance. [after *Strath Spey* a Scottish locality]

strati-, a combining form of **stratum:** *stratiform.*

stra·tic·u·late (strə tik′yə lit, -lāt′), *adj.* (of a geological formation) comprised of thin, continuous strata. [STRATI- + -CULE + -ATE[1]] —**stra·tic′u·la′tion,** *n.*

strat·i·fi·ca·tion (strat′ə fə kā′shən), *n.* **1.** the act or an instance of stratifying. **2.** a stratified state or appearance: *the stratification of ancient ruins from eight different periods.* **3.** *Sociol.* the hierarchical or vertical division of society according to rank, caste, or class: *stratification of feudal society.* **4.** *Geol.* **a.** formation of strata; deposition or occurrence in strata. **b.** a stratum. [< ML *strātificātiōn-* (s. of *strātificātiō*). See STRATI-, -FICATION]

Stratification (def. 4)

strat·i·form (strat′ə fôrm′), *adj.* **1.** *Geol.* occurring as a bed or beds; arranged in strata. **2.** *Anat.* noting a cartilage occurring in thin layers in bones. **3.** *Meteorol.* (of a cloud) having predominantly horizontal development. Cf. **cumuliform.** [STRATI- + -FORM]

strat·i·for·mis (strat′ə fôr′mis), *adj. Meteorol.* (of a cloud with cumuliform elements) occurring in a very extensive horizontal layer. [< NL: STRATIFORM]

strat·i·fy (strat′ə fī′), *v.,* **-fied, -fy·ing.** —*v.t.* **1.** to form or place strata or layers. **2.** to preserve or germinate (seeds) by placing them between layers of earth. **3.** *Sociol.* to arrange in a hierarchical order, esp. according to graded status levels. —*v.i.* **4.** to form strata. **5.** *Geol.* to lie in beds or layers. **6.** *Sociol.* to develop hierarchically, esp. as graded status levels. [modeled on NL *stratificāre,* equiv. to *strati-* STRATI- + *-ficāre* -FY]

stratig., stratigraphy.

stra·tig·ra·phy (strə tig′rə fē), *n.* a branch of geology dealing with the classification, nomenclature, correlation, and interpretation of stratified rocks. [STRATI-

+ -GRAPHY] —**stra·tig·ra·pher** (strə tig′rə fər), **stra·tig′ra·phist,** *n.* —**strat·i·graph·ic** (strat′ə graf′ik), **strat′i·graph′i·cal,** *adj.* —**strat′i·graph′i·cal·ly,** *adv.*

strato-, a combining form representing **stratus** (*stratocumulus*) or specialized as a combining form of **stratosphere** (*stratovision*). [< NL, comb. form repr. L *strātus* a spreading out. See STRATUS]

stra·toc·ra·cy (strə tok′rə sē), *n., pl.* **-cies.** a form of government in which power is vested in the army. [< Gk *stratό(s)* army + -CRACY] —**strat·o·crat** (strat′ə krat′), *n.* —**strat·o·crat·ic** (strat′ə krat′ik), *adj.*

stra·to·cu·mu·lus (strā′tō kyōō′myə ləs, strat′ō-), *n., pl.* **-lus.** a cloud of a class characterized by large dark, rounded masses, usually in groups, lines, or waves, the individual elements being larger than those in altocumulus and the whole being at a lower altitude, usually below 8000 feet. [STRATO- + -CUMULUS]

stratocu′mulus castella′nus, *pl.* **stratocumulus castellanus.** *Meteorol.* a stratocumulus cloud some elements of which have summits shaped like crenelated towers.

stratocu′mulus castella′tus, *pl.* **stratocumulus castellatus.** *Meteorol.* See **stratocumulus castellanus.**

stra′tocu′mulus floc′cus, *pl.* **stratocumulus floccus.** *Meteorol.* a stratocumulus cloud some elements of which have summits in the shape of small cumuliform tufts or masses.

stratocu′mulus lenticular′is, *pl.* **stratocumulus lenticularis.** *Meteorol.* a stratocumulus cloud having sharply outlined lenticular shapes and sometimes showing irisation.

stratocu′mulus stratifor′mis, *pl.* **stratocumulus stratiformis.** *Meteorol.* a stratocumulus cloud having great horizontal extent.

strat·o·pause (strat′ə pôz′), *n. Meteorol.* the boundary or transition layer between the stratosphere and mesosphere. [STRATO- + PAUSE]

strat·o·sphere (strat′ə sfēr′), *n.* **1.** the region of the upper atmosphere extending upward from the tropopause to about 15 miles above the earth, characterized by little vertical change in temperature. **2.** (formerly) all of the earth's atmosphere lying outside the troposphere. **3.** any great height or degree, as the highest point of a graded scale. [STRAT(UM + ATM)OSPHERE] —**strat·o·spher·ic** (strat′ə sfer′ik), **strat′o·spher′i·cal,** *adj.*

strat·o·vi·sion (strat′ə vizh′ən), *n.* the transmission of television and FM programs from an airplane flying in the stratosphere, increasing the area over which broadcasts may be received. [STRATO- + (TELE) VISION]

Strat·ton (strat′ᵊn), *n.* **Charles Sherwood** ("*Tom Thumb*"), 1838–83, U.S. midget who performed in the circus of P. T. Barnum.

stra·tum (strā′təm, strat′əm, strä′təm), *n., pl.* **stra·ta** (strā′tə, strat′ə, strä′tə), **stra·tums. 1.** a layer of material, naturally or artificially formed, often one of a number of parallel layers placed one upon another: *a stratum of ancient foundations.* **2.** one of a number of portions or divisions likened to layers or levels: *an allegory with many strata of meaning.* **3.** *Geol.* a single bed of sedimentary rock, generally consisting of one kind of matter representing continuous deposition. **4.** *Biol.* a layer of tissue; lamella. **5.** *Ecol.* (in a plant community) a layer of vegetation, usually of the same or similar height. **6.** a layer of the ocean or the atmosphere distinguished by natural or arbitrary limits. **7.** *Sociol.* a level or grade of a people or population with reference to social position, education, etc.: *the lowest stratum of society.* [< L: lit., a cover; n. use of neut. of *strātus.* See STRATUS] —**stra′tous,** *adj.*

stra·tus (strā′təs, strat′əs), *n., pl.* **-tus.** a cloud of a class characterized by a gray, horizontal layer with a uniform base, found at a lower altitude than altostratus, usually below 8000 feet. [< NL, L, ptp. of *sternere* to spread, equiv. to *strā-* (preterit, ptp. s. of *sternere*) + *-tus* ptp. suffix]

stra′tus frac′tus, *pl.* **stratus fractus.** *Meteorol.* a stratus cloud that is ill-formed, ragged, usually small, and rapidly changing.

stra′tus nebulo′sus, *pl.* **stratus nebulosus.** *Meteorol.* a stratus cloud having very indistinct details.

straucht (sträᴋʜt), *adj. Scot.* straight. Also, **straught** (sträᴋʜt).

Straus (strous; *Ger.* shtrous), *n.* **Os·car** (os′kər; *Ger.* ôs′kär), 1870–1954, Austrian composer.

Strauss (strous; *Ger.* shtrous), *n.* **1. Da·vid Frie·drich** (dä′vēt frē′drikh), 1808–74, German theologian, philosopher, and author. **2. Jo·hann** (yō′hän), 1804–49, Austrian orchestra conductor and composer. **3.** his son **Johann,** 1825–99, Austrian orchestra conductor and composer. **4. Rich·ard** (rich′ərd; *Ger.* riᴋʜ′ärt), 1864–1949, German orchestra conductor and composer.

stra·vage (strə vāg′), *v.i.,* **-vaged, -vag·ing. 1.** *Scot. and North Eng.* to wander aimlessly. **2.** to saunter; stroll. Also, **stra·vaig** (strə vāg′). [by aphesis < ML *extrāvag(ārī)* (to) wander out of bounds. See EXTRAVAGANT] —**stra·vaig′er,** *n.*

Stra·vin·sky (strə vin′skē; *Russ.* strä vēn′ski), *n.* **I·gor Fë·do·ro·vich** (ē′gôr fyô′də rō′vich; *Russ.* e′gôr fyô′do rô′vich), 1882–1971, U.S. composer, born in Russia.

straw (strô), *n.* **1.** a single stalk or stem, esp. of certain species of grain, chiefly wheat, rye, oats, and barley. **2.** a mass of such stalks, esp. after drying and threshing, used as fodder. **3.** material, fibers, etc., made from such stalks, as used for making hats, baskets, etc. **4.** the value of one such stalk; trifle; least bit: *not to care a straw.* **5.** a tube, usually of paper or glass, for sucking up a beverage from a container: *to sip lemonade through a straw.* **6.** anything of possible but dubious help in a desperate circumstance. **7.** a straw hat. **8. catch, clutch,** or **grasp at a straw, at straws,** or **at any straw** or **straws,** to seize at any chance, no matter how slight, of saving oneself from calamity. —*adj.* **9.** of, pertaining to, containing, or made of straw: *a straw hat.* **10.** of little value or consequence; worthless. **11.** sham; fictitious. [ME; OE *strēaw;* c. G *Stroh;* akin to STREW] —**straw′less,** *adj.* —**straw′like′,** *adj.*

straw·ber·ry (strô′ber′ē, -bə rē), *n., pl.* **-ries. 1.** the fruit of any stemless, rosaceous herb of the genus *Fragaria,* consisting of an enlarged fleshy receptacle bearing achenes on its exterior. **2.** the plant bearing it. [ME; OE *strēawberige.* See STRAW, BERRY]

straw′berry bass′ (bas), the black crappie. See under **crappie.**

straw′berry blonde′, 1. reddish blonde. **2.** a woman with reddish-blonde hair.

straw′berry bush′, wahoo[1] (def. 1).

straw′berry dish′, a shallow, circular fruit dish with a fluted or pierced border.

straw′berry gua′va, a shrub or small tree, *Psidium cattleianum,* of Brazil, having smooth, grayish-brown bark, leathery leaves, white flowers, and white-fleshed, purplish-red fruit.

straw′berry mark′, a small, reddish, slightly raised birthmark.

straw·ber·ry-rasp·ber·ry (strô′ber′ē raz′ber′ē, -bə rē-, -bə rē), *n.* an arching, prickly plant, *Rubus illecebrosus,* of Japan, having an herbaceous stem, white, fragrant flowers, and large, edible, scarlet fruit. Also called **balloon-berry.**

straw′berry roan′, a horse with a reddish coat that is liberally flecked with white hairs.

straw′berry shrub′, any of several shrubs of the genus *Calycanthus,* having fragrant, dark-brownish or purplish-red flowers.

straw′berry toma′to, 1. the small, edible, tomato-like fruit of a solanaceous plant, *Physalis pruinosa.* **2.** the plant itself.

straw′berry tree′, an evergreen, ericaceous shrub or tree, *Arbutus Unedo,* of southern Europe, bearing a scarlet, strawberrylike fruit.

straw·board (strô′bōrd′, -bôrd′), *n.* coarse, yellow paperboard made of straw pulp, used in packing, for making boxes, etc. [STRAW + BOARD]

straw′ boss′, *U.S. Informal.* a member of a work crew, as in a factory or logging camp, who acts as a boss; assistant foreman.

straw′ col′or, a pale yellow similar to the color of straw. —**straw′-col′ored,** *adj.*

straw·flow·er (strô′flou′ər), *n.* **1.** any of several everlasting flowers, esp. an Australian herb, *Helichrysum bracteatum,* having heads of chaffy yellow, orange, red, or white flowers. **2.** Also called **cornflower, wood daffodil.** a bellwort, *Uvularia grandiflora,* having yellow flowers. [STRAW + FLOWER]

straw·hat (strô′hat′), *adj.* of or pertaining to a summer theater situated outside an urban or metropolitan area: *strawhat theater; strawhat circuit.* [so called from the wearing of straw hats in summer]

straw′ man′, 1. a mass of straw formed to resemble a man, as for a doll or scarecrow. **2.** a person used by another to disguise his own activities, as a perjured witness. **3.** an unimportant person, object, or discussion: *Your argument is a straw man intended to divert us from the real issues.*

straw′ vote′, *U.S.* an unofficial vote taken to obtain an indication of the general trend of opinion on a particular issue.

straw′ wine′, a usually rich or sweet wine produced from grapes partially dried on the vine or picked and dried in the sun on a bed of straw or reeds.

straw·worm (strô′wûrm′), *n.* **1.** caddisworm. **2.** jointworm. [STRAW + WORM]

straw·y (strô′ē), *adj.,* **straw·i·er, straw·i·est. 1.** of, containing, or resembling straw. **2.** strewed or thatched with straw. [STRAW + -Y[1]]

stray (strā), *v.i.* **1.** to deviate from the direct course, leave the proper place, or go beyond the proper limits, esp. without a fixed course or purpose; ramble: *to stray from the main road.* **2.** to wander; roam: *The new puppy strayed from room to room.* **3.** to go astray; deviate, as from a moral, religious, or philosophical course: *to stray from the teachings of the church.* **4.** to digress or become distracted. —*n.* **5.** a domestic animal found wandering at large or without an owner. **6.** any homeless or friendless person or animal. **7.** a person or animal that strays: *the strays of a flock.* **8. strays,** *Radio.* static. —*adj.* **9.** straying or having strayed, as a domestic animal. **10.** found or occurring apart from others or as an isolated or casual instance; incidental or occasional. **11.** *Radio.* undesired: *stray capacitance.* [ME *stray(en),* aph. var. of *astraien, estraien* < MF *estraie(r)* < VL **extrāgāre* for ML *extrāvagārī* to wander out of bounds. See EXTRAVAGANT] —**stray′er,** *n.*
—**Syn. 1.** rove, range. **2.** meander. **3.** err.

stray′ line′, *Naut.* a length of log line immediately next to the log chip of a chip log and not included in the reckoning of knots.

streak (strēk), *n.* **1.** a long, narrow mark, smear, band of color, or the like: *streaks of mud.* **2.** a flash of lightning; bolt. **3.** a portion or layer of something, distinguished by color or nature from the rest; a vein or stratum: *streaks of fat in meat.* **4.** a vein, strain, or admixture of anything: *a streak of humor.* **5.** *U.S. Informal.* a spell or run: *a winning streak; a streak of good luck.* **6.** *Mineral.* the line of powder obtained by scratching a mineral or rubbing it upon a hard, rough white surface, often differing in color from the mineral in the mass, and forming an important distinguishing character. **7.** *Bacteriol.* the inoculation of a medium with a loop which contains the material to be inoculated, by passing the loop in a direct or zigzag line over the medium, without scratching the surface. **8.** *Plant Pathol.* **a.** an elongated, narrow, superficial lesion on stems or leaf veins, becoming brown and necrotic. **b.** any disease characterized by such lesions. **9.** *Informal.* a fast runner or worker. **10. blue streak.** See **blue streak.** —*v.t.* **11.** to mark with a streak or streaks; form streaks on: *sunlight streaking the water with gold; frost streaking the windows.* **12.** to dispose, arrange, smear, spread, etc., in the form of a streak or streaks: *to streak cold germs on a slide for microscopic study.* —*v.i.* **13.** to become streaked. **14.** to run, go, work, etc., rapidly. **15.** to flash, as lightning. [ME *strek(e),* akin to *strik(e),* OE *strica* STROKE[1], line, mark; c. G *Strich,* Goth *striks* stroke, L *strig-* (see STRIGIL)] —**streaked·ly** (strēkt′lē, strē′kid lē), *adv.* —**streaked′ness,** *n.* —**streak′er,** *n.* —**streak′like′,** *adj.*

streak·y (strē′kē), *adj.,* **streak·i·er, streak·i·est. 1.** occurring in streaks or a streak. **2.** marked with or characterized by streaks. **3.** *Informal.* varying or uneven in quality. [STREAK + -Y[1]] —**streak′i·ly,** *adv.* —**streak′i·ness,** *n.*

stream (strēm), *n.* **1.** a body of water flowing in a channel or watercourse, as a river, rivulet, or brook. **2.** a steady current in water, as in a river or the ocean: *to row against the stream; the Gulf Stream.* **3.** any flow of water or other liquid or fluid: *streams of blood.* **4.** a current or flow of air, gas, or the like. **5.** a beam or trail of light: *A stream of moonlight fell from the clouds.* **6.** a continuous flow or succession of anything: *a stream of words.* **7.** prevailing direction; drift: *the stream of opinion.* —*v.i.* **8.** to flow, pass, or issue in a stream, as water, tears, blood, etc. **9.** to send forth or throw off a stream; run or flow (often fol. by *with*): *eyes streaming with tears.* **10.** to extend in a beam or trail, as light: *Sunlight streamed in through the windows.* **11.** to move or proceed continuously like a flowing stream, as a procession. **12.** to wave or float outward, as a flag in the wind. **13.** to hang in a loose, flowing manner, as long hair. —*v.t.* **14.** to send forth or discharge in a stream: *The wound streamed blood.* **15.** to cause to stream or float outward, as a flag. **16.** to overspread or suffuse with a stream or streams (fol. by *with*): *His face was streaming with sweat and tears.* **17.** *Naut.* to place (an object) in the water at the end of a line attached to a vessel. [ME *streem,* OE *strēam;* c. G *Strom,* Icel *straumr;* akin to SERUM] —**stream′less,** *adj.* —**stream′like′,** *adj.*
—**Syn. 1.** rill, run, streamlet, runnel. STREAM, CURRENT refer to a steady flow. In this use they are interchangeable. In the sense of running water, however, a STREAM is a flow which may be as small as a brook or as large as a river: *A number of streams have their sources in mountains.* CURRENT refers to the most rapidly moving part of the stream: *This river has a swift current.* **2.** flow, tide. **6.** torrent, rush. **8.** pour.

stream·er (strē′mər), *n.* **1.** something that streams: *streamers of flame.* **2.** a long, narrow flag or pennant. **3.** a long, flowing ribbon, feather, or the like, used for ornament, as in dress. **4.** any long, narrow piece or thing, as a spray of a plant or a strip of cloud. **5.** a stream of light, esp. one appearing in some forms of the aurora borealis. **6.** *Elect.* an electric discharge in a narrow stream from a point of high potential on a charged body. **7.** banner (def. 7). [ME *stremer.* See STREAM, -ER[1]]

stream′er fly′, *Angling.* an artificial fly having a wing or wings extending beyond the crook of the fishhook.

stream′ func′tion, *Mech.* a function that expresses the flow of a fluid in a plane, across a line joining a fixed and a movable point as a variable determined by the position of the movable point.

stream·ing (strē′ming), *n.* **1.** the act or an instance of flowing. **2.** *Biol.* flowing of protoplasm within a cell; cyclosis. [late ME *streming.* See STREAM, -ING[1]] —**stream′ing·ly,** *adv.*

stream′ing poten′tial, *Physical Chem.* the potential produced in the walls of a porous membrane or a capillary tube by forcing a liquid through it.

stream·let (strēm′lit), *n.* a small stream; rivulet. [STREAM + -LET]

stream·line (strēm′līn′), *n., v.,* **-lined, -lin·ing.** —*n.* **1.** a teardrop line of contour offering the least possible resistance to a current of air, water, etc. **2.** the path of a particle that is flowing steadily and without turbulence in a fluid past an object. —*v.t.* **3.** to make streamlined. **4.** to alter (a routine, process, plan, organization, etc.) in order to make it more efficient, esp. by simplifying. [STREAM + LINE[1]]

stream·lined (strēm′līnd′), *adj.* **1.** having a surface designed to offer the least possible resistance to a current of air, water, etc., by allowing the uninterrupted flow of gas or fluid. **2.** designed or organized to give maximum efficiency; compact. **3.** modernized; up-to-date. [STREAMLINE + -ED[2]]

stream′line flow′, the flow of a fluid past an object such that the velocity at any fixed point in the fluid is constant or varies in a regular manner. Cf. **turbulent flow.**

stream·lin·er (strēm′lī′nər), *n.* something that is streamlined, esp. a locomotive or passenger train. [STREAMLINE + -ER[1]]

stream′ of con′sciousness, *Psychol.* thought regarded as a succession of states constantly moving forward in time.

stream-of-con·scious·ness (strēm′əv kon′shəs nis), *adj.* of, pertaining to, or characterized by a manner of writing in which a character's thoughts or perceptions are presented as occurring in random form, without regard for logical sequences, syntactic structure, distinctions between various levels of reality, or the like: *a stream-of-consciousness novel; a stream-of-consciousness technique.*

stream·way (strēm′wā′), *n.* the bed of a stream. [STREAM + WAY]

stream·y (strē′mē), *adj.,* **stream·i·er, stream·i·est. 1.** abounding in streams or watercourses: *streamy meadows.* **2.** flowing in a stream; streaming. [late ME *stremy.* See STREAM, -Y[1]] —**stream′i·ness,** *n.*

Strea·tor (strē′tər), *n.* a city in N Illinois. 16,868 (1960).

streek (strēk), *Brit. Dial.* —*v.t.* **1.** to stretch (one's limbs), as on awakening or by exercise. **2.** to extend (one's hand or arm), as in reaching for or offering an object. **3.** to stretch out or prepare (a corpse) for burial. —*v.i.* **4.** to fall or lie prostrate. **5.** to move quickly, esp. to advance. [ME (north) *streke,* var. of *strecchen* to STRETCH] —**streek′er,** *n.*

streek·ing (strē′king), *n. Brit. Dial.* the act of stretching one's limbs, as on awakening or by exercise. [ME *streekynge.* See STREEK, -ING[1]]

street (strēt), *n.* **1.** a public thoroughfare, usually paved, in a village, town, or city, including the sidewalk or sidewalks. **2.** such a thoroughfare together with adjacent buildings, lots, etc.: *Houses, lawns, and trees composed a very pleasant street.* **3.** the roadway of such a thoroughfare, as distinguished from the sidewalk: *to cross a street.* **4.** a main way or thoroughfare, as distinguished from a lane, alley, or the like. **5.** the inhabitants or frequentors of a street: *The whole street gossiped about the new neighbors.* **6. the Street,** *Slang.* **a.** the section of a city associated with a given profession or trade, esp. when concerned with business or finance, as Wall Street. **b.** the principal theater and entertainment district of any of a number of U.S. cities. **7. up one's street,** *Brit.* See **alley**[1] (def. 7). [ME; OE strēt, strēt; c. D *straat*, G *Strasse*; all << L (*via*) *strāta* paved (road); see STRATUS] —**street′less,** *adj.* —**street′like′,** *adj.*

—**Syn. 1.** roadway, concourse. STREET, ALLEY, AVENUE, BOULEVARD all refer to public ways or roads in municipal areas. A STREET is a road in a village, town, or city, esp. a road lined with buildings. An ALLEY is a narrow street or footway, esp. at the rear of or between rows of buildings or lots. An AVENUE is properly a prominent street, often one bordered by fine residences and impressive buildings, or with a row of trees on each side. A BOULEVARD is a beautiful, broad street, lined with rows of stately trees, esp. used as a promenade. In some cities STREET and AVENUE are used interchangeably, the only difference being that those running one direction (say, North and South) are given one designation and those crossing them are given the other.

Street (strēt), *n.* a walled plain in the third quadrant of the face of the moon: about 35 miles in diameter.

Street, The, a painting (1907) by Ernst Ludwig Kirchner.

street′ Ar′ab, 1. a homeless child who lives by begging or stealing. **2.** any homeless, usually destitute person who roams the streets.

street·car (strēt′kär′), *n.* *U.S.* a public vehicle running regularly along certain streets, usually on rails, as a trolley car or trolley bus. [STREET + CAR[1]]

Street′car Named′ Desire′, A, a play (1947) by Tennessee Williams.

street′ certif′icate, a certificate showing ownership of a specified number of shares of stock: endorsed by the owner and guaranteed by a broker, it may be traded without formal transfer on the books of the corporation issuing the stock.

street′ clean′er, a sanitation worker who cleans streets or sidewalks.

street′ dress′, a dress, more formal than a housedress, appropriate for general wear in public, as for shopping, meetings, etc.

street′ game′, a game originally played on a city street or other paved surface.

street·light (strēt′līt′), *n.* a light, usually supported by a lamppost, for illuminating a street, road, etc. [STREET + LIGHT[1]]

street′ name′, *Stock Exchange.* a broker who holds securities registered in his name instead of in the name of the customer, esp. for convenience in executing transfers and in pledging for borrowing in margin accounts.

street′ or′derly, *Brit.* See **street cleaner.**

street′ rail′way, a company that operates streetcars or buses.

Street′ Scene′, a play (1929) by Elmer Rice.

street′ ur′chin, a neglected or homeless child who roams the streets, often begging or stealing.

street·walk·er (strēt′wô′kər), *n.* a prostitute who solicits on the streets. [STREET + WALKER] —**street′walk′ing,** *n.*

Stre·ga (strā′gə), *n.* *Trademark.* a spicy, orange-flavored liqueur made in Italy.

strength (strengkth, strength), *n.* **1.** the quality or state of being strong; bodily or muscular power; vigor. **2.** mental power, force, or vigor. **3.** moral power, firmness, or courage. **4.** power by reason of influence, authority, resources, numbers, etc. **5.** number, as of men or ships in a force or body: *a regiment with a strength of 3000.* **6.** effective force, potency, or cogency, as of inducements or arguments: *the strength of his plea.* **7.** power of resisting force, strain, wear, etc. **8.** vigor of action, language, feeling, etc. **9.** the effective or essential properties characteristic of a beverage, chemical, or the like: *The alcoholic strength of brandy far exceeds that of wine.* **10.** a particular proportion of these properties; intensity, as of light, color, sound, flavor, or odor: *coffee of normal strength.* **11.** something or someone that makes strong or is a source of power or encouragement: *The Bible was her strength and joy.* **12.** power to rise or remain firm in prices: *Stocks continued to show strength. The pound declined in strength.* **13. on the strength of,** on the basis of; relying on: *He was accepted for college on the strength of good personal recommendations.* [ME *strengthe*, OE *strengthu*, equiv. to *streng-* (mutated var. of STRONG) + *-thu* -TH[1]]

—**Syn. 4.** STRENGTH, POWER, FORCE, MIGHT suggest capacity to do something. STRENGTH is inherent capacity to manifest energy, to endure, and to resist. POWER is capacity to do work and to act. FORCE is the exercise of power: *One has the power to do something. He exerts force when he does it. He has sufficient strength to complete it.* MIGHT is power or strength in a great or overwhelming degree: *the might of an army.* **9.** potency. **10.** brightness, loudness, vividness, pungency.

strength′ deck′, *Naut.* **1.** the uppermost deck that serves to strengthen the hull of a vessel. **2.** any deck that serves to strengthen a hull.

strength·en (strengk′thən, streng′-), *v.t.* **1.** to make stronger; give strength to. —*v.i.* **2.** to gain strength; grow stronger. [ME *strengthne(n)*. See STRENGTH, -EN[1]] —**strength′en·er,** *n.* —**strength′en·ing·ly,** *adv.*

stren·u·ous (stren′yo͞o əs), *adj.* **1.** vigorous, energetic, or zealously active: *a strenuous person; a strenuous intellect.* **2.** characterized by vigorous exertion, as action, efforts, life, etc.: *a strenuous exercise; a strenuous afternoon of hunting.* **3.** demanding or requiring vigorous exertion; laborious: *To think clearly and deeply is a strenuous task.* [< L *strēnuus*; see -OUS] —**stren′u·ous·ly,** *adv.* —**stren′u·ous·ness, stren·u·os·i·ty** (stren′yo͞o·os′i tē), *n.*

—**Syn. 1.** forceful. See **active.** —**Ant. 3.** easy.

strep (strep), *Informal.* —*n.* **1.** streptococcus. —*adj.* **2.** streptococcal: *strep throat.* [by shortening]

strep·i·tous (strep′i təs), *adj.* boisterous; noisy. Also, **strep′i·tant.** [< L *strepit(us)* noise + -OUS]

strepto-, a learned borrowing from Greek meaning "twined," used in the formation of compound words: *streptococcus.* [comb. form of Gk *streptós* pliant, twisted, twined, equiv. to *strep-* (var. s. of *stréphein* to twist) + *-tos* ptp. suffix]

strep·to·coc·cus (strep′tə kok′əs), *n., pl.* **-coc·ci** (-kok′sī). *Bacteriol.* any of several spherical or oval bacteria of the genus *Streptococcus*, occurring in pairs or chains, certain species of which are pathogenic for man, causing scarlet fever, tonsillitis, etc. [STREPTO- + COCCUS] —**strep·to·coc·cal** (strep′tə kok′əl), **strep·to·coc·cic** (strep′tə kok′sik), *adj.*

strep·to·dor·nase (strep′tō dôr′nās), *n.* *Biochem., Pharm.* a deoxyribonuclease, obtained from hemolytic streptococci, which, with streptokinase, is employed in medicine chiefly as an agent for the decomposition of blood clots and fibrinous and purulent matter resulting from injury or infection. [STREPTO- + D(E)O(XY)R(IBO)N(UCLE)ASE]

strep·to·ki·nase (strep′tō kī′nās, -kin′ās), *n.* *Pharm.* fibrinolysin (def. 2). [STREPTO- + KINASE]

strep·to·my·ces (strep′tə mī′sēz), *n., pl.* **-ces.** *Bacteriol.* any of several aerobic bacteria of the genus *Streptomyces*, certain species of which produce antibiotics. [< NL; see STREPTO-, MYC-]

strep·to·my·cin (strep′tō mī′sin), *n.* *Pharm.* an antibiotic, $C_{21}H_{39}N_7O_{12}$, produced by a soil actinomycete, *Streptomyces griseus*, and used in medicine in the form of its white, water-soluble sulfate salt, chiefly in the treatment of tuberculosis. Cf. **dihydrostreptomycin.** [STREPTO- + MYC- + -IN[2]]

strep·to·thri·cin (strep′tō thrī′sin), *n.* *Pharm.* an antibacterial substance produced by the soil fungus, *Actinomyces lavendulae.* [STREPTO- + *thric-* (var. of TRICH-) + -IN[2]]

Stre·se·mann (shtrā′zə män′), *n.* **Gus·taf** (go͝os′täf), 1878–1929, German statesman: Nobel peace prize 1926.

stress (stres), *n.* **1.** importance or significance attached to a thing; emphasis: *to lay stress upon good manners.* **2.** *Phonet.* emphasis in the form of prominent relative loudness of a syllable or a word as a result of special effort in utterance. **3.** *Pros.* accent or emphasis on syllables in a metrical pattern; beat. **4.** emphasis in melody, rhythm, etc.; beat. **5.** the physical pressure, pull, or other force exerted on one thing by another; strain. **6.** *Mech.* **a.** the action on a body of any system of balanced forces whereby strain or deformation results. **b.** the amount of stress, usually measured in number of pounds per square inch. **c.** a load, force, or system of forces producing a strain. **d.** the internal resistance or reaction of an elastic body to the external forces applied to it. **e.** the ratio of force to area. **7.** *Physiol.* any stimulus, as fear or pain, that disturbs or interferes with the normal physiological equilibrium of an organism. **8.** physical, mental, or emotional strain or tension: *Worry over his job and his wife's health put him under a great stress.* **9.** *Archaic.* strong or straining exertion. —*v.t.* **10.** to lay stress on; emphasize. **11.** *Phonet.* to pronounce (a syllable or a word) with prominent loudness: *Stress the first syllable of "runner." Stress the second word in "put up with."* Cf. **accent** (def. 15). **12.** to subject to stress or strain. **13.** *Mech.* to subject to stress. [ME *stresse*, aph. var. of *distresse* DISTRESS] —**stress′less,** *adj.* —**stress′less·ness,** *n.*

-stress, a feminine equivalent of **-ster:** *seamstress; songstress.* [-ST(E)R + -ESS]

stress·ful (stres′fəl), *adj.* full of stress or tension: *the stressful days before a war.* [STRESS + -FUL] —**stress′ful·ly,** *adv.*

stretch (strech), *v.t.* **1.** to draw out or extend (oneself, a body, limbs, wings, etc.) to the full length or extent (often fol. by *out*): *to stretch oneself out on the ground.* **2.** to hold out, reach forth, or extend (the hand or something held, the head, etc.). **3.** to extend, spread, or place (something) so as to reach from one point or place to another: *to stretch a rope across a road.* **4.** to draw tight or taut: *to stretch the strings of a violin.* **5.** to strain to the utmost, as by exertion: *She stretched herself to provide for the family.* **6.** to lengthen, widen, distend, or enlarge by tension: *to stretch a rubber band.* **7.** to draw out, extend, or enlarge unduly: *The jacket was stretched at the elbows.* **8.** to extend, force, or make serve beyond the normal or proper limits; strain: *to stretch the imagination; to stretch the facts; to stretch food to feed extra guests; to stretch money to keep within a budget.* **9.** to increase the quantity of (a beverage, food, paint, etc.) by dilution or admixing: *They caught the bartender stretching the gin with water.* **10.** *Radio and Television.* to prolong or slow down in order not to end too early: *to stretch a show; to stretch the action two minutes.* —*v.i.* **11.** to recline at full length (usually fol. by *out*): *to stretch out on a couch.* **12.** to extend the hand or to reach, as for something. **13.** to extend over a distance or area or in a particular direction: *The forest stretches for miles.* **14.** to extend in time: *His memory stretches back to his early childhood.* **15.** to stretch oneself by extending the limbs and straining the muscles to the utmost: *to stretch and yawn.* **16.** to become stretched, or admit of being stretched, to greater length, width, etc., as any elastic or ductile material. **17.** *Radio and Television.* to reduce the pace or slow down the action of a radio or television program. —*n.* **18.** the act or an instance of stretching. **19.** state of being stretched. **20.** a continuous length, distance, tract, or expanse: *a stretch of meadow.* **21.** *Horse Racing.* the backstretch or homestretch of a race track. **22.** *Baseball.* a short windup, usually used to keep base runners from taking too long a lead, in which the pitcher starts with his hands together at his waist, raises them to or above his head, brings them back to his waist, and, after a momentary pause, delivers the pitch. **23.** an extent in time; duration: *for a stretch of 10 years.* **24.** elasticity or capacity for extension. **25.** *Slang.* a term of imprisonment: *He's doing a stretch in the pen.* **26.** (*cap.*) a nickname for a tall, lanky person. —*adj.* **27.** made of synthetic or composite yarn having a sufficiently low denier to permit increased elasticity: *stretch fabrics; stretch socks; stretch girdle.* **28.** (of yarn) modified or twisted so as to afford high elasticity. [ME *strecche(n)*, OE *streccan*; c. D *strekken*, G *strecken*; akin to OE *stræc* firm, hard, MD *strac* stiff. See STARE, STARK] —**stretch′a·bil′i·ty,** *n.* —**stretch′a·ble,** *adj.*

—**Syn. 6.** See **lengthen. 11.** lie down. **20.** range, reach, compass. —**Ant. 6, 16.** shorten, shrink.

stretch·er (strech′ər), *n.* **1.** a kind of litter, usually of canvas stretched on a frame, for carrying the sick, wounded, or dead. **2.** one who or that which stretches. **3.** any of various instruments for extending, widening, distending, etc. **4.** a bar, beam, or fabricated material, serving as a tie or brace. **5.** *Masonry.* a brick or stone laid in a wall so that its longer edge is exposed or parallel to the surface. Cf. **header** (def. 4a). **6.** a simple wooden framework on which the canvas for an oil painting is stretched. **7.** *Furniture.* **a.** a framework connecting and bracing the legs of a piece of furniture. **b.** one member of this framework. **8.** a crosspiece that is set athwart and near the bottom in a small boat, and against which the feet of a rower are braced. **9.** one of the thin, sliding rods connecting the canopy and handle of an umbrella. **10.** a bar of wood, plastic, or metal for spreading the clews of a hammock. [late ME *stretcher*. See STRETCH, -ER[1]]

stretch·er-bear·er (strech′ər bâr′ər), *n.* a man who helps carry a stretcher, as in removing wounded from a battlefield.

stretch′er bond′. See **running bond.**

stretch′ing course′, (in brickwork) a course of stretchers. Cf. **heading course.**

stretch′ mill′, *Metalworking.* a mill for rolling and stretching seamless tubes, the rolls of each successive stand operating more quickly than those of the preceding.

stretch-out (strech′out′), *n.* *U.S.* **1.** a deliberate extension of time for meeting a production quota. **2.** a method of factory management by which employees do additional work without a commensurate increase in wages. [n. use of v. phrase *stretch out*]

stretch·y (strech′ē), *adj.,* **stretch·i·er, stretch·i·est. 1.** having a tendency to stretch, esp. excessively or unduly. **2.** capable of being stretched; elastic. **3.** (esp. of a pig) having a long body. [STRETCH + -Y[1]] —**stretch′i·ness,** *n.*

stret·ta (stret′ə), *n., pl.* **stret·te** (stret′ā), **stret·tas.** *Music.* **1.** a concluding passage played at a faster tempo. **2.** stretto. [< It; fem. of STRETTO]

stret·to (stret′ō), *n., pl.* **stret·ti** (stret′ē), **stret·tos.** *Music.* the close overlapping of statements of the subject in a fugue, each voice entering immediately after the preceding one. Also, **stretta.** [< It: lit., narrow < L *strict(us).* See STRICT, STRAIT]

streu·sel (*Ger.* shtroi′zəl; *Eng.* stroi′zəl, stro͞o′-), *n.* a topping for coffeecake, consisting of crumbs of blended sugar, cinnamon, flour, butter, and chopped nut meats. [< G: lit., a sprinkling; see STREW]

streu·sel·ku·chen (*Ger.* shtroi′zəl ko͞o′kHən; *Eng.* stroi′zəl ko͞o′kən, stro͞o′-), *n.* coffee cake topped with streusel. [< G; see STREUSEL, KUCHEN]

strew (stro͞o), *v.t.,* **strewed, strewn** or **strewed, strew·ing. 1.** to let fall in separate pieces or particles over a surface; scatter or sprinkle: *to strew seed in a garden bed.* **2.** to cover or overspread (a surface, place, etc.) with something scattered or sprinkled: *to strew a floor with sawdust.* **3.** to be scattered or sprinkled over (a surface): *Sawdust strewed the floor.* **4.** to spread widely: *to strew rumors among the troops.* [ME *strew(en)*, OE *strewian*; c. G *streuen*, Icel *strā* Goth *straujan*; akin to L *sternere* to spread (see STRATUS)] —**strew′er,** *n.*

—**Syn. 1.** broadcast. See **sprinkle.** —**Ant. 1.** gather, reap.

stri·a (strī′ə), *n., pl.* **stri·ae** (strī′ē). **1.** a slight or narrow furrow, ridge, stripe, or streak, esp. one of a number in parallel arrangement: *striae of muscle fiber.* **2.** *Geol.* any of a number of scratches or parallel grooves on the surface of a rock, resulting from the action of moving ice, as of a glacier. **3.** *Mineral.* any of a series of parallel lines or tiny grooves on the surface of a crystal, or on a cleavage face of a crystal, due to its molecular organization. **4.** Also called **strix.** *Archit.* a flute on the shaft of a column. [< L: furrow, channel]

stri·ate (*v.* strī′āt; *adj.* strī′it, -āt), *v.,* **-at·ed, -at·ing,** *adj.* —*v.t.* **1.** to mark with striae; furrow; stripe; streak. —*adj.* **2.** striated. [< L *striāt(us)* (ptp. of *striāre*), equiv. to *stri-* (see STRIA) + *-ātus* -ATE[1]]

stri·at·ed (strī′ā tid), *adj.* marked with striae; furrowed; striped; streaked. [STRIATE + -ED[2]]

stri·a·tion (strī ā′shən), *n.* **1.** striated condition or appearance. **2.** a stria; one of many parallel striae. [STRIATE + -ION]

strick (strik), *n.* **1.** a group of any of the major bast fibers prepared for conversion into sliver form. **2.** any of the pieces cut from a layer of carded and combed silk. [ME *strik*, perh. deriv. of OE *stric* a word of uncertain meaning; akin to STRIKE]

strick·en (strik′ən), *adj.* **1.** a pp. of **strike. 2.** hit or wounded by a weapon, missile, or the like. **3.** beset or afflicted, as with disease, trouble, or sorrow: *stricken areas; a stricken family.* **4.** deeply affected, as with grief, fear, or other emotions. **5.** characterized by or showing the effects of affliction, trouble, misfortune, a mental blow, etc.: *stricken features.* —**strick′en·ly,** *adv.*

Strick·land (strik′lənd), *n.* **William,** 1787–1854, U.S. architect and engineer.

strick·le (strik′əl), *n., v.,* **-led, -ling.** —*n.* **1.** a straightedge used for sweeping off heaped-up grain to the level of the rim of a measure. **2.** *Foundry.* a template rotated to generate a mold surface symmetrical about one axis. **3.** an implement for sharpening scythes, composed typically of a piece of wood smeared with grease and sand. —*v.t.* **4.** to sweep off or remove with a strickle. [ME *strikyll*, OE *stricel*; akin to STRIKE]

strick′le bar′, *Foundry.* a tool for trimming off excess sand at the top of a mold.

strict (strikt), *adj.* **1.** characterized by or acting in close conformity to requirements or principles: *a strict observance of rituals.* **2.** stringent or exacting in or in enforcing rules, requirements, obligations, etc.: *strict laws; a strict judge.* **3.** closely or rigorously enforced or maintained: *strict silence.* **4.** exact or precise: *a strict statement of facts.* **5.** extremely limited or conservative; narrowly or carefully limited: *a strict construction of the Constitution.* **6.** close, careful, or minute: *a strict search.* **7.** absolute, perfect, or complete: *told in strict confidence.* **8.** stern; severe; austere: *strict parents.* **9.** *Obs.* drawn tight or close. [< L *strict(us)*, equiv. to *stric-* (deriv. of *strig-*, var. s. of *stringere* to draw tight) + *-tus* ptp. suffix] —**strict′ness,** *n.*

—**Syn. 1.** narrow, illiberal, harsh, austere. STRICT, RIGID, RIGOROUS, STRINGENT imply inflexibility, severity, and an exacting quality. STRICT implies great exactness, esp. in the observance or enforcement of rules: *strict discipline.* RIGID, literally stiff or unbending, applies to that which is (often unnecessarily or narrowly) inflexible: *rigid economy.* RIGOROUS, with the same literal meaning, applies to that which is severe, exacting, and uncompromising, esp. in action or application: *rigorous self-denial.* STRINGENT applies to that which is vigorously exacting and severe: *stringent measures to suppress disorder.* **4.** accurate, scrupulous. —**Ant. 1.** flexible, lax.

stric·tion (strik′shən), *n.* the act of drawing tight, constricting, or straining. [< LL *strictiōn-* (s. of *strictiō*), equiv. to L *strict(us)* (see STRICT) + *-iōn-* -ION]

strict·ly (strikt′lē), *adv.* in a strict manner; precisely; stringently: *strictly speaking.* [STRICT + -LY]

strict′ly decreas′ing func′tion, *Math.* a function having the property that for any two points in the domain such that one is larger than the other, the image of the larger point is less than the image of the smaller point. Cf. **strictly increasing function.**

strict′ly increas′ing func′tion, *Math.* a function having the property that for any two points in the domain such that one is larger than the other, the image of the larger point is greater than the image of the smaller point. Cf. **strictly decreasing function.**

stric·ture (strik′chər), *n.* **1.** a remark or comment, esp. an adverse criticism: *The reviewer made several strictures upon the author's style.* **2.** an abnormal contraction of any passage or duct of the body. **3.** a restriction. **4.** *Archaic.* the act of enclosing or binding tightly. **5.** *Obs.* strictness. [< LL *strictūr(a)* tightening equiv. to L *strict(us)* (see STRICT) + *-ūra* -URE] —**stric′tured,** *adj.*

stride (strīd), *v.,* **strode, strid·den** (strid′ən), **strid·ing,** *n.* —*v.i.* **1.** to walk with long steps, as with vigor, haste, impatience, or arrogance. **2.** to take a long step: *to stride across a puddle.* **3.** to straddle. —*v.t.* **4.** to walk with long steps along, on, through, over, etc.: *to stride the deck.* **5.** to pass over or across in one long step: *to stride a ditch.* **6.** to straddle. —*n.* **7.** a striding manner or a striding gait. **8.** a long step in walking. **9.** (in animal locomotion) the act of progressive movement completed when all the feet are returned to the same relative position as at the beginning. **10.** the distance covered by such a movement: *He was walking a stride or two ahead of the others.* **11.** a regular or steady course, pace, etc.: *to hit one's stride.* **12.** a step forward in development or progress: *rapid strides in mastering algebra.* **13. take something in one's stride,** to deal with calmly; cope with successfully: *She was able to take her sudden rise to fame in her stride.* [ME *stride(n),* OE *strīdan;* c. D *strijden,* LG *strīden* to stride; akin to STRADDLE] —**strid′er,** *n.* —**strid′ing·ly,** *adv.*

stri·dent (strīd′ənt), *adj.* making or having a harsh sound; grating; creaking: *strident insects; strident hinges.* [< L *strīdent-* (s. of *strīdēns*), prp. of *strīd(ēre)* (to) make a harsh noise + *-ent-* -ENT] —**stri′dence, stri′den·cy,** *n.* —**stri′dent·ly,** *adv.*

stride′ pian′o, a style of jazz piano playing in which the right hand plays the melody while the left hand plays a single bass note or octave on the strong beat and a chord on the weak beat, developed in Harlem during the 1920's, partly from ragtime piano playing.

stri·dor (strī′dər), *n.* **1.** a harsh, grating, or creaking sound. **2.** *Pathol.* a harsh respiratory sound due to any of various forms of obstruction of the breathing passages. [< L, equiv. to *strīd-* to (see STRIDENT) + *-or* -OR[2]]

strid·u·late (strij′ə lāt′), *v.i.,* **-lat·ed, -lat·ing.** to produce a shrill, grating sound, as a cricket does, by rubbing together certain parts of the body; shrill. [back formation from *stridulation.* See STRIDUL(OUS), -ATION] —**strid′u·la′tion,** *n.* —**strid·u·la·to·ry** (strij′ə lə tôr′ē, -tōr′ē), *adj.*

strid·u·lous (strij′ə ləs), *adj.* **1.** Also, **strid′u·lant.** making or having a harsh or grating sound. **2.** *Pathol.* pertaining to or characterized by stridor. [< L *strīdulus,* equiv. to *strīd-* (see STRIDENT) + *-ulus* -ULOUS] —**strid′u·lous·ly,** *adv.* —**strid′u·lous·ness,** *n.*

strife (strīf), *n.* **1.** vigorous or bitter conflict, discord, or antagonism: *to be at strife.* **2.** a quarrel, struggle, or clash: *armed strife.* **3.** competition or rivalry: *the strife of the market place.* **4.** *Archaic.* strenuous effort. [ME *strif,* OF *(e)strif;* see STRIVE] —**strife′ful,** *adj.* —**strife′less,** *adj.*

—**Syn. 1.** difference, disagreement, contrariety, opposition. **2.** fight, conflict. —**Ant. 1, 2.** peace.

stri·ges (strī′jēz), *n.* pl. of **strix.**

strig·i·form (strij′ə fôrm′), *adj.* of, pertaining, or belonging to the order *Strigiformes,* comprising the owls. [< NL *Strigiform(ēs)* name of the order, equiv. to *strig-* (s. of *strix*) screech owl + *-i-* -I- + *-form-* -FORM]

strig·il (strij′əl), *n.* **1.** an instrument with a curved blade, used esp. by the ancient Greeks and Romans for scraping the skin at the bath and in the gymnasium. **2.** *Archit.* any of a series of decorative S-shaped flutings, esp. in Roman architecture. [< L *strigil(is),* equiv. to *strig-* (var. s. of *stringere* to touch lightly; see STREAK, STRIKE) + *-ilis* -ILE] —**strig·il·ate** (strij′ə lit, -lāt′), *adj.*

stri·gose (strī′gōs, stri gōs′), *adj.* **1.** *Bot.* set with stiff bristles of hairs; hispid. **2.** *Zool.* marked with fine, closely set ridges, grooves, or points. [< L *strig(a)* furrow, row of bristles (see STRIGIL) + -OSE[1]]

strike (strīk), *v.,* **struck; struck** or (*Obs.*) **strook; struck** or (*esp. for 31–34*) **strick·en** or (*Obs.*) **strook; strik·ing;** *n.* —*v.t.* **1.** to deal a blow or stroke to (a person or thing), as with the fist, a weapon, or a hammer; hit. **2.** to inflict, deliver, or deal (a blow, stroke, attack, etc.). **3.** to drive so as to cause impact: *to strike the hands together.* **4.** to thrust forcibly: *Brutus struck a dagger into the dying Caesar.* **5.** to produce (fire, sparks, light, etc.) by percussion, friction, etc. **6.** to cause (a match) to ignite by friction. **7.** (of some natural or supernatural agency) to smite or blast: *Lightning struck the spire. May God strike you dead!* **8.** to come into forcible contact or collision with; hit into or against: *The ship struck a rock.* **9.** to reach or fall upon (the senses), as light or sound: *A shrill peal of bells struck their ears.* **10.** to enter the mind of; occur to: *A happy thought struck him.* **11.** to catch or arrest (the sight, hearing, etc.): *the first object that strikes one's eye.* **12.** to impress strongly: *a picture that strikes one's fancy.* **13.** to impress in a particular manner: *How does it strike you?* **14.** to come across, meet with, or encounter suddenly or unexpectedly: *to strike the name of a friend in a newspaper.* **15.** to come upon or find (oil, ore, etc.) in drilling, prospecting, or the like. **16.** to send down or put forth (a root), as a plant, cutting, etc. **17.** to arrive at or achieve by or as by balancing: *to strike a balance; to strike a compromise.* **18.** to take apart or pull down (a structure or object, as a tent). **19.** to remove from the stage (the scenery and properties of an act or scene): *to strike a set.* **20.** *Naut.* **a.** to lower or take down (a sail, mast, etc.). **b.** to lower (a sail, flag, etc.) as a salute or as a sign of surrender. **c.** to lower (something) into the hold of a vessel by means of a rope and tackle. **21.** *Falconry.* to loosen (a hood) from the head of a hawk so that it may be instantly removed. **22.** *Angling.* **a.** to hook (a fish that has taken the bait) by making a sharp jerk on the line. **b.** (of a fish) to snatch at (the bait). **23.** to harpoon (a whale). **24.** (in technical use) to make level or smooth. **25.** to make level or even, as a measure of grain or salt, by drawing a strickle across the top. **26.** to efface, cancel, or cross out, with or as with the stroke of a pen (usually fol. by *out*): *to strike a passage out of a book.* **27.** to impress or stamp (a coin, medal, etc.) by printing or punching: *to strike a medal in commemoration.* **28.** to remove or separate with or as with a cut (usually fol. by *off*): *Illness struck him off from social contacts. The butcher struck off a chop.* **29.** *Masonry.* to finish (a mortar joint) with a stroke of the trowel. **30.** to indicate (the hour of day) by a stroke or strokes, as a clock: *to strike 12.* **31.** to afflict suddenly, as with disease, suffering, or death (often fol. by *down*): *The plague struck Europe. Apoplexy struck him down.* **32.** to overwhelm emotionally, as with terror, fear, etc.; affect deeply. **33.** to make blind, dumb, etc., suddenly, as if by a blow. **34.** to implant or induce (a feeling): *to strike fear into a person.* **35.** to start or move suddenly into (vigorous movement): *The horse struck a gallop.* **36.** to assume (an attitude or posture): *He likes to strike a noble pose.* **37.** to cause (chill, warmth, etc.) to pass or penetrate quickly. **38.** to come upon or reach in traveling or in a course of procedure: *We struck Rome before dark.* **39.** to make, conclude, or ratify (an agreement, treaty, etc.). **40.** to estimate or determine (a mean or average). **41.** to leave off (work) or stop (working) as a coercive measure, or as at the close of the day. **42.** (of a union or union member) **a.** to declare or engage in a suspension of (work) until an employer grants certain demands, such as pay increases, an improved pension plan, etc. **b.** to declare or engage in a suspension of work against (a factory, employer, industry, etc.) until certain demands are met. **43.** to draw (a straight line); paint the edge of an area with (a regular, usually straight line). **44.** *Law.* to choose from a given panel the persons to serve on (a jury).

—*v.i.* **45.** to deal or aim a blow or stroke, as with the fist, a weapon, or a hammer; make an attack. **46.** to knock, rap, or tap. **47.** to hit or dash on or against something, as a moving body does; come into forcible contact; collide. **48.** to run upon a bank, rock, or other obstacle, as a ship does. **49.** to fall, as light or sound does (fol. by *on* or *upon*). **50.** to make an impression on the mind, senses, etc., as something seen or heard. **51.** to come suddenly or unexpectedly (usually fol. by *on* or *upon*): *to strike on a new way of doing a thing.* **52.** to sound by percussion: *The clock strikes.* **53.** to be indicated by or as by such percussion: *The hour has struck.* **54.** to ignite or be ignited by friction, as a match. **55.** to make a stroke, as with the arms or legs in swimming or with an oar in rowing. **56.** to produce a sound, music, etc., by touching a string or playing upon an instrument. **57.** to take root, as a slip of a plant. **58.** to go, proceed, or advance, esp. in a new direction: *They struck out at dawn. They struck toward a new town.* **59.** *U.S. Navy.* to train for promotion to third-class petty-officer rank. **60.** (of a union or union member) to engage in a suspension of work until an employer or industry meets certain demands. **61.** *Naut.* **a.** to lower the flag or colors, esp. as a salute or as a sign of surrender. **b.** to run up the white flag of surrender. **62.** *Angling.* (of fish) to swallow or take the bait. **63. strike camp,** to dismantle and pack up equipment; prepare to move on; break camp: *The army struck camp and moved on.* **64. strike hands,** to conclude a bargain, as by shaking or joining hands; confirm an agreement: *They reached a price satisfactory to both of them, and struck hands on it.* **65. strike home, a.** to deal an effective blow. **b.** to have the intended effect; hit the mark: *The sermon on Christian charity struck home.* **66. strike in,** to interrupt suddenly; intervene: *I struck in with a suggestion.* **67. strike it rich, a.** to come upon a valuable mineral or oil deposit. **b.** to have sudden or unexpected financial success: *He struck it rich in real estate.* **68. strike off, a.** *Print.* to print: *They struck off 300 copies of the book.* **b.** to remove or cancel, as from a record, list, etc.: *His name was struck off the waiting list.* **c.** to produce rapidly and easily: *She struck off several letters and had no more work to do.* **69. strike oil.** See **oil** (def. 8). **70. strike out, a.** *Baseball.* to put out or be put out by a strike-out: *The pitcher walked two and struck out three. He struck out twice in three times at bat.* **b.** (of a person or effort) to fail: *His next two business ventures struck out.* **c.** to lose favor. **71. strike up, a.** to begin to play or to sing: *The orchestra struck up a waltz.* **b.** to set in operation; begin: *Strike up the band!* **c.** to bring into being; commence; begin: *to strike up an acquaintance.*

—*n.* **72.** the act or an instance of striking. **73.** a concerted stopping of work or withdrawal of workers' services, as to compel an employer to accede to workers' demands or in protest against terms or conditions imposed by an employer. **74.** Also called **strike plate, keeper.** a metal plate on a jamb holding the bolt of the lock on a door when closed. **75.** *Baseball.* **a.** a pitch that is swung at and missed by the batter. **b.** a pitch that passes through the strike zone and is not swung at by the batter. **c.** a foul tip caught by the catcher when there are already two strikes against the batter. **d.** a foul bunt when there are already two strikes against the batter. **e.** a ball hit foul and not caught on the fly when there are less than two strikes against the batter. **76.** *Bowling.* **a.** the knocking down of all of the pins with the first bowl. **b.** the score so made. Cf. **spare** (def 20). **77.** *Horol.* the striking mechanism of a timepiece. **78.** *Brewing.* the degree of excellence or strength of beer, ale, etc. **79.** *Angling.* **a.** a sharp jerk on the line, made in order to set the hook in the mouth of the fish. **b.** a pull on the line, made by the fish in the process of taking the bait. **80.** *Coining.* a quantity of coins struck at one time. **81.** *Geol.* **a.** the direction of the line formed by the intersection of the bedding plane of a bed or stratum of sedimentary rock with a horizontal plane. **b.** the direction or trend of a structural feature, as an anticlinal axis or the lineation resulting from metamorphism. **82.** the discovery of a rich vein or ore in mining, of petroleum in boring, etc. **83.** a board with a straight-edge for leveling brick clay in a mold. **84.** Also called **drive.** *Type Founding.* the copper die into which a character has been punched; an unjustified matrix. **85.** *Mil.* a planned attack, esp. by aircraft, on a target. **86. have two strikes against one,** to be in an unfavorable or a critical position: *With his age and his lack of education, I'm afraid he has two strikes against him in his search for a job.* [ME, OE *strīc(an);* c. G *streichen;* see STREAK, STROKE[1], STRIGIL] —**strike′less,** *adj.*

—**Syn. 1.** STRIKE, HIT, KNOCK imply suddenly bringing one body in contact with another. STRIKE suggests such an action in a general way: *to strike a child.* HIT is less formal than STRIKE, and often implies giving a single blow, but usually a strong one and definitely aimed: *to hit a baseball.* To KNOCK is to strike, often with a tendency to displace the object struck; it also means to strike repeatedly: *to knock someone down; to knock at a door.* See **beat.** —**Ant. 1.** miss.

strike-an′y·where match′ (strīk′en′ē hwâr′, -wâr′), a match that can be ignited by friction with any rough surface.

strike′ ben′efit, money paid to strikers by a union to enable them to subsist during a strike. Also called **strike pay.**

strike·board (strīk′bōrd′, -bôrd′), *n.* a board having one edge formed to the finish profile of a concrete pavement and moved along the fresh concrete of the pavement to give it such a profile. [STRIKE + BOARD]

strike·bound (strīk′bound′), *adj.* closed by a strike: *a strikebound factory.* [STRIKE + -BOUND[1]]

strike·break·er (strīk′brā′kər), *n.* one who takes part in breaking up a strike of workers, either by working or by furnishing workers. [STRIKE + BREAKER[1]]

strike·break·ing (strīk′brā′king), *n.* action directed at breaking up a strike of workers. [STRIKE + BREAKING]

strike′ fault′, *Geol.* a fault, the trend of which is parallel to the strike of the affected rocks.

strike-out (strīk′out′), *n.* *Baseball.* an out made by a batter to whom three strikes have been charged. [n. use of v. phrase *strike out*]

strike·o·ver (strīk′ō′vər), *n.* **1.** the act or an instance of typing over an error without erasing it. **2.** the typed-over portion, as a character: *The letter was full of strike-overs.* [n. use of v. phrase *strike over*]

strike′ pay′. See **strike benefit.**

strike′ plate′, strike (def. 74).

strik·er (strī′kər), *n.* **1.** one who or that which strikes. **2.** a worker who is on strike. **3.** manhelper. **4.** the clapper in a clock that strikes the hours or rings an alarm. **5.** *U.S. Army.* a private who acts as a voluntary paid servant to a commissioned officer. **6.** *U.S. Navy.* an enlisted man in training for a specific third-class petty-officer rating. **7.** one who strikes fish, whales, etc., with a spear or harpoon. **8.** *Whaling.* a harpoon. [ME; see STRIKE, -ER[1]]

strike′ zone′, *Baseball.* the area above home plate extending from the batter's knees to his shoulders.

strik·ing (strī′king), *adj.* **1.** that strikes. **2.** attractive; impressive: *a woman of striking beauty.* **3.** noticeable; conspicuous: *a striking lack of enthusiasm.* **4.** being on strike, as workmen. **5. a.** capable of attacking an enemy, esp. by air: *striking power.* **b.** within the extent of space through which it is possible to attack a target effectively: *striking distance.* [STRIKE + -ING[2]] —**strik′ing·ly,** *adv.* —**strik′ing·ness,** *n.*

strik′ing train′, *Horol.* the gear train of the striking mechanism of a timepiece. Cf. **going train.**

Strind·berg (strind′bûrg, strin′-; *Swed.* strin′bar′yə), *n.* **Jo·han Au·gust** (yo͞o′hän ou′go͞ost), 1849–1912, Swedish novelist, dramatist, and essayist.

string (string), *n., v.,* **strung; strung** or (*Rare*) **stringed; string·ing.** —*n.* **1.** a slender cord or thick thread used for binding or tying; line. **2.** something resembling a cord or thread. **3.** a narrow strip of flexible material, as cloth or leather, for tying parts together: *the strings of a bonnet.* **4.** a necklace consisting of a number of beads, pearls, or the like, threaded or strung on a cord; strand: *She wore a double string of pearls.* **5.** any series of things arranged or connected in a line or following closely one after another: *a string of islands; a string of questions.* **6.** *Journalism.* a compilation of clippings of a stringer's published writings, submitted in request of payment according to his space rate. **7.** a group of animals belonging to one owner or managed by one man: *a string of race horses.* **8.** (in a musical instrument) a tightly stretched cord or wire which produces a tone when caused to vibrate, as by plucking, striking, or friction of a bow. **9. strings, a.** stringed instruments, esp. those played with a bow. **b.** players on such instruments in an orchestra or band. **10.** a bowstring. **11.** a cord or fiber in a plant. **12.** the tough piece uniting the two parts of a pod: *the strings of beans.* **13.** *Archit.* **a.** a stringcourse. **b.** Also called **stringer.** one of the sloping sides of a stair, supporting the treads and risers. **14.** *Billiards, Pool.* **a.** a stroke made by each player from the head of the table to the opposite cushion and back, to determine, by means of the resultant positions of the cue balls, who shall open the game. **b.** Also called **string line.** a line from behind which the cue ball is placed after being out of play. **15.** a group of contestants or players listed in accordance with their skill: *He made the second string on the football team.* **16.** Usually, **strings.** *Informal.* conditions or limitations on a proposal: *a generous offer with no strings attached.* **17.** *Obs.* a ligament, nerve, or the like, in an animal body. **18. have two strings to one's bow,** to have two resources as security in case of the failure or ineffectiveness of one or the other: *What with his acting and singing, he has two strings to his bow.* **19. on a** or **the string,** *Slang.* subject to the whim of another; in one's power; dependent: *After keeping him on a string for two years, she finally married someone else.* **20. pull strings** or **wires, a.** to use one's influence or authority, usually in secret, in order to bring about a desired result. **b.** to gain or attempt to gain one's objectives by means of influential friends, associates, etc.: *He had his uncle pull strings to get him a promotion.*
—*v.t.* **21.** to furnish with or as with a string or strings: *to*

string a bonnet; to string a bow. **22.** to extend or stretch (a cord, thread, etc.) from one point to another. **23.** to thread on or as on a string: *to string beads.* **24.** to connect in or as in a line; arrange in a series or succession: *He knows how to string words together.* **25.** *Music.* **a.** to adjust the string of (a bow) or tighten the strings of (a musical instrument) to the required pitch. **b.** to equip (a bow or instrument) with new strings. **26.** to provide or adorn with something suspended or slung: *a room strung with festoons.* **27.** to deprive of a string or strings; strip the strings from: *to string beans.* **28.** to make tense, as the sinews, nerves, mind, etc. **29.** to kill by hanging (usually fol. by *up*). **30.** *Slang.* to fool or hoax. —*v.i.* **31.** to form into or move in a string or series: *The ideas string together coherently.* **32.** to form into a string or strings, as a glutinous substance does when pulled: *Good taffy doesn't break — it strings.* **33. string along,** *Slang.* **a.** Also, **string along with.** to be in agreement; keep faith; follow with confidence: *She found she couldn't string along with all their modern notions.* **b.** to keep (a person) waiting or in a state of uncertainty. **c.** to deceive; cheat; trick. **34. string out, a.** to extend; stretch out: *The parade strung out for miles.* **b.** to prolong: *The promised three days strung out to six weeks.* [ME, OE *streng;* c. D *streng,* G *Strang;* akin to L *stringere* to bind] —**string′less,** *adj.* —**string′like′,** *adj.*

string′ bass′ (bās). See **double bass.**

string′ bean′, **1.** any of various kinds of bean the unripe pods of which are used as food, usually after stripping off the fibrous thread along the side. **2.** the pod itself. **3.** *Informal.* a tall, thin person.

string·board (string′bōrd′, -bôrd′), *n.* a board or facing covering the ends of the steps in a staircase. [STRING + BOARD]

string′ correspond′ent, stringer (def. 6).

string·course (string′kōrs′, -kôrs′), *n. Archit.* a horizontal band or course of stone, etc., projecting beyond or flush with the face of a building, often molded and sometimes richly carved. Also called **belt course.** [STRING + COURSE]

S, Stringcourse

stringed (stringd), *adj.* **1.** fitted with strings (often used in combination): *a five-stringed banjo.* **2.** *Archaic.* produced or sounded by strings: *stringed melodies.* [STRING + -ED[3]]

stringed′ in′strument, a musical instrument having strings as the medium of sound production, played with the fingers or with a plectrum or a bow: *The guitar, the harp, and the violin are stringed instruments.*

strin·gen·cy (strin′jən sē), *n., pl.* **-cies.** **1.** stringent character or condition: *the stringency of poverty.* **2.** strictness; closeness; rigor: *the stringency of school discipline.* **3.** tightness; straitness: *stringency in the money market.* [STRING(ENT) + -ENCY]

strin·gen·do (strin jen′dō; *It.* strēn jen′dô), *adj., adv. Music.* (a musical direction) progressively quickening the tempo. [< It, equiv. to *string(ere)* to compress + *-endo* -ENT; see STRINGENT]

strin·gent (strin′jənt), *adj.* **1.** rigorously binding or exacting; strict; severe: *stringent laws.* **2.** compelling, constraining, or urgent: *stringent necessity.* **3.** convincing or forcible: *stringent arguments.* **4.** (of the money market) characterized by a shortage in money for loan or investment purposes; tight. [< L *stringent-* (s. of *stringēns*), prp. of *string(ere)* (to) draw tight; see -ENT] —**strin′gent·ly,** *adv.*
—**Syn. 1.** restrictive. See **strict. 3.** forceful, powerful, effective. —**Ant. 1.** flexible.

string·er (string′ər), *n.* **1.** one who or that which strings. **2.** a long horizontal timber connecting upright posts. **3.** *Archit.* string (def. 13b). **4.** *Naut.* **a.** any of the continuous, fore-and-aft girders strengthening the hull of a vessel, esp. along the side. **b.** Also called **string′er bar′.** an angle iron connecting a stringer strake to the ribs or plating of a hull. **5.** *Civ. Eng.* a longitudinal bridge girder for supporting part of a deck or railroad track between bents or piers. **6.** Also called **string correspondent.** *Journalism.* a part-time newspaper correspondent covering his local area for a paper published elsewhere: *The Los Angeles paper has a correspondent in San Francisco, but only a stringer in Seattle.* Cf. **staffer. 7.** a stout string, rope, etc., on which a fisherman strings the fish he has caught, by passing it through the gills and mouth, so that he may carry them or put them back in the water to keep them alive or fresh. [late ME; see STRING, -ER[1]]

string′er bead′, *Welding.* See under **bead** (def. 15).

string′er strake′, *Naut.* a strake of deck plating surrounding the deck area. Also called **string′er plate′.**

string·halt (string′hôlt′), *n. Vet. Pathol.* a nerve disorder in horses, causing exaggerated flexing movements of the hind legs in walking. Also, **springhalt.** [STRING + HALT[2]] —**string′halt′ed, string′halt′y,** *adj.* —**string′halt′ed·ness,** *n.*

string·hold·er (string′hōl′dər), *n.* an oblong piece of wood at the lower end of the body of a viol or other stringed instrument to which the strings are attached. [STRING + HOLDER]

string·ing (string′ing), *n.* a narrow band of inlay, as in a piece of furniture. [STRING + -ING[1]]

string′ line′, *Billiards, Pool.* string (def. 14b).

string·piece (string′pēs′), *n.* a long, usually horizontal piece of timber, beam, etc., for strengthening, connecting, or supporting a framework. [STRING + PIECE]

string′ play′er, one who plays an instrument of the violin family.

string′ quartet′, **1.** a musical composition, usually in three or four movements, for four stringed instruments, typically two violins, viola, and cello. **2.** a first violinist, second violinist, violist, and cellist forming a group for the performance of string quartets and similar music.

string′ tie′, a short, very narrow, and unflared necktie, usually tied in a bow.

string·y (string′ē), *adj.,* **string·i·er, string·i·est. 1.** resembling a string or strings; consisting of strings or stringlike pieces: *stringy weed; a stringy fiber.* **2.** coarsely or toughly fibrous, as meat. **3.** sinewy or wiry, as a person. **4.** ropy, as a glutinous liquid. [STRING + -Y[1]] —**string′i·ness,** *n.*

strip[1] (strip), *v.,* **stripped** or **stript, strip·ping.** —*v.t.* **1.** to deprive of covering: *to strip a fruit of its rind.* **2.** to deprive of clothing; make bare or naked. **3.** to take away or remove: *to strip a rind from a fruit; to strip fruit from trees.* **4.** to deprive or divest: *to strip a tree of its fruit.* **5.** to clear out or empty: *to strip a house of its contents.* **6.** to deprive of equipment; dismantle: *to strip a ship of rigging.* **7.** to dispossess, rob, or plunder: *to strip a man of his possessions.* **8.** to separate the leaves from the stalks of (tobacco). **9.** to remove the midrib, as from tobacco leaves. **10.** *Mach.* to break off the thread of (a screw, bolt, etc.) or the teeth of (a gear) as by applying too much force. **11.** to remove the mold from (an ingot). **12.** to draw the last milk from (a cow), esp. by a stroking and compressing movement. **13.** to draw out (milk) in this manner. **14.** *Photoengraving.* to remove (the emulsion from a film base) in order to place it on a glass plate for exposure to the metal plate. **15.** *Textiles.* **a.** to clean (a carding roller) by removing waste fibers. **b.** to transfer (fibers) from one carding roller to another. **c.** to remove (color) from a cloth in order to redye it another color. **d.** to remove color from (a cloth). **16.** *Bridge.* to lead successively winning cards from (a hand) in order to dispose of as many cards as necessary preparatory to surrendering the lead to an opponent so that any card that he plays will be to his disadvantage. **17.** *Chem.* **a.** to remove the most volatile components from, as by distillation or evaporation. **b.** to remove all or part of the dye from (yard or fabric being dyed), as by boiling or by treating with chemicals. —*v.i.* **18.** to strip something. **19.** to remove one's clothes. **20.** to perform a striptease. **21.** to become stripped: *Bananas strip easily.* [ME *strippe,* OE **strypp(an)* (cf. MHG *strupfen* to strip off); r. ME *stripe, strepe, strupe* < OE *(be)strȳp(an)* (to) rob, plunder; c. D *stroopen*]
—**Syn. 1.** uncover, peel, decorticate. **2.** denude. **7.** despoil. STRIP, DEPRIVE, DISPOSSESS, DIVEST imply more or less forcibly taking something away from someone. To STRIP is to take something completely (often violently) from a person or thing so as to leave in a destitute or powerless state: *to strip a man of all his property; to strip the bark from a tree.* To DEPRIVE is to take away forcibly or coercively what one has, or to withhold what one might have: *to deprive one of his income.* To DISPOSSESS is to deprive of the holding or use of something: *to dispossess the renters of a house.* DIVEST usually means depriving of rights, privileges, powers, or the like: *to divest a king of authority.* —**Ant. 6.** supply, furnish.

strip[2] (strip), *n., v.,* **stripped, strip·ping.** —*n.* **1.** a narrow piece, comparatively long and usually of uniform width: *a strip of cloth, metal, land, etc.* **2.** a continuous series of drawings or pictures illustrating incidents, conversation, etc., as a comic strip. **3.** *Aeron.* **a.** airstrip. **b.** See **landing strip. 4.** *Philately.* three or more stamps joined either in a horizontal or vertical row. **5.** *Theat.* striplight. **6.** *(sometimes cap.)* a road, street, or avenue, usually in a city or a main thoroughfare between outlying suburbs, densely lined on both sides by a large variety of retail stores, gas stations, restaurants, bars, etc.: *Sunset Strip in Los Angeles.* **7.** See **drag strip.** —*v.t.* **8.** to cut, tear, or form into strips. **9.** *Print.* to combine (a piece of film) with another, esp. for making a combination plate of lines and halftones. [late ME < MLG *strippe* strap; see STRIPE[1]]

strip′ crop′ping, the growing of different crops on alternate strips of ground that usually follow the contour of the land, in order to minimize erosion. Also called **strip farming, strip planting.**

stripe[1] (strīp), *n., v.,* **striped, strip·ing.** —*n.* **1.** a relatively long, narrow band of a different color, appearance, weave, material, or nature from the rest of a surface or thing: *the stripes of a zebra.* **2.** a fabric or material containing such a band or bands. **3.** a strip of braid, tape, or the like. **4. stripes,** a number or combination of such strips, worn on a military, naval, or other uniform as a badge of rank, service, good conduct, wounds, etc. **5.** a strip, or long, narrow piece of anything: *a stripe of beach.* **6.** a streak or layer of a different nature within a substance. **7.** style, variety, sort, or kind: *a man of quite a different stripe.* —*v.t.* **8.** to mark or furnish with a stripe or stripes. [ME < MD or MLG *strīpe,* in same sense] —**stripe′less,** *adj.*

stripe[2] (strīp), *n.* a stroke with a whip, rod, etc., as in punishment. [late ME, perh. special use of STRIPE[1] in sense of WALE[1]]

striped (strīpt, strī′pid), *adj.* having stripes or bands. [STRIPE[1] + -ED[3]]

striped′ bass′ (bas), an American game fish, *Roccus saxatilis,* having blackish stripes along each side.

striped′ go′pher, a ground squirrel marked with stripes, esp. the thirteen-lined ground squirrel.

strip′ed hye′na, a hyena, *Hyaena hyaena,* of northern Africa, Arabia, and India, having a grayish coat with blackish stripes.

striped′ kil′lifish, a killifish, *Fundulus majalis,* found along the Atlantic coast of the U.S., the female of which is marked with black stripes. Also called **mayfish.**

striped′ ma′ple, a maple, *Acer pennsylvanicum,* of northeastern North America, having white-striped bark. Also called **moosewood.**

striped′ mar′lin, a marlin, *Tetrapturus audax,* found in the Pacific Ocean, having the sides of the body marked with vertical stripes.

striped′ sper′mophile, *Zool.* See **thirteen-lined ground squirrel.**

striped′ squir′rel, any squirrel with stripes on its back, as a chipmunk.

strip·er (strī′pər), *n. Slang.* **1.** a naval officer who wears stripes on the sleeve of his uniform: *a four-striper.* **2.** an enlisted man of any of the armed services who wears stripes on his sleeve denoting years of service: *a six-striper.* [STRIPE[1] + -ER[1]]

stripe′ rust′, *Plant Pathol.* a disease of wheat, barley, rye, and other grasses, characterized by elongated pustules of yellow spores on the affected parts, caused by a rust fungus, *Puccinia glumarum.* Also called **yellow rust.**

stripe′ smut′, *Plant Pathol.* a disease of grasses, characterized by stripes of black spores on the leaves, caused by any of several smut fungi of the genera *Urocystis* and *Ustilago.*

strip′ farm′, a tract of land where strip cropping is done.

strip′ farm′ing. See **strip cropping.**

strip′ film′, a short length of film; filmstrip.

strip·ing (strī′ping), *n.* **1.** the act of decorating or otherwise providing with stripes: *The striping of the boat proceeded slowly.* **2.** a striped pattern: *the striping of the zebra; striping of different colors.* [STRIPE[1] + -ING[1]]

strip·light (strip′līt′), *n. Theat.* a row of lamps, provided with a reflector for floodlighting the stage, used as borderlights, footlights, backing lights, etc. [STRIP[2] + LIGHT[1]]

strip·ling (strip′ling), *n.* a youth. [late ME; see STRIP[2], -LING[1]]

strip′ map′, a map charting only the immediate territory to be traversed, which appears as a long, narrow strip.

strip′ min′ing, mining in an open pit after removal of the overburden.

strip·per (strip′ər), *n.* **1.** one who strips. **2.** that which strips, as an appliance or machine for stripping. **3.** Also called **ecdysiast, exotic dancer, stripteaser.** a woman who performs a striptease. **4.** a harvesting machine for stripping the seed heads from the stalks of grain. **5.** any of several rollers covered with card clothing that operate in combination with the worker rollers and the cylinder in the carding of fibers. [STRIP[1] + -ER[1]]

strip′ping liq′uor, any chemical for removing a coating from a metal surface.

strip′ plant′ing. See **strip cropping.**

strip′ pok′er, a game of poker in which the losers in a hand remove an article of clothing.

stript (stript), *v.* a pt. and pp. of **strip.**

strip·tease (strip′tēz′), *n., v.,* **-teased, -teas·ing.** —*n.* **1.** a burlesque act in which a woman dancer removes her garments one at a time to the accompaniment of music and sometimes patter. —*v.i.* **2.** to do a striptease. [STRIP[1] + TEASE]

strip·teas·er (strip′tē′zər), *n.* stripper (def. 3). [STRIPTEASE + -ER[1]]

strip·teuse (strip tœz′), *n. Chiefly Facetious.* stripper (def. 3). [STRIPT(EASE + DANS)EUSE]

strip·y (strī′pē), *adj.,* **strip·i·er, strip·i·est.** having or marked with stripes. [STRIPE[1] + -Y[1]]

strive (strīv), *v.i.,* **strove, striv·en** (striv′ən), **striv·ing. 1.** to exert oneself vigorously; try hard: *He strove to make himself understood.* **2.** to make strenuous efforts toward any goal: *to strive for success.* **3.** to contend in opposition, battle, or any conflict; compete. **4.** to struggle vigorously, as in opposition or resistance: *to strive against fate.* **5.** *Obs.* to rival; vie. [ME *strive(n)* < OF *(e)strive(r)* (to) quarrel, compete, strive < Gmc; cf. obs. D *strijven,* G *streben* to strive] —**striv′er,** *n.* —**striv′ing·ly,** *adv.*
—**Syn. 1.** See **try. 2.** toil. **3.** struggle, fight.

strix (striks), *n., pl.* **stri·ges** (strī′jēz), **strix·es.** *Archit.* stria (def. 4). [< L: furrow, channel; akin to STRIGIL]

stroam (strōm), *v.i. Brit. Dial.* to walk or stroll. Also, **strome.** [? b. ST(ROLL) + ROAM]

strobe (strōb), *n. Photog. Informal.* **1.** See **flash lamp** (def. 2). **2.** stroboscope (def. 2). —*adj.* **3.** stroboscopic. [shortening of STROBOSCOPE]

stro·bi·la (strō bī′lə), *n. Zool.* the entire body of a tapeworm. [< NL < Gk *strobílē,* fem. of *stróbilos* fir cone; see STROBILE]

strob·i·la·ceous (strob′ə lā′shəs), *adj.* **1.** resembling a strobile; conelike. **2.** bearing strobiles. [< NL *strobilaceus* < *strobil(us)* (< Gk *stróbilos* something twisted, fir cone) + *-aceus* -ACEOUS]

strob·ile (strob′il), *n. Bot.* **1.** the somewhat conical multiple fruit of the pine, fir, etc. **2.** a conelike mass of sporophylls found in certain club mosses and ferns. [< NL < Gk *strobílē* plug of lint shaped like a fir cone; see STROBILA] —**strob·i·loid** (strob′ə loid′), *adj.*

stro·bo·ra·di·o·graph (strō′bə rā′dē ə graf′, -gräf′, strob′ə-), *n.* a stroboscopic radiograph. [< Gk *strôbo(s)* action of whirling + RADIOGRAPH]

stro·bo·scope (strō′bə skōp′, strob′ə-), *n.* **1.** a device for studying the motion of a body, esp. one in rapid revolution or vibration, by making the motion appear to slow down or stop at frequent intervals, as by periodically illuminating the body or viewing it through widely spaced openings in a revolving disk. **2.** *Photog.* **a.** Also called **stro′boscop′ic lamp′.** a lamp capable of producing an extremely short, brilliant burst of light, for synchronization with a camera having a high shutter speed, in order to photograph a rapidly moving object, as a bullet, for such a short duration that it will appear to be standing still. **b.** the device and equipment for holding and firing such a lamp. **c.** an instantaneous, stop-motion photograph taken with such a lamp as a light source. [< Gk *strôbo(s)* action of whirling + -SCOPE] —**stro·bo·scop·ic** (strō′bə skop′ik, strob′ə-), **stro′bo·scop′i·cal,** *adj.* —**stro·bos·co·py** (strə bos′kə pē), *n.*

stro·bo·tron (strō′bə tron′, strob′ə-), *n. Electronics.* a glow lamp, used in stroboscopes, that gives very bright flashes of light in response to voltage pulses. [*strobo-* (see STROBOSCOPE) + -TRON]

strode (strōd), *v.* pt. of **stride.**

Stroess·ner (stres′nər), *n.* **Al·fre·do** (äl frā′thō), born 1912, Paraguayan general and statesman: president since 1954.

stro·ga·noff (strô′gə nôf′, strō′-), *adj.* (of meat) sautéed with onion, and cooked in a sauce of sour cream, seasonings, and, usually, mushrooms: *beef stroganoff.* [named after P. *Stroganoff,* 19th-century Russian count and diplomat]

stroke[1] (strōk), *n., v.,* **stroked, strok·ing.** —*n.* **1.** the act or an instance of striking, as with the fist, a weapon, a hammer, etc.; a blow. **2.** a hitting of or upon anything. **3.** a striking of a clapper or hammer, as on a bell. **4.** the sound produced by this. **5.** a throb or pulsation, as of the heart. **6.** something likened to a blow in its effect, as in causing pain, injury, or death; an attack of apoplexy or paralysis. **7.** a destructive discharge of lightning. **8.** a vigorous movement, as if in dealing a blow. **9.** *Sports.* a hitting of a ball, as the swinging hit

of tennis or the controlled jabbing or thrusting with the cue of pool and billiards. **10.** a single complete movement, esp. one continuously repeated in some process. **11.** *Mech.* **a.** one of a series of alternating continuous movements of something back and forth over or through the same line. **b.** the complete movement of a moving part, esp. a reciprocating part, in one direction. **c.** the distance traversed in the movement. **d.** a half revolution of an engine during which the piston travels from one extreme of its range to the other. **12.** *Swimming.* **a.** a type or method of swimming: *The crawl is a rapid stroke.* **b.** each of the successive movements of the arms and legs in propelling the body through the water. **13.** *Rowing.* **a.** a single pull of the oar. **b.** the manner or style of moving the oars. **c.** Also called **stroke oar.** the oarsman nearest to the stern of the boat, to whose strokes those of the other oarsmen must conform. **14.** a movement of a pen, pencil, brush, graver, or the like. **15.** a mark traced by or as if by one movement of a pen, pencil, brush, or the like. **16.** a distinctive or effective touch in a literary composition: *His style revealed the stroke of a master.* **17.** an act, piece, or amount of work, activity, etc.: *to refuse to do a stroke of work.* **18.** a vigorous attempt to attain some object: *a bold stroke for liberty.* **19.** a measure adopted for a particular purpose. **20.** a keystroke: *no more than 65 strokes to the line for business letters.* **21.** a feat or achievement: *a stroke of genius.* **22.** a sudden or chance happening, as of luck or fortune. **—*v.t.*** **23.** to mark with a stroke or strokes, as of a pen; cancel, as by a stroke of a pen. **24.** *Rowing.* **a.** to row as a stroke oar of (a boat or crew). **b.** to set the stroke for the crew of (a boat). **25.** *Masonry.* to dress (a stone) in a series of broad, shallow flutes; drove. **26.** *Sports.* to hit (a ball), as with a deliberate, smooth swing of a bat or club. [ME, OE **strāc* (whence *strācian* to STROKE[2]); c. G *Streich;* akin to STRIKE]
—Syn. 1. rap, tap, knock, pat. **1, 6.** See **blow**[1]. **5.** beat, thump; rhythm.

stroke[2] (strōk), *v.*, **stroked, strok·ing,** *n.* **—*v.t.*** **1.** to pass the hand or an instrument over (something) lightly or with little pressure; rub gently, as in soothing or caressing. **—*n.*** **2.** the act or an instance of stroking; a stroking movement. [ME, OE *strāc(ian);* c. G *streichen;* akin to STRIKE]

stroke′ hole′, *Golf.* (in a handicap match) a hole at which players with a handicap deduct a stroke from the number taken to play the hole.

stroke′ oar′, *Rowing.* **1.** the oar nearest to the stern of the boat. **2.** stroke[1] (def. 13c).

stroke′ play′, *Golf.* See **medal play.**

stroll (strōl), *v.i.* **1.** to walk leisurely as inclination directs; ramble; saunter; take a walk: *to stroll along the beach.* **2.** to wander or rove from place to place; roam: *strolling Gypsies.* **—*v.t.*** **3.** to saunter along or through: *to stroll the countryside.* **—*n.*** **4.** a leisurely walk; ramble; saunter: *a short stroll before supper.* [? akin to *streel* < Ir *straoill-* wander, loiter, trail]
—Syn. 1. stray, meander. **4.** promenade.

stroll·er (strō′lər), *n.* **1.** a person who takes a leisurely walk; saunterer. **2.** a wanderer; vagrant. **3.** an itinerant performer. **4.** a four-wheeled, often collapsible, chairlike carriage in which small children are pushed. [STROLL + -ER[1]]

stro·ma (strō′mə), *n., pl.* **-ma·ta** (-mə tə). **1.** *Anat.* **a.** the colorless, spongelike framework of an erythrocyte or other cell. **b.** the supporting framework, usually of connective tissue, of an organ, as distinguished from the parenchyma. **2.** (in certain fungi) a compact, somatic mass of fungous tissue, in or on which the fructifications may be developed. [< LL < Gk *strôma* bed-covering; akin to L *sternere, strātum;* see STRAW, STREW] **—stro·mat·ic** (strō mat′ik), **stro′mal, stro′ma·tous,** *adj.*

stro·ma·te·id (strō′mə tē′id), *n.* **1.** any of numerous marine fishes of the family *Stromateidae,* having a laterally compressed body and an expanded muscular esophagus, often lined with teeth. **—*adj.*** **2.** belonging or pertaining to the *Stromateidae.* [< NL *Stromateid(ae)* name of the family, equiv. to *Stromate(us)* name of the genus < Gk *Strōmateús* bed-covering of patchwork, a kind of fish, deriv. of *strōmat-* (s. of *strôma*) STROMA + NL *-idae* -ID[2]]

stro·ma·te·oid (strō′mə tē′oid), *adj.* **1.** resembling or related to the *Stromateidae.* **—*n.*** **2.** a stromateoid fish. [*stromate-* (see STROMATEID) + -OID]

Strom·bo·li (strom′bə lē; *It.* strôm′bô lē), *n.* **1.** an island off the NE coast of Sicily, in the Lipari group. **2.** an active volcano on this island. 3040 ft.

strome (strōm), *v.i.*, **stromed, strom·ing.** *Brit. Dial.* stroam.

stro·mey·er·ite (strō′mī ə rīt′), *n.* a mineral, silver and copper sulfide, AgCuS, steel-gray in color with a metallic luster. [named after Friedrich *Strohmeyer* (1776–1835), German chemist; see -ITE[1]]

strong (strông, strong), *adj.*, **strong·er** (strông′gər, strong′-), **strong·est** (strông′gist, strong′-), *adv.* **—*adj.*** **1.** having, showing, or able to exert great bodily or muscular power; physically vigorous or robust: *a strong boy.* **2.** accompanied or delivered by great physical, mechanical, etc., power or force: *a strong handshake; With one strong blow the machine stamped out a fender.* **3.** mentally powerful or vigorous: *He may be old, but his mind is still strong.* **4.** especially able, competent, or powerful in a specific field or respect: *She's very strong in mathematics. He's no good at bat, but he's a strong fielder.* **5.** of great moral power, firmness, or courage: *strong under temptation.* **6.** powerful in influence, authority, resources, or means of prevailing or succeeding: *a strong nation.* **7.** compelling; of great force, effectiveness, potency, or cogency: *strong reasons; strong arguments.* **8.** clear and firm; loud: *He has a strong voice.* **9.** having a great store of wealth or capable of managing money well: *The U.S. has a strong economy.* **10.** well-supplied or rich in something specific: *a strong hand in trumps.* **11.** having powerful means to resist attack, assault, or aggression: *a strong fortress; a strong defense.* **12.** able to resist strain, force, wear, etc.: *strong walls; strong cloth.* **13.** firm or uncompromising; unfaltering: *She has strong views about the United Nations. He has a strong sense of duty.* **14.** fervent; zealous; thoroughgoing: *He's a strong Democrat.* **15.** strenuous or energetic; vigorous: *strong efforts.* **16.** moving or acting with force or vigor: *strong winds.* **17.** distinct or marked; vivid, as impressions, resemblance or contrast, etc.: *He bears a strong resemblance to his grandfather.* **18.** intense, as light or color. **19.** having a large proportion of the effective or essential properties or ingredients; concentrated: *strong tea.* **20.** (of a beverage or food) containing alcohol or much alcohol: *strong drink; The fruitcake was too strong.* **21.** having a high degree of flavor or odor: *strong cheese; strong perfume.* **22.** having an unpleasant or offensive flavor or odor, esp. in the process of decay: *strong butter.* **23.** *Com.* characterized by steady or advancing prices: *The market resumed its strong pace after yesterday's setback.* **24.** *Gram.* **a.** (of Germanic verbs) having vowel change in the root in inflected forms, as the English verbs *sing, sang, sung; ride, rode, ridden.* **b.** (of Germanic nouns and adjectives) inflected with endings that are generally distinctive of case, number, and gender, as German *alter Mann* "old man." **c.** belonging to the morphophonemically less regular of two inflectional subtypes. **25.** (of a syllable in a verse) stressed. **26.** *Optics.* having great magnifying or refractive power: *a strong microscope.* **—*adv.*** **27.** strongly. [ME, OE; c. Icel *strangr,* MD *stranc;* akin to G *streng* severe, strict, L *stringere* to tie; see STRINGENT] **—strong′ish,** *adj.* **—strong′ness,** *n.*
—Syn. 1. mighty, sturdy, brawny, sinewy, hardy, muscular, stout, stalwart. **4.** potent, capable, efficient. **5.** valiant, brave. **7.** persuasive, cogent, impressive, conclusive. **9.** solid, firm, secure. **13.** unwavering, resolute. **14.** fervid, vehement. **17.** stark, sharp. **18.** brilliant, vivid. **21.** pungent, aromatic, sharp, piquant, hot, spicy, biting. **22.** smelly, rank. **—Ant. 1.** weak.

strong′ accumula′tion point′, *Math.* a point such that every neighborhood of the point contains infinitely many points of a given set. Cf. **accumulation point, strong derived set.**

strong-arm (strông′ärm′, strong′-), *Informal.* **—*adj.*** **1.** using, involving, or threatening the use of physical force or violence to gain an objective: *strong-arm methods.* **—*v.t.*** **2.** to use violent methods upon; assault. **3.** to rob by force.

strong·back (strông′bak′, strong′-), *n.* **1.** *Naut.* **a.** a longitudinal beam laid on a ship's boat as a support for a canvas cover when the boat is not in use. **b.** a bar laid across a port or other closure to secure it in a closed position. **c.** a movable beam for supporting part of a hatch cover. **d.** a transverse arched timber binding together the uprights of a hand-operated windlass. **e.** See **pudding boom. 2.** strongbark. [STRONG + BACK[1]]

strong·bark (strông′bärk′, strong′-), *n.* any of several tropical American shrubs or small trees of the genus *Bourreria,* esp. *B. ovata,* of southern Florida and the West Indies, having fragrant, white flowers. Also called **strongback.** [STRONG + BARK[2]]

strong·box (strông′boks′, strong′-), *n.* a strongly made, lockable box or chest for preserving valuable possessions, as money, jewels, or documents. [STRONG + BOX[1]]

strong′ breeze′, *Meteorol.* (on the Beaufort scale) a wind of 25–30 miles per hour.

strong′ derived′ set′, *Math.* the set of all strong accumulation points of a given set. Cf. **strong accumulation point.**

strong′ gale′, *Meteorol.* (on the Beaufort scale) a wind of 47–54 miles per hour.

strong·hold (strông′hōld′, strong′-), *n.* **1.** a well-fortified place; fortress. **2.** a place that serves as the center of a militant group, or one holding a controversial viewpoint: *The campus was a stronghold of liberalism.* [late ME; see STRONG, HOLD[1]]

strong·ly (strông′lē, strong′-), *adv.* **1.** in a strong manner; powerfully; forcibly; vigorously. **2.** with strength, speed, vigor, etc., to spare. [ME *strongliche,* OE *stranglīce.* See STRONG, -LY]

strong′ man′, **1.** one who performs remarkable feats of strength, as in a circus. **2.** the most powerful or influential person in an organization or business, by reason of skill in the formulation and execution of plans, work, etc. **3.** one who controls by force; dictator. **—strong′-man′,** *adj.*

strong-mind·ed (strông′mīn′did, strong′-), *adj.* **1.** having or showing an obstinate mind or vigorous mental powers. **2.** *Disparaging.* (of women) claiming mental and social equality with men. **—strong′-mind′ed·ly,** *adv.* **—strong′-mind′ed·ness,** *n.*

strong·point (strông′point′, strong′-), *n.* *Mil.* a heavily-fortified, tactically advantageous area in a defensive position. [STRONG + POINT]

strong·room (strông′ro͞om′, -ro͝om′, strong′-), *n.* *Chiefly Brit.* a fireproof, burglarproof room in which valuables are kept. [STRONG + ROOM]

Strongs·ville (strôngz′vil, strongz′-), *n.* a town in N Ohio. 8504 (1960).

strong-voiced (strông′voist′, strong′-), *adj.* having a loud, clear voice: *a strong-voiced radio announcer.*

strong-willed (strông′wild′, strong′-), *adj.* **1.** having a powerful will; resolute. **2.** stubborn; obstinate.

stron·gyle (stron′jil), *n.* any nematode of the family *Strongylidae,* parasitic as an adult in the intestine of mammals, esp. horses. Also, **stron′gyl.** [< NL *Strongyl(us)* name of type-genus < Gk *strongýlos* round, spherical] **—stron·gy·late** (stron′jə lāt′), *adj.*

stron·gy·lo·sis (stron′jə lō′sis), *n.* *Vet. Pathol.* a disease, esp. of horses, caused by an infestation by strongyles and characterized in serious cases by weakness and anemia. [< NL, equiv. to *Strongyl(us)* STRONGYLE + *-ōsis* -OSIS]

stron·ti·a (stron′shē ə, -shə), *n.* *Chem.* **1.** Also called **strontium oxide.** a white or grayish-white, amorphous powder, SrO, resembling lime in its general character: used chiefly in the manufacture of strontium salts. **2.** See **strontium hydroxide.** [alter. of STRONTIAN; see -IA]

stron·ti·an (stron′shē ən, -shən), *n.* **1.** strontianite. **2.** strontia. **3.** strontium. [short for *Strontian earth* mineral first found in *Strontian* parish, Argyllshire, Scotland]

stron·ti·an·ite (stron′shē ə nīt′, -shə nīt′), *n.* a mineral, strontium carbonate, $SrCO_3$, occurring in radiating, fibrous, or granular aggregates and crystals, varying from white to yellow and pale green: a minor ore of strontium. [STRONTIAN + -ITE[1]]

stron·ti·um (stron′shē əm, -shəm, -tē əm), *n.* *Chem.* a bivalent, metallic element whose compounds resemble those of calcium, found in nature only in the combined state, as in strontianite: used in fireworks, flares, and tracer bullets. *Symbol:* Sr; *at. wt.:* 87.62; *at. no.:* 38; *sp. gr.:* 2.6. [STRONT(IAN) + -IUM] **—stron·tic** (stron′tik), *adj.*

stron′tium hydrox′ide, *Chem.* a white, slightly water-soluble powder, $Sr(OH)_2$, or its crystalline octahydrate **(stron′tium hy′drate):** used chiefly in the refining of beet sugar. Also called **strontia.**

strontium 90, *Chem.* a harmful radioactive isotope of strontium, produced in certain nuclear reactions and paesent in their fallout. Also called **radiostrontium.**

stron′tium ox′ide, *Chem.* strontia (def. 1).

strook (stro͝ok), *v.* *Obs.* a pt. and pp. of **strike.**

strop (strop), *n., v.,* **stropped, strop·ping.** **—*n.*** **1.** a strip of leather or other flexible material or a long, narrow piece of wood having its faces covered with leather or an abrasive, or some similar device, used for sharpening razors. **2.** Also, **strap.** *Naut., Mach.* **a.** a rope or a band of metal surrounding and supporting a block, deadeye, etc. **b.** a metal band surrounding the pulley of a block to transmit the load on the pulley to its hook or shackle. **c.** a rope sling, as for handling cargo. **d.** a ring or grommet of rope. **—*v.t.*** **3.** to sharpen on or as on a strop. [ME, OE; c. D, LG *strop;* prob. < L *stropp(us)* strap]

stro·phan·thin (strō fan′thin), *n.* *Pharm.* a very poisonous, bitter glycoside or mixture of glycosides obtained from the dried, ripe seeds of a strophanthus, esp. *Strophanthus Kombe,* used as a cardiac stimulant. [STROPHANTH(US) + -IN[2]]

stro·phan·thus (strō fan′thəs), *n., pl.* **-thus·es. 1.** any apocynaceous shrub or small tree of the genus *Strophanthus,* chiefly of tropical Africa. **2.** the dried, ripe seed of any of these plants, which yields the drug strophanthin. [< NL < Gk *strophos* twine + *ánthos* flower]

stro·phe (strō′fē), *n.* **1.** the part of an ancient Greek choral ode sung by the chorus when moving from right to left. **2.** the movement performed by the chorus during the singing of this part. **3.** the first of the three series of lines forming the divisions of each section of a Pindaric ode. **4.** (in modern poetry) any separate section or extended movement in a poem, distinguished from a stanza in that it does not follow a regularly repeated pattern. [< Gk *strophḗ* a twist, turning about, akin to *stréphein* to turn; see STREPTO-]
—Syn. 3. See **verse.**

stroph·ic (strof′ik, strō′fik), *adj.* **1.** Also, **stroph′i·cal.** consisting of, pertaining to, or characterized by a strophe or strophes. **2.** *Music.* (of a song) having the same music for each successive stanza. Cf. **through-composed.** [STROPH(E) + -IC] **—stroph′i·cal·ly,** *adv.*

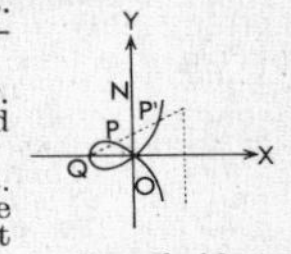

Stro·phi·us (strō′fē əs), *n.* *Class. Myth.* a king of Phocis who sheltered and reared Orestes.

stroph·oid (strof′oid, strō′foid), *n.* *Geom.* a plane curve generated by the loci of points *p* and *p′* on a straight line that intersects the *y*-axis at a point *n* and the minus *x*-axis at a fixed point *q,* such that *pn* = *np′* = *on,* as *on* changes, where *o* is the origin. Equation: $y^2 = \frac{x^2(x+a)}{(a-x)}$. [< Gk *strophos* twine + -OID, modeled on F *strophoïde*]

Strophoid

stroph·u·lus (strof′yə ləs), *n.* *Pathol.* a papular eruption of the skin in infants, occurring in several forms and usually harmless. Also called **gum rash, red gum, tooth rash.** [< NL < Gk *strophos* twine + L *-ulus* -ULE]

strop·per (strop′ər), *n.* **1.** one who strops. **2.** a mechanical instrument for honing double-edged blades for safety razors. [STROP + -ER[1]]

Stro·ther (struth′ər), *n.* a boy's given name.

stroud (stroud), *n.* a coarse woolen cloth, blanket, or garment formerly used by the British in bartering with the North American Indians. [named after *Stroud* in Gloucestershire, England, where woolens are made]

Strouds·burg (stroudz′bûrg), *n.* a town in E Pennsylvania. 6070 (1960).

strove (strōv), *v.* pt. of **strive.**

strow (strō), *v.,* **strowed, strown** or **strowed, strow·ing.** *Archaic.* strew. [ME *strow(en),* var. of *strewen* to STREW]

stroy (stroi), *v.t.* *Archaic.* to destroy. **—stroy′er,** *n.*

Stroz·zi (strôt′tsē), *n.* **Ber·nar·do** (ber när′dô), ("*Il Cappuccino*"), 1581–1644, Italian painter and engraver. Also, **Stroz·za** (strôt′tsä).

struck (struk), *v.* **1.** pt. and a pp. of **strike. —*adj.*** **2.** (of a factory, industry, etc.) closed or otherwise affected by a strike of workers.

struck·en (struk′ən), *v.* a pp. of **strike.**

struck′ joint′, *Masonry.* **1.** any of various mortar joints finished with a stroke of the trowel. **2.** a mortar joint sloping inward and downward from the face of the upper brick, stone, etc.

struck′ ju′ry, *Law.* a jury obtained by special agreement between the opposing attorneys, each taking turns in eliminating a member of the impaneled group until 12 members remain.

struck′ meas′ure, a measure, esp. of grain, even with the top of a receptacle.

struc·tur·al (struk′chər əl), *adj.* **1.** of or pertaining to structure; pertaining or essential to a structure. **2.** *Biol.* pertaining to organic structure; morphological. **3.** *Geol.* of or pertaining to geological structure, as of rock. **4.** *Chem.* pertaining to or showing the arrangement or mode of attachment of the atoms which constitute a molecule of a substance. Cf. **structural formula. 5.** resulting from or pertaining to political or economic structure. **6.** of, pertaining to, or based on the assumption that the elements of a field of study are naturally arranged in a systematic structure: *structural linguistics.* [STRUCTURE + -AL[1]] **—struc′tur·al·ly,** *adv.*

struc′tural for′mula, *Chem.* a chemical formula showing the diagrammatic linkage of the atoms in a molecule, as H–O–H. Cf. **empirical formula, molecular formula.**

struc′tural geol′ogy, the branch of geology dealing with the structure and distribution of rocks. Also called **geotectonic geology.**

struc·tur·al·ism (struk′chər ə liz′əm), *n.* **1.** See **structural psychology. 2.** any theory that embodies structural principles. [STRUCTURAL + -ISM] —**struc′tur·al·ist,** *n., adj.* —**struc′tur·al·is′tic,** *adj.*

struc′tural isom′erism, *Chem.* See under **isomerism** (def. 1).

struc′tural mill′, *Metalworking.* See **section mill.**

struc′tural psychol′ogy, psychology centering on the analysis of the structure or content of conscious mental states by introspective methods. Also called **structuralism.**

struc′tural shop′, *Shipbuilding.* See **plate shop.**

struc′tural steel′, 1. the variety of steel shapes rolled for use in construction. **2.** a steel having a composition suitable for such shapes.

struc·ture (struk′chər), *n., v.,* **-tured, -tur·ing.** —*n.* **1.** mode of building, construction, or organization; arrangement of parts, elements, or constituents: *a pyramidal structure.* **2.** something built or constructed, as a building, bridge, dam, etc. **3.** a complex system considered from the point of view of the whole rather than of any single part: *the structure of modern science.* **4.** anything composed of parts arranged together in some way; an organization. **5.** the relationship or organization of the component parts of a work of art or literature: *the structure of a poem.* **6.** *Biol.* mode of organization; construction and arrangement of tissues, parts, or organs. **7.** *Geol.* **a.** the attitude of a bed or stratum or of beds or strata of sedimentary rocks, as indicated by the dip and strike. **b.** the coarser composition of a rock, as contrasted with its texture. **8.** the manner by which atoms in a molecule are joined to each other, especially in organic chemistry where it is represented by a diagram or model of the molecular arrangement. **9.** *Sociol.* **a.** the system or complex of beliefs held by members of a social group. **b.** the system of relations between the constituent groups of a society. **c.** the relationship between or the interrelated arrangement of the social institutions of a society or culture, as of mores, marriage customs, family, etc. **d.** the pattern of relationships, as of status or friendship, existing among the members of a group or society. —*v.t.* **10.** to give a structure, organization, or arrangement to; construct a systematic framework for. [< L *structūr(a),* equiv. to *struc-* (var. s. of *struere* to put together) + *-t-* ptp. suffix + *ūra* -URE] —**struc′ture·less,** *adj.* —**struc′ture·less·ness,** *n.*
—**Syn. 1.** system, form, configuration. **2.** See **building.**

struc·tured (struk′chərd), *adj.* having and manifesting a clearly defined structure or organization. [STRUCTURE + -ED[3]]

stru·del (strōōd′əl; *Ger.* shtrōōd′əl), *n.* a pastry, usually consisting of a fruit, cheese, or other mixture, rolled in a blanket of paper-thin dough and baked. [< G: lit., eddy, whirlpool]

strug·gle (strug′əl), *v.,* **-gled, -gling,** *n.* —*v.i.* **1.** to contend with an adversary or opposing force. **2.** to contend resolutely with a task, problem, etc.; strive: *to struggle for existence.* **3.** to advance with violent effort: *to struggle through the snow.* —*v.t.* **4.** to bring, put, etc., by struggling: *He struggled the heavy box into a corner.* **5.** to make (one's way) with violent effort. —*n.* **6.** the act or process, or an instance of struggling. **7.** a war, fight, conflict, or contest of any kind. **8.** a task or goal requiring much effort to accomplish or achieve. [late ME *strugle,* equiv. to *strug-* (? b. STR(UT + T)UG) + *-le* -LE] —**strug′gler,** *n.* —**strug′gling·ly,** *adv.*
—**Syn. 1.** oppose, contest, fight, conflict. **7.** endeavor, exertion. **8.** encounter, skirmish. STRUGGLE, BRUSH, CLASH refer to a hostile meeting of opposing persons, parties, or forces. STRUGGLE implies vigorous bodily effort or violent exertion: *a hand-to-hand struggle.* A BRUSH is a brief, but smart, and often casual combat: *a brush between patrols.* CLASH implies a direct and sharp collision between opposing parties, efforts, interests, etc.: *a clash of opinions.*

strug′gle for exist′ence, the competition in nature among organisms of a population to maintain themselves in a given environment and to survive to reproduce others of their kind.

strum[1] (strum), *v.,* **strummed, strum·ming,** *n.* —*v.t.* **1.** to play on (a stringed musical instrument) by running the fingers lightly across the strings. **2.** to produce (notes, a melody, etc.) by such playing: *to strum a tune.* —*v.i.* **3.** to play on a stringed musical instrument by running the fingers lightly across the strings. —*n.* **4.** the act of strumming. **5.** the sound produced by strumming. [? b. STR(ING + TH)UMB] —**strum′mer,** *n.*

strum[2] (strum), *n.* a strainer, as at the inlet of a system of tubing. [?]

stru·ma (strōō′mə), *n., pl.* **-mae** (-mē). **1.** *Pathol.* **a.** scrofula. **b.** goiter. **2.** *Bot.* a cushionlike swelling on an organ, as that at one side of the base of the capsule in many mosses. [< L: scrofulous tumor]

Stru·ma (strōō′mä), *n.* a river in S Europe, flowing SE through SW Bulgaria and NE Greece into the Aegean. 225 mi. long.

stru·mec·to·my (strōō mek′tə mē), *n., pl.* **-mies.** *Surg.* **1.** excision of a scrofulous gland. **2.** excision of part or all of a goiter. [STRUM(A) + -ECTOMY]

stru·mose (strōō′mōs, strōō mōs′), *adj. Bot.* having a struma or strumae. [< L *strūmōs(us),* equiv. to *strūm(a)* STRUMA + *-ōsus* -OSE[1]]

stru·mous (strōō′məs), *adj.* affected with struma. [STRUM(A) + -OUS] —**stru′mous·ness,** *n.*

strum·pet (strum′pit), *n.* a prostitute; harlot. [ME < ?] —**strum′pet·like′,** *adj.*

strung (strung), *v.* pt. and pp. of **string.**

strunt (strunt, strōōnt), *Scot. and North Eng.* —*n.* **1.** the fleshy part or stump of a tail, esp. of a horse's tail. —*v.t.* **2.** to cut short, esp. to dock (the tail of a horse or sheep). [nasalized var. of STRUT[2]; cf. Norw *strunta* to walk stiffly]

strut[1] (strut), *v.,* **strut·ted, strut·ting,** *n.* —*v.i.* **1.** to walk with a vain, pompous bearing, as with head erect and chest thrown out, as if expecting to impress observers. —*v.t.* **2. strut one's stuff,** to dress, behave, perform, etc., one's best in order to impress others; show off. —*n.* **3.** the act of strutting. **4.** a strutting walk or gait. [ME *stroute,* OE *strūt(ian)* (to) stand out stiffly, struggle, deriv. of **strūt* (whence ME *strut* strife); akin to STRUT[2]] —**strut′ter,** *n.*
—**Syn. 1.** parade, flourish. STRUT and SWAGGER refer especially to carriage in walking. STRUT implies swelling pride or pompousness; to walk with a stiff, pompous, affected, self-conscious gait: *A turkey struts about the barnyard.* SWAGGER implies a domineering, sometimes jaunty, superiority or challenge, and a self-important manner: *to swagger down the street.*

strut[2] (strut), *n., v.,* **strut·ted, strut·ting.** —*n.* **1.** any of various structural members, as in trusses, primarily intended to resist longitudinal compression. See diags. under **king post, queen post.** —*v.t.* **2.** to brace or support by means of a strut or struts. [cf. LG *strutt* stiff]

Struth·ers (struth′ərz), *n.* a city in NE Ohio, near Youngstown. 15,631 (1960).

stru·thi·ous (strōō′thē əs), *adj.* resembling or related to the ostriches or other ratite birds. [< LL *struthi-* (shortened s. of *strūthiō* < Gk *strouthíō(n)* ostrich) + -OUS]

strut·ting (strut′ing), *adj.* walking or moving with a strut; walking pompously; pompous. [STRUT[1] + -ING[2]] —**strut′ting·ly,** *adv.*

Stru·ve (strōō′və), *n.* **1.** an irregularly shaped walled plain, having a dark floor, in the first quadrant of the face of the moon: about 55 miles long and 50 miles wide; Mare Struve. **2. O.,** Also called **Otto Struve.** an elliptical walled plain in the second quadrant of the moon: about 113 miles long and 96 miles wide.

strych·nic (strik′nik), *adj.* of, pertaining to, or obtained from strychnine. [< NL *Strychn(os)* (see STRYCHNINE) + -IC]

strych·nine (strik′nin, -nēn, -nīn), *n.* **1.** *Pharm.* a colorless, crystalline poison, $C_{21}H_{22}N_2O_2$, obtained chiefly by extraction from the seeds of nux vomica: used chiefly as an antidote for poisoning by depressant drugs because of its stimulating effect on the central nervous system, and to increase the appetite. **2.** a tree, *Strychnos Nux-vomica,* of India, having small, yellowish-white flowers in clusters nearly two inches wide, berrylike fruit, and seeds that yield strychnine. Also, **strych·ni·a** (strik′nē ə), **strych·ni·na** (strik′ni nə). [< F, equiv. to NL *Strychn(os)* < Gk: a kind of nightshade + F *-ine* -INE[2]]

strych·nin·ism (strik′ni niz′əm), *n. Pathol.* a condition induced by an overdose or by excessive use of strychnine. [STRYCHNINE + -ISM]

St. Si·mons (sī′mənz), a town in SE Georgia. 3199 (1960).

St. Swith′in's Day′ (swith′ənz), July 15, superstitiously regarded as a day which, should it rain or be fair, will be followed by 40 consecutive days of like weather.

St. Thomas, 1. an island in the Virgin Islands of the United States, in the E West Indies. 16,201 (1960); 32 sq. mi. **2.** former name of **Charlotte Amalie. 3.** Portuguese, **São Tomé.** an island in the republic of St. Thomas and Principe, in the Gulf of Guinea, off the W coast of Africa. 73,000; 318 sq. mi.

St. Thom′as and Prin′cipe, a republic in W Africa, in the Gulf of Guinea, comprising the islands of St. Thomas and Principe: a former overseas province of Portugal; independent since 1975. 80,000; 372 sq. mi.

St. Thom′as tree′, a shrub or small tree, *Bauhinia tomentosa,* of tropical Africa and Asia, having yellow flowers, with one of the petals chocolate-blotched.

Stu (stōō, styōō), *n.* a boy's given name, form of **Stewart** or **Stuart.** Also, **Stew.**

Stu·art (stōō′ərt, styōō′-), *n.* **1.** a member of the royal family which ruled in Scotland from 1371 to 1714 and in England from 1603 to 1714. **2. Charles Edward** (*"the Young Pretender"* or *"Bonnie Prince Charlie"*), 1720–80, grandson of James II. **3.** See **Darnley, Lord Henry. 4. Gilbert,** 1755–1828, U.S. painter. **5. James Ewell Brown** (*"Jeb"*), 1833–64, Confederate general in the Civil War. **6. James Francis Edward.** Also called **James III.** (*"the Old Pretender"*), 1688–1766, English prince. **7. Jesse Hilton,** born 1907, U.S. writer. **8. John, 3rd Earl of Bute,** 1713–92, British statesman: prime minister 1762–63. **9. Mary.** See **Mary Stuart. 10.** a town in SE Florida. 4791 (1960). **11.** a boy's given name. Also, **Stewart** (for defs. 3, 11).

stub[1] (stub), *n., v.,* **stubbed, stub·bing.** —*n.* **1.** a short projecting part. **2.** the end of a fallen tree, shrub, or plant left fixed in the ground; stump. **3.** a short remaining piece, as of a pencil, candle, or cigar. **4.** something unusually short, as a short, thick, or worn nail or a short-pointed, blunt pen. **5.** See **stub nail** (def. 2). **6.** (in a checkbook, receipt book, etc.) the inner end of each leaf, for keeping a record of the content of the part filled out and torn away. **7.** the returned portion of a ticket. **8.** *Bridge.* a part-score. —*v.t.* **9.** to strike accidentally against a projecting object: *I stubbed my toe against the step.* **10.** to clear of stubs, as land. **11.** to dig up by the roots; grub up (roots). [ME, OE *stubb;* c. MLG, MD *stubbe,* Icel *stubbi;* akin to Icel *stūfr* stump] —**stub′ber,** *n.*

stub[2] (stub), *adj.* stocky; squat. [special use of STUB[1]]

stub·bed (stub′id, stubd), *adj.* **1.** reduced to or resembling a stub; short and thick; stumpy. **2.** abounding in or rough with stubs. [STUB[1] + -ED[3]] —**stub′bed·ness,** *n.*

stub·ble (stub′əl), *n.* **1.** Usually, **stubbles.** the stumps of grain and other stalks left in the ground when the crop is cut. **2.** such stumps collectively. **3.** any short, rough growth, as of beard. [ME *stuble* < OF *(e)stuble* < VL **stupula,* L *stipula* STIPULE] —**stub′bled, stub′bly,** *adj.*

stub·born (stub′ərn), *adj.* **1.** unreasonably obstinate; obstinately perverse: *a stubborn child.* **2.** fixed or set in purpose or opinion; resolute: *a stubborn opponent of foreign aid.* **3.** obstinately maintained, as a course of action: *a stubborn resistance.* **4.** difficult to manage or suppress: *a stubborn horse; a stubborn pain.* **5.** hard, tough, or stiff, as stone or wood; difficult to shape or work. [ME *stiborn(e);* appar. < OE *stybb,* var. of *stubb* STUB + *-orn* adj. suffix (< ?)] —**stub′born·ly,** *adv.* —**stub′born·ness,** *n.*
—**Syn. 1.** contrary, intractable, refractory, unyielding, stiff, headstrong, obdurate. **2.** persevering. STUBBORN, DOGGED, OBSTINATE, PERSISTENT imply fixity of purpose or condition, and resistance to change. STUBBORN and OBSTINATE both imply resistance to advice, entreaty, remonstrance, or force; but STUBBORN implies more of innate quality and is the more frequently used when referring to inanimate things: *stubborn disposition; stubborn difficulties.* DOGGED implies pertinacity and grimness in doing something, esp. in the face of discouragements: *dogged determination.* PERSISTENT implies having staying or lasting qualities, resoluteness, and perseverance: *persistent questioning.* —**Ant. 1.** tractable. **2.** irresolute.

Stubbs (stubz), *n.* **William,** 1825–1901, English historian and bishop.

stub·by (stub′ē), *adj.,* **-bi·er, -bi·est. 1.** of the nature of or resembling a stub. **2.** short and thick or broad; thick-set or squat: *stubby fingers.* **3.** consisting of or abounding in stubs. **4.** bristly, as the hair or beard. [STUB[1] + -Y[1]] —**stub′bi·ness,** *n.*

stub′ mor′tise, *Carpentry.* a mortise extending only partly through a piece of wood.

stub′ nail′, 1. a short, thick nail. **2.** Also called **stub.** an old or worn horseshoe nail.

stub′ ten′on, *Carpentry.* a tenon fitting into a stub mortise.

stub′ track′. See **spur track.**

stuc·co (stuk′ō), *n., pl.* **-coes, -cos,** *v.,* **-coed, -co·ing.** —*n.* **1.** an exterior finish for masonry or frame walls, usually composed of cement, sand, and hydrated lime mixed with water and laid on wet. **2.** any of various fine plasters for decorative work, moldings, etc. **3.** any of various finishes made with cement, plaster, or mortar, as albarium. **4.** a wall, facing, molding, or other work made of such materials. —*v.t.* **5.** to cover or ornament with stucco. [< It < Gmc; cf. OHG *stucki* piece, crust, G *Stück,* OE *stycce*]

stuc·co·work (stuk′ō wûrk′), *n.* work made of stucco. [STUCCO + WORK] —**stuc′co·work′er,** *n.*

stuck (stuk), *v.* **1.** a pt. and pp. of **stick**[2]. **2. stuck on.** *Slang.* to be infatuated with (a person, place, or thing): *He met her only once and is already stuck on her.*

stuck-up (stuk′up′), *adj. Informal.* snobbishly conceited. —**stuck′-up′ness,** *n.*

stud[1] (stud), *n., v.,* **stud·ded, stud·ding.** —*n.* **1.** a boss, knob, nailhead, or other protuberance projecting from a surface or part, esp. as an ornament. **2.** any of various buttonlike, usually ornamental objects, mounted on a shank that is passed through an article of clothing to fasten it: *a collar stud.* **3.** any of a number of slender, upright members of wood, steel, etc., forming the frame of a wall or partition and covered with plasterwork, siding, etc. **4.** any of various projecting pins, lugs, or the like, on machines or other implements. **5.** *Horol.* the piece to which the fixed end of a hairspring is attached. —*v.t.* **7.** to set with or as with studs, bosses, or the like. **8.** to scatter over with things set at intervals: *The leather-covered door was studded with brass nails.* **9.** (of things) to be scattered over the surface of: *Stars stud the sky.* **10.** to set or scatter (objects) at intervals over a surface: *to stud raisins over a cake.* **11.** to furnish with or support by studs. [ME *stude,* OE *stud(u)* post; c. MHG *stud;* Icel *stoth* post]

stud[2] (stud), *n.* **1.** a studhorse or stallion. **2.** an establishment, as a farm, in which horses are kept for breeding. **3.** a number of horses, usually for racing or hunting, bred or kept by one owner. **4.** a male animal, as a bull, ram, etc., kept for breeding. **5.** a herd of animals kept for breeding. **6.** *Slang.* a carefree or independent young man. **7.** *Poker.* See **stud poker. 8. at** or **in stud,** (of a male animal) offered for the purpose of breeding. —*adj.* **9.** of, associated with, or pertaining to a studhorse or studhorses. **10.** retained for breeding purposes. [ME, OE *stōd;* c. Icel *stōth;* akin to STAND]

stud′ and mud′. See **wattle and daub.**

stud′ bolt′, a headless bolt threaded at each end.

stud·book (stud′bŏŏk′), *n.* a genealogical register of a stud; a book giving the pedigree of horses. [STUD[2] + BOOK]

stud·die (stud′ē, stŏŏd′ē), *n. Scot.* stithy. Also, **study.**

stud·ding (stud′ing), *n.* **1.** a number of studs, as in a wall or partition. **2.** timbers or manufactured objects for use as studs. [STUD[1] + -ING[1]]

stud·ding·sail (stud′ing sāl′; *Naut.* stun′səl), *n. Naut.* a light sail, sometimes set outboard of either of the leeches of a square sail and extended by booms. Also, **stunsail, stuns′l.** [*studding* (< ?) + SAIL]

stu·dent (stōōd′ənt, styōōd′-), *n.* **1.** a person formally engaged in learning, esp. one enrolled in a school or college; pupil: *a student at Yale.* **2.** any person who studies, investigates, or examines thoughtfully: *a student of human nature.* [late ME < L *student-* (s. of *studēns,* prp.), equiv. to *stud-* (root of *studēre* to take pains) + *-ent-* -ENT; r. *studiant* < MF] —**stu′dent·less,** *adj.* —**stu′dent·like′,** *adj.* —**stu′dent·ship′,** *n.*
—**Syn. 1, 2.** See **pupil**[1].

stu′dent coun′cil, a representative body composed chiefly of students chosen by their classmates to organize social and extracurricular activities and to participate in the government of a school or college.

stu′dent lamp′, an adjustable table lamp by which to read, write, or study.

Stu′dent Nonvi′olent Coor′dinating Commit′tee. See **SNCC.**

student's t test, *Statistics.* a test for determining whether or not an observed sample mean differs significantly from a hypothetical normal population mean.

stu′dent teach′er, a student who is studying to be a teacher and who, as part of his training, observes classroom instruction or does closely supervised teaching in an elementary or secondary school. Also called **intern, practice teacher, pupil teacher.** —**stu′dent teach′ing.**

stud′ fee′, the charge for the service of a male animal, as a horse, in breeding.

stud·fish (stud′fish′), *n., pl.* (*esp. collectively*) **-fish,** (*esp. referring to two or more kinds or species*) **-fish·es.** either of two bluish killifishes marked with orange spots, *Fundulus catenatus* **(northern studfish),** of the Tennessee and Cumberland rivers and Ozark Mountains region, or *Fundulus stellifer* **(southern studfish),** of the Alabama River. [STUD[1] + FISH]

stud·horse (stud′hôrs′), *n.* a stallion kept for breeding. [OE *stōdhors.* See STUD[2], HORSE]

stud·ied (stud′ēd), *adj.* **1.** marked by or suggestive of conscious effort; not spontaneous or natural; affected: *studied simplicity.* **2.** carefully considered: *a studied approval.* **3.** *Archaic.* learned. [STUDY[1] + -ED[2]] —**stud′ied·ly,** *adv.* —**stud′ied·ness,** *n.*
—**Syn. 1.** deliberate, considered. See **elaborate.**

stu·di·o (stōō′dē ō′, styōō′-), *n., pl.* **-di·os. 1.** the workroom or atelier of an artist, as a painter or sculptor. **2.** a room or place in which some form of art is pursued:

a music studio. **3.** a room or set of rooms specially equipped for broadcasting radio or television programs, making phonograph records, etc. **4.** all the buildings and adjacent land required or used by a company engaged in the production of motion pictures. **5.** See **studio apartment.** [< It: lit., STUDY[1]]

stu′dio apart′ment, **1.** an apartment consisting of one main room, a kitchen or kitchenette, and a bathroom. **2.** (formerly) a one-room apartment having a high ceiling and large windows.

stu′dio couch′, an upholstered couch, usually without a back, convertible into a double bed by sliding a bed frame out from beneath it and covering it with the mattress which forms the upper thickness of the upholstery.

stu·di·ous (sto͞o′dē əs, styo͞o′-), *adj.* **1.** disposed or given to study diligently: *a studious boy.* **2.** concerned with, characterized by, or pertaining to study: *studious tastes.* **3.** zealous, assiduous, or painstaking: *studious care.* **4.** carefully planned or maintained; studied: *a studious program to maintain peace.* **5.** *Chiefly Literary.* devoted to or favorable for study. [< L *studiōs(us),* equiv. to *studi(um)* (see STUDY[1]) + *-ōsus* -OUS] —**stu′di·ous·ly,** *adv.* —**stu′di·ous·ness,** *n.*

stud′ pok′er, *Cards.* **1.** a variety of poker in which each player is dealt one card face down in the first round and one card face up in each of the next four rounds, each of the last four rounds being followed by a betting interval. Cf. **seven-card stud. 2.** any similar variety of poker, as seven-card stud. [STUD[2] + POKER]

Studs Lon·i·gan (studz′ lon′ə gən), a trilogy of novels (1932–35) by James T. Farrell, consisting of *Young Lonigan, The Young Manhood of Studs Lonigan,* and *Judgment Day.*

stud·work (stud′wûrk′), *n.* **1.** the act or process of building with studding. **2.** structural work containing studding. [STUD[1] + WORK]

stud·y[1] (stud′ē), *n., pl.* **stud·ies,** *v.,* **stud·ied, stud·y·ing.** —*n.* **1.** application of the mind to the acquisition of knowledge, as by reading, investigation, or reflection: *long hours of study.* **2.** the cultivation of a particular branch of learning, science, or art: *the study of law.* **3.** Often, **studies.** a personal effort to gain knowledge: *to pursue one's studies.* **4.** something studied or to be studied: *Balzac's study was human nature.* **5.** research or a detailed examination and analysis of a subject, phenomenon, etc.: *He made a study of the transistor market for his firm.* **6.** a written account of such research, examination, or analysis: *He published a study of Milton's poetry.* **7.** a well-defined, organized branch of learning or knowledge. **8.** zealous endeavor or assiduous effort. **9.** the object of such endeavor or effort. **10.** deep thought, reverie, or a state of abstraction: *He was lost in study and did not hear us come in.* **11.** a room, in a house or other building, set apart for private study, reading, writing, or the like. **12.** Also called **étude.** *Music.* a composition that combines exercise in technique with a greater or lesser amount of artistic value. **13.** *Literature.* **a.** a literary composition executed for exercise or as an experiment in a particular method of treatment. **b.** such a composition dealing in detail with a particular subject, as a single main character. **14.** *Art.* something produced as an educational exercise, as a memorandum or record of observations or effects, or as a guide for a finished production: *He made a quick sketch of her hands as a study for the full portrait in oils.* **15.** a person, as an actor, considered in terms of his quickness or slowness in memorizing lines: *a quick study.* —*v.i.* **16.** to apply oneself to the acquisition of knowledge, as by reading, investigation, practice, etc. **17.** to apply oneself; endeavor. **18.** to think deeply, reflect, or consider. —*v.t.* **19.** to apply oneself to acquiring a knowledge of (a subject). **20.** to examine or investigate carefully and in detail: *to study the political situation.* **21.** to observe attentively; scrutinize: *to study a person's face.* **22.** to read carefully or intently: *to study a book.* **23.** to endeavor to learn or memorize, as a part in a play. **24.** to consider, as something to be achieved or devised. **25.** to think out, as the result of careful consideration or devising. [ME *studie* < OF *(e)studie* < L *studi(um),* equiv. to *stud-* (root of *studēre* to be busy with) + *-ium* -Y[3]] —**stud′i·a·ble,** *adj.* —**stud′i·er,** *n.*

—**Syn. 1.** inquiry, research, reading, thought, consideration. **7.** subject, field, area. **11.** library, den. **21.** STUDY, CONSIDER, REFLECT, WEIGH imply fixing the mind upon something, generally doing so with a view to some decision or action. STUDY implies an attempt to obtain a grasp of something by methodical or exhaustive thought: *to study a problem.* To CONSIDER is to fix the thought upon something and give it close attention before making a decision concerning it, or beginning an action connected with it: *consider ways and means.* REFLECT implies looking back quietly over past experience and giving it consideration: *reflect on similar cases in the past.* WEIGH implies a deliberate and judicial estimate, as by a balance: *weigh a decision.*

stud·y[2] (stud′ē, stŏŏd′ē), *n., pl.* **stud·ies.** *Scot.* stithy.

stud′y group′, an informal gathering of people who convene regularly to exchange ideas and information on a specific subject.

stud′y hall′, **1.** (in some schools) a room used solely or chiefly for studying. **2.** a period of time in a school day, set aside for study and doing homework, usually under the supervision of a teacher and in a room designated for this purpose.

stuff (stuf), *n.* **1.** the material of which anything is made: *a hard, crystalline stuff.* **2.** material to be worked upon or to be used in making something: *wood, steel, and other stuff for building.* **3.** material of some unspecified kind: *a cushion filled with some soft stuff.* **4.** *Chiefly Brit.* woven material or fabric. **5.** property, as personal belongings or equipment; things. **6.** something to be swallowed, as food, drink, or medicine. **7.** inward character, qualities, or capabilities: *to have good stuff in one.* **8.** *Informal.* action or talk of a particular kind: *kid stuff; Cut out the rough stuff.* **9.** worthless things or matter: *to clean the stuff out of a closet.* **10.** worthless or foolish ideas, talk, or writing: *a lot of stuff and nonsense.* **11.** *Sports Slang.* **a.** *Baseball.* the assortment of pitches that a pitcher uses in a game together with the ability to deliver them in the proper manner at the right speed to the desired spot: *He saved his best stuff for the tougher hitters in the line-up.* **b.** spin or speed imparted to a ball, as by a baseball pitcher, bowler, or tennis player: *a pitch with plenty of stuff.* **12.** *Informal.* journalistic, literary, artistic, dramatic, musical, or other compositions, or performances: *Bach composed some splendid stuff.* **13.** *Informal.* one's trade, skill, field, facts, etc.: *He knows his stuff.* **14.** *Papermaking.* refined and beaten wet pulp ready for spreading on the wire. —*v.t.* **15.** to fill (a receptacle), esp. by packing the contents closely together; cram full. **16.** to fill (an aperture, cavity, etc.) by forcing something into it. **17.** to fill or line with some kind of material as a padding or packing. **18.** to fill or cram (oneself, one's stomach, etc.) with food. **19.** to fill (poultry, meat, peppers, cabbage leaves, etc.) with seasoned bread crumbs or other savory matter. **20.** to fill the preserved skin of (a dead animal) with material, retaining its natural form and appearance for display. **21.** *U.S.* to put fraudulent votes into (a ballot box). **22.** to thrust or cram (something) into a receptacle, cavity, or the like. **23.** to pack tightly in a confined place; crowd together. **24.** to crowd (a vehicle, room, etc.) with persons. **25.** to clutter or fill (the mind) with facts, details, etc. **26.** (in leather manufacturing) to treat (a skin, hide, etc.) with a composition of tallow and other ingredients. **27.** to stop up or plug; block or choke (usually fol. by *up*). —*v.i.* **28.** to cram oneself with food; eat gluttonously; gorge. [ME < OF *(e)stoffe,* equiv. to *estoffe(r)* (to) stock, equip < MHG *stopfen* to stop up, fill, stuff; see STOP]

—**Syn. 1, 2, 3.** See **matter. 9.** waste, rubbish, trash. **10.** nonsense, twaddle, balderdash. **15.** crowd, press, stow. **27.** obstruct.

stuff-chest (stuf′chest′), *n.* *Papermaking.* the vat where pulp is stored and agitated before spreading on the wire.

stuffed′ der′ma, kishke.

stuffed′ shirt′, a pompous, self-satisfied, and inflexible person.

stuff·ing (stuf′ing), *n.* **1.** the act of one who or that which stuffs. **2.** that with which anything is or may be stuffed. **3.** seasoned bread crumbs or other filling used to stuff a chicken, turkey, etc., before cooking. **4.** *Informal.* internal parts; insides: *to beat the stuffing out of an opponent.* [STUFF + -ING[1]]

stuff′ing box′, *Mach.* a device for preventing leakage of gases or liquids along a reciprocating rod or rotating shaft at the point at which it leaves a cylinder, tank, ship hull, etc., consisting of a cylindrical box containing packing compressed around the rod or shaft.

stuff′ing nut′, a nut on a stuffing box that serves to condense the packing and so to tighten the seal. Also called **packing nut.**

stuff·y (stuf′ē), *adj.,* **stuff·i·er, stuff·i·est. 1.** close; poorly ventilated: *a stuffy room.* **2.** oppressive from lack of freshness: *stuffy air; a stuffy odor.* **3.** lacking in interest, as writing or discourse. **4.** affected with a sensation of obstruction in the respiratory passages: *a stuffy nose.* **5.** dull or tedious. **6.** self-important; pompous. **7.** rigid or old-fashioned in attitudes, esp. in matters of personal behavior. **8.** *Chiefly Brit.* old-fashioned; conservative. **9.** *Informal.* ill-tempered; sulky. [STUFF + -Y[1]] —**stuff′i·ly,** *adv.* —**stuff′i·ness,** *n.*

stui·ver (stī′vər), *n.* stiver.

Stu·ka (sto͞o′kə; *Ger.* shto͞o′kä), *n.* a German two-seated dive bomber with a single in-line engine, used by the Luftwaffe in World War II. [< G *Stu(rz)ka(mpfflugzeug)* dive bomber, equiv. to *Sturz* dive + *Kampf-Flugzeug* battle-plane]

stull (stul), *n.* *Mining.* **1.** a timber prop. **2.** a timber wedged in place between two walls of a stope as part of a protective covering or platform. [cf. G *Stollen* prop]

St. Ulmo's fire (ul′mōz). See **St. Elmo's fire.** Also called **St. Ulmo's light.**

stul·ti·fy (stul′tə fī′), *v.t.,* **-fied, -fy·ing. 1.** to make, or cause to appear, foolish or ridiculous. **2.** to render absurdly or wholly futile or ineffectual, esp. by degrading or frustrating means: *Menial work can stultify the mind.* **3.** *Law.* to allege or prove (oneself or another) to be of unsound mind. [< LL *stultificāre*), equiv. to *stult(us)* stupid + -I- + *-ficāre* -FY] —**stul′ti·fi·ca′tion,** *n.* —**stul′ti·fi′er,** *n.*

Stul·to·rum fe·ri·ae (stŏŏl tō′rŏŏm fā′ri ī′; *Eng.* stul tôr′əm fā′rē ā′), *Latin.* See **Feast of Fools.**

stum (stum), *n., v.,* **stummed, stumming.** —*n.* **1.** unfermented or partly fermented grape juice. **2.** wine in which increased fermentation has taken place because of the addition of stum. —*v.t.* **3.** to increase the fermentation of (wine) by adding stum. [< D *stom* dumb, dull; cf. F *vin muet,* G *stummer Wein,* in the same sense]

stum·ble (stum′bəl), *v.,* **-bled, -bling,** *n.* —*v.i.* **1.** to strike the foot against something, as in walking or running, so as to stagger or fall; trip. **2.** to walk or go unsteadily: *to stumble down a dark passage.* **3.** to make a slip, mistake, or blunder, esp. a sinful one: *to stumble over a question; to stumble and fall from grace.* **4.** to proceed in a hesitating or blundering manner, as in action or speech (often fol. by *along.*) **5.** to discover, arrive, or meet with accidentally or unexpectedly (usually fol. by *on, upon, across,* etc.): *They stumbled on a little village.* **6.** to falter or hesitate, as at an obstacle to progress or belief. —*v.t.* **7.** to cause to stumble; trip. **8.** to give pause to; puzzle or perplex. —*n.* **9.** the act of stumbling. **10.** a moral lapse or error. **11.** a slip or blunder. [ME; c. Norw *stumla* to grope and stumble in the dark; akin to STAMMER] —**stum′bler,** *n.* —**stum′bling·ly,** *adv.*

stum·ble·bum (stum′bəl bum′), *n.* *Slang.* **1.** a clumsy, second-rate prizefighter. **2.** a clumsy, incompetent person. [STUMBLE + BUM]

stum′bling block′, an obstacle or hindrance to progress, belief, or understanding.

stu·mer (sto͞o′mər, styo͞o′-), *n.* *Brit. Slang.* **1.** anything bogus or fraudulent. **2.** a horse that fails to win a race. **3.** a counterfeit coin or bill. **4.** See **rubber check.** [?]

stump (stump), *n.* **1.** the lower end of a tree or plant left after the main part falls or is cut off; a standing tree trunk from which the upper part and branches have been removed. **2.** the part of a limb of the body remaining after the rest has been cut off. **3.** a part of a broken or decayed tooth left in the gum. **4.** a short remnant, as of a candle; stub. **5.** any basal part remaining after the main or more important part has been removed. **6.** an artificial leg. **7.** Usually, **stumps.** *Informal.* legs: *Stir your stumps and get going out of here.* **8.** a short, stocky person. **9.** a heavy step or gait, as of a wooden-legged or lame person. **10.** the figurative place of political speechmaking: *to go on the stump.* **11.** *Furniture.* a support for the front end of the arm of a chair, sofa, etc. Cf. **post**[1] (def. 2). **12.** a short, thick roll of paper, soft leather, or some similar material, usually having a blunt point, for rubbing pencil, charcoal, or crayon drawing in order to achieve subtle gradations of tone in representing light and shade. **13.** *Cricket.* each of the three upright sticks which, with the two bails laid on top of them, form a wicket. **14. up a stump,** *Informal.* at a loss; embarrassed; perplexed: *Sociologists are up a stump over the sharp rise in juvenile delinquency and crime.* —*v.t.* **15.** to reduce to a stump; truncate; lop. **16.** to clear of stumps, as land. **17.** *Chiefly Southern U.S.* to stub, as one's toe. **18.** to nonplus, embarrass, or render completely at a loss: *This riddle stumps me.* **19.** *U.S. Informal.* to challenge or dare to do something. **20.** *Informal.* to make political campaign speeches to or in: *stump a state.* **21.** *Cricket.* (of the wicketkeeper) to put (a batsman) out by knocking down a stump or by dislodging a bail with the ball held in the hand at a moment when the batsman is off his ground. **22.** to tone or modify (a crayon drawing, pencil rendering, etc.) by means of a stump. —*v.i.* **23.** to walk heavily or clumsily, as if with a wooden leg: *Cap'n Eli stumped across the deck.* **24.** *Informal.* to make political campaign speeches; electioneer. [ME *stumpe;* c. MD *stomp(e),* G *Stumpf;* akin to STAMP] —**stump′less,** *adj.* —**stump′like′,** *adj.*

stump·age (stum′pij), *n.* **1.** standing timber with reference to its value. **2.** the right to cut such timber on the land of another. **3.** the value of such timber. [STUMP + -AGE]

stump′ bed′, a bed without posts.

stump·er (stum′pər), *n.* **1.** one who or that which stumps. **2.** an extremely difficult question, task, or problem. **3.** *Informal.* one who makes stump speeches. [STUMP + -ER[1]]

stump′ foot′, *Furniture.* a foot continuing the surfaces of a square leg in an outward flare.

stump′-jump plow′ (stump′jump′), a plow for use in newly cleared land, designed to permit the bottom to ride over roots and stumps.

stump·knock·er (stump′nok′ər), *n.* See **spotted sunfish.** [STUMP + KNOCKER]

stump′ speech′, a political campaign speech, esp. one made on a campaign tour.

stump·suck·er (stump′suk′ər), *n.* a horse that practices cribbing; windsucker; cribber. [STUMP + SUCKER]

stump′ topgal′lant mast′, *Naut.* an abbreviated topgallant mast ending abruptly above the upper topgallant yard on a vessel carrying no royals or other upper sails.

stump·y (stum′pē), *adj.,* **stump·i·er, stump·i·est. 1.** of the nature of or resembling a stump. **2.** short and thick; stubby; stocky. **3.** abounding in stumps: *a stumpy field.* [STUMP + -Y[1]] —**stump′i·ly,** *adv.* —**stump′i·ness,** *n.*

stun (stun), *v.,* **stunned, stun·ning,** *n.* —*v.t.* **1.** to deprive of consciousness or strength by or as if by a blow, fall, etc.: *The blow to his jaw stunned him for a moment.* **2.** to astonish; astound; amaze: *His wit stunned the audience.* **3.** to daze or bewilder by distracting noise. **4.** to injure the surface of (building stone) by scoring or bruising. —*n.* **5.** the act of stunning. **6.** condition of being stunned. [ME *ston(i)e(n), stune(n),* OE *stunian* to crash, resound (OF *estoner* to shake, make resound < ME); see ASTONISH]

—**Syn. 1.** dizzy. See **shock**[1]. **2.** overcome, overwhelm, confound. **3.** stupefy.

stung (stung), *v.* a pt. and pp. of **sting.**

stunk (stungk), *v.* a pt. and pp. of **stink.**

stun·ner (stun′ər), *n.* **1.** one who or that which stuns. **2.** *Chiefly Brit. Informal.* a person or thing of striking excellence, beauty, attractiveness, etc. [STUN + -ER[1]]

stun·ning (stun′ing), *adj.* **1.** causing, capable of causing, or liable to cause astonishment, bewilderment, or a loss of consciousness or strength: *a stunning blow.* **2.** of striking beauty or excellence: *What a stunning dress you're wearing!* [STUN + -ING[2]] —**stun′ning·ly,** *adv.*

stun·sail (stun′səl), *n.* studdingsail. Also, **stun′s'l.** [syncopated var. of STUDDINGSAIL]

stunt[1] (stunt), *v.t.* **1.** to stop or slow down the growth or development of; dwarf; hinder the increase or progress of: *A harsh climate stunted the trees. Brutal treatment in childhood stunted his personality.* —*n.* **2.** a stop or hindrance in growth or development. **3.** arrested development. **4.** a creature hindered from attaining its proper growth. **5.** *Plant Pathol.* a disease of plants, characterized by a dwarfing or stunting of the plant. [dial. adj. *stunt* dwarfed, stubborn (in ME, OE: stupid); c. MHG *stunz,* Icel *stuttr* short; akin to STINT[1]] —**stunt′ing·ly,** *adv.* —**stunt′y,** *adj.*

stunt[2] (stunt), *n.* **1.** a performance displaying a person's skill or dexterity, as in athletics; feat: *an acrobatic stunt.* **2.** any remarkable feat performed chiefly to attract attention: *The kidnaping was said to be a publicity stunt.* —*v.i.* **3.** to do a stunt or stunts. —*v.t.* **4.** to use in doing stunts: *to stunt an airplane.* [?]

stunt′ man′, *Motion Pictures.* a substitute who replaces an actor in scenes requiring hazardous or acrobatic feats. Also, *referring to a woman,* **stunt′ girl′.**

stu·pa (sto͞o′pə), *n.* a monumental pile of earth or other material, either dome-shaped or pyramidal, in memory of Buddha or a Buddhist saint, and commemorating some event or marking a sacred spot. [< Skt *stūpa-* topknot, top of the head, dome]

stupe[1] (sto͞op, styo͞op), *n.* two or more layers of flannel or other cloth soaked in hot water and applied to the skin as a counterirritant. [< L *stūp(a),* var. of *stuppa* < Gk *stýppē* flax, hemp, tow]

stupe[2] (sto͞op), *n.* *Slang.* a stupid person. [by shortening]

stu·pe·fa·cient (sto͞o′pə fā′shənt, styo͞o′-), *adj.* **1.** stupefying; producing stupor. —*n.* **2.** a drug or agent that produces stupor. [< L *stupefacient-* (s. of *stupefaciēns*) benumbing, equiv. to *stupe-* senseless + *-facient-* -FACIENT]

stu·pe·fac·tion (sto͞o′pə fak′shən, styo͞o′-), *n.* **1.** the act of stupefying. **2.** the state of being stupefied; stupor; numbness of the faculties. **3.** overwhelming amazement. [< NL *stupefactiōn-* (s. of *stupefactiō*) senseless state, equiv. to *stupe-* senseless + *fac-* make + *-tiōn-* -TION]

stu·pe·fac·tive (stōō′pə fak′tiv, styōō′-), *adj.* serving to stupefy. [< ML *stupefactīv(us)* < L *stupe* senseless + *fac-* make + *-t-* ptp. suffix + *-īvus* -IVE]

stu·pe·fy (stōō′pə fī′, styōō′-), *v.t.*, **-fied, -fy·ing. 1.** to put into a state of little or no sensibility; benumb the faculties of; put into a stupor. **2.** to stun, as with a narcotic, a shock, strong emotion, etc. **3.** to overwhelm with amazement; astound; astonish. [< MF *stupefi(er)*, equiv. to *stupe-* (< L *stupe-* senseless) + *-fier* -FY] **—stu·pe·fied·ness** (stōō′pə fīd′nis, -fī′id-, styōō′-), *n.* **—stu′pe·fi′er,** *n.*

stu·pe·fy·ing·ly (stōō′pə fī′ing lē, styōō′-), *adv.* in a stupefying manner; to the point of stupefaction or numbness: *a stupefyingly dull play.* [STUPEFYING + -LY]

stu·pen·dous (stōō pen′dəs, styōō-), *adj.* **1.** causing amazement; astounding; marvelous: *stupendous news.* **2.** amazingly large or great; immense: *a stupendous mass of information.* [< L *stupendus*, ger. of *stupēre* to be astonished] **—stu·pen′dous·ly,** *adv.* **—stu·pen′dous·ness,** *n.*
—Syn. 1. extraordinary. **2.** colossal, vast, gigantic, prodigious.

stu·pid (stōō′pid, styōō′-), *adj.* **1.** lacking ordinary activity and keenness of mind; slow-thinking; dull. **2.** characterized by, indicative of, or proceeding from mental dullness; foolish; senseless: *a stupid act.* **3.** tediously dull or uninteresting, esp. due to lack of meaning or sense: *to read a stupid book; to go to a stupid party.* **4.** in a state of stupor; stupefied: *to be stupid from fatigue.* **—n. 5.** *Informal.* a stupid person. [< L *stupid(us)*, equiv. to *stup-* senseless + *-idus* -ID[4]] **—stu′pid·ly,** *adv.* **—stu′pid·ness,** *n.*
—Syn. 1. witless, dumb. See **foolish. 3.** vapid, prosaic, tedious, uninteresting, boring, tiresome, heavy, pointless, inane, asinine. See **dull. —Ant. 1.** bright, clever.

stu·pid·i·ty (stōō pid′i tē, styōō-), *n.*, *pl.* **-ties** for 2. **1.** the state, quality, or fact of being stupid. **2.** a stupid act, notion, speech, etc. [< L *stupiditāt-* (s. of *stupiditās*), equiv. to *stupid(us)* STUPID + *-itāt-* -ITY]

stu·por (stōō′pər, styōō′-), *n.* **1.** suspension or great diminution of sensibility, as in disease or as caused by narcotics, intoxicants, etc.: *He lay there in a drunken stupor.* **2.** a state of suspended or deadened sensibility. **3.** mental torpor, or apathy; stupefaction. [< L: astonishment, insensibility, *stup-* senseless + *-or* -OR[1]] **—stu′por·ous,** *adj.*

stur·dy[1] (stûr′dē), *adj.*, **-di·er, -di·est. 1.** strongly built; stalwart; robust: *sturdy young athletes.* **2.** strong, as in substance, construction, texture, etc.: *sturdy walls.* **3.** firm; courageous; indomitable: *the sturdy defenders of the Alamo.* **4.** of strong or hardy growth, as a plant. [ME *stourdi* < OF *(e)stourdi* dazed, stunned, violent, reckless (ptp. of *estourdir* < ?)] **—stur′di·ly,** *adv.* **—stur′di·ness,** *n.*
—Syn. 1. hardy, muscular, brawny, sinewy, stout, strong, powerful. **3.** resolute, vigorous, determined, unconquerable. **—Ant. 1.** weak.

stur·dy[2] (stûr′dē), *n.* *Vet. Pathol.* gid. [< OF *estourdi* gid; see STURDY[1]] **—stur′died,** *adj.*

Sturgeon, *Acipenser oxyrhynchus* (Length to 12 ft.)

stur·geon (stûr′jən), *n.*, *pl.* (*esp. collectively*) **-geon,** (*esp. referring to two or more kinds or species*) **-geons.** any of various large ganoid fishes of the family *Acipenseridae*, found in fresh and salt waters of the North Temperate Zone: valued for their flesh and as a source of caviar and isinglass. [ME < AF < OF *(e)sturgeon* < Gmc; cf. OE *styria*, Icel *styrja*, OHG *sturio* (G *Stör*)]

Stur′geon Bay′, a town in NE Wisconsin. 7353 (1960).

Stur·gis (stûr′jis), *n.* **1.** a town in SW Michigan. 8915 (1960). **2.** a town in W South Dakota. 4639 (1960).

Sturm·ab·tei·lung (shtŏŏrm′äp′tī′lŏŏng), *n.* a political militia of the Nazi party, organized about 1923 and notorious for its violence and terrorism up to 1934 when it was purged and reorganized as an instrument of physical training and political indoctrination of German men; Brown Shirts. [< G, equiv. to *Sturm* storm, troop of storm troopers + *Abteilung* division, department]

Sturm und Drang (shtŏŏrm′ ŏŏnt dräng′), a style or movement of German literature of the latter half of the 18th century: characterized chiefly by impetuosity of manner, exaltation of individual sensibility and intuitive perception, opposition to established forms of society and thought, and extreme nationalism. [< G: lit., storm and stress]

sturt (stûrt), *Scot.* **—n. 1.** violent quarreling; loud dispute. **—v.i. 2.** to argue; dispute. **—v.t. 3.** to disturb, molest, or trouble. [metathetic var. of STRUT[1]] **—sturt·y,** *adj.*

stut·ter (stut′ər), *v.t., v.i.* **1.** to speak (words and sentences) in such a way that the rhythm is interrupted by repetitions, blocks or spasms, or prolongations of sounds or syllables, sometimes accompanied by contortions of the face and body. **—n. 2.** distorted speech characterized principally by blocks or spasms interrupting the rhythm. [*stut* (< ME *stutt(en)* (to) stutter; akin to STOIT) + -ER[6]; cf. D *stotteren*, MLG *stotern*, in same sense] **—stut′ter·er,** *n.* **—stut′ter·ing·ly,** *adv.*
—Syn. 1. See **stammer.**

Stutt·gart (stut′gärt, stŏŏt′-; *for 1 also Ger.* shtŏŏt′-gärt), *n.* **1.** a city in and the capital of Baden-Württemberg, in W West Germany. 640,500 (1963). **2.** a town in central Arkansas. 9661 (1960).

Stutt′gart disease′, *Pathol.* See **canine leptospirosis.** Also, **Stutt′gart's disease′.**

Stuy·ve·sant (stī′vi sənt), *n.* **Peter,** 1592–1672, Dutch colonial administrator in the Americas: last governor of New Netherlands 1646–64.

St. Vincent, 1. a British colony, comprised of St. Vincent Island and the N Grenadines, in the S Windward Islands, in the SE West Indies. 80,005 (1960); 150 sq. mi. *Cap.:* Kingstown. **2. Cape,** the SW tip of Portugal: naval battle 1797.

St. Vi·tus's dance (vī′tə siz), *Pathol.* chorea (def. 2). Also, **St. Vitus dance.** [named after *St. Vitus* (3rd century), patron saint of those afflicted with chorea]

S twist, a direction of the twist in yarns, from top left to bottom right, resembling the long stroke of the letter S. Cf. **Z twist.**

sty[1] (stī), *n.*, *pl.* **sties,** *v.*, **stied, sty·ing. —n. 1.** a pen or enclosure for swine; pigpen. **2.** any filthy place or abode. **3.** a place of bestial debauchery. **—v.t. 4.** to keep or lodge in or as in a sty. **—v.i. 5.** to live in or as in a sty. [ME, OE *stig*; c. Icel *stī*, D *stijg*, G *Steige*]

sty[2] (stī), *n.*, *pl.* **sties.** *Ophthalm.* a circumscribed inflammatory swelling, like a small boil, on the edge of the eyelid. Also, **stye.** [by false division of ME *styanye* sty (*styan*, OE *stīgend* sty, lit., rising + *ye* EYE) taken to be *sty on eye*]

Styg·i·an (stij′ē ən), *adj.* **1.** of or pertaining to the river Styx or to Hades. **2.** dark or gloomy. **3.** infernal; hellish. **4.** (of an oath or vow) binding; irrevocable; inviolable. [< L *Stygi(us)* < Gk *Stýgios* (*Styg-*, s. of *Stýx* STYX + *-ios* adj. suffix) + -AN]

styl-[1], var. of **stylo-**[1] before a vowel: *stylar.*

styl-[2], var. of **stylo-**[2] before a vowel: *stylite.*

sty·lar (stī′lər), *adj.* having the shape of an ancient style; resembling a pen, pin, or peg. [STYL-[1] + -AR[2]]

style (stīl), *n.*, *v.* **styled, styl·ing. —n. 1.** a particular kind, sort, or type, as with reference to form, appearance, or character: *the baroque style; The style of the house was too austere for their liking.* **2.** a particular, distinctive, or characteristic mode of action or manner of acting: *They do these things in a grand style.* **3.** a mode of living, as with respect to expense or display. **4.** an elegant, fashionable, or luxurious mode of living: *to live in style.* **5.** a mode of fashion, as in dress, esp. good or approved fashion; elegance; smartness. **6.** the mode of expressing thought in writing or speaking by selecting and arranging words, considered with respect to clearness, effectiveness, euphony, or the like, that is characteristic of a group, period, person, personality, etc.: *to write in the style of Faulkner; a familiar style; a pompous, pedantic style.* **7.** those components or features of a literary composition that have to do with the form of expression rather than the content of the thought expressed: *His writing is all style and no substance.* **8.** manner or tone adopted in discourse or conversation: *He has a patronizing style of addressing others.* **9.** a particular, distinctive, or characteristic mode or form of construction or execution in any art or work: *His painting is beginning to show a personal style.* **10.** a descriptive or distinguishing appellation, esp. a legal, official, or recognized title: *a firm trading under the style of Smith, Jones, & Co.* **11.** Also, **stylus. a.** an instrument of metal, bone, or the like, used by the ancients for writing on waxed tablets, having one end pointed for incising the letters and the other end blunt for rubbing out writing and smoothing the tablet. **b.** something resembling or suggesting such an instrument. **c.** a pointed instrument for drawing, etching, or writing. **12.** the gnomon of a sundial. **13.** a method of reckoning time. Cf. **New Style, Old Style** (def. 2). **14.** *Bot.* a narrow, usually cylindrical and more or less filiform extension of the ovary, which, when present, bears the stigma at its apex. See diag. under **flower. 15.** *Zool.* a small, slender, pointed process or part. **16.** the rules or customs of typography, punctuation, spelling, capitalization, etc., used by a newspaper, magazine, publishing house, etc., or in a specific publication. **—v.t. 17.** to call by a given title or appellation; denominate; name; call: *The Pope is styled His or Your Holiness.* **18.** to design in accordance with a given or new style: *to style an evening dress.* **19.** to bring into conformity with a specific style or give a specific style to: *Please style this manuscript.* **—v.i. 20.** to do decorative work with a style or stylus. [ME < L *styl(us)*, sp. var. of *stilus* tool for writing, hence, written composition, style; see STYLUS] **—style′less,** *adj.* **—style′less·ness,** *n.* **—style′like′,** *adj.* **—styl′er,** *n.*
—Syn. 2. method, approach. **5.** chic. See **fashion. 9.** touch, characteristic, mark. **17.** designate, address.

style·book (stīl′bŏŏk′), *n.* **1.** a book containing rules of usage in typography, punctuation, etc., employed by printers, editors, and writers. **2.** a book featuring styles, fashions, or the rules of styles. [STYLE + BOOK]

style ga·lant (*Fr.* stēl GA läN′), the rococo musical style characteristic of the middle 18th century in Europe. [< F: gallant style]

style′ sheet′, a listing of rules of usage in style, employed by a publishing house or in a publishing project. Cf. **stylebook** (def. 1).

sty·let (stī′lit), *n.* **1.** a stiletto or dagger. **2.** any similar sharp-pointed instrument. **3.** *Med.* **a.** a probe. **b.** a wire run through the length of a catheter, cannula, or needle to make it rigid or to clear it. **4.** *Zool.* style (def. 15). [< F < MF *stilet* < It *stilett(o)* STILETTO; *-y-* < L *stylus.* See STYLE, STYLUS]

sty·li·form (stī′lə fôrm′), *adj.* having the shape of an ancient style; stylar. [earlier *stiliform* < NL *stiliform(is)* < L *stil(us)* STYLUS + -I- + *-formis* -FORM]

styl·ise (stī′līz), *v.t.*, **-ised, -is·ing.** *Chiefly Brit.* stylize. **—styl′i·sa′tion,** *n.* **—styl′is·er,** *n.*

styl·ish (stī′lish), *adj.* characterized by or conforming to style or the fashionable standard; fashionably elegant; smart or chic: *a very stylish gown.* [STYLE + -ISH[1]] **—styl′ish·ly,** *adv.* **—styl′ish·ness,** *n.*

styl·ist (stī′list), *n.* **1.** a writer or speaker who is skilled in or who cultivates a literary style. **2.** one who designs clothing, interior decorations, etc. **3.** one who cultivates or maintains any particular style. [STYLE + -IST]

sty·lis·tic (stī lis′tik), *adj.* of or pertaining to style. Also, **sty·lis′ti·cal.** [STYLE + -ISTIC] **—sty·lis′ti·cal·ly,** *adv.*

sty·lite (stī′līt), *n.* *Eccles. Hist.* one of a class of solitary ascetics who lived on the top of high pillars or columns. [< LGK *stylítē(s)*, equiv. to *stýl(os)* STYL-[2] + *-ītes* -ITE[1]] **—sty·lit·ic** (stī lit′ik), *adj.*

styl·ize (stī′līz), *v.t.*, **-ized, -iz·ing.** to design in or cause to conform to a particular style, as of representation or treatment in art; conventionalize. Also, *esp. Brit.*, **stylise.** [STYLE + -IZE] **—styl′i·za′tion,** *n.* **—styl′iz·er,** *n.*

stylo-[1], a learned borrowing from Latin used to represent **style** or **styloid** in the formation of compound words: *stylography.* Also, *esp. before a vowel,* **styl-.** [comb. form of L *stilus.* See STYLUS, -O-]

stylo-[2], a learned borrowing from Greek meaning "column," "pillar," "tube," used in the formation of compound words: *stylolite.* Also, *esp. before a vowel,* **styl-.** [< Gk, comb. form of *stŷlos* pillar]

sty·lo·bate (stī′lə bāt′), *n.* *Archit.* (in a classical temple) a course of masonry, part of the stereobate, forming the foundation for a colonnade, esp. the outermost colonnade. [< L *stylobatē(s)*, *stylobata* < Gk, equiv. to *stŷlo(s)* STYLO-[2] + *-batēs* (*ba-* (s. of *bainein* to step) + *-tēs* suffix denoting agent)]

sty·lo·graph (stī′lə graf′, -gräf′), *n.* a fountain pen in which the writing point is a fine, hollow tube instead of a nib. Also called **sty′lograph′ic pen′.** [STYLO-[1] + -GRAPH]

sty·lo·graph·ic (stī′lə graf′ik), *adj.* **1.** of or pertaining to a stylograph. **2.** of, pertaining to, or used in stylography. Also, **sty′lo·graph′i·cal.** [STYLO-[1] + GRAPHIC] **—sty′lo·graph′i·cal·ly,** *adv.*

sty·log·ra·phy (stī log′rə fē), *n.* the art of writing, tracing, drawing, etc., with a style. [STYLO-[1] + -GRAPHY]

sty·lo·hy·oid (stī′lō hī′oid), *Anat.* **—adj. 1.** Also, **sty·lo·hy·oi·de·an** (stī′lō hī oi′dē ən). of, pertaining to, or situated between the styloid process of the temporal bone and the hyoid bone. **—n. 2.** Also **stylohyoideus.** a small, slender, stylohyoid muscle, the action of which elevates the hyoid bone. [< NL *stylohyoid(eus).* See STYLO-[1], HYOID]

sty·lo·hy·oi·de·us (stī′lō hī oi′dē əs), *n.*, *pl.* **-de·i** (-dē ī′). *Anat.* stylohyoid (def 2). [< NL]

sty·loid (stī′loid), *adj.* *Anat.* **1.** resembling a style; slender and pointed. **2.** pertaining to several bony processes on the temporal bone, radius, ulna, etc. [< NL *styloid(es).* See STYL-[1], -OID]

sty′loid proc′ess, *Anat.* a long, spinelike process of a bone, esp. the projection from the base of the temporal bone. See diag. under **skull.**

sty·lo·lite (stī′lə līt′), *n.* *Geol.* an irregular columnar structure in certain limestones, the columns being approximately at right angles to the bedding planes. [STYLO-[2] + -LITE] **—sty·lo·lit·ic** (stī′lə lit′ik), *adj.*

Sty·lo·nich·i·a (stī′lə nik′ē ə), *n.* a genus of marine and fresh-water ciliates, having the cilia fused into stiff projections that are used for locomotion. [< NL < Gk *styl-* STYL-[2] + *ónych-* (s. of *ónyx*) nail, claw + -IA]

sty·lo·po·di·um (stī′lə pō′dē əm), *n.*, *pl.* **-di·a** (-dē ə). *Bot.* a glandular disk or expansion surmounting the ovary in umbelliferous plants and supporting the styles. [STYLO-[1] + -PODIUM]

sty·lus (stī′ləs), *n.*, *pl.* **-li** (-lī), **-lus·es. 1.** a pointed instrument for writing on wax or other suitable surfaces; style. **2.** a needle used for cutting grooves in making a recording on a phonograph. **3.** a needle for reproducing the sounds of a phonograph record. **4.** any of various pointed wedges used to punch holes in paper or other material, as in writing Braille. **5.** any of various pointed, pen-shaped instruments used in drawing, artwork, etc. **6.** any of various kinds of pens for tracing a line automatically, as on a recording seismograph, electrocardiograph, etc. [< L *stilus* stake, pointed writing instrument; sp. with *-y-* from fancied derivation < Gk *stŷlos* column]

sty·mie (stī′mē), *n.*, *v.*, **-mied, -mie·ing. —n. 1.** *Golf.* (on a putting green) an instance of a ball's lying on a direct line between the cup and the ball of an opponent about to putt. **2.** a situation or problem presenting such difficulties as to discourage or defeat any attempt to deal with or resolve it. **—v.t. 3.** to hinder, block, or thwart. Also, **stimy, stymy.** [?]

Stym·pha′li·an birds′ (stim fā′lē ən, -fāl′yən), *Class. Myth.* a flock of annoying or dangerous birds of Arcadia that were driven away or killed by Hercules as one of his labors. Also called **Stym·pha·li·des** (stim-fā′li dēz′).

Stym·pha·lus (stim fā′ləs), *n.* *Class. Myth.* **1.** a king of Arcadia who was treacherously murdered by his militarily inferior enemy, Pelops. **2.** a lake in Arcadia where the Stymphalian birds dwelt.

sty·my (stī′mē), *n.*, *pl.* **-mies,** *v.t.*, **-mied, -my·ing.** stymie.

styp·sis (stip′sis), *n.* the employment or application of styptics. [< LL < Gk *stýpsis*, equiv. to *stýp-* (s. of *stýphein* to contract; see STYPTIC) + *-sis* -SIS]

styp·tic (stip′tik), *adj.* Also, **styp′ti·cal. 1.** contracting organic tissue; astringent; binding. **2.** checking hemorrhage or bleeding, as a drug; hemostatic. **—n. 3.** a styptic agent or substance. [late ME < LL *stýptic-(us)* < Gk *stypikós* contractile, equiv. to *stýp-* (see STYPSIS) + *-tikos* -TIC] **—styp·tic·i·ty** (stip tis′i tē), **styp′ti·cal·ness,** *n.*

styp′tic pen′cil, a pencil-shaped stick of a paste containing alum or a similar styptic agent, used to stanch the bleeding of minor cuts and abrasions, as those occurring in shaving.

Styr (stēr), *n.* a river in the W Soviet Union in Europe, in NW Ukraine, flowing N to the Pripet River. 300 mi. long.

sty·ra·ca·ceous (stī′rə kā′shəs), *adj.* belonging to the *Styracaceae*, or storax family of shrubs and trees. [*styrac-* (s. of STYRAX) + -ACEOUS]

sty′ra·lyl ac′etate (stī′rə lil, stēr′ə-), *Chem.* See **methylphenylcarbinyl acetate.** [STYR(AX) + -AL[3] + -YL]

sty·rax (stī′raks), *n.* any plant of the genus *Styrax*, comprising the storaxes. [var. of STORAX]

sty·rene (stī′rēn, stēr′ēn), *n.* *Chem.* a colorless, water-insoluble liquid, $C_6H_5CH{=}CH_2$, having a penetrating aromatic odor, usually prepared from ethylene and benzene or ethylbenzene, that polymerizes to a clear transparent material (**polystyrene**) and copolymerizes with other materials to form synthetic rubbers. Also called **cinnamene, phenylethylene, vinylbenzene.** [*styr-* (shortened s. of STYRAX) + -ENE]

sty′rene res′in, *Chem.* a transparent thermoplastic resin formed by polymerizing styrene.

Styr·i·a (stēr′ē ə), *n.* a province in SE Austria: formerly a duchy. 1,311,072 (1961); 6327 sq. mi. *Cap.:* Graz. German, **Steiermark.**

Sty·ron (stī′rən), *n.* **William,** born 1925, U.S. author.

stythe (stīth, stīth), *n.* *Brit. Mining.* chokedamp. [? OE *stithe* name of an unidentified plant, perh. an ill-smelling one]

Styx (stiks), *n. Class. Myth.* a river in the lower world, over which the souls of the dead were ferried by Charon, and by which the gods swore their most solemn oaths.

su-, var. of **sub-** before *sp: suspect.*

su·a·ble (so͞o′ə bəl), *adj.* liable to be sued; capable of being sued. [SUE + -ABLE] **—su′a·bil′i·ty,** *n.* **—su′a·bly,** *adv.*

Sua·kin (swä′kēn), *n.* a seaport in NE Sudan, on the Red Sea. 4228 (1956).

Suá·rez (swär′ez; *Sp.* swä′reth), *n.* **Fran·cis·co** (fran sis′kō; *Sp.* frän thēs′kô), 1548–1617, Spanish theologian and philosopher.

sua·sion (swā′zhən), *n.* **1.** the act of advising, urging, or attempting to persuade; persuasion. **2.** an instance of this; a persuasive effort. [< L *suāsiōn-* (s. of *suāsiō*), equiv. to *suās(us),* ptp. of *suādēre* to advise (*suād-* + *-tus* ptp. suffix) + *-iōn-* -ION] **—sua·sive** (swā′siv), *adj.* **—sua′sive·ly,** *adv.* **—sua′sive·ness,** *n.* **—sua·so·ry** (swā′sə rē), *adj.*

suave (swäv), *adj.* (of persons or their manner, speech, etc.) smoothly agreeable or polite; agreeably or blandly urbane. [< F < L *suāv(is)* sweet] **—suave′ly,** *adv.* **—suave′ness,** *n.*
—Syn. sophisticated, worldly. **—Ant.** blunt.

sua·vi·ter in mo·do, for·ti·ter in re (swä′wi-ter′ in mō′dō, fōr′ti ter′ in rā′; *Eng.* swav′i-tər in mō′dō, fôr′ti tər in rē′), *Latin.* gentle in manner, resolute in purpose.

suav·i·ty (swä′vi tē, swav′i-), *n., pl.* **-ties. 1.** a suave or smoothly agreeable quality. **2. suavities,** suave or courteous actions or manners; amenities. Also, **suave′ness.** [late ME < L *suāvitāt-* (s. of *suāvitās*), equiv. to *suāv-* (see SUAVE) + *-itāt-* -ITY]

sub (sub), *n., v.,* **subbed, sub·bing.** **—n. 1.** submarine. **2.** substitute. **3.** sublieutenant. **4.** subordinate. **5.** subaltern. **6.** *Brit.* an advance against one's wages, esp. one granted as a subsistence allowance. **7.** *Photog. Informal.* a substratum. **—v.i. 8.** to act as a substitute for another. **—v.t. 9.** *Photog. Informal.* to coat (a film or plate) with a substratum. [shortened form]

sub-, 1. a prefix meaning "under," "below," "slightly," and sometimes used with the notion of assistance, occurring in loan words from Latin (*subject; subtract; subvert; subsidy*), on this model used freely in combination with elements of any origin (*subarctic; subway; subdebutante; subteen*). **2.** *Chem.* **a.** a prefix indicating a basic compound: *subacetate; subcarbonate; subnitrate.* **b.** a prefix indicating that the element is present in a relatively small proportion, i.e., in a low oxidation state: *subchloride; suboxide.* Also, **su-, suc-, suf-, sug-, sum-, sup-, sus-.** [< L, comb. form repr. *sub* (prep.); akin to HYPO-]

sub., 1. subscription. **2.** substitute. **3.** suburban. **4.** subway.

sub·ac·e·tate (sub as′i tāt′), *n. Chem.* a basic salt of acetic acid. [SUB- + ACETATE]

sub·ac·id (sub as′id), *adj.* **1.** slightly or moderately acid or sour: *a subacid fruit.* **2.** (of a person or his speech, temper, etc.) somewhat biting or sharp. [SUB- + ACID] **—sub·a·cid·i·ty** (sub′ə sid′i tē), **sub·ac′id·ness,** *n.* **—sub·ac′id·ly,** *adv.*

sub·a·cute (sub′ə kyo͞ot′), *adj.* somewhat or moderately acute. [SUB- + ACUTE] **—sub′a·cute′ly,** *adv.*

su·ba·dar (so͞o′bə där′), *n.* (in India) **1.** a provincial governor of the Mogul empire. **2.** the chief native officer of a company of native troops in the British Indian Service. Also, **su′bah·dar′.** [< Urdu < Pers, equiv. to *sūba* province + *dār* holding, holder]

sub·a·gent (sub ā′jənt), *n.* **1.** a person whose duties as an agent are delegated to him by another agent. **2.** one who works for or under the supervision of an agent. [SUB- + AGENT]

sub·al·i·men·ta·tion (sub′al ə men tā′shən), *n. Pathol.* hypoalimentation. [SUB- + ALIMENTATION]

sub·al·pine (sub al′pīn, -pin), *adj.* **1.** pertaining to the regions at the foot of the Alps. **2.** *Bot.* growing on mountains below the limit of tree growth, and above the foothill, or montane, zone. [SUB- + ALPINE]

sub·al·tern (sub ôl′tərn *or, esp. for 3, 6,* sub′əl tûrn′), *adj.* **1.** lower in rank; subordinate: *a subaltern employee.* **2.** *Brit. Mil.* noting a commissioned officer below the rank of captain. **3.** *Logic.* **a.** noting the relation of one proposition to another when the first proposition is implied by the second but the second is not implied by the first. **b.** (in Aristotelian logic) denoting the relation of a particular proposition to a universal proposition having the same subject, predicate, and quality. **c.** of or pertaining to a proposition having either of these relations to another. **—n. 4.** one who has a subordinate position. **5.** *Brit. Mil.* a commissioned officer below the rank of captain. **6.** *Logic.* a subaltern proposition. [< L *subaltern(us),* equiv. to *sub-* SUB- + *alternus* ALTERNATE] **—sub′al·ter′ni·ty,** *n.*

sub·al·ter·nate (sub ôl′tər nit, -al′-), *adj.* **1.** subordinate; inferior. **2.** *Bot.* placed singly along an axis, but tending to become grouped oppositely. [< ML *subalternāt(us)* (ptp. of *subalternāre* to subordinate), equiv. to *subaltern(us)* SUBALTERN + *-ātus* -ATE[1]] **—sub·al·ter·na·tion** (sub ôl′tər nā′shən, -al′-), *n.*

sub·ant·arc·tic (sub′ant ärk′tik, -är′tik), *adj.* of, pertaining to, similar to, or being the region immediately north of the Antarctic Circle; subpolar. [SUB- + ANTARCTIC]

sub·ap·os·tol·ic (sub ap′ə stol′ik, sub′ap-), *adj.* of or pertaining to the period immediately succeeding that of the apostles. [SUB- + APOSTOLIC]

sub·aq·ual (sub ak′wəl), *adj. Geol.* (of soils, sediments, etc.) lying below the water table. Cf. **superaqual.** [SUB- + L *aqu(a)* water + -AL[1]]

sub·a·quat·ic (sub′ə kwat′ik, -ə kwot′-), *adj.* living or growing partly on land, partly in water. [SUB- + AQUATIC]

sub·a·que·ous (sub ā′kwē əs, -ak′wē-), *adj.* **1.** existing or situated under water. **2.** occurring or performed under water. **3.** used under water. [SUB- + AQUEOUS]

sub·a·rach·noid (sub′ə rak′noid), *adj. Anat.* of, pertaining to, or situated below the arachnoid membrane. [SUB- + ARACHNOID]

sub·arc·tic (sub ärk′tik, -är′tik), *adj.* of, pertaining to, similar to, or being the region immediately south of the Arctic Circle; subpolar. [SUB- + ARCTIC]

subarc′tic cur′rent. See **Aleutian current.**

sub·ar·id (sub ar′id), *adj.* moderately arid. [SUB- + ARID]

sub·as·sem·bly (sub′ə sem′blē), *n., pl.* **-blies.** a structural assembly, as of electronic or machine parts, forming part of a larger assembly. [SUB- + ASSEMBLY]

sub·as·trin·gent (sub′ə strin′jənt), *adj.* slightly astringent. [SUB- + ASTRINGENT]

sub·at·om (sub at′əm), *n. Chem.* any component of an atom. [SUB- + ATOM]

sub·a·tom·ic (sub′ə tom′ik), *adj. Physics.* **1.** of or pertaining to a process that occurs within an atom. **2.** noting or pertaining to a particle or particles contained in an atom, as electrons, protons, neutrons, etc. [SUB- + ATOMIC]

sub·au·di·tion (sub′ô dish′ən), *n.* **1.** the act or an instance of understanding or mentally supplying something not expressed. **2.** something mentally supplied; understood or implied meaning. [< LL *subaudītiōn-* (s. of *subaudītiō*) understanding, i.e., supplying an omitted word. See SUB-, AUDITION]

sub·au·ric·u·lar (sub′ô rik′yə lər), *adj. Anat.* situated below the ear. [SUB- + AURICULAR]

sub·ax·il·la·ry (sub ak′sə ler′ē), *adj. Bot.* situated or placed beneath an axil. [SUB- + AXILLARY]

sub·base (sub′bās′), *n.* **1.** *Archit.* the lowest part of a base, as of a column, which consists of two or more horizontal members. **2.** *Math.* a collection of subsets of a topological space having the property that every open set of a given topology can be written as the union of intersections of finite numbers of sets in the collection. Cf. **base**[1] (def. 13b). [SUB- + BASE[1]] **—sub·ba′sal,** *adj.*

sub·base·ment (sub′bās′mənt), *n.* a basement or one of a series of basements below the main basement of a building. [SUB- + BASEMENT]

sub·bass (sub′bās′), *n. Music.* a pedal stop producing the lowest tones of an organ. [SUB- + BASS[1]]

sub·bing (sub′ing), *n. Photog.* **1.** the act or process of applying a substratum. **2.** the material used for a substratum. [SUB + -ING[1]]

sub·branch (sub′branch′), *n.* a subordinate branch or a branch of a branch, as of a bank, business, or the like. [SUB- + BRANCH]

sub·cal·i·ber (sub kal′ə bər), *adj. Mil.* **1.** (of a projectile) having a diameter less than the caliber of the gun from which it is fired, the projectile being fitted with a disk large enough to fill the bore, or being fired from a tube attached to the inside or the outside of the gun. **2.** used in firing such a projectile: *a subcaliber gun.* [SUB- + CALIBER]

sub·car·bide (sub kär′bīd), *n. Chem.* a carbide containing less than the normal proportion of carbon. [SUB- + CARBIDE]

sub·car·ti·lag·i·nous (sub′kär tᵊlaj′ə nəs), *adj. Anat., Zool.* **1.** partially or incompletely cartilaginous. **2.** situated below or beneath cartilage. [SUB- + CARTILAGINOUS]

sub·cas·ing (sub kā′sing, sub′kā′-), *n. Carpentry.* a rough casing for a doorway or window. [SUB- + CASING]

sub·cat·e·go·ry (sub kat′ə gōr′ē, -gôr′ē), *n., pl.* **-ries.** a subordinate category or a division of a category. [SUB- + CATEGORY]

sub·ce·les·tial (sub′si les′chəl), *adj.* **1.** being beneath the heavens; terrestrial. **2.** mundane; worldly. **—n. 3.** a subcelestial being. [SUB- + CELESTIAL]

sub·cel·lar (sub′sel′ər), *n.* a cellar below the main cellar. [SUB- + CELLAR]

sub·cen·tral (sub sen′trəl), *adj.* near or almost to the center. [SUB- + CENTRAL] **—sub·cen′tral·ly,** *adv.*

subch., subchapter.

sub·chair·man (sub châr′mən), *n., pl.* **-men.** a subordinate or substitute chairman. [SUB- + CHAIRMAN]

sub·chas·er (sub′chā′sər), *n.* See **submarine chaser.** [SUB + CHASER]

sub·chlo·ride (sub klōr′īd, -id, -klôr′-), *n. Chem.* a chloride containing a relatively small proportion of chlorine, as mercurous chloride. [SUB- + CHLORIDE]

sub·cinc·to·ri·um (sub′singk tōr′ē əm, -tôr′-), *n., pl.* **-to·ri·a** (-tōr′ē ə, -tôr′-). *Rom. Cath. Ch.* an embroidered silk vestment resembling, but somewhat broader than, a maniple, worn by the pope on solemn occasions. Also, **succintorium.** [< LL; L *subcinct(us), succint(us)* SUCCINT + *-ōrium* -ORY[2]]

sub·class (sub′klas′, -kläs′), *n.* **1.** a primary division of a class. **2.** *Biol.* a category of related orders within a class. **—v.t. 3.** to place in a subclass. [SUB- + CLASS]

sub·clas·si·fy (sub klas′ə fī′), *v.t., v.i.,* **-fied, -fy·ing.** to arrange or be arranged in subclasses. [SUB- + CLASSIFY] **—sub′clas·si·fi·ca′tion,** *n.*

sub·cla·vate (sub klā′vāt), *adj. Zool.* somewhat club-shaped. [SUB- + CLAVATE]

sub·cla·vi·an (sub klā′vē ən), *Anat.* **—adj. 1.** situated or extending beneath the clavicle, as certain arteries, veins, etc. **2.** pertaining to such an artery, vein, or the like. **—n. 3.** a subclavian artery, vein, or the like. [< NL *subclāvi(us)* SUBCLAVIUS + -AN]

subcla′vian groove′, *Anat.* either of two shallow depressions on the first rib, one for the subclavian artery and the other for the subclavian vein.

sub·cla·vi·us (sub klā′vē əs), *n., pl.* **-vi·i** (-vē ī′). *Anat.* a small shoulder muscle, the action of which assists in depressing the shoulder. [< NL; see SUBCLAVIAN]

sub·cli·max (sub klī′maks), *n. Ecol.* the imperfect development of a climax community because of some factor, as repeated fires in a forest, which arrests the normal succession. [SUB- + CLIMAX]

sub·clin·i·cal (sub klin′i kəl), *adj. Med.* pertaining to a disease having symptoms so mild as to be unnoticeable in the usual clinical examination and tests. [SUB- + CLINICAL]

sub·co·lum·nar (sub′kə lum′nər), *adj.* almost or imperfectly columnar. [SUB- + COLUMNAR]

sub·com·mit·tee (sub′kə mit′ē), *n.* a secondary committee appointed out of a main committee. [SUB- + COMMITTEE]

---

sub·ab′bot, *n.*
sub′a·bil′i·ty, *n., pl.* **-ties.**
sub·ab′so·lute′, *adj.;* **-ly,** *adv.;* **-ness,** *n.*
sub′ac·a·dem′ic, *adj.*
sub′ac·a·dem′i·cal, *adj.;* **-ly,** *adv.*
sub′ac·count′, *n.*
sub′ac·e·tab′u·lar, *adj.*
sub′a·cid′u·lous, *adj.*
sub·ac′rid, *adj.;* **-ly,** *adv.;* **-ness,** *n.*
sub′a·crid′i·ty, *n.*
sub·ac′ro·drome′, *adj.*
sub′a·crod′ro·mous, *adj.*
sub′a·cro′mi·al, *adj.*
sub′a·cu′mi·nate, *adj.*
sub′a·cu′mi·na′tion, *n.*
sub·ad′di·tive, *adj.;* **-ly,** *adv.*
sub·ad′ja′cent, *adj.;* **-ly,** *adv.*
sub′ad·min′is·trate′, *v.t.,* **-trat·ed, -trat·ing.**
sub′ad·min′is·tra′tion, *n.*
sub′ad·min′is·tra′tive, *adj.;* **-ly,** *adv.*
sub′ad·min′is·tra′tor, *n.*
sub′a·dult′, *adj., n.;* **-ness,** *n.*
sub·ad′vo·cate, *n.*
sub·aer′ate, *v.t.,* **-at·ed, -at·ing.**
sub′aer·a′tion, *n.*
sub·aer′i·al, *adj.;* **-ly,** *adv.*
sub·af′flu·ence, *n.*
sub·af′flu·ent, *adj.;* **-ly,** *adv.*
sub′age′, *n.*
sub·a′gen·cy, *n., pl.* **-cies.**
sub·ag′gre·gate, *adj., n.;* **-ly,** *adv.*
sub′ag·gre·ga′tion, *n.*
sub·ag′gre·ga′tive, *adj.*
sub·a′la·ry, *adj.*
sub·a′late, *adj.*
sub·a′lat·ed, *adj.*
sub′al·ge·bra′ic, *adj.*
sub′al·ge·bra′i·cal, *adj.;* **-ly,** *adv.*
sub′al·ge·bra′ist, *n.*
sub′al·li′ance, *n.*
sub·al′mon·er, *n.*
sub·a′nal, *adj.*
sub′an·co′ne·al, *adj.*
sub-An·de′an, *adj.*
sub·an′gu·lar, *adj.;* **-ly,** *adv.;* **-ness,** *n.*
sub′an·gu·lar′i·ty, *n., pl.* **-ties.**
sub·an′gu·late, *adj.;* **-ly,** *adv.*
sub·an′gu·lat′ed, *adj.*
sub′an·gu·la′tion, *n.*
sub′an·tique′, *adj.;* **-ly,** *adv.;* **-ness,** *n.*
sub′an·tiq′ui·ty, *n., pl.* **-ties.**
sub′ap·par′ent, *adj.;* **-ly,** *adv.;* **-ness,** *n.*
sub′ap·pear′ance, *n.*
sub′ap·pressed′, *adj.*
sub′ap·pro·ba′tion, *n.*
sub·ap′pro·ba′tive, *adj.;* **-ness,** *n.*
sub′ap·pro′ba·to′ry, *adj.*
sub′ar·bo′re·al, *adj.*
sub′ar·bo′re·ous, *adj.*
sub′ar·bo·res′cent, *adj.*
sub′ar·bo·res′cence, *n.*
sub′ar·che·spo′ri·al, *adj.*
sub·ar′chi·tect′, *n.*
sub·ar′cu·ate, *adj.*
sub·ar′cu·at′ed, *adj.*
sub·ar′e·a, *n.*
sub·ar′e·al, *adj.*
sub·ar′mor, *n.*
sub′a·rous′al, *n.*
sub′ar·te′sian, *adj.*
sub·ar′ti·cle, *n.*
sub′ar·tic′u·late, *adj.;* **-ly,** *adv.;* **-ness,** *n.*
sub′ar·tic′u·la′tive, *adj.*
sub′ar·tic′u·la′tion, *n.*
sub·ar′y·te′noid, *adj.*
sub′ar·y·te·noi′dal, *adj.*
sub′as·cend′ing, *adj.*
sub′as·sem′blage, *n.*
sub′as·so′ci·a′tion, *n.*
sub′as·so′ci·a′tion·al, *adj.*
sub′as·so′ci·a′tive, *adj.;* **-ly,** *adv.*
sub′as·trag′a·lar, *adj.*
sub·as′tral, *adj.*
sub′-At·lan′tic, *adj.*
sub′at·ten′u·ate, *adj.*
sub′at·ten′u·at′ed, *adj.*
sub′at·ten′u·a′tion, *n.*
sub′at·tor′ney, *n., pl.* **-neys.**
sub′at·tor′ney·ship′, *n.*
sub′au·di·bil′i·ty, *n.*
sub·au′di·ble, *adj.;* **-ble·ness,** *n.;* **-bly,** *adv.*
sub·au′di·tor, *n.*
sub·au′ral, *adj.;* **-ly,** *adv.*
sub′au·ric′u·late, *adj.*
sub′au·to·mat′ic, *adj.*
sub′au·to·mat′i·cal·ly, *adv.*
sub·av′er·age, *adj.;* **-ly,** *adv.*
sub·ax′i·al, *adj.;* **-ly,** *adv.*
sub·ax′ile, *adj.*
sub·bail′ie, *n.*
sub·bail′iff, *n.*
sub·bail′i·wick, *n.*
sub·bal′last, *n.*
sub′band′, *n.*
sub′bank′, *n.*
sub′ba·sal′tic, *adj.*
sub·bea′dle, *n.*
sub·bi′as, *n.*
sub·bran′chi·al, *adj.*
sub′breed′, *n.*
sub′bri·gade′, *n.*
sub·brok′er, *n.*
sub·bro′mid, *n.*
sub·bro′mide, *n.*
sub·bron′chi·al, *adj.;* **-ly,** *adv.*
sub′bu′reau, *n., pl.* **-reaus, -reaux.**
sub·cae′cal, *adj.*
sub′cal·car′e·ous, *adj.*
sub′cal·lo′sal, *adj.*
sub·cam′pan′u·late, *adj.*
sub·can′cel·late′, *adj.*
sub·can′cel·lous, *adj.*
sub·can′did, *adj.;* **-ly,** *adv.;* **-ness,** *n.*
sub·cap′su·lar, *adj.*
sub·cap′tain, *n.*
sub·cap′tain·cy, *n.*
sub·cap′tain·ship′, *n.*
sub′car·bo·na′ceous, *adj.*
sub·car′di·nal, *adj.;* **-ly,** *adv.*
sub·car′i·nate′, *adj.*
sub·car′i·nat′ed, *adj.*
sub′-Car·pa′thi·an, *adj.*
sub′case′, *n.*
sub′cash′, *n.*
sub′cash·ier′, *n.*
sub′ca·si′no, *n., pl.* **-nos.**
sub′cast′, *n.*
sub′caste′, *n.*
sub′cause′, *n.*
sub·cav′i·ty, *n., pl.* **-ties.**
sub′cell′, *n.*
sub′cer·e·bel′lar, *adj.*
sub′cer′e·bral, *adj.*
sub·cham′ber·er, *n.*
sub·chan′cel, *n.*
sub′chap′ter, *n.*
sub·che′li·form′, *adj.*
sub′chief′, *n.*
sub·chon′dral, *adj.*
sub′cho′ri·oid′, *adj.*
sub′cho·ri·oi′dal, *adj.*
sub′cho·ri·on′ic, *adj.*
sub·cho′roid, *adj.*
sub′cho·roi′dal, *adj.*
sub-Chris′tian, *adj.*
sub·chron′ic, *adj.*
sub·chron′i·cal, *adj.;* **-ly,** *adv.*
sub·cir′cuit, *n.*
sub·cir′cu·lar, *adj.;* **-ly,** *adv.*
sub′cir·cu·lar′i·ty, *adj.*
sub·cit′y, *n., pl.* **-cit·ies.**
sub·civ′i·li·za′tion, *n.*
sub·civ′i·lized′, *adj.*
sub′clan′, *n.*
sub·claus′al, *adj.*
sub′clause′, *n.*
sub·cla′vate, *adj.*
sub′cla·vic′u·lar, *adj.*
sub′clerk′, *n.*
sub·clerk′ship′, *n.*
sub·cli′mate, *n.*
sub′cli·mat′ic, *adj.*
sub′clique′, *n.*
sub′col·lec′tor, *n.*
sub′col·lec′tor·ship′, *n.*
sub′col·le′gi·al, *adj.*
sub′col·le′giate, *adj.*
sub′com·mand′er, *n.*
sub′com·mand′er·ship′, *n.*
sub′com·men·da′tion, *n.*
sub′com·mend′a·to′ry, *adj.*
sub′com·mend′ed, *adj.*
sub′com·mis·sar′i·al, *adj.*
sub·com′mis·sar′y, *n., pl.* **-sar·ies.**
sub·com′mis·sar′y·ship′, *n.*
sub′com·mis′sion, *n.*
sub′com·mis′sion·er, *n.*
sub′com·mis′sion·er·ship′, *n.*

---

sub·com·pa·ny (sub′kum′pə nē), *n., pl.* **-nies.** See **subsidiary company.** [SUB- + COMPANY]

sub·con·scious (sub kon′shəs), *adj.* **1.** existing or operating in the mind beneath or beyond consciousness: *the subconscious self.* **2.** imperfectly or not wholly conscious: *subconscious motivations.* —*n.* **3.** the totality of mental processes of which the individual is not aware; unreportable mental activities. [SUB- + CONSCIOUS] —**sub·con′scious·ly,** *adv.* —**sub·con′scious·ness,** *n.*

sub·con·tig·u·ous (sub′kən tig′yo͞o əs), *adj.* almost touching; nearly contiguous. [SUB- + CONTIGUOUS]

sub·con·ti·nent (sub kon′tə nənt, sub′kon′-), *n.* **1.** a large, relatively self-contained land mass forming a subdivision of a continent: *the subcontinent of India.* **2.** a large land mass, as Greenland, that is smaller than any of the usually recognized continents. [SUB- + CONTINENT] —**sub·con·ti·nen·tal** (sub′kon tə nen′tᵊl), *adj.*

sub·con·tract (*n.* sub kon′trakt, sub′kon′-; *v.* sub′kən trakt′), *Law.* —*n.* **1.** a contract by which one agrees to render services or to provide materials necessary for the performance of another contract. —*v.t.* **2.** to make a subcontract for. —*v.i.* **3.** to make a subcontract. [SUB- + CONTRACT]

sub·con·trac·tor (sub kon′trak tər, sub′kon′-, sub′kən trak′tər), *n.* **1.** *Law.* a person who or business that contracts to provide some service or material necessary for the performance of another's contract. **2.** a person or business firm contracted to do part of another's work. [SUB- + CONTRACTOR]

sub·con·tra·oc·tave (sub′kon trə ok′tiv, -tāv), *n.* *Music.* the octave between the third and fourth C's below middle C. [SUB- + CONTRAOCTAVE]

sub·cor·tex (sub kôr′teks, sub′kôr′-), *n., pl.* **-ti·ces** (-ti sēz′). *Anat.* the portions of the brain situated beneath the cerebral cortex, considered as a whole. [SUB- + CORTEX]

sub·cor·ti·cal (sub kôr′ti kəl), *adj.* *Bot., Anat.* situated beneath the cortex. [SUB- + CORTICAL] —**sub·cor′ti·cal·ly,** *adv.*

sub·cos·ta (sub kos′tə, -kô′stə), *n., pl.* **-cos·tae** (-kos′tē, -kô′stē). a longitudinal vein in the anterior portion of the wing of an insect. [< NL; see SUB-, COSTA] —**sub·cos′tal,** *adj.*

sub·cov·er (sub′kuv′ər), *n.* *Math.* a set of subsets of a cover of a given set which also is a cover of the set. [SUB- + COVER]

sub·crit·i·cal (sub krit′i kəl), *adj.* *Physics.* pertaining to a state, value, or quantity that is less than critical, esp. to a mass of radioactive material. [SUB- + CRITICAL]

sub·cul·ture (*v.* sub kul′chər; *n.* sub′kul′chər), *v.,* **-tured, -tur·ing,** *n.* —*v.t.* **1.** *Bacteriol.* to cultivate (a bacterial strain) again on a new medium. —*n.* **2.** *Bacteriol.* a culture derived in this manner. **3.** *Sociol.* **a.** the cultural values and behavioral patterns distinctive of a particular group in a society. **b.** a group having social, economic, ethnic, or other traits distinctive enough to distinguish it from others within the same culture or society. [SUB- + CULTURE] —**sub·cul′tur·al,** *adj.* —**sub·cul′tur·al·ly,** *adv.*

sub·cur·rent (sub′kûr′ənt, -kur′-), *n.* a not clearly revealed or formulated direction of thought, intention, action, etc., underlying what is manifested: *His words, though ostensibly friendly, betrayed a subcurrent of hostility.* [SUB- + CURRENT]

sub·cu·ta·ne·ous (sub′kyo͞o tā′nē əs), *adj.* **1.** situated or lying under the skin, as tissue. **2.** performed or introduced under the skin, as an injection by a syringe. **3.** living below the several layers of the skin, as certain parasites. [< LL *subcutāneus.* See SUB-, CUTANEOUS] —**sub′cu·ta′ne·ous·ly,** *adv.* —**sub′cu·ta′ne·ous·ness,** *n.*

sub·dea·con (sub dē′kən, sub′dē′-), *n.* a member of the clerical order next below that of deacon. [ME *subdecon, -dekene* < ML *subdiācon(us).* See SUB-, DEACON]

sub·dea·con·ate (sub dē′kə nit), *n.* subdiaconate. [SUBDEACON + -ATE[1]]

sub·dean (sub′dēn′), *n.* *Chiefly Brit.* an assistant dean. [ME *subdene,* part adoption, part trans. of ML *subdecanus;* see SUB-, DEAN[1]] —**sub·dean′er·y,** *n.*

sub·deb (sub′deb′), *n.* *Informal.* **1.** a subdebutante. **2.** any girl in her teens. [shortened form]

sub·deb·u·tante (sub deb′yo͞o tänt′, -tant′), *n.* a young girl who has not yet made her debut into society. [SUB- + DEBUTANTE]

sub·de·lir·i·um (sub′di lēr′ē əm), *n., pl.* **-lir·i·ums, -lir·i·a** (-lēr′ē ə). *Med.* a mild delirium with lucid intervals. [SUB- + DELIRIUM]

sub·de·riv·a·tive (sub′di riv′ə tiv), *n.* a word derived from a derivative. [SUB- + DERIVATIVE]

sub·di·ac·o·nal (sub′dī ak′ə nᵊl), *adj.* of or pertaining to a subdeacon. [SUB- + DIACONAL]

sub·di·ac·o·nate (sub′dī ak′ə nit, -nāt′), *n.* **1.** the office or dignity of a subdeacon. **2.** a body of subdeacons. Also, **subdeaconate.** [SUB- + DIACONATE]

sub·dis·trict (sub′dis′trikt), *n.* a division of a district. [SUB- + DISTRICT]

sub·di·vide (sub′di vīd′, sub′di vīd′), *v.,* **-vid·ed, -vid·ing.** —*v.t.* **1.** to divide (that which has already been divided) into smaller parts; divide again after a first division. **2.** to divide into parts. **3.** to divide (a plot, tract of land, etc.) into building lots. —*v.i.* **4.** to become separated into divisions. [< LL *subdīvid(ere).* See SUB-, DIVIDE] —**sub′di·vid′a·ble,** *adj.* —**sub′di·vid′er,** *n.*

sub·di·vi·sion (sub′di vizh′ən), *n.* **1.** the act or fact of subdividing. **2.** a product of subdividing, as a section of a department. **3.** a portion of land divided into lots for real-estate development. [< LL *subdīvīsiōn-* (s. of *subdīvīsiō*), equiv. to *subdīvīs(us)* (ptp. of *subdīvīdere* to SUBDIVIDE) + *-iōn-* -ION]

sub·dom·i·nant (sub dom′ə nənt), *n.* **1.** *Music.* the fourth tone of a scale, next below the dominant. —*adj.* **2.** less than or not quite dominant. [SUB- + DOMINANT]

sub·du·al (səb do͞o′əl, -dyo͞o′-), *n.* **1.** the act or an instance of subduing. **2.** the state of being subdued. [SUBDUE + -AL[2]]

sub·duce (səb do͞os′, -dyo͞os′), *v.t.,* **-duced, -duc·ing.** *Obs.* to take away; remove. [< L *subdūce(re),* equiv. to *sub-* SUB- + *dūcere* to lead]

sub·duct (səb dukt′), *v.t.* *Archaic.* to take away; subtract. [< L *subduct(us),* equiv. to *subduc-* (see SUBDUCE) + *-tus* ptp. suffix] —**sub·duc′tion,** *n.*

sub·due (səb do͞o′, -dyo͞o′), *v.t.,* **-dued, -du·ing.** **1.** to conquer and bring into subjection: *Rome subdued Gaul.* **2.** to overpower by superior force; overcome. **3.** to bring under mental or emotional control, as by persuasion, intimidation, or the like; render submissive. **4.** to repress (feelings, impulses, etc.). **5.** to bring (land) under cultivation: *to subdue the wilderness.* **6.** to reduce the intensity, force, or vividness of (sound, light, color, etc.); tone down; soften. **7.** to allay (inflammation, infection, etc.). [late ME *so(b)due, -dewe* < AF **sodue(r)* (to) overcome < MF *soduire* to deceive, seduce < L *subdūcere* to SUBDUCE; meaning in E (and AF) < L *subdere*] —**sub·du′a·ble,** *adj.* —**sub·du′a·ble·ness,** *n.* —**sub·du′a·bly,** *adv.* —**sub·dued′ly,** *adv.* —**sub·dued′ness,** *n.* —**sub·du′er,** *n.* —**sub·du′ing·ly,** *adv.*
—**Syn. 1.** subjugate, vanquish. See **defeat. 3.** tame, break, discipline. **3, 4.** suppress. —**Ant. 4.** awaken, arouse. **6.** intensify.

sub·dued (səb do͞od′, -dyo͞od′), *adj.* **1.** quiet; inhibited; repressed; controlled: *After the argument he was much more subdued.* **2.** lowered in intensity or strength; reduced in fullness of tone, as a color or voice; muted: *subdued light; favoring subdued greens.* **3.** (of land) not marked by any striking features, as mountains or cliffs: *a subdued landscape.* [SUBDUE + -ED[2]]

sub·ed·it (sub ed′it), *v.t., v.i.* *Brit.* to edit and correct (a manuscript). [back formation from SUBEDITOR]

sub·ed·i·tor (sub ed′i tər), *n.* **1.** a subordinate or junior editor. **2.** *Brit.* a copyreader. [SUB- + EDITOR] —**sub·ed·i·to·ri·al** (sub′ed i tôr′ē əl, -tōr′-), *adj.* —**sub·ed′i·tor·ship′,** *n.*

sub·en·try (sub′en′trē), *n., pl.* **-tries.** an item shown or listed under a main entry, as in bookkeeping. [SUB- + ENTRY]

sub·ep·i·der·mal (sub′ep i dûr′məl), *adj.* lying or occurring beneath the epidermis; subcutaneous. [SUB- + EPIDERMAL]

sub·e·qua·to·ri·al (sub′ē kwə tôr′ē əl, -tōr′-, -ek-wə-), *adj.* of, pertaining to, or being a region near the equatorial region. [SUB- + EQUATORIAL]

su·be·re·ous (so͞o bēr′ē əs), *adj.* of the nature of or resembling cork; suberose. [< L *sūbereus,* equiv. to *sūber* cork + *-eus* -EOUS]

su·ber·ic (so͞o ber′ik), *adj.* of or pertaining to cork. [< L *sūber* cork + -IC]

suber′ic ac′id, *Chem.* a crystalline dibasic acid, $HOOC(CH_2)_6COOH$, obtained esp. from suberin, castor oil, and cork: used chiefly in the preparation of plastics and plasticizers.

su·ber·in (so͞o′bər in), *n.* *Bot.* a waxlike, fatty substance, occurring in cork cell walls and in or between other cells, that on alkaline hydrolysis yields chiefly suberic acid. [< L *sūber* cork + -IN[2]; cf. F *subérine*]

su·ber·ise (so͞o′bə rīz′), *v.t.,* **-ised, -is·ing.** *Chiefly Brit.* suberize.

su·ber·i·za·tion (so͞o′bər i zā′shən), *n.* *Bot.* the impregnation of cell walls with suberin, causing the formation of cork. Also, *esp. Brit.,* **su′ber·i·sa′tion.** [SUBERIZE + -ATION]

su·ber·ize (so͞o′bə rīz′), *v.t.,* **-ized, -iz·ing.** *Bot.* to convert into cork tissue. [< L *sūber* cork + -IZE]

su·ber·ose (so͞o′bə rōs′), *adj.* of the nature of cork; corklike; corky. Also, **su·ber·ous** (so͞o′bər əs). [< NL *sūberōs(us)* < L *sūber* cork + *-ōsus* -OSE[1]]

sub·fam·i·ly (sub fam′ə lē, -fam′lē, sub′fam′ə lē, -fam′lē), *n., pl.* **-lies. 1.** *Biol.* a category of related genera within a family. **2.** *Linguistics.* (in the classification of related languages within a family) a category of a higher order than a branch. Cf. **branch** (def. 6), **family** (def. 10). [SUB- + FAMILY]

sub·fe·brile (sub fē′brəl, -feb′rəl), *adj.* pertaining to or marked by a slight fever. [SUB- + FEBRILE]

sub·field (sub′fēld′), *n.* *Math.* a field that is a subset of a given field. [SUB- + FIELD]

sub·floor (sub′flôr′, -flōr′), *n.* a rough floor beneath a finish floor. Also called **blind floor.** [SUB- + FLOOR]

sub·floor·ing (sub flôr′ing, -flōr′-), *n.* material used for making a subfloor. [SUB- + FLOORING]

sub·freez·ing (sub′frē′zing), *adj.* below the freezing point. [SUB- + FREEZING]

sub·fusc (sub fusk′), *adj.* **1.** subfuscous; dusky. **2.** dark and dull; dingy; drab: *a subfusc mining town.* [< L *subfusc(us)* SUBFUSCOUS]

sub·fus·cous (sub fus′kəs), *adj.* slightly dark, dusky, or somber. [< L *subfuscus,* equiv. to *sub-* SUB- + *fuscus* FUSCOUS]

sub·gen·i·tal (sub jen′i tᵊl), *adj.* situated below the genitalia. [SUB- + GENITAL]

sub·ge·nus (sub jē′nəs), *n., pl.* **-gen·er·a** (-jen′ər ə), **-ge·nus·es.** *Biol.* a category of related species within a genus. [< NL; see SUB-, GENUS] —**sub·ge·ner·ic** (sub′jə ner′ik), *adj.*

sub·com′pen·sate′, *v.t.,* **-sat·ed, -sat·ing.**
sub′com·pen·sa′tion, *n.*
sub′com·pen·sa′tion·al, *adj.*
sub′com·pen′sa·tive, *adj.*
sub′com·pen′sa·to′ry, *adj.*
sub′com·plete′, *adj.;* **-ly,** *adv.;* **-ness,** *n.*
sub′com·ple′tion, *n.*
sub′com·pressed′, *adj.*
sub′con·cave′, *adj.;* **-ly,** *adv.;* **-ness,** *n.*
sub′con·cav′i·ty, *n., pl.* **-ties.**
sub′con·cealed′, *adj.*
sub′con·ces′sion, *n.*
sub′con·ces′sion·aire′, *n.*
sub′con·ces′sion·ar′y, *adj., n., pl.* **-ar·ies.**
sub′con·ces′sion·er, *n.*
sub′con·choi′dal, *adj.*
sub′con·fer′ence, *n.*
sub′con·fer·en′tial, *adj.*
sub′con·form′a·bil′i·ty, *n.*
sub′con·form′a·ble, *adj.;* **-ble·ness,** *n.;* **-bly,** *adv.*
sub·con′ic, *adj.*
sub·con′i·cal, *adj.;* **-ly,** *adv.*
sub′con·junc·ti′val, *adj.*
sub′con·junc′tive, *adj.;* **-ly,** *adv.*
sub·con′nate, *adj.*
sub′con·na′tion, *n.*
sub′con·nect′, *v.*
sub′con·nect′ed·ly, *adv.*
sub′con·niv′ent, *adj.*
sub·con′science, *n.*
sub′con′ser·va′tor, *n.*
sub′con·sid′er·a′tion, *n.*
sub′con·stel·la′tion, *n.*
sub·con′sul, *n.*
sub·con′su·lar, *adj.*
sub·con′sul·ship′, *n.*
sub′con·tained′, *adj.*
sub·con′test, *n.*
sub′con·trol′, *v.t.,* **-trolled, -trol·ling.**
sub′con·vex′, *adj.*
sub·con′vo·lute′, *adj.;* **-ly,** *adv.*
sub·cool′, *v.t.*
sub·cor′a·coid′, *adj.*
sub·cor′date, *adj.;* **-ly,** *adv.*
sub·cor′di·form′, *adj.*
sub′co·ri·a′ceous, *adj.*
sub·cor′ne·ous, *adj.*
sub·cor′nu·al, *adj.*
sub′cor·po·ra′tion, *n.*
sub′co·rym′bose, *adj.;* **-ly,** *adv.*
sub·coun′cil, *n.*
sub·cra′ni·al, *adj.;* **-ly,** *adv.*
sub′cre·a′tive, *adj.;* **-ly,** *adv.;* **-ness,** *n.*
sub′creek′, *n.*
sub·cre′nate, *adj.;* **-ly,** *adv.*
sub·cre′nat·ed, *adj.*
sub′crep·i·ta′tion, *n.*
sub′cre·scent′ic, *adj.*
sub′crest′, *n.*
sub·crim′i·nal, *adj.;* **-ly,** *adv.*
sub·cross′ing, *n.*
sub·cru′ci·form′, *adj.*
sub·crys′tal·line, *adj.*
sub·cu′bic, *adj.*
sub·cu′bi·cal, *adj.*
sub·cu′boid, *adj.*
sub′cu·boi′dal, *adj.*
sub·cul′trate, *adj.*
sub·cul′trat·ed, *adj.*
sub·cu′ne·us, *adj.*
sub·cu′rate, *n.*
sub′cu·ra′tor, *n.*
sub′cu·ra·to′ri·al, *adj.*
sub′cu·ra′tor·ship′, *n.*
sub′cu·tic′u·lar, *adj.*
sub′cy·a′ne·ous, *adj.*
sub·cy′a·nid, *n.*
sub·cy′a·nide′, *n.*
sub′cy·lin′dric, *adj.*
sub′cy·lin′dri·cal, *adj.*
sub·da′ta·ry, *n., pl.* **-ries.**
sub·date′, *v.t.,* **-dat·ed, -dat·ing.**
sub·deal′er, *n.*
sub′de·duc′i·ble, *adj.*
sub′def·i·ni′tion, *n.*
sub·del′e·gate, *n.*
sub·del′e·gate′, *v.t.,* **-gat·ed, -gat·ing.**
sub′del·e·ga′tion, *n.*
sub′del·ta′ic, *adj.*
sub·del′toid, *adj.*
sub·del·toi′dal, *adj.*
sub·dem′on·strate′, *v.t.,* **-strat·ed, -strat·ing.**
sub′dem·on·stra′tion, *n.*
sub·den′droid, *adj.*
sub′den·droi′dal, *adj.*
sub·den′tate, *adj.*
sub·den′tat·ed, *adj.*
sub′den·ta′tion, *n.*
sub′den·tic′u·late, *adj.*
sub′den·tic′u·lat′ed, *adj.*
sub′de·part′ment, *n.*
sub′de·part·men′tal, *adj.*
sub′de·pos′it, *n.*
sub′de·pos′i·to′ry, *n., pl.* **-ries.**
sub·de′pot, *n.*
sub′de·pressed′, *adj.*
sub·dep′u·ty, *n., pl.* **-ties.**
sub·der′mal, *adj.*
sub·der′mic, *adj.*
sub·dev′il, *n.*
sub·di′a·lect′, *n.*
sub′di·a·lec′tal, *adj.;* **-ly,** *adv.*
sub′di·a·pa′son, *n.*
sub′di·a·pa·son′ic, *adj.*
sub′di·a·phrag·mat′ic, *adj.*
sub′di·a·phrag·mat′i·cal·ly, *adv.*
sub′di·chot′o·my, *n., pl.* **-mies.**
sub·die′, *n.*
sub′di·lat′ed, *adj.*
sub′di·rec′tor, *n.*
sub′di·rec′tor·ship′, *n.*
sub·dis′coid, *adj.*
sub′dis·coi′dal, *adj.*
sub·dis′tich, *n.*
sub·dis′tich·ous, *adj.;* **-ly,** *adv.*
sub′dis·tinc′tion, *n.*
sub′dis·tinc′tive, *adj.;* **-ly,** *adv.;* **-ness,** *n.*
sub′di·vine′, *adj.;* **-ly,** *adv.;* **-ness,** *n.*
sub·doc′tor, *n.*
sub′dol·i·cho·ce·phal′ic, *adj.*
sub′dol·i·cho·ceph′a·lism, *n.*
sub′dol·i·cho·ceph′a·lous, *adj.*
sub′dol·i·cho·ceph′a·ly, *n.*
sub·dor′sal, *adj.;* **-ly,** *adv.*
sub·dru′id, *n.*
sub·ech′o, *n., pl.* **-ech·oes.**
sub′ec·to·der′mal, *adj.*
sub′ec·to·der′mic, *adj.*
sub′ef·fec′tive, *adj.;* **-ly,** *adv.;* **-ness,** *n.*
sub′e·lec′tion, *n.*
sub·el′e·ment, *n.*
sub′el·e·men′tal, *adj.;* **-ly,** *adv.*
sub′el·lip′tic, *adj.*
sub′el·lip′ti·cal, *adj.*
sub′e·lon′gate, *adj.*
sub′e·lon′gat·ed, *adj.*
sub′e·mar′gi·nate, *adj.*
sub′e·mar′gi·nat′ed, *adj.*
sub′en·do·car′di·al, *adj.*
sub′en·dorse′, *v.t.,* **-dorsed, -dors·ing.**
sub′en·dorse′ment, *n.*
sub′en·do·the′li·al, *adj.*
sub′en·gi·neer′, *n.*
sub′en·tire′, *adj.*
sub′en·ti′tle, *v.t.,* **-tled, -tling.**
sub′ep·i·glot′tal, *adj.*
sub′ep·i·glot′tic, *adj.*
sub′ep·i·the′li·al, *adj.*
sub·ep′och, *n.*
sub·e′qual, *adj.;* **-ly,** *adv.*
sub′e·qual′i·ty, *n., pl.* **-ties.**
sub′e·qui·lat′er·al, *adj.*
sub′e·rect′, *adj.;* **-ly,** *adv.;* **-ness,** *n.*
sub′es·cheat′or, *n.*
sub′e·soph′a·ge′al, *adj.*
sub′es·sen′tial, *adj.;* **-ly,** *adv.;* **-ness,** *n.*
sub·es′tu·a·rine, *adj.*
sub·ev′er·green′, *adj.*
sub′ex·am′in·er, *n.*
sub′ex·ec′u·tor, *n.*
sub′ex·ten′si·bil′i·ty, *n.*
sub′ex·ten′si·ble, *adj.;* **-ness,** *n.*
sub′ex·ter′nal, *adj.;* **-ly,** *adv.*
sub′face′, *n.*
sub·fa′ci·es′, *n.*
sub·fac′tor, *n.*
sub·fac′to·ry, *n., pl.* **-ries.**
sub·fal′cate, *adj.*
sub·fal′ci·al, *adj.*
sub·fal′ci·form′, *adj.*
sub·fas′ci·al, *adj.*
sub′fas·tig′i·ate, *adj.*
sub′fas·tig′i·at′ed, *adj.*
sub·fer′ry·man, *n., pl.* **-men.**
sub·fes′tive, *adj.;* **-ly,** *adv.;* **-ness,** *n.*
sub·fi′brous, *adj.*
sub·fig′ure, *n.*
sub·fis′sure, *n.*
sub·flex′u·ose′, *adj.*
sub·flex′u·ous, *adj.;* **-ly,** *adv.*
sub·flo′ra, *n.*
sub′flush′, *n.*
sub·fo′li·ar, *adj.*
sub·fo′li·ate, *adj.*
sub′fo·li·a′tion, *n.*
sub·fore′man, *n., pl.* **-men.**
sub·fore′man·ship′, *n.*
sub′form′, *n.*
sub′for·ma′tion, *n.*
sub·form′a·tive, *adj.;* **-ly,** *adv.;* **-ness,** *n.*
sub·fos′sil, *n.*
sub′fos·so′ri·al, *adj.*
sub·frac′tion, *n.*
sub·frac′tion·al, *adj.;* **-ly,** *adv.*
sub·frac′tion·ar′y, *adj.*
sub′frame′, *n.*
sub·fresh′man, *n., pl.* **-men.**
sub·fron′tal, *adj.;* **-ly,** *adv.*
sub·ful′gent, *adj.;* **-ly,** *adv.*
sub′fu·mi·ga′tion, *n.*
sub·func′tion, *n.*
sub·func′tion·al, *adj.;* **-ly,** *adv.*
sub·fu′si·form′, *adj.*
sub·gan′oid, *adj.*
sub·gape′, *v.i.,* **-gaped, -gap·ing.**
sub′ge·lat′i·ni·za′tion, *n.*
sub′ge·lat′i·noid′, *adj.*
sub′ge·lat′i·nous, *adj.;* **-ly,** *adv.;* **-ness,** *n.*
sub′ge·nic′u·late, *adj.*
sub′ge·nic′u·la′tion, *n.*
sub′gens′, *n., pl.* **-gen·tes.**
sub′ge·o·met′ric, *adj.*
sub′ge·o·met′ri·cal, *adj.;* **-ly,** *adv.*
sub·ger′mi·nal, *adj.;* **-ly,** *adv.*

sub·gla·cial (sub glā′shəl), *adj.* **1.** beneath a glacier: *a subglacial stream.* **2.** formerly beneath a glacier: *a subglacial deposit.* [SUB- + GLACIAL] —**sub·gla′cial·ly,** *adv.*

sub·grade (sub′grād′), *Civ. Eng., Building Trades.* —*n.* **1.** the prepared earth surface on which a pavement or the ballast of a railroad track is placed. —*adj.* **2.** beneath the finished ground level of a project. [SUB- + GRADE]

sub·group (sub′gro͞op′), *n.* **1.** a subordinate group; a division of a group. **2.** *Chem.* a vertical division of a group in the periodic table; family. **3.** *Math.* a subset of a group which is closed under the group operation and in which every element has an inverse in the subset. [SUB- + GROUP]

sub·gum (sub′gum′), *adj.* *Chinese or Chinese-American Cookery.* prepared with mixed vegetables, as with water chestnuts, mushrooms, and bean sprouts. [Cantonese Pidgin for mixed vegetable dishes]

sub·hal·ide (sub hal′īd, -hā′lid), *n.* *Chem.* a halide containing a relatively small proportion of the halogen, as mercurous chloride. [SUB- + HALIDE]

sub·har·mon·ic (sub′här mon′ik), *n.* *Physics.* an oscillation that has a frequency which is an integral submultiple of the frequency of a related oscillation. [SUB- + HARMONIC]

sub·head (sub′hed′), *n.* **1.** (in written or printed matter) a title or heading of a subdivision, as in a chapter, essay, or newspaper article. **2.** (in written or printed matter) a subordinate division of a title or heading. **3.** the immediate subordinate of the president or other head of an educational institution. Also, **sub′head′ing** (for defs. 1, 2). [SUB- + HEAD]

sub·he·dral (sub hē′drəl), *adj.* (of mineral crystals in igneous rocks) having a partial or incomplete crystal face or form. [SUB- + -HEDRAL]

sub·hu·man (sub hyo͞o′mən *or, often,* -yo͞o′-), *adj.* **1.** less than or not quite human. **2.** almost human: *In some respects, the porpoise is subhuman.* [SUB- + HUMAN]

sub·in·can·des·cent (sub′in kən des′ənt), *adj.* almost incandescent. [SUB- + INCANDESCENT]

sub·in·ci·sion (sub′in sizh′ən), *n.* the cutting open of the urethra along the underside of the penis, performed as part of a puberty ritual among some primitive tribes, esp. in central Australia. [SUB- + INCISION]

sub·in·de (sub in′dē), *adv.* (in prescriptions) frequently. [< L]

sub·in·dex (sub in′deks), *n., pl.* **-di·ces** (-di sēz′). *Math.* inferior (def. 10). [SUB- + INDEX]

sub·in·feu·date (sub′in fyo͞o′dāt), *v.t., v.i.,* **-dat·ed, -dat·ing.** to grant subinfeudation (to). Also, **sub′in·feud′.** [back formation from SUBINFEUDATION]

sub·in·feu·da·tion (sub′in fyo͞o dā′shən), *n.* *Feudal Law.* **1.** secondary infeudation; the granting of a portion of an estate by a feudal tenant to a subtenant, held from the tenant on terms similar to those of the grant to him. **2.** the tenure established. **3.** the estate or fief so created. [SUB- + INFEUDATION]

sub·in·feu·da·to·ry (sub′in fyo͞o′də tôr′ē, -tōr′ē), *n., pl.* **-ries.** one who holds by subinfeudation. [SUBINFEUDAT(ION) + -ORY¹]

sub·in·flu·ent (sub in′flo͞o ənt), *n.* *Ecol.* a plant or animal that has a lesser effect than an influent on the ecological processes within a community. [SUB- + INFLUENT]

sub·in·ter·val (sub in′tər vəl), *n.* *Math.* an interval that is a subset of a given interval. [SUB- + INTERVAL]

sub·ir·ri·gate (sub ir′ə gāt′), *v.t.,* **-gat·ed, -gat·ing.** to irrigate beneath the surface of the ground, as with water passing through a system of underground pipes or transmitted through the subsoil from ditches, etc. [SUB- + IRRIGATE] —**sub′ir·ri·ga′tion,** *n.*

su·bi·to (so͞o′bi tō′; *It.* so͞o′bē tō), *adv.* (as a musical direction) suddenly; abruptly: *subito pianissimo.* [< It < L, abl. sing. neut. of *subitus* sudden, equiv. to *sub-* SUB- + *-i-* (root of *-ire* to go) + *-tus* ptp. suffix]

subj., **1.** subject. **2.** subjective. **3.** subjectively. **4.** subjunctive.

sub·ja·cent (sub jā′sənt), *adj.* **1.** situated or occurring underneath or below; underlying. **2.** forming a basis. **3.** lower than but not directly under something. [< L *subjacent-* (s. of *subjacēns*) underlying (prp. of *subjacēre*), equiv. to *sub-* SUB- + *jac-* lie + *-ent-* -ENT] —**sub·ja′cen·cy,** *n.* —**sub·ja′cent·ly,** *adv.*

sub·ject (*n., adj.* sub′jikt; *v.* səb jekt′), *n.* **1.** that which forms a basic matter of thought, discussion, investigation, etc.: *a subject of conversation.* **2.** a branch of knowledge as a course of study: *He studied four subjects his first year at college.* **3.** a motive, cause, or ground: *a subject for complaint.* **4.** the theme of a sermon, book, story, etc. **5.** the principal melodic motive or phrase in a musical composition, esp. in a fugue. **6.** an object, scene, incident, etc., chosen by an artist for representation, or as represented in art. **7.** one who is under the dominion or rule of a sovereign. **8.** one who owes allegiance to a government and lives under its protection: *four subjects of Sweden.* **9.** such people collectively. **10.** *Gram.* (in English and many other languages) a syntactic unit that functions as one of the two main constituents of a simple sentence, the other being the predicate, and that consists of a noun, noun phrase, or noun substitute which often refers to the one performing the action or being in the state expressed by the predicate, as *He* in *He gave notice.* **11.** one who or that which undergoes or may undergo some action: *As a dissenter, he found himself the subject of the group's animosity.* **12.** a person or thing under the control or influence of another. **13.** a person as an object of medical, surgical, or psychological treatment or experiment. **14.** a cadaver used for dissection. **15.** *Logic.* that term of a proposition concerning which the predicate is affirmed or denied. **16.** *Philos.* **a.** that which thinks, feels, perceives, intends, etc., as contrasted with the objects of thought, feeling, etc. **b.** the self or ego. **17.** *Metaphysics.* that in which qualities or attributes inhere; substance. —*adj.* **18.** being under domination, control, or influence (often fol. by *to*). **19.** being under dominion, rule, or authority, as of a sovereign, state, or some governing power; owing allegiance or obedience (often fol. by *to*). **20.** open or exposed (usually fol. by *to*): *subject to ridicule.* **21.** being dependent or conditional upon something (usually fol. by *to*): *His consent is subject to your approval.* **22.** being under the necessity of undergoing something (usually fol. by *to*): *All men are subject to death.* **23.** liable; prone (usually fol. by *to*): *subject to headaches.* —*v.t.* **24.** to bring under domination, control, or influence (usually fol. by *to*). **25.** to bring under dominion, rule, or authority, as of a conqueror or a governing power (usually fol. by *to*). **26.** to cause to undergo the action of something specified; expose (usually fol. by *to*): *to subject metal to intense heat.* **27.** to make liable or vulnerable; lay open; expose (usually fol. by *to*): *to subject oneself to ridicule.* **28.** *Obs.* to place beneath something; make subjacent. [< L *subject(us)* thrown under (ptp. of *subicere*), hence as n. *subjectus* (masc.), person of inferior status, *subjectum* (neut.), basis; equiv. to *sub-* SUB- + *jec-* throw + *-tus* ptp. suffix; r. ME *suget* < OF] —**sub·ject′a·bil′i·ty,** *n.* —**sub·ject′a·ble,** *adj.* —**sub·ject′ed·ly,** *adv.* —**sub·ject′ed·ness,** *n.* —**sub′ject·less,** *adj.* —**sub′ject·like′,** *adj.*

—**Syn. 1.** SUBJECT, THEME, TOPIC are often interchangeable to express the material being considered in a speech or written composition. SUBJECT is a broad word for whatever is treated of in writing, speech, art, etc.: *the subject for discussion.* THEME and TOPIC are usually narrower and apply to some limited or specific part of a general subject. A THEME is often the underlying conception of a discourse or composition, perhaps not put into words but easily recognizable: *The theme of a need for reform runs throughout his work.* A TOPIC is the statement of what is to be treated in a section of a composition: *The topic is treated fully in this section.* **3.** reason, rationale. **18.** subordinate, subservient. **21.** contingent.

sub′ject cat′alog, *Library Science.* a catalog having entries listed by subject only.

sub·jec·ti·fy (səb jek′tə fī′), *v.t.,* **-fied, -fy·ing. 1.** to make subjective. **2.** to identify with (a subject) or interpret subjectively. Cf. **objectify.** [SUBJECT + -IFY] —**sub·jec′ti·fi·ca′tion,** *n.*

sub·jec·tion (səb jek′shən), *n.* **1.** the act of subjecting. **2.** the state or fact of being subjected. [ME < L *subjectiōn-* (s. of *subjectiō*) a throwing under, equiv. to *subject-* (see SUBJECT) + *-iōn-* -ION] —**sub·jec′tion·al,** *adj.*

sub·jec·tive (səb jek′tiv), *adj.* **1.** existing in the mind; belonging to the thinking subject rather than to the object of thought (opposed to *objective*). **2.** pertaining to or characteristic of an individual; personal; individual: *a subjective evaluation.* **3.** placing excessive emphasis on one's own moods, attitudes, opinions, etc.; unduly egocentric. **4.** *Philos.* relating to or of the nature of an object as it is known in the mind as distinct from a thing in itself. **5.** relating to properties or specific conditions of the mind as distinguished from general or universal experience. **6.** pertaining to the subject or substance in which attributes inhere; essential. **7.** *Gram.* **a.** pertaining to or constituting the subject of a sentence. **b.** (in English and certain other languages) noting a case specialized for that use, as *He* in *He hit the ball.* **c.** similar to such a case in meaning. Cf. **nominative. 8.** *Obs.* characteristic of a political subject; submissive. [< LL *subjectīv(us)* < L *subject(um)* (neut. of *subjectus;* see SUBJECT) + *-īvus* -IVE] —**sub·jec′tive·ly,** *adv.* —**sub·jec·tiv·i·ty** (sub′jek tiv′i tē), **sub·jec′tive·ness,** *n.*

—**Syn. 1.** mental. **6.** substantial, inherent.

subjec′tive ide′alism, *Philos.* a form of idealism asserting that all experience is of ideas created or distorted by the mind of the observer. Cf. **objective idealism.** —**subjec′tive ide′alist.**

subjec′tive spir′it, *Hegelianism.* spirit, insofar as it falls short of the attainments of objective spirit.

sub·jec·tiv·ism (səb jek′tə viz′əm), *n.* **1.** *Epistemology.* the doctrine that all knowledge is limited to experiences by the self, and that transcendent knowledge is impossible. **2.** *Ethics.* **a.** the theory that certain states of thought or feeling are the highest good. **b.** the doctrine that the good and the right can be distinguished and judged only by individual feeling. [SUBJECTIVE + -ISM] —**sub·jec′tiv·ist,** *n.* —**sub·jec′ti·vis′tic,** *adj.* —**sub·jec′ti·vis′ti·cal·ly,** *adv.*

sub′ject mat′ter, 1. the substance of a discussion, book, writing, etc., as distinguished from its form or style. **2.** the matter which is subject to some action. **3.** the matter out of which a thing is formed.

sub·join (səb join′), *v.t.* **1.** to add at the end, as of something said or written; append. **2.** to place in sequence or juxtaposition to something else. [< MF *subjoin(dre).* See SUB-, JOIN]

sub·join·der (səb join′dər), *n.* something subjoined, as an additional comment. [SUB- + *-joinder,* as in *rejoinder*]

sub ju·di·ce (sub jo͞o′di sē′; *Lat.* sub yo͞o′di ke′), before a judge or court; awaiting judicial determination. [< L]

sub·ju·gate (sub′jə gāt′), *v.t.,* **-gat·ed, -gat·ing. 1.** to bring under complete control or subjection; conquer; master. **2.** to make submissive or subservient; enslave. [< LL *subjugāt(us)* (ptp. of *subjugāre*), equiv. to *sub-* SUB- + *jug(um)* yoke + *-ātus* -ATE¹] —**sub·ju·ga·ble** (sub′jə gə bəl), *adj.* —**sub′ju·ga′tion,** *n.* —**sub′ju·ga′tor,** *n.*

—**Syn. 1, 2.** overcome, vanquish, reduce, overpower.

sub·junc·tion (səb jungk′shən), *n.* **1.** the act of subjoining. **2.** the state of being subjoined. **3.** something subjoined. [< LL *subjunctiōn-* (s. of *subjunctiō*) a subjoining. See SUB-, JUNCTION]

sub·junc·tive (səb jungk′tiv), *Gram.* —*adj.* **1.** (in English and certain other languages) noting or pertaining to a mood or mode of the verb that may be used for subjective, doubtful, hypothetical, or grammatically subordinate statements or questions, as the mood of *be* in *if this be treason.* Cf. **imperative** (def. 3), **indicative** (def. 2). —*n.* **2.** the subjunctive mood or mode. **3.** a verb in the subjunctive mood or form. [< LL *subjunctīv(us),* equiv. to *subjunct(us)* (ptp. of *subjungere* to subjoin), equiv. to *sub-* SUB- + *junc-* (< *jung-* join) + *-tus* ptp. suffix + *-īvus* -IVE] —**sub·junc′tive·ly,** *adv.*

—**Usage.** Speakers of standard English usually use the subjunctive in contrary to fact and other subordinate clauses where it applies, as *were* in *If I were king . . .,* and *I wish he were here.* Although the subjunctive seems to be disappearing from the speech of many, its proper use still marks the educated speaker.

sub·king·dom (sub king′dəm, sub′king′-), *n.* *Biol.* a category of related phyla within a kingdom. [SUB- + KINGDOM]

sub·la·bi·al (sub lā′bē əl), *adj.* situated below the lip or labium. [SUB- + LABIAL] —**sub·la′bi·al·ly,** *adv.*

sub·lap·sar·i·an·ism (sub′lap sâr′ē ə niz′əm), *n.* *Theol.* infralapsarianism. [< NL *sublapsāri(us)* (< L *sub-* SUB- + *laps(us)* a fall + *-ārius* -ARY) + -AN + -ISM] —**sub′lap·sar′i·an,** *adj., n.*

sub·lat·tice (sub′lat′is), *n.* *Math.* a set of elements of a lattice, in which each subset of two elements has a least upper bound and a greatest lower bound contained in the given set. [SUB- + LATTICE]

sub·lease (*n.* sub′lēs′; *v.* sub lēs′), *n., v.,* **-leased, -leas·ing.** —*n.* **1.** a lease granted by one who is himself a lessee of a property, as an apartment. —*v.t.* **2.** to grant a sublease of. **3.** to take or hold a sublease of. [SUB- + LEASE] —**sub·les·see** (sub′le sē′), *n.* —**sub·les·sor** (sub les′ôr, sub′le sôr′), *n.*

sub·let (*v.* sub let′; *n.* sub′let′, sub let′), *v.,* **-let, -let·ting,** *n.* —*v.t.* **1.** to sublease. **2.** to let under a subcontract: *to sublet work.* —*n.* **3.** a sublease. [SUB- + LET¹]

sub·le·thal (sub lē′thəl), *adj.* almost lethal or fatal: *a sublethal dose of poison.* [SUB- + LETHAL]

sub·lev·el (sub′lev′əl), *n.* *Mining.* a drift, dug through ore, into which overlying material, esp. from an upper layer of ore, is caved.

sub·lieu·ten·ant (sub′lo͞o ten′ənt), *n.* **1.** a subordinate lieutenant: not used in U.S. Armed Forces. **2.** *Brit.* a navy officer ranking next below a lieutenant. [SUB- + LIEUTENANT] —**sub′lieu·ten′an·cy,** *n.*

sub·li·mate (*v.* sub′lə māt′; *n., adj.* sub′lə mit, -māt′), *v.,* **-mat·ed, -mat·ing,** *n., adj.* —*v.t.* **1.** *Psychol.* to divert the energy of (a sexual or other biological impulse) from its immediate goal to one of a higher social, moral, or aesthetic nature or use. **2.** *Chem.* **a.** to sublime (a solid substance); extract by this process. **b.** to refine or purify (a substance). **3.** to make nobler or purer: *To read about great men sublimates ambition.* —*v.i.* **4.** to become sublimated; undergo sublimation. —*n.* **5.** *Chem.* **a.** the crystals, deposit, or material obtained when a substance is sublimated. **b.** See **mercuric chloride.** —*adj.* **6.** purified or exalted; sub-

sub·gla′brous, *adj.*
sub·gle′noid, *adj.*
sub·glo′boid, *adj.*
sub·glo′bose, *adj.;* **-ly,** *adv.*
sub′glo·bos′i·ty, *n.*
sub·glo′bous, *adj.*
sub·glob′u·lar, *adj.;* **-ly,** *adv.*
sub′glob·u·lar′i·ty, *n.*
sub·glos′sal, *adj.*
sub·glot′tal, *adj.;* **-ly,** *adv.*
sub·glot′tic, *adj.*
sub′glu·ma′ceous, *adj.*
sub′god′, *n.*
sub·gov′ern·ess, *n.*
sub·gov′er·nor, *n.*
sub·gov′er·nor·ship′, *n.*
sub·gran′u·lar, *adj.;* **-ly,** *adv.*
sub′gran·u·lar′i·ty, *n.*
sub′grin′, *n.*
sub·gu′lar, *adj.*
sub·gyre′, *n.*
sub·gy′rus, *n., pl.* **-gy·ri.**
sub′hall′, *n.*
sub·hatch′er·y, *n., pl.* **-er·ies.**
sub·head′quar′ters, *n.*
sub·head′wait′er, *n.*
sub·health′, *n.*
sub′hem·i·spher′ic, *adj.*
sub′hem·i·spher′i·cal, *adj.;* **-ly,** *adv.*
sub′he·pat′ic, *adj.*
sub′herd′, *n.*
sub·he′ro, *n., pl.* **-roes.**
sub′hex·ag′o·nal, *adj.*
sub′-Hi·ma·la′yan, *adj.*
sub·hir′sute, *adj.;* **-ness,** *n.*
sub·hooked′, *adj.*
sub′hor·i·zon′tal, *adj.;* **-ly,** *adv.;* **-ness,** *n.*
sub′house′, *n.*
sub·hu′mer·al, *adj.*
sub·hu′mid, *adj.*
sub·hy′a·lin, *adj.*
sub·hy′a·line, *adj.*
sub·hy′a·loid′, *adj.*
sub′hy·me′ni·al, *adj.*
sub′hy·me′ni·um, *n.*
sub·hy′oid, *adj.*
sub′hy·oid′e·an, *adj.*
sub′hy·poth′e·sis, *n., pl.* **-ses.**
sub′hys·te′ri·a, *n.*
sub′ic·ter′ic, *adj.*
sub′ic·ter′i·cal, *adj.*
sub′i·de′a, *n.*
sub′i·de′al, *n.*
sub·il′i·um, *n., pl.* **-il·i·a.**
sub·im′bri·cate, *adj.;* **-ly,** *adv.*
sub·im′bri·cat′ed, *adj.*
sub·im′bri·ca′tive, *adj.*
sub′im·posed′, *adj.*
sub′im·pressed′, *adj.*
sub′in·com·plete′, *adj.*
sub′in·fec′tion, *n.*
sub′in·fer′, *v.,* **-ferred, -fer·ring.**
sub′in·fe′ri·or, *adj.*
sub′in·flam·ma′tion, *n.*
sub′in·flam′ma·to′ry, *adj.*
sub′in·form′, *v.t.*
sub′in·i′tial, *v.t.*
sub′in·sert′, *v.t.*
sub′in·ser′tion, *n.*
sub′in·spec′tor, *n.*
sub′in·spec′tor·ship′, *n.*
sub′in·teg′u·men′tal, *adj.*
sub′in·teg′u·men′ta·ry, *adj.*
sub′in·ten′tion, *n.*
sub′in·ten′tion·al, *adj.;* **-ly,** *adv.*
sub′in·ter·ces′sor, *n.*
sub′in·ter′nal, *adj.;* **-ly,** *adv.*
sub′in·tes′ti·nal, *adj.*
sub·in′ti·mal, *adj.*
sub′in·tro·duce′, *v.t.,* **-duced, -duc·ing.**
sub′in·tro·duc′tion, *n.*
sub′in·tro·duc′tive, *adj.*
sub′in·tro·duc′to·ry, *adj.*
sub·in′vo·lute′, *adj.*
sub·in′vo·lut′ed, *adj.*
sub·i′o·dide′, *n.*
sub·i′tem, *n.*
sub′jack′, *n.*
sub′joint′, *n.*
sub′judge′, *n.*
sub′judge′ship′, *n.*
sub′ju·di′cial, *adj.;* **-ly,** *adv.*
sub′ju·di′ci·ar′y, *adj., n., pl.* **-ar·ies.**
sub·ju′gal, *adj.*
sub·jug′u·lar, *adj.*
sub·jun′ior, *adj.*
sub′king′, *n.*
sub′la·cin′i·ate, *adj.*
sub′la·cu′nose, *adj.*
sub′la·cus′trine, *adj.*
sub·la′nate, *adj.*
sub·lan′ce·o·late′, *adj.*
sub′la·ryn′gal, *adj.*
sub′la·ryn′ge·al, *adj.;* **-ly,** *adv.*
sub·lead′er, *n.*
sub·lec′tur·er, *n.*
sub′leg·is·la′tion, *n.*
sub·leg′is·la′ture, *n.*
sub′len·tic′u·lar, *adj.*
sub′len·tic′u·late, *adj.*
sub·li·brar′i·an, *n.*
sub′li·brar′i·an·ship′, *n.*
sub·li′cense, *n., v.t.,* **-censed, -cens·ing.**
sub′lid′, *n.*
sub·light′ed, *adj.*

limated. [< L *sublīmāt(us)* (ptp. of *sublīmāre* to elevate), equiv. to *sublīm(is)* SUBLIME -*ātus* -ATE[1]] —**sub·li·ma·ble** (sub′lə mə bəl), *adj.* —**sub′li·ma·ble·ness,** *n.* —**sub′li·ma′tion,** *n.* —**sub′li·ma′tion·al,** *adj.*

sub·lime (sə blīm′), *adj., n., v.,* **-limed, -lim·ing.** —*adj.* **1.** elevated or lofty in thought, language, etc.: *Paradise Lost is sublime poetry.* **2.** impressing the mind with a sense of grandeur or power; inspiring awe, veneration, etc.: *Switzerland has sublime scenery.* **3.** supreme or outstanding: *a sublime dinner.* **4.** *Archaic.* **a.** of lofty bearing. **b.** haughty. **5.** *Archaic.* raised high; high up. —*n.* **6.** that which is sublime: *the sublime in art.* **7.** the greatest degree or example (usually fol. by *of*): *Your answer is the sublime of stupidity.* —*v.t.* **8.** to make higher, nobler, or purer. **9.** *Chem.* **a.** to convert (a solid substance) by heat into a vapor, which on cooling condenses again to solid form, without apparent liquefaction. **b.** to cause to be given off by this or some analogous process. —*v.i.* **10.** *Chem.* to volatilize from the solid state to a gas, and then condense again as a solid without passing through the liquid state. [< L *sublīm(is)* high, equiv. to *sub-* SUB- + *-līm-* lintel + *-is* adj. suffix] —**sub·lime′ly,** *adv.* —**sub·lime′ness,** *n.* —**sub·lim′er,** *n.*
—**Syn. 1.** exalted, noble. **2.** magnificent, superb, august, grand, gorgeous, resplendent, imposing, majestic.

Sublime′ Porte′ (pōrt, pôrt), official name of **Porte.**

sub·lim·i·nal (sub lim′ə nᵊl, -lī′mə-), *adj. Psychol.* existing or operating below the threshold of consciousness; being or employing stimuli insufficiently intense to produce a discrete sensation but often being or designed to be intense enough to influence the mental processes or the behavior of the individual: *a subliminal stimulus; subliminal advertising.* [SUB- + L *līmin-* (s. of *līmen*) threshold + -AL[1]] —**sub·lim′i·nal·ly,** *adv.*

sub·lim·i·ty (sə blim′i tē), *n., pl.* **-ties** for 2. **1.** the state or quality of being sublime. **2.** a sublime person or thing. [< L *sublīmitāt-* (s. of *sublīmitās*) height, equiv. to *sublīm(is)* SUBLIME + *-itāt-* -ITY]

sub·lin·gual (sub ling′gwəl), *Anat.* —*adj.* **1.** situated under the tongue, or on the underside of the tongue. —*n.* **2.** a sublingual gland, artery, or the like. [< NL *sublinguāl(is)* < L *sub-* SUB- + *linguālis* LINGUAL]

sub·lit·er·a·ture (sub′lit′ər ə chər, -chŏŏr′, -li′trə-), *n.* **1.** writing below the standards of literature as an art form. **2.** a report or similar material written for immediate use and reproduced in an impermanent form. [SUB- + LITERATURE]

sub·lu·nar·y (sub′lōō ner′ē, sub lōō′nə rē), *adj.* **1.** situated beneath the moon or between the earth and the moon. **2.** characteristic of or pertaining to the earth; terrestrial. **3.** mundane or worldly: *fleeting, sublunary pleasure.* Also, **sub·lu·nar** (sub lōō′nər). [< LL *sublūnār(is)* < L *sub-* SUB- + *lūnāris* LUNAR]

sub·lux·a·tion (sub′luk sā′shən), *n. Med.* a partial dislocation, as of a joint; sprain. [< NL *subluxātiō* < L < *sub-* SUB- + *luxātiō* LUXATION]

sub·ma·chine′ gun′ (sub′mə shēn′), a lightweight automatic or semiautomatic gun, fired from the shoulder or hip. [SUB- + MACHINE GUN]

sub·man (sub′man′), *n., pl.* **-men.** a man of very low mental or physical capacity. [SUB- + MAN[1]]

sub·mar·gin·al (sub mär′jə nᵊl), *adj.* **1.** *Biol.* near the margin. **2.** below the margin. **3.** not worth cultivating, as land; less than satisfactory; unproductive. [SUB- + MARGINAL] —**sub·mar′gin·al·ly,** *adv.*

sub·ma·rine (*n.* sub′mə rēn′, sub′mə rēn′; *adj., v.* sub′mə rēn′), *n., adj., v.,* **-rined, -rin·ing.** —*n.* **1.** a ship that can be submerged and navigated under water, usually built for warfare and armed with torpedoes or guided missiles. **2.** something situated or living under the surface of the sea, as a plant or animal. **3.** See **hero sandwich.** —*adj.* **4.** situated, occurring, operating, or living under the surface of the sea. **5.** of, pertaining to, or carried on by submarine ships: *submarine warfare.* —*v.i.* **6.** *Slang.* to participate in the operating of a submarine. [SUB- + MARINE]

sub′marine chas′er, a small patrol vessel, between 100 and 200 feet long, designed for military operations against submarines. Also called **subchaser.**

sub·ma·rin·er (sub′mə rē′nər; səb mar′ə nər), *n.* a member of the crew of a submarine. [SUBMARINE + -ER[1]]

sub′marine sen′try, *Naut.* a kitelike object streamed beneath a vessel at a fixed depth, having a mechanism that sends it to the surface if it meets an obstruction.

sub·ma·trix (sub mā′triks), *n., pl.* **-tri·ces** (-tri sēz′), **-trix·es.** *Math.* a set of certain rows and columns of a given matrix. [SUB- + MATRIX]

sub·max·il·la (sub′mak sil′ə), *n., pl.* **-max·il·lae** (-mak sil′ē). *Anat., Zool.* the lower jaw or lower jawbone. [SUB- + MAXILLA]

sub·max·il·lar·y (sub mak′sə ler′ē, sub′mak sil′ə-rē), *adj.* of or pertaining to the lower jaw or lower jawbone. [SUB- + MAXILLARY]

submax′illary gland′, *Anat.* one of a pair of salivary glands: one gland is located on each side of and beneath the lower jaw.

sub·me·di·ant (sub mē′dē ənt), *n. Music.* the sixth tone of a scale, being midway between the subdominant and the upper tonic. Also called **superdominant.** [SUB- + MEDIANT]

sub·merge (səb mûrj′), *v.,* **-merged, -merg·ing.** —*v.t.* **1.** to put or sink below the surface of water or any other enveloping medium. **2.** to cover or overflow with water; immerse. —*v.i.* **3.** to sink or plunge under water, or beneath the surface of any enveloping medium. [< L *submerge(re),* equiv. to *sub-* SUB- + *mergere* to MERGE] —**sub·mer′gence,** *n.*
—**Syn. 1.** submerse, sink.

sub·merged (səb mûrjd′), *adj.* **1.** under the surface of water or any other enveloping medium. **2.** hidden or unknown: *There are many submerged facts which could have a bearing on the case.* **3.** poverty-stricken: *a program to aid the submerged socioeconomic groups.*

sub·mer·gi·ble (səb mûr′jə bəl), *adj.* submersible. [SUBMERGE + -IBLE] —**sub·mer′gi·bil′i·ty,** *n.*

sub·merse (səb mûrs′), *v.t.,* **-mersed, -mers·ing.** to submerge. [< L *submers(us)* (ptp. of *submergere* to SUBMERGE), equiv. to *sub-* SUB- + *merg-* dip + *-tus* ptp. suffix] —**sub·mer·sion** (səb mûr′zhən, -shən), *n.*

sub·mersed (səb mûrst′), *adj.* **1.** submerged. **2.** *Bot.* growing under water. [SUBMERSE + -ED[2]]

sub·mers·i·ble (səb mûr′sə bəl), *adj.* **1.** capable of being submersed. **2.** capable of functioning while submersed: *a submersible pump.* —*n.* **3.** a ship capable of submerging and operating under water; submarine. [SUBMERSE + -IBLE] —**sub·mers′i·bil′i·ty,** *n.*

sub·me·tal·lic (sub′mə tal′ik), *adj.* somewhat or imperfectly metallic. [SUB- + METALLIC]

sub·mi·cro·scop·ic (sub′mī krə skop′ik), *adj.* smaller than can be seen through a microscope. Also, **sub′mi·cro·scop′i·cal.** [SUB- + MICROSCOPIC] —**sub′mi·cro·scop′i·cal·ly,** *adv.*

sub·min·i·a·ture (sub min′ē ə chər), *n.* **1.** See **subminiature camera.** —*adj.* **2.** noting or pertaining to subminiature cameras, their accessories, and systems of photography. **3.** smaller than miniature, as certain electronic components. [SUB- + MINIATURE]

submin′iature cam′era, a very small, palm-sized still camera for taking photographs on 16-millimeter or similar film. Also called **subminiature.**

sub·min·i·a·tur·ize (sub min′ē ə chə rīz′), *v.t.,* **-ized, -iz·ing.** to design or manufacture (equipment, esp. electronic equipment) of a greatly reduced scale. [SUB- + MINIATURIZE] —**sub·min′i·a·tur·i·za′tion,** *n.*

sub·miss (səb mis′), *adj. Archaic.* submissive. [< L *submiss(us)* (ptp. of *submittere*), equiv. to *sub-* SUB- + *mitt-* send + *-tus* ptp. suffix]

sub·mis·sion (səb mish′ən), *n.* **1.** the act or an instance of submitting. **2.** the condition of having submitted. **3.** submissive conduct or attitude. **4.** something which is submitted, as an application. **5.** *Law.* an agreement between parties involved in a dispute, to abide by the decision of an arbitrator or arbitrators. [ME < L *submissiōn-* (s. of *submissiō*) a letting down. See SUB-, MISSION]

sub·mis·sive (səb mis′iv), *adj.* **1.** inclined or ready to submit; unresistingly or humbly obedient: *submissive servants.* **2.** marked by or indicating submission: *a submissive reply.* [SUBMISS + -IVE] —**sub·mis′sive·ly,** *adv.* —**sub·mis′sive·ness,** *n.*
—**Syn. 1.** tractable, compliant, pliant, amenable. **2.** passive, resigned, patient, docile, tame, subdued.

sub·mit (səb mit′), *v.,* **-mit·ted, -mit·ting.** —*v.t.* **1.** to yield in surrender, compliance, or obedience. **2.** to subject (esp. oneself) to imposed conditions, treatment, etc. **3.** to refer or present for the approval or decision of another or others: *to submit a plan; to submit an application.* **4.** to state or urge with deference; suggest or propose (usually fol. by a clause): *I submit that full proof should be required.* —*v.i.* **5.** to yield in surrender, compliance or obedience: *to submit to a conqueror.* **6.** to allow oneself to be subjected to something imposed or to be undergone: *to submit to medical treatment.* **7.** to defer to another's judgment, opinion, decision, etc.: *I submit to your superior judgment.* [< L *submitt(ere)* (to) lower, reduce, yield, equiv. to *sub-* SUB- + *mittere* to send] —**sub·mit′ta·ble, sub·mis·si·ble** (səb mis′ə bel), *adj.* —**sub·mit′tal,** *n.* —**sub·mit′ter,** *n.* —**sub·mit′ting·ly,** *adv.*
—**Syn. 1.** comply, bow, obey, agree, resign. See **yield.**
—**Ant. 1.** fight.

sub·mon·tane (sub mon′tān), *adj.* **1.** under or beneath a mountain or mountains. **2.** at or near the foot of mountains. **3.** pertaining or belonging to the lower slopes of mountains. [< LL *submontān(us),* equiv. to *sub-* SUB- + *mont-* (s. of *mōns*) mountain + *-ānus* -ANE] —**sub·mon′tane·ly,** *adv.*

sub·mul·ti·ple (sub mul′tə pəl), *n.* **1.** a number which is contained by another number an integral number of times without a remainder: *The number 3 is a submultiple of 12.* —*adj.* **2.** pertaining to or noting a quantity that is a submultiple. [SUB- + MULTIPLE]

sub·na·sal (sub nā′zəl), *adj. Anat.* situated beneath the nose. [SUB- + NASAL]

sub·net (sub′net′), *n. Math.* the abstraction, in topology, of a subsequence. [SUB- + NET[2]]

sub·ni·trate (sub nī′trāt), *n. Chem.* a basic salt of nitric acid. [SUB- + NITRATE] —**sub·ni′trat·ed,** *adj.*

sub·nor·mal (sub nôr′məl), *adj.* **1.** below the normal; less than or inferior to the normal: *a subnormal amount of rain.* **2.** being less than average in any psychological trait, as intelligence, personality, or emotional adjustment. —*n.* **3.** a subnormal person. **4.** *Geom.* that part of the *x*-axis of a curve cut off between the ordinate and a normal. [SUB- + NORMAL] —**sub′nor·mal′i·ty,** *n.*

sub·oc·cip·i·tal (sub′ok sip′i tᵊl), *adj.* situated below the occipital bone or the occipital lobe of the brain. [< NL *suboccipitāl(is);* see SUB-, OCCIPITAL]

sub·o·ce·an·ic (sub′ō shē an′ik), *adj.* **1.** occurring or existing below the floor of the ocean: *suboceanic oil.* **2.** of, pertaining to, or on the floor of the ocean: *suboceanic plants.* [SUB- + OCEANIC]

sub·or·bit·al (sub ôr′bi tᵊl), *adj.* **1.** not in orbit; not achieving an altitude and velocity resulting in a ballistic trajectory circling the earth at least once. **2.** *Anat.* situated below the orbit of the eye. [SUB- + ORBITAL]

sub·or·der (sub′ôr′dər), *n. Biol.* a category of related families within an order. [SUB- + ORDER]

sub·or·di·nal (sub ôr′dᵊnᵊl), *adj.* of, pertaining to, or ranked as a suborder. [SUB- + ORDINAL[1]]

sub·or·di·nar·y (sub ôr′dᵊner′ē), *n., pl.* **-nar·ies.** *Heraldry.* an ordinary other than an honorable ordinary, as a quarter, canton, inescutcheon, bordure, etc. Also called **secondary ordinary, subordinate ordinary.** [SUB- + ORDINARY]

sub·or·di·nate (*adj., n.* sə bôr′dᵊnit; *v.* sə bôr′dᵊnāt′), *adj., n., v.,* **-nat·ed, -nat·ing.** —*adj.* **1.** placed in or belonging to a lower order or rank. **2.** of less importance; secondary. **3.** subject to or under the authority of a superior. **4.** subservient; servile. **5.** subject; dependent. **6.** *Gram.* **a.** acting as a modifier, as *when I finished* which is subordinate to *They were glad* in *They were glad when I finished.* **b.** noting or pertaining to a subordinating conjunction. **7.** *Obs.* submissive. —*n.* **8.** a subordinate person or thing. —*v.t.* **9.** to place in a lower order or rank. **10.** to make secondary (usually fol. by *to*): *to subordinate work to pleasure.* **11.** to make subject, subservient, or dependent (usually fol. by *to*): *to subordinate passion to reason.* [< ML *subordināt(us)* (ptp. of *subordināre*) < L *sub-* SUB- + *ordin-* (s. of *ordō*) rank, order + *-ātus* -ATE[1]] —**sub·or′di·na′tion,** *n.* —**sub·or·di·na·tive** (sə bôr′dᵊnā′tiv, -bôr′dᵊnə-), *adj.*
—**Syn. 2.** ancillary. **8.** inferior, subject. **9.** subject, reduce. —**Ant. 2.** superior; primary.

subor′dinate clause′, *Gram.* a clause that modifies the principal clause, as "*when he arrived*" in the sentence "*I was there when he arrived.*" Cf. **main clause.**

subor′dinate conjunc′tion, *Gram.* a subordinating conjunction.

subor′dinate or′dinary, *Heraldry.* sub-ordinary.

subor′dinating conjunc′tion, *Gram.* a conjunction introducing a subordinate clause, as *when* in *They were glad when I finished.* Cf. **coordinating conjunction.** [SUBORDINATE + -ING[2]]

sub·or·di·na·tion·ism (sə bôr′dᵊnā′shə niz′əm), *n. Theol.* the doctrine that the first person of the Holy Trinity is superior to the second, and the second superior to the third. [SUBORDINATION + -ISM] —**sub·or′di·na′tion·ist,** *n.*

sub·orn (sə bôrn′), *v.t.* **1.** to bribe or induce (someone) unlawfully or secretly to perform some misdeed or to commit a crime. **2.** *Law.* to induce (a person, esp. a witness) to give false testimony. [< L *suborn(āre)* (to) instigate secretly, equiv. to *sub-* SUB- + *ornāre* to equip; see ADORN] —**sub·or·na·tion** (sub′ôr nā′shən), *n.* —**sub·or·na·tive** (sə bôr′nə tiv), *adj.* —**sub·orn′er,** *n.*

suborna′tion of per′jury, *Crim. Law.* the offense of bribing or otherwise persuading another to commit perjury.

Su·bo·ti·ca (*Serbo-Croatian.* sōō′bô ti tsä), *n.* a city in N Serbia in N Yugoslavia. 88,787. Hungarian, **Szabadka.**

sub·ox·ide (sub ok′sīd, -sid), *n. Chem.* the oxide of an element that contains the smallest proportion of oxygen. [SUB- + OXIDE]

sub·lin′e·ar, *adj.*
sub·lit′to·ral, *adj.*
sub·lob′u·lar, *adj.*
sub·long′, *adj.*
sub·lor′al, *adj.*
sub′lot, *n.*
sub·lum′bar, *adj.*
sub·lu′nate, *adj.*
sub·lu′nat·ed, *adj.*
sub·lus′trous, *adj.;* **-ly,** *adv.;* **-ness,** *n.*
sub′maid′, *n.*
sub·mam′ma·ry, *adj.*
sub·man′ag·er, *n.*
sub·man′ag·er·ship′, *n.*
sub·ma′ni·a, *n.*
sub′ma·ni′a·cal, *adj.;* **-ly,** *adv.*
sub′ma·nic, *adj.*
sub·man′or, *n.*
sub·mar′shal, *n.*
sub·mas′ter, *n.*
sub·max′i·mal, *adj.*
sub·mean′ing, *n.*
sub·me′di·al, *adj.;* **-ly,** *adv.*
sub·me′di·an, *adj.*
sub′me·di·a′tion, *n.*
sub′me·di·o′cre, *adj.*
sub·meet′ing, *n.*
sub·mem′ber, *n.*
sub·mem′bra·na′ceous, *adj.*
sub·mem′bra·nous, *adj.*
sub′me·nin′ge·al, *adj.*
sub·men′tal, *adj.*
sub′met·a·phor′ic, *adj.*
sub′met·a·phor′i·cal, *adj.;* **-ly,** *adv.*
sub·mil′i·ar′y, *adj.*
sub′mind′, *n.*
sub·min′i·mal, *adj.*
sub·min′is·trant, *adj.*
sub′mo·lec′u·lar, *adj.*
sub·mol′e·cule′, *n.*
sub·mort′gage, *n.*
sub·moun′tain, *adj.*
sub·mu′cous, *adj.*
sub·mu′cro·nate, *adj.*
sub·mu′cro·nat′ed, *adj.*
sub·mun′dane, *adj.*
sub·mu′ri·ate′, *n.*
sub·mus′cu·lar, *adj.;* **-ly,** *adv.*
sub·na′cre·ous, *adj.*
sub′nar·cot′ic, *adj.*
sub·nat′u·ral, *adj.;* **-ly,** *adv.;* **-ness,** *n.*
sub·neu′ral, *adj.*
sub·nod′u·lose′, *adj.*
sub·nod′u·lous, *adj.*
sub′no·ta′tion, *n.*
sub′no·ta′tion·al, *adj.*
sub′note′, *n.*
sub′no·to·chord′al, *adj.*
sub·nu′cle·us, *n., pl.* **-cle·i, -cle·us·es.**
sub·nude′, *adj.*
sub·num′ber, *n.*
sub′nu·tri′tious, *adj.;* **-ly,** *adv.;* **-ness,** *n.*
sub′ob·lique′, *adj.;* **-ly,** *adv.;* **-ness,** *n.*
sub′ob·scure′, *adj.;* **-ly,** *adv.;* **-ness,** *n.*
sub·ob′so·lete′, *adj.;* **-ly,** *adv.;* **-ness,** *n.*
sub′ob·tuse′, *adj.;* **-ly,** *adv.;* **-ness,** *n.*
sub·o′cean, *adj.*
sub·oc′u·lar, *adj.;* **-ly,** *adv.*
sub′oe·soph′a·ge′al, *adj.*
sub·of′fice, *n.*
sub·of′fi·cer, *n.*
sub′of·fi′cial, *n., adj.;* **-ly,** *adv.*
sub·ol′ive, *adj.*
sub′o·paque′, *adj.;* **-ly,** *adv.;* **-ness,** *n.*
sub·op′po·site, *adj.;* **-ly,** *adv.;* **-ness,** *n.*
sub·op′tic, *adj.*
sub·op′ti·cal, *adj.;* **-ly,** *adv.*
sub·op′ti·mum, *n., pl.* **-ma, -mums,** *adj.*
sub·o′ral, *adj.*
sub′or·bic′u·lar, *adj.;* **-ly,** *adv.*
sub′or·bic′u·lar′i·ty, *n.*
sub′or·bic′u·late, *adj.*
sub′or·bic′u·lat′ed, *adj.*
sub′or·gan′ic, *adj.*
sub′or·gan′i·cal·ly, *adv.*
sub·o′var′i·an, *adj.*
sub·o′vate, *adj.*
sub·o′ver·se·er, *n.*
sub·o′void, *adj.*
sub·pack′age, *n.*
sub′pa·go′da, *n.*
sub·pal′li·al, *adj.*
sub·pal′mate, *adj.*
sub·pal′mat·ed, *adj.*
sub·pan′el, *n.*
sub·par′, *adj.*
sub·par′a·graph′, *n.*
sub·par′al·lel, *adj.*
sub′par·a·lyt′ic, *adj.*
sub′pa·ri′e·tal, *adj.*
sub·par′lia·ment, *n.*
sub′part′, *n.*
sub′par·ti′tion, *n.*
sub′par·ti′tioned, *adj.*
sub′par·ti′tion·ment, *n.*
sub′par′ty, *n., pl.* **-ties.**
sub′pass′, *n.*
sub·pas′tor, *n.*
sub·pas′tor·ship′, *n.*
sub′pa·tel′lar, *adj.*
sub·pa′tron, *n.*
sub·pa′tron·al, *adj.*
sub·pa′tron·ess, *n.*
sub·pat′tern, *n.*
sub·pave′ment, *n.*
sub·pec′ti·nate′, *adj.*
sub·pec′ti·nat′ed, *adj.*
sub′pec·ti·na′tion, *n.*
sub·pec′to·ral, *adj.*
sub′pe·dun′cle, *n.*
sub′pe·dun′cled, *adj.*
sub′pe·dun′cu·lar, *adj.*
sub′pe·dun′cu·late, *adj.*
sub′pe·dun′cu·lat′ed, *adj.*
sub′pel·lu′cid, *adj.;* **-ly,** *adv.;* **-ness,** *n.*
sub·pel·lu·cid′i·ty, *n.*
sub·pel′tate, *adj.;* **-ly,** *adv.*

sub·phy·lum (sub fī′ləm), *n., pl.* **-la** (-lə). *Biol.* a category of related classes within a phylum. [< NL; see SUB-, PHYLUM] —**sub·phy′lar,** *adj.*

sub·pleu·ral (sub plo͝or′əl), *adj.* situated under the pleura. [SUB- + PLEURAL]

sub·plot (sub′plot′), *n.* a secondary plot in a play or other literary work which may highlight the main plot, contrast with it, or be almost unrelated. Cf. **counterplot** (def. 2). [SUB- + PLOT[1]]

sub·poe·na (sə pē′nə, səb-), *n., v.,* **-naed, -na·ing.** *Law.* —*n.* **1.** the usual process for the summoning of witnesses. —*v.t.* **2.** to serve with a subpoena. Also, **sub-pe′na.** [ME < L *sub poenā* under penalty]

sub·po·lar (sub pō′lər), *adj.* **1.** subantarctic. **2.** subarctic. [SUB- + POLAR]

sub·prin·ci·pal (sub prin′sə pəl, sub′prin′-), *n.* **1.** an assistant or deputy principal. **2.** *Carpentry.* an auxiliary rafter or additional supporting member. **3.** *Music.* (in an organ) a subbass of the open diapason class. [SUB- + PRINCIPAL]

sub·pur·lin (sub pûr′lin), *n.* a light structural member for carrying roofing materials, supported by and running at right angles to purlins. [SUB- + PURLIN]

sub·quar·ter (sub′kwôr′tər), *n. Heraldry.* one of the quarterings of a grand quarter. [SUB- + QUARTER]

sub·quar·ter·ly (sub kwôr′tər lē), *adv. Heraldry.* as one of the quarterings of a grand quarter: *a coat of arms borne subquarterly.* [SUB- + QUARTERLY]

sub·rail (sub′rāl′), *n.* (on a staircase with a closed string) a structural member receiving the lower ends of the balusters. Also called **shoe.** [SUB- + RAIL[1]]

sub·ra·tion·al (sub rash′ə nᵊl), *adj.* less than or almost rational. [SUB- + RATIONAL]

sub·re·gion (sub′rē′jən), *n.* a division or subdivision of a region, esp. a division of a zoogeographical region. [SUB- + REGION] —**sub·re′gion·al,** *adj.*

sub·rep·tion (səb rep′shən), *n.* **1.** *Canon Law.* a concealment of the pertinent facts in a petition, as for dispensation or favor, that in certain cases nullifies the grant. Cf. **obreption** (def. 2.). **2.** *Scots Law.* the act of obtaining something, as by escheat or by concealing pertinent facts. Cf. **abreption** (def. 2). **3.** a fallacious representation or an inference from it. [< LL *subreptiōn-* (s. of *subreptiō*) a stealing < L *subrept(us)* (ptp. of *subripere*), equiv. to *sub-* -SUB + *rep-* (var. of *rapseize*) + *-tus* ptp. suffix + *-iōn-* -ION] —**sub·rep·ti·tious** (sub′rep tish′əs), *adj.*

sub·ring (sub′ring′), *n. Math.* a subset of a ring which is a subgroup under addition and which is closed under multiplication. Cf. **ring**[1] (def. 7). [SUB- + RING[1]]

sub·ro·gate (sub′rō gāt′), *v.t.,* **-gat·ed, -gat·ing.** **1.** to put into the place of another; substitute for another. **2.** *Civil Law.* to substitute a claim against one person for a claim against another person, or transfer a security originally imposed on one piece of property to another piece of property. [< L *subrogāt(us)* (ptp. of *subrogāre* to nominate (someone) as a substitute), equiv. to *sub-* SUB- + *rog-* request + *-ātus* -ATE[1]] —**sub′ro·ga′tion,** *n.*

sub ro·sa (sub rō′zə), confidentially; secretly; privately. [< L: lit., under the rose, from the ancient use of the rose at meetings as a symbol of the sworn confidence of the participants]

sub·round (sub round′), *adj.* somewhat round or rounded. [SUB- + ROUND]

sub·rou·tine (sub′ro͞o tēn′), *n. Computer Technol.* a sequence of coded instructions directing a computer to perform a specific operation in the solution of a problem; part of a routine. [SUB- + ROUTINE]

sub·sam·ple (*n.* sub′sam′pəl; *v.* sub sam′pəl), *n., v.,* **-pled, -pling.** —*n.* **1.** a specimen from or a small part of a sample. —*v.t.* **2.** to take a subsample of. [SUB- + SAMPLE]

sub·scap·u·lar (sub skap′yə lər), *Anat.* —*adj.* **1.** situated beneath or on the deep surface of the scapula, as a muscle. —*n.* **2.** a subscapular muscle, artery, etc. [< NL *subscapulār(is),* equiv. to *sub-* SUB- + *scapulāris* SCAPULAR]

sub·scribe (səb skrīb′), *v.,* **-scribed, -scrib·ing.** —*v.t.* **1.** to promise, as by signing an agreement, to give or pay (a sum of money) as a contribution, payment, share, etc.: *He subscribed $6,000 for the new church.* **2.** to give or pay in fulfillment of such a promise. **3.** to express assent or adhesion to (a contract, statement, plan, will, etc.) by or as by signing one's name; attest by or as by signing. **4.** to write or inscribe (something) beneath or at the end of a thing: *to subscribe one's name to a document.* —*v.i.* **5.** to undertake, as by signing an agreement, to give or pay money for some special purpose. **6.** to obtain a subscription to a magazine, newspaper, etc. **7.** to give or pay money as a contribution, payment, etc. **8.** to sign one's name to something. **9.** to assent by or as if by signing one's name. **10.** to give consent or sanction: *I will not subscribe to popular fallacies.* [< L *subscrībe(be),* equiv. to *sub-* SUB- + *scrībere* to write] —**sub·scrib′a·ble,** *adj.* —**sub·scrib′er,** *n.* —**sub·scrib′er·ship′,** *n.*

sub·script (sub′skript), *adj.* **1.** written below (distinguished from *adscript, superscript*). **2.** inferior (def. 8). —*n.* **3.** *Math.* inferior (def. 11). **4.** any character, number, or symbol written next to and slightly below another. [< L *subscrīpt(us)* (ptp. of *subscrībere* to SUBSCRIBE), equiv. to *sub-* SUB- + *scrīp-* (var. of *scrīb-* write) + *-tus* ptp. suffix]

sub·scrip·tion (səb skrip′shən), *n.* **1.** a monetary contribution toward some cause, or a payment for shares, a magazine, etc. **2.** the right to receive a periodical for a sum paid, usually for an agreed number of issues. **3.** *Chiefly Brit.* the dues paid by a member of a club, society, etc. **4.** a fund raised through sums of money subscribed. **5.** a sum subscribed. **6.** the act of subscribing; the signing of one's name, as to a document. **7.** something written beneath or at the end of a thing. **8.** a signature attached to a paper. **9.** assent, agreement, or approval expressed verbally or by signing one's name. **10.** *Eccles.* assent to or acceptance of a body of principles or doctrines, the purpose of which is to establish uniformity. **11.** *Ch. of Eng.* formal acceptance of the Thirty-nine Articles of 1563 and the Book of Common Prayer. [< L *subscrīptiōn-* (s. of *subscrīptiō*) a writing beneath, equiv. to *subscrīpt(us)* (see SUBSCRIPT) + *-iōn-* -ION] —**sub·scrip·tive** (səb skrip′tiv), *adj.* —**sub·scrip′tive·ly,** *adv.*

subscrip′tion book′, a book in which the names of subscribers or contributors are recorded.

subscrip′tion edi′tion, **1.** an edition of one or more volumes for which a number of prospective purchasers place orders, usually in advance of publication. **2.** a specially designed edition offered to subscribers, usually on an installment or deferred payment plan, or on an installment or deferred delivery plan, or both.

subscrip′tion tel′evision, a type of closed-circuit television transmitted through private service lines to those who pay a subscription fee. Also called **pay TV.**

sub·sec·tion (sub sek′shən, sub′sek′-), *n.* a part or division of a section. [SUB- + SECTION]

sub·seg·ment (sub seg′mənt, sub′seg′-), *n.* a part or division of a segment. [SUB- + SEGMENT]

sub·sel·li·um (sub sel′ē əm), *n., pl.* **-sel·li·a** (-sel′ē ə). misericord (def. 3). [< L < *sub-* SUB- + *sell(a)* seat + *-ium* n. suffix]

sub·se·quence[1] (sub′sə kwəns), *n.* **1.** the state or fact of being subsequent. **2.** a subsequent occurrence, event, etc.; sequel. [SUBSEQU(ENT) + -ENCE]

sub·se·quence[2] (sub′sē′kwəns), *n. Math.* a sequence obtained from a given sequence by selecting terms from it and placing them in the order in which they occur in it. [SUB- + SEQUENCE]

sub·se·quent (sub′sə kwənt), *adj.* **1.** occurring or coming later or after: *subsequent events.* **2.** following in order or succession; succeeding: *a subsequent section in a treaty.* [< L *subsequent-* (s. of *subsequēns*) following (prp. of *subsequī*), equiv. to *sub-* SUB- + *sequ-* follow + *-ent-* -ENT] —**sub′se·quent·ly,** *adv.*

sub·se·rous (sub sēr′əs), *adj.* situated or occurring under a serous membrane. [SUB- + SEROUS]

sub·serve (səb sûrv′), *v.t.,* **-served, -serv·ing.** **1.** to be useful or instrumental in promoting (a purpose, action, etc.): *Light exercise subserves digestion.* **2.** *Obs.* to serve as a subordinate. [< L *subserv(īre),* equiv. to *sub-* SUB- + *servīre,* equiv. to *serv(us)* servant, slave + *-īre* inf. suffix]

sub·ser·vi·ent (səb sûr′vē ənt), *adj.* **1.** serving or acting in a subordinate capacity; subordinate. **2.** servile; excessively submissive; obsequious: *subservient persons; subservient conduct.* **3.** useful in promoting a purpose or end. [< L *subservient-* (s. of *subserviēns,* prp. of *subservīre* to -SUBSERVE), equiv. to *sub-* SUB- + *servi-* serve + *-ent* -ENT] —**sub·ser′vi·ence, sub·ser′vi·en·cy,** *n.* —**sub·ser′vi·ent·ly,** *adv.*

sub·set (sub′set′), *n.* **1.** a set that is a part of a larger set. **2.** *Math.* a particular set selected from the elements of a given set. [SUB- + SET]

sub·shrub (sub′shrub′), *n.* a plant consisting of a woody, perennial base with annual, herbaceous shoots. [SUB- + SHRUB] —**sub′shrub′by,** *adj.*

sub·side (səb sīd′), *v.i.,* **-sid·ed, -sid·ing.** **1.** to sink to a low or lower level. **2.** to become quiet, less active, or less violent; abate: *The laughter subsided.* **3.** to sink or fall to the bottom; settle; precipitate: *to cause coffee grounds to subside.* [< L *subsīde(re),* equiv. to *sub-* SUB- + *sīdere* to sit, settle; akin to L *sedēre* to be seated; see SIT] —**sub·sid·ence** (səb sīd′ᵊns, sub′si dᵊns), *n.* —**sub·sid′er,** *n.*

—**Syn. 1.** decline, descend, settle. **2.** diminish, lessen, wane, ebb. —**Ant. 1.** rise. **2.** increase.

sub·sid·i·ar·y (səb sid′ē er′ē), *adj., n., pl.* **-ar·ies.** —*adj.* **1.** serving to assist or supplement; auxiliary; supplementary. **2.** subordinate or secondary: *subsidiary issues.* —*n.* **3.** a subsidiary thing or person. **4.** See **subsidiary company. 5.** *Music.* a subordinate theme or subject. [< L *subsidiāri(us),* equiv. to *subsidi(um)* (see SUBSIDY) + *-ārius* -ARY] —**sub·sid·i·ar·i·ly** (səb sid′ē âr′ə lē, -sid′ē er′-), *adv.* —**sub·sid′i·ar′i·ness,** *n.*

subsid′iary coin′, a coin, esp. one made of silver, having a value less than that of the monetary unit. Cf. **minor coin.**

subsid′iary com′pany, a company whose controlling interest is owned by another company.

subsid′iary ledg′er, (in accounting) a ledger containing a group of detailed and related accounts the total of which is summarized in the control account.

sub·si·dize (sub′si dīz′), *v.t.,* **-dized, -diz·ing.** **1.** to furnish or aid with a subsidy. **2.** to purchase the assistance of by the payment of a subsidy. **3.** to secure the cooperation of by bribery; buy over. [SUBSID(Y) + -IZE] —**sub′si·diz′a·ble,** *adj.* —**sub′si·di·za′tion,** *n.* —**sub′si·diz′er,** *n.*

sub·si·dy (sub′si dē), *n., pl.* **-dies.** **1.** a direct pecuniary aid furnished by a government to a private industrial undertaking, a charity organization, or the like. **2.** a sum paid, often in accordance with a treaty, by one government to another to secure some service in return. **3.** a grant or contribution of money. **4.** money formerly granted by the English Parliament to the crown for special needs. [late ME *subsidie* < AF < L *subsidi(um)* auxiliary force, reserve, help, equiv. to *subsid-* stay behind (see SUBSIDE) + *-ium* n. suffix; see -Y[3]]

—**Syn. 1.** SUBSIDY, SUBVENTION are both grants of money, especially governmental, to aid private undertakings. A SUBSIDY is usually given to promote commerical enterprise: *a subsidy to manufacturers during a war.* A SUBVENTION is usually a grant to stimulate enterprises connected with science and the arts: *a subvention to a research chemist by a major company.*

sub·sist (səb sist′), *v.i.* **1.** to exist; continue in existence. **2.** to remain alive; live, as on food, resources, etc. **3.** to have existence in, or by reason of, something. **4.** to reside, lie, or consist (usually fol. by *in*). **5.** *Philos.* to have timeless or abstract existence, as a number, relation, etc. —*v.t.* **6.** to provide sustenance or support for; maintain. [< L *subsist(ere)* (to) remain, equiv. to *sub-* SUB- + *sistere* to stand, make stand] —**sub·sist′ing·ly,** *adv.*

sub·sist·ence (səb sis′təns), *n.* **1.** the state or fact of subsisting. **2.** the state or fact of existing. **3.** the providing of sustenance or support. **4.** means of supporting life; a living or livelihood. **5.** the source from which food and other items necessary to exist are obtained. **6.** *Philos.* **a.** the process of substance assuming individualization. **b.** the quality of having timeless or abstract existence. [late ME < LL *subsistentia,* equiv. to *subsist-* (see SUBSIST) + *-entia* -ENCE]

subsist′ence allow′ance, **1.** money given in advance to a new soldier, employee, etc., so that he may buy food, clothing, and pay for other necessities while awaiting his first pay. **2.** money paid a worker in addition to his salary to cover expenses he may incur in performing his job. **3.** money paid to members of the armed forces in lieu of meals; an allowance for food.

subsist′ence farm′ing, **1.** farming whose products are intended to provide for the basic needs of the farmer, with little surplus for marketing. **2.** farming that brings little or no profit to the farmer, allowing only for a marginal livelihood. Also, **subsist′ence ag′riculture.**

sub·sist·ent (səb sis′tənt), *adj.* **1.** subsisting, existing, or continuing in existence. **2.** inherent: *subsistent qualities of character.* [< L *subsistent-* (s. of *subsistēns,* prp.), equiv. to *subsist-* (see SUBSIST) + *-ent-* -ENT]

sub·pel′tat·ed, *adj.*
sub′pen·tag′o·nal, *adj.*
sub·per·i·car′di·ac′, *adj.*
sub′per·i·car′di·al, *adj.*
sub′per·i·cra′ni·al, *adj.*
sub·pe′ri·od, *n.*
sub′per·i·os′te·al, *adj.;* **-ly,** *adv.*
sub′per·i·to·ne′al, *adj.*
sub·per′ma·nent, *adj.;* **-ly,** *adv.*
sub·pet′i·o·late′, *adj.*
sub·pet′i·o·lat′ed, *adj.*
sub′pe·tro′sal, *adj.*
sub′pha·ryn′gal, *adj.*
sub′pha·ryn′ge·al, *adj.;* **-ly,** *adv.*
sub·phos′phate, *n.*
sub·phra′try, *n., pl.* **-tries.**
sub·phren′ic, *adj.*
sub·pi′al, *adj.*
sub·pi′lose, *adj.*
sub′pi·los′i·ty, *n.*
sub·pis′ton, *n.*
sub′pla·cen′ta, *n., pl.* **-tae, -tas.**
sub′pla·cen′tal, *adj.*
sub′plant′, *n.*
sub·plan′ti·grade′, *adj.*
sub·plex′al, *adj.*
sub·plow′, *n.*
sub·plow′, *v.*
sub′po·lyg′o·nal, *adj.;* **-ly,** *adv.*
sub-Pon′tine, *adj.*
sub′pool′, *n.*
sub·pop′u·lar, *adj.*
sub′pop·u·la′tion, *n.*
sub′por·phy·rit′ic, *adj.*
sub′port′, *n.*
sub′post′, *n.*
sub·post′mas′ter, *n.*
sub·post′mas′ter·ship′, *n.*
sub·post′script′, *n.*
sub′pre·cep′tor, *n.*
sub′pre·cep′to·ral, *adj.*
sub′pre·cep′tor·ate, *n.*
sub′pre·cep·to′ri·al, *adj.*
sub·pred′i·cate, *n.*
sub′pred·i·ca′tion, *n.*
sub·pred′i·ca′tive, *adj.*
sub′pre′fect, *n.*
sub′pre·fec·to′ri·al, *adj.*
sub′pre′fec·ture, *n.*
sub′pre·hen′sile, *adj.*
sub′pre·hen·sil′i·ty, *n.*
sub′pre·pū′tial, *adj.*
sub·pri′ma·ry, *adj.*
sub·pri′or, *n.*
sub·pri′or·ess, *n.*
sub·pri′or·ship′, *n.*
sub·prob′lem, *n.*
sub·proc′tor, *n.*
sub′proc·to′ri·al, *adj.*
sub·proc′tor·ship′, *n.*
sub′pro·fes′sion·al, *adj.;* **-ly,** *adv.*
sub′pro·fes′sor, *n.*
sub′pro·fes′sor·ate, *n.*
sub′pro·fes·so′ri·ate, *n.*
sub′pro·fes′sor·ship′, *n.*
sub·prof′it·a·ble, *adj.;* **-ble·ness,** *n.;* **-bly,** *adv.*
sub′pro·por′tion·al, *adj.;* **-ly,** *adv.*
sub′pro·stat′ic, *adj.*
sub′pro·tec′tor, *n.*
sub′pro·tec′tor·ship′, *n.*
sub·prov′ince, *n.*
sub′pro·vin′cial, *adj., n.*
sub′pu·bes′cent, *adj.*
sub·pu′bic, *adj.*
sub·pul′mo·nar′y, *adj.*
sub·pul′ver·iz′er, *n.*
sub′py·ram′i·dal, *adj.*
sub′pyr·a·mid′ic, *adj.*
sub′pyr·a·mid′i·cal, *adj.*
sub′-Pyr·e·ne′an, *adj.*
sub·pyr′i·form′, *adj.*
sub′quad·ran′gu·lar, *adj.*
sub·quad′rate, *adj.*
sub·qual′i·ty, *n., pl.* **-ties.**
sub·ques′tion, *n.*
sub·quin′que·fid′, *adj.*
sub′race′, *n.*
sub·ra′di·ance, *n.*
sub·ra′di·an·cy, *n.*
sub·ra′di·ate′, *adj.*
sub·ra′di·a′tive, *adj.*
sub·rad′i·cal, *adj.;* **-ness,** *n.*
sub·rad′u·lar, *adj.*
sub·ra′mose, *adj.*
sub·ra′mous, *adj.*
sub′range′, *n.*
sub·read′er, *n.*
sub·rea′son, *n.*
sub′re·bel′lion, *n.*
sub·rec′tal, *adj.*
sub′rec·tan′gu·lar, *adj.*
sub·rec′tor, *n.*
sub·rec′to·ry, *n., pl.* **-ries.**
sub′ref′er·ence, *n.*
sub·re′gent, *n.*
sub·reg′u·lar, *adj.*
sub′reg·u·lar′i·ty, *n.*
sub′re·la′tion, *n.*
sub′re·li′gion, *n.*
sub·ren′i·form′, *adj.*
sub′re·pand′, *adj.*
sub′re′pent, *adj.*
sub′re·port′, *n.*
sub·rep′u·ta·ble, *adj.;* **-bly,** *adv.*
sub·ret′i·nal, *adj.*
sub′re·trac′tile, *adj.*
sub·rhom′bic, *adj.*
sub·rhom′bi·cal, *adj.*
sub·rhom′boid, *adj.*
sub′rhom·boi′dal, *adj.*
sub·ric′tal, *adj.*
sub·rig′id, *adj.;* **-ly,** *adv.;* **-ness,** *n.*
sub′ri·gid′i·ty, *n.*
sub′root′, *n.*
sub·ros′tral, *adj.*
sub′ro·tund′, *adj.;* **-ly,** *adv.;* **-ness,** *n.*
sub′ro·tun′di·ty, *n.*
sub′rule′, *n.*
sub·rul′er, *n.*
sub·sa′cral, *adj.*
sub′sale′, *n.*
sub·sa′line, *adj.*
sub′sa·lin′i·ty, *n.*
sub′sa·tir′ic, *adj.*
sub′sa·tir′i·cal, *adj.;* **-ly,** *adv.;* **-ness,** *n.*
sub·sat′u·rat′ed, *adj.*
sub′sat·u·ra′tion, *n.*
sub·sched′ule, *n.*
sub′scheme′, *n.*
sub′school′, *n.*
sub·sci′ence, *n.*
sub·scle′ral, *adj.*
sub′scle·rot′ic, *adj.*
sub·scrip′ture, *n.*
sub′sec·re·tar′i·al, *adj.*
sub·sec′re·tar′y, *n., pl.* **-tar·ies.**
sub·sec′re·tar′y·ship′, *n.*
sub′sect′, *n.*
sub′se·cu′ri·ty, *n., pl.* **-ties.**
sub′sen·sa′tion, *n.*
sub·sen′su·al, *adj.;* **-ly,** *adv.*
sub·sen′su·ous, *adj.;* **-ly,** *adv.;* **-ness,** *n.*
sub′sept′, *n.*
sub·sep′tate, *adj.*
sub·se′ries, *n., pl.* **-ries.**
sub·ser′rate, *adj.*
sub·ser′rat·ed, *adj.*
sub·ses′sile, *adj.*
sub·sew′er, *n.*
sub′shaft′, *n.*
sub·sher′iff, *n.*
sub′shire′, *n.*
sub·sib′i·lance, *n.*
sub·sib′i·lan·cy, *n.*
sub·sib′i·lant, *adj., n.;* **-ly,** *adv.*
sub·sil′i·cate, *n.*
sub·sim′i·an, *adj.*
sub·sim′i·ous, *adj.*
sub·sim′ple, *adj.*
sub·sin′u·ous, *adj.*
sub·siz′ar, *n.*
sub·siz′ar·ship′, *n.*

sub·so·cial (sub sō′shəl), *adj.* without a definite social structure. [SUB- + SOCIAL] —**sub·so′cial·ly,** *adv.*

sub·soil (sub′soil′), *n.* the bed or stratum of earth or earthy material immediately under the surface soil. Also called **undersoil.** [SUB- + SOIL[1]]

sub·soil·er (sub′soi′lər), *n.* **1.** one who operates a subsoil plow. **2.** See **subsoil plow.** [SUBSOIL + -ER[1]]

sub′soil plow′, a plow for stirring the subsoil, usually without disturbing the surface.

sub·so·lar (sub sō′lər), *adj.* **1.** situated beneath the sun or between the earth and the sun. **2.** between the tropics. [SUB- + SOLAR]

sub·son·ic (sub son′ik), *adj.* **1.** noting or pertaining to a speed less than that of sound in air at the same height above sea level. **2.** infrasonic. [SUB- + SONIC]

sub·space (sub′spās′), *n.* *Math.* **1.** a subset of a given space. **2.** Also called **linear manifold.** a subset of a vector space which is itself a vector space. **3.** a subset of a topological space, having the relative topology. [SUB- + SPACE]

sub′space topol′ogy, *Math.* See **relative topology.**

sub spe·ci·e ae·ter·ni·ta·tis (sōōb spe′ki e′ ī ter′-ni tä′tis; *Eng.* sub spē′shē ē′ ē tûr′ni tā′tis), *Latin.* under the aspect of eternity: used esp. in the philosophy of Spinoza to designate perception of phenomena, as by God.

sub·spe·cies (sub spē′shēz, sub′spē′shēz), *n., pl.* **-cies.** a subdivision of a species, esp. a geographical or ecological subdivision. [SUB- + SPECIES]

sub·spe·cif·ic (sub′spi sif′ik), *adj.* **1.** of, pertaining to, or of the nature of a subspecies. **2.** less than specific. [SUB- + SPECIFIC] —**sub′spe·cif′i·cal·ly,** *adv.*

subst., **1.** substantive. **2.** substantively. **3.** substitute.

sub·stage (sub′stāj′), *n.* the component part of a microscope below the stage, for supporting a condenser, mirror, or other accessories. [SUB- + STAGE]

sub·stance (sub′stəns), *n.* **1.** that of which a thing consists; matter or material: *form and substance.* **2.** a species of matter of definite chemical composition: *a chalky substance.* **3.** the subject matter of thought, discourse, study, etc. **4.** the actual matter of a thing, as opposed to the appearance or shadow; reality. **5.** substantial or solid character or quality: *claims lacking in substance.* **6.** consistency; body: *soup without much substance.* **7.** the meaning or gist, as of speech or writing. **8.** something that has separate or independent existence. **9.** *Philos.* **a.** that which exists by itself and in which accidents or attributes inhere; that which receives modifications and is not itself a mode; that which is causally active; that which is more than an event. **b.** the essential part, or essence, of a thing. **c.** a thing considered as a continuing whole. **10.** possessions, means, or wealth: *to squander one's substance.* **11.** *Ling.* the articulatory or acoustic reality or the perceptual manifestation of a word or other construction (distinguished from *form*). **12.** a standard of weights for paper. **13. in substance, a.** concerning the essentials; substantially. **b.** actually; really: *That is in substance how it appeared to me.* [ME < L *substantia* essence (lit., that which stands under, i.e. underlies), equiv. to *sub-* SUB- + *-stant-* (s. of *stāns,* prp. of *stāre* to stand) + *-ia* -Y[3] (L *-antia* > -ANCE)] —**sub′stance·less,** *adj.*
—**Syn. 1.** See **matter. 3.** theme, subject. **3, 4, 7.** essence. **7.** significance, import, pith.

sub·stand·ard (sub stan′dərd), *adj.* **1.** below standard or less than adequate: *substandard housing conditions.* **2.** *Ling.* noting or pertaining to a dialect or variety of a language or a feature of usage that is often considered by others to mark its user as uneducated or socially inferior: *substandard English; substandard pronunciation.* **3.** *Insurance.* **a.** not measuring up to an insurer's regular standards in undertaking risks: *a substandard risk.* **b.** pertaining to insurance written to cover substandard risks. [SUB- + STANDARD]

sub·stan·tial (səb stan′shəl), *adj.* **1.** of ample or considerable amount, quantity, size, etc.: *a substantial sum of money.* **2.** of a corporeal or material nature; real or actual. **3.** of solid character or quality; firm, stout, or strong: *a substantial physique.* **4.** based on solid or firm essentials: *two stories in substantial agreement.* **5.** wealthy or influential: *one of the substantial men of the town.* **6.** of real worth, value, or effect: *substantial reasons.* **7.** pertaining to the substance, matter, or material of a thing. **8.** of or pertaining to the essence of a thing; essential, material, or important. **9.** being a substance; having independent existence. **10.** *Philos.* pertaining to or of the nature of substance rather than an accident or attribute. —*n.* **11.** something substantial. [ME *substancial* < LL *substantiāl(is)* < L *substanti(a)* SUBSTANCE + *-ālis* -AL[1]] —**sub·stan′ti·al′i·ty, sub·stan′tial·ness,** *n.* —**sub·stan′tial·ly,** *adv.*
—**Syn. 3.** stable, sound. **6.** valid, important. —**Ant. 1.** immaterial, ethereal.

sub·stan·tial·ism (səb stan′shə liz′əm), *n.* *Philos.* the doctrine that substantial noumena exist as a basis for phenomena. [SUBSTANTIAL + -ISM] —**sub·stan′-tial·ist,** *n.*

sub·stan·ti·ate (səb stan′shē āt′), *v.t.,* **-at·ed, -at·ing. 1.** to establish by proof or competent evidence: *to substantiate a charge.* **2.** to give substantial existence to: *to substantiate an idea through action.* **3.** to present as having substance; give body to; strengthen: *to substantiate a friendship.* [< NL *substantiāt(us)* (ptp. of *substantiāre*) < L *substanti(a)* SUBSTANCE + *-ātus* -ATE[1]] —**sub·stan′ti·a′tion,** *n.* —**sub·stan′ti·a′tive,** *adj.* —**sub·stan′ti·a′tor,** *n.*
—**Syn. 1.** prove, confirm, verify, validate.

sub·stan·ti·val (sub′stən tī′vəl), *adj.* noting, of, or pertaining to a substantive. [SUBSTANTIVE + -AL[1]] —**sub′stan·ti′val·ly,** *adv.*

sub·stan·tive (sub′stən tiv), *n.* *Gram.* **1.** a noun. **2.** a noun, pronoun, or other word or phrase having nominal function in sentences or inflected like a noun. **3.** (in Latin and other languages in which adjectives are inflected like nouns) a noun or adjective, as Latin *puella* "girl" and *bona* "good" in *Puella bona est* "The girl is good." —*adj.* **4.** *Gram.* **a.** pertaining to substantives. **b.** used in a sentence like a noun: *a substantive adjective.* **c.** expressing existence: *"to be" is a substantive verb.* **5.** having independent existence; independent. **6.** belonging to the real nature or essential part of a thing; essential. **7.** real or actual. **8.** of considerable amount or quantity. **9.** *Law.* pertaining to the rules of right which courts are called on to apply, as distinguished from rules of procedure (opposed to *adjective*). **10.** (of dye colors) attaching directly to the material without the aid of a mordant (opposed to *adjective*). [ME < L *substanti-* (s. of *substāns*) standing under (see SUBSTANCE) + *-īvus* -IVE] —**sub′stan·tive·ly,** *adv.* —**sub′stan·tive·ness,** *n.*

sub·sta·tion (sub′stā′shən), *n.* a subsidiary station, esp. a branch of a post office. [SUB- + STATION]

sub·stit·u·ent (sub stich′ōō ənt), *n.* **1.** *Chem.* an atom or atomic group which takes the place of another atom or group present in the molecule of the original compound. —*adj.* **2.** having been or capable of being substituted. [< L *substituent-* (s. of *substituēns* (prp.) putting in place of), equiv. to *substitu-* (see SUBSTITUTE) + *-ent-* -ENT]

sub·sti·tute (sub′sti tōōt′, -tyōōt′), *n., v.,* **-tut·ed, -tut·ing.** —*n.* **1.** a person or thing acting or serving in place of another. **2.** (formerly) one who, for payment, served in an army or navy in the place of a conscript. **3.** *Gram.* a word that functions as a replacement for any member of a class of words or constructions, as *do* in *I know but he doesn't.* **4.** *Naut.* repeater (def. 6). —*v.t.* **5.** to put (a person or thing) in the place of another. **6.** to take the place of; replace. —*v.i.* **7.** to act as a substitute. **8.** *Chem.* to replace one or more elements or groups in a compound by other elements or groups. [< L *substitūt(us)* (ptp. of *substituere* to put in place of), equiv. to *sub-* SUB- + *-stitū-*, var. of *statū-* cause to stand (see STATUS) + *-tus* ptp. suffix] —**sub′sti·tut′a·ble,** *adj.* —**sub′sti·tut′er,** *n.* —**sub′sti·tut′ing·ly,** *adv.* —**sub′sti·tu′tion,** *n.* —**sub′sti·tu′tion·al, sub·sti·tu·tion·ar·y** (sub′sti tōō′shə ner′ē, -tyōō′-), *adj.* —**sub′sti·tu′tion·al·ly,** *adv.*

sub·sti·tu·tive (sub′sti tōō′tiv, -tyōō′-), *adj.* **1.** serving as or capable of serving as a substitute. **2.** pertaining to or involving substitution. [SUBSTITUTE + -IVE] —**sub′sti·tu′tive·ly,** *adv.*

sub·strate (sub′strāt), *n.* **1.** a substratum. **2.** *Biochem.* the substance acted upon by an enzyme or ferment. [var. of SUBSTRATUM]

sub·strat·o·sphere (sub strat′ə sfēr′), *n.* (not used technically) the upper troposphere. [SUB- + STRATOSPHERE] —**sub·strat·o·spher·ic** (sub′strat ə sfer′ik), *adj.*

sub·stra·tum (sub strā′təm, -strat′əm, sub′strā′-təm, -strat′əm), *n., pl.* **-stra·ta** (-strā′tə, -strat′ə, -strā′tə, -strat′ə). **1.** that which is spread or laid under something else; a stratum or layer lying under another. **2.** something which underlies or serves as a basis or foundation. **3.** *Agric.* the subsoil. **4.** *Biol.* the base or material on which an organism lives. **5.** *Philos.* substance, considered as that which supports accidents or attributes. **6.** *Photog.* a layer of material placed directly on a film or plate as a foundation for the sensitive emulsion. [< NL; see SUB-, STRATUM] —**sub·stra′tive, sub·stra′tal,** *adj.*

sub·struc·tion (sub struk′shən), *n.* a foundation or substructure. [< L *substructiōn-* (s. of *substructiō*) foundation, equiv. to *substruct(us)* (ptp.) (*substruc-,* pt., ptp. s. of *substruere* to lay a foundation + *-tus* ptp. suffix) + *-iōn-* -ION] —**sub·struc′tion·al,** *adj.*

sub·struc·ture (sub struk′chər, sub′struk′-), *n.* **1.** a structure forming the foundation of a building or other construction. **2.** the foundations, piers, and abutments upon which the trusses or girders of the spans of a bridge rest. [SUB- + STRUCTURE] —**sub·struc′tur·al,** *adj.*

sub·sul·fate (sub sul′fāt), *n.* *Chem.* a basic salt of sulfuric acid. Also, **sub·sul′phate.** [SUB- + SULFATE]

sub·sume (səb sōōm′), *v.t.,* **-sumed, -sum·ing. 1.** to consider (an idea, term, proposition, etc.) as part of a more comprehensive one. **2.** to bring (a case, instance, etc.) under a rule. **3.** to take up into a more inclusive classification. [< NL *subsume(re)* < L *sub-* SUB- + *sumere* to take; see RESUME] —**sub·sum′a·ble,** *adj.*

sub·sump·tion (səb sump′shən), *n.* **1.** the act of subsuming. **2.** the state of being subsumed. **3.** that which is subsumed. **4.** a proposition subsumed under another. [< NL *subsumptiōn-* (s. of *subsumptiō*) a subjoining, equiv. to *subsumpt(us)* (ptp.) (*subsump-,* pt., ptp. s. of *subsumere* to SUBSUME + *-tus* ptp. suffix) + *-iōn-* -ION] —**sub·sump′tive,** *adj.*

sub·sur·face (sub sûr′fəs, sub′sûr′-), *adj.* below the surface, esp. of a body of water. [SUB- + SURFACE]

sub·sys·tem (sub′sis′təm, sub sis′-), *n.* a secondary or subordinate system. [SUB- + SYSTEM]

sub·tan·gent (sub tan′jənt), *n.* *Geom.* the part of the x-axis cut off between the ordinate of a given point of a curve and the tangent at that point. [SUB- + TANGENT]

sub·teen (sub′tēn′), *n.* **1.** a young person approaching his teens or adolescence. **2.** a range of even-numbered garment sizes, chiefly from 6–14, designed for girls under 13. [SUB- + TEEN[2]]

sub·tem·per·ate (sub tem′pər it), *adj.* pertaining to or occurring in the colder parts of the Temperate Zone. [SUB- + TEMPERATE]

sub·ten·ant (sub ten′ənt), *n.* one who rents land, a house, or the like, from a tenant. [SUB- + TENANT] —**sub·ten′an·cy,** *n.*

B
A C
Chord AC subtends arc ABC

sub·tend (səb tend′, sub-), *v.t.* **1.** *Geom.* to extend under or be opposite to: *a chord subtending an arc.* **2.** *Bot.* (of a leaf, bract, etc.) to enclose or embrace in its axil. **3.** to form or mark the outline or boundary of. [< L *subtend(ere)* (to) stretch beneath, equiv. to *sub-* SUB- + *tendere* to stretch; see TEND[1]]

sub·tense′ bar′ (səb tens′, sub-), *Survey.* a bar having near each end a target separated by an exactly known distance. It is laid horizontally over a point so that the distance from a station to the point can be determined by measuring the angle subtended by the distance between the targets. [< NL *subtens(a)* (*linea*) subtense (line), deriv. of *subtens(us)* (ptp. of *subtendere*). See SUBTEND, TENSE[1]]

sub·ten·ure (sub ten′yər), *n.* the tenure of a subtenant. [SUB- + TENURE]

subter-, a formal element occurring in loan words from Latin (*subterfuge*): used, with the meaning "under," "below," in the formation of compound words (*subternatural*). [< L *subter-* below, underhand, in secret, deriv. of *subter* (adv., prep.) underneath, equiv. to *sub-* SUB- + *-ter* comp. suffix (see FURTHER)]

sub·ter·fuge (sub′tər fyōōj′), *n.* an artifice or expedient used to evade a rule, escape a consequence, hide something, etc. [< LL *subterfug(ium)* < L *subterfug(ere)* (to) evade (equiv. to *subter-* SUBTER- + *fugere* to flee) + *-ium* n. suffix]

sub·ter·nat·u·ral (sub′tər nach′ər əl), *adj.* below what is natural; less than natural. [SUBTER- + NATURAL]

sub·ter·rane (sub′tə rān′, sub′tə rān′), *n.* a cave or subterranean room. Also, **sub′ter·rain′, sub·ter·rene** (sub′tə rēn′, sub′tə rēn′). [< L *subterrān(eus),* equiv. to *sub-* SUB- + *terr(a)* earth + *-āneus* composite adj. suffix, equiv. to *-ān(us)* -ANE + *-eus* -EOUS]

sub·ter·ra·ne·an (sub′tə rā′nē ən), *adj.* Also, **sub′-ter·ra′ne·ous. 1.** existing, situated, or operating below the surface of the earth; underground. **2.** existing or operating out of sight or secretly; hidden or secret. —*n.* **3.** one who or that which is subterranean. **4.** a subterrane. [< L *subterrāne(us)* (see SUBTERRANE) + -AN] —**sub′ter·ra′ne·an·ly, sub′ter·ra′ne·ous·ly,** *adv.*

sub·ter·res·tri·al (sub′tə res′trē əl), *adj.* underground; subterranean. [SUB- + TERRESTRIAL]

sub·tile (sut′əl, sub′til), *adj.* *Archaic.* subtle. [late ME < L *subtīle,* neut. of *subtīlis* fine (lit., finely woven), equiv. to *sub-* SUB- + *tēl(a)* web (< **texla;* see TEXT) + *-is* adj. suffix] —**sub′tile·ly,** *adv.* —**sub′tile·ness,** *n.*

sub·ti·lis (sub tī′lis), *adj.* (in prescriptions) fine; smooth. [< L]

sub·til·ise (sut′əlīz′, sub′tə līz′), *v.t., v.i.,* **-ised, -is·ing.** *Chiefly Brit.* subtilize. —**sub′til·i·sa′tion,** *n.* —**sub′til·is′er,** *n.*

sub·til·ize (sut′əlīz′, sub′tə līz′), *v.,* **-ized, -iz·ing.** —*v.t.* **1.** to elevate in character; sublimate. **2.** to make (the mind, senses, etc.) keen or discerning; sharpen. **3.** to introduce subtleties into or argue subtly about. **4.** to make thin, rare, or more fluid or volatile; refine. —*v.i.* **5.** to make subtle distinctions or to argue subtly. [< ML *subtīliz(āre),* equiv. to *subtīl(is)* SUBTLE + *-izāre* -IZE] —**sub′til·i·za′tion,** *n.* —**sub′til·iz′er,** *n.*

sub·til·ty (sut′əl tē, sub′til-), *n., pl.* **-ties.** *Archaic.* subtlety. Also, **sub·til·i·ty** (sub til′i tē).

sub·ti·tle (sub′tīt′əl), *n., v.,* **-tled, -tling.** —*n.* **1.** a secondary or subordinate title of a literary work, usually of explanatory character. **2.** a repetition of the leading words in the full title of a book at the head of the first page of text. **3.** *Motion Pictures.* **a.** (in sound motion pictures) the text of dialogue, speeches, etc., translated into another language and projected on the lower part of the screen. **b.** (in silent motion pictures) a title or caption. —*v.t.* **4.** to give a subtitle to. [SUB- + TITLE] —**sub·tit·u·lar** (sub tich′ə lər, -tit′yə-), *adj.*

sub·tle (sut′əl), *adj.* **1.** thin, tenuous, or rarefied, as a fluid or an odor. **2.** fine or delicate, often when likely to elude perception or understanding: *subtle irony.* **3.** delicate or faint and mysterious: *a subtle smile.* **4.** requiring mental acuteness, penetration, or discernment: *a subtle philosophy.* **5.** characterized by mental acuteness or penetration: *a subtle understanding.* **6.** cunning, wily, or crafty: *a subtle liar.* **7.** insidious in operation: *subtle poison.* **8.** skillful, clever, or ingenious: *a subtle painter.* [ME *sotil* < OF < L *subtīl(is)* SUBTILE (mute *b* of mod. sp. < L)] —**sub′tle·ness,** *n.* —**sub′tly,** *adv.*

sub·tle·ty (sut′əl tē), *n., pl.* **-ties. 1.** the state or quality of being subtle. **2.** delicacy or nicety of character or meaning; acuteness or penetration of mind; delicacy of discrimination. **3.** a fine-drawn distinction; refinement of reasoning: *the subtleties of logic.* **4.** something subtle. **5.** *Hist.* an elaborate confection, ornate in construction and ornamentation, sometimes edible but more often made and used as a decoration for a table or buffet. Also, **subtilty.** [ME *sutilte* < OF < L *subtīlitāt-* (s. of *subtīlitās*) fineness, equiv. to *subtīl(is)* SUBTILE + *-tāl-* -TY[2]]

sub·ton·ic (sub ton′ik), *n.* the seventh tone of a scale, being the next below the upper tonic. [SUB- + TONIC]

sub·to·pi·a (sub tō′pē ə), *n.* *Brit.* **1.** a visually displeasing, partly built-up area, lacking both the open-

sub·smile′, *n.*
sub·sneer′, *n.*
sub·sol′id, *n.*
sub′sort′, *n.*
sub′sort′, *v.*
sub·sort′er, *n.*
sub·sov′er·eign, *n., adj.*
sub·spat′u·late, *adj.*
sub·spe′cial·ist, *n.*
sub′spe·cial·i·za′tion, *n.*
sub·spe′cial·ize′, *v.,* -ized, -iz·ing.
sub·spe′cial·ty, *n., pl.* -ties.
sub′sphe′noid, *adj.*
sub′sphe·noi′dal, *adj.*
sub′sphere′, *n.*
sub·spher′ic, *adj.*
sub·spher′i·cal, *adj.*
sub·spi′nose, *adj.*
sub·spi′nous, *adj.*
sub·spi′ral, *adj.;* -ly, *adv.*
sub·sple′ni·al, *adj.*
sub′spon·ta′ne·ous, *adj.;* -ly, *adv.;* -ness, *n.*
sub·squad′ron, *n.*
sub′stand′ard·i·za′tion, *n.*
sub·stand′ard·ize′, *v.t.,* -ized, -iz·ing.
sub·ster′nal, *adj.*
sub′stock′, *n.*
sub′store′, *n.*
sub·store′room′, *n.*
sub·sto′ry, *n., pl.* -ries.
sub·stri′ate, *adj.*
sub·stri′at·ed, *adj.*
sub·sul′cus, *n., pl.* -ci.
sub·sul′fid, *n.*
sub·sul′fide, *n.*
sub·sul′phid, *n.*
sub·sul′phide, *n.*
sub′su·per·fi′cial, *adj.;* -ly, *adv.;* -ness, *n.*
sub·sure′ty, *n., pl.* -ties.
sub·syn′di·cate, *n.*
sub′syn·di·ca′tion, *n.*
sub·syn′od, *n.*
sub·syn′od·al, *adj.*
sub′syn·od′ic, *adj.*
sub′syn·od′i·cal, *adj.;* -ly, *adv.*
sub′syn·o′vi·al, *adj.*
sub·tar′sal, *adj.*
sub·tax′er, *n.*
sub·teg′mi·nal, *adj.*
sub′teg·u·men′tal, *adj.*
sub′teg·u·men′ta·ry, *adj.*
sub·tem′po·ral, *adj.*
sub′ten·tac′u·lar, *adj.*
sub·tep′id, *adj.;* -ly, *adv.;* -ness, *n.*
sub′te·pid′i·ty, *n.*
sub′te·rete′, *adj.*
sub·ter′mi·nal, *adj.;* -ly, *adv.*
sub′ter·ran′e·an·ize′, *v.t.,* -ized, -iz·ing.
sub′ter·ra′que·ous, *adj.*
sub′ter·ri·to′ri·al, *adj.*
sub·ter′ri·to′ry, *n., pl.* -ries.
sub·ter′tian, *adj.*
sub′te·tan′ic, *adj.*
sub′te·tan′i·cal, *adj.*
sub′text′, *n.*
sub′tha·lam′ic, *adj.*
sub·tho′ra·cal, *adj.*
sub′tho·rac′ic, *adj.*
sub′thrill′, *n.*

ness of the country and the coherence and sense of identity possible in a true suburb or other community. **2.** suburbia, considered as an ugly or unhappy place. [SUB + (U)TOPIA]

sub·top·ic (sub′top′ik, sub top′-), *n.* a topic that is included within another topic. [SUB- + TOPIC]

sub·tor·rid (sub tôr′id, -tor′-), *adj.* subtropical. [SUB- + TORRID]

sub·to·tal (sub tōt′ᵊl, sub′tōt′-), *n., adj., v.,* **-taled, -tal·ing** or (*esp. Brit.*) **-talled, -tal·ling.** —*n.* **1.** the total of a part of a group or column of figures, as in an accounting statement. —*adj.* **2.** somewhat less than complete; not total: *subtotal commitment.* —*v.t.* **3.** to determine a subtotal for (a column): *to subtotal the right-hand column.* —*v.i.* **4.** to determine a subtotal. [SUB- + TOTAL]

sub·tract (səb trakt′), *v.t.* **1.** to withdraw or take away, as a part from a whole. **2.** *Math.* to take (one number or quantity) from another; deduct. —*v.i.* **3.** to take away something or a part, as from a whole. [< L *subtract(us)* (ptp. of *subtrahere* to draw away from underneath), equiv. to *sub-* SUB- + *trac-* (pt., ptp. s. of *trahere* to draw) + *-tus* ptp. suffix] —**sub·tract′er,** *n.*
—**Syn. 1, 3.** SUBTRACT, DEDUCT express diminution in sum or quantity. To SUBTRACT suggests taking a part from a whole or a smaller from a larger: *to subtract the tax from one's salary.* To DEDUCT is to take away an amount or quantity from an aggregate or total so as to lessen or lower it: *to deduct a discount.* SUBTRACT is both transitive and intransitive, and has general or figurative uses; DEDUCT is always transitive and usually concrete and practical in application. —**Ant. 1, 2, 3.** add.

sub·trac·tion (səb trak′shən), *n.* **1.** the act or an instance of subtracting. **2.** *Math.* the operation or process of finding the difference between two numbers or quantities, denoted by the symbol −. [late ME < LL *subtractiōn-* (s. of *subtractiō*) a withdrawing, equiv. to *subtract-* (see SUBTRACT) + *-iōn-* -ION]

subtrac′tion sign′, *Math.* the symbol −, used in a mathematical expression to indicate the term that it precedes is to be subtracted from the term preceding the symbol in the expression, as in 5−3 where 3 is to be subtracted from 5.

sub·trac·tive (səb trak′tiv), *adj.* **1.** tending to subtract; having power to subtract. **2.** *Math.* (of a quantity) that is to be subtracted; having the minus sign (−). [SUBTRACT + -IVE]

subtrac′tive col′or, *Photog.* cyan, yellow, or magenta, as used in the subtractive process of color photography. Also called **subtrac′tive pri′mary.**

subtrac′tive proc′ess, a process of color photography in which the colors are formed by combination of cyan, yellow, and magenta lights. Cf. **additive process.**

sub·tra·hend (sub′trə hend′), *n.* *Math.* a number which is subtracted from another. Cf. **minuend.** [< L *subtrahend(um),* neut. ger. of *subtrahere;* see SUBTRACT]

sub·treas·ur·y (sub trezh′ə rē, sub′trezh′-), *n., pl.* **-ur·ies.** **1.** a subordinate or branch treasury. **2.** (formerly) any of the branch treasuries maintained by the U.S. government. [SUB- + TREASURY] —**sub·treas′ur·er,** *n.* —**sub·treas′ur·er·ship′,** *n.*

sub·trop·i·cal (sub trop′i kəl), *adj.* **1.** bordering on the tropics; nearly tropical. **2.** pertaining to or occurring in a region between tropical and temperate; subtorrid; semitropical. [SUB- + TROPICAL]

subtrop′ical high′, *Meteorol.* one of several highs, as the Azores and Pacific highs, that prevail over the oceans at about latitudes 30 degrees N and S. Cf. **high** (def. 40). Also called **subtrop′ical antic′yclone.**

sub·trop·ics (sub trop′iks), *n.pl.* subtropical regions. [SUB- + TROPICS]

sub·type (sub′tīp′), *n.* **1.** a subordinate type. **2.** a special type included within a more general type. [SUB- + TYPE] —**sub·typ·i·cal** (sub tip′i kəl), *adj.*

su·bu·late (sōō′byə lit, -lāt′), *adj.* **1.** awl-shaped. **2.** *Bot., Zool.* slender, more or less cylindrical, and tapering to a point. [< NL *subulat(us)* < L *subul(a)* awl + *-atus* -ATE¹]

Subulate leaves

sub·urb (sub′ûrb), *n.* **1.** a district lying immediately outside a city or town, esp. a smaller residential community. **2.** an outlying part. [late ME < L *suburb(ium),* equiv. to *sub-* SUB- + *urb(s)* city + *-ium* n. suffix] —**sub′urbed,** *adj.*

sub·ur·ban (sə bûr′bən), *adj.* **1.** pertaining to, inhabiting, or being in a suburb or the suburbs of a city or town. **2.** characteristic of a suburb or suburbs. —*n.* **3.** a suburbanite. **4.** a short overcoat for casual wear. **5.** See **station wagon.** [< L *suburbān(us),* equiv. to *sub-* SUB- + *urb(s)* city + *-ānus* -AN]

sub·ur·ban·ise (sə bûr′bə nīz′), *v.t.,* **-ised, -is·ing.** *Chiefly Brit.* suburbanize. —**sub·ur′ban·i·sa′tion,** *n.*

sub·ur·ban·ite (sə bûr′bə nīt′), *n.* one who lives in a suburb of a city or large town. [SUBURBAN + -ITE¹]

sub·ur·ban·ize (sə bûr′bə nīz′), *v.t.,* **-ized, -iz·ing.** to give suburban characteristics to: *to suburbanize a rural area.* Also, *esp. Brit.,* **suburbanise.** [SUBURBAN + -IZE] —**sub·ur′ban·i·za′tion,** *n.*

sub·ur·bi·a (sə bûr′bē ə), *n.* **1.** suburbs collectively. **2.** suburbanites collectively. **3.** the social or cultural aspects of life in suburbs. [SUBURB + -IA]

sub·ur·bi·car·i·an (sə bûr′bə kâr′ē ən), *adj.* **1.** being near the city of Rome. **2.** designating any of the dioceses surrounding the city of Rome, each of which is under the jurisdiction of a cardinal-bishop. [< LL *suburbicāri(us)* (< L *suburb(ium)* SUBURB + *-ic(us)* -IC + *-āri(us)* -ARY) + -AN]

sub·u·to·pi·a (sub′yōō tō′pē ə), *n.* *Brit.* a sprawling, nondescript, modern suburb: *The countryside is rapidly becoming a tasteless subutopia.* [SUB- + UTOPIA] —**sub′u·to′pi·an,** *n., adj.*

sub·vag·i·nal (sub vaj′ə nᵊl, -və jīn′ᵊl), *adj.* situated under a sheathing membrane. [SUB- + VAGINAL]

sub·vene (səb vēn′), *v.i.,* **-vened, -ven·ing.** to arrive or occur as a support or relief. [< L *subven(īre),* equiv. to *sub-* SUB- + *venīre* to come]

sub·ven·tion (səb ven′shən), *n.* **1.** a grant of money, esp. by a government or some other authority, in aid or support of some object, institution, or undertaking. **2.** the furnishing of aid or relief. [< LL *subventiōn-* (s. of *subventiō*) official grant in aid, equiv. to *subvent(us)* (ptp. of *subvenīre*) < *subven-* (see SUBVENE) + *-tus* ptp. suffix + *-iōn-* -ION] —**sub·ven′tion·ar′y,** *adj.*
—**Syn. 1.** See **subsidy.**

sub ver·bo (sōōb wer′bō; *Eng.* sub vûr′bō), *Latin.* (used as a direction to a reference) under the word or heading.

sub·ver·sion (səb vûr′zhən, -shən), *n.* **1.** the act or an instance of subverting. **2.** the state of being subverted; destruction. **3.** that which subverts or overthrows. [late ME < LL *subversiōn-* (s. of *subversiō*) an overthrowing. See SUB-, VERSION]

sub·ver·sive (səb vûr′siv), *adj.* **1.** tending to subvert; liable to cause subversion. —*n.* **2.** one who adopts subversive principles or policies. [< L *subvers(us)* (ptp. of *subvertere* to SUBVERT) + -IVE] —**sub·ver′sive·ly,** *adv.* —**sub·ver′siv·ism, sub·ver′sive·ness,** *n.*

sub·vert (səb vûrt′), *v.t.* **1.** to overthrow (something established or existing). **2.** to cause the downfall, ruin, or destruction of. **3.** to undermine the principles of; corrupt. [late ME *subvert(en)* < L *subvertere* to overthrow, equiv. to *sub-* SUB- + *vertere* to turn] —**sub·vert′er,** *n.*

sub·vis·i·ble (sub viz′ə bəl), *adj.* invisible unless viewed through a microscope. [SUB- + VISIBLE]

sub·vo·cal (sub vō′kəl), *adj.* mentally formulated as words, esp. without vocalization. [SUB- + VOCAL]

sub vo·ce (sōōb wō′ke; *Eng.* sub vō′sē), *Latin.* (used as a direction to a reference) under the specified word. [lit., under the voice, i.e., utterance]

sub·way (sub′wā′), *n.* **1.** *U.S.* an underground electric railroad, usually in a large city. **2.** *Chiefly Brit.* a short tunnel or underground passageway for pedestrians, automobiles, etc.; underpass. —*v.i.* **3.** to be transported by a subway: *We subwayed uptown.* [SUB- + WAY]

sub·ze·ro (sub zēr′ō), *adj.* **1.** indicating or recording lower than zero on some scale, esp. on the Fahrenheit scale: *a week of sub-zero temperatures.* **2.** characterized by or appropriate for sub-zero temperatures: *sub-zero climates; sub-zero clothing for the exploration.* [SUB- + ZERO]

sub·zone (sub′zōn′), *n.* a subdivision of a zone. [SUB- + ZONE] —**sub·zon′al, sub·zon′a·ry,** *adj.*

suc-, var. of **sub-** before *c: succeed.*

Su·ca·ryl (sōō′kə ril), *n.* *Trademark.* **1.** See **calcium cyclamate.** **2.** See **sodium cyclamate.**

suc·cah (sōō kä′; *Eng.* sōōk′ə), *n., pl.* **suc·coth** (sōō-kōt′), *Eng.* **suc·cahs.** *Hebrew.* sukkah.

suc·ce·da·ne·um (suk′si dā′nē əm), *n., pl.* **-ne·a** (-nē ə). a substitute. [< L, neut. sing. of *succedāneus* equiv. to *suc-* SUC- + *cēd(ere)* (to) come, go + *-āneus* composite adj. suffix, equiv. to *-ān(us)* -AN + *-eus* -EOUS] —**suc′ce·da′ne·ous,** *adj.*

suc·ceed (sək sēd′), *v.i.* **1.** to happen or terminate according to desire; turn out successfully; have the desired result: *Our efforts succeeded.* **2.** to have a given degree of success: *I have succeeded beyond my expectations.* **3.** to accomplish what is attempted or intended: *We succeeded in our efforts to start the car.* **4.** to attain success in some popularly recognized form, as wealth or standing: *The class voted him the one most likely to succeed.* **5.** to follow or replace another by descent, election, appointment, etc. (often fol. by *to*). **6.** to come next after something else in an order or series. —*v.t.* **7.** to come after and take the place of, as in an office or estate. **8.** to come next after in an order or series, or in the course of events; follow. [late ME < L *succēde(re)* (to) go (from) under, follow, prosper, equiv. to *suc-* SUC- + *cēdere* to go (see CEDE)] —**suc·ceed′a·ble,** *adj.* —**suc·ceed′er,** *n.* —**suc·ceed′ing·ly,** *adv.*
—**Syn. 1, 3, 4.** SUCCEED, FLOURISH, PROSPER, THRIVE mean to do well. To SUCCEED is to turn out well, to attain a goal: *It is everyone's wish to succeed in life.* To FLOURISH is to give evidence of success or a ripe development of power, reputation, etc.: *Culture flourishes among free people.* To PROSPER is to achieve and enjoy material success: *He prospered but was still discontented.* THRIVE suggests vigorous growth and development such as results from natural vitality or favorable conditions: *The children thrived in the sunshine.* **5.** See **follow.** —**Ant. 1, 3, 4.** fail. **8.** precede.

suc·cen·tor (sək sen′tər), *n.* *Eccles.* a precentor's deputy. [< LL, equiv. to *suc-* SUC- + *cent-,* var. of *cant-* (s. of *cantus,* ptp. of *canere* to sing) + *-or* -OR²]

suc·cès de scan·dale (syk sedᵊ skän dal′), *French.* success won by reason of topical, usually scandalous, subject matter rather than by merit and critical respect.

suc·cès d'es·time (syk se des tēm′), *French.* success won by reason of merit and critical respect rather than by popularity.

suc·cès fou (syk se fōō′), *French.* an extraordinarily great success.

suc·cess (sək ses′), *n.* **1.** the favorable or prosperous termination of attempts or endeavors. **2.** the attainment of wealth, position, honors, or the like. **3.** a successful performance or achievement: *The play was an instant success.* **4.** a thing or a person that is successful: *She was a great success at the party.* **5.** *Obs.* outcome. [< L *success(us)* (n.) deriv. of (ptp. of *succēdere:* see SUCCEED), equiv. to *suc-* SUC- + *cessus* (*ced-* come, go + *-tus* ptp. suffix)] —**suc·cess′less,** *adj.* —**suc·cess′less·ly,** *adv.* —**suc·cess′less·ness,** *n.*

suc·cess·ful (sək ses′fəl), *adj.* **1.** achieving or having achieved success. **2.** having attained wealth, position, honors, or the like. **3.** resulting in or attended with success. [SUCCESS + -FUL] —**suc·cess′ful·ly,** *adv.* —**suc·cess′ful·ness,** *n.*

suc·ces·sion (sək sesh′ən), *n.* **1.** the coming of one person or thing after another in order, sequence, or in the course of events: *many troubles in succession.* **2.** a number of persons or things following one another in order or sequence. **3.** the right, act, or process, by which one person succeeds to the office, rank, estate, or the like, of another. **4.** the order or line of those entitled to succeed one another. **5.** the descent or transmission of a throne, dignity, estate, or the like. **6.** *Ecol.* the progressive replacement of one community by another in developing towards a climax. [ME < L *successiōn-* (s. of *successiō*) a following (someone) in office, equiv. to *success-* (see SUCCESS) + *-iōn-* -ION] —**suc·ces′sion·al,** *adj.* —**suc·ces′sion·al·ly,** *adv.*
—**Syn. 2.** See **series.**

succes′sion of crops′, **1.** the continuous cultivation of a crop throughout a season by successive plantings or by the use of varieties with different rates of growth. **2.** the successive cultivation of short-lived crops.

suc·ces·sive (sək ses′iv), *adj.* **1.** following in order or in uninterrupted course: *three successive days.* **2.** following another in a regular sequence: *the second successive day.* **3.** characterized by or involving succession. [< ML *successīv(us),* equiv. to *success-* (see SUCCESS) + *-īvus* -IVE] —**suc·ces′sive·ly,** *adv.* —**suc·ces′sive·ness,** *n.*
—**Syn. 1.** SUCCESSIVE, CONSECUTIVE apply to things which follow one upon another. SUCCESSIVE refers to the position of one with reference to its following another: *discouraged by successive misfortunes.* CONSECUTIVE denotes a close and uninterrupted sequence, sometimes with the implication of an established order: *The army was finally routed by defeats on three consecutive days.*

suc·ces·sor (sək ses′ər), *n.* **1.** one who or that which succeeds or follows. **2.** one who succeeds another in an office, position, or the like. [< L, equiv. to *success-* (see SUCCESS) + *-or* -OR²; r. ME *successour* < AF] —**suc·ces′sor·al,** *adj.*

success′ sto′ry, an account, real or fictional, of the ascent to fame, fortune, etc., of a person of relatively obscure beginnings: *The actress's success story appeared in all the newspapers.*

suc·ci·nate (suk′sə nāt′), *n.* *Chem.* a salt or ester of succinic acid. [< F; see SUCCIN(IC), -ATE¹]

suc·cinct (sək singkt′), *adj.* **1.** expressed in few words; concise; terse. **2.** characterized by conciseness or verbal brevity. **3.** compressed into a small area, scope, or compass. **4.** *Archaic.* **a.** drawn up, as by a girdle. **b.** close-fitting. **c.** encircled, as by a girdle. [< L *succinct(us)* girt from below, tucked up, ready, concise, equiv. to *suc-* SUC- + *cinctus* (ptp.) (*cing-* gird + *-tus* ptp. suffix)] —**suc·cinct′ly,** *adv.* —**suc·cinct′ness,** *n.*

suc·cinc·to·ri·um (suk′singk tōr′ē əm, -tôr′-), *n., pl.* **-to·ri·a** (-tōr′ē ə, -tôr′ē ə). *Rom. Cath. Ch.* subcinctorium.

suc·cin·ic (sək sin′ik), *adj.* **1.** pertaining to or obtained from amber. **2.** *Chem.* of or derived from succinic acid. [< L *succin(um)* amber + -IC; cf. F *succinique*]

succin′ic ac′id, *Chem.* a colorless, crystalline, water-soluble solid, $HOOC(CH_2)_2COOH$, used chiefly in the manufacture of lacquers, dyes, and perfume.

suc·ci·nyl·sul·fa·thi·a·zole (suk′sə nᵊl sul′fə thī′ə-zōl′), *n.* *Pharm.* a white or yellowish-white, crystalline, very slightly water-soluble powder, $C_{13}H_{13}N_3O_5S_2 \cdot H_2O$, used chiefly in the treatment of bacillary dysentery. Also, **suc′ci·nyl·sul′pha·thi′a·zole′.** [SUCCIN(IC) + -YL + SULFATHIAZOLE]

suc·cor (suk′ər), *n.* **1.** help; relief; aid; assistance. **2.** one who or that which gives help, relief, aid, etc. —*v.t.* **3.** to help or relieve in difficulty, need, or distress; aid; assist. Also, *esp. Brit.,* **suc′cour.** [ME *sucur(en)* (v.) < OF *sucuri(r)* < L *succurrere* to go beneath, run to help, equiv. to *suc-* SUC- + *currere* to run (see CURRENT)] —**suc′cor·a·ble, suc′cour·a·ble,** *adj.* —**suc′cor·er, suc′cour·er,** *n.*
—**Syn. 1, 3.** support. **3.** See **help.**

suc·co·ry (suk′ə rē), *n., pl.* **-ries.** chicory. [< MLG *suckerie,* perh. < ML, b. L *succ(us)* juice + *(cich)orium* (< Gk *kichṓreia* (pl.) CHICORY); the plant's roots are full of sap]

sub·to′tem, *n.*
sub·to·tem′ic, *adj.*
sub·tow′er, *n.*
sub′trans·lu′cent, *adj.*
sub′trans·lu′cence, *n.*
sub′trans·lu′cen·cy, *n.*
sub′trans·par′ent, *adj.;* **-ly,** *adv.;* **-ness,** *n.*
sub′trans·ver′sal, *adj.;* **-ly,** *adv.*
sub′trans·verse′, *adj.;* **-ly,** *adv.*
sub·trap′e·zoid′, *adj.*
sub′trap·e·zoi′dal, *adj.*
sub·tread′, *n.*
sub·trench′, *n.*
sub′tri·an′gu·lar, *adj.*
sub′tri·an′gu·lar′i·ty, *n.*
sub′tri·an′gu·late, *adj.*
sub·trib′al, *adj.*
sub′tribe′, *n.*
sub·tri′fid, *adj.*
sub·trig′o·nal, *adj.*
sub′tri·he′dral, *adj.*
sub·trip′li·cate, *adj.*
sub·trip′li·cat′ed, *adj.*
sub′trip·li·ca′tion, *n.*
sub′tri·que′trous, *adj.*
sub·tro·chan·ter′ic, *adj.*
sub·troch′le·ar, *adj.*
sub′troch·le·ar′i·form′, *adj.*
sub·trun′cate, *adj.*
sub·trun′cat·ed, *adj.*
sub′trun·ca′tion, *n.*
sub′trunk′, *n.*
sub·tu′bi·form′, *adj.*
sub·tu′nic, *n.*
sub·tun′nel, *n.*
sub′tur·ric′u·late, *adj.*
sub′tur·ric′u·lat′ed, *adj.*
sub·tu′tor, *n.*
sub·tu′tor·ship′, *n.*
sub·twined′, *adj.*
sub′tym·pa·nit′ic, *adj.*
sub·ul′ti·mate, *adj.*
sub·um′bel·lar, *adj.*
sub·um′bel·late, *adj.*
sub·um′bel·lat′ed, *adj.*
sub′um·bel·lif′er·ous, *adj.*
sub′um·bil′i·cal, *adj.*
sub·um′bo·nal, *adj.*
sub·um′bo·nate, *adj.*
sub·un′ci·nal, *adj.*
sub·un′ci·nate, *adj.*
sub·un′ci·nat′ed, *adj.*
sub′un·e′qual, *adj.;* **-ly,** *adv.;* **-ness,** *n.*
sub·un′gual, *adj.*
sub·u′nit, *n.*
sub′u·ni·ver′sal, *adj.*
sub′u′ni·verse′, *n.*
sub′u·re′thral, *adj.*
sub·ur′sine, *adj.*
sub′va·ri′e·ty, *n., pl.* **-ties.**
sub·vas′sal, *n.*
sub·vas′sal·age, *n.*
sub′vein′, *n.*
sub·ven′tral, *adj.;* **-ly,** *adv.*
sub·ven′tri·cous, *adj.*
sub′ven·tric′u·lar, *adj.*
sub·ver′mi·form′, *adj.*
sub·ver′te·bral, *adj.*
sub·ver′te·brate, *n., adj.*
sub·ver′ti·cal, *adj.;* **-ly,** *adv.;* **-ness,** *n.*
sub′ver·tic′i·late, *adj.*
sub′ver·tic′i·lat′ed, *adj.*
sub′ve·sic′u·lar, *adj.*
sub·vest′ment, *n.*
sub·vic′ar, *n.*
sub·vic′ar·ship′, *n.*
sub·vil′lain, *n.*
sub·vir′ile, *adj.*
sub′vi·tal·i·sa′tion, *n.*
sub·vi′tal·ised′, *adj.*
sub′vi·tal·i·za′tion, *n.*
sub·vi′tal·ized′, *adj.*
sub·vit′re·ous, *adj.;* **-ly,** *adv.;* **-ness,** *n.*
sub·war′, *n.*
sub·ward′en, *n.*
sub·ward′en·ship′, *n.*
sub·wealth′y, *adj.*
sub′wink′, *n.*
sub·work′er, *n.*
sub·work′man, *n., pl.* **-men.**
sub′zy·go·mat′ic, *adj.*

suc·co·tash (suk′ə tash′), *n.* a cooked dish of kernels of corn mixed with beans and, often, with green and sweet red peppers. [< Narragansett *msiquatash,* lit., fragments]

suc·coth (so͞o kōt′), *n. Hebrew.* a pl. of **succah.**

Suc·coth (so͝ok′əs; *Heb.* so͞o kōt′), *n. Judaism.* Sukkoth.

suc·cu·ba (suk′yə bə), *n.* a succubus. [< LL: strumpet, equiv. to *suc-* -SUC + *cub-* (s. of *cubāre* to lie down) + *-a* fem. suffix]

suc·cu·bous (suk′yə bəs), *adj. Bot.* (of leaves) overlapping, with the base of each leaf covering part of that under it. Cf. **incubous.** [< L *succub(āre)* (to) lie under (see SUCCUBA) + -OUS]

suc·cu·bus (suk′yə bəs), *n., pl.* **-bi** (-bī′). **1.** a demon in female form, said to have sexual intercourse with men in their sleep. Cf. **incubus** (def. 1). **2.** any demon or evil spirit. **3.** a strumpet or prostitute. [late ME < ML, var. of SUCCUBA with masc. inflexion (deriv. of *incubus* INCUBUS) but unchanged meaning]

suc·cu·lent (suk′yə lənt), *adj.* **1.** full of juice; juicy. **2.** rich in desirable qualities. **3.** affording mental nourishment. **4.** (of a plant) having fleshy and juicy tissues. [< LL *succulent(us),* equiv. to *succu(s)* (var. of *sūcus*) juice + *-lentus* adj. suffix] —**suc′cu·lence, suc′cu·len·cy,** *n.* —**suc′cu·lent·ly,** *adv.*

suc·cumb (sə kum′), *v.i.* **1.** to give way to superior force; yield: *to succumb to despair.* **2.** to yield to disease, wounds, old age, etc.; die. [late ME < L *succumb(ere),* equiv. to *suc-* SUC- + *-cumbere,* var. of *cubāre* to lie down] —**suc·cumb′er,** *n.*

suc·cur·sal (sə kûr′səl), *adj.* subsidiary, esp. noting a religious establishment which is dependent upon a principal one. [< F *succursale,* equiv. to *succurs-* (< L *succurs(us)* (ptp. gone beneath, subordinate; see SUCCOR) + *-ale* -AL[1]]

suc·cuss (sə kus′), *v.t.* **1.** to shake up; shake. **2.** *Med.* to shake (a patient) in order to determine if a fluid is present in the thorax or elsewhere. [< L *succuss(us)* tossed up (ptp. of *succutere*), equiv. to *suc-* SUC- + *cut-* (root of *-cutere,* var. of *quatere* to shake) + *-tus* ptp. suffix]

suc·cus·sion (sə kush′ən), *n.* the act of succussing. [< L *succussiōn-* (s. of *succussiō*) a tossing up, equiv. to *succuss(us)* (see SUCCUSS) + *-iōn* -ION] —**suc·cus·sive** (sə kus′iv), *adj.*

such (such), *adj.* **1.** of the kind, character, degree, extent, etc., of that or those indicated or implied: *Such a man is dangerous.* **2.** of that particular kind or character: *The food, such as it was, was plentiful.* **3.** like or similar: *tea, coffee, and such commodities.* **4.** (used preceding an attributive adjective) so or in such a manner or degree: *such terrible deeds.* **5.** (used with omission of an indication of comparison) of so extreme a kind; so great, good, bad, etc.: *He is such a liar.* **6.** being as stated or indicated: *Such is the case.* **7.** being the person or thing or the persons or things indicated: *If any member be behind in his dues, such member shall be suspended.* **8.** not specified; such and such: *Allow such an amount for food, such an amount for rent, and the rest for other things.* —*pron.* **9.** such a person or thing or such persons or things: *kings, princes, and such.* **10.** the person or thing or the persons or things indicated: *He claims to be a friend but is not such.* **11. as such.** See **as**[1] (def. 22). **12. such as, a.** of the kind specified: *A plan such as you propose will never succeed.* **b.** for example: *He considers quiet pastimes, such as reading and chess, a bore.* [ME, OE *swilc;* c. G *solch,* Icel *slīkr,* Goth *swaleiks,* equiv. to *swa* so + *leiks* LIKE[1]]

such′ and such′, 1. definite or particular, but not named or specified: *They turned out to be such and such kind of people.* **2.** something or someone not specified: *You always have to know what to do if such and such should happen.* [late ME]

such·like (such′līk′), *adj.* **1.** of any such kind; similar. —*pron.* **2.** persons or things of such a kind. [late ME; see SUCH, LIKE[1]]

such·ness (such′nis), *n.* **1.** a fundamental, intrinsic, or characteristic quality or condition: *seraphic indifference to the suchness of his surroundings.* **2.** *Buddhism.* tathata. [SUCH + -NESS]

suck (suk), *v.t.* **1.** to draw into the mouth by action of the lips and tongue, thereby producing a partial vacuum: *to suck lemonade through a straw.* **2.** to draw (water, moisture, air, etc.) by or as if by suction: *Plants suck moisture from the earth. The pump sucked water from the basement.* **3.** to apply the lips or mouth to and draw upon by producing a partial vacuum, esp. for extracting fluid contents: *to suck an orange.* **4.** to apply the mouth to or take into the mouth and draw upon similarly: *to suck one's thumb.* **5.** to take into the mouth and dissolve by the action of the tongue, saliva, etc.: *to suck a piece of candy.* **6.** to render or bring to a specified condition by or as if by sucking. —*v.i.* **7.** to draw something in by producing a partial vacuum in the mouth, esp. to draw milk from the breast. **8.** to draw or be drawn by or as if by suction. **9.** (of a pump) to draw air instead of water, as when the water is low or a valve is defective. **10.** *Slang.* to behave in a fawning manner (usually fol. by *around*). **11. suck in,** *Slang.* to deceive; cheat; defraud: *She was sucked in by a confidence man.* **12. suck up to,** *Slang.* to toady to: *The workers are all sucking up to him because he's the one who decides who'll get the bonuses.* —*n.* **13.** the act or an instance of sucking. **14.** a sucking force. **15.** the sound produced by sucking. **16.** that which is sucked; nourishment drawn from the breast. **17.** a small drink; sip. **18.** a whirlpool. [ME *souk(en),* OE *sūcan;* c. L *sūgere;* akin to SOAK] —**suck′less,** *adj.*

suck·er (suk′ər), *n.* **1.** one who or that which sucks. **2.** *Informal.* a person easily cheated, deceived, or imposed upon. **3.** an infant or a young animal that is suckled, esp. a suckling pig. **4.** a part or organ of an animal adapted for sucking nourishment, or for adhering to an object as by suction. **5.** any of several fresh-water, mostly North American cyprinoid fishes of the family *Catostomidae,* often used for food. **6.** *Informal.* a lollipop. **7.** the piston of a pump which works by suction, or the valve of such a piston. **8.** a pipe or tube through which something is drawn or sucked. **9.** *Bot.* a shoot rising from a subterranean stem or root. —*v.t.* **10.** to strip off suckers or shoots from (a plant); remove superfluous shoots from (a plant). —*v.i.* **11.** to send out suckers or shoots, as a plant. [late ME; see SUCK, -ER[1]] —**suck′er·like′,** *adj.*

Sucker, *Catostomus commersoni* (Length to 2¼ ft.)

suck′er bait′, *Slang.* an enticement calculated to lure a person into a scheme in which he may be victimized.

suck·er·fish (suk′ər fish′), *n., pl.* **-fish·es,** (*esp. collectively*) **-fish.** remora. [SUCKER + FISH]

suck′er list′, *Slang.* a list of names and addresses of persons considered by a business, charity organization, or the like, to be likely purchasers or donors.

suck′et fork′ (suk′it), a utensil for sweetmeats of the 16th, 17th, and early 18th centuries, having fork tines at one end and a spoon bowl at the other end of a common stem. [alter. of *succade* < AF *sukade,* c. OF (northeast) *succade* + FORK]

suck·fish (suk′fish′), *n., pl.* (*esp. collectively*) **-fish,** (*esp. referring to two or more kinds or species*) **-fish·es.** **1.** remora (def. 1). **2.** a clingfish. [SUCK + FISH]

suck′ing louse′. See under **louse** (def. 1).

suck·le (suk′əl), *v.,* **-led, -ling.** —*v.t.* **1.** to nurse at the breast. **2.** to nourish or bring up. **3.** to put to suck. —*v.i.* **4.** to suck at the breast. [late ME; see SUCK, -LE]

suck·ler (suk′lər), *n.* **1.** an animal that suckles its young; mammal. **2.** a suckling. [SUCKLE + -ER[1]]

suck·ling (suk′ling), *n.* an infant or a young animal that is not yet weaned. [SUCK + -LING[1]]

Suck·ling (suk′ling), *n.* **Sir John,** 1609–42, English poet.

sucr-, var. of **sucro-** before a vowel.

su·crase (so͞o′krās), *n. Biochem.* invertase. [SUCR- + -ASE]

Su·cre (so͞o′kre), *n.* **1. An·to·nio Jo·sé de** (än tô′nyô hô se′ the), 1793–1830, Venezuelan general and South American liberator: 1st president of Bolivia 1826–28. **2.** a city in and the nominal capital of Bolivia, in the S part. 54,270 (est. 1962). **3.** (*l.c.*) a cupronickel coin and monetary unit of Ecuador, equal to 100 centavos and equivalent to about .0056 of a U.S. dollar. *Abbr.:* S.

su·cri·er (sy krē ā′), *n., pl.* **-cri·ers** (-krē ā′). *French.* a sugar bowl, often having a cover.

sucro-, a combining form meaning "sugar": *sucroclastic.* Also, *esp. before a vowel,* **sucr-.** [< F *sucr(e)* SUGAR + -O-]

su·crose (so͞o′krōs), *n. Chem.* a crystalline disaccharide, $C_{12}H_{22}O_{11}$, the sugar obtained from the sugar cane, the sugar beet, and sorghum, and forming the greater part of maple sugar; sugar. [SUCR- + -OSE[2]]

suc·tion (suk′shən), *n.* **1.** the act, process, or condition of sucking. **2.** the force that, by a pressure differential, attracts a substance to the region of lower pressure. **3.** the act or process of producing such a force. [< L *suctiōn-* (s. of *suctiō*) a sucking, equiv. to *suct(us)* (ptp. of *sūgere*) < *sug-* + *-tus* ptp. suffix + *-iōn-* -ION] —**suc′tion·al,** *adj.*

suc′tion cup′, a cup-shaped object of rubber, glass, plastic, etc., which, by producing a partial vacuum, can be made to adhere to or draw something to a surface.

suc′tion pump′, a pump for raising water or other fluids by suction, consisting essentially of a vertical cylinder in which a piston works up and down, both the cylinder and the pump having valves that control the flow of the fluid.

suc′tion stop′, *Phonet.* click (def. 3a).

Suc·to·ri·a (suk tōr′ē ə, -tôr′-), *n.* the class or order comprising the suctorians. [< NL; see SUCTORIAN]

suc·to·ri·al (suk tōr′ē əl, -tôr′-), *adj.* **1.** adapted for sucking or suction, as an organ; functioning as a sucker for imbibing or adhering. **2.** having sucking organs; imbibing or adhering by suckers. **3.** pertaining to or characterized by suction. [< NL *suctōri(us)* (see SUCTORIAN) + -AL[1]]

suc·to·ri·an (suk tōr′ē ən, -tôr′-), *n.* **1.** a suctorial animal. **2.** a protozoan of the class or order *Suctoria,* that live, as adults, attached by a stalk to the substrate and feed by means of long, suctorial tentacles. —*adj.* **3.** belonging or pertaining to the *Suctoria.* [< NL *Suctoria,* neut. pl. of *suctōrius* < L *suct(us)* (see SUCTION) + *-ōri(us)* -ORY[1] + -AN]

Su·da·fed (so͞o′də fed′), *n. Pharm., Trademark.* pseudoephedrine.

Su·dan (so͞o dan′), *n.* **1.** French, **Soudan.** a region in N Africa, S of the Sahara and Libyan deserts, extending from the Atlantic to the Red Sea. **2.** Formerly, **Anglo-Egyptian Sudan.** a republic in NE Africa, S of the United Arab Republic and bordering on the Red Sea: a former condominium of Egypt and Great Britain. 13,180,000 (est. 1964); 967,500 sq. mi. *Cap.:* Khartoum.

Su·da·nese (so͞od′ənēz′, -ənēs′), *n., pl.* **-nese,** *adj.* —*n.* **1.** a native or inhabitant of Sudan. —*adj.* **2.** of or pertaining to Sudan or its inhabitants. Also, **Soudanese.** [SUDAN + -ESE]

Sudan′ grass′, a sorghum, *Sorghum vulgare sudanensis,* introduced into the U.S. from Africa, grown for hay and pasture.

Su·dan·ic (so͞o dan′ik), *adj.* **1.** belonging to a residual category in former classifications of languages that consists of the non-Bantu, non-Hamitic languages of the Sudan. These have since been classified into families. **2.** of or pertaining to the Sudan or the Sudanese. [SUDAN + -IC]

su·dar·i·um (so͞o dâr′ē əm), *n., pl.* **-dar·i·a** (-dâr′ē ə). **1.** (in ancient Rome) a cloth, usually of linen, for wiping the face; handkerchief. **2.** (*sometimes cap.*) veronica (def. 2c). [< L, equiv. to *sūd-* (s. of *sūdāre* to sweat) + *-ārium* -ARY]

su·da·ti·o (so͞o dā′shē ō′), *n., pl.* **-da·ti·o·nes** (-dā′shē ō′nēz). (in an ancient Roman bath) a chamber, between the sudatorium and the calidarium, where sweat was removed. [< L, equiv. to *sūdāt(us)* (see SUDATORIUM) + *-iō* nom. n. suffix]

su·da·to·ri·um (so͞o′də tōr′ē əm, -tôr′-), *n., pl.* **-to·ri·a** (-tōr′ē ə, -tôr′-). a hot-air bath for inducing sweating. [< L < *sūdāre* (ptp. of *sūdāre* to sweat) + *-ōrium* -ORY[2]]

su·da·to·ry (so͞o′də tōr′ē, -tôr′ē), *adj., n., pl.* **-ries.** —*adj.* **1.** pertaining to or causing sweating. **2.** pertaining to a sudatorium. —*n.* **3.** a sudatorium. [< L *sūdātōri(us),* equiv. to *sūdāt(us)* (see SUDATORIUM) + *-ōrius* -ORY[1]]

Sud·bur·y (sud′ber′ē, -bə rē, -brē), *n.* a city in S Ontario, in S Canada. 80,120 (1961). —**Sud·bu·ri·an** (sud byo͝or′ē ən), *adj.*

sudd (sud), *n.* (in the White Nile) floating vegetable matter which often obstructs navigation. [< Ar: lit., an obstructing]

sud·den (sud′ən), *adj.* **1.** happening, coming, made, or done quickly, without warning, or unexpectedly: *a sudden attack; a sudden smile.* **2.** occurring without transition from the previous form, state, etc.; abrupt: *a sudden turn; a sudden slope.* **3.** *Archaic.* **a.** quickly made or provided. **b.** impetuous; rash. **4.** *Obs.* unpremeditated, as actions. —*adv.* **5.** *Poetic.* suddenly. —*n.* **6.** *Obs.* an unexpected occasion or occurrence. **7. all of a sudden,** without warning; unexpectedly; suddenly. Also, **on a sudden.** [< ME *sodain* < MF < L *subitān(eus)* going or coming stealthily, equiv. to *subit(us)* sudden, taking by surprise (see SUBITO) + *-āneus* adj. suffix, equiv. to *-ān-(us)* -AN + *-eus* -EOUS] —**sud′den·ly,** *adv.* —**sud′den·ness,** *n.*

—**Syn. 1, 2.** unforeseen, unanticipated. SUDDEN, UNEXPECTED, ABRUPT describe acts, events, or conditions for which there has been no preparation or gradual approach. SUDDEN refers to the quickness of an occurrence, although the event may have been expected: *a sudden change in the weather.* UNEXPECTED emphasizes the lack of preparedness for what occurs or appears: *an unexpected crisis.* ABRUPT characterizes something involving a swift adjustment; the effect is often unpleasant, unfavorable, or the cause of dismay: *He had an abrupt change in manner. The road came to an abrupt end.* —**Ant. 1, 2.** gradual, foreseen.

sud′den death′, *Sports.* an overtime period in which a tied contest is won and play is stopped immediately after one of the contestants scores, as in basketball, or goes ahead, as in golf.

Su·der·mann (zo͞o′dər män′), *n.* **Her·mann** (her′män), 1857–1928, German dramatist and novelist.

Su·de·ten (so͞o dāt′n; *Ger.* zo͞o dāt′n), *n.* **1.** Also, **Su·de·tes** (so͞o dē′tēz), Czech, **Su·de·ty** (so͝o′de ti). a mountain range in E central Europe, extending along the N boundary of the Czech Republic between the Elbe and Oder rivers. Highest peak, 5259 ft. **2.** a native or inhabitant of the Sudetenland. **3.** Sudetenland.

Su·de·ten·land (so͞o dāt′n land′; *Ger.* zo͞o dāt′n-länt′), *n.* a mountainous region in the N Czech Republic, including the Sudeten and the Erzgebirge: annexed by Germany 1938; returned to Czechoslovakia 1945. Also called **Sudeten.**

su·dor (so͞o′dōr; *Eng.* so͞o′dôr), *n. Latin.* sweat; perspiration.

su·dor·if·er·ous (so͞o′də rif′ər əs), *adj.* bearing or secreting sweat. [< LL *sūdōrifer* (< L *sūdor* sweat + *-i-* -I- + *-fer* -FER) + -OUS] —**su′dor·if′er·ous·ness,** *n.*

su·dor·if·ic (so͞o′də rif′ik), *adj.* **1.** causing sweat; diaphoretic. **2.** sudoriparous. —*n.* **3.** a sudorific agent. [< NL *sūdōrific(us)* < L *sūdor* sweat + *-i-* -I- + *-ficus* -FIC]

su·dor·ip·a·rous (so͞o′də rip′ər əs), *adj.* producing or secreting sweat. [< NL *sūdōriparus* < L *sūdor* sweat + *-i-* -I- + *-parus* -PAROUS]

Su·dra (so͞o′drə), *n.* a Hindu of the lowest caste, that of the workers. Cf. **Brahman** (def. 1), **Harijan, Kshatriya, untouchable** (def. 5), **Vaisya.** [< Skt *śūdra*]

suds (sudz), *n.* (*construed as pl.*) **1.** soapy water. **2.** foam; lather. **3.** *Slang.* beer. [? < MD *sudse* marsh; akin to SODDEN]

suds·y (sud′zē), *adj.,* **suds·i·er, suds·i·est.** **1.** consisting of, containing, or producing foamy lather. **2.** resembling or suggesting suds. [SUDS + -Y[1]]

sue (so͞o), *v.,* **sued, su·ing.** —*v.t.* **1.** to institute process in law against, or bring a civil action against: *to sue someone for damages or for breach of promise.* **2.** *Rare.* to make petition or appeal to **3.** *Archaic.* to woo or court. —*v.i.* **4.** to institute legal proceedings, or bring suit: *After the accident she threatened to sue.* **5.** to make petition or appeal: *to sue for peace.* **6.** *Archaic.* to court a woman. **7. sue out,** *Rare.* to make application for or apply for and obtain (a writ or the like) from a court of law. [ME *suen, siwen* < OF *sivre* < VL **sequere;* r. L *sequī* to follow] —**su′er,** *n.*

Sue (so͞o; *Fr.* sy), *n.* **1. Eu·gène** (œ zhen′), (*Marie Joseph Sue*), 1804–57, French novelist. **2.** a girl's given name, form of **Susan, Susanna, Susannah.**

suede (swād), *n., v.,* **sued·ed, sued·ing.** —*n.* **1.** kid or other leather finished with a soft, napped surface, on the flesh side or on the outer side after removal of a thin outer layer. **2.** Also called **suede′ cloth′.** a fabric with a napped surface suggesting this. —*v.t.* **3.** to treat so as to raise a nap on (leather, cloth, etc.). —*v.i.* **4.** to raise a nap on leather, cloth, etc. [< F (*gants de*) *Suède* (gloves from) Sweden]

sue·gee (so͞o′jē), *n. Naut.* soogee (def. 1).

Su·el·len (so͞o el′ən), *n.* a girl's given name.

Suess (sēs), *n.* a crater in the second quadrant of the face of the moon: about 4 miles in diameter.

su·et (so͞o′it), *n.* the hard fatty tissue about the loins and kidneys of beef, sheep, etc., used in cookery or processed to yield tallow. [late ME *sewet* < AF **suet,* equiv. to *su-, sew* (< L *sēbum* tallow) + *-et* -ET] —**su′et·y,** *adj.*

Sue·to·ni·us (swi tō′nē əs), *n.* (*Gaius Suetonius Tranquillus*) A.D. 75–150, Roman historian.

su′et pud′ding, a pudding made of chopped beef suet and flour, boiled or steamed in a cloth, often with other ingredients, as raisins, spices, etc.

Sue·vi·an (swā′vē ən), *n.* **1.** a member of an ancient Germanic people of uncertain origin, mentioned in the writings of Caesar and Tacitus. **2.** a member of a Germanic people that invaded France and Spain in the 5th century A.D. —*adj.* **3.** of or pertaining to the Suevians. [< L *Suēb(ī), Suēv(ī)* (of Gmc orig.; cf. G *Schwaben,* OE *Swǣfe*) + -IAN]

Su·ez (so͞o ez′, so͞o′ez), *n.* **1.** a seaport in the NE United Arab Republic, near the S end of the Suez Canal. 219,000 (est. 1962). **2. Gulf of,** a NW arm of the Red Sea, W of the Sinai Peninsula. **3. Isthmus of,** an isthmus in the NE United Arab Republic, joining Africa and Asia. 72 mi. wide.

Su′ez Canal′, a canal in the NE United Arab Republic, cutting across the Isthmus of Suez and connecting the Mediterranean and the Red Sea. 107 mi. long.

Su′ez Canal′ rud′der, *Naut.* See **salmon tail.**

suf-, var. of **sub-** before *f: suffer.*

suf., suffix. Also, **suff.**

Suff., **1.** Suffolk. **2.** suffragan.

suf·fer (suf′ər), *v.i.* **1.** to undergo or feel pain or distress: *The patient is still suffering.* **2.** to sustain injury, disadvantage, or loss: *One's health suffers from overwork. The business suffers from lack of capital.* **3.** to undergo a penalty, esp. of death: *The traitor was made to suffer for his acts.* **4.** to be the object of some action. **5.** *Obs.* to endure or hold out patiently. —*v.t.* **6.** to undergo, be subjected to, or endure (pain, distress, injury, loss, or anything unpleasant): *to suffer the pangs of conscience.* **7.** to undergo or experience (any action, process, or condition): *to suffer change.* **8.** to tolerate or allow: *I do not suffer fools gladly.* **9.** to allow or permit (to do or be as stated): *Suffer the little children to come unto me, and forbid them not.* [ME *suff(e)re(n)* < L *suffer(re),* equiv. to *suf-* SUF- + *fer-* bear; cf. OF *sofrir* < VL **sufferīre*] —**suf′fer·a·ble,** *adj.* —**suf′fer·a·ble·ness,** *n.* —**suf′fer·a·bly,** *adv.* —**suf′fer·er,** *n.*
—**Syn. 6.** sustain. **8.** stomach, stand, abide.

suf·fer·ance (suf′ər əns, suf′rəns), *n.* **1.** passive permission resulting from lack of interference; tolerance, esp. of something wrong or illegal (usually prec. by *on* or *by*). **2.** capacity to endure pain, hardship, etc.; endurance. **3.** *Archaic.* suffering; misery. **4.** *Archaic.* patient endurance. [ME *suffrance,* OF *soufrance,* < LL *sufferentia,* equiv. to *suffer-* SUFFER + *-entia* -ENCE, -ANCE]

suf′ferance wharf′, a wharf for merchant ships, managed under supervision of customs authorities.

suf·fer·ing (suf′ər ing, suf′ring), *n.* **1.** the act of one who or that which suffers. **2.** Often, **sufferings.** what is suffered by a person or a group of people: *the sufferings of the Jews.*
—**Syn. 1.** endurance, patience; agony, torment, torture; pain, distress.

Suf′ferings of Young′ Wer′ther, The. See **Sorrows of Werther, The.**

Suf·fern (suf′ərn), *n.* a town in SE New York. 5094 (1960).

suf·fice (sə fīs′, -fīz′), *v.,* **-ficed, -fic·ing.** —*v.i.* **1.** to be enough or adequate, as for needs, purposes, etc. —*v.t.* **2.** to be enough or adequate for; satisfy. [late ME *suffice(n)* < L *suffice(re),* equiv. to *suf-* SUF- + *-ficere,* var. of *facere* to make, do; r. ME *suffise(n)* < OF]

suf·fi·cien·cy (sə fish′ən sē), *n., pl.* **-cies.** **1.** the state or fact of being sufficient; adequacy. **2.** a sufficient number or amount; enough. **3.** adequate provision or supply, esp. of wealth. [< LL *sufficientia* < L *suffici-* (see SUFFICE) + *-entia* -ENCY]

suf·fi·cient (sə fish′ənt), *adj.* **1.** adequate for the purpose; enough: *sufficient proof; sufficient protection.* **2.** *Archaic.* competent. [late ME < L *sufficient-* (s. of *sufficiēns*) sufficing, equiv. to *suffici-* (see SUFFICE) + *-ent-* -ENT] —**suf·fi′cient·ly,** *adv.*

suf·fix (*n.* suf′iks; *v.* suf′iks, sə fiks′), *n.* **1.** *Gram.* an affix that follows the element to which it is added, as *-ly* in *kindly.* **2.** something added to the end of something else. —*v.t.* **3.** *Gram.* to add as a suffix. **4.** to affix at the end of something. **5.** to fix or put under. —*v.i.* *Gram.* **6.** to admit a suffix. **7.** to add a suffix. [< NL *suffix(um),* n. use of neut. of L *suffixus* (ptp. of *suffīgere* to fasten), equiv. to *suf-* SUF- + *fixus;* see FIX] —**suf·fix·al** (suf′ik səl), *adj.* —**suf·fix·ion** (sə fik′shən), *n.*

suf·flate (sə flāt′), *v.t.,* **-flat·ed, -flat·ing.** *Obs.* to inflate. [< L *sufflāt(us)* (ptp. of *sufflāre* to blow from below, blow up, inflate), equiv. to *suf-* SUF- + *flā-* blow + *-tus* ptp. suffix] —**suf·fla′tion,** *n.*

suf·fo·cate (suf′ə kāt′), *v.,* **-cat·ed, -cat·ing.** —*v.t.* **1.** to kill by preventing the access of air to the blood through the lungs or analogous organs, as gills; strangle. **2.** to impede the respiration of. **3.** to discomfort by a lack of fresh or cool air. **4.** to overcome or extinguish; suppress. —*v.i.* **5.** to become suffocated; stifle; smother. **6.** to be uncomfortable due to a lack of fresh or cool air. [< L *suffōcātus* (ptp. of *suffōcāre* to choke, stifle), equiv. to *suf-* SUF- + *fōc-* (var. of *fauc-,* s. of *faucēs* throat) + *-ātus* -ATE[1]] —**suf′fo·cat′ing·ly,** *adv.* —**suf′fo·ca′tion,** *n.* —**suf′fo·ca′tive,** *adj.*

Suf·folk (suf′ək), *n.* **1.** a county in E England, divided for administrative purposes into East Suffolk and West Suffolk. **2.** one of an English breed of sheep having a black face and legs, noted for mutton of high quality. **3.** one of an English breed of chestnut draft horses having a deep body and short legs. **4.** one of an English breed of small, black hogs. [OE *sūthfolk* south folk]

Suffr., suffragan.

suf·fra·gan (suf′rə gən), *adj.* **1.** assisting or auxiliary to, as applied to any bishop in relation to the archbishop or metropolitan who is his superior, or as applied to an assistant or subsidiary bishop who performs episcopal functions in a diocese but has no ordinary jurisdiction, as, in the Church of England, a bishop consecrated to assist the ordinary bishop of a see in part of his diocese. **2.** (of a see or diocese) subordinate to an archiepiscopal or metropolitan see. —*n.* **3.** a suffragan bishop. [late ME *suffragane* < ML *suffragān(eus)* voting, equiv. to *suffrāg(ium)* SUFFRAGE + *-āneus,* equiv. to *-ān(us)* -AN + *-eus* -EOUS]

suf·frage (suf′rij), *n.* **1.** the right to vote, esp. in a political election. **2.** a vote given in favor of a proposed measure, candidate, or the like. **3.** *Eccles.* a prayer, esp. a short intercessory prayer or petition. [late ME < L *suffrāg(ium)* voting tablet, vote, equiv. to L *suffrāg(āri)* (to) vote for, support + *-ium* n. suffix]

suf·fra·gette (suf′rə jet′), *n.* a woman advocate of female suffrage. [SUFFRAGE + -ETTE] —**suf′fra·get′tism,** *n.*

suf·fra·gist (suf′rə jist), *n.* an advocate of the grant or extension of political suffrage, esp. to women. [SUFFRAGE + -IST] —**suf′fra·gism,** *n.* —**suf′fra·gis′ti·cal·ly,** *adv.*

suf·fru·tes·cent (suf′ro͞o tes′ənt), *adj.* partially or slightly woody; subshrubby. [< NL *suffrutescent-* (s. of *suffrutescēns*) < L *suf-* SUF- + *frut-* (shortened s. of *frutex* shrub, bush) + *-escent-* -ESCENT]

suf·fru·ti·cose (sə fro͞o′tə kōs′), *adj.* woody at the base and herbaceous above. [< NL *suffruticōs(us)* < L *suf-* SUF- + *frutic-* (s. of *frutex* shrub, bush) + *-ōsus* -OSE[1]]

suf·fu·mi·gate (sə fyo͞o′mə gāt′), *v.t.,* **-gat·ed, -gat·ing.** to fumigate from below; apply fumes or smoke to. [< L *suffūmigāt(us),* equiv. to *suf-* SUF- + *fumigātus;* see FUMIGATE] —**suf·fu′mi·ga′tion,** *n.*

suf·fuse (sə fyo͞oz′), *v.t.,* **-fused, -fus·ing.** to overspread with or as with a liquid, color, etc. [< L *suffūs(us)* (ptp. of *suffundere*). See SUF-, FUSE[2]] —**suf·fused·ly** (sə fyo͞ozd′lē, -fyo͞o′zid-), *adv.* —**suf·fu·sion** (sə fyo͞o′zhən), *n.* —**suf·fu·sive** (sə fyo͞o′siv), *adj.*

Su·fi (so͞o′fē), *n., pl.* **-fis.** a member of an ascetic, retiring, and mystical Muslim sect. [< Ar, lit., (man) of wool, equiv. to *sūf* wool + *-ī* -EN[2]; named after his garb]

Su·fi (so͞o′fē), *n., pl.* **-fis.** a sovereign of the Safavi dynasty.

Su·fism (so͞o′fiz əm), *n.* the ascetic and mystical system of the Sufis. Also, **Su·fi·ism** (so͞o′fē iz′əm). [SUFI + -ISM] —**Su·fis′tic,** *adj.*

Sug (sho͝og), *n.* a boy's or girl's given name.

sug-, var. of **sub-** before *g: suggest.*

sug·ar (sho͝og′ər), *n.* **1.** a sweet, crystalline substance, $C_{12}H_{22}O_{11}$, obtained chiefly from the juice of the sugar cane and the sugar beet, and present in sorghum, maple sap, etc.: used extensively as an ingredient and flavoring of certain foods and as a fermenting agent in the manufacture of certain alcoholic beverages; sucrose. Cf. **beet sugar, cane sugar. 2.** *Chem.* a member of the same class of carbohydrates, as sucrose, glucose, and fructose. **3.** *Informal.* a term of endearment for a loved one; sweetheart; honey. **4.** a word formerly used in communications to represent the letter S. **5.** *Slang.* money. —*v.t.* **6.** to cover, sprinkle, mix, or sweeten with sugar. **7.** to make agreeable. —*v.i.* **8.** to form sugar or sugar crystals. **9.** to make maple sugar. **10. sugar off,** (in making maple sugar) to complete the boiling down of the syrup in preparation for granulation. [ME *sugre, sucre* < MF *sucre* < ML *succār(um)* < It *zucchero* < Ar *sakkar* << Skt *çarkarā*] —**sug′ar·less,** *adj.* —**sug′ar·like′,** *adj.*

sug′ar ap′ple, sweetsop.

sug′ar ba′sin, *Brit.* See **sugar bowl.**

sug′ar beet′, a beet, *Beta vulgaris,* having a white root, cultivated for the sugar it yields.

sug·ar·ber·ry (sho͝og′ər ber′ē), *n., pl.* **-ries.** a hackberry, *Celtis laevigata,* of the southern U.S. [SUGAR + BERRY]

sug·ar·bird (sho͝og′ər bûrd′), *n.* any of various honeycreepers that feed on nectar. [SUGAR + BIRD]

sug′ar bowl′, a small bowl, usually having a cover, for serving granulated sugar or sugar cubes.

sug·ar·bush (sho͝og′ər bo͝osh′), *n.* **1.** an evergreen shrub, *Rhus ovata,* of the desert regions of the southwestern U.S., having greenish-white flowers in short, dense spikes and hairy, dark red fruit. **2.** *U.S., Canada.* an orchard or grove of sugar maples. [SUGAR + BUSH[1]]

sug′ar can′dy, 1. a confection made by boiling pure sugar until it hardens. **2.** someone or something that is pleasing.

sug·ar-can·dy (sho͝og′ər kan′dē), *adj.* **1.** excessively sweet; saccharine: *They tried to sell their sugar-candy treatment of the story to the family magazines.* **2.** pertaining to or characteristic of someone or something that is pleasing.

sug′ar cane′, a tall grass, *Saccharum officinarum,* of tropical and warm regions, having a stout, jointed stalk, and constituting the chief source of sugar. —**sug′ar-cane′,** *adj.*

sug·ar-coat (sho͝og′ər kōt′), *v.t.* **1.** to cover with sugar: *to sugar-coat a pill.* **2.** to make (something difficult or distasteful) appear more pleasant or acceptable: *There was no way to sugar-coat the bad news.*

sug·ar-coat·ing (sho͝og′ər kō′ting), *n.* **1.** the act or process of covering something with sugar. **2.** a coating or layer of sugar or a sugary substance. **3.** a thing used to make something else considered unpleasant or disagreeable seem attractive or palatable.

sug′ar corn′. See **sweet corn.**

Sug′ar Creek′, a town in W Missouri. 2663 (1960).

sug′ar dad′dy, a wealthy, middle-aged man who spends freely on a young woman in return for her companionship or intimacy.

sug·ared (sho͝og′ərd), *adj.* **1.** covered, mixed, or sweetened with sugar. **2.** sweetened as if with sugar; made agreeable; honeyed, as words, speech, etc. [late ME *sugred.* See SUGAR, -ED[3]]

sug′ar grove′, *Midland U.S.* sugarbush (def. 2).

sug·ar·house (sho͝og′ər hous′), *n., pl.* **-hous·es** (-hou′ziz). a shed or other building where maple syrup or maple sugar is made. [SUGAR + HOUSE]

Sug′ar Land′, a town in S Texas. 2802 (1960).

sug′ar loaf′, 1. a large, approximately conical loaf or mass of hard refined sugar. **2.** anything resembling this in shape. **3.** an herb, *Clematis douglasi,* of the northwestern U.S., having solitary, tubular, purple-lined flowers.

sug·ar-loaf (sho͝og′ər lōf′), *adj.* resembling a sugar loaf. Also, **sug′ar-loafed′.**

Sug′arloaf Moun′tain, a mountain in SE Brazil in Rio de Janeiro, at the entrance to Guanabara Bay. 1280 ft. Portuguese, **Pão de Açúcar.**

sug′ar ma′ple, any of several maples having a sweet sap, esp. *Acer saccharum* (the State tree of New York, Vermont, West Virginia, and Wisconsin), yielding a hard wood used for making furniture and being the chief source of maple sugar. —**sug′ar-ma′ple,** *adj.*

sug′ar of lead′ (led), *Chem.* See **lead acetate.**

sug′ar of milk′, lactose.

sug′ar or′chard, *Chiefly New England.* sugarbush (def. 2).

sug′ar pine′, a tall pine, *Pinus Lambertiana,* of California, Oregon, etc., having cones twenty inches long.

sug·ar·plum (sho͝og′ər plum′), *n.* a small sweetmeat made of sugar with various flavoring and coloring ingredients; a bonbon. [SUGAR + PLUM[1]]

sug′ar sift′er. See **berry spoon.**

sug′ar sor′ghum, sorgo.

sug′ar spoon′, a small spoon for serving granulated sugar, resembling but having a wider bowl than a teaspoon.

sug·ar-tit (sho͝og′ər tit′), *n.* a piece of cloth containing moist sugar, wrapped to resemble a nipple and used to pacify an infant. Also, **sug·ar-teat** (sho͝og′ər tēt′).

sug′ar tongs′, small tongs used for serving cubed sugar.

sug·ar·y (sho͝og′ə rē), *adj.* **1.** of, containing, or resembling sugar. **2.** sweet; excessively sweet. **3.** dulcet; honeyed; cloying; deceitfully agreeable: *Her sugary words of greeting sounded insincere.* [SUGAR + -Y[1]] —**sug′ar·i·ness,** *n.*

sugg (sug), *v.i.* *Naut.* to roll with the movement of the sea when grounded: *They felt the ship sugg gently.* [var. of SWAG[1]]

sug·gest (səg jest′, sə-), *v.t.* **1.** to mention or introduce (an idea, proposition, plan, etc.) for consideration or possible action: *The architect suggested that the building be restored.* **2.** to propose (a person or thing) as suitable or possible for some purpose: *We suggested him for president.* **3.** (of things) to prompt the consideration, making, doing, etc., of: *The glove suggests that she was at the scene of the crime.* **4.** to bring before a person's mind indirectly or without plain expression: *I didn't tell him to leave, I only suggested it.* **5.** (of a thing) to call up in the mind (another thing) through association or natural connection of ideas: *The opening music suggests a still, moonlit night.* [< L *suggest(us)* brought up (ptp. of *suggerere*), equiv. to *sug-* SUG- + *ges-* (pt., ptp. s. of *gerere* to carry, display) + *-tus* ptp. suffix] —**sug·gest′ed·ness,** *n.* —**sug·gest′er,** *n.* —**sug·gest′ing·ly,** *adv.*
—**Syn. 2.** recommend, advise. **4.** indicate, imply. See **hint.**

sug·gest·i·ble (səg jes′tə bəl, sə-), *adj.* **1.** subject to or easily influenced by suggestion. **2.** that may be suggested. [SUGGEST + -IBLE] —**sug·gest′i·bil′i·ty, sug·gest′i·ble·ness,** *n.* —**sug·gest′i·bly,** *adv.*

sug·ges·tion (səg jes′chən, -jesh′-, sə-), *n.* **1.** the act of suggesting. **2.** the state of being suggested. **3.** something suggested, as a piece of advice: *We merely made the suggestion that she resign.* **4.** a slight trace: *He speaks English with just a suggestion of a foreign accent.* **5.** the calling up in the mind of one idea by another by virtue of some association or of some natural connection between the ideas. **6.** the idea thus called up. **7.** *Psychol.* **a.** the process of accepting a proposition for belief or action in the absence of the intervening and critical thought that would normally occur. **b.** a proposition for belief or action accepted in this way. **c.** the offering of a stimulus in such a way as to produce an uncritical response. [ME *suggestio(u)n* incitement to evil < ML *suggestiōn-* (s. of *suggestiō*) < L, equiv. to *suggest-* (see SUGGEST) + *-iōn-* -ION]
—**Syn. 1, 3.** See **advice.**

sug·ges·tive (səg jes′tiv, sə-), *adj.* **1.** that suggests; referring to other thoughts, persons, etc.: *His recommendation was suggestive of his wife's thinking, not his own.* **2.** rich in suggestions or recommendations: *a suggestive critical essay.* **3.** evocative; presented partially rather than comprehensively: *a suggestive lyric poem.* **4.** that suggests or implies something improper or indecent; risqué: *suggestive remarks.* [SUGGEST + -IVE] —**sug·ges′tive·ly,** *adv.* —**sug·ges′tive·ness,** *n.*
—**Syn. 1.** See **expressive.**

sugh (so͞okh, so͞of, sou), *n., v.t.* *Scot.* sough[2].

su·gi (so͞o′gē), *n., pl.* **-gi, -gis.** See **Japan cedar.** [< Jap]

Sui (swē), *n.* a dynasty ruling in China A.D. 589–618.

su·i·cid·al (so͞o′i sīd′əl), *adj.* **1.** pertaining to, involving, or suggesting suicide. **2.** tending or leading to suicide. **3.** foolishly or rashly dangerous: *He drives at a suicidal speed.* [SUICIDE + -AL[1]] —**su′i·cid′al·ly,** *adv.*

su·i·cide (so͞o′i sīd′), *n., v.,* **-cid·ed, -cid·ing.** —*n.* **1.** the intentional taking of one's own life. **2.** destruction of one's own interests or prospects: *Speculation in stocks can be financial suicide.* **3.** a person who intentionally takes his own life. —*v.i.* **4.** to commit suicide. —*v.t.* **5.** to kill (oneself). [< NL *suīcīd(ium),* *-cīda* < L *suī,* gen. sing. of refl. pron. + *-cīdium, -cīda* -CIDE]

su′icide clause′, a clause in a life-insurance policy stating that the insurer is required to pay only the reserve or the total premiums paid if the policyholder should commit suicide within a stated period.

su′icide squeeze′. See **squeeze play** (def. 1a). Also called **su′icide squeeze′ play′.**

su·i ge·ne·ris (so͞o′ī ge′ne ris; *Eng.* so͞o′ī jen′ər is), *Latin.* of his, her, its, or their own kind; unique.

su·i ju·ris (so͞o′ī jo͝or′is, so͞o′ē), *Law.* capable of managing one's affairs or assuming legal responsibility. Cf. **alieni juris.** [< L: of one's own right]

su·i·mate (so͞o′ī māt′, so͞o′ē-), *n.* *Chess.* self-mate. [< L *suī* of oneself + MATE[1]]

su·int (so͞o′int, swint), *n.* the natural grease of the wool of sheep, consisting of a mixture of fatty matter and potassium salts, used as a source of potash and in the preparation of ointments. [< F, equiv. to *su-* (*su-(er)* < L *sūdāre* to sweat) + *-int* < ?]

Suisse (swēs), *n.* French name of **Switzerland.**

suit (so͞ot), *n.* **1.** a set of clothing, armor, or the like, intended for wear together, esp. as outer garments. **2.** a set of men's garments of the same color and fabric, consisting of trousers, a fitted singlebreasted or double-breasted jacket, and sometimes a vest, worn with a dress shirt and necktie for business, for social occasions not requiring formal dress, etc. **3.** a similarly matched set consisting of a skirt and jacket, and sometimes a topcoat or blouse, worn by women. **4.** *Law.* the act, the process, or an instance of suing in a court of law; legal prosecution; lawsuit. **5.** *Cards.* **a.** one of the four sets or classes (spades, hearts, diamonds, and clubs) into which a common deck of playing cards is divided. **b.** the aggregate of cards belonging to one of these sets held in a player's hand at one time: *Spades were his long suit.* **c.** one of various sets or classes into which less common decks of cards are divided, as lances, hammers, etc., found in certain decks formerly used or used in fortune telling. **6.** suite (defs. 1–3, 5). **7.** the wooing or courting of a woman: *His suit was rejected at the insistance of her parents.* **8.** the act of making a petition or an appeal. **9.** a petition, as to a person of rank or station. **10.** Also called **set.** *Naut.* a complete group of sails for a boat. **11.** one of the seven classes into which a standard set of 28 dominoes may be divided by matching the numbers on half the face of each: a three suit contains the 3-blank, 3–1, 3–2, 3–3, 3–4, 3–5, and 3–6. Since each such suit contains one of each of the other possible suits, only one complete suit is available per game. **12. follow suit, a.** *Cards.* to play a card of the same suit as that led. **b.** to follow the example of another: *The little girl jumped over the fence, and her playmates followed suit.* **—***v.t.* **13.** to make appropriate, adapt, or accommodate, as one thing to another: *to suit the punishment to the crime.* **14.** to be appropriate or becoming to: *Blue suits you very well.* **15.** to be or prove satisfactory, agreeable, or acceptable to; satisfy or please: *The arrangements suit me.* **16.** to provide with a suit, as of clothing or armor; clothe; array. **—***v.i.* **17.** to be appropriate or suitable; accord. **18.** to be satisfactory, agreeable, or acceptable. [ME *siute, sute, suite* < AF, OF, akin to *sivre* to follow. see SUE, SUITE] **—suit′like′,** *adj.*

suit·a·ble (so͞o′tə bəl), *adj.* such as to suit; appropriate; fitting; becoming. [SUIT + -ABLE] **—suit′·a·bil′i·ty, suit′a·ble·ness,** *n.* **—suit′a·bly,** *adv.*

suit·case (so͞ot′kās′), *n.* an oblong valise. [SUIT + CASE[2]]

suit-dress (so͞ot′dres′), *n.* a costume ensemble for women, consisting of a dress and matching coat or jacket.

suite (swēt *or, for 3 often,* so͞ot), *n.* **1.** a number of things forming a series or set. **2.** a connected series of rooms to be used together: *a large suite at the Waldorf.* **3.** a set of furniture, esp. a set comprising the basic furniture necessary for one room: *bedroom suite.* **4.** a company of followers or attendants; a train or retinue. **5.** *Music.* **a.** an ordered series of instrumental dances, in the same or related keys, commonly preceded by a prelude. **b.** an ordered series of instrumental movements of any character. [< F, appar. metathetic var. of OF *siute* (see SUIT); akin to SUE, SUITOR]

suit·ed (so͞o′tid), *adj.* **1.** being appropriate: *He is particularly suited to such a job.* **2.** being compatible or consistent with: *His prose is suited to the essay style.* [SUIT + -ED[2]]

suit·ing (so͞o′ting), *n.* any fabric for making suits. [SUIT + -ING[1]]

suit·or (so͞o′tər), *n.* **1.** one who courts or woos a woman. **2.** *Law.* a petitioner or plaintiff. **3.** one who sues or petitions for anything. [late ME *s(e)utor, suitour* < AF < L *secūtor,* equiv. to *(secū-,* ptp. s. of *sequī* to follow + *-tus* ptp. suffix) + *-or* -OR[2]]

Sui·yüan (swē′yyän′), *n.* a former province in N China, now a part of Inner Mongolian Autonomous Area. *Cap.:* Kweihsui. 127,413 sq. mi.

su·jee-mu·jee (so͞o′jē mo͞o′jē), *n.* *Naut.* soogee (def. 1). Also, **su′ji-mu′ji.**

Su·kar·no (so͞o kär′nō), *n.* **Ach·med** (äk′med), 1901–1970, Indonesian statesman: president of the Republic of Indonesia 1945–67. Also, **Soekarno.**

su·ki·ya·ki (so͞o′kē yä′kē, so͝ok′ē-, skē yä′kē), *n.* a Japanese dish made with beef, chicken, or pork and usually containing soy sauce, bean curd, and greens, often cooked over direct heat at the table. [< Jap]

suk·kah (so͞o kä′; *Eng.* so͝ok′ə), *n., pl.* **suk·koth** (so͞o-kôt′, -kôs′), *Eng.* **suk·kahs.** *Hebrew.* a temporary structure made of boards, canvas, etc., and roofed with branches, esp. pine branches, built against or near a house or synagogue and used during the Jewish festival of Sukkoth chiefly as a dining area. Also, **succah.** [lit., booth]

suk·koth (so͞o kôt′, -kôs′), *n.* *Hebrew.* a pl. of **sukkah.**

Suk·koth (so͝ok′əs; *Heb.* so͞o kôt′, -kôs′), *n.* a Jewish festival, marked chiefly by the building of *sukkoth* and the use of the lulab and ethrog in the synagogue, that begins on the 15th day of the month of Tishri, is celebrated for nine days by Orthodox and Conservative Jews outside of Israel and for eight days by Reform Jews and by Jews in Israel, and celebrates the harvest and commemorates the period after the exodus from Egypt during which the Jews wandered in the wilderness and lived in huts. Also, **Succoth.** Also called **Feast of Booths, Feast of Tabernacles.** Cf. **Hoshana Rabbah, Shemini Atzereth, Simhath Torah.** [< Heb: booths]

Su·ky (so͞o′kē), *n.* a girl's given name, form of **Susanna** or **Susannah.**

Sulcate stem of horsetail, *Equisetum arvense*

Su·la·we·si (so͞o′lä wā′sē), *n.* Indonesian name of **Celebes.**

sul·cate (sul′kāt), *adj.* having long, narrow grooves or channels, as plant stems or furrowed or cleft, as hoofs. Also, **sul′cat·ed.** [< L *sulcāt(us)* (ptp. of *sulcāre* to plow). See SULCUS, -ATE[1]] **—sul·ca′tion,** *n.*

sul·cus (sul′kəs), *n., pl.* **-ci** (-sī). **1.** a furrow or groove. **2.** *Anat.* a groove or fissure, esp. a fissure between two convolutions of the brain. [L: furrow]

Su·lei·man (so͞o′lə män′, -lā-; so͞o′lā män′), *n.* (*"the Magnificent"*) 1495?–1566, sultan of the Ottoman Empire 1520–66. Also, **Soliman I, Solyman I.**

sulf-, a combining form of **sulfur:** *sulfarsphenamine.* Also, **sulfo-, sulph-.**

sul·fa (sul′fə), *Pharm.* **—***adj.* **1.** related chemically to sulfanilamide. **2.** pertaining to, consisting of, or involving a sulfa drug or drugs. **—***n.* **3.** See **sulfa drug.** Also, **sulpha.** [short for SULFANILAMIDE]

sulfa-, 1. *Pharm.* a combining form of sulfa drugs: *sulfathiazole.* **2.** *Chem.* a combining form of the sulfanilyl group. Also, **sulpha-,** *esp. before a vowel,* **sulf-, sulph-.** [see SULFA]

sul·fa·di·a·zine (sul′fə dī′ə zēn′, -zin), *n.* *Pharm.* a sulfanilamide derivative, $NH_2C_6H_4SO_2NHC_4H_3N_2$, used chiefly in the treatment of pneumococcal, staphylococcal, streptococcal, and gonococcal infections. Also, **sulphadiazine.** [SULFA- + DIAZINE]

sul′fa drug′, *Pharm.* any of a group of drugs closely related in chemical structure to sulfanilamide, having a bacteriostatic rather than a bacteriocidal effect: used in the treatment of various diseases, wounds, burns, and the like. Also called **sulfa.**

sul·fa·guan·i·dine (sul′fə gwan′i dēn′, -din, -gwä′-ni-), *n.* *Pharm.* a sulfa drug, $H_2NC_6H_4SO_2NHC(=NH)NH_2$, used chiefly in treating infections of the gastrointestinal tract. Also, **sulphaguanidine.** [SULFA- + GUANIDINE]

sul·fa·mer·a·zine (sul′fə mer′ə zēn′, -zin), *n.* *Pharm.* a sulfa drug, $C_{11}H_{12}N_4O_2S$, derived from sulfadiazine: used chiefly in the treatment of infections caused by meningococci. Also, **sulphamerazine.** [SULFA- + -MER + -AZINE]

sul·fa·nil·a·mide (sul′fə nil′ə mīd′, -mid), *n.* *Pharm.* a white, crystalline amide of sulfanilic acid, $NH_2C_6H_4SO_2NH_2$, used chiefly in the treatment of infections caused by hemolytic streptococci, gonococci, and the like. Also, **sulphanilamide.** [SULF- + *anil-* (abstracted from *anilic acid;* see ANIL) + AMIDE]

sul′fa·nil′ic ac′id (sul′fə nil′ik, sul′-), *Chem.* a grayish-white, crystalline, slightly water-soluble solid, the para form of $H_2NC_6H_4SO_3H \cdot H_2O$, used chiefly as an intermediate in the manufacture of dyes. Also, **sulphanilic acid.** [SULF- + *anilic* (see ANIL, -IC)]

sul·fan·i·lyl (sul fan′ə lil), *adj.* *Chem.* containing the sulfanilyl group. [SULFANIL(IC) + -YL]

sulfan′ilyl group′, *Chem.* the para form of the group $H_2NC_6H_4SO_2-$, derived from sulfanilic acid. Also called **sulfan′ilyl rad′ical.**

sulf·an·ti·mo·nide (sul fan′tə mə nīd′, -nid), *n.* *Chem.* any compound containing an antimonide and a sulfide. Also, **sulphantimonide.** [SULF- + *antimonide;* see ANTIMON(Y), -IDE]

sul·fa·pyr·a·zine (sul′fə pēr′ə zēn′, -zin), *n.* *Pharm.* a colorless, water-insoluble, crystalline sulfa drug, $C_{10}H_{10}N_4O_2S$, used chiefly in the treatment of infections caused by staphylococci or gonococci. Also, **sulphapyrazine.** [SULFA- + PYR- + AZINE]

sul·fa·pyr·i·dine (sul′fə pēr′i dēn′, -din), *n.* *Pharm.* a sulfanilamide derivative, $NH_2C_6H_4SO_2NHC_5H_4N$, formerly used for infections caused by pneumococci, now used primarily for a particular dermatitis. Also, **sulphapyridine.** [SULFA- + PYRIDINE]

sulf·ar·se·nide (sul fär′sə nīd′, -nid), *n.* *Chem.* any compound containing an arsenide and a sulfide. Also, **sulpharsenide.** [SULF- + ARSENIDE]

sulf·ars·phen·a·mine (sulf′ärs fen′ə mēn′, -min), *n.* *Pharm.* a yellow, water-soluble powder, $C_{14}H_{14}As_2N_2Na_2O_8S_2$, formerly used in the treatment of syphilis. [SULF + ARSPHENAMINE]

Sul·fa·sux·i·dine (sul′fə suk′si dēn′, -din), *n.* *Pharm., Trademark.* succinylsulfathiazole.

sul·fate (sul′fāt), *n., v.,* **-fat·ed, -fat·ing.** **—***n.* **1.** *Chem.* a salt or ester of sulfuric acid. **—***v.t.* **2.** to combine, treat, or impregnate with sulfuric acid, a sulfate, or sulfates. **3.** to convert into a sulfate. **4.** *Elect.* to form a deposit of lead-sulfate compound on the lead electrodes of a storage battery. **—***v.i.* **5.** to become sulfated. Also, **sulphate.** [earlier *sulphate* < NL *sulphātum.* See SULF-, -ATE[2]] **—sul·fa′tion,** *n.*

sul′fate pa′per, paper made from sulfate pulp.

sul′fate proc′ess, *Chem.* a process for making wood pulp by digesting wood chips in an alkaline liquor consisting chiefly of caustic soda together with sodium sulfate. Also called **kraft process.**

sul′fate pulp′, wood pulp made by the sulfate process.

sul·fa·thi·a·zole (sul′fə thī′ə zōl′, -zôl′, -zol′), *n.* *Pharm.* a sulfanilamide derivative, $NH_2C_6H_4SO_2NHC_3H_2NS$, formerly used in the treatment of pneumonia and staphylococcal infections, but now largely replaced because of its toxicity. Also, **sulphathiazole.** [SULFA- + THIAZOLE]

sul·fat·ize (sul′fə tīz′), *v.t.,* **-ized, -iz·ing.** to convert into a sulfate, as by the roasting of ores. Also, **sulphatize.** [SULFATE + -IZE] **—sul′fat·i·za′tion,** *n.*

sulf·hy·dryl (sulf hī′dril), *adj.* *Chem.* mercapto. [SULF- + HYDR-[2] + -YL]

sul·fide (sul′fīd), *n.* *Chem.* a compound of sulfur with a more electropositive element or, less often, a group. Also, **sulphide.** [SULF- + -IDE]

sul′fide dye′, *Chem.* See **sulfur dye.**

sul·fi·nyl (sul′fə nil), *adj.* *Chem.* containing the sulfinyl group; thionyl. Also, **sulphinyl.** [SULF- + -IN[2] + -YL]

sul′finyl group′, *Chem.* the bivalent group, >SO. Also called **sul′finyl rad′ical.**

sul·fi·sox·a·zole (sul′fi sok′sə zōl′, -zôl′, -zol′), *n.* *Pharm.* a white to yellowish, crystalline, slightly bitter, water-insoluble powder, $H_2NC_6H_4SO_2NHC_3NO(CH_3)_2$, used chiefly in the treatment of infections of the urinary tract. [SULF- + ISO- + OX- + AZOLE]

sul·fite (sul′fīt), *n.* *Chem.* a salt or ester of sulfurous acid. Also, **sulphite.** [SULF- + -ITE[1]] **—sul·fit·ic** (sul fit′ik), *adj.*

sul′fite pa′per, paper made from sulfite pulp.

sul′fite proc′ess, *Chem.* a process for making wood pulp by digesting wood chips in an acid liquor consisting of sulfurous acid and a salt, usually calcium bisulfite.

sul′fite pulp′, wood pulp made by the sulfite process.

sul·fo (sul′fō), *adj.* *Chem.* containing the sulfo group; sulfonic. [abstracted from SULFONIC]

sulfo-, var. of **sulf-,** esp. before a consonant: *sulfobenzoic acid.*

sul′fo group′, *Chem.* the univalent group, SO_3H-, derived from sulfuric acid. Also called **sulfo radical.**

Sul·fo·nal (sul′fə nal′, sul′fə nal′), *n.* *Pharm., Trademark.* sulfonmethane.

sul·fon·a·mide (sul fon′ə mīd′, sul′fə nam′id), *n.* *Pharm.* See **sulfa drug.** Also, **sulphonamide.** [sulfon- abstracted from SULFONIC + AMIDE]

sul·fo·nate (sul′fə nāt′), *n., v.,* **-nat·ed, -nat·ing.** *Chem.* **—***n.* **1.** an ester or salt derived from a sulfonic acid. **—***v.t.* **2.** to make into a sulfonic acid, as by treating an aromatic hydrocarbon with concentrated sulfuric acid. **3.** to introduce the sulfonic group into (an organic compound). Also, **sulphonate.** [SULFON(IC) + -ATE[2], r. -IC]

sul·fo·na·tion (sul′fə nā′shən), *n.* *Chem.* the process of attaching the sulfonic acid group, $-SO_3H$, directly to carbon in an organic compound. Also, **sulphonation.** [SULFONATE + -ION]

sul·fone (sul′fōn), *n.* *Chem.* any of a class of organic compounds containing the bivalent group, $-SO_2-$, united with two hydrocarbon groups. Also, **sulphone.** [SULF- + -ONE]

sul·fon·ic (sul fon′ik), *adj.* *Chem.* sulfo. Also, **sulphonic.** [SULFONE + -IC]

sulfon′ic ac′id, *Chem.* any of a large group of organic compounds of the structure RSO_2OH, which are strong acids that give neutral sodium salts: used in the synthesis of phenols, dyes, and other substances.

sul·fo·ni·um (sul fō′nē əm), *n.* *Chem.* the positively charged group, H_3S^+, its salts, or their substitute products, as trimethylsulfonium iodide, $(CH_3)_3SI$. Also, **sulphonium.** [NL, equiv. to *sulf-* SULF- + *-onium,* abstracted from AMMONIUM]

sul·fon·meth·ane (sul′fōn meth′ān, -fon-), *n.* *Pharm.* a crystalline organic compound, $(CH_3)_2C(SO_2C_2H_5)_2$, used chiefly as a mild hypnotic or sedative. [*sulfon-* abstracted from SULFON(IC) + METHANE]

sul·fo·nyl (sul′fə nil), *adj.* *Chem.* sulfuryl. [*sulfon-* abstracted from SULFON(IC) + -YL]

sul′fonyl chlo′ride, *Chem.* noting the group, $-SO_2Cl$, as in benzenesulfonyl chloride, $C_6H_5SO_2Cl$.

sul′fo rad′ical. See **sulfo group.**

sul·fur (sul′fər), *n.* **1.** Also, **sulphur.** *Chem.* a nonmetallic element that exists in several forms, the ordinary one being a yellow rhombic crystalline solid, and that burns with a blue flame and a suffocating odor: used esp. in making gunpowder and matches, in medicine, in vulcanizing rubber, etc. *Symbol:* S; *at. wt.:* 32.064; *at. no.:* 16; *sp. gr.:* 2.07 at 20° C. **2.** sulphur (def. 2). [ME *sulphur* < L, sp. var. of *sulfur*]

sul·fu·rate (sul′fyə rāt′, -fə-), *v.t.,* **-rat·ed, -rat·ing.** to combine, treat, or impregnate with sulfur, the fumes of burning sulfur, etc. Also, **sulphurate.** [< L *sulfurāt(us).* See SULFUR, -ATE[1]] **—sul′fu·ra′tion,** *n.* **—sul′fu·ra′tor,** *n.*

sul′furated pot′ash, *Pharm.* a yellowish-brown mixture consisting mainly of potassium polysulfides and potassium thiosulfate, used chiefly in treating chronic skin diseases. Also called **liver of sulfur.**

sul·fur-bot·tom (sul′fər bot′əm), *n.* sulphur-bottom.

sul′fur but′terfly, any of various yellow or orange butterflies of the family *Pieridae.*

sul′fur diox′ide, *Chem.* a colorless, nonflammable, water-soluble, suffocating gas, SO_2, formed when sulfur burns: used chiefly in the manufacture of chemicals such as sulfuric acid, in preserving fruits and vegetables, and in bleaching, disinfecting, and fumigating.

sul′fur dye′, *Chem.* any of the class of dyes produced by heating an organic compound, as an indophenol, with sulfur or sodium polysulfide, used chiefly to dye cotton. Also, **sulfide dye.**

sul·fu·re·ous (sul fyo͝or′ē əs), *adj.* **1.** consisting of, containing, or pertaining to sulfur. **2.** resembling sulfur, esp. in color. Also, **sulphureous.** [< L *sulfureus.* See SULFUR, -EOUS] **—sul·fu′re·ous·ly,** *adv.* **—sul·fu′re·ous·ness,** *n.*

sul·fu·ret (sul′fyə ret′), *n., v.,* **-ret·ed, -ret·ing** or (*esp. Brit.*) **-ret·ted, -ret·ting.** **—***n.* **1.** *Chem.* a sulfide. **—***v.t.* **2.** to treat or combine with sulfur. Also, **sulphuret.** [< NL *sulfuret(um)ē.* See SULF-, -URET]

sul′fureted hy′drogen, *Chem.* See **hydrogen sulfide.** Also, **sul′furetted hy′drogen.**

sul·fur-flow·er (sul′fər flou′ər), *n.* sulphur-flower.

sul·fu·ric (sul fyo͝or′ik), *adj.* *Chem.* of or containing sulfur, esp. in the hexavalent state. Also, **sulphuric.** [SULFUR + -IC; modeled on F *sulfurique*]

sulfu′ric ac′id, *Chem.* a clear, colorless to brownish, dense, oily, corrosive, water-miscible liquid, H_2SO_4, usually produced from sulfur dioxide: used chiefly in the manufacture of fertilizers, chemicals, explosives, dyestuffs, and in petroleum refining. Also called **oil of vitriol.**

sulfu′ric anhy′dride, *Chem.* See **sulfur trioxide.**

sulfu′ric e′ther, *Chem.* ether (def. 1).

sul·fu·rize (sul′fyə rīz′, -fə-), *v.t.,* **-rized, -riz·ing.** **1.** to combine, treat, or impregnate with sulfur. **2.** to fumigate with sulfur dioxide. Also, **sulphurize.** [< F *sulfuris(er).* See SULFUR, -IZE] **—sul′fu·ri·za′tion,** *n.*

sul·fur·ous (sul′fər əs, sul fyo͝or′əs), *adj.* **1.** relating to sulfur. **2.** of the yellow color of sulfur. **3.** containing tetravalent sulfur. Also, **sulphurous.** [< L *sulfurōs(us).* See SULFUR, -OUS] **—sul′fur·ous·ly,** *adv.* **—sul′·fur·ous·ness,** *n.*

sul′furous ac′id, *Chem.* a colorless liquid, H_2SO_3, having a suffocating odor, obtained by dissolving sulfur dioxide in water, known mainly by its salts, which are sulfites: used chiefly in organic synthesis and as a bleach.

sul′fur spring′, a spring the water of which contains naturally occurring sulfur compounds.

sul′fur triox′ide, *Chem.* an irritant, corrosive, low-melting solid, SO_3, obtained by the oxidation of sulfur dioxide as a liquid which reverts to the solid form unless stabilized: used as an intermediate in the manufacture of sulfuric acid. Also called **sulfuric anhydride.**

sul·fur·yl (sul′fə ril, -fyə ril), *adj.* *Chem.* containing the sulfuryl group, SO_2, as sulfuryl chloride; sulfonyl. Also, **sulphuryl.** [SULFUR + -YL]

sul′furyl chlo′ride, *Chem.* a colorless liquid, SO_2Cl_2, having a very pungent odor and corrosive to the skin and mucous membranes: used as a chlorinating or sulfonating agent.

sul′furyl group′, *Chem.* the bivalent group, SO_2, derived from sulfuric acid. Also called **sul′furyl rad′ical.**

sulk (sulk), *v.i.* **1.** to remain silent or hold oneself aloof in a sullen, ill-humored, or offended mood. **—***n.* **2.** a state or fit of sulking. **3. sulks,** ill-humor shown by sulking: *to be in the sulks.* **4.** Also, **sulk′er.** one who sulks. [back formation from SULKY]

sulk·y (sul′kē), *adj.,* **sulk·i·er, sulk·i·est,** *n., pl.* **sulk·ies.** **—***adj.* **1.** marked by or given to sulking;

sullenly ill-humored, resentful, or aloof. **2.** gloomy or dull: *sulky weather.* **—n. 3.** a light, two-wheeled, one-horse carriage for one person. [akin to OE *solcen-* lazy (in *solcennes* laziness), NFris *sulkig* sulky] **—sulk′i·ly,** *adv.* **—sulk′i·ness,** *n.*
—Syn. 1. moody, surly, morose, churlish. **—Ant. 1.** temperate, good-natured.

sull (sul), *Metall.* **—n. 1.** a film of oxide formed on wire as a means of protecting it and of holding the lubricant used when it is drawn. **—v.t. 2.** to treat (wire) so that a film of oxide will form on its surface. [back formation from SULLAGE]

Sul·la (sul′ə), *n.* (*Lucius Cornelius Sulla Felix*) 138–78 B.C., Roman general and statesman: dictator 82–79.

sul′la clo′ver (sul′ə). See **French honeysuckle.** [< Sp *zulla* + CLOVER]

sul·lage (sul′ij), *n.* **1.** refuse or waste; sewage. **2.** silt; sediment. **3.** *Metall.* scoria floating on molten metal in a ladle. [? < OE *sol* mud + -AGE; see SULKY]

sul·len (sul′ən), *adj.* **1.** showing irritation or ill humor by a gloomy silence or reserve. **2.** persistently and silently ill-humored; morose. **3.** indicative of gloomy ill humor. **4.** gloomy or dismal, as weather, sounds, etc. **5.** sluggish, as a stream. **6.** *Obs.* malignant, as planets or influences. [ME *solein* < ?] **—sul′len·ly,** *adv.* **—sul′len·ness,** *n.*
—Syn. 1. See **cross. 2.** sulky, moody, sour, bad-tempered. **4.** cheerless, clouded, overcast, somber, mournful, dark. **5.** slow, stagnant. **—Ant. 1, 2.** cheerful.

Sul·li·van (sul′ə vən), *n.* **1. Annie** (*Anne Mansfield Sullivan Macy*), 1866–1936, U.S. teacher of Helen Keller. **2. Sir Arthur (Seymour),** 1842–1900, English composer: collaborator with Sir William Gilbert. **3. Harry Stack** (stak), 1892–1949, U.S. psychiatrist and psychoanalyst. **4. John L(awrence),** 1858–1918, U.S. boxer: world heavyweight champion 1882–92. **5. Louis Henri,** 1856–1924, U.S. architect. **6.** a town in SW Indiana. 4979 (1960). **7.** a town in central Missouri. 4098 (1960). **8.** a town in central Illinois. 3946 (1960).

sul·ly (sul′ē), *v.*, **-lied, -ly·ing,** *n.*, *pl.* **-lies. —v.t. 1.** to soil, stain, or tarnish. **2.** to mar the purity or luster of; defile: *to sully a reputation.* **—v.i. 3.** to become sullied, soiled, or tarnished. **—n. 4.** *Obs.* a stain; soil. [OE *soli(an)* (to) become defiled akin to *sol* mud, slough] **—sul′li·a·ble,** *adj.*
—Syn. 1. taint, blemish, contaminate. **2.** dirty, disgrace, dishonor.

Sul·ly (sul′ē; *for 1 also Fr.* SY lē′), *n.* **1. Ma·xi·mi·lien de Bé·thune** (MAK sē mē lyAN′ də bā tYN′), **Duc de,** 1560–1641, French statesman. **2. Thomas,** 1783–1872, U.S. painter, born in England.

Sul·ly-Pru·dhomme (SY lē′PRY dôm′), *n.* **Re·né Fran·çois Ar·mand** (Rə nā′ FRÄN SWA′ AR mäN′), 1839–1907, French poet: Nobel prize 1901.

sulph-, var. of **sulf-** or **sulfa-.**

sul·pha (sul′fə), *adj.*, *n.* *Pharm.* sulfa.

sulpha-, var. of **sulfa-.** Also, *esp. before a vowel,* **sulph-.**

sul·pha·di·a·zine (sul′fə dī′ə zēn′, -zin), *n.* *Pharm.* sulfadiazine.

sul·pha·guan·i·dine (sul′fə gwan′i dēn′, -din, -gwä′ni-), *n.* *Pharm.* sulfaguanidine.

sul·pha·mer·a·zine (sul′fə mer′ə zēn′, -zin), *n.* *Pharm.* sulfamerazine.

sul·pha·nil·a·mide (sul′fə nil′ə mīd′, -mid), *n.* *Pharm.* sulfanilamide.

sul′pha·nil′ic ac′id (sul′fə nil′ik, sul′-), *Chem.* See **sulfanilic acid.**

sulph·an·ti·mo·nide (sul fan′tə mə nīd′, -nid), *n.* *Chem.* sulfantimonide.

sul·pha·pyr·a·zine (sul′fə pēr′ə zēn′, -zin), *n.* *Pharm.* sulfapyrazine.

sul·pha·pyr·i·dine (sul′fə pēr′i dēn′, -din), *n.* *Pharm.* sulfapyridine.

sulph·ar·se·nide (sul fär′sə nīd′, -nid), *n.* *Chem.* sulfarsenide.

sul·phate (sul′fāt), *n.*, *v.t.*, *v.i.*, **-phat·ed, -phat·ing.** sulfate. **—sul·pha′tion,** *n.*

sul·pha·thi·a·zole (sul′fə thī′ə zōl′, -zôl′, -zol′), *n.* *Pharm.* sulfathiazole.

sul·phat·ize (sul′fə tīz′), *v.t.*, **-ized, -iz·ing.** sulfatize. **—sul′phat·i·za′tion,** *n.*

sul·phide (sul′fīd), *n.* *Chem.* sulfide.

sul·phi·nyl (sul′fə nil), *adj.* *Chem.* sulfinyl.

sul·phite (sul′fīt), *n.* *Chem.* sulfite. **—sul·phit·ic** (sul fit′ik), *adj.*

sul·phon·a·mide (sul fon′ə mīd′, sul′fə nam′id), *n.* *Pharm.* sulfonamide.

sul·pho·nate (sul′fə nāt′), *n.*, *v.t.*, **-nat·ed, -nat·ing.** *Chem.* sulfonate.

sul·pho·na·tion (sul′fə nā′shən), *n.* *Chem.* sulfonation.

sul·phone (sul′fōn), *n.* *Chem.* sulfone.

sul·phon·ic (sul fon′ik), *adj.* *Chem.* sulfonic.

sul·pho·ni·um (sul fō′nē əm), *n.* *Chem.* sulfonium.

sul·phur (sul′fər), *n.* **1.** sulfur. **2.** yellow with a greenish tinge; lemon color. [var. of SULFUR]

Sul·phur (sul′fər), *n.* a town in S Oklahoma. 4737 (1960).

sul·phu·rate (sul′fyə rāt′, -fə-), *v.t.*, **-rat·ed, -rat·ing.** sulfurate. **—sul′phu·ra′tion,** *n.* **—sul′phu·ra′tor,** *n.*

sul·phur-bot·tom (sul′fər bot′əm), *n.* a grayish to bluish-gray whalebone whale, *Sibbaldus musculus,* of arctic seas, having yellowish underparts: the largest mammal that has ever lived. Also called **sulphur-bottom whale, sul′fur-bottom whale′, blue whale.**

sul·phu·re·ous (sul fyŏŏr′ē əs), *adj.* sulfureous. **—sul·phu′re·ous·ly,** *adv.* **—sul·phu′re·ous·ness,** *n.*

sul·phu·ret (sul′fyə ret′), *n.*, *v.t.*, **-ret·ed, -ret·ing** or (*esp. Brit.*) **-ret·ted, -ret·ting.** sulfuret.

sul·phur-flow·er (sul′fər flou′ər), *n.* an herb, *Eriogonum umbellatum,* of the western coast of the U.S., having leaves which are white-woolly on the underside and golden-yellow flowers. Also, **sulfur-flower.**

sul·phu·ric (sul fyŏŏr′ik), *adj.* *Chem.* sulfuric.

sul·phu·rize (sul′fyə rīz′, -fə-), *v.t.*, **-rized, -riz·ing.** *Chem.* sulfurize. **—sul′phu·ri·za′tion,** *n.*

sul·phur·ous (sul′fər əs, sul fyŏŏr′əs), *adj.* **1.** sulfurous. **2.** pertaining to the fires of hell; hellish or satanic. **3.** fiery or heated. [var. of SULFUROUS] **—sul′phur·ous·ly,** *adv.* **—sul′phur·ous·ness,** *n.*

Sul′phur Springs′, a town in NE Texas. 9160 (1960).

sul·phur·yl (sul′fə ril, -fyə ril), *adj.* *Chem.* sulfuryl.

sul·phy·dryl (sul fī′dril), *adj.* *Chem.* mercapto.

Sul·pi·cian (sul pish′ən), *n.* *Rom. Cath. Ch.* a member of a society of secular priests founded in France in 1642, engaged chiefly in training men to teach in seminaries. [< F *sulpicien,* after la Campagnie de Saint *Sulpice* + *-ien* -IAN]

Sul·pi·ci·us Gal·lus (sul pē′sē əs gal′əs), a crater in the first quadrant of the face of the moon: about 8 mi. in diameter.

sul·tan (sul′tᵊn), *n.* **1.** the sovereign of an Islamic country. **2.** (*cap.*) any of the former sovereigns of Turkey. [< ML *sultān(us)* < Ar *sulṭān* dominion, sovereign] **—sul·tan·ic** (sul tan′ik), *adj.* **—sul′tan-like′,** *adj.* **—sul′tan·ship′,** *n.*

sul·tan·a (sul tan′ə, -tä′nə), *n.* **1.** a wife or a concubine of a sultan. **2.** a sister, daughter, or mother of a sultan. **3.** a mistress, esp. of a king or other royal personage. **4.** *Chiefly Brit.* a small, seedless raisin. **5.** Also called **sultan′a bird′.** a purple gallinule, *Porphyrula martinica.* **6.** Also called **old amethyst.** a deep purplish-red color. [< It, fem. of *sultano* SULTAN]

sul·tan·ate (sul′tᵊnāt′), *n.* **1.** the office or rule of a sultan. **2.** the territory ruled over by a sultan. [SULTAN + -ATE¹]

sul·try (sul′trē), *adj.*, **-tri·er, -tri·est. 1.** oppressively hot and close or moist; sweltering: *a sultry day.* **2.** oppressively hot; emitting great heat: *the sultry sun.* **3.** characterized by or associated with sweltering heat: *sultry work in the fields.* **4.** characterized by or arousing heated temper or passion: *a sultry brunette.* [*sult(e)r* (var. of SWELTER) + -Y¹] **—sul′tri·ly,** *adv.* **—sul′tri·ness,** *n.*

Su·lu (sōō′lōō), *n.*, *pl.* **-lus,** (*esp. collectively*) **-lu.** a member of the most numerous and most highly cultivated tribe of Moros, found chiefly in the Sulu Archipelago.

Su′lu Archipel′ago, an island group in the SW Philippines, separating the Celebes Sea from the Sulu Sea. 390,000 (est. 1965); 1086 sq. mi. *Cap.:* Jolo.

Su′lu Sea′, a sea in the W Pacific, between the SW Philippines and Borneo.

Sulz·ber·ger (sulz′bûr gər), *n.* **Arthur Hays,** born 1891, U.S. newspaper publisher.

sum (sum), *n.*, *v.*, **summed, sum·ming. —n. 1.** the aggregate of two or more numbers, magnitudes, quantities, or particulars as determined by or as by the mathematical process of addition: *The sum of 6 and 8 is 14.* **2.** a particular aggregate or total, esp. with reference to money: *The expenses came to an enormous sum.* **3.** an indefinite amount or quantity, esp. of money: *to lend small sums.* **4.** a series of numbers or quantities to be added up. **5.** an arithmetical problem to be solved, or such a problem worked out and having the various steps shown. **6.** the total amount, or the whole. **7.** the substance or gist of a matter, comprehensively or broadly viewed or expressed: *The letter contains the sum of his opinions.* **8.** concise or brief form: *in sum.* **9.** *Math.* **a.** the limit of the sequence of partial sums of a given infinite series. **b.** union (def. 10a). **10.** a summary. **—v.t. 11.** to combine into an aggregate or total (often fol. by *up*). **12.** to ascertain the sum of, as by addition. **13.** to bring into or contain in a small compass (often fol. by *up*). **14. sum up, a.** to reckon: *He summed up his assets and liabilities.* **b.** to bring into or contain in a brief and comprehensive statement; summarize; recapitulate: *to sum up the case for the prosecution.* **c.** to form a quick estimate of: *He summed him up in a minute.* **—v.i. 15.** to amount (usually fol. by *to* or *into*): *Their expenses summed in the thousands.* [ME *summe* < L *summa* (n.), deriv. of *summa* (adj.), fem. of *summus* highest, superl. of *super(us)*; see SUPER] **—sum′less,** *adj.* **—sum′less·ness,** *n.*
—Syn. 1. See **number.**

sum-, var. of **sub-** before *m: summon.*

SUM, surface-to-underwater missile.

su·mac (shōō′mak, sōō′-), *n.* **1.** any of several anacardiaceous shrubs or small trees of the genus *Rhus.* **2.** a preparation of the dried and powdered leaves, bark, etc., of certain species of *Rhus,* esp. *R. coriaria* of southern Europe, used esp. in tanning. **3.** the wood of these trees. Also, **su′mach.** [ME < ML < Ar *summāq*]

Su·mac (sōō′mäk, -mak), *n.* **Y·ma** (ē′mä), (*Emperatriz Chavarri*), born 1927, U.S. singer, born in Peru.

su′mac wax′. See **Japan wax.**

sum′ and sub′stance, main idea, gist, or point: *the sum and substance of his argument.*

Su·ma·tra (sŏŏ mä′trə), *n.* a large island in the W part of Indonesia. 15,439,000 (est. 1961); 164,147 sq. mi. **—Su·ma′tran,** *adj.*, *n.*

Suma′tra cam′phor, borneol.

Sum·ba (sōōm′bä), *n.* one of the Lesser Sunda Islands, in Indonesia, S of Celebes. 250,852 (est. 1961); 4306 sq. mi. Also called **Sandalwood Island.** Dutch, **Soemba.**

Sum·ba·wa (sōōm bä′wä), *n.* one of the Lesser Sunda Islands, in Indonesia: destructive eruption in 1815 of Mt. Tambora. 194,819 (est. 1961); 5965 sq. mi. Dutch, **Soembawa.**

Su·mer (sōō′mər), *n.* an ancient region in southern Mesopotamia which contained a number of independent cities and city-states of which the first were established possibly as early as 5000 B.C.: conquered by the Elamites and about 2000 B.C. by the Babylonians: a number of its cities, as Ur, Uruk, Kish, and Lagash, are major archaeological sites in southern Iraq.

Su·me·ri·an (sōō mēr′ē ən, -mer′-), *adj.* **1.** of or pertaining to Sumer, its people, or their language. **—n. 2.** a native or inhabitant of Sumer. **3.** a language of unknown affinities that was the language of the Sumerians and had, in the late 4th and 3rd millenniums B.C., a well-developed literature that is preserved in pictographic and cuneiform writing and represents the world's oldest extant written documents. [SUMER + -IAN]

Su·me·rol·o·gy (sōō′mə rol′ə jē), *n.* the study of the history and language of the Sumerians. [SUMER + -O- + -LOGY] **—Su′me·rol′o·gist,** *n.*

su·mi (sōō′mē), *n.* *Japanese.* black ink made from a mixture of plant soot and glue solidified into sticks or cakes the ends of which are scraped or ground into, water, much used by calligraphers and painters.

su·mi-e (sōō′mē e′), *n.*, *pl.* **su·mi-e.** *Japanese.* (in fine arts) a monochrome painting executed in ink: *Zen painters were masters of* sumi-e. [< *sumi* SUMI + *e* painting]

sum·ma (sŏŏm′ə, sum′ə), *n.*, *pl.* **sum·mae** (sŏŏm′ī, sum′ē), **sum·mas. 1.** a comprehensive work or series of works covering, synthesizing, or summarizing a particular field or subject. **2.** a work or series of works that is a summary, synthesis, or synopsis of human knowledge. [< L; see SUM]

sum·ma·ble (sum′ə bəl), *adj.* *Math.* **1.** capable of being added. **2.** (of an infinite series, esp. a divergent one) capable of having a sum assigned to it by a method other than the usual one of taking the limit of successive partial sums. **3.** (of a function) possessing a finite Lebesgue integral. [SUM + -ABLE] **—sum′ma·bil′i·ty,** *n.*

sum·ma cum lau·de (sŏŏm′ə kŏŏm lou′dā, -də, -dē; sum′ə kum lô′dē), with highest praise: used in diplomas to grant the highest of three special honors for grades above the average. Cf. **cum laude, magna cum laude.** [< L]

sum·mand (sum′and, sum and′, sə mand′), *n.* a part of a sum. [< ML *summand(us),* ger. of *summāre* to total or sum, deriv. of *summ(a)* SUM]

Sum·ma·nus (sə mā′nəs), *n.* an ancient Roman god of thunderstorms.

sum·ma·rise (sum′ə rīz′), *v.t.*, **-rised, -ris·ing.** *Chiefly Brit.* summarize. **—sum′ma·ris′a·ble,** *adj.* **—sum′ma·ri·sa′tion,** *n.* **—sum′ma·ris′er,** *n.*

sum·ma·rize (sum′ə rīz′), *v.t.*, **-rized, -riz·ing. 1.** to make a summary of; state or express in a concise form. **2.** to constitute a summary of. [SUMMAR(Y) + -IZE] **—sum′ma·riz′a·ble,** *adj.* **—sum′ma·ri·za′tion,** *n.* **—sum′ma·riz′er, sum′mar·ist,** *n.*

sum·ma·ry (sum′ə rē), *n.*, *pl.* **-ries,** *adj.* **—n. 1.** a comprehensive and usually brief abstract, recapitulation, or compendium of previously stated facts or statements. **—adj. 2.** brief and comprehensive; concise. **3.** direct and prompt; unceremoniously fast: *to treat someone with summary dispatch.* **4.** (of legal proceedings, jurisdiction, etc.) conducted without, or exempt from the various steps and delays of a formal trial. [< L *summāri(um),* equiv. to *summ(a)* SUM + *-ārium* -ARY] **—sum·mar·i·ly** (sə mer′ə lē, sum′ər ə-), *adv.* **—sum′mar′i·ness,** *n.*
—Syn. 1. outline, précis. SUMMARY, BRIEF, DIGEST, SYNOPSIS are terms for a short version of a longer work. A SUMMARY is a brief statement or restatement of main points, esp. as a conclusion to a work: *the summary of a chapter.* A BRIEF is a detailed outline, by heads and subheads, of a discourse (usually legal) to be completed: *a brief for an argument.* A DIGEST is an abridgement of an article, book, etc., or an organized arrangement of material under heads and titles: *a magazine consisting of digests; a digest of Roman law.* A SYNOPSIS is usually a compressed statement of the plot of a novel, play, etc.: *a synopsis of* Hamlet. **2.** short, condensed, compact, succinct. **3.** curt, terse, peremptory.

sum′mary court′-martial, *U.S. Mil.* a court-martial composed of one commissioned officer, authorized to try minor offenses against military law.

sum′mary judg′ment, *Law.* a judgment, as in an action for debt, that is entered without the necessity of jury trial, based on affidavits of the creditor and debtor which convince the court that there is no arguable issue.

sum′mary proceed′ing, *Law.* a mode of trial authorized by statute to be held before a judge without the usual full hearing.

Sum·ma The·o·log·i·ca (sŏŏm′ə thē′ə loj′ə kə, sum′ə), a philosophical and theological work (1265–74) by St. Thomas Aquinas, consisting of an exposition of Christian doctrine.

sum·ma·tion (sə mā′shən), *n.* **1.** the act or process of summing. **2.** the result of this; an aggregate or total. **3.** a review or recapitulation of previously stated facts or statements, often with a final conclusion or conclusions drawn from them. **4.** *Law.* the final arguments of opposing attorneys before a case goes to the jury. [< ML *summātiōn-* (s. of *summātiō*), equiv. to *summāt(us)* (ptp. of *summāre* to SUM), equiv. to *summ-* + *-ātus* -ATE¹ + *-iōn-* -ION] **—sum·ma′tion·al,** *adj.*

summa′tion meth′od, *Math.* a method for associating a sum with a divergent series.

sum·mer¹ (sum′ər), *n.* **1.** the season between spring and autumn, in the Northern Hemisphere from the summer solstice to the autumnal equinox, and in the Southern Hemisphere from the winter solstice to the vernal equinox. **2.** the period comprising the months of June, July, and August in the U.S., and from the middle of May to the middle of August in Great Britain. **3.** a period of hot, usually sunny weather: *We had no real summer last year.* **4.** the hotter half of the year (opposed to *winter*): *They spend the summers in New Hampshire and the winters in Virginia.* **5.** the period of finest development, perfection, or beauty previous to any decline: *the summer of life.* **—adj. 6.** of, pertaining to, or characteristic of summer: *Iced tea is a summer drink.* **7.** suitable for or used during the summer: *summer clothes; summer sports.* **8.** having the weather or warmth of summer: *summer days in late October.* **—v.i. 9.** to spend or pass the summer: *He summered in Maine.* **—v.t. 10.** to keep, feed, or manage during the summer: *Sheep are summered in high pastures.* **11.** to make summerlike. [ME *sumer* < OE *sumor;* c. D *zomer,* G *Sommer,* Icel *sumar* summer, Skt *samā* half-year, year, OIr *sam,* Welsh *haf* summer] **—sum′mer·less,** *adj.*

sum·mer² (sum′ər), *n.* **1.** a principal beam or girder, as one running between girts to support joists. **2.** a stone laid upon a pier, column, or wall, from which one or more arches spring: usually molded or otherwise treated like the arch or arches springing from it. **3.** a beam or lintel. [ME *somer* < AF < OF *somier* packhorse, beam < VL **saumār(ius)* < L *sagm(a)* pack-saddle (< Gk) + *-ārius* -ARY]

Sum′mer and Smoke′, a play (1948) by Tennessee Williams.

sum′mer camp′, a camp providing facilities for sleeping and eating, and usually for learning or participating in swimming, boating, handicrafts, outdoor games, etc., esp. such a camp as attended by children for several weeks during the summer. Cf. **day camp.**

sum′mer complaint′, an acute condition of diarrhea, occurring during the hot summer months chiefly in infants and children, caused by bacterial contamination of food and associated with poor hygiene. Also called **sum′mer diarrhe′a.**

sum′mer floun′der, a flounder, *Paralichthys dentatus,* found in shallow waters from Cape Cod to South Carolina, valued as food.

sum′mer grape′, a high-climbing vine, *Vitis aestivalis,* of the eastern U.S., having leaves that are dull above and rusty beneath, and black, edible fruit. Also called **pigeon grape.**

sum·mer·house (sum′ər hous′), *n., pl.* **-hous·es** (-hou′ziz). a simple, often rustic structure in a park or garden, intended to provide a shady, cool place in the summer. [ME *sumer hous.* See SUMMER[1], HOUSE]

sum′mer kitch′en, an extra kitchen, usually detached from a house, for use in warm weather.

sum·mer·like (sum′ər līk′), *adj.* like or characteristic of summer; summery: *a spell of summerlike showers.* [SUMMER[1] + -LIKE]

sum·mer·ly (sum′ər lē), *adj.* summerlike; summery. [ME *sumerly,* OE *sumorlic.* See SUMMER[1], -LY] —**sum′mer·li·ness,** *n.*

sum·mer·sault (sum′ər sôlt′), *n., v.i.* somersault. Also, **summerset.**

sum′mer sau′sage, dried or smoked sausage that keeps without refrigeration.

sum′mer sa′vory. See under **savory**[2].

sum′mer school′, **1.** study programs offered by a high school, college, or university during the summer to those who wish to obtain their degrees more quickly, who must make up credits, or who wish to supplement their education. **2.** a school offering such programs.

Sum′mer Sea′. See **Mare Aestatis.**

sum·mer·set (sum′ər set′), *n., v.i.* somersault.

Sum·mer·side (sum′ər sīd′), *n.* a city on W central Prince Edward Island, in SE Canada. 7242 (1956).

sum′mer snow′flake, star-of-Bethlehem (def. 1).

sum′mer sol′stice, *Astron.* the solstice on or about June 21st that marks the beginning of summer in the Northern Hemisphere.

sum′mer squash′, any of several squashes of the variety *Cucurbita Pepo Melopepo,* which mature in the late summer or early autumn and which are used as a vegetable in an unripe state, before the rind and seeds become hard.

sum′mer stock′, **1.** the production of plays, musical comedy, etc., during the summer, often by a repertory group presenting a different production each week and on a limited budget, sometimes with members of the company sharing expenses and responsibilities. **2.** summer theaters collectively or their productions: *Summer stock usually begins about June 1.* **3.** such theaters or productions as a medium of entertainment or a source of employment: *She hates summer stock, but she makes a good living out of it.*

sum·mer-sweet (sum′ər swēt′), *n.* See **sweet pepperbush.**

sum′mer tan′ager, a tanager, *Piranga rubra,* of the U.S., the male of which is rose-red, the female olive-green above and yellow below.

sum′mer the′ater, a theater that operates during the summer, esp. in a suburban or resort area, usually offering a different play or musical comedy each week.

sum·mer·time (sum′ər tīm′), *n.* **1.** the summer season. **2.** *Brit.* See **daylight-saving time.** [late ME *somertime.* See SUMMER[1], TIME]

sum·mer·tree (sum′ər trē′), *n.* summer[2] (def. 1). [ME *somere tre.* See SUMMER[2], TREE]

Sum·mer·ville (sum′ər vil′), *n.* **1.** a town in NW Georgia. 4706 (1960). **2.** a town in SE South Carolina. 3633 (1960).

sum·mer·wood (sum′ər wo͝od′), *n.* the part of an annual ring of wood, characterized by compact, thick-walled cells, formed during the later part of the growing season. Also called **late wood.** Cf. **springwood.** [SUMMER[1] + WOOD[1]]

sum·mer·y (sum′ə rē), *adj.* of, like, or appropriate for summer: *summery weather; a summery dress.* [SUMMER[1] + -Y[1]] —**sum′mer·i·ness,** *n.*

sum·ming-up (sum′ing up′), *n., pl.* **sum·mings-up.** a summation or statement made for the purpose of reviewing the basic concepts or principles of an argument, story, explanation, testimony, or the like, and usually presented at the end. [n. use of v. phrase *sum up;* see -ING[2]]

sum·mit (sum′it), *n.* **1.** the highest point or part, as of a hill, a line of travel, or any object; top; apex. **2.** the highest point of attainment or aspiration: *the summit of one's ambition.* **3.** the highest state or degree. **4.** a meeting or conference between heads of state. **5.** the highest level of diplomatic or other governmental officials: *a meeting at the summit.* —*adj.* **6.** *Diplomacy.* between heads of state: *a summit conference.* [late ME *somete* < OF, equiv. to *som* top (< L *summ(um),* n. use of neut. of *summus* highest; see SUM) + *-ete* -IT] —**sum′mit·al,** *adj.* —**sum′mit·less,** *adj.*
—**Syn. 1.** peak, pinnacle. **2, 3.** acme, zenith, culmination. —**Ant. 1.** base.

Sum·mit (sum′it), *n.* a city in NE New Jersey. 23,677 (1960).

Sum′mit Hill′, a town in E Pennsylvania. 4386 (1960).

sum′mit-lev·el canal′ (sum′it lev′əl), a canal following the ascending and descending slopes of a rise, artificially supplied with water at the top. Also called **sum′mit canal′.**

sum·mon (sum′ən), *v.t.* **1.** to call or order to some duty, task, or performance; call upon to do something. **2.** to call for the presence of, as by command, message, or signal; call (usually fol. by *to, away, from,* etc.). **3.** to call or notify to appear at a specified place, esp. before a court: *to summon a defendant.* **4.** to authorize or order a gathering of; call together by authority, as for deliberation or action: *to summon parliament.* **5.** to call into action; rouse; call forth (often. fol. by *up*) *to summon up all one's courage.* **6.** to request, demand, or call upon (someone, an army, etc.) to surrender. [< ML *summon(ēre)* (to) summon (L: to remind unofficially, suggest), equiv. to *sum-* SUM- + *monēre* to remind, warn; r. ME *somon(en)* < OF *semond(re), somond(re)*] —**sum′mon·a·ble,** *adj.* —**sum′mon·er,** *n.*
—**Syn. 1-3.** See **call.**

sum·mons (sum′ənz), *n., pl.* **-mons·es,** *v.* —*n.* **1.** an authoritative command, message, or signal by which one is summoned. **2.** a request, demand, or call to do something: *a summons to surrender.* **3.** *Law.* **a.** a call or citation by authority to appear before a court or a judicial officer. **b.** the writ by which the call is made. **4.** an authoritative call or notice to appear at a specified place, as for a particular purpose or duty. **5.** a call issued for the meeting of an assembly or parliament. —*v.t.* **6.** to serve with a summons; summon. [ME *somons* < AF, OF *somonse* (n. use of fem. of *somons,* ptp. of *somondre* to summon) < VL **summonsa* (irreg. formation), r. L *summonita,* fem. ptp. of *summonēre;* see SUMMON]

sum·mum bo·num (so͝om′o͝om bō′no͞om; *Eng.* sum′əm bō′nəm), *Latin.* the highest or chief good.

Sum·ner (sum′nər), *n.* **1. Charles,** 1811–74, U.S. statesman. **2. James Batch·el·ler** (bach′ə lər), 1887–1955, U.S. biochemist: Nobel prize 1946. **3. William Graham,** 1840–1910, U.S. sociologist and economist. **4.** a town in central Washington. 5874 (1960). **5.** a boy's given name.

Sum′ner line′, *Navig.* a line of position that is established by drawing a line through all the points at which a given celestial body would be observed at the same altitude at the same time. [named after T. H. *Sumner,* 19th-century American naval captain]

su·mo (so͞o′mō), *n.* a form of wrestling in Japan in which a contestant wins by forcing his opponent out of the ring or by causing him to touch the ground with any part of his body except the feet, contestants usually being men of great height and weight who are hereditary participants in the profession. [< Jap *sumō*] —**su′mo·ist,** *n.*

sump (sump), *n.* **1.** a pit, well, or the like in which water or other liquid is collected. **2.** *Mach.* a chamber at the bottom of a machine, pump, circulation system, etc., into which a fluid drains before recirculation or in which wastes gather before disposal. **3.** *Mining.* **a.** a space where water is allowed to collect at the bottom of a shaft or below a passageway. **b.** a pilot shaft or tunnel pushed out in front of a main bore. **4.** *Brit.* crankcase. **5.** *Brit. Dial.* a swamp, bog, or muddy pool. [late ME *sompe* < MLG or MD *sump;* c. G *Sumpf;* akin to SWAMP]

sump′ pump′, a pump for removing liquid or wastes from a sump.

sump·ter (sump′tər), *n.* *Archaic.* a pack horse or mule. [ME *sompter* < OF *sometier* pack-horse driver < VL **saumatār(ius),* equiv. to L *sagmat-* (s. of *sagma;* see SUMMER[2]) + *-ārius* -ARY]

sump·tion (sump′shən), *n.* *Logic.* See **major premise.** [late ME *sumpcion* < L *sumptiōn-* (s. of *sumptiō*) a taking, equiv. to *sum-* (root of *sūmere* to take) + *-p-* (transition sound) + *-t-* (ptp. suffix) + *-iōn-* -ION. See ASSUMPTION, PRESUMPTION]

sump·tu·ar·y (sump′cho͞o er′ē), *adj.* pertaining to, dealing with, or regulating expense or expenditure. [< L *sumptuāri(us),* equiv. to *sumptu(s)* expense + *-ārius* -ARY; *sumptus* deriv. of *sumptus* taken, spent (ptp. of *sūmere*), equiv. to *sum-* + *-p-* (transition sound) + *-tus* ptp. suffix; see SUMPTION]

sump′tuary law′, **1.** a law regulating personal expenditures, esp. on food and dress, often perpetuating distinctions in social class. **2.** a law based on the police power of the state but regulating personal habits which offend the moral or religious beliefs of the community.

sump·tu·ous (sump′cho͞o əs), *adj.* **1.** entailing great expense, as from fine workmanship, choice materials, etc.; costly: *a sumptuous residence.* **2.** luxuriously fine; splendid or superb: *a sumptuous feast.* [late ME < L *sumptuōs(us),* equiv. to *sumptu(s)* expense (see SUMPTUARY) + *-ōsus* -OUS] —**sump′tu·ous·ly,** *adv.* —**sump′tu·ous·ness,** *n.*

Sum·ter (sum′tər, sump′-), *n.* **1.** a city in central South Carolina. 23,062 (1960). **2.** See **Fort Sumter.**

sum′ to′tal, **1.** complete numerical total: *He reckoned the sum total of his savings.* **2.** essence; substance: *The sum total of research in the field is contained in this report.*

Su·my (so͞o′mi), *n.* a city in the NE Ukraine, in the S Soviet Union in Europe. 123,000 (est. 1964).

sun (sun), *n., v.,* **sunned, sun·ning.** —*n.* **1.** the star that is the central body of the solar system, around which the planets revolve and from which they receive light and heat: its mean distance from the earth is about 93,000,000 miles, its diameter about 864,000 miles, and its mass about 330,000 times that of the earth; its period of surface rotation is about 26 days at its equator but longer in greater latitudes. **2.** the sun considered with reference to its position in the sky, its visibility, the season of the year, the time at which or the place where it is seen, etc. **3.** a self-luminous heavenly body; star. **4.** sunshine; the heat and light from the sun: *to be exposed to the sun.* **5.** a figure or representation of the sun, as a heraldic bearing usually surrounded with rays and marked with the features of a human face. **6.** something likened to the sun in brightness, splendor, etc. **7.** Also called **sun in splendor, sun in glory.** *Heraldry.* a representation of a sun tinctured or having conventional rays and usually having a human face. **8.** *Chiefly Literary.* **a.** clime; climate. **b.** glory; splendor. **9.** *Archaic.* **a.** a day. **b.** a year. **c.** sunrise or sunset: *They traveled hard from sun to sun.* **10. against the sun,** *Naut.* counterclockwise. **11. place in the sun,** a favorable or advantageous position; prominence; recognition: *The new generation of writers has achieved a place in the sun.* **12. under the sun,** on earth; anywhere: *the most beautiful city under the sun.* **13. with the sun,** *Naut.* clockwise. —*v.t.* **14.** to expose to the sun's rays. **15.** to warm, dry, etc., in the sunshine. **16.** to put, bring, make, etc., by exposure to the rays of the sun. —*v.i.* **17.** to expose oneself to the rays of the sun: *They were sunning in the yard.* [ME, OE *sunne;* c. G *Sonne,* Icel. *sunna,* Goth *sunno*] —**sun′like′,** *adj.*

Sun., Sunday. Also, **Sund.**

Sun′ Al′so Ris′es, The, a novel (1926) by Ernest Hemingway.

sun′-and-plan′et gear′ (sun′ən plan′it), *Mach.* a planetary epicyclic gear train.

Sun-and-planet gear

sun′ animal′cule, a heliozoan.

Su·nay (so͞o′nā′), *n.* **Cev·det** (jev′det′), born 1902, Turkish army officer and statesman: president since 1966.

sun·back (sun′bak′), *adj.* (of a garment) cut low to expose the back for sunbathing or coolness. [SUN + BACK[1]]

sun·baked (sun′bākt′), *adj.* **1.** baked by exposure to the sun, as pottery, bricks, etc. **2.** heated, dried-up, or hardened by the heat of the sun. [SUN + BAKED]

sun′ bath′, exposure of the body to the direct rays of the sun or a sun lamp.

sun·bathe (sun′bāth′), *v.i.,* **-bathed, -bath·ing.** to take a sun bath. [SUN + BATHE] —**sun′bath′er,** *n.*

sun·bath·ing (sun′bā′thing), *n.* the act or practice of taking a sun bath. [SUN + BATHING]

sun·beam (sun′bēm′), *n.* a beam or ray of sunlight. [ME *sunnebem,* OE *sun(ne)bēam.* See SUN, BEAM] —**sun′beamed′, sun′beam′y,** *adj.*

Sun·belt (sun′belt′), *n.* *Informal.* the southern and southwestern region of the U.S.

sun·ber·ry (sun′ber′ē, -bə rē), *n., pl.* **-ries.** wonderberry. [SUN + BERRY]

sun·bird (sun′bûrd′), *n.* any of various small, brilliantly colored, Old World birds of the family *Nectariniidae.* [SUN + BIRD]

sun′ bit′tern, a South American bird, *Eurypyga helias,* related to the rails, having variegated plumage.

sun·block (sun′blok′), *n.* **1.** a substance providing a high degree of protection against sunburn by obstructing the penetration of ultraviolet rays. **2.** a lotion or cream containing such a substance. Also, **sun′ block′.** [SUN + BLOCK]

sun·bon·net (sun′bon′it), *n.* a large bonnet of cotton or other light material shading the face and projecting down over the neck, worn by women and girls. [SUN + BONNET] —**sun′bon′net·ed,** *adj.*

sun·bow (sun′bō′), *n.* a bow or arc of prismatic colors like a rainbow, appearing in the spray of cataracts, waterfalls, fountains, etc. [SUN + BOW[2]]

sun·break (sun′brāk′), *n.* a projection from the side of a building for intercepting part of the sunlight falling upon the adjacent surface. Also, **sun′break′er.** [SUN + BREAK]

sun·burn (sun′bûrn′), *n., v.,* **-burned** or **-burnt, -burning.** —*n.* **1.** superficial inflammation of the skin caused by exposure to the rays of the sun or a sun lamp. **2.** the discoloration or tan so produced; sun tan. —*v.t., v.i.* **3.** to affect or be affected with sunburn. [SUN + BURN[1]]

sun·burst (sun′bûrst′), *n.* **1.** a burst of sunlight; a sudden shining of the sun through rifted clouds. **2.** a firework, piece of jewelry, ornament, or the like, resembling the sun with rays issuing in all directions. —*adj.* **3.** *Sewing.* sewn or made to resemble a sunburst; having the rays or lines of design flared from a central point: *sunburst pleats; sunburst tucks.* [SUN + BURST]

sun-cured (sun′kyo͝ord′), *adj.* cured or preserved by exposure to the rays of the sun.

Sund., Sunday.

sun·dae (sun′dē, -dā), *n.* a portion of ice cream with chocolate, fruit, or other syrup poured over it, and often topped with whipped cream, chopped nuts, or other additions. [? special use of *Sunday* (with distinctive sp.)]

Sun′da Is′lands (sun′də; *Du.* so͞on′dä), a chain of islands in the Malay Archipelago, including Borneo, Sumatra, Java, and Celebes **(Greater Sunda Islands);** and a group of smaller islands extending E from Java to Timor **(Lesser Sunda Islands).** Also, **Soenda Islands.**

sun′ dance′, a religious ceremony associated with the sun, practiced by North American Indians of the Plains, consisting of dancing attended with various symbolic rites and commonly including self-torture.

Sun′da Strait′, a strait between Sumatra and Java, connecting the Java Sea and the Indian Ocean. 20–65 mi. wide.

Sun·day (sun′dē, -dā), *n.* **1.** the first day of the week, observed as the Sabbath by most Christian sects. **2. a month of Sundays,** an indeterminate length of time, esp. a long time: *He hadn't taken a vacation in a month of Sundays.* —*adj.* **3.** of, pertaining to, or characteristic of Sunday. **4.** used, done, taking place, or being as indicated only on or as on Sundays: *a Sunday matinee; a Sunday driver.* [ME *sun(nen)day,* OE *sunnandæg,* trans. of L *diēs sōlis,* itself trans. of Gk *hēmera hēlíou* day of the sun; c. G *Sonntag*] —**Sun′day-like′,** *adj.*
—**Syn. 1.** SUNDAY, SABBATH are not properly synonyms. SUNDAY, kept as a day of special worship and of rest from business, is the first day of the week: *Palm Sunday.* The SABBATH, the day on which the fourth Commandment enjoins abstention from work of all kinds, is Saturday, the seventh day of the Jewish week; the name has been applied to Sunday by some Protestant religious bodies: *to observe the Sabbath.*

Sun·day (sun′dē, -dā), *n.* **William Ashley** (ash′lē), ("*Billy Sunday*"), 1862–1935, U.S. evangelist.

Sun′day Afternoon′ on La Grande′ Jatte′. See **Grande Jatte.**

Sun′day clothes′, *Informal.* one's best or newest clothing, as saved for Sundays and special occasions. Also called **Sun′day best′.**

Sun·day-go-to-meet·ing (sun′dē gō′tə mēt′ᵊn, -mē′ting, -dā-), *adj.* *Informal.* most presentable; best: *Sunday-go-to-meeting clothes.*

Sun′day Morn′ing, a poem (1923) by Wallace Stevens.

Sun′day paint′er, *Fine Arts.* a nonprofessional painter, usually unschooled and generally painting during spare time.

Sun′day punch′, **1.** *Boxing Informal.* the most powerful and effective punch of a boxer, esp. the punch used in trying to gain a knockout. **2.** anything, as an armed force, line of argument, etc., capable of inflicting a powerful blow on a hostile or opposing person or thing.

Sun·days (sun′dēz, -dāz), *adv.* on Sundays.

Sun′day School′, 1. a school, now usually in connection with a church, for religious instruction on Sunday. 2. the members of such a school. Also called **Sabbath School.**

sun′ deck′, a raised, open platform adjoining a house, hotel, etc., in a position exposed to the sun.

sun·der (sun′dər), *v.t.* 1. to separate; part; divide; sever. —*v.i.* 2. to become separated; part. [ME *sundr(en),* OE *-sundrian;* c. G *sondern,* Icel *sundra;* see ASUNDER] —**sun′der·a·ble,** *adj.* —**sun′der·er,** *n.*

sun·der·ance (sun′dər əns), *n.* separation; severance. [late ME *sandryans.* See SUNDER, -ANCE]

Sun·der·land (sun′dər lənd), *n.* a seaport in E Durham, in NE England. 189,629 (1961).

sun·dew (sun′do͞o′, -dyo͞o′), *n.* any of several small bog plants of the genus *Drosera,* having sticky hairs that trap insects. Also called **dew plant, rosa solis.** [< D *sondauw* (cf. G *Sonnentau*), trans. of L *rōs sōlis* dew of the sun]

Sundial

sun·di·al (sun′dī′əl, -dīl′), *n.* an instrument that indicates the time of day by means of the position, on a graduated plate or surface, of the shadow of the gnomon as it is cast by the sun. [SUN + DIAL]

sun′ disk′, 1. the disk of the sun. 2. a figure or representation of this, esp. in religious symbolism.

Sun disk, Ancient Egyptian (def. 2)

sun·dog (sun′dôg′, -dog′), *n.* 1. parhelion. 2. a small or incomplete rainbow. [?]

sun·down (sun′doun′), *n.* sunset, esp. the time of sunset. [SUN + DOWN[1]]

sun·down·er (sun′dou′nər), *n.* 1. *Chiefly Brit.* a highball taken after completing the day's work, usually at sundown. 2. *Australian.* a tramp or hobo, originally implying arrival at a station near sundown in order to avoid having to work in exchange for food and shelter. [SUNDOWN + -ER[1]]

sun·dress (sun′dres′), *n.* a dress with a bodice styled to expose the arms, shoulders, and back, for wear during hot weather. [SUN + DRESS]

sun-dried (sun′drīd′), *adj.* 1. dried in the sun, as bricks, raisins, etc. 2. dried up or withered by the sun.

sun·dries (sun′drēz), *n.pl.* sundry things or items, esp. small, miscellaneous items of small value. Cf. **notion** (def. 6). [n. pl. use of SUNDRY]

sun·drops (sun′drops′), *n., pl.* **-drops.** any of various onagraceous plants of the genus *Oenothera* (*Kneiffia*), related to the evening primrose. [SUN + DROP + -S[3]]

sun·dry (sun′drē), *adj.* 1. various or diverse: *sundry persons.* 2. **all and sundry,** everybody, collectively and individually: *Free samples were given to all and sundry.* [ME; OE *syndrig* private, separate, equiv. to *syndr-* (mutated var. of *sundor* ASUNDER) + *-ig* -Y[1]; akin to SUNDER] —**sun′dri·ly,** *adv.* —**sun′dri·ness,** *n.*

Sunds·vall (sunts′väl), *n.* a seaport in E Sweden, on the Gulf of Bothnia. 58,100 (1965).

sun·fast (sun′fast′, -fäst′), *adj.* not subject to fading in sunlight, as a dye, fabric, or garment. [SUN + FAST[1]]

sun·fish (sun′fish′), *n., pl.* (*esp. collectively*) **-fish,** (*esp. referring to two or more kinds or species*) **-fish·es.** 1. the ocean sunfish, *Mola mola.* 2. any of various other fishes of the family *Molidae.* 3. any of several small, fresh-water, spiny-rayed fishes of the genus *Lepomis,* of North America, having a deep, compressed body. [SUN + FISH]

sun·flow·er (sun′flou′ər), *n.* 1. any of several herbs of the genus *Helianthus,* as *H. annus* (the State flower of Kansas), having showy, yellow-rayed flowers, the seeds of which are used for stock feed, yield an edible oil, and are dried and eaten as snacks. 2. Also called **aster.** *U.S. Furniture.* a conventionalized flower motif carved in the center panels of a Connecticut chest. [trans. of L *flōs sōlis* flower of the sun]

sun′flower chest′. See **Connecticut chest.**

Sun′flower State′, Kansas (used as a nickname).

sung (sung), *v.* a pt. and pp. of **sing.**

Sung (so͝ong), *n.* a dynasty in China, A.D. 960–1279, characterized by a high level of achievement in painting, ceramics, and philosophy: overthrown by the Mongols.

Sun·ga·ri (so͞on gär′ē, so͝ong är′-), *n.* a river in NE China, flowing NW and NE through E and central Manchuria into the Amur River on the boundary of Siberia. 800 mi. long.

sun′ gear′, *Mach.* (in an epicyclic train) the central gear around which the planet gears revolve. Also called **sun wheel.**

Sung·kiang (so͝ong′gyäng′), *n.* a former province in NE China, now a part of the Inner Mongolian Autonomous Region. 79,151 sq. mi.

sun·glass[1] (sun′glas′, -gläs′), *n.* See **burning glass.** [SUN + GLASS]

sun·glass[2] (sun′glas′, -gläs′), *adj.* of or pertaining to sunglasses: *a new concept in sunglass styling.* [back formation from SUNGLASSES]

sun·glass·es (sun′glas′iz, -glä′siz), *n.pl.* spectacles with colored or tinted lenses which protect the eyes from the glare of sunlight. [SUN + GLASSES]

sun·glow (sun′glō′), *n.* a diffused, hazy light seen around the sun, caused by particles of foreign matter in the atmosphere. [SUN + GLOW]

sun-god (sun′god′), *n.* 1. the sun considered or personified as a deity. 2. a god identified or associated with the sun.

sun′ grebe′, finfoot.

sun′ hemp′, sunn.

sun′ in splen′dor, *Heraldry.* sun (def. 7). Also called **sun′ in glo′ry.**

sunk (sungk), *v.* 1. a pt. and pp. of **sink.** —*adj.* 2. *Naut.* (of a forecastle or poop) raised less than a full deck above the weather deck of a ship. 3. *Slang.* beyond help; done for; washed up: *If they catch you cheating, you're really sunk.*

sunk·en (sung′kən), *v.* 1. a pp. of **sink.** —*adj.* 2. having sunk or been sunk beneath the surface; submerged. 3. having settled to a lower level, as walls. 4. situated or lying on a lower level: *a sunken living room.* 5. hollow; depressed: *sunken cheeks.*

sunk′en gar′den, a formal garden set below the main level of the ground surrounding it. Also, **sunk′ gar′den.**

sun·ket (sung′kit, so͝ong′-), *n. Scot. and North Eng.* 1. something, esp. something to eat. 2. a table delicacy; fancy tidbit of food. [alter. of SOMEWHAT]

sunk′ fence′, a wall or other barrier set in a ditch to divide lands without marring the landscape.

sunk′ fore′castle, *Naut.* a forecastle structure raised less than full deck height above the weather deck.

sunk′ relief′, cavo-relievo.

sun′ lamp′, 1. a lamp which generates ultraviolet rays, used as a therapeutic device, for obtaining an artificial sun tan, etc. 2. a lamp used in motion-picture photography, having an arrangement of parabolic mirrors for directing and concentrating the light.

sun·less (sun′lis), *adj.* 1. lacking sun or sunlight; dark: *a sunless room.* 2. dismal; gloomy; cheerless: *a sunless smile.* [SUN + -LESS] —**sun′less·ly,** *adv.* —**sun′less·ness,** *n.*

sun′ let′ter, *Arabic Gram.* any letter, as tā, sīn, etc., representing a consonant that assimilates the *l* of a prefixed definite article. Cf. **moon letter.** [trans. of Ar *alhurūf ashshamsīya,* so called from the use of *shams* sun, to illustrate assimilation of *-l-* in *al* the]

sun·light (sun′līt′), *n.* sunshine. [ME *sonneliht.* See SUN, LIGHT[1]]

sun·lit (sun′lit′), *adj.* lighted by the sun. [SUN + LIT[1]]

sun′ moss′. See **rose moss.**

sunn (sun), *n.* 1. a tall, East Indian, fabaceous shrub, *Crotalaria juncea,* having slender branches and yellow flowers, and an inner bark which yields a hemplike fiber used for making ropes, sacking, etc. 2. the fiber. Also called **sunn′ hemp′, sun hemp.** [< Hindi *san* < Skt *śaṇa*]

Sun·na (so͝on′ə), *n.* the traditional portion of Muslim Law, claimed to be based on the words and acts of Muhammad, but not attributed directly to him. Also, **Sun′nah.** [< Ar *sunnah* way, path, rule]

Sun·nite (so͝on′īt), *n. Islam.* a member of one of the two great religious divisions of Islam, regarding the first four caliphs as legitimate successors of Muhammad and stressing the importance of Sunna as a basis for law. Also called **Sun·ni** (so͝on′ē). Cf. **Shiite.** [SUNN(A) + ITE[1]]

sun·ny (sun′ē), *adj.,* **-ni·er, -ni·est.** 1. abounding in sunshine: *a sunny day.* 2. exposed to, lighted, or warmed by the direct rays of the sun: *a sunny room.* 3. pertaining to or proceeding from the sun; solar. 4. resembling the sun. 5. cheery, cheerful, or joyous: *a sunny disposition.* [ME; see SUN, -Y[1]] —**sun′ni·ly,** *adv.* —**sun′ni·ness,** *n.*

sun′ny side′, 1. the part upon which sunlight falls: *the sunny side of the house.* 2. a pleasant or hopeful aspect or part: *the sunny side of life.* 3. some age less than one specified: *You're still on the sunny side of thirty.*

Sun·ny·side (sun′ē sīd′), *n.* a town in S Washington. 6208 (1960).

sun′ny-side up′ (sun′ē sīd′), (of an egg) fried without being turned over, so that the yolk is visible and liquid inside.

Sun·ny·vale (sun′ē vāl′), *n.* a city in central California, south of San Francisco. 52,898 (1960).

sun′ pan′, *Ceram.* a vat for drying slip, sometimes artificially heated.

sun′ par′lor, a porch or room with many windows exposed to sunshine; solarium.

sun′ pil′lar, *Astron.* a halo phenomenon in which a vertical streak of light appears above and below the sun, believed to be caused by the reflection of sunlight by ice crystals with vertical axes. Cf. **moon pillar.**

sun′ porch′, 1. a windowed porch or porchlike room having more window than wall area, intended to receive large amounts of sunlight. 2. an open pen, raised above the ground, for giving poultry light and air under sanitary conditions.

Sun′ Prai′rie, a town in S Wisconsin. 4008 (1960).

sun·proof (sun′pro͞of′), *adj.* impervious to sunlight or damage by the rays of the sun. [SUN + -PROOF]

sun·ray (sun′rā′), *n.* a ray of sunlight; sunbeam. [SUN + RAY[1]]

sun·rise (sun′rīz′), *n.* 1. the rise or ascent of the sun above the horizon in the morning. 2. the atmospheric and scenic phenomena accompanying this. 3. the time when half the sun has risen above the horizon. 4. the open or beginning stage of any period. [late ME, short for ME *sunrising*]

sun′rise serv′ice, (*sometimes caps.*) an outdoor religious service held at dawn on Easter morning.

sun′rise watch′, dogwatch (def. 2).

sun·room (sun′ro͞om′, -ro͝om′), *n.* a room designed to admit a large amount of sunlight; sun parlor or sun porch. [SUN + ROOM]

sun·set (sun′set′), *n.* 1. the setting or descent of the sun below the horizon in the evening. 2. the atmospheric and scenic phenomena accompanying this: *They went to the beach to watch the sunset.* 3. the time when the sun sets. 4. the close or final stage of any period. [ME; in OE: west]

Sun·set (sun′set′), *n.* a town in N Utah. 4235 (1960).

sun·shade (sun′shād′), *n.* 1. something used as a protection from the rays of the sun. 2. an awning in front of a store. 3. a parasol. [SUN + SHADE]

sun·shine (sun′shīn′), *n.* 1. the shining of the sun; direct light of the sun. 2. brightness or radiance; cheerfulness or happiness. 3. a source of cheer or happiness. 4. the effect of the sun in lighting and heating a place. 5. a place where the direct rays of the sun fall. [ME *sunnesin,* alter. of OE *sunnanscīma,* equiv. to *sunnan* sun's + *scīma* light] —**sun′shine′less,** *adj.* —**sun′shin′y,** *adj.*

Sun′shine State′, Florida (used as a nickname).

sun·spot (sun′spot′), *n.* one of the relatively dark patches which appear periodically on the surface of the sun, and effect terrestrial magnetism and certain other terrestrial phenomena. [SUN + SPOT] —**sun′spot′ted,** *adj.* —**sun′spot′ted·ness,** *n.*

sun′spot cy′cle, *Astron.* the cycle, averaging in duration slightly more than 11 years, in which the frequency of sunspots varies from a maximum to a minimum and back to a maximum again.

sun·stone (sun′stōn′), *n.* a reddish variety of oligoclase feldspar, used as a gem, having a red and bright-yellow play of color. [SUN + STONE]

sun·stroke (sun′strōk′), *n. Pathol.* a frequently fatal affection due to exposure to the sun's rays or to excessive heat, marked by sudden prostration, with or without fever, and symptoms resembling those of apoplexy. Also called **insolation, siriasis, thermic fever.** [SUN + STROKE[1]]

sun·struck (sun′struk′), *adj.* affected with sunstroke. [SUN + STRUCK]

sun·suit (sun′so͞ot′), *n.* a playsuit consisting of a halter and shorts. [SUN + SUIT]

sun′ tan′, 1. a browning or a brown color of the skin resulting from exposure to the rays of the sun or a sun lamp. 2. Also called **mayfair tan, merida.** a light to medium yellow-brown. 3. Also called **pastel orange.** a medium orange color. Also, **sun′tan′.**

sun·tans (sun′tanz′), *n.* (*construed as pl.*) a tan military uniform for summer wear. [special use of SUN TAN]

sun·up (sun′up′), *n.* sunrise, esp. the time of sunrise.

Sun′ Val′ley, a village in S central Idaho: winter resort.

sun′ vi′sor, a flap, usually of padded cardboard, acetate, or the like, which is attached above the windshield of an automobile and which can be swung down to protect the eyes from the sun's glare.

sun·ward (sun′wərd), *adv.* 1. Also, **sun′wards.** toward the sun. —*adj.* 2. directed toward the sun. [SUN + -WARD]

sun′ wheel′. See **sun gear.**

sun·wise (sun′wīz′), *adv.* 1. in the direction of the sun's apparent daily motion. 2. in a clockwise direction. [SUN + -WISE]

Sun·ya·ta (sho͞on′yə tä′), *n. Buddhism.* that which exists absolutely and without predication. Also, **Sun·ya** (sho͞on′yə). [< Skt *śūnyatā,* lit., vacuum deriv. of *śūnya* empty]

Sun Yat-sen (so͝on′ yät′sen′), 1867–1925, Chinese political and revolutionary leader.

su·o ju·re (so͞o′ō yo͞o′re; *Eng.* so͞o′ō jo͝or′ē), *Latin.* in one's own right.

su·o lo·co (so͞o′ō lō′kō), *Latin.* in one's own or rightful place.

Su·o·mi (so͞o′ ō′mē), *n.* Finnish name of **Finland.**

suo·ve·tau·ril·i·a (swō′vi tô ril′ē ə), *n.* (in ancient Rome) a sacrifice of a hog, a ram, and a bull. [< L, equiv. to *su(s)* swine + *ovi(s)* sheep + *taur(us)* bull + *-ilia (-il(is)* -ILE + *-ia* n. suffix)]

sup[1] (sup), *v.,* **supped, sup·ping.** —*v.i.* 1. to eat the evening meal; take supper. —*v.t.* 2. to provide with or entertain at supper. [ME *s(o)up(en)* < OF *soupe(r)* (to) take supper < Gmc; cf. OE *sūpan* to swallow, taste, sip. See SUP[2], SOP]

sup[2] (sup), *v.,* **supped, sup·ping,** *n.* —*v.t.* 1. to take (liquid food, or any liquid) into the mouth in small quantities, as from a spoon or a cup; sip. —*v.i.* 2. to take liquid into the mouth in small quantities, as by spoonfuls or sips. —*n.* 3. a mouthful or small portion of liquid food or of drink; sip. [ME *supp(en),* var. of *soupen,* OE *sūpan;* c. G *saufen* to drink. Cf. SIP, SOP, SUP[1], SOUP]

sup[3] (so͞op), *n. Math.* supremum.

sup-, var. of **sub-** before *p: suppose.*

sup., 1. superior. 2. superlative. 3. supine. 4. supplement. 5. supplementary. 6. supra.

Sup. Ct., 1. Superior Court. 2. Supreme Court.

su·per (so͞o′pər), *n.* 1. *Informal.* **a.** superintendent. **b.** supervisor. **c.** supernumerary. 2. *Com.* an article of a superior quality, grade, size, etc. 3. *Entomol.* the portion of a hive in which honey is stored. 4. *U.S. Informal.* supercalendered paper. —*adj. Informal.* 5. (of measurement) superficial. 6. superfine. 7. very good; first-rate; excellent. 8. of the highest degree, power, etc.: *a super bomb.* 9. of an extreme or excessive degree: *super secrecy.* [special use of SUPER-]

super-, a formal element occurring in loan words from Latin (*supersede*); used, with the meaning "above," "beyond," in the formation of compound words with second elements of any origin (*superman; superhighway; supersensitive; superstructure; supernatural*). [comb. form of L prep. and v. prefix *super* above, beyond, in addition, to an especially high degree]

su·per·a·ble (so͞o′pər ə bəl), *adj.* capable of being overcome; surmountable. [< L *superābil(is),* equiv. to *superā-* overcome (*super-* SUPER- + *-ā v.* suffix) + *-bilis* -BLE] —**su′per·a·bil′i·ty, su′per·a·ble·ness,** *n.* —**su′per·a·bly,** *adv.*

su·per·a·bound (so͞o′pər ə bound′), *v.i.* 1. to abound beyond something else. 2. to be very abundant or too abundant (usually fol. by *in* or *with*). [late ME < LL *superabund(āre),* equiv. to *super-* SUPER- + *abundāre* to ABOUND]

su·per·a·bun·dant (so͞o′pər ə bun′dənt), *adj.* exceedingly or excessively abundant; more than sufficient; excessive. [late ME < LL *superabundant-* (s. of *super-*

su′per·ab·hor′, *v.t.*
su′per·ab·nor′mal, *adj.;* **-ly,** *adv.*
su′per·a·bom′i·na·ble, *adj.;* **-ble·ness,** *n.;* **-bly,** *adv.*
su′per·a·bom′i·na′tion, *n.*
su′per·ab·stract′, *adj.;* **-ly,** *adv.;* **-ness,** *n.*
su′per·ab·surd′, *adj.;* **-ly,** *adv.;* **-ness,** *n.*
su′per·ab·surd′i·ty, *n.*
su′per·ac·com′mo·dat′ing, *adj.*
su′per·ac·com′plished, *adj.*
su′per·ac·crue′, *v.i.,* **-crued, -cru·ing.**
su′per·ac·cu′mu·late′, *v.i.,* **-lat·ed, -lat·ing.**
su′per·ac·cu′mu·la′tion, *n.*
su′per·ac′cu·rate, *adj.;* **-ly,** *adv.;* **-ness,** *n.*
su′per·a·chieve′ment, *n.*
su′per·a·cid′i·ty, *n.*
su′per·a·cid′u·lat′ed, *adj.*
su′per·ac·knowl′edg·ment, *n.*
su′per·ac′qui·si′tion, *n.*
su′per·a·cro′mi·al, *adj.*
su′per·ac′ti·vate′, *v.t.,* **-vat·ed, -vat·ing.**
su′per·ac′tive, *adj.;* **-ly,** *adv.;* **-ness,** *n.*
su′per·ac·tiv′i·ty, *n., pl.* **-ties.**
su′per·a·cute′, *adj.;* **-ly,** *adv.;* **-ness,** *n.*
su′per·a·dap′ta·ble, *adj.;* **-ble·ness,** *n.;* **-bly,** *adv.*

abundāns) superabounding. See SUPER-, ABUNDANT] —**su′per·a·bun′dance,** *n.* —**su′per·a·bun′dant·ly,** *adv.*

su·per·add (so͞o′pər ad′), *v.t.* to add over and above; join as a further addition; add besides. [< L *superadd(ere),* equiv. to *super-* SUPER- + *addere* to ADD] —**su·per·ad·di·tion** (so͞o′pər ə dish′ən), *n.* —**su′per·ad·di′tion·al,** *adj.*

su·per·aer·o·dy·nam·ics (so͞o′pər âr′ō dī nam′iks, -di-), *n.* (*construed as sing.*) the branch of aerodynamics that deals with gases at very low densities. [SUPER- + AERODYNAMICS]

su·per·a·gen·cy (so͞o′pər ā′jən sē), *n., pl.* **-cies.** a very large agency, esp. one in government which directs or oversees smaller agencies. [SUPER- + AGENCY]

su·per·an·nu·ate (so͞o′pər an′yo͞o āt′), *v.,* **-at·ed, -at·ing.** —*v.t.* **1.** to allow to retire from service or office on a pension because of age or infirmity. **2.** to set aside as out of date; remove as too old. —*v.i.* **3.** to be or become old, out of date, or retired. [back formation from SUPERANNUATED]

su·per·an·nu·at·ed (so͞o′pər an′yo͞o ā′tid), *adj.* **1.** retired because of age or infirmity. **2.** too old for use, work, service, or a position. **3.** antiquated or obsolete: *Even his friends make fun of his superannuated ideas.* [alter. (with *-u-* of ANNUAL) of ML *superannāt(us)* over a year old (said of cattle) + -ED²; *superannātus,* equiv. to *super ann(um)* beyond a year + *-ātus* -ATE¹]

su·per·an·nu·a·tion (so͞o′pər an′yo͞o ā′shən), *n.* **1.** the act of superannuating. **2.** the state of being superannuated. **3.** a pension or allowance to a superannuated person. [SUPERANNUATE + -ION]

su·per·aq·ual (so͞o′pər ak′wəl), *adj. Geol.* (of soils, sediments, etc.) lying just above the water table. Cf. **subaqual.** [SUPER- + AQU(A) + -AL¹]

su·perb (so͝o pûrb′, sə-), *adj.* **1.** admirably fine or excellent: *a superb performance.* **2.** sumptuous; rich; grand: *superb jewels.* **3.** of a proudly imposing appearance or kind; majestic: *a superb beauty; the superb vistas of the Grand Canyon.* [< L *superb(us)* proud, superior, excellent, equiv. to *super-* SUPER- + *-bus* suffix akin to *fuī* I have been, BE] —**su·perb′ly,** *adv.* —**su·perb′ness,** *n.*

—**Syn. 2.** elegant. See **magnificent.** —**Ant. 2.** inferior.

su·per·bomb (so͞o′pər bom′), *n.* a highly destructive bomb, esp. the hydrogen bomb. [SUPER- + BOMB]

su·per·cal·en·der (so͞o′pər kal′ən dər), *n.* **1.** a roll or set of rolls for giving a high, smooth finish to paper. —*v.t.* **2.** to finish (paper) in a supercalender. [SUPER- + CALENDER]

su·per·cal·i·frag·i·lis·tic·ex·pi·al·i·do·cious (so͞o′pər kal′ə fraj′ə lis′tik ek′spē al′ē dō′shəs), *n.* (used as a nonsense word by children to represent the longest word in English.)

su·per·cap·i·tal (so͞o′pər kap′i tᵊl), *n. Archit.* a member situated between a capital and the spring of an arch, as a dosseret. [SUPER- + CAPITAL²]

su·per·car·go (so͞o′pər kär′gō, so͞o′pər kär′-), *n., pl.* **-goes, -gos.** a merchant-ship officer who is in charge of the cargo and the commercial concerns of the voyage. [< Sp *sobrecargo* with *sobre-* over (< L *super*) Latinized; r. *supracargo* (with *supra-* for Sp *sobre-*); see CARGO]

su·per·cav·i·ta·tion (so͞o′pər kav′i tā′shən), *n. Naut.* cavitation leaving the trailing face of a propeller blade free of water. [SUPER- + CAVITATION]

su·per·charge (so͞o′pər chärj′), *v.t.,* **-charged, -charg·ing. 1.** to charge with an abundant or excessive amount, as of energy, emotion, tension, etc. **2.** to supply air to (an internal-combustion engine) at greater than atmospheric pressure. **3.** pressurize (def. 2). [SUPER- + CHARGE]

su·per·charg·er (so͞o′pər chär′jər), *n.* a mechanism for forcing air into an internal-combustion engine in order to increase fuel ignition and thereby engine power. [SUPERCHARGE + -ER¹]

su·per·cil·i·ar·y (so͞o′pər sil′ē er′ē), *adj. Anat., Zool.* **1.** of or pertaining to the eyebrow. **2.** having a conspicuous line or marking over the eye, as certain birds. **3.** situated on the frontal bone at the level of the eyebrow. [< NL *superciliar(is).* See SUPERCILIUM, -ARY]

su·per·cil·i·ous (so͞o′pər sil′ē əs), *adj.* haughtily disdainful or contemptuous, as a person, his expression, bearing, etc. [< L *superciliōs(us).* See SUPERCILIUM, -OUS] —**su′per·cil′i·ous·ly,** *adv.* —**su′per·cil′i·ous·ness,** *n.*

—**Syn.** arrogant, scornful. —**Ant.** humble.

su·per·cil·i·um (so͞o′pər sil′ē əm), *n., pl.* **-cil·i·a** (-sil′ē ə). *Archit.* **1.** the fillet above the cyma of a cornice. **2.** (on an Attic base) either of the fillets above and below the scotia. [< L: eyebrow, haughtiness, equiv. to *super-* SUPER- + *cilium* eyelid]

su·per·class (so͞o′pər klas′, -kläs′), *n. Biol.* **1.** a category of related classes within a subphylum. **2.** a subphylum. [SUPER- + CLASS]

su·per·co·lum·nar (so͞o′pər kə lum′nər), *adj. Archit.* **1.** existing above a column or columns: *a supercolumnar feature.* **2.** of, pertaining to, or characterized by supercolumniation: *a supercolumnar composition.* [SUPER- + COLUMNAR]

su·per·co·lum·ni·a·tion (so͞o′pər kə lum′nē ā′shən), *n. Archit.* the placing of one order of columns above another. [SUPER- + COLUMNIATION]

su·per·con·duc·tiv·i·ty (so͞o′pər kon′dək tiv′i tē), *n. Physics.* the phenomenon of almost perfect conductivity that is demonstrated by certain substances at low temperatures. [SUPER- + CONDUCTIVITY] —**su·per·con·duc·tion** (so͞o′pər kən duk′shən), *n.* —**su·per·con·duc·tive** (so͞o′pər kən duk′tiv), **su′per·con·duct′ing,** *adj.* —**su·per·con·duc·tor** (so͞o′pər kən duk′tər), *n.*

su·per·cool (so͞o′pər ko͞ol′), *v.t.* **1.** to cool (a liquid) below its freezing point without producing solidification or crystallization; undercool. —*v.i.* **2.** to become supercooled. [SUPER- + COOL]

su·per·crit·i·cal (so͞o′pər krit′i kəl), *adj.* **1.** extremely critical. **2.** *Physics.* pertaining to a mass of radioactive material in which the rate of a chain reaction increases with time. [SUPER- + CRITICAL] —**su′per·crit′i·cal·ly,** *adv.* —**su′per·crit′i·cal·ness,** *n.*

su·per·dom·i·nant (so͞o′pər dom′ə nənt), *n. Music.* submediant. [SUPER- + DOMINANT]

su·per·dread·nought (so͞o′pər dred′nôt′), *n.* a battleship of the dreadnought type but much larger and with superior armament. [SUPER- + DREADNOUGHT]

su·per·du·per (so͞o′pər do͞o′pər, -dyo͞o′-), *adj. Informal.* very super; marvelous or colossal. [rhyming compound with invented second element]

su·per·e·go (so͞o′pər ē′gō, -eg′ō), *n., pl.* **-gos.** *Psychoanal.* the part of the psychic apparatus which mediates between ego drives and social ideals, acting as a conscience which may be partly conscious and partly unconscious. [SUPER- + EGO]

su·per·el·e·vat·ed (so͞o′pər el′ə vā′tid), *adj. Civ. Eng.* (of a curve in a road, railroad track, etc.) banked. [SUPER- + ELEVATED]

su·per·el·e·va·tion (so͞o′pər el′ə vā′shən), *n.* bank¹ (def. 6). [SUPER- + ELEVATION]

su·per·em·i·nent (so͞o′pər em′ə nənt), *adj.* of superior eminence, rank, or dignity; distinguished, conspicuous, or worthy of note above others. [< L *superēminent-* (s. of *superēminēns*) overtopping. See SUPER-, EMINENT] —**su′per·em′i·nence,** *n.* —**su′per·em′i·nent·ly,** *adv.*

su·per·er·o·gate (so͞o′pər er′ə gāt′), *v.i.,* **-gat·ed, -gat·ing.** to do more than duty requires. [< LL *superērogāt(us)* (ptp. of *superērogāre* to pay out in addition), equiv. to *super-* SUPER- + *ērogātus* paid out, equiv. to *ērog-* (*ē-* E- + *rog-* ask) + *-ātus* -ATE¹] —**su′per·er′o·ga′tion,** *n.* —**su′per·er′o·ga′tor,** *n.*

su·per·e·rog·a·to·ry (so͞o′pər ə rog′ə tôr′ē, -tōr′ē), *adj.* **1.** going beyond the requirements of duty. **2.** greater than that required; superfluous. [< ML *superērogātōri(us).* See SUPEREROGATE, -ORY¹] —**su′per·e·rog′a·to′ri·ly,** *adv.*

su·per·ette (so͞o′pə ret′), *n.* a grocery store with some of the self-service features of a supermarket. [SUPER(MARKET) + -ETTE]

su·per·fam·i·ly (so͞o′pər fam′ə lē, -fam′lē), *n., pl.* **-lies.** *Biol.* a category of related families within an order or suborder. [SUPER- + FAMILY]

su·per·fe·cun·da·tion (so͞o′pər fē′kən dā′shən, -fek′ən-), *n.* the fertilization of two or more ova discharged at the same ovulation by successive acts of sexual intercourse. [SUPER- + FECUNDATION]

su·per·fe·ta·tion (so͞o′pər fē tā′shən), *n.* the fertilization of an ovum in a female mammal already pregnant. [< L *superfētāt(us)* (ptp. of *superfētāre* to conceive again while still pregnant), equiv. to *super-* SUPER- +

su′per·ad′e·quate, *adj.;* **-ly,** *adv.;* **-ness,** *n.*
su′per·ad·ja′cent, *adj.;* **-ly,** *adv.*
su′per·ad·min′is·tra′tion, *n.*
su′per·ad′mi·ra·ble, *adj.;* **-ble·ness,** *n.;* **-bly,** *adv.*
su′per·ad·mi·ra′tion, *n.*
su′per·a·dorn′, *adj.*
su′per·a·dorn′ment, *n.*
su′per·aer′i·al, *adj.;* **-ly,** *adv.*
su′per·aes·thet′i·cal, *adj.;* **-ly,** *adv.*
su′per·af·fil′i·a′tion, *n.*
su′per·af′flu·ence, *n.*
su′per·af′flu·ent, *adj.;* **-ly,** *adv.*
su′per·af·fu′sion, *n.*
su′per·ag·gra·va′tion, *n.*
su′per·ag′i·ta′tion, *n.*
su′per·a·grar′i·an, *adj.*
su′per·al′i·men·ta′tion, *n.*
su′per·al′ka·lin′i·ty, *n.*
su′per·al·low′ance, *n.*
su′per·am·bi′tion, *n.*
su′per·am·bi′tious, *adj.;* **-ly,** *adv.;* **-ness,** *n.*
su′per·an·gel′ic, *adj.*
su′per·an·gel′i·cal·ly, *adv.*
su′per·an′i·mal, *adj.*
su′per·an′i·mal′i·ty, *n.*
su′per·an·nu′i·ty, *n., pl.* **-ties.**
su′per·a·pol′o·gy, *n., pl.* **-gies.**
su′per·ap·pre′ci·a′tion, *n.*
su′per·a′que·ous, *adj.*
su′per·ar′bi·ter, *n.*
su′per·arc′tic, *adj.*
su′per·ar′du·ous, *adj.;* **-ly,** *adv.;* **-ness,** *n.*
su′per·ar′ro·gance, *n.*
su′per·ar′ro·gant, *adj.;* **-ly,** *adv.*
su′per·ar′ti·fi′cial, *adj.;* **-ly,** *adv.*
su′per·ar′ti·fi′ci·al′i·ty, *n.*
su′per·as′pi·ra′tion, *n.*
su′per·as·ser′tion, *n.*
su′per·as·so′ci·ate, *n.*
su′per·as·sume′, *v.t.,* **-sumed, -sum·ing.**
su′per·as·sump′tion, *n.*
su′per·as·ton′ish, *v.*
su′per·as·ton′ish·ment, *n.*
su′per·at·tach′ment, *n.*
su′per·at·tain′a·ble, *adj.;* **-ble·ness,** *n.;* **-bly,** *adv.*
su′per·at·tend′ant, *n., adj.*
su′per·at·trac′tion, *n.*
su′per·at·trac′tive, *adj.;* **-ly,** *adv.;* **-ness,** *n.*
su′per·au′di·tor, *n.*
su′per·av′er·age, *adj.;* **-ness,** *n.*
su′per·a·ward′, *n.*
su′per·ax′il·lar·y, *adj.*
su′per·be·lief′, *n.*
su′per·be·liev′a·ble, *adj.;* **-ble·ness,** *n.;* **-bly,** *adv.*
su′per·be·loved′, *adj.*
su′per·ben′e·fit, *n.*
su′per·be·nev′o·lence, *n.*
su′per·be·nev′o·lent, *adj.;* **-ly,** *adv.*
su′per·be·nign′, *adj.;* **-ly,** *adv.*
su′per·bi′as, *n.*
su′per·blessed′, *adj.*
su′per·bless′ed·ness, *n.*
su′per·blun′der, *n.*
su′per·bold′, *adj.;* **-ly,** *adv.;* **-ness,** *n.*
su′per·brain′, *n.*
su′per·brave′, *adj.;* **-ly,** *adv.;* **-ness,** *n.*
su′per·brute′, *n.*
su′per·build′, *v.*
su′per·bus′i·ly, *adv.*
su′per·bus′y, *adj.*
su′per·cab′i·net, *n.*
su′per·can′did, *adj.;* **-ly,** *adv.;* **-ness,** *n.*
su′per·ca′nine, *adj., n.*
su′per·ca·non′i·cal, *adj.*
su′per·can′on·i·za′tion, *n.*
su′per·can′o·py, *n., pl.* **-pies.**
su′per·ca′pa·bil′i·ty, *n., pl.* **-ties.**
su′per·ca′pa·ble, *adj.;* **-ble·ness,** *n.;* **-bly,** *adv.*
su′per·cap′tion, *n.*
su′per·car′pal, *adj.*
su′per·ca·tas′tro·phe, *n.*
su′per·cat′a·stroph′ic, *adj.*
su′per·cath′o·lic, *adj.*
su′per·ca·thol′i·cal·ly, *adj.*
su′per·caus′al, *adj.*
su′per·cau′tion, *n.*
su′per·ce·les′tial, *adj.;* **-ly,** *adv.*
su′per·cen′sure, *n.*
su′per·cer′e·bel′lar, *adj.*
su′per·ce·re′bral, *adj.;* **-ly,** *adv.*
su′per·cer′e·mo′ni·ous, *adj.;* **-ly,** *adv.;* **-ness,** *n.*
su′per·chem′i·cal, *adj., n.;* **-ly,** *adv.*
su′per·chiv′al·rous, *adj.;* **-ly,** *adv.;* **-ness,** *n.*
su′per·civ′il, *adj.;* **-ly,** *adv.*
su′per·civ′i·li·za′tion, *n.*
su′per·civ′il·ized′, *adj.*
su′per·claim′, *n.*
su′per·clas′si·fied′, *adj.*
su′per·co·in′ci·dence, *n.*
su′per·co·in′ci·dent, *adj.;* **-ly,** *adv.*
su′per·co·los′sal, *adj.;* **-ly,** *adv.*
su′per·com′bi·na′tion, *n.*
su′per·com′men·da′tion, *n.*
su′per·com′men·tar′y, *n., pl.* **-tar·ies.**
su′per·com′men·ta′tor, *n.*
su′per·com·mer′cial, *adj.;* **-ly,** *adv.;* **-ness,** *n.*
su′per·com′pe·ti′tion, *n.*
su′per·com·plex′, *adj.*
su′per·com·plex′i·ty, *n., pl.* **-ties.**
su′per·com′pre·hen′sion, *n.*
su′per·com·pres′sion, *n.*
su′per·con′fi·dence, *n.*
su′per·con′fi·dent, *adj.;* **-ly,** *adv.*
su′per·con′fir·ma′tion, *n.*
su′per·con·form′a·ble, *adj.;* **-ble·ness,** *n.;* **-bly,** *adv.*
su′per·con·form′ist, *n.*
su′per·con·form′i·ty, *n.*
su′per·con·fused′, *adj.*
su′per·con·fu′sion, *n.*
su′per·con·gest′ed, *adj.*
su′per·con·ges′tion, *n.*
su′per·con′se·crat′ed, *adj.*
su′per·con′se·quence′, *n.*
su′per·con·serv′a·tive, *adj.;* **-ly,** *adv.;* **-ness,** *n.*
su′per·con′sti·tu′tion·al, *adj.;* **-ly,** *adv.*
su′per·con′test, *n.*
su′per·con·test′, *v.t.*
su′per·con′tri·bu′tion, *n.*
su′per·con·trol′, *n.*
su′per·cor′dial, *adj.;* **-ly,** *adv.;* **-ness,** *n.*
su′per·cor′po·ra′tion, *n.*
su′per·cred′it, *n.*
su′per·cre·ta′ceous, *adj.*
su′per·crime′, *n.*
su′per·crim′i·nal, *adj., n.;* **-ly,** *adv.*
su′per·crit′ic, *n.*
su′per·crit′i·cal·ly, *adv.*
su′per·crowned′, *adj.*
su′per·cul′ti·vat′ed, *adj.*
su′per·cul′ture, *n.*
su′per·cu′ri·ous, *adj.;* **-ly,** *adv.;* **-ness,** *n.*
su′per·cy′cle, *n.*
su′per·cyn′i·cal, *adj.;* **-ly,** *adv.;* **-ness,** *n.*
su′per·dain′ty, *adj.*
su′per·dan′ger, *n.*
su′per·debt′, *n.*
su′per·de·clam′a·to′ry, *adj.*
su′per·dec′o·rat′ed, *adj.*
su′per·dec′o·ra′tion, *n.*
su′per·def′i·cit, *n.*
su′per·de′i·ty, *n., pl.* **-ties.**
su′per·de·jec′tion, *n.*
su′per·del′e·gate′, *n.*
su′per·del′i·cate, *adj.;* **-ly,** *adv.;* **-ness,** *n.*
su′per·de·mand′, *n.*
su′per·dem′o·crat′ic, *adj.*
su′per·dem′o·crat′i·cal·ly, *adv.*
su′per·de·mon′ic, *adj.*
su′per·dem′on·stra′tion, *n.*
su′per·den′si·ty, *n.*
su′per·de·pos′it, *n.*
su′per·de·sir′ous, *adj.;* **-ly,** *adv.*
su′per·de·vel′op·ment, *n.*
su′per·dev′il·ish, *adj.;* **-ly,** *adv.;* **-ness,** *n.*
su′per·de·vo′tion, *n.*
su′per·di′a·bol′i·cal, *adj.;* **-ly,** *adv.;* **-ness,** *n.*
su′per·dif′fi·cult, *adj.;* **-ly,** *adv.*
su′per·di·plo′ma·cy, *n.*
su′per·di·rec′tion, *n.*
su′per·dis′count, *n.*
su′per·dis·ten′tion, *n.*
su′per·dis′tri·bu′tion, *n.*
su′per·div′i·dend′, *n.*
su′per·di·vine′, *adj.*
su′per·di·vi′sion, *n.*
su′per·doc′tor, *n.*
su′per·dom′i·neer′ing, *adj.*
su′per·do·na′tion, *n.*
su′per·dose′, *n.*
su′per·dram′a·tist, *n.*
su′per·du′bi·ous, *adj.;* **-ly,** *adv.;* **-ness,** *n.*
su′per·du′pli·ca′tion, *n.*
su′per·du′ral, *adj.*
su′per·earth′ly, *adj.*
su′per·e·con′o·my, *n., pl.* **-mies.**
su′per·ed′u·cat′ed, *adj.*
su′per·ed′u·ca′tion, *n.*
su′per·ef·fec′tive, *adj.;* **-ly,** *adv.;* **-ness,** *n.*
su′per·ef′flu·ence, *n.*
su′per·ef′flu·ent, *adj.*
su′per·e·lab′o·rate, *adj.;* **-ly,** *adv.;* **-ness,** *n.*
su′per·e·las′tic, *adj.*
su′per·e·las′ti·cal·ly, *adv.*
su′per·e·lat′ed, *adj.*
su′per·el′e·gance, *n.*
su′per·el′e·gan·cy, *n., pl.* **-cies.**
su′per·el′e·gant, *adj.;* **-ly,** *adv.*
su′per·el′e·men′ta·ry, *adj.*
su′per·el′i·gi·bil′i·ty, *n.*
su′per·el′i·gi·ble, *adj.;* **-ble·ness,** *n.;* **-bly,** *adv.*
su′per·el′o·quence, *n.*
su′per·el′o·quent, *adj.;* **-ly,** *adv.*
su′per·em′pha·sis, *n.*
su′per·em′pha·size′, *v.t.,* **-sized, -siz·ing.**
su′per·en·dorse′, *v.t.,* **-dorsed, -dors·ing.**
su′per·en·dorse′ment, *n.*
su′per·en·dow′, *v.t.*
su′per·en′er·get′ic, *adj.*
su′per·en′er·get′i·cal·ly, *adv.*
su′per·en·force′ment, *n.*
su′per·en·grave′, *v.t.,* **-graved, -grav·ing.**
su′per·en·roll′ment, *n.*
su′per·ep′ic, *adj., n.*
su′per·ep′och, *n.*
su′per·e·quiv′a·lent, *adj., n.*
su′per·es·tab′lish, *v.t.*
su′per·es·tab′lish·ment, *n.*
su′per·e′ther, *n.*
su′per·eth′i·cal, *adj.;* **-ly,** *adv.;* **-ness,** *n.*
su′per·e′van·gel′i·cal, *adj.;* **-ly,** *adv.*
su′per·ev′i·dence, *n.*
su′per·ev′i·dent, *adj.;* **-ly,** *adv.*
su′per·ex·act′ing, *adj.*
su′per·ex·alt′, *v.t.*
su′per·ex′al·ta′tion, *n.*
su′per·ex·am′in·er, *n.*
su′per·ex·ceed′, *v.i.*
su′per·ex′cel·lence, *n.*
su′per·ex′cel·len·cy, *n.*
su′per·ex′cel·lent, *adj.;* **-ly,** *adv.*
su′per·ex·cep′tion·al, *adj.;* **-ly,** *adv.*
su′per·ex′ci·ta′tion, *n.*
su′per·ex·cit′ed, *adj.*
su′per·ex·cite′ment, *n.*
su′per·ex·cres′cence, *n.*
su′per·ex·cres′cent, *adj.;* **-ly,** *adv.*
su′per·ex·ert′, *v.t.*
su′per·ex·er′tion, *n.*
su′per·ex·pand′, *v.*
su′per·ex·pan′sion, *n.*
su′per·ex′pec·ta′tion, *n.*
su′per·ex·pen′di·ture, *n.*
su′per·ex·plic′it, *adj.;* **-ly,** *adv.*
su′per·ex′port, *n.*
su′per·ex·port′, *v.t.*
su′per·ex·pres′sion, *n.*
su′per·ex·pres′sive, *adj.;* **-ly,** *adv.;* **-ness,** *n.*
su′per·ex′qui·site, *adj.;* **-ly,** *adv.;* **-ness,** *n.*
su′per·ex·tend′, *v.*
su′per·ex·ten′sion, *n.*
su′per·ex·tol′, *v.t.*
su′per·ex·toll′, *v.t.*
su′per·ex·treme′, *adj.;* **-ly,** *adv.;* **-ness,** *n.*
su′per·ex·trem′i·ty, *n., pl.* **-ties.**
su′per·fan·tas′tic, *adj.*
su′per·fan·tas′ti·cal·ly, *adv.*
su′per·farm′, *n.*
su′per·fe·cun′di·ty, *n.*
su′per·fee′, *n.*
su′per·fem′i·nine, *adj.*
su′per·fem′i·nin′i·ty, *n.*
su′per·fer′vent, *adj.;* **-ly,** *adv.*

fētātus, equiv. to *fēt-* pregnant + *-ātus* -ATE¹] —**su′per·fe′tate**, *adj.*

su·per·fi·cial (so͞o′pər fish′əl), *adj.* **1.** of or pertaining to the surface: *superficial measurement.* **2.** being at, on, or near the surface: *a superficial wound.* **3.** external or outward: *a superficial resemblance.* **4.** concerned with or comprehending only what is on the surface or obvious: *a superficial observer.* **5.** shallow; not profound or thorough: *a superficial writer.* **6.** apparent rather than real. **7.** insubstantial or insignificant: *superficial improvements.* [< LL *superficiāl(is)*, equiv. to L *superficiē(s)* SUPERFICIES + *-ālis* -AL¹] —**su·per·fi·ci·al·i·ty** (so͞o′pər fish′ē al′i tē), **su′per·fi′cial·ness**, *n.* —**su′per·fi′cial·ly**, *adv.*

su·per·fi·ci·es (so͞o′pər fish′ē ēz′, -fish′ēz), *n.*, *pl.* **-ci·es.** **1.** the surface, outer face, or outside of a thing. **2.** the outward appearance, esp. as distinguished from the inner nature. [< L, equiv. to *super-* SUPER- + *-ficiēs*, var. of *faciēs* face]

su·per·fine (so͞o′pər fīn′), *adj.* **1.** extra fine; unusually fine: *a box of superfine sugar.* **2.** excessively refined; over-nice: *superfine manners.* [SUPER- + FINE¹]

su·per·flu·id (so͞o′pər flo͞o′id), *Physics.* —*n.* **1.** a fluid that exhibits frictionless flow, very high heat conductivity, and other unusual physical properties, helium below 2.186° K being the only known example. —*adj.* **2.** of or pertaining to a superfluid. [SUPER- + FLUID]

su·per·flu·i·ty (so͞o′pər flo͞o′i tē), *n.*, *pl.* **-ties.** **1.** the state of being superfluous. **2.** a superabundant or excessive amount. **3.** something superfluous, as a luxury. [late ME *superfluite* < OF < L *superfluitāt-* (s. of *superfluitās*). See SUPERFLUOUS, -ITY]

su·per·flu·ous (so͝o pûr′flo͞o əs), *adj.* **1.** being more than is sufficient or required; excessive. **2.** unnecessary or needless. **3.** *Obs.* possessing or spending more than enough; extravagant. [late ME < L *superfluus*, equiv. to *super-* SUPER- + *flu-* (s. of *fluere* to flow) + *-us* -OUS] —**su·per′flu·ous·ly**, *adv.* —**su·per′flu·ous·ness**, *n.*
—**Syn. 1.** extra; redundant.

Su·per·for·tress (so͞o′pər fôr′tris), *n.* *U.S. Mil.* a heavy, long-range, four-engined bomber, either the B-29 or the B-50. Also called **Su·per·fort** (so͞o′pər fôrt′, -fōrt′). [SUPER- + (FLYING) FORTRESS]

su·per·fuse (so͞o′pər fyo͞oz′), *v.t.*, **-fused, -fus·ing.** *Obs.* to pour. [< L *superfūs(us)* (ptp.) poured on or over, equiv. to *super-* SUPER- + *-fūsus*, equiv. to *fūd-* (root of *fundere* to pour) + *-tus* ptp. suffix] —**su·per·fu·sion** (so͞o′pər fyo͞o′zhən), *n.*

su·per·gal·ax·y (so͞o′pər gal′ək sē), *n.*, *pl.* **-ax·ies.** *Astron.* a system of galaxies. [SUPER- + GALAXY] —**su·per·ga·lac·tic** (so͞o′pər gə lak′tik), *adj.*

su·per·gene (so͞o′pər jēn′), *adj.* *Geol.* formed by descending waters, as mineral or ore deposits (opposed to *hypogene*). [SUPER- + *-gene*, as in *hypogene*]

su′per·gi′ant star′ (so͞o′pər jī′ənt), *Astron.* an exceptionally luminous star whose diameter is more than 100 times that of the sun, as Betelgeuse or Antares. [SUPER- + GIANT]

su·per·gla·cial (so͞o′pər glā′shəl), *adj.* **1.** on the surface of a glacier. **2.** believed to have been formerly on the surface of a glacier: *superglacial debris.* [SUPER- + GLACIAL]

su·per·gov·ern·ment (so͞o′pər guv′ərn mənt, -guv′ər-), *n.* **1.** a centralized organization formed by a group of governments to enforce justice or maintain peace. **2.** an internationally organized body designed to regulate the relations of its member states. **3.** any government having overwhelming and far-reaching powers. [SUPER- + GOVERNMENT]

su·per·heat (*n.* so͞o′pər hēt′; *v.* so͞o′pər hēt′), *n.* **1.** the state of being superheated. **2.** the amount of superheating. —*v.t.* **3.** to heat to an extreme degree or to a very high temperature. **4.** to heat (a liquid) above its boiling point without the formation of bubbles of vapor. **5.** to heat (a gas, as steam not in contact with water) to such a degree that its temperature may be lowered or its pressure increased without the conversion of any of the gas into liquid. [SUPER- + HEAT] —**su′per·heat′er**, *n.*

su·per·het·er·o·dyne (so͞o′pər het′ər ə dīn′), *Radio.* —*adj.* **1.** noting, pertaining to, or using a method of receiving radio signals by which the incoming modulated wave is changed by the heterodyne process to a lower, inaudible frequency and then submitted to stages of radio-frequency amplification with subsequent detection and audio-frequency amplification. —*n.* **2.** a superheterodyne receiver. [SUPER(SONIC) + HETERODYNE]

su′per·high fre′quency (so͞o′pər hī′), *Radio.* any frequency between 3,000 and 30,000 megacycles per second. *Abbr.:* SHF [SUPER- + HIGH FREQUENCY]

su·per·high·way (so͞o′pər hī′wā′), *n.* a highway designed for travel at high speeds, having more than one lane for each direction of traffic, a safety strip dividing the two directions, and cloverleaves to route the traffic on and off the highway. [SUPER- + HIGHWAY]

su·per·hive (so͞o′pər hīv′), *n.* *Entomol. Obs.* super (def. 3). [SUPER- + HIVE]

su·per·hu·man (so͞o′pər hyo͞o′mən *or, often,* -yo͞o′-), *adj.* **1.** above or beyond what is human; having a higher nature or greater powers than man has: *a superhuman being.* **2.** exceeding ordinary human power, achievement, experience, etc.: *a superhuman effort.* [< ML *superhūmān(us)*. See SUPER-, HUMAN] —**su·per·hu·man·i·ty** (so͞o′pər hyo͞o man′i tē *or, often,* -yo͞o-), **su′per·hu′man·ness**, *n.* —**su′per·hu′man·ly**, *adv.*

Su·pe·ri (so͞o′pə rī′), *n.pl.* (in ancient Rome) the gods.

su·per·im·pose (so͞o′pər im pōz′), *v.t.*, **-posed, -pos·ing.** **1.** to impose, place, or set over, above, or on something else. **2.** to put or join as an addition (usually fol. by *on* or *upon*). [SUPER- + IMPOSE] —**su·per·im·po·si·tion** (so͞o′pər im′pə zish′ən), *n.*

su·per·im·posed (so͞o′pər im pōzd′), *adj.* *Geol.* (of a stream or drainage system) having a course not adjusted to the structure of the rocks presently undergoing erosion but determined rather by a prior erosion cycle or by formerly overlying rocks or sediments. [SUPERIMPOSE + -ED²]

su·per·in·cum·bent (so͞o′pər in kum′bənt), *adj.* **1.** lying or resting on something else. **2.** situated above; overhanging. **3.** exerted from above, as pressure. [< L *superincumbent-* (s. of *superincumbēns*) lying on or over. See SUPER-, INCUMBENT] —**su′per·in·cum′bence**, **su′per·in·cum′ben·cy**, *n.* —**su′per·in·cum′bent·ly**, *adv.*

su·per·in·duce (so͞o′pər in do͞os′, -dyo͞os′), *v.t.*, **-duced, -duc·ing.** to bring in or induce as an added feature, circumstance, etc.; superimpose. [< L *superindūc(re)*. See SUPER-, INDUCE] —**su·per·in·duc·tion** (so͞o′pər in duk′shən), *n.*

su·per·in·tend (so͞o′pər in tend′, so͞o′prin-), *v.t.* **1.** to oversee and direct (work, processes, etc.). **2.** to exercise supervision over (an institution, district, place, etc.). [< LL *superintend(ere)*. See SUPER-, INTEND]
—**Syn.** supervise, manage, conduct, run; control.

su·per·in·tend·en·cy (so͞o′pər in ten′dən sē, so͞o′prin-), *n.*, *pl.* **-cies.** **1.** a district or place under a superintendent. **2.** the position or work of a superintendent. **3.** Also, **su′per·in·tend′ence.** the act or process of superintending; direction; supervision; oversight. [< ML *superintendentia*, equiv. to *superintend(ere)* (to) SUPERINTEND + *-entia* -ENCY]

su·per·in·tend·ent (so͞o′pər in ten′dənt, so͞o′prin-), *n.* **1.** one who oversees or directs some work, enterprise, establishment, organization, district, etc.; supervisor. **2.** a person who is responsible for an apartment house and represents the owner, esp. such a person who lives on the premises and acts as janitor and rent collector. —*adj.* **3.** superintending. [< ML *superintendent-* (s. of *superintendēns*) superintending. See SUPERINTEND, -ENT]

su·pe·ri·or (sə pēr′ē ər, so͝o-), *adj.* **1.** higher in station, rank, degree, etc.: *a superior officer.* **2.** above the average in excellence, merit, intelligence, etc.: *superior math students.* **3.** of higher grade or quality: *superior merchandise.* **4.** greater in quantity or amount: *superior numbers.* **5.** showing a consciousness or feeling of being better than or above others: *superior airs.* **6.** not yielding or susceptible (usually fol. by *to*): *to be superior to temptation.* **7.** higher in place or position: *We moved our camp to superior ground.* **8.** *Bot.* **a.** situated above some other organ. **b.** (of a calyx) seeming to originate from the top of the ovary. **c.** (of an ovary) free from the calyx. **9.** *Anat., Zool.* (of an organ or part) higher in place or position; situated above another. Cf. **inferior** (def. 6). **10.** *Print.* written or printed high on a line of text, as the "2" in a^2b; superscript. Cf. **inferior** (def. 8). **11.** *Astron.* **a.** (of a planet) having an orbit outside that of the earth. **b.** (of an inferior planet) noting a conjunction in which the sun is between the earth and the planet. —*n.* **12.** one superior to another or others. **13.** Also called **superscript.** *Print.* a letter, number, or symbol written or printed high on a line of text. Cf. **inferior** (def. 10). **14.** *Eccles.* the head of a monastery, convent, or the like. [ME < L, equiv. to *super(us)* situated above + *-ior* comp. suffix; see -ER⁴] —**su·pe′ri·or·ly**, *adv.*

Su·pe·ri·or (sə pēr′ē ər, so͝o-), *n.* **1. Lake,** a lake in the N central United States and S Canada: the northernmost of the Great Lakes; the largest body of fresh water in the world. 350 mi. long; 31,820 sq. mi.; greatest depth, 1290 ft.; 602 ft. above sea level. **2.** a port in NW Wisconsin, on Lake Superior. 33,563 (1960). **3.** a town in central Arizona. 4875 (1960). **4.** a town in S Nebraska. 2935 (1960).

supe′rior court′, **1.** the court of general jurisdiction found in many States of the United States. **2.** any court that has general jurisdiction above that of inferior courts.

supe′rior gen′eral, *pl.* **superiors general.** *Eccles.* the superior of an order or congregation.

supe′rior goods′, *Econ.* commodities that are more in demand as consumer income rises. Cf. **inferior goods.**

su·pe·ri·or·i·ty (sə pēr′ē ôr′i tē, -or′-, so͝o-), *n.* the quality or condition of being superior. [< ML *superiōritāt-* (s. of *superiōritās*). See SUPERIOR, -ITY]

superior′ity com′plex, an exaggerated feeling of superiority, often the mark of an overly assertive personality.

su·per·ja·cent (so͞o′pər jā′sənt), *adj.* lying above or upon something else. [< L *superjacent-* (s. of *superjacēns*) lying over or upon. See SUPER-, ADJACENT]

superl., superlative.

su·per·la·tive (sə pûr′lə tiv, so͝o-), *adj.* **1.** of the highest kind or order; surpassing all else or others; supreme; extreme: *superlative wisdom.* **2.** being more than is proper or normal; exaggerated in language or style. **3.** *Gram.* of, pertaining to, or noting the highest degree of the comparison of adjectives and adverbs, as *best,* the superlative form of *good.* Cf. **comparative** (def. 4), **positive** (def. 18). —*n.* **4.** a superlative person or thing. **5.** the utmost degree; acme. **6.** *Gram.* **a.** the superlative degree. **b.** a form in the superlative. [< LL *superlātīv(us)*, equiv. to L *superlāt(us)* hyperbolical (*super-* SUPER- + *-lātus* carried, ptp. of *ferre* to bear) + *-īvus* -IVE; r. ME *superlatif* < OF] —**su·per′la·tive·ly**, *adv.* —**su·per′la·tive·ness**, *n.*

su·per·lin·er (so͞o′pər lī′nər), *n.* an ocean liner of relatively great size or speed. [SUPER- + LINER¹]

su·per·load (so͞o′pər lōd′), *n.* a theoretical live load provided for in building codes or in engineering calculations. [SUPER- + LOAD]

su·per·lu·na·ry (so͞o′pər lo͞o′nə rē), *adj.* **1.** situated above or beyond the moon. **2.** celestial, rather than earthly. Also, **su′per·lu′nar.** [SUPER- + (SUB)LUNARY]

su·per·man (so͞o′pər man′), *n.*, *pl.* **-men.** **1.** a man of superhuman powers. **2.** an ideal superior being conceived by Nietzsche as the product of human evolution. **3.** a man who prevails by virtue of being a ruthless egoist of superior strength, cunning, and force of will. [SUPER- + MAN¹, trans. of G *Übermensch*]

su·per·mar·ket (so͞o′pər mär′kit), *n.* a large retail market that sells food and other household goods and that is usually operated on a self-service, cash-and-carry basis. [SUPER- + MARKET]

su·per·max·il·la (so͞o′pər mak sil′ə), *n.*, *pl.* **-max·il·lae** (-mak sil′ē). the upper jaw. [< NL; see SUPER-, MAXILLA] —**su·per·max·il·lar·y** (so͞o′pər mak′sə ler′ē, -mak sil′ə rē), *adj.*

su·per·mun·dane (so͞o′pər mun dān′), *adj.* above and beyond the nature or character of the worldly or terrestrial. [< ML *supermundān(us)*. See SUPER-, MUNDANE]

---

su′per·fi′bri·na′tion, *n.*
su′per·fi′nance, *n.*
su′per·fi·nance′, *n., v.,* **-nanced, -nanc·ing.**
su′per·fin′i·cal, *adj.*
su′per·fi′nite, *adj.; -ly, adv.; -ness, n.*
su′per·fis′sure, *n.*
su′per·fit′, *n., adj., v.,* **-fit·ted, -fit·ting.**
su′per·fleet′, *n.*
su′per·flex′ion, *n.*
su′per·flux′, *n.*
su′per·fo′li·a′ceous, *adj.*
su′per·fo′li·a′tion, *n.*
su′per·fol′ly, *n., pl.* **-lies.**
su′per·for′mal, *adj.; -ly, adv.; -ness, n.*
su′per·for·ma′tion, *n.*
su′per·for′mid·a·ble, *adj.; -ble·ness, n.; -bly, adv.*
su′per·for′tu·nate, *adj.; -ly, adv.*
su′per·fruc′ti·fied′, *adj.*
su′per·ful·fill′, *v.t.*
su′per·ful·fill′ment, *n.*
su′per·func′tion, *n.*
su′per·func′tion·al, *adj.*
su′per·gai′e·ty, *n.*
su′per·gal′lant, *adj.; -ly, adv.; -ness, n.*
su′per·ge·ner′ic, *adj.*
su′per·ge·ner′i·cal·ly, *adv.*
su′per·gen′er·os′i·ty, *n.*
su′per·gen′er·ous, *adj.; -ly, adv.*
su′per·gen′u·al, *adj.*
su′per·gi′ant, *adj.*
su′per·glo′ri·ous, *adj.; -ly, adv.; -ness, n.*
su′per·glot′tal, *adj.; -ly, adv.*
su′per·glot′tic, *adj.*
su′per·god′dess, *n.*
su′per·good′ness, *n.*
su′per·gov′ern, *v.t.*
su′per·grad′u·ate, *n.*
su′per·grant′, *n.*
su′per·grat′i·fi·ca′tion, *n.*
su′per·grat′i·fy′, *v.t.,* **-fied, -fy·ing.**
su′per·grav′i·tate′, *v.i.,* **-tat·ed, -tat·ing.**
su′per·grav′i·ta′tion, *n.*
su′per·guar′an·tee′, *n., v.,* **-teed, -tee·ing.**
su′per·gun′, *n.*
su′per·gyre′, *n.*
su′per·hand′some, *adj.*
su′per·heart′i·ly, *adv.*
su′per·heart′i·ness, *n.*
su′per·heart′y, *adj.*
su′per·her′e·sy, *n., pl.* **-sies.**
su′per·he′ro, *n., pl.* **-roes.**
su′per·he·ro′ic, *adj.*
su′per·he·ro′i·cal·ly, *adv.*
su′per·his·tor′ic, *adj.*
su′per·his·tor′i·cal, *adj.; -ly, adv.*
su′per·hu′man·ize′, *v.t.,* **-ized, -iz·ing.**
su′per·hyp′o·crite, *n.*
su′per·i·de′al, *adj., n.; -ly, adv.; -ness, n.*
su′per·ig′no·rant, *adj.; -ly, adv.*
su′per·il′lus·trate′, *v.t.,* **-trat·ed, -trat·ing.**
su′per·il′lus·tra′tion, *n.*
su′per·im·pend′, *v.i.*
su′per·im·per′son·al, *adj.; -ly, adv.*
su′per·im·ply′, *v.t.,* **-plied, -ply·ing.**
su′per·im·por′tant, *adj.; -ly, adv.*
su′per·im·prob′a·ble, *adj.; -ble·ness, n.; -bly, adv.*
su′per·im·proved′, *adj.*
su′per·in·cen′tive, *n., adj.*
su′per·in′cli·na′tion, *n.*
su′per·in·clu′sive, *adj.; -ly, adv.; -ness, n.*
su′per·in·com′pre·hen′si·ble, *adj.; -ble·ness, n.; -bly, adv.*
su′per·in·crease′, *v.t.,* **-creased, -creas·ing.**
su′per·in′crease, *n.*
su′per·in′de·pen′dence, *n.*
su′per·in′de·pen′dent, *adj.; -ly, adv.*
su′per·in·dict′ment, *n.*
su′per·in·dif′fer·ence, *n.*
su′per·in·dif′fer·ent, *adj.; -ly, adv.*
su′per·in·dig′nant, *adj.; -ly, adv.*
su′per·in′di·vid′u·al, *adj., n.; -ly, adv.*
su′per·in′di·vid′u·al·ism, *n.*
su′per·in′di·vid′u·al·ist, *n.*
su′per·in·dul′gence, *n.*
su′per·in·dul′gent, *adj.; -ly, adv.*
su′per·in·dus′tri·ous, *adj.; -ly, adv.; -ness, n.*
su′per·in′dus·try, *n., pl.* **-tries.**
su′per·in·fer′, *v.t.,* **-ferred, -fer·ring.**
su′per·in′fer·ence, *n.*
su′per·in′fin·ite, *adj.; -ly, adv.; -ness, n.*
su′per·in·firm′i·ty, *n., pl.* **-ties.**
su′per·in′flu·ence, *n., v.t.,* **-enced, -enc·ing.**
su′per·in·for′mal, *adj.; -ly, adv.*
su′per·in′for·mal′i·ty, *n., pl.* **-ties.**
su′per·in·fuse′, *v.t.,* **-fused, -fus·ing.**
su′per·in·gen′ious, *adj.; -ly, adv.; -ness, n.*
su′per·in′ge·nu′i·ty, *n., pl.* **-ties.**
su′per·in·i′ti·a·tive, *n.*
su′per·in·jec′tion, *n.*
su′per·in·jus′tice, *n.*
su′per·in′no·cence, *n.*
su′per·in′no·cent, *adj.; -ly, adv.*
su′per·in·quis′i·tive, *adj.; -ly, adv.; -ness, n.*
su′per·in·scribe′, *v.t.,* **-scribed, -scrib·ing.**
su′per·in·scrip′tion, *n.*
su′per·in·sist′, *v.i.*
su′per·in·sist′ence, *n.*
su′per·in·sist′ent, *adj.; -ly, adv.*
su′per·in′tel·lec′tu·al, *adj., n.; -ly, adv.*
su′per·in·tense′, *adj.; -ly, adv.; -ness, n.*
su′per·in·ten′si·ty, *n.*
su′per·in·tol′er·a·ble, *adj.; -ble·ness, n.; -bly, adv.*
su′per·in′un·da′tion, *n.*
su′per·in′vo·lu′tion, *n.*
su′per·ir′ri·ta·bil′i·ty, *n.*
su′per·ju·di′cial, *adj.; -ly, adv.*
su′per·ju′ris·dic′tion, *n.*
su′per·jus′ti·fi·ca′tion, *n.*
su′per·knowl′edge, *n.*
su′per·la·bo′ri·ous, *adj.; -ly, adv.; -ness, n.*
su′per·lac·ta′tion, *n.*
su′per·la·ryn′geal, *adj.; -ly, adv.*
su′per·le′ni·ent, *adj.; -ly, adv.*
su′per·lie′, *v.t.,* **-lied, -ly·ing.**
su′per·like′li·hood′, *n.*
su′per·line′, *n.*
su′per·lo′cal, *adj.; -ly, adv.*
su′per·log′i·cal, *adj.; -ly, adv.*
su′per·log′i·cal′i·ty, *n., pl.* **-ties.**
su′per·loy′al, *adj.; -ly, adv.*
su′per·luck′y, *adj.*
su′per·lux·u′ri·ous, *adj.; -ly, adv.; -ness, n.*
su′per·mag·nif′i·cent, *adj.; -ly, adv.*
su′per·mal′ate, *n.*
su′per·man′i·fest′, *v.t.*
su′per·mar′gin·al, *adj.; -ly, adv.*
su′per·ma·rine′, *adj.*
su′per·mar′ve·lous, *adj.; -ly, adv.; -ness, n.*
su′per·mas′cu·line, *adj.*
su′per·mas′cu·lin′i·ty, *n.*
su′per·ma·te′ri·al, *n.*
su′per·math′e·mat′i·cal, *adj.; -ly, adv.*
su′per·me·chan′i·cal, *adj.; -ly, adv.*
su′per·me′di·al, *adj.; -ly, adv.*
su′per·med′i·cine, *n.*
su′per·me′di·o′cre, *adj.*
su′per·men′tal, *adj.; -ly, adv.*
su′per·men·tal′i·ty, *n.*
su′per·met′ro·pol′i·tan, *adj.*
su′per·mil′i·tar′y, *adj.*
su′per·mix′ture, *n.*
su′per·mod′est, *adj.; -ly, adv.*
su′per·mois′ten, *v.t.*
su′per·mol′e·cule′, *n.*
su′per·mol′ten, *adj.*
su′per·mor′al, *adj.; -ly, adv.*
su′per·mo·rose′, *adj.; -ly, adv.; -ness, n.*
su′per·mo·til′i·ty, *n.*

su·per·nal (so͞o pûr′nəl), *adj.* **1.** being in or belonging to the heaven of divine beings; heavenly, celestial, or divine. **2.** lofty; of more than earthly or human excellence, powers, etc. **3.** being on high or in the sky or visible heavens. [late ME < MF, equiv. to *supern-* (< L *supern(us)* upper) + *-al* -AL[1]] —**su·per′nal·ly,** *adv.*

su·per·na·tant (so͞o′pər nāt′ənt), *adj.* floating above or on the surface. [< L *supernatant-* (s. of *supernatāns*) floating. See SUPER-, NATANT] —**su·per·na·ta·tion** (so͞o′pər nə tā′shən), *n.*

su·per·na·tion·al (so͞o′pər nash′ə nəl), *adj.* **1.** extremely or fanatically devoted to a nation. **2.** tending to involve, or extending authority over, more than one nation; international. [SUPER- + NATIONAL] —**su′per·na′tion·al·ly,** *adv.*

su·per·na·tion·al·ism (so͞o′pər nash′ə nəliz′əm), *n.* **1.** an extreme or fanatical loyalty or devotion to a nation. **2.** advocacy of the establishment of governments composed of more than one nation, each nation agreeing to surrender at least part of its national sovereignty to a superior governmental authority. **3.** advocacy of the establishment of organizations composed of groups from more than one nation, each of which agrees to surrender at least part of its authority to a superior, centralized authority. [SUPER- + NATIONALISM]

su·per·na·tion·al·ist (so͞o′pər nash′ə nəlist), *n.* one who is excessively or fanatically devoted to a nation; superpatriot. [SUPER- + NATIONALIST]

su·per·nat·u·ral (so͞o′pər nach′ər əl), *adj.* **1.** of, pertaining to, or being above or beyond what is natural; unexplainable by natural laws or phenomena; abnormal. **2.** of, pertaining to, or characteristic of God or a deity. **3.** of a superlative degree; preternatural: *a missile of supernatural speed.* **4.** of or relating to ghosts, goblins, or other unearthly beings; eerie; occult. —*n.* **5.** a being, place, object, occurrence, etc., considered as supernatural or of supernatural origin; that which is supernatural, or outside the natural order. **6.** behavior supposedly caused by the intervention of supernatural beings. **7.** direct influence or action of a god on earthly affairs. **8. the supernatural, a.** supernatural beings, behavior, and occurrences collectively. **b.** supernatural forces and the supernatural plane of existence: *Primitive people have a deep fear of the supernatural.* [< ML *supernātūrāl(is).* See SUPER-, NATURAL] —**su′per·nat′u·ral·ly,** *adv.* —**su′per·nat′u·ral·ness,** *n.*
—**Syn. 1.** superhuman. See **miraculous.**

su·per·nat·u·ral·ise (so͞o′pər nach′ər ə līz′), *v.t.,* **-ised, -is·ing.** *Chiefly Brit.* supernaturalize.

su·per·nat·u·ral·ism (so͞o′pər nach′ər ə liz′əm), *n.* **1.** supernatural character or agency. **2.** belief in the doctrine of supernatural or divine agency as manifested in the world, in human events, religious revelation, etc. [SUPERNATURAL + -ISM] —**su′per·nat′u·ral·ist,** *n., adj.* —**su′per·nat′u·ral·is′tic,** *adj.*

su·per·nat·u·ral·ize (so͞o′pər nach′ər ə līz′), *v.t.,* **-ized, -iz·ing. 1.** to make supernatural; give supernatural character or qualities to. **2.** to consider or interpret as supernatural. [SUPERNATURAL + -IZE]

su′pernat′ural vir′tue. See **theological virtue.**

su·per·nor·mal (so͞o′pər nôr′məl), *adj.* **1.** in excess of the normal or average: *supernormal faculties; supernormal production.* **2.** lying beyond normal or natural powers of comprehension: *supernormal intimations.* [SUPER- + NORMAL] —**su·per·nor·mal·i·ty** (so͞o′pər nôr mal′i tē), **su′per·nor′mal·ness,** *n.* —**su′per·nor′mal·ly,** *adv.*

su·per·no·va (so͞o′pər nō′və), *n., pl.* **-vae** (-vē), **-vas.** *Astron.* an extremely bright nova that emits from ten million to a hundred million times as much light as the sun, estimated to occur in a galaxy about once every 600 years. [SUPER- + NOVA]

su·per·nu·mer·ar·y (so͞o′pər no͞o′mə rer′ē, -nyo͞o′-), *adj., n., pl.* **-ar·ies.** —*adj.* **1.** being in excess of the usual, proper, or prescribed number; additional; extra. **2.** associated with a regular body or staff as an assistant or substitute in case of necessity. —*n.* **3.** a supernumerary or extra person or thing. **4.** a supernumerary official or employee. **5.** *Theat.* one who is not a member of a regular company and appears onstage without speaking lines or as part of a crowd; walk-on. [< LL *supernumerāri(us).* See SUPER-, NUMERARY]

su·per·or·der (so͞o′pər ôr′dər), *n. Biol.* a category of related orders within a class or subclass. [SUPER- + ORDER]

su·per·or·di·nate (*adj., n.* so͞o′pər ôr′dənit; *v.* so͞o′pər ôr′dənāt′), *adj., n., v.,* **-nat·ed, -nat·ing.** —*adj.* **1.** of higher degree in condition or rank. **2.** *Logic.* (of a universal proposition) related to a particular proposition containing the same terms. —*n.* **3.** a superordinate person or thing. —*v.t.* **4.** to elevate to superordinate position. [SUPER- + (SUB)ORDINATE]

su·per·or·di·na·tion (so͞o′pər ôr′dənā′shən), *n.* **1.** *Logic.* the relation between a universal proposition and a particular proposition containing the same terms. **2.** *Eccles.* the ordination by an official of his successor. [< eccl. L *superordinātiōn-* (s. of *superordinātiō*), equiv. to *superordināt(us)* (ptp. of *superordināre*; see SUPER-, ORDAIN, -ATE[1]) + *-iōn-* -ION]

su·per·or·gan·ic (so͞o′pər ôr gan′ik), *adj. Sociol., Anthropol.* of or pertaining to the structure of cultural elements within society conceived as independent of and superior to the individual members of society. [SUPER- + ORGANIC] —**su′per·or·gan′i·cism,** *n.* —**su′per·or·gan′i·cist,** *n.*

su·per·ox·ide (so͞o′pər ok′sīd, -sid), *n. Chem.* **1.** a compound containing the univalent ion, O_2^-. **2.** peroxide (def. 1a, b). Also called **hyperoxide.** [SUPER- + OXIDE]

su·per·par·a·site (so͞o′pər par′ə sīt′), *n.* hyperparasite. [SUPER- + PARASITE] —**su·per·par·a·sit·ic** (so͞o′pər par′ə sit′ik), *adj.* —**su′per·par′a·sit′ism,** *n.*

su·per·pa·tri·ot (so͞o′pər pā′trē ət, so͞o′pər pā′-; *esp. Brit.,* so͞o′pər pa′trē ət, so͞o′pər pa′-), *n.* a person who is patriotic to an extreme. [SUPER- + PATRIOT] —**su·per·pa·tri·ot·ic** (so͞o′pər pā′trē ot′ik; *esp. Brit.,* so͞o′pər pa′trē ot′ik), *adj.* —**su′per·pa′tri·ot′i·cal·ly,** *adv.* —**su′per·pa′tri·ot·ism,** *n.*

su·per·phos·phate (so͞o′pər fos′fāt), *n.* **1.** Also called **acid phosphate.** a mixture, prepared with sulfuric acid, of calcium acid phosphate and calcium sulfate, and containing about 20 percent of soluble phosphates available as P_2O_5, used chiefly as a fertilizer. **2.** Also called **triple superphosphate.** a mixture prepared with phosphoric acid and containing about 45 percent of soluble phosphates, used as a fertilizer. [SUPER- + PHOSPHATE]

su·per·phys·i·cal (so͞o′pər fiz′i kəl), *adj.* above or beyond what is physical; hyperphysical. [SUPER- + PHYSICAL]

su·per·pig·men·ta·tion (so͞o′pər pig′mən tā′shən), *n. Med.* excessive pigmentation in a part of the body. [SUPER- + PIGMENTATION]

su·per·pose (so͞o′pər pōz′), *v.t.,* **-posed, -pos·ing. 1.** to place above or upon something else, or one upon another. **2.** *Geom.* to place one figure in the space occupied by another, so that the two figures coincide throughout their whole extent. [< F *superpos(er).* See SUPER-, POSE[1]] —**su′per·pos′a·ble,** *adj.* —**su·per·po·si·tion** (so͞o′pər pə zish′ən), *n.*

superposi′tion prin′ciple, *Physics.* See **principle of superposition.**

su·per·pow·er (so͞o′pər pou′ər), *n.* **1.** power greater in scope or magnitude than that which is considered natural or which has previously existed. **2.** a political power capable of influencing, by virtue of its own conduct, the acts and policies of other nations. **3.** power, esp. mechanical or electric power, on an extremely large scale secured by the linking together of a number of separate power systems, with a view to more efficient and economical generation and distribution. [SUPER- + POWER] —**su′per·pow′ered,** *adj.*

su·per·race (so͞o′pər rās′), *n.* a race, class, or people allegedly superior to another or others. [SUPER- + RACE[2]]

su·per·ra·tion·al (so͞o′pər rash′ə nəl), *adj.* beyond the scope or range of reason; intuitional. [SUPER- + RATIONAL] —**su′per·ra′tion·al′i·ty,** *n.* —**su′per·ra′tion·al·ly,** *adv.*

su·per·re·gen·er·a·tion (so͞o′pər ri jen′ə rā′shən), *n. Electronics.* regeneration in which a signal is alternately amplified and quenched at a frequency slightly above the audible range to achieve high sensitivity with a single tube. [SUPER- + REGENERATION] —**su·per·re·gen·er·a·tive** (so͞o′pər ri jen′ə rā′tiv, -ər ə tiv), *adj.*

su′per roy′al, a size of printing paper, 20½ × 27½ inches in England and 22 × 28 inches in the U.S., and of drawing or writing paper, 19 × 27 inches. Also, *esp. Brit.,* **su′per-roy′al.**

su·per·sales·man (so͞o′pər sālz′mən, so͞o′pər sālz′-), *n., pl.* **-men. 1.** an extremely skillful and effective salesman. **2.** a person who is extremely skillful and effective at persuading others to agree to or approve an idea, course of action, or the like. [SUPER- + SALESMAN]

su·per·sales·man·ship (so͞o′pər sālz′mən ship′), *n.* salesmanship that is extremely skillful and effective. [SUPER- + SALESMANSHIP]

su·per·sat·u·rate (so͞o′pər sach′ə rāt′), *v.t.,* **-rat·ed, -rat·ing.** to increase the concentration of (a solution) beyond saturation; saturate abnormally. [SUPER- + SATURATE] —**su′per·sat′u·ra′tion,** *n.*

su·per·scribe (so͞o′pər skrīb′, so͞o′pər skrīb′), *v.t.,* **-scribed, -scrib·ing. 1.** to write (words, letters, one's name, etc.) above or on something: *to superscribe corrections on a text.* **2.** to inscribe or mark with writing at the top or on the outside or surface of; put an inscription above or on: *to superscribe the cover of a text with corrections.* [< L *superscrībe(re),* equiv. to *super-* SUPER- + *scrībere* to write; see SCRIBE[1]]

su·per·script (so͞o′pər skript′), *adj.* **1.** *Print.* superior (def. 10). —*n.* **2.** *Print.* superior (def. 13). **3.** *Obs.* an address on a letter; superscription. [< L *superscrīpt(us)* (ptp. of *superscrībere* to SUPERSCRIBE), equiv. to *super-* SUPER- + *scrīptus* written; see SCRIPT]

su·per·scrip·tion (so͞o′pər skrip′shən), *n.* **1.** the act of superscribing. **2.** that which is superscribed. **3.** an address on a letter, parcel, or the like. **4.** *Pharm.* the sign ℞, meaning "take," at the beginning of a prescription. [< LL *superscrīptiōn-* (s. of *superscrīptiō*) a writing above. See SUPERSCRIPT, -ION]

su·per·sede (so͞o′pər sēd′), *v.t.,* **-sed·ed, -sed·ing. 1.** to replace in power, authority, effectiveness, acceptance, use, etc., as by another person or thing. **2.** to set aside or cause to be set aside as void, useless, or obsolete, usually in favor of something mentioned; make obsolete: *They superseded the old statute with a new one.* **3.** to succeed to the position, function, office, etc., of; supplant. [< L *supersed(ēre)* (to) sit above or upon, forbear, equiv. to *super-* SUPER- + *sedēre* to SIT] —**su′per·sed′a·ble,** *adj.* —**su′per·sed′er,** *n.*
—**Syn. 1.** See **replace. 2.** void, overrule, annul, revoke, rescind.

su·per·se·de·as (so͞o′pər sē′dē əs, -as′), *n., pl.* **-de·as.** *Law.* a writ ordering a stoppage or suspension of a judicial proceeding, of the execution of a judgment, or of the enforcement of another writ. [< L, 2nd sing. pres. subj. of *supersedēre* to SUPERSEDE, the writ being so named because *supersedeas,* i.e., you shall desist, occurs in it]

su·per·se·dure (so͞o′pər sē′jər), *n.* **1.** the act of superseding. **2.** supersession. [SUPERSEDE + -URE]

su·per·sen·ior·i·ty (so͞o′pər sēn yôr′i tē, -yor′-), *n.* seniority that is granted or held without regard to age or service. [SUPER- + SENIORITY]

su·per·sen·si·ble (so͞o′pər sen′sə bəl), *adj.* being above or beyond perception by the senses; beyond the reach of the senses. [SUPER- + SENSIBLE] —**su′per·sen′si·bly,** *adv.*

su·per·sen·si·tise (so͞o′pər sen′si tīz′), *v.t.,* **-tised, -tis·ing.** *Chiefly Brit.* supersensitize. —**su′per·sen′si·ti·sa′tion,** *n.* —**su′per·sen′si·tis′er,** *n.*

su·per·sen·si·tive (so͞o′pər sen′si tiv), *adj.* **1.** extremely or excessively sensitive. **2.** *Elect.* of or pertaining to relays which operate on extremely small currents, below about 250 microamperes. **3.** hypersensitive (def. 2). [SUPER- + SENSITIVE] —**su′per·sen′si·tive·ness,** *n.*

su·per·sen·si·tize (so͞o′pər sen′si tīz′), *v.t.,* **-tized, -tiz·ing.** to render or make supersensitive. [SUPERSENSIT(IVE) + -IZE] —**su′per·sen′si·ti·za′tion,** *n.* —**su′per·sen′si·tiz′er,** *n.*

su·per·sen·so·ry (so͞o′pər sen′sə rē), *adj.* **1.** supersensible. **2.** independent of the organs of sense. [SUPER- + SENSORY]

su·per·sen·su·al (so͞o′pər sen′sho͞o əl), *adj.* **1.** beyond the range of the senses. **2.** spiritual. **3.** extremely sensual. [SUPER- + SENSUAL] —**su′per·sen′su·al·ism,** *n.* —**su′per·sen′su·al·ist,** *n.* —**su′per·sen′su·al·is′tic,** *adj.* —**su·per·sen·su·al·i·ty** (so͞o′pər sen′sho͞o al′i tē), *n.* —**su′per·sen′su·al·ly,** *adv.*

su·per·serv·ice·a·ble (so͞o′pər sûr′vi sə bəl), *adj.* overly disposed to be of service; officious. [SUPER- + SERVICEABLE] —**su′per·serv′ice·a·ble·ness,** *n.* —**su′per·serv′ice·a·bly,** *adv.*

su·per·ses·sion (so͞o′pər sesh′ən), *n.* **1.** the state of being superseded. **2.** supersedure. [< ML *supersessiōn-* (s. of *supersessiō*), deriv. of L *supersess(us)* (ptp. of *supersedēre*). See SUPERSEDE, SESSION]

su′per·mu·nic′i·pal, *adj.*
su′per·mys′te·ry, *n., pl.* **-ries.**
su′per·na′tion, *n.*
su′per·ne·ces′si·ty, *n., pl.* **-ties.**
su′per·neg′li·gence, *n.*
su′per·neg′li·gent, *adj.;* **-ly,** *adv.*
su′per·no′ta·ble, *adj.;* **-ble·ness,** *n.;* **-bly,** *adv.*
su′per·nu′mer·ous, *adj.;* **-ly,** *adv.;* **-ness,** *n.*
su′per·nu·tri′tion, *n.*
su′per·o·be′di·ence, *n.*
su′per·o·be′di·ent, *adj.;* **-ly,** *adv.*
su′per·o·bese′, *adj.*
su′per·ob·ject′, *v.i.*
su′per·ob·jec′tion, *n.*
su′per·ob·jec′tion·a·ble, *adj.;* **-bly,** *adv.*
su′per·ob′li·ga′tion, *n.*
su′per·ob′sti·nate, *adj.;* **-ly,** *adv.;* **-ness,** *n.*
su′per·oc·cip′i·tal, *adj.*
su′per·oc′u·lar, *adj.;* **-ly,** *adv.*
su′per·of·fen′sive, *adj., n.;* **-ly,** *adv.;* **-ness,** *n.*
su′per·of·fi′cious, *adj.;* **-ly,** *adv.;* **-ness,** *n.*
su′per·op′po·si′tion, *n.*
su′per·op′ti·mal, *adj.*
su′per·op′ti·mist, *n.*
su′per·o·ra′to·ri′cal, *adj.;* **-ly,** *adv.*
su′per·or′bit·al, *adj.*
su′per·or·dain′, *v.i.*
su′per·or′di·nar′y, *adj.*
su′per·or′gan·i·za′tion, *n.*
su′per·or′na·ment, *n.*
su′per·or′na·ment′, *v.t.*
su′per·or′na·men′tal, *adj.;* **-ly,** *adv.*
su′per·out′put′, *n.*
su′per·ox′a·late′, *n.*
su′per·ox′y·gen·ate′, *v.t.,* **-at·ed, -at·ing.**
su′per·ox′y·gen·a′tion, *n.*
su′per·par′a·mount′, *adj.*
su′per·par′lia·men′ta·ry, *adj.*
su′per·pas′sage, *n.*
su′per·pa′tience, *n.*
su′per·pa′tient, *adj.;* **-ly,** *adv.*
su′per·per′fect, *adj.;* **-ly,** *adv.*
su′per·per·fec′tion, *n.*
su′per·per′son, *n.*
su′per·per′son·al, *adj.;* **-ly,** *adv.*
su′per·pe·tro′sal, *adj.*
su′per·pet′rous, *adj.*
su′per·pi′e·ty, *n.*
su′per·pi′ous, *adj.;* **-ly,** *adv.;* **-ness,** *n.*
su′per·plau′si·ble, *adj.;* **-ble·ness,** *n.;* **-bly,** *adv.*
su′per·po·lite′, *adj.;* **-ly,** *adv.;* **-ness,** *n.*
su′per·pol′y·mer, *n.*
su′per·pop′u·lat′ed, *adj.;* **-ly,** *adv.;* **-ness,** *n.*
su′per·pop′u·la′tion, *n.*
su′per·pos′i·tive, *adj.;* **-ly,** *adv.;* **-ness,** *n.*
su′per·praise′, *n., v.t.,* **-praised, -prais·ing.**
su′per·pre·car′i·ous, *adj.;* **-ly,** *adv.;* **-ness,** *n.*
su′per·pre·cise′, *adj.;* **-ly,** *adv.;* **-ness,** *n.*
su′per·prep′a·ra′tion, *n.*
su′per·pre·pared′, *adj.*
su′per·prob′a·bil′i·ty, *n.*
su′per·pro·duce′, *v.,* **-duced, -duc·ing.**
su′per·pro′duce, *n.*
su′per·pro·duc′tion, *n.*
su′per·pro·por′tion, *n.*
su′per·pros′per·ous, *adj.*
su′per·pub·lic′i·ty, *n.*
su′per·pure′, *adj.*
su′per·pur·ga′tion, *n.*
su′per·pu′ri·ty, *n.*
su′per·qual′i·fy′, *v.,* **-fied, -fy·ing.**
su′per·quote′, *v.,* **-quot·ed, -quot·ing;** *n.*
su′per·rad′i·cal, *adj.;* **-ly,** *adv.;* **-ness,** *n.*
su′per·re·ac′tion, *n.*
su′per·re·fine′, *v.t.,* **-fined, -fin·ing.**
su′per·re·fined′, *adj.*
su′per·re·fine′ment, *n.*
su′per·re·flec′tion, *n.*
su′per·re·form′, *n., v.t.*
su′per·ref′or·ma′tion, *n.*
su′per·re′gal, *adj.;* **-ly,** *adv.*
su′per·reg·is·tra′tion, *n.*
su′per·reg·u·la′tion, *n.*
su′per·re·li′ance, *n.*
su′per·re·mu′ner·a′tion, *n.*
su′per·re′nal, *adj.*
su′per·re·quire′ment, *n.*
su′per·re·spect′a·bil′i·ty, *n.*
su′per·re·spect′a·ble, *adj.;* **-ble·ness,** *n.;* **-bly,** *adv.*
su′per·re·spon′si·bil′i·ty, *n.*
su′per·re·spon′si·ble, *adj.;* **-ble·ness,** *n.;* **-bly,** *adv.*
su′per·re·stric′tion, *n.*
su′per·re·ward′, *v.t., n.*
su′per·right′eous, *adj.;* **-ly,** *adv.;* **-ness,** *n.*
su′per·ro·man′tic, *adj.*
su′per·ro·man′ti·cal·ly, *adv.*
su′per·sac′er·do′tal, *adj.;* **-ly,** *adv.*
su′per·sa′cral, *adj.*
su′per·sa′cred, *adj.*
su′per·sac′ri·fice′, *n., v.t.*
su′per·safe′, *adj.;* **-ly,** *adv.;* **-ness,** *n.*
su′per·safe′ty, *n.*
su′per·sa·ga′cious, *adj.;* **-ly,** *adv.;* **-ness,** *n.*
su′per·saint′, *n.*
su′per·saint′ly, *adv.*
su′per·sanc′tion, *v.t., n.*
su′per·san′guine, *adj.*
su′per·san·guin′i·ty, *n.*
su′per·san′i·ty, *n.*
su′per·sar′casm, *n.*
su′per·sar·cas′tic, *adj.*
su′per·sar·cas′ti·cal·ly, *adv.*
su′per·sat′is·fac′tion, *n.*
su′per·sat′is·fy′, *v.t.,* **-fied, -fy·ing.**
su′per·scan′dal, *n.*
su′per·scan′dal·ous, *adj.;* **-ly,** *adv.*
su′per·schol′ar·ly, *adj.*
su′per·sci′en·tif′ic, *adj.*
su′per·sci′en·tif′i·cal·ly, *adv.*
su′per·sea′man, *n., pl.* **-men.**
su′per·se′cret, *n.*
su′per·se·cre′tion, *n.*
su′per·se·cre′tive, *adj.;* **-ly,** *adv.;* **-ness,** *n.*
su′per·sec′u·lar, *adj.;* **-ly,** *adv.*
su′per·se·cure′, *adj.;* **-ly,** *adv.;* **-ness,** *n.*
su′per·se·lec′tion, *n.*
su′per·sen′su·ous, *adj.;* **-ly,** *adv.;* **-ness,** *n.*
su′per·sen′ti·men′tal, *adj.;* **-ly,** *adv.*
su′per·sep′tal, *adj.*
su′per·se·raph′ic, *adj.*
su′per·se·raph′i·cal, *adj.;* **-ly,** *adv.*
su′per·se′ri·ous, *adj.;* **-ly,** *adv.;* **-ness,** *n.*
su′per·serv′ice, *n.*

su·per·smooth (so͞o′pər smo͞oth′), *adj.* (of a metal file) dead-smooth.

su·per·son·ic (so͞o′pər son′ik), *adj.* **1.** greater than the speed of sound waves through air. **2.** capable of achieving such speed: *a supersonic plane.* **3.** ultrasonic. [SUPER- + SONIC] —**su′per·son′i·cal·ly,** *adv.*

su·per·son·ics (so͞o′pər son′iks), *n.* (*construed as sing.*) the branch of science that deals with supersonic phenomena. [see SUPERSONIC, -ICS]

su·per·speed (so͞o′pər spēd′), *adj.* constructed or intended to function at a very high speed. [SUPER- + SPEED]

su·per·state (so͞o′pər stāt′), *n.* **1.** a state or a governing power presiding over states subordinated to it. **2.** an extremely powerful centralized government maintaining close control or supervision over its member states and their inhabitants. [SUPER- + STATE]

su·per·sti·tion (so͞o′pər stish′ən), *n.* **1.** a belief or notion, not based on reason or knowledge, in or of the ominous significance of a particular thing, circumstance, occurrence, proceeding, or the like. **2.** a system or collection of such beliefs. **3.** a custom or act based on such a belief. **4.** irrational fear of what is unknown or mysterious, esp. in connection with religion. **5.** any blindly accepted belief or notion: *He accepted the superstition that the party was always right.* [< L *superstitiōn-* (s. of *superstitiō*), equiv. to *superstit-* (s. of *superstes*) standing beyond, outliving (*super-* SUPER- + *stit-*, var. s. of *stāre* to STAND) + *-iōn-* -ION]

su·per·sti·tious (so͞o′pər stish′əs), *adj.* **1.** of the nature of, characterized by, or proceeding from superstition: *superstitious fears.* **2.** pertaining to or connected with superstition: *superstitious legends.* **3.** believing in, full of, or addicted to superstition: *a superstitious old woman.* [< L *superstitiōs(us)*, equiv. to *superstiti-* (shortened s. of *superstitiō* SUPERSTITION) + *-ōsus* -OUS] —**su′per·sti′tious·ly,** *adv.* —**su′per·sti′tious·ness,** *n.*

su·per·stra·tum (so͞o′pər strā′təm, -strat′əm), *n., pl.* **-stra·ta** (-strā′tə, -strat′ə), **-stra·tums.** an overlying stratum or layer. [SUPER- + STRATUM; cf. SUBSTRATUM]

su·per·struc·ture (so͞o′pər struk′chər), *n.* **1.** the part of a building or construction entirely above its foundation or basement. **2.** any structure built on something else. **3.** *Naut.* any construction built above the main deck of a vessel as an upward continuation of the sides. Cf. **deckhouse. 4.** the part of a bridge that rests on the piers and abutments. **5.** anything based on or rising from some foundation or basis: *a complex ideological superstructure based on two hypotheses.* [SUPER- + STRUCTURE] —**su′per·struc′tur·al,** *adj.*

su′perstructure deck′, *Naut.* the weather deck of an open-shelter-deck vessel.

su·per·sub·tle (so͞o′pər sut′əl), *adj.* extremely or excessively subtle; oversubtle. [SUPER- + SUBTLE] —**su′per·sub′tle·ty,** *n.*

su·per·tank·er (so͞o′pər tang′kər), *n.* a tanker with a capacity of over 75,000 tons. [SUPER- + TANKER]

su·per·tax (so͞o′pər taks′), *n.* **1.** *Chiefly Brit.* a tax in addition to a normal tax, as one upon income above a certain amount. **2.** *U.S.* a surtax. [SUPER- + TAX]

su·per·ton·ic (so͞o′pər ton′ik), *n.* *Music.* the second tone of a scale, being the next above the tonic. [SUPER- + TONIC]

su·per·tramp (so͞o′pər tramp′), *n.* *Naut.* a tramp freighter carrying at least 12,000 dead-weight tons of cargo. [SUPER- + TRAMP]

su·per·vene (so͞o′pər vēn′), *v.i.*, **-vened, -ven·ing. 1.** to take place or occur as something additional or extraneous (sometimes fol. by *on* or *upon*). **2.** to ensue. [< L *superven(īre)*, equiv. to *super-* SUPER- + *venīre* to come] —**su·per·ven·ience** (so͞o′pər vēn′yəns), **su·per·ven·tion** (so͞o′pər ven′shən), *n.* —**su·per·ven·ient** (so͞o′pər vēn′yənt), *adj.*

su·per·vise (so͞o′pər vīz′), *v.t.*, **-vised, -vis·ing.** to oversee (a process, work, workers, etc.) during execution or performance; superintend; have the oversight and direction of. [< ML *supervīs(us)* (ptp. of *supervidēre* to oversee), equiv. to *super-* SUPER- + *vīsus*, equiv. to *vīd-* see + *-tus* ptp. suffix]

su·per·vi·sion (so͞o′pər vizh′ən), *n.* the act or function of supervising; superintendence. [< ML *supervīsiōn-* (s. of *supervīsiō*) oversight, equiv. to *super-* SUPER- + *vīsiōn-* VISION]

su·per·vi·sor (so͞o′pər vī′zər), *n.* **1.** one who supervises workers or the work done by others; superintendent. **2.** *Educ.* an official responsible for assisting teachers in the preparation of syllabuses, in devising teaching methods, etc., in a department of instruction, esp. in public schools. **3.** *U.S.* an elected administrative officer in some States, often a member of a board governing a county. [< ML; see SUPERVISE, -OR²] —**su′per·vi′sor·ship′,** *n.*

su·per·vi·so·ry (so͞o′pər vī′zə rē), *adj.* of, pertaining to, or having supervision. [SUPERVISE + -ORY¹]

su·per·wom·an (so͞o′pər wo͝om′ən), *n., pl.* **-wom·en.** a woman of extraordinary or superhuman powers. [SUPER- + WOMAN]

su·pi·nate (so͞o′pə nāt′), *v.*, **-nat·ed, -nat·ing.** —*v.t.* **1.** to turn to a supine position; rotate (the hand or forearm) so that the palmar surface is upward. —*v.i.* **2.** to become supinated. [< L *supīnāt(us)* (ptp. of *supīnāre* to lay face up). See SUPINE, -ATE¹]

su·pi·na·tion (so͞o′pə nā′shən), *n.* **1.** rotation of the hand or forearm so that the palmar surface is facing upward (opposed to *pronation*). **2.** a comparable motion of the foot, consisting of adduction followed by inversion. **3.** the position assumed as the result of this rotation. [SUPINATE + -ION]

su·pi·na·tor (so͞o′pə nā′tər), *n.* *Anat.* a muscle used in supination. [< NL; see SUPINATE, -OR²]

su·pine (*adj.* so͞o pīn′; *n.* so͞o′pīn), *adj.* **1.** lying on the back, or with the face or front upward. **2.** inactive, passive, or inert, esp. from indolence or indifference. **3.** (of the hand) having the palm upward. —*n.* **4.** (in Latin) a noun form derived from verbs, appearing only in the accusative and the dative-ablative, as *dictū* in *mīrābile dictū*, "wonderful to say." **5.** (in English) the simple infinitive of a verb preceded by *to.* **6.** an analogous form in some other language. [< L *supīn(us)* lying face up, inactive] —**su·pine′ly,** *adv.* —**su·pine′ness,** *n.*

supp., supplement. Also, **suppl.**

Sup·pé (so͞o′pā; *Ger.* zo͞op′ā), *n.* **Franz von** (fränts fən), 1819–95, Austrian composer.

sup·pe·da·ne·um (sup′i dā′nē əm), *n., pl.* **-ne·a** (-nē ə). a shelf affixed to a cross for supporting the feet of the crucified. [< L, n. use of neut. of *suppedāneus* (adj.), equiv. to *sup-* SUP- + *ped-* (s. of *pēs*) foot + *-āneus, -um* -AN]

sup·per (sup′ər), *n.* **1.** the evening meal, esp. when dinner is served at midday. **2.** any light evening meal, esp. one taken late in the evening: *an after-the-theater supper.* —*adj.* **3.** of or pertaining to supper: *She washed the supper dishes.* **4.** for, during, or including supper: *a supper party.* [ME *sup(p)er* < OF *souper*, n. use of *souper* to SUP¹]

sup′per club′, a night club, esp. a small, luxurious one.

sup·per·less (sup′ər lis), *adj.* not having or not having eaten any supper. [SUPPER + -LESS]

sup·per·time (sup′ər tīm′), *n.* the time at which supper is served, usually between the hours of 5 and 7 P.M. [ME *soper tyme.* See SUPPER, TIME]

sup·plant (sə plant′, -plänt′), *v.t.* **1.** to displace or supersede, as one thing does another. **2.** to take the place of (another), as in office or favor, through force, scheming, strategy, or the like. **3.** to replace (one thing) by something else. [ME *supplante(n)* < L *supplantāre* to trip up, overthrow. See SUP-, PLANT] —**sup·plan·ta·tion** (sup′lan tā′shən), *n.* —**sup·plant′er,** *n.*
—**Syn. 1.** remove, succeed. See **replace.**

sup·ple (sup′əl), *adj.*, **-pler, -plest,** *v.*, **-pled, -pling.** —*adj.* **1.** bending readily without breaking or becoming deformed; pliant; flexible: *a supple bough.* **2.** characterized by ease in bending; limber; lithe: *a supple dancer; supple movements.* **3.** characterized by ease, responsiveness, and adaptability in mental action. **4.** compliant or yielding. **5.** obsequious; servile. —*v.t., v.i.* **6.** to make or become supple. [ME *souple* < OF: soft, yielding, lithe < L *supplic-* (s. of *supplex*) kneeling, bending under, submissive, equiv. to *sup-* SUP- + *plic-* PLY²] —**sup′ple·ly,** *adv.* —**sup′ple·ness,** *n.*
—**Syn. 1.** pliable, elastic. **2.** lissome. **3.** agreeable. —**Ant. 1.** rigid.

sup·ple·jack (sup′əl jak′), *n.* **1.** a strong, pliant cane or walking stick. **2.** any of various climbing shrubs with strong stems suitable for making walking sticks. [SUPPLE + JACK¹]

sup·ple·ment (*n.* sup′lə mənt; *v.* sup′lə ment′), *n.* **1.** something added to complete a thing, supply a deficiency, or reinforce or extend a whole. **2.** a part added to a book, document, etc., to supply additional or later information, correct errors, or the like. **3.** a part, usually of special character, issued as an additional feature of a newspaper or other periodical. **4.** *Math.* the quantity by which an angle or an arc falls short of 180° or a semicircle. —*v.t.* **5.** to complete, add to, or extend by a supplement; form a supplement or addition to. **6.** to supply (a deficiency). [late ME < L *supplēment(um)* that by which anything is made full, equiv. to *sup-* SUP- + *plē-* (s. of *plēre* to fill) + *-mentum* -MENT] —**sup′ple·ment′er,** *n.*
—**Syn. 1.** reinforcement, extension, addition, complement. **2.** addendum, epilogue, postscript. See **appendix. 5.** See **complement.**

120° B 60° D C A

Supplement (def. 4) Angle BCD, supplement of angle BCA

sup·ple·men·tal (sup′lə men′təl), *adj.* **1.** supplementary. **2.** (of a pleading, an affidavit, etc.) added to furnish what is lacking or missing. [SUPPLEMENT + -AL¹] —**sup′ple·men′tal·ly,** *adv.*

sup′plemen′tal plum′age, *Ornith.* the third plumage assumed by certain birds having three different plumages in their annual cycle of molts. Cf. **basic plumage, alternate plumage.**

sup·ple·men·ta·ry (sup′lə men′tə rē), *adj., n., pl.* **-ries.** —*adj.* **1.** Also, **supplemental.** of the nature of or forming a supplement; additional. —*n.* **2.** one who or that which is supplementary. [SUPPLEMENT + -ARY]

sup′plemen′tary an′gle, *Math.* either of two angles that added together produce an angle of 180°.

sup′plemen′tary stor′y, *Journalism.* follow-up (def. 3b).

sup·ple·men·ta·tion (sup′lə men tā′shən, -mən-), *n.* **1.** the act or process of supplementing. **2.** the state of being supplemented. **3.** that which supplements. [SUPPLEMENT + -ATION]

sup·ple·tion (sə plē′shən), *n.* *Gram.* the use in inflection or derivation of an allomorph that is not related in form to the primary allomorph of a morpheme, as the use of *better* as the comparative of *good.* [< ML *supplētiōn-* (s. of *supplētiō*) a filling up, equiv. to *supplēt(us)*, ptp. of *supplēre* to make complete, (*sup-* SUP- + *plē-*, s. of *plēre* to fill, + *-tus* ptp. suffix) + *-iōn-* -ION]

sup·ple·tive (sə plē′tiv, sup′li tiv), *adj.* *Gram.* **1.** serving as an inflected form of a word with a totally different stem, as *went*, the suppletive past of *go.* **2.** including one or more such forms: *a suppletive paradigm.* **3.** characterized by the use of such forms: *suppletive inflection.* [< ML *supplētīv(us)*, equiv. to L *supplēt(us)* (ptp. of *supplēre* to fill up; see SUPPLETION) + *-īvus* -IVE]

sup·ple·to·ry (sup′li tôr′ē, -tōr′ē), *adj.* supplying a deficiency. [< LL *supplētōri(us)*, equiv. to *supplēt-* (see SUPPLETION) + *-ōrius* -ORY¹] —**sup′ple·to′ri·ly,** *adv.*

sup·pli·ance¹ (sə plī′əns), *n.* the act, method, or process of supplying. [SUPPLY + -ANCE]

sup·pli·ance² (sup′lē əns), *n.* appeal; entreaty; plea; supplication: *The king would not hear her suppliance for mercy. He knelt in an attitude of suppliance.* Also, **suppliancy.** [SUPPLI(ANT) + -ANCE]

sup·pli·an·cy (sup′lē ən sē), *n., pl.* **-cies.** suppliance². [SUPPLI(ANT) + -ANCY]

sup·pli·ant (sup′lē ənt), *n.* **1.** one who supplicates; petitioner. —*adj.* **2.** supplicating. **3.** expressive of supplication, as words, actions, etc. [late ME < MF, prp. of *supplier* < L *supplicāre* to kneel, beseech. SUPPLICATE. See SUPPLE, -ANT] —**sup′pli·ant·ly,** *adv.* —**sup′pli·ant·ness,** *n.*

Suppliants, The, **1.** a tragedy (c490 B.C.) by Aeschylus. **2.** a tragedy (c420 B.C.) by Euripides.

sup·pli·cant (sup′lə kənt), *adj.* **1.** supplicating. —*n.* **2.** a suppliant. [< L *supplicant-* (s. of *supplicāns*, prp. of *supplicāre* to SUPPLICATE), equiv. to *supplic-* (see SUPPLE) + *-ant-* -ANT]

sup·pli·cate (sup′lə kāt′), *v.*, **-cat·ed, -cat·ing.** —*v.i.* **1.** to pray humbly; make humble and earnest entreaty or petition. —*v.t.* **2.** to pray humbly to; entreat or petition humbly. **3.** to seek or ask for by humble entreaty. [< L *supplicāt(us)* (ptp. of *supplicāre* to kneel), equiv. to *supplic-* (see SUPPLE) + *-ātus* -ATE¹] —**sup′pli·cat′ing·ly,** *adv.*
—**Syn. 2.** implore, crave, solicit, beseech. See **appeal.**

sup·pli·ca·tion (sup′lə kā′shən), *n.* the act of supplicating; humble prayer, entreaty, or petition. [late ME < L *supplicātiōn-* (s. of *supplicātiō*), lit., a kneeling. See SUPPLICATE, -ION]

sup·pli·ca·to·ry (sup′lə kə tôr′ē, -tōr′ē), *adj.* making or expressing supplication. [< ML *supplicātōri(us)*. See SUPPLICATE, -ORY¹]

sup·ply¹ (sə plī′), *v.*, **-plied, -ply·ing,** *n., pl.* **-plies.** —*v.t.* **1.** to furnish or provide (a person, establishment, place, etc.) with what is lacking or requisite (often fol. by *with*): *to supply someone clothing; to supply a community with electricity.* **2.** to furnish or provide (something wanting or requisite): *to supply electricity to a community.* **3.** to make up, compensate for, or satisfy (a deficiency, loss, need, etc.): *The TVA supplied the need for cheap electricity.* **4.** to fill or occupy as a substitute, as a vacancy, a pulpit, etc.: *During the summer local clergymen will supply the pulpit.* —*v.i.* **5.** to fill the place of another, esp. the pulpit of a church, temporarily or as a substitute: *Who will supply until the new minister arrives?* —*n.* **6.** the act of supplying,

su′per·se·vere′, *adj.*; **-ly,** *adv.*; **-ness,** *n.*
su′per·se·ver′i·ty, *n.*
su′per·ship′ment, *n.*
su′per·sig·nif′i·cant, *adj.*; **-ly,** *adv.*
su′per·si′lent, *adj.*; **-ly,** *adv.*
su′per·sim·plic′i·ty, *n.*
su′per·sim′pli·fy′, *v.t.*, **-fied, -fy·ing.**
su′per·sin·cer′i·ty, *n.*
su′per·sin′gu·lar, *adj.*
su′per·size′, *n.*
su′per·smart′, *adj.*; **-ly,** *adv.*; **-ness,** *n.*
su′per·soil′, *n.*
su′per·so′lar, *adj.*
su′per·sol′emn, *adj.*; **-ly,** *adv.*; **-ness,** *n.*
su′per·so·lem′ni·ty, *n.*
su′per·so·lic′it, *v.*
su′per·so·lic′i·ta′tion, *n.*
su′per·sov′er·eign, *adj.*, *n.*
su′per·sov′er·eign·ty, *n.*
su′per·spe′cial·ize′, *v.i.*, **-ized, -iz·ing.**
su′per·spe′cies, *n.*
su′per·spec′i·fi·ca′tion, *n.*
su′per·sphe′noid, *adj.*
su′per·sphe·noi′dal, *adj.*
su′per·spir′it·u·al, *adj.*; **-ly,** *adv.*
su′per·spir′it·u·al′i·ty, *n.*
su′per·squa·mo′sal, *adj.*
su′per·stage′, *n.*
su′per·stamp′, *n.*, *v.t.*
su′per·stand′ard, *n.*, *adj.*
su′per·states′man, *n.*, *pl.* **-men.**
su′per·stim′u·late′, *v.t.*, **-lat·ed, -lat·ing.**
su′per·stim·u·la′tion, *n.*
su′per·sto′i·cal, *adj.*; **-ly,** *adv.*
su′per·strain′, *n.*, *v.t.*
su′per·stren′u·ous, *adj.*; **-ly,** *adv.*; **-ness,** *n.*
su′per·strict′, *adj.*; **-ly,** *adv.*; **-ness,** *n.*
su′per·strong′, *adj.*
su′per·styl′ish, *adj.*; **-ly,** *adv.*; **-ness,** *n.*
su′per·sub′li·mat′ed, *adj.*
su′per·sub·sist′, *v.i.*
su′per·sub·stan′tial, *adj.*; **-ly,** *adv.*
su′per·sub′ti·lized′, *adj.*
su′per·suf·fi′cien·cy, *n.*
su′per·suf·fi′cient, *adj.*; **-ly,** *adv.*
su′per·sul′fate, *n.*
su′per·sul′fu·ret′ed, *adj.*
su′per·sul′fu·rize′, *v.t.*, **-ized, -iz·ing.**
su′per·sul′phate, *n.*
su′per·sul′phu·ret′ed, *adj.*
su′per·sul′phu·rize′, *v.t.*, **-ized, -iz·ing.**
su′per·sur·prise′, *n.*
su′per·sus·pi′cion, *n.*
su′per·sus·pi′cious, *adj.*; **-ly,** *adv.*; **-ness,** *n.*
su′per·sweet′, *adj.*; **-ly,** *adv.*; **-ness,** *n.*
su′per·sym·pa·thet′ic, *adj.*
su′per·sym′pa·thy, *n.*, *pl.* **-thies.**
su′per·syn′di·cate, *n.*
su′per·sys′tem, *n.*
su′per·tar′trate, *n.*
su′per·tem′po·ral, *adj.*
su′per·tempt′, *v.t.*
su′per·temp·ta′tion, *n.*
su′per·ten′sion, *n.*
su′per·ter·res′tri·al, *adj.*
su′per·thank′ful, *adj.*; **-ly,** *adv.*; **-ness,** *n.*
su′per·thor′ough, *adj.*; **-ly,** *adv.*; **-ness,** *n.*
su′per·tol′er·a′tion, *n.*
su′per·to′tal, *n.*
su′per·tow′er, *n.*
su′per·trag′e·dy, *n.*, *pl.* **-dies.**
su′per·trag′ic, *adj.*
su′per·trag′i·cal·ly, *adv.*
su′per·train′, *v.*
su′per·tran·scend′ent, *adj.*; **-ly,** *adv.*; **-ness,** *n.*
su′per·trea′son, *n.*
su′per·triv′i·al, *adj.*
su′per·tu′nic, *n.*
su′per·tu′te·lar′y, *adj.*
su′per·ug′ly, *adj.*
su′per·u′nit, *n.*
su′per·u′ni·ty, *n.*
su′per·u′ni·ver′sal, *adj.*; **-ly,** *adv.*; **-ness,** *n.*
su′per·u′ni·verse′, *n.*
su′per·ur′gen·cy, *n.*
su′per·ur′gent, *adj.*; **-ly,** *adv.*
su′per·val′ue, *n.*, *v.t.*, **-ued, -u·ing.**
su′per·vast′, *adj.*; **-ly,** *adv.*; **-ness,** *n.*
su′per·ve·nos′i·ty, *n.*
su′per·vest′ment, *n.*
su′per·vex·a′tion, *n.*
su′per·vic·to′ri·ous, *adj.*; **-ly,** *adv.*; **-ness,** *n.*
su′per·vic′to·ry, *n.*, *pl.* **-ries.**
su′per·vig′i·lance, *n.*
su′per·vig′i·lant, *adj.*; **-ly,** *adv.*
su′per·vig′or·ous, *adj.*; **-ly,** *adv.*; **-ness,** *n.*
su′per·vir′u·lent, *adj.*; **-ly,** *adv.*
su′per·vi′su·al, *adj.*; **-ly,** *adv.*
su′per·vi′tal, *adj.*; **-ly,** *adv.*; **-ness,** *n.*
su′per·vi·tal′i·ty, *n.*
su′per·vo·li′tion, *n.*
su′per·vo·lu′mi·nous, *adj.*; **-ly,** *adv.*
su′per·wa′ger, *n.*
su′per·wealth′y, *adj.*
su′per·wise′, *adj.*
su′per·world′li·ness, *n.*
su′per·world′ly, *adj.*
su′per·wrought′, *adj.*
su′per·yacht′, *n.*
su′per·zeal′ous, *adj.*; **-ly,** *adv.*; **-ness,** *n.*

furnishing, providing, satisfying, etc.: *to begin the supply of household help.* **7.** that which is supplied: *The storm cut off our water supply.* **8.** a quantity of something on hand or available, as for use; a stock or store: *Did you see our new supply of shirts?* **9.** Usually, **supplies.** a provision, stock, or store of food or other things necessary for maintenance: *to lay in supplies for the winter.* **10.** *Econ.* the quantity of a commodity that is in the market and available for purchase or that is available for purchase at a particular price. **11.** **supplies,** *Mil.* **a.** all items necessary for the equipment, maintenance, and operation of a military command, including food, clothing, arms, ammunition, fuel, materials, and machinery. **b.** procurement, distribution, maintenance, and salvage of supplies. **12.** one who fills a vacancy or takes the place of another, esp. temporarily. **13.** *Obs.* reinforcements. **14.** *Obs.* aid. [late ME *sup(p)lie(n)* < MF *souplie(r)*, var. of *soupleer* < L *supplēre* to fill up, equiv. to *sup-* SUP- + *plēre* to fill] **—sup·pli′a·ble,** *adj.* **—sup·pli′er,** *n.*
—Syn. 3. replenish, fulfill. **8.** inventory, reserve.

sup·ply[2] (sup′lē), *adv.* in a supple manner or way; supplely. [SUPPLE + -LY]

sup·ply-side (sə plī′sīd′), *adj. Econ.* of or pertaining to a theory that a nation can regain its economic stability and curb inflation by increasing its supply of goods and services, and that this can be achieved by reducing taxes and passing other legislation designed to encourage business investment and growth.

sup·ply-sid·er (sə plī′sī′dər), *n.* one who supports or advocates supply-side economics.

sup·port (sə pōrt′, -pôrt′), *v.t.* **1.** to bear or hold up (a load, mass, structure, part, etc.); serve as a foundation for. **2.** to sustain or withstand (weight, pressure, strain, etc.) without giving way; serve as a prop for. **3.** to undergo or endure, esp. with patience or submission; tolerate. **4.** to sustain (a person, the mind, spirits, courage, etc.) under trial or affliction: *His wife supported him throughout the ordeal.* **5.** to maintain (a person, family, establishment, institution, etc.) by supplying with things necessary to existence; provide for: *Can he support a family?* **6.** to uphold (a person, cause, policy, etc.) by aid, countenance, one's vote, etc.; back; second. **7.** to maintain or advocate (a theory, principle, etc.). **8.** to corroborate (a statement, opinion, etc.): *Leading doctors supported his testimony.* **9.** to act with or second (a leading actor), as on a stage; assist in performance: *The star was supported by a talented newcomer.* **—***n.* **10.** the act or an instance of supporting. **11.** the state of being supported. **12.** that which serves as a foundation, prop, brace, or stay. **13.** maintenance, as of a person or family, with necessaries, means, or funds: *His wife sued for support.* **14.** a thing that or a person who supports, as financially: *The pension was his only support. He was his mother's sole support.* **15.** a thing or a person that gives aid or assistance. **16.** an actor, actress, or group of entertainers performing with a leading actor: *The rest of the cast provided strong support.* **17.** the material, as canvas or wood, on which a picture is painted. [late ME *supporte(n)* < MF *supporte(r)* < ML *supportāre* to endure (L: to convey), equiv. to *sup-* SUP- + *portāre* to carry; see PORT[5]] **—sup·port′ing·ly,** *adv.* **—sup·port′less,** *adj.* **—sup·port′less·ly,** *adv.*
—Syn. 1, 6. SUPPORT, MAINTAIN, SUSTAIN, UPHOLD all mean to hold up and to preserve. To SUPPORT is to hold up or add strength to, literally or figuratively: *The columns support the roof.* To MAINTAIN is to support so as to preserve intact: *to maintain an attitude of defiance.* To SUSTAIN, a rather elevated word, suggests completeness and adequacy in supporting: *The court sustained his claim.* UPHOLD applies esp. to supporting or backing another, as in a statement, opinion, or belief: *to uphold the rights of a minority.* **3.** suffer, bear, stand, stomach. **6.** abet, further, encourage, forward; help, assist, succor. **8.** confirm. **13.** sustenance, subsistence, keep. See **living. 15.** help, aid.

sup·port·a·ble (sə pōr′tə bəl, -pôr′-), *adj.* capable of being supported; endurable; maintainable. [SUPPORT + -ABLE] **—sup·port′a·bil′i·ty, sup·port′a·ble·ness,** *n.* **—sup·port′a·bly,** *adv.*

sup·port·er (sə pōr′tər, -pôr′-), *n.* **1.** one who or that which supports. **2.** a device, usually of elastic cotton webbing, for supporting some part of the body, esp. a jockstrap. **3.** a garter, esp. one attached to a garter belt or girdle. **4.** an adherent, follower, backer, or advocate. **5.** *Heraldry.* either of two human or animal figures flanking and supporting an escutcheon in an achievement of arms. [late ME; see SUPPORT, -ER[1]]

sup·port·ive (sə pōr′tiv, -pôr′-), *adj.* **1.** giving support. **2.** *Med.* helping to maintain a normal physiological balance, as by the intravenous administration of required nutriment. [SUPPORT + -IVE]

suppos., (in prescriptions) a suppository. [< L *suppositōrium*]

sup·pos·al (sə pō′zəl), *n.* **1.** the act of supposing. **2.** that which is supposed; conjecture or notion. [late ME < MF *supposaille*. See SUPPOSE, -AL[2]]

sup·pose (sə pōz′), *v.*, **-posed, -pos·ing.** **—***v.t.* **1.** to assume (something), without reference to its being true or false, for the sake of argument or for the purpose of tracing the consequences: *Suppose the distance to be one mile.* **2.** (used in the imperative) to consider as a possibility suggested or an idea or plan proposed: *Suppose we wait until tomorrow.* **3.** to believe or assume as true, in the absence of positive knowledge or of evidence to the contrary: *It is supposed that the occurrence was an accident.* **4.** to take for granted, assume, or presume, without thought of possible error: *I supposed that you had gone.* **5.** to think, with reference to mere opinion: *What do you suppose he will do?* **6.** (of a proposition, theory, etc.) to make or involve the assumption of: *This theory supposes the existence of life on Mars.* **7.** (of facts, circumstances, etc.) to require logically; imply; presuppose: *The evidence supposes his presence near the scene.* **8.** to expect. **—***v.i.* **9.** to assume something; presume; think. [ME *suppose(n)* < OF *suppose(r)*, equiv. to *sup-* SUP- (< ML *suppōnere* to suppose) + *poser* to POSE[1]] **—sup·pos′a·ble,** *adj.* **—sup·pos′a·bly,** *adv.* **—sup·pos′er,** *n.*

sup·posed (sə pōzd′), *adj.* **1.** assumed as true, regardless of fact; hypothetical: *a supposed case.* **2.** accepted or believed as true, without positive knowledge: *the supposed site of an ancient temple.* **3.** merely thought to be such; imagined: *to sacrifice real for supposed gains.* [SUPPOSE + -ED[2]] **—sup·pos·ed·ly** (sə pō′zid lē), *adv.*

sup·pos·ing (sə pō′zing), *conj.* upon the supposition or premise that; in the event that. [ME; see SUPPOSE, -ING[1]]

sup·po·si·tion (sup′ə zish′ən), *n.* **1.** the act of supposing. **2.** that which is supposed; assumption; hypothesis. [late ME < L *suppositiōn-* (s. of *suppositiō* substitution; E meaning by assoc. with SUPPOSE), equiv. to *supposit(us)* (ptp. of *suppōnere* to substitute) + *-iōn-* -ION. See SUP-, POSITION] **—sup′po·si′tion·al,** *adj.* **—sup′po·si′tion·al·ly,** *adv.* **—sup′po·si′tion·less,** *adj.*

sup·po·si·tious (sup′ə zish′əs), *adj.* **1.** formed from or growing out of supposition: *suppositious evidence.* **2.** supposititious. [shortened form of SUPPOSITITIOUS]

sup·pos·i·ti·tious (sə poz′i tish′əs), *adj.* **1.** fraudulently substituted or pretended; spurious; not genuine. **2.** hypothetical. [< L *suppositicius*, equiv. to *supposit(us)* (ptp. of *suppōnere*; see SUPPOSITION) + *-icius* -ITIOUS] **—sup·pos′i·ti′tious·ly,** *adv.* **—sup·pos′i·ti′tious·ness,** *n.*

sup·pos·i·tive (sə poz′i tiv), *adj.* **1.** of the nature of or involving supposition; suppositional. **2.** suppositious or false. **3.** *Gram.* expressing or noting supposition, as the words *if, granting,* or *provided.* **—***n.* **4.** *Gram.* a suppositive word. [< LL *suppositīv(us)*, equiv. to *supposit(us)* (see SUPPOSITION) + *-īvus* -IVE] **—sup·pos′i·tive·ly,** *adv.*

sup·pos·i·to·ry (sə poz′i tōr′ē, -tôr′ē), *n., pl.* **-ries.** a solid, conical mass of medicinal substance for inserting into the rectum or vagina. [late ME < ML *suppositōri(um)*, equiv. to *supposit(us)* (see SUPPOSITITIOUS) + *-ōrium* -ORY[2]]

sup·press (sə pres′), *v.t.* **1.** to put an end to the activities of (a person, body of persons, etc.): *to suppress the Communist party.* **2.** to do away with by or as by authority; abolish; stop (a practice, custom, etc.). **3.** to keep in or repress (a feeling, smile, groan, etc.). **4.** to withhold from disclosure or publication (truth, evidence, a book, names, etc.). **5.** to stop or arrest (a flow, hemorrhage, cough, etc.). **6.** to vanquish or subdue (a revolt, rebellion, etc.); quell; crush. **7.** *Elect.* to reduce or eliminate (an irregular or undesired oscillation or frequency) in a circuit. [late ME < L *suppress(us)* pressed under (ptp. of *supprimere*), equiv. to *sup-* SUP- + *pressus*; see PRESS[1]] **—sup·press·ed·ly** (sə prest′lē, -pres′id lē), *adv.* **—sup·press′i·ble,** *adj.* **—sup·pres′sive,** *adj.* **—sup·pres′sive·ly,** *adv.* **—sup·pres′sor, sup·press′er,** *n.*

sup·pres·sion (sə presh′ən), *n.* **1.** the act of suppressing. **2.** the state of being suppressed. **3.** *Psychoanal.* conscious inhibition of an impulse. **4.** *Bot.* the absence of parts normally or usually present due to the action of frost, disease, or insects. **5.** *Radio, Electronics.* the elimination of a component of a varying emission, as the elimination of a frequency or group of frequencies from a signal. **6.** *Elect.* the reduction or elimination of irregular current oscillations or frequencies in a circuit. [< L *suppressiōn-* (s. of *suppressiō*) a pressing under. See SUPPRESS, -ION]

sup·pu·rate (sup′yə rāt′), *v.i.*, **-rat·ed, -rat·ing.** to produce or discharge pus, as a wound; maturate. [< L *suppurāt(us)* (ptp. of *suppurāre*), equiv. to *sup-* SUP- + *pur-* (s. of *pūs*) PUS + *-ātus* -ATE[1]]

sup·pu·ra·tion (sup′yə rā′shən), *n.* **1.** the process of suppurating. **2.** the matter produced by suppuration; pus. [< L *suppurātiōn-* (s. of *suppurātiō*) a forming of pus. See SUPPURATE, -ION]

sup·pu·ra·tive (sup′yə rā′tiv), *adj.* **1.** suppurating; characterized by suppuration. **2.** promoting suppuration. **—***n.* **3.** a medicine or application that promotes suppuration. [< ML *suppurātīv(us)* See SUPPURATE, -IVE]

supr., **1.** superior. **2.** supreme.

su·pra (so͞o′prə), *adv.* above, esp. when used in referring to parts of a text. Cf. **infra.** [< L (adv., prep.): on the upper side, above, over; akin to SUPER-]

supra-, a learned borrowing from Latin meaning "above," equivalent to **super-** but emphasizing location or position and used in the formation of compound words: *supraorbital; suprasegmental.*

su·pra·he·pat·ic (so͞o′prə hi pat′ik), *adj.* situated above the liver. [SUPRA- + HEPATIC]

su·pra·lap·sar·i·an (so͞o′prə lap sâr′ē ən), *n.* **1.** a person who believes in supralapsarianism. **—***adj.* **2.** of or pertaining to supralapsarians or supralapsarianism. [< NL *suprālapsāri(us)* (L *suprā-* SUPRA- + *laps(us)* a fall + *-ārius* -ARY) + -AN]

su·pra·lap·sar·i·an·ism (so͞o′prə lap sâr′ē ə niz′əm), *n. Theol.* the doctrine that the decree of election and reprobation, expressing the ultimate purpose of God, preceded the means by which this purpose was to be accomplished, namely, the decree of man's creation and the decree which permitted his fall (opposed to *infralapsarianism*). [SUPRALAPSARIAN + -ISM]

su·pra·lim·i·nal (so͞o′prə lim′ə nəl), *adj. Psychol.* existing or operating above the threshold of consciousness. [SUPRA- + LIMINAL] **—su′pra·lim′i·nal·ly,** *adv.*

su·pra·mo·lec·u·lar (so͞o′prə mə lek′yə lər), *adj.* **1.** having an organization more complex than that of a molecule. **2.** composed of an aggregate of molecules. [SUPRA- + MOLECULAR]

su·pra·na·sal (so͞o′prə nā′zəl), *adj.* situated above the nose or over the nasal bones. [SUPRA- + NASAL]

su·pra·na·tion·al (so͞o′prə nash′ə nəl), *adj.* outside or beyond the authority of one national government, as of a project or policy that is planned and controlled by a group of nations. [SUPRA- + NATIONAL] **—su′pra·na′tion·al·ism,** *n.*

su·pra·nat·u·ral (so͞o′prə nach′ər əl), *adj.* beyond what is natural; supernatural. [SUPRA- + NATURAL] **—su′pra·nat′u·ral·ism,** *n.* **—su′pra·nat′u·ral·ist,** *n.* **—su′pra·nat′u·ral·is′tic,** *adj.*

su·pra·or·bit·al (so͞o′prə ôr′bi təl), *adj.* situated above the eye socket. [< NL *suprāorbitāl(is)* equiv. to L *suprā-* SUPRA- + *orbit(a)* ORBIT + *-ālis* -AL[1]]

su·pra·pro·test (so͞o′prə prō′test), *n. Law.* an acceptance or a payment of a bill by a third person after protest for nonacceptance or nonpayment by the drawee. [alter. of It *sopra protesto* upon protest]

su·pra·ra·tion·al (so͞o′prə rash′ə nəl), *adj.* not understandable by reason alone; beyond rational comprehension. [SUPRA- + RATIONAL]

su·pra·re·nal (so͞o′prə rēn′əl), *Anat.* **—***adj.* **1.** situated above or on the kidney. **—***n.* **2.** a suprarenal part, esp. the suprarenal gland. [< NL *suprārēnāl(is)*. See SUPRA-, RENAL]

su′prare′nal gland′. See **adrenal gland.**

su·pra·ren·a·lin (so͞o′prə ren′əlin), *n. Pharm.* epinephrine. [SUPRARENAL + -IN[2]]

su·pra·seg·men·tal (so͞o′prə seg men′təl), *adj.* **1.** above, beyond, or in addition to a segment or segments. **2.** *Linguistics.* pertaining to or noting junctural or prosodic phonemic features. [SUPRA- + SEGMENTAL]

su·pra·tem·po·ral (so͞o′prə tem′pər əl), *adj. Anat.* situated above the upper part of the temporal bone or region. [SUPRA- + TEMPORAL[2]]

su·pra·vag·i·nal (so͞o′prə vaj′ə nəl, -və jīn′əl), *adj.* situated above the vagina or outside a sheathing membrane. [SUPRA- + VAGINAL]

su·prem·a·cist (sə prem′ə sist), *n.* one who believes in or advocates the supremacy of a particular group, esp. a racial group: *a white supremacist.* [SUPREMAC(Y) + -IST]

su·prem·a·cy (sə prem′ə sē, so͞o-), *n.* **1.** the state of being supreme. **2.** supreme authority or power. [SUPREME[1] + -ACY]

Su·prem·a·tism (sə prem′ə tiz′əm, so͞o-), *n.* (*sometimes l.c.*) *Fine Arts.* a nonrepresentational style of art developed in Russia in the early 20th century, characterized by severely simple geometric shapes or forms and an extremely limited palette. [*supremat-* (for *supremac-*, as in F *suprématie* SUPREMACY) + -ISM]

su·preme[1] (sə prēm′, so͞o-), *adj.* **1.** highest in rank or authority; paramount; sovereign; chief. **2.** of the highest quality, degree, character, importance, etc.: *supreme courage.* **3.** greatest, utmost, or extreme: *supreme disgust.* **4.** last or final, as of a person's life; ultimate. [< L *suprēm(us)*, superl. of *super(us)* upper] **—su·preme′ly,** *adv.* **—su·preme′ness,** *n.*

su·preme[2] (sə prēm′, -prām′, so͞o-), *n.* suprême (def. 3).

su·prême (sə prēm′, -prām′, so͞o-; *Fr.* sʏ prem′), *n.* **1.** Also called **sauce suprême.** a velouté made with a rich chicken stock. **2.** a dish prepared or served with this sauce. **3.** Also, **supreme. a.** a bowl or the like designed for the serving of cold foods in an inner container that is nestled in cracked ice. **b.** a dessert or appetizer served in such a container. **4.** *French Cookery.* the boned breast of chicken served with sauce suprême. [< F < L *suprēm(us)* SUPREME[1]]

Supreme′ Be′ing, the sovereign of the universe; God.

supreme′ command′er, the military, naval, or air officer commanding all allied forces in a theater of war.

Supreme′ Court′, *U.S.* **1.** the highest court of the nation. **2.** (in most States) the highest court of the State.

supreme′ judi′cial court′, (*often caps.*) *U.S.* the highest court in some States, as Massachusetts and Maine, usually having a chief justice and several associate justices.

supreme′ sac′rifice, the sacrifice of one's own life: *Many made the supreme sacrifice during the war.*

Supreme′ So′viet, the legislature of the Soviet Union, consisting of an upper house **(Soviet of the Union** or **Council of the Union),** whose delegates are elected on the basis of population, and a lower house **(Soviet of Nationalities** or **Council of Nationalities),** whose delegates are elected to represent the various nationalities. Also called **Supreme′ Coun′cil.**

su·pre·mum (sə prē′məm, so͞o-), *n. Math.* See **least upper bound.** Also called **sup.** [< NL: lit., SUPREME[1]]

Supt., superintendent. Also, **supt.**

suq (so͞ok), *n.* (in Muslim societies) a market place. Also, **souk.** [< Ar *sūq*]

sur (sûr), *prep. Law.* upon; on the basis of: *sur mortgage.* [< F < L *super* SUPER-]

Sur (so͝or), *n.* a town in S Lebanon, on the Mediterranean Sea: site of ancient port of Tyre.

sur-[1], a prefix corresponding to **super-** but mainly attached to stems not used as words and having figurative applications (*survive; surname*), used esp. in legal terms (*surrebuttal*). [ME < OF < L *super-* SUPER-]

sur-[2], var. of **sub-** before *r: surrogate.*

su·ra (so͝or′ə), *n. Islam.* any of the 114 chapters of the Koran. Also, **surah.** [< Ar *sūrah*, lit., row, step, rung]

Su·ra·ba·ya (so͝or′ə bä′yə), *n.* a seaport on NE Java: second largest city in Indonesia; naval base. 989,734 (est. 1961). Also, **Su′ra·ba′ja.** Dutch, **Soerabaja.**

su·rah[1] (so͝or′ə), *n.* a soft, twilled silk or rayon fabric. [appar. var. of SURAT]

su·rah[2] (so͝or′ə), *n. Islam.* sura.

Su·ra·jah Dow·lah (sə rä′jə dou′lə), Siraj-ud-daula.

Su·ra·kar·ta (so͝or′ə kär′tə), *n.* a city on central Java, in central Indonesia. 363,167 (1961). Formerly, **Solo.**

su·ral (so͝or′əl), *adj. Anat.* of or pertaining to the calf of the leg. [< NL *sūrāl(is)*, equiv. to L *sūr(a)* calf of the leg + *-ālis* -AL[1]]

Su·rat (so͞o rat′, so͝or′ət), *n.* a seaport in W Gujarat, in W India: first British settlement in India 1612. 288,000 (1961).

sur·base (sûr′bās′), *n. Archit.* a molding above a base, as that immediately above a baseboard, the crowning molding of a pedestal, etc. [SUR-[1] + BASE[1]]

sur′based arch′. See **drop arch** (def. 2).

sur·cease (sûr sēs′), *v.*, **-ceased, -ceas·ing,** *n. Archaic.* **—***v.i.* **1.** to cease from some action; desist. **2.** to come to an end. **—***v.t.* **3.** to cease from; leave off. **—***n.* **4.** cessation; end. [SUR-[1] + CEASE; r. late ME *sursese(n)* < MF *sursis* (ptp. of *surseoir* < L *supersedēre* to forbear; see SUPERSEDE) < L *supersess(us)* (ptp.), equiv. to *super-* SUPER- + *sed-* sit + *-tus* ptp. suffix]

sur·charge (*n.* sûr′chärj′, *v.* sûr chärj′, sûr′chärj′), *n., v.,* **-charged, -charg·ing.** **—***n.* **1.** an additional charge, tax, or cost. **2.** an excessive sum or price charged. **3.** an additional or excessive load or burden. **4.** *Philately.* **a.** an overprint which alters or restates the face value or denomination of a stamp to which it has been applied. **b.** a stamp bearing such an overprint. **5.** *Law.* act of surcharging. **6.** *Masonry.* the weight bearing on the extrados of an arch. —*v.t.* **7.** to subject to an additional or extra charge, tax, cost, etc. (for payment). **8.** to overcharge goods. **9.** to show an omission in (an account) of something that operates as a charge against the accounting party; to omit a credit toward (an account). **10.** *Philately.* to print a surcharge on (a stamp). **11.** to put an additional or excessive burden upon. [late ME < MF *surcharg(i)er.* See SUR-[1], CHARGE] —**sur·charg′er,** *n.*

sur·cin·gle (sûr′sing′gəl), *n.* **1.** a belt or girth that passes around the belly of a horse and over the blanket, pack, saddle, etc., and is buckled on the horse's back. **2.** a beltlike fastening for a garment, esp. a cassock. [late ME *surcengle* < MF, equiv. to *sur-* SUR-[1] + *cengle* belt < L; see CINGULUM]

sur·coat (sûr′kōt′), *n.* **1.** a garment worn over medieval armor, often embroidered with heraldic arms. **2.** an outer coat or other outer garment. [ME *surcote* < MF. See SUR-[1], COAT]

Surcoat (13th century)

sur·cu·lose (sûr′kyə lōs′), *adj. Bot.* producing suckers. [< L *surculōs(us),* equiv. to *surcul(us)* (*sūr(us)* branch, twig + *-culus* -CLE -CULE) + *-ōsus* -OSE[1]]

surd (sûrd), *adj.* **1.** *Phonet.* voiceless (opposed to *sonant*). **2.** *Math. Obs.* (of a quantity) not capable of being expressed in rational numbers; irrational. —*n.* **3.** *Phonet.* a voiceless consonant (opposed to *sonant*). **4.** *Math. Obs.* a surd quantity. [< L *surd(us)* dull-sounding, deaf]

sure (sho͝or), *adj.,* **sur·er, sur·est,** *adv.* —*adj.* **1.** free from apprehension or doubt as to the reliability, character, action, etc., of something (often fol. by *of*): *to be sure of one's data.* **2.** confident, as of something expected: *He was sure of ultimate success.* **3.** convinced, fully persuaded, or positive, as of something firmly believed: *to be sure of a person's guilt.* **4.** assured or certain beyond question: *His death is sure.* **5.** worthy of confidence; reliable: *a sure messenger.* **6.** firm or stable: *to stand on sure ground.* **7.** unfailing; never disappointing expectations: *a sure cure.* **8.** unerring; never missing, slipping, etc.: *a sure aim.* **9.** admitting of no doubt or question: *sure proof.* **10.** inevitable: *Death is sure.* **11.** destined; bound inevitably; certain: *He is sure to come.* **12.** *Obs.* secure; safe. **13. be sure,** to take care (to be or do as specified); be certain: *Be sure to close the windows.* **14. for sure,** as a certainty; surely: *It's going to be a good day, for sure.* **15. make sure,** to be or become absolutely certain: *I'm calling to make sure that you remember to come.* **16. sure enough,** *Informal.* as might have been supposed; actually; certainly: *Sure enough, the picnic was rained out.* **17. to be sure, a.** without doubt; surely; certainly. **b.** admittedly: *She sings well, to be sure, but she can't act.* —*adv. Informal.* **18.** surely; undoubtedly: *It sure is cold out.* **19.** inevitably: *He'll come, as sure as night follows day.* **20.** of course; yes: *Sure, I'll come.* [ME *sur(e)* < MF *sur,* OF *seur* < L *sēcūr(us)* SECURE] —**sure′ness,** *n.*

—**Syn. 1.** SURE, CERTAIN, CONFIDENT, POSITIVE indicate full belief and trust that something is true. SURE, CERTAIN, and POSITIVE are often used interchangeably. SURE, the simplest and most general, expresses mere absence of doubt. CERTAIN suggests that there are definite reasons which have freed one from doubt. CONFIDENT emphasizes the strength of the belief or the certainty of expectation felt. POSITIVE implies emphatic certainty, which may even become overconfidence or dogmatism. **5.** certain, trustworthy, honest. **6.** solid, steady. **8.** accurate, precise. **10.** unavoidable. —**Usage. 18.** Although many educated speakers use SURE when they mean SURELY—chiefly because it has become an idiomatic cliché—it is nonetheless considered to be somewhat less than standard usage and should not be used instead of SURELY except in informal situations.

sure-e·nough (sho͝or′i nuf′), *adj. Dial.* real; genuine.

sure-fire (sho͝or′fīər′), *adj. Informal.* sure to work; foolproof: *a sure-fire moneymaking scheme.*

sure-foot·ed (sho͝or′fo͝ot′id), *adj.* **1.** not likely to stumble, slip, or fall. **2.** proceeding surely; unerring: *his sure-footed pursuit of success.* —**sure′-foot′ed·ly,** *adv.* —**sure′-foot′ed·ness,** *n.*

sure·ly (sho͝or′lē), *adv.* **1.** firmly; unerringly; without missing, slipping, etc. **2.** undoubtedly, assuredly, or certainly: *The results are surely encouraging.* **3.** (in emphatic utterances that are not necessarily sustained by fact) assuredly: *Surely you are mistaken.* **4.** inevitably or without fail: *Slowly but surely the end approached.* —*interj.* **5.** (used to express disbelief, detachment, amusement, etc.) really; indeed: *Surely, you don't mean to go?* **6.** (used to express emphasis) without doubt; assuredly: *Surely, you must be mistaken!* **7.** (used to express affirmation) yes, indeed: *Will you go with us to the movies? Surely!* [ME *surly.* See SURE, -LY] —**Usage.** See **sure.**

sure′ thing′, *Informal.* **1.** that which is or is supposed to be a certain success, as a bet, business venture, etc.: *He thinks that investing in any musical comedy is a sure thing these days.* **2.** that which is inevitable in performance, development, or outcome: *With his psychological makeup, it's a sure thing that he'll refuse to work in a group.* **3.** surely; for sure; O.K.; roger (often used as an interjection): *Sure thing, Mrs. Brown, and should I send some parsnips, too?*

sure·ty (sho͝or′i tē, sho͝or′tē), *n., pl.* **-ties. 1.** security against loss or damage or for the fulfillment of an obligation, the payment of a debt, etc.; a pledge, guaranty, or bond. **2.** one who has made himself responsible for another, as a sponsor, godparent, or bondsman. **3.** the state or quality of being sure. **4.** certainty. **5.** that which makes sure; ground of confidence or safety. **6.** one who is legally responsible for the debt, default, or delinquency of another. **7.** assurance, esp. self-assurance. [ME *surte* < MF; OF *seurte* < L *sēcūritāt-* SECURITY]

sure·ty·ship (sho͝or′i tē ship′, sho͝or′tē-), *n. Law.* the relationship between the surety, the principal debtor, and the creditor. [SURETY + -SHIP]

surf (sûrf), *n.* **1.** the swell of the sea which breaks upon a shore or upon shoals. **2.** the mass or line of foamy water caused by the breaking of the sea upon a shore, esp. a shallow or sloping shore. **3.** a dance deriving from the twist. —*v.i.* **4.** to ride a surfboard. **5.** to float on the crest of a wave toward shore. **6.** to swim, play, or bathe in the surf. [earlier *suff,* var. of SOUGH[1]] —**surf′a·ble,** *adj.* —**surf′like′,** *adj.* —**Syn. 1.** See **wave.**

sur·face (sûr′fis), *n., adj., v.,* **-faced, -fac·ing.** —*n.* **1.** the outer face, outside, or exterior boundary of a thing; outermost or uppermost layer or area. **2.** any face of a body or thing: *the six surfaces of a cube.* **3.** extent or area of outer face; superficial area. **4.** the outward appearance, esp. as distinguished from the inner nature: *to look below the surface of a matter.* **5.** *Geom.* any figure having only two dimensions; part or all of the boundary of a solid. **6.** land or sea transportation, rather than air, underground, or undersea transportation. **7.** *Aeron.* an airfoil. —*adj.* **8.** of, on, or pertaining to the surface; external. **9.** apparent rather than real; superficial: *to be guilty of surface judgments.* **10.** of, pertaining to, or via land or sea: *surface travel; surface mail.* —*v.t.* **11.** to finish the surface of; give a particular kind of surface to; make even or smooth. —*v.i.* **12.** (of something submerged) to rise to the surface: *The submarine surfaced after four days.* **13.** *Mining.* **a.** to wash surface deposits of ore-bearing mineral. **b.** to mine at or near the surface. **14.** to work on or at the surface. [< F, equiv. to *sur-* SUR-[1] + *face* FACE, appar. modeled on L *superficies* SUPERFICIES] —**sur′face·less,** *adj.* —**sur′fac·er,** *n.*

sur′face-ac′tive a′gent (sûr′fis ak′tiv), *Chem.* any substance that when dissolved in water or an aqueous solution reduces its surface tension or the interfacial tension between it and another liquid. Also called **surfactant.**

sur′face bound′ary lay′er, *Meteorol.* the thin layer of air adjacent to the earth's surface, usually considered to be less than 300 feet high. Also called **sur′face lay′er, atmospheric boundary layer, friction layer, ground layer.**

sur′face condens′er, a device condensing steam or vapor by passing it over a cool surface.

sur′face den′sity, *Physics.* quantity, as of electric charge, per unit surface area.

sur′face in′tegral, *Math.* the limit, as the norm of the partition of a given surface into sections of area approaches zero, of the sum of the product of the areas times the value of a given function of three variables at some point on each section.

sur′face noise′, extraneous noise caused by physical wear or a physical flaw on a phonograph record or in a pick-up system, rather than by a flaw in the electronic or electrical system, when a record is played: often caused by a worn needle or record, a faulty cartridge, or by imperfect cutting of the record grooves.

sur′face of light′ and shade′, (in architectural shades and shadows) a surface in a plane tangent to the parallel rays from the theoretical light source, treated as a shade surface. Also called **light and shade surface.**

sur′face of projec′tion, the surface upon which an image or a set of points is projected.

sur′face of revolu′tion, *Math.* a surface formed by revolving a plane curve about a given line.

sur′face plate′, *Mach.* a flat plate used by machinists for testing surfaces which are to be made perfectly flat. Also called **planometer.**

sur·face-print·ing (sûr′fis prin′ting), *n.* planography.

sur′face ten′sion, *Physics.* the elasticlike force existing in the surface of a body, esp. a liquid, tending to minimize the area of the surface, caused by the irregular molecular forces at the surface and manifested in capillarity, the constriction of the surface of a liquid, and other such phenomena.

sur·face-to-air (sûr′fis to͞o âr′), *adj.* **1.** (of a missile, message, etc.) capable of traveling from the surface of the earth to a target in the atmosphere. —*adv.* **2.** from the surface of the earth to a target in the atmosphere: *an antimissile missile fired surface-to-air.*

sur·face-to-sur·face (sûr′fis tə sûr′fis), *adj.* **1.** (of a missile, message, etc.) capable of traveling from a base on the surface of the earth to a target also on the surface. —*adv.* **2.** from a base on the surface of the earth to a target on the surface.

sur·face-to-un·der·wa·ter (sûr′fis to͞o un′dər wô′tər, -wot′ər), *adj.* **1.** (of a missile, message, etc.) traveling from the surface of the earth to a target underwater: *a surface-to-underwater antisubmarine missile.* —*adv.* **2.** from the surface of the earth to a target underwater: *The rocket was fired surface-to-underwater.*

sur′face yeast′. See **top yeast.**

sur·fac·ing (sûr′fi sing), *n.* **1.** the action or process of giving a finished surface to something. **2.** the material with which something is surfaced. **3.** the act or an instance of rising to the surface of a body of water. **4.** the action or process of mining ore deposits at or near the surface. [SURFACE + -ING[1]]

sur·fac·tant (sər fak′tənt), *n. Chem.* See **surface-active agent.** [shortening of *surf(ace)-act(ive) a(ge)nt*]

surf·bird (sûrf′bûrd′), *n.* a shore bird, *Aphriza virgata,* of the Pacific coast of North and South America, related to the turnstones. [SURF + BIRD]

surf·board (sûrf′bōrd′, -bôrd′), *n.* **1.** a long, narrow board on which a person stands or lies prone in surfboarding. —*v.i.* **2.** to ride a surfboard. [SURF + BOARD]

surf·board·ing (sûrf′bōr′ding, -bôr′-), *n.* a sport in which a person stands or lies prone on a surfboard and rides the crest of a breaking wave toward the shore. [SURFBOARD + -ING[1]] —**surf′board′er,** *n.*

surf·boat (sûrf′bōt′), *n.* a strong, buoyant rowboat with high ends, adapted for passing through surf. [SURF + BOAT]

surf′ cast′ing, *Angling.* the act, technique, or sport of fishing by casting from the shoreline into the sea, usually using heavy-duty tackle.

surf′ duck′, a scoter, esp. the surf scoter.

sur·feit (sûr′fit), *n.* **1.** excess; an excessive amount: *a surfeit of speechmaking.* **2.** excess or overindulgence in eating or drinking. **3.** an uncomfortably full or crapulous feeling due to excessive eating or drinking. **4.** general disgust caused by excess or satiety. —*v.t.* **5.** to bring to a state of surfeit by excess of food or drink. **6.** to supply with anything to excess or satiety; satiate. —*v.i.* **7.** to eat or drink to excess. **8.** to suffer from the effects of overindulgence in eating or drinking. **9.** to indulge to excess in anything. [late ME *surfait* < MF *s(e)urfait* (n. use of ptp. of *surfaire* to overdo), equiv. to *sur-* SUR-[1] + *fait* < L *fact(us)* (see FACT), ptp. of *facere* to do]

surf·fish (sûrf′fish′), *n., pl.* (*esp. collectively*) **-fish,** (*esp. referring to two or more kinds or species*) **-fish·es. 1.** surfperch. **2.** any of several sciaenid fishes, as *Umbrina roncador,* found along the Pacific coast of North America. **3.** See **surf smelt.** [SURF + FISH]

surf·ing (sûr′fing), *n.* the act or sport of riding a surfboard. Also called **surfboarding, surf·rid·ing** (sûrf′rī′ding). [SURF + ING[1]] —**surf′er, surf′rid′er,** *n.*

surf·perch (sûrf′pûrch′), *n., pl.* (*esp. collectively*) **-perch,** (*esp. referring to two or more kinds or species*) **-perch·es.** any of several viviparous fishes of the family *Embiotocidae,* found in the shallow waters along the Pacific coast of North America. Also called **seaperch, surffish.** [SURF + PERCH[2]]

surf′ sco′ter, a large, North American scoter, *Melanitta perspicillata,* the adult male of which is black with two white patches on the head.

Surf·side (sûrf′sīd′), *n.* a town in SE Florida. 3157 (1960).

surf′ smelt′, a smelt, *Hypomesus pretiosus,* found in shallow waters from southern California to Alaska.

surf·y (sûr′fē), *adj.,* **surf·i·er, surf·i·est.** abounding with surf; forming or resembling surf. [SURF + -Y[1]]

surg., 1. surgeon. **2.** surgery. **3.** surgical.

surge (sûrj), *n., v.,* **surged, surg·ing.** —*n.* **1.** a strong forward movement, rush, or sweep, like that of swelling or rolling waves: *the onward surge of an angry mob.* **2.** a strong, swelling, wavelike volume or body of something: *A surge of smoke billowed from the windows.* **3.** the rolling swell of the sea. **4.** the swelling and rolling sea: *The surge crashed against the rocky coast.* **5.** a swelling wave; billow. **6.** *Meteorol.* **a.** a widespread change in atmospheric pressure that is in addition to cyclonic and normal diurnal changes. **b.** See **storm surge. 7.** *Elect.* **a.** a sudden rush or burst of current or voltage. **b.** a violent oscillatory disturbance. **8.** *Naut.* a slackening or slipping back, as of a rope or cable. **9.** *Mach.* **a.** an uneven flow and strong momentum given to a fluid, as water in a tank, resulting in a rapid, temporary rise in pressure. **b.** pulsating unevenness of motion in an engine or gas turbine. —*v.i.* **10.** to rise and fall, toss about, or move along like a ship on the waves: *to surge at anchor.* **11.** to rise, roll, move, or swell forward in or like waves: *The sea surged against the shore. The crowd surged around the accident.* **12.** to rise as if by a heaving or swelling force: *Blood surged to his face.* **13.** *Elect.* **a.** to increase suddenly, as current or voltage. **b.** to oscillate violently. **14.** *Naut.* **a.** to slack off or loosen a rope or cable around a capstan or windlass. **b.** to slip back, as a rope. **15.** *Mach.* to move with pulsating unevenness, as something driven by an engine or gas turbine. —*v.t.* **16.** to cause to surge or roll in or as in waves. **17.** *Naut.* to slacken (a rope). [? < L *surge(re)* (to) spring up, arise, stand up] —**surge′less,** *adj.*

surge′ cham′ber, *Mach.* a chamber for absorbing surge from a liquid or gas.

sur·geon (sûr′jən), *n.* a physician who specializes in surgery. [ME *surgien* < AF, alter. of OF *cirurgien* CHIRURGEON] —**sur′geon·less,** *adj.*

sur·geon·fish (sûr′jən fish′), *n., pl.* (*esp. collectively*) **-fish,** (*esp. referring to two or more kinds or species*) **-fish·es.** any tropical, coral-reef fish of the family *Acanthuridae,* with one or more spines near the base of the tail fin. [SURGEON + FISH; so called from the resemblance of its spines to a surgeon's instruments]

sur′geon gen′eral, *pl.,* **surgeons general. 1.** the chief of medical services in one of the armed forces. **2.** (*cap.*) the head of the U.S. Bureau of Public Health or, in some States, of a State health agency.

sur′geon's knot′, a knot resembling a reef knot, used by surgeons for tying ligatures and the like.

sur·ger·y (sûr′jə rē), *n., pl.* **-ger·ies** for 4, 5. **1.** the art, practice, or work of treating diseases, injuries, or deformities by manual operation or instrumental appliances. **2.** the branch of medicine concerned with such treatment. **3.** treatment, as an operation, performed by a surgeon. **4.** a room or place for surgical operations. **5.** *Brit.* **a.** the consulting office and dispensary of a general medical practitioner; doctor's office. **b.** the period of the day in which a doctor examines and consults with patients in his office; a doctor's office hours.

Surg. Gen., Surgeon General.

sur·gi·cal (sûr′ji kəl), *adj.* **1.** pertaining to or involving surgery. **2.** used in surgery. [SURG(EON) + -ICAL] —**sur′gi·cal·ly,** *adv.*

sur′gical nee′dle, a needle for suturing.

surg·y (sûr′jē), *adj.* billowy; surging or swelling. [SURGE + -Y[1]]

Su·ri·ba·chi (so͞or′ə bä′chē), *n.* an extinct volcano on Iwo Jima island: World War II battle 1945.

su·ri·cate (so͞or′ə kāt′), *n.* a small, burrowing, South African carnivore, *Suricata suricatta,* of a grayish color with dark bands across the back, related to the mongooses. [earlier *surikate* < F < D *surikat* macaque]

Suricate (Total length 21 in.; tail 8½ in.)

su·ri·mi (so͞o rē′mē), *n.* a paste of inexpensive fish shaped, colored, and flavored in imitation of lobster meat, crabmeat, etc. Also called **sea legs.** [< Japn: minced flesh]

Su′rinam cher′ry, 1. a myrtaceous tree, *Eugenia uniflora,* of Brazil. **2.** the yellow or red, edible, sour, cherrylike fruit of this tree. Also called **pitanga.**

Su·ri·name (so͞or′ə näm′, -nam′; *Du.* sʏ′rē nä′mə), *n.* a republic on the NE coast of South America: formerly a territory of the Netherlands; independent since 1975. 414,000; 60,230 sq. mi. *Cap.:* Paramaribo. Formerly, **Su·ri·nam** (so͞or′ə näm′, -nam′), **Dutch Guiana, Netherlands Guiana.**

Su′rinam toad′, a South American toad, *Pipa pipa,* the female of which carries the eggs and young in small depressions in its back until metamorphosis is completed.

sur·ly (sûr′lē), *adj.,* **-li·er, -li·est. 1.** churlishly rude or bad-tempered: *a surly waiter; a surly manner of speaking.* **2.** unfriendly or hostile; menacingly irritable: *a surly old lion.* **3.** dark or dismal; menacing; threatening: *a surly sky.* **4.** *Obs.* lordly; arrogant. —**sur′li·ly,** *adv.* —**sur′li·ness,** *n.*

sur·mise (*v.* sər mīz′; *n.* sər mīz′, sûr′mīz), *v.*, **-mised, -mis·ing,** *n.* —*v.t.* **1.** to think or infer without certain or strong evidence; conjecture; guess. —*v.i.* **2.** to conjecture or guess. —*n.* **3.** a matter of conjecture. **4.** an idea or thought of something as being possible or likely, although without any certain or strong evidence. **5.** a conjecture or opinion. [late ME *surmise(n)* < AF, MF *surmis(e)* (ptp. of *surmet(t)re* to accuse < L *supermittere* to throw upon), equiv. to *sur-* SUR-[1] + *mis(e)* < L *miss(us), -a,* equiv. to *mit-* send + *-tus, -ta* ptp. suffix] —**sur·mis′a·ble,** *adj.* —**sur·mised·ly** (sər mīzd′lē, -mī′zid-), *adv.* —**sur·mis′er,** *n.*
—**Syn. 1.** imagine, suppose, suspect. See **guess. 3.** possibility, likelihood.

sur·mount (sər mount′), *v.t.* **1.** to mount upon; get on the top of; mount upon and cross over: *to surmount a hill.* **2.** to get over or across (barriers, obstacles, etc.). **3.** to prevail over: *to surmount tremendous difficulties.* **4.** to be on top of or above: *a statue surmounting a pillar.* **5.** to furnish with something placed on top or above: *to surmount a tower with a spire.* **6.** *Obs.* **a.** to surpass in excellence. **b.** to exceed in amount. [late ME *surmounte(n)* < AF, MF *surmonte(r)* < ML *supermontāre.* See SUPER-, MOUNT[1]] —**sur·mount′a·ble,** *adj.* —**sur·mount′a·ble·ness,** *n.* —**sur·mount′er,** *n.*

sur·mul·let (sər mul′it), *n.* a goatfish, esp. one of the European species used for food. [< F *surmulet,* MF *sormulet,* equiv. to *sor* reddish brown (see SORREL[1]) + *mulet* MULLET]

sur·name (*n.* sûr′nām′; *v.* sûr′nām′, sûr nām′), *n., v.*, **-named, -nam·ing.** —*n.* **1.** Also called **last name.** the name that a person has in common with the other members of his family, as distinguished from his Christian or given name; family name. **2.** a name added to a person's name or names, as from birth or abode or from some characteristic or achievement; epithet. —*v.t.* **3.** to give a surname to; call by a surname. [ME; see SUR-[1], NAME; modeled on OF *surnom*]

sur·pass (sər pas′, -päs′), *v.t.* **1.** to go beyond in amount, extent, or degree; be greater than; exceed. **2.** to go beyond in excellence or achievement; be superior to; excel: *He surpassed his brother in sports.* **3.** to be beyond the range or capacity of; transcend: *misery that surpasses description.* [< MF *surpass(er),* equiv. to *sur-* SUR-[1] + *passer* to PASS] —**sur·pass′a·ble,** *adj.* —**sur·pass′er,** *n.*
—**Syn. 2.** beat, outstrip. See **excel.**

sur·pass·ing (sər pas′ing, -pä′sing), *adj.* **1.** of a large amount or high degree; exceeding, excelling, or extraordinary: *structures of surpassing magnificence.* —*adv.* **2.** *Archaic.* in a surpassing manner; extraordinarily. [SURPASS + -ING[2]] —**sur·pass′ing·ly,** *adv.* —**sur·pass′ing·ness,** *n.*

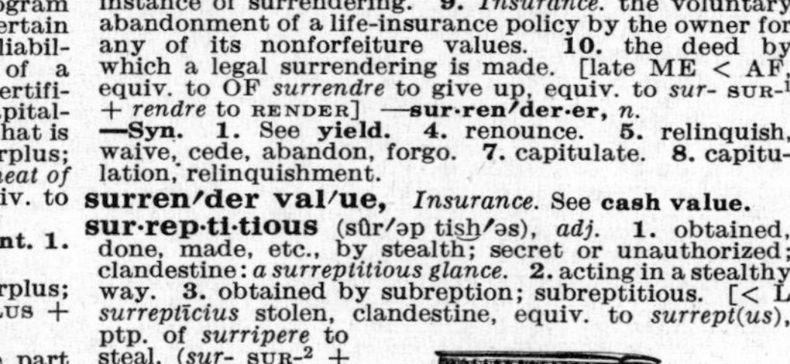
Surplice

sur·plice (sûr′plis), *n.* **1.** a loose-fitting, broad-sleeved white vestment, properly of linen, worn over the cassock by clergymen and choristers. **2.** a garment in which the two halves of the front cross each other diagonally. [ME *surplis* < AF *surpliz,* syncopated var. of OF *surpeliz* < ML *superpellīc(ium) (vestimentum)* over-pelt (garment), neut. of *superpellīcius* (adj.), equiv. to L *super-* SUPER- + *pellīc(us)* pelt-clad + *-ius* adj. suffix] —**sur′pliced,** *adj.*

sur·plus (sûr′plus, -pləs), *n.* **1.** that which remains above what is used or needed. **2.** an amount, quantity, etc., greater than needed. **3.** *U.S.* agricultural produce or a quantity of food grown by a nation or area in excess of its needs, esp. such a quantity of food purchased and stored by the government in its program of guaranteeing farmers a specific price for certain crops. **4.** *Accounting.* **a.** the excess of assets over liabilities accumulated throughout the existence of a business, excepting assets against which stock certificates have been issued; excess of net worth over capital-stock value. **b.** an amount of assets in excess of what is requisite to meet liabilities. —*adj.* **5.** being a surplus; being in excess of what is required: *the surplus wheat of America.* [late ME < OF < ML *superplus,* equiv. to *super-* SUPER- + *plus* PLUS]
—**Syn. 1.** superabundance. See **remainder.** —**Ant. 1.** deficiency.

sur·plus·age (sûr′plus ij), *n.* **1.** that which is surplus; an excess amount. **2.** an excess of words. [SURPLUS + -AGE]

sur′plus val′ue, (in Marxian economics) the part of the value of the product produced by labor that exceeds the wages paid, regarded as the profit of the capitalist.

sur·print (sûr′print′), *v.t.* **1.** to print over with additional marks or matter; overprint. **2.** to print (additional marks, a new address, etc.) over something already printed. —*n.* **3.** something surprinted. [SUR-[1] + PRINT]

sur·pris·al (sər prī′zəl), *n.* **1.** the act of surprising. **2.** the state of being surprised. **3.** a surprise. [SURPRISE + -AL[2]]

sur·prise (sər prīz′), *v.*, **-prised, -pris·ing,** *n.* —*v.t.* **1.** to strike with a sudden feeling of wonder that arrests the thoughts, as through unexpectedness or extraordinariness: *Her beauty surprised me.* **2.** to come upon suddenly and unexpectedly; catch in the act; take unawares: *She surprised the children raiding the cookie jar.* **3.** to hold a celebration or party for or to present a gift to unexpectedly: *They surprised her with a birthday party.* **4.** to attack suddenly or without warning; make an unexpected assault on (an unprepared army, fort, person, etc.): *a plan to surprise the enemy.* **5.** to elicit or bring out suddenly and without warning: *to surprise the facts from the witness.* **6.** to lead or bring unawares, as into doing something not intended: *to surprise a witness into telling the truth.* **7.** to discover suddenly; detect: *Looking up, I surprised a flush on her usually pallid face.* —*n.* **8.** the act or an instance of surprising. **9.** a completely unexpected occurrence, appearance, or statement: *The president's speech was a surprise to his advisors.* **10.** a celebration or party held for or a gift presented to someone who does not expect it: *He gave her a pearl ring as a surprise.* **11.** a sudden attack or assault, as on an army or a fort, made without warning. **12.** a coming upon unexpectedly; detecting or catching in the act; taking unawares. **13.** a state or feeling of sudden wonder, as something unexpected or extraordinary. **14.** something that excites this feeling, as an extraordinary occurrence. **15. take by surprise, a.** to come upon unawares; catch unprepared. **b.** to astonish; amaze: *The amount of the donation took us completely by surprise.* [late ME < AF, MF *surpris(e)* (ptp. of *surprendre* < ML *superprendere* to overtake, take unawares), equiv. to *sur-* SUR-[1] + *pris(e)* < L *prens(us), -sa,* equiv. to *prend-* take + *-tus, -ta* ptp. suffix] —**sur·pris·ed·ly** (sər prī′zid lē, -prīzd′-), *adv.* —**sur·pris′er,** *n.*
—**Syn. 1.** SURPRISE, ASTONISH, AMAZE, ASTOUND mean to strike with wonder because of unexpectedness, strangeness, unusualness, etc. To SURPRISE is to take unawares or to affect with wonder: *surprised at receiving a telegram.* To ASTONISH is to strike with wonder by something unlooked for, startling, or seemingly inexplicable: *astonished at someone's behavior.* To AMAZE is to astonish so greatly as to disconcert or bewilder: *amazed at an evidence of stupidity.* To ASTOUND is to so overwhelm with surprise that one is unable to think or act: *astounded by a sudden calamity.* **13.** amazement, astonishment.

surprise′ par′ty, 1. a party or celebration planned for someone without his knowledge and intended to surprise him. **2.** an occasion or event that will surprise someone: *There is a real surprise party waiting for him—his final paycheck.*

surprise′ piece′, *Horol.* (in a repeater) a device for preventing minutes from being struck during the minute after some larger division which the repeater strikes, as an hour or quarter-hour.

Surprise′ Sym′phony, the Symphony No. 94 in G major (1791) by Franz Josef Haydn.

sur·pris·ing (sər prī′zing), *adj.* **1.** causing surprise, wonder, or astonishment. **2.** unexpected. [SURPRISE + -ING[2]] —**sur·pris′ing·ly,** *adv.* —**sur·pris′ing·ness,** *n.*

sur·ra (sŏŏr′ə), *n.* *Vet. Pathol.* a highly fatal infectious disease of horses, camels, elephants, and dogs caused by a blood-infecting protozoan parasite, *Trypanosoma evansi,* transmitted by the bite of horseflies, characterized by fever, anemia, and emaciation. [< Marathi *sūra* heavy breathing sound]

Sur·re·al·ism (sə rē′ə liz′əm), *n.* (*often l.c.*) a style of art and literature developed principally in the 20th century, stressing the subconscious or nonrational significance of imagery arrived at by automatism or the exploitation of chance effects, unexpected juxtapositions, etc. [< F *surréalisme.* See SUR-[1], REALISM] —**Sur·re′al·ist,** *n., adj.* —**Sur·re′al·is′tic,** *adj.* —**Sur·re′al·is′ti·cal·ly,** *adv.*

sur·re·but·tal (sûr′ri but′əl), *n.* *Law.* the giving of evidence to meet a defendant's rebuttal. [SUR-[1] + REBUTTAL]

sur·re·but·ter (sûr′ri but′ər), *n.* *Law.* a plaintiff's reply to a defendant's rebutter. [SUR-[1] + REBUTTER]

sur·re·join·der (sûr′ri join′dər), *n.* *Law.* a plaintiff's reply to a defendant's rejoinder. [SUR-[1] + REJOINDER]

sur·ren·der (sə ren′dər), *v.t.* **1.** to yield (something) to the possession or power of another; deliver up possession of on demand or under duress: *to surrender a fort; He surrendered the stolen typewriter to the police.* **2.** to give (oneself) up, as to the police. **3.** to give (oneself) up to some influence, course, emotion, etc.: *He surrendered himself to a life of hardship.* **4.** to give up, abandon, or relinquish (comfort, hope, etc.): *The doctors surrendered all hope of his recovery.* **5.** to yield or resign (an office, privilege, etc.) in favor of another. **6.** *Obs.* to return: *to surrender thanks.* —*v.i.* **7.** to give oneself up, as into the power of another; submit or yield. —*n.* **8.** the act or an instance of surrendering. **9.** *Insurance.* the voluntary abandonment of a life-insurance policy by the owner for any of its nonforfeiture values. **10.** the deed by which a legal surrendering is made. [late ME < AF, equiv. to OF *surrendre* to give up, equiv. to *sur-* SUR-[1] + *rendre* to RENDER] —**sur·ren′der·er,** *n.*
—**Syn. 1.** See **yield. 4.** renounce. **5.** relinquish, waive, cede, abandon, forgo. **7.** capitulate. **8.** capitulation, relinquishment.

surren′der val′ue, *Insurance.* See **cash value.**

sur·rep·ti·tious (sûr′əp tish′əs), *adj.* **1.** obtained, done, made, etc., by stealth; secret or unauthorized; clandestine: *a surreptitious glance.* **2.** acting in a stealthy way. **3.** obtained by subreption; subreptitious. [< L *surreptīcius* stolen, clandestine, equiv. to *surrept(us),* ptp. of *surripere* to steal, (*sur-* SUR-[2] + *rep-,* var. of *rap-* snatch, RAPE[1] + *-tus* ptp. suffix) + *-icius* -ITIOUS] —**sur′rep·ti′tious·ly,** *adv.* —**sur′rep·ti′tious·ness,** *n.*

Surrey

sur·rey (sûr′ē, sur′ē), *n., pl.* **-reys.** a light, four-wheeled, two-seated carriage, with or without a top, for four persons. [after SURREY, the county]

Sur·rey (sûr′ē, sur′ē), *n.* **1. Earl of** (*Henry Howard*), 1517?–47, English poet. **2.** a county in SE England, bordering S London. 1,733,036 (1961); 722 sq. mi. *Co. seat:* Guildford.

sur·ro·gate (*n.* sûr′ə gāt′, -git, sur′-; *v.* sûr′ə gāt′, sur′-), *n., v.*, **-gat·ed, -gat·ing.** —*n.* **1.** one appointed to act for another; deputy. **2.** *U.S.* (in some States) a judicial officer having jurisdiction over the probate of wills, the administration of estates, etc. **3.** the deputy of an ecclesiastical judge, esp. of a bishop or his chancellor. **4.** a substitute. —*v.t.* **5.** to put into the place of another as a successor, substitute, or deputy; substitute for another. **6.** to subrogate. [< L *surrogāt(us),* assimilated var. of *subrogātus;* see SUBROGATE] —**sur′ro·gate·ship′,** *n.* —**sur′ro·ga′tion,** *n.*

sur·round (sə round′), *v.t.* **1.** to enclose on all sides; encompass: *She was surrounded by admirers.* **2.** to form an enclosure round; encircle: *A stone wall surrounds the estate.* **3.** to enclose (a body of troops, a fort or town, etc.) so as to cut off communication or retreat: *We have surrounded the enemy.* —*n.* **4.** *Archit.* a feature forming a border to an opening or panel. **5.** that which surrounds, as the area, border, etc., around an object or central space: *a surround of stately poplars; the flagstone surround of the fountain.* **6.** *Hunting.* **a.** a means of hunting in which wild animals are encircled and chased into a special spot which makes their escape impossible. **b.** the act of hunting by this means. **c.** the location encircled by hunters using this means. [SUR-[1] + ROUND; r. late ME *sourounde(n)* < AF *surounde(r),* MF *suronder* < LL *superundāre* to overflow, equiv. to L *super-* SUPER- + *undāre* to flood, deriv. of *und(a)* wave; see UNDULATE] —**sur·round′ed·ly,** *adv.* —**sur·round′er,** *n.*

sur·round·ing (sə roun′ding), *n.* **1.** that which surrounds. **2. surroundings,** environing things, circumstances, conditions, etc.; environment: *He was too sick to be aware of his surroundings.* **3.** the act of encircling or enclosing. —*adj.* **4.** enclosing or encircling. **5.** being the environment or adjacent area. [late ME (n.); see SURROUND, -ING[1], -ING[2]]

sur·roy·al (sûr roi′əl), *n.* See **crown antler.** [ME *surryal.* See SUR-[1], ROYAL]

sur·sum cor·da (sŏŏr′sŏŏm kōr′dä, kôr′-), **1.** *Rom. Cath. Ch.* part of a brief responsory before the preface of the Mass. **2.** *Anglican Ch.* the words "Lift up your hearts," addressed by the celebrant to the congregation before the preface. [< L]

Surt (sûrt, sŏŏrt), *n.* *Scand. Myth.* the guardian and ruler of Muspelheim, destined to defeat Frey at Ragnarok and destroy the world with fire. Also, **Sur·tr** (sŏŏr′tər)

sur·tax (*n.* sûr′taks′; *v.* sûr′taks′, sûr taks′), *n.* **1.** an additional or extra tax on something already taxed. **2.** one of a graded series of additional taxes levied on incomes exceeding a certain amount. Cf. **normal tax.** —*v.t.* **3.** to put an additional or extra tax on; charge with a surtax. [SUR-[1] + TAX; cf. SUPERTAX, F *surtaxe*]

Sur·tees (sûr′tēz), *n.* **Robert Smith,** 1805–64, English editor and writer.

sur·tout (sər to͞o′, -to͞ot′; *Fr.* SYR to͞o′), *n., pl.* **-touts** (-to͞oz′, -to͞ots′; *Fr.* -to͞o′), *adj.* —*n.* **1.** a man's close-fitting overcoat, esp. a frock coat. **2.** a hood with a mantle, worn by women. —*adj.* **3.** *Heraldry.* (of a charge or division of a shield) partly covering any other charge or division in the same area. [< F: lit., over all, equiv. to *sur-* SUR-[1] + *tout* everything]

Surt·sey (sûrt′sē; *Icel.* SYRT′sä), *n.* an island S of and belonging to Iceland: formed by an undersea volcano 1963. ab. ⅔ mi. long; 330 ft. high.

surv., 1. surveying. **2.** surveyor.

sur·veil·lance (sər vā′ləns, -vāl′yəns), *n.* **1.** a watch kept over a person, group, etc., esp. over a suspect, prisoner, or the like: *The suspects were under police surveillance.* **2.** supervision or superintendence. [< F, equiv. to *surveill(er)* (to) watch over (*sur-* SUR-[1] + *veiller* < L *vigilāre* to watch; see VIGIL) + *-ance* -ANCE]
—**Syn. 2.** care, control, management.

sur·veil·lant (sər vā′lənt, -vāl′yənt), *adj.* **1.** exercising surveillance. —*n.* **2.** one who exercises surveillance. [< F, equiv. to *surveill-* watch (see SURVEILLANCE) + *-ant* -ANT]

sur·vey (*v.* sər vā′; *n.* sûr′vā, sər vā′), *v., n., pl.* **-veys.** —*v.t.* **1.** to take a general or comprehensive view of or appraise, as a situation, area of study, etc. **2.** to view in detail, esp. to inspect, examine, or appraise formally or officially in order to ascertain condition, value, etc. **3.** to determine the exact form, boundaries, position, extent, etc., of (a tract of land, section of a country, etc.) by linear and angular measurements and the application of the principles of geometry and trigonometry. —*v.i.* **4.** to survey land; practice surveying. —*n.* **5.** the act or an instance of surveying or of taking a comprehensive view of something: *The course is a survey of Italian painting.* **6.** a formal or official examination of the particulars of something, made in order to ascertain condition, character, etc. **7.** a statement or description embodying the result of this: *They presented their survey to the board of directors.* **8.** a sampling, or partial collection, of facts, figures, or opinions taken and used to approximate or indicate what a complete collection and analysis might reveal: *The survey showed that 64 percent of the population owned more than one wristwatch.* **9.** the act of determining the exact form, boundaries, position, etc., as of a tract of land or section of a country, by linear measurements, angular measurements, etc. **10.** the plan or description resulting from such an operation. **11.** an agency for making determinations: *U.S. Coast and Geodetic Survey; U.S. Geological Survey.* [late ME *survei(en)* < AF *surveie(r),* MF *surve(i)r, -veoir* to oversee, equiv. to *sur-* SUR-[1] + *vee(i)r* < L *vidēre* to see] —**sur·vey′a·ble,** *adj.*
—**Syn. 2.** scan, observe, scrutinize. **6.** inspection.

survey., surveying.

sur·vey·ing (sər vā′ing), *n.* **1.** the science or scientific method of making surveys of land. **2.** the occupation of one who makes land surveys. **3.** the act of one who surveys: *The surveying required nearly two days.* [SURVEY + -ING[1]]

sur·vey·or (sər vā′ər), *n.* **1.** one whose occupation is surveying. **2.** an overseer or supervisor. **3.** *Chiefly Brit.* one who inspects something officially for the purpose of ascertaining condition, value, etc. **4.** (formerly) a U.S. customs official responsible for ascertaining the quantity and value of imported merchandise. [late ME *surveio(u)r* < AF, MF, equiv. to *survei-* (see SURVEY) + *-o(u)r* -OR[2]] —**sur·vey′or·ship′,** *n.*

survey′or's ar′row, *Survey.* See **chaining pin.**

survey′or's chain′. See under **chain** (def. 8a).

survey′or's com′pass, an instrument used by surveyors for measuring azimuths. Also called **survey′or's di′al.**

survey′or's lev′el, level (def. 9a).

survey′or's meas′ure, a system of units of length used in surveying land, based on the surveyor's chain of 66 feet and its 100 links of 7.92 inches.

sur·viv·al (sər vī′vəl), *n.* **1.** the act or fact of surviving, esp. under adverse or unusual circumstances. **2.** one who or that which survives or endures, esp. an ancient custom, observance, belief, or the like. —*adj.* **3.** of or pertaining to the food, clothing, equipment, etc., necessary to or aiding a person's survival in adverse or unusual circumstances. **4.** for use in keeping a person alive under adverse or unusual circumstances: *Astronauts may be equipped with survival masks and a portable oxygen supply.* [SURVIVE + -AL[2]]

surviv′al kit′, *Mil.* a package containing medical supplies, rations, and other vital equipment for use by a person forced to land in or parachute into the ocean, jungle, or other isolated or hostile territory.

sur·viv′al of the fit′test, *Biol.* the fact or the principle of the survival of the forms of animal and vegetable life best fitted for existing conditions, while related but less fit forms become extinct. Cf. **natural selection.**

sur·vive (sər vīv′), *v.*, **-vived, -viv·ing.** —*v.i.* **1.** to remain alive after the death of someone, the cessation of something, or the occurrence of some event; continue to live: *His wife and children survive. Few survived after the holocaust.* **2.** to remain or continue in existence or use: *Ancient farming methods still survive in the Middle East.* **3.** to get along or remain healthy, happy, and unaffected in spite of some occurrence: *So don't speak to me again, I'll survive.* —*v.t.* **4.** to continue to live or exist after the death, cessation, or occurrence of: *His wife survived him. He survived the operation but died the following year.* **5.** to endure or live through (an affliction, adversity, misery, etc.): *She's survived two divorces and the loss of her fortune.* [late ME < MF *surviv(re)* < L *supervīvere*, equiv. to *super-* SUPER- + *vīvere* to live; see VIVID] —**sur·viv′a·bil′i·ty,** *n.* —**sur·viv′a·ble,** *adj.*
—**Syn. 1.** persist, succeed. SURVIVE, OUTLIVE refer to remaining alive longer than someone else or after some event. SURVIVE usually means to succeed in keeping alive against odds, to live after some event which has threatened one: *to survive an automobile accident.* It is also used of living longer than another person (usually a relative), but, today, mainly in the passive, as in the fixed expression: *The deceased is survived by his wife and children.* OUTLIVE stresses capacity for endurance, the time element, and sometimes a sense of competition: *He outlived all his enemies.* It is also used, however, of a person or object that has lived or lasted beyond a certain point: *He has outlived his usefulness. This fan belt has outlived its usefulness.*

sur·vi·vor (sər vī′vər), *n.* **1.** one who or that which survives. **2.** *Law.* the one of two or more designated persons, as joint tenants or others having a joint interest, who outlives the other or others. [SURVIVE + -OR[2]]

sur·vi·vor·ship (sər vī′vər ship′), *n.* **1.** the state of being a survivor. **2.** *Law.* a right of a person to property on the death of another person having a joint interest: in the case of more than two joint tenants, the property passes to successive survivors. [SURVIVOR + -SHIP]

sus-, var. of **sub-** before *c, p, t*: *susceptible.*

Su·sa (so͞o′sä), *n.* a ruined city in W Iran: the capital of ancient Elam and later of Susiana; palaces of Darius and Artaxerxes; stele containing the Code of Hammurabi discovered here. Biblical name, **Shushan.**

Su·san (so͞o′zən), *n.* a girl's given name, form of **Susanna** or **Susannah.** Also, **Suzan.**

Su·san·na (so͞o zan′ə), *n.* **1.** a book of the Apocrypha, comprising the 13th chapter of Daniel in the Douay Bible. **2.** a girl's given name.

Su·san·nah (so͞o zan′ə), *n.* a girl's given name. Also, **Susanna.**

Su·sanne (so͞o zan′), *n.* a girl's given name, form of **Susanna** or **Susannah.**

Su·sa·no·wo (so͞o′sä nô′wô), *n.* *Japanese Myth.* the god of disorder.

Su·san·ville (so͞o′zən vil), *n.* a town in NE California. 5598 (1960).

sus·cep·tance (sə sep′təns), *n.* *Elect.* the imaginary component of admittance, equal to the quotient of the negative of the reactance divided by the sum of the squares of the reactance and resistance. *Symbol:* B [SUSCEPT(IBILITY) + -ANCE]

sus·cep·ti·bil·i·ty (sə sep′tə bil′i tē), *n., pl.* **-ties. 1.** state or character of being susceptible: *susceptibility to disease.* **2.** capability of being affected, esp. easily; capacity for receiving mental or moral impressions; tendency to be emotionally affected. **3. susceptibilities,** capacities for emotion; sensitive feelings; emotional vulnerability: *His susceptibilities are easily wounded.* **4.** *Elect.* the ratio of the magnetization produced in a substance to the magnetizing force. [< ML *susceptibilitāt-* (s. of *susceptibilitās*) equiv. to *susceptibil(is)* SUSCEPTIBLE + *-itāt-* -ITY]
—**Syn. 2.** See **sensibility.**

sus·cep·ti·ble (sə sep′tə bəl), *adj.* **1.** capable of receiving, admitting, undergoing, or being affected by, something (usually fol. by *of* or *to*): *susceptible of a high polish; susceptible to various interpretations.* **2.** accessible or especially liable or subject to some influence, mood, agency, etc. (usually fol. by *to*): *susceptible to colds; susceptible to flattery.* **3.** capable of being affected, esp. easily; readily impressed; impressionable. [< LL *susceptibil(is)*, equiv. to *suscept(us)*, ptp. of *suscipere* to take up, support, (*sus-* SUS- + *cep-* var. of *cap-* take, CAPTURE + *-tus* ptp. suffix) + *-ibilis* -IBLE] —**sus·cep′ti·ble·ness,** *n.* —**sus·cep′ti·bly,** *adv.*

sus·cep·tive (sə sep′tiv), *adj.* **1.** receptive. **2.** susceptible. [< LL *susceptīv(us)*, equiv. to *suscept(us)* (see SUSCEPTIBLE) + *-īvus* -IVE] —**sus·cep·tiv·i·ty** (sus′ep tiv′i tē), **sus·cep′tive·ness,** *n.*

Su·sette (so͞o zet′), *n.* a girl's given name, form of **Susanna** or **Susannah.**

su·shi (so͞o′shē), *n.* *Japanese Cookery.* a preparation of cooled cooked rice, dressed with seasoned vinegar, and often shaped into fingers, then garnished with a variety of raw seafood, vegetables, and seaweed. [< Jap]

Su·si·an (so͞o′zē ən), *n.* **1.** a native or inhabitant of Susa or Susiana. **2.** Elamite (def. 2). —*adj.* **3.** of or pertaining to Susa or Susiana. [SUS(A), SUS(IANA) + -IAN]

Su·si·a·na (so͞o′zē ā′nə, -an′ə), *n.* **1.** an ancient Persian province roughly coextensive with ancient Elam. **2.** Elam (def. 1).

Su·sie (so͞o′zē), *n.* a girl's given name, form of **Susanna** or **Susannah.** Also, **Su′si, Susy, Suzie, Suzy.**

sus·lik (sus′lik), *n.* **1.** a common ground squirrel or spermophile, *Citellus* (or *Spermophilus*) *citellus*, of Europe and Asia. **2.** the fur of this animal. Also, **souslik.** [< Russ]

Sus·lov (so͞os′lof), *n.* **Mi·kha·il An·dre·e·vich** (mi кнä ēl′ än dre′yə vich), born 1902, Russian government official: member of the Presidium since 1955.

sus·pect (*v.* sə spekt′; *n.* sus′pekt; *adj.* sus′pekt, sə spekt′), *v.t.* **1.** to believe to be guilty, false, counterfeit, undesirable, defective, bad, etc., with insufficient proof or with no proof. **2.** to believe to be rightly chargeable with something stated, usually something wrong or something considered as undesirable, on little or no evidence: *to suspect a person of murder.* **3.** to believe to be the case or to be likely; surmise: *I suspect his knowledge did not amount to much.* **4.** to have some hint or foreknowledge of: *The party was to be a surprise for her, but I think she suspects something.* —*v.i.* **5.** to believe something, esp. something evil, wrong, or undesirable, to be the case; have suspicion. —*n.* **6.** a person who is suspected, esp. one suspected of a crime, offense, or the like. —*adj.* **7.** suspected; open to or under suspicion. [late ME *suspecte(n)* < L *suspect(āre)*, equiv. to *su-* SU- + *spec-* (var. of *spic-* look) + *-t-* intensive suffix + *-āre* v. suffix] —**sus·pect′ed·ness,** *n.* —**sus·pect′er,** *n.* —**sus·pect′i·ble,** *adj.* —**sus′-pect·less,** *adj.*
—**Syn. 1.** distrust, mistrust, doubt. **3.** guess, conjecture, suppose. —**Ant. 5.** trust.

sus·pend (sə spend′), *v.t.* **1.** to hang by attachment to something above: *to suspend a chandelier from the ceiling.* **2.** to attach so as to allow free movement: *to suspend a door on a hinge.* **3.** to keep from falling, sinking, forming a deposit, etc., as if by hanging: *to suspend solid particles in a liquid.* **4.** to hold or keep undetermined; refrain from forming or concluding definitely: *to suspend one's judgment.* **5.** to defer or postpone: *to suspend sentence on a convicted person.* **6.** to cause to cease or bring to a stop or stay, usually for a time: *to suspend payment.* **7.** to cause to cease for a time from operation or effect, as a law, rule, privilege, or the like: *to suspend parking rules; to suspend ferry service.* **8.** to debar, usually for a limited time, from the exercise of an office or function or the enjoyment of a privilege: *The college suspended the student for a breach of discipline.* **9.** to keep in a mood or feeling of expectation or incompleteness; keep waiting in suspense: *Finish the story; don't suspend us in midair.* **10.** *Music.* to prolong (a note or tone) into the next chord. —*v.i.* **11.** to come to a stop, usually temporarily; cease from operation for a time. **12.** to stop payment; be unable to meet financial obligations. **13.** to hang or be suspended, as from another object: *The chandelier suspends from a gilded ceiling.* **14.** to be suspended, as in a liquid, gas, etc. [ME *suspend(en)* < L *suspende(re)* (to) hang up, equiv. to *sus-* SUS- + *pendere* to PEND; see SUSPENSE] —**sus·pend′i·bil′i·ty,** *n.* —**sus·pend′i·ble,** *adj.*
—**Syn. 4.** withhold. **5.** delay. **6.** hold up, intermit. See **interrupt.**

suspend′ed anima′tion, a state of temporary cessation of the vital functions.

sus·pend·er (sə spen′dər), *n.* **1.** Usually, **suspenders.** Also called, *esp. Brit.,* **braces.** *Chiefly U.S.* adjustable straps or bands worn over the shoulders with the ends buttoned or clipped to the waistband of the trousers to support them. **2.** *Brit.* garter. **3.** (in a suspension bridge) a hanging cable or chain connecting the deck with the suspension cable or chain. **4.** one who or that which suspends. [SUSPEND + -ER[1]] —**sus·pend′-er·less,** *adj.*

suspend′er belt′, *Brit.* See **garter belt.**

sus·pense (sə spens′), *n.* **1.** a state or condition of mental uncertainty or excitement, as in awaiting a decision or outcome, usually accompanied by a degree of apprehension or anxiety. **2.** a state of mental indecision. **3.** undecided or doubtful condition, as of affairs: *For a few days matters hung in suspense.* **4.** the state or condition of being suspended. [ME < ML *suspens(um)* deferment, suspension, uncertainty, n. use of neut. of L *suspens(us)* hung up, doubtful, in suspense (ptp. of *suspendere* to hang up, leave undecided), equiv. to *sus-* SUS- + *pensus*, equiv. to *pend-* hang + *-tus* ptp. suffix] —**sus·pense′ful,** *adj.*
—**Syn. 1.** doubt, incertitude. **2.** hesitation, hesitancy, vacillation, wavering, irresolution, misgiving. —**Ant. 1.** certainty. **2.** decision.

suspense′ account′, *Bookkeeping.* an account in which items are temporarily entered until their final disposition is determined.

sus·pen·si·ble (sə spen′sə bəl), *adj.* capable of being suspended. [< L *suspens(us)* (see SUSPENSE) + -IBLE] —**sus·pen′si·bil′i·ty,** *n.*

sus·pen·sion (sə spen′shən), *n.* **1.** the act of suspending. **2.** the state of being suspended. **3.** temporary abrogation or withholding, as of a law, privilege, decision, belief, etc. **4.** stoppage of payment of debts or claims because of financial inability or insolvency. **5.** *Chem.* **a.** the state in which the particles of a substance are mixed with a fluid but are undissolved. **b.** a substance in such a state. **6.** *Physical Chem.* a system consisting of small particles kept dispersed by agitation **(mechanical suspension)** or by the molecular motion in the surrounding medium **(colloidal suspension). 7.** something on or by which something else is suspended or hung. **8.** that which is suspended or hung. **9.** the arrangement of springs, shock absorbers, hangers, etc., in an automobile, railway car, etc., connecting the wheel-suspension units or axles to the chassis frame. **10.** *Elect.* a wire, filament, or group of wires, by which the conducting part of an instrument or device is suspended. **11.** *Music.* **a.** the prolongation of a tone in one chord into the following chord, usually producing a temporary dissonance. **b.** the tone so prolonged. **12.** *Rhet.* the heightening of interest by delay of the main subject or clause, especially by means of a series of parallel preceding elements. [< LL *suspensiōn-* (s. of *suspensiō*), equiv. to *suspens(us)* (see SUSPENSE) + *-iōn-* -ION]
—**Syn. 1-3.** intermission, interruption, discontinuance, cessation, abeyance, hiatus.

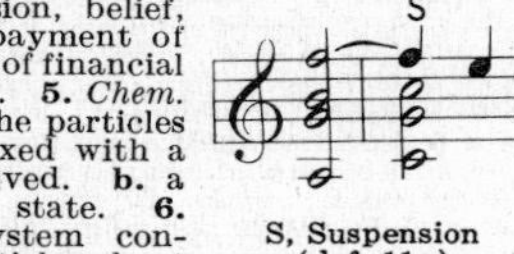

S, Suspension (def. 11a)

suspen′sion bridge′, a bridge having a deck suspended from cables anchored at their extremities and usually raised on towers.

suspen′sion points′, *Print.* a series of periods used as an ellipsis. Also called **breaks.**

sus·pen·sive (sə spen′siv), *adj.* **1.** pertaining to or characterized by suspension. **2.** undecided in mind. **3.** pertaining to or characterized by suspense. **4.** (of words, phrases, etc.) characterized by or expressing suspense; keeping the reader or listener in suspense. **5.** having the effect of suspending the operation of something. [< ML *suspensīv(us)*, equiv. to *suspens(us)* (see SUSPENSE) + *-īvus* -IVE] —**sus·pen′sive·ly,** *adv.* —**sus·pen′sive·ness,** *n.*

sus·pen·soid (sə spen′soid), *n.* *Physical Chem.* a sol having a solid disperse phase. Cf. **emulsoid.** [SUSPENS(ION) + (COLL)OID]

sus·pen·sor (sə spen′sər), *n.* a suspensory ligament, bandage, etc. [< ML; see SUSPENSE, -OR[2]]

sus·pen·so·ry[1] (sə spen′sə rē), *adj.* **1.** serving or fitted to suspend or hold up, as a ligament, muscle, bandage, etc. **2.** suspending the operation of something. [< L *suspens(us)* (see SUSPENSE) + -ORY[1]]

sus·pen·so·ry[2] (sə spen′sə rē), *n., pl.* **-ries.** a suspensory bandage, muscle, ligament, etc. [< L *suspens(us)* (see SUSPENSE) + -ORY[2]]

suspen′sory lig′ament, *Anat.* any of several tissues that suspend certain organs or parts of the body, esp. the transparent, delicate web of fibrous tissue that supports the crystalline lens. See diag. under **eye.**

sus. per coll., *Eng. Crim. Law.* (formerly) the notation made by a judge next to the name of one convicted of a capital crime. [< L *suspendātur per collum* let him be hanged by the neck]

sus·pi·cion (sə spish′ən), *n.* **1.** act of suspecting; belief in or imagination of the existence of guilt, falsity, a fault, a defect, or the like, on little or no evidence. **2.** state of mind or feeling of one who suspects: *Suspicion kept him awake all night long.* **3.** an instance of suspecting something or someone. **4.** state of being suspected: *under suspicion; above suspicion.* **5.** imagination of anything to be the case or to be likely; a vague notion of something. **6.** a slight trace, hint, or suggestion: *a suspicion of a smile.* —*v.t.* **7.** *Nonstandard.* to suspect. [late ME < L *suspīciōn-* (s. of *suspīciō*), equiv. to *suspic-* (var. of *suspic-*, base of *suspicere* to look from below, SUSPECT) + *-iōn-* -ION; r. ME *suspecioun* < AF << L *suspectiōn-* mistrust] —**sus·pi′cion·ful,** *adj.* —**sus·pi′cion·less,** *adj.*
—**Syn. 2.** doubt, mistrust, misgiving. SUSPICION, DISTRUST are terms for a feeling that appearances are not reliable. SUSPICION is the positive tendency to doubt the trustworthiness of appearances and therefore to believe that one has detected possibilities of something unreliable, unfavorable, menacing, or the like: *to feel suspicion about the honesty of a prominent man.* DISTRUST may be a passive want of trust, faith, or reliance in a person or thing: *to feel distrust of one's own ability.* **5.** idea, supposition, conjecture, guess. —**Ant. 2.** trust.

sus·pi·cion·al (sə spish′ə nəl), *adj.* of or pertaining to suspicion, esp. morbid or insane suspicions. [SUSPICION + -AL[1]]

sus·pi·cious (sə spish′əs), *adj.* **1.** tending to cause or excite suspicion; questionable: *suspicious behavior.* **2.** inclined to suspect, esp. inclined to suspect evil; distrustful: *a suspicious old maid.* **3.** full of or feeling suspicion. **4.** expressing or indicating suspicion: *a suspicious glance.* [ME < L *suspīciōs(us)*, equiv. to *suspīci-* (see SUSPICION) + *-ōsus* -OUS; r. ME *suspecious* < AF] —**sus·pi′cious·ly,** *adv.* —**sus·pi′cious·ness,** *n.*

sus·pi·ra·tion (sus′pə rā′shən), *n.* a long, deep sigh. [< L *suspīrātiōn-* (s. of *suspīrātiō*), equiv. to *suspīrāt(us)* (ptp. of *suspīrāre* to SUSPIRE) + *-iōn-* -ION]

sus·pire (sə spīər′), *v.*, **-pired, -pir·ing.** *Chiefly Literary.* —*v.i.* **1.** to sigh. **2.** to breathe. —*v.t.* **3.** to sigh; breathe with long, sighing breaths. [< L *suspīr(āre)*, equiv. to *su-* SU- + *spīrāre* to breathe]

Sus·que·han·na (sus′kwə han′ə), *n.* a river flowing S from central New York through E Pennsylvania and NE Maryland into Chesapeake Bay. 444 mi. long.

Susquehan′na De′pot, a town in NE Pennsylvania. 2591 (1960).

Sus·sex (sus′iks), *n.* **1.** a county in SE England; divided for administrative purposes into East Sussex and West Sussex. **2.** one of an English breed of red beef cattle. **3.** one of an English breed of chickens, raised chiefly for marketing as roasters.

Sus′sex span′iel, one of an English breed of short-legged spaniels having a golden liver-colored coat.

sus·tain (sə stān′), *v.t.* **1.** to support, hold, or bear up from below; bear the weight of, as a structure. **2.** to bear (a burden, charge, etc.). **3.** to undergo, experience, or suffer (injury, loss, etc.); endure without giving way or yielding. **4.** to keep (a person, the mind, the spirits, etc.) from giving way, as under trial or affliction. **5.** to keep up or keep going, as an action or process: *to sustain a conversation.* **6.** to supply with food, drink, and other necessities of life: *Charity sustained many poverty-stricken families.* **7.** to provide for (an institution or the like) by furnishing means or funds. **8.** to support (a cause or the like) by aid or approval. **9.** to uphold as valid, just, or correct, as a claim or the person making it: *The judge sustained the lawyer's objection.* **10.** to confirm or corroborate, as a statement: *Further investigation sustained my suspicions.* [ME *suste(i)n(en)* < AF, OF *susteni(r)* < L *sustinēre* to uphold, equiv. to *sus-* SUS- + *-tinēre*, var. of *tenēre* to hold] —**sus·tain′a·ble,** *adj.* —**sus·tain·ed·ly** (sə stā′nid lē, -stānd′-), *adv.* —**sus·tain′ing·ly,** *adv.* —**sus·tain′ment,** *n.*
—**Syn. 1.** carry. See **support. 3.** bear. **5.** maintain. **6.** nurture; back, abet, help. **10.** establish, ratify.

sus·tain·er (sə stā′nər), *n.* **1.** one who or that which sustains. **2.** *Rocketry.* (of a multistage rocket or guided missile) **a.** any stage that sustains flight after the burnout of the booster. **b.** the rocket engine or cluster of engines contained in such a stage. [late ME *sosteynere.* See SUSTAIN, -ER[1]]

sustain′ing pro′gram, a radio or television program without a commercial sponsor.

sus·te·nance (sus′tə nəns), *n.* **1.** means of sustaining life; nourishment. **2.** means of livelihood. **3.** the process of sustaining. **4.** the state of being sustained. [ME *sustena(u)nce* < AF, var. of OF *sostenance.* See SUSTAIN, -ANCE] —**sus′te·nance·less,** *adj.*

sus·ten·tac·u·lar (sus′tən tak′yə lər), *adj.* *Anat.* supporting. [< L *sustentācul(um)* a prop, support (*sustentā-*, see SUSTENTATION, + *-culum* suffix denoting means or instrument) + -AR[1]]

sus·ten·ta·tion (sus′ten tā′shən), *n.* **1.** maintenance in being or activity; the sustaining of life through vital processes. **2.** provision with means or funds for upkeep. **3.** means of sustaining life; sustenance. [ME < L *sustentātiōn-* (s. of *sustentātiō*) an upholding, equiv. to *sustentāt(us)* (ptp. of *sustentāre*, freq. of *sustinēre* to SUSTAIN + *-iōn-* -ION] —**sus·ten·ta·tive** (sus′tən tā′tiv, sə sten′tə tiv), *adj.* —**sus′ten·ta′tion·al,** *adj.*

sus·ten·tion (sə sten′shən), *n.* **1.** act of sustaining. **2.** state or quality of being sustained. [*susten-* (see SUSTAIN) + -TION, modeled on *detention, retention* (cf. *detain, retain*)] —**sus·ten·tive** (sə sten′tiv), *adj.*

sus·ti·ne·o a·las (sŏŏs tin′e ō′ ä′läs; *Eng.* su stin′ē ō′ ā′las), *Latin.* I sustain the wings: motto of the U.S. Air Force.

su·su (sōō′sōō′), *n.* an institutionalized kinship group among the Doubans, comprised of a woman, her brother, and the woman's children. [< Douban: lit., milk of the mother]

su·sur·rant (sŏŏ sûr′ənt), *adj.* softly murmuring; whispering. [< L *susurrant-* (s. of *susurrāns*) whispering (prp. of *susurrāre*). See SUSURRUS, -ANT]

su·sur·ra·tion (sōō′sə rā′shən), *n.* a soft murmur; whisper. [< LL *susurrātiōn-* (s. of *susurrātiō*), equiv. to *susurrāt(us)* (ptp. of *susurrāre;* see SUSURRANT) + *-iōn-* -ION]

su·sur·rous (sŏŏ sûr′əs), *adj.* full of whispering or rustling sounds. [SUSURR(US) + -OUS]

su·sur·rus (sŏŏ sûr′əs), *n., pl.* **-rus·es.** a soft murmuring or rustling sound; whisper. [< L: a whisper]

Su·sy (sōō′zē) *n.* a girl's given name, form of **Susanna** or **Susannah.** Also, **Susi, Susie, Suzie, Suzy.**

Su·sy-Q (sōō′zē kyōō′), *n.* a dance step, performed principally as part of the Big Apple, in which the feet, by alternating heel and toe movements, carry the dancer sideways. [?]

Suth·er·land (suth′ər lənd), *n.* **1. George,** 1862–1942, U.S. politician and jurist: associate justice of the U.S. Supreme Court 1922–38. **2. Joan,** born 1926, Australian soprano. **3.** Also called **Suth·er·land·shire** (suth′ər lənd shēr′, -shər). a county in N Scotland. 13,442 (1961); 2028 sq. mi. *Co. seat:* Dornoch.

Suth′erland Falls′, a waterfall in New Zealand, on SW South Island. 1904 ft. high.

Sut·lej (sut′lej), *n.* a river in S Asia, flowing W and SW from SW Tibet through NW India into the Indus River in W Pakistan. 900 mi. long.

sut·ler (sut′lər), *n.* a person who follows an army and sells provisions to the soldiers. [< obs. D *soeteler* (now *zoetelaar*), equiv. to *soetel(en)* (to) do befouling work (akin to SOOT) + *-er* -ER[1]] —**sut′ler·ship′,** *n.*

su·tra (sōō′trə), *n* **1.** *Hinduism.* a collection of aphorisms relating to some aspect of the conduct of life. **2.** Pali, **sut·ta** (sŏŏt′ə). *Buddhism.* any of the sermons of Buddha. **3.** one of the approximately 4000 rules or aphorisms that comprise Panini's grammar of Sanskrit. [< Skt *sūtra-* thread, connective cord, rule, technical manual]

Sut′ta Pit′aka (sŏŏt′ə), *Buddhism.* See under **Pali Canon.** [< Pali: doctrine, lit., teaching basket]

sut·tee (su tē′, sut′ē), *n.* **1.** a former Hindu practice whereby a widow immolated herself on the funeral pyre of her husband: abolished by the English in 1829. **2.** a Hindu widow who so immolated herself. [< Skt *satī* good woman, n. use of fem. of *sat* good (lit., being), prp. of *as* to be] —**sut·tee′ism,** *n.*

Sut·ter (sut′ər), *n.* **John Augustus,** 1803–80, U.S. frontiersman: owner of Sutter's Mill.

Sut′ter's Mill′, the location in central California, NE of Sacramento, near which gold was discovered in 1848, precipitating the gold rush of 1849. [after J. SUTTER, its owner]

Sutt·ner (zŏŏt′nər, sŏŏt′-; *Ger.* zŏŏt′nər), *n.* **Ber·tha von** (bûr′thə von; *Ger.* ber′tä fən), 1843–1914, Austrian writer: Nobel peace prize 1905.

Sut·ton Hoo (sut′ən hōō′), an archaeological site in Suffolk, England: a rowing boat, 80 feet long, discovered here and believed to have been buried A.D. c670 by Anglo-Saxons, possibly as a cenotaph in honor of a king.

su·ture (sōō′chər), *n., v.,* **-tured, -tur·ing.** —*n.* **1.** *Surg.* **a.** a joining of the lips or edges of a wound or the like by stitching or some similar process. **b.** a particular method of doing this. **c.** one of the stitches or fastenings employed. **2.** *Anat.* **a.** the line of junction of two bones, esp. of the skull, in an immovable articulation. **b.** the articulation itself. **3.** *Zool., Bot.* the junction or line of junction of contiguous parts, as the line of closure between the valves of a bivalve shell, a seam where carpels of a pericarp join, etc. **4.** a seam as formed in sewing; a line of junction between two parts. **5.** a sewing together or a joining as by sewing. —*v.t.* **6.** to unite by or as by a suture. [< L *sūtūr(a)* seam, suture, equiv. to *sūt(us)* (ptp. of *suere* to SEW) + *-ūra* -URE] —**su′tur·al,** *adj.* —**su′tur·al·ly,** *adv.*

su·um cui·que (sōō′ŏŏm kwē′kwe; *Eng.* sōō′əm kī′kwē, kwī′-), *Latin.* to each his own; to each what rightfully belongs to him.

Su·va (sōō′vä), *n.* a seaport in and the capital of Fiji, on Viti Levu island. 47,679 (est. 1963).

Su·vo·rov (sŏŏ vô′rof), *n.* **A·le·ksan·dr Va·si·le·vich** (ä′le ksän′dər vä sē′lə vich), (*Count Suvorov Rumnikski, Prince Itliski*), 1729–1800, Russian field marshal.

Su·wan·nee (sə won′ē, -wô′nē; swon′ē, swô′nē), *n.* a river in SE Georgia and N Florida, flowing SW to the Gulf of Mexico. 240 mi. long. Also, **Swanee.**

Su·zan (sōō′zən) *n.* a girl's given name, form of **Susanna** or **Susannah.** Also, **Susan.**

Su·zanne (sōō zan′) *n.* a girl's given name, French form of **Susanna** or **Susannah.** Also, **Su·zann′.**

su·ze·rain (sōō′zə rin, -rān′), *n.* **1.** a sovereign or a state exercising political control over a dependent state. **2.** *Hist.* a feudal overlord. —*adj.* **3.** characteristic of or being a suzerain. [< F, equiv. to *sus* above (< L *susum,* var. of *sursum,* contr. of *subversum,* neut. of *subversus* upturned; see SUB-, VERSE) + *(souv)erain* SOVEREIGN]

su·ze·rain·ty (sōō′zə rin tē, -rān′-), *n., pl.* **-ties.** the position or authority of a suzerain. [< F *suzeraineté,* MF *suserenete,* equiv. to *suseren* SUZERAIN + *-ete* -ITY]

Su·zie (sōō′zē), *n.* a girl's given name, form of **Susanna** or **Susannah.** Also, **Susi, Susie, Susy, Su′zy.**

S.V., Holy Virgin. [< L *Sancta Virgō*]

s.v., **1.** sub verbo. **2.** sub voce.

Sval·bard (sväl′bär), *n.* Norwegian name of **Spitsbergen.**

sva·ra·bhak·ti (sfär′ä bäk′tē; *Skt.* svə rə buk′ti), *n.* *Linguistics.* the process of inserting vowel sounds into a consonant cluster of a loan word to make it conform to the pattern of the speaker's language and, hence, more easily pronounceable, as in the Italian pronunciation (län′tse ke nek′kō) for German *Lands·knecht* (länts′knekht′). Cf. **epenthesis.** [< Skt, equiv. to *svara* vowel + *bhakti* apportionment]

Sved·berg (sved′bar′yə), *n.* **The(o·dor)** (tā′ō dôr′), born 1884, Swedish chemist: Nobel prize 1926.

svelte (svelt, sfelt), *adj.,* **svelt·er, svelt·est. 1.** slender, esp. gracefully slender in figure; lithe. **2.** suave; blandly urbane. [< F < It *svelt(o)* < VL **(e)xvellit(um)* pulled out (r. L *ēvulsum,* ptp. of *ēvellere*), equiv. to *ex-* EX- + *velli-* pull, pluck + *-tum* ptp. suffix]

Sverd·lovsk (sverd lôfsk′), *n.* a city in the W RSFSR, in the W Soviet Union in Asia, on the E slope of the central Ural Mountains: execution of Czar Nicholas and his family 1918. 917,000 (1965). Formerly, **Ekaterinburg.**

Sve·ri·ge (sve′rē ye), *n.* Swedish name of **Sweden.**

Sve·tam·ba·ra (shve täm′bər ə), *n.* one of the two principal Jain sects, its members wearing white and believing that women can attain salvation. Cf. **Digambara.** [< Skt: lit., white-clad]

Svet·la·na (svet′lä nä), *n.* a girl's given name.

Sviz·ze·ra (zvēt′tse rä), *n.* Italian name of **Switzerland.**

S.V.R., (in prescriptions) rectified spirit of wine (alcohol). [< L *spīritus vīnī rectificātus*]

SW, 1. southwest. **2.** southwestern. Also, **Sw**

Sw., 1. Sweden. **2.** Swedish.

S.W., 1. South Wales. **2.** southwest. **3.** southwestern.

S.W.A., South West Africa.

swab (swob), *n., v.,* **swabbed, swab·bing.** —*n.* **1.** a large mop used on shipboard for cleaning decks, living quarters, etc. **2.** a bit of sponge, cloth, cotton, or the like, sometimes fixed to a stick, for cleansing the mouth of a sick person or for applying medicaments, drying areas, etc. **3.** the material collected with a swab as a specimen for microscopic study. **4.** a brush or wad of absorbent material for cleaning the bore of a firearm. **5.** *Slang.* a clumsy fellow. —*v.t.* **6.** to clean with or as with a swab: *to swab the decks.* **7.** to take up or apply, as moisture, with or as if with a swab: *to swab soapy water from the decks.* **8.** to pass over a surface: *to swab a mop over the decks.* Also, **swob.** [back formation from SWABBER]

Swab., 1. Swabia. **2.** Swabian.

swab·ber (swob′ər), *n.* **1.** a person who uses a swab. **2.** *Slang.* swab (def. 5). **3.** a swab; mop. [< D *zwabber,* equiv. to *zwab-b(en)* (to) move back and forth + *-er* -ER[1]; cf. ME *swabben* to sway (< D or LG); akin to OE *swifan* to revolve, sweep, G *schweifen*]

Swa·bi·a (swā′bē ə), *n.* **1.** a medieval duchy in SW Germany: it comprised the area presently included in Baden-Württemberg and Bavaria. **2.** a district in SW Bavaria, in S West Germany. ab. 3900 sq. mi. *Cap.:* Augsburg. German, **Schwaben.** —**Swa′bi·an,** *adj., n.*

swad·dle (swod′əl), *v.,* **-dled, -dling,** *n.* —*v.t.* **1.** to bind (an infant, esp. a newborn infant) with long, narrow strips of cloth to prevent free movement; wrap tightly with clothes. **2.** to wrap (anything) round with bandages. —*n.* **3.** a long, narrow strip of cloth used for swaddling or bandaging. [ME *swathel,* OE *swæthel* swaddling band; akin to SWATHE]

swad′dling clothes′, 1. clothes consisting of long, narrow strips of cloth for swaddling an infant. **2.** long garments for an infant. **3.** the period of infancy or immaturity, as of a person, or incipience, as of a thing: *Utilization of atomic energy for peaceful purposes is still in swaddling clothes.* **4.** rigid supervision or restriction of actions or movements, as of the immature: *new nations that are freeing themselves of their swaddling clothes.* Also called **swad′dling bands′** (for defs. 1, 2).

Swa·de·shi (swə dā′shē), *n.* **1.** (formerly, in India) the encouragement of domestic production and the boycott of foreign, esp. British, goods as a step towards home rule. —*adj.* **2.** made in India. [< Bengali *svadesī,* equiv. to *sva-* self, own + *desī* native]

swag[1] (swag), *n., v.,* **swagged, swag·ging.** —*n.* **1.** a suspended wreath, garland, drapery, or the like, fastened up at or near each end and hanging down in the middle; festoon: *Swags of evergreens hung along the mantel. A swag of taffeta was draped across the bodice.* **2.** a wreath, spray, or cluster of foliage, flowers, or fruit. **3.** a festoon, esp. one very heavy toward the center. **4.** a swale. **5.** a swaying or lurching movement. —*v.i.* **6.** to move heavily or unsteadily from side to side or up and down; sway. **7.** to hang loosely and heavily; sink down. —*v.t.* **8.** to cause to sway, sink, or sag. **9.** to hang or adorn with swags. [prob. < Scand; cf. Norw *svagga* to sway]

swag[2] (swag), *n., v.,* **swagged, swag·ging.** —*n.* **1.** *Slang.* **a.** plunder; booty. **b.** money; valuables. **2.** *Australian.* a traveler's bundle containing personal belongings, cooking utensils, food, or the like, traditionally a large handkerchief of the sort a hobo carries over his shoulder on a stick or a blanket roll of the sort slung over a prospector's shoulder. —*v.i.* **3.** *Australian.* to travel about carrying one's bundle of personal belongings. [special uses of SWAG[1]]

swage (swāj), *n., v.,* **swaged, swag·ing.** —*n.* **1.** a tool for bending cold metal to a required shape. **2.** a tool, die, or stamp for giving a particular shape to metal on an anvil, in a stamping press, etc. **3.** See **swage block.** —*v.t.* **4.** to bend or shape by means of a swage. **5.** to reduce or taper (an object), as by forging or squeezing. [late ME *souage* < MF] —**swag′er,** *n.*

swage′ block′, an iron block containing holes and grooves of various sizes, used for heading bolts and shaping objects not easily worked on an anvil.

swag·ger (swag′ər), *v.i.* **1.** to walk or strut with a defiant or insolent air. **2.** to boast or brag noisily. —*v.t.* **3.** to bring, drive, force, etc., by blustering. —*n.* **4.** swaggering manner, conduct, or walk; ostentatious display of arrogance and conceit. [SWAG[1] + -ER[6]] —**swag′ger·er,** *n.*

—**Syn. 2.** bluster. **4.** boasting, bragging, affectation, braggadocio, bluster.

swag·ger·ing (swag′ər ing), *adj.* pertaining to, characteristic of, or behaving in the manner of one who swaggers. [SWAGGER + -ING[2]] —**swag′ger·ing·ly,** *adv.*

swag′ger stick′, a short, batonlike stick, usually leather-covered, sometimes carried by army officers, soldiers, etc.

swag·man (swag′mən), *n., pl.* **-men.** *Australian.* **1.** a tramp, hobo, or vagabond. **2.** anyone who carries a swag while traveling, as a camper or prospector. [SWAG[2] + MAN[1]]

swags·man (swagz′mən), *n., pl.* **-men.** *Australian.* swagman. [SWAG + 'S[1] + MAN[1]]

Swa·hi·li (swä hē′lē), *n., pl.* **-lis,** (*esp. collectively*) **-li. 1.** a member of a Bantu people of Zanzibar and the neighboring coast of Africa. **2.** the Bantu language of the Swahili people, used also as a lingua franca of E Africa and neighboring parts of the Congo. —**Swa·hi′li·an,** *adj.*

swain (swān), *n.* **1.** a lover. **2.** a country lad. **3.** a country gallant. [early ME *swein* servant < Scand; cf. Icel *sveinn* boy, lad, c. OE *swān,* OHG *swein*] —**swain′ish,** *adj.* —**swain′ish·ness,** *n.*

Swains·bor·o (swānz′bûr′ō, -bər ə), *n.* a town in central Georgia. 5943 (1960).

Swain′son's hawk′ (swān′sənz), a brownish American hawk, *Buteo swainsonii.* [named after W. *Swainson* (1789–1855), English naturalist]

Swain′son's thrush′. See **olive-backed thrush.** [see SWAINSON'S HAWK]

S.W.A.K., sealed with a kiss (written at the end of a love letter or on the back of its envelope). Also, **SWAK** (swak).

swale (swāl), *n.* **1.** a low place in a tract of land, usually moister and often having ranker vegetation than the adjacent higher land. **2.** a valleylike intersection of two slopes in a piece of land. [late ME; orig. a cool, shady, wet spot < Scand; cf. Icel *svalr* cool; akin to SWILL]

swal·let (swol′it), *n.* *Brit.* **1.** an underground stream. **2.** an opening through which a stream descends underground. [SWALL(OW)[1] + -ET]

swal·low[1] (swol′ō), *v.t.* **1.** to take into the stomach by drawing through the throat or esophagus with a voluntary muscular action, as food, drink, or other substances. **2.** to take in so as to envelop; withdraw from sight; assimilate or absorb; consume (often fol. by *up*): *The crowd swallowed him up.* **3.** *Informal.* to accept without question or suspicion. **4.** to accept without opposition; put up with: *to swallow an insult.* **5.** to suppress (emotion, a laugh, a sob, etc.) as if by drawing it down one's throat. **6.** to take back; retract: *to swallow one's words.* **7.** to enunciate poorly; mutter: *He swallowed the key phrases.* —*v.i.* **8.** to perform the act of swallowing. —*n.* **9.** the act or an instance of swallowing. **10.** a quantity swallowed at one time; a mouthful: *Take one swallow of brandy.* **11.** capacity for swallowing. **12.** Also called **crown, throat.** *Naut., Mach.* the space in a block, between the groove of the sheave and the shell, through which the rope runs. **13.** Also called **swal′low hole′.** a sinkhole. [ME *swalwen,* var. of *swelwen,* OE *swelgan;* c. G *schwelgen;* akin to Icel *svelgja*] —**swal′low·a·ble,** *adj.* —**swal′low·er,** *n.*

—**Syn. 1.** eat, gulp, drink. **2.** engulf, devour. **10.** gulp, draught, drink.

swal·low[2] (swol′ō), *n.* **1.** any of numerous small, long-winged, passerine birds of the family *Hirundinidae,* noted for their swift, graceful flight and for the extent and regularity of their migrations. Cf. **bank swallow, barn swallow, martin. 2.** any of several unrelated, swallowlike birds, as the chimney swift. [ME *swalwe,* OE *swealwe;* c. G *Schwalbe,* Icel *svala*] —**swal′low·like′,** *adj.*

swal′low dive′, *Chiefly Brit.* See **swan dive.**

swal·low·tail (swol′ō tāl′), *n.* **1.** the tail of a swallow or a deeply forked tail like that of a swallow. **2.** any of several butterflies of the genus *Papilio,* characterized by elongated hind wings that resemble the tail of a swallow, as *P. polyxenes* **(black swallowtail).** Cf. **spicebush swallowtail, tiger swallowtail, zebra swallowtail.** [SWALLOW[2] + TAIL[1]]

Tiger swallowtail, *Papilio glaucus* **(Wingspread to 4 in.)**

swal·low-tailed (swol′ō tāld′), *adj.* **1.** having a deeply forked tail like that of a swallow, as various birds. **2.** having an end or part suggesting a swallow's tail.

swal′low-tailed coat′, a man's fitted coat, as a dress coat, having the lower part cut away over the hips and descending in a pair of tapering skirts behind. See **tail coat.**

swal′low-tailed kite′, an American kite, *Elanoides forficatus,* having black upper parts, white head and underparts, and a long, deeply forked tail.

swal·low-tan·a·ger (swol′ō tan′ə jər), *n.* a tropical American, oscine bird, *Tersina viridis,* superficially resembling a tanager.

swal·low·wort (swol′ō wûrt′), *n.* **1.** the greater celandine, *Chelidonium majus.* **2.** any of several asclepiadaceous plants, esp. an herb, *Vincetoxicum officinale* (or *Cynanchum Vincetoxicum*), of Europe, having an emetic root formerly used as a counterpoison. [SWALLOW[2] + WORT[2]]

swam (swam), *v.* pt. of **swim.**

swa·mi (swä′mē), *n., pl.* **-mies. 1.** an honorific title given to a Hindu religious teacher. **2.** a person resembling a swami, esp. in authority, critical judgment, etc.; pundit: *The swamis are saying the stock market is due for a drop.* Also, **swamy.** [< Skt *svāmī* lord, master]

Swam·mer·dam (sväm′ər däm′), *n.* **Jan** (yän), 1637–80, Dutch anatomist and entomologist.

swamp (swomp), *n.* **1.** a tract of wet, spongy land; marshy ground. **2.** a tract of soft, wet ground having a growth of certain types of trees and other vegetation, but unfit for cultivation. —*v.t.* **3.** to flood or drench with water or the like. **4.** *Naut.* to sink or fill (a boat) with water. **5.** to plunge or cause to sink in or as if in a swamp. **6.** to overwhelm, esp. to overwhelm with an excess of something: *He swamped us with ideas and new plans.* **7.** to render helpless. **8.** to remove trees and underbrush from (a specific area), esp. to make or cleave a trail (often fol. by *out*). **9.** to trim (felled trees) into logs, as at a logging camp or sawmill. —*v.i.* **10.** to fill with water and sink, as a boat. **11.** to sink or be stuck in a swamp or something likened to a swamp. **12.** to be plunged into or overwhelmed with something, esp. something that keeps one busy, worried, etc.: *swamped with work.* [? < D *zwamp* fen; akin to SUMP and to MLG *swamp*, Dan *svamp*, Icel *svöppr* sponge] —**swamp′ish,** *adj.* —**swamp′less,** *adj.*

swamp′ an·drom′e·da (an drom′i də), a spreading shrub, *Lyonia ligustrina,* of the eastern U.S., having leafless, white flowers in terminal clusters. Also called **he-huckleberry, maleberry, privet andromeda.**

swamp′ azal′ea, an azalea, *Rhododendron viscosum,* of the eastern U.S., having fragrant, white to pink or sometimes red flowers. Also called **swamp honeysuckle, clammy azalea, clammy honeysuckle.**

swamp′ bay′. See **sweet bay** (def. 2).

swamp′ but′tonwood, the buttonbush.

swamp′ cab′bage. See **skunk cabbage.**

swamp′ cy′press. See **bald cypress.**

swamp′ dew′berry, a prostrate, vinelike plant, *Rubus hispidus,* of eastern North America, having bristly stems, a few small, white flowers, and sour fruit.

swamp·er (swom′pər), *n.* **1.** *Informal.* one who inhabits, works in, or is exceptionally familiar with swamps. **2.** a general handyman; common laborer; menial. **3.** one who trims felled trees into logs at a logging camp or sawmill. **4.** *Archaic.* the assistant driver of a mule train, camel caravan, or the like. [SWAMP + -ER[1]]

swamp′ fe′ver, *Pathol., Vet. Pathol.* **1.** leptospirosis. **2.** See **infectious anemia of horses. 3.** malaria.

swamp·fish (swomp′fish′), *n., pl.* **-fish·es,** (*esp. collectively*) **-fish.** a small fish, *Chologaster cornuta,* related to the cavefishes, found in the swamps and streams of the Atlantic coastal plain, having small but functional eyes and almost transparent skin. [SWAMP + FISH]

swamp′ hon′eysuckle, **1.** See **white swamp azalea. 2.** See **swamp azalea.**

swamp·land (swomp′land′), *n.* land or an area covered with swamps. [SWAMP + LAND]

swamp′ lau′rel, **1.** Also called **pale laurel.** a low shrub, *Kalmia polifolia,* of central and NW North America, having leaves that are white beneath, with the edges rolled under, and rose-colored flowers. **2.** See **sweet bay** (def. 2).

swamp′ lil′y, a lilylike herb, *Crinum americanum,* of the southeastern U.S., having clustered, white flowers.

swamp′ lo′cust. See **water locust.**

swamp′ loose′strife, a North American, woody, marsh herb, *Decodon verticillatus,* having clusters of magenta flowers in the leaf axils.

swamp′ mal′low, a rose mallow, *Hibiscus Moscheutos.*

swamp′ milk′weed, a coarse herb, *Asclepias incarnata,* found from eastern North America to Colorado, having ball-like clusters of rose-purple flowers, growing in swampy places. Also called **rose milkweed.**

swamp′ pink′, **1.** the swamp azalea, *Rhododendron viscosum.* **2.** the pinxter flower, *Rhododendron nudiflorum.* **3.** the grass pink, *Calopogon pulchellus.* **4.** a liliaceous herb, *Helonias bullata,* found in bogs of the eastern U.S., having fragrant pink flowers.

swamp′ priv′et, an oleaceous shrub, *Forestiera (Adelia) acuminata,* of the southern U.S.

swamp′ rose′, a shrub, *Rosa palustris,* of eastern North America, having pink flowers nearly two inches wide.

swamp′ spar′row, a North American finch, *Melospiza georgiana,* found in marshy areas.

swamp′ spleen′wort, a fern, *Athyrium pycnocarpon,* of eastern North America, having fronds from 18 to 24 inches long.

swamp′ sun′flower, a hairy, perennial herb, *Helianthus angustifolius,* of the swampy regions of the eastern U.S., having purple-centered, yellow-rayed flowers from two to three inches wide.

swamp′ tick′seed, a perennial herb, *Coreopsis rosea,* of the eastern U.S., having rose-pink flowers with yellow centers, growing in sunny, moist places.

swamp′ white′ oak′, an oak, *Quercus bicolor,* of eastern North America, yielding a hard, heavy wood used in shipbuilding, for making furniture, etc.

swamp·y (swom′pē), *adj.,* **swamp·i·er, swamp·i·est.** **1.** of the nature of, resembling, or abounding in swamps. **2.** found in swamps. [SWAMP + -Y[1]]

swa·my (swä′mē), *n., pl.* **-mies.** swami.

swan[1] (swon), *n.* **1.** any of several large, stately, aquatic birds of the subfamily *Anserinae,* of the family *Anatidae,* having a long, slender neck and usually pure-white plumage in the adult. Cf. **mute swan, trumpeter swan, whistling swan, whooper swan. 2.** a person or thing of unusual beauty, excellence, purity, or the like. **3.** a person who sings sweetly or a poet. **4.** (*cap.*) *Astron.* the constellation Cygnus. [ME, OE; c. G *Schwan,* Icel *svanr*] —**swan′like′,** *adj.*

Mute swan, *Cygnus olor* (Length 5 ft.)

swan[2] (swon), *v.i.* *U.S. Dial.* to swear: *I swan, that's a big one!* [? dial. (north) *I s'wan* I shall warrant; see WARRANT]

swan′ dive′, *Fancy Diving.* a forward dive in which the diver while in the air assumes a position with the arms outstretched at shoulder height and the legs straight and together, and enters the water with the arms stretched above the head. Also called, *esp. Brit.,* **swallow dive.**

Swa·nee (swon′ē, swô′nē), *n.* Suwannee.

swang (swang), *v.* *Archaic and Dial.* pt. of **swing**[1].

swan·herd (swon′hûrd′), *n.* one who tends swans. [ME; see SWAN[1], HERD[2]]

swank[1] (swangk), *n.* **1.** *Informal.* dashing smartness, as in dress or appearance; style. **2.** a swagger. —*adj.* **3.** *Informal.* pretentiously stylish. —*v.i.* **4.** to swagger in behavior; show off. [cf. Scot *swank* lively, prob. back formation from OE *swancor* lithe; akin to MD *swanc* supple, MHG *swanken* to sway]

swank[2] (swangk), *v.* a pt. of **swink.**

swank·y (swang′kē), *adj.,* **swank·i·er, swank·i·est.** *Informal.* **1.** swank. **2.** luxurious. [SWANK[1] + -Y[1]] —**swank′i·ly,** *adv.* —**swank′i·ness,** *n.*

Swan′ Lake′, The, a ballet (1876) by Tchaikovsky.

swan′ maid′en, any of a class of legendary maidens, in many Indo-European and Asian tales, capable of transforming themselves into swans, as by a robe or shift of swan's feathers or a magic ring or chain.

swan·ner·y (swon′ə rē), *n., pl.* **-ner·ies.** a place where swans are kept and raised. [SWAN[1] + -ERY]

Swan′ Riv′er dai′sy, a branching herb, *Brachycome iberidifolia,* of Australia, having blue, white, or rose-colored flowers.

Swan′ Riv′er everlast′ing, an herb, *Helipterum manglesi,* of Australia, having white or pink flowers.

swan's-down (swonz′doun′), *n.* **1.** the down or under plumage of a swan, used for trimming, powder puffs, etc. **2.** a fine, soft, thick woolen cloth. Also, **swans′down′.**

Swan·sea (swon′sē, -zē *for 1;* swon′sē *for 2*), *n.* **1.** a seaport in S Wales. 166,740 (1961). **2.** a town in SW Illinois. 3018 (1960).

swan′ shift′, *Teutonic Myth.* a garment of swan's feathers which, when worn, changes the wearer into a swan.

swan·skin (swon′skin′), *n.* **1.** the skin of a swan, with the feathers on. **2.** a twill-weave flannel, closely woven and napped, for work clothes. [SWAN[1] + SKIN]

swan's′ neck′, a shallow S-curve used in decorative work. Also, **swan′ neck′.**

swan's′ neck′ ped′iment, *Archit., Furniture.* a broken pediment, the outline of which consists of a pair of S-curves tangent to the cornice level at the ends of the pediment, rising to a pair of scrolls on either side of the center, where a finial often rises between the scrolls. Also, **swan′ neck′ ped′iment.**

Swan·son (swon′sən), *n.* **Gloria** (*Gloria Josephine May Swenson*), born 1899, U.S. actress.

swan′ song′, the last work, act, utterance, or achievement of a poet, group, period, etc., before death, retirement, disbanding, development into something else, etc.: *This building turned out to be the swan song of Victorian architecture.* [so called from the belief that the dying swan sings]

swan-up·ping (swon′up′ing), *n.* *Brit.* **1.** the taking up of young swans to mark them with nicks on the beak for identification by the owners. **2.** an annual expedition for this purpose on the Thames. [SWAN + *upping* (UP + -ING[1])]

swap (swop), *v.,* **swapped, swap·ping,** *n.* —*v.t.* **1.** to exchange, barter, or trade, as one thing for another: *He swapped his wrist watch for the radio.* —*v.i.* **2.** to make an exchange. —*n.* **3.** an exchange: *He got the radio in a swap.* Also, **swop.** [ME *swappe(n)* (to) strike, strike hands (in bargaining); c. dial. G *schwappen* to box (the ear)] —**swap′per,** *n.*

swa·raj (swə räj′), *n.* **1.** (in India) self-government. **2.** (*cap.*) (formerly, in British India) the political party supporting this principle over British rule. [< Skt *svarājya-,* equiv. to *sva-* self, one's own (cf. L *suus,* E SUICIDE) + *rāj-* king, ruler (cf. L *rex* king) + *-ya-* suffix making abstract n.] —**swa·raj′ism,** *n.* —**swa·raj′ist,** *n., adj.*

sward (swôrd), *n.* **1.** the grassy surface of land; turf. **2.** a stretch of turf; a growth of grass. —*v.t.* **3.** to cover with sward or turf. —*v.i.* **4.** to become covered with sward. [ME; OE *sweard* skin, rind; c. G *Schwarte* rind, OFris *swarde* scalp, MD *swaerde* skin]

sware (swâr), *v.* *Archaic.* pt. of **swear.**

swarf (swôrf), *n.* an accumulation of fine particles of metal or abrasive cut or ground from work by a machine tool or grinder. Also called **sludge.** [OE *(ge)swearf, gesweorf,* or ON *svarf,* akin to *sverfa* to file]

swarm[1] (swôrm), *n.* **1.** a body of honeybees which emigrate from a hive and fly off together, accompanied by a queen, to start a new colony. **2.** a body of bees settled together, as in a hive. **3.** a great number of things or persons, esp. in motion. **4.** *Biol.* a group or aggregation of free-floating or free-swimming cells or organisms. —*v.i.* **5.** to fly off together in a body from a hive to start a new colony, as bees. **6.** to move about, along, forth, etc., in great numbers, as things or persons. **7.** to congregate, hover, or occur in groups or multitudes; be exceedingly numerous, as in a place or area. **8.** (of a place) to be thronged or overrun; abound or teem (usually fol. by *with*): *The beach swarms with children on summer weekends.* **9.** *Biol.* to move or swim about in a swarm. —*v.t.* **10.** to swarm about, over, or in; throng; overrun. **11.** to produce a swarm of. [ME; OE *swearm;* c. G *Schwarm* swarm, Icel *svarmr* tumult] —**Syn. 3.** horde, host, mass. See **crowd. 7.** crowd, throng.

swarm[2] (swôrm), *v.t., v.i.* to climb by clasping with the legs and hands or arms and drawing oneself up; shin. [?]

swarm·er (swôr′mər), *n.* **1.** one of a number that swarm; one of a swarm. **2.** *Biol.* See **swarm spore.** [SWARM[1] + -ER[1]]

swarm′ spore′, *Biol.* any minute, motile, naked reproductive body.

swart (swôrt), *adj.* swarthy. Also, **swarth.** [ME; OE *sweart;* c. G *schwarz,* Icel *svatr,* Goth *swarts;* akin to L *sordes* filth] —**swart′ness,** *n.*

Swart (swôrt), *n.* **Charles Rob·berts** (rob′ərts), born 1894, South African statesman: president since 1961.

swarth[1] (swôrth), *n.* swart. [unexplained var.] —**swarth′ness,** *n.*

swarth[2] (swôrth), *n.* sward; greensward. [ME; OE *swearth,* var. of *sweard* skin, rind; see SWARD]

swarth[3] (swôrth), *adj.* *Archaic.* swarthy. [unexplained var. of SWART]

Swarth·more (swôrth′môr, -môr; *local* swoth′-), *n.* a town in SE Pennsylvania. 5753 (1960).

Swar·thout (swôr′thout), *n.* **Gladys,** born 1904, U.S. soprano.

swarth·y (swôr′thē, -thē), *adj.,* **swarth·i·er, swarth·i·est.** (of the skin, complexion, etc.) dark-colored: *a face made swarthy by the tropical sun; a short, swarthy man.* [unexplained var. of *swarty* (SWART + -Y[1])] —**swarth′i·ly,** *adv.* —**swarth′i·ness,** *n.* —**Syn.** See **dusky.**

Swartz′ Creek′ (swôrts), a town in central Michigan. 3006 (1960).

swartz·ite (swôrt′sīt), *n.* a mineral, $CaMg(UO_2)(CO_3)_3 \cdot 12H_2O$, occurring in green crystals: an ore of uranium. [named after C. K. *Swartz* (1861–1949), American geologist]

swash (swosh, swôsh), *v.i.* **1.** to splash, as things in water, or as water does: *Waves were swashing against the piers.* **2.** to dash around, as things in violent motion. **3.** to swagger. —*v.t.* **4.** to dash or cast violently, esp. to dash (water or other liquid) around, down, etc. —*n.* **5.** a swashing blow, stroke, or movement, or the sound of it. **6.** the surging or dashing, sometimes violent, of water, waves, etc. **7.** the sound made by such dashing: *the thunderous swash of the waves.* **8.** the ground over which water washes. **9.** a channel of water through or behind a sandbank. **10.** *Print.* an extending ornamental flourish, as on letters of certain fonts of italic or cursive type. —*adj.* **11.** *Print.* noting or pertaining to a character having a swash: *a swash letter.* [imit.] —**swash′ing·ly,** *adv.*

swash·buck·ler (swosh′buk′lər, swôsh′-), *n.* a swaggering swordsman, soldier, or adventurer; daredevil. Also, **swash′er.** [SWASH + BUCKLER]

swash·buck·ling (swosh′buk′ling, swôsh′-), *adj.* **1.** characteristic of or behaving in the manner of a swashbuckler. —*n.* **2.** the activities, deeds, or adventures of a swashbuckler. Also, **swash′buck′ler·ing.** [SWASHBUCKL(ER) + -ING[2], -ING[1]]

swash′ bulk′head, *Naut.* a partial bulkhead in a tanker, for decreasing the surge of a liquid cargo. Also called **swash plate.**

swash′ let′ter, an ornamental italic capital letter having a flourish extending beyond the body of the type.

swash′ plate′, **1.** *Mach.* an inclined circular plate on a rotating shaft for transferring force and motion to or from parts reciprocating in a direction parallel to the axis of shaft rotation. **2.** *Naut.* See **swash bulkhead.**

swas·ti·ka (swos′ti kə *or, esp. Brit.,* swas′-), *n.* **1.** a figure used as a symbol or an ornament in the Old World and in America since prehistoric times, consisting of a cross with arms of equal length, each arm having a continuation at right angles, and all four continuations extending either clockwise or counterclockwise. **2.** this figure with clockwise arms as the official emblem of the Nazi party and the Third Reich. [< Skt *svastika-* good luck sign, equiv. to *su-* good, well (c. Gk *eu-* EU-) + *as-* be + *ti-* abstract n. suffix + *-ka-* adj. suffix] —**swas′ti·kaed,** *adj.*

A B

Swastikas
A, Oriental and American Indian;
B, Nazi

swat[1] (swot), *v.,* **swat·ted, swat·ting,** *n.* —*v.t.* **1.** to hit; slap; smack. **2.** *Baseball.* to hit (a ball) a long distance. —*n.* **3.** a smart blow; slap; smack. **4.** *Baseball.* a long, usually extra-base, hit. Also, **swot.** [orig. var. of SQUAT] —**swat′ter,** *n.*

swat[2] (swot), *v.* *Dial.* pt. and pp. of **sweat.**

swat[3] (swot), *v.i.,* **swat·ted, swat·ting,** *n.* *Brit. Slang.* swot[2].

Swat (swät), *n.* **1.** a former princely state in NW India; now a part of Pakistan, in the province of West Pakistan. **2.** Also, **Swati.** a Muslim inhabitant of Swat.

swatch (swoch), *n.* **1.** a sample of cloth or other material. **2.** a sample, patch, or characteristic specimen of anything. [? akin to SWITCH]

swath (swoth, swôth), *n.* **1.** the space covered by the stroke of a scythe or the cut of a mowing machine. **2.** the piece or strip so cut. **3.** a line or ridge of grass, grain, or the like, cut and thrown together by a scythe or mowing machine. **4.** a strip, belt, or long and relatively narrow extent of anything. **5. cut a swath,** to make a pretentious display; attract notice: *The young doctor from the city cut a swath in the small community.* Also, **swathe.** [ME; OE *swæth* footprint; c. G *Schwade*]

swathe[1] (swoth, swāth), *v.,* **swathed, swath·ing,** *n.* —*v.t.* **1.** to wrap, bind, or swaddle with bands of some material; wrap up closely or fully. **2.** to bandage. **3.** to enfold or envelop, as wrappings do. **4.** to wrap (cloth, rope, etc.) around something. —*n.* **5.** a band of linen or the like in which something is wrapped; wrapping; bandage. [ME; late OE *swathian,* deriv. of OE *swæth bandage (in *swathium,* dat. pl.); c. Icel *svatha*] —**swath′a·ble, swathe′a·ble,** *adj.* —**swath′er,** *n.*

swathe[2] (swoth, swāth), *n.* swath.

Swa·ti (swä′tē), *n., pl.* **-tis,** (*esp. collectively*) **-ti.** Swat (def. 2).

Swa·tow (swä′tou′), *n.* a seaport in E Kwantung, in SE China. 280,400 (est. 1957).

swats (swats), *n.* (*construed as pl.*) *Scot.* sweet, new beer or ale. [cf. OE *swatan* beer (pl.)]

swat·ter (swä′tər, swô′-), *n.* **1.** one who or that which swats. **2.** See **fly swatter.** [SWAT[1] + -ER[1]]

S wave, a transverse earthquake wave that travels through the interior of the earth and is usually the second conspicuous wave to reach a seismograph. Also called **secondary wave.** Cf. **L wave, P wave.**

sway (swā), *v.i.* **1.** to move or swing to and fro, as something fixed at one end or resting on a support. **2.** to move or incline to one side or in a particular direction. **3.** to incline in opinion, sympathy, tendency, etc.: *He swayed toward conservatism.* **4.** to fluctuate or vacillate, as in opinion: *Her ideas swayed this way and that.* **5.** to wield power; exercise rule. —*v.t.* **6.** to cause to move to and fro or to incline from side to side. **7.** to cause to move to one side or in a particular direction. **8.** *Naut.* to hoist or raise (a yard, topmast, or the like) (usually fol. by *up*). **9.** to cause to fluctuate or vacillate. **10.** to cause (the mind, emotions, etc., or a person) to incline or turn in a specified way; influence. **11.** to cause to swerve, as from a purpose or a course of action: *He swayed them from their plan.* **12.** to dominate; direct. **13.** *Archaic.* **a.** to wield, as a weapon or scepter. **b.** to rule; govern. —*n.* **14.** the act of swaying; swaying move-

ment. **15.** rule; dominion: *He held all Asia in his sway.* **16.** dominating power or influence: *Many voters were under his sway.* [ME *sweye(n)* < Scand; cf. Icel *sveigja* to sway; akin to MLG *swājen* to sway] —**sway′a·ble,** *adj.* —**sway′er,** *n.* —**sway′ful,** *adj.* —**sway′ing·ly,** *adv.*
—**Syn. 1.** wave. See **swing**[1]. **3.** lean, bend, tend. **5.** reign, govern. **12.** control. **15.** sovereignty, authority, mastery. **16.** control, predominance, ascendancy.

sway-back (swā′bak′), *Vet. Pathol.* —*n.* Also, **sway′back′. 1.** an excessive downward curvature of the spinal column in the dorsal region, esp. of horses. **2.** Also called **enzootic ataxia.** a disease affecting the nerve tissue of young lambs, caused by a lack of copper in the diet of the ewes which bear them and characterized by a lack of muscular coordination. —*adj.* **3.** sway-backed. [SWAY + BACK[1]]

sway-backed (swā′bakt′), *adj. Vet. Pathol.* having the back sagged to an unusual degree; having a sway-back. Also, **sway-back.**

swayed (swād), *adj. Vet. Pathol.* sway-backed. [SWAY + -ED[2]]

Swa·zi (swä′zē), *n., pl.* **-zis,** (*esp. collectively*) **-zi.** a member of a Bantu tribe of Zulu descent found in SE Africa.

Swa·zi·land (swä′zē land′), *n.* a kingdom in SE Africa between S Mozambique and SE Transvaal in the Union of South Africa; formerly a British protectorate. 389,492 (1966); 6704 sq. mi. *Cap.:* Mbabane.

SWbS, See **southwest by south.**

SWbW, See **southwest by west.**

sweal (swēl), *v.i., v.t. Dial.* **1.** to melt, as a candle; waste away. **2.** to burn. [ME *swel(en),* OE *swǣlan* (trans.), *swelan* (intrans.), to burn; c. G *schwälen,* Icel *svæla* to burn out; akin to OE *swol* heat]

swear (swâr), *v.,* **swore** or (*Archaic*) **sware; sworn; swear·ing.** —*v.i.* **1.** to make a solemn declaration with an appeal to God or some superhuman being in confirmation of what is declared; make affirmation in a solemn manner by some sacred being or object, as the Deity or the Bible. **2.** to engage, attest, assert, or promise on oath or in a solemn manner; vow; bind oneself by oath (usually fol. by *to*). **3.** to give evidence or make any statement on oath or by solemn declaration (usually fol. by *to*). **4.** to use profane oaths or language, as in imprecation or anger or for mere emphasis: *Don't swear in front of the children.* —*v.t.* **5.** to declare, affirm, attest, etc., by swearing by a deity, some sacred object, etc. **6.** to affirm, assert, or say with solemn earnestness or great emphasis. **7.** to promise or undertake on oath or in a solemn manner; vow. **8.** to testify or state on oath or by solemn declaration; make oath to (something stated or alleged): *He swore it on the witness stand.* **9.** to take (an oath), as in order to give solemnity or force to a declaration, promise, etc. **10.** to administer an oath to; bind by an oath (usually fol. by *to*): *to swear someone to secrecy.* **11. swear by, a.** to name (a sacred being or thing) as one's witness or guarantee in swearing. **b.** *Informal.* to have confidence in; rely on: *He swears by his dentist.* **c.** to have certain knowledge of: *I thought I saw him leaving, but I couldn't swear by it.* **12. swear in,** to admit to office or service by administering an oath: *A new president will be sworn in today.* **13. swear off,** *Informal.* to promise or resolve to give up something, esp. intoxicating beverages: *He has sworn off drinking for Lent.* **14. swear out,** to secure (a warrant for arrest) by making an accusation under oath. [ME *swere(n),* OE *swerian;* G *schwören,* Icel *sverja;* akin to Goth *swaran* to swear; see ANSWER] —**swear′er,** *n.* —**swear′ing·ly,** *adv.*
—**Syn. 1.** declare, affirm, avow. **3.** depose, testify. **4.** imprecate. See **curse.**

swear·word (swâr′wûrd′), *n.* a word used in swearing or cursing; a profane or obscene word. [SWEAR + WORD]

sweat (swet), *v.,* **sweat** or **sweat·ed, sweat·ing,** *n.* —*v.i.* **1.** to excrete watery fluid through the pores of the skin, as from heat, exertion, etc.; perspire, esp. freely or profusely. **2.** to exude moisture, as green plants piled in a heap. **3.** to gather moisture from the surrounding air by condensation. **4.** (of moisture or liquid) to ooze or be exuded. **5.** *Informal.* to work hard. **6.** *Informal.* to experience distress, as from anxiety, vexation, or impatience. **7.** (of tobacco) to ferment. **8.** *Obs.* to suffer punishment.
—*v.t.* **9.** to excrete (perspiration, moisture, etc.) through the pores of the skin. **10.** to exude in drops or small particles: *The drying figs sweat tiny drops of moisture.* **11.** to send forth or get rid of with or like perspiration (often fol. by *out* or *off*). **12.** to wet or stain with perspiration. **13.** to cause (a person, a horse, etc.) to perspire. **14.** to cause to exude moisture, esp. as a step in some industrial process of treating or preparing: *to sweat tobacco leaves.* **15.** to earn, produce, or obtain (a result, promotion, compliment, etc.) by hard work. **16.** to cause to lose (weight) as by perspiring or hard work (often fol. by *off* or *out*): *The hard week's work sweat five pounds off him.* **17.** to cause, force, or bring pressure on (a person, an animal, etc.) to work hard. **18.** to employ (workers) at low wages, for long hours, or under other unfavorable conditions. **19.** *Slang.* **a.** to obtain or extort (money) from someone. **b.** to extort money from; fleece. **20.** *Slang.* to subject to severe questioning; give the third degree to. **21.** *Metall.* **a.** to heat (an alloy) in order to remove a constituent melting at a lower temperature than the alloy as a whole. **b.** to heat (solder or the like) until it melts. **c.** to join (metal objects) by heating them and pressing them together, usually with some solder between them. **22.** to remove bits of metal from (gold coins) by shaking them against one another, as in a bag. Cf. **clip**[1] (def. 3). **23.** to cause (tobacco) to ferment. **24. sweat blood,** *Slang.* **a.** to be under a strain; work strenuously. **b.** to wait anxiously; worry: *He was sweating blood while she was in the operating room.* **25. sweat** (something) **out,** *Slang.* **a.** to wait until the end of; endure. **b.** to work arduously at or toward (a goal, solution, etc.): *The director sweated out a camera angle with the cinematographer.*
—*n.* **26.** the process of sweating or perspiring, as from heat, exertion, or anxiety. **27.** that which is secreted from sweat glands; product of sweating. **28.** a state or a spell of sweating. **29.** *Informal.* hard work. **30.** *Informal.* a state of anxiety or impatience. **31.** a process of inducing sweating or perspiration, or of being sweated, as in medical or other special treatment. **32.** moisture or liquid matter exuded from something or gathered on a surface in drops or small particles. **33.** an exuding of moisture, as by a substance. **34.** an inducing of such exudation, as in some industrial process. **35.** a run given to a horse for exercise, as before a race. [ME *swete(n),* OE *swǣtan* to sweat, deriv. of *swāt* sweat; c. D *zweet,* G *Schweiss,* Icel *sveiti,* Skt *svedas;* akin to L *sūdor,* Gk *hidrōs*] —**sweat′less,** *adj.*
—**Syn. 27.** See **perspiration.**

sweat·band (swet′band′), *n.* a band lining the bottom of the inside of the crown of a hat or cap to protect it against sweat from the head. [SWEAT + BAND[2]]

sweat′ bee′, any of several bees of the family *Halictidae* that are attracted by perspiration.

sweat·box (swet′boks′), *n.* **1.** a device for sweating tobacco leaves, figs, raisins, etc. **2.** *Slang.* a box or cell in which a prisoner is punished or given the third degree. [SWEAT + BOX[1]]

sweat·ed (swet′id), *adj.* **1.** made by underpaid workers. **2.** underpaid and overworked. **3.** having poor working conditions. [SWEAT + -ED[2]]

sweat·er (swet′ər), *n.* **1.** a knitted jacket or jersey, in pullover or cardigan style, with or without sleeves, worn during athletic exercise, for warmth, or otherwise, as for casual wear with slacks or a skirt. **2.** one who or that which sweats. **3.** an employer who underpays and overworks employees. [SWEAT + -ER[1]]

sweat′er girl′, *Slang.* a girl or young woman with a shapely bosom, esp. one who wears tight sweaters to emphasize her bosom.

sweat′ gland′, *Anat.* one of the minute, coiled, tubular glands of the skin that secrete sweat.

sweat′ing sick′ness, a febrile epidemic disease that appeared in the 15th and 16th centuries: characterized by profuse sweating and frequently fatal in a few hours.

sweat′ing sys′tem, the practice of employing workers in sweatshops.

sweat′ pants′, loose-fitting trousers with close-fitting or elastic cuffs and a drawstring at the waist, worn esp. by athletes to prevent chilling or, while exercising, to induce sweating.

sweat′ shirt′, a loose, long-sleeved, collarless pullover, sometimes with close-fitting or elastic cuffs and a drawstring at the waist, worn esp. by athletes to prevent chilling or, while exercising, to induce sweating.

sweat·shop (swet′shop′), *n.* a shop employing workers at low wages, for long hours, and under unsanitary or otherwise unfavorable conditions. [SWEAT + SHOP]

sweat′ suit′, a set of garments consisting of sweat pants and a sweat shirt.

sweat·weed (swet′wēd′), *n.* See **marsh mallow.** [SWEAT + WEED[1]]

sweat·y (swet′ē), *adj.,* **sweat·i·er, sweat·i·est. 1.** covered, moist, or stained with sweat. **2.** causing sweat. **3.** laborious. [late ME *swety.* See SWEAT, -Y[1]] —**sweat′i·ly,** *adv.* —**sweat′i·ness,** *n.*

Swed., 1. Sweden. **2.** Swedish.

Swede (swēd), *n.* **1.** a native or inhabitant of Sweden. **2.** (*often l.c.*) *Chiefly Brit.* a rutabaga. [< MD or MLG; c. G *Schwede;* cf. OE *Swēon* (pl.), Icel *Svēar, Svíar,* L *Suīones*]

Swe·den (swēd′ən), *n.* a kingdom in N Europe, in the E part of the Scandinavian peninsula. 7,777,777 (est. 1966); 173,394 sq. mi. *Cap.:* Stockholm. Swedish, **Sverige.**

Swe·den·borg (swēd′ən bôrg′; *Sw.* svād′ən bôr′yə), *n.* **E·ma·nu·el** (i man′yo͞o əl; *Sw.* e mä′no͞o əl), (*Emanuel Swedberg*), 1688–1772, Swedish scientist and philosopher.

Swe·den·bor·gi·an (swēd′ən bôr′jē ən, -gē-), *adj.* **1.** pertaining to Emanual Swedenborg, to his religious doctrines, or to the body of followers adhering to these doctrines and constituting the Church of the New Jerusalem, or New Church. —*n.* **2.** a believer in the religious doctrines of Swedenborg. [SWEDENBORG + -IAN] —**Swe′den·bor′gi·an·ism, Swe′den·borg′ism,** *n.*

Swed·ish (swē′dish), *adj.* **1.** of or pertaining to Sweden, its inhabitants, or their language. —*n.* **2.** the people of Sweden collectively. **3.** a Germanic language, the language of Sweden and parts of Finland, closely related to Danish and Norwegian. [SWEDE + -ISH[1]]

Swed′ish massage′, a massage utilizing Swedish movements.

Swed′ish mile′, a unit of length equal to 10 kilometers.

Swed′ish move′ments, a system of muscular exercises for hygienic or therapeutic purposes.

Swed′ish Night′ingale, nickname of Jenny Lind.

Swed′ish put′ty, a waterproof patching compound consisting of spackle mixed with spar varnish.

Swed′ish tur′nip, rutabaga. [so called because introduced (into Great Britain) from Sweden]

Swee·linck (svā′lingk), *n.* **Jan Pie·ters** (yän pē′tərs) or **Jan Pie·ters·zoon** (yän pē′tər sōn′), 1562–1621, Dutch organist and composer. Also, **Swelinck.**

Swee′ney Among′ the Night′ingales (swē′nē), a poem (1919) by T. S. Eliot.

swee·ny (swē′nē), *n. Vet. Pathol.* atrophy of the shoulder muscles in horses. Also, **swinney.** [cf. dial. G *Schweine,* PaG *Schwinne* atrophy, OE *swindan* to pine away, disappear]

Swee·ny (swē′nē), *n.* a town in S Texas. 3087 (1960).

sweep[1] (swēp), *v.,* **swept, sweep·ing,** *n.* —*v.t.* **1.** to move or remove (dust, dirt, etc.) by passing a broom, brush, or the like, through, over, or back and forth over the surface occupied (often fol. by *away, out,* etc.): *to sweep away dust.* **2.** to clear or clean (a floor, room, chimney, etc.) of dirt, litter, or the like, by means of a broom or brush. **3.** to move, bring, take, etc., by or as by a steady, driving stroke or a series of short strokes or with continuous, forcible actions: *The wind swept the snow into drifts.* **4.** to pass or draw (something) over a surface, or about, along, etc., with a steady, continuous stroke or movement: *The painter swept a brush over his canvas.* **5.** to make (a path, opening, etc.) by clearing a space with or as with a broom: *to sweep a path through fallen leaves.* **6.** to clear (a surface, place, etc.) of something on or in it: *to sweep a sea of enemy ships.* **7.** to pass over (a surface, region, etc.) with a steady, driving movement or unimpeded course, as winds, floods, etc.: *sandstorms sweeping the plains.* **8.** to pass the gaze over (a region, area, etc.): *His gaze swept the countryside.* **9.** to direct (the eyes, gaze, etc.) over a region, surface, or the like: *He swept his eyes over the countryside.* **10.** to win a complete or overwhelming victory in (a contest): *Johnson swept the presidential election of 1964.* **11.** to win (every game, round, hand, etc., of a series of contests): *The Yanks swept the three-game series.* **12.** *Music.* **a.** to pass the fingers or bow over (a musical instrument, its strings or keys, etc.), as in playing. **b.** to bring forth (music) thus.
—*v.i.* **13.** to sweep a floor, room, etc., with or as with a broom: *A new broom sweeps clean.* **14.** to move steadily and strongly or swiftly (usually fol. by *along, down, by, into,* etc.). **15.** to pass in a swift but stately manner, as a person or a funeral cortege: *Proudly, she swept from the room.* **16.** to trail, as garments. **17.** to move or pass in a continuous course, esp. a wide curve or circuit: *His glance swept around the room.* **18.** to extend in a continuous or curving stretch, as a road, a shore, fields, etc.: *The road sweeps by the dunes.* **19.** to conduct an underwater search by towing a drag under the surface of the water, as for submarine mines, a lost anchor, or the like. **20.** *Aeron.* (of an airfoil or its leading or trailing edge) to project from the fuselage at an angle rearward or forward of a line perpendicular to the longitudinal axis of the aircraft.
—*n.* **21.** the act of sweeping, esp. a moving, removing, clearing, etc., by or as if by the use of a broom: *to get rid of all bad habits in one clean sweep.* **22.** the steady, driving motion or swift onward course of something moving with force or unimpeded: *the sweep of the wind and the waves.* **23.** a trailing movement, as of garments. **24.** a swinging or curving movement or stroke, as of the arm, a weapon, an oar, etc.: *a sweep of a scythe.* **25.** reach, range, or compass, as of something sweeping about: *the sweep of a road about a marsh.* **26.** a continuous extent or stretch: *a broad sweep of sand.* **27.** a curving, esp. widely or gently curving, line, form, part, or mass. **28.** matter removed or gathered by sweeping. **29.** a leverlike device for raising or lowering a bucket in a well, consisting essentially of a long pole pivoted on an upright post. **30.** a large oar used in small vessels, sometimes to assist the rudder in turning the vessel but usually to propel the craft. **31.** an overwhelming victory in a contest. **32.** a winning of all the games, rounds, hands, prizes, etc., in a contest or series of contests by one person, team, group, etc.: *The Japanese made a sweep of the Olympic judo contests.* **33.** *Football.* See **end run. 34.** one of the sails of a windmill. **35.** *Foundry.* a tool rotated within a sand mold to form cylindrical walls. **36.** *Agric.* any of the detachable triangular blades on a cultivator. **37.** *Chiefly Brit.* one employed to clean by sweeping, esp. a chimney sweeper. **38.** *Cards.* **a.** *Whist.* the winning of all the tricks in a hand. Cf. **slam**[2] (def. 1). **b.** *Casino.* a pairing or combining, and hence taking, of all the cards on the board. **39.** *Physics.* an irreversible process tending towards thermal equilibrium. [ME *swep(en);* cf. OE *geswēpa* sweepings, deriv. of *swāp(an)* (to) sweep; c. G *schweifen*] —**sweep′a·ble,** *adj.*

sweep[2] (swēp), *n. Slang.* a sweepstakes. Also, **sweeps.** [by shortening]

sweep·back (swēp′bak′), *n. Aeron.* the shape of, or the angle formed by, an airplane wing or other airfoil the leading or trailing edge of which slopes backward from the fuselage. [n. use of v. phrase *sweep back*]

sweep′ check′, *Ice Hockey.* a maneuver for depriving an opponent of the puck that consists of seizing it in the crook of one's stick and pulling it away with a movement in a long arc, the stick being held level or nearly level with the ice. Cf. **check** (def. 40).

sweep·er (swē′pər), *n.* **1.** one who or that which sweeps. **2.** See **carpet sweeper. 3.** a janitor. **4.** any of several fishes of the family *Pempheridae,* found in tropical seas, having an oblong, compressed body. [ME; see SWEEP[1], -ER[1]]

sweep′ hand′, *Horol.* a hand, usually a second hand, centrally mounted with the minute and hour hands of a timepiece and reaching to the edge of the dial.

sweep·ing (swē′ping), *adj.* **1.** of wide range or scope. **2.** moving or passing about over a wide area: *a sweeping glance.* **3.** moving, driving, or passing steadily and forcibly on. **4.** (of the outcome of a contest) decisive; overwhelming; complete: *a sweeping victory.* —*n.* **5.** the act of one who or that which sweeps. **6. sweepings,** matter swept out or up, as dust, refuse, etc.: *Put the sweepings in the dustpan.* [late ME (n.); see SWEEP[1], -ING[2], -ING[1]] —**sweep′ing·ly,** *adv.* —**sweep′ing·ness,** *n.*

sweep′ing score′, *Curling.* a line at each end of the rink parallel to the foot score and extending through the center of the tee.

sweeps (swēps), *n.* sweep[2].

sweep-sec·ond (swēp′sek′ənd), *n.* (on a timepiece) a second hand that is a sweep hand.

sweep·stake (swēp′stāk′), *n.* a sweepstakes.

sweep·stakes (swēp′stāks′), *n.* (*construed as sing. or pl.*) **1.** a race or other contest for which the prize consists of the stakes contributed by the various competitors. **2.** the prize itself. **3.** a lottery in which winning tickets are selected at random, as by a drawing, each winning-ticket number then being matched to one of the horses nominated for or entered in a specific race, and the amounts paid the winners being determined by the finishing order of the horses that run: *the Irish Sweepstakes; New Hampshire has a sweepstakes.* **4.** any gambling transaction in which each of a number of persons contributes a stake, and the stakes are awarded to one or several winners. [SWEEP[1] + STAKE[2] + -S[3]]

sweep·y (swē′pē), *adj.,* **sweep·i·er, sweep·i·est.** sweeping. [SWEEP[1] + -Y[1]]

sweer (swēr), *adj. Scot. and North Eng.* **1.** slothful; indolent. **2.** unwilling; reluctant. [ME *swer(e)*, OE *swǣr(e)* heavy, sluggish; c. G *schwer*]

sweet (swēt), *adj.* **1.** having the taste or flavor characteristic of sugar, honey, etc. **2.** producing one of the four basic taste sensations; not bitter, sour, or salt. **3.** not rancid or stale; fresh: *This milk is still sweet.* **4.** not salt or salted: *sweet butter.* **5.** pleasing to the ear; making a delicate, pleasant, or agreeable sound; musical. **6.** pleasing or fresh to the smell; fragrant; perfumed. **7.** pleasing or agreeable; yielding pleasure or enjoyment; delightful. **8.** pleasant in disposition or manners; amiable; kind or gracious, as a person, action, etc. **9.** dear; beloved; precious. **10.** easily managed; done or effected without effort. **11.** (of wine) not dry; containing unfermented, natural sugar. **12.** (of a cocktail) made with a greater proportion of vermouth than usual: *a sweet Manhattan.* **13.** sentimental, cloying, or unrealistic: *Those paintings of little kittens with pink bows are so sweet they're sickening.* **14.** (of air) fresh; free from odor, staleness, excess humidity, noxious gases, etc. **15.** free from acidity or sourness, as soil. **16.** *Chem.* **a.** devoid of corrosive or acidic substances. **b.** (of gasoline or the like) containing no sulfur compounds. **17.** (of jazz or big band music) performed with a regular beat, moderate tempo, lack of improvisation, and an emphasis on warm tone and clearly outlined melody. **18. sweet on,** *Informal.* infatuated with; in love with: *Gossip has it that the leading man is sweet on one of the chorus girls.* —*adv.* **19.** in a sweet manner; sweetly. —*n.* **20.** a sweet flavor, smell, or sound; sweetness. **21.** that which is sweet or causes or gives a sweet flavor, smell, or sound. **22. sweets,** *Informal.* **a.** candied sweet potatoes. **b.** (in direct address) sweetheart. **23. sweets,** pie, cake, candy, and other foods high in sugar content. **24.** *Chiefly Brit.* **a.** a piece of candy; sweetmeat or bonbon. **b.** a sweet dish or dessert, as a pudding or tart. **25.** something pleasant to the mind or feelings. **26.** a beloved person. **27.** (in direct address) darling; sweetheart. [ME, OE *swēte*; c. OS *swōti*, OHG *swuozi*, G *süss*; akin to Goth *suts*, D *zoet*, Icel *sætr*, Gk *hēdýs* sweet, L *suād(us)* persuasive, *suāvis* sweet] —**sweet′less,** *adj.* —**sweet′like′,** *adj.* —**sweet′ly,** *adv.* —**sweet′ness,** *n.*
—**Syn. 1.** sugary, honeyed, syrupy, saccharine. **3.** clean, new. **5.** melodious, mellifluous, harmonious, dulcet. **6.** redolent, aromatic, scented. **7.** pleasant, enjoyable. **8.** winning, lovable, charming. —**Ant. 1.** sour.

Sweet (swēt), *n.* **Henry,** 1845–1912, English philologist and linguist.

sweet′ al′mond oil′. See **almond oil** (def. 1).

sweet′ alys′sum, a cruciferous garden plant, *Lobularia maritima,* having small, white or violet flowers.

sweet-and-sour (swēt′ᵊn sour′, -sou′ər), *adj.* **1.** cooked with sugar and vinegar or lemon juice, and often with additional seasoning: *sweet-and-sour raisin sauce.* **2.** (in Oriental cooking) prepared with a seasoning of sugar, vinegar, soy sauce, garlic, cornstarch, and pepper: *sweet-and-sour pork.*

sweet′ bas′il. See under **basil.**

sweet′ bay′, **1.** the bay, or European laurel. **2.** Also called **beaver-tree, swamp bay, swamp laurel, white bay.** an American magnolia, *Magnolia virginiana,* having fragrant, white, globular flowers, common on the Atlantic coast.

sweet·bells (swēt′belz′), *n., pl.* **-bells.** (*construed as pl.*) See **pepper bush.** [SWEET + BELL¹ + -S³]

sweet′ birch′ oil′. See **methyl salicylate.**

sweet·bread (swēt′bred′), *n.* **1.** Also called **stomach sweetbread.** the pancreas of an animal, esp. a calf or a lamb, used for food. **2.** Also called **neck sweetbread, throat sweetbread.** the thymus gland of such an animal, used for food. [SWEET + BREAD]

sweet·bri·er (swēt′brī′ər), *n.* a rose, *Rosa Eglanteria,* of Europe and central Asia, having a tall stem, stout, hooked prickles often mixed with bristles, and single, pink flowers. Also, **sweet′bri′ar.** [SWEET + BRIER¹]

sweet′ cal′amus. See **sweet flag.**

sweet′ cassa′va. See under **cassava** (def. 1).

sweet′ cher′ry, **1.** a cherry, *Prunus avium,* characterized by reddish-brown bark and the pyramidal manner of growth. **2.** the red, purplish-black, or yellow, edible, sweet fruit of this tree.

sweet′ cic′ely, any of several umbelliferous plants, as a European herb, *Myrrhis odorata,* used as a potherb, or certain North American herbs of the genus *Osmorhiza.*

sweet′ ci′der. See under **cider.**

sweet′ clo′ver, melilot.

sweet′ colts′foot. See **winter heliotrope.**

sweet′ cone′flower, a perennial herb, *Rudbeckia subtomentosa,* of the midwestern U.S., having yellow flowers with brown centers.

sweet′ corn′, **1.** any of several varieties of corn, esp. *Zea Mays saccharata,* the grain or kernels of which are sweet and suitable for eating. **2.** the upright and tender ears of corn, esp. when used as a table vegetable; green corn.

sweet′ crab′ ap′ple. See **American crab.**

sweet·en (swēt′ᵊn), *v.t.* **1.** to make sweet, as by adding sugar. **2.** to make mild or kind; soften. **3.** to lessen the acridity or pungency of (a food) by prolonged cooking. **4.** to reduce the saltiness of (a food or dish) by diluting with water, milk, or other liquid. **5.** to make (the breath, room air, etc.) sweet or fresh, as with a mouth wash, spray, etc. **6.** to make (the stomach, soil, etc.) less acidic, as by taking certain preparations, spreading chemicals, etc. **7.** *Informal.* **a.** to enhance the value of (loan collateral) by including additional or especially valuable securities. **b.** to enhance the value or attractiveness of (any proposition, holding, etc.). **8.** *Poker Slang.* to increase (a pot) by adding stakes before opening. —*v.i.* **9.** to become sweet or sweeter. [SWEET + -EN¹] —**sweet′en·er,** *n.*

sweet·en·ing (swēt′ning, swēt′ning), *n.* **1.** something that sweetens food, beverages, etc., as sugar, saccharine, etc. **2.** the process of causing something to be or become sweet. [SWEETEN + -ING¹]

sweet′ false′ cam′omile, camomile (def. 2).

sweet′ fern′, a small, North American shrub, *Comptonia peregrina* (*Myrica asplenifolia*), having aromatic, fernlike leaves.

sweet′ flag′, an araceous plant, *Acorus Calamus,* having long, sword-shaped leaves and a pungent, aromatic rootstock. Also called **sweet calamus.**

sweet′ gale′, a shrub, *Myrica Gale,* growing in marshy places and having an aromatic odor. Also called **bog myrtle, moor myrtle.**

sweet′ grass′, **1.** any of several fragrant plants, as manna grass or the sweet flag. **2.** See **vanilla grass.**

sweet′ gum′, **1.** the American liquidambar, *Liquidambar Styraciflua.* **2.** the hard reddish-brown wood of this tree, used for making furniture. **3.** the amber balsam exuded by this tree, used in the manufacture of perfumes and medicines. Also called **red gum, copalm** (for defs. 1, 2).

sweet·heart (swēt′härt′), *n.* **1.** either of a pair of lovers in relation to the other. **2.** (often used as a term of endearment or in direct address) a beloved person. **3.** *Informal.* a generous, friendly, usually extroverted, person. [ME *swete herte.* See SWEET, HEART]

sweet′heart con′tract, *U.S. Slang.* a substandard contract made through collusion between dishonest management and labor representatives to pay low wages to union workers. Also called **sweet′heart agree′ment.**

Sweet′ Home′, a town in W Oregon. 3353 (1960).

sweet·ie (swē′tē), *n.* **1.** *Informal.* sweetheart (defs. 1, 2). **2.** Usually, **sweeties.** *Brit.* candy; sweets. [SWEET + -IE]

sweet·ing (swē′ting), *n.* **1.** a sweet variety of apple. **2.** *Archaic.* sweetheart. [ME *sweting.* See SWEET, -ING¹]

sweet·ish (swē′tish), *adj.* somewhat sweet. [SWEET + -ISH¹] —**sweet′ish·ly,** *adv.* —**sweet′ish·ness,** *n.*

sweet·leaf (swēt′lēf′), *n., pl.* **-leaves.** a shrub or small tree, *Symplocos tinctoria,* of the eastern coast of the U.S., having yellowish, fragrant flowers and orange or brown fruit. Also called **horse sugar.** [SWEET + LEAF]

sweet′ mar′joram, a fragrant herb, *Marjorana hortensis,* grown for its leaves for use in cookery.

sweet′ mar′ten, the European pine marten, *Martes martes.*

sweet·meat (swēt′mēt′), *n.* **1.** a sweet delicacy, prepared with sugar, honey, or the like, as preserves, candy, or, formerly, cakes or pastry. **2.** Usually, **sweetmeats.** any sweet delicacy of the confectionery or candy kind, as candied fruit, sugar-covered nuts, sugarplums, bonbons, balls or sticks of candy, etc. [ME *swete mete,* OE *swētmete.* See SWEET, MEAT]

sweet′ mock′ or′ange, the syringa, *Philadelphus coronarius.*

sweet′ness and light′, **1.** decorous charm combined with intelligence. **2.** extreme or excessive pleasantness; freedom from stress: *The ending to the movie is all sweetness and light.*

sweet′ oil′. See **olive oil.**

sweet′ olean′der, an evergreen shrub or small tree, *Nerium indicum,* found from Iran to Japan, having pink or white, sweet-scented flowers.

sweet′ or′ange. See under **orange** (def. 2).

sweet′ pea′, an annual climbing plant, *Lathyrus odoratus,* having sweet-scented flowers.

sweet′ pep′per, **1.** a variety of pepper, *Capsicum frutescens grossum,* having a mild-flavored, bell-shaped or somewhat oblong fruit. **2.** the fruit itself, used for stuffing, pickling, or as a vegetable. Also called **bell pepper.**

sweet′ pep′per·bush (pep′ər bo͝osh′), a shrub, *Clethra alnifolia,* of the eastern and southern coastal U.S., having numerous, erect clusters of very fragrant, pink flowers. Also called **spiked alder, summer-sweet.**

sweet′ pitaha′ya, pitahaya.

sweet′ pota′to, **1.** a convolvulaceous plant, *Ipomoea Batatas,* grown for its sweet, edible, tuberous roots. **2.** the root itself, used as a vegetable. **3.** *Informal.* ocarina.

sweet′ sca′bious. See under **scabious** (def. 1).

sweet-scent·ed (swēt′sen′tid), *adj.* having a pleasant and sweet smell; fragrant.

sweet′ shop′, *Brit.* a store that sells candy.

sweet·sop (swēt′sop′), *n.* **1.** a sweet, pulpy fruit having a thin, tuberculate rind, borne by an annonaceous tree or shrub, *Annona squamosa,* of tropical America. **2.** the tree or shrub. Also called **sugar apple.** [SWEET + SOP]

sweet′ sor′ghum, sorgo.

sweet′ spire′. See **Virginia willow.**

sweet′ spir′it of ni′tre, *Pharm.* See **ethyl nitrite spirit.** Also, **sweet′ spir′it of ni′ter.**

sweet′ sul′tan, an herb, *Centaurea moschata,* of the Orient, having solitary, fragrant, variously colored flowers.

sweet′ talk′, *Informal.* cajolery; soft soap.

sweet-talk (swēt′tôk′), *Informal.* —*v.i.* **1.** to use cajoling words. —*v.t.* **2.** to use cajoling words on in order to persuade; soft-soap: *They've been trying to sweet-talk the management into giving them more money.*

sweet-tem·pered (swēt′tem′pərd), *adj.* having a gentle and equable disposition; pleasant. —**sweet′-tem′pered·ness,** *n.*

sweet′ tooth′, a liking or craving for candy and other sweets.

sweet′ ver′nal grass′, a Eurasian meadow grass, *Anthoxanthum odoratum,* found throughout North America, having clusters of brownish-green flowers.

sweet′ vibur′num, the sheepberry, *Viburnum Lentago.*

Sweet·wa·ter (swēt′wô′tər, -wot′ər), *n.* a town in SE Tennessee. 4145 (1960).

sweet·weed (swēt′wēd′), *n.* See **marsh mallow.** [SWEET + WEED¹]

sweet′ wil′liam, a pink, *Dianthus barbatus,* having clusters of small, variously colored flowers. Also, **sweet′ Wil′liam.** Also called **bunch pink.**

sweet′ wil′liam catch′fly, an annual herb, *Silene Armeria,* of southern Europe, having pink flowers. Also called **none-so-pretty.**

sweet′ wood′ruff, a low, spreading, perennial herb, *Asperula odorata,* of Eurasia, having white flowers and fragrant foliage when dried, growing well in moist soil.

sweet′ worm′wood, a widely distributed herb, *Artemisia annua,* having scented leaves and yellow flowers.

sweet·wort (swēt′wûrt′), *n. Brit.* an infusion of unfermented malt. [SWEET + WORT²]

Swe·linck (svā′lingk), *n.* **Jan Pie·ters** (yän pē′tərs) or **Jan Pie·ters·zoon** (yän pē′tər sōn′). See **Sweelinck, Jan Pieters** or **Jan Pieterszoon.**

swell (swel), *v.,* **swelled, swelled** or **swol·len, swell·ing,** *n., adj.* —*v.i.* **1.** to grow in bulk, as by absorption of moisture, inflation, distention, addition of material in the process of growth, or the like; increase abnormally in size: *Her ankles swelled from standing.* **2.** to rise in waves, as the sea. **3.** to well up, as a spring or as tears. **4.** to bulge out or be protuberant, as a sail, the middle of a cask, etc. **5.** to grow in amount, degree, force, etc. **6.** to increase gradually in volume or intensity, as sound: *The sounds swelled and faded away.* **7.** to arise and grow within one, as a feeling or emotion. **8.** to become puffed up with pride; behave or talk arrogantly or pretentiously. —*v.t.* **9.** to cause to grow in bulk. **10.** to cause to increase gradually in loudness: *to swell a musical tone.* **11.** to cause (a thing) to bulge out or be protuberant. **12.** to increase in amount, degree, force, etc. **13.** to affect with a strong, expansive emotion. **14.** to puff up with pride. —*n.* **15.** the act of swelling or the condition of being swollen. **16.** an increase in bulk; inflation or distention. **17.** a part that bulges out; protuberant part. **18.** a wave, esp. when long and unbroken, or such waves collectively. **19.** a gradually rising elevation of the land. **20.** an increase in amount, degree, force, etc. **21.** a gradual increase in loudness of sound. **22.** *Music.* **a.** a gradual increase in loudness (crescendo) followed by a gradual decrease (diminuendo) in loudness or force of musical sound. **b.** the sign (< >) for indicating this. **c.** a device, as in an organ, by which the loudness of tones may be varied. **23.** a swelling of emotion within one. **24.** *Slang.* **a.** a fashionably dressed person; dandy. **b.** a socially prominent person. —*adj. Slang.* **25.** (of things) stylish; elegant: *a swell hotel.* **26.** (of persons) fashionably dressed or socially prominent. **27.** first-rate; fine: *We had a swell time at the picnic.* [ME; OE *swell(an)*; c. D *zwellen,* G *schwellen,* Icel *svella*; akin to Goth *(uf)swalleins* pride]
—**Syn. 1.** dilate, distend, expand. **4.** protrude. **7.** well up. **8.** strut. **9.** inflate, expand. **12.** augment. **16.** swelling. **17.** bulge, protuberance, prominence. **18.** sea, billow. **24.** blade. **26, 27.** grand. —**Ant. 1.** contract. **12.** decrease, diminish.

swell′ box′, a chamber containing a set of pipes in a pipe organ or of reeds in a reed organ, and having movable slats or shutters which can be opened or closed to increase or diminish tonal volume.

swelled′ head′, *Informal.* an inordinately grand opinion of oneself. —**swelled′-head′ed,** *adj.* —**swelled′-head′ed·ness,** *n.*

swell·fish (swel′fish′), *n., pl.* (*esp. collectively*) **-fish,** (*esp. referring to two or more kinds or species*) **-fish·es.** puffer (def. 2). [SWELL + FISH]

swell′ front′, *Furniture.* a horizontally convex front, as of a chest of drawers. Also called **bow front.** Cf. **bombé.**

swell·head (swel′hed′), *n. Informal.* a vain, arrogant person. [SWELL + HEAD] —**swell′head′ed,** *adj.* —**swell′head′ed·ness,** *n.*

swell·ing (swel′ing), *n.* **1.** the act of one who or that which swells. **2.** the condition of being or becoming swollen. **3.** a swollen part; a protuberance or prominence. **4.** *Pathol.* an abnormal enlargement or protuberance. [late ME; see SWELL, -ING¹]

swel·ter (swel′tər), *v.i.* **1.** to suffer or languish with oppressive heat; perspire profusely from heat. —*v.t.* **2.** to oppress or cause to languish with heat. **3.** *Archaic.* to exude, as venom. —*n.* **4.** a sweltering condition. [ME *swelt(e)r(en),* equiv. to *swelt(en)* (OE *sweltan* to die; c. Icel *svelta,* Goth *swiltan*) + *-eren* -ER⁶; akin to SWEAL]

swel·ter·ing (swel′tər ing), *adj.* **1.** suffering or languishing with oppressive heat. **2.** characterized by oppressive heat, as a place, a day, the weather, etc.; sultry. [SWELTER + -ING²] —**swel′ter·ing·ly,** *adv.*

swept (swept), *v.* **1.** pt. and pp. of **sweep.** —*adj.* **2.** (of a sword guard) made up of curved bars.

swept·back (swept′bak′), *adj. Aeron.* **1.** (of the leading edge of an airfoil) forming a markedly obtuse angle with the fuselage. **2.** (of an aircraft or winged missile) having wings of this type. [adj. use of v. phrase *swept back*]

swept′ deck′, *Shipbuilding.* See **laid deck.**

swept·wing (swept′wing′), *adj. Aeron.* (of an aircraft, winged missile, etc.) having sweptback wings. [SWEPT(BACK) + WING]

swerve (swûrv), *v.,* **swerved, swerv·ing,** *n.* —*v.i.* **1.** to turn aside abruptly in movement or direction; deviate suddenly from the straight or direct course. —*v.t.* **2.** to cause to turn aside: *Nothing could swerve him.* —*n.* **3.** an act of swerving; turning aside; deviation. **4.** that which swerves. [ME; OE *sweorf(an)* (to) rub, file; c. D *zwerven* to rove, Icel *sverfa* to file, OHG *swerban,* Goth *afswairban* to wipe off] —**swerv′a·ble,** *adj.* —**swerv′er,** *n.*
—**Syn. 1.** See **deviate.**

swev·en (swev′ən), *n. Archaic.* a vision; dream. [ME; OE *swefn*; akin to Icel *sofa* to sleep, L *somnus,* Gk *hýpnos* sleep]

S.W.G., standard wire gauge.

swift (swift), *adj.* **1.** moving or capable of moving with great speed or velocity; fleet; rapid: *a swift ship.* **2.** coming, happening, or performed quickly or without delay: *a swift decision.* **3.** quick or prompt to act or respond: *He is swift to jump to conclusions.* —*adv.* **4.** swiftly. —*n.* **5.** any of numerous long-winged, swallowlike birds of the family *Apodidae,* related to the hummingbirds and noted for their rapid flight. **6.** See **tree swift.** **7.** See **spiny lizard.** **8.** Also called **swift′ moth′, ghost moth.** any of several brown or gray moths of the family *Hepialidae,* noted for rapid flight. **9.** an adjustable device upon which a hank of yarn is placed in order to wind off skeins or balls. **10.** the main cylinder on a machine for carding flax. [ME, OE; akin to OE *swīfan* to revolve, Icel *svīfa* to rove; see SWIVEL] —**swift′ly,** *adv.* —**swift′ness,** *n.*
—**Syn. 1.** speedy. See **quick. 2.** expeditious. **3.** ready, eager, alert. —**Ant. 1.** slow.

Swift (swift), *n.* **Jonathan** ("*Isaac Bickerstaff*"), 1667–1745, English satirist and clergyman, born in Ireland.

Swift′ Cur′rent, a city in SW Saskatchewan, in S Canada. 10,612 (1960).

swift·er (swif′tər), *n.* **1.** *Naut.* **a.** a small line joining the outer ends of the bars of a capstan to confine them to their sockets while the capstan is being turned. **b.** the forward shroud of the lower rigging on either side of a mast. **c.** *Obs.* a rope used to encircle a boat lengthwise in order to strengthen and defend its sides. **2.** *Theat.* a taut steel line for sliding set pieces, flats, etc., on the stage. [*swift* to tie fast (< Scand; cf. Icel *svipta* to reef sails) + -ER[1]]

swift-foot·ed (swift′fo͝ot′id), *adj.* swift in running.

swift·let (swift′lit), *n.* any of several swifts of the genus *Collocalia*, of southeastern Asia, the East Indies, and Australia, certain species of which construct nests with saliva that are used in making bird's-nest soup. [SWIFT + -LET]

Swift's′ disease′, *Pathol.* acrodynia. [named after W. *Swift*, 20th-century Australian physician]

swig[1] (swig), *n., v.,* **swigged, swig·ging.** *Informal.* —*n.* **1.** an amount of liquid, esp. liquor, taken in one swallow; draught: *He took a swig from the flask.* —*v.t., v.i.* **2.** to drink heartily or greedily. [? akin to SWAG[1]] —**swig′ger,** *n.*

swig[2] (swig), *v.i.,* **swigged, swig·ging.** *Naut.* to haul on a rope while taking up its slack (sometimes fol. by *off* or *to*). [? var. of SWAG[1]]

swill (swil), *n.* **1.** liquid or partly liquid food for animals, esp. kitchen refuse given to swine; hogwash. **2.** kitchen refuse in general; garbage. **3.** any liquid mess, waste, or refuse; slop. **4.** a deep draught of liquor. —*v.i.* **5.** to drink greedily or excessively. —*v.t.* **6.** to drink (something) greedily or to excess; guzzle. **7.** to feed (animals) with swill: *to swill the hogs.* **8.** *Chiefly Brit. Informal.* to wash or cleanse by rinsing or flooding with water. [ME *swile(n)*, OE *swilian*, var. of *swillan*] —**swill′er,** *n.*

swim (swim), *v.,* **swam, swum, swim·ming,** *n.* —*v.i.* **1.** to move in water by movements of the limbs, fins, tail, etc. **2.** to float on the surface of water or some other liquid. **3.** to move, rest, or be suspended in air as if swimming in water. **4.** to move, glide, or go smoothly over a surface. **5.** to be immersed or steeped in or overflowed or flooded with a liquid: *eyes swimming with tears.* **6.** to be dizzy or giddy; have a whirling sensation; seem to whirl: *My head began to swim.* —*v.t.* **7.** to move along in or cross (a body of water) by swimming: *to swim a lake.* **8.** to perform (a particular stroke) in swimming: *to swim a sidestroke.* **9.** to cause to swim or float, as on a stream. **10.** to furnish with sufficient water to swim or float. —*n.* **11.** the act, an instance, or a period of swimming. **12.** a motion as of swimming; a smooth, gliding movement. **13.** a dance that is a modification of the watusi. **14. in the swim,** alert to or actively engaged in current affairs, social activities, etc.: *Despite her age, she tried to keep in the swim by visiting her former pupils and attending lectures.* [ME *swimm(en)*, OE *swimman*; c. G *schwimmen*, D *zwemmen*, Icel *svimma*] —**swim′ma·ble,** *adj.* —**swim′mer,** *n.*

swim′ blad′der. See **air bladder** (def. 2).

swim′ fin′, one of a pair of flippers.

swim′ mask′, mask (def. 2).

swim·mer·et (swim′ə ret′), *n.* (in many crustaceans) one of a number of abdominal limbs or appendages, usually adapted for swimming and for carrying eggs, as distinguished from other limbs adapted for walking or seizing. [SWIMMER + -ET]

swim·ming (swim′ing), *n.* **1.** the act of one who or that which swims. **2.** the skill or technique of one who swims. **3.** the sport or a contest based on the ability to swim. —*adj.* **4.** capable of, knowing how to, or in the act of propelling oneself in water by moving the limbs, fins, tail, etc. **5.** used in or for swimming: *swimming trunks.* **6.** immersed in or overflowing with water or some other liquid. **7.** having a sensation of dizziness or giddiness: *a swimming head.* [ME; OE *swimmende.* See SWIM, -ING[2], -ING[1]] —**swim′ming·ness,** *n.*

swim′ming bath′, *Brit.* See **swimming pool.**

swim′ming blad′der. See **air bladder** (def. 2).

swim′ming crab′, any of numerous, chiefly marine crabs, esp. of the family *Portunidae*, having the legs adapted for swimming.

swim′ming hole′, a place, as in a stream or creek, that is deep enough to use for swimming.

swim·ming·ly (swim′ing lē), *adv.* without difficulty; with great success: *She got along swimmingly in the exam.* [SWIMMING + -LY]

swim′ming pool′, a tank or large artificial basin, usually of concrete, for filling with water for swimming.

swim·suit (swim′so͞ot′), *n.* See **bathing suit.** [SWIM + SUIT]

Swin·burne (swin′bərn), *n.* **Algernon Charles,** 1837–1909, English poet and critic.

swin·dle (swin′dəl), *v.,* **-dled, -dling,** *n.* —*v.t.* **1.** to cheat (a person, business, etc.) out of money or other assets. **2.** to obtain by fraud or deceit. —*v.i.* **3.** to put forward plausible schemes or use unscrupulous trickery to defraud others; cheat. —*n.* **4.** the act of swindling or a fraudulent transaction or scheme. **5.** anything deceptive; a fraud: *This advertisement is a real swindle.* [back formation from *swindler* < G *Schwindler* giddy-minded, irresponsible person, promoter of wildcat schemes, cheat, deriv. of *schwindeln* to be dizzy (hence dizzy-minded, irresponsible), defraud, equiv. to *schwind-* (akin to OE *swindan* to languish) + *-eln* freq. suffix] —**swin′dle·a·ble,** *adj.* —**swin′dler,** *n.* —**swin′dling·ly,** *adv.*
—**Syn. 1.** cozen, dupe, trick, gull.

swin·dled (swin′dəld), *adj. Jewelry.* (of a gem) cut so as to retain the maximum weight of the original stone or to give a false impression of size, esp. by having the table too large. [SWINDLE + -ED[2]]

swin′dle sheet′, *Slang.* an expense account.

swine (swīn), *n., pl.* **swine. 1.** the domestic hog. **2.** any artiodactyl animal of the family, *Suidae*, of the Old World, or of the closely related New World family, *Tayassuidae*, comprising the peccaries. **3.** a coarse, gross, or brutishly sensual person. **4.** any contemptible man. [ME; OE *swīn*; c. G *Schwein* hog, L *suīnus* (adj.) porcine; akin to SOW[2]] —**swine′like′,** *adj.*

swine′ erysip′elas, *Vet. Pathol.* erysipelas (def. 2). Cf. **erysipeloid.**

swine′ fe′ver, *Vet. Pathol.* See **hog cholera.**

swine·herd (swīn′hûrd′), *n.* a man who tends swine. [ME; late OE *swȳnhyrde.* See SWINE, HERD[2]] —**swine′herd′ship,** *n.*

swine′ plague′, *Vet. Pathol.* a disease of hogs, caused by the bacterium *Pasteurella multocida*, characterized by an accompanying infection of pneumonia. Cf. **hemorrhagic septicemia.**

swine′ pox′, **1.** a variety of chicken pox. **2.** *Vet. Pathol.* a mild pox disease of swine, caused by a virus related to that of cowpox, characterized by the appearance of pustules in the skin, esp. of the abdomen.

swing[1] (swing), *v.,* **swung** or (*Archaic and Dial.*) **swang; swung; swing·ing;** *n., adj.* —*v.t.* **1.** to cause to move to and fro, sway, or oscillate, as something suspended from above: *to swing one's arms in walking.* **2.** to cause to move in alternate directions or in either direction around a fixed point, on an axis, or on a line of support, as a door on hinges. **3.** to move (the hand or something held) with an oscillating or rotary movement: *to swing one's fists; to swing a club around one's head.* **4.** *Aeron.* to pull or turn (a propeller) by hand, esp. in order to start the engine. **5.** to cause to move in a new direction, in a curve, as if around a central point, or in a curving course: *The driver swung the car into the driveway.* **6.** to suspend so as to hang freely, as a hammock or a door. **7.** *U.S. Informal.* to influence or manage as desired: *to swing votes; swing a business deal.* **8.** to direct, change, or shift (one's attention, interest, opinion, support, etc.). **9.** to turn (a ship or aircraft) to various headings in order to check compass deviation.
—*v.i.* **10.** to move or sway to and fro, as a pendulum or other suspended object. **11.** to move to and fro in a swing, as for recreation. **12.** to move in alternate directions or in either direction around a point, an axis, or a line of support, as a gate on its hinges. **13.** to move in a curve as if around a central point, as around a corner: *The highway swings to the east.* **14.** to move with a free, swaying motion, as soldiers on the march. **15.** to be suspended so as to hang freely, as a bell, hammock, etc. **16.** to move by grasping a support with the hands and drawing up the arms or using the momentum of the swaying body: *He swings through the air with the greatest of ease.* **17.** to change or shift one's attention, interest, opinion, condition, etc.: *He swung from mere indifference to outright scorn.* **18.** to hit at someone or something, with the hand or something grasped in the hand: *The prizefighter swung and missed. The batter swung and struck out.* **19.** *Slang.* **a.** to have or be characterized by a modern, lively, active, and knowledgeable attitude, life, or atmosphere; to be hip: *She may be 45, but she still swings. Las Vegas swings all year.* **b.** (of two persons) to be in rapport; accord in spirit, feeling, and temper: *Man, she may be ugly, but we swing.* **20.** *Informal.* to suffer death by hanging: *You'll swing for this.* **21. swing round the circle,** to tour an area on a political campaign.
—*n.* **22.** the act, manner, or progression of swinging; movement in alternate directions or in a particular direction: *a political swing to the left.* **23.** the amount or extent of such movement: *to correct the swing of a pendulum.* **24.** a curving movement or course. **25.** a moving of the body with a free, swaying motion, as in walking. **26.** a blow or stroke with the hand or an object grasped in the hands: *His even swing drove the ball 250 yards down the fairway.* **27.** a steady, marked rhythm or movement, as of verse or music. **28.** a regular upward or downward movement in the price of a commodity or of a security, or in any business activity. **29.** *Informal.* a work period coming between the regular day and night shifts. **30.** freedom of action: *to have free swing in carrying out a project.* **31.** active operation; progression: *to get into the swing of things.* **32.** something that is swung or that swings. **33.** a seat suspended from above by means of a loop of rope or between ropes or rods, on which one may sit and swing to and fro for recreation. **34.** the maximum diameter of the work machinable in a certain lathe or other machine tool. **35. in full swing,** *Informal.* working at the highest or most efficient speed; in active operation: *Automobile production is in full swing.*
—*adj.* **36.** of or pertaining to a swing. **37.** determining or capable of determining the outcome of an election, decision, etc.; deciding: *the swing vote in the primary.* **38.** designed or constructed to permit swinging or hanging. **39.** acting to relieve other workers when needed, as at night. [ME *swing(en)*, OE *swingan*; c. G *schwingen*] —**swing′a·ble,** *adj.*
—**Syn. 1.** wave. **10.** SWING, SWAY, OSCILLATE, ROCK suggest a movement back and forth. SWING expresses the comparatively regular motion to and fro of a body supported from the end or ends, esp. from above: *A lamp swings from the ceiling.* To SWAY is to swing gently and is used esp. of fixed objects or of persons: *Young oaks sway in the breeze.* OSCILLATE refers to the smooth, regular, alternating movement of a body within certain limits between two fixed points. ROCK indicates the slow and regular movement back and forth of a body, as on curved supports: *A cradle rocks.* **22.** sway, vibration, oscillation. **23.** range, scope, sweep, play.

swing[2] (swing), *n., adj., v.,* **swung, swing·ing.** —*n.* **1.** Also called **swing music.** a style of jazz, popular esp. in the 1930's and often arranged for a large dance band, marked by a smoother beat and more flowing phrasing than Dixieland and having less complex harmonies and rhythms than modern jazz. **2.** the rhythmic element that excites dancers and listeners to move in time to jazz music. —*adj.* **3.** of, pertaining to, playing, or characteristic of swing: *a swing record.* —*v.t.* **4.** to play (a piece of music) in the style of swing. [special use of SWING[1]]

Swing, The, a painting by Jean Honoré Fragonard.

swing·back (swing′bak′), *n.* (esp. in political affairs) a return or reversion, as to previous opinion, custom, etc.: *We must fight any swingback to isolationism.* [n. use of v. phrase *swing back*]

swing′ bridge′, a bridge that can open by pivoting on a central pier to let vessels pass.

swing′ door′. See **swinging door.**

swinge[1] (swinj), *v.t.,* **swinged, swinge·ing.** *Archaic.* to thrash; punish. [ME *swenge(n)* (to) shake, smite, OE *swengan*, caus. of *swingan* to swing or denominative of OE *sweng* a blow] —**swing·er** (swin′jər), *n.*

swinge[2] (swinj), *v.t.,* **swinged, swinge·ing.** *Dial.* to singe. [special use of SWINGE[1] by assoc. with SINGE]

swinge·ing (swin′jing), *adj. Chiefly Brit.* **1.** enormous; thumping. **2.** *Slang.* swinging (def. 3). **3.** *Slang.* swinging (def. 4). [SWINGE[1] + -ING[2]] —**swinge′ing·ly,** *adv.*

swing·er (swing′ər), *n.* **1.** one who or that which swings. **2.** *Slang.* a lively, active, and modern person. [SWING[1] + -ER[1]]

swing·ing (swing′ing), *adj., superl.* **-ing·est. 1.** characterized by or capable of swinging, being swung, or causing to swing. **2.** intended for swinging upon, by, from, or in: *the swinging devices in a playground.* **3.** *Slang.* excellent; first-rate. **4.** *Slang.* lively, active, and modern; hip. [SWING[1] + -ING[2]] —**swing′ing·ly,** *adv.*

swing′ing buoy′, *Naut.* a firmly anchored buoy to which a line can be attached in order to swing or head a vessel in a certain direction, as in putting it into a drydock or in checking compass deviation on board.

swing′ing com′pass, *Navig.* a portable compass used as a reference when making compass adjustments, swinging ship, etc.

swing′ing door′, a door that swings open on being pushed or pulled from either side and then swings closed by itself. Also called **swing door.**

swin·gle (swing′gəl), *n., v.,* **-gled, -gling.** —*n.* **1.** the swipple of a flail. **2.** a wooden instrument shaped like a large knife, for beating flax or hemp and scraping from it the woody or coarse portions. —*v.t.* **3.** to clean (flax or hemp) by beating and scraping with a swingle. [ME *swingel*, OE *swingell* rod (c. MD *swinghel*), equiv. to *swing-* (see SWING[1]) + *-el* instrumental suffix]

swin·gle·bar (swing′gəl bär′), *n.* a whiffletree. [SWINGLE + BAR[1]]

swing′ leg′, *Furniture.* a leg at the end of a hinged rail, swinging out to support a drop leaf. Cf. **gate leg.**

swin·gle·tree (swing′gəl trē′), *n.* a whiffletree. [late ME; see SWINGLE, TREE]

swing′ mu′sic, swing[2] (def. 1).

swing·o·ver (swing′ō′vər), *n.* a shift or transfer in attitude, opinion, or the like. [n. use of v. phrase *swing over*]

swing′ plow′. See **swivel plow.**

swing′ shift′, **1.** a work shift in industry from midafternoon until midnight. **2.** the group of workers on such a shift. —**swing′ shift′er.**

swing·tree (swing′trē′), *n.* a whiffletree. [late ME; appar. syncopated var. of SWINGLETREE]

swin·ish (swī′nish), *adj.* **1.** like or befitting swine; hoggish. **2.** brutishly gross or sensual. [ME; see SWINE, -ISH[1]] —**swin′ish·ly,** *adv.* —**swin′ish·ness,** *n.*

swink (swingk), *v.i.,* **swank** or **swonk, swonk·en, swink·ing,** *n. Brit. Archaic.* labor; toil. [ME *swink(en)*, OE *swincan*; akin to SWING[1]] —**swink′er,** *n.*

Swin·ner·ton (swin′ər tən), *n.* **Frank (Arthur),** born 1884, English novelist and critic.

swin·ney (swin′ē), *n. Vet. Pathol.* sweeny.

swipe (swīp), *n., v.,* **swiped, swip·ing.** —*n.* **1.** *Informal.* **a.** a strong, sweeping blow, as with a cricket bat or golf club. **b.** a sideswipe. **2.** a leverlike device for raising or lowering a weight, esp. a bucket in a well; sweep. **3.** *Informal.* one who rubs down horses in a stable; groom. —*v.t.* **4.** *Informal.* to strike with a sweeping blow. **5.** *Slang.* to steal: *He'll swipe anything that isn't nailed down.* —*v.i.* **6.** to make a sweeping stroke. [akin to SWEEP[1]; c. G *schweifen*]

swipes (swīps), *n.* (*construed as pl.*) *Brit. Informal.* **1.** poor, watery, or spoiled beer. **2.** malt liquor in general, esp. beer and small beer. [? n. pl. use of *swipe* to drink down at one gulp, var. of SWEEP[1]]

swip·ple (swip′əl), *n.* the freely swinging part of a flail, which falls upon the grain in threshing; swingle. Also, **swi′ple.** [ME *swipyl*, var. of *swepyl*, equiv. to *swep(en)* (to) SWEEP[1] + *-yl* instrumental suffix]

swirl (swûrl), *v.i.* **1.** to move around or along with a whirling motion; whirl; eddy. **2.** to be dizzy or giddy, or swim, as the head. —*v.t.* **3.** to cause to whirl; twist. —*n.* **4.** a swirling movement; whirl; eddy. **5.** a twist, as of hair around the head or of trimming on a hat. **6.** any curving, twisting line, shape, or form. **7.** confusion; disorder. [late ME (north) < Scand; cf. Norw *svirla*, c. D *zwirrelen* to whirl, G *schwirrlen* to totter; all < a root **swir-* (whence Dan *svirre* to whirl, G *schwirren* to whir) + freq. *l-* suffix] —**swirl′ing·ly,** *adv.*

swirl·y (swûr′lē), *adj.,* **swirl·i·er, swirl·i·est.** swirling, whirling, or twisted. [SWIRL + -Y[1]]

swish (swish), *v.i.* **1.** to move with or make a sibilant sound, as a slender rod cutting sharply through the air or as small waves washing on the shore. **2.** to rustle, as silk. —*v.t.* **3.** to flourish, whisk, etc., with a swishing movement or sound: *to swish a cane.* **4.** to bring, take, cut, etc., with or as with such a movement or sound: *to swish off the tops of plants with a cane.* **5.** to flog or whip. —*n.* **6.** a swishing movement or sound. **7.** a stock or rod for flogging or a stroke with this. **8.** *Slang.* a male homosexual with effeminate traits. —*adj.* **9.** *Slang.* swishy (def. 2). [imit.] —**swish′er,** *n.* —**swish′ing·ly,** *adv.*

swish·y (swish′ē), *adj.,* **swish·i·er, swish·i·est. 1.** causing, giving rise to, or characterized by a swishing sound or motion. **2.** Also, **swish.** *Slang.* exhibiting effeminate tendencies or characteristics. [SWISH + -Y[1]]

Swiss (swis), *adj.* **1.** of, pertaining to, associated with, or characteristic of Switzerland or its inhabitants. —*n.* **2.** a native or inhabitant of Switzerland. **3.** any thin, crisp fabric made in Switzerland, esp. Swiss muslin. **4.** Also called **Swiss cheese.** a firm, pale-yellow or whitish cheese containing many holes, made usually from half-skimmed cow's milk; Emmenthaler. [< F *Suisse* < MHG *Swiz*]

Swiss′ chard′. See under **chard.**

Swiss′ cheese′, Swiss (def. 4).

Swiss·er (swis′ər), *n.* Swiss (def. 2). [SWISS + -ER[1], modeled on SWITZER]

Swiss′ Guard′, a member of a corps of bodyguards protecting the pope, with membership restricted to natives of Switzerland.

Swiss′ la′pis, *Jewelry.* cracked quartz, stained blue in imitation of lapis lazuli.

Swiss′ mus′lin, a crisp, sheer muslin that is constructed in plain weave, bleached white, and often ornamented with raised dots or figures **(dotted swiss),** used chiefly in the manufacture of curtains and women's summer clothes.

Swiss′ steak′, a thick slice of steak dredged in flour and pounded, browned, and braised with tomatoes, onions, and other vegetables.

Swiss·vale (swis′vāl′), *n.* a city in SW Pennsylvania, on the Monongahela River. 15,089 (1960).

Swit., Switzerland.

switch (swich), *n.* **1.** a slender, flexible shoot, rod, etc., used esp. in whipping, beating, etc. **2.** the act of whipping or beating with or as with such an object; a stroke, lash, or whisking movement. **3.** a slender growing shoot, as of a plant. **4.** a hairpiece consisting of a bunch or tress of long hair or some substitute, fastened together at one end and worn by women to supplement their own hair. **5.** *Elect.* a device for turning on or off or directing an electric current, or making or breaking a circuit. **6.** *Railroads.* a track structure for diverting moving trains or rolling stock from one track to another, commonly consisting of a pair of movable rails. **7.** a turning, shifting, or changing: *a switch of votes to another candidate.* **8.** *Bridge.* a change to a suit other than the one played or bid previously. **9.** *Basketball.* a maneuver in which two teammates on defense shift assignments so that each guards the opponent usually guarded by the other. **10.** a tuft of hair at the end of the tail of some animals, as of the cow or lion. —*v.t.* **11.** to whip or beat with a switch or the like; lash: *He switched the boy with a cane.* **12.** to move, swing, or whisk (a cane, a fishing line, etc.) with a swift, lashing stroke. **13.** to shift or exchange: *The two boys switched their lunch boxes.* **14.** to turn, shift, or divert: *to switch conversation from a painful subject.* **15.** *Elect.* to connect, disconnect, or redirect (an electric circuit or the device it serves) by operating a switch (often fol. by *off* or *on*): *He switched on a light.* **16.** *Railroads.* **a.** to move or transfer (a train, car, etc.) from one set of tracks to another, as in a yard or at a terminal. **b.** to drop or add (cars) or to make up (a train). **17.** *Motion Pictures, Television.* to shift rapidly from one camera to another in order to change camera angles or shots. —*v.i.* **18.** to strike with or as with a switch. **19.** to change direction or course; turn, shift, or change. **20.** to exchange or replace something with another: *He used to smoke this brand of cigarettes, but he switched.* **21.** to be shifted, turned, etc., by means of a switch. **22.** *Basketball.* to execute a switch. **23.** *Bridge.* to lead a card of a suit different from the suit just led by oneself or one's partner. [earlier *swits, switz;* cf. LG (Hanoverian) *schwutsche* switch] —**switch′er,** *n.* —**switch′like′,** *adj.*

switch·back (swich′bak′), *n.* **1.** a highway, as in a mountainous area, having many hairpin curves. **2.** *Railroads.* a zigzag track arrangement for climbing a steep grade. **3.** *Brit.* See **roller coaster.** [SWITCH + BACK[2]]

switch·blade (swich′blād′), *n.* a pocketknife the blade of which is held by a spring and released by pressure on a button or other device on the handle of the knife. Also called **switch′blade knife′.** [SWITCH + BLADE]

switch·board (swich′bōrd′, -bôrd′), *n.* *Elect.* a structural unit containing mounting switches and instruments necessary to complete telephone circuits manually. [SWITCH + BOARD]

switch′ box′, a box, usually of metal, containing one or more electric switches.

switch′ cane′. See under **cane** (def. 5).

switch′ en′gine, *Railroads.* a locomotive for switching rolling stock in a yard.

switch·er·oo (swich′ə ro͞o′, swich′ə ro͞o′), *n., pl.* **-oos.** *Slang.* an unexpected or sudden change or reversal in attitude, character, position, action, etc. [SWITCHER + *-oo* suffix of appurtenance]

switch·gear (swich′gēr′), *n.* *Elect.* switching equipment used in an electric power station. Also, **switch′ gear′.** [SWITCH + GEAR]

switch-hit (swich′hit′), *v.i.,* **-hit, -hit·ting.** *Baseball.* to be able to bat from either side of the plate; to be able to bat both as a left-handed and as a right-handed batter.

switch′ hit′ter, *Baseball.* a player who switch-hits. Also, **switch′-hit′ter.**

switch·man (swich′mən), *n., pl.* **-men. 1.** one who has charge of a switch or switches on a railroad. **2.** one who assists in moving cars in a railway yard or terminal. [SWITCH + MAN[1]]

switch·o·ver (swich′ō′vər), *n.* a changeover. [n. use of v. phrase *switch over*]

switch′ plate′, a plate, usually of metal, ceramic, or plastic, covering a switch so that the knob or toggle protrudes.

switch′ plug′, a plug, as for an electric iron, equipped with an on-off switch.

switch·yard (swich′yärd′), *n.* a railroad yard in which rolling stock is distributed or made up into trains. [SWITCH + YARD[2]]

swith (swith), *adv.* **1.** *Chiefly Brit. Dial.* immediately; quickly. —*v.t.* **2.** *Scot.* to hurry; hasten. Also, **swithe.** [ME, OE *swithe* (adv.) strongly, equiv. to *swith* strong (c. Goth *swinths* strong, Icel *svinnr,* G *(ge)schwind* fast) + *-e* adv. suffix] —**swith′ly,** *adv.*

swith·er (swith′ər), *n.* *Brit. Dial.* a state of confusion, excitement, or perplexity. [cf. OE *swithrian* to retire, dwindle, fail]

Swith·in (swith′in, swith′-), *n.* **Saint,** died A.D. 862, English ecclesiastic: bishop of Winchester 852?–862. Also, **Swith′un.**

Switz., Switzerland.

Switz·er (swit′sər), *n.* Swiss (def. 2). [< MHG, equiv. to *Switz* Switzerland + *-er* -ER[1]]

Switz·er·land (swit′sər lənd), *n.* a republic in central Europe. 5,429,061 (1960). 15,944 sq. mi. *Cap.:* Bern. French, **Suisse.** German, **Schweiz.** Italian, **Svizzera.**

swiv·el (swiv′əl), *n., v.,* **-eled, -el·ing** or (*esp. Brit.*) **-elled, -el·ling.** —*n.* **1.** a fastening device which allows the thing fastened to turn round freely upon it, esp. to turn in a full circle. **2.** such a device consisting of two parts, each of which turns round independently, as a compound link of a chain, one part of which turns freely in the other by means of a headed pin or the like. **3.** a pivoted support allowing a gun to turn round in a horizontal plane. **4.** a swivel gun. **5.** a device attached to a loom and used as a shuttle to weave extra threads in the production of small figures, esp. dots. —*v.t.* **6.** to turn or pivot on or as on a swivel: *He swiveled his chair completely around.* **7.** to fasten by a swivel; furnish with a swivel. —*v.i.* **8.** to turn on or as on a swivel, pivot, or the like. [ME, equiv. to *swiv-* (akin to OE *swīfan* to revolve, Icel *svīfa* to turn) + *-el* instrumental suffix] —**swiv′el·like′,** *adj.*

swiv′el chair′, a chair whose seat turns round horizontally on a swivel.

swiv′el gun′, a gun mounted on a pedestal so that it can be turned from side to side or up and down.

swiv·el-hipped (swiv′əl hipt′), *adj.* characterized by an exaggeratedly swinging or extremely free motion of the hips.

swiv′el plow′, a plow equipped with a moldboard that can be reversed to turn the furrow to one side or the other. Also called **swing plow, turnwrest.**

swiv·el·tail (swiv′əl tāl′), *n.* thresher (def. 4). [SWIVEL + TAIL[1]]

swiv′el weav′ing, the process of weaving on a loom equipped with a swivel.

swiz·zle (swiz′əl), *n.* a tall drink, originating in Barbados, composed of full-flavored West Indian rum, lime juice, crushed ice, and sugar, and flavored with Falernum. [?]

swiz′zle stick′, a small rod for stirring highballs and cocktails in the glass.

swob (swob), *n., v.t.,* **swobbed, swob·bing.** swab.

swol·len (swō′lən), *v.* **1.** a pp. of **swell.** —*adj.* **2.** enlarged by or as by swelling; puffed up; tumid. **3.** turgid or bombastic. —**swol′len·ly,** *adv.* —**swol′len·ness,** *n.*

swoln (swōln), *adj.* *Archaic.* swollen.

swonk (swongk), *v.* a pt. of **swink.**

swonk·en (swong′kən), *v.* pp. of **swink.**

swoon (swo͞on), *v.i.* **1.** to faint; lose consciousness. **2.** to enter a state of hysterical rapture or ecstasy: *The teen-agers swooned at the sight of the singing star.* —*n.* **3.** a faint or fainting fit; syncope. [ME *swo(w)ne(n)* (to) faint, OE *(ge)swōgen* in a swoon] —**swoon′ing·ly,** *adv.*

swoop (swo͞op), *v.i.* **1.** to sweep through the air, as a bird or a bat, esp. down upon prey. **2.** to come down upon something in a sudden, swift attack (often fol. by *down* and *on* or *upon*): *The army swooped down on the town.* —*v.t.* **3.** to take, lift, scoop up, or remove with or as with one sweeping motion (often fol. by *up, away,* or *off*): *He swooped her up in his arms.* —*n.* **4.** the act or an instance of swooping; a sudden, swift descent. [var. (with close ō) of ME *swopen,* OE *swāpan* to sweep; c. G *schweifen*]

swoose (swo͞os), *n., pl.* **swoos·es, sweese.** a hybrid between a swan and a goose. [SW(AN[1] + G)OOSE]

swoosh (swo͝osh), *v.i.* **1.** to move with or make a rustling, swirling, or brushing sound. **2.** to pour out swiftly. —*v.t.* **3.** to cause to make or move with a rustling, swirling, or brushing sound. —*n.* **4.** a swirling or rustling sound or movement. [imit.]

swop (swop), *v.t., v.i.,* **swopped, swop·ping,** *n.* swap.

sword (sōrd, sôrd), *n.* **1.** a weapon having various forms but consisting typically of a long, straight or slightly curved blade, sharp-edged on one side or both sides, with one end pointed and the other fixed in a hilt or handle. **2.** this weapon as the symbol of military power, punitive justice, authority, etc.: *The pen is mightier than the sword.* **3.** a cause of death or destruction. **4.** war, combat, slaughter, or violence; military force or power: *He who lives by the sword shall perish by the sword.* **5. at swords' points,** mutually ready to begin hostilities; opposed: *Father and son are constantly at swords' points over the use of the car.* **6. cross swords, a.** to engage in combat; fight. **b.** to disagree violently; argue: *The members of the board of directors crossed swords in the selection of a new president.* **7. put to the sword,** to slay; execute: *The entire population of the town was put to the sword by the conqueror.* [ME; OE *sweord;* c. G *Schwert,* D *zwaard,* Icel *sverth*] —**sword′less,** *adj.* —**sword′like′,** *adj.*

sword′ bay′onet, a short sword that may be attached to the muzzle of a gun and used as a bayonet.

sword′ bean′, a twining vine, *Canavalia gladiata,* found in the tropics of the Eastern Hemisphere, having large, showy, pealike flowers and reddish-brown seeds. Also called **saber bean.**

sword-bear·er (sôrd′bâr′ər), *n.* *Brit.* an official who carries the sword of state on ceremonial occasions, as before the sovereign, a magistrate, or the like. [ME *swerd berer.* See SWORD, BEARER]

sword′ belt′, a military belt from which a sword may be hung.

sword·bill (sōrd′bil′, sôrd′-), *n.* a South American hummingbird, *Ensifera ensifera,* having a slender bill that is longer than its body. [SWORD + BILL[2]]

sword′ cane′, a cane or walking stick having a hollow shaft which serves as a sheath for a sword or dagger.

sword·craft (sōrd′kraft′, -kräft′, sôrd′-), *n.* **1.** skill in or the art of swordplay. **2.** military skill or power. [SWORD + CRAFT]

sword′ dance′, any of various dances, usually performed by men, in which swords are ceremonially flourished or are laid on the ground and danced around. —**sword′ danc′er.**

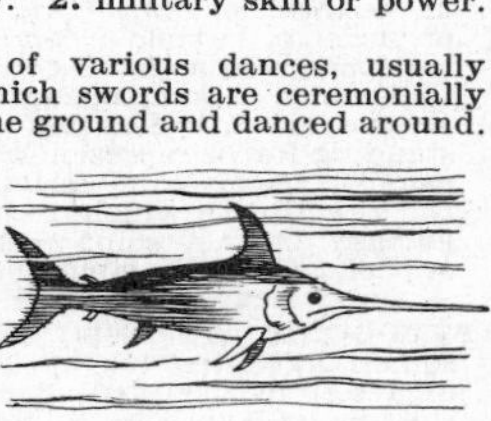

sword′ fern′, any fern of the genus *Nephrolepis,* esp. *N. exaltata,* characterized by sword-shaped, pinnate fronds.

Swordfish
(Length to 15 ft.)

sword·fish (sōrd′fish′, sôrd′-), *n., pl.* **-fish·es,** (*esp. collectively*) **-fish** for 1. **1.** a large, marine food fish, *Xiphias gladius,* having the upper jaw elongated into a swordlike structure. **2.** (*cap.*) *Astron.* the constellation Dorado. [SWORD + FISH]

sword′ grass′, any of various grasses or plants having swordlike or sharp leaves, as the sword lily.

sword′ knot′, a looped strap, ribbon, or the like, attached to the hilt of a sword as a support or ornament.

sword′ lil′y, a gladiolus.

sword·man (sōrd′mən, sôrd′-), *n., pl.* **-men.** swordsman. [ME *swerdman.* See SWORD, MAN[1]] —**sword′man·ship′,** *n.*

sword·play (sōrd′plā′, sôrd′-), *n.* the action or practice of wielding a sword; fencing. [SWORD + PLAY] —**sword′play′er,** *n.*

swords·man (sōrdz′mən, sôrdz′-), *n., pl.* **-men. 1.** one who uses or is skilled in the use of a sword. **2.** a fencer. **3.** a soldier. Also, **swordman.** [SWORD + 's[1] + MAN[1]] —**swords′man·ship′,** *n.*

sword·tail (sōrd′tāl′, sôrd′-), *n.* any of several small, brightly colored, viviparous, fresh-water fishes of the genus *Xiphophorous,* found in Central America, having the lower part of the caudal fin elongated into a swordlike structure: often kept in aquariums. [SWORD + TAIL[1]]

swore (swōr, swôr), *v.* a pt. of **swear.**

sworn (swōrn, swôrn), *v.* **1.** pp. of **swear.** —*adj.* **2.** having taken an oath: *a duly elected and sworn official.* **3.** bound by or as by an oath or pledge. **4.** avowed; affirmed: *He is my sworn enemy.*

swot[1] (swot), *v.t.* **swot·ted, swot·ting,** *n.* swat[1]. —**swot′ter,** *n.*

swot[2] (swot), *v.,* **swot·ted, swot·ting,** *n.* *Brit. Slang.* —*v.i.* **1.** to study or work hard. —*n.* **2.** a student who studies hard; grind. **3.** hard study or hard work; concentrated effort. [ME *swot,* OE *swāt* perspiration; see SWEAT]

swot·ter (swot′ər), *n.* *Brit. Slang.* swot[2].

swound (swound, swo͞ond), *v.i., n.* *Archaic.* swoon. [late ME, deriv. of *swoun* SWOON + meaningless *-d*]

'swounds (zwoundz, zoundz, zwo͞ondz), *interj.* *Obs.* zounds. [short for *God's wounds*]

Swoy·ers·ville (swoi′ərz vil), *n.* a town in central Pennsylvania. 6751 (1960).

Swtz., Switzerland.

swum (swum), *v.* pp. of **swim.**

swung (swung), *v.* a pt. and pp. of **swing.**

swung′ dash′, a mark of punctuation (~) used in place of a word or part of a word previously spelled out.

swy (swī), *n.* *Australian.* the game of two-up. [< G *zwei* two]

Sy (sī), *n.* a boy's given name, form of **Seymour, Simon, Sylvan,** or **Silas.**

sy-, var. of **syn-** before *s* followed by a consonant and before *z: systaltic, syzygy.*

Syb·a·ris (sib′ə ris), *n.* an ancient Greek city in S Italy: noted for its wealth and luxury; destroyed 510 B.C.

Syb·a·rite (sib′ə rīt′), *n.* **1.** an inhabitant of Sybaris. **2.** (*l.c.*) one devoted to luxury and pleasure. [< L *Sybarīt(a)* < Gk *Sybarítēs.* See SYBARIS, -ITE[1]] —**syb·a·rit·ism** (sib′ə rī tiz′əm), *n.*
—**Syn. 2.** sensualist.

Syb·a·rit·ic (sib′ə rit′ik), *adj.* **1.** of, pertaining to, or characteristic of the Sybarites. **2.** (*l.c.*) pertaining to or characteristic of a sybarite; loving luxury or sensuous pleasure: *to wallow in sybaritic splendor.* Also, **Syb′a·rit′i·cal.** [< L *Sybarīticus* < Gk *Sybaritikós,* equiv. to *Sybarít(ēs)* SYBARITE + *-ikos* -IC] —**Syb′a·rit′i·cal·ly,** *adv.*

Syb·il (sib′əl), *n.* a girl's given name. Also, **Sibyl, Sibylle, Sy′ble.**

syc·a·mine (sik′ə min, -mīn′), *n.* a tree mentioned in the New Testament, probably the black mulberry. [< L *sȳcamin(us)* < Gk *sykáminos* < Sem; cf. Heb *shiqmāh* mulberry tree, sycamore (*y* < Gk *sŷkon* fig)]

syc·a·more (sik′ə mōr′, -môr′), *n.* **1.** *U.S.* the plane tree or buttonwood, *Platanus occidentalis.* **2.** *Brit.* the sycamore maple. **3.** a tree, *Ficus Sycomorus,* of the Near East, related to the common fig, bearing an edible fruit. [ME *sicomore* < OF < L *sȳcomor(us)* < Gk *sykómoros,* equiv. to *sŷko(n)* fig + *móron* mulberry, appar. by folk etymology < Sem; cf. Heb *shiqmāh* sycamore]

Syc·a·more (sik′ə mōr′, -môr′), *n.* a town in N Illinois. 6961 (1960).

syc′amore ma′ple, a maple, *Acer Pseudo-Platanus,* of Europe and western Asia, grown as a shade tree.

syce (sīs), *n.* (in India) a groom; stableman. Also, **saice, sice.** [< Urdu *sā'is* < Ar]

sy·cee (sī sē′), *n.* fine uncoined silver in lumps of various sizes usually bearing a banker's or assayer's stamp or mark, used in China as a medium of exchange. Also called **sycee′ sil′ver.** [< dial. Chin *sai szi,* Cantonese for Mandarin *hsi sze* fine silk: so called because it can be made into wire as fine as silk thread]

Sy·chae·us (si kē′əs), *n.* *Rom. Legend.* a priest of Hercules and the husband of Dido: murdered for his wealth by his brother-in-law Pygmalion. Also called **Acerbas.**

sy·con (sī′kon), *n.* a type of sponge having a thick body wall that is folded to form many short canals leading to the spongocoel. Cf. **ascon, leucon.** [< NL < Gk *sŷkon* fig]

sy·co·ni·um (sī kō′nē əm), *n., pl.* **-ni·a** (-nē ə). *Bot.* a multiple fruit developed from a hollow fleshy receptacle containing numerous flowers, as in the fig. [< NL < Gk *sŷkon* fig + NL *-ium* -IUM]

sy·co·noid (sī′kə noid′), *adj.* pertaining to or resembling a sycon. [SYCON + -OID]

syc·o·phan·cy (sik′ə fən sē), *n.* **1.** self-seeking or servile flattery. **2.** the character or conduct of a sycophant. [< L *sycophantia* < Gk *sykophantía,* equiv. to *sykophant-* (see SYCOPHANT) + *-ia* -CY]

syc·o·phant (sik′ə fənt), *n.* a self-seeking, servile flatterer; fawning parasite. [< L *sycophant(a)* < Gk *sykophántēs* informer, lit., fig-shower (i.e., one who makes the fig sign; see FIG), equiv. to *sŷko(n)* fig + *phan-* (s. of *phaínein* to show) + *-tēs* agentive suffix] —**syc·o·phan·tic** (sik′ə fan′tik), **syc′o·phan′ti·cal, sy′co·phant′ish,** *adj.* —**syc′o·phan′ti·cal·ly, sy′co·phant′ish·ly,** *adv.*
—**Syn.** toady, yes man.

sy·co·sis (sī kō′sis), *n.* *Pathol.* an inflammatory disease of the hair follicles, characterized by a pustular eruption. [< NL < Gk *sýkōsis,* equiv. to *sŷk(on)* fig + *-ōsis* -OSIS]

Syd (sid), *n.* a boy's or girl's given name, form of **Sidney** or **Sydney.** Also, **Sid.**

Syd·ney (sid′nē), *n.* **1. Sir Philip.** See **Sidney, Sir Philip. 2.** a seaport in and the capital of New South Wales, in SE Australia. 2,183,388 with suburbs (1961). **3.** a seaport on NE Cape Breton Island, Nova Scotia, in SE Canada. 33,617 (1961). **4.** Also, **Sidney.** a boy's or girl's given name.

Sy·e·ne (sī ē′nē), *n.* ancient name of **Aswan.**

sy·e·nite (sī′ə nīt′), *n.* a granular igneous rock consisting chiefly of orthoclase and oligoclase with hornblende, biotite, or augite. [< L *syēnīte(s)* (lapis stone) of SYENE < Gk *syēnī́tēs* (*líthos*); see -ITE[1]] **—sy·e·nit·ic** (sī′ə nit′ik), *adj.*

syke[1] (sīk), *n. Heraldry.* fountain (def. 7). [ME (north): little stream, var. of *siche*, OE *sīc*]

syke[2] (sīk), *n. Scot. and North Eng.* sike.

syl-, var. of **syn-** before *l*: *syllepsis.*

Syl·a·cau·ga (sil′ə kô′gə), *n.* a city in central Alabama. 12,857 (1960).

Syl·e·us (sil′ē əs, sil′o͞os), *n. Class. Myth.* a king who forced all passing travelers to work in his vineyard: he was killed by Hercules.

syll., **1.** syllable. **2.** syllabus.

syl·la·bar·y (sil′ə ber′ē), *n., pl.* **-bar·ies. 1.** a list or catalog of syllables. **2.** a set of written symbols, each of which represents a syllable, used to write a given language: *the Japanese syllabary.* [< NL *syllabārі(um).* See SYLLABLE, -ARY]

syl·la·bi (sil′ə bī′), *n.* a pl. of **syllabus.**

syl·lab·ic (si lab′ik), *adj.* **1.** of, pertaining to, or consisting of a syllable or syllables. **2.** pronounced with careful distinction of syllables. **3.** of, pertaining to, or noting poetry based on a specific number of syllables, as distinguished from poetry depending on stresses or quantities. **4.** (of chanting) having each syllable sung to one note only. **5.** *Phonet.* syllable-forming or syllable-dominating; sonantal. **—*n.* 6.** *Phonet.* a syllabic sound. [< L *syllabic(us)* < Gk *syllabikós.* See SYLLABLE, -IC] **—syl·lab′i·cal·ly,** *adv.*

syl·lab·i·cate (si lab′ə kāt′), *v.t.,* **-cat·ed, -cat·ing.** to syllabify. [back formation from *syllabication* < ML *syllabicātiōn-* (s. of *syllabicātiō*). See SYLLABIC, -ATION] **—syl·lab′i·ca′tion,** *n.*

syl·lab·i·fy (si lab′ə fī′), *v.t.,* **-fied, -fy·ing.** to form or divide into syllables. [< ML *syllabificāre.* See SYLLABLE, -IFY] **—syl·lab′i·fi·ca′tion,** *n.*

syl·la·bise (sil′ə bīz′), *v.t.,* **-bised, -bis·ing.** *Chiefly Brit.* syllabize.

syl·la·bism (sil′ə biz′əm), *n.* **1.** the use of syllabic characters, as in writing. **2.** division into syllables. [< L *syllab(a)* SYLLABLE + -ISM]

syl·la·bize (sil′ə bīz′), *v.t.,* **-bized, -biz·ing.** to syllabify. [< ML *syllabiz(āre)* < Gk *syllabízein.* See SYLLABLE, -IZE]

syl·la·ble (sil′ə bəl), *n., v.,* **-bled, -bling. —*n.* 1.** a segment of speech typically produced with a single pulse of air pressure from the lungs, and consisting of a center of relatively great sonority with or without one or more accompanying sounds of relatively less sonority: *"Man," "eye," "strength," and "sixths" are English words of one syllable.* **2.** (in writing systems) a character or a set of characters representing more or less exactly such an element of speech. **3.** the least portion or amount of speech or writing; the least mention: *Do not breathe a syllable of all this.* **—*v.t.* 4.** to utter in syllables; articulate. **5.** to represent by syllables. **—*v.i.* 6.** to utter syllables; speak. [late ME *sillable* < AF; MF *sillabe* < L *syllab(a)* < Gk *syllabḗ*, equiv. to *syl-* SYL- + *lab-* (root of *lambánein* to take) + *-ē* n. suffix]

syl·la·bub (sil′ə bub′), *n.* **1.** sillabub. **2.** a glass for serving sillabub.

syl·la·bus (sil′ə bəs), *n., pl.* **-bus·es, -bi** (-bī′). **1.** an outline or other brief statement of the main points of a discourse, the subjects of a course of lectures, the contents of a curriculum, etc. **2.** *Law.* **a.** a short summary of the legal basis of a court's decision appearing at the beginning of a reported case. **b.** a book containing summaries of the leading cases in a legal field, used esp. by students. **3.** (*often cap.*) Also called **Syl′labus of Er′rors.** *Rom. Cath. Ch.* the list of 80 propositions condemned as erroneous by Pope Pius IX in 1864. [< NL < L *sittybus* or *sillybus* title-slip on a book < Gk *sittýba* or *sillybos* < ?]

syl·lep·sis (si lep′sis), *n., pl.* **-ses** (-sēz). *Gram.* the use of a word or expression to perform two syntactic functions, esp. to modify two or more words of which at least one does not agree in number, case, or gender, as the use of *are* in *Neither he nor we are willing.* [< L < Gk, equiv. to *syl-* SYL- + *lēp-* (var. of *lab-, lamb-,* s. of *lambánein* to take and of *syllabḗ* syllable) + *-sis* -SIS] **—syl·lep·tic** (si lep′tik), *adj.* **—syl·lep′ti·cal·ly,** *adv.*

syl·lo·gise (sil′ə jīz′), *v.i., v.t.,* **-gised, -gis·ing.** *Chiefly Brit.* syllogize. **—syl′lo·gi·sa′tion,** *n.* **—syl′lo·gis′er,** *n.*

syl·lo·gism (sil′ə jiz′əm), *n.* **1.** *Logic.* an argument the conclusion of which is supported by two premises, of which one **(major premise)** contains the term **(major term)** that is the predicate of the conclusion, and the other **(minor premise)** contains the term **(minor term)** that is the subject of the conclusion; common to both premises is a term **(middle term)** that is excluded from the conclusion. A typical form is "All A is B; all B is C; therefore all A is C." **2.** deductive reasoning. **3.** an extremely subtle, sophisticated, or deceptive argument. [< L *syllogism(us)* < Gk *syllogismós,* equiv. to *syllog-* (see SYLLOGIZE) + *-ismos* -ISM; r. ME *silogime* < OF]

syl·lo·gis·tic (sil′ə jis′tik), *adj.* Also, **syl′lo·gis′ti·cal. 1.** of or pertaining to a syllogism. **2.** like or consisting of syllogisms. **—*n.* 3.** the part of logic which deals with syllogisms. **4.** syllogistic reasoning. [< L *syllogistic(us)* < Gk *syllogistikós,* equiv. to *syllogist(ós)* verbid of *syllogízesthai* (see SYLLOGIZE) + *-ikos* -IC] **—syl′lo·gis′ti·cal·ly,** *adv.*

syl·lo·gize (sil′ə jīz′), *v.i., v.t.,* **-gized, -giz·ing.** to argue or reason by syllogism. [ME *silogyse(n)* < LL *syllogizā(re)* < Gk *syllogíz(esthai)* (to) reason, equiv. to *syl-* SYL- + *logízesthai* to reckon, infer, equiv. to *lóg(os)* discourse + *-izesthai* -IZE] **—syl′lo·gi·za′tion,** *n.* **—syl′lo·giz′er,** *n.*

sylph (silf), *n.* **1.** a slender, graceful girl or woman. **2.** one of a race of imaginary beings supposed to inhabit the air. [< NL *sylph(ēs)* (pl.), coined by Paracelsus; appar. b. *sylva* (var. sp. of L *silva* forest) + Gk *nýmphē* NYMPH] **—sylph′ic,** *adj.* **—sylph′like′, sylph′ish, sylph′y,** *adj.*

—Syn. 2. SYLPH, SALAMANDER, UNDINE (NYMPH), GNOME were imaginary beings inhabiting the four elements once believed to make up the physical world. All except the GNOMES were female. SYLPHS dwelt in the air and were light, dainty, and airy beings. SALAMANDERS dwelt in fire: *"a salamander that . . . lives in the midst of flames"* (Addison). UNDINES were water spirits: *By marrying a man, an undine could acquire a mortal soul.* (They were also called NYMPHS, though nymphs were ordinarily minor divinities of nature who dwelt in woods, hills, and meadows as well as in waters.) GNOMES were little old men or dwarfs, dwelling in the earth: *ugly enough to be king of the gnomes.*

sylph·id (sil′fid), *n.* **1.** a little or young sylph. **—*adj.* 2.** Also, **sylph·id·ine** (sil′fi din, -dīn′). of, pertaining to, or characteristic of a sylph. [< F *sylphide.* See SYLPH, -ID[1]]

Syl·phon (sil′fon), *n. Trademark.* a box or chamber of thin metal, partially evacuated of air, used in aneroid barometers, temperature and pressure regulators, etc.

syl·va (sil′və), *n., pl.* **-vas, -vae** (-vē). silva. [< L]

Syl·va (sil′və; *Rum.* sēl′vä), *n.* **Car·men** (kär′mən; *Rum* kär′men), pen name of Elizabeth, queen of Rumania.

syl·van (sil′vən), *adj.* **1.** of, pertaining to, or inhabiting the woods. **2.** consisting of or abounding in woods or trees; wooded; woody: *a shady, sylvan glade.* **3.** made of trees, branches, boughs, etc. **—*n.* 4.** a person dwelling in a woodland region. **5.** a mythical deity or spirit of the woods. Also, **silvan.** [< L *sylvān(us),* var. of *silvānus,* equiv. to *silv(a)* forest + *-ānus* -AN]

Syl·van·a (sil van′ə), *n.* a girl's given name, form of **Silvia** or **Sylvia.** Also, **Silvana.**

Syl·va·ni·a (sil vā′nē ə, -vān′yə), *n.* **1.** a town in NW Ohio. 5187 (1960). **2.** a town in E Georgia. 3469 (1960).

syl·van·ite (sil′və nīt′), *n.* a mineral, gold silver telluride, $(AuAg)Te_2$, silver-white with metallic luster, often occurring in crystals so arranged as to resemble written characters but sometimes bladed: an ore of gold. [named after (TRAN)SYLVAN(IA); see -ITE[1]]

Syl·va·nus (sil vā′nəs), *n., pl.* **-ni** (-nī). Silvanus.

Syl·ves·ter (sil ves′tər), *n.* **1.** a town in central Georgia. 3610 (1960). **2.** Also, **Silvester.** a boy's given name.

Sylvester I, Saint, died A.D. 335, pope 314–335. Also, **Silvester I,**

Sylvester II, (*Gerbert*) died 1003, French ecclesiastic: pope 999–1003. Also, **Silvester II.**

Sylves′ter's dialyt′ic meth′od, *Math.* See **dialytic method.** [named after J. J. *Sylvester* (1814–97), English mathematician]

Syl·vi·a (sil′vē ə), *n.* a girl's given name. Also, **Silvia.**

Syl′vi·an fis′sure (sil′vē ən), *Anat.* See **lateral fissure.** [named after *Sylvi(us),* Latinized form of Jacques *Dubois* (d. 1555), French anatomist; see -AN]

syl′vic ac′id (sil′vik), *Chem.* See **abietic acid.** [< F *sylvique* < L *silv(a)* a wood + *-ique* -IC]

syl·vi·cul·ture (sil′və kul′chər), *n.* silviculture. [*sylvi-* (s. of L *sylva, silva,* forest) + -I- + CULTURE]

syl·vite (sil′vīt), *n.* a common mineral, potassium chloride, KCl, colorless to milky-white or red, occurring in crystals, usually cubes, and masses with cubic cleavage, bitter in taste: the most important source of potassium. Also, **syl·vin, syl·vine** (sil′vin). [< L (*sal digestivus*) *Sylv(ii)* digestive salt of Sylvius (see SYLVIAN FISSURE) + -ITE[1]; r. *sylvine* < F]

sym-, var. of **syn-** before *b, p, m: symbol; symphony; symmetry.*

sym., **1.** symbol. **2.** *Chem.* symmetrical. **3.** symphony. **4.** symptom.

Sy·mae·this (si mē′this), *n. Class. Myth.* a sea nymph, the mother, by Faunus, of Aeis.

sym·bi·ont (sim′bī ont′, -bē-), *n. Biol.* an organism living in a state of symbiosis. [< Gk *symbioûnt-* (s. of *symbioûs*) aorist participle of *symbioûn* to live together; see SYMBIOSIS] **—sym·bi·on·tic** (sim′bī on′tik, -bē-), *adj.*

sym·bi·o·sis (sim′bī ō′sis, -bē-), *n., pl.* **-ses** (-sēz). *Biol.* the living together of two dissimilar organisms, esp. when this association is mutually beneficial. [< Gk *symbíōsis,* equiv. to *sym-* SYM- + *bio-* (s. of *bioûn* to live) + *-ōsis* -OSIS] **—sym·bi·ot·ic** (sim′bī ot′ik, -bē-), **sym′bi·ot′i·cal,** *adj.* **—sym′bi·ot′i·cal·ly,** *adv.*

sym·bol (sim′bəl), *n., v.,* **-boled, -bol·ing** or (*esp. Brit.*) **-bolled, -bol·ling. —*n.* 1.** something used for or regarded as representing something else; a material object representing something, often something immaterial; emblem, token, or sign. **2.** a letter, figure, or other character or mark or a combination of letters or the like used to represent something: *the algebraic symbol x; the chemical symbol Au.* **3.** a word, phrase, image, or the like, having a complex of associated meanings and perceived as having inherent value separable from that which is symbolized, as being part of that which is symbolized, and as performing its normal function of standing for or representing that which is symbolized: usually conceived as deriving its meaning chiefly from the structure in which it appears, and generally distinguished from a sign. **—*v.t.* 4.** to symbolize. [< L *symbol(um)* < Gk *sýmbolon* sign, equiv. to *sym-* SYM- + *-bolon,* neut. var. of *bolḗ, bólos* a throw]

sym·bol·ic (sim bol′ik), *adj.* **1.** serving as a symbol of something (often fol. by *of*). **2.** of, pertaining to, or expressed by a symbol. **3.** characterized by or involving the use of symbols: *a highly symbolic poem.* **4.** (in semantics, esp. formerly) pertaining to a class of words which expressed only relations (contrasted with *notional*). Also, **sym·bol′i·cal.** [< LL *symbolic(us)* < Gk *symbolikós.* See SYMBOL, -IC] **—sym·bol′i·cal·ly,** *adv.* **—sym·bol′i·cal·ness,** *n.*

symbol′ical books′, *Eccles.* the books of a religion containing the creeds, beliefs, etc. Also, **symbol′ic books′.**

symbol′ic code′, *Computer Technol.* pseudocode.

symbol′ic lan′guage, a specialized language dependent upon the use of symbols for communication and created for the purpose of achieving greater exactitude, as in symbolic logic, mathematics, etc.

symbol′ic log′ic. See **mathematical logic.**

sym·bol·ics (sim bol′iks), *n.* (*construed as sing.*) the branch of theology dealing with the study of the history and meaning of church creeds and confessions. [see SYMBOLIC, -ICS]

sym·bol·ise (sim′bə līz′), *v.t., v.i.,* **-ised, -is·ing.** *Chiefly Brit.* symbolize. **—sym′bol·i·sa′tion,** *n.*

sym·bol·ism (sim′bə liz′əm), *n.* **1.** the practice of representing things by symbols, or of investing things with a symbolic meaning or character. **2.** a set or system of symbols. **3.** symbolic meaning or character. **4.** the principles and practice of symbolists in art or literature. **5.** (*cap.*) a movement of the late 19th century in French art and literature. Cf. **symbolist** (defs. 3b, 4b). **6.** the use of any of certain special figures or marks of identification to signify a religious message or divine being, as the cross for Christ and the Christian faith. [SYMBOL + -ISM]

sym·bol·ist (sim′bə list), *n.* **1.** a person who uses symbols or symbolism. **2.** a person versed in the study or interpretation of symbols. **3.** *Literature.* **a.** a writer who seeks to express or evoke emotions, ideas, etc., by stressing the symbolic value of language, to which is ascribed a capacity for communicating otherwise inexpressible visions of reality. **b.** (*usually cap.*) a member of a group of chiefly French and Belgian poets of the latter part of the 19th century who sought to evoke aesthetic emotions by emphasizing the associative character of verbal, often private, images or by using synesthetic devices, as vowel sounds, presumably evocative of color. **4.** *Fine Arts.* **a.** an artist who seeks to symbolize or suggest particular ideas by the objects represented, the colors used, etc. **b.** (*usually cap.*) a member of a group of late 19th-century artists characterized by such procedures. Cf. **Nabis, Synthetism. 5.** (*often cap.*) *Eccles.* a person who rejects the doctrine of transubstantiation and views the Eucharist symbolically. **6.** a person who favors the use of symbols in religious services. **—*adj.* 7.** of or pertaining to symbolists or symbolism. [SYMBOL + -IST] **—sym′bol·is′tic, sym′bol·is′ti·cal,** *adj.* **—sym′bol·is′ti·cal·ly,** *adv.*

sym·bol·ize (sim′bə līz′), *v.,* **-ized, -iz·ing. —*v.t.* 1.** to be a symbol of; stand for or represent in the manner of a symbol. **2.** to represent by a symbol or symbols. **3.** to regard or treat as symbolic. **—*v.i.* 4.** to use symbols. [< NL *symboliz(āre).* See SYMBOL, -IZE] **—sym′bol·i·za′tion,** *n.*

sym·bol·o·gy (sim bol′ə jē), *n.* **1.** the study of symbols. **2.** the use of symbols; symbolism. [by haplology, *symbolo-* (comb. form of SYMBOL) + -LOGY] **—sym·bo·log·i·cal** (sim′bə loj′i kəl), *adj.* **—sym·bol′o·gist,** *n.*

Sy·ming·ton (sī′ming tən), *n.* **(William) Stuart,** born 1901, U.S. politician.

Sym·ma·chus (sim′ə kəs), *n.* **Saint,** died A.D. 514, pope 498–514.

sym·met·al·ism (sim met′əliz′əm), *n.* the use of two (or more) metals, such as gold and silver, combined in assigned proportions as a monetary standard. [SYM- + *-metallism,* as in *bimetallism*]

sym·met·ri·cal (si me′tri kəl), *adj.* **1.** characterized by or exhibiting symmetry; well-proportioned, as a body or whole; regular in form or arrangement of corresponding parts. **2.** *Geom.* **a.** noting two points in a plane such that the line segment joining the points is bisected by an axis: *points (1, 1) and (1, −1) are symmetrical with respect to the x-axis.* **b.** noting a set consisting of pairs of points having this relation with respect to the same axis. **c.** noting two points in a plane such that the line segment joining the points is bisected by a point or center: *the points (1, 1) and (−1, −1) are symmetrical with respect to (0, 0).* **d.** noting a set consisting of pairs of points having this relation with respect to the same center. **3.** Often, **symmetric.** *Math.* **a.** noting a square matrix that is equal to its transpose. **b.** noting a dyad or dyadic that is equal to its conjugate. **4.** *Bot.* **a.** divisible into two similar parts by more than one plane passing through the center; actinomorphic. **b.** (of a flower) having the same number of parts in each whorl. **5.** *Chem.* **a.** having a structure which exhibits a regular repeated pattern of the component parts. **b.** noting a benzene derivative in which three substitutions have occurred at alternate carbon atoms. **6.** *Pathol.* affecting corresponding parts simultaneously, as certain diseases. Also, **sym·met′ric.** [SYMMETR(Y) + -ICAL] **—sym·met′ri·cal·ly,** *adv.* **—sym·met′ri·cal·ness,** *n.*

symmet′ric dif′ference, *Math.* the union of the relative complements of two sets. Also called **Boolean sum.**

symmet′ric func′tion, *Math.* a polynomial in several indeterminates which stays the same under any permutation of the indeterminates. Also called **symmet′ric polyno′mial.**

symmet′ric group′, *Math.* the group of all permutations of a finite set. Cf. **alternating group.**

sym·me·trise (sim′i trīz′), *v.t.,* **-trised, -tris·ing.** *Chiefly Brit.* symmetrize. **—sym′me·tri·sa′tion,** *n.*

sym·me·trize (sim′i trīz′), *v.t.,* **-trized, -triz·ing.** to reduce to symmetry; make symmetrical. [SYMMETR(Y) + -IZE] **—sym′me·tri·za′tion,** *n.*

sym·me·try (sim′i trē), *n., pl.* **-tries. 1.** the correspondence in size, form, and arrangement of parts on opposite sides of a plane, line, or point; regularity of form or arrangement with reference to corresponding parts. **2.** the proper or due proportion of the parts of a body or whole to one another with regard to size and form; excellence of proportion. **3.** beauty based on or characterized by such excellence of proportion. **4.** *Math.* a rotation or translation of a plane figure which leaves the figure unchanged although its position may be altered. [< L *symmetria* < Gk *symmetría* commensurateness. See SYM-, -METRY]

—Syn. 1. consonance, concord, correspondence. SYMMETRY, BALANCE, PROPORTION, HARMONY are terms used, particularly in the arts, to denote qualities based upon a correspondence or agreement, usually pleasing, among the parts of a whole. SYMMETRY implies either a quantitative equality of parts (*the perfect symmetry of pairs of matched columns*) or a unified system of subordinate parts: *the symmetry of a well-ordered musical composition.* BALANCE implies equality of parts, often as a means of emphasis: *Balance in sentences may emphasize the contrast in ideas.* PROPORTION depends less upon equality of parts than upon that agreement among them that is determined by their relation to a whole: *The dimensions of the room gave a feeling of right proportion.* HARMONY, a technical term in music, may also suggest the pleasing quality that arises from a just ordering of parts in other forms of artistic composition: *harmony of line, color, mass, phrase, ideas.* **—Ant. 1.** asymmetry.

sym′metry ax′is of ro′tary inver′sion, *Crystall.* See **rotation-inversion axis.**

sym′metry ax′is of rota′tion, *Crystall.* See **rotation axis.**

sym′metry class′, *Crystall.* See **point group.**

sym′metry el′ement, *Crystall.* any of four points, lines, or planes of a crystal: a center of symmetry, a reflection plane, a rotation axis, or a rotation-inversion axis.

sym′metry plane′, *Crystall.* See **reflection plane.**

Sym·onds (sim′əndz), *n.* **John Add·ing·ton** (ad′ing-tən), 1840–93, English poet, essayist, and critic.

Sy·mons (sī′mənz), *n.* **Arthur,** 1865–1945, English poet and critic, born in Wales.

sym·pa·thec·to·mize (sim′pə thek′tə mīz′), *v.t.,* **-mized, -miz·ing.** *Surg.* to perform a sympathectomy on. [SYMPATHECTOM(Y) + -IZE]

sym·pa·thec·to·my (sim′pə thek′tə mē), *n., pl.* **-mies.** *Med.* **1.** surgery which interrupts a part of the nerve pathways of the sympathetic or involuntary nervous system, as that of the glands, heart, or smooth muscle. **2.** Also called **chemical sympathectomy.** a like interruption by chemical means. [SYMPATH(ETIC) + -ECTOMY]

sym·path·e·tec·to·my (sim path′i tek′tə mē), *n., pl.* **-mies.** *Med.* sympathectomy.

sym·pa·thet·ic (sim′pə thet′ik), *adj.* **1.** characterized by, proceeding from, exhibiting, or feeling sympathy; sympathizing; compassionate: *a sympathetic listener.* **2.** acting or affected by, of the nature of, or pertaining to a special natural sympathy or affinity; congenial: *With their many similar tastes, he found her a most sympathetic companion.* **3.** looking upon with favor (often fol. by *to* or *toward*): *He is sympathetic to the project.* **4.** *Anat., Physiol.* **a.** pertaining to that portion of the autonomic nervous system consisting of nerves and ganglia that arise from the thoracic and lumbar regions of the spinal cord, and functioning in opposition to the parasympathetic system, as in stimulating heartbeat, dilating the pupil of the eye, etc. **b.** *Obs.* pertaining to the autonomic nervous system in its entirety. **5.** *Physics.* noting or pertaining to vibrations, sounds, etc., produced by a body as the direct result of similar vibrations in a different body. [< NL *sympathēticus* < Gk *sympathētikós.* See SYM-, PATHETIC] —**sym′pa·thet′i·cal·ly,** *adv.*
—Syn. 1. commiserating, kind, tender, affectionate.

sym′pathet′ic con′tact, *Sociol.* behavior toward an individual based on his personal make-up instead of on his group membership. Cf. **categoric contact.**

sym′pathet′ic ink′, a fluid for producing writing that is invisible until brought out by heat, chemicals, etc.; invisible ink.

sympathet′ic introspec′tion, *Sociol.* a study of human conduct in which the investigator imagines himself engaged in that conduct.

sym′pathet′ic mag′ic, magic predicated on the belief that one thing or event can affect another at a distance as a consequence of a sympathetic connection between them. Cf. **contagious magic, imitative magic.**

sympathet′ic ophthal′mia, *Ophthalm.* a condition characterized by an acute inflammation of the iris and ciliary body of one eye due to injury or disease of the other eye.

sym′pathet′ic strike′. See **sympathy strike.**

sym′pathet′ic string′, a thin wire string, as in various obsolete musical instruments, designed to vibrate sympathetically with the bowed or plucked strings to reinforce the sound.

sym·pa·thin (sim′pə thin), *n.* *Biochem.* a hormonelike substance, secreted by sympathetic nerve endings, that serves to increase the heart rate, constrict the arterioles of the skin and mucous membranes, and dilate the arterioles of the skeletal and cardiac muscles. [SYMPATH(ETIC) + -IN[2]]

sym·pa·thise (sim′pə thīz′), *v.i.,* **-thised, -this·ing.** *Chiefly Brit.* sympathize. —**sym′pa·this′ing·ly,** *adv.*

sym·pa·thize (sim′pə thīz′), *v.i.,* **-thized, -thiz·ing.** **1.** to be in sympathy or agreement of feeling; share in a feeling or feelings (often fol. by *with*). **2.** to feel a compassionate sympathy, as for suffering or trouble (often fol. by *with*). **3.** to express sympathy or condole (often fol. by *with*). **4.** to be in approving accord, as with a person, cause, etc.: *to sympathize with a person's aims.* **5.** to agree, correspond, or accord. [< MF *sympathise(r),* equiv. to *sympath(ie)* SYMPATHY + *-iser* -ISE] —**sym′pa·thiz′ing·ly,** *adv.*

sym·pa·thiz·er (sim′pə thī′zər), *n.* **1.** one who sympathizes. **2.** *Ophthalm.* an eye that exhibits ophthalmia because of disease or injury of the other. Also, *esp. Brit.,* **sym′pa·this′er.** [SYMPATHIZE + -ER[1]]

sym·pa·thy (sim′pə thē), *n., pl.* **-thies.** **1.** harmony of or agreement in feeling, as between persons or on the part of one person with respect to another. **2.** the harmony of feeling naturally existing between persons of like tastes or opinion or of congenial dispositions. **3.** the fact or power of sharing the feelings of another, esp. in sorrow or trouble; fellow feeling, compassion, or commiseration. **4. sympathies,** feelings or impulses of compassion. **5.** favorable or approving accord; favor or approval: *He viewed the plan with sympathy and publicly backed it.* **6.** agreement, consonance, or accord. **7.** *Psychol.* a relationship between persons in which the condition of one induces a parallel or reciprocal condition in another. **8.** *Physiol. Rare.* the relation between parts or organs whereby a condition, affection, or disorder of one part induces some effect in another. [< L *sympathīa* < Gk *sympátheia,* equiv. to *sympathḗ(s)* (*sym-* SYM- + *-pathēs,* alter. of *páthos* suffering, sensation) + *-ia* -Y[3]]

sym′pathy strike′, a strike by a body of workers, not because of grievances against their own employer, but by way of endorsing and aiding another body of workers who are on strike or have been locked out. Also called **sympathetic strike.**

sym·pat·ric (sim pa′trik, -pā′-), *adj.* *Biol., Ecol.* originating in or occupying the same geographical area. [SYM- + Gk *pátr(ā)* fatherland (*patr-,* s. of *patḗr* father + *-ā* fem. n. suffix) + -IC]

sym·pet·al·ous (sim pet′əl əs), *adj.* *Bot.* gamopetalous. [SYM- + PETALOUS]

sym·pho·nette (sim′fə net′), *n.* a small symphony orchestra that usually specializes in playing short, familiar classical works or salon music. [SYMPHON(Y) + -ETTE]

sym·pho·ni·a (sim fō′nē ə), *n.* any of various medieval musical instruments, as the hurdy-gurdy. [< LL, L: SYMPHONY]

sym·phon·ic (sim fon′ik), *adj.* **1.** *Music.* of, for, pertaining to, or having the character of a symphony or symphony orchestra. **2.** of or pertaining to symphony or harmony of sounds. **3.** characterized by similarity of sound, as words. [SYMPHON(Y) + -IC] —**sym·phon′i·cal·ly,** *adv.*

symphon′ic po′em, *Music.* a form of tone poem, scored for a symphony orchestra, in which a literary or pictorial "plot" is treated with considerable program detail: originated by Franz Liszt in the mid-19th century and developed esp. by Richard Strauss.

sym·pho·nie con·cer·tante (*Fr.* saN fô nē′ kôN-seR täNt′), *pl.* **sym·pho·nies con·cer·tantes** (*Fr.* saN fô nē′ kôN seR täNt′). an 18th-century orchestral work having several solo instruments, resembling the concerto grosso in form, but sharing the stylistic characteristics of the Mannheim School. [< F: symphony in concert]

Sym·pho·nie Fan·tas·tique (*Fr.* saN fô nē′ fäN-tas tēk′), a programmatic symphony (1830–31) in five movements by Hector Berlioz.

Sym·pho·nie Pas·to·rale, La (*Fr.* lA saN fô nē pas tô RAl′). See **Pastoral Symphony, The.**

sym·pho·ni·ous (sim fō′nē əs), *adj.* harmonious; in harmonious agreement or accord. [SYMPHONY + -OUS] —**sym·pho′ni·ous·ly,** *adv.*

sym·pho·nise (sim′fə nīz′), *v.i.,* **-nised, -nis·ing.** *Chiefly Brit.* symphonize. —**sym′pho·ni·sa′tion,** *n.*

sym·pho·nist (sim′fə nist), *n.* a composer who writes symphonies. [SYMPHON(Y) + -IST]

sym·pho·nize (sim′fə nīz′), *v.i.,* **-nized, -niz·ing.** to play or sound together harmoniously. [SYMPHON(Y) + -IZE]

sym·pho·ny (sim′fə nē), *n., pl.* **-nies.** **1.** *Music.* **a.** an elaborate instrumental composition in three or more movements, similar in form to a sonata but written for an orchestra, and usually of far grander proportions and more varied elements. **b.** an instrumental passage occurring in a vocal composition, or between vocal movements in a composition. **c.** an instrumental piece, often in several movements, forming the overture to an opera or the like. **2.** See **symphony orchestra.** **3.** a concert performed by a symphony orchestra. **4.** anything characterized by a harmonious combination of elements, esp. an effective combination of colors. **5.** harmony of sounds. **6.** *Archaic.* agreement; concord. [ME *symfonye* < OF *symphonie* < L *symphōnia* concert < Gk *symphōnía* harmony. See SYM-, -PHONY]

sym′phony or′chestra, a large orchestra composed of wind, string, and percussion instruments and organized to perform symphonic compositions.

sym·phys·i·al (sim fiz′ē əl), *adj.* of, pertaining to, or noting a symphysis. Also, **sym·phys′e·al.** [SYMPHYSI(S) + -AL[1]]

sym·phy·sis (sim′fi sis), *n., pl.* **-ses** (-sēz′). **1.** *Anat., Zool.* **a.** the growing together, or the fixed or nearly fixed union, of bones, as that of the two halves of the lower jaw in man, or of the pubic bones in the anterior part of the pelvic girdle. **b.** a line of junction or articulation so formed. **2.** *Bot.* a coalescence or growing together of parts. [< NL < Gk *sýmphysis* a growing together, equiv. to *sym-* SYM- + *phýsis,* equiv. to *phý(ein)* (to) grow + *-sis* -SIS] —**sym·phys·tic** (sim fis′tik), *adj.*

Sym·pleg·a·des (sim pleg′ə dēz′), *n.pl.* *Class. Myth.* See **Clashing Rocks.**

sym·plo·ce (sim′plō sē), *n.* *Rhet.* the simultaneous use of anaphora and epistrophe. [< LL < Gk *symplokḗ* intertwining, combination, equiv. to *sym-* SYM- + *plokḗ,* equiv. to *plok-* (var. of *plek-,* s. of *plékein* to plait) + *-ē* n. suffix]

sym·po·di·um (sim pō′dē əm), *n., pl.* **-di·a** (-dē ə). *Bot.* an axis or stem which simulates a simple stem but is made up of the bases of a number of axes which arise successively as branches, one from another, as in the grapevine; pseudaxis. Cf. **monopodium.** [< NL < Gk *sym-* SYM- + *pódion* small foot, base; see PODIUM] —**sym·po′di·al,** *adj.* —**sym·po′di·al·ly,** *adv.*

Sympodium

sym·po·si·ac (sim pō′zē ak′), *adj.* **1.** of, pertaining to, or suitable for a symposium. **—n. 2.** a symposium. [< L *symposiac(us)* < Gk *symposiakós.* See SYMPOSIUM, -AC]

sym·po·si·arch (sim pō′zē ärk′), *n.* **1.** the president, director, or master of a symposium. **2.** a toastmaster. [< Gk *symposíarch(os).* See SYMPOSIUM, -ARCH]

sym·po·si·um (sim pō′zē əm), *n., pl.* **-si·ums, -si·a** (-zē ə). **1.** a meeting or conference for the discussion of some subject, esp. a meeting at which several speakers talk on or discuss a topic before an audience. **2.** a collection of opinions expressed or articles contributed by several persons on a given subject or topic. **3.** an account of a discussion meeting or of the conversation at it. **4.** (in ancient Greece and Rome) a convivial meeting, usually following a dinner, for drinking and intellectual conversation. **5.** (*cap., italics.*) a philosophical dialogue (4th century B.C.) by Plato, dealing with ideal love and the vision of absolute beauty. [< L < Gk *sympósion* a drinking together, equiv. to *sym-* SYM- + *po-* (var. s. of *pínein* to drink) + *-sion* composite n. suffix]

symp·tom (simp′təm), *n.* **1.** any phenomenon or circumstance accompanying something and serving as evidence of it. **2.** a sign or indication of something. **3.** *Pathol.* a phenomenon that arises from and accompanies a particular disease or disorder and serves as an indication of it. [< LL *symptom(a)* < Gk *sýmptōma* occurrence, that which falls together with something, equiv. to *sym-* SYM- + *ptō-* (var. s. of *píptein* to fall) + *-ma* n. suffix]

symp·to·mat·ic (simp′tə mat′ik), *adj.* **1.** pertaining to a symptom or symptoms. **2.** of the nature of or constituting a symptom; indicative (often fol. by *of*): *a condition symptomatic of cholera.* **3.** according to symptoms: *a symptomatic classification of disease.* Also, **symp′to·mat′i·cal.** [< LL *symptomatic(us),* equiv. to *symptōmat-* (s. of *symptōma*) SYMPTOM + *-icus* -IC] —**symp′to·mat′i·cal·ly,** *adv.*

symp′tomat′ic an′thrax, *Vet. Pathol.* blackleg.

symp·tom·a·tol·o·gy (simp′tə mə tol′ə jē), *n.* **1.** the branch of medical science dealing with symptoms. **2.** the collective symptoms of a patient or disease. Cf. **syndrome.** [< NL *symptōmatologia,* equiv. to *symptomat-* (s. of *symptōma*) SYMPTOM + *-o-* -O- + *-logia* -LOGY]

symp·tom·less (simp′təm lis), *adj.* having or showing no symptoms. [SYMPTOM + -LESS]

symp·to·sis (simp tō′sis), *n.* *Pathol.* **1.** local or general atrophy. **2.** wasting away; emaciation. [< Gk *sýmptōsis* a falling together, collapse, equiv. to *symptō-* (see SYMPTOM) + *-sis* -SIS]

syn-, a prefix occurring in loan words from Greek, having the same function as **co-** (*synthesis; synoptic*); used, with the meaning "with," "together," in the formation of compound words (*synsepalous*). Also, **sy-, syl-, sym-, sys-.** [< Gk, comb. form repr. *sýn*]

syn., **1.** synonym. **2.** synonymous. **3.** synonymy.

syn·aer·e·sis (si ner′i sis), *n.* *Phonet.* **1.** the contraction of two syllables or two vowels into one, esp. the contraction of two vowels so as to form a diphthong. **2.** synizesis. Also, **syneresis.** [< LL < Gk *synaíresis* act of taking together, equiv. to *syn-* SYN- + *haire-* (s. of *hairein* to take) + *-sis* -SIS]

syn·aes·the·sia (sin′is thē′zhə, -zhē ə, -zē ə), *n.* synesthesia. —**syn·aes·thet·ic** (sin′is thet′ik), *adj.*

syn·a·gogue (sin′ə gog′, -gôg′), *n.* **1.** a Jewish house of worship, usually having facilities for religious instruction. **2.** an assembly or congregation of Jews for the purpose of religious worship. Also, **syn′a·gog′.** [ME *synagoge* < eccl. L *synagōg(a)* < Gk *synagōgḗ* assembly, meeting, equiv. to *syn-* SYN- + *agōgḗ,* n. use of fem. of *agōgós* (adj.) gathering, deriv. of *ágein* to bring, lead; akin to L *agere* to drive] —**syn·a·gog·i·cal** (sin′ə goj′i-kəl), **syn·a·gog·al** (sin′ə gog′əl, -gô′gəl), *adj.*

syn·al·gia (sin al′jə, -jē ə), *n.* See **referred pain.** [SYN- + -ALGIA] —**syn·al′gic,** *adj.*

syn·a·loe·pha (sin′əlē′fə), *n.* the blending of two successive vowels into one. Also, **syn′a·le′pha, syn·a·le·phe** (sin′əlē′fē). [< NL < Gk *synaloiphḗ, synaliphḗ,* equiv. to *syn-* SYN- + *aloiph-, aliph-* (var. stems of *aleíphein* to smear) + *-ē* n. suffix]

Syn·a·non (sin′ə non′), *n.* a private organization assisting those who wish to be cured of narcotics addiction.

syn·apse (sin′aps, si naps′), *n.* *Physiol.* the region of contact between the axon of one neuron and the dendrite or cell body of another neuron, across which nerve impulses are transmitted in one direction only. [back formation from *synapses,* pl. of SYNAPSIS]

syn·ap·sis (si nap′sis), *n., pl.* **-ses** (-sēz). **1.** *Biol.* the conjugation of homologous chromosomes, one from each parent, during early meiosis. **2.** *Physiol.* synapse. [< NL < Gk *sýnapsis* junction, equiv. to *synap-* (s. of *synáptein* to make contact, equiv. to *syn-* SYN- + *háptein* to touch) + *-sis* -SIS] —**syn·ap·tic** (si nap′tik), **syn·ap′ti·cal,** *adj.* —**syn·ap′ti·cal·ly,** *adv.*

sy·nap·te (sē′näp tē′, sin′ap tē), *n.* *Eastern Ch.* a litany. Also called **ektene.** [< MGk, n. use of fem. of Gk *synapt(ós)* (adj.) joined together; see SYNAPSIS]

syn·ap·tene (si nap′tēn), *n.* *Biol.* zygotene. [*synapt-* (see SYNAPSIS) + -ENE]

syn·ar·thro·di·a (sin′är thrō′dē ə), *n., pl.* **-di·ae** (-dē ē′). synarthrosis. [< NL; see SYN-, ARTHRODIA] —**syn′ar·thro′di·al,** *adj.* —**syn′ar·thro′di·al·ly,** *adv.*

syn·ar·thro·sis (sin′är thrō′sis), *n., pl.* **-ses** (-sēz). *Anat.* immovable articulation; a fixed or immovable joint; suture. [< NL < Gk *synárthrōsis,* equiv. to *synarthrō-* (s. of *synarthroûsthai* to be joined by articulation, equiv. to *syn-* SYN- + *árthro(n)* joint + *-esthai* inf. suffix) + *-sis* -SIS]

sy·na·xa·ri·on (sē′nä ksä′Rē ôn; *Eng.* sin′ak sâr′-ē on′), *n., pl.* **sy·na·xa·ri·a** (sē′nä ksä′Rē ä; *Eng.* sin′ak sâr′ē ə). *Gk. Orth. Ch.* **1.** a summary of the life of a saint or of the particulars of a feast, read at the orthros. **2.** a book containing such summaries. [< eccl. L < MGk, equiv. to *sýnax(is)* SYNAXIS + *-arion* -ARY]

syn·ax·a·ri·um (sin′ak sâr′ē əm), *n., pl.* **-ax·a·ri·a** (-ak sâr′ē ə). synaxarion.

syn·ax·a·ry (si nak′sə rē), *n., pl.* **-ries.** synaxarion.

syn·ax·is (si nak′sis), *n., pl.* **syn·ax·es** (si nak′sēz). an assembly for religious worship, esp. for the celebration of the Eucharist. [< eccl. L < MGk, equiv. to *synág(ein)* (to) meet together (see SYNAGOGUE) + *-sis* -SIS]

sync (singk), *Informal.* **—n. 1.** synchronism; synchronization: *The picture and the sound track were out of sync.* **—v.i., v.t. 2.** to synchronize. [shortened form]

syn·carp (sin′kärp), *n.* *Bot.* **1.** an aggregate fruit. **2.** a collective fruit. [< NL *syncarp(ium),* equiv. to *syncarp(us)* SYNCARPOUS + *-ium* n. suffix]

syn·car·pous (sin kär′pəs), *adj.* *Bot.* **1.** of the nature of or pertaining to a syncarp. **2.** composed of or having united carpels. [< NL *syncarpus.* See SYN-, CARPOUS] —**syn·car·py** (sin′kär pē), *n.*

sync-gen·er·a·tor (singk′jen′ə rā′tər), *n.* *Television.* an electronic generator that supplies synchronizing pulses to television scanning and transmitting equipment. [SYNC + GENERATOR]

synchro-, a combining form of **synchronized** and **synchronous:** *synchroscope; synchrotron.*

syn·chro·cy·clo·tron (sing′krō sī′klə tron′, -sik′lə-), *n.* *Physics.* a type of cyclotron that synchronizes its accelerating voltage with particle velocity in order to compensate for the relativistic mass increase of the particle as it approaches the speed of light. Also called **FM cyclotron, syn′chro-cy′clo·tron′.** [SYNCHRO- + CYCLOTRON]

syn·chro·flash (sing′krə flash′), *adj.* of or pertaining to photography employing a device that synchronizes the photoflash with the shutter. [SYNCHRO- + FLASH]

syn·chro·mesh (sing′krə mesh′), *Auto.* **—adj. 1.** noting or pertaining to a synchronized shifting mechanism. —*n.* **2.** a synchronized shifting mechanism. **3.** any of the gears of such a mechanism. [SYNCHRO- + MESH]

syn·chro·nal (siŋ′krə nəl), *adj.* synchronous. [< NL *synchron(us)* SYNCHRONOUS + -AL[1]]

syn·chron·ic (sin kron′ik), *adj. Ling.* having reference to the facts of a linguistic system as it exists at one point in time; not using information about the history of words, sounds, grammar, etc.: *synchronic analysis; synchronic dialectology.* Also, **syn·chron′i·cal.** Cf. **diachronic.** [< LL *synchron(us)* SYNCHRONOUS + -IC] —**syn·chron′i·cal·ly,** *adv.*

syn·chro·nise (siŋ′krə nīz′), *v.i., v.t.,* **-nised, -nis·ing.** *Chiefly Brit.* synchronize. —**syn′chro·ni·sa′tion,** *n.* —**syn′chro·nis′er,** *n.*

syn·chro·nism (siŋ′krə niz′əm), *n.* **1.** coincidence in time; contemporaneousness; simultaneousness. **2.** the arrangement or treatment of synchronous things or events in conjunction, as in a history. **3.** a tabular arrangement of historical events or personages, grouped according to their dates. **4.** *Physics, Elect.* the state of being synchronous. [< ML *synchronism(us)* < Gk *synchronismós,* equiv. to *synchron(ós)* SYNCHRONOUS + *-ismos* -ISM] —**syn′chro·nis′tic, syn′chro·nis′ti·cal,** *adj.* —**syn′chro·nis′ti·cal·ly,** *adv.*

syn·chro·nize (siŋ′krə nīz′), *v.,* **-nized, -niz·ing.** —*v.i.* **1.** to occur at the same time or coincide or agree in time. **2.** to go on, move, operate, work, etc., at the same rate and exactly together; recur together. —*v.t.* **3.** to cause to indicate the same time, as one timepiece with another: *Synchronize your watches.* **4.** to cause to go on, move, operate, work, etc., at the same rate and exactly together: *They synchronized their steps and walked on together.* **5.** to cause to agree in time of occurrence; assign to the same time or period, as in a history. **6.** to adjust the periodicities of (two or more electrical or mechanical devices) so that the periods are equal or integral multiples or fractions of each other. [< Gk *synchroniz(ein)* (to) be contemporary with, equiv. to *synchron(os)* SYNCHRONOUS + *-izein* -IZE] —**syn′chro·ni·za′tion,** *n.* —**syn′chro·niz′er,** *n.*

syn′chronized shift′ing, *Auto.* gear shifting in which the gears to be meshed are made to rotate at the same speed.

syn·chron·o·scope (sin kron′ə skōp′), *n.* synchroscope. [< NL *synchron(us)* SYNCHRONOUS + -O- + -SCOPE]

syn·chro·nous (siŋ′krə nəs), *adj.* **1.** occurring at the same time; coinciding in time; contemporaneous; simultaneous. **2.** going on at the same rate and exactly together; recurring together. **3.** *Physics, Elect.* having the same frequency and zero phase difference. **4.** (of a computer) having each operation started by regularly timed signals from a master clock. [< LL *synchronus* < Gk *synchronós,* equiv. to *syn-* SYN- + *chrón(os)* time + *-os* adj. suffix] —**syn′chro·nous·ly,** *adv.* —**syn′chro·nous·ness,** *n.*

syn′chronous convert′er, *Elect.* a synchronous machine for converting alternating current to direct current, or vice versa, in which the armature winding is connected to collector rings and to a commutator.

syn′chronous machine′, *Elect.* an alternating-current machine in which the average speed of normal operation is exactly proportional to the frequency of the system to which it is connected.

syn′chronous speed′, *Elect.* the speed at which an alternating-current machine must operate to generate electromotive force at a given frequency.

syn·chro·scope (siŋ′krə skōp′), *n.* an instrument for determining the difference in phase between two related motions, as those of two aircraft engines or two electric generators. Also, **synchronoscope.** [SYNCHRO- + -SCOPE]

syn·chro·tron (siŋ′krə tron′), *n. Physics.* a type of cyclotron consisting of magnetic sections alternately spaced with sections in which the particles are electrostatically accelerated. [SYNCHRO- + -TRON]

syn′chro u′nit (siŋ′krō), *Elect.* a type of alternating-current motor designed to maintain continuously, at some remote location, the same rotational angle that may be imposed by force upon the electrically connected rotating element of a similar motor.

syn·clas·tic (sin klas′tik), *adj. Math.* (of a surface) having principal curvatures of similar sign at a given point. Cf. **anticlastic.** [SYN- + Gk *klast(ós)* broken + -IC]

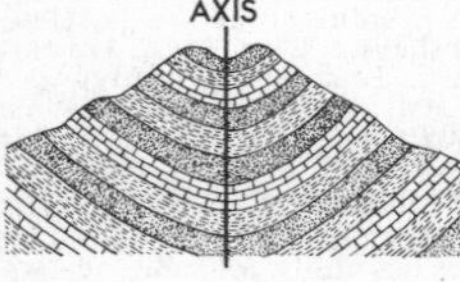

Synclinal folds

syn·cli·nal (sin klīn′əl, siŋ′kli nəl), *adj.* **1.** sloping downward in opposite directions so as to meet in a common point or line. **2.** *Geol.* **a.** inclining upward on both sides from a median line or axis, as a downward fold of rock strata. **b.** pertaining to such a fold. [SYN- + Gk *klīn(ein)* (to) lean + -AL[1]] —**syn·cli′nal·ly,** *adv.*

syn·cline (siŋ′klīn, sin′-), *n. Geol.* a synclinal fold. [back formation from SYNCLINAL]

syn·co·pate (siŋ′kə pāt′, sin′-), *v.t.,* **-pat·ed, -pat·ing.** **1.** *Music.* **a.** to place (the accents) on beats which are normally unaccented. **b.** to employ tones so affected in (a passage, piece, etc.). **2.** *Gram.* to contract (a word) by omitting one or more sounds from the middle, as in reducing *Gloucester* to *Gloster.* [< LL *syncopāt(us)* (ptp. of *syncopāre* to shorten by syncope). See SYNCOPE, -ATE[1]] —**syn′co·pa′tor,** *n.*

syn·co·pat·ed (siŋ′kə pā′tid, sin′-), *adj.* **1.** marked by syncopation: *syncopated rhythm.* **2.** cut short; abbreviated. [< LL *syncopāt(us).* See SYNCOPATE, -ED[2]]

syn·co·pa·tion (siŋ′kə pā′shən, sin′-), *n.* **1.** *Music.* a shifting of the normal accent, usually by stressing the normally unaccented beats. **2.** Also called **counterpoint, counterpoint rhythm.** *Pros.* the use of rhetorical stress at variance with the metrical stress of a line of verse, as in *Whether 'tis nobler in the mind to suffer. . . .* **3.** *Gram.* a syncope. [< ML *syncopātiōn-* (s. of *syncopātiō*), equiv. to LL *syncopāt(us)* (see SYNCOPATE) + *-iōn-* -ION]

Syncopation

syn·co·pe (siŋ′kə pē, -pē′, sin′-), *n.* **1.** *Gram.* the contraction of a word by omitting one or more sounds from the middle, as in the reduction of *never* to *ne'er.* **2.** *Pathol.* brief loss of consciousness associated with transient cerebral anemia, as in heart block, sudden lowering of the blood pressure, etc.; fainting. [late ME < LL < Gk *synkopḗ* a cutting short, equiv. to *syn-* SYN- + *kop-* (s. of *kóptein* to cut) + *-ē* n. suffix] —**syn·cop·ic** (sin kop′ik), **syn′co·pal,** *adj.*

syn·cre·tism (siŋ′kri tiz′əm, sin′-), *n.* **1.** the attempted reconciliation or union of different or opposing principles, practices, or parties, as in philosophy or religion. **2.** *Gram.* the merging, as by historical change in a language, of two or more categories in a specified environment into one, as, in nonstandard English, the use of *was* with both singular and plural subjects, while in standard English *was* is used with singular subjects (except for *you* in the second person singular) and *were* with plural subjects. [< NL *syncretism(us)* < Gk *synkrētismós* union of Cretans, hence a united front of two opposing parties against a common foe, deriv. of *synkrētíz(ein)* (to) SYNCRETIZE, with *-ismos* -ISM r. *-izein* -IZE] —**syn·cret·ic** (sin kret′ik), **syn·cret′i·cal, syn·cre·tis·tic** (siŋ′kri tis′tik, sin′-), **syn′cre·tis′ti·cal,** *adj.*

syn·cre·tize (siŋ′kri tīz′, sin′-), *v.t., v.i.,* **-tized, -tiz·ing.** to attempt to combine or unite, as different or opposing principles, parties, etc. [< NL *syncrētīz(āre)* < Gk *synkrētíz(ein)* (to) form a confederation, equiv. to *syn-* SYN- + *Krēt-* (s. of *Krḗs*) a Cretan + *-izein* -IZE; see SYNCRETISM]

syn·cri·sis (siŋ′kri sis, sin′-), *n. Rhet. Obs.* the comparison of opposites. [< LL < Gk *sýnkrisis* combination, comparison, equiv. to *syn-* SYN- + *kri-* (s. of *krī́nein* to separate) + *-sis* -SIS]

syn·cy·tium (sin sish′əm, -ē əm), *n., pl.* **-cy·tia** (-sish′ə, -ē ə). *Biol.* a multinucleate mass of protoplasm that is not differentiated into cells. [< NL; see SYN-, CYTO-, -IUM] —**syn·cy·tial** (sin sish′əl), *adj.*

synd., **1.** syndicate. **2.** syndicated.

syn·dac·tyl (sin dak′til), *adj.* **1.** having certain digits joined together. —*n.* **2.** a syndactyl animal. Also, **syn·dac′tyle.** [var. of SYNDACTYLUS] —**syn·dac·tyl·ism** (sin dak′təliz′əm), *n.*

syn·dac·ty·lus (sin dak′tələs), *n., pl.* **-ty·li** (-təlī′). *Med.* a person having united or webbed fingers or toes. [SYN- + Gk *dáktylos* finger, toe; see DACTYL]

syn·de·re·sis (sin′də rē′sis), *n.* **1.** innate knowledge of the basic principles of morality. **2.** *Christian Mysticism.* the essence of the soul which unites with God. Also, **synteresis.** [< ML < Gk *syntḗrēsis* a guarding, deriv. of *syntērein* to guard closely, equiv. to *syn-* SYN- + *tērein* to guard]

syn·de·sis (sin′di sis, sin dē′-), *n., pl.* **-ses** (-sēz′, -sēz). *Biol.* synapsis. [< NL < Gk, equiv. to *syn-* SYN- + *désis,* equiv. to *de-* (s. of *dein* to bind) + *-sis* -SIS]

syndesm-, a learned borrowing from Greek meaning "bond," "ligament," used in the formation of compound words: *syndesmosis.* [comb. form repr. Gk *sýndesmos* that which binds together, equiv. to *syn-* SYN- + *de-* (s. of *dein* to bind; see SYNDESIS) + *-smos,* var. of *-ismos* -ISM]

syn·des·mec·to·my (sin′dez mek′tə mē), *n., pl.* **-mies.** *Surg.* excision of part of a ligament. [SYNDESM- + -ECTOMY]

syn·des·mo·sis (sin′des mō′sis), *n., pl.* **-ses** (-sēz). *Anat.* a connection of bones by ligaments, fasciae, or membranes other than in a joint. [SYNDESM- + -OSIS] —**syn·des·mot·ic** (sin′des mot′ik), *adj.*

syn·det (sin′det), *n.* a synthetic detergent. [SYN(THETIC) + DET(ERGENT)]

syn·det·ic (sin det′ik), *adj.* **1.** serving to unite or connect; connective; copulative. **2.** conjunctive (def. 3c). Also, **syn·det′i·cal.** [< Gk *syndetik(ós),* equiv. to *sýndet(os)* bound together (*syn-* SYN- + *de-* (see SYNDESIS) + *-tos* verbal adj. suffix) + *-ikos* -IC] —**syn·det′i·cal·ly,** *adv.*

syn·dic (sin′dik), *n.* **1.** a person chosen to represent and transact business for a corporation, as a university. **2.** a civil magistrate having different powers in different countries. [< F < LL *syndic(us)* city official < Gk *sýndikos* counsel for defendant, equiv. to *syn-* SYN- + *dik-* (s. of *díkē*) justice + *-os* n. suffix] —**syn′dic·ship′,** *n.*

syn·di·cal (sin′di kəl), *adj.* **1.** noting or pertaining to a union of persons engaged in a particular trade. **2.** of or pertaining to syndicalism. [< F; see SYNDIC, -AL[1]]

syn·di·cal·ism (sin′di kə liz′əm), *n.* **1.** a form or development of trade unionism, originating in France, which aims at the possession of the means of production and distribution, and ultimately at the control of society, by the federated bodies of industrial workers, and which seeks to realize its purposes through general strikes, terrorism, sabotage, etc. **2.** an economic system in which workers own and manage industry. [< F *syndicalisme.* See SYNDICAL, -ISM] —**syn′di·cal·ist,** *adj., n.* —**syn′di·cal·is′tic,** *adj.*

syn·di·cate (*n.* sin′də kit; *v.* sin′də kāt′), *n., v.,* **-cat·ed, -cat·ing.** —*n.* **1.** a group of individuals or organizations combined or making a joint effort to undertake some specific duty or carry out specific transactions or negotiations: *The local furniture store is individually owned, but is part of a buying syndicate.* **2.** a combination of bankers or capitalists formed for the purpose of carrying out some project requiring large resources of capital, as the underwriting of an issue of stock or bonds. **3.** *Journalism.* **a.** an agency that buys articles, stories, columns, photographs, comic strips, or other features and distributes them for simultaneous publication in a number of newspapers or periodicals in different localities. Cf. **boiler plate** (def. 2). **b.** a business organization owning and operating a number of newspapers; newspaper chain. **4.** a group, combination, or association of gangsters controlling organized crime or one type of crime, esp. in one region of the country. **5.** a council or body of syndics. **6.** (formerly) a local organization of employers or employees in Italy during the fascist regime. —*v.t.* **7.** to combine into a syndicate. **8.** to publish simultaneously, or supply for simultaneous publication, in a number of newspapers or other periodicals in different places: *His column is syndicated in 120 papers.* [< MF *syndicat* office of syndic, board of syndics. See SYNDIC, -ATE[1]] —**syn′di·ca′tion,** *n.*

syn·drome (sin′drōm, sin′drə mē′), *n.* **1.** *Pathol., Psychiatry.* a group of symptoms that together are characteristic of a specific condition, disease, or the like. **2.** a group of related or coincident things, events, actions, etc. **3.** the pattern of symptoms which characterize or indicate a particular social condition. [< NL < Gk *syndromḗ* concurrence, combination, equiv. to *syn-* SYN- + *drom-* (var. s. of *dramein* to run) + *-ē* n. suffix] —**syn·drom·ic** (sin drom′ik), *adj.*

syne (sīn), *adv., prep., conj. Scot. and North Eng.* since. [ME (north), deriv. of *sithen* SITH]

syn·ec·do·che (si nek′də kē), *n. Rhet.* a figure of speech in which a part is used for the whole or the whole for a part, the special for the general or the general for the special, as in "ten sail" for ten ships or "a Croesus" for a rich man. [< L < Gk *synekdochḗ,* equiv. to *syn-* SYN- + *ekdochḗ* act of receiving from another, equiv. to *ek-* EC- + *doch-* (var. s. of *déchesthai* to receive) + *-ē* n. suffix] —**syn·ec·doch·ic** (sin′ek dok′ik), **syn′ec·doch′i·cal,** *adj.* —**syn′ec·doch′i·cal·ly,** *adv.*

syn·ech·i·a (si nek′ē ə, -nē′kē ə, sin′ə kī′ə), *n., pl.* **syn·ech·i·ae** (si nek′ē ē′, -nē′kē ē′, sin′ə kī′ē). *Med., Pathol.* any adhesion of parts of the body, as of the iris to the cornea. [< NL < Gk *synécheia* continuity, coherence, equiv. to *synechḗ(s)* (*syn-* SYN- + *ech-,* s. of *échein* to hold, + *-ēs* adj. suffix) + *-ia* -IA]

syn·e·chism (sin′ə kiz′əm), *n.* a tendency of philosophical thinking, stressing the importance of the idea of continuity: named and advocated by C. S. Peirce. [SYNECH(IA) + -ISM] —**syn′e·chist,** *n., adj.,* —**syn′e·chis′tic,** *adj.*

syn·e·cious (si nē′shəs), *adj.* synoicous. [SYN- + *eci-* (< Gk *oikía* house) + -OUS]

syn·e·col·o·gy (sin′ə kol′ə jē), *n.* the branch of ecology dealing with the relations between plant and animal communities and their environments. Cf. **autecology.** [SYN- + ECOLOGY] —**syn·ec·o·log·ic** (sin′ek ə loj′ik), **syn·ec·o·log′i·cal,** *adj.* —**syn′ec·o·log′i·cal·ly,** *adv.*

syn·ec·tics (si nek′tiks), *n.* (*construed as sing.*) the study of creative processes, esp. as applied to the solution of problems by a group of diverse individuals. [< LL *synectic(us)* < Gk *synektikós,* equiv. to *synéch(ein)* (see SYNECHIA) + *-tikos* -TIC; see -ICS]

synec′tics group′, a group of people of varied background that meets to attempt creative solutions of problems through the unrestricted exercise of imagination and the correlation of disparate elements.

syn·er·e·sis (si ner′i sis), *n.* **1.** synaeresis. **2.** *Physical Chem.* the contraction of a gel accompanied by the exudation of liquid. [var. of SYNAERESIS]

syn·er·get·ic (sin′ər jet′ik), *adj.* working together; cooperative. [< Gk *synergētik(ós),* equiv. to *syn-* SYN- + *-ergētikos;* see ENERGETIC]

syn·er·gism (sin′ər jiz′əm, si nûr′jiz-), *n.* **1.** *Theol.* the doctrine that the human will cooperates with the Holy Ghost in the work of regeneration. Cf. **monergism.** **2.** the joint action of agents, as drugs, which when taken together increase each other's effectiveness. [< NL *synergism(us)* < Gk *synerg(ós)* (*syn-* SYN- + *érg(on)* work + *-os* adj. suffix) + NL *-ismus* -ISM]

syn·er·gist (sin′ər jist, si nûr′-), *n.* **1.** *Theol.* one who holds the doctrine of synergism. **2.** *Physiol., Med.* a body organ, medicine, etc., that cooperates with another or others to produce or enhance an effect. **3.** *Chem., Pharm.* any admixture to a substance for increasing the effectiveness of one or more of its properties. [< NL *synergist(a)* < Gk *synerg(ós)* (see SYNERGISM) + NL *-ista* -IST]

syn·er·gis·tic (sin′ər jis′tik), *adj.* working together; synergetic. [SYNERG(ISM) or SYNERG(IST) + -ISTIC] —**syn′er·gis′ti·cal·ly,** *adv.*

syn·er·gy (sin′ər jē), *n., pl.* **-gies.** **1.** combined action. **2.** the cooperative action of two or more muscles, nerves, or the like. **3.** the cooperative action of two or more stimuli or drugs. **4.** *Rocketry.* the compromise between the optimum ascent trajectory of an escape rocket and the effects of gravitation and the atmosphere. [< NL *synergia* < Gk *synergía,* equiv. to *synerg(ós)* (see SYNERGISM) + *-ia* -Y[3]] —**syn·er·gic** (si nûr′jik), *adj.*

syn·e·sis (sin′i sis), *n. Gram.* a construction in which an expected grammatical agreement in form is replaced by an agreement in meaning, as in *the committee are,* where a plural verb is used with a singular noun. [< NL < Gk: understanding, intelligence, equiv. to *syn-* SYN- + (*h*)*e-* (s. of *hiénai* to throw, send) + *-sis* -SIS]

syn·es·the·sia (sin′is thē′zhə, -zhē ə, -zē ə), *n.* a sensation produced in one modality when a stimulus is applied to another modality, as when the hearing of a certain sound induces the visualization of a certain color. Also, **synaesthesia.** [< NL; see SYN-, ESTHESIA] —**syn·es·thet·ic** (sin′is thet′ik), *adj.*

sy·net·ic (si net′ik), *adj.* synoetic.

syn·fu·el (sin′fyōō′əl), *n.* See **synthetic fuel.** [SYN(THETIC) + FUEL]

syn·ga·my (siŋ′gə mē), *n. Biol.* union of gametes, as in fertilization or conjugation; sexual reproduction. [SYN- + -GAMY] —**syn·gam·ic** (sin gam′ik), **syn·ga·mous** (siŋ′gə məs), *adj.*

Synge (siŋ), *n.* **1. John Mill·ing·ton** (mil′iŋ tən), 1871–1909, Irish dramatist. **2. Richard Laurence Mil·ling·ton** (mil′iŋ tən), born 1914, English biochemist: Nobel prize 1952.

syn·gen·e·sis (sin jen′i sis), *n. Biol.* sexual reproduction. [< NL; see SYN-, GENESIS] —**syn·ge·net·ic** (sin′jə net′ik), *adj*

syn·i·ze·sis (sin′i zē′sis), *n. Phonet.* the combination into one syllable of two vowels (or of a vowel and a diphthong) that do not form a diphthong. Also called **synaeresis.** [< LL < Gk *synízēsis,* equiv. to *syn-* SYN- + (*h*)*iz-* (s. of *hízein* to sit) + *-ēsis* -ESIS]

syn·ne·ma (si nē′mə), *n., pl.* **-ma·ta** (-mə tə). *Bot.* a coremium having very compact condiophores. [< NL, equiv. to *syn-* SYN- + Gk *nêma* thread]

syn·od (sin′əd), *n.* **1.** an assembly of ecclesiastics or other church delegates convoked pursuant to the law of the church, for the discussion and decision of ecclesiastical affairs; ecclesiastical council. **2.** any council. [late ME < L *synod(us)* < Gk *sýnodos* meeting, equiv. to *syn-* SYN- + *hodós* way] —**syn′od·al,** *adj.*

syn·od·ic (si nod′ik), *adj. Astron.* pertaining to a conjunction, or to two successive conjunctions of the same bodies. Also, **syn·od′i·cal.** [< LL *synodic(us)* < Gk *synodikós.* See SYNOD, -IC] —**syn·od′i·cal·ly,** *adv.*

synod′ic month′. See under **month** (def. 5).

syn·o·et·ic (si net′ik), *adj.* being or associating with others, as in a community or other environment: *synoetic education.* Also, **synetic.** [< Gk]

syn·oi·cous (si noi′kəs), *adj. Bot.* having male and female flowers on one head, as in many composite plants. Also, **synecious, syn·oe·cious** (si nē′shəs). [< Gk *sýnoikos* dwelling in the same house, equiv. to *syn-* SYN- + *oik-* (s. of *oîkos, oikía* house, *oikein* to dwell) + *-os* -OUS] —**syn·oi′cous·ly, syn·oe′cious·ly,** *adv.* —**syn·oi′cous·ness, syn·oe′cious·ness,** *n.*

syn·o·nym (sin′ə nim), *n.* **1.** a word having the same or nearly the same meaning as another in the language, as *joyful, elated, glad.* **2.** a word or expression accepted as another name for something, as *Arcadia* for *pastoral simplicity.* **3.** *Bot., Zool.* a rejected scientific name, other than a homonym. [< LL *synonym(um)* < Gk *synṓnymon*, n. use of neut. of *synṓnymos* SYNONYMOUS; r. ME *sinonyme* < MF] —**syn′o·nym′ic, syn′o·nym′i·cal,** *adj.* —**syn·o·nym·i·ty** (sin′ə nim′i tē), *n.*

syn·on·y·mise (si non′ə mīz′), *v.t.*, **-mised, -mis·ing.** *Chiefly Brit.* synonymize.

syn·on·y·mize (si non′ə mīz′), *v.t.*, **-mized, -miz·ing.** to give synonyms for (a word, name, etc.); furnish with synonyms. [SYNONYM + -IZE]

syn·on·y·mous (si non′ə məs), *adj.* having the character of synonyms or a synonym; equivalent in meaning; expressing or implying the same idea. [< LL *synōnymus* < Gk *synṓnymos*, equiv. to *syn-* SYN- + *-ōnym-* -ONYM + *-os* -OUS] —**syn·on′y·mous·ly,** *adv.* —**syn·on′y·mous·ness,** *n.*

syn·on·y·my (si non′ə mē), *n., pl.* **-mies. 1.** the quality of being synonymous; equivalence in meaning. **2.** the study of synonyms. **3.** a set, list, or system of synonyms. **4.** *Bot., Zool.* **a.** a list of the scientific names for a particular species or other group, or for various species, etc., with discriminations or explanatory matter. **b.** these names collectively, whether listed or not. [< LL *synōnymia* < Gk. See SYNONYMOUS, -Y³]

synop., synopsis.

syn·oph·thal·mi·a (sin′of thal′mē ə), *n. Med.* cyclopia. [SYN- + OPHTHALMIA]

syn·op·sis (si nop′sis), *n., pl.* **-ses** (-sēz). **1.** a brief or condensed statement giving a general view of some subject. **2.** a compendium of heads or short paragraphs giving a view of the whole. **3.** a brief summary of the plot of a novel, motion picture, play, etc. [< LL < Gk *sýnopsis*, equiv. to *syn-* SYN- + *op-* (suppletive s. of *horân* to see; cf. AUTOPSY) + *-sis* -SIS]
—**Syn.** condensation, epitome, abstract, abridgment, précis. See **summary.**

syn·op·sise (si nop′sīz), *v.t.*, **-sised, -sis·ing.** *Chiefly Brit.* synopsize.

syn·op·size (si nop′sīz), *v.t.*, **-sized, -siz·ing.** to make a synopsis of; summarize. [SYNOPS(IS) + -IZE]

syn·op·tic (si nop′tik), *adj.* **1.** pertaining to or constituting a synopsis; affording or taking a general view of the principal parts of a subject. **2.** (*often cap.*) taking a common view: used chiefly in reference to the first three Gospels (**synop′tic Gos′pels**), Matthew, Mark, and Luke, from their similarity in content, order, and statement. **3.** (*often cap.*) pertaining to the synoptic Gospels. Also, **syn·op′ti·cal.** [< Gk *synoptik(ós)*, equiv. to *synop-* (see SYNOPSIS) + *-tikos* -TIC] —**syn·op′ti·cal·ly,** *adv.*

synop′tic chart′, a chart showing the distribution of meteorological conditions over a wide region at a given moment.

synop′tic meteorol′ogy, a branch of meteorology analyzing data taken simultaneously over a large area, for the purpose of weather forecasting.

syn·op·tist (si nop′tist), *n.* (*often cap.*) one of the authors (Matthew, Mark, or Luke) of the synoptic Gospels. [SYNOPT(IC) + -IST] —**syn′op·tis′tic,** *adj.*

syn·os·te·o·sis (si nos′tē ō′sis), *n., pl.* **-ses** (-sēz). *Anat.* synostosis.

syn·os·to·sis (sin′o stō′sis), *n., pl.* **-ses** (-sēz). *Anat.* union of separate bones into a single bone. [< NL; see SYN-, OSTOSIS] —**syn·os·tot·ic** (sin′o stot′ik), **syn′os·tot′i·cal,** *adj.* —**syn′os·tot′i·cal·ly,** *adv.*

syn·o·vi·a (si nō′vē ə), *n. Physiol.* a lubricating fluid resembling the white of an egg, secreted by certain membranes, as those of the joints. [< NL, equiv. to *syn-* SYN- + L *ov-* (s. of *ōvum* egg) + *-ia* -IA] —**syn·o′vi·al,** *adj.* —**syn·o′vi·al·ly,** *adv.*

syn·o·vi·tis (sin′ə vī′tis), *n. Pathol.* inflammation of a synovial membrane. [SYNOV(IA) + -ITIS] —**syn·o·vit·ic** (sin′ə vit′ik), *adj.*

syn·sac·rum (sin sak′rəm, -sā′krəm), *n., pl.* **-sac·ra** (-sak′rə, -sā′krə). *Ornith.* a dorsal ridge of bone in the pelvic region of birds, formed by the fusion of certain thoracic, lumbar, sacral, and caudal vertebrae. [SYN- + SACRUM] —**syn·sa′cral,** *adj.*

syn·sep·al·ous (sin sep′ə ləs), *adj. Bot.* gamosepalous. [SYN- + -SEPALOUS]

syn·tac·tic (sin tak′tik), *adj.* **1.** of or pertaining to syntax. **2.** consisting of or noting morphemes which are combined in the same order as they would be if they were separate words in a corresponding construction: Blackberry, *which consists of an adjective followed by a noun, is a syntactic compound.* Also, **syn·tac′ti·cal.** [< NL *syntactic(us)* < Gk *syntaktikós*, equiv. to *syntakt(ós)* ordered, arranged together, verbal of *syntássein* to arrange together (*syn-* SYN- + *tak-*, deriv. of *tag-* root of *tássein*, + *-tos* adj. suffix) + *-ikos* -IC] —**syn·tac′ti·cal·ly,** *adv.*

syntac′tic construc′tion, *Gram.* a construction which has no bound forms among its immediate constituents.

syn·tac·tics (sin tak′tiks), *n.* (*construed as sing.*) *Logic, Philos.* the branch of semiotics dealing with the formal properties of languages and systems of symbols. Also called **logical syntax.** [see SYNTACTIC, -ICS]

syn·tal·i·ty (sin tal′i tē), *n.* behavioral characteristics of a group perceived as parallel to or inferable from the personality structure of an individual. [SYN- + *-t-* connective + *-ality*, as in *personality*]

syn·tax (sin′taks), *n.* **1.** *Ling.* **a.** the study of the rules for the formation of grammatical sentences in a language. **b.** the study of the patterns of formation of sentences and phrases from words and suprasegmentals. **c.** the rules or patterns so studied: *English syntax.* **d.** a presentation of these: *a syntax of English.* **e.** an instance of these: *the syntax of a sentence.* **2.** *Logic.* **a.** that branch of modern logic which studies the various kinds of signs that occur in a system and the possible arrangements of those signs, complete abstraction being made of the meaning of the signs. **b.** the outcome of such a study when directed upon a specified language. **3.** *Obs.* a system. [short for earlier *syntaxis* < LL < Gk, equiv. to *syntak-* (var. of *syntag-*; see SYNTACTIC) + *-sis* -SIS]

syn′tax lan′guage, *Philos.* a metalanguage used to refer to the grammatical or other formal features of an object language.

syn·te·re·sis (sin′tə rē′sis), *n.* synderesis.

syn·the·sis (sin′thi sis), *n., pl.* **-ses** (-sēz′). **1.** the combining of the constituent elements of separate material or abstract entities into a single or unified entity (opposed to *analysis*). **2.** a complex whole formed by combining. **3.** *Chem.* the forming or building of a more complex substance or compound from elements or simpler compounds. **4.** a process of reasoning in which the conclusion is reached directly from given propositions and established or assumed principles. **5.** *Philos.* See under **Hegelian dialectic.** [< L < Gk *sýnthesis*, equiv. to *syn-* SYN- + *the-* (s. of *tithénai* to put, place) + *-sis* -SIS] —**syn′the·sist,** *n.*

syn·the·sise (sin′thi sīz′), *v.t.*, **-sised, -sis·ing.** *Chiefly Brit.* synthesize. —**syn′the·sis′er,** *n.*

syn′thesis gas′, *Chem.* any gaseous mixture consisting essentially of carbon monoxide and hydrogen, derived by the action of steam on coal or natural gas, used chiefly in the synthesis of hydrocarbons.

syn·the·size (sin′thi sīz′), *v.t.*, **-sized, -siz·ing. 1.** to form (a material or abstract entity) by combining parts or elements (opposed to *analyze*): *to synthesize a statement.* **2.** *Chem.* to combine (constituent elements) into a single or unified entity: *Scientists synthesize carbon and other matter under pressure to make diamonds.* **3.** to treat synthetically. Also, **synthetize.** [SYNTHES(IS) + -IZE] —**syn′the·si·za′tion,** *n.* —**syn′the·siz′er,** *n.*

syn·thet·ic (sin thet′ik), *adj.* Also, **syn·thet′i·cal. 1.** of, pertaining to, proceeding by, or involving synthesis (opposed to *analytic*). **2.** *Chem.* noting or pertaining to compounds formed by chemical reaction in a laboratory, as opposed to those of natural origin. **3.** (of a language) characterized by a relatively widespread use of affixes, rather than separate words, to express syntactic relationships: Latin is a synthetic language, while English is analytic. Cf. **analytic** (def. 2), **polysynthetic. 4.** not real or genuine; artificial; feigned: *a synthetic chuckle at a poor joke.* **5.** *Jewelry.* **a.** noting a gem mineral manufactured so as to be physically, chemically, and optically identical with the mineral as found in nature. **b.** noting a gem mineral manufactured and pigmented in imitation of a natural gemstone of that name. **c.** (not in technical use) noting any of certain imitation gemstones of nonprecious stones, glass, plastics, etc. —*n.* **6.** something made by a synthetic, or chemical, process. [< NL *synthetic(us)* < Gk *synthetikós*, equiv. to *synthet(ós)* placed together, verbid of *syntithénai* to put together (*syn-* SYN- + *the-*, s. of *tithénai*, + *-tos* adj. suffix) + *-ikos* -IC] —**syn·thet′i·cal·ly,** *adv.*

Synthet′ic Cub′ism, (*sometimes l.c.*) *Fine Arts.* the late phase of Cubism, characterized chiefly by an increased use of color and the imitation or introduction of a wide range of textures and material into painting. Cf. **Analytical Cubism.**

synthet′ic deter′gent, any synthetic substance, other than soap, that is an effective cleanser and functions equally well as a surface-active agent in hard or soft water.

synthet′ic divi′sion, a simplified procedure for dividing a polynomial by a linear polynomial.

synthet′ic fu′el, fuel in the form of liquid or gas manufactured from coal or in the form of oil extracted from shale or tar sands.

synthet′ic geom′etry, elementary geometry, as distinct from analytic geometry.

synthet′ic philos′ophy, the philosophy of Herbert Spencer, intended as a synthesis of all the sciences.

synthet′ic rub′ber, any of several substances similar to natural rubber in properties and uses, produced by the polymerization of an unsaturated hydrocarbon, as butylene or isoprene, or by the copolymerization of such hydrocarbons with styrene, butadiene, or the like.

syn·the·tise (sin′thi tīz′), *v.t.*, **-tised, -tis·ing.** *Chiefly Brit.* synthetize. —**syn′the·ti·sa′tion,** *n.* —**syn′the·tis′er,** *n.*

Syn·the·tism (sin′thi tiz′əm), *n.* (*sometimes l.c.*) *Fine Arts.* a style of painting developed toward the end of the 19th century, chiefly characterized by the use of flat, often strongly delineated shapes, bright colors, and a symbolic treatment of abstract ideas. Also called **Cloisonnisme.** Cf. **Nabis.** [< NL *synthetism(us)* < Gk *synthet-* (s. of *synthetízesthai* to combine; see SYNTHETIC) + *-ismos* -ISM]

syn·the·tize (sin′thi tīz′), *v.t.*, **-tized, -tiz·ing.** to synthesize. [< Gk *synthetíze(sthai)*; see SYNTHETISM, SYNTHETIC] —**syn′the·ti·za′tion,** *n.* —**syn′the·tiz′er,** *n.*

syn·thol (sin′thōl, -thôl, -thol), *n. Chem.* **1.** any of several processes for producing hydrocarbons by the interaction, under pressure, of hydrogen and carbon monoxide in the presence of a catalyst. **2.** any of certain hydrocarbons so produced. [SYNTH(ETIC) + -OL¹]

syn·ton·ic (sin ton′ik), *adj.* **1.** *Elect.* adjusted to oscillations of the same or a particular frequency. **2.** *Psychiatry.* of or denoting a personality characterized by normal emotional responsiveness to the environment. Also, **syn·ton′i·cal, syntonous.** [< Gk *sýnton(os)* attuned to, lit., stretched together (verbid of *synteínein* to harmonize), equiv. to *syn-* SYN- + *ton-* (var. s. of *teínein*; see TONE) + *-os* adj. suffix; + -IC] —**syn·ton′i·cal·ly,** *adv.*

syn·to·nise (sin′tə nīz′), *v.t.*, **-nised, -nis·ing.** *Chiefly Brit.* syntonize. —**syn′to·ni·sa′tion,** *n.*

syn·to·nize (sin′tə nīz′), *v.t.*, **-nized, -niz·ing.** to render syntonic; tune to the same frequency. [SYNTON(Y) + -IZE] —**syn′to·ni·za′tion,** *n.* —**syn′to·niz′er,** *n.*

syn·to·nous (sin′tə nəs), *adj.* syntonic. [< Gk *sýntonos* intense. See SYNTONIC, -OUS]

syn·to·ny (sin′tə nē), *n. Elect.* the state or condition of being syntonic. [< Gk *syntonía*, equiv. to *sýnton(os)* (see SYNTONIC) + *-ia* -Y³]

syn·troph·o·blast (sin trof′ə blast′), *n. Embryol.* the outer, syncytial layer of the trophoblast that erodes the uterine wall and forms the fetal part of the placenta. Cf. **cytotrophoblast.** [SYN- + TROPHOBLAST] —**syn·troph′o·blas′tic,** *adj.*

syn·type (sin′tīp′), *n. Biol.* a type specimen other than the holotype used in the description of a species. [SYN- + TYPE] —**syn·typ·ic** (sin tip′ik), *adj.*

syph (sif), *n. Slang.* syphilis (often prec. by *the*). [by shortening]

sy·pher (sī′fər), *v.t.* to join (boards having beveled edges) so as to make a flush surface. [sp. var. of CIPHER]

syph·i·lis (sif′ə lis), *n. Pathol.* a chronic infectious disease, caused by a spirochete, *Treponema pallidum*, usually venereal in origin but often congenital, and affecting almost any organ or tissue in the body, esp. the genitals, skin, mucous membranes, aorta, brain, liver, bones, and nerves. Cf. **primary syphilis, secondary syphilis, tertiary syphilis.** [< NL, coined by G. Fracastoro (1478–1553), Italian physician and poet, author of Latin poem *Syphilis*, with a shepherd *Syphilus* for chief character and first sufferer of the disease]

syph·i·li·sa·tion (sif′ə li zā′shən), *n. Chiefly Brit.* syphilization.

syph·i·lise (sif′ə līz′), *v.t.*, **-lised, -lis·ing.** *Chiefly Brit.* syphilize.

syph·i·lit·ic (sif′ə lit′ik), *adj.* **1.** pertaining to, noting, or affected with syphilis. —*n.* **2.** a person affected with syphilis. [< NL *syphilitic(us)*, equiv. to *syphilis* SYPHILIS + *-ticus* -TIC] —**syph′i·lit′i·cal·ly,** *adv.*

syph·i·li·za·tion (sif′ə li zā′shən), *n.* **1.** inoculation with syphilis-causing spirochetes. **2.** the condition of infection with syphilis. Also, *esp. Brit.*, **syphilisation.** [SYPHIL(IS) + -IZATION]

syph·i·lize (sif′ə līz′), *v.t.*, **-lized, -liz·ing.** to infect with syphilis. Also, *esp. Brit.*, **syphilise.** [SYPHIL(IS) + -IZE]

syph·i·loid (sif′ə loid′), *adj.* resembling syphilis. [SYPHIL(IS) + -OID]

syph·i·lol·o·gy (sif′ə lol′ə jē), *n.* the science dealing with the study of syphilis. [SYPHIL(IS) + -O- + -LOGY] —**syph′i·lol′o·gist,** *n.*

sy·phon (sī′fən), *n., v.t., v.i.* siphon.

Syr., **1.** Syria. **2.** Syriac. **3.** Syrian.

syr., *Pharm.* syrup.

Syr·a·cuse (sir′ə kyōōs′, sēr′-), *n.* **1.** a city in central New York. 216,038 (1960). **2.** Italian, **Siracusa.** a seaport in SE Sicily: ancient city founded by the Carthaginians 734 B.C.; battles 413 B.C., 212 B.C. 90,333 (1961). —**Syr′a·cu′san,** *adj., n.*

Syr Dar·ya (sēr där′yä), a river in the SW Soviet Union in Asia, flowing NW from the Tien Shan Mountains to the Aral Sea. 1300 mi. long. Ancient name, **Jaxartes.**

Syr·ette (si ret′), *n. Trademark.* a collapsible tube with an attached hypodermic needle for the subcutaneous administration of medication.

Syr·i·a (sēr′ē ə), *n.* **1.** Official name, **Syr′ian Ar′ab Repub′lic.** a republic in SW Asia at the E end of the Mediterranean: former province 1958–61 of the United Arab Republic. 5,179,684 (1962); 71,227 sq. mi. *Cap.:* Damascus. **2.** a territory mandated to France in 1922, including the present republics of Syria and Lebanon (Latakia and Djebel Druze were incorporated into Syria 1942): the French mandatory powers were nominally terminated as of January 1, 1944. **3.** an ancient country in W Asia, including the present Syria, Lebanon, Israel and adjacent areas: a part of the Roman Empire 64 B.C.–A.D. 636.

Syr·i·ac (sēr′ē ak′), *n.* a form of Aramaic used by various Eastern Churches. [< L *Syriac(us)* < Gk *Syriakós*. See SYRIA, -AC]

Syr·i·an (sēr′ē ən), *adj.* **1.** of or pertaining to Syria or its inhabitants. —*n.* **2.** a native or inhabitant of Syria. [late ME *Sirien* < MF. See SYRIA, -AN]

sy·rin·ga (sə ring′gə), *n.* **1.** any shrub of the genus *Philadelphus*, certain species of which are cultivated as ornamentals, esp. *P. coronarius*, having fragrant, white flowers. **2.** a lilac of the genus *Syringa*. [< NL < Gk *syring-* (s. of *sŷrinx* SYRINX) + *-a* n. suffix; name first given to mock-orange, the stems of which were used in pipe-making]

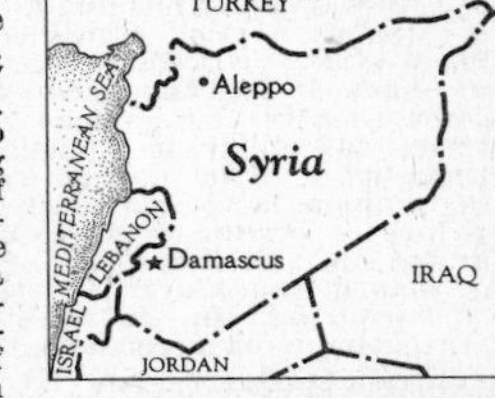
Syringe

sy·ringe (sə rinj′, sir′inj), *n., v.,* **-ringed, -ring·ing.** —*n.* **1.** *Med.* a small device consisting of a glass, metal, or hard rubber tube, narrowed at its outlet, and fitted with either a piston or a rubber bulb for drawing in a quantity of fluid and ejecting it in a stream, for cleaning wounds, injecting fluids into the body, etc. **2.** any similar device for pumping and spraying liquids through a small aperture. —*v.t.* **3.** to cleanse, wash, inject, etc., by means of a syringe. [back formation from LL *syringēs*, pl. of *syrinx* SYRINX; r. late ME *syring* < ML *syringa*] —**sy·ringe′ful,** *adj.*

sy·rin·ge·al (sə rin′jē əl), *adj. Ornith.* of, pertaining to, or connected with the syrinx. [*syringe-* (var. s. of SYRINX) + -AL¹]

sy·rin·go·my·e·li·a (sə ring′gō mī ē′lē ə), *n. Pathol.* a disease of the spinal cord in which the nerve tissue is replaced by a cavity filled with fluid. [*syringo-* (comb. form of Gk *sŷrinx* SYRINX) + *myelia* (MYEL- + -IA)] —**sy·rin·go·my·el·ic** (sə ring′gō mī el′ik), *adj.*

syr·inx (sir′ingks), *n., pl.* **sy·rin·ges** (sə rin′jēz), **syr·inx·es. 1.** *Ornith.* the vocal organ of birds, situated at or near the bifurcation of the trachea into the bronchi. **2.** (*cap.*) *Class. Myth.* a mountain nymph of Arcadia who was transformed, in order to protect her chastity from Pan, into the reed from which Pan then made the panpipe. **3.** a panpipe. **4.** a narrow corridor in an ancient Egyptian tomb. [(partly through L) < Gk: pipe, pipelike object]

syr·phid (sûr′fid), *n.* **1.** See **syrphid fly.** —*adj.* **2.** belonging or pertaining to the family *Syrphidae.* Also, **syr·phi·an** (sûr′fē-ən). [< Gk *sýrph(os)* gnat + -ID[2]]

Syrinx (of passerine bird) A, Tracheal rings B, Bronchial rings C, Right and left bronchi

syr′phid fly′, any of numerous beelike or wasplike flies of the family *Syrphidae* that feed on the nectar and pollen of flowers, and have larvae that feed on decaying vegetation or are predaceous on aphids. Also, **syr′phus fly′** (sûr′fəs). Also called **flower fly.**

Syr′tis Ma′jor (sûr′tis), an area in the northern hemisphere and near the equator of Mars, appearing as a dark region when viewed telescopically from the earth.

syr·up (sir′əp, sûr′-), *n.* **1.** any of various thick, sweet liquids prepared for table use from molasses, glucose, etc., water, and often a flavoring agent. **2.** any of various preparations consisting of fruit juices, water, etc., boiled with sugar: *a syrup of raspberries, sugar, and water.* **3.** *Pharm.* **a.** a concentrated sugar solution which contains medication or flavoring. **b.** Also called **simple syrup.** an official U.S.P. solution of 850 grams of sucrose and sufficient water to make a total volume of 1,000 cubic centimeters, used as a vehicle for medication. **4.** See **simple syrup** (def. 1). —*v.t.* **5.** to bring to the form or consistency of syrup. **6.** to cover, fill, or sweeten with syrup. Also, **sirup.** [< ML *syrup(us)* < Ar *sharāb* a drink; r. ME *sirop* < MF] —**syr′up·like′,** *adj.*

Syrphid fly, *Didea fuscipes* (Length ½ in.)

syr·up·y (sir′ə pē), *adj.* **1.** having the appearance or quality of syrup; thick or sweet: *syrupy coffee.* **2.** sentimental or overly sweet; mawkish: *a syrupy manner; a syrupy poem.* Also, **sirupy.** [SYRUP + -Y[1]]

sys-, var. of **syn-** before *s: syssarcosis.*

sys·sar·co·sis (sis′är kō′sis), *n., pl.* **-ses** (-sēz). *Anat.* the union of bones by muscle. [< NL < Gk *syssárkōsis,* equiv. to *syssark-,* s. of *syssarkoûthai* to be likewise overgrown with flesh (*sys-* SYS- + *sark-* SARC-) + *-ōsis* -OSIS]

syst., system.

sys·tal·tic (si stôl′tik, -stal′-), *adj. Physiol.* **1.** rhythmically contracting. **2.** of the nature of contraction. **3.** characterized by alternate contraction and dilatation, as the action of the heart. [< LL *systaltic(us)* < Gk *systaltikós,* equiv. to *systalt(ós)* contracted, verbid of *systéllein* to put together, (*sy-* SY- + *stal-,* var. s. of *stéllein* to place, + *-tos* adj. suffix) + *-ikos* -IC]

sys·tem (sis′təm), *n.* **1.** an assemblage or combination of things or parts forming a complex or unitary whole: *a mountain system; a railroad system.* **2.** any assemblage or set of correlated members: *a system of currency; a system of shorthand characters.* **3.** an ordered and comprehensive assemblage of facts, principles, doctrines, or the like, in a particular field of knowledge or thought: *a system of philosophy.* **4.** a coordinated body of methods or a complex scheme or plan of procedure: *a system of government; a winning system at bridge.* **5.** any formulated, regular, or special method or plan of procedure: *a system of marking, numbering, or measuring.* **6.** due method or orderly manner of arrangement or procedure: *There is no system in his work.* **7.** a number of heavenly bodies associated and acting together according to certain natural laws: *the solar system.* **8.** the world or universe. **9.** *Astron.* a hypothesis or theory of the disposition and arrangements of the heavenly bodies by which their phenomena, motions, changes, etc., are explained: *the Ptolemaic system; the Copernican system.* **10.** *Biol.* **a.** an assemblage of parts of organs of the same or similar tissues, or concerned with the same function: *the nervous system; the digestive system.* **b.** the entire human or animal body: *an ingredient toxic to the system.* **11.** one's personality, character, etc.: *to get the meanness out of one's system.* **12.** a method or scheme of classification: *the Linnean system of plants.* **13.** *Geol.* a major division of rocks comprising sedimentary deposits and igneous masses formed during a geological period. **14.** *Physical Chem.* a combination of two or more phases, as a binary system, each of which consists of one or more substances, that is attaining or is in equilibrium. **15.** *Checkers.* either of the two groups of 16 playing squares on four alternate columns. **16.** the structure or organization of society, business, or politics or of society in general: *She could never adapt herself to the system.* [< LL *systēm(a)* < Gk *sýstēma* whole compounded of several parts, equiv. to *sy-* SY- + *stē-* (var. s. of *histánai* to cause to stand; akin to L *stāre* to STAND) + *-ma* n. suffix denoting result of action] —**sys′tem·less,** *adj.*
—**Syn. 1.** organization. **6.** articulation. **8.** cosmos. **10b.** organism.

sys·tem·at·ic (sis′tə mat′ik), *adj.* **1.** having, showing, or involving a system, method, or plan: *a systematic course of reading; systematic efforts.* **2.** characterized by system or method; methodical: *a systematic person; systematic habits.* **3.** arranged in or comprising an ordered system: *systematic theology.* **4.** concerned with classification: *systematic botany.* **5.** pertaining to, based on, or in accordance with a system of classification: *the systematic names of plants.* Also, **sys′tem·at′i·cal.** [< LL *systēmatic(us)* < Gk *systēmatikós,* equiv. to *systemat-* (s. of *sýstēma*) SYSTEM + *-ikos* -IC] —**sys′tem·at′ic·ness,** *n.* —**sys′tem·at′i·cal·ly,** *adv.*
—**Syn. 2.** See **orderly.**

sys·tem·at·ics (sis′tə mat′iks), *n.* (*construed as sing.*) the study of systems or of classification. [see SYSTEMATIC, -ICS]

sys·tem·a·tise (sis′tə mə tīz′), *v.t.,* **-tised, -tis·ing.** *Chiefly Brit.* systematize. —**sys′tem·a·ti·sa′tion,** *n.* —**sys′tem·a·tis′er,** *n.*

sys·tem·a·tism (sis′tə mə tiz′əm), *n.* **1.** the practice of systematizing. **2.** adherence to system or method. [SYSTEMAT(IZE) + -ISM]

sys·tem·a·tist (sis′tə mə tist), *n.* **1.** a person who constructs a system. **2.** a naturalist engaged in classification. **3.** a person who adheres to system, order, or method. [< Gk *systemat-* (s. of *sýstēma*) SYSTEM + -IST]

sys·tem·a·tize (sis′tə mə tīz′), *v.t.,* **-tized, -tiz·ing.** to arrange in or according to a system; reduce to a system; make systematic. Also, **systemize.** [< Gk *systemat-* (s. of *sýstēma*) SYSTEM + -IZE] —**sys′tem·a·ti·za′tion,** *n.* —**sys′tem·a·tiz′er,** *n.*
—**Syn.** organize, order, articulate.

sys·tem·a·tol·o·gy (sis′tə mə tol′ə jē), *n.* the science of systems or their formation. [< Gk *systemat-* (s. of *sýstēma*) SYSTEM + -O- + -LOGY]

sys·tem·ic (si stem′ik), *adj.* **1.** of or pertaining to a system. **2.** *Physiol., Pathol.* **a.** pertaining to or affecting the entire bodily system or the body as a whole. **b.** pertaining to a particular system of parts or organs of the body. [SYSTEM + -IC] —**sys·tem′i·cal·ly,** *adv.*

sys·tem·ise (sis′tə mīz′), *v.t.,* **-ised, -is·ing.** *Chiefly Brit.* systemize. —**sys′tem·is′a·ble,** *adj.* —**sys′tem·i·sa′tion,** *n.* —**sys′tem·is′er,** *n.*

sys·tem·ize (sis′tə mīz′), *v.t.,* **-ized, -iz·ing.** to systematize. [SYSTEM + -IZE] —**sys′tem·iz′a·ble,** *adj.* —**sys′tem·i·za′tion,** *n.* —**sys′tem·iz′er,** *n.*

sys·tem·oid (sis′tə moid′), *adj. Pathol.* noting or pertaining to a tumor having a complex structure that resembles an organ. [SYSTEM + -OID]

sys′tems design′, **1.** the analyzing and subsequent organizing of a problem to make it suitable for solution or processing by electronic computers and other data-processing equipment. **2.** the organizing of a system of interrelated data-processing equipment to perform a given function or pattern of functions.

sys·to·le (sis′tə lē′, -lē), *n.* **1.** *Physiol.* the normal rhythmical contraction of the heart during which the blood in the chambers is forced onward. Cf. **diastole.** **2.** *Class. Pros.* the shortening of a syllable regularly long. [< Gk *systolḗ,* equiv. to *sy-* SY- + *stolḗ,* equiv. to *stol-* (var. s. of *stéllein* to send, place) + *-ē* n. suffix; cf. DIASTOLE, SYSTALTIC] —**sys·tol·ic** (si stol′ik), *adj.*

sys·tyle (sis′tīl), *adj. Archit.* having an intercolumniation of two diameters. See illus. under **intercolumniation.** [< L *systȳl(os)* < Gk *sýstȳlos,* equiv. to *sys-* SYS- + *stŷlos* column]

Syz·ran (siz′rän), *n.* a city in the RSFSR, in the E Soviet Union in Europe, on the Volga. 159,000 (est. 1962).

syz·y·gy (siz′i jē), *n., pl.* **-gies.** **1.** *Astron.* the conjunction or opposition of two heavenly bodies; a point in the orbit of a body, as the moon, at which it is in conjunction with or in opposition to the sun. **2.** *Class. Pros.* a group or combination of two feet, sometimes restricted to a combination of two feet of different kinds. **3.** any two related things, either alike or opposite. [< LL *syzygia* < Gk *syzygía* union, pair, equiv. to *sýzyg(os)* yoked together (*sy-* SY- + *zyg-,* root of *zeugnýnai* to yoke, + *-os* adj. suffix) + *-ia* -Y[3]] —**sy·zyg·i·al** (si zij′ē əl), **syz·y·get·ic** (siz′i jet′ik), **syz·y·gal** (siz′ə gəl), *adj.*

M, Syzygy of moon S, Sun; E, Earth

Sza·bad·ka (so′bot ko), *n.* Hungarian name of **Subotica.**

Szcze·cin (shche tsēn′), *n.* Polish name of **Stettin.**

Sze·chwan (se′chwän′; *Chin.* su′chwän′), *n.* a province in central China. 72,160,000 (est. 1957); 219,691 sq. mi. *Cap.:* Chengtu.

Sze·ged (se′ged), *n.* a city in S Hungary, on the Tisza River. 107,326 (est. 1963). German, **Sze·ge·din** (se′gə din).

Szell (sel), *n.* **George,** born 1897, U.S. pianist and conductor, born in Hungary.

Szent-Györ·gyi (sent jûr′jē; *Hung.* sent dyœr′dyi), *n.* **Al·bert** (al′bərt; *Hung.* ôl′bert), born 1893, U.S. biochemist, born in Hungary: Nobel prize for medicine 1937.

Szi·ge·ti (sig′i tē, si get′ē; *Hung.* si′ge tē), *n.* **Joseph,** born 1892, Hungarian violinist.

Szi·lard (sil′ärd), *n.* **Leo,** 1898–1964, U.S. physicist, born in Hungary.

Szold (zōld), *n.* **Henrietta,** 1860–1945, U.S. Zionist: founded Hadassah in 1912.

Szom·bat·hely (sôm′bät hā′, -he′yᵊ), *n.* a city in W Hungary: founded A.D. 48. 57,000 (est. 1962). German, **Steinamanger.**

Szy·ma·now·ski (shē′mä nôf′skē), *n.* **Ka·rol** (kä′rôl), 1882?–1937, Polish composer.

T

T, t (tē), *n., pl.* **T's** or **Ts, t's** or **ts. 1.** the 20th letter of the English alphabet, a consonant. **2.** any spoken sound represented by the letter *T* or *t*, as in *but, butter, tub,* etc. **3.** something having the shape of a T. **4.** a written or printed representation of the letter *T* or *t*. **5.** a device, as a printer's type, for reproducing the letter *T* or *t*. **6. to a T,** exactly; perfectly: *That job would suit you to a T.* Also, **to a tee.**

T, tesla; teslas.

T, 1. the 20th in order or in a series, or, when *I* is omitted, the 19th. **2.** (*sometimes l.c.*) the medieval Roman numeral for 160. Cf. **Roman numerals. 3.** absolute temperature. **4.** surface tension. **5.** *Photog.* See **T number. 6.** *Math.* a symbol followed by a subscript indicating the relation between points and closed sets in topological spaces.

t, *Statistics.* distribution.

't, a shortened form of *it*, before or after a verb, as in *'twas, 'tis, do't, see't.*

t-, *Chem.* tertiary.

-t, var. of **-ed** used in forming the past tense or past participle of certain verbs, usually occurring when the final consonant of the stem is voiceless and there is internal vowel change in the root: *slept.* [ptp.: ME, OE *-t, -(e)d,* OE *-od;* past tense: ME, OE *-te, -(e)de,* OE *-ode*]

T., 1. Territory. **2.** township. **3.** Tuesday.

t., 1. *Football.* tackle. **2.** taken from. **3.** tare. **4.** teaspoon. **5.** temperature. **6.** in the time of. [< L *tempore*] **7.** tenor. **8.** *Gram.* tense. **9.** territory. **10.** time. **11.** tome. **12.** ton. **13.** town. **14.** township. **15.** transitive.

ta (tä), *interj. Brit. Slang.* thank-you: *Ta very much for the gift.* [by infantile shortening and alter.]

tā (tä), *n.* the third letter of the Arabic alphabet. [< Ar]

tā (tä), *n.* the 16th letter of the Arabic alphabet. [< Ar]

Ta, *Chem.* tantalum.

Taal (täl), *n.* Afrikaans (usually prec. by *the*). [< D: language, speech; c. TALE]

Ta·al (tä äl′), *n.* an active volcano in the Philippines, on SW Luzon, on an island in Taal Lake: eruptions 1749, 1873, 1911. 1050 ft.

Ta·a·nith Es·ther (tä′ä nit es′tər; *Heb.* tä′ä nēt′ es tεr′), a Jewish fast day observed on the 13th day of the month of Adar in memory of Esther's fast of three days before petitioning her husband, King Ahasuerus of Persia, to spare the Jews from destruction by Haman. Also called **Fast of Esther.** [< Heb]

tab[1] (tab), *n., v.,* **tabbed, tab·bing. —*n.* 1.** a small flap, strap, loop, or similar appendage, as on a garment, used for pulling, hanging, decoration, etc. **2.** a tag or label. **3.** a small piece attached or intended to be attached, as to an automobile license plate. **4.** *Informal.* an unpaid bill, as for a meal in a restaurant; check. **5.** *Theat.* **a.** a small, often narrow, drop curtain, for masking part of the stage. **b.** See **tableau curtain. 6.** *Aeron.* a small airfoil hinged to the rear portion of a control surface, as to an elevator, aileron, or rudder. Cf. **trim tab. 7.** a small projection from a card, paper, or folder, used as an aid in filing. **8. keep tab** or **tabs on,** *Informal.* to keep an account of; check on; observe: *The police kept tabs on the suspect's activities.* **—*v.t.* 9.** to furnish or ornament with a tab or tabs. **10.** to name; designate; put a tab or tabs on.

tab[2] (tab), *n. Informal.* tabloid (def. 1). [by shortening]

Tab (tab), *n.* a boy's given name.

tab., 1. tables. **2.** (in prescriptions) tablet. [< L *tabella*]

tab·a·nid (tab′ə nid), *n.* **1.** any of numerous bloodsucking, dipterous insects of the family *Tabanidae,* comprising the deer flies and horse flies. **—*adj.* 2.** belonging or pertaining to the family *Tabanidae.* [back formation from NL *tabānidae,* based on L *tabā-n(us)* horse fly; see -IDAE]

tab·ard (tab′ərd), *n.* **1.** a loose outer garment, sleeveless or with short sleeves, worn by a knight over his armor and usually emblazoned with his arms. **2.** an official garment of a herald, emblazoned with the arms of his master. **3.** a coarse, heavy, short coat, with or without sleeves, formerly worn outdoors. [ME < OF *tabart*] **—tab′ard·ed,** *adj.*

Tabard (def. 2)

tab·a·ret (tab′ə rit), *n.* **1.** a durable silk or acetate fabric having alternating stripes of satin and moire, for drapery and upholstery. **2.** an embroidery frame. [? akin to TABBY[1]]

Ta·bas·co (tə bas′kō; *Sp.* tä väs′kō), *n.* a state in SE Mexico, on the Gulf of Campeche. 496,340 (1960); 9783 sq. mi. *Cap.:* Villa Hermosa.

Ta·bas·co (tə bas′kō), *n. Trademark.* a pungent condiment sauce prepared from the fruit of a variety of capsicum.

tab·bi·net (tab′ə net′), *n.* tabinet.

tab·by[1] (tab′ē), *n., pl.* **-bies,** *adj., v.,* **-bied, -by·ing. —*n.* 1.** a cat with a striped or brindled coat. **2.** a domestic cat, esp. a female one. **3.** an old maid; spinster. **4.** a spiteful female gossip or tattler. **5.** See **plain weave. 6.** a watered silk fabric, or any other watered material, as moreen. **—*adj.* 7.** striped or brindled. **8.** made of or resembling tabby. **—*v.t.* 9.** to give a wavy or watered appearance to, as silk. [back formation from F *tabis* (taken as pl.), MF *(a)tabis* silk cloth < ML *attābi* < Ar *'attābī,* short for *Al 'attābīya* quarter of Baghdad where first made, lit., the quarter of (Prince) 'Attab]

tab·by[2] (tab′ē), *n.* (in the southeastern U.S.) a building material composed of oyster shells, lime, and sand, mixed with salt water. [< Gullah *'tabi* < an African language]

Tab·by (tab′ē), *n.* a girl's given name, form of **Tabitha.**

tabel., (in prescriptions) tablet. [< L *tabella*]

ta·ber (tā′bər), *n. Music.* tabor.

tab·er·nac·le (tab′ər nak′əl), *n., v.,* **-led, -ling. —*n.* 1.** a temporary dwelling, as a tent or hut. **2.** a dwelling place. **3.** *Judaism.* the portable sanctuary in use by the Jews from the time of their wandering in the wilderness after the exodus from Egypt to the building of the Temple in Jerusalem by Solomon. Ex. 25–27. **4.** any place or house of worship, esp. one designed for a large congregation. **5.** a canopied niche or recess, as for an image or icon. **6.** *Eccles.* an ornamental receptacle for the reserved Eucharist, now generally found on the altar. **7.** the human body as the temporary abode of the soul. **8.** *Naut.* a raised support holding a mast in such a way that it can be readily lowered to the deck. **—*v.t., v.i.* 9.** to place or dwell in, or as in, a tabernacle. [ME < eccl. L *tabernācul(um)* tent, booth, double dim. of *taberna* hut, shed, TAVERN] **—tab·er·nac·u·lar** (tab′ər nak′yə lər), *adj.*

tab′ernacle mir′ror, a mirror of c1800, having columns and a cornice, usually gilt, with a painted panel over the mirror.

ta·bes (tā′bēz), *n. Pathol.* **1.** a gradually progressive emaciation. **2.** See **tabes dorsalis.** [< L: wasting, decay, akin to *tabēre* to waste away]

ta·bes·cent (tə bes′ənt), *adj.* that wastes away, emaciates, or becomes consumed. [< L *tabēscent-* (s. of *tabēscēns*) dwindling, wasting away (prp. of *tābēscere*). See TABES, -ESCENT] **—ta·bes′cence,** *n.*

ta′bes dor·sa′lis (dôr sā′lis), *Pathol.* syphilis of the spinal cord and its appendages, characterized by shooting pains and other sensory disturbances, and, in the later stages, by loss of control over the muscular movements, mainly in walking, and by paralysis. Also called **locomotor ataxia.** [< NL: lit., tabes of the back]

ta·bet (tā′bit), *n. Scot.* a physical sense or sensation. [?]

ta·bet·ic (tə bet′ik, -bē′tik), *Pathol.* **—*adj.* 1.** Also, **tab·id** (tab′id). pertaining to or affected with tabes. **—*n.* 2.** a person affected with tabes. [TABE(S) + -TIC]

ta·bi (tä′bē), *n., pl.* **-bi, -bis.** a covering for the foot, similar to a sock, having a separate pouchlike stall for the large toe, worn esp. in Japan, often with zoris. [< Jap]

tab·i·net (tab′ə net′), *n.* a fabric resembling poplin, made of silk and wool and usually given a watered finish. Also, **tabbinet.** [obs. *tabine* (perh. TABBY[1] + -INE[2]) + -ET]

Tab·i·tha (tab′ə thə), *n.* a girl's given name.

tab·la·ture (tab′lə chər), *n.* **1.** a tabular space, surface, or structure. **2.** *Music.* any of various systems of music notation, chiefly of the 15th and 17th centuries, using letters, numbers, or other signs to indicate the strings or frets to be played. [< F < It *tavolatur(a),* equiv. to *tavolat(o)* wooden floor, wainscoting (< L *tabulātum;* see TABULATE) + *-ura* -URE]

ta·ble (tā′bəl), *n., v.,* **-bled, -bling. —*n.* 1.** an article of furniture consisting of a flat, slablike top supported on one or more legs or other relatively narrow or isolated supports. **2.** such a piece of furniture specifically used for serving food to those seated at it. **3.** the food placed on a table to be eaten: *She sets a good table.* **4.** a group of persons at a table, as for a meal, game, or business transaction: *The table consisted of two diplomats, three actors, and a judge.* **5.** a flat or plane surface; a level area. **6.** a tableland or plateau. **7.** (*cap.*) *Astron.* the constellation Mensa. **8.** a flat and relatively thin piece of wood, stone, metal, or other hard substance, esp. one artificially shaped for a particular purpose. **9.** *Archit.* **a.** a course or band, esp. of masonry, having a distinctive form or position. **b.** a distinctively treated surface on a wall. **10.** a smooth, flat board or slab on which inscriptions may be put. **11. tables, a.** the tablets on which certain collections of laws were anciently inscribed, used most often of the Twelve Tables of Rome. **b.** the laws themselves. **12.** an arrangement of words, numbers, or signs, or combinations of them, as in parallel columns, to exhibit a set of facts or relations in a definite, compact, and comprehensive form; a synopsis or scheme. **13.** Also called **slab.** *Print.* (in a press) the flat metal surface over which the ink is distributed to attain its proper consistency. **14.** *Anat.* the inner or outer hard layer or any of the flat bones of the skull. **15.** *Music.* a sounding board. **16.** *Jewelry.* **a.** the upper horizontal surface of a faceted gem. **b.** a gem with such a surface. **17. on the table,** *U.S. Parl. Proc.* postponed. **18. turn the tables,** to cause a reversal of an existing situation, esp. with regard to persons or groups in opposition: *Fortune turned the tables and we won.* Also, **turn the tables on. 19. under the table, a.** drunk. **b.** as a bribe: *She gave money under the table to get the apartment.* **20. wait (on) table,** to work as a waiter; serve food: *He worked his way through college by waiting table.* **—*v.t.* 21.** to place (a card, money, etc.) on a table. **22.** to enter in or form into a table or list. **23.** *Parl. Proc.* **a.** *U.S.* to lay aside (a proposal, resolution, etc.) for future discussion, usually with a view to postponing or shelving the matter indefinitely. **b.** *Brit.* to present (a proposal, resolution, etc.) for discussion. **24.** *Carpentry.* to join (a timber) to another timber by letting projections on each into corresponding recesses or mortises on the other. [ME; OE *tablu, tabule,* var. of *tabula* < L: plank, tablet] **—ta′ble·less,** *adj.*

tab·leau (tab′lō, ta blō′), *n., pl.* **tab·leaux** (tab′lōz, ta blōz′), **tab·leaus. 1.** a picture, as of a scene. **2.** a picturesque grouping of persons or objects; a striking scene. **3.** a representation of a picture, statue, scene, etc., by one or more persons suitably costumed and posed. **4.** *Solitaire.* the portion of a layout on which addition of cards according to suit or denomination is usually permitted. [< F: board, picture, MF *tablel,* dim. of *table* TABLE]

tab′leau cur′tain, *Theat.* a curtain, often used as an act curtain, designed to be drawn aside and up to give a festooned or draped effect.

ta·bleau vi·vant (tᴀ blō′ vē väɴ′), *pl.* **ta·bleaux vi·vants** (tᴀ blō′ vē väɴ′). *French.* tableau (def. 3). [lit., living picture]

ta′ble board′, daily meals provided for pay.

ta·ble·cloth (tā′bəl klôth′, -kloth′), *n., pl.* **-cloths** (-klôthz′, -klothz′, -klôths′, -kloths′). a cloth for covering the top of a table, esp. during a meal. [TABLE + CLOTH]

ta′ble cut′, *Jewelry.* **1.** a variety of step cut in which a very large table is joined to the girdle with a bevel. **2.** an obsolete diamond cut in which the natural octahedral crystal of the diamond was used intact, the only cutting being in the formation of the table and culet.

ta·ble d'hôte (tab′əl dōt′, tä′bəl; *Fr.* tᴀ blᵊ dōt′), *pl.* **ta·bles d'hôte** (tab′əlz dōt′, tä′bəlz; *Fr.* tᴀ blᵊ dōt′). a meal of prearranged courses served at a fixed time and price to the guests at a hotel or restaurant. Cf. **à la carte, prix fixe.** [< F: lit., the host's table] —**ta′ble-d'hôte′,** *adj.*

ta′bled joint′, *Masonry.* a joint between two stones, one above the other, in which a raised area on the surface of one stone fits into a corresponding sunken area of the stone above or below. [ME *tablid.* See TABLE, -ED[3]]

ta′ble en′gine, a stationary vertical steam engine having a crankshaft below the cylinder driven by connecting rods returning from a crosshead above the cylinders.

ta·ble·ful (tā′bəl fo͝ol′), *n., pl.* **-fuls. 1.** the number of persons that can be seated at a table. **2.** the amount of food, dishes, etc., that a table can hold. [TABLE + -FUL]

ta·ble-hop (tā′bəl hop′), *v.i.,* **-hopped, -hop·ping.** *Informal.* to move about in a restaurant, night club, or the like, chatting with people at various tables. [TABLE + HOP[1]] —**ta′ble-hop′per,** *n.*

ta·ble·land (tā′bəl land′), *n.* an elevated and generally level region of considerable extent; plateau. [TABLE + LAND]

ta′ble lin′en, tablecloths, napkins, etc., used in setting a table.

Ta′ble Moun′tain, a mountain in the Republic of South Africa, near Cape Town. 3550 ft.

ta′ble salt′, salt (def. 1).

ta·ble·spoon (tā′bəl spo͞on′, -spo͝on′), *n.* **1.** a spoon larger than a teaspoon or a dessert spoon, used in serving food at the table and as a standard measuring unit in recipes. **2.** a unit of capacity, equal to ½ fluid ounce, or 3 household teaspoons. **3.** a tablespoonful. [TABLE + SPOON]

ta·ble·spoon·ful (tā′bəl spo͞on′fo͝ol′, -spo͝on′-), *n., pl.* **-fuls.** the quantity a tablespoon holds, equal to ½ fluid ounce. [TABLESPOON + -FUL]

tab·let (tab′lit), *n., v.,* **-let·ed, -let·ing** or **-let·ted, -let·ting.** —*n.* **1.** a number of sheets of writing paper, business forms, etc., fastened together at the edge; pad. **2.** a flat slab or surface, esp. one bearing or intended to bear an inscription, carving, or the like. **3.** a thin, flat leaf or sheet of slate, wax-coated wood, or other rigid material, used for writing or marking on, esp. one of a pair or set hinged or otherwise fastened together. **4.** **tablets,** the set as a whole. **5.** a small, flat, or flattish cake or piece of some solid or solidified substance, as a drug, chemical, soap, or the like. **6.** Also called **tabling.** a flat coping. —*v.t.* **7.** to furnish or mark with a tablet or plaque. **8.** to mark or inscribe (memoranda, notes, etc.) on a tablet. **9.** to form into tablets, cakes, pellets, etc. [ME *tablette* < MF *tablete.* See TABLE, -ET]

ta′ble talk′, 1. informal conversation at meals. **2.** a subject that is considered appropriate for conversation at meals.

tab′let chair′, a chair with one arm extending and expanding into a writing surface.

ta′ble ten′nis, a variety of tennis played on a table with small paddles and a hollow celluloid or plastic ball.

ta·ble·top (tā′bəl top′), *n.* **1.** a surface forming or suggesting the top of a table. **2.** a photograph of an arrangement of objects on top of a table. —*adj.* **3.** intended for use on the top of a table or the like. **4.** noting or pertaining to an arrangement of objects, esp. miniatures or models, as would be appropriate to the top of a table. [TABLE + TOP[1]]

ta′ble tri′pod, *Motion Pictures, Television.* a low mount or stand for a camera.

ta·ble·ware (tā′bəl wâr′), *n.* (collectively) the dishes, utensils, etc., used at the table. [TABLE + WARE[1]]

ta′ble wine′, a wine that contains not more than 14 percent alcohol and is usually served as an accompaniment to food.

ta·bling (tā′bling), *n.* **1.** tablet (def. 6). —*v.* **2.** prp. and gerund of **table.**

tab·li·num (ta blī′nəm), *n., pl.* **-na** (-nə). (in an ancient Roman house) a large, open room at the side of the peristyle farthest from the main entrance. [< L *tab(u)linum,* n. use of neut. of *tabulīnus* pertaining to tablets. See TABLE, -INE[1]]

tab·loid (tab′loid), *n.* **1.** a newspaper whose pages, usually five columns wide, are about one-half the size of a standard-sized newspaper page: left flat after printing rather than being folded horizontally at the middle as is a standard-sized newspaper. **2.** a small newspaper concentrating on sensational and lurid news, usually heavily illustrated. **3.** a short form or version; condensation; synopsis; summary. —*adj.* **4.** compressed or condensed in or as in a tabloid: *a tabloid article; a tabloid account of the adventure.* **5.** sensational, esp. when marked by vulgarity. [TABL(ET) + -OID] —**tab′loid·ism,** *n.*

Tab·loid (tab′loid), *n. Pharm., Trademark.* a compressed medicinal tablet.

ta·boo (tə bo͞o′, ta-), *adj., n., pl.* **-boos,** *v.,* **-booed, -boo·ing.** —*adj.* **1.** (among the Polynesians and other peoples of the South Pacific) separated or set apart as sacred or profane; forbidden for general use; placed under a prohibition or ban. —*n.* **2.** a prohibition or interdiction of anything; exclusion from use or practice. **3.** (among the Polynesians and other peoples of the South Pacific) **a.** the system, practice, or act whereby things are set apart as sacred, forbidden for general use, or placed under a prohibition or interdiction. **b.** the condition of being so set apart, forbidden, or interdicted. **4.** exclusion from social relations; ostracism. —*v.t.* **5.** to put under a taboo; prohibit or forbid. **6.** to ostracize (a person, group, etc.). Also, **tabu.** [< Tongan *tabu* set apart, inviolable]
—**Syn. 1.** prohibited, banned. **5.** See **forbid.**

ta·bor (tā′bər), *n.* **1.** a small drum formerly used to accompany oneself on a pipe or fife. —*v.i.* **2.** to play upon or as upon a tabor; drum. —*v.t.* **3.** to strike or beat, as on a tabor. Also, **ta′bour.** [ME < OF *tab(o)ur* << Pers *tabūrāk* drum. See TAMBOR] —**ta′bor·er, ta′bour·er,** *n.*

T, Tabor

Ta·bor (tā′bər), *n.* **Mount,** a mountain in N Israel, E of Nazareth. 1929 ft.

Ta·bo·ra (tä bōr′ə, -bôr′ə), *n.* a city in central Tanzania. 15,361 (1957).

tab·o·ret (tab′ə rit, tab′ə ret′), *n.* **1.** a low seat without back or arms, for one person; stool. **2.** a frame for embroidery. **3.** a small tabor. Also, **tab′ou·ret.** [var. of *tabouret* < F: lit., small drum. See TABOR, -ET]

tab·o·rin (tab′ər in), *n.* a small tabor. [< MF *tabourin.* See TABOR, -IN[1]]

Ta·bor·ite (tā′bə rīt′), *n.* (in the 15th century) a member of the militant body of Hussites maintaining a strict literal interpretation of the Scriptures. [named after *Tabor,* city in Bohemia where the radical party of Hussites had its headquarters + -ITE[1]]

tab·ret (tab′rit), *n.* **1.** a small tabor. **2.** *Obs.* one who plays upon this instrument. [late ME *taberett,* equiv. to *taber* (var. of TABOR) + *-ett* -ET]

Ta·briz (tä brēz′), *n.* a city in and the capital of Azerbaijan province, in NW Iran. 387,803 (est. 1963).

ta·bu (tə bo͞o′, ta-), *adj., n., v.t.* taboo.

tab·u·lar (tab′yə lər), *adj.* **1.** of, pertaining to, or arranged in a table or systematic arrangement by columns, rows, etc., as statistics. **2.** ascertained from or computed by the use of tables. **3.** having the form of a table, tablet, or tablature. **4.** flat and expansive, as tableland or a plateau. [< L *tabulār(is)* pertaining to a board or tablet. See TABLE, -AR[1]] —**tab′u·lar·ly,** *adv.*

ta·bu·la ra·sa (tab′yə lə rā′sə, rä′-; *Lat.* tä′bo͞o-lä′ rä′sä), *pl.* **ta·bu·lae ra·sae** (tab′yə lē′ rā′sē, rä′-; *Lat.* tä′bo͞o lī′ rä′sī). a mind not yet affected by experiences, impressions, etc. [< L: scraped tablet; clean slate]

tab′ular ice′berg, a large, flat-topped iceberg broken off from an ice shelf.

tab·u·lar·ise (tab′yə lə rīz′), *v.t.,* **-ised, -is·ing.** *Chiefly Brit.* tabularize. —**tab′u·lar·i·sa′tion,** *n.*

tab·u·lar·ize (tab′yə lə rīz′), *v.t.,* **-ized, -iz·ing.** to tabulate. [TABULAR + -IZE] —**tab′u·lar·i·za′tion,** *n.*

tab·u·late (*v.* tab′yə lāt′; *adj.* tab′yə lit, -lāt′), *v.,* **-lat·ed, -lat·ing,** *adj.* —*v.t.* **1.** to put or arrange in a tabular, systematic, or condensed form; formulate tabularly. —*v.i.* **2.** to set or operate the tabulator on a typewriter. —*adj.* **3.** shaped like a table or tablet; tabular. **4.** having transverse dissepiments, as certain corals. [< L *tabulāt(us)* boarded, planked. See TABLE, -ATE[1]] —**tab′u·la·ble,** *adj.* —**tab′u·la′tion,** *n.*

tab·u·la·tor (tab′yə lā′tər), *n.* **1.** one who or that which tabulates. **2.** a typewriter key for moving the carriage a set number of spaces to the left each time it is depressed, used for typing material in columns, for fixed indentions, and the like. Also called **tab, tab key.** [TABULATE + -OR[2]]

tac·a·ma·hac (tak′ə mə hak′), *n.* **1.** any of certain resinous substances, used in incenses, ointments, etc. **2.** any tree, as of the genera *Bursera* and *Protium,* yielding such a product. **3.** See **balsam poplar.** Also, **tac·a·ma·hac·a** (tak′ə mə hak′ə), **tacmahack.** [< Sp *tacama(ha)c(a)* < Nahuatl *tecomahca* smelling copal]

tace (tas, tās), *n. Armor.* tasset.

ta·cet (tä′ket, tā′sit), *v. imperative. Music.* be silent (directing an instrument or voice not to play or sing). [< L: lit., (it) is silent]

tache (tach), *n. Archaic.* a buckle; clasp. Also, **tach.** [late ME < MF < Gmc. See TACK[1]]

tach·e·om·e·ter (tak′ē om′i tər), *n. Survey.* tachymeter. [< F *tachéomètre* < *taché-* (< Gk *tácheos,* gen. sing. of *táchos* speed) + *-o-* -O- + *-mètre* -METER]

ta·chi (tä chē′), *n., pl.* **-chi.** a long, single-edged sword having a gentle curve and similar to the katana, which replaced it as the fighting sword of the samurai: now used as a ceremonial sword. [< Jap]

tach′i·na fly′ (tak′ə nə), any of numerous dipterous insects of the family *Tachinidae,* the larvae of which are parasitic on caterpillars, beetles, and other insects. [< NL *tachina* genus of flies < Gk *tachinē,* c. *tach(ŷs)* swift + *-inē,* fem. of *-inos* -INE[1]]

Ta Ch'ing (dä′ ching′), Ch'ing.

tach·i·ol (tak′ē ōl′, -ôl′, -ol′), *n. Chem.* See **silver fluoride.** [TACHY- + -OL[1]]

Ta·chisme (tᴀ kēsʹmᵊ), *n.* (*sometimes l.c.*) *Fine Arts.* a style of art in France concurrent with and related to Abstract Expressionism. [< F; see TACHY-, -ISM]

tachisto-, a learned borrowing from Greek meaning "swiftest," used in the formation of compound words: *tachistoscope.* Cf. **tacho-, tachy-.** [< Gk *táchisto(s),* superlative of *tachŷs* swift]

ta·chis·to·scope (tə kis′tə skōp′), *n. Psychol.* an apparatus for use in exposing visual stimuli, as pictures, letters, or words, for an extremely brief period, usually a tenth of a second: used esp. as an aid in increasing reading speed. [TACHISTO- + SCOPE] —**ta·chis·to·scop·ic** (tə kis′tə skop′ik), *adj.* —**ta·chis′to·scop′i·cal·ly,** *adv.*

tacho-, a learned borrowing from Greek meaning "speed," used in the formation of compound words: *tachometer.* Cf. **tachisto-, tachy-.** [comb. form repr. Gk *táchos;* akin to *tachŷs* swift]

tach·o·gram (tak′ə gram′), *n.* the record produced by the action of a tachometer. Also, **tachograph.** [TACHO- + -GRAM[1]]

tach·o·graph (tak′ə graf′, -gräf′), *n.* **1.** a recording tachometer. **2.** tachogram. [TACHO- + -GRAPH]

ta·chom·e·ter (ta kom′i tər, tə-), *n.* **1.** any of various instruments for measuring or indicating velocity or speed, as of a machine, a river, the blood, etc. **2.** an instrument measuring revolutions per minute, as of an engine. [TACHO- + -METER] —**tach·o·met·ri·cal·ly** (tak′ə me′trik lē), *adv.* —**ta·chom′e·try,** *n.*

tachy-, a learned borrowing from Greek meaning "swift," used in the formation of compound words: *tachygraphy.* Cf. **tachisto-, tacho-.** [< Gk, comb. form of *tachŷs*]

tach·y·aux·e·sis (tak′ē ôg zē′sis, -ôk sē′-), *n. Biol.* growth of a part at a faster rate than that of the whole organism. Cf. **bradyauxesis, isauxesis.** [< NL; see TACHY-, AUXESIS] —**tach·y·aux·et·ic** (tak′ē ôg zet′ik, -ôk set′-), *adj.*

tach·y·car·di·a (tak′ə kär′dē ə), *n. Med.* excessively rapid heart beat. [TACHY- + -CARDIA]

tach·y·graph (tak′ə graf′, -gräf′), *n.* **1.** tachygraphic writing. **2.** one who writes or is skilled in writing tachygraphy. [TACHY- + -GRAPH]

ta·chyg·ra·phy (ta kig′rə fē, tə-), *n.* the Greek and Roman handwriting used for rapid stenography and writing. [TACHY- + -GRAPHY] —**ta·chyg′ra·pher, ta·chyg′ra·phist,** *n.* —**tach·y·graph·ic** (tak′ə graf′ik), **tach′y·graph′i·cal,** *adj.* —**tach′y·graph′i·cal·ly,** *adv.*

tach·y·lyte (tak′ə līt′), *n.* a black, glassy form of basalt, readily fusible and of a high luster. Also, **tach′y·lite′.** [TACHY- + -LYTE[2]] —**tach·y·lit·ic** (tak′ə-lit′ik), *adj.*

ta·chym·e·ter (ta kim′i tər, tə-), *n. Survey.* any of several instruments for rapidly determining distances, directions, and differences of elevation, in a single operation, by various means, as by using stadia hairs or a gradienter to read a stadia rod. Also, **tacheometer.** [TACHY- + -METER]

ta·chym·e·try (ta kim′i trē, tə-), *n. Survey.* the science of measuring distances with a tachymeter. [< F *tachymétre.* See TACHY-, -METRY]

tach·y·phy·lax·is (tak′ə fi lak′sis), *n. Med.* immediate, temporary immunization against the effects of injection of a toxic extract owing to previous small injections of the same extract. Also, **tach·y·phy·lax·i·a** (tak′ə fə lak′sē ə). Also called **skeptophylaxis.** [TACHY- + Gk *phylak-* (s. of *phýlax* guard) + -SIS] —**tach·y·phy·lac·tic** (tak′ə fi lak′tik), *adj.*

tach·yp·ne·a (tak′ip nē′ə), *n. Med.* excessively rapid respiration. Also, **tach′yp·noe′a.** [TACHY- + *-pnea,* var. of *pnoea* < Gk *-pnoia,* gradational var. of *pneia* breath] —**tach′yp·ne′ic, tach′yp·noe′ic,** *adj.*

ta·chys·ter·ol (ta kis′tə rōl′, -rôl′, -rol′, tak′i-stēr′ōl, -ôl, -ol), *n. Biochem.* a water-insoluble sterol, $C_{28}H_{43}OH$, obtained by the ultraviolet irradiation of ergosterol or lumisterol, used in medicine chiefly in the treatment of hypoparathyroidism. [TACHY- + STEROL]

tach·y·tel·ic (tak′i tel′ik), *adj. Biol.* of or pertaining to evolution at a rate faster than the standard for a given group of plants or animals. Cf. **bradytelic, horotelic.** [TACHY- + TELIC] —**tach·y·tel·y** (tak′i-tel′ē), *n.*

tac·it (tas′it), *adj.* **1.** silent; saying nothing: *a tacit partner.* **2.** understood without being openly expressed; implied: *tacit approval.* **3.** unvoiced or unspoken: *a tacit prayer.* [< L *tacit(us)* silent, ptp. of *tacēre;* c. Goth *thahan;* akin to Icel *thegja*] —**tac′it·ly,** *adv.* —**tac′it·ness,** *n.*
—**Syn. 2.** unexpressed, unspoken, unsaid, implicit.
—**Ant. 2.** expressed.

Tac·i·te·an (tas′i tē′ən), *adj.* of or pertaining to Publius Cornelius Tacitus.

tac·i·turn (tas′i tûrn′), *adj.* **1.** inclined to silence; reserved in speech; reluctant to join in conversation. **2.** dour, stern, and silent in expression and manner. [< L *taciturn(us)* quiet, equiv. to *tacit(us)* silent + *-urnus* adj. suffix of time] —**tac′i·turn′ly,** *adv.*
—**Syn. 1.** silent, uncommunicative, reticent, quiet.

tac·i·turn·i·ty (tas′i tûr′ni tē), *n.* **1.** the state or quality of being reserved or reticent in conversation. **2.** *Scots Law.* a form of relinquishing a legal right through an unduly long delay, as by the silence of the creditor. [ME *taciturnite* < L *taciturnitāt-* (s. of *taciturnitās*), equiv. to *taciturn(us)* TACITURN + *-itāt-* -ITY]

Tac·i·tus (tas′i təs), *n.* **1. Pub·li·us Cornelius** (pub′lē əs), A.D. c55–c120, Roman historian. **2.** a walled plain in the fourth quadrant of the face of the moon: about 25 miles in diameter.

tack[1] (tak), *n.* **1.** a short, sharp-pointed nail, usually with a flat, broad head. **2.** a stitch, esp. a long stitch used in fastening seams, preparatory to a more thorough sewing. **3.** a fastening, esp. of a temporary kind. **4.** stickiness, as of nearly dry paint or glue or of gummed tape; adhesiveness. **5.** *Naut.* **a.** a rope for extending the weather clew of a course. **b.** the weather clew of a course. **c.** the lower forward corner of a fore-and-aft sail. See diag. under **sail. d.** a line secured to the lower outboard corner of a studdingsail to haul it to the end of the boom. **e.** the heading of a sailing vessel, when sailing close-hauled, with reference to the wind direction. **f.** a course run obliquely against the wind. **g.** one of the series of straight runs that make up the zigzag course of a ship proceeding to windward. **6.** a course of action or conduct, esp. one differing from some preceding or other course. **7.** one of the movements of a zigzag course on land. **8.** the gear used in equipping a horse, including saddle, bridle, martingale, etc. **9.** **on the wrong tack,** under a misapprehension; in error; astray: *His line of questioning began on the wrong tack.* —*v.t.* **10.** to fasten by a tack or tacks: *to tack a rug to the floor.* **11.** to secure by some slight or temporary fastening. **12.** to join together; unite; combine. **13.** to attach as something supplementary; append; annex (often fol. by *on* or *onto*). **14.** *Naut.* **a.** to change the course of (a sailing vessel) to the opposite tack. **b.** to navigate (a sailing vessel) by a series of tacks. **15.** to equip (a horse) with tack. —*v.i.* **16.** *Naut.* **a.** to change the course of a sailing vessel by bringing her head into the wind and then causing it to fall off on the other side: *He ordered us to tack at once.* **b.** (of a sailing vessel) to change course in this way. **c.** to proceed to windward by a series of courses as close to the wind as the vessel will sail, the wind being alternately on one bow and then on the other. **17.** to take or follow a zigzag course or route. **18.** to change one's course of action, conduct, ideas, etc. **19.** to equip a horse with tack (usually fol. by *up*): *Please tack up quickly.* [ME *tak* buckle, clasp, nail (later, tack); c. G *Zacke* prong, D *tak* twig. See TACHE] —**tack′er,** *n.* —**tack′less,** *adj.*

tack[2] (tak), *n.* food; fare. [?]

tack[3] (tak), *n. Scot. and North Eng.* **1.** a lease, esp. on farmland. **2.** a rented pasture. **3.** a catch, haul, or take of fish. [ME *tak* < Scand; cf. Icel *tak* chattels, seizure, grasp. See TAKE]

tack·et (tak′it), *n. Brit. Dial.* a nail or tack, esp. a hobnail. [ME *taket.* See TACK¹, -ET] —**tack′et·ed,** *adj.*

tack′ ham′mer, a light hammer for driving tacks, often magnetized to hold the tack to the head.

tack·le (tak′əl *or, for 2, 3,* tā′kəl), *n., v.,* **-led, -ling.** —*n.* **1.** equipment, apparatus, or gear, esp. for fishing: *fishing tackle.* **2.** a mechanism or apparatus, as a rope and block or a combination of ropes and blocks, for hoisting, lowering, and shifting objects or materials; purchase. **3.** any system of leverage using several pulleys. **4.** *Naut.* the gear and running rigging for handling a vessel or performing some task on a vessel. **5.** an act of tackling, as in football; a seizing or grasping. **6.** *Football.* **a.** either of the linemen stationed between a guard and an end. **b.** the position played by this lineman. **7.** (formerly) tack¹ (def. 8). —*v.t.* **8.** to undertake to handle, master, solve, etc.: *to tackle a difficult problem.* **9.** to deal with (a person) on some problem, issue, etc. **10.** to harness (a horse). **11.** *Football.* to seize, stop, or throw down (a ball-carrier). **12.** *Soccer, Field Hockey.* to block or impede the movement or progress of (an opponent having the ball) with the result of depriving him of the ball. —*v.i.* **13.** *Football.* to tackle an opponent having the ball. [ME *takel* gear < MLG; akin to TAKE] —**tack′ler,** *n.*

Tackles (def. 2)
A, Single whip; B, Runner; C, Gun tackle; D, Luff tackle; E, Single Spanish burton; F, Double Spanish burton

tack·ling (tak′ling), *n. Archaic.* equipment; tackle. [late ME; see TACKLE, -ING¹]

tack′ room′, a room in or near a stable for storing saddles, harnesses, and other tack.

tack·y¹ (tak′ē), *adj.,* **tack·i·er, tack·i·est.** adhesive; sticky. [TACK¹ + -Y¹] —**tack′i·ness,** *n.*

tack·y² (tak′ē), *adj.,* **tack·i·er, tack·i·est.** *Informal.* **1.** not tasteful or fashionable; dowdy; out-of-date. **2.** shabby in appearance: *a tacky, jerry-built housing development.* **3.** gaudy; flashy; showy. [?]

Ta·clo·ban (tä klō′bän), *n.* a seaport on NE Leyte, in the central Philippines. 56,703 (est. 1960).

tac·ma·hack (tak′mə hak′), *n.* tacamahac.

Tac·na-A·ri·ca (täk′nä ä rē′kä), *n.* a maritime region in W South America: long in dispute between Chile and Peru; annexed by Chile 1883; divided as a result of arbitration 1929 into a Peruvian department **(Tac′na)** and a Chilean department **(Arica).**

tac·node (tak′nōd), *n. Geom.* that point where two continuous, osculating branches of a curve have a common tangent. [< L *tac(tus)* touch (see TACT) + NODE]

ta·co (tä′kō; *Sp.* tä′kô), *n., pl.* **-cos** (-kōz; *Sp.* -kôs). a tortilla folded into a turnover or roll with a filling, usually fried. [< MexSp < Sp: bung, snack]

Ta·co·ma (tə kō′mə), *n.* **1.** a seaport in W Washington, on Puget Sound. 147,979 (1960). **2. Mount.** See **Rainier, Mount.** —**Ta·co′man,** *n.*

tac·o·nite (tak′ə nīt′), *n.* a low-grade iron ore, containing about 27 percent iron and 51 percent silica, found as a hard rock formation in the Lake Superior region. [*Tacon(ic)* mountain range (east of Hudson river) + -ITE¹]

tac·point (tak′point′), *n. Geom.* that point where two intersecting curves of the same family have a common tangent. [*tac-* (see TACNODE) + POINT]

Tac·quet (tä′kā, -kit), *n.* a crater in the first quadrant of the face of the moon: about 2 miles in diameter.

tact (takt), *n.* **1.** a keen sense of what to say or do to avoid giving offense; skill in dealing with difficult or delicate situations. **2.** a keen feeling or sense for what is appropriate, tasteful, or aesthetically pleasing; taste; discrimination. **3.** touch or the sense of touch. [< L *tact(us)* sense of touch < *tact-* (ptp. s. of *tangere* to touch) + *-us* n. suffix (4th decl.)]
—**Syn. 1.** perception, sensitivity; diplomacy, poise.

tact·ful (takt′fəl), *adj.* having or manifesting tact: *a tactful person; a tactful reply.* [TACT + -FUL] —**tact′ful·ly,** *adv.* —**tact′ful·ness,** *n.*
—**Syn.** adroit, skillful, clever, perceptive, sensitive. See **diplomatic.** —**Ant.** tactless.

tac·tic (tak′tik), *n.* **1.** tactics. **2.** a system or a detail of tactics. **3.** a plan, procedure, or expedient for promoting a desired end or result. —*adj.* **4.** of or pertaining to arrangement or order; tactical. [NL *tactic(us)* < Gk *taktikós* fit for arranging or ordering < *tak-* (verbid s. of *tássein, táttein* to arrange, put in order) + *-tikos* -TIC]

tac·ti·cal (tak′ti kəl), *adj.* **1.** of or pertaining to tactics, esp. military or naval tactics. **2.** characterized by skillful tactics or adroit maneuvering or procedure: *tactical movements.* **3.** of or pertaining to a maneuver or plan of action designed as an expedient toward gaining a desired end or temporary advantage. **4.** expedient; prudent; calculated; politic. [TACTIC + -AL¹] —**tac′ti·cal·ly,** *adv.*

tac′tical u′nit, *Mil.* a group organized to function in combat as a self-contained unit.

tac·ti·cian (tak tish′ən), *n.* a person who is adept in planning tactics. [TACTIC + -IAN]

tac·tics (tak′tiks), *n.* **1.** (*usually construed as sing.*) the art or science of disposing military or naval forces for battle and maneuvering them in battle. **2.** (*construed as pl.*) the maneuvers themselves. **3.** (*construed as pl.*) mode of procedure for gaining advantage or success. [see TACTIC, -ICS]
—**Syn. 1.** See **strategy.**

tac·tile (tak′til, -tīl), *adj.* **1.** of, pertaining to, endowed with, or affecting the sense of touch. **2.** perceptible to the touch; tangible. [< L *tactil(is)* tangible < *tact-* (ptp. s. of *tangere* to touch) + *-ilis* -ILE] —**tac·til′i·ty,** *n.*

tac·tion (tak′shən), *n.* touch; contact. [< L *tactiōn-* (s. of *tactiō*) a touching, equiv. to *tact-* (ptp. s. of *tangere* to touch) + *-iōn-* -ION]

tact·less (takt′lis), *adj.* lacking tact; showing no tact; undiplomatic; offendingly blunt: *a tactless remark.* [TACT + -LESS] —**tact′less·ly,** *adv.* —**tact′less·ness,** *n.*

tac·tu·al (tak′cho͞o əl), *adj.* **1.** of or pertaining to the sense of touch. **2.** communicating or imparting the sensation of contact; arising from or due to touch. [< L *tactu(s)* touch (see TACT) + -AL¹] —**tac′tu·al·ly,** *adv.*

tac·tus (täk′to͝os), *n.* the basic metrical unit in medieval music. [L: touch; see TACT]

Ta·cu·ba·ya (tä′ko͞o bä′yä), *n.* a former city in the Federal District of Mexico: now a SW district of Mexico City; national observatory.

tad (tad), *n. U.S. Informal.* a small child, esp. a boy. [short for TADPOLE]

Tad (tad), *n.* a boy's given name, form of **Thaddeus** or **Theodore.**

Tad·e·ma (tad′ə mə), *n.* **Sir Lawrence Alma-.** See **Alma-Tadema, Sir Lawrence.**

Ta·djik (tä′jik), *n., pl.* **-djik** for 1. **1.** Tajik. **2.** Tadzhikistan.

Tad·mor (tăd′môr), *n.* Biblical name of **Palmyra.**

tad·pole (tad′pōl′), *n.* the aquatic larva or immature form of frogs, toads, etc., esp. after the enclosure of the gills and before the appearance of the forelimbs and the resorption of the tail. [late ME *taddepol* < *tadde* TOAD + *pol* POLL¹ (head)]

Tadpoles in early stages of growth

Ta·dzhik (tä′jik), *n., pl.* **-dzhik** for 1. **1.** Tajik. **2.** Tadzhikistan.

Ta·dzhik·i·stan (te jik′ə stan′, -stän′, -jē′kə-, tä-; *Russ.* tə ji kyi stän′), *n.* a republic in central Asia, N of Afghanistan. 5,112,000; 55-240 sq. mi. *Cap.:* Dushanbe. Also, **Tajikistan.** Formerly, **Tadzhik′ So′viet So′cialist Repub′lic.**

tae (tā), *prep. Scot.* to.

tae·di·um vi·tae (tī′dē o͝om′ wē′tī; *Eng.* tē′dē əm vī′tē), *Latin.* a feeling that life is unbearably wearisome. [lit., tedium of life]

Tae·gu (tī′go͞o′), *n.* a city in SE South Korea: commercial center. 676,692 (1960). Japanese, **Taikyu.**

Tae·jon (tī′jon′), *n.* a city in W South Korea. 228,987 (1960). Japanese, **Taiden.**

tael (tāl), *n.* **1.** liang. **2.** any of various other similar units of weight in the Far East. **3.** a Chinese money of account, being the value of this weight of standard silver. [< Pg < Malay *tahil* weight]

ta'en (tān), *v. Archaic.* taken. [ME *(y)tan, tane, tain,* var. of TAKEN]

tae·ni·a (tē′nē ə), *n., pl.* **-ni·ae** (-nē ē′). **1.** *Class. Antiq.* a headband or fillet. **2.** *Archit.* (on a Doric entablature) a fillet or band separating the frieze from the architrave. **3.** *Anat.* a ribbonlike structure, as certain bands of white nerve fibers in the brain. **4.** any tapeworm of the genus *Taenia,* parasitic in man and other mammals. Also, **tenia.** [< L < Gk *tainía* band, ribbon]

tae·ni·a·cide (tē′nē ə sīd′), *Med.* —*adj.* **1.** Also, **tae′ni·a·cid′al, teniacidal.** destroying tapeworms. —*n.* **2.** an agent that destroys tapeworms. Also, **teniacide.** [TAENIA + -CIDE]

tae·ni·a·fuge (tē′nē ə fyo͞oj′), *Med.* —*adj.* **1.** expelling tapeworms, as a medicine. —*n.* **2.** an agent or medicine for expelling tapeworms from the body. Also, **teniafuge.** [TAENIA + -FUGE]

tae·ni·a·sis (tē nī′ə sis), *n. Pathol.* infestation with tapeworms. Also, **teniasis.** [TAENI(A) + -ASIS]

tae·nid·i·um (tē nid′ē əm), *n., pl.* **-nid·i·a** (-nid′ē ə). (of an insect) a circular or spiral fiber that supports the wall of a trachea. [< NL < Gk *tainídion,* dim. of *tainía* TAENIA] —**tae·nid′i·al,** *adj.*

tae·nite (tē′nīt), *n.* a mineral, an alloy of nickel and iron, found in iron meteorites. [TAEN(IA) + -ITE¹]

taf·fa·rel (taf′ər əl, -ə rel′), *n. Archaic.* taffrail. Also, **taf′fe·rel.** [< MD *tafereel,* var. (by dissimilation) of *tafeleel* < F (dial.) *tavlet* TABLEAU]

taf·fe·ta (taf′i tə), *n.* **1.** a medium-weight or lightweight fabric of acetate, nylon, rayon, or silk, usually smooth, crisp, and lustrous, plain-woven, and with a fine crosswise rib effect. **2.** any of various other fabrics of silk, linen, wool, etc., in use at different periods. —*adj.* **3.** of or resembling taffeta. [ME *taffata* < ML << Pers *tāftah* silken or linen cloth, n. use of ptp. of *tāftan* to twist, spin]

T, Taffrail

taf′feta weave′. See **plain weave.**

taff·rail (taf′rāl′), *n. Naut.* **1.** the upper part of the stern of a vessel. **2.** a rail above the stern of a vessel. [syncopated var. of TAFFAREL; *-ai-* repr. D *-ee-*]

taf·fy (taf′ē), *n.* **1.** a candy made of sugar or molasses boiled down, often with butter, nuts, etc. **2.** *Informal.* flattery. Also, *esp. Brit.,* **toffee, toffy.** [var. of TOFFEE]

taf·i·a (taf′ē ə), *n.* a type of rum made in Haiti from lower grades of molasses, refuse sugar, or the like. Also, **taf′fi·a.** [< F (WInd Creole dial.); aph. var. of *ratafia* RATAFIA]

Ta·fi·lelt (tä fē′lelt), *n.* an oasis in SE Morocco, ab. 200 sq. mi. Also, **Ta·fi·la·let** (tä′fē lä′let).

Taft (taft), *n.* **1. Lo·ra·do** (lə rā′dō), 1860–1936, U.S. sculptor. **2. Robert A(l·phon·so)** (al fon′sō), 1889–1953, U.S. lawyer and political leader (son of William Howard). **3. William Howard,** 1857–1930, 27th president of the U.S. 1909–13; Chief Justice of the U.S. Supreme Court 1921–30. **4.** a town in central California. 3822 (1960). **5.** a town in S Texas. 3463 (1960).

Taft′-Hart′ley Act′ (taft′härt′lē), *U.S.* an act of Congress (1947) which supersedes but continues most of the provisions of the National Labor Relations Act and which, in addition, provides for an eighty-day injunction against strikes that endanger public health and safety and bans closed shops, featherbedding, secondary boycotts, jurisdictional strikes, and certain other union practices.

tag¹ (tag), *n., v.,* **tagged, tag·ging.** —*n.* **1.** a piece or strip of strong paper, leather, or the like, for attaching by one end to something as a mark or label: *The price is on the tag.* **2.** any small hanging or loosely attached part or piece; tatter. **3.** a loop of material sewn on a garment so that it can be hung up. **4.** a metal, plastic, or other hard substance at the end of a shoelace, cord, or the like. **5.** *Angling.* a small piece of tinsel, or the like, tied to the shank of a hook at the body of an artificial fly. **6.** the tail end or concluding part, as of a proceeding. **7.** the last words of a speech, scene, act, etc., as in a play; a curtain line. **8.** (in computer programming) sentinel (def. 4). **9.** an addition to a speech or writing, as the moral of a fable. **10.** a quotation added for special effect. **11.** a descriptive word or phrase applied to a person, group, organization, etc., as a label or means of identification; epithet: *After the accident, they gave him the tag of murderer.* **12.** a trite phrase or saying; cliché. **13.** a traffic ticket. **14.** a curlicue in writing. **15.** a lock of hair. **16.** a matted lock of wool on a sheep. **17.** *Fox Hunting.* the white tip of the tail of a fox. **18.** *Obs.* the rabble. —*v.t.* **19.** to furnish with a tag or tags; attach a tag to. **20.** to accuse of a violation, esp. of a traffic law; give a traffic ticket to: *He was tagged for speeding. The policeman tagged the cars for parking on the wrong side of the street.* **21.** to append as a tag, addition, or afterthought, to something else. **22.** to attach or give an epithet to; label. **23.** to hold answerable or accountable for something; attach blame to: *The pitcher was tagged with the loss of the game. The firm tagged him with the loss of the account.* **24.** to set a price on; fix the cost of: *The dealer tagged the boat at $500 less than the suggested retail price.* **25.** *Informal.* to follow closely: *I tagged him to an old house at the outskirts of town.* **26.** to remove the tags of wool from (a sheep). —*v.i.* **27.** to follow closely; go along or about as a follower: *to tag after someone; to tag along behind someone.* [late ME *tagge;* c. MLG, Norw *tagge,* Sw *tagg* pointed protruding part; akin to TACK¹] —**tag′like′,** *adj.*

tag² (tag), *n., v.,* **tagged, tag·ging.** —*n.* **1.** a children's game in which one player chases the others till he touches one of them, who then takes his place as pursuer. **2.** *Baseball.* the act or an instance of tagging a base runner. —*v.t.* **3.** to touch in or as in the game of tag. **4.** *Baseball.* **a.** to touch (a base runner) with the ball held in the hand or glove. **b.** *Slang.* to hit (a pitched ball) solidly. **c.** *Slang.* to make a number of hits or runs as specified in batting against (a pitcher): *They tagged him for two hits in the first and three hits and two runs in the third.* **5.** *Boxing.* to strike (an opponent) with a powerful blow. **6. tag up,** *Baseball.* (of a base runner) to touch the base occupied before attempting to advance a base, after the catch of a fly ball: *He tagged up and scored from third on a long fly to center.* [? special use of TAG¹]

Ta·ga·log (tä gä′log, tag′ə log′), *n., pl.* **-logs,** (*esp. collectively*) **-log** for 1. **1.** a member of a Malayan people native to Luzon, in the Philippines. **2.** the principal Indonesian language of the Philippines.

Ta·gan·rog (tä′gän rôk′), *n.* **1.** a seaport in the S Soviet Union in Europe, on the Gulf of Taganrog. 220,000 (est. 1962). **2. Gulf of,** an arm of the Sea of Azov.

tag·board (tag′bōrd′, -bôrd′), *n.* a strong cardboard suitable for tags or posters. [TAG¹ + BOARD]

tag′ boat′, a small rowboat usually towed astern of a larger vessel.

tag′ day′, *U.S.* a day on which contributions to a fund are solicited, each contributor receiving a tag.

tag′ end′, **1.** the last or final part of something: *They came in at the tag end of the performance.* **2.** a random scrap, fragment, or remnant.

Tag·gard (tag′ərd), *n.* **Genevieve,** 1894–1948, U.S. poet.

tag·ger (tag′ər), *n.* **1.** one who or that which tags. **2. taggers,** *Metall.* iron or tin plate in very thin sheets. [TAG¹ + -ER¹]

ta·glia·ri·ni (tal′yə rē′nē; *It.* tä′lyä rē′nē), *n.* pasta in long, flat, slender pieces, narrower than tagliatelle. [< It < *tagliar(e)* (to) cut < LL *tāliāre* + It *-ini* m. pl. dim. suffix < L *-inus* -INE¹]

ta·glia·tel·le (täl′yə tel′ē, *It.* tä′lyä tel′le), *n.* a kind of pasta, made with egg, in long, flat pieces. [< It: flat noodles < *tagliat-* (ptp. s. of *tagliare* to cut < LL *tāliāre;* see TAILOR) + *-elle,* pl. of *-ella* dim. suffix]

Ta·glia·vi·ni (tä′lyä vē′nē), *n.* **Fer·ruc·cio** (feʀ-ʀo͞ot′chô), born 1913, Italian tenor.

tag′ line′, **1.** the last line of a play, story, speech, etc., used to clarify or dramatize a point. **2.** a phrase or catchword that becomes identified or associated with a person, group, product, etc., through repetition: *Entertainers often develop tag lines, as Ted Lewis's "Is everybody happy?"* **3.** *Mach.* (on a crane) a cable for steadying a suspended bucket at the rear.

tag·lock (tag′lok′), *n.* a matted lock of wool or hair. [TAG¹ + LOCK²]

tag·meme (tag′mēm), *n. Linguistics.* any of the minimal units of grammatical construction, embodying distinctive word order, grammatical agreement, and choice of determiners. The phrase *the second old white house* is a tagmeme illustrating fixed word order. Cf. **glosseme, morpheme.** [< Gk *tágm(a)* arrangement < *táss(ein)* (to) arrange + -EME]

tag·me·mic (tag mē′mik), *adj. Linguistics.* **1.** of or pertaining to tagmemes. **2.** of or pertaining to tagmemics. [TAGMEME + -IC]

tag·me·mics (tag mē′miks), *n.* (*construed as sing.*) *Linguistics.* the study of tagmemes and tagmemic systems. [TAGMEME + -ICS]

Ta·gore (tə gōr′, -gôr′, tä′gôr), *n.* **Sir Ra·bin·dra·nath** (rə bēn′drə nät′), 1861–1941, Hindu poet: Nobel prize 1913.

tag·rag (tag′rag′), *n.* **1.** riffraff; rabble. **2.** a tatter. [TAG¹ + RAG¹]

tag′ team′, *Professional Wrestling.* a team of two wrestlers who compete one at a time against either member of another such team, the wrestlers in the ring changing places with those outside by tagging them.

Ta·gus (tā′gəs), *n.* a river in SW Europe, flowing W through central Spain and Portugal to the Atlantic at Lisbon. 566 mi. long. Spanish, **Tajo.** Portuguese, **Tejo.**

Ta·hi·ti (tə hē′tē, tä-, tī′tē), *n.* the principal island of the Society Islands, in the S Pacific. 44,710 (1956); 402 sq. mi. *Cap.:* Papeete. Formerly, **Otaheite.**

Ta·hi·tian (tə hē′shən, -tē ən, tä-), *adj.* **1.** of or pertaining to Tahiti, its inhabitants, or their language. —*n.* **2.** a native or inhabitant of Tahiti. **3.** the Polynesian language of Tahiti. [TAHITI + -AN]

Tah·le·quah (tä′lə kwä′), *n.* a town in E Oklahoma. 5840 (1960).

Ta·hoe (tä′hō, tā′-), *n.* **Lake,** a lake in E California and W Nevada, in the Sierra Nevada Mountains: resort. ab. 200 sq. mi.; 6225 ft. above sea level.

Ta·ho·ka (tə hō′kə), *n.* a town in NW Texas. 3012 (1960).

tahr (tär), *n.* any of several wild goats of the genus *Hemitragus,* as *H. jemlahicus* **(Himalayan tahr),** having a long mane and short, stout, recurving horns. Also, **thar.** [< Nepali *thār*]

tah·sil·dar (tə sēl där′), *n.* (in India) a collector for, or official of, the revenue department. Also, **tah·seel·dar′.** [< Urdu < Pers < *taḥṣīl* collection (< Ar) + *-dār* agent suffix]

tai (tī), *n., pl.* **tai.** any of several sparoid fishes found in the Pacific Ocean, as *Pagrosomus major* **(red tai),** a food fish of Japan. [< Jap]

Tai (tī, tä′ē), *n., adj.* Thai.

Tai·chung (tī′jo͝ong′), *n.* a city in W Taiwan. 336,280 (est. 1963). Japanese, **Tai·chu** (tī′cho͞o′).

Tai·den (tī den′), *n.* Japanese name of **Taejon.**

Ta·if (tä′if), *n.* a city in W Saudi Arabia. 50,000 (est. 1956).

tai·ga (tī′gə), *n.* the coniferous, evergreen forests of subarctic lands, covering vast areas of northern North America and Eurasia. [< Russ < Turkic; akin to Turk *dağ* mountain]

taig·lach (tāg′ləKH, tīg′-), *n.* (*construed as sing. or pl.*) teiglach.

Tai·ho·ku (tī′hô ko͞o′), *n.* Japanese name of **Taipeh.**

Tai·kyu (tī kyo͞o′), *n.* Japanese name of **Taegu.**

tail[1] (tāl), *n.* **1.** the hindmost part of an animal, esp. that forming a distinct, flexible appendage to the trunk. **2.** something resembling or suggesting this in shape or position: *the tail of a kite.* **3.** the hinder, bottom, or end part of anything; the rear. **4.** a final or concluding part of a sentence, conversation, social gathering, etc.; conclusion; end: *The tail of the speech was boring. Toward the tail of the concert I'd begun to get tired.* **5.** the inferior or unwanted part of anything. **6.** a long braid or tress of hair. **7.** *Astron.* the luminous stream extending from the head of a comet. **8.** the reverse of a coin (opposed to *head*). **9.** an arrangement of objects or persons extending as or as if a tail. **10.** a line of persons awaiting their turns at something; queue. **11.** a retinue; train. **12.** *Aeron.* the after portion of an airplane or the like. **13.** *Mach.* (in an engine) an extension of a crosshead to which the connecting rod is attached. **14.** the lower part of a pool or stream. **15. tails, a.** See **tail coat. b.** full-dress attire. **c.** *Distilling.* alcohol obtained in the final distillation. Cf. **head** (def. 22). **16.** the exposed portion of a piece of roofing, as a slate. **17.** *Carpentry.* lookout (def. 7a). **18.** *Print.* the lower portion of a type, as of g, y, Q, etc. **19.** *Informal.* a person who trails or keeps a close surveillance of another, as a detective, spy, etc.: *The police decided to put a tail on the suspect.* **20.** *Slang.* the buttocks or rump. **21.** *Slang* (*vulgar*). coitus or a woman considered as an object of coitus. **22. turn tail, a.** to turn one's back on, as in aversion or fright. **b.** to run away from (difficulty, opposition, etc.); flee: *The sight of superior forces made the attackers turn tail.* **23. with one's tail between one's legs,** utterly humiliated; defeated; cowed: *They were forced to retreat with their tails between their legs.* —*adj.* **24.** coming from behind: *a tail breeze.* **25.** being in the back or rear: *a tail light.* —*v.t.* **26.** to form or furnish with a tail. **27.** to form or constitute the tail or end of (a procession, retinue, etc.). **28.** to terminate; come after or behind; follow like a tail. **29.** to join or attach (one thing) at the tail or end of another. **30.** *Building Trades.* to fasten (a beam, stone, etc.) by one end (usually fol. by *in* or *into*). **31.** to dock the tail of (a horse, dog, etc.). **32.** *Informal.* to follow in order to hinder escape of or to observe: *to tail a suspect.* —*v.i.* **33.** to form, or move or pass in, a line or column suggestive of a tail: *The hikers tailed up the narrow path.* **34.** (of a boat) to have or take a position with the stern in a particular direction. **35.** *Informal.* to follow close behind: *She always tails after her sister.* **36.** *Building Trades.* (of a beam, stone, etc.) to be fastened by one end (usually fol. by *in* or *into*). **37.** to disappear gradually or merge into: *The shouting and yelling of children at play tailed into silence as the afternoon began to wane. The path tails off into the woods.* [ME; OE *tægl;* c. Icel *tagl* horse's tail, Goth *tagl* hair, MHG *zagel* tail, MLG *tagel* rope-end] —**tail′less,** *adj.* —**tail′less·ly,** *adv.* —**tail′less·ness,** *n.* —**tail′like′,** *adj.*

tail[2] (tāl), *n.* **1.** *Law.* the limitation of an estate to a person and the heirs of his body, or some particular class of such heirs. **2.** *Print., Bookbinding.* the bottom of a page or book. —*adj.* **3.** *Law.* limited to a specified line of heirs; being in tail. [ME *taille* (n.) (< MF see TAILLE); late ME *taille* (adj.) < AF: cut, shaped, limited, ptp. of *tailler,* equiv. to OF *tailler* < LL *tāliāre.* See TAILOR[1]] —**tail′less,** *adj.*

tail·back (tāl′bak′), *n.* *Football.* **1.** the offensive back who lines up farthest behind the line of scrimmage, as in a single wingback or double wingback formation. **2.** the position played by this back. [TAIL[1] + BACK[1]]

tail·band (tāl′band′), *n.* a band sewn or glued to the tail of a book. Cf. **headband** (def. 3). [TAIL[1] + BAND[2]]

tail′ bay′, (in a roof or floor frame) the space between the outermost principal and the adjacent wall or gable. Cf. **case bay.**

tail′ beam′, tailpiece (def. 4a).

tail·board (tāl′bōrd′, -bôrd′), *n.* the tailgate, esp. of a wagon or truck. [TAIL[1] + BOARD]

tail′ coat′. a man's fitted coat, cutaway over the hips and descending in a pair of tapering skirts behind, usually black and worn as part of full evening dress. Also, **tail′coat′.** Also called **tails, dress coat, swallow-tailed coat.**

tail′ cone′, *Rocketry.* a cone-shaped component at the rear of a jet engine, rocket, or missile, usually serving as an exhaust pipe.

tailed′ frog′, a frog, *Ascaphus truei,* of the northwestern U.S. and adjacent Canada, the male of which has its cloaca modified into a taillike copulatory organ. Also called **bell toad, ribbed toad, tailed′ toad′.**

tail′ end′, **1.** the hinder or rear part of anything. **2.** the concluding or final part or section; tag end: *the tail end of a lecture.*

tail·er (tā′lər), *n.* one who or that which tails. [TAIL[1] + -ER[1]]

tail·first (tāl′fûrst′), *adv.* with the tail or rear part foremost. [TAIL[1] + FIRST]

tail·gate[1] (tāl′gāt′), *n., v.,* **-gat·ed, -gat·ing.** —*n.* **1.** the board or gate at the back of a wagon, truck, station wagon, etc., which can be removed or let down for convenience in loading or unloading. —*v.i.* **2.** to follow or drive hazardously close to the rear of another vehicle. —*v.t.* **3.** to follow or drive hazardously close to the rear of (another vehicle). [TAIL[1] + GATE]

tail·gate[2] (tāl′gāt′), *n.* *Jazz.* a style of playing the trombone, esp. in Dixieland jazz, distinguished esp. by the use of melodic counterpoint and long glissandi. [so called from the usual seat of trombonists in trucks carrying musicians during a parade]

tail·gat·er (tāl′gā′tər), *n.* a musician who plays trombone in tailgate style. [TAILGATE[2] + -ER[1]]

tail′ grab′, *Rocketry.* a mechanism which restrains a missile on its launch pad until the vehicle develops a desired amount of thrust.

tail·ing (tā′ling), *n.* **1.** the part of a projecting stone or brick tailed or inserted in a wall. **2. tailings, a.** *Building Trades.* gravel, aggregate, etc., failing to pass through a given screen. **b.** the residue of any product, as in mining; leavings. [TAIL[1] + -ING[1]]

tail′ joist′, tailpiece (def. 4a).

taille (tāl; *Fr.* tä′yə), *n., pl.* **tailles** (tālz; *Fr.* tä′yə). **1.** *French Hist.* a tax that was levied by a king or seigneur on his subjects or on lands held under him and that became solely a royal tax in the 15th century from which the lords and later the clergy were exempt. **2.** (in dressmaking) the waist or bodice of a garment. **3.** *Obs.* the shape of one's body from shoulders to waist; figure; build. [< F: lit., a cutting, verbid of *tailler,* OF *taillier* to cut, limit, tax; see TAILOR[1]]

tail′less air′plane, **1.** an airplane having an empennage that consists of a vertical fin and rudder, without horizontal stabilizers, and using elevons for vertical control. **2.** *Rare.* See **flying wing.**

tail·leur (tä yûr′), *n.* a tailored or tailor-made costume for women. [F: lit., tailor; see TAILLE, -OR[2]]

tail·light (tāl′līt′), *n.* a light, usually red, at the rear of an automobile, train, etc. Also, *Brit.,* **tail′ lamp′.** [TAIL[1] + LIGHT[1]]

tai·lor[1] (tā′lər), *n.* **1.** a person whose occupation is the making, mending, or altering of suits, coats, and other outer garments. —*v.i.* **2.** to do the work of a tailor. —*v.t.* **3.** to make by tailor's work. **4.** to fit or furnish with clothing. **5.** to fashion or adapt to a particular taste, purpose, need, etc.: *to tailor one's actions to those of another.* **6.** *Chiefly U.S. Mil.* to make (a uniform) to order; cut (a ready-made uniform) so as to cause to fit more snugly; taper. [ME < AF *taillour,* equiv. to OF *tailleor* < LL *tāliātōrem, acc. of *tāliātor cutter < *tāliāt(us)* cut, shaped (ptp. of *tāliāre,* deriv. of L *tālea* a cutting, lit., heel-piece; see TALLY) + *-or* -OR[2]] —**tai′lor·less,** *adj.*

tai·lor[2] (tā′lər), *n.* a stroke of a bell indicating someone's death; knell. [alter. by folk etymology of TELLER]

tai·lor·bird (tā′lər bûrd′), *n.* any of several small, Asian, passerine birds, esp. of the genus *Orthotomus,* that stitch leaves together to form and conceal their nests. [TAILOR[1] + BIRD]

tai·lored (tā′lərd), *adj.* **1.** (of a woman's garment) in a simple or plain style with fitted lines. Cf. **dressmaker** (def 2). **2.** having simple, straight lines and a neat appearance: *tailored slip covers.* [TAILOR[1] + -ED[2]]

tai·lor·ing (tā′lər ing), *n.* **1.** the business or work of a tailor. **2.** the skill or craftsmanship of a tailor. [TAILOR[1] + -ING[1]]

tai·lor-made (*adj.* tā′lər mād′; *n.* tā′lər mād′, -mād′), *adj.* **1.** tailored. **2.** custom-made; made-to-order; made-to-measure: *an expensive tailor-made suit.* **3.** fashioned to a particular taste, purpose, demand, etc.: *a musical comedy tailor-made for the popular audience.* —*n.* **4.** Usually, **tailor-mades.** a tailor-made garment.

tai·lor-make (tā′lər māk′), *v.t.,* **-made, -mak·ing.** to make or adjust to meet the needs of the particular situation, individual, object, etc.: *to tailor-make the tour.*

tail·piece (tāl′pēs′), *n.* **1.** a piece added at the end; an end piece or appendage. **2.** *Print.* a small decorative design at the end of a chapter or at the bottom of a page. **3.** (in a musical instrument of the viol family) a triangular piece of wood, usually of ebony, to which the lower ends of the strings are fastened. **4.** *Building Trades.* **a.** Also called **tail beam, tail joist.** a relatively short beam or rafter inserted in a wall by tailing and supported by a header. **b.** lookout (def. 7a). **5.** *Furniture.* (in certain Windsor chairs) a rearward extension of the seat supporting two struts bracing the back. Cf. **fiddle brace back.** [TAIL[1] + PIECE]

tail·pipe (tāl′pīp′), *n.* an exhaust pipe located at the rear of a vehicle, as a car or jet-engine airplane. [TAIL[1] + PIPE[1]]

tail′ plane′, *Aeron. Chiefly Brit.* See **horizontal stabilizer.**

tail·race (tāl′rās′), *n.* **1.** the race, flume, or channel leading away from a water wheel or the like. **2.** *Mining.* the channel for conducting tailings or refuse away in water. [TAIL[1] + RACE[1]]

tails (tālz), *adj., adv.* (of a coin) with the reverse facing up: *On the next toss, the coin came up tails.* Cf. **heads.** [TAIL[1] + -S[1]]

tail·shaft (tāl′shaft′, -shäft′), *n.* *Naut.* the aftermost end of a propeller shaft, where the propeller is fixed. [TAIL[1] + SHAFT]

tail′ skid′, *Aeron.* a runner under the tail of an airplane.

tail·spin (tāl′spin′), *n.* **1.** spin (def. 18). **2.** a sudden and helpless collapse into failure, confusion, or the like. Also, **tail′ spin′.** [TAIL[1] + SPIN]

tail·stock (tāl′stok′), *n.* a movable or sliding support for the dead center of a lathe or grinder. See illus. under **lathe.** [TAIL[1] + STOCK]

tail·wa·ter (tāl′wô′tər, -wot′ər), *n.* the water in a tailrace. [TAIL[1] + WATER]

tail·wind (tāl′wind′), *n.* a wind coming from directly behind a moving aircraft or vessel. [TAIL[1] + WIND[1]]

Tai·myr′ Penin′sula (tī mēr′), a peninsula in the N Soviet Union in Asia, between the Kara and Nordenskjöld seas. Also, **Tai·mir′ Penin′sula.**

tain (tān), *n.* **1.** a thin tin plate. **2.** tin foil for the backs of mirrors. [< F: silvering, foil, aph. var. of *étain* tin]

Tai·nan (tī′nän′), *n.* a city in SW Taiwan. 375,101 (est. 1963).

Taine (tān; *Fr.* ten), *n.* **Hip·po·lyte A·dolphe** (ē pô lēt′ A dôlf′), 1828–93, French literary critic and historian.

Tai·no (tī′nō), *n., pl.* **-nos,** (*esp. collectively*) **-no** for 1. **1.** a member of an extinct Arawakan Indian tribe of the West Indies. **2.** the language of the Taino.

taint (tānt), *n.* **1.** a trace of something bad, offensive, or harmful. **2.** a trace of infection, contamination, or the like. **3.** a trace of dishonor or discredit. **4.** *Obs.* color; tint. —*v.t.* **5.** to modify by or as if by a trace of something offensive or deleterious. **6.** to infect, contaminate, or corrupt. **7.** to sully or tarnish (a person's name, reputation, etc.). **8.** *Obs.* to color or tint. —*v.i.* **9.** to become tainted. [ME *taynt* (aph. var. of *attaint* struck, attainted, ptp. of ATTAIN) + late ME *taynt* < AF *teint(er)* (to) color, dye, tinge, v. use of ptp. of *teindre* < L *tingere* to TINGE]
—**Syn. 1.** blemish, stain, defect, spot, flaw, fault. **6.** defile, pollute, poison. **7.** blemish, stain.

taint·less (tānt′lis), *adj.* free from or without taint; pure; innocent. [TAINT + -LESS] —**taint′less·ly,** *adv.* —**taint′less·ness,** *n.*

tai·pan[1] (tī′pan), *n.* (in China) the head or owner of a foreign business establishment. [< Chin (Peking) *tai pan*]

tai·pan[2] (tī′pan), *n.* a highly venomous elapid snake, *Oxyuranus scutellatus,* of New Guinea and northern Australia, that grows to a length of from 10 to 11 feet. [< native Austral]

Tai·pei (tī′pā′; *Chin.* tī′bā′), *n.* a city in and the capital of Taiwan, in the N part: provisional capital of the Republic of China. 1,076,649 (1965). Also, **Tai′peh′.** Japanese, **Taihoku.**

Tai·ping (tī′ping′), *n.* a person who participated in the unsuccessful rebellion **(Tai′ping′ Rebel′lion),** 1850–64, led by Hung Hsiu-ch'üan, who attempted to overthrow the Manchu dynasty. [< Chin, equiv. to *t'ai* great + *p'ing* peace]

Tai·ra (tī′rä′), *n.* a member of a powerful family in Japan which ruled the country 1160–85.

Tai·sho (tī′shô′), *n.* *Japanese Hist.* the designation of the period of the reign of Emperor Yoshihito, 1912–26. [< Jap: great righteousness]

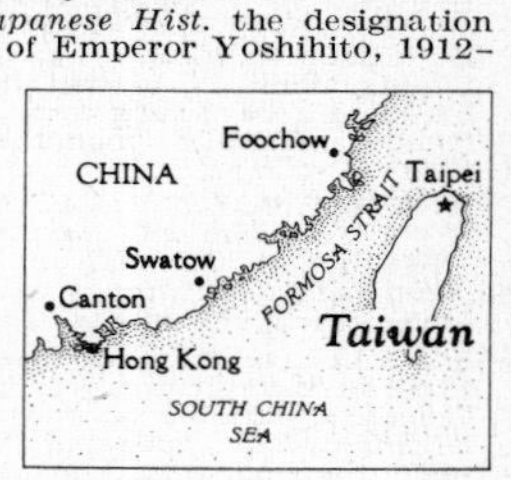

T'ai Tsung (tī′ dzo͝ong′), (*Li Shih-min*), A.D. 597–649, Chinese emperor of the T'ang dynasty 627–649.

Tai·wan (tī′wän′), *n.* a Chinese island separated from the SE coast of China by Formosa Strait: a possession of Japan 1895–1945; restored to China 1945; seat of the Republic of China since 1949. *Cap.:* Taipei. Also called **Formosa.**

Tai·wan·ese (tī′wä nēz′, -nēs′), *adj., n., pl.* **-ese.** —*adj.* **1.** of or pertaining to Taiwan or its people. —*n.* **2.** a native or inhabitant of Taiwan. [TAIWAN + -ESE]

Tai′wan′ Strait′. See **Formosa Strait.**

Tai·yüan (tī′yyän′), *n.* a city in and the capital of Shansi, in N China: a walled city. 1,020,000 (est. 1957). Also called **Yangkü.**

Ta·iz (ta iz′), *n.* a city in S Yemen. 25,000 (est. 1961). Also, **Ta'izz′.**

taj (täzh, täj), *n.* a high, conical cap worn in Muslim countries. [< Ar *tāj* < Pers]

Ta·jik (tä′jik), *n., pl.* **-jik.** **1.** a person of Iranian descent in Tadzhikistan and vicinity. **2.** Tadzhikistan. Also, **Tadjik, Tadzhik.**

Taj Ma·hal (täj′ mə häl′, täzh′), a white marble mausoleum built at Agra, India, by the Mogul emperor Shah Jahan (fl. 1628–58) for his favorite wife. [< Urdu: crown (i.e., finest) of buildings; reminiscent of queen's title: *mumtāz-i-mahall* Exalted One of the abode < Pers]

Ta·jo (tä′hô), *n.* Spanish name of **Tagus.**

Ta·ka·ma·tsu (tä′kä mä′tso͞o), *n.* a seaport on NE Shikoku, in SW Japan. 241,843 (1964).

Ta·kao (tä kou′), *n.* Kaohsiung.

take (tāk), *v.,* **took, tak·en, tak·ing,** *n.* —*v.t.* **1.** to get into one's hands, possession, control, etc., by force or artifice: *to take a bone from a snarling dog.* **2.** to seize or capture: *to take an enemy town; to take a prisoner.* **3.** to catch or get (fish, game, etc.), esp. by killing: *to take a dozen trout on a good afternoon.* **4.** to hold, grasp, or grip: *to take a book in one's hand; to take a child by the hand.* **5.** to get into one's hold or possession by voluntary action: *to take a cigarette out of a box; to take a pen and begin to write.* **6.** to pick from a number; select: *Take whichever you wish.* **7.** to receive and accept willingly (something given or offered): *to take a compliment with a smile; to take a present.* **8.** to receive or be the recipient of (something bestowed, administered, etc.): *to take first prize.* **9.** to accept and act upon or comply with: *to take advice; to take a dare.* **10.** to receive or adopt (a person) into

some relation: *to take someone in marriage; to take new members once a year.* **11.** to receive, react, or respond to in a specified manner: *Although she kept calm, she took his death hard.* **12.** to receive as a payment or charge: *He took five dollars for the use of his car.* **13.** to gain for use by payment, lease, etc.: *to take a box at the opera; to take a beach house for a month.* **14.** to secure regularly or periodically by payment: *to take a magazine.* **15.** to get or obtain from a source; derive: *The book takes its title from Dante.* **16.** to extract or quote: *He took whole passages straight from Dickens.* **17.** to obtain or exact as compensation for some wrong: *to take revenge.* **18.** to receive into the body or system, as by swallowing or inhaling: *to take a pill before breakfast; to take a breath of fresh air.* **19.** to have for one's benefit or use: *to take a meal; to take a nap; to take a bath.* **20.** to use as a flavoring agent in a food or beverage: *to take sugar in one's coffee.* **21.** to be subjected to; undergo: *to take a heat treatment.* **22.** to undergo or endure with equanimity or without an appreciable weakening of one's resistance: *to take a joke; unable to take punishment.* **23.** to enter into the enjoyment of (recreation, a holiday, etc.): *to take a vacation.* **24.** to carry off or remove: *to take something that belongs to another; to take the pins out of one's hair.* **25.** to remove by death: *The flood took many families.* **26.** to end (a life): *He took his own life.* **27.** to subtract or deduct: *If one takes 2 from 5, that leaves 3.* **28.** to carry with one: *Take your lunch with you. Are you taking an umbrella?* **29.** to convey in a means of transportation: *We took them for a ride in the country.* **30.** (of a vehicle) to convey or transport: *Will this bus take me across town?* **31.** (of a road, path, etc.) to serve as a means of conducting to or through some place or region: *Fifth Avenue took us through the center of town. These stairs will take you up to the attic.* **32.** to conduct or escort: *to take someone out for dinner; to take a girl to a dance.* **33.** to bring about a change in the state or condition of: *His ambition and perseverance took him quickly to the top of his field.* **34.** to set about or succeed in getting over, through, or around (some obstacle); clear; negotiate: *The horse took the hedge easily. He took the corner at top speed.* **35.** to come upon suddenly; catch: *to take someone by surprise.* **36.** to get or contract; catch: *He took cold over the weekend. I took a chill.* **37.** to attack or affect, as with a disease: *suddenly taken with a fit of coughing.* **38.** to be capable of attaining as a result of some action or treatment: *Most leathers take a high polish.* **39.** to absorb or become impregnated with; be susceptible to: *Waxed paper will not take ink. This cloth takes dye.* **40.** to attract and hold: *The pretty ribbon took her eye. The urgent voice took his attention.* **41.** to captivate or charm: *She took his fancy. He was greatly taken with her naïveté.* **42.** to require: *It takes courage to do that. The climb took all our strength.* **43.** to employ for some specified or implied purpose: *to take measures to check an evil.* **44.** to have recourse to as a means of transportation: *to take a car to the ferry.* **45.** to get on or board (a means of transportation) at a given time or in a given place: *He takes the train at New Milford.* **46.** to proceed to occupy: *to take a seat.* **47.** to occupy; fill (time, space, etc.): *His hobby takes most of his spare time. The machine takes a lot of room.* **48.** to use up; consume: *This car takes a great deal of oil. He took ten minutes to solve the problem.* **49.** to avail oneself of: *He took the opportunity to leave. He took the time to finish it properly.* **50.** to do, perform, execute, etc.: *to take a walk; to take a swing at someone.* **51.** to go into or enter: *Take the next road to the left.* **52.** to adopt and enter upon (a way, course, etc.): *to take the path of least resistance.* **53.** to act or perform: *to take a role in a play; to take the part of the hero.* **54.** to make (a reproduction, picture, or photograph): *to take home movies of the children.* **55.** to make a picture, esp. a photograph, of: *The photographer took us sitting down.* **56.** to write down: *to take a letter in shorthand; to take notes at a lecture.* **57.** to apply oneself to; study: *to take ballet; She took four courses in her freshman year.* **58.** to deal with; treat: *to take things in their proper order.* **59.** to proceed to handle in some manner: *to take a matter under consideration.* **60.** to assume or undertake (a function, duty, job, etc.): *The mayor took office last month.* **61.** to assume or adopt (a symbol, badge, or the like) as a token of office: *to take the veil; to take the throne.* **62.** to assume the obligation of; be bound by: *to take an oath.* **63.** to assume or adopt as one's own: *to take someone's part in an argument; He took the side of the speaker.* **64.** to assume or appropriate as if by right: *to take credit for another's work; She took the blame for his failure.* **65.** to determine by inquiry, examination, measurement, scientific observation, etc.: *to take someone's pulse; to take the ratings of certain television programs by a survey.* **66.** to make or carry out for purposes of yielding such a determination: *to take someone's measurements; to take a seismographic reading.* **67.** to begin to have; experience (a certain feeling or state of mind): *to take pride in one's appearance.* **68.** to form and hold in the mind: *to take a gloomy view.* **69.** to grasp or apprehend mentally; understand; comprehend: *Do you take my meaning, sir?* **70.** to understand in a specified way: *You must not take his remark as an insult.* **71.** to grasp the meaning of (a person): *if we take him correctly.* **72.** to accept the statements of: *to take someone at his word.* **73.** to assume as a fact: *I take it that you will be there.* **74.** to regard or consider: *He was taken to be wealthy.* **75.** *Chess.* to capture (a piece). **76.** *Slang.* to cheat or victimize: *They really take people in that shop.* **77.** *Slang.* to have sexual intercourse with. **78.** *Gram.* to be used with (a certain form, accent, case, mood, etc.): *Certain Latin verbs take the ablative.* **79.** *Law.* to acquire property, as on the happening of an event: *They take a fortune under the will.* **80.** *Baseball.* (of a batter) to allow (a pitch) to go by without swinging at it: *He took a third strike.*
—*v.i.* **81.** to catch or engage, as a mechanical device: *He turned the key and heard a click as the catch took.* **82.** to strike root or begin to grow, as a plant. **83.** to adhere, as ink, dye, color, etc. **84.** to win favor or acceptance, as person or thing: *Watch the people to see how my speech takes. There's one actor who took with the public.* **85.** to have the intended result or effect, as a medicine, inoculation, etc.: *The vaccination took.* **86.** to enter into possession, as of an estate. **87.** to detract (usually fol. by *from*). **88.** to apply or devote oneself: *He took to his studies.* **89.** to make one's way; proceed; go. **90.** to fall or become: *He took sick and had to go home.* **91.** to admit of being photographed in a particular manner: *a model who takes exceptionally well.* **92.** to admit of being moved or separated: *This crib takes apart for easy storage.* **93. take after, a.** to resemble (another person, as a parent) physically, temperamentally, etc.: *Each relative had a different opinion as to whom the baby took after.* **b.** Also, **take off after, take out after.** to follow; chase: *The detective took after the burglars.* **94. take back, a.** to regain possession of: *to take back one's lawnmower.* **b.** to return, as for exchange: *It was defective, and so she took it back to the store.* **c.** to allow to return; accept: *She said she would never take him back again.* **d.** to cause to remember: *It takes one back to the old days.* **e.** to retract: *to take back one's statement.* **95. take down, a.** to move from a higher to a lower level or place. **b.** to pull apart or take apart; dismantle; disassemble. **c.** to write down; record. **d.** to diminish the pride or arrogance of; humble: *to take someone down a notch or two.* **96. take for, a.** to assume to be: *I took it for the truth.* **b.** to assume falsely to be; mistake for: *to be taken for a foreigner.* **97. take in, a.** to permit to enter; admit. **b.** to alter (an article of clothing) so as to make smaller. **c.** to provide lodging for. **d.** to include; encompass. **e.** to grasp the meaning of; comprehend. **f.** to furl (a sail). **g.** to deceive; trick; cheat. **h.** to observe; notice. **i.** *Chiefly Brit.* to subscribe to: *to take in a magazine.* **98. take it, a.** to acquiesce to; accept: *I'll take it on your say-so.* **b.** *Slang.* to be able to resist or endure hardship, abuse, etc.: *He can't take it the way he used to.* **c.** to understand: *I take it that you're not interested.* **99. take it out of,** *Informal.* **a.** to exhaust; enervate: *Every year the winter takes it out of him.* **b.** to exact payment for; penalize: *They took it out of his pay.* **100. take it out on,** *Informal.* to cause someone else to suffer for one's own misfortune or dissatisfaction: *Just because you're angry about the outcome you don't have to take it out on me!* **101. take off, a.** to remove: *to take off one's coat.* **b.** to lead away: *The child was taken off by kidnapers.* **c.** *Informal.* to depart; leave: *He took off yesterday for California.* **d.** to leave the ground, as an airplane. **e.** to withdraw, as from service: *He was taken off the night shift.* **f.** to remove by death; kill: *Millions were taken off by the Black Plague.* **g.** to make a likeness or copy of; reproduce. **h.** to subtract, as a discount; deduct: *to take 20 percent off the list price.* **i.** *Informal.* to imitate; mimic; burlesque. **102. take on, a.** to hire; employ. **b.** to undertake; assume: *to take on new responsibilities.* **c.** to acquire: *The situation begins to take on a new light.* **d.** to accept a challenge; contend against: *to take on a bully.* **e.** *Informal.* to show great emotion; become excited: *There's no need to take on so.* **103. take out, a.** to withdraw; remove: *to take out a handkerchief.* **b.** to procure by application: *to take out an insurance policy.* **c.** to escort; invite: *He takes out my sister now and then.* **d.** to set out; start: *They took out for the nearest beach.* **104. take over, a.** to assume management of or responsibility for: *The first officer took over the ship when the captain suffered a heart attack.* **b.** *Slang.* to cheat; victimize: *That salesman really took her over when he sold her that used car.* **105. take to, a.** to devote or apply oneself to; become habituated to: *to take to drink.* **b.** to respond favorably to; begin to like: *They took to each other at once.* **c.** to go to: *to take to one's bed.* **d.** to have recourse to; resort to: *She took to nagging to get her own way.* **106. take up, a.** to occupy oneself with the study or practice of: *She took up sewing in her spare time.* **b.** to lift or pick up: *He took up the fallen leaves with a rake.* **c.** to occupy; cover: *A grand piano would take up half of our living room.* **d.** to consume; use up; absorb: *Traveling to her job takes up a great deal of time.* **e.** to begin to advocate or support: *He has taken up another struggling artist.* **f.** to continue; resume: *We took up where we had left off.* **g.** to reply to in order to reprove: *The author takes up his critics in the preface of his latest book.* **h.** to assume: *He took up the duties of the presidency.* **107. take upon oneself,** to assume as a responsibility or obligation: *She has taken it upon herself to speak personally with the parents of all her students.* **108. take up with,** *Informal.* to become friendly with; keep company with: *He took up with a girl of whom his family disapproved.*
—*n.* **109.** the act of taking. **110.** that which is taken. **111.** the quantity of fish, game, etc., taken at one time. **112.** *Slang.* money taken in, esp. profits. **113.** *Journalism.* a portion of copy assigned to a linotype operator or compositor, usually part of a story or article. **114.** *Motion Pictures.* **a.** a scene, or a portion of a scene, photographed without any interruption or break. **b.** an instance of such continuous operation of the camera. **115.** a recording of a musical performance. **116.** *Med.* a successful inoculation. **117. on the take,** *Slang.* **a.** in search of personal profit at the expense of others. **b.** accepting bribes. [ME *take(n)*, late OE *tacan* < Scand (cf. Icel *taka* to take); c. MD *taken* to grasp; akin to Goth *tekan* to touch] —**tak′a·ble, take′a·ble,** *adj.* —**tak′er,** *n.*
—**Syn. 1.** acquire, secure, procure. See **bring. 6.** choose. **22.** bear, stand, tolerate. **41.** delight, attract, interest, engage, bewitch, allure. **42.** need, demand. **43.** use. **65.** ascertain. **73.** suppose, presume. —**Ant. 1.** give.

take-all (tāk′ôl′), *n.* *Plant Pathol.* a disease of wheat, rye, barley and oats, characterized by the blackening and decaying of the base of the stems, caused by a fungus, *Ophiobolus graminis.*

take·down (tāk′doun′), *adj.* **1.** made or constructed so as to be easily dismantled or disassembled. —*n.* **2.** the act of taking down. **3.** a firearm designed to be swiftly disassembled or assembled. **4.** the point of separation of two or more of the parts of a takedown firearm or other device. **5.** *Informal.* the act of being humbled. Also, **take′-down′.** [adj., n. use of v. phrase *take down*]

take′-home pay′ (tāk′hōm′), the amount of salary remaining after all deductions, esp. tax deductions, have been made.

take-in (tāk′in′), *n.* *Informal.* a deception, fraud, or imposition. [n. use of v. phrase *take in*]

tak·en (tā′kən), *v.* pp. of **take.**

take·off (tāk′ôf′, -of′), *n.* **1.** a taking or setting off; the leaving of the ground, as in leaping or in beginning a flight in an airplane. **2.** the place or point at which a person or thing takes off. **3.** a humorous or satirical imitation; burlesque. **4.** *Mach.* a shaft geared to a main shaft for running auxiliary machinery. **5.** a branch connection to a pipe, electric line, etc. Also, **take′-off′.** [n. use of v. phrase *take off*]

take·out (tāk′out′), *n.* **1.** the act or fact of taking out. **2.** something taken out or made to be taken out: *Few good restaurants depend on takeouts for their income.* **3.** a section, as of a magazine, that may be removed intact, usually consisting of a story, article, or set of art reproductions of special interest. **4.** *Mach.* a device for removing a manufactured product from a machine after processing. **5.** *Cards.* **a.** *Bridge.* a bid in a suit or denomination different from the one bid by one's partner. **b.** *Poker.* the minimum wager with which a player can begin. [n. use of v. phrase *take out*]

take′out dou′ble, *Bridge.* See **informatory double.**

take·o·ver (tāk′ō′vər), *n.* the act of seizing, appropriating, or arrogating authority, control, management, etc. Also, **take′-o′ver.** [n. use of v. phrase *take over*]

tak·er-in (tā′kər in′), *n.* licker-in.

take-up (tāk′up′), *n.* **1.** the act of taking up. **2.** *Mach.* **a.** uptake (def. 3). **b.** any of various devices for taking up slack, winding in, or compensating for the looseness of parts due to wear. **3.** the contraction of fabric resulting from the wet operations in the finishing process, esp. fulling. [n. use of v. phrase *take up*]

tak·ing (tā′king), *n.* **1.** the act of one who or that which takes. **2.** the state of being taken. **3.** that which is taken. **4. takings,** receipts. **5.** *Archaic.* a state of agitation or distress. —*adj.* **6.** captivating, winning, or pleasing. **7.** *Obs.* infectious or contagious. [ME *takyng* (n.). See TAKE, -ING[1], -ING[2]] —**tak′ing·ly,** *adv.* —**tak′ing·ness,** *n.*

Ta·ko′ma Park′ (tə kō′mə), a city in central Maryland. 16,799 (1960).

Ta·ko·ra·di (tä′kō rä′dē), *n.* a seaport in SW Ghana. 40,937 (1960).

Ta·ku (tä′ko͞o′), *n.* a fortified city in E Hopeh, in NE China, E of Tientsin: battles 1860, 1900.

tal., (in prescriptions) such; like this. [< L *tālis*]

Ta·lae·me·nes (tə lē′mə nēz′), *n.* (in the *Iliad*) the father of Mesthles and Antiphus.

tal·a·poin (tal′ə poin′), *n.* a small, yellowish guenon monkey, *Cercopithecus talapoin,* of western Africa. [< F; special use (orig. jocular) of *talapoin* Buddhist monk << Mongolian *tala pôi* my lord (title, proper to such monks)]

Ta·la·ra (tä lä′rä), *n.* a seaport in NW Peru. 12,985 (1950).

ta·lar·i·a (tə lâr′ē ə), *n.pl.* *Class. Myth.* the wings or winged sandals on the feet of Hermes, or Mercury. [< L, neut. pl. of *tālāris* < *tāl(us)* ankle + *āris* -AR[1]]

Ta·las·si·o (tə las′ē ō′), *n.* a god invoked at ancient Roman weddings, esp. in epithalamiums.

Ta·la·ve·ra de la Rei·na (tä′lä ve′rä de lä rā′nä), a city in central Spain, on the Tagus River: British and Spanish defeat of the French 1809. 21,728 (est. 1960).

ta·la·yot (tə lä′yōt), *n.* any of the round or square prehistoric stone towers found in the Balearic Islands, possibly modeled after the nuraghi in Sardinia. [< Catalan *talaiot*]

tal·bot (tôl′bət, tal′-), *n.* *Heraldry.* a hound with long pendent ears. [ME: dog's name, orig. man's nickname < OF]

Tal·bot (tôl′bət *or, for 3,* tal′-), *n.* **1. Charles, Duke of Shrewsbury,** 1660–1718, British statesman: prime minister 1714. **2. William Henry Fox,** 1800–77, English pioneer in photography. **3.** a boy's given name.

talc (talk), *n., v.,* **talcked** or **talced** (talkt), **talck·ing** or **talc·ing** (tal′king). —*n.* **1.** Also, **tal·cum** (tal′kəm). a green-to-gray, soft mineral, hydrous magnesium silicate, $H_2Mg_3(SiO_3)_4$, unctuous to the touch, and occurring usually in foliated masses or compact, used in making lubricants, talcum powder, electrical insulation, etc. —*v.t.* **2.** to treat or rub with talc. [< ML *talc(um)* < Ar *ṭalq* mica < Pers *talk*]

Tal·ca (täl′kä), *n.* a city in central Chile. 69,864 (est. 1959).

Tal·ca·hua·no (täl′kä wä′nō), *n.* a seaport in central Chile. 102,323 (est. 1963).

talc·ose (tal′kōs, tal kōs′), *adj.* containing or composed largely of talc. Also, **talc·ous** (tal′kəs). [TALC + -OSE[1]]

tal′cum pow′der (tal′kəm), powdered talc or soapstone. [< ML *talcum* TALC]

tale (tāl), *n.* **1.** a narrative that relates the details of some real or imaginary event, incident, or case; story: *a tale about Lincoln's dog.* **2.** a literary composition having the form of such a narrative: *Chaucer's* Canterbury Tales. **3.** a falsehood; lie. **4.** a rumor or piece of gossip, often malicious or untrue. **5.** the full number or amount. **6.** *Archaic.* enumeration; count. **7.** *Obs.* talk; discourse. [ME; OE *talu* series, list, narrative, story; c. D *taal* speech, language, G *Zahl* number, Icel *tala* number, speech. See TELL[1]]
—**Syn. 1.** account, fable, fiction. **3.** fib.

tale·bear·er (tāl′bâr′ər), *n.* a person who spreads gossip that is likely to cause trouble or harm. [TALE + BEARER] —**tale′bear′ing,** *adj., n.*

tal·ent (tal′ənt), *n.* **1.** a special natural ability or aptitude: *a talent for drawing.* **2.** a capacity for achievement or success; ability: *young men of talent.* **3.** a talented person: *The cast includes many of the theater's major talents.* **4.** a group of persons with special ability: *an exhibition of watercolors by the local talent.* **5.** a power of mind or body considered as given to a person for use and improvement: so called from the parable in Matt. 25:14–30. **6.** any of various ancient units of weight, as a unit of Palestine and Syria equal to 3000 shekels, or a unit of Greece equal to 6000 drachmas. **7.** any of various ancient Hebrew or Attic monetary units equal in value to that of a talent weight of gold, silver, or other metal. **8.** *Obs.* inclination or disposition. [ME,

OE *talente* < L *talenta,* pl. of *talentum* < Gk *tálanton* balance, weight, monetary unit; in obs. sense desire < ML *talentum*]
—Syn. 1. capability, gift, genius. See **ability.**

tal·ent·ed (tal′ən tid), *adj.* having talent or special ability; gifted. [TALENT + -ED[3]]

tal′ent scout′, a person whose business it is to recognize and recruit persons of marked aptitude for a certain field or occupation, esp. a field of entertainment.

tal′ent show′, a theatrical show in which a series of usually amateur or aspiring singers, dancers, comedians, instrumentalists, etc., perform in the hope of gaining recognition.

Tale′ of a Tub′, A, **1.** a satire in prose (1704) by Swift. **2.** a comedy in verse (1633) by Ben Jonson.

Tale′ of Gen′ji, The (gen′jē), **1.** a novel (1001–20?) by Lady Murasaki, dealing with Japanese court life. **2.** any of four profusely illustrated Japanese narrative scrolls (c1100–50) containing this novel.

Tale′ of Two′ Cit′ies, A, a historical novel (1859) by Dickens.

ta·ler (tä′lər), *n., pl.* **-ler, -lers.** thaler.

ta·les (tā′lēz), *n. Law.* **1.** (*construed as pl.*) persons chosen to serve on the jury when the original panel is insufficiently large: originally selected from among those present in court. **2.** (*construed as sing.*) the order or writ summoning them. [< ML *tālēs* (*dē circumstantibus*) such (of the bystanders)]

tales·man (tālz′mən, tā′lēz mən), *n., pl.* **-men.** a person summoned as one of the tales. [TALES + MAN[1]]

Tales′ of a Way′side Inn′, a series of narrative poems (1863–74) by Longfellow, including *Paul Revere's Ride.*

Tales′ of Hoff′man, The, an opera (1880) by Jacques Offenbach.

tale·tell·er (tāl′tel′ər), *n.* **1.** a person who tells tales or stories; narrator. **2.** a person who tells falsehoods. **3.** a telltale. [TALE + TELLER] **—tale′tell′ing,** *adj., n.*

tali-, a learned borrowing from Latin meaning "ankle," used in the formation of compound words: *taligrade.* [comb. form repr. L *tālus*]

Ta·lien (dä′lyen′), *n.* Chinese name of **Dairen.**

Tal·i·es·in (tal′ē es′in), *n.* **1.** fl. A.D. c550, Welsh bard. **2.** Also called **Talies′in North′.** a country house and architectural school near Spring Green, Wisconsin, built 1911 for Frank Lloyd Wright and rebuilt in its general present form in 1925.

Talies′in West′, a country house at Scottsdale, Arizona, built after 1936 as the winter home of Frank Lloyd Wright: remarkable construction of wood and canvas with massive rubble masonry.

tal·i·grade (tal′ə grād′), *adj. Zool.* walking on the outer side of the foot. [TALI- + -GRADE]

tal·i·on (tal′ē ən), *n.* See **lex talionis.** [< L *tāliōn-* (s. of *tāliō*), equiv. to *tāl(is)* such + *-iōn-* -ION; r. late ME *talioun* < AF]

tal·i·ped (tal′ə ped′), *adj.* **1.** (of a foot) twisted or distorted out of shape or position. **2.** (of a person) clubfooted. **—***n.* **3.** a taliped person or animal. [TALI- + -PED]

tal·i·pes (tal′ə pēz′), *n.* **1.** a clubfoot. **2.** the condition of being clubfooted. [TALI- + L *pēs* foot]

tal·i·pot (tal′ə pot′), *n.* a tall palm, *Corypha umbraculifera,* of southern India and Ceylon, having large leaves used for making fans and umbrellas, for covering houses, and in place of writing paper. Also, **tal′ipot palm′.** [< Malayan *tālipat* < Skt *tālapattra* < *tāla* fanpalm + *pattra* leaf]

tal·is·man (tal′is mən, -iz-), *n., pl.* **-mans. 1.** a stone, ring, or other object, engraved with figures or characters supposed to possess occult powers and worn as an amulet or charm. **2.** any amulet or charm. **3.** anything whose presence exercises a remarkable or powerful influence on human feelings or actions. [< F or Sp << Ar *tilsam* < Gk *télesma* < *teles-* (var. s. of *telein* to complete, perform) + *-ma* n. suffix] **—tal·is·man·ic** (tal′is man′ik, -iz-), **tal′is·man′i·cal,** *adj.* **—tal′is·man′i·cal·ly,** *adv.*

talk (tôk), *v.i.* **1.** to communicate or exchange ideas, information, etc., by speaking: *to talk about poetry.* **2.** to consult or confer: *Talk with your adviser.* **3.** to spread a rumor or tell a confidence; gossip. **4.** to chatter or prate. **5.** to employ speech; perform the act of speaking: *to talk very softly; to talk into a microphone.* **6.** to deliver a speech, lecture, etc.: *The professor talked on the uses of comedy in the tragedies of Shakespeare.* **7.** to give or reveal confidential or incriminating information: *The police made the suspect talk. After a long interrogation, the spy finally talked.* **8.** to communicate ideas by means other than speech, as by writing, signs, or signals. **9.** to make sounds imitative or suggestive of speech. **—***v.t.* **10.** to express in words; utter: *to talk sense.* **11.** to use (a specified language or idiom) in speaking or conversing: *They talk French together for practice.* **12.** to discuss: *to talk politics.* **13.** to bring, put, drive, influence, etc., by talk: *to talk a person to sleep.* **14. talk around,** to bring someone over to one's way of thinking; persuade: *She sounded adamant over the phone, but I may still be able to talk her around.* **15. talk at, a.** to direct remarks meant for a person to another in his presence; speak indirectly to. **b.** to talk incessantly to; importune: *Be sure not to sit next to her at the party, because she'll talk at you all evening about her charities.* **16. talk away,** to spend or consume time in talking: *We talked away the tedious hours in the hospital.* **17. talk back,** to reply to (a command, request, etc.) in a rude or disrespectful manner: *Her father never allowed them to talk back.* **18. talk big,** *Informal.* to speak boastingly; brag: *He always talked big, but never amounted to anything.* **19. talk down, a.** to overwhelm by force of argument or by loud and persistent talking; subdue by talking. **b.** to speak disparagingly of; belittle. **c.** Also, **talk in.** to give instructions by radio for a ground-controlled landing to a pilot who is unable to make a conventional landing because of snow, fog, etc. **20. talk down to,** to speak condescendingly to; patronize: *They sensed that she was talking down to them, and nothing she said had any effect.* **21. talk of,** to debate as a possibility; discuss: *The two companies have been talking of a merger.* **22. talk one's head** or **ear off,** *Slang.* to bore or weary someone by excessive talk; talk incessantly: *All I wanted was a chance to read my book, but my seatmate talked my ear off.* **23. talk out, a.** to talk until conversation is exhausted. **b.** to attempt to reach a settlement by discussion: *We arrived at a compromise by talking out the problem.* **c.** *Brit. Politics.* to thwart the passage of (a bill, motion, etc.) by prolonging discussion until the session of Parliament adjourns. Cf. **filibuster** (def. 6). **24. talk over, a.** to weigh in conversation; consider; discuss. **b.** to cause someone to change his opinion; convince by talking: *He became an expert at talking people over to his views.* **25. talk to death, a.** to impede or prevent the passage of (a bill) through filibustering. **b.** to talk at great length; talk unceasingly: *She's the worst bore I've ever met and will talk anyone to death.* **26. talk up, a.** to promote interest in; discuss enthusiastically. **b.** to speak without hesitation; speak distinctly and openly: *If you don't talk up now, you may not get another chance.* **—***n.* **27.** the act of talking; speech; conversation, esp. of a familiar or informal kind. **28.** an informal speech or lecture. **29.** a conference: *They held a series of talks in an attempt to solve the problem.* **30.** report or rumor; gossip: *There is a lot of talk going around about her.* **31.** a subject or occasion of talking, esp. of gossip: *Her wild escapades are the talk of the neighborhood.* **32.** mere empty speech: *That's just a lot of talk.* **33.** a way of talking: *a halting, lisping talk.* **34.** language, dialect, or lingo. **35.** signs or sounds imitative or suggestive of speech, as the noise made by loose parts in a mechanism. [ME *talk(i)en,* deriv. (with *-k* suffix) of TALE; c. EFris *talken*] **—talk′a·bil′i·ty,** *n.* **—talk′a·ble,** *adj.* **—talk′er,** *n.*
—Syn. 1. See **speak. 2.** discuss. **4.** prattle. **27.** discourse. **29.** colloquy, dialogue, parley, confabulation. **32.** prattle, words.

talk·a·thon (tô′kə thon′), *n.* an unusually long speech or discussion, esp. on a matter of public interest, as a Congressional filibuster, a televised question-and-answer session with a political candidate, etc. [TALK + *-athon,* modeled on *marathon*]

talk·a·tive (tô′kə tiv), *adj.* inclined to talk a great deal: *One drink and she became gay and talkative.* [TALK + -ATIVE] **—talk′a·tive·ly,** *adv.* **—talk′a·tive·ness,** *n.*
—Syn. wordy, verbose, prolix. TALKATIVE, GARRULOUS, LOQUACIOUS agree in referring to one who talks a great deal. TALKATIVE is a mildly unfavorable word applied to one who is in the habit of talking a great deal and often without significance: *a talkative child.* The GARRULOUS person talks with wearisome persistence about personal and trivial things: *a garrulous old woman.* A LOQUACIOUS person, intending to be sociable, talks continuously and at length: *a loquacious hostess.*

talk-back (tôk′bak′), *n. Radio and Television.* a communications system enabling those in the studio to hear control-room personnel through a loudspeaker. [n. use of v. phrase *talk back*]

talk′ between′ ships′. See **TBS**

talk·fest (tôk′fest′), *n.* a lengthy conversation, discussion, or debate. [TALK + -FEST]

talk·ie (tô′kē), *n. Informal.* See **talking picture.** [TALK + (MOV)IE]

talk′ing book′, a phonograph record or tape recording of readings of a literary work, magazine article, etc., made esp. for use by the blind.

talk′ing chief′, a noble who serves as public spokesman for the chief in some Polynesian tribes.

talk′ing machine′, a phonograph.

talk′ing pic′ture, a motion picture with accompanying synchronized speech, singing, etc.

talk′ing point′, a fact or feature that aids or supports one side, as in an argument, competition, or the like.

talk·ing-to (tô′king to͞o′), *n., pl.* **-tos.** *Informal.* a scolding.

talk·y (tô′kē), *adj.,* **talk·i·er, talk·i·est. 1.** having or containing superfluous or purposeless talk, conversation, or dialogue, esp. so as to impede action or progress: *a talky play that bored the audience.* **2.** inclined to talk a great deal; talkative. [TALK + -Y[1]]

tall (tôl), *adj.* **1.** having a relatively great height; of more than average stature: *a tall boy; tall grass.* **2.** having stature or height as specified: *a man six feet tall.* **3.** *Informal.* **a.** large in amount or degree; considerable: *a tall price; Swinging that deal is a tall order.* **b.** extravagant; difficult to believe: *a tall tale.* **c.** high-flown; grandiloquent: *He engages in so much tall talk, one never really knows what he's saying.* **4.** having more than usual length; long and relatively narrow: *He carried a tall walking stick.* **5.** *Archaic.* valiant. **6.** *Obs.* **a.** seemly; proper. **b.** fine; handsome. [ME: big, bold, comely, proper, ready, OE *getæle* (pl.) quick, ready, competent; c. OHG *gizal* quick] **—tall′ness,** *n.*
—Syn. 2. See **high. —Ant. 1.** short.

Tal·la·de·ga (tal′ə dē′gə), *n.* a city in central Alabama, E of Birmingham. 17,742 (1960).

tal·lage (tal′ij), *n.* **1.** a tax paid by a feudal tenant to his lord. **2.** a compulsory tax levied by the Norman and early Angevin kings of England upon the demesne lands of the crown and upon all royal towns. [ME *taillage* < OF < *taill(ier)* (to) cut, tax (see TAILOR) < LL *tāliāre* to cut; see -AGE]

Tal·la·has·see (tal′ə has′ē), *n.* a city in and the capital of Florida, in the N part. 48,174 (1960).

Tal·la·poo·sa (tal′ə po͞o′sə), *n.* a town in NW Georgia. 2744 (1960).

Tal·las·see (tal′ə sē′), *n.* a town in central Alabama. 4934 (1960).

tall·boy (tôl′boi′), *n.* **1.** *Eng. Furniture.* **a.** a chest of drawers supported by a low stand. Cf. **highboy. b.** a chest-on-chest. **2.** a tall chimney pot. **3.** a tall-stemmed goblet. [TALL + BOY]

tall′ but′tercup, a buttercup, *Ranunculus acris,* having a tall stem and yellow flowers, found in fields and meadows.

tall′-case clock′ (tôl′kās′), a pendulum clock tall enough to stand on the floor; a grandfather's or grandmother's clock.

Tall·chief (tôl′chēf′), *n.* **Maria,** born 1925, U.S. ballet dancer.

tall′ coreop′sis, a perennial herb, *Coreopsis tripteris,* of eastern North America, having yellow flowers, growing up to eight feet high.

tall′ drink′, a beverage consisting essentially of liquor and a sparkling soda, fruit juice, or the like, to which may be added other ingredients, served in a tall glass, usually with ice.

Tal·ley·rand-Pé·ri·gord (tal′ē rand′per′ə gôr′; *Fr.* TA le RÄN′pā RE gôR′), *n.* **Charles Mau·rice de** (shARl mō RĒS′ də), **Prince de Bé·né·vent** (də bā nā vÄN′), 1754–1838, French statesman.

tall′ fes′cue. See **meadow fescue.**

Tal·linn (tä′lin, tal′in), *n.* a seaport in and the capital of Estonia, on the Gulf of Finland. 499,800. Also, **Tal′lin.** Formerly, Russian, **Revel;** German, **Reval.**

Tal·lis (tal′is), *n.* **Thomas,** c1505–85, English organist and composer, esp. of church music. Also, **Tallys, Talys.**

tall·ish (tô′lish), *adj.* rather tall. [TALL + -ISH[1]]

tal·lith (tä′lis; *Heb.* tä lēt′), *n., pl.* **ta·li·thim** (tä lē′sim; *Heb.* tä lē tēm′). *Judaism.* a shawllike garment of wool, silk, or the like, with fringes or zizith at the four corners, worn around the shoulders by Orthodox and Conservative (sometimes also Reform) Jewish males, as during the morning service. [< Heb: a cover]

Tallith

tal·lith ka·tan (tä lēt′ kä tän′), *Hebrew.* See **arba kanfoth.**

tall′ mead′ow rue′, a meadow rue, *Thalictrum polygamum.*

tall′ oat′ grass′, an oatlike European grass, *Arrhena therum elatius,* naturalized in North America, having rough leaves and a purplish-green flowering panicle. Also called **tall′ mead′ow oat′.**

tall′ oil′ (täl), a resinous secondary product resulting from the manufacture of chemical wood pulp: used in the manufacture of soaps, paints, etc. [< Sw *tallolja* < *tall* pine (c. Icel. *thöll* young pine tree) + *olja* oil]

tal·low (tal′ō), *n.* **1.** the fatty tissue or suet of animals. **2.** the harder fat of sheep, cattle, etc., separated by melting from the fibrous and membranous matter naturally mixed with it, and used to make candles, soap, etc. **3.** any of various similar fatty substances: *vegetable tallow.* **—***v.t.* **4.** to smear with tallow. [ME *talow, talgh;* c. G *Talg* (< LG)]

tal·low·pot (tal′ō pot′), *n. Railroads Slang.* a locomotive fireman. [lit., pot(full) of tallow, i.e., of sweat charged with fat; firemen sweat so profusely that they are thought to lose their tallow (slang for fat)]

tal·low-shrub (tal′ō shrub′), *n.* See **wax myrtle.**

tal·low·y (tal′ō ē), *adj.* resembling tallow in consistency, color, etc.; fatty: *a tallowy mass of moistened powder; tallowy skin.* Also, **tal′low·like′.** [late ME *talwy.* See TALLOW, -Y[1]] **—tal′low·i·ness,** *n.*

tall′ sun′flower. See **giant sunflower.**

Tal·lu·lah (tə lo͞o′lə), *n.* **1.** a town in NE Louisiana. 9413 (1960). **2.** a girl's given name.

tal·ly (tal′ē), *n., pl.* **-lies,** *v.,* **-lied, -ly·ing. —***n.* **1.** Also called **tal′ly stick′.** a stick of wood with notches cut to indicate the amount of a debt or payment, often split lengthwise across the notches, the debtor retaining one piece and the creditor the other. **2.** anything on which a score or account is kept. **3.** a notch or mark made on or in a tally. **4.** an account or reckoning; a record of debit and credit, of the score of a game, or the like. **5.** a number or group of items recorded. **6.** a mark made to register a certain number of items, as four consecutive vertical lines with a diagonal line through them to indicate a group of five. **7.** a number of objects serving as a unit of computation. **8.** a ticket, label, or mark used as a means of identification, classification, etc. **9.** anything corresponding to another thing as a counterpart or duplicate. **—***v.t.* **10.** to mark or enter on a tally; register; record. **11.** to count or reckon up. **12.** to furnish with a tally or identifying label. **13.** to cause to correspond or agree. **—***v.i.* **14.** to correspond, as one part of a tally with the other; accord or agree: *Does his story tally with John's?* [late ME *taly* < ML *talia,* var. of L *tālea* rod, cutting, lit., heel-piece, deriv. of *tālus* heel] **—tal′li·er,** *n.*
—Syn. 4. inventory, score, register, count, enumeration, roster, catalogue, list. **10.** enroll, list, enter. **11.** enumerate, calculate.

tal·ly·ho (*n., v.* tal′ē hō′; *interj.* tal′ē hō′), *n., pl.* **-hos,** *interj., v.* **-hoed** or **-ho'd, -ho·ing. —***n.* **1.** *Chiefly Brit.* a mail coach or a four-in-hand pleasure coach. **2.** a cry of "tallyho." **—***interj.* **3.** the cry of a huntsman on first sighting the fox. **—***v.t.* **4.** to arouse by crying "tallyho," as to the hounds. **—***v.i.* **5.** to utter a cry of "tallyho." [cf. F *tayau* hunter's cry]

tal·ly·man (tal′ē mən), *n., pl.* **-men. 1.** a person who tallies or keeps account of something. **2.** *Brit.* an owner of or salesman for a tallyshop. [TALLY + MAN[1]]

tal′ly plan′, *Brit.* See **installment plan.**

Tal·lys (tal′is), *n.* **Thomas.** See **Tallis, Thomas.**

tal′ly sheet′, a sheet for checking, counting, or scoring, as of cargo loaded or unloaded. Also, **tal′ly card′.**

tal·ly·shop (tal′ē shop′), *n. Brit.* a store specializing in selling merchandise on the hire-purchase system. [TALLY + SHOP]

Tal·mud (täl′mo͝od, -məd, tal′-), *n.* the collection of Jewish law and tradition consisting of the Mishnah and the Gemara and being either the edition produced in Palestine A.D. c400 or the larger, more important one produced in Babylonia A.D. c500. [< Heb: orig., instruction] **—Tal·mud·ic** (täl mo͞o′dik, -myo͞o′-, -mo͝od′ik, -mud′-, tal-), **Tal·mud′i·cal,** *adj.* **—Tal′mud·ism,** *n.*

Tal·mud·ist (täl′mo͝o dist, tal′mə-), *n.* **1.** one of the writers or compilers of the Talmud. **2.** a person who accepts or supports the doctrines of the Talmud. **3.** a person versed in the Talmud. [TALMUD + -IST]

Tal·mud To·rah (täl′mo͝od tō′Rə; *Eng.* täl′mo͝od tôr′ə, tōr′ə, -məd, tal′-), *Hebrew.* **1.** (in the U.S.) a Jewish parochial school, holding classes at the end of the secular school day, for teaching Hebrew, Bible, Jewish history, and the rudiments of Jewish religion, culture, and tradition to students of elementary school age. **2.** (in Europe) a Jewish school, supported and administered by the community, for teaching Hebrew, Bible, and prayers in the Jewish liturgy to children of elementary school age unable to pay for such instruction.

tal·on (tal′ən), *n.* **1.** a claw, esp. of a bird of prey. **2.** the shoulder on the bolt of a lock against which the key presses in sliding the bolt. **3.** *Cards.* **a.** the cards left over after the deal; stock. **b.** *Solitaire.* wastepile. [late ME *taloun* < AF equiv. to OF *talon* < LL *tālōn-, s. of *tālō for L tālus heel] —**tal′oned,** *adj.*

Ta·los (tā′los), *n.* *Class. Myth.* **1.** the inventive nephew of Daedalus, by whom he was jealously slain. **2.** a man of brass made by Hephaestus for Minos as a guardian of Crete.

tal·pa·ta·te (täl′pä tä′tā), *n.* *Geol.* **1.** a rock composed chiefly of calcite mixed with ash or gravel. **2.** an inferior soil composed chiefly of loose or consolidated ash. [< AmerSp, var. of *tepetate* < Nahuatl *tepetatl*]

tal. qual., of ordinary or average quality. [< L *tālis quālis*]

Tal·thyb·i·us (tal thib′ē əs), *n.* *Class. Myth.* a herald of Agamemnon who related much tragic news, always with compassion.

ta·luk (tä′lo͝ok, tä lo͝ok′), *n.* (in India) **1.** a hereditary estate. **2.** a subdivision of a revenue district. Also, **ta·lu·ka, ta·loo·ka** (tä lo͞o′kə). [< Urdu *ta'alluq* estate < Ar]

ta·lus[1] (tā′ləs), *n., pl.* **-li** (-lī). *Anat.* the uppermost of the proximal row of bones of the tarsus; anklebone. [< L: ankle, anklebone, die (OL *taxlus). See TASSEL[1]]

ta·lus[2] (tā′ləs), *n., pl.* **-lus·es.** **1.** a slope. **2.** *Geol.* a sloping mass of rocky fragments at the base of a cliff. **3.** *Fort.* the slope of the face of a work. [< F: pseudo-learned alter. of OF *talu* slope < LL *tālūtum, deriv. of L tālus ankle]

Tal·ys (tal′is), *n.* **Thomas.** See **Tallis, Thomas.**

tam (tam), *n.* tam-o'-shanter.

Tam (tam), *n.* a boy's given name.

Ta·ma (tā′mə), *n.* a town in central Iowa. 2925 (1960).

tam·a·ble (tā′mə bəl), *adj.* able to be tamed. Also, **tameable.** [TAME + -ABLE] —**tam′a·bil′i·ty, tam′a·ble·ness,** *n.*

ta·ma·le (tə mä′lē), *n.* a Mexican dish made of minced and seasoned meat that has been packed in cornmeal dough, wrapped in corn husks, and steamed. [back formation from MexSp *tamales*, pl. of *tamal* < Nahuatl *tamalli*]

Ta·ma·le (tə mä′lē), *n.* a city in N Ghana. 16,164 (1948).

ta·man·dua (tä′män dwä′), *n.* an arboreal, tropical American anteater, *Tamandua tetradactyla*, having a prehensile tail. Also, **ta·man·du** (tam′ən do͞o′). [< Pg < Tupi: lit., ant-trapper]

Ta·mar (tā′mər), *n.* the daughter of David and half-sister of Absalom. II Sam. 13. Also, *Douay Bible*, **Thamar.**

ta·ma·ra (tə mär′ə), *n.* *Italian Cookery.* a powdered mixture of cinnamon, cloves, coriander, aniseed, and fennel seed. [?]

Ta·ma·ra (tə mar′ə, -mär′ə), *n.* a girl's given name.

tam·a·rack (tam′ə rak′), *n.* **1.** an American larch, *Larix laricina*, yielding a useful timber. **2.** any of several related, very similar trees. **3.** the wood of these trees. [< Algonquian]

ta·ma·rao (tä′mə rou′), *n., pl.* **-raos.** tamarau.

ta·ma·rau (tä′mə rou′), *n.* a small wild buffalo, *Bubalus (Anoa) mindorensis*, of Mindoro in the Philippines, having thick, brown hair and short, massive horns. Also, **tamarao, timarau.** [< Tagalog]

tam·a·rin (tam′ə rin), *n.* any of various South American marmosets of the genus *Callithrix* and allied genera. [< F < Carib (Galibi dial.)]

Tamarin, *Saguinus oedipus* (Total length 22 in.; tail 1 ft.)

tam·a·rind (tam′ə rind), *n.* **1.** the pod of a large, tropical, caesalpiniaceous tree, *Tamarindus indica*, containing seeds enclosed in a juicy acid pulp that is used in beverages and food. **2.** the tree itself. [< ML *tamarindus* << Ar *tamr-hindī* date of India]

tam·a·risk (tam′ə risk), *n.* any Old World, tropical plant of the genus *Tamarix*, esp. *T. gallica*, an ornamental Mediterranean shrub or small tree having slender, feathery branches. [ME *tamarisc(us)* < LL, var of L *tamarix*]

ta·mas (tum′əs), *n.* *Hinduism.* See under **guna.** [< Skt: darkness] —**ta·mas·ic** (tə mas′ik), *adj.*

ta·ma·sha (tə mä′shə), *n.* (in the East Indies) a spectacle; entertainment. [< Urdu < Ar *tamāshā* a stroll]

Tam·a·sine (tam′ə sēn′), *n.* a girl's given name, form of **Thomasin, Thomasina, Thomasine.**

Ta·ma·tave (tä′mä täv′), *n.* a seaport on E Madagascar. 39,627 (1960).

Ta·mau·li·pas (tä′mou lē′päs), *n.* a state in NE Mexico, bordering on the Gulf of Mexico. 1,024,182 (1960); 30,731 sq. mi. *Cap.:* Ciudad Victoria.

Ta·ma·yo (tä mä′yō), *n.* **Ru·fi·no** (ro͞o fē′nō), born 1899, Mexican painter.

tam·bac (tam′bak), *n.* tombac.

Tam·bo (tam′bō), *n.* See **Mr. Tambo.**

tam·bor (tam′bôr, tam bôr′), *n.* See **rasphead rockfish.** [< Sp: drum (see TAMBOUR); so named from a fancied likeness to a drum]

Tam·bo·ra (täm′bō rä′, -bō-), *n.* an active volcano in Indonesia, on N Sumbawa: eruption 1815. 9042 ft.

tam·bour (tam′bo͝or), *n.* **1.** *Music.* a drum. **2.** a drum player. **3.** a circular frame consisting of two hoops, one fitting within the other, in which cloth is stretched for embroidering. **4.** embroidery done on such a frame. **5.** *Furniture.* a flexible shutter used as a desk top or in place of a door, composed of a number of closely set wood strips attached to a piece of cloth, the whole sliding in grooves along the sides or at the top and bottom. **6.** *Archit.* drum[1] (def. 11). **7.** *Masonry.* a drum of a column. **8.** *Court Tennis.* a sloping buttress opposite the penthouse, on the hazard side of the court. —*v.t., v.i.* **9.** to embroider on a tambour. [late ME: drum < MF << Ar *ṭanbūr* lute, confused with Pers *tabūrāk* drum. See TABOR]

T, Tambour (in bedside stand)

tam·bou·rin (tam′bo͝o rin; *Fr.* tän bo͞o raN′), *n., pl.* **-rins** (-rinz; *Fr.* -RAN′). **1.** a long narrow drum of Provence. **2.** an old Provençal dance in duple meter, accompanied by a drone bass or by a steady drumbeat. **3.** the music for this dance. [< F < Pr *tamborin*, dim. of *tambor* TAMBOUR]

tam·bou·rine (tam′bə rēn′), *n.* a small drum consisting of a circular frame with a skin stretched over it and several pairs of metal jingles attached to the frame, played by striking with the knuckles, shaking, and the like. [late ME *tamboryne* < MFlem *tamborijn* small drum < MF *tambourin* or ML *tamborīnum*. See TAMBOUR, -INE[1]] —**tam′bou·rin′ist,** *n.*

Tambourine

Tam·bov (täm bôf′), *n.* a city in the RSFSR, in the central Soviet Union in Europe, SE of Moscow. 199,000 (est. 1964).

tam·bu·ra (tam bo͝or′ə), *n.* an Asian musical instrument of the lute family having a small, round body and a long neck. Also, **tam·bou′ra, tam·bur** (täm bo͝or′), **tampur, tanbur.** [< Pers *ṭanbūr* < Ar *ṭunbūr*]

Tam·bur·laine (tam′bər lān′), *n.* Tamerlane.

Tam′burlaine the Great′, a drama in blank verse (1587?) by Christopher Marlowe.

tame (tām), *adj.,* **tam·er, tam·est,** *v.,* **tamed, tam·ing.** —*adj.* **1.** changed from the wild or savage state; domesticated: *a tame bear.* **2.** without the savageness or fear of humans normal in wild animals; gentle, fearless, or without shyness, as if domesticated: *That lion acts as tame as a house cat.* **3.** tractable, docile, or submissive, as a person, the disposition, etc. **4.** lacking in excitement; dull; insipid: *a very tame party.* **5.** spiritless or pusillanimous. **6.** not to be taken very seriously; without real power, importance, etc.: *Don't mind him; he's just our tame genius.* **7.** brought into service; rendered useful and manageable; under control, as natural resources, a source of power, etc. **8.** cultivated or improved by cultivation, as a plant, its fruit, etc. —*v.t.* **9.** to make tame; domesticate; make tractable; subdue. **10.** to deprive of courage, ardor, or interest. **11.** to soften; tone down. **12.** to harness or control; render useful, as a source of power. **13.** to cultivate, as land, plants, etc. [ME; OE *tam*; c. D *tam*, Icel *tamr*, G *zahm*; akin to OE *temman*, Icel *temja*, Goth *gatamjan*, L *domāre* to tame] —**tame′ly,** *adv.* —**tame′ness,** *n.* —**tam′er,** *n.*
—**Syn. 3.** meek, subdued. **4.** flat, empty, vapid, boring, tedious, uninteresting. **5.** cowardly, dastardly. **9.** break. **11.** calm, mollify. —**Ant. 1.** wild.

tame·a·ble (tā′mə bəl), *adj.* tamable. —**tame′a·bil′i·ty, tame′a·ble·ness,** *n.*

tame·less (tām′lis), *adj.* untamed or untamable. [TAME + -LESS] —**tame′less·ly,** *adv.* —**tame′less·ness,** *n.*

Tam·er·lane (tam′ər lān′), *n.* (*Timur Lenk*) 1336?–1405, Tartar conqueror in southern and western Asia: ruler of Samarkand 1369–1405. Also, **Tamburlaine.** Also called **Timour, Timur.**

Tam·il (tam′əl, tum′-), *n., pl.* **-ils,** (*esp. collectively*) **-il,** *adj.* —*n.* **1.** a member of a people of Dravidian stock of southern India and Ceylon. **2.** the Dravidian language of the Tamils, spoken in India from Madras southward and in Ceylon on the N and E coasts. —*adj.* **3.** of or pertaining to the Tamils or their language.

Tam′ing of the Shrew′, The, a comedy (1594?) by Shakespeare.

tam·is (tam′ē, -is), *n., pl.* **tam·ises** (tam′ēz, -i siz). a worsted cloth mesh constructed in open weave, used as a sieve or strainer. Also, **tammy.** [< F: sieve < ?; cf. OE *temes* sieve, c. MLG *temes*, MD *temse*, OHG *zemisa*]

Tamm (täm), *n.* **I·gor Ev·ge·nie·vich** (ē′gor ev ge′nye vich), born 1895, Russian physicist: Nobel prize 1958.

Tam·ma·ny (tam′ə nē), *adj.* **1.** pertaining to, involving, or characteristic of the membership or methods of Tammany Hall. —*n.* **2.** See **Tammany Hall.** —**Tam′ma·ny·ism,** *n.* —**Tam′ma·ny·ite′,** *n.*

Tam′many Hall′, **1.** a powerful Democratic political organization in New York City, founded in 1789 as a fraternal benevolent society (**Tam′many Soci′ety**). **2.** the building in which the Tammany organization had its headquarters. [named after *Tammany* (var. of *Tamanen, Tammenund*), 17th-century Delaware Indian chief, later facetiously canonized as patron saint of U.S.]

Tam·mer·fors (täm′mər fôrs′), *n.* Swedish name of **Tampere.**

Tamm·lie (tam′lē), *n.* a girl's given name.

Tam·muz (tä′mo͝oz; *for 1 also Heb.* tä mo͞oz′; *for 2 also* tam′uz), *n.* **1.** a month of the Jewish calendar. Cf. **Jewish calendar.** **2.** a Sumerian and Babylonian shepherd god, originally king of Erech, confined forever in the afterworld as a substitute for his consort Inanna or Ishtar. [< Heb]

tam·my[1] (tam′ē), *n.* a fabric of mixed fibers, constructed in plain weave and often heavily glazed, used in the manufacture of linings and undergarments. Also, **tam′mie.** [? back formation from obs. F *tamise* kind of glossy cloth (taken as pl.)]

tam·my[2] (tam′ē), *n., pl.* **-mies.** tamis.

Tam·my (tam′ē), *n.* a girl's given name, Scandinavian form of **Tamasine.** Also, **Tam′mie.**

ta·mo (tä′mō), *n., pl.* **-mos.** the light, yellowish-brown wood of a Japanese ash, *Fraxinus mandschurica*, used for making furniture. [< Jap]

tam-o'-shan·ter (tam′ə shan′tər), *n.* a cap of Scottish origin, usually made of wool, having a round, flat top that projects all around the head and has a pompon at its center. Also called **tam.** [named after the hero of *Tam O'Shanter*]

Tam O'Shan·ter (tam′ ə shan′tər), a narrative poem (1791) by Robert Burns.

tamp (tamp), *v.t.* **1.** to force in or down by repeated, rather light, strokes: *He tamped the tobacco in his pipe.* **2.** (in blasting) to fill (the hole made by the drill) with earth or the like after the powder or explosive has been introduced. [? back formation from *tampin* (obs. var. of TAMPION), taken as prp. (*-in* -ING[2])]

Tam-o'-shanter

Tam·pa (tam′pə), *n.* a seaport in W Florida, on Tampa Bay: fishing resort. 274,970 (1960). —**Tam′pan,** *n.*

Tam′pa Bay′, an inlet of the Gulf of Mexico, in W Florida. ab. 27 mi. long.

tam·per[1] (tam′pər), *v.i.* **1.** to meddle, esp. for the purpose of altering, damaging, or misusing (usually fol. by *with*). **2.** to engage secretly or improperly in something. **3.** to engage in underhand or corrupt dealings, as in order to influence improperly (usually fol. by *with*). [prob. var. of TEMPER (v.)] —**tam′per·er,** *n.*

tam·per[2] (tam′pər), *n.* one who or that which tamps. [TAMP + -ER[1]]

Tam·pe·re (täm′pe re), *n.* a city in SW Finland. 139,416 (est. 1965). Swedish, **Tammerfors.**

Tam·pi·co (tam pē′kō; *Sp.* täm pē′kô), *n.* a seaport in SE Tamaulipas, in E Mexico. 119,427 (1960). —**Tam·pi′can,** *n.*

tam·pi·on (tam′pē ən), *n.* a plug or stopper placed in the muzzle of a piece of ordnance when not in use, to keep out dampness and dust. Also, **tompion.** [late ME *tampyon*, var. of *tampon* < MF, nasalized var. of OF *tapon*, deriv. of *tape* plug < Gmc. See TAP[2]]

tam·pon (tam′pon), *n.* **1.** *Med.* a plug of cotton or the like for insertion into an orifice, wound, etc., chiefly for stopping hemorrhages. **2.** a two-headed drumstick for playing rolls. —*v.t.* **3.** *Surg.* to fill or plug with a tampon. [< F; see TAMPION]

tam·pon·ade (tam′pə nād′), *n.* **1.** *Med.* the use of a tampon, as to stop a hemorrhage. **2.** Also called **cardiac tamponade, heart tamponade.** *Pathol.* a condition in which the heart is compressed because of an accumulation of fluid in the pericardium. Also, **tam·pon·age** (tam′pə nij). [TAMPON + -ADE[1]]

tam·pur (täm po͝or′), *n.* tambura.

tam-tam (tum′tum′, tam′tam′), *n.* **1.** a gong with indefinite pitch. **2.** tom-tom. [var. of TOM-TOM]

Tam·worth (tam′wûrth′), *n.* one of an English breed of red hogs, raised chiefly for bacon. [after *Tamworth*, in Staffordshire, England where it was developed]

Tam·worth (tam′wûrth′), *n.* a city in E Australia. 18,984 (1961).

tan (tan), *v.,* **tanned, tan·ning,** *n., adj.* —*v.t.* **1.** to convert (a hide) into leather, esp. by soaking or steeping in a bath prepared from tanbark or synthetically. **2.** to make brown by exposure to ultraviolet rays, as of the sun. **3.** *Informal.* to thrash; spank. —*v.i.* **4.** to become tanned. **5.** **tan one's hide,** *Informal.* to beat soundly; thrash: *She threatened to tan our hides if she found us on her property again.* —*n.* **6.** the brown color imparted to the skin by exposure to the sun or open air. **7.** yellowish brown; light brown. **8.** tanbark. —*adj.* **9.** of the color of tan; yellowish-brown. **10.** used in or relating to tanning processes, materials, etc. [ME *tanne(n)*, late OE *tannian* < ML *tannāre*, deriv. of *tannum* oak bark, tanbark < Gmc; cf. OHG *tanna* oak, fir, akin to D *den* fir] —**tan′na·ble,** *adj.* —**tan′nish,** *adj.*

tan, tangent.

ta·na (tä′nə), *n.* thana.

Ta·na (tä′nä), *n.* **1.** a river in E Africa, in Kenya, flowing SE to the Indian Ocean. 500 mi. long. **2. Lake.** Also, **Lake Tsana.** a lake in NW Ethiopia: the source of the Blue Nile. 1100 sq. mi.

Ta·nach (tä näkh′), *n.* *Hebrew.* the Old Testament, being the three Jewish divisions of the Pentateuch or Torah, the Prophets or Nebiim, and the Hagiographa or Ketubim, taken as a whole. [vocalization of Heb *TNK* for *Tōrāh* law + *Nebhī'im* prophets + *Kethūbhim* (other) writings]

tan·a·ger (tan′ə jər), *n.* any of numerous small, usually brightly colored, passerine birds of the family *Thraupidae*, of the New World. [< NL *tanagra*, metathetic var. of Tupi *tangara*]

Scarlet tanager, *Piranga erythromelas* (Length 7 in.)

Tan·a·gra (tan′ə grə), *n.* a town in ancient Greece, in Boeotia: terra-cotta figurines; Spartan victory over the Athenians 457 B.C.

Tan′agra figurine′, a small terra-cotta statuette produced from the late 4th to the 3rd century B.C. in Tanagra, Boeotia, and found chiefly in tombs. Also, **Tan′agra fig′ure.**

tan·a·grine (tan′ə grin), *adj.* of or pertaining to the tanagers; belonging to the tanager family. [< NL *tanagr(a)* TANAGER + -INE[1]]

Ta·na·na (tan′ə nä′), *n.* a river flowing NW from E Alaska to the Yukon River. ab. 650 mi. long.

Ta·na·na·rive (tä nä nä rēv′), *n.* a city in and the capital of Madagascar, in the central part. 247,917 (1960). Also called **Antananarivo.**

Tan·a·quil (tan′ə kwil), *n.* a legendary queen of Rome who prophesied the future greatness of Servius Tullius and helped him to gain the throne after the murder of her husband by a political faction.

tan·bark (tan′bärk′), the bark of the oak, hemlock, etc., bruised and broken by a mill and used in tanning hides. [TAN + BARK[2]]

tan′bark oak′, any oak that yields tanbark, esp. an evergreen oak, *Lithocarpus densiflora*, of the Pacific coast of the U.S.

tan′ bay′. See **loblolly bay.**

tan·bur (tän bo͝or′), *n.* tambura.

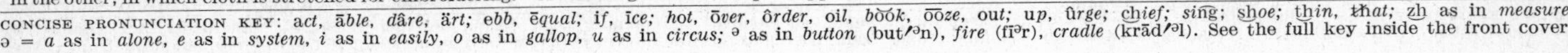

Tan·cred (tang′krid), *n.* 1078?–1112, Norman leader in the 1st Crusade.

T and A, tonsillectomy and adenoidectomy.

tan·dem (tan′dəm), *adv.* **1.** one following or behind the other: *to drive horses tandem.* **2. in tandem, a.** in single file: *They swam in tandem.* **b.** in association or partnership. —*adj.* **3.** having animals, seats, parts, etc., arranged tandem or one behind another. —*n.* **4.** a team of horses so harnessed. **5.** a two-wheeled carriage with a high driver's seat, drawn by two or more horses. **6.** any of various mechanisms having a tandem arrangement. [special use (orig. facetious) of L *tandem* at length, finally < *tam* so far + *-dem* demonstrative suffix]

Tandem

tan′dem bi′cycle, a bicycle for two or more persons, having seats and corresponding sets of pedals arranged in tandem, esp. popular in the 19th century.

tan·dem-com·pound (tan′dəm kom′pound), *adj.* (of a compound engine or turbine) having high-pressure and low-pressure units in tandem. Cf. **cross-compound.**

Tan·djung·pan·dan (tän′jŏŏng pän′dän), *n.* a town on NW Billiton, in central Indonesia.

Ta·ne (tä′nā), *n.* a Polynesian god of fertility.

Ta·ney (tô′nē), *n.* **Roger Brooke,** 1777–1864, U.S. jurist: Chief Justice of the U.S. 1836?–64.

tang[1] (tang), *n.* **1.** a strong taste or flavor. **2.** the distinctive flavor or quality of a thing. **3.** a pungent or distinctive odor. **4.** a smack, touch, or suggestion of something; slight trace. **5.** a long and slender projecting strip, tongue, or prong forming part of an object, as a chisel, file, knife, etc., and serving as a means of attachment for another part, as a handle or stock. **6.** a surgeonfish. —*v.t.* **7.** to furnish with a tang. [ME *tange* < Scand; cf. Icel *tangi* pointed object; akin to TONGS]
—**Syn. 1.** savor. **4.** taste, hint.

tang[2] (tang), *n.* **1.** a sharp ringing or twanging sound; clang. —*v.t., v.i.* **2.** to ring or twang; clang. [imit. See TING[1]]

Tang (täng), *n.* a dynasty in China, A.D. 618–907, marked by territorial expansion, the invention of printing, and the high development of poetry. Also, **T'ang.** [< Chin (Peking) *T'ang*]

tan·ga (tang gä′), *n.* **1.** either of two former coins of India, one gold and one silver, issued by various Muslim rulers. **2.** a former coin of Portuguese India, equal to the 10th part of a rupee. **3.** a former silver coin of Tibet of varying weight and fineness. Also, **tangka.** [< Hindi *ṭangā*]

Tan·ga (tang′gə), *n.* a seaport in NE Tanzania. 38,053 (1957).

Tan·gan·yi·ka (tan′gən yē′kə, tang′-), *n.* **1.** a former country in E Africa: formed the larger part of German East Africa; British trusteeship **(Tan′ganyi′ka Ter′ritory)** 1946–61; became independent 1961; now the mainland part of Tanzania. 9,798,000 (est. 1963); 361,800 sq. mi. *Cap.:* Dar es Salaam. **2. Lake,** a lake in central Africa, between the Republic of the Congo and Tanganyika: the longest fresh-water lake in the world. ab. 450 mi. long; 30–40 mi. wide; 12,700 sq. mi. —**Tan′gan·yi′kan,** *adj., n.*

Tanganyi′ka and Zan′zibar, United Republic of, former name of **Tanzania.**

tan·ge·lo (tan′je lō′), *n., pl.* **-los. 1.** a hybrid citrus tree produced by crossing the tangerine and the grapefruit. **2.** the tart fruit of this tree. [TANG(ERINE) + (POM)ELO]

tan·gen·cy (tan′jən sē), *n.* state of being tangent. [TANG(ENT) + -ENCY]

tan·gent (tan′jənt), *adj.* **1.** in immediate physical contact; touching. **2.** *Geom.* touching at a single point, as a tangent in relation to a curve or surface. **3.** in contact along a single line or element, as a plane with a cylinder. —*n.* **4.** *Geom.* a line or a plane that touches a curve or a surface at a point so that it is closer to the curve in the vicinity of the point than any other line or plane drawn through the point. **5.** *Trig.* **a.** (in a right triangle) the ratio of the side opposite a given angle to the side adjacent to the angle. **b.** (of an angle) a trigonometric function equal to the ratio of the ordinate of the end point of the arc to the abscissa of this end point, the origin being at the center of the circle on which the arc lies and the initial point of the arc being on the x-axis. *Abbr.:* tan, tg, tgn **c.** (originally) a straight line perpendicular to the radius of a circle at one end of an arc and extending from this point to the produced radius which cuts off the arc at its other end. **6.** *Survey.* **a.** the straight portion of a survey line between curves, as in railroad or highway alignment. **b.** Also called **tan′gent dis′tance.** the distance to either end of a curve from the point at which its tangents would intersect if prolonged. **7.** the upright metal blade, fastened on the inner end of a clavichord key, that rises and strikes the string when the outer end of the key is depressed. **8. off on** or **at a tangent,** digressing suddenly from one course of action or thought and turning to another: *The speaker flew off on a tangent.* [< L *tangent-* (s. of *tangēns,* prp. of *tangere* to touch) in phrase *līnea tangēns* touching line; see -ENT]
—**Syn. 1.** meeting, abutting.

tan·gen·tial (tan jen′shəl), *adj.* **1.** pertaining to or of the nature of a tangent; being or moving in the direction of a tangent. **2.** merely touching; slightly connected. **3.** divergent or digressive: *He is always injecting tangential issues into a discussion.* Also, **tan·gen·tal** (tan jen′tᵊl). [TANGENT + -IAL] —**tan·gen′tial·ly, tan·gen′tal·ly,** *adv.*

tangen′tial mo′tion, *Astron.* the component of the linear motion of a star with respect to the sun, measured along a line perpendicular to its line of sight and expressed in miles or kilometers per second. Cf. **proper motion** (def. 1), **radial motion.**

tan·gent-saw (tan′jənt sô′), *v.t.,* **-sawed, -sawed** or **-sawn, -saw·ing.** plain-saw.

tan·ge·rine (tan′jə rēn′), *n.* **1.** a small, loose-skinned variety of mandarin orange. **2.** the tree bearing this fruit. **3.** deep orange; reddish orange. —*adj.* **4.** of the color tangerine; reddish-orange. [TANG(I)ER + -INE[1]]

tan·gi·ble (tan′jə bəl), *adj.* **1.** capable of being touched; discernible by the touch; material or substantial. **2.** real or actual, rather than imaginary or visionary: *the tangible benefits of sunshine.* **3.** definite; not vague or elusive: *no tangible grounds for suspicion.* **4.** (of an asset) having actual physical existence, as real estate, chattels, etc., and therefore capable of being assigned a value in monetary terms. —*n.* **5.** something tangible, esp. a tangible asset. [< L *tangibil(is)* < *tang(ere)* (to) touch + *-ibil(is)* -IBLE] —**tan′gi·bil′i·ty, tan′gi·ble·ness,** *n.* —**tan′gi·bly,** *adv.*
—**Syn. 1.** palpable, corporeal. **2.** certain, genuine, perceptible. **3.** specific.

Tan·gier (tan jēr′), *n.* a seaport in N Morocco, on the W Strait of Gibraltar: capital of the former Tangier Zone. 141,714 (1960).

Tangier′ Zone′, a former internationalized zone on the Strait of Gibraltar: became a part of Morocco 1956. Cf. **Morocco** (def. 1).

tang·i·le (tang′ə lē), *n.* tanguile.

tang·ka (təng kä′), *n.* tanga.

tan·gle (tang′gəl), *v.,* **-gled, -gling,** *n.* —*v.t.* **1.** to bring together into a mass of confusedly interlaced or intertwisted threads, strands, or other like parts; snarl. **2.** to involve in something that hampers, obstructs, or overgrows: *The bushes were tangled with vines.* **3.** to catch and hold in or as in a net or snare. —*v.i.* **4.** to be or become tangled. **5.** *Informal.* to come into conflict; fight or argue: *I don't want to tangle with him over the new ruling.* —*n.* **6.** a tangled condition. **7.** a tangled or confused mass or assemblage of something. **8.** a confused jumble: *a tangle of contradictory statements.* **9.** *Informal.* a conflict; disagreement: *He got into a tangle with the Governor.* [ME *tangil,* nasalized var. of *tagil* entangle < Scand; cf. Sw (dial.) *taggla* to disarrange] —**tan′gle·ment,** *n.* —**tan′gler,** *n.* —**tan′gly,** *adv.*

tan·gle·ber·ry (tang′gəl ber′ē), *n., pl.* **-ries.** a huckleberry, *Gaylussacia frondosa,* of the eastern U.S. Also called **blue huckleberry, dangleberry.** [TANGLE + BERRY]

tan·gled (tang′gəld), *adj.* **1.** snarled, interlaced, or mixed up: *tangled thread.* **2.** very complicated, intricate, or involved: *tangled bureaucratic procedures.* [TANGLE + -ED[2]]

Tan·gle·wood (tang′gəl wŏŏd′), *n.* See under **Lenox.**

tan·go (tang′gō), *n., pl.* **-gos,** *v.,* **-goed, -go·ing.** —*n.* **1.** a ballroom dance of Spanish-American origin, danced by couples, and having many varied steps, figures, and poses. **2.** music for this dance. **3.** a word used in communications to represent the letter *T.* —*v.i.* **4.** to dance the tango. [< AmerSp < ?]

tan·go·re·cep·tor (tang′gō ri sep′tər), *n.* *Physiol., Biol.* a receptor stimulated by touch. [< L *tang(ere)* (to) touch + -O- + RECEPTOR]

tan·gram (tang′grəm), *n.* a Chinese puzzle consisting of a square cut into five triangles, a square, and a rhomboid, which can be combined so as to form a great variety of other figures. [? *tang* < Chin (Cantonese) *t'ang* Chinese + -GRAM[1]]

tang·ui·le (täng′ə lē), *n.* **1.** a Philippine mahogany, *Shorea polysperma.* **2.** the hard, reddish-brown wood of this tree, used for making furniture. Also, **tangile.** [< Tagalog *tanĝili*]

Tan·guy (tän gē′), *n.* **Yves** (ēv), 1900–55, French painter, in the U.S. after 1939.

tang·y (tang′ē), *adj.,* **tang·i·er, tang·i·est.** having a tang. [TANG[1] + -Y[1]]

tanh, hyperbolic tangent. [TAN(GENT) + H(YPERBOLIC)]

Tan·ia (tan′yə), *n.* a girl's given name, form of **Tatiana.** Also, **Tanya.**

Ta·nis (tā′nis), *n.* an ancient city in Lower Egypt, in the Nile delta. Biblical, **Zoan.**

tan·ist (tan′ist, thô′nist), *n.* *Hist.* the successor apparent to a Celtic chief, usually the oldest or worthiest of his kin, chosen by election among the tribe during the chief's lifetime. [< Ir, Gaelic *tānaiste* second, substitute, heir by election]

tan·ist·ry (tan′i strē, thô′ni-), *n.* the system among various Celtic tribes of choosing a tanist. [TANIST + -RY]

Tan·jore (tan jôr′, -jōr′), *n.* a city in E Madras, in SE India. 114,572 (est. 1964).

tank (tangk), *n.* **1.** a large receptacle, container, or structure for holding a liquid or gas: *tanks for storing oil.* **2.** a natural or artificial pool, pond, or lake. **3.** *Mil.* an armored, self-propelled combat vehicle, armed with cannon and machine guns and moving on a caterpillar tread. **4.** *Slang.* a prison cell or enclosure for more than one occupant, as for prisoners awaiting a hearing. —*v.t.* **5.** to put or store in a tank. [< Gujarati *tānkh* reservoir, lake + Pg *tanque* pond, lit., something dammed up, verbid of VL **tancare* to dam up, hem in] —**tank′less,** *adj.* —**tank′like′,** *adj.*

Tank (def. 3)

tan·ka (täng′kə), *n., pl.* **-kas, -ka.** *Pros.* a Japanese poem consisting of 31 syllables in 5 lines, with 5 syllables in the first and third lines and 7 in the others.

tank·age (tang′kij), *n.* **1.** the capacity of a tank or tanks. **2.** the act or process of storing liquid in a tank. **3.** the fee charged for such storage. **4.** the residue from tanks in which carcasses and other offal have been steamed and the fat has been rendered, used as a fertilizer. [TANK + -AGE]

tank·ard (tang′kərd), *n.* a large drinking cup, usually with a handle and a hinged cover. [ME bucket; cf. MD *tanckaert,* MF *tanquart*]

tank′ car′, **1.** *Railroads.* a car containing one or more tanks for the transportation of liquids, gases, or granular solids. **2.** See **tank truck.**

tank′ destroy′er, a high-speed, self-propelled, armored combat vehicle with antitank cannon.

tanked (tangkt), *adj.* **1.** put or stored in a tank. **2.** *Slang.* drunk. [TANK + -ED[2]]

tank·er (tang′kər), *n.* a ship, airplane, or truck designed to carry oil or other liquid in bulk. [TANK + -ER[1]]

tank′ farm′, an area or expanse of land used for holding oil-storage tanks.

Tankard (18th century)

tank′ farm′ing, hydroponics.

tank′ fight′er, *Boxing Slang.* a boxer known for his false shows of being knocked down or out in bouts the results of which have been prearranged.

tank·ful (tangk′fŏŏl), *n., pl.* **-fuls.** as much as a tank will hold. [TANK + -FUL]

tank′ locomo′tive, a steam locomotive carrying its own fuel and water without the use of a tender.

tank·ship (tangk′ship′), *n.* a ship for carrying bulk cargoes of liquids; tanker. [TANK + -SHIP]

tank′ suit′, a simple one-piece bathing suit for women, usually of cotton or wool knit.

tank′ town′, **1.** a town where trains stop to take on a supply of water. **2.** any small, unimportant, or uninteresting town.

tank′ trail′er, a trailer truck constructed to transport liquids or gases.

tank′ truck′, a truck constructed for transporting large quantities of liquid or gas. Also called **tank car.**

tan·na (tä′nä), *n., pl.* **tan·na·im** (tä nä′im). (*often cap.*) *Judaism.* one of a group of Jewish scholars, active in Palestine during the 1st and 2nd centuries A.D., whose teachings relating to Jewish law and tradition are found chiefly in the Mishnah. Cf. **amora, sabora.** [< Heb: teacher] —**tan·na·i·tic** (tä′nə it′ik), *adj.*

tan·nage (tan′ij), *n.* **1.** the act or process of tanning. **2.** the product of tanning; that which is tanned. [TAN + -AGE]

tan·nate (tan′āt), *n.* *Chem.* a salt of tannic acid. [TANN(IN) + -ATE[2]]

Tan·nen·berg (tän′ən berkh′), *n.* a village formerly in East Prussia, now in N Poland: decisive German victory over the Russians 1914.

tan·ner[1] (tan′ər), *n.* a person whose occupation it is to tan hides. [ME, OE *tannere.* See TAN, -ER[1]]

tan·ner[2] (tan′ər), *n.* *Brit. Slang.* a sixpenny piece. [?]

Tan·ner·us (tan′ər əs), *n.* a crater in the fourth quadrant of the face of the moon: about 20 miles in diameter.

tan·ner·y (tan′ə rē), *n., pl.* **-ner·ies.** a place where tanning is carried on. [TAN + -ERY]

Tann·häu·ser (tan′hoi′zər, -hou′-; *Ger.* tän′hoi′zər), *n.* **1.** a Middle High German lyric poet of the 13th century. A well-known legend tells of his stay with Venus in the Venusberg and his later repentance. **2.** (*italics*) an opera (1845) by Richard Wagner.

tan·nic (tan′ik), *adj.* *Chem.* of, pertaining to, or derived from tan or its tanning principle. [TANN(IN) + -IC]

tan′nic ac′id, *Chem.* See under **tannin.**

tan·nin (tan′in), *n.* *Chem.* any of a group of astringent vegetable principles or compounds, as the reddish compound which gives the tanning properties to oak bark or the whitish compound which occurs in large quantities in nutgalls **(common tannin, tannic acid).** [earlier *tanin* < F. See TAN, -IN[2]]

tan·ning (tan′ing), *n.* **1.** the process or art of converting hides or skins into leather. **2.** a browning or darkening of the skin, as by exposure to the sun. **3.** *Informal.* a thrashing; whipping. [late ME; see TAN, -ING[1]]

Tan′nu Tu′va Peo′ple's Repub′lic (tan′ōō tōō′və), former name of **Tuva Autonomous Soviet Socialist Republic.** Also called **Tan′nu Tu′va.** —**Tan′nu Tu′van.**

tan′ oak′. See **tanbark oak.**

Ta·no·an (tä′nō ən), *n.* a language family of which the three surviving languages are spoken in several pueblos, including Taos, in northern New Mexico near the Rio Grande. [*Tano* Pueblo Indian group + -AN]

tan·rec (tan′rek), *n.* tenrec.

tan·sy (tan′zē), *n., pl.* **-sies.** any composite plant of the genus *Tanacetum,* esp. a strong-scented, weedy, Old World herb, *T. vulgare,* having corymbs of yellow flowers. [late ME < OF *tanesie,* aph. var. of *atanesie* < ML *athanasia* < Gk: immortality < *a-* A-[6] + *-thanasia* mortality. See THANATOS, -Y[3]]

tan′sy rag′wort, a European, perennial herb, *Senecio Jacobaea,* naturalized in North America, having numerous yellow flowers.

Tan·ta (tän′tä), *n.* a city in the N United Arab Republic, in the Nile delta. 209,500 (est. 1962).

tan·ta·late (tan′tᵊlāt′), *n.* *Chem.* a salt of any tantalic acid. [TANTAL(UM) + -ATE[2]]

tan·tal·ic (tan tal′ik), *adj.* *Chem.* of or pertaining to tantalum, esp. in the pentavalent state. [TANTAL(UM) + -IC]

tantal′ic ac′id, *Chem.* an acid, $HTaO_3$, which forms complex salts or tantalates.

tan·ta·lise (tan′tᵊlīz′), *v.t.,* **-lised, -lis·ing.** *Chiefly Brit.* tantalize. —**tan′ta·li·sa′tion,** *n.* —**tan′ta·lis′er,** *n.*

tan·ta·lite (tan′tᵊlīt′), *n.* a mineral, iron tantalate, $FeTa_2O_6$, usually containing manganese and columbium, occurring in heavy black crystals: the principal ore of tantalum. [TANTAL(UM) + -ITE[1]]

tan·ta·lize (tan′tᵊlīz′), *v.t.*, **-lized, -liz·ing.** to torment with, or as with, the sight of something desired but out of reach; tease by arousing expectations that are repeatedly disappointed. Also, *esp. Brit.*, **tantalise.** [TANTAL(US) + -IZE] —**tan′ta·li·za′tion,** *n.* —**Ant.** satisfy.

tan·ta·liz·ing (tan′tᵊlī′ziŋ), *adj.* having or exhibiting that which provokes or arouses expectation, interest, or desire, esp. that which remains unobtainable or beyond one's reach: *a tantalizing taste of success.* Also, *esp. Brit.*, **tan′ta·lis′ing.** [TANTALIZE + -ING[2]] —**tan′ta·liz′·ing·ly;** *esp. Brit.*, **tan′ta·lis′ing·ly,** *adv.*

tan·ta·lous (tan′tᵊləs), *adj. Chem.* containing trivalent tantalum. [TANTAL(UM) + -OUS]

tan·ta·lum (tan′tᵊləm), *n. Chem.* a gray, hard, rare, metallic element occurring in columbite and usually associated with niobium (used, because of its resistance to corrosion by most acids, for chemical, dental, and surgical instruments and apparatus). *Symbol:* Ta; *at. wt.:* 180.948; *at. no.:* 73; *sp. gr.:* 16.6. [< NL; named after TANTALUS]

Tan·ta·lus (tan′tᵊləs), *n.*, *pl.* **-lus·es** for 3. **1.** *Class. Myth.* a Phrygian king, sometimes thought to be a son of Zeus, who for his crimes was condemned to remain in Tartarus, standing, thirsty and hungry, chin deep in water, with fruit-laden branches hanging above his head: whenever he tried to drink or eat, the water and fruit receded out of reach. **2.** a Pisan king, the first husband of Clytemnestra. **3.** (*l.c.*) *Chiefly Brit.* a stand or rack containing visible decanters, esp. of wines or liquors, secured by a lock.

tan·ta·mount (tan′tə mount′), *adj.* equivalent, as in value, force, effect, or signification: *His angry speech was tantamount to a declaration of war.* [adj. use of obs. n., itself n. use of obs. verb < AF *tant amunter* or It *tanto montare* to amount to as much. See TANTO, AMOUNT] —**Syn.** See **equal.**

tan·ta·ra (tan′tər ə, tan tar′ə, -tär′ə), *n.* **1.** a blast of a trumpet or horn. **2.** any similar sound. [< L (*tara*)*tantara;* imit.]

tan·tiv·y (tan tiv′ē), *adv., adj., n., pl.* **-tiv·ies,** *interj.* —*adv.* **1.** at full gallop: *to ride tantivy.* —*adj.* **2.** swift; rapid. —*n.* **3.** a gallop; rush —*interj.* **4.** (used as a hunting cry when the chase is at full speed.) [?]

tant mieux (täɴ myœ′), *French.* so much the better.

tan·to[1] (tän′tō; *It.* tän′tô), *adv. Music.* (of a musical direction) too much; so much. [It < L *tantum* so much]

tan·to[2] (tän tō′; *Jap.* tän tô′), *n., pl.* **-to.** a Japanese dagger having a tsuba and usually having a gentle curve and decorated mounts similar to those of a sword. [< Jap < *tan* short + *to* sword]

tant pis (täɴ pē′), *French.* so much the worse.

Tan·tra (tun′trə), *n.* **1.** (*italics*) *Hinduism.* any of several books of esoteric doctrine regarding rituals, disciplines, meditation, etc., composed in the form of dialogues between Shiva and his Shakti; Agama. **2.** Also called **Tantrism** (tun′triz əm). the philosophy or doctrine of these books, regarding the changing, visible world as the creative dance or play of the Divine Mother and regarding enlightenment as the realization of the essential oneness of one's self and of the visible world with Shiva-Shakti, the Godhead: influential in some schools of Mahayana Buddhism, esp. in Tibet. [< Skt: lit., warp, essence < *tanoti* he weaves]

Tan·tri·ka (tun′trə kə), *n.* **1.** Also called **Tan·trist** (tun′trist). an adherent of Tantra. —*adj.* **2.** of or pertaining to Tantra. Also, **Tan·tric, Tan·trik** (tun′trik). [var. of *Tantric.* See TANTRA, -IC]

tan·trum (tan′trəm), *n.* a violent demonstration of rage or frustration; a sudden burst of ill temper. [?]

Tan·ya (tan′yə), *n.* a girl's given name, form of **Tatiana.** Also, **Tania.**

Tan·za·ni·a (tan′zə nē′ə, tan zan′ē ə; *Swahili* tän zä nē′ä), *n.* a republic in E Africa, comprising the former country of Tanganyika and the islands of Zanzibar and Pemba, and adjacent small islands: formed 1964. 10,179,000 (est. 1965); 362,820 sq. mi. *Cap.:* Dar es Salaam. Formerly, **United Republic of Tanganyika and Zanzibar.**

Tao (dou, tou), *n.* **1.** (in philosophical Taoism) that in virtue of which all things happen or exist. **2.** the rational basis of human activity or conduct. **3.** a universal, regarded as an ideal attained to a greater or lesser degree by those embodying it. [< Chin: the way]

TAO, *Pharm., Trademark.* triacetyloleandomycin.

Tao·ism (dou′iz əm, tou′-), *n.* **1.** the philosophical system evolved by Lao-tzu and Chuang-tzu, advocating a life of complete simplicity and naturalness and of noninterference with the course of natural events, in order to attain a happy existence in harmony with the Tao. **2.** Also called **Hsüan Chiao.** a popular Chinese religion, purporting to be based on the doctrines of Lao-tzu but actually highly eclectic in nature and characterized by a pantheon of many gods, by superstition, and by the practice of alchemy, divination, and magic. [TAO + -ISM] —**Tao′ist,** *n., adj.* —**Tao·is′tic,** *adj.*

Taos (tous), *n., pl.* **Taos. 1.** a Tanoan language spoken in two villages in New Mexico. **2.** a member of an American Indian people occupying a pueblo in New Mexico. **3.** a town in N New Mexico: resort; art colony. 2163 (1960).

Tao Te Ching (dou′ de jiŋ′), the philosophical book in verse supposedly written by Lao-tzu. Also called **Lao-tzu, Lao-tse.**

t'ao t'ieh (tou′ tye′), the face of a mythical animal with a gaping mouth appearing as a motif in ancient Chinese art. [< Chin (Peking)]

tap[1] (tap), *v.*, **tapped, tap·ping,** *n.* —*v.t.* **1.** to strike with a light but audible blow or blows; hit with repeated, slight blows: *He tapped the door twice.* **2.** to make, put, etc., by tapping: *to tap a nail into a wall.* **3.** to strike (the fingers, a foot, a pencil, etc.) upon or against something, esp. with repeated light blows: *Stop tapping your feet!* **4.** to add a thickness of leather to the sole or heel of (a boot or shoe), as in repairing. **5.** *Basketball.* to strike (a ball in the air) in the direction of a teammate or of the basket. —*v.i.* **6.** to strike lightly but audibly, as to attract attention. **7.** to strike light blows. —*n.* **8.** a light but audible blow: *a tap on the shoulder.* **9.** the sound made by this. **10.** a thickness of leather added to the sole or heel of a boot or shoe, as in repairing. **11.** a piece of metal attached to the toe or heel of a shoe, as for reinforcement or for making the tapping of a dancer more audible. **12.** *Basketball.* an act or instance of tapping the ball: *Hanson got the tap from our center, who, 6′9″ tall, couldn't lose a jump ball.* [late ME *tappe*(*n*), var. of early ME *teppen;* prob. imit.] —**tap′pa·ble,** *adj.*

tap[2] (tap), *n., v.*, **tapped, tap·ping.** —*n.* **1.** a cylindrical stick, long plug, or stopper for closing an opening through which liquid is drawn, as in a cask; spigot. **2.** a faucet or cock. **3.** the liquor drawn through a particular tap. **4.** *Brit.* a taphouse or taproom. **5.** a tool for cutting screw threads into the cylindrical surface of a round opening. **6.** *Surg.* the withdrawal of fluid: *spinal tap.* **7.** a hole made in tapping, as one in a pipe to furnish connection for a branch pipe. **8.** *Elect.* a connection brought out of a winding at some point between its extremities, for controlling the voltage ratio. **9.** *Archaic.* a particular kind or quality of drink. **10. on tap, a.** ready to be drawn and served, as liquor from a cask. **b.** furnished with a tap or cock, as a barrel containing liquor. **c.** *Informal.* ready for immediate use; available: *There are numerous other projects on tap.* —*v.t.* **11.** to draw liquid from (a vessel or container). **12.** to draw off (liquid) by removing or opening a tap or by piercing a container. **13.** to draw the tap or plug from or pierce (a cask or other container). **14.** to penetrate, open up, reach into, etc., for the purpose of using something or drawing something off; begin to use: *to tap one's resources.* **15.** to connect into secretly so as to receive the message being transmitted: *to tap a telephone wire or telephone.* **16.** to furnish (a cask, container, pipe, etc.) with a tap. **17.** to cut a screw thread into the surface of (an opening). **18.** to open outlets from (power lines, highways, pipes, etc.). [ME *tappe,* OE *tæppa;* c. D *tap,* OHG *zapfo;* Icel *tappi*] —**tap′pa·ble,** *adj.*

ta·pa (tä′pə), *n.* **1.** the bark of the paper mulberry. **2.** Also, **ta′pa cloth′.** a cloth of the Pacific islands made by pounding this or similar barks flat and thin, used for clothing and floor covering. [< Polynesian]

tap·a·cu·lo (tap′ə ko͞o′lō), *n., pl.* **-los.** any of several Central and South American, passerine birds of the family *Rhinocryptidae,* related to the antbirds but having reduced powers of flight. [< AmerSp: lit., one that covers its hindparts < Sp *tapa*(*r*) (to) conceal < *tapa* lid (< Gmc) + *culo* backside < L *cūlus*]

Ta·pa·jós (tä′pə zhôs′), *n.* a river flowing NE through central Brazil to the Amazon. 500 mi. long.

ta·pas (tup′əs), *n. Yoga.* conditioning of the body through the proper kinds and amounts of diet, rest, recreation, etc., to bring it to the greatest possible state of health and activity. [< Skt: lit., heat]

tap′ bell′, a signal bell giving a single ring, as one announcing the approach to a certain floor of an elevator.

tap′ bolt′, a bolt for driving into a tapped hole in metal.

tap′ cin′der, *Metall.* bulldog (def. 3).

tap′ dance′, a dance in which the rhythm or rhythmical variation is audibly tapped out with the toe or heel by a dancer wearing shoes with special hard soles or with taps.

tap-dance (tap′dans′, -däns′), *v.i.*, **-danced, -danc·ing.** to perform a tap dance. —**tap′-danc′er,** *n.*

tape (tāp), *n., v.*, **taped, tap·ing.** —*n.* **1.** a long, narrow strip of linen, cotton, or the like, used for tying garments, binding seams or carpets, etc. **2.** a long, narrow strip of paper, metal, etc. **3.** See **tape measure. 4.** a string stretched across the finishing line in a race and broken by the winning contestant as he crosses. **5.** the ribbon of white paper on which a ticker prints quotations or news. **6.** See **magnetic tape.** —*v.t.* **7.** to furnish with a tape or tapes. **8.** to tie up, bind, or attach with tape. **9.** to measure with or as if with a tape measure. **10.** to tape-record. [ME, unexplained var. of *tappe,* OE *tæppe* strip (of cloth), lit., part torn off; akin to MLG *teppen* to tear, pluck] —**tap′er,** *n.* —**tape′less,** *adj.* —**tape′-like′,** *adj.*

tape′ deck′, a simplified tape recorder, lacking a power amplifier and speaker of its own.

tape′ grass′, a fresh-water plant, *Vallisneria spiralis,* that has long, ribbonlike leaves and grows under water. Also called **eelgrass, wild celery.**

tape′ machine′, a tape recorder.

tape·man (tāp′mən), *n., pl.* **-men.** *Survey.* a person who holds and positions a tape in taking measurements.

tape′ meas′ure, a long, flexible strip or ribbon of cloth, metal, etc., marked with subdivisions of the foot or meter and used for measuring. Also called **tape·line** (tāp′līn′).

tape′ play′er, a compact electrical device for playing back tape recordings.

ta·per (tā′pər), *v.i.* **1.** to become smaller or thinner toward one end. **2.** to grow gradually lean. —*v.t.* **3.** to make gradually smaller toward one end. **4.** to reduce gradually. **5. taper off, a.** to become gradually slenderer toward one end. **b.** to cease by degrees; decrease; diminish: *The storm is beginning to taper off now. I haven't stopped smoking entirely, but I'm tapering off to three cigarettes a day.* —*n.* **6.** gradual diminution of width or thickness in an elongated object. **7.** gradual decrease of force, capacity, etc. **8.** anything having a tapering form, as a spire, obelisk, etc. **9.** a candle, esp. a very slender one. **10.** a long wick coated with wax, tallow, or the like, as for use in lighting candles or gas. [ME, OE, var. of *tapur,* dissimilated var. of **papur* PAPER] —**ta′per·er,** *n.* —**ta′per·ing·ly,** *adv.*

tape-re·cord (tāp′ri kôrd′), *v.t.* to record on magnetic tape.

tape′ record′er, an electrical device for recording and playing back sound on magnetic tape.

tape′ record′ing, 1. a magnetic tape on which speech, music, etc., have been recorded. **2.** the act of recording on magnetic tape.

ta′per jack′. See **wax jack.**

ta·per·stick (tā′pər stik′), *n.* a candlestick designed to hold tapers. [TAPER + STICK[1]]

tap·es·tried (tap′i strēd), *adj.* **1.** furnished or covered with tapestries. **2.** represented in tapestry, as a story.

tap·es·try (tap′i strē), *n., pl.* **-tries,** *v.*, **-tried, -try·ing.** —*n.* **1.** a fabric consisting of a warp upon which colored threads are woven by hand to produce a design, often pictorial, used for wall hangings, furniture coverings, etc. **2.** a machine-woven reproduction of this. —*v.t.* **3.** to furnish, cover, or adorn with tapestry. [late ME *tapst*(*e*)*ry, tapistry* < MF *tapisserie* carpeting. See TAPIS, -ERY] —**tap′es·try·like′,** *adj.*

tap′estry Brus′sels. See under **Brussels carpet.**

tap′estry moth′. See **carpet moth.**

ta·pe·tum (tə pē′təm), *n., pl.* **-ta** (-tə). **1.** *Bot.* a layer of cells often investing the archespore in a developing sporangium and absorbed as the spores mature. **2.** *Anat., Zool.* any of certain membranous layers or the like, as in the choroid or retina. [< NL, special use of ML *tapētum* coverlet (L, only pl.) < Gk *tapēt-* (s. of *tápēs*) carpet, rug] —**ta·pe′tal,** *adj.*

tape·worm (tāp′wûrm′), *n.* any of various flat or tapelike worms of the class *Cestoda,* lacking any alimentary canal, and parasitic when adult in the alimentary canal of man and other vertebrates: usually characterized by having the larval and adult stages in different hosts. [TAPE + WORM]

taph·e·pho·bi·a (taf′ə fō′bē ə), *n. Psychiatry.* an abnormal fear of being buried alive. [< Gk *taphḗ* grave + -PHOBIA]

Ta·phi·ae (tā′fē ī′), *n.* (*construed as pl.*) (in ancient geography) a group of islands in the Ionian Sea. Also called **Teleboides.**

tap·hole (tap′hōl′), *n. Metall.* a hole in a blast furnace, steelmaking furnace, etc., through which molten metal or slag is tapped off. [TAP[2] + HOLE]

tap·house (tap′hous′), *n., pl.* **-hous·es** (-hou′ziz). *Brit.* an inn or tavern where liquor is kept on tap for sale. [TAP[2] + HOUSE]

tap-in (tap′in′), *n. Basketball.* a field goal made by striking a ball in the air into the basket, usually from close range. Also called **tip-in.** [n. use of v. phrase *tap in*]

tap′ing pin′, *Survey.* See **chaining pin.** Also called **tap′ing ar′row.**

tap·i·o·ca (tap′ē ō′kə), *n.* a food substance prepared from cassava in granular, flake, pellet (**pearl tapioca**), or flour form, used in puddings, as a thickener, etc. [< Pg < Tupi *tipioca,* lit., juice (of cassava) squeezed out, i.e., pulp after squeezing]

tap·i·o·ca-plant (tap′ē ō′kə plant′, -plänt′), *n.* the cassava, *Manihot esculenta.*

tapio′ca snow′. See **snow pellets.**

tap·i·o·lite (tap′ē ə līt′), *n.* a mineral, a tetragonal oxide of iron, manganese, niobium, and tantalum, dimorphous with orthorhombic tantalite: an ore of tantalum. [< Sw *tapiolit,* named after *Tapio,* a Finnish woodland god; see -LITE]

Tapir (South American), *Tapirus terrestris* (3 ft. high at shoulder; length 6½ ft.)

ta·pir (tā′pər), *n., pl.* **-pirs,** (*esp. collectively*) **-pir.** any of several large, stout, hoofed quadrupeds of the family *Tapiridae,* of Central and South America, the Malay Peninsula, and Sumatra, somewhat resembling swine and having a long, flexible snout. [< Tupi *tapira*]

tap·is (tap′ē, tap′is, ta pē′), *n., pl.* **tap·is. 1.** a carpet, tapestry, or other covering. **2. on the tapis,** under consideration or discussion: *A new housing development for that area is on the tapis.* [< MF; OF *tapiz* << Gk *tapētion-* < *tapēt-* (s. of *tápēs*) carpet + *-ion* dim. suffix]

ta·pis vert (ta pē ver′), *pl.* **ta·pis verts** (ta pē ver′). *French.* an unbroken expanse of lawn used as a major element of a landscape design. [lit., green carpet]

Tap·ley (tap′lē), *n.* a boy's given name.

tapped′ joint′, *Masonry.* a convex mortar joint made by laying down a slightly excessive amount of mortar, then tapping a brick down upon it.

tap·per[1] (tap′ər), *n.* **1.** one who or that which taps or strikes lightly. **2.** a telegraph key. [TAP[1] + -ER[1]]

tap·per[2] (tap′ər), *n.* **1.** one who or that which taps, as trees for the sap or juice, a blast furnace, cask, or other container for their contents, etc. **2.** a person who cuts screw threads into the surface of a circular opening, as of a pipe, nut, etc. [OE *tæppere.* See TAP[2], -ER[1]]

tap·pet (tap′it), *n. Mach.* a sliding rod, intermittently struck by a cam, for moving another part, as a valve. [TAP[1] + -ET]

tap·ping[1] (tap′iŋ), *n.* **1.** the act of one who or that which taps or strikes lightly. **2.** the sound produced by this. [late ME; see TAP[1], -ING[1]]

tap·ping[2] (tap′iŋ), *n.* **1.** the act of tapping casks, telephone conversations, etc. **2.** that which is drawn by tapping. **3.** paracentesis. [TAP[2] + -ING[1]]

tap′ping screw′. See **self-tapping screw.**

tap·pit-hen (tap′it hen′), *n. Scot.* **1.** a hen with a crest or topknot. **2.** a tankard, esp. a large one, with a knob or ornament projecting from the top of its lid. [*tappit* (Scot var. of *topped;* see TOP[1]) + HEN]

tap·room (tap′ro͞om′, -ro͝om′), *n. Chiefly Brit.* a room, as in a hotel, inn, or tavern, in which liquor is sold by the drink; barroom. [TAP[2] + ROOM]

tap·root (tap′ro͞ot′, -ro͝ot′), *n. Bot.* a main root descending downward from the radicle and giving off small lateral roots. [TAP[2] + ROOT[1]]

taps (taps), *n. Mil.* a signal by bugle or drum, sounded at night as an order to extinguish all lights, and sometimes performed as a postlude to a military funeral. [TAP[1] + -S[3]]

tap·sal-tee·rie (tap′səl tēr′ē), *adv., adj., n. Scot.* topsy-turvy. Also, **tap·sie-tee·rie** (tap′sē tēr′ē). [var. form]

tap·ster (tap′stər), *n.* a bartender. [ME; OE *tæppestre.* See TAP[2], -STER]

tap′ wa′ter, water, obtained directly from a faucet or tap, that has not been specially purified, distilled, or otherwise treated.

tar[1] (tär), *n., v.*, **tarred, tar·ring,** *adj.* —*n.* **1.** any of various dark-colored viscid products obtained by the destructive distillation of certain organic substances, as coal, wood, etc. **2.** coal-tar pitch. **3. beat, knock,** or **whale the tar out of,** to beat mercilessly: *The thief had knocked the tar out of the old man and left him for dead.* —*v.t.* **4.** to smear or cover with or as with tar. **5. tar and**

feather, a. to coat (a person) with tar and feathers as a punishment or humiliation. **b.** to punish severely: *She should be tarred and feathered for what she has done.* **—***adj.* **6.** of or characteristic of tar. **7.** covered or smeared with tar; tarred. **8. tarred with the same brush,** possessing the same shortcomings: *The whole family is tarred with the same brush.* [ME *tarr(e), ter(re),* OE *teru* (nom.), *terwes* (gen.); c. D, G *teer,* Icel *tjara;* akin to TREE]

tar[2] (tär), *n. Informal.* a sailor. [? short for TARPAULIN] **—Syn.** seafarer, gob. See **sailor.**

Tar·a (tar′ə), *n.* a village in the NE Republic of Ireland, NW of Dublin: home of the ancient Irish Kings **(Hill of Tara).**

tar·a·did·dle (tar′ə did′əl), *n. Informal.* **1.** a small lie; fib. **2.** pretentious nonsense. Also, **tarradiddle.** [?]

Ta·rai (tə rī′), *n.* Terai.

Tar·a·nis (tar′ə nis), *n.* an ancient thunder-god, sometimes identified by the Romans with Jupiter.

ta·ran·tass (tä′rän täs′), *n.* a large, four-wheeled Russian carriage mounted without springs on two parallel longitudinal wooden bars. Also, **ta′ran·tas′.** [< Russ *tarantas*]

tar·an·tel·la (tar′ən tel′ə), *n.* **1.** a rapid, whirling southern Italian dance in very quick sextuple, originally quadruple, meter, usually performed by a single couple, and formerly supposed to be a remedy for tarantism. **2.** a popular dance derived from it. **3.** a piece of music either for the dance or in its rhythm. [< It, after *Taranto* TARANTO + *-ella* n. suffix. See TARANTISM]

tar·ant·ism (tar′ən tiz′əm), *n.* a nervous condition characterized by an uncontrollable impulse to dance, esp. as prevalent in southern Italy from the 15th to the 17th century, popularly attributed to the bite of the tarantula. Cf. **tarantula** (def. 3). [< NL *tarantism(us).* See TARANTO, -ISM] **—tar′ant·ist,** *n.*

Ta·ran·to (tä′rän tô), *n.* **1.** Ancient name, **Tarentum.** a fortified seaport in SE Italy, on the Gulf of Taranto: founded by the Greeks in the 8th century B.C.; naval base. 191,515 (1961). **2. Gulf of,** an arm of the Ionian Sea, in S Italy. 85 mi. long.

Tarantula, *Dugesiella hentzi* (Body length 2 in.)

ta·ran·tu·la (tə ran′chə lə), *n., pl.* **-las, -lae** (-lē′). **1.** any of several large, hairy spiders of the family *Theraphosidae,* as *Dugesiella hentzi,* of the southwestern U.S., having a painful but not highly venomous bite. **2.** any of various related spiders. **3.** a large wolf spider, *Lycosa tarantula,* of southern Europe, having a bite once thought to be the cause of tarantism. [< ML < It *tarantola.* See TARANTO, -ULE]

Ta·ra·po·to (tä′rä pô′tô), *n.* a city in N Peru. 9249 (1950).

Ta·ras Bul·ba (tar′əs bōōl′bə; *Russ.* tä räs′ bōōl′-bä), a historical novel (1839) by Gogol.

ta·ra·ta (tə rä′tə), *n.* a tree, *Pittosporum eugenioides,* of New Zealand, having fragrant, yellow flowers. [< Maori]

ta′ra vine′ (tär′ə, tar′ə), a leafy, woody vine, *Actinidia arguta,* of Japan and eastern Asia, having brownish-white flowers and yellowish, sweet, edible fruit. [*tara* < Jap]

Ta·ra·wa (tä rä′wä, tä′rä wä′), *n.* one of the Gilbert and Ellice Islands, in the central Pacific: U.S. victory over Japanese forces after severe fighting, November, 1943. 7911 (est. 1963); 14 sq. mi.

ta·rax·a·cum (tə rak′sə kəm), *n. Pharm.* the dried roots of any of several composite plants of the genus *Taraxacum,* as the dandelion, *T. officinale,* or *T. laevigatum,* used in medicine, in powdered or fluidextract form, chiefly as a tonic and aperient. [< NL < Ar *ṭarakhshaqūn* wild chicory < Pers *tarkhashqūn* wild endive]

Tar·bell (tär′bel′), *n.* **Ida Minerva,** 1857–1944, U.S. author.

Tarbes (tarb), *n.* a city in and the capital of Hautes-Pyrénées, in SW France. 50,715 (1962).

tar·boosh (tär bōōsh′), *n.* a tasseled cap of cloth or felt, usually red, that is worn by Muslim men either by itself or as the inner part of the turban. Also, **tar·bush′.** [< Ar *ṭarbūsh*]

Tar·bor·o (tär′bûr′ō, -bur′ō, -bər ə), *n.* a town in central North Carolina. 8411 (1960).

tar·brush (tär′brush′), *n.* **1.** a brush for applying tar. **2.** *Slang, Usually Offensive.* Negro ancestry. [TAR[1] + BRUSH[1]]

tar·butt·ite (tär′bə tīt′), *n.* a mineral, basic zinc phosphate, $Zn_3P_2O_8 \cdot Zn(OH)_2$, occurring in the form of sheaflike aggregates. [named after Percy C. *Tarbutt* 20th-century Australian mining official; see -ITE[1]]

Tar·che·ti·us (tär kē′tē əs), *n. Rom. Legend.* a king of Alba Longa.

Tar·chon (tär′kən), *n. Rom. Legend.* the founder of the Etruscan race.

Tarde (tard), *n.* **Ga·bri·el** (ga brē el′), 1843–1904, French sociologist.

Tar·dieu (tar dyœ′), *n.* **An·dré Pierre Ga·bri·el A·mé·dée** (än drā′ pyer ga brē el′ a mā dā′), 1876–1945, French statesman.

tar·di·grade (tär′də grād′), *adj.* **1.** slow in pace or movement. **2.** belonging or pertaining to the phylum *Tardigrada.* **—***n.* **3.** any microscopic, chiefly herbivorous invertebrate of the phylum, *Tardigrada,* related to the arthropods, living in water, on mosses, lichens, etc. [< L *tardigrad(us)* slow-paced. See TARDY, -GRADE]

tar·do (tär′dō; *It.* tär′dô), *adj.* slow (used as a musical direction). [< It: slow < L *tardus*]

tar·dy (tär′dē), *adj.,* **-di·er, -di·est. 1.** late; behind time; not on time: *How tardy were you today?* **2.** moving or acting slowly; slow; sluggish. **3.** delaying through reluctance. [abstracted from late ME *tarditee* < L *tarditās,* equiv. to *tardi-* (comb. form of *tardus* slow) + *-tās* -TY[2]; r. late ME *tardive* < MF] **—tar′di·ly,** *adv.* **—tar′di·ness,** *n.*
—Syn. 1. backward, slack. **3.** reluctant, dilatory. **—Ant. 1.** prompt.

tare[1] (târ), *n.* **1.** any of various vetches, esp. *Vicia sativa.* **2.** the seed of a vetch. **3.** *Bible.* a noxious weed, probably the darnel. [ME: vetch; akin to D *tarwe* wheat]

tare[2] (târ), *n., v.,* **tared, tar·ing. —***n.* **1.** the weight of the wrapping, receptacle, or conveyance containing goods. **2.** a deduction from the gross weight to allow for this. **3.** the weight of a vehicle without cargo, passengers, etc. **4.** a counterweight used in chemical analysis to balance the weight of a container. **5.** a word formerly used in communications to represent the letter T. **—***v.t.* **6.** to ascertain, note, or allow for the tare of. [late ME < MF (equiv. to ML, It, Pr, Sp, Pg *tara,* Sp *atara*) << Ar *ṭarḥah* what one throws away < *ṭaraha* to throw away]

tare[3] (târ), *v. Archaic.* pt. and pp. of **tear.**

tar·ent·ism (târ′ən tiz′əm), *n.* tarantism.

Ta·ren·tum (tə ren′təm), *n.* **1.** ancient name of **Taranto. 2.** a town in central Pennsylvania. 8232 (1960).

targe (tärj), *n. Archaic.* a small, round shield; a target or buckler. [ME < OF < Scand (cf. Icel *targa* round shield; c. OHG *zarga* rim, ring); r. OE *targe, targa* < Scand]

tar·get (tär′git), *n.* **1.** an object, usually marked with concentric circles, to be aimed at in shooting practice or contests. **2.** any object used for this purpose. **3.** anything fired at. **4.** *Fencing.* the portion of a fencer's body where a touch can be scored. **5.** a goal to be reached. **6.** an object of abuse, scorn, derision, etc.; butt. **7.** a disk-shaped signal, as at a railroad switch, indicating the position of a switch. **8.** *Survey.* **a.** the sliding sight on a leveling rod. **b.** any marker on which sights are taken. **9.** a small shield, usually round, carried by a foot soldier; buckler. **—***v.t.* **10.** to use, set up, or designate as a target or goal. **11.** to make a target of (an object, person, city, etc.) for attack or bombardment. [late ME < MF *targuete,* var. of *targete* small shield. See TARGE, -ET] **—tar′get·less,** *adj.*

tar′get date′, the date set or aimed at for the commencement, fulfillment, or completion of some effort: *The target date for the moon shot is 1970.*

tar·get·eer (tär′gi tēr′), *n.* a soldier armed with a sword and buckler. [TARGET + -EER]

tar′get ri′fle, a rifle designed esp. for shooting at targets.

Tar·gi·ta·us (tär′ji tā′əs), *n. Class. Myth.* a son of Zeus who was the first to inhabit Scythia.

Tar·gum (tär′gōōm; *Heb.* tär gōōm′), *n., pl.* **Tar·gums,** *Heb.* **Tar·gu·mim** (tär′gōō mēm′). a translation or paraphrase in Aramaic of a book or division of the Old Testament. [< Aram: paraphrase, interpretation] **—Tar·gum′ic,** *adj.* **—Tar′gum·ist,** *n.*

Târ·gu-Mu·res (tɪr′gōō mōō′resh), *n.* a city in central Rumania. 75,450 (est. 1964).

Tar·heel (tär′hēl′), *n.* a native or inhabitant of North Carolina (the **Tarheel State**) (used as a nickname). [TAR[1] + HEEL[1]; point of nickname uncertain]

Tar′heel State′, North Carolina (used as a nickname).

tar·iff (tar′if), *n.* **1.** an official list or table showing the duties or customs imposed by a government on imports or exports. **2.** the schedule or system of duties so imposed. **3.** any duty or rate of duty in such a list or schedule. **4.** any table of charges, as of a railroad, bus line, etc. **5.** *Brit.* the bill of fare in a restaurant or hotel. **—***v.t.* **6.** to subject to a tariff. **7.** to put a valuation on according to a tariff. [earlier *tariffa* < It < Ar *ta'rīfa* information, akin to *'arafa* to make known] **—tar′iff·less,** *adj.*

Ta·ri·ja (tä rē′hä), *n.* a city in S Bolivia. 19,561 (est. 1959).

Ta·rim (tä′rēm′), *n.* a river in NW China, in Sinkiang province. ab. 1300 mi. long.

Ta′rim′ Ba′sin, a region in W China between the Tien Shan and Kunlun mountain ranges. ab. 350,000 sq. mi.

Tar·king·ton (tär′king tən), *n.* **(Newton) Booth,** 1869–1946, U.S. novelist and playwright.

Tar·lac (tär′läk), *n.* a city on central Luzon, in the N Philippines. 64,597 (1960).

tar·la·tan (tär′lə tən), *n.* a thin, open, stiff cotton fabric, not washable. Also, **tar′le·tan.** [< F *tarlatane,* dissimilated var. of *tarnatane* kind of cloth orig. imported from India < ?]

Tarl·ton (tärl′tən), *n.* **Richard,** died 1588, English actor.

Tar·mac (tär′mak), *n.* **1.** *Trademark.* a bituminous binder, similar to tarmacadam, for surfacing roads, airport runways, parking areas, etc. **2.** (*l.c.*) *Brit.* **a.** a road, airport runway, parking area, etc., paved with Tarmac, tarmacadam, or a layer of tar. **b.** a layer or covering of Tarmac, tarmacadam, or tar.

tar·mac·ad·am (tär′mə kad′əm), *n.* a paving material consisting of coarse crushed stone covered with a mixture of tar and bitumen. [TAR[1] + MACADAM]

tarn (tärn), *n.* a small mountain lake or pool. [ME *terne* < Scand; cf. Icel *tjörn* pond, pool]

Tarn (tarn), *n.* a department in S France. 319,560 (1962); 2232 sq. mi. *Cap.:* Albi.

'tar·nal (tär′nəl), *Dial.* **—***adj.* **1.** damned; blamed; cussed. **—***adv.* **2.** damned. [dial. var. of ETERNAL] **—'tar′nal·ly,** *adv.*

tar·na·tion (tär nā′shən), *Dial.* **—***interj.* **1.** damnation. **—***n.* **2.** damnation; hell (used as a euphemism): *Where in tarnation is that boy?* **—***adv.* **3.** damned. [TARN(AL) + (DAM)NATION]

Tar·ne (tär′nē), *n.* (in the *Iliad*) Sardis.

Tarn-et-Ga·ronne (tar′nā ga rôn′), *n.* a department in S France. 319,560 (1962); 1440 sq. mi. *Cap.:* Montauban.

tar·nish (tär′nish), *v.t.* **1.** to dull the luster of (a metallic surface), esp. by oxidation; discolor. **2.** to diminish or destroy the purity of; stain; sully: *The scandal tarnished his reputation.* **—***v.i.* **3.** to grow dull or discolored; lose luster. **4.** to become sullied. **—***n.* **5.** a tarnished coating. **6.** tarnished condition; discoloration; alteration of the luster of a metal. **7.** a stain or blemish. [< MF *terniss-,* long s. of *ternir* to dull, deaden; deriv. of *terne* dull, wan < HG; cf. OHG *tarni,* c. OS *derni,* OE *dierne* hidden, obscure; see -ISH[2]] **—tar′nish·a·ble,** *adj.*
—Syn. 2. taint, blemish, soil. **—Ant. 1.** brighten.

tarn·kap·pe (tärn′kap′ə), *n.* (in the *Nibelungenlied*) a cloak, seized from the Nibelungs by Siegfried, which renders the wearer invisible and gives him the strength of 12 men. [< G < *Tarn* mask, camouflage + *Kappe* hooded cloak (see CAP)]

Tar·no·pol (*Pol.* tär nô′pôl; *Russ.* tär′no pol′yə), *n.* Ternopol.

Tar·nów (tär′nōōf), *n.* a city in SE Poland, E of Cracow. 74,000 (est. 1963).

ta·ro (tär′ō, târ′ō), *n., pl.* **-ros. 1.** either of two stemless, araceous plants, *Colocasia esculenta* or *C. antiquorum,* cultivated in tropical regions, in the Pacific islands and elsewhere, for the tuberous, starchy, edible root. **2.** the root of either of these plants. [< Polynesian]

ta·ro·ga·to (tär′ō gə tō′), *n., pl.* **-tos.** a Hungarian woodwind instrument with a conical bore and originally with a double-reed mouthpiece but now with a clarinet mouthpiece. [< Hung]

ta·rok (tə rok′), *n.* a card game dating probably from the Renaissance and still popular in central Europe, originally played with a special pack of 78 cards but now usually played with 32 cards of a regular pack together with 22 tarots. [< obs. It *tarocc(o),* OIt]

ta·rot (ta rō′), *n. Cards.* any of a set of 22 playing cards bearing allegorical representations, used as trump cards in tarok and for fortunetelling. [back formation from *taroto* (pl.) < MF < It *tarocchi,* pl. of *tarocco* < ?]

tarp (tärp), *n. Informal.* tarpaulin. [by shortening]

tar·pan (tär pan′), *n.* a wild horse, *Equus przewalskii,* of central Asia, believed to be a subspecies of the domestic horse. Also called **Przewalski's horse.** [< Kirghiz]

tar·pau·lin (tär pô′lin, tär′pə lin), *n.* **1.** a protective covering of canvas or other material waterproofed with tar, paint, or wax. **2.** a hat, esp. a sailor's, made of or covered with such material. **3.** *Rare.* a sailor. [earlier *tarpauling.* See TAR[1], PALL[1], -ING[1]]

Tar·pe·ia (tär pē′ə), *n. Class. Myth.* a vestal virgin who betrayed Rome to the Sabines and was crushed under their shields when she claimed a reward.

Tar·pe·ian (tär pē′ən), *adj.* of, pertaining to, or noting a rock **(Tarpe′ian Rock′)** on the Capitoline Hill in Rome, from which criminals and traitors were hurled. [< L (*mons*) *Tarpēi(us)* Tarpeian (hill) + -AN]

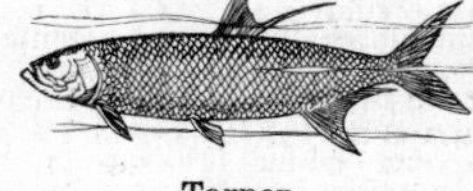

Tarpon (Length to 8 ft.)

tar·pon (tär′pən), *n., pl.* **-pons,** (*esp. collectively*) **-pon.** a large game fish, *Tarpon atlanticus,* found in the warmer waters of the Atlantic Ocean, having a compressed body and large, silvery scales. [?; c. D *tarpoen*]

Tar′pon Springs′ (tär′pon), a town in W Florida. 6768 (1960).

Tar·quin·i·us (tär kwin′ē əs), *n.* **1.** (*Lucius Tarquinius Priscus*) died 578 B.C., king of Rome 616–578. **2.** (*Lucius Tarquinius Superbus*) ("*the Proud*") died 498 B.C., king of Rome 534–510. Also, **Tar′quin.**

tar·ra·did·dle (tar′ə did′əl), *n.* taradiddle.

tar·ra·gon (tar′ə gon′, -gən), *n.* **1.** an Old World, aromatic plant, *Artemisia Dracunculus,* having aromatic leaves used for seasoning. **2.** the leaves themselves. Also called **estragon.** [earlier *taragon* < MF *targon,* var. of *tarc(h)on* < ML < MGk *tarchōn* < Ar *ṭarkhūn*]

Tar′rant City′ (tar′ənt), a town in central Alabama. 7810 (1960).

Tar·ra·sa (tär rä′sä), *n.* a city in NE Spain, N of Barcelona. 78,702 (1955).

tar·ri·ance (tar′ē əns), *n. Archaic.* **1.** delay. **2.** sojourn. [TARRY[1] + -ANCE]

tar·ry[1] (tar′ē), *v.,* **-ried, -ry·ing,** *n., pl.* **-ries. —***v.i* **1.** to remain or stay, as in a place; sojourn: *He tarried in Baltimore on his way to Washington.* **2.** to delay or be tardy in acting, starting, coming, etc.; linger or loiter. **3.** to wait. **—***v.t.* **4.** *Archaic.* to wait for. **—***n.* **5.** *Archaic.* a stay; sojourn. [ME *tarye*] **—tar′ri·er,** *n.*
—Syn. 1. rest, lodge, stop, abide. **3.** See **wait.** **—Ant. 1.** leave.

tar·ry[2] (tär′ē), *adj.,* **-ri·er, -ri·est.** of or like tar; smeared with tar. [TAR[1] + -Y[1]] **—tar′ri·ness,** *n.*

Tar·ry·town (tar′ē toun′), *n.* a village in SE New York, on the Hudson River: restored home of Washington Irving. 11,109 (1960).

tars-, var. of **tarso-** before a vowel: *tarsal.*

tar·sal (tär′səl), *adj.* **1.** of or pertaining to the tarsus of the foot. **2.** pertaining to the tarsi of the eyelids. **—***n.* **3.** a tarsal bone, joint, or the like. [TARS- + -AL[1]]

tar′ sand′, *Geol.* bituminous sand or sandstone from which petroleum can be obtained.

Tar·shish (tär′shish), *n.* an ancient country, of uncertain location, mentioned in the Bible. I Kings 10:22. Also, *Douay Bible,* **Tharsis.**

tar·si·a (tär′sē ə, tär sē′ə), *n.* intarsia. [< It: inlaid woodwork < *tars-* (< Gk *tarsós* frame) + *-ia* -IA]

tar·si·er (tär′sē ər), *n.* a small, arboreal, nocturnal primate of the genus *Tarsius,* of Indonesia and the Philippines, having a long thin tail and very large eyes. [< F < *tarse* TARSUS + *-ier* -ER[2]]

Tarsier, (Total length 13 in.; tail 8 in.)

Tar·ski (tär′skē), *n.* **Alfred,** born 1902, U.S. mathematician and logician, born in Poland.

tarso-, a combining form of **tarsus:** *tarsometatarsus.* Also, *esp. before a vowel,* **tars-.**

tar·so·met·a·tar·sus (tär′sō met′ə tär′səs), *n., pl.* **-si** (-sī). *Ornith.* the large bone in the lower leg of a bird with which the toe bones articulate, formed by the fusion of tarsal and metatarsal bones. [TARSO- + META-TARSUS] —**tar′so·met′a·tar′sal,** *adj.*

tar·sus (tär′səs), *n., pl.* **-si** (-sī). **1.** *Anat., Zool.* the proximal segment of the foot; the collection of bones between the tibia and the metatarsus, entering into the construction of the ankle joint. See diag. under **skeleton. 2.** the small plate of connective tissue along the border of an eyelid. **3.** tarsometatarsus. **4.** the distal part of the leg of an insect, usually subdivided in the adult into two to five segments. See diag. under **coxa.** [< NL < Gk *tarsós* the flat (of the foot)]

Tar·sus (tär′səs), *n.* a city in S Turkey, near the Mediterranean, on the Cydnus River: important seaport of ancient Cilicia; birthplace of Saint Paul. 57,035 (1965).

tart[1] (tärt), *adj.* **1.** sharp to the taste; sour or acid: *tart apples.* **2.** sharp in character, spirit, or expression; cutting; caustic: *a tart remark.* [ME; OE *teart* sharp, rough; akin to D *tarten* to defy, MHG *traz* defiance] —**tart′ish,** *adj.* —**tart′ish·ly,** *adv.* —**tart′ly,** *adv.* —**tart′ness,** *n.*

tart[2] (tärt), *n.* **1.** *U.S.* a small pie filled with cooked fruit or other sweetened preparation, usually having no top crust. **2.** a covered pie containing fruit or the like. **3.** *Chiefly Brit. Slang.* a girl or woman, esp. one of questionable morals. **4.** *Slang.* a prostitute. [late ME *tarte* < MF; cf. ML *tarta*]

Tartan

Tar·ta·gal (tär′tä gäl′), *n.* a city in N Argentina. 8539 (1947).

tar·tan[1] (tär′tᵊn), *n.* **1.** a woolen or worsted cloth woven with stripes of different colors and widths crossing at right angles, worn chiefly by the Scottish Highlanders, each clan having such a distinctive plaid. **2.** a design of such a plaid known by the name of the clan wearing it. **3.** any plaid. —*adj.* **4.** of, pertaining to, or resembling tartan. **5.** made of tartan. [var. of *tertane* < MF *tertaine* (OF *tiretaine*) linsey-woolsey]

tar·tan[2] (tär′tᵊn), *n.* a single-masted vessel with a lateen sail and a jib, used in the Mediterranean. Also, **tar·tan·a** (tär tan′ə, -tä′nə). [earlier *tartane* < F < Ar *tartaneh* transport ship]

tar·tar (tär′tər), *n.* **1.** a hard, brownish or brownish-yellow deposit on the teeth, consisting of salivary secretion, food particles, and various salts, as calcium carbonate and phosphate. **2.** the deposit from wines, potassium bitartrate. **3.** the intermediate product of cream of tartar, obtained from the crude form, argol. [ME < ML *tartar(um)* < Gk *tártaron;* r. ME *tartre* < MF]

Tar·tar (tär′tər), *n.* **1.** a member of any of the various tribes, chiefly Mongolian and Turkish, who, originally under the leadership of Genghis Khan, overran Asia and much of eastern Europe in the Middle Ages. **2.** a member of the descendants of this people variously intermingled with other races and tribes, now inhabiting parts of the European and W and central Asian Soviet Union. **3.** Tatar (def. 1). **4.** (*often l.c.*) a savage, intractable person. **5.** (*l.c.*) a shrew or vixen. **6. catch a Tartar,** to deal with someone or something that proves unexpectedly troublesome or powerful. Also, **catch a tartar.** —*adj.* **7.** of or pertaining to a Tartar or Tartars. **8.** Tatar (def. 3). Also, **Tatar** (for defs. 1, 2, 4–7). [late ME < ML *Tartar(us)* (? var. of **Tātārus* < Pers *Tātār,* by assoc. with TARTARUS); r. ME *Tartre* < MF] —**Tar′tar·ly,** *adv.*

Tar·tar (tär′tər), *n. Obs.* Tartarus.

tar·tar·at·ed (tär′tə rā′tid), *adj. Chem.* tartrated.

Tar′tar Auton′omous So′viet So′cialist Repub′lic. See **Tatar Autonomous Soviet Socialist Republic.**

Tar·tar·e·an (tär târ′ē ən), *adj.* of or pertaining to Tartarus; infernal. [< L *Tartare(us)* of TARTARUS (see -EOUS) + -AN]

tar′tar emet′ic, *Chem., Pharm.* a white, water-soluble, sweet and metallic-tasting, poisonous powder or granules, $K(SbO)C_4H_4O_6 \cdot \frac{1}{2}H_2O$, used as a mordant for dyeing textiles and leather, and in medicine as an expectorant, diaphoretic, and for inducing vomiting. Also called **antimony potassium tartrate, potassium antimonyl tartrate.**

Tar·tar·i·an (tär târ′ē ən), *adj.* of, pertaining to, or characteristic of a Tartar or the Tartars; Tartar. [TARTAR + -IAN]

Tartar′ian as′ter, a Siberian aster, *Aster tataricus,* having blue to purple flowers.

Tartar′ian dog′wood, an Asian dogwood, *Cornus alba,* having bright red twigs and white flowers.

Tartar′ian hon′eysuckle, an Asian honeysuckle, *Lonicera tatarica,* having white to pink flowers. Also called **bush honeysuckle, garden fly honeysuckle.**

tar·tar·ic (tär târ′ik, -tär′-), *adj.* pertaining to or derived from tartar. [TARTAR + -IC]

tartar′ic ac′id, *Chem.* an organic compound, $HOOC(CHOH)_2COOH$, existing in four isomeric forms, the common or dextrorotatory isomer being a white, crystalline, water-soluble powder or transparent crystals: used in effervescent beverages, baking powders, confections, photography, and tanning.

tar·tar·ize (tär′tə rīz′), *v.t.,* **-ized, -iz·ing.** *Chem.* to impregnate, combine, or treat with tartar or potassium bitartrate. [TARTAR + -IZE] —**tar′tar·i·za′tion,** *n.*

tar·tar·ous (tär′tər əs), *adj.* consisting of or containing tartar. [TARTAR + -OUS]

tar′tar sauce′, a mayonnaise dressing, usually with chopped pickles, onions, olives, capers, and green herbs added. Also, **tar′tare sauce′.** [< F *sauce tartare*]

tar′tar steak′, chopped beefsteak seasoned with salt and pepper and served uncooked, often with a raw egg and garnished with capers, onions, etc. Also, **tar′tare steak′.** Also called **steak tartare.**

Tar·ta·rus (tär′tər əs), *n. Class. Myth.* **1.** a sunless abyss, below Hades, in which Zeus imprisoned the Titans. **2.** a place in Hades for the punishment of the wicked. **3.** the underworld in general.

Tar·ta·ry (tär′tə rē), *n.* the historical name of a region of indefinite extent in E Europe and Asia: designates the area overrun by the Tartars in the Middle Ages. Also, **Tatary.** [ME *Tartarye* < MF *Tartarie* < ML *Tartaria.* See TARTAR, -Y[3]]

Tar·ti·ni (tär tē′nē), *n.* **Giu·sep·pe** (jo͞o zep′pe), 1692–1770, Italian violinist and composer.

tart·let (tärt′lit), *n. Brit.* a small pie. [TART[2] + -LET]

tar·trate (tär′trāt), *n. Chem.* a salt or ester of tartaric acid. [*tartr-* (comb. form repr. TARTAR) + -ATE[2]]

tar·trat·ed (tär′trā tid), *adj. Chem.* formed into a tartrate; combined with tartaric acid. Also, **tartarated.** [TARTRATE + -ED[3]]

tar·tra·zine (tär′trə zēn′, -zin), *n. Chem.* a type of yellow dye used in food materials. [*tartr-* (comb. form. repr. TARTAR) + AZINE]

Tar·tu (tär′to͞o), *n.* a city in SE Estonia, in the W Soviet Union. 74,000 (1959). German, **Dorpat.** Russian, **Yurev.**

Tar·tufe (tär to͞of′, -to͝of′; *Fr.* tar tyf′), *n., pl.* **-tufes** (-to͞ofs′, -to͝ofs′; *Fr.* -tyf′). Tartuffe.

Tar·tuffe (tär to͞of′, -to͝of′; *Fr.* tar tyf′), *n., pl.* **-tuffes** (-to͞ofs′, -to͝ofs′; *Fr.* -tyf′) for 2. **1.** (*italics*) a comedy (1664–69) by Molière. **2.** (*often l.c.*) a hypocritical pretender to piety.

Tar·tuf·fer·y (tär to͞of′ə re, -to͞o′fə-), *n.* behavior or character of a Tartuffe, esp. hypocritical piety. [< F *tartufferie.* See TARTUFFE, -RY]

Ta·run·tius (tə run′shəs), *n.* a crater in the first quadrant of the face of the moon: about 38 miles in diameter.

tar·weed (tär′wēd′), *n.* any of several resinous or gummy, composite plants of the genera *Grindelia* and *Media.* [TAR[1] + WEED[1]]

Tar·zan (tär′zən, -zan), *n.* **1. the hero of a series of adventure stories by Edgar Rice Burroughs exemplifying superior physical strength, agility, and prowess.**

ta·sa·jil·lo (tä′sə hē′ō), *n., pl.* **-los.** a bushy or tree-like cactus, *Opuntia leptocaulis,* of the southwestern U.S., having slender spines and greenish-yellow flowers. [< MexSp, dim. of *tasajo* < Sp: piece of meat]

Ta·shi La·ma (tä′shē lä′mə), any of a succession of Tibetan monks and spiritual leaders, second in importance only to the Dalai Lama. Also called **Panchen Lama, Panchen Rimpoche.** [after *Tashi (Lumpo)* name of monastery of which this Lama is abbot]

Tash·kent (täsh kent′, tash-; *Russ.* tu shkyent′), *n.* **a city in and the capital of Uzbekistan, in the NE part. 2,073,000.**

Tash·lich (täsh′likh), *n. Hebrew.* a Jewish rite, performed on the afternoon usually of the first day of Rosh Hashanah, in which the participants symbolically cast off their sins by gathering along the banks of a river, stream, or the like, and reciting prayers of repentance. Also, **Tash′lik.** [lit., thou wilt cast]

ta·sim·e·ter (tə sim′i tər), *n.* an electric device for determining minute changes in temperature and the like by means of the changes in pressure caused by expanding or contracting solids. [< Gk *tâsi(s)* tension + -METER] —**tas·i·met·ric** (tas′ə me′trik), *adj.* —**ta·sim′e·try,** *n.*

task (task, täsk), *n.* **1.** a definite piece of work assigned to, falling to, or expected of a person; duty. **2.** any piece of work. **3.** a matter of considerable labor or difficulty. **4.** *Obs.* a tax or impost. **5. take to task,** to call to account; blame; censure: *The teacher took them to task for being noisy in her absence.* —*v.t.* **6.** to subject to severe or excessive labor or exertion; put a strain upon (powers, resources, etc.). **7.** to impose a task on. **8.** *Obs.* to tax. [ME < ML *tasca,* metathetic var. of *taxa* TAX] —**task′less,** *adj.*

—**Syn. 1, 2.** job, assignment.

Task, The, a poem (1785) by William Cowper.

task′ force′, 1. *Navy, Mil.* a temporary grouping of units under one commander, formed for the purpose of carrying out a specific operation or mission. **2.** a group or committee, usually of experts or specialists, formed for analyzing, investigating, or solving a specific problem.

task·mas·ter (task′mas′tər, täsk′mä′stər), *n.* **1.** one whose function it is to assign tasks to others, esp. burdensome tasks. **2.** a person who supervises rigorously the work of others. [TASK + MASTER] —**task′mas′ter·ship′,** *n.*

task·mis·tress (task′mis′tris, täsk′-), *n.* a female taskmaster. [TASK + MISTRESS]

task·work (task′wûrk′, täsk′-), *n.* **1.** work assigned or imposed as a task. **2.** unpleasant or disagreeable work. **3.** work paid for by the job; piecework. [late ME *taske werke.* See TASK, WORK]

AUSTRALIA
Sydney
Adelaide
Canberra
Melbourne
INDIAN OCEAN
PACIFIC OCEAN
Tasmania
Hobart

Tasm., Tasmania.

Tas·man (taz′mən; *Du.* täs′män′), *n.* **A·bel Jans·zoon** (ä′bəl yän′sōn), 1602?–59, Dutch navigator and explorer.

Tas·ma·ni·a (taz mā′nē ə), *n.* an island S of Australia: a state of the commonwealth of Australia. 350,340 (1961); 26,215 sq. mi. *Cap.:* Hobart. Formerly, **Van Diemen's Land.** —**Tas·ma′ni·an,** *adj., n.*

Tasma′nian dev′il, a small, ferocious, carnivorous marsupial, *Sarcophilus harrisii,* of Tasmania, having a black coat with white patches.

Tasma′nian wolf′, the thylacine. Also called **Tasma′nian ti′ger.**

Tasmanian devil (Total length 3 ft.; tail 10½ in.)

Tas′man Sea′ (taz′mən), a part of the Pacific Ocean between SE Australia and New Zealand.

tass (tas), *n. Chiefly Scot.* **1.** a cup or small goblet, esp. an ornamental one. **2.** the contents of a cup or goblet; a small draught, as of liquor. Also, **tassie.** [late ME *tasse* < MF < Ar *tass, tassah* basin < Pers *tast* cup]

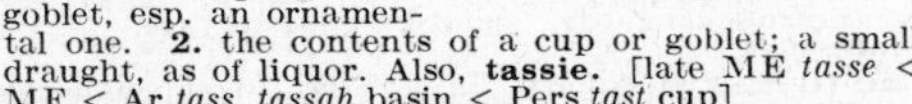

Tass (tas, täs), *n.* **a news-gathering agency of the former Soviet Union: merged with an alternative news service to form Itar-Tass (Russian Information Telegraph Agency). Also, TASS [< Russ. acronym from *T(elegráfnoe) a(géntstvo) S(ovétskogo) S(oyúza)* Telegraph Agency of the Soviet Union]**

tasse (tas), *n. Armor.* tasset.

tas·sel[1] (tas′əl), *n., v.,* **-seled, -sel·ing** or (*esp. Brit.*) **-selled, -sel·ling.** —*n.* **1.** a pendent ornament, originally a clasp consisting commonly of a bunch of threads, small cords, or strands hanging from a roundish knob or head. **2.** something resembling this, as the inflorescence of certain plants, esp. that at the summit of a stalk of corn. —*v.t.* **3.** to furnish or adorn with tassels. **4.** to form into a tassel or tassels. **5.** to remove the tassel from (growing corn) in order to improve the crop. —*v.i.* **6.** (of corn) to put forth tassels. [ME < OF: fastening for cloak < LL **tassell(us),* b. L *tessella* (dim. of *tessera* die for gaming) and *taxillus* (dim. of *tālus* die for gaming). See TASSELLATE, TALUS[1]] —**tas′sel·er;** *esp. Brit.,* **tas′sel·ler,** *n.* —**tas′sel·y;** *esp. Brit.,* **tas′sel·ly,** *adv.*

tas·sel[2] (tas′əl), *n. Obs.* tercel. [late ME, var. of *tarcel* TERCEL; cf. *cuss* for CURSE, etc.]

tas′sel flow′er, love-lies-bleeding.

tas′sel hy′acinth, a small, bulbous, perennial herb, *Muscari comosum,* of Eurasia, having blue or violet-colored flowers.

tas·set (tas′it), *n. Armor.* either of two pieces of plate armor hanging from the fauld to protect the upper parts of the thighs. Also, **tace, tasse.** [< F *tassette,* MF *tassete* < *tasse* pouch (< MHG *tasche,* lit., pendent object) + *-ete* -ET]

tass·ie (tas′ē), *n. Chiefly Scot.* tass. [TASS + -IE]

Tas·so (tas′ō; *It.* täs′sô), *n.* **Tor·qua·to** (tôr kwä′tô), 1544–95, Italian poet.

taste (tāst), *v.,* **tast·ed, tast·ing,** *n.* —*v.t.* **1.** to try or test the flavor or quality of (something) by taking some into the mouth: *to taste food.* **2.** to eat or drink a little of: *She barely tasted her dinner. He hadn't tasted food for three days.* **3.** to perceive or distinguish the flavor of: *to taste the wine in a sauce.* **4.** to have or get experience, esp. a slight experience: *these young men who had only begun to taste life.* **5.** *Dial.* to perceive in any way. **6.** *Archaic.* to enjoy or appreciate. **7.** *Obs.* **a.** to examine by touch; feel. **b.** to test or try. —*v.i.* **8.** to try the flavor or quality of something. **9.** to eat or drink a little (usually fol. by *of*): *She tasted of the cake.* **10.** to perceive or distinguish the flavor of anything. **11.** to have experience of something, however limited or slight. **12.** to have a particular flavor (often fol. by *of*): *The milk tastes sour. The bread tastes of mold.* **13.** to smack or savor (usually fol. by *of*): *The story tastes of treason.* —*n.* **14.** the act of tasting food or drink. **15.** the sense by which the flavor or savor of things is perceived when they are brought into contact with the tongue. **16.** sensation, flavor, or quality as perceived by this sense. **17.** a small quantity tasted; a morsel, bit, or sip. **18.** a relish, liking, or partiality for something: *a taste for music.* **19.** the sense of what is fitting, harmonious, or beautiful; the perception and enjoyment of what constitutes excellence in the fine arts, literature, etc. **20.** the sense of what is seemly, polite, tactful, etc., to say or do in a given social situation. **21.** one's personal attitude or reaction toward an aesthetic phenomenon or social situation, regarded as either good or bad. **22.** the ideas of aesthetic excellence or of aesthetically valid forms prevailing in a culture or personal to an individual: *I consulted only my own taste in decorating this room; a sample of Victorian taste.* **23.** the formal idiom preferred by a certain artist or culture; style; manner: *a façade in the Baroque taste.* **24.** a slight experience or a sample of something: *a taste of adventure.* **25.** *Obs.* test or trial. **26. to one's taste,** agreeable or pleasing to one: *He found no ties completely to his taste.* [ME *taste(n)* (to) touch, taste < OF *taster* to touch, explore by touching (MF also to taste); c. It. *tastare,* Pr, OSp *tastar;* < ?] —**tast′a·ble, taste′a·ble,** *adj.*

—**Syn. 1.** savor. **16.** TASTE, FLAVOR, SAVOR refer to a quality that is perceived when a substance is placed upon the tongue. TASTE is the general word: *the taste of roast beef.* FLAVOR is a characteristic taste, usually of a pleasing kind, and as of some ingredient put into the food: *lemon flavor.* SAVOR, much less common than TASTE or FLAVOR, implies pleasing scent as well as taste or flavor, and connotes enjoyment in tasting: *The sauce has an excellent savor.* **18.** fondness, disposition, appreciation, predisposition. **19.** discernment, perception, judgment. —**Ant. 18.** antipathy.

taste′ bud′, one of numerous small, flask-shaped bodies chiefly in the epithelium of the tongue, which are the end organs for the sense of taste.

taste·ful (tāst′fəl), *adj.* having, displaying, or in accordance with good taste: *He limited himself to a few tasteful remarks on marriage.* [TASTE + -FUL] —**taste′ful·ly,** *adv.* —**taste′ful·ness,** *n.*

taste·less (tāst′lis), *adj.* **1.** having no taste or flavor; insipid. **2.** dull; uninteresting. **3.** lacking in good taste; showing lack of good taste: *a tasteless remark about foreigners.* **4.** *Rare.* lacking the physical sense of taste. [TASTE + -LESS] —**taste′less·ly,** *adv.* —**taste′less·ness,** *n.*

tast·er (tā′stər), *n.* **1.** a person who tastes, esp. one skilled in distinguishing the qualities of liquors, tea, etc., by the taste. **2.** a container for taking samples or tasting. **3.** a wide shallow vessel, usually metal, for holding wine to be tasted, as by a professional taster. **4.** a pipette. **5.** a person employed or ordered to taste the food and drink prepared for a king, dictator, etc., to ascertain the presence of poison. **6.** a person able to taste phenylthiourea. [ME *tastour* < AF. See TASTE, -ER[1]]

tast·y (tā′stē), *adj.,* **tast·i·er, tast·i·est. 1.** good-tasting; savory: *a tasty canapé.* **2.** *Informal.* having or showing good taste; tasteful. [TASTE + -Y[1]] —**tast′i·ly,** *adv.* —**tast′i·ness,** *n.*

tat (tat), *v.i., v.t.,* **tat·ted, tat·ting.** to do, or make by, tatting. [back formation from TATTING]

TAT, See **Thematic Apperception Test.**

ta ta (tä tä′), *Chiefly Brit.* good-by. [?]

ta·ta·mi (tə tä′mē), *n., pl.* **-mi, -mis.** (in Japanese building) any of a number of thick, woven straw mats of uniform dimensions, about three feet by six feet, the placing of which determines the dimensions of an interior. [< Jap]

Ta·tar (tä′tər), *n.* **1.** any of several Turkic languages of W central Asia and E Europe. **2.** Tartar (defs. 1, 2, 4, 5, 6). —*adj.* **3.** of or pertaining to Tatar. **4.** Tartar (def. 7). Also, **Tartar** (for defs. 1, 3). [see TARTAR] —**Ta·tar·i·an** (tä târ′ē ən), **Ta·tar·ic** (tä tar′ik), *adj.*

Ta′tar Auton′omous Repub′lic, an autonomous republic in the E Russian Federation in Europe. 3,640,000; ab. 26,255 sq. mi. *Cap.:* Kazan. Also, **Tartar Autonomous Republic.**

Ta·ta·ry (tä′tə rē), *n.* Tartary.

tat·beb (tat′beb), *n.* (in ancient Egypt) a sandal. [vocalized alter. of Egypt *tbtbty* pair of sandals]

tate (tāt), *n. Scot. and North Eng.* a small tuft or handful, as of wool, hair, grass, or the like. [akin to TATTER; cf. dial. variants *tett, teat, tait, taut, tat,* and Icel (*ō*)*tōt* coarsest wool]

Tate (tāt), *n.* **1. Sir Henry,** 1819–99, English merchant and philanthropist: founder of the national art gallery of England. **2. (John Or·ley) Allen** (ôr′lē), 1899–1979, U.S. poet, critic, and editor. **3. Na·hum** (nā′əm, -həm), 1652–1715, English poet and playwright, born in Ireland: poet laureate 1692–1715.

ta·ter (tā′tər), *n. Dial.* potato. [by aphesis, and addition of hiatus-filling *r*]

Ta·tha·ga·ta (tə tä′gə tə), *n.* one of the names of Buddha. [< Skt *tathāgata* < *tathā* thus + *gata* gone < *gamati* he comes]

Ta·tha·ta (tut′ə tä′), *n. Buddhism.* the absoluteness of Sunya. Also called **Bhutatathata.** [< Pali *tathatā* < *tathā* thus < Skt]

Ta·tia·na (tä tyä′nä), *n.* a girl's given name.

Ta·tius (tā′shəs), *n. Rom. Legend.* a Sabine king who, following the rape of the Sabine women, attacked Rome and who eventually ruled with Romulus. Also, **Titus.**

Tat·ler, The (tat′lər), a triweekly periodical (1709–11) written, edited, and published by Richard Steele with the collaboration of Joseph Addison.

tat·ou·ay (tat′o͞o ā′, tä′to͞o ī′), *n.* an armadillo, *Tatoua unicintus,* of tropical South America. [< Sp *tatuay* < Pg < Guarani *tatu-ai,* equiv. to *tatu* armadillo + *ai* worthless (i.e., not edible)]

tat·pur·u·sha (tat po͝or′ə shə, tut-), *n. Linguistics.* a compound of two words in which the first is an attributive noun and the second a substantive, as *bookcase, aircraft, flowerpot,* etc. [< Skt *tatpuruṣa* his man, servant (repr. this type of compound) < *tat-* that one (neut. demonstrative pron.) + *puruṣa* man]

Ta′tra Moun′tains (tä′trə), a mountain range in N Slovakia and S Poland: a part of the central Carpathian Mountains. Highest peak, Gerlachovka, 8737 ft. Also called **High Tatra.**

tat·ter[1] (tat′ər), *n.* **1.** a torn piece hanging loose from the main part, as of a garment, flag, etc. **2.** a separate torn piece. **3. tatters,** torn or ragged clothing: *dressed in rags and tatters.* [late ME < Scand; cf. Icel *tötturr* rag, akin to OE *tætteca* rag, shred] —*v.t.* **4.** to tear or wear to tatters. —*v.i.* **5.** to become ragged. [back formation from TATTERED]

tat·ter[2] (tat′ər), *n.* one whose occupation is tatting. [TAT + -ER[1]]

tat·ter·de·mal·ion (tat′ər di māl′yən, -mal′-), *n.* a person in tattered clothing; a ragged fellow. [first written *tatter-de-mallian* and rhymed with *Italian;* see TATTER[1]; *-de-mallian* < ?]

tat·tered (tat′ərd), *adj.* **1.** torn to tatters; ragged: *a tattered flag.* **2.** wearing ragged clothing: *a tattered old man.* [TATTER[1] (n.) + -ED[3]]

tat·ter·sall (tat′ər sôl′), *n.* **1.** a fabric with brightly colored crossbars in a plaid pattern. —*adj.* **2.** made of this fabric: *a tattersall vest.* [after *Tattersall's,* London horse market, where brightly-colored blankets were used]

tat·tie (tat′ē), *n.* tatty[2].

tat·ting (tat′ing), *n.* **1.** the act or process of making a kind of knotted lace of cotton or linen thread with a shuttle. **2.** such lace. [?]

tat·tle (tat′əl), *v.,* **-tled, -tling,** *n.* —*v.i.* **1.** to let out secrets. **2.** to chatter, prate, or gossip. —*v.t.* **3.** to utter idly; disclose by gossiping. —*n.* **4.** act of tattling. **5.** idle talk; chatter; gossip. [late ME < MFlem *tatelen;* c. MLG *tatelen* to prattle, tattle] —**tat′tling·ly,** *adv.*

tat·tler (tat′lər), *n.* **1.** a person who tattles; telltale. **2.** any of several shore birds of the genus *Heteroscelus,* having a loud, whistling cry. **3.** any of various related shore birds having shrill cries, as the yellowlegs. **4.** a small bass, *Prionodes phoebe,* of the West Indies and Florida. [TATTLE + -ER[1]]

tat·tle·tale (tat′əl tāl′), *n.* **1.** a talebearer or informer, esp. among children. —*adj.* **2.** telltale; revealing: *a tattletale smear of lipstick on his collar.* [TATTLE + TALE]

tat·too[1] (ta to͞o′), *n., pl.* **-toos. 1.** a signal on a drum, bugle, or trumpet at night, for soldiers or sailors to go to their quarters. **2.** a knocking or strong pulsation: *My heart beat a tattoo on my ribs.* **3.** *Brit.* an outdoor military pageant or display. [earlier *taptoo* < D *taptoe,* lit., the tap(room) is to (i.e., shut)]

tat·too[2] (ta to͞o′), *n., pl.* **-toos,** *v.,* **-tooed, -too·ing.** —*n.* **1.** act or practice of marking the skin with indelible patterns, pictures, legends, etc., by making punctures in it and inserting pigments. **2.** a pattern, picture, legend, etc., so made. —*v.t.* **3.** to mark with tattoos. **4.** to put (designs or legends) on the skin. [< Marquesan *tatu;* r. *tattow* < Tahitian *tatau*] —**tat·too′er, tat·too′ist,** *n.*

tat tvam as·i (tat tvam as′ē, tut twum us′ē), *Sanskrit.* Thou art That (the statement, in the Upanishads, that Atman is identical with Brahman).

tat·ty[1] (tat′ē), *adj.* vulgar; crude; cheap. [perh. akin to OE *tætec* tatter, rag]

tat·ty[2] (tat′ē), *n., pl.* **-ties.** (in India) a screen, usually made of coarse, fragrant fibers, placed over a window or door and kept moistened with water in order to cool and deodorize the room. Also, **tattie.** [< Hindi *ṭaṭṭī*]

Ta·tum (tā′təm), *n.* **1. Art,** 1910–56, U.S. jazz pianist. **2. Edward Law·rie** (lôr′ē), 1909–75, U.S. biochemist: Nobel prize for medicine 1958.

tau (tô, tou), *n.* **1.** the 19th letter of the Greek alphabet (Τ, τ). **2.** the consonant sound represented by this letter. **3.** tav. [ME < L < Gk < Sem; cf. Heb *tāw*]

Tau·ber (tou′bər), *n.* **Richard,** 1892–1948, Austrian tenor, in England after 1940.

Tauch·nitz (toukн′nits), *n.* **Karl Chri·stoph Trau·gott** (kärl kris′tôf trou′gôt), 1761–1836, and his son, **Karl Chri·sti·an Phi·lipp** (kris′tē än′ fē′lip, fil′ip), 1798–1884, German printers and publishers.

tau′ cross′, a T-shaped cross. See illus. under **cross.**

taught (tôt), *v.* pt. and pp. of **teach.**

taunt[1] (tônt, tänt), *v.t.* **1.** to reproach in a sarcastic, insulting, or jeering manner; mock. **2.** to provoke by taunts; twit. —*n.* **3.** an insulting gibe or sarcasm; scornful reproach or challenge. **4.** *Obs.* an object of insulting gibes or scornful reproaches. [?] —**taunt′er,** *n.* —**taunt′ing·ly,** *adv.*
—**Syn. 1.** censure, upbraid, flout, insult. **2.** jeer. See **ridicule. 3.** jeer, scoff, derision, insult, censure, ridicule.

taunt[2] (tônt, tänt), *adj. Naut.* tall and well-stayed, as a mast. [akin to *ataunt* in phrase *all ataunt* fully rigged (said of a ship); cf. F *boire d'autant* to drink a great deal]

Taun·ton (tän′tən *for 1;* tôn′tən *for 2*), *n.* **1.** a city in SE Massachusetts. 41,132 (1960). **2.** a city in and the county seat of Somersetshire, in SW England. 35,178 (1961).

taupe (tōp), *n.* a dark brownish gray, sometimes slightly tinged with brown, purple, yellow, or green. [< F < L *talpa* mole]

taur-, var. of **tauro-** before a vowel: *taurine.*

Tau·ra (tôr′ə), *n.* a sterile cow sacred to the ancient Roman gods of the underworld.

Tau·rang·a (tou räng′ə), *n.* a city on the N coast of North Island, in N New Zealand. 7823 (1957).

tauri-, var. of **tauro-.**

tau·ri·form (tôr′ə fôrm′), *adj.* shaped like a bull or the head or horns of a bull. [< L *tauriform(is).* See TAURI-, -FORM]

tau·rine[1] (tôr′īn, -in), *adj.* **1.** of, pertaining to, or resembling a bull. **2.** pertaining to the zodiacal sign Taurus. [< L *taurīn(us).* See TAUR-, -INE[1]]

tau·rine[2] (tôr′ēn, -in), *n. Chem.* a neutral crystalline substance, $H_2NCH_2CH_2SO_3H$, obtained from the bile of oxen and other animals, from muscles, lung tissue, etc., and as a decomposition product of taurocholic acid: used in biochemical research. [TAUR(OCHOLIC) + -INE[2]]

tauro-, a learned borrowing from Latin and Greek meaning "bull," used in the formation of compound words: *taurocholic.* Also, **taur-, tauri-.** [comb. form repr. L *taurus,* Gk *taûros*]

tau·ro·bo·li·um (tôr′ə bō′lē əm), *n., pl.* **-li·a** (-lē ə). **1.** the sacrifice of a bull, followed by the baptism of neophytes in the blood, as practiced anciently in the rites of Mithras or Cybele. **2.** *Fine Arts.* a representation of the killing of a bull, as in Mithraic art. [< LL < Gk *taurobólion* < *tauroból(os)* bull sacrifice (*taûro(s)* bull + *bólos* a cast, throw, akin to *bolḗ* a wound, *bállein* to throw) + *-ion* dim. suffix]

tau·ro·cho·lic (tôr′ə kō′lik, -kol′ik), *adj. Chem.* of or derived from taurocholic acid. [TAURO- + CHOLIC]

tau′rocho′lic ac′id, *Chem.* an acid, $C_{26}H_{45}NO_7S$, occurring as a sodium salt in the bile of carnivorous animals, which on hydrolysis yields taurine and cholic acid.

tau·rom·a·chy (tô rom′ə kē), *n.* the art or technique of bullfighting. [< Sp *tauromaquia* < Gk *tauromachía.* See TAURO-, -MACHY] —**tau·ro·ma·chi·an** (tôr′ə mā′kē ən), *adj.*

tau·ro·ma·quia (tou′rô mä′kyä), *n. Spanish.* tauromachy.

Tau·rus (tôr′əs), *n., gen.* **Tau·ri** (tôr′ī) for 1. **1.** *Astron.* the Bull, a zodiacal constellation between Gemini and Aries, containing the bright star Aldebaran. **2.** the second sign of the zodiac. See illus. under **zodiac.** [< L]

Tau·rus (tôr′əs), *n.* a mountain range in S Turkey: highest peak, 12,251 ft.

Taus·sig (tou′sig), *n.* **Frank William,** 1859–1940, U.S. economist.

taut (tôt), *adj.* **1.** tightly drawn; tense; not slack. **2.** emotionally or mentally strained or tense: *taut nerves.* **3.** in good order or condition; tidy; neat. [earlier *taught,* ME *tought;* akin to TOW[1]] —**taut′ly,** *adv.* —**taut′ness,** *n.*

taut·ed (tä′tit), *adj. Scot.* tangled or matted together, esp. wood or hair. [*taut* (var. of TATE) + -ED[3]]

taut·en (tôt′ən), *v.t., v.i.* to make or become taut. [TAUT + -EN[1]]

tauto-, a learned borrowing from Greek meaning "same," used in the formation of compound words: *tautomerism.* [< Gk, comb. form of *tautó,* contr. of *tò autó* the same]

tau·to·chrone (tô′tə krōn′), *n. Geom.* the curve traced by a body moving without friction under the force of gravity such that the time required to reach a fixed point is the same regardless of the starting point. [< F; see TAUTO-, CHRON-]

tau·tog (tô tog′, -tôg′), *n.* a black labrid fish, *Tautoga onitis,* found along the North Atlantic coast of the U.S. [< Narragansett *tautauog,* pl. of *tautau* sheepshead]

tau·tol·o·gise (tô tol′ə jīz′), *v.i.,* **-gised, -gis·ing.** *Chiefly Brit.* tautologize.

tau·tol·o·gism (tô tol′ə jiz′əm), *n. Rare.* **1.** the use of tautology. **2.** a tautology. [TAUTOLOG(Y) + -ISM]

tau·tol·o·gize (tô tol′ə jīz′), *v.i.,* **-gized, -giz·ing.** to use tautology. [TAUTOLOG(Y) + -IZE]

tau·tol·o·gy (tô tol′ə jē), *n., pl.* **-gies. 1.** needless repetition of an idea, esp. in words other than those of the immediate context, without imparting additional force or clearness, as in "widow woman." **2.** an instance of such repetition: *Anything he either says or writes is always filled with tautologies.* **3.** *Logic.* **a.** a law that can be shown on the basis of certain rules to exclude no logical possibilities. **b.** an instance of such a law. [< LL *tautologia* < Gk. See TAUTO-, -LOGY] —**tau·to·log·i·cal** (tôt′əloj′i kəl), **tau′to·log′ic,** *adj.* —**tau′to·log′i·cal·ly, tau·tol′o·gous·ly,** *adv.* —**tau·tol′o·gist,** *n.*

tau·to·mer (tô′tə mər), *n. Chem.* a compound that exhibits tautomerism. [back formation from TAUTOMERISM]

tau·tom·er·ism (tô tom′ə riz′əm), *n. Chem.* the ability of certain organic compounds to react in isomeric structures which differ from each other in the position of a hydrogen atom and a double bond. The individual tautomers are in equilibrium, and some pairs of tautomeric isomers have been isolated. [TAUTO- + (ISO)MERISM] —**tau·to·mer·ic** (tô′tə mer′ik), *adj.*

tau·tom·er·ize (tô tom′ə rīz′), *v.,* **-ized, -iz·ing.** —*v.i.* **1.** to undergo tautomerism. —*v.t.* **2.** to cause to undergo tautomerism. [TAUTOMER(ISM) + -IZE] —**tau·tom′er·iz′a·ble,** *adj.* —**tau·tom′er·i·za′tion,** *n.*

tau·to·nym (tô′tə nim), *n. Bot., Zool.* a scientific name in which the generic and the specific names are the same, as *Chloris chloris* (the greenfinch). [< Gk *tautṓnym(os),* equiv. to *taut(o)-* TAUTO- + *-onymos* -ONYM] —**tau′to·nym′ic, tau·ton·y·mous** (tô ton′ə məs), *adj.* —**tau·ton′y·my,** *n.*

tav (täf, tôf), *n.* **1.** the 23rd letter of the Hebrew alphabet. **2.** the consonant sound represented by this letter. [< Heb, var. of *tāw* TAU]

Ta·var·es (tə vâr′ēz), *n.* a town in central Florida 2724 (1960).

Ta·vel (tä vel′), *n.* a dry rosé wine from the Rhone region of France.

tav·ern (tav′ərn), *n.* **1.** a place where liquors are sold to be consumed on the premises. **2.** a public house for travelers and others; inn. [ME *taverne* < OF < L *taberna* hut, inn, wine shop] —**tav′ern·less,** *adj.*
—**Syn. 1.** bar; pub. **2.** hostelry. See **hotel.**

tav·ern·er (tav′ər nər), *n.* **1.** *Archaic.* the owner of a tavern. **2.** *Obs.* a frequenter of taverns. [ME < AF, equiv. to OF *tavernier.* See TAVERN, -ER[2]]

Tav·ern·er (tav′ər nər), *n.* **John,** c1495–1548?, English organist and composer.

tav′ern ta′ble, a short table having a narrow, deep apron and legs connected by a box stretcher.

taw[1] (tô), *n.* **1.** a choice or fancy marble used as a shooter. **2.** a game in which marbles are arranged in the center of a circle drawn or scratched on the ground, the object being to knock out as many as possible from the circle; ringer. **3.** Also, **taw′ line′.** the line from which the players shoot. —*v.i.* **4.** to shoot a marble. [? special use of OE *getawu* tools, private parts (? whence testes)]

taw[2] (tô), *v.t.* **1.** to prepare or dress (some raw material) for use or further manipulation. **2.** to transform the skin of an animal into white leather by the application of minerals, emulsions, etc. **3.** *Archaic.* to flog; thrash. [ME *tawe(n),* OE *tawian;* c. D *touwen,* Goth *taujan*] —**taw′er,** *n.*

taw[3] (täf, tôf), *n.* tav.

taw·dry (tô′drē), *adj.,* **-dri·er, -dri·est.** (of finery, trappings, etc.) gaudy; showy and cheap. [short for (*Sain*)*t Audrey* lace, i.e., lace bought at her fair in Ely] —**taw′dri·ly,** *adv.* —**taw′dri·ness,** *n.*
—**Syn.** flashy, meretricious. —**Ant.** elegant.

taw·ie (tô′ē), *adj. Scot.* docile; easy to manage. [TAW[2] (in obs. sense mistreat, abuse) + *-ie* -Y[1]]

taw·ney (tô′nē), *adj.,* **-ni·er, -ni·est,** *n.* tawny.

Taw·ney (tô′nē, tā′-), *n.* **Richard Henry,** 1880–1962, English historian, born in Calcutta.

taw·ny (tô′nē), *adj.,* **-ni·er, -ni·est,** *n.* —*adj.* **1.** of a dark yellowish or dull yellowish-brown color. —*n.* **2.** a shade of brown tinged with yellow; dull yellowish brown. [ME *tauny* < AF *taune* < MF *tane,* ptp. of *taner* to TAN] —**taw′ni·ly,** *adv.* —**taw′ni·ness,** *n.*

taw·pie (tô′pē), *Scot.* —*n.* **1.** a foolish or thoughtless girl or young woman. —*adj.* **2.** (of girls and women) giddy; foolish. [*tawp* (< Scand; cf. Norw, Sw dial. *tåp* simpleton) + -IE]

taw·py (tô′pē), *n., pl.* **-pies,** *adj. Scot.* tawpie.

taws (tôz, täz), *n., pl.* **taws.** *Chiefly Scot.* **1.** a whip or leather thong used to drive a spinning top. **2.** a leather whip having its tip divided into smaller strips, used to punish students. [pl. of *taw* < Scand; cf. Icel *tang* string, rope, c. OE *tēag* TIE]

taw·yer (tô′yər), *n.* one who taws. [ME *tawiere;* OE *tawi(an)* (to) TAW[2] + *-ere* -ER[1]]

tax (taks), *n.* **1.** a sum of money demanded by a government for its support or for specific facilities or services, levied upon incomes, property, sales, etc. **2.** a burdensome charge, obligation, duty, or demand. —*v.t.* **3.** (of a government) **a.** to demand a tax from (a person, business, etc.). **b.** to demand a tax in consideration of the possession or occurrence of (income, goods, sales, etc.), usually in proportion to the value of money involved. **4.** to lay a burden on; make serious demands on: *to tax one's resources.* **5.** to take to task; censure; reprove; accuse: *to tax one with laziness.* **6.** *Informal.* to charge: *What did he tax you for that?* **7.** *Archaic.* to estimate or determine the amount or value of. [ME *taxe(n)* < ML *taxāre* to tax, appraise, L: to appraise, handle, freq. of *tangere* to touch] —**tax′er,** *n.* —**tax′ing·ly,** *adv.* —**tax′less,** *adj.* —**tax′less·ly,** *adv.* —**tax′less·ness,** *n.*
—**Syn. 1.** duty, impost, levy.

tax-, var. of **taxo-** before a vowel: *taxeme.* Also, **taxi-.**

tax·a·ble (tak′sə bəl), *adj.* **1.** capable of being taxed; subject to tax: *a taxable gain.* —*n.* **2.** Usually, **taxables.** persons, items of property, etc., that are subject to tax. [ME; see TAX, -ABLE] —**tax′a·bil′i·ty, tax′a·ble·ness,** *n.* —**tax′a·bly,** *adv.*

tax·a·ceous (tak sā′shəs), *adj.* belonging to the *Taxaceae,* or yew family of trees and shrubs. [< NL *taxāceus* < L *tax(us)* yew + *-āceus* -ACEOUS]

tax·a·tion (tak sā′shən), *n.* **1.** the act of taxing. **2.** the fact of being taxed. **3.** a tax imposed. **4.** the revenue raised by taxes. [< ML *taxātiōn-* (s. of *taxātiō*) an appraising (see TAX, -ATION); r. ME *taxacioun* < AF] —**tax·a′tion·al,** *adj.*

tax-de·duct·i·ble (taks′di duk′tə bəl), *adj.* noting an item, the value or cost of which is deductible from the gross amount on which a tax is calculated.

tax′ deduc′tion, a deduction from the gross amount on which a tax is calculated.

tax·eme (tak′sēm), *n. Ling.* a feature of the arrangement of elements in a construction, as selection, order, phonetic modification, or modulation. [TAX- + -EME] —**tax·e′mic,** *adj.*

tax-ex·empt (taks′ig zempt′), *adj.* **1.** not subject or liable to taxation: *tax-exempt imports.* **2.** providing income that is not taxable: *tax-exempt municipal bonds.*

tax·gath·er·er (taks′gath′ər ər), *n.* a person who collects taxes. [TAX + GATHERER] —**tax′gath′er·ing,** *n.*

tax·i (tak′sē), *n., pl.* **tax·is** or **tax·ies,** *v.,* **tax·ied, tax·i·ing** or **tax·y·ing.** —*n.* **1.** a taxicab. —*v.i.* **2.** to ride or travel in a taxicab. **3.** (of an airplane) to move over the surface of the ground or water under its own power. —*v.t.* **4.** to cause (an airplane) to taxi. [short for TAXICAB]

taxi-, var. of **taxo-:** *taxidermy.* Also, **tax-.**

tax·i·cab (tak′sē kab′), *n.* a public passenger vehicle, esp. an automobile, usually fitted with a taximeter. [TAXI(METER) + CAB]

tax′i danc′er, a girl or woman employed, as by a dance hall, to dance with patrons who pay a fee for each dance or for a set period of time. [so called because such a dancer, like a taxi, is hired for the occasion]

tax·i·der·my (tak′si dûr′mē), *n.* the art of preparing and preserving the skins of animals and of stuffing and mounting them in lifelike form. [TAX- + Gk *-dermia;* see -DERM, -Y³] —**tax′i·der′mal, tax′i·der′mic,** *adj.* —**tax′i·der′mist,** *n.*

Tax·i·la (tak′sə lə), *n.* an archaeological site near Rawalpindi, West Pakistan: ruins of three successive cities on the same site, dating from about the 7th century B.C. to about the 7th century A.D.: Buddhist center.

tax·i·me·ter (tak′sē mē′tər, tak sim′i tər), *n.* a device fitted to a taxicab or other vehicle, for automatically computing and indicating the fare due. [alter. of *taxameter* < G < *Taxa* (< ML: tax, charge) + *-meter* -METER]

tax·i·plane (tak′sē plān′), *n.* an airplane available for chartered or unscheduled trips. [TAXI(CAB + AIR)-PLANE]

tax·is¹ (tak′sis), *n.* **1.** arrangement or order, as in one of the physical sciences. **2.** *Biol.* movement of an organism in a particular direction in response to an external stimulus. **3.** *Surg.* the replacing of a displaced part, or the reducing of a hernial tumor or the like, by manipulation without cutting. **4.** *Archit.* the adaptation to the purposes of a building of its various parts. [< NL < Gk *táxis,* equiv. to *tak-* (var. s. of *tássein* to arrange, put in order) + *-sis* -SIS]

tax·is² (tak′sēs), *n.* a pl. of **taxi.**

-taxis, a combining form of **taxis¹:** *heterotaxis.* Cf. **tax-, taxo-, -taxy.**

tax′i strip′, *Aeron.* a narrow taxiway.

tax·ite (tak′sīt), *n.* *Petrog.* a lava appearing to be formed from fragments, because of its parts having different colors, textures, etc. [TAX- + -ITE¹] —**tax·it·ic** (tak sit′ik), *adj.*

tax·i·way (tak′sē wā′), *n.* any surface area of an airport used for taxiing airplanes to and from a runway, parking apron, terminal, etc. [TAXI (V.) + WAY]

taxo-, a combining form of **taxis¹:** *taxonomy.* Also, **tax-, taxi-.**

tax·on (tak′son), *n., pl.* **tax·a** (tak′sə). a taxonomic category, as a species, genus, etc. [back formation from TAXONOMY]

tax·on·o·my (tak son′ə mē), *n.* **1.** the science or technique of classification. **2.** the science dealing with the identification, naming, and classification of organisms. [F *taxonomie.* See TAXO-, -NOMY] —**tax·o·nom·ic** (tak′sə nom′ik), **tax′o·nom′i·cal,** *adj.* —**tax′o·nom′i·cal·ly,** *adv.* —**tax·on′o·mist, tax·on′o·mer,** *n.*

tax·paid (taks′pād′), *adj.* salaried or paid for by taxes: *taxpaid teachers; taxpaid highways.* [TAX + PAID]

tax·pay·er (taks′pā′ər), *n.* **1.** a person who pays a tax or is subject to taxation. **2.** a temporary building that yields rent sufficient only to pay the taxes on the property on which it stands. [TAX + PAYER] —**tax′pay′ing,** *n.*

tax′ rate′, the percentage of the value of a property to be paid as a tax.

tax′ sale′, the sale of real property, as land, usually at auction by a public authority, in order to pay delinquent taxes assessed upon its owner.

tax′ stamp′, a stamp required to be affixed to certain products, documents, etc., before they change hands to indicate that a tax has been paid.

tax′ ti′tle, *Law.* a title, acquired by the purchaser at a forced sale of property for nonpayment of taxes.

tax·us (tak′səs), *n., pl.* **tax·us.** any plant of the genus *Taxus,* comprising the yews. [< L: yew, yew-tree]

-taxy, var. of **-taxis:** *heterotaxy.* [< Gk *-taxia.* See TAXIS¹, -Y³]

Tay (tā), *n.* **1.** a river flowing through central Scotland into the Firth of Tay. 118 mi. long. **2. Firth of,** an estuary of the North Sea, off the coast of central Scotland. 25 mi. long.

Ta·yg·e·te (tā ij′i tē), *n.* *Class. Myth.* one of the Pleiades and the mother, by Zeus, of Lacedaemon.

Tay·lor (tā′lər), *n.* **1. Alan John Percivale,** born 1906, English historian. **2. Bay·ard** (bī′ərd, bā′-), (*James Bayard*), 1825–78, U.S. poet, novelist, and travel writer. **3. Brook,** 1685–1731, English mathematician. **4. Edward,** 1644?–1729, American physician, clergyman, and poet; born in England. **5. Frederick Winslow,** 1856–1915, U.S. inventor. **6. Jeremy,** 1613–67, English prelate and theological writer. **7. John W.,** 1784–1854, U.S. politician: Speaker of the House 1820–21, 1825–27. **8. (Joseph) Deems** (dēmz), 1885–1966, U.S. composer, music critic, and author. **9. Maxwell (Davenport),** born 1901, U.S. army general and diplomat: chief of staff 1955–59; chairman of Joint Chiefs of Staff 1962–64. **10. Myron Charles,** 1874–1959, U.S. lawyer, industrialist, and diplomat. **11. Paul (Bel·ville)** (bel′vil), born 1930, U.S. dancer and choreographer. **12. Tom,** 1817–80, English playwright and editor. **13. Zachary** ("*Old Rough and Ready*"), 1784–1850, 12th president of the U.S. 1849–50: major general during the Mexican War and commander of the army of the Rio Grande 1846. **14.** a town in central Texas. 9434 (1960). **15.** a town in NE Pennsylvania. 6148 (1960). **16.** a walled plain in the fourth quadrant of the face of the moon: about 25 miles in diameter. **17.** a boy's given name.

Tay·lor·ism (tā′lə riz′əm), *n.* a modified form of Calvinism that maintains that man has a free will, and that makes a distinction between depravity, as the tendency to commit sins, and sin, as a voluntary choice of evil actions. Also called **New Haven theology.** [after Nathaniel William *Taylor* (1786–1858), American theologian + -ISM] —**Tay·lor·ite** (tā′lə rīt′), *n.*

Tay′lor se′ries, *Math.* an approximation of a given function f at a particular point x by a power series in which the terms are given by $\frac{f^{(n)}(x_0)(x-x_0)^n}{n!}$, where $f^{(n)}(x_0)$ is the derivative of order n evaluated at a convenient reference point x_0. Cf. **Maclaurin series.** [named after Brook TAYLOR]

Tayra (Total length 3½ ft.; tail 1½ ft.)

Tay·lor·ville (tā′lər vil), *n.* a town in central Illinois. 8801 (1960).

tay·ra (tī′rə), *n.* an animal, *Tayra barbara,* of the weasel family, ranging from Mexico to tropical South America. [< Sp, var. of *taira* < Tupi]

Tay′-Sachs′ disease′ (tā′saks′), *Pathol.* a rare, fatal disease, occurring chiefly in infants and children, esp. of Jewish extraction and of eastern European origin, characterized by a red spot on the retina, gradual blindness, and loss of weight, and believed to be of genetic origin. [named after W. *Tay* (1843–1927), English physician, and B. *Sachs* (1858–1944), American neurologist]

taz·za (tät′sə; *It.* tät′tsä), *n., pl.* **-zas,** *It.* **-ze** (-tse). a shallow, saucerlike, ornamental bowl, often having handles and usually on a high base or pedestal. [< It < Ar *ṭassah* basin. See TASS]

TB, **1.** tubercle bacillus. **2.** tuberculosis. Also **T.B.**

Tb, *Chem.* terbium.

Tb, **1.** tubercle bacillus. **2.** tuberculosis.

t.b., **1.** trial balance. **2.** tubercle bacillus. **3.** tuberculosis.

T-bar (tē′bär′), *n.* (in construction work) a rolled metal bar or beam with a cross section resembling a T. Also called **tee.** See illus. under **shape.**

T-bev·el (tē′bev′əl), *n.* *Carpentry.* an instrument for laying out angles, consisting of two straightedges joined at one end by a pivot with a setscrew.

Tbi·li·si (tə bə lē′sē; *Russ.* tbyi lyē′syi), *n.* a city in and the capital of the Georgian Republic, in the SE part, on the Kura. 1,194,000. Formerly, **Tiflis.**

T.B.O., *Theat.* total blackout.

T′-bone steak′ (tē′bōn′), a loin steak having some tenderloin, characterized by its T-shaped bone.

TBS, *Naut.* talk between ships: a radiotelephone for short-range communication between vessels. [*T(alk) B(etween) S(hips)*]

tbs., tablespoon; tablespoons. Also, **tbsp.**

TC, Trustee Council (of the United Nations).

Tc, *Chem.* technetium.

tc., tierce; tierces.

TCBM, transcontinental ballistic missile.

Tchad (chAd), *n.* French name of **Chad.**

Tchai·kov·sky (chī kôf′skē; *Russ.* chī kôf′ski), *n.* **Peter Il·yich** (il′yich) or **Pë·tr Il·ich** (pyô′tər il-yēch′), 1840–93, Russian composer. Russian, **Chaikovski.** Also, **Tschaikovsky, Tschaikowsky.**

Tche·by·cheff′ equa′tion (chə bə shôf′), *Math.* a differential equation of the form $(1 - x^2)\frac{d^2y}{dx^2} - x\frac{dy}{dx} + n^2y = 0$, where n is any nonnegative integer. [named after Pafrutii L. *Tchebycheff* (1821–94), Russian mathematician]

Tchebycheff′ polyno′mial, *Math.* a polynomial solution of the Tchebycheff equation, of the form $Tn(x) = \cos(n\cos^{-1}x)$, where n is an integer.

Tche·khov (chek′ôf, -of; *Russ.* che′KHof), *n.* **Anton Pa·vlo·vich** (än tôn′ pä vlô′vich). See **Chekhov.**

Tche·rep·nin (chə rep′nin; *Russ.* che rep′nin), *n.* **1. Al·ex·an·der** (al′ig zan′dər; *Russ.* ä li ksän′dər), born 1899, Russian pianist and composer, in the U.S. **2.** his father, **Ni·cho·las** (nē′ko läs), 1873–1945, Russian composer and conductor.

tcher·vo·netz (cher vô′nits), *n., pl.* **-von·tzi** (-vôn′tsē). chervonets.

tchr., teacher.

TCS, traffic control station.

TD, touchdown; touchdowns.

T/D, time deposit.

T.D., **1.** Traffic Director. **2.** Treasury Department.

TDN, totally digestible nutrients. Also, **t.d.n.**

TDY, See **temporary duty.**

te (tā), *n.* *Music.* ti¹.

Te, *Chem.* tellurium.

Te (de), *n.* (in philosophical Taoism) the virtue or power inherent in a person or thing existing in harmony with the Tao. Also, **Teh.** [< Chin *te* virtue]

tea (tē), *n.* **1.** the dried and prepared leaves of a shrub, *Thea sinensis,* from which a somewhat bitter, aromatic beverage is prepared by infusion in hot water. **2.** the shrub itself, extensively cultivated in China, Japan, India, etc., and having fragrant white flowers. **3.** the beverage so prepared, served hot or iced. **4.** any kind of leaves, flowers, etc., so used, or any plant yielding them. **5.** any of various infusions prepared from the leaves, flowers, etc., of other plants, and used as beverages or medicines. **6.** See **beef tea. 7.** *Brit.* any meal, whether a light snack or one consisting of several courses, eaten in the late afternoon or in the evening; any meal other than dinner, eaten after the middle of the afternoon. **8.** an afternoon reception at which tea is served. **9.** *Slang.* marijuana. **10. one's cup of tea,** suitable, appropriate, or attractive to one: *Horror movies and westerns are just not my cup of tea.* [< Chin (Amoy dial.) *t'e;* c. Mandarin *ch'a*] —**tea′less,** *adj.*

Tea′ Act′, *Amer. Hist.* an act of the British Parliament (1773) that created a monopoly unfair to American tea merchants: the chief cause of the Boston Tea Party.

tea′ bag′, a container of thin paper or cloth holding a measured amount of tea leaves for making an individual serving of tea.

tea′ ball′, a perforated metal ball in which tea leaves are placed to be immersed in hot water to make tea.

tea′ bas′ket, *Brit.* a lunch basket or picnic hamper.

tea·ber·ry (tē′ber′ē, -bə rē), *n., pl.* **-ries.** the spicy red fruit of the American wintergreen, *Gaultheria procumbens.* [TEA + BERRY]

tea′ bis′cuit, a small, round, soft biscuit, usually shortened and sweetened.

tea′ break′, *Chiefly Brit.* an intermission from work, usually in the middle of the morning or afternoon, for a cup of tea, a snack, etc.

tea′ cad′dy, *Brit.* a small box, can, or chest for holding tea leaves.

tea·cake (tē′kāk′), *n.* **1.** (in the U.S.) a small cake, cooky, tart, or the like, for serving with tea or punch. **2.** (in England) a light, flat, sweet cake with raisins, usually buttered and served hot with tea. [TEA + CAKE]

tea·cart (tē′kärt′), *n.* See **tea wagon.** [TEA + CART]

teach (tēch), *v.,* **taught, teach·ing.** *n.* —*v.t.* **1.** to impart knowledge of or skill in; give instruction in: *He teaches mathematics.* **2.** to impart knowledge or skill to; give instruction to: *He teaches a large class.* —*v.i.* **3.** to impart knowledge or skill; give instruction. —*n.* **4.** *Slang.* teacher. [ME *teche(n),* OE *tǣcan;* akin to TOKEN]
—**Syn. 1, 2, 3.** coach. **2, 3.** instruct, tutor, educate, inform, enlighten, discipline, train, drill, school, indoctrinate.

Teach (tēch), *n.* **Edward** ("*Blackbeard*"), died 1718, English pirate and privateer in the Americas. Also, **Thatch, Thach.**

teach·a·ble (tē′chə bəl), *adj.* **1.** capable of being instructed, as a person; docile. **2.** capable of being taught, as a subject. [TEACH + ABLE] —**teach′a·bil′i·ty, teach′a·ble·ness,** *n.* —**teach′a·bly,** *adv.*

teach·er (tē′chər), *n.* a person who teaches or instructs, esp. as a profession; instructor. [ME *techer.* See TEACH, -ER¹] —**teach′er·less,** *adj.* —**teach′er·ship′,** *n.*

teach′er bird′, *U.S. Dial.* the ovenbird, *Seiurus aurocapillus.*

teach′ers col′lege, a four-year college offering courses for the training of primary and secondary school teachers and granting the bachelor's degree and often advanced degrees.

teach-in (tēch′in′), *n., pl.* **teach-ins.** a prolonged period of lectures, speeches, etc., conducted without interruption by members of the faculty and invited guests at an American college as a technique of social protest, first used to protest U.S. involvement in South Vietnam.

teach·ing (tē′ching), *n.* **1.** the act or profession of one who teaches. **2.** that which is taught. **3.** Often, **teachings.** doctrines or precepts: *the teachings of Lao-tsu.* [ME *teching.* See TEACH, -ING¹]

teach′ing aid′, material used by a teacher to supplement classroom instruction or to stimulate the interest of students.

teach′ing el′der, a minister in a Presbyterian church.

teach′ing fel′low, a holder of a teaching fellowship.

teach′ing fel′lowship, a fellowship providing a student in a graduate school with free tuition and expenses and stipulating that he assume some teaching duties in return.

teach′ing hos′pital, a hospital associated with a medical college and offering clinical and other facilities to those in various areas of medical study, as students, interns, and residents.

teach′ing machine′, a mechanical, electrical, or other automatic device that presents the user with items of information in planned sequence, registers his response to each item, and immediately informs him of the acceptability of his response.

tea′ clip′per, *Naut.* a clipper of the middle 19th century, having fast lines and engaged primarily in carrying tea from India or China to Europe or the east coast of the United States.

tea′ co′zy, cozy (def. 3).

tea·cup (tē′kup′), *n.* **1.** a cup in which tea is served, usually of small or moderate size. **2.** a teacupful. [TEA + CUP]

tea·cup·ful (tē′kup fŏŏl′), *n., pl.* **-fuls.** as much as a teacup will hold, equal to four fluid ounces. [TEACUP + -FUL]

tea′ dance′, a dance held at teatime.

tea′ gar′den, a tea plantation.

Tea·gar·den (tē′gär′dᵊn), *n.* **Wel·don John** (wel′dᵊn), (*Jack*), 1905–64, U.S. jazz trombonist and singer.

tea′ gown′, a semiformal gown of fine material, esp. one styled with soft, flowing lines, worn for afternoon social occasions.

Teague (tēg), *n.* a town in central Texas. 2728 (1960).

tea·house (tē′hous′), *n., pl.* **-hous·es** (-hou′ziz). a restaurant or other establishment, esp. in the Orient, where tea and refreshments are served. [TEA + HOUSE]

teak (tēk), *n.* **1.** a large, East Indian, verbenaceous tree, *Tectona grandis,* yielding a hard, durable, resinous, yellowish-brown wood used for shipbuilding, making furniture, etc. **2.** the wood of this tree. **3.** any of various similar trees or woods. [earlier *teke* < Pg *teca* < Malayalam *tēkka*]

tea·ket·tle (tē′ket′ᵊl), *n.* a portable kettle with a cover, spout, and handle, used for boiling water. [TEA + KETTLE]

teak·wood (tēk′wŏŏd′), *n.* the wood of the teak. [TEAK + WOOD¹]

teal (tēl), *n., pl.* **-teals,** (*esp. collectively*) **-teal. 1.** any of several small, fresh-water ducks. Cf. **blue-winged teal, green-winged teal. 2.** Also called **teal′ blue′.** a medium to dark greenish blue. [ME *tele;* akin to D *taling,* MLG *telink*]

tea′ lead′ (led), hard, stiff sheet lead, originally used as a lining for tea chests.

tea-leaf (tē′lēf′), *n., pl.* **-leaves** (-lēvz′). *Chiefly Brit. Slang.* a thief. [rhyming slang]

team (tēm), *n.* **1.** a number of persons associated in some joint action, esp. one of the sides in a game or contest: *a team of football players.* **2.** two or more horses, oxen, or other animals harnessed together to draw a vehicle, plow, or the like. **3.** one or more draft animals together with the harness and vehicle drawn. **4.** *Archaic.* a family of young animals, esp. ducks or pigs. **5.** *Obs.* offspring or progeny; race or lineage. —*v.t.* **6.** to join together in a team. **7.** to convey or transport by means of a team. —*v.i.* **8.** to drive a team. **9.** to gather or join in a team, a band, or a cooperative effort (usually fol. by *up, together,* etc.). —*adj.* **10.** of, pertaining to, or performed by a team: *a team sport; team effort.* [ME *teme,* OE *tēam* childbearing, brood, offspring, set of draft beasts; c. D *toom* bridle, reins, G *Zaum,* Icel *taumr*]

tea′ mak′er, a perforated, spoonlike object used as a tea strainer and having a hinged, convex lid.

team·er (tē′mər), *n.* a teamster. [TEAM + -ER[1]]

Team·er (tē′mər), *n.* a boy's given name.

team·mate (tēm′māt′), *n.* a member of the same team. [TEAM + MATE[1]]

team·ster (tēm′stər), *n.* one who drives a team or a truck for hauling, esp. as an occupation. [TEAM + -STER]

team·work (tēm′wûrk′), *n.* **1.** cooperative or coordinated effort on the part of a group of persons acting together as a team or in the interests of a common cause. **2.** work done with a team. [TEAM + WORK]

Tea·neck (tē′nek′), *n.* a town in NE New Jersey. 42,085 (1960).

tea-of-heav·en (tē′əv hev′ən), *n.* a shrub, *Hydrangea serrata,* of Japan and Korea, having flat or slightly arched clusters of blue or white flowers.

tea′ par′ty, a social gathering, usually in the afternoon, at which tea and light refreshments are served.

tea·pot (tē′pot′), *n.* a container with a lid, spout, and handle, in which tea is made and from which it is poured. [TEA + POT[1]]

tea·poy (tē′poi), *n.* **1.** a small three-legged table or stand. **2.** a small table for use in serving tea. [< Hindi *tīpāī,* alter. (with *t-* from *tir-* < Skt *tri* three) of Pers *sīpāē* three-legged stand]

tear[1] (tēr), *n.* **1.** a drop of the saline, watery fluid continually secreted by the lacrimal glands between the surface of the eye and the eyelid, serving to moisten and lubricate these parts and keep them clear of foreign particles. **2.** this fluid appearing in or flowing from the eye as the result of emotion, esp. grief. **3.** something resembling or suggesting a tear, as a drop of a liquid or a tearlike mass of a solid substance, esp. having a spherical or globular shape at one end and tapering to a point at the other. **4.** *Glassmaking.* a decorative air bubble enclosed in a glass vessel; air bell. **5. tears,** grief; sorrow. **6. in tears,** in the act of weeping: *The new bride was in tears over her unsuccessful dinner.* —*v.i.* **7.** to fill up and overflow with tears, as the eyes. [ME *teer,* OE (WS) *tēar* (Vernerian var. of *teagor*), equiv. to *tæher* (north); c. OHG *zahar,* Icel *tār* Goth *tagr,* Gk *dákry,* etc.]

tear[2] (târ), *v.,* **tore** or (*Archaic*) **tare; torn** or (*Archaic*) **tare; tear·ing;** *n.* —*v.t.* **1.** to pull apart or in pieces by force, esp. so as to leave ragged or irregular edges. **2.** to pull or snatch violently; wrench away with force: *to tear wrappings from a package; to tear a book from someone's hands.* **3.** to distress greatly: *anguish that tears the heart.* **4.** to divide or disrupt: *a country torn by civil war.* **5.** to wound or injure by or as if by rending; lacerate. **6.** to produce or effect by rending: *to tear a hole in one's coat.* **7.** to remove by force: *to be unable to tear oneself from a place.* —*v.i.* **8.** to become torn. **9.** to make a tear or rent. **10.** to move with violence or great haste: *Right after the explosion, he tore out into the street.* **11. tear at,** to pluck violently at; attempt to tear: *The wind tore at the newly planted saplings.* **12. tear down, a.** to pull down; destroy; demolish. **b.** to disparage or discredit: *She enjoys tearing down her friends when they aren't around.* **13. tear into,** *Informal.* **a.** to attack impulsively and heedlessly: *He tore into the food with a will.* **b.** to attack verbally: *She tore into him for being late for dinner.* **14. tear off,** *Slang.* to perform or do, esp. rapidly or casually: *to tear off a poem; tear off a set of tennis.* **15. tear up, a.** to tear into small shreds: *He tore up the drawings because she had criticized them.* **b.** to cancel or annul: *to tear up a contract.* —*n.* **16.** act of tearing. **17.** a rent or fissure. **18.** a rage or passion; violent flurry or outburst. **19.** *Slang.* a spree. [ME *tere(n),* OE *teran;* c. D *teren,* G *zehren* to consume, Goth *(dis)tairan* to destroy, Gk *dérein* to flay, etc.] —**tear′a·ble,** *adj.* —**tear′a·ble·ness,** *n.* —**tear′er,** *n.*

—**Syn. 1.** TEAR, REND, RIP mean to pull apart. To TEAR is to split the fibers of something by pulling apart, usually so as to leave ragged or irregular edges: *to tear open a letter.* REND implies force or violence in tearing apart or in pieces: *to rend one's clothes in grief.* RIP implies vigorous tearing asunder, esp. along a seam or line: *to rip the sleeves out of a coat.* **3.** shatter, afflict. **4.** split. **5.** cut, mangle. **17.** rip.

tear′ bomb′ (tēr), a bomb or grenade containing tear gas. Also called **tear shell, tear grenade.**

tear·down (târ′doun′), *n.* a taking apart; disassembly. [n. use of v. phrase *tear down*]

tear·drop (tēr′drop′), *n.* **1.** a tear or something suggesting a tear: *A single teardrop rolled down her face.* **2.** something shaped like a drop of a thin liquid, having a globular form at the bottom, tapering to a point at the top. [TEAR[1] + DROP]

tear·ful (tēr′fəl), *adj.* **1.** full of tears; weeping. **2.** causing tears: *the tearful story of his poverty.* [TEAR[1] + -FUL] —**tear′ful·ly,** *adv.* —**tear′ful·ness,** *n.*

tear′ gas′ (tēr), a gas that makes the eyes smart and water, thus producing a temporary blindness, used in modern warfare, to quell riots, etc.

tear-gas (tēr′gas′), *v.t.,* **-gassed, -gas·sing.** to subject to tear gas.

tear′ grenade′ (tēr). See **tear bomb.**

tear·ing (târ′ing), *adj.* violent or hasty: *with tearing speed.* [TEAR[2] + -ING[2]] —**tear′ing·ly,** *adv.*

tear-jerk·er (tēr′jûr′kər), *n.* *Informal.* a pathetic story, play, movie, or the like; an excessively sentimental tale. Also, **tear′jerk′er.**

tear·less (tēr′lis), *adj.* **1.** not weeping or shedding tears. **2.** unable to shed tears. [TEAR[1] + -LESS] —**tear′less·ly,** *adv.* —**tear′less·ness,** *n.*

tea·room (tē′ro͞om′, -ro͝om′), *n.* a room or shop where tea and other refreshments are served to customers.

tea′ rose′, *Hort.* any of several cultivated varieties of roses having a scent resembling that of tea.

tear′ sheet′ (târ), a sheet or page torn from a magazine, journal, or the like, esp. one containing an advertisement and sent to the advertiser as proof of publication.

tear′ shell′ (tēr). See **tear bomb.**

tear-stained (tēr′stānd′), *adj.* **1.** marked or wet with tears. **2.** showing traces of tears or signs of having wept.

tear·y (tēr′ē), *adj.,* **tear·i·er, tear·i·est. 1.** of or like tears. **2.** tearful. [ME *tery.* See TEAR[1], -Y[1]] —**tear′i·ly,** *adv.*

Teas·dale (tēz′dāl′), *n.* **Sara,** 1884–1933, U.S. poet.

tease (tēz), *v.,* **teased, teas·ing,** *n.* —*v.t.* **1.** to irritate or provoke with persistent petty distractions, trifling raillery, or other annoyance, often in sport. **2.** to pull apart or separate the adhering fibers of (wool or the like), as in combing or carding; comb or card, as wool; shred. **3.** to ruffle (the hair) by holding it at the ends and combing toward the scalp so as to give body to a hairdo. **4.** to raise a nap on (cloth) with teasels; teasel. —*v.i.* **5.** to provoke or disturb a person or animal by importunity or persistent petty annoyances. —*n.* **6.** a person who teases or annoys. **7.** the act of teasing; state of being teased. [ME *tese(n),* OE *tǣsan* to pull, tear, comb; c. MLG *tesen,* OHG *zeisan* to pluck] —**teas′a·ble,** *adj.* —**teas′a·ble·ness,** *n.* —**teas′ing·ly,** *adv.*

—**Syn. 1.** trouble, disturb, vex; harass. See **bother.** —**Ant. 1.** mollify.

tea·sel (tē′zəl), *n., v.,* **-seled, -sel·ing** or (*esp. Brit.*) **-selled, -sel·ling.** —*n.* **1.** any dipsacaceous herb of the genus *Dipsacus,* having prickly leaves and flower heads. **2.** the dried flower head or bur of the herb *D. fullonum,* used for teasing or teaseling cloth. **3.** any mechanical contrivance used for teaseling. —*v.t.* **4.** to raise a nap on (cloth) with teasels; dress by means of teasels. Also, **teazel, teazle.** [ME *tesel,* OE *tǣsel;* akin to TEASE] —**tea′sel·er;** *esp. Brit.,* **tea′sel·ler,** *n.*

tea′sel gourd′, a prickly-stemmed vine, *Cucumis dipsaceus,* of Arabia, having burlike, bristly fruit. Also called **hedgehog gourd.**

teas·er (tē′zər), *n.* **1.** one who or that which teases. **2.** *Theat.* a drapery or flat piece across the top of the proscenium arch which masks the flies and which, together with the tormentors, forms a frame for the stage opening. **3.** *Print., Journ.* kicker (def. 7). [TEASE + -ER[1]]

tea′ serv′ice, 1. a set of chinaware for preparing and drinking hot beverages, esp. tea. **2.** a set of silver or other metalware for preparing and serving hot beverages, esp. tea. Also called **tea′ set′.**

tease′ ten′on. See **teaze tenon.**

tea′ shop′, 1. a tearoom. **2.** *Brit.* a restaurant that specializes in serving light meals and snacks; lunchroom.

tea·spoon (tē′spo͞on′, -spo͝on′), *n.* **1.** a small spoon generally used to stir tea, coffee, etc. **2.** a teaspoonful. [TEA + SPOON]

tea·spoon·ful (tē′spo͞on fo͝ol′, -spo͝on-), *n., pl.* **-fuls.** as much as a teaspoon can hold, equal to one fluid dram. [TEASPOON + -FUL]

teat (tēt, tit), *n.* **1.** the protuberance on the breast or udder in female mammals, except the monotremes, through which the milk ducts discharge; nipple or mammilla. **2.** something resembling a teat. [ME *tete* < OF < Gmc; see TIT[2]]

tea′ ta′ble, a small table for holding a tea service and cups, plates, etc., for several people. —**tea′-ta′ble,** *adj.*

tea·tast·er (tē′tā′stər), *n.* a person whose profession is tasting and grading samples of tea. [TEA + TASTER]

tea·time (tē′tīm′), *n.* the time at which tea is served or taken, usually in the late afternoon. [TEA + TIME]

tea′ tow′el, a dishtowel.

tea′ tray′, a tray for carrying or holding articles used in serving tea. Also called **teacart.**

tea′ tree′, a tall shrub or small tree, *Leptospermum scoparium,* of New Zealand and Australia, having silky foliage when young, and bell-shaped, white flowers. [so called from the use of its leaves as an infusion]

tea′ wag′on, a small table on wheels for carrying articles for use in serving tea. Also called **teacart.**

tea·zel (tē′zəl), *n., v.t.,* **-zeled, -zel·ing** or (*esp. Brit.*) **-zelled, -zel·ling.** teasel.

teaze′ ten′on (tēz), *Carpentry.* a tenon having a stepped outline, cut on the top of a post to receive two horizontal timbers, one of which meets the other at a right angle. Also, **tease tenon.** [*teaze,* var. of TEASE]

tea·zle (tē′zəl), *n., v.t.,* **-zled, -zling.** teasel.

Te·bal·di (tə bäl′dē; *It.* te bäl′dē), *n.* **Re·na·ta** (rə nä′tə; *It.* re nä′tä), born 1922, Italian operatic soprano.

Te·bet (tā′vəs; *Heb.* tā bet′), *n.* a month of the Jewish calendar. Also, **Tevet.** Cf. **Jewish calendar.** [ME *tebeth* < LL < Heb]

tec·as·sir (tek′ə sēr′), *n.* a gallery in a mosque, esp. one for women. [< Turk]

tech., **1.** technical. **2.** technology.

tech·ne·ti·um (tek nē′shē əm, -shəm), *n.* **1.** *Chem.* an element of the manganese family, not found in nature, but obtained in the fission of uranium or by the bombardment of molybdenum. *Symbol:* Tc; *at. wt.:* 99; *at. no.:* 43; *sp. gr.:* 11.5. [Gk *technēt(ós)* artificial (lit., made, verbid of *technâsthai;* see TECHNO-) + -IUM]

tech·nic (tek′nik *or, for 1,* tek nēk′), *n.* **1.** technique. **2.** a technicality. **3. technics,** (*construed as sing. or pl.*) the study or science of an art or of arts in general, esp. the mechanical or industrial arts. —*adj.* **4.** technical. [(n.): earlier *technica* < Gk *techniká,* neut. pl. of *technikós* of art and craft, equiv. to *téchn(ē)* art, craft + *-ikos* -IC; (adj.): < Gk *technik(ós)*]

tech·ni·cal (tek′ni kəl), *adj.* **1.** belonging or pertaining to an art, science, or the like: *technical skill.* **2.** peculiar to or characteristic of a particular art, science, profession, trade, etc.: *technical details.* **3.** using terminology or treating subject matter in a manner peculiar to a particular field, as a writer or a book: *a technical report.* **4.** skilled in or familiar in a practical way with a particular art, trade, etc., as a person. **5.** pertaining to or connected with the mechanical or industrial arts and the applied sciences: *a technical school.* **6.** so considered from a point of view in accordance with a stringent interpretation of the rules: *a military engagement ending in a technical defeat.* **7.** noting a market in which prices are determined largely by supply and demand and other such internal factors rather than by general business, economic, or psychological factors that influence market activity: *technical weakness or strength.* [TECHNIC + -AL] —**tech′ni·cal·ly,** *adv.* —**tech′ni·cal·ness,** *n.*

tech·ni·cal·i·ty (tek′nə kal′i tē), *n., pl.* **-ties. 1.** technical character. **2.** the use of technical methods or terms. **3.** something that is technical; a technical point, detail, or expression. [TECHNICAL + -ITY]

tech′nical knock′out, *Boxing.* the termination of a bout by the referee when it is the judgment of the attending physician, a boxer's seconds, or the referee that a boxer cannot continue fighting without sustaining severe or disabling injury. *Abbr.:* TKO, T.K.O.

tech′nical ser′geant, 1. *U.S. Air Force and Marine Corps.* a noncommissioned officer ranking below a master sergeant and above a staff sergeant. **2.** *U.S. Army.* (formerly) a noncommissioned officer below a master sergeant and above a staff sergeant: now corresponds to sergeant first class.

tech·ni·cian (tek nish′ən), *n.* **1.** a person who is trained or skilled in the technicalities of a subject. **2.** a person who is skilled in the technique of an art, as music or painting. **3.** *U.S. Army.* (formerly) one of several grades above private, given to specialists who are enlisted men: now called specialist. [TECHNIC + -IAN; see -ICIAN]

Tech·ni·col·or (tek′nə kul′ər), *n.* **1.** *Trademark.* a system of making color motion pictures by means of superimposing the three primary colors to produce a final colored print. —*adj.* **2.** (*often l.c.*) flamboyant or lurid, as in color, meaning, detail, etc.

tech·nique (tek nēk′), *n.* **1.** the manner and ability with which an artist, writer, dancer, athlete, or the like, employs the technical skills of his particular art or field of endeavor. **2.** the body of specialized procedures and methods used in any specific field, esp. in an area of applied science. **3.** method of performance; way of accomplishing. **4.** technical skill; ability to apply procedures or methods so as to effect a desired result. **5.** *Informal.* method of projecting personal charm, appeal, etc.: *He has the greatest technique with women.* [< F: technical (adj.), technic (n.) < Gk; see TECHNIC]

techno-, a learned borrowing from Greek where it meant "art," "skill," used in the formation of compound words to refer to "technique," "technology," etc.: *technography.* [comb. form repr. Gk *téchnē* art, skill. See TECHNIC]

tech·noc·ra·cy (tek nok′rə sē), *n., pl.* **-cies. 1.** a theory and movement, prominent about 1932, advocating control of industrial resources, reform of financial institutions, and reorganization of the social system, based on the findings of technologists and engineers. **2.** a system of government in which this theory is applied. **3.** any application of this theory. [TECHNO- + -CRACY] —**tech·no·crat** (tek′nə krat′), *n.* —**tech′no·crat′ic,** *adj.*

tech·nog·ra·phy (tek nog′rə fē), *n.* the description and study of the arts and sciences in their geographical and ethnic distribution and historical development. [TECHNO- + -GRAPHY]

technol., technology.

tech·no·log·i·cal (tek′nə loj′i kəl), *adj.* **1.** of or pertaining to technology; relating to science and industry. **2.** *Econ.* caused by technical advances in production methods: *technological unemployment.* Also, **tech′no·log′ic.** [TECHNOLOG(Y) + -ICAL] —**tech′no·log′i·cal·ly,** *adv.*

tech·nol·o·gy (tek nol′ə jē), *n.* **1.** the branch of knowledge that deals with industrial arts, applied science, engineering, etc. **2.** the terminology of an art, science, etc.; technical nomenclature. **3.** a technological process, invention, method, or the like. **4.** the sum of the ways in which a social group provide themselves with the material objects of their civilization. [< Gk *technología* systematic treatment. See TECHNO-, -LOGY] —**tech·nol′o·gist,** *n.*

Tech. Sgt., Technical Sergeant.

tech·y (tech′ē), *adj.,* **tech·i·er, tech·i·est.** tetchy. —**tech′i·ly,** *adv.* —**tech′i·ness,** *n.*

Tec·mes·sa (tek mes′ə), *n.* *Class. Myth.* the daughter of King Teuthras of Thrace, carried off by Telamonian Ajax when he defeated her father in war. She bore Ajax a son, Eurysaces.

Tec·ton (tek′ton), *n.* (in the *Iliad*) a carpenter, the father of Phereclus.

tec·ton·ic (tek ton′ik), *adj.* **1.** of or pertaining to building or construction; constructive; architectural. **2.** *Geol.* **a.** pertaining to the structure of the earth's crust. **b.** referring to the forces or conditions within the earth that cause movements of the crust, as earthquakes, folds, faults, or the like. **c.** designating the results of such movements: *tectonic valleys.* [< LL *tectonic(us)* < Gk *tektonikós* pertaining to construction < *tekton-* (s. of *téktōn*) carpenter + *-ikos* -IC] —**tec·ton′i·cal·ly,** *adv.*

tec·ton·ics (tek ton′iks), *n.* (*construed as sing.*) **1.** the science or art of assembling, shaping, or ornamenting materials in construction; the constructive arts in general. **2.** structural geology. [see TECTONIC, -ICS]

tec·trix (tek′triks), *n., pl.* **tec·tri·ces** (tek′tri sēz′, tek trī′sēz). *Ornith.* covert (def. 8). [< NL, fem. of L *tector* < *tect(us)* covered (ptp. of *tegere*) + *-or* -OR[2]; see -TRIX] —**tec·tri·cial** (tek trish′əl), *adj.*

Te·cum·seh (ti kum′sə), *n.* **1.** Also, **Te·cum·tha** (ti-kum′thə). 1768?–1813, American Indian chief of the Shawnee tribe. **2.** a town in SE Michigan. 7045 (1960). **3.** a town in central Oklahoma. 2630 (1960).

ted (ted), *v.t.,* **ted·ded, ted·ding.** to spread out for drying, as newly mown hay. [late ME *tedde,* OE **teddan;* c. Icel *tethja* to manure, OHG *zettan* to spread, Gk *dateisthai* to divide]

Ted (ted), *n.* **1.** *Brit. Slang.* See **Teddy boy. 2.** a boy's given name, form of **Edward, Theodor,** or **Theodore.** [*Ted* by false analysis of *(tha)t Ed(ward);* later used for *Theodore*]

ted·der (ted′ər), *n.* **1.** a person who teds. **2.** an implement that turns and loosens hay after mowing in order to hasten drying. [late ME *teddere.* See TED, -ER[1]]

Ted·der (ted′ər), *n.* **Arthur William, 1st Baron,** 1890–1967, British Royal Air Force marshal and educator, born in Scotland.

ted·dy (ted′ē), *n., pl.* **-dies.** Often, **teddies.** a one-piece undergarment, consisting of a chemise and loose-fitting underpants, worn by women. Also called **envelope chemise.** [?]

Ted·dy (ted′ē), *n.* **1.** a boy's given name, form of **Edward, Theodor,** or **Theodore. 2.** a girl's given name, form of **Theodora.** Also, **Ted′die.**

CONCISE ETYMOLOGY KEY: <, descended or derived from; >, whence; b., blend of, blended; c., cognate with; deriv., derivative; equiv., equivalent; imit., imitative; m., modification of; obl., oblique; r., replacing; s., stem; sp., spelling; trans., translation; ?, origin unknown, perhaps; *, hypothetical. See the full key inside the front cover.

ted′dy bear′, a toy bear, esp. a stuffed one. [named after Theodore Roosevelt, called *Teddy* who is said to have saved the life of a bear cub while hunting]

Ted′dy boy′, (*often l.c.*) *Informal.* a rebellious British youth affecting the dress of the reign of Edward VII.

Ted′dy girl′, (*often l.c.*) *Informal.* **1.** a rebellious British girl affecting the dress of the reign of Edward VII. **2.** a girl companion of Teddy boys.

Te De·um (tā dā′o͞om, tē dē′əm), **1.** (*italics*) an ancient Latin hymn of praise to God, in the form of a psalm, sung regularly at matins in the Roman Catholic Church and, usually, in an English translation, at Morning Prayer in the Anglican Church, as well as on special occasions as a service of thanksgiving. **2.** a musical setting of this hymn. **3.** a service of thanksgiving in which this hymn forms a prominent part. [first two words of the hymn, which begins: *Tē Deum laudāmus* we praise thee God]

te·di·ous (tē′dē əs, tē′jəs), *adj.* **1.** marked by tedium; long and tiresome: *tedious tasks; a tedious journey.* **2.** wordy so as to cause weariness or boredom, as a speaker or writer; prolix. [late ME < ML, LL *taediōs(us).* See TEDIUM, -OUS] —**te′di·ous·ly,** *adv.* —**te′di·ous·ness,** *n.* —**Syn. 1.** wearing, boring, tiring, monotonous, dull.

te·di·um (tē′dē əm), *n.* the quality or state of being wearisome; irksomeness; tediousness. [< L *taedium*]

tee[1] (tē), *n.* **1.** the letter *T* or *t.* **2.** something shaped like a T, as a three-way joint used in fitting pipes together. **3.** T-bar. **4.** the mark aimed at in various games, as curling. **5. to a tee.** See **T, t** (def. 6). —*adj.* **6.** having a crosspiece at the top; shaped like a T.

tee[2] (tē), *n., v.,* **teed, tee·ing.** —*n.* **1.** *Golf.* **a.** Also called **teeing ground.** the starting place, usually a hard mound of earth, at the beginning of play for each hole. **b.** a small wooden, plastic, metal, or rubber peg from which the ball is driven, as in teeing off. **2.** *Football.* a device on which the ball may be placed to raise it off the ground preparatory to kicking. —*v.t.* **3.** *Golf.* to place (the ball) on a tee. **4. tee off, a.** *Golf.* to strike the ball from a tee. **b.** *Slang.* to reprimand severely; scold: *He teed off on his son for wrecking the car.* **c.** *Slang.* to begin: *They teed off the program with a medley of songs.* **d.** *Baseball, Softball Slang.* to make many runs and hits, esp. extra-base hits: *teeing off for six runs on eight hits, including three doubles and a home run.* **e.** *Baseball, Softball Slang.* to hit (a pitched ball) hard and far: *He teed off on a fast ball and drove it into the bleachers.* **f.** *Boxing Slang.* to strike with a powerful blow, esp. to the head: *He maneuvered his opponent into a corner and teed off on him with an overhand right.* **5. teed off,** *Slang.* irritated; disgusted: *She was teed off because her dinner guests arrived an hour late.* [?]

tee′ing ground′, *Golf.* tee[2] (def. 1a).

teel (tēl), *n.* til.

teem[1] (tēm), *v.i.* **1.** to abound or swarm; be prolific or fertile (usually fol. by *with*). **2.** *Obs.* to be or become pregnant; bring forth young. —*v.t.* **3.** *Obs.* to produce (offspring). [ME *teme(n),* OE *tēman, tīeman* to produce (offspring). See TEAM] —**teem′er,** *n.*

teem[2] (tēm), *v.t., v.i.* to empty or pour out; discharge. [ME *teme(n)* < Scand; cf. Icel *tæma* to empty, *tōmr* empty, c. OE *tōm* free from]

teem·ing (tē′ming), *adj.* **1.** abounding or swarming with something, as with people: *We elbowed our way through the teeming station.* **2.** prolific or fertile. [TEEM[1] + -ING[2]] —**teem′ing·ly,** *adv.* —**teem′ing·ness,** *n.*

teen[1] (tēn), *n.* **1.** *Archaic.* suffering; grief. **2.** *Obs.* injury; harm. [ME *tene,* OE *tēona;* c. OFris *tiona,* OS *tiono,* Icel *tjōn*]

teen[2] (tēn), *adj.* **1.** teen-age. —*n.* **2.** a teen-ager. [by shortening]

-teen, a suffix used to form cardinal numerals from thirteen to nineteen. [ME, OE *-tēne,* comb. form of TEN; c. D *-tien,* G *-zehn*]

Tee·na (tē′nə), *n.* a girl's given name, form of **Albertina, Bettina,** or **Christina.** Also, **Tina.**

teen-age (tēn′āj′), *adj.* of, pertaining to, or characteristic of a teen-ager. Also, **teen′age′, teen′-aged′, teen′aged′.** [TEEN + AGE]

teen-ag·er (tēn′ā′jər), *n.* a person in his or her teens. Also, **teen′ag′er.**

teens (tēnz), *n. pl.* the numbers 13 through 19, esp. in a progression, as the 13th through the 19th years of a lifetime or of a given or implied century. [independent pl. use of -TEEN]

teen·sy-ween·sy (tēn′sē wēn′sē), *adj.* *Baby Talk.* tiny; small. Also, **teent′sy-weent′sy, teen′sie-ween′sie.** [alter. of TEENY-WEENY]

tee·ny (tē′nē), *adj.,* **-ni·er, -ni·est.** *Informal.* tiny. [b. TINY + WEE]

tee·ny·bop·per (tē′nē bop′ər), *n.* *Disparaging.* a young, teenage girl of the late 1960's who affects the dress and behavior of hippies and sometimes imitates their actions. [TEEN[2] + -Y[2] + BOPPER]

tee·ny-wee·ny (tē′nē wē′nē), *adj.* *Baby Talk.* tiny; small. Also, **tee′nie-wee′nie.** [TEENY + WEENY]

tee·pee (tē′pē), *n.* tepee.

Tees (tēz), *n.* a river in N England, flowing E along the boundary between Durham and Yorkshire to the North Sea. 70 mi. long.

tee′ shirt′, T-shirt.

tee·ter (tē′tər), *Chiefly U.S.* —*v.i.* **1.** to seesaw. **2.** to move unsteadily. —*v.t.* **3.** to tip (something) up and down; move unsteadily. —*n.* **4.** a seesaw. **5.** a seesaw motion; wobble. Also called **tee·ter-tot·ter** (tē′tər tot′ər) (for defs. 1, 4). [northern var. of ME *titeren* < Scand; cf. Icel *titra;* c. G *zittern* to tremble, quiver]

tee·ter·board (tē′tər bōrd′, -bôrd′), *n.* a seesaw; teeter. [TEETER + BOARD]

teeth (tēth), *n.* pl. of **tooth.** —**teeth′less,** *adj.*

teethe (tēth), *v.i.,* **teethed, teeth·ing.** *Dentistry.* to grow teeth; cut one's teeth. [late ME *teth,* OE **tēthan* (only ptp. is recorded). See TEETH]

teeth·er (tē′thər), *n.* a device for a baby to bite on during teething. Cf. **teething ring.** [TEETHE + -ER[1]]

teeth·ing (tē′thing), *n.* *Dentistry.* eruption of the deciduous teeth, esp. the phenomena associated with their eruption. [TEETHE + -ING[1]]

teeth′ing ring′, a circular ring, usually of plastic, ivory, bone, etc., on which a teething baby may bite.

teeth·ridge (tēth′rij′), *n.* *Phonet.* See **alveolar ridge.** [TEETH + RIDGE]

tee·to·tal (tē tōt′əl), *adj., v.* **-taled, -tal·ing** or (*esp. Brit.*) **-talled, -tal·ling.** —*adj.* **1.** of or pertaining to, advocating, or pledged to total abstinence from intoxicating drink. **2.** *Informal.* absolute; complete. —*v.i.* **3.** to practice teetotalism. [reduplicated var. of TOTAL, coined by R. Turner, of Preston, England, in 1833, in a speech advocating total abstinence from alcoholic drinks] —**tee·to′tal·ly,** *adv.*

tee·to·tal·er (tē tōt′əl ər), *n.* a person who abstains totally from intoxicating drink. Also, **tee·to′tal·ist;** *esp. Brit.,* **tee·to′tal·ler.** [TEETOTAL + -ER[1]]

tee·to·tal·ism (tē tōt′əliz′əm), *n.* the principle or practice of total abstinence from intoxicating drink. [TEETOTAL + -ISM]

tee·to·tum (tē tō′təm), *n.* **1.** any small top spun with the fingers. **2.** a kind of die having four sides, each marked with a different initial letter, spun with the fingers in an old game of chance. [earlier *T totum,* alter. of *totum* (name of toy < L *tōtum,* neut. of *tōtus* all) by prefixing its initial letter, which stood on one side of the toy]

teff (tef), *n.* a fragrant grass, *Eragrostis abyssinica,* of North Africa, grown as an ornamental and as a cereal grain. [< Amharic *tēf*]

te·fil·lin (tə fil′in; *Heb.* tə fē lēn′), *n. pl.* *Judaism.* the phylacteries. Also, **tephillin.** [< Heb *tephillīn,* akin to *tephillāh* prayer]

Tef·lon (tef′lon), *n.* *Trademark.* polytetrafluoroethylene.

Tef·nut (tef′no͝ot), *n.* *Egyptian Religion.* the goddess of moisture and sister of Shu.

teg (teg), *n.* **1.** *Chiefly Brit.* a two-year-old doe. **2.** *Stockbreeding.* **a.** a two-year-old sheep that has not been shorn. **b.** the wool shorn from such a sheep. **3.** *Brit. Dial.* a yearling sheep. Also, **tegg.** [?]

Te·ge·a (tē′jē ə), *n.* an ancient city in SE Arcadia, Greece.

Te·ge·a·tes (ti jē′ə tēz′), *n.* *Class. Myth.* a son of Lycaon for whom Tegea was named.

teg·men (teg′mən), *n., pl.* **-mi·na** (-mə nə). **1.** a cover, covering, or integument. **2.** *Bot.* the delicate inner integument or coat of a seed. **3.** (of certain orthopterous insects) one of a pair of leathery forewings that form a protective covering for the hind wings. [< L: covering, syncopated var. of *tegumen* < *tegu-* (var. s. of *tegere* to cover) + *-men* n. suffix] —**teg·mi·nal** (teg′mə nəl), *adj.*

Te·gu·ci·gal·pa (te go͞o′se gäl′pä), *n.* a city in and the capital of Honduras, in the S part. 134,075 (1961).

teg·u·la (teg′yə lə), *n., pl.* **-lae** (-lē′). (in certain insects) a scalelike lobe at the base of the forewing. [< L: tile]

teg·u·lar (teg′yə lər), *adj.* **1.** pertaining to or resembling a tile. **2.** consisting of or arranged like tiles. [< L *tēgu(la)* tile + -AR[1]] —**teg′u·lar·ly,** *adv.*

teg·u·ment (teg′yə mənt), *n.* a covering or investment; integument. [< L *tegument(um)* < *tegu-* (see TEGMEN) + *-mentum* -MENT] —**teg·u·men·tal** (teg′yə men′təl), **teg·u·men·ta·ry** (teg′yə men′tə rē), *adj.*

te·gu·ri·um (tə gyo͝or′ē əm), *n., pl.* **-gu·ri·a** (-gyo͝or′ē ə). (in ancient Roman architecture) a double-sloped roof covering a sarcophagus. [< LL: lit., hut, akin to *tegere* to cover]

Te·gy·ri·us (tə jī′rē əs), *n.* *Class. Myth.* a Thracian king.

Teh (de), *n.* Te.

Te·hach·a·pi (tə hach′ə pē), *n.* a town in central California. 3161 (1960).

te-hee (tē hē′), *interj., n., v.,* **-heed, -hee·ing.** —*interj.* **1.** the sound of a tittering laugh. —*n.* **2.** a titter; snicker. —*v.i.* **3.** to titter; snicker. [ME; OE *tæg tæg;* imit.]

Te·he·ran (te′hə ran′, -rän′, tē′ə-, tā′ə-; *Pers.* te hrän′), *n.* a city in and the capital of Iran, in the N part: wartime conference of Roosevelt, Churchill, and Stalin 1943. 2,317,116 (est. 1963). Also, **Tehran′.**

Te·hil·lim (tə hil′im; *Heb.* tə hē lēm′), *n.* *Hebrew.* the Book of Psalms.

Te·huan·te·pec (tə wän′tə pek′; *Sp.* te wän′te pek′), *n.* **1. Isthmus of,** an isthmus in S Mexico, between the Gulf of Tehuantepec and the Gulf of Campeche. 125 mi. wide at its narrowest point. **2. Gulf of,** an inlet of the Pacific, off the S coast of Mexico. ab. 300 mi. wide.

te·huan·te·pec·er (tə wän′tə pek′ər), *n.* a strong, squally, northerly wind in the Gulf of Tehuantepec. [TEHUANTEPEC + -ER[2]]

Te·huel·che (te wel′che), *n., pl.* **-ches,** (*esp. collectively*) **-che.** a member of an Indian people of Patagonia. [< Araucanian: lit., southeasterners] —**Tehuel′che·an,** *adj.*

Teich′mann's crys′tals (tīk′mənz), *Biochem.* hemin. [named after L. *Teichmann*-Stawiarski (d. 1895), German anatomist]

Tei·de (tā′the), *n.* **Pi·co de** (pē′kô de), a volcanic peak in the Canary Islands, on Tenerife. 12,190 ft. Also called **Pico de Tenerife, Pico de Teneriffe, Pico de Teyde.**

te ig·i·tur (tā ij′i to͝or′), *Church Latin.* thee therefore: the first words in the canon of the Mass in the Roman rite and in some other Latin liturgies.

teig·lach (tāg′ləKH, -läKH, tig′-), *n.* (*construed as sing. or pl.*) a confection consisting of small balls of dough boiled in a syrup of honey, sugar, and spices. Also, **taiglach.** [< Yiddish *teyglekh,* dim. of *teyg* dough < MHG *teig,* OHG *teic*]

teil (tēl), *n.* the European linden. See under **linden.** [< MF (OF *til*); r. *tilie* < L *tilia* linden]

teind (tēnd), *Scot. and North Eng.* —*adj.* **1.** tenth. —*n., v.t., v.i.* **2.** tithe. [ME *te(i)nd,* earlier *tende,* OE **tēonda;* c. OS *tehando,* Icel *tiunda,* Goth *taihunda* tenth]

Tei·re·si·as (tī re′sē əs), *n.* Tiresias.

Te·jo (te′zho͞o), *n.* Portuguese name of **Tagus.**

Tek·a·kwith·a (tek′ə kwith′ə), *n.* **Ka·te·ri** (kä′tə-rē) or **Catherine,** 1656–80, U.S. Indian ascetic.

tek·non·y·my (tek non′ə mē), *n.* the practice, among certain primitive peoples, of giving to the parent the name of the child. [< Gk *tékn(on)* child + *ōnym(a)* name + -Y[3]] —**tek·non′y·mous,** *adj.* —**tek·non′y·mous·ly,** *adv.*

tek·tite (tek′tīt), *n.* *Geol.* any of several kinds of small glassy bodies, in various forms, occurring in Australia and elsewhere, the exact origin of which is unknown. [< Gk *tēkt(ós)* molten + -ITE[1]]

tek·to·sil·i·cate (tek′tō sil′ə kit, -kāt′), *n.* *Mineral.* any of the three-dimensional silicates, each tetrahedral group of which shares all its oxygen atoms with neighboring groups, the ratio of silicon to oxygen being one to two. Cf. **cyclosilicate, inosilicate, nesosilicate, sorosilicate.** [< Gk *tēktó(s)* molten + SILICATE]

TEL, *Chem.* tetraethyllead.

tel-[1], var. of **tele-**[1]: *telesthesia.* Properly, this form should occur wherever the following element begins with a vowel; however, **teleo-** is more frequently found.

tel-[2], var. of **tele-**[2]: *telencephalon.* For form, see **tel-**[1].

tel., **1.** telegram. **2.** telegraph. **3.** telephone.

Te·la (te′lä), *n.* a seaport in N Honduras. 13,619 (1961).

tel·aes·the·sia (tel′is thē′zhə, -zhē ə, -zē ə), *n.* telesthesia.

Tel A·mar·na (tel′ ə mär′nə). See **Tell el Amarna.**

tel·a·mon (tel′ə mon′), *n., pl.* **tel·a·mo·nes** (tel′ə-mō′nēz). *Archit.* atlas (def. 9). [< L < Gk: bearer, support; identified with TELAMON]

Tel·a·mon (tel′ə mən), *n.* *Class. Myth.* an Argonaut and friend of Hercules, and the father of Ajax and Teucer.

Tel·a·mo·ni·an A′jax (tel′ə mō′nē ən), Ajax (def. 1).

tel·an·gi·ec·ta·sis (tel an′jē ek′tə sis), *n., pl.* **-ses** (-sēz′). *Pathol.* chronic dilatation of the capillaries and other small blood vessels, as seen in the faces of alcoholics, those exposed to raw, cold climates, and certain congenital sufferers. [< NL < Gk *tél(os)* end + *angeî(on)* receptacle + *éktasis* extension] —**tel·an·gi·ec·tat·ic** (tel an′jē ek tat′ik), *adj.*

Tel·an·thro·pus (tə lan′thrə pəs, tel′an thrō′pəs), *n.* a genus of fossil hominids, known from two fragmentary lower jaws found in the region of Swartkrans, near Johannesburg, South Africa. [< NL; see TEL-[1], ANTHROPO-]

tel·au·to·gram (tel ô′tə gram′), *n.* the reproduction made by a TelAutograph. [TEL-[1] + AUTO + -GRAM[1]]

Tel·Au·to·graph (tel ô′tə graf′, -gräf′), *n.* *Trademark.* a form of telegraph for reproducing handwriting, drawings, etc., the movements of a pen or pencil at one end of the line being reproduced in a pen or pencil at the other end by a system of electromagnets. —**tel·au′to·graph′ic,** *adj.* —**tel·au·tog·ra·phy** (tel′ô tog′rə-fē), *n.*

Tel A·viv (tel′ ə vēv′), *n.* a city in W central Israel: one of the centers of Jewish immigration following World War II. 334,900. Official name, **Tel Aviv-Jaffa.** —**Tel′ A·viv′i·an.**

Tel·chi·nes (tel kī′nēz), *n.* (*construed as pl.*) *Class. Myth.* a group of malicious beings, magicians and craftsmen, who lived on Rhodes.

tel·e (tel′ē), *n.* *Brit. Informal.* television. Also, **telly.** [by shortening]

tele-[1], a learned borrowing from Greek meaning "distant," especially "transmission over a distance," used in the formation of technical terms: *telegraph.* Also, **tel-, telo-.** [comb. form repr. Gk *tēle* far]

tele-[2], a learned borrowing from Greek meaning "end," "complete," used in the formation of compound words: *telestich.* Also, **tel-, teleo-, telo-.** [comb. form repr. Gk *télos* end, and *téleios* perfected]

tele., television.

Tel·e·boi·des (tel′ə boi′dēz), *n.* (*construed as pl.*) Taphiae.

tel·e·cast (tel′ə kast′, -käst′), *v.,* **-cast** or **-cast·ed, -cast·ing,** *n.* —*v.t., v.i.* **1.** to broadcast by television. —*n.* **2.** a television broadcast. [TELE(VISION + BROAD)CAST] —**tel′e·cast′er,** *n.*

tel·e·cin·e (tel′i sin′ē, tel′i sin′ē), *n.* *Television.* **1.** a studio from which all nonlive elements, as film, slides, etc., are transmitted to a television show. **2.** the material, esp. motion pictures, transmitted from this studio. **3.** the equipment that transmits this material. [TELE-[1] + CINE(MATOGRAPH)]

tel·e·com·mu·ni·ca·tion (tel′ə kə myo͞o′nə kā′shən), *n.* Often, **telecommunications.** (*construed as sing.*) the science or technology of communication by telephone, telegraph, etc. [TELE-[1] + COMMUNICATION]

tel·e·course (tel′ə kōrs′, -kôrs′), *n.* a course of study conducted over television. [TELE(VISION) + COURSE]

tel·e·du (tel′i do͞o′), *n.* a small dark brown mammal, *Mydaus javensis,* of the mountains of Java, Sumatra, and Borneo, having a white stripe down the back, and ejecting a fetid secretion when alarmed or in danger. [< Malay]

tel·e·film (tel′ə film′), *n.* a motion picture produced for broadcast by television. [TELE-[1] + FILM]

teleg., **1.** telegram. **2.** telegraph. **3.** telegraphy.

te·le·ga (tə leg′ə), *n.* a Russian cart of rude construction, having four wheels and no springs. [< Russ]

tel·e·gen·ic (tel′ə jen′ik), *adj.* having physical qualities or characteristics that televise well; videogenic. [TELE-[1] + (PHOTO)GENIC] —**tel′e·gen′i·cal·ly,** *adv.*

tel·eg·no·sis (tel′əg nō′sis, tel′əg-), *n.* supernatural or occult knowledge; clairvoyance. [TELE-[1] + -GNOSIS] —**tel·eg·nos·tic** (tel′əg nos′tik, tel′əg-), *adj.*

Te·leg·o·nus (tə leg′ə nəs), *n.* *Class. Myth.* **1.** a son of Odysseus and Circe who unknowingly killed his father and who eventually married Penelope. **2.** a son of Proteus and the husband of Io who was killed by Hercules in a wrestling match.

te·leg·o·ny (tə leg′ə nē), *n.* *Genetics.* the supposed influence of a previous sire upon the progeny subsequently borne by the same mother to other sires. [TELE-[1] + -GONY] —**tel·e·gon·ic** (tel′ə gon′ik), *adj.*

tel·e·gram (tel′ə gram′), *n.* a message or communication sent by telegraph; a telegraphic dispatch. [TELE-[1] + -GRAM[1]] —**tel′e·gram′mic, tel·e·gram·mat·ic** (tel′ə grə mat′ik), *adj.*

tel·e·graph (tel′ə graf′, -gräf′), *n.* **1.** an apparatus, system, or process for transmitting messages or signals to a distant place, esp. by means of an electric device consisting essentially of a sending instrument and a distant receiving instrument connected by a conducting wire or other communications channel. **2.** *Naut.* an apparatus, usually mechanical, for transmitting and receiving orders between the bridge of a vessel and the engine room or some other part of the engineering department. **3.** a telegraphic message. —*v.t.* **4.** to transmit or send (a message) by telegraph. **5.** to send a message to (a person) by telegraph. **6.** *Informal.* to divulge or indicate unwittingly to one's opponent (one's next offensive move); broadcast: *He telegraphed his punch and his opponent was able to parry it.* —*v.i.* **7.** to send a message by telegraph. [TELE-¹ + -GRAPH] —**te·leg·ra·pher** (tə leg′rə fər); *esp. Brit.*, **te·leg′ra·phist,** *n.* —**tel′e·graph′ic, tel′e·graph′i·cal,** *adj.* —**tel′e·graph′i·cal·ly,** *adv.*

tel′egraph bu′oy, a buoy placed over an underwater telegraph cable.

tel·e·graph·ese (tel′ə gra fēz′, -fēs′, tel′ə gra fēz′, -fēs′), *n.* a style of writing or speaking distinguished by the omissions, abbreviations, and combinations that are characteristic of telegrams. Example: EXPECT ARRIVE SIX EVENING. [TELEGRAPH + -ESE]

te·leg·ra·phone (tə leg′rə fōn′), *n.* **1.** an early magnetic sound-recording device for use with wire, tape, or disks. **2.** a device that connects into a telephone and automatically records a caller's message if the telephone remains unanswered. [< Dan *telegraphon.* See TELE-¹, GRAPHO-, -PHONE]

tel′egraph plant′, an East Indian tick trefoil, *Desmodium gyrans,* noted for the spontaneous, jerking, signallike motions of its leaflets.

te·leg·ra·phy (tə leg′rə fē), *n.* the art or practice of constructing or operating telegraphs. [TELE-¹ + -GRAPHY]

Tel·e·gu (tel′ə go͞o′), *n., pl.* **-gus,** (*esp. collectively*) **-gu,** *adj.* Telugu.

tel·e·ki·ne·sis (tel′ə ki nē′sis, -kī), *n.* the production of motion in a body, apparently without the application of material force: a power long claimed by spiritualistic mediums. [TELE-¹ + Gk *kínēsis* movement] —**tel·e·ki·net·ic** (tel′ə ki net′ik, -kī-), *adj.*

Tel el A·mar·na (tel′ el ə mär′nə). See **Tell el Amarna.**

Te·lem·a·chus (tə lem′ə kəs), *n.* *Class. Myth.* the son of Odysseus and Penelope who helped Odysseus to kill the suitors of Penelope.

Te·le·mann (tā′lə män′), *n.* **Ge·org Phi·lipp** (gā ôrk′ fē′lip, fil′ip), 1681–1767, German composer.

tel·e·mark (tel′ə märk′), *n.* (*sometimes cap.*) *Skiing.* a turn in which a skier places one ski far forward of the other and gradually angles the tip of the forward ski inward in the direction to be turned. [named after *Telemark,* a Norwegian county]

tel·e·me·chan·ics (tel′ə mə kan′iks), *n.* (*construed as sing.*) the science or practice of operating mechanisms by remote control.

te·lem·e·ter (tə lem′i tər, tel′ə mē′tər), *n.* **1.** any of certain devices or attachments for determining distances by measuring the angle subtending a known distance. **2.** *Elect.* the complete measuring, transmitting, and receiving apparatus for indicating, recording, or integrating at a distance, by electrical translating means, the value of a quantity. —*v.t.* **3.** to transmit (radio signals, data, etc.) automatically and at a distance, as between a ground station and an artificial satellite, space probe, or the like, esp. in order to record information, operate guidance apparatus, etc. [TELE-¹ + -METER] —**tel·e·met·ric** (tel′ə me′trik), *adj.* —**tel′e·met′ri·cal·ly,** *adv.* —**te·lem·e·try** (tə lem′i trē), *n.*

tel·e·mo·tor (tel′ə mō′tər), *n.* a mechanical, electrical, or hydraulic system by which power is applied at or controlled from a distant point, esp. such a system actuating a ship's rudder. [TELE-¹ + MOTOR]

Te·le·mus (tē′lə məs), *n.* *Class. Myth.* a seer who warned Polyphemus that Odysseus would blind him.

tel·en·ceph·a·lon (tel′en sef′ə lon′), *n., pl.* **-lons, -la** (-lə). *Anat.* the anterior section of the forebrain comprising the cerebrum and related structures. [TEL-² + ENCEPHALON] —**tel·en·ce·phal·ic** (tel′en sə fal′ik), *adj.*

teleo-, var. of **tele-²**: *teleology.*

tel′eolog′ical ar′gument, *Metaphys.* the argument for the existence of God based on the assumption that order in the universe implies an orderer and cannot be a natural feature of the universe. Also called **argument from design, tel′eolog′ical proof′.**

tel·e·ol·o·gy (tel′ē ol′ə jē, tē′lē-), *n.* *Philos.* **1.** the doctrine that final causes exist. **2.** the study of the evidences of design or purpose in nature. **3.** such design or purpose. **4.** the belief that purpose and design are a part of or are apparent in nature. **5.** (in vitalist philosophy) the doctrine that phenomena are guided not only by mechanical forces but that they also move toward certain goals of self-realization. [< NL *teleologia.* See TELEO-, -LOGY] —**tel·e·o·log·i·cal** (tel′ē ə loj′i-kəl, tē′lē-), **tel′e·o·log′ic,** *adj.* —**tel′e·o·log′i·cal·ly,** *adv.* —**tel′e·ol′o·gism,** *n.* —**tel′e·ol′o·gist,** *n.*

tel·e·ost (tel′ē ost′, tē′lē-), *adj.* **1.** belonging or pertaining to the *Teleostei,* a group of bony fishes including most living species. —*n.* **2.** a teleost fish. [< NL, back formation from *teleostei,* (pl.). See TELE-², OSTEO-] —**tel′e·os′te·an,** *adj., n.*

te·lep·a·thist (tə lep′ə thist), *n.* **1.** a student of or believer in telepathy. **2.** a person having telepathic power. [TELEPATH(Y) + -IST]

te·lep·a·thy (tə lep′ə thē), *n.* communication between minds by some means other than sensory perception. [TELE-¹ + -PATHY] —**tel·e·path·ic** (tel′ə-path′ik), *adj.* —**tel′e·path′i·cal·ly,** *adv.*

teleph., telephony.

Tel·e·phas·sa (tel′ə fas′ə), *n.* *Class. Myth.* the wife of Agenor and the mother of many children, among them Cadmus and Europa.

tel·e·phone (tel′ə fōn′), *n., v.,* **-phoned, -phon·ing.** —*n.* **1.** an apparatus, system, or process for transmission of sound or speech to a distant point, esp. by an electric device. —*v.t.* **2.** to speak to or summon (a person) by telephone. **3.** to send (a message) by telephone. —*v.i.* **4.** to send a message by telephone. [TELE-¹ + -PHONE] —**tel′e·phon′er,** *n.*

tel′ephone book′, a book, directory, or the like, usually containing an alphabetical list of telephone subscribers in a city or other area, together with their addresses and telephone numbers. Also called **tel′ephone direc′tory.**

tel′ephone booth′, a more or less soundproof booth containing a public telephone. Also called, *esp. Brit.,* **tel′ephone box′.**

tel′ephone pole′, a utility pole for supporting telephone wires.

tel′ephone receiv′er, a device, as in a telephone, that converts changes in an electric current into sound.

tel·e·phon·ic (tel′ə fon′ik), *adj.* **1.** of, pertaining to, or happening by means of a telephone system. **2.** carrying sound to a distance by artificial means. [TELE-¹ + PHONIC] —**tel′e·phon′i·cal·ly,** *adv.*

tel·e·pho·no·graph (tel′ə fō′nə graf′, -gräf′), *n.* a device that connects into a telephone and makes a phonograph record of the conversation. [TELE(PHONE) + PHONOGRAPH]

te·leph·o·ny (tə lef′ə nē), *n.* **1.** the construction or operation of telephones or telephonic systems. **2.** a system of telecommunications in which telephonic equipment is employed in the transmission of speech or other sound between points, with or without the use of wires. [TELEPHONE + -Y³]

tel·e·pho·to (tel′ə fō′tō), *adj.* **1.** noting or pertaining to telephotography. **2.** (cap.) *Trademark.* noting or pertaining to a lens construction for producing a relatively large image with a focal length shorter than that required by an ordinary lens producing an image of the same size. [(def. 1) short for TELEPHOTOGRAPH]

tel·e·pho·to·graph (tel′ə fō′tə graf′, -gräf′), *n.* **1.** a picture transmitted by wire or radio. **2.** *Rare.* a photograph taken with a telephoto lens. [TELE-¹ + PHOTOGRAPH]

tel·e·pho·tog·ra·phy (tel′ə fə tog′rə fē), *n.* **1.** photography of distant objects, using a Telephoto lens. **2.** the art of electrically reproducing photographs or facsimiles over a communications channel. [TELE-¹ + PHOTOGRAPHY] —**tel·e·pho·to·graph·ic** (tel′ə fō′tə-graf′ik), *adj.*

tel·e·pho·tom·e·ter (tel′ə fō tom′i tər), *n.* **1.** an instrument for measuring the amount of light emanating from a distant object. **2.** transmissometer. [TELE-¹ + PHOTOMETER]

Tel·e·phus (tel′ə fəs), *n.* *Class. Myth.* a son of Hercules and Auge who became king of Mysia and who charted the course that the Greeks followed to Troy.

tel·e·plasm (tel′ə plaz′əm), *n.* *Parapsychol.* a hypothetical emanation from the body of a medium which serves as the means for telekinesis. [TELE-¹ + -PLASM] —**tel′e·plas′mic,** *adj.*

tel·e·play (tel′ə plā′), *n.* a play written or adapted for broadcast on television. [TELE(VISION) + PLAY]

tel·e·port (tel′ə pôrt′, -pōrt′), *v.t.* to transport (a body) by telekinesis. [TELE-¹ + PORT⁵] —**tel′e·por·ta′tion, tel′e·por′tage,** *n.*

tel·e·print·er (tel′ə prin′tər), *n.* a teletypewriter. [TELE(TYPE) + PRINTER]

Tel·e·prompt·er (tel′ə promp′tər), *n.* *Trademark.* an off-camera device for unrolling a magnified script so that it is visible to the performers or speakers on a television program.

tel·e·ran (tel′ə ran′), *n.* *Electronics.* a system of aircraft navigation using radar to map the sky above an airfield, which, together with the map of the airfield itself and other pertinent data, is transmitted by television to the airplane approaching the field. [short for *Tele(vision) R(adar) A(ir) N(avigation)*]

tel·e·scope (tel′i skōp′), *n., adj., v.,* **-scoped, -scop·ing.** —*n.* **1.** an optical instrument for making distant objects appear nearer and larger, of two principal forms, one **(refracting telescope)** consisting essentially of an objective lens and an eyepiece or combination of lenses that magnify the image formed by the objective, and the other **(reflecting telescope)** having a concave mirror instead of an objective lens. **2.** (*cap.*) *Astron.* the constellation Telescopium. —*adj.* **3.** consisting of parts which fit and slide one within another. —*v.t.* **4.** to force together, one into another, or force into something else, in the manner of the sliding tubes of a jointed telescope. **5.** to shorten or condense: *to telescope the events of five hundred years into one history lecture.* —*v.i.* **6.** to slide together, or into something else, in the manner of the tubes of a jointed telescope. **7.** to be driven one into another, as railroad cars in a collision. **8.** to be or become shortened or condensed. [TELE-¹ + -SCOPE; r. *telescopium* (< NL) and *telescopio* (< It)]

tel·e·scop·ic (tel′i skop′ik), *adj.* **1.** of, pertaining to, or of the nature of a telescope. **2.** obtained by means of a telescope: *a telescopic view of the moon.* **3.** seen by a telescope; visible only through a telescope. **4.** far-seeing: *a telescopic eye.* **5.** consisting of parts which slide one within another like the tubes of a jointed telescope and are thus capable of being extended or shortened. Also, **tel′e·scop′i·cal.** [TELESCOPE + -IC] —**tel′e·scop′i·cal·ly,** *adv.*

Tel·e·sco·pi·um (tel′i skō′pē əm), *n., gen.* **-pi·i** (-pē ī′). *Astron.* the Telescope, a small southern constellation between Ara and Corona Austrinus. [< NL; see TELESCOPE, -IUM]

te·les·co·py (tə les′kə pē), *n.* **1.** the use of the telescope. **2.** telescopic investigation. [TELESCOPE + -Y³] —**te·les′co·pist,** *n.*

tel·e·sis (tel′i sis), *n.* *Sociol.* deliberate, purposeful utilization of the processes of nature and society to obtain particular goals. [< Gk: completion]

tel·e·spec·tro·scope (tel′i spek′trə skōp′), *n.* a telescope with an attached spectroscope for analyzing the spectra of light from celestial bodies. [TELE-¹ + SPECTROSCOPE]

Te·les·pho·rus (tə les′fər əs), *n.* **1.** pope A.D. 125?–136?. **2.** the god of recovery from illness: worshiped with Asclepius and often depicted in ancient art, as a child.

tel·e·ster·e·o·scope (tel′i ster′ē ə skōp′, -stēr′-), *n.* a binocular optical instrument used for stereoscopic viewing of distant objects; a small range finder. [TELE-¹ + STEREOSCOPE]

tel·es·te·ri·on (tel′i stēr′ē on′), *n., pl.* **tel·es·te·ri·a** (tel′i stēr′ē ə). (in ancient Greece) a building in which religious mysteries were celebrated. [< Gk *telestḗrion* place for initiation < *telestḗr* initiator or initiated person + *-ion* suffix of place]

tel·es·the·sia (tel′is thē′zhə, -zhē ə, -zē ə), *n.* sensation or perception received at a distance without the normal operation of the recognized sense organs. Also, **telaesthesia.** [TEL-¹ + ESTHESIA] —**tel·es·thet·ic** (tel′is thet′ik), **tel′aes·thet′ic,** *adj.*

te·les·tich (tə les′tik, tel′i stik′), *n.* *Pros.* a poem in which the last letters of successive lines form a word, a phrase, or the consecutive letters of the alphabet. Cf. **acrostic.** [TELE-² + STICH]

tel·e·ther·mom·e·ter (tel′ə thər mom′i tər), *n.* any of various thermometers that indicate or record temperatures at a distance, as by means of an electric current. [TELE-¹ + THERMOMETER] —**tel′e·ther·mom′e·try,** *n.*

tel·e·thon (tel′ə thon′), *n.* a television broadcast lasting several hours, esp. one soliciting support for a charity. [TELE-¹ + *-thon,* modeled after *marathon*]

Tel·e·type (tel′i tīp′), *n., v.,* **-typed, -typ·ing.** —*n.* **1.** *Trademark.* a teletypewriter. **2.** (*l.c.*) a network of teletypewriters with their connecting lines, switchboards, etc. —*v.t.* **3.** (*l.c.*) to send by Teletype. —*v.i.* **4.** (*l.c.*) to operate a Teletype.

Tel·e·type·set·ter (tel′i tīp′set′ər, tel′i tīp′-), *n.* *Trademark.* an apparatus, actuated by punched paper tape, that fits over the keyboard of a slugcasting machine, as the Linotype, for operating it automatically. *Abbr.:* TTS —**tel′e·type′set′ting,** *n.*

tel·e·type·writ·er (tel′i tīp′rī′tər, tel′i tīp′-), *n.* a telegraphic apparatus by which signals are sent by striking the letters and symbols of the keyboard of an instrument resembling a typewriter and are received by a similar instrument which automatically prints them in types corresponding to the keys struck. [TELE-¹ + TYPEWRITER]

tel·e·typ·ist (tel′i tī′pist), *n.* a person who operates a teletypewriter. [TELE-¹ + TYPIST]

te·leu·to·so·rus (tə lo͞o′tə sôr′əs, -sōr′-), *n., pl.* **-so·ri** (-sōr′ī, -sôr′ī). *Bot.* (formerly) telium. [< NL < Gk *teleut(ḗ)* + -o- end + SORUS]

te·leu·to·spore (tə lo͞o′tə spōr′, -spôr′), *n.* *Bot.* (formerly) teliospore. [< Gk *teleut(ḗ)* completion, end + -o- + -SPORE] —**te·leu·to·spor·ic** (tə lo͞o′tə-spōr′ik, -spôr′-), *adj.*

tel·e·van·ge·list (tel′i van′jə list), *n.* an evangelist who conducts regular religious services on television. [b. TELEVISION and EVANGELIST]

tel·e·view (tel′ə vyo͞o′), *v.t., v.i.* to view with a television receiver. [TELE-¹ + VIEW] —**tel′e·view′er,** *n.*

tel·e·vise (tel′ə vīz′), *v.t., v.i.,* **-vised, -vis·ing.** to send or receive by television. [back formation from TELEVISION]

tel·e·vi·sion (tel′ə vizh′ən), *n.* **1.** the broadcasting of a still or moving image via radiowaves to receivers which project it on a picture tube for viewing at a distance from the point of origin. **2.** the process involved. **3.** the field of television broadcasting. **4.** a set for receiving television broadcasts. [TELE-¹ + VISION] —**tel·e·vi·sion·al** (tel′ə vizh′ə nəl), *adj.* —**tel′e·vi′sion·al·ly,** *adv.* —**tel·e·vi·sion·ar·y** (tel′ə vizh′ə ner′ē), *adj.*

tel′evision sta′tion. See **station** (def. 11).

tel·e·vi·sor (tel′ə vī′zər), *n.* an apparatus for transmitting or receiving television. [TELEVISE + -OR²]

Tel·ex (tel′eks), *n.* (*often l.c.*) a two-way teleprinter service channeled through a public telecommunications system for instantaneous, direct communication between private subscribers at remote locations. [*tel(eprinter) ex(change)*]

tel·fer (tel′fər), *n., adj., v.t.* telpher. —**tel′fer·age,** *n.*

tel·ford (tel′fərd), *adj.* noting a form of road pavement composed of compacted and rolled stones of various sizes. [after Thomas *Telford* (1757–1834), Scottish engineer]

tel·har·mo·ni·um (tel′här mō′nē əm), *n.* a musical keyboard instrument operating by alternating currents of electricity which, on impulse from the keyboard, produce music at a distant point via telephone lines. [TEL-¹ + HARMONIUM]

tel·ic (tel′ik), *adj.* **1.** *Gram.* **a.** expressing end or purpose: *a telic clause.* **b.** perfective: *the Semitic telic aspect.* **2.** tending to a definite end. Cf. **atelic.** [< Gk *telik(ós)* final. See TEL-², -IC] —**tel′i·cal·ly,** *adv.*

te·li·o·spore (tē′lē ə spōr′, -spôr′, tel′ē-), *n.* *Bot.* a spore of certain rust fungi, which carries the fungus through the winter and which, on germination, produces the promycelium. [*telio-* (comb. form of TELIUM) + -SPORE] —**te′li·o·spor′ic,** *adj.*

te·li·um (tē′lē əm, tel′ē-), *n., pl.* **te·li·a** (tē′lē ə, tel′ē ə). *Bot.* the sorus of the rust fungi, bearing teliospores. [< NL < Gk *téleion,* neut. of *téleios* perfected] —**te′li·al,** *adj.*

tell¹ (tel), *v.,* **told, tell·ing.** —*v.t.* **1.** to give an account or narrative of; narrate; relate (a story, tale, etc.): *to tell the story of Lincoln's childhood.* **2.** to make known by speech or writing (a fact, news, information, etc.); communicate. **3.** to announce or proclaim. **4.** to utter (the truth, a lie, etc.). **5.** to express in words (thoughts, feelings, etc.). **6.** to reveal or divulge (something secret or private). **7.** to say plainly or positively: *I cannot tell just what was done.* **8.** to discern (a distant person or thing) so as to be able to identify or describe: *Can you tell who that is over there?* **9.** to discern or distinguish: *You could hardly tell the difference between them.* **10.** to inform (a person) of something: *He told me his name.* **11.** to assure emphatically: *I won't, I tell you!* **12.** to bid, order, or command: *Tell him to stop.* **13.** to mention one after another, as in enumerating; count or set one by one or in exact amount: *to tell the cattle in a herd.* —*v.i.* **14.** to give an account or report: *He told of his many misfortunes.* **15.** give evidence or be an indication: *The ruined temples told of an ancient culture, long since passed from existence.* **16.** to disclose something secret or private; play the informer (usually fol. by *on*): *to tell on a naughty sister.* **17.** to say positively: *Who can tell what tomorrow will bring?* **18.** to have force or effect; operate effectively: *a contest in which every stroke tells.* **19.** to produce a marked or severe effect: *The strain was telling on his health.* **20.** *Brit. Dial.* to talk or chat. **21.** **tell off, a.** to separate from the whole and assign to a particular duty. **b.** *Informal.* to rebuke severely; scold: *It was about time that someone told him off.* [ME *telle(n),* OE *tellan* to relate, count; c. D *tellen* to reckon, count, Icel *telja* to count, say, OHG *zellen.* See TALE]

—**Syn. 1.** recount, describe, report. **2.** impart. **3.** publish. **4.** speak. **6.** disclose, betray; acknowledge.

tell² (tel), *n.* an artificial mound consisting of the accumulated remains of one or more ancient settlements (often used in Egypt and the Middle East as part of a place name). [< Ar *tall* hillock]

Tell (tel), *n.* **Wil·helm** (vil′helm). See **William Tell.**

Tell′ Cit′y, a town in S Indiana. 6609 (1960).

Tell el A·mar·na (tel′ el ə mär′nə), a village in central United Arab Republic, on the Nile: site of the ancient Egyptian city of Akhetaton; extensive excavations. Also, **Tell′-el-A·mar′na, Tel el Amarna, Tel Amarna.**

tell·er (tel′ər), *n.* **1.** a person who or that which tells, relates, or communicates; narrator. **2.** a person employed in a bank to receive or pay out money over the counter. **3.** a person who tells, counts, or enumerates, as one appointed to count votes in a legislative body. [ME; see TELL[1], -ER[1]] —**tell′er·ship′,** *n.*

Tel·ler (tel′ər), *n.* **Edward,** born 1908, U.S. physicist, born in Hungary.

Tél·lez (*Sp.* tel′yeth), *n.* **Ga·bri·el** (*Sp.* gä′vrē el′). See **Tirso de Molina.**

tel·lin (tel′in), *n.* any marine bivalve mollusk of the genus *Tellina*, having a thin, rounded, white, yellow, pink, or purple shell. [< NL *Tellina* name of the genus < Gk *tellī́nē* a shellfish]

tell·ing (tel′ing), *adj.* **1.** having force or effect; effective; striking: *a telling blow.* **2.** revealing; indicative of much otherwise unnoticed: *a telling analysis of motivation in business.* [TELL[1] + -ING[2]] —**tell′ing·ly,** *adv.*

Tel·loh (te lō′), *n.* a village in SE Iraq, between the lower Tigris and Euphrates: site of the ancient Sumerian city of Lagash. Also, **Tel·lo′.**

tell·tale (tel′tāl′), *n.* **1.** a person who heedlessly or maliciously reveals private or confidential matters; tattler; talebearer. **2.** a thing serving to reveal or disclose something. **3.** any of various indicating or registering devices, as a time clock. **4.** *Music.* a gauge on an organ for indicating the air pressure. **5.** an indicator showing the position of a ship's rudder. **6.** a row of strips hung over a track to warn trainmen atop freight trains when they are approaching a low bridge, tunnel, or the like. **7.** *Yachting.* (on a sailboat) a feather, string, or similar device, often attached to the port and starboard shrouds and to the backstay to indicate the relative direction of the wind. **8.** *Squash.* a narrow piece of metal across the front wall of a court, parallel to and 17 inches above the base: a ball that hits upon or below this is an out. —*adj.* **9.** that reveals or betrays what is not intended to be known: *a telltale blush.* **10.** giving notice or warning of something, as a mechanical device. [TELL[1] + TALE] —**tell′tale′ly,** *adv.*

tell′tale com′pass, *Naut.* See **hanging compass.**

tellur-, *Chem.* a prefix indicating the presence of tellurium: *tellurite.*

tel·lu·rate (tel′yə rāt′), *n.* *Chem.* a salt of a telluric acid, as of H_2TeO or H_6TeO_6. [TELLUR- + -ATE[2]]

tel·lu·ri·an[1] (te lo͝or′ē ən), *adj.* **1.** of or characteristic of the earth or its inhabitants; terrestrial. —*n.* **2.** an inhabitant of the earth. [< L *tellūri-* (s. of *tellūs*) earth + -AN]

tel·lu·ri·an[2] (te lo͝or′ē ən), *n.* tellurion.

tel·lu·ric[1] (te lo͝or′ik), *adj.* **1.** of or pertaining to the earth; terrestrial. **2.** of or proceeding from the earth or soil. [< L *tellūri-* (s. of *tellūs*) earth + -IC]

tel·lu·ric[2] (te lo͝or′ik), *adj.* **1.** *Chem.* of or containing tellurium, esp. in the hexavalent state. **2.** containing tellurium in a higher valence state than the corresponding tellurous compound. [TELLUR- + -IC]

tel·lu·ride (tel′yə rīd′, -rid), *n.* *Chem.* a binary compound of tellurium with an electropositive element or group. [TELLUR- + -IDE]

tel·lu·ri·on (tə lo͝or′ē on′), *n.* an apparatus for showing the manner in which the diurnal rotation and annual revolution of the earth and the obliquity of its axis produce the alternation of day and night and the changes of the seasons. Also, **tellurian.** [< L *tellūr-* (s. of *tellūs*) earth + Gk *-on*, neut. of *-os* adj. suffix]

tel·lu·rite (tel′yə rīt′), *n.* **1.** *Chem.* a salt of tellurous acid, as sodium tellurite, Na_2TeO_3. **2.** a rare mineral, tellurium dioxide, TeO_2. [TELLUR- + -ITE[1]]

tel·lu·ri·um (te lo͝or′ē əm), *n.* *Chem.* a rare, lustrous, brittle, crystalline, silver-white element resembling sulfur in its properties, and usually occurring in nature combined with gold, silver, or other metals of high atomic weight: used in the manufacture of alloys and as a coloring agent in glass and ceramics. *Symbol:* Te; *at. wt.:* 127.60; *at. no.:* 52; *sp. gr.:* 6.24. [< L *tellūr-* (s. of *tellūs*) earth + (URAN)IUM]

tel·lu·rize (tel′yə rīz′), *v.t.*, **-rized, -riz·ing.** to mix or cause to combine with tellurium. [TELLUR- + -IZE]

tel·lu·rous (tel′yər əs, te lo͝or′əs), *adj.* *Chem.* containing tetravalent tellurium. [TELLUR- + -OUS]

Tel·lus (tel′əs), *n.* an ancient Roman goddess of the earth and of marriages and fertility, identified with the Greek goddess Gaea.

tel·ly (tel′ē), *n.*, *pl.* **-lies.** *Brit. Informal.* **1.** television. **2.** a television receiving set. [by shortening and alter.]

telo-[1], var. of **tele-[1]**: *telodynamic.*

telo-[2], var. of **tele-[2]**: *telophase.*

tel·o·dy·nam·ic (tel′ō dī nam′ik, -di-), *adj.* pertaining to the transmission of power over considerable distances, as by means of endless wire ropes on pulleys. [TELO-[1] + DYNAMIC]

tel·o·lec·i·thal (tel′ō les′i thəl), *adj.* *Embryol.* having an accumulation of yolk near the vegetal pole, as the large-yolked eggs or ova of reptiles and birds. [TELO-[2] + Gk *lékith(os)* yolk + -AL[1]]

tel·o·phase (tel′ə fāz′), *n.* *Biol.* the final stage of mitosis in which new nuclei are formed. [TELO-[2] + PHASE] —**tel′o·pha′sic,** *adj.*

tel·o·tax·is (tel′ə tak′sis), *n.* *Biol.* movement of an organism toward or away from only one of a number of simultaneous stimuli. [TELO-[2] + -TAXIS]

tel·pher (tel′fər), *n.* **1.** a traveling unit, car, or carrier in a telpherage. —*adj.* **2.** of or pertaining to a system of telpherage. —*v.t.* **3.** to transport by means of a telpherage. Also, **telfer.** [alter. of *telephore.* See TELE-[1] + -PHORE]

tel·pher·age (tel′fər ij), *n.* a transportation system in which cars or carriers are suspended from or run on wire cables or the like, esp. one operated by electricity. Also, **telferage.** [TELPHER + -AGE]

Tel·phu·sa (tel fyo͞o′sə), *n.* *Class. Myth.* a spring nymph of Boeotia who cunningly advised Apollo to erect a temple and oracle at Delphi where she knew he would have to subdue the Python.

tel·son (tel′sən), *n.* the last segment, or an appendage of the last segment, of certain arthropods, as the middle flipper of a lobster's tail. [< Gk: boundary, limit] —**tel·son·ic** (tel son′ik), *adj.*

Tel·star (tel′stär′), *n.* *Trademark.* one of a series of low-altitude, active communications satellites for testing broadband microwave communications and satellite tracking techniques in space. [TEL-[1] + STAR]

Tel·u·gu (tel′o͞o go͞o′), *n.*, *pl.* **-gus,** (*esp. collectively*) **-gu,** *adj.* —*n.* **1.** a Dravidian language spoken in SE India in the region N of Madras. **2.** a member of the people speaking this language. —*adj.* **3.** of Telugu or the Telugu. Also, **Telegu.**

tem·blor (tem′blər, -blôr; *Sp.* tem blôr′), *n.*, *pl.* **-blors,** *Sp.* **-blo·res** (-blô′res). *Chiefly U.S.* a tremor; earthquake. [< Sp: lit., a quaking < *tembl(ar)* (to) quake (? b. L *timēre* to fear and LL *tremulāre* to quake; see TREMBLE) + *-or* -OR[1]]

tem·e·nos (tem′ə nos′), *n.*, *pl.* **-ne** (-nē′). (in ancient Greece) a sacred enclosure or precinct, esp. one containing a temple or dedicated to a god. [< Gk: lit., something cut off, set apart, akin to *témnein* to cut]

Tem·e·nus (tem′ə nəs), *n.* *Class. Myth.* **1.** a son of Aristomachus who was allotted the city of Argos for his participation in the Heraclidae invasion of Peloponnesus. **2.** a son of Pelasgus believed to have reared Hera.

tem·er·ar·i·ous (tem′ə râr′ē əs), *adj.* reckless; rash. [< L *temerārius* < *temer(e)* blindly, heedlessly + *-ārius* -ARY] —**tem′er·ar′i·ous·ly,** *adv.* —**tem′er·ar′i·ous·ness,** *n.*

te·mer·i·ty (tə mer′i tē), *n.* reckless boldness; rashness. [late ME *temeryte* < L *temeritās* hap, chance, rashness < *temer(e)* by chance, rashly + *-itās* -ITY] —**Syn.** audacity, effrontery, foolhardiness.

Te·mes·vár (te′mesh vär), *n.* Hungarian name of **Timisoara.**

temp., **1.** temperature. **2.** temporary. **3.** in the time of. [< L *tempore*]

Tem·pe (tem′pē), *n.* **1. Vale of,** a valley in E Greece, in Thessaly, between Mounts Olympus and Ossa. **2.** a city in central Arizona, near Phoenix. 24,897 (1960).

Tem·pel (tem′pəl), *n.* a walled plain in the first quadrant of the face of the moon: about 23 miles in diameter.

Tem·pel·hof (tem′pəl hōf′), *n.* a district of S West Berlin: international airport.

tem·per (tem′pər), *n.* **1.** a particular state of mind or feelings. **2.** habit of mind, esp. with respect to irritability or patience, outbursts of anger, or the like; disposition: *an even temper.* **3.** heat of mind or passion, shown in outbursts of anger, resentment, etc. **4.** calm disposition or state of mind: *to be out of temper.* **5.** a substance added to something to modify its properties or qualities. **6.** *Metall.* **a.** the degree of hardness and strength imparted to a metal, as by quenching, heat treatment, or cold working. **b.** the percentage of carbon in tool steel. **c.** the operation of tempering. **7.** *Archaic.* a middle course; compromise. **8.** *Obs.* the constitution or character of a substance. —*v.t.* **9.** to moderate or mitigate: *to temper justice with mercy.* **10.** to soften or tone down. **11.** to bring to a proper, suitable, or desirable state by or as by blending or admixture: **12.** to moisten, mix, and work up into proper consistency, as clay or mortar. **13.** *Metall.* **a.** to impart strength or toughness to (steel or cast iron) by heating it to some temperature below the transformation point, maintaining it there for some time, then cooling it under controlled conditions. **b.** (formerly) to impart strength and toughness to (steel) by quenching it at a temperature above the transformation point sufficiently to cool the surfaces partly, withdrawing it to allow the interior to reheat the surfaces, then quenching it again to environmental temperature. **14.** to produce internal stresses in (glass) by sudden cooling from low red heat; toughen. **15.** to tune (a keyboard instrument, as a piano, organ, etc.) so as to make the tones available in different keys or tonalities. **16.** to modify (color) by mixing with a medium. **17.** *Archaic.* to combine or blend in due proportions. **18.** *Archaic.* to pacify. —*v.i.* **19.** to be or become tempered. [ME *tempre(n)*, OE *temprian* < L *temperāre* to divide or proportion duly, temper] —**tem′per·a·bil′i·ty,** *n.* —**tem′per·a·ble,** *adj.* —**tem′per·er,** *n.*

—**Syn. 1.** nature, condition. **2.** humor. See **disposition. 3.** irritation. **4.** equanimity, coolness, composure. **10.** See **modify.**

tem·per·a (tem′pər ə), *n.* **1.** a technique of painting in which an emulsion consisting of water and pure egg yolk or a mixture of egg and oil is used as a binder or medium, characterized by its lean film-forming properties and rapid drying rate. **2.** a painting executed in this technique. **3.** a water paint used in this technique in which the egg-water or egg-oil emulsion is used as a binder. Cf. **distemper[2]** (defs. 1, 2). [< It, short for *pingere a tempera* painting in distemper. See TEMPER]

tem·per·a·ment (tem′pər ə mənt, -prə mənt), *n.* **1.** the individual peculiarity of physical organization by which the manner of thinking, feeling, and acting of every person is permanently affected; natural disposition. **2.** unusual personal make-up manifested by peculiarities of feeling, temper, action, etc., with disinclination to submit to conventional rules or restraints. **3.** the combination of the four cardinal humors, the relative proportions of which were supposed to determine physical and mental constitution. **4.** *Music.* **a.** the tuning of a keyboard instrument, as the piano, organ, etc., so that the instrument may be played in all keys without further tuning. **b.** a particular system of doing this. **5.** *Archaic.* act of tempering or moderating. **6.** *Archaic.* climate. **7.** *Obs.* temperature. [late ME < L *temperāment(um)* due mixture < *temperā(re)* (to) mix properly + *-mentum* -MENT]

tem·per·a·men·tal (tem′pər ə men′tᵊl, -prə men′-), *adj.* **1.** having or exhibiting a strongly marked, individual temperament. **2.** moody, irritable, or sensitive: *a temperamental actress.* **3.** given to erratic behavior. **4.** of or pertaining to temperament; constitutional: *temperamental differences.* [TEMPERAMENT + -AL[1]] —**tem′per·a·men′tal·ly,** *adv.*

tem·per·ance (tem′pər əns, tem′prəns), *n.* **1.** moderation or self-restraint in action, statement, etc.; self-control. **2.** habitual moderation in the indulgence of a natural appetite or passion, esp. in the use of alcoholic liquors. **3.** total abstinence from alcoholic liquors. [ME *temperaunce* < AF < L *temperantia* self-control. See TEMPER, -ANCE]

tem·per·an′tia tray′ (tem′pə ran′shə), a pewter tray of the 17th century, having a figure symbolic of temperance, in relief, with the legend "Temperantia," meaning "self-control." Also called **temperan′tia sal′ver.**

tem·per·ate (tem′pər it, tem′prit), *adj.* **1.** moderate or self-restrained; not extreme in opinion, statement, etc.: *a temperate response to an insulting challenge.* **2.** moderate as regards indulgence of appetite or passion, esp. in the use of alcoholic liquors. **3.** not excessive in degree, as things, qualities, etc. **4.** moderate in respect to temperature. [ME *temperat* < L *temperāt(us)*, ptp. of *temperāre* to control. See TEMPER, -ATE[1]] —**tem′per·ate·ly,** *adv.* —**tem′per·ate·ness,** *n.*

—**Syn. 1.** continent, sober, dispassionate. —**Ant. 1.** unrestrained.

Tem′perate Zone′, *Geog.* the part of the earth's surface lying between the tropic of Cancer and the Arctic Circle in the Northern Hemisphere or between the tropic of Capricorn and the Antarctic Circle in the Southern Hemisphere.

tem·per·a·ture (tem′pər ə chər, -prə chər), *n.* **1.** a measure of the warmth or coldness of an object or substance with reference to some standard value. The temperature of two systems is the same when the systems are in thermal equilibrium. **2.** *Physiol., Pathol.* **a.** the degree of heat in a living body, esp. the human body. **b.** the excess of this above the normal: in man this is about 98.6°F or about 37°C. **3.** *Obs.* mildness, as of the weather. **4.** *Obs.* temperament. [< L *temperātūra* a tempering. See TEMPERATE, -URE]

tem′perature gra′dient, *Meteorol.* rate of change of temperature with distance.

Tem′per·a·ture-Hu·mid′i·ty In′dex (tem′pər ə chər hyo͞o mid′i tē *or, often,* -yo͞o-, -prə chər-), a number representing an estimate of the effect of temperature and moisture on humans, computed by multiplying the sum of dry-bulb and wet-bulb temperature readings by 0.4 and adding 15, with 65 assumed as the highest comfortable Index. *Abbr.:* T.H.I.

tem′per col′or, *Metall.* any of the colors appearing on the surface of clean, unoxidized steel heated in air, from pale yellow at the coolest to dark blue at the hottest: used as an approximate indication of temperature.

tem·pered (tem′pərd), *adj.* **1.** having a temper or disposition of a specified character (usually used in combination): *a good-tempered child.* **2.** *Music.* tuned in accordance with some other temperament than just or pure temperament, esp., tuned in equal temperament. **3.** made less intense or violent, esp. by the influence of something good or benign: *justice tempered with mercy.* [TEMPER + -ED[2]]

tem′per pin′, *Scot.* **1.** the pin or screw regulating the tightness of the band of a spinning wheel. **2.** disposition; temper.

tem·pest (tem′pist), *n.* **1.** an extensive current of wind rushing with great velocity and violence, esp. one attended with rain, hail, or snow; a violent storm. **2.** a violent commotion, disturbance, or tumult. —*v.t.* **3.** to affect by or as by a tempest; disturb violently. [ME *tempeste* < OF < VL **tempesta* for L *tempestās* season, weather, storm < *tempes-* (var. of *tempus* time) + *-tās* -TY[2]]

Tempest, The, a comedy (1611) by Shakespeare.

Tem·pes·ta·tes (tem′pi stā′tēz), *n.pl.* the ancient Roman goddesses of storms.

tem·pest-tossed (tem′pist tôst′, -tost′), *adj.* buffeted about, as by adversities. Also, **tem′pest-tost′.**

tem·pes·tu·ous (tem pes′cho͞o əs), *adj.* **1.** characterized by or subject to tempests: *the tempestuous ocean.* **2.** of the nature of or resembling a tempest: *a tempestuous wind.* **3.** tumultuous; turbulent: *a tempestuous period in history.* [< L *tempestuōs(us)*, deriv. of *tempestus*, var. of *tempestās* TEMPEST; see -OUS] —**tem·pes′tu·ous·ly,** *adv.* —**tem·pes′tu·ous·ness,** *n.*

—**Syn. 2.** violent, stormy.

tem·pi (tem′pē), *n.* a pl. of **tempo.**

Tem·plar (tem′plər), *n.* **1.** a member of a religious military order founded by Crusaders in Jerusalem about 1118, and suppressed in 1312. **2.** a barrister or other person occupying chambers in the Temple, London. **3.** a member of the Masonic order, Knights Templars. Also called **Knight Templar.** [< ML *templār(ius)* (see TEMPLE, -AR[2]); r. ME *templer* < AF (see -ER[2])]

tem·plate (tem′plit), *n.* **1.** templet. **2.** Also called **safe.** a marble base for a toilet. [TEM(PLET) + PLATE[1]]

tem·ple[1] (tem′pəl), *n.* **1.** an edifice or place dedicated to the service or worship of a deity or deities. **2.** (*usually cap.*) any of the three successive houses of worship in Jerusalem in use by the Jews in Biblical times, the first built by Solomon, the second by Zerubbabel, and the third by Herod. **3.** a synagogue, usually a Reform or Conservative one. **4.** an edifice erected as a place of public worship; a church, esp. a large or imposing one. **5.** any place or object in which God dwells, as the body of a Christian. I Cor. 6:19. **6.** (in France) a Protestant church. **7.** *Mormonism.* a building devoted to administering sacred ordinances, principally that of eternal marriage. **8.** a building, usually large or pretentious, devoted to some public use: *a temple of music.* **9.** (*cap.*) either of two establishments of the medieval Templars, one in London and the other in Paris. **10.** (*cap.*) either of two groups of buildings (**Inner Temple** and **Middle Temple**) on the site of the Templars' former establishment in London, occupied by two of the Inns of Court. **11.** a building used by the Templars in the U.S. **12.** a building used by any of various fraternal orders. [ME, var. of *tempel*, OE < L *templum* space demarcated by an augur for taking auspices, temple] —**tem′pled,** *adj.* —**tem′ple·like′,** *adj.*

tem·ple[2] (tem′pəl), *n.* **1.** the flattened region on either side of the forehead in man. **2.** a corresponding region in certain animals. **3.** either of the sidepieces of a pair of spectacles, extending back above the ears. [ME < MF < VL **tempula* < L *tempora* the temples, pl. (taken as fem. sing.) of *tempus* period of time, orig. a part (of space or time) marked out or cut off; akin to TEMENOS]

tem·ple[3] (tem′pəl), *n.* a device in a loom for keeping the cloth stretched to the proper width during the weaving. [late ME *tempylle* < MF *temple* < L *templum* purlin, small piece of timber. See TEMPLE[1]]

Tem·ple (tem′pəl), *n.* **1. Sir William,** 1628–99, English essayist and diplomat. **2.** a city in central Texas. 30,419 (1960). **3.** a boy's given name.

Temple, The, a collection of poems (1633) by George Herbert.

Tem′ple Cit′y, a town in SW California, near Los Angeles. 31,838 (1960).

Tem′ple of Ar′temis, the large and imposing temple at Ephesus, dedicated to Artemis. Cf. **Seven Wonders of the World.**

tem·plet (tem′plit), *n.* **1.** a pattern, mold, or the like, usually consisting of a thin plate of wood or metal, serving as a gauge or guide in mechanical work. **2.** *Building.* a horizontal piece, as of timber or stone, in a wall, to receive and distribute the pressure of a girder, beam, or the like. **3.** *Shipbuilding.* either of two wedges in each of the temporary blocks forming the support for the keel of a ship while building. **4.** *Aerial Photogrammetry.* any object having lines, slots, or straightedges to represent lines radiating from the center of a photograph, used for graphic triangulation. Also, **template.** [< F, dim. of *temple* TEMPLE[3]; see -ET]

Tem′ple Ter′race, a town in W Florida. 3812 (1960).

tem·plon (tem′plon), *n.* *Rare.* iconostasis. [< MGk *témplon* reredos, iconostasis < L *templum* temple[1]]

tem·po (tem′pō), *n., pl.* **-pos, -pi** (-pē). **1.** *Music.* relative rapidity or rate of movement, usually indicated by such terms as *adagio, allegro,* etc., or by reference to the metronome. **2.** characteristic rate, rhythm, or pattern of work or activity: *the tempo of city life.* **3.** *Chess.* the gaining or losing of time and effectiveness relative to one's continued mobility or developing position, esp. with respect to the number of moves required to gain an objective: *Black gained a tempo.* [< It < L *tempus* time]

tem·po·ral[1] (tem′pər əl, tem′prəl), *adj.* **1.** of or pertaining to time. **2.** pertaining to or concerned with the present life or this world; worldly: *temporal joys.* **3.** enduring for a time only; temporary; transitory (opposed to *eternal*). **4.** *Gram.* **a.** of, pertaining to, or expressing time: *a temporal adverb.* **b.** of or pertaining to the tenses of a verb. **5.** secular, lay, or civil, as opposed to ecclesiastical. —*n.* Usually, **temporals. 6.** a temporal possession, estate, or the like; temporality. **7.** something that is temporal; a temporal matter or affair. [ME < L *temporāl(is)* < *tempor-* (s. of *tempus*) time + *-ālis* -AL[1]] —**tem′po·ral·ly,** *adv.* —**tem′po·ral·ness,** *n.*

tem·po·ral[2] (tem′pər əl, tem′prəl), *Anat.* —*adj.* **1.** of, pertaining to, or situated near the temple or a temporal bone. —*n.* **2.** any of several parts in the temporal region, esp. the temporal bone. [< L *temporāl(is)* < *tempor-* (s. of *tempus*) TEMPLE[2] + *-ālis* -AL[1]]

tem′poral bone′, *Anat.* either of a pair of compound bones, forming part of the sides and base of the skull. See diag. under **skull.**

tem′poral hour′, *Astron.* a unit of time used in the Roman and Ottoman empires that divided the daylight into an equal number of hours, resulting in long summer hours and short winter hours.

tem·po·ral·i·ty (tem′pə ral′i tē), *n., pl.* **-ties. 1.** temporal character or nature; temporariness. **2.** something temporal. **3.** Usually, **temporalities.** a temporal possession, revenue, or the like, as of the church or clergy. [ME *temporalite* < L *temporālitās.* See TEMPORAL[1], -ITY]

tem′poral lobe′, *Anat.* the lateral lobe of each cerebral hemisphere, in front of the occipital lobe.

tem·po·ra mu·tan·tur, nos et mu·ta·mur in il·lis (tem′pō rä′ mōō tän′tōōr, nōs et mōō tä′mōōr in il′ēs; *Eng.* tem′pər ə myōō tan′tər, nōs et myōō tā′mər in il′is), *Latin.* the times change and we change with them.

tem·po·rar·y (tem′pə rer′ē), *adj.* lasting, existing, serving, or effective for a time only; not permanent: *a temporary need; a temporary job.* [< L *temporāri(us)* < *tempor-* (s. of *tempus*) time + *-ārius* -ARY] —**tem·po·rar·i·ly** (tem′pə râr′ə lē, tem′pə rer′-), *adv.* —**tem′po·rar′i·ness,** *n.*

—**Syn.** impermanent, passing. TEMPORARY, TRANSIENT, TRANSITORY agree in referring to that which is not lasting or permanent. TEMPORARY implies an arrangement established with no thought of continuance but with the idea of being changed soon: *a temporary structure.* TRANSIENT describes that which is in the process of passing by, and which will therefore last or stay only a short time: *a transient condition.* TRANSITORY describes an innate characteristic by which a thing, by its very nature, lasts only a short time: *Life is transitory.* —**Ant.** permanent.

tem′porary du′ty, duty of limited duration performed with an organization other than the one to which a person is normally attached or assigned. *Abbr.:* TDY

tem′porary life′ annu′ity, *Insurance.* an annuity that ceases upon the death of the annuitant or upon the expiration of a period of time, whichever occurs first.

tem·po·rise (tem′pə rīz′), *v.i.,* **-rised, -ris·ing.** *Chiefly Brit.* temporize. —**tem′po·ri·sa′tion,** *n.* —**tem′po·ris′er,** *n.* —**tem′po·ris′ing·ly,** *adv.*

tem·po·rize (tem′pə rīz′), *v.i.,* **-rized, -riz·ing. 1.** to be indecisive or evasive to gain time or delay acting. **2.** to comply with the time or occasion; yield temporarily or ostensibly to prevailing opinion or circumstances. **3.** to treat or parley so as to gain time (usually fol. by *with*). **4.** to come to terms (usually fol. by *with*). **5.** to effect a compromise (usually fol. by *between*). [< ML *temporiz(āre)* (to) hang back, delay < *tempor-* (s. of *tempus*) time + *-izāre* -IZE] —**tem′po·ri·za′tion,** *n.* —**tem′po·riz′er,** *n.* —**tem′po·riz′ing·ly,** *adv.*

temporo-, a combining form of **temporal**[2]: *temporomaxillary.* [< L *tempor-* (s. of *tempus*) TEMPLE[2] + -o-]

tem·po·ro·max·il·lar·y (tem′pə rō mak′sə ler′ē, -mak sil′ə rē), *adj. Anat.* of, pertaining to, or situated near the temporal and maxillary bones. [TEMPORO- + MAXILLARY]

temps le·vé (*Fr.* täN lə vā′), *pl.* **temps le·vés** (*Fr.* täN lə vā′). *Ballet.* a small hop on one foot, with the other foot raised off the floor. [< F]

temps li·é (*Fr.* täN lē ā′), *pl.* **temps li·és** (*Fr.* täN lē ā′). *Ballet.* a series of systematized and connected arm and leg movements done for practice. [< F]

tempt (tempt), *v.t.* **1.** to induce or persuade by enticement or allurement, as to do something unwise, wrong, or immoral. **2.** to allure, appeal strongly to, or invite: *The offer tempts me.* **3.** to render strongly disposed to do something: *The book tempted me to read more on the subject.* **4.** to try to dispose or incite; assail with enticements, esp. to evil. **5.** to put to the test in a venturesome way; risk provoking; provoke: *to tempt one's fate.* **6.** *Obs.* to try or test. [ME *tempt(en)* < L *temptāre* to test, tempt] —**tempt′a·ble,** *adj.*

—**Syn. 1.** TEMPT, SEDUCE may both mean to allure or entice to something unwise or wicked. TO TEMPT is to attract by holding out the probability of gratification or advantage, often in the direction of that which is wrong or unwise: *to tempt a man with a bribe.* TO SEDUCE is literally to lead astray, sometimes from that which absorbs one or demands attention, but oftener, in a moral sense, from rectitude, chastity, etc.: *to seduce a person away from loyalty.* **2.** inveigle, decoy, lure. —**Ant. 1.** dissuade.

temp·ta·tion (temp tā′shən), *n.* **1.** act of tempting; enticement or allurement. **2.** something that tempts, entices, or allures. **3.** fact or state of being tempted, esp. to evil. **4.** an instance of it. [ME *temptacion* < L *temptātiōn-* (s. of *temptātiō*) a testing. See TEMPT, -ATION] —**temp·ta′tion·al,** *adj.*

tempt·er (temp′tər), *n.* **1.** one who or that which tempts, esp. to evil. **2. the Tempter,** Satan; the devil. [ME *temptour* < L *temptātōr-* (s. of *temptātor*). See TEMPT, -ATOR]

tempt·ing (temp′ting), *adj.* that tempts; enticing or inviting. [TEMPT + -ING[2]] —**tempt′ing·ly,** *adv.* —**tempt′ing·ness,** *n.*

—**Syn.** attractive, alluring, seductive. —**Ant.** repellent.

tempt·ress (temp′tris), *n.* a female tempter. [TEMPT(E)R + -ESS]

tem·pu·ra (tem′pōō rä′, tem pōōr′ə), *n. Japanese Cookery.* seafood or vegetables dipped in batter and deep-fried. [< Jap: fried food]

tem·pus e·dax re·rum (tem′pōōs e′daks rā′rōōm; *Eng.* tem′pəs ē′daks rēr′əm), *Latin.* time, devourer of all things.

tem·pus fu·git (tem′pōōs fōō′git; *Eng.* tem′pəs fyōō′jit), *Latin.* time flies.

Te·mu·co (te mōō′kō), *n.* a city in S Chile. 111,980 (1960).

ten (ten), *n.* **1.** a cardinal number, nine plus one. **2.** a symbol for this number, as 10 or X. **3.** a set of this many persons or things. **4.** a playing card with ten pips. **5.** Also called **ten's place.** *Math.* **a.** (in a mixed number) the position of the second digit to the left of the decimal point. **b.** (in a whole number) the position of the second digit from the right. **6. take ten,** *Informal.* to rest from what one is doing, esp. for ten minutes. —*adj.* **7.** amounting to ten in number. [ME, OE *tēn(e),* OE also *tīen(e);* c. D *tien,* G *zehn,* Icel *tíu,* Goth *taihun,* L *decem,* Gk *déka,* Skt *daśa*]

ten-, an element occurring in loan words from Latin (*tenant*), used, with the meaning "hold," in the formation of technical terms: *tenaculum.* [< L *ten(ēre)* (to) hold]

ten., **1.** tenor. **2.** *Music.* tenuto.

ten·a·ble (ten′ə bəl), *adj.* **1.** capable of being held, maintained, or defended, as against attack or dispute: *a tenable theory.* **2.** capable of being occupied, possessed, held, or enjoyed, as under certain conditions: *a research grant tenable for two years.* [< F: that can be held < *ten-* (< L *tenēre* to hold); see TEN- + *-able* -ABLE] —**ten′a·bil′i·ty, ten′a·ble·ness,** *n.* —**ten′a·bly,** *adv.*

ten·ace (ten′ās′), *n.* *Whist, Bridge.* a sequence of two high cards that lack an intervening card to be in consecutive order, as the ace and queen. Cf. **major tenace, minor tenace.** [< Sp *tenaza(s)* tongs, tenace (in card games), deriv. of *tenaz* < L *tenāc-* (s. of *tenāx*) TENACIOUS; cf. ML *tenācēs* forceps]

te·na·cious (tə nā′shəs), *adj.* **1.** holding fast; characterized by keeping a firm hold (often fol. by *of*): *a tenacious grip on my arm; tenacious of old habits.* **2.** highly retentive: *a tenacious memory.* **3.** pertinacious, persistent, stubborn, or obstinate. **4.** adhesive or sticky; viscous or glutinous. **5.** holding together; cohesive; not easily pulled asunder; tough. [TENACI(TY) + -OUS] —**te·na′cious·ly,** *adv.* —**te·na′cious·ness,** *n.*

—**Syn. 3.** opinionated, dogged. **4.** clinging.

te·nac·i·ty (tə nas′i tē), *n.* the quality or property of being tenacious. [< L *tenācitās* < *tenāci-* (s. of *tenāx*) holding fast + *-tās* -TY[2]]

—**Syn.** See **perseverance.**

te·nac·u·lum (tə nak′yə ləm), *n., pl.* **-la** (-lə). **1.** *Surg.* a small sharp-pointed hook set in a handle, used for seizing and picking up parts in operations and dissections. **2.** *Entomol.* a clasplike appendage on the abdomen of a springtail which holds the furcula or springing device in place. [< LL: holding-tool < *tenāc-* (s. of *tenāx*) holding fast (see TEN-) + *-ulum* suffix denoting instrument]

te·naille (te nāl′), *n.* *Fort.* an outwork containing one or two reentering angles, raised in the main ditch between two bastions and immediately in front of a curtain. Also, **te·nail′.** [< MF: lit., forceps, pincers < LL *tenācula,* (pl.). See TENACULUM]

te·na·im (tə nä ēm′; *Eng.* tə nô′im), *n.* (*construed as sing. or pl.*) *Yiddish.* the terms of a Jewish marriage, as the wedding date, amount of the bride's dowry, etc., or an agreement containing such terms, made by the parents of an engaged couple at the engagement party. [lit., agreements]

ten·an·cy (ten′ən sē), *n., pl.* **-cies. 1.** a holding, as of lands, by any kind of title; occupancy of land, a house, or the like, under a lease or on payment of rent; tenure. **2.** the period of a tenant's occupancy. **3.** occupancy or enjoyment of a position, post, situation, etc.: *his tenancy as professor of history at the state university.* **4.** *Archaic.* a piece of land held by a tenant; holding. [TENANT + -CY; cf. ML *tenantia,* var. of *tenentia;* see -ANCY]

ten·ant (ten′ənt), *n.* **1.** a person who holds land, a house, or the like, of another for a period of time, as by payment of rent; lessee. **2.** *Law.* a person who holds or possesses for a time lands, tenements, or personalty of another, usually for rent. **3.** an occupant or inhabitant of any place. —*v.t.* **4.** to hold or occupy as a tenant; dwell in; inhabit. —*v.i.* **5.** to dwell or live (usually fol. by *in*). —*adj.* **6.** *Rare.* tenent. [ME *tena(u)nt* < AF; MF *tenant,* n. use of prp. of *tenir* to hold < L *tenēre;* see TEN-, -ANT] —**ten′ant·a·ble,** *adj.* —**ten′ant·less,** *adj.* —**ten′ant·like′,** *adj.*

ten′ant farm′er, one who farms the land of another and pays rent with cash or with a portion of the produce.

ten′ant in chief′, a feudal vassal who holds his land directly from the king. Also, **ten′ant-in-chief′.** Also called **ten′ant in cap′i·te** (kap′i tē).

ten·ant·ry (ten′ən trē), *n.* **1.** tenants collectively; the body of tenants on an estate. **2.** state or condition of being a tenant. [ME; see TENANT, -RY]

ten′-cent store′ (ten′sent′, -sent′), five-and-ten (def. 1).

tench (tench), *n., pl.* **tench·es,** (*esp. collectively*) **tench.** a fresh-water cyprinoid fish, *Tinca tinca,* found in Europe. [ME *tenche* < MF, OF < LL *tinca*]

Ten′ Command′ments, the precepts spoken by God to Israel, delivered to Moses on Mount Sinai; the Decalogue. Ex. 20; 24:12,34; Deut. 5.

tend[1] (tend), *v.i.* **1.** to be disposed or inclined in action, operation, or effect to do something: *The particles tend to unite.* **2.** to be disposed toward an idea, emotion, way of thinking, etc.: *She tends to be sad. His religious philosophy tends toward pantheism.* **3.** to incline in operation or effect; lead or conduce, as to some result or resulting condition: *measures tending to improved working conditions; Governments are tending toward democracy.* **4.** (of a journey, course, road, etc.) to lead or be directed in a particular direction (usually fol. by *to, toward,* etc.): *a path tending toward the beach.* [ME *tende(n)* < MF *tendre* < L *tendere* to stretch, extend, proceed]

tend[2] (tend), *v.t.* **1.** to attend to by work or services, care, etc.: *to tend a fire.* **2.** to look after; watch over and care for; minister to or wait on with service: *to tend the sick.* **3.** *Naut.* to handle or attend to (a rope). —*v.i.* **4.** to attend by action, care, etc. (usually fol. by *to*). **5. tend on** or **upon,** *Archaic.* to attend or wait upon; minister to; serve: *She tended on the sick and dying with infinite compassion.* [ME *tende(n),* aph. var. of ATTEND]

tend·ance (ten′dəns), *n.* **1.** attention; care; ministration, as to the sick. **2.** *Archaic.* attendants. [aph. var. of ATTENDANCE]

ten·den·cious (ten den′shəs), *adj.* tendentious. —**ten·den′cious·ly,** *adv.* —**ten·den′cious·ness,** *n.*

ten·den·cy (ten′dən sē), *n., pl.* **-cies. 1.** natural or prevailing disposition to move, proceed, or act in some direction or toward some point, end, or result: *the tendency of falling bodies toward the earth.* **2.** an inclination, bent, or predisposition to something: *a tendency to talk too much.* **3.** a special and definite purpose in a novel or other literary work. [< ML *tendentia.* See TEND[1], -ENCY]

—**Syn. 1.** TENDENCY, DIRECTION, TREND, DRIFT refer to inclination or line of action or movement. A TENDENCY is an inclination toward a certain line of action (whether or not the action follows), and is often the result of inherent qualities, nature, or habit: *a tendency to procrastinate.* DIRECTION is the line along which an object or course of action moves, often toward some set point or intended goal: *The change is in the direction of improvement.* TREND emphasizes simultaneous movement in a certain direction of a number of factors, although the course or goal may not be clear for any single feature: *Business indicators showed a downward trend.* DRIFT emphasizes gradual development as well as direction: *the drift of his argument.* **2.** proclivity, leaning.

tend′ency tone′, a tone that is harmonically or melodically unstable and tends naturally to resolve itself either upward or downward.

ten·den·tious (ten den′shəs), *adj.* having or showing a definite tendency, bias, or purpose: *a tendentious novel.* Also, **tendencious, ten·den·tial** (ten den′shəl). [< ML *tendenti(a)* TENDENCY + -OUS] —**ten·den′tious·ly, ten·den′tial·ly,** *adv.* —**ten·den′tious·ness,** *n.*

ten·der[1] (ten′dər), *adj.* **1.** soft or delicate in substance; not hard or tough: *a tender steak.* **2.** weak or delicate in constitution; not strong or hardy. **3.** young or immature: *children of tender age.* **4.** delicate or soft in quality: *tender blue.* **5.** delicate, soft, or gentle: *the tender touch of her hand.* **6.** easily moved to sympathy or compassion; kind: *a tender heart.* **7.** affectionate or loving; sentimental or amatory: *a tender glance.* **8.** considerate or careful; chary or reluctant (usually fol. by *of*). **9.** acutely or painfully sensitive: *a tender bruise.* **10.** readily made uneasy: *a tender conscience.* **11.** yielding readily to force or pressure; easily broken; fragile. **12.** of a delicate or ticklish nature; requiring careful or tactful handling: *a tender subject.* **13.** *Naut.* crank[2] (def. 1). —*v.t.* **14.** to make tender. **15.** *Archaic.* to regard or treat tenderly. [ME, var. of *tendre* < OF < L *tenerum, teneram,* acc. of *tener* tender] —**ten′der·ly,** *adv.* —**ten′der·ness,** *n.*

ten·der[2] (ten′dər), *v.t.* **1.** to present formally for acceptance; make formal offer of: *to tender one's resignation.* **2.** to offer or proffer. **3.** *Law.* to offer, as money or goods, in payment of a debt or other obligation, esp. in exact accordance with the terms of the law and of the obligation. —*n.* **4.** the act of tendering; an offer of something for acceptance. **5.** that which is tendered or offered, esp. money, as in payment for something. **6.** *Com.* an offer made in writing by one party to another to execute certain work, supply certain commodities, etc., at a given cost; bid. **7.** *Law.* an offer, as of money or goods, in payment or satisfaction of a debt or other obligation. [earlier *tendre,* n. use of AF *tendre* to extend, offer. See TEND[1]] —**ten′der·er,** *n.*

—**Syn. 1.** See **offer. 4.** proposal, proffer.

ten·der[3] (ten′dər), *n.* **1.** a person who tends; a person who attends to or takes charge of someone or something. **2.** an auxiliary vessel employed to attend one or more other vessels, as for supplying provisions. **3.** a small rowboat or motorboat carried or towed by a yacht. **4.** *Railroads.* a car attached to a steam locomotive for carrying fuel and water. [late ME; aph. var. of ATTENDER]

ten·der·a·ble (ten′dər ə bəl), *adj.* capable of being tendered or offered in payment, as money or goods. [TENDER[2] + -ABLE] —**ten′der·a·bil′i·ty,** *n.*

ten·der·foot (ten′dər fōōt′), *n., pl.* **-foots, -feet** (-fēt′). **1.** a raw, inexperienced person; novice. **2.** a newcomer to the ranching and mining regions of the western U.S., unused to hardships. **3.** one in the lowest rank of the Boy Scouts of America or Girl Scouts of America. [TENDER[1] + FOOT]

ten·der-heart·ed (ten′dər här′tid), *adj.* soft-hearted; sympathetic. —**ten′der-heart′ed·ly,** *adv.* —**ten′der-heart′ed·ness,** *n.*

ten·der·ise (ten′də rīz′), *v.t.,* **-ised, -is·ing.** *Chiefly Brit.* tenderize. —**ten′der·i·sa′tion,** *n.* —**ten′der·is′er,** *n.*

Ten′der Is′ the Night′, a novel (1934) by F. Scott Fitzgerald.

ten·der·ize (ten′də rīz′), *v.t.,* **-ized, -iz·ing.** to make (meat) tender, as by pounding or by means of a chemical process or treatment. [TENDER[1] + -IZE] —**ten′der·i·za′tion,** *n.* —**ten′der·iz′er,** *n.*

ten·der·loin (ten′dər loin′), *n.* **1.** (in beef or pork) the tender meat of the muscle running through the sirloin and terminating before the ribs. **2.** a cut of beef lying between the sirloin and ribs. **3.** (*cap.*) **a.** (formerly) a district in New York City noted for corruption and vice: so called because police there could eat well from their bribes. **b.** a similar district in any U.S. city. [TENDER[1] + LOIN]

ten′der peren′nial, trumpets.

ten·di·nous (ten′də nəs), *adj.* **1.** of the nature of or resembling a tendon. **2.** consisting of tendons. [< early NL *tendin-* (r. ML *tendōn-*, s. of *tendō*) TENDON + -OUS]

ten·don (ten′dən), *n.* **1.** *Anat.* a cord or band of dense, tough, inelastic, white, fibrous tissue, serving to connect a muscle with a bone or part; sinew. **2.** a reinforcing strand in prestressed concrete. [< ML *tendōn-* (s. of *tendō*) < Gk *ténōn* sinew (with *-d-* from L *tendere* to stretch)]

ten·dril (ten′dril), *n.* *Bot.* a filiform, leafless organ of climbing plants, often growing in spiral form, which attaches itself to or twines round some other body, so as to support the plant. [earlier *tendrel*, var. (? by dissimilation) of ME *tendren, tendron* < MF *tendron* shoot, sprout, cartilage] —**ten′dril·lar, ten′dril·ous,** *adj.* —**ten′dril·ly,** *adv.*

T, Tendrils of fox grape, *Vitis Labrusca*

Ten·e·brae (ten′ə brā′), *n.* (*construed as sing. or pl.*) *Rom. Cath. Ch.* the office of matins and lauds for Thursday, Friday, and Saturday of Holy Week, sung respectively on the afternoon of Wednesday, Thursday, and Friday of that week, at which the Crucifixion is commemorated by the gradual extinguishment of candles. [< L: lit., darkness]

ten·e·brif·ic (ten′ə brif′ik), *adj.* producing darkness. [< L *tenebr(ae)* darkness + -I- + -FIC]

Ten·e·brism (ten′ə briz′əm), *n.* (*sometimes l.c.*) *Fine Arts.* a style of painting developed in the late 16th century, characterized chiefly by a systematic and dramatic use of chiaroscuro in which large areas of the picture are worked in dark tonal values sharply contrasted by lighter tones representing an oblique source of light and providing the illusion of forms emerging from shadow. [< L *tenebr(ae)* shadows, darkness + -ISM] —**Ten′e·brist,** *n., adj.*

ten·e·brous (ten′ə brəs), *adj.* dark; gloomy; obscure. Also, **te·neb·ri·ous** (tə neb′rē əs). [late ME < L *tenebrōs(us)*. See TENEBRAE, -OUS] —**ten′e·brous·ness, te·neb′ri·ous·ness,** *n.*

Ten·e·dos (ten′i dos′, -dōs′; *Gk.* ten′e thôs), *n.* an island in the Aegean, near the entrance to the Dardanelles, belonging to Turkey. Also called **Bozcaada.**

1080 (ten′ā′tē). See **sodium fluoroacetate.**

ten·e·ment (ten′ə mənt), *n.* **1.** any house or building to live in; dwelling house. **2.** See **tenement house. 3.** a portion of a house or building occupied by a tenant as a separate dwelling. **4.** any habitation, abode, or dwelling place. **5.** any species of permanent property, as lands, houses, rents, an office, a franchise, etc., that may be held of another. **6. tenements,** freehold interests in things immovable considered as subjects of property. [ME < ML *tenēment(um)* < L *tenē(re)* (to) hold + *-mentum* -MENT] —**ten·e·men·tal** (ten′ə men′tᵊl), **ten·e·men·ta·ry** (ten′ə men′tə rē), *adj.* —**ten′e·ment·ed,** *adj.*

ten′ement house′, an apartment house, esp. one in the poorer, crowded parts of a large city.

ten·ent (ten′ənt), *adj.* *Zool.* adapted for holding or clinging, as certain hairs on the feet of insects or spiders. [< L *tenent-* (s. of *tenēns*) prp. of *tenēre* to hold; see -ENT]

Ten·er·ife (ten′ə rif′, -rēf′; *Sp.* te′ne rē′fe), *n.* **1.** the largest of the Canary Islands, off the NW Coast of Africa. 321,949 (1950); 794 sq. mi. *Cap.:* Santa Cruz de Tenerife. **2. Pico de** (pē′kô de). See **Teide, Pico de.** Also, **Ten·er·iffe′.**

Ten·es (ten′es), *n.* *Class. Myth.* a son of Cycnus and Proclea who was banished by his father and set adrift in a chest when Phylonome, his stepmother, falsely accused him of trying to seduce her.

te·nes·mus (tə nez′məs, -nes′-), *n.* *Pathol.* the urgent feeling of need to urinate or defecate, without the ability to do so. [< L *tenent-* (s. of *tenēns*) prp. of *tenēre* to hold; see -ENT]

ten·et (ten′it, tē′nit), *n.* any opinion, principle, doctrine, dogma, etc., held as true. [< L: he holds] —**Syn.** belief, position.

ten·fold (*adj.* ten′fōld′; *adv.* ten′fōld′), *adj.* **1.** comprising ten parts or members. **2.** ten times as great or as much. —*adv.* **3.** in tenfold measure: *good deeds rewarded tenfold.* [ME; OE *tienfeald*. See TEN, -FOLD]

ten′-gal·lon hat′ (ten′gal′ən), a broad-brimmed hat with a high crown, as that worn in the western and southwestern U.S.; cowboy hat. Cf. **sombrero.** [so called from its size]

Ten·gri Khan (teng′grē kän′, KHän′), a mountain in central Asia, on the boundary between the Soviet Union and China: highest peak of the Tien Shan Mountains. ab. 23,950 ft.

Ten·gri Nor (teng′grē nôr′, nôr′), a salt lake in E Tibet, NW of Lhasa. ab. 700 sq. mi.; 15,186 ft. above sea level.

te·ni·a (tē′nē ə), *n., pl.* **-ni·ae** (-nē ē′). taenia.

te·ni·a·cide (tē′nē ə sīd′), *Med.* —*adj.* **1.** Also, **te′ni·a·ci′dal.** taeniacide. —*n.* **2.** taeniacide.

te·ni·a·fuge (tē′nē ə fyōōj′), *adj., n.* *Med.* taeniafuge.

te·ni·a·sis (ti nī′ə sis), *n.* *Pathol.* taeniasis.

Ten·iers (ten′yərz; *Flem.* tə nērs′; *Fr.* te nyā′), *n.* **1. David** ("*the Elder*"), 1582–1649, Flemish painter and engraver. **2.** his son, **David** ("*the Younger*"), 1610–90, Flemish painter.

Tenn., Tennessee.

ten·nant·ite (ten′ən tīt′), *n.* a mineral, copper arsenic sulfide, approximately Cu_3AsS_3, usually containing some antimony and grading into tetrahedrite: an ore of copper. [named after Smithson *Tennant* (1761–1815), English chemist; see -ITE[1]]

ten·né (ten′ē), *n.* **1.** *Heraldry.* a tincture or color of tawny orange: *a fess tenné.* [< late MF, var. of *tanné*, ptp. of *tanner* to TAN]

ten·ner (ten′ər), *n.* *Informal.* **1.** *U.S.* a 10-dollar bill. **2.** *Brit.* a 10-pound note. [TEN + -ER[1]]

Ten·nes·see (ten′i sē′), *n.* **1.** a State in the SE United States. 3,567,089 (1960); 42,246 sq. mi. *Cap.:* Nashville. *Abbr.:* Tenn. **2.** a river flowing from E Tennessee through N Alabama, W Tennessee, and SW Kentucky into the Ohio near Paducah. 652 mi. long. **3.** a boy's or girl's given name.

Ten·nes·se·an (ten′i sē′ən), *adj.* **1.** of, pertaining to, or characteristic of the State of Tennessee or its inhabitants. —*n.* **2.** a native or inhabitant of the State of Tennessee. Also, **Ten′nes·see′an.** [TENNESSEE + -AN]

Ten′nessee Val′ley Author′ity. See **TVA.**

Ten′nessee Walk′ing Horse′, one of a breed of saddle horses developed largely from Standardbred and Morgan stock. Also called **Plantation Walking Horse.**

Ten′nessee war′bler, a North American wood warbler, *Vermivora peregrina*, having a gray head, a greenish back, and white underparts.

Ten·niel (ten′yəl), *n.* **Sir John,** 1820–1914, English caricaturist and illustrator.

ten·nis (ten′is), *n.* a game played on a rectangular court by two players or two pairs of players equipped with rackets, in which a ball is driven back and forth over a low net that divides the court in half. Cf. **lawn tennis.** [late ME *tenetz* < AF, impv. pl. of *tenir* to hold < L *tenēre*]

Tennis court

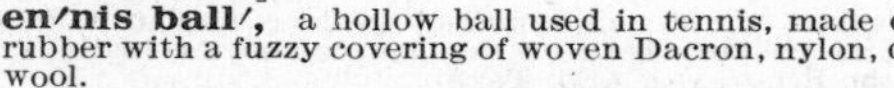

ten′nis ball′, a hollow ball used in tennis, made of rubber with a fuzzy covering of woven Dacron, nylon, or wool.

ten′nis el′bow, irritation of the synovial membrane, or joint rotary area, of the elbow, caused by immoderate motions while playing tennis or other sports.

ten′nis shoe′, a sports shoe with a rubber sole (usually pebbled) and a canvas upper that laces over the instep.

Ten·ny·son (ten′i sən), *n.* **Alfred, Lord** (*1st Baron*), 1809–92, English poet: poet laureate 1850–92.

Ten·ny·so·ni·an (ten′i sō′nē ən), *adj.* of, pertaining to, or characteristic of Tennyson or his writings. [TENNYSON + -IAN]

teno-, a learned borrowing from Greek meaning "tendon," used in the formation of compound words: *tenotomy.* [comb. form repr. Gk *ténōn*]

Te·noch·ti·tlán (te nôch′tē tlän′), *n.* the capital of the Aztec empire: founded in 1325; destroyed by the Spaniards in 1521; now the site of Mexico City.

ten·on (ten′ən), *n.* **1.** a projection formed on the end of a timber or the like for insertion into a mortise of the same dimensions. —*v.t.* **2.** to provide with a tenon. **3.** to join by or as by a tenon. **4.** to join securely. [late ME < MF *tenon* < *ten(ir)* to hold (< L *tenēre*) + *-on* n. suffix] —**ten′on·er,** *n.*

ten·o·ni·tis (ten′ə nī′tis), *n.* *Pathol.* inflammation of a tendon. Also, **tenositis.** [< Gk *ténōn* tendon + -ITIS]

ten·or (ten′ər), *n.* **1.** the course of thought or meaning which runs through something written or spoken; purport; drift. **2.** continuous course, progress, or movement. **3.** *Rhet.* the subject of a metaphor, as "she" in "She is a rose". Cf. **vehicle** (def. 7). **4.** *Music.* **a.** the adult male voice intermediate between the bass and the alto or countertenor. **b.** a part sung by or written for such a voice, esp. the next to the lowest part in four-part harmony. **c.** a singer with such a voice. **d.** an instrument corresponding in compass to this voice, esp. the viola. **e.** the lowest-toned bell of a peal. **5.** *Obs.* quality, character, or condition. —*adj.* **6.** *Music.* of, pertaining to, or having the compass of, a tenor. [< ML, L: course, etc. < *ten(ēre)* to hold + *-or* -OR[1]; r. ME *ten(o)ur* < AF] —**ten′or·less,** *adj.*

ten′or clef′, *Music.* a sign locating middle C on the next to the top line of the staff.

ten′or horn′, *n.* a musical brass wind instrument with valves; the tenor member of the cornet family.

ten·o·rite (ten′ə rīt′), *n.* a mineral, cupric oxide, CuO, occurring in veins of copper in black, minute scales. [named after G. *Tenore* (d. 1861), President of Naples Academy; see -ITE[1]]

te·nor·rha·phy (tə nôr′ə fē, -nor′-), *n., pl.* **-phies.** *Surg.* suture of a tendon. [TENO- + -RRHAPHY]

ten·o·si·tis (ten′ə sī′tis), *n.* *Pathol.* tenonitis.

te·not·o·my (tə not′ə mē), *n., pl.* **-mies.** *Surg.* the cutting or division of a tendon. [TENO- + -TOMY] —**te·not′o·mist,** *n.*

ten·pen·ny (ten′pen′ē, -pə nē), *adj.* **1.** noting a nail three inches in length. **2.** worth 10 cents. [TEN + PENNY]

ten′ percent′er, *Slang.* an agent, esp. an actor's agent, whose fee is 10 percent of his client's salary. Also, **ten′-per·cent′er.**

ten·pin (ten′pin′), *n.* **1.** one of the pins used in tenpins. **2. tenpins,** (*construed as sing.*) a form of bowling, played with ten wooden pins at which a ball is bowled to knock them down. [TEN + PIN]

ten·pound·er (ten′poun′dər), *n.* **1.** ladyfish (def. 1). **2.** the machete, *Elops affinis.* [TEN + POUNDER[2]]

ten·rec (ten′rek), *n.* any of several insectivorous mammals of the family *Tenrecidae*, of Madagascar, having a long, pointed snout, certain species of which are spiny and tailless. Also, **tanrec.** [< F < Malagasy *tàndraka*]

Tenrec, *Tenrec ecaudatus* (Length 14 in.)

tense[1] (tens), *adj.,* **tens·er, tens·est,** *v.,* **tensed, tens·ing.** —*adj.* **1.** stretched tight, as a cord, fiber, etc.; drawn taut; rigid. **2.** in a state of mental or nervous strain; high-strung; taut: *a tense person.* **3.** characterized by a strain upon the nerves or feelings: *a tense moment.* **4.** *Phonet.* pronounced with relatively tense tongue muscles. Cf. **lax**[2] (def. 7), **narrow** (def. 10a). —*v.t., v.i.* **5.** to make or become tense. [< L *tēns(us)* stretched, taut, ptp. of *tendere;* see TEND[1]] —**tense′ly,** *adv.* —**tense′ness,** *n.* —**Ant. 1–3.** relaxed.

tense[2] (tens), *n.* **1.** a category of verbal inflection found in some languages that specifies the time and length of occurrence of the action or state expressed by the verb. **2.** a set of such categories or constructions in a particular language. **3.** the time, as past, future, etc., expressed by such a category. **4.** such categories or constructions, or their meanings collectively. [ME *tens* < MF < L *tempus* time] —**tense′less,** *adj.* —**tense′less·ly,** *adv.* —**tense′less·ness,** *n.*

ten·seg·ri·ty (ten seg′ri tē), *n.* *Archit.* **1.** the property of skeleton structures that employ continuous tension members and discontinuous compression members in such a way that each member operates with the maximum efficiency and economy. —*adj.* **2.** noting any of a series of structures developed by R. Buckminster Fuller that embody this property. [TENSE[1] + (IN)TEGRITY]

ten·si·ble (ten′sə bəl), *adj.* capable of being stretched; tensile. [< NL *tensibil(is).* See TENSE[1], -IBLE] —**ten′si·bil′i·ty, ten′si·ble·ness,** *n.* —**ten′si·bly,** *adv.*

ten·sile (ten′səl, -sil *or, esp. Brit.,* -sīl), *adj.* **1.** of or pertaining to tension: *tensile strain.* **2.** capable of being stretched or drawn out; ductile. [< NL *tensil(is).* See TENSE[1], -ILE] —**ten·sil′i·ty, ten′sile·ness,** *n.* —**ten′sile·ly,** *adv.*

ten′sile strength′, the resistance of a material to longitudinal stress, measured by the minimum amount of longitudinal stress required to rupture the material.

ten·sim·e·ter (ten sim′i tər), *n.* an instrument for measuring vapor pressure. [TENSI(ON) + -METER]

ten·si·om·e·ter (ten′sē om′i tər), *n.* **1.** an instrument for measuring longitudinal stress in wires, structural beams, etc. **2.** an instrument for measuring the surface tension of a liquid. [TENSIO(N) + -METER]

ten·sion (ten′shən), *n.* **1.** the act of stretching or straining. **2.** the state of being stretched or strained. **3.** mental or emotional strain; intense, suppressed suspense, anxiety, or excitement. **4.** a strained relationship between individuals, groups, nations, etc. **5.** (not in current use) pressure, esp. of a vapor. **6.** *Mech.* **a.** the longitudinal deformation of an elastic body that results in its elongation. **b.** the force producing such deformation. **7.** *Elect.* electromotive force; potential. **8.** *Mach.* a device for stretching or pulling something. **9.** a device to hold the proper tension on the material being woven in a loom. —*v.t.* **10.** *Building Trades.* to subject (a cable, tendon, or the like) to tension, esp. for a specific purpose. [< LL *tensiōn-* (s. of *tensiō*) a stretching. See TENSE[1], -ION] —**ten′sion·al,** *adj.* —**ten′sion·less,** *adj.*

ten·si·ty (ten′si tē), *n.* the state of being tense. [< ML *tensitās.* See TENSE[1], -ITY]

ten·sive (ten′siv), *adj.* stretching or straining. [TENS(ION) + -IVE; cf. F *tensif*]

ten·son (ten sōn′), *n.* a Provençal poem taking the form of a dialogue between two persons. [< F; OF *tençon* < Pr *tensoun, tenso* contest, dispute < L *tensiōn-* (s. of *tensio*); see TENSION]

ten's′ place′, ten (def. 5).

ten·sor (ten′sər, -sôr), *n.* **1.** *Anat.* a muscle that stretches or tightens some part of the body. **2.** *Math.* a set of functions that are transformed in a particular way when changing from one coordinate system to another. [< NL: stretcher. See TENSE[1], -OR[2]] —**ten·so·ri·al** (ten sōr′ē əl, -sôr′-), *adj.*

ten-spot (ten′spot′), *n.* *Slang.* **1.** a playing card the face of which bears ten pips. **2.** a ten-dollar bill.

ten-strike (ten′strīk′), *n.* **1.** *Tenpins.* a strike. **2.** *Informal.* any stroke or act which is completely successful.

tent[1] (tent), *n.* **1.** a portable shelter of skins, coarse cloth, or esp. canvas supported by one or more poles and usually extended by ropes fastened to pegs in the ground. —*v.t.* **2.** to provide with or lodge in tents; cover as with a tent. —*v.i.* **3.** to live in a tent; encamp. [ME *tente* < OF < L *tenta*, fem. of *tentus* extended, stretched, ptp. of *tendere*, cf. *tentōrium* tent] —**tent′less,** *adj.* —**tent′like′,** *adj.*

tent[2] (tent), *n.* *Brit.* a dark, sweet wine from Spain. [alter. of Sp *tinto* dark red. See TINT[1]]

tent[3] (tent), *Scot. and North Eng.* —*n.* **1.** attention; care. —*v.t.* **2.** to give or pay attention to; heed. **3.** to tend; look after; attend to the care and safety of. **4.** to observe. [ME, aph. var. of *attent* < OF *atente* attention, intention < L *attenta*, fem. of *attentus*, ptp. of *attendere* to ATTEND]

tent[4] (tent), *Surg. Obs.* —*n.* **1.** a probe. **2.** a roll or pledget, usually of soft absorbent material, as lint or gauze, for dilating an orifice, keeping a wound open, etc. —*v.t.* **3.** to keep (a wound) open with a tent. [ME *tente* a probe < MF, verbid of *tenter* < L *tentāre*, var. of *temptāre* to probe. See TEMPT]

ten·ta·cle (ten′tə kəl), *n.* **1.** *Zool.* any of various slender, flexible processes or appendages in animals, esp. invertebrates, which serve as organs of touch, prehension, etc.; feeler. **2.** *Bot.* a sensitive filament or process, as one of the glandular hairs of the sundew. [< NL *tentācul(um)*, L *tentā(re)* (var. of *temptāre* to feel, probe) + *-culum* instrumental suffix] —**ten·tac·u·lar** (ten tak′yə lər), *adj.* —**ten′ta·cle·like′, ten·tac′u·loid′,** *adj.*

ten·ta·cled (ten′tə kəld), *adj.* having tentacles. Also, **ten·tac·u·lat·ed** (ten tak′yə lā′tid). [TENTACLE + -ED[3]]

tent·age (ten′tij), *n.* tents collectively; equipment or supply of tents. [TENT[1] + -AGE]

ten·ta·tion (ten tā′shən), *n.* a method of making mechanical adjustments or the like by a succession of trials. [< L *tentātiōn-* (s. of *tentātiō*) trial, var. of *temptātiō.* See TEMPTATION]

ten·ta·tive (ten′tə tiv), *adj.* **1.** of the nature of or made or done as a trial, experiment, or attempt; experimental: *a tentative report on his findings.* **2.** unsure; not definite or positive; hesitant: *a tentative smile on her face.* [< ML *tentātīv(us)* < L *tentāt(us)* tried (ptp. of *tentāre,* var. of *temptāre*) + *-īvus* -IVE] —**ten′ta·tive·ly,** *adv.* —**ten′ta·tive·ness,** *n.*

tent′ bed′, a field bed having a canopy in the form of a tent.

tent′ cat′erpillar, the larva of any of several moths of the genus *Malacosoma,* that live gregariously in tentlike silken webs and feed on the leaves of orchard and shade trees.

tent·ed (ten′tid), *adj.* **1.** covered with or living in a tent or tents. **2.** shaped like a tent. [TENT[1] + -ED[3]]

ten·ter[1] (ten′tər), *n.* **1.** a framework on which cloth in the process of manufacture is stretched so it may set or dry evenly. **2.** *Obs.* a tenterhook. —*v.t.* **3.** to stretch (cloth) on a tenter or tenters. —*v.i.* **4.** to be capable of being tentered. [ME *tente* to stretch (< L *tentus,* var. of *tensus* TENSE[1]) + -ER[1]; r. ME *teyntur* < ?]

ten·ter[2] (ten′tər), *n.* *Brit.* a person who tends, or has the care of, something, esp. a machine in a factory. [TENT[3] + -ER[1]]

ten·ter·hook (ten′tər ho͝ok′), *n.* **1.** one of the hooks or bent nails which hold cloth stretched on a tenter. **2. on tenterhooks,** in a state of uneasy suspense or painful anxiety: *The movie keeps one on tenterhooks until the very last moment.* [TENTER[1] + HOOK]

tent′ fly′, fly[1] (def. 27).

tenth (tenth), *adj.* **1.** next after ninth; being the ordinal number for 10. **2.** being one of 10 equal parts. —*n.* **3.** a 10th part, esp. of one ($^1/_{10}$). **4.** the 10th member of a series. **5.** *Music.* **a.** a tone distant from another tone by an interval of an octave and a third. **b.** the interval between such tones. **c.** the harmonic combination of such tones. **6.** Also called **tenth's′ place′.** (in decimal notation) the position of the first digit to the right of the decimal point. [ME *tenthe.* See TEN, -TH[2], TITHE] —**tenth′ly,** *adv.*

tent·ie (ten′tē), *adj.,* **tent·i·er, tent·i·est.** *Scot.* tenty.

tent·mak·er (tent′mā′kər), *n.* one who makes tents. [TENT[1] + MAKER]

ten·to·ri·um (ten tōr′ē əm, -tôr′-), *n., pl.* **-to·ri·a** (-tōr′ē ə, -tôr′-). (of an insect) the endoskeleton of the head. [< NL < L *tent(us)* (ptp. of *tendere* to stretch; see TEND[1]) + *-ōrium* -ORY[2]] —**ten·to′ri·al,** *adj.*

tent′ show′, an exhibition or performance, esp. a circus, presented in a tent.

tent′ stitch′, a short, slanting stitch used in embroidery. Cf. **gros point** (def. 1), **petit point** (def. 1).

tent·y (ten′tē), *adj.,* **tent·i·er, tent·i·est.** *Scot.* watchful; attentive. Also, **tentie.** [TENT[3] + -Y[1]]

ten·u·is (ten′yo͞o is), *n., pl.* **ten·u·es** (ten′yo͞o ēz′). *Gk. Grammar.* an unaspirated, voiceless plosive. [< L: thin, fine, slender]

te·nu·i·ty (tə no͞o′i tē, -nyo͞o′-, te-), *n.* **1.** the state of being tenuous. **2.** slenderness. **3.** thinness of consistency; rarefied condition. [< L *tenuitās* thinness. See TENUI(S), -TY[2]]

ten·u·ous (ten′yo͞o əs), *adj.* **1.** thin or slender in form. **2.** thin in consistency; rare or rarefied. **3.** of slight importance or significance; unsubstantial: *He holds a rather tenuous position in history.* **4.** lacking a sound basis; poorly supported; weak: *a tenuous claim to the land.* **5.** lacking in clarity; vague: *He gave a rather tenuous account of his past life.* [TENU(ITY) + -OUS] —**ten′u·ous·ly,** *adv.* —**ten′u·ous·ness,** *n.* —**Syn. 1.** attenuated. **3.** insignificant, unimportant, trivial, trifling. —**Ant. 1.** thick. **3.** important, substantial.

ten·ure (ten′yər), *n.* **1.** the holding or possessing of anything: *the tenure of an office.* **2.** the holding of property, esp. real property, of a superior in return for services to be rendered. **3.** the period or term of holding something. **4.** status granted to an employee, usually after a probationary period, assuring him of the permanency of his position or employment. [ME < AF; OF *teneure* < VL **tenitura* < **tenit(us)* held (for L *tentus,* ptp. of *tenēre*) + *-ura* -URE] —**ten·u·ri·al** (ten yo͝or′ē əl), *adj.* —**ten·u′ri·al·ly,** *adv.*

te·nu·to (tə no͞o′tō; *It.* te no͞o′tô), *adj., n., pl.* **-tos,** *It.* **-ti** (-tē). *Music.* —*adj.* **1.** (a musical direction, of a note, chord, or rest) held to the full time value. —*n.* **2.** a note, chord, or rest held longer than its normal duration; a hold. **3.** the sign indicating this. [< It: held (ptp. of *tenere*) < VL **tenutus* for L *tentus*]

ten′-weeks′ stock′ (ten′wēks′), an annual stock, *Matthiola incana annua,* having spikes of white, lilac, or crimson flowers.

Ten′ Years′ War′, a popular insurrection in Cuba (1868–78) against Spanish rule.

Ten·zing (ten′zing), *n.* (*Norgay*) born 1913?, Nepalese mountain climber who scaled Mt. Everest 1953.

te·o·cal·li (tē′ə kal′ē; *Sp.* te′ô kä′yē), *n., pl.* **-cal·lis** (-kal′ēz; *Sp.* -kä′yēs). a ceremonial structure of the Aztecs, consisting of a truncated terraced pyramid supporting a temple. [< Nahuatl < *teo(tl)* god + *calli* house]

te·o·sin·te (tē′ə sin′tē), *n.* a tall annual grass, *Euchlaena mexicana,* of Mexico and Central America, closely related to corn, and sometimes cultivated as a fodder plant. [< MexSp < Nahuatl *teo(tl)* god + *centli,* dry ear of maize]

tep′a·ry bean′ (tep′ə rē), a twining or bushy, annual herb, *Phaseolus acutifolius latifolius,* of Mexico and Arizona, having white or light violet-colored flowers and yellow, brown, white, or bluish-black seeds, grown as a food plant in dry regions. [?]

te·pe (tep′ē; *Turk.* te′pe), *n.* (in Turkey, Iran, and Iraq) tell[2]. [< Turk: hill]

te·pee (tē′pē), *n.* a tent or wigwam of the American Indians. Also, **teepee, tipi.** [< Siouan *tipi* tent < *ti* to dwell + *pi* used for]

tep·e·fy (tep′ə fī′), *v.t., v.i.,* **-fied, -fy·ing.** to make or become tepid or lukewarm. [< L *tepe-* (s. of *tepēre* to be tepid) + -FY] —**tep·e·fac·tion** (tep′ə fak′shən), *n.*

Te·pe Gaw·ra (*Turk.* te′pe gou-rä′), an archaeological site in N Iraq, near Mosul: excavations have revealed that numerous settlements have occupied this site since c5000 B.C.

Tepee

te·phil·lin (tə fil′in; *Heb.* tə fē-lēn′), *n.pl. Judaism.* tefillin.

teph·ra (tef′rə), *n.pl.* clastic volcanic material, as scoria, dust, etc., ejected during an eruption. [< Gk: ashes]

teph·rite (tef′rīt), *n.* *Petrog.* a basaltic rock consisting essentially of pyroxene and plagioclase with nepheline or leucite. [< Gk *tephr(ós)* ash-colored + -ITE[1]] —**teph·rit·ic** (tef rit′ik), *adj.*

teph·ro·ite (tef′rō īt′), *n.* a mineral, silicate of manganese, Mn_2SiO_4, occurring in orthorhombic crystals. [< G *Tephroit* < Gk *tephr(ós)* ash gray + *-it* -ITE[1]]

Te·pic (te pēk′), *n.* a city in W Mexico. 53,499 (1960).

tep·id (tep′id), *adj.* moderately warm; lukewarm: *tepid water.* [late ME < L *tepid(us)* lukewarm] —**te·pid′i·ty, tep′id·ness,** *n.* —**tep′id·ly,** *adv.*

tep·i·dar·i·um (tep′i dâr′ē əm), *n., pl.* **-dar·i·a** (-dâr′ē ə). (in an ancient Roman bath) a room having a lukewarm bath. [< L; see TEPID, -ARY]

TEPP, *Chem.* See **tetraethyl pyrophosphate.**

te·qui·la (tə kē′lə), *n.* **1.** a strong liquor from Mexico, distilled from fermented mash of an agave. **2.** the plant itself, *Agave tequilana.* [after *Tequila,* a district in Mexico]

ter (tûr), *adv.* (in prescriptions) three times. [< L]

ter-, a learned borrowing from Latin meaning "thrice," used in the formation of compound words: *tercentennial.* [< L, comb. form of *ter;* akin to *tres* THREE]

ter., **1.** (in prescriptions) rub. [< L *tere*] **2.** terrace. **3.** territory.

ter·a·cy·cle (ter′ə sī′kəl), *n.* one trillion cycles. *Abbr.:* Tc [< Gk *téra(s)* monster (see TERATO-) + CYCLE]

Te·rah (tēr′ə), *n.* the father of Abraham. Gen. 11:25–32. Also, *Douay Bible,* **Thare.**

Te·rai (tə rī′), *n.* a marshy lowland area in N India and S Nepal, between the Ganges and the foothills of the Himalayas. Also, **Tarai.**

terai′ hat′, a felt sun helmet with a high crown and wide brim, worn esp. in the subtropics. [after *Terai,* region in India where first worn]

ter·a·phim (ter′ə fim), *n.pl., sing.* **ter·aph** (ter′əf). idols or images reverenced by the ancient Hebrews and kindred peoples, apparently as household gods. [< Heb (pl.); r. ME *theraphym* < L *theraphim* (Vulgate) < Gk *theraphin* (Septuagint)]

te·rass (tə ras′), *n.* trass.

terat-, var. of **terato-** before a vowel: *teratoid.*

ter·a·tism (ter′ə tiz′əm), *n.* **1.** love or worship of the monstrous. **2.** *Biol.* a monstrosity. [TERAT- + -ISM]

terato-, a learned borrowing from Greek meaning "monster," used in the formation of compound words: *teratology.* Also, *esp. before a vowel,* **terat-.** [< Gk *térat-* (s. of *téras*) monster, marvel + -o-]

ter·a·to·gen·e·sis (ter′ə tō jen′i sis), *n.* *Biol.* the production of monsters or monstrous growths. [TERATO- + GENESIS] —**ter·a·to·ge·net·ic** (ter′ə tō jə net′ik), *adj.*

ter·a·tog·e·ny (ter′ə toj′ə nē), *n.* teratogenesis. —**ter·a·to·gen·ic** (ter′ə tō jen′ik), *adj.* [TERATO- + -GENY]

ter·a·toid (ter′ə toid′), *adj.* *Biol.* resembling a monster. [TERAT- + -OID]

ter·a·tol·o·gy (ter′ə tol′ə jē), *n.* *Biol.* the science or study of monstrosities or abnormal formations in animals or plants. [TERATO- + -LOGY] —**ter·a·to·log·i·cal** (ter′ə təloj′i kəl), *adj.* —**ter′a·tol′o·gist,** *n.*

ter·a·to·sis (ter′ə tō′sis), *n.* *Biol.* teratism (def. 2). [< NL; see TERAT-, -OSIS]

ter·bi·a (tûr′bē ə), *n.* *Chem.* an amorphous white powder, TbO_3. Also called **ter′bium ox′ide.** [< NL: TERBI(UM + ERBI)A]

ter·bi·um (tûr′bē əm), *n.* *Chem.* a rare-earth, metallic element present in certain minerals, and yielding colorless salts. *Symbol:* Tb; *at. no.:* 65; *at. wt.:* 158.924; *sp. gr.:* 8.25. [named after (*Yt*)*terb(y),* name of Swedish town where found + -IUM. See YTTERBIUM] —**ter′bic,** *adj.*

ter′bium met′al, *Chem.* any of a subgroup of rare-earth metals, of which the cerium and yttrium metals comprise the other two subgroups. Cf. **rare-earth element.**

Ter Borch (tər bôrḵh′), *n.* **Ge·rard** (gā′rärt), 1617–81, Dutch painter. Also, **Ter·borch′, Ter·burg** (tər bo͝orḵh′).

terce (tûrs), *n.* *Eccles.* tierce (def. 3). [late ME var. of TIERCE]

Ter·cei·ra (ter sā′rə), *n.* a Portuguese island in the Azores, in the N Atlantic. 86,443 (1950); 153 sq. mi. *Cap.:* Angra do Heroismo.

ter·cel (tûr′səl), *n.* *Falconry.* the male of a hawk, esp. of a gerfalcon or peregrine. Also, **terce·let** (tûrs′lit), **tiercel.** [ME < MF < LL **tertiol(us)* < L *terti(us)* third + *-olus* dim. suffix; said to be so named because only a third of birds of species are male]

ter·cen·te·nar·y (tûr sen′tᵊner′ē, tûr′sen ten′ə rē), *adj., n., pl.* **-nar·ies.** —*adj.* **1.** pertaining to 300 years or a period of 300 years. **2.** marking the completion of such a period: *a tercentenary celebration.* —*n.* **3.** a 300th anniversary or its celebration. Also, **ter′cen·ten′ni·al.** [TER- + CENTENARY]

ter·cet (tûr′sit, tûr set′), *n.* **1.** *Pros.* a group of three lines rhyming together or connected by rhyme with the adjacent group or groups of three lines. **2.** *Music.* triplet (def. 5). [< F < It *terzetto,* dim. of *terzo* third < L *tertius.* See -ET]

ter·e·bene (ter′ə bēn′), *n.* *Chem.* a mixture of terpenes that occurs as a colorless liquid, used in medicine chiefly as an expectorant. [TEREB(INTH) + -ENE]

te·reb·ic (te reb′ik, -rē′bik), *adj.* *Chem.* of or derived from terebic acid. Also, **terebinic.** [TEREB(INTH) + -IC]

tereb′ic ac′id, *Chem.* an acid, $C_7H_{10}O_4$, formed by the oxidation of certain terpenes and historically important in the discovery of the structures of many terpenes.

ter·e·bin·ic (ter′ə bin′ik), *adj.* *Chem.* terebic. [TEREBIN(TH) + -IC]

ter′ebin′ic ac′id, *Chem.* See **terebic acid.**

ter·e·binth (ter′ə binth), *n.* an anacardiaceous tree, *Pistacia Terebinthus,* of the Mediterranean regions, yielding Chian turpentine. [< L *terebinth(us)* < Gk *terébinthos* turpentine tree; r. ME *therebinte* < MF]

ter·e·bin·thi·nate (ter′ə bin′thə nāt′), *adj.* of, pertaining to, or resembling turpentine. [TEREBINTHINE + -ATE[1]]

ter·e·bin·thine (ter′ə bin′thin), *adj.* **1.** terebinthinate. **2.** of or pertaining to the terebinth. [TEREBINTH + -INE[1]]

te·re·do (te rē′dō), *n., pl.* **-re·dos, -re·di·nes** (-red′ᵊnēz′). a shipworm of the genus *Teredo.* [< L < Gk *terēdōn* wood-boring worm]

te·re·fah (tə rä fä′; *Eng.* tə rā′fə, trā′-), *adj.* *Hebrew.* unfit for use with respect to Jewish law; not kosher: *a terefah animal;* terefah *food.* Also, **trefah, tref.**

Ter·ence (ter′əns), *n.* **1.** (*Publius Terentius Afer*) c190–159? B.C., Roman playwright. **2.** Also, **Terrence.** a boy's given name.

Te·ren·tia (tə ren′shə), *n.* a girl's given name.

ter·eph·thal·ate (ter′ef thal′āt, -it, tə ref′thə lāt′), *n.* *Chem.* a salt or ester of terephthalic acid. [TEREPHTHAL(IC ACID) + -ATE[2]]

ter′eph·thal′ic ac′id (ter′ef thal′ik, ter′-), *Chem.* a white, crystalline, water-insoluble solid, C_6H_4-$(COOH)_2$, the para isomer of phthalic acid: used chiefly in the manufacture of resins and textile fibers.

Te·re·sa (tə rē′sə, -zə; *for 2 also Sp.* te re′sä), *n.* **1.** **Mother** (*Agnes Gonxha Bojaxhiu*), born 1910, Albanian nun: Nobel peace prize 1979 for work in the slums of Calcutta, India. **2. Saint.** See **Theresa, Saint.** **3.** a girl's given name, form of **Theresa.**

Te·resh·ko·va (te resh kô′vä), *n.* **Va·len·ti·na Vla·di·mi·rov·na** (vä′len tē′nä vlä dē′mi rôv′nä), born 1937, Russian cosmonaut: first woman to make orbital space flight.

Te·re·sian (tə rē′zhən), *n.* **1.** a member of the reformed order of barefooted Carmelites, founded in Spain in 1562. —*adj.* **2.** of or pertaining to St. Teresa or the Teresians. [*Teres(a)* + -IAN]

Te·re·si·na (ti ri zē′nə), *n.* a port in NE Brazil, on the Parnahiba River. 100,006 (1960). Formerly, **Therezina.**

te·rete (tə rēt′, ter′ēt), *adj.* **1.** slender and smooth, with a circular transverse section. **2.** cylindrical or slightly tapering. [earlier *teret* < L *teret-* (s. of *teres*) smooth and round, akin to *terere* to rub]

Te·re·us (tēr′ē əs, tēr′yo͞os), *n.* *Class. Myth.* a Thracian prince, the husband of Procne, who raped his sister-in-law Philomela and was changed into a hoopoe as a punishment.

ter·gal (tûr′gəl), *adj.* of or pertaining to the tergum. [TERG(UM) + -AL[1]]

ter·gite (tûr′jīt), *n.* **1.** a dorsal sclerite of an arthropod. **2.** the dorsal sclerite of an abdominal segment of an insect. [TERG(UM) + -ITE[1]]

ter·gi·ver·sate (tûr′ji vər sāt′), *v.i.,* **-sat·ed, -sat·ing.** **1.** to change repeatedly one's attitude or opinions with respect to a cause, subject, etc. **2.** to turn renegade. [< L *tergiversāt(us)* (ptp. of *tergiversārī* to turn one's back) < *tergi-* (comb. form of *tergum* back) + *versātus,* ptp. of *versāre,* freq. of *vertere* to turn; see -ATE[1]] —**ter′gi·ver·sa′tion,** *n.* —**ter′gi·ver·sa′tor, ter·gi·ver·sant** (tûr′ji vûr′sənt), *n.* —**ter·gi·ver·sa·to·ry** (tûr′ji vûr′sə tōr′ē, -tôr′ē), *adj.*

ter·gum (tûr′gəm), *n., pl.* **-ga** (-gə). *Zool.* the dorsal surface of a body segment of an arthropod. [< L: the back]

Ter·hune (tər hyo͞on′), *n.* **Albert Pay·son** (pā′sən), 1872–1942, U.S. novelist and short-story writer.

ter·i·ya·ki (ter′i yä′kē), *n.* *Japanese Cookery.* meat or fish marinated in seasoned soy sauce and grilled. [< Jap]

term (tûrm), *n.* **1.** a word or group of words serving as the specific name of something, esp. in a special field, as *atom* in physics, *quietism* in theology, *adze* in carpentry, or *district leader* in politics. **2.** any word or group of words considered as a member of a construction or utterance. **3.** the time or period through which something lasts. **4.** a period of time to which limits have been set: *elected for a term of four years.* **5.** each of certain stated periods of the year into which instruction is regularly organized for students or pupils in universities, colleges, and schools. **6.** an appointed or set time or date, as for the payment of rent, interest, wages, etc. **7. terms, a.** conditions with regard to payment, price, charge, rates, wages, etc.: *reasonable terms.* **b.** conditions or stipulations limiting what is proposed to be granted or done: *the terms of a treaty.* **c.** footing or standing; relations: *on good terms with someone.* **d.** *Obs.* state, situation, or circumstances. **8.** *Algebra, Arith.* each of the members of which an expression, a series of quantities, or the like, is composed, as one of two or more parts of an algebraic expression. **9.** *Logic.* **a.** the subject or predicate of a categorical proposition. **b.** the word or expression denoting the subject or predicate of a categorical proposition. **10.** Also called **terminus.** a figure, esp. of Terminus, in the form of a herm, used by the ancient Romans as a boundary marker; terminal figure. **11.** *Law.* **a.** an estate or interest in land or the like, to be enjoyed for a fixed period. **b.** the duration of an estate. **c.** each of the periods during which certain courts of law hold their sessions. **12.** termination of pregnancy; parturition. **13.** *Archaic.* **a.** end, conclusion, or termination. **b.** boundary or limit. **14. bring to terms,** to force to agree to stated demands or conditions; bring into submission: *After a long struggle, we brought them to terms.* **15. come to terms, a.** to reach an agreement; make an arrangement: *to come to terms with a creditor.* **b.** to become resigned or accustomed: *to come to terms with one's existence.* **16. eat one's terms,** *Brit. Informal.* to study for the bar; be a law student. —*v.t.* **17.** to apply a particular term or name to; name; call; designate. [ME *terme* < OF < L *term(inus)* boundary, limit, end; akin to Gk *térmōn* limit] —**term′ly,** *adv.*

term., **1.** terminal. **2.** termination.

ter·ma·gant (tûr′mə gənt), *n.* **1.** a violent, turbulent, or brawling woman. **2.** (*cap.*) a mythical deity popularly believed in the Middle Ages to be worshiped by the Muslims and introduced into the morality play as a violent, overbearing personage in long robes. —*adj.* **3.** violent; turbulent; brawling; shrewish. [ME *Termagaunt,* earlier *Tervagaunt,* alter. of OF *Tervagan* (see def. 2)] —**ter′ma·gant·ly,** *adv.*
—**Syn. 1.** shrew, virago.

term′ day′, a fixed or appointed day, as for the payment of money due; a quarter day. [ME *term dai*]

term·er (tûr′mər), *n.* a person who is serving a term, esp. in prison (usually used in combination): *a first-termer.* [TERM + -ER[1]]

ter·mi·na·ble (tûr′mə nə bəl), *adj.* **1.** that may be terminated. **2.** (of an annuity) coming to an end after a certain term. [obs. *termine* (< L *termināre* to end) + -ABLE] —**ter′mi·na·bil′i·ty, ter′mi·na·ble·ness,** *n.* —**ter′mi·na·bly,** *adv.*

ter·mi·nal (tûr′mə nᵊl), *adj.* **1.** situated at or forming the end or extremity of something: *a terminal feature of a vista.* **2.** occurring at or forming the end of a series, succession, or the like; closing; concluding. **3.** pertaining to or lasting for a term or definite period; occurring at fixed terms or in every term: *terminal payments.* **4.** pertaining to, situated at, or forming the terminus of a railroad. **5.** *Bot.* growing at the end of a branch or stem, as a bud, inflorescence, etc. **6.** *Archit.* noting a figure, as a herm or term, in the form of a bust upon a gaine. **7.** pertaining to or placed at a boundary, as a landmark. **8.** occurring at or causing the end of life: *terminal cancer; a terminal disease.* —*n.* **9.** a terminal part of structure; end or extremity. **10.** *Railroads.* a major assemblage of station, yard, maintenance, and repair facilities, as at a terminus, at which trains originate or terminate, or at which they are distributed or combined. **11.** *Computer Technol.* any device for entering information into a computer or receiving information from it, as a keyboard with video display unit or a printer, either adjoining the computer or at some distance from it. **12.** *Elect.* **a.** the mechanical device by means of which an electric connection to an apparatus is established. **b.** the point of current entry to, or point of current departure from any conducting component in an electric circuit. **13.** *Archit.* **a.** a herm or term. **b.** a carving or the like at the end of something, as a finial. [late ME < L *terminālis* < *termin(us)* end, limit + *-ālis* -AL[1]] —**ter′mi·nal·ly,** *adv.*
—**Syn. 1, 2.** final, ending, ultimate.

ter′minal leave′, the final leave granted to a member of the armed forces just before discharge, equal to the total unused leave accumulated during active service.

ter′minal mar′ket, an organized market in a city into which large quantities of agricultural produce, livestock, etc., are shipped for distribution and sale.

ter′minal moraine′ a moraine formed at the terminus of a glacier.

ter′minal veloc′ity, *Physics.* **1.** the velocity at which a falling body moves through a medium, as air, when the force of resistance of the medium is equal in magnitude and opposite in direction to the force of gravity. **2.** *Rocketry, Ballistics.* **a.** the greatest speed that a rocket, missile, etc., attains after burnout or after leaving the barrel of a gun. **b.** the speed of a missile or projectile on impact with its target. **3.** the maximum velocity of a body falling through a viscous fluid.

ter·mi·nate (tûr′mə nāt′), *v.,* **-nat·ed, -nat·ing.** —*v.t.* **1.** to bring to an end; put an end to: *to terminate a contract.* **2.** to occur at or form the conclusion of: *The countess's soliloquy terminates the play.* **3.** to bound or limit spatially; form or be situated at the extremity of. —*v.i.* **4.** to end, conclude, or cease. **5.** (of a train, bus, or other public conveyance) to end a scheduled run at a certain place: *This train terminates at New York.* **6.** to come to an end (often fol. by *at, in,* or *with*). **7.** to issue or result (usually fol. by *in*). [v. use of late ME *terminate* (adj.) limited < L *terminātus*), ptp. of *termināre.* See TERM, -ATE[1]] —**ter′mi·na′tive,** *adj.* —**ter′mi·na′tive·ly,** *adv.*
—**Syn. 1, 2.** end, finish, conclude, close, complete.

ter·mi·na·tion (tûr′mə nā′shən), *n.* **1.** the act of terminating; fact of being terminated. **2.** the place at which or the part in which anything terminates; bound or limit. **3.** an end or extremity; close or conclusion. **4.** an issue or result. **5.** *Gram.* a suffix or ending. [late ME *terminacion* < L *terminātiōn-* (s. of *terminātiō*) decision. See TERMINATE, -ION] —**ter′mi·na′tion·al,** *adj.*

ter·mi·na·tor (tûr′mə nā′tər), *n.* **1.** one who or that which terminates. **2.** *Astron.* the dividing line between the illuminated and the unilluminated part of a satellite or planet, esp. the moon. [< LL; see TERMINATE, -OR[2]]

ter·mi·na·to·ry (tûr′mə nə tôr′ē, -tōr′ē), *adj.* pertaining to or forming the extremity or boundary; terminal; terminating. [TERMINATE + -ORY[1]]

ter·min·ism (tûr′mə niz′əm), *n.* *Philos.* an extreme form of nominalism in which universals have no existence, either as essences or as concepts. [TERMIN(US) + -ISM] —**ter′mi·nist,** *n., adj.* —**ter′mi·nis′tic,** *adj.*

ter·mi·nol·o·gy (tûr′mə nol′ə jē), *n., pl.* **-gies. 1.** the system of terms belonging or peculiar to a science, art, or specialized subject; nomenclature: *the terminology of botany.* **2.** the science of terms, as in particular sciences or arts. [< ML *termin(us)* TERM + -O- + -LOGY] —**ter·mi·no·log·i·cal** (tûr′mə nᵊloj′i kəl), *adj.* —**ter′mi·no·log′i·cal·ly,** *adv.* —**ter′mi·nol′o·gist,** *n.*

term′ insur′ance, life insurance for a stipulated term of years only, the beneficiary being paid the face value of the policy upon death during the term, but nothing being paid upon survival at the completion of the term.

ter·mi·nus (tûr′mə nəs), *n., pl.* **-ni** (-nī′), **-nus·es. 1.** the end or extremity of anything. **2.** either end of a railroad line. **3.** *Brit.* the station or the town at the end of a railway or bus route. **4.** the point toward which anything tends; goal or end. **5.** a boundary or limit. **6.** a boundary post or stone. **7.** (*cap.*) the ancient Roman god of boundaries and landmarks. **8.** *Archit.* term (def. 10). [< L: boundary, limit, end]

ter·mi·nus ad quem (teʀ′mi no͞os′ äd kwem′; *Eng.* tûr′mə nəs ad kwem′), *Latin.* the end to which; aim; goal; finishing point.

ter·mi·nus a quo (teʀ′mi no͞os′ ä kwō′; *Eng.* tûr′mə nəs ā kwō′), *Latin.* the end from which; beginning; starting point.

ter·mi·tar·i·um (tûr′mi târ′ē əm), *n., pl.* **-tar·i·a** (-târ′ē ə). a termites' nest. [< NL *termit(ēs),* pl. of *termes* TERMITE + -ARIUM]

ter·mi·ta·ry (tûr′mi ter′ē), *n., pl.* **-ries.** termitarium. [TERMITE + -ARY]

Termite (worker), *Termes flavipes* (Length ¼ in.)

ter·mite (tûr′mīt), *n.* any of numerous pale-colored, soft-bodied, chiefly tropical, social insects of the order *Isoptera* that feed on wood, some being highly destructive to buildings, furniture, etc. Also called **white ant.** [back formation from *termites,* pl. of NL *termes* white ant, L: wood-eating worms]

ter·mit·ic (tər mit′ik), *adj.* of, pertaining to, produced by, or infested with termites. [TERMITE + -IC]

term·less (tûrm′lis), *adj.* **1.** not limited; unconditional. **2.** boundless; endless. [TERM + -LESS]

term·or (tûr′mər), *n.* *Law.* one who has an estate for a term of years or for life. [TERM + -OR[2]; r. ME *termur* < AF *termer* (see -ER[2])]

term′ pa′per, a long essay, report, or the like, written by a student as an assignment over the course of a term or semester.

term′ pol′icy, *Insurance.* a policy whose period of coverage is in excess of one year, usually paying a reduced premium rate, as in fire insurance.

tern[1] (tûrn), *n.* any of numerous aquatic birds of the subfamily *Sterninae* of the family *Laridae,* related to the gulls but usually having a more slender body and bill, smaller feet, a long, deeply forked tail, and a more graceful flight, esp. those of the genus *Sterna,* as *S. hirundo* **(common tern),** of Europe and America, having white, black, and gray plumage. [< Dan *terne* or Norw *terna;* c. Icel *therna*]

Tern, *Sterna hirundo* (Length 15 in.; wingspread 2½ ft.)

tern[2] (tûrn), *n.* **1.** a set of three. **2.** three winning numbers drawn together in a lottery. **3.** a prize won by drawing these. **4.** *Naut.* a fore-and-aft-rigged schooner having three masts. [ME *terne* < MF < It *terno* < L *ternī* three each, triad, akin to *ter* thrice]

ter·na (ter′nə, tûr′-), *n.* *Rom. Cath. Ch.* a list of three names submitted to the pope as recommended to fill a vacant bishopric or benefice. [short for eccl. L *terna nomina* three names together. See TERN[2]]

ter·na·ry (tûr′nə rē), *adj., n., pl.* **-ries.** —*adj.* **1.** consisting of or involving three; threefold; triple. **2.** third in order or rank. **3.** based on the number three. **4.** *Chem.* **a.** consisting of three different elements or groups. **b.** (formerly) consisting of three atoms. **5.** *Math.* having three variables. **6.** *Metall.* (of an alloy) having three principal constituents. —*n.* **7.** a group of three. [late ME < LL *ternāri(us)* made up of three. See TERN[2], -ARY]

ter′nary form′, a musical form in three sections, with the third usually an exact repetition of the first.

ter·nate (tûr′nit, -nāt), *adj.* **1.** consisting of three; arranged in threes. **2.** *Bot.* **a.** consisting of three leaflets, as a compound leaf. **b.** having leaves arranged in whorls of three, as a plant. [< NL *ternāt(us).* See TERN[2], -ATE[1]] —**ter′nate·ly,** *adv.*

A B

Ternate leaves A, Laburnum, *Laburnum laburnum;* B, Rosinweed, Silphium trifoliatum

Ter·na·te (teʀ nä′te), *n.* an island in E Indonesia, W of Halmahera: important source of spices. 53 sq. mi.

terne′ met′al (tûrn), an alloy of lead and tin used for plating. [TERNE(PLATE) + METAL]

terne·plate (tûrn′plāt′), *n.* steel plate coated with terne metal. [obs. *terne* (< F: dull; see TARNISH) + PLATE[1]]

tern′ foot′, *Furniture.* a foot ending in three scrolls.

Ter·ni (teʀ′nē), *n.* a city in central Italy. 95,207 (1961).

ter·ni·on (tûr′nē ən), *n.* **1.** a set or group of three; triad. **2.** *Bookbinding.* three gathered sheets folded in two for binding together. [< L *terniōn-* (s. of *terniō*) triad. See TERN[2], -ION]

Ter·no·pol (teʀ′no pôl′yᵊ), *n.* a city in the W Ukraine, in the SW Soviet Union in Europe: formerly in Poland. 52,000 (1959).

ter·pene (tûr′pēn), *n.* *Chem.* **1.** (originally) any of a class of monocyclic hydrocarbons of the formula $C_{10}H_{16}$, obtained from plants. **2.** this class or any of its oxygenated derivatives, any hydrocarbon from the same source having the formula C_5H_8 **(hemiterpene),** the formula $C_{10}H_{16}$ with an aliphatic structure **(acyclic terpene)** or two-ringed structure **(bicyclic terpene),** the formula $C_{15}H_{24}$ **(sesquiterpene),** etc., and any of their oxygenated derivatives. [alter. of TEREBENE, with *p* from TURPENTINE] —**ter′pene·less,** *adj.* —**ter·pe·nic** (tûr pē′nik), *adj.*

ter·pin·e·ol (tûr pin′ē ōl′, -ôl′, -ol′), *n.* *Chem.* any of several unsaturated, cyclic, tertiary alcohols having the formula $C_{10}H_{17}OH$, occurring in nature in many essential oils or prepared synthetically: used chiefly in the manufacture of perfumes. [*terpine* (TERP(ENE) + -INE[2]) + -OL[2]]

ter′pin hy′drate (tûr′pin), *Pharm.* a white, crystalline powder, $C_{10}H_{20}O_2 \cdot H_2O$, usually used in the form of an elixir, and often in combination with codeine, as an expectorant for coughing. [TERP(ENE) + -IN[2]]

Terp·sich·o·re (tûrp sik′ə rē), *n.* **1.** *Class. Myth.* the Muse of dancing and choral song. **2.** (*l.c.*) choreography; the art of dancing. [< L < Gk *Terpsichórē,* n. use of fem. of *terpsíchoros* dance-liking; see CHORUS]

terp·si·cho·re·an (tûrp′sə kə rē′ən, tûrp′sə kôr′ē ən, -kōr′-), *adj.* **1.** pertaining to dancing. **2.** (*cap.*) of or pertaining to Terpsichore. —*n.* **3.** *Informal.* a dancer. [TERPSICHORE + -AN]

terr., **1.** terrace. **2.** territory.

ter·ra (ter′ə), *n.* earth; land. [< L]

ter′ra al′ba (al′bə), any of various white, earthy or powdery substances, as pipe clay, gypsum, kaolin, or magnesia. [< L: white earth]

ter·race (ter′əs), *n., v.,* **-raced, -rac·ing.** —*n.* **1.** a raised level with a vertical or sloping front or sides faced with masonry, turf, or the like, esp. one of a series of levels rising one above another. **2.** the top of such a construction, used as a platform, garden, road, etc. **3.** a nearly level strip of land with a more or less abrupt descent along the margin of the sea, a lake, or a river. **4.** the flat roof of a house. **5.** an open, often paved area connected to a house and serving as an outdoor living area. **6.** *Chiefly Brit.* **a.** a row of houses on or near the top of a slope. **b.** a residential street following the top of a slope. —*v.t.* **7.** to form into or furnish with a terrace or terraces. [earlier *terrasse* < MF < ML *terrācea* heap of earth, n. use of fem. of L **terrāceus.* See TERRA, -ACEOUS] —**ter′race·less,** *adj.* —**ter′rac·er,** *n.*

ter·rac·ing (ter′ə siŋ), *n.* **1.** something formed as a terrace. **2.** a system of terraces. **3.** the act or process of making terraces. [TERRACE + -ING[1]]

ter′ra cot′ta (kot′ə), **1.** an earthenware, naturally brownish-orange in color but often glazed in various colors, used for architectural ornaments and facings, structural units, and as a material for sculpture. **2.** made of terra cotta. **3.** a brownish-orange color like that of much terra cotta. [< It: lit., baked earth < L *terra cocta*]

ter·ra-cot·ta (ter′ə kot′ə), *adj.* made of or having the color of terra cotta.

ter·rae fi·li·us (teʀ′ʀī fē′lē o͝os′; *Eng.* ter′ē fil′ē-əs), *pl.* **ter·rae fi·li·i** (teʀ′ʀī fē′lē ē′; *Eng.* ter′ē fil′ē-ī′). *Latin.* **1.** an Oxford University student formerly delegated to give a satirical oration. Cf. **prevaricator** (def. 2). **2.** *Archaic.* a person of lowly parentage. [lit., son of earth, i.e., man of unknown origin]

ter′ra fir′ma (fûr′mə), firm or solid earth; dry land (as opposed to water or air). [< L]

ter·rain (tə rān′, ter′ān), *n.* **1.** a tract of land, esp. as considered with reference to its natural features, military advantages, etc. **2.** *Geol.* terrane. [< F << VL **terrān(um),* n. use of neut. of **terrānus* of land. See TERRA, -AN]

ter·ra in·cog·ni·ta (teʀ′ʀä in kôg′ni tä′; *Eng.* ter′ə in kog′ni tə, in′kog nē′-), *Latin.* an unknown or unexplored land, region, or subject.

ter·ra·ma·ra (ter′ə mär′ə), *n., pl.* **-ma·re** (-mär′ē). a lake dwelling or settlement of lake dwellings, esp. those whose remains survive in mounds in the Po valley of N Italy. [< dial. It < *terra* earth + *mara,* dissimilated var. of It *marna* MARL]

Ter·ra Ma·ter (ter′ə mā′tər), *Rom. Religion.* Tellus.

Ter·ra·my·cin (ter′ə mī′sin), *n.* *Pharm., Trademark.* oxytetracycline.

ter·rane (tə rān′, ter′ān), *n.* *Geol.* any rock formation or series of formations. Also, **terrain.** [sp. var. of TERRAIN]

ter·ra·pin (ter′ə pin), *n.* **1.** any of several edible, North American turtles of the family *Emydidae,* found in fresh or brackish waters, esp. the diamondback terrapin. **2.** any of various similar turtles. [earlier *torope* < Algonquian (Va.); see -IN[1]]

ter·ra·que·ous (ter ā′kwē əs, -ak′wē-), *adj.* consisting of land and water, as the earth. [TERR(A) + AQUEOUS]

ter·rar·i·um (te râr′ē əm), *n., pl.* **-rar·i·ums, -rar·i·a** (-râr′ē ə). **1.** a vivarium for land animals (distinguished from *aquarium*). **2.** a glass container, chiefly or wholly enclosed, for growing plants. [TERR(A) + -ARIUM]

ter·ras (tə ras′), *n.* trass.

ter·ra ver·de (ter′ə ver′dā; *It.* teʀ′ʀä veʀ′de). See **green earth.** [< It]

ter·raz·zo (tə raz′ō, -räz′ō; *It.* teʀ ʀät′tsô), *n.* a mosaic flooring or paving composed of chips of broken stone, usually marble, and cement, polished when in place. [< It: balcony, terraced or flat roof]

Ter·re Haute (ter′ə hōt′, ter′ē hut′), a city in W Indiana, on the Wabash River. 72,500 (1960).

Ter·rel (ter′əl), *n.* a boy's given name.

Ter′rell Hills′ (ter′əl), a town in central Texas. 5572 (1960).

Ter·rence (ter′əns), *n.* a boy's given name. Also, **Terence.**

ter·rene (te rēn′, tə-), *adj.* **1.** earthly; worldly. **2.** earthy. —*n.* **3.** the earth. **4.** a land or region. [ME < L *terrēn(us)* pertaining to earth. See TERRA, -ENE] —**ter·rene′ly,** *adv.*

terre·plein (ter′plān′), *n.* *Fort.* the top platform or horizontal surface of a rampart, used as a support for cannon. [< F < ML *terrā plēnus,* lit., full with earth, i.e., a fill. See TERRA, PLENUM]

ter·res·tri·al (tə res′trē əl), *adj.* **1.** pertaining to, consisting of, or representing the earth. **2.** of or pertaining to land as distinct from water. **3.** *Bot.* **a.** growing on land; not aquatic. **b.** growing in the ground; not epiphytic or aerial. **4.** *Zool.* living on the ground; not aquatic, arboreal, or aerial. **5.** of or pertaining to the earth or this world; worldly; mundane. —*n.* **6.** an inhabitant of the earth, esp. a human being. [late ME < L *terrestri(s)* pertaining to earth + -AL[1]] —**ter·res′tri·al·ly,** *adv.*
—**Syn. 1.** terrene. See **earthly.** —**Ant. 1.** celestial.

terres′trial globe′. See under **globe** (def. 3).

terres′trial tel′escope, a refracting telescope having inverting lenses or an eyepiece that presents an erect image.

ter·ret (ter′it), *n.* one of the round loops or rings on the saddle of a harness, through which the driving reins pass. See illus. under **harness.** [late ME *teret,* unexplained var. of ME *toret* < MF, OF *tor* ring (see TOUR) + *-et* -ET]

terre verte (ter′ vert′), **1.** a grayish-green color. **2.** See **green earth.** [< F: lit., green earth]

Ter·ri (ter′ē), *n.* a girl's given name, form of **Theresa.** Also, **Terry.**

ter·ri·bi·li·tà (teʀ′rē bē′lē tä′; *Eng.* ter′ə bē′li tä′), *n. Italian.* (in fine arts) a quality of overwhelming power or energy perceived in a work of art: *Michelangelo's* Last Judgment *had that* terribilità *valued so highly by the 16th century.* [< It: lit., terribleness]

ter·ri·ble (ter′ə bəl), *adj.* **1.** distressing; severe: *a terrible winter.* **2.** extremely bad; horrible: *terrible coffee; a terrible movie.* **3.** exciting or fitted to excite terror or great fear; dreadful; awful. [late ME < L *terribil(is)* < *terr(ēre)* (to) frighten + *-ibilis* -IBLE] —**ter′ri·ble·ness,** *n.*
—**Syn. 3.** fearful, frightful, appalling, dire, horrible, horrifying, terrifying, horrendous, horrid. —**Ant. 3.** delightful.

ter·ri·bly (ter′ə blē), *adv.* **1.** in a terrible manner. **2.** *Informal.* extremely: *It's terribly late. He dances terribly well.* [TERRIBLE + -LY]

ter·ric·o·lous (te rik′ə ləs), *adj. Bot., Zool.* living on or in the ground. [< L *terri-* (comb. form of *terra* earth) + -COLOUS]

ter·ri·er[1] (ter′ē ər), *n.* **1.** one of any of several breeds of usually small dogs, used originally to pursue game and drive it out of its hole or burrow. **2.** (*cap.*) *U.S.* a surface-to-air, two-stage antiaircraft missile. [< MF, short for *chien terrier,* lit., dog of the earth (ML *terrārius;* see TERRA, -IER); so called because used to start badgers from their burrows; r. late ME *terrere* < AF]

ter·ri·er[2] (ter′ē ər), *n. Law.* a book or document in which are described the site, boundaries, acreage, tenants, etc., of certain lands. [< MF, short for *registre terrier* register of land (see TERRA, -IER); r. late ME *terrere* < AF]

ter·rif·ic (tə rif′ik), *adj.* **1.** *Informal.* extraordinarily great, intense, or good: *terrific speed; a terrific dive.* **2.** causing terror; terrifying. [< L *terrific(us)* frightening < *terr(ēre)* to frighten + *-i-* -I- + *-ficus* -FIC] —**ter·rif′i·cal·ly,** *adv.*
—**Syn. 1.** fine, excellent, extraordinary, remarkable.

ter·ri·fy (ter′ə fī′), *v.t.,* **-fied, -fy·ing.** to fill with terror; make greatly afraid. [< LL *terrifi(cāre)* < *terr(ēre)* (to) frighten + *-ificāre* -IFY] —**ter′ri·fi′er,** *n.* —**ter′ri·fy′ing·ly,** *adv.*
—**Syn.** See **frighten, afraid.**

ter·rig·e·nous (te rij′ə nəs), *adj.* **1.** produced by the earth. **2.** *Geol.* noting or pertaining to sediments on the sea bottom derived directly from the neighboring land, or to the rocks formed primarily by the consolidation of such sediments. [< L *terrigenus* < *terr(a)* earth + *-i-* -I- + *-genus* -GENOUS]

ter·rine (tə rēn′), *n.* **1.** a casserole made of pottery. **2.** a delicacy of meat, game, or fish, cooked in this casserole and served cold. **3.** a tureen. [< F; see TUREEN]

ter·ri·to·ri·al (ter′i tôr′ē əl, -tōr′-), *adj.* **1.** of or pertaining to territory or land. **2.** of, pertaining to, associated with, or restricted to a particular territory or district; local. **3.** pertaining or belonging to the territory of a state or ruler. **4.** (*cap.*) of or pertaining to a Territory of the U.S. **5.** (*cap.*) *Mil.* organized on a local basis for home defense: *the British Territorial Army.* —*n.* **6.** (*cap.*) a member of the British Territorial Army. **7.** a soldier in a territorial army. [< LL *territoriāl(is).* See TERRITORY, -AL[1]] —**ter′ri·to′ri·al·ly,** *adv.*

ter·ri·to·ri·al·ise (ter′i tôr′ē ə līz′, -tōr′-), *v.t.,* **-ised, -is·ing.** *Chiefly Brit.* territorialize. —**ter′ri·to′ri·al·i·sa′tion,** *n.*

ter·ri·to·ri·al·ism (ter′i tôr′ē ə liz′əm, -tōr′-), *n.* **1.** the principle of the predominance of the landed classes. **2.** Also called **territo′rial sys′tem.** the theory of church policy according to which the supreme ecclesiastical authority is vested in the civil power. [TERRITORIAL + -ISM] —**ter′ri·to′ri·al·ist,** *n.*

ter·ri·to·ri·al·i·ty (ter′i tôr′ē al′i tē, -tōr′-), *n.* **1.** territorial quality, condition, or status. **2.** the behavior of an animal in defending its territory. [TERRITORIAL + -ITY]

ter·ri·to·ri·al·ize (ter′i tôr′ē ə līz′, -tōr′-), *v.t.,* **-ized, -iz·ing. 1.** to extend by adding new territory. **2.** to reduce to the status of a territory. [TERRITORIAL + -IZE] —**ter′ri·to′ri·al·i·za′tion,** *n.*

territo′rial wa′ters, the waters of a littoral state that are regarded as under the jurisdiction of the state: commonly, those waters within three miles of the shore. Also, **territo′rial wa′ter.** Also called **marine belt.** Cf. **high sea.**

ter·ri·to·ry (ter′i tôr′ē, -tōr′ē), *n., pl.* **-ries. 1.** any tract of land; region or district. **2.** the land and waters belonging to or under the jurisdiction of a state, sovereign, etc. **3.** any separate tract of land belonging to a state. **4.** (*cap.*) *Govt.* **a.** *U.S.* (formerly) a region or district not admitted to the Union as a State but having its own legislature, with a governor and other officers appointed by the President and confirmed by the Senate. **b.** some similar district elsewhere, as in Canada and Australia. **5.** a field or sphere of action, thought, etc.; domain or province of something: *Don't ask me to do something that is not in my territory.* **6.** the region or district assigned to a representative, agent, or the like, as for making sales. **7.** the area which an animal defends against intruders of the same species. [late ME < L *territōri(um)* land round a town, district < *terr(a)* land + *-i-* -I- + *-tōrium* abstracted from other words in *-tōrium* with local sense; see -ORY[2]]

ter′ritory wool′, the wool of sheep raised west of the Mississippi River, esp. in Washington and the Rocky Mountain States. Also called **modock wool, range wool, western wool.** Cf. **bright wool.**

ter·ror (ter′ər), *n.* **1.** intense, sharp, overmastering fear: *to be frantic with terror.* **2.** a feeling, instance, or cause of intense fear: *to be a terror to evildoers.* **3.** any period of frightful violence or bloodshed likened to the Reign of Terror in France. **4.** any terrorist group, program, etc. **5.** *Informal.* a person or thing that is especially annoying or unpleasant. [< L *terr(ēre)* (to) frighten + *-or* -OR[1]; r. ME *terrour* < AF] —**ter′ror·ful,** *adj.* —**ter′ror·less,** *adj.*
—**Syn. 1.** alarm, dismay, consternation. TERROR, HORROR, PANIC, FRIGHT all imply extreme fear in the presence of danger or evil. TERROR implies an intense fear which is somewhat prolonged and may refer to imagined or future dangers: *frozen with terror.* HORROR implies a sense of shock at a danger which is also evil, and the danger may be to others rather than to oneself: *to recoil in horror.* PANIC and FRIGHT both imply a sudden shock of fear. FRIGHT is usually of short duration: *a spasm of fright.* PANIC is uncontrolled and unreasoning fear, often groundless, which may be prolonged: *The mob was in a panic.* —**Ant. 1.** calm.

ter·ror·ise (ter′ə rīz′), *v.t.,* **-ised, -is·ing.** *Chiefly Brit.* terrorize. —**ter′ror·i·sa′tion,** *n.* —**ter′ror·is′er,** *n.*

ter·ror·ism (ter′ə riz′əm), *n.* **1.** the use of terrorizing methods. **2.** the state of fear and submission so produced. **3.** a terroristic method of governing or of resisting a government. [TERROR + -ISM]

ter·ror·ist (ter′ər ist), *n.* **1.** a person who uses or favors terrorizing methods. **2.** (formerly) a member of a political group in Russia aiming at the demoralization of the government by terror. **3.** an agent or partisan of the revolutionary tribunal during the Reign of Terror in France. [TERROR + -IST; cf. F *terroriste*] —**ter′ror·is′tic,** *adj.*

ter·ror·ize (ter′ə rīz′), *v.t.,* **-ized, -iz·ing. 1.** to fill or overcome with terror. **2.** to dominate or coerce by intimidation. [TERROR + -IZE] —**ter′ror·i·za′tion,** *n.* —**ter′ror·iz′er,** *n.*
—**Syn. 1, 2.** See **frighten.**

ter·ror-strick·en (ter′ər strik′ən), *adj.* overwhelmed by terror; terrified.

ter·ry (ter′ē), *n., pl.* **-ries,** *adj.* —*n.* **1.** the loop formed by the pile of a fabric when left uncut. **2.** Also, **ter′ry cloth′.** a pile fabric with loops on both sides, as in a Turkish towel. —*adj.* **3.** having the pile loops uncut: *terry velvet.* [? var. of TERRET]

Ter·ry (ter′ē), *n.* **1. Ellen (Alicia** or **Alice),** 1848?–1928, English actress. **2.** a boy's given name, form of **Terrence** or **Theodore. 3.** Also, **Terri.** a girl's given name, form of **Theresa.**

Ter·sanc·tus (tûr saŋk′təs, ter-), *n.* Sanctus (def. 1). [< NL: lit., thrice holy (trans. of LGk *triságios*) < L *ter* thrice + *sanctus* holy; see SAINT-]

terse (tûrs), *adj.* **ters·er, ters·est.** neatly or effectively concise; brief and pithy, as language: *a terse review of the novel.* —**terse′ly,** *adv.* —**terse′ness,** *n.* [< L *ters(us),* ptp. of *tergēre* to rub off, wipe off, clean, polish]

ter·tial (tûr′shəl), *Ornith.* —*adj.* **1.** pertaining to any of a set of flight feathers situated on the basal segment of a bird's wing. —*n.* **2.** a tertial feather. [< L *terti(us)* third + -AL[1]]

ter·tian (tûr′shən), *adj.* **1.** *Pathol.* (of a fever, ague, etc.) characterized by paroxysms which recur every other day. —*n.* **2.** *Pathol.* a tertian fever or ague. **3.** a Jesuit during his tertianship. [ME *terciane* < L (*febris*) *tertiāna* tertian (fever) < *terti(us)* third + *-āna,* fem. of *-ānus* -AN]

ter·tian·ship (tûr′shən ship′), *n.* (in the Jesuit order) a period of strict discipline before the taking of final vows, beginning one or two years after ordination. [TERTIAN + -SHIP]

ter·ti·ar·y (tûr′shē er′ē, tûr′shə rē), *adj., n., pl.* **-ar·ies.** —*adj.* **1.** of the third order, rank, formation, etc.; third. **2.** *Chem.* **a.** noting or containing a carbon atom united to three other carbon atoms. **b.** formed by replacement of three atoms or groups. **3.** (*cap.*) *Geol.* noting or pertaining to the period forming the earlier part of the Cenozoic era, occurring from 1,000,000 to 70,000,000 years ago, characterized by the introduction and development of mammals other than man. Cf. **Neocene, Paleocene.** See table under **era. 4.** *Ornith.* tertial. **5.** *Eccles.* noting or pertaining to a branch, or third order, of certain religious orders which consists of lay members living in community **(regular tertiaries)** or living in the world **(secular tertiaries).** —*n.* **6.** (*cap.*) *Geol.* the Tertiary period or system. **7.** *Ornith.* a tertial feather. **8.** (*often cap.*) *Eccles.* a member of a tertiary branch of a religious order. **9.** See **tertiary color.** [< L *tertiāri(us)* of third part or rank < *terti(us)* third + *-ārius* -ARY]

ter′tiary col′or, a color, as gray or brown, produced by mixing two secondary colors.

ter′tiary syph′ilis, *Pathol.* the third stage of syphilis, characterized by involvement of the internal organs, esp. the brain, spinal cord, heart, and liver.

ter·ti·um quid (tûr′shē əm kwid′; *Lat.* teʀ′tē o͝om′ kwid′), something related in some way to two things, but distinct from both; something intermediate between two things. [< L, trans. of Gk *tríton ti* some third thing]

ter·ti·us (tûr′shē əs), *adj.* (in prescriptions) third. [< L]

Ter·tul·li·an (tər tul′ē ən, -tul′yən), *n.* (*Quintus Septimius Florens Tertullianus*) A.D. c160–c230, Carthaginian theologian.

ter·va·lent (tûr vā′lənt), *adj. Chem.* **1.** trivalent. **2.** possessing three different valences, as cobalt with valences 2, 3, and 4. [TER- + VALENT] —**ter·va′lence, ter·va′len·cy,** *n.*

ter·za ri·ma (tert′sə rē′mə; *It.* teʀ′tsä ʀē′mä), *n. Pros.* an Italian form of iambic verse consisting of eleven-syllable lines arranged in tercets, the middle line of each tercet rhyming with the first and last lines of the following tercet. [< It: third rhyme]

tesch·en·ite (tesh′ə nīt′), *n.* a coarse-grained igneous rock consisting of a plagioclase feldspar and of olivine with idiomorphic crystals of augite. [named after *Teschen* (German name of Czech *Těšín,* town in Czechoslovakia) + -ITE[1]]

tes·la (tes′lə), *n.* a unit of magnetic induction equal to one weber per square meter. *Abbr.:* T [named after N. TESLA]

Tes·la (tes′lə), *n.* **Ni·ko·la** (nik′ō lə), 1856–1943, U.S. physicist and inventor, born in Croatia.

Tes′la coil′, *Elect.* an air-core transformer used to produce high voltages of high-frequency alternating currents. Also called **Tes′la transform′er.** [named after its inventor, N. TESLA]

TESOL (tē′sôl), *n.* **1.** teaching English to speakers of other languages. **2.** Teachers of English to Speakers of Other Languages.

Tess (tes), *n.* a girl's given name, form of **Theresa.** Also, **Tes′sie.**

tes·se·late (tes′ə lāt′), *v.t.,* **-lat·ed, -lat·ing,** *adj.* tessellate.

tes·sel·late (*v.* tes′ə lāt′; *adj.* tes′ə lit, -lāt′), *v.,* **-lat·ed, -lat·ing,** *adj.* —*v.t.* **1.** to form of small squares or blocks, as floors, pavements, etc.; form or arrange in a checkered or mosaic pattern. —*adj.* **2.** tessellated. [< L *tessellāt(us)* mosaic < *tessell(a)* small square stone (dim. of *tessera* TESSERA) + *-ātus* -ATE[1]]

tes·sel·lat·ed (tes′ə lā′tid), *adj.* **1.** of, pertaining to, or like a mosaic. **2.** arranged in or having the appearance of a mosaic; checkered. Also, **tes′se·lat′ed.** [TESSELLATE + -ED[2]]

tes·sel·la·tion (tes′ə lā′shən), *n.* **1.** the art or practice of tessellating. **2.** tessellated form or arrangement. **3.** tessellated work. Also, **tes′se·la′tion.** [TESSELLATE (V.) + -ION]

Tesserae (def. 1)

tes·ser·a (tes′ər ə), *n., pl.* **tes·ser·ae** (tes′ə rē′). **1.** each of the small pieces used in mosaic work. **2.** a small square of bone, wood, or the like, used in ancient times as a token, tally, ticket, due, etc. [< L < Gk (Ionic) *tésseres* four]

tes·ser·act (tes′ə rakt′), *n.* the generalization of a cube to four dimensions. [< Gk *tésser(es)* four + *akt(ís)* ray]

Tes·sin (te sēn′), *n.* German name of **Ticino.**

tes·si·tu·ra (tes′i to͝or′ə; *It.* tes′sē to͞o′ʀä), *n., pl.* **-tu·ras,** *It.* **-tu·re** (-to͞o′ʀe). the general range of pitch of a voice or of musical composition. [< It: lit., texture < L *textūra* TEXTURE]

Tess′ of the D′Ur′ber·villes (dûr′bər vilz), a novel (1891) by Thomas Hardy.

test[1] (test), *n.* **1.** the means by which the presence, quality, or genuineness of anything is determined; a means of trial. **2.** the trial of the quality of something: *to put to the test.* **3.** a particular process or method for trying or assessing. **4.** *Educ.* a form of examination for evaluating the performance and capabilities of a student or class. **5.** *Psychol.* **a.** a set of standardized questions, problems, or tasks designed to elicit responses for use in measuring the traits, capacities, or achievements of an individual. **b.** a measurement technique based on such standardized criteria as specified. **6.** *Chem.* **a.** the process of detecting the presence of an ingredient in a substance, or of determining the nature of a substance, commonly by the addition of a reagent. **b.** the reagent used. **c.** an indication or evidence of the presence of an ingredient, or of the nature of a substance, obtained by such means. **7.** *Brit.* a cupel for refining or assaying metals. —*v.t.* **8.** to subject to a test of any kind; try. **9.** *Chem.* to subject to a chemical test. **10.** *Metall.* to assay or refine in a cupel. —*v.i.* **11.** to undergo a test or trial; try out for: *She is testing for Juliet.* **12.** to perform on a test: *People test better in comfortable conditions.* **13.** to conduct a test: *to test for diabetes; The mike is off—we're just testing.* [ME: cupel < MF < L *testū* earthen pot with lid; akin to TEST[2]] —**test′a·bil′i·ty,** *n.* —**test′a·ble,** *adj.* —**test′ing·ly,** *adv.*
—**Syn. 1.** proof, assay. See **trial. 8.** assay, prove, examine.

test[2] (test), *n.* **1.** *Zool.* the hard, protective shell or covering of certain invertebrates, as echinoderms or tunicates. **2.** *Bot.* testa. [< L *testa* tile, shell, covering. See TEST[1]]

Test., Testament.

tes·ta (tes′tə), *n., pl.* **-tae** (-tē). *Bot.* the outer, usually hard, integument or coat of a seed. [< L; see TEST[2]]

tes·ta·cean (te stā′shən), *adj. Zool.* having a shell or test. [< L *testāce(us)* shell-covered + -AN]

tes·ta·ceous (te stā′shəs), *adj.* **1.** of, pertaining to, or derived from shells. **2.** having a test or shell-like covering. **3.** *Bot., Zool.* of a brick-red, brownish-red, or brownish-yellow color. [< L *testāceus* shell-covered < *test(a)* (see TEST[2]) + *-āceus* -ACEOUS]

test′ act′, 1. any law requiring a person to belong to the established church of a country as a condition for holding public office. **2.** (*caps.*) *Eng. Hist.* the statute (1673) requiring all military officers and public officials to take an oath of allegiance to the Crown, receive the sacraments of the Church of England, and reject the doctrine of transubstantiation. It was repealed in 1828.

tes·ta·cy (tes′tə sē), *n.* state of being testate. [TESTA(TE) + -CY]

tes·ta·ment (tes′tə mənt), *n.* **1.** *Law.* **a.** a will, esp. one that relates to the disposition of one's personal property. **b.** will[2] (def. 8). **2.** a covenant, esp. between God and man. **3.** either of the two major portions of the Bible: the Mosaic or old covenant or dispensation, or the Christian or new covenant or dispensation. **4.** (*cap.*) the New Testament, as distinct from the Old Testament. **5.** (*cap.*) a copy of the New Testament. [ME: will < L *testāment(um)* < *testā(rī)* (eccl. L: covenant, mistranslation of Gk *diathḗkē*) (to) bear witness (see TESTATE) + *-mentum* -MENT]

tes·ta·men·ta·ry (tes′tə men′tə rē), *adj.* **1.** of, pertaining to, or of the nature of a testament or will. **2.** given, bequeathed, done, or appointed by will. **3.** set forth or contained in a will. Also, **tes′ta·men′tal.** [late ME < L *testāmentāri(us).* See TESTAMENT, -ARY]

tes·tate (tes′tāt), *adj.* having made and left a valid will. [late ME < L *testāt(us),* ptp. of *testārī* to bear witness, make a will, deriv. of *testis* witness]

tes·ta·tor (tes′tā tər, te stā′tər), *n.* **1.** one who makes a will. **2.** one who has died leaving a valid will. [< L; see TESTATE, -OR[2]; r. late ME *testatour* < AF]

tes·ta·trix (te stā′triks), *n., pl.* **tes·ta·tri·ces** (te stā′tri sēz′, tes′tə trī′sēz). a female testator. [< LL; fem. of TESTATOR]

test′ ban′, an agreement by nations producing nuclear bombs to refrain from testing them in the atmosphere. —**test′-ban′,** *adj.*

test′ blank′, *Educ., Psychol.* a typed or printed test form containing questions or tasks to be responded to.

test′ case′, 1. a typical case whose court decision may be interpreted as a precedent for application in future similar cases. **2.** a legal action taken, sometimes deliberately by agreement of both parties, with a special view to determining the position of the law on some matter, as the constitutionality of a statute.

test·ee (te stē′), *n.* one who is tested, as by a scholastic examination. [TEST[1] + -EE]

test·er[1] (tes′tər), *n.* one who or that which tests. [TEST[1] + -ER[1]]

tes·ter[2] (tes′tər), *n.* a canopy, as over a bed, altar, etc. [ME < ML *testrum* canopy of a bed; akin to L *testa* covering. See TEST[2]]

tes·ter[3] (tes′tər), *n.* the teston of Henry VIII. [earlier *testorn,* var. of TESTON, with *-r-* from MF *testart* teston]

tes·tes (tes′tēz), *n.* pl. of **testis.**

tes·ti·cle (tes′ti kəl), *n.* testis. [< L *testicul(us).* See TESTIS, -CLE]

tes·tic·u·lar (te stik′yə lər), *adj.* **1.** of or pertaining to the testes. **2.** *Bot.* testiculate. [< L *testicul(us)* TESTICLE + -AR[1]]

tes·tic·u·late (te stik′yŏŏ lit), *adj. Bot.* **1.** shaped like a testis. **2.** having tubers shaped like testes, as certain orchids. [< LL *testiculāt(us).* See TESTICLE, -ATE[1]]

tes·ti·ère (tes′tē âr′), *n. Armor.* chanfron. [ME < OF, equiv. to ML *testera* head covering < *test(a)* head + *-era* n. suffix]

tes·ti·fi·ca·tion (tes′tə fə kā′shən), *n.* act of testifying or giving testimony. [late ME *testificacion* < L *testificātiōn-* (s. of *testificātiō*) a bearing witness. See TESTIFY, -ATION]

tes·ti·fy (tes′tə fī′), *v.,* **-fied, -fy·ing.** —*v.i.* **1.** to bear witness; give or afford evidence. **2.** to make solemn declaration. **3.** *Law.* to give testimony under oath or solemn affirmation, usually in court. —*v.t.* **4.** to bear witness to; affirm as fact or truth; attest. **5.** to give or afford evidence of in any manner. **6.** to declare, profess, or acknowledge openly. **7.** *Law.* to state or declare under oath or affirmation, usually in court. [ME *testifye* < L *testificārī* to bear witness < *testi(s)* witness + *-ficārī* -FY] —**tes′ti·fi′er,** *n.*

tes·ti·mo·ni·al (tes′tə mō′nē əl), *n.* **1.** a written declaration certifying to a person's character, conduct, or qualifications, or to the value, excellence, etc., of a thing; a letter or written statement of recommendation. **2.** something given or done as an expression of esteem, admiration, or gratitude. —*adj.* **3.** pertaining to or serving as a testimonial: *a testimonial dinner for the retiring dean.* [late ME < LL *testimōniāl(is).* See TESTIMONY, -AL[1]]

tes·ti·mo·ni·al·ise (tes′tə mō′nē ə līz′), *v.t.,* **-ised, -is·ing.** *Chiefly Brit.* testimonialize.

tes·ti·mo·ni·al·ize (tes′tə mō′nē ə līz′), *v.t.,* **-ized, -iz·ing.** to honor (someone) by giving or doing something testimonial. [TESTIMONIAL + -IZE]

tes·ti·mo·ny (tes′tə mō′nē), *n., pl.* **-nies. 1.** *Law.* the statement or declaration of a witness under oath or affirmation, usually in court. **2.** evidence in support of a fact or statement; proof. **3.** open declaration or profession, as of faith. **4.** Usually, **testimonies.** the precepts of God. **5.** the Decalogue as inscribed on the two tables of the law, or the ark in which the tables were kept. Ex. 16:34; 25:16. **6.** *Archaic.* a declaration of disapproval; protest. [late ME < L *testimōni(um)* < *testi(s)* witness + *-mōnium* -MONY]
—**Syn. 1.** deposition, attestation. See **evidence. 2.** corroboration. **3.** affirmation.

tes′timony meet′ing, a meeting at which persons give testimonies of religious faith and related religious experiences. Also called **experience meeting.**

tes·tis (tes′tis), *n., pl.* **-tes** (-tēz). *Anat., Zool.* the male gonad or reproductive gland, either of two oval glands located in the scrotum. [< L]

test′ match′, 1. a group of cricket games played between all-star teams of Australia and England to determine the champion. **2.** a similar game or group of games played between all-star teams of other countries.

test′ meal′, *Med.* any meal of a specific type and quantity, given to stimulate gastric secretion and removed from the stomach after a period of time and examined for digestive changes.

tes·ton (tes′tən, te stōōn′), *n.* **1.** a former silver coin of France, equal at various times to between 10 and $14^1/_2$ sols, bearing on the obverse a bust of the reigning king. **2.** a former silver coin of England, issued by Henry VIII and Edward VI, and bearing on the obverse the bust of the reigning king: equal originally to 10 pence, later to sixpence. **3.** Also, **tes·to·ne** (te stō′nā). a former silver coin of Milan, first issued in 1468, bearing on the obverse a bust of the Duke of Milan. Also, **testoon** (te stōōn′). [< F < It *testone,* aug. of *testa* head < L; see TESTA]

tes·tos·ter·one (te stos′tə rōn′), *n.* **1.** *Biochem.* the sex hormone, $C_{19}H_{28}O_2$, secreted by the testes, that stimulates the development of masculine characteristics. **2.** *Pharm.* a commercially prepared form of this compound, originally isolated from bull's testes and now also produced synthetically, used in medicine chiefly for treatment of testosterone deficiency and for certain gynecological conditions. [*testo-* (comb. form of TESTIS) + STER(OL) + -ONE]

test′ pa′per, 1. *U.S.* the paper bearing answers given on an examination. **2.** *Chem.* paper impregnated with a reagent, as litmus, which changes color when acted upon by certain substances.

test′ pat′tern, *Television.* a geometric design broadcast to receivers for testing the quality of transmission, often identifying the transmitting station and channel.

test′ pi′lot, a pilot employed to fly newly-built aircraft through maneuvers designed to produce stresses in excess of normal so as to determine the strength, maneuverability, etc., of the aircraft.

test′ stand′, *Rocketry.* a device that restrains a missile or rocket during a captive test.

test′ tube′, a hollow cylinder of thin glass with one end closed, used in chemical and biological experimentation and analysis.

test-tube (test′tōōb′, -tyōōb′), *adj.* **1.** produced in or as in a test tube; synthetic or experimental. **2.** generated by artificial insemination: *a test-tube baby.*

tes·tu·di·nal (te stōōd′ᵊnᵊl, -styōōd′-), *adj.* pertaining to or resembling a tortoise or tortoise shell. Also, **tes·tu·di·nar·i·an** (te stōōd′ᵊnâr′ē ən, -styōōd′-). [< L *testūdin-* (s. of *testūdō*) tortoise + -AL[1]]

tes·tu·di·nate (te stōōd′ᵊnit, -ᵊnāt′, -styōōd′-), *adj.* **1.** formed like the carapace of a tortoise; arched; vaulted. **2.** chelonian. —*n.* **3.** a turtle. [< LL *testūdināt(us).* See TESTUDINAL, -ATE[1]]

tes·tu·do (te stōō′dō, -styōō′-), *n., pl.* **tes·tu·di·nes** (te stōōd′ᵊnēz′, -styōōd′-). **1.** *Fort.* **a.** (among the ancient Romans) a movable shelter with a strong and usually fireproof arched roof, used for protection of soldiers in siege operations. **b.** a shelter formed by overlapping oblong shields, held by soldiers above their heads. **2.** *Pathol.* an encysted tumor. **3.** (in Roman architecture) a vault, esp. one of relatively low rise. [late ME (in medical sense) < L: lit., tortoise; akin to TEST[2]]

Testudo (def. 1b)

tes·ty (tes′tē), *adj.,* **-ti·er, -ti·est.** irritably impatient; touchy. [late ME *testi,* alter. of MF *testu* headstrong; r. ME *testif* < MF. See TEST[2], -IVE] —**tes′ti·ly,** *adv.* —**tes′ti·ness,** *n.*
—**Syn.** tetchy, edgy, snappish, cross, irascible. —**Ant.** composed.

te·tan·ic (tə tan′ik), *adj.* **1.** *Pathol.* pertaining to, of the nature of, or characterized by tetanus. **2.** *Med.* noting a remedy which acts on the nerves and through them on the muscles, and which, if taken in overdoses, causes tetanic spasms of the muscles and death. Cf. **tetany.** Also, **te·tan′i·cal.** [< L *tetanic(us)* < Gk *tetanikós* < *tétan(os)* spasm, TETANUS + *-ikos* -IC] —**te·tan′i·cal·ly,** *adv.*

tet·a·nise (tet′ᵊnīz′), *v.t.,* **-nised, -nis·ing.** *Chiefly Brit.* tetanize. —**tet′a·ni·sa′tion,** *n.*

tet·a·nize (tet′ᵊnīz′), *v.t.,* **-nized, -niz·ing.** *Physiol.* to induce tetanus in (a muscle). [TETAN(US) + -IZE] —**tet′a·ni·za′tion,** *n.*

tet·a·nus (tet′ᵊnəs), *n.* **1.** *Pathol.* an infectious, often fatal disease, caused by a specific bacterium that enters the body through wounds, and characterized by more or less violent tonic spasms and rigidity of many or all the voluntary muscles, esp. those of the neck and lower jaw. Cf. **lockjaw. 2.** Also called **tet′anus bacil′lus.** *Bacteriol.* the bacterium, *Clostridium tetani,* causing this disease. **3.** *Physiol.* a state of sustained contraction of a muscle, during which the muscle does not relax to its initial length or tension, induced by a rapid succession of stimuli. [< L < Gk *tétanos* spasm (of muscles), tetanus] —**tet′a·noid′,** *adj.*

tet·a·ny (tet′ᵊnē), *n. Pathol.* a state marked by severe, intermittent tonic contractions and muscular pain, frequently due to a deficiency of calcium salts. [< NL *tetania.* See TETANUS, -Y[3]]

tetarto-, a learned borrowing from Greek meaning "one fourth," used in the formation of compound words: *tetartohedral.* [comb. form repr. Gk *tétartos;* akin to L *quartus*]

te·tar·to·he·dral (ti tär′tō hē′drəl), *adj.* (of a crystal) having one fourth the planes or faces required by the maximum symmetry of the system to which it belongs. [TETARTO- + -HEDRAL] —**te·tar′to·he′dral·ly,** *adv.* —**te·tar′to·he′drism,** *n.*

tetched (techt), *adj.* touched; slightly mad. [late ME *techyd* marked (confused in sense with *touched* a little crazy) < *teche* mark, spot, blemish, taint (< MF, OF < Gmc; akin to TOKEN) + *-ed* -ED[3]]

tetch·y (tech′ē), *adj.,* **tetch·i·er, tetch·i·est.** irritable; touchy. Also, **techy.** [? *tetch* (see TETCHED) + -Y[1]] —**tetch′i·ly,** *adv.* —**tetch′i·ness,** *n.*

tête-à-tête (tāt′ə tāt′; *Fr.* te tA tet′), *adj., n., pl.* **tête-à-têtes,** *Fr.* **tête-à-tête,** *adv.* —*adj.* **1.** of, between, or for two persons together without others. —*n.* **2.** a private conversation or interview, usually between two people. **3.** Also called **siamoise, vis-à-vis.** a sofa shaped, in plan, like an S so two people are able to converse face to face. —*adv.* **4.** (of two persons) together in private: *to sit tête-à-tête.* [< F: lit., head to head]

tête-bêche (tet besh′), *n. Philately.* (of a pair) reversed in relation to each other. [< F < *tête* head + *bêche,* reduced from *bêchevet* head (of bed) the wrong way]

tête-de-pont (*Fr.* tet də pôN′), *n., pl.* **têtes-de-pont** (*Fr.* tet də pôN′). *Fort.* bridgehead. [< F]

teth (tet, tes), *n.* **1.** the ninth letter of the Hebrew alphabet. **2.** the consonant sound represented by this letter. [< Heb]

teth·er (teth′ər), *n.* **1.** a rope, chain, or the like, by which an animal is fastened to a fixed object so as to limit its range of movement. **2.** the utmost length to which one can go in action; the utmost extent or limit of ability or resources. **3. at the end of one's tether,** at the end of one's resources, patience, or strength: *A succession of illnesses had brought him to the end of his tether.* —*v.t.* **4.** to fasten or confine with or as with a tether. [ME *tethir* < Scand; cf Icel *tjōthr,* c. D *tuier*]

teth·er·ball (teth′ər bôl′), *n.* a game for two persons played with rackets or wooden paddles, in which each player, standing on each side of a post from the top of which a ball is suspended by a cord, hits the ball in a direction opposite to that in which the other player hits it, the object being to coil the cord completely around the post. [TETHER + BALL[1]]

Te·thys (tē′this), *n.* **1.** *Class. Myth.* a Titaness, a daughter of Uranus and Gaea, the wife of Oceanus and mother of the Oceanids and river gods. **2.** *Astron.* one of the nine satellites of Saturn.

Te·ton (tēt′ᵊn), *n., pl.* **-tons,** (*esp. collectively*) **-ton** for 1. **1.** a member of a Dakota people of the western U.S. **2.** a dialect of the Dakota language.

Te′ton Range′, a mountain range in NW Wyoming and SE Idaho: a part of the Rocky Mountains. Highest peak, Grand Teton, ab. 13,700 ft.

tetr-, var. of **tetra-** before a vowel: *tetryl.*

tet·ra (te′trə), *n.* any of several tropical, fresh-water fishes of the family *Characidae,* often kept in aquariums. [shortening of NL *tetragonopterus.* See TETRAGON, -O-, -PTEROUS]

tetra-, a learned borrowing from Greek meaning "four," used in the formation of compound words: *tetrabranchiate.* Also, *esp. before a vowel,* **tetr-.** [< Gk, comb. form of *téttara*]

tet·ra·ba·sic (te′trə bā′sik), *adj. Chem.* **1.** (of an acid) having four atoms of hydrogen replaceable by basic atoms or groups. **2.** containing four basic atoms or groups having a valence of one. [TETRA- + BASIC] —**tet·ra·ba·sic·i·ty** (te′trə bā sis′i tē), *n.*

tet·ra·brach (te′trə brak′), *n. Class. Pros.* a metrical foot or word of four short syllables. [< Gk *tetrábrachys* having four short syllables. See TETRA-, BRACHY-]

tet·ra·bran·chi·ate (te′trə brang′kē it, -āt′), *adj.* belonging or pertaining to the *Tetrabranchiata,* a subclass or order of cephalopods with four gills, including the pearly nautilus and numerous fossil forms. [TETRA- + BRANCHIATE]

tet·ra·bro·mo·flu·o·res·ce·in (te′trə brō′mō flōō′ə res′ē in, -flŏŏ res′-, -flō res′-, -flô res′-), *n. Chem.* eosin (def. 1). [TETRA- + BROMO- + FLUORESCEIN]

tet·ra·caine (te′trə kān′), *n. Pharm.* a white, water-soluble, crystalline solid, $C_{15}H_{24}N_2O_2$, used usually in the form of its hydrochloride, chiefly as a local and as a spinal anesthetic. [TETRA- + (PRO)CAINE]

tet·ra·cene (te′trə sēn′), *n. Chem.* a solid compound, ONNHC(=NH)N=NNHC(=NH)NH$_2$, that because of its ability to be readily detonated is used for initiating the detonation of high explosives, as of TNT. Also, **tetrazene.** [alter. of TETRAZENE]

tet·ra·chlo·ride (te′trə klōr′īd, -id, -klôr′-), *n. Chem.* a chloride containing four atoms of chlorine. [TETRA- + CHLORIDE]

tet·ra·chlo·ro·eth·y·lene (te′trə klōr′ō eth′ə lēn′, -klôr′-), *n. Chem.* a colorless, nonflammable, nonexplosive liquid, $Cl_2C{=}CCl_2$, used as a solvent, esp. in dry-cleaning. Also called **perchloroethylene.** [TETRA- + CHLOROETHYLENE]

tet·ra·chlo·ro·meth·ane (te′trə klōr′ō meth′ān, -klôr′-), *n. Chem.* See **carbon tetrachloride.** [TETRA- + CHLOROMETHANE]

tet·ra·chord (te′trə kôrd′), *n. Music.* a diatonic series of four tones, the first and last separated by a perfect fourth. [< Gk *tetráchord(os)* having four strings. See TETRA-, CHORD[1]] —**tet′ra·chor′dal,** *adj.*

te·trac·id (te tras′id), *n. Chem.* a base or alcohol containing four hydroxyl groups. [TETR- + ACID]

tet·ra·coc·cus (te′trə kok′əs), *n., pl.* **-coc·ci** (-kok′sī). *Bacteriol.* a spherical bacterium occurring in square groups of four. [TETRA- + -COCCUS]

tet·ra·cy·cline (te′trə sī′klīn, -klin), *n. Pharm.* an antibiotic, $C_{22}H_{24}H_2O_8$, derived from chlortetracycline: used in medicine, usually in the form of its hydrochloride, chiefly to treat a broad variety of infections. [TETRA- + CYCL- + -INE]

Tet·ra·cyn (te′trə sin), *n. Pharm., Trademark.* a form of tetracycline.

tet·rad (te′trad), *n.* **1.** a group of four. **2.** the number four. **3.** *Chem.* a tetravalent or quadrivalent element, atom, or group. [< Gk *tetrad-* (s. of *tetrás*) group of four]

tet·ra·drach·ma (te′trə drak′mə), *n.* a silver coin of ancient Greece, equal to four drachmas. Also, **tet·ra·drachm** (te′trə dram′). [TETRA- + DRACHMA] —**tet′ra·drach′mal,** *adj.*

te·trad·y·mite (te trad′ə mīt′), *n.* a mineral, bismuth telluride and sulfide, Bi_2Te_2S, occurring in soft-gray to black foliated masses. [< Gk *tetrádym(os)* fourfold (see TETRA-, DIDYMOUS) + -ITE[1]; modeled on G *Tetradymit*]

tet·ra·dy·na·mous (te′trə dī′nə məs), *adj. Bot.* having four long and two short stamens, as a cruciferous flower. [TETRA- + Gk *-dynamos* < *dýnam(is)* power + *-os* -OUS]

tet·ra·eth·yl (te′trə eth′əl), *adj. Chem.* containing four ethyl groups. [TETRA- + ETHYL]

tet·ra·eth·yl·lead (te′trə eth′əl led′), *n. Chem.* a colorless, oily, water-insoluble, poisonous liquid, $(C_2H_5)_4Pb$, used as an antiknock agent in gasoline. Also called **lead tetraethyl, TEL** [TETRAETHYL + LEAD[1]]

tetraeth′yl pyrophos′phate, *Chem.* a colorless to amber, hygroscopic, poisonous liquid, $(C_2H_5)_4P_2O_7$, used as an insecticide and as a rodenticide. Also called **TEPP**

tet′ra·eth·yl·thi·u′ram disul′fide (te′trə eth′əl-thī yŏŏr′əm, -thī′yə ram′, te′-), *Pharm.* disulfiram. [TETRAETHYL + THIOUR(EA) + AM(YL)]

tet·ra·flu·o·ro·eth·yl·ene (te′trə flōō′ə rō eth′ə-lēn′, -flŏŏr′ō-, -flōr′-, -flôr′-), *n. Chem.* a colorless, water-insoluble, flammable gas, C_2F_4, used in the synthesis of certain polymeric resins. [TETRA- + FLUORO- + ETHYLENE]

tet·ra·gon (te′trə gon′), *n. Rare.* a plane figure having four angles or sides; a quadrangle or quadrilateral. [< Gk *tetrágōn(on)* quadrangle. See TETRA-, -GON]

te·trag·o·nal (te trag′ə nᵊl), *adj.* **1.** pertaining to or having the form of a tetragon. **2.** *Crystall.* noting or pertaining to the tetragonal system. [TETRAGON + -AL[1]] —**te·trag′o·nal·ly,** *adv.* —**te·trag′o·nal·ness,** *n.*

tetrag′onal sys′tem, *Crystall.* a system of crystallization in which all three axes are at right angles to one another and the two equal lateral axes differ in length from the vertical axis.

tetrag′onal trisoctahe′dron, a trisoctahedron the faces of which are quadrilaterals.

tet·ra·gram (te′trə gram′), *n.* a word of four letters. [< LGk *tetrágramm(on),* n. use of neut. of *tetrágrammos* having four letters < *tetra-* TETRA- + *grámm(a)* letter + *-os* adj. suffix]

Tet·ra·gram·ma·ton (te′trə gram′ə ton′), *n.* the Hebrew word for God that consists of the four letters *yod, he, vav,* and *he,* that is transliterated consonantally usually as *YHVH,* and that is pronounced at present as *Adonai* or *Elohim* in substitution of the original, now forbidden pronunciation. [late ME < Gk, n. use of neut. of *tetragrámmatos* having four letters < *tetra-* TETRA- + *grammat-* (s. of *grámma*) letter + *-os* adj. suffix]

tet·ra·he·dral (te′trə hē′drəl), *adj.* **1.** pertaining to or having the form of a tetrahedron. **2.** having four lateral planes in addition to the top and bottom. [TETRAHEDR(ON) + -AL[1]] —**tet′ra·he′dral·ly,** *adv.*

tet·ra·he·drite (te′trə hē′drīt), *n.* a steel-gray or blackish mineral with a brilliant metallic luster, essentially copper and antimony sulfide, approximately Cu_3SbS_3, but often containing other elements, as silver, occurring in tetrahedral crystals and massive: an important ore of silver. [TETRAHEDR(ON) + -ITE[1], modeled on G *Tetraedrit*]

Tetrahedron

tet·ra·he·dron (te′trə hē′drən), *n., pl.* **-drons, -dra** (-drə). **1.** *Geom.* a solid contained by four plane faces; a triangular pyramid. **2.** any of various objects resembling a tetrahedron in the distribution of its faces or apexes. [TETRA- + -HEDRON, modeled on LGk *tetráedron,* n. use of neut. of *tetráedros* four-sided]

tet·ra·hy·drate (te′trə hī′drāt), *n. Chem.* a hydrate that contains four molecules of water, as potassium sodium tartrate, $KNaC_4H_4O_6{\cdot}4H_2O$. [TETRA- + HYDRATE] —**tet′ra·hy′drat·ed,** *adj.*

tet·ra·hy·dric (te′trə hī′drik), *adj.* *Chem.* (esp. of alcohols and phenols) tetrahydroxy. [TETRA- + -HYDRIC]

tet·ra·hy·dro·pyr·role (te′trə hī′drō pi rōl′, -pir′ōl), *n.* *Chem.* pyrrolidine. [TETRA- + HYDRO-[2] + PYRROLE]

tet·ra·hy·drox·y (te′trə hī drok′sē), *adj.* *Chem.* (of a molecule) containing four hydroxyl groups. [TETRA- + HYDROXY]

tet′ra·hy·drox′y·a·dip′ic ac′id (te′trə hī drok′sē ə dip′ik, te′trə hī drok′-), *Chem.* See **mucic acid.** [TETRA- + HYDROXY- + ADIPIC ACID]

tet·ra·hy·droz·o·line (te′trə hī droz′ə lēn′), *n.* *Pharm.* a compound, $C_{13}H_{16}N_2$, used in the form of its hydrochloride in the treatment of nasal congestion and certain conditions of eye irritation. [TETRA- + HYDRO-[2] + (IMIDA)ZOL + -INE[2]]

tet·ra·i·o·do·pyr·role (te′trə ī ō′dō pi rōl′, -pir′ōl), *n.* *Pharm.* a yellowish, crystalline powder, C_4HI_4N, used as an antiseptic. [TETRA- + IODO- + PYRROLE]

tet·ra·lite (te′trə līt′), *n.* *Chem.* tetryl. [TETRA- + -LITE]

te·tral·o·gy (te tral′ə jē), *n., pl.* **-gies.** **1.** a series of four related dramas, operas, novels, etc. **2.** a group of four dramas, three tragic and one satiric, performed consecutively at the festival of Dionysus in ancient Athens. [< Gk *tetralogía.* See TETRA-, -LOGY]

tetral′ogy of Fal·lot′ (fa lō′), *Pathol.* a congenital malformation of the heart characterized by an abnormal opening in the interventricular septum, misplacement of the aorta so that it receives blood from both ventricles instead of only the left ventricle, narrowing of the pulmonary artery, and enlargement of the right ventricle. [TETRALOGY (referring to four distinct defects) + Étienne *Fallot,* French physician who named the disease in 1888]

tet·ra·mer (te′trə mər), *n.* **1.** a molecule composed of four identical, simpler molecules. **2.** a polymer derived from four identical monomers. [TETRA- + -MER(E)]

Tetramerous flower

te·tram·er·ous (te tram′ər əs), *adj.* **1.** consisting of or divided into four parts. **2.** *Bot.* (of flowers) having four members in each whorl. [< NL *tetramerus* < Gk *tetramerḗs* having four parts < *tetra-* TETRA- + *mér(os)* part + *-ēs* adj. suffix] —**te·tram′er·ism,** *n.*

te·tram·e·ter (te tram′i tər), *adj.* **1.** *Pros.* having four measures. —*n.* **2.** *Pros.* a tetrameter verse. **3.** *Class. Pros.* a line consisting of four dipodies or eight feet in trochaic, iambic, or anapestic meter. [< L *tetrametr(us)* < Gk *tetrámetros* having four measures. See TETRA-, METER[2]]

tet·ra·meth·yl·di·ar·sine (te′trə meth′əl dī′är sēn′, -dī är′sēn, -sin), *n.* *Chem.* cacodyl (def. 2). [TETRA- + METHYL + DI-[1] + ARSINE]

te·tran·drous (te tran′drəs), *adj.* *Bot.* having four stamens. [TETR- + -ANDROUS]

tet·ra·ni·trate (te′trə nī′trāt), *n.* *Chem.* a compound containing four nitrate groups. [TETRA- + NITRATE]

tet·ra·ni·tro·meth·ane (te′trə nī′trō meth′ān), *n.* *Chem.* a colorless, volatile, water-insoluble, toxic liquid, $C(NO_2)_4$, prepared by the reaction of fuming nitric acid with benzene, acetic anhydride, or acetylene: used chiefly as an oxidizer in rocket propellants. [TETRA- + NITRO- + METHANE]

tet·ra·pet·al·ous (te′trə pet′əl əs), *adj.* *Bot.* having four petals. [TETRA- + PETALOUS]

tet·ra·ple·gi·a (te′trə plē′jē ə), *n.* *Pathol.* quadriplegia. [TETRA- + -PLEGIA]

tet·ra·ploid (te′trə ploid′), *adj.* **1.** having a chromosome number that is four times the basic or haploid number. —*n.* **2.** a tetraploid cell or organism. [TETRA- + -PLOID] —**tet′ra·ploi′dy,** *n.*

tet·ra·pod (te′trə pod′), *n.* an object, as a caltrop, having four projections radiating from one central node, with each forming an angle of 120° with any other, so that no matter how the object is placed on a relatively flat surface, three of the projections will form a supporting tripod and the fourth will point directly upward. [< NL *tetrapod(us)* < Gk *tetrapod-* (s. of *tetrápous*) four-footed. See TETRA-, -POD]

te·trap·o·dy (te trap′ə dē), *n., pl.* **-dies.** *Pros.* a measure consisting of four feet. [< Gk *tetrapodía.* See TETRA-, -POD, -Y[3]] —**tet·ra·pod·ic** (te′trə pod′ik), *adj.*

te·trap·ter·ous (te trap′tər əs), *adj.* **1.** *Zool.* having four wings or winglike appendages. **2.** *Bot.* having four winglike appendages. [< Gk *tetrápteros.* See TETRA-, -PTEROUS]

Tetrapterous fruit
A, Silverbell tree, *Halesia Carolina;* B, Transverse section

tet·ra·py·lon (te′trə pī′lon), *n., pl.* **-la** (-lə). a structure having four gateways as features of an architectural composition. [< Gk, n. use of neut. of *tetrápylos* having four gates. See TETRA-, PYLON]

te·trarch (tē′trärk, te′-), *n.* **1.** any ruler of a fourth part, division, etc. **2.** a subordinate ruler. **3.** one of four joint rulers or chiefs. **4.** the ruler of the fourth part of a country or province in the ancient Roman Empire. [< LL *tetrarcha,* var. of L *tetrarchēs* < Gk *tetrárchēs* < *tetr-* TETR- + *arch(ós)* leader + *-ēs* adj. suffix] —**te·trarch·ate** (tē′trär kāt′, -kit, te′trär-), **te·trar·chy** (tē′trär kē, te′trär-), *n.* —**te·trar·chic** (ti trär′kik), **te·trar′chi·cal,** *adj.*

tet·ra·spo·ran·gi·um (te′trə spō ran′jē əm, -spô-), *n., pl.* **-gi·a** (-jē ə). *Bot.* a sporangium containing four asexual spores. [TETRA- + SPORANGIUM]

tet·ra·spore (te′trə spōr′, -spôr′), *n.* *Bot.* one of the four asexual spores produced within a tetrasporangium. [TETRA- + SPORE] —**tet·ra·spor·ic** (te′trə spōr′ik, -spor′-), **tet·ra·spor·ous** (te′trə spôr′əs, -spor′-, ti-tras′pər-), *adj.*

tet·ra·stich (te′trə stik, te tras′tik), *n.* *Pros.* a strophe, stanza, or poem consisting of four lines. [< L *tetrastichon* < Gk, n. use of neut. of *tetrástichos.* See TETRASTICHOUS] —**tet·ra·stich·ic** (te′trə stik′ik), **te·tras·ti·chal** (te tras′ti kəl), *adj.*

te·tras·ti·chous (te tras′ti kəs), *adj.* *Bot.* **1.** arranged in a spike of four vertical rows, as flowers. **2.** having four such rows of flowers, as a spike. [< NL *tetrastichus* < Gk *tetrástichos* having four lines or rows. See TETRA-, STICH]

tet·ra·style (te′trə stīl′), *adj.* *Archit.* **1.** having four columns. **2.** (of a classical temple or building in the style of one) having four columns on one or both fronts. [< L *tetrastȳl(on)* < Gk, n. use of neut. of *tetrástȳlos* having four pillars < *tetra-* TETRA- + *stŷl(os)* pillar + *-os* adj. suffix]

tet·ra·sty·los (te′trə stī′los), *n.* *Archit.* a tetrastyle building, as a classical temple. [< L; see TETRASTYLE]

tet·ra·syl·la·ble (te′trə sil′ə bəl), *n.* *Pros.* a word or line of verse of four syllables. [TETRA- + SYLLABLE] —**tet·ra·syl·lab·ic** (te′trə si lab′ik), **tet′ra·syl·lab′i·cal,** *adj.*

tet·ra·tom·ic (te′trə tom′ik), *adj.* *Chem.* **1.** having four atoms in the molecule. **2.** having a valence of four. **3.** containing four replaceable atoms or groups. [TETR- + ATOMIC]

tet·ra·va·lent (te′trə vā′lənt, te trav′ə-), *adj.* *Chem.* **1.** having a valence of four, as Pt^{+4}. **2.** quadrivalent. [TETRA- + VALENT] —**tet′ra·va′lence, tet′ra·va′len·cy,** *n.*

tet·ra·zene (te′trə zēn′), *n.* *Chem.* either of two isomeric compounds, $H_2NN{=}NNH_2$ or $HN{=}NNHNH_2$, known only in the form of their derivatives. **2.** tetracene. [TETR- + AZ- + -ENE]

Te·traz·zi·ni (te′trə zē′nē; *It.* te′trät tsē′nē), *n.* **Lu·i·sa** (lo͞o ē′zä), 1874–1940, Italian operatic soprano.

tet·rode (te′trōd), *n.* *Electronics.* a vacuum tube containing four electrodes, usually a plate, two grids, and a cathode. [TETR- + -ODE[1]]

te·trox·ide (te trok′sīd, -sid), *n.* *Chem.* an oxide whose molecule contains four atoms of oxygen. [TETR- + OXIDE]

tet·ryl (te′tril), *n.* *Chem.* a yellow, crystalline, water-insoluble solid, $(O_2N)_3C_6H_2N(CH_3)NO_2$, used as a chemical indicator and, militarily, as a detonator and bursting charge in small-caliber projectiles. Also, **tetralite.** Also called **nitramine, trinitrophenylmethylnitramine.** [TETR- + -YL]

tet·ter (tet′ər), *n.* *Pathol.* any of various cutaneous diseases, as herpes, eczema, impetigo, etc. [ME; OE *teter;* c. Skt *dadru* kind of skin disease]

Te·tuán (te twän′), *n.* a seaport in N Morocco, on the Mediterranean: former capital of the Spanish zone of Morocco. 101,352 (1960).

Tet·zel (tet′səl), *n.* **Jo·hann** (yō′hän), 1465?–1519, German monk and antagonist of Martin Luther. Also, **Tezel.**

Teu·cer (to͞o′sər, tyo͞o′-), *n.* *Class. Myth.* **1.** the son of Scamander and Idaea, the first king of Troy. **2.** a natural son of Telamon and half brother of Great Ajax: he was a noted archer in the Trojan War.

Teu·cri·an (to͞o′krē ən, tyo͞o′-), *adj.* **1.** of or pertaining to the ancient Trojans or to Teucer. —*n.* **2.** one of the ancient Trojans. [TEUC(E)R + -IAN]

teugh (to͞okh, tyo͞okh), *adj.* *Scot.* tough. —**teugh′ly,** *adv.* —**teugh′ness,** *n.*

Teut., **1.** Teuton. **2.** Teutonic.

Teu·this (to͞o′this, tyo͞o′-), *n.* *Class. Myth.* an Arcadian general who wounded the disguised Athena while she was trying to effect a reconciliation between him and Agamemnon: he was punished with disease and a pestilence on his fields. Also called **Ornytus.**

Teu·thras (to͞o′thrəs, tyo͞o′-), *n.* *Class. Myth.* **1.** a Mysian king who killed a boar sacred to Artemis: he was punished with disease and madness. **2.** a king of Phrygia and the father of Tecmessa. **3.** (in the *Iliad*) a Magnesian ally of the Greeks who was slain by Hector in the Trojan War.

Teu·to·bur·ger Wald (*Ger.* toi′tō bo͝or′gər vält′), a chain of wooded hills in N West Germany, in Westphalia: German defeat of the Romans A.D. 9.

Teu·ton (to͞ot′ən, tyo͞ot′-), *n.* **1.** a member of a Germanic people or tribe first mentioned in the 4th century B.C. and supposed to have dwelt in Jutland. **2.** a native of Germany or a person of German origin. —*adj.* **3.** Teutonic. [< L *Teuton(ēs), Teutonī* (pl.) tribal name < Gmc]

Teu·ton·ic (to͞o ton′ik, tyo͞o-), *adj.* **1.** of or pertaining to the ancient Teutons. **2.** of, pertaining to, or characteristic of the Teutons or Germans; German. **3.** noting or pertaining to the northern European stock which includes the German, Dutch, Scandinavian, British, and related peoples. **4.** (of languages) Germanic. **5.** Nordic. —*n.* **6.** Germanic. [TEUTON + -IC] —**Teu·ton′i·cal·ly,** *adv.*

Teu·ton·i·cism (to͞o ton′i siz′əm, tyo͞o-), *n.* **1.** the character or spirit of the Teutons, esp. the Germans. **2.** a Teutonic characteristic. **3.** a Germanism. [TEUTONIC + -ISM]

Teuton′ic Or′der, a religious military order founded c1190 in the Holy Land by German crusaders for charitable pursuits, and later employed against the Slavic and Baltic peoples in the eastward expansion of medieval Germany. Also called **Teuton′ic Knights′.**

Teu·ton·ise (to͞ot′əniz′, tyo͞ot′-), *v.t., v.i.,* **-ised, -is·ing.** *Chiefly Brit.* Teutonize. —**Teu′ton·i·sa′tion,** *n.*

Teu·ton·ism (to͞ot′əniz′əm, tyo͞ot′-), *n.* the culture of the Teutons. [TEUTON + -ISM] —**Teu′ton·ist,** *n.*

Teu·ton·ize (to͞ot′əniz′, tyo͞ot′-), *v.t., v.i.,* **-ized, -iz·ing.** to make or become Teutonic. [TEUTON + -IZE] —**Teu′ton·i·za′tion,** *n.*

Te·ve·re (te′ve re), *n.* Italian name of the **Tiber.**

Te·vet (tā′vās), *n.* Tebet.

tew (to͞o, tyo͞o), *Brit. Dial.* —*v.i.* **1.** to work hard and seriously. —*v.t.* **2.** taw[2]. —*n.* **3.** worry. [ME *tewe,* var. of *tawe,* TAW[2]]

tew·el (to͞o′əl, tyo͞o′-), *n.* *Obs.* a vent or flue. [ME: vent, anus < MF, OF *tuel* pipe, tube < *tu-* (? < Gmc; cf. D *tuit* spout) + *-el* dim. suffix]

Tewkes·bur·y (to͞oks′ber′ē, -bə rē, tyo͞oks′-), *n.* a town in N Gloucestershire, in W England: final defeat of the Lancastrians in the Wars of the Roses 1471. 5814 (1961).

Tex., **1.** Texan. **2.** Texas.

Tex·ar·kan·a (tek′sär kan′ə), *n.* **1.** a city in NE Texas. 30,218 (1960). **2.** a city in SW Arkansas: contiguous with but politically independent of Texarkana, Texas. 19,788 (1960). **3.** Texarkana, Arkansas, and Texarkana, Texas, considered as a unit.

tex·as (tek′səs), *n.* *U.S. Naut.* **1.** a deckhouse on a texas deck for the accommodation of officers. **2.** See **texas deck.** [after TEXAS, from the fact that the officers' accommodation was the most spacious on the Mississippi steamboats where cabins were named after States]

Tex·as (tek′səs), *n.* a State in the S United States. 9,579,677 (1960); 267,339 sq. mi. *Cap.:* Austin. *Abbr.:* Tex. —**Tex′an,** *adj., n.*

Tex′as armadil′lo. See **nine-banded armadillo.**

Tex′as buck′thorn. See **Texas jujube.**

Tex′as Cit′y, a city in SE Texas, on Galveston Bay. 32,065 (1960).

tex′as deck′, *U.S. Naut.* the uppermost deck of an inland or western river steamer. [see TEXAS]

Tex′as fe′ver. See **tick fever.**

Tex′as Independ′ence Day′, March 2, observed in Texas as the anniversary of the declaration in 1836 of the independence of Texas from Mexico and also as the birthday of Sam Houston.

Tex′as ju′jube, a stiff, spiny, much-branched shrub, *Zizyphus maritiana,* of the southwestern U.S. and northern Mexico, having small, black, edible fruit. Also called **lote bush, Texas buckthorn.**

Tex′as lea′guer, *Baseball.* a pop fly that falls safely between converging infielders and outfielders.

Tex′as long′horn, one of a nearly extinct breed of long-horned beef cattle of the southwestern U.S., which were developed from cattle introduced into North America from Spain.

Tex′as Rang′ers, the mounted police force of the State of Texas, originally a semiofficial group of settlers organized to fight the Indians.

Tex′as sage′, a perennial, slightly woody, hairy herb, *Salvia coccinea,* of the southeastern U.S. and tropical America, having scarlet flowers.

Tex′as spar′row, a fringilline bird, *Arremonops rufivirgatus,* of the lower Rio Grande valley, dull olive-green above with yellow on the wing edgings and dull brown stripes on the head.

Tex′as Tow′er, an offshore radar-equipped platform supported by foundations sunk into the floor of the ocean, used as part of a system for warning against air attacks.

text (tekst), *n.* **1.** the main body of matter in a manuscript, book, newspaper, etc., as distinguished from notes, appendixes, headings, illustrations, etc. **2.** the original words of an author or speaker, as opposed to a translation, paraphrase, commentary, or the like: *The newspaper published the whole text of the speech.* **3.** the actual wording of anything written or printed: *You have not kept to the text of my remarks.* **4.** any of the various forms in which a writing exists: *The text is a medieval transcription.* **5.** the wording adopted by an editor as representing the original words of an author: *the authoritative text of Catullus.* **6.** any theme or topic; subject: *The weather was the text of our conversation.* **7.** the words of a song or the like. **8.** a textbook. **9.** a short passage of Scripture, esp. one chosen in proof of a doctrine or as the subject of a sermon: *The text he chose was the* Sermon on the Mount. **10.** the letter of the Holy Scripture, or the Scriptures themselves. **11.** *Print.* **a.** See **black letter.** **b.** type, as distinguished from illustrations, margins, etc. [ME < ML *text(us)* wording, L: structure (of an utterance), texture (of cloth); see TEXTURE] —**text′less,** *adj.*

text·book (tekst′bo͝ok′), *n.* a book used by students as a standard work for a particular branch of study. [TEXT + BOOK]

text·book·ish (tekst′bo͝ok′ish), *adj.* suggesting a textbook, esp. in literary style or composition. [TEXTBOOK + -ISH[1]]

text′ edi′tion, a special edition of a book for distribution to schools or colleges, subject to a special rate of discount, sometimes without a dust jacket (distinguished from *trade edition*).

text′ hand′, handwriting characterized by large neat letters.

tex·tile (teks′til, -tīl), *n.* **1.** any material that is woven. **2.** a material, as a fiber or yarn, used in or suitable for weaving: *Glass can be used as a textile.* —*adj.* **3.** woven or capable of being woven: *textile fabrics.* **4.** of or pertaining to weaving: *the textile industries.* [< L *textil(is)* woven, *textile* woven fabric < *text(us)* woven (ptp. of *texere* to weave) + *-ilis, -ile* -ILE]

text rec., *Bible.* See **received text.** Also, **Text. Rec.** [< L *textus receptus*]

tex·tu·al (teks′cho͞o əl), *adj.* **1.** of or pertaining to the text: *textual errors.* **2.** based on or conforming to the text, as of the Scriptures: *a textual interpretation of the Bible.* [late ME < ML *textu(s)* wording (see TEXT) + -AL[1]; r. ME *textuel* < MF] —**tex′tu·al·ly,** *adv.*

tex′tual crit′icism. See **lower criticism.** —**tex′tual crit′ic.**

tex·tu·al·ism (teks′cho͞o ə liz′əm), *n.* strict adherence to the text, esp. of the Scriptures. [TEXTUAL + -ISM]

tex·tu·al·ist (teks′cho͞o ə list), *n.* **1.** a person who adheres closely to the text, esp. of the Scriptures. **2.** a person who is well versed in the text of the Scriptures. [TEXTUAL + -IST]

tex·tu·ar·y (teks′cho͞o er′ē), *adj., n., pl.* **-ar·ies.** —*adj.* **1.** of or pertaining to the text; textual. —*n.* **2.** a textualist. [< ML *textu(s)* wording (see TEXT) + -ARY]

tex·ture (teks′chər), *n., v.,* **-tured, -tur·ing.** —*n.* **1.** the characteristic structure of the interwoven or intertwined threads, strands, or the like, which make up a textile fabric: *rough texture.* **2.** the characteristic physical structure given to a material, an object, etc., by the size, shape, arrangement, and proportions of its parts: *soil of a sandy texture; Chocolate cake has a heavier texture than angel food cake.* **3.** an essential part or quality; essence. **4.** *Fine Arts.* **a.** the characteristic visual and tactile quality of the surface of a work of art resulting from the way in which the materials are used. **b.** the imitation of the tactile quality of represented objects. **5.** anything produced by weaving; woven fabric. —*v.t.* **6.** to make by or as by weaving. **7.** to give texture or a particular texture to. [late ME < L *textūra* web, equiv. to *text(us)* woven (ptp. of *texere*) + *-ūra* -URE] —**tex′tur·al,** *adj.* —**tex′tur·al·ly,** *adv.* —**tex′ture·less,** *adj.*

tex′ture paint′, a finish paint having an insoluble additive, as sand, for giving a slightly rough textural effect.

Tey·de (tā′thē), *n.* **Pi·co de** (pē′kô thē). See **Teide, Pico de.**

Tez·cat·li·po·ca (tes kät′li pō′kä), *n.* an Aztec god.

Te·zel (tet′səl), *n.* **Johann.** See **Tetzel, Johann.**

T formation, *Football.* an offensive formation in which the quarterback lines up directly behind the center, with the fullback about three yards behind the quarterback and the halfbacks on opposite sides of and about one yard from the fullback.

tfr., transfer.

tg, tangent.

t.g., *Biol.* type genus.

tgn, tangent.

Th, *Chem.* thorium.

Th 227, *Chem.* radioactinium. Also, **Th-227**

-th[1], a suffix referring to condition, quality, or action, formerly used to form abstract nouns from words (*warmth*) or from stems related to words (*depth; length*). [ME *-th(e),* OE *-thu, -tho, -th;* c. Icel *-th,* Goth *-itha*]

-th[2], a suffix used in the formation of ordinal numbers (*fourth, tenth*), in some cases, added to altered stems of the cardinal (*fifth; twelfth*). [ME *-(e)the, -te,* OE *-(o)tha, -(o)the;* c. Icel *-thi, -di,* L *-tus,* Gk *-tos*]

-th[3], var. of **-eth**[1]: *doth.*

Th., Thursday.

T.H., Territory of Hawaii.

thā (thä), *n.* the fourth letter of the Arabic alphabet. [< Ar]

Thach (thach), *n.* **Edward.** See **Teach, Edward.**

thack (thak), *n., v.t. Brit. Dial.* thatch. Also, **thak.** [ME *thak,* OE *thæc* roof; c. D *dak,* G *Dach,* Icel *thak;* see THATCH]

Thack·er·ay (thak′ə rē), *n.* **William Make·peace** (māk′pēs′), 1811–63, English novelist, born in India. —**Thack′er·ay·an,** *adj., n.*

Thad·de·us (thad′ē əs), *n.* a boy's given name.

thae (thā), *pron., adj. Scot. and North Eng.* **1.** those. **2.** these. [ME, OE *thā,* pl. of *thæt* THAT]

Thai (tī, tä′ē), *n.* **1.** Also called **Thai·land·er** (tī′lan′dər). a native or descendant of a native of Thailand. **2.** Also called **Siamese.** a member of the Kadai family of languages and the official language of Thailand. **3.** a group of languages, including Shan, Lao, and the Thai, that are spoken over a wide area of SE Asia and constitute a branch of the Kadai family of languages. —*adj.* **4.** of, designating, or pertaining to the Thai languages or to the peoples that speak them. **5.** of or pertaining to Thailand; Siamese. Also, **Tai.**

Thai·land (tī′lənd), *n.* a kingdom in SE Asia: official name of Siam 1939–45 and since 1949. 35,000,000 (est. 1970); 198,242 sq. mi. *Cap.:* Bangkok. Formerly, **Siam.**

thairm (thârm), *n. Scot.* tharm.

Tha·is (thā′is *for 1; Fr.* tä ēs′ *for 2, 3*), *n.* **1.** fl. late 4th century A.D., Athenian hetaera: mistress of Alexander the Great and Ptolemy I. **2.** (*italics*) a novel (1890) by Anatole France. **3.** (*italics*) an opera (1894) by Jules Massenet, based on this novel.

thak (thak), *n., v.t. Brit. Dial.* thack.

Tha·kur (tä′ko͝or), *n.* chief or master (used as a term of respectful address among the Kshatriya caste in India). [< Hindi *ṭhākur* < Skt *ṭhakkura*]

thal·a·men·ceph·a·lon (thal′ə men sef′ə lon′), *n., pl.* **-lons, -la** (-lə). *Anat.* the diencephalon. [THALAM(US) + ENCEPHALON] —**thal·a·men·ce·phal·ic** (thal′ə men′sə fal′ik), *adj.*

tha·la·mi·um (thə lā′mē əm), *n., pl.* **-mi·a** (-mē ə). thalamus (def. 3). [< NL; dim. of THALAMUS]

thal·a·mot·o·my (thal′ə mot′ə mē), *n., pl.* **-mies.** *Surg.* an operation for destroying part of the thalamus, usually by means of an electrode. [THALAM(US) + -O- + -TOMY]

thal·a·mus (thal′ə məs), *n., pl.* **-mi** (-mī′). **1.** *Anat.* the middle part of the diencephalon through which sensory impulses pass to reach the cerebral cortex. **2.** *Bot.* **a.** a receptacle or torus. **b.** thallus. **3.** Also called **thalamium.** an apartment for women in an ancient Greek house. [< NL; L *thalamus* bedroom < Gk *thálamos*] —**tha·lam·ic** (thə lam′ik), *adj.* —**tha·lam′i·cal·ly,** *adv.*

Tha·las·sa (thə las′ə), *n. Class. Myth.* the personification of the sea.

tha·las·sic (thə las′ik), *adj.* **1.** of or pertaining to the seas and oceans, but esp. to smaller bodies of water, as seas and gulfs, as distinguished from large oceanic bodies. **2.** growing, living, or found in the sea; marine. [< Gk *thálass(a)* sea + -IC]

thal·as·sog·ra·phy (thal′ə sog′rə fē), *n.* oceanography, esp. that branch dealing with smaller bodies of water, as bays, sounds, gulfs, etc. [< Gk *thálass(a)* sea + -O- + -GRAPHY] —**thal′as·sog′ra·pher,** *n.* —**tha·las·so·graph·ic** (thə las′ə graf′ik), **tha·las′so·graph′i·cal,** *adj.*

tha·ler (tä′lər), *n., pl.* **-ler, -lers.** any of various former large coins of various German states; dollar. Also, **taler.** [< G; see DOLLAR]

Tha·les (thā′lēz), *n.* **1.** c640–546? B.C., Greek philosopher, born in Miletus. **2.** a crater in the first quadrant of the face of the moon: about 18 miles in diameter.

Tha·li·a (thə lī′ə, thā′lē ə, thāl′yə), *n. Class. Myth.* **1.** the Muse of comedy and idyllic poetry. **2.** one of the Graces. [< L < Gk, special use of *tháleia* blooming; akin to THALLUS]

tha·lid·o·mide (thə lid′ə mīd′, tha-), *n. Chem.* a crystalline, slightly water-soluble solid, $C_{13}H_{10}N_2O_4$, formerly used as a tranquilizer, sedative, or hypnotic: when taken during pregnancy it was discovered to affect normal growth of the fetus and result in abnormally shortened limbs of the newborn. [THAL(IC) + (IM)IDO- + (*glutar*)*imide* (GLUT(EN) + (TART)AR(IC) + -IMIDE)]

thal·lic (thal′ik), *adj. Chem.* of or containing thallium, esp. in the trivalent state. [THALL(IUM) + -IC]

thal·li·um (thal′ē əm), *n. Chem.* a soft, malleable, rare, bluish-white, metallic element: used in the manufacture of alloys, and, in the form of its salts, in rat poisons. *Symbol:* Tl; *at. wt.:* 204.37; *at. no.:* 81; *sp. gr.:* 11.85 at 20°C. [< NL, equiv. to *thall-* (< Gk *thallós* green stalk) + *-ium* -IUM; named after green line in its spectrum]

thal′lium oxysul′fide, *Chem.* a light-sensitive compound, Tl_2SO, used in photoelectric cells.

thal′lium sul′fate, *Chem.* a colorless, crystalline, water-soluble, poisonous solid, Tl_2SO_4, used chiefly as an insecticide and rodenticide. Also, **thallous sulfate.**

Thal·lo (thal′ō), *n. Class. Myth.* the goddess of spring flowers, considered by the ancient Athenians as one of the Horae.

thal·loid (thal′oid), *adj. Bot.* resembling or consisting of a thallus. [THALL(US) + -OID]

thal·lo·phyte (thal′ə fīt′), *n.* any plant of the phylum or division *Thallophyta,* comprising the algae, fungi, and lichens, in which the plant body of the larger species is typically a thallus. [< NL *thallophyt(a)* (pl.). See THALLUS, -O-, -PHYTE] —**thal·lo·phyt·ic** (thal′ə fit′ik), *adj.*

thal·lous (thal′əs), *adj. Chem.* containing univalent thallium. Also, **thal·li·ous** (thal′ē əs). [THALL(IUM) + -OUS]

thal′lous sul′fate, *Chem.* See **thallium sulfate.**

thal·lus (thal′əs), *n., pl.* **thal·li** (thal′ī), **thal·lus·es.** *Bot.* a simple vegetative plant body undifferentiated into true leaves, stem, and root: the plant body of typical thallophytes. [< NL < Gk *thallós* young shoot, twig]

thal′o·fide cell′ (thal′ə fīd′), a photoconductive cell containing thallium oxysulfide and sensitive only to red and short infrared waves. [THAL(LIUM) + O(XYGEN) + (SUL)F(UR) + -IDE; coinage influenced by FIDE(LITY)]

thal·weg (täl′veg, -vāk), *n.* **1.** a line, as drawn on a map, connecting the lowest points of a valley. **2.** *Chiefly Internat. Law.* the middle of the main navigable channel of a waterway that serves as a boundary line between states. [< G < *Thal* valley (c. DALE) + *Weg* WAY]

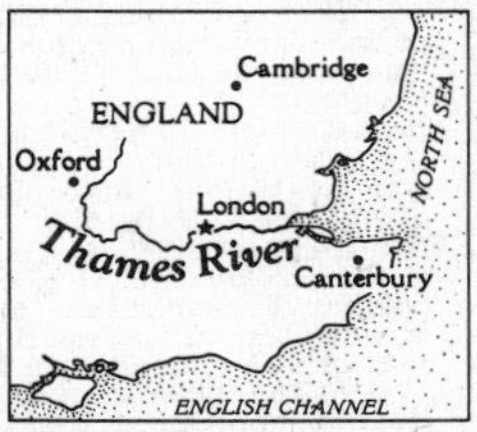

Tha·mar (thā′mər), *n. Douay Bible.* Tamar.

Thames (temz *for 1, 2;* thāmz, tāmz, temz *for 3*), *n.* **1.** a river in S England, flowing E through London to the North Sea. 209 mi. long. **2.** a river in SE Canada, in Ontario province, flowing SW to Lake St. Clair. 160 mi. long. **3.** an estuary in SE Connecticut, flowing S past New London to Long Island Sound. 15 mi. long.

Thames′ ton′nage (temz), *Naut.* the tonnage of a yacht as computed by a system of measurement **(Thames′ meas′urement)** according to which tonnage equals one ninety-fourth of the product of the length minus the breadth multiplied by one half of the breadth squared.

Tha·mus (thā′məs), *n. Class. Myth.* an Egyptian sailor who was bound for Italy when he heard a voice announce the death of Pan.

Tham·y·ris (tham′ə ris), *n. Class. Myth.* a Thracian poet and musician deprived of his creative ability and rendered blind and mute by the Muses as a punishment for his arrogance.

than (than; *unstressed* thən), *conj.* **1.** (used after comparative adjectives and adverbs, and certain other words, such as *other, otherwise, else,* etc., to introduce the second member of a comparison, both members being usually of the same case): *He is taller than I am.* **2.** (used after some adverbs and adjectives expressing choice or diversity, such as *anywhere, different, other, otherwise,* etc., to introduce an alternative or denote a difference in kind, place, style, identity, etc.): *I had no choice other than that. You won't find such freedom anywhere than in the U.S.* **3.** when: *We barely arrived than it was time to leave.* —*prep.* **4.** in relation to; by comparison with (usually fol. by a pronoun in the objective case): *He is a person than whom I can imagine no one more courteous.* [ME, OE *than(ne)* than, then, when; c. G *dann, denn,* Goth *than.* See THEN] —**Usage. 2.** See **different.**

tha·na (tä′nə), *n. Anglo-Indian.* **1.** a police station. **2.** (formerly) a military base. Also, **tana.** [< Hindi *thānā* < Skt *sthāna* a place]

than·age (thā′nij), *n.* **1.** the tenure by which lands were held by a thane. **2.** the land so held. **3.** the office, rank, or jurisdiction of a thane. [late ME < AL *thanag(ium).* See THANE, -AGE]

thanato-, a learned borrowing from Greek meaning "death," used in the formation of compound words: *thanatophobia.* [comb. form repr. Gk *thánatos*]

than·a·to·pho·bi·a (than′ə tə fō′bē ə), *n. Psychiatry.* an abnormal fear of death. [THANATO- + -PHOBIA]

than·a·top·sis (than′ə top′sis), *n.* **1.** a view or contemplation of death. **2.** (*cap., italics*) a poem (1817) by William Cullen Bryant. [THANATO- + -OPSIS]

Than·a·tos (than′ə tos′), *n.* an ancient Greek personification of death. —**Than·a·tot·ic** (than′ə tot′ik), *adj.*

thane (thān), *n.* **1.** *Early Eng. Hist.* a member of any of several classes of men ranking between earls and ordinary freemen, and holding lands of the king or lord by military service. **2.** *Scot. Hist.* a person, ranking with an earl's son, holding lands of the king; the chief of a clan, who became one of the king's barons. Also, **thegn.** [late ME, sp. var. (Scot) of ME *thain, thein,* OE *thegn;* c. Icel *thegn* subject, G *Degen* warrior, hero, Gk *téknon* child]

Than·et (than′it), *n.* **1. Oc·tave** (ok′tiv, -tāv), pen name of Alice French. **2. Isle of,** an island in SE England, forming the NE tip of Kent county. 42 sq. mi.

thank (thangk), *v.t.* **1.** to express gratitude, appreciation, or acknowledgment to: *Thank you for the beautiful red necktie.* **2. have oneself to thank,** to be personally to blame; have responsibility for: *The citizens have only themselves to thank for corruption in government.* —*n.* **3.** Usually, **thanks.** a grateful feeling or acknowledgment of a benefit, favor, or the like, expressed by words or otherwise: *to return a borrowed book with thanks.* **4. thanks,** I thank you (a common elliptical expression used in acknowledging a favor, service, courtesy, or the like). **5. thanks to,** because of; owing to: *Thanks to good organization and hard work, the church bazaar was a great success.* [ME *thanke(n),* OE *thancian* (c. D, G *danken*), deriv. of *thanc* gratitude, orig. thoughtfulness, thought. See THINK[1]] —**thank′er,** *n.*

thank·ee (thangk′ē), *interj. Chiefly Dial.* thank-you. [by alter.]

thank·ful (thangk′fəl), *adj.* feeling or expressing gratitude or appreciation. [ME; OE *thancful.* See THANK, -FUL] —**thank′ful·ly,** *adv.* —**thank′ful·ness,** *n.* —**Syn.** beholden, obliged. See **grateful.**

thank·less (thangk′lis), *adj.* **1.** not likely to be appreciated or rewarded; unappreciated: *a thankless job.* **2.** not feeling or expressing gratitude or appreciation; ungrateful: *a thankless child.* [THANK + -LESS] —**thank′less·ly,** *adv.* —**thank′less·ness,** *n.*

thanks·giv·er (thangks′giv′ər), *n.* one who gives thanks. [THANK + -S[3] + GIVER]

thanks·giv·ing (thangks′giv′ing), *n.* **1.** the act of giving thanks; grateful acknowledgment of benefits or favors, esp. to God. **2.** an expression of thanks, esp. to God. **3.** a public celebration in acknowledgment of divine favor or kindness. **4.** a day set apart for giving thanks to God. **5.** (*cap.*) *U.S.* See **Thanksgiving Day.** [THANK + -S[3] + GIVING]

Thanksgiv′ing Day′, 1. (in the United States) a national holiday for giving thanks to God, now observed on the fourth Thursday of November. **2.** (in Canada) a national holiday for giving thanks to God, observed on the second Monday of October.

thank·wor·thy (thangk′wûr′thē), *adj.* deserving gratitude. [THANK + WORTHY]

thank-you (thangk′yo͞o′), *adj.* expressing one's gratitude or thanks: *a thank-you note.* [adj. use of v. phrase *thank you*]

Thant (thant, thont), *n.* **U** (o͞o), born 1909, Burmese statesman: secretary-general of the United Nations 1962–71.

Thap·sus (thap′səs), *n.* an ancient town on the coast of Tunisia: decisive victory of Caesar 46 B.C.

thar (tär), *n.* tahr.

Thar′ Des′ert (tûr, tär), a desert in NW India and S West Pakistan. ab. 100,000 sq. mi. Also called **Indian Desert.**

Thar·e (thâr′ə), *n. Douay Bible.* Terah.

Thar·ge·li·a (thär jē′lē ə), *n.* (*sometimes construed as pl.*) an annual festival held in ancient Athens in honor of Apollo, Artemis, and the Horae, in which two condemned criminals were driven from the city and killed or banished in a ceremony of purification.

tharm (thärm), *n. Scot.* **1.** intestine. **2.** catgut as a material, as a fiddle string. Also, **thairm.** [ME, OE; c. Icel *tharmr,* G *Darm* gut, Gk *tórmos* hole]

Thar·sis (thär′sis), *n. Douay Bible.* Tarshish.

Tha·sos (thā′sôs), *n.* a Greek island in the N Aegean. 15,208 (1951); ab. 170 sq. mi. —**Tha·si·an** (thā′shē ən, -shən, -sē ən), *adj., n.*

that (that; *unstressed* thət), *pron. and adj., pl.* **those;** *adv.; conj.* —*pron.* **1.** (used to indicate a person, thing, idea, state, event, time, remark, etc., as pointed out or present, before mentioned, supposed to be understood, or by way of emphasis): *That is her mother.* **2.** (used to indicate one of two or more persons, things, etc., already mentioned, referring to the one more remote in place, time, or thought; opposed to *this*): *This is Alexandra and that is Nicky.* **3.** (used to indicate one of two or more persons, things, etc., already mentioned, implying a contrast or contradistinction; opposed to *this*): *This suit fits better than that.* **4.** (used as the subject or object of a relative clause, esp. one defining or restricting the antecedent, sometimes replaceable by *who, whom,* or *which*): *the horse that he bought.* **5.** (used as the object of a preposition, the preposition standing at the end of a relative clause): *the farm that I spoke of.* **6.** (used in various special or elliptical constructions): *Fool that he is.* **7. at that, a.** in spite of something; nevertheless: *Although perhaps too elaborate, it seemed like a good plan at that.* **b.** in addition; besides: *It was a long wait, and an exasperating one at that.* **8. that is,** (by way of explanation, clarification, or an example); more accurately: *He's very fat, that is, he weighs 273 pounds.* Also, **that is to say. 9. that's that,** *Informal.* there is no more to be said or done; that is finished: *I'm not going, and that's that!* **10. with that,** following that; thereupon: *With that, he turned on his heel and fled.* —*adj.* **11.** (used to indicate a person, place, thing, or degree as indicated, mentioned before, present, or as well-known or characteristic): *That woman is her mother. Those little mannerisms of hers make me sick.* **12.** (used to indicate the more remote in time, place, or thought of two persons, things, etc., already mentioned; opposed to *this*): *This room is his and that one is mine.* **13.** (used to imply mere contradistinction; opposed to *this*): *not this house, but that one.* **14. that way,** *Informal.* in love or very fond of (usually fol. by *about* or *for*): *The star and her director are that way. I'm that way about coffee.* —*adv.* **15.** (used with adjectives and adverbs of quantity or extent) to the extent or degree indicated: *that much; The fish was that big.* **16.** *Dial.* (used to modify an adjective or another adverb) to such an extent: *He was that weak he could hardly stand.* **—conj. 17.** (used to introduce a subordinate clause as the subject or object of the principal verb or as the necessary complement to a statement made, or a clause expressing cause or reason, purpose or aim, result or consequence, etc.): *That he will come is certain.* **18.** (used elliptically to introduce a sentence or exclamatory clause expressing desire, surprise, indignation, or other strong feeling): *That boy!* [ME, OE *thæt;* c. D *dat,* G *das(s),* Icel *that,* Gk *tó,* Skt *tād*]

that-a-way (ᵺat′ə wā′), *adv.* *Informal.* **1.** in or toward the direction pointed out: *The outlaws went that-away when they rode out of town.* **2.** in the manner indicated: *You secure the wrench to the bolt that-away.* [alter. of *that way*]

thatch (thach), *n.* **1.** Also, **thatching.** a material, as straw, rushes, leaves, or the like, used to cover roofs, grain stacks, etc. **2.** a covering of such a material. **3.** any of various palms, the leaves of which are used for thatching. **4.** the hair covering the head: *a thatch of unruly red hair.* **—v.t. 5.** to cover with or as with thatch. [ME *thacch(en),* var. (with *a* from THACK) of *thecchen,* OE *theccan* to cover, hide; c. D *dekken,* G *decken,* Icel *thekja;* see DECK] **—thatch′er,** *n.* **—thatch′less,** *adj.* **—thatch′y,** *adj.*

Thatch (thach), *n.* **Edward.** See **Teach, Edward.**

Thatch·er (thach′ər), *n.* **Margaret (Hilda),** born 1925, British leader of the Conservative party since 1975; prime minister since 1979.

thatch·ing (thach′ing), *n.* thatch (def. 1). [ME *thecchyng.* See THATCH, ING[1]]

thatch′ palm′, any of several fan palms, esp. of the genera *Sabal, Thrinax,* or *Coccothrinax,* the leaves of which are used for thatching.

that's (ᵺats), **1.** contraction of *that is: That's mine.* **2.** contraction of *that has: That's got more leaves.*

Thau·mas (thou′məs), *n.* *Class. Myth.* the father of the Harpies.

thaumato-, a learned borrowing from Greek meaning "miracle," "wonder," used in the formation of compound words: *thaumatology.* [< Gk, comb. form of *thaumat-* (s. of *thaûma*)]

thau·ma·tol·o·gy (thô′mə tol′ə jē), *n.* the study or description of miracles. [THAUMATO- + -LOGY]

thau·ma·trope (thô′mə trōp′), *n.* a card with different pictures on opposite sides (as a horse on one side and a rider on the other), which, when twirled rapidly, causes the pictures to appear as if combined, thus illustrating the persistence of visual impressions. [THAUMA(TO)- + -TROPE] **—thau·ma·trop·i·cal** (thô′mə trop′i kəl), *adj.*

thau·ma·turge (thô′mə tûrj′), *n.* a worker of wonders or miracles. Also, **thau′ma·tur′gist.** [back formation from THAUMATURGIC]

thau·ma·tur·gic (thô′mə tûr′jik), *adj.* **1.** pertaining to a thaumaturge or to thaumaturgy. **2.** having the powers of a thaumaturge. Also, **thau′ma·tur′gi·cal.** [< NL *thaumaturgic(us)* < *thaumaturg(us)* wonder-worker (< Gk *thaumatourgós* < *thaumat-* THAUMATO- + *-ourgos;* see -URGY) + *-icus* -IC]

thau·ma·tur·gy (thô′mə tûr′jē), *n.* the working of wonders or miracles; magic. [< Gk *thaumatourgía.* See THAUMATO-, -URGY]

thaw (thô), *v.i.* **1.** to pass or change from a frozen to a liquid or semiliquid state; melt. **2.** to be freed from the physical effect of frost or extreme cold (sometimes fol. by *out*): *Sit by the fire and thaw out.* **3.** (of the weather) to become warm enough to melt ice and snow: *It will probably thaw today.* **4.** to become less formal, reserved, or aloof: *He thawed at their kindness.* **5.** to become less hostile or tense: *International relations thawed.* **—v.t. 6.** to cause to change from a frozen to a liquid or semiliquid state; melt. **7.** to free from the physical effect of frost or extreme cold; bring to a more normal temperature, esp. to room temperature: *She took two steaks out of the freezer and thawed them several hours before putting them in the broiler.* **8.** to make less cold, formal, or reserved. **9.** to make less tense or hostile. **—n. 10.** the act or process of thawing. **11.** the act or fact of becoming less formal, reserved, or aloof. **12.** a reduction or easing in tension or hostility. **13.** (in winter or in areas where freezing weather is the norm) weather warm enough to melt ice and snow. **14.** a period of such weather: *We had a two-week thaw in January.* **15. the thaw,** the first day in the year when ice in harbors, rivers, etc., breaks up or loosens enough to begin flowing to the sea, allowing navigation: *The Anchorage thaw came on May 18th.* [ME *thawe(n),* OE *thawian;* c. D *dooien,* Icel *theyja*] **—thaw′less,** *adj.* **—Syn. 1.** See **melt. 2, 8.** warm. **—Ant. 1.** freeze.

Thay·er (thā′ər, thâr), *n.* **1. Sylvanus,** 1785–1872, U.S. army officer and educator. **2. William Roscoe,** 1859–1923, U.S. historian and author.

Th.B., Bachelor of Theology. [< L *Theologicae Baccalaureus*]

Th.D., Doctor of Theology. [< L *Theologicae Doctor*]

the[1] (*stressed* ᵺē; *unstressed before a consonant* ᵺə; *unstressed before a vowel* ᵺē), *definite article.* **1.** (used, esp. before a noun, with a specifying or particularizing effect, as opposed to the indefinite or generalizing force of the indefinite article *a* or *an*): *the book you gave me; Come into the house.* **2.** (used to mark a proper noun, natural phenomenon, ship, building, time, point of the compass, branch of endeavor, or field of study as something well-known or unique): *the Alps; the* Queen Elizabeth; *the past; the West.* **3.** (used with or as part of a title): *the Duke of Wellington; the Reverend John Smith.* **4.** (used to mark a noun as indicating the best-known, most approved, most important, most satisfying, etc.): *the skiing center of the U.S.; If you're going to work hard, now is the time.* **5.** (used to mark a noun as being used generically): *The dog is a quadruped.* **6.** (used in place of a possessive pronoun, to note a part of the body or a personal belonging): *He wouldn't be able to play football until the leg mended.* **7.** (used before adjectives that are used substantively, to note an individual, a class or number of individuals, or an abstract idea): *to visit the sick; from the sublime to the ridiculous.* **8.** (used before a modifying adjective to specify or limit its modifying effect): *He took the wrong road and drove miles out of his way.* **9.** (used to indicate one particular decade of a lifetime or of a century): *the gay nineties and the roaring twenties.* **10.** (one of many of a class or type, as of a manufactured item, as opposed to an individual one): *Did you listen to the radio last night?* **11.** enough: *He saved until he had the money for a new car. She didn't have the courage to leave.* **12.** (used distributively, to note any one separately); for, to, or in each; a or an: *at one dollar the pound.* [ME, OE, uninflected var. of demonstrative pronoun. See THAT]

the[2] (ᵺə, ᵺē), *adv.* **1.** (used to modify an adjective or adverb in the comparative degree and to signify "in or by that," "on that account," "in or by so much," or "in some or any degree"): *He is taking more care of himself and looks the better.* **2.** (used in correlative constructions to modify an adjective or adverb in the comparative degree, in one instance with relative force and in the other with demonstrative force, and signifying "by how much . . . by so much" or "in what degree . . . in that degree"): *the more the merrier; The bigger they are, the harder they fall.* [ME; OE *thē, thȳ,* instrumental case of demonstrative pronoun. See THAT]

the-, var. of **theo-** before a vowel: *thearchy.*

The·a (thē′ə), *n.* **1.** *Class. Myth.* a companion of Artemis who, after being ravished by Aeolus, was changed by Poseidon into a mare named Euippe. **2.** a girl's given name.

the·a·ceous (thē ā′shəs), *adj.* belonging to the *Theaceae,* or tea family of plants. [< NL *the(a)* tea + -ACEOUS]

The·ae·te·tus (thē ā′ti təs, -ē′ti-), *n.* a crater in the first quadrant of the face of the moon: about 16 miles in diameter.

the·an·throp·ic (thē′an throp′ik), *adj.* of or pertaining to both God and man; both divine and human. [THE- + ANTHROP- + -IC]

the·an·thro·pism (thē an′thrə piz′əm), *n.* **1.** the doctrine of the union of the divine and human natures, or the manifestation of God as man in Christ. **2.** the attribution of human nature to the gods. [THE- + ANTHROP- + -ISM] **—the·an′thro·pist,** *n.*

the·ar·chy (thē′är kē), *n., pl.* **-chies. 1.** the rule or government of God or of a god. **2.** an order or system of deities. [< eccl. Gk *thearchía.* See THE-, -ARCHY] **—the·ar′chic,** *adj.*

The·a·ri·ca (thē′ə rē′kə), *n.* a boy's given name.

theat., theater.

the·a·ter (thē′ə tər, thēə′-), *n.* **1.** a building, part of a building, or outdoor area for housing dramatic presentations, stage entertainments, or motion-picture shows. **2.** the audience at a theatrical or motion-picture performance: *The theater wept.* **3.** a theatrical or acting company. **4.** a room or hall, fitted with tiers of seats rising like steps, used for lectures, anatomical demonstrations, etc.: *Students crowded into the operating theater.* **5. the theater,** dramatic performances as a branch of art; the drama: *an actress devoted to the theater.* **6.** dramatic works collectively, as of literature, a nation, or an author (often prec. by *the*): *the theater of Ibsen.* **7.** the quality or effectiveness of dramatic performance: *good theater; bad theater; pure theater.* **8.** a place of action; field of operations. **9.** a natural formation of land rising by steps or gradations. Also, **theatre.** [ME *theatre* < L *theātr(um)* < Gk *théātron* seeing place, theater < *theâ(sthai)* (to) view + *-tron* -TRON]

the·a·ter·go·er (thē′ə tər gō′ər, thēə′-), *n.* a playgoer. Also, **the′a·tre·go′er.** [THEATER + GOER]

the·a·ter-in-the-round (thē′ə tər in ᵺə round′, thēə′-), *n.* See **arena theater.** Also, **the′atre-in-the-round′.**

the′ater of opera′tions, the part of the theater of war, including a combat zone and a communications zone, that is engaged in military operations and their support.

the′ater of war′, the entire area in which ground, sea, and air forces may become directly employed in war operations, and which includes the theater of operations and the zone of interior.

The·a·tine (thē′ə tin), *n.* **1.** a member of a congregation of regular clerics, founded in Italy in 1524 to combat Protestantism and promote higher morality among Roman Catholics. **2.** a member of a congregation of nuns, founded in Italy in 1583 under the direction of the Theatine fathers. [< NL *Theatin(us)* < L *Teatinus* of Chieti, Italy, where one of the founders held the archbishopric]

the·a·tre (thē′ə tər, thēə′-), *n.* theater.

Thé·â·tre-Fran·çais (*Fr.* tā ä′trə frän se′), *n.* See **Comédie Française.**

The′atre of the Absurd′, (*sometimes l.c.*) an avant-garde style of playwriting and theatrical presentation in which standard or naturalistic conventions of plot, characterization, and thematic structure are ignored or distorted for expressive, ideational, or aesthetic reasons, and in which the irrational or fictive nature of reality and man's essential isolation in the world are often stressed. Also, **The′ater of the Absurd′.**

the·at·ri·cal (thē a′tri kəl), *adj.* Also, **the·at′ric. 1.** of or pertaining to the theater, or dramatic or scenic representations: *theatrical performances.* **2.** suggestive of the theater or of acting; artificial, pompous, spectacular, or extravagantly histrionic: *a theatrical display of grief.* **—n. 3. theatricals, a.** dramatic performances, now esp. as given by amateurs. **b.** professional actors: *a family of renowned theatricals.* [< LL *theātric(us)* (see THEATRICS) + -AL[1]] **—the·at·ri·cal·i·ty** (thē a′tri kal′i tē), **the·at′ri·cal·ness,** *n.* **—the·at′ri·cal·ly,** *adv.*

the·at·ri·cal·ise (thē a′tri kə līz′), *v.t.,* **-ised, -is·ing.** *Chiefly Brit.* theatricalize. **—the·at′ri·cal·i·sa′tion,** *n.*

the·at·ri·cal·ism (thē a′tri kə liz′əm), *n.* conduct suggesting theatrical actions or mannerisms, esp. of an extravagant or exhibitionist sort. [THEATRICAL + -ISM]

the·at·ri·cal·ize (thē a′tri kə līz′), *v.t.,* **-ized, -iz·ing. 1.** to put into dramatic or theatrical form; dramatize. **2.** to express or represent in a spectacular or extravagantly histrionic manner. [THEATRICAL + -IZE] **—the·at′ri·cal·i·za′tion,** *n.*

the·a·tri·cian (thē′ə trish′ən), *n.* one skilled or versed in the art of the drama. [THEATER + -ICIAN]

the·at·ri·cism (thē a′tri siz′əm), *n.* theatricalism. [THEATRIC(S) + -ISM]

the·at·rics (thē a′triks), *n.* **1.** (*construed as sing.*) the art of staging plays and other stage performances. **2.** (*construed as pl.*) exaggerated, artificial, or histrionic mannerisms, actions, or words. [*theatric* < LL *theātric(us)* < Gk *theātrikós.* See THEATER, -ICS]

The·ba·id (thē′bā id, -bē-), *n.* **1.** the ancient region surrounding Thebes, in Egypt. **2.** (*italics*) an epic poem composed about A.D. 80–92 by Statius.

the·ba·ine (thē′bə ēn′, thi bā′ēn, -in), *n.* *Chem.* a white, crystalline, slightly water-soluble, poisonous alkaloid, $C_{19}H_{21}NO_3$, present in opium in small quantities, but having a strychninelike rather than a narcotic effect. [< NL *thēba(ia)* opium of Thebes, Egypt (alter. of L *Thēbaea,* fem. of *Thēbaeus* Theban) + -INE[2]]

The·be (thē′bē), *n.* *Class. Myth.* a daughter of Asopus and Metope who was abducted by Zeus.

Thebes (thēbz), *n.* **1.** an ancient ruined city in Upper Egypt, on the Nile: a former capital of Egypt. **2.** a city of ancient Greece, in Boeotia: a rival of ancient Athens. **—The·ba·ic** (thi bā′ik), *adj.* **—The·ban** (thē′bən), *adj., n.*

MEDITERRANEAN SEA
Alexandria
Memphis
EGYPT
Nile River
RED SEA
Thebes
1580-1085 B.C.

The·bit (thē′bit), *n.* a crater in the third quadrant of the face of the moon: about 30 miles in diameter.

the·ca (thē′kə), *n., pl.* **-cae** (-sē). **1.** a case or receptacle. **2.** *Bot.* **a.** a sac, cell, or capsule. **b.** a sporangium. **3.** *Anat., Zool.* a case or sheath enclosing an organ, structure, etc., as the horny covering of an insect pupa. [< L < Gk *thēkē* case, cover, akin to *tithénai* to place, put] **—the′cal,** *adj.*

the·cate (thē′kit, -kāt), *adj.* having or being contained in a theca. [THEC(A) + -ATE[1]]

the·ci·um (thē′shē əm, -sē əm), *n., pl.* **-ci·a** (-shē ə, -sē ə). *Bot.* hymenium. [< NL < Gk *thēkíon,* dim. of *thēkē* THECA] **—the′ci·al,** *adj.*

Thec·la (thek′lə), *n.* a girl's given name. Also, **Thekla.**

thé dan·sant (tā dän sän′), *pl.* **thés dan·sants** (tā dän sän′). *French.* See **tea dance.**

thee (ᵺē), *pron.* **1.** the objective and dative case of **thou:** *With this ring I thee wed. I shall bring thee a mighty army.* **2.** thou (now used chiefly by the Friends). [ME; OE *thē* (orig. dat.; later dat. and acc.); c. LD *di,* G *dir,* Icel *thēr.* See THOU]

thee·lin (thē′lin), *n.* *Biochem.* estrone. [irreg. < Gk *thēl(ys)* female + -IN[2]]

thee·lol (thē′lōl, -lôl, -lol), *n.* *Biochem.* estriol. [THEEL(IN) + -OL[1]]

theft (theft), *n.* **1.** the act of stealing; the wrongful taking and carrying away of the personal goods or property of another; larceny. **2.** an instance of this. **3.** *Archaic.* something stolen. [ME; OE *thēfth, thēofth;* see THIEF, -TH[1]; c. Icel *thȳfth,* obs. D *diefte*]

theft′ insur′ance, insurance against loss or damage of property resulting from theft.

theft·proof (theft′prōōf′), *adj.* safe against thieves. [THEFT + PROOF]

thegn (thān), *n.* thane. **—thegn′ly,** *adj.*

The·ia (thē′ə, thī′ə), *n.* *Class. Myth.* a Titaness, the daughter of Gaea and Uranus, and mother by her brother Hyperion of Eos, Helios, and Selene. Also, **Thia.**

Thei·ler (thī′lər), *n.* **Max,** 1899–1972, South African medical scientist, in the U.S. after 1922: Nobel prize for medicine 1951.

the·ine (thē′ēn, -in), *n.* caffeine, esp. in tea. [< NL *the(a)* TEA + -INE[2]]

their (ᵺâr; *unstressed* ᵺər), *pron.* **1.** a form of the possessive case of **they** used as an attributive adjective, before a noun: *their home; their rights as citizens; their departure for Rome.* **2.** *Nonstandard.* (used after an indefinite singular antecedent in place of the definite masculine form "his" or the definite feminine form "her"): *Someone left their book on the table.* Cf. **theirs.** [ME < Scand; cf. Icel *theirra* of those. See THEY] **—Usage.** See **me.**

their'n (ᵺârn), *pron.* *Dial.* theirs. Also, **theirn.** [THEIR + *n,* as in MINE, THINE]

theirs (ᵺârz), *pron.* **1.** a form of the possessive case of **they** used as a predicate adjective, after a noun or without a noun: *Are you a friend of theirs? It is theirs.* **2.** *Nonstandard.* (used after an indefinite singular antecedent in place of the definite masculine form "his" or the definite feminine form "hers"): *I have my book; does each student have theirs?* **3.** that which belongs to them: *Theirs is the largest house on the block.*

their·selves (ᵺâr′selvz′), *pron.* *Nonstandard.* themselves. [formed on analogy of MYSELF]

the·ism (thē′iz əm), *n.* **1.** the belief in one God as the creator and ruler of the universe, without rejection of revelation (distinguished from *deism*). **2.** belief in the existence of God or gods (opposed to *atheism*). [THE- + -ISM] **—the·ist** (thē′ist), *n., adj.* **—the·is′tic, the·is′ti·cal,** *adj.* **—the·is′ti·cal·ly,** *adv.*

Theiss (tīs), *n.* German name of **Tisza.**

Thek·la (thek′lə), *n.* a girl's given name. Also, **Thecla.**

the·li·tis (thi lī′tis), *n.* *Pathol.* inflammation of the nipple. [< Gk *thēl(ē)* nipple + -ITIS]

Thel·ma (thel′mə), *n.* a girl's given name.

the·lyt·o·kous (thi lit′ə kəs), *adj.* pertaining to or produced by thelytoky. Also, **thel·y·ot·o·kous** (thel′ē ot′ə kəs). [< Gk *thēlytókos.* See THELYTOKY, -OUS]

the·lyt·o·ky (thi lit′ə kē), *n.* parthenogenesis in which only females are produced. Also, **thel·y·ot·o·ky** (thel′ē ot′ə kē). [< Gk *thēlytokía* < *thēly(s)* female + *tók(os)* parturition, offspring + *-ia* -Y[3]]

them (ᵺem; *unstressed* ᵺəm), *pron.* **1.** the objective case of **they:** *We saw them yesterday.* **2.** the dative case of **they:** *I gave them the books.* **—adj. 3.** *Nonstandard.* those: *He don't want them books.* [ME *theym* < Scand; cf. Icel *theim* to those. See THEY]

the·ma (thē′mə), *n., pl.* **-ma·ta** (-mə tə). theme (def. 5). [< L]

the·mat·ic (thē mat′ik), *adj.* **1.** of or pertaining to a theme. **2.** *Gram.* **a.** (of a word or words) of, pertaining to, or producing a theme or themes. **b.** (of a letter) pertaining to the theme or stem. The thematic vowel is the vowel that ends the stem and precedes the inflectional ending of a word form, as *i* in Latin *audiō* "I hear." [< Gk *thematikós* of the subject, stem (Grammar) < *themat-* (s. of *théma*) THEME + *-ikos* -IC] **—the·mat′i·cal·ly,** *adv.*

The·mat′ic Ap·per·cep′tion Test′, *Psychol.* a projective technique in which stories told by a subject about each of a series of pictures are assumed to reveal dominant needs or motivations. *Abbr.:* TAT

theme (thēm), *n.* **1.** a subject of discourse, discussion, meditation, or composition; topic: *The need for world peace was the theme of the meeting.* **2.** a short, informal essay, esp. a school composition. **3.** *Music.* **a.** a principal melodic subject in a musical composition. **b.** a short melodic subject from which variations are developed. **4.** *Gram.* the element common to all or most of the forms of an inflectional paradigm, often consisting of a root with certain formative elements or modifications. Cf. **stem**[1] (def. 14). **5.** Also, **thema.** an administrative division of the Byzantine Empire. [ME *t(h)eme* < ML, L *thema* (pronounced *tema*) < Gk: proposition, deposit, akin to *tithénai* to put, set down] —**theme′less,** *adj.*
—**Syn. 1.** thesis, text. See **subject. 2.** paper.

theme′ song′, **1.** a melody in an operetta or musical comedy so emphasized by repetition as to dominate the presentation. **2.** a melody identifying or identified with a radio or television program, dance band, etc., usually played at the beginning of each program. **3.** *Informal.* an expression, comment, or subject of conversation that a person or group uses habitually.

The·mis (thē′mis), *n.* *Class. Myth.* a Titaness, the daughter of Uranus and Gaea and the mother of the Moerae and the Horae.

The·mis·te (thə mis′tē), *n.* *Class. Myth.* a daughter of Laomedon and Eurydice, and the mother of Anchises.

The·mis·to (thə mis′tō), *n.* *Class. Myth.* a wife of Athamas who killed herself when she discovered she had mistakenly brought about the death of her children while jealously plotting against Ino, her husband's former wife.

The·mis·to·cles (thə mis′tə klēz′), *n.* 527?–460? B.C., Athenian statesman.

them·selves (them selvz′), *pron. pl.* **1.** an emphatic form of **them** or **they:** *The authors themselves left the theater.* **2.** a reflexive form of **them:** *They washed themselves quickly.* **3.** *Nonstandard.* (used after an indefinite singular antecedent in place of the definite masculine "himself" or the definite feminine "herself"): *No one who ignores the law can call themselves a good citizen.* **4.** their usual, normal, characteristic selves: *After a hot meal and a few hours rest, they were themselves again.* [(ME *thamself*) THEM + SELVES; r. *themself;* see SELF]
—**Usage.** See **myself.**

then (then), *adv.* **1.** at that time: *Prices were lower then.* **2.** immediately or soon afterward: *The rain stopped and then began again.* **3.** next in order of time: *We ate, then we started home.* **4.** at the same time: *At first the water seemed blue, then gray.* **5.** next in order of place: *Standing beside Charlie is Hazel, then Uncle Harry, then Aunt Agatha.* **6.** in addition; besides; also: *I love my job, and then it pays so well.* **7.** in that case; as a consequence; in those circumstances: *If you are ill, then you must stay in bed.* **8.** since that is so; as it appears; therefore: *You have, then, found the mistake? You are leaving tonight then.* **9. but then,** but on the other hand: *I found their conversation very dull, but then I have different tastes.* **10. then and there,** at that moment; at once: *She began throwing things then and there.* Also, **there and then.** —*adj.* **11.** being; being such; existing or being at the time indicated: *the then prime minister.* —*n.* **12.** that time: *We have not been back since then. Till then, farewell.* [ME, var. of *thenne,* OE *thænne.* See THAN]
—**Syn. 8.** See **therefore.**

the·nar (thē′när), *n.* **1.** *Anat.* the fleshy mass of the outer side of the palm of the hand. **2.** the fleshy prominence or ball of muscle at the base of the thumb. —*adj.* **3.** of or pertaining to the thenar. [< NL < Gk: palm of hand or sole of foot]

the·nard·ite (thə när′dīt, tə-), *n.* a mineral, sodium sulfate, Na_2SO_4, occurring in white crystals and masses, esp. in salt lakes and arid regions. [named after L. J. *Thénard* (1777–1857), French chemist; see -ITE[1]]

The·nard's′ blue′ (thə närdz′, tə-). See **cobalt blue.** [see THENARDITE]

thence (thens), *adv.* **1.** from that place: *I went first to Paris and thence to Rome.* **2.** from that time; thenceforth: *He fell ill and thence was seldom seen.* **3.** from that source: *Thence came all our troubles.* **4.** from that fact or reason; therefore: *We were young, and thence optimistic.* [ME *thennes* < *thenne* (earlier *thenene,* OE *thanon(e)* thence) + *-es* -s[1]]

thence·forth (thens′fōrth′, -fôrth′, thens′fōrth′, -fôrth′), *adv.* from that time or place onward. Also, **thence·for·ward** (thens′fôr′wərd), **thence′for′wards.** [ME *thennes forth,* OE *thanonforth.* See THENCE, FORTH]

theo-, a learned borrowing from Greek meaning "god," used in the formation of compound words: *theocrat.* Also, *esp. before a vowel,* **the-.** [< Gk, comb. form of *theós*]

The·o·bald (thē′ə bôld′), *n.* **Lewis,** 1688–1744, English author.

The·o·bold (thē′ə bōld′), *n.* a boy's given name.

the·o·bro·mine (thē′ə brō′mēn, -min), *n.* *Pharm.* a white, crystalline, water-insoluble, poisonous powder, $C_7H_8N_4O_2$, an isomer of theophylline and lower homologue of caffeine, occurring in tea and obtained from the cacao bean: used chiefly as a diuretic, myocardial stimulant, and vasodilator. [< NL *theobrom(a)* genus of trees typified by cacao (< Gk *theo-* THEO- + *brôma* food) + -INE[2]]

the·o·cen·tric (thē′ə sen′trik), *adj.* having God as the focal point of thoughts, interests, and feelings: *theocentric philosophy.* [THEO- + -CENTRIC] —**the·o·cen·tric·i·ty** (thē′ō sen tris′i tē), *n.* —**the′o·cen′trism, the·o·cen·tri·cism** (thē′ō sen′tri siz′əm), *n.*

The·o·cly·me·nus (thē′ə klī′mə nəs), *n.* *Class. Myth.* **1.** (in the *Odyssey*) a seer who foretold the return of Odysseus and the death of Penelope's suitors. **2.** a son of Proteus and Psamathe who succeeded his father as king of Egypt.

the·oc·ra·cy (thē ok′rə sē), *n., pl.* **-cies. 1.** a form of government in which God or a deity is recognized as the supreme civil ruler, His laws being interpreted by the ecclesiastical authorities. **2.** a system of government by priests claiming a divine commission. **3.** a commonwealth or state under such a form or system of government. [< Gk *theokratía.* See THEO-, -CRACY] —**the·o·crat·ic** (thē′ə krat′ik), **the′o·crat′i·cal,** *adj.* —**the′o·crat′i·cal·ly,** *adv.*

the·oc·ra·sy (thē ok′rə sē), *n.* **1.** a mixture of religious forms and deities by worshipers. **2.** union of the personal soul with God, as in Neoplatonism. [< Gk *theokrāsía* < *theo-* THEO- + *krâs(is)* a mingling + *-ia* -Y[3]]

the·o·crat (thē′ə krat′), *n.* **1.** a person who rules, governs as a representative of God or a deity, or is a member of the ruling group in a theocracy, as a divine king or a high priest. **2.** a person who favors theocracy. [back formation from *theocratic* < Gk *theokrat(ía)* THEOCRACY + -IC]

The·oc·ri·tus (thē ok′ri təs), *n.* fl. c270 B.C., Greek poet. —**The·oc·ri·te·an** (thē ok′ri tē′ən), **The·oc′ri·tan,** *adj.*

the·od·i·cy (thē od′i sē), *n., pl.* **-cies.** a vindication of the divine attributes, particularly holiness and justice, in establishing or allowing the existence of physical and moral evil. [THEO- + Gk *dík(ē)* justice + -Y[3], modeled on F *théodicée,* a coinage of Leibniz] —**the·od′i·ce′an,** *adj.*

the·od·o·lite (thē od′əlīt′), *n.* **1.** *Survey.* a precision instrument having a telescopic sight for establishing horizontal and sometimes vertical angles. Cf. **transit** (def. 5). **2.** phototheodolite. [< NL *theodolit(us)* < ?] —**the·od·o·lit·ic** (thē od′əlit′ik), *adj.*

Theodolite
A, Telescope; B, Illuminating mirror for reading altitudes; C, Horizontal level; D, Reflector for collimation level; E, Leveling screw; F, Illuminating mirror for reading azimuths; G, Circular level; H, Eyepiece for optical centering

The·o·do·ra (thē′ə dōr′ə, -dôr′ə), *n.* **1.** A.D. 508–548, Byzantine empress: consort of Justinian I. **2.** a girl's given name.

The·o·dore (thē′ə dōr′, -dôr′), *n.* a boy's given name. Also, **The′o·dor′.**

Theodore I, died A.D. 649, pope 642–649.

Theodore II, pope A.D. 897.

The·od·o·ric (thē od′ə rik), *n.* **1.** A.D. 454?–526, king of the Ostrogoths and founder of the Ostrogothic monarchy in Italy: ruler of Italy 493–526. **2.** a boy's given name.

The·o·do·si·a (thē′ə dō′shē ə, -shə), *n.* a girl's given name.

The·o·do·sian (thē′ə dō′shən, -shē ən), *adj.* **1.** of or pertaining to Theodosius I who made Christianity the official state religion of the Roman Empire. **2.** of or pertaining to Theodosius II who issued the earliest collection of the imperial laws **(Theodo′sian Code′).** [THEODOS(IUS) + -IAN]

The·o·do·si·us I (thē′ə dō′shē əs, -shəs), ("*the Great*") A.D. 346?–395, Roman emperor of the Eastern Roman Empire 379–395.

Theodosius II, A.D. 401–450, emperor of the Eastern Roman Empire 408–450.

the·og·o·ny (thē og′ə nē), *n., pl.* **-nies. 1.** the origin of the gods. **2.** an account of this; a genealogical account of the gods. [< Gk *theogonía.* See THEO-, -GONY] —**the·o·gon·ic** (thē′ə gon′ik), *adj.* —**the·og′o·nist,** *n.*

theol., **1.** theologian. **2.** theological. **3.** theology.

the·ol·a·try (thē ol′ə trē), *n.* worship of a deity. [< Gk *theolatreía.* See THEO-, -LATRY]

the·o·log (thē′ə lôg′, -log′), *n.* *Informal.* theologue.

the·o·lo·gian (thē′ə lō′jən, -jē ən), *n.* one versed in theology, esp. Christian theology; divine. [THEOLOGY + -AN; r. late ME *theologien* < MF]

the·o·log·i·cal (thē′ə loj′i kəl), *adj.* **1.** of, pertaining to, or involved with theology: *a theological student.* **2.** based upon the nature and will of God as revealed to man. Also, **the′o·log′ic.** [< ML *theologicāl(is)* < *theologic(us)* (< Gk *theologikós;* see THEOLOGY, -IC) + *-ālis* -AL[1]] —**the′o·log′i·cal·ly,** *adv.*

theolog′ical vir′tue, (esp. among the scholastics) any virtue infused into the human intellect and will by a special grace of God, specifically one of the three graces: faith, hope, or charity. Also called **supernatural virtue.** Cf. **natural virtue.**

the·ol·o·gise (thē ol′ə jīz′), *v.i., v.t.,* **-gised, -gis·ing.** *Chiefly Brit.* theologize. —**the·ol′o·gi·sa′tion,** *n.* —**the·ol′o·gis′er,** *n.*

the·ol·o·gize (thē ol′ə jīz′), *v.,* **-gized, -giz·ing.** —*v.i.* **1.** to theorize or speculate upon theological subjects. —*v.t.* **2.** to make theological; treat theologically. Also, *esp. Brit.,* **theologise.** [< ML *theologiz(āre).* See THEOLOGY, -IZE] —**the·ol′o·gi·za′tion,** *n.* —**the·ol′o·giz′er,** *n.*

the·o·logue (thē′ə lôg′, -log′), *n.* *Informal.* a theological student. Also, **theolog.** [< L *theolog(us)* < Gk *theológos.* See THEO-, LOGO-]

the·ol·o·gy (thē ol′ə jē), *n., pl.* **-gies. 1.** the field of study, thought, and analysis which treats of God, His attributes, and His relations to the universe; the science or study of divine things or religious truth; divinity. **2.** a particular form, system, branch, or course of this science or study. [< LL *theologia* < Gk. See THEO-, -LOGY]

theol′ogy of cri′sis. See **crisis theology.**

the·om·a·chy (thē om′ə kē), *n., pl.* **-chies.** a battle with or among the gods. [< LL *theomachia* < Gk. See THEO-, -MACHY]

the·o·ma·ni·a (thē′ō mā′nē ə, -mān′yə), *n.* *Psychiatry.* insanity in which a person believes himself to be God or especially chosen by God, as to found a religious order. [< NL; see THEO-, -MANIA] —**the′o·ma′ni·ac′,** *n.*

the·o·mor·phic (thē′ə môr′fik), *adj.* having the form or likeness of God. [< Gk *theómorph(os);* see THEO-, -MORPHOUS, -MORPHIC] —**the′o·mor′phism,** *n.*

The′on Jun′ior (thē′on, -ən), a crater in the fourth quadrant of the face of the moon: about 10 miles in diameter.

The·on·o·ë (thē on′ō ē′), *n.* *Class. Myth.* **1.** a daughter of Thestor who was abducted by pirates and sold as a concubine. **2.** a prophetess and daughter of King Proteus: according to Euripides, she aided the escape of Menelaus and Helen from Egypt.

The′on Sen′ior, a crater in the fourth quadrant of the face of the moon: about 11 miles in diameter.

the·op·a·thy (thē op′ə thē), *n.* religious emotion excited by the contemplation of God. [THEO- + (SYM)PATHY] —**the·o·pa·thet·ic** (thē′ə pə thet′ik), **the·o·path·ic** (thē′ə path′ik), *adj.*

The·oph·a·ne (thē of′ə nē′), *n.* *Class. Myth.* a maiden changed into a ewe by Poseidon: she bore him the ram with the Golden Fleece.

the·oph·a·ny (thē of′ə nē), *n., pl.* **-nies.** a manifestation or appearance of God or a god to man. [< LL *theophania* < LGk *theopháneia.* See THEO-, -PHANY] —**the·o·phan·ic** (thē′ə fan′ik), **the·oph′a·nous,** *adj.*

The·oph·i·la (thē of′ə lə), *n.* a girl's given name.

The·oph·i·lus (thē of′ə ləs), *n.* **1.** a walled plain in the 4th quadrant of the face of the moon: about 65 miles in diameter. **2.** a boy's given name.

The·o·phras·tus (thē′ə fras′təs), *n.* 372?–287 B.C., Greek philosopher. —**The·o·phras·tian** (thē′ə fras′chən), *adj.*

the·o·phyl·line (thē′ə fil′ēn, -in), *n.* *Pharm.* a white, crystalline, slightly water-soluble, poisonous alkaloid, $C_7H_8N_4O_2$, an isomer of theobromine, extracted from tea leaves or produced synthetically: used, chiefly in the form of aminophylline, to relieve bronchial spasms in asthma, in the treatment of certain heart conditions, and as a diuretic. [*theo-,* irreg. comb. form repr. NL *thea* TEA) + -PHYLL + -INE[2]]

theophyl′line eth′yl·ene·di·a·mine′ (eth′ə lēn-dī′ə mēn′, -dī am′in), *Pharm.* aminophylline. [ETHYLENE + DIAMINE]

theor., theorem.

the·or·bo (thē ôr′bō), *n., pl.* **-bos.** an obsolete bass lute with two sets of strings attached to separate peg boxes, one above the other, on the neck. [< It *teorba,* var. of *tiorba,* special use of Venetian *tiorba,* var. of *tuorba* traveling bag << Turk *torba* bag; so called from the bag it was carried in] —**the·or′bist,** *n.*

Theorbo

The·o·rell (tā′ō rel′), *n.* **Ax·el Hu·go Te·o·dor** (äk′səl hōō′gō te′ô dôr′), born 1903, Swedish biochemist: Nobel prize for medicine 1955.

the·o·rem (thē′ə rəm, thēr′əm), *n.* **1.** *Math.* a theoretical proposition, statement, or formula embodying something to be proved from other propositions or formulas. **2.** a rule or law, esp. one expressed by an equation or formula. **3.** *Logic.* a proposition that can be deduced from the premises or assumptions of a system. **4.** an idea, belief, method, or statement generally accepted as true or worthwhile without proof: *There is an old theorem that sitting in a draft will give a person a cold.* [< LL *theōrēm(a)* < Gk *theṓrēma* spectacle, hence, subject for contemplation, thesis (to be proved) < *theōr(eîn)* (to) view + *-ēma* -EME] —**the·o·re·mat·ic** (thē′ər ə mat′ik, thēr′ə-), *adj.* —**the′o·re·mat′i·cal·ly,** *adv.*

the′orem of the mean′, *Math.* See **mean value theorem.**

the·o·ret·i·cal (thē′ə ret′i kəl), *adj.* **1.** of, pertaining to, or consisting in theory; not practical (distinguished from *applied*). **2.** existing only in theory; hypothetical. **3.** given to, forming, or dealing with theories; speculative. Also, **the′o·ret′ic.** [< LL *theōrētic(us)* < Gk *theōrētikós* < *theōrēt(ós)* to be seen (verbid of *theorein* to view) + *-ikos* -IC + -AL[1]] —**the′o·ret′i·cal·ly,** *adv.*

theoret′ical arith′metic, arithmetic (def. 2).

theoret′ical specif′ic im′pulse, *Rocketry.* See **specific impulse** (def. 2).

the·o·re·ti·cian (thē′ər i tish′ən, thēr′i-), *n.* one who deals with or is expert in the theoretical side of a subject: *a military theoretician.* [THEORETIC(S) + -IAN]

the·o·ret·ics (thē′ə ret′iks), *n.* *(construed as sing.)* the theoretical or speculative part of a science or subject. [see THEORETIC(AL), -ICS]

the·o·rise (thē′ə rīz′), *v.i.,* **-rised, -ris·ing.** *Chiefly Brit.* theorize. —**the′o·ri·sa′tion,** *n.* —**the′o·ris′er,** *n.*

the·o·rist (thē′ə rist), *n.* **1.** one who theorizes. **2.** one who deals mainly with the theory of a subject: *a theorist in medical research.* [THEOR(Y) + -IST]

the·o·rize (thē′ə rīz′), *v.i.,* **-rized, -riz·ing.** to form a theory or theories. Also, *esp. Brit.,* **theorise.** [< ML *theōriz(āre).* See THEORY, -IZE] —**the′o·ri·za′tion,** *n.* —**the′o·riz′er,** *n.*

the·o·ry (thē′ə rē, thēr′ē), *n., pl.* **-ries. 1.** a coherent group of general propositions used as principles of explanation for a class of phenomena: *Newton's theory of gravitation.* **2.** a proposed explanation whose status is still conjectural, in contrast to well-established propositions that are regarded as reporting matters of actual fact. **3.** *Math.* a body of principles, theorems, or the like, belonging to one subject: *number theory.* **4.** the branch of a science or art which deals with its principles or methods, as distinguished from its practice: *music theory.* **5.** a particular conception or view of something to be done or of the method of doing it; a system of rules or principles. **6.** contemplation or speculation. **7.** guess or conjecture. [< LL *theōria* < Gk *theōría* a viewing, contemplating (< *theōr(eîn)* (to) view + *-ia* -Y[3])]
—**Syn. 1.** THEORY, HYPOTHESIS are both often used colloquially to mean an untested idea or opinion. A THEORY properly is a more or less verified or established explanation accounting for known facts or phenomena: *the theory of relativity.* A HYPOTHESIS is a conjecture put forth as a possible explanation of certain phenomena or relations, which serves as a basis of argument or experimentation by which to reach the truth: *This idea is offered only as a hypothesis.* **2.** guess, scheme.

the′ory of equa′tions, *Math.* the branch of mathematics dealing with methods of finding the solutions to algebraic equations.

the′ory of games′. See **game theory.**

the′ory of relativ′ity, *Physics.* relativity (def. 2).

theos., 1. theosophical. 2. theosophy.

Theosoph′ical Soci′ety, a society founded by Madame Blavatsky and others, in New York in 1875, advocating a world-wide eclectic religion based largely on Brahmanic and Buddhistic teachings.

the·os·o·phy (thē os′ə fē), *n.* 1. any of various forms of philosophical or religious thought in which claim is made to a mystical insight into the divine nature or to a special divine revelation. 2. the system of belief and practice of the Theosophical Society. [< ML *theosophia* < LGk. See THEO-, -SOPHY] —**the·o·soph·i·cal** (thē′ə sof′i kəl), **the′o·soph′ic,** *adj.* —**the′o·soph′i·cal·ly,** *adv.* —**the·os′o·phism,** *n.* —**the·os′o·phist,** *n.*

The·o·to·co·pou·los (the′ô tô kô′po͞o lôs), *n.* **Do·men·i·kos** (thô men′ē kôs). See **El Greco.**

The·o·to·kos (thē′ə tok′əs), *n.* a title of the Virgin Mary as the Mother of the incarnate Son of God. Also, **The′o·to′cos.** [< Gk *theotókos* < *theo-* THEO- + *tókos* parturition]

The·ox·e·ni·us (thē′ok sē′nē əs), *n.* *Class. Myth.* an epithet of Apollo, meaning "god of strangers."

The·ra (thēr′ə), *n.* a Greek island in the S Aegean, in the Cyclades group. 30 sq. mi. Also, **Thira.** Formerly, **Santorin, Santorini.**

the·ra·lite (thēr′ə līt′), *n.* a coarse-grained, phaneritic rock composed of labradorite, nepheline, and augite. [< Gk *thḗra* prey + -LITE; said to be so called because success in hunting it down was thought to be certain]

therapeut., 1. therapeutic. 2. therapeutics. Also, **therap.**

ther·a·peu·tic (ther′ə pyo͞o′tik), *adj.* of or pertaining to the treating or curing of disease; curative. Also, **ther′a·peu′ti·cal.** [< NL *therapeutic(us)* < Gk *therapeutikós* < *therapeu-* (s. of *therapeúein* to attend, treat medically) + *-tikos* -TIC] —**ther′a·peu′ti·cal·ly,** *adv.*

therapeu′tic abor′tion, abortion induced when pregnancy endangers the mother's health. Also called **justifiable abortion.**

ther·a·peu·tics (ther′ə pyo͞o′tiks), *n.* (*construed as sing.*) the branch of medicine concerned with the remedial treatment of disease. [see THERAPEUTIC, -ICS]

ther·a·pist (ther′ə pist), *n.* 1. a person, as a doctor, skilled in therapeutics. 2. a person trained in the use of physical methods, as exercises, heat treatments, etc., in treating or rehabilitating the sick or wounded or in helping patients overcome physical defects. 3. a person trained in the use of psychological methods for rehabilitating the sick or wounded or in helping patients overcome psychological problems. Also, **ther·a·peu·tist** (ther′ə pyo͞o′tist). [THERAP(Y) + -IST]

The·rap·ne (thə rap′nē), *n.* *Class. Myth.* a girl who gave her name to the grounds on which the Dioscuri were buried.

ther·a·py (ther′ə pē), *n., pl.* **-pies.** 1. the treatment of disease, as by some remedial or curative process. 2. a curative power or quality. 3. physical treatment for curing or rehabilitating a patient or to overcome a physical defect, as by exercise, heat treatments, etc. 4. treatment of the psychologically or socially maladjusted in order to rehabilitate them into society, as by psychoanalysis, providing congenial tasks, etc. 5. any act, hobby, task, program, etc., that relieves tension. [< NL *therapīa* < Gk *therapeía* healing]

Ther·a·va·da (ther′ə vä′də), *n.* *Buddhism.* Hinayanist name for **Hinayana.**

Ther·a·va·din (ther′ə väd′ən), *n.* *Buddhism.* Hinayanist.

ther·blig (thûr′blig), *n.* (in time and motion study) any of the basic elements involved in completing a given manual operation or task that can be subjected to analysis. [anagram of F. B. *Gilbreth* (1868–1924), American engineer]

there (t͟hâr), *adv.* 1. in or at that place (opposed to *here*): *He is there now.* 2. at that point in an action, speech, etc.: *He stopped there for applause.* 3. in that matter, particular, or respect: *His anger was justified there.* 4. into or to that place; thither: *We went there last year.* 5. (used by way of calling attention to something or someone): *There they go.* 6. (used in interjectional phrases to express approval, encouragement, etc.): *There's a good boy!* 7. in or at that place where you are: *Well, hi there.* —*pron.* 8. (used to introduce a sentence or clause in which the verb comes before its subject or has no complement): *There is no hope.* 9. that place: *He comes from there too.* 10. that point. —*n.* 11. that state or condition: *I'll introduce you to her, but you're on your own from there on.* —*adj.* 12. (used after a demonstrative pronoun or after a noun modified by a demonstrative adjective, for emphasis): *Ask that man there.* 13. *Nonstandard.* (used between a demonstrative adjective and the noun it modifies, for emphasis): *Ask that there man.* —*interj.* 14. an exclamation used to express satisfaction, relief, encouragement, consolation, etc.: *There! It's done.* [ME; OE *thǣr*; c. D *daar*, OHG *dār*; akin to Goth, Icel *thar*; all with adv. suffix *-r*. See THAT]

there-, a prefix meaning "that (place)," "that (time)," etc., used in combination with certain adverbs and prepositions: *thereafter.*

there·a·bout (t͟hâr′ə bout′), *adv.* 1. about or near that place or time: *last June or thereabout.* 2. about that number, amount, etc. Also, **there′a·bouts′.** [ME *ther aboute*, OE *thǣr abūtan.* See THERE, ABOUT]

there·af·ter (t͟hâr′af′tər, -äf′-), *adv.* 1. after that in time or sequence; afterwards: *Thereafter they did not speak.* 2. *Obs.* accordingly. [ME *ther after*, OE *thǣr æfter.* See THERE, AFTER]

there·a·gainst (t͟hâr′ə genst′ *or, esp. Brit.,* -gānst′). *adv.* *Archaic.* against that. [late ME *ther agenst* (see THERE, AGAINST); r. ME *thereageyns*]

there·at (t͟hâr′at′), *adv.* 1. at that place or time; there: *Seeing the gate, they entered thereat.* 2. because of that; thereupon. [ME *ther at*, OE *thǣr æt.* See THERE, AT]

there·by (t͟hâr′bī′, t͟hâr′bī′), *adv.* 1. by that; by means of that. 2. in that connection or relation: *Thereby hangs a tale.* 3. by or near that place. 4. *Scot.* about that number, quantity, or degree. [ME *therby*, OE *thǣrbī.* See THERE, BY]

there·for (t͟hâr′fôr′), *adv.* for or in exchange for that or this; for it: *a refund therefor.* [ME *therfor.* See THERE, FOR]

there·fore (t͟hâr′fôr′, -fōr′), *adv.* in consequence of that; as a result; consequently: *I think; therefore I am.* [ME *ther(e)fore*, var. of *therfor* THERFOR]

—**Syn.** hence, whence. THEREFORE, WHEREFORE, ACCORDINGLY, CONSEQUENTLY, SO, THEN agree in introducing a statement resulting from, or caused by, what immediately precedes. THEREFORE (for this or that reason) and WHEREFORE (for which reason) imply exactness of reasoning; they are esp. used in logic, law, mathematics, etc., and in a formal style of speaking or writing. ACCORDINGLY (in conformity with the preceding) and CONSEQUENTLY (as a result, or sequence, or effect of the preceding) are less formal. So (because the preceding is true or this being the case) and THEN (since the preceding is true) are conversational in tone.

there·from (t͟hâr′frum′, -from′), *adv.* from that place, thing, etc. [ME; see THERE, FROM]

there·in (t͟hâr′in′), *adv.* 1. in or into that place or thing. 2. in that matter, circumstance, etc. [ME *therin*, OE *thǣrin.* See THERE, IN]

there·in·af·ter (t͟hâr′in af′tər, -äf′-), *adv.* afterward in that document. [THEREIN + AFTER]

there·in·to (t͟hâr′in′to͞o, t͟hâr′in to͞o′), *adv.* 1. into that place or thing. 2. into that matter, circumstance, etc. [ME *thar into.* See THERE, INTO]

ther·e·min (ther′ə min), *n.* a musical instrument with electronic tone generation, the pitch and tone volume being controlled by the distance between the player's hands and two metal rods serving as antennas. [named after Leo *Theremin* (b. 1896), Russian inventor] —**ther′e·min′ist,** *n.*

there·of (t͟hâr′uv′, -ov′), *adv.* 1. of that or it. 2. from or out of that origin or cause. [ME *therof*, OE *thǣrof.* See THERE, OF]

there·on (t͟hâr′on′, -ôn′), *adv.* 1. on or upon that or it. 2. immediately after that; thereupon. [ME *ther on*, OE *thǣron.* See THERE, ON]

there·out (t͟hâr′out′), *adv.* *Archaic.* out of that; thence. [ME *theroute*, OE *thǣr ūte.* See THERE, OUT]

there's (t͟hârz), 1. contraction of *there is*: *There's the hotel we were looking for.* 2. contraction of *there has*: *There's been entirely too much conversation on the subject.*

The·re·sa (tə rē′sə, -zə; *Sp.* te re′sä), *n.* 1. **Saint.** Also, **Teresa.** Also called **There′sa of Á′vi·la** (ä′vē-lä′). 1515–82, Spanish Carmelite nun, mystic, and writer. 2. a girl's given name.

Thé·rèse (tā rez′), *n.* a girl's given name, French form of **Theresa.**

Thé·rèse Ra·quin (*Fr.* tā rez ra kan′), a novel (1868) by Emile Zola.

There′ Shall′ Be′ No′ Night′, a play (1940) by Robert E. Sherwood.

there·to (t͟hâr′to͞o′), *adv.* 1. to that place, thing, etc. 2. to that matter, circumstance, etc. 3. *Archaic.* in addition to that. Also, **there·un·to** (t͟hâr′un to͞o′, t͟hâr′un′to͞o). [ME *therto*, OE *thǣrtō.* See THERE, TO]

there·to·fore (t͟hâr′tə fōr′, -fôr′), *adv.* before or until that time. [ME *ther tofore.* See THERE, HERETOFORE]

there·un·der (t͟hâr′un′dər), *adv.* 1. under or beneath that. 2. under the authority of or in accordance with that. [ME *therunder*, OE *thǣrunder.* See THERE, UNDER]

there·up·on (t͟hâr′ə pon′, -pôn′, t͟hâr′ə pon′, -pôn′), *adv.* 1. immediately following that. 2. in consequence of that. 3. upon that or it. 4. with reference to that. [ME *ther uppon.* See THERE, UPON]

there·with (t͟hâr′with′, -with′), *adv.* 1. with that. 2. in addition to that. 3. following upon that; thereupon. [ME *ther(e)with*, OE *thǣrwith.* See THERE, WITH]

there·with·al (t͟hâr′with ôl′, -with-), *adv.* 1. together with that; in addition to that. 2. following upon that. [ME *ther withal.* See THERE, WITHAL]

The·re·zi·na (*Port.* te′re zē′nə), *n.* former name of **Teresina.**

the·ri·ac (thēr′ē ak′), *n.* 1. molasses; treacle. 2. a paste formerly used as an antidote to poison, esp. snake venom, made from 60 or 70 different drugs pulverized and mixed with honey. Also, **the·ri·a·ca** (thə rī′ə kə). [< LL *thēriac(a)* antidote to poison < Gk *thēriakḗ*, fem. of *thēriakós* < *thēri(on)* wild beast + *-akos* -AC; r. ME *tiriake*, OE *tȳriaca* < ML] —**the·ri′a·cal,** *adj.*

the·ri·an (thēr′ē ən), *adj.* 1. belonging or pertaining to the group *Theria*, comprising the marsupial and placental mammals and their extinct ancestors. —*n.* 2. a therian animal. [< NL *Theri(a)* name of the group (< Gk *thēría*, pl. of *thērion* wild beast) + -AN]

the·ri·an·throp·ic (thēr′ē an throp′ik), *adj.* 1. being partly bestial and partly human in form. 2. of or pertaining to deities conceived or represented in such form. [< Gk *thēri(on)* beast + ANTHROP- + -IC] —**the·ri·an·thro·pism** (thēr′ē an′thrə piz′əm), *n.*

the·rid·i·id (thə rid′ē id, ther′i dī′id), *n.* 1. a spider of the family *Theridiidae*, comprising the comb-footed spiders. —*adj.* 2. belonging or pertaining to the family *Theridiidae.* [< NL *Theridiid(ae)* name of the family < Gk *thēri(on)* beast + NL *-idae* -ID[2]]

The·rim·a·chus (thə rim′ə kəs), *n.* *Class. Myth.* the eldest son of Hercules and Megara, killed by his father in a fit of madness.

the·ri·o·mor·phic (thēr′ē ə môr′fik), *adj.* (of deities) thought of or represented as having the form of beasts. Also, **the′ri·o·mor′phous.** [< Gk *thēriómorph(os)* beast-shaped (< *thērio(n)* wild beast + *-morphos* -MORPHOUS) + -IC] —**the′ri·o·morph′,** *n.*

The·ri·tas (thə rī′təs), *n.* *Class. Myth.* Ares: so called because his nurse was named Thero.

therm[1] (thûrm), *n.* *Physics.* any of several units of heat, as one equivalent to 1000 large calories or 100,000 Btu. Also, **therme.** [< Gk *thérm(ē)* heat]

therm[2] (thûrm), *n.* *Archaic.* a public bath. [< MF *therme(s)* (pl.) < L *thermae* hot baths < Gk *thérmai*, pl. of *thérmē* heat]

therm-, var. of **thermo-** before a vowel: *thermesthesia.*

-therm, var. of **thermo-** as final element in compound words: *isotherm.*

therm., thermometer.

Ther·ma (thûr′mə), *n.* ancient name of **Salonika.**

ther·mae (thûr′mē), *n.* (*construed as pl.*) 1. hot springs; hot baths. 2. a public bathing establishment of the ancient Greeks or Romans. [< L; see THERM[2]]

therm·aes·the·sia (thûrm′is thē′zhə, -zhē ə, -zē ə), *n.* thermesthesia.

ther·mal (thûr′məl), *adj.* 1. Also, **thermic.** of, pertaining to, or caused by heat or temperature: *thermal capacity.* 2. of, pertaining to, or of the nature of thermae: *thermal waters.* —*n.* 3. *Meteorol.* a rising air current caused by heating from the underlying surface, esp. such a current when not producing a cloud. [THERM- + -AL[1]] —**ther′mal·ly,** *adv.*

ther′mal bar′rier, *Aeronaut., Rocketry.* the high temperatures produced by the friction between a supersonic object and the earth's atmosphere which limit the speed of an airplane or rocket. Also called **heat barrier.**

ther′mal conductiv′ity, *Physics.* the amount of heat per unit time per unit area that can be conducted through a plate of unit thickness of a given material, the faces of the plate differing by one unit of temperature.

ther′mal diffu′sion, *Physical Chem.* the separation of constituents, often isotopes, of a fluid under the influence of a temperature gradient. Also, **thermodiffusion.**

ther′mal effi′ciency, *Thermodynamics.* the ratio of the work output of a heat engine to the heat input expressed in the same units of energy.

ther′mal equilib′rium, *Thermodynamics.* 1. the relationship between two systems connected only by a diathermic wall. 2. the relationship between two isolated systems the states of which are such that no net transfer of energy would occur between them if they were connected by a diathermic wall.

therm·al·ge·si·a (thûrm′al jē′zē ə), *n.* *Med.* pain caused by heat. [THERM- + ALGESIA]

ther′mal spring′, a spring with waters of a temperature higher than that of the surrounding locale.

ther′mal u′nit, a unit of heat energy or of the equivalent of heat energy in work.

therm·an·es·the·sia (thûrm′an is thē′zhə), *n.* *Pathol.* loss of ability to feel cold or heat; loss of the sense or feeling of temperature. Also, **thermoanesthesia.** [THERM- + ANESTHESIA]

Ther·ma·si·a (thər mā′sē ə), *n.* *Class. Myth.* an epithet of Demeter, meaning "warmth."

therme (thûrm), *n.* *Physics.* therm[1].

therm·el (thûr′mel), *n.* thermocouple. [THERM- + EL(ECTRIC)]

therm·es·the·sia (thûrm′is thē′zhə), *n.* *Physiol.* ability to feel cold or heat; sensitiveness to heat. Also, **thermaesthesia.** [THERM- + ESTHESIA]

ther·mic (thûr′mik), *adj.* thermal (def. 1). [THERM- + -IC]

ther′mic fe′ver, *Pathol.* sunstroke.

Ther·mi·dor (thûr′mi dôr′; *Fr.* ter mē dôr′), *n.* (in the French Revolutionary calendar) the 11th month of the year, extending from July 19th to August 17. Also called **Fervidor.** [< F < Gk *thérmē* heat + *dôr(on)* gift]

Ther·mi·do·ri·an (thûr′mi dōr′ē ən, -dôr′-), *n.* 1. a member of the French moderate group who participated in the downfall of Robespierre and his followers on the 9th Thermidor (July 27th), 1794. 2. a supporter of the reactionary movement following this coup d'état on the 9th Thermidor. Also, **Ther′mi·do′re·an.** [< F *thermidorien.* See THERMIDOR, -IAN]

therm·i·on (thûrm′ī′ən, thûr′mē ən), *n.* *Physics.* an ion emitted by incandescent material. [THERM- + ION]

therm·i·on·ic (thûrm′ī on′ik, thûr′mē-), *adj.* *Physics.* of or pertaining to thermions. [THERMION + -IC] —**therm′i·on′i·cal·ly,** *adv.*

therm′ion′ic cur′rent, an electric current produced by the flow of thermions.

therm·i·on·ics (thûrm′ī on′iks, thûr′mē-), *n.* (*construed as sing.*) the branch of physics that deals with thermionic phenomena. [see THERMIONIC, -ICS]

therm′ion′ic tube′, *Electronics.* a vacuum tube in which the cathode is heated electrically to cause the emission of electrons by thermal agitation. Also called **hot-cathode tube;** *Brit.,* **thermionic valve.**

therm′ion′ic valve′, *Brit.* 1. See **vacuum tube.** 2. See **thermionic tube.**

ther·mis·tor (thər mis′tər), *n.* *Electronics.* a resistor whose action depends upon the changes of resistance of its constituent material with changes of temperature. [THERM- + (TRANS)ISTOR]

Ther·mit (thûr′mit), *n.* *Trademark.* thermite.

ther·mite (thûr′mīt), *n.* a mixture of finely-divided metallic aluminum and ferric oxide that when ignited produces extremely high temperatures as the result of the union of the aluminum with the oxygen of the oxide: used in welding, incendiary bombs, etc. [THERM- + -ITE[1]]

thermo-, a learned borrowing from Greek meaning "heat," "hot," used in the formation of compound words: *thermoplastic.* Also, **therm-, -therm.** [< Gk, comb. form of *thermós* hot, *thérmē* heat]

ther·mo·am·me·ter (thûr′mō am′mē tər), *n.* *Elect.* an ammeter that measures amperage by means of a thermocouple. [THERMO- + AMMETER]

ther·mo·an·es·the·sia (thûr′mō an′is thē′zhə), *n.* *Pathol.* thermanesthesia.

ther·mo·bar·o·graph (thûr′mō bar′ə graf′, -gräf′), *n.* *Physics.* a device consisting of a thermograph and a barograph, for simultaneously recording the temperature and pressure of a gas. [THERMO- + BAROGRAPH]

ther·mo·ba·rom·e·ter (thûr′mō bə rom′i tər), *n.* 1. an instrument for measuring atmospheric pressure, and sometimes altitude, from its effect upon the boiling point of a liquid. 2. a form of barometer so constructed that it may also be used as a thermometer. [THERMO- + BAROMETER]

ther·mo·chem·is·try (thûr′mō kem′i strē), *n.* the branch of chemistry dealing with the relationship between chemical action and heat. [THERMO- + CHEMISTRY] —**ther′mo·chem′i·cal,** *adj.* —**ther′mo·chem′i·cal·ly,** *adv.* —**ther′mo·chem′ist,** *n.*

ther·mo·cline (thûr′mə klīn′), *n.* (of an ocean or certain lakes) a layer of water where the temperature gradient is greater than that of the warmer layer above and the colder layer below. Cf. **epilimnion, hypolimnion.** [THERMO- + Gk *klī́nē* bed] —**ther′mo·clin′al,** *adj.*

ther·mo·cou·ple (thûr′mə kup′əl), *n.* *Physics.* a device that consists of the junction of two dissimilar metallic conductors, as copper and iron, in which an electromotive force is induced when the conductors are maintained at different temperatures, the force being related to the temperature difference: used to determine the temperature of a third substance by connecting it to the junction of the metals and measuring the electromotive force produced. Also called **thermel, thermoelectric couple, thermoelectric thermometer.** [THERMO- + COUPLE]

ther·mo·cur·rent (thûr′mō kûr′ənt, -kur′-), *n.* a thermoelectric current. [THERMO- + CURRENT]

ther·mo·dif·fu·sion (thûr′mō di fyo͞o′zhən), *n. Physical Chem.* See **thermal diffusion.** [THERMO- + DIFFUSION]

ther·mo·dur·ic (thûr′mə do͝or′ik, -dyo͝or′ik), *adj. Bacteriol.* (of certain microorganisms) able to survive high temperatures, as during pasteurization. [THERMO- + L *dūr(āre)* (to) last + -IC]

thermodynam., thermodynamics.

ther·mo·dy·nam·ic (thûr′mō dī nam′ik), *adj.* **1.** of or pertaining to thermodynamics. **2.** using or producing heat. Also, **ther′mo·dy·nam′i·cal.** [THERMO- + DYNAMIC] —**ther′mo·dy·nam′i·cal·ly,** *adv.*

ther′modynam′ic poten′tial, *Thermodynamics.* See **Gibbs free energy.**

ther·mo·dy·nam·ics (thûr′mō dī nam′iks, -di-), *n.* (*construed as sing.*) the science concerned with the relations between heat and mechanical energy or work, and the conversion of one into the other: modern thermodynamics deals with the properties of systems for the description of which temperature is a necessary coordinate. [THERMO- + DYNAMICS] —**ther′mo·dy·nam′i·cist,** *n.*

ther′modynam′ic sys′tem, *Physics.* a system whose states of equilibrium can be specified by a few macroscopic properties.

ther·mo·e·las·tic (thûr′mō i las′tik), *adj. Physics.* pertaining to the thermodynamic effects produced by deformation of an elastic substance. [THERMO- + ELASTIC]

ther·mo·e·lec·tric (thûr′mō i lek′trik), *adj.* of, pertaining to, or involving the direct relationship between heat and electricity. Also, **ther′mo·e·lec′tri·cal.** [THERMO- + ELECTRIC] —**ther′mo·e·lec′tri·cal·ly,** *adv.*

ther′moelec′tric cou′ple, *Physics.* thermocouple.

ther′moelec′tric effect′, *Physics.* the production of an electromotive force in a thermocouple. Also called **Seebeck effect.**

ther·mo·e·lec·tric·i·ty (thûr′mō i lek tris′i tē, -ē′lek-), *n.* electricity generated by heat or temperature difference, as in a thermocouple. [THERMO- + ELECTRICITY]

ther′moelec′tric thermom′eter, *Physics.* thermocouple.

ther·mo·e·lec·trom·e·ter (thûr′mō i lek trom′i tər), *n. Elect.* an instrument for measuring a charge or voltage by means of the heat it produces in a resistance. [THERMO- + ELECTROMETER]

ther′mo·e·lec′tro·mo′tive force′ (thûr′mō i lek′trə mō′tiv, thûr′-), the electromotive force developed by a thermoelectric effect. [THERMO- + ELECTROMOTIVE]

ther·mo·e·lec·tron (thûr′mō i lek′tron), *n. Physics.* an electron emitted by an incandescent material. [THERMO- + ELECTRON] —**ther′mo·e·lec·tron′ic,** *adj.*

ther·mo·gal·va·nom·e·ter (thûr′mō gal′və nom′i tər), *n. Elect.* a thermoammeter for measuring small currents, consisting of a thermocouple connected to a direct-current galvanometer. [THERMO- + GALVANOMETER]

ther·mo·gen·e·sis (thûr′mō jen′i sis), *n.* the production of heat, esp. in an animal body by physiological processes. [THERMO- + GENESIS] —**ther·mo·ge·net·ic** (thûr′mō jə net′ik), *adj.*

ther·mo·gen·ic (thûr′mə jen′ik), *adj.* causing or pertaining to the production of heat. [THERMO- + -GENIC]

ther·mog·e·nous (thər moj′ə nəs), *adj.* producing heat; thermogenetic. [THERMO- + -GENOUS]

ther·mo·ge·og·ra·phy (thûr′mō jē og′rə fē), *n.* the study of the geographical variation and distribution of temperature. [THERMO- + GEOGRAPHY]

ther·mo·graph (thûr′mə graf′, -gräf′), *n.* a self-registering thermometer. [THERMO- + -GRAPH]

ther·mog·ra·phy (thər mog′rə fē), *n.* a technique for imitating an engraved appearance, as on business cards, announcements, stationery, or the like, by dusting printed areas with a powder which adheres only to the wet ink, and fusing the ink and powder to the paper by heat. [THERMO- + -GRAPHY] —**ther·mog′ra·pher,** *n.* —**ther·mo·graph·ic** (thûr′mə graf′ik), *adj.* —**ther′mo·graph′i·cal·ly,** *adv.*

ther·mo·la·bile (thûr′mō lā′bil), *adj. Biochem.* subject to destruction or loss of characteristic properties by the action of moderate heat, as certain toxins and ferments (opposed to *thermostable*). [THERMO- + LABILE] —**ther·mo·la·bil·i·ty** (thûr′mō lə bil′i tē), *n.*

ther·mo·lu·mi·nes·cence (thûr′mō lo͞o′mə nes′əns), *n. Physics.* phosphorescence produced by the heating of a substance. [THERMO- + LUMINESCENCE]

ther·mo·lu·mi·nes·cent (thûr′mō lo͞o′mə nes′ənt), *adj.* pertaining to or characterized by thermoluminescence. [THERMO- + LUMINESCENT]

ther·mol·y·sis (thər mol′i sis), *n.* **1.** *Physiol.* the dispersion of heat from the body. **2.** *Chem.* dissociation by heat. [THERMO- + -LYSIS] —**ther·mo·lyt·ic** (thûr′mə lit′ik), *adj.*

ther·mo·mag·net·ic (thûr′mō mag net′ik), *adj.* **1.** *Physics.* of or pertaining to the effect of heat on the magnetic properties of a substance. **2.** of or pertaining to the effect of a magnetic field on a conductor of heat. [THERMO- + MAGNETIC]

ther·mom·e·ter (thər mom′i tər), *n.* an instrument for measuring temperature, often consisting of a sealed glass tube that contains a column of liquid, as mercury, which expands and contracts, or rises and falls, with temperature changes, the temperature being read where the top of the column coincides with a calibrated scale marked on the tube or its frame. [THERMO- + -METER] —**ther·mo·met·ric** (thûr′mə me′trik), **ther′mo·met′ri·cal,** *adj.* —**ther′mo·met′ri·cal·ly,** *adv.*

F C R

Thermometers
F, Fahrenheit
C, Centigrade (Celsius)
R, Réaumur

thermomet′ric titra′tion, *Chem.* titration in which the end point is determined by measuring the temperature of a solution.

ther·mom·e·try (thər mom′i trē), *n.* **1.** the branch of physics dealing with the measurement of temperature. **2.** the science of the construction and use of thermometers. [THERMO- + -METRY]

ther·mo·mo·tive (thûr′mə mō′tiv), *adj.* **1.** pertaining to motion produced by heat. **2.** pertaining to a thermomotor. [THERMO- + MOTIVE]

ther·mo·mo·tor (thûr′mə mō′tər), *n.* an engine operated by heat, esp. one driven by the expansive force of heated air. [THERMO- + MOTOR]

ther·mo·nu·cle·ar (thûr′mō no͞o′klē ər, -nyo͞o′-), *adj.* of, pertaining to, or involving a thermonuclear reaction: *thermonuclear power.* [THERMO- + NUCLEAR]

ther′monu′clear bomb′. See **hydrogen bomb.**

ther′monu′clear reac′tion, *Chem., Physics.* a nuclear-fusion reaction that takes place between the nuclei of a gas, esp. hydrogen, heated to a temperature of several million degrees.

Ther·mo·pane (thûr′mə pān′), *n. Trademark.* a hermetically sealed double glazing.

ther·mo·phile (thûr′mə fīl′, -fil), *n.* a thermophilic bacterium. [THERMO- + -PHILE]

ther·mo·phil·ic (thûr′mə fil′ik), *adj.* (of bacteria) growing best at temperatures between 50° and 60°C, and capable of growth between temperatures of 45° to 75°C. [THERMO- + -PHILE + -IC]

ther·mo·phone (thûr′mə fōn′), *n.* an electroacoustic transducer that forms sound waves by the expansion and contraction of the air adjacent to a conductor that varies in temperature according to the magnitude of the current passing through it. [THERMO- + (TELE)PHONE]

ther·mo·phos·pho·res·cence (thûr′mō fos′fə res′əns), *n. Physics.* thermoluminescence. [THERMO- + PHOSPHORESCENCE] —**ther′mo·phos′pho·res′cent,** *adj.*

ther·mo·pile (thûr′mə pīl′), *n. Physics.* a device consisting of a number of thermocouples joined in series, used for generating thermoelectric current or for detecting and measuring radiant energy, as from a star. [THERMO- + PILE[1]]

ther·mo·plas·tic (thûr′mə plas′tik), *adj.* **1.** soft and pliable whenever heated, as some plastics, without any change of the inherent properties. —*n.* **2.** a plastic of this type. [THERMO- + PLASTIC] —**ther·mo·plas·tic·i·ty** (thûr′mō pla stis′i tē), *n.*

Ther·mop·o·lis (thər mop′ə lis), *n.* a town in central Wyoming. 3955 (1960).

Ther·mop·y·lae (thər mop′ə lē′), *n.* a pass in E Greece, between the cliffs of Mt. Oeta and the Gulf of Lamia: Persian defeat of the Spartans 480 B.C.

ther·mo·re·cep·tor (thûr′mō ri sep′tər), *n. Physiol., Biol.* a receptor stimulated by changes in temperature. [THERMO- + RECEPTOR]

Ther·mos (thûr′məs), *n. Trademark.* See **vacuum bottle.**

ther·mo·scope (thûr′mə skōp′), *n.* a device for giving an approximation of the temperature change of a substance by noting the corresponding change in its volume. [THERMO- + -SCOPE] —**ther·mo·scop·ic** (thûr′mə skop′ik), **ther′mo·scop′i·cal,** *adj.* —**ther′mo·scop′i·cal·ly,** *adv.*

ther·mo·sen·si·tive (thûr′mō sen′si tiv), *adj. Chem.* readily affected by heat or a change in temperature. [THERMO- + SENSITIVE]

ther·mo·set·ting (thûr′mō set′ing), *adj.* pertaining to a type of plastic, as the urea resins, which sets when heated and cannot be remolded. [THERMO- + SETTING]

ther·mo·si·phon (thûr′mō sī′fən, -fon), *n.* an arrangement of siphon tubes which induce the circulation of water in a heating apparatus. [THERMO- + SIPHON]

ther·mo·sphere (thûr′mə sfēr′), *n.* the region of the upper atmosphere in which temperature increases continuously with altitude, encompassing essentially all of the atmosphere above the mesosphere. [THERMO- + SPHERE]

ther·mo·sta·ble (thûr′mə stā′bəl), *adj. Biochem.* capable of being subjected to a moderate degree of heat without loss of characteristic properties, as certain toxins and ferments (opposed to *thermolabile*). [THERMO- + STABLE[2]] —**ther′mo·sta·bil′i·ty,** *n.*

ther·mo·stat (thûr′mə stat′), *n.* a device, including a relay actuated by thermal conduction or convection, that functions to establish and maintain a desired temperature automatically or signals a change in temperature for manual adjustment. [THERMO- + -STAT] —**ther′mo·stat′ic,** *adj.* —**ther′mo·stat′i·cal·ly,** *adv.*

ther·mo·stat·ics (thûr′mə stat′iks), *n.* (*construed as sing.*) *Rare.* the branch of physics dealing with thermal equilibrium. [THERMO- + STATICS]

ther·mo·tank (thûr′mə tangk′), *n.* a tank containing a number of heated or chilled tubes for heating or cooling air passing through it. [THERMO- + TANK]

ther·mo·tax·is (thûr′mə tak′sis), *n.* **1.** *Biol.* movement of an organism toward or away from a source of heat. **2.** *Physiol.* the regulation of the bodily temperature. [THERMO- + TAXIS] —**ther·mo·tac·tic** (thûr′mə tak′tik), **ther′mo·tax′ic,** *adj.*

ther·mo·ten·sile (thûr′mə ten′səl, -sil *or, esp. Brit.,* -sīl), *adj. Rare.* pertaining to tensile strength as affected by changes of temperature. [THERMO- + TENSILE]

ther·mo·ther·a·py (thûr′mō ther′ə pē), *n.* treatment of disease by means of heat, either moist or dry. [THERMO- + THERAPY]

ther·mot·ro·pism (thər mo′trə piz′əm), *n. Biol.* oriented growth of an organism in response to heat. [THERMO- + -TROPISM] —**ther·mo·trop·ic** (thûr′mə trop′ik), *adj.*

-thermy, a combining form referring to heat, used in the formation of nouns: *diathermy.* [< NL *-thermia;* see -THERM, -Y[3]]

The·ro (thēr′ō), *n. Class. Myth.* a nurse of Ares. Cf. **Theritas.**

the·roid (thēr′oid), *adj.* having animal propensities or characteristics; brutish. [< Gk *thēroeid(ēs)* < *thēr* wild beast + *-oeidēs* -OID]

the·ro·phyte (thēr′ə fīt′), *n. Bot.* a plant living only one year or one growing season. [< Gk *théro(s)* summer + -PHYTE]

Ther·san·der (thər san′dər), *n. Class. Myth.* one of the Epigoni who later fought as a Greek ally in the Trojan War.

Ther·sil·o·chus (thər sil′ə kəs), *n.* (in the *Iliad*) a Trojan ally killed by Achilles.

Ther·si·tes (thər sī′tēz), *n.* (in the *Iliad*) a Greek known for his ugliness, deformity, and foul-mouthed, quarrelsome nature: he accused Agamemnon of greed and Achilles of cowardice during the Trojan War. [< L < Gk < *thérs(os)* (dial. var. of *thársos* audacity) + *-ītēs* -ITE[1]]

ther·sit·i·cal (thər sit′i kəl), *adj.* scurrilous; foul-mouthed; grossly abusive. [THERSIT(ES) + -ICAL]

Thes., Thessalonians.

the·sau·ro·sis (thē′sô rō′sis), *n. Pathol.* a metabolic disorder characterized by an excessive storage of normal or foreign substances in certain cells, as phosphatides, fats, iron, carbohydrates, protein, and other material. Also, **the·sau·ris·mo·sis** (thi sôr′iz mō′sis, -is-). Also called **storage disease.** [< NL < Gk *thēsaur(ós)* storeroom, receptacle for storage (see THESAURUS) + *-ōsis* -OSIS]

the·sau·rus (thi sôr′əs), *n., pl.* **-sau·ri** (-sôr′ī). **1.** a dictionary, encyclopedia, or other comprehensive reference book, esp. a dictionary of synonyms and antonyms. **2.** a storehouse, repository, or treasury. **3.** *Computer Technol.* an index to information stored in a computer, consisting of a comprehensive list of subjects concerning which information may be retrieved by using the proper key terms. [< L < Gk *thēsaurós* treasure, treasury]

these (thēz), *pron., adj.* pl. of **this.**

The·seus (thē′sē əs, -so͞os), *n. Class. Myth.* an Attic hero, the son of Aegeus, the husband of Phaedra, and the father of Hippolytus. His adventures included the killing of the robbers Procrustes, Sciron, and Sinis, the slaying of the Minotaur, battles against the Amazons and the Centaurs, and the attempt to abduct Persephone. —**The·se·an** (thi sē′ən), *adj.*

the·sis (thē′sis), *n., pl.* **-ses** (-sēz). **1.** a proposition stated or put forward for consideration, esp. one to be discussed and proved or to be maintained against objections: *He vigorously defended his thesis concerning the causes of war.* **2.** a subject for a composition or essay. **3.** a dissertation on a particular subject in which one has done original research, as one presented by a candidate for a diploma or degree, esp. a master's degree. **4.** *Music.* the downward stroke in conducting; downbeat. Cf. **arsis** (def. 1). **5.** *Pros.* **a.** a part of a metrical foot that does not bear the ictus or stress. **b.** (less commonly) the part of a metrical foot that bears the ictus. Cf. **arsis** (def. 2). **6.** *Philos.* See under **Hegelian dialectic.** [ME < L < Gk: a setting down, something set down < *the-* (s. of *tithénai* to put, set down) + *-sis* -SIS]

the′sis play′, a play that develops or defends a particular thesis.

Thes·mi·a (thes′mē ə), *n. Class. Myth.* an epithet of Demeter, meaning "goddess of law."

Thes·mo·pho·ri·a (thes′mə fôr′ē ə, -fōr′-), *n.* (*sometimes construed as pl.*) an annual ancient Greek festival celebrated by women in honor of Demeter, a goddess of agriculture and the family. —**Thes′mo·pho′ri·an, Thes·mo·phor·ic** (thes′mə fôr′ik, -for′-), *adj.*

Thes·moph·o·rus (thes mof′ər əs), *n. Class. Myth.* an epithet of Demeter, meaning "lawgiver."

Thes·pi·ae (thes′pē ē′), *n. Class. Myth.* a city at the foot of Mount Helicon where the Muses performed their games.

Thes·pi·an (thes′pē ən), *adj.* **1.** of or characteristic of Thespis. **2.** (*often l.c.*) pertaining to tragedy or to the dramatic art in general. **3.** of or pertaining to Thespiae. —*n.* **4.** (*sometimes l.c.*) a tragedian; an actor or actress. [THESPI(S) + -AN]

Thes′pian Li′on, *Class. Myth.* a lion that attacked the flocks of Amphitryon and was killed by Hercules.

Thes′pian Maids′, *Class. Myth.* the Muses. Cf. **Thespiae.**

Thes·pis (thes′pis), *n.* fl. 6th century B.C., Greek poet.

Thes·pi·us (thes′pē əs), *n. Class. Myth.* the founder of the city of Thespiae and the father, by Megamede, of 50 daughters.

Thes·pro·ti (thes prō′tī), *n. pl.* the first inhabitants of ancient Epirus. Also, **Thes·pro·tians** (thes prō′shənz).

Thes·pro·tia (thes prō′shə), *n.* (in ancient geography) a coastal district in SW Epirus. Also, **Thes·pro·tis** (thes prō′tis).

Thess., Thessalonians.

Thes·sa·lo·ni·an (thes′ə lō′nē ən), *adj.* **1.** of or pertaining to Thessalonike or its inhabitants. —*n.* **2.** a native or inhabitant of Thessalonike. [THESSALONI(KE) + -AN]

Thes·sa·lo·ni·ans (thes′ə lō′nē ənz), *n.* (*construed as sing.*) either of two books of the New Testament, I Thessalonians and II Thessalonians, written by Paul. *Abbr.:* Thes., Thess.

Thes·sa·lo·ni·ke (thes′ä lô nē′ke), *n.* official name of **Salonika.** Ancient, **Thes·sa·lon·i·ca** (thes′ə lon′ə kə, -ə lō nī′kə).

Thes·sa·lus (thes′ə ləs), *n. Class. Myth.* **1.** a son of Hercules and Chalciope who became king of Thessaly. **2.** a son of Jason and Medea.

Thes·sa·ly (thes′ə lē), *n.* a region in E Greece: a former division of ancient Greece. 695,385 (1961); 5208 sq. mi. —**Thes·sa·li·an** (the sā′lē ən), *adj., n.*

Thes·ti·us (thes′tē əs), *n. Class. Myth.* an Aetolian king fathered by Ares.

Thes·tor (thes′tər), *n. Class. Myth.* the father of Calchas, Leucippe, and Theonoë.

the·ta (thā′tə, thē′-), *n.* **1.** the eighth letter of the Greek alphabet (Θ, θ). **2.** the consonant sound represented by this letter. [< Gk < Sem. See TETH]

thet·ic (thet′ik), *adj.* positive; dogmatic. Also, **thet′i·cal.** [< Gk *thetikós*, equiv. to *thet(ós)* placed, set (verbid of *tithénai* to lay down) + *-ikos* -IC] —**thet′i·cal·ly,** *adv.*

The·tis (thē′tis), *n. Class. Myth.* a Nereid, the wife of Peleus and the mother of Achilles.

the·ur·gy (thē′ûr jē), *n., pl.* **-gies. 1.** a system of magic practiced by the Egyptian Platonists and others professing to have communication with and aid from beneficent deities. **2.** the working of a divine or supernatural agency in human affairs or the effects brought about among men by such agency. [< L *theūrgia* < Gk *theourgeía* magic. See THE-, -URGY] —**the·ur′gic, the·ur′gi·cal,** *adj.* —**the·ur′gi·cal·ly,** *adv.* —**the′ur·gist,** *n.*

thew (thyōō), *n.* **1.** Usually, **thews.** muscle or sinew. **2. thews,** physical strength. [ME; OE *thēaw* custom, usage; c. OHG *thau* (later *dau*) discipline; akin to L *tuērī* to watch] —**thew′y,** *adj.*

thew·less (thyōō′lis), *adj.* **1.** cowardly; timid. **2.** *Scot.* thowless. [ME *theweles.* See THEW, -LESS]

they (thā), *pron. pl., poss.* **their** or **theirs,** *obj.* **them. 1.** nominative plural of **he, she,** and **it. 2.** people in general: *They say he's rich.* **3.** *Nonstandard.* (used with an indefinite singular antecedent in place of the definite masculine "he" or the definite feminine "she"): *Whoever is of voting age, whether they are interested in politics or not, should vote.* [ME < Scand; cf. Icel *their* those, c. OE *thā*, pl. of *thæt* THAT]

they'd (thād), **1.** contraction of *they had.* **2.** contraction of *they would.*

they'll (thāl), **1.** contraction of *they will.* **2.** contraction of *they shall.*

they're (thâr), contraction of *they are.*

they've (thāv), contraction of *they have.*

thi-, var. of **thio-** (*thiazine*), properly occurring before a vowel but not systematically employed (cf. *thioaldehyde*).

T.H.I., Temperature-Humidity Index.

Thi·a (thī′ə), *n.* Theia.

thi′a·ce′tic ac′id (thī′ə sē′tik, -ə set′ik, thī′-), *Chem.* See **thioacetic acid.**

Thial·fi (thyäl′vē), *n. Scand. Myth.* the fastest of men and the servant of Thor.

thi·a·mine (thī′ə mēn′, -min), *n. Biochem.* a white, crystalline, water-soluble compound of the vitamin-B complex, containing a thiazole and a pyrimidine group, $C_{12}H_{17}ClN_4OS$, essential for normal functioning of the nervous system, a deficiency of which results chiefly in beriberi and other nerve disorders: occurring in many natural sources, as green peas, liver, and esp. the seed coats of cereal grains, the commercial product of which is chiefly synthesized in the form of its chloride (**thi′amine chlo′ride** or **thi′amine hydrochlo′ride**) for therapeutic administration. Also, **thi·a·min** (thī′ə min). Also called **vitamin B_1, aneurin, aneurine.** [THI- + AMINE]

thi·a·sos (thī′ə sos′), *n., pl.* **-soi** (-soi′). thiasus.

thi·a·sus (thī′ə səs), *n., pl.* **-si** (-sī′). **1.** (in ancient Greece) a group or society worshiping and holding ceremonies in honor of a particular patron deity, usually Dionysus. **2.** *Class. Myth.* the group of maenads, satyrs, etc., following Dionysus. [< Gk *thíasos* Dionysiac revel]

Thia·zi (thyät′sē), *n. Scand. Myth.* a giant who carried away Idun and the apples of youth from Asgard. Also, **Thiat′si, Thjazi, Thjatsi.**

thi·a·zine (thī′ə zēn′, -zin), *n. Chem.* any of a class of compounds containing a ring composed of one atom each of sulfur and nitrogen and four atoms of carbon. [THI- + AZINE]

thi·a·zole (thī′ə zōl′), *n. Chem.* **1.** a colorless, slightly water-miscible liquid, C_3H_3NS, having a disagreeable odor. **2.** any of various derivatives of this substance, used as dyes or reagents. [THI- + AZOLE]

Thi·bet (ti bet′), *n.* Tibet. —**Thi·bet′an,** *adj., n.*

thick (thik), *adj.* **1.** having relatively great extent from one surface or side to the opposite; not thin: *a thick slice.* **2.** measured, as specified, between opposite surfaces, from top to bottom, or in a direction perpendicular to that of the length and breadth; (of a solid having three general dimensions) measured across its smallest dimension: *a board one inch thick.* **3.** close-packed; compact; dense: *a thick forest.* **4.** numerous, abundant, or plentiful. **5.** filled, covered, or abounding (usually fol. by *with*): *tables thick with dust.* **6.** profound, mysterious, or deep, as darkness. **7.** husky, hoarse, muffled, or not clear in sound: *a thick voice.* **8.** markedly so (as specified): *He has a thick German accent.* **9.** not distinctly articulated: *The patient's speech is still quite thick.* **10.** having relatively great consistency; viscous: *a thick syrup.* **11.** containing much solid matter in suspension or solution: *thick, muddy water.* **12.** (of mist, smoke, etc.) having the component particles densely aggregated. **13.** (of the weather, air, etc.) dense or close, as with fog, mist, haze, or smoke: *The air was so thick we could scarcely breathe.* **14.** *Informal.* close in friendship; intimate. **15.** mentally slow; stupid; dull: *He can handle routine tasks, but he's rather thick.* **16.** disagreeably excessive or exaggerated: *They thought it a bit thick when he called himself a genius.* **17.** *Archaic.* dull of sense perception. —*adv.* **18.** in a thick manner. **19.** close together; closely packed: *The roses grew thick along the path.* **20.** in a manner to produce something thick: *Slice the cheese thick.* **21. lay it on thick,** *Informal.* to praise excessively; flatter: *He's laying it on thick because he wants you to do him a favor.* —*n.* **22.** that which is thick. **23.** the thickest, densest, or most crowded part; the place, time, stage, etc., of greatest activity or intensity: *in the thick of the fight.* **24. through thick and thin,** under favorable and unfavorable conditions; steadfastly: *We have been friends for 20 years, through thick and thin.* [ME *thikke,* OE *thicce;* c. D *dik,* G *dick;* akin to Icel *thykkr,* Ir *tiugh*] —**thick′ly,** *adv.*

thick·en (thik′ən), *v.t., v.i.* **1.** to make or become thick or thicker. **2.** to make or grow more intense, profound, intricate, or complex: *The plot thickens.* [late ME *thikne* < Scand; cf. Icel *thykkna.* See THICK, -EN[1]]

thick·en·er (thik′ə nər), *n.* **1.** that which thickens. **2.** an apparatus for the sedimentation and removal of solids suspended in various liquids. [THICKEN + -ER[1]]

thick·en·ing (thik′ə ning), *n.* **1.** a making or becoming thick. **2.** a thickened part or area; swelling. **3.** something used to thicken; thickener. [THICKEN + -ING[1]]

thick·et (thik′it), *n.* a thick or dense growth of shrubs, bushes, or small trees; a thick coppice. [OE *thiccet,* equiv. to *thicce* THICK + *-et* n. suffix] —**thick′et·ed, thick′et·y,** *adj.*

thick·head (thik′hed′), *n.* **1.** a stupid person; blockhead. **2.** Also called **whistler.** any of several Old World, oscine birds of the genus *Pachycephala,* found chiefly on various islands in the Pacific Ocean, related to the flycatchers, and having a melodious whistling call. [THICK + HEAD]

thick·head·ed (thik′hed′id), *adj.* **1.** (of animals) having a thick head. **2.** (of persons) dull-witted; stupid. [THICK + -HEADED] —**thick′head′ed·ly,** *adv.* —**thick′-head′ed·ness,** *n.*

thick·ish (thik′ish), *adj.* rather thick. [THICK + -ISH[1]]

thick-knee (thik′nē′), *n.* any of several crepuscular or nocturnal birds of the family *Burhinidae,* of the Old World and tropical America, having a thickened joint between the femoral and tibiotarsal bones. Also called **stone curlew.**

thick·leaf (thik′lēf′), *n., pl.* **-leaves** (-lēvz′). any succulent herb or shrub of the genus *Crassula.* [THICK + LEAF]

thick·ness (thik′nis), *n.* **1.** state or quality of being thick. **2.** the measure of the smallest dimension of a solid figure: *a board of two-inch thickness.* **3.** the thick part or body of something: *the thickness of the leg.* **4.** a layer, stratum, or ply: *three thicknesses of cloth.* —*v.t.* **5.** to bring (a piece, as a board) to a uniform thickness. [ME *thiknesse,* OE *thicnes.* See THICK, -NESS]

thick′ness piece′, *Theat.* a narrow flat or board used in scenic construction to give the illusion of depth or solidity to a door, wall, window, or the like.

thick′ reg′ister, *Music.* See **chest register.**

thick·set (*adj.* thik′set′; *n.* thik′set′), *adj.* **1.** set thickly or in close arrangement; dense: *a thickset hedge.* **2.** studded, or furnished thickly; closely packed: *a sky thickset with stars.* **3.** heavily or solidly built; stocky: *a thickset young man.* —*n.* **4.** a thicket. [ME *thikke sette* thickly set. See THICK (adv.), SET]

thick-skinned (thik′skind′), *adj.* **1.** having a thick skin. **2.** insensitive or hardened to criticism, reproach, rebuff, etc. [THICK + SKINNED]
—**Syn. 1.** pachydermatous. **2.** insensitive, obtuse, callous.

thick-skulled (thik′skuld′), *adj.* stupid; dull.

thick′-tailed ray′ (thik′tāld′), *Ichthyol.* any ray of the suborder *Sarcura,* having a relatively thick, fleshy tail, including the guitarfishes and the skates.

thick-witted (thik′wit′id), *adj.* lacking intelligence; thickheaded; dull; stupid. —**thick′-wit′ted·ly,** *adv.* —**thick′-wit′ted·ness,** *n.*

thief (thēf), *n., pl.* **thieves.** a person who steals, esp. secretly or without open force; one guilty of theft or larceny. [ME; OE *thēof;* c. D *dief,* G *Dieb,* Icel *thjōfr,* Goth *thiufs*]
—**Syn.** burglar, pickpocket, highwayman. THIEF, ROBBER refer to one who steals. A THIEF takes the goods or property of another by stealth without the latter's knowledge: *a horse thief; like a thief in the night.* A ROBBER trespasses upon the house, property, or person of another, and makes away with things of value, even at the cost of violence: *A robber held up two women on the street.*

thief′ ant′, a small red ant, *Solenopsis molesta,* that nests in the walls of the nest of a larger species from which it steals eggs and young larvae.

Thief′ Riv′er Falls′, a town in NW Minnesota. 7151 (1960).

Thiens·ville (thēnz′vil), *n.* a town in E Wisconsin. 2507 (1960).

Thiers (tyer′), *n.* **Louis A·dolphe** (lwē A dôlf′), 1797–1877, French statesman: president 1871–73.

thieve (thēv), *v.,* **thieved, thiev·ing.** —*v.t.* **1.** to take by theft; steal. —*v.i.* **2.** to act as a thief; commit theft; steal. [OE *thēofian,* deriv. of *thēof* THIEF] —**thiev′ing·ly,** *adv.*

thieve·less (thēv′lis), *adj. Scot.* **1.** not cordial, affectionate, or emotional; cold. **2.** thowless. [? misreading of *theueless,* sp. var. of THEWLESS]

thiev·er·y (thē′və rē), *n., pl.* **-er·ies. 1.** the act or practice of thieving; theft. **2.** something taken by theft. [THIEVE + -ERY]

Thieves' Car′nival, a comedy (1937) by Jean Anouilh. French, **Le Bal des Voleurs.**

thiev·ish (thē′vish), *adj.* **1.** given to thieving. **2.** of, pertaining to, or characteristic of a thief; stealthy: *a furtive, thievish look.* [late ME *thevisch, thefyische.* See THIEF, -ISH[1]] —**thiev′ish·ly,** *adv.* —**thiev′ish·ness,** *n.*

thig (thig), *v.t., v.i.,* **thigged, thig·ging.** *Scot.* to beg (alms, food, etc.); solicit (gifts). [ME *thigge* < Scand; cf. OSw *thiggja* to beg, c. OE *thicgan* to accept, receive] —**thig′ger,** *n.*

thigh (thī), *n.* **1.** the part of the lower limb in man between the hip and the knee. **2.** the corresponding part of the hind limb of other animals; the femoral region. **3.** (in birds) **a.** the true femoral region which is hidden by the skin or feathers of the body. **b.** the segment below, containing the fibula and tibia. **4.** *Entomol.* the femur. [ME; OE *thēoh;* c. D *dij,* OHG *dioh,* Icel *thjō*]

thigh·bone (thī′bōn′), *n.* femur (def. 1). [late ME *the bane.* See THIGH, BONE[1]]

thig·mo·tax·is (thig′mə tak′sis), *n. Biol.* movement of an organism toward or away from any object that provides a mechanical stimulus; stereotaxis. [< Gk *thigm(a)* touch + -O- + -TAXIS] —**thig·mo·tac·tic** (thig′mə tak′tik), *adj.*

thig·mo·tro·pism (thig mo′trə piz′əm), *n. Biol.* oriented growth of an organism in response to mechanical contact. [< Gk *thigm(a)* touch + -O- + -TROPISM] —**thig·mo·trop·ic** (thig′mə trop′ik), *adj.*

thill (thil), *n.* either of the pair of shafts of a vehicle between which a single animal is harnessed to pull it. [ME *thille* shaft, OE: plank. See DEAL[2]]

thim·ble (thim′bəl), *n.* **1.** a small cap, usually of metal or plastic, worn over the finger to protect it when pushing a needle through cloth in sewing. **2.** *Mech.* any of various devices or attachments likened to this. **3.** *Naut.* a metal ring with a concave groove on the outside, used to line the outside of a ring of rope forming an eye. **4.** a sleeve of sheet metal passing through the wall of a chimney, for holding the end of a stovepipe or the like. [ME *thym(b)yl,* OE *thȳmel;* akin to Icel *thumall* thumb of a glove. See THUMB] —**thim′ble·like′,** *adj.*

thim·ble·ber·ry (thim′bəl ber′ē), *n., pl.* **-ries.** any of several American raspberries bearing a thimble-shaped fruit, esp. the black raspberry, *Rubus occidentalis.* [THIMBLE + BERRY]

thim·ble·flow·er (thim′bəl flou′ər), *n.* an annual herb, *Rudbeckia bicolor,* found in the pine woods of the southern U.S., having yellow flowers with black disks. [THIMBLE + FLOWER]

thim·ble·ful (thim′bəl fŏŏl′), *n., pl.* **-fuls.** as much as a thimble will hold; a small quantity, esp. of liquid. [THIMBLE + -FUL]

thim·ble·rig (thim′bəl rig′), *n., v.,* **-rigged, -rig·ging.** —*n.* **1.** a sleight-of-hand swindling game in which the operator palms a pellet or pea while appearing to cover it with one of three thimblelike cups, and then, moving the cups about, offers to bet that no one can tell under which cup the pellet or pea lies. —*v.t.* **2.** to cheat by or as by the thimblerig. [THIMBLE + RIG] —**thim′ble·rig′ger,** *n.*

thim·ble·weed (thim′bəl wēd′), *n.* any of various plants having a thimble-shaped fruiting head, as the anemone, *Anemone virginiana,* and the rudbeckia, *Rudbeckia laciniata.* [THIMBLE + WEED[1]]

Thim·bu (tim′bōō), *n.* a city in and the capital of Bhutan, in the W part.

thi·mer·o·sal (thī mûr′ə sal′, -mer′-), *n. Pharm.* a cream-colored, crystalline, water-soluble powder, $C_9H_9HgNaO_2S$, used chiefly as an antiseptic; sodium ethylmercurithiosalicylate. [? THI- + MER(CURY) + -O- + SAL(ICYLATE)]

thin (thin), *adj.,* **thin·ner, thin·nest,** *adv., v.,* **thinned, thin·ning.** —*adj.* **1.** having relatively little extent from one surface or side to the opposite; not thick: *thin ice.* **2.** of small cross section in comparison with the length; slender: *a thin wire.* **3.** having little flesh; spare; lean: *a thin man.* **4.** having the constituent or individual parts relatively few and not close together; not dense; sparse: *thin vegetation.* **5.** scant; not abundant or plentiful. **6.** having relatively slight consistency, as a liquid; fluid; rare or rarefied, as air. **7.** without solidity or substance; unsubstantial; slight; flimsy: *a very thin plot for such a long book; a thin excuse.* **8.** lacking fullness or volume; weak and shrill: *a thin voice; The sound was too thin.* **9.** faint or feeble; without force or a sincere effort: *a thin smile.* **10.** lacking body, richness, or strength: *a thin wine.* **11.** lacking in chroma; of light tint. **12.** *Photog.* (of a developed negative) lacking in density or contrast through underdevelopment or underexposure. —*adv.* **13.** in a thin manner. **14.** sparsely; not densely. **15.** in a manner to produce something thin: *Slice the ham thin.* —*v.t.* **16.** to make thin or thinner (often fol. by *down, out,* etc.). —*v.i.* **17.** to become thin or thinner; become reduced or diminished (often fol. by *down, out, off,* etc.): *The crowd is thinning out.* [ME, OE *thynne;* c. D *dun,* G *dünn,* Icel *thunnr;* akin to OIr *tana,* L *tenuis* thin, Gk *tany-* long] —**thin′ly,** *adv.* —**thin′ness,** *n.*
—**Syn. 3.** slim, slender, skinny, lank, scrawny. THIN, GAUNT, LEAN, SPARE agree in referring to one having little flesh. THIN applies often to one in an unnaturally reduced state, as from sickness, overwork, lack of food, or the like: *a thin, dirty little waif.* GAUNT suggests the angularity of bones prominently displayed in a thin face and body: *to look ill and gaunt.* LEAN usually applies to a person or animal that is naturally thin: *looking lean but healthy after an outdoor vacation.* SPARE implies a muscular leanness with no diminution of vitality: *Lincoln was spare in body.* **5.** meager. **7.** weak. **16.** dilute. —**Ant. 1.** thick. **3.** fat. **5.** abundant.

thine (thīn), *pron.* **1.** the possessive case of **thou** used as a predicate adjective, after a noun or without a noun. **2.** the possessive case of **thou** used as an attributive adjective before a noun beginning with a vowel or vowel sound: *thine eyes; thine honor.* Cf. **thy. 3.** that which belongs to thee: *Thine is the power and the glory.* [ME, OE *thīn;* c. Icel *thinn,* Goth *theins,* G *dein.* See THOU]

thing[1] (thing), *n.* **1.** a material object without life or consciousness; an inanimate object. **2.** some entity, object, or creature which is not or cannot be specifically designated or precisely described: *The stick had a brass thing on it.* **3.** an abstract quality or entity; that which is or may become an object of thought, whether material or ideal, animate or inanimate, actual, possible, or imaginary: *things of the spirit.* **4.** Often, **things.** matters; affairs: *Things are going well now.* **5.** a fact, circumstance, situation, or state of affairs: *It is a curious thing. We've got to end this thing before it gets out of hand.* **6.** an action, deed, event, or performance: *to do great things; His death was a horrible thing.* **7.** a particular, respect, or detail: *perfect in all things; to see each thing in its proper proportion.* **8.** aim; objective: *The thing is to reach this line with the ball.* **9.** an article of clothing or apparel, esp. one suited for a particular occasion or worn over or with other clothing while outdoors: *She didn't have a thing to wear. Come on in and let me take your things.* **10. things, a.** implements, utensils, or other articles for service: *I'll wash the breakfast things.* **b.** personal possessions or belongings: *Pack your things and go!* **11.** a task; chore: *I've got a lot of things to do today.* **12.** a living being or creature: *His daughter's a pretty little thing. We have a parakeet, but the poor thing won't make a sound.* **13.** a thought, idea, word, statement, or thesis: *I have just one thing to say to you.* **14.** a particular kind or type of material or substance: *She loves chocolate things.* **15.** *Informal.* a peculiar attitude or feeling toward something; mental quirk; phobia: *She has a thing about cats.* **16.** *Slang.* something special or unique that one feels disposed to do: *to do her thing; to find your own thing.* **17.** that which is signified or represented, as distinguished from a word, symbol, or idea representing it. **18.** *Law.* anything that may be the subject of a property right. **19. make a good thing of,** *Informal.* to turn (a situation, experience, etc.) to one's own profit; benefit by: *She made a good thing of her spare-time hobbies.* **20. not to get a thing out of, a.** to be unable to obtain information or news from: *The police couldn't get a thing out of him. I don't get a thing out of his lectures.* **b.** to fail to appreciate, understand, or derive aesthetic pleasure from: *My wife likes opera, but I don't get a thing out of it.* **21. the thing, a.** that which is correct or fashionable: *That café is the thing now.* **b.**

that which is expedient or necessary: *The thing to do is to tell them the truth.* [ME, OE; c. D *ding*, G *Ding* thing; earlier, meeting. See THING[2]]

thing[2] (thing, ting), *n.* (in Scandinavian countries) a public meeting or assembly, esp. a legislative assembly or a court of law. Also, **ting.** Cf. **thingstead.** [< Icel: assembly; c. THING[1], D *ding*, G *Ding*; akin to Goth *theihs* time]

thing·a·ma·bob (thing′ə mə bob′), *n.* *Informal.* thingumbob.

T hinge, cross-garnet.

thing-in-it·self (thing′in it self′), *n., pl.* **things-in-them·selves** (thingz′in *th*em selvz′). *Kantianism.* reality as it is apart from experience; what remains to be postulated after space, time, and all the categories of the understanding are assigned to consciousness. Cf. **noumenon** (def. 3). [trans. of G *Ding an sich*]

thing·stead (thing′sted, ting′-), *n.* the meeting place of a Scandinavian assembly. Cf. **thing**[2]. [THING[2] + STEAD]

thing·u·ma·jig (thing′ə mə jig′), *n.* *Informal.* thingumbob; thingamabob.

thing·um·bob (thing′əm bob′), *n.* *Informal.* a gadget or other thing for which the speaker does not know or has forgotten the name. Also, **thingamabob, thing·a·ma·jig** (thing′ə mə jig′), **thing·u·ma·bob** (thing′ə mə-bob′), **thingumajig.** [*thingum* (facetious Latinized var. of THING[1]) + BOB[2]]

think[1] (thingk), *v.,* **thought, think·ing,** *adj.* —*v.t.* **1.** to form or conceive in the mind; have in the mind as an idea, image, conception, etc. **2.** to meditate; ponder; analyze or examine with the intellect, as to reach a decision or conclusion (sometimes fol. by *over*): *He was thinking what it could mean. Think it over.* **3.** to have the mind preoccupied with or full of (a particular subject or the like). **4.** to form or have an idea or conception of (a thing, fact, circumstance, etc.). **5.** to bear in mind, recollect, or remember. **6.** to have in mind as a plan, intent, or purpose; intend. **7.** to hold as an opinion; believe; suppose: *They thought that the earth was flat.* **8.** to consider or regard (something) to be as specified: *He thought the lecture very interesting.* **9.** to anticipate or expect: *I did not think to find you here.* —*v.i.* **10.** to use the mind, esp. the intellect, actively; cogitate, meditate, or reason. **11.** to reflect upon the matter in question: *Think carefully before you begin.* **12.** to remember (usually fol. by *of*): *I can't think of his name.* **13.** to consider or regard someone or something as suitable or possible (usually fol. by *of*): *He thought about taking her to dinner and then the theater. We're thinking of you as a replacement for the man who quit.* **14.** to conceive of or regard someone or something as a specific kind or type (usually fol. by *of*): *He thought of her as a friend. She thought of golf as a waste of time.* **15.** to have consideration or regard (usually fol. by *of*): *to think of others first.* **16.** to make a mental discovery; form or have a plan (usually fol. by *of*): *He thought of it first.* **17.** to have a belief or opinion as indicated. **18. think better of,** to pursue a wiser or more sensible course after further thought; change one's mind; reconsider: *She considered emigrating to Australia, but thought better of it.* **19. think fit,** to consider advisable or appropriate: *By all means, take a vacation if you think fit.* **20. think nothing of.** See **nothing** (def. 13). **21. think of, a.** to form or have an idea or mental image; conceive of; imagine. **b.** to have an opinion or judgment of. **c.** to consider; anticipate: *When one thinks of what the future may bring, one is both worried and hopeful.* **22. think out** or **through, a.** to think about until a conclusion is reached; understand or solve by thinking. **b.** to devise by thinking; contrive: *He thought out a plan for saving time.* **23. think twice,** to weigh carefully before acting; consider: *I would think twice before taking on such a responsibility.* **24. think up,** to devise or contrive by thinking: *Can you think up an arrangement of furniture for this room?* —*adj.* **25.** of or pertaining to thinking or thought. **26.** *Informal.* stimulating or challenging to the intellect or mind: *the think book of the year.* Cf. **think piece.** [ME *thinke*, var. of *thenke(n)*, OE *thencan*; c. D, G *denken*, Icel *thekkja*, Goth *thagkjan*. See THANK]
—**Syn. 1.** imagine, picture. **2.** reflect, muse. **5.** recall.

think[2] (thingk), *v.i.,* **thought, think·ing.** *Obs.* to seem or appear (usually used impersonally with a dative as the subject). Cf. **methinks.** [ME *thinke*, OE *thyncan*; c. D *dunken*, G *dünken*, Icel *thykkja*, Goth *thugkjan*]

think·a·ble (thing′kə bəl), *adj.* **1.** capable of being thought; conceivable. **2.** that may be considered as possible or likely. [THINK[1] + -ABLE] —**think′a·ble·ness,** *n.* —**think′a·bly,** *adv.*

think·er (thing′kər), *n.* **1.** a person who thinks, as in a specified way or manner: *Your child is a slow thinker.* **2.** a person who has cultivated or exercised to an unusually great extent the capacity or faculty of thinking, as a philosopher, theorist, or scholar: *the great thinkers.* [ME *thenkare*. See THINK[1], -ER[1]]

Thinker, The, a bronze statue (1879–89) by Rodin.

think·ing (thing′king), *adj.* **1.** rational; reasoning: *Man is a thinking animal.* **2.** thoughtful; reflective; studious: *Her statements made thinking men blanch.* —*n.* **3.** thought; judgment, reflection: *clear thinking; There is nothing either good or bad but thinking makes it so.* [ME *thenking* (n.). See THINK[1], -ING[2], -ING[1]] —**think′ing·ly,** *adv.*

think′ing cap′, a state of mind marked by reflection or concentration: *If we put on our thinking caps, we may come up with the answer.*

think′ piece′, *Journalism.* an article analyzing and giving the background of a news event, often with the author's opinions and forecast for the future. Also called **dope story.** Cf. **editorial, news story.**

think′ tank′, *Informal.* a research institute or other organization of scholars, social or physical scientists, etc., esp. one employed by government to solve complex problems or predict future developments in military and social areas. Also called **think′ fac′tory.**

thin·ner[1] (thin′ər), *n.* **1.** one who or that which thins. **2.** a volatile liquid, as turpentine, used to dilute paint, varnish, rubber cement, etc., to the desired or proper consistency. **3.** a person who adds thinners to paints, varnishes, etc. **4.** one specialized in weeding plants, pruning shrubbery, thinning fruit, etc. [THIN + -ER[1]]

thin·ner[2] (thin′ər), *adj.* comparative of thin.

thin·nish (thin′ish), *adj.* somewhat thin. [THIN + -ISH[1]]

thin′ reg′ister, *Music.* See **head register.**

thin-skinned (thin′skind′), *adj.* **1.** having a thin skin. **2.** sensitive to criticism, reproach, rebuff, or the like; easily offended; touchy: *a thin-skinned prima donna.* —**thin′-skinned′ness,** *n.*

Thin′ Snow′, The, a novel (1944–47) by Tanizaki. Japanese, **Sasame-yuki.**

thi·o (thī′ō), *adj.* *Chem.* containing sulfur, esp. in place of oxygen. [< Gk *theion* sulfur]

thio-, a learned borrowing from Greek meaning "sulfur": used in chemical nomenclature to indicate the replacement of part or all of the oxygen atoms in a compound by sulfur; often used to designate sulfur analogues of oxygen compounds. Also, *esp. before a vowel,* **thi-.** [comb. form repr. Gk *theion*]

thi·o·ac·et·am·ide (thī′ō as′i tam′īd, -id, -ə set′ə-mīd′, -mid), *n.* *Chem.* a colorless, crystalline, water-soluble solid, CH_3CSNH_2, used chiefly in analytical chemistry as a source of hydrogen sulfide. [THIO- + ACETAMIDE]

thi·o·a·ce·tic (thī′ō ə sē′tik, -set′ik), *adj.* *Chem.* of or derived from thioacetic acid. Also, **thiolacetic.** [THIO- + ACETIC]

thi′oace′tic ac′id, *Chem.* a yellow, fuming, pungent liquid, CH_3COSH, used as a reagent and tear gas. Also, **thiacetic acid.**

thi′o ac′id, *Chem.* an acid in which part or all of the oxygen has been replaced by sulfur.

thi·o·al·de·hyde (thī′ō al′də hīd′), *n.* *Chem.* any of a class of compounds formed by the action of hydrogen sulfide on aldehydes, and regarded as aldehydes with the oxygen replaced by sulfur. [THIO- + ALDEHYDE]

thi′o·al′lyl e′ther (thī′ō al′il). See **allyl sulfide.**

thi·o·an·ti·mo·nate (thī′ō an′tə mə nāt′), *n.* *Chem.* a salt of thioantimonic acid. [THIO- + ANTIMONATE]

thi′o·an·ti·mo′nic ac′id (thī′ō an′tə mō′nik, -mon′-ik, thī′-), *Chem.* a hypothetical acid, H_3SbS_4, known only in the form of its salts. [THIO- + ANTIMONIC]

thi′o·an·ti·mo′ni·ous ac′id (thī′ō an′tə mō′nē əs, thī′-), *Chem.* any of four hypothetical acids, H_3SbS_3, $HSbS_2$, $H_4Sb_2S_5$, or $H_2Sb_4S_7$, known only in the form of their salts. [THIO- + ANTIMONIOUS]

thi·o·an·ti·mo·nite (thī′ō an′tə mə nīt′), *n.* *Chem.* a salt of a thioantimonious acid. [THIO- + ANTIMONITE]

thi·o·ar·se·nate (thī′ō är′sə nāt′), *n.* *Chem.* a salt of thioarsenic acid. [THIO- + ARSENATE]

thi′o·ar·sen′ic ac′id (thī′ō är sen′ik, thī′-), *Chem.* any of three hypothetical acids, H_3AsS_4, $HAsS_3$, or $H_4As_2S_7$, known only in the form of their salts. [THIO- + ARSENIC]

thi′o·ar·se′ni·ous ac′id (thī′ō är sē′nē əs, thī′-), *Chem.* any of four hypothetical acids, H_3AsS_3, $HAsS_2$, $H_4As_2S_5$, or $H_6As_4S_9$, known only in the form of their salts. [THIO- + ARSENIOUS]

thi·o·ar·se·nite (thī′ō är′sə nīt′), *n.* *Chem.* a salt of a thioarsenious acid. [THIO- + ARSENITE]

thi·o·ba·cil·lus (thī′ō bə sil′əs), *n., pl.* **-cil·li** (-sil′ī). *Bacteriol.* any of several rod-shaped bacteria of the genus *Thiobacillus,* found in soil, sewage, etc. [THIO- + BACILLUS]

thi·o·car·bam·ide (thī′ō kär bam′īd, -id), *n.* *Chem.* thiourea. [THIO- + CARBAMIDE]

thi·o·cy·a·nate (thī′ō sī′ə nāt′), *n.* *Chem.* a salt or ester of thiocyanic acid, as sodium thiocyanate, NaSCN. [THIO- + CYANATE]

thi·o·cy·an·ic (thī′ō sī an′ik), *adj.* *Chem.* of or derived from thiocyanic acid. [THIO- + CYANIC]

thi′ocyan′ic ac′id, *Chem.* an unstable acid, HSCN, known chiefly in the form of its salts.

thi·o·cy·a·no (thī′ō sī′ə nō′), *adj.* *Chem.* containing the thiocyano group. [back formation from *thiocyanogen.* See THIO-, CYANOGEN]

thi·o·cy·an·o·gen (thī′ō sī an′ə jən), *adj.* *Chem.* thiocyano. [THIO- + CYANOGEN]

thiocy′ano group′, *Chem.* the univalent group, -SCN, derived from thiocyanic acid; thiocyanogen. Also called **thiocy′ano rad′ical.**

Thi·od·a·mas (thī od′ə məs), *n.* *Class. Myth.* a Dryopian king slain by Hercules for refusing him one of his oxen.

thi·o·es·ter (thī′ō es′tər), *n.* *Chem.* an ester of a mercaptan. [THIO- + ESTER]

thi′o·eth·yl al′cohol (thī′ō eth′əl, thī′ō eth′əl), *Chem.* mercaptan (def. 2). [THIO- + ETHYL]

Thi·o·kol (thī′ō kōl′, -kôl′, -kol′), *n.* *Trademark.* any of a group of durable synthetic rubber products derived from an organic halide, as ethylene dichloride, $ClCH_2$-CH_2Cl, and an alkaline polysulfide, as sodium polysulfide: used chiefly in the manufacture of sealants, adhesives, and hoses for gasoline and oil.

thi·ol (thī′ōl, -ôl, -ol), *Chem.* —*n.* **1.** mercaptan. —*adj.* **2.** mercapto. [THI- + -OL[1]]

thi·ol·a·ce·tic (thī′ōl ə sē′tik, -set′ik, -ôl-, -ol-), *adj.* *Chem.* thioacetic.

thi·ol·ic (thī ol′ik), *adj.* *Chem.* of, pertaining to, or characteristic of the thiol, or mercapto, group. [THIOL + -IC]

thi·o·nate (thī′ə nāt′), *n.* *Chem.* a salt or ester of a thionic acid. [< Gk *theion* sulfur + -ATE[2]] —**thi′o·na′tion,** *n.*

thi·on·ic (thī on′ik), *adj.* *Chem.* of or pertaining to sulfur. [< Gk *theion* sulfur + -IC]

thion′ic ac′id, *Chem.* any of the five acids of sulfur of the type $H_2S_nO_6$, where *n* is from two to six.

thi·o·nin (thī′ə nin), *n.* *Chem.* a dark, crystalline thiazine derivative, used as a violet dye, as in staining microscopic objects. [< Gk *theion* sulfur + -IN[2]]

Thi·o·nine (thī′ə nēn′, -nin), *n.* *Trademark.* thionin.

thi·o·nyl (thī′ə nil), *adj.* *Chem.* sulfinyl. [< Gk *theion* sulfur + -YL]

thi′onyl chlo′ride, *Chem.* a clear, pale yellow or red, fuming, corrosive liquid, $SOCl_2$, used chiefly in organic synthesis.

thi·o·pen·tal (thī′ə pen′təl), *n.* *Pharm.* a barbiturate, $C_{11}H_{18}N_2O_2S$, used in the form of its yellowish-white, hygroscopic sodium powder, and usually administered intravenously: used chiefly as an anesthetic in surgery. Also called **thi′open′tal so′dium.** [THIO- + PENT- + -AL[3]]

thi·o·pen·tone (thī′ə pen′tōn), *n.* *Pharm., Brit.* thiopental. Also called **thi′open′tone so′dium.** [THIO- + PENT- + -ONE]

thi·o·phene (thī′ə fēn′), *n.* *Chem.* a water-insoluble, colorless liquid, C_4H_4S, resembling benzene, occurring in crude coal-tar benzene and prepared by high-temperature interaction of butane and sulfur: used chiefly as a solvent and in organic synthesis. Also, **thi·o·phen** (thī′ə fen′). [THIO- + *-phene,* final var. of PHEN-]

thi·o·phe·nol (thī′ə fē′nōl, -nol), *n.* *Chem.* a colorless, foul-smelling liquid, C_6H_5SH, used chiefly in organic synthesis. [THIO- + PHENOL]

thi′o salt′, *Chem.* a salt of a thio acid.

thi·o·sin·am·ine (thī′ə si nam′in), *n.* *Chem.* a white, crystalline, water-soluble, bitter-tasting powder, CH_2=$CHCH_2NHCSNH_2$, occurring in mustard oil, having a feeble garlicike odor: used chiefly in organic synthesis. Also called **allylthiourea.** [THIO- + Gk *sín(āpi)* mustard + -AMINE]

thi·o·sul·fate (thī′ō sul′fāt), *n.* *Chem.* a salt or ester of thiosulfuric acid. [THIO- + -SULFATE]

thi·o·sul·fu·ric (thī′ō sul fyo͝or′ik), *adj.* *Chem.* of or derived from thiosulfuric acid. [THIO- + SULFURIC]

thi′osulfu′ric ac′id, *Chem.* an acid, $H_2S_2O_3$, which may be regarded as sulfuric acid with one oxygen atom replaced by sulfur.

thi·o·u·ra·cil (thī′ō yo͝or′ə sil), *n.* *Pharm.* a white, slightly water-soluble, bitter, crystalline powder $C_4H_4N_2OS$, used chiefly in treating hyperthyroidism by reducing the activity of the thyroid gland. [THIO- + *uracil* (UR-[1] + AC(ETIC) + -IL)]

thi·o·u·re·a (thī′ō yo͞o rē′ə, -yo͝or′ē ə), *n.* *Chem.* a colorless, crystalline, bitter-tasting, water-soluble solid, $CS(NH_2)_2$, derived from urea by replacement of the oxygen with sulfur: used chiefly in photography, inorganic synthesis, and to accelerate the vulcanization of rubber. Also called **thiocarbamide.** [< NL; see THIO-, UREA]

thir (*th*ûr, *th*ər), *pron.* *Scot. and North Eng.* these. [ME (north)]

Thi·ra (thē′rä), *n.* Thera.

third (thûrd), *adj.* **1.** next after the second; being the ordinal number for three. **2.** being one of three equal parts. **3.** *Auto.* of, pertaining to, or operating at the gear transmission ratio at which the drive shaft speed is greater than that of second gear for a given engine crankshaft speed, but not so great as that of fourth gear, if such exists: *third gear.* **4.** rated, graded, or ranked one level below the second: *He's third engineer on the ship.* —*n.* **5.** a third part, esp. of one (1/3). **6.** the third member of a series. **7.** *Auto.* third gear: *Don't try to start driving a car when it's in third.* **8.** a person or thing next after second in rank, precedence, order: *The writer of the best essay will receive a gold medal, the second a silver, and the third a bronze.* **9.** Usually, **thirds.** *Law.* **a.** the third part of the personal property of a deceased husband, which under certain circumstances goes absolutely to the widow. **b.** a widow's dower. **10.** *Music.* **a.** a tone on the third degree from a given tone (counted as the first). **b.** the interval between such tones. **c.** the harmonic combination of such tones. **11.** *Baseball.* See **third base. 12.** Usually, **thirds.** *Com.* a product or goods below second quality. Cf. **first** (def. 21), **second**[1] (def. 23). [ME *thirde*, OE (north) *thirda*, var. of *thridda*; c. D *derde*, G *dritte*, Goth *thridja*, Icel *thrithi*, Gk *trítos*, L *tertius*, Skt *tritíya*. See THREE] —**third′ly,** *adv.*

third′ base′, *Baseball.* **1.** the third in counterclockwise order of the bases from home plate. **2.** the playing position of the fielder covering the area of the infield near this base.

third′ base′man, *Baseball.* the player whose position is third base.

third′ class′, **1.** the class, grade, or rank immediately below the second. **2.** the least costly class of accommodations on trains, in hotels, etc. Cf. **tourist class. 3.** (in the U.S. postal system) the class of mail consisting of merchandise not exceeding 16 ounces, and written or printed material, as books, manuscripts, circulars, or the like, not sealed against postal inspection. **4.** *Brit.* the lowest of three grades of baccalaureate degree conferred by some British universities.

third-class (thûrd′klas′, -kläs′), *adj.* **1.** of the lowest or poorest class or quality; inferior. **2.** least costly and luxurious: *a third-class coach.* —*adv.* **3.** by third-class conveyance; by means of the third-class: *to travel third-class.*

Third′-Class Car′riage, The, a painting (1862?) by Honoré Daumier.

third′ degree′, **1.** *Chiefly U.S.* intensive questioning or rough treatment, esp. by the police, in order to get information or a confession. **2.** the degree of master mason in Freemasonry. —**third′-de·gree′,** *adj.*

third-de·gree (thûrd′də grē′), *v.t.,* **-greed, -gree·ing.** to subject to the third degree.

third′-degree burn′, *Pathol.* See under **burn**[1] (def. 39).

third′ dimen′sion, **1.** the additional dimension by which a solid object is distinguished from a planar projection of itself or from any planar object. **2.** that which heightens the reality, vividness, or significance of a factual account, sequence of happenings, etc.: *The illustrations added a third dimension to the story.*

third′ ear′, *Slang.* an informer.

third′ estate′, the third of the three estates or political orders: the commons in France or England. Cf. **estate** (def. 5).

third′ eye′lid. See **nictitating membrane.**

third′ fin′ger, the finger next to the little finger; ring finger.

third′ force′, one or more nations, political parties, etc., occupying or advocating an intermediate position between two other forces representing opposite extremes.

third·hand (*adj.* thûrd′hand′; *adv.* thûrd′hand′), *adj.* **1.** previously used or owned by two successive people. **2.** (loosely) secondhand, esp. in poor condition. **3.** obtained through two intermediates successively; twice removed from the original source. —*adv.* **4.** being used or after being used or owned by two other people successively: *He bought the guitar thirdhand.* **5.** by way of several intermediate sources; indirectly. [THIRD + HAND]

Third′ Interna′tional, an ultraradical and communist organization (1919–43), founded in Moscow, uniting Communist groups of various countries and advocating the attainment of their ends by violent revolution. Also called **Communist International.** Cf. **international** (def. 6).

third′ law′ of mo′tion, *Physics.* See under **law of motion.**

third′ law′ of thermodynam′ics. See under **law of thermodynamics** (def. 1).

third′ man′, 1. *Cricket.* **a.** the position of a fielder on the off side between slip and point. **b.** the fielder occupying this position. **2.** *Lacrosse.* **a.** the position of a player, first in the line of defense between center and goal. **b.** the player occupying this position.

third′ mate′, the officer of a merchant vessel next in command beneath the second mate. Also called **third′ of′ficer.**

Third′ of May′, The, a painting (1814–15) by Francisco Goya.

third′ par′ty, 1. any party to an incident, case, quarrel, etc., who is incidentally involved. **2.** (in a two-party system) a political party formed as a dissenting or independent group from members of one or both of the two prevailing major parties.

third′ par′ty proce′dure, *Law.* impleader.

third′ per′son, *Gram.* **1.** the person that is used by the speaker of an utterance in referring to anything or to anyone other than himself or the one or ones to whom he is speaking. **2.** a linguistic form or the group of linguistic forms referring to this grammatical person, as certain verb forms, pronouns, etc.: "*He goes*" *contains a pronoun and a verb form in the third person.* **3.** in or referring to such a grammatical person or linguistic form: "*He,*" "*she,*" "*it,*" *and* "*they*" *are third person pronouns, singular and plural, nominative case.*

third′ posi′tion, *Ballet.* a position in which the feet overlap at the heels with the toes pointing out in opposite directions to the left and right. See illus. under **first position.**

third′ rail′, a metal conductor, in the form of a supplementary rail, laid beside the two regular rails of the track of an electric railroad to carry the electric current. Cf. **shoe** (def. 9).

third-rate (thûrd′rāt′), *adj.* **1.** of the third rate or class. **2.** distinctly inferior: *a third-rate performance.* —**third′-rat′er,** *n.*

Third′ Reich′, Germany during the Nazi regime 1933–45. Cf. **Reich.**

Third′ Repub′lic, the republic established in France in 1870 and terminating with the Nazi occupation in 1940.

third′ sex′, homosexuals.

third′ stream′, a style of music that uses features of both jazz and classical music in an attempt to develop a new and distinctive musical idiom.

Third′ World′, (*sometimes l.c.*) the group of developing nations, esp. of Asia and Africa, that do not align themselves with, or are not committed to, the policies of either the United States or the Soviet Union.

thirl (thûrl), *v.t., v.i. Brit. Dial.* **1.** to pierce. **2.** to thrill. [ME *thirle,* OE *thyr(e)lian,* deriv. of *thyrel* hole. See NOSTRIL]

thirl·age (thûr′lij), *n. Scots Law.* **1.** an obligation imposed on tenants of certain lands, requiring them to bring their grain to a particular mill for grinding. **2.** the price paid for such grinding. [metathetic var. of ME (Scot) *thrillage* bondage. See THRALL, -AGE]

thirst (thûrst), *n.* **1.** a sensation of dryness in the mouth and throat caused by need of liquid. **2.** the physical condition resulting from this need, in any of various degrees: *They almost died of thirst.* **3.** strong or eager desire; craving: *a thirst for knowledge.* —*v.i.* **4.** to feel thirst; be thirsty. **5.** to have a strong desire. [ME *thirst(en)* (v.), OE *thyrstan,* deriv. of *thurst* (n.); c. D *dorst,* G *Durst,* Icel *thorsti,* Goth *thaurstei;* modern *thirst* (n.) has its *-i-* from v. or adj.; see THIRSTY, TOAST] —**thirst′er,** *n.* —**thirst′less,** *adj.* —**thirst′less·ness,** *n.*
—**Syn. 3.** eagerness, hankering, yearning, hunger.

thirst·y (thûr′stē), *adj.,* **thirst·i·er, thirst·i·est. 1.** feeling or having thirst; craving liquid. **2.** needing moisture, as land; parched; dry or arid: *the thirsty soil.* **3.** eagerly desirous; eager: *thirsty for news.* **4.** *Informal.* causing thirst: *Digging is thirsty work.* [ME *thirsti,* OE *thyrstig;* akin to D *dorstig,* G *durstig,* Skt *tṛṣitás* thirsty] —**thirst′i·ly,** *adv.* —**thirst′i·ness,** *n.*

thir·teen (thûr′tēn′), *n.* **1.** a cardinal number, 10 plus 3. **2.** a symbol for this number, as 13 or XIII. **3.** a set of this many persons or things. —*adj.* **4.** amounting to 13 in number. [ME *thrittene,* OE *thrēotēne;* c. D *dertien,* G *dreizehn,* Icel *threttān.* See THREE, -TEEN]

thir′teen′-lined ground′ squir′rel (thûr′tēn′līnd′), a brownish ground squirrel, *Citellus tridecemlineatus,* of prairie regions of the U.S., having cream-colored stripes extending along its back and sides. Also called **thir′teen′-lined go′pher, striped spermophile.**

thir·teenth (thûr′tēnth′), *adj.* **1.** next after the twelfth; being the ordinal number for 13. **2.** being one of 13 equal parts. —*n.* **3.** a thirteenth part, esp. of one (1/13). **4.** the thirteenth member of a series. [THIRTEEN + -TH²; r. ME *thrittenthe* (see THREE, TENTH), OE *thryttēotha* (see TITHE)]

thir·ti·eth (thûr′tē ith), *adj.* **1.** next after the twenty-ninth; being the ordinal number for 30. **2.** being one of 30 equal parts. —*n.* **3.** a thirtieth part, esp. of one (1/30). **4.** the thirtieth member of a series. [THIRTY + -TH²; r. ME *thrittythe,* OE *thritegtha*]

thir·ty (thûr′tē), *n., pl.* **-ties,** *adj.* —*n.* **1.** a cardinal number, 10 times 3. **2.** a symbol for this number, as 30 or XXX. **3.** a set of this many persons or things. **4.** *Print., Journalism.* 30-dash. **5. thirties, a.** the part of a series which falls between thirty and forty, as in computation of age, time, temperature, etc.: *She looks to be somewhere in her late thirties.* **b.** the period of the fourth decade of a century: *the styles of the thirties.* —*adj.* **6.** amounting to 30 in number. [ME *thritty,* OE *thrītig,* equiv. to *thrī* THREE + *-tig* -TY¹; c. D *dertig,* G *dreissig,* Icel *thrjātīu*]

30-dash (thûr′tē dash′), *n. Print., Journalism.* the symbol —30—, —XXX—, —O—, etc., often used to mark the end of a piece of copy, story, etc.

thir·ty-eight (thûr′tē āt′), *n.* **1.** a cardinal number, 30 plus 8. **2.** a symbol for this number, as 38 or XXXVIII. **3.** a set of this many persons or things. —*adj.* **4.** amounting to 38 in number.

thir·ty-eighth (thûr′tē ātth′), *adj.* **1.** next after the thirty-seventh; being the ordinal number for 38. **2.** being one of 38 equal parts. —*n.* **3.** a thirty-eighth part, esp. of one (1/38). **4.** the thirty-eighth member of a series.

thir·ty-fifth (thûr′tē fifth′), *adj.* **1.** next after the thirty-fourth; being the ordinal number for 35. **2.** being one of 35 equal parts. —*n.* **3.** a thirty-fifth part, esp. of one (1/35). **4.** the thirty-fifth member of a series.

thir·ty-first (thûr′tē fûrst′), *adj.* **1.** next after the thirtieth; being the ordinal number for 31. **2.** being one of 31 equal parts. —*n.* **3.** a thirty-first part, esp. of one (1/31). **4.** the thirty-first member of a series.

thir·ty-five (thûr′tē fīv′), *n.* **1.** a cardinal number, 30 plus 5. **2.** a symbol for this number, as 35 or XXXV. **3.** a set of this many persons or things. —*adj.* **4.** amounting to 35 in number.

thir·ty-four (thûr′tē fôr′, -fōr′), *n.* **1.** a cardinal number, 30 plus 4. **2.** a symbol for this number, as 34 or XXXIV. **3.** a set of this many persons or things. —*adj.* **4.** amounting to 34 in number.

thir·ty-fourth (thûr′tē fôrth′, -fōrth′), *adj.* **1.** next after the thirty-third; being the ordinal number for 34. **2.** being one of 34 equal parts. —*n.* **3.** a thirty-fourth part, esp. of one (1/34). **4.** the thirty-fourth member of a series.

thir·ty-nine (thûr′tē nīn′), *n.* **1.** a cardinal number, 30 plus 9. **2.** a symbol for this number, as 39 or XXXIX. **3.** a set of this many persons or things. —*adj.* **4.** amounting to 39 in number.

Thir′ty-nine Ar′ticles, the 39 points of doctrine of the Church of England, promulgated in their final form in 1571.

thir·ty-ninth (thûr′tē nīnth′), *adj.* **1.** next after the thirty-eighth; being the ordinal number for 39. **2.** being one of 39 equal parts. —*n.* **3.** a thirty-ninth part, esp. of one (1/39). **4.** the thirty-ninth member of a series.

thir·ty-one (thûr′tē wun′), *n.* **1.** a cardinal number, 30 plus 1. **2.** a symbol for this number, as 31 or XXXI. **3.** a set of this many persons or things. —*adj.* **4.** amounting to 31 in number.

thir·ty·pen·ny (thûr′tē pen′ē), *adj.* noting a nail 4½ inches long. *Symbol:* 30d [THIRTY + -PENNY]

thir·ty-sec·ond (thûr′tē sek′ənd), *adj.* **1.** next after the thirty-first; being the ordinal number for 32. **2.** being one of 32 equal parts. —*n.* **3.** a thirty-second part, esp. of one (1/32). **4.** the thirty-second member of a series.

thir′ty-sec′ond note′, *Music.* a note having 1/32 of the time value of a whole note; demi-semiquaver. See illus. under **note.**

thir′ty-sec′ond rest′, *Music.* a rest equal in value to a thirty-second note. See illus. under **rest¹.**

thir·ty-sev·en (thûr′tē sev′ən), *n.* **1.** a cardinal number, 30 plus 7. **2.** a symbol for this number, as 37 or XXXVII. **3.** a set of this many persons or things. —*adj.* **4.** amounting to 37 in number.

thir·ty-sev·enth (thûr′tē sev′ənth), *adj.* **1.** next after the thirty-sixth; being the ordinal number for 37. **2.** being one of 37 equal parts. —*n.* **3.** a thirty-seventh part, esp. of one (1/37). **4.** the thirty-seventh member of a series.

thir·ty-six (thûr′tē siks′), *n.* **1.** a cardinal number, 30 plus 6. **2.** a symbol for this number, as 36 or XXXVI. **3.** a set of this many persons or things. —*adj.* **4.** amounting to 36 in number.

thir·ty-sixth (thûr′tē siksth′), *adj.* **1.** next after the thirty-fifth; being the ordinal number for 36. **2.** being one of 36 equal parts. —*n.* **3.** a thirty-sixth part, esp. of one (1/36). **4.** the thirty-sixth member of a series.

thir·ty-third (thûr′tē thûrd′), *adj.* **1.** next after the thirty-second; being the ordinal number for 33. **2.** being one of 33 equal parts. —*n.* **3.** a thirty-third part, esp. of one (1/33). **4.** the thirty-third member of a series.

thir·ty-three (thûr′tē thrē′), *n.* **1.** a cardinal number, 30 plus 3. **2.** a symbol for this number, as 33 or XXXIII. **3.** a set of this many persons or things. —*adj.* **4.** amounting to 33 in number.

thir·ty-two (thûr′tē to͞o′), *n.* **1.** a cardinal number, 30 plus 2. **2.** a symbol for this number, as 32 or XXXII. **3.** a set of this many persons or things. —*adj.* **4.** amounting to 32 in number.

thir·ty-two·mo (thûr′tē to͞o′mō), *n., pl.* **-mos,** *adj.* —*n.* **1.** Also called **trigesimo-secundo.** a book size of about 3¼ × 5½ inches, determined by printing on sheets which are folded to form 32 leaves or 64 pages. *Abbr.:* 32mo, 32° **2.** a book of this size. —*adj.* **3.** printed, folded, or bound as a thirty-twomo; trigesimo-secundo. Also, **thir′ty·two′mo.** [THIRTY-TWO + -MO]

Thir′ty Years′′ War′, the war, often regarded as a series of wars (1618–48), in central Europe, initially involving a conflict between German Protestants and Catholics and later including political rivalries with France, Sweden, and Denmark opposing the Holy Roman Empire and Spain.

this (this), *pron. and adj., pl.* **these** (thēz); *adv.* —*pron.* **1.** (used to indicate a person, thing, idea, state, event, time, remark, etc., as present, near, just mentioned or pointed out, supposed to be understood, or by way of emphasis): *This is my hat.* **2.** (used to indicate one of two or more persons, things, etc., already mentioned, referring to the one nearer in place, time, or thought; opposed to *that*): *This is Liza and that is Amy.* **3.** (used to indicate one of two or more persons, things, etc., already mentioned, implying a contrast or contradistinction; opposed to *that*): *I'd take that instead of this.* **4. with this,** following this; hereupon: *With this, he threw down his glass and left the table.* —*adj.* **5.** (used to indicate a person, place, thing, or degree as present, near, just indicated or mentioned, or as well-known or characteristic): *These people are my friends. This problem has worried me for a long time.* **6.** (used to indicate the nearer in time, place, or thought of two persons, things, etc., already mentioned; opposed to *that*). **7.** (used to imply mere contradistinction; opposed to *that*). —*adv.* **8.** (used with adjectives and adverbs of quantity or extent) to the extent or degree indicated: *this far; this softly.* [ME, OE; c. G *dies,* Icel *thissi*]

This·be (thiz′bē), *n.* **1.** *Class. Myth.* See **Pyramus and Thisbe. 2.** a girl's given name.

Thi·so·a (thī sō′ə), *n. Class Myth.* an Arcadian nymph who tended the infant Zeus.

this·tle (this′əl), *n.* **1.** any of various prickly, composite plants having showy, purple flower heads, esp. of the genus *Cirsium,* as an herb, *C. lanceolatum,* and the Scottish thistle, *Onopordum acanthium,* considered as the national emblem of Scotland. **2.** any of various other prickly plants. [ME, OE *thistel;* c. D *distel,* G *Distel,* Icel *thistill*] —**this′tle-like′,** *adj.*

Thistle, *Onopordum acanthium* (Height to 9 ft.)

this′tle but′terfly, any nymphalid butterfly of the genus *Vanessa,* as the red admiral or painted lady.

this·tle·down (this′əl doun′), *n.* the mature, silky pappus of a thistle. [THISTLE + DOWN²]

this·tly (this′lē, -ə lē), *adj.* **1.** filled with or having many thistles. **2.** suggesting a growth of thistles, esp. in being difficult or painful to handle: *a thistly set of problems.* [THISTLE + -Y¹]

thith·er (thith′ər, thith′-), *adv.* **1.** Also, **thith·er·ward** (thith′ər wərd, thith′-), **thith′er·wards.** to or toward that place or point; there. —*adj.* **2.** on the farther or other side or in the direction away from the person speaking; farther; more remote. [late ME, var. of ME, OE *thider,* alter. of OE *thæder* (*-i-* from *hider* HITHER); akin to Icel *thathra* there, Goth *thathro* thence, Skt *tátra* there, thither]

thith·er·to (thith′ər to͞o′, thith′-, thith′ər to͞o′, thith′-), *adv. Rare.* up to that time; until then. [late ME *thidir to.* See THITHER, TO]

thix·ot·ro·py (thik so′trə pē), *n. Chem.* the property exhibited by certain gels of becoming liquid when stirred or shaken. [< Gk *thíx(is)* touch + -o- + -TROPY] —**thix·o·trop·ic** (thik′sə trop′ik), *adj.*

Thja·zi (thyät′sē), *n.* Thiazi. Also, **Thjat′si.**

Th.M., Master of Theology.

tho (thō), *conj., adv. Informal.* though. Also, **tho′.**

Tho·as (thō′əs), *n. Class. Myth.* **1.** Also called **Thoön.** one of the Gigantes who was killed by Hercules. **2.** a son of Hypsipyle and Jason. **3.** a son of Ariadne and either Dionysus or Theseus who became a king of Tauris and the benefactor of Iphigenia. **4.** (in the *Iliad*) a suitor of Helen who aided the Greek forces in the Trojan War.

Thokk (thôk), *n. Scand. Myth.* an old giantess, possibly Loki in disguise, who was the only being to refuse to weep for the dead Balder, thus comdemning him to eternity in Niflheim. Also, **Thock, Thok.**

thole¹ (thōl), *n.* a pin, or either of two pins, inserted into a gunwale to provide a fulcrum for an oar. Also called **thole·pin** (thōl′pin′). [ME *tholle,* OE *tholl;* c. LG *dolle,* Icel *thollr;* akin to Icel *thǫll* young fir-tree]

Thole¹

thole² (thōl), *v.t.,* **tholed, thol·ing.** *Chiefly Scot.* to suffer; bear; endure. [ME; OE *thol(ian);* c. Icel *thola,* Goth *thulan;* akin to L *tolerāre,* Gk *tlênai* to bear, endure]

thole³ (thōl), *n.* (in an ancient Greek temple) a place where sacrifices were left. [Anglicized var. of THOLUS]

thol·o·bate (thol′ə bāt′), *n. Archit.* the substructure supporting a dome or cupola. [< Gk *thólo(s)* THOLOS + *-batēs* one that goes]

tho·los (thō′los), *n., pl.* **-loi** (-loi). **1.** (in classical architecture) **a.** a circular building. **b.** a small, round structure, as a lantern. **c.** a circular subterranean tomb, lined with masonry. **2.** a subterranean domed tomb chamber of the Mycenaean age. [< Gk: lit., rotunda]

tho·lus (thō′ləs), *n., pl.* **-li** (-lī). tholos. [< L < Gk *thólos*]

Thom·as (tom′əs *for 1, 2 4–13;* tô mä′ *for 3*), *n.* **1.** an apostle who demanded proof of Christ's Resurrection. John 20:24–29. **2. Augustus,** 1857–1934, U.S. playwright, journalist, and actor. **3. (Charles Louis) Am·broise** (sharl lwē äN brwaz′), 1811–96, French composer. **4. Dyl·an (Mar·lais)** (dil′ən mär′lā), 1914–53, Welsh poet and short-story writer. **5. George Henry,** 1816–70, Union general in the U.S. Civil War. **6. John,** 1724–76, American physician and general in the American Revolution. **7. John (Curtis),** born 1941, U.S. athlete. **8. Norman (Mat·toon)** (mə to͞on′), 1884–1968, U.S. socialist leader and political writer. **9. Seth,** 1785–1859, U.S. clock designer and manufacturer. **10. Theodore,** 1835–1905, U.S. orchestra conductor, born in Germany. **11. William Isaac,** 1863–1947, U.S. sociologist. **12.** See **doubting Thomas. 13.** a boy's given name.

Thom·as à Beck·et (tom′əs ə bek′it), **Saint.** See **Becket, Saint Thomas à.**

Thom·as à Kem·pis (tom′əs ə kem′pis). See **Kempis, Thomas à.**

Thom′as Aqui′nas (tom′əs), **Saint.** See **Aquinas, Saint Thomas.**

Thom·as of Er·cel·doune (tom′əs əv ûr′səl do͞on′), ("*Thomas the Rhymer*"), c1220–97?, Scottish poet.

Thom·as of Wood·stock (tom′əs əv wo͝od′stok′), **Duke of Gloucester,** 1355–97, English prince (son of Edward III).

Thom·as·ton (tom′ə stən), *n.* **1.** a town in central Georgia. 9336 (1960). **2.** a town in W Connecticut. 3579 (1960). **3.** a town on NW Long Island, in SE New York. 2767 (1960).

Thom·as·ville (tom′əs vil), *n.* **1.** a city in S Georgia. 18,246 (1960). **2.** a city in central North Carolina. 15,190 (1960). **3.** a town in SW Alabama. 3182 (1960).

tho·mi·sid (thō′mi sid), *n.* **1.** a spider of the family *Thomisidae,* comprising the crab spiders. —*adj.* **2.** belonging or pertaining to the family *Thomisidae.* [< NL *Thomisid(ae)* name of the family, irreg. < Gk *thōminx* string + NL *-idae* -ID²]

Tho·mism (tō′miz əm, thō′-), *n.* the theological and philosophical system of Thomas Aquinas. [THOM(AS) AQUINAS) + -ISM] —**Tho′mist,** *n., adj.* —**Tho·mis′tic,** *adj.*

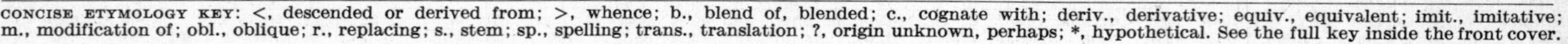

CONCISE ETYMOLOGY KEY: <, descended or derived from; >, whence; b., blend of, blended; c., cognate with; deriv., derivative; equiv., equivalent; imit., imitative; m., modification of; obl., oblique; r., replacing; s., stem; sp., spelling; trans., translation; ?, origin unknown, perhaps; *, hypothetical. See the full key inside the front cover.

Thomp·son (tomp′sən, tom′-), *n.* **1. Benjamin, Count Rumford,** 1753–1814, English physicist and diplomat, born in the U.S. **2. Francis** 1859–1907, English poet. **3. Sir John Sparrow David,** 1844–94, Canadian statesman: prime minister 1892–94. **4. Randall,** born 1899, U.S. composer and teacher. **5. Sylvia,** born 1902, English novelist, born in Scotland.

Thomp′son seed′less, **1.** a yellow, seedless variety of grape used in producing raisins. **2.** the vine bearing this fruit, grown in California. Also called **Thomp′son seed′less grape′.** [named after W. B. *Thompson* (1869–1930), American horticulturist]

Thomp′son submachine′ gun′, a portable, .45-caliber, automatic weapon designed to be fired from the shoulder or hip. Also called **Tommy gun.** [named after J. T. *Thompson* (1860–1940), American army officer who aided in its invention]

Thom·sen (tom′sən), *n.* **Chris·tian Jür·gen·sen** (kʀɪs′tyän yoor′gən sən), 1788–1865, Danish archaeologist.

Thom·son (tom′sən), *n.* **1. Elihu,** 1853–1937, U.S. inventor, born in England. **2. Sir George Paget,** born 1892, English physicist (son of Sir Joseph John): Nobel prize 1937. **3. James,** 1700–48, English poet, born in Scotland. **4. James** ("*B.V.*"), 1834–82, English poet. **5. John Arthur,** 1861–1933, Scottish scientist and author. **6. Sir Joseph John,** 1856–1940, English physicist: Nobel prize 1906. **7. Virgil,** born 1896, U.S. composer and music critic. **8. Sir William.** See **Kelvin, 1st Baron. 9.** a town in E Georgia. 4522 (1960).

Thom′son effect′, *Physics.* the tendency of unevenly heated segments of a strip of a specific metal to increase or decrease in temperature differences when an electric current is passed through the strip: in some metals heat will flow from the hotter to the colder sections, decreasing the temperature differences, in other metals it will flow from the colder to the hotter sections increasing the differences, and in still other metals no heat transfer will take place. Also called **Kelvin effect.** [named after Sir William Thomson]

thong (thông, thong), *n.* **1.** a narrow strip of hide or leather, used as a fastening, as the lash of a whip, etc. **2.** a similar strip of some other material, as for fastening sandals. [ME; OE *thwong;* akin to Icel *thvengr* strap, *thvinga* to compel]

thong′ leath′er, whang (def. 3b).

Tho·ön (thō′on), *n.* *Class. Myth.* **1.** Thoas (def. 1). **2.** (in the *Iliad*) a Trojan who was killed by Antilochus while attacking the Greek wall.

Thor (thôr), *n.* **1.** *Scand. Myth.* the god of thunder, rain, and farming, represented as riding a chariot drawn by goats and wielding the hammer Mjölnir: the defender of the Aesir, destined to kill and be killed by the Midgard Serpent. **2.** *U.S.* a surface-to-surface intermediate range ballistic missile powered by a single liquid-propellant rocket engine. **3.** a boy's given name. [OE *Thōr* < WScand; cf. Icel *Thōrr,* c. ODan *Thūr,* lit., THUNDER]

thorac-, var. of **thoraco-** before a vowel: *thoracic.*

tho·ra·cec·to·my (thôr′ə sek′tə mē, thōr′-), *n., pl.* **-mies.** *Surg.* costectomy. [THORAC- + -ECTOMY]

tho·rac·ic (thō ras′ik, thô-), *adj.* of or pertaining to the thorax. Also, **tho·ra·cal** (thôr′ə kəl, thōr′-). [< ML *thōrăcic(us)* < Gk *thōrākikós.* See THORAC-, -IC]

thorac′ic duct′, *Anat.* the main trunk of the lymphatic system, passing along the spinal column in the thoracic cavity, and conveying a large amount of lymph and chyle into the venous circulation.

thoracico-, a combining form of **thoracic:** *thoracicolumbar.*

tho·rac·i·co·lum·bar (thō ras′i kō lum′bər, thô-), *adj.* pertaining to the thoracic and lumbar areas of the body. Also, **tho·ra·co·lum·bar** (thôr′ə kō lum′bər, thōr′-). [THORACICO- + LUMBAR]

thoraco-, a combining form of **thorax:** *thoracoplasty.* Also, *esp. before a vowel,* **thorac-.** [comb. form repr. Gk *thōrāk-* (s. of *thṓrāx*) + chest + -o-]

tho·ra·cop·a·gus (thôr′ə kop′ə gəs, thōr′-), *n.* *Pathol.* a fetal monster consisting of twins joined at the thorax. [< NL; see THORACO-, -PAGUS]

tho·ra·co·plas·ty (thôr′ə kō plas′tē, thōr′-), *n., pl.* **-ties.** *Surg.* the operation removing selected portions of the bony chest wall or ribs to compress part of the underlying lung or an abnormal pleural space, usually in the treatment of tuberculosis. [THORACO- + -PLASTY]

tho·ra·cos·to·my (thôr′ə kos′tə mē, thōr′-), *n., pl.* **-mies.** *Surg.* incision through the chest wall into the pleural cavity, usually for draining. [THORACO- + -STOMY]

tho·ra·cot·o·my (thôr′ə kot′ə mē, thōr′-), *n., pl.* **-mies.** *Surg.* incision into the chest wall. [THORACO- + -TOMY]

tho·rax (thôr′aks, thōr′-), *n., pl.* **tho·rax·es, tho·ra·ces** (thôr′ə sēz′, thōr′-). **1.** the part of the trunk in man and higher vertebrates between the neck and the abdomen, containing the cavity, enclosed by the ribs, sternum, and certain vertebrae, in which the heart, lungs, etc., are situated; chest. **2.** a corresponding part in other animals. **3.** (in insects) the portion of the body between the head and the abdomen. See diag. under **insect.** [late ME < L < Gk *thṓrāx* breastplate, part of body which this covers]

Tho·ra·zine (thôr′ə zēn′, thōr′-), *n.* *Pharm., Trademark.* chlorpromazine.

Thor·burn (thôr′bûrn′), *n.* a boy's given name.

Tho·reau (thôr′ō, thōr′ō, thə rō′), *n.* **Henry David,** 1817–62, U.S. naturalist and author. —**Tho·reau·vi·an** (thə rō′vē ən), *adj.*

Tho·rez (tô rez′), *n.* **Mau·rice** (mô rēs′), 1900–64, French Communist party leader.

tho·ri·a (thôr′ē ə, thōr′-), *n.* *Chem.* a white, heavy, water-insoluble powder, ThO_2, used chiefly in incandescent mantles, as the Welsbach gas mantle which also contains one-percent ceria. Also called **thorium oxide, thorium dioxide.** [THORI(UM) + *-a,* modeled on *magnesia*]

tho·ri·a·nite (thôr′ē ə nīt′, thōr′-), *n.* a rare mineral, mainly thoria, ThO_2, but also containing uranium, cerium, and other rare-earth metals, occurring in small, black, cubic crystals, notable for its radioactivity: a minor source of thorium. [*thorian* (THORIA + -AN) + -ITE[1]]

tho·rite (thôr′īt, thōr′-), *n.* a rare mineral, thorium silicate, $ThSiO_4$, occurring in the form of yellow or black crystals. [*thor-* (as in THORIA, THORIUM) + -ITE[1], modeled on Sw *thorit*]

tho·ri·um (thôr′ē əm, thōr′-), *n.* *Chem.* a grayish-white, lustrous, somewhat ductile and malleable, radioactive, metallic element present in monazite: used as a source of nuclear energy, in sun-lamp and vacuum-tube filament coatings, and in alloys. *Symbol:* Th; *at. wt.:* 232.038; *sp. gr.:* 11.2. Cf. **thoria.** [THOR + -IUM] —**thor·ic** (thôr′ik, thor′-), *adj.*

tho′rium ox′ide, *Chem.* thoria. Also called **tho′rium diox′ide.**

tho′rium se′ries, *Chem.* the radioactive series that starts with thorium and ends with a stable isotope of lead of mass number 208.

thorn (thôrn), *n.* **1.** a sharp excrescence on a plant, esp. a sharp-pointed aborted branch; spine; prickle. **2.** any of various thorny shrubs or trees, esp. the hawthorns of the genus *Crataegus.* **3.** the wood of any of these trees. **4.** the runic character þ for *th* as in *thin,* borrowed into the Latin alphabet as used for Old English and Icelandic. **5.** something that wounds, annoys, or causes discomfort. **6. thorn in one's flesh** or **side,** a source of continual irritation or suffering: *That boy has been a thorn in every teacher's side since he entered the school.* —*v.t.* **7.** to prick with a thorn; vex. [ME, OE; c. D *doorn,* G *Dorn,* Icel *thorn,* Goth *thaurnus*] —**thorn′less,** *adj.* —**thorn′less·ness,** *n.* —**thorn′like′,** *adj.*

Thorn (tôrn), *n.* German name of **Torun.**

thorn′ ap′ple (thôrn), **1.** any poisonous, solanaceous plant of the genus *Datura,* the species of which bear capsules covered with prickly spines, esp. the jimson weed, *D. Stramonium.* **2.** the fruit of certain hawthorns of the genus *Crataegus.*

thorn·back (thôrn′bak′), *n.* **1.** a European skate, *Raja clavata,* with short spines on the back and tail. **2.** a California ray, *Platyrhinoidis triseriatus,* belonging to the guitarfish group. [THORN + BACK[1]]

Thorn·dike (thôrn′dīk′), *n.* **1. Ashley Horace,** 1871–1933, U.S. literary historian and teacher. **2. Edward Lee,** 1874–1949, U.S. psychologist and lexicographer. **3. (Everett) Lynn,** born 1882, U.S. historian and scholar (brother of Ashley Horace Thorndike). **4. Dame Sybil,** born 1882, English actress. **5.** a boy's given name.

Thorn·dyke (thôrn′dīk′), *n.* a boy's given name. Also, **Thorndike.**

Thorne (thôrn), *n.* a boy's given name.

thorn·head (thôrn′hed′), *n.* any of several scorpaenid fishes of the genus *Sebastolobus,* found in the deep waters of the North Pacific. [THORN + HEAD]

Thorn·ton (thôrn′tən, -tən), *n.* **1. William,** 1759–1828, U.S. architect, born in the British Virgin Islands. **2.** a town in NE Illinois. 2895 (1960). **3.** a boy's given name.

thorn·y (thôr′nē), *adj.,* **thorn·i·er, thorn·i·est. 1.** abounding in or characterized by thorns; spiny; prickly. **2.** thornlike. **3.** overgrown with thorns or brambles. **4.** painful; vexatious: *a thorny predicament.* **5.** full of difficulties, complexities, or controversial points: *a thorny question.* [ME; OE *thornig.* See THORN, -Y[1]] —**thorn′i·ly,** *adv.* —**thorn′i·ness,** *n.*

thorn′y lo′cust, a spiny shrub or small tree, *Robinia neo-mexicana,* of the southwestern U.S., having numerous branches, and downy leaflets when young.

thor·o (thûr′ō, thur′ō), *adj., adv.* *Informal.* thorough.

tho·ron (thôr′on, thōr′-), *n.* *Chem.* a radioactive element that is an isotope of radon, produced by the disintegration of thorium. *Symbol:* Tn; *at. wt.:* 220; *at. no.:* 86. [THOR(IUM) + -ON]

thor·ough (thûr′ō, thur′ō), *adj.* **1.** carried out through the whole of something; fully executed; complete: *a thorough search; thorough enjoyment.* **2.** utter; complete; perfect: *a thorough fool.* **3.** marked by close attention to accuracy and detail: *a thorough analysis of the problem.* **4.** extremely attentive to accuracy and detail; painstaking: *a thorough housewife.* **5.** having full command or mastery of an art, talent, etc.: *a thorough actress.* **6.** *Archaic.* extending or passing through. —*adv., prep.* **7.** *Archaic.* through. —*n.* **8.** (*cap.*) *Eng. Hist.* the administrative policies of the Earl of Stafford and Archbishop Laud during the reign of Charles I: so called because they were uncompromisingly carried out. [ME; OE *thuruh,* var. of *thurh* THROUGH] —**thor′ough·ly,** *adv.* —**thor′ough·ness,** *n.*
—**Syn. 1.** unqualified, total. —**Ant. 1.** partial.

thor′ough bass′ (bās), *Music.* **1.** a bass part written out in full throughout an entire piece, and accompanied by figures that indicate the successive chords of the harmony. **2.** the science or method of indicating harmonies by such figures. **3.** harmonic composition in general.

thor′ough brace′, either of two strong braces or bands of leather supporting the body of a coach or other vehicle and connecting the front and back springs.

thor·ough·bred (thûr′ō bred′, -ə bred′, thur′-), *adj.* **1.** of pure or unmixed breed, stock, or race, as a horse or other animal; bred from the purest and best blood. **2.** (*sometimes cap.*) of or pertaining to the Thoroughbred breed of horses. **3.** (of human beings) having qualities resembling those of a thoroughbred horse; high-spirited; mettlesome; elegant or graceful. **4.** thoroughly educated or trained. —*n.* **5.** (*cap.*) one of a breed of horses, to which all race horses belong, originally developed in England by crossing Arabian stallions with European mares. **6.** a thoroughbred animal. **7.** a well-bred or thoroughly trained person. [THOROUGH + BRED] —**thor′ough·bred′ness,** *n.*

thor·ough·fare (thûr′ō fâr′, -ə fâr′, thur′-), *n.* **1.** a road, street, or the like, that leads at each end into another street. **2.** a major road or highway. **3.** a passage or way through: *no thoroughfare.* **4.** a strait, river, or the like, affording passage. [ME *thurghfare.* See THOROUGH, FARE]

thor·ough·go·ing (thûr′ō gō′ing, -ə gō′-, thur′-), *adj.* **1.** doing things thoroughly. **2.** carried out to the full extent; thorough. **3.** complete; unqualified: *a thoroughgoing knave.* [THOROUGH + GOING] —**thor′ough·go′ing·ly,** *adv.* —**thor′ough·go′ing·ness,** *n.*

thor·ough·paced (thûr′ō pāst′, -ə pāst′, thur′-), *adj.* **1.** trained to go through all the possible paces, as a horse. **2.** thoroughgoing, complete, or perfect. [THOROUGH + PACED]

thor·ough·pin (thûr′ō pin′, -ə pin′, thur′-), *n.* *Vet. Pathol.* an abnormal swelling just above the hock of a horse, usually appearing on both sides of the leg and sometimes causing lameness. [THOROUGH + PIN]

thor′ough stone′, perpend[1].

thor·ough·wort (thûr′ō wûrt′, -ə wûrt′, thur′-), *n.* boneset. [THOROUGH + WORT[2]]

thorp (thôrp), *n.* *Archaic.* a hamlet; village. Also, **thorpe.** [ME, OE; c. G *Dorf,* Icel *thorp* village, Goth *thaurp* field]

Thorpe (thôrp), *n.* **James Francis** ("*Jim*"), 1888–1953, U.S. athlete.

thort·veit·ite (tôrt vī′tīt, thôrt-), *n.* a grayish-green, crystalline ore containing about 40 percent scandium oxide. [< G *Thortveitit,* named after Olaus *Thortveit,* 20th-century Norwegian mineralogist; see -ITE[1]]

Thor·vald·sen (tôôr′väl′sən), *n.* **Al·bert Ber·tal** (äl′bert bar′təl), 1770–1844, Danish sculptor. Also, **Thor·wald·sen** (tôôr′väl′sən).

those (thōz), *pron., adj.* pl. of **that.** [late ME *those, thoos,* pl. of THAT, earlier ME *thoos,* OE *thās,* pl. of THIS]

Thoth (thōth, tōt), *n.* *Egyptian Religion.* the god of wisdom, learning, and magic, the inventor of numbers and letters, and scribe of all the gods, represented as a man with the head either of an ibis or of a baboon: identified by the Greeks with Hermes.

Thoth

Thot·mes I (thot′mes). See **Thutmose I.** Also, **Thoth·mes I** (thoth′mēz, -mes, tot′-, thoth′-).

Thotmes II. See **Thutmose II.** Also, **Thothmes II.**

Thotmes III. See **Thutmose III.** Also, **Thothmes III.**

thou[1] (thou), *pron., sing., nom.* **thou;** *poss.* **thy** or **thine;** *obj.* **thee;** *pl., nom.* **you** or **ye;** *poss.* **your** or **yours;** *obj.* **you** or **ye;** *v.* —*pron.* **1.** *Archaic* (*except in some elevated or ecclesiastical prose*), *Poetic,* or *Brit. Dial.* the personal pronoun of the second person singular in the nominative case (used to denote the person or thing addressed): *Thou shalt not kill.* —*v.t.* **2.** to address as "thou." —*v.i.* **3.** to use "thou" in discourse. [ME; OE *thū;* c. G, MD *du,* Icel *thū,* Goth *thu,* Ir *tu,* Welsh, Cornish *ti,* L *tū,* Doric Gk *tý,* Lith *tu,* OSlav *ty;* akin to Skt *tvam*]

thou[2] (thou), *n., pl.* **thous,** (*as after a numeral*) **thou.** *Slang.* one thousand dollars, pounds, etc. [by shortening]

though (thō), *conj.* **1.** (used in introducing a subordinate clause, which is often marked by ellipsis) notwithstanding that; in spite of the fact that: *Though he tried very hard, he failed the course.* **2.** even if; granting that (often prec. by *even*). **3. as though,** as if: *It seems as though the place is deserted.* —*adv.* **4.** for all that; however. [ME, var. of *thoh* < Scand; cf. Icel *thō* < proto-Norse **thauh,* c. Goth *thauh,* OE *thēah,* G *doch*]
—**Usage.** Among some purists there is a traditional objection to the use of THOUGH in place of ALTHOUGH as a conjunction. However, the latter (earlier *all though*) was originally an emphatic form of the former, and there is nothing in modern English usage to justify such a distinction.

thought[1] (thôt), *n.* **1.** the product of mental activity; that which one thinks: *a body of thought.* **2.** a single act or product of thinking; idea or notion: *to collect one's thoughts.* **3.** the act or process of thinking; mental activity: *Thought as well as action wearies us.* **4.** the capacity or faculty of thinking, reasoning, imagining, etc.: *All his thought went into his work.* **5.** a consideration or reflection: *Thought of death terrified him.* **6.** meditation, contemplation, or recollection: *deep in thought; lost in thought.* **7.** intention, design, or purpose, esp. a half-formed or imperfect intention: *We had some thought of going to Alaska.* **8.** anticipation or expectation: *I had no thought of seeing you here.* **9.** consideration, attention, care, or regard: *She took no thought of her appearance.* **10.** a judgment, opinion, or belief: *According to his thought, all violence is evil.* **11.** the intellectual activity or the ideas, opinions, etc., characteristic of a particular place, class, or time: *Greek thought.* **12.** a very small amount; a touch; bit; trifle: *The steak is a thought underdone.* [ME *thoght,* OE *(ge)thōht;* c. D *gedachte;* akin to THANK, THINK[1]]
—**Syn. 2.** concept, opinion, judgment, belief. See **idea. 3.** reflection, cogitation.

thought[2] (thôt), *v.* pt. and pp. of **think.**

thought·ful (thôt′fəl), *adj.* **1.** occupied with or given to thought; contemplative; meditative; reflective: *in a thoughtful mood.* **2.** characterized by or manifesting careful thought: *a thoughtful essay.* **3.** careful, heedful, or mindful: *to be thoughtful of one's safety.* **4.** showing consideration for others; considerate. [ME; see THOUGHT[1], -FUL] —**thought′ful·ly,** *adv.* —**thought′ful·ness,** *n.*
—**Syn. 1.** pensive. **3.** regardful, discreet, prudent, wary, circumspect. **4.** attentive, solicitous. THOUGHTFUL, CONSIDERATE mean taking thought for the comfort and the good of others. THOUGHTFUL implies providing little attentions, offering services, or in some way looking out for the comfort or welfare of others: *It was thoughtful of you to send the flowers.* CONSIDERATE implies sparing others annoyance or discomfort, and being careful not to hurt their feelings: *not considerate, only polite.*

thought·less (thôt′lis), *adj.* **1.** not thinking enough; careless or heedless: *thoughtless of his health.* **2.** characterized by or showing lack of thought: *a shallow, thoughtless book.* **3.** lacking in consideration for others; inconsiderate; tactless: *a thoughtless remark.* **4.** devoid of or lacking capacity for thought. [THOUGHT[1] + -LESS] —**thought′less·ly,** *adv.* —**thought′less·ness,** *n.*
—**Syn. 1.** negligent, neglectful, unobservant, reckless, flighty, giddy. **3.** inattentive, remiss.

thought-out (thôt′out′), *adj.* produced by or showing the results of much thought: *a carefully thought-out argument.*

thought′ transfer′ence, transference of thought by extrasensory means from the mind of one individual to another; telepathy.

thou·sand (thou′zənd), *n., pl.* **-sands,** (*as after a numeral*) **-sand,** *adj.* —*n.* **1.** a cardinal number, 10 times 100. **2.** a symbol for this number, as 1000 or M. **3.** a great number or amount. **4.** Also, **thou′sand's place′. a.** (in a mixed number) the position of the fourth digit to the left of the decimal point. **b.** (in a whole number) the position of the fourth digit from the right. —*adj.* **5.** amounting to 1000 in number. [ME; OE *thūsend;* c. D *duizend,* OHG *dūsunt,* Icel *thūsund,* Goth *thūsindi*]

Thou′sand and One′ Nights′, The. See **Arabian Nights' Entertainments.**

thou·sand·fold (*adj.* thou′zənd fōld′; *adv.* thou′zənd fōld′), *adj.* **1.** having a thousand elements or parts. **2.** a thousand times as great or as much. —*adv.* **3.** Also, **thou′sand·fold′ly.** in a thousandfold manner or measure. [ME *thousand folde,* OE *thūsendfealde.* See THOUSAND, -FOLD]

Thou′sand Is′land dress′ing, a seasoned mayonnaise, often containing chopped pickles, pimientos, sweet peppers, hard-boiled eggs, etc.

Thou′sand Is′lands, a group of about 1500 islands in S Canada and the N United States, in the St. Lawrence River at the outlet of Lake Ontario: summer resorts.

Thou′sand Oaks′, a town in S California. 2934 (1960).

thou·sandth (thou′zəndth), *adj.* **1.** last in order of a series of a thousand. **2.** being one of a thousand equal parts. —*n.* **3.** a thousandth part, esp. of one (1/1000). **4.** the thousandth member of a series. **5.** Also, **thou′sandth's place′.** (in decimal notation) the position of the third digit to the right of the decimal point. [THOUSAND + -TH[2]]

thow·less (thou′lis), *adj. Scot.* listless; without energy or spirit. Also, **thewless, thieveless.** [ME *thowles* (Scot), var. of THEWLESS]

Thrace (thrās), *n.* **1.** an ancient region of varying extent in the E part of the Balkan Peninsula: later a Roman province; now in Bulgaria, Turkey, and Greece. **2.** a modern region corresponding to the S part of the Roman province: now divided between Greece (**Western Thrace**) and Turkey (**Eastern Thrace**).

Thra·cian (thrā′shən), *adj.* **1.** of or pertaining to Thrace or its inhabitants. —*n.* **2.** a native or inhabitant of Thrace. **3.** an Indo-European language that was the language of ancient Thrace. [< L *Thrāci(us)* of Thrace (< Gk *Thrāikios* < *Thrāik(ē)* THRACE + *-ios* adj. suffix) + -AN]

Thra·co-Phryg·i·an (thrā′kō frij′ē ən), *n.* **1.** a hypothetical branch of Indo-European implying a special genetic affinity between the meagerly attested Thracian and Phrygian languages. —*adj.* **2.** of, belonging to, or pertaining to Thraco-Phrygian. [*Thraco-* < Gk *Thrāiko-,* comb. form of *Thrāikē* Thrace; see PHRYGIAN]

Thrale (thrāl), *n.* **Hester Lynch** (*Hester Lynch Piozzi*), 1741–1821, Welsh writer and friend of Samuel Johnson.

thrall (thrôl), *n.* **1.** a person who is in bondage; bondman; slave. **2.** a person who is morally or mentally enslaved by some power, influence, or the like: *He was the thrall of morbid fantasies.* **3.** slavery; thralldom. —*v.t.* **4.** *Archaic.* to put or hold in thralldom; enslave. —*adj.* **5.** *Archaic.* subjected to bondage; enslaved. [ME; OE *thrǣl* < Scand; cf Icel *thrǣll* slave]

thrall·dom (thrôl′dəm), *n.* the state of being a thrall; bondage; slavery; servitude. Also, **thral′dom.** [ME *thraldom.* See THRALL, -DOM]

thrang (thrang), *n., v.i., v.t., adj. Scot.* throng.

thrash (thrash), *v.t.* **1.** to beat soundly in punishment; flog. **2.** to defeat thoroughly: *The home team thrashed the visitors.* **3.** *Naut.* to force (a close-hauled sailing vessel under heavy canvas) against a strong wind or sea. **4.** thresh. —*v.i.* **5.** to toss, or plunge about wildly or violently. **6.** *Naut.* to make way against the wind, tide, etc.; beat. **7.** thresh. **8. thrash out** or **over.** See **thresh** (def. 5). —*n.* **9.** the act or an instance of thrashing; beating; blow. **10.** thresh. **11.** *Swimming.* the upward and downward movement of the legs, as in the crawl. [var. of THRESH]
—**Syn. 1.** maul, drub. See **beat.**

thrash·er (thrash′ər), *n.* **1.** one who or that which thrashes. **2.** any of several long-tailed, thrushlike birds, esp. of the genus *Toxostoma,* related to the mockingbirds. Cf. **brown thrasher. 3.** thresher (def. 3). [THRASH + -ER[1]]

thrash·ing (thrash′ing), *n.* **1.** a flogging; whipping. **2.** the act of one who or that which thrashes. **3.** a pile or quantity of threshed grain or the grain threshed at one time. [THRASH + -ING[1]]

thra·son·i·cal (thrā son′i kəl), *adj.* boastful; vainglorious. [< L *Thrasōn-* (s. of *Thrasō,* braggart in Terence's play *Eunuchus*) + -ICAL] —**thra·son′i·cal·ly,** *adv.*

Thras·y·bu·lus (thras′ə byōō′ləs), *n.* died c389 B.C., Athenian patriot and general.

Thras·y·de·mus (thras′i dē′məs), *n.* (in the *Iliad*) the squire of Sarpedon: he was slain by Patroclus. Also, **Thras·y·mel·us** (thras′ə mel′əs).

Thras·y·me·des (thras′ə mē′dēz), *n. Class. Myth.* a son of Nestor who commanded the Greek sentries and fought bravely in the Trojan War.

thrave (thrāv), *n. Chiefly Scot.* **1.** a measure for grain or straw, usually 24 sheaves. **2.** a large number. [late ME < EScand; cf. MSw *thrave,* akin to OE, ME, *threfe* < WScand; cf. Icel *threfi*]

thraw (thrô, thrä), *v.t.* **1.** *Brit. Dial.* to throw. **2.** *Scot.* **a.** to twist; distort. **b.** to oppose; thwart; vex. —*v.i.* **3.** *Scot.* to disagree; object. —*adj.* **4.** *Scot.* thrawn (def. 1). [ME *thrawe,* OE *thrawu* THROE]

thrawn (thrôn, thrän), *adj. Scot.* **1.** twisted; crooked; distorted. **2.** contrary; peevish; perverse. **3.** unpleasant; sullen. [Scot. and dial. var of THROWN] —**thrawn′ly,** *adv.* —**thrawn′ness,** *n.*

thread (thred), *n.* **1.** a fine cord of flax, cotton, or other fibrous material spun out to considerable length, esp. when composed of two or more filaments twisted together. **2.** twisted filaments or fibers of any kind used for sewing. **3.** one of the lengths of yarn forming the warp or weft of a woven fabric. **4.** a filament or fiber of glass or other ductile substance. **5.** *Ropemaking.* **a.** any of a number of fibers twisted into a yarn. **b.** a yarn, esp. as enumerated in describing small stuff. **6.** something having the fineness or slenderness of a filament, as a thin continuous stream of liquid, a fine line of color, or a thin seam or ore: *a thread of smoke.* **7.** the helical ridge of a screw. **8.** that which runs through the whole course of something, connecting successive parts, as the sequence of events in a narrative: *He lost the thread of the story.* **9.** something conceived as being spun or continuously drawn out, as the course of life fabled to be spun, measured, and cut by the Fates. —*v.t.* **10.** to pass the end of a thread through the eye of (a needle). **11.** to fix (beads, pearls, etc.) upon a thread that is passed through; string. **12.** to pass continuously through the whole course of (something); pervade: *A joyous quality threaded the whole symphony.* **13.** to make one's way through (a narrow passage, forest, crowd, etc.). **14.** to make (one's way) thus: *He threaded his way through the crowd.* **15.** to form a thread on or in (a bolt, hole, etc.). **16.** to place and arrange thread, yarn, etc., in position on (a sewing machine, loom, textile machine, etc.). —*v.i.* **17.** to thread one's way, as through a passage or between obstacles: *They threaded carefully along the narrow pass.* **18.** to move in a threadlike course; wind or twine. **19.** *Cookery.* (of boiling syrup) to form a fine thread when poured from a spoon. [ME *threed,* OE *thrǣd;* c. D *draad,* Icel *thrathr* thread, G *Draht* wire. See THROW] —**thread′er,** *n.* —**thread′less,** *adj.* —**thread′like′,** *adj.*

thread·bare (thred′bâr′), *adj.* **1.** having the nap worn off so as to lay bare the threads of the warp and woof, as a fabric, garment, etc. **2.** meager, scanty, or poor: *a threadbare emotional life.* **3.** hackneyed; trite; ineffectively stale: *threadbare arguments.* **4.** wearing threadbare clothes; shabby or poor: *a threadbare old man.* [ME *thredbare.* See THREAD, BARE[1]] —**thread′bare′ness,** *n.*
—**Syn. 3.** shopworn, stereotyped.

thread′ blight′, *Plant Pathol.* a disease of woody plants, characterized by thick, threadlike strands of mycelium on the undersides of the leaves and branches, caused by a fungus, *Pellicularia koleroga.*

thread·ed (thred′id), *adj.* ornamented with a threadlike pattern: *silk threaded with gold.* [THREAD + -ED[3]]

thread′ed glass′, glass decorated with a pattern produced by variegated glass filaments.

thread′ escutch′eon, a raised metal rim around a keyhole.

thread·fin (thred′fin′), *n.* any spiny-rayed fishes of the family *Polynemidae,* having the lower part of the pectoral fin composed of numerous, separate, filamentous rays. [THREAD + FIN]

thread·fish (thred′fish′), *n., pl.* (*esp. collectively*) **-fish,** (*esp. referring to two or more kinds or species*) **-fish·es.** any of several carangid fishes of the genus *Alectis,* esp. *A. crinitus,* having the front rays of the dorsal and anal fins greatly elongated. [THREAD + FISH]

thread′ in′sert, *Mach., Building Trades.* a thin, threaded steel liner for reinforcing threads cut in weaker materials or for replacing worn threads.

thread′-leg·ged bug′ (thred′leg′id, -legd′), any of certain insects of the family *Reduviidae,* characterized by an elongated, slender body and long frail legs, the front pair of which are raptorial.

thread′-line fish′ing (thred′līn′), *Angling.* spinning (def. 2).

thread′ mark′, a thin threading in paper currency to make counterfeiting difficult.

thread′ rope′, cordage ½ inch or less in thickness.

thread′ silk′, silk yarn produced by a silk throwster.

thread·worm (thred′wûrm′), *n.* any of various nematode worms, esp. a pinworm. [THREAD + WORM]

thread·y (thred′ē), *adj.,* **thread·i·er, thread·i·est. 1.** consisting of or resembling a thread or threads; fibrous; filamentous. **2.** stringy or viscid, as a liquid. **3.** (of the pulse) thin and feeble. **4.** (of sound, the voice, etc.) lacking fullness; weak; feeble. [THREAD + -Y[1]] —**thread′i·ness,** *n.*

threap (thrēp), *Scot. and North Eng.* —*n.* **1.** an argument; quarrel. **2.** a hostile charge; accusation. —*v.t.* **3.** to rebuke; scold. —*v.i.* **4.** to argue; bicker. [ME *threpe,* OE *thrēapian* to blame] —**threap′er,** *n.*

threat (thret), *n.* **1.** a declaration of an intention or determination to inflict punishment, injury, death, or loss on someone in retaliation for, or conditionally upon, some action or course; menace: *He confessed under the threat of imprisonment.* **2.** an indication of probable evil, violence, or loss to come; something that gives indication of causing evil or harm; warning: *The threat of a storm was in the air.* —*v.t., v.i.* **3.** *Archaic.* to threaten. [ME *threte,* OE *thrēat* pressure, oppression; c. Icel *thraut* hardship, bitter end; akin to OE *thrēatian* to press, threaten, *thrēotan* to vex, *thrīetan* to compel] —**threat′ful,** *adj.* —**threat′ful·ly,** *adv.* —**threat′less,** *adj.*

threat·en (thret′ən), *v.t.* **1.** to utter a threat against; menace: *He threatened the boy with a beating.* **2.** to be a menace or source of danger to: *Sickness threatened her peace of mind.* **3.** to offer (a punishment, injury, etc.) by way of a threat: *They threatened swift retaliation.* **4.** to give an ominous indication of: *The clouds threaten rain.* —*v.i.* **5.** to utter or use threats. **6.** to indicate impending evil or mischief. [ME *thretne(n),* OE *thrēatnian,* var. of *thrēatian* to press, threaten. See THREAT, -EN[1]] —**threat′en·er,** *n.* —**threat′en·ing·ly,** *adv.*
—**Syn. 2.** endanger. **4.** presage, portend, impend, augur, forebode, foreshadow. **6.** See **imminent.** —**Ant. 2.** protect, defend.

three (thrē), *n.* **1.** a cardinal number, 2 plus 1. **2.** a symbol for this number, as 3 or III. **3.** a set of this many persons or things. **4.** a playing card, die face, or half of a domino face with three pips. —*adj.* **5.** amounting to three in number. [ME; OE *thrēo,* var. of *thrīo,* fem., neut. of *thrī(e);* c. D *drie,* G *drei,* Icel *thrír,* Goth *threis,* Gk *treîs,* L *trēs,* Ir *trí,* Skt *tri, trāyas*]

three-a-cat (thrē′ə kat′), *n. Games.* two-a-cat played with three bases and three batters. Also, **three o' cat, three old cat.**

three-and-a-half·pen·ny (thrē′ənd ə hāf′pen′ē, -hāf′-), *adj. Carpentry.* noting a shingle nail 1⅜ inches long. *Abbr.:* 3½d

three′-arm protrac′tor (thrē′ärm′), *Survey.* a device having three straightedges so hinged that they can form two angles simultaneously, used in graphic resection. Also called **station pointer.**

three-bag·ger (thrē′bag′ər), *n. Baseball Slang.* See **three-base hit.**

three′-ball match′ (thrē′bôl′), *Golf.* a match between three players each of whom plays his own ball.

three′-base hit′ (thrē′bās′), *Baseball.* a base hit that enables a batter to reach third base safely. Also called **triple.**

three-col·or (thrē′kul′ər), *adj.* **1.** having or characterized by the use of three colors. **2.** noting or pertaining to a photomechanical process for making reproductions of paintings, artwork, etc., usually by making three printing plates, each corresponding to a primary color, by the halftone process, and printing superimposed impressions from these plates in three correspondingly colored inks.

three-cor·nered (thrē′kôr′nərd), *adj.* **1.** having three corners: *a three-cornered hat.* **2.** pertaining to or involving three persons, parties, or things: *The candidates deadlocked in a three-cornered tie.* [ME *thre cornerid.* See THREE, CORNERED]

Three′-cornered Hat′, The, **1.** a novel (1874) by Pedro Antonio de Alarcón. Spanish, **El Sombrero de Tres Picos. 2.** a ballet (1919) by de Falla.

3-D (thrē′dē′), *adj. Informal.* **1.** of, pertaining to, or representing something in three dimensions; three-dimensional: *3-D movies.* —*n.* **2.** a three-dimensional form or appearance: *My dreams are always in 3-D.*

three-deck·er (thrē′dek′ər), *n.* **1.** any ship having three decks, tiers, etc. **2.** (formerly) one of a class of sailing warships that carried guns on three decks. **3.** a sandwich made of three slices of bread interlaid with two layers of filling. **4.** something having three layers, levels, or tiers. Also called **triple-decker** (for defs. 3, 4).

three-di·men·sion·al (thrē′di men′shə nəl), *adj.* **1.** having, or seeming to have, the dimension of depth as well as width and height. **2.** (in a literary work) fully developed: *The story came alive chiefly because the characters were vividly three-dimensional.* —**three′-di·men′sion·al′i·ty,** *n.*

Three′ Fires′, *Buddhism.* the three causes of suffering, or dukkha, given as hate, greed or restlessness, and dullness of mind: they are extinguished in Nirvana.

three-fold (thrē′fōld′), *n.* a unit of stage scenery consisting of three flats hinged together.

three·fold (thrē′fōld′), *adj.* **1.** comprising three parts, members, or aspects; triple: *a threefold program.* **2.** three times as great or as much; treble: *a threefold return on an investment.* —*adv.* **3.** in threefold manner or measure; trebly. [ME *threfold,* OE *thrifeald.* See THREE, -FOLD]

three′fold block′. See **treble block.**

three′fold pur′chase, a tackle composed of a fall rove through two treble blocks so as to give a mechanical advantage of six or seven, neglecting friction, depending on whether hauling is done on the running or the standing block.

three′-four′ time′ (thrē′fôr′, -fōr′). See **three-quarter time.**

three-gait·ed (thrē′gā′tid), *adj. Manège.* noting a horse trained to walk, trot, and canter, as for pleasure riding and showing. Cf. **five-gaited.**

three′-is′land ship′ (thrē′ī′lənd), a freight ship having a forecastle, midship house, and poop.

three-leg·ged (thrē′leg′id, -legd′), *adj.* **1.** *Informal.* (of a schooner) having three masts. **2.** having three legs: *a three-legged stool.*

three′-legged race′, a race between a number of paired contestants, each contestant having one leg tied to the adjacent leg of his partner.

Three′ Lives′, a group of three character studies (1909) by Gertrude Stein, consisting of *The Good Anna, Melanctha,* and *The Gentle Lena.*

three-mast·ed (thrē′mas′tid, -mä′stid), *adj. Naut.* having three masts.

three-mast·er (thrē′mas′tər, -mä′stər), *n. Naut.* a sailing ship with three masts.

three′-mile lim′it (thrē′mīl′), *Internat. Law.* the limit of the marine belt of three miles which is included within the jurisdiction of the state possessing the coast.

Three′ Musketeers′, The, a historical novel (1844) by Alexandre Dumas père. French, **Les Trois Mousquetaires.**

three′ of a kind′, *Poker.* a set of three cards of the same denomination.

three old cat (thrē′ ə kat′), three-a-cat. Also, **three′ o' cat′.**

three′-part time′ (thrē′pärt′), *Music.* See **triple time.**

three·pence (thrip′əns, threp′-, thrup′-; thrē′pens′), *n.* **1.** (*construed as sing. or pl.*) *Brit.* a sum of three pennies. **2.** a cupronickel coin of the United Kingdom, a quarter of a shilling, equal to three pennies and equivalent to .035 of a U.S. dollar. Also, **thrippence, thruppence.** [THREE + PENCE]

three·pen·ny (thrip′ə nē, threp′-, thrup′-; thrē′pen′ē), *adj.* **1.** of the amount or value of threepence. **2.** of little worth. **3.** *Carpentry.* **a.** noting a nail 1¼ inches long. **b.** noting a fine nail 1⅛ inches long. *Abbr.:* 3d [THREE + PENNY]

Three′pen·ny Op′era, The (thrē′pen′ē), a comic opera (1928) by Kurt Weill. German, **Die Dreigroschenoper.**

three-phase (thrē′fāz′), *adj. Elect.* **1.** noting or pertaining to a circuit, system, or device which is energized by three electromotive forces which differ in phase by one third of a cycle or 120°. **2.** having three phases.

three-piece (thrē′pēs′), *adj.* **1.** *Clothing.* consisting of three matching or harmonious pieces, as an ensemble of coat, skirt, and blouse for a woman or a suit of a jacket, vest, and pair of trousers for a man. **2.** having three parts. —*n.* **3.** a three-piece ensemble or suit. Cf. **coordinate** (def. 6).

three-ply (thrē′plī′), *adj.* consisting of three thicknesses, laminations, strands, or the like.

three′-point land′ing (thrē′point′), *Aeron.* an aircraft landing in which the two wheels of the main landing gear and the tail or nose wheel touch the ground simultaneously.

three-post·er (thrē′pō′stər), *n.* a three-masted sailing vessel.

three-quar·ter (thrē′kwôr′tər), *adj.* **1.** consisting of or involving three quarters of a whole or of the usual length: *three-quarter portrait; a blouse with a three-quarter sleeve.* **2.** (of the face) midway between the full-faced view and profile: *a three-quarter view.* Also, **three-quar·ters** (thrē′kwôr′tərz).

three′-quar′ter ar′mor, plate armor that leaves the legs exposed below the knees.

three′-quar′ter bind′ing, *Bookbinding.* a binding in which the material used for the back extends further over the covers than in half binding.

three′-quar′ter nel′son, *Wrestling.* a hold in which a wrestler, from a kneeling position behind his prone opponent, applies a half nelson with one arm, passes the other arm under the opponent's body on the near side, and locks the arms at the fingers or wrist on the back of the opponent's neck. Cf. **nelson.**

three′-quar′ter time′, *Music.* the meter of a musical composition having a time signature of ¾ and three quarter notes or their equivalents in each measure. Also called **three-four time, waltz time.**

three′-quar′ter turn′ stair′, a staircase requiring a three-quarter turn at each landing for continued ascent or descent.

three′-ring cir′cus (thrē′ring′), **1.** a circus having three adjacent rings in which performances take place simultaneously. **2.** something spectacular, tumultuous, entertaining, or full of confused action: *Our family reunions are always three-ring circuses.* Also, **three′-ringed′ cir′cus.**

Three′ Riv′ers, 1. a city in S Quebec, in SE Canada, on the St. Lawrence. 53,477 (1961). French, **Trois-Rivières. 2.** a town in SW Michigan. 7092 (1960). **3.** a town in S Massachusetts. 3082 (1960).

three R's, 1. reading, 'riting, and 'rithmetic, regarded as the fundamentals of education. **2.** the fundamentals, basic knowledge, or skills of any system or field: *the three R's of good government.*

three·score (thrē′skōr′, -skôr′), *adj.* being or containing three times twenty; sixty. [ME *thre scoor.* See THREE, SCORE]

Three′ Signs′ of Be′ing, *Buddhism.* the three characteristics of every living thing, which are anicca, or impermanence, dukkha, or suffering, and anatta, or the absence of a personal and immortal soul.

Three′ Sis′ters, a play (1901) by Anton Chekhov.

three·some (thrē′səm), *adj.* **1.** consisting of three; threefold. **2.** performed or played by three persons. —*n.* **3.** three forming a group. **4.** something in which three persons participate, as certain games. **5.** *Golf.* a match in which one contestant, playing his own ball, competes against two opponents who play, alternately, with one ball. [ME *thresum.* See THREE, -SOME[2]]

three-spot (thrē′spot′), *n.* a playing card, upward face of a die, or a domino half bearing three pips.

three-square (thrē′skwâr′), *adj.* having an equilateral triangular cross section, as certain files. [late ME *thre square.* See THREE, SQUARE]

three-stick·er (thrē′stik′ər), *n.* *Informal.* a sailing vessel having three masts.

three′-thorned aca′cia (thrē′thôrnd′). See **honey locust** (def. 1).

three′-toed wood′pecker (thrē′tōd′), **1.** either of two woodpeckers of the genus *Picoïdes,* of the Northern Hemisphere, having only three toes on each foot. **2.** any of various similar, tropical, Old World woodpeckers.

three′-toothed cinque′foil (thrē′tōōtht′, -tōōthd′), an herbaceous perennial, *Potentilla tridentata,* of eastern North America, having three leaflets, dark shiny green on the upper side, with three teeth, and small, white flowers in loose clusters.

three′ u′nities, the. See under **unity** (def. 9).

three′-way bulb′ (thrē′wā′), a light bulb that can be switched to three successive degrees of illumination.

three-wheel·er (thrē′hwē′lər, -wē′-), *n.* a vehicle equipped with three wheels, as a tricycle, a motorcycle with a sidecar, and some small, experimental, or early-model cars.

threm·ma·tol·o·gy (threm′ə tol′ə jē), *n.* *Biol.* the science of breeding or propagating animals and plants under domestication. [< Gk *thremmato-* (comb. form of *thrémma* nursling) + -LOGY]

thre·node (thrē′nōd, thren′ōd), *n.* threnody. [< Gk *thrên(os)* dirge + -ODE[1]]

thren·o·dy (thren′ə dē), *n., pl.* **-dies.** a poem, speech, or song of lamentation, esp. for the dead; dirge; funeral song. [< Gk *thrēnōidía* < *thrên(os)* dirge + *-ōid(ē)* song (see ODE) + *-ia* -Y[3]] —**thre·no·di·al** (thri nō′dē əl), **thre·nod·ic** (thri nod′ik), *adj.* —**thren·o·dist** (thren′ə-dist), *n.*

thre·o·nine (thrē′ə nēn′, -nin), *n.* *Biochem.* an essential amino acid, $CH_3CHOHCH(NH_2)COOH$, obtained by the hydrolysis of proteins. [*threon-* (alter. of Gk *erythrôn,* neut. of *erythrós* red; see ERYTHRO-) + -INE[2]]

thresh (thresh), *v.t.* **1.** to separate the grain or seeds from (a cereal plant or the like) by some mechanical means, as by beating with a flail or by the action of a threshing machine. **2.** to beat as if with a flail. —*v.i.* **3.** to thresh wheat, grain, etc. **4.** to deliver blows as if with a flail. **5. thresh out or over,** to talk over thoroughly and vigorously in order to reach a decision, conclusion, or understanding: discuss exhaustively: *They were threshing out their problems until far into the night.* —*n.* **6.** the act of threshing. Also, **thrash.** [ME *thresche(n),* OE *threscan;* c. G *dreschen,* Goth *thriskan;* akin to Icel *thriskja,* D *dorsen*]

thresh·er (thresh′ər), *n.* **1.** one who or that which threshes. **2.** one who separates grain or seeds from wheat, rye, etc., by beating with a flail or operating a threshing machine. **3.** Also, **thrasher.** Also called **thresh′er shark′,** a large shark of the genus *Alopias,* esp. *A. vulpinus,* which threshes the water with its long tail to drive together the small fish on which it feeds. [ME *thressher.* See THRESH, -ER[1]]

thresh′ing machine′, *Agric.* a machine for removing the grains and seeds from straw and chaff.

thresh·old (thresh′ōld, thresh′hōld), *n.* **1.** the sill of a doorway. **2.** the entrance to a house or building. **3.** any place or point of entering or beginning: *the threshold of a new career.* **4.** Also called **limen.** *Psychol., Physiol.* the point at which a stimulus is of sufficient intensity to begin to produce an effect: *the threshold of consciousness; threshold of pain.* [ME *threschold,* OE *threscold, threscwald;* c. Icel *threskǫldr,* dial. Sw *träskvald;* akin to THRESH in old sense trample, tread; *-old, -wald* unexplained]

threw (thrōō), *v.* a pt. of **throw.**

Thri·ae (thrī′ī), *n. pl.* *Class. Myth.* three nymphs of Parnassus who nursed the infant Apollo and taught Hermes to foretell the future.

Thri·am·bus (thrī am′bəs), *n.* *Class. Myth.* an epithet of Dionysus.

thrice (thrīs), *adv.* **1.** three times, as in succession; on three occasions, or in three ways. **2.** in threefold quantity or degree. **3.** very; greatly; extremely. [ME *thries* < obs. *thrie* thrice (OE *thrīga*) + *-s* -S[1]]

thrift (thrift), *n.* **1.** economical management; economy; frugality. **2.** Also called **sea pink.** any alpine and maritime, plumbaginaceous plant of the genus *Armeria,* having pink or white flowers, esp. *A. maritima,* noted for its vigorous growth. **3.** any of various allied plants. **4.** vigorous growth, as of a plant. **5.** *Obs.* prosperity. [ME < Scand; cf. Icel *thrift* prosperity. See THRIVE]

thrift·less (thrift′lis), *adj.* **1.** without thrift; improvident; wasteful. **2.** *Archaic.* useless or pointless. [ME: unsuccessful. See THRIFT, -LESS] —**thrift′less·ly,** *adv.* —**thrift′less·ness,** *n.*

thrift·shop (thrift′shop′), *n.* a retail store that sells second-hand goods at reduced prices. [THRIFT + SHOP]

thrift·y (thrif′tē), *adj.,* **thrift·i·er, thrift·i·est. 1.** practicing thrift or economical management; frugal: *a thrifty housewife.* **2.** thriving, prosperous, or successful. **3.** thriving physically; growing vigorously. [ME; see THRIFT, -Y[1]] —**thrift′i·ly,** *adv.* —**thrift′i·ness,** *n.*
—**Syn. 1.** sparing, saving. See **economical. 3.** flourishing. —**Ant. 1.** wasteful.

thrill (thril), *v.t.* **1.** to affect with a sudden wave of keen emotion or excitement, as to produce a tremor or tingling sensation through the body. **2.** to cause to vibrate or quiver: *The harpist thrilled the strings.* **3.** to utter or send forth tremulously, as a melody. —*v.i.* **4.** to affect one with a wave of emotion or excitement; produce a thrill. **5.** to be stirred by a tremor or tingling sensation of emotion or excitement: *He thrilled at the thought of home.* **6.** to move tremulously; vibrate; quiver. —*n.* **7.** a tremor or tingling sensation passing through the body as the result of sudden keen emotion or excitement: *A thrill ran down his spine.* **8.** that which produces or is capable of producing such a sensation: *a story full of thrills.* **9.** an experience containing such a sensation; a thrilling experience: *It was a thrill to see Paris again.* **10.** a vibration or quivering. **11.** *Pathol.* an abnormal tremor or vibration, as in the respiratory system. [ME; metathetic var. of THIRL] —**thrill′ful,** *adj.*

thrill·er (thril′ər), *n.* **1.** one who or that which thrills. **2.** *Informal.* an exciting, suspenseful play or story, esp. a mystery story. [THRILL + -ER[1]]

thrill·ing (thril′ing), *adj.* **1.** producing sudden, strong, and deep emotion or excitement. **2.** producing a tremor, as by chilling. **3.** vibrating; trembling; quivering. [THRILL + -ING[2]] —**thrill′ing·ly,** *adv.*

thrip·pence (thrip′əns), *n.* threepence.

thrips (thrips), *n., pl.* **thrips.** any of several minute insects of the order *Thysanoptera,* that have long, narrow wings fringed with hairs and that infest and feed on a wide variety of plants. [< NL < Gk: woodworm < *thrip-* (? c. DRIVE) + *-s* nom. sing. ending]

thrive (thrīv), *v.i.,* **throve** or **thrived, thrived** or **thriv·en** (thriv′ən), **thriv·ing. 1.** to prosper; be fortunate or successful; increase in property or wealth; grow richer or rich. **2.** to grow or develop vigorously; flourish: *The children thrived in the country.* [ME *thrive(n)* < Scand; cf. Icel *thrīfask* to thrive, reflexive of *thrīfa* to grasp] —**thriv′er,** *n.* —**thriv′ing·ly,** *adv.*
—**Syn. 1.** advance. See **succeed.** —**Ant. 1, 2.** languish.

thro (thrōō), *prep.* *Archaic.* through. Also, **thro′.**

throat (thrōt), *n.* **1.** the passage from the mouth to the stomach or to the lungs, including the fauces, pharynx, esophagus, larynx, and trachea. **2.** some analogous or similar narrowed part or passage. **3.** the front of the neck below the chin and above the collarbones. **4.** the narrow opening between a fireplace and its flue or smoke chamber, often closed by a damper. **5.** *Naut., Mach.* swallow[1] (def. 11). **6.** *Naut.* **a.** Also called **nock.** the forward upper corner of a quadrilateral fore-and-aft sail. **b.** jaw[1] (def. 6). **7.** the forward edge of the opening in the vamp of a shoe. **8.** *Welding.* the distance from the exterior surface of a fillet weld to the angle at which the surfaces joined by the weld meet. **9. cut one's own throat,** to bring about one's own ruin: *He cut his own throat by being nasty to the boss.* **10. cut someone's throat,** to ruin someone, esp. financially, by competing unfairly: *You'll cut his throat if you move into his territory.* **11. jump down someone's throat,** *Slang.* to give someone a scolding; berate: *Wait and let me finish before you jump down my throat.* **12. lump in one's throat,** a tight or uncomfortable feeling in the throat, as a reaction to an emotion: *The sight of the infant brought a lump to her throat.* **13. ram (something) down someone's throat,** *Informal.* to force someone to agree to or accept something: *I'll think about it for a few days, so don't try to ram it down my throat.* **14. stick in one's throat,** to be difficult of expression; cause to hesitate: *The words of sympathy stuck in her throat.* Also, **stick in one's craw.** —*v.t.* **15.** to make a throat in; provide with a throat. **16.** to utter or express from or as from the throat; utter throatily. [ME, OE *throte,* OE *throta, throtu;* akin to OHG *drozza* throat, Icel *throti* swelling. See THROTTLE] —**throat′less,** *adj.*

throat·latch (thrōt′lach′), *n.* a strap that passes under a horse's throat and helps to hold a bridle or halter in place. See illus. under **harness.** [THROAT + LATCH]

throat′ mi′crophone, a microphone worn around the throat and actuated by vibrations of the larynx, used when background noise would obscure the sound of speech, as in an airplane cockpit.

throat′ seiz′ing. See **cuckold's knot.**

throat′ sweet′bread, sweetbread (def. 2).

throat·y (thrō′tē), *adj.,* **throat·i·er, throat·i·est.** produced or modified in the throat, as sounds; guttural, husky, or hoarse. [THROAT + -Y[1]] —**throat′i·ly,** *adv.* —**throat′i·ness,** *n.*

throb (throb), *v.,* **throbbed, throb·bing,** *n.* —*v.i.* **1.** to beat with increased force or rapidity, as the heart under the influence of emotion or excitement; palpitate. **2.** to feel or exhibit emotion: *He throbbed at the happy thought.* **3.** to pulsate; vibrate: *The cello throbbed.* —*n.* **4.** the act of throbbing. **5.** a violent beat or pulsation, as of the heart. **6.** any pulsation or vibration: *the throb of the engines.* [ME *throbbant* (adj.) throbbing < ?] —**throb′-ber,** *n.* —**throb′bing·ly,** *adv.* —**throb′less,** *adj.*
—**Syn. 3.** See **pulsate.**

throe (thrō), *n.* **1.** a violent spasm or pang; paroxysm. **2.** a sharp attack of emotion. **3. throes, a.** any violent convulsion or struggle: *the throes of battle.* **b.** the agony of death. **c.** the pains of childbirth. [ME *throwe,* alter. of *thrawe* (*-o-* from OE *thrōwian* to suffer, be in pain), OE *thrawu;* c. Icel *thrā* (in *līkthrā* leprosy); akin to Ir *trū* wretch]

throm·bec·to·my (throm bek′tə mē), *n., pl.* **-mies.** *Surg.* removal of a blood clot from a blood vessel. [THROMB- + -ECTOMY]

throm·bin (throm′bin), *n.* *Biochem.* the substance or ferment that causes the coagulation of blood. [THROMB(US) + -IN[2]]

thrombo-, a learned borrowing from Greek meaning "clot (of blood)," used in the formation of compound words: *thrombocyte.* Also, *esp. before a vowel,* **thromb-.** [< Gk, comb. form of *thrómbos* clot, lump]

throm·boc·la·sis (throm bok′lə sis), *n.* *Med.* thrombolysis. [THROMBO- + Gk *klásis* fracture] —**throm·bo·clas·tic** (throm′bə klas′tik), *adj.*

throm·bo·cyte (throm′bə sīt′), *n.* *Anat.* one of the minute, nucleate cells which aid coagulation in the blood of those vertebrates that do not have blood platelets. [THROMBO- + -CYTE] —**throm·bo·cyt·ic** (throm′bə-sit′ik), *adj.*

throm·bo·gen (throm′bə jen′), *n.* *Biochem.* prothrombin. [THROMBO- + -GEN]

throm·bo·ki·nase (throm′bō kī′nās, -kin′ās), *n.* *Biochem.* thromboplastin. [THROMBO- + KINASE]

Throm·bo·ly·sin (throm′bō lī′sin), *n.* *Pharm., Trademark.* fibrinolysin (def. 2).

throm·bol·y·sis (throm bol′i sis), *n.* *Med.* the dissolving or breaking up of a thrombus. Also called **thromboclasis.** [THROMBO- + -LYSIS] —**throm·bo·lyt·ic** (throm′bə lit′ik), *adj.*

throm·bo·phle·bi·tis (throm′bō fli bī′tis), *n.* *Pathol.* the presence of a thrombus in a vein accompanied by irritation of the vessel wall. Cf. **phlebothrombosis.** [< NL; see THROMBO-, PHLEBITIS]

throm·bo·plas·tic (throm′bə plas′tik), *adj.* *Biochem.* causing or accelerating blood-clot formation. [THROMBO- + -PLASTIC] —**throm′bo·plas′ti·cal·ly,** *adv.*

throm·bo·plas·tin (throm′bə plas′tin), *n.* **1.** *Biochem.* any of the class of lipoproteins, containing cephalin or other phospholipids, that are found in most animal tissue, esp. in the blood platelets, and that serve to convert prothrombin to thrombin in the presence of calcium ions. **2.** *Pharm.* a commercial form of this substance, obtained from the brains of cattle, used chiefly as a local hemostatic and as a laboratory reagent in blood prothrombin tests. Also called **thrombokinase.** [THROMBO- + -PLAST + -IN[2]]

throm·bo·sis (throm bō′sis), *n.* *Pathol.* intravascular coagulation of the blood in any part of the circulatory system, as in the heart, arteries, veins, or capillaries. [< NL < Gk: a curdling. See THROMB-, -OSIS] —**throm·bot·ic** (throm bot′ik), *adj.*

throm·bus (throm′bəs), *n., pl.* **-bi** (-bī). *Pathol.* a fibrinous clot that forms in and obstructs a blood vessel, or that forms in one of the chambers of the heart. [< NL < Gk *thrómbos* clot, lump]

throne (thrōn), *n., v.,* **throned, thron·ing.** —*n.* **1.** the chair or seat occupied by a sovereign, bishop, or other exalted personage on ceremonial occasions, usually raised on a dais and covered with a canopy. **2.** the office or dignity of a sovereign: *He came to the throne by succession.* **3.** the occupant of a throne; sovereign. **4.** sovereign power or authority: *to address one's pleas to the throne.* **5.** an episcopal office or authority: *the diocesan throne.* **6.** See **mercy seat** (def. 2). **7. thrones,** an order of angels. Cf. **angel** (def. 1). **8.** *Navig.* a lug for supporting an astrolabe. —*v.t., v.i.* **9.** to sit on or as on a throne. [ME < L *thron(us)* < Gk *thrónos* high seat; r. ME *trone* < OF] —**throne′less,** *adj.*

throne′ room′, **1.** a chamber, usually containing a throne, used by a sovereign for audiences. **2.** the location of actual power or authority, as in a particular government or business organization.

throng (thrông, throng), *n.* **1.** a multitude of people crowded or assembled together; a crowd. **2.** a great number of things crowded or considered together: *a throng of memories.* **3.** *Chiefly Scot.* pressure, as of work. —*v.i.* **4.** to assemble, collect, or go in large numbers; crowd. —*v.t.* **5.** to crowd or press upon; jostle. **6.** to fill or occupy with or as with a crowd: *He thronged the picture with stars.* **7.** to bring or drive together into or as into a crowd, heap, or collection. **8.** to fill by crowding or pressing into: *They thronged the small room.* —*adj.* *Scot. and North Eng.* **9.** filled with people or objects; crowded. **10.** (of time) filled with things to do; busy. [ME; OE *gethrang;* c. D *drang,* G *Drang* pressure, Icel *thrōng* throng; akin to obs. *thring* to press]
—**Syn. 1.** horde, host; assemblage. See **crowd.**

thro·nos (thrō′nos), *n., pl.* **-noi** (-noi). an ancient Greek chair, usually highly ornamented, having a high seat and back and rectangular turned or carved legs ending in animal feet. [< Gk; see THRONE]

Throop (trōōp), *n.* a town in NE Pennsylvania. 4732 (1960).

thros·tle (thros′əl), *n.* **1.** *Brit., Chiefly Literary.* the song thrush. **2.** a machine for spinning wool, cotton, etc., in which the twisting and winding are simultaneous and continuous. [ME, OE; c. D *drossel,* G *Drossel;* akin to Icel *thrōstr,* L *turdus* thrush]

throt·tle (throt′əl), *n., v.,* **-tled, -tling.** —*n.* **1.** a lever, pedal, handle, etc., for controlling or manipulating a

throttle valve. **2.** See **throttle valve. 3.** the throat, gullet, or windpipe, as of a horse. [prob. dim. of ME *throte* THROAT; cf. G *Drossel*]
—*v.t.* **4.** to stop the breath of by compressing the throat; strangle. **5.** to choke or suffocate in any way. **6.** to compress by fastening something tightly around. **7.** to silence or check as if by choking: *His message was throttled by censorship.* **8.** *Mach.* **a.** to obstruct or check the flow of (a fluid), as to control the speed of an engine. **b.** to reduce the pressure of (a fluid) by passing it from a smaller area to a larger one. [late ME *throtel*, freq. of *throte(n)* (to) cut the throat of (someone), strangle, deriv. of THROAT] **—throt′tler,** *n.*

Throt·tle·bot·tom (throt′ᵊl bot′əm), *n.* (*sometimes l.c.*) a harmless incompetent in public office. [named after Alexander *Throttlebottom*, character in *Of Thee I Sing* (1932), musical comedy by George S. Kaufman and Morris Ryskind]

throt′tle lev′er, throttle (def. 1).

throt′tle valve′, a valve for throttling the working fluid of an engine, refrigerator, etc.

through (thro͞o), *prep.* **1.** in at one end, side, or surface and out at the other: *to pass through a tunnel; We drove through Denver without stopping. Sun came through the window.* **2.** past: *to go through a stop sign without stopping.* **3.** from one to the other of; between or among the individual members or parts of: *to swing through the trees; This book has passed through many hands.* **4.** over the surface of, by way of, or within the limits or medium of: *to travel through a country: He flies through the air with the greatest of ease.* **5.** during the whole period of; throughout: *He worked through the night.* **6.** having reached the end of: *to be through one's work.* **7.** to and including: *from 1900 through 1950.* **8.** having finished successfully: *to get through an examination.* **9.** by the means or instrumentality of; by the way or agency of: *It was through him they found out.* **10.** by reason of or in consequence of: *to run away through fear.* **11.** in at the first step of a process, treatment, or method of handling, passing through subsequent steps or stages in order, and finished, accepted, or out of the last step or stage: *The body of a car passes through 147 stages on the production line. The new tax bill finally got through Congress.* **—***adv.* **12.** in at one end, side, or surface and out at the other: *to push a needle through; We don't live here, we're just passing through.* **13.** all the way; along the whole distance: *This train goes through to Boston.* **14.** throughout: *soaking wet through.* **15.** from the beginning to the end: *to read a letter through.* **16.** to the end: *to carry a matter through.* **17.** to a favorable or successful conclusion: *He barely managed to pull through.* **18.** having completed an action, process, relationship, etc.: *Please be still until I'm through.* **19. through and through, a.** through the whole extent of; thoroughly: *wet and cold through and through.* **b.** from beginning to end; in all respects: *an aristocrat through and through.* **20. through with, a.** finished with. **b.** at the end of all relations or dealings with: *My sister again insists that she's through with men.* **—***adj.* **21.** passing or extending from one end, side, or surface to the other. **22.** traveling, conveying, or extending through the whole of a long distance with little or no interruption: *a through train.* **23.** (of a road, route, way, course, etc. or of a ticket, routing order, etc.) admitting continuous or direct passage; having no interruption, obstruction, or hindrance: *a through highway; through ticket.* **24.** (of a bridge truss) having a deck or decks within the depth of the structure. Cf. **deck** (def. 12). [ME, metathetic var. of *thourgh*, OE *thurh*; c. G *durch*; akin to OE *therh*, Goth *thairh* through, OHG *derh* perforated, OE *thyrel* full of holes (adj.), hole (n.). See THIRL, NOSTRIL]
—Syn. 9. See **by.**

through′ bass′ (bās). See **thorough bass.**

through-com·posed (thro͞o′kəm pōzd′), *adj.* having different music for each verse: *a through-composed song.* Cf. **strophic** (def. 2).

through·ly (thro͞o′lē), *adv.* *Archaic.* thoroughly. [late ME; see THROUGH, -LY]

through-oth·er (thro͞o′uth′ər), *adj.* *Chiefly Scot.* confused. Also, **through-ith·er** (thro͞o′ith′ər).

through·out (thro͞o out′), *prep.* **1.** in or to every part of; everywhere in: *They searched throughout the house.* **2.** from the beginning to the end of: *He was bored throughout the play.* **—***adv.* **3.** in every part: *rotten throughout.* **4.** at every moment or point: *Follow my plan throughout.* **5.** from the beginning to the end: *to read a book throughout.* [ME *throw out*, OE *thurh ūt*. See THROUGH, OUT]

through·put (thro͞o′po͝ot′), *n.* the quantity or amount of raw material processed within a given time, esp. the work done by an electronic computer in a given period of time. Also, **thruput.** [n. use of v. phrase *put through*, modeled on *output*]

through′ stone′, perpend[1].

through′ street′, a street on which the traffic has the right of way over vehicles entering or crossing at intersections. Cf. **stop street.**

Through′ the Look′ing-Glass, a story for children (1871) by Lewis Carroll: the sequel to *Alice's Adventures in Wonderland.*

through·way (thro͞o′wā′), *n.* thruway.

throve (thrōv), *v.* a pt. of **thrive.**

throw (thrō), *v.,* **threw, thrown, throw·ing,** *n.* **—***v.t.* **1.** to propel or cast in any way, esp. to project or propel from the hand by a sudden forward motion or straightening of the arm and wrist: *to throw a ball.* **2.** to hurl or project (a missile), as a gun does. **3.** to project or cast (light, a shadow, etc.). **4.** to project (the voice): *He threw his voice so that all might hear.* **5.** to make it appear that one's voice is coming from a place different from its source, as in ventriloquism: *When he threw his voice we all thought someone had been locked in the trunk.* **6.** to direct or send forth (words, a glance, etc.). **7.** to put or cause to go or come into some place, position, condition, etc., as if by hurling: *to throw a man into prison; to throw a bridge across a river; to throw troops into action.* **8.** to put on, off, or away hastily: *to throw a shawl over one's shoulders.* **9.** *Mach.* **a.** to move (a lever or the like) in order to connect or disconnect parts of an apparatus or mechanism: *to throw the switch.* **b.** to connect, engage, disconnect, or disengage by such a procedure: *to throw the current.* **10.** to shape on a potter's wheel: *He threw the clay into a vase.* **11.** to exert or bring to bear (influence, resources, or power or authority of any kind): *Throw all your energy into your work. The FBI threw every available agent into the case.* **12.** to deliver a blow or punch: *He threw a hard left jab to his opponent's chin.* **13.** *Cards.* to play (a card). **14.** to cause to fall to the ground, esp. to hurl to the ground, as an opponent in wrestling. **15.** *Informal.* to lose (a game, race, or other contest) intentionally, as for a bribe. **16.** to cast (dice). **17.** to make (a cast) at dice. **18.** (of an animal, as a horse) to cause (someone) to fall off; unseat: *The horse threw his rider twice.* **19.** (of domestic animals) to bring forth (young). **20.** *Textiles.* to twist (filaments) without attenuation in the production of yarn or thread. **21.** *Informal.* to overcome with astonishment or confusion; astonish; confuse: *It was her falsetto voice on top of it all that really threw me.* **22.** *Obs.* to turn on a lathe. **—***v.i.* **23.** to cast, fling, or hurl a missile or the like. **24. throw away, a.** to dispose of; discard. **b.** to employ wastefully; squander. **c.** to fail to use; miss (a chance, opportunity, etc.): *He threw away a college education and a professional career.* **25. throw back, a.** to retard the development or advancement of: *His illness threw him back a year at school.* **b.** to force into a state of dependence. **c.** to return to; hark back. **d.** to revert to a type found in one's ancestry; manifest atavism: *Her red hair and blue eyes throw back to her great-grandmother.* **26. throw cold water on.** See **cold** (def. 18). **27. throw down the gauntlet** or **glove.** See **gauntlet**[1] (def. 4). **28. throw in,** *Informal.* **a.** to add as a bonus or gratuity: *They throw in breakfast with the room.* **b.** to bring into (a discussion, plan, etc.) as an addition; interpolate: *The chairman threw in an amusing anecdote to relieve the tension.* **c.** *Cards.* to abandon (a hand). **29. throw in the sponge.** See **sponge** (def. 12). **30. throw in the towel.** See **towel** (def. 2). **31. throw off, a.** to free oneself of; cast aside: *to throw off the yoke of slavery.* **b.** to escape from or delay, as a pursuer. **c.** to give off; discharge. **d.** to perform or produce with ease: *The entertainer threw off a few songs and jokes to begin the show.* **e.** to confuse; fluster: *Thrown off by jeers, she forgot her lines.* **32. throw oneself at (someone)** or **at (someone's head),** (of a woman) to strive to attract the interest or attention of, esp. in order to win the love or admiration of: *She throws herself at any man who will look at her.* **33. throw oneself into,** to engage in with energy or enthusiasm: *She threw herself into making costumes for her daughter's dance recital.* **34. throw oneself on** or **upon (someone),** to commit oneself to another's mercy, generosity, support, etc.; trust in: *The members of his wife's family have all thrown themselves on him.* **35. throw out, a.** to cast away; remove; discard. **b.** to bring up for consideration; propose: *The committee threw out a few suggestions.* **c.** to put out of mind; reject: *We can throw out that scheme.* **d.** *Baseball.* to cause to be out by throwing the ball to a fielder, esp. an infielder, in time to prevent a batter or runner from reaching base safely: *The shortstop backhanded the ball and threw the batter out at first.* **e.** to eject from a place; remove, esp. forcibly: *He started making a disturbance so the bartenders threw him out.* **36. throw over,** to forsake; abandon: *She threw over her first husband for a richer man.* **37. throw the bull.** See **bull**[3] (def. 2). **38. throw together, a.** to make in a hurried and haphazard manner. **b.** to cause to associate: *Many races and nationalities have been thrown together in the American melting pot.* **39. throw up, a.** to give up; relinquish. **b.** to build hastily. **c.** to vomit. **d.** to point out, as an error; criticize. **e.** (of a hawk) to fly suddenly upward.
—*n.* **40.** the act or an instance of throwing or casting; cast; fling. **41.** the distance to which anything is or may be thrown: *a stone's throw.* **42.** *Informal.* a venture or chance: *It was his last throw.* **43.** *Mach.* **a.** the distance between the center of a crankshaft and the center of the crankpins, equal to one half of the piston stroke. **b.** the distance between the center of a crankshaft and the center of an eccentric. **c.** the movement of a reciprocating part in one direction. **44.** (in a motion-picture theater) the distance between the projector and the screen. **45.** (in an auditorium or the like) the distance between a loudspeaker and the audience. **46.** length of a beam of light: *a spotlight with a throw of 500 feet.* **47.** a scarf, boa, or the like. **48.** *Theat.* **a.** the distance to which a spotlight can be projected. **b.** the area illuminated by a spotlight. **49.** a light blanket, as for use when reclining on a sofa; afghan. **50.** a cast of dice. **51.** the number thrown with a pair of dice. **52.** *Wrestling.* the act, method, or an instance of throwing an opponent. **53.** *Geol., Mining.* the amount of vertical displacement produced by a fault. [ME *throw(en)*, *thrawen*, OE *thrāwan* to twist, turn; c. D *draaien*, G *drehen* to turn, spin, twirl, whirl; akin to L *terere*, Gk *teírein* to rub away]
—Syn. 1. fling, launch, send. THROW, CAST, PITCH, TOSS imply projecting something through the air. THROW is the general word, often used with an adverb which indicates direction, destination, etc.: *to throw a rope to him, the paper away.* CAST is a formal word for THROW, archaic except as used in certain idiomatic expressions (*to cast a net, black looks; cast down;* the compound *broadcast*, etc.): *to cast off a boat.* PITCH implies throwing with some force and definite aim: *to pitch a baseball.* To TOSS is to throw lightly, as with an underhand or sidewise motion, or to move irregularly up and down or back and forth: *to toss a bone to a dog.*

throw·a·way (thrō′ə wā′), *n.* any advertisement, as a folder or a broadside, passed out on streets, slipped under doors, etc. [n. use of v. phrase *throw away*]

throw·back (thrō′bak′), *n.* **1.** an act of throwing back. **2.** a setback or check. **3.** the reversion to an ancestral or earlier type or character; atavism. **4.** an example of this. [n. use of v. phrase *throw back*]

throw·er (thrō′ər), *n.* **1.** one who or that which throws. **2.** flinger (def. 2). [late ME; see THROW, -ER[1]]

throw′ing stick′, **1.** a slinglike device used in various primitive societies for propelling a weapon, as a spear, javelin, or the like. **2.** *Australian.* boomerang.

thrown (thrōn), *v.* a pp. of **throw.**

thrown′ silk′, raw silk that has been reeled and twisted into yarn. Also called, *Brit.*, **net silk.**

throw′ rug′. See **scatter rug.**

throw·ster (thrō′stər), *n.* one who throws silk or man-made filaments. [late ME *throwestre.* See THROW, -STER]

thru (thro͞o), *prep., adv., adj.* *Informal.* through.

thrum[1] (thrum), *v.,* **thrummed, thrum·ming,** *n.* **—***v.i.* **1.** to play on a stringed instrument, as a guitar, by plucking the strings, esp. in an idle, monotonous, or unskillful manner. **2.** to sound when thrummed on, as a guitar or similar stringed instrument. **3.** to drum or tap idly with the fingers. **—***v.t.* **4.** to play (a stringed instrument, or a melody on it) by plucking the strings, esp. in an idle, monotonous, or unskillful manner. **5.** to drum or tap idly on. **6.** to recite or tell in a monotonous way. **—***n.* **7.** the act or sound of thrumming; dull, monotonous sound. [imit.] **—thrum′mer,** *n.*

thrum[2] (thrum), *n., v.,* **thrummed, thrum·ming.** **—***n.* **1.** one of the ends of the warp threads in a loom, left unwoven and remaining attached to the loom when the web is cut off. **2. thrums,** the row or fringe of such threads. **3.** any short piece of waste thread or yarn; tuft, tassel, or fringe of threads, as at the edge of a piece of cloth. **4.** Often, **thrums.** *Naut.* short bits of rope yarn used for making mats. **—***v.t.* **5.** *Naut.* to insert short pieces of rope yarn through (canvas) and thus give it a rough surface, as for wrapping about a part to prevent chafing. **6.** *Archaic.* to furnish or cover with thrums, ends of thread, or tufts. [ME *throm* end-piece, OE *-thrum* ligament; c. OHG *drum* end-piece; akin to Icel *thröm(r)* brim, edge, L *terminus*, Gk *térma* end]

thrum·my (thrum′ē), *adj.,* **-mi·er, -mi·est.** of or abounding in thrums; shaggy or tufted. [THRUM[2] + -Y[1]]

thrump (thrump), *n.* a thumping, rumbling sound, usually repetitive: *the thrump of artillery echoing through the valley.* [imit.]

thrup·pence (thrup′əns), *n.* threepence.

thru·put (thro͞o′po͝ot′), *n.* throughput.

thrush[1] (thrush), *n.* **1.** any of numerous, cosmopolitan, passerine birds of the family *Turdidae*, many species of which are noted as songbirds. **2.** any of various unrelated, superficially similar birds, as the water thrushes. **3.** *Slang.* a female professional singer, esp. of popular songs. [ME *thrusche*, OE *thrysce*; c. OHG *drosca*] **—thrush′like′,** *adj.*

Wood thrush, *Hylocichla mustelina* (Length 8 in.)

thrush[2] (thrush), *n.* **1.** *Pathol.* a disease, esp. in children, characterized by whitish spots and ulcers on the membranes of the mouth, fauces, etc., caused by a parasitic fungus, *Candida albicans.* **2.** (in horses) a diseased condition of the frog of the foot. [akin to Dan *trøske*, Sw *torsk*]

thrust (thrust), *v.,* **thrust, thrust·ing,** *n.* **—***v.t.* **1.** to push forcibly; shove; put or drive with force: *He thrust his way through the crowd. She thrust a dagger into his back.* **2.** to impose acceptance of; put boldly into some position, condition, etc.: *to thrust oneself into a conversation between others; to thrust a dollar into the waiter's hand.* **3.** to stab or pierce, as with a sword: *She thrust his back with a dagger.* **4.** to extend; present: *He thrust his fist in front of my face.* **—***v.i.* **5.** to push against something. **6.** to push or force one's way, as against obstacles or through a crowd. **7.** to make a thrust, lunge, or stab at something. **—***n.* **8.** the act or an instance of thrusting; a forcible push or drive; lunge or stab. **9.** *Mach.* a linear reactive force exerted by a propeller, propulsive gases, etc., to propel a vessel, aircraft, etc. **10.** *Geol.* a compressive strain in the crust of the earth, which, in its most characteristic development, produces reversed or thrust faults. **11.** *Mech.* a pushing force or pressure exerted by a thing or a part against a contiguous one. **12.** *Archit.* the downward and outward force exerted by an arch on each side. **13.** an organized military attack; assault; offensive. [ME *thrust(en)*, *thrysten* < Scand; cf. Icel *thrȳsta* to thrust]
—Syn. 6. shove.

thrust′ augmenta′tion, *Rocketry.* an increase in the thrust of a jet or rocket engine, as by afterburning or reheating.

thrust′ bear′ing, *Mach.* a bearing designed to absorb thrusts parallel to the axis of revolution.

thrust′ coeffi′cient, *Rocketry.* the ratio of the thrust of a rocket engine, operating under given conditions, to the product of the mean pressure in the combustion chamber and the cross-sectional area of the throat of the nozzle.

thrust′ deduc′tion, *Naut.* a decrease in the effective thrust of a propeller caused by the movement aft of water past the run of the hull.

thrust·er (thrus′tər), *n.* **1.** one who or that which thrusts. **2.** *Fox Hunting.* a bold rider who keeps in the front of the field, following hounds in the most direct way. [THRUST + -ER[1]]

thrust′ fault′, *Geol.* a fault along an inclined plane in which the side or hanging wall appears to have moved upward with respect to the lower side or footwall (contrasted with *gravity fault*).

thru·way (thro͞o′wā′), *n.* a limited-access toll highway providing a means of direct transportation between distant areas for high-speed automobile traffic. Also, **throughway.** [THRU + WAY]

Thrym (thrym), *n.* *Scand. Myth.* a giant who, having demanded Freya in return for the stolen hammer of Thor, was killed by Thor, who came disguised as Freya.

thrym·sa (thrim′zə, -sə), *n.* an Anglo-Saxon gold coin of the 7th century. [OE (gen. pl.), alter. of *trymesa* (by influence of *thrie* three), gen. pl. of *trymes* < LL *tremis* a coin < L *trē(s)* three + *-mis*, as in *semis*]

Thu·cyd·i·des (tho͞o sid′i dēz′), *n.* c460–c400 B.C., Greek historian.

thud (thud), *n., v.,* **thud·ded, thud·ding.** **—***n.* **1.** a dull sound, as of a heavy blow or fall. **2.** a blow causing such a sound. **—***v.t., v.i.* **3.** to beat or strike with a dull sound of heavy impact. [ME *thudd(en)*, OE *thyddan* to strike, press] **—thud′ding·ly,** *adv.*

thug (thug), *n.* **1.** a cruel or vicious ruffian, robber, or murderer. **2.** (*sometimes cap.*) one of a former group of professional robbers and murderers in India, who strangled their victims. [< Hindi *thag,* lit., rogue, cheat] —**thug·ger·y** (thug′ə rē), *n.* —**thug′gish,** *adj.*

thug·gee (thug′ē), *n.* (*sometimes cap.*) (in India) robbery and strangulation committed by thugs. [< Hindi *thagī*]

thu·ja (tho͞o′jə), *n.* **1.** any tree of the genus *Thuja,* comprising the arborvitaes. **2.** the wood of the sandarac tree. Also, **thuya.** [< NL, ML *thuia,* for MGk *thyía,* mistake for Gk *thýa* kind of African tree]

Thu·le (tho͞o′lē *for 1, 2;* tyo͞o′lē *for 3*), *n.* **1.** the ancient Greek and Latin name for an island or region variously identified as one of the Shetland Islands, Iceland, Norway, etc.: supposed to be the most northerly region of the world. **2.** See **ultima Thule. 3.** a settlement in NW Greenland: site of U.S. air base. 603 (1962). [< L < Gk *Thoúlē;* r. ME, OE *Tyle* < L *Thȳlē* < Gk]

Thu·le (to͞o′lē), *adj.* of or pertaining to an Eskimo culture flourishing from A.D. 500–1400, and extending throughout the Arctic from Greenland to Alaska. [named after THULE, Greenland]

thu·li·a (tho͞o′lē ə), *n. Chem.* a dense, greenish-white powder, TmO_3, that on gentle heating exhibits a reddish incandescence. Also called **thu′lium ox′ide.** [< NL, L *Thūl(ē)* THULE + *-ia* -IA]

thu·li·um (tho͞o′lē əm), *n. Chem.* a rare-earth metallic element found in the minerals euxenite, gadolinite, etc. *Symbol:* Tm; *at. wt.:* 168.934; *at. no.:* 69; *sp. gr.:* 9.32. [< NL < *thūl-* (see THULE) + *-ium* -IUM]

thumb (thum), *n.* **1.** the short, thick, inner digit of the hand in man, next to the forefinger. **2.** the corresponding digit in other animals; pollex. **3.** the part of a glove or mitten for containing this digit. **4.** *Archit.* an ovolo or echinus molding. **5. all thumbs,** awkward; clumsy; bungling: *She knocked over three vases and seems to be all thumbs.* **6. thumbs down,** a gesture or expression of dissent or disapproval: *We turned thumbs down to that suggestion.* **7. thumbs up,** a gesture or expression of assent or approval. **8. under one's thumb,** under the power or influence of; subordinate to. Also, **under the thumb of.** —*v.t.* **9.** to soil or wear with the thumbs in handling, as the pages of a book. **10.** to glance through (the pages of a book, leaflet, etc.) quickly. **11.** to play (a guitar or other instrument) with or as with the thumbs. **12.** (of a hitchhiker) to solicit or get (a ride) by pointing the thumb in the desired direction of travel. **13. thumb one's nose,** to put one's thumb to one's nose and extend the fingers, as a crudely defiant or contemptuous gesture. [ME; OE *thūma;* c. D *duim,* OS, OHG *dūmo* (G *Daumen*), OSw *thumi;* akin to L *tumēre* to swell. See TUMOR] —**thumb′less,** *adj.* —**thumb′like′,** *adj.*

thumb·er (thum′ər), *n. Informal.* a hitchhiker. [THUMB + -ER[1]]

thumb′ glass′, a drinking glass having external indentations to allow it to be firmly grasped.

thumb′ in′dex, a series of labeled notches cut along the fore edge of a book, to indicate the divisions or sections.

thumb-in·dex (thum′in′deks), *v.t.* to provide (a book) with a thumb index.

thumb·kin (thum′kin), *n.* an instrument of torture for the thumbs; thumbscrew. Also, **thumb·i·kin** (thum′ə kin), **thumb′i·kins.** [THUMB + -KIN]

thumb·nail (thum′nāl′), *n.* **1.** the nail of the thumb. **2.** anything quite small or brief, as a drawing, a short essay, etc. **3.** *Print.* a small, rough dummy. **4.** Also called **porkchop.** *Journ., Print.* a half-column portrait in a newspaper. —*adj.* **5.** quite small or brief; concise: *a thumbnail description of Corsica.* —*v.t.* **6.** to make a thumbnail sketch or description of. [THUMB + NAIL]

thumb·piece (thum′pēs′), *n.* a lever over the hinge on the lid of a tankard, pressed by the thumb to raise the lid. Also called **billet.** [THUMB + PIECE]

thumb·screw (thum′skro͞o′), *n.* **1.** a screw, the head of which is so constructed that it may be turned easily with the thumb and a finger. **2.** Often, **thumbscrews.** an old instrument of torture by which one or both thumbs were compressed. [THUMB + SCREW]

thumbs-down (thumz′doun′), *n. Informal.* an act or instance of dissent, disapproval, or the like. Cf. **thumb** (def. 6).

thumb·stall (thum′stôl′), *n.* a protective sheath of rubber, leather, or the like, for the thumb. [THUMB + STALL[1]]

thumb-suck·er (thum′suk′ər), *n.* one who habitually sucks his thumb. —**thumb′-suck′ing,** *n.*

thumb·tack (thum′tak′), *n.* **1.** a tack with a large, flat head, designed to be thrust into a board or other fairly soft object by the pressure of the thumb. —*v.t.* **2.** to attach or tack by means of a thumbtack. [THUMB + TACK[1]]

thump (thump), *n.* **1.** a blow with something thick and heavy, producing a dull sound; a heavy knock. **2.** the sound made by such a blow. —*v.t.* **3.** to strike or beat with something thick and heavy, so as to produce a dull sound; pound. **4.** (of an object) to strike against (something) heavily and noisily. **5.** *Informal.* to thrash severely. —*v.i.* **6.** to strike, beat, or fall heavily, with a dull sound. **7.** to walk with heavy steps; pound. **8.** to palpitate or beat violently, as the heart. [imit.] —**thump′er,** *n.*

thump·ing (thum′ping), *adj.* **1.** of, like, or pertaining to a thump. **2.** *Informal.* very large; strikingly great, immense, or exceptional: *a thumping victory at the polls.* [THUMP + -ING[2]] —**thump′ing·ly,** *adv.*

Thun (to͞on), *n.* **1.** a city in central Switzerland, on the Aar River, near the Lake of Thun. 26,700 (est. 1959). **2. Lake of.** German, **Thuner See.** a lake in central Switzerland, formed by a widening in the course of the Aar River. 10 mi. long.

thun·der (thun′dər), *n.* **1.** a loud, explosive, resounding noise produced by the explosive expansion of air heated by a lightning discharge. **2.** *Archaic.* a thunderbolt. **3.** any loud, resounding noise: *the thunder of applause.* **4.** a threatening or startling utterance, denunciation, or the like. **5. steal someone's thunder, a.** to use for one's own purposes and without the knowledge or permission of the originator the inventions or ideas of another. **b.** to destroy the effect of a performance, remark, etc., by anticipating it. —*v.i.* **6.** to give forth thunder (often used impersonally with *it* as the subject): *It thundered last night.* **7.** to make a loud, resounding noise like thunder: *The artillery thundered in the hills.* **8.** to utter loud or vehement denunciations, threats, or the like. **9.** to speak in a very loud tone. **10.** to move or go with a loud noise or violent action: *The train thundered through the village.* —*v.t.* **11.** to strike, drive, inflict, give forth, etc., with loud noise or violent action. [ME; OE *thunor;* c. D *donder,* G *Donner;* Icel *thōrr* Thor, lit., thunder; akin to OE *thunian,* L *tonāre* to thunder] —**thun′der·er,** *n.* —**thun′der·ful,** *adj.* —**thun′der·less,** *adj.*

thun·der·a·tion (thun′də rā′shən), *interj.* an exclamation of surprise or petulance. [THUNDER + -ATION]

thun·der·bird (thun′dər bûrd′), *n.* (in the folk belief of certain western American Indians) a huge, eaglelike bird capable of producing thunder, lightning, and rain. [THUNDER + BIRD]

thun·der·bolt (thun′dər bōlt′), *n.* **1.** a flash of lightning with the accompanying thunder. **2.** an imaginary bolt or dart conceived as the material destructive agent cast to earth in a flash of lightning: *the thunderbolts of Jove.* **3.** any of various fossils, stones, or mineral concretions formerly supposed to have been cast to earth with lightning. **4.** something very destructive, terrible, severe, sudden, or startling: *The catastrophe struck like a thunderbolt.* **5.** one who acts with fury or with sudden and resistless force. [late ME *thondre bolte.* See THUNDER, BOLT[1]]

thun·der·clap (thun′dər klap′), *n.* a crash of thunder. [ME *thonder clappe.* See THUNDER, CLAP]

thun·der·cloud (thun′dər kloud′), *n.* cumulonimbus. Also, **thun′der·clouds′.** [THUNDER + CLOUD]

thun·der·head (thun′dər hed′), *n. Meteorol.* **1.** incus (def. 2). **2.** cumulonimbus. **3.** the upper portion of a cumulus congestus. [THUNDER + HEAD]

thun·der·ing (thun′dər ing), *adj.* **1.** of, pertaining to, or accompanied by thunder. **2.** producing a noise or effect like thunder. **3.** *Informal.* very great; extraordinary: *a thundering amount of work.* —*n.* **4.** thunder. [ME *thundring,* OE *thunring* thunder. See THUNDER, -ING[2], -ING[1]] —**thun′der·ing·ly,** *adv.*

thun·der·ous (thun′dər əs), *adj.* producing thunder or a loud noise like thunder: *thunderous applause.* Also, **thundery.** [THUNDER + -OUS] —**thun′der·ous·ly,** *adv.*

thun·der·peal (thun′dər pēl′), *n.* a crash of thunder. [THUNDER + PEAL]

thun·der·show·er (thun′dər shou′ər), *n.* a shower accompanied by thunder and lightning. [THUNDER + SHOWER]

thun·der·squall (thun′dər skwôl′), *n.* a combined squall and thunderstorm. [THUNDER + SQUALL[1]]

thun·der·stick (thun′dər stik′), *n.* bull-roarer. [THUNDER + STICK[1]]

thun·der·stone (thun′dər stōn′), *n.* any of various stones, fossils, etc., formerly popularly believed to have fallen as thunderbolts. [THUNDER + STONE]

thun·der·storm (thun′dər stôrm′), *n.* a transient storm of lightning and thunder, usually with rain and gusty winds, sometimes with hail or snow, produced by cumulonimbus clouds. Also called **electrical storm.** [THUNDER + STORM]

thun′derstorm cir′rus. See **cirrus spissatus.**

thun·der·struck (thun′dər struk′), *adj.* **1.** struck by a thunderbolt. **2.** overcome with consternation; confounded; astounded: *He was thunderstruck by the news of his promotion.* Also, **thun·der·strick·en** (thun′dər strik′ən). [THUNDER + STRUCK]

thun·der·y (thun′də rē), *adj.* thunderous. [THUNDER + -Y[1]]

Thü·nen (to͞o′nən), *n.* **Jo·hann Hein·rich von** (yō′hän hīn′riKH fən), 1783–1850, German economic theorist.

Thu·ner See (to͞o′nər zā′), German name of Lake of Thun.

Thur., Thursday.

Thur·ber (thûr′bər), *n.* **James (Gro·ver)** (grō′vər), 1894–1961, U.S. writer, caricaturist, and illustrator.

Thur·gau (to͞or′gou), *n.* a canton in NE Switzerland. 166,420 (1960); 388 sq. mi. *Cap.:* Frauenfeld.

thu·ri·ble (tho͝or′ə bəl), *n.* a censer. [late ME *turrible, thoryble* < L *t(h)ūribul(um)* censer < *thūri-* (s. of *thūs*) incense + *-bulum* instrumental suffix]

thu·ri·fer (tho͝or′ə fər), *n.* one who carries the thurible in religious ceremonies. [< NL, n. use of L *t(h)ūrifer* (adj.), < *t(h)uri-* (s. of *t(h)ūs*) incense + *-fer* bearing, making; see -FER]

Thu·rin·ger (tyo͝or′in jər, tho͝or′-, thûr′-, tir′-), *n.* a mildly seasoned cervelat, either fresh or smoked. Also, **Thü′ringer.** [< G, short for *Thüringerwurst* Thuringian sausage]

Thu·rin·gi·a (tho͝o rin′jē ə, -jə), *n.* a former state in central Germany: formed originally from duchies and principalities. German, **Thü·ring·en** (tY′ring ən). —**Thu·rin′gi·an,** *adj., n.*

Thurin′gian For′est, a forested mountain region in central East Germany: a resort area. German, **Thü·ring·er Wald** (tY′ring ər vält′).

Thur·low (thûr′lō), *n.* **Edward, 1st Baron,** 1731–1806, British statesman: Lord Chancellor 1778–92.

thurm (thûrm), *v.t.* to carve (a piece of wood, as a post or table leg) across the grain so as to produce an effect of turning. [? metathetic var. of THRUM[2]]

Thur·mont (thûr′mont), *n.* a town in N Maryland. 2802 (1960).

Thurs., Thursday.

Thurs·day (thûrz′dē, -dā), *n.* the fifth day of the week, following Wednesday. *Abbr.:* Th., Thur., Thurs. [ME; OE *Thursdæg* < ODan *Thūrsdagr,* lit., Thor's day; r. OE *Thunres dæg,* c. D *donderdag,* G *Donnerstag* (all repr. Gmc trans. of LL *diēs Jovis*). See THOR, THUNDER, DAY]

Thurs′day Is′land, an island in Torres Strait between NE Australia and New Guinea; part of Queensland: pearl fishing. 2140 (1955); 1½ sq. mi.

Thurs·days (thûrz′dēz, -dāz), *adv.* on Thursdays; every Thursday.

Thur′so's Land′ing (thûr′sōz), a narrative poem (1932) by Robinson Jeffers.

Thur·ston (thûr′stən), *n.* a boy's given name.

thus (thus), *adv.* **1.** in the way just indicated; in this way: *Stated thus, the problem seems trivial.* **2.** in such or the following manner; so: *Thus it came to pass—.* **3.** in accordance with this; accordingly; consequently: *It is late, and thus you must go.* **4.** to this extent or degree: *thus far.* **5.** as an example; for instance. [ME, OE; c. D *dus*]

thus·ly (thus′lē), *Informal.* thus. [THUS + -LY] —**Usage.** Since THUS is an adverb, THUSLY is avoided by careful speakers as a grammatical tautology.

Thus′ Spake′ Zarathus′tra, a philosophical work in poetic form (1883) by Friedrich Nietzsche. German, **Also Sprach Zarathustra.**

Thut·mo·se I (tho͞ot mō′sə, -mōs′), *n.* fl. c1500 B.C., Egyptian ruler. Also, **Thotmes I, Thothmes I, Thutmo·sis I** (tho͞ot mō′sis).

Thutmose II, fl. c1495 B.C., Egyptian ruler, son of Thutmose I, half brother of Thutmose III. Also, **Thotmes II, Thothmes II, Thutmosis II.**

Thutmose III, fl. c1475 B.C., Egyptian ruler: conqueror of the Middle East. Also, **Thotmes III, Thothmes III, Thutmosis III.**

thu·ya (tho͞o′yə), *n.* thuja.

thwack (thwak), *v.t.* **1.** to strike or beat vigorously with something flat; whack. —*n.* **2.** a sharp blow with something flat; whack. [imit.] —**thwack′er,** *n.*

thwart (thwôrt), *v.t.* **1.** to oppose successfully; prevent from accomplishing a purpose. **2.** to frustrate or baffle (a plan, purpose, etc.). **3.** *Archaic.* **a.** to cross. **b.** to extend across. —*n.* **4.** a seat across a boat, esp. one used by an oarsman. **5.** a transverse member spreading the gunwales of a canoe or the like. —*adj.* **6.** passing or lying crosswise or across; cross; transverse. **7.** *Archaic.* perverse; obstinate. **8.** adverse; unfavorable. —*prep., adv.* **9.** across; athwart. [ME *thwert* (adv.) < Scand; cf. Icel *thvert* across, neut. of *thverr* transverse, c. OE *thweorh* crooked, cross, Goth *thwairhs* cross, angry] —**thwart′ed·ly,** *adv.* —**thwart′er,** *n.*
—**Syn. 1.** hinder, obstruct. THWART, FRUSTRATE, BAFFLE imply preventing one, more or less completely, from accomplishing a purpose. THWART and FRUSTRATE apply to purposes, actions, plans, etc., BAFFLE, to the psychological state of the person thwarted. THWART suggests stopping one by opposing him, blocking him, or in some way running counter to his efforts. FRUSTRATE implies rendering all attempts or efforts useless or ineffectual, so that nothing ever comes of them. BAFFLE suggests causing defeat by confusing, puzzling, or perplexing, so that a situation seems too hard a problem to understand or solve.

Thwing (twing), *n.* **Charles Franklin,** 1853–1937, U.S. educator and Congregational clergyman.

thy (thī), *pron.* the possessive case of *thou* (used as an attributive adjective before a noun beginning with a consonant sound): *thy table.* Cf. **thine.** [ME; var. of THINE]

Thy·a·ti·ra (thī′ə tī′rə), *n.* ancient name of **Akhisar.**

Thyes′tean ban′quet, *Literary.* a dinner at which human flesh is eaten.

Thy·es·tes (thī es′tēz), *n. Class. Myth.* a son of Pelops and brother and rival of Atreus: he unknowingly ate the flesh of his own sons, which Atreus served to him at a dinner in punishment for his having committed adultery with Atreus' wife, Aërope: Thyestes then pronounced a curse on the house of Atreus. —**Thy·es·te·an** (thī es tē′ən, thī′e stē′ən), **Thy·es′ti·an,** *adj.*

Thy·iad (thī′yad), *n., pl.* **-iads, -ia·des** (-yə dēz′). bacchante. [< L *Thyiad-* (s. of *Thyias*) < Gk < *thý(ein)* (to) seethe]

Thylacine
(Total length 6 ft.; tail 2 ft.)

thy·la·cine (thī′lə sīn′, -sin), *n.* a carnivorous, wolflike marsupial, *Thylacinus cynocephalus,* of Tasmania, tan-colored, with black stripes across the back. [< NL *Thȳlacīn(us)* < *thȳlac-* (< Gk *thýlakos* pouch) + *-īnus* -INE[1]]

Thym·brae·us (thim brē′əs), *n. Class. Myth.* one of the twin sons of Laocoön.

thyme (tīm; *spelling pron.* thīm), *n.* any menthaceous plant of the genus *Thymus,* as a low subshrub, *T. vulgaris,* a common garden herb having aromatic leaves used for seasoning. [ME < L *thym(um)* < Gk *thýmon*]

thym·e·lae·a·ceous (thim′ə lē ā′shəs), *adj.* belonging to the *Thymelaeaceae,* a family of chiefly Old World trees, shrubs, and herbs comprising the mezereon, leatherwood, etc. [< NL *Thymelae(a)* genus name (< Gk *thymelaía* < *thým(on)* THYME + *elaía* olive-tree) + -ACEOUS]

thym·ic[1] (tī′mik), *adj.* pertaining to or derived from thyme. [THYME + -IC]

thym·ic[2] (thī′mik), *adj.* of or pertaining to the thymus. [THYM(US) + -IC]

thy·mine (thī′mēn, -min), *n. Biochem.* a white, crystalline, water-insoluble pyrimidine, $C_5H_6N_2O_2$, derived from thymus DNA, used chiefly in medical and biochemical research. [THYM(IC)[2] + -INE[2]]

Thy·moe·tes (thi mē′tēz), *n. Class. Myth.* **1.** a Trojan elder who counseled Priam and suggested that the Trojan Horse be brought into the city. **2.** an Athenian king who gained the throne by killing his brother.

thy·mol (thī′mōl, -mol), *n. Chem., Pharm.* a colorless, crystalline, slightly water-soluble solid, $(CH_3)_2CHC_6H_3(CH_3)OH$, having a pungent, aromatic taste and odor, obtained from the oil distilled from thyme or prepared

CONCISE PRONUNCIATION KEY: *act, āble, dâre, ärt; ebb, ēqual; if, īce; hot, ōver, ôrder, oil, bo͝ok, o͞oze, out; up, ûrge; chief; sing; shoe; thin, that; zh as in measure.* ə = *a* as in *alone, e* as in *system, i* as in *easily, o* as in *gallop, u* as in *circus;* ᵊ as in *button* (but′ᵊn), *fire* (fīᵊr), *cradle* (krād′ᵊl). See the full key inside the front cover.

synthetically: used chiefly in perfumery, embalming, preserving biological specimens, and in medicine as a fungicide, antiseptic, and sometimes as an anthelmintic. Also called **thyme′ cam′phor, thym′ic ac′id** (tī′mik). [THYME + -OL[2]]

thy·mus (thī′məs), *n., pl.* **-mus·es, -mi** (-mī). *Anat.* a glandular body or ductless gland of uncertain function found in vertebrate animals, lying in the thorax near the base of the neck in man and becoming vestigial in the adult. Also called **thy′mus gland′.** [< NL < Gk *thýmos* sweetbread, lit., thymelike excrescence]

thym·y (tī′mē), *adj.,* **thym·i·er, thym·i·est.** of, pertaining to, resembling, or characteristic of thyme: *a thymy fragrance.* [THYME + -Y[1]]

Thy·o·ne (thī′ō nē′), *n. Class. Myth.* the name given to Semele by her son, Dionysus, when he took her from the underworld and ascended with her to Olympus.

Thy·o·ne·us (thī′ə nē′əs), *n. Class. Myth.* an epithet of Dionysus, meaning "son of Thyone."

thyr-, a combining form of **thyroid:** *thyroxine.* Also, **thyreo-, thyro-.**

Thy·ra·tron (thī′rə tron′), *n. Electronics, Trademark.* a gas-filled, hot-cathode tube in which one or more control electrodes initiate, but do not limit and cannot interrupt, the flow of electrons.

thy·ro·ad·e·ni·tis (thī′rō ad′ənī′tis), *n. Pathol.* thyroiditis. [THYRO- + ADENITIS]

thy·ro·ar·y·te·noid (thī′rō ar′i tē′noid, -ə rit′ənoid′), *adj. Anat.* of, pertaining to, or connecting the thyroid and arytenoid cartilages of the larynx. [THYRO- + ARYTENOID]

thy·ro·car·di·tis (thī′rō kär dī′tis), *n. Pathol.* any affection of the heart muscle, as tachycardia, occurring with hyperthyroidism. [THYRO- + CARDITIS]

thy·roid (thī′roid), *adj.* **1.** of or pertaining to the thyroid gland. **2.** of or pertaining to the largest cartilage of the larynx, forming the projection known in men as the Adam's apple. —*n.* **3.** See **thyroid gland. 4.** the thyroid cartilage. **5.** an artery, vein, etc., in the thyroid region. **6.** *Med.* a preparation made from the thyroid glands of certain animals, used in treating hypothyroid conditions. [var. of *thyreoid* < Gk *thyreoeidḗs* shield-shaped < *thyre(ós)* oblong shield (lit., doorlike object < *thyr(a)* DOOR + *-eos* -EOUS) + *-oeidēs* -OID] —**thy′roid·less,** *adj.*

thy·roid·ec·to·mize (thī′roi dek′tə mīz′), *v.t.,* **-mized, -miz·ing.** *Surg.* to perform a thyroidectomy on. [THYROIDECTOM(Y) + -IZE]

thy·roid·ec·to·my (thī′roi dek′tə mē), *n., pl.* **-mies.** *Surg.* excision of all or a part of the thyroid gland. [THYROID + -ECTOMY]

thy′roid gland′, *Anat.* a bilobate endocrine gland on each side of the trachea, connected below the larynx by a thin isthmus of tissue, the secretion of which regulates the rates of metabolism and body growth.

thy·roid·i·tis (thī′roi dī′tis), *n. Pathol.* inflammation of the thyroid gland. Also, **thyroadenitis.** [THYROID + -ITIS]

thy·roi·dot·o·my (thī′roi dot′ə mē), *n., pl.* **-mies.** *Surg.* incision of the thyroid gland. Also, **thyrotomy.** [THYROID + -O- + -TOMY]

thy·ro·ri·on (thī rōr′ē on′, -rôr′-), *n., pl.* **-ro·ri·a** (-rōr′ē ə, -rôr′-). (in an ancient Greek house) a passage between the entrance and the peristyle. [< LGk *thyrōreíon* porter's lodge < Gk *thyrōn* hall + *-eion* n. suffix]

thy·ro·sis (thī rō′sis), *n.* any condition resulting from abnormal functioning of the thyroid gland. [THYR- + -OSIS]

thy·ro·tome (thī′rə tōm′), *n. Surg.* an instrument for cutting the thyroid cartilage. [THYRO- + -TOME]

thy·rot·o·my (thī rot′ə mē), *n., pl.* **-mies.** *Surg.* **1.** incision or splitting of the thyroid cartilage; laryngotomy. **2.** thyroidotomy. Cf. **thyroidectomy.** [THYRO- + -TOMY]

thy·ro·tox·ic (thī′rō tok′sik), *adj. Pathol.* of or pertaining to a condition caused by excessive thyroid hormone in the system, usually resulting from overactivity of the thyroid gland. [THYRO- + TOXIC] —**thy·ro·tox·ic·i·ty** (thī′rō tok sis′i tē), *n.*

thy·ro·tox·i·co·sis (thī′rō tok′sə kō′sis), *n. Pathol.* a condition caused by overactivity of the thyroid gland, characterized by tremors, rapid pulse, enlargement of the thyroid, protrusion of the eyes, loss of weight, etc. [THYRO- + TOXICOSIS]

thy·rox·ine (thī rok′sēn, -sin), *n.* **1.** *Biochem.* the hormone of the thyroid gland, $C_{15}H_{11}O_4NI_4$, which regulates the metabolic rate. **2.** *Pharm.* a commerical form of this compound, obtained from the thyroid glands of animals or synthesized, used in the treatment of hypothyroidism. Also, **thy·rox·in** (thī rok′sin). [THYR- + *-oxine,* abstracted from *toxine* TOXIN]

thyr·soid (thûr′soid), *adj. Bot.* having somewhat the form of a thyrsus. Also, **thyr·soi′dal.** [< Gk *thyrsoeid(ḗs)* thyrsuslike. See THYRSUS, -OID]

thyr·sus (thûr′səs), *n., pl.* **-si** (-sī). **1.** Also, **thyrse** (thûrs). *Bot.* a form of mixed inflorescence, as in the lilac, in which the primary ramification is centripetal or indeterminate, and the secondary and successive ramifications are centrifugal or determinate. **2.** *Gk. Antiq.* a staff tipped with a pine cone and sometimes twined with ivy and vine branches, borne by Dionysus and his votaries. [< L < Gk *thýrsos* Bacchic staff, stem of plant]

thy·sa·nu·ran (thī′sə nŏŏr′ən, -nyŏŏr′-, this′ə-), *adj.* **1.** belonging or pertaining to the order *Thysanura,* comprising the bristletails. —*n.* **2.** a thysanuran insect. [< NL *Thysanur(a)* (< Gk *thýsan(os)* tassel + *ourá* tail) + -AN] —**thy′sa·nu′rous,** *adj.*

thy·self (thī self′), *pron.* **1.** an emphatic appositive to *thou* or *thee.* **2.** a substitute for reflexive *thee.* [ME *thi self;* r. OE *thē self.* See THEE, THY, SELF]

Thys·sen (tis′ən), *n.* **Fritz** (frits), 1873–1951, German industrialist.

ti[1] (tē), *n., pl.* **tis.** *Music.* **1.** the syllable for the seventh tone of a diatonic scale. **2.** (in the fixed system of solmization) the tone B. Also, **te.** Cf. **sol-fa** (def. 1). [substituted for *si* to avoid confusion with the sharp of *sol.* See GAMUT]

ti[2] (tē), *n., pl.* **tis.** a tropical, palmlike plant, *Cordyline australis.* Also called **tuft tree, cabbage tree.** [< Polynesian]

Ti, *Chem.* titanium.

Ti·a·hua·na·co (tē′ə wə nä′kō), *adj.* of or pertaining to a pre-Incan culture existing c300 B.C.–A.D. c900, chiefly in Peru and Bolivia, characterized by the use of megalithic masonry carved with geometric and animal designs, stone statues, polychrome pottery, and bronze artifacts. Also, **Ti·a·hua·na·cu** (tē′ə wə nä′kōō). —**Ti′a·hua·na′can,** *n.*

Ti·a Jua·na (tē′ə wä′nə; *Sp.* tē′ä hwä′nä), Tijuana.

Tia·mat (tyä′mät), *n.* an Akkadian goddess, the consort of Apsu and mother of the gods.

Tian Shan (tyän′ shän′). See **Tien Shan.**

ti·ar·a (tē ar′ə, -är′ə, -âr′ə), *n.* **1.** a jeweled, ornamental coronet worn by women. **2.** *Rom. Cath. Ch.* a headpiece consisting of three coronets on top of which is an orb and a cross, worn by the pope, or carried before him during certain nonliturgical functions. **3.** the position, authority, and dignity of the pope. **4.** a high headdress, or turban, worn by the ancient Persians and others. [< L < Gk: kind of turban] —**ti·ar′aed,** *adj.* —**ti·ar′a·like′,** *adj.*

Tib·bett (tib′it), *n.* **Lawrence (Mer·vil)** (mûr′vil), 1896–1960, U.S. baritone.

Ti·ber (tī′bər), *n.* a river in central Italy, flowing through Rome into the Mediterranean. 244 mi. long. Italian, **Tevere.**

Ti·be·ri·as (tī bēr′ē əs), *n.* **Sea of.** See **Galilee, Sea of.**

Ti·ber·i·nus (tī′bə rī′nəs), *n.* the ancient Roman god of the Tiber.

Ti·be·ri·us (tī bēr′ē əs), *n.* (*Tiberius Claudius Nero Caesar*) 42 B.C.–A.D. 37, Roman emperor 14–37.

Ti·bet (ti bet′), *n.* a country in S Asia, N of the Himalayas: under the suzerainty of China: the highest country in the world, average elevation, ab. 16,000 ft. 1,270,000 (est. 1957); 471,660 sq. mi. *Cap.:* Lhasa. Also, **Thibet.** Chinese, **Sitsang.**

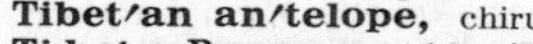

Ti·bet·an (ti bet′ən, tib′i tən), *adj.* **1.** of or pertaining to Tibet, its inhabitants, or their language. —*n.* **2.** a member of the native Mongolian race of Tibet. **3.** the Sino-Tibetan language of Tibet, esp. in its standard literary form. Also, **Thibetan.** [TIBET + -AN]

Tibet′an an′telope, chiru.

Ti·bet·o-Bur·man (ti bet′ō bûr′mən), *n.* a subfamily of Sino-Tibetan languages, including esp. Tibetan and Burmese. [TIBET + -O- + BURM(A) + -AN]

tib·i·a (tib′ē ə), *n., pl.* **tib·i·ae** (tib′ē ē′), **tib·i·as. 1.** *Anat.* the inner of the two bones of the leg, extending from the knee to the ankle and articulating with the femur and the talus; shinbone. See diag. under **skeleton. 2.** *Zool.* **a.** a corresponding bone in a horse or other hoofed quadruped, extending from the stifle to the hock. **b.** (in insects) the fourth segment of the leg, between the femur and tarsus. See diag. under **coxa.** [< L: shinbone] —**tib′i·al,** *adj.*

tib·i·o·tar·sus (tib′ē ō tär′səs), *n., pl.* **-si** (-sī). *Ornith.* the main bone of the leg of a bird, between the femur and tarsometatarsus, formed by the fusion of several tarsal bones with the tibia. [TIBI(A) + -O- + TARSUS] —**tib′i·o·tar′sal,** *adj.*

Ti·bul·lus (ti bul′əs), *n.* **Al·bi·us** (al′bē əs), c54–c19 B.C., Roman poet.

Ti·bur (tī′bər), *n.* ancient name of **Tivoli.**

tic (tik), *n. Pathol.* **1.** a sudden, spasmodic, painless, involuntary muscular contraction, as of the face. **2.** See **tic douloureux.** [< F; c. It *ticche*]

-tic, a suffix occurring in adjectives of Greek origin (*analytic*), used esp. in the formation of adjectives from nouns with stems in *-sis: hematotic; neurotic.* [< Gk *-tikos;* cf. -IC]

ti·cal (ti käl′, -kôl′, tē′kəl), *n., pl.* **-cals, -cal. 1.** a former Thai unit of weight, equal to 231.5 grains, or about half an ounce. **2.** a former silver coin and monetary unit of Siam, equal to 100 satang: replaced in 1928 by the baht. **3.** baht. [< Siamese < Pg < Malay *tikal*]

tic dou·lou·reux (tik′ dōō′lōō rōō′; *Fr.* tēk′ dōō lōō rœ′), *Pathol.* paroxysmal darting pain and muscular twitching in the face, evoked by rubbing certain points of the face. Also called **facial neuralgia, trifacial neuralgia, trigeminal neuralgia.** [< F: lit., painful tic]

Tice (tīs), *n.* a town in SW Florida. 4377 (1960).

Ti·ci·no (tē chē′nō), *n.* a canton in S Switzerland. 195,566 (1960); 1086 sq. mi. *Cap.:* Bellinzona. German, **Tessin.**

tick[1] (tik), *n.* **1.** a slight, sharp recurring click, tap, or beat, as of a clock. **2.** *Chiefly Brit. Informal.* a moment or instant. **3.** a small dot, mark, or check, as used to mark off an item on a list, serve as a reminder, call attention to something, etc. **4.** *Manège.* a jumping fault consisting of a light touch of a fence with one or more feet. —*v.i.* **5.** to emit or produce a tick, like that of a clock. **6.** to pass as with ticks of a clock: *The hours ticked by.* —*v.t.* **7.** to sound or announce by a tick or ticks: *The clock ticked the minutes.* **8.** to mark with a tick or ticks; check (usually fol. by *off*): *to tick off the items on the memo.* **9.** *Manège.* (of a horse) to hit (a jump) lightly without knocking it down. **10. what makes one tick,** the motive or explanation of one's behavior: *The biographer failed to show what made Herbert Hoover tick.* [late ME *tek* little touch; akin to D *tik(je)* a touch, pat, Norw *tikka* to touch or shove slightly. See TICKLE]

tick[2] (tik), *n.* **1.** any of numerous bloodsucking arachnids of the order *Acarina,* including the families *Ixodidae* and *Argasidae,* somewhat larger than the related mites and having a barbed proboscis for attachment to the skin of warm-blooded vertebrates. **2.** See **sheep tick.** [ME *teke, tyke,* OE *ticia* (? for *tiica* or *ticca*); akin to LG *tieke,* G *Zecke*]

Dog tick, *Dermacentor variabilis* (Length ¼ in.)

tick[3] (tik), *n.* **1.** the cloth case of a mattress, pillow, etc., containing hair, feathers, or the like. **2.** *Informal.* ticking. Also called **bedtick.** [ME *tikke, teke, tyke* (c. D *tijk,* G *Zieche*) << L *tēca, thēca* < Gk *thḗkē* case]

tick[4] (tik), *n. Chiefly Brit. Informal.* **1.** a score or account. **2. on tick,** on credit or trust: *We bought our telly on tick.* [short for TICKET]

tick′ bird′, any of various birds that feed on ticks, as an oxpecker.

Tick·ell (tik′əl), *n.* **Thomas,** 1686–1740, English poet and translator.

tick·er (tik′ər), *n.* **1.** one who or that which ticks. **2.** a telegraphic receiving instrument which automatically prints stock prices, market reports, etc., on a tape. **3.** *Slang.* a watch. **4.** *Slang.* the heart. [TICK[1] + -ER[1]]

tick′er-tape parade′ (tik′ər tāp′), a parade honoring a visiting dignitary, hero, or the like, in which ticker tapes, confetti, shredded newspapers, etc., are showered into the streets from buildings along the route over which the parade passes.

tick·et (tik′it), *n.* **1.** a slip, usually of paper or cardboard, serving as evidence that the holder has paid his fare or admission or is entitled to some service, right, or the like: *a railroad ticket; a theater ticket.* **2.** a written or printed slip of paper, cardboard, etc., affixed to something to indicate its nature, price, or the like; label or tag. **3.** *U.S.* a list of candidates nominated by a political party or faction. **4.** a summons issued for a traffic or parking violation. **5.** the license of a ship's officer or of an aviation pilot. **6.** *Banking.* a preliminary recording of transactions prior to their entry in more permanent books of account. **7.** *Informal.* the proper or advisable thing: *That's the ticket. Warm milk and toast is just the ticket for you.* **8.** *Rare.* a short note, notice, or memorandum. **9.** *Archaic.* a placard. —*v.t.* **10.** to attach a ticket to; distinguish by means of a ticket; label. **11.** *U.S.* to furnish with a ticket, as on the railroad. [earlier *tiket* < MF *etiquet* memorandum. See ETIQUETTE] —**tick′et·less,** *adj.*

tick′et a′gency, an agency dealing in the sale of tickets, esp. theater tickets.

tick′et a′gent, one who sells tickets, as for theater seats, train accommodations, etc.

tick′et of′fice, an office or booth at which tickets are sold, as for a play, a film, travel accommodations, etc.

tick′et of leave′, *pl.* **tickets of leave.** *Brit.* (formerly) a permit allowing a convict to leave prison, under certain restrictions, and go to work before his full term had been served, somewhat similar to a certificate of parole. Also, **tick′et-of-leave′.**

tick′et-of-leave′ man′, *Brit.* (formerly) a convict granted a ticket of leave.

tick·et-por·ter (tik′it pōr′tər, -pôr′-), *n. Brit.* a licensed porter who wears a badge or ticket for purposes of identification.

tick·et·y-boo (tik′i tē bōō′), *adj. Chiefly Brit. Informal.* fine; O.K. [perh. childish formation on the phrase *that's the ticket*]

tick′ fe′ver, any fever transmitted by ticks, as Rocky Mountain spotted fever, which attacks man, or Texas fever, which is confined to some animals, as cattle.

tick·ing (tik′ing), *n.* **1.** a strong cotton fabric, usually twilled, used esp. in making ticks. **2.** a similar cloth in satin weave or Jacquard, used esp. for mattress covers. [TICK[3] + -ING[1]]

tick·le (tik′əl), *v.,* **-led, -ling,** *n.* —*v.t.* **1.** to touch or stroke lightly with the fingers, a feather, etc., so as to excite a tingling or itching sensation in; titillate. **2.** to poke in some sensitive part of the body so as to excite spasmodic laughter. **3.** to excite agreeably; gratify: *to tickle someone's vanity.* **4.** to excite amusement in: *The clown tickled the kids.* **5.** to get, move, etc., by or as by tickling: *She tickled him into saying yes.* —*v.i.* **6.** to be affected with a tingling or itching sensation, as from light touches or strokes: *I tickle all over.* **7.** to produce such a sensation. **8. tickled pink,** *Informal.* greatly pleased: *She was tickled pink that someone had remembered her birthday.* —*n.* **9.** the act or an instance of tickling. **10.** a tickling sensation. [ME *tikele(n);* freq. of TICK[1] (in obs. sense) to touch lightly]

tick·ler (tik′lər), *n.* **1.** one who or that which tickles. **2.** a memorandum book, card file, or the like, kept to refresh the memory as to appointments, payments due, etc. **3.** *Accounting.* a single-entry account arranged according to the due dates of obligations. **4.** *Electronics.* a small coil in the anode circuit of an electron tube, inductively coupled to a grid circuit to provide feedback. [TICKLE + -ER[1]]

tick′ler coil′, *Radio.* the coil by which the plate circuit of a vacuum tube is inductively coupled with the grid circuit in the process of regeneration.

tick·lish (tik′lish), *adj.* **1.** sensitive to tickling. **2.** requiring careful or delicate handling or action; difficult; risky: *a ticklish situation.* **3.** extremely sensitive; touchy: *Father is ticklish about being interrupted.* **4.** unstable or easily upset, as a boat; unsteady. [TICKLE + -ISH[1]] —**tick′lish·ly,** *adv.* —**tick′lish·ness,** *n.*

Tick·nor (tik′nər, -nôr), *n.* **George,** 1791–1871, U.S. literary historian and educator.

tick·seed (tik′sēd′), *n.* **1.** any of various plants having seeds resembling ticks, as a coreopsis or the bugseed. **2.** See **tick trefoil.** [TICK[2] + SEED]

tick′seed sun′flower, any of various species of bur marigold, esp. *Bidens trichosperma* and *B. coronata,* having flowers with conspicuous yellow rays.

tick·tack (tik′tak′), *n.* **1.** a repetitive sound, as of ticking, tapping, knocking, clicking, etc.: *the ticktack of high heels in the corridor.* **2.** a device for making a tapping sound, as against a window or door in playing a practical joke. —*v.i.* **3.** to make a repeated ticking or tapping sound: *Sleet ticktacked against the window panes.* Also, tictac. [imit. See TICK[1]]

tick-tack-toe (tik′tak tō′), *n.* **1.** a simple game in which one player marks down only crosses and another only ciphers, each alternating in filling in marks in any of the nine compartments of a figure formed by two vertical lines crossed by two horizontal lines, the winner being the first to fill in three of his marks in any row or diagonal. **2.** a children's game consisting of trying, with the eyes shut, to bring a pencil down upon one of a set of circled numbers, as on a slate, the number hit being scored. Also, **tick-tack-too** (tik′tak to͞o′), **tic-tac-toe, tit-tat-toe.** [imit. of sound]

tick·tock (tik′tok′), *n.* **1.** an alternating ticking sound, as that made by a clock. —*v.i.* **2.** to emit or produce a ticking sound, like that of a clock. Also, **tictoc.** [imit.]

tick′ tre′foil, any leguminous plant of the genus *Desmodium,* having trifoliolate leaves and jointed pods with hooked hairs by which they adhere to objects.

Ti·con·der·o·ga (tī′kon də rō′gə), *n.* a village in NE New York, on Lake Champlain: site of French fort captured by the English 1759 and by Americans under Ethan Allen 1775. 3568 (1960).

tic·tac (tik′tak′), *n., v.i.,* **-tacked, -tack·ing.** ticktack.

tic-tac-toe (tik′tak tō′), *n.* tick-tack-toe.

tic·toc (tik′tok′), *n., v.i.,* **-tocked, -tock·ing.** ticktock.

t.i.d., (in prescriptions) three times a day. [< L *ter in diē*]

tid·al (tīd′əl), *adj.* **1.** of, pertaining to, characterized by, or subject to tides: *a tidal current.* **2.** dependent on the state of the tide as to time of departure: *a tidal steamer.* [TIDE[1] + -AL[1]] —**tid′al·ly,** *adv.*

tid′al ba′sin, an artificial body of water open to a river, etc., subject to tidal action.

tid′al bench′ mark′, a bench mark used as a reference for tidal observations.

ti′dal da′tum, (in a hydrographic survey) a curved surface representing one phase of a tide, usually mean low water, taken as a datum level. Also called **datum plane.**

tid′al flat′, tideland that is flat or nearly flat and often muddy or marshy.

tid′al light′, a light placed at the entrance of a harbor to indicate the depth of the water and the direction of tidal flow.

tid′al wave′, 1. (not in technical use) a large, destructive ocean wave, produced by a seaquake, hurricane, or strong wind. Cf. **tsunami. 2.** either of the two great wavelike swellings of the ocean surface that move around the earth on opposite sides and give rise to tides, caused by the attraction of the moon and sun. **3.** any widespread or powerful movement, opinion, or tendency: *a tidal wave of public indignation.*

tid·bit (tid′bit′), *n.* **1.** a delicate bit or morsel of food. **2.** a choice or pleasing bit of anything, as news or gossip. Also, *esp. Brit.,* **titbit.** [TIDE[1] (in sense of feast day) + BIT[2]]

tid·dly (tid′lē), *adj. Chiefly Brit. Slang.* slightly drunk; tipsy. [dial.: little (OE *tīdlic* timely). See TIDE[1], -LY]

tid·dly·winks (tid′lē wiŋgks′), *n.* (*construed as sing.*) a game played on a flat surface, in which players attempt to snap small plastic disks into a cup by pressing the edges of the disks with larger ones. Also, **tid·dle·dy·winks** (tid′əl dē wiŋgks′). [pl. of *tiddlywink* (TIDDLY + dial. *wink,* var. of WINCH), referring to the counter used to snap the pieces into place]

tide[1] (tīd), *n., v.,* **tid·ed, tid·ing.** —*n.* **1.** the periodic rise and fall of the waters of the ocean and its inlets, produced by the attraction of the moon and sun, and occurring about every 12 hours. **2.** the inflow, outflow, or current of water at any given place resulting from the waves of tides. **3.** See **flood tide. 4.** a stream or current. **5.** anything that alternately rises and falls, increases and decreases, etc.: *the tide of the seasons.* **6.** current, tendency, or drift, as of events, ideas, action, etc.: *the tide of international events.* **7.** any extreme or critical period or condition: *The tide of her illness is at its height.* **8.** a season or period in the course of the year, day, etc. (now used chiefly in combination): *wintertide; eventide.* **9.** *Eccles.* a period of time that includes and follows an anniversary or festival, etc. **10.** *Archaic.* a suitable time or occasion. **11.** *Obs.* an extent of time. **12. turn the tide,** to reverse the course of events, esp. from one extreme to another: *The Battle of Saratoga turned the tide of the American Revolution.* —*v.i.* **13.** to flow as the tide; flow to and fro. **14.** to float or drift with the tide. —*v.t.* **15.** to carry, as the tide does. **16. tide over, a.** to assist in getting over a period of difficulty or distress. **b.** to surmount (a difficulty, obstacle, etc.); survive. [ME; OE *tīd* time, hour; c. D *tijd,* Icel *tīth,* G *Zeit;* akin to TIME] —**tide′ful,** *adj.* —**tide′less,** *adj.* —**tide′less·ness,** *n.* —**tide′like′,** *adj.*

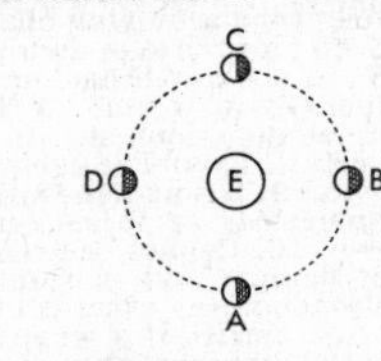

Tide
S, Sun; E, Earth;
A, C, Moon at neap tide;
B, D, Moon at spring tide

tide[2] (tīd), *v.i.,* **tid·ed, tid·ing.** *Archaic.* to happen or befall. [ME; OE (*ge*)*tīda*(*n*) (to) happen. See BETIDE]

tide-bound (tīd′bound′), *adj. Naut.* (of a vessel) grounded or otherwise confined at low tide.

tide′ gage′, a gauge for measuring the level of the tide: usually equipped with a marigraph. Also, **tide′ gauge′.** Also called **tide register.**

tide′ gate′, 1. a gate through which water flows when the tide is in one direction and which closes automatically when the tide is in the opposite direction. **2.** a restricted passage, as a strait, through which the tide flows swiftly.

tide·head (tīd′hed′), *n.* the inland limit of the tide. [TIDE[1] + HEAD]

tide·land (tīd′land′), *n.* land alternately exposed and covered by the ordinary ebb and flow of the tide. [TIDE[1] + LAND]

tide′ lock′, a lock at the entrance to a tidal basin.

tide·mark (tīd′märk′), *n.* **1.** the point which something or someone has reached, receded below, or risen above: *He has reached the tidemark of his prosperity.* **2.** a mark left by the highest or lowest point of a tide. **3.** a mark made to indicate the highest or lowest point of a tide. [TIDE[1] + MARK[1]]

tide′ pole′. See **tide staff.**

tide′ race′, 1. a swift tidal current. **2.** a tideway.

tide′ reg′ister. See **tide gage.**

tide·rip (tīd′rip′), *n.* a rip caused by conflicting tidal currents or by a tidal current crossing a rough bottom. [TIDE[1] + RIP[2]]

tide·rode (tīd′rōd′), *adj. Naut.* (of a moored vessel) riding with the force of the tide. Cf. **windrode.** [TIDE[1] + *rode,* dial. ptp. of RIDE]

tide′ staff′, a tide gage consisting of a vertical, graduated rod. Also called **tide pole.**

tide′ ta′ble, a table listing the predicted times and heights of the tides for specific dates and places.

tide·wait·er (tīd′wā′tər), *n.* (formerly) a customs inspector who boarded ships at dockside to enforce the customs regulations. [TIDE[1] + WAITER]

tide·wa·ter (tīd′wô′tər, -wot′ər), *n.* **1.** water affected by the flow and ebb of the tide. **2.** the water covering tideland at flood tide. **3.** seacoast. [TIDE[1] + WATER]

tide·way (tīd′wā′), *n.* **1.** a channel in which a tidal current runs. **2.** the rush of a tidal current through a channel or stream. **3.** tideland. Also, **tide′ way′.** [TIDE[1] + WAY]

ti·dings (tī′diŋgz), *n.* (*sometimes construed as sing.*) news, information, or intelligence: *sad tidings.* [ME; OE *tīdung;* c. D *tijding,* G *Zeitung* news; akin to Icel *tīthindi.* See TIDE[2], -ING[1]]

ti·dy (tī′dē), *adj.,* **-di·er, -di·est,** *v.,* **-died, -dy·ing,** *n., pl.* **-dies.** —*adj.* **1.** neat, orderly, or trim, as in appearance, dress, etc.: *a tidy room; a tidy person.* **2.** clearly organized and systematic: *a tidy mind; a tidy way of working.* **3.** tolerably good, acceptable: *They worked out a tidy arrangement agreeable to all.* **4.** *Informal.* considerable: *a tidy sum.* —*v.t., v.i.* **5.** to make tidy or neat (often fol. by *up*). —*n.* **6.** any of various articles for keeping things tidy, as various boxlike devices with small drawers and compartments. **7.** an antimacassar. [ME *tidi, tidy* seasonable, hence good; c. D *tijdig.* See TIDE[1], -Y[1]] —**ti′di·ly,** *adv.* —**ti′di·ness,** *n.* —**Ant. 1.** messy, sloppy.

ti·dy·tips (tī′dē tips′), *n., pl.* **-tips.** a showy, composite plant, *Layia elegans,* of California, having flowers with bright yellow rays. [TIDY + TIP[1] + -S[3]]

tie (tī), *v.,* **tied, ty·ing,** *n.* —*v.t.* **1.** to bind, fasten, or attach with a cord, string, or the like, drawn together and knotted: *to tie a tin can on a dog's tail.* **2.** to draw together the parts of with a knotted string or the like: *to tie a bundle tight.* **3.** to fasten by tightening and knotting the string or strings of: *to tie one's shoes.* **4.** to draw or fasten together into a knot, as a cord: *to tie one's shoelace.* **5.** to form by looping and interlacing, as a knot or bow. **6.** to fasten, join, or connect in any way. **7.** *Angling.* to design and make (an artificial fly). **8.** to bind or join closely or firmly: *Great affection tied them.* **9.** *Informal.* to unite in marriage. **10.** to confine, restrict, or limit: *The weather tied him to the house.* **11.** to bind or oblige, as to do something. **12.** to make the same score as; equal in a contest. **13.** *Music.* to connect (notes) by a tie. —*v.i.* **14.** to make a tie, bond, or connection. **15.** to make or be the same score; be equal in a contest: *The teams tied for first place in the league.* **16. tie down,** to limit one's activities; confine; curtail: *He finds that a desk job ties him down.* **17. tie in, a.** *Survey.* to establish the position of (a point not part of a survey control). **b.** to connect or be connected; be consistent: *His story ties in with the facts.* **18. tie off,** to tie a cord or suture around (a vein, blood vessel, or the like) so as to stop the flow within. **19. tie one on,** *Slang.* to get drunk: *Charlie sure tied one on last night!* **20. tie the knot.** See **knot**[1] (def. 12). **21. tie up, a.** to fasten securely by tying. **b.** to wrap; bind. **c.** to hinder; impede. **d.** to bring to a stop; make inactive. **e.** to invest or place (money) in such a way as to render unavailable for other uses. **f.** to place (property) under such conditions or restrictions as to prevent sale or alienation. **g.** to moor a ship. **h.** to engage or occupy completely: *I can't see you now, I'm all tied up.* —*n.* **22.** that with which anything is tied. **23.** a cord, string, or the like, used for tying, fastening, binding, or wrapping something. **24.** a necktie. **25.** a low shoe fastened with a lace. **26.** a knot, esp. an ornamental one; bow. **27.** anything that fastens, secures, or unites. **28.** a bond or connection of affection, kinship, business, mutual interest, etc. between two or more people, groups, nations, or the like: *family ties; The ties between Britain and the U.S. are strong.* **29.** a state of equality in the result of a contest, as in points scored, votes obtained, etc., among competitors: *The game ended in a tie.* **30.** a match or contest in which this occurs. **31.** any of various structural members, as beams or rods, for keeping two objects, as rafters or the haunches of an arch, from spreading or separating. **32.** *Music.* a curved line connecting two notes on the same line or space to indicate that the sound is to be sustained for their joint value, not repeated. **33.** *Railroads.* any of a number of closely spaced transverse beams, usually of wood, for holding the rails forming a track at the proper distance from each other and for transmitting train loads to the ballast and roadbed; sleeper. **34.** bride[2] (def. 1). **35.** *Survey.* a measurement made to determine the position of a survey station with respect to a reference mark or other isolated point. **36.** *Naut.* tye. [ME *tie*(*n*), OE *tīegan* (v.), *tēag* (n.); c. Icel *taug* rope, *teygja* to draw. See TUG, TOW[1]] —**Syn. 6.** unite, link, knit, yoke, lock. **11.** obligate, constrain. **23.** rope, band, ligature. **24.** cravat. —**Ant. 1.** loose, loosen.

Ties (def. 32)

tie-and-dye (tī′ən dī′), *n.* See **tie dyeing.**

tie·back (tī′bak′), *n.* **1.** a strip or loop of material, heavy braid, or the like, used for holding a curtain back to one side. **2.** a curtain having such a device. [n. use of v. phrase *tie back*]

tie′ beam′, a horizontal timber or the like for connecting two structural members to keep them from spreading apart, as a beam connecting the feet of two principal rafters in a roof truss.

Tieck (tēk), *n.* **Lud·wig** (lo͞ot′viкн, lo͞od′-), 1773–1853, German writer.

tie·clasp (tī′klasp′, -kläsp′), *n.* an ornamental metal clasp for securing the two ends of a necktie to a shirt front. [TIE + CLASP]

tied′ house′, *Brit.* **1.** a public house or tavern owned by or under contract to a brewery whose brands of beer, ale, etc., it sells exclusively. **2.** Also called **tied′ cot′tage.** a house owned by an employer and rented to an employee.

tie-down (tī′doun′), *n.* **1.** a device for tying something down. **2.** the act of tying something down. [n. use of v. phrase *tie down*]

tie′ dye′ing, a process of hand-dyeing fabrics, portions of the fabric being tightly bound with thread to resist the dye solution. Also called **tie-and-dye.**

tie-in (tī′in′), *adj.* **1.** pertaining to or designating a sale in which the buyer in order to get the item desired must also purchase one or more other, usually undesired, items. **2.** of or pertaining to two or more products advertised, sold, obtained, or allotted together: *I bought the table and the store gave me the lamp free on a tie-in deal.* —*n.* **3.** a tie-in sale or advertisement. **4.** an item in a tie-in sale or advertisement. **5.** any direct or indirect link, relationship, or connection: *There is a tie-in between smoking and cancer.* [adj., n. use of v. phrase *tie in*]

tie′ line′, *Telephony.* (in a PBX system) a line that connects two or more extensions.

tie·mann·ite (tē′mə nīt′), *n.* a mineral, mercuric selenide, HgSe, occurring in the form of a compact mass of gray crystals. [named in 1855 after W. *Tiemann,* German scientist who found it; see -ITE[1]]

Tien Shan (tyen′ shän′), a mountain range in central Asia, in China and the Soviet Union. Highest peak, Tengri Khan, ab. 23,950 ft. Also, **Tian Shan.**

Tien·tsin (tin′tsin′; *Chin.* tyen′jin′), *n.* a port in E Hopeh, in NE China. 3,220,000 (est. 1957).

tie′-off rail′ (tī′ôf′, -of′). See **trim rail.**

tie·pin (tī′pin′), *n.* a straight pin, usually with an ornamented head and a sheath or clasp for its point, for holding together the ends of a necktie or to pin them to a shirt front. Also called **scarfpin.** [TIE + PIN]

tie′ point′, *Survey.* an isolated point tied into a survey, as a reference mark.

Tie·po·lo (tē ep′ə lō′; *It.* tye′pô lô), *n.* **Gio·van·ni Bat·ti·sta** (jō vä′nē bə tē′stə; *It.* jô vän′nē bät tē′stä), 1696–1770, and his son, **Giovanni Do·me·ni·co** (də men′ə kō′; *It.* dô me′nē kô), 1727–1804, Italian painters.

tier[1] (tēr), *n.* **1.** one of a series of rows or ranks rising one behind or above another, as of seats in an amphitheater, boxes in a theater, guns in a man-of-war, or oars in an ancient galley. **2.** one of a number of galleries, as in a theater. **3.** a layer; level; stratum: *The wedding cake had six tiers.* **4.** *Australian.* a mountain range. —*v.t.* **5.** to arrange in tiers. —*v.i.* **6.** to rise in tiers. [earlier also *tire, tyre, teare* < MF, OF *tire, tiere* order, row, rank < Gmc; cf. OE, OS *tīr,* OFrankish **tēri,* OHG *zēri* glory, adornment]

ti·er[2] (tī′ər), *n.* **1.** one who or that which ties. **2.** *Naut.* a short rope or band for securing a furled sail. **3.** *U.S. Dial.* a child's apron or pinafore. [TIE + -ER[1]]

tierce (tērs), *n.* **1.** an old measure of wine capacity equivalent to one third of a pipe, or 42 wine gallons. **2.** a cask or vessel holding this quantity. **3.** Also, **terce.** *Eccles.* the third of the seven canonical hours, or the service for it, originally fixed for the third hour of the day (or 9 A.M.). **4.** *Fencing.* the third of eight defensive positions. **5.** *Piquet.* a sequence of three cards of the same suit, as an ace, king, and queen (**tierce major**), or a king, queen, and jack (**tierce minor**). **6.** *Obs.* a third or third part. [ME < MF, fem. of *tiers* < L *tertius* third]

tierced (tērst), *adj. Heraldry.* (of an escutcheon) divided vertically or horizontally into three equal parts; party, or parted, per tierce: *an escutcheon tierced in pale.* [TIERCE + -ED[3]; cf. F *tiercé*]

tierce de Pi·car·die (*Fr.* tyers də pē kar dē′). See **Picardy third.**

tier·cel (tēr′səl), *n. Falconry.* tercel.

tierce′ ma′jor. See under **tierce** (def. 5).

tierce′ mi′nor. See under **tierce** (def. 5).

tierce′ point′, the crown of a pointed arch. [< F *tiers-point,* lit., third point]

tier·ce·ron (tēr′sər ən), *n.* (in a ribbed vault) a diagonal rib, other than an ogive, springing from a point of support. See illus. under **vault.** [< F < *tierce* TIERCE + *-r-* (< ?) + *-on* -OON]

tie′ rod′, 1. an iron or steel rod serving as a structural tie, esp. one keeping the lower ends of a roof truss, arch, etc., from spreading. **2.** *Auto.* a rod connecting the wheels which turn to steer a vehicle.

Tier·ra del Fue·go (tyer′rä del fwe′gô), a group of islands at the S tip of South America, separated from the mainland by the Strait of Magellan: the eastern part (9765, est. 1953; 8074 sq. mi.) belongs to Argentina and the western part (4768, 1952; 19,402 sq. mi.) belongs to Chile.

tiers é·tat (tyer zā ta′), *French.* See **third estate.**

tier′ ta′ble, a stand having a number of round shelves, one on top of the other.

tie′ tack′, a pin having an ornamental head, pinned through the ends of a necktie to hold it against a shirt.

Tiet′ze's exten′sion the′orem (tēt′səz), *Math.* the theorem that given any function, continuous and bounded on a closed set in the plane, there is a function, continuous and bounded in the plane, which has the same value as the given function at each point of the set. [named after its discoverer]

tie-up (tī′up′), *n.* **1.** a temporary stoppage or slowing of business, traffic, telephone service, etc., as due to a strike, storm, accident, etc. **2.** the act or state of tying up or the state of being tied up. **3.** an involvement, connection, or entanglement: *the tie-up between the two companies; his tie-up with the crime syndicate.* **4.** a mooring place; place where a boat may be tied up. **5.** See **Jacquard harness.** [n. use of v. phrase *tie up*]

tiff[1] (tif), *n.* **1.** a slight or petty quarrel. **2.** a slight fit of annoyance, bad mood, or the like. —*v.i.* **3.** to have a petty quarrel. **4.** to be in a tiff. [?]

tiff[2] (tif), *n. Archaic.* **1.** liquor. **2.** a sip of liquor. [?]

tiff[3] (tif), *v.i.* (in Anglo-Indian use) to take tiffin; eat lunch. [back formation from TIFFIN, taken as var. of **tiffing* lunching]

tif·fa·ny (tif′ə nē), *n., pl.* **-nies.** a sheer, mesh fabric constructed in plain weave, originally made of silk but now often made of cotton and man-made fibers. [prob. < obs. F *tiphanie* Epiphany < LL *theophania.* See THEOPHANY]

Tif·fa·ny (tif′ə nē), *n.* **1. Charles Lewis,** 1812–1902, U.S. jeweler. **2.** his son **Louis Com·fort** (kum′fərt), 1848–1933, U.S. painter and decorator, esp. of glass. **3.** a boy's or girl's given name.

Tif′fany glass′. See **Favrile glass.** [named after L. C. TIFFANY]

Tif′fany set′ting, *Jewelry.* a setting, as in a ring, in which the stone is held with prongs. [named after C. L. TIFFANY]

tif·fin (tif′in), *Brit.* —*n.* **1.** lunch. —*v.i.* **2.** to eat lunch. —*v.t.* **3.** to provide lunch for; serve lunch to. [var. of **tiffing* lunching. See TIFF[2]]

Tif·fin (tif′in), *n.* a city in N Ohio. 21,478 (1960).

Tif·lis (tif′lis; *Russ.* tif lēs′), *n.* a city in and the capital of the Georgian Republic, in the SW Soviet Union in Europe. 805,000 (1965). Official name, **Tbilisi.**

Tif·ton (tif′tən), *n.* a town in central Georgia. 9903 (1960).

ti·ger (tī′gər), *n., pl.* **-gers,** (*esp. collectively for 1, 2, 5*) **-ger. 1.** a large, carnivorous, tawny-colored, black-striped feline, *Panthera tigris,* of Asia, ranging in several races from India and the Malay Peninsula to Siberia. **2.** the cougar, jaguar, thylacine, or other animal resembling the tiger. **3.** a person resembling a tiger in fierceness, courage, etc. **4.** *U.S.* an additional cheer (often the word *tiger*) at the end of a round of cheering. **5.** any of several strong, voracious fishes, as a sand shark. [ME *tigre,* OE *tigras* (pl.) < L *tigris, tigris* < Gk *tigris*] —**ti′ger·like′,** *adj.*

Tiger
(Total length 10 ft.; tail 3 ft.)

ti′ger bee′tle, any of numerous active, usually brightly colored beetles of the family *Cicindelidae* that prey on other insects.

ti′ger bit′tern, any of several tropical American herons of the genus *Tigrisoma,* having plumage barred with black, brown, and white.

ti′ger cat′, 1. any of several felines, as the ocelot, margay, etc., that resemble the tiger in coloration or ferocity but are smaller. **2.** a spotted marsupial cat, *Dasyurops maculatus.* **3.** a domestic cat having a striped coat resembling that of a tiger.

ti·ger·eye (tī′gər ī′), *n.* tiger's-eye.

ti·ger·fish (tī′gər fish′), *n., pl.* (*esp. collectively*) **-fish,** (*esp. referring to two or more kinds or species*) **-fish·es.** a large, voracious, freshwater game fish, *Hydrocyon lineatus,* found in Africa. [TIGER + FISH]

ti·ger·ish (tī′gər ish), *adj.* **1.** tigerlike, as in power, fierceness, courage, coloration, etc. **2.** fiercely cruel; bloodthirsty; relentless. Also, **tigrish.** [TIGER + -ISH[1]] —**ti′ger·ish·ly,** *adv.* —**ti′ger·ish·ness,** *n.*

ti′ger lil′y, 1. a lily, *Lilium tigrinum,* having dull-orange flowers spotted with black, and small bulbs or bulbils in the axils of the leaves. **2.** any lily, esp. *L. pardalinum,* of similar coloration.

ti′ger liz′ard, a lacertid lizard, *Nucras delalandi,* of southern Africa, having a gray or brown body marked with black spots and bars.

ti′ger moth′, any of numerous moths of the family *Arctiidae,* many of which have conspicuously striped or spotted wings.

ti′ger sal′amander, a salamander, *Ambystoma tigrinum,* common in North America, having a dark body marked with yellowish spots or bars.

ti·ger's-eye (tī′gərz ī′), *n.* **1.** a golden-brown chatoyant stone used for ornament, formed by the alteration of crocidolite, and consisting essentially of quartz colored by iron oxide. **2.** a glass coating or glaze giving the covered object the appearance of this stone. Also, **tigereye.**

ti′ger shark′, a large shark, *Galeocerdo cuvier,* found in warm seas, noted for its voracious habits.

ti′ger snake′, a highly venomous elapid snake, *Notechis scutatus,* of Australia and Tasmania, that grows to a length of six feet.

ti′ger swal′lowtail, a yellow swallowtail butterfly, *Papilio glaucus,* of eastern North America, having the forewings striped with black.

tight (tīt), *adj.* **1.** firmly or closely fixed in place; not easily moved; secure: *a tight knot.* **2.** drawn or stretched so as to be tense; taut. **3.** affording little or no extra room; fitting closely, esp. too closely: *a tight collar.* **4.** difficult to deal with or manage: *to be in a tight situation.* **5.** of such close or compacted texture, or fitted together so closely, as to be impervious to water, air, steam, etc.: *a good, tight roof.* **6.** concise; terse: *a tight style of writing.* **7.** firm; rigid: *his tight control of the company.* **8.** packed closely or full; affording little leeway: *a tight schedule.* **9.** *Informal.* nearly even; close: *a tight race.* **10.** *Informal.* parsimonious; stingy. **11.** *Slang.* drunk; tipsy. **12.** *Com.* (of a commodity) difficult to obtain. **13.** (of the stock market) characterized by scarcity or eager demand. **14.** *Journalism.* (of a newspaper) having more news available than is required for or utilizable in a particular issue. **15.** *Baseball Informal.* inside (def. 19). **16.** *Chiefly Dial.* competent or skillful. **17.** *Chiefly Dial.* **a.** tidy. **b.** neatly or well built or made. —*adv.* **18.** Also, **tight′ly.** in a tight manner; closely; firmly; securely; tensely: *Shut the door tight. The shirt fit tight across the shoulders.* [late ME, sandhi var. of *thight* dense, solid, OE *-thīht* (as in *magathīht* belly-strong); c. Icel *thēttr* tight, D, G *dicht* tight, close, dense] —**tight′ness,** *n.*
—**Syn. 10.** close, niggardly, mean, grasping, frugal, sparing.

tight·en (tīt′ən), *v.t., v.i.* to make or become tight or tighter. [TIGHT + -EN[1]] —**tight′en·er,** *n.*

tight-fist·ed (tīt′fis′tid), *adj.* parsimonious; stingy; tight.

tight-knit (tīt′nit′), *adj.* well-organized and integrated.

tight-lipped (tīt′lipt′), *adj.* **1.** having the lips drawn tight. **2.** not speaking or saying much; taciturn.

tight·rope (tīt′rōp′), *n., v.,* **-roped, -rop·ing.** —*n.* **1.** a rope or wire cable stretched tight, on which acrobats perform feats of balancing. —*v.i.* **2.** to walk, move, or proceed on or as on a tight rope: *He tightroped through enemy territory.* —*v.t.* **3.** to make (one's way, course, etc.) on or as on a tightrope. [TIGHT + ROPE]

tights (tīts), *n.* (*construed as pl.*) **1.** a skin-tight garment for the lower part of the body and the legs, worn by acrobats, dancers, gymnasts, etc., now often made of stretch fabric. **2.** a leotard with legs and, sometimes, feet. [n. use of TIGHT; see -S[3]]

tight·wad (tīt′wod′), *n. Informal.* a close-fisted or stingy person. [TIGHT + WAD[1]]

Tig·lath-pi·le·ser I (tig′lath pi lē′zər, -pī-), died 1102? B.C., king of Assyria c1115–1102?.

Tiglath-pileser III, died 727 B.C., king of Assyria 745–727.

tig·lic (tig′lik), *adj. Chem.* of or derived from tiglic acid. Also, **tig·lin·ic** (ti glin′ik). [< NL *tigl(ium)* croton-oil plant (said to be < Gk *tīl(os)* watery excrement + NL *-ium* -IUM) + -IC]

tig′lic ac′id, *Chem.* a slightly water-soluble, poisonous compound, $CH_3CH{=}C(CH_3)COOH$, derived from croton oil and occurring as a thick, syrupy liquid or in colorless crystals: used chiefly in medicine.

ti·glon (tī′glən), *n.* the offspring of a male tiger and a female lion. [TIG(ER) + L(I)ON]

Ti·gré (tē grā′), *n.* a former kingdom in E Africa: now a province in N Ethiopia. *Cap.:* Aduwa.

ti·gress (tī′gris), *n.* **1.** a female tiger. **2.** a fierce or cruel woman. [earlier *tigresse* < F; see TIGER, -ESS]

Ti·gris (tī′gris), *n.* a river in SW Asia, flowing SE from SE Turkey through Iraq, joining the Euphrates to form the Shatt-al-Arab. 1150 mi. long.

ti·grish (tī′grish), *adj.* tigerish.

Ti·hwa (*Chinese.* dē′hwä′), *n.* Urumchi.

Ti·jua·na (tē′ə wä′nə; *Sp.* tē hwä′nä), *n.* a city in NW Mexico, on the Mexico-U.S. border. 222,534 (est. 1963). Also, **Tia Juana.**

tike (tīk), *n.* tyke.

ti·ki (tē′kē), *n.* **1.** (in Polynesian mythology) the first man on earth. **2.** a carved representation of an ancestor, worn as a pendant around the neck in some Polynesian cultures. [< Maori and Marquesan]

til (til, tēl), *n.* the sesame plant. Also, **teel.** [< Hindi: sesame]

til·ak (til′ək), *n., pl.* **-ak, -aks.** a distinctive spot of colored powder or paste worn on the forehead by Hindu men and women as a religious symbol. [< Skt *tilaka*]

Til·burg (til′bûrg; *Du.* til′bœʀKH), *n.* a city in the S Netherlands. 141,580 (1962).

til·bur·y (til′ber′ē, -bə rē), *n., pl.* **-ries.** a light two-wheeled carriage without a top. [named after its inventor, a 19th-century English coach-builder]

Til·da (til′də), *n.* a girl's given name, form of **Matilda.**

til·de (til′də), *n.* **1.** a diacritic (˜) placed over a letter, as in Spanish over the first *n* in *mañana* to indicate a palatal nasal sound. **2.** a similar mark used in some texts, esp. certain dictionaries, to indicate the omission of a word, syllable, or phrase: *The inflected forms of "walk" are "walk, ~ed, ~ing."* [< Sp < L *titul(us)* superscription. See TITLE]

Til·den (til′dən), *n.* **1. Samuel Jones,** 1814–86, U.S. statesman. **2. William Ta·tem, Jr.** (tā′təm), 1893–1953, U.S. tennis player. **3.** a boy's given name.

Til·dy (til′dē), *n.* **Zol·tán** (zôl′tän), 1889–1961, Hungarian statesman: premier 1945–46; president 1946–48.

tile (tīl), *n., v.,* **tiled, til·ing.** —*n.* **1.** a thin slab or bent piece of baked clay, sometimes painted or glazed, used for various purposes, as to form one of the units of a roof covering, pavement, revetment, etc. **2.** any of various similar slabs or pieces, as of stone or metal. **3.** tiles collectively. **4.** a pottery tube or pipe used for draining land. **5.** any of various hollow or cellular units of burnt clay or other materials, as gypsum or cinder concrete, for building walls, partitions, floors, and roofs, or for fireproofing steelwork or the like. **6.** *Informal.* a stiff hat or high silk hat. —*v.t.* **7.** to cover with or as with tiles. [ME; OE *tīgele* (c. G *Ziegel*) < L *tēgul(a)*] —**tile′like′,** *adj.*

tiled (tīld), *adj.* **1.** covered or furnished with tiles. **2.** barred to outsiders, as nonmembers of a lodge. [ME; see TILE, -ED[3]]

tile·fish (tīl′fish′), *n., pl.* (*esp. collectively*) **-fish,** (*esp. referring to two or more kinds or species*) **-fish·es. 1.** a large, brilliantly-colored food fish, *Lopholatilus chamaeleonticeps,* found in the Atlantic Ocean. **2.** any of several related fishes of the family *Branchiostegidae.* [TILE + FISH]

til·er (tī′lər), *n.* **1.** one who lays tiles. **2.** Also, **tyler.** the doorkeeper of a Masonic lodge. [ME; see TILE, -ER[1]]

til·er·y (tī′lə rē), *n., pl.* **-er·ies.** a factory or kiln for making tiles. [TILE + -ERY]

til·i·a·ceous (til′ē ā′shəs), *adj.* belonging to the *Tiliaceae,* or linden family of plants. [< LL *tiliāceus* < L *tili(a)* lime tree + *-āceus* -ACEOUS]

til·ing (tī′ling), *n.* **1.** the operation of covering with tiles. **2.** tiles collectively. **3.** a tiled surface. [late ME *tylynge.* See TILE, -ING[1]]

till[1] (til), *prep.* **1.** up to the time of; until: *to fight till death.* **2.** before (used in negative constructions): *He did not come till today.* **3.** near or at a specified time: *till evening.* **4.** *Scot. and North Eng.* **a.** to. **b.** unto. —*conj.* **5.** to the time that or when; until. **6.** before (used in negative constructions). [ME; OE (north) *til* < Scand; cf. Icel *til* to, akin to OE *till* station, G *Ziel* goal. See TILL[2]]

till[2] (til), *v.t.* **1.** to labor, as by plowing, harrowing, etc., upon (land) for the raising of crops; cultivate. **2.** to plow. —*v.i.* **3.** to cultivate the soil. [ME *tile(n),* OE *tilian* to strive after, get, till; c. D *telen* to breed, cultivate, G *zielen* to aim (at)] —**till′a·ble,** *adj.*

till[3] (til), *n.* **1.** a drawer, box or the like, as in a shop or bank in which money is kept. **2.** a drawer, tray, or the like, as in a cabinet or chest, for keeping valuables. **3.** an arrangement of drawers or pigeonholes, as on a desk top. [late ME *tylle,* n. use of *tylle* to draw, OE *-tyllan* (in *fortyllan* to seduce); akin to L *dolus* trick, Gk *dólos* bait (for fish), any cunning contrivance, treachery]

till[4] (til), *n.* **1.** *Geol.* glacial drift consisting of an unassorted mixture of clay, sand, gravel, and boulders. **2.** a stiff clay. [?]

till[5] (til), *n.* (in early hand printing presses) the transverse beam, supported by the main upright frame, through which the vertical screw is threaded. [? < G *Tülle* socket]

till·a·ble (til′ə bəl), *adj.* able to be tilled; arable. [TILL[2] + -ABLE]

till·age (til′ij), *n.* **1.** the operation, practice, or art of tilling land. **2.** tilled land. [TILL[2] + -AGE]

Til·la·mook (til′ə mo͝ok′), *n.* a town in NW Oregon. 4244 (1960).

til·lands·i·a (ti lan′dzē ə), *n.* any tropical and subtropical American bromeliaceous plants of the genus *Tillandsia,* most of which are epiphytic on trees, as Spanish moss. [named after E. *Tillands,* 17th-century Finno-Swedish botanist; see -IA]

till·er[1] (til′ər), *n.* one who tills; farmer. [ME *tiliere.* See TILL[2], -ER[1]]

till·er[2] (til′ər), *n. Naut.* a bar or lever fitted to the head of a rudder, for turning the rudder in steering. [late ME < AF *teiler* weaver's beam, AL *tēlār(ium)* < L *tēl(a)* warp + *-ārium* -ARY] —**till′er·less,** *adj.*

till·er[3] (til′ər), *n.* **1.** a plant shoot which springs from the root or bottom of the original stalk. **2.** a sapling. —*v.i.* **3.** (of a plant) to put forth new shoots from the root or around the bottom of the original stalk. [OE *telgor* twig, shoot; akin to *telge* rod, Icel *tjalga* branch, *telgja* to cut]

till·er·man (til′ər mən), *n., pl.* **-men.** one who steers a boat or has charge of a tiller. [TILLER[2] + MAN[1]]

Till Eu·len·spie·gel (til′ oi′lən shpē′gəl), a semifictitious German peasant of the 14th century whose practical jokes yielded many stories. Also, **Tyll Eulenspiegel.**

Til·lich (til′ik; *Ger.* til′ɪKH), *n.* **Paul Jo·han·nes** (pôl yō han′is; *Ger.* poul yō hän′is), 1886–1965, U.S. philosopher and theologian, born in Germany.

Til·lie (til′ē), *n.* a girl's given name, form of **Matilda.** Also, **Til′li, Tilly.**

till·ite (til′īt), *n.* a rock composed of consolidated till. [TILL[4] + -ITE[1]]

till′ mon′ey, *Banking.* money set aside for use by a teller, as distinguished from money kept in the vault.

Til·lot·son (til′ət sən), *n.* **John,** 1630–94, English clergyman: archbishop of Canterbury 1691–94.

Til·ly (til′ē), *n.* **1. Count Jo·han Tser·claes von** (yō′hän tseʀ kläs′ fən), 1559–1632, German general in the Thirty Years' War. **2.** a girl's given name, form of **Matilda.**

til·ly-val·ly (til′ē val′ē), *interj. Archaic.* (esp. in exclamations of annoyance or impatience) fiddlesticks! Also, **til·ly-fal·ly** (til′ē fal′ē). [?]

Til·sit (til′zit), *n.* **1.** former name of **Sovetsk. 2.** a semihard, light yellow cheese made from whole milk, similar in flavor to mild Limburger.

tilt[1] (tilt), *v.t.* **1.** to cause to lean, incline, slope, or slant. **2.** to rush at or charge, as in a joust. **3.** to hold poised for attack, as a lance. **4.** to move (a camera) up or down on its vertical axis for photographing or televising a moving character, object, or the like. —*v.i.* **5.** to move into or assume a sloping position or direction. **6.** to strike, thrust, or charge with a lance or the like (usually fol. by *at*). **7.** to engage in a joust, tournament, or similar contest. **8.** (of a camera) to move on its vertical axis: *The camera tilts downward for an overhead shot.* **9. tilt at windmills,** to contend against imaginary opponents or injustices. Also, **fight with windmills.** —*n.* **10.** the act or an instance of tilting. **11.** the state of being tilted; a sloping position. **12.** a slope. **13.** a joust or any other contest. **14.** a dispute; controversy. **15.** a thrust of a weapon, as at a tilt or joust. **16.** (in aerial photography) the angle formed by the direction of aim of a camera and a perpendicular to the surface of the earth. **17. full tilt,** with full force or speed; directly: *The car came at us full tilt along the deserted road.* [ME *tylte(n)* (to) upset, tumble < Scand; cf. dial. Norw *tylta* to tiptoe, *tylten* unsteady; akin to OE *tealt* unsteady, *tealtian* to totter, amble, MD *touteren* to sway] —**tilt′a·ble,** *adj.* —**tilt′er,** *n.*

tilt[2] (tilt), *n.* **1.** a cover of coarse cloth, canvas, etc., as for a wagon. **2.** an awning. —*v.t.* **3.** to furnish with a tilt. [ME, var. of *tild,* OE *teld;* c. G *Zelt* tent, Icel *tjald* tent, curtain]

tilt′ an′gle, *Rocketry.* the angle a missile makes with the vertical as it curves along its trajectory.

tilth (tilth), *n.* **1.** the act or operation of tilling land; tillage. **2.** the state of being tilled or under cultivation. **3.** the physical condition of soil in relation to plant growth. **4.** land which is tilled or cultivated. [ME, OE. See TILL[2], -TH[1]]

tilt′ ham′mer, a drop hammer used in forging, consisting of a heavy head at one end of a pivoted lever.

tilt·head (tilt′hed′), *n. Photog.* a tripod head permitting full horizontal rotation and a large amount of vertical rotation. [TILT[1] + HEAD]

tilt′ing chest′, a medieval chest decorated with a representation of a tournament.

tilt′ing lev′el, *Survey.* a level having a micrometer screw for precise adjustment of the telescope.

Til·ton (til′tən), *n.* a town in E Illinois. 2598 (1960).

tilt′-top ta′ble (tilt′top′), a pedestal table having a top that can be tilted vertically.

tilt·yard (tilt′yärd′), *n.* a courtyard or other area for tilting. [TILT[1] + YARD[2]]

Tim (tim), *n.* a boy's given name, form of **Timothy.**

Tim., *Bible.* Timothy.

Ti·mae·us (tī mē′əs), *n.* a crater in the second quadrant and extending into the first quadrant of the face of the moon: about 22 miles in diameter.

Ti·mae·us (tī mē′əs), *n.* a philosophical dialogue (4th century B.C.) by Plato, containing his cosmogony and having a Pythagorean astronomer as its protagonist.

Ti·man·dra (tī man′drə), *n. Class. Myth.* a daughter of Tyndareus and Leda, and the sister of Clytemnestra and Helen: as were her sisters, she was cursed by Aphrodite and fated to become an adulteress.

ti·ma·rau (tē′mə rou′), *n.* tamarau.

Tim·a·ru (tim′ə rōō′), *n.* a seaport on the E coast of South Island, in S New Zealand. 26,424 (1961).

tim·bal (tim′bəl), *n.* **1.** a kettledrum. **2.** *Entomol.* a vibrating membrane in certain insects, as the cicada. Also, **tymbal.** [< F, MF *timbale* < OF *timb(re)* drum (see TIMBRE) + MF *(attab)al* < Sp *atabal* < Ar *ṭabl* drum]

tim·bale (tim′bəl; *Fr.* taN bAl′), *n., pl.* **-bales** (-bəlz; *Fr.* -bAl′). **1.** Also, **tim′bale case′.** a small shell made of batter, fried usually in a timbale iron. **2.** a preparation, usually richly sauced, as of minced meat, fish, or vegetables, served in such a mold or other crust. [< F: lit., kettledrum. See TIMBAL]

tim′bale i′ron, a metal mold made in any of several shapes and usually provided with a long handle, for deep-frying timbales.

tim·ber (tim′bər), *n.* **1.** the wood of growing trees suitable for structural uses. **2.** growing trees themselves. **3.** wooded land. **4.** wood, esp. when suitable or adapted for various building purposes. **5.** a single piece of wood forming part of a structure or the like: *A timber fell from the roof.* **6.** *Naut.* (in a ship's frame) one of the curved pieces of wood that spring upward and outward from the keel; rib. **7.** personal character or quality: *He's being talked up as presidential timber.* **8.** *Sports Slang.* a wooden hurdle, as a gate, fence, etc., over which a horse must jump in equestrian sports. —*v.t.* **9.** to furnish with timber. **10.** to support with timber. —*interj.* **11.** a lumberjack's call to warn those in the vicinity that a cut tree is about to fall to the ground. [ME, OE; orig. house, building material; c. Icel *timbr* timber, G *Zimmer* room; akin to Goth *timrjan,* Gk *démein* to build. See DOME] —**tim′ber·less,** *adj.* —**tim′ber·y,** *adj.*

tim′ber bamboo′, a woody-stemmed grass, *Phyllostachys reticulata,* of China, having bristly sheathed leaves, bluish-green beneath.

tim′ber cruis′er, cruiser (def. 5).

tim·bered (tim′bərd), *adj.* **1.** made of or furnished with timber. **2.** covered with growing trees; wooded: *timbered acres.* [late ME *timbred.* See TIMBER, -ED[3]]

tim·ber·head (tim′bər hed′), *n. Naut.* **1.** the top end of a timber, rising above the deck and serving for belaying ropes. **2.** a bollard resembling this in position and use. [TIMBER + HEAD]

tim′ber hitch′, a knot or hitch on a spar or the like, made by taking a turn on the object, wrapping the end around the standing part of the rope, then several times around itself.

tim·ber-hitch (tim′bər hich′), *v.t.* to fasten by means of a timber hitch.

tim·ber·ing (tim′bər ing), *n.* **1.** building material of wood. **2.** timberwork. [ME *timbrung.* See TIMBER, -ING[1]]

tim·ber·jack (tim′bər jak′), *n.* one whose occupation is logging; logger. [TIMBER + JACK[1]]

tim·ber·land (tim′bər land′), *n.* land covered with timber-producing forests. [TIMBER + LAND]

tim′ber lim′it, *Canadian.* See **timber line.**

tim′ber line′, **1.** the altitude above sea level at which timber ceases to grow. **2.** the arctic or antarctic limit of tree growth. —**tim′ber-line′,** *adj.*

tim′ber mill′, a sawmill producing timbers, as for building purposes.

tim′ber rat′tlesnake, a rattlesnake, *Crotalus horridus,* of the eastern U.S., usually having the body marked with wide, V-shaped bands. Also called **banded rattlesnake.**

tim′ber wolf′, the American gray wolf *Canis lupus,* esp. the subspecies *C. lupus occidentalis,* formerly common in northern North America but now restricted to heavily forested parts of Canada and the northern U.S.

tim·ber·work (tim′bər wûrk′), *n.* structural work formed of timbers. [ME *timberwerk.* See TIMBER, WORK]

tim′ber yard′, *Brit.* a lumberyard.

tim·bre (tim′bər; *Fr.* taN′brə), *n.* **1.** *Acoustics, Phonet.* the characteristic quality of a sound, independent of pitch and loudness, from which its source or manner of production can be inferred. Timbre depends on the relative strengths of the components of different frequencies, which are determined by resonance. **2.** *Music.* the characteristic quality of sound produced by a particular instrument or voice; tone color. [< F: sound (orig. of bell), MF: bell, timbrel, drum, OF: drum < MGk *tímban(on),* var. of Gk *týmpanon* drum]

tim·brel (tim′brəl), *n.* a tambourine or similar instrument. [ME *timbre* drum (see TIMBRE) + *-el* dim. suffix] —**tim′·breled, tim′brelled,** *adj.*

Tim·buk·tu (tim′buk-tōō′, tim buk′tōō), *n.* **1.** a town in central Mali, in W Africa, near the Niger River. 6000 (est. 1961). French, **Tombouctou. 2.** any faraway place.

time (tīm), *n., adj., v.,* **timed, tim·ing.** —*n.* **1.** the system of those sequential relations that any event has to any other, as past, present, or future; indefinite and continuous duration regarded as that in which events succeed one another. **2.** duration regarded as belonging to the present life as distinct from the life to come or from eternity; finite duration. **3.** a system or method of measuring or reckoning the passage of time: *mean time; apparent time; Greenwich time.* **4.** a limited period or interval, as between two successive events: *a long time.* **5.** a particular period considered as distinct from other periods: *Youth is the best time of life.* **6.** Often, **times. a.** a period in the history of the world, or contemporary with the life or activities of a notable person: *prehistoric times; in Lincoln's time.* **b.** the period or era now or previously present: *a sign of the times; How times have changed!* **c.** a period considered with reference to its events or prevailing conditions, tendencies, ideas, etc.: *hard times; a time of war.* **7.** a prescribed or allotted period, as of one's life, for payment of a debt, etc. **8.** the end of a prescribed or allotted period, as of one's life, a period of gestation, etc.: *When her time came she was delivered of a boy. His time had come, but there was no one left to mourn over him.* **9.** a period with reference to personal experience of a specified kind: *to have a good time; a hot time in the old town tonight.* **10.** a period of work of an employee, or the pay for it; working hours or days or an hourly or daily pay rate. **11.** *Informal.* a term of enforced duty or imprisonment: *to serve time in the army; do time in prison.* **12.** the period necessary for or occupied by something: *The time of the baseball game was two hours and two minutes. The bus takes too much time, so I'll take a plane.* **13.** leisure time; sufficient or spare time: *to have time for a vacation; I have no time to stop now.* **14.** a particular or definite point in time, as indicated by a clock: *What time is it?* **15.** a particular part of a year, day, etc.; season or period: *lunch time; Christmas time.* **16.** an appointed, fit, due, or proper instant or period: *a time for sowing; the time when the sun crosses the meridian; There is a time for everything.* **17.** the particular point in time when an event is scheduled to take place: *train time; curtain time.* **18.** an indefinite, frequently prolonged period or duration in the future: *Time will tell if what we have done here today was right.* **19.** the right occasion or opportunity: *to watch one's time.* **20.** each occasion of a recurring action or event: *to do a thing five times; It's Mickey Mantle's time at bat.* **21. times,** used as a multiplicative word in phrasal combinations expressing how many instances of a quantity or factor are taken together: *four times five; five times faster.* **22.** *Drama.* one of the three unities. Cf. **unity** (def. 9). **23.** *Pros.* a unit or a group of units in the measurement of meter. **24.** *Music.* **a.** tempo; relative rapidity of movement. **b.** the metrical duration of a note or rest. **c.** proper or characteristic tempo. **d.** the general movement of a particular kind of musical composition with reference to its rhythm, metrical structure, and tempo. **e.** the movement of a dance or the like to music so arranged: *waltz time.* **25.** *Mil.* rate of marching, calculated on the number of paces taken per minute: *double time; quick time.* **26.** *Embryol.* the period of gestation. **27.** *Manège.* each completed action or movement of the horse. **28. against time,** in an effort to finish something within a limited period: *We worked against time to get out the newspaper.* **29. ahead of time,** before the time due; early: *The building was completed ahead of time.* **30. at one time, a.** once; in a former time: *At one time we were all animals.* **b.** at the same time; at once: *They all tried to talk at one time.* **31. at the same time,** nevertheless; yet: *She is entertaining, but, at the same time, somewhat tiresome.* **32. at times,** at intervals; occasionally: *At times the city becomes intolerable.* **33. beat (someone's) time,** *Slang.* to compete for or win the person, esp. a woman, being dated or courted by another; prevail over a rival: *He accused his brother of trying to beat his time.* **34. behind the times,** old-fashioned; dated: *These attitudes are behind the times.* **35. for the time being,** temporarily; for the present: *Let's forget about it for the time being.* **36. from time to time,** on occasion; occasionally; at intervals: *She comes to see us from time to time.* **37. gain time,** to postpone in order to make preparations or gain an advantage; delay the outcome of: *He hoped to gain time by putting off signing the papers for a few days more.* **38. in good time, a.** at the right time; on time; punctually. **b.** in advance of the right time; early: *We arrived at the appointed spot in good time.* **39. in no time,** in a very brief time; almost at once: *Working together, they cleaned the entire house in no time.* **40. in time, a.** early enough: *to come in time for dinner.* **b.** in the future; eventually: *In time he'll see what is right.* **c.** in the correct rhythm or tempo: *There would always be at least one child who couldn't keep in time with the music.* **41. keep time, a.** to record time, as a watch or clock does. **b.** to mark or observe the tempo. **c.** to perform rhythmic movements in unison. **42. kill time,** to occupy oneself with some activity to make time pass quickly: *While I was waiting, I killed time counting the cars on the freight trains.* **43. make time, a.** to move quickly, esp. in an attempt to recover lost time. **b.** to travel at a particular speed. **c.** *Slang.* to date, court, or have a love affair with (a woman). **44. many a time,** again and again; frequently: *Many a time they didn't have enough to eat and went to bed hungry.* **45. mark time, a.** to suspend progress temporarily, as to await developments; fail to advance. **b.** *Mil.* to move the feet alternately as in marching, but without advancing. **46. on (one's) own time,** during one's free time; without payment: *He worked out more efficient production methods on his own time.* **47. on time, a.** at the specified time; punctually. **b.** to be paid for within a designated period of time, as in installments: *Many people are never out of debt because they buy everything on time.* **48. out of time,** not in the proper rhythm: *His singing was out of time with the music.* **49. pass the time of day,** to converse briefly with or greet someone: *The women would stop in the market to pass the time of day.* **50. take one's time,** to be slow or leisurely; dawdle: *Speed was important here, but he just took his time.* **51. take time by the forelock,** to take prompt advantage of an opportunity; act swiftly and in time. **52. time after time,** again and again; repeatedly; often: *I've told him time after time not to slam the door.* **53. time and time again,** repeatedly; often: *Time and time again I told her to stop smoking.* Also, **time and again. 54. time of life,** (one's) age: *At your time of life you must be careful not to overdo things.* **55. time of (one's) life,** *Informal.* an extremely enjoyable experience: *They had the time of their lives on their trip to Europe.* —*adj.* **56.** of, pertaining to, or showing the passage of time. **57.** (of an explosive device) containing a clock so that it will detonate at the desired moment: *a time bomb.* **58.** *Com.* payable a stated period of time after presentment: *time drafts or notes.* **59.** of or pertaining to purchases on the installment plan, or with payment postponed. —*v.t.* **60.** to ascertain or record the time, duration, or rate of: *to time a race.* **61.** to fix the duration of: *The proctor timed the test at 15 minutes.* **62.** to fix the interval between (actions, events, etc.): *They timed their strokes at six per minute.* **63.** to regulate as to time, as a train, a clock, etc. **64.** to appoint or choose the moment or occasion for; schedule: *He timed the attack perfectly.* **65.** to mark the rhythm or measure of, as in music. **66.** *Music.* to classify (notes or syllables) according to meter, accent, rhythm, etc. —*v.i.* **67.** to keep time; sound or move in unison. [ME; OE *tīma;* c. Icel *tīmi;* akin to TIDE[1]]

—**Syn. 4.** period, interval, term, spell, span, space. **6.** epoch, era, season, age, date.

time′ and a half′, a rate of pay for overtime work equal to one and one half times the regular hourly wage.

time′ and mo′tion stud′y, the systematic investigation and analysis of the motions and the time required to perform a specific operation or task with a view to seeking more efficient methods of production as well as setting time standards. Also called **time study, motion study.**

time′ ball′, a visual time signal consisting of a ball, raised on a mast a little before an important time of day, as noon, and allowed to drop on the stroke of the hour.

time′ belt′. See **time zone.**

time′ bill′, a bill of exchange payable at a specified date.

time-bind·ing (tīm′bīn′ding), *n.* the distinctively human attribute of preserving memories and records of experiences for the use of subsequent generations.

time′ bomb′, **1.** a bomb so arranged as to explode at a certain time. **2.** a situation, condition, etc., resembling such a bomb in having disastrous consequences resulting from long preparation.

time′ cap′sule, a receptacle containing documents or objects typical of the current period, placed in the earth or in a cornerstone for discovery in the future.

time·card (tīm′kärd′), *n.* a card for recording the time at which an employee arrives at and departs from his place of employment. [TIME + CARD[1]]

time′ clock′, a clock with an attachment which may be manually activated to stamp or otherwise record the exact time on a card or tape, used to keep a record of the time of something, as of the arrival and departure of employees.

time′ con′stant, *Elect.* the time required for a changing quantity in a circuit, as voltage or current, to rise or fall approximately .632 of the difference between its old and new value after an impulse has been applied that induces such a change: equal in seconds to the inductance of the circuit in henries divided by its resistance in ohms.

time-con·sum·ing (tīm′kən sōō′ming), *adj.* (of an action) requiring or wasting much time.

time′ cop′y, *Journalism.* written material set in type and held for future use. Cf. **filler** (def. 8).

time′ depos′it, *Banking.* a deposit that can be withdrawn by the depositor only after he has given advance notice or after an agreed period of time has elapsed.

time′ dis′count, a discount allowed for payment of an invoice or bill before it falls due.

time′ draft′, a draft payable within a specified number of days after it is presented.

time′ expo′sure, *Photog.* a long exposure in which the shutter is opened and closed by hand or by a mechanism other than the automatic mechanism of the shutter. —**time′-ex·po′sure,** *adj.*

time-hon·ored (tīm′on′ərd), *adj.* revered or respected because of antiquity and long continuance: *a time-honored custom.* Also, *esp. Brit.,* **time′-hon′oured.**

time′ immemo′rial, **1.** Also called **time out of mind.** time in the distant past beyond memory or record: *Those carvings have been there from time immemorial.* **2.** *Law.* time beyond legal memory, fixed by statute in England as prior to the beginning of the reign of Richard I (1189).

time·keep·er (tīm′kē′pər), *n.* **1.** one who or that which keeps time. **2.** an official appointed to time, regulate, and record the duration of a sports contest or its component parts, as to give the official time of a race, assure that a round of boxing is ended exactly on time, or announce to football, basketball, hockey, etc., teams the amount of time left to play. **3.** a timepiece: *This watch is a good timekeeper.* **4.** a person employed to keep account of the hours of work done by others. **5.** one who beats time in music. [TIME + KEEPER] —**time′keep′ing,** *n.*

time-lag (tīm′lag′), *n.* the period of time between two closely related events, phenomena, etc., as between stimulus and response, or between cause and effect: *a time-lag between the declaration of war and full war production.*

time′ lamp′, an oil lamp of the 17th and 18th centuries, burning at a fixed rate and having a reservoir graduated in units of time.

time′-lapse photog′raphy (tīm′laps′), the photographing on motion-picture film of a slow and continuous process, as the growth of a plant, at regular intervals, esp. by exposing a single frame at a time, for projection at a higher speed.

time·less (tīm′lis), *adj.* **1.** without beginning or end; eternal; everlasting. **2.** referring or restricted to no particular time: *the timeless beauty of great music.* [TIME + -LESS] —**time′less·ly,** *adv.* —**time′less·ness,** *n.*

time′ lim′it, a period of time within which an action or procedure must be done or completed.

time′ loan′, a loan repayable at a specified date. Cf. **call loan.**

time′ lock′, a lock, as for the door of a bank vault, equipped with a mechanism that makes it impossible to operate the lock within certain hours.

time·ly (tīm′lē), **—adj. 1.** occurring at a suitable time; seasonable; opportune; well-timed: *a timely warning.* **2.** *Archaic.* early. **—adv. 3.** seasonably; opportunely. **4.** *Archaic.* early or soon. [ME *tim(e)-liche*, OE *tīmlīc*. See TIME, -LY] **—time′li·ness,** *n.*
—Syn. 1. See **opportune.**

time′ mon′ey, funds loaned or available to be loaned for repayment within a designated period of time, usually in installments.

time′ note′, a note payable within a specified number of days after it is presented.

ti·me·o Da·na·os et do·na fe·ren·tes (tim′e ō′ dä′nä ōs′ et dō′nä fe ren′tes; *Eng.* tim′ē ō′ dan′ā ōs′ et dō′nə fə ren′tēz), *Latin.* I fear the Greeks even when they bear gifts; I fear treacherous persons even when they appear to be friendly. Vergil's *Aeneid: I,* 2:49.

time′ of day′, 1. a definite time as shown by a timepiece; the hour: *Can you tell me the time of day?* **2.** the current time; the present: *The younger generation in this time of day encounters problems quite different from those of past generations.* **3.** an interval of time during the day: *He stopped by just to pass the time of day.* **4.** *Informal.* a minimum of attention: *He wouldn't even give her the time of day.*

Time′ of Your Life′, The, a play (1939) by William Saroyan.

time·ous (tī′məs), *adj. Scot.* **1.** early. **2.** timely. [TIME + -OUS; r. late ME (Scot) *tymys;* see -ISH[1]] **—time′ous·ly,** *adv.*

time-out (tīm′out′), *n.* **1.** Also called **time′ out′.** a brief suspension of activity; intermission or break. **2.** *Sports.* a short interruption in a regular period of play during which a referee or other official stops the clock so that the players may rest, deliberate, make substitutions, etc.

time′ out of mind′. See **time immemorial** (def. 1).

time·piece (tīm′pēs′), *n.* **1.** an apparatus for measuring and recording the progress of time; chronometer. **2.** a clock or a watch. [TIME + PIECE]

time·pleas·er (tīm′plē′zər), *n. Obs.* a timeserver. [TIME + PLEASER]

tim·er (tī′mər), *n.* **1.** one who or that which times. **2.** one who measures or records time. **3.** a device for indicating or measuring elapsed time, as a stop watch. **4.** a device for controlling machinery, appliances, or the like in a specified way at a predetermined time: *She put the roast in the oven and set the timer to cook it for two hours.* **5.** (in an internal-combustion engine) a set of points actuated by a cam, which causes the spark for igniting the charge at the instant required. [TIME + -ER[1]]

Time′ Remem′bered, a comedy (1945) by Jean Anouilh. French, **Léocadia.**

time·sav·ing (tīm′sā′ving), *adj.* (of methods, devices, etc.) reducing the time spent or required to do something. [TIME + SAVING] **—time′sav′er,** *n.*

time·serv·er (tīm′sûr′vər), *n.* a person who shapes his conduct to conform with the opinions of the time or of persons in power, esp. for selfish ends. [TIME + SERVER] **—time′serv′ing,** *adj., n.* **—time′serv′ing·ness,** *n.*

time′ shar′ing, a system or service in which a number of subscribers at remote locations simultaneously use a single multiple-access computer. **—time′-shar′ing,** *adj.*

time′ sheet′, a sheet or card recording the hours worked by an employee, made esp. for accounting purposes.

time′ sig′nal, a signal sent electrically or by radio, to indicate a precise moment of time as a means of checking or regulating timepieces.

time′ sig′nature, *Music.* a numerical or other indication at the beginning of a piece showing the meter.

Times′ Square′, a wide intersection extending from 43rd to 47th Streets in central Manhattan, New York City, where Broadway and Seventh Avenue intersect: theaters, restaurants, etc.

time′ stud′y. See **time and motion study.**

time·ta·ble (tīm′tā′bəl), *n.* **1.** a schedule showing the times at which railroad trains, airplanes, etc., arrive and depart. **2.** any schedule or plan, designating the times at or within which certain things occur or are scheduled to occur: *a timetable of coming musical events; a timetable of space research.* **3.** *Brit.* **a.** a university or college catalogue listing all classes taught during a school semester, along with the time that each class is held, the teacher's name, etc. **b.** a student's class schedule or course of study during a school semester. [TIME + TABLE]

time′ train′, *Horol.* See **going train.**

time·work (tīm′wûrk′), *n.* work done and paid for by the hour or day. Cf. **piecework.** [TIME + WORK] **—time′work′er,** *n.*

time·worn (tīm′wōrn′, -wôrn′), *adj.* **1.** worn or impaired by time. **2.** showing the effects of age or antiquity; antiquated: *a timeworn story.* [TIME + WORN]

time′ zone′, one of the 24 regions or divisions of the globe approximately coinciding with meridians at successive hours from the observatory at Greenwich, England. Also called **time belt.**

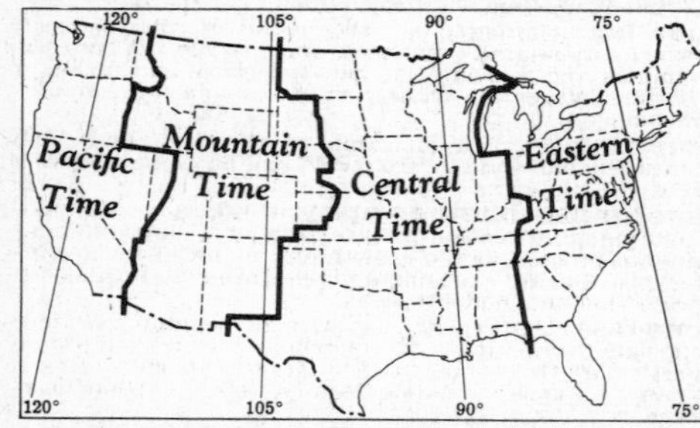

Time zones of the continental United States

tim·id (tim′id), *adj.* **1.** lacking in self-assurance, courage, or fearlessness; easily alarmed; timorous; shy. **2.** characterized by or indicating fear: *a timid approach to a problem.* [< L *timid(us)* fearful, < *tim(ēre)* (to) fear + *-idus* -ID[4]] **—ti·mid′i·ty, tim′id·ness,** *n.* **—tim′id·ly,** *adv.*
—Syn. 1. fearful, faint-hearted. See **cowardly.**

tim·ing (tī′ming), *n.* **1.** *Theat.* **a.** a synchronizing of the various parts of a production for theatrical effect. **b.** the result or effect thus achieved. **c.** (in acting) the act of adjusting one's tempo of speaking and moving for dramatic effect. **2.** *Sports.* the control of the speed of a stroke, blow, etc., in order that it may reach its maximum at the proper moment. **3.** selecting the best time or speed for doing something in order to achieve the desired or maximum result: *Her timing was bad when she asked her husband for a new coat just a day after she wrecked the car.* **4.** the act or an instance of observing and recording the elapsed time of an act, contest, process, etc. [TIME + -ING[1]]

tim′ing belt′, an endless belt bearing teeth for engaging sprockets on two mechanisms requiring precise synchronization.

tim′ing chain′, a chain for driving the camshaft of an internal-combustion engine from the crankshaft.

Ti·mi·șoa·ra (tē′mē shwä′rä), *n.* a city in W Rumania. 152,230 (est. 1964). Hungarian, **Temesvár.**

Ti·moch·a·ris (ti mok′ər is), *n.* a crater in the second quadrant of the face of the moon: about 25 miles in diameter.

ti·moc·ra·cy (tī mok′rə sē), *n., pl.* **-cies. 1.** a form of government in which love of honor is the dominant motive of the rulers. **2.** a form of government in which a certain amount of property is requisite as a qualification for office. [earlier *timocratie* < Gk *tīmokratía* < *tīmo-* (comb. form of *tīmḗ* honor, worth) + *-kratia* -CRACY] **—ti·mo·crat·ic** (tī′mə krat′ik), **ti′mo·crat′i·cal,** *adj.*

Ti·mo·le·on (ti mō′lē ən), *n.* a walled plain in the first quadrant of the face of the moon, in the libration area: about 80 miles in diameter.

Ti·mon (tī′mən), *n.* c320–c230 B.C., Greek philosopher.

Ti′mon of Ath′ens a tragedy (1605–8?) by Shakespeare.

Ti·mor (tē′môr), *n.* **1.** an island in the Malay Archipelago: largest and easternmost of the Lesser Sunda Islands; W half belongs to Indonesia, E half belongs to Portugal. **2.** Also called **Indonesian Timor.** Formerly, **Netherlands Timor.** the W part of this island. 569,927 (est. 1961); 5765 sq. mi. **3.** Also called **Portuguese Timor.** a Portuguese overseas territory comprising the E part of this island. 496,000 (est. 1959); 7330 sq. mi. *Cap.:* Dili.

tim·or·ous (tim′ər əs), *adj.* **1.** full of fear; fearful: *The noise made them timorous.* **2.** subject to fear; timid. **3.** characterized by or indicating fear: *a timorous whisper.* [late ME < ML *timōrōs(us)* (L *timōr-* (s. of *timor*) fear + *-ōsus* -OUS); r. late ME *tymerous, tumerous,* etc. < MF *temerous*] **—tim′or·ous·ly,** *adv.* **—tim′or·ous·ness,** *n.*
—Syn. 1. See **cowardly.**

Ti′mor Sea′, an arm of the Indian Ocean, between Timor and NW Australia.

Ti·mo·shen·ko (tim′ə sheng′kō; *Russ.* tə′mo shen′ko), *n.* **Se·mion Kon·stan·ti·no·vich** (si myôn′ kôn′stän tē′no vich), 1895–1970, Russian general.

tim·o·thy (tim′ə thē), *n., pl.* **-thies.** a coarse grass, *Phleum pratense,* having cylindrical spikes, used as fodder. Also, **tim′othy grass′.** [named after *Timothy* Hanson, American farmer who grew this grass and spread its cultivation in early 18th century]

Tim·o·thy (tim′ə thē), *n.* **1.** a disciple and companion of the apostle Paul, to whom Paul is supposed to have addressed two Epistles. **2.** either of these Epistles, I Timothy or II Timothy. **3.** a boy's given name.

Ti·mour (ti mŏŏr′), *n.* Tamerlane. Also, **Ti·mur′.**

tim·pa·ni (tim′pə nē), *n.pl.* (*often construed as sing.*) a set of kettledrums, esp. as used in an orchestra or band. Also, **tympani.** [< It, pl. of *timpano* kettledrum < L *tympan(um)* < Gk *týmpanon*] **—tim′pa·nist,** *n.*

Tim·rod (tim′rod), *n.* **Henry,** 1828–67, U.S. poet.

ti·mu·cu (ti mōō′kə, tim′yə kyōō′), *n.* a needlefish, *Strongylura timucu,* found in warm, western Atlantic waters. [var. of *Timoco, Timucua,* Florida Indian tribe, which may have been named after the fish]

tin (tin), *n., adj., v.,* **tinned, tin·ning. —n. 1.** *Chem.* a low-melting, malleable, ductile metallic element nearly approaching silver in color and luster: used in plating and in making alloys, tinfoil, and soft solders. *Symbol:* Sn; *at. wt.:* 118.69; *at. no.:* 50; *sp. gr.:* 7.31 at 20°C. **2.** See **tin plate. 3.** *Chiefly Brit.* **a.** any shallow pan, esp. one used in baking. **b.** any pot, box, can, or other container or vessel made of tin or tin plate. **c.** a hermetically-sealed can containing food. **4.** *Brit. Slang.* money. **—adj. 5.** made or consisting of tin or tin plate. **6.** mean; worthless; counterfeit: *a tin god.* **7.** indicating the tenth event of a series, as a wedding anniversary. **—v.t. 8.** *Metall.* **a.** to cover or coat with tin. **b.** to coat with soft solder. **9.** *Chiefly Brit.* to preserve or pack (esp. food) in cans; can. [ME, OE; c. D, Icel *tin,* G *Zinn*] **—tin′like′,** *adj.*

Ti·na (tē′nə), *n.* a girl's given name, form of **Albertina, Bettina,** or **Christina.** Also, **Teena.**

tin·a·mou (tin′ə mōō′), *n.* any of several birds of the family *Tinamidae,* of South and Central America, related to the ratite birds but superficially resembling the gallinaceous birds. [< F < Carib *tinamu* (Galibi dial.)]

tin′ ash′, *Chem.* See **stannic oxide.**

tin′ beard′, *Slang.* an artificial beard made of crepe hair that has not been properly blended into the facial make-up of an actor.

tin′ brass′, any of various brasses to which tin has been added, as admiralty metal.

tin·cal (tiŋ′käl, -kôl), *n.* the former Oriental name of crude native borax. [< Malay *tingkal*]

tin′ can′, 1. a sealed or covered metal can for food or other perishables, esp. one made of tin-plated sheet steel. **2.** *U.S. Navy Slang.* a destroyer.

tinct (tiŋkt), *v.t.* **1.** *Obs.* to tinge or tint, as with color. **2.** *Obs.* to imbue. **—adj. 3.** *Archaic. Literary.* tinged; colored; flavored. **—n. 4.** *Literary.* tint; tinge; coloring. [< L *tinct(us),* ptp. of *tingere* to dye, color, tinge]

tinct., tincture.

tinc·to·ri·al (tiŋk tōr′ē əl, -tôr′-), *adj.* pertaining to coloring or dyeing. [< L *tinctōri(us)* of or related to dipping, dyeing (see TINCT, -ORY[1]) + -AL[1]] **—tinc·to′ri·al·ly,** *adv.*

tinc·ture (tiŋk′chər), *n., v.,* **-tured, -tur·ing. —n. 1.** *Pharm.* a solution of alcohol or of alcohol and water, containing animal, vegetable, or chemical drugs. **2.** a slight infusion, as of some element or quality: *A tincture of education had softened his rude manners.* **3.** a trace; a smack or smattering; a tinge: *a tincture of irony.* **4.** *Heraldry.* any of the colors, metals, or furs used for the fields, charges, etc., of an escutcheon or achievement of arms. **5.** *Obs.* a dye or pigment. **—v.t. 6.** to impart a tint or color to; tinge. **7.** to imbue or infuse with something. [< LL *tinctūr(a)* dyeing. See TINCT, -URE]

Tin·dal (tin′dəl), *n.* **1. Matthew,** c1655–1733, English deist. **2.** Also, **Tin′dale. William.** See **Tyndale, William.**

tin·der (tin′dər), *n.* **1.** a highly flammable material or preparation formerly used for catching the spark from a flint and steel struck together for fire or light. **2.** any dry substance that readily takes fire from a spark. [ME; OE *tynder;* akin to Icel *tundr,* G *Zunder,* OE *-tendan* (as in *ātendan* to set on fire), Goth *tundnan* to catch fire, G *-zünden* in *entzünden* to kindle] **—tin′der-like′,** *adj.*

tin·der·box (tin′dər boks′), *n.* **1.** a box for holding tinder, usually fitted with a flint and steel. **2.** one who or that which is highly excitable, inflammable, etc.; a potential source of widespread violence: *Berlin is the tinderbox of Europe.* [TINDER + BOX[1]]

tin·der·y (tin′də rē), *adj.* resembling tinder; highly inflammable or inflammatory. [TINDER + -Y[1]]

tin′ disease′. See **tin pest.**

tine[1] (tīn), *n.* a sharp, projecting point or prong, as of a fork. Also, *esp. Brit.,* **tyne.** [late ME *tyne,* ME, OE *tind;* c. Icel *tindr,* OHG *zint*] **—tined,** *adj.*

tine[2] (tīn), *v.,* **tined** or **tint** (tint), **tin·ing.** *Chiefly Scot.* **—v.t. 1.** to lose. **—v.i. 2.** to be lost; die. [ME < Scand; cf. Icel *týna* to lose, destroy. See TEEN[1]]

tin·e·a (tin′ē ə), *n. Pathol.* any of several skin diseases caused by fungi; ringworm. [< NL; in L: gnawing worm] **—tin′e·al,** *adj.*

tin′ea bar′bae (bär′bē), *Pathol.* See **barber's itch.** [< NL: tinea of the beard]

tin′ ear′, *Slang.* **1.** See **cauliflower ear. 2.** an inability to distinguish all or certain sounds or tones: *He has a tin ear, so he keeps still when the rest of the class sings.*

tin·e·id (tin′ē id), *n.* **1.** a moth of the family *Tineidae,* comprising the clothes moths. **—adj. 2.** belonging or pertaining to the family *Tineidae.* [< NL *Tineid(ae).* See TINEA, -ID[2]]

tin′ fish′, *Slang.* a torpedo.

tin′ foil′, tin, or an alloy of tin and lead, in the form of a thin sheet, much used as a wrapping for drugs, confectionery, tobacco, etc. **—tin′-foil′,** *adj.*

ting[1] (tiŋ), *v.t., v.i.* **1.** to cause to make or to make a high, clear, ringing sound. **—n. 2.** a tinging sound. [imit.; see TANG[2]]

ting[2] (tiŋ), *n.* thing[2]. [< Dan, Norw, Sw; c. Icel *thing* THING[2]]

ting-a-ling (tiŋ′ə liŋ′), *n.* a repeated tinkling sound, as of a small bell. [imit. rhyming compound]

tinge (tinj), *v.,* **tinged, tinge·ing** or **ting·ing,** *n.* **—v.t. 1.** to impart a trace or slight degree of some color to; tint. **2.** to impart a slight taste or smell to. **—n. 3.** a slight degree of coloration. **4.** a slight admixture, as of some qualifying property or characteristic; trace; smattering: *a tinge of garlic; a tinge of anger.* [late ME < L *ting(ere)* (to) dye, color]

tin·glass (tin′glas′, -gläs′), *n. Obs.* bismuth. [TIN + GLASS]

tin′ glaze′, *Ceram.* a glaze containing ashes or oxide of tin, white unless colored with a mixture of metallic oxides.

tin-glazed (tin′glāzd′), *adj.* (of a ceramic object) covered with a tin glaze.

tin·gle (tiŋ′gəl), *v.,* **-gled, -gling,** *n.* **—v.i. 1.** to have a sensation of slight prickles, stings, or tremors, as from cold, a sharp blow, excitement, etc.: *I tingle all over.* **2.** to cause such a sensation: *The scratch tingles.* **—n. 3.** a tingling sensation. **4.** the tingling action of cold, a blow, excitement, etc. [ME; var. of TINKLE] **—tin′gler,** *n.* **—tin′gling·ly,** *adv.*

Ting·ley (tiŋ′lē), *n.* **Katherine Augusta West·cott** (west′kot), 1847–1929, U.S. theosophist leader.

tin·gly (tiŋ′glē), *adj.,* **-gli·er, -gli·est.** tingling or causing a tingling sensation. [TINGLE + -Y[1]]

tin′ God′, 1. a self-important, dictatorial person in a position of authority, as an employer, military officer, critic, teacher, etc. **2.** a person who considers himself infallible and tries to impose his judgments, beliefs, standards of behavior, etc., on those subordinate to him. Also, **tin′ god′.**

tin′ hat′, *Slang.* a steel helmet worn by soldiers.

tin·horn (tin′hôrn′), *Slang.* **—n. 1.** someone, esp. a gambler, who pretends to be important but actually has little ability, influence, or money. **—adj. 2.** cheap and insignificant; small-time: *a tinhorn racket.* [TIN + HORN]

Tin·i·a (tin′ē ə), *n.* the chief god of the Etruscans, with powers similar to those of Zeus.

tink·er (tiŋ′kər), *n.* **1.** a mender of pots, kettles, pans, etc., usually an itinerant. **2.** an unskillful or clumsy worker; bungler. **3.** one skilled in various minor kinds of mechanical work; jack-of-all-trades. **4.** the act or an instance of tinkering: *Let me have a tinker at that motor.* **5.** *Scot., Irish Eng.* **a.** a gypsy. **b.** any itinerant worker. **c.** wanderer. **d.** beggar. **6.** a small mackerel, *Pneumatophorus grex*, found off the Atlantic coast of the U.S. —*v.i.* **7.** to do the work of a tinker. **8.** to work unskillfully or clumsily at anything. **9.** to busy oneself with a thing without useful results: *Stop tinkering with that clock and take it to the repair shop.* —*v.t.* **10.** to mend as a tinker. **11.** to repair in an unskillful, clumsy, or makeshift way. [ME *tinkere*, syncopated var. of *tinekere* worker in tin]

tink′er's dam′, **1.** Also, **tink′er's damn′.** something worthless or trivial; nothing at all: *It's not worth a tinker's dam. I don't care a tinker's damn.* **2.** (in plumbing) a barrier for retaining molten solder within a certain area until it has cooled.

tink′er's weed′. See **horse gentian.**

tin·kle (tiŋ′kəl), *v.*, **-kled, -kling,** *n.* —*v.i.* **1.** to give forth or make a succession of short, light, ringing sounds, as a small bell. **2.** to run one's fingers lightly over a keyboard instrument or to play such an instrument simply or badly. —*v.t.* **3.** to cause to tinkle or jingle: *The goat tinkled its bell every time it raised its head. Who's tinkling the piano?* **4.** to make known, call attention to, attract, or summon by tinkling. —*n.* **5.** a tinkling sound or tune. **6.** the act or an instance of tinkling. **7.** *Informal.* a telephone call: *Give me a tinkle before you leave for Europe.* [ME, freq. of obs. *tink* (v.) to clink; imit.]

tin·kler (tiŋ′klər), *n.* *Brit. Dial.* tinker (defs. 1, 4, 5). [ME]

tin·kling (tiŋ′kliŋ), *n.* a short, light, ringing sound or succession of such sounds, as of a small bell. [TINKLE + -ING[1]] —**tin′kling·ly,** *adv.*

tin·kly (tiŋ′klē), *adj.*, **-kli·er, -kli·est.** tinkling or producing a tinkling sound. [TINKLE + -Y[1]]

Tin′ley Park′ (tin′lē), a town in NE Illinois. 6392 (1960).

tin′ liz′zie (liz′ē), *Slang.* a small, cheap automobile.

tin·man (tin′mən), *n.*, *pl.* **-men.** a tinsmith. [TIN + MAN[1]]

tinned (tind), *adj.* **1.** coated or plated with tin. **2.** *Chiefly Brit.* preserved or packed in a can, as food; canned. [TIN + -ED[3]]

tin·ner (tin′ər), *n.* a tinsmith. [TIN + -ER[1]]

tin·ner·y (tin′ə rē), *n.*, *pl.* **-ner·ies.** tinworks.

Tin·nev′el·ly sen′na (ti nev′ə lē, tin′ə vel′ē). See under **senna** (def. 2). [named after *Tinnevelly*, southern district of Madras, India]

tin·ni·ent (tin′ē ənt), *adj.* having a ringing or clinking sound. [< L *tinnient-* (s. of *tinniēns*), prp. of *tinnīre;* prob. of imit. orig.]

tin·ning (tin′iŋ), *n.* **1.** the act or technique of coating with tin. **2.** the act or technique of coating with soft solder. **3.** *Chiefly Brit.* the process, technique, or business of preserving or packing foodstuffs in tins; canning. [TIN + -ING]

tin′ning stack′, (in tin-plating) a row of baths containing molten tin and grease alternately.

tin·ni·tus (ti nī′təs), *n.* *Pathol.* a ringing or similar sensation of sound in the ears. [< L: a tinkling < *tinnīt-* (ptp. s. of *tinnīre* to tinkle) + *-us* n. suffix, 4th decl.]

tin·ny (tin′ē), *adj.*, **-ni·er, -ni·est.** **1.** of or like tin. **2.** containing tin. **3.** lacking in timbre or resonance; sounding thin or twangy: *a tinny piano.* **4.** not strong or durable. **5.** having the taste of tin. [TIN + -Y[1]] —**tin′ni·ly,** *adv.* —**tin′ni·ness,** *n.*

tin′ o′pener, *Brit.* See **can opener.**

tin-pan (tin′pan′), *adj.* harsh, tinny, or clanging; noisy. Also, **tin′-pan′ny.**

Tin′-Pan Al′ley, **1.** the district of a city, esp. New York City, where most of the popular music is published. **2.** the composers or publishers of popular music as a group.

tin′ pants′, *U.S.* heavy waterproof trousers, usually of paraffin-soaked canvas, worn by loggers and fishermen.

tin′ pest′, the powdering of tin exposed to temperatures of 13°C or lower, caused by allotropic transformation. Also called **tin disease.**

tin′ plate′, thin iron or steel sheet coated with tin. Also, **tin′plate′.**

tin-plate (tin′plāt′), *v.t.*, **-plat·ed, -plat·ing.** to coat (iron or steel sheet) with tin. —**tin′ plat′er.**

tin-pot (tin′pot′), *adj.* inferior; paltry; shoddy. [from the believed inferior quality of a *tin pot*]

tin′ pyri′tes, *Mineral.* stannite.

tin·sel (tin′səl), *n.*, *adj.*, *v.*, **-seled, -sel·ing** or (*esp. Brit.*) **-selled, -sel·ling.** —*n.* **1.** a glittering metallic substance, as copper, brass, etc., in thin sheets, used in pieces, strips, threads, etc., to produce a sparkling effect cheaply. **2.** a metallic yarn, usually wrapped around a core yarn of silk, rayon, or cotton, for weaving brocade or lamé. **3.** anything showy or attractive with little or no real worth; showy pretense: *The actress was tired of the fantasy and tinsel of her life.* **4.** *Obs.* a fabric, formerly in use, of silk or wool interwoven with threads of gold, silver, or, later, copper. —*adj.* **5.** consisting of or containing tinsel. **6.** showy; gaudy; tawdry. —*v.t.* **7.** to adorn with tinsel. **8.** to adorn with anything glittering. **9.** to make showy or gaudy. [by aphesis < MF *estincelle* (OF *estincele*) a spark, flash < VL **stincilla*, metathetic var. of L *scintilla* SCINTILLA; first used attributively in phrases *tinsel satin, tinsel cloth*] —**tin′sel-like′,** *adj.*

tin·sel·ly (tin′sə lē), *adj.* cheap and gaudy. [TINSEL + -Y[1]]

tin·sel·ry (tin′səl rē), *n.* cheap and pretentious display. [TINSEL + -RY]

tin·smith (tin′smith′), *n.* one who makes or repairs tinware or items of other light metals. [TIN + SMITH]

tin′ sol′dier, a miniature toy soldier of cast metal, usually of lead.

tin′ spir′it, Often, **tin spirits.** any of a group of solutions containing tin salts, used in dyeing.

tin·stone (tin′stōn′), *n.* cassiterite. [TIN + STONE]

tint[1] (tint), *n.* **1.** a color or a variety of a color; hue. **2.** a color diluted with white; a color of less than maximum purity, chromo, or saturation. **3.** a delicate or pale color. **4.** *Engraving.* a uniform shading, as that produced by series of fine parallel lines. **5.** Also called **tint′ block′.** *Print.* a faintly or lightly colored background upon which an illustration or the like is to be printed. **6.** any of various commercial dyes for the hair. —*v.t.* **7.** to apply a tint or tints to; color slightly or delicately; tinge. [var. of TINCT] —**tint′er,** *n.*

tint[2] (tint), *v.* a pt. and pp. of **tine**[2].

tin·tack (tin′tak′), *n.* *Brit.* a short nail made of tin-plated iron. [TIN + TACK[1]]

Tin·tag′el Head′, (tin taj′əl), a cape in SW England, on the W coast of Cornwall.

Tin′tern Ab′bey (tin′tərn), (*Lines Composed a Few Miles Above Tintern Abbey*) a poem (1798) by Wordsworth.

tin·tin·nab·u·lar (tin′ti nab′yə lər), *adj.* of or pertaining to bells or bell ringing. Also, **tin·tin·nab·u·lar·y** (tin′ti nab′yə ler′ē), **tin′tin·nab′u·lous.** [< L *tintinnābul(um)* bell (< *tintinnā(re)* (to) ring + *-bulum* instrumental suffix) + -AR[1]]

tin·tin·nab·u·la·tion (tin′ti nab′yə lā′shən), *n.* the ringing or sound of bells. [< L *tintinnābul(um)* bell (see TINTINNABULAR) + -ATION]

tint·less (tint′lis), *adj.* without tint or tints; colorless. [TINT[1] + -LESS] —**tint′less·ness,** *n.*

tint·om·e·ter (tin tom′i tər), *n.* a precision instrument for comparing tints or colors with those used as arbitrary standards. [TINT + -O- + -METER] —**tint·o·met·ric** (tin′tə me′trik), *adj.* —**tint·om′e·try,** *n.*

Tin·to·ret·to (tin′tə ret′ō; *It.* tēn′tô ret′tô), *n.* **Il** (ēl), (*Jacopo Robusti*), 1518–94, Venetian painter.

tin·type (tin′tīp′), *n.* a positive photograph made on a sensitized sheet of enameled tin or iron; ferrotype. [TIN + -TYPE]

tin·ware (tin′wâr′), *n.* articles made of tin plate. [TIN + WARE[1]]

tin-white (tin′hwīt′, -wīt′), *adj.* white, as the color of tin; bluish-white. [TIN + WHITE]

tin·work (tin′wûrk′), *n.* **1.** something made of tin. **2.** such things collectively. [TIN + WORK]

tin·works (tin′wûrks′), *n.*, *pl.* **-works.** (*construed as sing. or pl.*) an establishment for the mining or processing of tin or for the making of tinware. [TIN + WORKS]

ti·ny (tī′nē), *adj.*, **-ni·er, -ni·est.** very small; minute; wee. [late ME *tine* very small (< ?) + -Y[1]] —**ti′ni·ly,** *adv.* —**ti′ni·ness,** *n.*
—**Syn.** little, diminutive, teeny.

-tion, a suffix occurring in words of Latin origin, used to form abstract nouns from verbs or stems not identical with verbs, whether as expressing action (*revolution; commendation*), or a state (*contrition; starvation*), or associated meanings (*relation; temptation*). Also, **-ation, -cion, -ion, -sion, -xion.** [< L *-tiōn-* (s. of *-tiō*) < *-t(us)* ptp. suffix + *-iōn-* -ION]

-tious, a suffix originally occurring in adjectives borrowed from Latin (*fictitious*); on this model, used with stems of other origin (*bumptious*). Also, **-ious, -ous.** [< L *-tiōs(us)*, equiv. to *-t(us)* ptp. suffix + *-iōsus* -IOUS]

tip[1] (tip), *n.*, *v.*, **tipped, tip·ping.** —*n.* **1.** a slender or pointed end or extremity, esp. of anything long or tapered: *the tips of the fingers.* **2.** the top, summit, or apex: *the tip of the mountain.* **3.** a small piece or part, as of metal, leather, etc., forming or covering the extremity of something: *a cane with a rubber tip.* **4.** Also called **tip-in, tip-on.** an insert, as an illustration, map, or errata slip, pasted to a page of a book, magazine, etc., usually along the binding margin. **5.** a small, delicate tool made of fine hair cemented between two cards, for applying gold leaf. —*v.t.* **6.** to furnish with a tip. **7.** to serve as or form the tip of. **8.** to mark or adorn the tip of. **9.** to remove the tip or stem of (berries or certain fruits or vegetables). **10. tip in,** *Bookbinding.* to paste the inner margin of (a map, illustration, or other plate) into a signature before gathering. [ME; cf. D, LG, Dan *tip*, Sw *tipp*, G *zipf-* in *Zipfel* tip] —**tip′less,** *adj.*

tip[2] (tip), *v.*, **tipped, tip·ping,** *n.* —*v.t.* **1.** to cause to assume a slanting or sloping position; incline; tilt. **2.** to overturn, upset, or overthrow (often fol. by *over*). **3.** to remove or lift (one's hat or cap) in salutation. **4.** *Brit.* to dump or dispose of by dumping: *The lorry tipped the coal. The maid tipped the rubbish.* —*v.i.* **5.** to assume a slanting or sloping position; incline. **6.** to tilt up at one end and down at the other; slant. **7.** to be overturned or upset: *The car tipped into the ditch.* **8.** to tumble or topple (usually fol. by *over*): *The lamp on the table tipped over.* —*n.* **9.** the act of tipping. **10.** the state of being tipped. **11.** *Brit.* a dump for refuse, as that from a mine. [earlier *tipe*, ME *type* to upset, overturn] —**tip′pa·ble,** *adj.*

tip[3] (tip), *n.*, *v.*, **tipped, tip·ping.** —*n.* **1.** a small present of money given directly to someone for performing a service or menial task; gratuity: *He gave the waiter a dollar as a tip.* **2.** a piece of private or secret information, as for use in betting, speculating, a news story, etc.: *a tip from a bookie.* **3.** a useful hint or idea; a basic, practical fact: *tips on painting.* —*v.t.* **4.** to give a small gratuity to. —*v.i.* **5.** to give a gratuity: *He tipped lavishly.* **6. tip off,** *Informal.* **a.** to give private or secret information about or to inform. **b.** to warn of impending danger or trouble; caution beforehand: *The moonshiners had been tipped off that they were about to be raided.* [? special use of TIP[4]] —**tip′less,** *adj.* —**tip′pa·ble,** *adj.*

tip[4] (tip), *n.*, *v.*, **tipped, tip·ping.** —*n.* **1.** a light, smart blow; tap. **2.** *Baseball.* a batted ball that glances off the bat. Cf. **foul tip.** —*v.t.* **3.** to strike or hit with a light, smart blow; tap. **4.** *Baseball.* to strike (the ball) with a glancing blow. [? < LG; cf. G *tippen* to tap < LG]

ti′ palm′, ti[2].

tip-and-run (tip′ənd run′, -ənd-), *adj.* *Brit.* marked by or having resort to a rapid escape after a sudden, brief attack: *tip-and-run tactics.* [TIP[4] + RUN]

tip·burn (tip′bûrn′), *n.* *Plant Pathol.* a disease of lettuce, potatoes, and other plants, characterized by browning of the tips and edges of the leaves, resulting from any of several environmental factors, as excessive heat and humidity. [TIP[1] + BURN[1]]

tip·cart (tip′kärt′), *n.* a cart with a body that can be tipped or tilted to empty it of its contents. [TIP[2] + CART]

tip·cat (tip′kat′), *n.* **1.** a game in which a short piece of wood, tapered at both ends, is struck lightly at one end with a bat, causing the wood to spring into the air so that it can be batted for a distance. **2.** Also called **pussy.** the tapered piece of wood used in this game. [TIP[2] + CAT]

Ti·phys (tī′fis), *n.* *Class. Myth.* the steersman of the Argonauts.

ti·pi (tē′pē), *n.*, *pl.* **-pis.** tepee.

tip-in[1] (tip′in′), *n.* *Basketball.* tap-in.

tip-in[2] (tip′in′), *n.* tip[1] (def. 4).

tip-off (tip′ôf′, -of′), *n.* *Informal.* **1.** the act of tipping off. **2.** a hint or warning: *They got a tip-off on the raid.* [n. use of v. phrase *tip off*]

tip-on (tip′on′, -ôn′), *n.* tip[1] (def. 4).

Tipp′ Cit′y (tip), a town in W Ohio. 4267 (1960).

Tip·pe·ca·noe (tip′ə kə nōō′), *n.* **1.** nickname of William Henry Harrison. **2.** a river in N Indiana, flowing SW to the Wabash: battle 1811. 200 mi. long.

tip·per (tip′ər), *n.* one who or that which tips: *The waiters liked him for being a big tipper.* [TIP[3] + -ER[1]]

Tip·per·ar·y (tip′ə râr′ē), *n.* **1.** a county in Munster province, in the S Republic of Ireland. 123,822 (1961); 1643 sq. mi. *Co. seat:* Clonmel. **2.** a town in this county. 5148 (1951).

tip·pet (tip′it), *n.* **1.** a scarf, usually of fur or wool, for covering the neck, or the neck and shoulders, and usually having ends hanging down in front. Cf. **stole**[2] (def. 2). **2.** *Eccles.* a band of silk or the like worn around the neck with the ends pendent in front. Cf. **stole**[2] (def. 1). **3.** a long, narrow, pendent part of a hood, sleeve, etc. **4.** *Angling.* **a.** a short length of gut, nylon, or the like, for tying an artificial fly to the leader. **b.** a branch of the shaft of a bird feather, serving as the tail of an artificial fly. [ME; see TIP[1], -ET]

tip′ping cen′ter, *Naval Archit.* See **center of flotation.**

tip·ple[1] (tip′əl), *v.*, **-pled, -pling,** *n.* —*v.t.* **1.** to drink (intoxicating liquor), esp. repeatedly, in small quantities. —*v.i.* **2.** to drink intoxicating liquor, esp. habitually or to some excess. —*n.* **3.** intoxicating liquor. [back formation from ME *tipeler* tapster < *tipel-* TAP[2] (c. D *tepel* teat) + *-er* -ER[1]. See TIPSY]

tip·ple[2] (tip′əl), *n.* **1.** a device that tilts or overturns a freight car to dump its contents. **2.** a place where loaded cars are emptied by tipping. [n. use of *tipple* to tumble, freq. of TIP[2]]

tip·pler[1] (tip′lər), *n.* one who tipples intoxicating liquor. [TIPPLE[1] + -ER[1]]

tip·pler[2] (tip′lər), *n.* one who works at a tipple, as at a mine. [TIPPLE[2] + -ER[1]]

tip·py (tip′ē), *adj.*, **-pi·er, -pi·est.** (of an object) liable to tip over. [TIP[2] + -Y[1]]

tip·py·toe (tip′ē tō′), *n.*, *v.i.*, **-toed, -to·ing,** *adj.*, *adv.* *Informal.* tiptoe. [by alter.]

tip′ sheet′, a publication containing the latest information, tips, and predictions for a particular business, stock-market conditions, horse racing results, etc.

tip·staff (tip′staf′, -stäf′), *n.*, *pl.* **-staves** (-stāvz′, -stavz′, -stävz′), **-staffs.** **1.** an attendant or crier in a court of law. **2.** a staff tipped with metal, formerly carried as a badge of office, as by a constable. **3.** any official who carried such a staff. [*tipp(ed)* (see TIP[1], -ED[3]) + STAFF]

tip·ster (tip′stər), *n.* *Informal.* one who makes a business of furnishing tips, as for betting or speculation. [TIP[3] + -STER]

tip·sy (tip′sē), *adj.*, **-si·er, -si·est.** **1.** slightly intoxicated or drunk. **2.** characterized by or due to intoxication: *a tipsy lurch.* **3.** tipping, unsteady, or tilted, as if from intoxication. [obs. *tip* strong drink (? back formation from TIPPLE[1]) + *-sy* adj. suffix. Cf. obs. *bumpsy* in same sense] —**tip′si·ly,** *adv.* —**tip′si·ness,** *n.*

tip′sy cake′, *Brit.* wine-soaked sponge cake with a custard filling.

tip·toe (tip′tō′), *n.*, *v.*, **-toed, -to·ing,** *adj.*, *adv.* —*n.* **1.** the tip or end of a toe. **2. on tiptoe, a.** on the tips of one's toes. **b.** expectant; eager: *With Christmas coming, the children were on tiptoe.* **c.** stealthily; cautiously: *The concert had already begun, so he entered the back of the hall on tiptoe.* —*v.i.* **3.** to move or go on tiptoe, as with caution or stealth: *She tiptoed out of the room.* —*adj.* **4.** characterized by standing or walking on tiptoe. **5.** straining upward. **6.** eagerly expectant. **7.** cautious; stealthy. —*adv.* **8.** eagerly or cautiously; on tiptoe. [ME *tiptoon* (pl.). See TIP[1], TOE]

Tip·ton (tip′tən), *n.* **1.** a town in central Indiana. 5604 (1960). **2.** a town in E Iowa. 2862 (1960).

tip·top (tip′top′), *n.* **1.** the extreme top or summit. **2.** *Informal.* the highest point or degree: *the very tiptop of physical condition.* **3.** *Chiefly Brit. Informal.* the highest social class. —*adj.* **4.** situated at the very top. **5.** *Informal.* of the highest quality: *a tiptop meal.* —*adv.* **6.** in a tiptop manner; very well: *It's shaping up tiptop.* [gradational compound; see TIP[1], TOP[1]]

tip′-up ta′ble (tip′up′), a pedestal table having a top folding downward in two leaves. [adj. use of v. phrase *tip up*]

Ti′pu Sa′hib (tip′ōō), 1750–99, sultan of Mysore 1782–99.

ti·rade (tī′rād, tə rād′), *n.* **1.** a prolonged outburst of bitter, outspoken denunciation: *a tirade against smoking.* **2.** a long, vehement speech: *a tirade in the Senate.* **3.** a passage dealing with a single theme or idea, as in poetry: *the stately tirades of Corneille.* [< F: lit., a stretch, (continuous) pulling < It *tirata*, n. use of fem. of *tirato*, ptp. of *tirare* to draw, pull, fire (a shot)]
—**Syn. 2.** harangue

ti·rail·leur (tē RA yœR′), *n.*, *pl.* **-leurs** (-yœR′). *French.* **1.** skirmisher; sharpshooter. **2.** one of the native infantry units formerly organized by the French in North Africa, Senegal, and Indochina.

Ti·ra·na (tē RÄ′nä), *n.* a city in and the capital of Albania, in the central part. 156,950 (est. 1964). Albanian, **Ti·ra·në** (tē Rä′nə).

tire[1] (tīər), *v.*, **tired, tir·ing,** *n.* —*v.t.* **1.** to reduce or exhaust the strength of, as by exertion; make weary; fatigue: *The long walk tired him.* **2.** to exhaust the interest, patience, etc., of, as by long continuance or by dullness; make weary; bore: *Your stories tire me.* —*v.i.* **3.** to have the strength reduced or exhausted, as by labor or exertion; become fatigued; be sleepy. **4.** to have one's appreciation, interest, patience, etc., exhausted; become or be weary; become bored (usually fol. by *of*): *He soon tired of playing billiards.* —*n.* **5.** *Brit. Dial.* fatigue. [late ME (Scot) *tyre*, OE *tȳr(ian)*, var. of *tēorian* to weary, be wearied]
—**Syn. 2.** exasperate, bore, irk.

CONCISE PRONUNCIATION KEY: *act, āble, dâre, ärt; ebb, ēqual; if, īce; hot, ōver, ôrder, oil, bŏŏk, ōōze, out; up, ûrge; chief; sing; shoe; thin, that;* zh as in *measure.* ə = *a* as in *alone*, *e* as in *system*, *i* as in *easily*, *o* as in *gallop*, *u* as in *circus;* ə as in *button* (but′ən), *fire* (fīər), *cradle* (krād′əl). See the full key inside the front cover.

tire[2] (tīər), *n., v.,* **tired, tir·ing.** —*n.* **1.** a ring or band of rubber, either solid or hollow and inflated, or of metal, placed over the rim of a wheel to provide traction, resistance to wear, or other desirable properties. **2.** a metal band attached to the outside of the felloes and forming the tread of a wagon wheel. —*v.t.* **3.** to furnish with tires. Also, *Brit.,* **tyre.** [late ME *tyre;* special use of TIRE[3]]

tire[3] (tīər), *v.,* **tired, tir·ing,** *n. Archaic.* —*v.t.* **1.** to attire or array. **2.** to dress (the head or hair), esp. with a headdress. —*n.* **3.** attire or dress. **4.** a headdress. [ME; aph. var. of ATTIRE]

tire[4] (tīər), *v.,* **tired, tir·ing.** *Obs.* —*v.i.* **1.** to tear flesh greedily; prey (upon). **2.** to concentrate (upon) in thought or action. —*v.t.* **3.** to tear greedily. [< MF *tire(r)* (to) draw, pull, shoot]

tire[5] (tīər), *n. Obs.* a volley of cannon. [< MF, verbid of *tirer* to TIRE[4]]

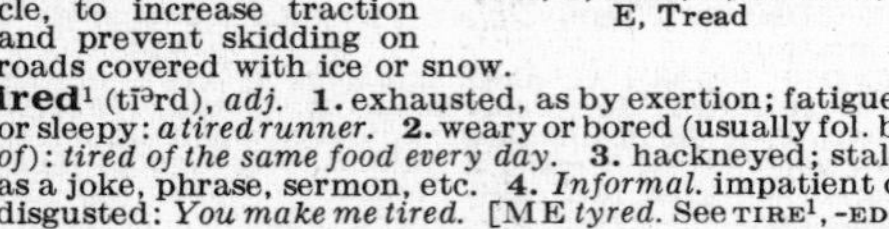

Tire[2] (Cross Section)
A, Rim of wheel; B, Inner tube; C, Bead; D, Sidewall; E, Tread

tire′ chain′, a chain fitting over the tire of a car, truck, or other vehicle, to increase traction and prevent skidding on roads covered with ice or snow.

tired[1] (tīərd), *adj.* **1.** exhausted, as by exertion; fatigued or sleepy: *a tired runner.* **2.** weary or bored (usually fol. by *of*): *tired of the same food every day.* **3.** hackneyed; stale, as a joke, phrase, sermon, etc. **4.** *Informal.* impatient or disgusted: *You make me tired.* [ME *tyred.* See TIRE[1], -ED[2]] —**Syn. 1.** enervated. TIRED, EXHAUSTED, FATIGUED, WEARIED, WEARY suggest a condition in which a large part of one's energy and vitality has been consumed. One who is TIRED has used up a considerable part of his bodily or mental resources: *to feel tired at the end of the day.* One who is EXHAUSTED is completely drained of energy and vitality, usually because of arduous or long-sustained effort: *exhausted after a hard run.* One who is FATIGUED has consumed energy to a point where rest and sleep are demanded: *feeling rather pleasantly fatigued.* One who is WEARIED has been under protracted exertion or strain which has gradually worn out his strength: *wearied by a long vigil.* WEARY suggests a more permanent condition than wearied: *weary of struggling against misfortunes.* —**Ant. 1.** rested; energetic, tireless.

tired[2] (tīərd), *adj.* having a tire or tires. [TIRE[2] + -ED[3]]

tire′ i′ron, a short length of steel with one end flattened to form a blade, used as a crowbar for removing tires from wheel rims.

tire·less (tīər′lis), *adj.* untiring; indefatigable: *a tireless worker.* [TIRE[1] + -LESS]

Ti·re·si·as (tī rē′sē əs, -shē əs), *n. Class. Myth.* a blind prophet, usually said to have been blinded because he saw Athena bathing, and then to have been awarded the gift of prophecy as a consolation for his blindness, and said to have lived both as a man and as a woman.

tire·some (tīər′səm), *adj.* **1.** causing or liable to cause a person to tire; wearisome: *a tiresome job.* **2.** annoying or vexatious. [TIRE[1] + -SOME[1]] —**Syn. 1.** dull, fatiguing, humdrum. —**Ant. 2.** interesting.

tire·wom·an (tīər′wŏŏm′ən), *n., pl.* **-wom·en.** *Archaic.* a lady's maid. [TIRE[3] + WOMAN]

Ti·rich Mir (tē′rich mēr′), a mountain in N West Pakistan, on the border of Afghanistan: highest peak of the Hindu Kush Mountains. 25,230 ft.

tir′ing room′, *Archaic.* a dressing room, esp. in a theater. [aph. var. of *attiring room*]

tirl (tûrl), *Scot.* —*n.* **1.** a wheel, cam, or any revolving mechanism or piece of machinery. **2.** an allotted time for action which comes in rotation to each member of a group; turn. —*v.t.* **3.** to rotate; turn; twirl. —*v.i.* **4.** to make a rattling noise by spinning or revolving. [metathetic var. of TRILL]

ti·ro (tī′rō), *n., pl.* **-ros.** tyro.

Tir·ol (tir′ol, tī′rōl, tī rōl′; *Ger.* tē rōl′), *n.* Tyrol.

Ti·ro·le·an (ti rō′lē ən), *adj., n.* Tyrolean.

Tir·o·lese (tir′ə lēz′, -lēs′), *adj., n., pl.* **-lese.** Tyrolese.

Ti·ros (tī′rōs), *n. U.S.* one of a series of satellites for transmitting television pictures of the earth's cloud cover.

Tir·pitz (tir′pits), *n.* **Al·fred von** (äl′frāt fən), 1849–1930, German admiral and statesman.

tir·ri·vee (tûr′ə vē′), *n. Scot.* a tantrum. [?]

Tir·so de Mo·li·na (tēr′sô de mô lē′nä), (*Gabriel Téllez*) 1571?–1648, Spanish dramatist.

Tir·than·ka·ra (tir tung′kər ə), *n. Jainism.* one of 24 persons who have attained personal immortality through enlightenment. [< Skt *tīrthankara,* lit., passage-making]

Ti·ru·chi·ra·pal·li (tir′ōō chi rə pul′ē), *n.* a city in central Madras, in S India, on the Cauvery River. 249,900 (1961). Formerly, **Trichinopoly.**

Tir·yns (tir′inz), *n.* an ancient city in Greece, in Peloponnesus: destroyed in 486 B.C. by the Argives; excavated ruins include Cyclopean walls forming part of a great fortress.

'tis (tiz), a contraction of *it is.*

Ti·sam·e·nus (ti sam′ə nəs), *n. Class. Myth.* **1.** a son of Orestes and Hermione who ruled in Sparta until he was killed by the invading Heraclidae. **2.** a leader of the Boeotians at Troy. **3.** a seer whose prophetic powers aided several Spartan victories.

ti·sane (ti zan′; *Fr.* tē zan′), *n., pl.* **-sanes** (-zanz′; *Fr.* -zan′). **1.** (*italics.*) *French.* aromatic or herb-flavored tea. **2.** *Obs.* a ptisan. [< F]

Tisch·en·dorf (tish′ən dôrf′), *n.* **Lo·be·gott Frie·drich Kon·stan·tin von** (lō′bə gôt′ frē′drikh kôn′stän tēn′ fən), 1815–74, German biblical critic.

Ti·se·li·us (tə sā′lē ōōs′), *n.* **Ar·ne** (är′nə), born 1902, Swedish biochemist: Nobel prize 1948.

Tish·ab b'Ab (tē shä′ bə äb′), a Jewish fast day observed on the ninth day of the month of Ab in memory of the destruction in Jerusalem of the First and Second Temples. Also, **Tish·ah b'Av** (tish′ə bôv′). Also called **Ninth of Ab.** [< Heb: ninth (day) of Ab]

Tish·ri (tish′rā, -rē; *Heb.* tēsh rē′), *n.* a month of the Jewish calendar. Cf. **Jewish calendar.** [< Heb]

Ti·siph·o·ne (ti sif′ə nē′), *n. Class. Myth.* one of the Furies.

Ti·so (tē′sō), *n.* **Jo·sef** (yô′sef), 1887–1947, Slovakian Roman Catholic clergyman and politician.

'Tis′ Pit′y She's′ a Whore′, a tragedy (1633) by John Ford.

Tis·se·rand (tē′sə rän′, tēs rän′; *Fr.* tēsə rän′), *n.* a walled plain in the first quadrant of the face of the moon: about 21 miles in diameter.

Tis·sot (tē sō′), *n.* **James Jo·seph Jacques** (zham zhō zef′ zhäk, zhämz), 1836–1902, French painter.

tis·sue (tish′ōō), *n., v.,* **-sued, -su·ing.** —*n.* **1.** *Biol.* an aggregate of similar cells and cell products forming a definite kind of structural material in an animal or plant. **2.** a woven fabric, esp. one of light or gauzy texture, originally woven with gold or silver: *a blouse of a delicate tissue.* **3.** an interwoven or interconnected series or mass: *a tissue of falsehoods.* **4.** any of several kinds of soft gauzy papers used for various purposes: *cleansing tissue; toilet tissue.* **5.** See **tissue paper. 6.** a piece of thin writing paper on which carbon copies are made. —*v.t. Archaic.* **7.** to weave, esp. with threads of gold and silver. **8.** to clothe or adorn with tissue. [ME *tissew,* var. of *tissu* < MF, OF, n. use of ptp. of *tistre* to weave < L *texere*] —**tis′su·al,** *adj.* —**tis′su·ey,** *adj.*

tis′sue cul′ture, 1. the science of cultivating animal tissue in a prepared medium. **2.** the process itself.

tis′sue pa′per, a very thin, almost transparent paper used for wrapping delicate articles, covering illustrations in books, copying letters, etc.

tiss·wood (tis′wŏŏd′), *n.* a tall tree, *Halesia monticola,* of the southeastern U.S., having white flowers in clusters. [*tiss* (< ?) + WOOD[1]]

tis·win (tiz wēn′), *n.* a fermented beverage made by the Apache Indians. Also, **tizwin.** [< MexSp *tesguino, tecuin* < Nahuatl *tecuini* heartbeat]

Ti·sza (tē′so), *n.* a river in S central Europe, flowing from the Carpathian Mountains through E Hungary and NE Yugoslavia into the Danube N of Belgrade. 800 mi. long. German, **Theiss.**

tit[1] (tit), *n.* **1.** a titmouse. **2.** any of various other small birds. **3.** *Archaic.* a girl or young woman; hussy. **4.** *Archaic.* a small or poor horse; nag. [ME *tite-* (in *titemose* TITMOUSE); c. Norw *tite* titmouse; akin to Icel *tittr* tack, pin. See TIT[2]]

tit[2] (tit), *n.* **1.** a teat. **2.** a female breast. [ME *titte,* OE *titt;* c. MLG, MD *titte,* G *Zitze,* Norw *titta;* akin to TIT[1]]

tit[3] (tit), *n.* See **tit for tat.** [? var. of TIP[4]]

Tit., Titus.

tit., title.

Ti·tan (tīt′ən), *n.* **1.** *Class. Myth.* **a.** any of the sons of Uranus and Gaea, including Coeus, Crius, Cronus, Hyperion, Iapetus, and Oceanus. **b.** Also, **Ti′tan·ess.** any of the sisters of these, including Mnemosyne, Phoebe, Rhea, Tethys, Themis, and Thia. **c.** any of the offspring of the children of Uranus and Gaea. **2. the Titan,** Helios. **3.** *Astron.* one of the nine satellites of Saturn. **4.** (*usually l.c.*) a person or thing of enormous size, strength, power, influence, etc.: *a titan of industry.* **5.** *U.S.* a surface-to-surface, two-stage intercontinental ballistic missile, with the booster powered by two liquid-propellant rocket engines and with one liquid-propellant rocket engine as sustainer. —*adj.* **6.** (*l.c.*) titanic. [late ME: the sun < L < Gk]

ti·tan·ate (tīt′ənāt′), *n. Chem.* a salt of titanic acid. [TITAN(IUM) + -ATE[2]]

Ti·tan·esque (tīt′ənesk′), *adj.* Titanlike; Titanic. [< F]

ti·ta·ni·a (tī tā′nē ə), *n.* synthetic rutile, TiO_2, used as a gem. [< NL; see TITANIUM, -IA]

Ti·ta·ni·a (ti tā′nē ə, tī-), *n.* **1.** (in Shakespeare's *Midsummer Night's Dream*) the wife of Oberon and the queen of fairyland. **2.** *Astron.* one of the five satellites of Uranus. **3.** *Class. Myth.* a poetic epithet variously applied to Diana, Pyrrha, Latona, and Circe.

ti·tan·ic[1] (tī tan′ik, ti-), *adj. Chem.* of or containing titanium, esp. in the tetravalent state. [TITAN(IUM) + -IC]

ti·tan·ic[2] (tī tan′ik), **1.** (*cap.*) of, pertaining to, or characteristic of the Titans. **2.** Also, **titan.** of enormous size, strength, power, etc.; gigantic. [< Gk *Titanik(ós).* See TITAN, -IC] —**ti·tan′i·cal·ly,** *adv.*

titan′ic ac′id, *Chem.* **1.** See **titanium dioxide. 2.** any of various acids derived from titanium dioxide.

titan′ic ox′ide, *Chem.* See **titanium dioxide.**

ti·tan·if·er·ous (tīt′ənif′ər əs), *adj.* containing or yielding titanium. [TITANI(UM) + -FEROUS]

Ti·tan·ism (tīt′əniz′əm), *n.* (*sometimes l.c.*) the characteristic Titan spirit or quality, esp. of revolt against tradition, convention, and established order. [TITAN + -ISM]

ti·tan·ite (tīt′ənīt′), *n. Mineral.* sphene. [< G *Titanit.* See TITANIUM, -ITE[1]]

ti·ta·ni·um (tī tā′nē əm), *n. Chem.* a dark-gray or silvery, lustrous, very hard, light, corrosion-resistant, metallic element, occurring combined in various minerals: used in metallurgy to remove oxygen and nitrogen from steel and to toughen it. *Symbol:* Ti; *at. wt.:* 47.90; *at. no.:* 22; *sp. gr.:* 4.5 at 20°C. [TITAN + -IUM]

tita′nium diox′ide, *Chem.* a white, water-insoluble powder, TiO_2, used chiefly in white pigments, plastics, ceramics, and for delustering synthetic fibers. Also called **tita′nium ox′ide, titanic acid, titanic oxide.**

tita′nium white′, a pigment used in painting, consisting chiefly of titanium dioxide and noted for its brilliant white color, covering power, and permanence.

Ti·tan·om·a·chy (tīt′ənom′ə kē), *n. Class. Myth.* the unsuccessful revolt of the family of Iapetus against Zeus, put down with the aid of the Cyclopes and the Hecatonchires and the advice of Prometheus. [< Gk *tītānomachía.* See TITAN, -O-, -MACHY]

ti·tan·o·saur (tī tan′ə sôr′, tīt′ənə sôr′), *n.* any amphibious, herbivorous dinosaur of the genus *Titanosaurus,* from the Cretaceous period. [< NL *Tītānosaur(us).* See TITAN, -O-, -SAUR]

ti·tan·ous (tī tan′əs, ti-), *adj. Chem.* containing trivalent titanium. [TITAN(IUM) + -OUS]

tit·bit (tit′bit′), *n. Chiefly Brit.* tidbit. [rhyming compound, by alter.]

ti·ter (tī′tər, tē′-), *n. Chem.* the strength of a solution as determined by titration with a standard substance. Also, *esp. Brit.,* **titre.** [< F *titre* title, qualification, fineness of alloyed gold or silver < L *titulus* TITLE]

tit·fer (tit′fər), *n. Chiefly Brit. Slang.* See **tit for tat** (def. 2). [rhyming slang, shortening of *tit for tat*]

tit′ for tat′, 1. with an equivalent given in retaliation, as a blow for a blow, repartee, etc.: *He answered their insults tit for tat.* **2.** Also, **titfer.** *Chiefly Brit. Slang.* a hat. [? var. of earlier *tip for tap*]

tith·a·ble (tī′thə bəl), *adj.* subject to the payment of tithes. [late ME *tythable.* See TITHE, -ABLE]

tithe (tīth), *n., v.,* **tithed, tith·ing.** —*n.* **1.** Sometimes, **tithes.** the tenth part of agricultural produce or personal income set apart as an offering to God or for works of mercy, or the same amount regarded as an obligation or tax for the support of the church, priesthood, or the like. **2.** any tax, levy, or the like, of one-tenth. **3.** a tenth part or any indefinitely small part of anything. [ME *ti(ghe)the,* OE *teogotha* tenth] —*v.t.* **4.** to give or pay a tithe or tenth of (produce, money, etc.). **5.** to give or pay tithes on (crops, income, etc.). **6.** to exact a tithe from (a person, community, parish, etc.). **7.** to levy a tithe on (crops, income, etc.). —*v.i.* **8.** to give or pay a tithe. Also, *Brit.,* **tythe.** [ME *tithe(n),* OE *te(o)g(o)thian* to take the tenth of] —**tithe′less,** *adj.*

tithe′ barn′, *Brit.* (formerly) a barn built on church or parish property to hold the tithes of neighboring farmers.

tith·er (tī′thər), *n.* **1.** one who gives or pays tithes, as to a church. **2.** one who advocates payment of tithes. **3.** one who collects tithes. [ME; see TITHE, -ER[1]]

tith·ing (tī′thing), *n.* **1.** a tithe. **2.** a giving or an exacting of tithes. **3.** a company of householders, originally 10 in number, in the old English system of frankpledge. **4.** a rural division in England, originally regarded as one tenth of a hundred, descended from this system. [ME; OE *tigething.* See TITHE, -ING[1]]

Ti·tho·nus (ti thō′nəs), *n. Class. Myth.* a son of Laomedon, beloved by Eos (Aurora): he asked Eos for and was granted immortality, but finding himself immortally old he asked her to take back the gift and was metamorphosed into a grasshopper.

ti·ti[1] (tē tē′), *n., pl.* **-tis.** any of various small reddish or grayish monkeys of the genus *Callicebus,* of South America. [< Sp < Aymaran]

ti·ti[2] (tē′tē), *n., pl.* **-tis.** any of the cyrillaceous shrubs or small trees of the southern U.S., esp. *Cliftonia monophylla* **(black titi)** and *Cyrilla racemiflora* **(white titi),** having glossy leaves and racemes of fragrant white flowers. [< AmerInd]

Ti·tian (tish′ən), *n.* **1.** (*Tiziano Vecellio*) c1477–1576, Italian painter. **2.** (*l.c.*) a reddish-brown or golden-brown color: *titian hair.* —**Ti′tian·esque′,** *adj.*

Ti·ti·ca·ca (tē′tē kä′kä), *n.* **Lake,** a lake on the boundary between S Peru and W Bolivia, in the Andes: the largest lake in South America; the highest large lake in the world. 3200 sq. mi.; 12,508 ft. above sea level.

tit·il·late (tit′əlāt′), *v.t.,* **-lat·ed, -lat·ing. 1.** to tickle; excite a tingling or itching sensation in, as by touching or stroking lightly. **2.** to excite agreeably: *to titillate the fancy.* [< L *titillāt(us),* ptp. of *titillāre* to tickle; see -ATE[1]] —**tit′il·lat′ing·ly,** *adv.* —**tit′il·la′tion,** *n.* —**tit′il·la′tive,** *adj.*

tit·i·vate[1] (tit′ə vāt′), *v.,* **-vat·ed, -vat·ing.** *Informal.* —*v.t.* **1.** to make smart or spruce: *She titivated her old dress with a new belt.* —*v.i.* **2.** to make oneself smart or spruce. Also, **tittivate.** [earlier *tidivate* (TIDY + (ELE)VATE; i.e., tidy up)] —**tit′i·va′tion,** *n.* —**tit′i·va′tor,** *n.*

tit·i·vate[2] (tit′ə vāt′), *v.t.,* **-vat·ed, -vat·ing.** titillate. [by alter.]

tit·lark (tit′lärk′), *n.* any of several small, larklike birds, esp. a pipit. [TIT[1] + LARK[1]]

ti·tle (tīt′əl), *n., v.,* **-tled, -tling.** —*n.* **1.** the distinguishing name of a book, poem, picture, piece of music, or the like. **2.** a descriptive heading or caption, as of a chapter, section, or other part of a book. **3.** See **title page. 4.** a descriptive or distinctive appellation, esp. one belonging to a person by right of rank, office, attainment, etc.: *the title of Lord Mayor.* **5.** *Sports.* the championship: *He won the title three years in a row.* **6.** an established or recognized right to something. **7.** a ground or basis for a claim. **8.** anything that provides a ground or basis for a claim. **9.** *Law.* **a.** legal right to the possession of property, esp. real property. **b.** the ground or evidence of such right. **c.** the instrument constituting evidence of such right. **d.** a unity combining all of the requisites to complete legal ownership. **e.** a division of a statute, lawbook, etc., esp. one larger than an article or section. **f.** (in pleading) the designation of one's basis for judicial relief; the cause of action sued upon, as contract, tort, etc. **10.** *Eccles.* **a.** a fixed sphere of work and source of income, required as a condition of ordination. **b.** any of certain Roman Catholic churches in Rome, the nominal incumbents of which are cardinals. **11.** Usually, **titles.** *Motion Pictures, Television.* **a.** a subtitle in the viewer's own language: *The Italian movie has English titles.* **b.** any written matter inserted into the film or program, esp. the list of actors, technicians, writers, etc., contributing to it; credits. —*v.t.* **12.** to furnish with a title; designate by an appellation; entitle. [ME, var. of *titel,* OE *titul* < L *titul(us)* superscription, title] —**Syn. 4.** designation, denomination. See **name. 12.** denominate, term, call, style.

ti′tle cat′alog, *Library Science.* a catalog whose entries are listed by title only.

ti′tled (tīt′əld), *adj.* having a title, esp. of nobility: *a titled family.* [TITLE + -ED[3]]

ti′tle deed′, a deed or document containing or constituting evidence of ownership.

ti′tle en′try, *Library Science.* a catalog entry of a book, document, etc., by title, usually arranged alphabetically by the first word other than an article.

ti·tle·hold·er (tīt′əl hōl′dər), *n.* **1.** one who holds a title. **2.** *Sports.* one who holds a championship; present champion. [TITLE + HOLDER]

ti′tle insur′ance, insurance protecting the owner or mortgagee of real estate from lawsuits or claims arising from a defective title.

ti′tle lin′ing, *Print.* a system for aligning type in which the baseline is established close to the edge of the body, used esp. for titles set in capitals which have no descenders. Cf. **art lining, standard lining.**

ti′tle page′, the page at the beginning of a volume which indicates the title, author's or editor's name, and the publication information, usually the publisher and the place and date of publication.

ti′tle role′, (in a play, opera, etc.) the role or character from which the title is derived: *She sang the title role in* Carmen.

ti·tlist (tīt′list), *n. Sports.* a titleholder; champion. [TITLE + -IST]

tit·mouse (tit′mous′), *n., pl.* **-mice** (-mīs′). any of numerous small, passerine birds of the family *Paridae,* esp. of the genus *Parus,* having soft, thick plumage and a short, stout, conical bill. Cf. **tufted titmouse.** [ME *tit(e)-mose* (see TIT[1]); *mose,* OE *māse* titmouse; c. G *Meise* titmouse, Icel *meis-* in *meisingr* kind of bird; modern *-mouse* by folk etymology]

Tufted titmouse, ***Parus bicolor*** **(Length 6 in.)**

Ti·to (tē′tō), *n.* **1. Marshal** (*Josip Broz*), 1891–1980, president of Yugoslavia 1953–80. **2.** a boy's given name.

Ti·to·grad (tē′tō grad′), *n.* a city in and the capital of Montenegro, in S Yugoslavia. 17,000 (est. 1959). Formerly, **Podgorica, Podgoritsa.**

Ti·to·ism (tē′tō iz′əm), *n.* a form of communism associated with Tito, characterized by disaffection from or rebellion against the domination by the Soviet Union of communist states outside of Russia. [TITO + -ISM] —**Ti′to·ist,** *adj., n.*

Ti·tov (tē′tof), *n.* **Vi·ta·li Ni·ko·la·ye·vich** (vi tä′li ni ko lä′ye vich), born 1907, Russian government official: member of the Presidium since 1961.

ti·trant (tī′trənt), *n. Chem.* the reagent added in a titration. [TIT(E)R + -ANT]

ti·trate (tī′trāt, ti′-), *v.t., v.i.,* **-trat·ed, -trat·ing.** *Chem.* to ascertain the quantity of a given constituent present in (a solution) by adding a liquid reagent of known strength and measuring the volume necessary to convert the constituent to another form. [TIT(E)R + -ATE[1]] —**ti·trat′a·ble, ti·tra·ble** (tī′trə bəl), *adj.* —**ti·tra′tion,** *n.*

ti·tre (tī′tər, tē′-), *n. Chiefly Brit.* titer.

tit-tat-toe (tit′tat tō′), *n.* tick-tack-toe.

tit·ter (tit′ər), *v.i.* **1.** to laugh in a half-restrained, self-conscious, or affected way, as from nervousness or in ill-suppressed amusement. —*n.* **2.** a tittering laugh. [? < Scand; cf. Icel *titra* to quiver, Sw (dial.) *tittra* to giggle] —**tit′ter·er,** *n.* —**tit′ter·ing·ly,** *adv.* —**Syn. 1.** snicker, snigger, giggle, laugh.

tit·tie (tit′ē), *n. Scot. Informal.* titty[1].

tit·ti·vate (tit′ə vāt′), *v.t., v.i.,* **-vat·ed, -vat·ing.** *Informal.* titivate. —**tit′ti·va′tion,** *n.* —**tit′ti·va′tor,** *n.*

tit·tle (tit′əl), *n.* **1.** a dot or other small mark in writing or printing, used as a diacritic, punctuation, etc. **2.** a very small part or quantity; a particle, jot, or whit: *He said he didn't care a tittle.* [ME *titel,* OE *titul* < ML *titul(us)* mark over letter or word. See TITLE]

tit·tle-tat·tle (tit′əl tat′əl), *n., v.,* **-tled, -tling.** —*n.* **1.** gossip or chatter. —*v.i.* **2.** to gossip or chatter. [gradational compound based on *tittle* to whisper, gossip] —**tit′tle-tat′tler,** *n.*

tit·tup (tit′əp), *n., v.,* **-tuped, -tup·ing** or (*esp. Brit.*) **-tupped, -tup·ping.** *Chiefly Brit.* —*n.* **1.** an exaggerated prancing, bouncing movement or manner of moving. —*v.i.* **2.** to move, esp. to walk, in an exaggerated prancing or bouncing way, as a spirited horse. [dial. *tit* a jerk, twitch (ME *titte*) + (GALL)OP] —**tit′tup·py,** *adj.*

tit·ty[1] (tit′ē), *n., pl.* **-ties.** *Scot. Informal.* sister. Also, **tittie.** [? < Scand; cf. Norw *titta* young girl, a nursery word like obs. Scot *titta* father]

tit·ty[2] (tit′ē), *n., pl.* **-ties.** a teat. [TIT[2] + -Y[2]]

tit·u·ba·tion (tich′o͝o bā′shən), *n. Pathol.* a disturbance of body equilibrium in standing or walking, resulting in an uncertain gait and trembling, esp. resulting from diseases of the cerebellum. [< L *titubātiōn-* (s. of *titubātiō*) a staggering < *titubāt(us),* ptp. of *titubāre* to stagger + *-iōn-* -ION] —**tit·u·bant** (tich′o͝o bənt), *adj.*

tit·u·lar (tich′ə lər, tit′yə-), *adj.* **1.** of, pertaining to, or of the nature of a title. **2.** having a title, esp. of rank. **3.** existing or being such in title only; nominal; having the title but none of the associated duties, powers, etc.: *He is only the titular head of the company.* **4.** from whom or which a title or name is taken: *His titular Saint is Michael.* **5.** designating any of the Roman Catholic churches in Rome whose nominal incumbents are cardinals. —*n.* **6.** one who bears a title. **7.** one from whom or that from which a title or name is taken. **8.** *Eccles.* one entitled to a benefice but not required to perform its duties. [< L *titul(us)* TITLE + -AR[1]] —**tit·u·lar·i·ty** (tich′ə lar′i tē, tit′yə-), *n.* —**tit′u·lar·ly,** *adv.*

tit·u·lar·y (tich′ə ler′ē, tit′yə-), *adj., n., pl.* **-lar·ies.** titular. [< L *titul(us)* TITLE + -ARY]

Ti·tus (tī′təs), *n.* **1.** a disciple and companion of the apostle Paul, to whom Paul is supposed to have addressed an Epistle. **2.** this New Testament Epistle. **3.** (*Flavius Sabinus Vespasianus*) A.D. 40?–81, Roman emperor 79–81. **4.** Tatius. **5.** a boy's given name.

Ti′tus An·dron′i·cus (an dron′ə kəs), a tragedy (1594) ascribed in part to Shakespeare.

Ti·tus·ville (tī′təs vil), *n.* **1.** a town in NW Pennsylvania: first oil well in U.S. drilled 1859. 8356 (1960). **2.** a town in central Florida. 6410 (1960).

Tit·y·us (tit′ē əs), *n. Class. Myth.* a giant, the son of Zeus and Elara, tortured for having attacked Leto.

Ti·u (tē′o͞o), *n. Eng. Myth.* a god of the sky and of war, the equivalent of Tyr in Scandinavian mythology.

Tiv (tiv), *n.* a Benue-Congo language of Nigeria, spoken near the lower course of the Benue River.

Tiv·o·li (tiv′ə lē; *It.* tē′vô lē), *n.* **1.** a town in central Italy, E of Rome: ruins of Roman villas. 34,235 (1961). Ancient, **Tibur. 2.** a park and entertainment center in Copenhagen, Denmark.

tiz·win (tiz wēn′), *n.* tiswin.

tiz·zy (tiz′ē), *n., pl.* **-zies. 1.** *Informal.* a dither. **2.** *Brit. Obs.* a sixpence. [?]

Tji·re·bon (chir′ē bôn′), *n.* a seaport on N Java, in S central Indonesia. 158,299 (1961).

TKO, *Boxing.* See **technical knockout.** Also, **T.K.O.**

Tl, *Chem.* thallium.

TL, trade-last.

TL., lira (def. 2).

T/L, time loan.

T.L., **1.** trade-last. **2.** trade list.

Tla·loc (tlä lōk′), *n.* the Aztec god of rain.

Tlal·pan (tläl pän′), *n.* a city in S Mexico: near site of Cuicuilco mound. 18,141 (1956).

Tlax·ca·la (tläs kä′lä), *n.* a state in SE central Mexico. 347,334 (1960); 1554 sq. mi. *Cap.:* Tlaxcala.

Tlem·cen (tlem sen′), *n.* a city in NW Algeria. 53,233 (1954). Also, **Tlem·sen′.**

Tle·pol·e·mus (tlə pol′ə məs), *n. Class. Myth.* a son of Hercules and Astyocheia who was killed by Sarpedon during the Trojan War.

Tlin·git (tliŋ′git), *n., pl.* **-gits,** (*esp. collectively*) **-git. 1.** a member of any of a number of American Indian peoples of the coastal regions of southern Alaska and northern British Colombia. **2.** the language of the Tlingit, a Na-Dene language related to Athapaskan.

Tlin·kit (tliŋ′kit), *n., pl.* **-kits,** (*esp. collectively*) **-kit.** Tlingit.

t.l.o., *Insurance.* total loss only.

Tm, *Chem.* thulium.

t.m., true mean.

T-man (tē′man′), *n., pl.* **T-men.** *U.S. Informal.* a special investigator of the Department of the Treasury.

tme·sis (tə mē′sis, mē′sis), *n.* the interpolation of one or more words between the parts of a compound word, as *be thou ware* for *beware.* [< L < Gk: a cutting < *tmē-* (var. s. of *témnein* to cut) + *-sis* -SIS]

Tmo·lus (təmō′ləs), *n. Class. Myth.* a Lydian king killed by a wild bull after having ravished a maiden in the temple of Artemis.

Tn, *Chem.* thoron.

tn., ton.

TNB, *Chem.* trinitrobenzene, esp. the 1,3,5- isomer.

Tng., training.

TNT, *Chem.* a yellow, crystalline, water-insoluble, flammable solid, $CH_3C_6H_2(NO_2)_3$, derived from toluene by nitration, a high explosive unaffected by ordinary friction or shock: used chiefly in military and other explosive devices, and as an intermediate in the preparation of dyestuffs and photographic chemicals. Also, **T.N.T.** Also called **trinitrotoluene, trinitrotoluol, methyltrinitrobenzene.**

T number, *Photog.* one of a series of calibrations of lens openings according to the intensity of the light actually transmitted by the lens. *Abbr.:* T

to (to͞o; *unstressed* to͝o, tə), *prep.* **1.** (used for expressing motion or direction toward a point, person, place, or thing approached and reached, as opposed to *from*): *He came to the house.* **2.** (used for expressing direction or motion or direction toward something) in the direction of; toward: *from north to south.* **3.** (used for expressing limit of movement or extension): *He grew to six feet.* **4.** (used for expressing contact or contiguity) on; against; beside; upon: *a right uppercut to the jaw; Apply varnish to the surface.* **5.** (used for expressing a point of limit in time) before; until: *to this day; It is ten minutes to six. We work from nine to five.* **6.** (used for expressing aim, purpose, or intention): *going to the rescue.* **7.** (used for expressing destination or appointed end): *sentenced to jail.* **8.** (used for expressing agency, result, or consequence): *to his dismay; The flowers opened to the sun.* **9.** (used for expressing a resulting state or condition): *He tore it to pieces.* **10.** (used for expressing the object of inclination or desire): *They drink to his health.* **11.** (used for expressing the object of a right or claim): *claimants to an estate.* **12.** (used for expressing limit in degree, condition, or amount): *wet to the skin; goods amounting to $1000; Tomorrow's high will be 75 to 80°.* **13.** (used for expressing addition or accompaniment) with: *He added insult to injury. They danced to the music. Where is the top to this box?* **14.** (used for expressing attachment or adherence): *He held to his opinion.* **15.** (used for expressing comparison or opposition): *inferior to last year's crop; The score is eight to seven.* **16.** (used for expressing agreement or accordance) according to; by: *a position to one's liking; to the best of my knowledge.* **17.** (used for expressing reference, reaction, or relation): *What will he say to this?* **18.** (used for expressing a relative position): *parallel to the roof.* **19.** (used for expressing a proportion of number or quantity) in; making up: *12 to the dozen; 20 miles to the gallon.* **20.** (used for indicating or supplying the dative case, for connecting a verb with its complement, or for indicating or limiting the application of an adjective, noun, or pronoun): *Give it to me. I refer to your work.* **21.** (used as the ordinary sign or accompaniment of the infinitive, as in expressing motion, direction, purpose, etc., in ordinary uses with a substantive object.) **22.** *Math.* raised to the power indicated: *Three to the fourth is 81* ($3^4 = 81$). —*adv.* **23.** toward a point, person, place, or thing, implied or understood. **24.** toward a contact point or closed position: *Pull the door to.* **25.** toward a matter, action, or work: *We turned to with a will.* **26.** into a state of consciousness; out of unconsciousness: *after he came to.* **27. to and fro,** toward and from some place or thing; moving alternately in opposite directions: *The wind was whipping the playground swings to and fro.* [ME, OE *tō;* c. D *te, toe,* G *zu*]

Toad, ***Bufo americanus*** **(Length 3 to 4 in.)**

t.o., **1.** turnover. **2.** turn over.

toad (tōd), *n.* **1.** any of numerous tailless amphibians, esp. of the family *Bufonidae,* that have dry, warty skin and that are chiefly terrestrial, entering water only during the breeding season. **2.** any of various toadlike animals, as certain lizards. **3.** a person or thing as an object of disgust or aversion. [ME *tode,* OE *tāde, tādi(g)e*] —**toad′ish, toad′like′,** *adj.* —**toad′ish·ness,** *n.* —**toad′less,** *adj.*

toad·eat·er (tōd′ē′tər), *n.* a toady. [TOAD + EATER]

toad·fish (tōd′fish′), *n., pl.* (*esp. collectively*) **-fish,** (*esp. referring to two or more kinds or species*) **-fish·es. 1.** any of several thick-headed, wide-mouthed fishes of the family *Batrachoididae,* as *Opsanus tau* **(oyster toadfish),** found along the Atlantic coast of the U.S. **2.** puffer (def. 2). [TOAD + FISH]

toad·flax (tōd′flaks′), *n.* **1.** a common, European, scrophulariaceous plant, *Linaria vulgaris,* having showy yellow-and-orange flowers, naturalized as a weed in the U.S. **2.** any plant of the same genus. [TOAD + FLAX]

toad-in-the-hole (tōd′in thə hōl′), *n. Brit. Cookery.* a dish consisting of sausage or beef baked in a coating of batter.

toad′ lil′y, 1. a hairy, perennial herb, *Tricyrtis hirta,* of Japan, having purple- and black-spotted white flowers. **2.** Also called **checkered lily, guinea-hen flower, snake's-head.** an herb, *Fritillaria meleagris,* of Eurasia, having purplish or maroon checkered and veined flowers.

toad's-mouth (tōdz′mouth′, -mouth′), *n., pl.* **-mouths** (-mouthz′). snapdragon.

toad′ spit′tle, cuckoo-spit (def. 1).

toad·stone (tōd′stōn′), *n.* any of various stones or stonelike objects, formerly supposed to have been formed in the head or body of a toad, worn as jewels or amulets. [TOAD + STONE]

toad·stool (tōd′sto͞ol′), *n.* **1.** any of various fleshy fungi having a stalk with an umbrellalike cap, esp. the agarics. **2.** a poisonous agaric, as distinguished from an edible one. **3.** any of various other fleshy fungi, as the puffballs, coral fungi, etc. [ME *tadstol.* See TOAD, STOOL]

toad·y (tō′dē), *n., pl.* **toad·ies,** *v.,* **toad·ied, toad·y·ing.** —*n.* **1.** an obsequious sycophant; a fawning flatterer. —*v.t.* **2.** to be the toady to. —*v.i.* **3.** to be a toady. [TOAD + -Y[2]] —**toad′y·ish,** *adj.* —**toad′y·ism,** *n.* —**Syn. 1.** fawner, yes-man, parasite, sycophant, apple polisher.

To Althe′a, from Pris′on, a poem (1643?) by Richard Lovelace.

to-and-fro (to͞o′ən frō′), *adj., n., pl.* **-fros,** *adv.* —*adj.* **1.** back-and-forth: *to-and-fro motion.* —*n.* **2.** a continuous or regular movement backward and forward; an alternating movement, flux, flow, etc.: *the to-and-fro of the surf.* —*adv.* **3.** to (def. 27).

To′ a Sky′lark, a poem (1820) by Shelley.

toast[1] (tōst), *n.* **1.** sliced bread that has been browned by heat. —*v.t.* **2.** to brown, as bread or cheese, by exposure to heat. **3.** to heat or warm thoroughly at a fire: *She toasted her feet at the fireplace.* —*v.i.* **4.** to become toasted. [ME *toste(n)* < MF *toste(r)* < L *tōst(us)* for **torsitus,* ptp. of *torrēre* to roast, parch; akin to Goth *thaursus,* Icel *thurr* dry. See TORRID, THIRST]

toast[2] (tōst), *n.* **1.** a person, event, sentiment, or the like, in honor of whom another or others raise their glasses in salutation and then drink. **2.** a salutation or a few words of congratulation, good wishes, appreciation, remembrance, etc., uttered immediately before drinking to such a person, event, etc. **3.** a call on another or others to drink to some person or thing. **4.** the act or an instance of thus drinking: *They drank a toast to the queen.* **5.** a person who is celebrated as with the spirited homage of a toast: *She was the toast of five continents.* —*v.t.* **6.** to propose as a toast. **7.** to drink to the health of or in honor of; propose a toast to or in honor of. —*v.i.* **8.** to propose or drink a toast. [fig. use of TOAST[1] (n.), the lady's name giving flavor to the drink comparable to that given by spiced toast]

toast·er[1] (tōs′tər), *n.* **1.** one who toasts something. **2.** an instrument or appliance for toasting bread, muffins, etc. [TOAST[1] + -ER[1]]

toast·er[2] (tōs′tər), *n.* one who proposes or joins in a toast to someone or something. [TOAST[2] + -ER[1]]

toast′ing fork′, a long-handled fork used for cooking or toasting frankfurters, marshmallows, bread, etc., usually over an open fire.

toast·mas·ter (tōst′mas′tər, -mä′stər), *n.* **1.** one who presides at a dinner and introduces the after-dinner speakers. **2.** one who proposes or announces toasts. Also, *referring to a woman,* **toast·mis·tress** (tōst′mis′tris). [TOAST[2] + MASTER]

toast·y (tō′stē), *adj.,* **toast·i·er, toast·i·est. 1.** characteristic of or resembling toast: *toasty aromas.* **2.** comfortably or cozily warm. [TOAST[1] + -Y[1]]

tob (tōb), *n.* tobe.

Tob., Tobit.

to·bac·co (tə bak′ō), *n., pl.* **-cos, -coes. 1.** any solanaceous plant of the genus *Nicotiana,* esp. one of those species, as *N. Tabacum,* whose leaves are prepared for smoking or chewing or as snuff. **2.** the prepared leaves, as used in cigarettes, cigars, and pipes. **3.** any of various similar plants of other genera. [< Sp *tabaco* < Arawak (? < Guarani): a pipe for smoking the plant, or roll of leaves smoked, or the plant] —**to·bac′co·less,** *adj.*

tobac′co heart′, *Pathol.* a functional disorder of the heart, characterized by a rapid and often irregular pulse, caused by excessive use of tobacco.

tobac′co horn′worm, the larva of a hawk moth, *Protoparce sexta,* that feeds on the leaves of tobacco and other solanaceous plants. Also called **tobac′co worm′.**

to·bac·co·nist (tə bak′ə nist), *n.* a dealer in tobacco, esp. an owner of or clerk in a store that sells pipe tobaccos, cigarettes, and cigars. [TOBACCO + hiatus-filling -n- + -IST]

Tobac′co Road′, **1.** a novel (1932) by Erskine Caldwell. **2.** a play (1933) by Jack Kirkland, based on this novel.

To·ba·go (tō bā′gō), *n.* an island in the SE West Indies, off the NE coast of Venezuela: formerly a British colony in the Federation of the West Indies; now part of the independent republic of Trinidad and Tobago. 35,600 (est. 1957); 116 sq. mi. —**To·ba·go·ni·an** (tō′bə gō′nē ən, -gōn′yən), *n.*

to-be (tə bē′), *adj.* future; soon to be the thing specified (usually used in combination): *bride-to-be.*

tobe (tōb), *n.* the principal outer garment in some parts of north and central Africa, consisting of a length of cloth that is sewn into a long loose skirt or is draped around the body and fastened over one shoulder. Also, **tob.** [< Ar *thawb* garment]

To·bey (tō′bē), *n.* **Mark,** 1890–1976, U.S. painter.

To·bi (tō′bē), *n.* **1.** a boy's given name, form of **Tobias. 2.** a girl's given name. Also, **To′bie, Toby.**

To·bi·as (tō bī′əs), *n.* **1.** the son of Tobit. **2.** *Douay Bible.* Tobit. **3.** a boy's given name.

to·bi·ra (tə bī′rə), *n.* a shrub, *Pittosporum Tobira,* of China and Japan, having leathery leaves, fragrant, greenish-white flower clusters, densely hairy fruit, and lemon-scented foliage. [< Jap: lit., door]

To·bit (tō′bit), *n.* **1.** a book of the Apocrypha. **2.** a devout Jew whose story is recorded in this book. Also, *Douay Bible,* **Tobias.**

to·bog·gan (tə bog′ən), *n.* **1.** a long, narrow, flat-bottomed sled made of a thin board curved upward and backward at the front, often with low hand rails on the sides, used esp. in the sport of coasting over snow or ice. —*v.i.* **2.** to use, or coast on, a toboggan. **3.** to fall rapidly, as prices, one's fortune, etc. [< CanF *tabagane,* etc. < Micmac *tobâgun* something used for dragging] —**to·bog′gan·er, to·bog′gan·ist,** *n.*

To·bol (to bôl′yᵊ), *n.* a river in the W Soviet Union in Asia, flowing NE to the Irtish River. 800 mi. long.

To·bolsk (to bôlsk′), *n.* a town in the W RSFSR, in the W Soviet Union in Asia, on the Irtish River near the confluence of the Tobol. 46,700 (1959).

to·by¹ (tō′bē), *n., pl.* **-bies. 1.** Also, **Toby, To′by jug′.** a mug in the form of a stout old man wearing a three-cornered hat. **2.** *U.S. Slang.* a long, slender, cheap cigar. [abbrev. of *Tobias*]

to·by² (tō′bē), *n., pl.* **-bies.** *Brit. Slang.* a road or highway. [< Gypsy *tobar,* prob. m. IrGael *bóthar*]

Toby (18th century)

To·by (tō′bē), *n., pl.* **-bies** for 3. **1.** a boy's given name, form of **Tobias. 2.** a girl's given name. **3.** toby. Also, **Tobi, Tobie** (for defs. 1, 2).

To·can·tins (tō′kän tēns′), *n.* a river in E Brazil, flowing N to the Pará River. 1700 mi. long.

toc·ca·ta (tə kä′tə; *It.* tôk kä′tä), *n. pl.* **-te** (-tē; *It.* -te). *Music.* a composition in the style of an improvisation, for the piano, organ, or other keyboard instrument, intended to exhibit the player's technique. [< It: lit., touched, ptp. fem. of *toccare* to TOUCH]

Toc·co·a (tə kō′ə), *n.* a town in NE Georgia. 7303 (1960).

Toch (tôkʜ), *n.* **Ernst** (ernst), 1887–1964, Austrian composer.

To·char·i·an (tō kâr′ē ən, -kär′-), *n.* **1.** a member of a central Asian people of high culture, who were assimilated with other peoples about the 11th century A.D. **2.** the language of the Tocharians, an extinct Indo-European language, records of which date from A.D. c600–c1000. —*adj.* **3.** of or pertaining to the Tocharians or their language. Also, **Tokharian.** [< Gk *Tochár(oi)* Tocharians + -IAN]

toch·er (tokʜ′ər), *Scot. and North Eng.* —*n.* **1.** a dowry; marriage settlement given to the groom by the bride or her family. —*v.t.* **2.** to provide with a dowry. [< Ir *tochar,* var. of *tachar* a providing, provision]

to·co·dy·na·mom·e·ter (tō′kō dī′nə mom′i tər, tok′ō-), *n.* tokodynamometer.

to·col·o·gy (tō kol′ə jē), *n.* obstetrics. Also, **tokology.** [< Gk *tóko(s)* child(birth) + -LOGY]

to·com·e·ter (tō kom′i tər), *n.* tokodynamometer. [by shortening]

to·coph·er·ol (tō kof′ə rōl′, -rôl′, -rol′), *n.* *Biochem.* one of several alcohols that comprise the dietary factor known as vitamin E, occurring in wheat-germ oil, lettuce or spinach leaves, egg yolk, etc. Cf. **vitamin E.** [< Gk *tóko(s)* child(birth) + *phér(ein)* (to) carry, bear + -OL¹]

To·co·pil·la (tô′kô pē′yä), *n.* a seaport in N Chile. 19,353 (1952).

Tocque·ville (tōk′vil, tok′-; *Fr.* tôk vēl′), *n.* **A·le·xis Charles Hen·ri Mau·rice Clé·rel de** (A lek sē′ sharl äɴ rē′ mō rēs′ klā rel′ də), 1805–59, French statesman and author.

toc·sin (tok′sin), *n.* **1.** a signal, esp. of alarm, sounded on a bell or bells. **2.** a bell used to sound an alarm. [< F < Pr *tocasenh* < *toca(r)* (to) TOUCH, strike + *senh* sign, bell < L *sign(um)* sign, in ML, also bell]

tod¹ (tod), *n.* **1.** an English unit of weight, chiefly for wool, commonly equal to 28 pounds but varying locally. **2.** a load. **3.** a bushy mass, esp. of ivy. [late ME *todde;* akin to EFris *todde* small load, Icel *toddi* piece, slice]

tod² (tod), *n.* *Scot. and North Eng.* **1.** a fox. **2.** a crafty, foxy person. [early ME]

Tod (tod), *n.* a boy's given name. Also, **Todd.**

to·day (tə dā′), *n.* **1.** this present day: *Today is beautiful.* **2.** this present time or age: *the world of today.* —*adv.* **3.** on this present day: *I will do it today.* **4.** at the present time; in these days: *Today you seldom see horses.* Also, **to-day′.** [ME; OE *tō dæg.* See TO, DAY]

Todd (tod), *n.* **1. Sir Alexander Ro·ber·tus** (rō bûr′təs), born 1907, Scottish chemist: Nobel prize 1957. **2. David,** 1855–1939, U.S. astronomer and teacher. **3.** a boy's given name.

tod·dle (tod′ᵊl), *v.,* **-dled, -dling,** *n.* —*v.i.* **1.** to go with short, unsteady steps, as a child or an old person. —*n.* **2.** the act of toddling. **3.** an unsteady gait. [b. TO(TTER + WA)DDLE] —**tod′dler,** *n.*

tod·dy (tod′ē), *n., pl.* **-dies. 1.** a drink made of alcoholic liquor and hot water, sweetened and sometimes spiced with cloves. **2.** *Rare.* the drawn sap, esp. when fermented, of any of several toddy palms, used as a drink. [var. of *tarrie* < Hindi *tārī* palmyra palm juice < *tār* palmyra palm (< Skt *pāla*) + -ī suffix of appurtenance]

tod′dy palm′, an Indo-Malayan palm, *Caryota urens,* yielding toddy.

tod′dy ta′ble, a small stand of the 18th century, used for holding drinks.

Tod in Ve·ne·dig, Der (*Ger.* dər tōt′ in ve nā′dikʜ). See **Death in Venice.**

to-do (tə do͞o′), *n., pl.* **-dos.** *Informal.* bustle; fuss; *They made a great to-do over the dinner.* [n. use of infinitive phrase; see TO, DO¹, ADO]

—**Syn.** See **ado.**

Todt (tōt), *n.* **Fritz** (frits), 1891–1942, German military engineer.

to·dy (tō′dē), *n., pl.* **-dies.** any of several small, insectivorous, West Indian birds of the family *Todidae,* related to the motmots and kingfishers, having brightly colored green and red plumage. [< NL *Todī,* pl. of *Todus* genus name; L: name of some small bird]

toe (tō), *n., v.,* **toed, toe·ing.** —*n.* **1.** one of the terminal digits of the foot in man. **2.** an analogous part in certain animals. **3.** the forepart of the foot or hoof of a horse or the like. **4.** the forepart of anything worn on the foot, as of a shoe, stocking, etc. **5.** a part resembling a toe in shape or position. **6.** *Railroads.* the end of a frog in front of the point and in the direction of the switch. **7.** *Mach.* **a.** a journal or part placed vertically in a bearing, as the lower end of a vertical shaft. **b.** a curved partial cam lifting the flat surface of a follower and letting it drop; wiper. **8.** the edge of either leg of an angle iron. **9.** *Golf.* the outer end of the head of a club. **10. on one's toes,** *Informal.* energetic; alert; ready: *The spirited competition kept them on their toes.* **11. step** or **tread on (someone's) toes,** to offend (a person); encroach on (another's) territory or sphere of responsibility: *The new employee stepped on a lot of toes when he suggested reorganizing the office.* —*v.t.* **12.** to furnish with a toe or toes. **13.** to touch or reach with the toes: *The pitcher toed the mound, wound up, and threw a fast ball.* **14.** to kick with the toe. **15.** *Golf.* to strike (the ball) with the toe of the club. **16.** *Carpentry.* **a.** to drive (a nail) obliquely. **b.** to toenail. —*v.i.* **17.** to stand, walk, etc., with the toes in a specified position: *to toe in.* **18.** to tap with the toe, as in dancing. **19. toe the line.** See **line**¹ (def. 68). [ME; OE *tā;* c. G *Zeh(e),* Icel *tā,* D *teen;* akin to L *digitus* DIGIT] —**toe′less,** *adj.* —**toe′like′,** *adj.*

toe′ box′, a piece of stiffened material, as leather, placed between the lining and the toecap of a shoe.

toe·cap (tō′kap′), *n.* a piece of leather or other material covering the toe of a shoe. [TOE + CAP]

toe′ crack′, a sand crack on the front of the hoof of a horse.

toed (tōd), *adj.* **1.** having a toe or toes: *five-toed; a toed clog; stockings that are toed.* **2.** *Carpentry.* **a.** (of a nail) driven obliquely. **b.** toenailed. [TOE + -ED³]

toe′ dance′, a dance performed on the tips of the toes.

toe-dance (tō′dans′, -däns′), *v.i.,* **-danced, -danc·ing.** to perform a toe dance. [v. use of n. phrase TOE DANCE] —**toe′ danc′er.**

toe′ hold′, 1. a small ledge or niche just large enough to support the toes, as in climbing. **2.** any slight or initial support, influence, advantage, progress, or the like: *His knowledge of Latin gave him a toehold for learning French.* **3.** a batten nailed to a sloping roof as a support for workmen. **4.** *Wrestling.* a hold in which an opponent's foot is twisted.

toe-in (tō′in′), *n.* the slight forward convergence given to the front wheels of an automobile to improve steering qualities. [n. use of v. phrase *toe in*]

toe·nail (tō′nāl′), *n.* **1.** a nail of a toe. **2.** *Carpentry.* a nail driven obliquely. **3.** *Print. Slang.* a parenthesis. —*v.t.* **4.** *Carpentry.* to secure with oblique nailing. [TOE + NAIL]

toe′ rail′, *Naut.* a raised strip of planking around the edge of the deck of a yacht.

toe·shoe (tō′sho͞o′), *n.* *Ballet.* a heelless dance slipper fitted with a thick, leather-covered wooden toe to enable the ballet dancer to toe-dance. [TOE + SHOE]

toff (tof), *n.* *Brit. Informal.* a stylishly dressed, fashionable person, esp. one who is or wants to be considered a member of the upper class. [? var. of TUFT]

tof·fee (tô′fē, tof′ē), *n.* *Chiefly Brit.* taffy (def. 1). Also, **tof′fy.**

tof·fee-nosed (tô′fē nōzd′, tof′ē-), *adj.* *Brit. Slang.* stuck-up; conceited; pretentious: *a toffee-nosed butler; a toffee-nosed shop.*

toft (tôft, toft), *n.* *Brit. Dial.* **1.** the site of a house and its outbuildings. **2.** a house site and its adjoining arable land. [ME, late OE < Scand; cf. Icel *topt* homestead]

to·fu (tō′fo͞o), *n.* a soft, bland, white cheeselike food made from curdled soybean milk, high in protein content, used originally in Oriental cookery but now in a wide variety of soups and main dishes. [< Jap]

tog (tog), *n., v.,* **togged, tog·ging.** —*n.* **1.** a coat. **2.** Usually, **togs.** clothes. —*v.t.* **3.** to dress (often fol. by *out* or *up*). [appar. short for obs. *tog(e)man(s)* cloak, coat < *toge* (late ME < L *toga* TOGA) + *-mans* obs. cant suffix < ?]

to·ga (tō′gə), *n., pl.* **-gas, -gae** (-jē). **1.** (in ancient Rome) the loose outer garment worn by citizens when appearing in public. **2.** a robe of office, a professorial gown, or some other distinctive garment. [< L: lit., a covering. See TEGMEN] —**to·gaed** (tō′gəd), *adj.*

Toga (def. 1)

to·gate (tō′gāt), *adj.* dressed in a toga. [< L *togāt(us).* See TOGA, -ATE¹]

to·gat·ed (tō′gā tid), *adj.* **1.** characteristic of peace; peaceful: *the togated rule of Rome.* **2.** clad in a toga. [< L *togāt(us)* clad in a toga (see TOGATE) + -ED²]

to·ga vi·ri·lis (tō′gə vi rī′lis; *Lat.* tō′gä wi rē′lis), *pl.* **to·gae vi·ri·les** (tō′jē vi rī′lēz; *Lat.* tō′gī wi-rē′les). the white toga assumed by boys in ancient Rome at the end of their 14th year. [< L; see TOGA, VIRILE]

to·geth·er (to͝o geth′ər), *adv.* **1.** into or in one gathering, company, mass, place, or body: *to call the people together.* **2.** into or in union, proximity, contact, or collision, as two or more things: *to sew things together.* **3.** into or in relationship, association, business, or agreement, etc., as two or more persons: *to bring strangers together.* **4.** taken or considered collectively or conjointly: *This one cost more than all the others together.* **5.** (of a single thing) into or in a condition of unity, compactness, or coherence: *to squeeze a thing together; The argument does not hang together well.* **6.** at the same time; simultaneously: *You cannot have both together.* **7.** without intermission or interruption; continuously; uninterruptedly: *for days together.* **8.** in cooperation; with united action; conjointly: *to undertake a task together.* **9.** with mutual action; mutually; reciprocally: *to confer together; to multiply two numbers together.* [late ME; earlier *togedere, togadere,* OE *tōgædere;* c. OFris *togadera.* See TO, GATHER]

to·geth·er·ness (to͝o geth′ər nis), *n.* **1.** the quality, state, or condition of being together. **2.** warm fellowship, as among members of a family. [TOGETHER + -NESS]

tog·ger·y (tog′ə rē), *n.* *Informal.* clothes; garments; togs. [TOG + -ERY]

tog·gle (tog′əl), *n., v.,* **-gled, -gling.** —*n.* **1.** a pin, bolt, or rod placed transversely through a chain, an eye or loop in a rope, etc., as to bind it temporarily to another chain or rope similarly treated. **2.** a toggle joint, or a device having one. **3.** an ornamental, rod-shaped button for inserting into a large buttonhole, loop, or frog, used esp. on sports clothes. **4.** *Theat.* **a.** Also called **tog′gle rail′.** a wooden batten across the width of a flat, for strengthening the frame. **b.** Also called **tog′gle i′ron.** a metal device for fastening a toggle rail to a frame. —*v.t.* **5.** to furnish with a toggle or toggles. **6.** to bind or fasten with a toggle or toggles. [? var. of TACKLE] —**tog′gler,** *n.*

tog′gle bolt′, an anchor bolt having two hinged wings, ordinarily held open by a spring, for engaging the rough sides of a hole drilled in masonry or the inner surface of a hollow wall.

tog′gle joint′, *Mach.* any of various devices consisting basically of a rod which can be inserted into an object and then manipulated so that the inserted part spreads, becomes offset, or turns at a right angle to the exterior part, allowing it to be used as a support, handle, linkage, lever, etc.

Toggle joint

tog′gle mo′tion, the motion of a toggle joint.

tog′gle switch′, *Elect.* a switch in which a projecting knob or arm, moving through a small arc, causes the contacts to open or close an electric circuit suddenly, as commonly used in most homes.

To·gliat·ti (tô lyät′tē), *n.* **Pal·mi·ro** (päl mē′rô), 1893–1964, Italian Communist Party leader.

To·go (tô′gô *for 1, 2;* tō′gō *for 3*), *n.* **1. Hei·ha·chi·ro** (hā′hä-chē′rô), **Count** 1847–1934, Japanese admiral. **2. Shi·ge·no·ri** (shē′ge nô′rē), 1882–1950, Japanese political leader and diplomat. **3. Republic of,** an independent country in W Africa; formerly a French mandate 1922–46 and trusteeship 1946–60 in E Togoland. 1,424,300 (est. 1960); 21,830 sq. mi. *Cap.:* Lomé.

To·go·land (tō′gō land′), *n.* a former German protectorate in W Africa, on the Gulf of Guinea: E part is now the Republic of Togo; W part, a British mandate 1922–46 and trusteeship 1946–57, is now part of Ghana. —**To′go·land′er,** *n.*

To·go·lese (tō′gə lēz′, -lēs′, -gō-), *n. pl.* **-lese,** *adj.* —*n.* **1.** a native or inhabitant of the Republic of Togo. —*adj.* **2.** of, pertaining to, or characteristic of the Togolese or the Republic of Togo. [TOGO + *-lese,* as in *Congolese*]

togue (tōg), *n., pl.* **togues,** (*esp. collectively*) **togue.** *Canadian.* See **lake trout.** [< CanF]

To His Coy′ Mis′tress, a poem (1650?) by Andrew Marvell.

to·hu·bo·hu (tō′ho͞o bō′ho͞o), *n.* chaos; disorder; confusion. [< Heb *tōhū wā-bhōhū*]

toil¹ (toil), *n.* **1.** hard and continuous work; exhausting labor or effort. **2.** a laborious task. **3.** *Archaic.* battle; strife; struggle. —*v.i.* **4.** to engage in hard and continuous work; labor arduously: *those who toil in the vineyard.* **5.** to move or travel with difficulty, weariness, or pain. —*v.t.* **6.** to accomplish or produce by toil. [ME *toile* (n.), *toil(en)* (v.) < AF *toil* contention, *toil(er)* (v.) to contend < L *tudiculāre* to stir up, beat < *tudicul(us)* stick for stirring or beating < *tudi-* (s. of *tundere* to beat) + *-culus* -CULE] —**toil′er,** *n.*

—**Syn. 1.** exertion, travail, pains. See **work. 4.** strive, moil. —**Ant. 1.** indolence, sloth.

toil² (toil), *n.* **1.** Usually, **toils.** a net or series of nets in which game known to be in the area is trapped or into which game outside of the area is driven. **2.** *Obs.* any snare or trap for wild beasts. [< F *toile* < L *tēl(a)* web]

toile (twäl), *n.* any of various transparent linens and cottons. [< F: linen cloth, canvas. See TOIL²]

toile de Jouy (*Fr.* twAl də zhwē′), a cotton or linen fabric characterized by monochromatic prints on a light background. Also called **Jouy print.** [< F: lit., cloth of *Jouy* (-en-Josar) France]

toi·let (toi′lit), *n.* **1.** a bathroom fixture consisting of a bowl, usually with a detachable, hinged seat and lid, and a device for flushing with water, used for defecation and urination. **2.** a bathroom. **3.** See **toilet bowl. 4.** a dressing room, esp. one containing a bath. **5.** the act or process of dressing, including bathing, arranging the hair, etc.: *to make one's toilet; busy at her toilet.* **6.** See **toilet set. 7.** *Archaic.* See **dressing table. 8.** the dress or costume of a person; any particular costume: *toilet of white silk.* **9.** *Surg.* the cleansing of the part or wound after an operation, esp. in the peritoneal cavity. Also, **toilette** (for defs. 5, 8). [< F *toilette* small cloth, doily, dressing-table < *toile* TOIL² + *-ette* -ET]

toi′let bowl′, the ceramic bowl of a toilet.

toi′let pa′per, a soft, light-weight, sanitized paper used in bathrooms for personal cleanliness. Also called **toi′let tis′sue, bathroom tissue.**

toi′let pow′der, a fine powder sprinkled or rubbed over the skin, esp. after bathing.

toi·let·ry (toi′li trē), *n., pl.* **-ries.** an article or substance used in dressing or making up. [TOILET + -RY]

toi′let seat′, a detachable, ringlike seat of wood or plastic hinged to the top of a toilet bowl.

toi′let set′, the articles used in dressing, as a mirror, brush, comb, etc., esp. when of a matching design.

toi·lette (toi let′; *Fr.* twA let′), *n., pl.* **-lettes** (-lets′; *Fr.* -let′). toilet (defs. 5, 8).

toi′let train′ing, the training of a very young child to control and regulate bowel and bladder movements and use the toilet.

toi′let wa′ter, a scented liquid used as a light perfume; cologne.

toil·ful (toil′fəl), *adj.* characterized by or involving toil; laborious; toilsome. [TOIL[1] + -FUL] **—toil′ful·ly,** *adv.*

toil·some (toil′səm), *adj.* characterized by or involving toil; laborious or fatiguing. [TOIL[1] + -SOME[1]] **—toil′some·ly,** *adv.* **—toil′some·ness,** *n.*

toil·worn (toil′wōrn′, -wôrn′), *adj.* **1.** worn by toil: *toilworn hands.* **2.** worn out or aged by toil: *a toilworn farmer.* [TOIL[1] + WORN]

toise (toiz), *n.* an old French unit of length equivalent to 6.395 feet or 1.949 meters. [< MF < LL *tēs(a)* < L *tensa* (*bracchia*) outstretched (arms), neut. pl., taken as fem. sing. See TENSE[1]]

To·jo (tō′jō), *n.* **Hi·de·ki** (hē′de kē′), 1885–1948, Japanese general.

to·kay (tō kā′), *n.* a gecko, *Gecko gecko,* of the Malay Archipelago and southeastern Asia. [< Malay *toke*]

Tokay
(Length to 14 in.)

To·kay (tō kā′), *n.* **1.** an aromatic wine made from Furmint grapes grown in the district surrounding Tokay, a town in NE Hungary. **2.** *Hort.* **a.** a large, red variety of grape, grown for table use. **b.** the vine bearing this fruit, grown in California. **3.** a sweet, strong white wine made in California. [< Hung]

to·ken (tō′kən), *n.* **1.** something meant or serving to represent or indicate some fact, event, feeling, etc.; sign: *to wear black as a token of mourning.* **2.** a characteristic indication or mark of something; symbol: *His shabby suit is a token of his poverty.* **3.** a memento; souvenir; keepsake: *The seashell was a token of their trip to Atlantic City.* **4.** something used to indicate authenticity, authority, etc.; emblem; badge: *He wore his robes as a token of office.* **5.** Also called **to′ken coin′.** a stamped piece of metal, issued as a limited medium of exchange, as for bus fares, at a nominal value much greater than its commodity value. **6.** anything of only nominal value similarly used, as paper currency. **7.** an item, idea, person, etc., representing a group; a part as representing the whole; sample; indication. **8. by the same token, a.** in proof of which. **b.** moreover; furthermore: *She had never seen such poverty before, and by the same token could not quite believe it.* **9. in token of,** as a sign of; in evidence of: *He gave her a ring in token of his love.* **—*v.t.* 10.** to be a token of; signify; symbolize. **—*adj.* 11.** serving as a token: *a token gift.* **12.** slight; perfunctory; minimal: *token resistance.* [ME; OE *tāc(e)n;* c. Icel *teikn,* Goth *taikn,* G *Zeichen* sign, mark. See TEACH]

to·ken·ism (tō′kə niz′əm), *n.* the practice of admitting a very limited number of Negroes into business organizations, schools, etc., in token conformity with legislation and public opinion regarding civil rights. [TOKEN + -ISM]

to′ken pay′ment, a small payment binding an agreement or acknowledging a debt.

To·khar·i·an (tō kâr′ē ən, -kär′-), *n.* Tocharian.

to·ko·dy·na·mom·e·ter (tō′kō dī′nə mom′i tər), *n.* an obstetrical instrument used during labor to measure the pressure within the uterus. Also, **tocodynamometer.** Also called **tocometer.** [< Gk *tók(os)* child(birth) + -O- + DYNAMOMETER]

to·kol·o·gy (tō kol′ə jē), *n.* tocology.

to·ko·no·ma (tō′kə nō′mə), *n.* (in Japanese architecture) a shallow alcove for the display of kakemonos or flower arrangements. [< Jap]

To·ku·ga·wa (tō′kōō gä′wä), *n.* a member of a powerful family in Japan which ruled as shoguns, 1603–1867.

tok·us (tuk′əs, tō′kəs, tōkh′əs), *n. Slang.* the buttocks. [< Yiddish < Heb *taḥath* under]

To·ku·shi·ma (tō′kōō shē′mä), *n.* a seaport on NE Shikoku, in SW Japan. 195,764 (1964).

To·ky·o (tō′kē ō′; *Jap.* tō′kyō), *n.* a seaport in and the capital of Japan, on Tokyo Bay: one of the world's three largest cities; destructive earthquake and fire 1923; signing of the Japanese surrender document aboard the U.S.S. *Missouri,* September 2, 1945. 11,468,516. Also, **To′ki·o′.** Formerly, **Yeddo, Yedo, Edo. —To′ky·o·ite′,** *n.*

To′kyo Bay′, an inlet of the Pacific, in SE Honshu Island of Japan. 30 mi. long; 20 mi. wide.

to·la (tō′lä), *n.* a unit of weight in India: the government tola is 180 ser and equals 180 English grains, the weight of a silver rupee. [< Hindi < Skt *tulā* balance, scale, weight]

to·lan (tō′lan), *n. Chem.* a crystalline, water-insoluble, solid, unsaturated compound, $C_6H_5C{\equiv}CC_6H_5$, used chiefly in organic synthesis. Also called **diphenylacetylene.** [var. of *tolane.* See TOLUENE, -ANE]

tol·booth (tōl′bōōth′, -bōōth′), *n., pl.* **-booths** (-bōōthz′). **1.** *Chiefly Scot.* **a.** a town jail. **b.** a town hall or guild hall, esp. a place where tolls are paid. **2.** tollbooth.

tol·bu·ta·mine (tol byōō′tə mēn′), *n. Pharm.* a white, crystalline, water-insoluble powder, $C_{12}H_{18}N_2O_3S$, used in the treatment of mild cases of diabetes mellitus. [TOL(U) + BUT(YL) + AMINE]

told (tōld), *v* **1.** pt. and pp. of **tell. 2. all told,** counting everyone or everything; in all: *There were 50 guests all told.*

tole[1] (tōl), *n.* enameled or lacquered metalware, usually with gilt decoration, often used, esp. in the 18th century, for trays, lampshades, etc. Also, **tôle.** [< F *tôle* sheet of iron, plate, dial. var. of *table* TABLE]

tole[2] (tōl), *v.t.,* **toled, tol·ing.** toll[1] (defs. 5, 6).

To·le·do (tə lē′dō; *for 1, 3, 6, also Sp.* tô le′thô), *n.* **1. Fran·cis·co de** (frän sēs′kô de), c1515–84?, Spanish administrator: viceroy of Peru 1569–81. **2.** a port in NW Ohio, on Lake Erie. 318,003 (1960). **3.** a city in central Spain, on the Tagus River: the capital of Spain under the Romans. 38,136 (est. 1960). **4.** a town in W Oregon. 3053 (1960). **5.** a town in central Iowa. 2850 (1960). **6.** a sword or sword blade of finely tempered steel, as formerly made in Toledo, Spain.

tol·er·a·ble (tol′ər ə bəl), *adj.* **1.** capable of being tolerated; endurable: *His arrogance is no longer tolerable.* **2.** fairly good; not bad. **3.** *Informal.* in fair health. [late ME < L *tolerābil(is)* < *tolerā(re)* (to) endure + *-bilis* -BLE] **—tol′er·a·ble·ness, tol′er·a·bil′i·ty,** *n.* **—tol′er·a·bly,** *adv.*
—Syn. 1. bearable, supportable. **2.** passable, middling, indifferent, so-so.

tol·er·ance (tol′ər əns), *n.* **1.** a fair and objective attitude toward those whose opinions, practices, race, religion, nationality, etc. differ from one's own; freedom from bigotry. **2.** a fair and objective attitude toward opinions and practices which differ from one's own. **3.** interest in and concern for ideas, opinions, practices, etc., foreign to one's own; a liberal, undogmatic viewpoint. **4.** the act or capacity of enduring; endurance: *My tolerance of noise is limited.* **5.** *Med.* the power of enduring or resisting the action of a drug, poison, etc.: *a tolerance to antibiotics.* **6.** *Mach.* **a.** the permissible range of variation in a dimension of an object. Cf. **allowance** (def. 8). **b.** the permissible variation of an object or objects in some characteristic such as hardness, weight, or quantity. **7.** Also called **allowance.** *Coining.* a permissible deviation in the fineness and weight of coin, owing to the difficulty of securing exact conformity to the standard prescribed by law. [late ME < L *tolerantia.* See TOLERANT, -ANCE]
—Syn. 1. patience, sufferance, forbearance; liberality, impartiality, open-mindedness. TOLERANCE, TOLERATION agree in allowing the right of something that one does not approve. TOLERANCE suggests a liberal spirit toward the views and actions of others: *tolerance toward religious minorities.* TOLERATION implies the allowance or sufferance of conduct with which one is not in accord: *toleration of graft.*

tol′erance lim′its, *Statistics.* a pair of numbers obtained from a sample such that it can be stated with a given degree of probability that the numbers will include between them at least a specified percentage of values of a variable in the population; quality control limits on the sample values of a variable.

tol·er·ant (tol′ər ənt), *adj.* **1.** inclined or disposed to tolerate; showing tolerance; forbearing: *tolerant of errors.* **2.** favoring toleration: *a tolerant church.* **3.** *Med.* able to endure or resist the action of a drug, poison, etc. [< L *tolerant-* (s. of *tolerāns*), prp. of *tolerāre* to bear. See TOLERATE, -ANT] **—tol′er·ant·ly,** *adv.*

tol·er·ate (tol′ə rāt′), *v.t.,* **-at·ed, -at·ing. 1.** to allow the existence, presence, practice or act of without prohibition or hindrance; permit. **2.** to endure without repugnance; put up with: *I can tolerate laziness, but not sloth.* **3.** *Med.* to endure or resist the action of (a drug, poison, etc.). **4.** *Obs.* to experience, undergo, or sustain, as pain or hardship. [< L *tolerāt(us),* ptp. of *tolerāre* to bear (akin to THOLE[2]); see -ATE[1]] **—tol′er·a′tive,** *adj.* **—tol′er·a′tor,** *n.*
—Syn. 2. support, endure, accept.

tol·er·a·tion (tol′ə rā′shən), *n.* **1.** the act or an instance of tolerating, esp. of what is not actually approved; forbearance: *The police were ordered to show toleration toward the marchers.* **2.** allowance, by a government, of the exercise of religions other than the religion officially established or recognized; recognition of the right of private judgment in matters of faith and worship. [< L *tolerātiōn-* (s. of *tolerātiō*). See TOLERATE, -ION] **—tol′er·a′tion·ism,** *n.* **—tol′er·a′tion·ist,** *n.*
—Syn. 1. See **tolerance.**

Tolera′tion Act′, *Eng. Hist.* See **Act of Toleration.**

To′ Let′, a novel (1921) by John Galsworthy. Cf. **Forsyte Saga, The.**

tole·ware (tōl′wâr′), *n.* articles made of tole. [TOLE[1] + WARE[1]]

tol·i·dine (tol′i dēn′, -din), *n. Chem.* any of several isomeric derivatives of biphenyl containing two methyl and two amino groups, esp. the ortho isomer which is used as a reagent and in the preparation of dyes. [TOL(UENE) + -ID[3] + -INE[2]]

To·li·ma (tô lē′mä), *n.* a volcano in W Colombia, in the Andes. 18,438 ft.

toll[1] (tōl), *v.t.* **1.** to cause (a large bell) to sound with single strokes slowly and regularly repeated, as for summoning a congregation to church, or esp. for announcing a death. **2.** to sound or strike (a knell, the hour, etc.) by such strokes: *In the distance Big Ben tolled five.* **3.** to announce by this means; ring a knell for (a dying or dead person). **4.** to summon or dismiss by tolling. **5.** to lure or decoy (game) by arousing curiosity. **6.** to allure; entice: *He tolls us on with fine promises.* **—*v.i.* 7.** to sound with single strokes slowly and regularly repeated, as a bell. **—*n.* 8.** act of tolling a bell. **9.** one of the strokes made in tolling a bell. **10.** the sound made. Also, **tole** (for defs. 5, 6). [ME *toll(en);* akin to OE *-tyllan,* in *fortyllan* to attract, allure]

toll[2] (tōl), *n.* **1.** a payment or fee exacted by the state, the local authorities, etc., for some right or privilege, as for passage along a road or over a bridge. **2.** (formerly, in England) the right to take such payment. **3.** a payment made for a long-distance telephone call. **4.** a tax, duty, or tribute, as for services, use of facilities, etc. **5.** the extent of loss, damage, suffering, etc., resulting from some action or calamity: *The toll was 300 persons dead or missing.* **6.** a compensation for services, as for grinding corn or for transportation or transmission. **7.** *Chiefly Dial.* grain retained by a miller in payment for his services. **—*v.t.* 8.** to collect (something) as toll. **9.** to impose a tax or toll on (a person). **—*v.i.* 10.** to collect toll; levy toll. [ME, OE (c. D *tol,* Icel *tollr,* G *Zoll*), assimilated var. of OE *toln* < LL *tolōn(ēum),* for *telōnēum* < Gk *telōneion* tollhouse, akin to *telōnēs* tax collector, *télos* tax]
—Syn. 3. tariff, levy, impost, exaction.

toll·age (tō′lij), *n.* **1.** toll; tax. **2.** exaction or payment of toll. [TOLL[2] + -AGE]

toll′ bar′, a barrier, esp. a gate, across a road or bridge, where toll is collected.

toll·booth (tōl′bōōth′, -bōōth′), *n., pl.* **-booths** (-bōōthz′). **1.** a booth, as at a bridge or the entrance to a toll road, where a toll is collected. **2.** *Chiefly Scot.* tolbooth. [ME *tolbothe.* See TOLL[2], BOOTH]

toll′ bridge′, a bridge at which a toll is charged.

toll′ call′, any telephone call involving a higher base rate than that fixed for a local message.

toll′ collec′tor, 1. a person or device collecting tolls at a tollgate. **2.** a device at a tollgate for registering the number of tolls collected.

toll·er[1] (tō′lər), *n.* **1.** one who or that which tolls. **2.** Also called **tolling dog.** a small dog trained to entice ducks into shooting range or a trap. **3.** one who tolls a bell. **4.** a bell used for tolling; a tolling bell. [ME, OE *tollere.* See TOLL[1], -ER[1]]

toll·er[2] (tō′lər), *n.* See **toll collector** (def. 1). [ME; OE *tollere.* See TOLL[2], -ER[1]]

Tol·ler (tô′lər, tol′ər; *Ger.* tô′lər), *n.* **Ernst** (ûrnst; *Ger.* ernst), 1893–1939, German dramatist.

Tol·le·son (tol′i sən), *n.* a town in central Arizona. 3886 (1960).

toll·gate (tōl′gāt′), *n.* a gate where toll is collected. [TOLL[2] + GATE]

toll·gath·er·er (tōl′gath′ər ər), *n.* a person who collects tolls, taxes, or other imposts. [ME *tol gaderer.* See TOLL[2], GATHERER]

toll·house (tōl′hous′), *n., pl.* **-hous·es** (-hou′ziz). a house or booth at a tollgate, occupied by a tollkeeper. [late ME *tolhowse.* See TOLL[2], HOUSE]

toll′house cook′y, a crisp cooky containing bits of chocolate and sometimes chopped nuts.

toll′ing dog′, toller[1] (def. 2).

toll·keep·er (tōl′kē′pər), *n.* the collector at a tollgate. [TOLL[2] + KEEPER]

toll′ line′, a telephone line for long-distance calls.

toll·man (tōl′mən), *n., pl.* **-men.** a tollkeeper. [TOLL[2] + MAN[1]]

toll′ road′, a road or highway on which a toll is exacted.

toll′ thor′ough, *Brit.* a payment exacted by a municipal government for the right to use a highway, bridge, or the like; toll.

toll′ trav′erse, *Brit.* a payment made for the right to cross privately owned property.

tol·ly (tol′ē), *n., pl.* **-lies.** *Brit. Slang.* candle (def. 1). [alter. of TALLOW]

Tol·stoy (tol′stoi, tōl′-; *Russ.* tol stoi′), *n.* **Lev** (*Russ.* lef) or **Leo Ni·ko·la·e·vich** (*Russ.* ni ko lä′yə vich), **Count,** 1828–1910, Russian novelist and social critic. Also, **Tol′stoi. —Tol′stoy·an, Tol′stoi·an,** *adj., n.* **—Tol′stoy·ism,** *n.* **—Tol′stoy·ist,** *n.*

Tol·tec (tol′tek), *n., pl.* **-tecs,** (*esp. collectively*) **-tec,** *adj.* **—*n.* 1.** a member of an Indian people living in central Mexico before the advent of the Aztecs and traditionally credited with laying the foundation of Aztec culture. **—*adj.* 2.** Also, **Tol′tec·an.** of or pertaining to the Toltecs.

to·lu (tô lōō′, tə-), *n.* a fragrant yellowish-brown balsam or resin obtained from a South American tree, *Myroxylon balsamum,* used in medicine as a stomachic and expectorant, and in perfumery. Also called **tolu balsam, balsam of tolu, tolu resin.** [after *Tolu* (now Santiago de Tolu) in Columbia, where balsam is obtained]

tol·u·ate (tol′yōō āt′), *n. Chem.* a salt or ester of any of the three isomeric toluic acids. [TOLU(ENE) + -ATE[2]]

tolu′ bal′sam, tolu.

To·lu·ca (tô lōō′kä), *n.* **1.** a city in and the capital of Mexico state, in S central Mexico. 71,026 (1960). **2.** an extinct volcano in central Mexico, in Mexico state. 15,026 ft.

To Lu·cas′ta, Go′ing to the Wars′ (lōō kas′tə), a poem (1649) by Richard Lovelace.

tol·u·ene (tol′yōō ēn′), *n. Chem.* a colorless, water-insoluble, flammable liquid, $C_6H_5CH_3$, having a benzenelike odor, obtained chiefly from coal tar and petroleum: used as a solvent in the manufacture of benzoic acid, benzaldehyde, TNT, and other organic compounds. Also called **methylbenzene, phenylmethane.** [TOLU + -ENE]

tol′uene trichlo′ride, *Chem.* benzotrichloride.

tol′uene triflu′oride, *Chem.* benzotrifluoride.

to·lu·ic (tə lōō′ik, tol′yōō ik), *adj. Chem.* of or derived from toluic acid. [TOLU(ENE) + -IC]

tolu′ic ac′id, *Chem.* any of three isomeric acids having the formula $CH_3C_6H_4COOH$: derivatives of toluene.

tol·u·ide (tol′yōō īd′, -id), *n. Chem.* an amide of the structure $RCONHC_6H_4CH_3$. Also, **tol·u·id** (tol′yōō id). [TOLU(IDINE) + -IDE]

to·lu·i·dine (tə lōō′i dēn′, -din), *n. Chem.* any of three isomeric amines having the formula $CH_3C_6H_4NH_2$, derived from toluene: used in the dye and drug industries. Cf. **meta-toluidine, ortho-toluidine, para-toluidine.** [TOLU(ENE) + -ID[3]]

To·lum·ni·us (tə lum′nē əs), *n. Rom. Legend.* an augur who warned Turnus against fighting Aeneas singlehandedly.

tol·u·ol (tol′yōō ōl′), *n. Chem.* **1.** toluene. **2.** the commercial form of toluene. [TOLU + -OL[2]]

tolu′ res′in, tolu.

tolu′ tree′, a South American, leguminous tree, *Myroxylon balsamum,* yielding tolu.

tol·u·yl (tol′yōō il), *adj. Chem.* containing the toluyl group. [TOLU(ENE) + -YL]

tol′uyl group′, *Chem.* any of three univalent isomeric groups having the formula $CH_3C_6H_4CO\text{–}$, derived from toluic acids. Also called **tol′uyl rad′ical.**

tol·yl (tol′il), *adj. Chem.* containing a tolyl group; cresyl. [TOL(UENE) + -YL]

tol′yl group′, *Chem.* any of three univalent, isomeric groups having the formula $CH_3C_6H_4\text{–}$, derived from toluene. Also called **tol′yl rad′ical.** Cf. **meta[2], ortho, para[2].**

tom (tom), *n.* **1.** the male of various animals: *tom turkey.* **2.** a tomcat. [special use of TOM]

Tom (tom), *n.* **1.** See **Uncle Tom.** **2.** a boy's given name, form of **Thomas.**

To·mah (tō′mə), *n.* a town in central Wisconsin. 5321 (1960).

tom·a·hawk (tom′ə hôk′), *n.* **1.** a light ax used by the North American Indians as a weapon and tool. **2.** any of various similar weapons or implements. **3.** (in Australia) a stone hatchet used by the aborigines. **4. bury the tomahawk.** See **hatchet** (def. 4). —*v.t.* **5.** to attack, wound, or kill with or as with a tomahawk. [earlier *tomahack* < Algonquian (Virginia dial.)] —**tom′a·hawk′er,** *n.*

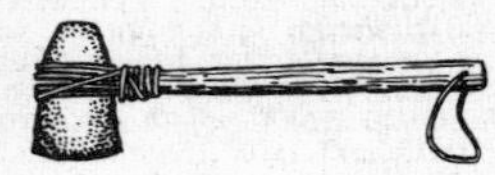

Tomahawk (def. 1)

Tom·a·hawk (tom′ə hôk′), *n.* a town in N Wisconsin. 3348 (1960).

tom·al·ley (tom′al′ē), *n., pl.* **-leys.** *Cookery.* the liver of a lobster. [earlier *taumali* < Carib]

to·man (tə män′), *n.* a coin of Iran, equal to 10 rials and equivalent to about .13 of a U.S. dollar. [< Pers *tōmān, tūmān,* of Mongolian orig.]

Tom′ and Jer′ry, a hot drink made of rum and water or milk, beaten eggs, spices, and sugar. [named after the principal characters in *Life in London* (1821) by Pierce Egan (d. 1849), English writer]

to·ma·til·lo (tō′mə tē′ō, -tēl′yō), *n., pl.* **-loes, -los.** an annual herb, *Physalis ixocarpa,* of Mexico, having yellow flowers with five blackish spots in the throat and bluish, sticky berries in a purple-veined calyx. Also called **Mexican ground cherry.** [< Sp, dim. of *tomate* TOMATO]

to·ma·to (tə mā′tō, -mä′-), *n., pl.* **-toes. 1.** a widely cultivated, solanaceous perennial plant, *Lycopersicon esculentum,* bearing a mildly acid, pulpy fruit, commonly red, sometimes yellow, used as a vegetable. **2.** the fruit itself. **3.** any plant of the same genus. **4.** its fruit. **5.** *Slang.* a girl or woman. [earlier *tomate* < Sp < Nahuatl *tomatl*]

toma′to as′pic, aspic[1] (def. 2).

toma′to egg′plant. See **scarlet eggplant.**

toma′to horn′worm, the larva of a hawk moth, *Protoparce quinquemaculata,* that feeds on the leaves of tomato, potato, and other solanaceous plants. Also called **potato worm.**

tomb (to͞om), *n.* **1.** an excavation in earth or rock for the burial of a corpse; a grave or other burial place. **2.** a mausoleum, burial chamber, or the like. **3.** a monument for housing a corpse or a structure erected in memory of a dead person. **4.** any sepulchral structure. —*v.t.* **5.** to place in or as in a tomb; entomb; bury. [early ME *tumbe* < AF, equiv. to OF *tombe* < LL *tumba* < Gk *týmbos* burial mound; akin to L *tumēre* to swell. See TUMOR, TUMULUS, THUMB] —**tomb′al,** *adj.* —**tomb′less,** *adj.* —**tomb′like′,** *adj.*

tom·bac (tom′bak), *n.* an alloy, used to imitate gold, containing from 70 to 92 percent copper with zinc and sometimes tin and other materials forming the remainder. Also, **tambac.** [< D *tombak* < Pg *tambaca* < Malay *tambāga* copper < Skt *tāmraka;* r. earlier *tombaga* < Malay, as above]

Tom·bal·ba·ye (tôm′bäl bä′ye), *n.* **Fran·çois** (*Fr.* fräN swa′), born 1918, African statesman: president of the Republic of Chad since 1960.

Tom·big·bee (tom big′bē), *n.* a river flowing S through NE Mississippi and SW Alabama to the Mobile River. 525 mi. long.

tom·bo·la (tom′bə lə), *n. Brit.* house (def. 19). [< It < *tombol(are)* (to) tumble < *tombare* to fall < VL **tumbāre* to fall, of imit. orig.]

tom·bo·lo (tom′bə lō′), *n., pl.* **-los.** a sand bar connecting an island to the mainland or to another island. [< It < L *tumul(us)* mound. See TUMULUS]

Tom·bouc·tou (tôN bo͞ok to͞o′), *n.* French name of **Timbuktu.**

tom·boy (tom′boi′), *n.* a carefree, romping, boisterous girl. [TOM + BOY] —**tom′boy′ish,** *adj.* —**tom′boy′ish·ly,** *adv.* —**tom′boy′ish·ness,** *n.*

tomb·stone (to͞om′stōn′), *n.* a stone marker, usually inscribed, on a tomb or grave. [TOMB + STONE]

tom·cat (tom′kat′), *n., v.,* **-cat·ted, -cat·ting.** —*n.* **1.** a male cat. **2.** *Slang.* a man who goes whoring. —*v.i.* **3.** *Slang.* to look for a sexual partner; go whoring; cat. [TOM + CAT[1]]

tom·cod (tom′kod′), *n., pl.* (*esp. collectively*) **-cod,** (*esp. referring to two or more kinds or species*) **-cods. 1.** either of two small cods, *Microgadus tomcod,* of the Atlantic Ocean, or *M. proximus,* of the Pacific Ocean. **2.** any of various similar fishes. [TOM (THUMB) + COD[1]]

Tom′ Col′lins, a tall drink containing gin, lemon or lime juice, and carbonated water, sweetened and served with ice. [said to have been named after its inventor]

Tom′, Dick′, and Har′ry, *Slang.* the common man; people generally; everyone: *They invited every Tom, Dick, and Harry to the party.*

tome (tōm), *n.* **1.** a volume forming a part of a larger work. **2.** any book, esp. a very heavy, large, or learned one. [< F < L *tom(us)* < Gk *tómos* slice, piece, roll of paper, book, akin to *témnein* to cut]

-tome, a learned borrowing from Greek meaning "cutting," used esp. in the formation of scientific terms: *microtome; osteotome.* Cf. **-tomic[1], tomo-, -tomous, -tomy.** [comb. form repr. Gk *tomḗ* a cutting; *tómos* a cut, slice; *-tomon,* neut. of *-tomos* -cutting]

to·men·tose (tə men′tōs, tō′men tōs′), *adj. Bot., Entomol.* closely covered with down or matted hair. [< NL *tōmentōs(us).* See TOMENT(UM), -OSE[1]]

to·men·tum (tə men′təm), *n., pl.* **-ta** (-tə). *Bot.* pubescence consisting of longish, soft, entangled hairs pressed close to the surface. [< NL, special use of L *tōmentum* stuffing (of wool, hair, etc.) for cushions]

tom·fool (tom′fo͞ol′), *n.* **1.** a grossly foolish or stupid person; a silly fool. —*adj.* **2.** being or characteristic of a tomfool. [ME *Thome fole* Tom the fool] —**tom′fool′ish,** *adj.* —**tom′fool′ish·ness,** *n.*

tom·fool·er·y (tom′fo͞o′lə rē), *n., pl.* **-er·ies. 1.** foolish or silly behavior. **2.** a silly act, matter, or thing. [TOMFOOL + -ERY]

-tomic[1], a combination of **-tome** and **-ic** used to form adjectives from nouns with stems in **-tome:** *microtomic.*

-tomic[2], a combination of **-tomy** and **-ic** used to form adjectives from nouns with stems in **-tomy:** *dichotomic.*

to·mi·um (tō′mē əm), *n., pl.* **-mi·a** (-mē ə). the cutting edge of a bird's bill. [< NL < Gk *tóm(os)* a cutting (see TOME) + NL *-ium* neut. n. suffix] —**to′mi·al,** *adj.*

Tom′ Jones′, a novel (1749) by Henry Fielding.

Tom·lin·son (tom′lin sən), *n.* **Henry Major,** 1873–1958, English journalist and novelist.

Tom·ma·si·ni (tom′ə sē′nē; *It.* tôm′mä zē′nē), *n.* **Vi·cen·zo** (vē chen′dzō), 1880–1950, Italian composer.

tom·my (tom′ē), *n., pl.* **-mies. 1.** (*sometimes cap.*) See **Tommy Atkins. 2.** *Brit. Slang.* bread, esp. brown bread, or rations, as formerly distributed to troops and workers. [by shortening]

Tom·my (tom′ē), *n.* **1.** a boy's given name, form of **Thomas. 2.** Also, **Tom′mie, Tom′mye.** a girl's given name, form of **Thomasin.**

Tom′my At′kins, *pl.* **Tommy Atkins. 1.** any private of the British army. **2.** *Brit.* one of the rank and file of any organization or group.

Tom′my gun′, 1. See **Thompson submachine gun. 2.** *Informal.* any submachine gun. [by shortening]

tom·my·rot (tom′ē rot′), *n.* nonsense; utter foolishness. [*tommy* simpleton (see TOMFOOL) + ROT]

tomo-, a combining form meaning "a cut," "section," used in the formation of compound words: *tomography.* [comb. form repr. Gk *tómos* a cut, section; cf. -TOME]

Tom o'Bed·lam (tom′ ə bed′ləm), *pl.* **-lams.** a roving beggar afflicted with or feigning madness.

to·mo·gram (tō′mə gram′), *n. Med.* the x-ray photograph obtained by tomography. [TOMO- + -GRAM[1]]

to·mo·graph (tō′mə graf′, -gräf′), *n.* a machine for making tomograms; an x-ray machine. [TOMO- + -GRAPH] —**to·mo·graph·ic** (tō′mə graf′ik), *adj.*

to·mog·ra·phy (tə mog′rə fē), *n. Med.* x-ray photography of a selected plane in the body. [TOMO- + -GRAPHY]

To·mo·na·ga (tô′mô nä′gä), *n.* **Shi·ni·chi·ro** (shi′ni-chi′rô), born 1906, Japanese physicist: Nobel prize 1965.

to·mor·row (tə môr′ō, -mor′ō), *n.* **1.** the day following today: *Tomorrow is supposed to be sunny.* **2.** a future period or time: *the stars of tomorrow.* —*adv.* **3.** on the morrow; on the day following today: *Come tomorrow at this same time.* **4.** at some future time: *We shall rest easy tomorrow if we work for peace today.* Also, **to-mor′row.** [ME *to morwe(n),* OE *to morgen(ne).* See TO, MORROW]

-tomous, a suffix of adjectives indicating a cut or division of a certain kind: *dichotomous.* [-TOME or -TOMY + -OUS]

tom·pi·on (tom′pē ən), *n.* tampion.

Tomp·kins (tomp′kinz), *n.* **Daniel D.,** 1774–1825, U.S. politician and jurist: vice-president of the U.S. 1817–25.

Tom′ Saw′yer, (*The Adventures of Tom Sawyer*) a novel (1876) by Mark Twain.

Tomsk (tômsk), *n.* a city in the central RSFSR, in the SW Soviet Union in Asia, E of the Ob River. 293,000 (est. 1964).

Toms′ Riv′er (tomz), a town in E New Jersey. 6062 (1960).

Tom′ Swift′ie (swif′tē), a play on words that follows an unvarying pattern and relies for its humor on a punning relationship between the way an adverb describes a speaker and at the same time refers significantly to the import of the speaker's statement, as in "*I know who turned off the lights,*" *Tom hinted darkly.* [named after a narrative mannerism characteristic of the *Tom Swift* American series of adventure novels for boys]

tom·tate (tom′tāt), *n. Ichthyol.* a grunt, *Bathystoma aurolineatum,* found off the West Indies and Florida. [?]

Tom′ Thumb′, 1. a diminutive hero of folk tales. **2.** an extremely small person; dwarf. **3.** nickname of Charles Sherwood Stratton.

tom·tit (tom′tit′), *n. Brit. Dial.* **1.** a titmouse. **2.** any of various other small birds, as the wren. [TOM (THUMB) + TIT[1]]

tom-tom (tom′tom′), *n.* **1.** an American Indian or Oriental drum of indefinite pitch, commonly played with the hands. **2.** a dully repetitious drumbeat or similar sound. Also, **tam-tam.** [< Hindi *tamtam,* repetitive compound; imit.]

Tom-tom

-tomy, a suffix meaning "a cutting," used esp. in relation to a surgical operation (*appendectomy, lithotomy, phlebotomy*) or sometimes a division (*dichotomy*). Cf. **-tome, -tomic[2], tomo-, -tomous.** [repr. Gk *-tomía;* see -TOME, -Y[3]]

ton[1] (tun), *n.* **1.** a unit of weight, equivalent to 2000 pounds avoirdupois **(short ton)** in the U.S. and 2240 pounds avoirdupois **(long ton)** in Great Britain. **2.** Also called **freight ton.** a unit of volume for freight that weighs one ton, varying with the type of freight measured, as 40 cubic feet of oak timber, 20 bushels of wheat, etc. **3.** See **metric ton. 4.** See **displacement ton. 5.** a unit of volume used in transportation by sea, commonly equal to 40 cubic feet **(shipping ton** or **measurement ton). 6.** a unit of internal capacity of ships, equal to 100 cubic feet **(register ton). 7.** Often, **tons.** *Informal.* a great quantity; a lot: *a ton of jokes; tons of wedding presents.* [ME; var. of TUN]

ton[2] (*Fr.* tôN), *n., pl.* **tons** (*Fr.* tôN). **1.** high fashion; stylishness. **2.** the current fashion, style, or vogue. [< F < L *ton(us).* See TONE] —**ton·ish, ton·nish** (ton′ish), *adj.* —**ton′ish·ly, ton′nish·ly,** *adv.* —**ton′ish·ness, ton′nish·ness,** *n.*

-ton, a suffix formerly used to form nouns from adjectives: *simpleton, singleton.* [var. of dial. *tone* ONE. See TOTHER]

ton·al (tōn′əl), *adj. Music.* pertaining to tonality (opposed to *modal*). [< ML *tonāl(is).* See TONE, -AL[1]] —**ton′al·ly,** *adv.*

ton·al·ist (tōn′əlist), *n.* one who works with or uses tonality, esp. one who uses traditional tonality rather than atonality in composing music. [TONAL + -IST]

to·nal·i·ty (tō nal′i tē), *n., pl.* **-ties. 1.** *Music.* **a.** the sum of relations, melodic and harmonic, existing between the tones of a scale or musical system. **b.** a particular scale or system of tones; a key. **2.** (in painting, graphics, etc.) the system of tones or tints, or the color scheme, of a picture. [TONAL + -ITY] —**to·nal′i·tive,** *adj.*

to-name (to͞o′nām′), *n. Chiefly Scot.* **1.** a nickname, esp. one to distinguish a person from others of the same name. **2.** a surname. [ME; OE *tōnama.* See TO, NAME]

Ton·a·wan·da (ton′ə won′də), *n.* a city in NW New York, near Buffalo. 21,561 (1960).

ton·do (ton′dō; *It.* tôn′dô), *n., pl.* **-di** (-dē). a round painting or relief. [< It: plate, circle, round painting < *tondo* (adj.) round < (*ro*)*tundo* < L *rotund(us);* see ROTUND]

tone (tōn), *n., v.,* **toned, ton·ing.** —*n.* **1.** any sound considered with reference to its quality, pitch, strength, source, etc.: *shrill tones.* **2.** quality or character of sound. **3.** vocal sound; the sound made by vibrating muscular bands in the larynx. **4.** a particular quality, way of sounding, modulation, or intonation of the voice as expressive of some meaning, feeling, spirit, etc.: *a tone of command.* **5.** an accent peculiar to a person, people, locality, etc., or a characteristic mode of sounding words in speech. **6.** stress of voice on a syllable of a word. **7.** *Ling.* a musical pitch or movement in pitch serving to distinguish two words otherwise composed of the same sounds, as in Chinese. **8.** *Music.* **a.** a musical sound of definite pitch, consisting of several relatively simple constituents called partial tones, the lowest of which is called the fundamental tone and the others harmonics or overtones. **b.** an interval equivalent to two semitones; a whole tone; a whole step. **c.** any of the nine melodies or tunes to which Gregorian plainsong psalms are sung. **9.** value; a quality of color with reference to the degree of absorption or reflection of light; a tint or shade. **10.** hue; that distinctive quality by which colors differ from one another in addition to their differences indicated by chroma, tint, shade; a slight modification of a given color: *green with a yellowish tone.* **11.** *Art.* the prevailing effect of harmony of color and values. **12.** *Physiol.* **a.** the normal state of tension or firmness of the organs or tissues of the body. **b.** that state of the body or of an organ in which all its functions are performed with healthy vigor. **c.** normal sensitivity to stimulation. **13.** a normal healthy mental condition. **14.** a particular mental state or disposition; spirit, character, or tenor. **15.** a particular style or manner, as of writing or speech; mood: *the macabre tone of Poe's stories.* **16.** prevailing character or style, as of manners, morals, or philosophical outlook: *the liberal tone of the 1930's.* **17.** style, distinction, or elegance: *That girl has real tone!* —*v.t.* **18.** to sound with a particular tone. **19.** to give the proper tone to (a musical instrument). **20.** to modify the tone or general coloring of. **21.** to give the desired tone to (a painting, drawing, etc.). **22.** *Photog.* to change the color of (a print), esp. by chemical means. **23.** to render as specified in tone or coloring. **24.** to modify the tone or character of. **25.** to give or restore physical or mental tone to. —*v.i.* **26.** to take on a particular tone; assume color or tint. **27. tone down, a.** *Painting.* to subdue; make (a color) less intense in hue. **b.** to become or cause to become softened or moderated: *The newspaper toned down its attack.* **28. tone up, a.** to give a higher or stronger tone to. **b.** to gain or cause to gain in tone or strength: *This exercise is fine for toning up little-used muscles.* **29. tone with** or **in with,** to harmonize in tone or coloring; blend: *The painting tones with the rest of the room.* [ME < L *ton(us)* < Gk *tónos* strain, tone, mode, lit., a stretching, akin to *teínein* to stretch] —**tone′less,** *adj.* —**tone′less·ly,** *adv.* —**tone′less·ness,** *n.*
—**Syn. 1.** See **sound[1].**

tone′ arm′, the free-swinging bracket of a phonograph containing the pickup. Also called **pickup arm.**

tone′ clus′ter, *Music.* a group of adjacent notes played on a keyboard instrument typically with the fist, forearm, or elbow, similar groupings also occurring in orchestral music.

tone′ col′or, *Music.* quality of tone; timbre.

tone′ control′, a manual control used to adjust the relative responses of an amplifier to high, low, and intermediate audio frequencies.

tone-deaf (tōn′def′), *adj. Pathol.* afflicted with tone deafness.

tone′ deaf′ness, *Pathol.* an inability to distinguish differences in pitch in musical sounds when producing or hearing them.

to·ne·la·da (*Sp.* tô′ne lä′ᵺä; *Port.* tô′nə lä′də, tô′ni-lä′dä), *n., pl.* **-das** (*Sp.* -ᵺäs; *Port.* -dəsh, -däs). a unit of weight corresponding to a ton and varying in value, equal in Brazil to nearly 1750 pounds, in Spain to nearly 2030 pounds. [< Sp, Pg < *tonel* old measure of weight (< Catalan *tonell* cask; see TUNNEL) + *-ada* -ADE[1]]

tone′ lan′guage, a language, as Swedish, Chinese, Yoruba, or Serbo-Croatian, in which words that are otherwise phonologically identical are distinguished by having different pitches or pitch contour.

ton·eme (tō′nēm), *n.* a phoneme consisting of a contrastive feature of tone in a tone language: *Swedish has two tonemes.* [TONE + -EME]

tone′ paint′ing, musical description, by harmonic, melodic, or rhythmic means, of the words of a text or the story elements in program music.

tone′ po′em, *Music.* an instrumental composition intended to portray a particular story, scene, mood, etc. Cf. **program music.**

ton·er (tō′nər), *n.* **1.** one who or that which tones. **2.** a highly concentrated organic pigment containing little or no inert matter. **3.** a worker for a paint manufacturer who tests the color and quality of paint. [TONE + -ER[1]]

tone′ row′, *Music.* a series of tones in which no tone is duplicated, and in which the tones may appear in the same sequence. Also called **twelve-tone row;** *esp. Brit.,* **note row.**

to·net·ic (tō net′ik), *adj.* noting or pertaining to the phonetic study of tone in language. [TONE + (PHO)NETIC] —**to·net′i·cal·ly,** *adv.*

to·net·ics (tō net′iks), *n.* (*construed as sing.*) the phonetic study of tone in language. [TONE + (PHO)NETICS] —**to·ne·ti·cian** (tō′ni tish′ən), *n.*

to·nette (tō net′), *n.* a small end-blown flute of simple construction and narrow range. [TONE + -ETTE]

ton-force (tun′fōrs′, -fôrs′), *n.* two thousand pound-force. *Abbr.:* tonf

tong[1] (tông, tong), *n.* **1.** tongs. —*v.t.* **2.** to lift, seize, gather, hold, or handle with tongs, as logs or oysters. —*v.i.* **3.** to use, or work with, tongs. [ME, OE; c. D *tang*, G *Zange* pair of tongs or pincers; akin to Gk *dáknein* to bite]

tong[2] (tông, tong), *n.* **1.** (in China) an association, society, or political party. **2.** (among Chinese living in the U.S.) a fraternal organization or secret society, formerly believed to engage extensively in criminal activities. [< Chin *t'ang* meeting place]

ton·ga (tong′gə), *n.* a light, two-wheeled, horse-drawn vehicle used in India. [< Hindi *tāṅgā*]

Ton·ga (tong′gə), *n.* a Polynesian kingdom consisting of three groups of islands in the S Pacific, NE of New Zealand: a British protectorate. 69,439 (est. 1963); ab. 270 sq. mi. *Cap.:* Nukualofa. Also called **Ton′ga Is′lands, Friendly Islands.**

Ton·gan (tong′gən), *n.* **1.** a native or inhabitant of Tonga. **2.** a Polynesian language, the language of the Tongans. —*adj.* **3.** of or pertaining to Tonga, its people, or their language. [TONG(A) + -AN]

Tong·king (tong′king′), *n.* Tonkin.

tong·man (tong′mən), *n., pl.* **-men.** a member of a Chinese tong. [TONG[2] + MAN]

tongs (tôngz, tongz), *n.* (*usually construed as pl.*) any of various implements consisting of two arms hinged, pivoted, or otherwise fastened together, for seizing, holding, or lifting something (usually used with *pair of*). [see TONG[1]]

tongue (tung), *n., v.* **tongued, tongu·ing.** —*n.* **1.** the usually movable organ in the floor of the mouth in man and most vertebrates, functioning in eating, in tasting, and, in man, in speaking. **2.** an analogous organ in invertebrate animals. **3.** the tongue of an animal, as an ox, beef, or sheep, used for food, often prepared by smoking or pickling. **4.** the human tongue as the organ of speech. **5.** the faculty or power of speech: *Have you lost your tongue?* **6.** speech or talk, esp. mere glib or empty talk. **7.** manner or character of speech: *a flattering tongue.* **8.** the language of a particular people, region, or nation: *the Hebrew tongue.* **9.** a dialect. **10.** Often, **tongues.** a people or nation distinguished by its language. Is. 66:18; Rev. 5:9. **11.** an object that resembles an animal's tongue in shape, position, or function. **12.** a strip of leather under the lacing or fastening of a shoe. **13.** a piece of metal suspended inside a bell that strikes against the side producing a sound; clapper. **14.** a vibrating reed or similar structure in a musical instrument, as in a clarinet, or in part of a musical instrument, as in an organ reed pipe. **15.** the pole extending from a carriage or other vehicle between the animals drawing it. **16.** a projecting strip along the center of the edge or end of a board, for fitting into a groove in another board. **17.** a narrow strip of land extending into a body of water; cape. **18.** a section of ice projecting outward from the submerged part of an iceberg. **19.** *Mach.* a long, narrow projection on a machine. **20.** that part of a railroad switch which is shifted to direct the wheels of a locomotive or car to one or the other track of a railroad. **21.** the pin of a buckle, brooch, etc. **22. find one's tongue,** to regain one's powers of speech; recover one's poise: *She wanted to say something, but couldn't find her tongue.* **23. give tongue, a.** *Fox Hunting.* (of a hound) to bay while following a scent. **b.** to utter one's thoughts; speak: *He wouldn't give tongue to his suspicions.* **24. hold one's tongue,** to refrain from or cease speaking; keep silent: *She never has the sense to hold her tongue at the right time.* **25. lose one's tongue,** to lose the power of speech, esp. temporarily. **26. on the tip of one's tongue, a.** on the verge of being uttered. **b.** unable to be recalled; barely escaping one's memory: *The answer was on the tip of my tongue, but I couldn't think of it.* **27. slip of the tongue,** a mistake in speaking, as an inadvertent remark: *His slip of the tongue cost him a friend when he said "I won't do it" instead of "I want to do it."* **28. with one's tongue in one's cheek,** mockingly; insincerely. Also, **with tongue in cheek, tongue in cheek.** —*v.t.* **29.** to articulate (tones played on a flute, cornet, etc.) by strokes of the tongue. **30.** *Carpentry.* **a.** to cut a tongue on (a board). **b.** to join or fit together by a tongue-and-groove joint. **31.** to touch with the tongue. **32.** to reproach or scold. **33.** to articulate or pronounce. **34.** *Archaic.* to speak or utter. —*v.i.* **35.** to tongue tones played on a flute, cornet, etc. **36.** to talk, esp. idly or foolishly; chatter; prate. **37.** to project like a tongue or tongues. [ME, OE *tunge*; c. D *tong*, Icel *tunga*, G *Zunge*, Goth *tuggo*; akin to L *lingua* (earlier *dingua*)] —**tongue′less,** *adj.* —**tongue′like′,** *adj.*

Tongue-and-groove joint

tongue′-and-groove′ joint′ (tung′ən grōōv′), *Carpentry.* a joint between two boards in which a raised area on the edge of one board fits into a corresponding groove in the edge of the other to produce a flush surface.

tongue′ cov′er, a loose-leaf binding having a flap of the cover concealing the binding posts.

tongue′ depres′sor, a broad, thin piece of wood used by doctors to hold down the patient's tongue during an examination of the mouth and throat. Also called **tongue′ blade′.**

tongue·fish (tung′fish′), *n., pl.* (*esp. collectively*) **-fish,** (*esp. referring to two or more kinds or species*) **-fish·es.** any of several flatfishes of the family *Cynoglossidae*, having both eyes on the left side of the head and a pointed tail. [TONGUE + FISH]

tongue′ graft′. See **whip graft.**

tongue-lash (tung′lash′), *v.t., v.i.* to scold severely.

tongue-lash·ing (tung′lash′ing), *n.* a severe scolding or reprimand: *The judge gave the juvenile delinquents a tongue-lashing.*

tongue′ sole′, tonguefish.

tongue-tie (tung′tī′), *n., v.,* **-tied, -ty·ing.** —*n.* **1.** impeded motion of the tongue caused esp. by shortness of the frenum, which binds it to the floor of the mouth. —*v.t.* **2.** to make tongue-tied. [back formation from TONGUE-TIED]

tongue-tied (tung′tīd′), *adj.* **1.** unable to speak, as from shyness, embarrassment, or surprise. **2.** affected with tongue-tie. [TONGUE + TIED]

tongue′ twist′er, a word or sequence of words difficult to pronounce, especially rapidly, because of alliteration or a slight variation of consonant sounds, as "Good blood, bad blood" or "The Leith police dismisseth us."

tongue′ worm′. See **acorn worm.**

tongu·ing (tung′ing), *n.* *Music.* the manipulation of the tongue in playing a wind instrument to interrupt the tone and produce a staccato effect. [TONGUE + -ING[1]]

tongu′ing-and-groov′ing plane′ (tung′ing ən-grōō′ving), *Carpentry.* a plane for cutting the edges of boards into tongues and grooves.

To·ni (tō′nē), *n.* a girl's given name, form of **Antoinette** or **Antonia.**

ton·ic (ton′ik), *n.* **1.** a medicine that invigorates or strengthens: *a spring tonic of sulphur and molasses.* **2.** anything invigorating physically, mentally, or morally: *His cheerful greeting was a real tonic.* **3.** *Music.* the first degree of the scale; the keynote. **4.** carbonated quinine water for mixing with alcoholic drinks to make highballs. **5.** *Chiefly Eastern New Eng.* See **soft drink.** —*adj.* **6.** pertaining to, maintaining, increasing, or restoring the tone or health of the body or an organ, as a medicine. **7** invigorating physically, mentally, or morally. **8.** *Physiol., Pathol.* **a.** pertaining to tension, as of the muscles. **b.** marked by continued muscular tension: *a tonic spasm.* **9.** using differences in tone or pitch to distinguish between words that are otherwise phonemically identical: *a tonic language.* **10.** pertaining to tone or accent in speech. **11.** *Phonet.* accented, esp. with primary accent. **12.** *Music.* **a.** of or pertaining to a tone or tones. **b.** pertaining to or founded on the keynote, or first tone, of a musical scale: *a tonic chord.* [< Gk *tonik(ós)* pertaining to stretching or tones. See TONE, -IC] —**ton′i·cal·ly,** *adv.*

ton′ic ac′cent, vocal accent, or syllabic stress, in pronunciation or speaking.

to·nic·i·ty (tō nis′i tē), *n.* **1.** tonic quality or condition. **2.** the state of bodily tone. **3.** *Physiol.* the normal elastic tension of living muscles, arteries, etc., by which the tone of the system is maintained. [TONIC + -ITY]

ton′ic sol-fa′, a system of singing characterized by emphasis upon tonality or key relationship, in which tones are indicated by the initial letters of the syllables of the *sol-fa* system rather than by conventional staff notation.

ton′ic spasm′, *Med.* See under **spasm** (def. 1).

to·night (tə nīt′), *n.* **1.** this present or coming night, the night of this present day. —*adv.* **2.** on this present night; on the night of this present day. **3.** *Obs.* during last night. Also, **to-night′.** [ME, OE *tō niht*. See TO, NIGHT]

ton·ite (tō′nīt), *n.* *Chem.* an explosive consisting of guncotton, a nitrate, and a nitro compound, used chiefly in blasting powders and grenades. [< L *ton(āre)* (to) thunder + -ITE[1]]

ton′ka bean′ (tong′kə), **1.** the fragrant, black almond-shaped seed of a tall, leguminous tree of the genus *Dipteryx* (or *Coumarouna*), esp. *D. odorata*, of tropical South America, used in perfumes and snuff, and as a substitute for vanilla. **2.** the tree itself. [*tonka* ? < Tupi

ton′ka bean′ cam′phor, coumarin.

Ton·ka·wa (tong′kə wô′), *n.* a town in N Oklahoma. 3415 (1960).

Ton·kin (ton′kin′, tong′kin′), *n.* **1.** a former state in N French Indochina, now part of North Vietnam. **2. Gulf of,** an arm of the South China Sea, W of Hainan. 300 mi. long. Also, **Tongking, Ton·king** (ton′king′, tong′-).

Ton·le Sap (ton′lā säp′), a lake in W Cambodia, draining into the Mekong River.

ton·let (tun′lit), *n.* *Armor.* a skirt of plates. Also called **jamboy, lamboy.** [< F *tonnelet* keg < MF, prob. dim. of *tonel* cask, from the resemblance to the arrangement of staves]

ton-mile (tun′mīl′), *n.* a unit of freight transportation measurement equivalent to a ton of freight transported one mile. —**ton′-mile′age,** *n.*

tonn., tonnage.

ton·nage (tun′ij), *n.* **1.** the capacity of a merchant vessel, expressed either in units of weight, as deadweight tons, or of volume, as gross tons. **2.** ships collectively considered with reference to their carrying capacity or together with their cargoes. **3.** a duty on ships or boats at so much per ton of cargo or freight, or according to the capacity in tons. Also, **tunnage.** [ME: duty < OF. See TON[1], -AGE]

ton′nage deck′, *Naut.* **1.** the upper deck in a vessel with only two decks. **2.** the second deck above the inner bottom in a vessel with more than two decks.

ton′nage hatch′, a nonwatertight hatch on a cargo vessel, opening into the weather deck in order to exclude the shelter deck beneath from the net tonnage: used on an open-shelter-deck ship.

ton′nage length′, *Naut.* the length of the tonnage deck of a vessel, measured inside the hull along the fore-and-aft centerline.

ton′nage o′pening, *Naut.* any of various openings, as doorways or hatchways, enclosed by nonpermanent or nonwatertight means in order to create a theoretical open space exempt from taxation. Cf. **open space.**

ton′nage well′, *Naut.* an open area beneath a tonnage hatch, enclosed by nonwatertight partitions.

tonne (tun), *n.* See **metric ton.** *Abbr.:* t

ton·neau (tu nō′), *n., pl.* **-neaus, -neaux** (-nōz′). **1.** a rear part or compartment of an automobile body, containing seats for passengers. **2.** a complete automobile body having such a rear part. **3.** millier. [< F: kind of vehicle; also, cask; OF *tonel* cask. See TUNNEL]

Tön·nies (tœ′nəs), *n.* **Fer·di·nand** (fer′dē nänt′), 1855–1936, German sociologist.

to·nom·e·ter (tō nom′i tər), *n.* **1.** an instrument for measuring the frequencies of tones, as a tuning fork or a graduated set of tuning forks. **2.** any of various physiological instruments, as for measuring the tension within the eyeball, or for determining blood pressure. **3.** *Physical. Chem.* an instrument for measuring vapor pressure. [< Gk *tóno(s)* tension, tone + -METER] —**ton·o·met·ric** (ton′ə me′trik, tō′nə-), *adj.* —**to·nom′e·try,** *n.*

tons′ bur′den, *Naut.* the number of long tons of capacity of a vessel; the deadweight tonnage of a vessel.

ton·sil (ton′səl), *n.* *Anat.* a prominent oval mass of lymphoid tissue on each side of the fauces. [< L *tōnsill(ae)* (pl.) the tonsils] —**ton′sil·lar, ton′sil·ar, ton·sil·lar·y** (ton′sə ler′ē), *adj.*

A, Tonsil
B, Adenoids

ton·sil·lec·tome (ton′sə lek′tōm), *n.* *Surg.* an instrument for performing a tonsillectomy. [< L *tōnsill(ae)* tonsils + -ECTOME]

ton·sil·lec·to·my (ton′sə lek′tə mē), *n., pl.* **-mies.** *Surg.* the operation of excising or removing one or both tonsils. [< L *tōnsill(ae)* tonsils + -ECTOMY]

ton·sil·li·tis (ton′sə lī′tis), *n.* *Pathol.* inflammation of a tonsil or the tonsils. [< L *tōnsill(ae)* tonsils + -ITIS] —**ton·sil·lit·ic** (ton′sə lit′ik), *adj.*

ton·sil·lot·o·my (ton′sə lot′ə mē), *n., pl.* **-mies.** *Surg.* incision or excision of a portion of a tonsil. [< L *tōnsill(ae)* tonsils + -o- + -TOMY]

ton·so·ri·al (ton sōr′ē əl, -sôr′-), *adj.* *Often Facetious.* of or pertaining to a barber or his work: *the tonsorial shop.* [< L *tōnsōri(us)* of shaving (< *tōns(us)*, ptp. of *tondēre* to shave + *-ōrius* -ORY[1]) + -AL[1]]

ton·sure (ton′shər), *n., v.,* **-sured, -sur·ing.** —*n.* **1.** act of cutting the hair or shaving the head. **2.** the shaving of the head or of some part of it as a religious practice or rite, esp. in preparation for entering the priesthood or a monastic order. **3.** the part of a cleric's head, usually the crown, left bare by shaving the hair. **4.** state of being shorn. —*v.t.* **5.** to confer the ecclesiastical tonsure upon. **6.** to subject to tonsure. [ME < L *tōnsūr(a)* a shearing < *tōns(us)* (ptp. of *tondēre* to shear, clip, shave) + *-ūra* -URE]

ton·tine (ton′tēn, ton tēn′), *n.* **1.** an annuity scheme in which subscribers share a common fund with the benefit of survivorship, the survivors' shares being increased as the subscribers die, until the whole goes to the last survivor. **2.** the annuity shared. **3.** the share of each subscriber. **4.** the number of subscribers. **5.** any of various forms of life insurance in which the chief beneficiaries are those whose policies are in force at the end of a specified period **(ton′tine pe′riod).** [< F; named after Lorenzo *Tonti*, Neapolitan banker who started the scheme in France about 1653. See -INE[1]]

to·nus (tō′nəs), *n.* *Physiol.* a normal state of continuous slight tension in muscle tissue which facilitates its response to stimulation. [< NL, special use of L *tonus* < Gk *tónos* TONE]

ton·y (tō′nē), *adj.,* **ton·i·er, ton·i·est.** *Slang.* high-toned; stylish: *a tony nightclub.* [TONE + -Y[1]]

To·ny (tō′nē), *n., pl.* **-nies.** one of a group of awards made annually, by the American Theater Wing, a professional school for the performing arts, for achievements in theatrical production and performance. [after the nickname of Antoinette Perry]

To·ny (tō′nē), *n.* **1.** a boy's given name, form of **Anthony. 2.** a girl's given name, form of **Antoinette** or **Antonia.**

too (tōō), *adv.* **1.** in addition; also; furthermore; moreover: *young, clever, and rich too.* **2.** to an excessive extent or degree; beyond what is desirable, fitting, or right: *too sick to travel.* **3.** more, as specified, than should be. **4.** extremely: *only too glad to be of assistance.* **5.** used as an affirmative to contradict a negative statement: *I am too!* [sp. var. of TO (adv.)]

too·dle-oo (tōōd′ᵊlōō′), *interj.* *Informal.* good-by; so long. [? *toodle* (var. of dial. *tootle* to TODDLE) + *-oo* interjection]

Too·el·e (tōō el′ə), *n.* a town in NW Utah. 9133 (1960).

took (tŏŏk), *v.* pt. of **take.**

Tooke (tŏŏk), *n.* **(John) Horne** (hôrn), 1736–1812, English politician and philologist.

tool (tōōl), *n.* **1.** an implement, esp. one held in the hand, for performing or facilitating mechanical operations, as a hammer, saw, file, etc. **2.** any instrument of manual operation. **3.** the cutting or machining part of a lathe, planer, drill, or similar machine. **4.** the machine itself; a machine tool. **5.** anything used as a tool. **6.** a person manipulated by another for his own ends; cat's-paw. **7.** the design or ornament impressed upon the cover of a book. —*v.t.* **8.** to work or shape with a tool. **9.** to work decoratively with a hand tool. **10.** to ornament (the cover of a book) with a bookbinder's tool. **11.** to drive or ride in (a car or other vehicle): *He tooled the jeep skillfully along the jungle path.* —*v.i.* **12.** to work with a tool or tools. **13.** to drive or ride in a vehicle: *tooling along the freeway in her new convertible.* **14. tool up,** to install machinery designed for performing a particular job: *The auto manufacturers are tooling up for next year's models.* [ME; OE *tōl*; c. Icel *tōl* tools; akin to TAW[2]] —**tool′er,** *n.* —**tool′less,** *adj.*

—**Syn. 1.** TOOL, IMPLEMENT, INSTRUMENT, UTENSIL refer to contrivances for doing work. A TOOL is a contrivance held in and worked by the hand, for assisting the work of (especially) mechanics or laborers: *a carpenter's tools.* An IMPLEMENT is any tool or contrivance designed or used for a particular purpose: *agricultural implements.* An INSTRUMENT is anything used in doing a certain work or producing a certain result, esp. such as requires delicacy, accuracy, or precision: *surgical or musical instruments.* A UTENSIL is especially an article for domestic use: *kitchen utensils.* When used figuratively of human agency, TOOL is generally used in a contemptuous sense; INSTRUMENT, in a neutral or good sense: *a tool of unscrupulous men; an instrument of Providence.*

tool·box (tōōl′boks′), *n.* **1.** a box or case in which tools are kept. **2.** an attached mechanism, as on planing machines, lathes, etc., which carries the cutting tools. [TOOL + BOX[1]]

tool′ engineer′ing, the branch of engineering having to do with planning the tooling and processes required for manufacturing certain products, with the design and manufacture of the tools, dies, and jigs required, and with the control of the production processes. —**tool′ engineer′.**

tool·hold·er (tōōl′hōl′dər), *n.* a device for holding a tool or tools. [TOOL + HOLDER]

tool·house (tōōl′hous′), *n., pl.* **-hous·es** (-hou′ziz). toolshed. [TOOL + HOUSE]

tool·ing (tōō′ling), *n.* **1.** work done with a tool or tools; tooled ornamentation, as on wood, stone, leather, etc. **2.** *Mach.* **a.** a number of tools, as in a particular factory. **b.** the planning and arrangement of tools for a particular manufacturing process. [TOOL + -ING[1]]

tool·mak·er (tōōl′mā′kər), *n.* a workman skilled in the building and reconditioning of tools, jigs, and related devices used in a machine shop. [TOOL + MAKER] —**tool′mak′ing,** *n.*

tool′ post′, an upright for holding a lathe tool.

tool·room (tōōl′rōōm′, -rŏŏm′), *n.* a room, as in a machine shop, in which tools are stored, repaired, produced, etc., for the workmen of the shop. [TOOL + ROOM]

tool·shed (tōōl′shed′), *n.* a small building where tools are stored, often in the backyard of a house. Also called **toolhouse.** [TOOL + SHED[1]]

tool′ sub′ject, *Educ.* a subject that, when mastered, equips students with a skill useful in studying other subjects: *Grammar is a tool subject for English composition.*

toom (tōōm), *Scot. and North Eng.* —*adj.* **1.** empty; vacant. —*v.t.* **2.** to empty or drain (a vessel), esp. by drinking the contents. [ME *tome,* OE *tōm;* c. Icel *tōmr*]

Toombs (tōōmz), *n.* **Robert,** 1810–85, U.S. lawyer, orator, and Confederate statesman and army officer.

toon (tōōn), *n.* **1.** a meliaceous tree, *Toona ciliata* (or *Cedrela Toona*), of the East Indies and Australia, yielding an aromatic red wood resembling but softer than mahogany, used for furniture, carving, etc. **2.** the wood. [< Hindi *tūn* < Skt *tunna*]

toot[1] (tōōt), *v.i.* **1.** (of a horn) to give forth its characteristic sound. **2.** to make a sound resembling that of a horn or the like. **3.** to sound or blow a horn or other wind instrument. **4.** (of grouse) to give forth a characteristic cry or call. —*v.t.* **5.** to cause (a horn or other wind instrument) to sound. **6.** to sound (notes, music, etc.) on a horn or the like. —*n.* **7.** an act or sound of tooting. [akin to LG, G *tuten,* D *toeten,* Sw *tuta* in same sense; orig. imit.] —**toot′er,** *n.*

toot[2] (tōōt), *n.* *Informal.* act or instance of drunken revelry; binge; spree. [?]

tooth (tōōth), *n., pl.* **teeth,** *v.,* **toothed** (tōōtht, tōōthd), **tooth·ing** (tōō′thing, -thing). —*n.* **1.** (in most vertebrates) one of the hard bodies or processes usually attached in a row to each jaw, serving for the prehension and mastication of food, as weapons of attack or defense, etc., and in mammals typically composed chiefly of dentin surrounding a sensitive pulp and covered on the crown with enamel. **2.** (in invertebrates) any of various similar or analogous processes occurring in the mouth or alimentary canal, or on a shell. **3.** any projection resembling or suggesting a tooth. **4.** one of the projections of a comb, rake, saw, etc. **5.** *Mach.* **a.** any of the uniform projections on a gear or rack by which it drives, or is driven by, a gear, rack, or worm. **b.** any of the uniform projections on a sprocket by which it drives or is driven by a chain. **6.** *Bot.* one of the toothlike divisions of the peristome of mosses. **7.** a sharp, distressing, or destructive attribute or agency. **8.** taste, relish, or liking. **9.** a surface, as on a grinding wheel, sharpening stone, etc., slightly roughened so as to increase friction with another part. **10.** a rough surface created on a paper made for charcoal drawing, water color, or the like, or on canvas for oil painting. **11. by the skin of one's teeth,** barely: *He got away by the skin of his teeth. I missed getting the prize by the skin of my teeth.* **12. cast** or **throw in one's teeth,** to reproach someone for (an action): *History will ever throw this blunder in his teeth.* **13. cut one's teeth on,** to do at the beginning of one's education, career, etc., or in one's youth: *The hunter boasted of having cut his teeth on tigers.* **14. in the teeth of, a.** so as to face or confront; straight into or against: *in the teeth of the wind; in the teeth of the storm.* **b.** in defiance of; in opposition to: *He maintained his stand in the teeth of public opinion.* **15. long in the tooth,** old; elderly: *She's a bit long in the tooth to play the part of a young girl.* **16. put teeth in** or **into,** to establish or increase the effectiveness of: *The proposed amendment will put teeth into the law.* **17. set one's teeth,** to become resolute; prepare for difficulty: *He set his teeth and prepared to separate the combatants.* **18. set** or **put one's teeth on edge, a.** to induce an unpleasant sensation. **b.** to repel; irritate: *The noise of the machines sets my teeth on edge.* **19. show one's teeth,** to become hostile or threatening; exhibit anger: *She had always seemed friendly until suddenly she began to show her teeth.* **20. to the teeth,** entirely; fully: *armed to the teeth; dressed to the teeth in furs and jewels.* —*v.t.* **21.** to furnish with teeth. **22.** to cut teeth upon. —*v.i.* **23.** to interlock, as cogwheels. [ME; OE *tōth;* c. D *tand,* Icel *tönn,* G *Zahn;* akin to Goth *tunthus,* L *dēns,* Gk *odoús,* Skt *dan*] —**tooth′like′,** *adj.*
—**Syn. 5.** sprocket. **8.** fondness, partiality, predilection.

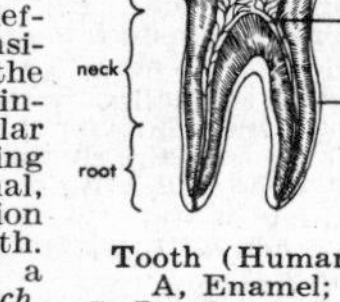

Tooth (Human)
A, Enamel;
B, Dentin; C, Pulp;
D, Cementum

tooth·ache (tōōth′āk′), *n.* a pain in or about a tooth. [ME *tothache,* OE *tōthæce.* See TOOTH, ACHE] —**tooth′ach′y,** *adj.*

tooth′ache grass′, a tall grass, *Ctenium aromaticum,* of the southern U.S., having a pungent taste.

tooth′ache tree′, **1.** the prickly ash, *Zanthoxylum americanum.* **2.** the Hercules'-club, *Zanthoxylum Clava-Herculis.*

tooth′ and nail′, with all one's resources or energy; fiercely: *We fought tooth and nail but lost.*

tooth′ ax′, an ax for dressing stone, having two serrated edges.

tooth·brush (tōōth′brush′), *n.* a small brush with a long handle, for cleaning the teeth. [TOOTH + BRUSH[1]]

tooth′ chis′el, *Masonry.* See **claw chisel.**

toothed′ whale′, any whale of the suborder *Odontoceti,* having conical teeth in one or both jaws and feeding on fish, squid, etc. Cf. **whalebone whale.**

tooth·less (tōōth′lis), *adj.* **1.** lacking teeth, as a person or animal. **2.** without a serrated edge, as a saw. **3.** lacking in force or sharpness; dull; ineffectual: *a toothless argument; toothless leadership.* [ME; see TOOTH, -LESS] —**tooth′less·ly,** *adv.* —**tooth′less·ness,** *n.*

tooth·like (tōōth′līk′), *adj.* of or suggestive of a tooth or teeth. [TOOTH + -LIKE]

tooth·paste (tōōth′pāst′), *n.* a dentifrice in the form of paste. [TOOTH + PASTE]

tooth·pick (tōōth′pik′), *n.* a small pointed piece of wood, plastic, etc., for removing substances, esp. food particles, from between the teeth. [TOOTH + PICK[2]]

tooth′ pow′der, a dentifrice in the form of a powder.

tooth′ rash′, *Pathol.* strophulus.

tooth′ shell′, **1.** any marine mollusk of the class *Scaphopoda,* having a curved, tapering shell that is open at both ends. **2.** the shell itself. Also called **tusk shell.**

tooth·some (tōōth′səm), *adj.* **1.** pleasing to the taste; palatable: *a toothsome dish.* **2.** pleasing or desirable, as fame, power, etc. **3.** voluptuous; sexually alluring: *The heroine was a toothsome blonde.* [TOOTH + -SOME[1]] —**tooth′some·ly,** *adv.* —**tooth′some·ness,** *n.*

tooth·wort (tōōth′wûrt′), *n.* **1.** a European, orobanchaceous plant, *Lathraea Squamaria,* having a rootstock covered with toothlike scales. **2.** any cruciferous plant of the genus *Dentaria,* having toothlike projections upon the creeping rootstock. **3.** a tender, spreading shrub, *Plumbago scandens,* of tropical America, having white flowers. [TOOTH + WORT[2]]

tooth·y (tōō′thē, -thē), *adj.,* **tooth·i·er, tooth·i·est.** **1.** having or displaying conspicuous teeth: *a toothy smile to advertise a dentifrice.* **2.** savory; appetizing; toothsome. **3.** possessing a rough surface: *toothy paper.* **4.** *Archaic.* sharp or caustic: *toothy commentary.* [TOOTH + -Y[1]] —**tooth′i·ly,** *adv.* —**tooth′i·ness,** *n.*

too·tle (tōōt′əl), *v.,* **-tled, -tling,** *n.* —*v.i.* **1.** to toot gently or repeatedly on a flute or the like. —*n.* **2.** the sound so made. [TOOT + -LE] —**too′tler,** *n.*

too-too (tōō′tōō′), *adj.* **1.** excessively and tastelessly affected: *The movie was simply too-too.* —*adv.* **2.** in an excessively and tastelessly affected manner. [redupl. of TOO]

toots (tŏŏts), *n.* *Informal.* an affectionate or flippant form of address for a girl or woman; honey; baby. [back formation from TOOTSY]

toot·sy (tŏŏt′sē), *n., pl.* **-sies.** *Informal.* **1.** a foot. **2.** toots. [dial. *toot* foot (lit., something that peeps or sticks out, n. use of *toot* to protrude, OE *tōtian*) + *-sy* hypocoristic suffix]

toot·sy-woot·sy (tŏŏt′sē wŏŏt′sē), *n., pl.* **toot·sy-woot·sies.** *Informal.* toots. [redupl. of TOOTSY]

Too·woom·ba (tə wŏŏm′bə), *n.* a city in SE Queensland, in E Australia. 50,134 (1961).

top[1] (top), *n., adj., v.,* **topped, top·ping.** —*n.* **1.** the highest or loftiest point or part of anything; apex; summit. **2.** the uppermost or upper part, surface, etc., of anything. **3.** the higher end of anything on a slope. **4.** *Brit.* **a.** a part considered as higher: *the top of the street.* **b.** high gear of an automobile. **5.** the part of a plant above ground, as distinguished from the root. **6.** Usually, **tops.** one of the tender tips of the branches or shoots of plants. **7.** that part of anything which is first or foremost; beginning: *Let's take it from the top again, and this time do it right.* **8.** the highest or leading place, position, rank, etc.: *at the top of the class.* **9.** the highest point, pitch, or degree: *to talk at the top of one's voice.* **10.** one who or that which occupies the highest or leading position. **11.** the best or choicest part: *the top of all creation.* **12.** a covering or lid, as of a box, automobile, carriage, etc. **13.** the head. **14.** *Naut.* a platform surrounding the head of a lower mast on a ship, and serving as a foothold, a means of extending the upper rigging, etc. **15.** *Chem.* that part of a mixture under distillation which volatilizes first. **16.** *Bridge.* **a.** the best card of a suit in a player's hand. **b.** (in duplicate bridge) the best score on a hand. **17.** *Sports* **a.** a stroke that hits the ball above its center. **b.** the forward spin given to the ball by such a stroke. **18.** *Baseball.* **a.** the first half of an inning. **b.** the first three batters in the batting order. **19.** *Textiles.* **a.** a cluster of textile fibers, esp. tow, put on a distaff. **b.** a strand of the long wool fibers in sliver form, separated from noil by combing and wound into a large ball. **c.** a similar strand of rayon. **20.** *Jewelry.* crown (def. 29). **21.** *Archaic.* the most perfect example or type: *the top of all honors.* **22. blow one's top,** *Slang.* **a.** to become enraged; lose one's temper. **b.** to go mad; become insane: *We thought that he must have blown his top to make such a fool of himself.* **23. on top,** successful; victorious; dominant: *In the entertainment field there are few who can stay on top indefinitely.* **24. on top of, a.** over or upon. **b.** in addition to; over and above. **c.** close upon; following upon: *Gale winds came on top of the floods.* **d.** in complete control: *on top of the problem.* **25. on top of the world,** *Informal.* **a.** successful. **b.** elated: *The sea and the warm sun made us feel on top of the world.* **26. over the top,** *Mil.* over the top of the parapet before a trench, as in issuing to charge against the enemy. **27. the tops,** *Informal.* (used predicatively) foremost in favor, ability, rank, etc.; the best or most praiseworthy: *His performance was the tops.* Also, **tops.** —*adj.* **28.** pertaining to, situated at, or forming the top; highest; uppermost; upper: *the top shelf.* **29.** highest in degree; greatest: *to pay top prices.* **30.** foremost, chief, or principal: *to win top honors in a competition.* —*v.t.* **31.** to furnish with a top; put a top on. **32.** to be at or constitute the top of. **33.** to reach the top of. **34.** to rise above: *The sun had topped the horizon.* **35.** to exceed in height, amount, number, etc. **36.** to surpass, excel, or outdo: *That tops everything!* **37.** to come up to or go beyond the requirements of (a part or character). **38.** to surmount with something specified: *to top a pedestal with a statue; to top a sundae with whipped cream.* **39.** to remove the top of; crop; prune: *to top a tall tree.* **40.** to get or leap over the top of (a fence, barrier, etc.). **41.** *Chem.* to distill off only the most volatile part of a mixture. **42.** *Sports.* **a.** to strike (the ball) above its center, giving it a forward spin. **b.** to make (a stroke) by hitting the ball in this manner. **43.** to top-dress (land). **44.** *Obs.* to have coitus with (a woman). **45. top out,** to finish the top of (a masonry structure). —*v.i.* **46.** to rise aloft. **47. top off,** to climax or complete, esp. in an exceptional manner; finish: *They topped off the evening with a ferryboat ride at midnight.* [ME, OE; c. D *top,* G *Zopf,* Icel *toppr* top, tuft]
—**Syn. 1.** zenith, acme, peak, pinnacle, vertex. **39.** lop.
—**Ant. 1.** bottom.

top[2] (top), *n.* **1.** a child's toy, often inversely conical, with a point on which it is made to spin. **2. sleep like a top,** to sleep soundly: *After a day of hiking and swimming we slept like tops.* [ME, OE; c. Fris, Flem *top*]

top-, var. of **topo-** before a vowel: *toponym.*

to·paz (tō′paz), *n.* **1.** a mineral, a fluosilicate of aluminum, usually occurring in prismatic orthorhombic crystals of various colors, and used as a gem. **2.** a yellow variety of quartz; false topaz; common topaz. **3.** either of two South American hummingbirds, *Topaza pella* or *T. pyra,* having chiefly red and crimson plumage and a yellowish-green throat with a topaz sheen. [< L *topaz(us)* < Gk *tópazos;* r. ME *topace* < OF < L *topaz(us)*] —**to·paz·ine** (tō′pə zēn′, -zin), *adj.*

To·paze (tō′paz), *n.* a girl's given name.

To·paze (tô päz′), *n.* a satirical comedy (1928) by Marcel Pagnol.

to·paz·o·lite (tō paz′ə līt′), *n.* a yellow or olive-green variety of andradite garnet found in Piedmont. [*topazo-* (comb. form repr. Gk *tópazos* TOPAZ) + -LITE]

to′paz quartz′, citrine (def. 2).

top′ banan′a, *Slang.* a leading comedian in musical comedy, burlesque, vaudeville, etc.: *For many years he was top banana on the circuit.*

top′ boot′, a high boot, esp. one having a cuff of a different material, color, etc., from the rest of the boot.

top·cas·tle (top′kas′əl), *n.* a large fighting top used in medieval ships. [ME *top-castel.* See TOP[1], CASTLE]

top′ cin′der, *Metall.* bulldog (def. 3).

top·coat (top′kōt′), *n.* **1.** a lightweight overcoat. **2.** an outer coat; an overcoat. [TOP[1] + COAT]

top′ cross′, *Genetics.* the progeny of the cross of a variety with one inbred line.

top′ dog′, *Informal.* a person, group, or nation that has, usually as a result of winning in a competition, acquired a position of highest authority: *He was determined to be top dog at the swimming meet.*

top-dog (top′dôg′, -dog′), *adj.* of or pertaining to the highest authority: *a top-dog position.* [adj. use of TOP DOG]

top′ draw′er, the highest level in rank, excellence, or importance: *a debutante strictly out of the top drawer.*

top-dress (top′dres′), *v.t.* to manure (land) on the surface. [TOP[1] + DRESS]

top′ dress′ing, **1.** a dressing of manure on the surface of land. **2.** the action of one who top-dresses. **3.** a top layer of gravel, crushed rock, etc., on a roadway. —**top′ dress′er.**

tope[1] (tōp), *v.,* **toped, top·ing.** —*v.i.* **1.** to drink alcoholic liquor habitually and to excess. —*v.t.* **2.** to drink (liquor) habitually and to excess. [var. of obs. *top* to drink, in phrase *top off,* equiv. to *tip off* to drink (a full helping) at a draught; special use of *top* to tilt. See TOPPLE]

tope[2] (tōp), *n.* **1.** a small shark, *Galeorhinus galeus,* found along the European coast. **2.** any of various related sharks of small to medium size. [akin to *toper* dogfish (Norfolk dial.)]

tope[3] (tōp), *n.* (in Buddhist countries) a dome-shaped monument, usually for religious relics. [< Hindi *tōp*]

Tope[3] (East Indian)

to·pec·to·my (tə pek′tə mē), *n., pl.* **-mies.** *Surg.* excision of part of the cerebral cortex for the relief of unmanageable pain or esp. as a treatment for certain kinds of mental disease. [TOP- + -ECTOMY]

to·pee (tō pē′, tō′pē), *n.* (in India) a lightweight helmet or sun hat of sola pith. Also, **topi.** [< Hindi: hat]

To·pe·ka (tə pē′kə), *n.* a city in and the capital of Kansas, in the NE part, on the Kansas River. 119,484 (1960).

To·pe·li·us (tŏŏ pā′lē us′), *n.* **Za·ka·ri·as** (sä′kä rē′äs), 1818–98, Finnish poet and novelist.

top·er (tō′pər), *n.* a hard drinker or chronic drunkard. [TOPE[1] + -ER[1]]

top·er's-plant (tō′pərz plant′, -plänt′), *n.* See **salad burnet.**

top·flight (top′flīt′), *adj.* outstandingly excellent, superior, or expert; first-rate: *a topflight performer.* [TOP[1] + FLIGHT[1]]

top·flight·er (top′flī′tər), *n.* *Informal.* a leading expert. [TOPFLIGHT + -ER[1]]

top·full (top′fŏŏl′), *adj.* full to the utmost; brimful. [TOP[1] + FULL]

top·gal·lant (top′gal′ənt; *Naut.* tə gal′ənt), *Naut.* —*n.* **1.** See **topgallant sail. 2.** *Archaic.* a top at the head of a topmast. —*adj.* **3.** of or pertaining to a topgallant mast. [TOP[1] + GALLANT]

topgal′lant bul′warks, *Naut.* bulwarks above the main bulwarks and rail of a vessel, terminating in a smaller rail (**topgal′lant rail′**).

topgal′lant fore′castle, *Naut.* **1.** a partial weather deck on top of a forecastle superstructure; forecastle deck. **2.** *Rare.* a forecastle superstructure.

topgal′lant mast′, *Naut.* **1.** a mast fixed to the head of a topmast on a square-rigged vessel. **2.** a section of an extended topmast on which the topgallant yards are carried.

topgal′lant sail′, *Naut.* a sail or either of two sails set on the yard or yards of a topgallant mast. Also called **topgallant.**

CONCISE ETYMOLOGY KEY: <, descended or derived from; >, whence; b., blend of, blended; c., cognate with; deriv., derivative; equiv., equivalent; imit., imitative; m., modification of; obl., oblique; r., replacing; s., stem; sp., spelling; trans., translation; ?, origin unknown, perhaps; *, hypothetical. See the full key inside the front cover.

top′ graft′ing, *Hort.* grafting in the top, as of a tree, in order to replace with a more desired variety or form.

toph (tōf), *n. Geol.* tufa (def. 1). Also, **tophe.** [< L *tōph(us)*, misspelling of *tōfus* TUFA]

top·ham·per (top′ham′pər), *n. Naut.* **1.** the light upper sails and their gear and spars, sometimes used to refer to all spars and gear above the deck. **2.** any unnecessary weight, either aloft or about the upper decks. [TOP[1] + HAMPER[1]]

top′ hat′, a tall, cylindrical hat with a stiff brim usually slightly curved on the sides, worn by men esp. on formal occasions. Cf. **beaver**[1] (def. 4), **opera hat, silk hat.**

top-hat (top′hat′), *adj.* of or pertaining to polite or fashionable society. [adj. use of TOP HAT]

top-heav·y (top′hev′ē), *adj.* **1.** having the top disproportionately heavy; liable to fall from too great weight above. **2.** relatively much heavier above the center or waist than below: *a top-heavy woman; a top-heavy flagpole.* **3.** *Finance.* **a.** having a financial structure overburdened with securities that have priority in the payment of dividends. **b.** overcapitalized. [TOP[1] + HEAVY] **—top′-heav′i·ly,** *adv.* **—top′-heav′i·ness,** *n.*

To·phet (tō′fet), *n. Bible.* **1.** a place in the valley of Hinnom, near Jerusalem, where, contrary to the law, children were offered as sacrifices, esp. to Moloch. It was later used as a dumping ground for refuse. **2.** the place of punishment for the wicked after death; hell. **3.** some place, condition, etc., likened to hell. Also, **To·pheth** (tō′fet). [ME << Heb *Tōpheth* a place-name]

top-hole (top′hōl′), *adj. Brit. Slang.* first-rate. [TOP[1] + HOLE]

to·phus (tō′fəs), *n., pl.* **-phi** (-fī). *Pathol.* a calcareous concretion formed in the soft tissue about a joint, in the pinna of the ear, etc., esp. in gout; a gouty deposit. [< L; see TOPH] **—to·pha·ceous** (tə fā′shəs), *adj.*

to·pi[1] (tō pē′, tō′pē), *n., pl.* **-pis.** topee.

to·pi[2] (tō′pē), *n., pl.* **-pis.** an antelope, *Damaliscus korigum eureus*, of eastern central Africa, having bluish-black and yellow markings. [< Mandingo]

to·pi·ar·y (tō′pē er′ē), *adj., n., pl.* **-ar·ies.** *Hort.* **—***adj.* **1.** (of a plant) clipped or trimmed into fantastic shapes. **2.** of or pertaining to such trimming. **—***n.* **3.** topiary work; the topiary art. **4.** a garden containing such work. [< L *topiāri(us)* pertaining to landscape-gardening or to ornamental gardens < *topi-* (< Gk *tópi(on)*, dim. of *tópos* place) + *-ārius* -ARY]

Topi
(3½ ft. high at shoulder; total length 6 ft.; tail 1 ft.)

top·ic (top′ik), *n.* **1.** a subject of conversation or discussion: *to provide a topic for discussion.* **2.** the subject or theme of a discourse or of one of its parts. **3.** *Rhet., Logic.* a general field of considerations from which arguments can be drawn. **4.** a general rule or maxim. [< L *topic(a)* (pl.) < Gk *(tà) topiká* name of work by Aristotle (lit., things pertaining to commonplaces) < *tóp(oi)* commonplaces + *-ika*, neut. pl. of *-ikos* -IC; see TOPO-]
—Syn. 2. thesis, subject-matter. See **subject.**

top·i·cal (top′i kəl), *adj.* **1.** pertaining to or dealing with matters of current or local interest: *a topical reference.* **2.** pertaining to the subject of a discourse, composition, or the like. **3.** of a place; local. **4.** *Med.* of, pertaining to, or applied to a particular part of the body; local: *a topical anesthetic.* [< Gk *topik(ós)* local, pertaining to commonplaces (see TOPO-, -IC) + -AL[1]] **—top′i·cal·ly,** *adv.*

top·i·cal·i·ty (top′ə kal′i tē), *n., pl.* **-ties** for 2. **1.** state or quality of being topical. **2.** a detail or matter of current or local interest. [TOPICAL + -ITY]

top′ic sen′tence, an introductory sentence that expresses the essential idea of a paragraph or larger section. Also, **top′ical sen′tence.**

top·kha·na (tōp′kä nə), *n. Anglo-Indian.* a building where artillery, ammunition, etc., are made, repaired, and stored. [< Hindi, Urdu *tōpkhānā*]

top′ kick′, *Mil. Slang.* a first sergeant.

top·knot (top′not′), *n.* **1.** a tuft of hair growing on the top of the head. **2.** a knot of hair so worn in some styles of hairdressing. **3.** a knot or bow of ribbon worn on the top of the head. **4.** a tuft or crest of feathers on the head of a bird. [TOP[1] + KNOT[1]]

top·less (top′lis), *adj.* **1.** lacking a top: *a topless bathing suit.* **2.** extremely high: *a topless mountain.* **3.** *Obs.* without a peer. [TOP[1] + -LESS]

top-lev·el (top′lev′əl), *adj. Informal.* at a high level: *a top-level conference.*

top·line (top′līn′), *adj.* **1.** so important as to be named at or near the top of a newspaper item, advertisement, or the like: *a topline actress; topline news.* **2.** of the highest reputation, importance, etc.: *a topline business firm.* [TOP[1] + LINE[1]]

top·lin·er (top′lī′nər), *n. Chiefly Brit.* a topline person, esp. an actor. [TOPLINE + -ER[1]]

top·loft·y (top′lôf′tē, -lof′-), *adj. Informal.* condescending; haughty. [TOP[1] + LOFTY] **—top′loft′i·ly,** *adv.* **—top′loft′i·ness,** *n.*

top·man (top′mən), *n., pl.* **-men.** *Naut.* a man stationed for duty in a top. [TOP[1] + MAN]

top·mast (top′mast′, -mäst′; *Naut.* top′məst), *n. Naut.* the mast next above a lower mast, usually formed as a separate spar from the lower mast and used to support the yards or rigging of a topsail or topsails. [TOP[1] + MAST[1]]

top·maul (top′môl′), *n.* a heavy hammer with a steel or wooden head, used in shipbuilding. [TOP[1] + MAUL]

top·min·now (top′min′ō), *n., pl.* (*esp. collectively*) **-now,** (*esp. referring to two or more kinds or species*) **-nows.** any of several small, surface-swimming cyprinodont fishes of the egg-laying family *Cyprinodontidae* and the live-bearing family *Poeciliidae.* [TOP[1] + MINNOW]

top·most (top′mōst′ *or, esp. Brit.,* -məst), *adj.* highest; uppermost. [TOP[1] + -MOST]

top·notch (top′noch′), *adj. Informal.* first-rate: *a topnotch job.* [TOP[1] + NOTCH]

topo-, a learned borrowing from Greek meaning "place," used in the formation of compound words: *topography.* Also, *esp. before a vowel,* **top-.** [comb. form of Gk *tópos* place, commonplace]

top′ of house′, *Naut.* See **flying bridge.**

topog., **1.** topographical. **2.** topography.

to·pog·ra·pher (tə pog′rə fər), *n.* **1.** a specialist in topography. **2.** one who describes the surface features of a place or region. [< Gk *topográph(os)* topographer (see TOPO-, -GRAPH) + -ER[1]]

top′ograph′ic map′, a map showing topographic features, usually by means of contour lines.

to·pog·ra·phy (tə pog′rə fē), *n., pl.* **-phies.** **1.** the detailed mapping or charting of the features of a relatively small area, district, or locality. **2.** the detailed description, esp. by means of surveying, of particular localities, as cities, towns, estates, etc. **3.** the relief features or surface configuration of an area. **4.** the features, relations, or configuration of a structural entity. **5.** a schema of a structural entity, as of the mind, field of study, society, etc., reflecting a division into distinct areas having a specific relation or a specific position relative to one another: *economic topography; cultural topography.* [late ME *topographye* < LL *topographia* < Gk. See TOPO-, -GRAPHY] **—top·o·graph·ic** (top′ə graf′ik), **top′o·graph′i·cal,** *adj.* **—top′o·graph′i·cal·ly,** *adv.*

topolog′ical equiv′alence, *Math.* the property of two topological spaces such that there is a homeomorphism from one to the other.

top′olog′ical group′, *Math.* a set that is a group and a topological space and for which the group operation and the map of an element to its inverse are continuous functions.

topolog′ical invar′iant, *Math.* a property of a topological space which is a property of every space related to the given space by a homeomorphism.

top′olog′ical space′, *Math.* a set with a collection of subsets or open sets satisfying the properties that the union of open sets is an open set, the intersection of two open sets is an open set, and the given set and the empty set are open sets.

to·pol·o·gy (tə pol′ə jē), *n., pl.* **-gies** for 3. *Math.* **1.** the study of those properties of geometric forms that remain invariant under certain transformations, as bending, stretching, etc. **2.** Also called **point set topology.** the study of limits in sets considered as collections of points. **3.** a collection of open sets making a given set a topological space. Also called **analysis situs** (for defs. 1, 2). [TOPO- + -LOGY] **—top·o·log·ic** (top′ə loj′ik), **top′o·log′i·cal,** *adj.* **—top′o·log′i·cal·ly,** *adv.* **—to·pol′o·gist,** *n.*

top·o·nym (top′ə nim), *n.* **1.** a place name. **2.** a name derived from the name of a place. [TOP- + (SYN)ONYM]

to·pon·y·my (tə pon′ə mē), *n.* **1.** the study of toponyms. **2.** *Anat.* the nomenclature of the regions of the body. [TOPONYM + -Y[3]] **—top·o·nym·ic** (top′ə nim′ik), **top′o·nym′i·cal,** *adj.*

top·o·type (top′ə tīp′), *n. Biol.* a specimen from the type locality. [TOPO- + -TYPE] **—top·o·typ·ic** (top′ə tip′ik), **top′o·typ′i·cal,** *adj.*

Top·pe·nish (top′ə nish), *n.* a town in S Washington. 5667 (1960).

top·per (top′ər), *n.* **1.** one who or that which tops. **2.** a woman's loose topcoat, usually knee-length or shorter. **3.** *Informal.* See **top hat.** **4.** *Brit. Slang.* **a.** anything excellent or well-liked. **b.** anyone admired or well-liked. [TOP[1] + -ER[1]]

top·ping (top′ing), *n.* **1.** act of one who or that which tops. **2.** a distinct part forming a top to something. **3.** something put on a thing at the top to complete it. **4. toppings,** that which is removed in topping or cropping plants, as branches. **—***adj.* **5.** rising above something else; overtopping. **6.** very high in rank, degree, etc. **7.** *Chiefly Brit. Informal.* excellent; wonderful. [TOP[1] + -ING[1], -ING[2]]

top′ping lift′, *Naut.* a line for raising and supporting a spar, as a yard or boom. Also called **lift.**

top·ple (top′əl), *v.,* **-pled, -pling.** **—***v.i.* **1.** to fall forward, as from having too heavy a top; pitch; tumble down. **2.** to lean over or jut, as if threatening to fall. **—***v.t.* **3.** to cause to topple. **4.** to overthrow, as from a position of authority: *The revolution toppled the king from his throne.* [earlier *top* to tilt, topple (see TOPE[1]) + -LE]

top·rail (top′rāl′), *n.* the uppermost rail of the back of a chair or the like; a crest rail. [TOP[1] + RAIL[1]]

top′ round′, a cut of beef taken from inside the round, which is below the rump and above the upper leg. Cf. **bottom round.**

tops (tops), *adj.* **1.** ranked among the highest, as in ability, performance, comprehensiveness, quality, etc.: *His work is tops. That car is tops.* **—***n.* **2. the tops,** a person or thing that is outstanding: *He's the tops.* [pl. of TOP[1]]

top·sail (top′sāl′; *Naut.* top′səl), *n. Naut.* a sail, or either of a pair of sails, set immediately above the lowermost sail of a mast and supported by a topmast. See diag. under **ship.** [ME *topseil.* See TOP[1], SAIL]

top′sail schoon′er, a sailing vessel fore-and-aft-rigged on all of two or more masts with square sails above the foresail, and often with a square sail before the foresail. Cf. **main-topsail schooner.**

top-se·cret (top′sē′krit), *adj. U.S. Govt., Mil.* (of information, a document, etc.) **1.** bearing the classification *top-secret.* **2.** limited to persons authorized to use information, documents, etc., so classified. Cf. **classification** (def. 5). [TOP[1] + SECRET]

top′ ser′geant, *Mil. Slang.* a first sergeant.

top·side (top′sīd′), *n.* **1.** the upper side. **2.** Usually, **topsides.** *Naut.* the outer surface of a hull above the water. **3.** *Chiefly Brit.* a cut of beef similar to a U.S. rump roast. Cf. **silverside** (def. 1). **4.** *Brit.* the top or outer side of a round of beef; beef from the outer thigh of a butchered cow. **—***adj.* **5.** of, pertaining to, or located on the topside. **—***adv.* **6.** Also, **top′sides′.** up on the deck: *He left the engine room and went topside.* **7.** to, toward, or at topside. [TOP[1] + SIDE[1]]

top′ slice′, *Mining.* (in top slicing) one of several masses of ore, side-by-side, successively extracted and caved.

top′ slic′ing, *Mining.* mining of thick orebodies in a series of stopes from top to bottom, the roof being caved with its timbers as each stope is exhausted.

top·smelt (top′smelt′), *n., pl.* **-smelts,** (*esp. collectively*) **-smelt.** a silversides, *Atherinops affinis,* found along the Pacific coast of North America, used as food. Also called **baysmelt.** [TOP[1] + SMELT[2]]

top·soil (top′soil′), *n.* **1.** the surface or upper part of the soil. **—***v.t.* **2.** to cover (land) with topsoil. [TOP[1] + SOIL[1]]

top′ spin′, a spinning motion imparted to a ball that causes it to rotate forward.

top·sy-tur·vy (top′sē tûr′vē), *adv., adj., n., pl.* **-vies.** **—***adv.* **1.** with the top where the bottom should be; upside down. **2.** in or into a reversed condition or order. **3.** in or into a state of confusion or disorder. **—***adj.* **4.** turned upside down; inverted; reversed: *The mirror gave me a topsy-turvy reflection.* **5.** confused or disorderly: *The teacher returned to a topsy-turvy classroom.* **—***n.* **6.** inversion of the natural order. **7.** a state of confusion or disorder. [? var. of *top syd turvye* topside down (with loss of *d* before *t*); *turvy,* var. of *tervy,* equiv. to obs. *terve* to turn over (c. OHG *zerben*) + -Y[1]] **—top′sy-tur′vi·ly,** *adv.* **—top′sy-tur′vi·ness,** *n.*

top·sy-tur·vy·dom (top′sē tûr′vē dəm), *n.* a state of affairs or a region in which everything is topsy-turvy. [TOPSY-TURVY + -DOM]

top′ tim′ber, *Naut.* a timber forming the upper, straighter portion of a frame in a wooden hull, generally secured side by side with another longer or shorter top timber so that the two butt at their lower ends against a pair of futtocks in a broken joint.

top′ yeast′, a carbon-producing yeast whose cells rise to the surface as froth during fermentation. Also called **surface yeast.**

toque (tōk), *n.* **1.** a velvet hat with a narrow, sometimes turned-up brim, a full crown, and usually a plume, worn esp. in 16th-century France. **2.** a brimless and close-fitting hat for women, in any of several shapes. **3.** tuque. [< F; r. earlier *toock, towk* (< Pg *touca* coif), *tock, tocque* (< It *tocca* cap), *toke* (< Sp *toca* headdress); all perh. < Basque *tauka* hat]

Toque

tor (tôr), *n.* a rocky pinnacle; a peak of a bare or rocky mountain or hill. [ME; OE *torr* < Celt; cf. Gael *torr* hill, mound, Ir *torr,* Welsh *twr* heap, pile]

To·rah (tôr′ə, tôr′ə; *Heb.* tō rä′), *n.* **1.** the Pentateuch, being the first of the three Jewish divisions of the Old Testament. Cf. **Tanach.** **2.** the Old Testament itself. **3.** the entire body of Jewish law as contained chiefly in the Old Testament and the Talmud. Also, **To′ra.** [< Heb *tōrāh* instruction, law]

to·ran (tôr′ən, tôr′-), *n.* (in Indian Buddhist and Hindu architecture) a gateway having two or three lintels between two posts. Also, **to·ra·na** (tôr′ə nə, tôr′-). [< Hindi < Skt *toraṇa*]

tor·ban·ite (tôr′bə nīt′), *n.* a dark-brown oil shale containing a large amount of carbonaceous matter. [named after *Torbane (Hill),* in Linlithgowshire, Scotland + -ITE[1]]

tor·bern·ite (tôr′bər nīt′), *n.* a mineral, hydrated copper uranium phosphate, $CuU_2P_2O_{12}{\cdot}12H_2O$, occurring in square tabular crystals of a bright-green color: a minor ore of uranium; copper uranite. Also called **chalcolite.** [named after *Torbern* Bergman (1735–84), Swedish chemist; see -ITE[1]]

Tor·bert (tôr′bərt), *n.* a boy's given name.

torc (tôrk), *n.* torque (def. 4).

torch[1] (tôrch), *n.* **1.** a light to be carried in the hand, consisting of some combustible substance, as resinous wood, or of twisted flax or the like, soaked with tallow or other flammable substance. **2.** something considered as a source of illumination, enlightenment, guidance, etc.: *the torch of learning.* **3.** any of various lamplike devices which produce a hot flame and are used for soldering, burning off paint, etc. **4.** *Brit.* a flashlight. **5. carry the** or **a torch for,** *Slang.* to be in love, esp. to suffer from unrequited love: *He still carries a torch for his ex-wife.* **—***v.i.* **6.** to burn or flare up like a torch. **—***v.t.* **7.** to subject to the flame or light of a torch, as in order to burn, sear, solder, or illuminate. [ME *torche* < OF < VL **torca* something twisted. See TORQUE] **—torch′less,** *adj.* **—torch′like′,** *adj.*

torch[2] (tôrch), *v.t.* to point (the joints between roofing slates) with a mixture of lime and hair. [< F *torch(er)* (to) plaster with a mixture of clay and chopped straw, deriv. of *torche* a twist of straw. See TORCH[1]]

torch·bear·er (tôrch′bâr′ər), *n.* **1.** one who carries a torch. **2.** a leader in a movement, campaign, etc.: *a torchbearer of democracy.* [TORCH[1] + BEARER]

tor·chère (tôr shâr′), *n.* a tall stand for a candelabrum. [< F < *torche* TORCH[1] + *-ère,* fem. of *-er* -ER[2]]

tor·chier (tôr chēr′), *n.* a floor lamp for indirect lighting, having its source of light within a reflecting bowl. Also, **tor·chiere′.** [var. of TORCHÈRE]

torch·light (tôrch′līt′), *n.* the light of a torch or torches. [TORCH[1] + LIGHT[1]]

torch′ lil′y, a desert plant, *Doryanthes excelsa,* of California and Florida, having a tall central stalk topped by large, showy, clusters of red flowers.

tor′chon lace′ (tôr′shon; *Fr.* tôr shôN′), **1.** a bobbin-made linen or cotton lace with loosely twisted threads in simple, open patterns. **2.** a machine-made imitation of this. [*torchon* < F: duster, dishcloth, lit., something to wipe with < *torch(er)* (to) wipe (see TORCH[2]) + *-on* n. suffix]

torch′ sing′er, a singer, esp. a woman, who specializes in singing torch songs.

torch′ song′, a popular song concerned with unhappiness or failure in love.

torch·wood (tôrch′wo͝od′), *n.* **1.** any of various resinous woods suitable for making torches, as the wood of the rutaceous tree, *Amyris balsamifera,* of Florida, the West Indies, etc. **2.** any of the trees yielding these woods. [TORCH[1] + WOOD[1]]

torch·y (tôr′chē), *adj.,* **torch·i·er, torch·i·est.** of, pertaining to, or characteristic of a torch song or a torch singer. [TORCH[1] + -Y[1]]

Tor·de·sil·las (tôr′the sē′lyäs), *n.* a town in NW Spain, SW of Valladolid: treaty (1494) defining the colonial spheres of Spain and Portugal. 4515 (1950).

tore[1] (tôr, tōr), *v.* pt. of **tear**[2].

tore[2] (tôr, tōr), *n.* a torus. [< F < L *tor(us)*]

tor·e·a·dor (tôr′ē ə dôr′; *Sp.* tô′re ä ᵺôr′), *n.* a bullfighter; torero. [< Sp < *toread(o)* (ptp. of *torear* to bait a bull, deriv. of *toro* bull < L *taur(us)*, akin to STEER[2]; *-ado* < L *-ātus* -ATE[1]) + *-or* -OR[2]]

Tor′eador Fres′co, The, a mural (c1500 B.C.) from Minoan Crete.

tor′eador pants′, close-fitting slacks that extend below the knee, worn by women esp. for sports.

To·rel·li (tô rel′ē; *It.* tô rel′lē), *n.* **Giu·sep·pe** (jo͞o zep′pe), 1650?–1708, Italian composer and violinist.

to·re·ro (tə râr′ō; *Sp.* tô re′rô), *n., pl.* **-re·ros** (-râr′ōz; *Sp.* -re′rôs). a bullfighter, esp. a matador. [< Sp < LL *taurār(ius)* < L *taur(us)* bull (see STEER[2]) + *-ārius* -ER[2]]

to·reu·tic (tə ro͞o′tik), *adj.* of or pertaining to toreutics or the objects produced by this technique. [< Gk *toreutik(ós)* < *toreú(ein)* (to) bore, chase, emboss (< *toreús* graving tool) + *-tikos* -TIC]

to·reu·tics (tə ro͞o′tiks), *n.* (*construed as sing.*) the art or technique of decorating metal or other material, esp. by embossing or chasing. [see TOREUTIC, -ICS]

to·ri (tôr′ē, tōr′ē), *n.* pl. of **torus.**

tor·ic (tôr′ik, tor′-), *adj.* **1.** noting or pertaining to a lens with a surface forming a portion of a torus, used for eyeglasses. **2.** *Geom. Rare.* toroidal. [TOR(US) + -IC]

to·ri·i (tôr′ē ē′, tōr′-), *n., pl.* **to·ri·i.** a form of decorative gateway or portal in Japan, consisting of two upright wooden posts connected at the top by two horizontal crosspieces, commonly found at the entrance to Shinto temples. [< Jap]

Torii

to·rin′go crab′ ap′ple (tə riṅg′gō), a shrub, *Malus sieboldi,* of Japan, having pink or deep rose-colored flowers and pea-shaped, red or brownish-yellow fruit. [*toringo* < Jap: crab-apple tree]

To·ri·no (tô rē′nô), *n.* Italian name of **Turin.**

tor·ment (*v.* tôr ment′; *n.* tôr′ment), *v.t.* **1.** to afflict with great bodily or mental suffering; pain: *to be tormented with violent headaches.* **2.** to worry or annoy excessively: *to torment one with questions.* **3.** to throw into commotion; stir up; disturb. —*n.* **4.** a state of great bodily or mental suffering; agony; misery. **5.** something that causes great bodily or mental pain or suffering. **6.** a source of pain, anguish, trouble, worry, or annoyance. **7.** *Archaic.* **a.** an instrument of torture, as the rack or the thumbscrew. **b.** the infliction of torture by means of such an instrument. **c.** the torture inflicted. [ME *torment(en)* (v.), *torment* (n.) < LL *torment(āre)* (v.), L *torment(um)* (n.), lit., an instrument (of torture) worked by twisting, earlier **torquementum.* See TORQUE, -MENT] —**tor·ment′ed·ly,** *adv.* —**tor·ment′ing·ly,** *adv.* —**tor·ment′ing·ness,** *n.*
—**Syn. 1.** harry, hector, vex, distress, agonize. TORMENT, RACK, TORTURE suggest causing great physical or mental pain, suffering, or harassment. To TORMENT is to harass as by incessant repetition of vexations or annoyances: *to be tormented with a toothache.* To RACK is to affect with such pain as that suffered by one stretched on a rack; to concentrate with painful effort: *to rack one's brains.* To TORTURE is to afflict with acute and more or less protracted suffering: *to torture one by keeping him in suspense.* **2.** plague, pester, tease, provoke, needle, trouble, fret. **4.** torture, distress, anguish. —**Ant. 1.** please.

tor·men·til (tôr′men til), *n.* a low, rosaceous herb, *Potentilla Tormentilla,* of Europe, having small, bright-yellow flowers, and a strongly astringent root used in medicine and in tanning and dyeing. [ME *tormentille* < ML *tormentill(a)* < L *torment(um)* TORMENT + *-illa* dim. suffix]

tor·men·tor (tôr men′tər), *n.* **1.** one who or that which torments. **2.** *Theat.* a curtain or framed structure behind the proscenium at both sides of the stage, for screening the wings from the audience. **3.** *Motion Pictures.* a sound-deadening screen used during the taking of scenes to prevent echo and reverberation. Also, **tor·ment′er.** [ME *tormento(u)r* < AF; OF *tormenteor* < LL **tormentātōr-.* See TORMENT, -OR[2]]

torn (tōrn, tôrn), *v.* pp. of **tear**[2].

tor·na·do (tôr nā′dō), *n., pl.* **-does, -dos. 1.** a localized, violently destructive windstorm occurring over land, esp. in the Midwestern U.S., and characterized by a long, funnel-shaped cloud extending toward the ground and made visible by condensation and debris. Cf. **waterspout** (def. 3). **2.** a violent squall or whirlwind of small extent, as one of those occurring during the summer on the west coast of Africa. **3.** a violent outburst, as of emotion or activity. [appar. by metathesis < Sp *tronada* thunderstorm, n. use of fem. of *tronado,* ptp. of *tronar* < L *tonāre* to thunder; r. 16th-century *ternado,* with unexplained *e*] —**tor·nad·ic** (tôr nad′ik), *adj.* —**tor·na′do·like′,** *adj.*

torna′do belt′, the part of the U.S. in which tornadoes occur most frequently, roughly the area within a 500-mile radius of southern Missouri.

torna′do cloud′, tuba (def. 2).

torna′do lan′tern. See **hurricane lantern.**

tor·nar·i·a (tôr nâr′ē ə), *n., pl.* **-nar·i·as, -nar·i·ae** (-nâr′ē ē′). the ciliate, free-swimming larva of certain hemichordates. [< NL equiv. to L *torn(us)* lathe + *-āria* -ARIA]

tor·nil·lo (tôr nil′ō; *Sp.* tôr nēl′yô), *n., pl.* **-nil·los** (-nil′ōz; *Sp.* -nēl′yôs). See **screw bean.** [< Sp: screw, clamp < *torn(o)* lathe, gyration (< L *tornus* lathe < Gk *tórnos*) + *-illo* dim. suffix (< L *-illum*)]

to·ro (tô′rô), *n., pl.* **-ros** (-rôs). *Spanish.* a bull, *Bos taurus africanus* (*ibericus*), bred esp. for combat in the bull ring.

to·ro bra·vo (tô′rô brä′vô), *pl.* **to·ros bra·vos** (tô′rôs brä′vôs). *Spanish.* toro. [lit., fierce bull]

to·roid (tōr′oid, tôr′-), *n. Geom.* **1.** a surface generated by the revolution of any closed plane curve or contour about an axis lying in its plane. **2.** the solid enclosed by such a surface. [TOR(US) + -OID]

to·roi·dal (tō roid′ᵊl, tô-, tōr′oidᵊl, tôr′-), *adj. Geom.* of or pertaining to a torus; toric. [TOROID + -AL[1]] —**to·roi′dal·ly,** *adv.*

To·ron·to (tə ron′tō), *n.* **1.** a city in and the capital of Ontario, in SE Canada, on Lake Ontario. 633,318. **2.** a town in E Ohio. 7780 (1960). —**To·ron·to′ni·an,** *adj., n.*

to·rose (tôr′ōs, tōr′-, tō rōs′, tô-), *adj.* **1.** *Bot.* cylindrical, with swellings or constrictions at intervals; knobbed. **2.** *Zool.* bulging. Also, **to·rous** (tôr′əs, tōr′-). [< L *torōs(us)* bulging, full of muscle < *tor(us)* muscle + *-ōsus* -OSE[1]]

tor·pe·do (tôr pē′dō), *n., pl.* **-does,** *v.,* **-doed, -do·ing.** —*n.* **1.** a self-propelled, cigar-shaped missile containing explosives and often equipped with a homing device, launched from a submarine or other warship, for destroying enemy surface ships. **2.** any of various submarine explosive devices for destroying hostile ships, as a mine. **3.** a cartridge of gunpowder, dynamite, or the like, exploded in an oil well to facilitate the extraction of oil from the well. **4.** a detonating device for fastening to the top of a rail to be exploded by the pressure of a locomotive or car to give an audible signal to members of a train crew. **5.** any of various other explosive devices, as a firework which consists of an explosive wrapped up with gravel in a piece of tissue paper and which detonates when thrown forcibly on the ground or against a hard surface. **6.** *U.S. Slang.* a gangster who hires himself out as a murderer. **7.** an electric catfish, *Malapterurus electricus,* found in tropical central Africa and the Nile valley. **8.** Also, **torpe′do fish′.** an electric ray, esp. *Torpedo nobiliana,* found in the Atlantic Ocean. —*v.t.* **9.** to attack, hit, damage, or destroy with or as with a torpedo or torpedoes. **10.** to explode a torpedo in (an oil well) to facilitate the extraction of oil. —*v.i.* **11.** to attack, damage, or sink a ship with torpedoes. [< L *torpēdō* numbness, torpidity, crampfish < *torpē(re)* (to) be stiff (see TORPID) + *-dō* state or condition of] —**tor·pe′do·like′,** *adj.*

torpe′do boat′, a small, fast, highly maneuverable boat used for torpedoing enemy shipping.

tor·pe′do-boat destroy′er (tôr pē′dō bōt′), a vessel somewhat larger than the ordinary torpedo boat, designed for destroying torpedo boats or as a more powerful form of torpedo boat.

torpe′do bod′y, a body for an open automobile having a more or less continuous surface from front to back.

tor·pe·do·man (tôr pē′dō man′, -mən), *n., pl.* **-men** (-men′, -mən). a petty officer or warrant officer responsible for the maintenance, use, and repair of underwater weapons and equipment. [TORPEDO + MAN]

torpe′do tube′, a tube through which a self-propelled torpedo is launched, usually by the explosion of a charge of powder.

tor·pid[1] (tôr′pid), *adj.* **1.** inactive or sluggish, as a bodily organ. **2.** slow; dull; apathetic; lethargic. **3.** dormant, as a hibernating or estivating animal. [< L *torpid(us)* numb < *torp(ēre)* (to) be stiff or numb + *-idus* -ID[4]] —**tor·pid′i·ty, tor′pid·ness,** *n.* —**tor′pid·ly,** *adv.*
—**Syn. 2.** indolent. **3.** See **inactive.** —**Ant. 1.** energetic.

tor·pid[2] (tôr′pid), *n.* **1.** an eight-oared, clinker-built boat used for races at Oxford University during the Lenten term. **2.** one of the crew in these races. **3.** **torpids,** the races themselves. [special use of TORPID[1]]

tor·por (tôr′pər), *n.* **1.** a state of suspended physical powers and activities. **2.** sluggish inactivity or inertia. **3.** dormancy, as of a hibernating animal. **4.** lethargic dullness or indifference; apathy. [< L: numbness < *torp(ēre)* (to) be stiff or numb + *-or* -OR[1]]
—**Syn. 3.** sleepiness, slumber, drowsiness. **4.** stolidity, listlessness, indifference.

tor·por·if·ic (tôr′pə rif′ik), *adj.* causing torpor. [TORPOR + -I- + -FIC]

tor·quate (tôr′kwit, -kwāt), *adj. Zool.* ringed about the neck, as with feathers or a color; collared. [< L *torquāt(us)* adorned with a necklace < *torqu(ēs)* twisted neck-chain + *-ātus* -ATE[1]]

Tor·quay (tôr kē′), *n.* a municipal borough in S Devonshire, in SW England: seaside resort. 53,915 (1961).

torque (tôrk), *n.* **1.** *Mech.* that which produces or tends to produce torsion or rotation; the moment of a force or system of forces tending to cause rotation. **2.** *Mach.* the measured ability of a rotating element, as of a gear or shaft, to overcome turning resistance. **3.** *Optics.* the rotational effect on plane-polarized light passing through certain liquids or crystals. **4.** Also, **torc.** a collar, necklace, or similar ornament consisting of a twisted narrow band, usually of precious metal, worn esp. by the ancient Gauls and Britons. [back formation from TORQUES, the *s* being taken as pl. sign]

torque′ convert′er, *Mach.* a fluid coupling in which three or more rotors are used, one of which can be checked so that output torque is augmented and output speed diminished.

Tor·que·ma·da (tôr′ke mä′ᵺä), *n.* **To·más de** (tô mäs′ de), 1420–98, Spanish inquisitor general.

tor·ques (tôr′kwēz), *n. Zool.* a ringlike band or formation about the neck, as of feathers, hair, or integument of distinctive color or appearance; a collar. [< L: twisted necklace or collar, equiv. to *torquē(re)* (to) twist (akin to Gk *trépein*) + *-s* nom. sing. ending]

torque′ wrench′, a wrench having a dial or other indicator showing the amount of torque being applied.

torr (tôr), *n.* a unit of pressure, being the pressure necessary to support a column of mercury one millimeter high at 0°C and standard gravity, equal to 1333.2 microbars. [named after Evangelista TORR(ICELLI)]

Tor·rance (tôr′əns, tor′-), *n.* a city in SW California, SW of Los Angeles. 100,991 (1960).

Tor·re del Gre·co (tôr′re del gre′kô), a city in SW Italy, near Naples. 77,851 (1961).

tor·re·fy (tôr′ə fī′, tor′-), *v.t.,* **-fied, -fy·ing. 1.** to subject to fire or intense heat; parch, roast, or scorch. **2.** *Pharm.* to dry or parch (drugs) with heat. **3.** to roast, as metallic ores. Also, **torrify.** [< L *torrefacere* to make dry or hot < *torrē(re)* (to) dry up, parch, scorch + *facere* -FY; see TORRID] —**tor·re·fac·tion** (tôr′ə fak′shən, tor′-), *n.*

Tor·rence (tôr′əns, tor′-), *n.* **(Frederic) Ridge·ly** (rij′lē), 1875–1950, U.S. poet, playwright, and editor.

Tor·rens (tôr′ənz, tor′-), *n.* **Lake,** a salt lake in Australia, in E South Australia. 130 mi. long; 25 ft. below sea level.

Tor′rens sys′tem, (in Australia, England, Canada, certain States of the U.S., etc.) a system of registration of land titles in which the titles are settled consequent to establishment and validation by a legal proceeding, designed chiefly to make title insurance unnecessary and to facilitate transfers. [named after Sir Robert *Torrens* (1814–84), British administrator in Australia]

tor·rent (tôr′ənt, tor′-), *n.* **1.** a stream of water flowing with great rapidity and violence. **2.** a rushing, violent, or abundant and unceasing stream of anything: *a torrent of lava.* **3.** a violent downpour of rain. **4.** a violent, tumultuous, or overwhelming flow: *a torrent of abuse.* —*adj.* **5.** torrential. [< L *torrent-* (s. of *torrēns*) seething, lit., burning, prp. of *torrēre* to burn, parch; see -ENT]

tor·ren·tial (tô ren′shəl, to-, tə-), *adj.* **1.** pertaining to or having the nature of a torrent. **2.** resembling a torrent in rapidity or violence. **3.** falling in torrents: *torrential rains.* **4.** produced by the action of a torrent. **5.** violent, vehement, or impassioned. **6.** overwhelming; extraordinarily copious. [TORRENT + -IAL] —**tor·ren′tial·ly,** *adv.*

Tor·re·ón (tôr′re ôn′), *n.* a city in N Mexico. 205,931 (est. 1963).

Tor·res Bo·det (tôr′res bô ᵺet′), **Jai·me** (hī′me), born 1902, Mexican poet, statesman, and diplomat.

Tor′res Strait′ (tôr′iz, tor′-), a strait between NE Australia and S New Guinea. 80 mi. wide.

Tor·ri·cel·li (tôr′i chel′ē; *It.* tôr′rē chel′lē), *n.* **Evan·ge·li·sta** (e vän′je lē′stä), 1608–47, Italian physicist. —**Tor′ri·cel′li·an,** *adj.*

Tor·ri·cel·li (tôr′i chel′ē, tōr′-), *n.* a formation consisting of two adjoining walled plains in the fourth quadrant of the face of the moon: one about 12 miles in diameter and the other about 5 miles in diameter.

tor·rid (tôr′id, tor′-), *adj.* **1.** subject to parching or burning heat, esp. of the sun, as regions: *the torrid sands of the Sahara.* **2.** oppressively hot, parching, or burning, as climate, weather, air, etc. **3.** ardent; passionate: *a torrid love story.* [< L *torrid(us)* dried up, parched < *torr(ēre)* (to) parch, burn (see TORRENT, THIRST) + *-idus* -ID[4]] —**tor·rid′i·ty, tor′rid·ness,** *n.* —**tor′rid·ly,** *adv.*
—**Syn. 1.** tropical. **2.** scorching, fiery. —**Ant. 1.** arctic. **2.** frigid. **3.** cool.

Tor′rid Zone′, the part of the earth's surface between the tropics of Cancer and Capricorn.

tor·ri·fy (tôr′ə fī′, tor′-), *v.t.,* **-fied, -fy·ing.** torrefy.

Tor·ring·ton (tôr′iṅg tən, tor′-), *n.* **1.** a city in NW Connecticut. 30,045 (1960). **2.** a town in SE Wyoming. 4188 (1960).

tor·sade (tôr säd′), *n.* **1.** a twisted cord. **2.** any ornamental twist, as of velvet. [< F: twisted fringe < *tors* twisted (see TORSE) + *-ade* -ADE[1]]

torse (tôrs), *n. Heraldry.* a wreath of twisted silks of two alternating tinctures, usually a metal and a color, depicted supporting a crest or coronet, often upon a helmet. [< MF: wreath, n. use of fem. of *tors* twisted < LL *tors(us),* ptp., r. L *tortus,* ptp. of *torquēre* to twist]

tor·sel (tôr′səl), *n. Building Trades.* a beam or slab of wood, stone, iron, etc., laid on a masonry wall to receive and distribute the weight from one end of a beam. [alter. of TASSEL[1]]

tor·si (tôr′sē), *n.* a pl. of **torso.**

tor·si·bil·i·ty (tôr′sə bil′i tē), *n.* **1.** capability of being twisted. **2.** resistance to being twisted. **3.** capacity to return to original shape after being twisted. [TORSI(ON) + (A)BILITY]

tor·sion (tôr′shən), *n.* **1.** act of twisting. **2.** resulting state. **3.** *Mech.* **a.** the twisting of a body by two equal and opposite torques. **b.** the internal torque so produced. **4.** *Math.* **a.** the degree of departure of a curve from a plane. **b.** a number measuring this. [late ME *torcion* < medical L *torsiōn-* (s. of *torsiō*) a griping or wringing of the bowels < LL *tors(us)* twisted (see TORSE) + *-iōn-* -ION] —**tor′sion·al,** *adj.* —**tor′sion·al·ly,** *adv.*

tor′sion bal′ance, an instrument for measuring small forces, as electric attraction or repulsion, by determining the amount of torsion or twisting they cause in a slender wire or filament.

tor′sion bar′, a metal bar having elasticity when subjected to torsion: used as a spring in various machines.

tor′sion-free group′ (tôr′shən frē′), *Math.* a group in which every element other than the identity has infinite order.

tor′sion group′, *Math.* a group in which every element has finite order.

tor′sion pen′dulum, *Horol.* a pendulum the weight of which is rotated alternately in opposite directions through a horizontal plane by the torsion of the suspending rod or spring: used for clocks intended to run a long time between windings.

torsk (tôrsk), *n., pl.* **torsks,** (*esp. collectively*) **torsk. 1.** a cod. **2.** cusk (def. 1). [< Norw; ONorw *thorskr* akin to *thurr* dry. See THIRST]

tor·so (tôr′sō), *n., pl.* **-sos, -si** (-sē). **1.** the trunk of the human body. **2.** a sculptured form representing the trunk of a nude female or male figure. **3.** something mutilated or incomplete. [< It: stalk, trunk of statue < L *thyrs(us)* < Gk *thýrsos* wand, stem]

tor′so mur′der, a murder in which the body of the victim is dismembered at the torso.

tort (tôrt), *n. Law.* a wrongful act, not including a breach of contract or trust, which results in injury to another's person, property, reputation, or the like, and for which the injured party is entitled to compensation. [ME < legal L *tort(um)* wrong, injustice, n. use of neut. of L *tortus* twisted, crooked, dubious, ptp. of *torquēre* to twist, wring]

torte (tôrt; *Ger.* tôr′tə), *n., pl.* **tortes** (tôrts), *Ger.* **tor·ten** (tôr′tᵊn). a rich cake, esp. one containing little or no flour, usually made with eggs, crumbs, and ground nuts. [< G << LL *tōrt(a)* round cake (of bread) < ?]

tor·teau (tôr tō′), *n., pl.* **-teaus** (-tōz′). *Heraldry.* a roundel gules. [< MF; r. late ME *tortel* < ML *tortell(a),* equiv. to LL *tōrt(a)* TORTE + *-ella* dim. suffix. See TORTILLA]

tort-fea·sor (tôrt′fē′zər, -zôr, -fē′-), *n. Law.* one who commits a tort. [< AF *tortfesor* wrongdoer, equiv. to F *tortfaiseur.* See TORT, FEASANCE, -OR[2]]

tor·ti·col·lis (tôr′tə kol′is), *n. Pathol.* a condition in which the neck is twisted and the head inclined to one side, caused by spasmodic contraction of the muscles of the neck. Also called **wryneck.** [< NL, equiv. to L *tort(us)* twisted (see TORT) + *-i-* -I- + *coll(um)* neck + *-is* 3rd decl. nom. sing. suffix]

tor·tile (tôr′til), *adj.* twisted; coiled. [< L *tortil(is)* < *tort(us)* twisted (see TORT) + *-ilis* -ILE]

tor·til·la (tôr tē′ə; *Sp.* tôr tē′yä), *n., pl.* **-til·las** (-tē′əz; *Sp.* -tē′yäs). *Mexican Cookery.* a thin, round, unleavened bread prepared from corn meal, baked on a flat plate of iron, earthenware, or the like. [< Sp, equiv. to *tort(a)* cake (see TORTE) + *-illa* < L, dim. suffix]

Tortil′la Flat′, a novel (1935) by John Steinbeck.

tor·til·lon (tôr′tē on′, -ōn′; *Fr.* tôr tē yôN′), *n., pl.* **-til·lons** (-tē onz′, -ōnz′; *Fr.* -tē yôN′). a stump made of paper twisted to a point. [< F: lit., something twisted < *tortill(er)* (to) twist (see TORT) + *-on* n. suffix]

tor·tious (tôr′shəs), *adj.* *Law.* of the nature of or pertaining to a tort. [ME *torcious* < AF < *torci(on)* TORSION + *-ous* -OUS; meaning influenced by TORT] —**tor′tious·ly,** *adv.*

tor·toise (tôr′təs), *n.* **1.** a turtle, esp. a terrestrial turtle. **2.** a very slow person or thing. **3.** testudo (def. 1). [var. of earlier (15th-century) *tortuse, tortose, tortuce,* ME *tortuca* < ML << LL *tartarūcha* (fem.) of Tartarus (< Gk *tartaroûchos*), the tortoise being regarded as an infernal animal; ML form influenced by L *tortus* crooked, twisted (see TORT)]

tor′toise bee′tle, any of several turtle-shaped leaf beetles, as *Chelymorpha cassidea* **(milkweed tortoise beetle).**

tor·toise-core (tôr′təs kōr′, -kôr′), *n.* (in the prehistoric Levalloisian culture) a flint core so shaped in advance that a usable flake could be detached with a single blow.

tor′toise plant′, elephant's-foot.

tor′toise shell′, **1.** a horny substance of a mottled brown and yellow coloration, composing the plates that form the carapace of a hawksbill turtle, used for making combs and ornamental articles, inlaying, etc. **2.** any synthetic substance made to appear like natural tortoise shell. **3.** Also, **tor′toise-shell but′terfly.** any of several nymphalid butterflies of the genus *Nymphalis,* as *N. californica,* having variegated markings of red, yellow, or orange on the wings.

tor·toise-shell (tôr′təs shel′), *adj.* **1.** mottled or variegated like tortoise shell, esp. with yellow and brown and sometimes other colors. **2.** made of tortoise shell.

tor′toise-shell tur′tle. See **hawksbill turtle.**

Tor·to·la (tôr tō′lə), *n.* the principal island of the British Virgin Islands, in the NE West Indies.

tor·to·ni (tôr tō′nē), *n.* **1.** a kind of ice cream or frozen mousse made with eggs and heavy cream, often containing chopped cherries or topped with minced almonds or crumbled macaroons. **2.** See **biscuit tortoni.** [? named after an Italian caterer in Paris in the 19th century]

tor·tri·cid (tôr′tri sid), *n.* **1.** any of numerous moths of the family *Tortricidae,* characterized by broad wings and forewings each with a truncated tip, the larvae of which are usually leaf rollers. —*adj.* **2.** belonging or pertaining to the family *Tortricidae.* [back formation from NL *Tortrīcidae* genus name < *tortrīc-* (s. of *tortrix,* fem. of L *tortor* torturer, lit., twister; see TORT, -OR[2]) + *-idae* -ID[2]]

Tor·tu·ga (tôr to͞o′gə), *n.* an island off the N coast of and belonging to Haiti: formerly a pirate stronghold. 23 mi. long; 70 sq. mi. French, **La Tortue.**

tor·tu·os·i·ty (tôr′cho͞o os′i tē), *n., pl.* **-ties.** **1.** state of being tortuous; twisted form or course; crookedness. **2.** a twist, bend, or crook. **3.** a twisting or crooked part, passage, or thing. [< LL *tortuōsitās.* See TORTUOUS, -ITY]

tor·tu·ous (tôr′cho͞o əs), *adj.* **1.** full of twists, turns, or bends; twisting, winding, or crooked: *a tortuous path through the woods.* **2.** not direct or straightforward, as in a course of procedure, thought, speech, or writing. **3.** deceitfully indirect or morally crooked, as proceedings, methods, policy, etc. **4.** *Geom. Obs.* not in one plane, as a curve, such as a helix, which does not lie in a plane. [late ME < L *tortuōs(us)* < *tortu(s)* a twisting (4th decl.; see TORT) + *-ōsus* -OUS] —**tor′tu·ous·ly,** *adv.* —**tor′tu·ous·ness,** *n.*
—**Syn. 1.** bent, sinuous, serpentine. **2.** evasive, roundabout, circuitous, indirect.

tor·ture (tôr′chər), *n., v.,* **-tured, -tur·ing.** —*n.* **1.** the act of inflicting excruciating pain, as punishment or revenge, as a means of getting a confession or information, or for sheer cruelty. **2.** a method of inflicting such pain. **3.** Often, **tortures.** the pain or suffering caused or undergone. **4.** extreme anguish of body or mind; agony. **5.** a cause of severe pain or anguish. —*v.t.* **6.** to subject to torture. **7.** to afflict with severe pain of body or mind: *My back tortures me.* **8.** to force or extort by torture: *We'll torture the truth from his lips!* **9.** to twist, force, or bring into some unnatural position or form: *trees tortured by storms.* **10.** to distort or pervert (language, meaning, etc.). [< LL *tortūr(a)* a twisting, torment, torture. See TORT, -URE] —**tor′tur·a·ble,** *adj.* —**tor′tured·ly,** *adv.* —**tor′tur·er,** *n.* —**tor′ture·some,** *adj.* —**tor′tur·ous,** *adj.* —**tor′tur·ing·ly,** *adv.* —**tor′tur·ous·ly,** *adv.* —**Syn. 6.** See **torment.**

tor·u·lo·sis (tôr′yə lō′sis), *n.* *Pathol.* cryptococcosis. [< NL *Torul(a)* name of a genus (dim. of TORUS) + -OSIS]

To·ruń (tô′ro͞on′y[ə]), *n.* a city in N Poland, on the Vistula. 110,000 (est. 1963). German, **Thorn.**

to·rus (tôr′əs, tōr′-), *n., pl.* **to·ri** (tôr′ī, tōr′ī). **1.** *Archit.* a large convex molding, more or less semicircular in profile, commonly forming the lowest member of the base of a column, or that directly above the plinth (when present), sometimes occurring as one of a pair separated by a scotia and fillets. **2.** *Geom.* **a.** Also called **anchor ring.** a doughnut-shaped surface generated by the revolution of a conic, esp. a circle, about an exterior line lying in its plane. **b.** the solid enclosed by such a surface. **3.** *Bot.* **a.** the receptacle of a flower. **b.** a thickening of the wall membrane in the bordered pits occurring in the tracheid cells of the wood of many conifers. **4.** *Anat.* a rounded ridge; a protuberant part. [< L: bulge, rounded molding]

Torus (def. 2)

to′rus pal·a·ti′nus (pal′ə tī′nəs), *Anat.* a rounded ridge on the hard palate. [< NL; see TORUS, PALATINE[2]]

To·ry (tôr′ē, tōr′ē), *n., pl.* **-ries,** for 1–4, *adj.* —*n.* **1.** a member of a political party in Great Britain from the late 17th century to about 1832 that favored the authority of the king over Parliament and the preservation of the existing social and political order: succeeded by the Conservative party. **2.** (*often l.c.*) an advocate of conservative principles; one opposed to reform or radicalism. **3.** a person who supported the British cause in the American Revolution; a loyalist. **4.** (in the 17th century) one of a class of dispossessed Irishmen, nominally royalists, who became outlaws and were noted for their outrages and cruelties. **5.** a boy's given name. —*adj.* **6.** of, belonging to, or characteristic of the Tories. **7.** being a Tory. **8.** (*sometimes l.c.*) opposed to radicalism; conservative. [< Ir *tōraidhe, tōiridhe* highwayman, persecuted person < *tōir* chase, pursuit + *-idhe* n. suffix]

To·ry·ish (tôr′ē ish, tōr′-), *adj.* of, pertaining to, or resembling a Tory. [TORY + -ISH]

To·ry·ism (tôr′ē iz′əm, tōr′-), *n.* **1.** the act or fact of being a Tory. **2.** the principles and beliefs of Tories. [TORY + -ISM]

Tos·ca (tos′kə; *It.* tôs′kä), *n.* an opera (1900) by Giacomo Puccini.

Tos·ca·na (tôs kä′nä), *n.* Italian name of **Tuscany.**

Tos·ca·ni·ni (tos′kə nē′nē; *It.* tôs′kä nē′nē), *n.* **Ar·tu·ro** (är to͞or′ō; *It.* är to͞o′rô), 1867–1957, U.S. orchestra conductor, born in Italy.

tosh[1] (tosh), *n.* *Brit. Slang.* nonsense; bosh. [? b. TRASH + BOSH]

tosh[2] (tosh), *Scot.* —*v.t.* **1.** to make neat or tidy. —*adj.* **2.** neat; tidy. [?] —**tosh′ly,** *adv.*

tosh′ nail′ing. See **blind nailing.**

toss (tôs, tos), *v.,* **tossed** or (*Poetic*) **tost; toss·ing;** *n.* —*v.t.* **1.** to throw, pitch, or fling, esp. to throw lightly or carelessly: *to toss a piece of paper into the wastebasket.* **2.** to throw or send from one to another, as in play: *to toss a ball.* **3.** to throw or pitch with irregular or careless motions; fling or jerk about: *The ship was tossed by waves. A tree tosses its branches in the wind.* **4.** to agitate, disturb, or disquiet. **5.** to throw, raise, or jerk upward suddenly: *She tossed her head disdainfully.* **6.** to speak or express in a sudden offhand manner; interject: *He gleefully tossed irrelevancies into their serious discussion.* **7.** to throw (a coin) into the air in order to decide something by the side turned up when it falls (sometimes fol. by *up*). **8.** to stir or mix lightly and gently (a salad) until the ingredients are coated with the dressing. **9.** *Metall.* to purify (tin) by pouring it in a molten state from ladle to ladle so as to allow air to oxidize the impurities. —*v.i.* **10.** to pitch, rock, sway, or move irregularly, as a ship on a rough sea or a flag or plumes in the breeze. **11.** to fling or jerk oneself or move restlessly about, esp. on a bed or couch: *to toss in one's sleep.* **12.** to throw something. **13.** to throw a coin into the air in order to decide something by the way it falls (sometimes fol. by *up*). **14.** to go with a fling of the body: *to toss out of a room in a fit of anger.* **15. toss off, a.** to accomplish quickly or easily. **b.** to consume rapidly, esp. to drink something up in one swallow: *He generally tosses off a cocktail or two before dinner.* **16. toss up,** *Informal.* to vomit. —*n.* **17.** act of tossing. **18.** a pitching about or up and down. **19.** a throw or pitch. **20.** a tossing of a coin to decide something; toss-up. **21.** the distance to which something is or may be thrown. **22.** a sudden fling or jerk of the body, esp. a quick upward or backward movement of the head. [appar. < Scand; cf. dial. Sw *tossa* to spread, strew] —**toss′er,** *n.* —**toss′ing·ly,** *adv.*
—**Syn. 1.** See **throw.**

tossed′ sal′ad, a salad consisting of one or more greens, tomatoes, onion slices, etc., with a dressing, and mixed with a large fork and spoon.

toss·pot (tôs′pot′, tos′-), *n.* a tippler; drunkard. [TOSS + POT]

toss-up (tôs′up′, tos′-), *n.* **1.** the tossing up of a coin to decide something by its fall. **2.** *Informal.* an even choice or chance: *It's a tossup whether he'll come or not.* [n. use of v. phrase *toss up*]

tost (tôst, tost), *v.* a pt. and pp. of **toss.**

tot[1] (tot), *n.* **1.** a small child. **2.** *Chiefly Brit.* a small portion of a beverage, esp. a dram of liquor. **3.** a small quantity of anything. [? short for TOTTERER]

tot[2] (tot), *v.,* **tot·ted, tot·ting,** *n.* —*v.t., v.i.* **1.** to add; total (often fol. by *up*). —*n.* **2.** a total. **3.** act of adding. **4.** *Brit. Informal.* a column of numbers to be added. [< L: so much, so many]

to·tal (tōt′[ə]l), *adj., n., v.,* **-taled, -tal·ing** or (*esp. Brit.*) **-talled, -tal·ling.** —*adj.* **1.** constituting or comprising the whole; entire; whole: *the total expenditure.* **2.** of or pertaining to the whole of something: *the total effect of a play.* **3.** complete in extent or degree; absolute; unqualified; utter: *a total failure.* —*n.* **4.** the total amount; sum; aggregate: *to add the several items to find the total; costing a total of $200.* **5.** the whole; an entirety: *the impressive total of Mozart's achievement.* —*v.t.* **6.** to bring to a total; add up. **7.** to reach a total of; amount to. —*v.i.* **8.** to amount (often fol. by *to*). [ME < ML *tōtāl(is)* < L *tōt(us)* entire + *-ālis* -AL[1]]
—**Syn. 1.** complete. **4, 5.** gross, entirety, totality. **5.** See **whole.**

to′tal an′gular momen′tum quan′tum num′ber, *Physics.* See **angular momentum quantum number.**

to′tal bas′es, *Baseball.* the number of bases reached by a batter as a result of base hits.

to′tal deprav′ity, the doctrine that man's entire nature, including his reason, is utterly corrupt or sinful as a result of the Fall, and that man is therefore completely dependent on God for regeneration.

to′tal differen′tial, *Math.* a function that is obtained from a given function of several variables, $w = f(x, y, z)$, and that expresses the increment in the given function as the sum of the products of the partial derivatives with respect to each variable times the corresponding increment, written as $dw = \frac{\delta f}{\delta x}dx + \frac{\delta f}{\delta y}dy + \frac{\delta f}{\delta z}dz$. Cf. **differential** (def. 8).

to′tal eclipse′, an eclipse in which the surface of the eclipsed body is completely obscured. Cf. **annular eclipse.**

to′tal heat′, *Thermodynamics.* enthalpy.

to′tal im′pulse, *Rocketry.* a measure of the maximum momentum that a given reaction engine and fuel supply can impart to a vehicle, equal to the product of the average thrust in pounds and the period of firing in seconds.

to′tal inter′nal reflec′tion. See **total reflection.**

to·tal·ise (tōt′[ə]līz′), *v.t.,* **-ised, -is·ing.** *Chiefly Brit.* totalize. —**to′tal·i·sa′tion,** *n.*

to·tal·i·tar·i·an (tō tal′i târ′ē ən), *adj.* **1.** of or pertaining to a centralized government in which those in control grant neither recognition nor tolerance to parties of differing opinion. Cf. **authoritarian** (def. 3). —*n.* **2.** an adherent of totalitarian principles. [TOTALIT(Y) + -ARIAN]
—**Syn. 1.** arbitrary, oppressive, tyrannical.

to·tal·i·tar·i·an·ism (tō tal′i târ′ē ə niz′əm), *n.* **1.** the practices and principles of a totalitarian regime: *the totalitarianism of Nazi Germany.* **2.** absolute control by the state or a governing branch of a highly centralized institution: *Totalitarianism aims at suppressing initiative as well as individualism.* **3.** the character or quality of an autocratic or authoritarian individual, group, or government: *They suffered under the totalitarianism of the father in their patriarchal household.* [TOTALITARIAN + -ISM]

to·tal·i·tar·i·an·ize (tō tal′i târ′ē ə nīz′), *v.t.,* **-ized, -iz·ing.** to make totalitarian. [TOTALITARIAN + -IZE]

to·tal·i·ty (tō tal′i tē), *n., pl.* **-ties.** **1.** state of being total; entirety. **2.** that which is total; the total amount; a whole. **3.** *Astron.* total obscuration in an eclipse. [TOTAL + -ITY]

To·tal·i·za·tor (tōt′[ə]li zā′tər), *n.* *Trademark.* **1.** an apparatus for registering and indicating the total of operations, measurements, etc. **2.** a parimutuel machine.

to·tal·ize (tōt′[ə]līz′), *v.t.,* **-ized, -iz·ing.** to make total; combine into a total. Also, *esp. Brit.,* **totalise.** [TOTAL + -IZE] —**to′tal·i·za′tion,** *n.*

to·tal·iz·er (tōt′[ə]lī′zər), *n.* **1.** one who or that which totals. **2.** a totalizator. **3.** a machine for adding and subtracting. [TOTALIZE + -ER[1]]

to·tal·ly (tōt′[ə]lē), *adv.* wholly; entirely; completely: *His statement is totally accurate.* [TOTAL + -LY]

to′tally or′dered set′, *Math.* a set in which a relation, as less than or equal to, holds for all pairs of elements of the set. Also called **chain, linearly ordered set, simply ordered set.** Cf. **partially ordered set, well-ordered set.**

to′tal quan′tum num′ber, *Physics.* See **principal quantum number.**

to′tal recall′, the ability to remember with complete, detailed accuracy.

to′tal reflec′tion, *Optics.* the effect that occurs when light meets the interface between the medium in which it is traveling and a medium of smaller refractive index at an angle of incidence greater than the critical angle, all light being reflected back to the first medium. Also called **total internal reflection.**

to·ta·quine (tō′tə kwēn′, -kwin), *n.* *Pharm.* a yellowish-white to gray, water-insoluble powder obtained from cinchona bark, used in medicine chiefly as an antimalarial. [var. of *totaquina* < NL < L *tōta* (fem. of *tōtus* all) + Sp *quina* cinchona bark < Kechua *kina* bark]

tote (tōt), *v.,* **tot·ed, tot·ing,** *n.* *Informal.* —*v.t.* **1.** to carry, as on one's back or in one's arms: *to tote a bundle.* **2.** to carry on one's person: *to tote a gun.* **3.** to transport or convey, as on a vehicle or boat. —*n.* **4.** act or course of toting. **5.** that which is toted. **6.** See **tote bag.** [? < Angolese *tota* to pick up, carry] —**tot′a·ble,** *adj.* —**tot′er,** *n.*

tote′ bag′, a capacious women's handbag, used esp. for carrying packages or small items. Also called **tote.**

tote′ board′, *Informal.* a Totalizator.

tote′ box′, a box for holding and carrying tools, machine parts, etc.

to·tem (tō′təm), *n.* **1.** a natural object or an animate being, as an animal or bird, assumed as the emblem of a clan, family, or group. **2.** an object or natural phenomenon with which a primitive family or sib considers itself closely related. **3.** a representation of such an object serving as the distinctive mark of the clan or group. [< Ojibwa *ototeman* his brother-sister kin] —**to·tem·ic** (tō tem′ik), *adj.* —**to·tem′i·cal·ly,** *adv.*

to·tem·ism (tō′tə miz′əm), *n.* **1.** the practice of having totems. **2.** the system of tribal division according to totems. [TOTEM + -ISM]

to·tem·ist (tō′tə mist), *n.* a member of a clan, family, or group distinguished by a totem. [TOTEM + -IST] —**to′tem·is′tic,** *adj.*

to′tem pole′, a pole or post carved and painted with totemic figures, erected by Indians of the northwest coast of North America, esp. in front of their houses.

tote′ road′, an unpaved road for carrying supplies, as to a camp, clearing, etc.

To′ the Light′house, a novel (1927) by Virginia Woolf.

toth·er (tuth′ər), *adj., pron.* *Dial.* that other; the other. Also, **t'oth′er.** [ME *the tother* for *thet other,* var. of *that other* the other]

toti-, a learned borrowing from Latin meaning "entire," "entirely," used in the formation of compound words: *totipalmation.* [comb. form repr. L *tōtus*]

to·ti·dem ver·bis (tō′ti dem′ wer′bēs; *Eng.* tot′i dem′ vûr′bis), *Latin.* with just so many words; in these words.

Totem pole

to·tient (tō′shənt), *n.* *Math.* See **Euler's phi-function.** [irreg. < L *totiēs, totiēns,* modeled after *quotient*]

tot·ing (tō′tiŋ), *n. Southern U.S.* **1.** the taking home of food by a domestic from his employer: *Toting was a fringe benefit of the job.* **2.** the food so taken. [TOTE + -ING¹]

to·ti·pal·mate (tō′tə pal′mit, -māt), *adj. Ornith.* having all four toes fully webbed. [TOTI- + PALMATE]

to·ti·pal·ma·tion (tō′tə pal mā′shən), *n.* totipalmate condition or formation. [TOTI- + PALMATION]

to·tis vi·ri·bus (tō′tēs wē′ʀi bo͞os′; *Eng.* tō′tis vir′ə bəs), *Latin.* with all one's might.

tot·i·tive (tot′i tiv), *n. Math. Obs.* any integer that is less than a given integer and has no factor, except unity, in common with it. [irreg. < L *tot* so many + -ITIVE]

Totipalmate foot

Tot·le·ben (tôt′le ben, tot le′-), *n.* **Franz E·du·ard I·va·no·vich** (fränts e′do͞o äʀt′ i vä′no vich), **Count,** 1818–84, Russian military engineer and general.

to·to cae·lo (tō′tō kī′lō; *Eng.* tō′tō sē′lō), *Latin.* by the entire extent of the heavens; diametrically.

Tot·ten·ham (tot′ᵊnəm), *n.* a city in E Middlesex, in SE England, N of London. 113,126 (1961).

tot·ter (tot′ər), *v.i.* **1.** to walk or go with faltering steps, as if from extreme weakness. **2.** to sway or rock on the base or ground, as if about to fall: *a tottering tower; a tottering government.* **3.** to shake or tremble: *a tottering load.* —*n.* **4.** act of tottering; an unsteady movement or gait. [ME *toter(en)* (to) swing, perh. back formation from OE *totrida* a swing, lit., a rider (*rida*) on a projecting part (*tot*); cf. Icel *tota* toe (of a shoe), *toti* snout] —**tot′ter·er,** *n.*
—**Syn. 1.** See **stagger. 2.** waver. **3.** oscillate, quiver.

tot·ter·ing (tot′ər iŋ), *adj.* **1.** walking unsteadily or shakily, as a person. **2.** lacking security or stability; threatening to collapse; precarious: *a tottering empire; a tottering building.* [TOTTER + -ING²] —**tot′ter·ing·ly,** *adv.*

tot·ter·y (tot′ə rē), *adj.* tottering; shaky. [TOTTER + -Y¹]

tou·can (to͞o′kan, to͞o kän′), *n.* **1.** any of several usually brightly colored, fruit-eating birds of the family *Ramphastidae,* of tropical America, having a very large bill. **2.** (*cap.*) *Astron.* the constellation Tucana. [< F < Pg *tucano* < Tupi *tucana*]

Red-billed toucan, *Ramphastos monilis* (Length 22 in.)

tou·can·et (to͞o′kə net′, to͞o′kə-net′), *n.* any of several small, greenish toucans, as *Aulacorhynchus prasinus* **(emerald toucanet),** of Central America. [TOUCAN + -ET]

touch (tuch), *v.t.* **1.** to put the hand, finger, etc., on or into contact with (something) to feel it: *She touched the crown fearfully.* **2.** to come into contact with and perceive (something), as the hand or the like does. **3.** to bring (the hand, finger, etc., or something held) into contact with something. **4.** to give a slight tap or pat to with the hand, finger, etc.; strike or hit gently or lightly. **5.** to come into or be in contact with. **6.** *Geom.* (of a line or surface) to be tangent to. **7.** to be adjacent to or border on. **8.** to come up to; reach; attain. **9.** (usually used with a negative) to attain equality with; compare with: *a style that cannot touch that of Shakespeare.* **10.** to mark by strokes of the brush, pencil, or the like. **11.** to mark or relieve slightly, as with color: *a gray dress touched with blue.* **12.** to stop at (a place), as a ship: *The ship touched shore several times during the cruise.* **13.** to treat or affect in some way by contact. **14.** to affect as if by contact; tinge; imbue. **15.** to affect with some feeling or emotion, esp. tenderness, pity, gratitude, etc.: *Their sufferings touched his heart.* **16.** to handle, use, or have to do with in any way: *He won't touch another drink.* **17.** to deal with or treat in speech or writing. **18.** to refer or allude to. **19.** to pertain or relate to: *a critic in all affairs touching the kitchen.* **20.** to be a matter of importance to; make a difference to; affect: *This grave decision touches all of us.* **21.** *Metall.* to stamp (metal) as being of standard purity. **22.** *Slang.* to apply to for money, or succeed in getting money from: *He touched me for a sawbuck.* **23.** *Slang.* to steal from. **24.** *Archaic.* to strike the strings, keys, etc., of (a musical instrument) so as to cause it to sound. **25.** *Archaic.* to play or perform (an air, notes, etc.) on a musical instrument.
—*v.i.* **26.** to place the hand, finger, etc., on or in contact with something. **27.** to come into or be in contact. **28.** to make a stop or a short call at a place, as a ship or those on board (usually fol. by *at*). **29. touch down,** (of an airplane) to come into contact with the ground; land. **30. touch off, a.** to represent or characterize precisely. **b.** to cause to ignite or explode. **c.** to give rise to; initiate: *This incident will undoubtedly touch off another international crisis.* **31. touch on** or **upon,** to mention a subject briefly or casually; treat of in passing: *In his lecture he touched on the major aspects of the controversy.* **32. touch up, a.** to modify or improve (a painting, photograph, etc.) by adding small strokes or making slight changes. **b.** to rouse by or as by striking: *This should touch up your memory.*
—*n.* **33.** the act or state of touching; state or fact of being touched. **34.** that sense by which anything material is perceived by means of the contact with it of some part of the body. **35.** the sensation or effect caused by touching something, regarded as a quality of the thing: *an object with a slimy touch.* **36.** a coming into or being in contact. **37.** mental or moral perception, sensitivity, or understanding: *The dean has a marvelous touch in dealing with the students.* **38.** ability, skill, or dexterity; knack. **39.** *Fencing.* the contact of the point of a foil or épée or the point or edge of the blade of a saber with a specified portion of the opponent's body, counting as one point for the scorer. **40.** a close relation of communication, agreement, sympathy, or the like: *to be in touch with public opinion.* **41.** a slight stroke or blow. **42.** a slight attack, as of illness or disease: *a touch of rheumatism.* **43.** a slight added action or effort in doing or completing any piece of work. **44.** manner of execution in artistic work. **45.** act or manner of touching or fingering a musical instrument, esp. a keyboard instrument, so as to bring out its tones. **46.** the mode of action of the keys of an instrument. **47.** *Change Ringing.* a partial series of changes on a peal of bells. **48.** a stroke or dash, as with a brush, pencil, or pen. **49.** a detail in any artistic work. **50.** a slight amount of some quality, attribute, etc.: *a touch of sarcasm in his voice.* **51.** a slight quantity or degree: *a touch of salt.* **52.** a distinguishing characteristic or trait: *the touch of the master.* **53.** quality or kind in general. **54.** act of testing anything. **55.** something that serves as a test; touchstone. **56.** *Slang.* **a.** the act of approaching someone for money as a gift or a loan. **b.** the obtaining of money in this manner. **c.** the money obtained. **d.** a person considered from the standpoint of the relative ease with which he will lend money: *I can always hit her for ten—she's a soft touch.* **57.** *Slang.* theft. **58.** *Metall.* **a.** an official mark put upon precious metal after testing to indicate its purity. **b.** a die, stamp, or the like for impressing such a mark. **59.** *Soccer.* the area outside the touchlines. **60.** *Rugby.* either of the touchlines or the area outside of the touchlines. **61. put the touch on,** *Informal.* to try to borrow money from: *Willie put the touch on me for another fin last night.* [ME *to(u)che* < OF *tochie(r)* < VL **toccāre* to knock, strike, touch, based on an imitation of a knocking sound] —**touch′a·ble,** *adj.* —**touch′a·ble·ness,** *n.* —**touch′er,** *n.* —**touch′less,** *adj.*
—**Syn. 1.** handle, feel. **13.** impress. **15.** move, strike, stir, melt, soften. **19.** concern, regard, affect. **41.** pat, tap. **51.** hint, trace, suggestion.

touch′ and go′, 1. quick action or movement: *the touch and go of city traffic.* **2.** a precarious or delicate state of affairs: *It was touch and go there for a while during the Battle of the Coral Sea.*

touch-and-go (tuch′ən gō′), *adj.* **1.** hasty, sketchy, or desultory. **2.** risky; precarious: *After the snow began to fall, the mountain climbers really had a touch-and-go descent.* [n. use of v. phrase; see TOUCH, GO]

touch·back (tuch′bak′), *n. Football.* a play in which the ball is downed after having been kicked into the end zone by the opposing team or having been recovered or intercepted there, or in which it has been kicked beyond the end zone. Cf. **safety** (def. 6a). [TOUCH + BACK²]

touch·down (tuch′doun′), *n.* **1.** *Football.* the act or an instance of scoring six points by being in possession of the ball on or behind the opponent's goal line. **2.** *Rugby.* act of a player who touches the ball on or to the ground inside of his own in-goal. [TOUCH + DOWN¹]

tou·ché (to͞o shā′), *interj.* **1.** *Fencing.* (an expression used to indicate a hit or touch.) **2.** (an expression used for acknowledging a telling remark or rejoinder.) [< F: lit., touched]

touched (tucht), *adj.* **1.** moved; stirred. **2.** slightly crazy; unbalanced: *touched in the head.* [TOUCH + -ED²]

touch′ foot′ball, an informal variety of football in which the touching, usually with both hands, of a ball-carrier by a member of the opposing team results in a down.

touch·hole (tuch′hōl′), *n.* the vent in the breech of an old-time firearm or cannon through which the charge was ignited. [TOUCH + HOLE]

touch·ing (tuch′iŋ), *adj.* **1.** affecting; moving; pathetic: *a touching scene of farewell.* **2.** that touches. —*prep.* **3.** in reference or relation to; concerning; about: *He addressed them touching future plans.* [TOUCH + -ING²] —**touch′ing·ly,** *adv.* —**touch′ing·ness,** *n.*
—**Syn. 1.** piteous; impressive. **2.** tangent.

touch-in-goal (tuch′in gōl′), *n. Rugby.* the area at each end of the field outside of a touch-in-goal line.

touch′-in-goal′ line′, *Rugby.* either of the two touchlines at each end of the field between the goal line and the dead-ball line.

touch·line (tuch′līn′), *n. Rugby, Soccer.* any of the outer lines bordering the playing field. [TOUCH + LINE¹]

touch′ mark′. See **touch** (def. 58a).

touch-me-not (tuch′mē not′), *n.* any of several plants of the genus *Impatiens,* esp. *I. noli-me-tangere,* bearing pods that, when ripe, burst on being touched, scattering the seeds. Cf. **jewelweed.**

touch′ nee′dle, (in assaying) any of a series of gold or silver needles of various known degrees of purity, rubbed on a touchstone to make a mark compared for color with a mark made by a specimen. [TOUCH + NEEDLE]

touch′ pa′per, paper saturated with potassium nitrate to make it burn slowly, used for igniting explosives and fireworks.

touch′ plate′, a pewter plate belonging to a guild of pewterers and bearing samples of the touch marks of all pewterers belonging to the guild.

touch·stone (tuch′stōn′), *n.* **1.** a black siliceous stone used to test the purity of gold and silver by the color of the streak produced on it by rubbing it with either metal. **2.** a test or criterion for the qualities of a thing. [TOUCH + STONE]
—**Syn. 2.** standard, measure, model, pattern.

touch′ sys′tem, a system of typing in which each finger is trained to operate one or more specified keys, thereby enabling a person to type without looking at the keyboard. Cf. **hunt and peck.**

touch-tack·le (tuch′tak′əl), *n.* See **touch football.**

touch·wood (tuch′wo͝od′), *n.* **1.** wood converted into an easily ignitible substance by the action of certain fungi, and used as tinder; punk. **2.** amadou. [TOUCH + WOOD¹]

touch·y (tuch′ē), *adj.,* **touch·i·er, touch·i·est. 1.** apt to take offense on slight provocation; irritable: *He is very touchy when sick.* **2.** requiring caution, tactfulness, or expert handling; precarious; risky: *a touchy subject; a touchy situation in Africa.* **3.** sensitive to touch. **4.** easily ignited, as tinder. [var. of TECHY, by assoc. with TOUCH] —**touch′i·ly,** *adv.* —**touch′i·ness,** *n.*
—**Syn. 1.** testy, irascible, edgy, snappish, cranky, techy.

Toug·gourt (to͞o go͞ort′), *n.* a city in NE Algeria. 17,380 (1954).

tough (tuf), *adj.* **1.** strong and durable; not easily broken or cut. **2.** not brittle or tender. **3.** difficult to masticate, as food: *a tough steak.* **4.** of viscous consistency, as liquid or semiliquid matter: *tough molasses.* **5.** capable of great endurance; sturdy; hardy: *tough troops.* **6.** not easily influenced, as a person; unyielding; stubborn: *a tough man to work for.* **7.** hardened; incorrigible: *a tough criminal.* **8.** difficult to perform, accomplish, or deal with; hard, trying, or troublesome: *a tough problem.* **9.** hard to bear or endure: *tough luck.* **10.** vigorous; severe; violent: *a tough struggle.* **11.** *U.S.* vicious; rough; rowdyish: *a tough character; a tough neighborhood.* —*n.* **12.** *U.S.* a ruffian; rowdy. [ME; OE *tōh;* cf. D *taai,* G *zäh(e)*] —**tough′ly,** *adv.* —**tough′ness,** *n.*
—**Syn. 1.** firm, strong, hard. **5.** durable. **6.** inflexible. —**Ant. 1.** fragile. **5.** feeble, weak.

tough′ cake′. See **tough pitch copper.**

tough·en (tuf′ən), *v.t., v.i.* to make or become tough or tougher. [TOUGH + -EN¹] —**tough′en·er,** *n.*

tough·ie (tuf′ē), *n. Informal.* **1.** a tough person, esp. one who is belligerent. **2.** a difficult problem or situation: *That math test was a real toughie!* **3.** a harsh or blunt book, movie, etc. Also, **toughy.** [TOUGH + -IE]

tough·ish (tuf′ish), *adj.* being somewhat tough. [TOUGH + -ISH¹]

tough-mind·ed (tuf′mīn′did), *adj.* **1.** characterized by a practical, unsentimental attitude or point of view: *a tough-minded man who often misses the finer points.* **2.** strong-willed; vigorous; not easily swayed. —**tough′-mind′ed·ly,** *adv.* —**tough′-mind′ed·ness,** *n.*

tough′ pitch′, *Metall.* the state of refined copper when it is soft, malleable, and flexible.

tough′ pitch′ cop′per, copper refined in a reverberatory furnace to a state of tough pitch, containing from 0.02 to 0.05 percent oxygen. Also called **tough cake.**

tough·y (tuf′ē), *n., pl.* **tough·ies.** toughie.

tou·jours per·drix (to͞o zho͞or peʀ dʀē′), *French.* too much of a good thing. [lit., always partridge]

Toul (to͞ol), *n.* a fortress town in NE France, on the Moselle: siege 1870. 15,031 (1962).

Tou·lon (to͞o lôɴ′), *n.* a seaport in SE France: naval base. 172,586 (1962).

Tou·louse (to͞o lo͞oz′), *n.* a city in and the capital of Haute-Garonne, in S France, on the Garonne River. 330,570 (1962).

Tou·louse-Lau·trec (to͞o lo͞os′lō trek′, -lə-; *Fr.* to͞o-lo͞oz′lō tʀek′), *n.* **Hen·ri Ma·rie Ray·mond de** (äɴ ʀē′ ma ʀē′ ʀā môɴ′ də), 1864–1901, French painter and lithographer.

tou·pee (to͞o pā′, -pē′), *n.* **1.** a man's wig. **2.** a patch of false hair for covering a bald spot. **3.** (formerly) a curl or an artificial lock of hair on the top of the head, esp. as a crowning feature of a periwig. [var. of *toupet* < F, equiv. to OF *to(u)p* tuft (< Gmc; see TOP¹) + *-et* -ET]

tour (to͝or), *v.i.* **1.** to travel from place to place. **2.** to travel from city to city with a theatrical company. —*v.t.* **3.** to travel through (a place). **4.** (of a manager) to send or take (a theatrical company, its production, etc.) from city to city. —*n.* **5.** a traveling around from place to place. **6.** a long journey including the visiting of a number of places in sequence. **7.** a journey of a theatrical company from town to town to fulfill engagements: *to go on tour.* **8.** *Chiefly Mil.* a period of duty at one place. [ME < MF < L *tor(nus)* < Gk *tórnos* tool for making a circle. See TURN]
—**Syn. 1, 3.** visit. **6.** trip, tour, expedition. See **excursion.**

tou·ra·co (to͝or′ə kō′), *n., pl.* **-cos.** any of several large, brightly colored birds of the family *Musophagidae,* of Africa, having a helmetlike crest. Also, **turaco.** [< WAfr]

Tou·raine (to͞o ren′; *Fr.* to͞o ʀen′), *n.* a former province in W France. *Cap.:* Tours.

Tou·rane (to͞o rän′), *n.* a seaport in E South Vietnam. 97,652 (est. 1957).

tour·bil·lion (to͝or bil′yən), *n.* **1.** a whirlwind or something resembling a whirlwind. **2.** a firework that rises spirally. **3.** *Horol.* a frame for the escapement of a timepiece, esp. a watch, geared to the going train in such a way as to rotate the escapement about once a minute in order to minimize positional error. Cf. **karrusel.** [late ME *turbilloun* < MF *to(u)rbillon* < LL **turbiliōnem,* dissimilated var. of **turbiniōnem,* acc. of **turbiniō* whirlwind. See TURBINE]

Tour·coing (to͞oʀ kwaɴ′), *n.* a city in N France, near the Belgian border. 90,105 (1962).

tour de force (to͝or′ də fōrs′, -fôrs′; *Fr.* to͞oʀ də fôʀs′), *pl.* **tours de force** (to͝or′ də fōrs′, -fôrs′; *Fr.* to͞oʀ də fôʀs′). **1.** an exceptional achievement by an artist, author, or the like, that is unlikely to be equaled by him or anyone else; stroke of genius: *Herman Melville's* Moby Dick *was a tour de force.* **2.** a particularly adroit maneuver or technique in handling a difficult situation: *The way the president got his bill through the senate was a tour de force.* **3.** a feat requiring unusual strength, skill, or ingenuity. [< F: feat of strength or skill]

Tou·ré (*Fr.* to͞o ʀā′), *n.* **Sé·kou** (sā′ko͞o), born 1922, African political leader: president of the Republic of Guinea since 1958.

tou·relle (to͞o ʀel′; *Eng.* to͝o rel′), *n., pl.* **-relles** (-ʀel′; *Eng.* -relz′). *French.* turret (defs. 1, 2).

tour en l'air (*Fr.* to͞oʀ äɴ leʀ′), *pl.* **tours en l'air** (*Fr.* to͞oʀ zäɴ leʀ′). *Ballet.* a turn executed in the air. [< F: turn in the air]

tour′ing car′, an open automobile designed for five or more passengers.

tour·ism (to͝or′iz əm), *n.* **1.** the activity or practice of touring, esp. for pleasure. **2.** the occupation of providing local transportation, entertainment, lodging, food, etc., for tourists. [TOUR + -ISM]

tour·ist (to͝or′ist), *n.* **1.** a person who makes a tour, esp. for pleasure. **2.** See **tourist class.** —*adv.* **3.** in tourist-class accommodations, or by tourist-class conveyance: *to travel tourist.* [TOUR + -IST]

our′ist car′, a railroad sleeping car, usually having seats that can be converted into berths.

our′ist class′, the least costly class of accommodations on regularly scheduled ships and airplanes. Cf. third class (def. 2). —**tour′ist-class′**, *adj., adv.*

our′ist court′, motel.

our′ist home′, a private home with rooms for rent, usually for one night, to tourists, travelers, etc.

our·is·tic (to͝o ris′tik), *adj.* of, pertaining to, or typical of tourists or tourism: *She embarked on her itinerary with high touristic fervor.* Also, **tour·is′ti·cal.** [TOURIST + -IC] —**tour·is′ti·cal·ly,** *adv.*

our·is·try (to͝or′i strē), *n.* **1.** tourists collectively: *the yearly invasion of American touristry.* **2.** the fact or practice of touring. [TOURIST + -RY]

our′ist trap′, a business, as a restaurant, shop, hotel, or the like, that takes advantage of tourists by overcharging.

our·ist·y (to͝or′i stē), *adj. Often Disparaging.* **1.** of or pertaining to tourists: *a touristy attitude.* **2.** popular with or catering to tourists: *The beach was touristy in summer.* [TOURIST + -Y[1]]

our je·té (*Fr.* to͞or zhə tā′), *pl.* **tours je·tés** (*Fr.* to͞or zhə tā′). *Ballet.* a movement in which the dancer leaps from one foot, makes a half turn in the air, and lands on the other foot. [< F: lit., flung turn]

our·ma·line (to͝or′mə lin, -lēn′), *n.* a mineral, essentially a complex silicate containing boron, aluminum, etc., usually black but having various colored, transparent varieties used as gems. Also, **tour·ma·lin** (to͝or′mə lin), **turmaline.** [earlier *tourmalin* < G *Turmalin* < Sinhalese *toramalli* carnelian; see -IN[2]] —**tour·ma·lin·ic** (to͝or′mə lin′ik), *adj.*

Tour·nai (to͝or nā′; *Fr.* to͞or nā′), *n.* a city in W Belgium, on the Scheldt River. 33,197 (est. 1964). Also, **Tour·nay′.**

our·na·ment (to͝or′nə mənt, tûr′-), *n.* **1.** a trial of skill in some game, in which competitors play a series of contests: *a chess tournament.* **2.** a meeting for contests in a variety of sports, as between teams of different nations. **3.** *Hist.* **a.** a contest or martial sport in which two opposing parties of mounted and armored combatants fought for a prize, with blunted weapons and in accordance with certain rules. **b.** a meeting at an appointed time and place for the performance of knightly exercises and sports. [ME *tornement* < OF *torneiement* < *tornei(er)* (to) TOURNEY + *-ment* -MENT]

our·ne·dos (to͝or′ni dō′, to͝or′ni dō′; *Fr.* to͞or nə-dō′), *n., pl.* **-dos** (-dōz′, -dōz′; *Fr.* -dō′). small slices of fillet of beef, round and thick, served with a variety of sauces and garnished. [< F < *tourn(er)* (to) TURN + *dos* (< L *dors(um)* back)]

Tour·neur (tûr′nər), *n.* **Cyril,** 1575?–1626, English dramatist.

our·ney (to͝or′nē, tûr′-), *n., pl.* **-neys,** *v.,* **-neyed, -ney·ing.** —*n.* **1.** a tournament. —*v.i.* **2.** to contend or engage in a tournament. [ME *tourney(en)* < OF *torneie(r)* < VL **tornidiare* to wheel, keep turning. See TURN]

our·ni·quet (tûr′nə kit, to͝or′-), *n.* **1.** *Surg.* any device for arresting bleeding by forcibly compressing a blood vessel, as a pad pressed down by a screw, a bandage tightened by twisting, etc. **2.** a device for pulling the parts of a wooden piece of furniture together, consisting of a pair of twisted cords passed around the parts. [< F < *tourn(er)* (to) TURN]

our·nois (to͝or nwä′; *Fr.* to͞or NWA′), *adj.* (of coins) minted in Tours, France: *livre tournois.* [late ME *Tourneys* < F *tournois* of Tours < L *turōnēnsis* < *Turōn(ēs)* TOURS + *-ēnsis* -ESE]

Tours (to͝or; *Fr.* to͞or), *n.* a city in and the capital of Indre-et-Loire, in W France, on the Loire River: Charles Martel defeated the Saracens near here A.D. 732. 96,472 (1962).

touse (touz; *Scot.* to͞oz, to͞os), *v.,* **toused, tous·ing,** *n. Chiefly Dial.* —*v.t.* **1.** to handle roughly; dishevel. —*v.i.* **2.** to struggle; tussle. —*n.* **3.** a commotion; rumpus. [ME *-t(o)use(n)*; c. OFris *tūsen* to rend, G *zausen* to tousle]

tou·sle (tou′zəl), *v.,* **-sled, -sling,** *n.* —*v.t.* **1.** to handle roughly. **2.** to disorder or dishevel: *The wind tousled our hair.* —*n.* **3.** a disheveled or rumpled mass, esp. of hair. **4.** a disordered, disheveled, or tangled condition. Also, **touzle.** [late ME *tousel;* c. LG *tūseln.* See TOUSE, -LE]

tou·sled (tou′zəld), *adj.* disordered or disheveled: *tousled hair; tousled clothes.* [TOUSLE + -ED[2]]

tous-les-mois (to͞o′lə mwä′), *n.* a large-grained farinaceous food resembling arrowroot, obtained from a South American canna, *Canna edulis,* and used in baby food. [< F: all the months, prob. alter. of French Antilles *toloman,* native name]

Tous·saint L'Ou·ver·ture (*Fr.* to͞o saN′ lo͞o vertyr′), (*Francis Dominique Toussaint*) 1743–1803, Haitian military and political leader.

tout (tout), *Informal.* —*v.i.* **1.** to solicit business, employment, votes, or the like importunately. **2.** *Horse Racing.* to act as a tout. —*v.t.* **3.** to solicit support for importunately. **4.** to describe flatteringly or proclaim: *a politician touted as a friend of the people.* **5.** to give a tip on (a race horse, etc.), esp. in order to indicate a probable winner. **6.** *Horse Racing.* **a.** to provide information on (a horse) running in a particular race, esp. for a fee. **b.** to spy on (a horse in training) in order to gain information for the purpose of betting. **7.** to watch; spy on. —*n.* **8.** one who solicits business, employment, support, or the like importunately. **9.** *Horse Racing.* **a.** one who gives information on a horse, esp. for a fee. **b.** *Chiefly Brit.* one who spies on a horse in training for the purpose of betting. [late ME *tute* to look out, peer; akin to OE *tōtian* to peep out. See TOOTSY]

tout à fait (to͞o tA fe′), *French.* entirely. [lit., wholly to fact]

tout à l'heure (to͞o tA lœr′), *French.* **1.** presently; very soon. **2.** just a moment ago; just now. [lit., wholly to the hour]

tout à vous (to͞o tA vo͞o′), *French.* sincerely yours. [lit., wholly to you]

tout com·pren·dre, c'est tout par·don·ner (to͞o kôN präN′drᵊ, se to͞o PAR dô nā′), *French.* to understand all is to forgive all.

tout de suite (to͞ot swēt′), *French.* at once; immediately. [lit., wholly consecutively]

tout en·sem·ble (to͞o täN säN′blᵊ), *French.* **1.** all together. **2.** the assemblage of parts or details, as in a work of art, considered as forming a whole; the ensemble.

tout·er (tou′tər), *n. Informal.* a tout. [TOUT + -ER[1]]

tout le monde (to͞olᵊ mōND′), *French.* the whole world; everyone; everybody.

tou·zle (tou′zəl), *v.t.,* **-zled, -zling,** *n.* tousle.

to·va·rich (to vä′rishch; *Eng.* tō vär′ish), *n. Russian.* **1.** comrade (used as a term of address by members of the Communist Party of the Soviet Union). **2.** one who lives in the U.S.S.R. Also, **to·va′rish, to·va′risch.**

To·vey (tō′vē), *n.* **Sir Donald Francis,** 1875–1940, English musical scholar, pianist, and composer.

tow[1] (tō), *v.t.* **1.** to drag or pull (a car, boat, etc.) by means of a rope, chain, or other device; haul. —*n.* **2.** act of towing. **3.** state of being towed. **4.** something being towed. **5.** a truck, boat, etc., which tows. **6.** a rope, chain, or other device for towing. **7.** See **ski tow. 8. in tow, a.** in the condition of being towed. **b.** under one's guidance; in one's charge. **c.** as a follower, admirer, or companion: *a playboy who always has a glamour girl in tow.* **9. under tow,** in the condition of being towed; in tow. [ME *towe(n),* OE *togian* to pull by force, drag; c. MHG *zogen* to draw, tug, drag. See TUG] —**tow′a·ble,** *adj.*
—**Syn. 1.** trail, draw, tug.

tow[2] (tō), *n.* **1.** the fiber of flax, hemp, or jute prepared for spinning by scutching. **2.** the shorter, less desirable flax fibers separated from line fibers in hackling. **3.** man-made filaments prior to spinning. —*adj.* **4.** made of tow: *tow cloth.* [ME; OE *tōw-* (in *tōwlīc* pertaining to thread, *tōwhūs* spinning house); akin to Icel *tō* wool]

tow[3] (tō), *n. Scot.* a rope. [late ME (Scot); OE *toh-* (in *tohline* towline); c. Icel *tog* towline. See TOW[1]]

tow·age (tō′ij), *n.* **1.** act of towing. **2.** state of being towed. **3.** the price or charge for towing. [TOW[1] + -AGE]

To·wan·da (tə won′də), *n.* a town in NE Pennsylvania. 4293 (1960).

to·ward (*prep.* tōrd, tôrd, tə wôrd′; *adj.* tōrd, tôrd), *prep.* Also, **to·wards′. 1.** in the direction of: *to walk toward the river.* **2.** with a view to obtaining or having; for: *They're saving money toward a new house.* **3.** in the area or vicinity of; near: *His cabin is toward the top of the hill.* **4.** turned to; facing: *His back was toward me.* **5.** shortly before; close to: *toward midnight.* **6.** as a help or contribution to: *to give money toward a person's expenses.* **7.** with respect to; as regards: *his attitude toward capital punishment.* —*adj.* **8.** that is to come soon; imminent. **9.** going on; in progress; afoot: *There is work toward.* **10.** propitious; favorable. **11.** *Obs.* promising or apt, as a student. **12.** *Obs.* compliant; docile. [ME; OE *tōweard.* See TO, -WARD]

to·ward·ly (tōrd′lē, tôrd′-), *adj. Archaic.* **1.** apt to learn; promising. **2.** docile; tractable. **3.** propitious; seasonable. [TOWARD + -LY] —**toward·li·ness, to′ward·ness,** *n.*

tow·boat (tō′bōt′), *n.* **1.** a diesel-powered or steam-powered boat used esp. on inland waterways to push groups of barges lashed to it in front or on one side or both. **2.** tugboat. [TOW[1] + BOAT]

tow′ car′, wrecker (def. 3).

tow·el (tou′əl), *n., v.,* **-eled, -el·ing** or (*esp. Brit.*) **-elled, -el·ling.** —*n.* **1.** an absorbent cloth or paper for wiping and drying something wet, esp. one for the hands, face, or body after washing or bathing. **2. throw in the towel,** *Slang.* to concede defeat; give up; yield: *He vowed he would never throw in the towel.* —*v.t.* **3.** to wipe or dry with a towel. **4.** *Brit. Slang.* to thrash; beat. [ME < OF *toaille* cloth for washing or wiping < WGmc **thwahliō* > OHG *dwahilla,* akin to *dwahal* bath; c. Goth *thwahl,* OE *thwæhl, thwēal,* etc.]

tow·el·ing (tou′ə ling), *n.* a narrow fabric of cotton or linen, in plain, twill, or huck weave, used for hand or dish towels. Also, *esp. Brit.,* **tow′el·ling.** [TOWEL + -ING[1]]

tow′el rack′, a rack consisting of one or more bars on which towels or washcloths are hung.

tow·er[1] (tou′ər), *n.* **1.** a building or structure high in proportion to its lateral dimensions, either isolated or forming part of a building. **2.** such a structure used as or intended for a stronghold, fortress, prison, etc. **3.** any of various fully enclosed fireproof housings for vertical communications, as staircases, between the stories of a building. **4.** any structure, contrivance, or object that resembles or suggests a tower. **5.** a tall, movable structure used in ancient and medieval warfare in storming a fortified place. —*v.i.* **6.** to rise or extend far upward, as a tower; reach or stand high: *The city's skyscrapers tower above its bustling humanity.* **7.** to rise above or surpass others: *He towers above his fellow students in mathematical ability.* **8.** *Falconry.* (of a hawk) to rise straight into the air; to ring up. [ME *tour,* earlier *tur, tor* < OF < L *turr(is)* (but note OE *tor(r),* var. of *tūr*) < Gk *týrris,* var. of *týrsis* tower] —**tow′er·less,** *adj.* —**tow′er·like′,** *adj.*

tow·er[2] (tō′ər), *n.* one who or that which tows.

tow′er bolt′. See **barrel bolt.**

tow·er·ing (tou′ər ing), *adj.* **1.** very high or tall; lofty: *a towering oak.* **2.** surpassing others; very great: *a towering figure in American poetry.* **3.** rising to an extreme degree of violence or intensity: *a towering rage.* **4.** beyond the proper or usual limits; inordinate; excessive: *towering pride; towering ambitions.* [TOWER[1] + -ING[2]] —**tow′er·ing·ly,** *adv.*
—**Syn. 1.** elevated. See **high.** —**Ant. 1.** short.

tow·er·man (tou′ər mən), *n., pl.* **-men. 1.** a person who works in a switch tower and, by means of a signal box, directs the movement of trains. **2.** a person in the control tower of an airport who directs incoming and outgoing flights of airplanes. [TOWER[1] + MAN]

tow·er-mill (tou′ər mil′), *n.* a windmill of which only the cap rotates to face the sails into the wind. [TOWER[1] + MILL[1]]

Tow′er of Ba′bel. See under **Babel.** (def. 1).

Tow′er of Lon′don, a historic fortress in London, England: originally a royal palace, later a prison, now a group of buildings containing an arsenal and museum, etc.

tow′er of si′lence, a circular stone platform, typically 30 feet in height, on which the Parsees of India leave their dead to be devoured by vultures. Also called **dakhma.**

tow·er·y (tou′ə rē), *adj.* **1.** having towers: *a towery city.* **2.** very tall; lofty: *towery oaks.* [TOWER[1] + -Y[1]]

tow·head (tō′hed′), *n.* **1.** a head of very light blond, almost white, hair. **2.** a person with such hair. **3.** a sand bar in a river, esp. a sand bar with a stand of cottonwood trees. [TOW[2] + HEAD] —**tow′-head′ed,** *adj.*

tow·hee (tou′hē, tō′hē), *n.* any of several long-tailed, North American finches of the genus *Pipilo.* Also called **tow′hee bun′ting.** [imit.]

tow·line (tō′lin′), *n.* a line, hawser, or the like, by which anything is or may be towed. [TOW[1] + LINE[1], but note OE *tohline;* see TOW[3]]

tow·mond (tou′mənd), *n. Scot.* twelvemonth. Also, **tow·mont** (tou′mənt). [late ME (Scot) *towlmonyth* < Scand; cf. Icel. *tōlfmānathr* twelvemonth]

town (toun), *n.* **1.** a thickly populated area, usually smaller than a city and larger than a village, having fixed boundaries and certain local powers of government. **2.** a densely populated area of considerable size, as a city or borough. **3.** *U.S.* (esp. in New England) a municipal corporation with less elaborate organization and powers than a city. **4.** *U.S.* a township; used in most States but not in New England. **5.** any urban area, as contrasted with its surrounding countryside. **6.** the inhabitants of a town; townspeople; citizenry. **7.** the particular town or city in mind or referred to: *living on the outskirts of town; to be out of town.* **8.** a nearby or neighboring city; the chief town or city in a district: *I am staying at a friend's apartment in town.* **9.** the main business or shopping area in a town or city; downtown. **10.** *Brit.* **a.** a village or hamlet in which a periodic market or fair is held. **b.** *Dial.* any village or hamlet. **11.** *Scot.* a farmstead. **12. go to town,** *Slang.* **a.** to be successful. **b.** to do or plan well, efficiently, or speedily: *The engineers really went to town on those plans.* **c.** to lose restraint or inhibition; overindulge. **13. on the town, a.** supported by the public charity of the state or community; on relief. **b.** *Slang.* in quest of entertainment in a city's night clubs, bars, etc.; out to have a good time: *a bunch of college boys out on the town.* **14. paint the town.** See **paint** (def. 16). —*adj.* **15.** of, pertaining to, characteristic of, or belonging to a town: *town laws; town government; town constable.* [ME *toun, tun,* OE *tūn* walled or fenced place (whence courtyard, farm, village); c. Icel *tūn* homefield, G *Zaun* fence, Ir *dūn* fort] —**town′less,** *adj.*
—**Syn. 1.** See **community.** —**Ant. 1.** country.

Town (toun), *n.* **Ith·i·el** (ith′ē əl), 1784–1844, U.S. architect.

town′ car′, an automobile having an enclosed rear seat separated by a glass partition from the open driver's seat.

town′ clerk′, a town official who keeps the records, issues licenses, calls the town meeting, and acts as secretary of a town.

town′ cri′er, a person employed by a town to make public announcements or proclamations, usually by shouting in the streets.

town·er (tou′nər), *n.* one who lives in a town or city. [TOWN + -ER[1]]

Townes (tounz), *n.* **Charles Hard,** born 1915, U.S. physicist and educator: Nobel prize for physics 1964.

town′ hall′, a hall or building belonging to a town, used for the transaction of the town's business, for public debate, etc., and often also as a place of public assembly.

town′ house′, 1. a house in the city, esp. as distinguished from a house in the country owned by the same person. **2.** a rather luxurious private house in a large city, occupied entirely by one family.

town·ish (tou′nish), *adj.* **1.** of or pertaining to qualities or features typical of or befitting a town or city. **2.** (of persons) characterized by the attitudes, opinions, manners, etc., of town or city living: *Although a country boy, he was thoroughly townish in outlook.* [ME *townysche.* See TOWN, -ISH[1]] —**town′ish·ly,** *adv.* —**town′ish·ness,** *n.*

town′ meet′ing, 1. a general meeting of the inhabitants of a town. **2.** a meeting of the qualified voters of a town for the transaction of public business.

town′ plan′ning. See **city planning.** —**town′ plan′ner.**

town·scape (toun′skāp′), *n.* **1.** a scene, either pictorial or natural, of a town or city: *The townscape from this window is pretty dismal. He paints nothing but townscapes these days.* **2.** the planning and building of structures in a town or city, with special concern for aesthetically pleasing results. [TOWN + *-scape,* modeled on LANDSCAPE]

Town′send av′alanche (toun′zənd), *Physics.* avalanche (def. 3). [named after J. S. E. *Townsend* (1868–1957), Irish physicist]

Town′send plan′, *U.S.* a pension plan, proposed in 1934 but never passed, that would have awarded $200 monthly to persons over 60 who were no longer gainfully employed, provided that such allowance was spent in the U.S. within 30 days. [named after Francis E. *Townsend* (1867–1960), American reformer, its proposer]

Town′send's sol′itaire, a brownish bird, *Myadestes townsendi,* of western North America. [named after John Kirk Townsend (1809–51), American ornithologist]

towns·folk (tounz′fōk′), *n.pl.* townspeople. [TOWN + 'S[1] + FOLK]

Town′shend Acts′ (toun′zənd), *Amer. Hist.* acts of the British Parliament in 1767, esp. the act that placed duties on tea, paper, lead, paint, etc., imported into the American colonies. [named after Charles *Townshend* (1725–67), English statesman, their sponsor]

town·ship (toun′ship), *n.* **1.** (in the U.S. and Canada) an administrative division of a county, with varying corporate powers. **2.** (in U.S. surveys of public land) a region or district approximately six miles square, containing 36 sections. **3.** *Eng. Hist.* **a.** one of the local divisions or districts of a large parish, each containing a village or small town, usually with a church of its own. **b.** the manor, parish, etc., itself. **c.** its inhabitants. **4.** *Australian.* **a.** a small town or settlement serving as the business center of a rural area. **b.** the business center of a town or suburb. [late ME *township* community, OE *tūnscipe* village community. See TOWN, -SHIP]

town′ship line′, one of two parallel lines running east and west that define the north and south borders of a township. Cf. **range line, township** (def. 2).

towns·man (tounz′mən), *n., pl.* **-men.** **1.** a native or inhabitant of a town. **2.** a native or inhabitant of one's own or the same town. **3.** (in New England) a selectman. [ME, OE *tūnesman* fellow member of a township. See TOWN, 'S[1], MAN[1]]

towns·peo·ple (tounz′pē′pəl), *n.pl.* **1.** the inhabitants or citizenry of a town. **2.** people who were raised in a town or city (in contrast with country-bred people). Also called **townsfolk.** [TOWN + 'S[1] + PEOPLE]

Towns·ville (tounz′vil), *n.* a seaport on the E coast of Queensland, in E Australia. 51,143 (1961).

towns·wom·an (tounz′wo͝om′ən), *n., pl.* **-wom·en.** a woman inhabitant of a town. [TOWN + 'S[1] + WOMAN]

town talk (toun′tôk′ *for 1;* toun′tôk′ *for 2*), **1.** the usual talk, gossip, or rumors, as in a village, town, etc.: *The excitement about the new power plant was merely town talk.* **2.** the subject of gossip, rumor, or the like: *They've been the town talk ever since their elopement.*

town·wear (toun′wâr′), *n.* tailored, usually dark-colored, and somewhat formal dress, appropriate for business, the theater, etc. [TOWN + WEAR]

tow·path (tō′path′, -päth′), *n., pl.* **-paths** (-pathz′, -päthz′). a path along the bank of a canal or river, for use in towing boats. [TOW[1] + PATH]

tow·rope (tō′rōp′), *n.* a rope, hawser, or the like, used in towing boats. [TOW[1] + ROPE]

tow′rope horse′power, *Naval Archit.* See **effective horsepower.**

tow·ser (tou′zər), *n.* **1.** a big dog. **2.** *Informal.* a big, crude person, esp. one who is very energetic: *He is a towser for work and perfect for the job.* [TOUSE + -ER[1]]

Tow·son (tou′sən), *n.* a town in central Maryland, near Baltimore. 19,090 (1960).

tow′ truck′, wrecker (def. 3). Also called **tow car.**

tow·y (tō′ē), *adj.* of the nature of or resembling the fiber tow. [TOW[2] + -Y[1]]

tox-, var. of **toxo-** before a vowel: *toxemia.*

tox., toxicology.

tox·al·bu·min (tok′sal byo͞o′mən), *n.* *Biochem.* any poisonous protein occurring in certain bacterial cultures or plants and in snake venoms. [TOX- + ALBUMIN]

tox·a·phene (tok′sə fēn′), *n.* *Chem.* an amber, waxy, water-insoluble solid, whose principal constituent is chlorinated camphene, used as an insecticide and as a rodenticide. [TOX- + (C)A(M)PHENE]

tox·e·mi·a (tok sē′mē ə), *n.* *Pathol.* a condition of illness due to a presence in the bloodstream of toxins, caused by the ingestion of foods contaminated with poisons, by self-produced toxins, as in toxemia of pregnancy, or especially by toxic metabolic by-products from pathogenic microorganisms of a local infection. Also, **tox·ae′mi·a.** [TOX- + -EMIA]

tox·e·mic (tok sē′mik, -sem′ik), *adj.* *Pathol.* **1.** pertaining to or of the nature of toxemia. **2.** affected with toxemia. Also, **tox·ae′mic.** [TOXEM(IA) + -IC]

tox·ic (tok′sik), *adj.* **1.** of, pertaining to, affected with, or caused by a toxin or poison: *a toxic condition.* **2.** acting as or having the effect of a poison; poisonous: *a toxic drug.* [< LL *toxic(us)* poisonous, n. use of L *toxicum* poison < Gk *toxikón* (orig. short for *toxikòn phármakon,* lit., bow poison, i.e., poison used on arrows), equiv. to *tóx(on)* bow + *-ikon,* neut. of *-ikos* -IC] —**tox′i·cal·ly,** *adv.*

toxic-, var. of **toxico-** before a vowel: *toxicity.*

tox·i·cant (tok′sə kənt), *adj.* **1.** poisonous; toxic. —*n.* **2.** a poison. [< ML *toxicant-* (s. of *toxicāns*), prp. of *toxicāre* to poison. See TOXIC, -ANT]

tox·i·ca·tion (tok′sə kā′shən), *n.* poisoning. [< ML *toxicātiōn-* (s. of *toxicātiō*), equiv. to *toxicāt(us)* poisoned (ptp. of *toxicāre;* see TOXIC, -ATE[1]) + *-iōn-* -ION]

tox·ic·i·ty (tok sis′i tē), *n., pl.* **-ties.** quality, relative degree, or specific degree of being toxic or poisonous: *an experiment to determine the toxicity of arsenic in relation to other poisons.* [TOXIC + -ITY]

toxico-, a combining form of **toxic:** *toxicology.* Also, *esp. before a vowel,* **toxic-.** Cf. **toxo-.**

tox·i·co·gen·ic (tok′sə kō jen′ik), *adj.* *Pathol.* generating or producing toxic products or poisons. [TOXICO- + -GENIC]

toxicol., toxicology.

tox·i·col·o·gy (tok′sə kol′ə jē), *n.* the science dealing with the effects, antidotes, detection, etc., of poisons. [TOXICO- + -LOGY] —**tox·i·co·log·i·cal** (tok′sə kə loj′i kəl), **tox′i·co·log′ic,** *adj.* —**tox′i·co·log′i·cal·ly,** *adv.* —**tox′i·col′o·gist,** *n.*

tox·i·co·sis (tok′sə kō′sis), *n.* *Pathol.* an abnormal condition produced by the action of a poison. [TOXIC + -OSIS]

tox′ic-shock′ syn′drome (tok′sik shok′), a rare, sometimes fatal, disease contracted by and developing rapidly in women, esp. those under 30, who use tampons during menstruation: characterized by high fever, vomiting, and diarrhea, and thought to be caused by the release and rapid spread of bacterial infection in the vagina. Also called **TSS.**

tox·in (tok′sin), *n.* any of a group of poisonous, usually unstable compounds generated by microorganisms or plants or of animal origin. Certain toxins are produced by specific pathogenic microorganisms and are the causative agents in various diseases, as tetanus, diphtheria, etc.; some are capable of inducing the production of antibodies in certain animals. Cf. **antitoxin, endotoxin, exotoxin, phytotoxin, ptomaine, toxoid, venom, zootoxin.** [TOX(IC) + -IN[2]]
—**Syn.** See **poison.**

tox·in-an·ti·tox·in (tok′sin an′ti tok′sin, -an′tē-), *n.* *Immunol.* a mixture of toxin and antitoxin, formerly used to induce active immunity against certain diseases, esp. diphtheria.

tox·i·pho·bi·a (tok′sə fō′bē ə), *n.* *Psychiatry.* an abnormal fear of being poisoned. [TOXI(CO)- + -PHOBIA]

toxo-, var. of **toxico-:** *toxoplasma.* Also, *esp. before a vowel,* **tox-.**

tox·oid (tok′soid), a toxin rendered nontoxic by treatment with chemical agents or by physical means and used for administration into the body in order to produce specific immunity by stimulating the production of antibodies. [TOX- + -OID]

tox·oph·i·lite (tok sof′ə līt′), *n.* a devotee of archery; archer. [*Toxophil(us)* bow-lover (coined by Roger Ascham < Gk *tóxo(n)* bow + *-philos* -PHILE) + -ITE[1]] —**tox·oph·i·lit·ic** (tok sof′ə lit′ik), *adj.* —**tox·oph′i·ly,** *n.*

tox·o·plas·mo·sis (tok′sō plaz mō′sis), *n.* *Vet. Pathol.* an infection caused by the protozoan parasite *Toxoplasma gondii,* affecting dogs, cats, and other animals, and sometimes man. [TOXO- + -PLASM + -OSIS] —**tox′o·plas′mic,** *adj.*

tox·o·so·zin (tok′sō sō′zin), *n.* *Biochem.* any sozin that destroys bacterial poisons. [TOXO- + SOZIN]

toy (toi), *n.* **1.** an object, often a small representation of something familiar, as an animal, object, person, etc., for children or others to play with; plaything. **2.** a thing or matter of little or no value or importance; a trifle. **3.** a small article of little value but prized as a souvenir or for some other special reason; trinket; knickknack; bauble. **4.** something diminutive, esp. in comparison with like objects. **5.** an animal of a breed or variety noted for smallness of size: *The winning poodle at the dog show was a toy.* **6.** a close-fitting cap of linen or wool, with flaps coming down to the shoulders, formerly worn by women in Scotland. **7.** a simple, light piece of music, esp. of 16th or 17th century England, written for the virginal. **8.** *Obs.* amorous dallying. —*adj.* **9.** made or designed for use as a toy: *a toy gun.* **10.** of or resembling a toy, esp. in size. —*v.i.* **11.** to play; sport: *He toyed with his soldiers all morning.* **12.** to act idly or without seriousness; trifle: *Stop toying with your food!* **13.** to dally amorously; to flirt or make love without serious intention. [ME *toye* dalliance] —**toy′er,** *n.* —**toy′less,** *adj.* —**toy′like′,** *adj.*
—**Syn. 12.** loiter, delay, dawdle. **13.** jest.

To·ya·ma (tô′yä mä′), *n.* a city on W Honshu, in central Japan. 217,550 (1964).

toy′ dog′, one of any of several breeds of very small dogs, as the Yorkshire terrier, Toy spaniel, etc.

toy′ fish′, any of various tiny aquarium fishes.

Toyn·bee (toin′bē), *n.* **Arnold J(oseph),** 1889–1975, English historian.

To·yo·ha·shi (tô′yô hä′shē), *n.* a seaport on S Honshu, in central Japan. 228,734 (1964).

to·yon (tō′yən), *n.* an evergreen, rosaceous shrub or small tree, *Photinia* (*Heteromeles*) *arbutifolia,* of California, having white flowers and bright-red berries. Also called **Christmasberry.** [var. of *tollon* < MexSp]

tp., **1.** township. **2.** troop.

t.p., **1.** title page. **2.** *Survey.* See **turning point** (def. 3).

tpd, tons per day.

tph, tons per hour.

tpi, **1.** teeth per inch. **2.** turns per inch.

TPI test, *Med.* the treponema pallidum immobilization test, a highly specific test for syphilis.

tpm, tons per minute.

tr., **1.** tare. **2.** tincture. **3.** trace. **4.** train. **5.** transaction. **6.** transitive. **7.** translated. **8.** translation. **9.** translator. **10.** transpose. **11.** treasurer. **12.** *Music.* trill. **13.** trustee.

T.R., **1.** in the time of the king. [< L *tempore regis*] **2.** See **Roosevelt, Theodore. 3.** tons registered. **4.** trust receipt.

tra·be·at·ed (trā′bē ā′tid), *adj.* *Archit.* **1.** constructed with a beam or on the principle of a beam, as an entablature or flat ceiling. **2.** denoting a form of architecture or system of construction employing beams or lintels exclusively. Also, **tra·be·ate** (trā′bē it, -āt′). [*trabeat(ion)* structure with beams (< L *trabē(s)* beam + -ATION) + -ED[3]] —**tra′be·a′tion,** *n.*

tra·bec·u·la (trə bek′yə lə), *n., pl.* **-lae** (-lē′). **1.** *Anat., Bot.* a structural part resembling a small beam or crossbar. **2.** *Bot.* one of the projections from the cell wall which extends across the cell cavity of the ducts of certain plants, or the plate of cells across the cavity of the sporangium of a moss. [< NL; in L: little beam, equiv. to *trabē(s)* beam + *-cula* -CULE] —**tra·bec′u·lar, tra·bec·u·late** (trə bek′yə lit, -lāt′), *adj.*

Trab·zon (*Turkish.* träb zôn′), *n.* official name of **Trebizond.**

trace[1] (trās), *n., v.,* **traced, trac·ing.** —*n.* **1.** a surviving mark, sign, or evidence of the former existence, influence, or action of some agent or event; vestige: *traces of a high civilization among the ruins.* **2.** a barely discernible indication or evidence of some quantity, quality, characteristic, expression, etc.: *the trace of a smile; a trace of anger in his tone.* **3.** an extremely small amount of some chemical component: *a trace of copper in its composition.* **4. traces,** the series of footprints left by an animal. **5.** the track left by the passage of a man, animal, or object: *the trace of his skates on the ice.* **6.** *Meteorol.* precipitation of less than .005 in. **7.** a trail or path, esp. through wild or open territory, made by the passage of people, animals, or vehicles. **8.** Also called **engram.** *Psychol.* a structural change in the nervous system effected by an experience, considered to be the physical basis of memory. **9.** a tracing, drawing, or sketch of something. **10.** a lightly drawn line, as the record drawn by a self-registering instrument. **11.** *Math.* the intersection of two planes, or of a plane and a surface. **12.** the visible line or lines produced on the screen of a cathode ray tube by the deflection of the electron beam. **13.** *Obs.* a footprint. —*v.t.* **14.** to follow the footprints, track, or traces of. **15.** to follow, make out, or determine the course or line of, esp. by going backward from the latest evidence, nearest existence, etc.: *to trace a river to its source; to trace one's ancestry to the Pilgrims.* **16.** to follow (footprints, evidence, the history or course of something, etc.). **17.** to follow the course, development, or history of: *to trace a political movement.* **18.** to ascertain by investigation; find out; discover: *The police were unable to trace the whereabouts of the missing girl.* **19.** to draw (a line, outline, figure, etc.). **20.** to make a plan, diagram, or map of. **21.** to copy (a drawing, plan, etc.) by following the lines of the original on a superimposed transparent sheet. **22.** to mark or ornament with lines, figures, etc. **23.** to make an impression or imprinting of (a design, pattern, etc.). **24.** (of a self-registering instrument) to print in a curved, broken, or wavy-lined manner. **25.** to put down in writing. —*v.i.* **26.** to go back in history, ancestry, or origin; date back in time: *Her family traces back to Paul Revere.* **27.** to follow a course, trail, etc.; make one's way. **28.** (of a self-registering instrument) to print a record in a curved, broken, or wavy-lined manner. [late ME < MF *trac(i)e(r)* < VL **tractiāre,* deriv. of L *tractus,* ptp. of *trahere* to draw, drag. See TRACT[1]]
—**Syn. 1.** TRACE, VESTIGE agree in denoting marks or signs of something, usually of the past. TRACE, the broader term, denotes any mark or slight indication of something past or present: *a trace of ammonia in water.* VESTIGE is more limited and refers to some slight, though actual, remains of something that no longer exists: *vestiges of one's former wealth.* **2.** hint, suggestion, taste, touch. **5.** spoor, trail, record. **14.** trail. —**Ant. 3.** abundance, plethora.

trace[2] (trās), *n.* **1.** either of the two straps, ropes, or chains by which a carriage, wagon, or the like is drawn by a harnessed horse or other draft animal. See illus. under **harness. 2.** *Obs.* a piece in a machine, as a bar, transferring the movement of one part to another part, being hinged to each. **3. kick over the traces,** to throw off restraint; become independent or defiant: *He kicked over the traces and ran off to join the navy.* [ME *trais* < MF, pl. of *trait* strap for harness, action of drawing < L *tract(us)* a drawing, dragging; see TRACT[1]]

trace·a·ble (trā′sə bəl), *adj.* **1.** capable of being traced. **2.** logically attributable or ascribable (usually fol. by *to*): *Their winning record was traceable to good coaching.* [TRACE[1] + -ABLE] —**trace′a·bil′i·ty, trace′a·ble·ness,** *n.* —**trace′a·bly,** *adv.*

trace′ el′ement, *Biochem.* an element found in plants and animals in minute quantities and believed to be a critical factor in physiological processes. Also called **microelement.**

trace·less (trās′lis), *adj.* not having or leaving a trace: *a traceless crime.* [TRACE[1] + -LESS] —**trace′less·ly,** *adv.*

trac·er (trā′sər), *n.* **1.** one who or that which traces. **2.** a person whose business or work is the tracing of missing property, parcels, persons, etc. **3.** an inquiry form sent from point to point to trace a missing shipment, parcel, or the like, as in a transportation system. **4.** any of various devices for tracing drawings, plans, etc. **5.** Also called **trac′er ammuni′tion.** ammunition containing a chemical substance that causes a projectile to trail smoke or fire so as to make its path visible and indicate a target to other firers, esp. at night. **6.** the chemical substance contained in such ammunition. **7.** a substance, usually radioactive, traced through a biological, chemical, or physical system in order to study the system. [TRACE[1] + -ER[1]]

trac′er bul′let, a bullet containing a tracer so that when fired a trail of smoke or fire marks its path, used esp. in automatic weapons.

trac·er·ied (trā′sə rēd), *adj.* ornamented or decorated with tracery. [TRACERY + -ED[3]]

trac·er·y (trā′sə rē), *n., pl.* **-er·ies. 1.** ornamental work consisting of ramified ribs, bars, or the like, as in the upper part of a Gothic window, in panels, screens, etc. **2.** any delicate, interlacing work of lines, threads, etc., as in carving, embroidery, etc.; network. [TRACE[1] + -ERY]

Window tracery

trache-, var. of **tracheo-** before a vowel: *tracheitis.*

tra·che·a (trā′kē ə *or, esp. Brit.,* trə kē′ə), *n., pl.* **tra·che·ae** (trā′kē ē′ *or, esp. Brit.,* trə kē′ē). **1.** *Anat., Zool.* the tube in man and other air-breathing vertebrates extending from the larynx to the bronchi, serving as the principal passage for conveying air to and from the lungs; the windpipe. See diag. under **lung. 2.** (in insects and other arthropods) one of the air-conveying tubes of the respiratory system. **3.** *Bot.* vessel (def. 5). [< ML < Gk *trācheia,* short for *artēría trācheîa* rough artery, i.e. windpipe]

tra·che·al (trā′kē əl *or, esp. Brit.,* trə kē′əl), *adj.* **1.** *Anat., Zool.* pertaining to or connected with the trachea or tracheae. **2.** *Bot.* of the nature of or composed of tracheae or vessels. [TRACHE(A) + -AL[1]]

tra·che·ate (trā′kē āt′, -it *or, esp. Brit.,* trə kē′it), *adj.* **1.** (of an arthropod) having tracheae. —*n.* **2.** a tracheate arthropod. [< NL *Tracheāt(a)* name of the class, n. use of neut. pl. of *tracheātus.* See TRACHE-, -ATE[1]]

tra·che·a·tion (trā′kē ā′shən), *n.* the arrangement of tracheae in insects and other arthropods. [TRACHE(A) + -ATION]

tra·che·id (trā′kē id), *n.* *Bot.* an elongated, tapering xylem cell having lignified, pitted, intact walls, adapted for conduction and support. Cf. **vessel** (def. 5). [TRACHE(A) + -ID[3]] —**tra·che·i·dal** (trə kē′i dəl, trā′kē id′əl), *adj.*

tra·che·i·tis (trā′kē ī′tis), *n.* *Pathol.* inflammation of the trachea. [TRACHE(A) + -ITIS]

tra·che·li·um (trə kē′lē əm), *n., pl.* **-li·a** (-lē ə). (in classical architecture) any member between the hypotrachelium and the capital of a column. [< NL < Gk *trāchēl(os)* neck + L *-ium* neut. n. suffix]

tracheo-, a combining form of **trachea:** *tracheotomy.* Also, *esp. before a vowel,* **trache-.**

tra·che·o·bron·chi·al (trā′kē ō brong′kē əl), *adj.* *Anat.* of, pertaining to, or affecting the trachea and bronchi. [TRACHEO- + BRONCHIAL]

tra·che·o·phyte (trā′kē ə fīt′), *n.* any plant of the division *Tracheophyta,* characterized by a vascular system and comprising the pteridophytes and spermatophytes. [< NL *Tracheophyta* name of the division. See TRACHEO-, -PHYTE]

tra·che·os·co·py (trā′kē os′kə pē), *n.* *Med.* examination of the interior of the trachea, as with a laryngoscope. [TRACHEO- + -SCOPY] —**tra·che·o·scop·ic** (trā′kē ə skop′ik), *adj.* —**tra′che·os′co·pist,** *n.*

tra·che·os·to·my (trā′kē os′tə mē), *n., pl.* **-mies.** *Surg.* the formation of an artificial opening, either permanent or semipermanent, into the trachea. [TRACHEO- + -STOMY]

tra·che·ot·o·my (trā′kē ot′ə mē), *n., pl.* **-mies.** *Surg.* the operation of cutting into the trachea. [TRACHEO- + -TOMY] —**tra′che·ot′o·mist,** *n.*

tra·chle (träʹkhəl), *n., v.* **-chled, -chling.** *Scot.* —*n.* **1.** an exhausting effort, esp. walking or working. **2.** an exhausted or bedraggled person. —*v.t.* **3.** to fatigue; tire; wear out. **4.** to bedraggle. Also, **trauchle.** [? < WFlem *tragel(en)* (to) walk laboriously (intr.) drag (trans.)]

tra·cho·ma (trə kō′mə), *n. Ophthalm.* a contagious inflammation of the conjunctiva and cornea, characterized by the formation of granulations and scarring. [< Gk *trā́khōma* roughness, equiv. to *trākh(ýs)* rough + *-ōma* -OMA] —**tra·chom·a·tous** (trə kom′ə təs, -kō′mə-), *adj.*

trachy-, a learned borrowing from Greek meaning "rough," used in the formation of compound words: *trachycarpous.* [comb. form repr. Gk *trākhýs*]

tra·chy·ba·salt (trā′kē bə sôlt′, -bas′ôlt, -bā′sôlt, trak′ē-), *n.* a fine-grained igneous rock containing sanidine and calcic plagioclase, occurring in lava. [TRACHY- + BASALT]

tra·chy·car·pous (trā′kē kär′pəs, trak′ē-), *adj. Bot.* having rough-skinned fruit. [TRACHY- + -CARPOUS]

tra·chy·sper·mous (trā′kē spûr′məs, trak′ē-), *adj. Bot.* having seeds with a rough coat. [TRACHY- + -SPERMOUS]

tra·chyte (trā′kīt, trak′īt), *n.* a fine-grained igneous rock consisting essentially of alkali feldspar and one or more subordinate minerals, as hornblende or mica: the volcanic equivalent of syenite. [< F < Gk *trākhýt(ēs)* roughness] —**trach·y·toid** (trak′i toid′, trā′ki-), *adj.*

tra·chyt·ic (trə kit′ik), *adj. Petrog.* of or pertaining to the nearly parallel arrangement of feldspar crystals in the groundmass of volcanic rocks. [TRACHYTE + -IC]

trac·ing (trā′siŋ), *n.* **1.** the act of one who or that which traces. **2.** that which is produced by tracing. **3.** a copy of a drawing, map, plan, etc., made by tracing on a transparent sheet placed over the original. **4.** the record made by a self-registering instrument. [TRACE[1] + -ING[1]]

trac′ing pa′per, a thin, transparent paper for tracing.

trac′ing tape′, (on a building site) one of several lines stretched between batter boards to outline the foundations.

track (trak), *n.* **1.** a structure consisting of a pair of parallel lines of rails with their crossties, etc., to provide a road for railroad trains. **2.** a wheel rut. **3.** evidence, as a mark or a series of marks, that something has passed. **4.** Usually, **tracks.** footprints or other marks left by an animal, person, or vehicle: *a lion's tracks; car tracks.* **5.** a path made or beaten by or as by the feet of men or animals; trail: *to follow the track of a murderer.* **6.** a line of travel or motion: *the track of a bird.* **7.** a course or route followed. **8.** a course of action, conduct, or procedure: *He couldn't solve the problem because he started out on the wrong track.* **9.** a path or course made or laid out for some particular purpose. **10.** a series or sequence of events or ideas. **11.** something associated with making a track, as the wheel span of a vehicle, the tread of a tire, etc. **12.** *Sports.* **a.** a course laid out for running or racing. **b.** the group of sports performed on a track, as running or hurdling, as distinguished from field events. **c.** both track and field events as a whole. **13.** *Auto.* the distance between the centers of the treads of either the front or rear wheels of a vehicle, measured along the ground in inches. **14.** *Computer Technol.* a series of binary cells on the magnetic drum or tape of a computer, so arranged as to allow data to be read from one cell at a time. **15. in one's tracks,** *Informal.* in the spot in which one is or is standing at the moment: *He stopped dead in his tracks, listening for the sound to be repeated.* **16. keep track of,** to follow the course or progress of; keep informed about: *She kept track of some of her college friends and met one of them for lunch every week.* **17. lose track of,** to fail to keep informed about; neglect to keep a record: *He soon lost track of how much money he had spent.* **18. make tracks,** *Informal.* to go or depart in a hurry: *to make tracks for the store before closing time.* **19. off the track,** departing from the objective or the subject at hand; astray: *She can't tell a story without getting off the track.* **20. on the track of,** in search or pursuit of; close upon: *They are on the track of a solution to the problem.* **21. on the wrong** or **right side of the tracks,** from a poor or wealthy part of a community or of society: *The magazine revealed that she had been born on the wrong side of the tracks.* —*v.t.* **22.** to follow or pursue the track, traces, or footprints of. **23.** to follow (a track, course, etc.). **24.** to make one's way through; traverse. **25.** *U.S.* **a.** to leave footprints on (often fol. by *up* or *on*): *Don't track up my clean floor with your muddy shoes!* **b.** to make a trail of footprints with (dirt, snow, or the like): *The dog tracked mud all over the living room rug.* **26.** to furnish with a track or tracks, as for railroad trains. **27.** *Railroads.* to have (a certain distance) between wheels, runners, rails, etc. —*v.i.* **28.** to follow or pursue a track or trail. **29.** to run in the same track, as the wheels of a vehicle. **30.** to be in alignment, as one gearwheel with another. **31.** to have a specified span between wheels or runners: *The car's wheels track about five feet.* **32.** *Motion Pictures, Television.* dolly (def. 8). **33. track down,** to pursue until caught or captured; follow: *tracking down a killer.* [late ME *trak* < MF *trac,* perh. < Scand; cf. Icel *traðk* trodden spot, Norw *trakke* to trample; akin to TREAD] —**track′a·ble,** *adj.* —**track′er,** *n.*

—**Syn. 3.** trace, record, spoor. **22.** stalk, hunt.

track·age (trak′ij), *n.* **1.** the whole quantity of track owned by a railroad. **2.** the right of one railroad company to use the tracks of another. **3.** the money paid for this right. [TRACK + -AGE]

track′ and field′, a sport, performed indoors or outdoors, made up of several events, as running, pole-vaulting, broad-jumping, etc.

track-and-field (trak′ən fēld′), *adj.* of, pertaining to, or participating in the sports of running, pole-vaulting, broad-jumping, etc.: *Jim Thorpe was perhaps the greatest of all track-and-field athletes.*

track′ brake′, a mechanism that slows or stops a vehicle by pressing against the track rather than the wheels.

track′ing shot′, *Motion Pictures, Television.* See **dolly shot.**

track·lay·er (trak′lā′ər), *n.* See **section hand.** [TRACK + LAYER]

track·less (trak′lis), *adj.* **1.** without a track, as a snow-covered meadow. **2.** not making or leaving a track: *The horsemen knew that the rain would render their route trackless.* **3.** not on tracks: *a trackless vehicle.* [TRACK + -LESS] —**track′less·ly,** *adv.* —**track′less·ness,** *n.*

track′less trol′ley. See **trolley bus.**

track·man (trak′mən), *n., pl.* **-men.** *U.S.* **1.** a man who assists in inspecting, installing, or maintaining railroad tracks. **2.** trackwalker. [TRACK + MAN[1]]

track′ meet′, a series of athletic contests such as running, jumping, etc.

track′ shoe′, 1. the part of a track-brake mechanism that slows or stops a vehicle. **2.** a light, heelless, leather shoe having either steel spikes for use outdoors on a cinder or dirt track, or a rubber sole for use indoors on a board floor.

track′ shot′. See **dolly shot.**

track·walk·er (trak′wô′kər), *n. U.S.* a man employed to walk over and inspect a certain section of railroad track at intervals. Also called **trackman.** [TRACK + WALKER]

tract[1] (trakt), *n.* **1.** an expanse or area of land, water, etc.; region; stretch. **2.** *Anat.* **a.** a definite region or area of the body, esp. a group, series, or system of related parts or organs: *the digestive tract.* **b.** a bundle of nerve fibers having a common origin and destination. **3.** a stretch or period of time; interval; lapse. **4.** *Rom. Cath. Ch.* an anthem consisting of verses of Scripture, sung after the gradual in the Mass from Septuagesima until the day before Easter and on certain other occasions, taking the place of the alleluias and the verse which ordinarily accompany the gradual. **5.** *Ornith.* a pteryla. [late ME *tracte* < L *tract(us)* stretch (of space or time), a drawing out, n. use of *tractus,* ptp. of *trahere* to draw]

—**Syn. 1.** district, territory.

tract[2] (trakt), *n.* a brief treatise, pamphlet, or leaflet for general distribution, usually on a religious or political topic. [late ME *tracte* < L *tract(ātus)* TRACTATE]

—**Syn.** essay, homily, disquisition.

trac·ta·ble (trak′tə bəl), *adj.* **1.** easily managed; docile; yielding: *tractable persons; a tractable disposition.* **2.** easily worked, shaped, or otherwise handled; malleable. [< L *tractābil(is),* equiv. to *tractā(re)* (to) handle, deal with (freq. of *trahere* to draw) + *-bilis* -BLE] —**trac′ta·bil′i·ty, trac′ta·ble·ness,** *n.* —**trac′ta·bly,** *adv.*

—**Syn. 1.** manageable, willing, governable. —**Ant. 1.** stubborn.

Trac·tar·i·an (trak târ′ē ən), *n.* **1.** one of the supporters of Tractarianism; a supporter of the Oxford movement. —*adj.* **2.** of or pertaining to Tractarianism or Tractarians. [TRACT[2] + -ARIAN]

Trac·tar·i·an·ism (trak târ′ē ə niz′əm), *n.* the religious opinions and principles of the Oxford movement, esp. in its early phase, given in a series of ninety papers called *Tracts for the Times,* published at Oxford, England, 1833–41. [TRACTARIAN + -ISM]

trac·tate (trak′tāt), *n.* a treatise; tract. [late ME < L *tractāt(us)* handling, treatment, treatise, n. use of *tractātus,* ptp. of *tractāre* to handle, treat, freq. of *trahere* to draw]

trac·tile (trak′til), *adj.* **1.** that can be drawn out in length; ductile. **2.** capable of being drawn. [< LL *tractil(is).* See TRACT[1], -ILE] —**trac·til′i·ty,** *n.*

trac·tion (trak′shən), *n.* **1.** the adhesive friction of a body on some surface, as a wheel on a rail or a tire on a road. **2.** action of drawing a body, vehicle, train, or the like, along a surface, as a road, track, railroad, waterway, etc. **3.** *Med.* the deliberate and prolonged pulling of a muscle, organ, or the like, as by weights, to correct dislocation, relieve pressure, etc. **4.** transportation by means of railroads. **5.** act of drawing or pulling. **6.** state of being drawn. **7.** attracting power or influence; attraction. [< ML *tractiōn-* (s. of *tractiō*) act of drawing. See TRACT[1], -ION] —**trac′tion·al,** *adj.*

trac′tion en′gine, a locomotive operating on surfaces other than tracks and pulling heavy loads, as fallen logs.

trac·tive (trak′tiv), *adj.* having or exerting traction; drawing. [< L *tract(us)* (see TRACT[1]) + -IVE]

trac′tive ef′fort, the force, measured in pounds, exerted by a locomotive or other powered vehicle on its driving wheels.

trac·tor (trak′tər), *n.* **1.** a powerful motor-driven vehicle with large, heavy treads, used for pulling farm machinery, other vehicles, etc. **2.** a short truck with a body containing only a cab for the driver, used to haul detachable trailers. **3.** one who or that which draws or pulls. **4.** something used for drawing or pulling. **5.** a self-propelled vehicle for pulling a trailer or semitrailer to form a tractor-trailer. **6.** a propeller mounted at the front of an airplane, thus exerting a pull. **7.** Also called **trac′tor air′plane.** an airplane with a propeller so mounted. [< ML; see TRACT[1], -OR[2]]

trac·tor-trail·er (trak′tər trā′lər), *n.* a combination trucking unit consisting of a tractor and a trailer or semitrailer.

trac·trix (trak′triks), *n., pl.* **trac·tri·ces** (trak trī′sēz, trak′tri sēz′). *Geom.* the path of a particle pulled by a flexible, inextensible string whose end follows a line; involute of a catenary. Equation: $x = a \log(a \pm \sqrt{a^2 + y^2} \mp \sqrt{a^2 - y^2})$. [< NL < *tract(us)* (ptp. of *trahere* to drag, haul; see TRACT[1]) + *-trix* -TRIX]

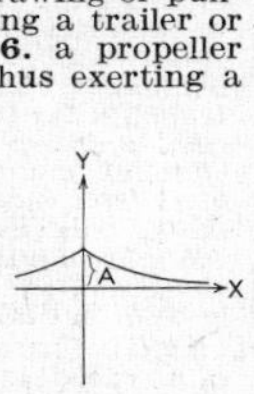

Tractrix

tract′ soci′ety, a society that publishes and distributes religious pamphlets.

Tra·cy (trā′sē), *n.* **1. Spencer,** 1900–67, U.S. actor. **2.** a town in SW Minnesota. 2862 (1960). **3.** a boy's or girl's given name.

trade (trād), *n., v.,* **trad·ed, trad·ing,** *adj.* —*n.* **1.** act or process of buying, selling, or exchanging commodities, at either wholesale or retail prices, within a country or between countries: *domestic trade; foreign trade.* **2.** a purchase, sale, or exchange. **3.** any occupation pursued as a business or livelihood. **4.** some line of skilled manual or mechanical work; craft: *the trade of a carpenter; printer's trade.* **5.** people engaged in a particular line of business: *a lecture of interest only to the trade.* **6.** market: *an increase in the tourist trade.* **7.** a field of business activity: *a magazine for the furniture trade.* **8.** the body of customers of a business establishment. **9. trades.** See **trade wind** (def. 1). —*v.t.* **10.** to buy and sell; barter; traffic in. **11.** to exchange: *to trade seats with a person.* —*v.i.* **12.** to carry on trade. **13.** to traffic (usually fol. by *in*): *a tyrant who trades in human lives.* **14.** to make an exchange. **15.** to make one's purchases; shop; buy: *I trade at Mr. Martin's store exclusively.* **16. trade in,** to give (a used article) as payment to be credited toward a purchase: *We trade in our car every three years.* **17. trade on** or **upon,** to turn to one's advantage, esp. selfishly or unfairly; exploit: *He made his fortune by trading on the weaknesses of others.* **18. trade up,** to exchange a less valuable or desirable item for a more valuable or desirable one. —*adj.* **19.** of or pertaining to trade or commerce. **20.** used by, serving, or intended for a particular trade: *trade journal.* **21.** Also, **trades.** composed of members of a trade: *trade council.* [ME: course, path, track < MLG, MD < OS *trada;* c. OHG *trata;* akin to TREAD] —**trad′a·ble, trade′a·ble,** *adj.* —**trade′less,** *adj.*

—**Syn. 1.** business, barter, dealing. TRADE, COMMERCE, TRAFFIC refer to the exchanging of commodities for other commodities or money. TRADE is the general word: *a brisk trade between the nations.* COMMERCE applies to trade on a large scale and over an extensive area: *international commerce.* TRAFFIC may refer to a particular kind of trade; but it usually suggests the travel, transportation, and activity associated with or incident to trade: *the opium traffic; heavy traffic on the railroads.* **2.** swap. **3.** vocation, métier, employment, living, craft, avocation. See **occupation. 10.** TRADE, BARGAIN, BARTER, SELL refer to exchange or transfer of ownership for some kind of material consideration. TRADE conveys the general idea, but often means to exchange articles of more or less even value: *to trade with Argentina.* BARGAIN suggests a somewhat extended period of coming to terms: *to bargain about the price of a horse.* BARTER applies esp. to exchanging goods, wares, labor, etc., with no transfer of money for the transaction: *to barter wheat for machinery.* SELL implies transferring ownership, usually for a sum of money: *to sell a car.*

trade′ accept′ance, a bill of exchange drawn by the seller of goods on the buyer, and accepted by the buyer for payment at a future date.

trade′ associa′tion, an association of merchants, businessmen, or manufacturers in a particular business or trade, organized to promote their common interests.

trade′ bal′ance. See **balance of trade.**

trade′ book′, a book published in a form designed for the general public and available through an ordinary book dealer, as distinguished from a limited edition, textbook edition, etc., of the same book.

trade′ coun′cil, a central council comprised of local trade unions. Also, **trades council.**

trade′ dis′count, *Com.* a deduction from the list price of goods, granted by a manufacturer or wholesaler to a retailer.

trade′ dol′lar, a silver coin of the U.S., containing slightly more silver than the standard dollar, issued from 1873 to 1885 for trade with the Orient.

trade′ edi′tion, an edition of a book printed for the general public (distinguished from *text edition*).

trade′ guild′, a medieval guild composed of tradesmen.

trade-in (trād′in′), *n.* **1.** goods given in whole or, usually, part payment of a purchase: *We used our old car as a trade-in for the new one.* **2.** a business transaction involving a trade-in. —*adj.* **3.** of or pertaining to the valuation of goods used in a trade-in: *trade-in value; trade-in price.* **4.** of or pertaining to such a business transaction: *trade-in terms.* [n. use of v. phrase *trade in*]

trade-last (trād′last′, -läst′), *n. Informal.* a flattering remark relayed to the person so complimented by someone who heard it, in exchange for the report of a similar compliment made about himself. *Abbr.:* T.L.

trade·mark (trād′märk′), *n.* **1.** the name, symbol, figure, letter, word, or mark adopted and used by a manufacturer or merchant in order to designate his goods and to distinguish them from any others. A trademark is usually registered with a governmental agency to assure its use exclusively by the owner of the mark. —*v.t.* **2.** to stamp or otherwise place a trademark designation upon. **3.** to register the trademark of. [TRADE + MARK[1]]

trade′ name′, 1. a word or phrase used in trade whereby a business or enterprise or a particular class of goods is designated, but which is not technically a trademark, either because it is not susceptible of exclusive appropriation as a trademark or because it is not affixed to goods sold in the market. **2.** the name by which an article or substance is known to the trade. **3.** the name or style under which a firm does business.

trade-off (trād′ôf′, -of′), *n.* tossup (def. 2). [n. use of v. phrase *trade off*]

trad·er (trā′dər), *n.* **1.** a person who trades; a merchant or businessman. **2.** a ship used in trade, esp. foreign trade. **3.** a member of a stock exchange trading for himself and not for his customers. [TRADE + -ER[1]] —**trad′er·ship′,** *n.*

trade′ ref′erence, an individual or company in business to which one is referred for information concerning an applicant's credit standing.

trade′ route′, any route usually taken by merchant ships, caravans, etc.

trad·es·can·ti·a (trad′is kan′shē ə, -shə), *n.* any plant of the genus *Tradescantia,* comprising the spiderworts. [< NL; named after (John) *Tradescant* (1608–62), English gardener to Charles I; see -IA]

trade′ school′, a high school giving instruction chiefly in the skilled trades.

trades′ coun′cil. See **trade council.**

trade′ se′cret, a secret process, technique, method, etc., used to advantage in a trade, business, profession, etc.

trades·folk (trādz′fōk′), *n.pl.* tradesmen; tradespeople. [TRADE + 's[1] + FOLK]

trades·man (trādz′mən), *n., pl.* **-men. 1.** a man engaged in trade. **2.** a worker skilled in a particular craft; artisan; craftsman. **3.** *Chiefly Brit.* a shopkeeper. [TRADE + 's[1] + MAN[1]]

trades·peo·ple (trādz′pē′pəl), *n.pl.* **1.** those persons who are engaged in trade; tradesmen. **2.** *Chiefly Brit.* **a.** tradesmen. **b.** shopkeepers collectively. Also, **tradesfolk.** [TRADE + 's[1] + PEOPLE]

trades·wom·an (trādz′wo͝om′ən), *n., pl.* **-wom·en.** a woman engaged in trade. [TRADE + 's[1] + WOMAN]

trade′ un′ion, 1. a union of craftsmen or workers in related crafts, as distinguished from general workers, or a union including all workers in an industry. **2.** See **labor union.** —**trade′-un′ion,** *adj.*

trade′ un′ionism, **1.** the system, methods, or practice of trade or labor unions. **2.** trade unions collectively. Also, **trade′-un′ion·ism, trades′-un′ion·ism.**

trade′ un′ionist, **1.** a member of a trade union. **2.** one who favors or advocates trade unionism. Also, **trade′-un′ion·ist, trades′-un′ion·ist.**

trade′ wind′, **1.** Also **trade′ winds′.** Also called **trades.** the nearly constant easterly winds that dominate most of the tropics and subtropics throughout the world, blowing mainly from the northeast in the Northern Hemisphere, and from the southeast in the Southern Hemisphere. **2.** *Archaic.* any wind that blows in one regular course, or continually in the same direction.

trade′-wind rig′ (trād′wind′), *Naut.* a rig for a small boat, having one or two sails sheeted to the tiller in such a way as to keep the boat before the wind.

trad′ing post′, **1.** a store established in an unsettled or thinly settled region by a trader or trading company, in which inhabitants of the region may exchange local products for the goods they wish to purchase. **2.** *Stock Exchange.* the station on the floor of an exchange where a particular stock or bond is traded.

trad′ing stamp′, a stamp with a certain value given as a premium by a retailer to a customer, specified quantities of these stamps being exchangeable for various articles.

tra·di·tion (trə dish′ən), *n.* **1.** the handing down of statements, beliefs, legends, customs, etc., from generation to generation, esp. by word of mouth or by practice: *a story that has come down to us by popular tradition.* **2.** that which is so handed down: *the traditions of the Eskimos.* **3.** *Theol.* **a.** (among Jews) an unwritten body of laws and doctrines, or any one of them, held to have been received from Moses and handed down orally from generation to generation. **b.** (among Christians) a body of teachings, or any one of them, held to have been delivered by Christ and His apostles but not committed to writing. **4.** *Law.* act of handing over something to another, esp. in a formal legal manner; delivery; transfer. [ME *tradicion* < L *trāditiōn-* (s. of *trāditiō*) a handing over or down, transfer, surrender, betrayal, equiv. to *trādit(us)* given over, ptp. of *trādere,* (*trā-,* var. of *trāns-* TRANS- + *-ditus,* var. of *datus* given; see DATE[1]) + *-iōn-* -ION] —**tra·di′tion·less,** *adj.*

tra·di·tion·al (trə dish′ə nəl), *adj.* **1.** of or pertaining to tradition. **2.** handed down by tradition. **3.** in accordance with tradition. **4.** of, pertaining to, or characteristic of the older styles of jazz, esp. New Orleans style, Chicago style, Kansas City style, and Dixieland. Cf. **mainstream** (def. 3). Also, **tra·di·tion·ar·y** (trə dish′ə ner′ē) (for defs. 1–3). [< ML *trāditiōnāl(is).* See TRADITION, -AL[1]] —**tra·di′tion·al′i·ty,** *n.* —**tra·di′tion·al·ly,** *adv.*

tra·di·tion·al·ism (trə dish′ə nəlizm), *n.* **1.** adherence to tradition as authority, esp. in matters of religion. **2.** a system of philosophy according to which all knowledge of religious truth is derived from divine revelation and received by traditional instruction. [TRADITIONAL + -ISM] —**tra·di′tion·al·ist,** *n., adj.* —**tra·di′tion·al·is′tic,** *adj.*

tradi′tional log′ic, formal logic based on syllogistic formulas, esp. as developed by Aristotle.

tra·di·tion·ist (trə dish′ə nist), *n.* **1.** a traditionalist. **2.** one who records, transmits, or is versed in traditions. [TRADITION + -IST]

trad·i·tive (trad′i tiv), *adj.* traditional. [TRADIT(ION) + -IVE]

trad·i·tor (trad′i tər), *n., pl.* **trad·i·to·res** (trad′i-tôr′ēz, -tôr′-). an early Christian who betrayed his fellows at the time of the Roman persecutions. [ME < L: traitor, equiv. to *trādit(us)* delivered, betrayed (ptp. of *trādere;* see TRADITION) + *-or* -OR[2]]

tra·duce (trə do͞os′, -dyo͞os′), *v.t.,* **-duced, -duc·ing.** to speak maliciously and falsely of; slander; defame; malign: *to traduce someone's character.* [< L *trādūce(re),* var. of *trānsdūcere* to transfer, display, expose, equiv. to *trāns-* TRANS- + *dūcere* to lead] —**tra·duce′ment,** *n.* —**tra·duc′er,** *n.* —**tra·duc′ing·ly,** *adv.*
—**Syn.** vilify, abuse, asperse, depreciate, decry, disparage. —**Ant.** praise.

tra·du·cian·ism (trə do͞o′shə niz′əm, -dyo͞o′-), *n.* *Theol.* the doctrine that the human soul is propagated along with the body. Cf. **creationism** (def. 1). [< eccl. L *trāduciān(us)* believer in inheritance of original sin or of soul (*trāduci-,* s. of *trādux* lineage (L: vine led across for propagation; see TRADUCE) + *-ānus* -AN) + -ISM] —**tra·du′cian·ist, tra·du′cian,** *n., adj.* —**tra·du′cian·is′tic,** *adj.*

Tra·fal·gar (trə fal′gər; *Sp.* trä′fäl gär′), *n.* **Cape,** a cape on the SW coast of Spain, W of Gibraltar: British naval victory over the French and Spanish fleets 1805.

traf·fic (traf′ik), *n., v.,* **-ficked, -fick·ing.** —*n.* **1.** the movement of vehicles, ships, persons, etc., in an area, along a street, through an air lane, over a water route, etc.: *the heavy traffic on Main Street.* **2.** the vehicles, persons, etc., moving in an area, along a street, etc. **3.** the transportation of goods for the purpose of trade, by sea, land, or air: *ships of traffic.* **4.** trade; buying and selling; commercial dealings. **5.** trade between different countries or places; commerce. **6.** the business done by a railroad or other carrier in the transportation of freight or passengers. **7.** the aggregate of freight, passengers, telephone or telegraph messages, etc., handled, esp. in a given period. **8.** communication, dealings, or contact between persons or groups: *traffic between the Democrats and the Republicans.* **9.** mutual exchange or communication: *a traffic in ideas.* **10.** trade or dealing in some specific commodity or service, often of an illegal nature: *the vast traffic in narcotics.* —*v.i.* **11.** to carry on traffic, trade, or commercial dealings. **12.** to trade or deal in a specific commodity or service, often of an illegal nature (usually fol. by *in* when accompanied by an object): *They arrested him when they could prove that he trafficked in opium.* [earlier *traffyk* < MF *trafique* (n.), *trafique(r)* (v.) < It *traffic(o)* (n.), *trafficare* (v.)] —**traf′fick·er,** *n.* —**traf·fic·less,** *adj.*
—**Syn. 4.** See **trade.**

traf·fic·a·bil·i·ty (traf′ə kə bil′i tē), *n.* **1.** the condition of soil or terrain with regard to its being traveled over, as by men, vehicles, or machinery: *The invasion would have to cope with the problem of trafficability.* **2.** the skill of maneuvering over a terrain: *The division's trafficability was essential in its victory.* [TRAFFICABLE + -ITY]

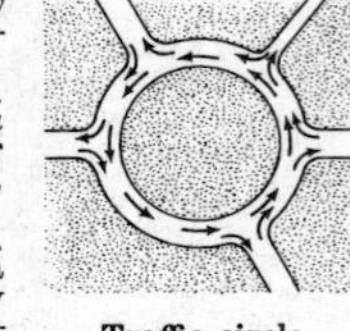
Traffic circle

traf·fic·a·ble (traf′ə kə bəl), *adj.* **1.** that can be traveled upon: *a trafficable road.* **2.** suitable for marketing, commercial dealings, etc. [TRAFFIC + -ABLE]

traf·fi·ca·tor (traf′ə kā′tər), *n.* *Brit.* a directional signal on a vehicle for indicating which way it is going to turn. [TRAFFIC + (INDIC)ATOR]

traf′fic cir′cle, a circular arrangement placed at the intersection of two or more roads in order to facilitate the passage of vehicles from one road to another. Also called **rotary;** *Brit.,* **roundabout.**

traf′fic cop′, *Informal.* a policeman who directs the flow of motor vehicles, usually at an intersection.

traf′fic court′, a court that passes on alleged violations of traffic laws.

traf′fic is′land, a raised or marked-off area between lanes of a roadway, used by pedestrians to get out of the flow of traffic, as a place for traffic signals, for separating lanes, etc.

traf′fic jam′, a slowing down or stopping of vehicles on a highway, caused by a detour, an accident, overcrowding, etc. —**traf′fic-jammed′,** *adj.*

traf′fic light′, a set of electrically operated signal lights used to direct or control traffic at intersections. Also called **traf′fic sig′nal, traf′fic control′ sig′nal.**

traf′fic man′ager, **1.** one who supervises the transportation of goods for his employer. **2.** a person in a transportation company who sets rates or fares, schedules space, etc., for freight or passengers. **3.** (in business management) an office employee, esp. an executive, responsible for routing items of business within a company for appropriate action by various departments.

traf′fic pat′tern, *Aeron.* a system of courses about an airfield that aircraft are assigned to fly when taking off, landing, or preparing to land.

Traf·ford (traf′ərd), *n.* a town in SW Pennsylvania. 4330 (1960).

trag·a·canth (trag′ə kanth′), *n.* **1.** a mucilaginous substance derived from various low, spiny, Asian shrubs of the genus *Astragalus,* esp. *A. gummifer:* used to impart firmness to pills and lozenges, stiffen calicoes, etc. **2.** the plants themselves. [< L *tragacantha* goat's thorn < Gk *tragákantha,* equiv. to *trág(os)* goat + *ákantha* thorn. See TRAGEDY, ACANTHO-]

tra·ge·di·an (trə jē′dē ən), *n.* **1.** an actor especially noted for his performances in tragedy. **2.** a writer of tragedy. [TRAGEDY + -AN; r. ME *tragedien* < MF]

tra·ge·di·enne (trə jē′dē en′), *n.* an actress especially noted for her performances in tragedy. [< F, fem. of *tragédien* TRAGEDIAN]

trag·e·dy (traj′i dē), *n., pl.* **-dies.** **1.** a dramatic composition, often in verse, dealing with a serious or somber theme, typically that of a noble person whose character is flawed by a single weakness, as pride, envy, etc., which causes him to break a divine law or moral precept and which leads inevitably to his downfall or destruction. **2.** that branch of the drama which is concerned with this form of composition. **3.** the art and theory of writing and producing tragedies. **4.** any literary composition, as a novel, dealing with a somber theme carried to a tragic conclusion. **5.** the tragic element of drama, of literature generally, or of life. **6.** a lamentable, dreadful, or fatal event or affair; calamity; disaster: *the tragedy of war; the tragedy of the President's assassination.* [ME *tragedie* < ML *tragēdia,* var. of L *tragoedia* < Gk *tragōidía,* equiv. to *trág(os)* goat + *ōidḗ* song (see ODE) + *-ia* -Y[3]; reason for name variously explained]

trag·ic (traj′ik), *adj.* **1.** characteristic or suggestive of tragedy: *tragic solemnity.* **2.** extremely mournful, melancholy, or pathetic: *a tragic plight.* **3.** dreadful, calamitous, disastrous, or fatal: *a tragic event.* **4.** of, pertaining to, characterized by, or of the nature of tragedy: *the tragic drama.* **5.** acting in or writing tragedy: *a tragic actor; a tragic poet.* **6. the tragic,** the element or quality of tragedy in literature, art, drama, etc.: *lives that had never known anything but the tragic.* Also, **trag′i·cal.** [< L *tragic(us)* < Gk *tragikós* of tragedy, equiv. to *trág(os)* goat + *-ikos* -IC] —**trag′i·cal·ly,** *adv.* —**trag′i·cal·ness,** *n.*
—**Syn. 2.** distressing, pitiful. —**Ant. 1–3.** comic.

trag′ic flaw′, *Literature.* the defect in the character of a tragic hero causing his downfall; hamartia.

trag′ic i′rony, dramatic irony in tragic drama.

trag·i·com·e·dy (traj′i kom′i dē), *n., pl.* **-dies.** **1.** a dramatic or other literary composition combining elements of both tragedy and comedy. **2.** an incident, or series of incidents, of mixed tragic and comic character. [< LL *tragicōmoedia,* syncopated var. of L *tragicocōmoedia.* See TRAGIC, -O-, COMEDY] —**trag·i·com·ic** (traj′i kom′ik), **trag′i·com′i·cal,** *adj.* —**trag′i·com′i·cal·ly,** *adv.*

Trag′icom′edy of Ca·lis′to and Mel·i·be′a, The (kə lis′tō; mel′ə bē′ə). See **La Celestina.**

tra·gi·on (trā′gē on′), *n., pl.* **-gi·a** (-gē ə), **-gi·ons.** *Craniom.* a point in the depth of the notch just above the tragus of the ear. [TRAG(US) + -ION]

trag·o·pan (trag′ə pan′), *n.* any of several Asian pheasants of the genus *Tragopan,* having two fleshy, erectile horns on the head and wattles on the throat. [< NL, special use of L *tragopān* fabulous Ethiopian bird < Gk, equiv. to *trágo(s)* goat + *pân* PAN]

tra·gus (trā′gəs), *n., pl.* **-gi** (-jī). *Anat.* a fleshy prominence at the front of the external opening of the ear. See diag. under **ear.** [< LL < Gk *trágos* hairy part of ear, lit., he-goat]

Tra·herne (trə hûrn′), *n.* **Thomas,** 1637?–74, English writer.

traik (trāk), *v.i.* *Scot.* **1.** to become ill or lose one's good health. **2.** to stroll, wander, or stray. [< Scand; cf. Norw *trǣkes* to become tired or worn out]

trail[1] (trāl), *v.t.* **1.** to drag or let drag along the ground or other surface; draw or drag along behind. **2.** to bring or have floating after itself or oneself: *a racing car trailing clouds of dust.* **3.** to follow the track, trail, or scent of; track. **4.** *U.S. Informal.* to follow along behind (another or others), as in a race. **5.** to mark out, as a track. **6.** *U.S.* to tread down or make a path through (grass or the like). **7.** to draw out, as speech; protract. **8.** *Mil.* to carry (a firearm, etc.) in the right hand in an oblique position, with the muzzle forward and the butt near the ground. **9.** *Ceram.* to pour (slip) on a biscuit so as to produce a pattern. —*v.i.* **10.** to be drawn or dragged along the ground or some other surface, as when hanging from something moving: *Her long bridal gown trailed across the church floor.* **11.** to hang down loosely from something. **12.** to stream from or float after something moving, as dust, smoke, sparks, etc., do. **13.** to follow as if drawn along. **14.** to fish by trailing a line from a moving boat; troll. **15.** to go slowly, lazily, or wearily along. **16.** to pass or extend in a straggling line. **17.** to change gradually or wander from a course, so as to become weak, ineffectual, etc. (usually fol. by *off* or *away*): *Her voice trailed off into silence. The conversation trailed off into absurdities.* **18.** to arrive or be last: *She finally trailed in at 10 o'clock.* **19.** to be losing in a contest: *The home team was trailing 20 to 15.* **20.** to creep or crawl, as a serpent. **21.** to follow a track or scent, as of game. **22.** (of a plant) to extend itself in growth along the ground and over objects encountered, resting on these for support rather than taking root or clinging by tendrils, etc. —*n.* **23.** a path or track made across a wild region, over rough country, or the like, by the passage of men or animals: *to follow the trail.* **24.** the track, scent, or the like, left by an animal, person, or thing, esp. as followed by a hunter, hound, or other pursuer. **25.** something that is trailed or that trails behind, as the train of a skirt or robe. **26.** a stream of dust, smoke, light, people, vehicles, etc., behind something moving. **27.** *Artillery.* the part of a gun carriage that rests on the ground when the piece is unlimbered. **28.** *Naut.* trailboard. **29. trail arms,** *Mil.* **a.** to hold a rifle in the right hand at an oblique angle, with the muzzle forward and the butt a few inches off the ground. **b.** a command to trail arms. [ME *trail(en),* OE *trǣglian* to tear off, drag; c. MD *traghelen* to drag; akin to Latvian *dragāt* to tear off, drag] —**trail′ing·ly,** *adv.* —**trail′less,** *adj.*
—**Syn. 3.** trace, hunt. **23.** See **path. 24.** spoor.

trail[2] (trāl), *n.* a running vine, leaf, or tendril ornament, as in a Gothic molding. [special use of TRAIL[1]]

trail·blaz·er (trāl′blā′zər), *n.* **1.** one who blazes a trail for others to follow through unsettled country or wilderness; pathfinder. **2.** a pioneer in any field of endeavor: *a trailblazer in aerodynamics.* [TRAIL[1] + BLAZE[2] + -ER[1]] —**trail′blaz′ing,** *adj.*

trail·board (trāl′bōrd′, -bôrd′), *n.* *Naut.* an ornamented board extending on each side of the bow of a vessel from a figurehead or the like to abaft the hawse. Also called **trail.** [TRAIL[1] + BOARD]

trail′ boss′, (in Western U.S.) a person responsible for driving a herd of cattle.

trail·er (trā′lər), *n.* **1.** one who or that which trails. **2.** a large van or wagon drawn by an automobile, truck, or tractor, used esp. in hauling freight by road. **3.** a vehicle attached to an automobile and used as a mobile home or place of business, usually equipped with furniture, kitchen facilities, etc. **4.** a trailing plant. **5.** an advertisement for a forthcoming motion picture, shown as part of the program of a motion-picture theater. **6.** blank film at the end of a reel or strip of film, for winding off the film in a motion-picture camera or projector. Cf. **leader** (def. 13). **7.** *Ceram.* a can with a spout, used in slip trailing. [TRAIL[1] + -ER[1]]

trail′er camp′, an area where house trailers may be parked, usually having running water, electrical outlets, etc. Also called **trail′er court′, trail′er park′.**

trail′er car′, *Railroads.* **1.** a second flatcar used for transporting an object or objects of excessive weight or length. **2.** a passenger car, not self-propelled, included in a train of self-propelled cars.

trail′ herd′, (in Western U.S.) a herd of cattle driven along a trail, esp. from their home range to market.

trail′ing arbu′tus, arbutus (def. 2).

trail′ing edge′, *Aeron.* the rear edge of a propeller blade or airfoil.

trail′ing ev′ergreen, a low, fleshy herb, *Sedum sarmentosum,* of northern China and Japan, having bright yellow flowers.

trail′ing fuch′sia, a shrub, *Fuchsia procumbens,* of New Zealand, having long-stalked leaves and orange and purple flowers, used in hanging baskets.

trail′ing phlox′, camla.

Traill's′ fly′catcher (trālz). See **alder flycatcher.** [named after Thomas S. *Traill* (d. 1862), English encyclopedist]

trail′ man′, a cowboy on horseback who helps in driving a cattle herd.

trail·man (trāl′mən), *n., pl.* **-men.** trailsman. [TRAIL[1] + MAN[1]]

trail′ rope′, a guide rope on an aerostat.

trails·man (trālz′mən), *n., pl.* **-men.** a person who follows a trail. Also, **trailman.** [TRAIL[1] + 's[1] + MAN]

train (trān), *n.* **1.** *Railroads.* a self-propelled, connected group of rolling stock. **2.** a line or procession of persons, vehicles, animals, etc., traveling together. **3.** *Mil.* an aggregation of vehicles, animals, and men accompanying an army to carry supplies, baggage, ammunition, etc. **4.** a series or row of objects or parts. **5.** *Mach.* a connected set of three or more rotating elements, usually gears, through which force is transmitted, or motion or torque changed. **6.** order, esp. proper order: *Matters were in good train.* **7.** something that is drawn along; a trailing part. **8.** an elongated part of a skirt or robe trailing behind on the ground. **9.** a trail or stream of something from a moving object. **10.** a line or succession of persons or things following after. **11.** a body of followers or attendants; retinue. **12.** a succession or series of proceedings, events, circumstances, etc. **13.** the series of results or circumstances following or proceeding from an event, action, etc.; aftermath:

Disease came in the train of war. **14.** a succession of connected ideas; a course of reasoning: *to lose one's train of thought.* **15.** *Astron.* **a.** the trace of light created by a meteor falling through the earth's atmosphere. **b.** the tail of a comet. **16.** a line of combustible material, as gunpowder, for leading fire to an explosive charge. **17.** *Physics.* a succession of wave fronts, oscillations, or the like. —*v.t.* **18.** to develop or form the habits, thoughts, or behavior of (a child or other person) by discipline and instruction: *to train an unruly boy.* **19.** to make proficient by instruction and practice, as in some art, profession, or work: *to train soldiers.* **20.** to make (a person) fit by proper exercise, diet, practice, etc., as for some athletic feat or contest. **21.** to discipline and instruct (an animal), as in the performance of tasks or tricks. **22.** to treat or manipulate so as to bring into some desired form, position, direction, etc. **23.** *Hort.* to bring (a plant, branch, etc.) into a particular shape or position, by bending, pruning, or the like. **24.** to bring to bear on some object; point, aim, or direct, as a firearm, camera, telescope, eye, etc. **25.** *Archaic.* to entice; allure. —*v.i.* **26.** to give the discipline and instruction, drill, practice, etc., designed to impart proficiency or efficiency. **27.** to undergo discipline and instruction, drill, etc. **28.** to get oneself into condition for an athletic feat or contest through exercise, diet, practice, etc. **29.** to travel or go by train: *to train to New York.* [late ME *traine* < MF *train(er)*, OF *trahiner* < LL **tragināre*, deriv. of **tragina* something dragged or drawn (cf. ML *tragīna* carriage), akin to L *trahere* to draw] —**train′a·ble,** *adj.* —**train′er,** *n.* —**train′less,** *adj.*
—**Syn. 3.** convoy. **6.** array, arrangement. **10.** file, column. **19.** exercise, drill, practice, teach, school.

train·band (trān′band′), *n.* *Eng. Hist.* one of the trained bands or forces of citizen soldiers organized in London and elsewhere in the 16th, 17th, and 18th centuries. [TRAIN(ED) + BAND[1]]

trained′ nurse′. See **graduate nurse.**

train·ee (trā nē′), *n.* **1.** a person receiving training, esp. vocational training; apprentice. **2.** an enlisted person undergoing military training. [TRAIN + -EE]

train·ing (trā′ning), *n.* **1.** the education, instruction, or discipline of one who or that which trains: *When his training is finished, he will come home. He broke training and was disqualified from the Olympics.* **2.** the status or condition of one who has been trained: *Only athletes in top training may compete.* —*adj.* **3.** of, pertaining to, or used in or for training: *Follow the training manual.* [late ME (n.); see TRAIN, ING[1], -ING[2]]
—**Syn. 1.** See **education.**

train′ing aid′, a mechanical contrivance used to supplement other forms and methods of training: *Motion pictures and slides were used as training aids.*

train′ing col′lege, *Brit.* a college where students are trained to be teachers in elementary and secondary schools; a teachers college.

train′ing pants′, briefs or shorts of cotton with added thickness, worn by a young child as a garment transitional between diapers and ordinary underwear.

train′ing school′, **1.** a school that provides training in some art, profession, or vocation. **2.** an institution for the detention and education of juvenile delinquents.

train′ing ship′, a ship equipped for training men in seamanship, as for naval service.

train′ing wall′, an artificial embankment or wall for directing the course of a stream.

train·line (trān′līn′), *n.* a pipe or hose distributing compressed air through a train for operation of the brakes. Also called **trainpipe.** [TRAIN + LINE[1]]

train·man (trān′mən), *n., pl.* **-men.** a member of the crew that operates a railroad train, usually an assistant to the conductor, such as a brakeman or flagman. [TRAIN + MAN[1]]

train·mas·ter (trān′mas′tər, -mä′stər), *n.* one who has charge of operations over one portion of a railroad. [TRAIN + MASTER]

train′ oil′, oil obtained from the blubber of whales or from seals, walruses, or other marine animals. [earlier *trane* train oil (< MD: whale oil, drop, tear; c. G *Träne* tear)]

train·pipe (trān′pīp′), *n.* trainline. [TRAIN + PIPE[1]]

train·shed (trān′shed′), *n.* (in a railroad station) a shelter completely covering railroad tracks and their adjoining platforms. [TRAIN + SHED[1]]

train·sick (trān′sik′), *adj.* ill with train sickness. [TRAIN + SICK[1]]

train′ sick′ness, a feeling of nausea and dizziness, sometimes accompanied by vomiting, as a result of the motion of the train in which one is traveling. Cf. **motion sickness.**

traipse (trāps), *v.,* **traipsed, traips·ing,** *n.* *Informal.* —*v.i.* **1.** to walk aimlessly or idly: *We traipsed all over town.* —*v.t.* **2.** *Dial.* to walk over; tramp: *to traipse the fields.* —*n.* **3.** *Dial.* a tiring walk. Also, **trapes.** [earlier *trapse*, unexplained var. of *trape*, non-nasalized var. of TRAMP]

trait (trāt), *n.* **1.** a distinguishing characteristic or quality, esp. of one's personal nature: *several bad traits of character.* **2.** a pen or pencil stroke. **3.** a stroke, touch, or strain, as of some quality: *a trait of pathos; a trait of ready wit.* [< MF: lit., something drawn < L *tract(us)*. See TRACT[1]]
—**Syn. 1.** peculiarity, mark, attribute, property.

trai·tor (trā′tər), *n.* **1.** one who betrays a person, a cause, or any trust. **2.** one who betrays his country by violating his allegiance; one guilty of treason. Also, *referring to a woman,* **trai·tress** (trā′tris). [ME *traitur* < OF < L *trāditōrem*, acc. of *trāditor* betrayer. See TRADITOR] —**trai′tor·ship′,** *n.*

trai·tor·ous (trā′tər əs), *adj.* **1.** having the character of a traitor; treacherous; perfidious. **2.** characteristic of a traitor. **3.** of the nature of treason; treasonable: *a traitorous act.* [TRAITOR + -OUS] —**trai′tor·ous·ly,** *adv.* —**trai′tor·ous·ness,** *n.*
—**Syn. 1–3.** disloyal, treasonous, faithless.

Tra·jan (trā′jən), *n.* (*Marcus Ulpius Nerva Trajanus*) A.D. 53?–117, Roman emperor 98–117.

tra·ject (trə jekt′), *v.t.* *Archaic.* to transport, transmit, or transpose. [< L *trāject(us)* (ptp. of *trāicere* to cast, throw over or across), equiv. to *trā-* (var. of *trāns-* TRANS-) + *-jec-* (var. of *jac-*, s. of *iacere* to throw) + *-tus* ptp. suffix] —**tra·jec′tion,** *n.*

tra·jec·to·ry (trə jek′tə rē), *n., pl.* **-ries.** **1.** the curve described by a projectile, rocket, or the like in its flight. **2.** the path described by a body moving under the action of given forces. **3.** *Geom.* a curve or surface which cuts all the curves or surfaces of a given system at a constant angle. [< NL *trājectōria*, n. use of fem. of ML *trājectōrius* casting over. See TRAJECT, -ORY[1]] —**tra·jec·tile** (trə jek′tᵊl, -tīl), *adj.* —**tra·jec·tion** (trə jek′shən), *n.*

Tra·lee (trə lē′), *n.* a city in and the county seat of Kerry, in the SW Republic of Ireland. 10,723 (1961).

Tralles (trälz), *n.* a walled plain in the first quadrant of the face of the moon: about 28 miles in diameter.

tram[1] (tram), *n., v.,* **trammed, tram·ming.** —*n.* **1.** *Brit.* a streetcar. **2.** a tramway; tramroad. **3.** Also called **tramcar.** a truck or car on rails for carrying loads in a mine. **4.** the vehicle or cage of an overhead carrier. —*v.t., v.i.* **5.** to convey or travel by tram. [< MFlem: shaft of a cart or wheelbarrow; akin to L *trabs* beam, tree] —**tram′less,** *adj.*

tram[2] (tram), *n., v.,* **trammed, tram·ming.** —*n.* **1.** trammel (def. 3). **2.** *Mach. Obs.* correct position or adjustment: *The spindle is in tram.* —*v.t.* **3.** *Mach.* to adjust (something) correctly. [short for TRAMMEL]

tram[3] (tram), *n.* silk that has been slightly or loosely twisted, used weftwise in weaving silk fabrics. Cf. **organzine.** [var. of *trame* < F < L *trāma* weft, akin to *trāns* across. See TRANS-]

tram·car (tram′kär′), *n.* **1.** *Brit. Archaic.* tram[1] (def. 1). **2.** *Mining.* tram[1] (def. 3). [TRAM[1] + CAR[1]]

tram·line (tram′līn′), *n.* *Brit.* **1.** a streetcar system. **2.** a streetcar route or track. [TRAM[1] + LINE[1]]

tram·mel (tram′əl), *n., v.,* **-meled, -mel·ing** or (*esp. Brit.*) **-melled, -mel·ling.** —*n.* **1.** Usually, **trammels.** hindrances or impediments to free action; restraints: *the trammels of custom.* **2.** an instrument for drawing ellipses. **3.** Also called **tram.** a device used to align or adjust parts of a machine. **4.** See **trammel net.** **5.** a fowling net. **6.** a contrivance hung in a fireplace to support pots, kettles, etc., over the fire. **7.** a fetter or shackle, esp. one used in training a horse to amble. —*v.t.* **8.** to involve or hold in trammels; hamper; restrain. **9.** to catch or entangle in or as in a net. [late ME *tramayle* < MF *tramail*, var. of *tremail* three-mesh net < LL *trēmacul(um)*, equiv. to L *trē(s)* three + *macula* mesh] —**tram′mel·er;** *esp. Brit.,* **tram′mel·ler,** *n.*
—**Syn. 1.** drag, hobble, curb, inhibition. **8.** hinder, impede, obstruct, encumber.

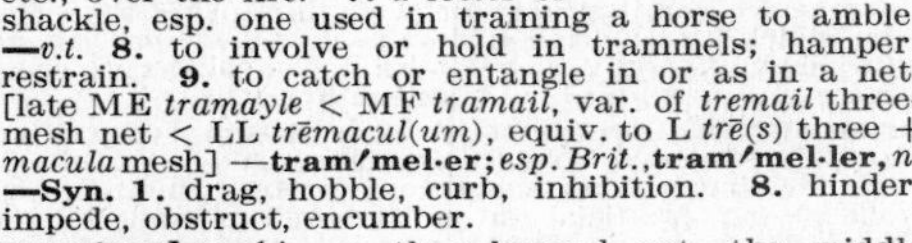
Trammel (def. 2)

tram′mel net′, a three-layered net, the middle layer of which is fine-meshed, the others coarse-meshed, so that fish attempting to pass through the net will become entangled in one or more of the meshes.

tra·mon·ta·na (trä′mon tä′nə, -tan′ə; *It.* trä′mōn-tä′nä), *n., pl.* **-nas,** *It.* **-ne** (-ne). **1.** a cold wind from the north or northeast that blows in the western Mediterranean. **2.** any north wind issuing from a mountainous region. [< It, n. use of fem. of *tramontano* TRAMONTANE]

tra·mon·tane (trə mon′tān, tram′ən tān′), *adj.* Also, **transmontane.** **1.** being or situated beyond the mountains. **2.** beyond the Alps as viewed from Italy; transalpine. **3.** of, pertaining to, or coming from the other side of the mountains. **4.** foreign; barbarous. —*n.* **5.** one who lives beyond the mountains: formerly applied by the Italians to the peoples beyond the Alps, and by the latter to the Italians. **6.** a foreigner; outlander; barbarian. **7.** a violent, polar wind from the northwest that blows in southern France. [< It *tramontano* < L *trānsmontān(us)* beyond the mountains. See TRANS-, MOUNT[2], -AN]

tramp (tramp), *v.i.* **1.** to tread or walk with a firm, heavy, resounding step. **2.** to tread heavily or trample (usually fol. by *on* or *upon*): *to tramp on a person's toes.* **3.** to walk steadily; march; trudge. **4.** to go on a walking excursion or expedition; hike. **5.** to go about as a vagabond or tramp. **6.** to make a voyage on a tramp steamer. —*v.t.* **7.** to tramp or walk heavily or steadily through or over. **8.** to traverse on foot: *to tramp the streets.* **9.** to tread or trample underfoot: *to tramp grapes in order to make wine.* **10.** to travel over as a tramp. **11.** to run (a ship) as a tramp steamer. —*n.* **12.** act of tramping. **13.** a firm, heavy, resounding tread. **14.** the sound made by such a tread. **15.** a long, steady walk; trudge. **16.** a walking excursion or expedition; hike. **17.** a person who travels about on foot from place to place, esp. a vagabond living on occasional jobs or gifts of money or food. **18.** a sexually promiscuous girl or woman. **19.** a freight vessel that does not run regularly between fixed ports, but takes a cargo wherever shippers desire. **20.** a piece of iron affixed to the sole of a shoe. [ME *tramp(en)* (to) stamp; c. LG *trampen;* akin to Goth *ana-trimpan* to press hard upon. See TRAIPSE, TRAMPLE] —**tramp′er,** *n.* —**tramp′ish,** *adj.* —**tramp′ish·ly,** *adv.* —**tramp′ish·ness,** *n.*
—**Syn. 17.** vagrant, bum, hobo.

tram·ple (tram′pəl), *v.,* **-pled, -pling,** *n.* —*v.i.* **1.** to tread or step heavily and noisily; stamp. **2.** to tread heavily, roughly, or crushingly (usually fol. by *on, upon,* or *over*): *to trample on a flower bed.* **3.** to act in a harsh, domineering, or cruel manner, as if treading roughly (usually fol. by *on, upon,* or *over*): *to trample on another's feelings; to trample on an oppressed people.* —*v.t.* **4.** to tread heavily, roughly, or carelessly on or over; tread underfoot. **5.** to domineer harshly over; crush: *to trample law and order.* **6.** to put out or extinguish by trampling (usually fol. by *out*): *to trample out a fire.* —*n.* **7.** act of trampling. **8.** sound of trampling. [ME *trample(n)* (to) stamp (c. G *trampeln*), freq. of TRAMP] —**tram′pler,** *n.*

tram·po·line (tram′pə lēn′, tram′pə lin), *n.* a sheet of canvas attached by resilient cords or springs to a horizontal frame several feet above the floor, used by acrobats and gymnasts as a springboard in tumbling. [var. of *trampolin* < Sp < It *trampolino* springboard, equiv. to *trampol(i)* stilts (< Gmc; see TRAMPLE) + *-ino* -INE[1]] —**tram′po·lin·er, tram′po·lin′ist,** *n.*

Trampoline

tramp′ steam′er, tramp (def. 19).

tram·road (tram′rōd′), *n.* (in a mine) a small railroad for trams. [TRAM[1] + ROAD]

tram·way (tram′wā′), *n.* **1.** a crude railroad of wooden rails, or wooden rails capped with metal treads. **2.** *Brit.* tramline. **3.** *Mining.* a track, usually elevated, or roadway for mine haulage. **4.** Also called **aerial railway, aerial tramway, cable tramway, ropeway.** a system for hauling passengers and freight in vehicles suspended from a cable or cables supported by a series of towers, hangers, etc. **5.** *Naut.* railway (def. 4). [TRAM[1] + WAY]

trance[1] (trans, träns), *n., v.,* **tranced, tranc·ing.** —*n.* **1.** a half-conscious state, seemingly between sleeping and waking, in which ability to function voluntarily may be suspended. **2.** a dazed or bewildered condition. **3.** a state of complete mental absorption or deep musing. **4.** an unconscious, cataleptic, or hypnotic condition. **5.** *Spiritualism.* a temporary state in which a medium, with suspension of personal consciousness, is controlled by an intelligence from without and used as a means of communication, as from the dead. —*v.t.* *Archaic.* **6.** to put in a trance; stupefy. **7.** to entrance; enrapture. [ME *traunce* state of extreme dread, swoon, dazed state < MF *transe*, lit., passage (from life to death), deriv. of *transir* to go across, pass over < L *trānsīre*, equiv. to *trāns-* TRANS- + *-īre* to go] —**tranced·ly** (transt′lē, tran′sid lē), *adv.* —**trance′like′,** *adj.*

trance[2] (trans, träns), *n., v.* **tranced, tranc·ing.** *Scot.* —*n.* **1.** a passageway, as a hallway, alley, or the like. —*v.i.* **2.** to move or walk rapidly or briskly. Also, **transe.** [special use of TRANCE[1], perh. inspired by L *trānsitus* passage. See TRANSIT]

tranche (träNsh), *n.* *French.* slice.

tran·chet (trän shā′; *Fr.* träN she′), *n., pl.* **-chets** (-shāz′; *Fr.* -she′). *Archaeol.* a flint implement in the form of a chisel, found at Neolithic sites. [< F < *tranch(er)* (to) cut (see TRENCH) + *-et* -ET]

tranfd., transferred.

tran·gam (trang′gəm), *n.* *Archaic.* an odd gadget; gewgaw; trinket. [?]

trank (trangk), *n.* **1.** the piece of leather from which one glove is cut. **2.** the cut or shaped trank, not including thumb, gussets, and fourchettes. [?]

tran·quil (trang′kwil), *adj.* **1.** free from commotion or tumult; peaceful; quiet; calm: *a tranquil country place.* **2.** free from or unaffected by disturbing emotions; unagitated; serene; placid: *a tranquil life.* [earlier *tranquill* < L *tranquill(us)* quiet, calm, still] —**tran′quil·ly,** *adv.* —**tran′quil·ness,** *n.*
—**Syn. 1.** See **peaceful.** —**Ant. 1.** agitated.

tran·quil·ize (trang′kwə līz′), *v.t., v.i.,* **-ized, -iz·ing.** to make or become tranquil. Also, **tranquil·lize;** *esp. Brit.,* **tranquillise.** [TRANQUIL + -IZE] —**tran′quil·i·za′tion,** *n.*

tran·quil·iz·er (trang′kwə lī′zər), *n.* **1.** one who or that which tranquilizes. **2.** a drug that has a sedative or calming effect without inducing sleep. Also, **tran′quil·liz′er;** *esp. Brit.,* **tran′quil·lis′er.** [TRANQUILIZE + -ER[1]]

tran·quil·lise (trang′kwə līz′), *v.t., v.i.,* **-lised, -lis·ing.** *Chiefly Brit.* tranquilize. —**tran′quil·li·sa′tion,** *n.*

Tran·quil·li·ta·tis (trang kwil′ē tä′tis), *n.* **Mare.** See **Mare Tranquillitatis.**

tran·quil·li·ty (trang kwil′i tē), *n.* quality or state of being tranquil; calmness; peacefulness; quiet; serenity. Also, **tran·quil′i·ty.** [ME *tranquillite* < L *tranquillitās*. See TRANQUIL, -ITY]

Tran·quil·li·ty (trang kwil′i tē), *n.* **Sea of.** See **Mare Tranquillitatis.**

tran·quil·lize (trang′kwə līz′), *v.t., v.i.,* **-lized, -liz·ing.** tranquilize.

trans-, **1.** a prefix occurring in loan words from Latin (*transcend; transfix*); on this model, used with the meaning "across," "beyond," "through," in combination with elements of any origin: *transisthmian; trans-Siberian.* **2.** *Chem.* a prefix denoting a geometric isomer having a pair of identical atoms or groups on the opposite sides of two atoms linked by a double bond. **3.** *Astron.* a prefix denoting something farther from the sun (than a given planet): *transmartian; transplutonian.* Cf. **cis-** (def. 2). [< L, comb. form of *trāns* (adv. and prep.)]

trans., **1.** transaction; transactions. **2.** transfer. **3.** transferred. **4.** transformer. **5.** transit. **6.** transitive. **7.** translated. **8.** translation. **9.** translator. **10.** transparent. **11.** transportation. **12.** transpose. **13.** transverse.

trans·act (tran sakt′, -zakt′), *v.t.* **1.** to carry on or conduct (business, negotiations, activities, etc.) to a conclusion or settlement. —*v.i.* **2.** to carry on or conduct business, negotiations, etc.: *He was ordered to transact only with the highest authorities.* [< L *trānsact(us)* carried out, accomplished (ptp. of *transigere*), equiv. to *trāns-* TRANS- + *ag(ere)* (to) drive, lead + *-tus* ptp. suffix] —**trans·ac′tor,** *n.*
—**Syn. 1.** enact, conclude, settle, manage, negotiate, conduct. See **perform.**

trans·ac·tion (tran sak′shən, -zak′-), *n.* **1.** act of transacting; fact of being transacted. **2.** an instance or process of transacting something. **3.** that which is transacted, esp. a business agreement. **4. transactions,** the published reports of the proceedings, as papers read, addresses delivered, discussions, etc., at the meetings of a learned society or the like. [late ME < L *trānsactiōn-* (s. of *trānsactiō*) completion, transaction. See TRANSACT, -ION] —**trans·ac′tion·al,** *adj.* —**trans·ac′tion·al·ly,** *adv.*

trans·al·pine (trans al′pin, -pīn, tranz-), *adj.* **1.** situated beyond the Alps. esp. as viewed from Italy. **2.** passing or extending across or through the Alps: *transalpine tunnel; transalpine railway.* **3.** of, pertaining to, or characteristic of peoples or lands beyond the Alps. —*n.* **4.** a native or inhabitant of a country beyond the Alps. [< L *trānsalpīn(us)* across the Alps, equiv. to *trāns-* TRANS- + *Alp(ēs)* the Alps + *-inus* -INE[1]]

Transal′pine Gaul′. See under **Gaul** (def. 1).

trans·am·i·nase (trans am′ə nās′, tranz-), *n.* *Biochem.* any of a class of enzymes, occurring in most plant and animal tissue, that cause transamination; aminopherase. [TRANSAMIN(ATION) + -ASE]

trans′-A·dri·at′ic, *adj.* **trans′-Af′ri·can,** *adj.* **trans′-Al·ge′ri·an,** *adj.* **trans′-Al·le·ghe′ni·an,** *adj.* **trans′-A·mer′i·can,** *adj.*

trans·am·i·na·tion (trans am′ə nā′shən, tranz-), *n.* *Biochem., Chem.* the transfer of an amino group from one compound to another. [TRANS- + AMIN(O) + -ATION]

trans·an·nu·lar (trans an′yə lər, tranz-), *adj.* *Chem.* of or pertaining to tautomerism in cyclic compounds that is characterized by the migration of an atom or group from one position in the ring to another. [TRANS- + ANNULAR]

trans·arc·tic (trans ärk′tik, tranz-), *adj.* across or beyond the arctic. [TRANS- + ARCTIC]

trans·at·lan·tic (trans′ət lan′tik, tranz′-), *adj.* **1.** crossing or reaching across the Atlantic: *a transatlantic liner; transatlantic communications.* **2.** situated beyond the Atlantic. [TRANS- + ATLANTIC] —**trans′at·lan′ti·cal·ly,** *adv.*

trans·ca·lent (trans kā′lənt), *adj.* pervious to heat; permitting the passage of heat. [TRANS- + L *calent-* (s. of *calēns*), prp. of *calēre* to be hot; see -ENT] —**trans·ca·len·cy** (trans kā′lən sē), *n.*

Trans·cau·ca·sia (trans′kô kā′zhə, -shə), *n.* a region in SE Europe, S of the Caucasus Mountains, between the Black and Caspian seas: constituted a republic 1922–36 (**Trans·cau·ca′sian So′cialist Fed′erated-So′viet Repub′lic**); area now includes the republics of Armenia, Azerbaijan, and Georgia. —**Trans·cau·ca·sian** (trans′kô kā′zhən, -shən, -kazh ən, -kash′-), *adj., n.*

trans·ceiv·er (tran sē′vər), *n.* *Radio.* a transmitter and receiver combined in one unit. [TRANS(MITTER) + (RE)CEIVER]

tran·scend (tran send′), *v.t.* **1.** to rise above or go beyond the limits of; overpass; exceed: *to transcend the limits of common thought; kindness that transcends mere courtesy.* **2.** to outdo or exceed in excellence, elevation, extent, degree, etc.; surpass; excel. **3.** *Theol.* (of the Deity) to be above and independent of (the universe, time, etc.). —*v.i.* **4.** to be transcendent; excel; surpass: *His competitive nature made him want to transcend.* [ME < L *transcend(ere)* (to) surmount, equiv to *trāns-* TRANS- + *scandere* to climb] —**tran·scend′ing·ly,** *adv.* —**Syn. 2.** outstrip.

tran·scend·ence (tran sen′dəns), *n.* quality or state of being transcendent. Also, **tran·scend′en·cy.** [< ML *transcendentia.* See TRANSCENDENT, -ENCE]

tran·scend·ent (tran sen′dənt), *adj.* **1.** going beyond ordinary limits; surpassing; exceeding. **2.** superior or supreme. **3.** *Theol.* (of the Deity) transcending the universe, time, etc. Cf. **immanent** (def. 3). **4.** *Philos.* **a.** *Scholasticism.* above all possible modes of the infinite. **b.** *Kantianism.* transcending experience; not realizable in human experience. Cf. **transcendental** (defs. 5a, c). **c.** (in modern realism) referred to, but beyond, direct apprehension; outside consciousness. —*n.* *Math.* **5.** a transcendental function. [< L *transcendent-* (s. of *transcendēns*), prp. of *transcendere.* See TRANSCEND, -ENT] —**tran·scend′ent·ly,** *adv.* —**tran·scend′ent·ness,** *n.*

tran·scen·den·tal (tran′sen den′tᵊl), *adj.* **1.** transcendent, surpassing, or superior. **2.** being beyond ordinary or common experience, thought, or belief; supernatural. **3.** abstract or metaphysical. **4.** idealistic, lofty, or extravagant. **5.** *Philos.* **a.** beyond the contingent and accidental in human experience, but not beyond all human knowledge. Cf. **transcendent** (def. 4b). **b.** pertaining to certain theories, etc., explaining what is objective as the contribution of the mind. **c.** *Kantianism.* of, pertaining to, based upon, or concerned with a priori elements in experience, which condition human knowledge. Cf. **transcendent** (def. 4b). **6.** *Math.* **a.** (of a quantity or number) not a root of any algebraic equation having integral coefficients. **b.** (of a function) not expressible by the operations of addition, subtraction, multiplication or division, as $y = \sin x$. **c.** (of an equation) involving transcendental functions. —*n.* **7.** *Math.* a transcendental number, as π or e. **8.** **transcendentals,** *Scholasticism.* categories which have universal application as being, one, true, good. [< ML *transcendentāl(is).* See TRANSCENDENT, -AL[1]] —**tran′scen·den·tal′i·ty,** *n.* —**tran′scen·den′tal·ly,** *adv.*

transcenden′tal aesthet′ic, (in Kantian epistemology) the study of space and time as the a priori forms of perception.

transcenden′tal analyt′ic, *Kantianism.* (in transcendental logic) the study of the means by which the mind categorizes data from the sensory manifold.

transcenden′tal dialec′tic, *Kantianism.* (in transcendental logic) the study of the fallacious attribution of objective reality to the perceptions by the mind of external objects. Cf. **dialectic** (def. 8).

tran′scenden′tal e′go, (in Kantian epistemology) that part of the self that is the subject and never the object.

tran·scen·den·tal·ise (tran′sen den′tᵊlīz′), *v.t.,* **-ised, -is·ing.** *Chiefly Brit.* transcendentalize. —**tran′scen·den′tal·i·sa′tion,** *n.*

tran·scen·den·tal·ism (tran′sen den′tᵊliz′əm), *n.* **1.** transcendental character, thought, or language. **2.** Also called **transcenden′tal philos′ophy.** any philosophy based upon the doctrine that the principles of reality are to be discovered by the study of the processes of thought, or a philosophy emphasizing the intuitive and spiritual above the empirical: in America, associated with the name of Emerson. [< G *Transcendentalism(us).* See TRANSCENDENTAL, -ISM] —**tran′scen·den′tal·ist,** *n., adj.*

tran·scen·den·tal·is·tic (tran′sen den′tᵊlis′tik), *adj.* **1.** transcendentalist. **2.** adhered to or held by a transcendentalist. [TRANSCENDENTALIST + -IC]

tran·scen·den·tal·ize (tran′sen den′tᵊlīz′), *v.t.,* **-ized, -iz·ing.** **1.** to cause to become transcendent. **2.** to cause to become transcendental; idealize. Also, *esp. Brit.,* **transcendentalise.** [TRANSCENDENTAL + -IZE] —**tran′scen·den′tal·i·za′tion,** *n.*

tran′scenden′tal log′ic, (in Kantian epistemology) the study of the mind with reference to its perceptions of external objects and to the objective truth of such perceptions. Cf. **transcendental analytic, transcendental dialectic.**

transcenden′tal u′nity of appercep′tion, (in Kantian epistemology) the meaningful organization, within the consciousness, of individual objects of perception.

trans·con·duct·ance (trans′kən duk′təns), *n.* *Electronics.* **1.** the ratio of a small change in anode current of an electron tube at a certain level of output to the corresponding small change of control-electrode voltage, usually expressed in mhos or micromhos. **2.** (loosely) the amplification factor of a tube divided by its anode resistance. [TRANS- + CONDUCTANCE]

trans·con·ti·nen·tal (trans′kon tᵊnen′tᵊl), *adj.* **1.** passing or extending across a continent: *a transcontinental railroad; a transcontinental television network.* **2.** on the other, or far, side of a continent. [TRANS- + CONTINENTAL] —**trans′con·ti·nen′tal·ly,** *adv.*

tran·scribe (tran skrīb′), *v.t.,* **-scribed, -scrib·ing.** **1.** to make a written or typewritten copy of (dictated material, notes taken during a lecture, or other spoken material): *to transcribe shorthand notes; to transcribe her minutes of the meeting.* **2.** to make an exact copy of (a document, text, etc.). **3.** to write out in another language or alphabet; translate or transliterate: *to transcribe a passage in English into the phonetic alphabet; to transcribe Russian books into English.* **4.** *Phonet.* to represent speech sounds in written phonetic or phonemic symbols. **5.** *Radio.* to make a recording of (a program, announcement, etc.) for broadcasting. **6.** *Music.* to arrange (a composition) for a medium other than that for which it was originally written. [< L *transcrīb(ere)* (to) copy off, equiv. to *trāns-* TRANS- + *scrībere* to write. See SHRIVE, SCRIBE] —**tran·scrib′er,** *n.*

tran·script (tran′skript), *n.* **1.** a written, typewritten, or printed copy; something transcribed or made by transcribing. **2.** an exact copy or reproduction, esp. one having an official status. **3.** a form of something as rendered from one alphabet or language into another. **4.** an official report supplied by a scholar or college on the record of an individual student, listing subjects studied, credits and grades received, etc. [late ME < L *transcript(um)* thing copied (neut. of ptp. of *transcrībere* to TRANSCRIBE); r. ME *transcrit* < OF; see SCRIPT]

tran·scrip·tion (tran skrip′shən), *n.* **1.** act of transcribing. **2.** a transcript; copy. **3.** *Music* **a.** the arrangement of a composition for a medium other than that for which it was originally written. **b.** a composition so arranged. **4.** *Chiefly Radio.* a phonograph record. [< L *trānscriptiōn-* (s. of *trānscriptiō*). See TRANSCRIPT, -ION] —**trans·scrip′tion·al,** *adj.* —**tran·scrip′tion·al·ly,** *adv.* —**tran·scrip·tive** (tran skrip′tive), *adj.* —**tran·scrip′tive·ly,** *adv.*

trans·crys·tal·line (trans kris′tᵊlin, -tᵊlīn′), *adj.* *Crystall.* situated within or passing through the crystals of a substance. Cf. **intercrystalline.** [TRANS- + CRYSTALLINE]

trans·cur·rent (trans kûr′ənt, -kur′-), *adj.* running or extending across or transversely. [< L *trānscurrent-* (s. of *trānscurrēns*) running across, prp. of *trānscurrere.* See TRANS-, CURRENT]

trans·di·a·lect (trans dī′ə lekt′, tranz-), *v.t.* to translate (speech, writing, etc.) into a different dialect. [TRANS- + DIALECT]

trans·duc·er (trans do͞o′sər, -dyo͞o′-, tranz-), *n.* a device that receives energy from one system and retransmits it, often in a different form, to another. [*transduce* to transfer (see TRADUCE) + -ER[1]]

transe (träns), *n., v.i.,* **transed, tran·sing.** *Scot.* trance[2].

tran·sect (tran sekt′), *v.t.* to cut across; dissect transversely. [TRANS- + -SECT] —**tran·sec′tion,** *n.*

trans·el·e·ment (trans el′ə mənt, tranz-), *v.t.* to change the elements of; transmute. [< ML *transelement(āre),* equiv. to L *trāns-* TRANS- + *element(um)* ELEMENT + *-āre* v. suffix]

trans·el·e·ment·ate (trans el′ə mən tāt′, tranz-), *v.t.,* **-at·ed, -at·ing.** transelement. [< ML *transelementāt(us),* ptp. of *transelementāre.* See TRANSELEMENT, -ATE[1]] —**trans·el′e·men·ta′tion,** *n.*

trans·em·pir·i·cal (trans′em pir′i kəl, tranz′-), *adj.* beyond the range of experiential knowledge. [TRANS- + EMPIRICAL]

tran·sen·na (tran sen′ə), *n., pl.* **-sen·nae** (-sen′ē). (in early Christian architecture) an openwork screen of stone or metal enclosing a shrine. [< L *trā(n)senna,* lit., cross-work]

tran·sept (tran′sept), *n.* *Archit.* **1.** any major transverse part of the body of a church, usually crossing the nave at the entrance to the choir and often similar to the nave in cross section and appearance. **2.** an arm of this, on either side of the central aisle of a church. [< AL *transept(um).* See TRANS-, SEPTUM] **tran·sep′tal,** *adj.* —**tran·sep′tal·ly,** *adv.*

trans·es·ter·i·fi·ca·tion (trans′ə ster′ə fə kā′shən, tranz′-), *n.* *Chem.* a reaction between an ester of one alcohol and a second alcohol to form an ester of the second alcohol and an alcohol from the original ester, as that of methyl acetate and ethyl alcohol to form ethyl acetate and methyl alcohol; interesterification. [TRANS- + ESTERIFICATION]

trans·e·unt (tran′sē ənt), *adj.* *Philos.* (of a mental act) producing an effect outside of the mind. Also, **transient.** Cf. **immanent** (def. 2). [< L *trānseunt-,* oblique s. of *trānsiēns* passing beyond; see TRANSIENT]

transf., **1.** transfer. **2.** transferred. **3.** transformer.

transfd., transferred.

trans·fer (*v.* trans fûr′, trans′fər; *n.* trans′fər), *v.,* **-ferred, -fer·ring,** *n.* —*v.t.* **1.** to convey or remove from one place, person, etc., to another: *He transferred the package from one hand to the other.* **2.** to cause to pass from one person to another, as thought, qualities, power, etc.; transmit. **3.** *Law.* to make over the possession or control of: *to transfer a title to land.* **4.** to imprint, impress, or otherwise convey (a drawing, design, pattern, etc.) from one surface to another. —*v.i.* **5.** to remove oneself from one place to another: *I intend to transfer from our New York office to our London branch.* **6.** to withdraw from one school, college, or the like, and enter another: *He transferred from Rutgers to Tulane.* **7.** to be moved from one place to another: *The entire military unit will transfer to overseas duty.* **8.** to change by means of a transfer from one bus, train, or the like, to another. —*n.* **9.** means or system of transferring. **10.** act of transferring; fact of being transferred. **11.** a point or place for transferring. **12.** a ticket, issued with or without extra charge, entitling a passenger to continue his journey on another bus, train, or the like. **13.** a drawing, design, pattern, or the like, that is or may be transferred to another surface, usually by direct contact. **14.** one who changes or is changed from one college, military unit, business department, etc., to another. **15.** *Law.* a conveyance, by sale, gift, or otherwise, of real or personal property, to another. **16.** *Finance.* act of having the ownership of a stock or registered bond transferred on the books of the issuing corporation or its agent. **17.** Also called **transfer of training.** *Psychol.* a change, positive or negative, in ability or willingness to perform certain acts, resulting from prior learning of a related kind. Cf. **generalization** (def. 4). [ME *transferre* < L, equiv. to *trāns-* TRANS- + *ferre* to bear, carry] —**trans·fer′a·bil′i·ty,** *n.* —**trans·fer′a·ble, trans·fer′ra·ble,** *adj.* —**trans·fer′rer,** *n.*

trans′fer a′gent, a person, bank, or trust company officially designated to act for a corporation in executing and recording the transfers of its stock from one legal owner to another.

trans·fer·al (trans fûr′əl), *n.* transference; transfer. Also, **transferral.** [TRANSFER + -AL[2]]

trans·fer·ase (trans′fə rās′), *n.* *Biochem.* any of the class of enzymes, as the transaminases or the transpeptidases, that catalyze the transfer of an organic group from one compound to another. [TRANSFER + -ASE]

trans′fer com′pany, a company that transports people or luggage for a relatively short distance, esp. between two points, as the terminals of two railroad lines.

trans·fer·ee (trans′fə rē′), *n.* **1.** one who is transferred or removed, as from one place to another. **2.** *Law.* one to whom a transfer is made, as of property. [TRANSFER + -EE]

trans·fer·ence (trans fûr′əns, trans′fər əns), *n.* **1.** act or process of transferring; fact of being transferred. **2.** *Psychoanal.* **a.** reproduction of emotions, esp. those experienced in childhood toward a person other than the one toward whom they were initially experienced. **b.** displacement (def. 7). [< NL *trānsferentia.* See TRANSFER, -ENCE]

transfer′ence num′ber, *Physical Chem.* that fraction of the total electric current, passed through a solution, carried by the anions or cations. Also called **transport number.**

trans·fer·en·tial (trans′fə ren′shəl), *adj.* of, pertaining to, or involving transference. [< NL *trānsferenti(a)* TRANSFERENCE + -AL[1]]

trans′fer of train′ing, *Psychol.* transfer (def. 17)

trans·fer·or (trans fûr′ər), *n.* *Law.* one who makes a transfer, as of property. [TRANSFER + -OR[2]]

trans·fer·ral (trans fûr′əl), *n.* transferal.

trans·fig·u·ra·tion (trans′fig yə rā′shən, trans-fig′-), *n.* **1.** act of transfiguring. **2.** state of being transfigured. **3.** the supernatural and glorified change in the appearance of Jesus on the mountain. Matt. 17:1–9. **4.** (*cap.*) the church festival commemorating this, observed on August 6. [ME *transfiguracion* < eccl. L *trānsfigūrātiōn-* (s. of *trānsfigūrātiō*) change of shape. See TRANS-, FIGURATION]

trans·fig·ure (trans fig′yər), *v.t.,* **-ured, -ur·ing.** **1.** to change in outward form or appearance; transform, change, or alter. **2.** to change so as to glorify, exalt, or idealize. [ME < L *trānsfigūr(āre)* (to) change in shape. See TRANS-, FIGURE] —**trans·fig′ure·ment,** *n.* —**Syn. 2.** transmute, renew.

trans·fi·nite (trans fī′nīt), *adj.* **1.** going beyond or surpassing the finite. —*n.* **2.** See **transfinite number.** [TRANS- + FINITE]

transfi′nite num′ber, *Math.* an infinite cardinal or ordinal number.

trans·fix (trans fiks′), *v.t.,* **-fixed** or **fixt, fix·ing.** **1.** to pierce through with or as if with a pointed weapon; impale. **2.** to hold or fasten with or on something that pierces. **3.** to make or hold motionless with amazement, awe, terror, etc. [< L *trānsfīx(us)* pierced through (ptp. of *trānsfīgere*), equiv. to *trāns-* TRANS- + *fīxus* (*fīg-* pierce + *-sus* ptp. suffix)] —**trans·fix·ion** (trans-fik′shən), *n.*

trans′-An·de′an, *adj.*
trans-An′dine, *adj.*
trans′-Ant·arc′tic, *adj.*
trans-Ap′en·nine′, *adj.*
trans′a·quat′ic, *adj.*
trans′-A·ra′bi·an, *adj.*
trans′-A·si·at′ic, *adj.*
trans·au′di·ent, *adj.*
trans′-Aus·tral′ian, *adj.*
trans-Aus′tri·an, *adj.*
trans-Bal′kan, *adj.*
trans-Bal′tic, *adj.*
trans·bay′, *adj.*
trans·bor′der, *adj.*
trans′-Ca·na′di·an, *adj.*
trans′-Car·pa′thi·an, *adj.*
trans-Cas′pi·an, *adj.*
trans·change′, *v.t.,* **-changed, -chang·ing.**
trans·chang′er, *n.*
trans·chan′nel, *adj.*
trans·col′or, *adj.*
trans′col·or·a′tion, *n.*
trans·col′our, *adj.*
trans′col·our·a′tion, *n.*
trans·con′dy·lar, *adj.*
trans′con·dy·loid′, *adj.*
trans-Con′go, *adj.*
trans′-Cor·dil·le′ran, *adj.*
trans·cor′po·re′al, *adj.*
trans·cul′tur·al, *adj.;* **-ly,** *adv.*
trans·cur′sive, *adj.;* **-ly,** *adv.*
trans′cur·va′tion, *n.*
trans-Dan·u′bi·an, *adj.*
trans·der′mic, *adj.*
trans·des′ert, *adj.*
trans′di·a·phrag·mat′ic, *adj.*
trans′di·ur′nal, *adj.*
trans′-E·gyp′tian, *adj.*
trans·el′e·ment′, *n.*
trans′el·e·men′tal, *adj.*
trans′el·e·men′ta·ry, *adj.*
trans′e·qua·to′ri·al, *adj.;* **-ly,** *adv.*
trans′es·sen′ti·ate′, *v.t.,* **-at·ed, -at·ing.**
trans′-Eu·phra′tes, *adj.*
trans′ex·pe′ri·en′tial, *adj.*
trans·fash′ion, *n.*
trans·fea′ture, *v.t.,* **-tured, -tur·ing.**
trans′fil·tra′tion, *n.*
trans·flu′ent, *adj.*
trans·flu′vi·al, *adj.*
trans·flux′, *n.*

trans·form (*v.* trans fôrm′; *n.* trans′fôrm), *v.t.* **1.** to change in form, appearance, or structure; metamorphose. **2.** to change in condition, nature, or character; convert. **3.** to change into another substance; transmute. **4.** *Elect.* **a.** to increase or decrease (the voltage and current characteristics of an alternating-current circuit), as by means of a transformer. **b.** to decrease (the voltage and current characteristics of a direct-current circuit), as by means of a transformer. **5.** *Math.* to change the form of (a figure, expression, etc.) without in general changing the value. **6.** *Physics.* to change into another form of energy. **—*v.i.* 7.** to undergo a change in form, appearance, or character; become transformed. **—*n.* 8.** *Math.* **a.** a mathematical quantity obtained from a given quantity by an algebraic, geometric, or functional transformation. **b.** the transformation itself. **9.** the result of a transformation. **10.** a transformation. **11.** *Grammar, Logic.* transformation (def. 5). [ME *transforme* < L *trānsformā(re)* (to) change in shape. See TRANS-, FORM] **—trans·form′a·ble,** *adj.* **—trans·form·a·tive** (trans fôr′mə tiv), *adj.*

—Syn. 1. transfigure. TRANSFORM, CONVERT mean to change one thing into another. TRANSFORM suggests changing from one form, appearance, structure, or type to another: *to transform soybeans into oil and meal by pressure.* CONVERT suggests so changing the characteristics as to change the use or purpose: *to convert a barn into a house.*

trans·for·ma·tion (trans′fər mā′shən), **1.** act or process of transforming; state of being transformed. **2.** change in form, appearance, nature, or character. **3.** *Theat.* a seemingly miraculous change in the appearance of scenery or actors in view of the audience. **4.** a wig or hairpiece for a woman. **5.** *Grammar, Logic.* Also called **transform.** one of a set of algebraic formulas used to express the relations between elements, sets, etc., that form parts of a given system, as of the grammar of a language. **6.** *Math.* **a.** the act, process, or result of transforming or mapping. **b.** function (def. 4a). [late ME < LL *trānsformātiōn-* (s. of *trānsformātiō*) change of shape. See TRANS-, FORMATION] **—trans′for·ma′tion·al,** *adj.*

transforma′tional gram′mar, a system of grammatical analysis that uses transformations to express the relations between elements in a sentence, clause, or phrase, or between different forms of a word, phrase, etc., as between the passive and active forms of a verb.

trans·for·ma·tion·ist (trans′fôr mā′shə nist), *n.* transformist. [TRANSFORMATION + -IST]

transforma′tion point′, *Metall.* a temperature at which the transformation of one microconstituent to another begins or ends during heating or cooling. Also called **transforma′tion tem′perature.**

transforma′tion range′, *Metall.* the temperature range within which austenite forms when a ferrous metal is heated, or within which it disappears when the metal is cooled.

trans·form·er (trans fôr′mər), *n.* **1.** one who or that which transforms. **2.** *Elect.* an electric device consisting essentially of two or more windings wound on the same core, which by electromagnetic induction transforms electric energy from one set of one or more circuits to another set of one or more circuits such that the frequency of the energy remains unchanged while the voltage and current usually change. [TRANSFORM + -ER[1]]

trans·form·ism (trans fôr′miz əm), *n.* *Biol.* **1.** the doctrine of gradual transformation of one species into another by descent with modification through many generations. **2.** such transformation itself. **3.** any doctrine or instance of evolution. [TRANSFORM + -ISM, modeled on F *transformisme*]

trans·form·ist (trans fôr′mist), *n.* one who adheres to transformism. [TRANSFORM + -IST, modeled on F *transformiste*] **—trans′form·is′tic,** *adj.*

trans·fuse (trans fyōōz′), *v.t.,* **-fused, -fus·ing. 1.** to transfer or pass from one source to another; transmit; impart; instill: *to transfuse a love of literature to one's students.* **2.** to diffuse into or through; permeate; infuse. **3.** *Med.* **a.** to transfer (blood) from the veins or arteries of one person or animal into those of another. **b.** to inject, as a saline solution, into a blood vessel. **4.** *Archaic.* to pour from one container into another. [late ME < L *trānsfūs(us)* decanted, ptp. of *trānsfundere.* See TRANS-, FUSE[2]] **—trans·fus′er,** *n.* **—trans·fus′i·ble, trans·fus′a·ble,** *adj.* **—trans·fu·sive** (trans fyōō′siv), *adj.*

trans·fu·sion (trans fyōō′zhən), *n.* **1.** act or process of transfusing. **2.** *Med.* **a.** the direct transferring of blood, plasma, or the like from one person or animal into another. **b.** the injecting of bottled blood or a solution of a salt, sugar, etc., into a blood vessel. [< L *trānsfūsiōn-* (s. of *trānsfūsiō*) decanting, intermingling, equiv. to *trānsfūs(us)* (see TRANSFUSE) + *-iōn-* -ION]

trans·gress (trans gres′, tranz-), *v.t.* **1.** to pass over or go beyond (a limit, boundary, etc.): *to transgress the bounds of prudence.* **2.** to go beyond the limits imposed by (a law, command, etc.); violate; infringe; break: *those who transgress the will of God.* **—*v.i.* 3.** to break or violate a law, command, moral code, etc.; offend; sin (usually fol. by *against*). [< L *trānsgress(us)* having stepped across (ptp. of *trānsgredī*), equiv. to *trāns-* TRANS- + *gressus,* equiv. to *gred-* (var. of *grad-* step; see GRADE) + *-tus* ptp. suffix] **—trans·gres′sive,** *adj.* **—trans·gres′sive·ly,** *adv.* **—trans·gres′sor,** *n.*

—Syn. 2. contravene, disobey. **3.** err, trespass. **—Ant. 2.** obey.

trans·gres·sion (trans gresh′ən, tranz-), *n.* act of transgressing; violation of a law, command, etc.; sin. [late ME < L *trānsgressiōn-* (s. of *trānsgressiō*) a stepping across. See TRANSGRESS, -ION]

tran·ship (tran ship′), *v.t., v.i.,* **-shipped, -ship·ping.** transship **—tran·ship′ment,** *n.*

trans·hu·mance (trans hyōō′məns *or, often,* -yōō′-), *n.* the seasonal migration of livestock, and the people who tend them, between lowlands and adjacent mountains. [< F, equiv. to *transhum(er)* (to) shift ground (modeled on Sp *trashumar;* see TRANS-, HUMUS) + *-ance* -ANCE] **—trans·hu′mant,** *adj.*

tran·sience (tran′shəns, -zhəns), *n.* transient state or quality. Also, **tran′sien·cy.** [TRANSI(ENT) + -ENCE]

tran·sient (tran′shənt, -zhənt), *adj.* **1.** not lasting, enduring, or permanent; transitory. **2.** lasting only a short time; existing briefly; temporary: *transient authority.* **3.** staying only a short time: *the transient guests at a hotel.* **4.** *Philos.* transeunt. **—*n.* 5.** one who or that which is transient, esp. a temporary guest, boarder, or the like. **6.** *Math.* a function which tends to zero as the independent variable tends to infinity. [alter. of earlier *transeunt* (see TRANSEUNT), with *-ie-* from L *transiēns* (nom. sing.) passing, prp. of *transīre* to pass by, lit., go across; see -ENT] **—tran′sient·ly,** *adv.* **—tran′sient·ness,** *n.*

—Syn. 2. fleeting, flitting, flying, fugitive, evanescent. See **temporary. —Ant. 2.** permanent.

tran′sient modula′tion, *Music.* a modulation of a temporary nature. Also called **passing modulation.**

tran·sil·i·ent (tran sil′ē ənt, -sil′yənt), *adj.* leaping or passing from one thing or state to another. [< L *trānsilient-* (s. of *trānsiliēns*) leaping across, prp. of *trānsilīre,* equiv. to *trāns-* TRANS- + *-sili-* (var. s. of *salīre* to leap) + *-ent-* -ENT] **—tran·sil′i·ence,** *n.*

trans·il·lu·mi·nate (trans′i lōō′mə nāt′, tranz′-), *v.t.,* **-nat·ed, -nat·ing. 1.** to cause light to pass through. **2.** *Med.* to throw a strong light through (an organ or part) as a means of diagnosis. [TRANS- + ILLUMINATE] **—trans′il·lu′mi·na′tion,** *n.* **—trans′il·lu′mi·na′tor,** *n.*

tran·sis·tor (tran zis′tər), *n.* **1.** *Electronics.* a device, utilizing a semiconductor, for controlling the flow of current between two terminals by means of variations of current flow between one of these terminals and a third terminal. It performs functions similar to those of a vacuum tube without requiring current to heat a cathode. **2.** *Informal.* a transistorized radio. [TRANS(FER) + (RES)ISTOR]

tran·sis·tor·ize (tran zis′tə rīz′), *v.t.,* **-ized, -iz·ing.** *Electronics.* to equip with or convert to a circuit employing transistors. [TRANSISTOR + -IZE]

trans·it (tran′sit, -zit), *n., v.,* **-it·ed, -it·ing. —*n.* 1.** act or fact of passing across or through; passage from one place to another. **2.** conveyance or transportation from one to another, as of persons or goods: *the problem of rapid transit in large cities; the transit system of Baltimore.* **3.** a transition or change. **4.** *Astron.* **a.** the passage of a heavenly body across the meridian of a given location or through the field of a telescope. **b.** the passage of Mercury or Venus across the disk of the sun, or of a satellite or its shadow across the face of its primary. **c.** See **meridian circle. 5.** *Survey.* **a.** Also called **transit instrument.** an instrument, as a theodolite, having a telescope that can be transited, used for measuring horizontal and sometimes vertical angles. **b.** *U.S.* a repeating transit theodolite. **6.** (*cap.*) *U.S.* one of a series of satellites for providing positional data to ships and aircraft. **—*v.t.* 7.** to pass across or through. **8.** *Survey.* to turn (the telescope of a transit) in a vertical plane to reverse its direction; plunge. **9.** *Astron.* to cross (a meridian, celestial body, etc.). **—*v.i.* 10.** to pass over or through something; make a transit. **11.** *Astron.* to make a transit across a meridian, celestial body, etc. [late ME < L *trānsit(us)* a going across, passage, n. use of *trānsitus* crossed (ptp. of *trānsīre*), equiv. to *trāns-* TRANS- + *-i-* go + *-tus* ptp. suffix]

tran·sit·a·ble (tran′si tə bəl, -zi-), *adj.* capable of being crossed or passed over. [TRANSIT + -ABLE]

trans′it cir′cle, *Astron.* See **meridian circle.**

trans′it in′strument, 1. *Astron.* See **meridian circle. 2.** *Survey.* transit (def. 5).

tran·si·tion (tran zish′ən, -sish′-), *n.* **1.** movement or passage from one position, state, stage, subject, concept, etc., to another; change: *the transition from a monarchy to a democracy.* **2.** a passage or change of this kind: *the transition from adolescence to adulthood.* **3.** *Music.* **a.** a passing from one key to another; modulation. **b.** a brief modulation; a modulation used in passing. **c.** a sudden, unprepared modulation. **4.** a passage from one scene to another by sound effects, music, etc., as in a television program, theatrical production, or the like. [< L *trānsitiōn-* (s. of *trānsitiō*) a going across, equiv. to *trānsit(us)* (see TRANSIT) + *-iōn-* -ION] **—tran·si′tion·al, tran·si·tion·a·ry** (tran zish′ə ner′ē), *adj.* **—tran·si′tion·al·ly,** *adv.*

transi′tion el′ement, *Chem.* any element in either of the three series of elements with atomic numbers 21–30, 39–48, 57–80, and 89–103, that in a given suborbital has less than a full quota of electrons.

transi′tion probabil′ity, *Math.* the probability of going from a given state to the next state in a Markov process.

tran·si·tive (tran′si tiv, -zi-), *adj.* **1.** *Gram.* having the nature of a transitive verb. **2.** characterized by or involving transition; transitional; intermediate. **3.** passing over to or affecting something else; transeunt. **4.** *Math.* noting a relation in which one element in relation to a second element and the second in relation to a third element implies the first element is in relation to the third element, as the relation "less than or equal to." **—*n.* 5.** *Gram.* See **transitive verb.** [< LL *trānsitīv(us),* equiv. to L *trānsit(us)* (see TRANSIT) + *-īvus* -IVE] **—tran′si·tive·ly,** *adv.* **—tran′si·tive·ness, tran′si·tiv′i·ty,** *n.*

tran′sitive verb′, *Gram.* a verb accompanied by a direct object and from which a passive can be formed, as *deny, rectify, elect.*

trans·it·man (tran′sit mən, -zit-), *n., pl.* **-men.** *Survey.* one who makes observations with a transit. [TRANSIT + MAN[1]]

trans′it num′ber, an identifying number assigned by a banking organization to a bank and printed on its checks.

tran·si·to·ry (tran′si tôr′ē, -tōr′ē, -zi-), *adj.* **1.** not lasting, enduring, permanent, or eternal. **2.** lasting only a short time; brief; short-lived; temporary. [ME *transitorie* < eccl. L *trānsitōri(us)* fleeting (see TRANSIT, -ORY[1]); r. ME *transitoire* < MF] **—tran·si·to·ri·ly** (tran′si tôr′ə lē, -tôr′-, tran′si tôr′-, -tôr′-, -zi-), *adv.* **—tran′si·to′ri·ness,** *n.*

—Syn. 2. See **temporary. —Ant. 2.** permanent.

tran·si·tron (tran′si tron′, -zi-), *n.* *Electronics.* a pentode with a negative transconductance, used in oscillator circuits. [? TRANSI(TION) + -TRON]

trans′it theod′olite, a theodolite having a telescope that can be transited.

Trans-Jor·dan (trans jôr′dᵊn, tranz-), *n.* a former territory and kingdom (1946–49) in SW Asia: now the major part of the kingdom of Jordan.

transl., 1. translated. **2.** translation. **3.** translator.

trans·late (trans lāt′, tranz-, trans′lāt, tranz′-); *v.,* **-lat·ed, -lat·ing. —*v.t.* 1.** to turn (something written or spoken) from one language into another: *to translate English books into Spanish.* **2.** to change the form, condition, nature, etc., of; transform; convert: *to translate wishes into deeds.* **3.** to explain in terms that can be more easily understood; interpret. **4.** to bear, carry, or move from one place, position, etc., to another; transfer. **5.** *Mech.* to cause (a body) to move without rotation or angular displacement; subject to translation. **6.** *Telegraphy.* to retransmit or forward (a message), as by a relay. **7.** *Eccles.* **a.** to move (a bishop) from one see to another. **b.** to move (a see) from one place to another. **c.** to move (relics) from one place to another. **8.** to convey or remove to heaven without natural death. **9.** *Math.* to perform a translation (on a set, function, etc.). **10.** *Archaic.* to exalt in spiritual or emotional ecstasy; enrapture. **—*v.i.* 11.** to provide or make a translation; act as translator. **12.** to admit of translation; to be capable of translation: *The Greek expression does not translate easily into English.* [ME < L *trānslāt(us)* transferred (ptp. of *transferre*), equiv. to *trāns-* TRANS- + *-lātus* carried, borne (ptp. of *ferre* to BEAR[1]), earlier **tlātus,* equiv. to **tlā-* (akin to THOLE[2]) + *-tus* ptp. suffix] **—trans·lat′a·bil′i·ty, trans·lat′a·ble·ness,** *n.* **—trans·lat′a·ble,** *adj.* **—trans·la·tor** (trans lā′tər, tranz-, trans′lā tər, tranz′-), **trans·lat′er,** *n.*

trans·la·tion (trans lā′shən, tranz-), *n.* **1.** the rendering of something into another language. **2.** a version in a different language: *a French translation of Hamlet.* **3.** change or conversion to another form, appearance, etc.; transformation: *a swift translation of thought into action.* **4.** act or process of translating; state of being translated. **5.** *Mech.* motion in which all particles of a body move with the same velocity along parallel paths. **6.** *Telegraphy.* the retransmitting or forwarding of a message, as by relay. **7.** *Math.* a function obtained from a given function by adding the same constant to each value of the variable of the given function and moving the graph of the function a constant distance to the right or left. [< L *trānslātiōn-* (s. of *trānslātiō*) a transferring, equiv. to *trānslāt(us)* (see TRANSLATE) + *-iōn-* -ION; r. ME *translacioun* < AF] **—trans·la′tion·al,** *adj.* **—trans·la′tion·al·ly,** *adv.*

—Syn. 2. TRANSLATION, PARAPHRASE, VERSION refer to a rewording of something. A TRANSLATION is a rendering of the same ideas in a different language from the original: *a translation from Greek into English.* A PARAPHRASE is a free rendering of the sense of a passage in other words, usually in the same language: *a paraphrase of a poem.* A VERSION is a translation, esp. of the Bible, or else an account of something illustrating a particular point of view: *the Douay Version.*

transla′tion of ax′es (ak′sēz), *Math.* the process of replacing the axes in a Cartesian coordinate system with a new set of axes, parallel to the first, used to write equations of curves not centered about the origin.

trans·la·tive (trans lā′tiv, tranz-; trans′lā-, tranz′-), *adj.* **1.** of or pertaining to the transfer of something from one person, position, or place to another. **2.** of translation; serving to translate. **3.** *Gram.* noting a case, as in Finnish, whose distinctive function is to indicate a change from one state into another. **—*n.* 4.** the translative case. [< L *trānslātīv(us),* equiv. to *trānslāt(us)* (see TRANSLATE) + *-īvus* -IVE]

trans·lit·er·ate (trans lit′ə rāt′, tranz-), *v.t.,* **-at·ed, -at·ing.** to change (letters, words, etc.) into corresponding characters of another alphabet or language: *to transliterate the Greek* χ *as ch.* [TRANS(LATE) + OB)LITERATE] **—trans·lit′er·a′tion,** *n.* **—trans·lit′er·a′tor,** *n.*

trans·lo·cate (trans lō′kāt, tranz-), *v.t.,* **-cat·ed, -cat·ing.** to move or transfer from one place to another; cause to change location; displace; dislocate. [TRANS- + LOCATE] **—trans′lo·ca′tion,** *n.*

trans·lu·cent (trans lōō′sənt, tranz-), *adj.* **1.** permitting light to pass through but diffusing it so that persons, objects, etc., on the opposite side are not clearly visible (distinguished from *opaque*): *Frosted window-glass is translucent but not transparent.* **2.** easily understandable; lucid: *His explanation of symbolic logic was absolutely translucent.* **3.** *Rare.* clear; transparent. [< L *trānslūcent-* (s. of *trānslūcēns*) shining through, prp. of *trānslūcēre.* See TRANS-, LUCENT] **—trans·lu′cence, trans·lu′cen·cy,** *n.* **—trans·lu′cent·ly,** *adv.*

—Syn. 1. See **transparent. —Ant. 1.** opaque.

trans·lu·cid (trans lōō′sid, tranz-), *adj.* translucent. [< L *trānslūcid(us)* clear, transparent. See TRANS-, LUCID]

trans·lu·ci·dus (trans lōō′si dəs, tranz-), *adj.* *Meteorol.* (of a cloud) sufficiently transparent as not to obscure the sun, moon, or higher clouds. [< NL; see TRANSLUCID]

trans·lu·nar·y (trans′lōō ner′ē, tranz′-; trans lōō′nə rē, tranz-), *adj.* **1.** situated beyond or above the moon; superlunary. **2.** celestial, rather than earthly. **3.** ideal; visionary. Also, **trans·lu·nar** (trans′lōō′nər, tranz′-; trans lōō′nər, tranz-). [TRANS- + *lunary* < L *lūnāri(s)* LUNAR; see -ARY]

trans·ma·rine (trans′mə rēn′, tranz′-), *adj.* **1.** being on or coming from the opposite side of the sea or ocean. **2.** being or crossing over the sea or ocean. [< L *trānsmarīn(us).* See TRANS-, MARINE]

trans·meth·yl·a·tion (trans′meth ə lā′shən, tranz′-), *n.* *Chem.* the transfer of a methyl group from one compound to another. [TRANS- + METHYLATION]

trans·fron′tal, *adj.*
trans/fron·tier′, *adj.*
trans′-Ger·man′ic, *adj.*
trans-Gram′pi·an, *adj.*
trans′-Him′a·lay′an, *adj.*
trans′-His·pan′ic, *adj.*
trans·hu′man, *adj.*
trans′-I·be′ri·an, *adj.*
trans·il′i·ac′, *adj.*
trans-In′di·an, *adj.*
trans′in·di·vid′u·al, *adj.*
trans-In′dus, *adj.*
trans·in′su·lar, *adj.*
trans′-I·ra′ni·an, *adj.*
trans′-I·raq′, *adj.*
trans·isth′mi·an, *adj.*
trans-Jo′vi·an, *adj.*
trans′-Li·be′ri·an, *adj.*
trans-Lib′y·an, *adj.*
trans·light′, *n.*
trans·make′, *v.t.,* **-made, -mak·ing.**
trans′-Man·chu′ri·an, *adj.*
trans·mar′gi·nal, *adj.;* **-ly,** *adv.*
trans-Mar′tian, *adj.*
trans′ma·te′ri·al, *adj.*
trans′-Med·i·ter·ra′ne·an, *adj.*
trans·men′tal, *adj.;* **-ly,** *adv.*
trans′me·rid′i·o·nal, *adj.;* **-ly,** *adv.*

trans·mi·grant (trans mī′grənt, tranz-; trans′mə grənt, tranz′-), *n.* **1.** one who or that which transmigrates. **2.** a person passing through a country or place on his way from his own country to a country in which he intends to settle. **—***adj.* **3.** passing from one place or state to another. [< L *trānsmigrant-* (s. of *trānsmigrāns*), prp. of *trānsmigrāre* to depart, migrate. See TRANS-, MIGRANT]

trans·mi·grate (trans mī′grāt, tranz-), *v.*, **-grat·ed, -grat·ing.** **—***v.i.* **1.** to move or pass from one place to another. **2.** to migrate from one country to another in order to settle there. **3.** (of the soul) to be reborn at death in another body. **—***v.t.* **4.** to cause to transmigrate, as a soul; transfer. [late ME < L *trānsmigrāt(us)* moved off (ptp. of *trānsmigrāre*). See TRANS-, MIGRATE] **—trans·mi′gra·tor,** *n.* **—trans·mi·gra·to·ry** (trans mī′grə tōr′ē, -tôr′ē, tranz-), **trans·mi′gra·tive,** *adj.*

trans·mi·gra·tion (trans′mī grā′shən, tranz′-), *n.* **1.** act of transmigrating. **2.** the passage of a soul at death into another body; metempsychosis. Cf. **reincarnation.** [ME *transmigracion* < LL *trānsmigrātiōn-* (s. of *trānsmigrātiō*) removal. See TRANS-, MIGRATION]

trans·mis·si·ble (trans mis′ə bəl, tranz-), *adj.* capable of being transmitted. [< L *trānsmiss(us)* transmitted (see TRANSMISSION) + -IBLE] **—trans·mis′si·bil′i·ty,** *n.*

trans·mis·sion (trans mish′ən, tranz-), *n.* **1.** act or process of transmitting. **2.** fact of being transmitted. **3.** that which is transmitted. **4.** *Mach.* **a.** transference of force between machines or mechanisms, often with changes of torque and speed. **b.** a compact, enclosed unit of gears or the like for this purpose, as in an automobile. **5.** *Radio.* the broadcasting of electromagnetic waves from the transmitting station to the receiving station. [< L *trānsmissiōn-* (s. of *trānsmissiō*) a sending across, equiv. to *trānsmiss(us)* sent across (ptp. of *trānsmittere*) + *-iōn-* -ION. See TRANS-, MISSION] **—trans·mis·sive** (trans mis′iv, tranz-), *adj.* **—trans·mis′sive·ly,** *adv.* **—trans·mis′sive·ness,** *n.*

transmis′sion stop′ sys′tem. See **T-stop system.**

trans-Mis·sis·sip·pi (trans′mis i sip′ē, tranz′-), *adj.* across or beyond the Mississippi River. [TRANS- + MISSISSIPPI]

trans·mis·som·e·ter (trans′mi som′i tər, tranz′-), *n.* *Meteorol.* an instrument for measuring visibility or the transmission of light in the atmosphere. Also called **hazemeter, telephotometer, transmittance meter.** [TRANSMISS(ION) + -O- + -METER]

trans·mit (trans mit′, tranz-), *v.*, **-mit·ted, -mit·ting.** **—***v.t.* **1.** to send or forward, as to a recipient or destination; dispatch; convey. **2.** to communicate, as information, news, etc. **3.** to pass or spread (disease, infection, etc.) to another: *A carrier of a disease may transmit the infection to others without being ill himself.* **4.** to pass on (a genetic character) from parent to offspring: *The mother transmitted her red hair to her daughter.* **5.** *Physics.* **a.** to cause (light, heat, sound, etc.) to pass through a medium. **b.** to convey or pass along (an impulse, force, motion, etc.). **c.** to permit (light, heat, etc.) to pass through: *Glass transmits light.* **6.** *Radio.* to emit (electromagnetic waves). **—***v.i.* **7.** to send a signal by wire or radio waves. **8.** to pass on a right or obligation to heirs or descendants. [ME *transmitte* < L *trānsmitte(re)* (to) send across, equiv. to *trāns-* TRANS- + *mittere* to send] **—trans·mit′ta·ble, trans·mit′ti·ble,** *adj.* **—Syn. 1.** transfer, remit. **2.** bear. See **carry.**

trans·mit·tal (trans mit′əl, tranz-), *n.* transmission. [TRANSMIT + -AL[2]]

trans·mit·tance (trans mit′əns, tranz-), *n.* **1.** transmission. **2.** *Physics.* the ratio of the radiant flux transmitted through and emerging from a body to the total flux incident on it: equivalent to one minus the absorptance. [TRANSMIT + -ANCE]

transmit′tance me′ter, transmissometer.

trans·mit·ter (trans mit′ər, tranz-), *n.* **1.** one who or that which transmits. **2.** Also called **transmit′ting set′.** *Radio.* a device for sending electromagnetic waves; that part of a broadcasting apparatus which generates and modulates the radiofrequency current and conveys it to the antenna. **3.** that part of a telephonic or telegraphic apparatus converting sound waves or mechanical movements into corresponding electric waves or impulses. [TRANSMIT + -ER[1]]

trans·mog·ri·fy (trans mog′rə fī′, tranz-), *v.t.*, **-fied, -fy·ing.** to change in appearance or form, esp. strangely or grotesquely; transform. [vulgar or humorous coinage] **—trans·mog′ri·fi·ca′tion,** *n.*

trans·mon·tane (trans mon′tān, tranz-), *adj.* tramontane. [< L *trānsmontān(us)* TRAMONTANE]

trans·mun·dane (trans′mun dān′, tranz′-; trans mun′dān, tranz-), *adj.* reaching beyond or existing outside the physical or visible world. [TRANS- + L *mund(us)* world + -ANE]

trans·mu·ta·tion (trans′myōō tā′shən, tranz′-), *n.* **1.** act or process of transmuting. **2.** fact or state of being transmuted. **3.** change into another nature, substance, form, or condition. **4.** *Biol.* the transformation of one species into another. Cf. **transformism. 5.** *Physics.* any process in which a nuclide is transformed into a different nuclide, usually one of a different element. **6.** *Alchemy.* the supposed conversion of base metals into metals of greater value, esp. into gold or silver. [ME *transmutacion* < L *trānsmūtātiōn-* (s. of *trānsmūtātiō*) a changing, shifting, equiv. to *trānsmūtāt(us)* changed (ptp. of *trānsmūtāre*) + *-iōn-* -ION. See TRANSMUTE, -ATION] **—trans′mu·ta′tion·al, trans·mut·a·tive** (trans myōō′tə tiv, tranz-), *adj.* **—trans′-mu·ta′tion·ist,** *n.*

trans·mute (trans myōōt′, tranz-), *v.t., v.i.*, **-mut·ed, -mut·ing.** to change from one nature, substance, form, or condition into another; transform. [ME < L *trānsmūt(āre)* (to) shift, equiv. to *trāns-* TRANS- + *mūtāre* to change. See MUTABLE, etc.] **—trans·mut′a·bil′i·ty, trans·mut′a·ble·ness,** *n.* **—trans·mut′a·ble,** *adj.* **—trans·mut′a·bly,** *adv.* **—trans·mut′er,** *n.* **—Syn.** metamorphose, convert, alter.

trans·na·tion·al (trans nash′ə nəl, tranz-), *adj.* going beyond national boundaries or solely national interests: *a transnational program for improving the economy of Europe.* [TRANS- + NATIONAL]

trans·o·ce·an·ic (trans′ō shē an′ik, tranz′-), *adj.* **1.** extending across or traversing the ocean: *a transoceanic cable; a transoceanic voyage.* **2.** situated or living beyond the ocean: *the transoceanic nations of Europe; transoceanic peoples.* [TRANS- + OCEANIC]

tran·som (tran′səm), *n.* **1.** a crosspiece separating a door or the like from a window or fanlight above it. **2.** a window above such a crosspiece. **3.** a crossbar of wood or stone, dividing a window horizontally. **4.** a window so divided. **5.** *Naut.* **a.** a flat termination to a stern, above the water line. **b.** framework running athwartships in way of the sternpost of a steel or iron vessel, used as a support for the frames of the counter. **6.** *Artillery.* a metal piece connecting the sidepieces of the tail or the cheeks of a gun carriage. [late ME < L *trāns(tr)um* cross-beam (with loss of second *-tr-* by dissimilation), equiv. to *trāns-* TRANS- + *-trum* instrumental suffix] **—tran′somed,** *adj.*

T, Transom (def. 5a)

tran′som light′, a window above the transom of a doorway.

tran′som win′dow, 1. a window divided by a transom. **2.** See **transom light.**

tran·son·ic (tran son′ik), *adj.* *Chiefly Aeron.* close to the speed of propagation of sound; moving at 700–780 miles per hour at sea level. Also, **transsonic.** [TRANS- + SONIC]

transon′ic bar′rier. See **sound barrier.**

transp., 1. transparent. **2.** transportation.

trans·pa·cif·ic (trans′pə sif′ik), *adj.* **1.** passing or extending across the Pacific. **2.** beyond or on the other side of the Pacific. [TRANS- + PACIFIC]

trans·pa·dane (trans′pə dān′, trans pā′dān), *adj.* on the farther side, esp. the northern side of the Po River. [< L *trānspadān(us)* beyond the Po, equiv. to *trāns-* TRANS- + *Pad(us)* Po + *-ānus* -ANE]

trans·par·en·cy (trans pâr′ən sē, -par′-), *n., pl.* **-cies. 1.** Also, **trans·par′ence.** quality or state of being transparent. **2.** something transparent, esp. a picture, design, or the like on glass or some translucent substance, made visible by light shining through from behind. **3.** *Photog.* the proportion of the light that is passed through the emulsion on an area of a photographic image. [< ML *trānsparentia.* See TRANSPARENT, -ENCY]

trans·par·ent (trans pâr′ənt, -par′-), *adj.* **1.** having the property of transmitting rays of light through its substance so that bodies situated beyond or behind can be distinctly seen (opposed to *opaque,* and usually distinguished from *translucent*). **2.** admitting the passage of light through interstices. **3.** so sheer as to permit light to pass through; diaphanous. **4.** open; frank; candid: *the man's transparent earnestness.* **5.** easily seen through, recognized, or detected: *his transparent excuses.* **6.** manifest; obvious: *a story with a transparent plot.* **7.** *Obs.* shining through, as light. [late ME < ML *trānspārent-* (s. of *trānspārēns*) showing through (prp. of *trānspārēre*), equiv. to L *trāns-* TRANS- + *pārent-* (s. of *pārēns*) appearing (prp. of *pārēre*); see -ENT] **—trans·par′ent·ly,** *adv.* **—trans·par′ent·ness,** *n.*
—Syn. 1. clear, pellucid, limpid, crystalline. TRANSPARENT, TRANSLUCENT agree in describing material that light rays can pass through. That which is TRANSPARENT allows objects to be seen clearly through it: *Clear water is transparent.* That which is TRANSLUCENT allows light to pass through, diffusing it, however, so that objects beyond are not distinctly seen: *Ground glass is translucent.* **—Ant. 1.** opaque. **4.** secretive.

trans·pep·ti·da·tion (trans pep′ti dā′shən), *n.* *Biochem.* the process of transferring an amino acid or group of amino acids from one compound to another. [TRANS- + PEPTIDE + -ATION]

tran·spic·u·ous (tran spik′yōō əs), *adj.* transparent. [< NL *trānspicuus,* equiv. to *trāns-* TRANS- + *(per)spicuus* transparent; see PERSPICUOUS] **—tran·spic′u·ous·ly,** *adv.*

trans·pierce (trans pērs′), *v.t.*, **-pierced, -pierc·ing.** to pierce through; penetrate; pass through. [TRANS- + PIERCE; cf. F *transpercer*]

tran·spire (tran spīər′), *v.*, **-spired, -spir·ing.** **—***v.i.* **1.** to occur; happen; take place. **2.** to emit or give off waste matter, etc., through the surface, as of the body, of leaves, etc. **3.** to escape, as moisture, odor, etc., through or as if through pores. **4.** to be revealed or become known. **—***v.t.* **5.** to emit or give off (waste matter, watery vapor, an odor, etc.) through the surface, as of the body, of leaves, etc. [TRANS- + obs. *spire* to breathe < L *spīr(āre)*; cf. F *transpirer*] **—tran·spir′a·ble,** *adj.* **—tran·spi·ra·tion** (tran′spə rā′shən), *n.* **—tran·spir·a·to·ry** (tran spīər′ə tōr′ē, -tôr′ē), *adj.*

trans·plan·e·tar·y (trans plan′i ter′ē), *adj.* farther from the sun than a given planet. [TRANS- + PLANETARY]

trans·plant (*v.* trans plant′, -plänt′; *n.* trans′plant′, -plänt′), *v.t.* **1.** to remove (a plant) from one place and plant it in another. **2.** *Surg.* to transfer (an organ, a portion of tissue, etc.) from one part of the body to another or from one person or animal to another. **3.** to move from one place to another. **4.** to bring (a family, colony, etc.) from one country, region, etc., to another for settlement; relocate. **—***n.* **5.** act or process of transplanting. **6.** something transplanted. [late ME < LL *trānsplant(āre),* equiv. to L *trāns-* TRANS- + *plantāre* to PLANT] **—trans·plant′a·ble,** *adj.* **—trans′plan·ta′tion,** *n.* **—trans·plant′er,** *n.*

tran·spon·der (tran spon′dər), *n.* a radio or radar transceiver, used in radar beacons, that automatically transmits a reply promptly on reception of a certain signal. Also, **tran·spon′dor.** [TRANS(MITTER) + (RES)PONDER]

trans·po·ni·ble (trans pō′nə bəl), *adj.* capable of being transposed. [< L *trānspōn(ere)* (to) transfer, remove (*trāns-* TRANS- + *pōnere* to place) + -IBLE] **—trans′po·ni·bil′i·ty,** *n.*

trans·pon·tine (trans pon′tin, -tīn), *adj.* **1.** across or beyond a bridge. **2.** on the southern side of the Thames in London. [TRANS- + L *pont-* (s. of *pōns*) bridge + -INE[1]]

trans·port (*v.* trans pōrt′, -pôrt′; *n.* trans′pōrt′, -pôrt′), *v.t.* **1.** to carry, move, or convey from one place to another. **2.** to carry away by strong emotion; enrapture. **3.** to send into banishment, esp. to a penal colony. **4.** *Obs.* to kill. **—***n.* **5.** act of transporting or conveying; conveyance. **6.** a means of transporting or conveying, as a truck, bus, etc. **7.** a ship or plane employed for transporting soldiers, military stores, etc. **8.** an airplane carrying freight or passengers as part of a transportation system. **9.** a system of public travel. **10.** transportation (def. 4). **11.** strong emotion; ecstatic joy, bliss, etc. **12.** a convict sent into banishment, esp. to a penal colony: *The country had been colonized largely by transports.* [late ME < L *trānsport(āre)* (to) carry across. See TRANS-, PORT[5]] **—trans·port′a·ble,** *adj.* **—trans·port′a·bil′i·ty,** *n.* **—trans·port′ed·ly,** *adv.* **—trans·port′er,** *n.* **—trans·port′ive,** *adj.*
—Syn. 1. See **carry. 3.** banish, exile. **7.** freighter, tanker, troopship, oiler. **11.** rapture, ecstasy, happiness.

trans·por·ta·tion (trans′pər tā′shən), *n.* **1.** act of transporting. **2.** state of being transported. **3.** means of transport or conveyance. **4.** the business of conveying people, goods, etc. **5.** price of travel or transport by public conveyance; fare. **6.** *U.S.* tickets or permits for transport or travel. **7.** banishment, as of a criminal to a penal colony; deportation. [TRANSPORT + -ATION]

trans·port·ed (trans pōr′tid, -pôr′-), *adj.* **1.** emotionally moved; ecstatic: *He was transported by the music, as if in another world.* **2.** taken or carried from one place to another. [TRANSPORT + -ED[2]]

transport′er bridge′, a bridge for carrying passengers and vehicles by means of a platform suspended from a trolley.

trans′port num′ber, *Physical Chem.* See **transference number.**

trans·pos·al (trans pō′zəl), *n.* transposition. [TRANSPOSE + -AL[2]]

trans·pose (trans pōz′), *v.*, **-posed, -pos·ing.** **—***v.t.* **1.** to change the relative position, order, or sequence of; cause to change places; interchange: *to transpose the third and fourth letters of a word; to transpose several words in a sentence.* **2.** *Algebra.* to bring (a term) from one side of an equation to the other, with corresponding change of sign. **3.** *Music.* to reproduce in a different key, by raising or lowering in pitch. **4.** *Archaic.* to transfer or transport. **5.** *Obs.* to transform; transmute. **—***v.i.* **6.** to perform a piece of music in a key other than the one in which it is written: *Accompanists must learn to transpose at sight.* **—***n.* **7.** *Math.* a matrix formed from a given matrix by interchanging rows and columns. [ME < MF *transpos(er).* See TRANS-, POSE[1]] **—trans·pos′a·bil′i·ty,** *n.* **—trans·pos′a·ble,** *adj.* **—trans·pos′er,** *n.*
—Syn. 1, 3. rearrange. **2.** invert.

trans′posed con′jugate, *Math.* adjoint (def. 2).

transpos′ing in′strument, a musical instrument played at a pitch different from that indicated in the score.

trans·po·si·tion (trans′pə zish′ən), *n.* **1.** act of transposing; state of being transposed. **2.** a transposed form of something. **3.** *Photog.* the process of reversing the tonality of an image, as from negative to positive. **4.** *Math.* a permutation of a set of elements which interchanges two elements and leaves the remaining elements in their original positions. [< ML *trānspositiōn-* (s. of *trānspositiō*). See TRANS-, POSITION] **—trans′po·si′tion·al, trans·pos·i·tive** (trans poz′i tiv), *adj.*

trans·rec·ti·fi·ca·tion (trans rek′tə fə kā′shən, tranz-), *n.* *Elect., Electronics.* rectification occurring in one circuit as a result of the application of an alternating voltage to another circuit. [TRANS- + RECTIFICATION]

trans·rec·ti·fi·er (trans rek′tə fī′ər, tranz-), *n.* *Electronics.* a device, usually a vacuum tube, that provides transrectification. [TRANS- + RECTIFIER]

trans·ship (trans ship′), *v.*, **-shipped, -ship·ping.** **—***v.t.* **1.** to transfer from one ship, truck, freight car, or other conveyance to another. **—***v.i.* **2.** to change from one ship or other conveyance to another. Also, **tranship.** [TRANS- + SHIP] **—trans·ship′ment,** *n.*

Trans′-Si·be′ri·an Rail′road (trans′sī bēr′ē ən, trans′-), a railroad traversing Siberia and Manchuria, from Chelyabinsk in the Ural Mountains to Vladivostok: constructed by the Russian government 1891–99. over 4000 mi. long.

trans·son·ic (trans son′ik), *adj.* transonic.

trans′-Mis·sis·sip′pi, *adj.*
trans′-Mis·sis·sip′pi·an, *adj., n.*
trans·mold′, *v.t.*
trans′-Mon·go′li·an, *adj.*
trans·mon′tane, *adj.*
trans·mould, *v.t.*
trans·mun′dane, *adj.*
trans·mus′cle, *n.*
trans·mu′tu·al, *adj.*; -ly, *adv.*
trans·na′tion·al, *adj.*; -ly, *adv.*
trans·nat′ur·al, *adj.*
trans′-Nep·tu′ni·an, *adj.*
trans-Ni′ger, *adj.*
trans·nor′mal, *adj.*; -ly, *adv.*
trans·oc′u·lar, *adj.*
trans·or′bit·al, *adj.*
trans′o·var′i·an, *adj.*
trans·pal′mar, *adj.*
trans′-Pan·a·ma′ni·an, *adj.*
trans′-Par·a·guay′an, *adj.*
trans′pa·ri′e·tal, *adj.*
trans·par′ish, *adj.*
trans·pas′sion·al, *adj.*
trans·pa′tron·ized, *v.t.*, -ized, -iz·ing.
trans·pen′e·tra·ble, *adj.*
trans′pen·e·tra′tion, *n.*
trans′pen·in′su·lar, *adj.*
trans′per·i·to·ne′al, *adj.*; -ly, *adv.*
trans-Per′sian, *adj.*
trans·per′son·al, *adj.*; -ly, *adv.*
trans·phys′i·cal, *adj.*; -ly, *adv.*
trans·pleu′ral, *adj.*; -ly, *adv.*
trans·po′lar, *adj.*
trans·pour′, *v.t.*
trans·proc′ess, *n.*
trans·pul′mo·nar′y, *adj.*
trans′-Pyr·e·ne′an, *adj.*
trans·ra′tion·al, *adj.*; -ly, *adv.*
trans·re′al, *adj.*
trans-Rhen′ish, *adj.*
trans·riv′er·ine′, *adj.*
trans′-Sa·har′a, *adj.*
trans′-Sa·har′an, *adj.*
trans′-Sa·tur′ni·an, *adj.*
trans′seg·men′tal, *adj.*; -ly, *adv.*
trans·sen′su·al, *adj.*; -ly, *adv.*
trans·sep′tal, *adj.*
trans′se·pul′chral, *adj.*
trans-Sev′ern, *adj.*
trans·shape′, *v.t.*, -shaped, -shap·ing.
trans·shift, *v.*
trans′-Si·be′ri·an, *adj.*
trans·sol′id, *adj.*
trans·stel′lar, *adj.*
trans-Styg′i·an, *adj.*
trans′tha·lam′ic, *adj.*
trans′tho·rac′ic, *adj.*
trans-Ti′ber, *adj.*
trans′-Ti·be′ri·an, *adj.*
trans·tra′che·al, *adj.*

tran·sub·stan·ti·ate (tran′səb stan′shē āt′), *v.t.*, **-at·ed, -at·ing.** **1.** to change from one substance into another; transmute. **2.** *Theol.* to change (the substance of bread and wine) into the substance of body and blood of Christ, only the external form or appearance of the bread and wine remaining. [v. use of late ME *transsubstanciate* (adj.) < ML *trānssubstantiāt(us)*, ptp. of *trānssubstantiāre*. See TRANS-, SUBSTANCE, -ATE[1]] —**tran′sub·stan′tial,** *adj.* —**tran′sub·stan′tial·ly,** *adv.*

tran·sub·stan·ti·a·tion (tran′səb stan′shē ā′shən), *n.* **1.** the changing of one substance into another. **2.** *Theol.* (in the Eucharist) the conversion of the whole substance of the bread and wine into the body and blood of Christ, only the external appearance of bread and wine remaining (a doctrine of the Roman Catholic Church). [ME *transubstanciacioun* < ML *trānssubstantiātiōn-* (s. of *trānssubstantiātiō*). See TRANSUBSTANTIATE, -ION] —**tran′sub·stan′ti·a′tion·al·ist,** *n.*

tran·su·date (tran′sōō dāt′), *n.* transudation. [< NL *trānsūdāt(us)*, ptp. of *trānsūdāre* to TRANSUDE; see -ATE[1]]

tran·su·da·tion (tran′sōō dā′shən), *n.* **1.** act or process of transuding. **2.** a substance which has transuded. [< NL *trānsūdātiōn-* (s. of *trānsūdātiō*). See TRANSUDATE, -ION] —**tran·su·da·tive** (tran sōō′də tiv), **tran·su′da·to′ry,** *adj.*

tran·sude (tran sōōd′), *v.i.*, **-sud·ed, -sud·ing.** to pass or ooze through pores or interstices, as a fluid. [< NL *trānsūd(āre)* equiv. to L *trāns-* TRANS- + *sūdāre* to SWEAT]

trans·u·ran·ic (trans′yŏŏ ran′ik, tranz′-), *adj.* *Chem., Physics.* noting or pertaining to an element having a higher atomic number than uranium. Those presently known, and having atomic numbers from 93 to 103, are neptunium, plutonium, americium, curium, berkelium, californium, einsteinium, fermium, mendelevium, nobelium, and lawrencium. Also, **trans·u·ra·ni·an** (trans′yŏŏ rā′ nē ən, tranz′-), **trans′u·ra′ni·um.** [TRANS- + URANIC]

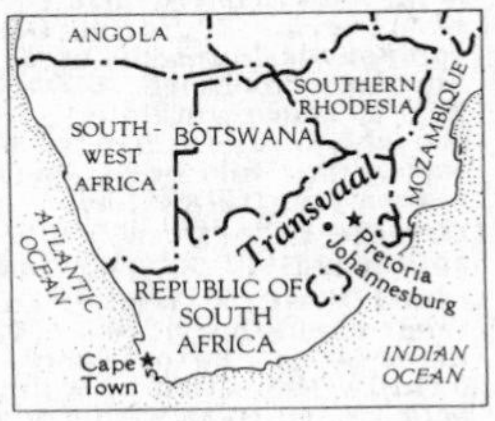

Trans·vaal (trans väl′, tranz-), *n.* a province in the NE Republic of South Africa. 6,225,052 (1960); 110,450 sq. mi. *Cap.:* Pretoria. Formerly, **South African Republic.** —**Trans·vaal′er,** *n.* —**Trans·vaal′i·an,** *adj.*

Trans′vaal jade′, a green grossularite, used as a gem: not a true jade. Also called **garnet jade, South African jade.**

trans·val·ue (trans val′yōō, tranz-), *v.t.*, **-ued, -u·ing.** to reestimate the value of, esp. on a basis differing from accepted standards; reappraise; reevaluate. [TRANS- + VALUE] —**trans′val·u·a′tion,** *n.*

trans·vec·tion (trans vek′shən, tranz-), *n.* *Rare.* act of transporting, as of a witch by a devil through the air. [< L *trānsvectiōn-* (s. of *trānsvectiō*) a carrying over, equiv. to *trānsvect(us)* carried over (ptp. of *trānsvehere*) + *-iōn-* -ION. See TRANS-, VECTOR]

trans·ver·sal (trans vûr′səl, tranz-), *adj.* **1.** transverse. —*n.* **2.** *Geom.* a line intersecting two or more lines. [late ME < ML *trānsversāl(is)*. See TRANSVERSE, -AL[1]] —**trans·ver′sal·ly,** *adv.*

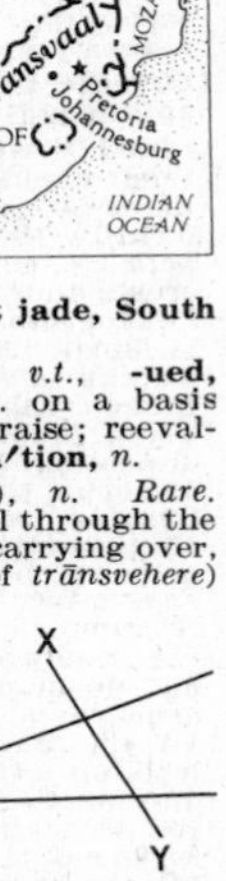

XY, Transversal (def. 2)

trans·verse (trans vûrs′, tranz-; trans′vûrs, tranz′-), *adj.* **1.** lying or being across or in a cross direction; cross; athwart. **2.** (of a flute) having a mouth hole in the side of the tube, near its end, across which the player's breath is directed. Cf. **end-blown.** —*n.* **3.** something which is transverse. **4.** *Naut.* See **web frame. 5.** *Geom.* See **transverse axis. 6.** a direct city route or road that cuts through a park or other area of light traffic; shortcut. [< L *trānsvers(us)* going or lying across, athwart. See TRAVERSE] —**trans·verse′ly,** *adv.* —**trans·verse′ness,** *n.*

trans′verse ax′is, *Geom.* **1.** the axis of a hyperbola that passes through the two foci. **2.** the segment of such an axis included between the vertices of the hyperbola. See diag. under **hyperbola.**

transverse′ magnifica′tion, *Optics.* See **lateral magnification.**

transverse′ presenta′tion, *Obstet.* presentation in which the fetus is turned with its long axis across the mouth of the uterus, at right angles to the axis of the birth canal. Also called **crossbirth.**

trans′verse proc′ess, a process which projects from the sides of a vertebra.

trans′verse sec′tion. See **cross section.**

transverse′ vibra′tions, *Physics.* periodic disturbances for which the particle oscillations of the medium are perpendicular to the direction of propagation.

trans′verse wave′, *Physics.* a wave in which the direction of displacement is perpendicular to the direction of propagation, as a surface wave of water. Cf. **longitudinal wave.**

trans·ves·tism (trans ves′tiz əm, tranz-), *n.* the practice of wearing clothing appropriate to the opposite sex, often as a manifestation of homosexuality. Also, **trans·ves·ti·tism** (trans ves′ti tiz′əm, tranz-). [*transvest* to clothe across, i.e. in violation of custom (now obs.; see TRANS-, VEST) + -ISM; modeled on G *Transvestismus*] —**trans·ves′tic,** *adj.* —**trans·ves·tite** (trans ves′tīt, tranz-), *n.*

Tran·syl·va·ni·a (tran′sil vā′nē ə, -vān′yə), *n.* a region and former province in central Rumania: formerly part of Hungary. 24,027 sq. mi. —**Tran′syl·va′ni·an,** *adj.*, *n.*

Tran′sylva′nian Alps′, a mountain range in S Rumania, forming a SW extension of the Carpathian Mountains. Highest peak, Mt. Negoiul, 8345 ft.

trant·er (tran′tər), *n.* *Brit. Dial.* a peddler, hawker, or carrier using a horse and cart. [alter. of earlier *traunter* < ML *travetār(ius)*, perh. < L *transvect(us)* (see TRANSVECTION) + *-ārius* -ER[1]]

trap[1] (trap), *n.*, *v.*, **trapped** or (*Archaic*) **trapt; trap·ping.** —*n.* **1.** a contrivance used for catching game or other animals, as a mechanical device that springs shut suddenly, a pitfall, or a snare. **2.** any device, stratagem, trick, or the like for catching a person unawares. **3.** any of various devices for removing undesirable substances from a moving fluid, vapor, etc., as water from steam or cinders from coal gas. **4.** an arrangement in a pipe, as a double curve or a U-shaped section, in which liquid remains and forms a seal for preventing the passage or escape of air or of gases through the pipe from behind or below. **5. traps,** the percussion instruments of a jazz or dance band. **6.** *Trapshooting, Skeet.* a device for hurling clay pigeons into the air. **7.** the piece of wood, shaped somewhat like a shoe hollowed at the heel, and moving on a pivot, used in playing the game of trapball. **8.** the game of trapball. **9.** *Chiefly Brit.* a carriage, esp. a light, two-wheeled one. **10.** See **trap door. 11.** *Sports.* **a.** act or instance of trapping a ball. **b.** *Football.* mousetrap (def. 2). **12.** *Slang.* mouth: *Keep your trap shut.* —*v.t.* **13.** to catch in a trap; ensnare: *to trap foxes.* **14.** to catch by stratagem, artifice, or trickery. **15.** to furnish or set with traps. **16.** to provide (a drain or the like) with a trap. **17.** to stop and hold by a trap, as air in a pipe. **18.** *Sports.* **a.** to catch (a ball) as it rises after having just hit the ground: *The outfielder thought he had caught it on the fly, but the umpire ruled that he had trapped it.* **b.** *Baseball.* to catch (a base runner) away from a base, usually by a throw: *He was trapped off first by a quick throw from the catcher.* **c.** mousetrap. (def. 3). —*v.i.* **19.** to set traps for game: *He was busy trapping.* **20.** to engage in the business of trapping animals for their furs. **21.** *Trapshooting, Skeet.* to work the trap. [ME *trappe*, OE *træppe;* c. MD, MFlem *trappe* trap; akin to OE *treppan* to tread, G *Treppe* staircase, ladder, D *trap* step, kick, stair, ladder] —**trap′like′,** *adj.*

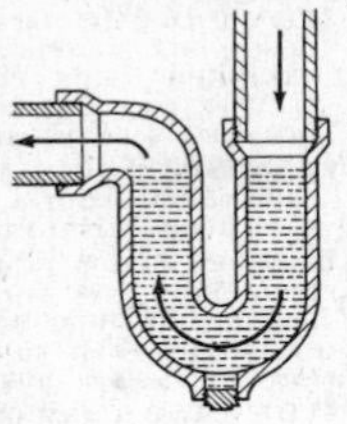

Trap[1] (def. 4)

—**Syn. 1, 2.** TRAP, PITFALL, SNARE apply to literal or figurative contrivances for deceiving and catching animals or people. Literally, a TRAP is a mechanical contrivance for catching animals, the main feature usually being a spring: *a trap baited with cheese for mice.* Figuratively, TRAP suggests the scheme of one person to take another by surprise and gain an advantage from him: *a trap for the unwary.* A PITFALL is (usually) a concealed pit arranged for the capture of large animals or of men who may fall into it; figuratively, it is any concealed danger, error, or source of disaster: *to catch elephants in a pitfall.* A SNARE is a device for entangling birds, rabbits, etc., with intent to capture; figuratively, it implies enticement and inveiglement: *a snare for small animals.* **2.** ambush, artifice, maneuver. **13.** entrap. **14.** ambush, outmaneuver.

trap[2] (trap), *n.*, *v.*, **trapped, trap·ping.** —*n.* **1. traps,** *Informal.* personal belongings; baggage. **2.** *Obs.* a cloth or covering for a horse; caparison. —*v.t.* **3.** to furnish with or as with trappings; caparison. [ME *trappe* < ?]

trap[3] (trap), *n.* *Geol.* any of various fine-grained, dark-colored igneous rocks having a more or less columnar structure, esp. some form of basalt. Also called **traprock.** [< Sw *trapp*, var. of *trappa* stair (so named from their looks) < MLG *trappe.* See TRAP[1]]

trap[4] (trap), *n.* *Scot.* a ladder or ladderlike device used to reach a loft, attic, etc. [< D; MD *trappe.* See TRAP[1]]

tra·pan (trə pan′), *n.*, *v.t.*, **-panned, -pan·ning.** *Archaic.* trepan[2]. —**tra·pan′ner,** *n.*

Tra·pa·ni (trä′pä nē), *n.* a seaport in NW Sicily. 75,537 (1961).

trap·ball (trap′bôl′), *n.* **1.** an old game in which a ball placed on the hollowed end of a trap is thrown into the air by striking the other end of the trap with a bat and then driven to a distance with the bat. **2.** the ball used in this game. [TRAP[1] + BALL[1]]

trap′ car′, a railroad car used at a terminal for collecting and distributing freight.

trap′ cut′, *Jewelry.* See **step cut.**

trap′ door′, **1.** a door or the like, flush, or nearly so, with the surface of a floor, ceiling, roof, etc. **2.** the opening which it covers. —**trap′-door′,** *adj.*

trap′-door spi′der, any of several burrowing spiders of the family *Ctenizidae*, that construct a tubular nest with a hinged lid.

trapes (trāps), *v.i.*, *v.t.*, *n.* traipse.

tra·peze (tra pēz′), *n.* **1.** an apparatus consisting of a short horizontal bar attached to the ends of two suspended ropes. **2.** (on a small sailboat) a device by which a person can hold himself almost completely outboard while hiking. [< F, special use of *trapèze* TRAPEZIUM]

trapeze′ art′ist, one who performs, esp. professionally, on a trapeze. Also called **tra·pez′ist.**

trapeze′ dress′, a semifitted, unbelted dress that widens gradually from the shoulder to the hem.

tra·pe·zi·form (trə pē′zə fôrm′), *adj.* formed like a trapezium. [TRAPEZI(UM) + -FORM]

tra·pe·zi·um (trə pē′zē əm), *n.*, *pl.* **-zi·ums, -zi·a** (-zē ə). **1.** *Geom.* **a.** (in Euclidean geometry) any rectilinear quadrilateral plane figure not a parallelogram. **b.** a quadrilateral plane figure of which no two sides are parallel. **c.** *Brit.* trapezoid (def. 1a). **2.** *Anat.* the greater multangular bone. See under **multangulum.** [< NL < Gk *trapézion* kind of quadrilateral, lit., small table, equiv. to *trápez(a)* table (aph. var. of **tetrapeza* object having four feet, equiv. to *tetra-* four + *péza* foot) + *-ion* dim. suffix] —**tra·pe′zi·al,** *adj.*

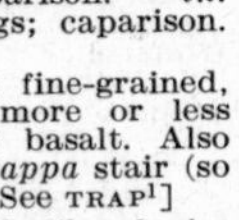

Trapezium (def. 1b)

tra·pe·zi·us (trə pē′zē əs), *n.*, *pl.* **-us·es.** *Anat.* a broad, flat muscle on each side of the upper and back part of the neck, shoulders, and thorax, the action of which raises, or rotates, or draws back the shoulders, and pulls the head backward or to one side. [< NL, short for *trapezius musculus* trapeziform muscle]

trapezo-, a learned borrowing from Greek meaning "table," "trapezium," used in the formation of compound words: *trapezohedron.* [comb. form of Gk *trápeza* table, *trapézion* trapezium]

tra·pe·zo·he·dron (trə pē′zə hē′drən, trap′i-), *n.*, *pl.* **-drons, -dra** (-drə). *Crystall.* a crystal form having all faces trapeziums. [TRAPEZO- + -HEDRON] —**tra·pe′zo·he′dral,** *adj.*

trap·e·zoid (trap′i zoid′), *n.* **1.** *Geom.* **a.** a quadrilateral plane figure having two parallel and two nonparallel sides **b.** *Brit.* trapezium (def. 1b). **2.** *Anat.* the lesser multangular bone. See under **multangulum.** —*adj.* **3.** Also, **trap′e·zoi′dal.** *Geom.* of, pertaining to, or having the form of a trapezoid. [< NL *trapezoīd(ēs)* < LGk *trapezoeidḗs* trapezium-like. See TRAPEZO-, -OID]

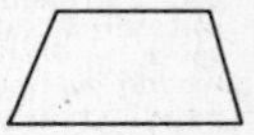

Trapezoid (def. 1a)

trap′ezoi′dal rule′, *Math.* a numerical method for evaluating the area between a curve and an axis by approximating the area with the areas of trapezoids.

trap·e·zoph·o·ron (trap′i zof′ə ron′), *n.*, *pl.* **-zoph·o·ra** (-zof′ər ə). one of two or more sculptured supports for a classical table top, usually decorated with human or animal members, as heads, wings, or legs. [< Gk: table-bearer, equiv. to *trapezo-* TRAPEZO- + *-phoron*, neut. of *-phoros* -PHOROUS]

Trappe, La (*Fr.* LA TRAP′). See **La Trappe.**

trap·per (trap′ər), *n.* **1.** one who traps. **2.** a person whose business is the trapping of animals for their furs. **3.** *Mining.* one who opens and closes doors that regulate the flow of air through an opening in a mine. [TRAP[1] + -ER[1]]

trap·pings (trap′ingz), *n.* (*construed as pl.*) **1.** articles of equipment or dress, esp. of an ornamental character. **2.** conventional or characteristic articles of dress or adornment. **3.** Sometimes, **trapping.** an ornamental covering for a horse; caparison. [ME; see TRAP[2], -ING[1]]

Trap·pist (trap′ist), *n.* **1.** *Rom. Cath. Ch.* a member of a branch of the Cistercian order, observing the extremely austere reformed rule established at La Trappe in 1664. —*adj.* **2.** of or pertaining to the Trappists. [< F *trappiste*, based on the name of the monastery. See LA TRAPPE, -IST]

Trap′pist cheese′, a semisoft, mild, yellow cheese from whole milk, made by Trappist monks. Also called **Gethsemane cheese.**

trap′ play′, *Football.* mousetrap (def. 2).

trap·py (trap′ē), *adj.*, **-pi·er, -pi·est. 1.** difficult or tricky: *It was a long, treacherous march over trappy terrain.* **2.** catching one unawares: *trappy pitfalls.* **3.** (of horses) moving with the legs lifted high in a short and rapid manner. [TRAP[1] + -Y[1]]

trap·rock (trap′rok′), *n.* trap[3]. [TRAP[3] + ROCK]

trap·shoot·ing (trap′shōō′ting), *n.* the sport of shooting at clay pigeons hurled into the air from a trap. Cf. **skeet.**[1] [TRAP[1] + SHOOTING] —**trap′-shoot′er,** *n.*

trap′ shot′, *Sports.* See **half volley.**

trapt[1] (trapt), *v.* *Archaic.* a pt. and pp. of **trap**[1].

trapt[2] (trapt), *v.* *Archaic.* pp. of **trap**[2].

tra·pun·to (trə pōōn′tō), *n.*, *pl.* **-tos.** quilting having an embossed design produced by outlining the pattern with single stitches and then padding it with yarn or cotton. [< It: embroidery; as adj., embroidered, lit., pricked through (ptp. of *trapungere*), equiv. to *tra-* (< L *trā-*, var. of *trāns-* TRANS-) + *-punto* < L *punct(us)*, equiv. to *pung-* (s. of *pungere* to prick) + *-tus* ptp. suffix; see PUNCTURE]

Tras·en·tine (traz′ən tēn′), *n.* *Pharm., Trademark.* adiphenine.

trash[1] (trash), *n.* **1.** anything worthless or useless; rubbish. **2.** foolish or pointless ideas, talk, or writing; nonsense. **3.** a worthless or disreputable person. **4.** such persons collectively. **5.** literary or artistic material of poor or inferior quality. **6.** broken or torn bits, as twigs, splinters, rags, or the like. **7.** that which is broken or lopped off from anything in preparing it for use. **8.** the refuse of sugar cane after the juice has been expressed. —*v.t.* **9.** to remove the outer leaves of (a growing sugar cane plant). **10.** to free from superfluous twigs or branches. [ME *trasches* (pl.), appar. c. Norw *trask* rubbish; akin to OE *trus* brushwood, Icel *tros* rubbish]

trash[2] (trash), *v.t.* **1.** *Obs.* to hinder; retard; restrain. **2.** *Obs.* to hold (a dog or other animal) in check by a cord or leash. —*n.* **3.** *Brit. Dial.* a cord or leash for holding an animal, esp. a hunting dog, in check. [? var. of TRACE[2]]

trash′ can′, a container for the disposal of dry waste matter. Cf. **garbage can.**

trash′ rack′, a grating for retaining floating objects from water entering a penstock.

trash·y (trash′ē), *adj.*, **trash·i·er, trash·i·est. 1.** of the nature of trash; inferior in quality; rubbishy; useless or worthless. **2.** (of a field) strewn or encumbered with trash, esp. the withered vegetation from an earlier crop. [TRASH[1] + -Y[1]] —**trash′i·ly,** *adv.* —**trash′i·ness,** *n.*

Tra·si·me·no (trä′sē me′nô), *n.* a lake in central Italy, in Umbria near Perugia: Romans defeated by Hannibal 217 B.C. ab. 50 sq. mi. Also called **Lake of Perugia.** Latin, **Tras·i·me·nus** (tras′ə mē′nəs).

trass (tras), *n.* a rock common along the Rhine, composed chiefly of comminuted pumice or other volcanic material, used for making hydraulic cement. Also, **terass, terras.** [< D *tras*, earlier *tarasse* < early It *terrazza* worthless earth. See TERRACE]

trau·chle (trä′кнəl), *n.*, *v.t.*, **-chled, -chling.** *Scot.* trachle.

trau·ma (trou′mə, trô′-), *n.*, *pl.* **-ma·ta** (-mə tə), **-mas. 1.** *Pathol.* **a.** a body injury produced by violence or any thermal, chemical, etc., extrinsic agent. **b.** the condition produced by this; traumatism. **2.** *Psychiatry.* a startling experience which has a lasting effect on mental life; a shock. [< Gk *traûma* wound]

trau·mat·ic (trə mat′ik, trô-, trou-), *adj.* **1.** of, pertaining to, or produced by a trauma or wound. **2.** adapted to the cure of wounds. [< LL *traumatic(us)*

< Gk *traumatikós* pertaining to wounds, equiv. to *traumat-* (s. of *traûma* TRAUMA) + *-ikos* -IC] —**trau·mat′i·cal·ly,** *adv.*

traumat′ic neuro′sis, *Psychiatry.* a neurosis caused by physical injury or severe emotional stress.

trau·ma·tism (trô′mə tiz′əm, trou′-), *n. Pathol.* **1.** any abnormal condition produced by a trauma. **2.** the trauma or wound itself. [< LGk *traumatismós* a wounding. See TRAUMATIC, -ISM]

trau·ma·tize (trô′mə tīz′, trou′-), *v.t.*, **-tized, -tiz·ing. 1.** *Pathol.* to injure (tissues) by force or by thermal, chemical, electrical, etc., agents. **2.** *Psychiatry.* to cause a trauma in (a person's mind): *to be traumatized by a childhood experience.* [< Gk *traumatíz(ein)* (to) wound. See TRAUMATIC, -IZE] —**trau′ma·ti·za′tion,** *n.*

trav., 1. traveler. **2.** travels.

tra·vail (trə vāl′, trav′āl, trav′əl), *n.* **1.** painfully difficult or burdensome work; toil. **2.** pain, anguish, suffering, etc., resulting from mental or physical hardship. **3.** the labor and pain of childbirth. —*v.i.* **4.** to suffer the pangs of childbirth; be in labor. **5.** *Archaic.* to toil or exert oneself. [ME *travaill(en)* < OF *travaill(i)e(r)* (to) torment < VL **trepaliāre* to torture, deriv. of LL *trepāli(um)* torture chamber, lit., instrument of torture made with three stakes. See TRI-, PALE[3]]
—**Syn. 1.** labor, work, moil. **2.** torment, agony.

Trav·an·core (trav′ən kōr′, -kôr′), *n.* a former state in SW India: merged 1949 with Cochin to form a new state (**Trav′ancore and Co′chin**); reorganized 1956 to form the larger part of Kerala state. Cf. **Cochin.**

trave[1] (trāv), *n. Archit.* **1.** a crossbeam. **2.** a section or bay formed by crossbeams. [< MF *trave* < L *trab(em)*, acc. of *trabs* beam, timber]

trave[2] (trāv), *n.* a device to inhibit a wild or untrained horse or one being shod. [ME; OE *træf* framework, building, heathen temple < L *trab-* (s. of *trabs*) structure made of timbers]

trav·el (trav′əl), *v.*, **-eled, -el·ing** or (*esp. Brit.*) **-elled, -el·ling,** *n.* —*v.i.* **1.** to go from one place to another, as by car, train, plane, or ship; take a trip; journey: *to travel for pleasure.* **2.** to move or go from one place or point to another. **3.** to proceed or advance in any way. **4.** to go from place to place as a representative of a business firm. **5.** to associate or consort with: *He travels with a wealthy crowd. She travels in good company.* **6.** *Informal.* to move with speed. **7.** to move in a fixed course, as a piece of mechanism. **8.** to pass, or be transmitted, as light, sound, etc. **9.** *Basketball.* walk (def. 7). —*v.t.* **10.** to travel, journey, or pass through or over, as a country, district, road, etc. **11.** to journey or traverse (a specified distance): *We traveled a hundred miles today.* **12.** to cause to journey; ship: *to travel logs downriver; to travel stock to market.* —*n.* **13.** act of traveling; journeying, esp. in distant or foreign places: *the difficulties of travel in midwinter; to discuss future travel to Mars.* **14. travels, a.** journeys; wanderings: *to set out on one's travels.* **b.** journeys as the subject of a written account or literary work: *a book of travels.* **c.** such an account or work. **15.** the coming and going of persons or conveyances along a way of passage; traffic: *an increase in travel on state roads.* **16.** *Mach.* **a.** the complete movement of a moving part, esp. a reciprocating part, in one direction, or the distance traversed; stroke. **b.** length of stroke. **17.** movement or passage in general: *to reduce the travel of food from kitchen to customer's table.* [ME *travaill(en)* (to) journey; special use of TRAVAIL] —**trav′el·a·ble;** *esp. Brit.,* **trav′el·la·ble,** *adj.*

trav′el a′gency, a business that accommodates travelers, as by securing tickets, arranging for reservations, giving information, etc. Also called **trav′el bu′reau.**

trav′el a′gent, one who works in a travel agency and arranges accommodations at hotels or with transportation facilities, prepares an itinerary, etc., for a client.

trav·eled (trav′əld), *adj.* **1.** having traveled, esp. to distant places; experienced in travel. **2.** used by travelers: *a heavily traveled road.* **3.** *Geol.* moved to a distance from the original site, as a boulder. Also, *esp. Brit.,* **travelled.** [late ME; see TRAVEL, -ED[2]]

trav·el·er (trav′ə lər, trav′lər), *n.* **1.** one who or that which travels. **2.** one who travels or has traveled in distant places or foreign lands. **3.** See **traveling salesman. 4.** *Chiefly Brit.* a commercial traveler or traveling salesman. **5.** a piece of mechanism constructed to move in a fixed course. **6.** *Textiles.* (in ring spinning) a small metal device that moves rapidly around the ring and guides the yarn onto the revolving bobbin. **7.** *Naut.* **a.** a metal ring or thimble fitted to move freely on a rope, spar, or rod. **b.** Also called **horse.** the rope, spar, or rod itself. **c.** a ring block, or other fitting, either attached to the sheet of a fore-and-aft sail or through which the sheet is rove, that slides from side to side on a metal rod fastened to the deck. **8.** Also, **trav′eler cur′tain.** *Theat.* a transverse curtain opened by being drawn from both sides of the proscenium. Also, *esp. Brit.,* **traveller.** [ME *travaillour.* See TRAVEL, -ER[1]]

trav′eler's check′, a check, usually one of a set, sold by a bank or the like, that may be cashed by countersigning in the presence of a payee and is widely accepted by financial and commercial firms.

trav·el·er's-joy (trav′əl ərz joi′, trav′lərz-), *n.* a woody vine, *Clematis Vitalba,* of Europe and northern Africa, having long-plumed fruit and slightly fragrant, white flowers. Also called **old-man's-beard, withywind.**

trav·el·er's-tree (trav′ə lərz trē′, trav′lərz-), *n.* a bananalike tree, *Ravenala madagascariensis,* of the Malagasy Republic, having large leaves, the petioles of which contain a clear, watery sap.

trav′eling bag′, a small bag, as a valise or suitcase, usually made of leather, having an oblong shape, and used chiefly to hold clothes.

trav′eling block′, (in a hoisting tackle) the block hooked to and moving with the load.

trav′eling sales′man, a representative of a business firm who travels in an assigned territory soliciting orders for his company's products or services. Also called **commercial traveler.**

trav′eling-wave′ tube′ (trav′ə liṅg wāv′, trav′liṅg-), *Electronics.* an electron tube used in microwave communications systems, having an electron beam directed coaxially through a wire helix to produce amplification.

trav·elled (trav′əld), *adj. Chiefly Brit.* traveled.

trav·el·ler (trav′ə lər, trav′lər), *n. Chiefly Brit.* traveler.

trav·e·logue (trav′ə lôg′, -log′), *n.* **1.** a lecture describing travels, usually illustrated by photographs, exhibited items, etc. **2.** a motion picture describing travels, esp. one shown in theaters. Also, **trav′e·log′.** [TRAVEL + (MONO)LOGUE]

trav′el shot′, *Motion Pictures, Television.* a camera shot taken from a mobile platform, dolly, or the like, that keeps within range of a moving subject.

trav′el time′, time spent traveling for a job, as from home to work or from one designated point to another in the course of business, often paid for by the employer: *You can figure my travel time to and from the office at two hours daily.*

trav·erse (trav′ərs, trə vûrs′), *v.*, **-ersed, -ers·ing,** *n., adj., adv.* —*v.t.* **1.** to pass or move over, along, or through. **2.** to go to and fro over or along. **3.** to extend across or over: *A covered bridge traverses the stream.* **4.** to go up, down, or across (a rope, mountain, hill, etc.) at an angle: *The climbers traversed the east face of the mountain with ease.* **5.** to cause to move laterally. **6.** to look over, examine, or consider carefully; review; survey. **7.** to go counter to; obstruct; oppose; thwart. **8.** to contradict or deny. **9.** *Law.* **a.** (in the law of pleading) to deny formally (an allegation of fact set forth in a previous pleading). **b.** to join issue upon. **10.** to turn and point (a gun) in any direction. **11.** *Naut.* to brace (a yard) fore and aft. —*v.i.* **12.** to pass along or go across something; cross; cross over: *traversing along the open road; a point in the river where we could traverse.* **13.** to turn laterally, as a gun. **14.** *Fencing.* to glide the blade toward the hilt of the contestant's foil while applying pressure to the blade. [ME *travers(en)* < MF *traverse(r)* (to) cross < LL *trānsversāre,* deriv. of L *trānsvers(us)* TRANSVERSE. See TRANS-, VERSUS]
—*n.* **15.** act of passing across, over, or through. **16.** something that crosses, obstructs, or thwarts; obstacle. **17.** a transversal or similar line. **18.** a place where one may traverse or cross; crossing. **19.** *Archit.* a transverse gallery or loft of communication in a church or other large building. **20.** a bar, strip, rod, or other structural part placed or extending across; crosspiece; crossbar. **21.** a railing, lattice, or screen serving as a barrier. **22.** *Naut.* **a.** the zigzag track of a vessel compelled by contrary winds or currents to sail on different courses. **b.** each of the runs in a single direction made in such sailing. **23.** *Fort.* **a.** a defensive barrier, parapet, or the like, placed transversely. **b.** a defensive barrier thrown across the terreplein or the covered way of a fortification to protect it from enfilade fire. **24.** *Gunnery.* the horizontal turning of a gun so as to make it point in any required direction. **25.** *Mach.* **a.** the motion of a lathe tool or grinding wheel along a piece of work. **b.** a part moving along a piece of work in this way, as the carriage of a lathe. **26.** *Survey.* a series of distances and angles or bearings connecting successive instrument stations of a survey. **27.** *Law.* a formal denial of some matter of fact alleged by the other side. —*adj.* **28.** lying, extending, or passing across; transverse. —*adv.* **29.** *Obs.* across; crosswise; transversely. [ME *travers(e)* (n.) < MF *traverse* (<< L *trānsversa* something lying across, fem. of *trānsversus*) and *travers* (<< L *trānsversum* passage across, neut. of *trānsversus.* See v.)] —**tra·vers′a·ble,** *adj.* —**tra·vers′al,** *n.* —**tra·vers′er,** *n.*
—**Syn. 1.** cross. **6.** inspect. **7.** hinder, impede. **8.** counter, gainsay, dispute, challenge.

trav′erse board′, a circular board formerly used in navigation, marked with 32 radii representing points of the compass, with each radius having a group of holes for pegs indicating the number of hours or half-hours sailed on each course.

Trav′erse Cit′y (trav′ərs), a city in NW Michigan. 18,432 (1960).

trav′erse rod′, a horizontal rod upon which drapes slide to open or close when pulled by cords.

trav·er·tine (trav′ər tin, -tēn′), *n.* a form of limestone deposited by springs, esp. hot springs, used in Italy for building. Also, **trav·er·tin** (trav′ər tin). [< It *travertin(o),* equiv. to *tra-* across (< L *trāns-* TRANS-) + *(ti)vertino* < L *Tīburtīn(us),* equiv. to *Tīburt-* (s. of *Tībur*s) the Tiburtine territory + *-inus* -INE[1]]

trav·es·ty (trav′i stē), *n., pl.* **-ties,** *v.,* **-tied, -ty·ing.** —*n.* **1.** a literary or artistic burlesque of a serious work or subject, characterized by grotesque or ludicrous incongruity of style, treatment, subject matter, etc. **2.** a literary or artistic composition so inferior in quality as to seem merely a grotesque imitation of its model. **3.** any grotesque or debased likeness or imitation: *a travesty of justice.* —*v.t.* **4.** to make a travesty on; turn (a serious work or subject) to ridicule by burlesque imitation or treatment. **5.** to imitate grotesquely or absurdly. [< F *travesti* disguised, ptp. of *travestir* < It *travestire* to disguise, equiv. to *tra-* (< L *trāns-* TRANS-) + *vestire* to clothe < L *vestīre;* see VEST]

Tra·vi·a·ta, La (*It.* lä trä vyä′tä; *Eng.* lä trä′vē ä′tə), an opera (1853) by Giuseppe Verdi.

tra·vi·at·ed (trā′vē ā′tid), *adj.* (of a ceiling) divided transversely. [var. of *travated* < It *travat(o)* (*trav(e)* beam, TRAVE[1] + *-ato* -ATE[1]) + -ED[3]]

tra·vois (trə voi′), *n., pl.* **-vois** (-voiz′). a transport device, formerly used by the Plains Indians, consisting of two poles joined by a frame and drawn by an animal. [pseudo-F for *travoy* (rhyming with *boy*), repr. var. pronunciation of F *travail* TRAVE[2] < ?]

trawl (trôl), *n.* **1.** Also called **trawl′ net′.** a strong fishing net for dragging along the sea bottom. **2.** Also called **trawl′ line′.** a buoyed line used in sea fishing, having numerous short lines with baited hooks attached at intervals. —*v.i.* **3.** to fish with a net whose edge is dragged along the sea bottom to catch the fish living there. **4.** to fish with a trawl line. **5.** to troll. —*v.t.* **6.** to catch with a trawl net or a trawl line. **7.** to drag (a trawl net). **8.** to troll. [late ME *trawelle* < MD *traghel* dragnet, *traghelen* to drag; c. TRAIL[1]] —**trawl′a·bil′i·ty,** *n.* —**trawl′a·ble,** *adj.*

trawl·er (trô′lər), *n.* **1.** one who trawls. **2.** any of various types of vessels used in fishing with a trawl net. [TRAWL + -ER[1]]

tray[1] (trā), *n.* **1.** a flat, shallow container or receptacle made of wood, metal, etc., usually with slightly raised edges, used for carrying, holding, or displaying articles of food, glass, china, etc. **2.** a removable receptacle of this shape in a cabinet, box, trunk, or the like, sometimes forming a drawer. **3.** a tray and its contents: *to have a breakfast tray in one's room; to examine a tray of diamonds.* [ME; OE *trēg, trīg;* c. OSw *trō* corn measure; akin to TREE]

tray[2] (trā), *n. Australian Slang.* a coin worth threepence. Also called **tray′ bit′.** [see TREY]

tray′ ag′riculture, hydroponics.

tray′ ta′ble, a folding stand for supporting a tray.

treach·er·ous (trech′ər əs), *adj.* **1.** characterized by faithlessness or readiness to betray trust; disloyal; perfidious; traitorous. **2.** deceptive, untrustworthy, or unreliable. **3.** unstable or insecure, as footing. **4.** dangerous; hazardous: *the treacherous ascent up the face of the mountain.* [ME *trecherous* < AF, equiv. to *trecher* deceiver (*trech-* deceive + *-er* -ER[2]) + *-ous* -OUS. Cf. F *tricheur* trickster] —**treach′er·ous·ly,** *adv.* —**treach′er·ous·ness,** *n.*
—**Syn. 1.** unfaithful, faithless, treasonous. **2.** deceitful.
—**Ant. 1.** loyal. **2.** reliable.

treach·er·y (trech′ə rē), *n., pl.* **-er·ies. 1.** violation of faith; betrayal of trust; treason. **2.** an act of perfidy, faithlessness, or treason. [ME *trecherie* < MF, OF *trech(ier)* (to) deceive + *-erie* -ERY]
—**Syn. 1.** See **disloyalty.** —**Ant. 1.** loyalty.

trea·cle (trē′kəl), *n.* **1.** *Brit.* **a.** molasses, esp. that which is drained from the vats used in sugar refining. **b.** Also called **golden syrup.** a mild mixture of molasses, corn syrup, etc., used in cooking or as a table syrup. **2.** contrived or unrestrained sentimentality: *a movie plot of the most shameless treacle; an Irish tenor with a voice of pure treacle.* **3.** *Pharm. Obs.* any of various medicinal compounds, formerly used as antidotes for poisonous bites or for poisons. **4.** *Obs.* a sovereign remedy. [ME, var. of *triacle* antidote < MF, OF < L *thēriaca* < Gk *thēriakḗ,* n. use of fem. of *thēriakós,* equiv. to *thēri(on)* reptile (*thḗr* wild beast + *-ion* dim. suffix) + *-akos* -AC] —**trea·cly** (trē′klē), *adj.*

trea·cle·ber·ry (trē′kəl ber′ē), *n., pl.* **-ries.** See **wild spikenard.** [TREACLE + BERRY]

tread (tred), *v.,* **trod** or (*Archaic*) **trode; trod·den** or **trod; tread·ing;** *n.* —*v.t.* **1.** to step or walk on, about, in, or along. **2.** to trample or crush underfoot. **3.** to form by the action of walking or trampling: *to tread a path.* **4.** to treat with disdainful harshness or cruelty; crush; oppress. **5.** to perform by walking or dancing: *to tread a measure.* **6.** (of a male bird) to copulate with (a female bird). —*v.i.* **7.** to set down the foot or feet in walking; step; walk. **8.** to step, walk, or trample so as to press, crush, or injure something (usually fol. by *on* or *upon*): *to tread on grapes; to tread on a person's foot.* **9.** (of a male bird) to copulate. **10. tread on someone's toes** or **corns,** to offend or irritate someone: *I'm sorry if I'm treading on anyone's toes, but I thought it was an awful book.* **11. tread the boards** or **stage,** to play a role on the stage; act, esp. professionally: *He recalled with nostalgia the days when he had trod the boards.* **12. tread water,** *Swimming.* to maintain the body erect in the water with the head above the surface usually by a pumping up-and-down movement of the legs and sometimes the arms. —*n.* **13.** action of treading, stepping, or walking. **14.** the sound of footsteps. **15.** manner of treading or walking. **16.** a single step as in walking. **17.** any of various things or parts on which a person or thing treads, stands, or moves. **18.** the part of the under surface of the foot or of a shoe that touches the ground. **19.** the horizontal upper surface of a step in a stair, on which the foot is placed. **20.** *Naut.* **a.** the length of the keel of a vessel. **b.** the width of this from front to back. **21.** the part of a wheel, tire, or runner which bears on the road, rail, etc. **22.** the pattern raised on or cut into the face of a rubber tire. **23.** *Railroads.* that part of a rail in contact with the treads of wheels. [ME *tred(en),* OE *tredan;* c. D *treden,* G *treten;* akin to Goth *trudan,* Icel *trotha*] —**tread′er,** *n.*

trea·dle (tred′əl), *n., v.,* **-dled, -dling.** —*n.* **1.** a lever or the like worked by continual action of the foot to impart motion to a machine. **2.** a platform, as on a bus, trolleycar, etc., for actuating an exit door. —*v.i.* **3.** to work a treadle. [ME, OE *tredel* stairstep, lit., something that one treads or steps on. See TREAD] —**trea·dler** (tred′lər), *n.*

tread·mill (tred′mil′), *n.* **1.** an apparatus for producing rotary motion by the weight of men or animals, treading on a succession of moving steps or a belt that forms a kind of continuous path, as around the periphery of a pair of horizontal cylinders. **2.** a monotonous, wearisome routine of work or other activity in which there is little or no satisfactory progress. [TREAD + MILL[1]]

tread·plate (tred′plāt′), *n.* a metal plate having a raised pattern to give traction to a foot or wheel moving upon it. [TREAD + PLATE[1]]

treas., 1. treasurer. **2.** treasury. Also, **Treas.**

trea·son (trē′zən), *n.* **1. a.** violation by a subject of his allegiance to his sovereign or to the state; high treason. **b.** *U.S.* such a violation directed against the United States, and consisting "only in levying war against them, or in adhering to their enemies, giving them aid and comfort" (*Constitution of the U.S.,* III. 3. 1.). **2.** *Rare.* the betrayal of a trust or confidence; breach of faith; treachery. [ME *tre(i)so(u)n* < AF; OF *traïson* < L *trāditiōn-* (s. of *trāditiō*) a handing over, betrayal. See TRADITION]
—**Syn. 1.** TREASON, SEDITION mean disloyalty or treachery to one's country or its government. TREASON is any attempt to overthrow the government or impair the well-being of a state to which one owes allegiance; the crime of giving aid or comfort to the enemies of one's government. SEDITION is any act, writing, speech, etc., directed unlawfully against state authority, the government, or constitution, or calculated to bring it into contempt or to incite others to hostility, ill will or disaffection; it does not amount to treason and therefore is not a capital offense. **2.** See **disloyalty.**

trea·son·a·ble (trē′zə nə bəl), *adj.* **1.** of the nature of treason. **2.** involving treason; traitorous. [ME *tresonabill.* See TREASON, -ABLE] —**trea′son·a·ble·ness,** *n.* —**trea′son·a·bly,** *adv.*

trea·son·ous (trē′zə nəs), *adj.* treasonable. [TREASON + -OUS] —**trea′son·ous·ly,** *adv.*

treasr., treasurer.

treas·ure (trezh′ər), *n., v.,* **-ured, -ur·ing.** —*n.* **1.** wealth or riches stored or accumulated, esp. in the form of precious metals, money, jewels, or plate. **2.** wealth, rich materials, or valuable things. **3.** any thing or person greatly valued or highly prized: *This book was his chief treasure.* —*v.t.* **4.** to retain carefully or keep in store, as in the mind. **5.** to regard or treat as precious; prize; cherish. **6.** to put away for security or future use, as money; lay up in store. [early ME *tresor* < OF < L *thēsaur(us)* storehouse, hoard. See THESAURUS] —**treas′ur·a·ble,** *adj.* —**treas′ure·less,** *adj.*
—**Syn. 1, 6.** hoard. **5.** value, esteem, cling to.

treas′ure house′, **1.** a building, room, or chamber used as a storage place for valuables; treasury. **2.** a place, source, or the like, where many things of value or worth may be found: *Reading is the key to the treasure house of ideas.* Also, **treasure-house.**

treas·ure-house (trezh′ər hous′), *n., pl.* **-hous·es** (-hou′ziz). See **treasure house.**

treas′ure hunt′, a game in which each person or team attempts to be first in finding an object or series of objects that have been hidden, using written directions or clues.

Treas′ure Is′land, **1.** (*italics.*) a novel (1883) by R. L. Stevenson. **2.** a town in W Florida. 3506 (1960). **3.** a man-made island in San Francisco Bay, in W California: naval base. 380 acres.

treas·ur·er (trezh′ər ər), *n.* **1.** one who is in charge of treasure or a treasury. **2.** an officer of a corporation, association, club, or the like who is in charge of the receipt, care, and disbursement of money. **3.** an officer of a state, city, etc., entrusted with the receipt, care, and disbursement of public money. [ME *tresorer* < AF < LL *thēsaurār(ius).* See THESAURUS, -ER[2]] —**treas′ur·er·ship′,** *n.*

Treas′urer of the Unit′ed States′, the official in the Department of the Treasury charged with the responsibility of issuing and redeeming paper currency as well as for the receipt, safekeeping, and disbursement of the federal government's money.

treas·ure-trove (trezh′ər trōv′), *n.* **1.** *Law.* any money, bullion, or the like, of unknown ownership, found hidden in the earth or any other place. **2.** anything of the nature of treasure that one finds; a valuable discovery: *Mother's attic was a treasure-trove when we were furnishing our apartment.* [< AF *tresor trové* treasure found. See TREASURE, TROVER]

treas·ur·y (trezh′ə rē), *n., pl.* **-ur·ies.** **1.** a place where the funds of the government, of a corporation, or the like are deposited, kept, and disbursed. **2.** funds or revenue of a government, public or private corporation, etc. **3.** (*cap.*) the department of government which has control over the collection, management, and disbursement of the public revenue. **4.** a building, room, chest, or other place for the preservation of treasure or valuable objects. **5.** a collection or supply of excellent or highly prized writings, works of art, etc.: *a treasury of American poetry.* [ME *tresorie* < OF. See TREASURE, -Y[3]]

treas′ury bill′, an obligation of the U.S. government represented by promissory notes in denominations ranging from $1000 to $1,000,000, with a maturity of about 90 days but bearing no interest, and sold periodically at a discount on the market.

treas′ury bond′, any of various interest-bearing bonds issued by the U.S. Treasury Department, usually maturing over a long period of time.

treas′ury certif′icate, an obligation of the U.S. government represented by certificates in denominations ranging from $1,000 to $1,000,000, maturing in one year or less with interest periodically payable by the redemption of coupons.

treas′ury note′, a note or bill issued by the U.S. Department of the Treasury, receivable as legal tender for all debts except as otherwise expressly provided.

treas′ury of mer′its, *Rom. Cath. Ch.* the superabundant store of merits and satisfactions, comprising those of Christ, the Virgin Mary, and the saints. Also called **treas′ury of the Church′.**

treat (trēt), *v.t.* **1.** to act or behave toward (a person) in some specified way: *to treat someone with respect.* **2.** to consider or regard in a specified way, and deal with accordingly: *to treat a matter as unimportant.* **3.** to deal with (a disease, patient, etc.) in order to relieve or cure. **4.** to deal with in speech or writing; discuss. **5.** to deal with, develop, or represent artistically, esp. in some specified manner or style: *to treat a theme realistically.* **6.** to subject to some agent or action in order to bring about a particular result: *to treat a substance with an acid.* **7.** to entertain; give hospitality to: *He treats visiting dignitaries in the lavish surroundings of his country estate.* **8.** to provide food, entertainment, gifts, etc., at one's own expense: *When he treated her to dinner he treated himself to an entertaining evening.* —*v.i.* **9.** to deal with a subject in speech or writing; discourse (often fol. by *of*): *a work which treats of the caste system in India.* **10.** to give, or bear the expense of, a treat: *Is it my turn to treat?* **11.** to carry on negotiations with a view to a settlement; discuss terms of settlement; negotiate. —*n.* **12.** an entertainment of food, drink, amusement, etc., given by way of compliment or as an expression of friendly regard. **13.** anything that affords particular pleasure or enjoyment. **14.** act of treating. **15.** one's turn to treat. [ME *trete(n)* < OF *tretie(r), traitie(r)* < L *tractāre* to drag, handle, treat, deriv. of *tract(us)* drawn, ptp. of *trahere* to DRAG. See TRACT[1]] —**treat′a·ble,** *adj.* —**treat′er,** *n.*
—**Syn. 5.** handle. **11.** bargain, settle. **12.** party.

trea·tise (trē′tis), *n.* **1.** a book or writing that treats of some particular subject. **2.** a formal and systematic exposition in writing of the principles of a subject, generally longer and more detailed than an essay. [ME *tretis* < AF *tretiz.* See TREAT]

treat·ment (trēt′mənt), *n.* **1.** act or manner of treating. **2.** action or behavior toward a person, animal, etc. **3.** management in the application of medicines, surgery, etc. **4.** literary or artistic handling, esp. with reference to style. **5.** subjection to some agent or action. [TREAT + -MENT]

trea·ty (trē′tē), *n., pl.* **-ties.** **1.** a formal agreement between two or more states in reference to peace, alliance, commerce, or other international relations. **2.** the formal document embodying such an international agreement. **3.** any agreement or compact. **4.** *Archaic.* negotiation with a view to settlement. **5.** *Obs.* entreaty. [ME *trete* < AF < L *tractāt(us)* TRACTATE] —**trea′ty·less,** *adj.*

trea′ty port′, *Hist.* any of the ports in China, Japan, or Korea through which trade with foreign countries was permitted by special treaty.

Treb·bia (treb′byä), *n.* a river in N Italy, flowing N into the Po at Piacenza: Romans defeated by Hannibal near here 218 B.C. 70 mi. long.

Treb·i·zond (treb′i zond′), *n.* **1.** a medieval empire in NE Asia Minor 1204–1461. **2.** Official name, **Trabzon.** a seaport in NE Turkey, on the Black Sea: an ancient Greek colony; capital of the medieval empire of Trebizond. 65,598 (1965).

Treb′izond date′, oleaster.

tre·ble (treb′əl), *adj., n., v.,* **-bled, -bling.** —*adj.* **1.** threefold; triple. **2.** *Music.* **a.** of or pertaining to the highest part in harmonized music; soprano. **b.** of the highest pitch or range, as a voice part, voice, singer, or instrument. **c.** high in pitch; shrill. —*n.* **3.** *Music.* **a.** the treble or soprano part. **b.** a treble voice, singer, or instrument. **4.** a high or shrill voice or sound. **5.** the highest-pitched peal of a bell. —*v.t., v.i.* **6.** to make or become three times as much or as many; triple. [ME < MF < L *tripl(us)* TRIPLE] —**tre·bly** (treb′lē), *adv.*

tre′ble block′, a block with three pulleys or sheaves. Also called **threefold block.**

tre′ble clef′, *Music.* a sign which locates the G above middle C, placed on the second line of the staff, counting up; G clef. See illus. under **clef.** Also called **violin clef.**

tre′ble staff′, *Music.* a staff, bearing a treble clef.

Tre·blin·ka (tʀe bleng′kä; *Eng.* trə bling′kə), *n.* a Nazi concentration camp in Poland, near Warsaw.

treb·u·chet (treb′yo͝o shet′), *n.* a medieval engine of war having a pivoted beam with a heavy weight at one end and a sling for a missile at the other, the sling being pulled down for loading and released suddenly for shooting. Also, **tre·buck·et** (trē′buk′it). [ME < MF, equiv. to *trebuch(er)* (to) overturn, fall, equiv. to *tre(s)* across, over (< L *trāns-* TRANS- + *buc* trunk of body < Gmc; cf. OE *būc* belly) + *-et* -ET]

tre·cen·to (trā chen′tō; *It.* tʀe chen′tô), *n.* (*often cap.*) the 14th century, with reference to Italy, and esp. to its art or literature. [< It, short for *mille trecento* a thousand three hundred] —**tre·cen′tist,** *n.*

tre cor·de (trā kôr′dā; *It.* tʀe kôʀ′de), with the soft pedal released (a musical direction in piano playing). Cf. **una corda.** [< It: lit., three strings]

tre·de·cil·lion (trē′di sil′yən), *n., pl.* **-lions,** (*as after a numeral*) **-lion,** *adj.* —*n.* **1.** a cardinal number represented in the United States and France by one followed by 42 zeros, and in Great Britain and Germany, by one followed by 78 zeros. —*adj.* **2.** amounting to one tredecillion in number. [< L *tre(s)* THREE + DECILLION] —**tre′de·cil′lionth,** *adj., n.*

tree (trē), *n., v.,* **treed, tree·ing.** —*n.* **1.** a perennial plant having a permanent, woody, self-supporting main stem or trunk, ordinarily growing to a considerable height, and usually developing branches at some distance from the ground. **2.** any of various shrubs, bushes, and herbaceous plants, as the banana, resembling a tree in form and size. **3.** something resembling a tree in shape, as a clothes tree, crosstree, etc. **4.** See **family tree.** **5.** a pole, post, beam, bar, handle, or the like, as one forming part of some structure. **6.** See **boot tree.** **7.** a saddletree. **8.** a treelike group of crystals, as one forming in an electrolytic cell. **9.** a gallows or gibbet. **10.** *Archaic.* the cross on which Christ was crucified. **11.** See **Christmas tree.** **12. up a tree,** *Informal.* in a difficult or embarrassing situation; at a loss; stumped: *Her obstinacy has me up a tree.* —*v.t.* **13.** to drive into or up a tree, as a hunted animal or a man pursued by an animal. **14.** *Informal.* to put into a difficult position. **15.** to stretch or shape on a tree, as a boot. **16.** to furnish (a structure) with a tree. [ME; OE *trēo(w)*; c. OFris, Icel *trē,* OS *treo,* Goth *triu*; akin to Gk *drŷs* oak, Skt, Avestan *dru* wood] —**tree′less,** *adj.* —**tree′less·ness,** *n.* —**tree′like′,** *adj.*

Tree (trē), *n.* **Sir Herbert Beer·bohm** (bēr′bōm), (*Herbert Beerbohm*), 1853–1917, English actor and theater manager; brother of Max Beerbohm.

tree′ azal′ea, a shrub, *Azalea arborescens,* of mountainous areas of southeastern U.S., having funnel-shaped, fragrant, white or pinkish flowers, hairy on the outside.

tree′ cel′andine. See **plume poppy.**

tree′ crab′. See **coconut crab.**

tree′ creep′er. See under **creeper** (def. 5).

tree′ crick′et. See under **cricket**[1] (def. 1).

treed (trēd), *adj.* **1.** planted with trees; wooded: *a treed hillside.* **2.** driven up a tree: *a treed animal.* **3.** fitted with trees: *treed boots.* [TREE + -ED[3]]

tree′ duck′, any of several long-legged ducks of the genus *Dendrocygna,* certain species of which nest in trees, as *D. bicolor* (**fulvous tree duck**) of the New and Old World tropics. Also called **whistling duck.**

tree′ farm′, a tree-covered area managed as a business enterprise under a plan of reforestation that makes continuous production of timber possible.

tree′ fern′, any of various ferns, mostly tropical and chiefly of the family *Cyatheaceae,* which attain the size of trees, sending up a straight trunklike stem with foliage at the summit.

tree·fish (trē′fish′), *n., pl.* **-fish·es,** (*esp. collectively*) **-fish.** a rockfish, *Sebastodes serriceps,* found in southern California, marked with black bands. [TREE + FISH]

tree′-form frame′ (trē′fôrm′), a rigid frame having a pair of inclined girders branching from each column, as to form principals of a roof.

tree′ frog′, any of various arboreal frogs, esp. of the family *Hylidae,* usually having adhesive disks at the tip of each toe.

tree′ german′der, an evergreen, bushy herb, *Teucrium fruticans,* of southern Europe, having blue flowers in sparse clusters.

tree′ heath′, the brier, *Erica arborea.*

tree·hop·per (trē′hop′ər), *n.* any of numerous hemopterous jumping insects of the family *Membracidae,* which have an enlarged prothorax and feed on the juices of plants. [TREE + HOPPER]

tree′ house′, a small house, esp. one for children to play in, built or placed up in the branches of a tree.

tree′ hy′rax, an arboreal hyrax of the genus *Dendrohyrax,* of central and southern Africa.

tree′ kangaroo′, any arboreal kangaroo of the genus *Dendrolagus,* of Queensland, Australia, and New Guinea.

tree′ lawn′, a strip of grass-covered ground between the sidewalk and the curb, often planted with shade trees.

tree·lined (trē′līnd′), *adj.* having a line of trees: *a treelined road.* [TREE + LINE[1] + -ED[2]]

tree′ lung′wort. See **Virginia cowslip.**

tree′ lu′pine, a shrubby tree, *Lupinus arboreus,* of California, having hairy, finger-shaped leaflets and fragrant, sulphur-yellow flowers.

tree′ myr′tle, an evergreen, treelike shrub, *Ceanothus arboreus,* of the California coast and islands, having fragrant, pale-blue flowers. Also called **island myrtle.**

tre·en (trē′ən), *adj.* **1.** made entirely of wood. —*n.* **2.** treenware. [ME; OE *trēowen.* See TREE, -EN[2]]

tree·nail (trē′nāl′, tren′əl, trun′əl), *n.* a wooden pin for fastening together timbers, as those of ships. Also, **trenail, trunnel.** [ME *trenayl.* See TREE, NAIL]

tre·en·ware (trē′ən wâr′), *n.* household utensils, dishes, etc., made entirely of wood. [TREEN + WARE[1]]

tree′ of heav′en, an Asiatic, simarubaceous tree, *Ailanthus altissima,* having rank-smelling flowers, often planted as a shade tree. Also called **stinkweed.**

tree′ of Jes′se, a pictorial or sculpted image of a family tree representing the genealogy of Christ. Also called **Jesse tree.**

tree′ of knowl′edge of good′ and e′vil, the tree in the Garden of Eden bearing the forbidden fruit that was tasted by Adam and Eve. Gen. 2:17; 3:6–24. Also called **tree′ of knowl′edge.**

tree′ of life′, **1.** a tree in the Garden of Eden which yielded food giving everlasting life. Gen 2:9; 3:22. **2.** a tree in the heavenly Jerusalem with leaves for the healing of the nations. Rev. 22:2. **3.** See **arbor vitae.**

tree′ of sad′ness. See **night jasmine** (def. 1).

tree′ pe′ony. See **Japanese tree peony.**

Tree′ Plant′ers State′, Nebraska (used as a nickname).

tree′ post′. See **king post** (def. 1).

tree′ shrew′, any of several insectivorous, arboreal mammals of the family *Tupaiadae,* of southern Asia and adjacent islands, resembling a squirrel and having a long snout.

tree′ spar′row, **1.** a European weaverbird, *Passer montanus,* related to the English sparrow. **2.** a North American finch, *Spizella arborea,* common in winter in the northern U.S.

tree′ sur′gery, the repair of damaged trees, as by the removal of diseased parts, filling of cavities, and prevention of further decay, and by strengthening branches with braces. —**tree′-sur′geon,** *n.*

tree′ swal′low, a bluish-green and white swallow, *Iridoprocne bicolor,* of North and Central America, that nests in tree cavities.

tree′ swift′, any of several birds of the family *Hemiprocnidae,* of India and the Malay Archipelago, related to the true swifts, but differing in having erectile crests and the habit of perching in trees. Also called **crested swift.**

tree′ toad′. See **tree frog.**

tree′ tobac′co, a treelike herb, *Nicotiana glauca,* of South America, having blue-green foliage, heart-shaped leaves, and white, greenish-yellow, or purple flowers, the corolla yellow, grown as an ornamental.

tree·top (trē′top′), *n.* the top or uppermost branches of a tree. [TREE + TOP[1]]

tree′ yuc′ca. See **Joshua tree.**

tre·fah (tʀā fä′; *Eng.* trā′fə), *adj. Hebrew.* terefah. Also, **tref** (*Eng.* trāf).

tref·lé (tref lā′), *adj. Heraldry.* botonée. [< F, deriv. of *trefle* TREFOIL]

tre·foil (trē′foil), *n.* **1.** any leguminous plant of the genus *Trifolium,* having usually digitate leaves of three leaflets and reddish, purple, yellow, or white flower heads, comprising the common clovers. **2.** any of various similar plants. **3.** an ornamental figure or structure resembling a trifoliolate leaf. **4.** such an ornamental figure used by the Girl Scouts as its official emblem. —*adj.* **5.** of, pertaining to, or shaped like a trefoil. [late ME < AF *trifoil* < L *trifol(ium)* triple leaf, the three-leaved plant, clover, equiv. to *tri-* TRI- + *folium* leaf]

Trefoils (def. 3)

tre′foil arch′, *Archit.* an arch having the intrados on either side of the center formed like a cusp. See illus. under **arch.**

tre′foil knot′, a knot having the form of a trefoil.

tre·ha·la (tri hä′lə), *n.* an edible, sugary substance secreted by certain Asiatic beetles of the genus *Larinus,* forming their pupal covering. [< NL < Turk *tigala* < Pers *tighāl*]

tre·ha·lose (trē′hə lōs′), *n. Chem.* a white, crystalline disaccharide, $C_{12}H_{22}O_{11}$, found in yeast, certain fungi, etc., and used to identify certain bacteria. [TREHAL(A) + -OSE[2]]

treil·lage (trā′lij), *n.* latticework; a lattice or trellis. [< F, equiv. to *treille* vine-arbor, trellis (see TREILLE) + *-age* -AGE]

treille (trāl), *n. Heraldry.* trellis (def. 4). [late ME < OF: bower < ML *trelia,* var. of L *trichila.* See TRELLIS]

Trein·ta y Tres (tʀān′tä ē tʀes′), a city in E Uruguay. 19,400 (est. 1954).

Treitsch·ke (tʀīch′kə), *n.* **Hein·rich von** (hīn′ʀiKH fən), 1834–96, German historian.

trek (trek), *v.,* **trekked, trek·king,** *n.* —*v.i.* **1.** to travel or migrate, esp. slowly or with difficulty. **2.** *South Africa.* to travel by ox wagon. —*v.t.* **3.** *South Africa.* (of a draft animal) to draw (a vehicle or load). —*n.* **4.** a journey or trip, esp. one involving difficulty or hardship. **5.** *South Africa.* a migration or expedition, as by ox wagon. **6.** *South Africa.* a stage of a journey, esp. by ox wagon, between one stopping place and the next. [< D *trekk(en)* (to) draw, travel] —**trek′ker,** *n.*

Tre·law·ney (tri lô′nē), *n.* **Edward John,** 1792–1881, English adventurer and author.

Tre·lew (tʀe le′o͞o), *n.* a city in E Argentina. 5880 (1947).

trel·lis (trel′is), *n.* **1.** a frame or structure of latticework; lattice. **2.** a framework of this kind used as a support for growing vines, climbing plants, etc. **3.** a summerhouse, gazebo, arch, etc., made chiefly or completely of lattice work. **4.** Also, **treille.** *Heraldry.* a charge of bendlets overlying bendlets sinister, the whole being cloué at the crossings. —*v.t.* **5.** to furnish with a trellis. **6.** to enclose in a trellis. **7.** to train or support on a trellis: *trellised vines.* **8.** to form into or like a trellis; interlace. [late ME *trelis* < MF < LL *trilīcius* (r. L *trilīx*) woven with three threads, equiv. to L *tri-* TRI- + *līci(um)* thread + *-us* adj. suffix] —**trel′lis·like′,** *adj.*

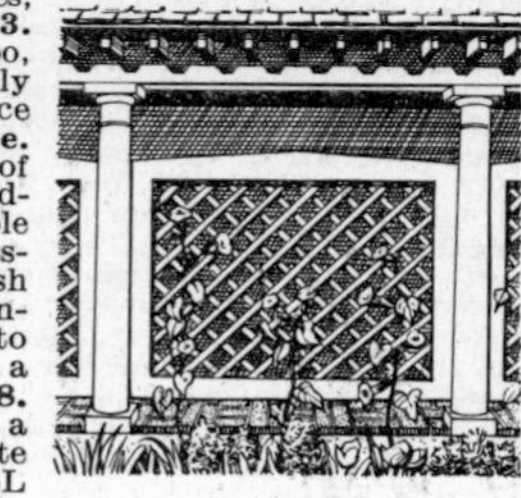
Trellis

trel·lised (trel′ist), *adj.* *Armor.* noting armor having diagonally crisscrossed strips of leather enframing metal plates, the whole being sewn to a flexible backing. [TRELLIS + -ED³]

trel·lis·work (trel′is wûrk′), *n.* latticework. [TRELLIS + WORK]

Trem·a·to·da (trem′ə tō′də, trē′mə-), *n.* the class comprising the trematodes. [< NL; see TREMATODE]

trem·a·tode (trem′ə tōd′, trē′mə-), *n.* any parasitic platyhelminth or flatworm of the class *Trematoda,* having one or more external suckers; fluke. [< NL *Trematod(a)* class name < Gk *trēmatṓd(ēs)* having holes, equiv. to *trēmat-* (s. of *trēma*) hole + *-ōdēs* -ODE¹]

trem·ble (trem′bəl), *v.,* **-bled, -bling,** *n.* —*v.i.* **1.** to shake involuntarily with quick, short movements, as from fear, excitement, weakness, cold, etc.; quake; quiver; shake: *She trembled at his voice. He stood there trembling in the snow.* **2.** to be troubled or concerned with fear, apprehension, or the like. **3.** (of things) to be affected with vibratory motion. **4.** to be tremulous, as light, sound, etc.: *His voice trembled as he spoke.* —*n.* **5.** act of trembling. **6.** a state or fit of trembling. **7. trembles,** (*construed as sing.*) **a.** *Pathol.* any condition or disease characterized by continued trembling or shaking, as ague. **b.** See **milk sickness. c.** *Vet. Pathol.* a toxic condition of cattle and sheep caused by the eating of white snakeroot and characterized by muscular tremors. [ME < MF *trembl(er)* < ML *tremulāre,* deriv. of L *tremul(us)* TREMULOUS; r. ME *trem(e)le(n)* < ML *tremulāre*] —**trem′bling·ly,** *adv.*
—**Syn. 1.** shudder. See **shake. 3.** oscillate.

trem·bler (trem′blər), *n.* **1.** one who or that which trembles. **2.** an oscine bird, *Cinclocerthia ruficauda,* of the Lesser Antilles, related to the thrashers, noted for its habit of trembling violently. [TREMBLE + -ER¹]

trem·bly (trem′blē), *adj.* **-bli·er, -bli·est.** quivering; tremulous; shaking. [TREMBLE + -Y¹]

tre·men·dous (tri men′dəs), *adj.* **1.** *Informal.* extraordinarily great in size, amount, or intensity: *a tremendous ocean liner; tremendous talent; a tremendous blow to his morale.* **2.** dreadful or awful, as in character or effect; exciting fear; frightening; terrifying. **3.** *Informal.* extraordinary in excellence: *a tremendous piano player; a tremendous time at the dance.* [< L *tremendus* dreadful, to be shaken by, equiv. to *trem(ere)* (to) shake, quake + *-endus* fut. pass. part. suffix] —**tre·men′dous·ly,** *adv.* —**tre·men′dous·ness,** *n.*
—**Syn. 1.** See **huge.**

trém·ie (trem′ē; *Fr.* trā mē′), *n., pl.* **trém·ies** (trem′ēz; *Fr.* trā mē′). a funnellike device lowered into water to deposit concrete. [< F: hopper < L *trimodia* three-peck measure, equiv. to *tri-* TRI- + *mod(ius)* measure of grain + *-ia* -IA]

tre·mis·sis (tri mis′is), *n., pl.* **-mis·ses** (-mis′ēz). **1.** Also called **triens.** a gold coin of the Eastern Roman Empire, the third part of a solidus, first issued in the 3rd century B.C. **2.** a Merovingian gold coin imitating this. [< LL, equiv. to L *tre(s)* three + *-missis* as in *semissis,* equiv. to *semis* SEMI- + *as* AS²]

trem·o·lant (trem′ə lənt), *adj.* **1.** having a tremulous or vibrating tone, as certain pipes of an organ. —*n.* **2.** an organ pipe producing a tremolant tone. [< G < It *tremolant(e)* TREMULANT]

trem·o·lite (trem′ə līt′), *n.* a white or grayish variety of amphibole, $Ca_2Mg_5Si_8O_{22}(OH)_2$, usually occurring in bladed crystals. [named after *Tremol(a),* valley in Switzerland; see -ITE¹] —**trem·o·lit·ic** (trem′ə lit′ik), *adj.*

trem·o·lo (trem′ə lō′), *n., pl.* **-los.** *Music.* **1.** a tremulous or vibrating effect produced on certain instruments and in the human voice, as to express emotion. **2.** a mechanical device in an organ by which such an effect is produced. [< It: trembling < L *tremul(us)* TREMULOUS]

trem·or (trem′ər, trē′mər), *n.* **1.** involuntary shaking of the body or limbs, as from disease, fear, weakness, excitement, etc.; a fit of trembling. **2.** any tremulous or vibratory movement; vibration: *The earth tremors lasted all night.* **3.** a trembling or quivering effect, as of light. **4.** a quavering sound, as of the voice. [ME < L: a trembling, equiv. to *trem(ere)* (to) tremble + *-or* -OR¹] —**trem′or·less,** *adj.* —**trem′or·less·ly,** *adv.* —**trem′or·ous,** *adj.*
—**Syn. 1.** shudder, shiver, quaver, quiver. **3.** oscillation.

trem·u·lant (trem′yə lənt), *adj.* trembling; tremulous. [< ML *tremulant-* (s. of *tremulāns*) prp. of *tremulāre* to TREMBLE; see -ANT]

trem·u·lous (trem′yə ləs), *adj.* **1.** (of persons, the body, etc.) characterized by trembling, as from fear, nervousness, weakness, etc. **2.** timid; timorous; fearful. **3.** (of things) vibratory, shaking, or quivering. **4.** (of writing) done with a trembling hand. [< L *tremulus,* equiv. to *trem(ere)* (to) tremble + *-ulus* adj. suffix denoting qualities] —**trem′u·lous·ly,** *adv.* —**trem′u·lous·ness,** *n.*
—**Syn. 2.** frightened; afraid

tre·nail (trē′nāl′, tren′əl, trun′əl), *n.* treenail.

trench (trench), *n.* **1.** *Fort.* a long, narrow excavation in the ground, the earth from which is thrown up in front to serve as a shelter from the enemy's fire, etc. **2. trenches,** a system of such excavations, with their embankments, etc. **3.** a deep furrow, ditch, or cut. **4.** *Phys. Geog.* a long, steep-sided, narrow depression in the ocean floor. —*v.t.* **5.** to surround or fortify with a trench or trenches; entrench. **6.** to cut a trench or trenches in. **7.** to set or place in a trench. **8.** to form (a furrow, ditch, etc.) by cutting into or through something. **9.** to make a cut in; cut into; carve. **10.** *Obs.* to sever or slash. —*v.i.* **11.** to dig a trench or trenches. **12.** *Obs.* to enter so as to affect intimately (usually fol. by *into* or *unto*). **13. trench on** or **upon, a.** to encroach or infringe on. **b.** to come close to; verge on: *His remarks were trenching on poor taste.* [ME *trenche* path made by cutting < OF: act of cutting, a cut, deriv. of *trenchier* to cut < VL **trincāre* for L *truncāre* to lop; see TRUNCATE]

Trench (trench), *n.* **Richard Chen·e·vix** (shen′ə vē), 1807–86, English clergyman and scholar, born in Ireland.

trench·ant (tren′chənt), *adj.* **1.** incisive or keen, as language or a person; caustic; cutting: *trenchant wit.* **2.** vigorous; effective; energetic: *a trenchant policy of political reform.* **3.** clearly or sharply defined; clear-cut; distinct. **4.** *Archaic.* sharp-edged: *a trenchant blade.* [ME *tranchaunt* < AF, equiv. to OF *trenchant,* prp. of *trenchier* to cut. See TRENCH, -ANT] —**trench′an·cy,** *n.* —**trench′ant·ly,** *adv.*
—**Syn. 1.** sharp, biting, acute.

Tren·chard (tren′chärd, -chərd), *n.* **Hugh Montague, 1st Viscount,** 1873–1956, British Royal Air Force marshal.

trench′ coat′, a waterproof overcoat styled along military lines, belted, usually double-breasted, and with straps on the shoulders and lower sleeves, capacious pockets, etc.

trench·er (tren′chər), *n.* **1.** one who digs trenches. **2.** *Archaic.* **a.** a rectangular or circular flat piece of wood on which meat, or other food, is served or carved. **b.** such a piece of wood and the food on it. **c.** food; the pleasures of good eating. [ME *trenchour* something to cut with or on < AF, equiv. to MF *trencheoir.* See TRENCH, -ORY²]

trench·er·man (tren′chər mən), *n., pl.* **-men. 1.** one who has a hearty appetite; a heavy eater. **2.** *Archaic.* a hanger-on; parasite. [TRENCHER + MAN¹]

trench′ fe′ver, *Pathol.* a lice-spread recurrent fever, often suffered by soldiers in trenches in World War I, caused by a rickettsia transmitted by the body louse.

trench′ foot′, *Pathol.* a disease of the feet due to exposure to cold and wet, common among soldiers serving in trenches.

trench′ing plane′. See **grooving plane.**

trench′ knife′, a short knife for stabbing, sometimes equipped with brass knuckles as a guard, used in modern warfare in hand-to-hand combat.

trench′ mor′tar, a portable, muzzle-loaded mortar, usually having a smooth bore, fired at high angles of elevation to reach concealed enemy targets.

trench′ mouth′. See **Vincent's angina.** [so called from the high incidence among soldiers in the trenches]

trench′ war′fare, combat in which each side occupies a system of protective trenches.

trend (trend), *n.* **1.** the general course or prevailing tendency; drift: *trends in the teaching of foreign languages; the trend of events.* **2.** style; vogue: *the new trend in women's apparel.* **3.** the general direction followed by a road, river, coastline, or the like. —*v.i.* **4.** to have a general tendency, as events, conditions, etc. **5.** to tend to take a particular direction; extend in some direction indicated. **6.** to veer or turn off in a specified direction, as a river, mountain range, etc.: *At that latitude the river trends toward the southeast.* [ME *trend(en),* OE *trendan;* akin to OE *trinde* ball, D *trent* circumference, Sw *trind* round. See TRINDLE, TRUNDLE]
—**Syn. 1.** See **tendency. 5.** stretch, run, incline.

Treng·ga·nu (treng gä′nōō), *n.* a state in Malaysia, on the SE Malay Peninsula. 317,049 (est. 1961); 5050 sq. mi. *Cap.:* Kuala Trengganu.

Trent (trent), *n.* **1.** Italian, **Trento.** Ancient, **Tridentum.** a city in N Italy, on the Adige River. 74,766 (1961). **2. Council of,** the ecumenical council of the Roman Catholic Church that met at Trent intermittently from 1545 to 1563, and defined church doctrine and condemned the Reformation. **3.** a river in central England, flowing NE from Staffordshire to the Humber. 170 mi. long.

tren·tal (tren′təl), *n.* *Rom. Cath. Ch.* a series of 30 Requiems celebrated one each day for 30 consecutive days. [ME < ML *trentāle* < VL **trenta,* var. of L *trīgintā* thirty + *-āle* -AL². Cf. OF *trentel*]

trente et qua·rante (tränt′ ā kə ränt′; *Fr.* träN tā KA RäNt′), *n.* See **rouge et noir.** [< F]

Tren·ti·no-Al·to A·di·ge (tren tē′nô äl′tô ä′dē je), a region in NE Italy. 785,491 (1961); 5256 sq. mi.

Tren·to (tren′tō), *n.* Italian name of **Trent.**

Tren·ton (tren′tən), *n.* **1.** a city in and the capital of New Jersey, in the W part, on the Delaware River: Washington defeated the Hessians here 1776. 114,167 (1960). **2.** a city in SE Michigan, S of Detroit. 18,439 (1960). **3.** a town in N Missouri. 6262 (1960). **4.** a town in NW Tennessee. 4225 (1960). **5.** a town in SW Ohio. 3064 (1960). —**Tren·to·ni·an** (tren tō′nē ən), *n.*

tre·pan¹ (tri pan′), *n., v.,* **-panned, -pan·ning.** —*n.* **1.** a tool for cutting shallow holes by removing a core. **2.** *Surg.* an obsolete form of the trephine resembling a carpenter's bit and brace. —*v.t.* **3.** *Mach.* **a.** to cut circular disks out of plate stock using a rotating cutter. **b.** to cut a concentric groove around a bored or drilled hole. **4.** to operate upon with a trepan; perforate by a trepan; trephine. [late ME *trepane* < ML *trepan(um)* crown saw < Gk *trýpanon* borer, akin to *trýpa* hole, *trypân* to bore] —**trep·a·na·tion** (trep′ə nā′shən), *n.* —**tre·pan′ner,** *n.*

tre·pan² (tri pan′), *n., v.,* **-panned, -pan·ning.** *Archaic.* —*n.* **1.** one who ensnares or entraps others. **2.** a stratagem; a trap. —*v.t.* **3.** to ensnare or entrap. **4.** to entice. **5.** to cheat or swindle. Also, **trapan.** [earlier *trapan,* equiv. to TRAP¹ + *-an* < ?] —**trep·a·na·tion** (trep′ə nā′shən), *n.* —**tre·pan′ner,** *n.*

tre·pang (tri pang′), *n.* any of various wormlike holothurians or sea cucumbers, as *Holothuria edulis,* used as food in China. [< Malay *tripang*]

tre·phine (tri fīn′, -fēn′), *n., v.,* **-phined, -phin·ing.** *Surg.* —*n.* **1.** a small circular saw with a center pin mounted on a strong hollow metal shaft to which is attached a transverse handle: used in surgery to remove circular disks of bone from the skull. —*v.t.* **2.** to operate upon with a trephine. [sp. var. of *trefine,* orig. *trafine,* b. *trapan* (var. of TREPAN¹) + L phrase *trēs fīnēs* the three ends (the inventor's explanation)] —**treph·i·na·tion** (tref′ə nā′shən), *n.*

trep·i·da·tion (trep′i dā′shən), *n.* **1.** tremulous fear, alarm, or agitation; perturbation. **2.** trembling or quivering movement; vibration; tremor. **3.** *Pathol.* rapid, repeated, muscular flexion and extension of muscles of the extremities or lower jaw; clonus. [< L *trepidātiōn-* (s. of *trepidātiō*), equiv. to *trepidāt(us)* hurried, alarmed (ptp. of *trepidāre;* see INTREPID, -ATE¹) + *-iōn-* -ION]
—**Syn. 1.** trembling, fright. **2.** quivering, shaking, oscillation.

trep·o·ne·ma (trep′ə nē′mə), *n., pl.* **-mas, -ma·ta** (-mə tə). any of several anaerobic spirochetes of the genus *Treponema,* certain species of which are parasitic in and pathogenic for man and warm-blooded animals. [< NL: genus name < Gk *trép(ein)* (to) turn + *-o-* + *nēma* thread] —**trep·o·nem·a·tous** (trep′ə nem′ə təs), **trep′o·ne′mal,** *adj.*

trep·o·ne·ma·to·sis (trep′ə nē′mə tō′sis), *n.* *Pathol.* an infection caused by an organism of the genus *Treponema,* as syphilis, pinta, bejel, and yaws. [< NL *Treponemat-* (s. of *Treponema;* see TREPONEMA) + -OSIS]

trep·o·ne·mi·a·sis (trep′ə nə mī′ə sis), *n.* *Pathol.* infection with treponema; syphilis. [TREPONEM(A) + -IASIS]

tres (tres), *adj.* (in prescriptions) three. [< L]

tres·pass (tres′pəs), *n.* **1.** *Law.* **a.** an unlawful act causing injury to the person, property, or rights of another, committed with force or violence, actual or implied. **b.** a wrongful entry upon the lands of another. **c.** the action to recover damages for such an injury. **2.** an encroachment or intrusion. **3.** an offense, sin, or wrong. —*v.i.* **4.** *Law.* to commit a trespass. **5.** to encroach on a person's privacy, time, etc.; infringe (usually fol. by *on* or *upon*). **6.** to commit a transgression or offense; transgress; offend; sin. [ME *trespas* < OF, deriv. of *trespasser,* equiv. to *tres-* (< L *trāns-* TRANS-) + *passer* to PASS] —**tres′pass·er,** *n.*
—**Syn. 2.** invasion, infringement. **3.** transgression, error, fault, misdeed; crime, misdemeanor. **4, 5.** TRESPASS, ENCROACH, INFRINGE, INTRUDE imply overstepping boundaries and assuming possession of others' property or crowding onto the right of others. To TRESPASS is to pass unlawfully within the boundaries of another's property: *Hunters trespass on a farmer's fields.* To ENCROACH is to creep, as it were, gradually and often stealthily, upon territory, rights, or privileges, so that a footing is imperceptibly established: *The sea slowly encroached upon the land.* To INFRINGE is to break in upon or invade rights, customs, or the like, by violating or disregarding them: *to infringe upon a patient.* To INTRUDE is to thrust oneself into the presence of a person or into places or circumstances where one is not welcome: *to intrude into a private conversation.*

Très Riches Heures du Duc de Ber·ry, Les (lā tre rēsh̲ zœr′ dʏ dʏk də be rē′), a book of hours (1413–16) illustrated with miniatures by the Limbourg brothers.

tress (tres), *n.* **1.** Usually, **tresses.** long locks or curls of unbraided or unbound hair, esp. those of a woman. **2.** *Archaic.* a plait or braid of hair, esp. of a woman. [ME *tresse* < MF: plait or braid of hair, equiv. to ML *treccia,* var. of *trica* < Gk *trícha* threefold; see TRI-]

tressed (trest), *adj.* **1.** (of the hair) arranged or formed into tresses; braided; plaited. **2.** having tresses (usually used in combination): *auburn-tressed; golden-tressed.* [ME; see TRESS, -ED³]

tres·sure (tresh′ər), *n.* **1.** *Heraldry.* a narrower diminutive of the orle, usually ornamented with fleurs-de-lis at the edges and often doubled. **2.** *Numis.* an ornamental border enclosing the type on a coin or medal. [late ME < MF, equiv. to *tress(er)* (to) braid, plait (deriv. of *tresse* TRESS) + *-ure* -URE; r. ME *tressour* < MF *tresseor, tressoir*] —**tres′sured,** *adj.*

tress·y (tres′ē), *adj.,* **tress·i·er, tress·i·est.** *Archaic.* resembling or having tresses. [TRESS + -Y¹]

tres·tine (tres′tīn), *n.* See **royal antler.** Also, **trez-tine.** [? < L *trēs* three + TINE]

tres·tle (tres′əl), *n.* **1.** a frame typically composed of a horizontal bar or beam rigidly joined or fitted at each end to the top of a transverse A-frame, used as a barrier, a transverse support for planking, etc.; horse. **2.** *Civ. Eng.* **a.** one of a number of bents, having sloping sides of framework or piling, for supporting the deck or stringers of a bridge. **b.** a bridge made of these. [ME *trestel* < MF; OF *trestre* (by dissimilation) < L *trānstr(um)* crossbeam. See TRANSOM]

Trestle

tres′tle ta′ble, 1. a table having transverse slabs or rigid frames for supports, and usually strengthened by a long stretcher. **2.** a table composed of a movable top supported by trestles.

tres·tle·tree (tres′əl trē′), *n.* *Naut.* either of a pair of timbers or metal shapes lying along the tops of the hounds or cheeks of a mast to support crosstrees or a top. [TRESTLE + TREE]

tres·tle·work (tres′əl wûrk′), *n.* a structural system composed of trestles. [TRESTLE + WORK]

tret (tret), *n.* (formerly) an allowance for waste, after deduction for tare. [< AF, var. of *trait* TRAIT]

Tre·ta Yu·ga (*Skt.* trā′tä yōō′gə), *Hinduism.* the second Yuga, not as good as the Satya Yuga but better than the Dvapara Yuga. [< Skt, equiv. to *tretā* third throw of the dice + *yuga* YUGA]

Tre·vel·yan (tri vel′yən, -vil′-), *n.* **1. George Macaulay,** 1876–1962, English historian. **2.** his father **Sir George Otto,** 1838–1928, English biographer, historian, and statesman.

Treves (trēvz), *n.* Trier. French, **Trèves** (tʀev).
tre·vette (trə vet′), *n.* trivet[2]. Also, **tre·vet′.** [var. of *trevat* < ?]
Tre·vi·so (tʀe vē′zô), *n.* a city in NE Italy. 75,185 (1961).
Trev·i·thick (trev′ə thik), *n.* **Richard,** 1771–1833, English engineer.
Trev·or (trev′ər), *n.* a boy's given name.
Trev·or·ton (trev′ər tən), *n.* a town in central Pennsylvania. 2597 (1960).
Trew (trōō), *n.* a girl's given name. Also, **True.**
trews (trōōz), *n.* (*construed as pl.*) close-fitting tartan trousers, worn esp. by certain Scottish regiments. [< Ir and ScotGael *triubhas* < OF *trebus* breeches]
trey (trā), *n.* a playing card or a die having three pips. [ME < MF *trei(s)* < L *trēs* three]
trez·tine (trez′tīn), *n.* See **royal antler.**
trf, 1. transfer. 2. tuned radio frequency.
tri-, a learned borrowing from Latin or Greek meaning "three," used in the formation of compound words: *triacid; triatomic.* [ME < L, comb. form repr. L *trēs, tria,* Gk *treîs, tria* three]
tri·a·ble (trī′ə bəl), 1. subject or liable to judicial trial. 2. *Obs.* that may be tried, attempted, or tested. [late ME < AF. See TRY, -ABLE] —**tri′a·ble·ness,** *n.*
tri·ac·e·tate (trī as′i tāt′), *n.* *Chem.* an acetate containing three acetate groups. [TRI- + ACETATE]
tri·a·ce·tyl·o·le·an·do·my·cin (trī′ə sēt′ᵊl ō′lē an′-də mī′sin, -set′ᵊl-, trī as′i tᵊl-), *n.* *Pharm.* a white, crystalline, slightly water-soluble broad-spectrum antibiotic, $C_{41}H_{67}NO_{15}$, prepared from oleandomycin by acetylation: used in the treatment of both Gram-positive and Gram-negative infections. [TRI- + ACETYL + OLEANDOMYCIN]
tri·ac·id (trī as′id), *adj.* *Chem.* 1. capable of combining with three molecules of a monobasic acid: *a triacid base.* 2. noting acid salts containing three replaceable hydrogen atoms. [TRI- + ACID]
tri·ad (trī′ad), *n.* 1. a group of three, esp. of three closely related or associated persons or things. 2. *Chem.* **a.** an element, atom, or group having a valence of three. Cf. **monad** (def. 2), **dyad** (def. 3). **b.** a group of three closely related compounds or elements, as isomers or halides. 3. *Music.* a chord of three tones, esp. one consisting of a given tone with its major or minor third and its perfect, augmented, or diminished fifth. [< L *triad-* (s. of *trias*) < Gk. See TRI-, -AD] —**tri·ad′ic,** *adj.* —**tri·ad′i·cal·ly,** *adv.* —**tri′ad·ism,** *n.*
tri·a·del·phous (trī′ə del′fəs), *adj.* *Bot.* (of stamens) united by the filaments into three sets or bundles. [TRI- + Gk *adelphós* brother]
tri·age (trē äzh′), *n., adj., v.,* **-aged, ag·ing.** —*n.* 1. the process of sorting victims, as of a battle or disaster, to determine priority or appropriate place of medical treatment. 2. the determination of priorities for action in an emergency. —*adj.* 3. of, pertaining to, or performing the task of triage: *a triage officer.* —*v.t.* 4. to act on or in by triage: *to triage a crisis.* [< F: lit., sorting, selecting]
tri·a junc·ta in u·no (tʀē′ä yōōngk′tä in ōō′nō; *Eng.* trī′ə jungk′tə in yōō′nō), *Latin.* three united in one: motto of the Order of the Bath.
tri·al (trī′əl, trīl), *n.* 1. *Law.* **a.** the examination before a judicial tribunal of the facts put in issue in a cause, often including issues of law as well as of fact. **b.** the determination of a person's guilt or innocence by due process of law. 2. act of trying, testing, or putting to the proof. 3. test; proof. 4. an attempt or effort to do something. 5. a tentative or experimental action in order to ascertain results; experiment. 6. state or position of a person or thing being tried or tested; probation. 7. subjection to suffering or grievous experiences; a distressed or painful state: *comfort in the hour of trial.* 8. an affliction or trouble. 9. a trying, distressing, or annoying thing or person. 10. *Ceram.* a piece of ceramic material used to try the heat of a kiln and the progress of the firing of its contents. —*adj.* 11. of, pertaining to, or employed in a trial. 12. done or made by way of trial, test, proof, or experiment. 13. used in testing, experimenting, etc. 14. acting or serving as a sample, experimental specimen, etc.: *a trial offer.* [TRY + -AL[2]]
—**Syn. 2, 3, 5.** examination, proof. TRIAL, EXPERIMENT, TEST imply an attempt to find out something or to find out about something. TRIAL is the general word for a trying of anything: *articles sent for ten days' free trial.* EXPERIMENT looks to the future, and is a trial conducted to prove or illustrate the truth or validity of something, or an attempt to discover something new: *an experiment in chemistry.* TEST is a stronger and more specific word, referring to a trial under approved and fixed conditions, or a final and decisive trial as a conclusion of past experiments: *a test of a new type of airplane.* 4. endeavor, essay, struggle. 7. grief, tribulation, distress, sorrow, trouble, hardship. See **affliction.**
Trial, The, a novel (1924) by Franz Kafka. German, **Der Prozess.**
tri′al and er′ror, experimentation or investigation in which various methods or means are tried and faulty ones eliminated in order to find the correct solution or to achieve the desired result or effect. —**tri′al-and-er′ror,** *adj.*
tri′al bal′ance, *Bookkeeping.* a statement of all the open debit and credit items, made preliminary to balancing a double-entry ledger.
tri′al balloon′, 1. a statement, program, or the like issued publicly as a means of determining reactions in advance: *The senator's remark was a trial balloon for a new law he wanted to propose.* 2. See **pilot balloon.**
tri′al dock′et, *U.S.* docket (def. 3b).
tri′al horse′, *Informal.* an opponent that performs against a superior foe in a workout or exhibition, rather than in an official competition: *They played mostly trial horses during spring training.*
tri′al ju′ry. See **petty jury.**
tri′al law′yer, a lawyer who specializes in appearing before a court of law on behalf of his clients.
tri′al mar′riage, a nonconjugal relationship in which a man and woman agree to live together for a specified period of time, esp. in the expectation of having the period terminate in legal marriage. Cf. **companionate marriage.**
tri′al run′, a preliminary performance of action in order to ascertain results, as of the operation of a ship, the effectiveness of a play, etc.; an initial and tentative trial or test of something.

Tri·an·da (trē än′də; *Gk.* tʀē än′dä), *n.* a town on the Greek island of Rhodes, in the Aegean Sea: built on the site of ancient Ialysus. Also, **Trianta.**
tri·an·gle (trī′ang′gəl), *n.* 1. a closed plane figure having three sides and three angles. 2. a flat triangular piece, usually of plastic, with straight edges, used in connection with a T square for drawing perpendicular lines, geometric figures, etc. 3. any three-cornered or three-sided figure, object, or piece: *a triangle of land.* 4. a musical percussion instrument that consists of a steel rod bent into triangular shape, open at one corner, and is struck with a small, straight steel rod. 5. a group of three; triad. 6. a situation involving three persons, esp. one in which two men are in love with the same woman. 7. (*cap.*) *Astron.* the constellation Triangulum. [ME < L *triangul(um),* n. use of neut. of *triangulus* three-cornered. See TRI-, ANGLE[1]] —**tri′an·gled,** *adj.*

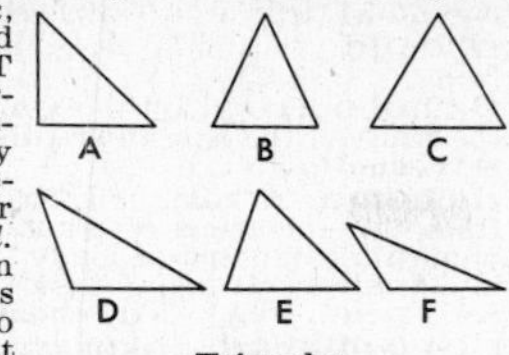

Triangles
A, Right angle; B, Isosceles; C, Equilateral; D, Obtuse; E, Acute; F, Scalene

tri′angle inequal′ity, *Math.* the theorem that the absolute value of the sum of two quantities is less than or equal to the sum of the absolute values of the quantities.
tri·an·gu·lar (trī ang′gyə lər), *adj.* 1. pertaining to or having the form of a triangle; three-cornered. 2. having a triangle as base or cross section: *a triangular prism.* 3. comprising three parts or elements; triple. 4. pertaining to or involving a group of three, as three persons, parties, or things. [< L *triangulār(is),* equiv. to *triangul(um)* TRIANGLE + *-āris* -AR[1]] —**tri·an·gu·lar·i·ty** (trī ang′gyᵊ lar′i tē), *n.* —**tri·an′gu·lar·ly,** *adv.*
trian′gular ma′trix, *Math.* a square matrix in which either all the entries above the principal diagonal, or all the entries below the principal diagonal, are zero.
tri·an·gu·late (*adj.* trī ang′gyə lit, -lāt′; *v.* trī ang′gyə lāt′), *adj., v.,* **-lat·ed, -lat·ing.** —*adj.* 1. composed of or marked with triangles. —*v.t.* 2. to make triangular. 3. to divide into triangles. 4. to survey (an area) by triangulation. [< ML *triangulāt(us),* ptp. of *triangulāre* to make triangles. See TRIANGLE, -ATE[1]] —**tri·an′gu·late·ly,** *adv.* —**tri·an′gu·la′tor,** *n.*
tri·an·gu·la·tion (trī ang′gyə lā′shən), *n.* *Survey., Navig.* 1. a technique for establishing the distance between any two points, or the relative position of two or more points, by using such points as vertices of a triangle or series of triangles, such that each triangle has a side of known or measurable length (**base** or **base line**) that permits size of the angles of the triangle and the length of its other two sides to be established by observations taken either upon or from the two ends of the base line. 2. the triangles thus formed and measured. [< ML *triangulātiōn-* (s. of *triangulātiō*) the making of triangles. See TRIANGULATE, -ION]

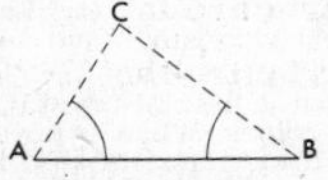

Triangulation
A,B, Points known; C, Point visible from both A and B, the position of which is plotted by measuring angles A and B

Tri·an·gu·lum (trī ang′gyə ləm), *n., gen.* **-li** (-lī′). *Astron.* the Triangle, a northern constellation between Pisces and Perseus. [< L]
Tri·an·gu·lum Aus·tra·le (trī ang′gyə ləm ô strā′lē), *gen.* **Tri·an·gu·li Aus·tra·lis** (trī ang′gyə lī′ ô strā′lis). *Astron.* the Southern Triangle, a southern constellation between Pavo and Circinus. [< L]
Tri·an·ta (*Gk.* tʀē än′dä), *n.* Trianda.
tri·ap·si·dal (trī ap′si dᵊl), *adj.* *Archit.* having three apses. [TRI- + APSIDAL]
tri·ar·chy (trī′är kē), *n., pl.* **-chies.** 1. government by three persons. 2. a set of three joint rulers; a triumvirate. 3. a country divided into three governments. 4. a group of three countries or districts, each under its own ruler. [< Gk *triarchía* triumvirate. See TRI-, -ARCHY]
tri·ar·yl (trī ar′il), *adj.* *Chem.* containing three aryl groups. [TRI- + ARYL]
tri·ar·yl·meth′ane dye′ (trī ar′il meth′ān), *Chem.* any of the class of dyes containing three aryl groups attached to a central carbon atom: used chiefly for dyeing cotton, wool, and silk. [TRIARYL + METHANE]
Tri·as (trī′əs), *n.* Triassic. [< LL < Gk. See TRIAD]
Tri·as·sic (trī as′ik), *Geol.* —*adj.* 1. noting or pertaining to a period of the Mesozoic era, occurring from 180,000,000 to 220,000,000 years ago; characterized by volcanic activity and the advent of dinosaurs and marine reptiles. See table under **era.** —*n.* 2. the Triassic period or system. Also, **Trias.** [TRIAS + -IC; so called because it has three subdivisions]
tri·ath·lon (trī′ath′lon), *n.* 1. an athletic competition comprising three events, usually swimming, bicycling, and distance running. 2. a women's track-and-field contest including the 100-meter dash, high jump, and shot put. [TRI- + (DEC)ATHLON]
tri·at′ic stay′ (trī at′ik), *Naut.* a backstay for the head of a fore-and-aft-rigged topmast, running down to the head of the lower mast next aft. Also called **freshwater stay.** [? TRI- + -ATE[1] + -IC]
tri·a·tom·ic (trī′ə tom′ik), *adj.* *Chem.* 1. having three atoms in a molecule. 2. having three replaceable hydrogen atoms. 3. having three replaceable hydroxyl groups. [TRI- + ATOMIC] —**tri′a·tom′i·cal·ly,** *adv.*
tri·ax·i·al (trī ak′sē əl), *adj.* having three axes. [TRI- + AXIAL] —**tri·ax′i·al′i·ty,** *n.*
tri·a·zine (trī′ə zēn′, -zin, trī az′ēn, -in), *n.* *Chem.* 1. any of a group of three compounds containing three nitrogen and three carbon atoms arranged in a six-membered ring and having the formula $C_3H_3N_3$. 2. any of a number of their derivatives. [TRI- + AZINE]
tri·a·zo (trī az′ō, -ā′zō), *adj.* *Chem.* azido. [TRI- + AZO-]
tri·a·zo·ic (trī′ə zō′ik), *adj.* *Chem.* hydrazoic. [TRI- + AZOIC]
tri·a·zole (trī′ə zōl′, trī az′ōl), *n.* *Chem.* 1. any of a group of four compounds containing three nitrogen and two carbon atoms arranged in a five-membered ring and having the formula $C_2H_3N_3$. 2. any of a number of their derivatives. [TRI- + AZOLE] —**tri·a·zol·ic** (trī′ə zol′ik), *adj.*

trib·ade (trib′əd), *n.* a woman who practices tribadism, esp. a female homosexual who assumes the male role. [< F < L *tribad-* (s. of *tribas*) < Gk: lit., rubbing, equiv. to *trīb(ein)* (to) rub + *-ad-* -ADE[2]] —**tri·bad·ic** (tri bad′ik), *adj.*
trib·a·dism (trib′ə diz′əm), *n.* lesbianism. [TRIBADE + -ISM]
trib·al (trī′bəl), *adj.* of, pertaining to, or characteristic of a tribe or tribes: *tribal customs; a tribal dance.* [TRIBE + -AL[1]] —**trib′al·ly,** *adv.*
trib·al·ism (trī′bə liz′əm), *n.* 1. the customs and beliefs of tribal life and society. 2. strong loyalty to one's own tribe, party, or group. [TRIBAL + -ISM] —**trib′al·ist,** *n.*
tri·ba·sic (trī bā′sik), *adj.* *Chem.* 1. (of an acid) having three atoms of hydrogen replaceable by basic atoms or groups. 2. containing three basic atoms or groups, each having a valence of one, as tribasic sodium phosphate, Na_3PO_4. [TRI- + BASIC] —**tri·ba·sic·i·ty** (trī′bā sis′i tē), *n.*
triba′sic so′dium phos′phate. See **sodium phosphate** (def. 3).
trib·ble (trib′əl), *n.* *Papermaking.* a large frame with wires stretched across it on which paper is hung for drying. [? var. of *thripple* framework for hauling hay, orig. for drying it, late ME *therrepyll;* cf. OE *thierran* to dry]
tribe (trīb), *n.* 1. any aggregate of people united by ties of descent from a common ancestor, community of customs and traditions, adherence to the same leaders, etc. 2. a local division of an aboriginal people. 3. a division of some other people. 4. a class or type of animals, plants, articles, or the like. 5. *Stockbreeding.* a group of animals, esp. cattle, descended through the female line from a common female ancestor. 6. *Biol.* **a.** a category in the classification of plants and animals usually between a family and a genus or sometimes between an order and a family. **b.** any group of plants or animals. 7. a company, group, or number of persons. 8. *Facetious.* **a.** *Often Disparaging.* a class or set of persons. **b.** a family. 9. *Rom. Hist.* **a.** any one of three divisions of the people representing the Latin, Sabine, and Etruscan settlements. **b.** any of the later political divisions of the people, after 450 B.C. numbering 20, and after 241 B.C. numbering 35. 10. *Gk. Hist.* a phyle. [ME < L *trib(us)* tribe, orig. each of the three divisions of the Roman people; see TRI-] —**tribe′less,** *adj.*
tribe·let (trīb′lit), *n.* a tribe having few members, esp. one that is a component of a larger tribal organization. [TRIBE + -LET]
tribes·man (trībz′mən), *n., pl.* **-men.** a member of a tribe. [TRIBE + 's[1] + MAN[1]]
tribes·peo·ple (trībz′pē′pəl), *n.pl.* the members of a tribe. [TRIBE + 's[1] + PEOPLE]
tribo-, a learned borrowing from Greek meaning "friction," used in the formation of compound words: *triboelectricity.* [comb. form repr. Gk *trībein* to rub]
tri·bo·e·lec·tric·i·ty (trī′bō i lek tris′i tē, -ē′lek-, trib′ō-), *n.* *Elect.* electricity generated by friction. [TRIBO- + ELECTRICITY] —**tri·bo·e·lec·tric** (trī′bō i-lek′trik, trib′ō-), *adj.*
tri·bo·lu·mi·nes·cence (trī′bō lōō′mə nes′əns, trib′-ō-), *n.* *Physics.* luminescence produced by friction, usually within a crystalline substance. [TRIBO- + LUMINESCENCE]
tri·bo·lu·mi·nes·cent (trī′bō lōō′mə nes′ənt, trib′-ō-), *adj.* pertaining to or characterized by triboluminescence. [TRIBO- + LUMINESCENT]
tri·brach (trī′brak, trib′rak), *n.* 1. *Pros.* a foot of three short syllables. 2. *Survey.* a three-armed frame on an instrument stand, resting on leveling screws, for supporting an alidade, target, etc. [< L *tribrach(ys)* < Gk *tribrachys,* equiv. to *tri-* TRI- + *brachýs* short; see BRACHY-] —**tri·brach′ic,** *adj.* —**tri·brach′i·al,** *adj.*
tri·bro·mo·ac·et·al·de·hyde (trī brō′mō as′i tal′-də hīd′), *n.* *Pharm.* bromal. [TRI- + BROMO- + ACETALDEHYDE]
tri·bro·mo·eth·a·nol (trī brō′mō eth′ə nōl′, -nôl′, -nol′), *n.* *Pharm.* a white, crystalline powder, CBr_3CH_2OH, used as a basal anesthetic, usually by rectal administration. Also called **tribromoethyl alcohol.** [TRI- + BROMO- + ETHANOL]
tri·bro′mo·eth′yl al′cohol (trī brō′mō eth′əl, -brō′-), *Pharm.* tribromoethanol. [TRI- + BROMO- + ETHYL]
trib·u·la·tion (trib′yə lā′shən), *n.* 1. grievous trouble; severe trial or suffering. 2. an instance of this; an affliction, trouble, etc. [ME < L *trībulātiōn-* (s. of *trībulātiō*) distress, trouble, equiv. to *trībulāt(us)* oppressed (ptp. of *trībulāre*), lit., threshed (*trībul(um)* threshing sledge, equiv. to *trī-,* perf. s. of *terere* to rub, crush, + *-bulum* n. suffix of instrument + *-ātus* -ATE[1]) + *-iōn-* -ION]
—**Syn. 1.** affliction, hardship, distress, adversity, suffering.
tri·bu·nal (trī byōōn′ᵊl, tri-), *n.* 1. a court of justice. 2. a place or seat of judgment. 3. Also called **tribune.** a raised platform for the seats of magistrates, as in an ancient Roman basilica. [< L: judgment seat, equiv. to *tribūn(us)* TRIBUNE[1] + *-āl(e),* neut. of *-ālis* -AL[1]]
trib·u·nate (trib′yə nit, -nāt′), *n.* *Hist.* 1. the office of tribune. 2. a body of tribunes. [< L *tribūnāt(us)* the office of a tribune. See TRIBUNE[1], -ATE[1]]
trib·une[1] (trib′yōōn *or, esp. Brit.,* trī′byōōn), *n.* 1. a person who upholds or defends the rights of the people. 2. *Rom. Hist.* **a.** any of various administrative officers, esp. one of 10 officers elected to protect the interests and rights of the plebeians from the patricians. **b.** any of the six officers of a legion who rotated in commanding the legion during the year. [ME < L *tribūn(us),* orig., the head of a TRIBE] —**trib′une·ship′,** *n.* —**trib·u·ni·tial, trib·u·ni·cial** (trib′yə nish′əl), *adj.*
trib·une[2] (trib′yōōn), *n.* 1. a raised platform for a speaker; a dais, rostrum, or pulpit. 2. a raised part, or gallery, with seats, as in a church. 3. (in a Christian basilica) the bishop's throne in a corresponding recess or apse. 4. the apse itself. 5. tribunal (def. 3). [< ML *tribūn(a);* r. L *tribūnāle* TRIBUNAL]
trib·u·tar·y (trib′yə ter′ē), *n., pl.* **-tar·ies,** *adj.* —*n.* 1. a stream contributing its flow to a larger stream or other body of water. 2. a person or nation that pays tribute in acknowledgment of subjugation or the like. —*adj.* 3. (of a stream) flowing into a larger stream or

other body of water. **4.** furnishing subsidiary aid; contributory; auxiliary. **5.** paying or required to pay tribute. **6.** paid as tribute. **7.** subject; subjugated; subordinate: *a tributary nation.* [ME < L *tribūtāri(us)* of tribute. See TRIBUTE, -ARY] —**trib′u·tar′i·ly,** *adv.*

trib·ute (trib′yo͞ot), *n.* **1.** a gift, testimonial, compliment, given as due or in acknowledgment of gratitude, esteem, or regard. **2.** a stated sum or other valuable consideration paid by one sovereign or state to another in acknowledgment of subjugation or as the price of peace, security, protection, or the like. **3.** a rent, tax, or the like, as that paid by a subject to a sovereign. **4.** any exacted or enforced payment or contribution. **5.** obligation or liability to make such payment. [ME *tribut* < L *tribūt(um)* a levied payment (n. use of neut. of ptp. of *tribuere* to assign, allot), equiv. to *tribū-* (ptp. s. of *tribuere*) + *-tum,* neut. of *-tus* ptp. suffix]
—**Syn. 1.** recognition, commendation, eulogy. **4.** levy, toll, impost, duty.

tri·car·pel·lar·y (trī kär′pə ler′ē), *adj. Bot.* having three carpels. [TRI- + CARPELLARY]

trice[1] (trīs), *n.* a very short time; a moment; an instant: *to come back in a trice.* [late ME *tryse;* special use of TRICE[2]]

trice[2] (trīs), *v.t.,* **triced, tric·ing.** *Naut.* **1.** to pull or haul with a rope. **2.** to haul up and fasten with a rope (usually fol. by *up*). [ME < MD *trīsen* to hoist; equiv. to *trīse* pulley + *-en* inf. suffix]

tri·cen·ten·ni·al (trī′sen ten′ē əl), *adj., n.* tercentenary. [TRI- + CENTENNIAL]

tri·ceps (trī′seps), *n., pl.* **-ceps·es** (-sep siz), **-ceps.** *Anat.* a muscle having three heads or points of origin, esp. the muscle on the back of the arm, the action of which extends the elbow. [< L: three-headed, equiv. to *tri-* TRI- + *-ceps* headed, akin to *caput* head]

Tri·cer·a·tops (trī ser′ə tops′), *n.* a genus of ceratopsian dinosaurs, of the late Cretaceous period, having a bony crest on the neck, a long horn over each eye, and a shorter horn on the nose. [< NL, equiv. to *tricerat-* (see TRI-, CERAT-) + Gk *ōps* eye]

Triceratops,
Triceratops elatus
(8 ft. high at shoulder; total length 20 ft.; horns 3¼ ft.; skull 8 ft.)

trich-, var. of **tricho-** before a vowel: *trichite.*

tri·chi·a·sis (tri kī′ə sis), *n. Pathol.* a condition in which the eyelashes grow inwardly. [< LL < Gk *trichíasis.* See TRICH-, -IASIS]

tri·chi·na (tri kī′nə), *n., pl.* **-nae** (-nē). a nematode, *Trichinella spiralis,* the adults of which live in the intestine and produce embryos which encyst in the muscle tissue, esp. in pigs, rats, and man. [< NL < Gk *trichína,* n. use of fem. of *tríchinos* of hair. See TRICH-, -INE[1]]

trich·i·ni·a·sis (trik′ə nī′ə sis), *n. Pathol.* trichinosis. [TRICHIN(A) + -IASIS]

trich·i·nise (trik′ə nīz′), *v.t.,* **-nised, -nis·ing.** *Chiefly Brit.* trichinize. —**trich′i·ni·sa′tion,** *n.*

trich·i·nize (trik′ə nīz′), *v.t.,* **-nized, -niz·ing.** *Pathol.* to infect with trichinae. [TRICHIN(A) + -IZE] —**trich′i·ni·za′tion,** *n.*

Trich·i·nop·o·ly (trik′ə nop′ə lē), *n.* former name of **Tiruchirapalli.**

trich·i·no·sis (trik′ə nō′sis), *n. Pathol.* a disease resulting from infestation with *Trichinella spiralis,* occurring in man, caused by ingestion of infested undercooked pork, and characterized by fever, muscle weakness, diarrhea, etc. Also, **trichiniasis.** [TRICHIN(A) + -OSIS]

trich·i·nous (trik′ə nəs), *adj. Pathol.* **1.** pertaining to or of the nature of trichinosis. **2.** infected with trichinae. [TRICHIN(A) + -OUS]

trich·i·on (trik′ē on′), *n., pl.* **trich·i·a** (trik′ē ə), **trich·i·ons.** *Physical Anthropol.* the point of intersection of the normal hairline and the middle line of the forehead. [< Gk *tríchion,* dim. of *thríx* hair (see TRICH-) + *-ion* dim. suffix]

trich·ite (trik′īt), *n. Petrog.* any of various minute, hairlike mineral bodies occurring in certain vitreous igneous rocks, esp. obsidian. [TRICH- + -ITE[1]] —**tri·chit·ic** (tri kit′ik), *adj.*

tri·chlo·ride (trī klōr′īd, -id, -klôr′-), *n. Chem.* a chloride having three atoms of chlorine, as ferric chloride, $FeCl_3$. [TRI- + CHLORIDE]

tri·chlo·ro·ac·e·tal·de·hyde (trī klōr′ō as′i tal′də hīd′, -klôr′-), *n. Chem.* chloral (def. 1). Also called **tri·chlo′ro·a·ce′tic ac′id al′dehyde** (trī klōr′ō ə sē′tik, -set′ik, -klôr′-, -klōr′-, -klôr′-). [TRI- + CHLORO-[2] + ACETALDEHYDE]

tri·chlo·ro·eth·yl·ene (trī klōr′ō eth′ə lēn′, -klôr′-), *n. Chem.* a colorless, poisonous liquid, $CHClCCl_2$, used chiefly as a degreasing agent for metals and as a solvent, esp. in dry cleaning, for fats, oils, and waxes. [TRI- + CHLORO-[2] + ETHYLENE]

tri·chlo·ro·flu·o·ro·meth·ane (trī klōr′ō flo͞o′ə rō meth′ān, -flo͝or′ō-, -flōr′-, -flôr′-, -klôr′-), *n. Chem.* chlorotrifluoromethane.

tri·chlo·ro·meth·ane (trī klōr′ō meth′ān, -klôr′-), *n. Chem.* chloroform (def. 1). [TRI- + CHLORO-[2] + METHANE]

tri·chlo·ro·meth′yl chlorofor′mate (trī klōr′ō meth′əl, -klôr′-), *Chem.* diphosgene. [TRI- + CHLORO-[2] + METHYL]

tri·chlo·ro·ni·tro·meth·ane (trī klōr′ō nī′trō meth′ān, -klôr′-), *n. Chem.* chloropicrin. [TRI- + CHLORO-[2] + NITROMETHANE]

tri·chlo′ro·phe·nox·y·a·ce′tic ac′id (trī klōre′fə nok′sē ə sē′tik, -set′ik, -klôr′-, -klōr′-, -klôr′-), *Chem.* a light-tan, water-insoluble solid, $Cl_3C_6H_2OCH_2CO_2H$, used chiefly for killing weeds. Also called **2, 4, 5-T.** [TRI- + CHLORO-[2] + PHEN- + OXY-[2] + ACETIC]

tricho-, a learned borrowing from Greek meaning "hair," used in the formation of compound words: *trichocyst.* Also, *esp. before a vowel,* **trich-.** [< Gk *tricho-,* comb. form of *thríx, thrichós*]

trich·o·cyst (trik′ə sist′), *n. Zool.* an organ of offense and defense embedded in the outer protoplasm of many infusorians, consisting of a small elongated sac containing a fine, hairlike filament capable of being ejected. [TRICHO- + CYST] —**trich′o·cyst′ic,** *adj.*

trich·o·gyne (trik′ə jīn′, -jin), *n. Bot.* a hairlike prolongation of a carpogonium, serving as a receptive organ for the spermatium. [TRICHO- + -GYNE] —**trich·o·gyn·i·al** (trik′ə jin′ē əl), **trich′o·gyn′ic,** *adj.*

trich·oid (trik′oid), *adj.* resembling hair; hairlike. [TRICH- + -OID]

tri·chol·o·gy (tri kol′ə jē), *n.* the science dealing with the study of the hair and its diseases. [TRICHO- + -LOGY] —**tri·chol′o·gist,** *n.*

tri·chome (trī′kōm, trik′ōm), *n.* **1.** *Bot.* an outgrowth from the epidermis of plants, as a hair. **2.** a microorganism composed of many filamentous cells arranged in strands or chains. [< Gk *tríchōm(a)* growth of hair. See TRICH-, -OMA] —**tri·chom·ic** (tri kom′ik), *adj.*

trich·o·mon·ad (trik′ə mon′ad), *n.* any flagellate protozoan of the genus *Trichomonas,* parasitic in man or animals. [< NL *Trichomonad-* (s. of *Trichomonas*) genus name. See TRICHO-, MONAD] —**trich·o·mon·a·dal** (trik′ə mon′ə dəl), **trich·o·mon·al** (trik′ə mon′əl, -mōn′-, tri kom′ə nəl), *adj.*

trich·o·mo·ni·a·sis (trik′ə mə nī′ə sis), *n.* **1.** *Pathol.* infestation with a trichomonad. **2.** *Pathol.* vaginitis characterized by a persistent discharge and itching, caused by the trichomonad *Trichomonas vaginalis.* **3.** *Vet. Pathol.* **a.** a venereal disease of domestic cattle, characterized by pus in the uterine cavity, sterility, and abortion, caused by the trichomonad *T. fetus.* **b.** a disease of birds, characterized by diarrhea, and caused by one of several trichomonads. [TRICHOMON(AD) + -IASIS]

trich·o·not·id (trik′ə not′id), *n.* **1.** any fish of the family *Trichonotidae,* comprising the sand divers. —*adj.* **2.** belonging or pertaining to the family *Trichonotidae.* [< NL *Trichonotid(ae)* name of the family, equiv. to *tricho-* TRICHO- + Gk *nōtid(anós)* a kind of small shark]

Trich·o·nym·pha (trik′ə nim′fə), *n.* a genus of flagellate protozoans that live in the intestine of wood-eating termites, transforming the cellulose in the wood into soluble carbohydrates that can be utilized by the insect. [< NL; see TRICHO-, NYMPHA]

tri·cho·sis (tri kō′sis), *n. Pathol.* any disease of the hair. [TRICH- + -OSIS]

tri·chot·o·my (tri kot′ə mē), *n., pl.* **-mies. 1.** division into three parts, classes, categories, etc. **2.** an instance of such a division, as in thought, structure, or object. **3.** the three-part division of man into body, spirit, and soul. [TRICHO- + -TOMY] —**trich·o·tom·ic** (trik′ə tom′ik), **tri·chot′o·mous,** *adj.* —**tri·chot′o·mous·ly,** *adv.*

tri·chro·ic (trī krō′ik), *adj. Crystall.* manifesting trichroism. [TRI- + -CHROIC]

tri·chro·ism (trī′krō iz′əm), *n. Crystall.* pleochroism of a biaxial crystal such that it exhibits three different colors when viewed from three different directions under transmitted light. [TRICHRO(IC) + -ISM]

tri·chro·mat (trī′krō mat′, -krə-), *n. Ophthalm.* a person who has trichromatic vision. [back formation from TRICHROMATIC]

tri·chro·mat·ic (trī′krō mat′ik, -krə-), *adj.* **1.** pertaining to the use or combination of three colors, as in printing or in color photography. **2.** pertaining to, characterized by, or involving three colors. **3.** *Ophthalm.* of, pertaining to, or exhibiting trichromatism. Also, **tri·chro·mic** (trī krō′mik). [TRI- + CHROMATIC]

tri·chro·ma·tism (trī krō′mə tiz′əm), *n.* **1.** quality or condition of being trichromatic. **2.** the use or combination of three colors, as in printing or photography. **3.** *Ophthalm.* Also, **tri·chro·ma·top·si·a** (trī krō′mə top′sē ə). normal vision, in which the retina responds to all colors. Cf. **monochromatism** (def. 2), **dichromatism** (def. 2). [TRICHROMAT(IC) + -ISM]

tri·cit·y (trī′sit′ē, -sit′ē), *adj.* **1.** of or pertaining to a metropolitan area consisting of three separate but interdependent cities: *an instance of tri-city cooperation.* —*n.* **2.** any one of three such cities.

trick (trik), *n.* **1.** a crafty or underhanded device, stratagem, or the like, intended to deceive or cheat; artifice; ruse; wile. **2.** a deceptive appearance; illusion: *It must have been some visual trick caused by the flickering candlelight.* **3.** a roguish or mischievous act; practical joke; prank: *He likes to play tricks on his friends.* **4.** a mean, foolish, childish, or disgraceful action. **5.** a clever or ingenious device or expedient; adroit technique: *a rhetorical trick; the tricks of the trade.* **6.** the art or knack of doing something skillfully: *You seem to have mastered the trick of making others laugh.* **7.** a clever or dexterous feat intended to entertain, amuse, exhibit skill, etc.: *He taught his dog some amazing tricks; tricks in horsemanship.* **8.** a feat of jugglery, magic, or legerdemain: *a magician's tricks; card tricks.* **9.** a characteristic or habitual manner or way of acting; behavioral peculiarity; trait; habit; mannerism. **10.** a turn; stint; tour of duty: *I relieved the helmsman after he had completed his trick at the wheel.* **11.** *Cards.* **a.** the group or set of cards played and won in one round. **b.** a point or scoring unit. **c.** a card that is a potential winner. Cf. **honor trick. 12.** *Informal.* a child or young girl: *a pretty little trick.* **13.** a specific period when a person is to perform a particular action; turn of duty; shift. **14.** *Slang.* **a.** a prostitute's customer. **b.** a business transaction between a prostitute and a customer. **15.** *Heraldry.* **a.** a preliminary sketch of a coat of arms. **b.** See **engraver's trick. 16. do** or **turn the trick,** to achieve the desired effect or result: *Another turn of the pliers should do the trick.* —*adj.* **17.** of, pertaining to, characterized by, or involving tricks: *trick shooting; trick riding.* **18.** designed or used for tricks: *a trick chair; a trick horse.* —*v.t.* **19.** to deceive by trickery. **20.** *Heraldry.* to indicate the tinctures of (a coat of arms) with engraver's tricks. **21.** to cheat or swindle (usually fol. by *out of*). **22.** to beguile by trickery (usually fol. by *into*). **23.** to dress, array, or deck, esp. ostentatiously or decoratively (often fol. by *out* or *up*). —*v.i.* **24.** to practice trickery or deception; cheat. **25.** to play tricks; trifle (usually fol. by *with*). [late ME *trik* < ONF *trique* deceit, deriv. of *trikier* to deceive < VL **triccare,* var. of L *trīcārī* to play tricks] —**trick′er,** *n.* —**trick′ing·ly,** *adv.* —**trick′less,** *adj.*
—**Syn. 1.** deception. TRICK, ARTIFICE, RUSE, STRATAGEM, WILE are terms for crafty or cunning devices that are intended to deceive. TRICK, the general term, refers usually to an underhanded act designed to cheat someone, but it sometimes refers merely to a pleasurable deceiving of the senses: *to win by a trick.* Like TRICK, but to a greater degree, ARTIFICE emphasizes the cleverness, ingenuity, or cunning with which the proceeding is devised: *an artifice of diabolical ingenuity.* RUSE and STRATAGEM emphasize the purpose for which the trick is designed; RUSE is the more general term of the two, and STRATAGEM sometimes implies a more elaborate procedure or a military application: *He gained entrance by a ruse. His stratagem gave them command of the hill.* WILE emphasizes the disarming effect of the trick upon those who are deceived: *His wiles charmed them into trusting him.* **19.** See **cheat.**

trick·er·y (trik′ə rē), *n., pl.* **-er·ies. 1.** use or practice of tricks or stratagems to deceive; artifice; deception. **2.** a trick used to deceive. [TRICK + -ERY]
—**Syn. 1.** See **deceit.**

trick·ish (trik′ish), *adj.* tricky. [TRICK + -ISH[1]] —**trick′ish·ly,** *adv.* —**trick′ish·ness,** *n.*

trick′ knee′, a condition of the knee in which the joint suddenly stiffens or abandons its support.

trick·le (trik′əl), *v.,* **-led, -ling,** *n.* —*v.i.* **1.** to flow or fall by drops, or in a small, gentle stream: *Tears trickled down her cheeks.* **2.** to come, go, or pass bit by bit, slowly, or irregularly: *Subscriptions trickled into the office. The guests trickled out of the room.* —*v.t.* **3.** to cause to trickle. —*n.* **4.** a trickling flow or stream. **5.** a small, slow, or irregular quantity of anything coming, going, or proceeding: *a trickle of visitors throughout the day.* [ME; sandhi var. of obs. *strickle,* equiv. to STRIKE (in obs. sense, flow) + -LE] —**trick′ling·ly,** *adv.*

trick′ or treat′, a game or sport engaged in by children on Halloween, in which they call on neighbors, using this phrase, and threaten to play a trick on them if a treat is not forthcoming.

trick-or-treat (trik′ər trēt′), *v.i.* to become involved or take part in trick or treat. —**trick′-or-treat′er,** *n.*

trick·some (trik′səm), *adj.* **1.** tricksy (def. 1). **2.** tricky (def. 1). [TRICK + -SOME[1]]

trick·ster (trik′stər), *n.* **1.** a deceiver; cheat; fraud. **2.** one who plays tricks. **3.** a supernatural figure appearing in various guises and typically engaging in mischievous activities, important in the folklore and mythology of many primitive peoples and usually conceived as a culture hero. [TRICK + -STER] —**trick′ster·ing,** *n.*

trick·sy (trik′sē), *adj.,* **-si·er, -si·est. 1.** Also, **tricksome.** given to tricks; mischievous; playful; prankish. **2.** *Archaic.* tricky; crafty; wily. **3.** *Archaic.* difficult to handle or deal with. **4.** *Archaic.* fashionably trim; spruce; smart. [? *tricks* (pl. of TRICK) + -Y[1]] —**trick′si·ly,** *adv.* —**trick′si·ness,** *n.*

trick-track (trik′trak′), *n.* a variety of backgammon. Also, **tictrac.** [< F *trictrac;* so called in imitation of the clicking sound made in moving the pieces]

trick′ wheel′, *Naut.* a wheel independently actuating the steering mechanism of a ship, for use in case the steering engine fails.

trick·y (trik′ē), *adj.,* **trick·i·er, trick·i·est. 1.** given to or characterized by deceitful tricks; crafty; wily. **2.** skilled in clever tricks or dodges. **3.** deceptive, uncertain, or difficult to deal with or handle. [TRICK + -Y[1]] —**trick′i·ly,** *adv.* —**trick′i·ness,** *n.*
—**Syn. 1.** artful, sly, shrewd. **2.** skillful, cunning, adroit. **3.** doubtful, unsure, unpredictable, unreliable, perilous.

tri·clad (trī′klad), *n.* a planarian. [back formation from NL *Tricladida* name of order. See TRI-, CLAD(O)-, -IDA]

tri·clin·ic (trī klin′ik), *adj. Crystall.* noting or pertaining to a system of crystallization in which the three axes are unequal and intersect at oblique angles. [TRI- + Gk *klín(ein)* (to) lean, slope + -IC]

tri·clin·i·um (trī klin′ē əm), *n., pl.* **-clin·i·a** (-klin′ē ə). *Rom. Hist.* **1.** a couch extending along three sides of a table, for reclining on at meals. **2.** a dining room, esp. one containing such a couch. [< L < Gk *triklínion,* dim. of *triklīnos* having three couches (adj.), dining-room so furnished (n.), equiv. to *tri-* TRI- + *klīn(ē)* couch + *-os* adj. suffix; see CLINIC]

tric·o·lette (trik′ə let′), *n.* a knitted fabric made of silk or man-made yarn, used in the manufacture of wearing apparel. [TRICO(T + FLANNE)LETTE]

tri·col·or (trī′kul′ər), *adj.* **1.** Also, **tri′col′ored;** *esp. Brit.,* **tri′col′oured.** having three colors. —*n.* **2.** a flag having three colors. **3.** the national flag of France, adopted during the French Revolution, consisting of three vertical bands of blue, white, and red. Also, *esp. Brit.,* **tri′col′our.** [< LL *tricolor,* equiv. to *tri-* TRI- + *-color* colored]

tri′color cam′era, a camera for taking color photographs by exposing three separation negatives simultaneously by splitting the light from the subject by means of prisms and mirrors, and exposing through appropriate filters.

tri·corn (trī′kôrn), *adj.* **1.** having three horns or hornlike projections; three-cornered. —*n.* **2.** Also, **tri′corne.** a hat with the brim turned up on three sides; cocked hat. [< L *tricorn(is)* having three horns, equiv. to *tri-* TRI- + *corn(u)* HORN + *-is* adj. suffix]

tri·cor·nered (trī′kôr′nərd), *adj.* having three corners; tricorn. [TRI- + CORNERED]

tri·cos·tate (trī kos′tāt), *adj. Bot., Zool.* having three ribs, costae, or raised lines. [TRI- + COSTATE]

tri·cot (trē′kō; *Fr.* trē kō′), *n.* **1.** a warp-knit fabric, usually of nylon, with each side different. **2.** a kind of worsted cloth. [< F: knitting, knitted fabric, sweater, deriv. of *tricoter* to knit << Gmc; akin to G *stricken* to knit]

tric·o·tine (trik′ə tēn′), *n.* See **cavalry twill.** [< F, equiv. to *tricot* TRICOT + *-ine* -INE[1]]

tri·cre·sol (trī krē′sōl, -sôl, -sol), *n. Chem.* a mixture of the three isomeric cresols. [TRI- + CRESOL]

tri·crot·ic (trī krot′ik), *adj. Physiol.* **1.** having three arterial beats for one heartbeat, as certain pulses. **2.** pertaining to such a pulse. [< Gk *tríkrot(os)* with triple beat (*tri-* TRI- + *krótos* beat) + -IC] —**tri·cro·tism** (trī′krə tiz′əm, trik′rə-), *n.*

tric·trac (trik′trak′), *n.* ticktrack.

tri·cus·pid (trī kus′pid), *adj.* **1.** Also, **tri·cus′pi·dal.** having three cusps or points, as a tooth. Cf. **bicuspid. 2.** *Anat.* of, pertaining to, or affecting the tricuspid valve. —*n.* **3.** *Anat.* a tricuspid part, as a tooth. [< L *tricuspid-* (s. of *tricuspis*) having three points. See TRI-, CUSPID]

tri·cus·pi·date (trī kus′pi dāt′), *adj. Anat.* having three cusps or flaps. [TRICUSPID + -ATE[1]]

tricus′pid valve′, *Anat.* the valve, consisting of three triangular flaps of tissue between the right auricle and ventricle of the heart, that prevents the blood from flowing back into the auricle. Cf. **mitral valve.**

tri′cy·an′ic ac′id (trī′sī an′ik, trī′-). See **cyanuric acid.** [TRI- + CYANIC ACID]

tri·cy·cle (trī′si kəl), *n.* **1.** a child's vehicle having one large front wheel and two small rear wheels, propelled by foot pedals. **2.** a velocipede with three wheels propelled by pedals or hand levers. **3.** a three-wheeled motorcycle. [< F; see TRI-, CYCLE]

tri·cy·clic (trī sī′klik, -sik′lik), *adj.* pertaining to or embodying three cycles. [TRI- + CYCLIC]

trid., (in prescriptions) three days. [< L *trīduum*]

Tri·dac·na (tri dak′nə), *n.* a genus of giant clams found on reefs in the South Pacific, attaining a diameter of 4 feet or more, and weighing over 500 pounds. [< NL, L: oyster < Gk *trídakn(os)* eaten at three bites, equiv. to *tri-* TRI- + *dakn-*, equiv. to *dákn(ein)* (to) bite + *-a* fem. n. suffix]

tri·dac·tyl (trī dak′tᵊl, -til), *adj. Zool.* having three fingers or toes, as certain reptiles. [TRI- + DACTYL]

tri′darn cup′board (trī′därn), a Welsh cupboard of the late 17th and 18th centuries, having two sections, closing with doors, supporting an open, canopied upper section for displaying vessels, plates, etc. [< Welsh, equiv. to *tri-* TRI- + *darn* piece; see DARN[1]]

Trident held by Poseidon

tri·dent (trīd′ᵊnt), *n.* **1.** a three-pronged instrument or weapon. **2.** *Rom. Hist.* a three-pronged spear used by a retiarius in gladiatorial combats. **3.** *Class. Myth.* the three-pronged spear forming a characteristic attribute of the sea god Poseidon, or Neptune. **4.** a fish spear having three prongs. —*adj.* **5.** Also, **tri·den·tal** (trī den′tᵊl). having three prongs or tines. [< L *trident-* (s. of *tridēns*) having three teeth. See TRI-, DENT[2]]

tri·den·tate (trī den′tāt), *adj.* having three teeth or toothlike parts or processes. [TRIDENT + -ATE[1]]

Tri·den·tine (trē den′tin, -tīn, tri-), *adj.* **1.** of or pertaining to the city of Trent. **2.** of or pertaining to the Council of Trent. **3.** conforming to the decrees and doctrines of the Council of Trent. [< ML *Tridentīnus*, adj. use of L *Tridentīnus* tribesman of the Tridentini. See TRADENTUM, -INE[1]]

Tri·den·tum (trī den′təm), *n.* ancient name of Trent, Italy.

tri·di·men·sion·al (trī′di men′shə nᵊl), *adj.* having three dimensions. [TRI- + DIMENSIONAL] —**tri′di·men′sion·al′i·ty,** *n.*

trid·y·mite (trid′ə mīt′), *n. Mineral.* a polymorph of quartz occurring in the form of small crystals, commonly twinned, in siliceous volcanic rocks. [< G *Tridymit*, equiv. to *tridym-* (Gk *trídym(os)* triple, equiv. to *tri-* TRI- + *(di)dymos* DIDYMOUS) + *-it* -ITE[1]]

tri·e·cious (trī ē′shəs), *adj. Bot.* trioecious. —**tri·e′cious·ly,** *adv.*

tried (trīd), *v.* **1.** a pt. and pp. of **try.** —*adj.* **2.** tested and proved good, dependable, or trustworthy. **3.** subjected to hardship, worry, trouble, or the like.

tri·en·ni·al (trī en′ē əl), *adj.* **1.** occurring every three years. **2.** lasting three years. —*n.* **3.** a third anniversary. **4.** something that appears or occurs every three years. **5.** a period of three years; triennium. [TRIENNI(UM) + -AL[1]] —**tri·en′ni·al·ly,** *adv.*

tri·en·ni·um (trī en′ē əm), *n., pl.* **-en·ni·ums, -en·ni·a** (-en′ē ə). a period of three years. [< L: period of three years, equiv. to *trienni(s)* pertaining to three years (*tri-* TRI- + *-ennis*, akin to *annus* year) + *-um* neut. n. suffix]

tri·ens (trī′enz), *n., pl.* **tri·en·tes** (trī en′tēz). **1.** a copper coin of ancient Rome, issued during the Republic, a third part of an as. **2.** tremissis (def. 1). [< L: third part]

tri·er (trī′ər), *n.* one who or that which tries or tests; tester. [TRY + -ER[1]]

Trier (trēr), *n.* a city in W West Germany, on the Moselle River: extensive Roman ruins; cathedral. 87,400 (1963). Also called **Treves.** French, **Trèves.**

tri·er·arch (trī′ə rärk′), *n. Gk. Hist.* **1.** the commander of a trireme. **2.** (in Athens) a citizen who, singly, or jointly with other citizens, was required to fit out a trireme for the public service. [< Gk *triḗrarch(os)*, equiv. to *triḗr(ēs)* having three banks of oars (adj.), trireme (n.) + *archós* commander. See TRI-, -ARCH]

tri·er·ar·chy (trī′ə rär′kē), *n., pl.* **-chies.** *Gk. Hist.* **1.** the office of a trierarch. **2.** trierarchs collectively. **3.** (in Athens) the duty of fitting out or furnishing triremes for the public service. [< Gk *triērarchía*. See TRIERARCH, -Y[3]]

Tries·neck·er (trēz′nek ər), *n.* a crater in the first quadrant of the face of the moon: about 14 miles in diameter.

Tri·este (trē est′; *It.* trē es′te), *n.* **1.** a seaport in NE Italy, on the Gulf of Trieste. 237,472. **2. Free Territory of,** an area bordering the N Adriatic: originally a part of Italy; designated a free territory by the UN 1947; N zone, including the city of Trieste, 86 sq. mi. administered by the U.S. and Great Britain from 1947 until it was turned over to Italy in 1954; S zone 199 sq. mi. incorporated into Yugoslavia; now part of Slovenia. **3. Gulf of,** an inlet at the N end of the Adriatic, in NE Italy. 20 mi. wide.

tri·eth·yl (trī eth′əl), *adj. Chem.* containing three ethyl groups. [TRI- + ETHYL]

tri·eth·yl·a·mine (trī eth′əl ə mēn′, -eth′əl ə mēn′, -am′in), *n. Chem.* a colorless, flammable liquid, $(C_2H_5)_3N$, used chiefly as a solvent in chemical syntheses. [TRI- + ETHYL + AMINE]

trieth′yl orthofor′mate, *Chem.* a colorless liquid, $HC(OC_2H_5)_3$, used chiefly in organic synthesis. Also called **aethon.**

tri·fa·cial (trī fā′shəl), *adj.* trigeminal. [TRI- + FACIAL]

trifa′cial neural′gia, *Pathol.* See **tic douloureux.**

tri·fid (trī′fid), *adj.* cleft into three parts or lobes. [< L *trifid(us)* split in three. See TRI-, -FID]

Trifid foot

tri′fid foot′, *Furniture.* a pad foot having the form of three connected lobes emerging from the leg. Also called **drake foot.**

tri·fle (trī′fəl), *n., v.,* **-fled, -fling.** —*n.* **1.** an article or thing of very little value. **2.** a matter, affair, or circumstance of trivial importance or significance. **3.** a small, inconsiderable, or trifling sum of money. **4.** a small quantity or amount of anything; a little: *He's still a trifle angry.* **5.** a literary, musical, or artistic work of a light or trivial character having no great or lasting merit; bagatelle. **6.** a kind of pewter of medium hardness. **7. trifles,** articles made of this. **8.** *English Cookery.* a dessert consisting of custard or some substitute, and usually containing cake soaked in wine or liqueur, and jam, fruit, or the like. —*v.i.* **9.** to deal lightly or without due seriousness or respect (usually fol. by *with*): *He was in no mood to be trifled with.* **10.** to amuse oneself; dally (usually fol. by *with*). **11.** to play or toy by handling or fingering (usually fol. by *with*): *He sat trifling with a pen.* **12.** to act or talk in an idle or frivolous way. **13.** to pass time idly or frivolously; waste time; idle. —*v.t.* **14.** to pass or spend (time) idly or frivolously (usually fol. by *away*). [ME *trufle* idle talk < OF; ME *treoflen* to mock < OF *trufler* to make sport of] —**tri′fler,** *n.*
—**Syn. 1.** bauble, toy. **9, 10.** play, toy. **12.** gossip, chatter. **14.** fritter.

tri·fling (trī′fling), *adj.* **1.** of very little importance; trivial; insignificant: *a trifling matter.* **2.** of small value, cost, or amount: *a trifling sum.* **3.** frivolous; shallow; light: *trifling conversation.* **4.** *U.S. Dial.* mean; worthless. —*n.* **5.** idle or frivolous conduct, talk, etc. **6.** foolish delay or waste of time. [late ME; see TRIFLE, -ING[2], -ING[1]] —**tri′fling·ly,** *adv.* —**tri′fling·ness,** *n.*
—**Syn. 1.** unimportant, nugatory, slight, inconsequential, immaterial. See **petty. 2.** negligible, piddling. —**Ant. 1.** important.

tri·flu·o·per·a·zine (trī flo͞o′ə per′ə zēn′), *n. Pharm.* a compound, $C_{21}H_{24}F_3N_3S$, used in the form of its dihydrochloride as a tranquilizer. [TRI- + FLUO- + *(pi)perazine* (comb. form repr. L *piper* pepper) + -AZ + -INE[2]]

tri·flu·o·ride (trī flo͞o′ə rīd′, -flo͞or′īd, -flôr′-, -flōr′-), *n. Chem.* a fluoride containing three atoms of fluorine. [TRI- + FLUORIDE]

tri·flu·o·ro·chlo·ro·meth·ane (trī flo͞o′ə rō klôr′ō-meth′ān, -klōr′-, -flo͞or′ō, -flôr′-, -flōr′-), *n. Chem.* chlorotrifluoromethane. [TRI- + FLUOR- + -O- + CHLORO-[2] + METHANE]

tri·fo·cal (*adj.* trī fō′kəl; *n.* trī fō′kəl, trī′fō′kəl), *adj.* **1.** *Optics.* having three foci. **2.** (of an eyeglass lens) having three portions, one for near, one for intermediate, and one for far vision. —*n.* **3. trifocals,** eyeglasses with trifocal lenses. [TRI- + FOCAL]

tri·fo·li·ate (trī fō′lē it, -āt′), *adj.* **1.** having three leaflets, leaflike parts, lobes, or foils; trefoil. **2.** *Bot.* trifoliolate. Also, **tri·fo′li·at′ed.** [TRI- + FOLIATE]

trifo′liate or′ange, a spiny, Chinese orange tree, *Poncirus trifoliata*, used as a stock in grafting and for hedges.

tri·fo·li·o·late (trī fō′lē ə lāt′), *adj. Bot.* **1.** having three leaflets, as a compound leaf. **2.** having leaves with three leaflets, as a plant. [TRI- + FOLIOLATE]

tri·fo·li·um (trī fō′lē əm), *n.* any plant of the genus *Trifolium*, comprising the trefoils. [< L: triple leaf. See TRI-, FOLIUM]

Triforium

tri·fo·ri·um (trī fōr′ē əm, -fôr′-), *n., pl.* **-fo·ri·a** (-fōr′ē ə, -fôr′-). *Archit.* (in a church) the wall at the side of the nave, choir, or transept, corresponding to the space between the vaulting or ceiling and the roof of an aisle, often having a blind arcade or an opening in a gallery. [< AL, special use of ML *triforium* kind of gallery, lit., something with three openings, equiv. to L *tri-* TRI- + *for-* opening + *-ium* n. suffix (neut. of *-ius* adj. suffix)] —**tri·fo′ri·al,** *adj.*

tri·form (trī′fôrm′), *adj.* **1.** formed of three parts; in three divisions. **2.** existing or appearing in three different forms. **3.** combining three different forms. Also, **tri′formed′.** [< L *triform(is)*. See TRI-, -FORM]

tri·fur·cate (*v.* trī fûr′kāt; *adj.* trī fûr′kit, -kāt), *v.,* **-cat·ed, -cat·ing,** *adj.* —*v.i.* **1.** to divide into three forks or branches. —*adj.* **2.** Also, **tri·fur′cat·ed.** divided into three forks or branches. [TRI- + FURCATE] —**tri′fur·ca′tion,** *n.*

trig[1] (trig), *adj., v.,* **trigged, trig·ging.** —*adj. Chiefly Brit.* **1.** neat, trim, smart, or spruce. **2.** in good physical condition; sound; well. —*v.t.* **3.** *Brit. Dial.* to make trim, smart, etc. (often fol. by *up* or *out*). [ME < Scand; cf. Icel *tryggr* loyal, safe; c. Goth *triggws* true, faithful. See TRUE] —**trig′ness,** *n.*
—**Syn. 1.** tidy, orderly.

trig[2] (trig), *v.,* **trigged, trig·ging,** *n.* —*v.t. Dial.* **1.** to support or prop, as with a wedge. **2.** to act as a check on (the moving of wheels, vehicles, etc.). —*n.* **3.** a wedge or block used to prevent a wheel, cask, or the like, from rolling. [? < Scand; cf. Icel *tryggja* to make fast, secure]

trig., **1.** trigonometric. **2.** trigonometrical. **3.** trigonometry.

tri·ga (trē′gə, trī′-), *n., pl.* **tri·gae** (trē′gī, trī′jē). *Class. Antiq.* a two-wheeled chariot drawn by a team of three horses. Cf. **biga, quadriga.** [< LL *trīga* contr. of L *trijuga*, equiv. to *tri-* TRI- + *juga*, pl. of *jugum* YOKE]

trig·a·mous (trig′ə məs), *adj.* **1.** of or pertaining to trigamy or a trigamist. **2.** *Bot.* having staminate, pistillate, and hermaphrodite flowers in the same flower head. [< Gk *trígamos* thrice married. See TRIGAMY, -OUS]

trig·a·my (trig′ə mē), *n.* **1.** the state of having three wives or three husbands at one time. **2.** the state of having been lawfully married to three wives or three husbands at different times. [< LL *trigamia* < Gk, equiv. to *trígam(os)* thrice-married + *-ia* -Y[3]. See TRI-, -GAMY] —**trig′a·mist,** *n.*

trig·a·tron (trig′ə tron′), *n. Electronics.* an electronic switch consisting of two main electrodes and an auxiliary trigger electrode in a gas-filled tube. The gas is normally nonconducting but its resistance breaks down when a sufficiently strong pulse is sent through the trigger electrode. [TRIG(GER) + *-a-* connective vowel + -TRON]

tri·gem·i·nal (trī jem′ə nᵊl), *Anat.* —*adj.* **1.** of or pertaining to the trigeminal nerve. —*n.* **2.** See **trigeminal nerve.** [< NL *trigemin(us)*, L: triple (*tri-* TRI- + *geminus* twin, double) + -AL[1]]

trigem′inal nerve′, *Anat.* either one of the fifth pair of cranial nerves, consisting of motor fibers that innervate the muscles of mastication, and of sensory fibers that conduct impulses from the head and face to the brain.

trigem′inal neural′gia, *Pathol.* See **tic douloureux.**

Tri·gère (tri zhâr′, -jâr′; *Fr.* trē zher′), *n.* **Pauline,** born 1912, U.S. fashion designer, born in France.

tri·ges·i·mo·se·cun·do (trī jes′ə mō′sə kun′dō), *n., pl.* **-dos,** *adj. Bookbinding.* thirty-twomo. [< L: thirty-second]

trig·ger (trig′ər), *n.* **1.** a small projecting tongue in a firearm, which when pressed by the finger, actuates the mechanism that discharges the weapon. **2.** a device, as a lever, the pulling or pressing of which releases a detent or spring. **3.** anything, as an act, event, etc., that serves as a stimulus and initiates or precipitates a reaction or series of reactions. **4.** *Informal.* triggerman. **5. quick on the trigger,** *Informal.* quick to act or respond; impetuous; alert: *The youngsters were quick on the trigger, and it was all she could do to keep up with them.* —*v.t.* **6.** to initiate or precipitate (a chain of events, scientific reaction, psychological process, etc.): *Their small protest triggered a mass demonstration.* **7.** to fire or explode (a gun, missile, etc.) by pulling a trigger or releasing a triggering device: *He accidentally triggered his rifle.* [earlier *tricker* < D *trekker*, equiv. to *trekk(en)* (to) pull + *-er* -ER[1]] —**trig′ger·less,** *adj.*

trig′ger fin′ger, **1.** any finger, usually the forefinger, that presses the trigger of a gun. **2.** either forefinger, depending on which hand is dominant.

trig·ger·fish (trig′ər fish′), *n., pl.* (*esp. collectively*) **-fish,** (*esp. referring to two or more kinds or species*) **-fish·es.** any of various compressed, deep-bodied fishes of the genus *Balistes* and allied genera, chiefly found in tropical seas, having an anterior dorsal fin with three stout spines. [TRIGGER + FISH]

trig·ger-hap·py (trig′ər hap′ē), *adj. Informal.* **1.** ready to fire a gun at the least provocation, regardless of the situation or probable consequences: *a trigger-happy hoodlum.* **2.** heedless and foolhardy in matters of great importance and recklessly advocating action that can result in war: *Some called him a trigger-happy candidate.* **3.** eager to point out the mistakes or shortcomings of others; aggressively or wantonly critical: *He's a trigger-happy editor with a nervous blue pencil.*

trig·ger·man (trig′ər mən, -man′), *n., pl.* **-men** (-mən, -men′). *Informal.* **1.** a gangster who specializes in committing murder with a gun. **2.** a bodyguard, esp. of a gangster. Also called **trigger.** [TRIGGER + MAN[1]]

trig′ger mech′anism, a physiological or psychological process caused by a stimulus and resulting in a usually severe reaction.

tri·glyc·er·ide (trī glis′ə rīd′, -ər id), *n. Chem.* an ester obtained from glycerol by the esterification of three hydroxyl groups with fatty acids. Cf. **glyceride.** [TRI- + GLYCERIDE]

tri·glyph (trī′glif′), *n. Archit.* a structural member of a Doric frieze, separating two consecutive metopes, and consisting typically of a rectangular block with two vertical grooves or glyphs, and two chamfers or half grooves at the sides, together counting as a third glyph, and leaving three flat vertical bands on the face of the block. [< L *triglyph(us)* < Gk *tríglyphos* thrice-grooved, equiv. to *tri-* TRI- + *glyph(ḗ)* GLYPH + *-os* adj. suffix] —**tri′glyphed′,** *adj.* —**tri·glyph′ic, tri·glyph′i·cal,** *adj.*

tri·go (trē′gō; *Sp.* trē′gô), *n., pl.* **-gos** (-gōz; *Sp.* -gôs). wheat; field of wheat. [< Sp < L *trīticum* wheat, equiv. to *trīt(us)* ground, rubbed to pieces (ptp. of *terere*) + *-icum* -IC]

tri·gon (trī′gon), *n.* **1.** *Astrol.* the position or aspect of two planets 120° distant from each other. **2.** an ancient Greek stringed instrument with a triangular shape. **3.** *Archaic.* a triangle. [< L *trigōn(um)* triangle < Gk *trígōnon*, n. use of neut. of *trígōnos* three-angled. See TRI-, -GON]

trigon., **1.** trigonometric. **2.** trigonometrical. **3.** trigonometry.

trig·o·nal (trig′ə nᵊl), *adj.* **1.** of, pertaining to, or shaped like a triangle; having three angles; triangular. **2.** *Crystall.* having threefold symmetry. [TRIGON + -AL[1]] —**trig′o·nal·ly,** *adv.*

trig′onal trisoctahe′dron, a trisoctahedron whose faces are triangles.

tri·gone (trī′gōn), *n. Anat.* a triangular part or area. Also, **trigonum.** [< F < L *trigōnum* triangle]

trig·o·nom·e·ter (trig′ə nom′i tər), *n.* an instrument for solving plane right-angled triangles by inspection. [TRIGONO(METRY) + -METER]

trig·o·no·met·ri·a (trig′ə nə me′trē ə), *n.* an obsolete instrument for triangulation by graphic means. [< NL: lit., triangle measuring. See TRIGON, -METRY]

trig′onomet′ric equa′tion, *Math.* an equation involving trigonometric functions of unknown angles, as $\cos B = \frac{1}{2}$.

trig′onomet′ric func′tion, *Math.* **1.** Also called **circular function.** a function, as sine, cosine, etc., expressed as the ratio of the sides of a right triangle. **2.** any function involving only trigonometric functions and constants.

trig′onomet′ric se′ries, *Math.* an infinite series involving sines and cosines of increasing integral multiples of a variable.
trig·o·nom·e·try (trig′ə nom′i trē), *n.* the branch of mathematics that deals with the relations between the sides and angles of plane or spherical triangles, and the calculations based on them. [< NL *trigōnometria* TRIGONOMETRIA] —**trig·o·no·met·ric** (trig′ə nə me′trik), **trig′o·no·met′ri·cal,** *adj.* —**trig′o·no·met′ri·cal·ly,** *adv.*
trig·o·nous (trig′ə nəs), *adj.* having three angles or corners, as a stem, seed, etc.; triangular. [< L *trigōnus* triangular < Gk *trígōnos.* See TRI-, -GON, -OUS]
tri·go·num (trī gō′nəm), *n., pl.* **-na** (-nə). *Anat.* trigone. [< L: triangle. See TRIGON]
tri·graph (trī′graf, -gräf), *n.* a group of three letters representing a single speech sound, as *eau* in *beau.* [TRI- + -GRAPH] —**tri·graph′ic,** *adj.*
tri·he·dral (trī hē′drəl), *adj.* **1.** *Geom.* having, or formed by, three planes meeting in a point: *a trihedral angle.* —*n.* **2.** the figure formed by three lines of different planes, meeting at a point. [TRI- + -HEDRAL]
tri·he·dron (trī hē′drən), *n., pl.* **-drons, -dra** (-drə). *Geom.* the figure determined by three planes meeting in a point. [TRI- + -HEDRON]
tri·hy·drate (trī hī′drāt), *n.* *Chem.* a hydrate that contains three molecules of water, as potassium pyrophosphate, $K_4P_2O_7 \cdot 3H_2O$. [TRI- + HYDRATE] —**tri·hy′drat·ed,** *adj.*
tri·hy·dric (trī hī′drik), *adj.* *Chem.* (esp. of alcohols and phenols) trihydroxy. [TRI- + -HYDRIC]
tri·hy·drox·y (trī′hī drok′sē), *adj.* *Chem.* containing three hydroxyl groups. [TRI- + HYDROX(YL) + -Y[1]]
tri·i·o·do·meth·ane (trī′ī ō′dō meth′ān), *n.* *Chem.* iodoform. [TRI- + IODO- + METHANE]
tri·ju·gate (trī′jŏŏ gāt′, tri jōō′git, -gāt), *adj.* *Bot.* having three pairs of leaflets. Also, **tri·ju·gous** (trī′jŏŏ gəs, trī jōō′-). [TRI- + JUGATE]
trike (trīk), *n.* *Informal.* tricycle. [by shortening and alter.]
Tril·a·fon (tril′ə fon′), *n.* *Pharm., Trademark.* perphenazine.
tri·lat·er·al (trī lat′ər əl), *adj.* having three sides. [< L *trilater(us)* three-sided + -AL[1]. See TRI-, LATERAL] —**tri·lat′er·al′i·ty,** *n.* —**tri·lat′er·al·ly,** *adv.*
tri·lat·er·a·tion (trī lat′ə rā′shən), *n.* *Survey.* a method of determining the relative positions of three or more points by treating these points as vertices of a triangle or triangles of which the angles and sides can be measured. [TRILATER(AL) + -ATION]
tril·by (tril′bē), *n., pl.* **-bies.** *Chiefly Brit.* a hat of soft felt with an indented crown. Also, **tril′by hat′.** [short for *Trilby hat,* named after heroine of *Trilby,* novel by G. du Maurier]
Tril·by (tril′bē), *n.* a girl's given name.
tri·lem·ma (trī lem′ə), *n.* a situation, analogous to a dilemma, in which there are three almost equally undesirable alternatives: *His trilemma consisted in not knowing whether to acknowledge receipt, deny it, or simply leave.* **2.** *Logic.* a form of argument in which three choices are presented, each of which is indicated to have consequences that may be unfavorable. [TRI- + *-lemma* (as in DILEMMA)]
tri·lin·e·ar (trī lin′ē ər), *adj.* of, pertaining to, or bounded by three lines. [TRI- + LINEAR]
tri·lin·gual (trī ling′gwəl), *adj.* **1.** employing, speaking, or involving three languages. —*n.* **2.** an inscription in three languages. [< L *trilingu(is)* triple-tongued + -AL[1]. See TRI-, LINGUAL] —**tri·lin′gual·ism,** *n.* —**tri·lin′gual·ly,** *adv.*
tri·lit·er·al (trī lit′ər əl), *adj.* **1.** using or consisting of three letters. **2.** (of Semitic roots) consisting of three consonants. —*n.* **3.** a triliteral word or root. [TRI- + LITERAL]
tri·lit·er·al·ism (trī lit′ər ə liz′əm), *n.* the characteristic presence of triliteral roots in a language, as in the Semitic languages. [TRILITERAL + -ISM]
tri·lith·on (trī lith′on, trī′lə thon′), *n.* a prehistoric structure consisting of two upright stones supporting a horizontal stone. Also, **tri·lith** (trī′lith). [< Gk *trílithon,* neut. of *trílithos* having three stones. See TRI-, -LITH]
trill[1] (tril), *v.t.* **1.** to sing with a vibratory effect of voice, esp. in the manner of a shake or trill. **2.** to play with like effect on an instrument. **3.** *Phonet.* to produce (a trill). **4.** (of birds, insects, etc.) to sing or utter in a succession of rapidly alternating sounds. —*v.i.* **5.** to resound vibrantly, or with a rapid succession of sounds, as the voice, song, laughter, etc. **6.** to utter or make a sound or succession of sounds resembling such singing, as a bird, frog, grasshopper, person laughing, etc. **7.** to execute a shake or trill with the voice or on a musical instrument. **8.** *Phonet.* to execute a trill, esp. with the tongue, as while singing, talking, or whistling. —*n.* **9.** act or sound of trilling. **10.** *Music.* a rapid alternation of two adjacent tones; a shake. **11.** a similar sound, or succession of sounds, uttered or made by a bird, an insect, a person laughing, etc. **12.** *Phonet.* **a.** an uttered, sung, whispered, or whistled sequence of repetitive, rapid, vibratory movements produced in any free articulator or membrane by a rush of air expelled from the lungs and often causing a corresponding sequence of contacts between the vibrating articulator and another organ or surface. **b.** a speech sound produced by such a trill. [< It *trill(o)* quaver or warble in singing << Gmc; cf. D *trillen* to vibrate, late ME *trille* to shake or rock (something)]

Trill[1] (def. 10)

trill[2] (tril), *Archaic.* —*v.i.* **1.** to flow in a thin stream; trickle. —*v.t.* **2.** to cause to flow in a thin stream. [ME *trille* to make (something) turn; to roll, flow (said of tears, water) < Scand; cf. Dan *trille* to roll (said, e.g., of tears and of a wheelbarrow). See TRILL[1]]
Tril·ling (tril′ing), *n.* **Lionel,** born 1905, U.S. critic and author.
tril·lion (tril′yən), *n., pl.* **-lions,** (*as after a numeral*) **-lion,** *adj.* —*n.* **1.** a cardinal number represented, in the U.S. and France, by one followed by 12 zeros, and, in Great Britain and Germany, by one followed by 18 zeros. —*adj.* **2.** amounting to one trillion in number. [< F, c. It *trillione,* equiv. to *tr(i)*- TRI- + *(m)illione* MILLION] —**tril′lionth,** *n., adj.*
tril·li·um (tril′ē əm), *n.* any liliaceous herb of the genus *Trillium,* having a whorl of three leaves from the center of which rises a solitary flower. [< NL: genus name, appar. alter. (by Linnaeus) of Sw *trilling* triplet, alluding to the foliation]
tri·lo·bate (trī lō′bāt, trī′lə bāt′), *adj.* having three lobes. Also, **tri·lo′bat·ed.** [TRI- + LOBATE]

Trilobate leaf

tri·lobed (trī′lōbd′), *adj.* trilobate. [TRI- + LOBED]
tri·lo·bite (trī′lə bīt′), *n.* any marine arthropod of the extinct group *Trilobita,* from the Paleozoic era, having a flattened, oval body varying in length from an inch or less to two feet: one of the earliest known fossils. [< NL *Trilobītes* < Gk *trílob(os)* three-lobed (see TRI-, LOBE) + *-ītes* -ITE[1]] —**tri·lo·bit·ic** (trī′lə bit′ik), *adj.*

Trilobite, *Griffithides bufo* (Length 1¼ in.)

tri·loc·u·lar (trī lok′yə lər), *adj.* *Bot., Zool.* having three loculi, chambers, or cells. [TRI- + LOCULAR]
tril·o·gy (tril′ə jē), *n., pl.* **-gies.** **1.** a series or group of three plays, novels, operas, etc., that, although individually complete, are closely related in theme, sequence, or the like. **2.** (in ancient Greek drama) a series of three complete and usually related tragedies performed at the festival of Dionysus and forming a tetralogy with the satyr play. **3.** a group of three related things. [< Gk *trilogía.* See TRI-, -LOGY]
trim (trim), *v.,* **trimmed, trim·ming,** *n., adj.,* **trim·mer, trim·mest,** *adv.* —*v.t.* **1.** to put into a neat or orderly condition by clipping, paring, pruning, etc.: *to trim a hedge.* **2.** to remove by clipping, paring, pruning, or the like (often fol. by *off*): *to trim off loose threads from a ragged edge.* **3.** to modify (opinions, views, etc.) according to expediency. **4.** to cut down (an object, as a piece of wood) to a required smoothness or shape. **5.** *Aeron.* to level off (an airship or airplane) in flight. **6.** *Naut.* **a.** to distribute the load of (a ship) so that it sits well in the water. **b.** to stow or arrange, as cargo. **c.** to adjust (the sails or yards) with reference to the direction of the wind and the course of the ship. **7.** *Theat.* to adjust (flied scenery) with reference to its proper or designated place and height for a stage set. **8.** to decorate or adorn with ornaments or embellishments: *to trim a dress with fur; to trim a Christmas tree.* **9.** to arrange goods in (a store window, showcase, etc.) as a display. **10.** to prepare or adjust (a lamp, fire, etc.) for proper burning. **11.** *Informal.* **a.** to rebuke or reprove. **b.** to beat or thrash. **c.** to defeat. **12.** *Archaic.* to dress or array (often fol. by *up*). **13.** *Obs.* to equip. —*v.i.* **14.** *Naut.* **a.** to assume a particular position or trim in the water, as a vessel. **b.** to adjust the sails or yards with reference to the direction of the wind and the course of the ship. **15.** to pursue a neutral or cautious policy between parties. **16.** to accommodate one's views to the prevailing opinion for reasons of expediency. —*n.* **17.** condition, order, or fitness of a person or thing for action, work, use, etc. **18.** *Naut.* **a.** the set of a ship in the water, esp. the most advantageous one. **b.** the balance of a ship. **c.** the difference between the draft at the bow of a vessel and that at the stern. **d.** the condition of a ship with reference to her fitness for sailing. **e.** the adjustment of the sails, rigging, etc., with reference to the direction of the wind and the course of the ship. **f.** the condition of a submarine as regards buoyancy. **19.** a person's dress, adornment, or appearance. **20.** material used for decoration or embellishment; decorative trimming. **21.** decoration of a store window for the display of merchandise; window dressing. **22.** a trimming by cutting, clipping, or the like. **23.** a haircut which restores the previous cut to neatness without changing the hair style. **24.** that which is cut off or eliminated. **25.** *Aeron.* the attitude of an airplane with respect to all three axes, at which balance occurs in forward flight under no controls. **26.** *Building Trades.* finished woodwork or the like used to decorate or border openings or wall surfaces, as cornices, baseboards, moldings, etc. **27.** *Auto.* **a.** the upholstery, knobs, handles, and other equipment inside a motor car. **b.** ornamentation on the exterior of an automobile, esp. in metal or a contrasting color. —*adj.* **28.** pleasingly neat or smart in appearance: *trim lawns.* **29.** in good condition or order. **30.** *Archaic.* properly prepared or equipped. **31.** *Obs.* good, excellent, or fine. —*adv.* **32.** trimly. [OE *trymman, trymian* to strengthen, prepare, deriv. of *trum* strong, active; akin to Ir *dron* strong, Gk *drȳmós* coppice, L *dūrus* hard. See TREE] —**trim′ness,** *n.*
—**Syn. 1.** shear, shave, cut, lop. **3.** adjust, arrange. **8.** deck, bedeck, ornament, embellish, garnish. **20.** adornment, embellishment, garnish. **28.** compact, trig, spruce.
tri·ma·ran (trī′mə ran′), *n.* a vessel similar to a catamaran but having three separate hulls. [TRI- + *-maran* (as in CATAMARAN)]
tri·mer (trī′mər), *n.* *Chem.* **1.** a molecule composed of three identical, simpler molecules. **2.** a polymer derived from three identical monomers. [< Gk *trimer(ēs)* having three parts. See TRI-, -MER] —**tri·mer·ic** (trī mer′ik), *adj.*
trim·er·ous (trim′ər əs), *adj.* **1.** *Bot.* (of flowers) having three members in each whorl. **2.** *Entomol.* having three segments or parts. [< NL *trimerus,* equiv. to *trimer-* (< Gk *trimer(ēs)* TRIMER) + *-us* -OUS]
tri·mes·ter (trī mes′tər), *n.* **1.** a term or period of three months. **2.** one of the three approximately equal terms into which the year is divided by some colleges, schools, etc. [< F *trimestre* < L *trimēstris* of three months, equiv. to *tri-* TRI- + *-mēstris,* var. of *mēnstruus* monthly. See MENSTRUAL] —**tri·mes′tral, tri·mes′tri·al,** *adj.*
tri·me·tal·lic (trī′mə tal′ik), *adj.* **1.** of three metals. **2.** *Engraving.* (of an offset plate) consisting of a face layer of chromium, stainless steel, or chemically prepared aluminum over a layer of copper with a strengthening back-up layer of steel or other metal. [TRI- + METALLIC]
trim·e·ter (trim′i tər), *Pros.* —*n.* **1.** a verse of three measures or feet. —*adj.* **2.** consisting of three measures or feet. **3.** *Class. Pros.* composed of six feet or three dipodies. [< L *trimetr(us)* having three measures < Gk *trímetros.* See TRI-, METER[2]]
tri·meth·yl·ene (trī meth′ə lēn′), *n.* *Chem.* cyclopropane. [TRI- + METHYLENE]
tri·meth·yl·gly·cine (trī meth′əl glī′sēn, -glī sēn′) *n.* *Chem.* betaine. [TRI- + METHYL + GLYCINE]
tri·met·ric (trī me′trik), *adj.* **1.** pertaining to or consisting of a trimeter or trimeters. **2.** *Crystall.* orthorhombic. Also, **tri·met′ri·cal.** [TRIMET(E)R + -IC]
trimet′ric projec′tion, *Geom.* a three-dimensional projection with three different linear scales at arbitrary angles.
tri·met·ro·gon (trī me′trə gon′), *adj.* of or pertaining to a system of aerial photography using three cameras, one pointed directly downward and the others at 60° to it. [TRI- + Gk *métro(n)* measure + -GON]
trim·ly (trim′lē), *adv.* in a trim manner. Also, **trim.** [TRIM + -LY]
trim·mer[1] (trim′ər), *n.* **1.** one who or that which trims. **2.** a tool or machine for trimming, clipping, paring, or pruning. **3.** a machine for trimming lumber. **4.** *Building Trades.* **a.** a joist or rafter supporting one of the ends of a header at the edge of a wellhole. **b.** a wall tile or floor tile for finishing an edge or angle. **5.** an apparatus for stowing, arranging, or shifting cargo, coal, or the like. **6.** one who has no firm position, opinion, or policy, esp. in politics. **7.** one who is committed to no particular political party, accommodating himself to one side or another as expediency may dictate. [TRIM + -ER[1]]
trim·mer[2] (trim′ər), *adj.* comparative of **trim.**
trim·ming (trim′ing), *n.* **1.** anything used or serving to decorate or complete: *the trimmings of a Christmas tree.* **2.** a decorative or ornamental fitting, embellishment, etc., which gives a finished appearance; garnish. **3.** Usually, **trimmings.** an accompaniment or garnish to a main dish: *roast turkey with all the trimmings.* **4.** **trimmings,** pieces cut off in trimming, clipping, paring, or pruning. **5.** act of one who or that which trims. **6.** *Informal.* a rebuking or reproving. **7.** *Informal.* a beating or thrashing. **8.** *Informal.* a defeat: *our team took quite a trimming.* [TRIM + -ING[1]]
trim′ming tab′, *Aeron.* See **trim tab.**
tri·mod·al (trī mōd′əl), *adj.* *Statistics.* (of a distribution) having three modes. [TRI- + MODAL] —**tri′mod·al′i·ty,** *n.*
tri·mo·lec·u·lar (trī′mə lek′yə lər), *adj.* *Chem.* pertaining to or having three molecules. [TRI- + MOLECULAR]
tri·month·ly (trī munth′lē), *adj.* occurring, taking place, done, or acted upon every three months. [TRI- + MONTHLY]
tri·morph (trī′môrf), *n.* *Crystall.* **1.** a substance existing in three structurally distinct forms; a trimorphous substance. **2.** any of the three forms. [< Gk *trímorph(os)* having three forms. See TRI-, -MORPH]
tri·mor·phism (trī môr′fiz əm), *n.* **1.** *Zool.* the occurrence of three forms distinct in structure, coloration, etc., among animals of the same species. **2.** *Bot.* the occurrence of three different forms of flowers, leaves, etc., on the same plant or on distinct plants of the same species. **3.** *Crystall.* the property of some substances of crystallizing in three structurally distinct forms. **4.** the property or condition of occurring in three distinct forms. [< Gk *trímorph(os)* of three forms (see TRIMORPH) + -ISM] —**tri·mor′phic, tri·mor′phous,** *adj.*

Trimorphism (def. 2) A, Long style; B, Intermediate style; C, Short style

tri·mo·tor (trī′mō′tər), *n.* an airplane that has three motors. [TRI- + MOTOR]
tri·mo·tored (trī mō′tərd), *adj.* having three engines. [TRIMOTOR + -ED[3]]
trim′ rail′, *Theat.* the lower row of pins or cleats on a pin rail, used for tying off or fastening lines after lowering scenery into position. Also called **tie-off rail.**
trim′ size′, the final size of a product after its unnecessary parts have been cut off or removed: *The pages were not yet trim size.*
trim′ tab′, *Aeron.* an independently controlled tab set in the trailing edge of a control surface, as an elevator, aileron, or rudder, to hold it in a position suitable for stabilizing the aircraft in a flight attitude. Also, **trimming tab.**
Tri·mur·ti (tri mŏŏr′tē), *n.* (in later Hinduism) a trinity consisting of Brahma the Creator, Vishnu the Preserver, and Shiva the Destroyer. [< Skt, equiv. to *tri* THREE + *mūrti* shape]
Tri·na·cri·a (tri nā′krē ə), *n.* ancient name of **Sicily.**
Tri·na·cri·an (tri nā′krē ən, trī-), *adj.* *Archaic.* Sicilian. [< L *Trinacri(s)* TRINACRIA + -AN]
tri·nal (trīn′əl), *adj.* threefold; triple; trine. [< LL *trīnāl(is).* See TRINE, -AL[1]]
tri·na·ry (trī′nə rē), *adj.* consisting of three parts, or proceeding by three; ternary. [< LL *trīnāri(us)* of three kinds, equiv. to *trīn(ī)* three apiece (*tri-* three + *-nī* each) + *-ārius* -ARY]
tri·na·tion (trī nā′shən), *n.* celebration of Mass three times on the same day by the same priest. [< NL *trīnāt(us)* (ptp. of *trīnāre* to triple, ? deriv. of L *trīnī* three apiece) + -ION]
Trin·co·ma·lee (tring′kō mə lē′), *n.* a seaport in E Ceylon. 26,356 (1953). Also, **Trin′co·ma·li′.**
trin·dle (trin′dəl, trin′əl), *n., v.,* **-dled, -dling.** —*n.* **1.** *Bookbinding.* one of several flat pieces of wood or metal shaped like a tuning fork without the handle, passed between the cords and the boards of a book to flatten the back and fore edge preparatory to trimming. **2.** *Archaic.* a wheel, esp. of a wheelbarrow. **3.** *Obs.* a

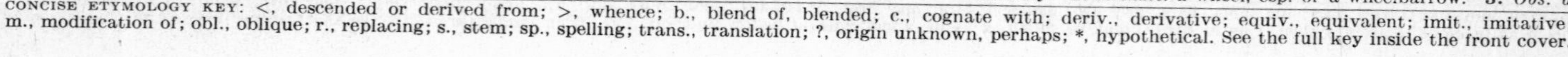

kind of wax taper which has been rolled or coiled. —*v.t., v.i.* **4.** *Obs.* to roll; trundle. [ME *trindel,* OE *tryndel* circle, ring; akin to LG *tründeln* to roll. See TREND]

trine (trīn), *adj.* **1.** threefold; triple. **2.** *Astrol.* of or pertaining to the trigon aspect of two planets distant from each other 120°, or the third part of the zodiac. —*n.* **3.** a set or group of three; triad. **4.** (*cap.*) the Trinity. **5.** *Astrol.* the trine aspect of two planets. [ME < L *trīn(us),* equiv. to *trī-* three + *-nus* -fold]

trine′ immer′sion, a form of baptism in which the candidate is immersed three times, once for each person of the Trinity.

trin·gle (tring′gəl), *n.* a narrow, straight molding, as a fillet. [< F: curtain rod, rod, alter. of MF *tingle;* cf. MD *tingel* lathe]

Trin·i·dad (trin′i dad′; *Sp.* trē′nē thäth′), *n.* **1.** an island in the SE Lesser Antilles, in the E West Indies, off the NE coast of Venezuela: formerly a British colony in the Federation of the West Indies; now part of Trinidad and Tobago. 794,624 (1960); 1864 sq. mi. **2.** a city in central Bolivia. 15,000 (est. 1965). —**Trin′i·dad′i·an,** *adj., n.*

Trin′idad and Toba′go, an independent republic in the West Indies, comprising the islands of Trinidad and Tobago: member of the British Commonwealth. 949,000 (est. 1964); 1980 sq. mi. *Cap.:* Port-of-Spain.

Trin·i·tar·i·an (trin′i târ′ē ən), *adj.* **1.** believing in the doctrine of the Trinity. **2.** pertaining to Trinitarians, or believers in the doctrine of the Trinity. **3.** belonging or pertaining to the religious order of Trinitarians. **4.** of or pertaining to the Trinity. **5.** (*l.c.*) forming a trinity; threefold; triple. —*n.* **6.** one who believes in the doctrine of the Trinity. **7** a member of the "Order of the Holy Trinity," a religious order founded in 1198 to redeem Christian captives of the Muslims. [< NL *trīnitāri(us)* of the Trinity (see TRINITY, -ARY) + -AN]

Trin·i·tar·i·an·ism (trin′i târ′ē ə niz′əm), *n.* the belief in, or doctrine of, the Trinity. [TRINITARIAN + -ISM]

trinitro-, *Chem.* a combination of **tri-** and **nitro-:** *trinitrotoluene.*

tri·ni·tro·ben·zene (trī nī′trō ben′zēn, -ben zēn′), *n. Chem.* any of three yellow crystalline compounds having the formula $C_6H_3(NO_2)_3$, capable of more explosive power and requiring more impact than TNT. Also called **TNB.** [TRINITRO- + BENZENE]

tri·ni·tro·cre·sol (trī nī′trō krē′sōl, -sôl, -sol), *n. Chem.* a yellow, crystalline compound, $CH_3C_6H(OH)(NO_2)_3$, used in high explosives. [TRINITRO- + CRESOL]

tri·ni·tro·glyc·er·in (trī nī′trō glis′ər in), *n. Chem.* nitroglycerin. [TRINITRO- + GLYCERIN]

tri·ni·tro·phen·yl·meth·yl·ni·tra·mine (trī nī′trō fen′əl meth′əl nī′trə mēn′, -nī tram′in, -fēn′-), *n. Chem.* tetryl. [TRINITRO- + PHENYL + METHYL + NITRAMINE]

tri·ni·tro·tol·u·ene (trī nī′trō tol′yo͞o ēn′), *n. Chem.* See **TNT.** Also, **tri·ni·tro·tol·u·ol** (trī nī′trō tol′yo͞o ōl′, -ol′). [TRINITRO- + TOLUENE]

Trin·i·ty (trin′i tē), *n., pl.* **-ties** for 2, 4. **1.** Also called **Blessed Trinity, Holy Trinity.** the union of three persons (Father, Son, and Holy Ghost) in one Godhead, or the threefold personality of the one Divine Being. **2.** a representation of this in art. **3.** See **Trinity Sunday. 4.** (*l.c.*) a group of three; triad. **5.** (*l.c.*) state of being threefold or triple. [ME *trinite* < OF < LL *trīnitāt-* (s. of *trīnitās*) triad, trio, trinity, equiv. to *trīn(us)* threefold (see TRINE) + *-itāt-* -ITY]

trin′ity lil′y. See **great white trillium.**

Trin′ity Sun′day, the Sunday after Pentecost, observed as a festival in honor of the Trinity.

trin·ket (tring′kit), *n.* **1.** a small ornament, piece of jewelry, etc., usually of little value. **2.** anything of trivial value. —*v.i.* **3.** to deal secretly or surreptitiously. [?]

trin·ket·er (tring′ki tər), *n.* a person who deals secretly or surreptitiously. [TRINKET + -ER¹]

trin·ket·ry (tring′ki trē), *n.* trinkets collectively. [TRINKET + -RY]

trin·kum (tring′kəm), *n. Brit. Dial.* a trinket. [jocular alter. of TRINKET]

tri·nod·al (trī nōd′əl), *adj. Bot.* having three nodes or joints. [< L *trinōd(is)* having three knots (*tri-* TRI- + *nōd(us)* NODE + *-is* adj. suffix) + -AL¹]

tri·no·mi·al (trī nō′mē əl), *adj.* **1.** *Algebra.* consisting of or pertaining to three terms. **2.** *Biol.* **a.** pertaining to a scientific name comprising three terms, as of genus, species, and subspecies or variety. **b.** characterized by the use of such names. —*n.* **3.** *Algebra.* an expression which is a sum or difference of three terms, as $3x + 2y + z$ or $3x^3 + 2x^2 + x$. **4.** *Biol.* a trinomial name as *Rosa gallica pumila.* [TRI- + (BI)NOMIAL] —**tri·no′mi·al·ly,** *adv.*

tri·o (trē′ō), *n., pl.* **tri·os. 1.** a musical composition for three voices or instruments. **2.** a company of three singers or players. **3.** a subordinate division of a minuet, scherzo, march, etc., usually in a contrasted key and style (perhaps originally written for three instruments or in three parts). **4.** any group of three persons or things. [< It, equiv. to *tri-* TRI- + *(du)o* two]

tri·ode (trī′ōd), *n. Electronics.* a vacuum tube containing three elements, usually plate, grid, and cathode. [TRI- + (ELECTR)ODE]

tri·oe·cious (trī ē′shəs), *adj. Bot.* of or pertaining to a species having male, female, and hermaphrodite flowers on different plants. Also, **triecious.** [< NL *trioeci(a)* pl. name of the order (< Gk *tri-* TRI- + *oikía,* pl. of *oíkion,* equiv. to *oîk(os)* house + *-ion* dim. suffix) + -OUS] —**tri·oe′cious·ly,** *adv.*

tri·o·le·in (trī ō′lē in), *n. Chem.* olein (def. 1). [TRI- + OLEIN]

tri·o·let (trī′ə lit), *n.* a short poem of fixed form, having a rhyme scheme of *ab, aa, abab,* and having the first line repeated as the fourth and seventh lines, and the second line repeated as the eighth. [< F: lit., little trio]

tri·ox·ide (trī ok′sīd, -sid), *n. Chem.* an oxide containing three oxygen atoms, as As_2O_3. [TRI- + OXIDE]

trip¹ (trip), *n., v.,* **tripped, trip·ping.** —*n.* **1.** a journey or voyage: *to win a trip to Paris.* **2.** a journey, voyage, or run made by a boat, train, bus, or the like, between two points: *It's a short trip from Baltimore to Washington.* **3.** See **round trip** (defs. 1, 2). **4.** a single journey or course of travel taken as part of one's duty, work, etc.: *his daily trip to the bank.* **5.** a stumble; misstep. **6.** a sudden impeding or catching of a person's foot so as to throw him down, esp. in wrestling. **7.** a slip, mistake, error, or blunder. **8.** an error or lapse in conduct or etiquette. **9.** a light, nimble step or movement of the feet. **10.** *Mach.* **a.** Also called **trip dog.** a projecting object mounted on a moving part for striking a control lever to stop, reverse, or otherwise control the actions of some machine, as a milling machine or printing press. **b.** a sudden release or start. **11.** a catch of fish taken by a fishing vessel in a single voyage. **12.** *Slang.* **a.** an instance or period of being under the influence of a hallucinogenic drug, esp. LSD. **b.** the euphoria, illusions, etc., experienced during such a period. —*v.i.* **13.** to stumble: *to trip over a child's toy.* **14.** to make a slip, error, or mistake, as in conversation, conduct, action, etc. **15.** to step lightly or nimbly; skip; dance. **16.** to go with a light, quick step or tread: *She tripped gaily across the room.* **17.** to make a journey or excursion. **18.** to tip or tilt. **19.** *Naut.* (of a boom) to roll under water in a seaway. **20.** *Horol.* (of a tooth on an escape wheel) to slide past the face of the pallet by which it is supposed to be locked and strike the pallet in such a way as to move the balance or pendulum improperly. —*v.t.* **21.** to cause to stumble (often fol. by *up*): *The rug tripped him up.* **22.** to cause to fail; hinder, obstruct, or overthrow. **23.** to cause to make a slip or error: *to trip up a witness by artful questions.* **24.** to catch in a slip or error. **25.** to tip or tilt. **26.** *Naut.* **a.** to break out (an anchor) by turning it over or lifting it from the bottom by a line **(tripping line)** attached to its crown. **b.** to tip or turn (a yard) from a horizontal to a vertical position. **c.** to lift (an upper mast) before lowering. **27.** to operate, start, or set free (a mechanism, weight, etc.) by suddenly releasing a catch, clutch, or the like. **28.** *Mach.* to release or operate suddenly (a catch, clutch, etc.). **29.** wedge (def. 13). **30.** to tread or dance lightly upon (the ground, floor, etc.). **31.** *Archaic.* to perform with a light or tripping step, as a dance. **32. trip the light fantastic,** to go dancing. [ME *trippen* to step lightly < MD (whence also MF *triper;* note single *p*); akin to OE *treppan* to tread]

—**Syn. 1.** excursion, tour, jaunt, junket. TRIP, EXPEDITION, JOURNEY, PILGRIMAGE, VOYAGE are terms for a course of travel made to a particular place, usually for some specific purpose. TRIP is the general word, indicating going any distance and returning, by walking or any means of locomotion, for either business or pleasure, and in either a hurried or a leisurely manner: *a trip to Europe; a vacation trip; a bus trip.* An EXPEDITION, made often by an organized company, is designed to accomplish a specific purpose: *an archaeological expedition.* JOURNEY indicates a trip of considerable length, wholly or mainly by land, for business or pleasure or other reasons, and is now applied to travel which is more leisurely or more fatiguing than a trip; a return is not necessarily indicated: *the long journey to Siam.* A PILGRIMAGE is made as to a shrine, from motives of piety or veneration: *a pilgrimage to Lourdes.* A VOYAGE is travel by water or air, usually for a long distance and for business or pleasure; if by water, leisure is indicated: *a voyage around the world.* **7.** lapse, oversight. **14.** bungle, blunder, err.

trip² (trip), *n. Brit. Dial.* a group of animals, as sheep, goats, fowl, etc.; flock. [ME; appar. special use of TRIP¹ in the sense of a group moving together, hence gang, flock]

tri·pal·mi·tin (trī pal′mi tin), *n. Chem.* palmitin. [TRI- + PALMITIN]

tri·part·ed (trī pär′tid), *adj.* divided into three parts. Also, **tri′part′.** [late ME: alter. of TRIPARTITE; see -ED²]

tri·par·tite (trī pär′tīt), *adj.* **1.** divided into or consisting of three parts: *the tripartite occupation of West Germany.* **2.** *Bot.* divided into three parts by incisions which extend nearly to the base, as a leaf. **3.** involving, participated in, or made by three parties: *a tripartite treaty signed by Argentina, Brazil, and Chile.* [late ME < L *tripartīt(us)* divided into three parts, *tri-* TRI- + *partītus,* ptp. of *partīre* to divide. See PART, -ITE²]

Tripartite leaf

tripar′tite and fret′ty, *Heraldry.* (of a cross) having the limbs divided into three longitudinal strips each, intermingled in the manner of those in a cross parted and fretty.

tri·par·ti·tion (trī′pär tish′ən, trip′ər-), *n.* division into three parts. [TRI- + PARTITION]

trip′ dog′, trip¹ (def. 10a).

tripe (trīp), *n.* **1.** the first and second divisions of the stomach of a ruminant, esp. oxen, sheep, or goats, used as food. Cf. **honeycomb tripe, plain tripe. 2.** *Slang.* something, esp. speech or writing, that is false or worthless; rubbish. **3.** *Theat. Brit.* a length of electric cable connecting a stage pocket to lighting units located on a pipe batten. [ME < OF < ?]

tri·pe·dal (trī′pi dəl, trī pēd′əl, trip′i dəl), *adj.* having three feet. [< L *tripedāl(is).* See TRI-, PEDAL]

tri·pel·en·na·mine (trī′pe len′ə mēn′, -min), *n. Pharm.* a white, crystalline, antihistamine powder, $C_{16}H_{21}N_3$, used chiefly in the form of its citrate or hydrochloride esp. for the treatment of allergic disorders. [TRI- + P(YRIDINE) + E(THY)LENE + (DI)AMINE]

tri·per·son·al (trī pûr′sə nəl), *adj.* (*sometimes cap.*) consisting of or existing in three persons, as the Godhead. [TRI- + PERSONAL]

tri·per·son·al·i·ty (trī′pûr sə nal′i tē), *n.* (*sometimes cap.*) condition of being tripersonal; existence in three persons, as the Godhead. [TRIPERSONAL + -ITY]

tri·pet·al·ous (trī pet′əl əs), *adj. Bot.* having three petals. [TRI- + PETALOUS]

trip·ham·mer (trip′ham′ər), *n.* **1.** *Mach.* a heavy hammer raised and then let fall by means of some tripping device, as a cam. —*adj.* **2.** of, resembling, or characteristic of the repetitive and forceful pounding of a triphammer: *He was subjected to triphammer interrogation by the police detectives.* Also, **trip′ ham′mer.** [TRIP¹ + HAMMER]

tri·phen·yl·meth·ane (trī fen′əl meth′ān, -fēn′-), *n. Chem.* a colorless, crystalline, solid compound containing three benzene rings, $(C_6H_5)_3CH$, from which many dyes are derived. [TRI- + PHENYL + METHANE]

triphen′ylmeth′ane dye′, *Chem.* any of a great number of dyes, as crystal violet, fuchsin, and rosaniline, produced from triphenylmethane by replacement of the ring hydrogen atoms with hydroxy, amino, sulfo, or other atoms or groups.

tri·phib·i·an (trī fib′ē ən), *adj. Mil.* **1.** skilled in combat equally on land, sea, and in the air. **2.** (of an aircraft) equipped to take off from land, water, snow, or ice. **3.** triphibious. —*n.* **4.** a person who is triphibian. **5.** a triphibian airplane. [TRI- + (AM)PHIBIAN]

tri·phib·i·ous (trī fib′ē əs), *adj.* employing or involving land, naval, and air forces in a combined operation. Also, **triphibian.** [TRI- + (AM)PHIBIOUS]

tri·phos·phate (trī fos′fāt), *n. Chem.* a phosphate containing the group $P_3O_{10}^{5-}$. [TRI- + PHOSPHATE]

triph·thong (trif′thông, -thong, trip′-), *n.* **1.** *Phonet.* a monosyllabic speech-sound sequence perceived as being made up of three differing vowel qualities, as the pronunciation of *our,* esp. in r-dropping dialects. **2.** (not in technical use) a trigraph. [< NL *triphthong(us)* < MGk *tríphthongos* with three vowels, equiv. to *tri-* TRI- + *phthóngos* voice, sound] —**triph·thong·al** (trif thông′gəl, -thong′-, trip-), *adj.*

triph·y·lite (trif′ə līt′), *n.* a mineral, a rare phosphate of lithium, iron, and manganese, usually occurring in masses of a bluish or greenish color. Also called **triph·y·line** (trif′ə lēn′, -lin). [TRI- + PHYLE + -ITE¹; r. *triphyline* < G *Triphylin*]

tri·phyl·lous (trī fil′əs), *adj. Bot.* having three leaves. [TRI- + -PHYLLOUS]

tri·pin·nate (trī pin′āt), *adj. Bot.* bipinnate, as a leaf, with the divisions also pinnate. Also, **tri·pin′nat·ed.** [TRI- + PINNATE] —**tri·pin′nate·ly,** *adv.*

Tri·pit·a·ka (tri pit′ə kə), *n. Buddhism.* See **Pali Canon.** [< Skt, equiv. to *tri-* TRI- + *pitaka* basket]

tri·plane (trī′plān′), an airplane with three supporting wings, one above another (a design used mainly in the early history of the airplane). [TRI- + PLANE¹]

tri·ple (trip′əl), *adj., n., v.,* **-pled, -pling.** —*adj.* **1.** threefold; consisting of three parts: *a triple knot.* **2.** of three kinds; threefold in character or relationship. **3.** three times as great. **4.** *Internat. Law.* tripartite. —*n.* **5.** an amount, number, etc., three times as great as another. **6.** a group, set, or series of three; something threefold; triad. **7.** *Baseball.* See **three-base hit. 8.** *Bowling.* three strikes in succession. —*v.t.* **9.** to make triple. **10.** *Baseball.* to cause to come into home plate by a three-base hit: *to triple a runner home; to triple a run in.* —*v.i.* **11.** to become triple. **12.** *Baseball.* to make a three-base hit. [late ME < L *triplus,* equiv. to *tri-* TRI- + *(du)plus* DUPLE] —**tri·ply** (trip′lē), *adv.*

Tri′ple Alli′ance, 1. the alliance (1882–1915) of Germany, Austria-Hungary, and Italy. **2.** a league (1717) of France, Great Britain, and the Netherlands against Spain. **3.** a league (1668) of England, Sweden, and the Netherlands against France.

tri′ple bond′, *Chem.* a chemical linkage consisting of three covalent bonds between two atoms of a molecule, represented in chemical formulas by three lines or six dots, as CH≡CH or CH⋮⋮CH.

tri′ple coun′terpoint, *Music.* invertible counterpoint involving three transposable voices.

tri·ple-deck·er (trip′əl dek′ər), *n.* three-decker (defs. 3, 4).

tri′ple dress′er, *Furniture.* a dresser having three drawers across for most of its height.

Tri′ple Entente′, 1. an informal understanding among Great Britain, France, and Russia based on a Franco-Russian military alliance (1894), an Anglo-French entente (1904), and an Anglo-Russian entente (1907). It was considered a counterbalance to the Triple Alliance but was terminated when the Bolsheviks came into control in Russia in 1917. **2.** the member nations of this entente.

tri·ple-ex·pan·sion (trip′əl ik span′shən), *adj.* noting a power source, esp. a steam engine, using the same fluid at three successive stages of expansion to do work in three or more cylinders.

tri′ple fugue′, *Music.* **1.** a fugue with a subject and two countersubjects developed simultaneously. **2.** a fugue with three subjects which are developed at first successively and finally together.

tri·ple-head·er (trip′əl hed′ər), *n. Sports.* a set of three games, as of basketball, each game being played in the same arena on the same day and often between different pairs of teams.

tri′ple in′tegral, *Math.* the limit, as the norm of the partition of a given solid in space into rectangular solids approaches zero, of the sum of the product of the increment in each variable of a given function of three variables times the value of the function at some point in each solid.

tri′ple meas′ure, *Music.* See **triple time.**

tri·ple-nerved (trip′əl nûrvd′), *adj. Bot.* noting a leaf in which two prominent nerves emerge from the middle nerve a little above its base.

tri′ple play′, *Baseball.* a play in which three putouts are made.

tri′ple point′, *Physics.* the particular temperature and pressure at which the solid, liquid, and gaseous phases of a given substance are all at equilibrium with one another.

tri′ple rhyme′. See under **feminine rhyme.**

tri′ple rhythm′, *Pros.* a rhythmic pattern created by a succession of trisyllabic feet.

tri′ple sca′lar prod′uct, *Math.* See **scalar triple product.**

tri·ple-space (trip′əl spās′), *v.t., v.i.,* **-spaced, -spacing.** to type by setting the space regulator on a typewriter so as to have two blank lines between each typed line.

tri′ple superphos′phate, superphosphate (def. 2).

tri·plet (trip′lit), *n.* **1.** one of three children or offspring born at the same birth. **2. triplets,** three offspring born at one birth. **3.** any group or combination of three. **4.** *Pros.* three successive verses or lines, esp. when rhyming and of the same length; a stanza of three lines. **5.** Also called **tercet.** *Music.* a group of three notes to be performed in the time of two ordinary notes of the same kind. **6.** an assembled imitation gem with three parts, the center one giving the color, the top and bottom, sometimes genuine, supplying the wearing qualities. **7. triplets,** (in some card games) three cards of the same denomination. [TRIPLE + -ET]

tri·ple·tail (trip′əl tāl′), *n.* a large food fish, *Lobotes surinamensis,* found in the warmer waters of the Atlantic Ocean and the Mediterranean Sea, with the lobes of its dorsal and anal fins extending backward and with the caudal fin suggesting a three-lobed tail. [TRIPLE + TAIL[1]]

tri′ple threat′, **1.** an expert in three different fields or in three different skills in the same field. **2.** *Football.* a back who is proficient at running, passing, and punting: *The triple threat is a rare find for coaches.*

tri′ple time′, *Music.* time or rhythm characterized by three beats to the measure with an accent on the first beat. Also called **triple measure, triplex.**

tri′plet lil′y, an herb, *Brodiaea laxa,* of California, having purple or white flowers. Also called **Ithuriel's-spear.**

tri·ple·ton (trip′əl tən), *n.* *Chiefly Bridge.* a set of three cards of the same suit in a hand as dealt. [TRIPLE + -TON. See DOUBLETON, SINGLETON]

tri′ple voile′, a lightweight, sheer voile of silk or man-made fibers constructed in plain or novelty weaves. Cf. **ninon.**

tri·plex (trip′leks, trī′pleks), *adj.* **1.** threefold; triple. —*n.* **2.** something triple. **3.** *Music.* See **triple time. 4.** an apartment having three floors. [< L: threefold, equiv. to *tri-* TRI- + *-plex,* nom. sing. of *-plic-* -fold; see PLY[2]]

trip·li·cate (*v.* trip′lə kāt′; *adj., n.* trip′lə kit, -kāt′), *v.,* **-cat·ed, -cat·ing,** *adj., n.* —*v.t.* **1.** to make threefold; triple. **2.** to make or produce in triplicate; provide an original and two copies. —*adj.* **3.** produced in or consisting of three copies or parts; threefold; triple: *triplicate contracts.* —*n.* **4.** one of three identical things. **5. in triplicate,** in three copies, esp. identical copies: *Please type the letter in triplicate.* [< L *triplicātus* (ptp. of *triplicāre* to triple), equiv. to *triplic-* (s. of *triplex*) TRIPLEX + *-ātus* -ATE[1]] —**trip′li·ca′tion,** *n.*

tri·plic·i·ty (tri plis′i tē), *n., pl.* **-ties. 1.** quality or state of being triple; threefold character or condition. **2.** a group or combination of three; triad. **3.** *Astrol.* a set of three signs of the zodiac. [ME *triplicite* < LL *triplicitās* threefold state. See TRIPLEX, -ITY]

trip′ line′, **1.** (in lumbering) a line for freeing a dog hook from a log at a distance. **2.** haulback.

trip·lite (trip′līt), *n.* a dark-brown, massive mineral, fluorophosphate of iron and manganese. [< G *Triplit.* See TRIPLE, -ITE[1]]

trip·lo·blas·tic (trip′lō blas′tik), *adj.* having three primary germ layers, as the embryos of vertebrates. [< Gk *triplō(os)* threefold + *blastik(ós)* budding. See TRI-, -BLAST, -IC]

trip·loid (trip′loid), *Biol.* —*adj.* **1.** having a chromosome number that is three times the basic or haploid number. —*n.* **2.** a triploid cell or organism. [TRIPLE + -OID] —**trip′loi·dy,** *n.*

tri·pod (trī′pod), *n.* **1.** a stool, table, pedestal, etc., with three legs. **2.** a three-legged stand or support, as for a camera, telescope, etc. **3.** the oracular seat of the priestess of Apollo at Delphi. [< L *tripod-* (s. of *tripūs*) < Gk *tripod-* (s. of *trípous*) three-footed. See TRI-, -POD]

trip·o·dal (trip′ə dəl), *adj.* **1.** pertaining to or having the form of a tripod. **2.** having three feet or legs. [TRIPOD + -AL[1]]

tri·pod·ic (trī pod′ik), *adj.* having or using three feet or legs. [TRIPOD + -IC]

trip·o·dy (trip′ə dē), *n., pl.* **-dies.** *Pros.* a measure of three feet. [< Gk *tripodía.* See TRI-, -POD, -Y[3]]

Trip·o·li (trip′ə lē; *It.* trē′pô lē), *n.* **1.** Also, **Tripolitania.** one of the former Barbary States of N Africa: later a province of Turkey; now a part of Libya. **2.** a seaport in and the capital of Libya, in the NW part. 212,577 (1964). **3.** a seaport in N Lebanon, on the Mediterranean. 160,000 (est. 1965). **4.** (*l.c.*) any of several siliceous substances, as rottenstone and infusorial earth, used chiefly in polishing.

Trip·o·li·ta·ni·a (trip′ə li tā′nē ə; *It.* trē′pô lē tä′nyä), *n.* Tripoli (def. 1).

tri·pos (trī′pos), *n., pl.* **-pos·es.** (at Cambridge University, England) any of various final honors examinations. [< L, pseudo-Hellenization of *tripūs* tripod]

trip·pant (trip′ənt), *adj.* *Heraldry.* (of a deer or the like) represented in the act of walking: *a stag trippant.* [alter. of TRIPPING; see -ANT]

trip·per (trip′ər), *n.* **1.** one who or that which trips. **2.** *Mach.* **a.** a tripping mechanism; a trip. **b.** an apparatus causing a signal or other operating device, to be tripped or activated. **3.** *Brit. Informal.* one who goes on a pleasure trip or excursion; excursionist. [TRIP[1] + -ER[1]]

trip·pet (trip′it), *n.* *Mach.* a projection, cam, or the like, for striking some other part at regular intervals. [late ME *trypet.* See TRIP[1], -ET]

trip·ping (trip′ing), *adj.* **1.** light and quick, as a step, pace, etc. **2.** proceeding with a light, easy movement or rhythm. [TRIP[1] + -ING[2]] —**trip′ping·ly,** *adv.*

trip′ping line′, *Naut.* See under **trip**[1] (def. 25a).

trip·tane (trip′tān), *n.* *Chem.* a colorless liquid, $CH_3C(CH_3)_2CH(CH_3)CH_3$, having high antiknock properties as a fuel: used chiefly as an admixture to airplane gasolines. [short for *trimethyl butane* (with $b > p$ before *t*). See TRI-, METHYL]

trip·ter·al (trip′tər əl), *adj.* (of a classical building) having a triple pteron. [< Gk *trípter(os)* having three wings (see TRI-, -PTEROUS) + -AL[1]]

trip·ter·ous (trip′tər əs), *adj.* *Bot.* three-winged; having three wings or winglike expansions. [TRI- + -PTEROUS]

Trip·tol·e·mus (trip tol′ə məs), *n.* *Class. Myth.* a favorite of Demeter and the inventor of the plow and patron of agriculture, connected with the Eleusinian mysteries. Also, **Trip·tol′e·mos.**

trip·tych (trip′tik), *n.* **1.** *Art.* a set of three panels or compartments side by side, bearing pictures, carvings, or the like. **2.** a hinged, three-leaved tablet, written on, in ancient times, with a stylus. [< Gk *tríptych(os)* of three plates, equiv. to *tri-* TRI- + *ptych-* (s. of *ptýx*) plate + *-os* adj. suffix]

Tri·pu·ra (trip′ər ə), *n.* a union territory in NE India. 1,142,005 (1961); 4033 sq. mi. *Cap.:* Agartala.

tri·que·tra (trī kwē′trə, -kwe′-), *n.* **1.** a geometrical figure having three points, esp. one formed of three intersecting ellipses: *The triquetra was often used in ancient art to symbolize a triune deity.* **2.** *Rare.* a triskelion. [< NL, n. use of fem. of L *triquetrus* TRIQUETROUS] —**tri·quet·ric** (trī kwe′trik), *adj.*

tri·que·trous (trī kwē′trəs, -kwe′-), *adj.* **1.** three-sided; triangular. **2.** having a triangular cross section. [< L *triquetrus* triangular, equiv. to *tri-* TRI- + *-quetrus* cornered]

tri·ra·di·ate (trī rā′dē āt′), *adj.* having or consisting of three rays or raylike processes. Also, **tri·ra′di·at′ed.** [TRI- + RADIATE (adj.)] —**tri·ra′di·ate·ly,** *adv.*

tri·ra·di·us (trī rā′dē əs), *n., pl.* **-di·i** (-dē ī′), **-di·us·es.** *Physical Anthropol.* a Y-shaped group of ridges on the palm of the hand at the base of each finger. [TRI- + RADIUS]

Tri·rat·na (trē rut′nə), *n.* (*construed as pl.*) *Buddhism.* the three components of Buddhism, which are the Buddha, or teacher, the dharma, or teaching, and the Sangha, or priesthood. [< Skt: three jewels, equiv. to *tri* three + *ratna* jewel]

tri·reme (trī′rēm), *n.* *Class. Hist.* a galley with three rows or tiers of oars on each side, one above another, used chiefly as a warship. [< L *trirēm(is)* having three banks of oars, equiv. to *tri-* TRI- + *rēm(us)* oar + *-is* adj. suffix]

Trireme (Cross section)

Tri·sa (trē′sə), *n.* a girl's given name.

tri·sac·cha·ride (trī sak′ə rīd′, -ər id), *n.* *Chem.* a carbohydrate composed of three monosaccharide units, and hydrolyzable to a monosaccharide or a mixture of monosaccharides. [TRI- + SACCHARIDE]

tri·sect (trī sekt′), *v.t.* to divide into three parts, esp. into three equal parts. [TRI- + -SECT] —**tri·sec·tion** (trī sek′shən), *n.* —**tri·sec′tor,** *n.*

trisec′tion of the an′gle, *Geom.* the problem, insoluble by means of Euclidean geometry, of constructing an equal to one-third of a given angle.

tri·sep·al·ous (trī sep′ə ləs), *adj.* *Bot.* having three sepals. [TRI- + SEPALOUS]

tri·sep·tate (trī sep′tāt), *adj.* *Bot., Zool.* having three septa. [TRI- + SEPTATE]

tri·se·ri·al (trī sēr′ē əl), *adj.* **1.** arranged in three series or rows. **2.** *Bot.* having only three verticils. [TRI- + SERIAL]

tris·kel·i·on (tri skel′ē on′, -ən), *n., pl.* **tris·kel·i·a** (tri skel′ē ə). a symbolic figure consisting of three legs, arms, or branches radiating from a common center, as the device of Sicily and the Isle of Man. Also, **tris·kele** (tris′kēl). [< Gk *triskel(ḗs)* three-legged (*tri-* TRI- + *skél(os)* leg + *-ēs* adj. suffix) + *-ion* dim. suffix]

Triskelion

tris·mus (triz′məs, tris′-), *n., pl.* **-mus·es.** *Pathol.* **1.** a spasm of the jaw muscles that makes it difficult to open the mouth. **2.** lockjaw. [< NL < Gk *trismós* a grinding] —**tris′mic,** *adj.*

tris·oc·ta·he·dron (tris ok′tə hē′drən), *n., pl.* **-drons, -dra** (-drə). a solid bounded by 24 identical faces in groups of three, each group corresponding to one face of an octahedron. [< Gk *trís* thrice + OCTOHEDRON] —**tris·oc′ta·he′dral,** *adj.*

tri·some (trī′sōm), *n.* *Genetics.* a trisomic individual. [TRI- + -SOME[3]]

tri·so·mic (trī sō′mik), *adj.* *Genetics.* having one chromosome in addition to the usual diploid number. [TRISOME + -IC] —**tri·so·my** (trī′sō mē), *n.*

tri·spast (trī′spast), *n.* an ancient hoist or hauling device having three blocks. [< L *trispast(os)* < Gk *trís-pastos* (*órganon*) triple (pulley), equiv. to *tri-* TRI- + *spá(ein)* (to) draw, pull]

tri·sper·mous (trī spûr′məs), *adj.* *Bot.* having three seeds. [TRI- + SPERMOUS]

Tris·ta (tris′tə), *n.* a girl's given name.

Tris·tan (tris′tən; *Ger.* tʀis′tän), *n.* a boy's given name, form of **Tristram.** Also, **Tris·tam** (tris′təm).

Tris·tan da Cu·nha (tris′tən də ko͞on′yə), a group of three volcanic islands in the S Atlantic, belonging to Great Britain: volcanic eruption 1961. 40 sq. mi.

Tris·tan und I·sol·de (*Ger.* tris′tän o͝ont ē zôl′de; *Eng.* tris′tən and i zōl′də), a music drama (composed, 1857–59; première, 1865) by Richard Wagner.

tri·state (trī′stāt′), *adj.* **1.** pertaining to a territory made up of three adjoining states: *a tri-state league.* **2.** pertaining to the three adjoining parts of such states: *the tri-state region of Missouri, Kansas, and Nebraska.*

triste (trēst), *adj.* *French.* sad; sorrowful; melancholy.

tris·tesse (trēs tes′), *n.* *French.* sadness; sorrow; melancholy.

tris·te·za (tri stā′zə), *n.* *Plant Pathol.* a disease of certain citrus trees, characterized by yellowed leaves, wilting, defoliation, and dieback, caused by a virus. [< AmerSp, lit., sadness < L *tristitia.* See TRISTESSE]

trist·ful (trist′fəl), *adj.* *Archaic.* full of sadness; sorrowful. [late ME; see TRISTE, -FUL] —**trist′ful·ly,** *adv.* —**trist′ful·ness,** *n.*

tris·tich (tris′tik), *n.* *Pros.* a strophe, stanza, or poem consisting of three lines. [TRI- + STICH] —**tris·tich′-ic,** *adj.*

tris·tich·ous (tris′tə kəs), *adj.* **1.** arranged in three rows. **2.** *Bot.* arranged in or characterized by three vertical rows. [< Gk *trístichos* of three rows or verses. See TRI-, -STICHOUS]

Tris·tram (tris′trəm), *n.* **1.** one of the knights of the Round Table, whose love for Iseult, wife of King Mark, is the subject of many romances. **2.** a boy's given name. Also, **Tristan, Tris·trem** (tris′trəm), **Tristam.**

Tris′tram Shan′dy (shan′dē), a novel (1759–67) by Laurence Sterne.

tri·sty·lous (trī stī′ləs), *adj.* *Bot.* having three styles. [TRI- + STYLE + -OUS] —**tri′sty·ly,** *n.*

tri·sul·fide (trī sul′fīd, -fid), *n.* *Chem.* a sulfide containing three sulfur atoms. [TRI- + SULFIDE]

tri·syl·la·ble (trī sil′ə bəl, tri-), *n.* a word of three syllables, as *pendulum.* [TRI- + SYLLABLE, modeled on Gk *trisýllabos* having three syllables] —**tri·syl·lab·ic** (trī′si lab′ik, tris′i-), **tri′syl·lab′i·cal,** *adj.* —**tri′-syl·lab′i·cal·ly,** *adv.* —**tri·syl′lab·ism,** *n.*

trit., triturate.

trit·an·ope (trīt′ᵊnōp′), *n.* *Ophthalm.* a person who has tritanopia. [back formation from TRITANOPIA]

trit·an·o·pi·a (trīt′ᵊnō′pē ə), *n.* *Ophthalm.* a defect of vision in which the retina fails to respond to blue and yellow. [< NL < *trit-* (< Gk *trít(os)* third) + *an-* AN-[1] + *-opia* -OPIA] —**trit·an·op·ic** (trīt′ᵊnop′ik), *adj.*

trite (trīt), *adj.,* **trit·er, trit·est. 1.** lacking in freshness or effectiveness because of constant use or excessive repetition; hackneyed; stale: *the trite phrases in his letter.* **2.** characterized by hackneyed expressions, ideas, etc.: *The commencement address was trite and endlessly long.* **3.** *Archaic.* rubbed or worn by use. [< L *trītus* worn, common, equiv. to *trī-* (ptp. s. of *terere* to rub, wear down) + *-tus* ptp. suffix] —**trite′ly,** *adv.* —**trite′ness,** *n.* —**Syn. 1.** ordinary. See **commonplace.** —**Ant. 1.** original

tri·the·ism (trī′thē iz′əm), *n.* *Theol.* belief in three Gods, esp. in the doctrine that the three persons of the Trinity (Father, Son, and Holy Ghost) are three distinct Gods, each an independent center of consciousness and determination. [TRI- + THEISM] —**tri′the·ist,** *n., adj.* —**tri′the·is′tic, tri′the·is′ti·cal,** *adj.*

tri·thing (trī′thing), *n.* riding[2]. [ME, var. of *thrithing* < Scand; see RIDING[2]]

trit·i·um (trit′ē əm, trish′əm), *n.* *Chem.* an isotope of hydrogen having an atomic weight of three. [< NL < *trit-* (< Gk *trítos* third, equiv. to *tri-* TRI- + *-tos* adj. suffix) + *-ium* -IUM]

Tri·to·ge·nei·a (trī′tō jə nī′ə), *n.* *Class. Myth.* Athena: so called because it was near lake Tritonis that she was born from the head of Zeus.

tri·ton (trī′ton), *n.* *Physics.* a positively-charged particle consisting of a proton and two neutrons, equivalent to the nucleus of an atom of tritium. Cf. **deuteron.** [< Gk *tríton,* neut. of *trítos* third < *trí-* TRI- + *-t-* adj. suffix + *-on* neut. nom.]

Tri·ton (trīt′ᵊn), *n.* **1.** *Class. Myth.* **a.** a son of Poseidon and Amphitrite, represented as having the head and trunk of a man and the tail of a fish, and as using a conch-shell trumpet. **b.** any of a number of minor sea deities attendant upon the major sea gods. **2.** *Astron.* one of the two satellites of Neptune. **3.** (*l.c.*) any of various marine gastropods of the family *Tritonidae,* esp. of the genus *Triton,* having a large, spiral, often beautifully colored shell. **4.** (*l.c.*) the shell of a triton. —**Tri·ton·ic** (trī ton′ik), *adj.*

tri·tone (trī′tōn′), *n.* *Music.* an interval consisting of three whole tones; an augmented fourth. [< ML *tritonus* < Gk *trítonos* having three tones. See TRI-, TONE]

Tri·to·nis (trī tō′nis), *n.* (in ancient geography) a mythical lake near the Mediterranean coast of Libya.

trit·u·ra·ble (trich′ər ə bəl), *adj.* that may be triturated. [TRITUR(ATE) + -ABLE]

trit·u·rate (trich′ə rāt′), *v.,* **-rat·ed, -rat·ing,** *n.* —*v.t.* **1.** to reduce to fine particles or powder by rubbing, grinding, bruising, or the like; pulverize. —*n.* **2.** a triturated substance. **3.** trituration (def. 3). [< LL *trītūrātus* (ptp. of *trītūrāre* to thresh) < L *trītūr(a)* a threshing (*trītus* rubbed, crushed (see TRITE) + *-ūra* -URE) + *-ātus* -ATE[1]] —**trit′u·ra′tor,** *n.*

trit·u·ra·tion (trich′ə rā′shən), *n.* **1.** act of triturating. **2.** state of being triturated. **3.** *Pharm.* **a.** a mixture of a medicinal substance with sugar of milk, triturated to an impalpable powder. **b.** any triturated substance. [< LL *trītūrātiōn-* (s. of *trītūrātiō*), equiv. to *trītūrāt(us)* threshed (see TRITURATE) + *-iōn-* -ION]

tri·umph (trī′əmf), *n.* **1.** the act, fact, or condition of being victorious or triumphant; victory; conquest. **2.** a significant success or noteworthy achievement; instance or occasion of victory. **3.** exultation resulting from victory; joy over success. **4.** *Rom. Hist.* the ceremonial entrance into Rome of a victorious commander with his army, spoils of war, and captives, authorized by the senate in honor of an important military or naval victory. Cf. **ovation** (def. 2). **5.** *Obs.* a public pageant, spectacle, or the like. —*v.i.* **6.** to gain a victory; be victorious; win. **7.** to gain mastery; prevail: *to triumph over fear.* **8.** to be successful; achieve success. **9.** to exult over victory; rejoice over success. **10.** to be elated or glad; rejoice proudly; glory. **11.** to celebrate a triumph, as a victorious Roman commander. —*v.t.* **12.** *Obs.* to conquer; triumph over. [ME *triumphe,* OE *triumpha* < L *triumphus,* OL *triumpus;* cf. Gk *thríambos* Dionysiac procession] —**tri′umph·er,** *n.*
—**Syn. 1.** success. See **victory. 3.** jubilation, celebration. **6.** succeed. —**Ant. 1.** defeat, loss.

tri·um·phal (trī um′fəl), *adj.* **1.** of, pertaining to, celebrating, or commemorating a triumph or victory: *a triumphal banquet; a triumphal ode.* **2.** triumphant (def. 2). [late ME < L *triumphālis.* See TRIUMPH, -AL[1]]

trium′phal arch′, **1.** a monumental archway, often erected in permanent materials as a commemorative structure, straddling the line of march of a victorious army during a triumphal procession. **2.** an architectural motif resembling in its composition an ancient Roman triumphal arch, having one high central archway flanked by side elements composed of lower arches, compartments, bas-reliefs, etc., the whole usually adorned by a huge order.

tri·um·phant (trī um′fənt), *adj.* **1.** having achieved victory or success; victorious; successful. **2.** exulting over victory; rejoicing over success; exultant. **3.** *Archaic.* triumphal (def. 1). **4.** *Obs.* splendid; magnificent. [< L *triumphant-,* s. of *triumphāns,* prp. of *triumphāre* to triumph. See TRIUMPH, -ANT] —**tri·um′phant·ly,** *adv.*

tri·um·vir (trī um′vər), *n., pl.* **-virs, -vi·ri** (-və rī′). **1.** *Rom. Hist.* one of three officers or magistrates mutually exercising the same public function. **2.** one of three persons associated in any office or position of authority. [< L: lit., one man of three, back formation from *trium virōrum* of three men] —**tri·um′vi·ral,** *adj.*

tri·um·vi·rate (trī um′vər it, -və rāt′), *n.* **1.** *Rom. Hist.* the office or magistracy of a triumvir. **2.** a government of three officers or magistrates functioning jointly. **3.** a coalition of three magistrates or rulers for joint administration. **4.** any association of three in office or authority. **5.** any group or set of three. [< L *triumvirātus.* See TRIUMVIR, -ATE[1]]

tri·une (trī′yo͞on), *adj.* **1.** three in one; constituting a trinity in unity, as the Godhead. —*n.* **2.** (*cap.*) the Trinity. [TRI- + L *ūn(us)* one]

tri·un·gu·lin (trī ung′gyə lin), *n.* the first larval instar of certain insects that undergo hypermetamorphosis, esp. the meloid beetles. [TRI- + UNGUL(A) + -IN[1]]

tri·u·ni·tar·i·an (trī yo͞o′ni târ′ē ən), *n.* Trinitarian. [TRIUNE + -*itarian* as in UNITARIAN]

tri·u·ni·ty (trī yo͞o′ni tē), *n., pl.* **-ties.** Trinity (defs. 4,5). [TRIUNE + -ITY]

tri·va·lent (trī vā′lənt, triv′ə lənt), *adj. Chem.* having a valence of three. [TRI- + VALENT] —**tri·va′lence, tri·va′len·cy,** *n.*

triva′lent car′bon, *Chem.* a carbon atom that utilizes only three of its four valences, as most free radicals.

tri·valve (trī′valv′), *adj.* **1.** having three valves, as a shell. —*n.* **2.** a trivalve shell. [TRI- + VALVE]

Tri·van·drum (tri van′drəm), *n.* a city in and the capital of Kerala, in S India: Vishnu pilgrimage center. 239,800 (1961).

triv·et[1] (triv′it), *n.* **1.** a small metal plate with short legs, esp. one put under a hot platter or dish to protect a table. **2.** a three-footed or three-legged stand or support, esp. one of iron placed over a fire to support cooking vessels or the like. [ME *trevet,* OE *trefet,* appar. b. of OE *thrifēte* three-footed and L *triped-,* s. of *tripēs* three-footed (with VL *-e-* for L *-i-*)]

triv·et[2] (triv′it), *n.* a special knife for cutting pile loops, as of velvet or carpets. Also, **trevet, trevette, triv′ette.** [?]

triv·i·a (triv′ē ə), *n.pl.* matters or things that are very unimportant, inconsequential, or inessential; trifles; trivialities. [appar. back formation from TRIVIAL]

Triv·i·a (triv′ē ə), *n.* (in Roman religion) Hecate: so called because she was the goddess of the crossroads. [< L, fem. of *trivius* (adj.), deriv. of *trivium* place where three roads meet < *tri-* TRI- + *-vium* < *via* way, road]

triv·i·al (triv′ē əl), *adj.* **1.** of very little importance or value; trifling; insignificant: *Don't bother me with trivial matters.* **2.** commonplace; ordinary. **3.** *Biol.* (of names of animals and plants) specific, as distinguished from *generic.* **4.** *Math.* **a.** noting a solution of an equation in which the value of every variable of the equation is equal to zero. **b.** (of a topology or topological space) having the property that the only two open sets are the whole space and the empty set; indiscrete. [ME < L *triviālis* belonging to the crossroads, (hence) common < *tri-* TRI- + *vi(a)* road + *-ālis* -AL[1]] —**triv′i·al·ly,** *adv.* —**triv′i·al·ness,** *n.*
—**Syn. 1.** unimportant, nugatory, slight, immaterial, inconsequential, frivolous. See **petty.** —**Ant. 1.** important.

triv·i·al·ise (triv′ē ə līz′), *v.t.,* **-ised, -is·ing.** *Chiefly Brit.* trivialize. —**triv′i·al·i·sa′tion,** *n.*

triv·i·al·ism (triv′ē ə liz′əm), *n.* **1.** trivial character. **2.** something trivial. [TRIVIAL + -ISM]

triv·i·al·i·ty (triv′ē al′i tē), *n., pl.* **-ties. 1.** something trivial; a trivial matter, affair, remark, etc.: *cocktail conversation marked by trivialities.* **2.** Also, **trivialness.** trivial quality or character. [TRIVIAL + -ITY]

triv·i·al·ize (triv′ē ə līz′), *v.t.,* **-ized, -iz·ing.** to make trivial; cause to become unimportant, trifling, etc. Also, *esp. Brit.,* **trivialise.** [TRIVIAL + -IZE] —**triv′i·al·i·za′tion,** *n.*

triv·i·um (triv′ē əm), *n., pl.* **triv·i·a** (triv′ē ə). (during the Middle Ages) the lower division of the seven liberal arts, comprising grammar, rhetoric, and logic. Cf. **quadrivium.** [< ML, special use of L *trivium* public place, lit., place where three roads meet. See TRIVIAL]

tri·week·ly (trī wēk′lē), *adv., adj., n., pl.* **-lies.** —*adv.* **1.** every three weeks. **2.** three times a week. —*adj.* **3.** occurring or appearing three times a week. **4.** occurring or appearing every three weeks. —*n.* **5.** a triweekly publication. [TRI- + WEEKLY]

-trix, a feminine suffix of agent-nouns corresponding to masculine *-tor: aviatrix.* Cf. **-tress, -ess, -or**[2]. [< L, fem. of *-tor,* equiv. to *-t(us)* ptp. ending + *-or* -OR[2]]

Trix·ie (trik′sē), *n.* a girl's given name, form of **Beatrix.** Also, **Trix′y.**

Tro·as (trō′as), *n.* a region in NW Asia Minor surrounding ancient Troy. Also called **The Tro·ad** (trō′ad).

tro·bar clus (trō bär′ klo͞os′), a complex and obscure style of writing adopted by some 12th-century Provençal poets. [< Pr: lit., closed composition]

Tro′bri·and Is′lands (trō′brē änd′, -ənd), a group of islands north of the eastern end of New Guinea: part of the Australian Territory of New Guinea. 100,000 (est. 1961); 170 sq. mi.

tro·car (trō′kär), *n. Surg.* a sharp-pointed instrument enclosed in a cannula, used for withdrawing fluid from a cavity, as the abdominal cavity, etc. Also, **trochar.** [earlier *trocart* < F, lit., three-sided, equiv. to *tro-* (var. of *trois* three) + *cart,* var. of *carre* side < L *quadra* something square]

troch., (in prescriptions) troche.

tro·cha·ic (trō kā′ik), *Pros.* —*adj.* **1.** pertaining to the trochee. **2.** consisting of or employing a trochee or trochees. —*n.* **3.** a trochee. **4.** Usually, **trochaics.** a verse or poem written in trochees. [< L *trochaic(us)* < Gk *trochaïkós,* equiv. to *trocha(ios)* TROCHEE + *-ikos* -IC] —**tro·cha′i·cal·ly,** *adv.*

tro·chal (trō′kəl), *adj. Zool.* resembling a wheel. [< Gk *troch(ós)* wheel + -AL[1]]

tro·chan·ter (trō kan′tər), *n.* **1.** *Anat., Zool.* a prominence or process on the upper part of the femur of many vertebrates serving for the attachment of muscles, and in man being situated on the outer side of the bone (**greater trochanter**) and on the inner side (**lesser trochanter**). **2.** *Entomol.* (in an insect) the usually small second segment of the leg, between the coxa and femur. See diag. under **coxa.** [< NL < Gk *trochantḗr* ball on which the hip bone turns in its socket. See TROCHE] —**tro·chan·ter·ic** (trō′kən ter′ik), **tro·chan′ter·al,** *adj.*

tro·char (trō′kär), *n. Surg.* trocar.

tro·che (trō′kē), *n. Pharm.* a small tablet or lozenge, usually a circular one, made of medicinal substance worked into a paste with sugar and mucilage or the like, and dried. [back formation from *troches,* earlier *tro(s)-ches,* late ME *trocis* (taken as pl.) < MF *trocisse* < L *trochiscus* < Gk *trochískos,* equiv. to *troch(ós)* wheel (akin to *tréchein* to run) + *-iskos* dim. suffix]

tro·chee (trō′kē), *n. Pros.* a foot of two syllables, a long followed by a short in quantitative meter, or a stressed followed by an unstressed in accentual meter. [< L *trochae(us)* < Gk *trochaîos* running, equiv. to *troch-* (var. s. of *tréchein* to run) + *-aios* adj. suffix]

troch·el·minth (trok′əl minth), *n.* any invertebrate of the phylum *Trochelminthes* (now usually broken up into several phyla), comprising the rotifers, gastrotrichs, and several other forms. [back formation from NL *trochelminthes* phylum name < Gk *troch(ós)* wheel + *helminth-* HELMINTH]

troch·i·lus[1] (trok′ə ləs), *n., pl.* **-li** (-lī′). **1.** a hummingbird. **2.** *Rare.* **a.** any of several small, Old World warblers, as the willow warbler, *Phylloscopus trochilus.* **b.** See **crocodile bird.** [< L < Gk *trochílos* Egyptian courser (crocodile bird), equiv. to *troch-* (var. s. of *tréchein* to run) + *-ilos* dim. suffix]

troch·i·lus[2] (trok′ə ləs), *n., pl.* **-li** (-lī′). *Archit.* scotia. [< L: molding, lit., runner < Gk *trochílos.* See TROCHILUS[1]]

Troch·i·lus (trok′ə ləs), *n. Class. Myth.* a priest of the mysteries at Argos and father of Eubuleus and Triptolemus.

troch·le·a (trok′lē ə), *n., pl.* **-le·ae** (-lē ē′). *Anat.* a pulleylike structure or arrangement of parts affording a smooth surface upon which another part glides, as a tendon or bone. [< L: pulley block or sheave < Gk *trochiléa.* See TROCHILUS[1]]

troch·le·ar (trok′lē ər), *adj.* **1.** *Anat.* of, pertaining to, or connected with a trochlea. **2.** *Physiol., Anat.* pulleylike. **3.** *Bot.* circular and contracted in the middle so as to resemble a pulley. —*n.* **4.** See **trochlear nerve.** Also, **troch·le·ar·i·form** (trok′lē ar′ə fôrm′). [TROCHLE(A) + -AR[1]]

troch′lear nerve′, *Anat.* either one of the fourth pair of cranial nerves, consisting of motor fibers that innervate the superior oblique muscle of the upper part of the eyeball.

Trochoid
A, b>a
B, b<a

tro·choid (trō′koid), *n.* **1.** *Geom.* a curve traced by a point on a radius or an extension of the radius of a circle which rolls, without slipping, on a curve, another circle, or a straight line. Equation: $x = a\theta - b\sin\theta$, $y = a - b\cos\theta$. —*adj.* **2.** rotating on an axis, as a wheel. [< Gk *trochoeidḗs* round like a wheel. See TROCHE, -OID] —**tro·choi′dal,** *adj.* —**tro·choi′dal·ly,** *adv.*

troch·o·phore (trok′ə fōr′, -fôr′), *n. Zool.* a ciliate, free-swimming larva common to several groups of invertebrates. [< Gk *trochó(s)* wheel + -PHORE]

trod (trod), *v.* a pt. and pp. of **tread.**

trod·den (trod′ən), *v.* a pp. of **tread.**

trode (trōd), *v. Archaic.* pt. and pp. of **tread.**

Troe·zen (trē′zən), *n.* (in ancient geography) a town in E Peloponnesus near the coast of the Saronic Gulf, regarded in mythology as the birthplace of Theseus.

trof·fer (trof′ər), *n.* a trough-shaped reflector holding one or more fluorescent lamps. [*troff* (var. of TROUGH) + -ER[1]]

trog·lo·dyte (trog′lə dīt′), *n.* **1.** a cave man or cave dweller. **2.** a person living in seclusion. **3.** one unacquainted with affairs of the world. **4.** a person of degraded, primitive, or brutal character. [< L *trōglodyta* < Gk *trōglodýtēs* one who creeps into holes, cave dweller, equiv. to *trōglo-* (comb. form of *trṓglē* a gnawed hole; see TROGON) + *dý(ein)* (to) creep into + *-tēs* agent suffix] —**trog·lo·dyt·ic** (trog′lə dit′ik), **trog′lo·dyt′i·cal,** *adj.* —**trog′lo·dyt′ism,** *n.*

tro·gon (trō′gon), *n.* any of several brilliantly colored birds of the family *Trogonidae,* esp. of the genus *Trogon,* of tropical and subtropical regions. [< NL < Gk *trṓgōn,* prp. of *trṓgein* to gnaw] —**tro·gon·oid** (trō′gə noid′), *adj.*

troi·ka (troi′kə), *n.* **1.** a Russian carriage or wagon drawn by a team of three horses abreast. **2.** a team of three horses driven abreast. **3.** any group of three persons, nations, etc., acting equally in unison to exert influence, control, or the like. [< Russ < *troe* THREE + *-ka* n. suffix]

tro·i·lite (trō′ə līt′, troi′līt), *n.* a mineral, iron sulfide, FeS, occurring in meteorites. [named after D. *Troili,* 18th-century Italian savant who described a meteorite containing it. See -ITE[1]]

Troi·lus (troi′ləs, trō′ə-), *n. Class. and Med. Legend.* a warrior son of Priam, mentioned by Homer and Vergil and later represented as the lover of Cressida.

Troi′lus and Cres′sida, a satiric comedy (1598–1602?) by Shakespeare.

Troi′lus and Cri·sey′de (kri sā′də), a narrative poem (1385?) by Chaucer.

tro′i·lus but′terfly (trō′ə ləs). See **spicebush swallowtail.**

trois (trwä), *n. French.* the number 3.

Trois Mous·que·taires, Les (*Fr.* lā trwä mo͞os kə ter′). See **Three Musketeers, The.**

Trois-Ri·vières (trwa rē vyer′), *n.* French name of **Three Rivers.**

Tro·jan (trō′jən), *adj.* **1.** of or pertaining to ancient Troy or its inhabitants. —*n.* **2.** a native or inhabitant of Troy. **3.** a person who shows pluck, determination, or energy: *to work like a Trojan.* [ME, OE *Trōiān* < L *Trōiānus,* equiv. to *Trōi(a)* TROY + *-ānus* -AN]

Tro′jan group′, *Astron.* a group of asteroids oscillating about either of two points, equidistant from the sun and Jupiter, that forms an equilateral triangle with the sun and Jupiter.

Tro′jan Horse′, **1.** *Class. Myth.* a gigantic hollow and wooden horse, left by the Greeks upon their pretended abandonment of the siege of Troy. The Trojans, induced to regard the horse as a sacrifice to Athena, opened the city gates and took it into Troy. Greek soldiers concealed in the horse opened the gates to the Greek army at night and conquered the city. **2.** one who or that which is designed to undermine or destroy from within.

Tro′jan War′, *Class. Myth.* a ten-years' war waged by the confederated Greeks, under the Greek king Agamemnon, against the Trojans, to avenge the abduction of Helen, wife of the Greek king Menelaus, by Paris, son of the Trojan king Priam, and ending in the plundering and burning of Troy.

Tro′jan Wom′en, The, a tragedy (415 B.C.) by Euripides.

troke (trōk), *n., v.,* **troked, trok·ing.** *Scot.* —*n.* **1.** truck[2] (defs. 4-7). —*v.t., v.i.* **2.** truck[2] —**trok′er,** *n.*

tro·land (trō′lənd), *n. Ophthalm.* photon (def. 2). [named after L. T. *Troland,* (1889–1932), American psychologist and physicist]

troll[1] (trōl), *v.t.* **1.** to sing or utter in a full, rolling voice. **2.** to sing in the manner of a round or catch. **3.** to fish by trolling. **4.** to move (the line or bait) in doing this. **5.** to cause to turn round and round; roll. **6.** *Obs.* to hand around, as a bowl of liquor at table. —*v.i.* **7.** to sing with a full, rolling voice; give forth full, rolling tones. **8.** to be uttered or sounded in such tones. **9.** to fish with a moving line, working the line up and down with a rod, as in fishing for pike, or trailing the line behind a slow-moving boat. **10.** to roll; turn round and round. **11.** *Archaic.* to move nimbly, as the tongue in speaking. —*n.* **12.** a song whose parts are sung in succession; a round. **13.** act of trolling. **14.** a lure used in trolling for fish. **15.** the fishing line containing the lure and hook for use in trolling. [ME *trolle(n)* to roll, stroll < MF *troller* to run here and there < MHG *trollen* walk or run with short steps] —**troll′er,** *n.*

troll[2] (trōl), *n.* (in Scandinavian folklore) any of a race of supernatural beings, sometimes conceived as giants and sometimes as dwarfs, inhabiting caves or subterranean dwellings. [< Scand; cf. Icel *troll* giant, demon]

trol·ley (trol′ē), *n., pl.* **-leys,** *v.,* **-leyed, -ley·ing.** —*n.* **1.** a trolley car. **2.** a pulley or truck traveling on an overhead track and serving to support and move a suspended object. **3.** a grooved metallic wheel or pulley carried on the end of a pole (**trol′ley pole′**) by an electric car or locomotive, and held in contact with an overhead conductor, usually a suspended wire (**trol′ley wire′**), from which it collects the current for the propulsion of the car or locomotive. **4.** any of various devices for collecting current for such a purpose, as a bowlike structure (**bow trolley**) sliding along an overhead wire, or a device (**underground trolley**) for taking current from the underground wire or conductor used by some electric railways. **5.** a small truck or car operated on a track, as in a mine, factory, etc. **6.** *Brit.* **a.** any of various low carts or vehicles, as a railway handcar, costermonger's cart, etc. **b.** a serving cart, as one used to serve tea and cakes. **7. off one's trolley,** *Slang.* **a.** in a confused mental state. **b.** insane: *He's been off his trolley for years, but his family refuses to have him committed.* —*v.t., v.i.* **8.** to convey or go by trolley. Also, **trolly.** [TROLL[1] (n.) + -EY[2]] —**trol′ley·less,** *adj.*

trol′ley bus′, a passenger bus operating on tires and having an electric motor which draws power from overhead wires. Also called **trackless trolley, trolley coach.**

trol′ley car′, a streetcar propelled electrically by current taken by means of a trolley from a conducting wire strung overhead or running beneath a slot between the tracks.

trol′ley coach′. See **trolley bus.**

trol′ley line′, **1.** the route of a trolley car or trolley bus. **2.** a public or private transportation system using cars or trolley buses.

trol·lop (trol′əp), *n.* **1.** an untidy or slovenly woman; slattern. **2.** an immoral or promiscuous woman, esp. a prostitute. [earlier *trollops;* akin to TROLL[1]] —**trol′lop·y,** *adj.*

Slide trombone

Trol·lope (trol′əp), *n.* **Anthony,** 1815–82, English novelist. —**Trol·lop·i·an, Trol·lop·e·an** (trə lop′ē ən, -lō′pē-, trol′ə pē′-), *adj., n.*

trol·ly (trol′ē), *n., pl.* **-lies,** *v.t., v.i.,* **-lied, -ly·ing.** trolley.

trom·ba ma·ri·na (trom′bə mə rē′nə; *It.* trôm′bä mä rē′nä), *pl.* **trom·be ma·ri·ne** (trom′bā mə rē′nā; *It.* trôm′be mä rē′ne). See **trumpet marine.** [< It: lit., waterspout]

trom·bi·di·a·sis (trom′bə dī′ə sis), *n. Vet. Pathol.* the condition of being infested with chiggers. Also, **trom·bi·di·o·sis** (trom′bi dē ō′sis). [<NL *trombid(ium)* genus name + -IASIS]

trom·bone (trom bōn′, trom′bōn), *n.* a musical wind instrument consisting of a cylindrical metal tube expanding into a bell and bent twice in U shape, usually equipped with a slide (**slide trombone**). [< It, equiv. to *tromb(a)* trumpet (< OHG *trumba*) + *-one* aug. suffix] —**trom·bon·ist** (trom′bō nist, trom bō′-), *n.*

trom·mel (trom′əl), *n.* a rotary, cylindrical or conical screen for sorting ores, coal, gravel, etc., according to size. [< G *Trommel* drum]

tro·mom·e·ter (trō mom′i tər), *n.* an instrument for recording and measuring minor tremors in the earth. [< Gk *trómo(s)* terror, fright + -METER] —**trom·o·met·ric** (trom′ə me′trik), **trom′o·met′ri·cal,** *adj.* —**tro·mom′e·try,** *n.*

Tromp (trômp), *n.* **Cor·ne·lis** (kôr nā′lis), 1629–91, and his father, **Maar·ten Har·perts·zoon** (mär′tən här′pərt sōn′), 1597–1653, Dutch admirals.

Trompes (def. 2)
A, At exterior angle
B, At interior angle

trompe (tromp), *n.* **1.** *Metall.* a device formerly used for inducing a blast of air upon the hearth of a forge by means of a current of falling water. **2.** *Masonry.* a squinchlike structure for supporting an eccentric load having the form of a part of a cone, a sphere, or a cloistered vault. [< F: lit., TRUMP[3]]

CONCISE PRONUNCIATION KEY: *act, āble, dâre, ärt; ebb, ēqual; if, īce; hot, ōver, ôrder, oil, bo͝ok, o͞oze, out; up, ûrge; chief; sing; shoe; thin, that;* zh as in *measure.* ə = *a* as in *alone,* e as in *system,* i as in *easily,* o as in *gallop,* u as in *circus;* ə as in *button* (but′ən), *fire* (fīər), *cradle* (krād′əl). See the full key inside the front cover.

trompe l'oeil (trômp/ lā/; *Fr.* trônp lœ/yᵊ), 1. visual deception, esp. in paintings in which objects are rendered in extremely fine detail emphasizing the illusion of tactile and spatial qualities. 2. a painting, mural, or panel of wallpaper designed to create such an effect. [< F: lit., trick of the eye]

Troms·ö (troms/sō; *Nor.* trōōms/œ), *n.* a seaport in N Norway. 10,931 (est. 1959).

-tron, a learned borrowing from Greek denoting an instrument, used in the formation of compound words: *cyclotron.* [< Gk *-tron*]

tro·na (trō/nə), *n.* a mineral, grayish or yellowish hydrous sodium carbonate and bicarbonate, $Na_2CO_3·NaHCO_3·2H_2O$, occurring in dried or partly evaporated lake basins. [< Sw < Ar *ṭrōn*, aph. var. of *naṭrūn* NATRON]

Trond·heim (trôn/hām), *n.* a seaport in central Norway, on Trondheim Fiord. 56,669 (est. 1959). Formerly, **Nidaros, Trond·hjem** (trôn/yem).

Trond/heim Fiord/, an inlet of the North Sea, extending into N Norway. 80 mi. long.

trondh·jem·ite (tron/ye mīt/), *n.* *Mineral.* a coarse-grained igneous rock composed of quartz, plagioclase feldspar, and a small amount of biotite. [*Trondhjem,* (NOW TRONDHEIM) + -ITE[1]]

trone (trōn), *n.* *Scot. and North Eng.* a large pair of scales, a spring balance, or other weighing device located in a town or market place to weigh goods and merchandise. [ME (Scot) < AF << L *trutina* < Gk *trytánē* balance, scales]

troop (trōōp), *n.* 1. an assemblage of persons or things; company; band. 2. a great number or multitude: *A whole troop of children swarmed through the museum.* 3. *Mil.* an armored cavalry or cavalry unit consisting of two or more platoons and a headquarters group. 4. **troops,** a body of soldiers, police, etc.: *Mounted troops quelled the riot.* 5. a unit of Boy Scouts or Girl Scouts usually having a maximum of 32 members under the guidance of an adult leader. 6. a herd, flock, or swarm. 7. *Archaic.* a band or troupe of actors. —*v.i.* 8. to gather in a company; flock together. 9. to come, go, or pass in great numbers; throng. 10. to walk, as if in a march; go: *troop down to breakfast.* 11. to walk, march, or pass in rank or order: *The students trooped into the auditorium.* 12. to associate or consort (usually fol. by *with*). 13. *Brit. Mil.* to carry the flag or colors in a ceremonial way before troops. 14. *Obs.* to assemble or form into a troop or troops. [< F *troupe* back formation from *troupeau* herd < VL **troppellus* < LL *tropp(us)* flock (< Gmc; see THORP) + L *-ellus* dim. suffix]
—**Syn.** 1. body, group, crowd. See **company.** 2. crowd, herd, flock, swarm, throng. 7. TROOP, TROUPE both mean a band, company, or group. TROOP has various meanings as indicated in the definitions above. With the spelling TROUPE the word has the specialized meaning of a company of actors, singers, or acrobats. 8. collect. 9. swarm.

troop/ car/rier, 1. a transport airplane used for carrying troops and their equipment. 2. an armored vehicle, often amphibious and mounted with light weapons, for transporting infantry troops and equipment.

troop·er (trōō/pər), *n.* 1. a horse-cavalry soldier. 2. a mounted policeman; a policeman on horseback. 3. See **State trooper.** 4. a cavalry horse. 5. *Chiefly Brit.* a troopship. 6. **like a trooper,** with great energy, enthusiasm, or display: *He swears like a trooper.* [TROOP + -ER[1]]

troop·ship (trōōp/ship/), *n.* a ship for the conveyance of military troops; transport. [TROOP + SHIP]

troost·ite[1] (trōō/stīt), *n.* *Mineral.* a variety of willemite, $Zn_2(SiO_4)$, having some of the zinc replaced by manganese. [named after G. *Troost* (1776–1850), American metallurgist + -ITE[1]] —**troost·it·ic** (trōō stit/ik), *adj.*

troost·ite[2] (trōō/stīt), *n.* a microconstituent of hardened and tempered steel, consisting of a very fine aggregate of ferrite and cementite. [named after L. J. *Troost* (d. 1911), French chemist + -ITE[1]] —**troost·it·ic** (trōō stit/ik), *adj.*

troost·o·mar·tens·ite (trōō/stō mär/tᵊn zīt/), *n.* bainite. Also called **troost·ite-mar·tens·ite** (trōō/stīt-mär/tᵊn zīt/). [TROOST(ITE)[2] + -O- + MARTENSITE]

trop (trō), *adv.* *French.* too; too many; very much.

trop-, var. of **tropo-** before a vowel: *tropism.*

Tro·pae·an (trə pē/ən), *n.* *Class. Myth.* an epithet of Zeus, meaning "giver of victory." [< Gk *tropaî(os)* lit., of a turning or change, hence, for defeat (*tropḗ* a turn + *-aios* adj. suffix) + -AN; see TROPHY]

tro·pae·o·lin (trō pē/ə lin), *n.* *Chem.* any of a number of orange or yellow azo dyes of complex molecular structure. Also, **Tropeolin.** [TROPAEOL(UM) + -IN[2]]

tropaeolin D, *Chem.* See **methyl orange.**

tro·pae·o·lum (trō pē/ə ləm), *n.*, *pl.* **-lums, -la** (-lə). any plant of the genus *Tropaeolum,* comprising the nasturtiums. [< NL < L *tropae(um)* TROPHY + *-olum,* neut. of -OLUS dim. suffix]

tro·pae·um (trō pē/əm), *n.*, *pl.* **-pae·a** (-pē/ə). a monument erected in ancient Greece or, esp., Rome to commemorate a military or naval victory. Also, **trophaeum.** [< L; see TROPHY]

tro·pai·on (trō pī/on), *n.*, *pl.* **-pai·a** (-pī/ə). a tropaeum, esp. in Greece. [< Gk; see TROPHY]

-tropal, a suffix identical in meaning with **-tropic,** used to form adjectives from stems in **-trope.** [-TROPE + -AL[1]]

trope (trōp), *n.* 1. *Rhet.* a. any literary or rhetorical device, as metaphor, metonymy, synecdoche, and irony, which consists in the use of words in other than their literal sense. b. an instance of this. Cf. **figure of speech.** 2. a phrase, sentence, or verse formerly interpolated in a liturgical text to amplify or embellish. 3. (in the philosophy of Santayana) the principle of organization according to which matter moves to form an object during the various stages of its existence. [< L *tropus* figure in rhetoric < Gk *trópos* turn, turning, turn or figure of speech, akin to *trépein* to turn]

-trope, var. of **tropo-,** occurring as the final element in compound words: *heliotrope.* Cf. **-tropal, -tropic, -tropism, -tropous, -tropy.**

tro·pe·o·lin (trō pē/ə lin), *n.* *Chem.* tropaeolin.

tropeolin D, *Chem.* See **methyl orange.**

troph-, var. of **tropho-** before a vowel: *trophic.*

tro·phae·um (trō fē/əm), *n.*, *pl.* **-phae·a** (-fē/ə). tropaeum.

troph·al·lax·is (trof/ə lak/sis), *n.*, *pl.* **-lax·es** (-lak/sēz). (among social insects) the exchange of nutriments or other secretions between members of a colony. [TROPH- + Gk *állaxis* exchange, equiv. to *allak-* (verbid s. of *allássein* to change; see ALLO-) + *-sis* -SIS] —**troph·al·lac·tic** (trof/ə lak/tik), *adj.*

tro·phi (trō/fē), *n.pl.* *Entomol.* the mouth parts of an insect, including the labrum, mandibles, maxillae, labium, and hypopharynx. [< NL < Gk *trophoí,* pl. of *trophós* feeder, nurse, akin to *tréphein* to nourish]

troph·ic (trof/ik), *adj.* *Physiol.* of or pertaining to nutrition; concerned in nutritive processes. [< Gk *trophikós* pertaining to food; see TROPH-, -IC] —**troph/i·cal·ly,** *adv.*

tro·phied (trō/fēd), *adj.* adorned with trophies. [TROPHY + -ED[3]]

tropho-, a learned borrowing from Greek meaning "nourishment," used in the formation of compound words: *trophoplasm.* Also, *esp. before a vowel,* **troph-.** [comb. form of Gk *trophḗ* nourishment, food; akin to *tréphein* to feed, nourish]

troph·o·blast (trof/ə blast/), *n.* *Embryol.* the extra-embryonic part of a blastocyst, which chiefly nourishes the embryo or which develops into fetal membranes with nutritive functions. [TROPHO- + -BLAST] —**troph/o·blas/tic,** *adj.*

Tro·pho·ni·us (trə fō/nē əs), *n.* *Class. Myth.* 1. an earth-god. 2. a master builder whom Apollo rewarded with a peaceful death for having built the temple at Delphi.

troph·o·plasm (trof/ə plaz/əm), *n.* *Biol.* the kind of protoplasm that is regarded as forming the nutritive part of a cell. [TROPHO- + -PLASM] —**troph/o·plas/mic, troph·o·plas·mat·ic** (trof/ə plaz mat/ik), *adj.*

troph·o·zo·ite (trof/ə zō/īt), *n.* *Zool.* a protozoan in the initial stage of asexual reproduction. [TROPHO- + -ZO(ON) + -ITE[1]]

tro·phy (trō/fē), *n.*, *pl.* **-phies.** 1. anything taken in war, hunting, competition, etc., esp. when preserved as a memento; spoil, prize, or award. 2. anything serving as a token or evidence of victory, valor, skill, etc. 3. a carving, painting, or other representation of objects associated with or symbolic of victory or achievement. 4. any memento or memorial. 5. a memorial erected by certain ancient peoples, esp. the Greeks and Romans, in commemorating a victory in war and consisting of arms or other spoils taken from the enemy and hung upon a tree, pillar, or the like. [earlier *trophe* < F *trophée* < L *trop(h)aeum* < Gk *trópaion,* n. use of neut. of *trópaios,* Attic var. of *tropaîos* of turning or putting to flight, equiv. to *trop(ḗ)* a turning (akin to *trépein* to turn) + *-aios* adj. suffix. See TROPE] —**tro/phy·less,** *adj.*

-trophy, a combining form referring to nourishment or growth, used in the formation of compound words: *hypertrophy.* [< Gk *-trophía* nutrition < *troph(ḗ)* food + *-ia* -Y[3]]

tro/phy room/, a room in which a person or group keeps and displays trophies, as for bowling, golf, etc.

trop·ic (trop/ik), *n.* 1. *Geog.* a. either of two corresponding parallels of latitude on the terrestrial globe, one **(tropic of Cancer)** about 23½° N, and the other **(tropic of Capricorn)** about 23½° S of the equator, being the boundaries of the Torrid Zone. See diag. under **zone.** b. **the tropics,** the regions lying between and near these parallels of latitude; the Torrid Zone and neighboring regions. 2. *Astron.* a. either of two circles on the celestial sphere, one lying in the same plane as the tropic of Cancer, the other in the same plane as the tropic of Capricorn. b. *Obs.* either of the two solstitial points, at which the sun reaches its greatest distance north and south of the celestial equator. —*adj.* 3. of, pertaining to, characteristic of, or occurring in the tropics; tropical: *romance under the tropic skies of Old Mexico.* [ME < L *tropicus* < Gk *tropikós* pertaining to a turn, equiv. to *tróp(os)* turn + *-ikos* -IC]

-tropic, a combination of **-trope** and **-ic,** used in the formation of adjectives from stems in **-trope:** *geotropic.* Also, **-tropal.** [see TROPIC]

trop·i·cal (trop/i kəl *for 1–3;* trō/pi kəl *for 4*), *adj.* 1. pertaining to, characteristic of, occurring in, or inhabiting the tropics, esp. the humid tropics: *tropical flowers.* 2. designed for use in the tropics or in very hot weather: *tropical-weight woolens.* 3. of or pertaining to either or both of the astronomical tropics. 4. pertaining to, characterized by, or of the nature of a trope or tropes; metaphorical. [TROPIC + -AL[1]] —**trop/i·cal/i·ty,** *n.* —**trop/i·cal·ly,** *adv.*

trop/ical cy/clone, a cyclone that originates over a tropical ocean area and can develop into the destructive storm known in the U.S. as a hurricane, in the western Pacific region as a typhoon, and elsewhere by other names. Cf. **baguio, cordonazo, extratropical cyclone, hurricane** (def. 1), **willy-willy.**

trop/ical fish/, any of numerous small, usually brightly colored fishes indigenous to the tropics that are kept and bred in aquariums.

trop·i·cal·ise (trop/i kə līz/), *v.t.*, **-ised, -is·ing.** *Chiefly Brit.* tropicalize. —**trop/i·cal·i·sa/tion,** *n.*

trop·i·cal·ize (trop/i kə līz/), *v.t.*, **-ized, -iz·ing.** 1. to make tropical, as in character, appearance, etc. 2. to adapt or make suitable for use in tropical regions, esp. in regard to protection against the destructive effects of moisture and fungi. [TROPICAL + -IZE] —**trop/i·cal·i·za/tion,** *n.*

trop/ical med/icine, the branch of medicine dealing with the study and treatment of diseases and other conditions occurring in the tropics.

trop/ical year/, year (def. 4b).

trop/ic bird/, any of several totipalmate sea birds of the family *Phaethontidae,* found chiefly in tropical regions, having white plumage with black markings and a pair of greatly elongated central tail feathers.

trop/ic of Can/cer. See under **tropic** (def. 1a).

trop/ic of Cap/ricorn. See under **tropic** (def. 1a).

tro·pine (trō/pēn, -pin), *n.* *Chem.* a white, crystalline, hygroscopic, water-soluble, poisonous alkaloid, $C_8H_{15}NO$, obtained chiefly by the hydrolysis of atropine or hyoscyamine. [aph. var. of ATROPINE]

tro·pism (trō/piz əm), *n.* *Biol.* an orientation of an organism, usually by growth rather than by movement, in response to an external stimulus. [separate use of -TROPISM] —**tro·pis·mat·ic** (trō/piz mat/ik), *adj.* —**tro·pis·tic** (trō pis/tik), *adj.*

-tropism, a combination of **-trope** and **-ism,** used in the formation of nouns from stems in **-trope:** *heliotropism.*

tropo-, a learned borrowing from Greek meaning "turn," "turning," often indicating a change, or an attraction to a given thing, used in the formation of compound words: *tropophilous.* Also, *esp. before a vowel,* **trop-.** Cf. **-trope, -tropism, -tropy, -tropal, -tropic, -tropous.** [comb. form repr. Gk *trópos* turn, *tropḗ* turning]

tro·pol·o·gy (trō pol/ə jē), *n.*, *pl.* **-gies** for 2. 1. the use of figurative language in speech or writing. 2. a treatise on figures of speech or tropes. 3. the use of a Scriptural text so as to give it a moral interpretation or significance apart from its direct meaning. [< LL *tropologi(a)* < Gk. See TROPO-, -LOGY] —**trop·o·log·ic** (trop/ə loj/ik), **trop/o·log/i·cal,** *adj.* —**trop/o·log/i·cal·ly,** *adv.*

trop·o·pause (trop/ə pôz/), *n.* *Meteorol.* the boundary, or transitional layer, between the troposphere and the stratosphere. [TROPO- + PAUSE]

tro·poph·i·lous (trō pof/ə ləs), *adj.* *Ecol.* adapted to a climate with alternate growing and rest periods, as a plant. [TROPO- + -PHILOUS]

trop·o·phyte (trop/ə fīt/), *n.* a tropophilous plant. [TROPO- + -PHYTE] —**trop·o·phyt·ic** (trop/ə fit/ik), *adj.*

trop·o·sphere (trop/ə sfēr/), *n.* *Meteorol.* the inner layer of the atmosphere, varying in height between about 6 miles and 12 miles, within which there is a steady fall of temperature with increasing altitude and within which nearly all cloud formations occur and weather conditions manifest themselves. [TROPO- + SPHERE] —**trop·o·spher·ic** (trop/ə sfer/ik), *adj.*

-tropous, a combination of **-trope** and **-ous,** used in the formation of adjectives from nouns ending in **-trope:** *heterotropous.* Cf. **-tropic, -tropal.** [< Gk *-tropos* pertaining to a turn]

-tropy, a combination of **-trope** and **-y,** used in the formation of nouns: *allotropy.* Cf. **-tropism.** [< Gk *-tropía.* See -TROPE, -Y[3]]

Tros (trōs), *n.* *Class. Myth.* a son of Erichthonius and the husband of Callirrhoë. The Trojans were named in his honor.

Tros·sachs (tros/əks), *n.* a valley in central Scotland, in Perth county, near Loch Katrine.

trot[1] (trot), *v.*, **trot·ted, trot·ting,** *n.* —*v.i.* 1. (of a horse) to go at a gait between a walk and a run, in which the legs move in diagonal pairs, but not quite simultaneously, so that when the movement is slow one foot at least is always on the ground, and when fast all four feet are momentarily off the ground at once. 2. to go at a quick, steady pace; move briskly; bustle; hurry. —*v.t.* 3. to cause to trot. 4. to ride at a trot. 5. to lead at a trot. 6. to execute by trotting. 7. **trot out,** *Informal.* a. to bring forward for inspection. b. to bring to the attention of; introduce; submit: *He trots out his old jokes at every party.* —*n.* 8. the gait of a horse, dog, or other quadruped, when trotting. 9. the sound made by an animal when trotting. 10. the jogging gait of a human being, between a walk and a run. 11. *Harness Racing.* a race for trotters. 12. brisk, continuous movement or activity: *I've been on the trot all afternoon.* 13. *U.S. Slang.* a literal translation used illicitly in doing schoolwork; crib; pony. 14. *Informal.* a toddling child. 15. *Disparaging.* an old woman. 16. **the trots,** *Slang.* diarrhea. [ME *trotte(n)* < MF *troter* < Gmc; akin to OHG *trottōn* to tread, whence MHG *trotten* to run]

trot[2] (trot), *n.* 1. a trotline. 2. a short line with hooks, attached to the trotline. [short for TROTLINE]

troth (trôth, trōth), *n.* *Archaic.* 1. faithfulness, fidelity, or loyalty: *by my troth.* 2. truth or verity: *in troth.* 3. one's word or promise, esp. in engaging oneself to marry. [ME *trowthe, trouthe,* OE *trēowth.* See TRUTH] —**troth/less,** *adj.*

troth·plight (trôth/plīt/, trōth/-), *Archaic.* —*n.* 1. engagement to be married; betrothal. —*v.t.* 2. to betroth. —*adj.* 3. betrothed. [ME *trouth plight* having plighted troth, betrothed; see TROTH, PLIGHT[2]]

trot·line (trot/līn/), *n.* a strong fishing line strung across a stream, or deep into a river, having individual hooks attached by smaller lines at intervals. [TROT[1] + LINE[1]]

Trot·sky (trot/skē; *Russ.* trôt/ski), *n.* **Leon** (*Lev,* or *Leib, Davidovich Bronstein*), 1879–1940, Russian revolutionary and writer: minister of war 1918–25. Also, **Trot/ski.**

Trot·sky·ism (trot/skē iz/əm), *n.* the form of communism advocated by Leon Trotsky, based on an immediate, world-wide revolution by the proletariat. [TROTSKY + -ISM]

Trot·sky·ite (trot/skē it/), *n.* 1. a supporter of Trotsky or Trotskyism. —*adj.* 2. of or pertaining to Trotsky or Trotskyism. Also, **Trot/sky·ist.** [Leon TROTSKY + -ITE[1]]

Trot/skyist Interna/tional. See **Fourth International.**

trot·ter (trot/ər), *n.* 1. an animal that trots, esp. a horse bred and trained for harness racing. 2. a person who moves about briskly and constantly. 3. the foot of an animal, esp. of a sheep or pig, used as food. [ME; see TROT[1], -ER[1]]

trot/ting race/, a horserace using trotters.

trot·ty (trot/ē), *adj.* resembling a trot. [TROT[1] + -Y[1]]

Trot·wood (trot/wōōd/), *n.* a town in W Ohio. 4992 (1960).

tro·tyl (trō/til, -tēl), *n.* *Chem.* See **TNT.** [(TRINI)-TROT(OLUENE) + -YL]

trou·ba·dour (trōō/bə dōr/, -dôr/, -dōōr/), *n.* 1. one of a class of medieval lyric poets who flourished principally in southern France from the 11th to 13th centuries, and wrote songs and poems of a complex metrical form in langue d'oc, chiefly on themes of courtly love. Cf. **trouvère.** 2. any wandering singer or minstrel. [< F < Pr *trobador,* equiv. to *trob(ar)* to find, compose (see TROVER) + *-ador* < L *-ātor;* see -ATOR]

Trou·betz·koy (trōō/bit skoi/; *Russ.* trōō bet skoi/), *n.* **N(i·co·lai) S(er·ge·ie·vich)** (ni ko lī/ ser ge/yə vich). See **Trubetzkoy, N(icolai) S(ergeievich).**

trou·ble (trub′əl), *v.*, **-bled, -bling,** *n.* —*v.t.* **1.** to disturb the mental calm and contentment of; worry; distress; agitate. **2.** to put to inconvenience, exertion, pains, or the like: *May I trouble you to shut the door?* **3.** to cause bodily pain, discomfort, or disorder to; afflict: *Her arthritis troubles her greatly.* **4.** to annoy, vex, or bother: *Don't trouble her with petty complaints now.* **5.** to disturb, agitate, or stir up so as to make turbid, as water, wine, etc.: *A heavy gale troubled the ocean waters.* —*v.i.* **6.** to put oneself to inconvenience, extra effort, or the like. **7.** to be distressed or agitated mentally; worry: *She always troubled over her son's solitariness.* —*n.* **8.** difficulty, annoyance, or harassment: *It would be no trouble at all to advise you.* **9.** unfortunate or distressing position, circumstance, or occurrence; misfortune: *Financial trouble may threaten security.* **10.** civil disorder, disturbance, or conflict: *political trouble in the new republic; labor troubles.* **11.** a physical disorder, disease, ailment, etc.; ill health: *heart trouble; stomach trouble.* **12.** mental or emotional disturbance or distress; worry: *Trouble and woe were her lot in life.* **13.** an instance of this: *some secret trouble weighing on his mind; a wife who shares all her husband's troubles.* **14.** effort, exertion, or pains in doing something; inconvenience endured in accomplishing some action, deed, etc.: *The results were worth the trouble it took.* **15.** something or someone that is a cause or source of disturbance, distress, annoyance, etc. **16.** a personal habit or trait that is a disadvantage or a cause of mental distress: *Her greatest trouble is oversensitivity.* **17. in trouble,** being pregnant out of wedlock (used as a euphemism). [ME *trouble(n)* < OF *troubler* < VL **turbulare,* deriv. of **turbulus* turbid, back formation from L *turbulentus* TURBULENT] —**trou′bled·ly,** *adv.* —**trou′bled·ness,** *n.* —**trou′bler,** *n.* —**trou′bling·ly,** *adv.*
—**Syn. 1.** concern, upset, confuse. **4.** pester, plague, fret, torment, hector, harass, badger. **12.** concern, grief, agitation, care, suffering. **14.** effort. See **care. 15.** trial, tribulation, affliction, misfortune. —**Ant. 1.** mollify; delight.

trou′bled wa′ters, a confused or chaotic state of affairs: *The situation was terrible, but like many politicians he was attracted by troubled waters.*

trou·ble·mak·er (trub′əl mā′kər), *n.* a person who causes difficulties, distress, worry, etc., for others, esp. one who does so habitually as a matter of malice. [TROUBLE + MAKER] —**trou′ble·mak′ing,** *n.*

trou′ble man′, troubleshooter (def. 2).

trou·ble·proof (trub′əl pro͞of′), *adj.* not easily disturbed, disabled, injured, or put out of working order. [TROUBLE + -PROOF]

trou·ble·shoot (trub′əl sho͞ot′), *v.*, **-shoot·ed** or **-shot, -shoot·ing.** —*v.i.* **1.** to act or be employed as a troubleshooter: *He troubleshoots for a large industrial firm.* —*v.t.* **2.** to deal with in the capacity of a troubleshooter. Also, **trou′ble-shoot′.** [back formation from TROUBLESHOOTER]

trou·ble·shoot·er (trub′əl sho͞o′tər), *n.* **1.** a person with special skill in resolving disputes, impasses, etc., as in business, national, or international affairs: *a diplomatic troubleshooter in the Far East.* **2.** Also called **trouble man.** an expert in discovering and eliminating the cause of trouble in mechanical equipment, power lines, etc. Also, **trou′ble-shoot′er.** [TROUBLE + SHOOTER]

trou·ble·some (trub′əl səm), *adj.* **1.** causing trouble, annoyance, or difficulty; vexatious: *a troublesome situation; a troublesome person.* **2.** laborious; difficult. **3.** *Archaic.* full of distress or affliction. [TROUBLE + -SOME[1]] —**trou′ble·some·ly,** *adv.* —**trou′ble·some·ness,** *n.*
—**Syn. 1.** perplexing, galling, harassing. **2.** arduous, hard, burdensome. —**Ant. 2.** easy.

trou′ble spot′, an area in which trouble exists or is expected to develop: *There are several diplomatic trouble spots in Africa.*

trou·blous (trub′ləs), *adj.* *Archaic.* **1.** characterized by trouble; unsettled: *troublous times.* **2.** causing disturbance; restless: *a troublous preacher.* **3.** turbulent; stormy: *a troublous sea.* **4.** causing annoyance; troublesome. [late ME *troub(e)lous,* equiv. to *trouble* turbid (< MF < VL **turbulus;* see TROUBLE) + -OUS] —**trou′blous·ly,** *adv.* —**trou′blous·ness,** *n.*

trou-de-loup (tro͞od′ᵊlo͞o′), *n., pl.* **trous-de-loup** (tro͞od′ᵊlo͞o′). *Mil.* a conical or pyramidal pit with a pointed stake fixed vertically in the center, rows of which are dug in front of a fortification to hinder an enemy's approach, formerly used chiefly against cavalry. [< F: lit., wolfhole]

trough (trôf, trof; *dial.* trôth, troth), *n.* **1.** a long, narrow, open receptacle, usually boxlike in shape, used chiefly to hold water or food for animals. **2.** any of several similarly shaped receptacles used for various commercial or household purposes. **3.** a channel or conduit for conveying water, as a gutter under the eaves of a building for carrying away rain water. **4.** any long depression or hollow, as between two ridges or waves. **5.** *Meteorol.* an elongated area of relatively low pressure. [ME; OE *trōh;* c. D, G, Icel *trog*] —**trough′like′,** *adj.*

trough′ roof′. See **M roof.**

trough′ shape′, a broad channel iron. Also called **trough′ i′ron.**

trounce (trouns), *v.t.*, **trounced, trounc·ing. 1.** to beat severely; thrash. **2.** to punish. **3.** to defeat. [?] —**trounc′er,** *n.*

troupe (tro͞op), *n.*, *v.*, **trouped, troup·ing.** *Theat.* —*n.* **1.** a company, band, or group of singers, actors, or other performers, esp. one that travels about. —*v.i.* **2.** to travel as a member of a theatrical company; barnstorm. [< F. See TROOP]
—**Syn. 1.** See **troop.**

troup·er (tro͞o′pər), *n.* **1.** an actor, esp. a member of a touring company. **2.** a veteran actor. **3.** anyone loyal to a job or undertaking: *He's a good trouper, even when the going is rough.* [TROUPE + -ER[1]]

troup·i·al (tro͞o′pē əl), *n.* any of several American birds of the family *Icteridae,* esp. one with brilliantly colored plumage, as *Icterus icterus,* of South America. [< F *troupiale* (so called from its gregariousness). See TROOP, -IAL]

trou·ser (trou′zər), *adj.* **1.** of or pertaining to trousers or a trouser: *trouser cuffs; a trouser seam.* —*n.* **2.** a leg of a pair of trousers. [back formation from TROUSERS]

trou·sers (trou′zərz), *n.* (*construed as pl.*) **1.** Sometimes, **trouser.** Also called **pants.** a usually loose-fitting outer garment for the lower part of the body, having individual leg portions that reach typically to the ankle but sometimes to any of various other points from the upper leg down, worn esp. by men and boys. Cf. **Bermuda shorts, breeches, knickers** (def. 1), **short** (def. 36a), **slacks. 2.** pantalets. [*trouse* (var. of TREWS) + (DRAW)ERS] —**trou′ser·less,** *adj.*

trous·seau (tro͞o′sō, tro͞o sō′), *n., pl.* **-seaux** (-sōz, -sōz′), **-seaus.** a bride's outfit of clothing, household linen, etc., which she brings with her at marriage. [< F < MF *troussel* small bundle. See TRUSSELL]

trout (trout), *n., pl.* (*esp. collectively*) **trout,** (*esp. referring to two or more kinds or species*) **trouts. 1.** any of several game fishes of the genus *Salmo,* related to the salmon. Cf. **brown trout, cutthroat trout, rainbow trout. 2.** any of various game fishes of the salmon family of the genera *Salvelinus* and *Cristovomer.* Cf. **brook trout** (def. 1), **char[2], Dolly Varden** (def. 4), **lake trout. 3.** any of several unrelated fishes, as a bass, *Micropterus salmoides,* a drum of the genus *Cynoscion,* or a greenling of the genus *Hexagrammos.* [ME *trou(h)te,* OE *truht* < L *tructa* < Gk *trṓktēs* gnawer, a seafish, equiv. to *trōg(ein)* (to) gnaw + *-tēs* agent n. suffix] —**trout′less,** *adj.* —**trout′like′,** *adj.*

Brook trout, *Salvelinus fontinalis* (Length 1½ ft.)

trout·perch (trout′pûrch′), *n., pl.* **-perch·es,** (*esp. collectively*) **-perch.** a North American, fresh-water fish, *Percopsis omiscomaycas,* exhibiting characteristics of both trouts and perches. [TROUT + PERCH[2]]

trou·vaille (tro͞o vä′yᵊ), *n., pl.* **-vailles** (-vä′yᵊ). *French.* a lucky find; godsend; windfall.

Trou·ve·lot (tro͞o′və lō′), *n.* a crater in the first quadrant of the face of the moon: about 5½ miles in diameter.

trou·vère (tro͞o vâr′; *Fr.* tro͞o vᴇʀ′), *n., pl.* **-vères** (-vârz′; *Fr.* -vᴇʀ′). one of a class of medieval poets who flourished in northern France during the 12th and 13th centuries, wrote in langue d'oïl, and composed chiefly the *chansons de geste* and works on the themes of courtly love. Also, **trouveur.** Cf. **troubador** (def. 1). [< F; OF *troveor,* equiv. to *trov(er)* (to) find, compose (see TROVER) + *-eor* < L *-ātor* -ATOR]

trou·veur (tro͞o vûr′; *Fr.* tro͞o vœʀ′), *n., pl.* **-veurs** (-vûrz′; *Fr.* -vœʀ′). trouvère.

Trou·ville (tro͞o vēl′), *n.* a seaport in NW France, on the English Channel: resort. 6822 (1962). Also called **Trouville-sur-Mer** (tro͞o vēl′syʀ mer′).

Tro·va·to·re, Il (il trō′və tôr′ē; *It.* ēl trô′vä tô′ʀe), an opera (1853) by Giuseppe Verdi.

tro·ver (trō′vər), *n.* *Law.* an action for the recovery of the value of personal property wrongfully converted by another to his own use. [< MF, OF: to find, orig., stir up < L *turbāre* to disturb. See TURBID]

trow[1] (trō), *v.i.* *Archaic.* to believe, think, or suppose. [ME *trowe(n),* OE *trēow(i)an* to believe, deriv. of *trēow* belief; akin to Icel *trūa,* G *trauen,* Goth *trauan* to trust, believe. See TRUST, TRUE]

trow[2] (trō), *n.* a river barge used in the British Isles. [ME; OE *trog,* var. of *troh* kind of boat (dugout) TROUGH]

trow·el (trou′əl), *n., v.,* **-eled, -el·ing** or (*esp. Brit.*) **-elled, -el·ling.** —*n.* **1.** any of various tools having a flat blade with a handle, used for depositing and working mortar, plaster, etc. **2.** a similar tool with a curved, scooplike blade, used in gardening for taking up plants, turning up earth, etc. —*v.t.* **3.** to apply, shape, or smooth with or as with a trowel. [ME < OF *truelle* < LL *truella,* equiv. to L *tru(a)* ladle + *-ella* dim. suffix] —**trow′el·er;** *esp. Brit.,* **trow′el·ler,** *n.*

troy (troi), *adj.* expressed or computed in troy weight. [ME *troye,* named after TROYES, France, where it was standard]

Troy (troi), *n.* **1.** Latin, **Ilium.** Greek, **Ilion.** an ancient ruined city in NW Asia Minor: the seventh of nine settlements on the same site; besieged by the Greeks for ten years. **2.** a city in E New York, on the Hudson River. 67,492 (1960). **3.** a city in SE Michigan, near Detroit. 19,058 (1960). **4.** a city in S Alabama. 10,234 (1960). **5.** a boy's given name.

Troyes (tʀwä), *n.* a city in and the capital of Aube, in NE France, on the Seine: treaty. 68,898 (1962).

Tro·yon (tʀwa yôɴ′), *n.* **Con·stant** (kôɴ stäɴ′), 1813–65, French painter.

troy′ weight′, a system of weights in use for precious metals and gems (formerly also for bread, grain, etc.): 24 grains = 1 pennyweight; 20 pennyweights = 1 ounce; 12 ounces = 1 pound. The grain, ounce, and pound are the same as in apothecaries' weight, the grain alone being the same as in avoirdupois weight. The troy pound is no longer a standard weight in Great Britain.

trp, *Mil.* troop.

tru·an·cy (tro͞o′ən sē), *n., pl.* **-cies** for 2. **1.** the act or state of being truant. **2.** an instance of being truant: *His parents were questioned about his many truancies.* Also, **truantry.** [TRUAN(T) + -CY]

tru·ant (tro͞o′ənt), *n.* **1.** a student who stays away from school without permission. **2.** a person who shirks or neglects his duty. —*adj.* **3.** absent from school without permission. **4.** neglectful of duty or responsibility; idle. **5.** of, pertaining to, or characteristic of a truant. —*v.i.* **6.** to be truant. [ME < OF: vagrant, beggar < Celt; cf. Welsh *truan* wretched, wretch] —**tru′ant·ly,** *adv.*

tru′ant of′fi·cer, a public-school official who investigates unauthorized absences from school. Also called **attendance officer.**

tru·ant·ry (tro͞o′ən trē), *n., pl.* **-ries.** truancy. [TRUANT + -RY]

Tru·betz·koy (tro͞o′bit skoi′; *Russ.* tro͞o bet skoi′), *n.* **N(i·ko·lai) S(er·ge·ie·vich)** (ni ko lī′ sᴇʀ ge′yə vich), 1890–1938, Russian linguist in Austria. Also, **Tru′betz·koi′, Troubetzkoy.**

truce (tro͞os), *n.* **1.** a suspension of hostilities for a specified period of time by mutual agreement of the warring parties; cease-fire; armistice. **2.** an agreement or treaty establishing this. **3.** respite, relief, or freedom, as from trouble, pain, etc. [ME *trewes,* pl. of *trewe,* OE *trēow* belief, pledge, treaty. See TROW[1]] —**truce′less,** *adj.*

Tru·cial O·man (tro͞o′shəl ō män′), former name of a group of Arab sheikdoms under British protection on the S coast **(Tru′cial Coast′)** of the Persian Gulf. Also called **Tru′cial Sheik′doms, Tru′cial States′.** Formerly, **Pirate Coast.** Official name, since 1971, **United Arab Emirates.**

truck[1] (truk), *n.* **1.** any of various forms of vehicle for carrying goods and materials, usually consisting of a single self-propelled unit but also often composed of a trailer vehicle hauled by a tractor unit. **2.** any of various wheeled frames used for transporting heavy objects. **3.** Also called **hand truck.** a barrowlike frame with low wheels, a ledge at the bottom, and handles at the top, used to move heavy luggage, packages, cartons, etc. **4.** a low, rectangular frame on which heavy boxes, crates, trunks, etc., are moved; a dolly. **5.** a tiered framework on casters. **6.** a group of two or more pairs of wheels in one frame, for supporting one end of a railroad car, locomotive, etc. **7.** *Brit.* a freight car having no top. **8.** a small wooden wheel, cylinder, or roller, as on certain old-style gun carriages. **9.** *Naut.* a circular or square piece of wood fixed on the head of a mast or the top of a flagstaff, usually containing small holes for signal halyards. —*v.t.* **10.** to transport by a truck or trucks. **11.** to put on a truck. **12.** dolly (def. 8). —*v.i.* **13.** to convey articles or goods on a truck. **14.** to drive a truck. **15.** dolly (defs. 9, 10). —*adj.* **16.** of, pertaining to, or for a truck or trucks: *a truck drive; truck tires.* [back formation from *truckle* wheel. See TRUCKLE[2]]

truck[2] (truk), *n.* **1.** *U.S.* vegetables raised for the market. **2.** miscellaneous articles of little worth; odds and ends. **3.** *Informal.* trash or rubbish: *That's a lot of truck.* **4.** *Informal.* dealings: *I'll have no truck with him.* **5.** barter. **6.** a bargain or deal. **7.** the payment of wages in goods instead of money. **8.** See **truck system.** —*v.t.* **9.** to exchange; trade; barter. —*v.i.* **10.** to exchange commodities; barter. **11.** to traffic; have dealings. [ME *trukien* < OF *troquer* to exchange]

truck[3] (truk), *n.* **1.** a shuffling jitterbug step. —*v.i.* **2.** to dance with such steps. [special use of TRUCK[1]]

truck·age (truk′ij), *n.* **1.** conveyance by a truck or trucks. **2.** the charge for this. [TRUCK[1] + -AGE]

truck′ crop′, a vegetable crop raised on a truck farm.

truck·driv·er (truk′drī′vər), *n.* a person who drives a truck. [TRUCK[1] + DRIVER]

truck·er[1] (truk′ər), *n.* **1.** a person who drives a truck; truckdriver. **2.** a person whose business is trucking goods. [TRUCK[1] + -ER[1]]

trucker[2] (truk′ər), *n.* *U.S.* a truck farmer. [TRUCK[2] + -ER[1]]

truck′ farm′, *U.S.* a farm for the growing of vegetables for the market. Also called **truck′ gar′den;** *esp. Brit.,* **market garden.** Cf. **market garden.** —**truck′ farmer.** —**truck′ farming.**

truck·ing[1] (truk′ing), *n.* the art or business of conveying articles or goods on trucks. [TRUCK[1] + ING[1]]

truck·ing[2] (truk′ing), *n.* **1.** *U.S.* the growing of vegetables for the market. **2.** commercial bartering. [TRUCK[2] + -ING[1]]

truck′ing shot′. See **dolly shot.** Also, **truck shot.**

truck′ job′ber, a jobber or wholesaler who makes his calls carrying his goods on a truck, thereby enabling him to take and deliver orders on the same call. Also called **wagon jobber.**

truck·le[1] (truk′əl), *v.i.*, **-led, -ling.** to submit or yield obsequiously or tamely (usually fol. by *to*): *Don't truckle under to unreasonable demands.* [special use of obs. *truckle* to sleep on truckle bed. See TRUCKLE[2]] —**truck′ler,** *n.* —**truck′ling·ly,** *adv.*

truck·le[2] (truk′əl), *n.* **1.** See **truckle bed. 2.** *Obs.* a pulley. [late ME *trocle* sheave, roller < AF < L *trochlea* pulley. See TROCHLEA]

truck′le bed′, a low bed moving on casters, usually pushed under another bed when not in use. Also called **trundle bed.**

truck·load (truk′lōd′), *n.* **1.** a full or almost full load on a truck. **2.** the minimum weight legally required for making shipments at a rate **(truck′load rate′)** below that charged for shipments under the minimum. [TRUCK[1] + LOAD]

truck·man (truk′mən), *n., pl.* **-men. 1.** a truck driver. **2.** a man who is in the business of trucking goods, produce, etc. [TRUCK[1] + MAN[1]]

truck′ shot′. See **dolly shot.**

truck′ sys′tem, the system of paying wages in goods instead of money. Also called **truck.**

truck′ trac′tor, *Auto.* a motor truck with a short body and no cargo space, for hauling semitrailers.

truck′ trail′er, *Auto.* a trailer designed to be drawn by a truck tractor or other motor truck.

truc·u·lent (truk′yə lənt, tro͞o′kyə-), *adj.* **1.** fierce; cruel; savagely brutal. **2.** brutally harsh; vitriolic; scathing: *his truculent criticism of her work.* **3.** aggressively hostile; belligerent. [< L *truculentus,* equiv. to *trucu-* (comb. form of *trux* savage, grim) + *-lentus* -LENT] —**truc′u·lence, truc′u·len·cy,** *n.* —**truc′u·lent·ly,** *adv.*
—**Syn. 1.** See **fierce.** —**Ant. 1.** amiable, gentle.

Tru·deau (tro͞o dō′), *n.* **Pi·erre Elliot** (pē âr′), born 1919, Canadian statesman: prime minister 1968–79 and 1980–84.

trudge (truj), *v.*, **trudged, trudg·ing,** *n.* —*v.i.* **1.** to walk. **2.** to walk laboriously or wearily: *trudge up the mountain.* —*v.t.* **3.** to walk laboriously or wearily along or over: *He trudged the deserted road for hours.* —*n.* **4.** a laborious or tiring walk; tramp. [? TR(EAD + DR)UDGE] —**trudg′er,** *n.* —**Syn. 2.** tramp. See **pace[1].**

trudg·en (truj′ən), *n.* *Swimming.* a stroke in which a double overarm motion and a scissors kick are used. Also called **trudg′en stroke′.** [named after John *Trudgen* (1852–1902), British swimmer]

Tru·dy (tro͞o′dē), *n.* a girl's given name, form of **Gertrude.** Also, **Tru′di, Tru′die.**

true (tro͞o), *adj.*, **tru·er, tru·est,** *n., adv., v.,* **trued, tru·ing** or **true·ing.** —*adj.* **1.** being in accordance with

the actual state or conditions; conforming to reality or fact; not false: *a true story.* **2.** real; genuine; authentic: *true gold; true feelings.* **3.** sincere; not deceitful: *a true interest in someone's welfare.* **4.** firm in allegiance; loyal; faithful; steadfast: *a true friend.* **5.** being or reflecting the essential or genuine character of something: *the true meaning of his statement.* **6.** conforming to or consistent with a standard, pattern, or the like: *a true copy.* **7.** exact; precise; accurate; correct: *a true balance.* **8.** of the right kind; such as it should be; proper: *to arrange things in their true order.* **9.** properly so called; rightly answering to a description: *true statesmanship.* **10.** legitimate or rightful: *the true heir.* **11.** reliable, unfailing, or sure: *a true sign.* **12.** exactly or accurately shaped, formed, fitted, or placed, as a surface, instrument, or part of a mechanism. **13.** *Biol.* conforming to the type, norm, or standard of structure of a particular group; typical: *The lion is a true cat.* **14.** *Stockbreeding.* purebred. **15.** *Navig.* (of a bearing, course, etc.) determined in relation to true north. **16.** *Archaic.* truthful. **17.** *Archaic.* honest; honorable; upright. **—***n.* **18.** exact or accurate formation, position, or adjustment: *to be out of true.* **19. the true,** that which is true; truth. **—***adv.* **20.** in a true manner; truly; truthfully. **21.** exactly or accurately. **22.** in conformity with the ancestral type: *to breed true.* **23. come true,** to have the expected result; become a reality: *She couldn't believe that her dream would ever come true.* **—***v.t.* **24.** to make true; shape, adjust, place, etc., exactly or accurately. [ME *trewe,* OE *trēowe* loyal, trusty, honest (see TROW[1], TRUCE); akin to G *treu,* D *trouw,* Goth. *triggws,* Icel *tryggr*] **—true′ness,** *n.*
—Syn. 1. factual, veracious. See **real. 3.** honest. **4.** trustworthy; staunch, constant, steady, unwavering. **7.** faithful, just.

True (tro͞o), *n.* a girl's given name. Also, **Trew.**

true′ anom′aly, *Astron.* the anomaly of a planet; its angular distance from perihelion or aphelion.

true′ bill′, *Law.* a bill of indictment endorsed by a grand jury, after investigation, as being sufficiently supported by evidence to justify a hearing of the case.

true′ blue′, **1.** a nonfading blue dye or pigment. **2.** one who is true-blue. **3.** (in the 17th century) the color adopted by the Covenanters in contradistinction to the royal red.

true-blue (tro͞o′blo͞o′), *adj.* unwaveringly loyal or faithful; staunch; unchangingly true.

true·born (tro͞o′bôrn′), *adj.* genuinely or authentically so because of birth: *a trueborn son of Ireland; a trueborn Parisian.* [TRUE + BORN]

true·bred (tro͞o′bred′), *adj.* **1.** marked by qualities of good breeding and education; well-bred. **2.** thoroughbred or purebred: *a truebred Lippizaner.* [TRUE + BRED]

true′ bug′, bug[1] (def. 1).

true′ course′, *Navig.* a course whose bearing is given relative to the geographical meridian. Cf. **compass course, magnetic course.**

true′ fly′, fly[2] (def. 1).

true′ fres′co, fresco (def. 1).

true·heart·ed (tro͞o′här′tid), *adj.* **1.** faithful; loyal. **2.** honest; sincere. Also, **true′-heart′ed.** [late ME *true hartyd;* see HEART, -ED[3]] **—true′heart′ed·ness, true′-heart′ed·ness,** *n.*

true′ jade′, jadeite or nephrite.

true′ lev′el, an imaginary surface everywhere perpendicular to the plumb line, or line of gravity.

true-life (tro͞o′līf′), *adj.* similar to everyday life; realistic: *true-life episodes.*

true·love (tro͞o′luv′), *n.* **1.** a sweetheart; a truly loving or loved person. **2.** the herb Paris, *Paris quadrifolia,* having a whorl of four leaves suggesting a truelove knot. [ME *trewe love,* OE *trēow lufu.* See TRUE, LOVE]

true′love knot′, a complicated ornamental knot, esp. a double knot having two interlacing bows, regarded as an emblem of true love or interwoven affections. Also called **true′ lov′er's knot′, true′-lov′er's knot′.**

true′ north′, *Navig.* the direction of the north pole from a given point.

true·pen·ny (tro͞o′pen′ē), *n., pl.* **-nies.** *Archaic.* trusty, honest fellow. [TRUE + PENNY]

true′ rib′, *Anat.* one member of the first seven pairs of ribs that are attached in man to the sternum by costal cartilages.

true′ time′, apparent solar time; the time as shown by a sundial.

true′ vo′cal cords′, *Anat.* the lower pair of vocal cords, the edges of which can be drawn tense and made to vibrate by the passage of air from the lungs, thus producing vocal sound. Also called **vocal folds.** Cf. **false vocal cord, vocal cords.**

truffe (TRYF), *n.* *French.* **1.** truffle. **2.** *Slang.* peasant; boor.

truf·fle (truf′əl, tro͞o′fəl), *n.* **1.** any of several subterranean, edible, ascomycetous fungi of the genus *Tuber.* **2.** any of various similar fungi of other genera. [appar. < Vaudois (Swiss) *trufla* << LL **tūfera* < Oscan-Umbrian *tūfer,* c. L *tūber* truffle. See TUBER[1]] **—truf′fled,** *adj.*

trug (trug, tro͝og), *n.* *Brit.* **1.** a shallow basket for carrying flowers, vegetables, etc., made from strips of wood. **2.** a shallow, wooden milk pan. **3.** a wooden tray for holding mortar. [?]

tru·ism (tro͞o′iz əm), *n.* a self-evident, obvious truth. [TRUE + -ISM] **—tru·is′tic, tru·is′ti·cal,** *adj.*
—Syn. cliché, platitude.

Tru·jil·lo (tro͞o hē′ō; *Sp.* tro͞o hē′yô), *n.* **1. Ra·fa·el Le·o·ni·das** (raf′ā el′ lē on′i dəs; *Sp.* rä′fä el′ le′ō-nē′thäs), *(Rafael Leonidas Trujillo Molina),* 1891–1961, Dominican general and politician: president 1930–38, 1942–52. **2.** a seaport in NW Peru. 100,130 (1961).

Truk′ Is′lands (truk), a group of the Caroline Islands, in the N Pacific: an important Japanese naval base in World War II. ab. 17,000; ab. 50 sq. mi.

trull (trul), *n.* a prostitute; strumpet. [< G *Trulle,* var. of *Trudel* loose woman]

trul·li·sa·tio (tro͞o′li sä′shō), *n., pl.* **-tios.** (formerly in fresco painting) the first coat of rough plaster laid on a wall. Also called **rough cast, scratch coat.** Cf. **arriccio, intonaco.** [< It < L *trullissātiōn-* (s. of *trullissātiō*) < *trullissāt(us)* (ptp. of *trullissāre* to plaster < *trull(a)* trowel + *-iss(āre)* v. suffix) + *-iōn-* -ION]

tru·ly (tro͞o′lē), *adv.* **1.** in accordance with fact or truth; truthfully. **2.** exactly; accurately; correctly. **3.** rightly; properly; duly. **4.** legitimately; by right. **5.** really; genuinely; authentically. **6.** indeed; verily. **7.** sincerely: *yours truly.* **8.** *Archaic.* faithfully; loyally. [ME *treuli,* OE *trēowlīce.* See TRUE, -LY]

Tru·man (tro͞o′mən), *n.* **1. Harry S,** born 1884, 33rd president of the U.S. 1945–53. **2.** a boy's given name.

Tru′man Doc′trine, the policy of President Truman, as advocated in his address to Congress on March 12, 1947, to provide military and economic aid to Greece and Turkey and, by extension, to any country threatened by communism or any totalitarian ideology.

Tru·mann (tro͞o′mən), *n.* a town in NE Arkansas. 4511 (1960).

Trum·bull (trum′bəl), *n.* **1. John,** 1756–1843, U.S. painter (son of Jonathan Trumbull). **2. Jonathan,** 1710–85, U.S. statesman.

tru·meau (tro͞o mō′; *Fr.* TRY mō′), *n., pl.* **-meaux** (-mōz′; *Fr.* -mō′). **1.** a mirror having a painted or carved panel above or below the glass in the same frame. **2.** *Archit.* a column supporting a tympanum of a doorway at its center. [< F]

trump[1] (trump), *n.* **1.** *Cards.* **a.** any playing card of a suit that for the time outranks the other suits, such a card being able to take any card of another suit. **b.** Often, **trumps.** (*construed as sing.*) the suit itself. **2.** *Informal.* a fine person; brick. **—***v.t.* **3.** *Cards.* to take with a trump. **4.** to excel; surpass; outdo. **—***v.i.* **5.** *Cards.* **a.** to play a trump. **b.** to take a trick with a trump. **6. trump up,** to devise deceitfully or dishonestly, as an accusation; fabricate: *Try as they might, they were unable to trump up a convincing case against him.* [unexplained var. of TRIUMPH] **—trump′less,** *adj.*

trump[2] (trump), *Archaic or Poetic.* **—***n.* **1.** trumpet. **2.** its sound. **—***v.i.* **3.** to blow a trumpet. [ME *trompe* < OF < OHG *trumpa,* var. of *trumba* trumpet]

trump card (trump′ kärd′ *for 1;* trump′ kärd′ *for 2*), **1.** *Cards.* trump[1] (def. 1a). **2.** *Informal.* something that gives one person or group the advantage over another: *The surprise witness was his trump card.*

trumped-up (trumpt′up′), *adj.* spuriously devised; fraudulent; fabricated: *He was arrested on some trumped-up charge.* [special use of TRUMP[1]; see -ED[2]]

Trum·pel·dor (trum′pəl dôr′), *n.* **Joseph,** 1880–1920, Palestinian hero and Zionist leader, born in Russia.

trump·er·y (trum′pə rē), *n., pl.* **-ries,** *adj.* **—***n.* **1.** something without use or value; rubbish; trash; worthless stuff. **2.** nonsense; twaddle: *His usual conversation is pure trumpery.* **3.** *Archaic.* worthless finery. **—***adj.* **4.** of little or no value; trifling, worthless; rubbishy; trashy. [late ME *trompery* deceit < MF *tromperie,* equiv. to *tromp(er)* to deceive + *-erie* -ERY]

trum·pet (trum′pit), *n.* **1.** *Music.* **a.** any of a family of brass wind instruments with a powerful, penetrating tone, consisting of a tube commonly curved once or twice around on itself and having a cup-shaped mouthpiece at one end and a flaring bell at the other. **b.** an organ stop having a tone resembling that of a trumpet. **c.** a trumpeter. **2.** something used as or resembling a trumpet, esp. in sound. **3.** a sound like that of a trumpet. **4.** the loud shrill cry of an animal, esp. an elephant. **5.** See **ear trumpet. 6. trumpets,** any of several pitcher plants of the southeastern U.S. **—***v.i.* **7.** to blow a trumpet. **8.** to emit a loud, trumpetlike cry, as an elephant. **—***v.t.* **9.** to sound on a trumpet. **10.** to utter with a sound like that of a trumpet. **11.** to proclaim loudly or widely. [ME *trumpette, trompette* < F, equiv. to *trompe* TRUMP[2] + *-ette* -ET] **—trum′pet·less,** *adj.* **—trum′pet·like′,** *adj.*

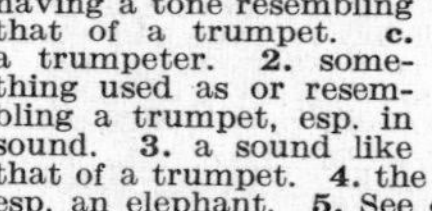

Trumpet (def. 1a)

trum′pet creep′er, any climbing, bignoniaceous plant of the genus *Campsis,* esp. *C. radicans,* of the southern U.S., having large, red, trumpet-shaped flowers.

trum·pet·er (trum′pi tər), *n.* **1.** a person who plays a trumpet; trumpet player. **2.** a person who proclaims or announces something with a trumpet. **3.** a soldier, usually in a mounted unit, whose duty is to sound the required trumpet calls. **4.** one who proclaims, commends, or extols something loudly or widely; eulogizer. **5.** any of several large, South American birds of the family *Psophiidae,* esp. *Psophia crepitans,* related to the cranes and rails, having a loud, harsh, prolonged cry. **6.** See **trumpeter swan. 7.** one of a breed of domestic pigeons. [TRUMPET + -ER[1]]

trum′peter swan′, a large, North American, wild swan, *Olor buccinator,* having a sonorous cry.

trum·pet·fish (trum′pit fish′), *n., pl.* (*esp. collectively*) **-fish,** (*esp. referring to two or more kinds or species*) **-fish·es.** any of several fishes of the family *Aulostomidae,* having a long, tubular snout, as the slender, brown-flecked *Aulostomus maculatus,* found on both sides of the tropical Atlantic Ocean. [TRUMPET + FISH]

trum′pet flow′er, **1.** any of various plants with pendent flowers shaped like a trumpet. **2.** See **trumpet creeper. 3.** See **trumpet honey suckle. 4.** the flower of any of these plants.

trum′pet hon′eysuckle, an American honeysuckle, *Lonicera sempervirens,* having large, tubular flowers, deep-red outside and yellow within. Also called **coral honeysuckle.**

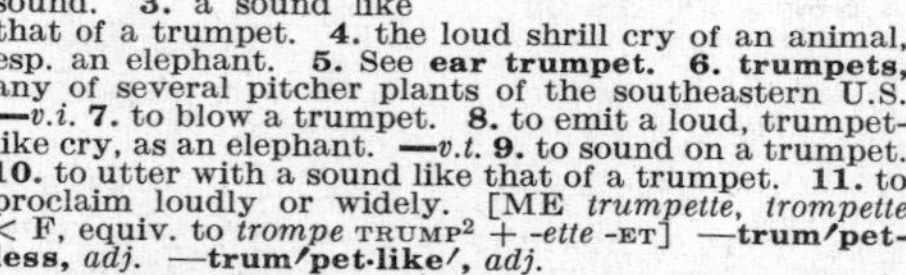

Trumpet legs

trum·pet-leaf (trum′pit lēf′), *n., pl.* **-leaves.** trumpets.

trum′pet leg′, *Furniture.* a turned leg that flares upward and outward from a narrow lower end.

trum′pet marine′, an obsolete musical instrument having a long, wooden, pyramid-shaped body, characteristically with one string that is touched with the finger to produce harmonics and is bowed between the touching finger and the upper end. Also called **nun's fiddle, tromba marina, trumscheit.**

trum·pet·ry (trum′pi trē), *n.* **1.** the manner of playing the trumpet: *The character of modern trumpetry has changed.* **2.** the sound, esp. the blaring sound, of trumpets. **3.** trumpets collectively. [TRUMPET + -RY]

trum·pets (trum′pits), *n., pl.* **-pets.** a showy, herbaceous perennial, *Sarracenia flava,* of the southeastern U.S., having prominently veined, crimson-throated, yellow-green leaves and yellow flowers from two to four inches wide. Also called **tender perennial, trumpet-leaf, yellow pitcher plant.** [pl. of TRUMPET]

trum·pet-tree (trum′pit trē′), *n.* a tropical American, moraceous tree, *Cecropia peltata,* having hollow, jointed stems and branches used in making certain wind instruments. Also called **trumpetwood.**

trum′pet turn′ing, *Furniture.* the turning of a piece to give a trumpetlike, flaring form.

trum′pet vine′. See **trumpet creeper.**

trum·pet·weed (trum′pit wēd′), *n.* any of several eupatoriums, as a boneset, *Eupatorium perfoliatum,* and the joe-pye weeds, *E. maculatum* and *E. purpureum.* [TRUMPET + WEED[1]]

trum·pet·wood (trum′pit wo͝od′), *n.* trumpet-tree. [TRUMPET + WOOD[1]]

trum·scheit (tro͝om′shīt), *n.* See **trumpet marine.** [< G *Trummscheit,* equiv. to *Trumm-* < OHG *trumba* trumpet (see TRUMP[2]) + *scheit* piece of wood, board]

truncate (trung′kāt), *v.,* **-cat·ed, -cat·ing,** *adj.* **—***v.t.* **1.** to shorten by cutting off a part; cut short: *Truncate detailed explanations.* **—***adj.* **2.** truncated. **3.** *Biol.* **a.** square or broad at the end, as if cut off transversely. **b.** lacking the apex, as certain spiral shells. [< L *truncātus* lopped (ptp. of *truncāre*), equiv. to *truncus* TRUNK + *-ātus* -ATE[1]] **—trun′cate·ly,** *adv.*

Truncate leaf

trun·cat·ed (trung′kā tid), *adj.* **1.** shortened by or as if by having a part cut off; cut short: *an unnecessarily truncated essay.* **2.** (of a geometric figure or solid) having the apex, vertex, or end cut off by a plane: *a truncated cone or pyramid.* **3.** *Crystall.* **a.** (of a crystal) having angles or edges cut off or replaced by a single plane. **b.** (of one of the edges or corners) cut off or replaced by a modifying plane which makes equal angles with the adjacent similar planes. **4.** *Biol.* truncate (def. 3). **5.** *Pros.* (of a line of verse) lacking at the beginning or end one or more unstressed syllables needed to fill out the metrical pattern. [TRUNCATE + -ED[2]]

Truncated cone

trun·ca·tion (trung kā′shən), *n.* **1.** the act or process of truncating. **2.** the quality or state of being truncated. **3.** *Pros.* the omission of one or more unaccented syllables at the beginning or the end of a line of verse. [< LL *truncātiōn-* (s. of *truncātiō*) < L *truncātus* (see TRUNCATE) + *-iōn-* -ION]

trun·cheon (trun′chən), *n.* **1.** *Chiefly Brit.* the club carried by a policeman; billy. **2.** a staff representing an office or authority; baton. **3.** *Obs.* a club or cudgel. **4.** *Obs.* the shaft of a spear. **—***v.t.* **5.** *Archaic.* to beat with a club. [ME *tronchon* fragment < MF < LL **trunciōn-,* s. of **trunciō* lit., a lopping. See TRUNK, -ION]

trun·dle (trun′dəl), *v.,* **-dled, -dling,** *n.* **—***v.t.* **1.** to cause (a circular object) to roll along; roll. **2.** to convey or move in a wagon, cart, or other wheeled vehicle; wheel: *The farmer trundled his produce to market in a rickety wagon.* **3.** *Archaic.* to cause to rotate; twirl; spin. **—***v.i.* **4.** to roll along. **5.** to move or run on a wheel or wheels. **6.** to travel in a wheeled vehicle: *He got into his car and trundled downtown.* **7.** to move or walk with a rolling gait. **—***n.* **8.** a small wheel, roller, or the like. **9.** a lantern wheel. **10.** each of the bars of a lantern wheel. **11.** a truck or carriage on low wheels. [var. of TRINDLE] **—trun′dler,** *n.*

trun′dle bed′. See **truckle bed.**

trun·dle·tail (trun′dəl tāl′), *n.* *Archaic.* a dog with a curly tail; a mongrel. [TRUNDLE + TAIL[1]]

trunk (trungk), *n.* **1.** the main stem of a tree, as distinct from the branches and roots. **2.** a large, sturdy box or chest for holding or transporting clothes, personal effects, or other articles. **3.** a large compartment in an automobile in which luggage, a spare tire, and other articles may be kept. **4.** the body of man or an animal excluding the head and limbs; torso. **5.** *Ichthyol.* the part of a fish between the head and the anus. **6.** *Archit.* **a.** the shaft of a column. **b.** the dado or die of a pedestal. **7.** the main channel, artery, or line in a river, railroad, highway, canal, or other tributary system. **8.** *Telephony, Telegraphy.* **a.** a telephone line or channel between two central offices or switching devices that is used in providing telephone connections between subscribers generally. **b.** a telegraph line or channel between two main or central offices. **9.** *Anat.* the main body of an artery, nerve, or the like, as distinct from its branches. **10. trunks, a.** brief shorts, loose-fitting or tight, worn by men chiefly for boxing, swimming, and track. **b.** *Obs.* See **trunk hose. 11.** the long, flexible, cylindrical nasal appendage of the elephant. **12.** *Mach.* **a.** (in a steam engine) a tube, attached to the piston and passing through a stuffing box, permitting the connecting rod to be attached directly to the piston. **b.** a cylinder serving as a dashpot. **13.** *Naut.* **a.** a large enclosed passage through the decks or bulkheads of a vessel, for cooling, ventilation, or the like. **b.** any of various watertight casings in a vessel, as the vertical one above the slot for a centerboard in the bottom of a boat. **14.** a conduit; shaft; chute. **15.** *Obs.* any of various pipes or tubes, as a speaking tube, a blowgun, or a telescope. **—***adj.* **16.** of, pertaining to, or noting a main channel or line, as of a railroad, river, etc. [late ME *trunke* < L *truncus* stem, trunk, stump, n. use of *truncus* (adj.) lopped] **—trunk′less,** *adj.*

trunk′ bu′oy, *Naut.* a mooring buoy having a cylindrical, steel body enclosing a central, watertight trunk.

trunk′ cab′in, a cabin of a yacht that presents a long, low profile with a relatively unbroken line fore and aft. Cf. **doghouse** (def. 3).

trunk′ call′, *Chiefly Brit.* a long-distance phone call.

trunk′-decked ves′sel (trungk′dekt′), *Naut.* a bulk-carrying freighter having its tanks or hatches ending in raised, narrow compartments on the fore-and-aft line to allow for expansion of liquids, to minimize surging or shifting of cargo, etc.

Trunk cabin

trunk′ di′al, *Horol.* a dial concealing all the works of a spring-driven clock except the lower part of the pendulum, which is housed in a downward extension of the case.

trunk′ en′gine, 1. an engine having a trunk piston or pistons. 2. a double-acting steam engine having a connecting rod passing through a trunk to the piston.

trunk·fish (trungk′fish′), *n., pl.* (*esp. collectively*) **-fish,** (*esp. referring to two or more kinds or species*) **-fish·es.** any plectognath fish of the family *Ostraciontidae,* found in warm seas, having a boxlike body encased in bony, polygonal plates. Also called **boxfish.** [TRUNK + FISH]

trunk·ful (trungk′fo͝ol′), *n., pl.* **-fuls.** 1. the full capacity of a trunk. 2. *Informal.* a full or abundant supply: *a trunkful of soap; a trunkful of opinions.* [TRUNK + -FUL]

trunk′ hose′, full, baglike breeches covering the body from the waist to the middle of the thigh or lower, worn in the 16th and 17th centuries.

trunk′ line′, 1. a major long-distance transportation line. 2. trunk (def. 8).

trunk′ pis′ton, *Mach.* a piston with a long skirt to take the side thrust, as in an automobile engine.

trun·nel (trun′əl), *n.* treenail.

trun·nion (trun′yən), *n.* 1. either of the two cylindrical projections on a cannon, one on each side for supporting the cannon on its carriage. 2. any of various similar supports for machinery. [< F *trognon* trunk, stump, core (of fruit)] —**trun′nioned,** *adj.*

truss (trus), *v.t.* 1. to tie, bind, or fasten. 2. to make fast with skewers, thread, or the like, as the wings or legs of a fowl in preparation for cooking. 3. to furnish or support with a truss or trusses. 4. to tie or secure (the body) closely or tightly; bind (often fol. by *up*). 5. *Falconry.* (of a falcon) to grasp (prey) firmly. —*n.* 6. *Engineering, Building Trades.* a. any of various structural frames based on the geometric rigidity of the triangle and composed of straight members subject only to longitudinal compression, tension, or both, and so disposed as to make the frame rigid under anticipated loads: functions as a beam or cantilever to support bridges, roofs, etc. Cf. **complete** (def. 7), **incomplete** (def. 3), **redundant** (def. 5c). b. any of various structural frames constructed on principles other than the geometric rigidity of the triangle or deriving stability from other factors, as the rigidity of joints, the abutment of masonry, or the stiffness of beams. 7. *Med.* an apparatus consisting of a pad usually supported by a belt for maintaining a hernia in a reduced state. 8. *Hort.* a. a compact terminal cluster or head of flowers growing upon one stalk. b. a compact cluster of fruit, as of tomatoes. 9. *Naut.* a device for supporting a standing yard, having a pivot permitting the yard to swing horizontally when braced. 10. a collection of things tied together or packed in a receptacle; bundle; pack. 11. *Chiefly Brit.* a bundle of hay or straw, esp. one containing about 56 pounds of old hay, 60 pounds of new hay, or 36 pounds of straw. [ME *trusse(n)* < OF *tr(o)usser,* var. of *torser* < VL **torciare,* deriv. of **torca* bundle, TORCH] —**truss′er,** *n.*

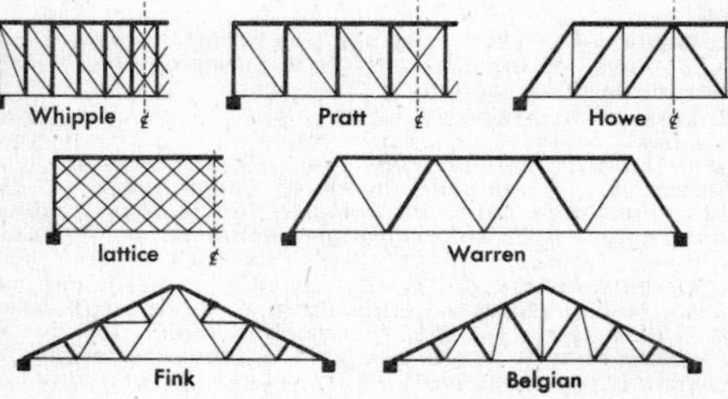

Trusses (def. 6)

truss′ bridge′, a bridge in which the loads are supported by trusses.

trussed (trust), *adj. Heraldry.* close (def. 52). [TRUSS + -ED²]

trussed′ beam′, a wooden beam reinforced with truss rods.

trussed′ joist′, any of various joists, as a bar joist, constructed in the form of a truss.

trus·sell (trus′əl), *n.* the upper of two dies for coining by hand. Cf. **pile⁵.** Also, **trus′sel.** [ME < MF *troussel,* equiv. to *trousse* bundle (see TRUSS) + *-el* < L *-ellus* dim. suffix]

truss′ hoop′, 1. a hoop placed around the staves of a barrel to secure them in place. 2. *Naut.* a metal band attaching a truss to its yard or to its mast. Also, **truss′-hoop′.**

truss·ing (trus′ing), *n.* 1. the members that form a truss. 2. a structure consisting of trusses. 3. trusses collectively. [TRUSS + -ING¹]

truss′ rod′, *Building Trades.* 1. a tie rod in a truss. 2. a diagonal iron or steel reinforcement in a wooden beam. 3. any iron or steel rod serving as a tension member.

Truss·ville (trus′vil), *n.* a town in central Alabama. 2510 (1960).

trust (trust), *n.* 1. reliance on the integrity, strength, ability, surety, etc., of a person or thing; confidence. 2. confident expectation of something; hope. 3. confidence in the certainty of future payment for property or goods received; credit: *to sell merchandise on trust.* 4. one on whom or that on which one relies: *God is my trust.* 5. the condition of one to whom something has been entrusted. 6. the obligation or responsibility imposed on one in whom confidence or authority is placed: *a position of trust.* 7. charge; custody; care: *to leave valuables in someone's trust.* 8. something committed or entrusted to one's care for use or safekeeping, as an office, duty, or the like; responsibility; charge. 9. *Law.* a fiduciary relationship in which one person (the trustee) holds the title to property (the trust estate or trust property) for the benefit of another (the beneficiary). 10. *Com.* a. an illegal combination of industrial or commercial companies in which the stock of the constituent companies is controlled by a central board of trustees, thus making it possible to manage the companies so as to minimize production costs, control prices, destroy competition, etc. b. any large industrial or commercial corporation or combination having a monopolistic or semimonopolistic control over the production of some commodity or service. 11. *Archaic.* reliability. 12. **in trust,** in the position of being left in the care or guard of another: *She left money to her uncle to keep in trust for her children.* —*adj.* 13. *Law.* of or pertaining to trusts or a trust. —*v.i.* 14. to rely upon or place confidence in someone or something (usually fol. by *in* or *to*): *to trust in another's honesty; trusting to luck.* 15. to have confidence; hope: *Things work out if one only trusts.* 16. to sell merchandise on credit. —*v.t.* 17. to have trust or confidence in; rely on. 18. to believe. 19. to expect confidently; hope (usually fol. by a clause or infinitive as object): *trusting the job would soon be finished; trusting to find oil on the land.* 20. to commit or consign with trust or confidence. 21. to permit to remain or go somewhere or to do something without fear of consequences: *She does not trust her children out of her sight.* 22. to invest with a trust; entrust with something. 23. to give credit to (a person) for goods, services, etc., supplied: *Will you trust us till payday?* 24. **trust to,** to rely on; trust: *Never trust to luck!* [ME < Scand; cf. Icel *traust* trust, c. G *Trost* comfort] —**trust′a·bil′i·ty,** *n.* —**trust′a·ble,** *adj.* —**trust′er,** *n.*

—**Syn.** 1. certainty, belief, faith. TRUST, ASSURANCE, CONFIDENCE imply a feeling of security. TRUST implies instinctive unquestioning belief in and reliance upon something: *to have trust in one's parents.* CONFIDENCE implies conscious trust because of good reasons, definite evidence, or past experience: *to have confidence in the outcome of events.* ASSURANCE implies absolute confidence and certainty: *to feel an assurance of victory.* 8. commitment, commission. 17. depend on. 18. credit. 20. entrust.

trust′ account′, 1. an account of property established with a trust company by a grantor, for distribution while he is still alive or after his death. 2. Also called **trustee′ account′.** *Banking U.S.* a savings account over which the depositor, as trustee, has sole control during his lifetime, after which any balance in the account becomes payable to the beneficiary.

trust′ bust′er, a federal official who seeks to dissolve business trusts, esp. through vigorous application of antitrust regulations.

trust′ com′pany, a company or corporation organized to exercise the functions of a trustee, but usually engaging also in other banking and financial activities.

trus·tee (tru stē′), *n., v.* **-teed, -tee·ing.** *Law.* —*n.* 1. a person, usually one of a body of persons, appointed to administer the affairs of a company, institution, etc. 2. a person who holds the title to property for the benefit of another. 3. (in New England) a garnishee. 4. a trusty. —*v.t.* 5. to place in the hands of a trustee or trustees. 6. (in New England) to garnish. [TRUST + -EE]

trustee′ in bank′ruptcy, *Law.* a person appointed by a court to administer the property of a bankrupt.

trustee′ proc′ess, *Law.* (in New England) garnishment (def. 2).

trus·tee·ship (tru stē′ship), *n.* 1. *Law.* the office or function of a trustee. 2. the administrative control of a territory granted to a country by a body (**Trustee′ship Coun′cil**) of the United Nations. 3. See **trust territory.** [TRUSTEE + -SHIP]

trust·ful (trust′fəl), *adj.* full of trust; free of distrust, suspicion, etc.; confiding: *a trustful friend.* [TRUST + -FUL] —**trust′ful·ly,** *adv.* —**trust′ful·ness,** *n.*

trust′ fund′, money, securities, property, etc., held in trust.

trust·ing (trus′ting), *adj.* that trusts; confiding; trustful: *a trusting child.* [TRUST + -ING²] —**trust′ing·ly,** *adv.* —**trust′ing·ness,** *n.*

trust·less (trust′lis), *adj.* 1. not worthy of trust; faithless; unreliable; false: *He was trustless when money was involved.* 2. distrustful; suspicious: *a doorman trustless of all strangers.* [TRUST + -LESS] —**trust′less·ly,** *adv.* —**trust′less·ness,** *n.*

trus·tor (trus′tər, tru stôr′), *n. Law.* a person who creates a trust. [TRUST + -OR²]

trust′ ter′ritory, a territory under the administrative control of a country designated by the United Nations.

trust·wor·thy (trust′wûr′thē), *adj.* deserving of trust or confidence; dependable; reliable: *The treasurer was not entirely trustworthy.* [TRUST + -WORTHY] —**trust′wor′thi·ly,** *adv.* —**trust′wor′thi·ness,** *n.*

—**Syn.** true, accurate, honest, faithful. See **reliable.**

trust·y (trus′tē), *adj.,* **trust·i·er, trust·i·est,** *n., pl.* **trust·ies.** —*adj.* 1. that may be trusted or relied on; trustworthy; reliable. 2. *Archaic.* trustful. —*n.* 3. a person who or that which is trusted. 4. a well-behaved and trustworthy convict to whom special privileges are granted. [TRUST + -Y¹] —**trust′i·ly,** *adv.* —**trust′i·ness,** *n.*

truth (tro͞oth), *n., pl.* **truths** (tro͞othz). 1. true or actual state of a matter: *He tried to find out the truth.* 2. conformity with fact or reality; verity: *the truth of a statement.* 3. a verified or indisputable fact, proposition, principle, or the like: *mathematical truths.* 4. state or character of being true. 5. actuality or actual existence. 6. (*often cap.*) ideal or fundamental reality apart from and transcending perceived experience: *the basic truths of life.* 7. agreement with a standard or original. 8. honesty; integrity; truthfulness. 9. an obvious or accepted fact; truism; platitude. 10. accuracy, as of position or adjustment. 11. *Archaic.* fidelity or constancy. 12. **in truth,** in reality; in fact; actually: *In truth, moral decay hastened the decline of the Roman Empire.* [ME *treuthe,* OE *trēowth* (c. Icel *tryggth* faith). See TRUE, -TH¹] —**truth′less,** *adj.* —**truth′less·ness,** *n.*

—**Syn.** 1. fact. 2. veracity. 8. sincerity, candor, frankness. 10. precision, exactness. —**Ant.** 1. falsehood. 2, 4, 8. falsity.

truth′ claim′, *Pragmatism.* a hypothesis not yet verified by experience.

truth·ful (tro͞oth′fəl), *adj.* 1. telling the truth, esp. habitually: *a truthful person.* 2. conforming to truth: *a truthful statement.* 3. corresponding with reality: *a truthful portrait.* [TRUTH + -FUL] —**truth′ful·ly,** *adv.* —**truth′ful·ness,** *n.*

truth-func·tion (tro͞oth′fungk′shən), *n. Logic.* a statement so constructed from other statements that its truth-value depends only on the truth-values of the other statements rather than on their meanings. —**truth′-func′tion·al,** *adj.* —**truth′-func′tion·al·ly,** *adv.*

truth′ or con′sequences, a game in which each contestant is asked a question and upon failure to answer or give a correct answer receives a penalty imposed by the leader or the group.

Truth′ or Con′sequences, a town in SW New Mexico. 4269 (1960).

truth′ se′rum, a drug, as the twilight-sleep-producing scopolamine, or esp. in intravenous solution, either of two barbiturates, amobarbital or thiopental, used in psychological investigation of a therapeutic or criminological nature. Also, **truth′ drug′.** Cf. **narcoanalysis.**

truth-val·ue (tro͞oth′val′yo͞o), *n. Logic.* (of a proposition) either the property of being true or the property of being false.

try (trī), *v.,* **tried, try·ing,** *n., pl.* **tries.** —*v.t.* 1. to attempt to do or accomplish: *Try it before you say it's simple.* 2. to test the effect or result of (often fol. by *out*): *to try a new method; to try out an idea.* 3. to endeavor to evaluate by experiment or experience: *to try a new field; to try a new book.* 4. to test the quality, value, fitness, accuracy, etc., of: *Will you try this spoonful and tell me what you think of it?* 5. to attempt to open (a door, window, etc.) in order to find out whether it is locked: *Try all the doors before leaving.* 6. *Law.* to examine and determine judicially, as a cause; determine judicially the guilt or innocence of (a person). 7. to put to a severe test; subject to strain, as of endurance, patience, affliction, trouble, etc.; tax: *to try one's patience.* 8. to melt down (fat, blubber, etc.) to obtain the oil; render (usually fol. by *out*). 9. *Archaic.* a. to determine the truth or right of (a quarrel or question) by test or battle (sometimes fol. by *out*). b. to find to be right by test or experience. 10. *Obs.* to extract by heat, as metal from ore; refine; purify. —*v.i.* 11. to make an attempt or effort; strive: *Try to complete the examination.* 12. *Naut.* to lie to in heavy weather under just sufficient sail to head into the wind. 13. **try it, that,** etc., **on,** *Chiefly Brit. Informal.* a. to put on airs: *She's been trying it on ever since the inheritance came through.* b. to be forward or presumptuous, esp. with a member of the opposite sex: *She avoided him after he'd tried it on with her.* 14. **try on,** to put on an article of clothing in order to judge its appearance and fit: *You can't really tell how it will look until you try it on.* 15. **try out,** to use experimentally; test. 16. **try out for,** to compete for (a position, membership, etc.): *Over a hundred boys came to try out for the football team.* 17. **try up,** *Carpentry.* to plane a shaving from a whole length of (a piece of wood). —*n.* 18. an attempt; an effort: *to have a try at something.* 19. *Rugby.* a score of three points earned by advancing the ball to or beyond the opponents' goal line. 20. **the old college try,** *Informal.* a sincere effort: *I gave it the old college try and finally landed a decent job.* [ME *trie(n)* to try (a legal case) < AF *trier,* equiv. to OF *trier* to sift, cull]

—**Syn.** 1, 11. TRY, ATTEMPT, ESSAY, ENDEAVOR, STRIVE imply putting forth effort toward a specific end. TRY is the verb in most general use, transitively and intransitively: *Try doing your best. Try with all you have.* ATTEMPT, a transitive verb, is more formal and often carries the idea of more effort: *He attempted to deceive me.* ESSAY, also transitive, is still more formal; it emphasizes an effort made in order to test: *to essay a task.* ENDEAVOR, usually intransitive, suggests resolve and continuous effort, esp. in the face of difficulties: *to endeavor to overcome obstacles.* STRIVE, intransitive, implies hard and earnest exertion to accomplish something difficult or laborious: *to strive mightily at a task.*

Try·gon (trī′gon), *n. Class. Myth.* the nurse of the infant Asclepius.

try′ hole′, *Metall.* (in a blast furnace) a hole at the top admitting a rod for finding the level of the stock.

try·ing (trī′ing), *adj.* extremely annoying, difficult, or the like; straining one's patience and good will to the limit: *a trying day; a trying experience.* [TRY + -ING²] —**try′ing·ly,** *adv.* —**try′ing·ness,** *n.*

try′ing plane′, *Carpentry.* a plane for trying up wood.

try·ma (trī′mə), *n., pl.* **-ma·ta** (-mə tə). *Bot.* a drupaceous nut having a fibrous or fleshy epicarp which is ultimately dehiscent, as in the walnut and hickory. [< NL < Gk, hole, equiv. to *trȳ(ein)* (to) rub down, wear away + *-ma* n. suffix marking result]

try·out (trī′out′), *n.* a trial or test to ascertain fitness for some purpose. [n. use of v. phrase *try out*]

tryp·a·fla·vine (trip′ə flā′vin, -vēn, trī′pə-), *n. Chem.* See **acriflavine hydrochloride.** [< Gk *trȳpa* hole + -FLAVIN(E)]

tryp′afla′vine neu′tral, *Chem.* acriflavine.

tryp·a·no·so·ma (trip′ə nə sō′mə, tri pan′ə-), *n., pl.* **-ma·ta** (-mə tə). trypanosome.

tryp·a·no·some (trip′ə nə sōm′, tri pan′ə-), *n.* any minute, flagellate protozoan of the genus *Trypanosoma,* parasitic in the blood or tissues of man and other vertebrates, usually transmitted by insects, often causing serious diseases, as African sleeping sickness in man, and many diseases in domestic animals. [< Gk *trȳpano-* (comb. form of *trȳpanon* borer) + -SOME³] —**tryp′a·no·so′mal, tryp·a·no·som·ic** (trip′ə nə som′ik), *adj.*

tryp·a·no·so·mi·a·sis (trip′ə nō sō mī′ə sis, tri pan′-ō-), *n. Pathol.* any infection caused by a trypanosome. [TRYPANOSOM(E) + -IASIS]

tryp·ars·am·ide (tri pär′sə mīd′, -mid), *n. Pharm.* a white, water-soluble, crystalline powder, $C_8H_{10}O_4N_2$-$AsNa \cdot \frac{1}{2}H_2O$, used chiefly in treating African sleeping sickness and syphilis of the central nervous system. [formerly a trademark]

tryp·sin (trip′sin), *n. Biochem.* a proteolytic enzyme of the pancreatic juice, capable of converting proteins into peptone. [for *tripsin < Gk *trips(is)* friction (*trīb(ein)* (to) rub + *-sis* -SIS) + -IN[2]; so called because first obtained by rubbing] —**tryp·tic** (trip′tik), *adj.*

tryp·sin·ize (trip′si nīz′), *v.t.*, **-ized, -iz·ing.** to cause trypsin to act upon. [TRYPSIN + -IZE]

tryp·to·phan (trip′tə fan′), *n. Biochem.* a colorless, crystalline, aromatic essential amino acid, (C_8H_6N)-$CH_2CH(NH_2)COOH$, occurring in the seeds of some leguminous plants, released from proteins by tryptic digestion, and important in the nutrition of animals. Also, **tryp·to·phane** (trip′tə fān′). [< *trypto-* (comb. form of Gk *triptós* rubbed) + -PHAN(E)]

try·sail (trī′sāl′; *Naut.* trī′səl), *n. Naut.* a triangular or quadrilateral sail having its luff hooped or otherwise bent to a mast, used for lying to or keeping a vessel headed into the wind; spencer. [TRY + SAIL]

try′sail mast′, *Naut.* a small auxiliary mast fastened just abaft the mainmast or foremast of a sailing vessel to enable the gaff of a fore-and-aft sail to be raised higher than the yard of a course on the foremast or mainmast or to permit the luff of such a sail to be hooped to the mast: used esp. on the mainmast of the snow or with spencers. Also called **snowmast, spencer mast.**

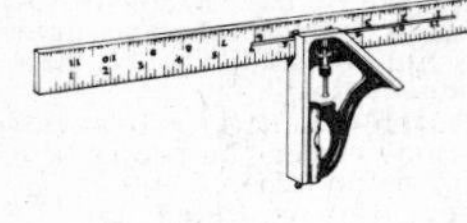

Try square

try′ square′, a device for testing the squareness of carpentry work or the like, or for laying out right angles, consisting of a pair of straightedges fixed at right angles to one another.

tryst (trist, trīst), *n.* **1.** an appointment to meet at a certain time and place, esp. one made somewhat secretly by lovers. **2.** an appointed meeting. **3.** an appointed place of meeting. —*v.t. Chiefly Scot.* **4.** to make an appointment or arrange a meeting with. —*v.i. Chiefly Scot.* **5.** to make an appointment or agreement. [ME *triste* set hunting-station < OF < Gmc; cf. Goth *trausti* agreement, arrangement, akin to ME *trist* confidence (OE **tryst*). See TROW[1], TRUST] —**tryst′er,** *n.*
—**Syn. 1, 2.** assignation. **1–3.** rendezvous.

tryst′ing place′, a place for a meeting, esp. a secret meeting of lovers; rendezvous.

TS, **1.** tool shed. **2.** top secret.

tsa·di (tsä′dē), *n.* sadhe.

Tsa·na (tsä′nä), *n.* **Lake.** See **Tana, Lake.**

tsar (zär, tsär), *n.* czar.

tsar·dom (zär′dəm, tsär′-), *n.* czardom.

tsar·e·vitch (zär′ə vich, tsär′-), *n.* czarevitch.

tsa·rev·na (zä rev′nə, tsä-), *n.* czarevna.

tsa·ri·na (zä rē′nə, tsä-), *n.* czarina.

tsar·ism (zär′iz əm, tsär′-), *n.* czarism.

tsar·ist (zär′ist, tsär′-), *adj., n.* czarist.

tsa·ris·tic (zä ris′tik, tsä-), *adj.* czarist.

Tsa·rit·syn (tsä rit′sin), *n.* former name of **Volgograd.**

tsa·rit·za (zä rit′sə, tsä-), *n.* czaritza.

Tschai·kov·sky (chī kôf′skē), *n.* **Peter Il·yich** (il′yich). See **Tchaikovsky, Peter Ilyich.** Also, **Tschai·kow′sky, Chaikovski.**

tscher·no·sem (*Russ.* cher′noz-yôm′), *n.* a soil common in cool or temperate semiarid climates, very black and rich in humus and carbonates. Also, **chernozem, tscher′no·zem′.** [< Russ: lit., black earth, equiv. to *cherno-*, for *cherny* black + *zem* earth]

Tsetse fly, *Glossina morsitans* (Length ¼ in.)

Tse·li·no·grad (tse′li no gräd), *n.* a city in N central Kazakhstan, in Asia. 276,000. Formerly, **Akmolinsk.**

tset′se fly′ (tset′sē, tset′-), any of several bloodsucking, African flies of the genus *Glossina* that act as a vector of sleeping sickness and other trypanosome infections of man and domestic animals. Also, **tzetze fly.** Also called **tset′se, tzetse.** [< Bantu (Bechuana)]

T.S.F., wireless telegraph. [< F *t(élégraphie) s(ans) f(il)*]

T.Sgt., Technical Sergeant.

T-shirt (tē′shûrt′), *n.* a lightweight, often knitted, pull-over shirt, close-fitting and with a round neckline and short sleeves, worn esp. as an undershirt by men and boys but also used as an outer garment for leisure and work by both sexes. Also, **tee-shirt.** [named from its shape]

Tshom·be (chom′bā), *n.* **Mo·ïse Ka·pen·da** (mō ēs′ kə pen′də), born 1919, African political leader in the Republic of the Congo.

tsi, tons per square inch.

T sill, *Carpentry.* a sill for a building frame, composed of a plate resting on a basement wall, supporting the studs on its outer half and having an outer joist or header running behind the studs as the outer edge of the floor.

Tsim·shi·an (chim′shē ən, tsim′-), *n., pl.* **-ans,** (*esp. collectively*) **-an.** a member of an American Indian people of the coastal region of British Columbia.

Tsi·nan (jē′nän′), *n.* a city in and the capital of Shantung, in NE China. 862,000 (est. 1957).

Tsing·hai (ching′hī′), *n.* Chinghai.

Tsing·tao (tsing′tou′; *Chin.* ching′dou′), *n.* a seaport in E Shantung, in E China. Municipal district, 1,121,000 (est. 1957). Cf. **Kiaochow.**

Tsing·yuan (ching′yyän′), *n.* a city in N Hopeh, in NE China. 197,000 (est. 1957). Formerly, **Paoting.**

Tsin·kiang (jin′gyäng′), *n.* a seaport in SE Fukien, in SE China, on Formosa Strait. 107,700 (1953). Formerly, **Chuanchow.**

Tsin·ling Shan (chin′ling′ shän′), a mountain range in central China: highest peak over 12,000 ft.

Tsiol·kov·sky (tsyôl kôf′skē), *n.* **1. Kon·stan·tin E·duar·do·vich** (kon stän tēn′ e dŏŏ är′do vich), 1857–1935, Russian inventor and rocket expert. **2.** a crater on the averted hemisphere or far side of the moon.

Tsi·ra·na·na (tsē rä′nä nä), *n.* **Phil·i·bert** (fil′ə-bərt), born 1912?, president of the Malagasy Republic since 1960.

Tsi·tsi·har (tsē′tsē′här′; *Chin.* chē′chē′här′), *n.* a city in NW Heilungkiang, in NE China. 668,000 (est. 1957). Also, **Chichihar, Chichihaerh, Tsi′tsi′haerh′.**

tsk (*pronounced as an alveolar click; spelling pron.* tisk), *interj.* **1.** (used as an exclamation of contempt, disdain, impatience, etc.) **2.** for shame! —*n.* **3.** an exclamation of "tsk." —*v.i.* **4.** to utter the exclamation "tsk." Also, **tsk′-tsk′.**

T square on drawing board

tsp., **1.** teaspoon. **2.** teaspoonful.

T square, a T-shaped ruler, used primarily in mechanical drawing, having a short crosspiece which slides along the edge of the drawing board as a guide to the perpendicular longer section in making parallel lines, right angles, etc. and as a support for triangles.

T′-stop sys′tem (tē′stop′), *Photog.* a system of stops calibrated by T numbers. Also called **transmission stop system.** Cf. **f-stop system.**

tsu·ba (tsŏŏ′bə; *Jap.* tsŏŏ bä′), *n., pl.* **-ba.** the metal plate, usually elliptical, serving as the guard of a Japanese sword or knife, having an opening for the tang of the blade, a blank area, or seppa dai, sometimes bearing the maker's signature, and sometimes one or two lateral openings, or riobitsus, for a kogai, a kozuka, or both. [< Jap]

Tsu·ga (sōō′gə, tsōō′-), *n.* the genus comprising the hemlock tress. [NL < Jap: larch]

tsu·na·mi (tsŏŏ nä′mē), *n.* an unusually large sea wave produced by a seaquake or undersea volcanic eruption. [< Jap: *tsu* harbor + *nami* wave] —**tsu·na·mic** (tsŏŏ nä′mik, -nam′ik), *adj.*

tsu·ru·gi (tsŏŏ rōō′gē; *Jap.* tsŏŏ rŏŏ′gē), *n.* ken[2].

Tsu·shi·ma (tsōō′shē mä′), *n.* two adjacent Japanese islands between Korea and Kyushu: Russian fleet defeated by Japanese fleet 1905. 66,206 (1963); 271 sq. mi.

Tsu′shima cur′rent, a warm ocean current flowing northward along the west coast of Japan.

Tsu′shima Strait′, a channel between the Tsushima islands and the East China Sea: sometimes considered part of the Korea Strait. ab. 60 mi. long; 40 mi. wide.

tsu′tsu·ga·mu′shi disease′ (tsōō′tsə gə mōō′shē, tsōō′-), *Pathol.* See **Japanese river fever.** [< Jap *tsutsugamushi* a name for the *mushi* (insect) that carries the disease]

Tswa·na (tswä′nə, sä′-), *n., pl.* **-nas,** (*esp. collectively*) **-na.** **1.** a member of a numerous Negro people of Bechuanaland and neighboring parts of South Africa, having an agricultural and pastoral economy. **2.** the language of the Tswana, a Bantu language.

TTS, Teletypesetter.

TTY, teletypewriter.

Tu, *Chem. Obs.* thulium.

Tu., Tuesday.

T.U., **1.** toxic unit. **2.** Trade Union. **3.** Training Unit. **4.** transmission unit.

t.u., trade union.

Tu·a·mo′tu Archipel′ago (tōō′ä mô′tōō), a group of French islands in the S Pacific. 5617 (1951); 332 sq. mi. Also called **Low Archipelago, Paumotu Archipelago.**

Tua·reg (twä′reg), *n.* **1.** a Berber or Hamitic-speaking member of the Moslem nomads of the Sahara. **2.** the language of the Tuaregs, an Afro-Asian language of the Berber subfamily. [< Berber *Twāreg*, pl. of *Tārgwi*]

Tuatara (Length to 2½ ft.)

tu·a·ta·ra (tōō′ə tä′rə), *n.* a nocturnal, lizardlike reptile, *Sphaenodon punctatum*, of islands near the coast of New Zealand: the only surviving rhynchocephalian. Also, **tu·a·te·ra** (tōō′ə tâ′rə). [< Maori < *tua* dorsal + *tara* spine]

Tu·a·tha De Da·nann (thōō′ə hə dā dä′nən), *Irish Legend.* a race of gods or demigods who defeated the Fomorians and ruled Ireland during a golden age. Also, **Tu′atha de Da′naan, Tu′atha De′.**

tub (tub), *n., v.,* **tubbed, tub·bing.** —*n.* **1.** a bathtub. **2.** a broad, round, open, wooden container, usually made of staves held together by hoops and fitted around a flat bottom. **3.** any of various containers resembling or suggesting a tub: *a tub for washing clothes.* **4.** the amount a tub will hold. **5.** *Offensive.* a short and fat person. **6.** *Naut.* **a.** a cylindrical band encircling a mast for securing a hoisting yard or forward end of a gaff so that it can slide. **b.** *Disparaging.* an old, slow, or clumsy vessel. **7.** *Brit. Informal.* a bath in a bathtub. **8.** *Mining.* an ore car; tram. —*v.t.* **9.** to place or keep in a tub. **10.** *Brit. Informal.* to bathe in a bathtub. —*v.i.* **11.** *Brit. Informal.* to bathe oneself in a bathtub. **12.** *Informal.* to undergo washing, esp. without damage, as a fabric: *This cotton print tubs well.* [ME *tubbe* < MFlem *tobbe*, c. LG *tubbe*] —**tub′-ba·ble,** *adj.* —**tub′ber,** *n.* —**tub′-like′,** *adj.*

Tuba (def. 1a)

tu·ba (tōō′bə, tyōō′-), *n., pl.* **-bas, -bae** (-bē). **1.** *Music.* **a.** a valved, brass wind instrument having a low range. **b.** an organ reed stop of large scale with tones of exceptional power. **c.** an ancient Roman trumpet. **2.** Also called **funnel cloud, pendant cloud, tornado cloud.** *Meteorol.* a rapidly whirling, funnel-shaped cloud form hanging from a cloud base, esp. that of a cumulonimbus or cumulus. Cf. **tornado** (def. 1), **waterspout** (def. 3). [< L: trumpet; akin to TUBE]

tub·al (tōō′bəl, tyōō′-), *adj. Anat.* pertaining to a tube, as a Fallopian tube. [TUBE + -AL[1]]

Tu·bal-cain (tōō′bəl kān′, tyōō′-), *n.* the son of Lamech and Zillah: the progenitor of metalworkers. Gen. 4:22. Also, **Tu′bal·cain′.**

tu·bate (tōō′bāt, tyōō′-), *adj.* having or forming a tube or tubes; tubular. [TUBE + -ATE[1]]

tub′ boat′, a canal boat for hauling freight, having a rectangular shape.

tub·by (tub′ē), *adj.,* **-bi·er, -bi·est.** **1.** short and fat: *a tubby child.* **2.** having a dull, thumping sound; without resonance. [TUB + -Y[1]] —**tub′bi·ness,** *n.*

tub′ chair′, *English Furniture.* an easy chair having a semicircular back and, with the wings or arms, forming a single upholstered piece.

tube (tōōb, tyōōb), *n., v.,* **tubed, tub·ing.** —*n.* **1.** a hollow, usually cylindrical body of metal, glass, rubber, or other material, used esp. for conveying or containing liquids or gases. **2.** a small, collapsible, cylinder of metal or plastic sealed at one end and having a capped opening at the other from which paint, toothpaste, or some other semifluid substance may be squeezed. **3.** *Anat., Zool.* any hollow, cylindrical vessel or organ: *the bronchial tubes.* **4.** *Bot.* **a.** any hollow, elongated body or part. **b.** the united lower portion of a gamopetalous corolla or a gamosepalous calyx. **5.** the tubular tunnel in which an underground railroad runs. **6.** *Informal.* the railroad itself. **7.** See **inner tube.** **8.** *Electronics.* See **vacuum tube.** **9.** *Archaic.* a telescope. —*v.t.* **10.** to furnish with a tube or tubes. **11.** to convey or enclose in a tube. **12.** to form into the shape of a tube; make tubular. [< L *tub(us)* pipe] —**tube′less,** *adj.* —**tube′like′,** *adj.*

tube-eye (tōōb′ī′, tyōōb′ī′), *n., pl.* **-eyes.** a pelagic fish, *Stylephorus chordatus*, related to the ribbonfishes, having vertically tubular eyes.

tube′ foot′, one of numerous small, tubular processes on the body surface of most echinoderms, used for locomotion and grasping.

tube′less tire′, a rubber balloon tire made as a single piece without an inner tube.

tube·nose (tōōb′nōz′, tyōōb′-), *n.* tubesnout. [TUBE + NOSE]

tube′ of force′, *Elect., Magnetism.* a tubular space bounded by lines of force or induction.

tu·ber[1] (tōō′bər, tyōō′-), *n.* **1.** *Bot.* a fleshy, usually oblong or rounded thickening or outgrowth, as the potato, of a subterranean stem or shoot, bearing minute scalelike leaves with buds or eyes in their axils from which new plants may arise. **2.** *Anat.* a rounded swelling or protuberance; a tuberosity; a tubercle. [< L: bump, swelling. See TRUFFLE] —**tu′ber·less,** *adj.* —**tu′ber·oid′,** *adj.*

tu·ber[2] (tōō′bər, tyōō′-), *n.* one who or that which forms, installs, or operates with tubes. [TUBE + -ER[1]]

tube′ rail′way, *Chiefly Brit.* an underground electric railway.

tu·ber·cle (tōō′bər kəl, tyōō′-), *n.* **1.** a small rounded projection or excrescence, as on a bone, on the surface of the body in various animals, or on a plant. **2.** *Pathol.* **a.** a small, firm, rounded nodule or swelling. **b.** such a swelling as the characteristic lesion of tuberculosis. [< L *tūberculum.* See TUBER[1], -CLE]

Tubercle bacillus
A, Bacillus
B, Blood cell

tu′bercle bacil′lus, the bacterium, *Mycobacterium tuberculosis*, causing tuberculosis.

tubercul-, var. of **tuberculo-** before a vowel: *tuberculin.*

tu·ber·cu·lar (tŏŏ bûr′kyə lər, tyŏŏ-), *adj.* **1.** pertaining to tuberculosis; tuberculous. **2.** of, pertaining to, or of the nature of a tubercle or tubercles. **3.** characterized by or having tubercles. —*n.* **4.** a tuberculous person. [< L *tūbercul(um)* TUBERCLE + -AR[1]] —**tu·ber′cu·lar·ly,** *adv.*

tu·ber·cu·lar·ise (tŏŏ bûr′kyə lə rīz′, tyŏŏ-), *v.t., v.i.,* **-ised, -is·ing.** *Chiefly Brit.* tubercularize. —**tu·ber′cu·lar·i·sa′tion,** *n.*

tu·ber·cu·lar·ize (tŏŏ bûr′kyə lə rīz′, tyŏŏ-), *v.,* **-ized, -iz·ing.** —*v.i.* **1.** to form tubercles. **2.** to become affected with tuberculosis. —*v.t.* **3.** to cause to have tubercles. **4.** to cause to have tuberculosis. **5.** to inoculate with tuberculin; tuberculinize. Also, **tuberculize;** *esp. Brit.,* **tubercularise, tuberculise.** [TUBERCULAR + -IZE] —**tu·ber′cu·lar·i·za′tion,** *n.*

tu·ber·cu·late (tŏŏ bûr′kyə lit, -lāt′, tyŏŏ-), *adj.* **1.** Also, **tu·ber′cu·lat′ed, tuberculose.** having tubercles. **2.** tubercular. [< NL *tuberculātus*, equiv. to *tūbercul(um)* TUBERCLE + *-ātus* -ATE[1]] —**tu·ber′cu·la′tion,** *n.*

tu·ber·cule (tōō′bər kyōōl′, tyōō′-), *n. Bot.* a nodule, esp. on the roots of certain legumes. [< L *tūberculum.* See TUBER[1], -CULE]

tu·ber·cu·lin (tŏŏ bûr′kyə lin, tyŏŏ-), *n. Med.* a sterile liquid prepared from cultures of the tubercle bacillus, used in the diagnosis and treatment of tuberculosis. [TUBERCUL- + -IN[2]]

tu·ber·cu·lin·ise (tŏŏ bûr′kyə lə nīz′, tyŏŏ-), *v.t., v.i.,* **-ised, -is·ing.** *Chiefly Brit.* tuberculinize. —**tu·ber′cu·lin·i·sa′tion,** *n.*

tu·ber·cu·lin·ize (tŏŏ bûr′kyə lə nīz′, tyŏŏ-), *v.,* **-ized, -iz·ing.** —*v.t.* **1.** to inoculate with tuberculin. **2.** to cause to form tubercles. —*v.i.* **3.** to form tubercles. [TUBERCULIN + -IZE] —**tu·ber′cu·lin·i·za′tion, tu·ber′cu·li·na′tion,** *n.*

tuber′culin test′, a test for tuberculosis in which a hypersensitive reaction to a given quantity of tuberculin indicates a past or present tubercular condition.

tu·ber·cu·lise (tŏŏ bûr′kyə līz′, tyŏŏ-), *v.t., v.i.,* **-lised, -lis·ing.** *Chiefly Brit.* tuberculize. —**tu·ber′cu·li·sa′tion,** *n.*

tu·ber·cu·lize (tŏŏ bûr′kyə līz′, tyŏŏ-), *v.t., v.i.,* **-lized, -liz·ing.** tubercularize. [TUBERCUL- + -IZE] —**tu·ber′cu·li·za′tion,** *n.*

tuberculo-, a combining form representing **tubercle:** *tuberculosis.* Also, *esp. before a vowel,* **tubercul-.** [< L *tūbercul(um)* tubercle + -o-]

tu·ber·cu·lo·cele (tŏŏ bûr′kyə lō sēl′, tyŏŏ-), *n. Pathol.* tuberculosis of the testis. [TUBERCULO- + -CELE]

tu·ber·cu·loid (to͝o bûr′kyə loid′, tyo͞o-), *adj.* **1.** resembling a tubercle. **2.** resembling tuberculosis. [TUBERCUL- + -OID]

tu·ber·cu·lo·ma (to͝o bûr′kyə lō′mə, tyo͞o-), *n., pl.* **-mas, -ma·ta** (-mə tə). *Pathol.* a tubercle of a caseous, or cheeselike, nature. [< NL; See TUBERCUL-, -OMA]

tu·ber·cu·lose (to͝o bûr′kyə lōs′, tyo͞o-), *adj.* tuberculate. [< NL *tuberculosus;* see TUBERCUL-, -OSE[1]]

tu·ber·cu·lo·sis (to͝o bûr′kyə lō′sis, tyo͞o-), *n. Pathol.* **1.** an infectious disease that may affect almost any tissue of the body, esp. the lungs, caused by the organism *Mycobacterium tuberculosis,* and characterized by tubercles. **2.** this disease when affecting the lungs; pulmonary phthisis; consumption. Also called **TB.** [< NL; see TUBERCUL-, -OSIS]

tu·ber·cu·lous (to͝o bûr′kyə ləs, tyo͞o-), *adj.* **1.** tubercular. **2.** affected with tuberculosis: *a hospital for tuberculous people.* [TUBERCUL- + -OUS] —**tu·ber′cu·lous·ly,** *adv.*

tu·ber·cu·lum (to͝o bûr′kyə ləm, tyo͞o-), *n., pl.* **-la** (-lə). a tubercle. [< NL]

tu′ber fern′, a tropical, erect fern, *Nephrolepis cordifolia,* having sharply toothed and numerously segmented fronds.

tube·rose[1] (to͞ob′rōz′, tyo͞ob′-, to͞o′bə rōz′, tyo͞o′-), *n.* a bulbous, amaryllidaceous plant, *Polianthes tuberosa,* cultivated for its spike of fragrant, creamy-white, lily-like flowers. [< L *tūberōsa,* fem. of *tūberōsus* TUBEROSE[2]]

tu·ber·ose[2] (to͞o′bə rōs′, tyo͞o′-), *adj.* tuberous. [< L *tūberōsus* knobby. See TUBER, -OSE[1]]

tu·ber·os·i·ty (to͞o′bə ros′i tē, tyo͞o′-), *n., pl.* **-ties.** a rough projection or protuberance of a bone, as for the attachment of a muscle. [< L *tūberōsitās.* See TUBEROSE[2], -ITY]

tu·ber·ous (to͞o′bər əs, tyo͞o′-), *adj.* **1.** characterized by the presence of rounded or wartlike prominences or tubers. **2.** of the nature of such a prominence. **3.** *Bot.* bearing tubers. **4.** having the nature of or resembling a tuber. Also, **tuberose.** [< L *tūberōsus* knobby. See TUBER[1], -OUS]

tu′berous root′, a true root so thickened as to resemble a tuber, but bearing no buds or eyes. —**tu′ber·ous-root′ed,** *adj.*

tube·snout (to͞ob′snout′, tyo͞ob′-), *n.* a slender, marine fish, *Aulorhynchus flavidus,* found along the coast from southern California to Alaska, having a long, tubelike snout. Also called **tubenose.** [TUBE + SNOUT]

tubi-, a combining form representing **tube:** *tubiform.* [< L *tub(us)* + -I-]

tu·bi·form (to͞o′bə fôrm′, tyo͞o′-), *adj.* shaped like a tube. [TUBI- + -FORM]

tub·ing (to͞o′bing, tyo͞o′-), *n.* **1.** material in the form of a tube: *glass tubing.* **2.** tubes collectively. **3.** a piece of tube: *two feet of copper tubing.* [TUBE + -ING[1]]

Tu Bi·she·bat (to͞o′ bē shə bät′), *Judaism.* the 15th day of the month of Shebat, observed in Israel by planting trees and outside of Israel chiefly by eating Israeli fruits and contributing money for planting trees in Israel. Also, **Tu Bi·she·vat** (to͞o′ bē shə vät′, -shvät′). Also called **Hamishah Asar Bishebat.** [< NHeb: fifteen + Heb *bi* in + *shebat* fifth month]

tub·man (tub′mən), *n., pl.* **-men.** *Old Eng. Law.* a barrister in the Court of Exchequer who had precedence in motions over every other barrister except the postman. Cf. **postman**[2]. [TUB + MAN]

Tub·man (tub′mən), *n.* **William Va·can·a·rat Shad·rach** (və kan′ə rat′), born 1895, president of Liberia since 1944.

tu·boid (to͞o′boid, tyo͞o′-), *adj.* having or approximating a tubular form. [TUB(I)- + -OID]

tu·bu·lar (to͞o′byə lər, tyo͞o′-), *adj.* **1.** of or pertaining to a tube or tubes. **2.** characterized by or consisting of tubes. **3.** having the form or shape of a tube; tubiform. **4.** *Physiol., Pathol.* noting a respiratory sound resembling that produced by a current of air passing through a tube. [< NL *tubulāris;* see TUBULE, -AR[1]] —**tu′bu·lar′i·ty,** *n.* —**tu′bu·lar·ly,** *adv.*

tu′bular skate′, a type of ice skate consisting of a steel blade set into an aluminum tube and connected to the shoe by tubular supports, used for both hockey and racing skates. Cf. **hockey skate, racing skate.**

tu·bu·late (*adj.* to͞o′byə lit, -lāt′, tyo͞o′-; *v.* to͞o′byə-lāt′, tyo͞o′-), *adj., v.,* **-lat·ed, -lat·ing.** —*adj.* **1.** Also, **tu′bu·lat′ed.** shaped like or having a tube. —*v.t.* **2.** to form into or furnish with a tube. [< L *tubulātus;* see TUBULE, -ATE[1]] —**tu′bu·la′tion,** *n.* —**tu′bu·la′tor,** *n.*

tu·bule (to͞o′byo͞ol, tyo͞o′-), *n.* a small tube; a minute tubular structure. [< L *tubulus,* equiv. to *tub(us)* pipe + *-ulus* -ULE]

tubuli-, a combining form of **tubule** or **tubular:** *tubuliflorous.* [TUBULE + -I-]

Tu·bu·li·den·ta·ta (to͞o′byə li den tā′tə, -tä′-, tyo͞o′-), *n.* the order comprising the aardvarks. [< NL; see TUBULI-, DENTATE]

tu·bu·li·flo·rous (to͞o′byə lə flôr′əs, -flōr′-, tyo͞o′-), *adj. Bot.* having the corolla tubular in all the perfect flowers of a head, as certain composite plants. [TUBULI- + -FLOROUS]

tu·bu·lous (to͞o′byə ləs, tyo͞o′-), *adj.* **1.** containing or consisting of tubes. **2.** having the form of a tube; tubular. **3.** *Bot.* having tubular flowers. [< NL *tubulōsus.* See TUBULE, -OUS] —**tu′bu·lous·ly,** *adv.*

tu·bu·lure (to͞o′byə lər, tyo͞o′-), *n.* a short tubular opening, as in a glass jar or at the top of a retort. [< F; see TUBULE, -URE]

tu·bu·phone (to͞o′byə fōn′, tyo͞o′-), *n.* an instrument resembling a glockenspiel but with metal tubes instead of bars. [< L *tubu(s)* TUBE + -PHONE]

tub′ wheel′, a vertical water turbine turned by the fall of water on vanes mounted spirally on a central barrel.

T.U.C., *Brit.* Trades Union Congress.

Tu·can·a (to͞o kan′ə, -kä′nə, -kā′-, tyo͞o-), *n., gen.* **-can·ae** (-kan′ē, -kä′nē, -kā′-). *Astron.* the Toucan, a southern constellation between Octans and Phoenix. [< NL]

tu·chun (do͞o′jyn′), *n. Chinese Hist.* the title of a military governor of a province during the period 1916–25; a war lord. [< Chin: lit., overseer of troops]

tuck[1] (tuk), *v.t.* **1.** to put into a small, close, or concealing place: *Tuck the money into your wallet.* **2.** to thrust in the loose end or edge of (a garment, covering, etc.) so as to hold closely in place (usually fol. by *in, up, under,* etc.): *Tuck in your blouse. Tuck the edge of the sheet under the mattress.* **3.** to cover snugly in or as in this manner: *She tucked the children into bed.* **4.** to pull up into a fold or folds; draw up into a folded arrangement (usually fol. by *in, up,* etc.): *to tuck up one's skirts; to tuck one's knees under one's chin.* **5.** *Needlework.* to sew tucks in. **6.** to pass (a strand) above or below another one. **7.** *Slang.* to eat or drink (usually fol. by *in, away,* etc.): *He tucked away a big meal.* —*v.i.* **8.** to draw together; contract; pucker. **9.** *Needlework.* to make tucks. —*n.* **10.** something tucked or folded in. **11.** *Sewing.* a fold, or one of a series of folds, made by doubling cloth upon itself and stitching parallel with the edge of the fold, used for decoration or for shortening or fitting a garment. **12.** *Sports.* **a.** (in fancy diving) a dive in which the diver bends his knees and pulls his thighs close to the chest. **b.** (in tumbling) the drawing of the knees close to the chest. Cf. **layout** (def. 10b), **pike**[7]. **13.** *Naut.* **a.** the part of a vessel where the after ends of the outside planking or plating unite at the sternpost. **b.** the operation of placing one of the unlaid strands of a rope between other such strands, as in splicing. **14.** (in tying knots) the operation of passing one strand above or below another. **15.** *Brit. Slang.* food. [ME *t(o)uke(n)* to stretch (cloth), torment, OE *tūcian* to torment; akin to MLG *tucken* to tug, G *zucken* to jerk. See TOW[1]]

tuck[2] (tuk), *n. Archaic.* a rapier or estoc. [earlier *tocke,* appar. sandhi var. of obs. *stock* sword < It *stocco* < G *Stock* stick, c. STOCK]

tuck[3] (tuk), *n. Chiefly Scot.* a drumbeat or the sound of one beat on a drum. [ME *tukke* to beat, sound (said of a drum) < MF (north.) *toker* to strike, touch. See TOUCH]

Tuck (tuk), *n.* **Friar.** See **Friar Tuck.**

tuck·a·hoe (tuk′ə hō′), *n.* **1.** Also called **Indian bread.** the edible, underground sclerotium of the fungus *Poria cocos,* found on the roots of trees in the southern United States. **2.** (*usually cap.*) a Virginian, esp. one inhabiting the lowland E of the Blue Ridge. [< Algonquian (Va. dial.) *tockawhoughe* it is globular]

Tuck·a·hoe (tuk′ə hō′), *n.* a town in SE New York. 6423 (1960).

tuck′a·way ta′ble (tuk′ə wā′), a table having a support folding into one plane and a tilting or drop-leaf top.

tuck′ box′, *Brit.* a box containing fruit, candy, etc., as a gift from home to a schoolboy.

tuck·er[1] (tuk′ər), *n.* **1.** a person who or that which tucks. **2.** a piece of linen, muslin, or the like, worn by women about the neck and shoulders. **3.** chemisette. **4.** *Australian.* food. [ME *tokere.* See TUCK[1], -ER[1]]

tuck·er[2] (tuk′ər), *v.t. U.S. Informal.* to weary; tire; exhaust (often fol. by *out*): *The game tuckered him out.* [TUCK[1] + -ER[6]]

Tuck·er (tuk′ər), *n.* **1. Richard,** born 1915, U.S. opera singer. **2. Sophie** (*Sophie Abruza*), 1884–1966, U.S. actress, born in Russia.

tuck·er-bag (tuk′ər bag′), *n. Australian.* any bag used to carry food, esp. by travelers and ranch hands in the bush.

tuck·er-box (tuk′ər boks′), *n. Australian.* any box used to store or carry food, esp. by travelers and ranch hands in the bush.

tuck·et (tuk′it), *n.* a trumpet fanfare. [TUCK[3] + -ET]

tuck-point (tuk′point′), *v.t.* to finish (masonry) with tuck pointing.

tuck′ point′ing, *Masonry.* pointing which has an ornamental fillet of putty, lime, or chalk projecting from the mortar joint. Also called **tuck′ and pat′ point′ing.** —**tuck′-point′er,** *n.*

tuck-shop (tuk′shop′), *n. Brit. Slang.* a shop where food is sold, esp. pastry, candy, or the like.

tu·co-tu·co (to͞o′kō to͞o′kō), *n., pl.* **-cos.** any of several burrowing rodents of the genus *Ctenomys,* of South America. [< AmerSp *tucotuco,* imit. of its cry]

Tuc·son (to͞o′son, to͞o son′), *n.* a city in S Arizona: health resort. 212,892 (1960).

Tu·cu·mán (to͞o′ko͞o män′), *n.* a city in NW Argentina. 287,004 (1960).

Tu·cum·car·i (to͞o′kəm kâr′ē), *n.* a town in E New Mexico. 8143 (1960).

-tude, a suffix appearing in abstract nouns (generally formed from Latin adjectives or participles) of Latin origin (*latitude; altitude*); on this model, used in the formation of new nouns: *platitude.* [< L *-tūdo,* whence also F *-tude*]

Tu·dor (to͞o′dər, tyo͞o′-), *adj.* **1.** pertaining or belonging to the English royal house of Tudor. **2.** of, pertaining to, or characteristic of the periods of the reigns of the Tudor sovereigns: *Tudor architecture.* —*n.* **3.** a member of the royal family which ruled in England from 1485 to 1603. **4. Antony,** born 1909, English choreographer and dancer.

Tu′dor arch′, a four-centered arch, the inner pair of curves having a radius much greater than that of the outer pair. See illus. under **arch.**

tu·e·bor (to͞o ē′bôr; *Eng.* to͞o ē′bôr, tyo͞o-), *v. Latin.* I will defend: motto on the coat of arms of Michigan.

Tues., Tuesday.

Tues·day (to͞oz′dē, -dā, tyo͞oz′-), *n.* the third day of the week, following Monday. [ME *tewesday,* OE *tīwesdæg* (c. OHG *ziestac,* Icel *tȳsdagr,* etc.), orig. phrase *Tīwes daeg* Tiw's day, translating L *diēs Martis* day of Mars. See TIW, DAY]

Tues·days (to͞oz′dēz, -dāz, tyo͞oz′-), *adv.* on Tuesdays.

tu·fa (to͞o′fə, tyo͞o′-), *n. Geol.* **1.** Also, **toph, tophe.** Also called **calcareous tufa, calc-tufa, calc-tuff.** a porous limestone formed from calcium carbonate deposited by springs or the like. Cf. **travertine. 2.** (not in technical use) tuff. [< It *tufo* < L *tōfus*] —**tu·fa·ceous** (to͞o fā′shəs, tyo͞o-), *adj.*

tuff[1] (tuf), *adj. Slang.* remarkably excellent; first-rate; great.

tuff[2] (tuf), *n. Geol.* a fragmental rock consisting of the smaller kinds of volcanic detritus, usually more or less stratified. Also called **volcanic tuff.** [< F *tuf* < It *tufo.* See TUFA] —**tuff·a·ceous** (tuf ā′shəs), *adj.*

tuft (tuft), *n.* **1.** a bunch or cluster of small, usually soft and flexible parts, as feathers, hairs, etc., attached or fixed closely together at the base and loose at the upper ends. **2.** a small clump of bushes, trees, etc. **3.** a cluster of short-stalked flowers, leaves, etc., growing from a common point. **4.** a cluster of cut threads, used as a decorative finish attached to the tying or holding threads of mattresses, quilts, upholstery, etc. **5.** a covered or finished button designed for similar use. **6.** a cluster of short, fluffy threads, used to decorate cloth, as for a bedspread, robe, bath mat, window curtain, etc. **7.** a gold tassel on the cap formerly worn at English universities by titled undergraduates. **8.** a titled undergraduate at an English university. —*v.t.* **9.** to furnish or decorate with a tuft or tufts. **10.** to arrange in a tuft or tufts. **11.** *Upholstery.* to draw together (a cushion or the like) by passing a thread through at regular intervals, the depressions thus produced being usually ornamented with tufts or buttons. —*v.i.* **12.** to form into or grow in a tuft or tufts. [ME, var. of *toft(e)* < MF *tofe* (< Frankish *tupfa* TOP[1]) + inorganic *-t*] —**tuft′er,** *n.*

tuft·ed (tuf′tid), *adj.* **1.** furnished or decorated with tufts. **2.** formed into or growing in a tuft or tufts. [TUFT + -ED[3]]

tuft′ed duck′, an Old World, wild duck, *Aythya fuligula,* having a tufted head.

tuft′ed tit′mouse, a gray titmouse, *Parus bicolor,* of the eastern and midwestern U.S., having a crested head. See illus. under **titmouse.**

tuft·hunt·er (tuft′hun′tər), *n.* **1.** (at Oxford or Cambridge Universities) a person who seeks the acquaintance of titled undergraduates. **2.** any toady; sycophant. [TUFT (defs. 7, 8) + HUNTER] —**tuft′hunt′ing,** *adj., n.*

tuft·ing (tuf′ting), *n.* **1.** the act or process of making tufts. **2.** tufts collectively, esp. as decoration. [TUFT + -ING[1]]

tuft′ tree′, ti[2].

tuft·y (tuf′tē), *adj.,* **tuft·i·er, tuft·i·est. 1.** abounding in tufts. **2.** covered or adorned with tufts. **3.** growing in or forming tufts. [TUFT + -Y[1]] —**tuft′i·ly,** *adv.*

Tu Fu (do͞o′ fo͞o′), A.D. 712–770, Chinese poet.

tug (tug), *v.,* **tugged, tug·ging,** *n.* —*v.t.* **1.** to pull at with force, vigor, or effort. **2.** to move by pulling forcibly; drag; haul. **3.** to tow (a vessel) by means of a tugboat. —*v.i.* **4.** to pull with force or effort: *to tug at a stuck drawer.* **5.** to strive hard; labor; toil. —*n.* **6.** act or instance of tugging; pull; haul. **7.** a strenuous contest between opposing forces, groups, or persons; struggle: *the tug of young minds in a seminar.* **8.** tugboat. **9.** that by which something is tugged, as a rope, chain, etc. **10.** (on a harness) **a.** trace[2] (def. 1). **b.** any of various supporting or pulling parts. [ME *toggen,* akin to OE *togian* to TOW[1]] —**tug′ger,** *n.* —**tug′less,** *adj.*

tug·boat (tug′bōt′), *n.* a small, powerful boat for towing or pushing ships, barges, etc. [TUG + BOAT]

tug′ of war′, 1. an athletic contest between two teams at opposite ends of a rope, each team trying to drag the other over a line. **2.** a hard-fought, critical struggle for supremacy.

tu·i (to͞o′ē), *n.* a black, New Zealand honey-eater, *Prosthemadera novae-zealandiae,* having a patch of white feathers on each side of the throat. Also called **parson bird.** [< Maori]

Tui·ler·ies (twē′lə rēz; *Fr.* twēlᵊ rē′), *n.* a former royal palace in Paris: begun by Catherine de Médicis in 1564; burned by supporters of the Commune in 1871. The gardens that formed part of the palace grounds remain as a public park (**Tui′leries Gar′dens**).

tuille (twēl), *n.* (loosely) a tasset. [late ME *toile* < MF *tuille,* var. of *teuille* < L *tēgula* TILE]

Tu·i·nal (to͞o′i nôl′), *n. Pharm., Trademark.* a combination of amobarbital and secobarbital used as a prompt and sustained sedative and hypnotic.

tu·i·tion (to͞o ish′ən, tyo͞o-), *n.* **1.** the charge or fee for instruction: *The college will raise its tuition again next year.* **2.** teaching or instruction, as of pupils: *a school offering private tuition in languages.* **3.** *Archaic.* guardianship or custody. [late ME *tuicion* a looking after, guarding < L *tuitiōn-* (s. of *tuitiō*), equiv. to *tuit(us)* watched over (ptp. of *tuērī*) + *-iōn-* -ION] —**tu·i′tion·al, tu·i·tion·ar·y** (to͞o ish′ə ner′ē, tyo͞o-), *adj.* —**tu·i′tion·less,** *adj.*

Tu·la (to͞o′lä, -lə), *n.* **1.** a city in the W RSFSR, in the central Soviet Union in Europe, S of Moscow. 360,000 (est. 1964). **2.** a girl's given name.

tu·la·di (to͞o′lə dē), *n., pl.* (*esp. collectively*) **-di,** (*esp. referring to two or more kinds or species*) **-dis.** *Canadian.* See **lake trout.** [< CanF *touladi* < dial. Cree]

Tu·lar·e (to͞o lâr′ē, to͞o lâr′), *n.* a city in central California. 13,824 (1960).

tu·la·re·mi·a (to͞o′lə rē′mē ə), *n. Pathol., Vet. Pathol.* a disease of rabbits, squirrels, etc., caused by a bacterium, *Pasteurella tularensis* (or *Bacterium tularense*), transmitted to man by insects or by the handling of infected animals, resembling the plague and taking the form in man of an irregular fever lasting several weeks. Also, **tu′la·rae′mi·a.** Also called **deer fly fever, Pahvant Valley plague, rabbit fever.** [*Tulare,* California county where first found + -EMIA] —**tu′la·re′mic, tu′la·rae′mic,** *adj.*

Tu·la·ro·sa (to͞o′lə rō′sə), *n.* a town in S New Mexico. 3200 (1960).

tu·le (to͞o′lē; *Sp.* to͞o′le), *n., pl.* **-les** (-lēz; *Sp.* -les). either of two large bulrushes, *Scirpus lacustris* or *S. californicus,* found in California and adjacent regions in inundated lands and marshes. [< Sp < Nahuatl *tullin*]

Tu·lé·ar (*Fr.* ty lā ar′), *n.* a city in SW Madagascar. 33,850 (1960).

tu′le perch′. See under **perch**[2] (def. 3).

Tu·lia (to͞ol′yə), *n.* a town in NW Texas. 4410 (1960).

tu·lip (to͞o′lip, tyo͞o′-), *n.* **1.** any liliaceous plant of the genus *Tulipa,* cultivated in many varieties, and having large, showy, usually erect, cup-shaped or bell-shaped flowers of various colors. **2.** a flower or bulb of such a plant. [earlier *tulipa* < NL, appar. back formation from It *tulipano* (taken as adj.) < Turk *tülbend* turban (from a fancied likeness); see TURBAN] —**tu′lip·like′,** *adj.*

tu·lip·o·ma·ni·a (to͞o′li pə mā′nē ə, -mān′yə, tyo͞o′-), *n.* a mania for planting and growing tulips, esp. such a mania widespread in Holland in the 1630's. [TULIP + -O- + -MANIA] —**tu′lip·o·ma′ni·ac′,** *n.*

tu′lip or′chid, a tropical American plant, *Cattleya citrina,* having solitary, tuliplike, white-edged, yellow flowers, growing in trees.

tu′lip pop′py, an annual herb, *Papaver glaucum,* of Syria and Iran, having bluish-green stem leaves and scarlet, cup-shaped flowers.

tu′lip tree′, a North American, magnoliaceous tree, *Liriodendron Tulipifera,* having tuliplike flowers and yielding a wood used in making furniture: the State tree of Indiana, Kentucky, and Tennessee. Also called **tu′lip pop′lar.**

tu·lip·wood (to͞o′lip wo͝od′, tyo͞o′-), *n.* **1.** the wood of the tulip tree. **2.** any of various striped or variegated woods of other trees. **3.** any of these trees. [TULIP + WOOD[1]]

tulle (to͞ol; *Fr.* tyl), *n.* a thin, fine net of acetate, nylon, rayon, or silk, for millinery, dresses, etc. [< F, named after TULLE, France, where first made]

Tulle (to͞ol; *Fr.* tyl), *n.* a city in and the capital of Corrèze, in S central France. 20,790 (1962).

Tul·li·a (tul′ē ə), *n.* **1.** *Rom. Legend.* the wife of Tarquin and the daughter of Servius Tullius, whom she helped to assassinate. **2.** a girl's given name.

tul·li·bee (tul′ə bē′), *n.* a deep-bodied, Canadian cisco, *Coregonus artedi tullibee.* [< CanF *toulibi* < Algonquian (Ojibwa or Cree) *otonabi* mouth water, equiv. to *oton* its mouth + *abi* water, liquid]

Tul·li·us (tul′ē əs), *n.* **Servius.** See **Servius Tullius.**

Tul·ly (tul′ē), *n.* See **Cicero, Marcus Tullius.**

Tul·sa (tul′sə), *n.* a city in NE Oklahoma: center of a rich oil-producing region. 261,685 (1960). —**Tul′san,** *n.*

Tu·luá (to͞ol wä′), *n.* a city in W Colombia. 151,370 (est. 1964).

tul·war (tul′wär, tul wär′), *n.* any of several Indian sabers. [< Hindi *talwār, tarwār* < Skt *taravāri*]

tum (tum), *v.t.,* **tummed, tum·ming.** to tease (wool) in the preliminary carding operation, or to open out the fibers prior to carding. [?]

Tu·ma·co (to͞o mä′kō), *n.* a seaport in SW Colombia. 12,692 (1961).

Tum·bes (to͞om′bes), *n.* a seaport in NW Peru. 10,046 (est. 1957).

tum·ble (tum′bəl), *v.,* **-bled, -bling,** *n.* —*v.i.* **1.** to fall helplessly down, end over end, as by losing one's footing, support, or equilibrium; plunge headlong: *to tumble down the stairs.* **2.** to roll end over end, as in falling: *The stones tumbled down the hill.* **3.** to fall or decline rapidly; drop: *Prices on the stock market tumbled today.* **4.** to perform gymnastic feats of skill and agility, as leaps, somersaults, etc. **5.** to fall suddenly from a position of power or authority; suffer overthrow: *As one dictator tumbles, another is rising to take his place.* **6.** to fall in ruins, as from age or decay; collapse; topple: *The walls of the old mansion tumbled down upon the intruders.* **7.** to roll about by turning one way and another; pitch about; toss. **8.** to stumble or fall (usually fol. by *over*): *to tumble over a sled.* **9.** to go, come, get, etc., in a hasty and confused way: *The people tumbled out of the theater. He tumbled hurriedly into his clothes.* **10.** *Informal.* to understand or become aware of some fact or circumstance (often fol. by *to*): *He finally tumbled to what they were doing.* **11.** *Rocketry.* (of a missile) to rotate without control end over end. —*v.t.* **12.** to cause to fall or roll end over end; throw over or down. **13.** to throw or toss about; disorder or disarray, as in handling, searching, etc. **14.** to put in a disordered or rumpled condition. **15.** to throw, cast, put, send, etc., in a precipitate, hasty, or rough manner. **16.** to cause to fall from a position of authority or power; overthrow; topple: *They tumbled him from his throne.* **17.** to cause to fall or collapse in ruins: *The wreckers tumbled the walls of the building.* **18.** to subject to the action of a tumbling box. —*n.* **19.** an act of tumbling or falling. **20.** a gymnastic or acrobatic feat. **21.** an accidental fall; spill. **22.** a drop in value, as of stocks. **23.** a fall from a position of power or authority: *The great man finally took a tumble.* **24.** a response indicating interest, affection, etc.: *She wouldn't give me a tumble.* **25.** tumbled condition; disorder or confusion. **26.** a confused heap: *a tumble of papers, ashes, pens, and keys on his desk.* [ME *tum(b)le(n)* to dance in acrobatic style (c. D *tuimelen,* LG *tummeln,* etc.), freq. of ME *tomben,* OE *tumbian,* c. Icel *tumba,* akin to OHG *tūmōn* to reel (? < OLG). Cf. F *tomber* to fall < Gmc]

tum·ble·bug (tum′bəl bug′), *n.* any of several dung beetles that roll balls of dung in which they deposit their eggs and in which the young develop. [TUMBLE + BUG]

tum′ble cart′, a horse-drawn cart having two solid wheels. Also called **tum′ble car′.**

tum·ble-down (tum′bəl doun′), *adj.* dilapidated; ruined; rundown: *He lived in a tumble-down shack.*

tum′ble home′, *Naut.* an inward and upward slope of the middle body of a vessel. Also called **falling home.**

tum·bler (tum′blər), *n.* **1.** one who performs leaps, somersaults, and other bodily feats. **2.** (in a lock) any locking or checking part which, when lifted or released by the action of a key or the like, allows the bolt to move. **3.** a stemless drinking glass having a flat bottom and no handle. **4.** (in a gunlock) a leverlike piece that by the action of a spring forces the hammer forward when released by the trigger. **5.** *Mach.* **a.** a part moving a gear into place in a selective transmission. **b.** a single cog or cam on a rotating shaft, transmitting motion to a part with which it engages. **6.** a tumbling box or barrel. **7.** a person who operates a tumbling box or barrel. **8.** one of a breed of dogs resembling a small greyhound, used formerly in hunting rabbits. **9.** one of a breed of domestic pigeons, noted for the habit of tumbling backward in flight. **10.** a toy, usually representing a fat, squatting figure, which is weighted and rounded at the bottom so as to rock when touched. **11.** a tumbrel or tumble cart. [TUMBLE + -ER[1]. Cf. LG *tümeler* drinking-cup, kind of pigeon]

tum′bler gear′, *Mach.* a transmission having gears actuated by a tumbler.

tum·ble·weed (tum′bəl wēd′), *n.* *U.S.* any of various plants, as an amaranth, *Amaranthus graecizans,* whose branching upper part becomes detached from the roots in autumn and is driven about by the wind. [TUMBLE + WEED[1]]

tum·bling (tum′bling), *n.* the act, practice, or art of performing acrobatic tumbles, usually on a mat or the ground. [TUMBLE + -ING[1]]

tum′bling bar′rel, a rotating drum for subjecting materials or small manufactured objects, loosely placed inside, to a tumbling action, as to mix materials or to polish objects by friction with one another or with an abrasive.

tum′bling box′, a box, pivoted at two corners, used in the manner of a tumbling barrel.

tum·brel (tum′brəl), *n.* **1.** one of the carts used during the French Revolution to convey victims to the guillotine. **2.** a dumpcart, esp. one for carrying dung. **3.** *Obs.* a two-wheeled covered cart accompanying artillery for carrying tools, ammunition, etc. Also, **tum′bril.** [late ME *tumberell* ducking-stool < ML *tumberellus* < OF *tumberel* dump-cart, equiv. to *tomber* to fall (see TUMBLE) + *-rel* -REL]

tu·me·fa·ci·ent (to͞o′mə fā′shənt, tyo͞o′-), *adj.* tumefying; causing to swell. [< L *tumefacient-,* s. of *tumefaciēns* causing to swell (prp. of *tumefacere*). See TUMEFY, -ENT]

tu·me·fac·tion (to͞o′mə fak′shən, tyo͞o′-), *n.* the act of making or becoming swollen or tumid. [< medical L *tumefactiōn-* (s. of *tumefactiō* a causing to swell), equiv. to *tumefact(us)* made to swell, swollen (ptp. of *tumefacere* TUMEFY) + *-iōn-* -ION]

tu·me·fy (to͞o′mə fī′, tyo͞o′-), *v.t., v.i.,* **-fied, -fy·ing.** to make or become swollen or tumid. [back formation from *tumefied,* Anglicization of L *tumefactus* caused to swell (ptp. of *tumefacere*) < *tume(re)* (to) swell + *-factus* made, done; see FACT, -FY, -ED[2]]

tu·mes·cent (to͞o mes′ənt, tyo͞o-), *adj.* **1.** swelling; slightly tumid. **2.** exhibiting or affected with many ideas or emotions; teeming. **3.** pompous and pretentious, esp. in the use of language; bombastic. [< L *tumescent-* (s. of *tumescēns* beginning to swell, prp. of *tumescere*), equiv. to *tum(ēre)* (to) swell + *-escent-* -ESCENT] —**tu·mes′cence,** *n.*

tu·mid (to͞o′mid, tyo͞o′-), *adj.* **1.** swollen, or affected with swelling, as a part of the body. **2.** pompous or inflated, as language; turgid; bombastic. **3.** seeming to swell; bulging. [< L *tumidus* swollen, equiv. to *tum(ēre)* (to) swell + *-idus* -ID[4]] —**tu·mid′i·ty, tu′mid·ness,** *n.* —**tu′mid·ly,** *adv.*

—**Syn. 1.** distended, turgid. **2.** inflated. —**Ant. 1.** deflated.

tum·mel·er (to͝om′ə lər), *n.* *U.S. Informal.* **1.** a male entertainer, as formerly employed by resorts in the Catskill Mountains, who combined the duties of a comedian, activities director, and master of ceremonies to keep the guests amused throughout the day. **2.** any lively, prankish, or mischievous man. Also, **tum′mul·er.** [< Yiddish; cf. G *tummeln,* to bustle about, romp, exercise, *Tummelplatz* playground. See TUMBLE, -ER[1]]

tum·my (tum′ē), *n., pl.* **-mies.** *Informal.* stomach: *The baby had a pain in his tummy. A girdle gives extra support for the tummy.* [nursery form: *(s)tummi(ck),* dial. var. of STOMACH]

tu·mor (to͞o′mər, tyo͞o′-), *n.* **1.** a swollen part; swelling; protuberance. **2.** *Pathol.* an abnormal or diseased swelling in any part of the body, esp. a more or less circumscribed overgrowth of new tissue that is autonomous, differs more or less in structure from the part in which it grows, and serves no useful purpose; neoplasm. **3.** *Archaic.* **a.** inflated pride; haughtiness. **b.** pompous language; bombast. Also, *esp. Brit.,* **tu′mour.** [< L: a swelling, swollen state, equiv. to *tum(ēre)* (to) swell + *-or* -OR[1]] —**tu′mor·like′,** *adj.* —**tu′mor·ous, tu′mor·al,** *adj.*

tump (tump, to͞omp), *n.* *Brit. Dial.* **1.** a small mound, hill, or rise of ground. **2.** a clump of grass, shrubs, or trees, esp. rising from a swamp or bog. **3.** a heap or stack, as a haystack. [? nasalized var. of TOP[1]]

tump·line (tump′līn′), *n.* a strap or sling passed around the chest or forehead to help support a pack carried on a person's back. [< *tump,* of Algonquian orig. + LINE[1]]

tu·mu·lar (to͞o′myə lər, tyo͞o′-), *adj.* of, pertaining to, resembling, or characterized by a tumulus or tumuli. [< L *tumul(us)* mound + -AR[1]]

tu·mu·lous (to͞o′myə ləs, tyo͞o′-), *adj.* having mounds; full of mounds; tumular. Also, **tu·mu·lose** (to͞o′myə lōs′, tyo͞o′-). [< L *tumulōsus* < *tumul(us)* TUMULUS + *-ōsus* -OUS]

tu·mult (to͞o′məlt, tyo͞o′-), *n.* **1.** violent and noisy commotion or disturbance of a crowd or mob; uproar: *The tumult reached its height during the premier's speech.* **2.** a general outbreak, riot, uprising, or other disorder: *The tumult moved toward the embassy.* **3.** highly distressing agitation of mind or feeling; turbulent mental or emotional disturbance: *His placid façade failed to conceal the tumult of his mind.* [late ME *tumult(e)* < L *tumultus* an uproar, lit., a rising, equiv. to *tum(ēre)* (to) swell (with anger) + *-ul-* formative suffix (see TUMULUS) + *-tus* suffix of action and its result]

—**Syn. 1.** disorder, turbulence. See **ado. 2.** revolt, revolution, mutiny. **3.** excitement, perturbation.

tu·mul·tu·ar·y (to͞o mul′cho͞o er′ē, tyo͞o-), *adj.* **1.** tumultuous; turbulent. **2.** confused; disorderly; haphazard: *tumultuary habits of studying.* [< L *tumultuārius* pertaining to bustle or hurry, equiv. to *tumultu(s)* TUMULT + *-ārius* -ARY[1]]

tu·mul·tu·ous (to͞o mul′cho͞o əs, tyo͞o-), *adj.* **1.** full of tumult or riotousness; marked by disturbance and uproar: *a tumultuous celebration.* **2.** raising a great clatter and commotion; disorderly or noisy: *a tumultuous crowd of students.* **3.** highly disturbed or agitated, as the mind or emotions; distraught; turbulent. [< L *tumultuōsus,* equiv. to *tumultu(s)* TUMULT + *-ōsus* -OUS] —**tu·mul′tu·ous·ly,** *adv.* —**tu·mul′tu·ous·ness,** *n.*

—**Syn. 1.** uproarious, turbulent, violent. **2.** boisterous. **3.** unquiet. —**Ant. 1.** calm. **2, 3.** quiet.

tu·mu·lus (to͞o′myə ləs, tyo͞o′-), *n., pl.* **-lus·es, -li** (-lī′). **1.** a domelike swelling or mound formed in congealed lava. **2.** barrow[2] (def. 1). [< L: mound, swelling, equiv. to *tum(ēre)* (to) swell + *-ulus* suffix of place]

Tum·wa·ter (tum′wô′tər, -wot′ər), *n.* a town in W Washington. 3885 (1960).

tun (tun), *n., v.,* **tunned, tun·ning.** —*n.* **1.** a large cask for holding liquids, esp. wine, ale, or beer. **2.** a measure of capacity for wine, etc., usually equivalent to 252 wine gallons. **3.** *Chiefly Brit.* a chimney stack. —*v.t.* **4.** to put into or store in a tun or tuns. [ME, OE *tunne,* c. D *ton,* G *Tonne* (< LG), Icel *tunna*]

Bluefin tuna, *Thunnus thynnus* (Length to 14 ft.)

Tun., Tunisia.

tu·na[1] (to͞o′nə), *n., pl.* (*esp. collectively*) **-na,** (*esp. referring to two or more kinds or species*) **-nas. 1.** any of several large food and game fishes of the family *Scombridae,* found in temperate and tropical seas. Cf. **albacore, bluefin tuna, yellowfin tuna. 2.** any of various related fishes. **3.** Also called **tu′na fish′.** the flesh of the tuna, used as food. [< AmerSp, var. of Sp *atún* < Ar *tūn* < Gk *thýnnos* TUNNY]

tu·na[2] (to͞o′nə, tyo͞o′-), *n.* **1.** any of various prickly pears, esp. either of two erect, treelike species, *Opuntia Tuna* or *O. megacantha,* of Mexico, bearing a sweet, edible fruit. **2.** the fruit. [< Sp < Taino]

tun·a·ble (to͞o′nə bəl, tyo͞o′-), *adj.* **1.** capable of being tuned. **2.** *Archaic.* harmonious; tuneful; melodious. Also, **tuneable.** [TUNE + -ABLE] —**tun′a·ble·ness,** *n.* —**tun′a·bly,** *adv.*

Tun′bridge Wells′ (tun′brij′), a city in SW Kent, in SE England: mineral springs; resort. 39,855 (1961).

tun·dish (tun′dish′), *n.* *Metall.* **1.** (in a vacuum induction furnace) a trough through which molten metal flows under vacuum to a mold chamber. **2.** Also called **pouring box, pouring basket, pouring basin.** a refractory-lined vessel having holes for distributing metal being teemed into ingot molds. [ME; see TUN, DISH]

tun·dra (tun′drə, to͝on′-), *n.* one of the vast, nearly level, treeless plains of the arctic regions of Europe, Asia, and North America. [< Russ: marshy plain]

tune (to͞on, tyo͞on), *n., v.,* **tuned, tun·ing.** —*n.* **1.** a succession of musical sounds forming an air or melody, with or without the harmony accompanying it. **2.** a musical setting of a hymn, poem, psalm, etc., usually in four-part harmony. **3.** state of being in the proper pitch: *to be in tune.* **4.** agreement in pitch; unison; harmony. **5.** proper adjustment, as of radio instruments or circuits with respect to frequency. **6.** harmonious relationship; accord; agreement. **7.** *Archaic.* frame of mind; mood. **8.** *Obs.* a tone or sound. **9. call the tune,** to decide matters of policy; control: *He was technically running the business, but his father still called the tune.* **10. change (one's) tune,** to reverse one's views; change one's mind: *She changed her tune about children when she married and had her own.* **11. sing a different tune,** to change one's opinion, attitude, behavior, etc.: *He will sing a different tune when he has to earn his own money.* **12. to the tune of,** *Informal.* at a price or cost of (a specified amount): *In order to expand, they will need capital to the tune of six million dollars.* —*v.t.* **13.** to adjust (a musical instrument) to a correct or given standard of pitch (often fol. by *up*). **14.** to adapt (the voice, song, etc.) to a particular tone, to the expression of a particular feeling, or the like. **15.** to bring into harmony. **16.** to adjust (a motor, mechanism, or the like) for proper functioning. **17.** *Radio.* **a.** to adjust (a circuit, frequency, or the like) so as to bring it into resonance with another circuit, a given frequency, or the like. **b.** to adjust (a receiving apparatus) so as to make it in accord in frequency with a transmitting apparatus whose signals are to be received. **c.** to adjust a receiving apparatus so as to receive (the signals of a particular transmitting station). **18.** to put into or cause to be in a receptive condition, mood, etc.; bring into harmony or agreement. **19.** *Archaic.* **a.** to utter, sound, or express musically. **b.** to play upon (a lyre). —*v.i.* **20.** to put a musical instrument in tune (often fol. by *up*). **21.** to give forth a musical sound. **22.** to be in harmony or accord; become responsive. **23. tune in,** to adjust a radio so as to receive signals. **24. tune out,** to adjust a radio so as to avoid the signals of a transmitting station. **25. tune up, a.** to cause a group of musical instruments to be brought to the same pitch. **b.** to begin to sing. **c.** to bring into proper operating order, as a motor: *Before starting on our trip we should have the car tuned up.* [ME; unexplained var. of TONE]

—**Syn. 18.** harmonize, balance. **21.** chime.

tune·a·ble (to͞o′nə bəl, tyo͞o′-), *adj.* tunable. —**tune′a·ble·ness,** *n.* —**tune′a·bly,** *adv.*

tune·ful (to͞on′fəl, tyo͞on′-), *adj.* **1.** full of melody; melodious: *tuneful compositions.* **2.** producing musical sounds or melody. [TUNE + -FUL] —**tune′ful·ly,** *adv.* —**tune′ful·ness,** *n.*

—**Syn. 1.** musical, harmonious, dulcet, sweet. —**Ant. 1.** discordant.

tune·less (to͞on′lis, tyo͞on′-), *adj.* **1.** unmelodious; unmusical. **2.** making or giving no music; silent: *In the corner stood a tuneless old piano.* [TUNE + -LESS] —**tune′less·ly,** *adv.*

tun·er (to͞o′nər, tyo͞o′-), *n.* **1.** one who or that which tunes. **2.** the portion of a radio receiver producing an output suitable for feeding into a detector and adjustable for selecting a desired signal. [TUNE + -ER[1]]

tune·smith (to͞on′smith′, tyo͞on′-), *n.* *Informal.* a person who composes popular music or songs. [TUNE + SMITH]

tune-up (to͞on′up′, tyo͞on′-), *n.* an adjustment, as of a motor, to improve working order or condition: *The car needs a tune-up badly.* [n. use of v. phrase *to tune up*]

Tun′gar Tube′ (tung′gər), *Electronics, Trademark.* a gas-filled tube having a hot cathode and a graphite disk as anode, used as a rectifier in battery-charging circuits. Also called **Tun′gar rec′tifier.**

tun·go (tung′gō), *n., pl.* **-gos.** *n.* *Australian.* rat-kangaroo. [from SAustral native name]

tung′ oil′ (tung), a yellow drying oil derived from the seeds of a tung tree, *Aleurites Fordii,* used in varnishes, linoleum, etc. [half translation, half adoption of Chinese *yu t'ung* oil of TUNG TREE]

tung′-oil tree′ (tung′oil′). See **tung tree.**

tung·state (tung′stāt), *n.* *Chem.* a salt of any tungstic acid. Also called **wolframate.** [TUNGST(EN) + -ATE[2]]

tung·sten (tung′stən), *n.* *Chem.* a rare, metallic element having a bright-gray color, a metallic luster, and a high melting point, 3410°C, and found in wolframite, tungstite, and other minerals: used in alloys of high-speed cutting tools, electric-lamp filaments, etc. *Symbol:* W; *at. wt.:* 183.85; *at. no.:* 74; *sp. gr.:* 19.3. [< Sw: *tung* heavy + *sten* stone] —**tung·sten·ic** (tung sten′ik), *adj.*

tung′sten lamp′, an incandescent electric lamp in which the filament is made of tungsten.

tung′sten steel′, an alloy steel containing tungsten.

tung′sten triox′ide, *Chem.* a heavy, canary-yellow, water-insoluble powder, WO_3, used in the manufacture of tungstates. Also called **tung′sten ox′ide, tung′stic ac′id hydrox′ide, tung′stic anhy′dride.**

tung·stic (tuŋ′stik), *adj.* *Chem.* of or containing tungsten, esp. in the pentavalent or hexavalent state. [TUNGST(EN) + -IC]

tung′stic ac′id, *Chem.* **1.** a hydrate of tungsten trioxide, $H_2WO_4 \cdot H_2O$, used in the manufacture of tungsten-lamp filaments. **2.** any of a group of acids derived from tungsten by the addition of acid to a soluble tungstate or to a mixture of a tungstate and a silicate, phosphate, etc.

tung·stite (tuŋ′stīt), *n.* a native tungsten trioxide, WO_3, a yellow or yellowish-green mineral usually occurring in a pulverulent form. [TUNGST(EN) + -ITE[1]]

Tung·ting (do͝oŋ′tiŋ′), *n.* a lake in S China, in Hunan province. 1450 sq. mi.

tung′ tree′, any of several euphorbiaceous trees of the genus *Aleurites*, esp. *A. Fordii*, of China, bearing seeds that yield tung oil. Also called **tung-oil tree.**

Tun·gus (to͝on go͞oz′), *n., pl.* **-gus·es,** (*esp. collectively*) **-gus. 1.** a member of a Mongoloid people living in eastern Siberia and including several nomadic tribes. **2.** the northern group of Tungusic languages. Also, **Tunguz.**

Tun·gus·ic (to͝on go͞oz′ik), *n.* **1.** a branch of the Altaic family of languages, including Manchu. —*adj.* **2.** of or pertaining to the Tunguses or Tungusic. [TUNGUS + -IC]

Tun·gus·ka (to͝on go͞os′kä), *n.* any of three tributaries of the Yenesei River in the central Soviet Union in Asia: includes the Lower Tunguska 2000 mi. long; the Upper Tunguska or the lower course of the Angara; and the Stony Tunguska ab. 975 mi. long.

Tun·guz (to͝on go͞oz′), *n., pl.* **-guz·es,** (*esp. collectively*) **-guz.** Tungus.

tu·nic (to͞o′nik, tyo͞o′-), *n.* **1.** *Chiefly Brit.* a coat worn as part of a military or other uniform. **2.** a gownlike outer garment, with or without sleeves and sometimes belted, worn by the ancient Greeks and Romans. **3.** a woman's upper garment, either loose or close-fitting and extending over the skirt to the hips or below. **4.** a garment with a short skirt, worn by women for sports. **5.** *Eccles.* a tunicle. **6.** *Anat., Zool.* any covering or investing membrane or part, as of an organ. **7.** *Bot.* a natural integument. [OE *tunice* (occurs in acc. case *tunican*) < L *tunica*]

tu·ni·ca (to͞o′nə kə, tyo͞o′-), *n., pl.* **-cae** (-sē′). *Anat., Zool., Bot.* a tunic. [< NL, special use of L *tunica* tunic]

tu·ni·cate (to͞o′nə kit, -kāt′, tyo͞o′-), *n.* **1.** *Zool.* any marine chordate of the subphylum *Tunicata*, having a saclike body enclosed in a thick membrane or tunic, from which protrude two openings or siphons for the ingress and egress of water. —*adj.* Also, **tu′ni·cat′ed. 2.** (esp. of the *Tunicata*) having a tunic or covering. **3.** of or pertaining to the tunicates. **4.** *Bot.* having or consisting of a series of concentric layers, as a bulb. [< L *tunicātus* wearing a tunic. See TUNIC, -ATE[1]]

tu′nic flow′er. See **saxifrage pink.**

tu·ni·cle (to͞o′ni kəl, tyo͞o′-), *n.* *Eccles.* a vestment worn over the alb by subdeacons, as at the celebration of the Mass, and by bishops. [ME < L *tunicula*, equiv. to *tunic(a)* tunic + *-ula*; see -ULE, -CLE]

tun′ing fork′, a steel instrument consisting of a stem with two prongs, producing a musical tone of definite, constant pitch when struck, and serving as a standard for tuning musical instruments, making acoustical experiments, and the like.

Tuning fork

Tu·nis (to͞o′nis, tyo͞o′-), *n.* **1.** a city in and the capital of Tunisia, in the NE part. 678,000 with suburbs. (est. 1965). **2.** one of the former Barbary States in N Africa, once notorious for its pirates: constitutes modern Tunisia.

Tu·ni·sia (to͞o nē′zhə, -shə, -nizh′ə, -nish′ə), *n.* a republic in N Africa, on the Mediterranean: a French protectorate until 1956. 4,494,000 (est. 1963); 48,330 sq. mi. *Cap.:* Tunis. —**Tu·ni′sian,** *adj., n.*

tun·ka (tuŋ′kə), *n.* See **wax gourd.** [< Chin *tung* winter + *kua* gourd]

Tun·ker (tuŋ′kər), *n.* Dunker.

tun·nage (tun′ij), *n.* tonnage.

tun·nel (tun′əl), *n., v.,* **-neled, -nel·ing** or (*esp. Brit.*) **-nelled, -nel·ling.** —*n.* **1.** an underground passage. **2.** a passageway, as for trains, automobiles, etc., through or under an obstruction, as a city, mountain, river, harbor, or the like. **3.** an approximately horizontal gallery or corridor in a mine. **4.** the burrow of an animal. **5.** *Dial.* a funnel. **6.** *Obs.* the flue of a chimney. —*v.t.* **7.** to construct a passageway through or under: *to tunnel a mountain.* **8.** to make or excavate (a tunnel or underground passage): *to tunnel a passage under a river.* **9.** to move or proceed by or as by boring a tunnel: *The river tunneled its way through the mountain.* **10.** to pierce or hollow out, as with tunnels. —*v.i.* **11.** to make a tunnel or tunnels: *to tunnel through the Alps.* [late ME *tonel* < MF *tonele, tonnelle* funnel-shaped net, fem. of *tonnel* cask, dim. of *tonne* TUN] —**tun′nel·er;** *esp. Brit.,* **tun′nel·ler,** *n.* —**tun′nel·like′,** *adj.*

tun′nel disease′, *Pathol.* **1.** See **caisson disease. 2.** hookworm (def. 2).

tun′nel of love′, a ride in an amusement park consisting of a dark, narrow, covered passageway through which small cars or boats are mechanically conveyed, usually frequented by couples.

tun′nel vault′. See **barrel vault.**

tun′nel vi′sion, 1. *Psychiatry.* a hysterical condition characterized by a constricted field of vision that is the same size throughout the range of accommodation. **2.** a drastically narrowed field of vision, as in looking through a tube.

Tun·ney (tun′ē), *n.* **James Joseph** ("*Gene*"), born 1897, U.S. boxer: world heavyweight champion 1926–28.

tun·ny (tun′ē), *n., pl.* **-nies,** (*esp. collectively*) **-ny.** *Chiefly Brit.* tuna[1]. [< ML *tunnīna* false tunny (by apocope), n. use of fem. of *tunnīnus* tunnylike, equiv. to *tunn(us)* tunny (var. of L *thynnus* < Gk *thýnnos*) + *-īnus* -INE[1]]

Tuo·ne·la (twô′ne lə), *n.* *Finnish Myth.* the afterworld, an island on which the sun and moon never shine. Also called **Manala.**

tup (tup), *n., v.,* **tupped, tup·ping.** —*n.* **1.** *Chiefly Brit.* a male sheep; ram. **2.** the head of a falling hammerlike mechanism, as of a steam hammer or pile driver. —*v.t.* **3.** *Chiefly Brit.* (of a ram) to copulate with (a ewe). —*v.i. Chiefly Brit.* **4.** (of a ram) to copulate with a ewe. **5.** (of a ewe) to be in estrus; be ready to copulate with a ram. [ME *tope, tupe* ram]

tu·pe·lo (to͞o′pə lō′), *n., pl.* **-los. 1.** any of several cornaceous trees of the genus *Nyssa*, esp. the black gum, *N. sylvatica*, or *N. aquatica*, of deep swamps and river bottoms of the southern U.S. **2.** the strong, tough wood of any of these trees, esp. in commercial use. [< Creek *(i)to opelwa* swamp tree]

Tu·pe·lo (tyo͞o′pə lō′), *n.* a city in NE Mississippi. 17,221 (1960).

Tu·pi (to͞o pē′, to͞o′pē), *n., pl.* **-pis,** (*esp. collectively*) **-pi. 1.** a member of any of several related Indian peoples living in the valleys of various Brazilian rivers, esp. the Amazon. **2.** a language belonging to the Tupi-Guarani family of languages and spoken in northern Brazil by the Tupi Indians. Also, **Tu·pí′.** —**Tu·pi′an,** *adj.*

Tu·pi-Gua·ra·ni (to͞o pē′gwär′ə nē′, to͞o′pē-), *n.* a family of Indian languages including Tupi, Guarani, lingua geral, and many others of central South America. —**Tu·pi-Gua·ra·ni·an** (to͞o′pē gwə rä′nē ən), *adj., n.*

Tu·po·lev (to͞o pô′ləf), *n.* **An·drei Ni·co·la·ye·vich** (än drā′ ni ko lä′yə vich), born 1888, Russian engineer and aircraft designer.

tup·pence (tup′əns), *n.* *Brit.* twopence. [16th-century *tuppens*. See TWO, PENCE]

tup·pen·ny (tup′ə nē), *adj.* twopenny (defs. 1–3).

Tup·per (tup′ər), *n.* **Sir Charles,** 1821–1915, Canadian statesman: prime minister 1896.

Tup′per Lake′, a town in N New York. 5200 (1960).

Tu·pun·ga·to (to͞o′po͞on gä′tô), *n.* a mountain between Argentina and Chile, in the Andes. ab. 21,490 ft.

tuque (to͞ok, tyo͞ok), *n.* a heavy stocking cap worn in Canada. Also, **toque.** [< CanF, var. of F *toque* TOQUE]

tu quo·que (to͞o kwō′kwe; *Eng.* to͞o kwō′kwē, tyo͞o), *Latin.* thou too: a retort by one charged with a crime accusing an opponent who has brought the charges with a similar crime.

Tu·ra (to͞o′RÄ), *n.* **Co·si·mo** (kô′zē mô), c1430–98?, Italian painter.

tu·ra·co (to͝or′ə kō′), *n., pl.* **-cos.** touraco.

Tu·ran·dot (to͝or′ən dot′, -dōt′, to͝or′ən dō′), *n.* an opera by Giacomo Puccini (completed in 1926 by Franco Alfano).

Tu·ra·ni·an (to͝o rā′nē ən, tyo͝o-), *adj.* **1.** belonging or pertaining to a group of Asian peoples or languages comprising nearly all of those which are neither Indo-European nor Semitic; allophylian. **2.** *Obs.* Ural-Altaic. —*n.* Also called **allophylian. 3.** a member of any of the races speaking a Turanian, esp. a Ural-Altaic, language. **4.** a member of any of the Ural-Altaic races. [< Pers *Tūrān* Turkestan + -IAN]

tu·ran·ose (to͝or′ə nōs′, tyo͝or′-), *n.* *Biochem.* a white, water-soluble disaccharide, $C_{12}H_{22}O_{11}$, found in certain trisaccharides, as melezitose, and yielding glucose and fructose upon hydrolysis. [< G *turanos*, lit., pertaining to Turkestan < Pers *Tūrān* Turkestan + G *-os* -OSE[1]; so called because obtained thence]

tur·ban (tûr′bən), *n.* **1.** a man's headdress worn chiefly by Muslims in the eastern Mediterranean basin and southern Asia, consisting of a long cloth of silk, linen, cotton, etc., wound either about a cap or directly around the head. **2.** any headdress resembling this. **3.** any of various off-the-face hats for women that are close-fitting, of a soft fabric, and brimless or having a narrow, sometimes draped, brim. [earlier *torbant*, var. of *tulbant* < Turk (var. of *tülbend*) < Pers *dulband*] —**tur′baned,** *adj.* —**tur′ban·less,** *adj.* —**tur′ban·like′,** *adj.*

Turban

tur′ban squash′, a turban-shaped variety of winter squash, *Cucurbita maxima turbaniformis.*

tur·ba·ry (tûr′bə rē), *n., pl.* **-ries. 1.** land, or a piece of land, where turf or peat may be dug or cut. **2.** *Law.* the right to cut turf or peat on a common land or on another person's land. [ME *turbarye* < ML *turbaria* < *turba* TURF + *-aria* -ARY[1]]

tur·bel·lar·i·an (tûr′bə lâr′ē ən), *adj.* **1.** belonging to the *Turbellaria*, a class of platyhelminths or flatworms, mostly aquatic, and having cilia on the body surface. —*n.* **2.** a turbellarian platyhelminth. [< NL *Turbellāria* (< L *turbell(ae)* a stir, row (pl. dim. of *turba* turmoil) + *-āria*, neut. pl. of *-ārius* -ARY) + -AN]

tur·bid (tûr′bid), *adj.* **1.** not clear or transparent because of stirred-up sediment or the like; clouded; opaque; obscured: *the turbid waters near the waterfall.* **2.** thick or dense, as smoke, clouds, etc. **3.** confused; muddled; disturbed. [< L *turbidus* disturbed, equiv. to *turb(āre)* (to) disturb (deriv. of *turba* turmoil) + *-idus* -ID[4]] —**tur·bid′i·ty, tur′bid·ness,** *n.* —**tur′bid·ly,** *adv.*

tur·bi·dim·e·ter (tûr′bi dim′i tər), *n.* a device for measuring the turbidity of water or other liquids. [TURBID + -I- + -METER] —**tur′bi·dim′e·try,** *n.* —**tur·bi·di·met·ric** (tûr′bi di me′trik), *adj.* —**tur′bi·di·met′ri·cal·ly,** *adv.*

turbid′ity cur′rent, *Geol.* a turbid, dense current of sediments in suspension moving along the slope and bottom of a lake or ocean. Also called **density current.**

tur·bi·nal (tûr′bə nəl), *adj.* **1.** turbinate. —*n.* **2.** *Anat.* a turbinate bone. [< L *turbin-* (s. of *turbō* a whirlwind, a top) + -AL[1]]

tur·bi·nate (tûr′bə nit, -nāt′), *adj.* Also, **tur′bi·nat′ed. 1.** scroll-like; whorled; spiraled. **2.** *Anat.* of or pertaining to certain scroll-like, spongy bones of the nasal passages in man and other vertebrates. **3.** inversely conical. —*n.* **4.** a turbinate shell. **5.** Also called **nasal concha.** *Anat.* a turbinate bone. [< L *turbinātus* shaped like a top, equiv. to *turbin-* (s. of *turbō* a top) + *-ātus* -ATE[1]] —**tur′bi·na′tion,** *n.*

tur·bine (tûr′bin, -bīn), *n.* any of various machines having a rotor, usually with vanes or blades, driven by the pressure, momentum, or reactive thrust of a moving fluid, as steam, water, hot gases, or air, either occurring in the form of free jets or as a fluid passing through and entirely filling a housing around the rotor. Cf. **impulse turbine, reaction turbine.** [< F < L *turbin-*, s. of *turbō* something that spins, e.g., a top, a spindle; akin to TURBID]

tur′bine ven′tilator, a ventilator, usually mounted on the roof of a building, deck of a vessel, etc., having at its head a globular, vaned rotor that is rotated by the wind, conveying air through a duct to and from a chamber below.

tur·bit (tûr′bit), *n.* one of a breed of domestic pigeons having a stout, roundish body, a short head and beak, and a ruffled breast and neck. [var. of TURBOT; appar. because, like the fish, the bird is toplike in outline]

tur·bo (tûr′bō), *n., pl.* **-bos. 1.** turbine. **2.** turbosupercharger. [by shortening]

turbo-, a combining form of **turbine:** *turbojet.* [TURB(INE) + -O-]

tur·bo-e·lec·tric (tûr′bō i lek′trik), *adj.* noting, pertaining to, or utilizing machinery including a generator driven by a turbine: *turbo-electric engine; turbo-electric propulsion.*

tur·bo·fan (tûr′bō fan′), *n.* a jet engine having a large impeller that takes in air, part of which is used in combustion of fuel, the remainder being mixed with the products of combustion to form a low-velocity exhaust jet. [TURBO- + FAN[1]]

tur·bo·jet (tûr′bō jet′), *n.* **1.** See **turbojet engine. 2.** an airplane equipped with one or more turbojet engines. [TURBO- + JET[1]]

tur′bo·jet en′gine, a jet-propulsion engine in which air from the atmosphere is compressed for combustion by a turbine-driven compressor.

tur·bo·prop (tûr′bō prop′), *n.* **1.** See **turbo-propeller engine. 2.** an airplane equipped with one or more turbo-propeller engines. [TURBO- + PROP[3]]

tur′bo-pro·pel′ler en′gine (tûr′bō prə pel′ər), *Aeron.* a jet engine with a turbine-driven propeller that produces thrust augmenting the thrust of the jet exhaust. Also called **propjet engine, turboprop, tur′boprop en′gine.**

tur·bo-ram′jet en′gine (tûr′bō ram′jet′), a combination engine that can be operated as a turbojet or ramjet engine.

tur·bo·su·per·charged (tûr′bō so͞o′pər chärjd′), *adj.* equipped with a turbosupercharger. [TURBO- + SUPERCHARGED]

tur·bo·su·per·charg·er (tûr′bō so͞o′pər chär′jər), *n.* a supercharger driven by a turbine turned by a stream of exhaust gases from the engine. [TURBO- + SUPERCHARGER]

tur·bot (tûr′bət), *n., pl.* (*esp. collectively*) **-bot,** (*esp. referring to two or more kinds or species*) **-bots. 1.** a European flatfish, *Psetta maxima*, having a diamond-shaped body. **2.** any of several other flatfishes. **3.** a triggerfish. [ME *turbut* < AF (equiv. to OF *tourbot*) < ML *turb(o)* turbot (in L, top; appar. applied to the fish because of its outline; see TURBINE) + *-ut*, equiv. to F *-ot* n. suffix]

tur·bu·lence (tûr′byə ləns), *n.* **1.** the quality or state of being turbulent; violent disorder or commotion. **2.** *Hydraulics.* the haphazard secondary motion caused by eddies within a moving fluid. **3.** *Meteorol.* irregular motion of the atmosphere, as that indicated by gusts and lulls in the wind. Also, **tur′bu·len·cy.** [< LL *turbulentia.* See TURBULENT, -ENCE]

tur·bu·lent (tûr′byə lənt), *adj.* **1.** being in a state of agitation or tumult; disturbed: *turbulent feelings or emotions.* **2.** characterized by, or showing disturbance, disorder, etc.: *the turbulent years.* **3.** given to acts of violence and aggression: *the turbulent young soldiers.* [< L *turbulentus* restless, equiv. to *turbu-* (comb. form of *turba* turmoil) + *-lentus* full of] —**tur′bu·lent·ly,** *adv.*

tur′bulent flow′, the flow of a fluid past an object such that the velocity at any fixed point in the fluid varies irregularly. Cf. **streamline flow.**

Tur·co (tûr′kō), *n., pl.* **-cos.** *Often Disparaging.* (formerly) an Algerian serving in the light infantry of the French army; a Zouave. [< F < It: lit., Turk]

Turco-, a combining form of **Turkish.** Also, **Turko-.** [< F < It]

Tur·co·man (tûr′kə mən), *n., pl.* **-mans. 1.** Turkoman. **2.** Turkmen.

Tur·co·phile (tûr′kə fīl′), *n.* **1.** one who favors or admires Turkey, Turkish customs, or Turks. —*adj.* **2.** tending to favor Turkey or Turkish customs. Also, **Tur·co·phil** (tûr′kə fil), **Turkophile, Turkophil.** [TURCO- + -PHILE]

Tur·co·phobe (tûr′kə fōb′), *n.* one who has a morbid fear of Turks. Also, **Turkophobe.** [TURCO- + -PHOBE] —**Tur′co·pho′bi·a,** *n.*

turd (tûrd), *n.* *Slang* (*vulgar*). a piece of excrement. [ME; OE *tord*]

tur·di·form (tûr′də fôrm′), *adj.* having the form of a thrush. [< NL *turdiformis* < L *turd(us)* THRUSH + -I- + *-formis* FORM]

tur·dine (tûr′dīn, -din), *adj.* belonging or pertaining to the family *Turdidae*, comprising the true thrushes. [< L *turd(us)* THRUSH + -INE[1]]

tu·reen (to͝o rēn′, tyo͝o-), *n.* a large, deep, covered dish for serving soup, stew, or other foods. [earlier *terrene* < F *terrine* earthenware dish, n. use of fem. of LL **terrinus* earthen < L *terr(a)* earth + *-īnus* -INE[1]]

Tu·renne (ty REN′), *n.* **Hen·ri de la Tour d'Au·vergne de** (äN Rē′ də lA to͞oR′ dō veRN′yə də), 1611–75, French general and marshal.

turf (tûrf), *n., pl.* **turfs,** (*esp. Brit.*) **turves;** *v.* —*n.* **1.** a layer of matted earth formed by grass and plant roots. **2.** *Chiefly Brit.* a piece cut or torn from the surface of grassland; sod. **3.** peat, esp. as material for fuel. **4.** a block or piece of peat dug for fuel. **5.** *Slang.* the neighborhood over which a street gang asserts its authority. **6. the turf, a.** the track over which horse races are run. **b.** the practice or sport of racing horses. —*v.t.* **7.** to cover with turf or sod. **8.** *Brit. Slang.* to remove from a desirable office or position; expel; kick out: *He was turfed from leadership of the group.* [ME, OE, c. D *turf,* G *Torf* (< LG), Icel *torf,* akin to Skt *darbha* tuft of grass. See TURBARY] —**turf′less,** *adj.* —**turf′like′,** *adj.*

turf′ing dai′sy, a low, perennial herb, *Matricaria tchihatchewi,* of Asia Minor, having white, daisylike flowers.

turf·man (tûrf′mən), *n., pl.* **-men.** a person who is extremely devoted to horse racing. [TURF + MAN[1]]

turf·y (tûr′fē), *adj.,* **turf·i·er, turf·i·est. 1.** covered with or consisting of grassy turf. **2.** resembling turf; turflike. **3.** of the nature of or abounding in peat. **4.** of, pertaining to, or characteristic of horse racing. [TURF + -Y[1]] —**turf′i·ness,** *n.*

Tur·ge·nev (tŏŏr ge′nyəf), *n.* **I·van Ser·ge·e·vich** (i vän′ ser ge′yə vich), 1818–83, Russian novelist. Also, **Tur·ge′niev.**

tur·gent (tûr′jənt), *adj. Obs.* swelling; swollen; turgid. [< L *turgent-* (s. of *turgēns* swelling, prp. of *turgēre*), equiv. to *turg-* swell + *-ent-* -ENT] —**tur′·gen·cy,** *n.* —**tur′gent·ly,** *adv.*

tur·ges·cent (tûr jes′ənt), *adj.* becoming swollen; swelling. [< L *turgescent-* (s. of *turgescēns* beginning to swell, prp. of *turgescere*), equiv. to *turg(ēre)* (to) swell + *-escent-* -ESCENT] —**tur·ges′cence, tur·ges′cen·cy,** *n.*

tur·gid (tûr′jid), *adj.* **1.** swollen; distended; tumid. **2.** inflated, overblown, or pompous; bombastic: *turgid language.* [< L *turgidus,* equiv. to *turg(ēre)* (to) swell + *-idus* -ID[4]] —**tur·gid′i·ty, tur′gid·ness,** *n.* —**tur′·gid·ly,** *adv.*

tur·gite (tûr′jīt), *n.* an iron ore, a hydrated ferric oxide, related to limonite but containing less water. [*Turg(inak)* mine in Soviet Union + -ITE[1]]

tur·gor (tûr′gər), *n.* **1.** *Plant Physiol.* the normal distention or rigidity of plant cells, resulting from the pressure exerted from within against the cell walls by the cell contents. **2.** the state of being swollen or distended. [< LL < L *turg(ēre)* (to) swell (out) + *-or* -OR[1]]

Tur·got (tyr gō′), *n.* **Anne Ro·bert Jacques** (an rō ber′ zhäk), 1727–81, French statesman, financier, and economist.

Tu·rin (tŏŏr′in, tyŏŏr′-, tŏŏ rin′, tyŏŏ-), *n.* a city in NW Italy, on the Po: capital of the Kingdom of Italy 1860–65. 1,019,230 (1961). Italian, **Torino.**

Tu·ri·na (tōō rē′nä), *n.* **Joa·quín** (hwä kēn′), 1882–1949, Spanish composer and pianist.

Turk (tûrk), *n.* **1.** a native or inhabitant of Turkey. **2.** (formerly) a native or inhabitant of the Ottoman Empire. **3.** a Muslim, esp. a subject of the Sultan of Turkey. **4.** a member of any of the peoples speaking Turkic languages. **5.** one of a breed of Turkish horses closely related to the Arabian horse. **6.** any Turkish horse. **7.** *Informal.* a cruel, brutal, and domineering man. **8.** See **Young Turk.** [ME < Turkish *Türk;* cf. ML *Turcus,* MGk *Toûrkos,* MF *Turc,* It *Turco,* Pers *turk*]

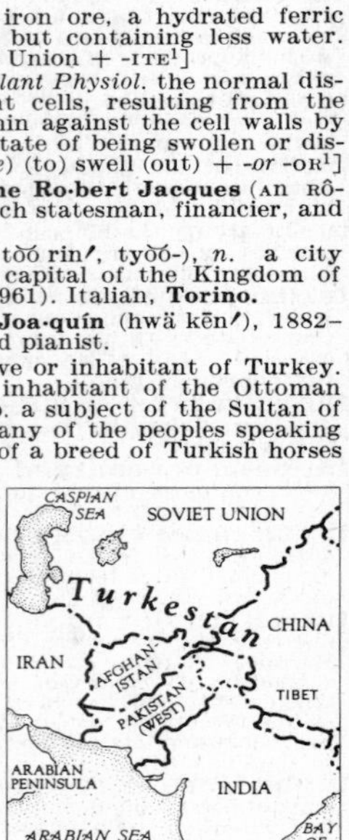

Turk., 1. Turkey. **2.** Also, **Turk** Turkish.

Tur·ke·stan (tûr′ki stan′, -stän′), *n.* a vast region in W and central Asia, E of the Caspian Sea: includes territory in the S central part of Sinkiang province in China **(Eastern Turkestan** or **Chinese Turkestan),** a strip of N Afghanistan, and the area **(Russian Turkestan)** comprising the republics of Kazakstan, Kinghizia, Tadzhikistan, Turkmenistan, and Uzbekistan. Also, **Turkistan.**

tur·key (tûr′kē), *n., pl.* **-keys,** *(esp. collectively)* **-key. 1.** a large, gallinaceous bird of the family *Meleagrididae,* esp. *Meleagris gallopava,* of America, that typically has green, reddish-brown, and yellowish-brown plumage of a metallic luster and that is domesticated in most parts of the world. **2.** the flesh of this bird, used as food. **3.** See **ocellated turkey. 4.** *Slang.* a person or thing of little appeal; dud. **5.** *Slang.* a poor and unsuccessful theatrical production; flop. **6.** *Bowling Slang.* three strikes in succession. **7. talk turkey,** *Informal.* to talk frankly; mean business: *Let's stop kidding around now and talk turkey.* [short for *Turkey cock* and *Turkey hen* cock and hen of Turkey, first applied to guinea fowl, later (by confusion) to the American bird]

Turkey (Domestic)

Tur·key (tûr′kē), *n.* a republic in W Asia and SE Europe. 31,391,207 (1965); 296,184 sq. mi. (286,928 sq. mi. in Asia; 9257 sq. mi. in Europe). *Cap.:* Ankara. Cf. **Ottoman Empire.**

tur′key buz′zard. See **turkey vulture.**

tur′key cock′, 1. the male of the turkey. **2.** a strutting, pompous, conceited person.

tur′key corn′. See **squirrel corn.**

tur·key·fish (tûr′kē fish′), *n., pl. (esp. collectively)* **-fish,** *(esp. referring to two or more kinds or species)* **-fish·es.** lionfish (def. 1). [TURKEY + FISH]

tur′key oak′, any of several oaks, as *Quercus Cerris,* of Eurasia, or *Q. laevis* and *Q. incana,* of the southern U.S., that grow on dry, sandy barrens.

Tur′key red′, 1. a bright red produced in fabrics by madder, alizarin, or synthetic dyes. **2.** cotton cloth of this color. **3.** See **Adrianople red.**

tur′key shoot′, 1. a contest, usually at a festive gathering, in which rifles are fired for marksmanship at live turkeys or other moving targets. **2.** any competitive match similar to a turkey shoot.

tur′key trot′, a round dance, danced by couples, properly to ragtime, the step being a springy walk with little or no bending of the knees, and accompanied by a swinging motion of the body with shoulder movements up and down.

tur·key-trot (tûr′kē trot′), *v.i.,* **-trot·ted, -trot·ting.** to dance the turkey trot.

tur′key vul′ture, a blackish-brown vulture, *Cathartes aura,* of Central and South America and the southern U.S., having a bare, red head and neck. Also called **turkey buzzard.**

Tur·ki (tûr′kē, tŏŏr′-), *n.* **1.** the Turkic languages of central Asia, taken collectively. —*adj.* **2.** of or pertaining to Turki or to the peoples speaking these languages. [< Pers, equiv. to *turk* TURK + *-ī* suffix of appurtenance]

Tur·kic (tûr′kik), *n.* **1.** a branch of the Altaic language family comprising languages of central and southwest Asia and eastern Europe, as Turkish, Azerbaijani, Turkmen, Uzbek, Kirghiz, and Yakut. —*adj.* **2.** of or pertaining to Turkic. Also called **Turko-Tatar.** [TURK + -IC]

Turk·ish (tûr′kish), *adj.* **1.** of, pertaining to, characteristic of, or derived from Turkey or the Turks. **2.** of or pertaining to the language of Turkey. **3.** (loosely) Turkic. —*n.* **4.** the language of Turkey; Ottoman Turkish. **5.** (loosely) Turkic. [TURK + -ISH[1]] —**Turk′·ish·ly,** *adv.* —**Turk′ish·ness,** *n.*

Turk′ish bath′, a bath in which the bather, after copious perspiration in a steam room, is washed, massaged, etc.

Turk′ish cres′cent, crescent (def. 7).

Turk′ish delight′, a candy made of fruit juice and gelatin, cubed and dusted with sugar. Also called **Turk′·ish paste′.**

Turk′ish Em′pire. See **Ottoman Empire.**

Turk′ish knot′. See **Ghiordes knot.**

Turk′ish pound′, the Turkish lira.

Turk′ish rug′, any of a large variety of handwoven rugs produced in Turkey, characterized by coarse, heavy yarn and a long, uneven pile. Also called **Turk′·ish car′pet.**

Turk′ish tobac′co, an aromatic tobacco, grown chiefly in Turkey and Greece, used in cigarettes.

Turk′ish tow′el, a thick, cotton towel with a long nap usually composed of uncut loops. Also, **turk′ish tow′el.**

Turk′ish tu′lip, a bulbous herb, *Tulipa acuminata,* of Turkey, having yellow flowers with red lines.

Turk·ism (tûr′kiz əm), *n.* the culture, beliefs, principles, practices, etc., of the Turks. [TURK + -ISM]

Tur·ki·stan (tûr′ki stan′, -stän′), *n.* Turkestan.

Turk·man (tûrk′mən), *n., pl.* **-men.** a native or inhabitant of Turkmenistan. [alter. of TURKOMAN] —**Turk·me·ni·an** (tûrk mē′nē ən), *adj.*

Turk·men (tûrk′men), *n.* the language of the Turkman people, a Turkic language spoken mostly east of the Caspian Sea in the Turkmen S.S.R. but also in parts of European Russia, Iran, and the Caucasus. Also, **Turkoman, Turcoman.** [< Pers *Turkmēn* Turkoman]

Turk·me·ni·stan (tûrk′me nə stan′, -stän′), *n.* a republic in central Asia, bordering the Caspian Sea, Iran, and Afghanistan. 3,534,000; 188,417 sq. mi. *Cap.:* Ashkhabad. Also called **Turkomen.** Formerly, **Turk′men So′viet So′cialist Repub′lic.**

Turko-, var. of **Turco-.** [appar. back formation from TURKOMAN]

Tur·ko·man (tûr′kə mən), *n., pl.* **-mans. 1.** a member of a Turkish people consisting of a group of tribes which inhabit the region near the Aral Sea and parts of Iran and Afghanistan. **2.** Turkmen. Also, **Turcoman.** [< ML *Turcomannus* < Pers *turkumān* Turklike person < *turk* Turk + *-u-* + *mān(dan)* (to) resemble]

Tur′koman rug′, any of a number of handwoven rugs produced by the Turkomans and characterized by coarse warp and filling yarn, a short, even pile made with the Sehna knot, and a variety of geometric, marine, and serpentine designs. Also called **Tur′koman car′pet.**

Tur·ko·men (tûr′kə men′, -mən), *n.* Turkmenistan.

Tur·ko·phile (tûr′kə fīl′), *n., adj.* Turcophile. Also, **Tur·ko·phil** (tûr′kə fil). [TURKO- + -PHILE]

Tur·ko·phobe (tûr′kə fōb′), *n.* Turcophobe. [TURKO- + -PHOBE] —**Tur′ko·pho′bi·a,** *n.*

Tur·ko-Ta·tar (tûr′kō tä′tər), *n., adj.* Turkic.

Turks′ and Cai′cos Is′lands (tûrks; kī′kōs), two groups of islands in the SE Bahamas: a dependency of Jamaica. 5716 (est. 1960); ab. 166 sq. mi. *Cap.:* Grand Turk.

Turk's′-cap lil′y (tûrks′kap′), either of two lilies, *Lilum Martagon* or *L. superbum,* having nodding flowers with the perianth segments strongly revolute. Also called **Martagon lily.**

Turk's-head (tûrks′hed′), *n.* a turbanlike knot of small cords, made around a rope, spar, etc.

Turk's′-head cac′tus, a cactus, *Melocactus communis,* of Jamaica, having needlelike spines and a cylindrical body with a tawny red, fezlike terminal part bearing red flowers. Also called **Turk's′-cap cac′tus.**

Tur·ku (tŏŏr′kōō), *n.* a seaport in SW Finland. 138,299 (est. 1965). Swedish, **Åbo.**

turle′ knot′ (tûrl), *Angling.* a special kind of knot for tying a leader, esp. of gut, to an eyed hook or fly. [named after Major W. G. *Turle,* 19th-century English angler]

Tur·lock (tûr′lok′), *n.* a town in central California. 9116 (1960).

tur·ma·line (tûr′mə lēn′), *n.* tourmaline.

tur·mer·ic (tûr′mər ik), *n.* **1.** the aromatic rhizome of an East Indian, zingiberaceous plant, *Curcuma longa.* **2.** a powder prepared from it, used as a condiment, as in curry powder, or as a yellow dye, a medicine, etc. **3.** the plant itself. **4.** any of various similar substances or plants. [earlier *tarmaret* < ML *terra merita* merited earth, unexplained name for curcuma]

tur′meric pa′per, paper treated with turmeric: used to indicate the presence of alkalis, which turn it brown, or of boric acid, which turns it reddish-brown.

tur·moil (tûr′moil), *n.* **1.** a state of great commotion, confusion, or disturbance; tumult; agitation; disquiet: *mental turmoil caused by difficult decisions.* **2.** *Obs.* harassing labor. [TUR(N) + MOIL]
—**Syn. 1.** turbulence, disorder, uproar. See **agitation.**
—**Ant. 1.** order, quiet.

turn (tûrn), *v.t.* **1.** to cause to move around on an axis or about a center; rotate: *to turn a wheel.* **2.** to cause to move around or partly around, as for the purpose of opening, closing, tightening, etc.: *to turn a key; to turn the cap of a jar.* **3.** to reverse the position or placement of: *to turn a page; to turn an egg; to turn a person around.* **4.** to bring the lower layers of (sod, soil, etc.) to the surface, as in plowing. **5.** to change the position of, by or as by rotating; move into a different position: *to turn the handle one notch.* **6.** to change or alter the course of; divert; deflect: *He turned the blow with his arm.* **7.** to change the tendency or trend of: *She skillfully turned the conversation away from so unpleasant a subject.* **8.** to reverse the progress of; cause to retreat: *The police turned the advancing rioters by firing over their heads.* **9.** to change or alter the nature, character, or appearance of: *Worry turned his hair gray.* **10.** to change or convert (usually fol. by *into* or *to*): *to turn water into ice; to turn tears into laughter.* **11.** to render or make by some change: *Fear turned him cowardly and craven.* **12.** to change the color of (leaves). **13.** to cause to become sour, ferment, or the like: *Warm weather turns milk.* **14.** to cause (the stomach) to reject food, liquid, etc.; affect with nausea. **15.** to change from one language or form of expression to another; translate. **16.** to put or apply to some use or purpose: *He turned his mind to practical matters.* **17.** to go or pass around or to the other side of: *to turn a street corner.* **18.** to get beyond or pass (a certain age, time, amount, etc.): *His son just turned four.* **19.** to direct, aim, or set toward, away from, or in a specified direction: *to turn the car toward the center of town; to turn one's back to the audience.* **20.** to direct (the eyes, face, etc.) another way; avert. **21.** to shape (a piece of metal, wood, etc.) into rounded form with a cutting tool while rotating on a lathe. **22.** to bring into a rounded or curved form in any way. **23.** to shape artistically or gracefully, esp. in rounded form. **24.** to form or express gracefully: *to turn a phrase well.* **25.** to direct (thought, attention, desire, etc.) toward or away from something. **26.** to cause to go; send; drive: *to turn a person from one's door.* **27.** to revolve in the mind; ponder (often fol. by over): *He turned the idea over a couple of times before acting on it.* **28.** to persuade (a person) to change or reorder the course of his life. **29.** to cause to be prejudiced against: *to turn a son against his father.* **30.** to maintain a steady flow or circulation of (money or articles of commerce). **31.** to reverse or remake (a garment or some part of a garment) so that the inner side becomes the outer: *His wife turns his shirt collars when they get frayed.* **32.** to pour from one container into another by inverting. **33.** to curve, bend, or twist. **34.** to twist out of position; wrench: *He turned his ankle.* **35.** to bend back or blunt (the edge of a blade). **36.** to perform (a gymnastic feat) by rotating or revolving: *to turn a somersault.* **37.** to disturb the mental balance of; distract; derange. **38.** to disorder or upset the placement or condition of: *He turned the room upside down.* **39.** *Obs.* **a.** to convert. **b.** to pervert.
—*v.i.* **40.** to move around on an axis or about a center; rotate. **41.** to move partly around through the arc of a circle, as a door on a hinge. **42.** to hinge or depend (usually fol. by *on* or *upon*): *The question turns on this point.* **43.** to direct or set one's course toward, away from, or in a particular direction. **44.** to direct the face or gaze toward or away from someone or something. **45.** to direct one's thought, attention, desire, etc., toward or away from someone or something. **46.** to give or apply one's interest, attention, effort, etc., to something; pursue: *He turned to the study and practice of medicine.* **47.** to change or reverse a course so as to go in a different or the opposite direction: *to turn to the right.* **48.** to change position so as to face in a different or the opposite direction. **49.** to change or reverse position or posture as by a rotary motion. **50.** to shift the body about as if on an axis: *to turn on one's side while sleeping.* **51.** to assume a curved form; bend. **52.** to become blunted or dulled by bending, as the cutting edge of a knife, saw, etc. **53.** to be affected with nausea, as the stomach. **54.** to be affected with giddiness or dizziness; have a sensation of whirling or reeling. **55.** to adopt religion, a manner of life, etc., esp. as differing from a previous position or attitude: *He turned to Christianity in his old age.* **56.** to change or transfer one's loyalties; defect: *He turned from the Democrats and joined the Republicans.* **57.** to make a sudden, usually unexpected change or reversal of position in order to resist or attack: *The big cats suddenly turned on their trainer.* **58.** to change an attitude or policy: *to turn in favor of someone; to turn against a person.* **59.** to change or alter, as in nature, character, or appearance. **60.** to become sour, rancid, fermented, or the like, as milk, butter, etc. **61.** to change color: *The leaves began to turn in August.* **62.** to change so as to be; become: *a lawyer turned poet; to turn pale.* **63.** to become mentally unbalanced or distracted. **64.** to put about or tack, as a ship. **65.** *Journalism.* (of copy) to run either from the bottom of the last column on one page to the top of the first column on the following page or from one column on a page to the expected place in the next column on the page (opposed to *jump*). **66. turn back, a.** to retrace or cause to retrace one's footsteps. **b.** to fold (a blanket, sheet of paper, etc.) on itself: *Turn back the page to keep the place.* **67. turn down, a.** to turn over; fold down. **b.** to lower in intensity; lessen. **c.** to refuse or reject (a person, request, etc.): *The Marine Corps turned him down.* **68. turn in, a.** to hand in; submit: *to turn in a resignation.* **b.** to inform on or

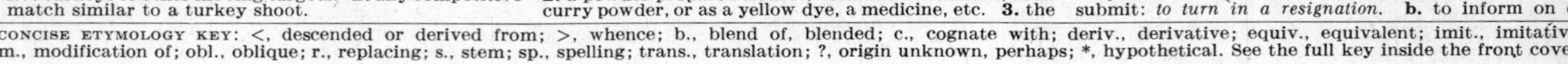

deliver up: *She promptly turned him in to the police.* **c.** to turn from one path or course into another; veer. **d.** *Informal.* to go to bed; retire: *I never turn in before eleven o'clock.* **e.** *Naut.* to wrap a rope or the like around and seize it to (a deadeye, bee, etc.). **69. turn into, a.** to walk or drive a vehicle into (a street, store, etc.): *He turned into the dead-end street. He turned into the saloon at the corner.* **b.** to be changed, transformed, or converted into: *He has turned into a very pleasant fellow. The caterpillar turned into a butterfly.* **70. turn off, a.** to stop the flow of (water, gas, etc.), as by closing a faucet or valve. **b.** to extinguish (a light). **c.** to divert; deflect. **d.** to diverge or branch off, as a side road from a main road. **e.** to drive a vehicle or walk onto (a side road) from a main road: *You turn off at 96th Street. Turn off the highway on the dirt road.* **f.** *Slang.* to stop listening: *You could see him turn off as she kept up her chatter.* **g.** *Chiefly Brit.* to discharge an employee. **71. turn on, a.** to cause (water, gas, etc.) to flow, as by opening a valve. **b.** to switch on (a light). **c.** to put into operation; activate. **d.** to start suddenly to affect or show: *She turned on the charm and won him over.* **e.** *Slang.* to induce (a person) to start taking a narcotic drug. **f.** *Slang.* to take a narcotic drug. **g.** Also, **turn upon.** to become suddenly hostile to: *The dog turned on its owner.* **72. turn one's hand to.** See **hand** (def. 73). **73. turn out, a.** to extinguish (a light). **b.** to produce as the result of labor: *She turned out four tapestries a year.* **c.** to drive out; dismiss; discharge: *a premier turned out of office.* **d.** to fit out; dress; equip. **e.** to result; issue. **f.** to come to be; become ultimately. **g.** to be found or known; prove. **h.** *Informal.* to be present at; appear. **i.** *Informal.* to get out of bed. **j.** *Naut.* to order (a seaman or seamen) from quarters for duty. **k.** *Naut.* to let out (a reef of sail). **74. turn over, a.** to move or be moved from one side to another. **b.** to put in reverse position; invert. **c.** to consider; meditate; ponder. **d.** to transfer; give. **e.** to start (an engine): *He turned over the car motor.* **f.** (of an engine) to start: *The motor turned over without any trouble.* **g.** *Com.* to purchase and then sell (goods or commodities). **h.** *Com.* to do business or sell goods to the amount of (a specified sum). **i.** *Com.* to invest or recover (capital) in some transaction or in the course of business. **75. turn the tables.** See **table** (def. 18). **76. turn the tide.** See **tide**[1] (def. 12). **77. turn to, a.** to apply to for aid; appeal to: *When he was starting out as an artist he turned to his friends for loans.* **b.** to begin to attend to or work at: *After the storm we turned to and cleaned up the debris.* **c.** to change to: *The ice turned to water.* **78. turn up, a.** to fold (material, a hem, cuffs, etc.) up or over in order to alter a garment. **b.** to bring to the surface by digging: *to turn up a shovelful of earth.* **c.** to uncover; find. **d.** to intensify or increase. **e.** to happen; occur: *Let's wait and see what turns up.* **f.** to appear; arrive: *He turned up at the last moment.* **g.** to be recovered: *I'm sure your watch will turn up eventually.* **h.** to come to notice; be seen. —*n.* **79.** a movement of partial or total rotation: *a slight turn of the handle.* **80.** act of changing or reversing position or posture as by a rotary movement: *a turn of the head.* **81.** a time or opportunity for action which comes in due rotation or order to each of a number of persons, animals, etc.: *It's my turn to pay the bill.* **82.** act of changing or reversing the course or direction: *to make a turn to the right.* **83.** a place or point at which such a change occurs. **84.** a place where a road, river, or the like, turns; bend: *About a mile ahead, you'll come to a turn in the road.* **85.** a single revolution, as of a wheel. **86.** act of turning so as to face or go in a different direction. **87.** direction, drift, or trend: *The conversation took an interesting turn.* **88.** any change, as in nature, character, condition, affairs, circumstances, etc.; alteration; modification: *a turn for the better.* **89.** the point or time of change. **90.** the time during which a workman or a set of workmen is at work in alternation with others. **91.** that which is done by each of a number of persons acting in rotation or succession. **92.** rounded or curved form. **93.** the shape or mold in which something is formed or cast. **94.** a passing or twisting of one thing around another, as of a rope around a mast. **95.** state or manner of being twisted. **96.** a single circular or convoluted shape, as of a coiled or wound rope. **97.** a small latch operated by a turning knob or lever. **98.** style, as of expression or language. **99.** a distinctive form or style imparted: *a happy turn of expression.* **100.** a short walk, ride, or the like, out and back, esp. by different routes: *Let's go for a turn in the car.* **101.** natural inclination, bent, tendency, or aptitude: *the turn of his mind.* **102.** a spell or period of work; shift. **103.** a spell or bout of action or activity, esp. in wrestling. **104.** an attack of illness or the like. **105.** an act of service or disservice: *He once did her a good turn. She repaid it with a bad turn.* **106.** requirement, exigency, or need: *This will serve your turn.* **107.** treatment or rendering, esp. with reference to the form or content of a work of literature, art, etc.; twist: *He gave the story a new turn.* **108.** *Informal.* a nervous shock, as from fright or astonishment: *It certainly gave her quite a turn to see him.* **109.** *Stock Exchange.* a complete securities transaction which includes both a purchase and sale. **110.** *Music.* a melodic embellishment or grace, commonly consisting of a principal tone with two auxiliary tones, one above and the other below it. **111.** *Chiefly Brit.* an individual stage performance, esp. in a vaudeville theater or music hall. **112.** *Mil.* a drill movement by which a formation changes fronts. **113.** a contest or round; a bout, as in wrestling. **114. at every turn,** in every case or instance; constantly: *She met with kindness at every turn.* **115. by turns,** one after another; in rotation or succession; alternately: *They did their shopping and cleaning by turns.* **116. hand's turn,** a period or piece of work: *It won't be necessary for you to do a hand's turn yourself, but rather to supervise.* **117. in turn,** in due order of succession: *Each generation in turn must grapple with the same basic problems.* **118. on the turn,** on the verge or in the process of turning; changing: *She said she hoped to be alive to see the century on the turn.* **119. out of turn,** **a.** not in the correct succession; out of proper order. **b.** at an unsuitable time; imprudently; indiscreetly: *He spoke out of turn, and destroyed the cordial atmosphere of the meeting.* **120. take turns,** to succeed one another in order; rotate; alternate: *They took turns walking the dog.* **121. to a turn,** to just the proper degree; to perfection: *The steak was done to a turn.* **122. turn and turn about** or **turn about,** by turns: *They fought the fire, turn and turn about, until daybreak.* [ME *turnen*, OE *turnian* < L *tornāre* to turn in a lathe, round off, deriv. of *tornus* lathe < Gk *tórnos* tool for making circles] —**turn′a·ble,** *adj.*

—**Syn. 9.** metamorphose, transmute, transform. **23, 24.** fashion, mold. **40.** TURN, REVOLVE, ROTATE, SPIN indicate moving in a more or less rotary, circular fashion. TURN is the general and popular word for motion on an axis or around a center, but it is used also of motion that is less than a complete circle: *A gate turns on its hinges.* REVOLVE refers esp. to movement in an orbit around a center, but is sometimes exchangeable with ROTATE, which refers only to the motion of a body around its own center or axis: *The moon revolves about the earth. The earth revolves (or rotates) on its axis.* To SPIN is to rotate very rapidly: *The blades of an electric fan spin.* **79.** spin, gyration, revolution. **88.** deviation, bend, twist, vicissitude, variation. **101.** talent, proclivity. TURN, CAST, TWIST are colloquial in use and imply a bent, inclination, or habit. TURN means a tendency or inclination for something: *a turn for art.* CAST means an established habit of thought, manner or style: *a melancholy cast.* TWIST means a bias: *a twist for conservatism; a twist against liquor.*

turn·a·bout (tûrn′ə bout′), *n.* **1.** act of turning in a different or opposite direction. **2.** a change of opinion, loyalty, etc. **3.** *Brit.* merry-go-round. **4.** a reciprocal action; doing to someone exactly as he has done to another: *Turnabout is fair play.* **5.** *Obs.* a person who changes things; a radical. [n. use of v. phrase *turn about*]

turn′-and-bank′ in′dicator (tûrn′ən baŋk′), *Aeron.* See **bank-and-turn indicator.**

turn′-and-slip′ in′dicator (tûrn′ən slip′). See **bank-and-turn indicator.**

turn·a·round (tûrn′ə round′), *n.* **1.** the total time consumed in the round trip of a ship, aircraft, vehicle, etc. **2.** turnabout. **3.** change of allegiance, opinion, mood, policy, etc. **4.** a place or area having sufficient room for a vehicle to turn around. [n. use of v. phrase *turn around*]

turn·buck·le (tûrn′buk′əl), *n.* a link or sleeve with a swivel at one end and an internal screw thread at the other, or with an internal screw thread at each end, one right-handed and the other left-handed, used as a means of uniting or coupling, and of tightening, two parts, as the ends of two rods. [TURN + BUCKLE]

Turnbuckle (Open)

turn′ but′ton, button (def. 6).

turn·coat (tûrn′kōt′), *n.* a person who changes to the opposite party or faction, reverses his principles, etc.; renegade. [TURN + COAT]

turn·down (tûrn′doun′), *adj.* that is or may be turned down; folded or doubled down: *a turndown collar.* [from v. phrase *turn down*]

turned′ com′ma, *Brit.* See **quotation mark.** Also called **inverted comma.**

turned-on (tûrnd′on′, -ôn′), *adj. Slang.* **1.** lively and chic; switched-on. **2.** full of or characterized by excitement. **3.** under the influence of a narcotic or hallucinogen, as marijuana.

turn·er[1] (tûr′nər), *n.* **1.** one who or that which turns or is employed in turning. **2.** a person who fashions or shapes objects on a lathe. [ME; see TURN, -ER[1]]

turn·er[2] (tûr′nər, tŏŏr′-), *n.* a member of a turnverein; a tumbler or gymnast. [< G *Turner* gymnast, deriv. of *turnen* to exercise < F *tourner* to TURN]

Tur·ner (tûr′nər), *n.* **1. Frederick Jackson,** 1861–1932, U.S. historian. **2. Joseph Mallord William,** 1775–1851, English painter. **3. Nat,** 1800–31, American Negro slave leader. **4.** a walled plain in the third quadrant of the face of the moon: about 7 miles in diameter.

Tur′ners Falls′, a town in NW Massachusetts. 4917 (1960).

turn·er·y (tûr′nə rē), *n., pl.* **-er·ies. 1.** the process or art of forming or shaping objects on a lathe. **2.** objects or articles fashioned on a lathe collectively. **3.** a workshop where such work is done. [TURNER[1] + -Y[3]]

turn·hall (tûrn′hôl′), *n.* a hall or building in which turners or gymnasts practice or perform. [< G *Turnhalle*, equiv. to *turn(en)* (to) practice gymnastics + *Halle* hall]

turn′ in′dicator, *Aeron.* a flight instrument that indicates the angular rate of turn of an aircraft about its vertical axis. Cf. **bank-and-turn indicator.**

turn·ing (tûr′niŋ), *n.* **1.** the act of one who or that which turns. **2.** the act of reversing position. **3.** the place or point at which anything bends or changes direction. **4.** the forming of objects on a lathe. **5.** an object, as a spindle, turned on a lathe. **6.** the act of shaping or forming something: *the skillful turning of verses.* [ME, OE; see TURN, -ING[1]]

turn′ing en′gine. See **jacking engine.**

turn′ing piece′, a wooden pattern for an arch built without centering.

turn′ing point′, **1.** a point at which a decisive change takes place; critical point; crisis. **2.** a point at which something changes direction, esp. a high or low point on a graph. **3.** *Survey.* (in leveling or plane-tabling) a point temporarily located and marked in order to establish the elevation or position of a surveying instrument at a new station. *Abbr.:* T.P.

tur·nip (tûr′nip), *n.* **1.** the thick, fleshy, edible root of either of two cruciferous plants, the white-fleshed *Brassica Rapa*, or the yellow-fleshed rutabaga. **2.** the plant itself. **3.** the root of this plant used as a vegetable. [earlier *turnepa* < TURN (with reference to its neatly rounded shape) + *nepe* NEEP] —**tur′nip·like′,** *adj.*

tur′nip-root·ed cel′ery (tûr′nip rōō′tid), celeriac.

turn·key (tûrn′kē′), *n., pl.* **-keys.** one who has charge of the keys of a prison; jailer. [TURN + KEY[1]]

turn·off (tûrn′ôf′, -of′), *n.* **1.** a small road that branches off from a larger one, esp. a ramp or exit leading off a major highway: *He took the wrong turnoff and it took him about 15 minutes before he could get back on the turnpike.* **2.** a place at which one diverges from or changes a former course. **3.** act of turning off. **4.** the finished product of a certain manufacturing process, as weaving. **5.** the quantity of fattened livestock distributed to market. [n. use of v. phrase *to turn off*]

Turn′ of the Screw′, The, a short novel (1898) by Henry James.

turn·out (tûrn′out′), *n.* **1.** the gathering of persons who come to an exhibition, party, spectacle, or the like: *They had a large turnout at the meeting.* **2.** quantity of production; output. **3.** the act of turning out. **4.** manner or style in which a person or thing is equipped, dressed, etc. **5.** equipment; outfit. **6.** a short side track or passage which enables trains, automobiles, etc., to pass one another. **7.** *Ballet.* the turning out of the legs from the hips, with the feet back to back or heel to heel. **8.** *Railroads.* a track structure composed of a switch, a frog, and closure rails, permitting a train to leave a given track for a branching or parallel track. Cf. **crossover** (def. 3). **9.** *Brit.* **a.** a labor strike. **b.** a worker who is on strike; striker. [n. use of v. phrase *turn out*]

turn·o·ver (tûrn′ō′vər), *n.* **1.** the act or result of turning over; upset. **2.** change or movement of people as tenants, customers, etc., in, out, or through a place: *The restaurant did a lively business and had a rapid turnover.* **3.** the aggregate of worker replacements in a given period in a given business or industry. **4.** the ratio of the labor turnover to the average number of employees in a given period. **5.** the total amount of business done in a given time. **6.** the rate at which items are sold, esp. with reference to the depletion of stock and replacement of inventory: *Things are slow now, but they expect an increased turnover next month.* **7.** the number of times that capital is invested and reinvested in a line of merchandise during a specified period of time. **8.** the turning over of the capital or stock of goods involved in a particular transaction or course of business. **9.** rate of processing or the amount of material which has undergone a particular process in a given period of time, as in manufacturing. **10.** a change from one position, opinion, etc., to another, often to one that is opposed to that previously held. **11.** a reorganization of a political organization, business, etc., esp. one involving a change or shift of personnel. **12.** a baked pastry with a sweet or savory filling in which half the dough is turned over the filling and the edges sealed to form a semicircle or triangle. —*adj.* **13.** that is or may be turned over. **14.** having a part that turns over, as a collar. [n. use of v. phrase *turn over*]

turn·pike (tûrn′pīk′), *n.* **1.** a high-speed highway, esp. one maintained by tolls. **2.** (formerly) a barrier set across such a highway to stop passage until a toll has been paid; tollgate. [late ME *turnepike* road barrier. See TURN, PIKE[2]]

turn·plate (tûrn′plāt′), *n. Brit.* a railroad turntable. [TURN + PLATE[1]]

turn·screw (tûrn′skrōō′), *n. Chiefly Brit.* a screwdriver.

turn·sole (tûrn′sōl′), *n.* **1.** any of several plants regarded as turning with the movement of the sun. **2.** heliotrope (def. 2). **3.** a European euphorbiaceous plant, *Chrozophora tinctoria*, yielding a purple dye. **4.** a purple dye prepared from the turnsole herb *Chrozophora tinctoria;* litmus. [ME *turnesole* < MF *tournesol* the dye got from the plant < It *tornasole* the plant *tornare* to turn + *sole* sun]

turn·spit (tûrn′spit′), *n.* **1.** a spit that rotates or can be rotated. **2.** a mechanically or manually operated device for turning a spit on which meat is roasted. **3.** a person who turns a spit. **4.** a small dog having a long body and short legs, used formerly to work a treadmill that turned a spit. [TURN + SPIT[2]]

turn·stile (tûrn′stīl′), *n.* **1.** a structure of four horizontally revolving arms pivoted atop a post and set in a gateway or opening in a fence to allow the controlled passage of people. **2.** a similar device set up in an entrance to bar passage until a charge is paid, to record the number of persons passing through, etc. [TURN + STILE]

turn·stone (tûrn′stōn′), *n.* **1.** any of several small, limicoline birds of the genus *Arenaria*, characterized by the habit of turning over stones in search of food. **2.** a New World turnstone, *Arenaria interpres*, having a chestnut and black back, a black breast, and a white abdomen. [TURN + STONE]

turn′ sto′ry, *Journalism.* a story that runs from the bottom of the last column of one page to the top of the first column of the following page.

turn·ta·ble (tûrn′tā′bəl), *n.* **1.** the rotating disk on which the record in a phonograph rests. **2.** *Railroads.* a rotating, track-bearing platform pivoted in the center, used for turning locomotives and cars around. **3.** a rotating stand used in sculpture, metalwork, and ceramics. [TURN + TABLE]

turn·up (tûrn′up′), *n.* **1.** that which is turned up or which turns up: *The escapee's turnup is expected soon.* **2.** *Brit.* a cuff on a pair of trousers. **3.** *Chiefly Brit.* fight; row; disturbance. —*adj.* **4.** that is or may be turned up. [n. use of v. phrase *turn up*]

Tur·nus (tûr′nəs), *n. Rom. Legend.* an Italian king and rival of Aeneas for Lavinia. He was finally killed by Aeneas.

turn·ver·ein (tûrn′və rīn′; *Ger.* tŏŏrn′fer īn′), *n.* an athletic club, esp. of gymnasts. [< G: gymnastic club, equiv. to *turn(en)* (to) practice gymnastics + *Verein* union]

turn·wrest (tûrn′rest′), *n.* See **swivel plow.** Also, **turn·wrist** (tûrn′rist′). [TURN + WREST]

tur·pen·tine (tûr′pən tīn′), *n., v.,* **-tined, -tin·ing.** —*n.* **1.** any of various oleoresins derived from coniferous trees, esp. the longleaf pine, *Pinus palustris*, and yielding a volatile oil and a resin when distilled. **2.** Also called **Chian turpentine.** an oleoresin exuding from the terbinth, *Pistacia Terebinthus.* **3.** See **oil of turpentine.** —*v.t.* **4.** to treat with turpentine; apply turpentine to. **5.** to gather or take crude turpentine from (trees). [late ME, r. ME *ter(e)bentyn(e)* < ML *ter(e)bentīna* < L *terebinthina*, n. use of fem. of *terebinthīnus* of the turpentine tree, equiv. to *terebinth(us)* turpentine tree (< Gk *terébinthos*) + *-īnus* -INE[1]] —**tur·pen·tin·ic** (tûr′pən tin′ik), **tur·pen·tin·ous** (tûr′pən tin′əs, -tī′nəs), **tur·pen·tin·y** (tûr′pən tī′nē), *adj.*

tur·peth (tûr′pith), *n.* **1.** the root of a convolvulaceous plant, *Operculina turpethum*, of the East Indies, formerly used as a purgative. 2. the plant itself. 3. Also called **tur′peth min′eral.** *Chem.* See **mercuric subsulfate.** [< ML *turpethum* < Ar *turbid;* r. late ME *tubit* < MF < Ar *turbid*]

Tur·pin (tûr′pin), *n.* **Richard** (*Dick*), 1706–39, English highwayman.

tur·pi·tude (tûr′pi to͞od′, -tyo͞od′), *n.* 1. vile, shameful, or base character; depravity. 2. a vile or depraved act. [late ME < L *turpitūdō*, equiv. to *turpi(s)* base, vile + *-tūdō* -TUDE]

tur·quoise (tûr′koiz, -kwoiz), *n.* 1. Also, **tur′quois.** an opaque mineral, a basic hydrous copper aluminum phosphate often containing a small amount of iron, sky-blue or greenish-blue in color, cut cabochon as a gem. Cf. **bone turquoise.** 2. Also called **tur′quoise blue′.** a greenish blue or bluish green. [< F: Turkish (stone) < *Turc* TURK + *-oise*, fem. of *-ois* -ESE; r. ME *turkeis* < MF]

tur·ret (tûr′it, tur′-), *n.* 1. a small tower, usually one forming part of a larger structure. 2. a small tower at an angle of a building, as of a castle or fortress, frequently beginning some distance above the ground. 3. Also called **turrethead.** a pivoted attachment on a lathe or the like for holding a number of tools, each of which can be presented to the work in rapid succession by a simple rotating movement. 4. *Navy, Army.* a low, towerlike, heavily armored structure, usually revolving horizontally, within which guns are mounted. 5. *Fort.* a tall structure, usually moved on wheels, formerly employed in breaching or scaling a fortified place, a wall, or the like. [ME *turet* < MF *turete* < OF *tur* tower (< L *turris*) + *-ete* -ET] —**tur′ret·less,** *adj.*

Turret (def. 2)

tur′ret clock′, an outside clock having two or more faces with dials.

tur′ret deck′, *Naut.* a narrow weather deck on a turret-deck vessel.

tur′ret-deck′ ves′sel (tûr′it dek′, tur′-), *Naut.* a freighter having a hull with sides rising from an abrupt tumble home to a narrow weather deck. Also, **tur′ret-decked′ ves′sel** (tûr′it dekt′, tur′-).

tur·ret·ed (tûr′i tid, tur′-), *adj.* 1. furnished with a turret or turrets. 2. having a turretlike part or parts. 3. *Zool.* having whorls in the form of a long or towering spiral, as certain shells. [TURRET + -ED³]

Turreted shell

tur·ret·head (tûr′it hed′, tur′-), *n.* *Mach.* turret (def. 3). [TURRET + HEAD]

tur′ret lathe′, a lathe fitted with a turret.

turri-, a learned borrowing from Latin meaning "tower," used in the formation of compound words: *turrilite.* [comb. form of L *turris* tower]

tur·ri·cal (tûr′i kəl), *adj.* of, pertaining to, or resembling a turret. [TURR(I)- tower + -ICAL]

tur·ric·u·late (tə rik′yə lit, -lāt′), *adj.* furnished with or resembling a turret or turrets. Also, **tur·ric′u·lat′ed.** [< L *turricula* little tower (dim. of *turris* + -ATE¹]

tur·ri·lite (tûr′ə līt′), *n.* an ammonoid of the genus *Turrilites*, of the Cretaceous period, having a turreted shell. [< NL; see TURRI-, -LITE]

Tur·sha (tûr′shə), *n.* an ancient people of the Mediterranean region, variously identified with the Lydians, Etruscans, or Trojans.

tur·tle¹ (tûr′tᵊl), *n., pl.* **-tles,** (*esp. collectively*) **-tle,** *v.,* **-tled, -tling.** —*n.* 1. any reptile of the order *Chelonia*, comprising aquatic and terrestrial species having the trunk enclosed in a shell consisting of a dorsal carapace and a ventral plastron. 2. (not used technically) an aquatic turtle as distinguished from a terrestrial one. Cf. **tortoise** (def. 1). 3. *Naut.* a vertical pocket in a spinnaker, for containing most of the sail, formed by closing the halves of a zipper sewn near the leeches: used esp. in yacht races to facilitate spreading the spinnaker by opening the zipper to allow the sail to billow out. 4. **turn turtle, a.** *Naut.* to capsize or turn over completely in foundering. **b.** to overturn; upset: *Several of the sports cars turned turtle in the course of the race.* —*v.i.* 5. to catch turtles, esp. as a business. [adaptation (influenced by TURTLE²) of F *tortue* < VL **tortūca* (> Sp *tortuga*), formed on L *tort(us)* twisted]

Box turtle, *Terrapene carolina* (Length 6 in.)

tur·tle² (tûr′tᵊl), *n.* *Archaic.* a turtledove. [ME, OE, var. of *turtur* turtledove < L < sound imit.]

tur·tle·back (tûr′tᵊl bak′), *n.* 1. Also called **tur′tle-deck′.** an arched protection erected over the deck of a steamer at the bow, and often at the stern also, to guard against damage from heavy seas. 2. *Archaeol.* a rough stone implement having one or both faces slightly convex. 3. *Furniture.* an oval or elliptical boss. [TURTLE¹ + BACK¹]

tur·tle·dove (tûr′tᵊl duv′), *n.* 1. any of several small to medium-sized, Old World doves of the genus *Streptopelia*, esp. *S. turtur*, of Europe, having a long, graduated tail. 2. *U.S. Dial.* See **mourning dove.** 3. a sweetheart or beloved mate. [ME *turtildove*, equiv. to *turtil* TURTLE² + *dove* DOVE¹]

tur·tle·head (tûr′tᵊl hed′), *n.* any scrophulariaceous herb of the genus *Chelone*, of North America. [TURTLE¹ + HEAD, so called from the appearance of its flower]

tur·tle·neck (tûr′tᵊl nek′), *n.* 1. a high, close-fitting collar, often rolled or turned down, appearing esp. on pull-over sweaters. 2. a sweater with such a collar. [TURTLE¹ + NECK]

tur′tle peg′, a weapon for piercing and capturing turtles, consisting of a sharp-pointed, metal head fastened to a cord and mounted on a shaft, the shaft being disengaged from the head in pulling in the turtle.

turt·let (tûrt′lit), *n.* a young or small turtle. [TUR-TL(E)¹ + -ET]

turves (tûrvz), *n.* *Chiefly Brit.* pl. of **turf.**

Tus·ca·loo·sa (tus′kə lo͞o′sə), *n.* a city in W Alabama. 63,370 (1960).

Tus·can (tus′kən), *adj.* 1. of, pertaining to, or characteristic of Tuscany, its people, or their dialect. 2. *Archit.* noting or pertaining to one of the five classical orders: developed in Rome, it is basically a simplified Roman Doric, with unfluted columns and with no decoration other than moldings. See illus. under **order.** Cf. **composite** (def. 3), **Corinthian** (def. 4), **Doric** (def. 3), **Ionic** (def. 1). —*n.* 3. the standard literary form of the Italian language. 4. any Italian dialect of Tuscany. 5. a native of Tuscany. [ME < L *Tuscānus* Etruscan, equiv. to *tusc(i)* the Etruscans + *-ānus* -AN]

Genoa ITALY ADRIATIC SEA MEDITERRANEAN SEA Florence Tuscany ELBA CORSICA Rome TYRRHENIAN SEA

Tus′can a′trium, (in an ancient Roman house) an atrium with no columns surrounding the compluvium.

Tus·ca·ny (tus′kə nē), *n.* a region in W central Italy: formerly a grand duchy. 3,267,374 (1961); 8879 sq. mi. Italian, **Toscana.**

Tus·ca·ro·ra (tus′kə rōr′ə, -rôr′ə), *n., pl.* **-ras,** (*esp. collectively*) **-ra.** 1. a member of an Indian people living originally in North Carolina and later, after their admission into the Iroquois confederacy, in New York. 2. an Iroquoian language, the language of the Tuscarora people.

tusch·e (to͝osh; *Ger.* to͝osh′ə), *n.* a greaselike liquid used in lithography as a medium receptive to lithographic ink, and in etching and silk-screen as a resist. [< G *Tusche*, back formation of *tuschen* to lay on color or ink < F *toucher* to touch]

Tus·co·la (tus kō′lə), *n.* a town in central Illinois. 3875 (1960).

Tus·cu·lum (tus′kyə ləm), *n.* an ancient city of Latium, SE of Rome: Roman villas, esp. that of Cicero. —**Tus′cu·lan,** *adj.*

Tus·cum·bi·a (tus kum′bē ə), *n.* a town in NW Alabama. 8994 (1960).

tush¹ (tush), *interj.* 1. (used as an exclamation of impatience, disdain, contempt, etc.) —*n.* 2. an exclamation of "tush." [sound imit.]

tush² (tush), *n.* 1. one of the four canine teeth of the horse. 2. a tusk. [ME, OE *tusc.* See TUSK] —**tushed,** *adj.*

tush·ie (to͝osh′ē), *n.* *Informal, Babytalk.* the buttocks. Also, **tushy.** [hypocristic alter. of TOKUS; see -IE]

tush·y (to͝osh′ē), *n., pl.* **tush·ies.** tushie.

tusk (tusk), *n.* 1. (in certain animals) a tooth developed to great length, usually one of a pair, as in the elephant, walrus, wild boar, etc., but singly in the narwhal. 2. a long, pointed, or protruding tooth. 3. a projection resembling the tusk of an animal. 4. Also called **gain.** *Carpentry.* a diagonally cut shoulder at the end of a timber for strengthening a tenon. —*v.t.* 5. to dig up or tear off with the tusks. 6. to gore with a tusk. —*v.i.* 7. to dig up or thrust at the ground with the tusks. [ME; OE *tusc* (also, *tux*), c. OFris *tusk;* akin to TOOTH] —**tusk′less,** *adj.* —**tusk′like′,** *adj.*

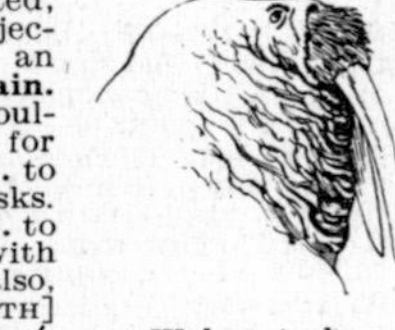

Walrus tusks

Tus·ke·gee (tus kē′gē), *n.* a city in E Alabama: location of Tuskegee Institute. 1750 (1960).

tusk·er (tus′kər), *n.* an animal with tusks, as an elephant or a wild boar. [TUSK + -ER¹]

tusk′ shell′. See **tooth shell.**

tusk′ ten′on, *Carpentry.* a tenon formed with a tusk.

tus·sah (tus′ə), *n.* 1. a tan silk from India. Cf. **Shantung** (def. 3). 2. the silkworm of an oriental moth of the genus *Antheraea*, as *A. mylitta*, that produces this silk. Also, **tus′seh, tus·ser** (tus′ər), **tussor, tussore, tussur.** Also called **wild silk.** [earlier *tusser* < Hind *tasar* shuttle < Skt *tasara, trasara* kind of silkworm]

tus·sal (tus′əl), *adj.* *Pathol.* pertaining to tussis, or cough. [< L *tuss(is)* cough + -AL¹]

tus·sis (tus′is), *n.* *Pathol.* a cough. [< L: cough]

tus·sive (tus′iv), *adj.* *Pathol.* of or pertaining to a cough. [< L *tuss(is)* cough + -IVE]

tus·sle (tus′əl), *v.,* **-sled, -sling,** *n.* —*v.i.* 1. to struggle or fight roughly or vigorously; wrestle; scuffle. —*n.* 2. a rough physical contest or struggle; scuffle. 3. any vigorous or determined struggle, conflict, etc.: *I had quite a tussle with that chemistry exam.* [var. of earlier *touse* to tease, pull (ME *-tuse(n)*) + -LE]

tus·sock (tus′ək), *n.* a tuft or clump of growing grass or the like. [appar. akin to MHG *zūsach* thicket, deriv. of *zūse* lock (of hair), brushwood. See TOUSLE, -OCK] —**tus′socked,** *adj.*

tus′sock cat′erpillar, the larva of a tussock moth.

tus′sock moth′, any of several moths of the family *Lymantriidae*, the larvae of which have characteristic tufts of hair on the body and feed on the leaves of various deciduous trees.

tus·sock·y (tus′ə kē), *adj.* 1. abounding in tussocks. 2. forming tussocks. [TUSSOCK + -Y¹]

tus·sor (tus′ər), *n.* tussah.

tus·sore (tus′ōr, -ôr), *n.* tussah.

tus·sur (tus′ər), *n.* tussah.

tut (*pronounced as an alveolar click; spelling pron.* tut), *interj., n., v.,* **tut·ted, tut·ting.** —*interj.* 1. (used as an exclamation of contempt, disdain, impatience, etc.) 2. for shame! —*n.* 3. an exclamation of "tut." —*v.i.* 4. to utter the exclamation "tut." Also, **tut-tut.**

Tut·ankh·a·men (to͞ot′ängk ä′mən), *n.* 14th century B.C., a king of Egypt of the 18th dynasty. Also, **Tut′ankh·a′mon, Tut′ankh·a′mun, Tut·enkh·a·mon** (to͞ot′engk ä′mən).

tu·te·lage (to͞ot′ᵊlij, tyo͞ot′-), *n.* 1. the act of guarding, protecting, or guiding; office or function of a guardian; guardianship. 2. instruction; teaching; guidance: *His Latin facility grew under private tutelage.* 3. the state of being under a guardian or a tutor. [< L *tūtēla* watching + -AGE]

tu·te·lar·y (to͞ot′ᵊler′ē, tyo͞ot′-), *adj., n., pl.* **-lar·ies.** —*adj.* 1. having the position of guardian or protector of a person, place, or thing: *tutelary saint.* 2. of or pertaining to a guardian or guardianship. —*n.* 3. one who has tutelary powers, as a saint, deity, guardian, or the like. Also, **tu·te·lar** (to͞ot′ᵊlər, tyo͞ot′-). [< L *tūtēlārius* guardian; see -ARY]

tu·te·nag (to͞ot′ᵊnag′, tyo͞ot′-), *n.* a nickel silver containing about 45 percent copper, with varying proportions of nickel and zinc and often smaller amounts of other metals. [< Mahratti *tuttināg*, appar. < Skt *tuttha-* sulfate of copper + *nāga* tin, lead]

tu·tor (to͞o′tər, tyo͞o′-), *n.* 1. a person employed to instruct another in some branch or branches of learning, esp. a private instructor. 2. a teacher of academic rank lower than instructor in some American universities and colleges. 3. a teacher without institutional connection who assists students in preparing for examinations. 4. one of a class of officers in a university or college, esp. at Oxford and Cambridge, having immediate supervision, as to studies, residence, etc., of undergraduates assigned to them. 5. the guardian of a boy or girl below age of puberty or majority. —*v.t.* 6. to act as a tutor to; teach or instruct, esp. privately. 7. to have the guardianship, instruction, or care of. 8. to instruct underhandedly; coach: *to tutor a witness before he testifies.* 9. *Archaic.* to train, school, or discipline. 10. *Archaic.* to admonish or reprove. —*v.i.* 11. to act as a tutor or private instructor. 12. to study privately with a tutor. [ME < L, protector, equiv. to *tūt(us)* (ptp. of *tuērī* to guard) + *-or* -OR²] —**tu′tor·ship,** *n.*

tu·tor·age (to͞o′tər ij, tyo͞o′-), *n.* 1. the office, authority, or care of a tutor. 2. the charge for instruction by a tutor. [TUTOR + -AGE]

tu·to·ri·al (to͞o tôr′ē əl, -tôr′-, tyo͞o-), *adj.* 1. pertaining to or exercised by a tutor: *tutorial functions or authority.* —*n.* 2. a class in which a tutor gives intensive instruction in some subject to an individual student or a small group of students. [< L *tūtōri(us)* of a guardian + -AL¹]

tuto′rial sys′tem, a system of education, esp. in some colleges, in which instruction is given personally by tutors, who also act as general advisers of a small group of students in their charge.

tu·toy·er (to͞o′twä yā′, tyo͞o′-; *Fr.* TY TWA YĀ′), *v.t.,* **-toy·ered** or **-toy·ed** (-twä yād′), **-toy·er·ing** (-twä yā′ing). to treat or speak to (someone) with familiarity, esp. upon short acquaintance when a more formal address would be more appropriate. [< F, to address as "tu" and "toi" (the familiar sing. forms for "you" in French)]

tut·ti (to͞o′tē; *It.* to͞ot′tē), *adj., n., pl.* **-tis.** *Music.* —*adj.* 1. all; all the voices or instruments together. 2. intended for or performed by all (or most of) the voices or instruments together, as a passage or movement in concert music (opposed to *solo*). —*n.* 3. a tutti passage or movement. 4. the tonal product or effect of a tutti performance. [< It, pl. of *tutto* all]

tut·ti-frut·ti (to͞o′tē fro͞o′tē), *n.* 1. a preserve of chopped mixed fruits, often with brandy syrup. 2. a variety of fruits, usually candied and minced, used in ice cream, confections, etc. [< It: lit., all the fruits]

tut·to (to͞o′tō; *It.* to͞ot′tô), *adj.* *Music.* all; entire. [< It: all, whole < L *totus*]

tut-tut (*pronounced as two alveolar clicks; spelling pron.* tut′tut′), *interj., n., v.i.,* **-tut·ted, -tut·ting.** tut.

tut·ty (tut′ē), *n.* an impure oxide of zinc obtained from the flues of smelting furnaces, or a similar substance occurring as a native mineral, used chiefly as a polishing powder. [ME *tutie* < late OF < ML *tūtia* < Ar *tūtiyā* oxide of zinc, ? < Pers]

tu·tu (to͞o′to͞o; *Fr.* TY TY′), *n., pl.* **-tus** (-to͞oz; *Fr.* -TY′). a short, full skirt, usually made of several layers of tarlatan or tulle, worn by ballerinas. [< F]

Tu·tu (to͞o′to͞o), *n.* **Desmond (Mpi·lo)** (əm pē′lō), born 1931, South African Anglican clergyman and civil-rights activist: Nobel peace prize 1984; archbishop of Cape Town since 1986.

Tu·tu·i·la (to͞o′to͞o ē′lä), *n.* the largest of the islands of American Samoa: excellent harbor at Pago Pago. 17,250 (1960); 53 sq. mi. —**Tu′tu·i′lan,** *adj., n.*

Tu′va Auton′omous Re·pub′lic (to͞o′və), an autonomous republic in the Russian Federation in Asia: formerly an independent republic in Mongolia. 309,000; 65,810 sq. mi. *Cap.:* Kyzyl. Also, **Tuvin′ian Auton′omous Repub′lic.** Formerly, **Tannu Tuva People's Republic, Tannu Tuva.**

tu-whit tu-whoo (to͝o hwit′ to͝o hwo͞o′, -wit′, -wo͞o′), (imitation of the cry of an owl).

tux·e·do (tuk sē′dō), *n., pl.* **-dos.** See **dinner jacket.** Also, **Tux·e′do.** [short for *Tuxedo coat*, named after country club at Tuxedo Park, N.Y.]

Tux·tla Gu·tiér·rez (to͞os′tlä go͞o tyeR′Res), *n.* a city in and the capital of Chiapas, in SE Mexico. 28,260 (1960). Also called **Tuxtla.**

tu·yère (twē yâr′, to͞o-, twēr; *Fr.* TY YeR′), *n., pl.* **tu·yères** (twē yârz′, to͞o-, twērz′; *Fr.* TY YeR′). *Metall.* an opening through which the blast of air enters a blast furnace, cupola forge, or the like, to facilitate combustion. Also, **tu·yer** (twē yâr′, to͞o-, twēr).

TV, 1. television. 2. *Slang.* transvestite.

TVA, *U.S. Govt.* Tennessee Valley Authority: a three-member board, created in 1933, charged with developing the Tennessee River and its tributaries to promote their use for cheap electric power, irrigation, flood control, navigation, etc. Since 1933 many projects have been constructed including 20 dams.

TV dinner, a quick-frozen meal, usually consisting of meat, a potato, and a vegetable, packaged in a partitioned tray of aluminum foil and requiring only heating before serving.

Tver (tvâr; *Russ.* tveR), *n.* a city in the W Russian Federation in Europe, NW of Moscow, on the Volga. 447,000. Formerly (1934–90), **Kalinin.**

TV table. See **snack table.**

twa (twä, twô), *n., adj.* *Scot.* two.

twad·dle (twod′ᵊl), *n., v.,* **-dled, -dling.** —*n.* 1. trivial, feeble, silly, or tedious talk or writing: *twaddle expected of a 13-year-old, not of a man.* —*v.i.* 2. to talk in a trivial, feeble, silly, or tedious manner; prate

Boring everyone and impressing no one, he twaddled on. —*v.t.* **3.** to utter as twaddle. [var. of *twattle*, b. TWIDDLE and TATTLE] —**twad′dler,** *n.* —**twad′dly,** *adj.*

twain (twān), *adj., n. Archaic.* two. [ME *twayn* < OE *twēgen;* c. obs. G *zween*]

Twain (twān), *n.* **Mark,** pen name of Samuel Langhorne Clemens.

twang (twang), *v.i.* **1.** to give out a sharp, vibrating sound, as the string of a musical instrument when plucked. **2.** to produce such a sound by plucking a stringed musical instrument. **3.** to have a sharp, nasal tone, as the human voice. —*v.t.* **4.** to cause to make a sharp, vibrating sound, as a string of a musical instrument. **5.** to produce (music) by plucking the strings of a musical instrument. **6.** to pluck the strings of (a musical instrument): *to twang a guitar.* **7.** to speak with a sharp, nasal tone. **8.** to pull the string of (an archer's bow). **9.** to let fly (an arrow). —*n.* **10.** the sharp, ringing sound produced by plucking or suddenly releasing a tense string. **11.** a sound resembling this. **12.** act of plucking or picking: *He gave his guitar strings a twang.* **13.** a sharp, nasal tone, as of the human voice. [sound imit.]

twan·gle (twang′gəl), *n., v.t., v.i.,* **-gled, -gling.** twang. [TWANG + -LE]

twang·y (twang′ē), *adj.,* **twang·i·er, twang·i·est.** **1.** having the sharp, vibrating tone of a plucked string. **2.** having a nasal voice quality. [TWANG + -Y[1]] —**twang′i·ness,** *n.*

'twas (twuz, twoz; *unstressed* twəz), contraction of *it was.*

twat·tle (twot′əl), *v.i., v.t.,* **-tled, -tling,** *n. Brit. Dial.* twaddle.

tway·blade (twā′blād′), *n.* any of various orchidaceous plants, esp. of the genera *Listera, Ophrys,* or *Liparis,* characterized by two nearly opposite broad leaves. [*tway* (apocopate form of OE *twēgen* twain) + BLADE]

tweak (twēk), *v.t.* **1.** to seize and pull with a jerk and twist: *to tweak someone's ear; to tweak someone's nose.* **2.** to pull or pinch the nose of, esp. gently: *He tweaked the baby on greeting.* —*n.* **3.** act of tweaking; a sharp, twisting pull or jerk. [akin to TWITCH]

tweed (twēd), *n.* **1.** a coarse wool cloth in a variety of weaves and colors, either hand-spun and hand-woven in Scotland, or reproduced, often by machine, elsewhere. **2. tweeds,** garments made of this cloth. **3.** a paper having a rough surface, used esp. for certain photographic prints. [appar. back formation from Scot *tweedling* twilling (now obs.) < ?]

Tweed (twēd), *n.* **1. William Mar·cy** (mär′sē) ("*Boss Tweed*"), 1823–78, U.S. politician. **2.** a river flowing E from S Scotland along part of the NE boundary of England into the North Sea. 97 mi. long. **3.** a boy's given name.

Tweed·dale (twēd′dāl′), *n.* Peebles.

twee·dle (twēd′əl), *v.,* **-dled, -dling.** —*v.i.* **1.** to produce high-pitched, modulated sounds, as a singer, bird, musical instrument, etc. **2.** to perform lightly upon a musical instrument. —*v.t.* **3.** to lure by or as by music: *The Pied Piper tweedled the children into following him.*

Twee·dle·dum and Twee·dle·dee (twēd′əl dum′ ən twēd′əl dē′), two persons or things nominally different but practically the same; a nearly identical pair. [humorous imit. coinage, appar. first applied as nicknames to Handel and Bononcini, with reference to their musical rivalry, deriv. of *tweedle* imit. word for a shrill note]

Tweeds·muir (twēdz′myŏŏr), *n.* **Baron.** See **Buchan, John.**

tweed·y (twē′dē), *adj.,* **tweed·i·er, tweed·i·est.** **1.** made of or resembling tweed, as in texture, appearance, or the like. **2.** wearing or favoring tweeds, esp. as a mark of a leisurely, casual way of life, as at college or in the country: *a tweedy sportswoman.* **3.** accustomed to or preferring casual or outdoor life: *a large and tweedy colony of civil servants and government officials.* [TWEED + -Y[1]]

'tween (twēn), *prep.* **1.** contraction of *between.* —*n.* **2.** Also, **tween, tweeny.** a youngster between 10 and 12 years of age, considered too old to be a child and too young to be a teenager. [ME *twene,* deriv. of *atwene*]

'tween′ deck′, *Naut.* any space between two continuous decks in the hull of a vessel, as between a shelter deck and a freeboard deck.

tween·y (twē′nē), *n., pl.* **tween·ies.** **1.** *U.S.* 'tween (def. 2). **2.** *Brit. Informal.* a maid who assists other servants; an apprentice or auxiliary maid. [(BE)TWEEN + -Y[2]]

tweese (twēz), *v.t.,* **tweesed, twees·ing,** *n.* tweeze[2].

tweet (twēt), *n.* **1.** the weak chirp of a young or small bird. —*v.i.* **2.** to chirp. [imit.]

tweet·er (twē′tər), *n.* a small loudspeaker designed for the reproduction of high-frequency sounds. [TWEET + -ER[1]]

tweet·er-woof·er (twē′tər wŏŏf′ər), *n.* a loudspeaker, usually coaxial, in which the tweeter is mounted in and in front of the cone of the woofer.

tweeze[1] (twēz), *v.t.,* **tweezed, tweez·ing.** to pluck, as with tweezers. [back formation from TWEEZERS]

tweeze[2] (twēz), *n. Obs.* a case of instruments, as that of a surgeon. Also, **tweese.** [< (*e*)*twees*(*e*) < F *étuis;* pl. of *étui* < OF *etuier* to keep < L *studiāre* to care for]

tweez·er (twē′zər), *n.* tweezers.

tweez·ers (twē′zərz), *n. pl.* small pincers or nippers for plucking out hairs, taking up small objects, etc. [pl. of *tweezer* (after *scissors, pincers,* etc.), equiv. to TWEEZE[2] + -ER[1]]

Tweezers

twelfth (twelfth), *adj.* **1.** next after the eleventh; being the ordinal number for 12. **2.** being one of 12 equal parts. —*n.* **3.** a twelfth part, esp. of one (1/12). **4.** the twelfth member of a series. [ME *twelfthe, twelfte* < OE *twelfta,* equiv. to *twelf* TWELVE + *-ta* -TH[2]]

Twelfth-day (twelfth′dā′), *n.* the 12th day after Christmas, January 6, on which the festival of the Epiphany is celebrated, formerly observed as the last day of the Christmas festivities.

Twelfth-night (twelfth′nīt′), *n.* **1.** the evening before Twelfth-day, formerly observed with various festivities. **2.** the evening of Twelfth-day itself. [ME; OE *twelftan niht*]

Twelfth′ Night′, a comedy (1602) by Shakespeare.

Twelfth·tide (twelfth′tīd′), *n.* the season of Twelfth-night and Twelfth-day. [TWELFTH + TIDE[1]]

twelve (twelv), *n.* **1.** a cardinal number, 10 plus 2. **2.** a symbol for this number, as 12 or XII. **3.** a set of this many persons or thing. **4. the Twelve,** the 12 apostles chosen by Christ. —*adj.* **5.** amounting to 12 in number. [ME *twelve,* inflected form of *twelf,* OE *twelfe,* lit., (ten and) two leave, i.e. two left over; c. OFris *twel*(*e*)*f,* Goth *twalif,* OHG *zwelif,* Icel *tólf;* cf. Lith *dvýlika*]

twelve·fold (twelv′fōld′), *adj.* **1.** having twelve sections, aspects, divisions, kinds, etc. **2.** being twelve times more, larger, greater, etc., as a given quantity size, intensity, or the like. —*adv.* **3.** twelve times in amount or degree: *Its potential destructive power was increased twelvefold.* [OE *twelf-feald.* See TWELVE, -FOLD]

twelve′-mile lim′it (twelv′mīl′), the offshore boundary of a state, extending 12 miles at sea. Cf. **three-mile limit.**

twelve·mo (twelv′mō), *n., pl.* **-mos,** *adj.* duodecimo. [TWELVE + (DUODECI)MO]

twelve·month (twelv′munth′), *n. Chiefly Brit.* a year. [ME *twelfmoneth.* See TWELVE, MONTH] —**twelve′-month′ly,** *adv.*

twelve-note row (twelv′nōt′ rō′), *Chiefly Brit.* See **tone row.**

twelve·pen·ny (twelv′pen′ē), *adj.* noting a nail 3¼ inches long. *Abbr.:* 12d [TWELVE + -PENNY]

Twelv·er (twel′vər), *n. Islam.* Imamite. [TWELVE + -ER[1]]

Twelve′ Ta′bles, the, the tablets on which were engraved short statements of legal principles drawn up by the decemvirs in 451 and 450 B.C., largely declaratory of the contemporary practices and rules that were the most important in the affairs of Roman daily life.

twelve-tone (twelv′tōn′), *adj. Music.* **1.** based on or incorporating the twelve-tone technique: *twelve-tone music.* **2.** using or advocating the twelve-tone technique: *a twelve-tone composer.*

twelve′-tone′ row′ (rō). See **tone row.** Also, *esp. Brit.,* **twelve-note row.**

twelve′-tone′ technique′, *Music.* a modern system of tone relationships in which the 12 tones of an octave are not centered around any one tone, but are unified by a selected order of tones for a given composition.

twen·ti·eth (twen′tē ith), *adj.* **1.** next after the nineteenth; being the ordinal number for 20. **2.** being one of 20 equal parts. —*n.* **3.** a twentieth part, esp. of one (1/20). **4.** the twentieth member of a series. [ME *twentithe* < OE *twentigotha.* See TWENTY, -TH[2]]

twen·ty (twen′tē), *n., pl.* **-ties,** *adj.* —*n.* **1.** a cardinal number, 10 times 2. **2.** a symbol for this number, as 20 or XX. **3.** a set of this many persons or things. **4. twenties,** the numbers 20 through 29, esp. the 20th through the 29th year of a lifetime or of a given or implied century: *We now look back on the twenties with nostalgia.* —*adj.* **5.** amounting to 20 in number. [ME; OE *twēntig;* c. OFris *tw*(*e*)*intich,* OHG *zweinzug* (G *zwanzig*), Goth *twai tigjus* two tens]

twen·ty-eight (twen′tē āt′), *n.* **1.** a cardinal number, 20 plus 8. **2.** a symbol for this number, as 28 or XXVIII. **3.** a set of this many persons or things. —*adj.* **4.** amounting to 28 in number.

twen·ty-eighth (twen′tē ātth′), *adj.* **1.** next after the twenty-seventh; being the ordinal number for 28. **2.** being one of 28 equal parts. —*n.* **3.** a twenty-eighth part, esp. of one (1/28). **4.** the twenty-eighth member of a series.

twen·ty-fifth (twen′tē fifth′), *adj.* **1.** next after the twenty-fourth; being the ordinal number for 25. **2.** being one of 25 equal parts. —*n.* **3.** a twenty-fifth part, esp. of one (1/25). **4.** the twenty-fifth member of a series.

twen·ty-first (twen′tē fûrst′), *adj.* **1.** next after the twentieth; being the ordinal number for 21. **2.** being one of 21 equal parts. —*n.* **3.** a twenty-first part, esp. of one (1/21). **4.** the twenty-first member of a series.

twen·ty-five (twen′tē fīv′), *n.* **1.** a cardinal number, 20 plus 5. **2.** a symbol for this number, as 25 or XXV. **3.** a set of this many persons or things. —*adj.* **4.** amounting to 25 in number.

twen·ty-five·pen·ny (twen′tē fīv′pen′ē), *adj.* noting a nail 4¼ inches long. *Abbr.:* 25d [TWENTY-FIVE + -PENNY]

twen·ty·fold (twen′tē fōld′), *adj.* **1.** having twenty sections, aspects, divisions, kinds, etc. **2.** being twenty times as large, great, many, etc. —*adv.* **3.** twenty times in amount or degree. [OE *twentigfeald.* See TWENTY, -FOLD]

twen·ty-four (twen′tē fōr′, -fôr′), *n.* **1.** a cardinal number, 20 plus 4. **2.** a symbol for this number, as 24 or XXIV. **3.** a set of this many persons or things. —*adj.* **4.** amounting to 24 in number.

twen·ty-four·mo (twen′tē fōr′mō, -fôr′-), *n., pl.* **-mos,** *adj.* —*n.* **1.** a book size of about 3⅝ × 5⅛ inches, determined by printing on sheets folded to form 24 leaves or 48 pages. **2.** a book of this size. *Abbr.:* 24mo, 24° —*adj.* **3.** in twenty-fourmo. Also called **vigesimo-quarto.** [TWENTY-FOUR + (DUODECI)MO]

twen·ty-fourth (twen′tē fōrth′, -fôrth′), *adj.* **1.** next after the twenty-third; being the ordinal number for 24. **2.** being one of 24 equal parts. —*n.* **3.** a twenty-fourth part, esp. of one (1/24). **4.** the twenty-fourth member of a series.

twen·ty·mo (twen′tē mō′), *n., pl.* **-mos,** *adj.* —*n.* **1.** a book size of about 3 × 5 inches, determined by printing on sheets folded to form 20 leaves or 40 pages. **2.** a book of this size. *Abbr.:* 20mo, 20° —*adj.* **3.** in twentymo. Also called **vigesimo.** [TWENTY + (DUODECI)MO]

twen·ty-nine (twen′tē nīn′), *n.* **1.** a cardinal number, 20 plus 9. **2.** a symbol for this number, as 29 or XXIX. **3.** a set of this many persons or things. —*adj.* **4.** amounting to 29 in number.

twen·ty-ninth (twen′tē nīnth′), *adj.* **1.** next after the twenty-eighth; being the ordinal number for 29. **2.** being one of 29 equal parts. —*n.* **3.** a twenty-ninth part, esp. of one (1/29). **4.** the twenty-ninth member of a series.

twen·ty-one (twen′tē wun′), *n.* **1.** a cardinal number, 20 plus 1. **2.** a symbol for this number, as 21 or XXI. **3.** a set of this many persons or things. **4.** Also called **blackjack.** a gambling game at cards, in which the object is to obtain from the dealer cards whose values add up to, or close to, 21 but which do not exceed it. —*adj.* **5.** amounting to 21 in number.

twen·ty·pen·ny (twen′tē pen′ē), *adj.* noting a nail four inches long. *Abbr.:* 20d [TWENTY + -PENNY]

twen′ty ques′tions, an oral game in which one player selects a word or object which the other players attempt to guess by asking up to twenty questions that can be answered with a yes or a no.

twen·ty-sec·ond (twen′tē sek′ənd), *adj.* **1.** next after the twenty-first; being the ordinal number for 22. **2.** being one of 22 equal parts. —*n.* **3.** a twenty-second part, esp. of one (1/22). **4.** the twenty-second member of a series.

twen·ty-sev·en (twen′tē sev′ən), *n.* **1.** a cardinal number 20 plus 7. **2.** a symbol for this number, as 27 or XXVII. **3.** a set of this many persons or things. —*adj.* **4.** amounting to 27 in number.

twen·ty-sev·enth (twen′tē sev′ənth), *adj.* **1.** next after the twenty-sixth; being the ordinal number for 27. **2.** being one of 27 equal parts. —*n.* **3.** a twenty-seventh part, esp. of one (1/27). **4.** the twenty-seventh member of a series.

twen·ty-six (twen′tē siks′), *n.* **1.** a cardinal number, 20 plus 6. **2.** a symbol for this number, as 26 or XXVI. **3.** a set of this many persons or things. —*adj.* **4.** amounting to 26 in number.

Twen′ty-six Men′ and a Girl′, a short story (1899) by Maxim Gorki.

twen·ty-sixth (twen′tē siksth′), *adj.* **1.** next after the twenty-fifth; being the ordinal number for 26. **2.** being one of 26 equal parts. —*n.* **3.** a twenty-sixth part, esp. of one (1/26). **4.** the twenty-sixth member of a series.

twen·ty-third (twen′tē thûrd′), *adj.* **1.** next after the twenty-second; being the ordinal number for 23. **2.** being one of 23 equal parts. —*n.* **3.** a twenty-third part, esp. of one (1/23). **4.** the twenty-third member of a series.

Twen′ty Thou′sand Leagues′ Un′der the Sea′, a novel (1870) by Jules Verne.

twen·ty-three (twen′tē thrē′), *n.* **1.** a cardinal number, 20 plus 3. **2.** a symbol for this number, as 23 or XXIII. **3.** a set of this many persons or things. —*adj.* **4.** amounting to 23 in number.

twen·ty-twen·ty (twen′tē twen′tē), *adj. Ophthalm.* having normal visual acuity.

twen·ty-two (twen′tē to͞o′), *n.* **1.** a cardinal number, 20 plus 2. **2.** a symbol for this number, as 22 or XXII. **3.** a set of this many persons or things. —*adj.* **4.** amounting to 22 in number.

.22 (twen′tē to͞o′), *pl.* **.22s, .22's.** a pistol, rifle, or cartridge of .22-caliber, or having a diameter of .22 inches or of 22 millimeters.

'twere (twûr; *unstressed* twər), contraction of *it were.*

twerp (twûrp), *n. Slang.* an insignificant or despicable fellow: *Her father thinks her boyfriend is just a twerp.* Also, **twirp.** [?]

Twi (chwē, chē), *n.* a dialect that is spoken and written in Ghana, belongs to the Kwa group of languages, and is mutually intelligible with Fanti.

twi-, a word element meaning "two," "twice": *twibill.* [ME, OE; c. G *zwie-* (OHG *zwi-*), L *bi-.* See TWO]

twi·bill (twī′bil′), *n.* **1.** a mattock with one arm like that of an adz and the other like that of an ax. **2.** *Archaic.* a double-bladed battle-ax. [ME, OE. See TWI-, BILL[3]]

twice (twīs), *adv.* **1.** two times, as in succession: *Write twice a week.* **2.** on two occasions; in two instances: *I phoned him twice.* **3.** in twofold quantity or degree; in double the amount or degree: *twice as much.* [ME *twies,* equiv. to *twie* twice (OE *twiga*) + *-s* -s[1]]

twice-laid (twīs′lād′), *adj.* **1.** made from strands of used rope. **2.** made from makeshift or used material.

twic·er (twī′sər), *n.* **1.** *Slang.* a two-time loser. **2.** *Brit. Slang.* an employee of a printing establishment who works both as a compositor and as a pressman. **3.** *Brit., Australian.* **a.** a deceiver. **b.** a crook. [TWICE + -ER[1]]

twice-told (twīs′tōld′), *adj.* having been told before; related two times. [late ME]

Twice′-Told Tales′, a collection of short stories (1837, enlarged 1842) by Nathaniel Hawthorne.

Twick·en·ham (twik′ə nəm), *n.* a city in S Middlesex, in SE England, on the Thames, near London. 100,822 (1961).

twid·dle (twid′əl), *v.,* **-dled, -dling,** *n.* —*v.t.* **1.** to turn about or play with lightly or idly, esp. with the fingers; twirl. —*v.i.* **2.** to play or trifle idly with something; fiddle. **3.** to turn about lightly; twirl. **4. twiddle one's thumbs,** to do nothing; be idle: *Business was slack, and the salesmen were twiddling their thumbs.* —*n.* **5.** the act of twiddling; turn; twirl. [TW(ITCH + F)IDDLE] —**twid′dler,** *n.*

twi·er (twī′ər), *n. Obs.* tuyère.

twig[1] (twig), *n.* **1.** a slender shoot of a tree or other plant. **2.** a small offshoot from a branch or stem. **3.** a small, dry, woody piece fallen from a branch: *a fire of twigs.* **4.** *Anat.* one of the minute branches of a blood vessel or nerve. [ME; OE *twig, twigge,* orig. (something) divided in two; akin to OHG *zwīg* (G *Zweig*), D *twijg;* cf. Skt *dvikās* double] —**twig′less,** *adj.* —**twig′like′,** *adj.*

twig[2] (twig), *v.,* **twigged, twig·ging.** *Brit.* —*v.t.* **1.** to look at; observe: *Now, twig the man climbing there, will you?* **2.** to see; perceive: *Do you twig the difference in colors?* **3.** to understand. —*v.i.* **4.** to understand. [? < Celt]

twig[3] (twig), *n. Brit.* style; fashion. [?]

twig′ blight′, *Plant Pathol.* blight affecting the twigs of a plant.

twig′ bor′er, any of several insects, as the larvae of a small moth, *Anarsia lineatella* (**peach twig borer**), that bore into the twigs of plants.

twig′ gir′dler. See under **girdler** (def. 2).

twig·gy (twig′ē), *adj.,* **-gi·er, -gi·est.** **1.** of, pertaining to, or resembling twigs. **2.** full of twigs. [TWIG[1] + -Y[1]]

twi·light (twī′līt′), *n.* **1.** the soft, diffused light from the sky when the sun is below the horizon, either from daybreak to sunrise or, more commonly, from sunset to nightfall. **2.** the period in the morning or, more commonly, in the evening during which this light prevails. **3.** a terminal period, esp. after full development, success, etc.: *the twilight of his life.* **4.** a state of uncertainty, vagueness, or gloom. —*adj.* **5.** of, pertaining to, or resembling twilight; dim; obscure: *in the twilight hours.* **6.** appearing or flying at twilight; crepuscular. [ME; see TWI-, LIGHT] —**twi′light′y,** *adj.*

Twi′light of the Gods′, *Teutonic Myth.* Ragnarok; Götterdämmerung.

twi′light sleep′, *Med.* a state of semiconsciousness, usually produced by hypodermic injections of scopolamine and morphine, used chiefly to effect relatively painless childbirth.

twi′light zone′, **1.** the lowest level of the ocean to which light can reach. **2.** an ill-defined area between two distinct conditions, categories, etc., usually comprising certain features of both; an indefinite boundary: *a twilight zone between fantasy and reality.*

twill (twil), *n.* **1.** a fabric constructed in twill weave. **2.** See **twill weave.** —*v.t.* **3.** to weave in the manner of a twill. **4.** to weave in twill construction. [Scot and north var. of *twilly,* ME *twyle,* OE *twili(c),* half trans., half adoption of L *bilīc(em)* having double thread. See TWI-]

'twill (twil), a contraction of *it will.*

twill′ weave′, one of the basic weave structures in which the filling threads are woven over one warp yarn and under two or more others, producing a characteristic diagonal pattern. Also called **twill.** Cf. **plain weave, satin weave.**

Twill weave

T.W.I.M.C., to whom it may concern.

twin[1] (twin), *n., adj., v.,* **twinned, twin·ning.** —*n.* **1.** either of two children or animals brought forth at a birth. **2.** either of two persons or things closely related to or closely resembling each other. **3.** Also called **hemitrope.** *Crystall.* a compound crystal consisting of two or more parts or crystals definitely oriented each to the other; macle. **4. Twins,** *Astron., Astrol.* the constellation or sign of Gemini. —*adj.* **5.** being two, or one of two, children or animals born at the same birth: *twin sisters.* **6.** being two persons or things closely related to or closely resembling each other. **7.** being one of a pair; identical: *a twin bracelet; a twin peak.* **8.** consisting of two similar parts or elements joined or connected: *a twin vase.* **9.** *Bot., Zool.* occurring in pairs; didymous. **10.** *Crystall.* of the nature of a twin; hemitrope. **11.** *Obs.* twofold or double. —*v.t.* **12.** to bring together in close relationship; pair; couple. **13.** to furnish a counterpart to; match. **14.** *Crystall.* to form into a twin. **15.** *Obs.* to conceive or bring forth twins. —*v.i.* **16.** to bring forth twins. **17.** *Obs.* to be paired or coupled. [ME; OE *(ge)twinn;* akin to OFris *twine,* Goth *twaihnai,* Icel *tvinn(r)* double]

twin[2] (twin), *v.t., v.i.,* **twinned, twin·ning.** *Scot.* twine[2].

twin′ bed′, a single bed, esp. one of a matching pair in a bedroom.

twin·ber·ry (twin′ber′ē, -bə rē), *n., pl.* **-ries. 1.** the partridgeberry, *Mitchella repens.* **2.** a North American honeysuckle shrub, *Lonicera involucrata,* having involucrate flowers of various colors. [TWIN[1] + BERRY]

twin′ bill′, *Sports.* a doubleheader, as in baseball.

twin·born (twin′bôrn′), *adj.* born at the same birth. [TWIN[1] + BORN]

Twin′ Cit′ies, the cities of St. Paul and Minneapolis.

twine[1] (twīn), *n., v.,* **twined, twin·ing.** —*n.* **1.** a strong thread or string composed of two or more strands twisted together. **2.** act of twining, twisting, or interweaving. **3.** a coiled or twisted object or part; convolution. **4.** a twist or turn in anything. **5.** a knot or tangle. —*v.t.* **6.** to twist together; interwind; interweave. **7.** to form by or as by twisting together: *to twine a wreath.* **8.** to twist (one strand, thread, or the like) with another; interlace. **9.** to insert with a twisting or winding motion (usually fol. by *in* or *into*): *She twined her fingers in her hair.* **10.** to clasp or enfold (something) around something else; place by or as by winding (usually fol. by *about, around,* etc.): *She twined her arms about him.* **11.** to cause (a person, object, etc.) to be encircled with something else; wreathe; wrap: *She twined the bridal arch with flowers.* —*v.i.* **12.** to wind about something; twist itself in spirals (usually fol. by *about, around,* etc.): *Strangling vines twined about the tree.* **13.** to wind in a sinuous or meandering course. [ME; OE *twīn,* lit., a double or twisted thread; c. D *twijn;* akin to Icel *tvinni,* G *Zwirn* thread, twine] —**twine′a·ble,** *adj.* —**twin′er,** *n.*

Twining stems

twine[2] (twīn), *v.t., v.i.,* **twined, twin·ning.** *Scot.* to separate; part. Also, **twin.** [ME *twinne(n),* deriv. of *twin* TWIN[1]]

twin-en·gine (twin′en′jən), *adj.* having two engines of equal power as prime movers: *a twin-engine airplane.*

Twin′ Falls′, **1.** a city in S Idaho. 20,126 (1960). **2.** a waterfall near here, on the Snake River. ab. 180 ft. high.

twin·flow·er (twin′flou′ər), *n.* either of two slender, creeping, evergreen, caprifoliaceous plants, *Linnaea borealis,* of Europe, or *L. americana,* of North America, having pink or purplish nodding flowers borne in pairs on threadlike peduncles. [TWIN[1] + FLOWER]

twinge (twinj), *n., v.,* **twinged, twing·ing.** —*n.* **1.** a sudden, sharp pain: *On damp days, he's often bothered by a twinge of rheumatism.* **2.** a sharp mental or emotional pain or prick; pang: *a twinge of guilt; twinges of sorrow.* —*v.t.* **3.** to affect (the body or mind) with a sudden, sharp pain or pang. **4.** *Obs.* to pinch; tweak; twitch. —*v.i.* **5.** to have or feel a sudden, sharp pain. [ME *twenge(n),* OE *twengan* to pinch]

twi-night (twī′nīt′), *adj.* *Baseball.* pertaining to or noting a doubleheader in which the first game begins late in the afternoon and the second game begins in the evening under lights. [TWI(LIGHT) + NIGHT]

twi-night·er (twī′nī′tər), *n.* *Baseball Informal.* a twi-night doubleheader. [TWI-NIGHT + -ER[1]]

Twi·ning (twī′niŋ), *n.* **Nathan Farragut,** born 1897, U.S. Air Force officer.

twink[1] (twiŋk), *v.i., v.t., n.* **1.** wink. **2.** twinkle. [ME *twinke(n);* c. G *zwinken* to wink; akin to TWINKLE]

twink[2] (twiŋk), *v.t.* *Brit. Dial.* to punish. [?]

twink[3] (twiŋk), *Obs.* —*v.i.* **1.** to clink; tinkle. **2.** to twitter; chirp. —*v.t.* **3.** to chirp. [imit.]

twin′ kill′ing, *Baseball Slang.* See **double play.**

twin·kle (twiŋ′kəl), *v.,* **-kled, -kling,** *n.* —*v.i.* **1.** to shine with a flickering gleam of light, as a star, distant light, etc. **2.** to sparkle in the light: *The diamond on her finger twinkled in the firelight.* **3.** (of the eyes) to be bright with amusement, pleasure, etc. **4.** to move flutteringly and quickly, as flashes of light; flit. **5.** *Archaic.* to wink; blink. —*v.t.* **6.** to emit (light) in intermittent gleams or flashes. **7.** *Archaic.* to wink (the eyes or eyelids). —*n.* **8.** a flickering or intermittent brightness or light. **9.** a scintillating brightness in the eyes; sparkle. **10.** the time required for a wink; twinkling. **11.** *Archaic.* a wink. [ME *twinkle(n),* OE *winclian*] —**twin′kler,** *n.*

twin·kling (twiŋ′kliŋ), *n.* **1.** the act of shining with intermittent gleams of light. **2.** the time required for a wink; an instant. **3.** *Archaic.* winking; a wink. [ME; see TWINKLE, -ING[1]]

twin-leaf (twin′lēf′), *n., pl.* **-leaves.** a berberidaceous plant, *Jeffersonia diphylla,* of the eastern U.S., having solitary white flowers and leaves divided into pairs of leaflets.

twin′-lens re′flex cam′era. See under **reflex camera.**

twin′-lens cam′era (twin′lenz′), *Photog.* a camera having two separately mounted lenses coordinated to eliminate parallax errors or for making stereoptic photographs.

twinned (twind), *adj.* **1.** born two at one birth. **2.** closely or intimately associated, joined, or united; coupled; paired. [TWIN[1] + -ED[3]]

twin·ning (twin′iŋ), *n.* **1.** the bearing of two children at one birth. **2.** the coupling of two persons or things; union. **3.** *Crystall.* the union of crystals to form a twin. [ME *twynnynge.* See TWIN[1], -ING[1]]

Twins·burg (twinz′bûrg), *n.* a town in NE Ohio. 4098 (1960).

twin-screw (twin′skrōō′), *adj.* *Naut.* (of a vessel) having two screw propellers, which usually revolve in opposite directions.

twin′ spin′naker rig′, *Naut.* a trade-wind rig having a spinnaker set on each side of the mast.

twirl (twûrl), *v.t.* **1.** to cause to rotate rapidly; spin; revolve; whirl. **2.** to twiddle: *to twirl my thumbs.* **3.** to wind idly, as about something. **4.** *Baseball Slang.* to pitch. —*v.i.* **5.** to rotate rapidly; whirl. **6.** to turn quickly so as to face or point in another direction. **7.** *Baseball Slang.* to pitch. —*n.* **8.** act of rotating rapidly; a rapid spinning or turning; spin; whirl. **9.** something convoluted or having a spiral shape; coil; curl; convolution. [TW(IST + WH)IRL]

twirl·er (twûr′lər), *n.* **1.** one who or that which twirls. **2.** *Baseball Slang.* a pitcher. [TWIRL + -ER[1]]

twirp (twûrp), *n.* twerp.

twist (twist), *v.t.* **1.** to combine, as two or more strands or threads, by winding together; intertwine. **2.** to form by or as by winding strands together: *Several fibers were used to twist the rope.* **3.** to entwine (one thing) with another; interlace (something) with something else; interweave; plait. **4.** to wind or coil (something) about something else; encircle; entwine; wreathe. **5.** to alter in shape, as by turning the ends in opposite directions, so that parts previously in the same straight line and plane are located in a spiral curve: *The sculptor twisted the form into an arabesque. He twisted his body around to look behind him.* **6.** to turn sharply or wrench out of place; sprain: *He twisted his ankle.* **7.** to pull, tear, or break off by turning forcibly: *She twisted the arm off her doll.* **8.** to distort (the features) by tensing or contracting the facial muscles; contort: *He twisted his face in a wry smile.* **9.** to distort the meaning or form of; pervert: *He twisted my sentence about to suit his own purpose.* **10.** to cause to become mentally or emotionally distorted; warp: *The loss of his business twisted his whole outlook on life.* **11.** to form into a coil, knot, or the like by winding, rolling, etc.: *to twist the hair into a knot.* **12.** to bend tortuously. **13.** to cause to move with a rotary motion, as a ball pitched in a curve. **14.** to turn (something) from one direction to another, as by rotating, revolving, etc.: *He twisted his chair to face the window.* **15.** to combine or associate intimately. —*v.i.* **16.** to be or become intertwined. **17.** to wind or twine about something. **18.** to writhe or squirm. **19.** to take a spiral form or course; wind, curve, or bend. **20.** to turn or rotate, as on an axis; revolve, as about something. **21.** to turn so as to face in another direction. **22.** to turn, coil, or bend into a spiral shape. **23.** to change shape under forcible turning or twisting. **24.** to move with a progressive rotary motion, as a ball pitched in a curve. **25.** to dance the twist. —*n.* **26.** a deviation in direction; curve; bend; turn. **27.** action of turning or rotating on an axis; rotary motion; spin. **28.** anything formed by or as by twisting or twining parts together. **29.** act or process of twining strands together, as in thread, yarn, or rope. **30.** a twisting awry or askew. **31.** distortion or perversion, as of meaning or form. **32.** a peculiar attitude or bias; eccentric turn or bent of mind; eccentricity. **33.** spiral disposition, arrangement, or form. **34.** spiral movement or course. **35.** an irregular bend; crook; kink. **36.** a sudden, unanticipated change of course, as of events. **37.** a treatment, method, idea, system, etc., esp. one differing from that which preceded: *He gave the old plot a new twist.* **38.** the changing of the shape of anything by or as by turning the ends in opposite directions. **39.** the stress causing this alteration; torque. **40.** the resulting state. **41.** a twisting or torsional action, force, or stress; torsion. **42.** a strong, twisted silk thread, heavier than ordinary sewing silk, for working buttonholes and for other purposes. **43.** the direction of twisting in weaving yarn; S twist or Z twist. **44.** a loaf or roll of dough twisted and baked. **45.** a strip of citrus peel that has been twisted and placed in a drink to add flavor. **46.** a kind of tobacco manufactured in the form of a rope or thick cord. **47.** a vigorous dance performed by couples and characterized by strongly rhythmic gyrations and flailings of the arms, legs, and torso. **48.** the degree of spiral formed by the grooves in a rifled firearm or cannon. **49.** *Obs.* a wrench. [ME *twiste(n)* (to) divide, deriv. of *twist* divided object, rope, OE *-twist;* c. D *twisten* to quarrel, G *Zwist* a quarrel. See TWI-] —**twist′a·bil′i·ty,** *n.* —**twist′a·ble,** *adj.* —**twist′ed·ly,** *adv.* —**twist′ing·ly,** *adv.*
—**Syn. 20.** spin. **32.** See **turn.**

twist′ drill′, *Mach.* a drill with one or more deep helical grooves in the body.

twist′ed eg′lantine, woodbine (def. 1).

twist′ed stom′ach worm′. See **stomach worm.**

twist·er (twis′tər), *n.* **1.** one who or that which twists. **2.** a ball pitched or moving with a spinning motion. **3.** *U.S. Informal.* a whirlwind or tornado. **4.** *Chiefly Brit. Informal.* a deceitful, unscrupulous person. [TWIST + -ER[1]]

twist′ turn′ing, the turning of table legs, or the like, in the form of a helix. —**twist′-turned′,** *adj.*

twit[1] (twit), *v.,* **twit·ted, twit·ting,** *n.* —*v.t.* **1.** to taunt, tease, ridicule, etc., with references to anything embarrassing; gibe at. **2.** to reproach or upbraid. —*n.* **3.** act of twitting. **4.** a derisive reproach; taunt; gibe. [aph. var. of obs. *atwite,* ME *atwiten,* OE *ætwītan* to taunt, equiv. to *æt-* AT + *wītan* to blame]

twit[2] (twit), *n.* a weak or thin place in yarn caused by uneven spinning. [?]

twitch (twich), *v.t.* **1.** to tug or pull at with a quick, short movement; pluck: *She twitched him by the sleeve.* **2.** to jerk rapidly: *The rider twitched the reins a couple of times.* **3.** to move (a part of the body) with a sudden, jerking motion. **4.** to pinch or pull at sharply and painfully; give a smarting pinch to; nip. —*v.i.* **5.** to move spasmodically or convulsively; jerk; jump. **6.** to give a sharp, sudden pull; tug; pluck (usually fol. by *at*): *She constantly twitched at her skirt.* **7.** to ache or hurt with a sharp, shooting pain; twinge: *That back tooth twitches a bit.* —*n.* **8.** a quick, jerky movement of the body, or of some part of it. **9.** involuntary, spasmodic movement of a muscle: *Have you ever noticed that twitch he gets in his left eye when he's nervous?* **10.** a short, sudden pull or tug; jerk. **11.** a bodily or mental twinge, as of pain, conscience, etc.; pang. **12.** a loop or noose placed over the muzzle of a horse and tightened by twisting a stick or handle to which it is attached, used as a restraining device during a painful operation. [ME *twicche(n);* akin to OE *twiccian* to pluck; c. G *zwicken* to pinch] —**twitch′er,** *n.* —**twitch′ing·ly,** *adv.*

twitch′ grass′. See **couch grass.** [m. *quitch grass*]

twit·ter (twit′ər), *v.i.* **1.** to utter a succession of small, tremulous sounds, as a bird. **2.** to talk lightly and rapidly, esp. of trivial matters; chatter: *The room was filled with happy ladies twittering over their tea.* **3.** to titter; giggle. **4.** to tremble with excitement or the like; be in a flutter. —*v.t.* **5.** to express or utter by twittering. —*n.* **6.** act of twittering. **7.** a twittering sound. **8.** a state of tremulous excitement. [ME *twiter;* akin to G *zwitschern*] —**twit′ter·er,** *n.* —**twit′ter·ing·ly,** *adv.*

Twit′tering Machine′, The, a watercolor (1922) by Paul Klee.

twit·ter·y (twit′ə rē), *adj.* **1.** given to or characterized by twittering. **2.** tremulous; shaky. [TWITTER + -Y[1]]

'twixt (twikst), *prep.* contraction of *betwixt.*

two (tōō), *n.* **1.** a cardinal number, 1 plus 1. **2.** a symbol for this number, as 2 or II. **3.** a set of this many persons or things. **4.** a playing card, die face, or half of a domino face with two pips. **5. in two,** into two separate parts, as halves: *A bolt of lightning split the tree in two.* **6. put two and two together,** to draw a correct conclusion from the given circumstances; infer: *It didn't require a great mind to put two and two together.* —*adj.* **7.** amounting to two in number. [ME; OE *twā;* c. G *zwei;* cf. L *duo,* Gk *dýo*]

two-a-cat (tōō′ə kat′), *n.* See **two old cat.**

two-bag·ger (tōō′bag′ər), *n.* *Baseball Slang.* See **two-base hit.**

two′-base hit′ (tōō′bās′), *Baseball.* a base hit that enables a batter to reach second base safely. Also called **double.**

two-beat (tōō′bēt′), *adj.* having four beats to the measure with the second and fourth beats accented: *two-beat jazz.*

two-bit (tōō′bit′), *adj.* *Slang.* **1.** costing twenty-five cents. **2.** inferior or unimportant; small-time: *a two-bit actor.*

two′ bits′, *Slang.* twenty-five cents.

two-by-four (tōō′bī fôr′, -fōr′, -bə-), *adj.* **1.** two units thick and four units wide, esp. in inches. **2.** *Slang.* unimportant; insignificant; two-bit: *Theirs was a petty, two-by-four operation.* **3.** *Informal.* lacking adequate space; cramped: *a small, two-by-four room.* —*n.* **4.** a timber measuring two by four inches in cross section.

two-col·or (tōō′kul′ər), *adj.* **1.** having or using two colors. **2.** noting or pertaining to a photomechanical process similar to the three-color process, but using only two primary or secondary colors.

two′-com·part·ment ves′sel (tōō′kəm pärt′mənt), *Naut.* a vessel having a floodable length equal to any two watertight compartments.

two-cy·cle (tōō′sī′kəl), *adj.* noting or pertaining to an internal-combustion engine in which a complete cycle in each cylinder requires two strokes, one to admit and compress air or an air-fuel mixture and one to ignite fuel, do work, and scavenge the cylinder. Cf. **four-cycle.**

two-di·men·sion·al (tōō′di men′shə nəl), *adj.* **1.** having the dimensions of height and width only: *a two-dimensional surface.* **2.** (of a work of art) having its elements organized in terms of a flat surface, esp. emphasizing the vertical and horizontal character of the picture plane: *the two-dimensional structure of a painting.* **3.** (in a literary work) shallow, unconvincing, or superficial in execution: *Character development in most popular modern novels is two-dimensional.* —**two′-di·men′sion·al′i·ty,** *n.* —**two′-di·men′sion·al·ly,** *adv.*

two-edged (tōō′ejd′), *adj.* **1.** having two edges, as a sword. **2.** cutting or effective both ways.

two-faced (to͞o′fāst′), *adj.* **1.** having two faces. **2.** deceitful; hypocritical. —**two-fac·ed·ly** (to͞o′fā′sid lē, -fāst′lē), *adv.* —**two′-fac′ed·ness,** *n.*

two′-fam·i·ly house′ (to͞o′fam′ə lē, -fam′lē), a specially designed house for occupation by two families in living quarters that are contiguous, as apartments one above the other on separate floors.

two-fer (to͞o′fər), *n.* *Theat.* a card or ticket entitling the holder to purchase one or two tickets to a theatrical performance at a reduced price. [from the phrase *two for* (the price of one, a nickel, etc.)]

two-fist·ed (to͞o′fis′tid), *adj.* **1.** having two fists and being able to use them. **2.** *U.S. Informal.* strong and vigorous.

two-fold (to͞o′fōld′), *n.* *Theat.* a unit of stage scenery consisting of two flats hinged together.

two·fold (to͞o′fōld′), *adj.* **1.** having two elements or parts. **2.** twice as great or as much; double. —*adv.* **3.** in twofold measure; doubly. [ME; see TWO, -FOLD] —**two′fold′ness,** *n.*

two′fold pur′chase, a purchase using a double standing block and a double running block so as to give a mechanical advantage of four or five, neglecting friction, depending on whether the hauling is on the standing block or the running block.

two-four (to͞o′fôr′, -fōr′), *adj.* *Music.* (of a meter) characterized by two quarter notes to each measure.

2, 4-d, See **dichlorophenoxyacetic acid.**

2, 4, 5-t, See **trichlorphenoxyacetic acid.**

Two′ Gen′tlemen of Vero′na, The, a comedy (1594–95) by Shakespeare.

two-hand·ed (to͞o′han′did), *adj.* **1.** having two hands. **2.** using both hands equally well; ambidextrous. **3.** involving or requiring the use of both hands: *a two-handed sword.* **4.** requiring the hands of two persons to operate: *a two-handed saw.* **5.** engaged in by two persons: *a two-handed game.* [late ME *too-honded*] —**two′-hand′ed·ly,** *adv.* —**two′-hand′ed·ness,** *n.*

Two′ Har′bors, a town in NE Minnesota. 4695 (1960).

two·leg·ged (to͞o′leg′id, -legd′), *adj.* having two legs. [TWO + LEG + -ED[3]]

two-mast·ed (to͞o′mas′tid, -mä′stid), *adj.* *Naut.* having two masts.

two-mast·er (to͞o′mas′tər, -mä′stər), *n.* *Naut.* a vessel rigged with two masts.

two′-name pa′per (to͞o′nām′), *Banking.* commercial paper having more than one obligor, usually a maker and endorser, both of whom are fully liable.

two old cat (to͞o′ ə kat′), *Games.* one old cat played with two batters. Also, **two′ o′ cat′, two-a-cat.**

two′ pair′, *Poker.* a set of two cards of the same denomination together with another matched set of different denomination from the first.

two′-part time′ (to͞o′pärt′), *Music.* See **duple time.**

two′-par·ty sys′tem (to͞o′pär′tē), *Govt.* a political system consisting chiefly of two major parties, more or less equal in strength.

two·pence (tup′əns), *n.* **1.** (*construed as sing. or pl.*) *Brit.* a sum of two pennies. **2.** a former copper coin of Great Britain, equal to two pennies, issued under George III. **3.** a former silver coin of England, equal to two pennies: issued only as maundy money after 1662. **4.** a trifle. Also, **tuppence.** [ME *two pens*]

two·pen·ny (tup′ə nē), *adj.* **1.** of the amount or value of twopence. **2.** involving an outlay of twopence. **3.** of very little value; trifling; worthless. **4.** noting a nail one inch long. *Abbr.:* 2d Also, **tuppenny** (for defs. 1–3). [TWO + -PENNY]

two-phase (to͞o′fāz′), *adj.* *Elect.* diphase.

two-piece (to͞o′pēs′), *adj.* **1.** having or consisting of two parts or pieces, esp. two matching pieces of a clothing ensemble: *a two-piece bathing suit.* —*n.* **2.** Also, **two′-piec′er.** a two-piece garment.

two-ply (to͞o′plī′), *adj.* consisting of two thicknesses, layers, strands, or the like.

two′-point perspec′tive (to͞o′point′). See under **linear perspective.**

Twor·kov (twôr′kof), *n.* **Jack,** born 1900, U.S. painter, born in Poland.

two-seat·er (to͞o′sē′tər), *n.* a vehicle accommodating two persons.

two-shot (to͞o′shot′), *n.* *Motion Pictures, Television.* a camera shot, as a close-up, of two persons.

Two′ Sic′ilies, a former kingdom in Sicily and S Italy which existed intermittently from 1130 to 1861.

two-sid·ed (to͞o′sī′did), *adj.* **1.** having two sides; bilateral. **2.** having two aspects or characters. —**two′-sid′ed·ness,** *n.*

two·some (to͞o′səm), *adj.* **1.** consisting of two; twofold. **2.** performed or played by two persons. —*n.* **3.** two together or in company; couple; duo. **4.** *Golf.* a match between two persons. [ME (north); see TWO, -SOME[2]]

two-spot (to͞o′spot′), *n.* **1.** a playing card or the upward face of a die that bears two pips; a domino one half of which bears two pips. **2.** *Slang.* a two-dollar bill.

two-step (to͞o′step′), *n.*, *v.*, **-stepped, -step·ping.** —*n.* **1.** a ballroom dance in duple meter, marked by sliding steps. **2.** a piece of music for, or in the rhythm of, this dance. —*v.i.* **3.** to dance the two-step.

two-stick·er (to͞o′stik′ər), *n.* *Informal.* a sailing vessel having two masts.

two′-thirds rule′ (to͞o′thûrdz′), *U.S.* a rule in the Democratic party, formerly effective 1832–1936, requiring a vote of at least two thirds of its national convention delegates to nominate a presidential and vice-presidential candidate.

two-time (to͞o′tīm′), *v.t.*, **-timed, -tim·ing.** *Slang.* to double-cross, esp. to be unfaithful to a lover or spouse. —**two′-tim′er,** *n.*

two′-time los′er, *Slang.* **1.** a person who has been sentenced to prison twice, esp. for a major crime in a state where a third sentence is mandatory life imprisonment. **2.** a person who has failed at the same endeavor twice, esp. one who has been divorced twice or who has gone bankrupt twice.

two′-toed ant′eater (to͞o′tōd′). See **silky anteater.**

two-tone (to͞o′tōn′), *adj.* having two colors or two shades of the same color: *a two-tone automobile.* Also, **two′-toned′.**

two′-top·sail schoon′er (to͞o′top′səl), *Naut.* **1.** See **main-topsail schooner.** **2.** any schooner having gaff topsails on two topmasts, all masts being fore-and-aft-rigged.

two-track (to͞o′trak′), *Dressage.* —*n.* **1.** an oblique movement of a horse in which the forehand and hindquarters move on two distinct parallel tracks and the body is bent uniformly in the direction of the movement. —*v.i.* **2.** (of a horse) to execute a two-track. —*v.t.* **3.** to cause (a horse) to two-track.

'twould (two͝od), contraction of *it would.*

two-up (to͞o′up′), *n.* a game in which two players bet that two coins tossed into the air will land either with matching or nonmatching sides facing up.

two-way (to͞o′wā′), *adj.* **1.** allowing persons or vehicles to travel in opposite directions at the same time; allowing movement in both directions. **2.** allowing or entailing communication or exchange between two persons, groups, countries, etc. **3.** entailing mutual agreement, responsibility, liability, etc. **4.** involving two participating persons, parties, etc.; two-sided: *a two-way race for the nomination.* **5.** capable of both receiving and sending signals: *a two-way radio.* **6.** capable of being used in two ways.

two-wheel·er (to͞o′hwē′lər, -wē′-), *n.* a vehicle, esp. a bicycle, having two wheels: *The boy changed his tricycle for a two-wheeler.*

Two′ Years′ Before′ the Mast′, an autobiographical novel (1840) by Richard Henry Dana.

twp., township.

TWS, *Teleg.* timed wire service.

TWX, teletypewriter exchange.

Ty (tī), *n.* a boy's given name.

-ty[1], a suffix of numerals denoting multiples of ten: *twenty; thirty.* [OE *-tig;* c. OFris *-tich,* Goth *-tigjus,* Icel *-tigr,* G *-zig*]

-ty[2], a suffix occurring in nouns of Latin origin, denoting quality, state, etc.: *unity; enmity.* [ME *-te(e)* < OF *-te* (m.), *-tet* (fem.) < L *-tāt-* (obl. of *-tās*)]

Ty., Territory.

Ty·burn (tī′bərn), *n.* a former place of public execution in London, England.

Ty′burn tree′, *Brit.* the gallows. [after TYBURN]

Ty·che (tī′kē), *n.* the ancient Greek goddess of fortune, identified by the Romans with Fortuna. [< Gk *týchē* luck, fortune]

ty·chism (tī′kiz əm), *n.* (in the philosophy of Peirce) the theory that chance has objective existence in the universe. [< Gk *tých(ē)* chance + -ISM] —**ty·chis′tic,** *adj.*

Ty·chi·us (tī′kē əs), *n.* (in the *Iliad*) the artisan who created the shield used by Telamonian Ajax.

Ty·cho (tī′kō), *n.* a crater in the third quadrant of the face of the moon, being the most prominent formation when the moon is full, and having the most extensive ray system: about 56 miles in diameter from crest to crest with walls rising about 12,000 feet from its floor; a central mountain about 5000 feet high.

ty·cho·po·tam·ic (tī′kō pə tam′ik), *adj.* (of a plant or animal) living or growing chiefly in still fresh water, and occasionally in flowing fresh water. [< Gk *tých(ē)* chance + -o- + POTAMIC]

ty·coon (tī ko͞on′), *n.* **1.** a businessman having great wealth and power. **2.** (*often cap.*) a title used with reference to the shogun of Japan. [< Jap *taikun* < Chin *tai* great (dial. var. of *ta*) + *kiun* prince]

Ty·de·us (tī′dē əs, -dyo͞os, tid′ē əs), *n.* *Class. Myth.* the father of Diomedes and one of the Seven Against Thebes.

Ty·di·des (ti dī′dēz), *n.* *Class. Myth.* a patronymic of Diomedes, the son of Tydeus.

tye (tī), *n.* *Naut.* a chain for hoisting a yard, as an upper topsail, upper topgallant, or royal yard at its middle, rigged in any of various ways and hauled upon by the halyard tackle. Also, **tie.** [ME; see TIE]

ty·ee (tī′ē), *n.* See **chinook salmon.** Also called **ty′ee salm′on.** [< AmerInd (Nootka) *ta-yi* elder brother]

Ty·fon (tī′fon), *n.* *Trademark.* typhon.

tyg (tig), *n.* a large ceramic drinking mug of the 17th century having as many as twelve handles. [?]

ty·ing (tī′ing), *v.* present participle of **tie.**

tyke (tīk), *n.* **1.** a cur; mongrel. **2.** *Chiefly Scot.* a low, contemptible fellow; boor. **3.** a child, esp. a small boy. **4.** any small child. Also, **tike.** [ME < Icel *tīk* bitch]

tyl·er (tī′lər), *n.* tiler (def. 2).

Ty·ler (tī′lər), *n.* **1. John,** 1790–1862, 10th president of the United States 1841–45. **2. Moses Coit** (koit), 1835–1900, U.S. historian and educator. **3. Wat** (wot) or **Walter,** died 1381, English rebel: leader of the peasants' revolt of 1381. **4.** a city in E Texas. 51,230 (1960).

Tyll Eu·len·spie·gel (til′ oi′lən shpē′gəl). See **Till Eulenspiegel.** Also, **Tyl Eulenspiegel.**

ty·lo·sis (tī lō′sis), *n.*, *pl.* **-ses** (-sēz). *Bot.* a bubblelike formation in the cavity of tracheids or vessels in the wood of trees, consisting of protoplasm intruded from adjacent parenchyma cells. [< Gk *týlōsis* act of making callous]

tym·bal (tim′bəl), *n.* timbal.

tym·pan (tim′pən), *n.* **1.** *Print.* a padlike device interposed between the platen or its equivalent and the sheet to be printed, in order to soften and equalize the pressure. **2.** See **tympanic membrane.** **3.** tympanum (defs. 2, 4). [< L *tympan(um)* TYMPANUM]

tym·pa·ni (tim′pə nē), *n. pl.* timpani.

tym·pan·ic (tim pan′ik), *adj.* pertaining or belonging to a tympanum, esp. the tympanum of the ear. [TYMPAN + -IC]

tympan′ic bone′, *Anat., Zool.* (in mammals) a bone of the skull, supporting the tympanic membrane and enclosing part of the tympanum or middle ear.

tympan′ic mem′brane, *Anat., Zool.* a membrane separating the tympanum or middle ear from the passage of the external ear; eardrum. See diag. under **ear.**

tym·pa·nist (tim′pə nist), *n.* a person who plays the drums or other percussion instruments in an orchestra. [< L *tympanista* < Gk *tympanistés,* equiv. to *tympan(ízein)* (to) beat a drum + *-istēs* -IST]

tym·pa·ni·tes (tim′pə nī′tēz), *n.* *Pathol.* distention of the abdominal wall, as in peritonitis, caused by the accumulation of gas or air in the intestine or peritoneal cavity. [< NL < Gk *tympanítēs* pertaining to a drum] —**tym·pa·nit·ic** (tim′pə nit′ik), *adj.*

tym·pa·ni·tis (tim′pə nī′tis), *n.* *Pathol.* inflammation of the middle ear; otitis media. [TYMPAN(UM) + -ITIS]

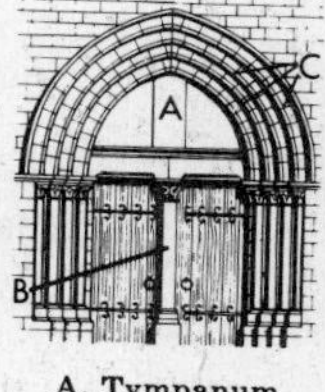

A, Tympanum (def. 2b); B, Trumeau; C, Orders of arches

tym·pa·num (tim′pə nəm), *n.*, *pl.* **-nums, -na** (-nə). **1.** *Anat., Zool.* **a.** See **middle ear.** **b.** See **tympanic membrane.** **2.** *Archit.* **a.** the recessed, usually triangular space enclosed between the horizontal and sloping cornices of a pediment, often decorated with sculpture. **b.** a similar space between an arch and the horizontal head of a door or window below. **3.** *Elect.* the diaphragm of a telephone. **4.** a drum or similar instrument. **5.** the stretched membrane forming a drumhead. **6.** a wheel for raising water, having scooplike passages taking in the water at the circumference of the wheel and discharging it at the center. [< L < Gk *týmpanon* drum]

tym·pa·ny (tim′pə nē), *n.* **1.** *Pathol.* tympanites. **2.** *Archaic.* inflated or pretentious style; bombast; turgidity. [< ML *tympanias* < Gk *tympanías*]

Tyn·dale (tin′dᵊl), *n.* **William,** c1492–1536, English religious reformer, translator of the Bible into English, and martyr. Also, **Tindal, Tindale.**

Tyn·dall (tin′dᵊl), *n.* **John,** 1820–93, English physicist.

Tyn′dall beam′, *Physical Chem.* the visible path of light produced by the scattering action of the particles in a colloidal solution on a beam of light passed through it. [named after John TYNDALL]

Tyn′dall effect′, *Physics.* the scattering and polarization of light passing through a system of particles, as a solution of colloidal particles. [named after John TYNDALL]

Tyn·dar·e·us (tin dâr′ē əs), *n.* *Class. Myth.* the husband of Leda and father of Clytemnestra and Castor.

Tyn·dar·i·dae (tin dar′i dē′), *n.* (*construed as pl.*) *Class. Myth.* a patronymic of Castor and Pollux.

tyne (tīn), *n.* *Chiefly Brit.* tine.[1]

Tyne (tīn), *n.* a river in NE England, in Northumberland, flowing E into the North Sea. ab. 30 mi. long.

Tyne·mouth (tīn′məth, tin′-), *n.* a seaport in SE Northumberland, in NE England, at the mouth of the Tyne River. 70,112 (1961).

Tyn·wald (tin′wəld), *n.* the legislature of the Isle of Man, consisting of the lieutenant governor, the council, and the House of Keys. [< ON *thingvǫll(r).* See THING[2]]

typ., **1.** typographer. **2.** typographic. **3.** typographical. **4.** typography.

typ·al (tī′pəl), *adj.* **1.** of, pertaining to, or constituting a type. **2.** serving as a type; representative; typical. [TYPE + -AL[1]]

type (tīp), *n.*, *v.*, **typed, typ·ing.** —*n.* **1.** a kind, class, or group that is distinguished by some particular characteristic. **2.** the general form, structure, style, or character common to or distinctive of a particular kind, class, or group. **3.** a person or thing embodying the characteristic qualities of a kind, class, or group; a representative specimen. **4.** *Print.* **a.** a rectangular piece or block, now usually of metal, having on its upper surface a letter or character in relief. **b.** such pieces or blocks collectively. **c.** a similar piece in a typewriter or the like. **d.** such pieces collectively. **e.** a printed character or printed characters: *a headline in large type.* **5.** *Biol.* **a.** a genus or species that most nearly exemplifies the essential characteristics of a higher group. **b.** the one or more specimens on which the description and naming of a species is based. **6.** *Agric.* **a.** the inherited features of an animal or breed that are favorable for any given purpose: *dairy type.* **b.** a strain, breed, or variety of animal, or a single animal, belonging to a specific kind. **7.** the pattern or model from which something is made. **8.** an image or figure produced by impressing or stamping, as the principal figure or device on either side of a coin or medal. **9.** a symbol of something in the future, as an Old Testament event serving as a prefiguration of a New Testament event. —*v.t.* **10.** to write on a typewriter; typewrite. **11.** to reproduce in type or in print. **12.** *Med.* to ascertain the type of (blood sample). **13.** to typecast. **14.** to be a type or symbol of; typify; symbolize; represent. **15.** to represent prophetically; foreshadow; prefigure. —*v.i.* **16.** to typewrite. [late ME < L *typus* < Gk *týpos* blow, impression] —**Syn. 1.** sort, classification, form, stamp. **3.** sample, example.

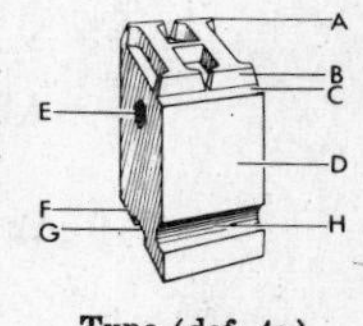

Type (def. 4a) A, Serif; B, Beard or neck; C, Shoulder; D, Body; E, Pin mark; F, Foot; G, Groove; H, Nick

-type, a suffix representing **type** (*prototype*), esp. used of photographic processes: *ferrotype.* Cf. **typo-.**

type·bar (tīp′bär′), *n.* (on a typewriter) one of a series of thin metal bars containing type and actuated by the keyboard. [TYPE + BAR[1]]

type-cast (tīp′kast′, -käst′), *v.*, **-cast, -cast·ing,** *adj.* *Print.* —*v.t.*, *v.i.* **1.** to cast (type). —*adj.* **2.** (of text to be printed) having the type already cast. —**type′-cast′er,** *n.*

type·cast (tīp′kast′, -käst′), *v.t.*, **-cast, -cast·ing.** *Theat.* **1.** to cast (a performer) in a role that requires characteristics of physique, manner, personality, etc., similar to those possessed by the performer. **2.** to cast (a performer) in a kind of role in which the public has become accustomed to seeing him as a result of previous successes. [TYPE + CAST]

Ty·pee (tī pē′), *n.* a novel (1846) by Herman Melville.

type·face (tīp′fās′), *n.* face (defs. 18b, c). [TYPE + FACE]

TYPE FACES IN COMMON USE

TEXT FACES

Baskerville	ABCDEFGHIJKLMNOPQRSTUVWXYZabcdefghijklmnopqrstuvwxyz1234567890 *ABCDEFGHIJKLMNOPQRSTUVWXYZabcdefghijklmnopqrstuvwxyz1234567890*
Bodoni	ABCDEFGHIJKLMNOPQRSTUVWXYZabcdefghijklmnopqrstuvwxyz1234567890 *ABCDEFGHIJKLMNOPQRSTUVWXYZabcdefghijklmnopqrstuvwxyz1234567890*
Caledonia	ABCDEFGHIJKLMNOPQRSTUVWXYZabcdefghijklmnopqrstuvwxyz1234567890 *ABCDEFGHIJKLMNOPQRSTUVWXYZabcdefghijklmnopqrstuvwxyz1234567890*
Century Schoolbook	ABCDEFGHIJKLMNOPQRSTUVWXYZabcdefghijklmnopqrstuvwxyz1234567890 *ABCDEFGHIJKLMNOPQRSTUVWXYZabcdefghijklmnopqrstuvwxyz1234567890*
Garamond	ABCDEFGHIJKLMNOPQRSTUVWXYZabcdefghijklmnopqrstuvwxyz1234567890 *ABCDEFGHIJKLMNOPQRSTUVWXYZabcdefghijklmnopqrstuvwxyz1234567890*
News Gothic Condensed	ABCDEFGHIJKLMNOPQRSTUVWXYZabcdefghijklmnopqrstuvwxyz1234567890
Primer	ABCDEFGHIJKLMNOPQRSTUVWXYZabcdefghijklmnopqrstuvwxyz1234567890 *ABCDEFGHIJKLMNOPQRSTUVWXYZabcdefghijklmnopqrstuvwxyz1234567890*
Times Roman	ABCDEFGHIJKLMNOPQRSTUVWXYZabcdefghijklmnopqrstuvwxyz1234567890 *ABCDEFGHIJKLMNOPQRSTUVWXYZabcdefghijklmnopqrstuvwxyz1234567890*

DISPLAY FACES

Albertus	ABCDEFGHIJKLMNOPQRSTUVWXYZabcdefghijklmnopqrstuvwxyz1234567890
Bank Script	*ABCDEFGHIJKLMNOPQRSTUVWXYZabcdefghijklmnopqrstuvwxyz1234567890*
Barnum	ABCDEFGHIJKLMNOPQRSTUVWXYZabcdefghijklmnopqrstuvwxyz1234567890
Bodoni Bold	**ABCDEFGHIJKLMNOPQRSTUVWXYZabcdefghijklmnopqrstuvwxyz1234567890** ***ABCDEFGHIJKLMNOPQRSTUVWXYZabcdefghijklmnopqrstuvwxyz1234567890***
Bodoni Ultra	**ABCDEFGHIJKLMNOPQRSTUVWXYZabcdefghijklmnopqrstuvw** ***ABCDEFGHIJKLMNOPQRSTUVWXYZabcdefghijklmnopqrstuv***
Bulmer	ABCDEFGHIJKLMNOPQRSTUVWXYZabcdefghijklmnopqrstuvwxyz1234567890 *ABCDEFGHIJKLMNOPQRSTUVWXYZabcdefghijklmnopqrstuvwxyz1234567890*
Lydian	ABCDEFGHIJKLMNOPQRSTUVWXYZabcdefghijklmnopqrstuvwxyz1234567890
Lydian Cursive	*ABCDEFGHIJKLMNOPQRSTUVWXYZabcdefghijklmnopqrstuvwxyz1234567890*
Microgramma Bold	**ABCDEFGHIJKLMNOPQRSTUVWXYZ1234567890**
Palatino	ABCDEFGHIJKLMNOPQRSTUVWXYZabcdefghijklmnopqrstuvwxyz1234567890 *ABCDEFGHIJKLMNOPQRSTUVWXYZabcdefghijklmnopqrstuvwxyz1234567890*
Peignot Medium	ABCDEFGHIJKLMNOPQRSTUVWXYZabcdefghijklmnopqrstuvwxyz1234567890
Stymie Medium	ABCDEFGHIJKLMNOPQRSTUVWXYZabcdefghijklmnopqrstuvwxyz1234567890 *ABCDEFGHIJKLMNOPQRSTUVWXYZabcdefghijklmnopqrstuvwxyz12345678*

type′ found′er, one engaged in the making of metallic types for printers. —**type′ found′ing.** —**type′-found′ry.**

type′ ge′nus, *Biol.* the genus that is formally held to be typical of the family or other higher group to which it belongs.

type-high (tīp′hī′), *adj.* *Print.* of a height equal to the distance from the foot to the face of a type: 0.918 inch.

type·hold·er (tīp′hōl′dər), *n.* *Print.* a small device for holding a few lines of type, used in stamping titles on book covers, or the like. Also called **pallet.** [TYPE + HOLDER]

type′ local′ity, *Biol.* the locality in which a type specimen was collected.

type′ met′al, an alloy for making printing types, consisting chiefly of lead and antimony, and sometimes small quantities of tin, copper, etc.

type·script (tīp′skript′), *n.* **1.** a typewritten copy of a literary composition, document, or the like, esp. as prepared for a printer. **2.** typewritten matter, as distinguished from handwritten or printed matter. [TYPE + SCRIPT (formed on model of *manuscript*)]

type·set (tīp′set′), *v.t.*, **-set, -set·ting,** *adj.* —*v.t.* **1.** to set (textual matter) in type. —*adj.* **2.** (of written, textual matter) set in type. [back formation from TYPESETTER]

type·set·ter (tīp′set′ər), *n.* **1.** a person who sets or composes type; compositor. **2.** a typesetting machine. [TYPE + SETTER]

type·set·ting (tīp′set′ing), *n.* **1.** the process or action of setting type. —*adj.* **2.** used or intended for setting type. [TYPE + SETTING]

type′ spe′cies, *Biol.* the species of a genus that is regarded as the best example of the generic characters; the species from which a genus is named.

type′ spec′imen, *Biol.* an individual animal or plant from which the description of a species has been prepared.

type·write (tīp′rīt′), *v.t.*, *v.i.*, **-wrote, -writ·ten, -writ·ing.** to write by means of a typewriter; type. [back formation from TYPEWRITER]

type·writ·er (tīp′rī′tər), *n.* **1.** a machine for writing mechanically in letters and characters like those produced by printers' types. **2.** *Print.* a type style which gives the appearance of typewritten copy. **3.** a typist. [TYPE + WRITER]

type·writ·ing (tīp′rī′ting), *n.* **1.** the act or art of using a typewriter. **2.** work done on a typewriter. [TYPEWRITE + -ING[1]]

type·writ·ten (tīp′rit′ən), *v.* pp. of **typewrite.**

typh-, var. of **typho-** before a vowel: *typhoid.*

typh·li·tis (tif lī′tis), *n.* *Pathol.* inflammation of the caecum. [< Gk *typhl(ós)* blind + -ITIS] —**typh·lit·ic** (tif lit′ik), *adj.*

typh·lol·o·gy (tif lol′ə jē), *n.* the sum of scientific knowledge concerning blindness. [< Gk *typhlo-* (comb. form of *typhlós* blind) + -LOGY]

typh·lo·sis (tif lō′sis), *n.* *Pathol.* blindness. [< Gk *typhl(ós)* blind + -OSIS disease]

typho- a combining form representing **typhus** and **typhoid**: *typhogenic.* Also, *esp. before a vowel,* **typh-.**

Ty·phoe·an (tī fē′ən), *adj.* of, pertaining to, or resembling Typhoeus. [TYPHOE(US) + -AN]

Ty·phoe·us (tī fē′əs), *n.* *Class. Myth.* a monster with a hundred serpents' heads, fiery eyes, and a terrifying voice. Zeus set him on fire with thunderbolts and flung him down into Tartarus under Mount Etna. Cf. **Typhon.**

ty·pho·gen·ic (tī′fə jen′ik), *adj.* *Pathol.* producing typhus or typhoid fever. [TYPHO- + -GENIC]

ty·phoid (tī′foid), *Pathol.* —*n.* **1.** Also called **ty′phoid fe′ver.** an infectious, often fatal, febrile disease, usually of the summer months, characterized by intestinal inflammation and ulceration, caused by the typhoid bacillus, which is usually introduced with food or drink. —*adj.* **2.** resembling typhus; typhous. **3.** typhoidal. [TYPH- + -OID]

ty·phoi·dal (tī foid′əl), *adj.* *Pathol.* of, pertaining to, or resembling typhoid. [TYPHOID + -AL[1]]

ty′phoid bacil′lus, the bacterium, *Salmonella typhosa,* causing typhoid fever.

ty·phoi·din (tī foi′din), *n.* *Med.* a culture of dead typhoid bacillus used by cutaneous inoculation to detect the presence of a typhoid infection. [TYPHOID + -IN[1]]

ty·pho·ma·lar·i·al (tī′fō mə lâr′ē əl), *adj.* *Pathol.* having the symptoms of both typhoid and malaria. [TYPHO- + MALARIAL]

ty·phon (tī′fon), *n.* *Naut.* a signal horn operated by compressed air or steam. [appar. after TYPHON]

Ty·phon (tī′fon), *n.* *Class. Myth.* a monster and a son of Typhoeus later confused with Typhoeus. —**Ty·pho·ni·an** (tī fō′nē ən), *adj.*

ty·phoon (tī fo͞on′), *n.* **1.** a tropical cyclone or hurricane of the western Pacific area and the China seas. **2.** a violent storm or tempest of India. **3.** (*cap., italics.*) a short story (1902) by Joseph Conrad. [< Chin *tai fung* great wind; influenced by Gk *typhôn* violent wind] —**ty·phon·ic** (tī fon′ik), *adj.*

ty·phus (tī′fəs), *n.* *Pathol.* an acute, infectious disease characterized by great prostration, severe nervous symptoms, and a peculiar eruption of reddish spots on the body: now regarded as due to a specific microorganism transmitted by lice and fleas. Also called **ty′phus fe′ver.** [< NL < Gk *týphos* vapor] —**ty′phous,** *adj.*

typ·i·cal (tip′i kəl), *adj.* **1.** of the nature of or serving as a type or representative specimen. **2.** conforming to a particular type. **3.** *Biol.* exemplifying most nearly the essential characteristics of a higher group in natural history, and forming the type: *the typical genus of a family.* **4.** characteristic or distinctive: *He has the mannerisms typical of his class.* **5.** pertaining to, of the nature of, or serving as a type or emblem; symbolic. Also, **typ′ic.** [< ML *typicāl(is),* equiv. to L *typic(us)* (< Gk *typikós,* equiv. to *týp(os)* TYPE + *-ikos* -IC) + *-ālis* -AL[1]] —**typ′i·cal·ly,** *adv.* —**typ′i·cal·ness, typ′i·cal′i·ty,** *n.*

ty·pi·con (tip′i kon′), *n.* *Eastern Ch.* the instructions for the orders of the services during the ecclesiastical year, contained in a manual. Also, **typikon.** [< MGk *typikón,* n. use of neut. of *typikós* according to rule, regular, Gk: conforming to type, TYPICAL]

typ·i·fy (tip′ə fī′), *v.t.*, **-fied, -fy·ing. 1.** to serve as the typical specimen of; exemplify. **2.** to serve as a symbol or emblem of; symbolize; prefigure. **3.** to represent by a type or symbol. [< L *typ(us)* TYPE + -IFY] —**typ′i·fi·ca′tion,** *n.* —**typ′i·fi′er,** *n.*

ty·pi·kon (tip′i kon′), *n.*, *pl.* **-ka** (-kə), **-kons.** typicon.

typ·ist (tī′pist), *n.* a person who operates a typewriter. [TYPE + -IST]

ty·po (tī′pō), *n.*, *pl.* **-pos.** *Informal.* See **typographical error.** [shortened form]

typo-, a combining form representing **type:** *typography, typology.* Cf. **-type.**

typo., **1.** typographer. **2.** typographic. **3.** typographical. **4.** typography.

typog., **1.** typographer. **2.** typographic. **3.** typographical. **4.** typography.

ty·pog·ra·pher (tī pog′rə fər), *n.* one skilled or engaged in typography. [TYPOGRAPH(Y) + -ER[1]]

ty·po·graph·ic (tī′pə graf′ik), *adj.* of or pertaining to typography. Also, **ty′po·graph′i·cal.** [< NL *typographic(us),* equiv. to ML *typograph(ia)* TYPOGRAPHY + *-icus* -IC] —**ty′po·graph′i·cal·ly,** *adv.*

typograph′ical er′ror, an error in printed or typewritten matter resulting from striking the improper key of a keyboard, from mechanical failure, or the like.

ty·pog·ra·phy (tī pog′rə fē), *n.* **1.** the art or process of printing with type. **2.** the work of setting and arranging types and of printing from them. **3.** the general character or appearance of printed matter. [< NL *typographia* < Gk *týpo(s)* type + *graphía* -GRAPHY]

ty·pol·o·gy (tī pol′ə jē), *n.* **1.** the doctrine or study of types or prefigurative symbols, esp. in scriptural literature. **2.** a systematic classification or study of types. **3.** symbolism. [TYPO- + -LOGY] —**ty·po·log·i·cal** (tī′pə loj′i kəl), **ty′po·log′ic,** *adj.* —**ty′po·log′i·cal·ly,** *adv.* —**ty·pol′o·gist,** *n.*

ty·poth·e·tae (tī poth′i tē′, tī′pə thē′tē), *n. pl.* printers, esp. master printers: used in the names of associations. [< NL < Gk *týpo(s)* type + *-thetai,* Latinized pl. of Gk *thétēs* THETE]

typp (tip), *n.* *Textiles.* a number representing the aggregate of thousands of yards of yarn weighing one pound. [*t(housand) y(ards) p(er) p(ound)*]

typw., **1.** typewriter. **2.** typewritten.

Tyr (tēr, tyr), *n.* *Scand. Myth.* the god of victory, usually regarded as the son of Odin and Frigg, who lost one hand when Fenrir was chained. He was destined to kill and to be killed by the dog Garm at Ragnarok.

ty·ran·ni·cal (ti ran′i kəl, tī-), *adj.* unjustly cruel, harsh, or severe; arbitrary or oppressive; despotic: *a tyrannical ruler.* Also, **ty·ran′nic.** [< L *tyrannic(us)* (< Gk *tyrannikós,* equiv. to *týrann(os)* TYRANT + *-ikos* -IC) + -AL[1]] —**ty·ran′ni·cal·ly,** *adv.* —**ty·ran′ni·cal·ness,** *n.*

—**Syn.** dictatorial; imperious, domineering.

ty·ran·ni·cide (ti ran′i sīd′, tī-), *n.* **1.** the act of killing a tyrant. **2.** a person who kills a tyrant. [< L *tyrrannicīda, -um.* See TYRANT, -CIDE] —**ty·ran′ni·cid′al,** *adj.*

tyr·an·nise (tir′ə nīz′), *v.i.*, *v.t.*, **-nised, -nis·ing.** *Chiefly Brit.* tyrannize. —**tyr′an·nis′er,** *n.* —**tyr′an·nis′ing·ly,** *adv.*

tyr·an·nize (tir′ə nīz′), *v.*, **-nized, -niz·ing.** —*v.i.* **1.** to exercise absolute power or control cruelly or oppressively (often fol. by *over*). **2.** to govern despotically, cruelly, or oppressively. **3.** to govern or reign as a tyrant. —*v.t.* **4.** to rule or govern tyrannically; treat oppressively. [< F *tyrannise(r)* < LL *tyrannizāre,* equiv. to *tyrann(us)* TYRANT + *-izāre* -IZE] —**tyr′an·niz′er,** *n.* —**tyr′an·niz′ing·ly,** *adv.*

ty·ran·no·saur (ti ran′ə sôr′, tī-), *n.* a carnivorous dinosaur of the genus *Tyrannosaurus,* from the late Cretaceous period of North America, that walked erect on its hind feet. [< NL *tyrrano-* (comb. form of L *tyrannus* tyrant) + -SAUR]

tyr·an·nous (tir′ə nəs), *adj.* tyrannical. [ME < L *tyrann(us)* TYRANT + -OUS] —**tyr′an·nous·ly,** *adv.* —**tyr′an·nous·ness,** *n.*

tyr·an·ny (tir′ə nē), *n.*, *pl.* **-nies. 1.** arbitrary or unrestrained exercise of power; despotic abuse of authority. **2.** the government or rule of a tyrant or absolute ruler. **3.** a state ruled by a tyrant or absolute ruler. **4.** oppressive or unjustly severe government on the part of any ruler. **5.** undue severity or harshness. **6.** a tyrannical act or proceeding. [ME *tyrannie* < OF < ML *tyrannia,* equiv. to L *tyrann(us)* TYRANT + *-ia* -Y[3]]

ty·rant (tī′rənt), *n.* **1.** a king or ruler who uses his power oppressively or unjustly. **2.** any person in a position of authority who exercises power oppressively or despotically. **3.** a tyrannical or compulsory influence. **4.** an absolute ruler, esp. one in ancient Greece or Sicily. [ME *tirant* < OF < L *tyrann(us)* < Gk *týrannos*]

—**Syn. 1.** despot, autocrat, dictator.

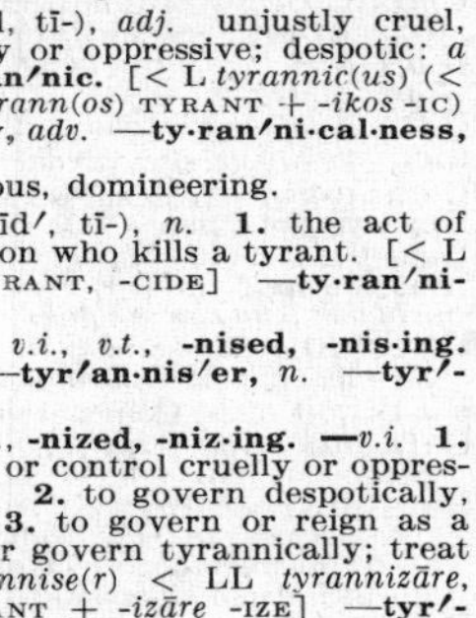

ty′rant fly′catcher, flycatcher (def. 2).

tyre (tīər), *n.*, *v.t.*, **tyred, tyr·ing.** *Brit.* tire[2].

Tyre (tīər), *n.* an ancient seaport of Phoenicia: one of the great cities of antiquity, famous for its navigators and traders; site of modern Sur.

Tyr·i·an (tir′ē ən), *adj.* **1.** of or pertaining to ancient Tyre or its people. **2.** of the color of Tyrian purple. [< L *tyri(us)* (< Gk *týri(os),* deriv. of *Týros* TYRE) + -AN]

Tyr′ian pur′ple, **1.** Also called **Tyr′ian dye′.** a highly prized purple dye of classical antiquity, originally obtained at great expense from a certain shellfish. It was later shown to be an indigo derivative and synthetically produced, and has been replaced by other synthetic dyes. **2.** a vivid, purplish red.

ty·ro (tī′rō), *n.*, *pl.* **-ros.** a beginner in learning anything; novice. Also, **tiro.** [< L *tīro* recruit] —**ty·ron·ic** (tī ron′ik), *adj.*

—**Syn.** neophyte, learner.

Ty·ro (tī′rō), *n.* *Class. Myth.* the daughter of Salmoneus and Alcidice, and the mother, by Poseidon, of Neleus and Pelias.

ty·ro·ci·dine (tī′rə sīd′ən, -sī′dēn), *n.* *Pharm.* a colorless, crystalline, slightly water-soluble, antibacterial substance, obtained from tyrothricin by extraction, and used chiefly in treating infections caused by Gram-positive bacteria. Also, **ty·ro·ci·din** (tī′rə sīd′ən). [TYRO- (SINE) + -CID(E) + -INE[1]]

Tyr·ol (tir′ol, tī′rōl, ti-rōl′; *Ger.* tē rōl′), *n.* **1.** an alpine region in W Austria and N Italy: a former Austrian crown land. **2.** a province in W Austria. 462,612 (1961); 4883 sq. mi. *Cap.:* Innsbruck. Also, **Tirol.**

Ty·ro·le·an (ti rō′lē ən), *adj.* **1.** of, pertaining to, or characteristic of the Tyrol or its inhabitants. —*n.* **2.** a native or inhabitant of the Tyrol. Also, **Tirolean, Tyrolese, Tirolese.** [TYROL + *-ean* (var. of -IAN)]

Tyr·o·lese (tir′ə lēz′, -lēs′), *adj.*, *n.*, *pl.* **-lese.** Tyrolean. Also, **Tirolese.** [TYROL + -ESE]

Ty·ro·li·enne (ti rō′lē en′, tī-; *Fr.* tē rô lyen′), *n.*, *pl.* **-li·ennes** (-lē enz′; *Fr.* -lyen′). **1.** a dance of the Tyrolean peasants. **2.** a song or melody, characteristically a yodel, suitable for such a dance. [< F, fem. of *tyrolien* pertaining to Tyrol]

Ty·rone (ti rōn′ *for 1, 2;* tī′rōn *for 3*), *n.* **1.** a county in W Northern Ireland. 133,919 (1961); 1218 sq. mi. *Co. seat:* Omagh. **2.** a town in central Pennsylvania. 7792 (1960). **3.** a boy's given name.

ty·ro·si·nase (tī′rō si nās′, tir′ō-), *n.* *Biochem.* an oxidizing enzyme, found in plant and animal tissues, that catalyzes the aerobic oxidation of tyrosine into melanin and other pigments. [TYROSINE + -ASE]

ty·ro·sine (tī′rə sēn′, -sin, tir′ə-), *n.* *Biochem.* a crystalline amino acid, $HOC_6H_4CH_2CH(NH_2)COOH$, resulting from the hydrolysis of proteins. [< Gk *tyrós* cheese + -INE[2]]

ty·ro·sin·o·sis (tī′rō si nō′sis, tir′ō-), *n.* *Pathol.* a condition characterized by abnormally large amounts of tyrosine in the urine, caused by faulty metabolism. [TYROSINE + -OSIS]

ty·ro·thri·cin (tī′rō thrī′sin, -thris′in), *n.* *Pharm.* a white to buff-colored, water-insoluble, antibiotic powder extracted from *Bacillus brevis* or other related soil bacilli, and consisting chiefly of a mixture of gramicidin and tyrocidine: used chiefly in external applications for treating local infections caused by Gram-positive bacteria. [< NL *Tyrothric-* (s. of *Tyrothrix*) name of genus of bacteria + -IN[2]]

Tyrr (tēr, tyr), *n.* Tyr.

Tyr·rhe′ni·an Sea′ (ti rē′nē ən), a part of the Mediterranean, bounded by W Italy, Corsica, Sardinia and Sicily.

Tyr·rhe·num (ti rē′nəm), *n.* **Mare.** See **Mare Tyrrhenum.**

Tyr·rhe·us (tī′rē əs, tī′ro͞os), *n.* *Rom. Legend.* a shepherd. The killing of his tame stag by Ascanius was a cause of the war between Aeneas' Trojans and the people of Latium. Also, **Tyr·rhus** (tī′rəs).

Tyr·tae·us (tûr tē′əs), *n.* fl. 7th century B.C., Greek poet.

Ty·rus (tī′rəs), *n.* a boy's given name.

Ty·son (tī′sən), *n.* a boy's given name.

Tyr·whitt-Wil·son (tir′it wil′sən), *n.* **Gerald Hugh, 14th Baron Ber·ners** (bûr′nərz), 1883–1950, English composer, painter, and author.

tythe (tīth), *n.*, *v.t.*, *v.i.*, **tythed, tyth·ing.** *Brit.* tithe.

Tyu·men (tyo͞o men′), *n.* a city in the SW RSFSR, in the W Soviet Union in Asia. 200,000 (est. 1964).

Ty·zine (tī′zēn), *n.* *Pharm., Trademark.* tetrahydrozoline.

tzad·dik (tsä dēk′; *Eng.* tsä′dik), *n.*, *pl.* **tza·di·kim** (tsä dē kēm′; *Eng.* tsä dik′im). *Hebrew.* zaddik.

tzar (zär, tsär), *n.* czar.

tzar·dom (zär′dəm, tsär′-), *n.* czardom.

tzar·e·vich (zär′ə vich, tsär′-), *n.* czarevitch.

tza·rev·na (zä rev′nə, tsä-), *n.* czarevna.

tza·ri·na (zä rē′nə, tsä-), *n.* czarina.

tzar·ism (zär′iz əm, tsär′-), *n.* czarism.

tzar·ist (zär′ist, tsär′-), *adj.*, *n.* czarist.

tza·ris·tic (zä ris′tic, tsä-), *adj.* czarist.

tza·rit·za (zä rit′sə, tsä-), *n.* czaritza.

tze·da·kah (tsə dä kä′; *Eng.* tsə dô′kə), *n.* *Hebrew.* charity or the giving of charity. Also, **zedakah.**

tzet′ze fly′ (tset′sē). See **tsetse fly.** Also called **tzetze.**

Tzi·gane (tsi gän′), *adj.* **1.** (*often l.c.*) of, consisting of, or pertaining to Gypsies: *Tzigane music.* —*n.* **2.** a Gypsy, esp. a Hungarian one. [< F < Russ *tzygan* (c. Ukr *tzigán*) < Hung *cigány* gypsy, Romany < ?]

Tzi·ga·ny (tsi gä′nē), *adj.*, *n.*, *pl.* **-nies.** Tzigane.

tzim·mes (tsim′is), *n.* **1.** *Jewish Cookery.* any of various sweetened combinations of vegetables, fruit, and sometimes meat, prepared as a casserole or stew. **2.** *Yiddish.* (*italics*) fuss; uproar; hullabaloo: *He made such a tzimmes over that mistake!*

tzi·tzith (tsit′sis; *Heb.* tsē tsēt′), *n.* (*construed as sing. or pl.*) *Judaism.* zizith.

Tzom Ge·dal·iah (tsôm′ gə däl′yə), a Jewish fast day observed on the third day of the month of Tishri in memory of the treacherous murder of Gedaliah, Jewish governor of Judah appointed by King Nebuchadnezzar of Babylonia. Also called **Fast of Gedaliah.**

U

U, u, (yo͞o), *n., pl.* **U's** or **Us, u's** or **us. 1.** the 21st letter of the English alphabet, a vowel. **2.** any spoken sound represented by the letter *U* or *u*, as in *curious, put, jug, quiet*, etc. **3.** something having the shape of a U. **4.** a written or printed representation of the letter *U* or *u*. **5.** a device, as a printer's type, for reproducing the letter *U* or *u*.

U (yo͞o), *pron. Informal.* you: *Shoes Fixed While U Wait.*

U (yo͞o), *adj. Informal.* characteristic of or appropriate to the upper class, esp. of Great Britain. [*u*(*pper class*)]

U (o͞o), *n.* a Burmese title of respect applicable to a man: used before the proper name.

U, 1. the 21st in order or in a series, or, when *I* is omitted, the 20th. **2.** *Chem.* uranium. **3.** *Thermodynamics.* See **internal engine. 4.** *Brit.* (used to designate a motion picture certified as fit for children as well as adults). Cf. **A, X.**

U-235, *Chem.* See **uranium 235.** Also, **U 235.**

U-238, *Chem.* See **uranium 238.** Also, **U 238.**

U-239, *Chem.* See **uranium 239.** Also, **U 239.**

U., 1. uncle. **2.** and. [< G *und*] **3.** uniform. **4.** union. **5.** unit. **6.** united. **7.** university. **8.** upper.

u., 1. and. [< G *und*] **2.** uniform. **3.** unit. **4.** upper. Also, **U.** (for defs. 1, 3).

ua·ka·ri (wä kär′ē), *n., pl.* **-ris.** any of several New World monkeys of the genus *Cacajao* having short tails. [< Tupi Guarani *uakari* a genus of monkeys]

UAM, underwater-to-air missile.

u·a ma·u ke e·a o ka a·i·na i ka po·no (o͞o′ä mä′o͞o kā ā′ä ō kä ä′ē nä′ ē kä pō′nō), *Hawaiian.* The life of the land is maintained by righteousness: motto of Hawaii.

u. & l.c., *Print.* upper and lower case.

U.A.R., United Arab Republic.

UAW, United Automobile Workers (full name: International Union of United Automobile, Aerospace, and Agricultural Implement Workers of America). Also, **U.A.W.**

U.B., United Brethren.

U·ban·gi (yo͞o bang′gē, o͞o bäng′-), *n.* **1.** a river in W central Africa, forming part of the boundary between the Republic of the Congo and the Central African Republic, flowing W and S into the Congo River. 700 mi. long. French, **Oubangi. 2.** a woman of the Sara tribe in the Central African Republic whose lips are pierced and stretched around flat wooden disks.

U·ban·gi-Sha·ri (yo͞o bang′gē shär′ē, o͞o bäng′-), *n.* former name of the **Central African Republic.** French, **Oubangi-Chari.**

U·be (o͞o′bē; *Jap.* o͞o bē′), *n.* a seaport on W Honshu, in W Japan. 161,905 (1964).

U·be·ra·ba (o͞o′bə rä′bə), *n.* a city in E Brazil. 72,053 (1960).

U·ber·lân·dia (o͞o′bər länn′dyə), *n.* a city in E Brazil. 71,717 (1960).

Ü·ber·mensch (y′bər mensh′), *n., pl.* **-mensch·en** (-men′shən). *German.* superman (def. 2).

u·bi (o͞o′bē), *conj.* (in prescriptions) where; wherever; whenever. [< L]

u·bi·e·ty (yo͞o bī′i tē), *n.* the property of having a definite location at any given time; state of existing and being localized in space. [< ML *ubietāt-*, equiv. to L *ubi* where + *-etāt-* -ety, var. of -ITY]

u·bi·que (o͞o bē′kwe; *Eng.* yo͞o bī′kwē), *adv. Latin.* everywhere.

U·biq·ui·tar·i·an (yo͞o bik′wi târ′ē ən), *Theol.* —*adj.* **1.** of or pertaining to the doctrine, esp. as advocated by Luther, that the body of Christ is omnipresent and therefore exists in the Eucharistic bread. —*n.* **2.** Also, **Ubiquarian, Ubiquist.** one who advocates this doctrine. [< ML *ubīquitāri*(*us*) being everywhere at once (see UBIQUITY, -ARY) + -AN] —**U·biq′ui·tar′i·an·ism,** *n.*

u·biq·ui·tous (yo͞o bik′wi təs), *adj.* present everywhere; being everywhere, esp. at the same time; omnipresent: *ubiquitous fog; ubiquitous little ants.* Also, **u·biq·ui·tar·y** (yo͞o bik′wi ter′ē). [UBIQUIT(Y) + -OUS] —**u·biq′ui·tous·ly,** *adv.* —**u·biq′ui·tous·ness,** *n.*
—**Syn.** See **omnipresent.**

u·biq·ui·ty (yo͞o bik′wi tē), *n.* **1.** state or capacity of being everywhere, esp. at the same time; omnipresence: *the ubiquity of magical beliefs.* **2.** (*cap.*) *Theol.* the omnipresence of God or Christ. [< F *ubiquité*, OF *ubiquite* < VL **ubiquitāt-*, equiv. to L *ubiqu*(*e*) everywhere + *-tāt-* -TY[2]]

u·bi su·pra (o͞o′bē so͞o′prä; *Eng.* yo͞o′bī so͞o′prə), *Latin.* See **u.s.** (def. 1).

U-boat (yo͞o′bōt′), *n.* a German submarine. [< G *U-Boot*, short for *Unterseeboot*, lit., undersea boat]

U bolt, a bar of iron bent into the form of the letter U, fitted with a screw thread and nut at each end.

U·bu Roi (*Fr.* Y BY RWA′), a satirical farce (1896) by Alfred Jarry.

U.C., 1. Upper Canada. **2.** Under Construction.

u.c., 1. *Music.* una corda. **2.** *Print.* upper case.

U·cal·e·gon (yo͞o kal′ə gon′), *n.* (in the *Iliad*) a counselor of Priam.

U·ca·ya·li (o͞o′kä yä′lē), *n.* a river in W South America, flowing N from E Peru and joining the Marañón to form the Amazon. 1200 mi. long.

Uc·cel·lo (o͞o chel′ō; *It.* o͞ot chel′lô), *n.* **Pa·o·lo** (pä′ô lô), (*Paolo di Dono*), 1397–1475, Italian painter.

U.C.V., United Confederate Veterans.

U·dae·us (yo͞o dē′əs), *n. Class. Myth.* one of the Sparti.

U·dai·pur (o͞o dī′po͝or, o͞o′dī po͝or′), *n.* **1.** a city in S Rajasthan, in NW India. 111,100 (1961). **2.** Also called **Mewar.** a former state in NW India: merged into Rajasthan state 1948.

U·dall (yo͞o′dôl *or, for 1,* yo͞od′əl), *n.* **1.** Also called **Uvedale. Nicholas,** 1505–56, English translator and playwright, esp. of comedy. **2. Stewart Lee,** born 1920, U.S. politician: Secretary of the Interior 1961–69.

U.D.C., United Daughters of the Confederacy.

ud·der (ud′ər), *n.* a mamma or mammary gland, esp. when baggy and with more than one teat, as in cows. [ME *uddre*, OE *ūder*; c. G *Euter*, L *über*, Gk *oûthar*, Skt *ūdhar*]

U·dele (yə del′), *n.* a girl's given name.

U·di·ne (o͞o′dē ne), *n.* a city in NE Italy. 85,205 (1961).

Udmurt′ Auton′omous Repub′lic (o͞od mo͞ort′), **an autonomous republic in the Russian Federation in Europe. 1,609,000; 16,250 sq. mi.** ***Cap.:*** **Izhevsk.**

u·do (o͞o′dō), *n., pl.* **u·dos.** a plant, *Aralia cordata*, cultivated esp. in Japan and China for its edible shoots. [< Jap]

u·dom·e·ter (yo͞o dom′i tər), *n.* a rain gauge; a pluviometer. [< F *udomètre* < L *ūd*(*us*) wet + F *-o-* -o- + *-mètre* -METER] —**u·do·met·ric** (yo͞o′də me′trik), *adj.* —**u·dom′e·try,** *n.*

U·don Tha·ni (o͞o′dôn′ tä′nē′), a city in NE Thailand. 10,000 (1961).

Ue·le (wā′lə), *n.* a river in central Africa flowing W from the NE Republic of the Congo to the Ubangi River. 700 mi. long.

U·fa (o͞o fä′), *n.* **a city in and the capital of the Bashkir Autonomous Republic, in the Russian Federation in Europe. 1,083,000.**

U.F.C., United Free Church (of Scotland).

UFO, unidentified flying object.

U·gan·da (yo͞o gan′də, o͞o gän′dä), *n.* an independent state in E Africa, between the NE Democratic Republic of the Congo and Kenya: member of the British Commonwealth; formerly a British protectorate. 7,190,000 (est. 1963); 93,981 sq. mi. *Cap.:* Kampala. —**U·gan′dan,** *adj., n.*

U·ga·rit (o͞o′gə rēt′), *n.* an ancient city in Syria, N of Latakia, on the site of modern Ras Shamra: destroyed by an earthquake c1350 B.C., rebuilt and destroyed again in the early part of the 12th century B.C.

U·ga·rit·ic (o͞o′gə rit′ik), *adj.* **1.** of or pertaining to Ugarit, its people, or their language. —*n.* **2.** Also, **U·ga·ri·tian** (o͞o′gə rish′ən). the language of the Ugaritic people, related to Hebrew and Phoenician and written in a cuneiform alphabet having 30 characters. [UGARIT + -IC]

ugh (o͝okh, ukh, u, o͝o; *spelling pron.* ug), *interj.* **1.** an exclamation expressing disgust, aversion, horror, or the like. —*n.* **2.** the sound of a cough, grunt, or the like.

ug·li·fy (ug′lə fī′), *v.t.,* **-fied, -fy·ing.** to make ugly. [UGLY + -FY] —**ug′li·fi·ca′tion,** *n.* —**ug′li·fi′er,** *n.*

ug·ly (ug′lē), *adj.,* **-li·er, -li·est. 1.** very unattractive or unpleasant to look at; offensive to the sense of beauty; displeasing in appearance. **2.** disagreeable; unpleasant; objectionable: *ugly tricks; ugly discords.* **3.** morally revolting: *ugly crime.* **4.** threatening trouble or danger: *ugly symptoms.* **5.** mean; hostile; quarrelsome: *an ugly mood; an ugly frame of mind.* **6.** (esp. of natural phenomena) unpleasant and dangerous: *ugly weather; an ugly sea.* [ME *ugly, uglike* < ON *uggilig*(*r*) fearful, dreadful, equiv. to *ugg*(*r*) + *-ligr* -LY] —**ug′li·ly,** *adv.* —**ug′li·ness,** *n.*
—**Syn. 1.** ill-favored, hard-featured, uncomely, unsightly, unlovely, homely. **3.** base, heinous, vile, monstrous, corrupt. **4.** disadvantageous, ominous. **5.** surly, spiteful. **6.** stormy, tempestuous. —**Ant. 1.** beautiful.

ug′ly cus′tomer, a hostile or dangerous person.

ug′ly duck′ling, an unattractive or unpromising child who becomes a beautiful or much-admired adult. [after the story of the same name by Hans Christian Andersen]

U·gri·an (o͞o′grē ən, yo͞o′-), *adj.* **1.** denoting or pertaining to a race or ethnological group including the Magyars and related peoples of western Siberia and the northeastern Soviet Union in Europe. —*n.* **2.** a member of any of the Ugrian peoples. **3.** Ugric. [< Russ *Ugri* (pl.) (ORuss *ugreninu* Hungarians) + -AN]

U·gric (o͞o′grik, yo͞o′-), *n.* **1.** a branch of the Uralic family of languages, consisting of Hungarian and two languages, Ostyak and Vogul, spoken in western Siberia. —*adj.* **2.** Ugrian. [UGR(IAN) + -IC]

Ugro-, a combining form of **Ugric:** *Ugro-Finnic.*

U·gro-Fin·nic (o͞o′grō fin′ik, yo͞o′-), *n., adj.* Finno-Ugric.

ug·some (ug′səm), *adj. Scot. and North Eng.* horrid; loathsome. [ME, equiv. to *ugg*(*en*) (to) fear, cause loathing + *-some* -SOME[1]] —**ug′some·ness,** *n.*

Uh·de (o͞o′də), *n.* **Fritz Karl Her·mann von** (frits kärl her′män fən), 1848–1911, German painter.

UHF, See **ultrahigh frequency.** Also, **uhf**

uh·lan (o͞o′län, yo͞o′lən), *n.* **1.** one of a group of lancers in a light-cavalry unit, first appearing in Europe in the Polish army. **2.** one of such a group as later developed into heavy cavalry in western European armies, esp. in Germany. Also, **ulan.** [< G < Pol *ulan* << Turk *oğlan* boy, lad]

Uh·land (o͞o′länt), *n.* **Jo·hann Lud·wig** (yō′hän lo͞ot′vikh, lo͞od′-), 1787–1862, German poet and writer.

Uh·richs·ville (yo͞or′iks vil), *n.* a town in E Ohio. 6201 (1960).

u.i., ut infra.

Ui·gur (wē′go͝or), *n.* **1.** a member of a Turkish people dominant in Mongolia and eastern Turkestan from the 8th to 12th centuries A.D. **2.** the Turkic language of the Uigurs, esp. in the period of their dominance. —*adj.* **3.** of, pertaining to, or characteristic of the Uigurs. Also, **Ui′ghur.** —**Ui·gu·ri·an** (wē go͝or′ē ən), **Ui·gu′ric,** *adj.*

u·in·ta·ite (yo͞o in′tə īt′), *n.* gilsonite. Also, **u·in′tah·ite′.** [named after the UINTA (MOUNTAINS); see -ITE[1]]

U·in′ta Moun′tains (yo͞o in′tə), a mountain range in NE Utah, part of the Rocky Mountains. Highest peak, Kings Peak, 13,498 ft.

uit·land·er (īt′lan′dər, oit′-; *Du.* œit′län′dər), *n.* (*often cap.*) a foreigner, esp. a British settler in the Boer republics prior to the formation of the Union of South Africa. [< SAfrD: outsider]

Ui·tzi·lo·poch·tli (wē′tsē lō pōch′tlē), *n.* the Aztec god of war and of the sun. Also, **Huitzilopochtli.** [< Nahuatl: humming-bird of the south]

U·ji·ji (o͞o jē′jē), *n.* a town in W Tanzania, on Lake Tanganyika: Stanley found Livingstone here 1871. 12,011 (1957).

Uj·pest (o͞o′ē pesht′), *n.* a suburb of Budapest, in N Hungary. 68,530 (est. 1954). German, **Neupest.**

U.K., United Kingdom.

u·kase (yo͞o′kās, yo͞o kāz′), *n.* **1.** (in czarist Russia) an edict or order of the czar having the force of law. **2.** any order or proclamation by an absolute or arbitrary authority. [< F < Russ *ukáz,* ORuss *ukázŭ,* equiv. to *u-* away + *-kaz-* show]

uke (yo͞ok), *n.* *Informal.* ukulele. [by shortening]

U·kert (yo͞o′kərt), *n.* a crater in the first quadrant of the face of the moon: about 14 miles in diameter.

U·ki·ah (yo͞o kī′ə), *n.* a town in NW California. 9900 (1960).

U·ki Gu·mo (*Jap.* o͞o′kē go͞o′mô). See **Drifting Cloud, The.**

u·ki·yo-e (o͞o kē′yô e′), *n.* a genre style of painting and printmaking developed in Japan from the 17th–19th centuries. [< Jap, equiv. to *ukiyo* world, life + *e* painting]

Ukr., Ukraine.

U·kra·i·na (o͞o krä ē′nä), *n.* the Russian name of **Ukraine.**

U·kraine (yo͞o krān′, -krīn′, yo͞o′krān), *n.* a constituent republic of the Soviet Union, in S Europe: rich agricultural region. 42,500,000 (est. 1960); ab. 223,000 sq. mi. *Cap.:* Kiev. Russian, **Ukraina.** Official name, **Ukrain′ian So′viet So′cialist Repub′lic.**

U·krain·i·an (yo͞o krā′nē ən, -krī′-), *adj.* **1.** of or pertaining to the Ukraine, its people, or their language. —*n.* **2.** a native or inhabitant of the Ukraine. **3.** Also called **Little Russian.** a Slavic language closely related to Russian. [UKRAINE + -IAN]

u·ku·le·le (yo͞o′kə lā′lē; *Hawaiian* o͞o′ko͞o lä′lā), *n.* a small guitarlike musical instrument associated chiefly with Hawaiian music. Also, **u′ke·le′le.** [< Hawaiian: lit., flea]

Ukulele

U·la (yo͞o′lə), *n.* a girl's given name. Also, **Eula.**

′u·la·ma (o͞o′lä mä′), *n.* (*construed as pl.*) ulema.

u·lan (o͞o′län, yo͞o′lən), *n.* uhlan.

U·lan Ba·tor (o͞o′län bä′tôr), a city in and the capital of the Mongolian People's Republic, in E central Asia: former holy city of Mongols. 195,300 (est. 1962). Chinese, **Kulun.** Formerly, **Urga.**

U·lan U·de (o͞o′län o͞o′də), a city in the SE RSFSR, in the S Soviet Union in Asia, near Lake Baikal. 209,000 (est. 1964).

Ul·bricht (o͝ol′brikht), *n.* **Wal·ter** (väl′tər), 1893–1973, chairman of the East German Council of State 1960–73.

ul·cer (ul′sər), *n.* **1.** *Pathol.* a sore open either to the surface of the body or to a natural cavity, and accompanied by the disintegration of tissue, the formation of pus, etc. **2.** any chronically corrupting or disrupting condition, element, etc. [ME < L *ulcer-* (s. of *ulcus*); c. Gk *hélkos*]

ul·cer·ate (ul′sə rāt′), *v.,* **-at·ed, -at·ing.** —*v.i.* **1.** to form an ulcer; become ulcerous: *His skin ulcerated after exposure to radioactive material.* —*v.t.* **2.** to cause an ulcer on or in: *Continued worry ulcerated his stomach.* [< L *ulcerāt(us)* (ptp. of *ulcerāre*) made sore, equiv. to *ulcer-* (see ULCER) + *-ātus* -ATE[1]] —**ul′cer·a′tion,** *n.*

ul·cer·a·tive (ul′sə rā′tiv, -sər ə tiv), *adj.* **1.** causing ulceration. **2.** of the nature of or characterized by ulceration. [< ML *ulcerātīv(us),* equiv. to L *ulcerāt(us)* (see ULCERATE) + *-īvus* -IVE]

ul·cer·ous (ul′sər əs), *adj.* **1.** of the nature of an ulcer or ulcers; characterized by the formation of ulcers. **2.** affected with an ulcer or ulcers. [< L *ulcerōs(us)* full of sores, ulcerous, equiv. to *ulcer-* a sore, ULCER + *-ōsus* -OUS] —**ul′cer·ous·ly,** *adv.* —**ul′cer·ous·ness,** *n.*

-ule, a suffix, usually having diminutive force, occurring in nouns of Latin origin (*granule*): used in combination with nouns of other origin (*neurotubule*). [< L *-ulus*]

u·le·ma (o͞o′lə mä′), *n.* (*construed as pl.*) the doctors of Muslim religion and law, esp. in Turkey. Also, **′ulama.** [< Ar *ulemā* learned men]

-ulent, an adjective suffix meaning "abounding in," occurring in words of Latin origin: *fraudulent.* [< L *-ulentus*]

u·lex·ite (yo͞o lek′sīt), *n.* a mineral, hydrous sodium and calcium borate, $NaCaB_5O_9 \cdot 8H_2O$, occurring in arid regions in the form of white acicular crystals. [named after George L. *Ulex,* German chemist; see -ITE[1]]

Ul·fi·las (ul′fi ləs), *n.* A.D. c311–c382, Christian bishop to the Goths: translated Bible into the Gothic language. Also, **Ul·fi·la** (ul′fi lə), **Wulfila.**

u·lig·i·nous (yo͞o lij′ə nəs), *adj.* *Bot.* growing in swamps or muddy places. Also, **u·lig·i·nose** (yo͞o lij′ə nōs′). [< L *ūlīginōs(us)* full of moisture, wet, equiv. to *ūligin-* (s. of *ūlīgō*) moisture + *-ōsus* -OUS]

ul·lage (ul′ij), *n.* **1.** the amount by which the contents fall short of filling a container, as a cask, bottle, etc. **2.** the quantity of wine, liquor, or the like, remaining in a container which has lost part of its contents by evaporation, leakage, or use. **3.** *Rocketry.* the volume of a loaded tank of liquid propellant in excess of the volume of the propellant; the space provided for thermal expansion of the propellant and the accumulation of gases evolved from it. [< AF *ulliage,* OF *ouillage,* etc., wine needed to fill a cask, equiv. to *(a)ouill(er)* (to) fill (a cask) (deriv. of *ouil* eye, hole < L *oculus*) + *-age* -AGE] —**ul′laged,** *adj.*

Ull·er (o͝ol′ər), *n.* *Teutonic Myth.* a stepson of Thor, a god of winter and sports, identified with various gods. Also, **Ullr, Ull′ur.**

Ulm (o͝olm), *n.* a port in E Baden-Württemberg, in S West Germany, on the Danube. 94,400 (1963).

ul·ma·ceous (ul mā′shəs), *adj.* belonging to the *Ulmaceae,* or elm family of trees and shrubs. [< NL *Ulmāce(ae)* name of genus (L *ulm(us)* elm tree + *-āceae* -ACEAE) + -OUS]

ul·na (ul′nə), *n., pl.* **-nae** (-nē), **-nas. 1.** *Anat.* the bone of the forearm on the side opposite to the thumb. Cf. **radius** (def. 7). See diag. under **skeleton. 2.** a corresponding bone in the forelimb of other vertebrates. [< L: elbow; c. Gk *ōlénē,* OE *eln* ELL[2]] —**ul′nar,** *adj.*

ulno-, a combining form of **ulna:** *ulnoradial.*

ul·no·ra·di·al (ul′nə rā′dē əl), *adj.* *Anat.* of, pertaining to, or involving the ulna and the radius. [ULNO- + RADIAL]

-ulose, var. of **-ulous,** used in scientific terminology: *granulose; ramulose.* [< L *-ulōsus.* See -ULE, -OSE[1]]

u·lot·ri·chous (yo͞o lo′trə kəs), *adj.* belonging to a group of people whose hair is woolly or crisply curly. [< NL *Ulotrich(ī)* (see ULOTRICHY) + -OUS]

u·lot·ri·chy (yo͞o lo′trə kē), *n.* *Physical Anthropol.* the condition of having woolly or crisply curly hair. [< NL *Ulotrich(ī)* name of the genus < Gk *oulótrich-* (s. of *oulóthrix*) with curly hair, equiv. to *oûl(os)* thick, fleecy + *trich-* (s. of *thríx*) hair + -Y[3]]

-ulous, an adjective suffix meaning "tending to": *granulous, credulous.* [< L *-ulōsus* or *-ulus.* See -ULE, -OUS]

Ul·pi·an (ul′pē ən), *n.* (*Domitius Ulpianus*) died A.D. 288?, Roman jurist.

Ul·ric (ul′rik), *n.* a boy's given name.

Ul·ri·ca (ul′rə kə), *n.* a girl's given name. Also, **Ul′ri·ka.**

Ul·ster (ul′stər), *n.* **1.** a former province in Ireland, now comprising Northern Ireland and a part of the Republic of Ireland. **2.** a province in N Republic of Ireland. 217,524 (1961); 3123 sq. mi. **3.** *Informal.* See **Northern Ireland. 4.** (*l.c.*) a long, loose, heavy overcoat, originally of Irish frieze, now also of any of various other woolen cloths.

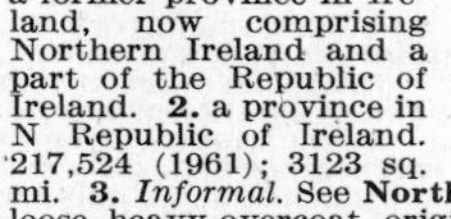

Ul·ster·man (ul′stər mən), *n., pl.* **-men.** a native or inhabitant of Ulster. [ULSTER + MAN[1]]

ult., **1.** ultimate. **2.** ultimately. **3.** ultimo.

ul·te·ri·or (ul tēr′ē ər), *adj.* **1.** being beyond what is seen or avowed; intentionally kept concealed: *ulterior motives.* **2.** coming at a subsequent time or stage: *ulterior action.* **3.** lying beyond or outside of some specified or understood boundary; more remote: *a suggestion ulterior to the purposes of the present discussion.* [< L: farther, comp. of *ulter*] —**ul·te′ri·or·ly,** *adv.*

ul·ti·ma (ul′tə mə), *n.* the last syllable of a word. [< L, fem. of *ultimus,* superl. of *ulter* far]

Ul·ti·ma (ul′tə mə), *n.* a girl's given name.

ul·ti·ma ra·ti·o re·gum (o͝ol′ti mä′ rä′tē ō′ rā′go͝om; *Eng.* ul′tə mə rā′shē ō′ rē′gəm), *Latin.* the final argument of kings (a resort to arms): motto engraved on the cannon of Louis XIV.

ul·ti·mate (ul′tə mit), *adj.* **1.** last; furthest or farthest; ending a process or series: *the ultimate point in a journey; the ultimate style in hats.* **2.** maximum; decisive; conclusive: *the ultimate authority; the ultimate weapon.* **3.** highest; not subsidiary: *ultimate goal in life.* **4.** basic; fundamental; representing a limit beyond which further progress, as in investigation or analysis, is impossible: *the ultimate particle; ultimate principles.* **5.** final; total: *the ultimate consequences; the ultimate cost of a project.* —*n.* **6.** the final point; final result. **7.** a fundamental fact or principle. [< LL *ultimāt(us)* having come to an end (ptp. of *ultimāre*), equiv. to L *ultim(us)* last, most distant (see ULTIMA) + *-ātus* -ATE[1]] —**ul′ti·mate·ly,** *adv.* —**ul′ti·mate·ness,** *n.*
—**Syn. 1.** extreme, remotest, uttermost. **2.** supreme. **5.** See **last**[1]. —**Ant. 5.** first.

ul′timate constit′uent, *Grammar.* an element of a construction that cannot be further divided into grammatical constituents: the morphemes of an utterance are usually considered to be its ultimate constituents. Cf. **immediate constituent.**

ul′timate strength′, *Engineering.* the quantity of the utmost tensile, compressive, or shearing stress that a given unit area of a certain material is expected to bear without failing. Also called **ul′timate stress′.**

ul·ti·ma Thu·le (ul′tə mə tho͞o′lē; *Lat.* o͝ol′ti mä′ to͞o′le), **1.** (*italics*) *Latin.* the highest degree attainable. **2.** the farthest point; the limit of any journey. **3.** the point believed by the ancients to be farthest north. Also called **Thule.** [lit., farthest Thule]

ul·ti·ma·tum (ul′tə mā′təm, -mä′-), *n., pl.* **-tums, -ta** (-tə). **1.** a final, uncompromising demand or set of terms issued by a party to a dispute, the rejection of which may lead to a severance of relations or to the use of force. **2.** a final proposal or statement of conditions. [< NL, LL, neut. of *ultimātus.* See ULTIMATE]

ul·ti·mo (ul′tə mō′), *adv.* in or of the month preceding the current one: *on the 12th ultimo. Abbr.:* ult., ulto. Cf. **proximo.** [< L *ultimō* (*mēnse* or *diē*) in the last (month) or on the last (day)]

ul·ti·mo·gen·i·ture (ul′tə mō jen′i chər), *n.* postremogeniture. [< L *ultimo-,* comb. form of *ultimus* (see ULTIMA) + GENITURE, modeled on *primogeniture*] —**ul·ti·mo·gen·i·tar·y** (ul′tə mō jen′i ter′ē), *adj.*

ulto., ultimo.

Ul·tor (ul′tôr), *n.* an ancient Roman epithet of Jupiter meaning "avenger."

ul·tra (ul′trə), *adj.* **1.** going beyond what is usual or ordinary; excessive; extreme. —*n.* **2.** an extremist, as in politics, religion, fashion, or the like. [< L *ultrā,* adv. and prep., beyond, on the other side, farther special use of abl. sing. fem. of *ulter* beyond]

ultra-, a combining form of **ultra:** *ultramarine.*

ul·tra·ba·sic (ul′trə bā′sik), *adj.* (of rocks) containing iron and magnesium, with little or no silica. [ULTRA- + BASIC]

ul·tra·cen·tri·fuge (ul′trə sen′trə fyo͞oj′), *n., v.,* **-fuged, -fug·ing.** *Physical Chem.* —*n.* **1.** a high-speed centrifuge for subjecting sols or solutions to forces many times that of gravity and producing concentration differences depending on the weight of the micelle or molecule. —*v.t.* **2.** to subject to the action of an ultracentrifuge. [ULTRA- + CENTRIFUGE] —**ul·tra·cen·trif·u·gal** (ul′trə sen trif′yə gəl), *adj.* —**ul′tra·cen·trif′u·gal·ly,** *adv.*

ul·tra·fil·ter (ul′trə fil′tər), *n.* *Physical Chem.* **1.** a filter for purifying sols, having a membrane with pores sufficiently small to prevent the passage of the suspended particles. —*v.t.* **2.** *Physical Chem.* to purify by means of an ultrafilter. **3.** *Math.* a filter in a topological space, having the property that no other filter exists in the space having among its subsets all the subsets in the given filter. [ULTRA- + FILTER] —**ul·tra·fil·tra·tion** (ul′trə fil trā′shən), *n.*

ul·tra·fil·trate (ul′trə fil′trāt), *n.* *Physical Chem.* a liquid that has been passed through an ultrafilter. [ULTRAFILT(E)R + -ATE[1]]

ul′tra·high fre′quency (ul′trə hī′, -hī′), *Radio.* any frequency between 300 and 3,000 megacycles per second. *Abbr.:* uhf, UHF [ULTRA- + HIGH] —**ul′tra·high′-fre′quen·cy,** *adj.*

ul·tra·ism (ul′trə iz′əm), *n.* **1.** extremism. **2.** an extremist point of view or act. [ULTRA- + -ISM] —**ul′tra·ist,** *n., adj.* —**ul′tra·is′tic,** *adj.*

ul·tra·ma·rine (ul′trə mə rēn′), *adj.* **1.** beyond the sea. **2.** of the color ultramarine. —*n.* **3.** a blue pigment consisting of powdered lapis lazuli. **4.** a similar artificial blue pigment. **5.** any of various other pigments. **6.** a deep-blue color. [< ML *ultrāmarīn(us),* equiv. to L *ultrā* ULTRA- + *marīnus* MARINE]

ul·tra·met·a·mor·phism (ul′trə met′ə môr′fiz əm), *n.* *Geol.* metamorphism during which the temperature of a rock exceeds its melting point. [ULTRA- + METAMORPHISM] —**ul′tra·met′a·mor′phic,** *adj.*

ul·tra·mi·cro·bal·ance (ul′trə mī′krō bal′əns), *n.* *Chem.* a balance for weighing precisely, to a hundredth of a microgram or less, minute quantities of material. [ULTRA- + MICROBALANCE]

ul·tra·mi·cro·chem·is·try (ul′trə mī′krō kem′i strē), *n.* the branch of microchemistry dealing with minute quantities of material weighing one microgram or less. [ULTRA- + MICROCHEMISTRY] —**ul′tra·mi′cro·chem′ist,** *n.* —**ul·tra·mi·cro·chem·i·cal** (ul′trə mī′krə kem′i kəl), *adj.*

ul·tra·mi·crom·e·ter (ul′trə mī krom′i tər), *n.* a micrometer calibrated to a very fine scale and capable of measuring extremely small magnitudes. [ULTRA- + MICROMETER]

ul·tra·mi·cro·scope (ul′trə mī′krə skōp′), *n.* an instrument that uses scattering phenomena to detect the position of objects too small to be seen by an ordinary microscope. [ULTRA- + MICROSCOPE] —**ul·tra·mi·cro·scop·ic** (ul′trə mī′krə skop′ik), **ul′tra·mi′cro·scop′i·cal,** *adj.*

ul·tra·mi·cros·co·py (ul′trə mī kros′kə pē), *n.* the use of the ultramicroscope. [ULTRA- + MICROSCOPY]

ul·tra·mod·ern (ul′trə mod′ərn), *adj.* beyond the merely modern; very advanced in ideas or techniques: *an ultramodern automobile.* [ULTRA- + MODERN] —**ul′tra·mod′ern·ism,** *n.* —**ul′tra·mod′ern·ist,** *n.*

ul·tra·mon·tane (ul′trə mon tān′), *adj.* **1.** beyond the mountains. **2.** of or pertaining to the area south of the Alps, esp. Italy. **3.** *Rom. Cath. Ch.* **a.** of, pertaining to, or advocating ultramontanism. **b.** of, pertaining to, or supporting the belief that the pope is the spiritual head of the Church in all countries. **4.** (formerly) north of the Alps; tramontane. —*n.* **5.** one who lives beyond the mountains. **6.** one living south of the Alps. **7.** *Rom. Cath. Ch.* one who supports ultramontanism. **8.** (formerly) one living to the north of the Alps. [< ML *ultrāmontān(us),* equiv. to L *ultrā* ULTRA- + *montānus* of, belonging to a MOUNTAIN]

ul·tra·mon·ta·nism (ul′trə mon′tə niz′əm), *n.* (*sometimes cap.*) the policy of the party in the Roman Catholic Church that favors increasing and enhancing the power and authority of the pope. Cf. **Gallicanism.** [< F *ultramontanisme,* equiv. to *ultramontain* ULTRAMONTANE + *-isme* -ISM] —**ul′tra·mon′ta·nist,** *n.*

ul·tra·mun·dane (ul′trə mun′dān, -mun dān′), *adj.* **1.** outside or beyond the earth or the orbits of the planets. **2.** outside the sphere of physical existence. [< L *ultrāmundān(us),* equiv. to L *ultrā* ULTRA- + *mundānus* MUNDANE]

ul·tra·na·tion·al·ism (ul′trə nash′ə nəliz′əm), *n.* excessive devotion to or advocacy of the interests of a nation, regardless of the effect on any other nations. [ULTRA- + NATIONALISM] —**ul′tra·na′tion·al,** *adj.*

ul·tra·na·tion·al·ist (ul′trə nash′ə nəlist), *n.* **1.** an advocate of ultranationalism. —*adj.* **2.** Also, **ul′tra·na′tion·al·is′tic.** of or pertaining to ultranationalism or ultranationalists. [ULTRA- + NATIONALIST] —**ul′tra·na′tion·al·is′ti·cal·ly,** *adv.*

ul·tra·net (ul′trə net′), *n.* *Math.* a net in a topological space which is residually in every set or its complement in the space. [ULTRA- + NET[1]]

ul·tra·red (ul′trə red′), *n.* (not in technical use) infrared. [ULTRA- + RED]

ul·tra·son·ic (ul′trə son′ik), *adj.* noting or pertaining to a frequency above the audio-frequency range. [ULTRA- + SONIC] —**ul′tra·son′i·cal·ly,** *adv.*

ul·tra·son·ics (ul′trə son′iks), *n.pl.* (*construed as sing.*) the branch of science that deals with ultrasonic phenomena. [see ULTRASONIC, -ICS]

ul·tra·struc·ture (ul′trə struk′chər), *n.* *Biol.* the submicroscopic, elemental structure of protoplasm. [ULTRA- + STRUCTURE] —**ul′tra·struc′tur·al,** *adj.*

Ul·tra·suede (ul′trə swād′), *n.* *Trademark.* a washable, synthetic, suedelike fabric.

ul·tra·trop·i·cal (ul′trə trop′i kəl), *adj.* **1.** outside the tropics. **2.** hotter than the average or usual tropical climate. [ULTRA- + TROPICAL]

ul·tra·vi·o·let (ul′trə vī′ə lit), *adj.* **1.** beyond the violet in the spectrum, corresponding to light having wavelengths shorter than 4000 angstrom units. **2.** pertaining to or producing light having such wavelengths. Cf. **infrared.** —*n.* **3.** ultraviolet radiation. [ULTRA- + VIOLET]

ul·tra vi·res (ul′trə vī′rēz), *Law.* beyond the legal power or authority of a corporation, corporate officer, etc. (opposed to *intra vires*). [< L: lit., beyond strength]

ul·tra·vi·rus (ul′trə vī′rəs), *n., pl.* **-rus·es.** an ultramicroscopic virus capable of passing through the finest bacterial filters. [ULTRA- + VIRUS]

u·lu (o͞o′lo͞o), *n.* a curved knife used by Eskimos. [< Inupik Eskimo *ulu* woman's knife]

U·lugh Beigh (o͞o′lo͝og bāg′, bā′), a crater in the second quadrant of the face of the moon, in the libration area: about 30 miles in diameter.

ul·u·lant (yo͞ol′yə lənt, ul′-), *adj.* howling; ululating. [< L *ululant-* (s. of *ululāns*), prp. of *ululāre.* See ULULATE, -ANT]

ul·u·late (yo͞ol′yə lāt′, ul′-), *v.i.,* **-lat·ed, -lat·ing. 1.** to howl, as a dog or a wolf; hoot, as an owl. **2.** to utter howling sounds, as in shrill, wordless lamentation; wail. **3.** to lament loudly and shrilly. [< L *ululāt(us)* howled, shrieked (ptp. of *ululāre*), equiv. to *ulul(a)* owl (imit.) + *-ātus* -ATE[1]] —**ul′u·la′tion,** *n.*

-ulus, a diminutive suffix occurring in loan words from Latin: *calculus.* [< L *-ulus;* cf. -ULE]

Ul·ya·novsk (o͞ol yä′nofsk), *n.* a city in the W RSFSR, in the E Soviet Union in Europe: birthplace of Lenin. 256,000 (est. 1964).

U·lys·ses (yo͞o lis′ēz; *Brit. also* yo͞o′li sēz′ *for 2*), *n.* **1.** Latin name for **Odysseus. 2.** (*italics*) a psychological novel (1922) by James Joyce. **3.** a town in SW Kansas 3157 (1960). **4.** a boy's given name.

-um, a formal element occurring in loan words from Latin: *rostrum; addendum.* [< L *-um,* neut. sing. nom. or acc. ending]

U·may·yad (o͞o mī′yad), *n.* Omayyad.

um·bel (um′bəl), *n. Bot.* an inflorescence in which a number of flower stalks or pedicels, nearly equal in length, spread from a common center. [< L *umbel(la)* a sunshade parasol, equiv. to *umb(ra)* a shadow, shade + *-ella* dim. suffix]

um·bel·late (um′bə lit, -lāt′), *adj.* having or forming an umbel or umbels. [< NL *umbellāt(us),* equiv. to L *umbell(a)* (see UMBEL) + *-ātus* -ATE[1]] —**um′bel·lar, um′bel·lat′ed,** *adj.* —**um′bel·late·ly,** *adj.*

um·bel·let (um′bə lit), *n.* an umbellule. [< L *umbell(a)* (see UMBEL) + -ET]

um·bel·lif·er·ous (um′bə lif′ər əs), *adj.* **1.** bearing an umbel or umbels. **2.** belonging or pertaining to the *Umbelliferae* (or *Ammiaceae*), a family of plants comprising the carrot, celery, parsnip, parsley, and other similar plants; apiaceous. [< NL *umbellifer* (*umbelli-,* comb. form of L *umbella* (see UMBEL) + *-fer* -FER) + -OUS]

um·bel·lule (um′bəl yo͞ol′, um bel′yo͞ol), *n.* one of the secondary umbels in a compound umbel. [< NL *umbellul(a),* equiv. to L *umbell(a)* (see UMBEL) + *-ula* -ULE] —**um·bel·lu·late** (um bel′yə lit, -lāt′), *adj.*

um·ber (um′bər), *n.* **1.** an earth consisting chiefly of a hydrated oxide of iron and some oxide of manganese, used in its natural state as a brown pigment or, after heating, as a reddish-brown pigment. **2.** the color of such a pigment; dark dusky brown or dark reddish brown. **3.** the European grayling, *Thymallus thymallus.* **4.** Also called **um′ber bird′.** *Rare.* hammerhead (def. 2). **5.** *Brit. Dial.* shade; shadow. —*adj.* **6.** of the color umber. —*v.t.* **7.** to color with or as if with umber. [ME *umbre, umber* shade, shadow < OF *umbre* < L *umbr(a)*]

Um·ber·to (*It.* o͞om bεr′tô), *n.* See **Humbert I.**

um·bil·i·cal (um bil′i kəl), *adj.* **1.** of, pertaining to, or characteristic of an umbilicus or umbilical cord. **2.** joined together by or as if by an umbilical cord; heavily dependent in a close relationship. **3.** adjacent to or located near the navel; central to the abdomen: *the umbilical region.* **4.** serving as or containing a conduit through which power is transferred, esp. to a unit which will be or is designed to be ultimately self-sufficient or independent: *an umbilical cable for launching a rocket; an umbilical plug for starting jet engines.* [< ML *umbilicāl(is),* equiv. to L *umbilic(us)* (see UMBILICUS) + *-ālis* -AL[1]] —**um·bil′i·cal·ly,** *adv.*

umbil′ical cord′, 1. *Anat.* a cord or funicle connecting the embryo or fetus with the placenta of the mother and transmitting nourishment from the mother. **2.** *Rocketry Slang.* **a.** an electrical cable for servicing, operating, or testing equipment in a rocket or missile, disconnected from it automatically immediately prior to launching. **b.** a strong life line connecting an astronaut working in space outside his vehicle to the vehicle, and supplying him with air, a communication system, etc.

umbil′ical her′nia, *Pathol.* a hernia of the umbilicus. Also called **omphalocele.**

um·bil·i·cate (um bil′ə kit, -kāt′), *adj.* **1.** having the form of an umbilicus or navel. **2.** having an umbilicus. Also, **um·bil′i·cat′ed.** [< L *umbilicāt(us),* equiv. to *umbilic(us)* (see UMBILICUS) + *-ātus* -ATE[1]]

um·bil·i·ca·tion (um bil′ə kā′shən), *n.* **1.** a central navellike depression. **2.** an umbilicate condition or formation. [UMBILIC(US) + -ATION]

um·bil·i·cus (um bil′ə kəs, um′bə lī′kəs), *n., pl.* **-bil·i·ci** (-bil′i sī′, -bə lī′sī). **1.** *Anat.* the depression in the center of the surface of the abdomen indicating the point of attachment of the umbilical cord to the embryo; navel. **2.** *Bot., Zool.* a navellike formation, as the hilum of a seed. [< L *umbilīcus* navel, middle, center; c. Gk *omphalós*]

um·bil·i·form (um bil′ə fôrm′), *adj.* having the form of an umbilicus. [UMBILI(CUS) + -FORM]

um′ble pie′ (um′bəl). See **humble pie** (def. 1).

um·bles (um′bəlz), *n.pl.* numbles.

um·bo (um′bō), *n., pl.* **um·bo·nes** (um bō′nēz), **um·bos. 1.** a boss on a shield, as one at the center of a circular shield. **2.** any similar boss or protuberance. **3.** *Zool.* the beak of a bivalve shell; the protuberance of each valve above the hinge. **4.** *Anat.* the depressed area on the outer surface of the tympanic membrane. [< L *umbō* boss (of a shield), knob, projecting part] —**um·bon·ic** (um bon′ik), *adj.*

um·bo·nal (um′bə nəl), *adj.* **1.** having the shape or appearance of an umbo; bosslike: *an umbonal structure.* **2.** of, pertaining to, or near the umbo: *the umbonal region.* Also, **um·bon·ic** (um bon′ik). [< L *umbōn-* (s. of *umbō*) UMBO + -AL[1]]

um·bo·nate (um′bə nit, -nāt′), *adj.* **1.** having an umbo or projecting boss. **2.** shaped like an umbo; having a rounded convex form: *an umbonate fungus.* [< L *umbōn-* (s. of *umbō*) (see UMBO) + -ATE[1]]

um·bra (um′brə), *n., pl.* **-brae** (-brē). **1.** shade; shadow. **2.** the invariable or characteristic accompaniment or companion of a person or thing. **3.** *Astron.* **a.** the complete or perfect shadow of an opaque body, as a planet, where the direct light from the source of illumination is completely cut off. Cf. **penumbra. b.** the dark central portion of a sunspot. **4.** a phantom or shadowy apparition, as of someone or something not physically present; ghost; spectral image. **5.** an evergreen tree, *Phytolacca dioica,* of southern California, that has white flowers and is grown as an ornamental. [< L: shade, shadow] —**um′bral,** *adj.*

um·brage (um′brij), *n.* **1.** offense; annoyance; displeasure: *to feel umbrage at a social snub; to give umbrage to someone; to take umbrage at someone's rudeness.* **2.** the slightest indication or vaguest feeling of suspicion, doubt, hostility, or the like. **3.** leaves which afford shade, as the foliage of trees. **4.** *Archaic.* shade or shadows, as cast by trees. **5.** *Archaic.* a shadowy appearance or semblance of something. [late ME < OF < L *umbrātic(um),* deriv. of *umbrātus* (ptp. of *umbrāre* to shade), equiv. to *umbr(a)* shade + *-āticum* -AGE]
—**Syn. 1.** pique, grudge, resentment.

um·bra·geous (um brā′jəs), *adj.* **1.** creating or providing shade; shady: *an umbrageous tree.* **2.** apt to take offense. [UMBRAGE + -OUS] —**um·bra′geous·ly,** *adv.* —**um·bra′geous·ness,** *n.*

um·brel·la (um brel′ə), *n.* **1.** a light, small, portable, usually circular cover for protection from sun or rain, consisting of a fabric held on a collapsible frame of thin ribs radiating from the top of a carrying stick or handle: *beach umbrella; rain umbrella.* **2.** the saucer- or bowl-shaped, gelatinous body of a jellyfish; the bell. **3.** something which covers or protects from above, as military aircraft safeguarding surface forces: *air umbrella.* **4.** any general kind of protection: *a price umbrella.* —*adj.* **5.** shaped like or intended to perform the function of an umbrella. **6.** having the quality or function of covering or applying simultaneously to a group of similar items or elements: *an umbrella patent; umbrella legislation.* [< It *ombrella* (influence of *ombra* shade < L *umbra*) < L *umbella.* See UMBEL] —**um·brel′la·less,** *adj.* —**um·brel′la·like′,** *adj.*

umbrel′la bird′, any of several South American birds of the genus *Cephalopterus,* as *C. ornatus,* having an umbrellalike crest above the head.

umbrel′la leaf′, a North American berberidaceous herb, *Diphylleia cymosa,* having either a large peltate, umbrellalike, lobed, basal leaf or two smaller similar leaves on a flowering stem.

umbrel′la palm′, an Australian feather palm, *Hedyscepe canterburyana,* characterized by the umbrellalike manner of growth of its leaves.

umbrel′la pine′, a Japanese evergreen tree, *Sciadopitys verticillata,* having linear leaves growing in umbrellalike whorls.

umbrel′la plant′, an herb, *Cyperus alternifolius,* of Africa, that has several stems from a mass of roots and an umbrella-shaped cluster of leaves at the top of each stem, and that grows in moist soil.

umbrel′la step′, (in the game of giant steps) a step executed by extending one foot forward and whirling on the heel. Cf. **baby step.**

umbrel′la tent′, a small tent with a metal frame consisting of ribs that radiate from a single supporting pole.

umbrel′la tree′, 1. an American magnolia, *Magnolia tripetala,* having large leaves in umbrellalike clusters. **2.** any of various other trees resembling an umbrella, as a tropical American moraceous tree, *Musanga Smithii.*

um·brette (um bret′), *n.* hammerhead (def. 2). [< NL *umbrett(a)* < F *ombrette* shade, shadow. See UMBRA, -ETTE]

Um·bri·a (um′brē ə; *It.* o͞om′brē ä′), *n.* **1.** an ancient district in central and N Italy. **2.** a region in central Italy. 788,546 (1961); 3270 sq. mi.

Um·bri·an (um′brē ən), *adj.* **1.** of or pertaining to Umbria, its inhabitants, or their language. —*n.* **2.** a native or inhabitant of Umbria. **3.** the extinct Italic language of the ancient Umbrians. [UMBRI(A) + -AN]

Um·bri·el (um′brē el′), *n. Astron.* one of the five satellites of Uranus.

um·brif·er·ous (um brif′ər əs), *adj.* casting or making shade. [< L *umbrifer* shade-bringing, shady (*umbri-,* comb. form of *umbra* shade + *-fer* -FER) + -OUS] —**um·brif′er·ous·ly,** *adv.*

um·brose (um′brōs), *adj. Archaic.* shady. [< L *umbrōs(us)* full of shade, shady, equiv. to *umbr(a)* shade + *-ōsus* -OSE[1]]

U·me·å (o͞o′me ô′), *n.* a city in NE Sweden, on the Gulf of Bothnia. 47,292 (1965).

u·mi·ak (o͞o′mē ak′), *n.* an open Eskimo boat that consists of a wooden frame covered with skins and provided with several thwarts: used for transport of goods and passengers. Also, **oomiak, oomiac, u′mi·ac′.** [< Greenland Eskimo: boat used exclusively for women]

Umiak

um·laut (o͝om′lout), *Gram.* —*n.* **1.** (of vowels in Germanic languages) assimilation in which a vowel is influenced by a following vowel or semivowel; apophony. **2.** a mark (¨) used as a diacritic over a vowel, as *ä, ö, ü,* to indicate a vowel sound different from that of the letter without the diacritic, esp. as so used in German. Cf. **dieresis.** —*v.t.* **3.** to modify by umlaut. **4.** to write an umlaut over. [< G, equiv. to *um-* about (changed) + *Laut* sound]

ump (ump), *n., v.t., v.i., Slang.* umpire. [shortened form]

umph (əm, əmf), *interj.* humph.

um·pir·age (um′pīər ij, -pər ij), *n.* **1.** the office or authority of an umpire. **2.** the decision of an umpire; arbitrament. [UMPIRE + -AGE]

um·pire (um′pīər), *n., v.,* **-pired, -pir·ing.** —*n.* **1.** a person selected to rule on the plays in a game. **2.** one selected to settle disputes about the application of settled rules or usages; a person agreed on by disputing parties to arbitrate their differences. —*v.t.* **3.** to act as umpire in (a game). **4.** to decide or settle (a controversy, dispute, or the like) as umpire; arbitrate. —*v.i.* **5.** to act as umpire. [ME *umpere,* var. of *noumpere* (cf. APRON) < OF *nomper, nonper* not equal (arbiter). See NON-, PEER[1]]
—**Syn. 1.** referee, arbiter, arbitrator. **2.** See **judge.**

ump·teen (ump′tēn′), *adj. Informal.* innumerable; many. Also, **ump·steen** (ump′stēn′), **umteen.** [*umpt(y),* var. of *-enty,* as in *twenty* + -TEEN]

ump·teenth (ump′tēnth′), *adj. Informal.* of an indefinitely large number in succession: *He was the umpteenth person to arrive.* Also, **um·teenth** (um′tēnth′). [UMPTEEN + -TH[2]]

UMT, See **universal military training.**

um·teen (um′tēn′), *adj.* umpteen.

UMW, United Mine Workers. Also, **U.M.W.**

un (ən), *pron. Dial.* one: *He's a bad un. Young uns.* Also, **'un.**

UN, United Nations. Also, **U.N.**

un-[1], a prefix meaning "not," freely used as an English formative, giving negative or opposite force in adjectives and their derivative adverbs and nouns (*unfair; unfairly; unfairness; unfelt; unseen; unfitting; unformed; unheard-of; un-get-at-able*), and less freely used in certain other nouns (*unfaith; unrest; unemployment*). [ME, OE *un-, on-;* c. D *on-,* Goth, G *un-,* Icel *ū-, ō-;* akin to L *in-,* Gk *an-, a-.* See A-[6], AN-[1]]
—**Syn.** See **in-[3].**

un-[2], a prefix freely used in English to form verbs expressing a reversal of some action or state, or removal, deprivation, release, etc. (*unbend; uncork; unfasten,* etc.), or to intensify the force of a verb already having such a meaning (*unloose*). [ME, OE *un-, on-;* c. Goth *and-,* D *ont-,* G *ent-;* akin to L *ante,* Gk *antí;* cf. ANTE-, ANTI-]

U·na (o͞o′nə, yo͞o′-), *n.* a girl's given name. Also, **Ona, Oona, Oonagh.**

un·a·bat·ed (un′ə bā′tid), *adj.* with undiminished force, power, or vigor. [UN-[1] + ABATED] —**un′a·bat′ed·ly,** *adv.*

un·a·ble (un ā′bəl), *adj.* lacking the necessary power, competence, etc., to accomplish some specified act: *He was unable to swim.* [ME; see UN-[1], ABLE]
—**Syn.** See **incapable.**

un·a·bridged (un′ə brijd′), *adj.* **1.** not abridged or shortened, as a book. —*n.* **2.** a dictionary which has not been reduced in size by omission of terms or definitions; the most comprehensive edition of a given dictionary. [UN-[1] + ABRIDGED]

un·ac·cent·ed (un ak′sen tid, un′ak sen′-) *adj.* not accented; unstressed. [UN-[1] + ACCENT + -ED[2]]

un·ac·com·mo·dat·ed (un′ə kom′ə dā′tid), *adj.* **1.** not accommodated; not adapted. **2.** not having accommodations. **3.** not furnished with something wanted or needed; not given satisfaction: *A businessman must avoid leaving his customers unaccommodated.* [UN-[1] + ACCOMMODATED]

un·ac·com·pa·nied (un′ə kum′pə nēd), *adj.* **1.** not accompanied; alone: *The shipment arrived unaccompanied by an invoice.* **2.** *Music.* without an accompaniment: *a sonata for unaccompanied violin.* [UN-[1] + ACCOMPANIED]

un·ac·com·plished (un′ə kom′plisht), *adj.* **1.** not accomplished; incomplete or not carried out: *Many tasks remain unaccomplished.* **2.** without accomplishments; inexpert: *an unaccomplished musician.* [UN-[1] + ACCOMPLISHED]

un·ac·count·a·ble (un′ə koun′tə bəl), *adj.* **1.** exempt from being called to account; not answerable: *As a*

un′a·ban′doned, *adj.*
un′a·ban′don·ing, *adj.*
un′a·based′, *adj.*
un′a·bash′a·ble, *adj.*
un′a·bashed′, *adj.*
un′a·bash′ed·ly, *adv.*
un′a·bas′ing, *adj.*
un′a·bat′a·ble, *adj.*
un′a·bat′ing, *adj.;* **-ly,** *adv.*
un′ab·bre′vi·at′ed, *adj.*
un·ab′di·cat′ed, *adj.*
un·ab′di·cat′ing, *adj.*
un·ab′di·ca′tive, *adj.*
un′ab·duct′ed, *adj.*
un′a·bet′ted, *adj.*
un′a·bet′ting, *adj.*
un′ab·horred′, *adj.*
un′ab·hor′rent·ly, *adv.*
un′a·bid′ing, *adj.;* **-ly,** *adv.;* **-ness,** *n.*
un·ab′ject, *adj.;* **-ly,** *adv.;* **-ness,** *n.*
un′ab·jec′tive, *adj.*
un′ab·jur′a·to′ry, *adj.*
un′ab·jured′, *adj.*
un·ab′la·tive, *adj.*
un·ab′ne·gat′ed, *adj.*
un·ab′ne·gat′ing, *adj.*
un′a·bol′ish·a·ble, *adj.*
un′a·bol′ished, *adj.*
un′a·bort′ed, *adj.*
un′a·bor′tive, *adj.;* **-ly,** *adv.;* **-ness,** *n.*
un′a·brad′ed, *adj.*
un′a·bra′sive, *adj.;* **-ly,** *adv.*
un·ab′ro·ga·ble, *adj.*
un·ab′ro·gat′ed, *adj.*
un·ab′ro·ga′tive, *adj.*
un′ab·rupt′ly, *adv.*
un′ab·scessed, *adj.*
un′ab·solved′, *adj.*
un′ab·sorb′a·ble, *adj.*
un′ab·sorbed′, *adj.*
un′ab·sorb′ent, *adj.*
un′ab·sorb′ing, *adj.;* **-ly,** *adv.*
un′ab·sorp′tive, *adj.;* **-ness,** *n.*
un′ab·ste′mi·ous, *adj.;* **-ly,** *adv.;* **-ness,** *n.*
un′ab·sten′tious, *adj.*
un′ab·stract′ed, *adj.;* **-ly,** *adv.;* **-ness,** *n.*
un′ab·strac′tive, *adj.;* **-ly,** *adv.*
un′a·bus′a·ble, *adj.*
un′a·bused′, *adj.*
un′a·bu′sive, *adj.;* **-ly,** *adv.;* **-ness,** *n.*
un′a·but′ting, *adj.*
un′ac·a·dem′ic, *adj.*
un′ac·a·dem′i·cal, *adj.;* **-ly,** *adv.*
un′ac·ced′ing, *adj.*
un′ac·cel′er·at′ed, *adj.*
un′ac·cel′er·a′tive, *adj.*
un′ac·cen′tu·at′ed, *adj.*
un′ac·cept′a·bil′i·ty, *n.*
un′ac·cep′ta·ble, *adj.;* **-ble·ness,** *n.;* **-bly,** *adv.*
un′ac·cept′ance, *n.*
un′ac·cept′ant, *adj.*
un′ac·cept′ed, *adj.*
un′ac·ces′si·bil′i·ty, *n.*
un′ac·ces′si·ble, *adj.;* **-bly,** *adv.*
un′ac·ces′sion·al, *adj.*
un′ac·ci·den′tal, *adj.;* **-ly,** *adv.*
un′ac·claimed′, *adj.*
un·ac′cli·mat′ed, *adj.*
un′ac·cli′ma·tised′, *adj.*
un′ac·cli′ma·tized′, *adj.*
un′ac·cliv′i·tous, *adj.*
un′ac·cliv′i·tous·ly, *adv.*
un′ac·com′mo·da·ble, *adj.*
un′ac·com′mo·dat′ing, *adj.;* **-ly,** *adv.*
un′ac·com′plish·a·ble, *adj.*
un′ac·cord′a·ble, *adj.*
un′ac·cord′ant, *adj.*
un′ac·cord′ed, *adj.*
un′ac·cost′a·ble, *adj.*
un′ac·cost′ed, *adj.*

CONCISE ETYMOLOGY KEY: <, descended or derived from; >, whence; b., blend of, blended; c., cognate with; deriv., derivative; equiv., equivalent; imit., imitative; m., modification of; obl., oblique; r., replacing; s., stem; sp., spelling; trans., translation; ?, origin unknown, perhaps; *, hypothetical. See the full key inside the front cover.

subordinate, he is unaccountable for errors in policy. **2.** unexplained; inexplicable; not in accordance with understood relations of cause and effect; strange: *The boat has an unaccountable tendency to yaw.* [UN-[1] + ACCOUNTABLE] **—un/ac·count/a·ble·ness, un/ac·count/a·bil/i·ty,** *n.* **—un/ac·count/a·bly,** *adv.*
—Syn. 1. unanswerable, irresponsible. **2.** incomprehensible, inscrutable, mysterious, unintelligible.

un·ac·count·ed-for (un/ə koun/tid fôr/), *adj.* not understood; unexplained: *The explosion probably resulted from some unaccounted-for failure of the automatic control mechanism.*

un·ac·cus·tomed (un/ə kus/təmd), *adj.* **1.** unusual; unfamiliar: *A brief after-dinner speech is an unaccustomed pleasure.* **2.** not habituated: *to be unaccustomed to hardships.* [UN-[1] + ACCUSTOMED] **—un/ac·cus/tomed·ness,** *n.*

u·na cor·da (ōō/nə kôr/də; *It.* ōō/nä kôR/dä), with the soft pedal depressed (a musical direction in piano playing). [< It: lit., one string, since depressing the soft pedal eliminates the hammers which would otherwise strike all the strings for that note]

u/na cor/da ped/al. See **soft pedal** (def. 1).

un·ad·vised (un/ad vīzd/), *adj.* **1.** without advice; uninformed: *A plea of guilty should not be accepted from a defendant unadvised of his legal rights.* **2.** imprudent; rash; ill-advised: *He purchased a business with unadvised haste.* [ME *onavised.* See UN-[1], ADVISED] **—un·ad·vis·ed·ly** (un/ad vī/zid lē), *adv.* **—un/ad·vis/ed·ness,** *n.*

un·aes·thet·ic (un/es thet/ik *or, esp. Brit.,* -ēs-), *adj.* offensive to the aesthetic sense; lacking in beauty or sensory appeal; unpleasant, as an object, design, arrangement, etc.: *an unaesthetic combination of colors.* Also, **unesthetic.** [UN-[1] + AESTHETIC]

un·af·fect·ed[1] (un/ə fek/tid), *adj.* **1.** free from affectation; sincere; genuine: *The man showed unaffected grief at the death of his former opponent.* **2.** unpretentious, as a personality or literary style. [UN-[1] + AFFECTED[2]] **—un/af·fect/ed·ly,** *adv.* **—un/af·fect/ed·ness,** *n.*
—Syn. 1. plain, natural, simple, honest, real, unfeigned, artless; naïve, guileless.

un·af·fect·ed[2] (un/ə fek/tid), *adj.* not affected, acted upon, or influenced; unchanged; unaltered: *The laboratory clock remained accurate, unaffected by the explosion.* [UN-[1] + AFFECTED[1]]
—Syn. unmoved, untouched, unimpressed, unstirred.

U·na·las·ka (ōō/nə las/kə, un/ə las/-), *n.* an island off the coast of SW Alaska, one of the Aleutian Islands: site of the Dutch Harbor naval base. ab. 75 mi. long.

un·al·ter·a·ble (un ôl/tər ə bəl), *adj.* not capable of being altered. Also, **inalterable.** [UN-[1] + ALTERABLE] **—un·al/ter·a·bly,** *adv.* **—un·al/ter·a·ble·ness,** *n.*

un-A·mer·i·can (un/ə mer/i kən), *adj.* not American; not characteristic of or proper to America; foreign or opposed to American character, usages, standards, etc. **—un/-A·mer/i·can·ism,** *n.*

U·na·mu·no (ōō/nə mōō/nō; *Sp.* ōō/nä mōō/nô), *n.* **Mi·guel de** (mē gel/ de), 1864–1936, Spanish philosopher, poet, novelist, and essayist.

un·a·neled (un/ə nēld/), *adj. Archaic.* not having received extreme unction. [UN-[1] + ANELED]

u·na·nim·i·ty (yōō/nə nim/i tē), *n.* state or quality of being unanimous; a consensus or undivided opinion: *The unanimity of the delegates was obvious on the first ballot.* [ME *unanimite* < MF < L *ūnanimitāt-* (s. of *ūnanimitās*), equiv. to *ūnanim(us)* UNANIMOUS + *-itāt-* -ITY]
—Syn. harmony, unity, unison, concert. **—Ant.** disagreement.

u·nan·i·mous (yōō nan/ə məs), *adj.* **1.** of one mind; in complete accord; agreed. **2.** characterized by or showing complete accord: *a unanimous vote.* [< L *ūnanim(us)* (*ūn(us)* one + *animus* mind, heart, feeling) + -OUS] **—u·nan/i·mous·ly,** *adv.* **—u·nan/i·mous·ness,** *n.*

un·an·swer·a·ble (un an/sər ə bəl), *adj.* **1.** not capable of being answered; not having a known or discoverable answer: *an unanswerable question.* **2.** not open to dispute or rebuttal; irrefutable; conclusive: *an unanswerable proof.* [UN-[1] + ANSWERABLE] **—un·an/swer·a·ble·ness,** *n.* **—un·an/swer·a·bly,** *adv.*

un·ap·peal·a·ble (un/ə pē/lə bəl), *adj.* **1.** not appealable to a higher court, as a cause. **2.** incapable of being appealed from as a judgment. [UN-[1] + APPEALABLE] **—un/ap·peal/a·ble·ness,** *n.* **—un/ap·peal/a·bly,** *adv.*

un·ap·proach·a·ble (un/ə prō/chə bəl), *adj.* **1.** not capable of being approached; remote; unreachable: *an unapproachable spot; an unapproachable person.* **2.** impossible to equal or rival: *an unapproachable mastery of a craft.* [UN-[1] + APPROACHABLE] **—un/ap·proach/a·ble·ness,** *n.* **—un/ap·proach/a·bly,** *adv.*

un·ap·pro·pri·at·ed (un/ə prō/prē ā/tid), *adj.* **1.** not set apart or voted for some purpose or use, as money, revenues, etc. **2.** not taken into possession by any person: *A portion of the free land in the West is still unappropriated.* [UN-[1] + APPROPRIATED]

un·apt (un apt/), *adj.* **1.** not appropriate; unfit; unsuitable: *an unapt answer.* **2.** not prone, likely, or disposed: *He is unapt to waste what he has accumulated with such effort.* **3.** deficient in aptitude or capacity; slow; dull: *His inability to reason made him an unapt student.* [ME; see UN-[1], APT] **—un·apt/ly,** *adv.* **—un·apt/ness,** *n.*

un·ar·gued (un är/gyōōd), *adj.* **1.** undisputed; not subject to argument or discussion: *an unargued right.* **2.** undebated; unopposed by argument; admitted: *an unargued objection.* [UN-[1] + ARGUED]

un·arm (un ärm/), *v.t.* to deprive or relieve of arms; disarm. [ME *unarme.* See UN-[2], ARM[2]]

un·armed (un ärmd/), *adj.* **1.** without weapons or armor. **2.** not having claws, thorns, scales, etc., as animals or plants. **3.** (of an artillery shell) not armed. [ME; see UN-[1], ARMED]

un/ac·count/ed, *adj.*
un/ac·cou/tered, *adj.*
un/ac·cou/tred, *adj.*
un/ac·cred/it·ed, *adj.*
un/ac·crued/, *adj.*
un/ac·cu/mu·la·ble, *adj.*
un/ac·cu/mu·lat/ed, *adj.*
un/ac·cu/mu·la/tive, *adj.;* **-ly,** *adv.;* **-ness,** *n.*
un·ac/cu·rate, *adj.;* **-ly,** *adv.;* **-ness,** *n.*
un/ac·cus/a·ble, *adj.*
un/ac·cused/, *adj.*
un/ac·cus/ing, *adj.;* **-ly,** *adv.*
un/ac·cus/tom, *v.t.*
un/a·cer/bic, *adj.*
un/a·cer/bi·cal·ly, *adv.*
un/a·ce/tic, *adj.*
un/a·chiev/a·ble, *adj.*
un/a·chieved/, *adj.*
un·ach/ing, *adj.;* **-ly,** *adv.*
un/a·cid/ic, *adj.*
un/a·cid/u·lat/ed, *adj.*
un/ac·knowl/edged, *adj.*
un/ac·knowl/edg·ing, *adj.*
un/a·cous/tic, *adj.*
un/a·cous/ti·cal, *adj.;* **-ly,** *adv.*
un/ac·quaint/ed, *adj.*
un/ac·qui·es/cent, *adj.;* **-ly,** *adv.*
un/ac·quir/a·ble, *adj.*
un/ac·quired/, *adj.*
un/ac·quis/i·tive, *adj.;* **-ly,** *adv.;* **-ness,** *n.*
un/ac·quit/ted, *adj.*
un/ac·ri·mo/ni·ous, *adj.;* **-ly,** *adv.;* **-ness,** *n.*
un·act/a·ble, *adj.*
un·act/ed, *adj.*
un·act/ing, *adj.*
un/ac·tin/ic, *adj.*
un·ac/tion·a·ble, *adj.*
un·ac/ti·vat/ed, *adj.*
un·ac/tu·at/ed, *adj.*
un/a·cu/mi·nous, *adj.*
un·ad/a·mant, *adj.*
un/a·dapt/a·ble, *adj.;* **-ness,** *n.*
un/a·dapt/ed, *adj.*
un/a·dap/tive, *adj.;* **-ly,** *adv.;* **-ness,** *n.*
un·add/a·ble, *adj.*
un·add/ed, *adj.*
un·add/i·ble, *adj.*
un/ad·dict/ed, *adj.*
un·ad/dled, *adj.*
un/ad·dressed/, *adj.*
un/ad·duce/a·ble, *adj.*
un/ad·duced/, *adj.*
un/ad·duc/i·ble, *adj.*
un/a·dept/, *adj.;* **-ly,** *adv.;* **-ness,** *n.*
un/ad·her/ing, *adj.*
un/ad·he/sive, *adj.;* **-ly,** *adv.;* **-ness,** *n.*
un/ad·ja/cent, *adj.;* **-ly,** *adv.*
un/ad·joined/, *adj.*
un/ad·join/ing, *adj.*
un/ad·journed/, *adj.*
un/ad·judged/, *adj.*
un/ad·ju/di·cat/ed, *adj.*
un/ad·junc/tive, *adj.;* **-ly,** *adv.*
un/ad·just/a·ble, *adj.;* **-bly,** *adv.*
un/ad·just/ed, *adj.*
un/ad·min/is·tered, *adj.*
un/ad·min/is·tra·ble, *adj.*
un/ad·min/is·tra/tive, *adj.;* **-ly,** *adv.*
un·ad/mir·a·ble, *adj.;* **-ble·ness,** *n.;* **-bly,** *adv.*
un/ad·mired/, *adj.*
un/ad·mir/ing, *adj.;* **-ly,** *adv.*
un/ad·mis/si·ble, *adj.;* **-ble·ness,** *n.;* **-bly,** *adv.*
un/ad·mis/sive, *adj.*
un/ad·mit/ted, *adj.;* **-ly,** *adv.*
un/ad·mon/ished, *adj.*
un/ad·mon/i·to/ry, *adj.*
un/a·dopt/a·ble, *adj.*
un/a·dopt/ed, *adj.*
un/a·dop/tion·al, *adj.*
un/a·dop/tive, *adj.;* **-ly,** *adv.*
un/a·dor/a·ble, *adj.;* **-ble·ness,** *n.;* **-bly,** *adv.*
un/a·dored/, *adj.*
un/a·dor/ing, *adj.;* **-ly,** *adv.*
un/a·dorn/a·ble, *adj.*
un/a·dorned/, *adj.*
un/a·dorn/ment, *n.*
un/a·droit/, *adj.;* **-ly,** *adv.;* **-ness,** *n.*
un·ad/u·lat/ing, *adj.*
un·ad/u·la·to/ry, *adj.*
un/a·dult/, *adj.*
un/a·dul/ter·ate, *adj.;* **-ly,** *adv.*
un/a·dul/ter·at/ed, *adj.;* **-ly,** *adv.*
un/a·dul/ter·ous, *adj.;* **-ly,** *adv.*
un/ad·vanc/ing, *adj.*
un/ad·van/taged, *adj.*
un/ad·van·ta/geous, *adj.;* **-ly,** *adv.;* **-ness,** *n.*
un/ad·ven/tur·ing, *adj.*
un/ad·ven/tur·ous, *adj.;* **-ly,** *adv.;* **-ness,** *n.*
un/ad·verse/, *adj.;* **-ly,** *adv.;* **-ness,** *n.*
un·ad/ver·tised/, *adj.*
un/ad·vis/a·ble, *adj.;* **-ble·ness,** *n.;* **-bly,** *adv.*
un·ad/vo·cat/ed, *adj.*
un·aer/at·ed, *adj.*
un/aes·thet/i·cal, *adj.;* **-ly,** *adv.*
un·af/fa·ble, *adj.;* **-ble·ness,** *n.;* **-bly,** *adv.*
un/af·fect/ing, *adj.*
un/af·fil/i·at/ed, *adj.*
un/af·firmed/, *adj.*
un/af·fixed/, *adj.*
un/af·flict/ed, *adj.;* **-ly,** *adv.;* **-ness,** *n.*
un/af·flict/ing, *adj.*
un/af·ford/ed, *adj.*
un/af·fright/ed, *adj.;* **-ly,** *adv.*
un/af·front/ed, *adj.*
un/a·fraid/, *adj.*
un·aged/, *adj.*
un/ag·glom/er·a/tive, *adj.*
un·ag/gra·vat/ed, *adj.*
un·ag/gra·vat/ing, *adj.*
un·ag/gre·gat/ed, *adj.*
un/ag·gres/sive, *adj.;* **-ly,** *adv.;* **-ness,** *n.*
un·ag/ile, *adj.;* **-ly,** *adv.*
un·ag/ing, *adj.*
un·ag/i·tat/ed, *adj.;* **-ly,** *adv.*
un/a·grar/i·an, *adj.*
un/a·greed/, *adj.*
un/ag·ri·cul/tur·al, *adj.;* **-ly,** *adv.*
un·aid/a·ble, *adj.*
un·aid/ed, *adj.;* **-ly,** *adv.*
un·aid/ing, *adj.*
un·aimed/, *adj.*
un·aim/ing, *adj.*
un·air/a·ble, *adj.*
un·aired/, *adj.*
un·air/i·ly, *adv.*
un·aisled/, *adj.*
un/a·lac/ri·tous, *adj.*
un/a·larmed/, *adj.*
un/a·larm/ing, *adj.;* **-ly,** *adv.*
un·al/co·hol·ised, *adj.*
un·al/co·hol·ized, *adj.*
un·al/der·man·ly, *adj.*
un/a·lert/ed, *adj.*
un·al/ien·a·ble, *adj.*
un·al/ien·at/ed, *adj.*
un·al/ien·at/ing, *adj.*
un/al·ge·bra/i·cal, *adj.*
un·a·lign/a·ble, *adj.*
un/a·ligned/, *adj.*
un/a·like/, *adj., adv.*
un/al·i·men/ta·ry, *adj.*
un/al·i·men/ta·tive, *adj.*
un/al·lay/a·ble, *adj.;* **-bly,** *adv.*
un/al·layed/, *adj.*
un/al·leged/, *adj.*
un/al·leg/ed·ly, *adv.*
un/al·le·gor/i·cal, *adj.;* **-ly,** *adv.*
un·al/le·go·rized/, *adj.*
un/al·ler/gic, *adj.*
un/al·le/vi·at/ed, *adj.;* **-ly,** *adv.*
un/al·le/vi·at/ing, *adj.;* **-ly,** *adv.*
un/al·le/vi·a/tive, *adj.*
un/al·lied/, *adj.*
un/al·lit/er·at/ed, *adj.*
un/al·lit/er·a/tive, *adj.*
un/al·lot/ted, *adj.*
un/al·low/a·ble, *adj.*
un/al·lowed/, *adj.*
un/al·loyed/, *adj.*
un/al·lured/, *adj.*
un/al·lur/ing, *adj.;* **-ly,** *adv.*
un/al·lu/sive, *adj.;* **-ly,** *adv.;* **-ness,** *n.*
un/al·pha·bet/ic, *adj.*
un/al·pha·bet/i·cal, *adj.*
un·al/pha·bet·ised/, *adj.*
un·al/pha·bet·ized/, *adj.*
un·al/ter·ing, *adj.*
un·al/ter·nat/ed, *adj.*
un·al/ter·nat/ing, *adj.*
un/a·mal/ga·ma·ble, *adj.*
un/a·mal/ga·mat/ed, *adj.*
un/a·mal/ga·mat/ing, *adj.*
un/a·mal/ga·ma/tive, *adj.*
un/a·massed/, *adj.*
un·am/a·tive, *adj.*
un·am/a·tive·ly, *adv.*
un/a·mazed/, *adj.*
un/a·maz/ed·ly, *adv.*
un/a·maz/ed·ness, *n.*
un·am/bi·ent, *adj.;* **-ly,** *adv.*
un/am·big/u·ous, *adj.;* **-ly,** *adv.;* **-ness,** *n.*
un/am·bi/tious, *adj.;* **-ly,** *adv.;* **-ness,** *n.*
un·am/bu·lant, *adj.*
un/a·mel/io·ra·ble, *adj.*
un/a·mel/io·rat/ed, *adj.*
un/a·mel/io·ra/tive, *adj.*
un/a·me/na·ble, *adj.;* **-bly,** *adv.*
un/a·mend/a·ble, *adj.*
un/a·mend/ed, *adj.*
un/a·mend/ing, *adj.*
un/a·merce/a·ble, *adj.*
un/a·merced/, *adj.*
un·a/mi·a·ble, *adj.;* **-ble·ness,** *n.;* **-bly,** *adv.*
un·am/i·ca·bil/i·ty, *n.*
un·am/i·ca·ble, *adj.;* **-ble·ness,** *n.;* **-bly,** *adv.*
un·am/mo·ni·at/ed, *adj.*
un·am/or·ous, *adj.;* **-ly,** *adv.;* **-ness,** *n.*
un·am/or·tized/, *adj.*
un·am/pli·fi/a·ble, *adj.*
un·am/pli·fied/, *adj.*
un·am/pu·tat/ed, *adj.*
un·am/pu·ta/tive, *adj.*
un/a·mus/a·ble, *adj.;* **-bly,** *adv.*
un/a·mused/, *adj.*
un/a·mus/ing, *adj.;* **-ly,** *adv.;* **-ness,** *n.*
un/a·nach/ro·nis/tic, *adj.*
un/a·nach/ro·nis/ti·cal, *adj.;* **-ly,** *adv.*
un/a·nach/ro·nous, *adj.;* **-ly,** *adv.*
un/a·nae/mic, *adj.*
un/an·a·log/i·cal, *adj.;* **-ly,** *adv.*
un/a·nal/o·gized/, *adj.*
un/a·nal/a·gous, *adj.;* **-ly,** *adv.;* **-ness,** *n.*
un/an·a·lyt/ic, *adj.*
un/an·a·lyt/i·cal, *adj.;* **-ly,** *adv.*
un·an/a·lyz/a·ble, *adj.;* **-bly,** *adv.*
un·an/a·lyzed/, *adj.*
un·an/a·lyz/ing, *adj.*
un/an·ar/chic, *adj.*
un/an·ar·chis/tic, *adj.*
un/a·nat/o·mis/a·ble, *adj.*
un/a·nat/o·mised/, *adj.*
un/a·nat/o·miz/a·ble, *adj.*
un/a·nat/o·mized/, *adj.*
un·an/chored, *adj.*
un/an·ec·do/tal, *adj.;* **-ly,** *adv.*
un/a·ne/mic, *adj.*
un·an/gered, *adj.*
un·an/gri·ly, *adv.*
un·an/gry, *adj.*
un·an/guished, *adj.*
un·an/gu·lar, *adj.;* **-ly,** *adv.;* **-ness,** *n.*
un·an/i·mat/ed, *adj.;* **-ly,** *adv.*
un·an/i·mat/ing, *adj.;* **-ly,** *adv.*
un/an·nealed/, *adj.*
un/an·nex/a·ble, *adj.*
un/an·nexed/, *adj.*
un/an·ni/hi·la·ble, *adj.*
un/an·ni/hi·lat/ed, *adj.*
un/an·ni/hi·la/tive, *adj.*
un/an·ni/hi·la·to/ry, *adj.*
un·an/no·tat/ed, *adj.*
un/an·nounced/, *adj.*
un/an·noyed/, *adj.*
un/an·noy/ing, *adj.;* **-ly,** *adv.*
un/an·nul/la·ble, *adj.*
un/an·nulled/, *adj.*
un/an·nun/ci·a·ble, *adj.*
un/an·nun/ci·a/tive, *adj.*
un/a·noint/ed, *adj.*
un·an/swer·ing, *adj.*
un·an·tag/o·nis/a·ble, *adj.*
un·an·tag/o·nised/, *adj.*
un·an·tag/o·nis/ing, *adj.*
un/an·tag/o·nis/tic, *adj.*
un·an·tag/o·niz/a·ble, *adj.*
un·an·tag/o·nized/, *adj.*
un·an·tag/o·niz/ing, *adj.*
un/an·thol/o·gized/, *adj.*
un/an·tic/i·pat/ed, *adj.*
un/an·tic/i·pat/ing, *adj.;* **-ly,** *adv.*
un/an·tic/i·pa/tive, *adj.*
un·an/ti·quat/ed, *adj.*
un·ant/lered, *adj.*
un·anx/ious, *adj.;* **-ly,** *adv.;* **-ness,** *n.*
un/a·pha/sic, *adj.*
un/a·pol/o·get/ic, *adj.*
un/a·pol/o·get/i·cal·ly, *adv.*
un/a·pol/o·giz/ing, *adj.*
un/a·pos/ta·tized/, *adj.*
un/a·pos/tro·phized/, *adj.*
un/ap·palled/, *adj.*
un/ap·pall/ing, *adj.;* **-ly,** *adv.*
un/ap·par/eled, *adj.*
un/ap·par/elled, *adj.*
un/ap·par/ent, *adj.;* **-ly,** *adv.;* **-ness,** *n.*
un/ap·pealed/, *adj.*
un/ap·peal/ing, *adj.;* **-ly,** *adv.*
un/ap·peas/a·ble, *adj.;* **-bly,** *adv.*
un/ap·peased/, *adj.*
un/ap·peas/ing, *adj.;* **-ly,** *adv.*
un/ap·pen/daged, *adj.*
un/ap·pend/ed, *adj.*
un/ap·per·ceived/, *adj.*
un/ap·per·cep/tive, *adj.*
un·ap/pe·tis/ing, *adj.;* **-ly,** *adv.*
un·ap/pe·tiz/ing, *adj.;* **-ly,** *adv.*
un/ap·plaud/a·ble, *adj.*
un/ap·plaud/ed, *adj.*
un/ap·plaud/ing, *adj.*
un/ap·plau/sive, *adj.*
un·ap/pli/a·ble, *adj.;* **-bly,** *adv.*
un·ap/pli·ca·bil/i·ty, *n.*
un·ap/pli·ca·ble, *adj.;* **-ble·ness,** *n.;* **-bly,** *adv.*
un·ap/pli·ca/tive, *adj.*
un/ap·plied/, *adj.*
un/ap·pli·qué/d, *adj.*
un/ap·point/a·ble, *adj.*
un/ap·point/ed, *adj.*
un/ap·por/tioned, *adj.*
un/ap·pos/a·ble, *adj.*
un·ap/po·site, *adj.;* **-ly,** *adv.;* **-ness,** *n.*
un/ap·praised/, *adj.*
un/ap·pre/ci·a·ble, *adj.;* **-bly,** *adv.*
un/ap·pre/ci·at/ed, *adj.*
un/ap·pre/ci·at/ing, *adj.*
un/ap·pre/ci·a/tive, *adj.;* **-ly,** *adv.;* **-ness,** *n.*
un/ap·pre·hend/a·ble, *adj.;* **-bly,** *adv.*
un/ap·pre·hend/ed, *adj.*
un/ap·pre·hend/ing, *adj.*
un/ap·pre·hen/si·ble, *adj.*
un/ap·pre·hen/sive, *adj.;* **-ly,** *adv.;* **-ness,** *n.*
un/ap·pren/ticed, *adj.*
un/ap·prised/, *adj.*
un/ap·proach/a·bil/i·ty, *n.*
un/ap·proached/, *adj.*
un/ap·proach/ing, *adj.*
un/ap·pro/pri·a·ble, *adj.*
un/ap·prov/a·ble, *adj.;* **-bly,** *adv.*
un/ap·proved/, *adj.*
un/ap·prov/ing, *adj.;* **-ly,** *adv.*
un·a/proned, *adj.*
un·ar/bi·trar/i·ly, *adv.*
un·ar/bi·trar/y, *adj.*
un·ar/bi·trat/ed, *adj.*
un·ar/bi·tra/tive, *adj.*
un·ar/bored, *adj.*
un·ar/boured, *adj.*
un·arched/, *adj.*
un·arch/ing, *adj.*
un·ar/chi·tect/ed, *adj.*
un/ar·chi·tec/tur·al, *adj.;* **-ly,** *adv.*
un·arch/ly, *adv.*
un·ar/du·ous, *adj.;* **-ly,** *adv.;* **-ness,** *n.*
un·ar/gu·a·ble, *adj.;* **-bly,** *adv.*
un/ar·gu·men/ta·tive, *adj.;* **-ly,** *adv.;* **-ness,** *n.*
un/a·ris/to·crat/ic, *adj.*
un/a·ris/to·crat/i·cal·ly, *adv.*
un/ar·ith·met/i·cal, *adj.;* **-ly,** *adv.*
un·ar/mored, *adj.*
un·ar/moured, *adj.*
un/ar·mo/ri·al, *adj.*
un/ar·o·mat/ic, *adj.*
un/ar·o·mat/i·cal·ly, *adv.*
un/a·rous/a·ble, *adj.*
un/a·roused/, *adj.*
un/a·rous/ing, *adj.*
un/ar·raign/a·ble, *adj.*
un/ar·raigned/, *adj.*
un/ar·ranged/, *adj.*
un/ar·rayed/, *adj.*
un/ar·rest/a·ble, *adj.*
un/ar·rest/ed, *adj.*
un/ar·rest/ing, *adj.*

un·a·shamed (un′ə shāmd′), *adj.* **1.** not ashamed; not restrained by embarrassment or consciousness of moral guilt: *He remained as dishonest as ever, unashamed even after his public reprimand.* **2.** open; unconcealed; unabashed: *He ate with unashamed gusto.* [UN-[1] + ASHAMED] —**un·a·sham·ed·ly** (un′ə shā′mid lē), *adv.* —**un′a·sham′ed·ness,** *n.*

un·as·sail·a·ble (un′ə sā′lə bəl), *adj.* **1.** not open to attack or assault, as by military force, argument, etc.: *unassailable fortifications; unassailable logic.* **2.** not subject to denial or loss: *Shakespeare's genius gives his works an unassailable position in literature.* [UN-[1] + ASSAILABLE] —**un′as·sail′a·ble·ness,** *n.* —**un′as·sail′a·bly,** *adv.*

un·as·sum·ing (un′ə so͞o′ming), *adj.* modest; unpretentious. [UN-[1] + ASSUMING] —**un′as·sum′ing·ly,** *adv.* —**un′as·sum′ing·ness,** *n.*

un·at·tached (un′ə tacht′), *adj.* **1.** not attached. **2.** not connected or associated with any particular body, group, organization, or the like; independent. **3.** not engaged or married. [UN-[1] + ATTACHED]

un·at·tend·ed (un′ə ten′did), *adj.* **1.** without attendance; lacking an audience, spectators, etc.: *an unattended meeting.* **2.** not accompanied; not associated with, as a concomitant effect or result: *a flash of lightning unattended by thunder.* **3.** not cared for or ministered to; not waited on, as an invalid. **4.** not accompanied, as by an attendant or companion; alone: *The queen was unattended.* **5.** not taken in charge; not attended; not watched over: *an unattended switchboard.* **6.** unheeded; not listened to; disregarded: *unattended warning signals.* **7.** not tended to; not done or carried out, as a task (usually fol. by *to*): *He left his studies unattended to.* [UN-[1] + ATTEND + -ED[2]]

u·nau (yo͞o nô′, o͞o nou′), *n.* a sloth, *Choloepus didactylus,* of tropical America, having two toes on each forelimb. [< F < Tupian; akin to Tupi *unáu*]

un·a·vail·ing (un′ə vā′ling), *adj.* ineffectual; futile. [UN-[1] + AVAIL + -ING[2]] —**un′a·vail′ing·ly,** *adv.*

un·a·ware (un′ə wâr′), *adj.* **1.** not aware; unconscious: *to be unaware of any change.* —*adv.* **2.** unawares. [ME *uniwar, ungewar;* c. OE *gewær* and *unwær.* See UN-[1], AWARE] —**un′a·ware′ly,** *adv.* —**un′a·ware′ness,** *n.*

un·a·wares (un′ə wârz′), *adv.* **1.** while not aware or conscious of a thing oneself; unknowingly or inadvertently. **2.** without warning; suddenly; unexpectedly: *to come upon someone unawares.* [UNAWARE + -S[1]]

un·backed (un bakt′), *adj.* **1.** without backing or support. **2.** not supported by bets: *an unbacked challenger.* **3.** not endorsed: *an unbacked product.* **4.** never having been mounted by a rider, as a horse. [UN-[1] + BACKED]

un·bal·ance (un bal′əns), *v.,* **-anced, -anc·ing,** *n.* —*v.t.* **1.** to throw or put out of balance. **2.** to disorder or derange, as the mind. —*n.* **3.** unbalanced condition. [UN-[2] + BALANCE]

un·bal·anced (un bal′ənst), *adj.* **1.** not balanced or not properly balanced. **2.** lacking steadiness and soundness of judgment. **3.** mentally disordered; deranged. **4.** (of an account) not adjusted; not brought to an equality of debits and credits. **5.** *Football.* of or pertaining to an offensive line formation having more than three linemen on one side of the center. Cf. **balanced** (def. 2). [UN-[1] + BALANCED]

un·bal·last·ed (un bal′ə stid), *adj.* **1.** not ballasted. **2.** not properly steadied or regulated. [UN-[1] + BALLASTED]

Un Bal·lo in Ma·sche·ra (o͞on bäl′lô ēn mä ske′rä), an opera (1859) by Verdi. English, **A Masked Ball.**

un·bar (un bär′), *v.t.,* **-barred, -bar·ring. 1.** to remove a bar or bars from. **2.** to open; unlock; unbolt: *to unbar a door.* [ME *unbarre(n).* See UN-[2], BAR[1]]

un·barbed (un bärbd′), *adj.* barbless. [UN-[1] + BARB[1] + -ED[3]]

un·bat·ed (un bā′tid), *adj.* **1.** not abated; undiminished; unlessened. **2.** *Archaic.* not blunted, as a lance or fencer's foil. [UN-[1] + BATED]

un·bear·a·ble (un bâr′ə bəl), *adj.* not bearable; unendurable; intolerable. [late ME; see UN-[1], BEARABLE] —**un·bear′a·ble·ness,** *n.* —**un·bear′a·bly,** *adv.*

un·be·com·ing (un′bi kum′ing), *adj.* unattractive; unsuitable, as an article of apparel, a fashion, habit, etc.; detracting from one's appearance, character, or reputation; creating an unfavorable impression: *an unbecoming hat; an unbecoming slouch; unbecoming language.* [UN-[1] + BECOMING] —**un′be·com′ing·ly,** *adv.* —**un′be·com′ing·ness,** *n.*
—**Syn.** unapt, unsuitable, unfit. See **improper.**

un·be·got·ten (un′bi got′ən), *adj.* **1.** not yet begotten; as yet unborn: *The consequences of this act will extend to our unbegotten children.* **2.** without a beginning; eternal. [UN-[1] + BEGOTTEN]

un·be·known (un′bi nōn′), *adj.* unknown; unperceived; without one's knowledge (usually fol. by *to*). Also, **un·be·knownst** (un′bi nōnst′). [UN-[1] + *beknown* (late ME *beknowe,* ptp. of *bynowe*); see BE-, KNOW]

un·be·lief (un′bi lēf′), *n.* state or quality of not believing; incredulity or skepticism, esp. in matters of doctrine or religious faith. [ME *unbelefe*]

un·be·liev·er (un′bi lē′vər), *n.* **1.** one who does not believe. **2.** one who does not accept any, or some particular, religious belief. [UN-[1] + BELIEVER]

un·be·liev·ing (un′bi lē′ving), *adj.* **1.** not believing; skeptical. **2.** not accepting any, or some particular, religious belief. [late ME; see UN-[1], BELIEVING] —**un′be·liev′ing·ly,** *adv.* —**un′be·liev′ing·ness,** *n.*

un·belt (un belt′), *v.t.* **1.** to remove the belt from. **2.** to remove by undoing a supporting belt: *to unbelt a sword.* [UN-[2] + BELT]

un·bend (un bend′), *v.,* **-bent** or (*Archaic*) **-bend·ed, -bend·ing.** —*v.t.* **1.** to release from the strain of effort or close application; relax by laying aside formality. **2.** to release from tension, as a bow. **3.** to straighten from a bent form or position. **4.** *Naut.* **a.** to loose or untie, as a sail, rope, etc. **b.** to unfasten from spars or stays, as sails. —*v.i.* **5.** to relax the strictness of formality or ceremony; act in an easy, genial manner: *Imagine him unbending!* **6.** to become unbent. [late ME; see UN-[2], BEND[1]] —**un·bend′a·ble,** *adj.*

un·bend·ing (un ben′ding), *adj.* not bending; rigid; unyielding; inflexible. [UN-[1] + BENDING] —**un·bend′ing·ly,** *adv.* —**un·bend′ing·ness,** *n.*

un·bent (un bent′), *v.* **1.** a pt. and pp. of **unbend.** —*adj.* **2.** not bent; unbowed. **3.** not forced to yield or submit.

un·bi·ased (un bī′əst), *adj.* not biased; unprejudiced; impartial. Also, *esp. Brit.,* **un·bi′assed.** [UN-[1] + BIASED] —**un·bi′ased·ly,** *adv.*
—**Syn.** fair, equitable, tolerant, neutral.

un·bid·den (un bid′ən), *adj.* **1.** not commanded; spontaneous. **2.** not bidden, asked, or summoned; uninvited. Also, **un·bid′.** [ME *unbiden,* OE *unbēden.* See UN-[1], BIDDEN]

un·bind (un bīnd′), *v.t.,* **-bound, -bind·ing. 1.** to release from bonds or restraint, as a prisoner; free. **2.** to unfasten or loose, as a bond or tie. [ME; OE *unbindan*; c. G *entbinden.* See UN-[2], BIND]

un·bit·ted (un bit′id), *adj.* **1.** not bitted or bridled. **2.** uncontrolled. [UN-[1] + BITTED]

un·blenched (un blencht′), *adj. Archaic.* undaunted. [UN-[1] + BLENCH[1] + -ED[2]]

un′ar·res′tive, *adj.*
un′ar·rived′, *adj.*
un′ar·riv′ing, *adj.*
un·ar′ro·gant, *adj.;* **-ly,** *adv.*
un·ar′ro·gat′ed, *adj.*
un·ar′ro·gat′ing, *adj.*
un·art′ful, *adj.;* **-ly,** *adv.;* **-ness,** *n.*
un·ar′ti·cled, *adj.*
un′ar·tic′u·late, *adj.;* **-ly,** *adv.*
un′ar·tic′u·lat′ed, *adj.*
un′ar·tic′u·la′tive, *adj.*
un′ar·tic′u·la·to′ry, *adj.*
un′ar·ti·fi′cial, *adj.;* **-ly,** *adv.*
un′ar·tis′tic, *adj.*
un′ar·tis′ti·cal·ly, *adv.*
un′as·cend′a·ble, *adj.*
un′as·cend′ant, *adj.*
un′as·cend′ed, *adj.*
un′as·cend′ent, *adj.*
un′as·cer·tain′a·ble, *adj.;* **-bly,** *adv.*
un′as·cer·tained′, *adj.*
un′as·cet′ic, *adj.*
un′as·cet′i·cal·ly, *adv.*
un′as·cribed′, *adj.*
un·ask′a·ble, *adj.*
un·ask′ing, *adj.;* **-ly,** *adv.*
un′as·persed′, *adj.*
un′as·per′sive, *adj.*
un·as′phalt·ed, *adj.*
un·as′pi·rat′ed, *adj.*
un′a·spir′ing, *adj.;* **-ly,** *adv.*
un′as·sailed′, *adj.*
un′as·sail′ing, *adj.*
un′as·sas′si·nat′ed, *adj.*
un′as·sault′a·ble, *adj.*
un′as·sault′ed, *adj.*
un′as·sayed′, *adj.*
un′as·say′ing, *adj.*
un′as·sem′bled, *adj.*
un′as·sent′ing, *adj.*
un′as·sen′tive, *adj.*
un′as·sert′ed, *adj.*
un′as·ser′tive, *adj.;* **-ly,** *adv.;* **-ness,** *n.*
un′as·sess′a·ble, *adj.*
un′as·sessed′, *adj.*
un′as·sib′i·lat′ed, *adj.*
un′as·sid′u·ous, *adj.;* **-ly,** *adv.;* **-ness,** *n.*
un′as·sign′a·ble, *adj.;* **-bly,** *adv.*
un′as·signed′, *adj.*
un′as·sim′i·la·ble, *adj.*
un′as·sim′i·lat′ed, *adj.*
un′as·sim′i·lat′ing, *adj.*
un′as·sim′i·la′tive, *adj.*
un′as·sist′ant, *adj.*
un′as·sist′ed, *adj.*
un′as·sist′ing, *adj.*
un′as·so′ci·a·ble, *adj.;* **-bly,** *adv.*
un′as·so′ci·at′ed, *adj.*
un′as·so′ci·a′tive, *adj.;* **-ly,** *adv.*
un′as·sort′ed, *adj.*
un′as·suage′a·ble, *adj.*
un′as·suag′ing, *adj.*
un′as·sua′sive, *adj.*
un′as·sum′a·ble, *adj.*
un′as·sumed′, *adj.*
un′as·sured′, *adj.*
un′as·sur′ed·ly, *adv.*
un′as·sur′ed·ness, *n.*
un′as·sur′ing, *adj.*
un′asth·mat′ic, *adj.*
un′as·ton′ished, *adj.*
un′ath·let′ic, *adj.*
un′ath·let′i·cal·ly, *adv.*
un′at·mos·pher′ic, *adj.*
un′a·toned′, *adj.*
un′a·ton′ing, *adj.*
un·at′ro·phied, *adj.*
un′at·tach′a·ble, *adj.*
un′at·tack′a·ble, *adj.*
un′at·tacked′, *adj.*
un′at·tain′a·bil′i·ty, *n.*
un′at·tain′a·ble, *adj.;* **-ble·ness,** *n.;* **-bly,** *adv.*
un′at·tained′, *adj.*
un′at·tain′ing, *adj.*
un′at·taint′ed, *adj.*
un′at·tem′pered, *adj.*
un′at·tempt′a·ble, *adj.*
un′at·tempt′ed, *adj.*
un′at·tempt′ing, *adj.*
un′at·tend′ance, *n.*
un′at·tend′ant, *adj.*
un′at·ten′tive, *adj.;* **-ly,** *adv.;* **-ness,** *n.*
un′at·ten′u·at′ed, *adj.;* **-ly,** *adv.*
un′at·test′ed, *adj.*
un′at·tired′, *adj.*
un′at·tract′a·ble, *adj.*
un′at·tract′ed, *adj.*
un′at·tract′ing, *adj.*
un′at·trac′tive, *adj.;* **-ly,** *adv.;* **-ness,** *n.*
un′at·trib′u·ta·ble, *adj.;* **-bly,** *adv.*
un′at·trib′u·tive, *adj.;* **-ly,** *adv.;* **-ness,** *n.*
un′at·tuned′, *adj.*
un·auc′tioned, *adj.*
un′au·da′cious, *adj.;* **-ly,** *adv.;* **-ness,** *n.*
un·au′dit·ed, *adj.*
un′au·di′tioned, *adj.*
un′aug·ment′a·ble, *adj.*
un′aug·ment′a·tive, *adj.*
un′aug·ment′ed, *adj.*
un′aus·pi′cious, *adj.;* **-ly,** *adv.*
un′aus·tere′, *adj.;* **-ly,** *adv.;* **-ness,** *n.*
un′-Aus·tral′ian, *adj.*
un-Aus′tri·an, *adj.*
un′au·then′tic, *adj.*
un′au·then′ti·cal, *adj.;* **-ly,** *adv.;* **-ness,** *n.*
un′au·then′ti·cat′ed, *adj.*
un′au·then·tic′i·ty, *n.*
un·au′thor·ised′, *adj.*
un′au·thor′i·ta′tive, *adj.;* **-ly,** *adv.;* **-ness,** *n.*
un·au′thor·ized′, *adj.*
un′au·tis′tic, *adj.*
un·au′to·graphed′, *adj.*
un′au·to·mat′ic, *adj.*
un′au·to·mat′i·cal·ly, *adv.*
un′au·tum′nal, *adj.*
un′a·vail′a·bil′i·ty, *n.*
un′a·vail′a·ble, *adj.;* **-ble·ness,** *n.;* **-bly,** *adv.*
un′a·vailed′, *adj.*
un′a·venge′a·ble, *adj.*
un′a·venged′, *adj.*
un′a·veng′ing, *adj.;* **-ly,** *adv.*
un·av′er·aged, *adj.*
un′a·verred′, *adj.*
un′a·vert′ed, *adj.*
un·av′id, *adj.;* **-ly,** *adv.;* **-ness,** *n.*
un′a·void′a·bil′i·ty, *n.*
un′a·void′a·ble, *adj.;* **-ble·ness,** *n.;* **-bly,** *adv.*
un′a·void′ing, *adj.*
un′a·vouched′, *adj.*
un′a·vow′a·ble, *adj.;* **-ble·ness,** *n.;* **-bly,** *adv.*
un′a·wak′a·ble, *adj.*
un′a·wake′, *adj.*
un′a·waked′, *adj.*
un′a·wak′en·ing, *adj.*
un′a·wak′ing, *adj.*
un′a·ward′a·ble, *adj.*
un′a·ward′ed, *adj.*
un·awed′, *adj.*
un·aw′ful, *adj.;* **-ness,** *n.*
un·awk′ward, *adj.;* **-ly,** *adv.;* **-ness,** *n.*
un·awned′, *adj.*
un·axed′, *adj.*
un′ax·i·o·mat′ic, *adj.*
un′ax·i·o·mat′i·cal·ly, *adv.*
un·ax′ised, *adj.*
un·ax′led, *adj.*
un·back′ward, *adj.*
un′bac·te′ri·al, *adj.*
un·badged′, *adj.*
un·badg′ered, *adj.*
un·badg′er·ing, *adj.*
un·baf′fled, *adj.*
un·baf′fling, *adj.;* **-ly,** *adv.*
un·bagged′, *adj.*
un·bail′a·ble, *adj.*
un·bailed′, *adj.*
un·bait′, *v.t.*
un·baked′, *adj.*
un·bal′ance·a·ble, *adj.*
un·bal′co·nied, *adj.*
un·bale′, *v.t.,* **-baled, -bal·ing.**
un·balked′, *adj.*
un·balk′ing, *adj.;* **-ly,** *adv.*
un·bal′lot·ed, *adj.*
un·band′age, *v.t.,* **-aged, -ag·ing.**
un·band′ed, *adj.*
un·ban′gled, *adj.*
un·ban′ished, *adj.*
un·bank′a·ble, *adj.;* **-ble·ness,** *n.;* **-bly,** *adv.*
un·banned′, *adj.*
un·ban′nered, *adj.*
un·ban′ter·ing, *adj.;* **-ly,** *adv.*
un·bap′tised, *adj.*
un·bap′tized, *adj.*
un·bar′ba·rise′, *v.t.,* **-rised, -ris·ing.**
un·bar′ba·rize′, *v.t.,* **-rized, -riz·ing.**
un·bar′ba·rous, *adj.;* **-ly,** *adv.;* **-ness,** *n.*
un·bar′bered, *adj.*
un·bar′gained, *adj.*
un·bark′ing, *adj.*
un·bar′ra·ble, *adj.*
un·bar′reled, *adj.*
un·bar′relled, *adj.*
un·bar′ren, *adj.;* **-ly,** *adv.;* **-ness,** *n.*
un·bar′ri·cade′, *v.t.,* **-cad·ed, -cad·ing.**
un·bar′tered, *adj.*
un·bar′ter·ing, *adj.*
un·base′, *adj.*
un·based′, *adj.*
un·bash′ful, *adj.;* **-ly,** *adv.;* **-ness,** *n.*
un·bas′ket·like′, *adj.*
un·bas′tard·ised′, *adj.*
un·bas′tard·ized′, *adj.*
un·bast′ed, *adj.*
un′bas·ti·na′doed, *adj.*
un·bathed′, *adj.*
un·bat′ing, *adj.*
un·bat′ted, *adj.*
un·bat′ter·a·ble, *adj.*
un·bat′tered, *adj.*
un·bat′tling, *adj.*
un·bay′, *v.t.*
un·beached′, *adj.*
un·bea′coned, *adj.*
un·bead′ed, *adj.*
un·beamed′, *adj.*
un·beam′ing, *adj.*
un·beard′, *v.t.*
un·beard′ed, *adj.*
un·bear′ing, *adj.*
un·beat′a·ble, *adj.*
un·beat′en, *adj.*
un·beaued′, *adj.*
un·beau′te·ous, *adj.;* **-ly,** *adv.;* **-ness,** *n.*
un·beau′ti·fied′, *adj.*
un·beau′ti·ful, *adj.;* **-ly,** *adv.*
un·beck′oned, *adj.*
un′be·cloud′ed, *adj.*
un′be·dab′bled, *adj.*
un′be·daubed′, *adj.*
un′be·decked′, *adj.*
un′be·dimmed′, *adj.*
un′be·di′zened, *adj.*
un′be·drag′gled, *adj.*
un′be·fit′ting, *adj.*
un′be·friend′ed, *adj.*
un·beg′gar·ly, *adj.*
un·begged′, *adj.*
un′be·grudged′, *adj.*
un′be·guiled′, *adj.*
un′be·guil′ing, *adj.*
un′be·hav′ing, *adj.*
un′be·head′ed, *adj.*
un′be·held′, *adj.*
un′be·hold′a·ble, *adj.*
un′be·hold′en, *adj.*
un′be·lied′, *adj.*
un·bel′li·cose′, *adj.*
un′bel·lig′er·ent, *adj.;* **-ly,** *adv.*
un′be·long′ing, *adj.*
un′be·loved′, *adj.*
un′be·moaned′, *adj.*
un·bench′, *v.t.*
un·ben′e·ficed, *adj.*
un′be·nef′i·cent, *adj.;* **-ly,** *adv.*
un′ben·e·fi′cial, *adj.;* **-ly,** *adv.;* **-ness,** *n.*
un·ben′e·fit·ed, *adj.*
un·ben′e·fit·ing, *adj.*
un′be·nev′o·lence, *n.*
un′be·nev′o·lent, *adj.;* **-ly,** *adv.*
un′be·nign′, *adj.;* **-ly,** *adv.*
un′be·nig′nant, *adj.;* **-ly,** *adv.*
un′be·nig′ni·ty, *n.*
un′be·numbed′, *adj.*
un′be·queath′a·ble, *adj.*
un′be·queathed′, *adj.*
un′be·reaved′, *adj.*
un′be·rouged′, *adj.*
un·berth′, *v.t.*
un′be·seech′ing, *adj.;* **-ly,** *adv.*
un′be·seem′ing, *adj.*
un′be·set′, *adj.*
un′be·sieged′, *adj.*
un′be·smeared′, *adj.*
un′be·smirched′, *adj.*
un′be·smut′ted, *adj.*
un′be·sought′, *adj.*
un′be·spo′ken, *adj.*
un′be·sprin′kled, *adj.*
un′be·stowed′, *adj.*
un·bet′, *adj.*
un′be·trayed′, *adj.*
un′be·tray′ing, *adj.*
un′be·trothed′, *adj.*
un·bet′tered, *adj.*
un·bev′eled, *adj.*
un·bev′elled, *adj.*
un′be·wailed′, *adj.*
un′be·wail′ing, *adj.*
un′be·wil′dered, *adj.;* **-ly,** *adv.*
un′be·wil′der·ing, *adj.;* **-ly,** *adv.*
un′be·witched′, *adj.*
un′be·witch′ing *adj.;* **-ly,** *adv.*
un′be·wrayed′, *adj.*
un·bib′u·lous, *adj.;* **-ly,** *adv.;* **-ness,** *n.*
un·bick′ered, *adj.*
un·bick′er·ing, *adj.*
un·bid′da·ble, *adj.*
un·big′a·mous, *adj.;* **-ly,** *adv.*
un·big′ot·ed, *adj.*
un·bil′ious, *adj.;* **-ly,** *adv.;* **-ness,** *n.*
un·bill′a·ble, *adj.*
un·billed′, *adj.*
un·bil′let·ed, *adj.*
un·binned′, *adj.*
un′bi·o·graph′i·cal, *adj.;* **-ly,** *adv.*
un′bi·o·log′i·cal, *adj.;* **-ly,** *adv.*
un·bird′like′, *adj.*
un·bit′, *v.t.,* **-bit·ted, -bit·ting,** *adj.*
un·bit′ing, *adj.*
un·bit′ten, *adj.*
un·bit′ter, *adj.*
un·blacked′, *adj.*
un·black′ened, *adj.*
un·blade′, *v.t.,* **-blad·ed, -blad·ing.**
un·blam′a·ble, *adj.;* **-ble·ness,** *n.;* **-bly,** *adv.*
un·blamed′, *adj.*
un·blam′ing, *adj.*
un·blanched′, *adj.*
un·blan′ket·ed, *adj.*
un·blas′phemed, *adj.*
un·blast′ed, *adj.*
un·bla′zoned, *adj.*
un·bleached′, *adj.*
un·bleach′ing, *adj.*
un·bled′, *adj.*
un·bleed′ing, *adj.*
un·blem′ish·a·ble, *adj.*
un·blem′ished, *adj.*
un·blem′ish·ing, *adj.*
un·blench′ing, *adj.;* **-ly,** *adv.*
un·blend′a·ble, *adj.*
un·blend′ed, *adj.*
un·blent′, *adj.*

un·blessed (un blest′), *adj.* **1.** excluded from or lacking a blessing. **2.** unhallowed. **3.** unhappy; wretched. Also, **un·blest′.** [ME; see UN-[1], BLESSED] —**un·bless·ed·ness** (un bles′id nis), *n.*

un·blink·ing (un bliŋg′kiŋg), *adj.* **1.** not blinking. **2.** without displaying response, as surprise, confusion, chagrin, etc.: *an unblinking reaction to the charges.* **3.** not varying or wavering; fearless; forthright: *unblinking devotion.* [UN-[1] + BLINKING] —**un·blink′ing·ly,** *adv.*

un·block (un blok′), *v.t.* **1.** to remove a block or obstruction from: *to unblock a channel; to unblock a person's credit.* **2.** *Bridge.* to play (a suit) so that the last card of the suit in one hand can provide access to the hand of the partnership having the longer holding in the suit. [UN-[2] + BLOCK] —**un·blocked′,** *adj.*

un·blush·ing (un blush′iŋg), *adj.* **1.** shameless: *unblushing flirtatiousness.* **2.** not blushing. [UN-[1] + BLUSHING] —**un·blush′ing·ly,** *adv.* —**un·blush′ing·ness,** *n.*

un·bod·ied (un bod′ēd), *adj.* **1.** incorporeal; disembodied. **2.** lacking a form; formless; shapeless. [UN-[1] + BODIED]

un·bolt (un bōlt′), *v.t.* **1.** to open (a door, window, etc.) by or as if by removing a bolt; unlock; unfasten. **2.** to release, as by the removal of threaded bolts: *He unscrewed the nuts and unbolted the inspection cover.* [UN-[2] + BOLT[1]]

un·bolt·ed[1] (un bōl′tid), *adj.* not fastened or secured, as with a bolt or bolts. [UN-[1] + BOLT[1] + -ED[2]]

un·bolt·ed[2] (un bōl′tid), *adj.* not sifted, as grain. [UN-[1] + BOLT[2] + -ED[2]]

un·boned (un bōnd′), *adj.* **1.** boneless. **2.** not having the bones removed: *an unboned chicken.* [UN-[1] + BONED]

un·bon·net (un bon′it), *v.i.* **1.** to uncover the head, as in respect. —*v.t.* **2.** to take off the bonnet from. [UN-[2] + BONNET]

un·bon·net·ed (un bon′i tid), *adj.* bareheaded. [UN-[1] + BONNET + -ED[2]]

un·born (un bôrn′), *adj.* **1.** not yet born; yet to come; future: *unborn generations.* **2.** not yet delivered; still existing in the mother's womb: *an unborn baby.* **3.** existing without birth or beginning. [ME; OE *unboren.* See UN-[1], BORN]

un·bos·om (un bo͝oz′əm, -bo͞o′zəm), *v.t.* **1.** to disclose (a confidence, secret, etc.). —*v.i.* **2.** to disclose one's thoughts, feelings, or the like, esp. in confidence. **3. unbosom oneself,** to disclose one's personal thoughts, feelings, etc., to another person; confide in someone: *She unbosomed herself to a complete stranger, since there was no one else to whom she could turn.* [UN[2] + BOSOM (v.)] —**un·bos′om·er,** *n.*

un·bound (un bound′), *v.* **1.** pt. and pp. of **unbind.** —*adj.* **2.** not bound, as a book. **3.** free; not attached, as by a chemical bond: *unbound electrons.*

un·bound·ed (un boun′did), *adj.* **1.** unlimited; boundless. **2.** unrestrained; uncontrolled: *unbounded enthusiasm.* [UN-[1] + BOUND[3] + -ED[3]] —**un·bound′ed·ly,** *adv.* —**un·bound′ed·ness,** *n.*
—**Syn. 1.** limitless, immense, vast, infinite, immeasurable. **2.** unconfined, immoderate.

un·bowed (un boud′), *adj.* **1.** not bowed or bent. **2.** not yielding or submitting, as to defeat; not subjugated: *Even when their country was occupied the people of Norway remained proud and unbowed.* [ME; see UN-[1] + BOWED]

un·brace (un brās′), *v.t.,* **-braced, -brac·ing. 1.** to remove the braces of. **2.** to free from tension; relax. **3.** to weaken. [ME *unbrace(n)* (to) free of clothing or armor. See UN-[2], BRACE]

un·braid (un brād′), *v.t.* to separate (anything braided, as hair) into the several strands. [UN-[2] + BRAID]

un·breathed (un brēthd′), *adj.* **1.** not breathed: *unbreathed air.* **2.** not disclosed; uncommunicated, as a secret. [UN-[1] + BREATHED]

un·bred (un bred′), *adj.* **1.** not taught or trained. **2.** not bred or mated, as a stock animal; not yet bred: *An unbred cow gives no milk.* [UN-[1] + BRED]

un·bri·dle (un brīd′əl), *v.t.,* **-dled, -dling. 1.** to remove the bridle from (a horse, mule, etc.). **2.** to free from restraint. [ME *unbridle(n).* See UN-[2], BRIDLE (v.)]

un·broke (un brōk′), *adj.* *Obs.* unbroken.

un·bro·ken (un brō′kən), *adj.* **1.** whole; intact. **2.** uninterrupted; continuous. **3.** not tamed, as a horse. **4.** undisturbed; unimpaired. [ME; see UN-[1], BROKEN] —**un·bro′ken·ly,** *adv.* —**un·bro′ken·ness,** *n.*
—**Syn. 1.** complete, entire.

un·buck·le (un buk′əl), *v.t.,* **-led, -ling.** to unfasten the buckle or buckles of. [ME *unbocle(n).* See UN-[2], BUCKLE]

un·build (un bild′), *v.t.,* **-built, -build·ing.** to demolish (something built); raze. [UN-[2] + BUILD]

un·bur·den (un bûr′dən), *v.t.* **1.** to free from a burden. **2.** to relieve (one's mind, conscience, etc.) by disclosure or confession of something. **3.** to cast off or get rid of, as a burden or something burdensome; disclose; reveal: *He unburdened the worries that plagued him.* [UN-[2] + BURDEN[1]]

un·but·ton (un but′ən), *v.t.* **1.** to free (buttons) from buttonholes; unfasten or undo. **2.** to unfasten by or as if by unbuttoning: *to unbutton a hatch; to unbutton a jacket.* **3.** to end a silence or disclose one's feelings, thoughts, etc., as if by undoing a button. —*v.i.* **4.** to unfasten a button or one's buttons. [ME *unboten(en).* See UN-[2], BUTTON]

un·called-for (un kôld′fôr′), *adj.* **1.** not called for; not required; superfluous; unwanted. **2.** unwarranted; unjustified; improper: *an uncalled-for criticism.*

un·can·ny (un kan′ē), *adj.* **1.** having or seeming to have a supernatural or inexplicable basis; beyond the ordinary or normal; extraordinary: *uncanny accuracy; an uncanny knack of foreseeing trouble.* **2.** mysterious; frightening, as by superstitious dread; uncomfortably strange: *Uncanny sounds filled the house.* [UN-[1] + CANNY] —**un·can′ni·ly,** *adv.* —**un·can′ni·ness,** *n.*
—**Syn. 2.** preternatural, odd. See **weird.** —**Ant. 2.** ordinary, natural.

un·ca·non·i·cal (un′kə non′i kəl), *adj.* **1.** not in accordance with canons or rules. **2.** not belonging to the canon of Scripture. [UN-[1] + CANONICAL] —**un′ca·non′i·cal·ly,** *adv.*

un·cap (un kap′), *v.,* **-capped, -cap·ping.** —*v.t.* **1.** to remove a cap or hat from (the head of a person). **2.** to remove (a cap or cover) from. —*v.i.* **3.** to remove the cap from the head, as in respect. [UN-[2] + CAP[1]]

un·ca·pa·ble (un kā′pə bəl), *adj.* *Obs.* incapable. [UN-[1] + CAPABLE]

un·cared-for (un kârd′fôr′), *adj.* **1.** not cared for; for which no liking, fondness, or affection is felt or shown: *uncared-for reminders of youth.* **2.** untended; neglected; unkempt: *The garden had an uncared-for look.*

un·case (un kās′), *v.t.,* **-cased, -cas·ing. 1.** to remove from a case; remove the case from. **2.** to remove the cover from; put on view. **3.** to make known; reveal. [UN-[2] + CASE[2]]

un·caused (un kôzd′), *adj.* not resulting from some antecedent cause; self-existent. [UN-[1] + CAUSED]

un·cer·e·mo·ni·ous (un′ser ə mō′nē əs), *adj.* **1.** without ceremony or ritual; informal: *an unceremonious*

un·blight′ed, *adj.;* **-ly,** *adv.;* **-ness,** *n.*
un·blind′fold′ed, *adj.*
un·blind′ing, *adj.*
un·bliss′ful, *adj.;* **-ly,** *adv.;* **-ness,** *n.*
un·blis′tered, *adj.*
un′block·ad′ed, *adj.*
un·blood′i·ly, *adv.*
un·blood′i·ness, *n.*
un·blood′y, *adj.*
un·bloomed′, *adj.*
un·blos′somed, *adj.*
un·blos′som·ing, *adj.*
un·blot′ted, *adj.*
un·bloused′, *adj.*
un·blown′, *adj.*
un·blued′, *adj.*
un·bluff′a·ble, *adj.*
un·bluffed′, *adj.*
un·bluff′ing, *adj.*
un·blun′der·ing, *adj.*
un·blunt′ed, *adj.*
un·blurred′, *adj.*
un·blus′ter·ous, *adj.;* **-ly,** *adv.*
un·board′ed, *adj.*
un·boast′ed, *adj.*
un·boast′ful, *adj.;* **-ly,** *adv.;* **-ness,** *n.*
un·boast′ing, *adj.*
un·bobbed′, *adj.*
un·bod′ing, *adj.*
un·bog′gy, *adj.*
un·boiled′, *adj.*
un·bois′ter·ous, *adj.;* **-ly,** *adv.;* **-ness,** *n.*
un·bold′, *adj.;* **-ly,** *adv.;* **-ness,** *n.*
un·bol′ster, *v.t.*
un·bol′stered, *adj.*
un·bombed′, *adj.*
un′bom·bard′ed, *adj.*
un′bom·bas′tic, *adj.*
un′bom·bas′ti·cal·ly, *adv.*
un·bond′a·ble, *adj.*
un·bond′ed, *adj.*
un·book′ish, *adj.;* **-ly,** *adv.;* **-ness,** *n.*
un·boot′ed, *adj.*
un·bor′dered, *adj.*
un·bored′, *adj.*
un·bor′ing, *adj.*
un·borne′, *adj.*
un·bor′rowed, *adj.*
un·bor′row·ing, *adj.*
un·bossed′, *adj.*
un′bo·tan′i·cal, *adj.*
un·both′ered, *adj.*
un·both′er·ing, *adj.*
un·bot′tle, *v.t.,* **-tled, -tling.**
un·bot′tom, *v.t.*
un·bought′, *adj.*
un·boun′te·ous, *adj.;* **-ly,** *adv.;* **-ness,** *n.*
un·boun′ti·ful, *adj.;* **-ly,** *adv.;* **-ness,** *n.*
un·bowd′ler·ized′, *adj.*
un·bow′ing, *adj.*
un·bowled′, *adj.*
un·box′, *v.t.*
un·boy′ish, *adj.;* **-ly,** *adv.;* **-ness,** *n.*
un·brace′let·ed, *adj.*
un·brack′et·ed, *adj.*
un·brag′ging, *adj.*
un′-Brah·min′i·cal, *adj.*
un·brailed′, *adj.*
un·branched′, *adj.*
un·branch′ing, *adj.*
un·brand′ed, *adj.*
un·bran′died, *adj.*
un·brave′, *adj.;* **-ly,** *adv.;* **-ness,** *n.*
un·braved′, *adj.*
un·brawl′ing, *adj.*
un·brawn′y, *adj.*
un·bra′zen, *adj.;* **-ly,** *adv.;* **-ness,** *n.*
un·breach′a·ble, *adj.;* **-ble·ness,** *n.;* **-bly,** *adv.*
un·breached′, *adj.*
un·bread′ed, *adj.*
un·break′a·ble, *adj.;* **-ble·ness,** *n.;* **-bly,** *adv.*
un·break′ing, *adj.*
un·breath′a·ble, *adj.*
un·breath′ing, *adj.*
un·breeched′, *adj.*
un·breez′y, *adj.*
un·brewed′, *adj.*
un·brib′a·ble, *adj.;* **-bly,** *adv.*
un·bribed′, *adj.*
un·brib′ing, *adj.*
un·bricked′, *adj.*
un·bridge′a·ble, *adj.*
un·bridged′, *adj.*
un·brief′, *adj.;* **-ly,** *adv.;* **-ness,** *n.*
un·briefed′, *adj.*
un·bright′, *adj.;* **-ly,** *adv.;* **-ness,** *n.*
un·bright′ened, *adj.*
un·bril′liant, *adj.;* **-ly,** *adv.;* **-ness,** *n.*
un·brim′ming, *adj.*
un·brined′, *adj.*
un·bris′tled, *adj.*
un·brit′tle, *adj.;* **-ness,** *n.*
un·broached′, *adj.*
un·broad′cast′, *adj.*
un·broad′cast′ed, *adj.*
un·broad′ened, *adj.*
un′bro·cad′ed, *adj.*
un·broiled′, *adj.*
un·bronzed′, *adj.*
un·brooch′, *v.t.*
un·brood′ed, *adj.*
un·brood′ing, *adj.*
un·broth′ered, *adj.*
un·broth′er·li·ness, *n.*
un·broth′er·ly, *adj., adv.*
un·brought′, *adj.*
un·browned′, *adj.*
un·brows′ing, *adj.*
un·bruised′, *adj.*
un·brush′a·ble, *adj.*
un·brushed′, *adj.*
un·bru′tal·ise′, *v.t.,* **-ised, -is·ing.**
un·bru′tal·ize′, *v.t.,* **-ized, -iz·ing.**
un·brut′ise, *v.t.,* **-ised, -is·ing.**
un·brut′ize, *v.t.,* **-ized, -iz·ing.**
un·bud′, *v.t.,* **-bud·ded, -bud·ding.**
un·budged′, *adj.*
un·budg′et·ed, *adj.*
un·budg′ing, *adj.*
un·buffed′, *adj.*
un·buf′fered, *adj.*
un·buf′fet·ed, *adj.*
un·bul′lied, *adj.*
un·bul′ly·ing, *adj.*
un·bumped′, *adj.*
un·bump′tious, *adj.;* **-ly,** *adv.;* **-ness,** *n.*
un·bunched′, *adj.*
un·bun′dled, *adj.*
un·bun′gling, *adj.*
un·buoy′ant, *adj.;* **-ly,** *adv.*
un·buoyed′, *adj.*
un′bu·reau·crat′ic, *adj.*
un′bu·reau·crat′i·cal·ly, *adv.*
un·bur′den·some, *adj.*
un·bur′glar·ized′, *adj.*
un·bur′ied, *adj.*
un′bur·lesqued′, *adj.*
un·bur′ly, *adj.*
un·burn′a·ble, *adj.*
un·burned′, *adj.*
un·burn′ing, *adj.*
un·bur′nished, *adj.*
un·burnt′, *adj.*
un·bur′rowed, *adj.*
un·burst′, *adj.*
un·burst′a·ble, *adj.*
un·bus′i·ly, *adv.*
un·busi′ness·like′, *adj.*
un·bus′kined, *adj.*
un·bus′tling, *adj.*
un·butch′ered, *adj.*
un·but′tered, *adj.*
un·but′tressed, *adj.*
un·buy′a·ble, *adj.*
un·buy′ing, *adj.*
un·cab′ined, *adj.*
un·ca′bled, *adj.*
un′ca·coph′o·nous, *adj.*
un·ca′denced, *adj.*
un′ca·jol′ing, *adj.*
un·cake′, *v.t.,* **-caked, -cak·ing.**
un′ca·lam′i·tous, *adj.;* **-ly,** *adv.*
un′cal·car′e·ous, *adj.*
un·cal′ci·fied′, *adj.*
un·cal′cined, *adj.*
un·cal′cu·la·ble, *adj.;* **-bly,** *adv.*
un·cal′cu·lat′ed, *adj.*
un·cal′cu·lat′ing, *adj.;* **-ly,** *adv.*
un·cal′cu·la′tive, *adj.*
un·cal′en·dared, *adj.*
un·cal′i·brat′ed, *adj.*
un·calk′, *v.t.*
un·calked′, *adj.*
un·called′, *adj.*
un·cal′lous, *adj.;* **-ly,** *adv.;* **-ness,** *n.*
un·cal′lused, *adj.*
un·calm′, *adj.;* **-ly,** *adv.;* **-ness,** *n.*
un·cal′ma·tive, *adj.*
un′cal·o·rif′ic, *adj.*
un′ca·lum′ni·a′tive, *adj.*
un′ca·lum′ni·ous, *adj.;* **-ly,** *adv.*
un·cam′bered, *adj.*
un·cam′ou·flaged′, *adj.*
un′cam·paign′ing, *adj.*
un·camped′, *adj.*
un·cam′phor·at′ed, *adj.*
un′ca·nal′ized, *adj.*
un·can′cel·a·ble, *adj.*
un·can′celed, *adj.*
un·can′cel·la·ble, *adj.*
un·can′celled, *adj.*
un·can′cer·ous, *adj.*
un·can′did, *adj.;* **-ly,** *adv.;* **-ness,** *n.*
un·can′died, *adj.*
un·can′dled, *adj.*
un·caned′, *adj.*
un·can′kered, *adj.*
un·canned′, *adj.*
un·can′on·i·sa′tion, *n.*
un·can′on·ise, *v.t.,* **-ised, -is·ing.**
un·can′on·i·za′tion, *n.*
un·can′on·ize, *v.t.,* **-ized, -iz·ing.**
un·can′o·pied′, *adj.*
un·can′toned, *adj.*
un·can′vassed, *adj.*
un′ca·pa′cious, *adj.;* **-ly,** *adv.;* **-ness,** *n.*
un′ca·par′i·soned, *adj.*
un·caped′, *adj.*
un·ca′per·ing, *adj.*
un·cap′i·tal·ised′, *adj.*
un′cap·i·tal·is′tic, *adj.*
un·cap′i·tal·ized′, *adj.*
un′ca·pit′u·lat′ed, *adj.*
un′ca·pit′u·la′ting, *adj.*
un′ca·pri′cious, *adj.;* **-ly,** *adv.;* **-ness,** *n.*
un′cap·siz′a·ble, *adj.*
un′cap·sized′, *adj.*
un·cap′suled, *adj.*
un·cap′tained, *adj.*
un·cap′tioned, *adj.*
un·cap′tious, *adj.;* **-ly,** *adv.;* **-ness,** *n.*
un·cap′ti·vat′ed, *adj.*
un·cap′ti·vat′ing, *adj.*
un·cap′ti·va′tive, *adj.*
un·cap′tur·a·ble, *adj.*
un·cap′tured, *adj.*
un·car′a·mel·ised′, *adj.*
un·car′a·mel·ized′, *adj.*
un·car′bon·at′ed, *adj.*
un·car′bon·ized′, *adj.*
un·car′bu·ret′ed, *adj.*
un·car′bu·ret′ted, *adj.*
un·card′ed, *adj.*
un·car′di·nal·ly, *adv.*
un′ca·ressed′, *adj.*
un′ca·ress′ing, *adj.;* **-ly,** *adv.*
un·car′i·ca·tured, *adj.*
un·car′ing, *adj.*
un′car·niv′o·rous, *adj.;* **-ly,** *adv.;* **-ness,** *n.*
un·car′oled, *adj.*
un·car′olled, *adj.*
un′ca·rous′ing, *adj.*
un·car′pen·tered, *adj.*
un·car′pet·ed, *adj.*
un·car′ried, *adj.*
un·cart′ed, *adj.*
un′car·tooned′, *adj.*
un·carved′, *adj.*
un·cas′cad′ed, *adj.*
un·cas′cad′ing, *adj.*
un·case′mat·ed, *adj.*
un·cashed′, *adj.*
un·cask′, *v.t.*
un·casked′, *adj.*
un·cas′ket·ed, *adj.*
un·cast′, *adj.*
un·cas′ti·gat′ed, *adj.*
un·cas′ti·ga′tive, *adj.*
un·cas′tled, *adj.*
un·cas′trat·ed, *adj.*
un·cas′u·al, *adj.;* **-ly,** *adv.;* **-ness,** *n.*
un·cat′a·loged′, *adj.*
un·cat′a·logued′, *adj.*
un′cat·a·stroph′ic, *adj.*
un′cat·a·stroph′i·cal·ly, *adv.*
un·catch′a·ble, *adj.*
un·cat′e·chized′, *adj.*
un′cat·e·gor′i·cal, *adj.;* **-ly,** *adv.;* **-ness,** *n.*
un·cat′e·go·rised′, *adj.*
un·cat′e·go·rized′, *adj.*
un·cat′e·nat′ed, *adj.*
un·ca′tered, *adj.*
un·ca′ter·ing, *adj.*
un′ca·thar′tic, *adj.*
un·cath′o·lic, *adj.*
un′ca·thol′i·cal, *adj.*
un′ca·thol′i·cise′, *v.t.,* **-cised, -cis·ing.**
un′cath·o·lic′i·ty, *n.*
un′ca·thol′i·cize′, *v.t.,* **-cized, -ciz·ing.**
un·caught′, *adj.*
un·caus′a·ble, *adj.*
un·caus′al, *adj.*
un·caus′a·tive, *adj.;* **-ly,** *adv.;* **-ness,** *n.*
un·caus′tic, *adj.*
un·caus′ti·cal·ly, *adv.*
un·cau′ter·ized′, *adj.*
un·cau′tioned, *adj.*
un·cau′tious, *adj.;* **-ly,** *adv.;* **-ness,** *n.*
un·cav′a·lier′, *adj.;* **-ly,** *adv.*
un·cav′ern·ous, *adj.;* **-ly,** *adv.*
un·cav′il·ing, *adj.*
un·cav′il·ling, *adj.*
un·cav′i·tied, *adj.*
un·ceased′, *adj.*
un·ceas′ing, *adj.;* **-ly,** *adv.;* **-ness,** *n.*
un·ced′ed, *adj.*
un·ceil′inged, *adj.*
un·cel′e·brat′ed, *adj.*
un·cel′e·brat′ing, *adj.*
un′ce·les′tial, *adj.*
un·cel′i·bate, *adj.*
un·cen′sor·a·ble, *adj.*
un·cen′sored, *adj.*
un′cen·so′ri·ous, *adj.;* **-ly,** *adv.;* **-ness,** *n.*
un·cen′sur·a·ble, *adj.*
un·cen′sured, *adj.*
un·cen′sur·ing, *adj.*
un·cen′tered, *adj.*
un·cen′tral, *adj.;* **-ly,** *adv.*
un·cen′tral·ised′, *adj.*
un·cen′tral·ized′, *adj.*
un·cen′tred, *adj.*
un·cen′tric, *adj.*
un·cen′tri·cal, *adj.*
un′cen·trip′e·tal, *adj.*
un′ce·phal′ic, *adj.*
un·ce′rat·ed, *adj.*
un·cer′e·bric, *adj.*
un′cer·e·mo′ni·al, *adj.;* **-ly,** *adv.*

monious observance of a holiday. **2.** abrupt, as with less than the normal courtesy; hasty; rude: *He turned on his heel with unceremonious abruptness.* [UN-[1] + CEREMONIOUS] —**un′cer·e·mo′ni·ous·ly,** *adv.* —**un′cer·e·mo′ni·ous·ness,** *n.*

un·cer·tain (un sûr′tən), *adj.* **1.** not definitely ascertainable or fixed, as in time of occurrence, number, dimensions, quality, or the like. **2.** not confident, assured, or free from hesitancy: *an uncertain smile.* **3.** not clearly or precisely determined; indefinite; unknown: *a manuscript of uncertain origin.* **4.** vague; indistinct; not perfectly apprehended: *an abstruse novel with uncertain themes.* **5.** subject to change; variable; capricious; unstable: *a person of uncertain opinions.* **6.** ambiguous; unreliable; undependable: *His loyalties are uncertain.* **7.** dependent on chance or unpredictable factors; doubtful; of unforeseeable outcome or effect. **8.** unsteady or flickering, as light; of changing intensity or quality. [ME; see UN-[1], CERTAIN] —**un·cer′tain·ly,** *adv.* —**un·cer′tain·ness,** *n.*
—**Syn. 1.** unsure, unpredictable. UNCERTAIN, INSECURE, PRECARIOUS imply a lack of predictability. That which is UNCERTAIN is doubtful or problematical; it often involves danger through an inability to predict or to place confidence in the unknown: *The time of his arrival is uncertain.* That which is INSECURE is not firm, stable, reliable, or safe, and hence is likely to give way, fail, or be overcome: *an insecure foundation, footing, protection.* PRECARIOUS suggests great susceptibility to failure, or exposure to imminent danger: *precarious means of existence.* **3.** unsettled, undetermined. **8.** irregular.

un·cer·tain·ty (un sûr′tən tē), *n., pl.* **-ties. 1.** the state of being uncertain; doubt; hesitancy: *His uncertainty gave impetus to his inquiry.* **2.** an instance of uncertainty, doubt, etc.: *His clearing of the throat meant uncertainty.* **3.** unpredictability; indeterminacy; indefiniteness. [ME; see UN-[1], CERTAINTY]

uncer′tainty prin′ciple, *Physics.* the principle of quantum mechanics, formulated by Heisenberg, that the accurate measurement of one of two related, observable quantities, as position and momentum or energy and time, produces uncertainties in the measurement of the other, such that the product of the uncertainties of both quantities is equal to or greater than $h/2\pi$, where h equals Planck's constant. Also called **indeterminacy principle, Heisenberg uncertainty principle.**

un·chain (un chān′), *v.t.* to free from or as from chains; set free. [UN-[2] + CHAIN]

un·chan·cy (un chan′sē, -chän′-), *adj. Chiefly Scot.* **1.** unlucky. **2.** dangerous. [UN-[1] + CHANCY]

un·charge (un chärj′), *v.t.,* **-charged, -charg·ing.** *Obs.* **1.** to free from a load; unload. **2.** to acquit. [ME; see UN-[2], CHARGE]

un·charged (un chärjd′), *adj.* not charged, esp. with electricity; electrically neutral: *an uncharged battery; an uncharged particle.* [ME; see UN-[1], CHARGED]

un·char·i·ta·ble (un char′i tə bəl), *adj.* deficient in charity; unkind; harsh; unforgiving; censorious; merciless: *an uncharitable attitude; an uncharitable remark.* [ME; see UN-[1], CHARITABLE] —**un·char′i·ta·ble·ness,** *n.* —**un·char′i·ta·bly,** *adv.*

un·chart·ed (un chär′tid), *adj.* not shown or located on a map; unexplored; unknown, as a place or region: *the uncharted depths of space.* [UN-[1] + CHART + -ED[2]]

un·char·tered (un chär′tərd), *adj.* **1.** without a charter. **2.** without regulation; lawless. [UN-[1] + CHARTER + -ED[2]]

un·chaste (un chāst′), *adj.* **1.** not chaste; not virtuous; not pure: *an unchaste woman.* **2.** characterized by sexual suggestiveness, transgression, or excess; lascivious; bawdy: *an unchaste exhibition.* [ME; see UN-[1], CHASTE] —**un·chaste′ly,** *adv.* —**un·chaste′ness, un·chas·ti·ty** (un chas′ti tē), *n.*

un·chris·tian (un kris′chən), *adj.* **1.** not Christian. **2.** unworthy of Christians. **3.** not conforming to Christian teaching or principles: *an unchristian haughtiness.* [UN-[1] + CHRISTIAN] —**un·chris′tian·ly,** *adv.*

un·church (un chûrch′), *v.t.* **1.** to expel (individuals) from a church; excommunicate. **2.** to deprive of the character and rights of a church. [UN-[2] + CHURCH]

un·churched (un chûrcht′), *adj.* not being a member of a church; not attending any church. [UN-[1] + CHURCH + -ED[2]]

un·ci·a (un′shē ə), *n., pl.* **-ci·ae** (-shē ē′). **1.** a bronze coin of ancient Rome, the 12th part of an as. **2.** (in prescriptions) an ounce of weight or volume. [< L; c. Gk *ounkía*]

un·ci·al (un′shē əl, -shəl), *adj.* **1.** designating, written in, or pertaining to a form of majuscule writing having more curves than capitals have and used chiefly in Greek and Latin manuscripts from about the 3rd to the 9th century A.D. —*n.* **2.** an uncial letter. **3.** uncial writing. **4.** a manuscript written in uncials. [< L *unciāl(is).* See UNCIA, -AL[1]] —**un′ci·al·ly,** *adv.*

Uncials (Latin), 8th century

un·ci·form (un′sə fôrm′), *adj.* **1.** hook-shaped. —*n.* **2.** *Anat.* hamate (def. 3). [< NL *unciform(is),* equiv. to L *unc(us)* a hook, barb (c. Gk *ónkos*) + *-formis* -FORM]

un′ciform proc′ess, *Anat.* a hooklike process of a bone, esp. the hamate.

un·ci·na·ri·a·sis (un′sə nə rī′ə sis), *n. Pathol.* hookworm (def. 2). [< NL *Uncinār(ia)* name of the genus (L *uncīn(us)* (see UNCINUS) + *-āria* -ARIA) + *-iasis* -IASIS]

Uncinate prickles

un·ci·nate (un′sə nit, -nāt′), *adj. Biol.* hooked; bent at the end like a hook. [< L *uncīnāt(us)* furnished with hooks, equiv. to *uncīn(us)* (see UNCINUS) + *-ātus* -ATE[1]]

un′cinate proc′ess, *Ornith.* a curved, bony process on certain ribs of birds that projects backward and overlaps the succeeding rib, serving to strengthen the thorax.

un·ci·nus (un sī′nəs), *adj. Meteorol.* (of a cloud) having elements in the form of a comma. [< NL, L: hooked < Gk *onkínos* hook, deriv. of *ónkos* barb (of an arrow)]

UNCIO, United Nations Conference on International Organization.

un·cir·cum·cised (un sûr′kəm sīzd′), *adj.* **1.** not circumcised. **2.** not Jewish; Gentile. **3.** heathen; unregenerate. [ME; see UN-[1], CIRCUMCISED]

un·cir·cum·ci·sion (un′sûr kəm sizh′ən), *n.* **1.** condition of being uncircumcised. **2.** people who are not circumcised; gentiles. Rom. 2:26. [UN-[1] + CIRCUMCISION]

un·civ·il (un siv′əl), *adj.* **1.** without good manners; unmannerly; rude; impolite; discourteous. **2.** uncivilized. [UN-[1] + CIVIL] —**un·ci·vil·i·ty** (un′si vil′i tē), **un·civ′il·ness,** *n.* —**un·civ′il·ly,** *adv.*
—**Syn. 1.** disrespectful, uncouth, boorish.

un·civ·i·lized (un siv′ə līzd′), *adj.* barbarous; unenlightened. Also, *esp. Brit.,* **un·civ′i·lised′.** [UN-[1] + CIVILIZED] —**un·civ·i·liz·ed·ly;** *esp. Brit.,* **un·civ·i·lis·ed·ly** (un siv′ə lī′zid lē, -līzd′-), *adv.* —**un·civ′i·liz′ed·ness;** *esp. Brit.,* **un·civ′i·lis′ed·ness,** *n.*

un·clad (un klad′), *v.* **1.** a pt. and pp. of **unclothe.** —*adj.* **2.** naked; nude; undressed.

un·clasp (un klasp′, -kläsp′), *v.t.* **1.** to undo the clasp or clasps of; unfasten. **2.** to release from the grasp: *to unclasp a sword handle.* —*v.i.* **3.** to become unclasped, as the hands, arms, etc. **4.** to release or relax the grasp. [UN-[2] + CLASP]

un·clas·si·cal (un klas′i kəl), *adj.* **1.** not classical or contrary to classical precepts. **2.** *Physics.* pertaining to a law, theory, or observation that cannot be expressed or understood in terms of Newtonian physics. [UN-[1] + CLASSICAL] —**un·clas′si·cal·ly,** *adv.*

un·clas·si·fied (un klas′ə fīd′), *adj.* **1.** not assigned to a class or category; not arranged according to characteristics: *Reported instances fall into two main types, with a few unclassified anomalies.* **2.** (of data, documents, etc.) not belonging to a category that is restricted for reasons of military security; not secret: *unclassified plans; unclassified information.* [UN-[1] + CLASSIFIED]

un·cle (ung′kəl), *n.* **1.** a brother of one's father or mother. **2.** an aunt's husband. **3.** a familiar title applied to any elderly man. **4.** *Slang.* a pawnbroker. **5.** a word formerly used in communications to represent the letter U. **6. say uncle,** *Slang.* to concede defeat; submit: *They ganged up on him in the schoolyard and made him say uncle.* [ME < AF *uncle,* OF *oncle* < L *avunculus* mother's brother, equiv. to *av(us)* grandfather + *-unculus* double dim. suffix] —**un′cle·less,** *adj.* —**un′cle·ship′,** *n.*

un·clean (un klēn′), *adj.* **1.** not clean; dirty. **2.** morally impure; evil; vile: *an unclean attitude.* **3.** *Chiefly Biblical.* having a physical or moral blemish so as to make impure according to the laws, esp. the dietary or ceremonial laws: *an unclean animal; unclean persons.* [ME *unclene,* OE *unclǣne.* See UN-[1], CLEAN] —**un·clean′ness,** *n.*
—**Syn. 1.** soiled, filthy. **2.** base, impure, unchaste, sinful, corrupt, polluted.

un·clean·ly[1] (un klēn′lē), *adv.* in an unclean manner. [ME *onclenlich,* OE *unclǣnlīc.* See UNCLEAN, -LY]

un·clean·ly[2] (un klen′lē), *adj.* not cleanly; unclean. [OE *unclǣnlīche.* See UN-[1], CLEANLY] —**un·clean′li·ness,** *n.*

un·clench (un klench′), *v.t., v.i.* to open or become opened from a clenched state. [ME *unclainte.* See UN-[2], CLENCH]

Un′cle Re′mus (rē′məs), a character in several books by Joel Chandler Harris: an old plantation Negro who tells animal tales to a little boy.

Un′cle Sam′, a personification of the government or people of the U.S.: represented as a tall, lean man with white chin whiskers, wearing a blue tailcoat, red-and-white-striped trousers, and a top hat with a band of stars. [extension of the initials U.S.]

Un′cle Tom′, (*sometimes l.c.*) *Contemptuous.* a Negro who is abjectly servile or deferential to whites. Also called **Tom.** [so called after the leading character in *Uncle Tom's Cabin*]

Un′cle Tom′ism (tom′iz əm), a policy of relationship between whites and Negroes involving a benevolent but patronizing attitude on the part of the whites and a willingly submissive attitude on the part of the Negroes. [UNCLE TOM + -ISM]

Un′cle Tom's′ Cab′in, an antislavery novel (1852) by Harriet Beecher Stowe.

Un′cle Van′ya (vän′yə), a play (1897) by Anton Chekhov.

un·clinch (un klinch′), *v.t., v.i.* to unclench.

un·cloak (un klōk′), *v.t.* **1.** to remove the cloak from. **2.** to reveal; expose: *His motives were uncloaked at last.* —*v.i.* **3.** to take off the cloak or the outer garments generally. [UN-[2] + CLOAK]

un·clog (un klog′), *v.t.,* **-clogged, -clog·ging.** to free of an obstruction or impediment: *to unclog a drain; to unclog a traffic artery.* [UN-[2] + CLOG]

un·close (un klōz′), *v.t., v.i.,* **-closed, -clos·ing.** to bring or come out of a closed state; open. [ME *unclose(n).* See UN-[2], CLOSE]

un·clothe (un klōth′), *v.t.,* **-clothed** or **-clad, -cloth·ing. 1.** to strip of clothes. **2.** to remove a covering from; lay bare, as by removing garments. [ME *unclothe(n).* See UN-[2], CLOTHE]

un·co (ung′kō), *adj., adv., n., pl.* **-cos.** *Scot. and North Eng.* —*adj.* **1.** remarkable; extraordinary. **2.** unusual; strange. **3.** uncanny. —*adv.* **4.** remarkably; extremely. —*n.* **5.** something extraordinary or unusual;

un′ce·rif′er·ous, *adj.*
un·cer′ti·fi′a·ble, *adj.;* **-ly,** *adv.*
un′cer·tif′i·cat′ed, *adj.*
un·cer′ti·fied′, *adj.*
un·cer′ti·fy′ing, *adj.*
un·cer′ti·tude′, *adj.*
un·chafed′, *adj.*
un·chaffed′, *adj.*
un·chaff′ing, *adj.*
un′cha·grined′, *adj.*
un·chain′a·ble, *adj.*
un·chained′, *adj.*
un·chair′, *v.t.*
un·chalked′, *adj.*
un·chalk′y, *adj.*
un·chal′lenge·a·ble, *adj.;* **-bly,** *adv.*
un·chal′lenged, *adj.*
un·chal′leng·ing, *adj.*
un·cham′bered, *adj.*
un·cham′fered, *adj.*
un·cham′pi·oned, *adj.*
un·chanced′, *adj.*
un·chance′a·ble, *adj.*
un·change′a·bil′i·ty, *n.*
un·change′a·ble, *adj.;* **-bly,** *adv.*
un·changed′, *adj.*
un·change′ful, *adj.;* **-ly,** *adv.;* **-ness,** *n.*
un·chang′ing, *adj.;* **-ly,** *adv.;* **-ness,** *n.*
un·chan′neled, *adj.*
un·chan′nel·ized′, *adj.*
un·chan′nelled, *adj.*
un·chant′ed, *adj.*
un·cha·ot′ic, *adj.*
un′cha·ot′i·cal·ly, *adv.*
un·chap′er·oned′, *adj.*
un·chap′let·ed, *adj.*
un·chapped′, *adj.*
un·chap′ter, *v.t.*
un·chap′tered, *adj.*
un·char′ac·tered, *adj.*
un·char′ac·ter·ised′, *adj.*
un′char·ac·ter·is′tic, *adj.*
un′char·ac·ter·is′ti·cal·ly, *adv.*
un·char′ac·ter·ized′, *adj.*
un·charge′a·ble, *adj.*
un·char′i·ly, *adv.*
un·char′i·ot, *v.t.*
un·char′i·ta·ble, *adj.;* **-ble·ness,** *n.;* **-bly,** *adv.*
un·charm′a·ble, *adj.*
un·charmed′, *adj.*
un·charm′ing, *adj.*
un·charred′, *adj.*
un·char′y, *adj.*
un·chased′, *adj.*
un·chas′tened, *adj.*
un′chas·tis′a·ble, *adj.*
un·chas′tised, *adj.*
un·chas′tis·ing, *adj.*
un·chat′ter·ing, *adj.*
un·chauf′feured, *adj.*
un′chau·vin·is′tic, *adj.*
un·cheap′ened, *adj.*
un·cheap′ly, *adv.*
un·cheat′ed, *adj.*
un·cheat′ing, *adj.*
un·check′a·ble, *adj.*
un·checked′, *adj.*
un·check′ered, *adj.*
un·check′mat′ed, *adj.*
un·cheer′a·ble, *adj.*
un·cheered′, *adj.*
un·cheer′ful, *adj.;* **-ly,** *adv.;* **-ness,** *n.*
un·cheer′i·ly, *adv.*
un·cheer′i·ness, *n.*
un·cheer′ing, *adj.*
un·cheer′y, *adj.*
un·chem′i·cal, *adj.;* **-ly,** *adv.*
un·cher′ished, *adj.*
un·cher′ish·ing, *adj.*
un·chest′ed, *adj.*
un·chev′roned, *adj.*
un·chew′a·ble, *adj.*
un·chewed′, *adj.*
un·chid′, *adj.*
un·chid′den, *adj.*
un·chid′ed, *adj.*
un·chid′ing, *adj.;* **-ly,** *adv.*
un·child′ish, *adj.;* **-ly,** *adv.;* **-ness,** *n.*
un·child′like′, *adj.*
un·chilled′, *adj.*
un·chim′ing, *adj.*
un·chinked′, *adj.*
un·chip′pa·ble, *adj.*
un·chipped′, *adj.*
un·chip′ping, *adj.*
un·chis′eled, *adj.*
un·chis′elled, *adj.*
un·chiv′al·ric, *adj.*
un·chiv′al·rous, *adj.;* **-ly,** *adv.;* **-ness,** *n.*
un·chiv′al·ry, *n.*
un·chlo′ri·dized′, *adj.*
un·chlo′ri·nat′ed, *adj.*
un·chok′a·ble, *adj.*
un·choked′, *adj.*
un·chol′er·ic, *adj.*
un·choos′a·ble, *adj.*
un·chopped′, *adj.*
un·cho′sen, *adj.*
un·chris′tened, *adj.*
un·Chris′tian·ise′, *v.t.,* **-ised, -is·ing.**
un·Chris′tian·ize′, *v.t.,* **-ized, -iz·ing.**
un·Chris′tian·like′, *adj.*
un·Chris′tian·ly, *adj.*
un·Christ′mas·like′, *adj.*
un′chro·mat′ic, *adj.*
un·chromed′, *adj.*
un·chron′ic, *adj.*
un·chron′i·cal·ly, *adv.*
un·chron′i·cled, *adj.*
un′chron·o·log′i·cal, *adj.;* **-ly,** *adv.*
un·church′ly, *adj.*
un·churl′ish, *adj.;* **-ly,** *adv.;* **-ness,** *n.*
un·churn′, *v.t.*
un·churned′, *adj.*
un·cil′i·at′ed, *adj.*
un·cinch′, *v.t.*
un·cinc′tured, *adj.*
un·cir′cled, *adj.*
un′cir·cu′i·tous, *adj.;* **-ly,** *adv.;* **-ness,** *n.*
un·cir′cu·lar, *adj.;* **-ly,** *adv.*
un·cir′cu·lar·ised′, *adj.*
un·cir′cu·lar·ized′, *adj.*
un·cir′cu·lat′ed, *adj.*
un·cir′cu·lat′ing, *adj.*
un·cir′cu·la·tive, *adj.*
un′cir·cum·loc′u·to′ry, *adj.*
un′cir·cum·scrib′a·ble, *adj.*
un·cir′cum·scribed′, *adj.*
un·cir′cum·spect′, *adj.;* **-ly,** *adv.;* **-ness,** *n.*
un′cir·cum·spec′tive, *adj.*
un′cir·cum·stan′tial, *adj.;* **-ly,** *adv.*
un′cir·cum·vent′ed, *adj.*
un·cit′a·ble, *adj.*
un·cite′a·ble, *adj.*
un·cit′ed, *adj.*
un·cit′ied, *adj.*
un·cit′i·zen·like′, *adj.*
un·cit′i·zen·ly, *adj.*
un·civ′ic, *adj.*
un·civ′i·lis′a·ble, *adj.*
un·civ′i·liz′a·ble, *adj.*
un·civ′i·lize′, *v.t.,* **-lized, -liz·ing.**
un·claimed′, *adj.*
un·claim′ing, *adj.*
un·clam′or·ous, *adj.;* **-ly,** *adv.;* **-ness,** *n.*
un·clamped′, *adj.*
un′clan·des′tine·ly, *adv.*
un·clan′nish, *adj.;* **-ly,** *adv.;* **-ness,** *n.*
un·clar′i·fied′, *adj.*
un·clar′i·fy′ing, *adj.*
un·clar′i·ty, *n.*
un·clash′ing, *adj.*
un·class′a·ble, *adj.*
un·classed′, *adj.*
un·clas′si·fi′a·ble, *adj.;* **-ble·ness,** *n.;* **-bly,** *adv.*
un·clas′si·fy′ing, *adj.*
un·clawed′, *adj.*
un·clayed′, *adj.*
un·clean′a·ble, *adj.*
un·cleaned′, *adj.*
un·cleans′a·ble, *adj.*
un·cleansed′, *adj.*
un·clear′, *adj.;* **-ly,** *adv.*
un·clear′a·ble, *adj.*
un·cleared′, *adj.*
un·clear′ing, *adj.*
un·cleav′a·ble, *adj.*
un·cleft′, *adj.*
un·cler′i·cal, *adj.;* **-ly,** *adv.*
un·clerk′ly, *adj.*
un·clev′er, *adj.;* **-ly,** *adv.;* **-ness,** *n.*
un′cli·mac′tic, *adj.*
un·cli′maxed, *adj.*
un·climb′a·ble, *adj.*
un·climbed′, *adj.*
un·climb′ing, *adj.*
un·cling′ing, *adj.*
un·clin′i·cal, *adj.*
un·clip′, *v.t.,* **-clipped, -clip·ping.**
un·clip′per, *n.*
un·clois′tered, *adj.*
un·clois′tral, *adj.*
un·clos′a·ble, *adj.*
un·clos′et·ed, *adj.*
un·clot′ted, *adj.*
un·cloud′ed, *adj.*
un·cloud′y, *adj.*
un·clo′ven, *adj.*
un·cloyed′, *adj.*
un·cloy′ing, *adj.*
un·clus′tered, *adj.*
un·clus′ter·ing, *adj.*
un·clutch′a·ble, *adj.*
un·clutched′, *adj.*
un·clut′ter, *v.t.*
un·clut′tered, *adj.*

novelty. **6. uncos,** news. **7.** *Obs.* a stranger. [var. of UNCOUTH]

un·coil (un koil′), *v.t., v.i.* to unwind from a coiled position. [UN-^{2} + COIL^1]

un·com·fort·a·ble (un kumf′tə bəl, -kum′fər tə bəl), *adj.* **1.** causing discomfort or distress; painful; irritating. **2.** in a state of discomfort; uneasy; conscious of stress or strain. [UN-^{1} + COMFORTABLE] **—un·com′fort·a·ble·ness,** *n.* **—un·com′fort·a·bly,** *adv.*

un·com·mer·cial (un′kə mûr′shəl), *adj.* **1.** not engaged in or involved with commerce or trade. **2.** not in accordance with commercial principles or practices. [UN-^{1} + COMMERCIAL]

un·com·mit·ted (un′kə mit′id), *adj.* not committed, esp. not pledged or bound to follow a prescribed course of action: *uncommitted delegates; uncommitted reserves.* [UN-^{1} + COMMITTED]

un·com·mon (un kom′ən), *adj.* **1.** not common; unusual; rare: *an uncommon word.* **2.** unusual in amount or degree; above the ordinary: *an uncommon amount of mail.* **3.** exceptional or remarkable; outstanding. [UN-^{1} + COMMON] **—un·com′mon·ness,** *n.*
—Syn. 1. scarce, infrequent; odd, singular, strange, peculiar, queer. **2.** extraordinary.

un·com·mon·ly (un kom′ən lē), *adv.* **1.** in an uncommon or unusual manner or degree. **2.** exceptionally; outstandingly. **3.** rarely; infrequently. [UNCOMMON + -LY]

un·com·mu·ni·ca·tive (un′kə myōō′nə kā′tiv, -nə kə tiv), *adj.* not disposed to impart information, opinions, etc.; reserved; taciturn. [UN-^{1} + COMMUNICATIVE] **—un′com·mu′ni·ca′tive·ly,** *adv.* **—un′com·mu′ni·ca′tive·ness,** *n.*

un·com·pro·mis·ing (un kom′prə mī′zing), *adj.* **1.** not admitting of compromise or adjustment of differences; making no concessions; inaccessible to flexible bargaining; unyielding: *an uncompromising attitude.* **2.** without reservation or exception; undeviating; absolute, as believing in or adhering to a principle, position, or the like: *an uncompromising abolitionist.* [UN-^{1} + COMPROMISING] **—un·com′pro·mis′ing·ly,** *adv.* **—un·com′pro·mis′ing·ness,** *n.*
—Syn. 1. rigid, firm, steadfast, obstinate.

un·con·cern (un′kən sûrn′), *n.* lack of concern; freedom from anxiety; absence of feeling or show of solicitude; indifference. [UN-^{1} + CONCERN]
—Syn. nonchalance, insouciance. See **indifference.**

un·con·cerned (un′kən sûrnd′), *adj.* **1.** not involved or interested; disinterested. **2.** not caring; unworried; free from solicitude or anxiety. [UN-^{1} + CONCERNED] **—un·con·cern·ed·ly** (un′kən sûr′nid lē), *adv.* **—un′con·cern′ed·ness,** *n.*

un·con·di·tion·al (un′kən dish′ə nəl), *adj.* **1.** not limited by conditions; absolute: *an unconditional promise.* **2.** *Math.* absolute (def. 11). [UN-^{1} + CONDITIONAL] **—un′con·di′tion·al·ly,** *adv.* **—un′con·di′tion·al·ness, un′con·di′tion·al′i·ty,** *n.*
—Syn. 1. complete, unqualified, categorical.

uncondi′tional conver′gence. *Math.* **1.** the property of a convergent infinite series that remains convergent when the terms are arranged in any order. **2.** See **absolute convergence.**

un·con·di·tioned (un′kən dish′ənd), *adj.* **1.** not subject to conditions; absolute. **2.** *Psychol.* not proceeding from or dependent on a conditioning of the individual; natural; innate. Cf. **conditioned** (def. 3). [UN-^{1} + CONDITIONED] **—un′con·di′tioned·ness,** *n.*

un·con·form·a·ble (un′kən fôr′mə bəl), *adj.* **1.** not conformable; not conforming. **2.** *Geol.* indicating discontinuity of any type in stratigraphic sequence. [UN-^{1} + CONFORMABLE] **—un′con·form′a·bil′i·ty,** *n.* **—un′con·form′a·bly,** *adv.*

un·con·form·i·ty (un′kən fôr′mi tē), *n., pl.* **-ties. 1.** lack of conformity; incongruity; inconsistency. **2.** *Geol.* **a.** a discontinuity in rock sequence indicating interruption of sedimentation, commonly accompanied by erosion of rocks below the break. **b.** the interface between such strata. [UN-^{1} + CONFORMITY]

un·con·nec·ted (un′kə nek′tid), *adj.* **1.** not connected; not joined together or attached: *an unconnected wire.* **2.** without connection; not related causally, logically, etc.; incoherent: *an unconnected account of the accident.* [UN-^{1} + CONNECTED] **—un′con·nect′ed·ly,** *adv.* **—un′con·nect′ed·ness,** *n.*

un·con·scion·a·ble (un kon′shə nə bəl), *adj.* **1.** not guided by conscience; unscrupulous. **2.** not in accordance with what is just or reasonable: *unconscionable behavior.* **3.** excessive; extortionate: *an unconscionable profit.* [UN-^{1} + CONSCIONABLE] **—un·con′scion·a·ble·ness,** *n.* **—un·con′scion·a·bly,** *adv.*

un·con·scious (un kon′shəs), *adj.* **1.** not conscious; without awareness, sensation, or cognition. **2.** temporarily devoid of consciousness. **3.** not endowed with mental faculties: *the unconscious stones.* **4.** not perceived at the level of awareness; occurring below the level of conscious thought: *an unconscious impulse.* **5.** not consciously realized, planned, or done; without conscious volition or intent: *an unconscious social slight.* **—***n.* **6. the unconscious,** *Psychoanal.* the part of the mind containing the psychic material of which the ego is unaware. [UN-^{1} + CONSCIOUS] **—un·con′scious·ly,** *adv.* **—un·con′scious·ness,** *n.*

un·con·sti·tu·tion·al (un′kon sti tōō′shə nəl, -tyōō′-), *adj.* not constitutional; unauthorized by or inconsistent with the constitution, as of a country. [UN-^{1} + CONSTITUTIONAL] **—un′con·sti·tu′tion·al·ism,** *n.* **—un′con·sti·tu′tion·al′i·ty,** *n.* **—un′con·sti·tu′tion·al·ly,** *adv.*

un·con·ven·tion·al (un′kən ven′shə nəl), *adj.* not conventional; not bound by or conforming to convention, rule, or precedent; free from conventionality:

un·coach′a·ble, *adj.*
un·coached′, *adj.*
un′co·ag′u·la·ble, *adj.*
un′co·ag′u·lat′ed, *adj.*
un′co·ag′u·la′ting, *adj.*
un′co·ag′u·la′tive, *adj.*
un′co·a·les′cent, *adj.*
un·coarse′, *adj.;* **-ly,** *adv.;* **-ness,** *n.*
un·coat′, *v.t.*
un·coax′a·ble, *adj.*
un′co·ax′al, *adj.*
un·coaxed′, *adj.*
un′co·ax′i·al, *adj.*
un·coax′ing, *adj.*
un·cob′bled, *adj.*
un·cocked′, *adj.*
un·cod′dled, *adj.*
un·cod′ed, *adj.*
un·cod′i·fied′, *adj.*
un′co·erced′, *adj.*
un·cof′fin, *v.t.*
un·co′gent, *adj.;* **-ly,** *adv.*
un·cogged′, *adj.*
un·cog′ni·sa·ble, *adj.*
un·cog′ni·za·ble, *adj.*
un·cog′ni·zant, *adj.*
un·cog′nized, *adj.*
un′cog·nos′ci·bil′i·ty, *n.*
un′cog·nos′ci·ble, *adj.*
un′co·he′sive, *adj.;* **-ly,** *adv.;* **-ness,** *n.*
un·coifed′, *adj.*
un′co·in·cid′ed, *adj.*
un′co·in′ci·dent, *adj.;* **-ly,** *adv.*
un′co·in′ci·den′tal, *adj.;* **-ly,** *adv.*
un′co·in·cid′ing, *adj.*
un·coked′, *adj.*
un′col·lab′o·ra′tive, *adj.;* **-ly,** *adv.*
un′col·laps′a·ble, *adj.*
un′col·lapsed′, *adj.*
un′col·laps′i·ble, *adj.*
un·col′lar, *v.t.,* **-lared, -lar·ing.**
un·col′lat·ed, *adj.*
un′col·lect′a·ble, *adj.*
un′col·lect′ed, *adj.*
un′col·lect′i·ble, *adj.*
un′col·lec′tive, *adj.;* **-ly,** *adv.*
un′col·le′giate, *adj.*
un′col·lo′qui·al, *adj.;* **-ly,** *adv.*
un′col·lu′sive, *adj.*
un′co·lo′ni·al, *adj.*
un·col′o·nise′, *v.t.,* **-nised, -nis·ing.**
un·col′o·nize′, *v.t.,* **-nized, -niz·ing.**
un·col′or·a·ble, *adj.;* **-bly,** *adv.*
un·col′ored, *adj.;* **-ly,** *adv.;* **-ness,** *n.*
un·col′our·a·ble, *adj.;* **-bly,** *adv.*
un·col′oured, *adj.;* **-ly,** *adv.;* **-ness,** *n.*
un·comb′a·ble, *adj.*
un·com′bat·a·ble, *adj.*
un·com′bat·ant, *adj.*
un·com′bat·ed, *adj.*
un·com′ba·tive, *adj.*
un·combed′, *adj.*
un′com·bin′a·ble, *adj.;* **-bly,** *adv.*
un·com′bi·na′tion·al, *adj.*
un·com′bi·na′tive, *adj.*
un′com·bined′, *adj.*
un′com·bin′ing, *adj.*
un′com·bus′ti·ble, *adj.*
un′com·bus′tive, *adj.*
un·come′ly, *adj.*
un·com′fort·ed, *adj.*
un·com′fort·ing, *adj.*
un·com′ic, *adj.*
un·com′i·cal, *adj.;* **-ly,** *adv.*
un′com·mand′ed, *adj.*
un′com·man′der·like′, *adj.*
un′com·mem′o·rat′ed, *adj.*
un′com·mem′o·ra′tive, *adj.;* **-ly,** *adv.*
un′com·menced′, *adj.*
un′com·mend′a·ble, *adj.;* **-bly,** *adv.*
un′com·mend′a·to′ry, *adj.*
un′com·men′su·rate, *adj.;* **-ly,** *adv.*
un·com′ment·ed, *adj.*
un·com′ment·ing, *adj.*
un·com·min′gled, *adj.*
un·com′mi·nut′ed, *adj.*
un′com·mis′er·at′ed, *adj.*
un′com·mis′er·at′ing, *adj.*
un′com·mis′er·a′tive, *adj.;* **-ly,** *adv.*
un′com·mis′sioned, *adj.*
un′com·mit′ting, *adj.*
un′com·mo′di·ous, *adj.*
un·com′mon·place′, *adj.*
un′com·mu′ni·cat′ing, *adj.*
un′com·mut′a·ble, *adj.*
un′com·mu′ta·tive, *adj.;* **-ly,** *adv.;* **-ness,** *n.*
un′com·mut′ed, *adj.*
un′com·pan′ion·a·ble, *adj.*
un′com·pan′ioned, *adj.*
un·com′pa·ra·ble *adj.;* **-bleness,** *n.;* **-bly,** *adv.*
un′com·pared′, *adj.*
un′com·pass′a·ble, *adj.*
un′com·pas′sion, *n.*
un′com·pas′sion·ate, *adj.;* **-ly,** *adv.;* **-ness,** *n.*
un′com·pas′sioned, *adj.*
un′com·pel′la·ble, *adj.*
un′com·pelled′, *adj.*
un′com·pel′ling, *adj.*
un′com·pen′di·ous, *adj.*
un·com′pen·sat′ed, *adj.*
un·com′pen·sat′ing, *adj.*
un′com·pen′sa·tive, *adj.*
un′com·pen′sa·to′ry, *adj.*
un·com′pe·tent, *adj.;* **-ly,** *adv.*
un′com·pet′i·tive, *adj.;* **-ly,** *adv.;* **-ness,** *n.*
un′com·piled′, *adj.*
un′com·pla′cent, *adj.;* **-ly,** *adv.*
un′com·plained′, *adj.*
un′com·plain′ing, *adj.;* **-ly,** *adv.*
un′com·plai′sance, *n.*
un′com·plai′sant, *adj.;* **-ly,** *adv.*
un′com·ple·men′tal, *adj.;* **-ly,** *adv.*
un′com·ple·men′ta·ry, *adj.*
un·com′ple·ment′ed, *adj.*
un′com·plet′a·ble, *adj.*
un′com·plete′, *adj.;* **-ly,** *adv.;* **-ness,** *n.*
un·com′plex′, *adj.;* **-ly,** *adv.;* **-ness,** *n.*
un′com·pli′a·ble, *adj.;* **-ble·ness,** *n.;* **-bly,** *adv.*
un′com·pli′ant, *adj.;* **-ly,** *adv.*
un·com′pli·cat′ed, *adj.*
un′com·pli·men′ta·ry, *adj.*
un·com′pli·ment′ed, *adj.*
un·com′pli·ment′ing, *adj.*
un′com·ply′ing, *adj.*
un′com·port′a·ble, *adj.*
un′com·pos′a·ble, *adj.*
un′com·pose′a·ble, *adj.*
un′com·posed′, *adj.*
un′com·pound′a·ble, *adj.*
un′com·pound′ed, *adj.*
un′com·pound′ing, *adj.*
un′com·pre·hend′ed, *adj.*
un′com·pre·hend′ing, *adj.;* **-ly,** *adv.*
un′com·pre·hen′si·ble, *adj.;* **-ble·ness,** *n.;* **-bly,** *adv.*
un′com·pre·hen′sion, *n.*
un′com·pre·hen′sive, *adj.;* **-ly,** *adv.;* **-ness,** *n.*
un′com·pressed′, *adj.*
un′com·press′i·ble, *adj.*
un·com′pro·mised′, *adj.*
un′com·pul′sive, *adj.;* **-ly,** *adv.*
un′com·pul′so·ry, *adj.*
un′com·put′a·ble, *adj.;* **-ble·ness,** *n.;* **-bly,** *adv.*
un′com·put′ed, *adj.*
un′con·cat′e·nat′ed, *adj.*
un′con·cat′e·nat′ing, *adj.*
un′con·ceal′ing, *adj.;* **-ly,** *adv.*
un′con·ced′ed, *adj.*
un′con·ced′ing, *adj.*
un′con·ceit′ed, *adj.;* **-ly,** *adv.*
un′con·ceived′, *adj.*
un·con′cen·trat′ed, *adj.;* **-ly,** *adv.*
un′con·cen′tra·tive, *adj.*
un′con·cen′tric, *adj.*
un′con·cen′tri·cal·ly, *adv.*
un′con·cep′tu·al, *adj.;* **-ly,** *adv.*
un′con·cert′a·ble, *adj.*
un′con·cert′ed, *adj.;* **-ly,** *adv.*
un′con·cil′i·a·ble, *adj.*
un′con·cil′i·at′ed, *adj.*
un′con·cil′i·at′ing, *adj.*
un′con·cil′i·a′tive, *adj.*
un′con·cil′i·a·to′ry, *adj.*
un′con·clud′a·ble, *adj.*
un′con·clud′ed, *adj.*
un′con·cord′ant, *adj.;* **-ly,** *adv.*
un′con·crete′, *adj.;* **-ly,** *adv.*
un′con·cret′ed, *adj.*
un′con·curred′, *adj.*
un′con·cur′rent, *adj.;* **-ly,** *adv.*
un′con·cur′ring, *adj.*
un′con·dem′na·ble, *adj.*
un′con·demned′, *adj.*
un′con·demn′ing, *adj.;* **-ly,** *adv.*
un′con·den′sa·ble, *adj.;* **-ble·ness,** *n.;* **-bly,** *adv.*
un′con·den·sa′tion·al, *adj.*
un′con·densed′, *adj.*
un′con·dens′ing, *adj.*
un′con·des·cend′ing, *adj.;* **-ly,** *adv.*
un′con·di′tion, *v.t.*
un·con·do′la·to′ry, *adj.*
un′con·doled′, *adj.*
un′con·dol′ing, *adj.*
un′con·doned′, *adj.*
un′con·don′ing, *adj.*
un′con·duc′ing, *adj.*
un′con·du′cive, *adj.;* **-ly,** *adv.;* **-ness,** *n.*
un′con·duct′ed, *adj.*
un′con·duct′i·ble, *adj.*
un′con·duc′tive, *adj.*
un′con·fect′ed, *adj.*
un′con·fed′er·at′ed, *adj.*
un′con·ferred′, *adj.*
un′con·fessed′, *adj.*
un′con·fess′ing, *adj.*
un′con·fid′ed, *adj.*
un·con′fi·dent, *adj.;* **-ly,** *adv.*
un′con·fid′ing, *adj.*
un′con·fin′a·ble, *adj.*
un′con·fined′, *adj.*
un′con·fin′ing, *adj.*
un′con·firm′, *v.t.*
un′con·firm′a·tive, *adj.*
un′con·firm′a·to′ry, *adj.*
un·con′fis·ca·ble, *adj.*
un·con′fis·cat′ed, *adj.*
un′con·fis′ca·to′ry, *adj.*
un′con·flict′ing, *adj.;* **-ly,** *adv.*
un′con·flic′tive, *adj.*
un′con·formed′, *adj.*
un′con·form′ing, *adj.*
un′con·found′, *v.t.*
un′con·found′ed·ly, *adv.*
un′con·found′ing, *adj.;* **-ly,** *adv.*
un′con·front′a·ble, *adj.*
un′con·front′ed, *adj.*
un′con·fus′a·ble, *adj.;* **-bly,** *adv.*
un′con·fused′, *adj.*
un′con·fus′ed·ly, *adv.*
un′con·fus′ing, *adj.*
un′con·fut′a·ble, *adj.*
un′con·fut′a·tive, *adj.*
un′con·fut′ed, *adj.*
un′con·fut′ing, *adj.*
un′con·geal′, *v.i.*
un′con·geal′a·ble, *adj.*
un·con·gen′ial, *adj.;* **-ly,** *adv.*
un′con·ge′ni·al′i·ty, *n.*
un′con·gest′ed, *adj.*
un′con·ges′tive, *adj.*
un′con·glom′er·at′ed, *adj.*
un′con·glu′ti·nat′ed, *adj.*
un′con·glu′ti·na′tive, *adj.*
un′con·grat′u·lat′ed, *adj.*
un′con·grat′u·lat′ing, *adj.*
un′con·grat′u·la·to′ry, *adj.*
un·con′gre·gat′ed, *adj.*
un′con·gre·ga′tion·al, *adj.*
un·con′gre·ga′tive, *adj.*
un′con·gres′sion·al, *adj.*
un·con′gru·ous, *adj.;* **-ly,** *adv.;* **-ness,** *n.*
un·con′i·cal, *adj.*
un′con·jec′tur·a·ble, *adj.*
un′con·jec′tur·al, *adj.*
un′con·jec′tured, *adj.*
un′con·joined′, *adj.*
un·con′ju·gal, *adj.*
un·con′ju·gat′ed, *adj.*
un′con·junc′tive, *adj.*
un′con·jured, *adj.*
un·conned′, *adj.*
un′con·nived′, *adj.*
un′con·niv′ing, *adj.*
un·con′no·ta′tive, *adj.*
un·con′quer·a·ble, *adj.;* **-bly,** *adv.*
un·con′quered, *adj.*
un′con·sci·en′tious, *adj.;* **-ly,** *adv.;* **-ness,** *n.*
un·con′se·crat′ed, *adj.*
un′con·se·cra′tion, *n.*
un·con′se·cra′tive, *adj.*
un′con·sec′u·tive, *adj.;* **-ly,** *adv.*
un′con·sen·ta′ne·ous, *adj.;* **-ly,** *adv.;* **-ness,** *n.*
un′con·sen′tient, *adj.*
un′con·sent′ing, *adj.*
un′con·serv′a·ble, *adj.*
un′con·serv′a·tive, *adj.;* **-ly,** *adv.;* **-ness,** *n.*
un′con·served′, *adj.*
un′con·serv′ing, *adj.*
un′con·sid′er·a·ble, *adj.;* **-ly,** *adv.*
un′con·sid′ered, *adj.*
un′con·sid′er·ing, *adj.*
un′con·sign′a·ble, *adj.*
un′con·signed′, *adj.*
un′con·so′ci·at′ed, *adj.*
un′con·sol′a·bil′i·ty, *n.*
un′con·sol′a·ble, *adj.;* **-bly,** *adv.*
un′con·sol′a·to′ry, *adj.*
un′con·soled′, *adj.*
un′con·sol′i·dat′ed, *adj.*
un′con·sol′i·dat′ing, *adj.*
un′con·sol′i·da′tion, *n.*
un′con·sol′ing, *adj.;* **-ly,** *adv.*
un·con′so·nant, *adj.*
un′con·spired′, *adj.*
un′con·spir′ing, *adj.;* **-ly,** *adv.*
un·con′stant, *adj.;* **-ly,** *adv.*
un·con′stel·lat′ed, *adj.*
un·con′ster·nat′ed, *adj.*
un·con′sti·pat′ed, *adj.*
un·con′sti·tut′ed, *adj.*
un′con·strain′a·ble, *adj.*
un′con·strained′, *adj.*
un′con·strain′ing, *adj.*
un′con·strict′ed, *adj.*
un′con·stric′tive, *adj.*
un′con·stru′a·ble, *adj.*
un′con·struct′ed, *adj.*
un′con·struc′tive, *adj.;* **-ly,** *adv.*
un′con·strued′, *adj.*
un′con·sult′a·ble, *adj.*
un′con·sult′a·tive, *adj.*
un′con·sul′ta·to′ry, *adj.*
un′con·sult′ed, *adj.*
un′con·sult′ing, *adj.*
un′con·sum′a·ble, *adj.*
un′con·sumed′, *adj.*
un′con·sum′ing, *adj.*
un′con·sum′mate, *adj.;* **-ly,** *adv.*
un·con′sum·mat′ed, *adj.*
un·con′sum·ma′tive, *adj.*
un′con·sump′tive, *adj.;* **-ly,** *adv.*
un·con′tact·ed, *adj.*
un′con·ta′gious, *adj.;* **-ly,** *adv.*
un′con·tained′, *adj.*
un′con·tam′i·na·ble, *adj.*
un′con·tam′i·nat′ed, *adj.*
un′con·tam′i·na′tive, *adj.*
un′con·temned′, *adj.*
un′con·temn′ing, *adj.;* **-ly,** *adv.*
un·con′tem·pla·ble, *adj.*
un·con′tem·plat′ed, *adj.*
un′con·tem′pla·tive, *adj.;* **-ly,** *adv.;* **-ness,** *n.*
un′con·tem′po·ra′ne·ous, *adj.;* **-ly,** *adv.;* **-ness,** *n.*
un′con·tem′po·rar′y, *adj.*
un′con·tempt′i·bil′i·ty, *n.*
un′con·tempt′i·ble, *adj.;* **-ble·ness,** *n.;* **-bly,** *adv.*
un′con·temp′tu·ous, *adj.;* **-ly,** *adv.;* **-ness,** *n.*
un′con·tend′ed, *adj.*
un′con·tend′ing, *adj.*
un′con·ten′tious, *adj.;* **-ly,** *adv.;* **-ness,** *n.*
un′con·test′a·bil′i·ty, *n.*
un′con·test′a·ble, *adj.;* **-ly,** *adv.*
un′con·test′ant, *n.*
un′con·test′ed, *adj.;* **-ly,** *adv.*
un′con·tig′u·ous, *adj.;* **-ly,** *adv.;* **-ness,** *n.*
un·con′ti·nence, *n.*
un·con′ti·nent, *adj.*
un′con·tin′gent, *adj.;* **-ly,** *adv.*
un′con·tin′u·al, *adj.;* **-ly,** *adv.*
un′con·tin′ued, *adj.*
un′con·tin′u·ous, *adj.;* **-ly,** *adv.*
un′con·tort′ed, *adj.;* **-ly,** *adv.*
un′con·tor′tioned, *adj.*
un′con·tor′tive, *adj.*
un·con′toured, *adj.*
un′con·tract′ed, *adj.*
un′con·trac′tile, *adj.*
un′con·tra·dict′a·ble, *adj.;* **-ly,** *adv.*
un′con·tra·dict′ed, *adj.;* **-ly,** *adv.*
un′con·tra·dic′tious, *adj.*
un′con·tra·dic′tive, *adj.*
un′con·tra·dic′to·ry, *adj.*
un′con·trast′a·ble, *adj.;* **-bly,** *adv.*
un′con·trast′ed, *adj.*
un′con·trast′ing, *adj.*
un′con·tras′tive, *adj.;* **-ly,** *adv.*
un′con·trib′ut·ed, *adj.*
un′con·trib′ut·ing, *adj.*
un′con·trib′u·tive, *adj.;* **-ly,** *adv.;* **-ness,** *n.*
un′con·trib′u·to′ry, *adj.*
un′con·trite′, *adj.*
un′con·trived′, *adj.*

an unconventional artist; an unconventional use of material. [UN-[1] + CONVENTIONAL] —**un′con·ven′tion·al·ly,** *adv.*

un·con·ven·tion·al·i·ty (un′kən ven′shə nal′i tē), *n., pl.* **-ties. 1.** disregard for convention; the state or quality of being inconsistent with customs, rules, etc.; originality. **2.** something unconventional, as an act. [UN-[1] + CONVENTIONALITY]

un·cork (un kôrk′), *v.t.* to draw the cork from. [UN-[2] + CORK]

un·cor·rect (un′kə rekt′), *v.t.* **1.** *Navig.* to convert (a true course) into a magnetic course. **2.** to convert (a magnetic course) into a compass course. [UN-[2] + CORRECT]

un·count·a·ble (un koun′tə bəl), *adj.* **1.** not countable; incapable of having the total precisely ascertained: *uncountable myriads of bacteria; uncountable kindnesses and small favors.* **2.** indefinitely large in number; infinite: *the uncountable days of eternity.* [UN-[1] + COUNTABLE]

un·count·ed (un koun′tid), *adj.* **1.** not counted. **2.** innumerable: *Uncounted generations of tiny creatures built the coral atolls.* [ME *uncountit.* See UN-[1], COUNT[1], -ED[2]]

un·cou·ple (un kup′əl), *v.,* **-pled, -pling.** —*v.t.* **1.** to release the coupling or link between; disconnect, as two things connected by a coupling; let go, as a connecting link: *to uncouple railroad cars.* —*v.i.* **2.** to become unfastened; let go: *The glider uncoupled from the tow plane.* [ME; see UN-[2], COUPLE]

un·cour·te·ous (un kûr′tē əs), *adj.* impolite; discourteous. [ME *uncurteis.* See UN-[1], COURTEOUS] —**un·cour′te·ous·ly,** *adv.* —**un·cour′te·ous·ness,** *n.*

un·court·ly (un kôrt′lē), *adj.* **1.** not courtly; rude. **2.** not conforming to the customs or usage of a royal court: *an uncourtly lack of respect for hereditary rank.* [UN-[1] + COURTLY] —**un·court′li·ness,** *n.*

un·couth (un ko͞oth′), *adj.* **1.** awkward, clumsy, or unmannerly: *uncouth behavior; an uncouth ruffian.* **2.** strange and ungraceful in appearance or form. **3.** unusual or strange. [ME; OE *uncūth* (*un-* UN-[1] + *cūth* known, ptp); c. D *onkond*] —**un·couth′ly,** *adv.* —**un·couth′ness,** *n.*

—**Syn. 1.** discourteous, rude, boorish, uncivil. **3.** odd, unfamiliar. —**Ant. 1.** courteous.

un·cov·e·nant·ed (un kuv′ə nən tid), *adj.* **1.** not agreed to or promised by covenant. **2.** not having joined in a covenant. [UN-[1] + COVENANT + -ED[3]]

un·cover (un kuv′ər), *v.t.* **1.** to lay bare; disclose; reveal. **2.** to remove the cover or covering from. **3.** to remove (a hat or other head covering). —*v.i.* **4.** to remove a cover or covering. **5.** to take off one's hat or other head covering as a gesture of respect. [ME *uncover(en).* See UN-[2], COVER]

un·cov·ered (un kuv′ərd), *adj.* **1.** having no cover or covering. **2.** having the head bare. **3.** not protected by security, as a note. [ME *uncovert.* See UN-[1], COVER, -ED[2]]

un·crit·i·cal (un krit′i kəl), *adj.* **1.** not inclined or able to judge, esp. by the application of comparative standards: *an uncritical reader.* **2.** undiscriminating; not applying or not guided by the standards of analysis: *an uncritical estimate; their uncritical acceptance of traditional values.* [UN-[1] + CRITICAL] —**un·crit′i·cal·ly,** *adv.*

un·crown (un kroun′), *v.t.* **1.** to deprive or divest of a crown. **2.** to reduce from dignity or preeminence. [ME *uncroun(en).* See UN-[2], CROWN]

un·crowned (un kround′), *adj.* **1.** not crowned; not having yet assumed the crown. **2.** having royal rank or power without occupying the royal office. [ME *uncrouned.* See UN-[1], CROWNED]

unct., (in prescriptions) smeared. [< L *unctus*]

unc·tion (ungk′shən), *n.* **1.** an act of anointing, esp. as a medical treatment or ritual symbol. **2.** *Relig.* **a.** the oil used in religious rites, as in anointing the sick or dying. **b.** the shedding of a divine or spiritual influence upon a person. **c.** the influence shed. **d.** See **extreme unction. 3.** something soothing or comforting. **4.** a soothing, sympathetic, and persuasive quality in discourse, esp. on religious subjects. **5.** a professional, conventional, or affected earnestness or fervor in utterance. [ME *unctioun* < L *unctiōn-* (s. of *unctiō*) anointing, besmearing, equiv. to *unct(us)* smeared, anointed (ptp. of *ungere, unquere*) + *-iōn-* -ION] —**unc′tion·less,** *adj.*

unc·tu·ar·i·um (ungk′cho͞o âr′ē əm), *n., pl.* **-ar·i·a** (-âr′ē ə). alipterion. [? < NL **unctuārium,* var. of L *unctōrium*]

unc·tu·ous (ungk′cho͞o əs), *adj.* **1.** of the nature of or characteristic of an unguent or ointment; oily; greasy. **2.** characterized by excessive piousness or moralistic fervor, esp. in an affected manner; excessively smooth, suave, or smug. **3.** having an oily or soapy feel, as certain minerals. [< ML *unctuōs(us),* equiv. to L *unct(um)* ointment, n. use of neut. of *unctus* (see UNCTION) + *-ōsus* -OUS] —**unc·tu·os·i·ty** (ungk′cho͞o os′i tē), **unc′tu·ous·ness,** *n.* —**unc′tu·ous·ly,** *adv.*

un·cul·ture (un kul′chər), *n.* the lack or absence of culture: *Much modern fiction is a product of unculture.* [UN-[1] + CULTURE]

un·curl (un kûrl′), *v.t., v.i.* to straighten out, as something curled. [UN-[2] + CURL]

un·cut (un kut′), *adj.* **1.** not cut. **2.** *Chiefly Brit.* untrimmed (def. 2). **3.** not shortened or condensed; unabridged: *an uncut version of the play.* **4.** in the original form; neither reduced in size nor given shape, as a diamond. [ME *unkitt.* See UN-[1], CUT]

un·damped (un dampt′), *adj.* **1.** not damped or dampened; undiminished, as in energy, vigor, etc.: *undamped spirits.* **2.** *Physics.* (of an oscillation) having constant or increasing amplitude. [UN-[1] + DAMP + -ED[2]]

Un·da·rum (un där′əm), *n.* **Mare.** See **Mare Undarum.**

un·daunt·ed (un dôn′tid), *adj.* **1.** undismayed; not discouraged; not forced to abandon purpose or effort: *undaunted by failure; undaunted by misfortune.* **2.** undiminished in courage or valor; not giving way to fear; intrepid: *Although outnumbered, he was undaunted.* [late ME; see UN-[1], DAUNT, -ED[2]] —**un·daunt′ed·ly,** *adv.* —**un·daunt′ed·ness,** *n.*

un·dé (un dā′), *adj. Heraldry.* wavy, esp. when the curves are relatively abrupt and close. Also, **un·dée′, undy.** [< AF (c. OF *onde*) < L *undāt(us)* (ptp. of *undāre* to make waves), equiv. to *und(a)* wave + *-ātus* -ATE[1]]

un·dec·a·gon (un dek′ə gon′), *n.* a polygon having 11 angle and 11 sides. [< L *undec(im)* eleven, equiv. to *ūn(us)* one + *decem* ten + *-a-* connective vowel + -GON]

un·de·ceive (un′di sēv′), *v.t.,* **-ceived, -ceiv·ing.** to free from deception, fallacy, or mistake. [UN-[2] + DECEIVE] —**un′de·ceiv′a·ble,** *adj.* —**un′de·ceiv′er,** *n.*

un·de·cid·ed (un′di sī′did), *adj.* **1.** not decided or determined. **2.** not having one's mind firmly made up; irresolute. [UN-[1] + DECIDED] —**un′de·cid′ed·ly,** *adv.* —**un′de·cid′ed·ness,** *n.*

un·de·cil·lion (un′di sil′yən), *n., pl.* **-lions,** (*as after a numeral*) **-lion,** *adj.* —*n.* **1.** a cardinal number represented in the United States and France by 1 followed by 36 zeros, and in Great Britain and Germany, by 1 followed by 66 zeros. —*adj.* **2.** amounting to one undecillion in number. [< L *undec(im)* eleven, equiv. to *ūn(us)* one + *decem* ten + *-illion,* as in *million*] —**un′de·cil′lionth,** *adj., n.*

un·de·fined (un′di fīnd′), *adj.* **1.** without fixed limits; indefinite in form, extent, or application:

---

un′con·triv′ing, *adj.*
un′con·trol′la·ble, *adj.;* **-bly,** *adv.*
un′con·trolled′, *adj.*
un′con·trol′ling, *adj.*
un′con·tro·ver′sial, *adj.;* **-ly,** *adv.*
un·con′tro·vert′ed, *adj.;* **-ly,** *adv.*
un′con·tro·vert′i·ble, *adj.;* **-bly,** *adv.*
un′con·tu·ma′cious, *adj.;* **-ly,** *adv.;* **-ness,** *n.*
un′con·ven′a·ble, *adj.*
un′con·vened′, *adj.*
un′con·ven′ing, *adj.*
un′con·verged′, *adj.*
un′con·ver′gent, *adj.*
un′con·verg′ing, *adj.*
un′con·vers′a·ble, *adj.*
un′con·ver′sant, *adj.*
un′con·ver·sa′tion·al, *adj.*
un′con·vert′ed, *adj.*
un′con·vert′i·bil′i·ty, *n.*
un′con·vert′i·ble, *adj.;* **-ble·ness,** *n.;* **-bly,** *adv.*
un′con·vict′ed, *adj.*
un′con·vict′ing, *adj.*
un′con·vic′tive, *adj.*
un′con·vinced′, *adj.*
un′con·vin′ci·ble, *adj.*
un′con·vinc′ing, *adj.;* **-ly,** *adv.*
un·con′vo·lute′, *adj.;* **-ly,** *adv.*
un·con′vo·lut′ed, *adj.*
un′con·voyed′, *adj.*
un′con·vulsed′, *adj.*
un′con·vul′sive, *adj.;* **-ly,** *adv.;* **-ness,** *n.*
un·cook′a·ble, *adj.*
un·cooked′, *adj.*
un·cooled′, *adj.*
un·coop′, *v.t.*
un′co·op′er·a′ting, *adj.*
un′co·op′er·a′tive, *adj.;* **-ly,** *adv.;* **-ness,** *n.*
un·coop′ered, *adj.*
un′co·or′di·nate, *adj.;* **-ly,** *adv.;* **-ness,** *n.*
un′co·or′di·nat′ed, *adj.*
un·cop′i·a·ble, *adj.*
un·cop′ied, *adj.*
un·co′pi·ous, *adj.*
un·cop′y·right′ed, *adj.*
un′co·quet′tish, *adj.;* **-ly,** *adv.;* **-ness,** *n.*
un·cor′dial, *adj.;* **-ly,** *adv.;* **-ness,** *n.*
un′cor·dial′i·ty, *n.*
un·core′, *v.t.,* **-cored, -cor·ing.**
un·corned′, *adj.*
un·cor′nered, *adj.*
un·cor′o·net′ed, *adj.*
un·cor′pu·lent, *adj.;* **-ly,** *adv.*
un′cor·rect′a·ble, *adj.;* **-ly,** *adv.*
un′cor·rect′ed, *adj.*
un′cor·rec′tive, *adj.*
un·cor′re·lat′ed, *adj.;* **-ly,** *adv.*
un′cor·rel′a·tive, *adj.;* **-ly,** *adv.;* **-ness,** *n.*
un′cor·rel′a·tiv′i·ty, *n.*
un′cor·res·pond′ing, *adj.;* **-ly,** *adv.*
un·cor′ri·dored, *adj.*
un′cor·rob′o·rant, *adj.*
un′cor·rob′o·rat′ed, *adj.*
un′cor·rob′o·ra′tive, *adj.;* **-ly,** *adv.*
un′cor·rob′o·ra·to′ry, *adj.*
un′cor·rod′ed, *adj.*
un·cor′ru·gat′ed, *adj.*
un′cor·rupt′, *adj.;* **-ly,** *adv.;* **-ness,** *n.*
un′cor·rupt′ed, *adj.;* **-ly,** *adv.;* **-ness,** *n.*
un′cor·rupt′i·ble, *adj.;* **-ble·ness,** *n.;* **-bly,** *adv.*
un′cor·rupt′ing, *adj.*
un′cor·rup′tive, *adj.*
un·cor′set·ed, *adj.*
un·cos′set·ed, *adj.*
un·cost′ly, *adj.*
un·cos′tumed, *adj.*
un·cot′toned, *adj.*
un·coun′seled, *adj.*
un·coun′selled, *adj.*
un·coun′te·nanced, *adj.*
un′coun·ter·act′ed, *adj.*
un′coun·ter·bal′anced, *adj.*
un·coun′ter·feit·ed, *adj.*
un′coun·ter·mand′a·ble, *adj.*
un′coun·ter·mand′ed, *adj.*
un′coun·ter·vailed′, *adj.*
un·coun′tri·fied′, *adj.*
un′cou·ra′geous, *adj.;* **-ly,** *adv.;* **-ness,** *n.*
un·court′ed, *adj.*
un·cour′te·sy, *n., pl.* **-sies.**
un·cour′ti·er·like′, *adj.*
un·court′ing, *adj.*
un·cov′et·ed, *adj.*
un·cov′et·ing, *adj.*
un·cov′et·ous, *adj.;* **-ly,** *adv.;* **-ness,** *n.*
un·cowed′, *adj.*
un·coy′, *adj.;* **-ly,** *adv.;* **-ness,** *n.*
un·cracked′, *adj.*
un·cra′dled, *adj.*
un·craft′i·ly, *adv.;* **-ness,** *n.*
un·craft′y, *adj.*
un·crag′gy, *adj.*
un·cramped′, *adj.*
un·cranked′, *adj.*
un·cran′nied, *adj.*
un·crat′ed, *adj.*
un′cra·vat′ted, *adj.*
un·cra′ven, *adj.*
un·crav′ing, *adj.;* **-ly,** *adv.*
un·creased′, *adj.*
un′cre·at′a·ble, *adj.*
un′cre·at′ed, *adj.*
un′cre·a′tive, *adj.;* **-ly,** *adv.;* **-ness,** *n.*
un′cre·a·tiv′i·ty, *n.*
un·crea′ture·ly, *adj.*
un′cre·den′tialed, *adj.*
un·cred′it, *v.t.*
un·cred′it·a·ble, *adj.;* **-ble·ness,** *n.;* **-bly,** *adv.*
un·cred′u·lous, *adj.;* **-ly,** *adv.;* **-ness,** *n.*
un·creep′ing, *adj.*
un·cre′o·sot′ed, *adj.*
un·crest′ed, *adj.*
un·crev′assed, *adj.*
un·crib′, *v.t.,* **-cribbed, -crib·bing.**
un·cried′, *adj.*
un·crim′i·nal, *adj.;* **-ly,** *adv.*
un·crip′pled, *adj.*
un·crit′i·cis′a·ble, *adj.;* **-bly,** *adv.*
un·crit′i·ciz′a·ble, *adj.;* **-bly,** *adv.*
un·crit′i·cized′, *adj.*
un·crit′i·ciz′ing, *adj.;* **-ly,** *adv.*
un·crook′ed, *adj.;* **-ly,** *adv.*
un·cropped′, *adj.*
un·cross′, *v.t., adj.;* **-ly,** *adv.*
un·cross′a·ble, *adj.*
un′cross-ex·am′ined, *adj.*
un·crowd′ed, *adj.*
un·cru′ci·fied′, *adj.*
un·crude′, *adj.;* **-ly,** *adv.;* **-ness,** *n.*
un·cru′di·ty, *n.*
un·cru′el, *adj.;* **-ly,** *adv.;* **-ness,** *n.*
un·crum′bled, *adj.*
un·crum′pled, *adj.*
un·crum′pling, *adj.*
un·crush′a·ble, *adj.*
un·crushed′, *adj.*
un·crust′ed, *adj.*
un·cry′ing, *adj.*
un·crys′taled, *adj.*
un·crys′talled, *adj.*
un·crys′tal·line, *adj.*
un·crys′tal·lis′a·ble, *adj.*
un·crys′tal·liz′a·ble, *adj.*
un·crys′tal·lized′, *adj.*
un·cu′bic, *adj.*
un·cu′bi·cal, *adj.;* **-ly,** *adv.;* **-ness,** *n.*
un·cudg′eled, *adj.*
un·cudg′elled, *adj.*
un·cuffed′, *adj.*
un·culled′, *adj.*
un·cul′pa·ble, *adj.*
un·cul′ti·va·ble, *adj.*
un·cul′ti·vat′a·ble, *adj.*
un·cul′ti·vat′ed, *adj.*
un′cul·ti·va′tion, *n.*
un·cul′tur·a·ble, *adj.*
un·cul′tured, *adj.*
un·cum′bered, *adj.*
un·cum′brous, *adj.;* **-ly,** *adv.;* **-ness,** *n.*
un·cu′mu·la′tive, *adj.*
un·cupped′, *adj.*
un·cur′a·ble, *adj.;* **-ble·ness,** *n.;* **-bly,** *adv.*
un·curb′, *v.t.*
un·curb′a·ble, *adj.*
un·curbed′, *adj.*
un·curd′, *v.t.*
un·cur′dled, *adj.*
un·cur′dling, *adj.*
un·cured′, *adj.*
un·cu′ri·ous, *adj.;* **-ly,** *adv.*
un·cur′rent, *adj.;* **-ly,** *adv.*
un·cur′ried, *adj.*
un·cursed′, *adj.*
un·curs′ing, *adj.*
un′cur·tail′a·ble, *adj.;* **-bly,** *adv.*
un′cur·tailed′, *adj.*
un·cur′tained, *adj.*
un·curved′, *adj.*
un·curv′ing, *adj.*
un·cush′ioned, *adj.*
un·cusped′, *adj.*
un·cus′tom·ar′i·ly, *adv.*
un·cus′tom·ar′y, *adj.*
un·cut′ta·ble, *adj.*
un·cyn′i·cal, *adj.;* **-ly,** *adv.*
un·dab′bled, *adj.*
un·dag′gled, *adj.*
un·dain′ti·ly, *adv.*
un·dain′ti·ness, *n.*
un·dain′ty, *adj.*
un·dal′ly·ing, *adj.*
un·dam′, *v.t.,* **-dammed, -dam·ming.**
un·dam′age·a·ble, *adj.*
un·dam′aged, *adj.*
un·dam′ag·ing, *adj.*
un·dam′asked, *adj.*
un·dam′ni·fied′, *adj.*
un·damp′ened, *adj.*
un·dance′a·ble, *adj.*
un·danc′ing, *adj.*
un·dan′dled, *adj.*
un·dan′gered, *adj.*
un·dan′ger·ous, *adj.;* **-ly,** *adv.*
un·dap′per, *adj.*
un·dap′pled, *adj.*
un·dared′, *adj.*
un·dar′ing, *adj.*
un·dark′en, *v.t.*
un·darned′, *adj.*
un·dat′a·ble, *adj.*
un·date′a·ble, *adj.*
un·dat′ed, *adj.*
un·daubed′, *adj.*
un·daugh′ter·ly, *adj.*
un·daunt′ing, *adj.*
un·dawned′, *adj.*
un·dawn′ing, *adj.*
un·dazed′, *adj.*
un·daz′ing, *adj.*
un·daz′zled, *adj.*
un·daz′zling, *adj.*
un·dead′ened, *adj.*
un·dead′locked′, *adj.*
un·deaf′, *adj.*
un·deal′a·ble, *adj.*
un·dealt′, *adj.*
un′de·based′, *adj.*
un′de·bat′a·ble, *adj.*
un′de·bat′ed, *adj.*
un′de·bat′ing, *adj.*
un′de·bauched′, *adj.*
un′de·bil′i·tat′ed, *adj.*
un′de·bil′i·tat′ing, *adj.*
un′de·bil′i·ta′tive, *adj.*
un·deb′it·ed, *adj.*
un′de·ca′dent, *adj.;* **-ly,** *adv.*
un′de·cay′a·ble, *adj.*
un′de·cayed′, *adj.*
un′de·cay′ing, *adj.*
un′de·ceased′, *adj.*
un′de·ceit′ful, *adj.*
un′de·cep′tive, *adj.;* **-ly,** *adv.;* **-ness,** *n.*
un′de·ci′pher·a·ble, *adj.;* **-bly,** *adv.*
un′de·ci′phered, *adj.*
un·decked′, *adj.*
un′de·claimed′, *adj.*
un′de·claim′ing, *adj.*
un′de·clam′a·to′ry, *adj.*
un′de·clar′a·ble, *adj.*
un′de·clar′a·tive, *adj.*
un′de·clared′, *adj.*
un′de·clin′a·ble, *adj.*
un′de·clined′, *adj.*
un′de·clin′ing, *adj.*
un′de·coct′ed, *adj.*
un′de·com·pos′a·ble, *adj.*
un′de·com·posed′, *adj.*
un′de·com·pound′ed, *adj.*
un·dec′o·rat′ed, *adj.*
un·dec′o·ra′tive, *adj.*
un·dec′o·rous, *adj.;* **-ly,** *adv.;* **-ness,** *n.*
un·de·cor′ti·cat′ed, *adj.*
un′de·creased′, *adj.*
un′de·creas′ing, *adj.;* **-ly,** *adv.*
un′de·creed′, *adj.*
un′de·crep′it, *adj.*
un′de·cre′tive, *adj.*
un·dec′re·to′ry, *adj.*
un′de·cried′, *adj.*
un·ded′i·cat′ed, *adj.*
un′de·duced′, *adj.*
un′de·duc′i·ble, *adj.*
un′de·duct′ed, *adj.*
un′de·duct′i·ble, *adj.*
un′de·duc′tive, *adj.;* **-ly,** *adv.*
un·deed′ed, *adj.*
un·deep′, *adj.;* **-ly,** *adv.*
un·deep′ened, *adj.*
un′de·face′a·ble, *adj.*
un′de·faced′, *adj.*
un′de·fal′cat·ed, *adj.*
un′de·fam′a·to′ry, *adj.*
un′de·famed′, *adj.*
un′de·fam′ing, *adj.*
un′de·fault′ed, *adj.*
un′de·fault′ing, *adj.*
un′de·feat′a·ble, *adj.;* **-ble·ness,** *n.;* **-bly,** *adv.*
un′de·feat′ed, *adj.;* **-ly,** *adv;* **-ness,** *n.*
un′de·fec′tive, *adj.;* **-ly,** *adv.;* **-ness,** *n.*
un′de·fend′a·ble, *adj.;* **-ble·ness,** *n.;* **-bly,** *adv.*
un′de·fend′ant, *adj.*
un′de·fend′ed, *adj.*
un′de·fend′ing, *adj.*
un′de·fensed′, *adj.*
un′de·fen′si·ble, *adj.;* **-ble·ness,** *n.;* **-bly,** *adv.*
un′de·fen′sive, *adj.;* **-ly,** *adv.;* **-ness,** *n.*
un′def·er·en′tial, *adj.;* **-ly,** *adv.*
un′de·fer′ra·ble, *adj.;* **-bly,** *adv.*
un′de·ferred′, *adj.*
un′de·fi′a·ble, *adj.;* **-bly,** *adv.*
un′de·fi′ant, *adj.;* **-ly,** *adv.*
un′de·fi′cient, *adj.;* **-ly,** *adv.*
un′de·fied′, *adj.*
un′de·filed′, *adj.*
un′de·fin′a·ble, *adj.*

CONCISE ETYMOLOGY KEY: <, descended or derived from; >, whence; b., blend of, blended; c., cognate with; deriv., derivative; equiv., equivalent; imit., imitative; m., modification of; obl., oblique; r., replacing; s., stem; sp., spelling; trans., translation; ?, origin unknown, perhaps; *, hypothetical. See the full key inside the front cover.

an undefined authority; an undefined feeling of sadness. **2.** not given meaning or significance, as by a definition; unexplained: *an undefined term.* [UN-[1] + DEFINED] —**un·de·fin·ed·ly** (un′di fī′nid lē, -fīnd′-), *adv.* —**un′de·fin′ed·ness,** *n.*

un·de·ni·a·ble (un′di nī′ə bəl), *adj.* **1.** not capable of being validly disputed or controverted; inescapable: *undeniable evidence of authenticity.* **2.** not open to refusal: *The mother had an undeniable claim on the child's affection.* **3.** unquestioned as to quality, merit, etc.; indisputably good: *undeniable character; an undeniable bargain.* [UN-[1] + DENIABLE] —**un′de·ni′a·ble·ness,** *n.* —**un′de·ni′a·bly,** *adv.*
—**Syn. 1.** incontrovertible, incontestable, unquestionable; obvious, evident, clear, certain, sure.

un·de·nom·i·na·tion·al (un′di nom′ə nā′shə nᵊl), *adj.* free from religious sects or denominationalism; not limited or belonging to any particular religious group or groups. [UN-[1] + DENOMINATIONAL] —**un′de·nom′i·na′tion·al·ly,** *adv.*

un·der (un′dər), *prep.* **1.** beneath and covered by: *under a table; under a tree.* **2.** below the surface of: *under water.* **3.** at a point or position lower or further down than: *to hit a man under the belt.* **4.** in the position or state of bearing, supporting, sustaining, enduring, etc.: *to sink under a heavy load.* **5.** beneath the heading or within the category of: *Classify the books under "Fiction" and "General."* **6.** as designated, indicated, or represented by: *to register under a new name.* **7.** below in degree, amount, etc.; less than: *purchased under cost.* **8.** below in rank; of less dignity, importance, or the like: *A corporal is under a sergeant.* **9.** subject to the authority, direction, or supervision of: *a bureau functioning under the prime minister.* **10.** subject to the instruction or advice of: *to study violin under Heifetz.* **11.** subject to the influence, condition, force, etc.: *under these circumstances; born under the sign of Taurus.* **12.** protected, controlled, or watched by: *under guard.* **13.** authorized, warranted, or attested by: *under one's hand or seal.* **14.** in accordance with: *under the provisions of the law.* **15.** during the rule, administration, or government of: *new laws passed under President Johnson.* **16.** in the state or process of: *under repair; a matter under consideration.* —*adv.* **17.** below or beneath something: *Go over the fence, not under.* **18.** beneath the surface. **19.** in a lower place. **20.** in a lower degree, amount, etc.: *selling blouses for $6 and under.* **21.** in a subordinate position or condition. **22.** in or into subjection or submission. **23. go under, a.** to give in; succumb; yield: *He tried desperately to fight off his drowsiness, but felt himself going under.* **b.** *Informal.* to fail in business: *After 20 years on the same corner he finally went under.* —*adj.* **24.** beneath. **25.** lower in position. **26.** lower in degree, amount, etc. **27.** lower in rank or condition. **28.** subject to the control, effect, etc., as of a person, drug, or force (used predicatively): *The hypnotist had his subject under at once. The patient was under as soon as he breathed the anesthetic.* [ME, OE; c. D *onder,* G *unter,* OIcel *undir,* L *infra* below]
—**Syn. 2.** See **below.**

under-, a prefixal attributive use of *under,* as to indicate place or situation below or beneath (*underbrush; undertow*); lower in grade or dignity (*undersheriff; understudy*); of lesser degree, extent, or amount (*undersized*); or insufficiency (*underfeed*).

un·der·act (un′dər akt′), *v.t., v.i.* to underplay. [UNDER- + ACT]

un·der·age[1] (un′dər āj′), *adj.* lacking the required age, esp. that of legal maturity. [UNDER- + AGE]

un·der·age[2] (un′dər ij), *n.* shortage; deficiency in amount. [UNDER- + -AGE]

un·der·arm (un′dər ärm′), *adj.* **1.** of, applicable to, or associated with the region under the arm or in the armpit. **2.** underhand: *an underarm pitch in softball.* —*adv.* **3.** underhand. [UNDER- + ARM[1]]

un·der·armed (un′dər ärmd′), *adj.* not having sufficient weapons. [UNDER- + ARMED]

un·der·bel·ly (un′dər bel′ē), *n., pl.* **-lies. 1.** the lower abdomen; posterior ventral area, as of an animal's body. **2.** the vital area most vulnerable to attack; the quarter in which defense is necessary but most difficult; the weakest point: *the soft underbelly of Europe.* [UNDER- + BELLY]

un·der·bid (un′dər bid′), *v.t.,* **-bid, -bid·ding.** to make a bid lower than that of (another bidder), as in seeking a contract to be awarded to the lowest bidder; make an offer at a lower price than (a competitive offer). [UNDER- + BID] —**un′der·bid′der,** *n.*

un·der·bod·ice (un′dər bod′is), *n.* a bodice worn under an outer bodice. [UNDER- + BODICE]

un·der·bod·y (un′dər bod′ē), *n., pl.* **-bod·ies. 1.** the bottom or underneath part, as of a mechanism or animal: *the underbody of a tank.* **2.** *Naut.* the portion of a hull that is normally under water. [UNDER- + BODY]

un·der·bred (un′dər bred′), *adj.* **1.** having inferior breeding or manners; vulgar. **2.** not of pure breed, as a horse. [UNDER- + BRED] —**un·der·breed·ing** (un′dər brē′ding), *n.*

un·der·brush (un′dər brush′), *n.* shrubs, small trees, etc., growing under large trees in a wood or forest. Also, **un·der·bush** (un′dər bo͝osh′). [UNDER- + BRUSH[2]]

un·der·buy (un′dər bī′), *v.,* **-bought, -buy·ing.** —*v.t.* **1.** to buy more cheaply than (another). **2.** to buy at less than the actual value. —*v.i.* **3.** to buy an insufficient quantity, as of supplies or stock in trade. [UNDER- + BUY]

un·der·cap·i·tal·ize (un′dər kap′i tᵊlīz′; *Brit. also* un′dər kə pit′ᵊlīz′), *v.t.,* **-ized, -iz·ing.** to provide an insufficient amount of capital for (a business enterprise). [UNDER- + CAPITALIZE]

un·der car·riage (un′dər kar′ij), *n.* **1.** the supporting framework underneath a vehicle, as an automobile, trailer, etc.; the structure to which the wheels, tracks, or the like, are attached or fitted. **2.** the portions of an aircraft that are below the body. [UNDER- + CARRIAGE]

un·der·cast (un′dər kast′, -käst′), *n.* **1.** *Mining.* a crossing of two passages, as airways, dug at the same level so that one descends to pass beneath the other without any opening into it. Cf. **overcast** (def. 9). **2.** an overcast layer of clouds viewed from above. [UNDER- + CAST]

un·der·cel·lar (un′dər sel′ər), *n.* a cellar beneath another cellar; subbasement. [UNDER- + CELLAR]

un·der·charge (*v.* un′dər chärj′; *n.* un′dər chärj′), *v.,* **-charged, -charg·ing,** *n.* —*v.t.* **1.** to charge (a purchaser) less than the proper or fair price. **2.** to charge (a stated amount) less than the proper price: *They undercharged several dollars for storing the goods.* **3.** to put an insufficient charge or load into. —*n.* **4.** a charge or price less than is proper or customary. **5.** an insufficient charge or load. [UNDER- + CHARGE]

un·der·class·man (un′dər klas′mən, -kläs′-), *n., pl.* **-men.** a freshman, sophomore, or junior in a secondary school or college. [UNDER- + CLASS + MAN[1]]

un·der·clay (un′dər klā′), *n.* *Geol.* a layer of argillite immediately underlying a bed of coal. [UNDER- + CLAY]

un·der·clothes (un′dər klōz′, -klōthz′), *n.pl.* clothes worn under outer clothes, esp. those worn next to the skin. Also called **underclothing.** [UNDER- + CLOTHES]

un·der·cloth·ing (un′dər klō′thing), *n.* **1.** underwear. **2.** underclothes. [UNDER- + CLOTHING]

un·der·coat (un′dər kōt′), *n.* **1.** a coat or jacket worn under another. **2.** *Zool.* a growth of short fur or hair lying beneath a longer growth. **3.** an undercoating. **4.** a coat of paint or the like applied under the finishing coat. **5.** a paint, sealer, or the like specially prepared for use underneath a finishing coat. —*v.t.* **6.** to apply an undercoating to. [UNDER- + COAT]

un·der·coat·ing (un′dər kō′ting), *n.* a protective seal applied to the underside of an automobile to reduce corrosion and vibration. [UNDERCOAT + -ING[1]]

un·der·cool (un′dər ko͞ol′), *v.t.* **1.** *Chem.* **a.** to cool less than necessary for a given process or purpose. **b.** to supercool. **2.** *Metall.* to cool (molten metal) without forming crystals to a temperature below that at which crystallization normally takes place: *Metal must be absolutely still to be undercooled.* [UNDER- + COOL]

un·der·cov·er (un′dər kuv′ər, un′dər kuv′-), *adj.* working or done out of public sight; secret: *an undercover agent.* [UNDER- + COVER]

un·der·croft (un′dər krôft′, -kroft′), *n.* a vault or chamber under the ground, esp. in a church. [ME; see UNDER, CROFT]

un·der·cur·rent (un′dər kûr′ənt, -kur′-), *n.* **1.** a current, as of air or water, that flows below the upper currents or surface. **2.** a tendency underlying or at variance with the obvious or superficial significance of words, actions, etc.: *Even in his most friendly remarks, one could sense an undercurrent of hostility.* [UNDER- + CURRENT]

un·der·cut (un′dər kut′), *v.,* **-cut, -cut·ting,** *n., adj.* —*v.t.* **1.** to cut under or beneath. **2.** to cut away material from so as to leave a portion overhanging, as in carving or sculpture. **3.** to sell at a lower price or work for a lower wage than another, as a competitor. **4.** *Golf.* to hit (the ball) so as to cause a backspin. **5.** *Tennis.* to slice (the ball) using an underhand motion. **6.** to cut (a sound recording) with grooves too shallow or with insufficient lateral motion of the stylus. —*v.i.* **7.** to undercut material, a competitor, a ball, etc. —*n.* **8.** a cut or a cutting away underneath. **9.** a notch cut in a tree to determine the direction in which the tree is to fall and to prevent splitting. **10.** *Golf.* a backspin. **11.** *Tennis.* a slice or cut made with an underhand motion. **12.** *Chiefly Brit.* a tenderloin of beef including the fillet. **13.** *Dentistry.* a tooth cavity prepared with a wide base for anchoring a filling securely. —*adj.* **14.** having or resulting from an undercut. [UNDER- + CUT]

un·der·de·vel·op (un′dər di vel′əp), *v.t.* to develop (something) short of the required amount: *to underdevelop film.* [UNDER- + DEVELOP] —**un′der·de·vel′op·ment,** *n.*

un·der·de·vel·ope (un′dər di vel′əp), *v.t.,* **-oped, -op·ing.** underdevelop. —**un′der·de·vel′ope·ment,** *n.*

un·der·de·vel·oped (un′dər di vel′əpt), *adj.* **1.** improperly or insufficiently developed: *a plan to aid all the underdeveloped nations of the world.* **2.** *Photog.* (of a negative) less developed than is normal, so as to produce a relatively dark positive lacking in contrast. [UNDER- + DEVELOP + -ED[2]]

un·der·do (un′dər do͞o′), *v.i., v.t.,* **-did, -done, -do·ing.** to do less than is usual or requisite. [UNDER- + DO[1]]

---

un′def′i·nite, *adj.;* **-ly,** *adv.;* **-ness,** *n.*
un′de·fin′i·tive, *adj.;* **-ly,** *adv.;* **-ness,** *n.*
un′de·flect′ed, *adj.*
un′de·flec′tive, *adj.*
un′de·form′a·ble, *adj.*
un′de·formed′, *adj.*
un′de·fraud′ed, *adj.*
un′de·frayed′, *adj.*
un·deft′, *adj.*
un′de·gen′er·a·cy, *n.*
un′de·gen′er·ate, *adj.*
un′de·gen′er·at′ed, *adj.*
un′de·gen′er·at′ing, *adj.*
un′de·gen′er·a′tive, *adj.*
un′de·grad′ed, *adj.*
un′de·grad′ing, *adj.*
un·de′i·fied′, *adj.*
un′de·is′ti·cal, *adj.*
un′de·ject′ed, *adj.;* **-ly,** *adv.;* **-ness,** *n.*
un′de·lay′a·ble, *adj.*
un′de·layed′, *adj.*
un′de·lay′ing, *adj.;* **-ly,** *adv.*
un′de·lec′ta·ble, *adj.;* **-bly,** *adv.*
un·del′e·gat′ed, *adj.*
un′de·let′ed, *adj.*
un′del·e·te′ri·ous, *adj.;* **-ly,** *adv.;* **-ness,** *n.*
un′de·lib′er·ate, *adj.;* **-ly,** *adv.;* **-ness,** *n.*
un′de·lib′er·at′ing, *adj.;* **-ly,** *adv.*
un′de·lib′er·a′tive, *adj.;* **-ly,** *adv.;* **-ness,** *n.*
un′de·li′cious, *adj.;* **-ly,** *adv.*
un′de·light′ed, *adj.;* **-ly,** *adv.*
un′de·light′ful, *adj.;* **-ly,** *adv.*
un′de·light′ing, *adj.*
un′de·lin′e·a·ble, *adj.*
un′de·lin′e·at′ed, *adj.*
un′de·lin′e·a′tive, *adj.*
un′de·lin′quent, *adj.;* **-ly,** *adv.*
un′de·lir′i·ous, *adj.;* **-ly,** *adv.*
un′de·liv′er·a·ble, *adj.*
un′de·liv′ered, *adj.*
un′de·lud′ed, *adj.;* **-ly,** *adv.*
un′de·lud′ing, *adj.*
un·del′uged, *adj.*
un′de·lu′sive, *adj.;* **-ly,** *adv.;* **-ness,** *n.*
un′de·lu′so·ry, *adj.*
un·delved′, *adj.*
un′de·mand′ed, *adj.*
un′de·mand′ing, *adj.*
un′de·mised′, *adj.*
un′dem·o·crat′ic, *adj.*
un′dem·o·crat′i·cal·ly, *adv.*
un′de·moc′ra·ti·sa′tion, *n.*
un′de·moc′ra·tise′, *v.t.,* **-tised, -tis·ing.**
un′de·moc′ra·ti·za′tion, *n.*
un′de·moc′ra·tize′, *v.t.,* **-tized, -tiz·ing.**
un′de·mol′ish·a·ble, *adj.*
un′de·mol′ished, *adj.*
un′de·mon′stra·ble, *adj.;* **-ble·ness,** *n.;* **-bly,** *adv.*
un·dem′on·strat′ed, *adj.*
un′dem·on·stra′tion·al, *adj.*
un′de·mon′stra·tive, *adj.;* **-ly,** *adv.;* **-ness,** *n.*
un′de·mure′, *adj.;* **-ly,** *adv.;* **-ness,** *n.*
un′de·mur′ring, *adj.*
un′de·nied′, *adj.*
un·den′i·zened, *adj.*
un′de·nom′i·nat′ed, *adj.*
un′de·not′a·ble, *adj.*
un′de·no′ta·tive, *adj.;* **-ly,** *adv.*
un′de·not′ed, *adj.*
un′de·nounced′, *adj.*
un·dent′ed, *adj.*
un′de·nud′ed, *adj.*
un′de·nun′ci·at′ed, *adj.*
un′de·nun′ci·a·to′ry, *adj.*
un′de·part′ed, *adj.*
un′de·part′ing, *adj.*
un′de·pend′a·bil′i·ty, *n.*
un′de·pend′a·ble, *adj.;* **-ble·ness,** *n.;* **-bly,** *adv.*
un′de·pend′ent, *adj.*
un′de·pict′ed, *adj.*
un′de·plet′ed, *adj.*
un′de·plored′, *adj.*
un′de·port′ed, *adj.*
un′de·pos′a·ble, *adj.*
un′de·posed′, *adj.*
un′de·pos′it·ed, *adj.*
un′de·praved′, *adj.*
un·dep′re·cat′ed, *adj.*
un·dep′re·cat′ing, *adj.;* **-ly,** *adv.*
un·dep′re·ca′tive, *adj.;* **-ly,** *adv.*
un′de·pre′ci·a·ble, *adj.*
un′de·pre′ci·at′ed, *adj.*
un′de·pre′ci·a′tive, *adj.*
un′de·pre′ci·a·to′ry, *adj.*
un′de·pressed′, *adj.*
un′de·press′i·ble, *adj.*
un′de·press′ing, *adj.*
un′de·pres′sive, *adj.;* **-ly,** *adv.;* **-ness,** *n.*
un′de·prived′, *adj.*
un′de·put′ed, *adj.*
un·dep′u·tized′, *adj.*
un′de·ranged′, *adj.*

---

un′der·ac′ci·dent, *n.*
un′der·ac·com′mo·dat′ed, *adj.*
un′der·a·chieve′ment, *n.*
un′der·a·chiev′er, *n.*
un′der·ac′tor, *n.*
un′der·ad·just′ment, *n.*
un′der·age′, *adj.*
un′der·a′gen·cy, *n.*
un′der·a′gent, *n.*
un′der·ag′i·ta′tion, *n.*
un′der·aim′, *n.*
un′der·al′der·man, *n., pl.* **-men.**
un′der·av′er·age, *adj.*
un′der·bail′iff, *n.*
un′der·bake′, *v.t.,* **-baked, -bak·ing.**
un′der·bal′ance, *v.t.,* **-anced, -anc·ing.**
un′der·bal′last, *v.t.*
un′der·bank′, *v.*
un′der·bar′ber, *n.*
un′der·bea′dle, *n.*
un′der·beak′, *n.*
un′der·beam′, *n.*
un′der·beat′, *n.*
un′der·beat′en, *adj.*
un′der·bev′el·ing, *n.*
un′der·bev′el·ling, *n.*
un′der·bil′low, *v.i.*
un′der·bish′op, *n.*
un′der·bish′op·ric, *n.*
un′der·boil′, *v.*
un′der·boom′, *v.*
un′der·bot′tom, *n.*
un′der·bough′, *n.*
un′der·box′, *n.*
un′der·brace′, *n.*
un′der·brace′, *v.t.,* **-braced, -brac·ing.**
un′der·branch′, *n.*
un′der·brew′, *v.t.*
un′der·bridge′, *v.t.,* **-bridged, -bridg·ing.**
un′der·bridge′, *n.*
un′der·brig′a·dier′, *n.*
un′der·bud′, *n.*
un′der·bud′, *v.,* **-bud·ded, -bud·ding.**
un′der·build′, *v.,* **-built, -build·ing.**
un′der·build′er, *n.*
un′der·build′ing, *n.*
un′der·bur′sar, *n.*
un′der·but′ler, *n.*
un′der·can′vass, *v.*
un′der·cap′, *n.*
un′der·cap′tain, *n.*
un′der·car′ry, *v.t.,* **-ried, -ry·ing.**
un′der·carve′, *v.t.,* **-carved, -carv·ing.**
un′der·case′, *n.*
un′der·cas′ing, *n.*
un′der·cause′, *n.*
un′der·ceil′ing, *n.*
un′der·cham′ber, *n.*
un′der·cham′ber·lain, *n.*
un′der·chan′cel·lor, *n.*
un′der·chant′er, *n.*
un′der·chap′, *n.*
un′der·chief′, *n.*
un′der·chin′, *n.*
un′der·chord′, *n.*
un′der·cir′cle, *v.t.,* **-cled, -cling.**
un′der·cir′cle, *n.*
un′der·cit′i·zen, *n.*
un′der·cit′i·zen·ry, *n., pl.* **-ries.**
un′der·clad′, *adj.*
un′der·clad′ding, *n.*
un′der·clerk′, *n.*
un′der·clerk′ship, *n.*
un′der·cloak′, *n.*
un′der·cloth′, *n.*
un′der·clothed′, *adj.*
un′der·clothes, *n.*
un′der·cloth′ing, *n.*
un′der·clutch′, *v.t.*
un′der·clutch′, *n.*
un′der·coach′man, *n., pl.* **-men.**
un′der·col·lect′or, *n.*
un′der·col′ored, *adj.*
un′der·com·mand′er, *n.*
un′der·com′ment, *n.*
un′der·com′ment, *v.*
un′der·con·cerned′, *adj.*
un′der·con′scious·ness, *n.*
un′der·con′sta·ble, *n.*
un′der·con·sume′, *v.t.,* **-sumed, -sum·ing.**
un′der·con·sump′tion, *n.*
un′der·cook′, *n., v.t.*
un′der·coop′er, *n.*
un′der·cor·rect′, *v.t.*
un′der·coun′te·nance, *n.*
un′der·course′, *n.*
un′der·course′, *v.,* **-coursed, -cours·ing.**
un′der·cour′ti·er, *n.*
un′der·crawl′, *v.i.*
un′der·crest′, *n.*
un′der·cri′er, *n.*
un′der·crust′, *n.*
un′der·crypt′, *n.*
un′der·cup′, *n.*
un′der·curl′, *n.*
un′der·curl′, *v.*
un′der·curve′, *n.*
un′der·curve′, *v.i.,* **-curved, -curv·ing.**
un′der·dea′con, *n.*
un′der·deal′ing, *n.*
un′der·de·greed′, *adj.*
un′der·dev′il, *n.*
un′der·di′a·logue′, *n.*
un′der·dig′, *v.,* **-dug, -dig·ging.**
un′der·dish′, *n.*
un′der·dis·tinc′tion, *n.*
un′der·dis·trib′u·tor, *n.*
un′der·dive′, *n.*
un′der·dive′, *v.i.,* **-dived** or **-dove, -dived, -div·ing.**
un′der·doc′tor, *n.*

---

un·der·dog (un′dər dôg′, -dog′), *n.* **1.** one who is expected to lose in a contest or conflict. **2.** a victim of social or political injustice: *The underdogs were beginning to express their protest.* [UNDER- + DOG]

un·der·done (un′dər dun′), *adj.* **1.** (of food) not thoroughly cooked; not cooked enough. **2.** *Chiefly Brit.* (of meat) rare. [UNDER- + DONE]

un·der·draft (un′dər draft′, -dräft′), *n.* *Metalworking.* a tendency of a rolled piece to curve downward after passing through a stand, occurring when the upper roll is faster than the lower. Cf. **overdraft** (def. 6). [UNDER- + DRAFT]

un·der·drain (*n.* un′dər drān′; *v.* un′dər drān′), *n.* **1.** a drain placed beneath the surface of cultivated fields, streets, etc. —*v.t.* **2.** to equip or supply with an underdrain or underdrains. [UNDER- + DRAIN]

un·der·drain·age (un′dər drā′nij), *n.* drainage of agricultural lands and removal of excess water and of alkali by drains buried beneath the surface. [UNDER- + DRAINAGE]

un·der·draw (un′dər drô′), *v.t.*, **-drew, -drawn, -draw·ing.** to line the underside of (a structure, as a floor) with plasterwork, boarding, or the like. [UNDER- + DRAW]

un·der·draw·ers (un′dər drôrz′), *n.* (*construed as pl.*) an undergarment for the lower part of the body, typically covering at least part of the legs. Cf. **drawer** (def. 2). [UNDER- + DRAWER]

un·der·dress (*v.* un′dər dres′; *n.* un′dər dres′), *v.*, **-dressed, -dress·ing,** *n.* —*v.i.* **1.** to clothe oneself less completely or formally than is usual or fitting for the circumstances. —*n.* **2.** garments, as underclothes, worn beneath others. **3.** an undergarment, as a slip, petticoat, or other underskirt, esp. one designed to be seen when worn, as beneath a redingote. [UNDER- + DRESS]

un·der·es·ti·mate (*v.* un′dər es′tə māt′; *n.* un′dər-es′tə mit, -māt′), *v.*, **-mat·ed, -mat·ing,** *n.* —*v.t.* **1.** to estimate at too low a value, rate, or the like. —*v.i.* **2.** to make an estimate lower than that which would be correct. —*n.* **3.** an estimate that is too low. [UNDER- + ESTIMATE] —**un′der·es′ti·ma′tion,** *n.*

un·der·ex·pose (un′dər ik spōz′), *v.t.*, **-posed, -pos·ing.** to expose either to insufficient light or to sufficient light for too short a period, as in photography. [UNDER- + EXPOSE]

un·der·ex·po·sure (un′dər ik spō′zhər), *n.* **1.** inadequate exposure, as of photographic film. **2.** a photographic negative or print which is imperfect because of insufficient exposure. [UNDER- + EXPOSURE]

un·der·feed (un′dər fēd′ *for 1;* un′der fēd′ *for 2*), *v.t.*, **-fed, -feed·ing. 1.** to feed insufficiently. **2.** to feed with fuel from beneath. [UNDER- + FEED]

un·der·fired (un′dər fīərd′), *adj.* supplied with fuel or heat from beneath. [UNDER- + FIRE + -ED[2]]

un·der·foot (un′dər fo͝ot′), *adv.* **1.** under the foot or feet; on the ground; underneath or below. —*adj.* **2.** lying under the foot or feet; in a position to be trodden upon. **3.** forming an obstruction, as to walking; in the way. [ME *underfot.* See UNDER-, FOOT]

un·der·fur (un′dər fûr′), *n.* the fine, soft, thick, hairy coat under the longer and coarser outer hair in certain animals, as seals, otters, and beavers. [UNDER- + FUR]

un·der·gar·ment (un′dər gär′mənt), *n.* an article of underwear. [UNDER- + GARMENT]

un·der·gird (un′dər gûrd′), *v.t.*, **-gird·ed** or **-girt, -gird·ing. 1.** to strengthen; secure, as by passing a rope or chain under and around: *to undergird a top-heavy load.* **2.** to give fundamental support; provide with a sound or secure basis: *Ethics are undergirded by faith.* [UNDER- + GIRD]

un·der·glaze (un′dər glāz′), *Ceram.* —*adj.* **1.** (of a color) applied to a piece before the piece is glazed. —*n.* **2.** color applied to a piece before it is glazed. [UNDER- + GLAZE]

un·der·go (un′dər gō′), *v.t.*, **-went, -gone, -go·ing. 1.** to be subjected to; experience; pass through: *to undergo surgery.* **2.** to endure; sustain; suffer: *to undergo sustained deprivation.* [ME *undergon.* See UNDER-, GO[1]] —**un′der·go′er,** *n.*
—**Syn. 1.** See **experience. 2.** bear, tolerate. —**Ant. 1.** avoid.

un·der·grad (un′dər grad′), *n.* *Informal.* an undergraduate. [by shortening]

un·der·grad·u·ate (un′dər graj′o͞o it), *n.* **1.** a student in a university or college who has not taken his first degree. —*adj.* **2.** having the standing of an undergraduate. **3.** of, for, pertaining to, or characteristic of undergraduates. [UNDER- + GRADUATE] —**un′der·grad′u·ate·ship′,** *n.*

un·der·grad·u·ette (un′dər graj′o͞o et′, -graj′o͞o-et′), *n.* *Brit. Informal.* a female undergraduate; coed. [UNDERGRADU(ATE) + -ETTE]

un·der·ground (*adv., adj.* un′dər ground′; *n.* un′dər ground′), *adv.* **1.** beneath the surface of the ground: *traveling underground by subway.* **2.** in concealment or secrecy; not openly: *subversion carried on underground.* —*adj.* **3.** existing, situated, operating, or taking place beneath the surface of the ground. **4.** used, or for use, underground. **5.** hidden or secret; not open: *underground political activities.* —*n.* **6.** the place or region beneath the surface of the ground. **7.** an underground space or passage. **8.** a secret organization fighting the established government or occupation forces, esp. one in a European country that was conquered or occupied by the Nazis or fascists before or during World War II. **9.** *Chiefly Brit.* **a.** a subway train or car. **b.** a subway system. [UNDER- + GROUND[1]]

un′derground rail′road, 1. Also called **un′derground rail′way.** a railroad running through a continuous tunnel, as under city streets; subway. **2.** *U.S. Hist.* (before the abolition of slavery) an arrangement among opponents of slavery for helping fugitive slaves to escape into Canada or other places of safety.

un′derground trol′ley. See under **trolley** (def. 4).

un·der·grown (un′dər grōn′, un′dər grōn′), *adj.* **1.** not grown to normal size or height: *sickly and undergrown cattle.* **2.** having an undergrowth: *an undergrown thicket tangled with creeping vines.* [ME; see UNDER-, GROWN]

un·der·growth (un′dər grōth′), *n.* **1.** low-lying vegetation or small trees growing beneath or among larger trees; underbrush. **2.** the condition of being undergrown or undersized. **3.** short, fine hair underlying longer, outer wool or fur. [UNDER- + GROWTH]

un·der·hand (un′dər hand′), *adj.* **1.** not open and aboveboard; secret and crafty or dishonorable: *The gamblers had an underhand deal with the chief of police.* **2.** executed with the hand below the level of the shoulder and the palm turned upward and forward: *an underhand delivery of a ball.* —*adv.* **3.** with the hand below the level of the shoulder and the palm turned upward and forward: *to bowl underhand.* **4.** secretly; stealthily; slyly. [ME *under hande,* OE *underhand.* See UNDER-, HAND]
—**Syn. 1.** stealthy, sly, clandestine, surreptitious.

un·der·hand·ed (un′dər han′did), *adj.* **1.** underhand. **2.** short-handed: *By the time of the Navy game, Army usually finds itself underhanded.* [UNDERHAND + -ED[2]] —**un′der·hand′ed·ly,** *adv.* —**un′der·hand′ed·ness,** *n.*

un·der·hung (un′dər hung′), *adj.* **1.** *Anat.* **a.** (of the lower jaw) projecting beyond the upper jaw. **b.** having the lower jaw so projecting. **2.** resting on a track beneath instead of being overhung, as a sliding door. [UNDER- + HUNG]

un′derhung rud′der, *Naut.* See **spade rudder.**

un·der·in·sur·ance (un′dər in sho͝or′əns), *n.* insurance purchased against damage or loss of property in an amount less than its true value, sometimes bought intentionally by the insured with full knowledge of the risk. [UNDER- + INSURANCE]

un·der·in·sured (un′dər in sho͝ord′), *adj.* insured for an amount less than the true value. [UNDER- + INSURED]

un·de·rived (un′di rīvd′), *adj.* not derived; fundamental, as an axiom or postulate; immediate. [UN-[1] + DERIVED] —**un·de·riv·ed·ly** (un′di rī′vid lē), *adv.* —**un′de·riv′ed·ness,** *n.*

un·der·laid (un′dər lād′), *adj.* **1.** placed or laid underneath, as a foundation or substratum. **2.** having an underneath layer (often fol by *with*): *a lace tablecloth underlaid with damask; courtesy underlaid with reserve.* —*v.* **3.** pt. and pp. of **underlay.**

un·der·lap (un′dər lap′), *v.t.*, **-lapped, -lap·ping.** to extend partly under. [UNDER- + LAP[2]]

un·der·lay (*v.* un′dər lā′; *n.* un′dər lā′), *v.*, **-laid, -lay·ing,** *n.* —*v.t.* **1.** to lay under or beneath: *The manufacturer underlays the chrome finish with a zinc coating.* **2.** to provide with something laid underneath; raise or support with something laid underneath. **3.** to extend across the bottom of. —*n.* **4.** something underlaid. **5.** *Print.* a piece or pieces of paper put under types or cuts to bring them to the proper height for printing. [ME; see UNDER-, LAY[1]]

un·der·lay·er (un′dər lā′ər), *n.* a layer lying beneath another; substratum. [UNDER- + LAYER]

un·der·lay·ment (un′dər lā′mənt), *n.* material laid between a subfloor and a finish floor of linoleum, asphalt tile, etc. [UNDERLAY + -MENT]

un·der·let (un′dər let′), *v.t.*, **-let, -let·ting. 1.** to let below the true value. **2.** to sublet. [UNDER- + LET[1]]

un·der·lie (*v.* un′dər lī′; *n.* un′dər lī′), *v.*, **-lay, -lain, -ly·ing,** *n.* —*v.t.* **1.** to lie under or beneath; be situated under. **2.** to be at the basis of; form the foundation of. **3.** *Gram.* to function as the root morpheme or original or basic form of (a derived form): *The form "boy" underlies "boyish."* **4.** *Finance.* to be primary to another right or security. —*n.* **5.** Also called **underset.** *Mining.* the angle made by a stull with a line perpendicular to a hanging wall at its point of support. [ME *underly,* OE *underlicgan.* See UNDER-, LIE[2]] —**un′der·li′er,** *n.*

un·der·line (*v.* un′dər līn′, un′dər līn′; *n.* un′dər-līn′), *v.*, **-lined, -lin·ing,** *n.* —*v.t.* **1.** to mark with a line or lines underneath; underscore. **2.** to indicate the importance of; emphasize, as by stressing or italicizing. —*n.* **3.** *Print.* a caption under an illustration. [UNDER- + LINE[1]] —**un·der·lin·e·a·tion** (un′dər lin′ē ā′shən), *n.*

un·der·ling (un′dər ling), *n.* a subordinate, esp. one of slight importance. [ME, OE. See UNDER-, -LING[1]]

un·der·lit (un′dər lit′), *adj.* poorly lighted. [UNDER- + LIT[1]]

un·der·ly·ing (un′dər lī′ing), *adj.* **1.** lying or situated beneath, as a substratum. **2.** fundamental; basic: *an underlying cause for all types of cancer.* **3.** implicit; discoverable only by close scrutiny or analysis: *an underlying seriousness in his witticisms.* **4.** (of a claim, mortgage, etc.) taking precedence; anterior; prior. —*v.* **5.** ppr. of **underlie.** [UNDERLIE + -ING[2]]

un·der·manned (un′dər mand′), *adj.* lacking a normal or sufficient work force, complement of troops, or the like; understaffed; short-handed. [UNDER- + MANNED]

un·der·mine (un′dər mīn′ *or, esp. for 2–4,* un′dər-mīn′), *v.t.*, **-mined, -min·ing. 1.** to make an excavation under; dig or tunnel beneath, as a military stronghold. **2.** to weaken or cause to collapse by removing underlying support, as by digging away or eroding the foundation. **3.** to injure or destroy by insidious activity or imperceptible stages, sometimes tending toward a sudden dramatic effect. **4.** to attack by indirect, secret, or underhand means; attempt to subvert by stealth. [ME *undermine(n).* See UNDER-, MINE[2]] —**un′der·min′er,** *n.* —**un′der·min′ing·ly,** *adv.*

un·der·most (un′dər mōst′), *adj., adv.* lowest, as in position, status, or the like. [UNDER- + -MOST]

un·der·neath (un′dər nēth′), *prep.* **1.** below the surface or level of; directly or vertically beneath; at or on the bottom of. **2.** under the control of; in a lower position in a hierarchy of authority: *Underneath the department heads are the junior executives and foremen.* **3.** hidden, disguised, or misrepresented, as by a false appearance or pretense: *Underneath his bluster is a timid nature. Underneath all this gossip is a single error of observation.* —*adv.* **4.** below; at a lower level or position; on the underside. —*adj.* **5.** lower; situated below or under. —*n.* **6.** the bottom; underside; lowest part. [ME *undernethe,* OE *underneoth(an).* See UNDER, BENEATH]

un·der·nour·ish (un′dər nûr′ish, -nur′-), *v.t.* to furnish with less than the food requirements for good health or normal development. [UNDER- + NOURISH] —**un′der·nour′ish·ment,** *n.*

un·dern·song (un′dərn sông′, -song′), *n.* *Eccles. Obs.* tierce (def. 3). [ME *undern,* OE: tierce + SONG, as in OE *undernsang*]

un·der·nu·tri·tion (un′dər no͞o trish′ən, -nyo͞o-), *n.* nutritional deficiency resulting from lack of food or from the inability of the body to convert or absorb it. [UNDER- + NUTRITION]

un·de·rog·a·to·ry (un′də rog′ə tôr′ē, -tôr′ē), *adj.* not derogatory. [UN-[1] + DEROGATORY]

un′de·rid′ed, *adj.*
un′de·ris′i·ble, *adj.*
un′de·ri′sive, *adj.;* **-ly,** *adv.;* **-ness,** *n.*
un′de·ri′so·ry, *adj.*
un′de·riv′a·ble, *adj.*
un′de·riv′a·tive, *adj.;* **-ly,** *adv.*
un′der·o′gat′ing, *adj.*
un′de·rog′a·tive, *adj.;* **-ly,** *adv.*

un′der·dose′, *n.*
un′der·dose′, *v.t.*, **-dosed, -dos·ing.**
un′der·dot′, *n.*
un′der·dot′, *v.t.*, **-dot·ted, -dot·ting.**
un′der·down′, *n.*
un′der·draught′, *n.*
un′der·dry′, *v.t.*, **-dried, -dry·ing.**
un′der·drum′ming, *n.*
un′der·eat′, *v.i.*, **-ate, -eat·en, -eat·ing.**
un′der·edge′, *n.*
un′der·ed′u·cat′ed, *adj.*
un′der·em·ploy′ment, *n.*
un′der·en·grav′er, *n.*
un′der·ex′er·cise′, *v.i.*, **-cised, -cis·ing.**
un′der·eye′, *n., v.t.*, **-eyed, -ey·ing.**
un′der·face′, *n.*
un′der·face′, *v.t.*, **-faced, -fac·ing.**
un′der·fac′tion, *n.*
un′der·fac′tor, *n.*
un′der·fac′ul·ty, *n.*
un′der·fal′con·er, *n.*
un′der·farm′er, *n.*
un′der·feath′er·ing, *n.*
un′der·fea′ture, *n.*
un′der·feel′ing, *n.*
un′der·fiend′, *n.*
un′der·fi·nance′, *v.t.*, **-nanced, -nanc·ing.**
un′der·fit′ting, *n.*
un′der·flame′, *n.*
un′der·flan′nel, *n.*
un′der·flood′, *v.*
un′der·flood′, *n.*
un′der·floor′, *n.*
un′der·floor′ing, *n.*
un′der·flow′, *n.*
un′der·fold′ed, *adj.*
un′der·foot′age, *n.*
un′der·foot′man, *n., pl.* **-men.**
un′der·form′, *n.*
un′der·for′ti·fy′, *v.t.*, **-fied, -fy·ing.**
un′der·frame′, *n.*
un′der·frame′work′, *n.*
un′der·fre′quen·cy, *n., pl.* **-cies.**
un′der·fringe′, *n.*
un′der·frock′, *n.*
un′der·fur′nish, *v.t.*
un′der·game′keep′er, *n.*
un′der·gaol′er, *n.*
un′der·garb′, *n.*
un′der·gar′den·er, *n.*
un′der·gar′nish, *v.t.*
un′der·gen′er·al, *n.*
un′der·gen′tle·man, *n., pl.* **-men.**
un′der·girth′, *n.*
un′der·gloom′, *n.*
un′der·glow′, *n.*
un′der·gnaw′, *v.t.*
un′der·god′, *n.*
un′der·gov′ern·ess, *n.*
un′der·gov′ern·ment, *n.*
un′der·gov′er·nor, *n.*
un′der·grain′ing, *n.*
un′der·grass′, *n.*
un′der·groan′, *n.*
un′der·growl′, *n.*
un′der·guard′, *n.*
un′der·guard′i·an, *n.*
un′der·gun′ner, *n.*
un′der·hab′it, *n.*
un′der·ham′mer, *n.*
un′der·hang′, *v.*, **-hung, -hang·ing.**
un′der·hang′man, *n., pl.* **-men.**
un′der·hatch′, *v.t.*
un′der·heat′, *v.t.*
un′der·heav′en, *n.*
un′der·help′, *n.*
un′der·hill′, *n.*
un′der·his′to·ry, *n.*
un′der·horse′, *v.t.*, **-horsed, -hors·ing.**
un′der·horse′man, *n., pl.* **-men.**
un′der·house′maid′, *n.*
un′der·hum′, *n.*
un′der·in′stru·ment, *n.*
un′der·is′sue, *n.*
un′der·jack′et, *n.*
un′der·jail′er, *n.*
un′der·jan′i·tor, *n.*
un′der·jaw′, *n.*
un′der·job′bing, *n.*
un′der·join′, *v.t.*
un′der·joint′, *n.*
un′der·judge′, *v.t.*, **-judged, -judg·ing.**
un′der·judge′, *n.*
un′der·jun′gle, *n.*
un′der·keep′er, *n.*
un′der·king′, *n.*
un′der·king′dom, *n.*
un′der·la′bor·er, *n.*
un′der·la′bour·er, *n.*
un′der·land′, *n.*
un′der·lash′, *n.*
un′der·laun′dress, *n.*
un′der·law′yer, *n.*
un′der·leath′er, *n.*
un′der·leg′ate, *n.*
un′der·les·see′, *n.*
un′der·lev′el, *adj.*
un′der·lid′, *n.*
un′der·lieu·ten′ant, *n.*
un′der·life′, *n.*
un′der·lift′, *n.*
un′der·light′, *n.*
un′der·lik′ing, *n.*
un′der·limbed′, *adj.*
un′der·lim′it, *n.*
un′der·lim′it, *v.t.*
un′der·line′man, *n., pl.* **-men.**
un′der·lin′en, *n.*
un′der·lip′, *n.*
un′der·load′, *v.t.*
un′der·lock′, *n.*
un′der·lodg′ing, *n.*
un′der·loft′, *n.*
un′der·made′, *adj.*
un′der·maid′, *n.*
un′der·mak′er, *n.*
un′der·man′, *v.t.*, **-manned, -man·ning.**
un′der·man′a·ger, *n.*
un′der·mark′, *n.*
un′der·mark′, *v.t.*
un′der·mar′shal, *n.*
un′der·mar′shal·man, *n., pl.* **-men.**
un′der·mast′ed, *adj.*
un′der·mas′ter, *n.*
un′der·mate′, *n.*
un′der·mean′ing, *n.*
un′der·meas′ure, *v.t.*, **-ured, -ur·ing;** *n.*
un′der·me′di·a′tor, *n.*
un′der·mel′o·dy, *n., pl.* **-dies.**
un′der·men′tioned, *adj.*
un′der·mill′er, *n.*
un′der·min′is·ter, *n.*
un′der·min′is·try, *n.*
un′der·mist′, *n.*
un′der·moat′ed, *adj.*
un′der·mor′al, *adj.*
un′der·mo′tion, *n.*
un′der·mount′, *n.*
un′der·moun′tain, *n.*
un′der·mu′sic, *adj.*
un′der·mus′lin, *n.*
un′der·name′, *n.*
un′der·named′, *adj.*
un′der·note′, *n.*
un′der·not′ed, *adj.*
un′der·nurse′, *n.*
un′der·nu·tri′tion, *n.*
un′der·of′fi·cer, *n.*
un′der·of·fi′cial, *adj.*
un′der·o·pin′ion, *n.*
un′der·or′gan·i·sa′tion, *n.*
un′der·or′gan·i·za′tion, *n.*
un′der·ox′i·dise′, *v.t.*, **-dised, -dis·ing.**
un′der·ox′i·dize′, *v.t.*, **-dized, -diz·ing.**

un·der·paint·ing (un′dər pān′tiŋ), *n.* the first coat of paint, esp. the initial painting on a canvas in which the major areas, tones, colors, and forms are indicated in mass. [UNDER- + PAINTING]

un·der·pants (un′dər pants′), *n.pl.* drawers or shorts worn under outer clothing, usually next to the skin. [UNDER- + PANTS]

un·der·part (un′dər pärt′), *n.* the lower part or side: *The underpart of the plane's fuselage scraped the treetops. The squirrel's underparts are lighter in color.* [UNDER- + PART]

un·der·pass (un′dər pas′, -päs′), *n.* a passage running underneath, esp. a passage for pedestrians or vehicles, or both, crossing under a railroad, road, etc. [UNDER- + PASS]

un·der·pay (un′dər pā′), *v.t.*, **-paid, -pay·ing.** to pay less than is deserved. [UNDER- + PAY[1]] —**un′der·pay′ment,** *n.*

un·der·pin (un′dər pin′), *v.t.*, **-pinned, -pin·ning. 1.** to prop up or support from below; strengthen, as by reinforcing a foundation. **2.** to replace or strengthen the foundation of (a building or the like). **3.** to furnish a foundation for; corroborate: *The author's conclusions are underpinned by references to experimental findings.* [UNDER- + PIN]

un·der·pin·ning (un′dər pin′iŋ), *n.* **1.** a system of supports beneath a wall or the like. **2. underpinnings,** underwear, esp. women's underwear. [UNDERPIN + -ING[1]]

un′der·pitch vault′ (un′dər pich′), a construction having a central vault intersected by vaults of lower pitch. See illus. under **vault.** Also called **Welsh vault.** [UNDER- + PITCH[1]]

un·der·play (un′dər plā′, un′dər plā′), *v.t.* **1.** to act (a part) sketchily. **2.** to act subtly and restrainedly. —*v.i.* **3.** to leave out of one's acting all subtlety and enriching detail. **4.** to achieve an effect in acting with a minimum of emphasis. [UNDER- + PLAY]

un·der·plot (un′dər plot′), *n.* a plot subordinate to another plot, as in a play or novel. [UNDER- + PLOT[1]]

un·der·praise (un′dər prāz′), *v.t.*, **-praised, -prais·ing.** to praise to a lesser degree or extent than the circumstances warrant. [UNDER- + PRAISE]

un·der·price (un′dər prīs′), *v.t.*, **-priced, -pric·ing. 1.** to price (goods or merchandise) lower than the standard price or fair value. **2.** to undercut (a competitor) by underselling him or setting prices below actual cost. [UNDER- + PRICE]

un·der·priv·i·leged (un′dər priv′ə lijd, -priv′lijd), *adj.* denied the enjoyment of the normal privileges or rights of a society because of low economic and social status. [UNDER- + PRIVILEGED]

un·der·pro·duc·tion (un′dər prə duk′shən), *n.* production that is less than normal or than is required by the demand. [UNDER- + PRODUCTION] —**un′der·pro·duc′tive,** *adj.*

un·der·proof (un′dər pro͞of′), *adj.* containing a smaller proportion of alcohol than proof spirit. [UNDER- + PROOF]

un·der·prop (un′dər prop′), *v.t.*, **-propped, -prop·ping.** to prop underneath; support; uphold. [UNDER- + PROP[1]] —**un′der·prop′per,** *n.*

un·der·quote (un′dər kwōt′), *v.t.*, **-quot·ed, -quot·ing. 1.** to offer (stocks, merchandise, etc.) at a price lower than the market price or some other quoted price; offer at a price reduced by (a specified amount). **2.** to quote a price lower than that of (a specified competitor). [UNDER- + QUOTE]

un·der·rate (un′dər rāt′), *v.t.*, **-rat·ed, -rat·ing.** to rate too low; underestimate. [UNDER- + RATE[1]]

un·der·ripe (un′dər rīp′), *adj.* not completely ripe, as fruit. [UNDER- + RIPE]

un·der·run (un′dər run′), *v.*, **-ran, -run, -run·ning,** *n.* —*v.t.* **1.** to run, pass, or go under. **2.** *Naut.* **a.** to pass beneath (a stretched rope, net, etc.) in a boat or the like for the purpose of inspection or repairs. **b.** to lay out (a tackle) in proper order and readiness. —*n.* **3.** that which runs or passes underneath, as a current. [UNDER- + RUN]

un·der·sat·u·rat·ed (un′dər sach′ə rā′tid), *adj.* *Chem.* unsaturated (def. 2). [UNDER- + SATURATED] —**un′der·sat′u·ra′tion,** *n.*

un·der·score (*v.* un′dər skōr′, -skôr′; *n.* un′dər skōr′, -skôr′), *v.*, **-scored, -scor·ing,** *n.* —*v.t.* **1.** to mark with a line or lines underneath; underline, as for emphasis. **2.** to stress; emphasize: *The recent tragedy underscores the danger of disregarding safety rules.* —*n.* **3.** a line drawn beneath something written or printed. **4.** music for a film soundtrack; background for a film or stage production. [UNDER- + SCORE]

un·der·sea (un′dər sē′), *adj.* **1.** located, carried on, or designed for use under the surface of the sea: *undersea life; an undersea voyage; an undersea vessel.* —*adv.* **2.** underseas. [UNDER- + SEA]

un·der·seas (un′dər sēz′), *adv.* beneath the surface of the sea. [UNDERSEA + -S[1]]

un·der·sec·re·tar·i·at (un′dər sek′ri târ′ē ət, un′dər sek′rə ter′-), *n.* a department or section of a ministry of which an undersecretary is in charge. [UNDER- + SECRETARIAT]

un·der·sec·re·tar·y (un′dər sek′ri ter′ē), *n., pl.* **-tar·ies.** a secretary subordinate to a principal secretary. [UNDER- + SECRETARY]

un·der·sell (un′dər sel′), *v.t.*, **-sold, -sell·ing. 1.** to sell more cheaply than competitive merchandise. **2.** to advertise with restraint; understate the merits of, as of merchandise offered to a prospective purchaser: *By underselling his product, he let his hearers convince themselves of its importance.* **3.** to sell for less than the actual value. [UNDER- + SELL] —**un′der·sell′er,** *n.*

un·der·serv·ant (un′dər sûr′vənt), *n.* a servant of inferior or subordinate rank. [UNDER- + SERVANT]

un·der·set (un′dər set′), *n.* **1.** a current of water below the surface and flowing in a direction contrary to the water on the surface. **2.** *Mining.* underlie (def. 5). [ME *undersett(en).* See UNDER, SET]
—**Syn. 1.** See **undertow.**

un·der·sher·iff (un′dər sher′if), *n.* a sheriff's deputy, esp. a deputy on whom the sheriff's duties devolve when the sheriff is incapacitated or when the office is vacant. [late ME; see UNDER-, SHERIFF] —**un′der·sher′iff·ship′,** *n.*

un·der·shirt (un′dər shûrt′), *n.* a collarless, usually pull-over undergarment for the torso, usually of cotton and either sleeveless and low-cut or with sleeves, worn chiefly by men and children. [UNDER- + SHIRT]

un·der·shoot (un′dər sho͞ot′, un′dər sho͞ot′), *v.*, **-shot, -shoot·ing.** —*v.t.* **1.** to shoot or launch a projectile that strikes under or short of (a target). **2.** *Aeron.* (of an aircraft or pilot) to land before reaching (a landing strip) because of a too rapid loss of altitude. —*v.i.* **3.** to shoot or launch a projectile so as to strike under or short of a target. [UNDER- + SHOOT]

un·der·shorts (un′dər shôrts′), *n.pl.* short underpants for men and boys. [UNDER- + SHORTS]

un·der·shot (un′dər shot′), *adj.* **1.** having the front teeth of the lower jaw projecting in front of the upper teeth, as a bulldog. **2.** driven by water passing beneath: *an undershot vertical water wheel.* —*v.* **3.** pt. and pp. of **undershoot.** [UNDER- + SHOT[2]]

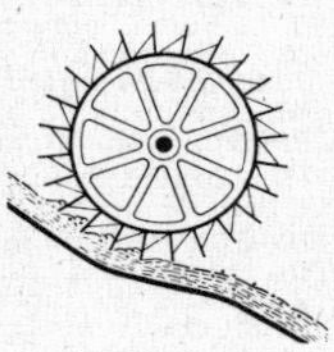

un′dershot wheel′, a water wheel on a horizontal axis turned by the force of water passing at the bottom against blades projecting from the rim.

Undershot wheel

un·der·shrub (un′dər shrub′), *n.* a low shrub. [UNDER- + SHRUB[1]]

un·der·side (un′dər sīd′), *n.* an under or lower side. [UNDER- + SIDE[1]]

un·der·sign (un′dər sīn′, un′dər sīn′), *v.t.* to sign one's name under or at the end of (a letter or document); affix one's signature to. [UNDER- + SIGN]

un·der·signed (*adj.* un′dər sīnd′; *n.* un′dər sīnd′), *adj.* **1.** whose signature appears at the end of a letter or document: *All of the undersigned persons are bound by the contract.* **2.** signed at the bottom or end of, as a writing: *The undersigned names guarantee the good faith of the statement.* —*n.* **3. the undersigned,** the person or persons signing a letter or document. [UNDER- + SIGN + -ED[2]]

un·der·size (un′dər sīz′), *adj.* **1.** undersized. **2.** (of screened minerals) passing through a sieve of given mesh. [UNDER- + SIZE[1]]

un·der·sized (un′dər sīzd′), *adj.* smaller than the usual or normal size. [UNDER- + SIZE[1] + -ED[3]]

un·der·skirt (un′dər skûrt′), *n.* a skirt, as a petticoat, worn under another skirt or a dress. [UNDER- + SKIRT]

un·der·sleeve (un′dər slēv′), *n.* a separate sleeve worn under the sleeve of a dress and visible through it or extending beyond it. [UNDER- + SLEEVE]

un·der·slung (un′dər sluŋ′), *adj.* **1.** suspended from an upper support, as the chassis of a vehicle from the axles. **2.** supported from above; placed or suspended below the source of support: *Conestoga wagons with underslung bundles and kettles.* **3.** having a center of gravity close to the bottom; squat; more massive at the bottom than the top: *The high wings and large fuselage give the plane an underslung look.* [UNDER- + SLUNG]

un·der·soil (un′dər soil′), *n.* subsoil. [UNDER- + SOIL[1]]

un·der·song (un′dər sông′, -soŋ′), *n.* **1.** the accompaniment of a song; a subordinate strain. **2.** a counter theme; a submerged suggestion not in harmony with the obviously stated: *An undersong of discontent runs through his praise.* [UNDER- + SONG]

un·der·sparred (un′dər spärd′), *adj.* *Naut.* having spars too small to carry the necessary sail. [UNDER- + SPAR[1] + -ED[3]]

un·der·spin (un′dər spin′), *n.* backspin. [UNDER- + SPIN]

un·der·staffed (un′dər staft′, -stäft′), *adj.* having an insufficient number of personnel: *The hospital is understaffed.* [UNDER- + STAFF[1] + -ED[3]]

un·der·stand (un′dər stand′), *v.*, **-stood, -stand·ing.** —*v.t.* **1.** to perceive the meaning of; grasp the idea of; comprehend: *The professor said he could not understand Kant.* **2.** to be thoroughly familiar with; apprehend clearly the character, nature, or subtleties of: *to understand a trade; to understand a poem.* **3.** to be conversant with, as words or symbols: *to understand Spanish; to understand shorthand.* **4.** to assign a meaning to; interpret: *I am at a loss to understand your rudeness. He understood her suggestion as a complaint.* **5.** to grasp the significance, implications, or importance of: *He does not understand responsibility. She understood his odd choice of words.* **6.** to regard as firmly communicated; take as agreed or settled: *I understand that you will repay this loan in 30 days.* **7.** to get knowledge of; learn or hear: *I understand that you are going out of town.* **8.** to accept as true; believe: *I understand that you are trying to be truthful, but you are wrong.* **9.** to construe in a particular way: *You are to understand the phrase literally.* **10.** to supply mentally, in reading or hearing, an omitted word or phrase needed to complete the meaning. —*v.i.* **11.** to perceive what is meant; grasp the information intended to be conveyed: *He told them about it in simple words, hoping they would understand.* **12.** to accept tolerantly or sympathetically: *If you cannot do it, I will understand.* **13.** to have knowledge or background, as on a particular subject: *He understands about boats.* **14.** to have a systematic interpretation or rationale, as in a field or area of knowledge: *He can repeat every rule in the book, but he just doesn't understand.* [ME; OE *understond(an)*; c. D *onderstaan.* See UNDER-, STAND]
—**Syn. 1.** See **know.**

un·der·stand·a·ble (un′dər stan′də bəl), *adj.* capable of being understood; comprehensible. [UNDERSTAND + -ABLE] —**un′der·stand′a·ble·ness, un′der·stand′a·bil′i·ty,** *n.* —**un′der·stand′a·bly,** *adv.*

un·der·stand·ing (un′dər stan′diŋ), *n.* **1.** mental process of one who comprehends; comprehension; personal interpretation: *His understanding is unequal to the task. My understanding of the word does not agree with yours.* **2.** intellectual faculties; intelligence; mind: *a quick understanding.* **3.** superior power of discernment; enlightened intelligence: *With his keen understanding he should have become a leader.* **4.** knowledge of or familiarity with a particular thing; skill in dealing with or handling something: *a clear understanding of gasoline engines; an understanding of accounting practice.* **5.** a state of cooperative or mutually tolerant relations between people: *To him, understanding and good will were the supreme virtues.* **6.** a mutual agreement, esp. of a private, unannounced, or tacit kind: *They had an understanding about who would do the dishes.* **7.** an agreement regulating joint activity or settling differences, often informal or preliminary in character: *After hours of negotiation, the envoys reached an understanding on the subjects to be discussed at the coming conference.* **8.** *Philos.* **a.** the power of abstract thought; logical power. **b.** *Kantianism.* the mental faculty resolving the sensory manifold into the transcendental unity of apperception. —*adj.* **9.** characterized by understanding; prompted by, based on, or demonstrating comprehension, intelligence, discernment, empathy, or the like: *an understanding attitude; understanding comments.* [ME *understandynge,*

un′der·pack′ing, *n.*
un′der·pain′, *n.*
un′der·par·tic′i·pa′tion, *n.*
un′der·part′ner, *n.*
un′der·peep′, *v.i.*
un′der·peer′, *v.i.*
un′der·pen′, *n.*
un′der·peo′pled, *adj.*
un′der·pet′ti·coat′, *n.*
un′der·pet′ti·coat′ed, *adj.*
un′der·pier′, *n.*
un′der·pi·las′ter, *n.*
un′der·pile′, *n.*
un′der·pitched′, *adj.*
un′der·plain′, *adj.*
un′der·plan′, *n.*
un′der·plant′, *v.t.*
un′der·plate′, *n.*
un′der·ply′, *n.*
un′der·point′, *n.*
un′der·point′, *v.i.*
un′der·pop′u·late′, *v.t.*, **-lat·ed, -lat·ing.**
un′der·pop′u·la′tion, *n.*
un′der·porch′, *n.*
un′der·por′ter, *n.*
un′der·pos·ses′sor, *n.*
un′der·pot′, *n.*
un′der·pow′ered, *adj.*
un′der·pre′fect, *n.*
un′der·pren′tice, *n.*
un′der·press′er, *n.*
un′der·pres′sure, *n.*
un′der·priest′, *n.*
un′der·prin′ci·pal, *n.*
un′der·pri′or, *n.*
un′der·prize′, *v.t.*, **-prized, -priz·ing.**
un′der·pro·duce′, *v.i.*, **-duced, -duc·ing.**
un′der·pro·duc′er, *n.*
un′der·pro·fi′cient, *adj.*
un′der·prompt′er, *n.*
un′der·pro·por′tioned, *adj.*
un′der·prop′o·si′tion, *n.*
un′der·pros′pect, *n.*
un′der·qual′i·fied′, *adj.*
un′der·queen′, *n.*
un′der·rang′er, *n.*
un′der·read′er, *n.*
un′der·re′al·ise′, *v.t.*, **-ised, -is·ing.**
un′der·re′al·ize′, *v.t.*, **-ized, -iz·ing.**
un′der·realm′, *n.*
un′der·re·ceiv′er, *n.*
un′der·reck′on, *v.t.*
un′der·rec′om·pense′, *v.t.*, **-pensed, -pens·ing;** *n.*
un′der·re′gion, *n.*
un′der·reg′is·tra′tion, *n.*
un′der·rep′re·sent′, *v.t.*
un′der·rep′re·sen·ta′tion, *n.*
un′der·re·spect′ed, *adj.*
un′der·rid′dle, *n.*
un′der·rigged′, *adj.*
un′der·ring′, *n.*
un′der·ri′pened, *adj.*
un′der·roar′er, *n.*
un′der·roast′, *v.t.*
un′der·robe′, *n.*
un′der·rogue′, *n.*
un′der·roll′er, *n.*
un′der·roof′, *n.*
un′der·room′, *n.*
un′der·root′ed, *adj.*
un′der·row′er, *n.*
un′der·rule′, *n.*
un′der·rule′, *v.*, **-ruled, -rul·ing.**
un′der·rul′er, *n.*
un′der·sac′ris·tan, *n.*
un′der·sat′is·fac′tion, *n.*
un′der·sat′u·ra′tion, *n.*
un′der·sav′ior, *n.*
un′der·saw′, *n.*
un′der·saw′, *v.t.*
un′der·saw′yer, *n.*
un′der·scheme′, *n.*
un′der·school′, *n.*
un′der·scoop′, *n.*
un′der·scoop′, *v.t.*
un′der·scribe′, *n.*
un′der·script′, *n.*
un′der·scru′pu·lous, *adj.*; **-ly,** *adv.*
un′der·seam′, *n.*
un′der·search′, *n.*
un′der·seat′ed, *adj.*
un′der·sec′re·tar′y·ship, *n.*
un′der·sect′, *n.*
un′der·see′, *v.i.*, **-saw, -seen, -see·ing.**
un′der·seed′ed, *adj.*
un′der·se′quence, *n.*
un′der·serv′ice, *n.*
un′der·sex′ton, *n.*
un′der·sheath′ing, *n.*
un′der·shep′herd, *n.*
un′der·shield′, *n.*
un′der·shine′, *n.*
un′der·shine′, *v.*, **-shone** or **-shined, -shin·ing.**
un′der·shire′, *n.*
un′der·shoe′, *n.*
un′der·shore′, *n.*
un′der·shore′, *v.t.*, **-shored, -shor·ing.**
un′der·short′en, *v.t.*
un′der·sight′, *n.*
un′der·sight′ed, *adj.*
un′der·sig′nal·man, *n., pl.* **-men.**
un′der·sill′, *n.*
un′der·skin′, *n.*
un′der·sky′, *n.*
un′der·sleep′, *v.i.*, **-slept, -sleep·ing.**
un′der·slept′, *adj.*
un′der·slip′, *n.*
un′der·sluice′, *n.*
un′der·so·ci′e·ty, *n.*
un′der·sole′, *n.*
un′der·sor′cer·er, *n.*
un′der·sort′, *n.*
un′der·soul′, *n.*
un′der·sound′, *n.*
un′der·sov′er·eign, *n.*
un′der·sow′, *n.*
un′der·span′, *n.*
un′der·spar′, *n.*
un′der·spec′i·fied′, *adj.*
un′der·spec′i·fy, *v.t.*, **-fied, -fy·ing.**
un′der·spe′cies, *n.*
un′der·spend′, *v.*, **-spent, -spend·ing.**
un′der·spin′ner, *n.*
un′der·splice′, *v.t.*, **-spliced, -splic·ing.**
un′der·spread′, *v.t.*, **-spread, -spread·ing.**
un′der·spring′, *n.*
un′der·spring′, *n., v.i.*, **-sprang** or **-sprung, -sprung, -spring·ing.**
un′der·sprout′, *n.*
un′der·sprout′, *v.i.*
un′der·staff′, *n.*
un′der·staffed′, *adj.*
un′der·stage′, *n.*
un′der·stain′, *n.*
un′der·stain′, *v.t.*
un′der·stamp′, *n.*
un′der·stamp′, *v.t.*

OE *understandincge* (n.). See UNDERSTAND, -ING[1], -ING[2] —**un/der·stand/ing·ly,** *adv.* —**un/der·stand/ing·ness,** *n.*

un·der·state (un/dər stāt/), *v.t.,* **-stat·ed, -stat·ing.** to state or represent less strongly or strikingly than the facts would bear out; set forth in restrained, moderate, or weak terms: *The casualty lists understate the extent of the disaster.* [UNDER- + STATE] —**un/der·state/ment,** *n.*

un·der·stock (*v.* un/dər stok/; *n.* un/dər stok/), *v.t.* **1.** to provide an insufficient quantity, as of merchandise, supplies, or livestock. —*n.* **2.** *Hort.* (in grafting) the rooted plant that receives the scion. [UNDER- + STOCK]

un·der·stood (un/dər sto͝od/), *v.* **1.** pt. and pp. of **understand.** —*adj.* **2.** agreed upon; known in advance; assented to: *It is the understood policy of this establishment to limit credit.* **3.** implied but not stated; left unexpressed: *The understood meaning of a danger sign is "Do not approach."*

un·der·strap·per (un/dər strap/ər), *n.* an underling. [UNDER- + STRAPPER]

un·der·stra·tum (un/dər strā/təm, -strat/əm), *n., pl.* **-stra·ta** (-strā/tə, -strat/ə), **-strat·ums.** a substratum. [UNDER- + STRATUM]

un·der·struc·ture (un/dər struk/chər), *n.* **1.** a structure serving as a support; a base or foundation: *The building has a strong understructure.* **2.** any thing, condition, etc., establishing support; a basis: *His argument rests on a sound understructure of knowledge.* [UNDER- + STRUCTURE]

un·der·stud·y (un/dər stud/ē), *v.,* **-stud·ied, -stud·y·ing,** *n., pl.* **-stud·ies.** —*v.t.* **1.** to study (a part) in order to replace the regular actor or actress when necessary. **2.** to act as understudy to (an actor or actress): *understudy the lead.* —*n.* **3.** a person trained and retained to act as substitute for an actor or actress. [UNDER- + STUDY]

un·der·sup·ply (un/dər sə plī/), *n.* a short supply or inadequate amount of something; less than is necessary or desirable. [UNDER- + SUPPLY[1]]

un·der·sur·face (un/dər sûr/fis), *n.* **1.** underside; bottom surface. —*adj.* **2.** submerged; under the surface, as of water, earth, etc.: *the undersurface speed of a submarine; undersurface development of a plant.* [UNDER- + SURFACE]

un·der·take (un/dər tāk/), *v.,* **-took, -tak·en, -tak·ing.** —*v.t.* **1.** to take on oneself, as a task, performance, etc.; attempt: *The butler undertook the duty of cooking.* **2.** to promise, agree, or obligate oneself to perform a task, duty, or the like: *The bride undertakes to love, honor, and obey her husband.* **3.** to warrant or guarantee (fol. by a clause): *The sponsors undertake that the candidate they propose meets all the requirements.* **4.** to take in charge; assume the duty of attending to: *The lawyer undertook the case without a fee.* **5.** *Obs.* to engage with, as in a duel. —*v.i.* **6.** *Archaic.* to take on oneself any task or responsibility. **7.** *Archaic.* to engage oneself by promise; give a guarantee, or become surety. [ME; see UNDER-, TAKE]

un·der·tak·er (un/dər tā/kər *for 1;* un/dər tā/kər *for 2*), *n.* **1.** one who undertakes something. **2.** Also called **mortician.** one whose business it is to prepare the dead for burial and to conduct funerals. [ME; see UNDERTAKE, -ER[1]] —**un/der·tak/er·ly,** *adj.*

un·der·tak·ing (un/dər tā/king *for 1–3;* un/dər-tā/king *for 4*), *n.* **1.** the act of one who undertakes any task or responsibility. **2.** a task, enterprise, etc., undertaken. **3.** a promise; pledge; guarantee. **4.** the business of an undertaker or funeral director. [ME; see UNDER, TAKING]

un·der·ten·ant (un/dər ten/ənt), *n.* a subtenant. [UNDER- + TENANT] —**un/der·ten/an·cy,** *n.*

un·der-the-coun·ter (un/dər *th*ə koun/tər), *adj.* **1.** pertaining to merchandise that is hidden or kept out of sight because of scarcity, illegality, impropriety, etc.: *under-the-counter sales of rationed goods.* **2.** illegal; unauthorized: *graft, bribery, and other under-the-counter dealings.*

un·der-the-ta·ble (un/dər *th*ə tā/bəl), *adj.* transacted in secret or in an underhanded manner.

un·der·things (un/dər thingz/), *n. pl.* women's underclothes. [UNDER- + THINGS]

un·der·throat·ing (un/dər thrō/ting), *n.* (on a cornice) a cove extended outward and downward to form a drip. [UNDER- + THROAT + -ING[1]]

un·der·thrust (un/dər thrust/), *n.* *Geol.* a thrust fault in which the footwall was the one that moved (opposed to *overthrust*). [UNDER- + THRUST]

un·der·tint (un/dər tint/), *n.* a subdued tint. [UNDER- + TINT]

un·der·tone (un/dər tōn/), *n.* **1.** a low or subdued tone: *to speak in undertones.* **2.** an unobtrusive or background sound: *There was an undertone of traffic noise in the recordings of street conversations.* **3.** an underlying quality or element; undercurrent: *There was an undertone of regret in his refusal.* **4.** a subdued color; a color modified by an underlying color. [UNDER- + TONE]

un·der·took (un/dər to͝ok/), *v.* pt. of **undertake.**

un·der·tow (un/dər tō/), *n.* **1.** the seaward, subsurface flow or draft of water from waves breaking on a beach. **2.** any strong current below the surface of a body of water, moving in a direction different from that of the surface current. [UNDER- + TOW[1]]

—**Syn. 2.** UNDERTOW, UNDERSET, RIPTIDE are terms for a usually strong undercurrent or flow of water in the ocean, contrary to the direction of surface water. UNDERTOW and another nautical term UNDERSET (a set or current contrary to the general set of the water, or contrary to the wind) came into notice early in the 19th century. The former is still in general use along the Atlantic coast; the latter now less well known. RIP, in use in the U.S. by the late 18th century, properly means a violently disturbed place in a body of water, usually by the meeting of opposing tides. Of recent years, in the form RIPTIDE, it has also been used, esp. on the Pacific coast, to mean much the same as UNDERTOW, dangerous to bathers where heavy surf prevails.

un·der·trick (un/dər trik/), *n.* *Bridge.* a trick that a declarer failed to win in relation to the number of tricks necessary to make his contract. Cf. **overtrick.** [UNDER- + TRICK]

un·der·trump (un/dər trump/), *v.t., v.i.* *Cards.* **1.** to trump with a lower trump than has already been played. [UNDER- + TRUMP[1]]

un·der·val·ue (un/dər val/yo͞o), *v.t.,* **-ued, -u·ing.** **1.** to value below the real worth; put too low a value on. **2.** to diminish in value; make of less value. **3.** to have insufficient regard or esteem for; hold too low an opinion of. [UNDER- + VALUE]

—**Syn. 1.** underrate, underestimate, depreciate.

un·der·vest (un/dər vest/), *n.* *Brit.* an undershirt. [UNDER- + VEST]

un·der·waist (un/dər wāst/), *n.* **1.** a blouse worn under another. **2.** such a blouse to which other undergarments are pinned or buttoned, worn by infants and small children. [UNDER- + WAIST]

un·der·wa·ter (un/dər wô/tər, -wot/ər), *adj.* **1.** existing or occurring under water. **2.** designed to be used under water. **3.** located below a ship's waterline. —*adv.* **4.** beneath the water: *to travel underwater.* —*n.* **5.** the water beneath the surface: *cold currents in the underwater.* **6. underwaters,** the depths, as of a sea, lake, etc. [UNDER- + WATER]

un·der·wear (un/dər wâr/), *n.* clothing worn next to the skin under outer clothes. Also called **underclothing.** [UNDER- + WEAR]

un·der·weight (*n.* un/dər wāt/; *adj.* un/dər wāt/), *n.* **1.** deficiency in weight below a standard or requirement. —*adj.* **2.** lacking the usual, required, or proper weight. [UNDER- + WEIGHT]

un·der·went (un/dər went/), *v.* pt. of **undergo.**

un·der·wing (un/dər wing/), *n.* **1.** one of the hind wings of an insect. **2.** any of several noctuid moths of the genus *Catocala,* characterized by red-, yellow-, or orange-banded hind wings. [UNDER- + WING]

un·der·wood (un/dər wo͝od/), *n.* **1.** woody shrubs or small trees growing among taller trees. **2.** a clump or stretch of such growth. [ME *underwode.* See UNDER-, WOOD[1]] —**un/der·wood/ed,** *adj.*

un·der·work (un/dər wûrk/), *v.,* **-worked, -work·ing.** —*v.t.* **1.** to do less work on than is necessary or required: *to underwork an idea.* **2.** to employ inadequately: *He underworks his mind and overworks his feet.* —*v.i.* **3.** to do less work than is normal or proper: *He is fat because he underworks and overeats.* [UNDER- + WORK] —**un/der·work/er,** *n.*

un·der·world (un/dər wûrld/), *n.* **1.** the criminal element of human society; the aggregate of those who habitually engage in crime or align themselves with known criminals. **2.** the imagined abode of departed souls or spirits; Hades. **3.** a region below the surface, as of the earth or a body of water. **4.** the opposite side of the earth; the antipodes. **5.** the world below the skies; the earth. [UNDER- + WORLD]

un·der·write (un/dər rīt/), *v.,* **-wrote, -writ·ten, -writ·ing.** —*v.t.* **1.** to write under or at the foot of, esp. under other written matter. **2.** to sign one's name, as to a document or the like. **3.** to subscribe to; concur with a statement, a decision, testimony, etc., by or as by signing one's name to it. **4.** to bind oneself to contribute a sum of money to an activity carried on by others; agree to pay any deficiency or loss, in order to encourage a favored activity: *Wealthy music lovers underwrote the cost of the experimental concerts.* **5.** to guarantee capital for; agree to finance, as a business venture. **6.** to guarantee the sale of (a security issue to be offered to the public for subscription). **7.** *Insurance.* **a.** to write one's name at the end of (a policy), thereby becoming liable in case of certain losses specified in the policy. **b.** to insure. **c.** to assume liability to the extent of (a specified sum) by way of insurance. **d.** to select or rate risks for insurance. —*v.i.* **8.** to underwrite something. **9.** to carry on the business of an underwriter. [late ME, trans. of L *subscribere* to write underneath, sign, subscribe. See SUBSCRIBE]

un·der·writ·er (un/dər rī/tər), *n.* **1.** one who underwrites policies of insurance or carries on insurance as a business. **2.** a person who underwrites shares or bonds. [UNDERWRITE + -ER[1]]

un·der·writ·ten (un/dər rit/ən), *v.* pp. of **underwrite.**

un·der·wrote (un/dər rōt/), *v.* pt. of **underwrite.**

un·de·signed (un/di zīnd/), *adj.* not planned beforehand; unpremeditated; unintentional: *an outcome which was undesigned but as satisfactory as the intended result.* [UN-[1] + DESIGN + ED[3]] —**un·de·sign·ed·ly** (un/di-zī/nid lē, -zīnd/-), *adv.*

un·de·sign·ing (un/di zī/ning), *adj.* not characterized by underhand schemes or selfish motives; without an ulterior design. [UN-[1] + DESIGNING] —**un/de·sign/ing·ly,** *adv.* —**un/de·sign/ing·ness,** *n.*

un·de·sir·a·ble (un/di zīər/ə bəl), *adj.* **1.** not desirable or attractive; objectionable; inappropriate or detrimental: *undesirable qualities; undesirable members of the community.* —*n.* **2.** one who or that which is undesirable; a person of doubtful or negative value to a group or to society in general: *a collection of malcontents, undesirables, and riffraff.* [UN-[1] + DESIRABLE] —**un/de·sir/a·ble·ness,** *n.* —**un/de·sir/a·bly,** *adv.*

undesir/able dis/charge. *U.S.* **1.** a discharge under other than honorable conditions of a person from military service by administrative action. **2.** a certificate of such a discharge.

un·de·vel·oped (un/di vel/əpt), *adj.* not developed. [UN-[1] + DEVELOP + -ED[2]]

---

un/de·scend/a·ble, *adj.*
un/de·scend/ed, *adj.*
un/de·scend/ent, *adj.*
un/de·scend/i·ble, *adj.*
un/de·scend/ing, *adj.*
un/de·scrib/a·ble, *adj.;* **-ble·ness,** *n.;* **-bly,** *adv.*
un/de·scribed/, *adj.*
un/de·scried/, *adj.*
un/de·scrip/tive, *adj.;* **-ly,** *adv.;* **-ness,** *n.*
un/de·scry/ing, *adj.*
un·des/e·crat/ed, *adj.*
un/de·sert/ed, *adj.*
un/de·served/, *adj.*
un/de·serv/ed·ly, *adv.*
un/de·serv/ing, *adj.;* **-ly,** *adv.;* **-ness,** *n.*
un·des/ic·cat/ed, *adj.*
un·des/ig·nat/ed, *adj.*
un·des/ig·na/tive, *adj.*
un/de·sired/, *adj.*
un/de·sir/ing, *adj.*
un/de·sir/ous, *adj.;* **-ly,** *adv.*
un/de·sist/ing, *adj.*
un/de·spaired/, *adj.*
un/de·spair/ing, *adj.;* **-ly,** *adv.*
un/des·patched/, *adj.*
un/de·spised/, *adj.*
un/de·spis/ing, *adj.*
un/de·spoiled/, *adj.*
un/de·spond/ent, *adj.;* **-ly,** *adv.*
un/de·spond/ing, *adj.;* **-ly,** *adv.*
un/des·pot/ic, *adj.*
un/des·pot/i·cal·ly, *adv.*
un·des/tined, *adj.*
un·des/ti·tute/, *adj.*
un/de·stroyed/, *adj.*
un/de·struct/i·ble, *adj.;* **-ble·ness,** *n.;* **-bly,** *adv.*
un/de·struc/tive, *adj.;* **-ly,** *adv.;* **-ness,** *n.*
un/de·tach/a·ble, *adj.*
un/de·tached/, *adj.*
un/de·tailed/, *adj.*
un/de·tain/a·ble, *adj.*
un/de·tained/, *adj.*
un/de·tect/a·ble, *adj.;* **-bly,** *adv.*
un/de·tect/ed, *adj.*
un/de·tect/i·ble, *adj.*
un/de·te/ri·o·rat/ed, *adj.*
un/de·te/ri·o·rat/ing, *adj.*
un/de·te/ri·o·ra/tive, *adj.*
un/de·ter/mi·na·ble, *adj.;* **-ble·ness,** *n.;* **-bly,** *adv.*
un/de·ter/mined, *adj.*
un/de·ter/min·ing, *adj.*
un/de·ter/ra·bil/i·ty, *n.*
un/de·ter/ra·ble, *adj.;* **-bly,** *adv.*
un/de·terred/, *adj.*
un/de·ter/ring, *adj.*
un/de·test/a·bil/i·ty, *n.*
un/de·test/a·ble, *adj.;* **-ble·ness,** *n.;* **-bly,** *adv.*
un/de·test/ed, *adj.*
un/de·test/ing, *adj.*
un/de·throned/, *adj.*
un·det/o·nat/ed, *adj.*
un/de·tract/ing, *adj.;* **-ly,** *adv.*
un/de·trac/tive, *adj.;* **-ly,** *adv.*
un/de·trac/to·ry, *adj.*
un/det·ri·men/tal, *adj.;* **-ly,** *adv.*
un·dev/as·tat/ed, *adj.*
un·dev/as·tat/ing, *adj.;* **-ly,** *adv.*
un/de·vel/op·a·ble, *adj.*
un/de·vel/op·ing, *adj.*
un/de·vel/op·men/tal, *adj.;* **-ly,** *adv.*
un·de/vi·a·ble, *adj.*
un·de/vi·at/ed, *adj.*
un·de/vi·at/ing, *adj.;* **-ly,** *adv.*
un·dev/il·ish, *adj.*
un·de/vi·ous, *adj.;* **-ly,** *adv.;* **-ness,** *n.*
un/de·vis/a·ble, *adj.*
un/de·vised/, *adj.*
un/de·vot/ed, *adj.*
un/de·vo/tion·al, *adj.*
un/de·voured/, *adj.*
un/de·vout/, *adj.;* **-ly,** *adv.;* **-ness,** *n.*
un·dewed/, *adj.*
un·dew/i·ly, *adv.*
un·dew/i·ness, *n.*
un·dew/y, *adj.*
un·dex/ter·ous, *adj.;* **-ly,** *adv.;* **-ness,** *n.*
un·dex/trous, *adj.;* **-ly,** *adv.;* **-ness,** *n.*

---

un/der·stay/, *n.*
un/der·stay/, *v.i.*
un/der·steer/, *v.t.*
un/der·stem/, *n.*
un/der·step/, *n.*
un/der·stew/ard, *n.*
un/der·stew/ard·ship/, *n.*
un/der·stim/u·lus, *n., pl.* **-li.**
un/der·strain/, *n.*
un/der·strap/, *n.*
un/der·strap/, *v.t.,* **-strapped, -strap·ping.**
un/der·stream/, *n.*
un/der·stress/, *n.*
un/der·stress/, *v.t.*
un/der·strew/, *v.t.,* **-strewed, -strewed** or **-strewn, -strew·ing.**
un/der·strife/, *n.*
un/der·strike/, *v.t.,* **-struck, -strick·en, -strik·ing.**
un/der·stuff/, *v.t.*
un/der·stuff/ing, *n.*
un/der·suit/, *n.*
un/der·suit/, *v.t.*
un/der·sup·ply/, *n.*
un/der·sup·ply/, *v.t.,* **-plied, -ply·ing.**
un/der·sup·port/, *n.*
un/der·swain/, *n.*
un/der·swamp/, *n.*
un/der·sward/, *n.*
un/der·swear/er, *n.*
un/der·sweep/, *v.t.,* **-swept, -sweep·ing.**
un/der·swell/, *v.i.*
un/der·swell/, *n.*
un/der·talk/, *n.*
un/der·tap/ster, *n.*
un/der·taxed/, *adj.*
un/der·teach/, *v.,* **-taught, -teach·ing.**
un/der·teach/er, *n.*
un/der·teamed/, *adj.*
un/der·tell/er, *n.*
un/der·ten/ure, *n.*
un/der·ter·res/tri·al, *adj.*
un/der·test/, *v.t.*
un/der·thane/, *n.*
un/der·thaw/, *v.*
un/der·thief/, *n.*
un/der·thought/, *n.*
un/der·tide/, *n.*
un/der·tid/ed, *adj.*
un/der·tie/, *n.*
un/der·tie/, *v.t.,* **-tied, -ty·ing.**
un/der·ti/tle, *n.*
un/der·trade/, *v.,* **-trad·ed, -trad·ing.**
un/der·trad/er, *n.*
un/der·train/, *v.t.*
un/der·trained/, *adj.*
un/der·treas/ur·er, *n.*
un/der·tribe/, *n.*
un/der·truck/, *n.*
un/der·truss/, *v.t.*
un/der·tub/, *n.*
un/der·tune/, *n.*
un/der·tune/, *v.t.,* **-tuned, -tun·ing.**
un/der·tu/nic, *n.*
un/der·tu/tor, *n.*
un/der·twig/, *n.*
un/der·ty/rant, *n.*
un/der·ush/er, *n.*
un/der·valve/, *n.*
un/der·vas/sal, *n.*
un/der·vault/ed, *adj.*
un/der·vault/ing, *n.*
un/der·veg/e·ta/tion, *n.*
un/der·ven/ti·late/, *v.t.,* **-lat·ed, -lat·ing.**
un/der·ven/ti·lat/ed, *adj.*
un/der·ven/ti·la/tion, *n.*
un/der·verse/, *n.*
un/der·vic/ar, *n.*
un/der·view/er, *n.*
un/der·vil/lain, *n.*
un/der·vi/tal·ized/, *adj.*
un/der·voice/, *n.*
un/der·wage/, *n.*
un/der·waist/coat/, *n.*
un/der·ward/en, *n.*
un/der·wash/, *n.*
un/der·watch/er, *n.*
un/der·wave/, *n.*
un/der·wav/ing, *n.*
un/der·weft/, *n.*
un/der·wheel/, *n.*
un/der·wind/, *n.*
un/der·witch/, *n.*
un/der·work/er, *n.*
un/der·work/man, *n., pl.* **-men.**
un/der·wrap/, *n.*
un/der·wrap/, *v.t.,* **-wrapped, -wrap·ping.**
un/der·wrought/, *adj.*
un/der·yield/, *n.*
un/der·yield/, *v.i.*
un/der·yoke/, *n.*
un/der·zeal/, *n.*
un/der·zeal/ot, *n.*
un/der·zeal/ous, *adj.;* **-ly,** *adv.;* **-ness,** *n.*

un·did (un did′), *v.* pt. of **undo.**

un·dies (un′dēz), *n.pl.* women's or children's underwear. [shortening and alter. of UNDERWEAR]

un·di·gest·i·ble (un′di jes′tə bəl, -dī-), *adj.* *Rare.* indigestible. [UN-[1] + DIGESTIBLE]

un·dine (un dēn′, un′dēn, -dīn), *n.* one of a group of female water spirits. According to Paracelsus, when an undine married a mortal and bore a child, she received a soul. [< NL *undina* (coined by Paracelsus), equiv. to L *und(a)* wave, water + *-īna* -INE[1]] **—Syn.** See **sylph.**

Un·dine (un dēn′, un′dēn), *n.* a girl's given name.

un·di·rect·ed (un′di rek′tid, -dī-), *adj.* **1.** not directed; not guided: *He wasted his time on undirected activity.* **2.** bearing no address, as a letter. [UN-[1] + DIRECTED]

un·dis·posed (un′di spōzd′), *adj.* **1.** not disposed of. **2.** not favorably inclined; not prepared; unwilling: *They are both disinclined to work and undisposed to starve.* [ME; see UN-[1], DISPOSED]

un·dis·so·ci·at·ed (un′di sō′shē ā′tid, -sē ā′-), *adj.* *Chem.* not dissociated, esp. into ions or into simpler molecules. [UN-[1] + DISSOCIATED]

un·dis·tin·guished (un′di sting′gwisht), *adj.* **1.** without apparent differences; having no distinguishing marks or features; indistinguishable: *As part of the crowd he was anonymous, undistinguished.* **2.** without distinction; not possessing any special merit; mediocre: *an undistinguished performance.* **3.** undetected; unobserved: *The magician's trunk appeared to float in midair, its supporting wires undistinguished against the black backdrop.* **4.** not divided according to a system or set of categories; unseparated: *The sorting process leaves many valuable specimens undistinguished from the rejects.* [UN-[1] + DISTINGUISHED]

un′di·vid′ed prof′its, (un′di vīd′id), earnings that have neither been distributed as dividends to stockholders nor transferred to the earned surplus account. [late ME; see UN[1], DIVIDED]

un·do (un dōō′), *v.t.*, **-did, -done, -do·ing. 1.** to reverse the doing of; cause to be as if never done: *Murder once done can never be undone.* **2.** to do away with; erase; efface: *The survivors set to work to undo the havoc done by the storm.* **3.** to bring to ruin or disaster; destroy: *He did wrong, and in the end his wrongs undid him.* **4.** to unfasten by releasing: *to undo a barred door; to undo a lock; to undo a jacket; to undo a zipper.* **5.** to untie or loose (a knot, rope, etc.): *He undid the cords that held the bundle together.* **6.** to open (a package, wrapping, etc.): *The child could not wait to undo the glittering paper that hid his present.* **7.** *Archaic.* to explain; interpret. [ME; OE *undōn;* c. D *ontdoen.* See UN-[2], DO[1]] **—un·do′a·ble,** *adj.* **—un·do′er,** *n.*

un·do·ing (un dōō′ing), *n.* **1.** the reversing of what has been done; annulling. **2.** a bringing to destruction, ruin, or disaster. **3.** a cause of destruction or ruin. **4.** the act of unfastening or loosing. [ME; see UNDO, -ING[1]]

un·done[1] (un dun′), *adj.* not done; not accomplished or completed. [ME *un-dun.* See UN-[1], DONE]

un·done[2] (un dun′), *v.* **1.** pp. of **undo.** **—adj. 2.** brought to destruction or ruin. **3.** unfastened.

un·dou·ble (un dub′əl), *v.t.*, **-bled, -bling.** to unfold; render single. [UN-[2] + DOUBLE]

un·doubt·ed (un dou′tid), *adj.* not called in question; accepted as beyond doubt; undisputed. [ME; see UN-[1], DOUBT, -ED[2]] **—un·doubt′ed·ly,** *adv.*

un·drape (un drāp′), *v.t.*, **-draped, -drap·ing.** to strip of drapery; uncover. [UN-[2] + DRAPE]

un·draw (un drô′), *v.*, **-drew, -drawn, -draw·ing.** **—***v.t.* **1.** to draw open or aside: *to undraw a curtain.* **—***v.i.* **2.** to be drawn open or aside. [ME: to withdraw; see UN-[2], DRAW]

un·dress (un dres′), *v.*, **-dressed** or **-drest, -dress·ing,** *n.*, *adj.* **—***v.t.* **1.** to take the clothes off (a person); disrobe. **2.** to strip or divest of or as if of a covering; expose: *to undress a pretense.* **3.** to remove the dressing from (a wound, sore, etc.). **—***v.i.* **4.** to take off one's clothes. **—***n.* **5.** dress of a style designed to be worn on other than highly formal or ceremonial occasions; informal dress, as opposed to full dress. **6.** dress of a style not designed to be worn in public; dishabille; negligée: *She couldn't receive guests in such a state of undress.* **—***adj.* **7.** of or pertaining to clothing of a style less formal than full dress: *undress uniform.* **8.** characterized by informality of dress, manners, or the like: *an undress dinner party.* [UN-[2] + DRESS]

un·dressed (un drest′), *adj.* **1.** not dressed; not specially prepared. **2.** (of leather) having a napped finish on the flesh side. [ME; see UN-[1], DRESSED]

un′dress u′niform, *Mil.*, *Navy.* a uniform worn on other than formal occasions.

Und·set (ōōn′set), *n.* **Sig·rid** (sig′rid; *Nor.* si′gʀi), 1882–1949, Norwegian novelist: Nobel prize 1928.

und so wei·ter (ōōnt zō vī′tər), *German.* and so forth; et cetera. *Abbr.:* usw, u.s.w.

un·due (un dōō′, -dyōō′), *adj.* **1.** unwarranted; excessive: *undue hardship; undue haste.* **2.** inappropriate; unjustifiable; improper: *undue influence.* **3.** not owed or currently payable. [ME *undewe.* See UN-[1], DUE]

un·du·lant (un′jə lənt, un′də-, -dyə-), *adj.* undulating; characterized by a wavelike motion or pattern: *an undulant dance; an undulant edge.* [UNDUL(ATE) + -ANT] **—un′du·lance,** *n.*

un′dulant fe′ver, *Pathol.* brucellosis.

un·du·late (*v.* un′jə lāt′, un′də-, -dyə-; *adj.* un′jə lit, -lāt′, un′də-, -dyə-), *v.*, **-lat·ed, -lat·ing,** *adj.* **—***v.i.* **1.** to move with a sinuous or wavelike motion; display a smooth rising-and-falling or side-to-side alternation of movement: *The flag undulates in the breeze. The snake undulated across the bare ground.* **2.** to have a wavy form or surface; bend with successive curves in alternate directions. **—***v.t.* **3.** to cause to move in waves. **4.** to give a wavy form to. **—***adj.* **5.** Also, **un′du·lat′ed.** wavy; bending with successive curves in alternate directions; having a wavelike or rippled form, surface, edge, etc. [< L *undulāt(us)* waved, equiv. to *undul(a)* (dim. of *unda* wave) + *-ātus* -ATE[1]] **—un′du·la′tor,** *n.*

un·du·la·tion (un′jə lā′shən, un′də-, -dyə-), *n.* **1.** an act of undulating; a wavelike motion. **2.** wavy form or outline. **3.** one of a series of wavelike bends, curves, or elevations. **4.** *Physics.* **a.** a wave. **b.** the motion of waves. [< NL **undulātiōn-* (s. of **undulātiō*), equiv. to L *und(a)* wave + *-ul-* -ULE + *-ātiōn-* -ATION]

un·du·la·to·ry (un′jə lə tôr′ē, -tōr′ē, un′də-, -dyə-), *adj.* **1.** Also, **un′du·lar.** moving in undulations. **2.** having the form or appearance of waves. Also, **un·du·la·tive** (un′jə lā′tiv, un′də-, -dyə-). [UNDULATE + -ORY[1]]

un′dulatory the′ory, *Physics.* See **wave theory.**

un·du·la·tus (un′dōō lā′təs, -dyōō-), *adj.* *Meteorol.* (of a cloud) consisting of elements arranged in wavelike rows or files. [< NL, L: waving, bending. See UNDULATE]

un·du·ly (un dōō′lē, -dyōō′-), *adv.* **1.** excessively: *unduly worried.* **2.** in an inappropriate, unjustifiable, or improper manner: *unduly critical.* [ME *undewely.* See UNDUE, -LY]

un·dy (un′dē), *adj.* *Heraldry.* undé.

un·dy·ing (un dī′ing), *adj.* deathless; immortal; unending. [ME; see UN-[1], DYING] **—un·dy′ing·ly,** *adv.* **—un·dy′ing·ness,** *n.*

un·earned (un ûrnd′), *adj.* **1.** not received in exchange for labor or services; not gained by lawful work or employment. **2.** not earned; unmerited; undeserved: *unearned promotion; an unearned compliment.* **3.** not yet earned: *Lenders are not permitted to take borrowers' unearned wages as collateral.* [UN-[1] + EARN[1] + -ED[2]]

un′di·a·bet′ic, *adj.*
un·di′ag·nosed′, *adj.*
un·di′a·gramed′, *adj.*
un·di′a·gram·mat′ic, *adj.*
un′di·a·gram·mat′i·cal, *adj.;* -ly, *adv.*
un·di′a·grammed′, *adj.*
un·di′aled, *adj.*
un·di′alled, *adj.*
un·di′a·lyzed′, *adj.*
un′di·a·met′ric, *adj.*
un′di·a·met′ri·cal, *adj.;* -ly, *adv.*
un·di′a·pered, *adj.*
un′di·aph′a·nous, *adj.;* -ly, *adv.;* -ness, *n.*
un′di·a·ton′ic, *adj.*
un′di·a·ton′i·cal·ly, *adv.*
un′di·chot′o·mous, *adj.;* -ly, *adv.*
un·dic′tat·ed, *adj.*
un′dic·ta·to′ri·al, *adj.;* -ly, *adv.*
un′di·dac′tic, *adj.*
un·dif′fer·ent, *adj.;* -ly, *adv.*
un′dif·fer·en′ti·a·ble, *adj.;* -bly, *adv.*
un′dif·fer·en′ti·at′ed, *adj.*
un·dif′fer·ing, *adj.*
un·dif′fi·cult′, *adj.;* -ly, *adv.*
un·dif′fi·dent, *adj.;* -ly, *adv.*
un′dif·fract′ed, *adj.*
un′dif·frac′tive, *adj.;* -ly, *adv.;* -ness, *n.*
un′dif·fused′, *adj.*
un′dif·fus′i·ble, *adj.*
un′dif·fu′sive, *adj.;* -ly, *adv.;* -ness, *n.*
un′di·gest′ed, *adj.*
un′di·gest′ing, *adj.*
un·dig′i·tat′ed, *adj.*
un·dig′ni·fied′, *adj.;* -ly, *adv.*
un′di·gres′sive, *adj.;* -ly, *adv.;* -ness, *n.*
un·diked′, *adj.*
un′di·lap′i·dat′ed, *adj.*
un′di·lat′a·ble, *adj.*
un′di·lat′ed, *adj.*
un′di·lat′ing, *adj.*
un′di·la′tive, *adj.*
un·dil′a·to′ri·ly, *adv.*
un·dil′a·to′ry, *adj.*
un·dil′i·gent, *adj.;* -ly, *adv.*
un′di·lute′, *adj.*
un′di·lut′ed, *adj.*
un′di·lut′ing, *adj.*
un′di·lu′vi·al, *adj.*
un′di·lu′vi·an, *adj.*
un·dim′, *adj.;* -ly, *adv.*
un′di·men′sioned, *adj.*
un·dim′er·ous, *adj.*
un′di·mid′i·at′ed, *adj.*
un′di·min′ish·a·ble, *adj.;* -ble·ness, *n.;* -bly, *adv.*
un′di·min′ished, *adj.*
un′di·min′ish·ing, *adj.*
un·dimmed′, *adj.*
un·dim′pled, *adj.*
un′di·plo′maed, *adj.*
un′dip·lo·mat′ic, *adj.*
un′dip·lo·mat′i·cal·ly, *adv.*
un·dipped′, *adj.*
un′di·rec′tion·al, *adj.*
un′dis·a′bled, *adj.*
un′dis·a·gree′a·ble, *adj.*
un′dis·ap·pear′ing, *adj.*
un′dis·ap·point′a·ble, *adj.*
un′dis·ap·point′ed, *adj.*
un′dis·ap·point′ing, *adj.*
un′dis·armed′, *adj.*
un′dis·as′trous, *adj.;* -ly, *adv.*
un′dis·band′ed, *adj.*
un′dis·barred′, *adj.*
un′dis·bursed′, *adj.*
un′dis·card′a·ble, *adj.*
un′dis·card′ed, *adj.*
un′dis·cern′a·ble, *adj.;* -bly, *adv.*
un′dis·cerned′, *adj.*
un′dis·cern′i·ble, *adj.;* -bly, *adv.*
un′dis·cern′ing, *adj.;* -ly, *adv.*
un′dis·charge′a·ble, *adj.*
un′dis·charged′, *adj.*
un·dis′ci·plin′a·ble, *adj.*
un·dis′ci·plined, *adj.*
un′dis·claimed′, *adj.*
un′dis·closed′, *adj.*
un′dis·col′ored, *adj.*
un′dis·col′oured, *adj.*
un′dis·com′fit·ed, *adj.*
un′dis·com·posed′, *adj.*
un′dis·con·cert′ed, *adj.*
un′dis·con·nect′ed, *adj.;* -ly, *adv.*
un′dis·con·tin′ued, *adj.*
un′dis·cord′ant, *adj.;* -ly, *adv.*
un′dis·cord′ing, *adj.*
un′dis·count′a·ble, *adj.*
un·dis′count·ed, *adj.*
un′dis·cour′age·a·ble, *adj.*
un′dis·cour′aged, *adj.*
un′dis·cour′ag·ing, *adj.;* -ly, *adv.*
un′dis·cov′er·a·ble, *adj.*
un′dis·cov′ered, *adj.*
un′dis·cred′it·a·ble, *adj.*
un′dis·cred′it·ed, *adj.*
un′dis·crim′i·nat′ed, *adj.*
un′dis·crim′i·nat′ing, *adj.;* -ly, *adv.*
un′dis·crim′i·na·to′ry, *adj.*
un′dis·cuss′a·ble, *adj.*
un′dis·cussed′, *adj.*
un′dis·dain′ing, *adj.*
un′dis·eased′, *adj.*
un′dis·es·tab′lished, *adj.*
un′dis·fig′ured, *adj.*
un′dis·fran′chised, *adj.*
un′dis·gorged′, *adj.*
un′dis·graced′, *adj.*
un′dis·guis′a·ble, *adj.*
un′dis·guised′, *adj.*
un′dis·gust′ed, *adj.*
un′dis·heart′ened, *adj.*
un′di·shev′eled, *adj.*
un′dis·hon′ored, *adj.*
un′dis·il·lu′sioned, *adj.*
un′dis·in·fect′ed, *adj.*
un′dis·in·her′it·a·ble, *adj.*
un′dis·in·her′it·ed, *adj.*
un′dis·joined′, *adj.*
un′dis·joint′ed, *adj.*
un′dis·lo·cat′ed, *adj.*
un′dis·lodged′, *adj.*
un′dis·man′tled, *adj.*
un′dis·may′a·ble, *adj.*
un′dis·mayed′, *adj.*
un′dis·missed′, *adj.*
un′dis·or′dered, *adj.*
un′dis·or′der·ly, *adj.*
un′dis·or′gan·ized′, *adj.*
un′dis·par′aged, *adj.*
un′dis·pas′sion·ate, *adj.;* -ly, *adv.*
un′dis·patch′a·ble, *adj.*
un′dis·patched′, *adj.*
un′dis·patch′ing, *adj.*
un′dis·pel′la·ble, *adj.*
un′dis·pelled′, *adj.*
un′dis·pen′sa·ble, *adj.*
un′dis·pensed′, *adj.*
un′dis·persed′, *adj.*
un′dis·pers′ing, *adj.*
un′dis·place′a·ble, *adj.*
un′dis·placed′, *adj.*
un′dis·play′a·ble, *adj.*
un′dis·played′, *adj.*
un′dis·play′ing, *adj.*
un′dis·prov′a·ble, *adj.*
un′dis·proved′, *adj.*
un′dis·put′a·ble, *adj.*
un′dis·pu·ta′tious, *adj.;* -ly, *adv.;* -ness, *n.*
un′dis·put′ed, *adj.;* -ly, *adv.*
un′dis·put′ing, *adj.*
un′dis·qual′i·fi′a·ble, *adj.*
un′dis·qual′i·fied′, *adj.*
un′dis·qui′et·ed, *adj.*
un′dis·rupt′ed, *adj.*
un′dis·sect′ed, *adj.*
un′dis·sem′bled, *adj.*
un′dis·sem′bling, *adj.;* -ly, *adv.*
un′dis·sem′i·nat′ed, *adj.*
un′dis·sent′ing, *adj.*
un′dis·sev′ered, *adj.*
un·dis′si·pat′ed, *adj.*
un′dis·sol′u·ble, *adj.*
un·dis′so·lute′, *adj.*
un′dis·solv′a·ble, *adj.*
un′dis·solved′, *adj.*
un′dis·solv′ing, *adj.*
un·dis′so·nant, *adj.;* -ly, *adv.*
un′dis·suad′a·ble, *adj.*
un·dis′tant, *adj.;* -ly, *adv.*
un′dis·taste′ful, *adj.*
un′dis·tem′pered, *adj.*
un′dis·tend′, *v.t.*
un′dis·tilled′, *adj.*
un′dis·tin′guish·a·ble, *adj.*
un′dis·tin′guish·ing, *adj.;* -ly, *adv.*
un′dis·tort′ed, *adj.;* -ly, *adv.*
un′dis·tort′ing, *adj.*
un′dis·tract′ed, *adj.;* -ly, *adv.;* -ness, *n.*
un′dis·tract′ing, *adj.;* -ly, *adv.*
un′dis·trained′, *adj.*
un′dis·traught′, *adj.*
un′dis·tressed′, *adj.*
un′dis·trib′ut·ed, *adj.*
un′dis·trust′ful, *adj.;* -ly, *adv.;* -ness, *n.*
un′dis·turb′a·ble, *adj.*
un′dis·turbed′, *adj.*
un′dis·turb′ing, *adj.;* -ly, *adv.*
un′dith·y·ram′bic, *adj.*
un′di·u·ret′ic, *adj.*
un′di·ur′nal, *adj.;* -ly, *adv.*
un′di·ver′gent, *adj.;* -ly, *adv.*
un′di·verg′ing, *adj.*
un′di·verse′, *adj.;* -ly, *adv.;* -ness, *n.*
un′di·ver′si·fied′, *adj.*
un′di·vert′ed, *adj.*
un′di·vert′i·ble, *adj.*
un′di·ver′tive, *adj.*
un′di·vest′ed, *adj.*
un′di·vid′a·ble, *adj.*
un′di·vid′ed, *adj.*
un′di·vid′ing, *adj.*
un′di·vin′a·ble, *adj.*
un′di·vined′, *adj.*
un′di·vin′ing, *adj.*
un′di·vis′i·ble, *adj.*
un′di·vi′sive, *adj.;* -ly, *adv.;* -ness, *n.*
un′di·vorce′a·ble, *adj.*
un′di·vorced′, *adj.*
un′di·vulge′a·ble, *adj.*
un′di·vulged′, *adj.*
un′di·vulg′ing, *adj.*
un·docked′, *adj.*
un·dock′et·ed, *adj.*
un·doc′tored, *adj.*
un·doc′tri·nal, *adj.;* -ly, *adv.*
un·doc′trined, *adj.*
un′doc·u·men′ta·ry, *adj.*
un·doc′u·ment·ed, *adj.*
un·dodged′, *adj.*
un′dog·mat′ic, *adj.*
un′dog·mat′i·cal, *adj.;* -ly, *adv.*
un·dol′or·ous, *adj.;* -ly, *adv.;* -ness, *n.*
un·domed′, *adj.*
un′do·mes′tic, *adj.*
un′do·mes′ti·ca·ble, *adj.*
un′do·mes′ti·cal·ly, *adv.*
un′do·mes′ti·cat′ed, *adj.*
un·dom′i·ciled′, *adj.*
un·dom′i·nat′ed, *adj.*
un·dom′i·na′tive, *adj.*
un′dom·i·neer′ing, *adj.*
un′do·min′i·cal, *adj.*
un·do′nat·ed, *adj.*
un·doped′, *adj.*
un·dot′ing, *adj.*
un·dot′ted, *adj.*
un·doubt′a·ble, *adj.*
un·doubt′ful, *adj.;* -ly, *adv.;* -ness, *n.*
un·doubt′ing, *adj.*
un·douched′, *adj.*
un·dough′ty, *adj.*
un·dow′eled, *adj.*
un·dow′elled, *adj.*
un·dow′ered, *adj.*
un·downed′, *adj.*
un·draft′a·ble, *adj.*
un·draft′ed, *adj.*
un·drag′oned, *adj.*
un′dra·gooned′, *adj.*
un·drain′a·ble, *adj.*
un·drained′, *adj.*
un′dra·mat′ic, *adj.*
un′dra·mat′i·cal, *adj.;* -ly, *adv.*
un·dram′a·tis′a·ble, *adj.*
un·dram′a·tiz′a·ble, *adj.*
un·dram′a·tized′, *adj.*
un·dra′per·ied, *adj.*
un·draw′a·ble, *adj.*
un·dread′ed, *adj.*
un·dread′ing, *adj.*
un·dreamed′, *adj.*
un·dream′ing, *adj.*
un·dream′like′, *adj.*
un·dreamt′, *adj.*
un·dredged′, *adj.*
un·drenched′, *adj.*
un·dried′, *adj.*
un·drift′ing, *adj.*
un·drill′a·ble, *adj.*
un·drilled′, *adj.*
un·drink′a·ble, *adj.*
un·drink′ing, *adj.*
un·driv′a·ble, *adj.*
un·driv′en, *adj.*
un·droop′ing, *adj.*
un·dropped′, *adj.*
un·drop′si·cal, *adj.*
un·dross′i·ly, *adv.*
un·dross′i·ness, *n.*
un·dross′y, *adj.*
un·drowned′, *adj.*
un·drubbed′, *adj.*
un·drugged′, *adj.*
un·drunk′, *adj.*
un·drunk′en, *adj.*
un·dry′, *adj.*
un·dry′a·ble, *adj.*
un·dry′ing, *adj.*
un′du·al·is′tic, *adj.*
un′du·al·is′ti·cal·ly, *adv.*
un·dubbed′, *adj.*
un·du′bi·ous, *adj.;* -ly, *adv.;* -ness, *n.*
un·du′bi·ta′tive, *adj.;* -ly, *adv.*
un·du′cal, *adj.*
un·duc′tile, *adj.*
un·dug′, *adj.*
un·dulled′, *adj.*
un·dumped′, *adj.*
un·dup′a·ble, *adj.*
un·duped′, *adj.*
un·du′pli·ca′tive, *adj.*
un·dur′a·bil′i·ty, *n.*
un·dur′a·ble, *adj.;* -ble·ness, *n.;* -bly, *adv.*
un·dust′ed, *adj.*
un·dust′y, *adj.*
un·du′te·ous, *adj.;* -ly, *adv.;* -ness, *n.*
un·du′ti·a·ble, *adj.*
un·du′ti·ful, *adj.;* -ly, *adv.*
un·dwarfed′, *adj.*
un·dwell′a·ble, *adj.*
un·dwin′dling, *adj.*
un·dy′a·ble, *adj.*
un·dyed′, *adj.*
un′dy·nam′ic, *adj.*
un′dy·nam′i·cal·ly, *adv.*
un·dy′na·mit′ed, *adj.*
un·ea′ger, *adj.;* -ly, *adv.;* -ness, *n.*

un′earned in′come, income received from property, as interest, dividends, or the like. Cf. **earned income.**

un′earned in′crement, the increase in the value of property, esp. land, due to natural causes, as growth of population, rather than to any labor or expenditure by the owner.

un·earth (un ûrth′), *v.t.* **1.** to dig or get out of the earth; dig up. **2.** to uncover or bring to light by search, inquiry, etc.: *The lawyer unearthed new evidence.* [ME *unerth(en).* See UN-[2], EARTH]

un·earth·ly (un ûrth′lē), *adj.* **1.** seeming not to belong to this earth or world: *unearthly beauty.* **2.** supernatural; ghostly; unnaturally strange; weird: *an unearthly scream.* **3.** out of the ordinary; extreme: *to get up at an unearthly hour.* [UN-[1] + EARTHLY] **—un·earth′li·ness,** *n.*
—Syn. 2. preternatural, spectral. See **weird. —Ant. 1.** terrestrial.

un·eas·y (un ē′zē), **-eas·i·er, -eas·i·est. 1.** not easy in body or mind; uncomfortable; restless; disturbed; perturbed. **2.** not easy in manner; constrained. **3.** not conducive to ease; causing bodily discomfort. [ME *unesy.* See UN-[1], EASY] **—un·ease′,** *n.* **—un·eas′i·ly,** *adv.* **—un·eas′i·ness,** *n.*

un·ed·u·cat·ed (un ej′o͝o kā′tid, -ed′yo͝o-), *adj.* not educated. [UN-[1] + EDUCATED]
—Syn. untutored, unschooled, untaught, uninstructed, unenlightened, uninformed, uncultivated. See **ignorant.**

un·e·lec·tri·fied (un′i lek′trə fīd′), *adj.* **1.** not furnished with or adapted to operation by the use of electric power. **2.** not electrified. [UN-[1] + ELECTRIFIED]

un·em·ploy·a·ble (un′em ploi′ə bəl), *adj.* **1.** unacceptable or unsuitable for employment: *The severely handicapped are not necessarily unemployable.* **—n. 2.** an unemployable individual. [UN-[1] + EMPLOYABLE] **—un′em·ploy′a·bil′i·ty,** *n.*

un·em·ployed (un′em ploid′), *adj.* **1.** not employed; without a job; out of work: *an unemployed secretary.* **2.** not currently in use: *unemployed productive capacity.* **3.** not productively used: *unemployed capital; unemployed skills.* **4. the unemployed,** persons who do not have jobs: *The problem of the unemployed is a significant factor in the economy.* [UN-[1] + EMPLOY + -ED[2]]
—Syn. 1. unoccupied, idle, at liberty, jobless.

un·em·ploy·ment (un′em ploi′mənt), *n.* the state of being unemployed, esp. involuntarily: *Automation poses a threat of unemployment for many unskilled workers.* [UN-[1] + EMPLOYMENT]

unemploy′ment compensa′tion, *U.S.* money paid, usually weekly, to an unemployed worker by a State or federal agency or by his employer or labor union during all or part of his term of unemployment.

un·e·qual (un ē′kwəl), *adj.* **1.** not equal; not of the same quantity, quality, value, rank, ability, merit, etc.: *Men are unequal in their capacities.* **2.** not adequate, as in amount, power, ability, etc. (usually fol. by *to*): *strength unequal to the task.* **3.** not evenly proportioned or balanced; not having the parts alike or symmetrical: *an unequal leaf.* **4.** not even or regular, as motion. **5.** uneven or variable in character, quality, etc. **6.** *Obs.* inequitable; unfair; unjust. **—n. 7. unequals,** persons or things not equal to each other: *A contest between obvious unequals often elicits sympathy for the loser.* [UN-[1] + EQUAL] **—un·e′qual·ly,** *adv.* **—un·e′qual·ness,** *n.*

un·e·qualed (un ē′kwəld), *adj.* not equaled; supreme; matchless: *an unequaled record of victories; He is unequaled as an architect.* Also, *esp. Brit.,* **un·e·qualled.** [UN-[1] + EQUALED]
—Syn. peerless, unrivaled, inimitable, incomparable.

un·e·quiv·o·cal (un′i kwiv′ə kəl), *adj.* **1.** not equivocal; unambiguous; clear; having only one possible meaning or interpretation: *Sometimes silence is an unequivocal indication of assent.* **2.** explicit; definite; not merely implied or suggested: *Calling a man a thief is an unequivocal charge of dishonesty.* **3.** absolute; unqualified; not subject to conditions or exceptions: *The cosigner of a note gives his unequivocal assurance that it will be paid when due.* **4.** conclusive; unquestionable; not subject to dispute or challenge: *Actually doing a thing is the only unequivocal proof of ability to do it.* [UN-[1] + EQUIVOCAL] **—un′e·quiv′o·cal·ly,** *adv.* **—un′e·quiv′o·cal·ness,** *n.*
—Syn. simple, direct, obvious, explicit, unmistakable.

un·err·ing (un ûr′ing, -er′-), *adj.* **1.** not erring; not going astray or missing the mark: *The captain set an unerring course for home.* **2.** undeviatingly accurate throughout, not containing any error or flaw: *He gave an unerring recital of the day's events.* **3.** unfailingly right; invariably precise or correct: *unerring taste; an unerring sense of pitch.* [UN-[1] + ERRING] **—un·err′ing·ly,** *adv.* **—un·err′ing·ness,** *n.*
—Syn. 2. definite, infallible.

Une Sai·son En Enfer (*Fr.* yn se zôN nä näN feR′). See **Season in Hell, A.**

UNESCO (yo͞o nes′kō), *n.* an agency of the United Nations charged with instituting and administering programs for cooperative, coordinated action by member states in education, science, and the arts. [*U(nited) N(ations) E(ducational), S(cientific, and) C(ultural) O(rganization)*]

un·es·sen·tial (un′ə sen′shəl), *adj.* **1.** not of prime importance; not indispensable. **—n. 2.** an unessential thing; nonessential. [UN-[1] + ESSENTIAL] **—un′es·sen′tial·ly,** *adv.*
—Syn. 2. unnecessary, dispensable, unimportant.

un·es·tab·lished (un′e stab′lisht), *adj.* **1.** not established. **2.** *Brit.* (of a worker or job) temporary, part-time, or having a special or unique routine. [UN-[1] + ESTABLISHED]

un·es·thet·ic (un′es thet′ik), *adj.* unaesthetic.

un·e·ven (un ē′vən), *adj.* **1.** not level or flat; rough; rugged: *The wheels bumped and jolted over the uneven*

un·ear′nest, *adj.;* **-ly,** *adv.;* **-ness,** *n.*
un·east′ern, *adj.*
un·eat′a·ble, *adj.*
un·eat′en, *adj.*
un·eat′ing, *adj.*
un·eaved′, *adj.*
un·ebbed′, *adj.*
un·ebb′ing, *adj.*
un′e·bul′lient, *adj.*
un′ec·cen′tric, *adj.*
un′ec·cen′tri·cal·ly, *adv.*
un′ec·cle′si·as′tic, *adj.*
un′ec·cle′si·as′ti·cal·ly, *adv.*
un·ech′oed, *adj.*
un′e·cho′ic, *adj.*
un·ech′o·ing, *adj.*
un′ec·lec′tic, *adj.*
un′ec·lec′ti·cal·ly, *adv.*
un′e·clipsed′, *adj.*
un′e·clips′ing, *adj.*
un′e·clip′tic, *adj.*
un′e·clip′ti·cal, *adj.;* **-ly,** *adv.*
un′e·co·nom′ic, *adj.*
un′e·co·nom′i·cal, *adj.;* **-ly,** *adv.*
un′e·con′o·miz′ing, *adj.*
un′ec·stat′ic, *adj.*
un′ec·stat′i·cal·ly, *adv.*
un′e·da′cious, *adj.;* **-ly,** *adv.*
un·ed′died, *adj.*
un·ed′dy·ing, *adj.*
un·edge′, *v.t.,* **-edged, -edg·ing.**
un·ed′i·ble, *adj.*
un′ed·i·fi′cial, *adj.*
un·ed′i·fied′, *adj.*
un·ed′i·fy′ing, *adj.*
un·ed′it·a·ble, *adj.*
un·ed′it·ed, *adj.*
un·ed′u·ca·ble, *adj.*
un·ed′u·ca′tive, *adj.*
un′e·duced′, *adj.*
un′ef·face′a·ble, *adj.*
un′ef·faced′, *adj.*
un′ef·fect′ed, *adj.*
un′ef·fect′i·ble, *adj.*
un′ef·fec′tive, *adj.;* **-ly,** *adv.;* **-ness,** *n.*
un′ef·fec′tu·at′ed, *adj.*
un′ef·fem′i·nate, *adj.;* **-ly,** *adv.*
un′ef·fer·ves′cent, *adj.;* **-ly,** *adv.*
un′ef·fete′, *adj.;* **-ness,** *n.*
un′ef·fi·ca′cious, *adj.;* **-ly,** *adv.*
un′ef·fi′cient, *adj.*
un′ef·ful′gent, *adj.;* **-ly,** *adv.*
un′ef·fused′, *adj.*
un′ef·fus′ing, *adj.*
un′ef·fu′sive, *adj.;* **-ly,** *adv.;* **-ness,** *n.*
un′e·go·is′ti·cal, *adj.;* **-ly,** *adv.*
un′e·go·tis′ti·cal, *adj.;* **-ly,** *adv.*
un′e·gre′gious, *adj.;* **-ly,** *adv.;* **-ness,** *n.*
un′e·jac′u·lat′ed, *adj.*
un′e·ject′ed, *adj.*
un′e·jec′tive, *adj.*
un′e·lab′o·rate, *adj.;* **-ly,** *adv.;* **-ness,** *n.*
un′e·lab′o·rat′ed, *adj.*
un′e·lapsed′, *adj.*
un′e·las′tic, *adj.*
un′e·las′ti·cal·ly, *adv.*
un′e·las·tic′i·ty, *n.*
un′e·lat′ed, *adj.*
un′e·lat′ing, *adj.*
un·el′bowed, *adj.*
un·eld′er·ly, *adj.*
un′e·lect′a·ble, *adj.*
un′e·lect′ed, *adj.*
un′e·lec′tive, *adj.*
un′e·lec′tric, *adj.*
un′e·lec′tri·cal, *adj.;* **-ly,** *adv.*
un′e·lec′tri·fy′ing, *adj.*
un′e·lec·tron′ic, *adj.*
un′el·ee·mos′y·nar′y, *adj.*
un·el′e·gant, *adj.;* **-ly,** *adv.*
un′el·e·men′tal, *adj.;* **-ly,** *adv.*
un′el·e·men′ta·ry, *adj.*
un·el′e·vat′ed, *adj.*
un′e·lic′it·a·ble, *adj.*
un′e·lic′it·ed, *adj.*
un′e·lid′ed, *adj.*
un′e·lid′i·ble, *adj.*
un′e·lim′i·nat′ed, *adj.*
un′el·lip′ti·cal, *adj.*
un′e·lon′gat·ed, *adj.*
un′e·loped′, *adj.*
un′e·lop′ing, *adj.*
un·el′o·quent, *adj.;* **-ly,** *adv.*
un′e·lu′ci·dat′ed, *adj.*
un′e·lu′ci·dat′ing, *adj.*
un′e·lu′ci·da′tive, *adj.*
un′e·lud′a·ble, *adj.*
un′e·lud′ed, *adj.*
un′e·lu′sive, *adj.;* **-ly,** *adv.;* **-ness,** *n.*
un′e·lu′so·ry, *adj.*
un′e·ma′ci·at′ed, *adj.*
un·em′a·na′tive, *adj.*
un′e·man′ci·pat′ed, *adj.*
un′e·man′ci·pa′tive, *adj.*
un′e·mas′cu·lat′ed, *adj.*
un′e·mas′cu·la′tive, *adj.*
un′e·mas′cu·la·to′ry, *adj.*
un′em·balmed′, *adj.*
un′em·banked′, *adj.*
un′em·bar′rassed, *adj.*
un′em·bat′tled, *adj.*
un′em·bayed′, *adj.*
un′em·bel′lished, *adj.*
un′em·bez′zled, *adj.*
un′em·bit′tered, *adj.*
un′em·bla′zoned, *adj.*
un′em·bossed′, *adj.*
un′em·bow′eled, *adj.*
un′em·bow′elled, *adj.*
un′em·bow′ered, *adj.*
un′em·brace′a·ble, *adj.*
un′em·braced′, *adj.*
un′em·broi′dered, *adj.*
un′em·broiled′, *adj.*
un·em′bry·o·nal, *adj.*
un′em·bry·on′ic, *adj.*
un′e·mend′a·ble, *adj.*
un′e·mend′ed, *adj.*
un′e·merged′, *adj.*
un′e·mer′gent, *adj.*
un′e·merg′ing, *adj.*
un·em′i·grant, *adj.*
un·em′i·grat′ing, *adj.*
un·em′i·nent, *adj.;* **-ly,** *adv.*
un′e·mis′sive, *adj.*
un′e·mit′ted, *adj.*
un′e·mit′ting, *adj.*
un′e·mo′tion·al, *adj.;* **-ly,** *adv.*
un′e·mo′tioned, *adj.*
un′e·mo′tive, *adj.;* **-ly,** *adv.;* **-ness,** *n.*
un′em·pan′eled, *adj.*
un′em·pan′elled, *adj.*
un·em′pha·sized′, *adj.*
un·em′pha·siz′ing, *adj.*
un′em·phat′ic, *adj.*
un′em·phat′i·cal·ly, *adv.*
un′em·pir′i·cal, *adj.;* **-ly,** *adv.*
un′em·poi′soned, *adj.*
un·em′pow′ered, *adj.*
un·emp′tied, *adj.*
un·emp′ty, *adj.*
un·em′u·la′tive, *adj.*
un·em′u·lous, *adj.*
un′e·mul′si·fied′, *adj.*
un′en·act′ed, *adj.*
un′en·am′eled, *adj.*
un′en·am′elled, *adj.*
un′en·am′ored, *adj.*
un′en·am′oured, *adj.*
un′en·camped′, *adj.*
un′en·chant′ed, *adj.*
un′en·cir′cled, *adj.*
un′en·closed′, *adj.*
un′en·com′passed, *adj.*
un′en·coun′ter·a·ble, *adj.*
un′en·coun′tered, *adj.*
un′en·cour′aged, *adj.*
un′en·cour′ag·ing, *adj.*
un′en·croached′, *adj.*
un′en·croach′ing, *adj.*
un′en·cum′bered, *adj.*
un′en·cum′ber·ing, *adj.*
un′en·cyst′ed, *adj.*
un·end′a·ble, *adj.*
un′en·dan′gered, *adj.*
un′en·deared′, *adj.*
un·end′ed, *adj.*
un′en·dem′ic, *adj.*
un·end′ing, *adj.;* **-ly,** *adv.*
un′en·dors′a·ble, *adj.*
un′en·dorsed′, *adj.*
un′en·dowed′, *adj.*
un′en·dow′ing, *adj.*
un′en·dued′, *adj.*
un′en·dur′a·bil′i·ty, *adj.*
un′en·dur′a·ble, *adj.;* **-bly,** *adv.*
un′en·dured′, *adj.*
un′en·dur′ing, *adj.;* **-ly,** *adv.*
un′en·er·get′ic, *adj.*
un′en·er·get′i·cal·ly, *adv.*
un·en′er·gized′, *adj.*
un·en′er·vat′ed, *adj.*
un′en·fee′bled, *adj.*
un·en′fi·lad′ed, *adj.*
un′en·force′a·ble, *adj.*
un′en·force′a·bil′i·ty, *n.*
un′en·forced′, *adj.*
un′en·forc′ed·ly, *adv.*
un′en·fran′chised, *adj.*
un′en·gaged′, *adj.*
un′en·gag′ing, *adj.*
un′en·gen′dered, *adj.*
un′en·gi·neered′, *adj.*
un·Eng′lish, *adj.*
un′en·graved′, *adj.*
un′en·gra′ven, *adj.*
un′en·grossed′, *adj.*
un′en·gross′ing, *adj.*
un′en·hanced′, *adj.*
un′en·ig·mat′ic, *adj.*
un′en·ig·mat′i·cal, *adj.;* **-ly,** *adv.*
un′en·joined′, *adj.*
un′en·joy′a·ble, *adj.;* **-ble·ness,** *n.;* **-bly,** *adv.*
un′en·joyed′, *adj.*
un′en·joy′ing, *adj.;* **-ly,** *adv.*
un′en·larged′, *adj.*
un′en·larg′ing, *adj.*
un′en·light′ened, *adj.*
un′en·light′en·ing, *adj.*
un′en·list′ed, *adj.*
un′en·liv′ened, *adj.*
un′en·liv′en·ing, *adj.*
un′en·no′bled, *adj.*
un′en·no′bling, *adj.*
un′e·nounced′, *adj.*
un′en·quired′, *adj.*
un′en·quir′ing, *adj.*
un′en·rap′tured, *adj.*
un′en·rich′a·ble, *adj.*
un′en·riched′, *adj.*
un′en·rich′ing, *adj.*
un′en·rolled′, *adj.*
un′en·shrined′, *adj.*
un′en·slaved′, *adj.*
un′en·snared′, *adj.*
un′en·sured′, *adj.*
un′en·tailed′, *adj.*
un′en·tan′gle·a·ble, *adj.*
un′en·tan′gled, *adj.*
un′en·tan′gling, *adj.*
un·en′ter·a·ble, *adj.*
un·en′tered, *adj.*
un·en′ter·pris′ing, *adj.;* **-ly,** *adv.*
un′en·ter·tain′a·ble, *adj.*
un′en·ter·tained′, *adj.*
un′en·ter·tain′ing, *adj.;* **-ly,** *adv.*
un′en·thralled′, *adj.*
un′en·thrall′ing, *adj.*
un′en·thused′, *adj.*
un′en·thu′si·asm, *n.*
un′en·thu′si·as′tic, *adj.*
un′en·thu′si·as′ti·cal·ly, *adv.*
un′en·tice′a·ble, *adj.*
un′en·ticed′, *adj.*
un′en·tic′ing, *adj.*
un′en·ti′tled, *adj.*
un′en·tombed′, *adj.*
un′en·to·mo·log′i·cal, *adj.*
un′en·tranced′, *adj.*
un′en·trapped′, *adj.*
un′en·treat′a·ble, *adj.*
un′en·treat′ed, *adj.*
un′en·treat′ing, *adj.*
un′en·trenched′, *adj.*
un′en·twined′, *adj.*
un′e·nu′mer·at′ed, *adj.*
un′e·nu′mer·a′tive, *adj.*
un′e·nun′ci·a·ble, *adj.*
un′e·nun′ci·at′ed, *adj.*
un′e·nun′ci·a′tive, *adj.*
un′en·vel′oped, *adj.*
un′en·ven′omed, *adj.*
un·en′vi·a·bil′i·ty, *n.*
un·en′vi·a·ble, *adj.;* **-bly,** *adv.*
un·en′vied, *adj.*
un·en′vi·ous, *adj.;* **-ly,** *adv.*
un′en·vi′roned, *adj.*
un·en′vy·ing, *adj.;* **-ly,** *adv.*
un·ep′au·let′ed, *adj.*
un·ep′au·let′ted, *adj.*
un′e·phem′er·al, *adj.;* **-ly,** *adv.*
un·ep′ic, *adj.*
un′ep·i·cu·re′an, *adj.*
un′ep·i·gram·mat′ic, *adj.*
un′ep·i·gram·mat′i·cal·ly, *adv.*
un·ep′i·logued′, *adj.*
un′e·pis′to·lar′y, *adj.*
un·ep′i·taphed′, *adj.*
un′ep·i·the′li·al, *adj.*
un′e·pit′o·mised′, *adj.*
un′e·pit′o·mized′, *adj.*
un·ep′och·al, *adj.*
un′eq·ua·bil′i·ty, *n.*
un·eq′ua·ble, *adj.;* **-ble·ness,** *n.;* **-bly,** *adv.*
un·e′qual·ise′, *v.t.,* **-ised, -is·ing.**
un·e′qual·ize′, *v.t.,* **-ized, -iz·ing.**
un′e·quat′ed, *adj.*
un′e·qua·to′ri·al, *adj.*
un′e·ques′tri·an, *adj.*
un′e·qui·an′gu·lar, *adj.*
un′e·qui·lat′er·al, *adj.;* **-ly,** *adv.*
un′e·qui·li′brat·ed, *adj.*
un·e′quine, *adj.*
un′e·quipped′, *adj.*
un′e·quiv′a·lent, *adj.;* **-ly,** *adv.*
un′e·quiv′o·cat′ing, *adj.*
un′e·rad′i·ca·ble, *adj.*
un′e·rad′i·cat′ed, *adj.*
un′e·rad′i·ca′tive, *adj.*
un′e·ras′a·ble, *adj.*
un′e·rased′, *adj.*
un′e·ras′ing, *adj.*
un′e·rect′, *adj.*
un′e·rect′ed, *adj.*
un·er′mined, *adj.*
un′e·rod′a·ble, *adj.*
un′e·rod′ed, *adj.*
un′e·rod′ent, *adj.*
un′e·rod′ing, *adj.*
un′e·ro′sive, *adj.*
un′e·rot′ic, *adj.*
un·er′rant, *adj.;* **-ly,** *adv.*
un′er·rat′ic, *adj.*
un·er′u·dite′, *adj.*
un′e·rupt′ed, *adj.*
un′e·rup′tive, *adj.*
un′es·cal′loped, *adj.*
un′es·cap′a·ble, *adj.;* **-bly,** *adv.*
un′es·caped′, *adj.*
un′es·cheat′a·ble, *adj.*
un′es·cheat′ed, *adj.*
un′es·chewed′, *adj.*
un′es·cort′ed, *adj.*
un′es·cutch′eoned, *adj.*
un′es·o·ter′ic, *adj.*
un′es·pied′, *adj.*
un′es·pous′a·ble, *adj.*
un′es·poused′, *adj.*
un′es·sayed′, *adj.*
un′es·tab′lish·a·ble, *adj.*
un′es·teemed′, *adj.*
un·es′ti·ma·ble, *adj.*
un·es′ti·mat′ed, *adj.*
un′es·topped′, *adj.*
un′es·tranged′, *adj.*
un·etched′, *adj.*
un′e·ter′nized, *adj.*
un′e·the′re·al, *adj.;* **-ly,** *adv.;* **-ness,** *n.*
un·eth′i·cal, *adj.;* **-ly,** *adv.*
un′eth·no·log′ic, *adj.*
un′eth·no·log′i·cal, *adj.;* **-ly,** *adv.*
un·eth′yl·at′ed, *adj.*
un′et·y·mo·log′ic, *adj.*
un′et·y·mo·log′i·cal, *adj.;* **-ly,** *adv.*
un′-Eu·cha·ris′tic, *adj.*
un′-Eu·cha·ris′ti·cal, *adj.;* **-ly,** *adv.*
un′eu·gen′ic, *adj.*
un′eu·gen′i·cal, *adj.;* **-ly,** *adv.*
un·eu′lo·gised′, *adj.*
un·eu′lo·gized′, *adj.*
un′eu·phe·mis′tic, *adj.*
un′eu·phe·mis′ti·cal, *adj.;* **-ly,** *adv.*
un′eu·phon′ic, *adj.*
un′eu·pho′ni·ous, *adj.;* **-ly,** *adv.;* **-ness,** *n.*
un′-Eu·ro·pe′an, *adj.*
un′e·vac′u·at′ed, *adj.*
un′e·vad′a·ble, *adj.*
un′e·vad′ed, *adj.*
un′e·vad′i·ble, *adj.*
un′e·vad′ing, *adj.*
un′e·val′u·at′ed, *adj.*
un′ev·a·nes′cent, *adj.;* **-ly,** *adv.*
un′e·van·gel′ic, *adj.*
un′e·van·gel′i·cal, *adj.;* **-ly,** *adv.*
un′e·van′gel·ised′, *adj.*
un′e·van′gel·ized′, *adj.*
un′e·vap′o·rat′ed, *adj.*
un′e·vap′o·ra′tive, *adj.*
un′e·va′sive, *adj.;* **-ly,** *adv.;* **-ness,** *n.*

surface. 2. irregular; varying; not uniform: *The shots rang out at uneven intervals. The book is uneven in quality.* 3. not equitable or fair; one-sided: *One of the combatants was so much stronger and more skillful that it was an uneven contest.* 4. not equally balanced; not symmetrical; not parallel in arrangement or distribution: *Uneven loading gave the ship a list to starboard. The pillars were uneven, so the roof was lower on one side.* 5. (of a number) odd; not divisible into two equal integers: *The numerals 3, 5, and 7 are uneven.* [ME; OE *unefen;* c. G *uneben.* See UN-[1], EVEN[1]] —**un·e′ven·ly,** *adv.* —**un·e′ven·ness,** *n.*

un·e·vent·ful (un′i vent′fəl), *adj.* not eventful; lacking in important or striking occurrences: *an uneventful day at the office.* [UN-[1] + EVENTFUL] —**un′e·vent′ful·ly,** *adv.* —**un′e·vent′ful·ness,** *n.*

un·ex·act·ing (un′ig zak′ting), *adj.* 1. not making excessive demands; easygoing: *an unexacting relationship.* 2. requiring or expecting no particular level of performance; easily satisfied; uncritical: *an unexacting supervisor.* [UN-[1] + EXACTING] —**un′ex·act′ing·ly,** *adv.*

un·ex·am·pled (un′ig zam′pəld, -zäm′-), *adj.* unprecedented; unparalleled; unlike anything previously known: *unexampled kindness; unexampled depravity.* [UN-[1] + EXAMPLE + -ED[2]]

un·ex·cep·tion·a·ble (un′ik sep′shə nə bəl), *adj.* not offering any basis for exception or objection; beyond criticism: *an unexceptionable record of achievement.* [UN-[1] + EXCEPTIONABLE] —**un′ex·cep′tion·a·ble·ness, un′ex·cep′tion·a·bil′i·ty,** *n.* —**un′ex·cep′tion·a·bly,** *adv.*

un·ex·cep·tion·al (un′ik sep′shə nəl), *adj.* 1. not exceptional; not unusual or extraordinary. 2. admitting of no exception to the general rule. 3. unexceptionable. [UN-[1] + EXCEPTIONAL] —**un′ex·cep′tion·al·ly,** *adv.*

un·ex·pect·ed (un′ik spek′tid), *adj.* not expected; unforeseen; surprising: *an unexpected pleasure; an unexpected development.* [UN-[1] + EXPECT + -ED[2]] —**un′ex·pect′ed·ly,** *adv.* —**un′ex·pect′ed·ness,** *n.*
—**Syn.** unanticipated. See **sudden.**

un·ex·pend·a·ble (un′ik spen′də bəl), *adj.* 1. essential; absolutely required; of sufficient importance to warrant special care and preservation: *Certain resources are unexpendable because our security depends on them.* 2. not capable of being expended; inexhaustible: *The sun is a source of unexpendable quantities of energy.* 3. not available for expenditure: *The principal of the trust fund is unexpendable under the terms of the trust agreement.* [UN-[1] + EXPENDABLE]

un·ex·pressed (un′ik sprest′), *adj.* 1. not expressed; not indicated or communicated, as in words, intimations, or the like: *an unexpressed desire.* 2. tacit; understood without explicit statement: *an unexpressed agreement.* [UN-[1] + EXPRESS + -ED[2]]

un·ex·pres·sive (un′ik spres′iv), *adj.* 1. not expressive; lacking in expression of meaning, feeling, etc.: *a bland and unexpressive person.* 2. *Obs.* inexpressible. [UN-[1] + EXPRESSIVE] —**un′ex·pres′sive·ly,** *adv.* —**un′ex·pres′sive·ness,** *n.*

un·faced (un fāst′), *adj.* *Crystall.* without crystal faces. [UN-[1] + FACED]

un·fail·ing (un fā′ling), *adj.* 1. not failing; not giving way; not falling short of expectation; completely dependable: *an unfailing source of electric power; an unfailing friend.* 2. inexhaustible; endless: *unfailing resources; unfailing good humor.* 3. unerring; infallible: *an unfailing guide; an unfailing indication.* [ME; see UN-[1], FAILING] —**un·fail′ing·ly,** *adv.* —**un·fail′ing·ness,** *n.*

un·fair (un fâr′), *adj.* 1. not fair; not conforming to approved standards, as of justice, honesty, ethics, or the like: *an unfair law; an unfair distinction; an unfair blow.* 2. disproportionate; undue; beyond what is proper or fitting: *an unfair share; an unfair advantage.* 3. characterized by irregular or unethical business or administrative practices, methods, etc.: *unfair competition; an unfair wage policy.* [ME; OE *unfæger;* c. OIcel *ūfagr.* See UN-[1], FAIR[1]] —**un·fair′ly,** *adv.* —**un·fair′ness,** *n.*

un′fair competi′tion, 1. acts done by a seller to confuse or deceive the public with intent to acquire a larger portion of the market, as by cutting prices below cost, misleading advertising, selling a spurious product under a false identity, etc. 2. the use of any such methods.

un′fair prac′tice, 1. See **unfair competition.** 2. any practice in business involving the general public or competing parties that is prohibited by statute and regulated by an appropriate government agency.

un·faith·ful (un fāth′fəl), *adj.* 1. not faithful; false to duty, obligation, or promises; faithless; disloyal. 2. guilty of adultery. 3. not accurate or complete, as a report, description, or the like; inexact: *an unfaithful account of a historical event.* 4. not upright; dishonest; not of good faith, as to a trust or position entailing financial responsibility: *an unfaithful employee.* 5. *Obs.* unbelieving; infidel. [ME *unfeithful.* See UN-[1], FAITHFUL] —**un·faith′ful·ly,** *adv.* —**un·faith′ful·ness,** *n.*
—**Syn.** 1. untrustworthy, deceitful, treacherous, recreant. 3. imprecise, untrue. 4. crooked.

un·fa·mil·iar (un′fə mil′yər), *adj.* 1. not familiar; not acquainted with or conversant about: *to be unfamiliar with a subject.* 2. different; unaccustomed; unusual; strange: *an unfamiliar treat.* [UN-[1] + FAMILIAR] —**un·fa·mil·i·ar·i·ty** (un′fə mil′ē ar′i tē), *n.* —**un′fa·mil′iar·ly,** *adv.*

un·fas·ten (un fas′ən, -fä′sən), *v.t.* 1. to release from or as from fastenings; detach. 2. to undo or open (something fastened). —*v.i.* 3. to become unfastened. [ME *unfastne(n).* See UN-[2], FASTEN]

un·fa·thered (un fä′thərd), *adj.* 1. having no father; fatherless. 2. of illegitimate or unknown paternity; bastard. 3. not ascribable to a particular author or source: *unfathered tales.* [UN-[1] + FATHER + -ED[3]]

un·fa·vor·a·ble (un fā′vər ə bəl), *adj.* 1. not favorable; contrary; adverse: *an unfavorable decision; an unfavorable wind.* 2. not propitious: *an unfavorable omen.* 3. unfortunate; undesirable; disadvantageous: *an unfavorable development; an unfavorable balance in international trade.* Also, *esp. Brit.,* **un·fa′vour·a·ble.** [ME; see UN-[1], FAVORABLE] —**un·fa′vor·a·ble·ness;** *esp. Brit.* **un·fa′vour·a·ble·ness,** *n.* —**un·fa′vor·a·bly;** *esp. Brit.* **un·fa′vour·a·bly,** *adv.*

Unfed′erated Ma′lay States′, a former group of five native states in the Malay Peninsula, under indirect British control and forming a part of the former Federation of Malaya: now part of the federation of Malaysia. 24,347 sq. mi.

un·feel·ing (un fē′ling), *adj.* 1. not feeling; devoid of feeling; insensible or insensate. 2. unsympathetic; callous: *an intelligent but unfeeling man.* [ME; OE *unfelende.* See UN-[1], FEELING] —**un·feel′ing·ly,** *adv.* —**un·feel′ing·ness,** *n.*
—**Syn.** 1. numb. 2. hard-hearted. See **hard.** —**Ant.** 2. sympathetic.

un·feigned (un fānd′), *adj.* not feigned; sincere; genuine. [ME *unfeynid.* See -UN[1], FEIGNED] —**un·feign·ed·ly** (un fā′nid lē), *adv.* —**un·feign′ed·ness,** *n.*

un·fet·ter (un fet′ər), *v.t.* 1. to release from fetters. 2. to free from restraint; liberate. [ME *unfeteren.* See UN-[2], FETTER]

un′e·ver′si·ble, *adj.*
un′e·vert′ed, *adj.*
un·e·vict′ed, *adj.*
un·ev′i·denced, *adj.*
un′ev·i·den′tial, *adj.*
un·e′vil, *adj.;* -ly, *adv.*
un′e·vinced′, *adj.*
un′e·vin′ci·ble, *adj.*
un′e·vis′cer·at′ed, *adj.*
un·ev′o·ca·ble, *adj.*
un′e·voc′a·tive, *adj.*
un′e·voked′, *adj.*
un′ev·o·lu′tion·al, *adj.*
un′ev·o·lu′tion·ar′y, *adj.*
un′e·volved′, *adj.*
un′ex·ac′er·bat′ed, *adj.*
un′ex·ac′er·bat′ing, *adj.*
un′ex·act′ed, *adj.*
un′ex·act′ing, *adj.*
un′ex·ag′ger·at′ed, *adj.*
un′ex·ag′ger·at′ing, *adj.*
un′ex·ag′ger·a′tive, *adj.*
un′ex·ag′ger·a·to′ry, *adj.*
un′ex·alt′ed, *adj.*
un′ex·alt′ing, *adj.*
un′ex·am′in·a·ble, *adj.*
un′ex·am′ined, *adj.*
un′ex·am′in·ing, *adj.*
un′ex·as′per·at′ed, *adj.*
un′ex·as′per·at′ing, *adj.*
un·ex′ca·vat′ed, *adj.*
un′ex·ceed′a·ble, *adj.*
un′ex·ceed′ed, *adj.*
un′ex·celled′, *adj.*
un′ex·cel′ling, *adj.*
un·ex′cel·lent, *adj.;* -ly, *adv.*
un′ex·cept′a·ble, *adj.*
un′ex·cept′ed, *adj.*
un′ex·cept′ing, *adj.*
un′ex·cep′tive, *adj.*
un′ex·cerpt′ed, *adj.*
un′ex·ces′sive, *adj.;* -ly, *adv.*
un′ex·change′a·ble, *adj.;* -ness, *n.*
un′ex·changed′, *adj.*
un·ex′cised, *adj.*
un′ex·cit′a·bil′i·ty, *n.*
un′ex·cit′a·ble, *adj.;* -ly, *adv.*
un′ex·cit′ed, *adj.*
un′ex·cit′ing, *adj.*
un′ex·claim′ing, *adj.*
un′ex·clud′a·ble, *adj.*
un′ex·clud′ed, *adj.*
un′ex·clud′ing, *adj.*
un′ex·clu′sive, *adj.;* -ly, *adv.;* -ness, *n.*
un′ex·cog′i·ta·ble, *adj.*
un′ex·cog′i·tat′ed, *adj.*
un′ex·cog′i·ta′tive, *adj.*
un′ex·com·mu′ni·cat′ed, *adj.*
un′ex·co′ri·at′ed, *adj.*
un′ex·cres′cent, *adj.;* -ly, *adv.*
un′ex·cret′ed, *adj.*
un′ex·cru′ci·at′ing, *adj.*
un′ex·cul′pa·ble, *adj.*
un·ex′cul·pat′ed, *adj.*
un′ex·cur′sive, *adj.;* -ly, *adv.*
un′ex·cus′a·ble, *adj.;* -bly, *adv.*
un′ex·cused′, *adj.*
un′ex·cus′ed·ly, *adv.*
un′ex·cus′ing, *adj.*
un·ex′e·crat′ed, *adj.*
un·ex′e·cut′a·ble, *adj.*
un·ex′e·cut′ed, *adj.*
un·ex′e·cut′ing, *adj.*
un′ex·ec′u·to′ri·al, *adj.*
un′ex·em′pla·ry, *adj.*
un′ex·empt′, *adj.*
un′ex·empt′a·ble, *adj.*
un′ex·empt′ed, *adj.*
un′ex·empt′ing, *adj.*
un·ex′er·cis′a·ble, *adj.*
un·ex′er·cised′, *adj.*
un′ex·ert′ed, *adj.*
un′ex·haled′, *adj.*
un′ex·haust′ed, *adj.;* -ly, *adv.*
un′ex·haus′tion, *n.*
un′ex·haus′tive, *adj.;* -ly, *adv.*
un′ex·hib′it·a·ble, *adj.*
un′ex·hib′it·ed, *adj.*
un′ex·hil′a·rat′ed, *adj.*
un′ex·hil′a·rat′ing, *adj.*
un′ex·hil′a·ra′tive, *adj.*
un′ex·hor′ta·tive, *adj.*
un′ex·hort′ed, *adj.*
un′ex·humed′, *adj.*
un·ex′i·gent, *adj.;* -ly, *adv.*
un·ex′i·gi·ble, *adj.*
un′ex·iled, *adj.*
un′ex·ist′ent, *adj.*
un′ex·is·ten′tial, *adj.;* -ly, *adv.*
un′ex·ist′ing, *adj.*
un′ex·on′er·at′ed, *adj.*
un′ex·on′er·a′tive, *adj.*
un′ex·or′bi·tant, *adj.;* -ly, *adv.*
un′ex·or′cised′, *adj.*
un′ex·ot′ic, *adj.*
un′ex·ot′i·cal·ly, *adv.*
un′ex·pand′a·ble, *adj.*
un′ex·pand′ed, *adj.*
un′ex·pand′ing, *adj.*
un′ex·pan′si·ble, *adj.*
un′ex·pan′sive, *adj.;* -ly, *adv.;* -ness, *n.*
un′ex·pect·a·bil′i·ty, *n.*
un′ex·pect′a·ble, *adj.;* -bly, *adv.*
un′ex·pect′ant, *adj.;* -ly, *adv.*
un′ex·pect′ing, *adj.;* -ly, *adv.*
un′ex·pec′to·rat′ed, *adj.*
un′ex·pe′di·ent, *adj.;* -ly, *adv.*
un·ex′pe·dit′a·ble, *adj.*
un·ex′pe·dit′ed, *adj.*
un′ex·pe·di′tious, *adj.;* -ly, *adv.;* -ness, *n.*
un′ex·pel′la·ble, *adj.*
un′ex·pelled′, *adj.*
un′ex·pend′ed, *adj.*
un′ex·pe′ri·enced, *adj.*
un′ex·pe′ri·en′tial, *adj.;* -ly, *adv.*
un′ex·per′i·men′tal, *adj.;* -ly, *adv.*
un′ex·per′i·ment′ed, *adj.*
un′ex·pert′, *adj.*
un·ex′pi·a·ble, *adj.*
un·ex′pi·at′ed, *adj.*
un′ex·pired′, *adj.*
un′ex·pir′ing, *adj.*
un′ex·plain′a·ble, *adj.;* -bly, *adv.*
un′ex·plained′, *adj.*
un′ex·plain′ed·ly, *adv.*
un′ex·plain′ing, *adj.*
un′ex·plan′a·to′ry, *adj.*
un·ex′pli·cat′ed, *adj.*
un·ex′pli·ca′tive, *adj.*
un′ex·plic′it, *adj.;* -ly, *adv.*
un′ex·plod′a·ble, *adj.*
un′ex·plod′ed, *adj.*
un′ex·ploit′a·ble, *adj.*
un′ex·ploit′a·tive, *adj.*
un′ex·ploit′ed, *adj.*
un′ex·plor′a·ble, *adj.*
un′ex·plor′a·tive, *adj.*
un′ex·plor′a·to′ry, *adj.*
un′ex·plored′, *adj.*
un′ex·plo′sive, *adj.;* -ly, *adv.;* -ness, *n.*
un′ex·po′ni·ble, *adj.*
un′ex·port′a·ble, *adj.*
un′ex·port′ed, *adj.*
un′ex·port′ing, *adj.*
un′ex·pos′a·ble, *adj.*
un′ex·posed′, *adj.*
un′ex·pos′tu·lat′ing, *adj.*
un′ex·pound′a·ble, *adj.*
un′ex·pound′ed, *adj.*
un′ex·press′a·ble, *adj.*
un′ex·press′ly, *adv.*
un′ex·pro′pri·a·ble, *adj.*
un′ex·pro′pri·at′ed, *adj.*
un′ex·punged′, *adj.*
un·ex′pur·gat′ed, *adj.*
un′ex·tend′a·ble, *adj.*
un′ex·tend′ed, *adj.;* -ly, *adv.*
un′ex·tend′i·ble, *adj.*
un′ex·ten′si·ble, *adj.*
un′ex·ten′u·at′ed, *adj.*
un′ex·ten′u·at′ing, *adj.*
un′ex·ter′mi·na·ble, *adj.*
un′ex·ter′mi·nat′ed, *adj.*
un′ex·tinct′, *adj.*
un′ex·tin′guish·a·ble, *adj.*
un′ex·tin′guished, *adj.*
un·ex′tir·pat′ed, *adj.*
un′ex·tolled′, *adj.*
un′ex·tort′a·ble, *adj.*
un′ex·tort′ed, *adj.*
un′ex·tract′a·ble, *adj.*
un′ex·tract′ed, *adj.*
un·ex′tra·dit′ed, *adj.*
un′ex·tra′ne·ous, *adj.;* -ly, *adv.*
un′ex·traor′di·nar′y, *adj.*
un′ex·trav′a·gant, *adj.;* -ly, *adv.*
un′ex·trav′a·sat′ed, *adj.*
un′ex·treme′, *adj.*
un·ex′tri·ca·ble, *adj.*
un·ex′tri·cat′ed, *adj.*
un′ex·trin′sic, *adj.*
un′ex·trud′ed, *adj.*
un′ex·u′ber·ant, *adj.;* -ly, *adv.*
un′ex·u′da·tive, *adj.*
un′ex·ud′ed, *adj.*
un′ex·ult′ant, *adj.;* -ly, *adv.*
un·eye′a·ble, *adj.*
un·fa′bled, *adj.*
un·fa′bling, *adj.*
un·fab′ri·cat′ed, *adj.*
un·fab′u·lous, *adj.;* -ly, *adv.*
un′fa·çad′ed, *adj.*
un·face′a·ble, *adj.*
un·fac′et·ed, *adj.*
un′fa·ce′tious, *adj.;* -ly, *adv.;* -ness, *n.*
un·fac′ile, *adj.;* -ly, *adv.*
un′fa·cil′i·tat′ed, *adj.*
un·fac′tion·al, *adj.*
un·fac′tious, *adj.;* -ly, *adv.*
un·fac′tor·a·ble, *adj.*
un·fac′tored, *adj.*
un·fac′tu·al, *adj.;* -ly, *adv.*
un·fad′a·ble, *adj.*
un·fad′ed, *adj.*
un·fad′ing, *adj.*
un·fagged′, *adj.*
un·fag′ot·ed, *adj.*
un·failed′, *adj.*
un·faint′ing, *adj.*
un·faint′ly, *adv.*
un·fak′a·ble, *adj.*
un·faked′, *adj.*
un′fal·la′cious, *adj.;* -ly, *adv.*
un·fall′en, *adj.*
un·fall′ing, *adj.*
un·fal′lowed, *adj.*
un·fal′si·fi′a·ble, *adj.*
un·fal′si·fied′, *adj.*
un·fal′ter·ing, *adj.;* -ly, *adv.*
un′fa·mil′iar·ized′, *adj.*
un′fa·nat′i·cal, *adj.;* -ly, *adv.*
un·fan′cied, *adj.*
un·fan′ci·ful, *adj.*
un·fan′cy, *adj.*
un·fanged′, *adj.*
un·fanned′, *adj.*
un′fan·tas′tic, *adj.*
un′fan·tas′ti·cal·ly, *adv.*
un·far′, *adj., adv.*
un·farced′, *adj.*
un·far′ci·cal, *adj.*
un·farm′a·ble, *adj.*
un·farmed′, *adj.*
un·farm′ing, *adj.*
un·fas′ci·ate′, *adj.*
un·fas′ci·at′ed, *adj.*
un·fas′ci·nat′ed, *adj.*
un·fas′ci·nat′ing, *adj.*
un·fash′ion·a·ble, *adj.;* -bly, *adv.*
un·fash′ioned, *adj.*
un·fas′ten·a·ble, *adj.*
un·fas′ten·er, *n.*
un′fas·tid′i·ous, *adj.;* -ly, *adv.;* -ness, *n.*
un·fast′ing, *adj.*
un′fa·tal·is′tic, *adj.*
un′fa·tal·is′ti·cal·ly, *adv.*
un·fat′ed, *adj.*
un·fa′ther·ly, *adj.*
un·fath′om·a·ble, *adj.*
un·fath′omed, *adj.*
un·fat′i·ga·ble, *adj.*
un′fa·tigued′, *adj.*
un′fa′ti′guing, *adj.*
un·fat′ted, *adj.*
un·fat′ty, *adj.*
un′fa·tu′i·tous, *adj.;* -ly, *adv.*
un·fau′cet·ed, *adj.*
un·fault′y, *adj.*
un·fa′vored, *adj.*
un·fa′vor·ing, *adj.*
un·fa′vor·ite, *adj.*
un·fa′voured, *adj.*
un·fa′vour·ing, *adj.*
un·fa′vour·ite, *adj.*
un·fawn′ing, *adj.*
un·fe′al·ty, *n.*
un·feared′, *adj.*
un·fear′ful, *adj.;* -ly, *adv.;* -ness, *n.*
un·fear′ing, *adj.*
un′fea·si·bil′i·ty, *n.*
un·fea′si·ble, *adj.;* -ble·ness, *n.;* -bly, *adv.*
un·feast′ed, *adj.*
un·feath′ered, *adj.*
un·fea′tured, *adj.*
un·fe′brile, *adj.*
un·fe′cund, *adj.*
un·fe′cun·dat′ed, *adj.*
un·fed′, *adj.*
un·fed′er·at′ed, *adj.*
un·fed′er·a′tive, *adj.;* -ly, *adv.*
un·feed′ble, *adj.;* -ble·ness, *n.;* -bly, *adv.*
un·feed′a·ble, *adj.*
un·feed′ing, *adj.*
un·feign′a·ble, *adj.*
un·feign′ing, *adj.;* -ly, *adv.*
un′fe·lic′i·tat′ed, *adj.*
un′fe·lic′i·tat′ing, *adj.*
un′fe·lic′i·tous, *adj.;* -ly, *adv.;* -ness, *n.*
un·fe′line, *adj.*
un·fell′a·ble, *adj.*
un·felled′, *adj.*
un′fe·lo′ni·ous, *adj.;* -ly, *adv.*
un·felt′, *adj.*
un·felt′ed, *adj.*
un·fe′male, *adj.*
un·fem′i·nine, *adj.;* -ly, *adv.*
un·fem′i·nise′, *v.t.,* -nised, -nis·ing.
un·fem′i·nist, *n.*
un·fem′i·nize′, *v.t.,* -nized, -niz·ing.
un·fence′, *v.t.,* -fenced, -fenc·ing.
un·fend′ed, *adj.*
un·fen′dered, *adj.*
un′fe·nes′tral, *adj.*
un′fe·nes′trat·ed, *adj.*
un·feoffed′, *adj.*
un′fer·ment′a·ble, *adj.*
un′fer·ment′a·tive, *adj.*
un′fer·ment′ed, *adj.*
un′fer·ment′ing, *adj.*
un′fe·ro′cious, *adj.;* -ly, *adv.*
un·fer′ret·ed, *adj.*
un·fer′ret·ing, *adj.*
un·fer′ried, *adj.*
un·fer′tile, *adj.*
un·fer′ti·lis′a·ble, *adj.*
un·fer′ti·lised′, *adj.*
un·fer′ti·lis′ing, *adj.*
un′fer·til′i·ty, *n.*
un·fer′ti·liz′a·ble, *adj.*
un·fer′ti·lized′, *adj.*
un·fer′ti·liz′ing, *adj.*
un·fer′vent, *adj.;* -ly, *adv.*
un·fer′vid, *adj.;* -ly, *adv.*
un·fes′tered, *adj.*
un·fes′ter·ing, *adj.*
un·fes′tive, *adj.;* -ly, *adv.*
un′fes·tooned′, *adj.*
un·fetched′, *adj.*
un·fetch′ing, *adj.*
un·fet′ed, *adj.*

un·fil·i·al (un fil′ē əl), *adj.* not befitting a son or daughter; violating the customary obligation of a child to a parent. [UN-[1] + FILIAL] —**un·fil′i·al·ly,** *adv.*

un·fin·ished (un fin′isht), *adj.* **1.** not finished; incomplete or unaccomplished. **2.** lacking some special finish or surface treatment, as polish, paint, etc. **3.** (of cloth) not sheared following the looming process. [UN-[1] + FINISHED] —**un·fin′ished·ness,** *n.*

unfin′ished wor′sted, men's suiting of worsted yarns, given a slight nap.

un·fit (un fit′), *adj.* **1.** not fit; not adapted or suited; unsuitable: *He was unfit for his office.* **2.** unqualified or incompetent. **3.** not physically fit or in due condition. —*v.t.* **4.** to render unfit or unsuitable; disqualify. [UN-[1] + FIT[1]] —**un·fit′ly,** *adv.* —**un·fit′ness,** *n.*
—**Syn. 1.** inappropriate, unapt. **2.** incapable.

un·fix (un fiks′), *v.t.,* **-fixed** or **-fixt, -fix·ing. 1.** to render no longer fixed; unfasten; detach; loosen; free. **2.** to unsettle, as the mind, traditions, habits, etc. [UN-[2] + FIT] —**un·fix·ed·ness** (un fik′sid nis, -fikst′-nis), *n.*

un·fledged (un flejd′), *adj.* **1.** not fledged; without feathers sufficiently developed for flight, as a young bird. **2.** immature; undeveloped; callow. [UN-[1] + FLEDGED]

un·flesh·ly (un flesh′lē), *adj.* not fleshly; not carnal or corporeal; spiritual. [UN-[1] + FLESHLY] —**un·flesh′li·ness,** *n.*

un·flinch·ing (un flin′ching), *adj.* not flinching; unshrinking: *He faced dangers with unflinching courage.* [UN-[1] + FLINCH[1] + -ING[2]] —**un·flinch′ing·ly,** *adv.*

un·fold (un fōld′), *v.t.* **1.** to bring out of a folded state; spread or open out: *Unfold your arms.* **2.** to spread out or lay open to view. **3.** to reveal or display. **4.** to reveal or disclose in words, esp. by careful or systematic exposition; set forth; explain. —*v.i.* **5.** to become unfolded; open. **6.** to develop. **7.** to become clear, apparent, or known: *The protagonist's character unfolds as the story reaches its climax.* [ME; OE *unfeald(an)*; c. G *entfalten.* See UN-[2], FOLD[1]] —**un·fold′a·ble,** *adj.* —**un·fold′er,** *n.* —**un·fold′ment,** *n.*

un·for·get·ta·ble (un′fər get′ə bəl), *adj.* impossible to forget; indelibly impressed on the memory: *scenes of unforgettable beauty.* [UN-[1] + FORGETTABLE] —**un′for·get′ta·ble·ness,** *n.* —**un·for·get′ta·bly,** *adv.*

un·formed (un fôrmd′), *adj.* **1.** not definitely shaped; shapeless or formless. **2.** undeveloped; crude. **3.** not formed; not created. [ME *unfourmed.* See UN-[1], FORM, -ED[2]]

un·for·tu·nate (un fôr′chə nit), *adj.* **1.** unlucky; not favored by fortune; meeting with unexpected reverses: *an unfortunate person; an unfortunate regiment.* **2.** unsuitable; inept; infelicitous: *an unfortunate phrase; an unfortunate suggestion.* **3.** untoward; unpropitious; unfavorable: *an unfortunate development; an unfortunate change in the weather.* **4.** unpromising; inauspicious; ill-starred: *an unfortunate decision; an unfortunate beginning.* **5.** bringing or inviting misfortune; deplorable; regrettable: *an unfortunate craving for liquor; an unfortunate personality.* **6.** eliciting sympathy or commiseration; lamentable; sad: *the unfortunate death of his partner; an unfortunate accident.* —*n.* **7.** Usually, **unfortunates.** people who are generally unfortunate. [UN-[1] + FORTUNATE] —**un·for′tu·nate·ly,** *adv.* —**un·for′tu·nate·ness,** *n.*
—**Syn. 1.** unsuccessful, hapless.

un·found·ed (un foun′did), *adj.* **1.** without foundation; not based on fact, realistic considerations, or the like: *unfounded suspicions.* **2.** not established; not endowed with the requisites for functioning: *the prophet of a religion as yet unfounded.* [UN-[1] + FOUND[2] + -ED[2]] —**un·found′ed·ly,** *adv.* —**un·found′ed·ness,** *n.*

un·freeze (un frēz′), *v.,* **-froze, -fro·zen, -freez·ing.** —*v.t.* **1.** to cause to thaw; melt. —*v.i.* **2.** to become unfrozen; thaw. [UN-[2] + FREEZE]

un·fre·quent·ed (un frē′kwən tid), *adj.* **1.** usually empty or nearly empty of people; characterized by scarcity of occupants or passers-by: *an unfrequented side street.* **2.** not habitually visited or gone to.

un·friend·ed (un fren′did), *adj.* without friends; not befriended. [UN-[1] + FRIEND + -ED[3]] —**un·friend′ed·ness,** *n.*

un·friend·ly (un frend′lē), *adj.,* **-li·er, -li·est,** *adv.* —*adj.* **1.** not amicable; without indications of friendly or kindly disposition; unsympathetic; aloof: *an unfriendly coldness of manner.* **2.** hostile; antagonistic: *He was so unpleasant he refused to shake hands when we were introduced—a most unfriendly act.* **3.** unfavorable; inhospitable or inimical, as an environment: *The area has been an unfriendly climate for those who believe in freedom of speech.* —*adv.* **4.** in an unfriendly manner. [ME *unfrendly.* See UN-[1], FRIENDLY] —**un·friend′li·ness,** *n.*

un·frock (un frok′), *v.t.* **1.** to deprive (a monk, priest, minister, etc.) of ecclesiastical rank, authority, and function; to depose from the rank of an ecclesiastic. **2.** to divest or strip of a frock. [UN-[2] + FROCK]

un·fruit·ful (un frōōt′fəl), *adj.* **1.** not providing satisfaction or leading to a desired result; unprofitable: *unfruitful efforts.* **2.** not producing offspring; sterile: *an unfruitful marriage.* **3.** not yielding good crops; infertile: *unfruitful acres.* **4.** not bearing fruit; fruitless; barren: *an unfruitful tree.* [ME; see UN-[1], FRUITFUL] —**un·fruit′ful·ly,** *adv.* —**un·fruit′ful·ness,** *n.*

un·furl (un fûrl′), *v.t.* **1.** to spread or shake out from a furled state, as a sail or a flag; unfold. —*v.i.* **2.** to become unfurled. [UN-[2] + FURL] —**un·furl′a·ble,** *adj.*

ung., (in prescriptions) ointment. [< L *unguentum*]

un·gain·ly (un gān′lē), *adj.* **1.** not graceful; awkward; clumsy; uncouth: *an ungainly child; ungainly prose style; ungainly trunk.* —*adv.* **2.** in an awkward manner. [ME *ungaynly* (adv.). See UN-[1], GAINLY] —**un·gain′li·ness,** *n.*

---

un·feu′dal, *adj.;* **-ly,** *adv.*
un·feu′dal·ise′, *v.t.,* **-ised, -is·ing.**
un·feu′dal·ize′, *v.t.,* **-ized, -iz·ing.**
un·fe′vered, *adj.*
un·fe′ver·ish, *adj.*
un·fib′bing, *adj.*
un·fi′bered, *adj.*
un·fi′bred, *adj.*
un·fi′brous, *adj.;* **-ly,** *adv.*
un·fick′le, *adj.*
un′fic·ti′tious, *adj.;* **-ly,** *adv.*
un′fi·del′i·ty, *n.*
un·fidg′et·ing, *adj.*
un′fi·du′cial, *adj.*
un·field′ed, *adj.*
un·fierce′, *adj.;* **-ly,** *adj.*
un·fier′y, *adj.*
un·fight′a·ble, *adj.*
un·fight′ing, *adj.*
un·fig′ur·a·ble, *adj.*
un·fig′ur·a·tive, *adj.*
un′fil·a·men′tous, *adj.*
un·filched′, *adj.*
un·file′, *v.t.,* **-filed, -fil·ing.**
un·filled′, *adj.*
un·fill′ing, *adj.*
un·filmed′, *adj.*
un·fil′ter·a·ble, *adj.*
un·fil′tered, *adj.*
un·fil′ter·ing, *adj.*
un·fil′trat·ed, *adj.*
un·fim′bri·at′ed, *adj.*
un·fin′a·ble, *adj.*
un′fi·nanced′, *adj.*
un·fine′, *adj.*
un·fine′a·ble, *adj.*
un·fined′, *adj.*
un·fin′i·cal, *adj.*
un·fin′ish·a·ble, *adj.*
un·fi′nite, *adj.*
un·fired′, *adj.*
un·fir′ing, *adj.*
un·firm′, *adj.;* **-ly,** *adv.;* **-ness,** *n.*
un·fis′cal, *adj.;* **-ly,** *adv.*
un·fish′a·ble, *adj.*
un·fished′, *adj.*
un·fis′sile, *adj.*
un·fis′tu·lous, *adj.*
un·fit′ta·ble, *adj.*
un·fit′ted, *adj.*
un·fit′ting, *adj.;* **-ly,** *adv.*
un·fix′a·ble, *adj.*
un·fix′at·ed, *adj.*
un·fix′a·tive, *adj.*
un·fix′i·ty, *n.*
un·flagged′, *adj.*
un·flag′ging, *adj.;* **-ly,** *adv.*
un′fla·gi′tious, *adj.*
un·fla′grant, *adj.;* **-ly,** *adv.*
un·flaked′, *adj.*
un·flak′ing, *adj.*
un·flak′y, *adj.*
un′flam·boy′ant, *adj.;* **-ly,** *adv.*
un·flam′ing, *adj.*
un·flanged′, *adj.*
un·flank′, *v.t.*
un·flap′ping, *adj.*
un·flared′, *adj.*
un·flar′ing, *adj.*
un·flash′ing, *adj.*
un·flash′y, *adj.*
un·flat′, *adj.*
un·flat′ted, *adj.*
un·flat′tened, *adj.*
un·flat′ter·a·ble, *adj.*
un·flat′tered, *adj.*
un·flat′ter·ing, *adj.;* **-ly,** *adv.*
un·flaunt′ed, *adj.*
un·flaunt′ing, *adj.;* **-ly,** *adv.*
un·fla′vored, *adj.*
un·fla′vor·ous, *adj.*
un·fla′voured, *adj.*
un·fla′vour·ous, *adj.*
un·flawed′, *adj.*
un·flayed′, *adj.*
un·flecked′, *adj.*
un·fleeced′, *adj.*
un·flee′ing, *adj.*
un·fleet′ing, *adj.*
un·fletched′, *adj.*
un·flexed′, *adj.*
un′flex·i·bil′i·ty, *n.*
un·flex′i·ble, *adj.;* **-bly,** *adv.*
un·flick′er·ing, *adj.;* **-ly,** *adv.*
un·flight′y, *adj.*
un·flip′pant, *adj.;* **-ly,** *adv.*
un′flir·ta′tious, *adj.;* **-ly,** *adv.;* **-ness,** *n.*
un·flitched′, *adj.*
un·float′a·ble, *adj.*
un·float′ing, *adj.*
un·flog′ga·ble, *adj.*
un·flogged′, *adj.*
un·flood′ed, *adj.*
un·floor′, *v.t.*
un·flor′id, *adj.*
un·floss′y, *adj.*
un·flounced′, *adj.*
un·floun′der·ing, *adj.*
un·floured′, *adj.*
un·flour′ish·ing, *adj.*
un·flout′ed, *adj.*
un·flow′ered, *adj.*
un·flow′er·ing, *adj.*
un·flow′er·y, *adj.*
un·flow′ing, *adj.*
un·flown′, *adj.*
un·fluc′tu·ant, *adj.*
un·fluc′tu·at′ing, *adj.*
un·flu′ent, *adj.;* **-ly,** *adv.*
un·fluffed′, *adj.*
un·fluff′y, *adj.*
un·flu′id, *adj.*
un·fluked′, *adj.*
un·flunked′, *adj.*
un′flu·o·res′cent, *adj.*
un·fluor′i·nat′ed, *adj.*
un·flur′ried, *adj.*
un·flushed′, *adj.*
un·flus′tered, *adj.*
un·flut′ed, *adj.*
un·flut′ter·a·ble, *adj.*
un·flut′tered, *adj.*
un·flut′ter·ing, *adj.*
un·flu′vi·al, *adj.*
un·fly′ing, *adj.*
un·foaled′, *adj.*
un·foamed′, *adj.*
un·foam′ing, *adj.*
un·fo′cused, *adj.*
un·fo′cus·ing, *adj.*
un·fo′cussed, *adj.*
un·fo′cus·sing, *adj.*
un·fogged′, *adj.*
un·fog′ging, *adj.*
un·fog′gy, *adj.*
un·foil′a·ble, *adj.*
un·foiled′, *adj.*
un·foist′ed, *adj.*
un·fo′li·aged, *adj.*
un·fo′li·at′ed, *adj.*
un·fol′low·a·ble, *adj.*
un·fol′lowed, *adj.*
un·fol′low·ing, *adj.*
un′fo·ment′ed, *adj.*
un·fond′, *adj.;* **-ly,** *adv.;* **-ness,** *n.*
un·fon′dled, *adj.*
un·fool′a·ble, *adj.*
un·fooled′, *adj.*
un·fool′ing, *adj.*
un·fool′ish, *adj.;* **-ly,** *adv.;* **-ness,** *n.*
un·for′aged, *adj.*
un′for·bear′ing, *adj.*
un′for·bid′den, *adj.*
un′for·bid′ding, *adj.*
un·force′a·ble, *adj.*
un·forced′, *adj.*
un·forc′ed·ly, *adv.*
un·force′ful, *adj.;* **-ly,** *adv.*
un·for′ci·ble, *adj.;* **-ble·ness,** *n.;* **-bly,** *adv.*
un·forc′ing, *adj.*
un·ford′a·ble, *adj.*
un·ford′ed, *adj.*
un′fore·bod′ed, *adj.*
un′fore·bod′ing, *adj.*
un·fore′cast′, *adj.*
un·fore′cast′ed, *adj.*
un′fore·gone′, *adj.*
un·for′eign, *adj.*
un′fore·know′a·ble, *adj.*
un′fore·known′, *adj.*
un′fo·ren′sic, *adj.*
un′fo·ren′si·cal·ly, *adv.*
un′fore·see′a·ble, *adj.;* **-ble·ness,** *n.;* **-bly,** *adv.*
un′fore·see′ing, *adj.*
un′fore·seen′, *adj.*
un′fore·short′ened, *adj.*
un′fore·stall′a·ble, *adj.*
un′fore·stalled′, *adj.*
un·for′est·ed, *adj.*
un′fore·tell′a·ble, *adj.*
un′fore·told′, *adj.*
un′fore·warned′, *adj.*
un·for′feit·a·ble, *adj.*
un·for′feit·ed, *adj.*
un·for′feit·ing, *adj.*
un′forge·a·bil′i·ty, *n.*
un·forge′a·ble, *adj.*
un·forged′, *adj.*
un′for·get′ful, *adj.;* **-ly,** *adv.;* **-ness,** *n.*
un′for·get′ting, *adj.*
un′for·giv′a·ble, *adj.;* **-ble·ness,** *n.;* **-bly,** *adv.*
un′for·giv′en, *adj.*
un′for·giv′ing, *adj.*
un′for·gone′, *adj.*
un′for·got′ten, *adj.*
un·fork′, *v.t.*
un′for·lorn′, *adj.*
un·for′mal·ised′, *adj.*
un′for·mal·is′tic, *adj.*
un·for′mal·ized′, *adj.*
un·form′a·tive, *adj.*
un·for′mi·da·ble, *adj.;* **-ble·ness,** *n.;* **-bly,** *adv.*
un·for′mu·lat′ed, *adj.*
un′for·mu·lis′tic, *adj.*
un′for·sak′en, *adj.*
un′for·sak′ing, *adj.*
un′for·sworn′, *adj.*
un′forth·right′, *adj.*
un·for′ti·fi′a·ble, *adj.*
un·for′ti·fied′, *adj.*
un′for·tu′i·tous, *adj.;* **-ly,** *adv.;* **-ness,** *n.*
un·for′ward, *adj.;* **-ly,** *adv.*
un·for′ward·ed, *adj.*
un′fos·sil·if′er·ous, *adj.*
un·fos′sil·ised′, *adj.*
un·fos′sil·ized′, *adj.*
un·fos′tered, *adj.*
un·fos′ter·ing, *adj.*
un·fought′, *adj.*
un·foul′, *adj.;* **-ly,** *adv.*
un·fouled′, *adj.*
un·found′, *adj.*
un·foun′dered, *adj.*
un·foun′der·ing, *adj.*
un·foun′tained, *adj.*
un·foxed′, *adj.*
un·fox′y, *adj.*
un·frac′tious, *adj.;* **-ly,** *adv.;* **-ness,** *n.*
un·frac′tured, *adj.*
un·frag′ile, *adj.*
un·frag′ment·ed, *adj.*
un·fra′grance, *n.*
un·fra′grant, *adj.;* **-ly,** *adv.*
un·frail′, *adj.*
un·fram′a·ble, *adj.;* **-ble·ness,** *n.;* **-bly,** *adv.*
un·frame′a·ble, *adj.*
un·framed′, *adj.*
un·fran′chised, *adj.*
un·frank′, *adj.;* **-ly,** *adv.;* **-ness,** *n.*
un′fra·ter′nal, *adj.;* **-ly,** *adv.*
un·frat′er·nised′, *adj.*
un·frat′er·nized′, *adj.*
un·frat′er·niz′ing, *adj.*
un·fraud′u·lent, *adj.;* **-ly,** *adv.*
un·fraught′, *adj.*
un·frayed′, *adj.*
un·fraz′zled, *adj.*
un·freak′ish, *adj.;* **-ly,** *adv.;* **-ness,** *n.*
un·freck′led, *adj.*
un·free′, *v.t.,* **-freed, -free·ing,** *adj.;* **-ly,** *adv.*
un·freez′a·ble, *adj.*
un·freight′ed, *adj.*
un-French′, *adj.*
un·fren′zied, *adj.*
un·fre′quent, *adj.;* **-ly,** *adv.*
un′fre·quent′a·ble, *adj.*
un′fre·quen′ta·tive, *adj.*
un·fret′ful, *adj.;* **-ly,** *adv.*
un·fret′ted, *adj.*
un·fret′ting, *adj.*
un·fret′ty, *adj.*
un·fri′a·ble, *adj.;* **-bleness,** *n.*
un·fric′a·tive, *adj.*
un·fric′tion·al, *adj.;* **-ly,** *adv.*
un·fric′tioned, *adj.*
un·fried′, *adj.*
un·fright′ed, *adj.*
un·fright′ened, *adj.*
un·fright′en·ing, *adj.*
un·fright′ful, *adj.*
un·frig′id, *adj.;* **-ly,** *adv.;* **-ness,** *n.*
un′fri·gid′i·ty, *n.*
un·frill′, *v.t.*
un·frill′y, *adj.*
un·fringe′, *v.t.,* **-fringed, -fring·ing.**
un·frisk′ing, *adj.*
un·frisk′y, *adj.*
un·frit′tered, *adj.*
un·friv′o·lous, *adj.;* **-ly,** *adv.;* **-ness,** *n.*
un·friz′zled, *adj.*
un·friz′zly, *adj.*
un·friz′zy, *adj.*
un·front′ed, *adj.*
un·frost′, *v.t.*
un·frost′ed, *adj.*
un·frost′y, *adj.*
un·frothed′, *adj.*
un·froth′ing, *adj.*
un·frounced′, *adj.*
un·fro′ward, *adj.;* **-ly,** *adv.*
un·frown′ing, *adj.*
un·fro′zen, *adj.*
un·fruc′ti·fied′, *adj.*
un·fruc′tu·ous, *adj.*
un·fru′gal, *adj.;* **-ly,** *adv.;* **-ness,** *n.*
un′fru·gal′i·ty, *n.*
un·fruit′y, *adj.*
un·frus′trat·a·ble, *adj.*
un·frus′trat·ed, *adj.*
un·fud′dled, *adj.*
un·fudged′, *adj.*
un·fu′eled, *adj.*
un·fu′elled, *adj.*
un·fu′gal, *adj.;* **-ly,** *adv.*
un·fu′gi·tive, *adj.;* **-ly,** *adv.*
un′ful·fill′a·ble, *adj.*
un′ful·filled′, *adj.*
un′ful·fill′ing, *adj.*
un·ful′gent, *adj.;* **-ly,** *adv.*
un·full′, *adj.*
un·full′y, *adv.*
un·ful′mi·nant, *adj.*
un·ful′mi·nat′ed, *adj.*
un·ful′mi·nat′ing, *adj.*
un·ful′some, *adj.*
un·fum′bled, *adj.*
un·fum′bling, *adj.*
un·fu′mi·gat′ed, *adj.*
un·fum′ing, *adj.*
un·func′tion·al, *adj.;* **-ly,** *adv.*
un·func′tion·ing, *adj.*
un′fun·da·men′tal, *adj.;* **-ly,** *adv.*
un·fund′a·ble, *adj.*
un·fund′ed, *adj.*
un′fu·ne′re·al, *adj.;* **-ly,** *adv.*
un·fun′gi·ble, *adj.*
un·fun′ni·ly, *adv.*
un·fun′ni·ness, *n.*
un·fun′ny, *adj.*
un·fur′be·lowed′, *adj.*
un·fur′bished, *adj.*
un·fur′cate, *adj.*
un·fur′nished, *adj.*
un·fur′ni·tured, *adj.*
un·furred′, *adj.*
un·fur′rowed, *adj.*
un·fused′, *adj.*
un′fu·si·bil′i·ty, *n.*
un·fu′si·ble, *adj.;* **-ness,** *n.*
un·fussed′, *adj.*
un·fuss′ing, *adj.*
un·fuss′i·ly, *adv.*
un·fuss′i·ness, *n.*
un·fuss′y, *adj.*
un·fu′tile, *adj.*
un′fu·tur·is′tic, *adj.*
un·ga′bled, *adj.*
un·gag′, *v.t.,* **-gagged, -gag·ging.**
un·gain′a·ble, *adj.*
un·gained′, *adj.*
un·gain′ful, *adj.;* **-ly,** *adv.*
un·gain′ing, *adj.*
un′gain·said′, *adj.*
un·gait′ed, *adj.*
un·gal′lant, *adj.;* **-ly,** *adv.*
un·galled′, *adj.*
un·gal′ler·ied, *adj.*
un·gall′ing, *adj.*
un·gal′lop·ing, *adj.*
un·gal′va·nized′, *adj.*
un·gam′bled, *adj.*
un·gam′bling, *adj.*
un·gam′boled, *adj.*
un·gam′bol·ing, *adj.*
un·gam′bolled, *adj.*
un·gam′bol·ling, *adj.*
un·game′like′, *adj.*
un·gam′y, *adj.*
un·ganged′, *adj.*
un·gan′grened, *adj.*
un·gan′gre·nous, *adj.*
un·gap′ing, *adj.*
un′ga·raged′, *adj.*
un·garbed′, *adj.*
un·gar′bled, *adj.*
un·gar′dened, *adj.*
un·gar′land, *v.t.*

Un·ga·va (ung gä′və, -gä′-), *n.* a region in NE Canada, comprising the larger part of the peninsula of Labrador: incorporated into Quebec province 1912.

un·gen·er·ous (un jen′ər əs), *adj.* **1.** stingy; niggardly; miserly: *an ungenerous portion; an ungenerous employer.* **2.** uncharitable; petty; small-minded; deficient in liberality or nobility of thought: *an ungenerous critic; an ungenerous impulse.* [UN-¹ + GENEROUS] —**un·gen·er·os·i·ty** (un jen′ə ros′i tē), *n.* —**un·gen′er·ous·ly,** *adv.*

Ung·er (o͝ong′ər), *n.* **Her·mann** (her′män), born 1886, German composer.

un·gird (un gûrd′), *v.t.*, **-gird·ed** or **-girt, -gird·ing.** **1.** to loosen or remove a girdle or belt from. **2.** to loosen or remove by unfastening a belt: *to ungird a sword.* [UN-² + GIRD; c. G *entgürten*]

un·girt (un gûrt′), *adj.* **1.** having a girdle loosened or removed. **2.** slack; relaxed; not taut or pulled together: *the ungirt thinking that often characterizes free verse.* [ME *ungyrt.* See UN-¹, GIRT¹]

un·glue (un glo͞o′), *v.t.*, **-glued, -glu·ing.** to separate or detach by or as if by overcoming an adhesive agent: *to unglue a sticker from a wall.* [UN-² + GLUE]

un·god·ly (un god′lē), *adj.*, **-li·er, -li·est.** **1.** not accepting God or a particular religious doctrine; irreligious; atheistic: *an ungodly era.* **2.** sinful; wicked; impious; not conforming to religious tenets or canons: *an ungodly life.* **3.** *Informal.* dreadful; insufferable: *an ungodly roar; an ungodly hour to drop in.* [UN-¹ + GODLY] —**un·god′li·ly,** *adv.* —**un·god′li·ness,** *n.*
—**Syn. 2.** profane, evil, corrupt, blasphemous.

un·got·ten (un got′ən), *adj.* **1.** not obtained or gained. **2.** *Obs.* not begotten. Also, **un·got′.** [ME; see UN-¹, GOTTEN]

un·gov·ern·a·ble (un guv′ər nə bəl), *adj.* impossible to govern, rule, or restrain; uncontrollable. [UN-¹ + GOVERNABLE] —**un·gov′ern·a·ble·ness,** *n.* —**un·gov′ern·a·bly,** *adv.*

un·grace·ful (un grās′fəl), *adj.* lacking charm or elegance; awkward; clumsy; uncouth. [UN-¹ + GRACEFUL] —**un·grace′ful·ly,** *adv.* —**un·grace′ful·ness,** *n.*

un·gra·cious (un grā′shəs), *adj.* **1.** discourteous; unpleasant; ill-mannered; rude: *ungracious behavior.* **2.** unpleasant; disagreeable; unrewarding: *an ungracious task.* **3.** thankless: *the hangman's ungracious skill.* **4.** *Obs.* ungraceful; unpleasing. [ME; see UN-¹, GRACIOUS] —**un·gra′cious·ly,** *adv.* —**un·gra′cious·ness,** *n.*

un·gram·mat·i·cal (un′grə mat′i kəl), *adj.* **1.** grammatically incorrect or awkward; expressed in a form that violates the rules or principles of grammar: *an ungrammatical sentence.* **2.** not conforming to accepted usage; not idiomatic. [UN-¹ + GRAMMATICAL] —**un′gram·mat′i·cal·ly,** *adv.*

un·grate·ful (un grāt′fəl), *adj.* **1.** unappreciative; not displaying gratitude; not giving due return or recompense for benefits conferred: *ungrateful heirs.* **2.** unpleasant; distasteful; repellent: *an ungrateful task.* [UN-¹ + GRATEFUL] —**un·grate′ful·ly,** *adv.* —**un·grate′ful·ness,** *n.*

un·grudg·ing (un gruj′ing), *adj.* not begrudging; not stinting; wholehearted: *an ungrudging supporter of charities.* [UN-¹ + GRUDGING] —**un·grudg′ing·ly,** *adv.*

ungt., (in prescriptions) ointment. [< L *unguentum*]

un·gual (ung′gwəl), *adj.* of, pertaining to, bearing, or shaped like a nail, claw, or hoof. [< L *ungu(is)* a nail, claw, hoof (c. Gk *ónyx*) + -AL¹]

un·guard·ed (un gär′did), *adj.* **1.** not guarded; unprotected; undefended. **2.** open; frank; guileless: *an unguarded manner.* **3.** exposed to attack or capture by the opponent without recourse by the player, as a card, chess piece, etc.: *an unguarded queen of clubs; an unguarded pawn.* **4.** not cautious or discreet; careless: *In an unguarded moment he had told her about his affair with Agatha.* **5.** without a safeguard, as a cover, barrier, shield, or the like, for protection: *an unguarded buzz saw.* [UN-¹ + GUARDED] —**un·guard′ed·ly,** *adv.* —**un·guard′ed·ness,** *n.*
—**Syn. 1.** defenseless. **4.** indiscreet.

un·guent (ung′gwənt), *n.* an ointment or salve, usually liquid or semiliquid, for application to wounds, sores, etc.: *a healing unguent.* [< L *unguent(um)*, equiv. to *unguent-* s. of *unguens* prp. of *ungu(ere)* (to) anoint + *-ent-* -ENT + *-um* n. suffix] —**un·guen·tar·y** (ung′gwən ter′ē), *adj.*

un·guen·tum (ung gwen′təm), *n., pl.* **-ta** (-tə). (in prescriptions) ointment. [< L]

un·guic·u·late (ung gwik′yə lit, -lāt′), *adj.* Also, **un·guic′u·lat′ed. 1.** bearing or resembling a nail or claw. **2.** *Zool.* having nails or claws, as distinguished from hoofs. **3.** *Bot.* having a clawlike base, as certain petals. —*n.* **4.** an unguiculate animal. [< NL *unguiculātus* < L *unguicul(us)* fingernail (*ungu(is)* (see UNGUIS) + *-i-* + *-I-* + *-culus* -CULE) + *-ātus* -ATE¹]

un·gui·nous (ung′gwi nəs), *adj.* resembling, containing, or consisting of fat or oil; greasy; oily. [< L *unguinōs(us)* < *unguin-* (s. of *unguen*) ointment + *-ōsus* -OUS]

un·guis (ung′gwis), *n., pl.* **-gues** (-gwēz). **1.** a nail, claw, or hoof. **2.** *Bot.* the clawlike base of certain petals. [< L *unguis* a nail, claw, hoof; c. Gk *ónyx*]

Ungula

un·gu·la (ung′gyə lə), *n., pl.* **-lae** (-lē′). **1.** *Geom.* a part cut off from a cylinder cone, or the like, by a plane oblique to the base. **2.** *Bot.* an unguis. [< L *ungula* a claw, hoof, talon, dim. of *unguis* UNGUIS]

un·gu·lar (ung′gyə lər), *adj.* pertaining to or of the nature of an ungula; ungual. [UNGUL(A) + -AR¹]

un·gu·late (ung′gyə lit, -lāt′), *adj.* **1.** having hoofs. **2.** belonging or pertaining to the *Ungulata*, a former group comprising all hoofed mammals. **3.** hooflike. —*n.* **4.** a hoofed mammal. [< LL *ungulāt(us)* having claws or hoofs. See UNGULA, -ATE¹]

un·guled (ung′gyo͞old), *adj. Heraldry.* (of an animal) represented as having hoofs of a different tincture from that of the body: *a stag argent unguled gules.* [UNGUL(A) + -ED³]

un·hair (un hâr′), *v.t.* **1.** to remove the hair from, as a hide in preparation for tanning. **2.** to remove the guard hairs from, as for a pelt or animal skin to be made into a garment. **3.** to give a fur a finer texture by removing the guard hairs and leaving the underfur. —*v.i.* **4.** to become hairless: *After soaking, the hides unhair easily.* [ME *unheere(n).* See UN-², HAIR] —**un·hair′er,** *n.*

un·hal·low (un hal′ō), *v.t.* to desecrate; profane. [UN-² + HALLOW¹]

un·hal·lowed (un hal′ōd), *adj.* **1.** not hallowed or consecrated; not regarded as holy or sacred: *unhallowed ground.* **2.** contrary to religious belief or practice; impious; unholy. **3.** of, appropriate to, or inspired by evil; wicked; sinful; damnable; fiendish: *unhallowed practices.* **4.** involving or associated with a breach of public morals; improper; indecent; licentious; lascivious. [ME *unhalewed;* see UN-¹, HALLOWED]

un·hand (un hand′), *v.t.* to take the hand or hands from; release from a grasp; let go: *Unhand that girl, you wretched coward!* [UN-² + HAND]

un·han·dled (un han′dəld), *adj.* **1.** not handled; not touched. **2.** (of animals) untamed; unbroken; untrained: *An unhandled tiger can upset the other cats and endanger the whole act.* **3.** not dealt with or in, as merchandise; not carried in stock. [UN-¹ + HANDLED]

un·hand·some (un han′səm), *adj.* **1.** lacking good looks; not attractive in physical appearance; plain or ugly. **2.** ungracious; discourteous; unseemly: *an unhandsome exchange of epithets.* **3.** ungenerous; illiberal: *an unhandsome return.* [UN-¹ + HANDSOME] —**un·hand′some·ly,** *adv.* —**un·hand′some·ness,** *n.*

un·hap·py (un hap′ē), *adj.*, **-pi·er, -pi·est. 1.** sad; miserable; wretched: *Why is she so unhappy?* **2.** unfortunate; unlucky: *an unhappy incident.* **3.** unfavorable; inauspicious: *an unhappy omen.* **4.** infelicitous; unsuitable: *an unhappy choice of words* **5.** *Obs.* causing trouble; reprehensible; troublesome. [ME: causing misfortune, objectionable; see UN-¹, HAPPY] —**un·hap′pi·ly,** *adv.* —**un·hap′pi·ness,** *n.*
—**Syn. 1.** sorrowful, downcast, cheerless, disconsolate, distressed, afflicted. **2.** hapless. **3.** unpropitious. **4.** inappropriate, inapt, inept.

un·har·ness (un här′nis), *v.t.* **1.** to strip of harness; detach the harness from (a horse, mule, etc.). **2.** *Archaic.* to divest of armor, as a knight or warhorse. [ME *onharnes(en).* See UN-², HARNESS]

un·hasp (un hasp′), *v.t.* to loosen the hasp of. [ME *unhasp(en).* See UN-², HASP]

un·gar′ment·ed, *adj.*
un·gar′nered, *adj.*
un·gar′nished, *adj.*
un·gar′ri·soned, *adj.*
un·gar′ru·lous, *adj.;* **-ly,** *adv.;* **-ness,** *n.*
un·gar′ter, *v.t.*
un·gashed′, *adj.*
un·gassed′, *adj.*
un·gat′ed, *adj.*
un·gath′ered, *adj.*
un·gaud′i·ly, *adv.*
un·gaud′i·ness, *n.*
un·gaud′y, *adj.*
un·gauged′, *adj.*
un·gaunt′let·ed, *adj.*
un′ga·zet′ted, *adj.*
un·gaz′ing, *adj.*
un·geared′, *adj.*
un′ge·lat′i·nized′, *adj.*
un′ge·lat′i·nous, *adj.;* **-ly,** *adv.;* **-ness,** *n.*
un·geld′ed, *adj.*
un·gen′er·a·ble, *adj.*
un·gen′er·al·ised′, *adj.*
un·gen′er·al·is′ing, *adj.*
un·gen′er·al·ized′, *adj.*
un·gen′er·al·iz′ing, *adj.*
un·gen′er·at′ed, *adj.*
un·gen′er·at′ing, *adj.*
un·gen′er·a′tive, *adj.*
un′ge·ner′ic, *adj.*
un′ge·ner′i·cal, *adj.;* **-ly,** *adv.*
un·gen′ial, *adj.;* **-ly,** *adv.;* **-ness,** *n.*
un·gen′i·tive, *adj.*
un′gen·teel′, *adj.*
un·gen′tile, *adj.*
un′gen·til′i·ty, *n.*
un·gen′tle, *adj.;* **-tle·ness,** *n.;* **-tly,** *adv.*
un·gen′tle·man·like′, *adj.*
un·gen′tle·man·ly, *adj.*
un·gen′u·ine, *adj.;* **-ly,** *adv.;* **-ness,** *n.*
un′ge·o·det′ic, *adj.*
un′ge·o·det′i·cal·ly, *adv.*
un′ge·o·graph′ic, *adj.*
un′ge·o·graph′i·cal, *adj.;* **-ly,** *adv.*
un′ge·o·log′i·cal, *adj.;* **-ly,** *adv.*
un′ge·o·met′ric, *adj.*
un′ge·o·met′ri·cal, *adj.;* **-ly,** *adv.*
un-Ger′man, *adj.*
un′ger·mane′, *adj.*
un·ger′mi·nant, *adj.*
un·ger′mi·nat′ed, *adj.*
un·ger′mi·nat′ing, *adj.*
un·ger′mi·na′tive, *adj.*
un′ges·tic′u·lar, *adj.*
un′ges·tic′u·lat′ing, *adj.*
un′ges·tic′u·la′tive, *adj.*
un′ges·tic′u·la·to′ry, *adj.*
un·ges′tur·al, *adj.*
un·ges′tur·ing, *adj.*
un·ghost′like′, *adj.*
un·ghost′ly, *adj.*
un·gid′dy, *adj.*
un·gift′ed, *adj.*
un·gild′ed, *adj.*
un·gilled′, *adj.*
un·gilt′, *adj.*
un·ginned′, *adj.*
un·gir′dle, *v.t.,* **-dled, -dling.**
un·girl′ish, *adj.;* **-ly,** *adv.;* **-ness,** *n.*
un·girthed′, *adj.*
un·giv′a·ble, *adj.*
un·giv′en, *adj.*
un·giv′ing, *adj.*
un·gla′cial, *adj.;* **-ly,** *adv.*
un·gla′ci·at·ed, *adj.*
un·glad′, *adj.;* **-ly,** *adv.*
un·glad′den, *v.t.*
un·glam′or·ous, *adj.;* **-ly,** *adv.;* **-ness,** *n.*
un·glam′our·ous, *adj.;* **-ly,** *adv.*
un·glan′du·lar, *adj.*
un·glar′ing, *adj.*
un·glassed′, *adj.*
un·glass′y, *adj.*
un·glazed′, *adj.*
un·gleam′ing, *adj.*
un·gleaned′, *adj.*
un·glee′ful, *adj.;* **-ly,** *adv.*
un·glib′, *adj.;* **-ly,** *adv.*
un·glid′ing, *adj.*
un·glimpsed′, *adj.*
un·glis′ten·ing, *adj.*
un·glit′ter·ing, *adj.*
un·glit′ter·y, *adj.*
un·gloat′ing, *adj.*
un·glob′u·lar, *adj.;* **-ly,** *adv.*
un·gloom′, *v.t.*
un·gloom′i·ly, *adv.*
un·gloom′y, *adj.*
un·glo′ri·fied′, *adj.*
un·glo′ri·fy′ing, *adj.*
un·glo′ri·ous, *adj.;* **-ly,** *adv.*
un·glos′sa·ried, *adj.*
un·glossed′, *adj.*
un·gloss′y, *adj.*
un·gloved′, *adj.*
un·glow′er·ing, *adj.;* **-ly,** *adv.*
un·glow′ing, *adj.*
un·glozed′, *adj.*
un′glu·ti·nos′i·ty, *n.*
un·glu′ti·nous, *adj.;* **-ly,** *adv.;* **-ness,** *n.*
un·glut′ted, *adj.*
un·glut′ton·ous, *adj.*
un·gnarled′, *adj.*
un·gnawed′, *adj.*
un·gnawn′, *adj.*
un·gnos′tic, *adj.*
un·goad′ed, *adj.*
un·god′like′, *adj.*
un·gog′gled, *adj.*
un·goi′tered, *adj.*
un·gold′en, *adj.*
un·good′ly, *adj., adv.*
un·gored′, *adj.*
un·gorged′, *adj.*
un·gos′sip·ing, *adj.*
un·gos′sip·y, *adj.*
un·goth′ic, *adj.*
un·gouged′, *adj.*
un·gout′y, *adj.*
un·gov′ern·a·bil′i·ty, *n.*
un·gov′erned, *adj.*
un·gov′ern·ing, *adj.*
un′gov·ern·men′tal, *adj.;* **-ly,** *adv.*
un·gowned′, *adj.*
un·grab′bing, *adj.*
un·graced′, *adj.*
un·gra′dat·ed, *adj.*
un·gra′dat·ing, *adj.*
un·grad′ed, *adj.*
un·grad′u·at′ed, *adj.*
un·grad′u·at′ing, *adj.*
un·grad′u·al, *adj.;* **-ly,** *adv.*
un·graft′ed, *adj.*
un·grain′a·ble, *adj.*
un·grained′, *adj.*
un·grand′, *adj.*
un·grant′a·ble, *adj.*
un·gran′u·lar, *adj.*
un·gran′u·lat′ed, *adj.*
un·graph′a·ble, *adj.*
un·graph′ic, *adj.*
un·graph′i·cal, *adj.;* **-ly,** *adv.*
un·graph′i·tized′, *adj.*
un·grap′pled, *adj.*
un·grap′pling, *adj.*
un·grasp′a·ble, *adj.*
un·grasped′, *adj.*
un·grasp′ing, *adj.*
un·grassed′, *adj.*
un·grass′y, *adj.*
un·grat′ed, *adj.*
un·grat′i·fi′a·ble, *adj.*
un·grat′i·fied′, *adj.*
un·grat′i·fy′ing, *adj.*
un·grat′ing, *adj.*
un·grat′i·tude′, *n.*
un′gra·tu′i·tous, *adj.;* **-ly,** *adv.;* **-ness,** *n.*
un·graved′, *adj.*
un·grav′eled, *adj.*
un·grav′elled, *adj.*
un·grav′el·ly, *adj.*
un·grave′ly, *adv.*
un·grav′en, *adj.*
un·grav′i·tat′ing, *adj.*
un′grav·i·ta′tion·al, *adj.*
un·grav′i·ta′tive, *adj.*
un·grayed′, *adj.*
un·grazed′, *adj.*
un·greased′, *adj.*
un·greas′y, *adj.*
un·greed′y, *adj.*
un·greened′, *adj.*
un·greet′ed, *adj.*
un′gre·gar′i·ous, *adj.;* **-ly,** *adv.;* **-ness,** *n.*
un·greyed′, *adj.*
un·grieved′, *adj.*
un·griev′ing, *adj.*
un·grilled′, *adj.*
un·grimed′, *adj.*
un·grind′a·ble, *adj.*
un·grip′, *v.,* **-gripped, -grip·ping.**
un·grit′ty, *adj.*
un·griz′zled, *adj.*
un·groan′ing, *adj.*
un·groined′, *adj.*
un·groomed′, *adj.*
un·grooved′, *adj.*
un·gross′, *adj.*
un′gro·tesque′, *adj.*
un·ground′, *adj.*
un·ground′a·ble, *adj.*
un·ground′ed, *adj.*
un·group′a·ble, *adj.*
un·grouped′, *adj.*
un·grov′el·ing, *adj.*
un·grov′el·ling, *adj.*
un·grow′ing, *adj.*
un·growl′ing, *adj.*
un·grown′, *adj.*
un·grudged′, *adj.*
un·grue′some, *adj.*
un·gruff′, *adj.*
un·grum′bling, *adj.*
un·grump′y, *adj.*
un′guar·an·teed′, *adj.*
un·guard′a·ble, *adj.*
un·guer′doned, *adj.*
un·guess′a·ble, *adj.*
un·guessed′, *adj.*
un·guid′a·ble, *adj.*
un·guid′ed, *adj.;* **-ly,** *adv.*
un·guile′ful, *adj.*
un·guil′lo·tined, *adj.*
un·gummed′, *adj.*
un·gush′ing, *adj.*
un·gus′ta·to′ry, *adj.*
un·gut′ted, *adj.*
un·gut′tur·al, *adj.;* **-ly,** *adv.;* **-ness,** *n.*
un·guyed′, *adj.*
un·guz′zled, *adj.*
un′gym·nas′tic, *adj.*
un·gy′rat·ing, *adj.*
un·gyved′, *adj.*
un·hab′it·a·ble, *adj.;* **-ble·ness,** *n.;* **-bly,** *adv.*
un·hab′it·ed, *adj.*
un′ha·bit′u·al, *adj.;* **-ly,** *adv.*
un′ha·bit′u·at′ed, *adj.*
un·hacked′, *adj.*
un·hack′led, *adj.*
un·hack′neyed, *adj.*
un·haft′, *v.t.*
un·hag′gled, *adj.*
un·hag′gling, *adj.*
un·hail′a·ble, *adj.*
un·hailed′, *adj.*
un·hair′i·ness, *n.*
un·hair′y, *adj.*
un·hale′, *adj.*
un·ha′loed, *adj.*
un′hal·lu′ci·nat′ed, *adj.*
un′hal·lu′ci·nat′ing, *adj.*
un′hal·lu′ci·na·to′ry, *adj.*
un·halt′ed, *adj.*
un·hal′tered, *adj.*
un·hal′ter·ing, *adj.*
un·halt′ing, *adj.;* **-ly,** *adv.*
un·halved′, *adj.*
un·ham′mered, *adj.*
un·ham′pered, *adj.*
un·ham′per·ing, *adj.*
un·hand′cuff′, *v.t.*
un·hand′i·capped′, *adj.*
un·hand′seled, *adj.*
un·hand′selled, *adj.*
un·hanged′, *adj.*
un·hang′ing, *adj.*
un·hanked′, *adj.*
un′ha·rangued′, *adj.*
un·har′assed, *adj.*
un·har′bored, *adj.*
un·har′boured, *adj.*
un·hard′en, *v.t.*
un·hard′en·a·ble, *adj.*
un·hard′ened, *adj.*
un·harked′, *adj.*
un·harm′a·ble, *adj.*
un·harmed′, *adj.*
un·harm′ful, *adj.;* **-ly,** *adv.*
un·harm′ing, *adj.*
un′har·mon′ic, *adj.*
un′har·mon′i·cal·ly, *adv.*
un′har·mo′ni·ous, *adj.;* **-ly,** *adv.*
un·har′mo·nise′, *v.t.,* **-nised, -nis·ing.**
un·har′mo·nize′, *v.t.,* **-nized, -niz·ing.**
un·harped′, *adj.*
un·harp′ing, *adj.*
un·har′ried, *adj.*
un·har′rowed, *adj.*
un·harsh′, *adj.;* **-ly,** *adv.*
un·har′vest·ed, *adj.*
un·hashed′, *adj.*
un·hast′ed, *adj.*
un·has′tened, *adj.*
un·hast′i·ly, *adv.*
un·hast′ing, *adj.*
un·hast′y, *adj.*
un′hatch·a·bil′i·ty, *n.*
un·hatch′a·ble, *adj.*
un·hatched′, *adj.*
un·hat′ed, *adj.*

UNHCR, United Nations High Commissioner for Refugees.

un·health·y (un hel′thē), *adj.*, **-health·i·er, -health·i·est.** **1.** not in a state of good or normal health; in an unsound, weak, or morbid condition. **2.** symptomatic of or resulting from bad health: *an unhealthy pallor.* **3.** not conducive to good health; noxious; unwholesome; not salubrious: *Night air was formerly considered unhealthy.* **4.** morally bad, harmful, or contaminating; inciting to corruption or depravity: *unhealthy examples for the young.* **5.** dangerous; risky; unwise; likely to result in injury or detriment: *Asking questions in this neighborhood can be unhealthy.* [UN-[1] + HEALTHY] —**un·health′i·ly,** *adv.* —**un·health′i·ness,** *n.*
—**Syn. 1.** sickly, delicate, frail, weak, feeble, afflicted. **3.** unhealthful, unsanitary, unhygienic, deleterious.

un·heard (un hûrd′), *adj.* **1.** not heard; not perceived by the ear. **2.** not given a hearing or audience. **3.** *Archaic.* unheard-of. [ME *unherd.* See UN-[1], HEARD]

un·heard-of (un hûrd′uv′, -ov′), *adj.* **1.** that was never heard of; unknown: *an unheard-of artist.* **2.** such as was never known before; unprecedented.

un·helm (un helm′), *v.t. Archaic.* to deprive of the helm or helmet. [ME *unhelm(en).* See UN-[2], HELM[2]]

un·hes·i·tat·ing (un hez′i tā′ting), *adj.* **1.** without hesitation; not delayed by uncertainty: *an unhesitating decision.* **2.** unwavering; unfaltering; steady: *an unhesitating adherence to duty.* [UN-[1] + HESITATING] —**un·hes′i·tat′ing·ly,** *adv.*

un·hinge (un hinj′), *v.t.*, **-hinged, -hing·ing.** **1.** to remove (a door or the like) from hinges. **2.** to open wide by or as if by removing supporting hinges: *to unhinge one's jaws.* **3.** to upset; unbalance; disorient; throw into confusion or turmoil: *to unhinge the mind.* **4.** to dislocate or disrupt the normal operation of; disorder: *to unhinge plans.* **5.** to detach or separate from something. **6.** to discompose; make uncertain; cause to waver or vacillate: *to unhinge supporters of conservative policies.* **7.** to unsettle; cause to change or fluctuate: *to unhinge fixed customs.* [UN-[2] + HINGE] —**un·hinge′ment,** *n.*

un·hitch (un hich′), *v.t.* to free from attachment; unfasten: *to unhitch a locomotive from a train.* [UN-[2] + HITCH]

un·ho·ly (un hō′lē), *adj.*, **-li·er, -li·est.** **1.** not holy; not sacred or hallowed. **2.** impious; sinful; wicked. **3.** dreadful; ungodly: *They got us out of bed at the unholy hour of three in the morning.* [ME; OE *unhālig* (c. D *onheilig,* OIcel *ūheilagr*). See UN-[1], HOLY] —**un·ho′li·ly,** *adv.* —**un·ho′li·ness,** *n.*

un·hood (un ho͝od′), *v.t.* **1.** to divest of a hood or covering. **2.** to remove from (a hawk) the hood used to blind it. [UN-[2] + HOOD]

un·hook (un ho͝ok′), *v.t.* **1.** to detach by or as if by releasing a hook: *to unhook a tractor from a trailer.* **2.** to unfasten or open by undoing a hook or hooks: *to unhook a door; to unhook a corset.* —*v.i.* **3.** to become unhooked. [UN-[2] + HOOK]

un·hoped-for (un hōpt′fôr′), *adj.* unexpected; unanticipated: *an unhoped-for piece of good luck.* [UN-[1] + *hoped-for* (HOPE + -ED[2])]

un·horse (un hôrs′), *v.t.*, **-horsed, -hors·ing.** **1.** to dislodge from the saddle; cause to fall from a horse, as in battle: *Sir Gawain unhorsed the strange knight.* **2.** to throw off or cause to fall, as by bucking; unseat. **3.** to defeat; overcome; dislodge, as from a position or office: *His vigorous campaign unhorsed his adversary.* **4.** *Archaic.* to deprive of a horse or horses; take a horse or horses from. [ME *unhorse(n).* See UN-[2], HORSE]

un·house (un houz′), *v.t.*, **-housed, -hous·ing.** to drive from a house or habitation; deprive of shelter. [ME *unhouse(n).* See UN-[2], HOUSE]

un·hou·seled (un hou′zəld), *adj. Archaic.* not having received the Eucharist. [UN-[1] + HOUSEL + -ED[2]]

un·hur·ried (un hûr′ēd, -hur′-), *adj.* not hurried; leisurely; deliberate: *an unhurried day; an unhurried decision.* [UN-[1] + HURRIED] —**un·hur·ried·ly** (un hûr′id lē, -ēd-, -hur′-), *adv.* —**un·hur′ried·ness,** *n.*

un·husk (un husk′), *v.t.* to free from or as if from a husk. [UN-[2] + HUSK]

uni-, a formal element occurring in loan words from Latin (*universe*): used, with the meaning "one," in the formation of compound words (*unicycle*). [< L *ūni-* comb. form of *ūnus* one + *-i-* -I-]

U·nião da Vi·tó·ria (o͞o nyouN′ dä vē tô′ryə), a city in S Brazil. 16,887 (1960).

U·ni·at (yo͞o′nē at′), *n.* a member of an Eastern church that is in union with the Roman Catholic Church, acknowledges the Roman pope as supreme in matters of faith, but maintains its own liturgy, discipline, and rite. Also, **U·ni·ate** (yo͞o′nē it, -āt′). [< Russ] —**u′ni·at·ism,** *n.*

u·ni·ax·i·al (yo͞o′nē ak′sē əl), *adj.* **1.** having one axis. **2.** *Crystall.* (of a crystal) having one direction in which no double refraction occurs. **3.** *Bot.* (of a plant) having a primary stem that does not branch and that terminates in a flower. [UNI- + AXIAL] —**u′ni·ax′i·al·ly,** *adv.*

u·ni·cam·er·al (yo͞o′nə kam′ər əl), *adj.* consisting of a single chamber, as a legislative assembly. [UNI- + CAMERAL[1]] —**u′ni·cam′er·al·ism,** *n.* —**u′ni·cam′er·al·ly,** *adv.*

UNICEF (yo͞o′ni sef′), *n.* an agency, created by the United Nations General Assembly in 1946, concerned with improving the health and nutrition of children and mothers throughout the world. [*U(nited) N(ations) I(nternational) C(hildren's) E(mergency) F(und)*]

u·ni·cel·lu·lar (yo͞o′ni sel′yə lər), *adj.* having or consisting of a single cell or individual structural unit. [UNI- + CELLULAR] —**u′ni·cel′lu·lar′i·ty,** *n.*

u′nicel′lular an′imal, a protozoan.

u·ni·col·or (yo͞o′nə kul′ər, yo͞o′nə kul′-), *adj.* having only one color. Also, **u′ni·col′ored;** *esp. Brit.,* **u′ni·col′our, u′ni·col′oured.** [UNI- + COLOR]

u·ni·corn (yo͞o′nə kôrn′), *n.* **1.** a mythical creature resembling a horse and having a single horn in the center of its forehead: often symbolic of chastity or purity, capable of being tamed by a virgin, and usually successful in evading capture. **2.** a heraldic representation of this animal, in the form of a horse with a lion's tail and with a long, straight, and spirally twisted horn. **3.** (*cap.*) *Astron.* the constellation Monoceros. **4.** Also, *Douay Bible,* **rhinoceros.** an animal mentioned in the Bible. Deut. 33:17. **5.** a former gold coin of Scotland, first issued by James III in 1486, having an obverse bearing the figure of a unicorn. [ME *unicorne* < LL *unicorn(is)* one-horned < L *uni-* UNI- + *cornu* HORN]

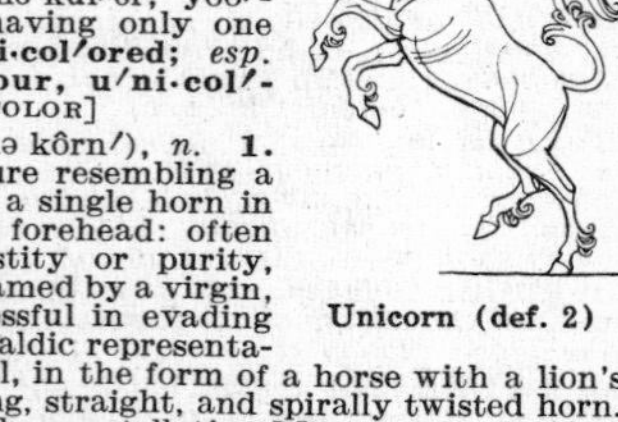
Unicorn (def. 2)

u′nicorn plant′, a North American herb, *Proboscidea (Martynia) louisianica,* bearing a woody capsule with a long, curved beak.

u·ni·cos·tate (yo͞o′nə kos′tāt, -kô′stāt), *adj.* **1.** having only one costa, rib, or ridge. **2.** *Bot.* (of a leaf) having only one primary or prominent rib, the midrib. [UNI- + COSTATE]

u·ni·cur·sal (yo͞o′nə kûr′səl), *adj. Math.* **1.** of or pertaining to a plane curve whose parametric equations, in terms of one parameter, are rational functions. **2.** (of a network of lines) capable of being traversed so that each line is traversed exactly once. [UNI- + L *curs(us)* COURSE + -AL[1]]

u·ni·cus·pid (yo͞o′nə kus′pid), *adj.* having but one cusp. [UNI- + CUSPID]

u·ni·cy·cle (yo͞o′ni sī′kəl), *n.* a vehicle designed to operate on one wheel, esp. a pedal-driven device kept upright and steered by body balance, commonly used by acrobats and other performers. [UNI- + CYCLE] —**u′ni·cy′clist,** *n.*

un·i·de·aed (un′ī dē′id), *adj.* characterized by a lack of ideation. [UN-[1] + IDEA + -ED[3]]

u·ni·di·rec·tion·al (yo͞o′ni di rek′shə nəl, -dī-), *adj.* operating or moving in one direction only; not changing direction: *a unidirectional flow.* [UNI- + DIRECTIONAL]

u·ni·face (yo͞o′nə fās′), *n. Numis.* a coin or medal having a blank reverse. [UNI- + FACE]

u·ni·fi·a·ble (yo͞o′nə fī′ə bəl), *adj.* capable of being unified. [UNIFY + -ABLE]

u·nif·ic (yo͞o nif′ik), *adj.* unifying; uniting: *the unific influence of a common language.* [UNI- + -FIC]

u·ni·fi·ca·tion (yo͞o′nə fə kā′shən), *n.* **1.** the process of unifying or uniting; union: *The unification of the 13 original colonies led to the drafting of the Constitution.* **2.** state or condition of being unified: *The unification of the manufacturing and distribution functions under one executive has advantages.* [UNI- + -FICATION, modeled on *purify, purification*]

u·ni·fi·lar (yo͞o′nə fī′lər), *adj.* having or involving only one thread, wire, or the like. [UNI- + FILAR]

u·ni·flag·el·late (yo͞o′nə flaj′ə lāt′), *adj.* having only one flagellum. [UNI- + FLAGELLATE]

u·ni·flor·ous (yo͞o′ni flōr′əs, -flôr′-), *adj. Bot.* having only one flower. [UNI- + -FLOROUS]

u′niflow en′gine (yo͞o′nə flō′), a double-acting steam engine exhausting from the middle of each cylinder at each stroke so that the motion of the steam from admission to exhaust is continuous in one direction. [UNI- + FLOW + ENGINE]

u·ni·fo·li·ate (yo͞o′nə fō′lē it, -āt′), *adj.* **1.** having only one leaf. **2.** unifoliolate. [UNI- + FOLIATE]

u·ni·fo·li·o·late (yo͞o′nə fō′lē ə lāt′), *adj. Bot.* **1.** compound in structure yet having only one leaflet, as the orange. **2.** bearing such leaves. [UNI- + FOLIOLATE]

Unifoliolate leaf

u·ni·form (yo͞o′nə fôrm′), *adj.* **1.** having a single form or pattern; consistently following a definite formula or set of rules; unchanging; consistent over the full range of occurrence: *uniform spelling.* **2.** unvarying in significant aspects; having no unpredictable discontinuities or irregularities; without diversity in characteristics or qualities, as in amount, degree, appearance, etc.: *uniform output; a uniform product; a uniform surface.* **3.** characterized by distinctive or distinguishing features or appearance; recognizable as a particular style, type, or design indicating membership in a distinct group: *the uniform markings of the species.* **4.** regular; even; undeviating; constant; invariant: *a uniform velocity; uniform intervals.* **5.** not diverse; without dissimilarities in application, operation, etc., consistent or identical everywhere: *uniform customs.* **6.** unchanging; the same from beginning to end, or alike from one instance to another; unvarying: *uniform kindness.* **7.** *Math.* occurring in a manner independent of some variable, parameter, function, etc.: *a uniform bound.* —*n.* **8.** a distinctive style or fashion of dress; a uniform design or characteristic pattern of clothing which identifies members of a group or organization. **9.** a single suit or outfit of a uniform style. **10.** a word used in com-

un·hate′ful, *adj.*
un·hat′ing, *adj.;* **-ly,** *adv.*
un·hauled′, *adj.*
un·haunt′ed, *adj.*
un·hawked′, *adj.*
un·hayed′, *adj.*
un·haz′ard·ed, *adj.*
un·haz′ard·ing, *adj.*
un·haz′ard·ous, *adj.;* **-ly,** *adv.*
un·hazed′, *adj.*
un·ha′zi·ly, *adv.*
un·ha′zi·ness, *n.*
un·ha′zy, *adj.*
un·head′ed, *adj.*
un·head′y, *adj.*
un·heal′a·ble, *adj.*
un·healed′, *adj.*
un·heal′ing, *adj.*
un·heaped′, *adj.*
un·hear′a·ble, *adj.*
un·hear′ing, *adj.*
un·heart′i·ly, *adv.*
un·heart′y, *adj.*
un·heat′a·ble, *adj.*
un·heat′ed, *adj.*
un·hea′then, *adj.*
un·heaved′, *adj.*
un·heav′en·ly, *adj.*
un·heav′i·ly, *adv.*
un·heav′i·ness, *n.*
un·heav′y, *adj.*
un·hec′tic, *adj.*
un·hec′ti·cal·ly, *adv.*
un·hec′tored, *adj.*
un·hedge′, *v.t.,* **-hedged, -hedg·ing.**
un′he·do·nis′tic, *adj.*
un·he·do·nis′ti·cal·ly, *adv.*
un·heed′ed, *adj.;* **-ly,** *adv.*
un·heed′ful, *adj.;* **-ly,** *adv.;* **-ness,** *n.*
un·heed′ing, *adj.;* **-ly,** *adv.*
un·heeled′, *adj.*
un·heft′ed, *adj.*
un·height′ened, *adj.*
un·held′, *adj.*
un·hel′met·ed, *adj.*
un·help′a·ble, *adj.*
un·helped′, *adj.*
un·help′ful, *adj.;* **-ly,** *adv.*
un·help′ing, *adj.*
un·helved′, *adj.*
un·hemmed′, *adj.*
un′her′ald·ed, *adj.*
un′he·ral′dic, *adj.*
un′her·ba′ceous, *adj.*
un·herd′ed, *adj.*
un′her′it·a·ble, *adj.*
un′her·met′ic, *adj.*
un′her·mit′ic, *adj.*
un′her·mit′i·cal, *adj.;* **-ly,** *adv.*
un′he·ro′ic, *adj.;* **-ness,** *n.*
un′he·ro′i·cal, *adj.;* **-ly,** *adv.;* **-ness,** *n.*
un·he′ro·like′, *adj.*
un·hes′i·tant, *adj.;* **-ly,** *adv.*
un·hes′i·ta′tive, *adj.;* **-ly,** *adv.*
un′heu·ris′tic, *adj.*
un′heu·ris′ti·cal·ly, *adv.*
un·hew′a·ble, *adj.*
un·hewed′, *adj.*
un·hewn′, *adj.*
un·hid′, *adj.*
un·hid′den, *adj.*
un·hid′e·ous, *adj.;* **-ly,** *adv.;* **-ness,** *n.*
un′hi·er·at′ic, *adj.*
un′hi·er·at′i·cal, *adj.;* **-ly,** *adv.*
un′hi·lar′i·ous, *adj.;* **-ly,** *adv.;* **-ness,** *n.*
un·hill′y, *adj.*
un·hin′der·a·ble, *adj.;* **-bly,** *adv.*
un·hin′dered, *adj.*
un·hin′der·ing, *adj.;* **-ly,** *adv.*
un·hint′ed, *adj.*
un·hipped′, *adj.*
un·hired′, *adj.*
un·hissed′, *adj.*
un′his·tor′ic, *adj.*
un′his·tor′i·cal, *adj.;* **-ly,** *adv.*
un·his′to·ried, *adj.*
un·his′to·ry, *n.*
un′his·tri·on′ic, *adj.*
un·hit′, *adj.*
un·hit′ta·ble, *adj.*
un·hoard′ed, *adj.*
un·hoard′ing, *adj.*
un·hoar′y, *adj.*
un·hoaxed′, *adj.*
un·hob′bling, *adj.*
un·hocked′, *adj.*
un·hoed′, *adj.*
un·hogged′, *adj.*
un·hoist′ed, *adj.*
un·hol′low, *adj.*
un·hol′lowed, *adj.*
un·home′li·ness, *n.*
un·home′ly, *adj.*
un′hom·i·cid′al, *adj.*
un′hom·i·let′ic, *adj.*
un′hom·i·let′i·cal, *adj.;* **-ly,** *adv.*
un′ho·mo·ge′ne·ous, *adj.;* **-ly,** *adv.;* **-ness,** *n.*
un′ho·mog′e·nized′, *adj.*
un′ho·mo·log′ic, *adj.*
un′ho·mo·log′i·cal, *adj.;* **-ly,** *adv.*
un′ho·mol′o·gized′, *adj.*
un′ho·mol′o·gous, *adj.*
un·honed′, *adj.*
un·hon′eyed, *adj.*
un·hon′ied, *adj.*
un·hon′ored, *adj.*
un·hon′oured, *adj.*
un·hood′winked′, *adj.*
un·hoofed′, *adj.*
un·hooped′, *adj.*
un·hoot′ed, *adj.*
un·hope′ful, *adj.;* **-ly,** *adv.*
un·hop′ing, *adj.;* **-ly,** *adv.*
un·hop′pled, *adj.*
un′ho·ri′zoned, *adj.*
un′hor·i·zon′tal, *adj.;* **-ly,** *adv.*
un·horned′, *adj.*
un′hor·o·scop′ic, *adj.*
un·hor′ri·fied, *adj.*
un·hor′ta·tive, *adj.;* **-ly,** *adv.*
un·hosed′, *adj.*
un·hos′pi·tal·ized′, *adj.*
un·hos′tile, *adj.;* **-ly,** *adv.*
un′hos·til′i·ty, *n.*
un·hot′, *adj.*
un·hound′ed, *adj.*
un·house′wife′ly, *adj.*
un·hu′bris′tic, *adj.*
un·hud′dle, *v.t.,* **-dled, -dling.**
un·hued′, *adj.*
un·hugged′, *adj.*
un·hull′, *v.t.*
un·hu′man, *adj.;* **-ly,** *adv.;* **-ness,** *n.*
un′hu·mane′, *adj.;* **-ly,** *adv.;* **-ness,** *n.*
un·hu′man·ise′, *v.t.,* **-ised, -is·ing.**
un′hu·man·is′tic, *adj.*
un′hu·man′i·tar′i·an, *adj.*
un·hu′man·ize′, *v.t.,* **-ized, -iz·ing.**
un·hum′ble, *adj.;* **-ble·ness,** *n.;* **-bly,** *adv.*
un·hum′bled, *adj.*
un·hu′mid, *adj.*
un′hu·mid′i·fied′, *adj.*
un′hu·mid′i·fy′ing, *adj.*
un′hu·mil′i·at′ed, *adj.*
un′hu·mil′i·at′ing, *adj.;* **-ly,** *adv.*
un·hu′mored, *adj.*
un·hu′mor·ous, *adj.;* **-ly,** *adv.*
un·hu′moured, *adj.*
un·hu′mour·ous, *adj.;* **-ly,** *adv.*
un·hung′, *adj.*
un·hunt′a·ble, *adj.*
un·hunt′ed, *adj.*
un·hur′dled, *adj.*
un·hurled′, *adj.*
un·hur′ry·ing, *adj.;* **-ly,** *adv.*
un·hurt′, *adj.*
un·hurt′ful, *adj.;* **-ly,** *adv.*
un·hurt′ing, *adj.*
un·hus′band·ed, *adj.*
un·hush′a·ble, *adj.*
un·hush′ing, *adj.*
un·husk′a·ble, *adj.*
un·husked′, *adj.*
un·hus′tled, *adj.*
un·hus′tling, *adj.*
un·hutched′, *adj.*
un′huz·zaed′, *adj.*
un·hy′drat·ed, *adj.*
un′hy·drau′lic, *adj.*
un′hy′dro·lized′, *adj.*
un′hy·gi·en′ic, *adj.*
un′hy·gi·en′i·cal·ly, *adv.*
un′hy·gro·met′ric, *adj.*
un′hy·me·ne′al, *adj.*
un·hymned′, *adj.*
un·hy′phen·a·ble, *adj.*
un·hy′phen·at′ed, *adj.*
un·hy′phened, *adj.*
un′hyp·not′ic, *adj.*
un′hyp·not′i·cal·ly, *adv.*
un·hyp′no·tis′a·ble, *adj.*
un·hyp′no·tise′, *v.t.,* **-tised, -tis·ing.**
un·hyp′no·tiz′a·ble, *adj.*
un·hyp′no·tize′, *v.t.,* **-tized, -tiz·ing.**
un′hyp·o·crit′i·cal, *adj.;* **-ly,** *adv.*
un′hy·poth′e·cat′ed, *adj.*
un′hy·po·thet′i·cal, *adj.;* **-ly,** *adv.*
un′hys·ter′i·cal, *adj.;* **-ly,** *adv.*
un′i·am′bic, *adj.*
un·ice′, *v.t.,* **-iced, -ic·ing.**
un′i·con′o·clas′tic, *adj.*
un′i·con′o·clas′ti·cal·ly, *adv.*
un′i·de′al, *adj.*
un′i·de′al·is′tic, *adj.*
un′i·de′al·is′ti·cal·ly, *adv.*
un′i·de′al·ised′, *adj.*
un′i·de′al·ized′, *adj.*
un·i′de·at′ed, *adj.*
un·i′de·at′ing, *adj.*
un′i·de·a′tion·al, *adj.*
un′i·den′ti·cal, *adj.;* **-ly,** *adv.*
un′i·den′ti·fi′a·ble, *adj.;* **-bly,** *adv.*
un′i·den′ti·fied′, *adj.*
un′i·den′ti·fy′ing, *adj.*
un′id·e·o·graph′ic, *adj.*
un′id·e·o·graph′i·cal, *adj.;* **-ly,** *adv.*
un′id·i·o·mat′ic, *adj.*
un′id·i·o·mat′i·cal·ly, *adv.*
un·i′dle, *adj.*
un·i′dling, *adj.*
un·i′dly, *adv.*
un·i·dol′a·trous, *adj.*
un·i′dol·ised′, *adj.*
un·i′dol·ized′, *adj.*
un·i·dyl′lic, *adj.*

munications to represent the letter U. —*v.t.* **11.** to make uniform, standard, or similar in character, treatment, etc.; give uniformity to. **12.** to clothe in or furnish with a uniform. [< L *uniform(is)*, equiv. to *uni-* UNI- + *-formis* -FORM] —**u′ni·form′less,** *adj.* —**u′ni·form′ly,** *adv.* —**u′ni·form′ness,** *n.*
—**Syn. 1.** invariable, constant, regular. **2.** undiversified, unvariegated, dun, plain. **4.** See **even.** —**Ant. 1.** irregular.

u·ni·for·mal·ize (yo͞o′nə fôr′mə līz′), *v.t.*, **-ized, -iz·ing.** *Rare.* to bring into uniformity. [UNIFORM + -AL[1] + -IZE] —**u′ni·for′mal·i·za′tion,** *n.*

U′niform Code′ of Mil′itary Jus′tice, the body of laws and legal procedures of the armed forces: replaced the Articles of War in 1951.

u′niform conver′gence, *Math.* the property of an indefinite sequence of functions in which the functional values of all terms of the sequence are eventually arbitrarily close to each other for any point in the domain under consideration.

u·ni·formed (yo͞o′nə fôrmd′), *adj.* wearing a uniform. [UNIFORM + -ED[3]]

u·ni·form·ise (yo͞o′nə fôr mīz′), *v.t.*, **-ised, -is·ing.** *Chiefly Brit.* uniformize. —**u′ni·form′i·sa′tion,** *n.*

u·ni·form·i·tar·i·an (yo͞o′nə fôr′mi târ′ē ən), *adj.* **1.** supporting, adhering to, conforming to, or derived from a theory or doctrine about uniformity, esp. on the subject of geology. **2.** *Geol.* of or pertaining to the thesis that early geological processes are not different from those observed now. —*n.* **3.** one who accepts or supports a uniformitarian theory. [UNIFORMIT(Y) + -ARIAN] —**u′ni·form′i·tar′i·an·ism,** *n.*

u·ni·form·i·ty (yo͞o′nə fôr′mi tē), *n., pl.* **-ties. 1.** the state or quality of being uniform; overall sameness or homogeneity; absence of diversity or variation: *uniformity of style.* **2.** conformity or agreement in structure, pattern, composition, etc.: *a uniformity of elements.* **3.** unvarying regularity or similarity; monotony: *the wearisome uniformity of TV commercials.* **4.** something uniform; an extent or expanse of a uniform character. [ME *uniformite* < MF *uniformite* < LL *ūniformitāt-* (s. of *ūniformitās*), equiv. to L *ūniform(is)* UNIFORM + *-itāt-* -ITY]

Uniform′ity Act′, *Eng. Hist.* See **Act of Uniformity.**

u·ni·form·ize (yo͞o′nə fôr mīz′), *v.t.*, **-ized, -iz·ing.** to bring into uniformity. Also, *esp. Brit.*, **uniformise.** [< F *uniformis(er).* See UNIFORM, -IZE] —**u′ni·form′i·za′tion,** *n.*

u′niformly contin′uous func′tion, a function on a set having the property that for any small number, a second number can be found such that when the distance between two points in the set is less than the second number, the difference in the function values at the two points is less than the first number. Cf. **continuous** (def. 3).

u·ni·fy (yo͞o′nə fī′), *v.t.*, **-fied, -fy·ing.** to form into a single unit; unite; reduce to unity by removing or reconciling differences, incompatible elements, or the like: *to unify conflicting theories; to unify a country.* [< LL *ūnificāre* < L *ūni-* UNI- + *-ficāre* -FY] —**u′ni·fi′er,** *n.*

Unijugate leaf

u·nij·u·gate (yo͞o nij′ə gāt′, yo͞o′ni jo͞o′git, -gāt), *adj. Bot.* (of a pinnate leaf) having only a single pair of leaflets. [< L *ūnijug(us)* having one yoke, equiv. to *ūni-* UNI- + *jug(um)* YOKE + -ATE[1]]

u·ni·lat·er·al (yo͞o′nə lat′ər əl), *adj.* **1.** relating to, occurring on, or involving one side only: *unilateral development.* **2.** concerned with, considering, or taking into account one side only, as of a question or subject: *a unilateral approach.* **3.** directed to, preponderating on, or tending toward one side: *unilateral distribution.* **4.** affecting, involving, or obligating only one side or party; not reciprocal: *unilateral commitment.* **5.** undertaken or done by or on behalf of one side, party, or faction only; not mutual: *a unilateral decision; unilateral benefit.* **6.** having only one side or surface; without a reverse side or inside, as a Möbius strip. **7.** *Law.* noting or pertaining to a contract under which one party makes a promise in exchange for a certain action on the part of another. **8.** *Bot.* having all the parts disposed on one side of an axis, as an inflorescence. **9.** through forebears of one sex only, as through either the mother's or father's line. Cf. **bilateral** (def. 5). **10.** *Phonet.* (of an *l*-sound) characterized by passage of air on only one side of the tongue. [< NL *ūnilaterāl(is).* See UNI-, LATERAL] —**u′ni·lat′er·al·ism, u′ni·lat′er·al′i·ty,** *n.* —**u′ni·lat′er·al·ly,** *adv.*

u·ni·lin·gual (yo͞o′nə liŋ′gwəl), *adj.* limited to a single language: *a unilingual person; a unilingual book; a unilingual bibliography.* [UNI- + LINGUAL]

u·ni·lobed (yo͞o′nə lōbd′), *adj.* having or consisting of a single lobe, esp. of the maxilla of an insect. [UNI- + LOBED]

u·ni·loc·u·lar (yo͞o′nə lok′yə lər), *adj. Bot., Zool.* having or consisting of only one loculus, chamber, or cell. [UNI- + LOCULAR]

u·ni·mod·u·lar (yo͞o′nə moj′ə lər, mod′yə-), *adj. Math.* (of a matrix) having its determinant equal to 1. [UNI- + MODULAR]

un·im·pas·sioned (un′im pash′ənd), *adj.* not impassioned; dispassionate; unemotional: *an unimpassioned point of view; an unimpassioned interpretation of a symphony.* [UN-[1] + IMPASSIONED] —**un′im·pas′sioned·ly,** *adv.*

un·im·peach·a·ble (un′im pē′chə bəl), *adj.* above suspicion; impossible to discredit; impeccable: *unimpeachable motives; unimpeachable authority; an unimpeachable witness.* [UN-[1] + IMPEACHABLE] —**un′im·peach′a·bil′i·ty, un′im·peach′a·ble·ness,** *n.* —**un′im·peach′a·bly,** *adv.*

un·im·pos·ing (un′im pō′ziŋ), *adj.* not imposing; unimpressive; not calculated to create a strong or favorable impression: *an unimposing spectacle; a man of unimposing stature.* [UN-[1] + IMPOSING]

un·im·proved (un′im pro͞ovd′), *adj.* **1.** not used to advantage; not turned to account; neglected: *an unimproved opportunity.* **2.** not developed to full potential, as of quality, usefulness, value, or the like: *unimproved resources; unimproved methods.* **3.** (of land) not fitted for a profitable use, as by clearing, cultivation, addition of facilities for dwelling or business purposes, or the like. **4.** (of a road) not made better for travel. **5.** (of the mind) not refined or educated, as by study, training, etc. **6.** (of animal or plant species) not made more useful or attractive by selective breeding or cultivation. **7.** not bettered in condition by the removal of some threat or unfavorable factor: *His health is unimproved.* **8.** not enhanced; not increased: *Our chance of success is unimproved.* [UN-[1] + IMPROVED]

un·in·cor·po·rat·ed (un′in kôr′pə rā′tid), *adj.* **1.** not chartered as a corporation; lacking the powers and immunities of a corporate enterprise: *an unincorporated business.* **2.** not chartered as a self-governing village or city; lacking the tax, police, and other powers conferred by the state on incorporated towns: *an unincorporated hamlet.* **3.** not combined into a single body or unit; not made part of; not included: *Many unincorporated research notes are appended to the text of the book.* [UN-[1] + INCORPORATED]

un·in·hib·it·ed (un′in hib′i tid), *adj.* **1.** not inhibited; not subjected to inhibition: *uninhibited freedom to act.* **2.** unconstrained; startling; shocking; not restrained or restricted, as by social convention, usage, or the like: *an uninhibited discussion of the causes of divorce; an uninhibited sunbather.* [UN-[1] + INHIBIT + -ED[2]] —**un′in·hib′it·ed·ly,** *adv.*

un·in·spired (un′in spīərd′), *adj.* not inspired; not creative or spirited; unimaginative; lifeless; dull; unremarkable: *an uninspired performance; an uninspired teacher.* [UN-[1] + INSPIRED]

un·in·struct·ed (un′in struk′tid), *adj.* **1.** not instructed; uninformed; uneducated. **2.** (of a person acting in a representative capacity) not furnished with orders on how to proceed or vote; uncommitted: *uninstructed convention delegates.* [UN-[1] + INSTRUCTED] —**un′in·struct′ed·ly,** *adv.*

un·in·tel·li·gent (un′in tel′i jənt), *adj.* **1.** deficient in intelligence; dull; stupid. **2.** not endowed with intelligence: *Viruses appear to be unintelligent life forms.* [UN-[1] + INTELLIGENT] —**un′in·tel′li·gence,** *n.* —**un′in·tel′li·gent·ly,** *adv.*

un·in·tel·li·gi·ble (un′in tel′i jə bəl), *adj.* not intelligible; not capable of being understood. [UN-[1] + INTELLIGIBLE] —**un′in·tel′li·gi·bil′i·ty, un′in·tel′li·gi·ble·ness,** *n.* —**un′in·tel′li·gi·bly,** *adv.*

un·in·ter·est·ed (un in′tər i stid, -tris tid, -tə res′tid), *adj.* **1.** having or showing no feeling of interest;

un′ig·nit′a·ble, *adj.*
un′ig·nit′ed, *adj.*
un′ig·nit′ing, *adj.*
un′ig·no·min′i·ous, *adj.*; **-ly,** *adv.*; **-ness,** *n.*
un·ig′no·rant, *adj.*; **-ly,** *adv.*
un′ig·nored′, *adj.*
un′ig·nor′ing, *adj.*
un′il·lud′ed, *adj.*; **-ly,** *adv.*
un′il·lumed′, *adj.*
un′il·lu′mi·nant, *adj.*
un′il·lu′mi·nat′ed, *adj.*
un′il·lu′mi·nat′ing, *adj.*
un′il·lu′mi·na′tive, *adj.*
un′il·lu′sioned, *adj.*
un′il·lu′sive, *adj.*
un′il·lu′so·ry, *adj.*
un·il′lus·trat′ed, *adj.*
un′il·lus′tra·tive, *adj.*
un′il·lus′tri·ous, *adj.*; **-ly,** *adv.*; **-ness,** *n.*
un·im′aged, *adj.*
un′im·ag′i·na·ble, *adj.*; **-ble·ness,** *n.*; **-bly,** *adv.*
un′im·ag′i·nar′y, *adj.*
un′im·ag′i·na′tive, *adj.*; **-ly,** *adv.*
un′im·ag′ined, *adj.*
un′im·bibed′, *adj.*
un′im·bib′ing, *adj.*
un′im·bued′, *adj.*
un·im′i·ta·ble, *adj.*
un·im′i·tat′ed, *adj.*
un·im′i·tat′ing, *adj.*
un·im′i·ta′tive, *adj.*
un′im·mac′u·late, *adj.*; **-ly,** *adv.*; **-ness,** *n.*
un·im′ma·nent, *adj.*; **-ly,** *adv.*
un′im·me′di·ate, *adj.*; **-ly,** *adv.*; **-ness,** *n.*
un′im·merged′, *adj.*
un′im·mersed′, *adj.*
un·im′mi·grat′ing, *adj.*
un·im′mi·nent, *adj.*
un·im′mo·lat′ed, *adj.*
un·im′mu·nised′, *adj.*
un·im′mu·nized′, *adj.*
un′im·mured′, *adj.*
un′im·pact′ed, *adj.*
un′im·pair′a·ble, *adj.*
un′im·paired′, *adj.*
un′im·part′ed, *adj.*
un′im·par′tial, *adj.*; **-ly,** *adv.*
un′im·part′i·ble, *adj.*
un′im·pas′sion·ate, *adj.*; **-ly,** *adv.*
un·im′pa′tient, *adj.*; **-ly,** *adv.*
un′im·pawned′, *adj.*
un′im·peached′, *adj.*
un′im·pearled′, *adj.*
un′im·ped′ed, *adj.*
un′im·ped′ing, *adj.*; **-ly,** *adv.*
un′im·pelled′, *adj.*
un′im·per′a·tive, *adj.*; **-ly,** *adv.*
un′im·pe′ri·al, *adj.*; **-ly,** *adv.*
un′im·pe′ri·al·is′tic, *adj.*
un′im·pe′ri·ous, *adj.*; **-ly,** *adv.*
un·im·per′ti·nent, *adj.*; **-ly,** *adv.*
un·im′ping·ing, *adj.*
un′im·plant′ed, *adj.*
un·im′pli·cat′ed, *adj.*
un′im·plic′it·ly, *adv.*
un′im·plied′, *adj.*
un′im·plor′a·ble, *adj.*
un′im·plored′, *adj.*
un′im·por′tant, *adj.*; **-ly,** *adv.*
un′im·port′ed, *adj.*
un′im·port′ing, *adj.*
un′im·por′tu·nate, *adj.*; **-ly,** *adv.*; **-ness,** *n.*
un·im′por·tuned′, *adj.*
un′im·posed′, *adj.*
un′im·pound′ed, *adj.*
un′im·pov′er·ished, *adj.*
un·im′pre·cat′ed, *adj.*
un·im′preg′nat·ed, *adj.*
un′im·pressed′, *adj.*
un′im·press′i·ble, *adj.*
un′im·press′i·bil′i·ty, *n.*
un′im·pres′sion·a·ble, *adj.*
un′im·pres′sive, *adj.*; **-ly,** *adv.*
un′im·print′ed, *adj.*
un′im·pris′on·a·ble, *adj.*
un′im·pris′oned, *adj.*
un′im·pro′pri·at′ed, *adj.*
un·im′pro·vised′, *adj.*
un′im·pugn′a·ble, *adj.*
un′im·pugned′, *adj.*
un′im·pul′sive, *adj.*; **-ly,** *adv.*
un′im·put′a·ble, *adj.*
un′im·put′ed, *adj.*
un′in·au′gu·rat′ed, *adj.*
un′in·car′cer·at′ed, *adj.*
un′in·car′nate, *adj.*
un′in·car′nat·ed, *adj.*
un′in·censed′, *adj.*
un′in·cep′tive, *adj.*; **-ly,** *adv.*
un′in·ces′tu·ous, *adj.*; **-ly,** *adv.*
un′in·cho′a·tive, *adj.*
un′in·ci·den′tal, *adj.*; **-ly,** *adv.*
un′in·cin′er·at′ed, *adj.*
un′in·cised′, *adj.*
un′in·ci′sive, *adj.*; **-ly,** *adv.*; **-ness,** *n.*
un′in·cit′ed, *adj.*
un′in·clin′a·ble, *adj.*
un′in·clined′, *adj.*
un′in·clin′ing, *adj.*
un′in·closed′, *adj.*
un′in·clud′a·ble, *adj.*
un′in·clud′ed, *adj.*
un′in·clud′i·ble, *adj.*
un′in·clu′sive, *adj.*
un′in·con·ven′ienced, *adj.*
un′in·creas′a·ble, *adj.*
un′in·creased′, *adj.*
un′in·creas′ing, *adj.*
un′in·crim′i·nat′ed, *adj.*
un′in·crim′i·nat′ing, *adj.*
un·in′cu·bat′ed, *adj.*
un′in·cum′bered, *adj.*
un′in·dem′ni·fied′, *adj.*
un′in·den′tured, *adj.*
un·in′dexed, *adj.*
un·in′di·cat′ed, *adj.*
un′in·dic′a·tive, *adj.*; **-ly,** *adv.*
un′in·dict′a·ble, *adj.*
un′in·dict′ed, *adj.*
un′in·dig′e·nous, *adj.*; **-ly,** *adv.*
un′in·dig′nant, *adj.*
un′in·di·vid′u·al·ized′, *adj.*
un′in·di·vid′u·at′ed, *adj.*
un′in·doc′tri·nat′ed, *adj.*
un′in·dorsed′, *adj.*
un′in·duced′, *adj.*
un′in·duc′i·ble, *adj.*
un′in·duct′ed, *adj.*
un′in·duc′tive, *adj.*
un′in·dulged′, *adj.*
un′in·dul′gent, *adj.*; **-ly,** *adv.*
un′in·dulg′ing, *adj.*
un·in′du·rate, *adj.*
un·in′du·ra′tive, *adj.*
un′in·dus′tri·al, *adj.*
un′in·dus′tri·al·ized′, *adj.*
un′in·dus′tri·ous, *adj.*; **-ly,** *adv.*
un′in·e′bri·at′ed, *adj.*
un′in·e′bri·at′ing, *adj.*
un′in·ert′, *adj.*; **-ly,** *adv.*
un′in·fat′u·at′ed, *adj.*
un′in·fect′a·ble, *adj.*
un′in·fect′ed, *adj.*
un′in·fec′tious, *adj.*; **-ly,** *adv.*; **-ness,** *n.*
un′in·fec′tive, *adj.*
un′in·fer′a·ble, *adj.*; **-bly,** *adv.*
un′in·fer·en′tial, *adj.*; **-ly,** *adv.*
un′in·fer′ra·ble, *adj.*; **-bly,** *adv.*
un′in·ferred′, *adj.*
un′in·fer′ri·ble, *adj.*; **-bly,** *adv.*
un′in·fest′ed, *adj.*
un′in·fil′trat·ed, *adj.*
un·in′fi·nite, *adj.*; **-ly,** *adv.*; **-ness,** *n.*
un′in·fixed′, *adj.*
un′in·flamed′, *adj.*
un′in·flam′ma·bil′i·ty, *n.*
un′in·flam′ma·ble, *adj.*
un′in·flat′ed, *adj.*
un′in·flect′ed, *adj.*
un′in·flec′tive, *adj.*
un′in·flict′ed, *adj.*
un·in′flu·enced, *adj.*
un·in′flu·enc·ing, *adj.*
un′in·flu·en′tial, *adj.*; **-ly,** *adv.*
un′in·fold′ed, *adj.*
un′in·form′a·tive, *adj.*
un′in·formed′, *adj.*
un′in·form′ing, *adj.*
un′in·fract′ed, *adj.*
un′in·fringed′, *adj.*
un′in·fu′ri·at′ed, *adj.*
un′in·fused′, *adj.*
un′in·fus′ing, *adj.*
un′in·fu′sive, *adj.*
un′in·gest′ed, *adj.*
un′in·ges′tive, *adj.*
un′in·graft′ed, *adj.*
un′in·grained′, *adj.*
un·in·gra′ti·at′ing, *adj.*
un′in·hab′it·a·bil′i·ty, *n.*
un′in·hab′it·a·ble, *adj.*
un′in·hab′it·ed, *adj.*
un′in·haled′, *adj.*
un′in·her′ent, *adj.*; **-ly,** *adv.*
un′in·her′it·a·bil′i·ty, *n.*
un′in·her′it·a·ble, *adj.*
un′in·her′it·ed, *adj.*
un′in·hib′it·ing, *adj.*
un′in·humed′, *adj.*
un′in·im′i·cal, *adj.*; **-ly,** *adv.*
un′in·iq′ui·tous, *adj.*; **-ly,** *adv.*; **-ness,** *n.*
un′in·i′tialed, *adj.*
un′in·i′tialled, *adj.*
un′in·i′ti·ate, *adj.*
un′in·i′ti·at′ed, *adj.*
un′in·i′ti·a′tive, *adj.*
un′in·ject′a·ble, *adj.*
un′in·ject′ed, *adj.*
un·in′jured, *adj.*
un·in′jur·ing, *adj.*
un′in·ju′ri·ous, *adj.*; **-ly,** *adv.*; **-ness,** *n.*
un·inked′, *adj.*
un′in·laid′, *adj.*
un′in·nate′, *adj.*; **-ly,** *adv.*; **-ness,** *n.*
un·in′no·cent, *adj.*; **-ly,** *adv.*
un′in·noc′u·ous, *adj.*; **-ly,** *adv.*; **-ness,** *n.*
un·in′no·vat′ing, *adj.*
un·in′no·va′tive, *adj.*
un′in·oc′u·la·ble, *adj.*
un′in·oc′u·lat′ed, *adj.*
un′in·oc′u·la′tive, *adj.*
un′in·quired′, *adj.*
un′in·quir′ing, *adj.*
un′in·quis′i·tive, *adj.*; **-ly,** *adv.*; **-ness,** *n.*
un′in·quis′i·to′ri·al, *adj.*; **-ly,** *adv.*
un′in·scribed′, *adj.*
un′in·sert′ed, *adj.*
un′in·sid′i·ous, *adj.*; **-ly,** *adv.*; **-ness,** *n.*
un′in·sin′u·at′ed, *adj.*
un′in·sin′u·at′ing, *adj.*
un′in·sin′u·a′tive, *adj.*
un′in·sist′ent, *adj.*; **-ly,** *adv.*
un·in′so·lat′ed, *adj.*
un·in′so·lat′ing, *adj.*
un′in·spect′ed, *adj.*
un′in·spir′a·ble, *adj.*
un′in·spir′ing, *adj.*; **-ly,** *adv.*
un′in·spir′it·ed, *adj.*
un′in·spis′sat·ed, *adj.*
un′in·stalled′, *adj.*
un·in′stanced, *adj.*
un′in·stat′ed, *adj.*
un·in′sti·gat′ed, *adj.*
un·in′sti·ga′tive, *adj.*
un′in·stilled′, *adj.*
un′in·stinc′tive, *adj.*; **-ly,** *adv.*; **-ness,** *n.*
un·in′sti·tut′ed, *adj.*
un·in′sti·tu′tion·al, *adj.*; **-ly,** *adv.*
un·in′sti·tu′tive, *adj.*; **-ly,** *adv.*
un′in·struct′i·ble, *adj.*
un′in·struct′ing, *adj.*
un′in·struc′tive, *adj.*; **-ly,** *adv.*
un′in·stru·men′tal, *adj.*; **-ly,** *adv.*
un·in′su·lar, *adj.*
un·in′su·late′, *v.t.*, **-lat·ed, -lat·ing.**
un′in·sult′a·ble, *adj.*
un′in·sult′ed, *adj.*
un′in·sult′ing, *adj.*
un′in·sur′a·bil′i·ty, *n.*
un′in·sur′a·ble, *adj.*
un′in·sured′, *adj.*
un·in′te·gra·ble, *adj.*
un·in′te·gral, *adj.*; **-ly,** *adv.*
un·in′te·grat′ed, *adj.*
un·in′te·gra′tive, *adj.*
un′in·tel·lec′tive, *adj.*
un′in·tel·lec′tu·al, *adj.*; **-ly,** *adv.*
un′in·tel·lec′tu·al′i·ty, *n.*
un′in·tend′ed, *adj.*; **-ly,** *adv.*
un′in·ten′si·fied′, *adj.*
un′in·ten′sive, *adj.*; **-ly,** *adv.*
un′in·tent′, *adj.*; **-ly,** *adv.*
un′in·ter′ca·lat′ed, *adj.*
un′in·ter·cept′ed, *adj.*
un′in·ter·cept′ing, *adj.*
un′in·ter·change′a·ble, *adj.*
un′in·ter·dict′ed, *adj.*
un·in′ter·est·ing, *adj.*; **-ly,** *adv.*
un′in·ter·ject′ed, *adj.*
un′in·ter·laced′, *adj.*
un′in·ter·leaved′, *adj.*
un′in·ter·lined′, *adj.*
un′in·ter·linked′, *adj.*
un′in·ter·locked′, *adj.*
un′in·ter·me′di·ate, *adj.*; **-ly,** *adv.*; **-ness,** *n.*
un′in·ter·min′gled, *adj.*
un′in·ter·mis′sive, *adj.*
un′in·ter·mit′ted, *adj.*
un′in·ter·mit′tent, *adj.*; **-ly,** *adv.*
un′in·ter·mit′ting, *adj.*
un·in′ter′nal·ized′, *adj.*
un′in·ter·na′tion·al, *adj.*
un′in·ter·plead′ed, *adj.*
un′in·ter′po·lat′ed, *adj.*
un′in·ter′po·la′tive, *adj.*
un′in·ter·posed′, *adj.*

indifferent. 2. not personally concerned in something. [UN-¹ + INTERESTED] —**un·in′ter·est·ed·ly,** *adv.* —**un·in′ter·est·ed·ness,** *n.*
—**Syn. 1.** See **disinterested. 2.** unconcerned.

u·ni·oc·u·lar (yo͞o′nē ok′yə lər), *adj.* monocular. [UNI- + OCULAR]

un·ion (yo͞on′yən), *n.* **1.** the act of uniting two or more things; the state of being united; combination; conjunction. **2.** something formed by uniting two or more things; combination. **3.** a number of persons, societies, states, or the like, joined or associated together for some common purpose: *student union; credit union; customs union.* **4.** the uniting of persons, parties, etc., in general agreement. **5.** a uniting of states or nations into one political body, as that of the American colonies at the time of the Revolution, that of England and Scotland in 1707, or that of Great Britain and Ireland in 1801. **6. the Union.** See **United States. 7.** a device emblematic of union, used in a flag or ensign, sometimes occupying the upper corner next to the staff or occupying the entire field. **8.** the act of uniting or of being united in marriage or sexual intercourse: *an ideal union; an illicit union.* **9.** a trade or labor union, or organization of workmen. **10.** *Math.* **a.** Also called **join, logical sum, sum.** the set consisting of elements contained in any two or more sets. *Symbol:* ∪ **b.** the least upper bound of two elements in a lattice. **11.** the process or result of merging or integration of disjoined, severed, or fractured elements, as the healing of a wound or broken bone, the growing together of the parts in a plant graft, the fusion of pieces in a welding process, or the like. **12.** the junction or location at which the merging process has taken place. **13.** *Brit.* (formerly) **a.** a number of parishes united for the administration of the poor laws. **b.** a workhouse erected and maintained by such a union. **14.** any of various contrivances for connecting parts of machinery or the like, esp. a fitting composed of three parts used to connect the ends of two pipes, neither of which can be turned. **15.** *Textiles.* **a.** a fabric of two kinds of yarn. **b.** a yarn of two or more fibers. [ME < MF < LL *ūnion-* (s. of *ūniō*), equiv. to L *ūn(us)* one + *-iōn-* -ION]
—**Syn. 1.** UNION, UNITY agree in referring to a oneness, either created by putting together, or by being undivided. A UNION is a state of being united, a combination, as the result of joining two or more things into one: *to promote the union between two families; the Union of England and Scotland.* UNITY is the state or inherent quality of being one, single, individual, and indivisible (often as a consequence of union): *to find unity in diversity; to give unity to a work of art.* **3.** coalition. **4.** association, confederacy. See **alliance. 8.** wedlock. —**Ant. 1, 2.** separation, division.

Union
A∪B

Un·ion (yo͞on′yən), *n.* **1.** a town in NE New Jersey. 51,499 (1960). **2.** a town in central Missouri. 3937 (1960).

Un′ion Beach′, a town in E New Jersey. 5862 (1960).

un′ion card′, a card identifying one as a member of a particular labor union.

un′ion cat′alog, a library catalog listing in alphabetical sequence the contents of several catalogs, often those of separate libraries. Also called **repertory catalog.**

Un′ion Cit′y, 1. a city in NE New Jersey. 52,180 (1960). **2.** a town in NW Tennessee. 8837 (1960). **3.** a town in W California. 6618 (1960). **4.** a town in E Indiana. 4047 (1960). **5.** a town in NW Pennsylvania. 3819 (1960).

Un·ion·dale (yo͞on′yən dāl′), *n.* a town on W Long Island, in SE New York. 20,041 (1960).

Un′ion Day′, a legal holiday in the Republic of South Africa commemorating the founding of the country on May 31, 1910.

un·ion·ise (yo͞on′yə nīz′), *v.t., v.i.,* **-ised, -is·ing.** *Chiefly Brit.* unionize. —**un′ion·i·sa′tion,** *n.*

un·ion·ism (yo͞on′yə niz′əm), *n.* **1.** the principle of union, esp. trade unionism. **2.** attachment to a union. **3.** (*cap.*) loyalty to the federal union of the United States of America, esp. at the time of the Civil War. [UNION + -ISM]

un·ion·ist (yo͞on′yə nist), *n.* **1.** one whose activities or beliefs are characterized by unionism. **2.** a member of a trade union. **3.** (*cap.*) an adherent of the federal union of the United States of America, esp. during the Civil War. **4.** *Brit. Politics.* (formerly) an upholder of the legislative union of Great Britain and Ireland; an opponent of home rule in Ireland. [UNION + -IST] —**un′ion·is′tic,** *adj.*

un·ion·ize (yo͞on′yə nīz′), *v.,* **-ized, -iz·ing.** —*v.t.* **1.** to form into a union. **2.** to organize into a trade union; bring into or incorporate in a trade union. **3.** to subject to the rules of a trade union. —*v.i.* **4.** to form a union. **5.** to join in a trade union. Also, *esp. Brit.,* **unionise.** [UNION + -IZE] —**un′ion·i·za′tion,** *n.*

un′ion jack′, 1. a jack consisting of the union of a national flag or ensign, as the U.S. jack, which has the white stars and blue field of the union of the U.S. national flag. **2.** any flag the overall design of which is a union. **3.** (*often cap.*) the British national flag.

un′ion la′bel, a tag or stamped imprint on a product indicating that it has been made by union labor.

un′ion lan′guage, an artificial language, as Shona, created by combining vocabulary and grammatical features of the members of a group of related dialects, and representing a compromise between them: used for education, published material, etc.

un′ion list′, a list of the materials on a designated subject available in a specific group of libraries.

un·ion-made (yo͞on′yən mād′), *adj.* produced by workers belonging to a labor union.

Un′ion of Bur′ma, official name of **Burma.**

Un′ion of South′ Af′rica, former name of the Republic of South Africa.

Un′ion of So′viet So′cialist Repub′lics, a former federal union of 15 constituent republics, in E Europe and W and N Asia, comprising the larger part of the former Russian Empire: dissolved in December 1991. 8,650,069 sq. mi. *Cap.:* Moscow. Also called **Russia, Soviet Union.** *Abbr.:* U.S.S.R., USSR.

un′ion shop′, 1. a shop, business establishment, or part thereof, in which terms and conditions of employment for all employees are fixed by agreement between the employer and a labor union. **2.** a shop, business, etc., in which membership in a union is made a condition of employment, but in which the employer may hire nonunion workers provided that they become members after a stated period, usually 30 days. Cf. **nonunion shop.**

un′ion suit′, a close-fitting undergarment, esp. worn by men and children, combining drawers and shirt in one piece.

Un·ion·town (yo͞on′yən toun′), *n.* a city in SW Pennsylvania. 17,942 (1960).

u·nip·ar·ous (yo͞o nip′ər əs), *adj.* **1.** *Zool.* producing only one egg or offspring at a time. **2.** *Bot.* (of a cyme) producing only one axis at each branching. [< NL *ūniparus.* See UNI-, -PAROUS]

u·ni·per·son·al (yo͞o′nə pûr′sə nəl), *adj.* **1.** consisting of or existing as one person only. **2.** *Gram.* used in only one person, esp. the third person singular, as certain verbs. [UNI- + PERSONAL] —**u′ni·per′son·al′i·ty,** *n.*

u·ni·pet·al·ous (yo͞o′nə pet′əl əs), *adj.* *Bot.* having only one petal. [UNI- + PETALOUS]

u·ni·pla·nar (yo͞o′nə plā′nər), *adj.* confined to a single plane or two-dimensional continuum: *uniplanar motion.* [UNI- + PLANAR]

u·ni·pod (yo͞o′nə pod′), *n.* something that is formed with a single leg or foot, as a one-legged support for a camera. [UNI- + -POD]

u·ni·po·lar (yo͞o′nə pō′lər), *adj.* **1.** *Physics.* having or pertaining to a single magnetic or electric pole. **2.** *Anat.* of or pertaining to a nerve cell in spinal and cranial ganglia in which the incoming and outgoing processes fuse outside the cell body. [UNI- + POLAR] —**u·ni·po·lar·i·ty** (yo͞o′nə pō lar′i tē), *n.*

u·nip·o·tent (yo͞o nip′ə tənt), *adj.* *Biol.* (of cells) capable of developing into only one type of cell or tissue.

u·ni·po·ten·tial (yo͞o′nə pə ten′shəl), *adj.* **1.** *Elect., Electronics.* having uniform electric potential throughout, as a hot cathode (**u′nipoten′tial cath′ode**) indirectly heated by a separate heater circuit so that there is no lateral change of voltage across the cathode due to resistance to a heating current. **2.** *Biol.* unipotent. [UNI- + POTENTIAL]

u·nique (yo͞o nēk′), *adj.* **1.** existing as the only one or as the sole example; single; solitary in type or characteristics: *a unique copy of an ancient manuscript.* **2.** having no like or equal; standing alone in quality; unequaled; unparalleled; incomparable: *Bach was unique in his handling of counterpoint.* **3.** impossible to duplicate within a stated or implied scope, as a geographical area or range of experience; unlikely to be matched; extremely rare: *a ruthlessness probably unique in European history; The yogi possesses a skill as unique in occidental communities as it is commonplace in the East.* **4.** limited in occurrence to a given class, situation, or area: *a species unique to Australia; a unique symptom of our times; The elephant's trunk is unique.* **5.** limited to a simple outcome or result; without alternative possibilities: *Certain types of problems have unique solutions.* —*n.* **6.** the embodiment of unique characteristics; the only specimen of a given kind: *The unique is also the improbable.* [< F < L *ūnic(us),* equiv. to *ūn(us)* one + *-icus* -IC] —**u·nique′ly,** *adv.* —**u·nique′ness,** *n.*
—**Syn. 2.** peerless. **3.** singular, strange, uncommon.

unique′ factoriza′tion domain′, *Math.* a commutative integral domain with a multiplicative identity having the property that every nonzero element can be factored into a unique product of prime elements. Also called **Gaussian domain.**

unique′ factoriza′tion the′orem. See **fundamental theorem of arithmetic.**

u·ni·sep·tate (yo͞o′ni sep′tāt), *adj.* having only one septum or partition, as a silicle. [UNI- + SEPTATE]

u·ni·sex (yo͞o′nə seks′), *adj.* of, noting, or engaged in a design, type, or style that is for use or wear by both sexes alike: *unisex clothes; a unisex shop.*

u·ni·sex·u·al (yo͞o′ni sek′sho͞o əl), *adj.* **1.** of or pertaining to one sex only. **2.** having only male or female organs in one individual, as an animal or a flower. [UNI- + SEXUAL] —**u′ni·sex′u·al′i·ty,** *n.* —**u′ni·sex′u·al·ly,** *adv.*

u·ni·son (yo͞o′ni sən, -zən), *n.* **1.** coincidence in pitch of two or more musical tones, voices, etc. **2.** the musical interval of a perfect prime. **3.** the performance of musical parts at the same pitch or at the octave. **4.** a sounding together in octaves, esp. of male and female voices or of higher and lower instruments of the same class. **5.** a process in which all elements behave in the same way at the same time; simultaneous or synchronous parallel action: *to march in unison.* **6. in unison,** in perfect accord; corresponding exactly: *My feelings on the subject are in unison with yours.* [< ML *ūnison(us)* of a single sound, equiv. to L *ūni-* UNI- + *sonus* sound]

u·nis·o·nous (yo͞o nis′ə nəs), *adj.* being in unison. Also, **u·nis′o·nal, u·nis′o·nant.** [< ML *ūnison(us)* (see UNISON) + -OUS]

u·ni·spi·ral (yo͞o′ni spī′rəl), *adj.* having one spiral. [UNI- + SPIRAL]

u·nit (yo͞o′nit), *n.* **1.** a single thing or person. **2.** any group of things or persons regarded as an entity: *They formed a cohesive unit.* **3.** one of the individuals or groups that together constitute a whole; one of the parts, elements, or the like into which a whole may be divided or analyzed. **4.** any magnitude regarded as an independent whole; a single, indivisible entity. **5.** any specified amount of a quantity, as of length, volume, force, momentum, or time, by comparison with which any other quantity of the same kind is measured or estimated. **6.** the least positive integer; one. **7.** Also called **unit's place. a.** (in a mixed number) the position of the first digit to the left of the decimal point. **b.** (in a whole number) the position of the first digit from the right of the decimal point. **8.** a machine or machines having a specified purpose; apparatus: *a heating unit.* **9.** *Educ.* the quantity of educational instruction, determined usually by a number of hours of classroom and, sometimes, laboratory work. **10.** *Mil.* an organized body of soldiers, varying in size and constituting a subdivision of a larger body. **11.** *Immunol., Pharm.* **a.** the measured amount of a substance necessary to cause a certain effect; a clinical unit used when a substance cannot readily be isolated in pure form and its activity determined directly. **b.** the amount necessary to cause a specific effect upon a specific animal or upon animal tissues. **12.** *Math.* **a.** an identity element. **b.** an element in a group, ring, etc., that possesses an inverse. [appar. back formation from UNITY]

Unit., Unitarian.

u·nit·age (yo͞o′ni tij), *n.* specification of the amount making up a unit in a system of measurement. [UNIT + -AGE]

u·ni·tar·i·an (yo͞o′ni târ′ē ən), *n.* **1.** one who maintains that God is one being, rejecting the doctrine of the Trinity, and emphasizing freedom in religious belief, tolerance of difference in religious opinion, character as the fundamental principle in religion, and the use of all religious history and experience interpreted by reason as a guide to conduct. **2.** (*cap.*) a member of a Christian denomination founded upon the doctrine that God is one being, and giving each congregation complete control over its affairs. **3.** an advocate of unity or centralization, as in government. —*adj.* **4.** (*cap.*) pertaining to the Unitarians or their doctrines; accepting Unitarianism; belonging to the Unitarians. **5.** unitary. [< NL *unitari(us)* (L *ūnit(ās)* UNITY + *-ārius* -ARY) + -AN]

U·ni·tar·i·an·ism (yo͞o′ni târ′ē ə niz′əm), *n.* **1.** the beliefs, principles, and practices of Unitarians. **2.** (*l.c.*) any system advocating unity or centralization, as in government. [UNITARIAN + -ISM]

u·ni·tar·y (yo͞o′ni ter′ē), *adj.* **1.** of or pertaining to a unit or units. **2.** of, pertaining to, characterized by, or aiming toward unity: *the unitary principles of contemporary nationalism.* **3.** of the nature of a unit; having the indivisible character of a unit; whole. **4.** serving as a unit, as of measurement or estimation. **5.** of or pertaining to the use of units: *a unitary method was applied.* **6.** *Govt.* of or pertaining to a system of government in which the executive, legislative, and judicial powers of each state in a body of states are vested in a central authority. [UNIT, UNIT(Y) + -ARY] —**u′ni·tar′i·ness,** *n.*

u′nitary ma′trix, *Math.* a matrix, the entries of which are complex numbers and which gives the identity matrix when multiplied by the transpose of the matrix whose entries are the conjugates of the entries of the given matrix.

u′nitary space′, *Math.* a vector space with an inner product having complex values defined on it.

u′nitary transforma′tion, *Math.* a transformation on a unitary space which preserves length.

un′in·ter·pos′ing, *adj.*
un′in·ter′pret·a·ble, *adj.*
un′in·ter′pre·ta′tive, *adj.*
un′in·ter′pret·ed, *adj.*
un′in·ter′pre·tive, *adj.;* **-ly,** *adv.*
un′in·terred′, *adj.*
un′in·ter′ro·ga·ble, *adj.*
un′in·ter′ro·gat′ed, *adj.*
un′in·ter·rog′a·tive, *adj.;* **-ly,** *adv.*
un′in·ter·rog′a·to′ry, *adj.*
un′in·ter·rupt′ed, *adj.;* **-ly,** *adv.;* **-ness,** *n.*
un′in·ter·rupt′ing, *adj.*
un′in·ter·rup′tive, *adj.*
un′in·ter·sect′ed, *adj.*
un′in·ter·sect′ing, *adj.*
un′in·ter·spersed′, *adj.*
un′in·ter·ven′ing, *adj.*
un·in′ter·viewed′, *adj.*
un′in·ter·volved′, *adj.*
un′in·ter·wo′ven, *adj.*
un′in·thralled′, *adj.*
un·in′ti·mate, *adj;* **-ly,** *adv.*
un·in′ti·mat′ed, *adj.*
un′in·tim′i·dat′ed, *adj.*
un′in·tim′i·dat′ing, *adj.*
un′in·toned′, *adj.*
un′in·tox′i·cat′ed, *adj.*
un′in·tox′i·cat′ing, *adj.*
un′in·trench′a·ble, *adj.*
un′in·trenched′, *adj.*
un·in′tri·cate, *adj.;* **-ly,** *adv.;* **-ness,** *n.*
un′in·trigued′, *adj.*
un′in·tri′guing, *adj.*
un′in·tro·duced′, *adj.*
un′in·tro·duc′i·ble, *adj.*
un′in·tro·duc′tive, *adj.*
un′in·tro·duc′to·ry, *adj.*
un′in·tro·mit′ted, *adj.*
un′in·tro·mit′tive, *adj.*
un′in·tro·spec′tive, *adj.;* **-ly,** *adv.*
un′in·tro·ver′sive, *adj.*
un′in·tro·vert′ed, *adj.*
un′in·trud′ed, *adj.*
un′in·trud′ing, *adj.;* **-ly,** *adv.*
un′in·tru′sive, *adj.;* **-ly,** *adv.*
un′in·trust′ed, *adj.*
un′in·tu′it·a·ble, *adj.*
un′in·tu·i′tion·al, *adj.*
un′in·tu′i·tive, *adj.;* **-ly,** *adv.*
un·in′un·dat′ed, *adj.*
un′in·ured′, *adj.*
un′in·urned′, *adj.*
un′in·vad′a·ble, *adj.*
un′in·vad′ed, *adj.*
un′in·vag′i·nat′ed, *adj.*
un′in·va′sive, *adj.*
un′in·vec′tive, *adj.*
un′in·veigh′ing, *adj.*
un′in·vei′gled, *adj.*
un′in·vent′ed, *adj.*
un′in·ven′tive, *adj.;* **-ly,** *adv.*
un′in·vert′ed, *adj.*
un′in·vert′i·ble, *adj.*
un′in·vest′a·ble, *adj.*
un′in·vest′ed, *adj.*
un′in·ves′ti·ga·ble, *adj.*
un′in·ves′ti·gat′ed, *adj.*
un′in·ves′ti·gat′ing, *adj.*
un′in·ves′ti·ga′tive, *adj.*
un′in·ves′ti·ga·to′ry, *adj.*
un′in·vid′i·ous, *adj.;* **-ly,** *adv.*
un′in·vig′or·at·ed, *adj.*
un′in·vig′or·at′ing, *adj.*
un′in·vig′or·a′tive, *adj.;* **-ly,** *adv.*
un′in·vin′ci·ble, *adj.;* **-ble·ness,** *n.;* **-bly,** *adv.*
un′in·vit′ed, *adj.*
un′in·vit′ing, *adj.;* **-ly,** *adv.;* **-ness,** *n.*
un′in·voc′a·tive, *adj.*
un·in′voiced, *adj.*
un′in·vok′a·ble, *adj.*
un′in·voked′, *adj.*
un·in′vo·lut′ed, *adj.*
un′in·volved′, *adj.*
un′in·wo′ven, *adj.*
un′in·wrapped′, *adj.*
un′in·wreathed′, *adj.*
un·i′on·ised′, *adj.*
un·i′on·ized′, *adj.*
un′i·ras′ci·bil′i·ty, *n.*
un′i·ras′ci·ble, *adj.*
un′i·ren′ic, *adj.*
un′ir·i·des′cent, *adj.;* **-ly,** *adv.*
un·i′roned, *adj.*
un′i·ron′i·cal, *adj.;* **-ly,** *adv.*
un′ir·ra′di·at·ed, *adj.*
un′ir·ra′di·a′tive, *adj.*
un·ir′ri·ga·ble, *adj.*
un·ir′ri·gat′ed, *adj.*
un·ir′ri·ta·ble, *adj.;* **-bly,** *adv.*
un·ir′ri·tant, *adj.*
un·ir′ri·tat′ed, *adj.*
un·ir′ri·tat′ing, *adj.*
un·ir′ri·ta′tive, *adj.*
un′ir·rupt′ed, *adj.*
un′ir·rup′tive, *adj.*
un·i′so·late′, *v.t.,* **-lat·ed, -lat·ing.**
un′i·so·la′tion·ist, *adj.*
un·i′so·la′tive, *adj.*
un′i·so·mer′ic, *adj.*
un′i·so·met′ri·cal, *adj.*
un′i·so·mor′phic, *adj.*
un′i·so·trop′ic, *adj.*
un′i·sot′ro·pous, *adj.*
un·is′su·a·ble, *adj.*
un·is′su·ant, *adj.*
un·is′sued, *adj.*
un′i·tal′i·cized′, *adj.*

u′nit car′rier. See **straddle truck.**

u′nit cell′, *Crystall.* the simplest unit of a regular lattice.

u′nit char′acter, *Genetics.* a character, usually controlled by a single gene, that is transmitted as a unit in heredity.

u′nit cost′, the cost of a specified unit of a product or service.

u·nite[1] (yo͞o nīt′), *v.,* **u·nit·ed, u·nit·ing.** —*v.t.* **1.** to join, combine, or incorporate so as to form a single whole or unit. **2.** to cause to hold together or adhere: *to unite two pieces of wood with glue.* **3.** to join in marriage. **4.** to associate (persons, ideas, feelings, etc.) by some bond or tie; connect closely. **5.** to have or exhibit in union or combination: *He unites generosity and forgiveness in himself.* —*v.i.* **6.** to become joined together or combined so as to form a single whole; become one. **7.** to become joined in marriage: *They were united in a civil ceremony.* **8.** to enter into alliance or association; join in action; act in concert or agreement; become one in opinion or feeling. [ME *unite(n)* < L *ūnīt(us)* joined together, united (ptp. of *ūnīre*), equiv. to *ūn(us)* one + *-ītus* -ITE[1]] —**u·nit′a·ble, u·nite′a·ble,** *adj.* —**u·nit′er,** *n.*
—**Syn. 1.** conjoin, couple, link, yoke. See **join. 2, 6.** amalgamate, compound, consolidate, weld, fuse, blend, mingle, merge. **3.** marry, wed. **6.** coalesce. —**Ant. 1.** divide. **2.** separate.

u·nite[2] (yo͞o′nīt, yo͞o nīt′), *n.* a former gold coin of England, equal to 20 shillings, issued under James I and Charles I. [from UNITE[1], referring to union of England and Scotland]

u·nit·ed (yo͞o nī′tid), *adj.* **1.** joined together; combined into one. **2.** of or produced by the joint action of two or more persons, things, etc.: *Their united effort was effective.* **3.** formed by the union of two or more things, bodies, etc. **4.** agreed; in harmony: *His parents were united in their decision to send him to college.* [UNITE[1] + -ED[2]] —**u·nit′ed·ly,** *adv.* —**u·nit′ed·ness,** *n.*

Unit′ed Ar′ab Emir′ates, an independent federation of seven Arab emirates, on the S Coast **(Pirate Coast)** of the Persian Gulf: formerly under British protection. 200,000 (est. 1972). 32,000 sq. mi. *Cap.:* Abu Dhabi. Formerly, **Trucial Coast, Trucial Oman, Trucial Sheikdoms, Trucial States.**

Unit′ed Ar′ab Repub′lic, 1. a former republic in NE Africa: formed in 1958 by the union of Egypt and Syria; Syria withdrew in 1961. **2.** former official name (1961–71) of Egypt.

Unit′ed Ar′ab States′, a former (1958–61) federation of the United Arab Republic (Egypt and Syria) and Yemen.

Unit′ed Breth′ren, a Protestant denomination, of Wesleyan beliefs and practices, founded in 1800.

unit′ed front′, 1. a coalition formed to oppose a force that menaces the interests, otherwise usually diverging, of all the members: *Russia and the western nations presented a united front against Germany in World War II.* **2.** See **popular front.**

Unit′ed King′dom, a kingdom in NW Europe, consisting of Great Britain and Northern Ireland: formerly comprising Great Britain and Ireland 1801–1922. 52,719,604 (1961); 93,377 sq. mi. *Cap.:* London. *Abbr.:* U.K. Official name, **Unit′ed King′dom o Great′ Brit′ain and North′ern Ire′land.**

Unit′ed Na′tions, 1. an international organization, consisting of 126 countries, with headquarters in New York City, formed to promote international peace, security, and cooperation under the terms of the charter signed in San Francisco in 1945. Cf. **General Assembly, Security Council. 2.** the nations that signed the joint declaration in Washington, D.C., January 2, 1942, pledging to employ full resources against the Axis powers, not to make a separate peace, etc.

Uni′ted Na′tions Chil′dren's Fund′. See **UNICEF.**

Unit′ed Na′tions Educa′tional, Scientif′ic, and Cul′tural Organiza′tion. See **UNESCO.**

Unit′ed Presbyte′rian, 1. a member of the United Presbyterian Church of North America, founded in Pittsburgh in 1858 by a union of two Presbyterian groups. **2.** a member of the United Presbyterian Church in the U.S.A., founded in Pittsburgh in 1958 by combining the United Presbyterian Church of North America with another Presbyterian body.

Unit′ed Press′ Interna′tional, a business organization of newspapers in the U.S., together with representatives abroad, for the reporting and interchange of news. *Abbr.:* UPI, U.P.I.

Unit′ed Prov′inces, 1. former name of **Uttar Pradesh. 2.** *Hist.* the seven northern provinces in the Low Countries that declared their independence from Spain in 1581 and laid the foundation for the establishment of the Netherlands.

Unit′ed Prov′inces of A′gra and Oudh′, former official name of **Uttar Pradesh.**

Unit′ed States′, a republic in North America, consisting of 50 States and the District of Columbia. 226,545,805; conterminous United States, 3,022,387 sq. mi.; with Alaska and Hawaii, 3,615,122 sq. mi. *Cap.:* Washington, D.C. *Abbr.:* U.S. Also called **United States of America, America.**

Unit′ed States′ Air′ Force′, the permanent military air force of the U.S., established as a separate branch of the armed forces in 1947. Prior to that date it was a component of the U.S. Army. *Abbr.:* USAF

Unit′ed States′ Ar′my, the permanent military force of the United States. (The term is generally used to refer to the Regular Army, though it also includes other normal peacetime components.) *Abbr.:* USA

Unit′ed States′ Employ′ment Serv′ice, *U.S. Govt.* the division of the Department of Labor that supervises and coordinates the activities of State employment agencies. *Abbr.:* USES

Unit′ed States′ Na′vy, the permanent naval force of the U.S., including the Navy, Marine Corps, and when under the command of the Navy, the U.S. Coast Guard. *Abbr.:* USN

Unit′ed States′ of Amer′ica. See **United States.** *Abbr.:* U.S.A.

Unit′ed States′ of Brazil′, official name of **Brazil.**

Unit′ed States′ of Indone′sia, former official name of the Republic of Indonesia.

u′nit el′ement, *Math.* identity (def. 7b).

u′nit fac′tor, *Biol.* a gene; a substance which functions as the hereditary unit for a single character.

u′nit invest′ment trust′. See **unit trust.**

u·ni·tive (yo͞o′ni tiv), *adj.* **1.** capable of causing unity or serving to unite. **2.** marked by or involving union. [< LL *ūnītīvus* uniting, equiv. to L *ūnīt(us)* (see UNITE) + *-īvus* -IVE] —**u′ni·tive·ly,** *adv.* —**u′ni·tive·ness,** *n.*

u′nit magnet′ic pole′, *Physics.* the unit of magnetic pole strength equal to the strength of a magnetic pole that repels a similar pole with a force of one dyne, the two poles being placed in a vacuum and separated by a distance of one centimeter.

u′nit price′, 1. rate[1] (def. 3). **2.** a price for a service or commodity that includes all extra costs incidental to the item: *the unit price of a wedding.*

u′nit rule′, *U.S.* (in national conventions of the Democratic party) a rule whereby some States vote as a unit, not recognizing minority votes within the delegation.

u′nit's place′, unit (def. 7).

u′nit stress′, *Engineering.* a stress upon a structure at a certain place, expressed in units of force per unit of cross-sectional area, as in pounds per square inch.

u′nit trust′, *(often cap.)* an investment company that holds a fixed group of securities in which each investor receives a share in the amount proportionate to his investment. Also called **fixed investment trust, fixed trust, unit investment trust.**

u·ni·ty (yo͞o′ni tē), *n., pl.* **-ties. 1.** the state of being one; oneness. **2.** one single thing; something complete in itself, or regarded as such. **3.** the oneness of a complex or organic whole or of an interconnected series; a whole or totality as combining all its parts into one. **4.** the state or fact of being united or combined into one, as of the parts of a whole; unification. **5.** absence of diversity; unvaried or uniform character. **6.** oneness of mind, feeling, etc., as among a number of persons; concord, harmony, or agreement. **7.** *Math.* **a.** the number one; a quantity regarded as one. **b.** identity[2] (def. 7b). **8.** (in literature and art) a relation of all the parts or elements of a work constituting a harmonious whole and producing a single general effect. **9.** one of the three principles of dramatic structure **(the three unities)** derived from Aristotelian aesthetics and formalized in the neoclassic canon in which a play is required to represent action as taking place in one day **(u′nity of time′)**, as occurring within one place **(u′nity of place′)**, and as having a single plot with a beginning, middle, and end **(u′nity of ac′tion)**. [ME *unite* < OF *unite* < L *ūnitāt-* (s. of *ūnitās*), equiv. to *ūn(us)* one + *-itāt-* -ITY]
—**Syn. 1.** singleness, singularity, individuality. See **union. 8.** concert, harmony, unison. —**Ant. 1.** diversity.

Univ., 1. Universalist. **2.** University.

univ., 1. universal. **2.** universally. **3.** university.

u·ni·va·lence (yo͞o′nə vā′ləns, yo͞o niv′ə-), *n. Chem.* the quality of being univalent. Also, **u′ni·va′len·cy.** [UNI- + VALENCE]

u·ni·va·lent (yo͞o′nə vā′lənt, yo͞o niv′ə-), *adj.* **1.** *Chem.* having a valence of one; monovalent. **2.** *Genetics.* (of a chromosome) single; unpaired; not possessing or joining its homologous chromosome in synapsis. [UNI- + -VALENT]

u·ni·valve (yo͞o′nə valv′), *adj.* Also, **u′ni·valved′, u·ni·val·vu·lar** (yo͞o′nə val′vyə lər). **1.** having one valve. **2.** (of a shell) composed of a single valve or piece. —*n.* **3.** a univalve mollusk or its shell. [UNI- + VALVE]

u·ni·var·i·ate (yo͞o′nə vâr′ē it), *adj. Statistics.* (of a distribution) having one variate. [UNI- + VARIATE]

u·ni·ver·sal (yo͞o′nə vûr′səl), *adj.* **1.** of, pertaining to, or characteristic of all or the whole: *universal experience of mankind.* **2.** applicable to many individuals or many single cases; general. **3.** affecting, concerning, or involving all: *universal military training.* **4.** used or understood by all: *a universal language.* **5.** existing or prevailing everywhere; present in all parts, places, etc.: *the universal calm of southern seas.* **6.** versed in or embracing many or all skills, branches of learning, etc.: *Leonardo da Vinci was a universal genius.* **7.** given or extended to all: *universal revelation.* **8.** of or pertaining to the universe, all nature, or all existing things: *universal cause.* **9.** characterizing all or most members of a class; generic. **10.** *Logic.* (of a proposition) asserted of every member of a class. **11.** *Mach.* noting any of various machines, tools, or devices widely adaptable in position, range of use, etc. **12.** *Metalworking.* **a.** (of metal plates and shapes) rolled in a universal mill. **b.** (of a rolling mill or rolling method) having or employing vertical edging rolls. —*n.* **13.** something that may be applied throughout the universe to many things, usually thought of as an entity which can be in many places at the same time. **14.** a trait or characteristic, as distinguished from a particular individual or event, that can be possessed in common by many distinct things, as the love of a mother for her young. **15.** *Logic.* a universal proposition. **16.** *Philos.* **a.** a general term or concept or the generic nature that such a term signifies; a Platonic idea or Aristotelian form. **b.** a metaphysical entity that is repeatable and remains unchanged in character in a series of changes or changing relations. **c.** *Hegelianism.* See **concrete universal.** [ME *universel* < MF < L *ūniversāl(is).* See UNIVERSE, -AL[1]] —**u′ni·ver′sal·ness,** *n.*

univer′sal affirm′ative, *Logic.* a proposition of the form "All S is P." *Symbol:* A, a

u′niver′sal chuck′, a chuck, as on a lathe headstock, having three stepped jaws moving simultaneously for precise centering of a workpiece of any of a wide range of sizes.

u′niver′sal class′, *Logic.* (in the theory of classes) the class that includes all other classes and is composed of all individuals composing these classes.

u′niver′sal cou′pling. See **universal joint.**

u′niver′sal gas′ con′stant, *Physics.* a constant, 8.314 joules per degree Kelvin, equal to the product of the pressure and the volume of one gram molecule of an ideal gas divided by the absolute temperature. Cf. **Boltzmann constant.** Also called **gas constant.**

u′niver′sal head′, (on a machine tool) a head for indexing or moving work or a tool through any vertical or horizontal angle.

u·ni·ver·sal·ise (yo͞o′nə vûr′sə līz′), *v.t.,* **-ised, -ising.** *Chiefly Brit.* universalize. —**u′ni·ver′sal·i·sa′tion,** *n.* —**u′ni·ver′sal·is′er,** *n.*

u·ni·ver·sal·ism (yo͞o′nə vûr′sə liz′əm), *n.* **1.** universal character; universality. **2.** universal range of knowledge, interests, or activities. **3.** *(cap.)* the doctrine that all men will finally be saved or be brought back to holiness and God. Cf. **apocatastasis** (def. 2). [UNIVERSAL + -ISM]

u·ni·ver·sal·ist (yo͞o′nə vûr′sə list), *n.* **1.** one characterized by universalism, as in knowledge, interests, or activities. **2.** *(cap.)* a member of a Christian denomination advocating Universalism. —*adj.* **3.** *(cap.)* Also, **U′ni·ver′sal·is′tic.** of or pertaining to Universalism or Universalists. [UNIVERSAL + -IST]

u·ni·ver·sal·i·ty (yo͞o′nə vər sal′i tē), *n., pl.* **-ties. 1.** character or state of being universal; existence or prevalence everywhere. **2.** relation, extension, or applicability to all. **3.** universal character or range of knowledge, interests, etc. [ME *universalite* < LL *ūniversālit(ās).* See UNIVERSAL, -ITY]

u·ni·ver·sal·ize (yo͞o′nə vûr′sə līz′), *v.t.,* **-ized, -iz·ing.** to make universal. Also, *esp. Brit.,* **universalise.** [UNIVERSAL + -IZE] —**u′ni·ver′sal·i·za′tion,** *n.* —**u′ni·ver′sal·iz′er,** *n.*

u′niver′sal joint′, *Mach.* a coupling between rotating shafts set at an angle to one another. Also called **universal coupling.**

Universal joint

u′niver′sal lan′guage, 1. an auxiliary language that is used and understood everywhere. **2.** any kind of expression that is used and understood everywhere: *Music is a universal language.*

u·ni·ver·sal·ly (yo͞o′nə vûr′sə lē), *adv.* in a universal manner; in every instance or place; without exception. [ME; see UNIVERSAL, -LY]

u′niver′sal mil′itary train′ing, a program for maintaining the supply of army manpower, requiring all young male citizens, excepting those exempt for specific reasons, as physical or mental defects, to serve for a period of active and reserve duty. *Abbr.:* UMT

u′niver′sal mill′, *Metalworking.* a rolling mill having both horizontal and vertical rolls.

u′niver′sal mo′tor, a series-wound motor, of one-half horsepower or less, using alternating or direct current.

u′niver′sal neg′ative, *Logic.* a proposition of the form "No S is P." *Symbol:* E, e

u′niver′sal plane′, *Carpentry.* an adjustable plane able to hold a large variety of cutters for forming moldings, chamfers, grooves, etc.

u′niver′sal plate′, metal plates rolled in a universal mill.

U′niver′sal Post′al Un′ion, an international organization, formed in Bern, Switzerland (1875), that administers and regulates international postal service. *Abbr.:* UPU Formerly, **General Postal Union.**

u′niver′sal quan′tifier, *Logic.* a quantifier indicating that the sentential function within its scope is true for all values of any variable included in the quantifier. Cf. **existential quantifier.**

u′niver′sal stage′, a small theodolite mounted on the stage of a microscope and used in the petrographic analysis of rocks.

u′niver′sal suf′frage, suffrage for all persons over a certain age, usually 21, who in other respects satisfy the requirements established by law.

univer′sal time′. See **Greenwich Time.**

u·ni·verse (yo͞o′nə vûrs′), *n.* **1.** the totality of known or supposed objects and phenomena; all existing things, including the earth and its creatures, the heavenly bodies, and all else throughout space; the cosmos; macrocosm. **2.** the whole world, esp. with reference to mankind: *It is a truth implicit throughout the universe.* **3.** a world or sphere in which something exists or prevails: *His private universe was bright and cheerful.* **4.** *Logic.* See **universe of discourse.** [< L *ūnivers(um),* neut. of *ūniversus,* equiv. to *ūni-* UNI- + *versus* (ptp. of *vertere* to turn)]

u′niverse of dis′course, *Logic.* the aggregate of all the objects, attributes, and relations assumed or implied in a given discussion.

u·ni·ver·si·ty (yo͞o′nə vûr′si tē), *n., pl.* **-ties.** an institution of learning of the highest level, having a college of liberal arts and a program of graduate studies together with several professional schools and faculties, as of theology, law, medicine, engineering, etc., and authorized to confer degrees. Continental European universities usually have only graduate or professional schools. [ME *universite* < OF < ML *ūniversitāt-* (s. of *ūniversitās*) < LL: guild, corporation < L: totality, equiv. to *ūnivers(us)* UNIVERSE + *-itāt-* -ITY] —**u·ni·ver·si·tar·i·an** (yo͞o′nə vûr′si târ′ē ən), *n., adj.*

U·ni·ver·si·ty (yo͞o′nə vûr′si tē), *n.* a town in N Mississippi. 3597 (1960).

Univer′sity Cit′y, a city in E Missouri, near St. Louis. 51,249 (1960).

univer′sity exten′sion, a system by which an institution provides educational programs, as evening classes, for students otherwise unable to attend. Cf. **extension courses.**

Univer′sity Heights′, a city in NE Ohio, near Cleveland. 16,641 (1960).

Univer′sity Park′, 1. a city in N Texas. 23,202 (1960). **2.** a town in central Maryland. 3098 (1960).

Univer′sity Wits′, a name given to an Elizabethan group of university-trained playwrights and pamphleteers, among them Robert Greene, John Lyly, Thomas Nash, and George Peele.

un·jaun·diced (un jôn′dist), *adj.* devoid of distorted or prejudiced views. [UN-[1] + JAUNDICED]

un·i′tem·ized′, *adj.*
un·it′er·at′ed, *adj.*
un·it′er·a′tive, *adj.*
un′i·tin′er·ant, *adj.*
un·jack′et·ed, *adj.*
un·jad′ed, *adj.*
un·jag′ged, *adj.*
un·jailed′, *adj.*
un·jam′, *v.t.,* **-jammed, -jam·ming.**
un′ja·panned′, *adj.*
un·jarred′, *adj.*
un·jar′ring, *adj.*
un·jaun′ty, *adj.*
un·jeal′ous, *adj.;* **-ly,** *adv.*

un·joint (un joint′), *v.t.* to sever or dislocate a joint or joints of; disjoint. [UN-2 + JOINT]

un·just (un just′), *adj.* **1.** not just; lacking in justice or fairness: *unjust criticism; an unjust prince; an unjust verdict.* **2.** *Archaic.* unfaithful or dishonest. [ME; see UN-1, JUST1] —**un·just′ly,** *adv.* —**un·just′ness,** *n.*
—**Syn. 1.** inequitable, partial, unfair, prejudiced, biased; undeserved, unmerited, unjustifiable.

Un·ke·los (ung′kə los′), *n.* Onkelos.

un·kempt (un kempt′), *adj.* **1.** not combed: *His hair is unkempt.* **2.** in an uncared-for, neglected, or untidy condition; disheveled; messy: *unkempt clothes; an unkempt lawn.* **3.** unpolished; rough; crude. [var. of *unkembed*; UN-1 + *kembed,* ptp. of obs. *kemb* to comb (< ME *kembe,* OE *cemban*; c. G *kämmen*)] —**un·kempt′ly,** *adv.* —**un·kempt′ness,** *n.*

un·kenned (un kend′; *Scot.* un kent′), *adj. Chiefly Scot.* unknown. [ME; see UN-1, KEN, -ED2]

un·ken·nel (un ken′əl), *v.,* **-neled, -nel·ing** or (*esp. Brit.*) **-nelled, -nel·ling.** —*v.t.* **1.** to drive or release from, as from a kennel: *to unkennel one's hounds before a hunt.* —*v.i.* **3.** to come out of a kennel, den, lair, or the like. [UN-2 + KENNEL]

un·kind (un kīnd′), *adj.* **1.** lacking in kindness or consideration. **2.** lacking in sympathy or mercy; severe. [ME; see UN-1, KIND1] —**un·kind′ly,** *adv.* —**un·kind′ness,** *n.*

un·kind·ly (un kīnd′lē), *adj.* **1.** not kindly; unkind; ill-natured. **2.** inclement or bleak, as weather, climate, etc. **3.** unfavorable for crops: *unkindly soil.* [ME; see UN-1, KINDLY] —**un·kind′li·ness,** *n.*

un·knight·ly (un nīt′lē), *adj.* **1.** unworthy of a knight. **2.** not like a knight. —*adv.* **3.** in a manner unworthy of a knight. [UN-1 + KNIGHTLY] —**un·knight′li·ness,** *n.*

un·knit (un nit′), *v.,* **-knit·ted** or **-knit, -knit·ting.** —*v.t.* **1.** to untie or unfasten (a knot, tangle, etc.); unravel (something knitted); undo. **2.** to weaken, undo, or destroy. **3.** to smooth out (something wrinkled). —*v.i.* **4.** to become undone. [ME *unknytte(n),* OE *uncnyttan.* See UN-2, KNIT] —**un·knit′ta·ble,** *adj.*

un·knot (un not′), *v.t.,* **-knot·ted, -knot·ting.** to untie by or as if by undoing a knot: *to unknot a tie.* [UN-2 + KNOT]

un·know·a·ble (un nō′ə bəl), *adj.* **1.** not knowable; incapable of being known or understood; transcending human knowledge or experience. —*n.* **2.** something that is unknowable. **3. the Unknowable,** the postulated reality lying behind all phenomena but not cognizable by any of the processes by which the mind cognizes phenomenal objects; thing-in-itself. [ME; see UN-1, KNOWABLE] —**un·know′a·ble·ness, un·know′a·bil′i·ty,** *n.* —**un·know′a·bly,** *adv.*

un·know·ing (un nō′ing), *adj.* not knowing; ignorant or unaware: *unknowing aid to the enemy.* [ME; see UN-1, KNOWING] —**un·know′ing·ly,** *adv.* —**un·know′ing·ness,** *n.*

un·known (un nōn′), *adj.* **1.** not known; not within the range of one's knowledge, experience, or understanding; strange; unfamiliar. **2.** not discovered, explored, identified, or ascertained: *the unknown parts of Antarctica.* —*n.* **3.** a person, thing, influence, area, factor, etc., that is unknown: *the many unknowns in modern medicine.* **4.** *Math.* a symbol representing an unknown quantity: in algebra, analysis, etc., frequently represented by a letter from the last part of the alphabet, as *x, y,* or *z.* [ME *unknow(e)n.* See UN-1, KNOWN] —**un·known′ness,** *n.*

Unknown′ Amer′ican, either of two unidentified soldiers in the U.S. armed forces, one killed during World War II and the other in the Korean War, both buried in Arlington National Cemetery in Virginia to represent all the unidentified dead of those wars. Cf. **Unknown Soldier.**

Un′known Sea′. See **Mare Incognito.**

Un′known Sol′dier, an unidentified soldier killed in battle and buried with honors, his tomb serving as a memorial to all the unidentified dead of a nation's armed forces. The tomb of the American Unknown Soldier, killed in World War I, is located in the Arlington National Cemetery in Virginia. Also called, *Brit.,* **Un′known War′rior.** Cf. **Unknown American.**

un·lace (un lās′), *v.t.,* **-laced, -lac·ing.** **1.** to loosen or undo the lacing or laces of (a pair of boots, a corset, etc.). **2.** to loosen or remove (the garment of) by or as if by undoing laces. [ME *unlace(n).* See UN-2, LACE]

un·lade (un lād′), *v.,* **-lad·ed, -lad·ing.** —*v.t.* **1.** to take the lading, load, or cargo from; unload. **2.** to discharge (a load or cargo). —*v.i.* **3.** to discharge a load or cargo. [ME *unlade(n).* See UN-2, LADE]

un·laid (un lād′), *adj.* **1.** not laid or placed: *It was suppertime and still the table was unlaid.* **2.** (of dead bodies) not laid to rest: *The dead were still unlaid.* **3.** untwisted, as a rope. [ME *unleyd.* See UN-1, LAID]

un·lash (un lash′), *v.t.* to loosen, unfasten, or detach, as something lashed or tied fast. [UN-2 + LASH2]

un·latch (un lach′), *v.t.* **1.** to unfasten (a door, window shutter, etc.) by lifting the latch. —*v.i.* **2.** to become unlatched; open through the lifting of a latch. [UN-2 + LATCH]

un·law·ful (un lô′fəl), *adj.* **1.** not lawful; contrary to law; illegal; not sanctioned by law. **2.** born out of wedlock; illegitimate. [ME *unlaweful.* See UN-1, LAWFUL] —**un·law′ful·ly,** *adv.* —**un·law′ful·ness,** *n.*
—**Syn. 1.** illicit. **2.** bastard, natural.

un·lay (un lā′), *v.t.,* **-laid, -lay·ing.** **1.** to separate (a strand) from a rope. **2.** to untwist (a rope) in order to separate its strands. [UN-2 + LAY1]

un·lead·ed (un led′id), *adj.* not separated or spaced with leads, as lines of type or printed matter. [UN-1 + LEAD2 + -ED3]

un·learn (un lûrn′), *v.t.* **1.** to forget or lose knowledge of. **2.** to discard or put aside certain knowledge as being false or binding: *He had to unlearn his preconceptions before meeting the community on its own terms.* —*v.i.* **3.** to lose or discard knowledge: *To unlearn as a result of mental laziness is one thing, and to unlearn for the sake of learning still more is quite another.* [ME *unlerne(n).* See UN-2, LEARN]

un·learn·ed (un lûr′nid), *adj.* **1.** not learned; not scholarly or erudite. **2.** uneducated; untaught; unschooled; ignorant. **3.** not acquired by instruction, study, etc. **4.** known without being learned. **5.** of or pertaining to uneducated persons. [ME *unlerned.* See UN-1, LEARNED] —**un·learn′ed·ly,** *adv.*

un·leash (un lēsh′), *v.t.* **1.** to release from or as if from a leash; set free to pursue or run at will; set loose. **2.** to abandon control of: *It was fearful when he unleashed his fury.* [UN-2 + LEASH]

un·leav·ened (un lev′ənd), *adj.* (of bread, cake, cookies, etc.) containing no leaven or leavening agent. [UN-1 + LEAVEN + -ED3]

un·less (un les′), *conj.* **1.** except under the circumstances that: *Mankind will survive unless universal war breaks out.* —*prep.* **2.** except; but; save: *Nothing will come of it, unless disaster.* [ME *onlesse,* equiv. to *on* ON (prep.) + *lesse* LESS; orig. meaning, for less (than)]

un·les·soned (un les′ənd), *adj.* not educated or trained. [UN-1 + LESSON + -ED3]

un·let·tered (un let′ərd), *adj.* **1.** not educated; uneducated; untutored; ignorant. **2.** not literate; illiterate. **3.** not marked with letters, as a tombstone. [ME; see UN-1, LETTERED]
—**Syn.** See **ignorant.**

un·li·censed (un lī′sənst), *adj.* **1.** having no license. **2.** done or undertaken without license or permission; unauthorized. **3.** unrestrained; unbridled. [UN-1 + LICENSED]

un·like (un līk′), *adj.* **1.** different, dissimilar, or unequal; not alike: *They contributed unlike sums to charity.* —*prep.* **2.** dissimilar to; different from: *She is unlike my sister in many ways.* **3.** not typical or characteristic of: *It is unlike her to enjoy herself so much.* —*n.* **4.** a person or thing differing from another or others. [ME *unlik.* See UN-1, -LIKE] —**un·like′ness,** *n.*
—**Syn. 1.** diverse, various, heterogeneous.

un·like·li·hood (un līk′lē hŏŏd′), *n.* the state of being unlikely; improbability. [UNLIKELY + -HOOD]

un·like·ly (un līk′lē), *adj.* **1.** not likely to be or occur; improbable; marked by doubt. **2.** holding little prospect of success; unpromising; likely to fail: *He is an unlikely candidate for reelection.* **3.** not ingratiating; objectionable. —*adv.* **4.** in an unlikely way. [ME *unlikli.* See UN-1, LIKELY] —**un·like′li·ness,** *n.*

un·lim·ber (un lim′bər), *v.t.* **1.** to detach (a gun) from its limber or prime mover. **2.** to make ready for use or action. —*n.* **3.** the act of changing a gun from traveling to firing position. [UN-2 + LIMBER2]

un·lim·it·ed (un lim′i tid), *adj.* **1.** not limited; unrestricted; unconfined: *unlimited trade.* **2.** boundless; limitless; infinite; vast: *To human eyes, the heavens appear unlimited.* **3.** without any qualification or exception: *Unlimited surrender is unconditional surrender.* [ME; see UN-1, LIMITED] —**un·lim′it·ed·ly,** *adv.* —**un·lim′it·ed·ness,** *n.*
—**Syn. 1.** unconstrained, unrestrained, unfettered. **2.** unbounded, extensive.

un·link (un lingk′), *v.t.* **1.** to separate the links of (a chain, linked bracelet, watchband, etc.); unfasten. **2.** to detach or separate by or as if by undoing one or more connecting links: *to unlink hands; to unlink a string of boxcars.* —*v.i.* **3.** to become detached. [UN-2 + LINK2]

un·list·ed (un lis′tid), *adj.* **1.** not listed; not entered in a list: *an unlisted telephone number.* **2.** (of a security) not admitted to trading privileges on an exchange. [UN-1 + LIST1 + -ED2]

un·live (un liv′), *v.t.,* **-lived, -liv·ing.** **1.** to undo or annul (past life, experiences, etc.). **2.** to live so as to undo the consequences of: *He wishes to unlive the crimes he has committed.* [UN-2 + LIVE1]

un·load (un lōd′), *v.t.* **1.** to take the load from; remove the cargo or freight from: *to unload a truck; to unload a cart.* **2.** to remove or discharge (a load, group of people, etc.): *The ship unloaded its passengers an hour after docking.* **3.** to remove the charge from (a firearm). **4.** to relieve of anything burdensome, oppressive, etc.: *He unloaded his responsibilities as quickly as possible.* **5.** to get rid of (shares of stock or the like) by sale in large quantities. —*v.i.* **6.** to unload something. [UN-2 + LOAD] —**un·load′er,** *n.*

un·lock (un lok′), *v.t.* **1.** to undo the lock of (a door, chest, etc.), esp. with a key: *He unlocked the door and*

---

un·jeered′, *adj.*
un·jeer′ing, *adj.*
un·jelled′, *adj.*
un·jel′lied, *adj.*
un·jeop′ard·ised′, *adj.*
un·jeop′ard·ized′, *adj.*
un·jest′ing, *adj.;* **-ly,** *adv.*
un′-Je·su·it′ic, *adj.*
un′-Je·su·it′i·cal, *adj.;* **-ly,** *adv.*
un·jew′eled, *adj.*
un·jew′elled, *adj.*
un·jilt′ed, *adj.*
un′jo·cose′, *adj.;* **-ly,** *adv.;* **-ness,** *n.*
un·joc′und, *adj.*
un·jogged′, *adj.*
un·jog′ging, *adj.*
un·join′, *v.*
un·join′a·ble, *adj.*
un·join′tured, *adj.*
un·jok′ing, *adj.;* **-ly,** *adv.*
un·jol′ly, *adj.*
un·jolt′ed, *adj.*
un·jos′tled, *adj.*
un′jour·nal·is′tic, *adj.*
un·jour′nal·ized′, *adj.*
un·jo′vi·al, *adj.;* **-ly,** *adv.*
un·joyed′, *adj.*
un·joy′ful, *adj.;* **-ly,** *adv.*
un·joy′ous, *adj.;* **-ly,** *adv.*
un·ju′bi·lant, *adj.;* **-ly,** *adv.*
un·judg′a·ble, *adj.*
un·judge′a·ble, *adj.*
un·judged′, *adj.*
un·judge′like′, *adj.*
un·judg′ing, *adj.*
un·ju′di·ca·ble, *adj.*
un·ju′di·ca′tive, *adj.*
un′ju·di′ci·a·ble, *adj.*
un′ju·di′cial, *adj.;* **-ly,** *adv.*
un·jug′gled, *adj.*
un·juic′i·ly, *adv.*
un·juic′y, *adj.*
un·jum′bled, *adj.*
un·jump′a·ble, *adj.*
un′ju·rid′ic, *adj.*
un′ju·rid′i·cal, *adj.;* **-ly,** *adv.*
un·jus′ti·fi′a·ble, *adj.;* **-ble·ness,** *n.;* **-bly,** *adv.*
un·jus′ti·fied′, *adj.*
un·ju′ve·nile, *adj.;* **-ly,** *adv.;* **-ness,** *n.*
un·keeled′, *adj.*
un·kept′, *adj.*
un·keyed′, *adj.*
un·kid′naped, *adj.*
un·kid′napped, *adj.*
un·killed′, *adj.*
un·kill′ing, *adj.*
un·kilned′, *adj.*
un·kind′heart′ed, *adj.*
un·kin′dled, *adj.*
un·kin′dling, *adj.*
un·kinged′, *adj.*
un·king′like′, *adj.*
un·king′ly, *adj., adv.*
un·kink′, *v.*
un·kissed′, *adj.*
un·knead′ed, *adj.*
un·kneel′ing, *adj.*
un·knelled′, *adj.*
un·knight′ed, *adj.*
un·knocked′, *adj.*
un·knock′ing, *adj.*
un·knot′ty, *adj.*
un·knowl′edge·a·ble, *adj.*
un·la′beled, *adj.*
un·la′belled, *adj.*
un·la′bi·al·ise′, *v.t.,* **-ised, -is·ing.**
un·la′bi·al·ize′, *v.t.,* **-ized, -iz·ing.**
un·la′bi·ate′, *adj.*
un·la′bored, *adj.*
un·la′bor·ing, *adj.*
un′la·bo′ri·ous, *adj.;* **-ly,** *adv.;* **-ness,** *n.*
un·la′boured, *adj.*
un·la′bour·ing, *adj.*
un·lac′er·at′ed, *adj.*
un·lac′er·at′ing, *adj.*
un·lack′eyed, *adj.*
un′la·con′ic, *adj.*
un·lac′quered, *adj.*
un·la′den, *adj.*
un·la′dled, *adj.*
un·lag′ging, *adj.*
un·lame′, *adj.*
un·lamed′, *adj.*
un·lam′en·ta·ble, *adj.*
un′la·ment′ed, *adj.*
un·lam′i·nat′ed, *adj.*
un′lam·pooned′, *adj.*
un·lanced′, *adj.*
un·land′ed, *adj.*
un·land′marked′, *adj.*
un·lan′guid, *adj.;* **-ly,** *adv.;* **-ness,** *n.*
un·lan′guish·ing, *adj.*
un·lan′terned, *adj.*
un·lapped′, *adj.*
un·lapsed′, *adj.*
un·laps′ing, *adj.*
un·lar′ce·nous, *adj.;* **-ly,** *adv.*
un·lard′ed, *adj.*
un·large′, *adj.*
un·las′soed, *adj.*
un·last′ing, *adj.*
un·lath′ered, *adj.*
un·Lat′in·ised, *adj.*
un·Lat′in·ized′, *adj.*
un·lat′ticed, *adj.*
un·laud′a·ble, *adj.;* **-ble·ness,** *n.;* **-bly,** *adv.*
un·laud′a·tive, *adj.*
un·laud′a·to′ry, *adj.*
un·laud′ed, *adj.*
un·laugh′ing, *adj.*
un·launched′, *adj.*
un·laun′dered, *adj.*
un·lau′reled, *adj.*
un·lau′relled, *adj.*
un·laved′, *adj.*
un·lav′ing, *adj.*
un·lav′ish, *adj.*
un·lav′ished, *adj.*
un·law′yer·like, *adj.*
un·lay′a·ble, *adj.*
un·leached′, *adj.*
un·leaf′, *v.t.*
un·leaf′like′, *adj.*
un·leak′a·ble, *adj.*
un·leak′y, *adj.*
un·lean′, *adj.*
un·learn′ing, *adj.*
un·leas′a·ble, *adj.*
un·leased′, *adj.*
un·leath′ered, *adj.*
un·leaved′, *adj.*
un·leav′en·a·ble, *adj.*
un·lech′er·ous, *adj.;* **-ly,** *adv.;* **-ness,** *n.*
un·lec′tured, *adj.*
un·led′, *adj.*
un·ledged′, *adj.*
un·left′, *adj.*
un·le′gal, *adj.;* **-ly,** *adv.;* **-ness,** *n.*
un·le′gal·ised′, *adj.*
un·le′gal·ized′, *adj.*
un·leg′i·ble, *adj.*
un·leg′is·lat′ed, *adj.*
un·leg′is·la′tive, *adj.;* **-ly,** *adv.*
un·lei′sured, *adj.*
un·lei′sure·ly, *adj.*
un·length′ened, *adj.*
un·le′ni·ent, *adj.;* **-ly,** *adv.*
un·lensed′, *adj.*
un·lent′, *adj.*
un·les′sened, *adj.*
un·let′, *adj.*
un·le′thal, *adj.;* **-ly,** *adv.*
un′le·thar′gic, *adj.*
un′le·thar′gi·cal, *adj.;* **-ly,** *adv.*
un·lev′el, *adj.;* **-ly,** *adv.;* **-ness,** *n.*
un·lev′eled, *adj.*
un·lev′elled, *adj.*
un·lev′i·a·ble, *adj.*
un·lev′ied, *adj.*
un·lev′i·gat′ed, *adj.*
un′lex·i·co·graph′i·cal, *adj.;* **-ly,** *adv.*
un·li′a·ble, *adj.*
un·li′beled, *adj.*
un·li′belled, *adj.*
un·li′bel·ous, *adj.;* **-ly,** *adv.*
un·li′bel·lous, *adj.;* **-ly,** *adv.*
un·lib′er·al, *adj.;* **-ly,** *adv.*
un·lib′er·al·ised′, *adj.*
un·lib′er·al·ized′, *adj.*
un·lib′er·at′ed, *adj.*
un′li·bid′i·nous, *adj.;* **-ly,** *adv.*
un′li·cen′ti·at′ed, *adj.*
un′li·cen′tious, *adj.;* **-ly,** *adv.;* **-ness,** *n.*
un·li′chened, *adj.*
un·lid′ded, *adj.*
un·life′like′, *adj.*
un·lift′a·ble, *adj.*
un·lift′ed, *adj.*
un·lift′ing, *adj.*
un·lig′a·tured, *adj.*
un·light′, *adj.*
un·light′ed, *adj.*
un·light′ened, *adj.*
un·lig′ni·fied′, *adj.*
un·lik′a·ble, *adj.;* **-ble·ness,** *n.;* **-bly,** *adv.*
un·like′a·ble, *adj.;* **-ble·ness,** *n.;* **-bly,** *adv.*
un·liked′, *adj.*
un·lik′ened, *adj.*
un·limed′, *adj.*
un·limned′, *adj.*
un·limp′, *adj.*
un·lin′e·al, *adj.*
un·lined′, *adj.*
un·lin′ger·ing, *adj.*
un·li′on·ised′, *adj.*
un·li′on·ized′, *adj.*
un·liq′ue·fi′a·ble, *adj.*
un·liq′ue·fied′, *adj.*
un′li·ques′cent, *adj.*
un·liq′uid, *adj.*
un·liq′ui·dat′ed, *adj.*
un·liq′ui·dat′ing, *adj.*
un·lisp′ing, *adj.*
un·lis′ten·ing, *adj.*
un·lit′, *adj.*
un·lit′er·al, *adj.;* **-ly,** *adv.*
un·lit′er·al·ised′, *adj.*
un·lit′er·al·ized′, *adj.*
un·lit′er·ar′y, *adj.*
un·lit′er·ate, *adj.*
un′lith·o·graph′ic, *adj.*
un·lit′i·gat′ed, *adj.*
un·lit′i·gat′ing, *adj.*
un·li·ti′gious, *adj.;* **-ly,** *adv.;* **-ness,** *n.*
un·lit′tered, *adj.*
un·liv′a·ble, *adj.;* **-ble·ness,** *n.*
un·live′a·ble, *adj.;* **-ble·ness,** *n.*
un·live′li·ness, *n.*
un·live′ly, *adj., adv.*
un·liv′er·ied, *adj.*
un·liv′ing, *adj.*
un·loaf′ing, *adj.*
un·loaned′, *adj.*
un·loan′ing, *adj.*
un·loath′, *adj.;* **-ly,** *adv.*
un·loathed′, *adj.*
un·loath′ful, *adj.*
un·loath′some, *adj.*
un·lob′bied, *adj.*
un·lob′by·ing, *adj.*
un·lobed′, *adj.*
un·lo′cal, *adj.;* **-ly,** *adv.*
un·lo′cal·is′a·ble, *adj.*
un·lo′cal·ise′, *v.t.,* **-ised, -is·ing.**
un·lo′cal·iz′a·ble, *adj.*
un·lo′cal·ize′, *v.t.,* **-ized, -iz·ing.**
un·lo′cat·ed, *adj.*
un·loc′a·tive, *adj.*
un′lo·co·mo′tive, *adj.*
un·lodged′, *adj.*
un·loft′y, *adj.*

stepped into the room. **2.** to open or release by or as if by undoing a lock. **3.** to open (anything firmly closed or joined): *to unlock the jaws.* **4.** to lay open; disclose: *She unlocked the secrets of her heart.* —*v.i.* **5.** to become unlocked. [UN-[2] + LOCK[1]] —**un·lock′a·ble,** *adj.*

un·looked (un lo͝okt′), *adj.* not examined, investigated, or heeded (usually fol. by *into, on,* or *at*): *a crime which remains unlooked into.* [UN-[1] + LOOK + -ED[2]]

un·looked-for (un lo͝okt′fôr′), *adj.* not expected, anticipated, or foreseen: *He was confronted with an unlooked-for situation.*

un·loose (un lo͞os′), *v.t.,* **-loosed, -loos·ing. 1.** to loosen or relax (the grasp, hold, fingers, etc.). **2.** to let loose or set free; release from bonds, shackles, fastenings, etc.; free from restraint. **3.** to undo or untie (a fastening, knot, etc.); unfasten. [ME *unloosen;* see UN-[2], LOOSE] —**un·loos′a·ble,** *adj.* —**un·loos′a·bly,** *adv.*

un·loos·en (un lo͞o′sən), *v.t.* to unloose; loosen. [ME *unlosnen;* see UN-[2], LOOSEN]

un·love·ly (un luv′lē), *adj.* **1.** not lovely; without beauty or charm; failing to please the senses. **2.** unattractive, unbecoming, harsh, or repellent in character; unpleasant; disagreeable; objectionable. [ME; see UN-[1], LOVELY] —**un·love′li·ness,** *n.*

un·luck·y (un luk′ē), *adj.,* **-luck·i·er, -luck·i·est. 1.** (of a person) not lucky; lacking good fortune; ill-fated. **2.** (of an event or circumstance) inauspicious; ominous. [UN-[1] + LUCKY] —**un·luck′i·ly,** *adv.* —**un·luck′i·ness,** *n.*
—**Syn.** hapless, unsuccessful, ill-omened.

un·made (un mād′), *adj.* **1.** not made. **2.** *Falconry.* unmanned (def. 2). [ME; see UN-[1], MADE]

un·make (un māk′), *v.t.,* **-made, -mak·ing. 1.** to cause to be as if never made; reduce to the original elements or condition; undo; take to pieces; destroy; ruin. **2.** to depose from office or authority; demote in rank. **3.** to change the essential point of (a book, play, etc.). **4.** to alter the opinion of (one's mind). **5.** to change or alter the character of. [ME *unmake(n).* See UN-[2], MAKE] —**un·mak′a·ble,** *adj.* —**un·mak′er,** *n.*

un·man (un man′), *v.t.,* **-manned -man·ning. 1.** to deprive of courage or fortitude; break down the manly spirit of: *Constant conflict finally unmanned him.* **2.** to deprive of virility; emasculate; castrate. **3.** *Archaic.* to deprive of the character of man. [UN-[2] + MAN]

un·man·ly (un man′lē), *adj.* **1.** not manly; not characteristic of or befitting a man; weak, timid, or cowardly. **2.** womanish; effeminate. —*adv.* **3.** *Archaic.* in an unmanly manner. [ME; see UN-[1], MANLY] —**un·man′li·ness,** *n.*

un·manned (un mand′), *adj.* **1.** without the physical presence of men in control: *an unmanned aircraft guided by remote control.* **2.** *Falconry.* (of a captured hawk) untrained for hunting with a master; unmade. [UN-[1] + MANNED]

un·man·nered (un man′ərd), *adj.* **1.** lacking good manners; rude or ill-bred. **2.** without affectation or insincerity; ingenuous: *He is a refreshingly unmannered person.* [UN-[1] + MANNERED]

un·man·ner·ly (un man′ər lē), *adj.* **1.** not mannerly; impolite; discourteous; coarse. —*adv.* **2.** *Archaic.* with ill manners. [ME: see UN-[1], MANNERLY] —**un·man′ner·li·ness,** *n.*

un·marked (un märkt′), *adj.* **1.** not marked. **2.** *Ling.* **a.** characterized by the absence of a feature that distinguishes the members of a minimal pair, as in /pâr/ and /bâr/. The first is the unmarked member because voice is lacking in the first phoneme. Cf. **marked** (def. 4a). **b.** characterized by the absence of a marker. [ME; see UN-[1], MARKED]

un·mask (un mask′, -mäsk′), *v.t.* **1.** to strip a mask or disguise from. **2.** to reveal the true character of; disclose; expose. **3.** *Mil.* to reveal the presence of (guns) by firing. —*v.i.* **4.** to put off one's mask; appear in true nature. [UN-[2] + MASK] —**un·mask′er,** *n.*

un·mean·ing (un mē′ning), *adj.* **1.** not meaning anything; devoid of intelligence, sense, or significance, as words or actions; pointless; empty. **2.** expressionless, vacant, or unintelligent, as the face; insipid. [UN-[1] + MEANING] —**un·mean′ing·ly,** *adv.* —**un·mean′ing·ness,** *n.*

un·mean·ing·ful (un mē′ning fəl), *adj.* not meaningful; without significance. [UN-[1] + MEANINGFUL] —**un·mean′ing·ful·ly,** *adv.* —**un·mean′ing·ful·ness,** *n.*

un·meas·ured (un mezh′ərd), *adj.* **1.** of undetermined or indefinitely great extent or amount; unlimited; measureless: *the unmeasured heavens.* **2.** unrestrained; intemperate: *unmeasured rage.* **3.** *Pros.* not metrical. [ME *unmesured.* See UN-[1], MEASURED] —**un·meas′ur·a·ble,** *adj.* —**un·meas′ur·a·ble·ness,** *n.* —**un·meas′ur·a·bly,** *adv.* —**un·meas′ured·ly,** *adv.* —**un·meas′ured·ness,** *n.*
—**Syn. 1.** immense, vast. **2.** unstinting, lavish; uncontrolled.

un·meet (un mēt′), *adj.* not meet; not fitting, suitable, or proper; not becoming or seemly. [ME *unmete,* OE *unmǣte.* See UN-[1], MEET[2]] —**un·meet′a·ble,** *adj.* —**un·meet′ly,** *adv.* —**un·meet′ness,** *n.*

un·men·tion·a·ble (un men′shə nə bəl), *adj.* **1.** not mentionable; inappropriate, unfit, or improper for mention, as in polite conversation; unspeakable. —*n.* **2.** something that is not to be mentioned: *That subject was classed among the unmentionables.* **3. unmentionables, a.** trousers or breeches. **b.** *Facetious.* undergarments. [UN-[1] + MENTIONABLE] —**un·men′tion·a·ble·ness,** *n.*

un·mer·ci·ful (un mûr′si fəl), *adj.* **1.** merciless; relentless; severe; cruel; unconscionable; pitiless. **2.** unsparingly great, extreme, or excessive, as amounts: *She talked for an unmerciful length of time.* [UN-[1] + MERCIFUL] —**un·mer′ci·ful·ly,** *adv.* —**un·mer′ci·ful·ness,** *n.*

un·mer·i·ta·ble (un mer′i tə bəl), *adj.* not worthy or deserving of merit. [UN-[1] + MERIT + -ABLE] —**un·mer′i·ta·bil′i·ty,** *n.*

un·mer·it·ing (un mer′i ting), *adj.* not meriting; unearned; undeserving. [UN-[1] + MERIT + -ING[2]]

un·mew (un myo͞o′), *v.t.* to set free (something mewed up); release, as from confinement. [UN-[2] + MEW[3]]

un·mind·ful (un mīnd′fəl), *adj.* not mindful; unaware; heedless; forgetful; careless; neglectful: *He was unmindful of his obligations.* [ME *unmyndeful.* See UN-[1], MINDFUL] —**un·mind′ful·ly,** *adv.* —**un·mind′ful·ness,** *n.*
—**Syn.** inattentive, negligent, unobservant.

un·logged′, *adj.*
un·log′i·cal, *adj.;* **-ly,** *adv.*
un′lo·gis′tic, *adj.*
un′lo·gis′ti·cal, *adj.*
un·lone′ly, *adj.*
un·longed′-for′, *adj.*
un·loop′, *v.t.*
un·loot′ed, *adj.*
un·lopped′, *adj.*
un′lo·qua′cious, *adj.;* **-ly,** *adv.*
un·los′a·ble, *adj.*
un·lost′, *adj.*
un·lot′ted, *adj.*
un·loud′ly, *adv.*
un·loung′ing, *adj.*
un·lov′a·ble, *adj.;* **-ble·ness,** *n.;* **-bly,** *adv.*
un·love′a·ble, *adj.;* **-ble·ness,** *n.;* **-bly,** *adv.*
un·loved′, *adj.*
un·lov′ing, *adj.*
un·low′ered, *adj.*
un·low′ly, *adj.*
un·loy′al, *adj.;* **-ly,** *adv.*
un·loy′al·ty, *n.*
un·lu′bri·cant, *adj.*
un·lu′bri·cat′ed, *adj.*
un·lu′bri·cat′ing, *adj.*
un·lu′bri·ca′tive, *adj.*
un′lu·bri′cious, *adj.*
un·lu′cent, *adj.*
un·lu′cid, *adj.;* **-ly,** *adv.;* **-ness,** *n.*
un·lu′cra·tive, *adj.*
un·lu′di·crous, *adj.;* **-ly,** *adv.;* **-ness,** *n.*
un·luffed′, *adj.*
un·lugged′, *adj.*
un′lu·gu′bri·ous, *adj.;* **-ly,** *adv.;* **-ness,** *n.*
un·lum′ber·ing, *adj.*
un′lu·mi·nes′cent, *adj.*
un′lu·mi·nif′er·ous, *adj.*
un·lu′mi·nous, *adj.;* **-ly,** *adv.;* **-ness,** *n.*
un·lumped′, *adj.*
un·lump′y, *adj.*
un·lu′nar, *adj.*
un·lu′nate, *adj.*
un·lu′nat·ed, *adj.*
un·lured′, *adj.*
un·lurk′ing, *adj.*
un·lush′, *adj.*
un·lust′ing, *adj.*
un·lus′tered, *adj.*
un·lus′tred, *adj.*
un·lust′ful, *adj.;* **-ly,** *adv.*
un·lus′trous, *adj.;* **-ly,** *adv.*
un·lust′y, *adj.*
un·lux′at·ed, *adj.*
un′lux·u′ri·ant, *adj.;* **-ly,** *adv.*
un′lux·u′ri·at′ing, *adj.*
un′lux·u′ri·ous, *adj.;* **-ly,** *adv.*
un·ly′ing, *adj.*
un·lyr′ic, *adj.*
un·lyr′i·cal, *adj.;* **-ly,** *adv.;* **-ness,** *n.*
un·mac′ad·am·ized′, *adj.*
un·mac′er·at′ed, *adj.*
un′ma·chin′a·ble, *adj.*
un·mach′i·nat′ed, *adj.*
un·mach′i·nat′ing, *adj.*
un′ma·chine′a·ble, *adj.*
un′ma·chined′, *adj.*
un·mad′, *adj.*
un·mad′ded, *adj.*
un·mad′dened, *adj.*
un·mag′i·cal, *adj.;* **-ly,** *adv.*
un′mag·is·te′ri·al, *adj.*
un′mag·nan′i·mous, *adj.;* **-ly,** *adv.;* **-ness,** *n.*
un′mag·net′ic, *adj.*
un′mag·net′i·cal, *adj.*
un·mag′net·ised′, *adj.*
un·mag′net·ized′, *adj.*
un·mag′ni·fied′, *adj.*
un·mag′ni·fy′ing, *adj.*
un·maid′en·like′, *adj.*
un·maid′en·li·ness, *n.*
un·maid′en·ly, *adj.*
un·mail′a·ble, *adj.*
un·mailed′, *adj.*
un·maim′a·ble, *adj.*
un·maimed′, *adj.*
un′main·tain′a·ble, *adj.*
un′main·tained′, *adj.*
un′ma·jes′tic, *adj.*
un′ma·jes′ti·cal·ly, *adv.*
un′ma·lar′i·al, *adj.*
un′mal·e·dic′tive, *adj.*
un′mal·e·dic′to·ry, *adj.*
un′ma·lev′o·lent, *adj.;* **-ly,** *adv.*
un′ma·li′cious, *adj.;* **-ly,** *adv.*
un′ma·lig′nant, *adj.;* **-ly,** *adv.*
un′ma·ligned′, *adj.*
un·mal′le·a·bil′i·ty, *n.*
un·mal′le·a·ble, *adj.*
un·malt′a·ble, *adj.*
un·malt′ed, *adj.*
un′mam·ma′li·an, *adj.*
un·man′a·cled, *adj.*
un·man′age·a·ble, *adj.;* **-ble·ness,** *n.;* **-bly,** *adv.*
un·man′aged, *adj.*
un·man′dat·ed, *adj.*
un·man′da·to′ry, *adj.*
un·maned′, *adj.*
un′ma·neu′vered, *adj.*
un·man′ful, *adj.;* **-ly,** *adv.;* **-ness,** *n.*
un·man′gled, *adj.*
un′ma·ni′a·cal, *adj.;* **-ly,** *adv.*
un·man′i·cured′, *adj.*
un·man′i·fest′, *adj.*
un′man·i·fes′ta·tive, *adj.*
un·man′i·fest′ed, *adj.*
un′ma·nip′u·la·ble, *adj.*
un′ma·nip′u·lat′a·ble, *adj.*
un′ma·nip′u·lat′ed, *adj.*
un′ma·nip′u·la′tive, *adj.*
un′ma·nip′u·la·to′ry, *adj.*
un·man′nish, *adj.;* **-ly,** *adv.;* **-ness,** *n.*
un′ma·noeu′vred, *adj.*
un·man′tled, *adj.*
un·man′u·al, *adj.;* **-ly,** *adv.*
un′man·u·fac′tur·a·ble, *adj.*
un′man·u·fac′tured, *adj.*
un′man·u·mit′ted, *adj.*
un′ma·nur′a·ble, *adj.*
un·map′pa·ble, *adj.*
un·mar′bel·ize′, *v.t.,* **-ized, -iz·ing.**
un·mar′bled, *adj.*
un·mar′ble·ize′, *v.t.,* **-ized, -iz·ing.**
un·march′ing, *adj.*
un·mar′gin·al, *adj.;* **-ly,** *adv.*
un·mar′gin·at′ed, *adj.*
un′ma·rine′, *adj.*
un·mar′i·time′, *adj.*
un·mark′a·ble, *adj.*
un·mar′ket·a·ble, *adj.*
un·mar′ket·ed, *adj.*
un·marled′, *adj.*
un·marred′, *adj.*
un·mar′riage·a·ble, *adj.*
un·mar′ried, *adj.*
un·mar′ring, *adj.*
un·mar′ry·ing, *adj.*
un·mar′shaled, *adj.*
un·mar′shalled, *adj.*
un·mar′tial, *adj.*
un·mar′tyred, *adj.*
un·mar′vel·lous, *adj.;* **-ly,** *adv.;* **-ness,** *n.*
un·mar′vel·ous, *adj.;* **-ly,** *adv.;* **-ness,** *n.*
un·mas′cu·line, *adj.;* **-ly,** *adv.*
un·mashed′, *adj.*
un·masked′, *adj.*
un·mask′ing, *adj.*
un·mas′sa·cred, *adj.*
un·massed′, *adj.*
un·mast′, *v.t.*
un·mas′ter·a·ble, *adj.*
un·mas′tered, *adj.*
un·mas′ter·ful, *adj.;* **-ly,** *adv.*
un·mas′ti·cat′ed, *adj.*
un·mas′ti·ca·to′ry, *adj.*
un·match′a·ble, *adj.*
un·matched′, *adj.*
un·match′ing, *adj.*
un·mate′, *v.t.,* **-mat·ed, -mat·ing.**
un′ma·te′ri·al, *adj.;* **-ly,** *adv.*
un′ma·te′ri·al·is′tic, *adj.*
un′ma·te′ri·al·is′ti·cal·ly, *adv.*
un′ma·te′ri·al·ised′, *adj.*
un′ma·te′ri·al·ized′, *adj.*
un′ma·ter′nal, *adj.;* **-ly,** *adv.*
un′math·e·mat′i·cal, *adj.;* **-ly,** *adv.*
un·mat′ing, *adj.*
un′ma·tric′u·lat′ed, *adj.*
un′mat·ri·mo′ni·al, *adj.;* **-ly,** *adv.*
un·mat′ted, *adj.*
un′ma·tur′a·tive, *adj.*
un′ma·ture′, *adj.;* **-ly,** *adv.*
un′ma·tured′, *adj.*
un′ma·tur′ing, *adj.*
un·maud′lin, *adj.;* **-ly,** *adv.*
un·mauled′, *adj.*
un′me·an′der·ing, *adj.;* **-ly,** *adv.*
un·meant′, *adj.*
un′me·chan′i·cal, *adj.;* **-ly,** *adv.*
un′mech·a·nis′tic, *adj.*
un·mech′a·nised′, *adj.*
un·mech′a·nized′, *adj.*
un·med′aled, *adj.*
un·med′alled, *adj.*
un·med′dled, *adj.*
un·med′dle·some, *adj.*
un·med′dling, *adj.;* **-ly,** *adv.*
un′me·di·ae′val, *adj.*
un·me′di·at′ed, *adj.*
un·me′di·at′ing, *adj.*
un·me′di·a′tive, *adj.*
un·med′i·ca·ble, *adj.*
un·med′i·cal, *adj.;* **-ly,** *adv.*
un·med′i·cat′ed, *adj.*
un·med′i·ca′tive, *adj.*
un′me·dic′i·nal, *adj.;* **-ly,** *adv.*
un′me·di·e′val, *adj.*
un·med′i·tat′ed, *adj.*
un·med′i·tat′ing, *adj.*
un·med′i·ta′tive, *adj.;* **-ly,** *adv.*
un′mel·an·chol′ic, *adj.*
un′mel·an·chol′i·cal·ly, *adv.*
un·mel′an·chol′y, *adj.*
un·mel′io·rat′ed, *adj.*
un′mel·lif′lu·ent, *adj.;* **-ly,** *adv.*
un′mel·lif′lu·ous, *adj.;* **-ly,** *adv.*
un·mel′low, *adj.*
un·mel′lowed, *adj.*
un′me·lod′ic, *adj.*
un′me·lod′i·cal·ly, *adv.*
un′me·lo′di·ous, *adj.;* **-ly,** *adv.;* **-ness,** *n.*
un·mel′o·dised′, *adj.*
un·mel′o·dized′, *adj.*
un′mel·o·dra·mat′ic, *adj.*
un′mel·o·dra·mat′i·cal·ly, *adv.*
un·melt′a·ble, *adj.*
un·melt′ed, *adj.*
un·melt′ing, *adj.*
un·mem′or·a·ble, *adj.*
un′me·mo′ri·al·ised′, *adj.*
un′me·mo′ri·al·ized′, *adj.*
un·mem′o·ried, *adj.*
un·men′aced, *adj.*
un·men′ac·ing, *adj.*
un·mend′a·ble, *adj.*
un′men·da′cious, *adj.;* **-ly,** *adv.*
un·mend′ed, *adj.*
un·me′ni·al, *adj.;* **-ly,** *adv.*
un·men′stru·at′ing, *adj.*
un·men′sur·a·ble, *adj.*
un·men′tal, *adj.;* **-ly,** *adv.*
un·men′tho·lat′ed, *adj.*
un·men′tioned, *adj.*
un·mer′can·tile, *adj.*
un·mer′ce·nar′i·ly, *adv.*
un·mer′ce·nar′i·ness, *n.*
un·mer′ce·nar′y, *adj.*
un·mer′cer·ized′, *adj.*
un·mer′chan·dised′, *adj.*
un·mer′chant·a·ble, *adj.*
un·mer′chant·ly, *adj., adv.*
un′mer·cur′i·al, *adj.;* **-ly,** *adv.;* **-ness,** *n.*
un′mer·e·tri′cious, *adj.;* **-ly,** *adv.;* **-ness,** *n.*
un·merge′, *v.t.,* **-merged, -merg·ing.**
un′me·rid′i·o·nal, *adj.;* **-ly,** *adv.*
un′me·ringued′, *adj.*
un·mer′it·ed, *adj.;* **-ly,** *adv.*
un′mer·i·to′ri·ous, *adj.;* **-ly,** *adv.;* **-ness,** *n.*
un·mer′ri·ly, *adv.*
un·mer′ry, *adj.*
un·mesh′, *v.t.*
un′mes·mer′ic, *adj.*
un′mes·mer′i·cal·ly, *adv.*
un·mes′mer·ised′, *adj.*
un·mes′mer·ized′, *adj.*
un·met′, *adj.*
un·met′aled, *adj.*
un·met′al·ised′, *adj.*
un·met′al·ized′, *adj.*
un·met′alled, *adj.*
un′me·tal′lic, *adj.*
un′me·tal′li·cal·ly, *adv.*
un′met·al·lur′gic, *adj.*
un′met·al·lur′gi·cal, *adj.;* **-ly,** *adv.*
un′met·a·mor′phic, *adj.*
un′met·a·mor′phosed, *adj.*
un′met·a·phys′ic, *adj.*
un′met·a·phys′i·cal, *adj.;* **-ly,** *adv.*
un·met′ed, *adj.*
un′me·te·or·o·log′ic, *adj.*
un′me·te·or·o·log′i·cal, *adj.;* **-ly,** *adv.*
un·me′tered, *adj.*
un′me·thod′ic, *adj.*
un′me·thod′i·cal, *adj.;* **-ly,** *adv.;* **-ness,** *n.*
un·meth′od·ised′, *adj.*
un·meth′od·ized′, *adj.*
un·meth′od·is′ing, *adj.*
un·meth′od·iz′ing, *adj.*
un·meth′yl·at′ed, *adj.*
un′me·tic′u·lous, *adj.;* **-ly,** *adv.;* **-ness,** *n.*
un·me′tred, *adj.*
un·met′ric, *adj.*
un·met′ri·cal, *adj.;* **-ly,** *adv.*
un·met′ri·fied′, *adj.*
un′met·ro·pol′i·tan, *adj.*
un′mi·as′mal, *adj.*
un′mi·as·mat′ic, *adj.*
un′mi·as·mat′i·cal, *adj.*
un′mi·as′mic, *adj.*
un′mi·ca′ceous, *adj.*
un′mi·cro′bi·al, *adj.*
un′mi·cro′bic, *adj.*
un′mi·cro·scop′ic, *adj.*
un′mi·cro·scop′i·cal·ly, *adv.*
un·mi′grant, *adj.*
un·mi′grat·ing, *adj.*
un·mi′gra·tive, *adj.*
un·mi′gra·to′ry, *adj.*
un·mil′dewed′, *adj.*
un·mil′i·tant, *adj.;* **-ly,** *adv.*
un′mil·i·ta·ris′tic, *adj.*
un′mil·i·ta·ris′ti·cal·ly, *adv.*
un·mil′i·ta·rised′, *adj.*
un·mil′i·ta·rized′, *adj.*
un·mil′i·tar′y, *adj.*
un·milked′, *adj.*
un·milled′, *adj.*
un·milt′ed, *adj.*
un·mim′e·o·graphed′, *adj.*
un′mi·met′ic, *adj.*
un′mi·met′i·cal·ly, *adv.*
un·mim′icked, *adj.*
un·minced′, *adj.*
un·minc′ing, *adj.*
un·mind′ing, *adj.*
un·mined′, *adj.*
un·min′er·al·ised′, *adj.*
un·min′er·al·ized′, *adj.*
un·min′gled, *adj.*
un·min′i·mised′, *adj.*
un·min′i·mized′, *adj.*
un·min′i·mis′ing, *adj.*
un·min′i·miz′ing, *adj.*
un·min′is·tered, *adj.*
un′min·is·te′ri·al, *adj.;* **-ly,** *adv.*
un·min′is·trant, *adj.*
un·min′is·tra′tive, *adj.*
un·mint′ed, *adj.*
un·min′ut·ed, *adj.*
un·mir′a·cled, *adj.*
un′mi·rac′u·lous, *adj.;* **-ly,** *adv.*
un·mired′, *adj.*
un·mir′rored, *adj.*
un·mirth′ful, *adj.;* **-ly,** *adv.*
un·mir′y, *adj.*
un′mis·an·throp′ic, *adj.*
un′mis·an·throp′i·cal, *adj.;* **-ly,** *adv.*
un·mis′chie·vous, *adj.;* **-ly,** *adv.*
un·mis′ci·ble, *adj.*
un·mi′ser·ly, *adj.*
un·mis·giv′ing, *adj.;* **-ly,** *adv.*
un′mis·guid′ed, *adj.;* **-ly,** *adv.*
un′mis·in·ter′pret·a·ble, *adj.*

un·mis·tak·a·ble (un′mi stā′kə bəl), *adj.* not mistakable; clear; evident; obvious. [UN-[1] + MISTAKABLE] —**un′mis·tak′a·ble·ness,** *n.* —**un′mis·tak′a·bly,** *adv.*

un·mi·ter (un mī′tər), *v.t.* to deprive of a miter; depose from the rank of a bishop. [UN-[2] + MITER]

un·mit·i·gat·ed (un mit′ə gā′tid), *adj.* **1.** not mitigated; not softened or lessened: *unmitigated suffering.* **2.** unqualified or absolute: *an unmitigated cad.* [UN-[1] + MITIGATED] —**un·mit′i·gat′ed·ly,** *adv.*

un·mi·tre (un mī′tər), *v.t.,* **-tred, -tring.** *Chiefly Brit.* unmiter.

un·mixed (un mikst′), *adj.* not mixed; pure: *an unmixed breed of cattle; unmixed joy.* Also, **un·mixt′.** [UN-[1] + MIXED] —**un·mix·ed·ly** (un mik′sid lē, -mikst′lē), *adv.* —**un·mix′ed·ness,** *n.*

un·mold (un mōld′), *v.t.* **1.** to destroy the mold or shape of. **2.** to take out of a mold: *to unmold a gelatin dessert.* Also, *esp. Brit.,* **un·mould′.** [UN-[2] + MOLD[1]] —**un·mold′a·ble;** *esp. Brit.,* **un·mould′a·ble,** *adj.*

un·moor (un mo͝or′), *v.t.* **1.** to loose (a vessel) from moorings or anchorage. **2.** to bring to the state of riding with a single anchor after being moored by two or more. —*v.i.* **3.** (of a vessel) to become unmoored. [ME *unmoor(en).* See UN-[2], MOOR[2]]

un·mor·al (un môr′əl, -mor′-), *adj.* neither moral nor immoral; amoral; nonmoral: *Nature is unmoral.* [UN-[1] + MORAL] —**un·mo·ral·i·ty** (un′mə ral′i tē, -mô-), *n.* —**un·mor′al·ly,** *adv.*
—**Syn.** See **immoral.**

un·mor·tise (un môr′tis), *v.t.,* **-tised, -tis·ing.** to unfasten or separate (something mortised).

unmoved′ mov′er, *Aristotelianism.* See **prime mover** (def. 3).

un·mov·ing (un mo͞o′ving), *adj.* **1.** not moving; still; motionless. **2.** not stirring the emotions.

un·muf·fle (un muf′əl), *v.,* **-fled, -fling.** —*v.t.* **1.** to strip of or free from that which muffles. —*v.i.* **2.** to throw off that which muffles. [UN-[2] + MUFFLE]

un·mu·si·cal (un myo͞o′zi kəl), *adj.* **1.** not musical; deficient in melody, harmony, rhythm, or tone. **2.** acoustically and aesthetically harsh on the ear; strident; dissonant; cacophonous. **3.** not fond of or skilled in music. [UN-[1] + MUSICAL] —**un·mu′si·cal·ly,** *adv.* —**un·mu′si·cal·ness,** *n.*

un·muz·zle (un muz′əl), *v.t.,* **-zled, -zling. 1.** to remove a muzzle from (a dog, cat, etc.). **2.** to free from restraint, as speech or expression. [UN-[2] + MUZZLE]

un·nail (un nāl′), *v.t.* to take out the nails from. [UN-[2] + NAIL]

un·named (un nāmd′), *adj.* **1.** without a name; nameless. **2.** not indicated or mentioned by name; unidentified; unspecified: *an unnamed lover.* [UN-[1] + NAMED]

un·nat·u·ral (un nach′ər əl), *adj.* **1.** not natural; not conforming to the natural constitution or character of a thing or person; at variance with or contrary to nature or the course of nature. **2.** lacking natural or proper instincts, feelings, habits, etc.; not in accordance with accepted modes of behavior; strange; perverse; abnormal: *The unnatural atmosphere of the place stifled him.* **3.** extremely cruel or evil; monstrous; inhuman: *His crimes against humanity were most unnatural.* **4.** artificial or affected; forced or strained; not genuine; contrived (opposed to *spontaneous*): *Their unnatural manner never failed to amuse him.* **5.** not conforming to normal expectations; unusual: *an unnatural relationship.* **6.** *Obs.* lacking a valid or natural claim; illegitimate. [ME; see UN-[1], NATURAL] —**un·nat′u·ral·ly,** *adv.* —**un·nat′u·ral·ness,** *n.*
—**Syn. 3.** inhuman, heartless, brutal. **5.** irregular, anomalous, aberrant. —**Ant. 3.** humane.

un·nec·es·sar·y (un nes′i ser′ē), *adj., n., pl.* **-sar·ies.** —*adj.* **1.** not necessary; needless; unessential. —*n.* **2. unnecessaries,** things which are not necessary or essential. [UN-[1] + NECESSARY] —**un·nec·es·sar·i·ly** (un nes′i sâr′ə lē, -nes′i ser′-), *adv.* —**un·nec′es·sar′i·ness,** *n.*

un·nerve (un nûrv′), *v.t.,* **-nerved, -nerv·ing.** to deprive of courage, strength, determination; render ineffectual; upset: *News of the trapeze artist's death unnerved all the other acrobats.* [UN-[2] + NERVE]
—**Syn.** discourage, shake, fluster, disconcert. —**Ant.** steel.

un·num·bered (un num′bərd), *adj.* **1.** countless; innumerable: *the unnumbered stars in the sky.* **2.** having no number or numbers as identification: *the unnumbered pages at the front of the book.* **3.** uncounted. [ME *unnoumbred.* See UN-[1], NUMBERED]

UNO, United Nations Organization. Also, **U.N.O.**

un·oc·cu·pied (un ok′yə pīd′), *adj.* **1.** (of buildings, apartments, etc.) **a.** without occupants; empty; vacant: *a shortage of unoccupied apartments.* **b.** (in real estate law) without occupants but not devoid of furniture or other goods (distinguished from *vacant*): *The landlord examined the expensive fixtures in the unoccupied apartment.* **2.** (of land) without inhabitants; desolate; deserted: *an unoccupied territory.* **3.** not held or controlled by invading forces: *The citizens looked back to the days when their land was unoccupied.* **4.** not busy or active; idle; not gainfully employed: *An unoccupied person can easily get into trouble.* [ME; see UN-[1], OCCUPIED]

un·o·pened (un ō′pənd), *adj.* **1.** not opened: *an unopened can of sardines.* **2.** (of a book) having uncut edges, or bolts, ready for slitting by hand. [UN-[1] + OPEN + -ED[2]]

un′mis·led′, *adj.*
un·miss′a·ble, *adj.*
un·missed′, *adj.*
un′mis·tak′en, *adj.*
un′mis·tak′ing, *adj.;* **-ly,** *adv.*
un′mis·trust′ed, *adj.*
un′mis·trust′ful, *adj.;* **-ly,** *adv.*
un′mis·trust′ing, *adj.*
un′mis·un·der·stand′a·ble, *adj.*
un′mis·un·der·stood′, *adj.*
un·mit′i·ga·ble, *adj.*
un·mit′i·ga′tive, *adj.*
un·mit′tened, *adj.*
un·mix′, *v.t.*
un·mix′a·ble, *adj.*
un·moaned′, *adj.*
un·moan′ing, *adj.*
un·moat′ed, *adj.*
un·mobbed′, *adj.*
un·mo′bile, *adj.*
un·mo′bi·lised′, *adj.*
un·mo′bi·lized′, *adj.*
un·mocked′, *adj.*
un·mock′ing, *adj.;* **-ly,** *adv.*
un·mod′eled, *adj.*
un·mod′elled, *adj.*
un·mod′er·at′ed, *adj.*
un·mod′er·at′ing, *adj.*
un·mod′ern, *adj.*
un′mo·der′ni·ty, *n.*
un·mod′ern·ised′, *adj.*
un·mod′ern·ized′, *adj.*
un·mod′est, *adj.;* **-ly,** *adv.*
un·mod′i·fi′a·ble, *adj.*
un·mod′i·fi′ca′tive, *adj.*
un·mod′i·fied′, *adj.*
un·mod′ish, *adj.;* **-ly,** *adv.*
un·mod′u·lat′ed, *adj.*
un·mod′u·la′tive, *adj.*
un·moiled′, *adj.*
un·mois′ten, *v.t.*
un·mold′ered, *adj.*
un·mold′er·ing, *adj.*
un·mold′y, *adj.*
un′mo·lest′ed, *adj.*
un′mo·lest′ing, *adj.*
un·mol′li·fi′a·ble, *adj.*
un·mol′li·fied′, *adj.*
un·mol′li·fy′ing, *adj.*
un·mol′ten, *adj.*
un′mo·men′tous, *adj.;* **-ly,** *adv.;* **-ness,** *n.*
un′mo·nar′chic, *adj.*
un′mo·nar′chi·cal, *adj.;* **-ly,** *adv.*
un′mo·nas′tic, *adj.*
un′mo·nas′ti·cal·ly, *adv.*
un·mon′e·tar′y, *adj.*
un′mo·nis′tic, *adj.*
un·mon′i·tored, *adj.*
un·mon′o·grammed′, *adj.*
un′mo·nop′o·lised′, *adj.*
un′mo·nop′o·lis′ing, *adj.*
un′mo·nop′o·lized′, *adj.*
un′mo·nop′o·liz′ing, *adj.*
un′mo·not′o·nous, *adj.;* **-ly,** *adv.*
un′mon·u·men′tal, *adj.*
un·mon′u·ment′ed, *adj.*
un·mood′y, *adj.*
un·moot′ed, *adj.*
un·mopped′, *adj.*
un′mor·al·is′tic, *adj.*
un·mor′al·is′ing, *adj.*
un·mor′al·iz′ing, *adj.*
un·mor′bid, *adj.;* **-ly,** *adv.;* **-ness,** *n.*
un·mor′dant, *adj.;* **-ly,** *adv.*
un·mor′i·bund′, *adj.;* **-ly,** *adv.*
un′mo·rose′, *adj.;* **-ly,** *adv.;* **-ness,** *n.*
un′mor·pho·log′i·cal, *adj.;* **-ly,** *adv.*
un·mor′tal, *adj.*
un·mor′tared, *adj.*
un·mort′gage, *v.t.,* **-gaged, -gag·ing.**
un·mort′gage·a·ble, *adj.*
un·mor′ti·fied′, *adj.*
un·mossed′, *adj.*
un·moss′y, *adj.*
un·moth′-eat′en, *adj.*
un·moth′ered, *adj.*
un·moth′er·ly, *adj.*
un·mo′tile, *adj.*
un·mo′tion·a·ble, *adj.*
un·mo′tioned, *adj.*
un·mo′tion·ing, *adj.*
un·mo′ti·vat′ed, *adj.*
un·mo′ti·vat′ing, *adj.*
un·mo′tored, *adj.*
un·mo′tor·ised′, *adj.*
un·mo′tor·ized′, *adj.*
un·mot′tled, *adj.*
un·mould′, *v.t.*
un·moul′dered, *adj.*
un·mould′er·ing, *adj.*
un·mould′y, *adj.*
un·mound′ed, *adj.*
un·mount′a·ble, *adj.*
un·moun′tain·ous, *adj.*
un·mount′ed, *adj.*
un·mount′ing, *adj.*
un·mourned′, *adj.*
un·mourn′ful, *adj.;* **-ly,** *adv.*
un·mourn′ing, *adj.*
un·mouth′a·ble, *adj.*
un·mouthed′, *adj.*
un·mov′a·ble, *adj.*
un·move′a·ble, *adj.*
un·moved′, *adj.*
un·mowed′, *adj.*
un·mown′, *adj.*
un·mu′ci·laged′, *adj.*
un·mud′ded, *adj.*
un·mud′died, *adj.*
un·mud′dled, *adj.*
un·mud′dy, *adj.*
un·mulct′ed, *adj.*
un·mul′ish, *adj.*
un·mulled′, *adj.*
un·mul′lioned, *adj.*
un·mul′ti·pli′a·ble, *adj.*
un·mul′ti·pli′ca·ble, *adj.*
un·mul′ti·pli·ca′tive, *adj.*
un·mul′ti·plied′, *adj.*
un·mul′ti·ply′ing, *adj.*
un·mum′bled, *adj.*
un·mum′bling, *adj.*
un·mum′mied, *adj.*
un·mum′mi·fied′, *adj.*
un·mum′mi·fy′ing, *adj.*
un·munched′, *adj.*
un′mun·dane′, *adj.;* **-ly,** *adv.*
un·mun′di·fied′, *adj.*
un′mu·nic′i·pal·ised′, *adj.*
un′mu·nic′i·pal·ized′, *adj.*
un′mu·nif′i·cent, *adj.;* **-ly,** *adv.*
un′mu·ni′tioned, *adj.*
un·mur′mured, *adj.*
un·mur′mur·ing, *adj.;* **-ly,** *adv.*
un·mur′mur·ous, *adj.;* **-ly,** *adv.*
un·mus′cled, *adj.*
un·mus′cu·lar, *adj.;* **-ly,** *adv.*
un′mu·si·cal′i·ty, *n.*
un′mu·si′cian·ly, *adj.*
un·mus′ing, *adj.*
un·musked′, *adj.*
un·mus′ter·a·ble, *adj.*
un·mus′tered, *adj.*
un·mut′a·ble, *adj.*
un·mu′tant, *adj.*
un·mu′tat·ed, *adj.*
un′mu·ta′tion·al, *adj.*
un·mu′ta·tive, *adj.*
un·mut′ed, *adj.*
un·mu′ti·lat′ed, *adj.*
un·mu′ti·la′tive, *adj.*
un·mu′ti·nous, *adj.;* **-ly,** *adv.;* **-ness,** *n.*
un·mut′tered, *adj.*
un·mut′ter·ing, *adj.;* **-ly,** *adv.*
un·mu′tu·al, *adj.;* **-ly,** *adv.*
un·mu′tu·al·ised′, *adj.*
un·mu′tu·al·ized′, *adj.*
un′my·op′ic, *adj.*
un′mys·te′ri·ous, *adj.;* **-ly,** *adv.;* **-ness,** *n.*
un·mys′tic, *adj.*
un·mys′ti·cal, *adj.;* **-ly,** *adv.;* **-ness,** *n.*
un·mys′ti·cise′, *v.t.,* **-cised, -cis·ing.**
un·mys′ti·cize′, *v.t.,* **-cized, -ciz·ing.**
un·mys′ti·fied′, *adj.*
un·myth′i·cal, *adj.;* **-ly,** *adv.*
un′myth·o·log′i·cal, *adj.;* **-ly,** *adv.*
un·na′cre·ous, *adj.*
un·nagged′, *adj.*
un·nag′ging, *adj.;* **-ly,** *adv.*
un′na·ïve′, *adj.;* **-ly,** *adv.*
un·na′ked, *adj.*
un·nam′a·ble, *adj.*
un·name′a·ble, *adj.*
un·napped′, *adj.*
un′nar·cis·sis′tic, *adj.*
un′nar·cot′ic, *adj.*
un·nar′rat·a·ble, *adj.*
un·nar′rat·ed, *adj.*
un·nar′ra·tive, *adj.*
un·nar′row, *adj.;* **-ly,** *adv.*
un·nar′rowed, *adj.*
un·nar′row-mind′ed, *adj.;* **-ly,** *adv.;* **-ness,** *n.*
un·na′sal, *adj.;* **-ly,** *adv.*
un·nas′cent, *adj.*
un·na′tion·al, *adj.;* **-ly,** *adv.*
un′na·tion·al·is′tic, *adj.*
un′na·tion·al·is′ti·cal·ly, *adv.*
un·na′tion·al·ised′, *adj.*
un·na′tion·al·ized′, *adj.*
un·na′tive, *adj.*
un·nat′u·ral·ise′, *v.t.,* **-ised, -is·ing.**
un·nat·u·ral·is′tic, *adj.*
un·nat′u·ral·ize′, *v.t.,* **-ized, -iz·ing.**
un·nau′se·at′ed, *adj.*
un·nau′se·at′ing, *adj.*
un·nau′ti·cal, *adj.*
un·nav′i·ga·bil′i·ty, *n.*
un·nav′i·ga·ble, *adj.;* **-ble·ness,** *n.;* **-bly,** *adv.*
un·nav′i·gat′ed, *adj.*
un·neat′, *adj.;* **-ly,** *adv.;* **-ness,** *n.*
un′ne·ces′si·tat′ed, *adj.*
un′ne·ces′si·tat′ing, *adj.*
un′ne·ces′si·tous, *adj.;* **-ly,** *adv.;* **-ness,** *n.*
un′nec·tar′e·ous, *adj.*
un′nec·tar′i·al, *adj.*
un·need′ed, *adj.*
un·need′ful, *adj.;* **-ly,** *adv.*
un·need′y, *adj.*
un′ne·far′i·ous, *adj.;* **-ly,** *adv.;* **-ness,** *n.*
un′ne·gat′ed, *adj.*
un′neg·lect′ed, *adj.*
un′ne·glect′ful, *adj.;* **-ly,** *adv.*
un·neg′li·gent, *adj.*
un′ne·go′ti·a·ble, *adj.*
un′ne·go′ti·at′ed, *adj.*
un-Ne′gro, *adj.*
un·neigh′bor·li·ness, *n.*
un·neigh′bor·ly, *adj.*
un·neigh′bour·li·ness, *n.*
un·neigh′bour·ly, *adj.*
un′ne·phrit′ic, *adj.*
un·ner′vous, *adj.;* **-ly,** *adv.;* **-ness,** *n.*
un·nes′tled, *adj.*
un·net′ted, *adj.*
un·net′tled, *adj.*
un·neu′ral, *adj.*
un′neu·ral′gic, *adj.*
un′neu·rot′ic, *adj.*
un′neu·rot′i·cal·ly, *adv.*
un·neu′tral, *adj.;* **-ly,** *adv.*
un·neu′tral·ise′, *v.t.,* **-ised, -is·ing.**
un′neu·tral′i·ty, *n.*
un·neu′tral·ize′, *v.t.,* **-ized, -iz·ing.**
un·new′, *adj.;* **-ness,** *n.*
un·nibbed′, *adj.*
un·nib′bled, *adj.*
un·nice′, *adj.;* **-ly,** *adv.;* **-ness,** *n.*
un·niched′, *adj.*
un·nicked′, *adj.*
un·nick′named′, *adj.*
un·nig′gard, *adj.;* **-ly,** *adv.*
un·nigh′, *adj.*
un′ni·hil·is′tic, *adj.*
un·nim′ble, *adj.;* **-ble·ness,** *n.;* **-bly,** *adv.*
un·nipped′, *adj.*
un·ni′tro·gen·ised′, *adj.*
un·ni′tro·gen·ized′, *adj.*
un′ni·trog′e·nous, *adj.*
un′noc·tur′nal, *adj.;* **-ly,** *adv.*
un·nod′ding, *adj.*
un·noised′, *adj.*
un·nois′i·ly, *adv.*
un·nois′y, *adj.*
un′no·mad′ic, *adj.*
un′no·mad′i·cal·ly, *adv.*
un·nom′i·nal, *adj.;* **-ly,** *adv.*
un·nom′i·nal·is′tic, *adj.*
un·nom′i·nat′ed, *adj.*
un·nom′i·na′tive, *adj.*
un·noosed′, *adj.*
un·nor′mal, *adj.;* **-ly,** *adv.;* **-ness,** *n.*
un·nor′mal·ised′, *adj.*
un·nor′mal·is′ing, *adj.*
un·nor′mal·ized′, *adj.*
un·nor′mal·iz′ing, *adj.*
un·nor′ma·tive, *adj.*
un·north′ern, *adj.*
un·nosed′, *adj.*
un·not′a·ble, *adj.*
un′no·ta′tion·al, *adj.*
un·notched′, *adj.*
un·not′ed, *adj.*
un·note′wor′thy, *adj.*
un·no′tice·a·ble, *adj.;* **-ble·ness,** *n.;* **-bly,** *adv.*
un·no′ticed, *adj.*
un·no′tic·ing, *adj.*
un·no′ti·fied′, *adj.*
un·not′ing, *adj.*
un·no′tion·al, *adj.;* **-ly,** *adv.*
un·no′tioned, *adj.*
un·nour′ish·a·ble, *adj.*
un·nour′ished, *adj.*
un·nour′ish·ing, *adj.*
un·nov′el, *adj.*
un′no·ver′cal, *adj.*
un·nu′cle·at′ed, *adj.*
un·nul′li·fied′, *adj.*
un·numbed′, *adj.*
un·nu′mer·at′ed, *adj.*
un′nu·mer′i·cal, *adj.*
un·nu′mer·ous, *adj.;* **-ly,** *adv.;* **-ness,** *n.*
un·nur′tured, *adj.*
un′nu·tri′tious, *adj.;* **-ly,** *adv.*
un·nu′tri·tive, *adj.*
un·nuz′zled, *adj.*
un·nymph′al, *adj.*
un′nym·phe′an, *adj.*
un·nymph′like′, *adj.*
un·oared′, *adj.*
un·ob′du·rate, *adj.;* **-ly,** *adv.;* **-ness,** *n.*
un′o·bese′, *adj.;* **-ly,** *adv.;* **-ness,** *n.*
un′o·beyed′, *adj.*
un′o·bey′ing, *adj.*
un·ob′fus·cat·ed, *adj.*
un′ob·ject′ed, *adj.*
un′ob·jec′ti·fied′, *adj.*
un′ob·jec′tion·a·ble, *adj.*
un′ob·jec′tion·al, *adj.*
un′ob·jec′tive, *adj.;* **-ly,** *adv.*
un′ob·jec′ti·vized′, *adj.*
un·ob′li·gat′ed, *adj.*
un·ob′li·ga′tive, *adj.*
un′ob·lig′a·to′ry, *adj.*
un′ob·liged′, *adj.*
un′ob·lig′ing, *adj.*
un′ob·lit′er·at′ed, *adj.*
un′ob·liv′i·ous, *adj.;* **-ly,** *adv.;* **-ness,** *n.*
un′ob·nox′i·ous, *adj.;* **-ly,** *adv.*
un′ob·scene′, *adj.;* **-ly,** *adv.;* **-ness,** *n.*
un′ob·scure′, *adj.;* **-ly,** *adv.;* **-ness,** *n.*
un′ob·scured′, *adj.*
un′ob·se′qui·ous, *adj.;* **-ly,** *adv.;* **-ness,** *n.*
un′ob·serv′a·ble, *adj.*
un′ob·serv′ant, *adj.;* **-ly,** *adv.*
un′ob·served′, *adj.*
un′ob·serv′ing, *adj.*
un′ob·sessed′, *adj.*
un·ob′so·lete′, *adj.*
un·ob′sti·nate, *adj.;* **-ly,** *adv.*
un′ob·struct′ed, *adj.*
un′ob·struc′tive, *adj.*
un·ob′stru·ent, *adj.;* **-ly,** *adv.*
un′ob·tain′a·ble, *adj.*
un′ob·tained′, *adj.*
un′ob·trud′ed, *adj.*
un′ob·trud′ing, *adj.*
un′ob·tru′sive, *adj.;* **-ly,** *adv.;* **-ness,** *n.*
un′ob·vert′ed, *adj.*
un·ob′vi·a·ble, *adj.*
un·ob′vi·at′ed, *adj.*
un·ob′vi·ous, *adj.;* **-ly,** *adv.;* **-ness,** *n.*
un′oc·ca′sion·al, *adj.;* **-ly,** *adv.*
un′oc·ci·den′tal, *adj.;* **-ly,** *adv.*
un′oc·clud′ed, *adj.*
un·oc′cu·pan·cy, *n.*
un′oc·cur′ring, *adj.*
un′o·ce·an′ic, *adj.*
un·oc′u·lar, *adj.*
un·o′di·ous, *adj.;* **-ly,** *adv.;* **-ness,** *n.*
un·o′dored, *adj.*
un′o·dor·if′er·ous, *adj.;* **-ly,** *adv.;* **-ness,** *n.*
un·o′dor·ous, *adj.;* **-ly,** *adv.;* **-ness,** *n.*
un′oec·u·men′ic, *adj.*
un′oec·u·men′i·cal, *adj.*
un′of·fend′a·ble, *adj.*
un′of·fend′ed, *adj.*
un′of·fend′ing, *adj.*
un′of·fen′sive, *adj.;* **-ly,** *adv.;* **-ness,** *n.*
un·of′fered, *adj.*
un·of′ficed, *adj.*
un·of′fi·cered, *adj.*
un′of·fi′cial, *adj.;* **-ly,** *adv.*
un′of·fi′ci·at′ed, *adj.*
un′of·fi′ci·at′ing, *adj.*
un′of·fi′cious, *adj.;* **-ly,** *adv.;* **-ness,** *n.*
un·o′gled, *adj.*
un·oiled′, *adj.*
un·oil′ing, *adj.*
un·oil′y, *adj.*
un·o′mened, *adj.*
un·om′i·nous, *adj.;* **-ly,** *adv.;* **-ness,** *n.*
un′o·mit′ted, *adj.*
un′om·nip′o·tent, *adj.;* **-ly,** *adv.*
un′om·nis′cient, *adj.;* **-ly,** *adv.*
un·o′ner·ous, *adj.;* **-ly,** *adv.;* **-ness,** *n.*
un′on·to·log′i·cal, *adj.*

un·or·gan·ized (un ôr′gə nīzd′), *adj.* **1.** not organized; without organic structure. **2.** not formed into an organized or systematized whole: *an unorganized essay; an unorganized team; an unorganized government.* **3.** without definite boundaries: *unorganized territory.* **4.** not having membership in a labor union: *The unorganized workers lacked a spokesman.* Also, *esp. Brit.,* **un·or′gan·ised′.** [UN-[1] + ORGANIZED]

unor′ganized fer′ment, an enzyme.

un·pack (un pak′), *v.t.* **1.** to undo or remove the contents of (a box, trunk, etc.). **2.** to remove (something) from a container, suitcase, etc. **3.** to unburden, as the mind; release; reveal: *He would unpack his grievances to any sympathetic listener.* **4.** to decipher or discern (the meaning of symbols, statements, etc.): *According to the critic, the poem could be unpacked to make sense.* **5.** to remove a pack or load from (a horse, vehicle, etc.). —*v.i.* **6.** to remove the contents of a container. [ME *unpakke(n).* See UN-[2], PACK] —**un·pack′er,** *n.*

un·paged (un pājd′), *adj.* (of a publication) having unnumbered pages. [UN-[1] + PAGE[1] + -ED[2]]

un·paid-for (un pād′fôr′), *adj.* not paid for.

un·par·al·leled (un par′ə leld′), *adj.* not paralleled; unequaled or unmatched; peerless; unprecedented; without a match or counterpart: *an unparalleled action; unparalleled athletic ability.* Also, *esp. Brit.,* **un·par′al·lelled′.** [UN-[1] + PARALLELED]
—**Syn.** matchless, unrivaled.

un·par·lia·men·ta·ry (un′pär lə men′tə rē), *adj.* not parliamentary; at variance with or contrary to the methods employed by parliamentary bodies. [UN-[1] + PARLIAMENTARY] —**un′par·lia·men′ta·ri·ly,** *adv.* —**un′par·lia·men′ta·ri·ness,** *n.*

un·peg (un peg′), *v.t.,* **-pegged, -peg·ging.** **1.** to remove the peg or pegs from. **2.** to open, unfasten, or unfix by or as if by removing a peg or pegs. **3.** to stop pegging the commodity price, exchange rate, etc. [UN-[2] + PEG]

un·pen (un pen′), *v.t.,* **-penned, -pen·ning.** to release from confinement. [UN-[2] + PEN[2]]

un·peo·ple (un pē′pəl), *v.t.,* **-pled, -pling.** to deprive of people; depopulate. [UN-[2] + PEOPLE]

un·peo·pled (un pē′pəld), *adj.* without people; uninhabited. [UN-[1] + PEOPLED]

un·pile (un pīl′), *v.,* **-piled, -pil·ing.** —*v.t.* **1.** to disentangle or remove from a piled condition: *to unpile boxes; to unpile a heap of stones.* —*v.i.* **2.** to become removed or separated from a piled condition: *The autumnal breeze caused the heaped-up leaves to unpile. The football players unpiled after each play.* [UN-[2] + PILE[1]]

un·pin (un pin′), *v.t.,* **-pinned, -pin·ning.** **1.** to remove a pin or pins from. **2.** to unfasten or loosen by or as if by removing a pin; detach. [UN-[2] + PIN]

un·plait (un plāt′), *v.t.* to alter from a plaited state; unbraid, as hair. [UN-[2] + PLAIT]

un·o′pen·ing, *adj.*
un·op′er·at′a·ble, *adj.*
un·op′er·at′ed, *adj.*
un/op′er·at′ic, *adj.*
un/op′er·at′i·cal·ly, *adv.*
un·op′er·at′ing, *adj.*
un·op′er·a′tive, *adj.*
un·o′pi·at′ed, *adj.*
un·o′pi·at′ic, *adj.*
un′o·pined′, *adj.*
un′o·pin′ion·at′ed, *adj.*
un′o·pin′ioned, *adj.*
un′op·por·tune′, *adj.;* **-ly,** *adv.;* **-ness,** *n.*
un′op·por·tun·is′tic, *adj.*
un′op·pos′a·ble, *adj.*
un′op·posed′, *adj.*
un′op·pos′ing, *adj.*
un′op·po·si′tion·al, *adj.*
un′op·pres′si·ble, *adj.*
un′op·pressed′, *adj.*
un′op·pres′sive, *adj.;* **-ly,** *adv.;* **-ness,** *n.*
un′op·pro′bri·ous, *adj.;* **-ly,** *adv.;* **-ness,** *n.*
un′op·pugned′, *adj.*
un·opt′ed, *adj.*
un′op·ti·mis′tic, *adj.*
un′op·ti·mis′ti·cal, *adj.;* **-ly,** *adv.*
un·op′tion·al, *adj.;* **-ly,** *adv.*
un·op′u·lence, *n.*
un·op′u·lent, *adj.;* **-ly,** *adv.*
un·o′ral, *adj.;* **-ly,** *adv.*
un′o·ra′tion·al, *adj.*
un′or·a·to′ri·al, *adj.*
un′or·a·to′ri·cal, *adj.;* **-ly,** *adv.*
un·orbed′, *adj.*
un·or′bi·tal, *adj.;* **-ly,** *adv.*
un·or′ches·trat′ed, *adj.*
un′or·dain′a·ble, *adj.*
un′or·dained′, *adj.*
un·or′der·a·ble, *adj.*
un·or′dered, *adj.*
un·or′der·ly, *adj.*
un·or′di·nal, *adj.*
un·or′di·nar′y, *adj.*
un′or·gan′ic, *adj.*
un′or·gan′i·cal·ly, *adv.*
un′or·gan·is′a·ble, *adj.*
un′or·gan·iz′a·ble, *adj.*
un′o·ri·en′tal, *adj.;* **-ly,** *adv.*
un′o·rig′i·nal, *adj.;* **-ly,** *adv.*
un·or′na·men′tal, *adj.;* **-ly,** *adv.*
un·or′na·ment′ed, *adj.*
un′or·nate′, *adj.;* **-ly,** *adv.;* **-ness,** *n.*
un′or·ni·tho·log′i·cal, *adj.*
un·or′phaned, *adj.*
un·or′tho·dox, *adj.;* **-ly,** *adv.*
un·or′tho·dox′y, *adj.*
un′or·tho·graph′i·cal, *adj.;* **-ly,** *adv.*
un·os′cil·lat′ing, *adj.*
un·os′cu·lat′ed, *adj.*
un′os·mot′ic, *adj.*
un·os′si·fied′, *adj.*
un·os′si·fy′ing, *adj.*
un′os·ten′si·ble, *adj.;* **-bly,** *adv.*
un′os·ten′sive, *adj.;* **-ly,** *adv.*
un′os·ten·ta′tious, *adj.;* **-ly,** *adv.*
un·oust′ed, *adj.*
un·out′lawed′, *adj.*
un·out′raged, *adj.*
un′out·spo′ken, *adj.*
un′out·worn′, *adj.*
un′o·ver·come′, *adj.*
un′o·ver·drawn′, *adj.*
un′o·ver·flow′ing, *adj.*
un′o·ver·hauled′, *adj.*
un′o·ver·looked′, *adj.*
un′o·ver·paid′, *adj.*
un′o·ver·pow′ered, *adj.*
un′o·ver·ruled′, *adj.*
un′o·vert′, *adj.*
un′o·ver·ta′ken, *adj.*
un′o·ver·thrown′, *adj.*
un′o·ver·whelmed′, *adj.*
un·ow′ing, *adj.*
un·owned′, *adj.*
un·ox′i·dat′ed, *adj.*
un·ox′i·da′tive, *adj.*
un·ox′i·dis′a·ble, *adj.*
un·ox′i·dised′, *adj.*
un·ox′i·diz′a·ble, *adj.*
un·ox′i·dized′, *adj.*
un·ox′y·gen·at′ed, *adj.*
un·ox′y·gen·ized′, *adj.*
un·paced′, *adj.*
un·pac′i·fi′a·ble, *adj.*
un′pa·cif′ic, *adj.*
un·pac′i·fied′, *adj.*
un·pac′i·fist, *adj.*
un′pac·i·fis′tic, *adj.*
un·pack′aged, *adj.*
un·pad′ded, *adj.*
un·pad′locked′, *adj.*
un·pa′gan, *adj.*
un·pa′gan·ize′, *v.t.,* **-ized, -iz·ing.**
un·pag′i·nal, *adj.*
un·pag′i·nat′ed, *adj.*
un·paid′, *adj.*
un·pained′, *adj.*
un·pain′ful, *adj.;* **-ly,** *adv.*
un·pain′ing, *adj.*
un·paint′ed, *adj.*
un·paired′, *adj.*
un·pal′at·a·ble, *adj.;* **-bly,** *adv.*
un·pal′a·tal, *adj.;* **-ly,** *adv.*
un′pa·la′tial, *adj.*
un·pale′, *adj.*
un·paled′, *adj.*
un·pal′i·sad′ed, *adj.*
un·pal′i·sa′doed, *adj.*
un·palled′, *adj.*
un·pal′li·at′ed, *adj.*
un·pal′li·a′tive, *adj.*
un·pal′pa·ble, *adj.;* **-bly,** *adv.*
un·pal′pi·tat′ing, *adj.*
un·pal′sied, *adj.*
un·pal′try, *adj.*
un·pam′pered, *adj.*
un·pan′e·gy·rised′, *adj.*
un·pan′e·gy·rized′, *adj.*
un·pan′eled, *adj.*
un·pan′elled, *adj.*
un·pan′ick·y, *adj.*
un·pan′niered, *adj.*
un·pan′o·plied, *adj.*
un′pan·the·is′tic, *adj.*
un′pan·the·is′ti·cal, *adj.;* **-ly,** *adv.*
un·pant′ing, *adj.*
un·pa′pal, *adj.*
un·pa′pered, *adj.*
un·pa·rad′ed, *adj.*
un′par·a·dox′al, *adj.*
un′par·a·dox′i·cal, *adj.;* **-ly,** *adv.*
un·par′a·graphed′, *adj.*
un·par′al·lel′, *adj.*
un·par′a·lysed′, *adj.*
un·par′a·lyzed′, *adj.*
un·par′a·phrased′, *adj.*
un′par·a·sit′ic, *adj.*
un′par·a·sit′i·cal, *adj.;* **-ly,** *adv.*
un·par′celed, *adj.*
un·par′cel·ing, *adj.*
un·par′celled, *adj.*
un·par′cel·ling, *adj.*
un·parched′, *adj.*
un·parch′ing, *adj.*
un·par′don·a·ble, *adj.;* **-bly,** *adv.*
un·par′doned, *adj.*
un·par′don·ing, *adj.*
un·pared′, *adj.*
un′pa·ren′tal, *adj.;* **-ly,** *adv.*
un′pa·ren′the·sised′, *adj.*
un′pa·ren′the·sized′, *adj.*
un′par·en·thet′ic, *adj.*
un′par·en·thet′i·cal, *adj.;* **-ly,** *adv.*
un·par′get·ed, *adj.*
un·parked′, *adj.*
un·park′ing, *adj.*
un·par′lia·ment′ed, *adj.*
un′pa·ro′chi·al, *adj.;* **-ly,** *adv.*
un·par′o·died, *adj.*
un′pa·rol′a·ble, *adj.*
un′pa·roled′, *adj.*
un·par′ried, *adj.*
un·par′ry·ing, *adj.*
un·parsed′, *adj.*
un′par·si·mo′ni·ous, *adj.;* **-ly,** *adv.*
un·par·ta′ken, *adj.*
un·par·tak′ing, *adj.*
un·part′ed, *adj.*
un·part′i·ble, *adj.*
un′par·tic′i·pant, *adj.*
un′par·tic′i·pat′ed, *adj.*
un′par·tic′i·pat′ing, *adj.*
un′par·tic′i·pa′tive, *adj.*
un′par·tic′u·lar, *adj.*
un′par·tic′u·lar·ised′, *adj.*
un′par·tic′u·lar·is′ing, *adj.*
un′par·tic′u·lar·ized′, *adj.*
un′par·tic′u·lar·iz′ing, *adj.*
un·par′ti·san, *adj.*
un′par·ti′tioned, *adj.*
un′par·ti·tive, *adj.*
un·par′ti·zan, *adj.*
un·passed′, *adj.*
un·pass′ing, *adj.*
un·pas′sion·ate, *adj.;* **-ly,** *adv.;* **-ness,** *n.*
un·pas′sioned, *adj.*
un·pas′sive, *adj.;* **-ly,** *adv.*
un·paste′, *v.t.,* **-past·ed, -past·ing.**
un·pas′teur·ised′, *adj.*
un·pas′teur·ized′, *adj.*
un·pas′to·ral, *adj.;* **-ly,** *adv.*
un·pas′tured, *adj.*
un·patched′, *adj.*
un·pat′ent, *adj.*
un·pat′ent·a·ble, *adj.*
un·pat′ent·ed, *adj.*
un′pa·ter′nal, *adj.;* **-ly,** *adv.*
un′pa·thet′ic, *adj.*
un′pa·thet′i·cal·ly, *adv.*
un′path·o·log′i·cal, *adj.;* **-ly,** *adv.*
un·pa′tient, *adj.;* **-ly,** *adv.*
un·pat′i·nat′ed, *adj.*
un′pa·tri·ar′chal, *adj.;* **-ly,** *adv.*
un′pa·tri′cian, *adj.*
un′pa·tri·ot′ic, *adj.*
un′pa·tri·ot′i·cal·ly, *adv.*
un′pa·tris′tic, *adj.*
un′pa·tris′ti·cal, *adj.;* **-ly,** *adv.*
un′pa·trolled′, *adj.*
un·pa′tron·is′a·ble, *adj.*
un·pa′tron·iz′a·ble, *adj.*
un·pa′tron·iz′ing, *adj.;* **-ly,** *adv.*
un·pat′ted, *adj.*
un·pat′terned, *adj.*
un·pat′tern·ized′, *adj.*
un·paus′ing, *adj.*
un·paved′, *adj.*
un′pa·vil′ioned, *adj.*
un·pav′ing, *adj.*
un·pawed′, *adj.*
un·pawned′, *adj.*
un·pay′a·ble, *adj.;* **-bly,** *adv.*
un·pay′ing, *adj.*
un·peace′a·ble, *adj.;* **-bly,** *adv.*
un·peace′ful, *adj.;* **-ly,** *adv.*
un·peaked′, *adj.*
un·pealed′, *adj.*
un·pearled′, *adj.*
un·peb′bled, *adj.*
un·pecked′, *adj.*
un·pec′u·lat′ing, *adj.*
un′pe·cul′iar, *adj.;* **-ly,** *adv.*
un′ped·a·gog′ic, *adj.*
un′ped·a·gog′i·cal·ly, *adv.*
un′pe·dan′tic, *adj.*
un′pe·dan′ti·cal, *adj.*
un·ped′dled, *adj.*
un·ped′es·tal, *v.t.,* **-taled, -tal·ing** or (*esp. Brit.*) **-talled, -tal·ling.**
un·ped′i·greed′, *adj.*
un·peel′a·ble, *adj.*
un·peeled′, *adj.*
un·peel′ing, *adj.*
un·pee′vish, *adj.;* **-ly,** *adv.;* **-ness,** *n.*
un′pe·jo′ra·tive, *adj.;* **-ly,** *adv.*
un·pelt′ed, *adj.*
un·pe′nal, *adj.;* **-ly,** *adv.*
un·pe′nal·ised′, *adj.*
un·pe′nal·ized′, *adj.*
un·pen′anced, *adj.*
un·pen′ciled, *adj.*
un·pen′cilled, *adj.*
un·pend′ant, *adj.*
un·pend′ent, *adj.*
un·pend′ing, *adj.*
un·pen′du·lous, *adj.;* **-ly,** *adv.;* **-ness,** *n.*
un·pen′e·tra·ble, *adj.;* **-bly,** *adv.*
un·pen′e·trant, *adj.*
un·pen′e·trat′ed, *adj.*
un·pen′e·trat′ing, *adj.;* **-ly,** *adv.*
un·pen′e·tra′tive, *adj.;* **-ly,** *adv.*
un·pen′i·tent, *adj.;* **-ly,** *adv.*
un′pen·i·ten′tial, *adj.;* **-ly,** *adv.*
un·pen′nied, *adj.*
un·pen′noned, *adj.*
un·pen′sion·a·ble, *adj.*
un·pen′sioned, *adj.*
un·pen′sion·ing, *adj.*
un·pent′, *adj.*
un′pe·nu′ri·ous, *adj.;* **-ly,** *adv.;* **-ness,** *n.*
un·pep′pered, *adj.*
un·pep′per·y, *adj.*
un′per·ceiv′a·ble, *adj.;* **-bly,** *adv.*
un′per·ceived′, *adj.*
un′per·ceiv′ing, *adj.*
un′per·cep′ti·ble, *adj.;* **-bleness,** *n.;* **-bly,** *adv.*
un′per·cep′tion·al, *adj.*
un′per·cep′tive, *adj.;* **-ly,** *adv.*
un′per·cep′tu·al, *adj.;* **-ly,** *adv.*
un·perched′, *adj.*
un′per·cip′i·ent, *adj.*
un·per′co·lat′ed, *adj.*
un′per·cussed′, *adj.*
un′per·cus′sive, *adj.*
un·per′dur·a·ble, *adj.;* **-bly,** *adv.*
un′per·emp′to·ri·ly, *adv.*
un′per·emp′to·ri·ness, *n.*
un′per·emp′to·ry, *adj.*
un·per′fect, *adj.*
un′per·fect′ed, *adj.*
un′per·fect′i·ble, *adj.*
un′per·fec′tive, *adj.;* **-ly,** *adv.;* **-ness,** *n.*
un′per·fid′i·ous, *adj.;* **-ly,** *adv.;* **-ness,** *n.*
un·per′fo·ra·ble, *adj.*
un·per′fo·rat′ed, *adj.*
un·per′fo·rat′ing, *adj.*
un·per′fo·ra′tive, *adj.*
un′per·form′a·ble, *adj.*
un′per·formed′, *adj.*
un′per·form′ing, *adj.*
un′per·fumed′, *adj.*
un·per′il·ous, *adj.;* **-ly,** *adv.*
un′pe·ri·od′ic, *adj.*
un′pe·ri·od′i·cal, *adj.;* **-ly,** *adv.*
un′pe·riph′er·al, *adj.;* **-ly,** *adv.*
un′per·i·phras′tic, *adj.*
un′per·i·phras′ti·cal·ly, *adv.*
un·per′ish·a·ble, *adj.*
un·per′ished, *adj.*
un·per′ish·ing, *adj.*
un·per′jured, *adj.*
un·per′jur·ing, *adj.*
un·per′ma·nent, *adj.;* **-ly,** *adv.*
un·per′me·a·ble, *adj.*
un·per′me·ant, *adj.*
un·per′me·at′ed, *adj.*
un·per′me·at′ing, *adj.*
un·per′me·a′tive, *adj.*
un′per·mis′si·ble, *adj.;* **-bly,** *adv.*
un′per·mis′sive, *adj.*
un′per·mit′ted, *adj.*
un′per·mit′ting, *adj.*
un′per·ni′cious, *adj.;* **-ly,** *adv.*
un′per·pen·dic′u·lar, *adj.;* **-ly,** *adv.*
un·per′pe·trat′ed, *adj.*
un′per·pet′u·a·ble, *adj.*
un′per·pet′u·at′ed, *adj.*
un′per·pet′u·at′ing, *adj.*
un′per·plexed′, *adj.*
un′per·plex′ing, *adj.*
un·per′se·cut′ed, *adj.*
un·per′se·cut′ing, *adj.*
un·per′se·cu′tive, *adj.*
un′per·sist′ing, *adj.*
un·per′son·a·ble, *adj.*
un·per′son·al, *adj.;* **-ly,** *adv.*
un·per′son·al·ised′, *adj.*
un·per′son·al·is′ing, *adj.*
un·per′son·al·ized′, *adj.*
un·per′son·al·iz′ing, *adj.*
un′per·son′i·fied′, *adj.*
un′per·son′i·fy′ing, *adj.*
un′per·spic′u·ous, *adj.;* **-ly,** *adv.;* **-ness,** *n.*
un′per·spired′, *adj.*
un′per·spir′ing, *adj.*
un′per·suad′a·ble, *adj.;* **-bly,** *adv.*
un′per·suad′ed, *adj.*
un′per·sua′si·ble, *adj.*
un′per·sua′sive, *adj.;* **-ly,** *adv.;* **-ness,** *n.*
un′per·tain′ing, *adj.*
un·per′ti·nent, *adj.;* **-ly,** *adv.*
un′per·turb′a·ble, *adj.*
un′per·turbed′, *adj.*
un′per·turb′ing, *adj.*
un′pe·ruked′, *adj.*
un′pe·rus′a·ble, *adj.*
un′pe·rused′, *adj.*
un′per·vad′ed, *adj.*
un′per·vad′ing, *adj.*
un′per·va′sive, *adj.;* **-ly,** *adv.;* **-ness,** *n.*
un′per·verse′, *adj.;* **-ly,** *adv.*
un′per·ver′sive, *adj.*
un′per·vert′ed, *adj.;* **-ly,** *adv.*
un·per′vi·ous, *adj.;* **-ly,** *adv.;* **-ness,** *n.*
un′pes·si·mis′tic, *adj.*
un′pes·si·mis′ti·cal·ly, *adv.*
un·pes′tered, *adj.*
un·pes′ter·ous, *adj.*
un·pes′ti·lent, *adj.;* **-ly,** *adv.*
un′pes·ti·len′tial, *adj.*
un·pet′aled, *adj.*
un·pet′alled, *adj.*
un′pe·ti′tioned, *adj.*
un·pet′ri·fied′, *adj.*
un·pet′ri·fy′ing, *adj.*
un·pet′ted, *adj.*
un·pet′ti·coat′ed, *adj.*
un·pet′u·lant, *adj.;* **-ly,** *adv.*
un·phased′, *adj.*
un′phe·nom′e·nal, *adj.;* **-ly,** *adv.*
un′phil·an·throp′ic, *adj.*
un′phil·an·throp′i·cal·ly, *adv.*
un′phil·o·log′ic, *adj.*
un′phil·o·log′i·cal, *adj.*
un′phil·o·soph′ic, *adj.*
un′phil·o·soph′i·cal, *adj.;* **-ly,** *adv.*
un′phleg·mat′ic, *adj.*
un′phleg·mat′i·cal, *adj.;* **-ly,** *adv.*
un′pho·net′ic, *adj.*
un′pho·net′i·cal, *adj.;* **-ly,** *adv.*
un·phos′pha·tised′, *adj.*
un·phos′pha·tized′, *adj.*
un′pho·to·graph′a·ble, *adj.*
un·pho′to·graphed′, *adj.*
un·phrased′, *adj.*
un·phys′i·cal, *adj.;* **-ly,** *adv.*
un′phys·i·o·log′i·cal, *adj.;* **-ly,** *adv.*
un′pic·a·resque′, *adj.*
un·pick′a·ble, *adj.*
un·picked′, *adj.*
un·pick′et·ed, *adj.*
un·pick′led, *adj.*
un′pic·to′ri·al, *adj.;* **-ly,** *adv.*
un′pic·to′ri·al·ise′, *v.t.,* **-ised, -is·ing.**
un′pic·to′ri·al·ize′, *v.t.,* **-ized, -iz·ing.**
un·pic′tured, *adj.*
un′pic·tur·esque′, *adj.;* **-ly,** *adv.;* **-ness,** *n.*
un·pieced′, *adj.*
un·pierce′a·ble, *adj.*
un·pierced′, *adj.*
un·pierc′ing, *adj.*
un·pi′e·ty, *n.*
un·pig′ment·ed, *adj.*
un·pil′fered, *adj.*
un·pil′laged, *adj.*
un·pil′lared, *adj.*
un·pil′lo·ried, *adj.*
un·pil′lowed, *adj.*
un·pi′lot·ed, *adj.*
un·pim′pled, *adj.*
un·pinched′, *adj.*
un·pin′ioned, *adj.*
un′pi·o·neer′ing, *adj.*
un·pi′ous, *adj.;* **-ly,** *adv.*
un·piped′, *adj.*
un·piqued′, *adj.*
un·pi′rat·ed, *adj.*
un′pi·rat′i·cal, *adj.;* **-ly,** *adv.*
un·pitched′, *adj.*
un·pit′e·ous, *adj.;* **-ly,** *adv.*
un·pit′i·a·ble, *adj.;* **-bly,** *adv.*
un·pit′ied, *adj.*
un·pit′i·ful, *adj.;* **-ly,** *adv.;* **-ness,** *n.*
un·pit′ted, *adj.*
un·pit′y·ing, *adj.*
un·pla′cat·ed, *adj.*
un·pla′ca·to′ry, *adj.*
un·placed′, *adj.*
un·plac′id, *adj.;* **-ly,** *adv.;* **-ness,** *n.*
un·pla′gi·a·rised′, *adj.*
un·pla′gi·a·rized′, *adj.*
un·plagued′, *adj.*
un·plan′, *v.t.,* **-planned, -planning.**
un·planed′, *adj.*
un·plan′ished, *adj.*
un·planked′, *adj.*
un·plant′a·ble, *adj.*
un·plant′ed, *adj.*
un·plashed′, *adj.*
un·plas′ter, *v.t.*
un·plas′tic, *adj.*
un·plat′ed, *adj.*
un·plat·i·tu′di·nous, *adj.;* **-ly,** *adv.;* **-ness,** *n.*
un·plat′ted, *adj.*
un·plau′si·ble, *adj.;* **-ble·ness,** *n.;* **-bly,** *adv.*

un·pleas·ant (un plez′ənt), *adj.* not pleasant; displeasing; disagreeable; offensive: *an unpleasant taste; an unpleasant situation; an unpleasant manner.* [UN-[1] + PLEASANT] —**un·pleas′ant·ly,** *adv.*
—**Syn.** unpalatable, unappetizing, obnoxious, noisome, repulsive, repellent.

un·pleas·ant·ness (un plez′ənt nis), *n.* **1.** the quality or state of being unpleasant. **2.** that which is displeasing or offensive, as certain experiences, events, or situations. **3.** a disagreement or quarrel: *Owing to the recent unpleasantness between them, the couple felt rather ill-at-ease.* **4.** an unpleasant feeling or sensation caused by disagreeable or painful stimuli. [UNPLEASANT + -NESS]

un·plug (un plug′), *v.t.*, **-plugged, -plug·ging.** to remove a plug or plugs from. [UN-[2] + PLUG]

un·plumbed (un plumd′), *adj.* **1.** not plumbed; not tested or measured with a plumb line. **2.** not understood or explored in depth, as an idea, theory, feeling, experience, etc. **3.** having no plumbing installations: *an unplumbed shack.* [UN-[1] + PLUMB + -ED[3]]

un′polished rice′, a partly refined rice, hulled and deprived of its germ but retaining some bran.

un·po·lite (un′pə līt′), *adj.* impolite. [UN-[1] + POLITE] —**un′po·lite′ly,** *adv.* —**un′po·lite′ness,** *n.*

un·pol·i·tic (un pol′i tik), *adj.* impolitic. [UN-[1] + POLITIC]

un·polled (un pōld′), *adj.* **1.** not polled; not registered, cast, or counted at the polls: *The unpolled vote would be taken into consideration at a later date.* **2.** not consulted or interviewed in a poll: *The show's rating was dubious, as numerous unpolled viewers expressed their unflattering opinion of the program.* [UN-[1] + POLL[1] + -ED[2]]

un·pop·u·lar (un pop′yə lər), *adj.* not popular; disliked, disapproved, or ignored by the public or by persons generally. [UN-[1] + POPULAR] —**un·pop·u·lar·i·ty** (un′pop yə lar′i tē), *n.* —**un·pop′u·lar·ly,** *adv.*

un·posed (un pōzd′), *adj.* not posed; not done for effect; natural or candid: *her unposed manner; an unposed photograph.* [UN-[1] + POSE[1] + -ED[2]]

un·prac·ti·ca·ble (un prak′tə kə bəl), *adj.* impracticable. [UN-[1] + PRACTICABLE] —**un′prac·ti·ca·bil′i·ty, un·prac′ti·ca·ble·ness,** *n.* —**un·prac′ti·ca·bly,** *adv.*

un·prac·ti·cal (un prak′ti kəl), *adj.* not practical; impractical; lacking practical usefulness or wisdom. [UN-[1] + PRACTICAL] —**un′prac·ti·cal′i·ty, un·prac′ti·cal·ness,** *n.* —**un·prac′ti·cal·ly,** *adv.*

un·prac·ticed (un prak′tist), *adj.* **1.** not trained or skilled; inexpert: *an unpracticed actor.* **2.** not practiced; not usually or generally used or done; not put in effect. Also, *esp. Brit.,* **un·prac′tised.** [UN-[1] + PRACTICED]

un·prec·e·dent·ed (un pres′i den′tid), *adj.* without previous instance; never before known or experienced; unexampled or unparalleled: *His action was unprecedented.* [UN-[1] + PRECEDENT[1] + -ED[2]] —**un·prec′e·dent′ed·ly,** *adv.* —**un·prec′e·dent′ed·ness,** *n.*

un·pre·dict·a·ble (un′pri dik′tə bəl), *adj.* **1.** not predictable; not to be foreseen or foretold: *Unpredictable events are often troublesome.* —*n.* **2.** something that is unpredictable: *The future is at best an unpredictable.* [UN-[1] + PREDICTABLE] —**un′pre·dict′a·bil′i·ty, un′pre·dict′a·ble·ness,** *n.* —**un′pre·dict′a·bly,** *adv.*

un·prej·u·diced (un prej′ə dist), *adj.* **1.** not prejudiced; without preconception; unbiased; impartial: *the unprejudiced view of the judge.* **2.** *Obs.* not damaged; unimpaired. [UN-[1] + PREJUDICED] —**un·prej′u·diced·ly,** *adv.* —**un·prej′u·diced·ness,** *n.*
—**Syn. 1.** See **fair**[1].

un·pre·ten·tious (un′pri ten′shəs), *adj.* not pretentious; simple; modest; unaffected; without ostentatious display, as of possessions or learning: *the unpretentious manner of Albert Einstein; an unpretentious summer resort.* [UN-[1] + PRETENTIOUS] —**un′pre·ten′tious·ly,** *adv.* —**un′pre·ten′tious·ness,** *n.*
—**Syn.** humble, unpretending, plain, open, easy.

un·priced (un prīst′), *adj.* **1.** not priced; having no price shown or set. **2.** beyond price; priceless. [UN-[1] + PRICED]

un·prin·ci·pled (un prin′sə pəld), *adj.* **1.** lacking or not based on moral scruples or principles: *an unprincipled person; unprincipled behavior.* **2.** not instructed in the principles of something (usually fol. by *in*). [UN-[1] + PRINCIPLED] —**un·prin′ci·pled·ness,** *n.*
—**Syn. 1.** tricky, dishonest. See **unscrupulous.**

un·print·a·ble (un prin′tə bəl), *adj.* improper or unfit for print, esp. because of obscenity or offensive nature. [UN-[1] + PRINTABLE] —**un·print′a·ble·ness,** *n.* —**un·print′a·bly,** *adv.*

un·pris·on (un priz′ən), *v.t.* to release from prison. [ME; see UN-[2], PRISON]

un·priz·a·ble (un prī′zə bəl), *adj.* not worthy to be prized; of little worth. [UN-[1] + PRIZABLE]

un·pro·fes·sion·al (un′prə fesh′ə nəl), *adj.* **1.** not professional; not pertaining to or characteristic of a profession. **2.** at variance with or contrary to professional standards or ethics; not befitting members of a profession, as language, behavior, etc.: *unprofessional conduct.* **3.** not belonging to a profession; nonprofessional. **4.** not done with professional competence, as a play staged or an opera performed by amateurs; amateurish. **5.** not engaged in as a means of livelihood or for any financial gain: *He qualified for the Olympics when his unprofessional status was proved.* —*n.* **6.** one who is not a professional; amateur. [UN-[1] + PROFESSIONAL] —**un′pro·fes′sion·al·ly,** *adv.*

un·prom·is·ing (un prom′i sing), *adj.* unlikely to be favorable or successful, as the weather, a situation, a career, etc. [UN-[1] + PROMISING] —**un·prom′is·ing·ly,** *adv.*

un·play′a·ble, *adj.*
un·played′, *adj.*
un·play′ful, *adj.*; **-ly,** *adv.*
un·play′ing, *adj.*
un·pleached′, *adj.*
un·plead′a·ble, *adj.*
un·plead′ed, *adj.*
un·plead′ing, *adj.*
un·pleas′a·ble, *adj.*
un·pleased′, *adj.*
un·pleas′ing, *adj.*
un·pleas′ur·a·ble, *adj.*
un·pleat′ed, *adj.*
un′ple·be′ian, *adj.*
un·pledged′, *adj.*
un·plen′ished, *adj.*
un·plen′te·ous, *adj.*; **-ly,** *adv.*
un·plen′ti·ful, *adj.*; **-ly,** *adv.*
un·pli′a·ble, *adj.*; **-ble·ness,** *n.*; **-bly,** *adv.*
un·pli′an·cy, *n.*
un·pli′ant, *adj.*; **-ly,** *adv.*; **-ness,** *n.*
un·plied′, *adj.*
un·plight′ed, *adj.*
un·plod′ding, *adj.*
un·plot′ted, *adj.*
un·plot′ting, *adj.*
un·ploughed′, *adj.*
un·plowed′, *adj.*
un·plucked′, *adj.*
un·plumb′, *adj.*
un·plumed′, *adj.*
un·plum′met·ed, *adj.*
un·plun′dered, *adj.*
un·plun′der·ous, *adj.*; **-ly,** *adv.*
un·plunged′, *adj.*
un·plu′ral·ised′, *adj.*
un′plu·ral·is′tic, *adj.*
un·plu′ral·ized′, *adj.*
un′plu·to·crat′ic, *adj.*
un′plu·to·crat′i·cal, *adj.*
un′pneu·mat′ic, *adj.*
un′pneu·mat′i·cal·ly, *adv.*
un·poached′, *adj.*
un·pock′et, *v.t.*
un·pod′ded, *adj.*
un′po·et′ic, *adj.*
un′po·et′i·cal, *adj.*; **-ly,** *adv.*
un′po·et′i·cised′, *adj.*
un′po·et′i·cized′, *adj.*
un·po′et·ized′, *adj.*
un·poign′ant, *adj.*; **-ly,** *adv.*
un·point′ed, *adj.*
un·point′ing, *adj.*
un·poised′, *adj.*
un·poi′son·a·ble, *adj.*
un·poi′soned, *adj.*
un·poi′son·ous, *adj.*; **-ly,** *adv.*
un·po′lar·ised′, *adj.*
un·po′lar·ized′, *adj.*
un·poled′, *adj.*
un′po·lem′ic, *adj.*
un′po·lem′i·cal, *adj.*; **-ly,** *adv.*
un′po·liced′, *adj.*
un·pol′ish·a·ble, *adj.*
un·pol′ished, *adj.*
un′po·lit′i·cal, *adj.*; **-ly,** *adv.*
un·pol′lard·ed, *adj.*
un·pol′lened, *adj.*
un′pol·lut′ed, *adj.*
un′pol·lut′ing, *adj.*
un·pol′y·mer·ised′, *adj.*
un·pol′y·mer·ized′, *adj.*
un·pomp′ous, *adj.*; **-ly,** *adv.*; **-ness,** *n.*
un·pon′der·a·ble, *adj.*
un·pon′dered, *adj.*
un·pon′der·ous, *adj.*; **-ly,** *adv.*; **-ness,** *n.*
un′pon·tif′i·cal, *adj.*; **-ly,** *adv.*
un·pooled′, *adj.*
un·pop′u·lar·ised′, *adj.*
un·pop′u·lar·ized′, *adj.*
un·pop′u·lat′ed, *adj.*
un·pop′u·lous, *adj.*; **-ly,** *adv.*; **-ness,** *n.*
un·por′ce·lain·ized′, *adj.*
un′por·no·graph′ic, *adj.*
un·po′rous, *adj.*; **-ness,** *n.*
un·port′a·ble, *adj.*
un′por·tend′ed, *adj.*
un′por·ten′tous, *adj.*; **-ly,** *adv.*; **-ness,** *n.*
un·por′ti·coed′, *adj.*
un·por′tion·a·ble, *adj.*
un·por′tioned, *adj.*
un·port′ly, *adj.*
un′por·tray′a·ble, *adj.*
un′por·trayed′, *adj.*
un·pos′ing, *adj.*
un·pos′i·tive, *adj.*; **-ly,** *adv.*; **-ness,** *n.*
un′pos·i·tiv·is′tic, *adj.*
un′pos·sess′a·ble, *adj.*
un′pos·sessed′, *adj.*
un′pos·sess′ing, *adj.*
un′pos·ses′sive, *adj.*; **-ly,** *adv.*; **-ness,** *n.*
un·post′ed, *adj.*
un·pos′tered, *adj.*
un·post′marked′, *adj.*
un′post·pon′a·ble, *adj.*
un′post·poned′, *adj.*
un·pos′tu·lat′ed, *adj.*
un·pot′, *v.t.*, **-pot·ted, -pot·ting.**
un·po′ta·ble, *adj.*
un·po′tent, *adj.*; **-ly,** *adv.*
un·pot′ted, *adj.*
un·pouched′, *adj.*
un·poul′ticed, *adj.*
un·pounced′, *adj.*
un·pound′ed, *adj.*
un·pour′a·ble, *adj.*
un·poured′, *adj.*
un·pout′ing, *adj.*; **-ly,** *adv.*
un·pow′dered, *adj.*
un′prag·mat′ic, *adj.*
un′prag·mat′i·cal, *adj.*; **-ly,** *adv.*
un·prais′a·ble, *adj.*
un·praised′, *adj.*
un·praise′ful, *adj.*
un·praise′wor′thy, *adj.*
un·prais′ing, *adj.*
un·pranked′, *adj.*
un·prat′ing, *adj.*
un·prayer′ful, *adj.*; **-ly,** *adv.*; **-ness,** *n.*
un·pray′ing, *adj.*
un·preached′, *adj.*
un·preach′ing, *adj.*
un′pre·car′i·ous, *adj.*; **-ly,** *adv.*; **-ness,** *n.*
un′pre·cau′tioned, *adj.*
un′pre·ced′ed, *adj.*
un′prec·e·den′tial, *adj.*
un′pre·cep′tive, *adj.*; **-ly,** *adv.*
un·pre′cious, *adj.*; **-ly,** *adv.*; **-ness,** *n.*
un·prec′i·piced, *adj.*
un′pre·cip′i·tant, *adj.*; **-ly,** *adv.*
un′pre·cip′i·tate′, *adj.*; **-ly,** *adv.*; **-ness,** *n.*
un′pre·cip′i·tat′ed, *adj.*
un′pre·cip′i·ta′tive, *adj.*; **-ly,** *adv.*
un′pre·cip′i·tous, *adj.*; **-ly,** *adv.*; **-ness,** *n.*
un′pre·cise′, *adj.*; **-ly,** *adv.*; **-ness,** *n.*
un′pre·ci′sive, *adj.*
un′pre·clud′a·ble, *adj.*
un′pre·clud′ed, *adj.*
un′pre·clu′sive, *adj.*; **-ly,** *adv.*
un′pre·co′cious, *adj.*; **-ly,** *adv.*; **-ness,** *n.*
un′pre·da′ceous, *adj.*; **-ly,** *adv.*; **-ness,** *n.*
un′pre·da′cious, *adj.*; **-ly,** *adv.*; **-ness,** *n.*
un·pred′a·to′ry, *adj.*
un′pre·des′tined, *adj.*
un·pred′i·ca·ble, *adj.*; **-ble·ness,** *n.*; **-bly,** *adv.*
un·pred′i·cat′ed, *adj.*
un·pred′i·ca′tive, *adj.*; **-ly,** *adv.*
un′pre·dict′ed, *adj.*
un′pre·dict′ing, *adj.*
un′pre·dic′tive, *adj.*; **-ly,** *adv.*
un′pre·dis·posed′, *adj.*
un′pre·dis·pos′ing, *adj.*
un′pre·empt′ed, *adj.*
un·preened′, *adj.*
un·pref′aced, *adj.*
un·pref′er·a·ble, *adj.*; **-ble·ness,** *n.*; **-bly,** *adv.*
un′pre·ferred′, *adj.*
un′pre·fig′ured, *adj.*
un′pre·fixed′, *adj.*
un′pre·fix′al, *adj.*; **-ly,** *adv.*
un·preg′nant, *adj.*
un′prej·u·di′cial, *adj.*; **-ly,** *adv.*
un′pre·lat′ic, *adj.*
un′pre·lud′ed, *adj.*
un′pre·ma·ture′, *adj.*; **-ly,** *adv.*; **-ness,** *n.*
un′pre·med′i·tat′ed, *adj.*
un′pre·mon′ished, *adj.*
un′pre·oc′cu·pied′, *adj.*
un′pre·or·dained′, *adj.*
un′pre·pared′, *adj.*
un′pre·par′ed·ly, *adv.*
un′pre·par′ed·ness, *n.*
un′pre·par′ing, *adj.*
un′pre·pon′der·at′ed, *adj.*
un′pre·pon′der·at′ing, *adj.*
un′pre·pos·sess′ing, *adj.*; **-ly,** *adv.*
un′pre·pos′ter·ous, *adj.*; **-ly,** *adv.*; **-ness,** *n.*
un·pres′aged′, *adj.*
un·pres·ag′ing, *adj.*
un·pre′sci·ent, *adj.*; **-ly,** *adv.*
un′pre·scind′ed, *adj.*
un′pre·scribed′, *adj.*
un′pre·sent′a·ble, *adj.*; **-ble·ness,** *n.*; **-bly,** *adv.*
un′pre·sent′a·tive, *adj.*
un′pre·sent′ed, *adj.*
un′pre·serv′a·ble, *adj.*
un′pre·served′, *adj.*
un′pres·i·den′tial, *adj.*; **-ly,** *adv.*
un′pre·sid′ing, *adj.*
un·pressed′, *adj.*
un·pres′sured, *adj.*
un′pre·sum′a·ble, *adj.*; **-bly,** *adv.*
un′pre·sumed′, *adj.*
un′pre·sum′ing, *adj.*
un′pre·sump′tive, *adj.*; **-ly,** *adv.*
un′pre·sump′tu·ous, *adj.*; **-ly,** *adv.*; **-ness,** *n.*
un′pre·tend′ed, *adj.*
un′pre·ter·mit′ted, *adj.*
un′pre·ter·nat′u·ral, *adj.*; **-ly,** *adv.*
un·pret′ti·fied′, *adj.*
un·pret′ti·ly, *adv.*
un·pret′ti·ness, *n.*
un·pret′ty, *adj.*
un′pre·vail′ing, *adj.*
un·prev′a·lent, *adj.*; **-ly,** *adv.*
un′pre·var′i·cat′ing, *adj.*
un′pre·vent′a·ble, *adj.*
un′pre·vent′a·tive, *adj.*
un′pre·vent′ed, *adj.*
un′pre·vent′i·ble, *adj.*
un′pre·ven′tive, *adj.*; **-ly,** *adv.*; **-ness,** *n.*
un·pre′viewed′, *adj.*
un·prey′ing, *adj.*
un·pricked′, *adj.*
un·prick′led, *adj.*
un·prick′ly, *adv.*
un·pride′ful, *adj.*; **-ly,** *adv.*
un·priest′like′, *adj.*
un·priest′ly, *adj.*, *adv.*
un·prig′gish, *adj.*
un·prim′, *adj.*; **-ly,** *adv.*; **-ness,** *n.*
un·primed′, *adj.*
un·prim′i·tive, *adj.*; **-ly,** *adv.*; **-ness,** *n.*
un′prim·i·tiv·is′tic, *adj.*
un·primmed′, *adj.*
un·prince′ly, *adj.*, *adv.*
un·print′ed, *adj.*
un′pris·mat′ic, *adj.*
un′pris·mat′i·cal *adj.*; **-ly,** *adv.*
un·pris′on·a·ble, *adj.*
un·pri′vate, *adj.*; **-ly,** *adv.*; **-ness,** *n.*
un·priv′i·leged, *adj.*
un·prized′, *adj.*
un·pro′bat·ed, *adj.*
un′pro·ba′tion·al, *adj.*
un′pro·ba′tion·ar′y, *adj.*
un·pro′ba·tive, *adj.*
un·probed′, *adj.*
un′prob·lem·at′ic, *adj.*
un′prob·lem·at′i·cal, *adj.*; **-ly,** *adv.*
un·proc′essed, *adj.*
un′pro·ces′sion·al, *adj.*
un′pro·claimed′, *adj.*
un′pro·cras′ti·nat′ed, *adj.*
un·pro′cre·ant, *adj.*
un·pro′cre·at′ed, *adj.*
un·proc′tored, *adj.*
un′pro·cur′a·ble, *adj.*
un′pro·cured′, *adj.*
un·prod′ded, *adj.*
un′pro·di′gious, *adj.*; **-ly,** *adv.*; **-ness,** *n.*
un′pro·duced′, *adj.*
un′pro·duc′i·ble, *adj.*
un′pro·duc′tive, *adj.*; **-ly,** *adv.*; **-ness,** *n.*
un′pro·duc·tiv′i·ty, *n.*
un′pro·fan′a·ble, *adj.*
un′pro·fane′, *adj.*; **-ly,** *adv.*; **-ness,** *n.*
un′pro·faned′, *adj.*
un′pro·fessed′, *adj.*
un′pro·fess′ing, *adj.*
un′pro·fes·so′ri·al, *adj.*; **-ly,** *adv.*
un·prof′fered, *adj.*
un·prof′it·a·bil′i·ty, *n.*
un·prof′it·a·ble, *adj.*; **-ble·ness,** *n.*; **-bly,** *adv.*
un·prof′it·ed, *adj.*
un·prof′it·eer′ing, *adj.*
un·prof′it·ing, *adj.*
un′pro·found′, *adj.*; **-ly,** *adv.*
un′pro·fuse′, *adj.*; **-ly,** *adv.*; **-ness,** *n.*
un·prog′nos′ti·cat′ed, *adj.*
un′prog·nos′ti·ca′tive, *adj.*
un′pro·gram·mat′ic, *adj.*
un′pro·gressed′, *adj.*
un′pro·gres′sive, *adj.*; **-ly,** *adv.*; **-ness,** *n.*
un′pro·hib′it·ed, *adj.*
un′pro·hib′i·tive, *adj.*; **-ly,** *adv.*
un′pro·ject′ed, *adj.*
un′pro·ject′ing, *adj.*
un′pro·jec′tive, *adj.*
un′pro·lif′er·ous, *adj.*
un′pro·lif′ic, *adj.*; **-ness,** *n.*
un′pro·lif′i·cal·ly, *adv.*
un′pro·lix′, *adj.*
un′pro·logued, *adj.*
un′pro·long′a·ble, *adj.*
un′pro·longed′, *adj.*
un′pro·mis′cu·ous, *adj.*; **-ly,** *adv.*; **-ness,** *n.*
un·prom′ised, *adj.*
un′pro·mot′a·ble, *adj.*
un′pro·mot′ed, *adj.*
un′pro·mo′tion·al, *adj.*
un′pro·mo′tive, *adj.*
un·prompt′, *adj.*; **-ly,** *adv.*; **-ness,** *n.*
un·prompt′ed, *adj.*
un·pro·mul′gat·ed, *adj.*
un′pro·nounce′a·ble, *adj.*
un′pro·nounced′, *adj.*
un′pro·nounc′ing, *adj.*
un·proof′read′, *adj.*
un·prop′a·ga·ble, *adj.*
un′prop·a·gan·dis′tic, *adj.*
un·prop′a·gat′ed, *adj.*
un·prop′a·ga′tive, *adj.*
un′pro·pelled′, *adj.*
un′pro·pel′lent, *adj.*
un·prop′er, *adj.*; **-ly,** *adv.*
un·prop′er·tied, *adj.*
un·proph′e·sied′, *adj.*
un′pro·phet′ic, *adj.*
un′pro·phet′i·cal, *adj.*; **-ly,** *adv.*
un′pro·pi′ti·a·ble, *adj.*
un′pro·pi′ti·at′ed, *adj.*
un′pro·pi′ti·at′ing, *adj.*
un′pro·pi′ti·a′tive, *adj.*
un′pro·pi′ti·a·to′ry, *adj.*
un′pro·pi′tious, *adj.*; **-ly,** *adv.*; **-ness,** *n.*
un′pro·por′tion·a·ble, *adj.*; **-bly,** *adv.*
un′pro·por′tion·al, *adj.*; **-ly,** *adv.*
un′pro·por′tion·ate, *adj.*; **-ly,** *adv.*
un′pro·por′tioned, *adj.*
un′pro·pos′a·ble, *adj.*
un′pro·posed′, *adj.*
un′pro·pos′ing, *adj.*
un′pro·pound′ed, *adj.*
un·propped′, *adj.*
un′pro·rogued′, *adj.*
un′pro·sa′ic, *adj.*; **-ness,** *n.*
un′pro·sa′i·cal, *adj.*; **-ly,** *adv.*
un′pro·scrib′a·ble, *adj.*
un′pro·scribed′, *adj.*
un′pro·scrip′tive, *adj.*; **-ly,** *adv.*
un·pros′pered, *adj.*
un·pros′per·ing, *adj.*
un·pros′per·ous, *adj.*; **-ly,** *adv.*; **-ness,** *n.*
un·pros′ti·tut′ed, *adj.*
un·pros′trat·ed, *adj.*
un′pro·tect′a·ble, *adj.*
un′pro·tect′ed, *adj.*
un′pro·tect′ing, *adj.*
un′pro·tec′tive, *adj.*; **-ly,** *adv.*
un·prot′es·tant, *adj.*
un′pro·test′ed, *adj.*
un′pro·test′ing, *adj.*; **-ly,** *adv.*
un′pro·tract′ed, *adj.*
un′pro·trac′tive, *adj.*
un′pro·trud′ed, *adj.*
un′pro·trud′ent, *adj.*
un′pro·trud′ing, *adj.*
un′pro·tru′si·ble, *adj.*
un′pro·tru′sive, *adj.*; **-ly,** *adv.*
un′pro·tu′ber·ant, *adj.*; **-ly,** *adv.*
un·proud′, *adj.*; **-ly,** *adv.*
un·prov′a·ble, *adj.*
un·proved′, *adj.*
un·prov′en, *adj.*
un′pro·ver′bi·al, *adj.*; **-ly,** *adv.*
un′pro·vid′a·ble, *adj.*
un′pro·vid′ed, *adj.*
un·prov′i·dent, *adj.*; **-ly,** *adv.*
un′prov·i·den′tial, *adj.*; **-ly,** *adv.*
un′pro·vin′cial, *adj.*; **-ly,** *adv.*
un·prov′ing, *adj.*
un′pro·vi′sion·al, *adj.*

un·pub′lished work′, *Law.* a literary work which, at the time of registration, has not been reproduced for sale or publicly distributed.

un·qual·i·fied (un kwol′ə fīd′), *adj.* **1.** not qualified; not fit; lacking the requisite qualifications: *He is unqualified for the presidency.* **2.** not modified, limited, or restricted in any way; without reservations: *unqualified praise.* **3.** absolute; complete; out-and-out: *an unqualified liar.* [UN-[1] + QUALIFIED] —**un·qual′i·fi′a·ble,** *adj.* —**un·qual′i·fied′ly,** *adv.* —**un·qual′i·fied′ness,** *n.*
—**Syn. 1.** unfit, incompetent. **2.** unmitigated. **3.** downright, thorough.

un·ques·tion·a·ble (un kwes′chə nə bəl), *adj.* **1.** not open to question; beyond doubt or dispute; indisputable; indubitable; undeniable; certain: *an unquestionable fact.* **2.** above criticism; unexceptionable: *a man of unquestionable principles.* [UN-[1] + QUESTIONABLE] —**un·ques′tion·a·ble·ness,** *n.* —**un·ques′tion·a·bly,** *adv.*

un·ques·tioned (un kwes′chənd), *adj.* **1.** not open to doubt or question; undisputed: *Dante's poetic mastery remains unquestioned.* **2.** not inquired into or investigated. **3.** not interrogated: *The eyewitness went unquestioned.* [UN-[1] + QUESTION + -ED[2]]

un·qui·et (un kwī′it), *adj.* **1.** agitated; restless; disordered; turbulent or tumultuous: *There was increased uncertainty in those unquiet times.* **2.** mentally or emotionally disturbed; vexed or perturbed; uneasy: *He felt unquiet and alone.* **3.** *Archaic.* not silent; noisy: *the cackling of unquiet women.* —*n.* **4.** a state of agitation, turbulence, disturbance, etc.: *Unquiet spread throughout the land.* [UN-[1] + QUIET[2]] —**un·qui′et·ly,** *adv.* —**un·qui′et·ness,** *n.*

un·quote (un kwōt′), *v.i.,* **-quot·ed, -quot·ing.** to close a quotation (often used with the word *quote,* which notes the opening of the quotation): *Jack said, quote, I never wore a hat, unquote.* [UN-[2] + QUOTE]

un·rav·el (un rav′əl), *v.,* **-eled, -el·ing** or (*esp. Brit.*) **-elled, -el·ling.** —*v.t.* **1.** to separate or disentangle the threads of (a woven or knitted fabric, a rope, etc.). **2.** to free from complication or difficulty; make plain or clear; solve: *to unravel a situation; to unravel a mystery.* —*v.i.* **3.** to become unraveled. [UN-[2] + RAVEL] —**un·rav′el·er;** *esp. Brit.,* **un·rav′el·ler,** *n.* —**un·rav′el·ment,** *n.*

un·read (un red′), *adj.* **1.** not read, as a letter, newspaper, etc.: *the unread classics.* **2.** lacking in knowledge gained by reading: *He disliked books and was for the most part unread.* **3.** having acquired little or no knowledge from reading: *Although a multimillionaire, he was still unread.* **4.** having little knowledge of a specific field: *While a brilliant literary critic, he remains almost totally unread in nuclear physics.* [ME *unred.* See UN-[1], READ[2]]

un·read·a·ble (un rē′də bəl), *adj.* **1.** not readable; undecipherable; scribbled: *His scrawl was almost unreadable.* **2.** not interesting to read; dull; tedious: *an unreadable treatise on ancient philosophy.* **3.** extraordinarily difficult to read or comprehend; obscure; incomprehensible: *an unreadable dream; an unreadable expression.* [UN-[1] + READABLE] —**un·read′a·bil′i·ty, un·read′a·ble·ness,** *n.* —**un·read′a·bly,** *adv.*

un·read·y (un red′ē), *adj.* **1.** not ready; not made ready: *The new stadium is as yet unready for use.* **2.** not in a state of readiness; unprepared: *He was emotionally unready for success.* **3.** lacking in presence of mind, as when a quick decision or a sharp answer is required: *Awkward situations often found him unready.* **4.** *Brit. Dial.* not dressed. **5.** not prompt or quick. [ME *unredy.* See UN-[1], READY] —**un·read′i·ness,** *n.*

un·re·al (un rē′əl, -rēl′), *adj.* **1.** not real or actual. **2.** imaginary; fanciful; illusory; delusory; fantastic. **3.** lacking in truth; not genuine; false; artificial: *His unreal conclusions were dressed in rhetoric.* [UN-[1] + REAL[1]] —**un·re′al·ly,** *adv.*
—**Syn.** sham, spurious, fictitious, illusive, theoretical, impractical, vague, fanciful.

un·re·al·i·ty (un′rē al′i tē), *n., pl.* **-ties. 1.** lack of reality; quality of being unreal: *the basic unreality of politics.* **2.** something that is unreal, invalid, imaginary, or illusory: *He appeared to be living in a world of unrealities.* **3.** incompetence or impracticality, esp. in everyday matters. [UN-[1] + REALITY]

un·re·al·iz·a·ble (un rē′ə lī′zə bəl), *adj.* **1.** incapable of being made actual or real, as an ideal, ambition, etc.: *His dream of military glory was unrealizable.* **2.** incapable of being sensed or understood; unthinkable. Also, *esp. Brit.,* **un′re·al·is′a·ble.** [UN-[1] + REALIZABLE]

un·re·al·ized (un rē′ə līzd′), *adj.* **1.** not made real or actual; not resulting in accomplishment, as a task, aim, etc.: *unrealized ambitions.* **2.** not known or suspected: *unrealized talent.* Also, *esp. Brit.,* **un·re′al·ised′.** [UN-[1] + REALIZED]

un·rea·son (un rē′zən), *n.* **1.** inability or unwillingness to think or act rationally, reasonably, or sensibly; irrationality. **2.** lack of reason or sanity; madness; confusion; disorder; chaos: *a world torn by unreason.* —*v.t.* **3.** to upset or disrupt the reason or sanity of: *The devious plot soon unreasoned the general.* [ME *un-reson.* See UN-[1], REASON]

un·rea·son·a·ble (un rē′zə nə bəl), *adj.* **1.** not reasonable or rational; acting at variance with or contrary to reason; not guided by reason, sound judgment, or good sense; irrational: *an unreasonable man.* **2.** not in accordance with practical realities, as attitude, behavior, etc.; inappropriate: *There was something of the Bohemian in his unreasonable way of life.* **3.** excessive, immoderate, or exorbitant; unconscionable: *an unreasonable price; unreasonable demands.* **4.** not having the faculty of reason. [ME *unresonabel.* See UN-[1], REASONABLE] —**un·rea′son·a·ble·ness,** *n.* —**un·rea′son·a·bly,** *adv.*
—**Syn. 1, 2.** senseless, foolish, silly. **2.** preposterous, absurd, stupid, nonsensical. **3.** extravagant.

un·rea·son·ing (un rē′zə ning), *adj.* not reasoning or exercising reason; reasonless; thoughtless; irrational: *an unreasoning fanatic.* [UN-[1] + REASONING] —**un·rea′son·ing·ly,** *adv.*

un·re·con·struct·ed (un′rē kən struk′tid), *adj.* **1.** stubbornly maintaining earlier positions, beliefs, etc.; not adjusted to new or current situations: *an unreconstructed Republican.* **2.** *U.S. Hist.* (of Southern States) not accepting the conditions for reinstatement in the Union after the Civil War. [UN-[1] + RECONSTRUCTED]

un·re·con·struc·ti·ble (un′rē kən struk′tə bəl), *adj.* that cannot be reconstructed. [UN-[1] + RECONSTRUCT + -IBLE]

un·re·cord·ed (un′ri kôr′did), *adj.* **1.** not recorded; not reported in an official record. **2.** not noted in historical documents: *an unrecorded event; an unrecorded tradition.* [UN-[1] + RECORD + -ED[2]]

un·reel (un rēl′), *v.t.* **1.** to unwind from or as if from a reel: *to unreel some wire; to unreel a tangled skein.* —*v.i.* **2.** to become unreeled. [UN-[2] + REEL[1]] —**un·reel′a·ble,** *adj.* —**un·reel′er,** *n.*

un·reeve (un rēv′), *v.,* **-rove** or **-reeved, -reev·ing.** —*v.t.* **1.** *Naut.* to withdraw (a rope) from a block, thimble, etc. —*v.i.* **2.** to unreeve a rope. **3.** (of a rope) to become unreeved. [UN-[2] + REEVE[2]]

un·re·fined (un′ri fīnd′), *adj.* **1.** not refined; not purified, as substances: *unrefined metal.* **2.** coarse or crude; lacking in refinement of taste, feeling, manners, language, etc. [UN-[1] + REFINED]
—**Syn. 1.** unpurified, crude, coarse. **2.** unpolished, uncultured, ill-bred, rude, boorish, vulgar, gross.

un·re·flect·ed (un′ri flek′tid), *adj.* **1.** not reflected on; not given consideration: *unreflected opinions.* **2.** not cast back, as light, heat, an image, etc.: *the unreflected heat of the sun; the unreflected glory of an illustrious ancestor.* [UN-[1] + REFLECT + -ED[2]]

un·re·flect·ing (un′ri flek′ting), *adj.* not reflecting; unthinking: *an unreflecting, self-satisfied man.* [UN-[1] + REFLECT + -ING[2]] —**un′re·flect′ing·ly,** *adv.*

un·re·flec·tive (un′ri flek′tiv), *adj.* not reflective; thoughtless; lacking in due deliberation; heedless; rash: *unreflective conclusions; unreflective behavior.* [UN-[1] + REFLECTIVE] —**un′re·flec′tive·ly,** *adv.*

un′pro·vi′sioned, *adj.*
un′pro·voc′a·tive, *adj.;* **-ly,** *adv.;* **-ness,** *n.*
un′pro·vok′a·ble, *adj.*
un′pro·voked′, *adj.*
un′pro·vok′ing, *adj.;* **-ly,** *adv.*
un·prowl′ing, *adj.*
un′prox·im′i·ty, *n.*
un·pru′dent, *adj.;* **-ly,** *adv.*
un′pru·den′tial, *adj.;* **-ly,** *adv.*
un·prun′a·ble, *adj.*
un·pruned′, *adj.*
un·pry′ing, *adj.*
un·psy′chic, *adj.*
un·psy′chi·cal·ly, *adv.*
un′psy·cho·log′i·cal, *adj.;* **-ly,** *adv.*
un′psy·cho·path′ic, *adj.*
un′psy·chot′ic, *adj.*
un·pub′lic, *adj.;* **-ly,** *adv.*
un·pub′li·cized′, *adj.*
un·pub′lish·a·ble, *adj.*
un·pub′lished, *adj.*
un·puck′ered, *adj.*
un·pud′dled, *adj.*
un·puffed′, *adj.*
un·puff′ing, *adj.*
un′pu·gil·is′tic, *adj.*
un′pug·na′cious, *adj.;* **-ly,** *adv.;* **-ness,** *n.*
un·pul′leyed, *adj.*
un·pulped′, *adj.*
un·pul′sat·ing, *adj.*
un·pul′sa·tive, *adj.*
un·pul′ver·a·ble, *adj.*
un·pul′ver·ised′, *adj.*
un·pul′ver·ized′, *adj.*
un·pul′vi·nate′, *adj.*
un·pul′vi·nat′ed, *adj.*
un·pum′meled, *adj.*
un·pum′melled, *adj.*
un·pump′a·ble, *adj.*
un·pumped′, *adj.*
un·punc′tate, *adj.*
un·punc′tat·ed, *adj.*
un·punc·til′i·ous, *adj.;* **-ly,** *adv.;* **-ness,** *n.*
un·punc′tu·al, *adj.;* **-ly,** *adv.;* **-ness,** *n.*
un·punc·tu·al′i·ty, *n.*
un·punc′tu·at′ed, *adj.*
un·punc′tu·at′ing, *adj.*
un·punc′tured, *adj.*
un·pun′ish·a·ble, *adj.*
un·pun′ished, *adj.*
un·pun′ish·ing, *adj.;* **-ly,** *adv.*
un·pu′ni·tive, *adj.*
un·pur′chas·a·ble, *adj.*
un·pur′chased, *adj.*
un·pure′, *adj.;* **-ly,** *adv.;* **-ness,** *n.*
un·pur′ga·tive, *adj.;* **-ly,** *adv.*
un·purge′a·ble, *adj.*
un·purged′, *adj.*
un·pu′ri·fied′, *adj.*
un·pu′ri·fy′ing, *adj.*
un·pu·ris′tic, *adj.*
un·pu′ri·tan, *adj.*
un′pu·ri·tan′ic, *adj.*
un′pu·ri·tan′i·cal, *adj.;* **-ly,** *adv.*
un·purled′, *adj.*
un′pur·loined′, *adj.*
un′pur·port′ed, *adj.*
un·pur′posed, *adj.*
un·pur′pose·ly, *adv.*
un·pur′pos·ing, *adj.*
un·pur′pos·ive, *adj.*
un′pur·su′a·ble, *adj.*
un′pur·su′ant, *adj.*
un′pur·sued′, *adj.*
un′pur·su′ing, *adj.*
un·pushed′, *adj.*
un·pu′ta·tive, *adj.;* **-ly,** *adv.*
un·pu′tre·fi′a·ble, *adj.*
un·pu′tre·fied′, *adj.*
un·pu′trid, *adj.;* **-ly,** *adv.;* **-ness,** *n.*
un′pu·trid′i·ty, *n.*
un·put′tied, *adj.*
un·puz′zle, *v.t.,* **-zled, -zling.**
un·quad′ded, *adj.*
un·quaffed′, *adj.*
un·quail′ing, *adj.*
un·quak′ing, *adj.*
un·qual′i·fy′ing, *adj.;* **-ly,** *adv.*
un·quan′ti·fied′, *adj.*
un·quan′ti·ta′tive, *adj.*
un·quar′an·tined′, *adj.*
un·quar′rel·ing, *adj.*
un·quar′rel·ling, *adj.*
un·quar′rel·some, *adj.*
un·quar′ried, *adj.*
un·quar′tered, *adj.*
un·quashed′, *adj.*
un·qua′ver·ing, *adj.*
un·quayed′, *adj.*
un·queen′ly, *adj.*
un·quell′a·ble, *adj.*
un·quelled′, *adj.*
un·quench′a·ble, *adj.*
un·quenched′, *adj.*
un·que′ried, *adj.*
un·quer′u·lous, *adj.;* **-ly,** *adv.;* **-ness,** *n.*
un·quest′ed, *adj.*
un·ques′tion·ing, *adj.*
un·quib′bling, *adj.*
un·quick′, *adj.;* **-ly,** *adv.;* **-ness,** *n.*
un·quick′ened, *adj.*
un·qui′et·a·ble, *adj.*
un·qui′et·ed, *adj.*
un·qui′et·ing, *adj.*
un·quilt′ed, *adj.*
un·quit′ted, *adj.*
un·quiv′ered, *adj.*
un·quiv′er·ing, *adj.*
un′quix·ot′ic, *adj.*
un′quix·ot′i·cal, *adj.;* **-ly,** *adv.*
un·quiz′za·ble, *adj.*
un·quizzed′, *adj.*
un·quiz′zi·cal, *adj.;* **-ly,** *adv.*
un·quot′a·ble, *adj.*
un·quot′ed, *adj.*
un·rab′bet·ed, *adj.*
un′rab·bin′ic, *adj.*
un′rab·bin′i·cal, *adj.*
un·rack′, *v.t.*
un·ra′di·ant, *adj.*
un·ra′di·at′ed, *adj.*
un·ra′di·a′tive, *adj.*
un·rad′i·cal, *adj.;* **-ly,** *adv.*
un′ra·di·o·ac′tive, *adj.*
un·raf′fled, *adj.*
un·raf′tered, *adj.*
un·raid′ed, *adj.*
un·railed′, *adj.*
un·rail′road′ed, *adj.*
un·rail′wayed′, *adj.*
un·rain′y, *adj.*
un·rais′a·ble, *adj.*
un·raise′a·ble, *adj.*
un·raised′, *adj.*
un·raked′, *adj.*
un·rak′ing, *adj.*
un·ral′lied, *adj.*
un·ral′ly·ing, *adj.*
un·ram′bling, *adj.*
un·ram′i·fied′, *adj.*
un·rammed′, *adj.*
un·ramped′, *adj.*
un·ranched′, *adj.*
un·ran′cid, *adj.*
un·ran′cored, *adj.*
un·ran′cor·ous, *adj.*
un·ran′coured, *adj.*
un·ran′cour·ous, *adj.*
un·rang′ing, *adj.*
un·ranked′, *adj.*
un·ran′kled, *adj.*
un·ran′sacked, *adj.*
un·ran′som·a·ble, *adj.*
un·ran′somed, *adj.*
un·rant′ing, *adj.*
un′ra·pa′cious, *adj.;* **-ly,** *adv.;* **-ness,** *n.*
un·raped′, *adj.*
un·rap′tured, *adj.*
un·rap′tur·ous, *adj.;* **-ly,** *adv.;* **-ness,** *n.*
un·rar′e·fied′, *adj.*
un·rash′, *adj.;* **-ly,** *adv.;* **-ness,** *n.*
un·rasped′, *adj.*
un·rasp′ing, *adj.*
un·rasp′y, *adj.*
un·rat′a·ble, *adj.*
un·rat′ed, *adj.*
un·rat′i·fied′, *adj.*
un·ra′tion·a·ble, *adj.*
un·ra′tion·al, *adj.;* **-ly,** *adv.*
un·ra′tion·al·ised′, *adj.*
un·ra′tion·al·is′ing, *adj.*
un·ra′tion·al·ized′, *adj.*
un·ra′tion·al·iz′ing, *adj.*
un·ra′tioned, *adj.*
un·rav′aged, *adj.*
un·rav′ing, *adj.*
un·rav′ished, *adj.*
un·rayed′, *adj.*
un·razed′, *adj.*
un·ra′zored, *adj.*
un·reach′a·ble, *adj.*
un·reached′, *adj.*
un′re·ac′tion·ar′y, *adj.*
un′re·ac′tive, *adj.*
un′re·al·is′tic, *adj.*
un′re·al·is′ti·cal·ly, *adv.*
un·re′al·ise′, *v.,* **-ised, -is·ing.**
un·re′al·ize′, *v.,* **-ized, -iz·ing.**
un·realmed′, *adj.*
un·reaped′, *adj.*
un·reared′, *adj.*
un·rea′soned, *adj.*
un′re·as·sur′ing, *adj.;* **-ly,** *adv.*
un·reav′ing, *adj.*
un·re′bat·ed, *adj.*
un′re·bel′lious, *adj.;* **-ly,** *adv.;* **-ness,** *n.*
un′re·buff′a·ble, *adj.*
un′re·buffed′, *adj.*
un′re·built′, *adj.*
un′re·buk′a·ble, *adj.*
un′re·buked′, *adj.*
un′re·but′ta·ble, *adj.*
un′re·but′ted, *adj.*
un′re·cal′ci·trant, *adj.*
un′re·call′a·ble, *adj.*
un′re·called′, *adj.*
un′re·cant′ed, *adj.*
un′re·cant′ing, *adj.*
un′re·cap′tured, *adj.*
un′re·ced′ing, *adj.*
un′re·ceipt′ed, *adj.*
un′re·ceiv′a·ble, *adj.*
un′re·ceiv′ing, *adj.*
un′re·cep′tive, *adj.;* **-ly,** *adv.;* **-ness,** *n.*
un′re·cep·tiv′i·ty, *n.*
un′re·ces′sive, *adj.;* **-ly,** *adv.*
un′re·cip′i·ent, *adj.*
un′re·cip′ro·cal, *adj.;* **-ly,** *adv.*
un′re·cip′ro·cat′ed, *adj.*
un′re·cip′ro·cat′ing, *adj.*
un·rec′i·ta′tive, *adj.*
un′re·cit′ed, *adj.*
un·reck′on, *v.t.*
un·reck′on·a·ble, *adj.*
un·reck′oned, *adj.*
un′re·claim′a·ble, *adj.*
un′re·claimed′, *adj.*
un′re·claim′ing, *adj.*
un′re·clined′, *adj.*
un′re·clin′ing, *adj.*
un·rec′luse, *adj.*
un′re·clu′sive, *adj.*
un·rec′og·nis′a·ble, *adj.;* **-bly,** *adv.*
un′re·cog′ni·to′ry, *adj.*
un·rec′og·niz′a·ble, *adj.;* **-bly,** *adv.*
un·rec′og·nized′, *adj.*
un·rec′og·niz′ing, *adj.*
un′re·col·lect′ed, *adj.*
un′rec·ol·lec′tive, *adj.*
un′rec·om·mend′a·ble, *adj.*
un′rec·om·mend′ed, *adj.*
un′rec·om·pens′a·ble, *adj.*
un·rec′om·pensed′, *adj.*
un·rec′on·cil′a·ble, *adj.;* **-ble·ness,** *n.;* **-bly,** *adv.*
un·rec′on·ciled′, *adj.*
un·rec′on·cil′ing, *adj.*
un·rec′on·dite′, *adj.*
un′rec·on·noi′tered, *adj.*
un′rec·on·noi′tred, *adj.*
un′re·con·sid′ered, *adj.*
un′re·cord′a·ble, *adj.*
un′re·count′a·ble, *adj.*
un′re·count′ed, *adj.*
un′re·cov′er·a·ble, *adj.*
un·rec′re·ant, *adj.*
un′rec·re·a′tion·al, *adj.*
un′re·crim′i·na′tive, *adj.*
un′re·cruit′a·ble, *adj.*
un′re·cruit′ed, *adj.*
un·rec′tan′gu·lar, *adj.;* **-ly,** *adv.*
un·rec′ti·fi′a·ble, *adj.*
un·rec′ti·fied′, *adj.*
un′re·cum′bent, *adj.;* **-ly,** *adv.*
un′re·cu′per·at′ed, *adj.*
un′re·cu′per·a′tive, *adj.;* **-ness,** *n.*
un′re·cu′per·a·to′ry, *adj.*
un′re·cur′rent, *adj.;* **-ly,** *adv.*
un′re·cur′ring, *adj.*
un·rec′u·sant, *adj.*
un′re·dact′ed, *adj.*
un′re·deem′a·ble, *adj.;* **-bly,** *adv.*
un′re·deem′ing, *adj.*
un′re·demp′tive, *adj.*
un′re·dress′a·ble, *adj.*
un′re·dressed′, *adj.*
un′re·duced′, *adj.*
un′re·duc′i·ble, *adj.;* **-bly,** *adv.*
un·reefed′, *adj.*
un·ref′er·enced, *adj.*
un′re·ferred′, *adj.*
un′re·filled′, *adj.*
un′re·fin′ing, *adj.*
un′re·fit′ted, *adj.*
un′re·form′a·ble, *adj.*
un′re·form′a·tive, *adj.*
un′re·formed′, *adj.*
un′re·form′ing, *adj.*
un′re·fract′ed, *adj.*
un′re·fract′ing, *adj.*
un′re·frac′tive, *adj.;* **-ly,** *adv.;* **-ness,** *n.*
un′re·frac′to·ry, *adj.*
un′re·frain′a·ble, *adj.*
un′re·frained′, *adj.*
un′re·frain′ing, *adj.*
un′re·fran′gi·ble, *adj.*
un′re·freshed′, *adj.*
un′re·fresh′ing, *adj.;* **-ly,** *adv.*
un′re·frig′er·at′ed, *adj.*
un′re·ful′gent, *adj.;* **-ly,** *adv.*
un′re·fund′a·ble, *adj.*
un′re·fund′ed, *adj.*
un′re·fund′ing, *adj.*
un′re·fus′a·ble, *adj.*
un′re·fused′, *adj.*
un′re·fus′ing, *adj.*
un′re·fut′a·ble, *adj.;* **-bly,** *adv.*
un′re·fut′ed, *adj.*
un′re·fut′ing, *adj.*
un′re·gain′a·ble, *adj.*
un′re·gained′, *adj.*
un·re′gal, *adj.;* **-ly,** *adv.*
un′re·galed, *adj.*
un′re·gard′a·ble, *adj.*
un′re·gard′ant, *adj.*
un′re·gard′ed, *adj.;* **-ly,** *adv.*

un·re·gen·er·ate (un′ri jen′ər it), *adj.* Also, **un·re·gen·er·at·ed** (un′ri jen′ə rā′tid). **1.** not regenerate; not renewed in heart and mind or reborn in spirit; unrepentant: *an unregenerate sinner.* **2.** refusing to believe in the existence of God: *an unregenerate atheist; an unregenerate skeptic.* **3.** unconvinced by or unconverted to a particular religion, sect, or movement; unreconstructed: *As far as the leaders of the cause were concerned, he was an unregenerate rebel.* **4.** persisting in the holding of prior convictions; opposing new ideas, causes, etc.; stubborn; obstinate: *an unregenerate reactionary.* **5.** not reformed; wicked; sinful; profligate; dissolute: *an unregenerate way of life.* —*n.* **6.** an unregenerate person. [UN-^{1} + REGENERATE] —**un·re·gen·er·a·cy** (un′ri jen′ər ə sē), *n.* —**un′re·gen′er·ate·ly,** *adv.*

un·re·lent·ing (un′ri len′ting), *adj.* **1.** not relenting; not yielding or swerving in determination or resolution, as of or from opinions, convictions, ambitions, ideals, etc.; inflexible: *an unrelenting stand on the school integration issue.* **2.** not easing or slackening in severity: *an unrelenting rain.* **3.** maintaining speed, effort, vigor, intensity, rate of advance, etc.: *The football team kept up their unrelenting attack. There was unrelenting progress under the new administration.* [UN-^{1} + RELENT + -ING^2] —**un′re·lent′ing·ly,** *adv.* —**un′re·lent′ing·ness,** *n.*
—**Syn. 1.** relentless, merciless, unmerciful, ruthless, pitiless, cruel, remorseless. **2.** unremitting, implacable, inexorable.

un·re·li·a·ble (un′ri lī′ə bəl), *adj.* not reliable; not to be relied or depended on. [UN-^{1} + RELIABLE] —**un′re·li′a·bil′i·ty, un′re·li′a·ble·ness,** *n.* —**un′re·li′a·bly,** *adv.*

un·re·li·gious (un′ri lij′əs), *adj.* **1.** irreligious. **2.** having no connection with or relation to religion; neither religious nor irreligious; nonreligious: *His thinking, while unreligious, did not oppose religion.* [ME; see UN-^{1}, RELIGIOUS] —**un′re·li′gious·ly,** *adv.*

un·re·mit·ted (un′rē mit′id), *adj.* **1.** not remitted, as a debt. **2.** unpardoned, as a sin. **3.** steadily maintained; uninterrupted; constant: *He gave the matter his unremitted attention.* [UN-^{1} + REMITTED]

un·re·mit·ted·ly (un′rē mit′id lē), *adv.* continuously; uninterruptedly; constantly. [UNREMITTED + -LY]

un·re·mit·tent (un′rē mit′ənt), *adj.* (esp. of a fever) unremitting. [UN-^{1} + REMITTENT] —**un′re·mit′tence, un′re·mit′ten·cy,** *n.* —**un′re·mit′tent·ly,** *adv.*

un·re·mit·ting (un′ri mit′ing), *adj.* not slackening or abating; incessant: *unremitting noise; unremitting toil; unremitting scholarship.* [UN-^{1} + REMITTING] —**un′re·mit′ting·ly,** *adv.* —**un′re·mit′ting·ness,** *n.*

un·rent (un rent′), *adj.* not rent; not torn, disturbed, pained, or the like: *unrent garments; unrent silence; unrent feelings.* [UN-^{1} + RENT^2]

un·re·pair (un′ri pâr′), *n.* lack of repair; disrepair; dilapidation. [UN-^{1} + REPAIR^1] —**un′re·paired′,** *adj.*

un·re·serve (un′ri zûrv′), *n.* absence of reserve; frankness; candor. [UN-^{1} + RESERVE]

un·re·served (un′ri zûrvd′), *adj.* **1.** not reserved; without reservation; full; entire; unqualified: *unreserved approval.* **2.** free from reserve; frank; open: *unreserved behavior.* [UN-^{1} + RESERVED] —**un·re·serv·ed·ly** (un′ri zûr′vid lē), *adv.* —**un′re·serv′ed·ness,** *n.*
—**Syn. 1.** complete, unlimited. **2.** ingenuous, candid, artless, guileless, sincere.

un·rest (un rest′), *n.* **1.** lack of rest; a restless, troubled, or uneasy state; disquiet: *He was aware of the unrest within himself.* **2.** strong, almost rebellious, dissatisfaction and agitation: *There was considerable unrest in the underdeveloped countries.* [ME; see UN-^{1}, REST^1] —**un·rest′ing,** *adj.*

un·re·straint (un′ri strānt′), *n.* absence of or freedom from restraint. [UN-^{1} + RESTRAINT]

un′restrict′ed propel′lant, *Rocketry.* a rocket propellant usable as fuel in more than one type of plane. Cf. **restricted propellant.**

un·rid·dle (un rid′əl), *v.t.,* **-dled, -dling.** to solve (a riddle, mystery, etc.). [UN-^{2} + RIDDLE^1]

un·rid·dled (un rid′əld), *adj.* not solved, as a riddle, mystery, etc. [UN-^{1} + RIDDLE^1 + -ED^2]

un·rig (un rig′), *v.t.,* **-rigged, -rig·ging. 1.** to strip of rigging, as a ship. **2.** to strip of equipment. **3.** *Chiefly Brit. Dial.* to undress. [UN-^{2} + RIG]

un·right·eous (un rī′chəs), *adj.* **1.** not righteous; not upright or virtuous; wicked; sinful; evil: *an unrighteous man.* **2.** not in accordance with right or justice; unfair or unjust: *an unrighteous law.* [ME *unrightwyse,* OE *unrihtwīs.* See UN-^{1}, RIGHTEOUS] —**un·right′eous·ly,** *adv.* —**un·right′eous·ness,** *n.*

un·rip (un rip′), *v.t.,* **-ripped, -rip·ping. 1.** to undo by ripping; cut or tear open; rip; take apart or detach. **2.** to make known; disclose; reveal. [UN-^{2} + RIP^1]

un·ripe (un rīp′), *adj.* **1.** not ripe; immature; not fully developed: *unripe fruit.* **2.** too early; premature. [ME *unrype,* OE *unripe.* See UN-^{1}, RIPE] —**un·ripe′ly,** *adv.* —**un·ripe′ness,** *n.*

un·ri·valed (un rī′vəld), *adj.* having no rival or competitor; having no equal; peerless; unparalleled; incomparable; supreme: *His work is unrivaled for the beauty of its prose. He viewed a landscape of unrivaled beauty.* Also, *esp. Brit.,* **un·ri′valled.** [UN-^{1} + RIVALED]

un·robe (un rōb′), *v.t., v.i.,* **-robed, -rob·ing.** to disrobe; undress. [UN-^{2} + ROBE]

un·roll (un rōl′), *v.t.* **1.** to open or spread out (something rolled or coiled): *The merchant quickly unrolled several types of fabric.* **2.** to lay open; display; reveal.

---

un′re·gard′ful, *adj.*
un′re·gen′er·a·ble, *adj.*
un′re·gen′er·at′ing, *adj.*
un′re·gen′er·a′tive, *adj.*
un·reg′i·men′tal, *adj.;* **-ly,** *adv.*
un·reg′i·ment′ed, *adj.*
un·reg′is·tra·ble, *adj.*
un·reg′is·tered, *adj.*
un′re·gres′sive, *adj.;* **-ly,** *adv.;* **-ness,** *n.*
un′re·gret′ful, *adj.;* **-ly,** *adv.;* **-ness,** *n.*
un′re·gret′ta·ble, *adj.;* **-bly,** *adv.*
un′re·gret′ted, *adj.*
un′re·gret′ting, *adj.*
un·reg′u·la·ble, *adj.*
un·reg′u·lar·ised′, *adj.*
un·reg′u·lar·ized′, *adj.*
un·reg′u·lat′ed, *adj.*
un·reg′u·la′tive, *adj.*
un·reg′u·la·to′ry, *adj.*
un′re·gur′gi·tat′ed, *adj.*
un′re·ha·bil′i·tat′ed, *adj.*
un′re·hears′a·ble, *adj.*
un′re·hearsed′, *adj.*
un′re·hears′ing, *adj.*
un·reign′ing, *adj.*
un·reined′, *adj.*
un′re·in·forced′, *adj.*
un′re·in·stat′ed, *adj.*
un′re·it′er·a·ble, *adj.*
un′re·it′er·at′ed, *adj.*
un′re·it′er·a′ting, *adj.*
un′re·it′er·a′tive, *adj.*
un′re·ject′a·ble, *adj.*
un′re·ject′ed, *adj.*
un′re·jec′tive, *adj.*
un′re·joiced′, *adj.*
un′re·joic′ing, *adj.*
un′re·ju′ve·nat′ed, *adj.*
un′re·ju′ve·nat′ing, *adj.*
un′re·laps′ing, *adj.*
un′re·lat′ed, *adj.*
un′re·lat′ing, *adj.*
un′re·la′tion·al, *adj.*
un·rel′a·tive, *adj.;* **-ly,** *adv.*
un′rel·a·tiv·is′tic, *adj.*
un′re·lax′a·ble, *adj.*
un′re·laxed′, *adj.*
un′re·lax′ing, *adj.*
un·re·layed, *adj.*
un′re·leas′a·ble, *adj.*
un′re·leased′, *adj.*
un′re·leas′i·ble, *adj.*
un′re·leas′ing, *adj.*
un·rel′e·ga·ble, *adj.*
un·rel′e·gat′ed, *adj.*
un′re·lent′ed, *adj.*
un·rel′e·vant, *adj.;* **-ly,** *adv.*
un′re·li′ant, *adj.*
un′re·liev′a·ble, *adj.*
un′re·lieved′, *adj.*
un′re·liev′ing, *adj.*
un′re·li′gioned, *adj.*
un′re·lin′quish·a·ble, *adj.*
un′re·lin′quished, *adj.*
un′re·lin′quish·ing, *adj.*
un·rel′ish·a·ble, *adj.*
un·rel′ished, *adj.*
un·rel′ish·ing, *adj.*
un′re·luc′tant, *adj.;* **-ly,** *adv.*
un′re·main′ing, *adj.*
un′re·mand′ed, *adj.*
un′re·mark′a·ble, *adj.*
un′re·marked′, *adj.*
un′re·mar′ried, *adj.*
un′re·me′di·a·ble, *adj.*
un·rem′e·died, *adj.*
un′re·mem′bered, *adj.*
un′re·mem′ber·ing, *adj.*
un′re·mind′ed, *adj.*
un′rem·i·nis′cent, *adj.;* **-ly,** *adv.*
un′re·miss′i·ble, *adj.*
un′re·mis′sive, *adj.*
un′re·mit′ta·ble, *adj.*
un′re·mon′strant, *adj.*
un′re·mon′strat·ed, *adj.*
un′re·mon′strat·ing, *adj.*
un′re·mon′stra·tive, *adj.*
un′re·morse′ful, *adj.;* **-ly,** *adv.;* **-ness,** *n.*
un′re·mote′, *adj.;* **-ly,** *adv.;* **-ness,** *n.*
un′re·mount′ed, *adj.*
un′re·mov′a·ble, *adj.;* **-ble·ness,** *n.;* **-bly,** *adv.*
un′re·moved′, *adj.*
un′re·mu′ner·at′ed, *adj.*
un′re·mu′ner·a′tive, *adj.;* **-ly,** *adv.*
un·ren′der·a·ble, *adj.*
un·ren′dered, *adj.*
un′re·new′a·ble, *adj.*
un′re·newed′, *adj.*
un′re·nounce′a·ble, *adj.*
un′re·nounced′, *adj.*
un′re·nounc′ing, *adj.*
un·ren′o·vat′ed, *adj.*
un·ren′o·va′tive, *adj.*
un′re·nowned′, *adj.*
un·rent′a·ble, *adj.*
un·rent′ed, *adj.*
un′re·nun′ci·a·ble, *adj.*
un′re·nun′ci·a′tive, *adj.*
un′re·nun′ci·a·to′ry, *adj.*
un′re·or′gan·ised′, *adj.*
un′re·or′gan·ized′, *adj.*
un′re·paid′, *adj.*
un′re·pay′a·ble, *adj.*
un′re·peal′a·bil′i·ty, *n.*
un′re·peal′a·ble, *adj.*
un′re·pealed′, *adj.*
un′re·peat′a·ble, *adj.*
un′re·peat′ed, *adj.*
un′re·pel′la·ble, *adj.*
un′re·pelled′, *adj.*
un′re·pel′lent, *adj.;* **-ly,** *adv.*
un′re·pent′ant, *adj.;* **-ly,** *adv.*
un′re·pent′ed, *adj.*
un′re·pent′ing, *adj.;* **-ly,** *adv.*
un′rep·e·ti′tious, *adj.;* **-ly,** *adv.;* **-ness,** *n.*
un′re·pet′i·tive, *adj.;* **-ly,** *adv.*
un′re·pined′, *adj.*
un′re·pin′ing, *adj.*
un′re·place′a·ble, *adj.*
un′re·placed′, *adj.*
un′re·plen′ished, *adj.*
un′re·plete′, *adj.;* **-ness,** *n.*
un′re·plev′in·a·ble, *adj.*
un′re·plev′ined, *adj.*
un′re·plev′is·a·ble, *adj.*
un′re·plied′, *adj.*
un′re·ply′ing, *adj.*
un′re·port′a·ble, *adj.*
un′re·port′ed, *adj.*
un′rep·or·to′ri·al, *adj.*
un′re·pose′, *n.*
un′re·posed′, *adj.*
un′re·pose′ful, *adj.;* **-ly,** *adv.;* **-ness,** *n.*
un′re·pos′ing, *adj.*
un′re·pos·sessed′, *adj.*
un′rep·re·hend′ed, *adj.*
un′rep·re·hen′si·ble, *adj.;* **-ble·ness,** *n.;* **-bly,** *adv.*
un′rep·re·sent′a·ble, *adj.*
un′rep·re·sen·ta′tion·al, *adj.*
un′rep·re·sent′a·tive, *adj.;* **-ly,** *adv.;* **-ness,** *n.*
un′rep·re·sent′ed, *adj.*
un′re·pressed′, *adj.*
un′re·press′i·ble, *adj.*
un′re·pres′sive, *adj.;* **-ly,** *adv.;* **-ness,** *n.*
un′re·priev′a·ble, *adj.*
un′re·prieved′, *adj.*
un′rep·ri·mand′ed, *adj.*
un′rep·ri·mand′ing, *adj.*
un′re·print′ed, *adj.*
un′re·proach′a·ble, *adj.;* **-ble·ness,** *n.;* **-bly,** *adv.*
un′re·proached′, *adj.*
un′re·proach′ful, *adj.;* **-ly,** *adv.;* **-ness,** *n.*
un′re·proach′ing, *adj.*
un·rep′ro·bat′ed, *adj.*
un·rep′ro·ba′tive, *adj.;* **-ly,** *adv.*
un′re·pro·duc′i·ble, *adj.*
un′re·pro·duc′tive, *adj.;* **-ly,** *adv.;* **-ness,** *n.*
un′re·prov′a·ble, *adj.*
un′re·proved′, *adj.*
un′re·prov′ing, *adj.*
un′re·pub′li·can, *adj.*
un′re·pu′di·a·ble, *adj.*
un′re·pu′di·at′ed, *adj.*
un′re·pu′di·a′tive, *adj.*
un′re·pug′nant, *adj.;* **-ly,** *adv.*
un′re·pulsed′, *adj.*
un′re·puls′ing, *adj.*
un′re·pul′sive, *adj.;* **-ly,** *adv.;* **-ness,** *n.*
un′re·put′a·ble, *adj.*
un′re·put′ed, *adj.*
un′re·qual′i·fied′, *adj.*
un′re·quest′ed, *adj.*
un′re·quired′, *adj.*
un·req′ui·site, *adj.;* **-ly,** *adv.;* **-ness,** *n.*
un′req·ui·si′tioned, *adj.*
un′re·quit′a·ble, *adj.*
un′re·quit′al, *n.*
un′re·quit′ed, *adj.*
un′re·quit′ing, *adj.*
un′re·scind′ed, *adj.*
un′re·scis′sa·ble, *adj.*
un′re·scis′so·ry, *adj.*
un·res′cu·a·ble, *adj.*
un·res′cued, *adj.*
un′re·searched′, *adj.*
un′re·sem′blant, *adj.*
un′re·sem′bling, *adj.*
un′re·sent′ed, *adj.*
un′re·sent′ful, *adj.;* **-ly,** *adv.;* **-ness,** *n.*
un′re·sent′ing, *adj.*
un·res′i·dent, *adj.*
un·res′i·den′tial, *adj.*
un′re·sid′u·al, *adj.*
un′re·signed′, *adj.*
un′re·sil′ient, *adj.;* **-ly,** *adv.*
un·res′in·ous, *adj.*
un′re·sist′a·ble, *adj.*
un′re·sist′ant, *adj.*
un′re·sist′ed, *adj.*
un′re·sist′i·ble, *adj.*
un′re·sist′ing, *adj.*
un′re·sis′tive, *adj.*
un·res′o·lute′, *adj.;* **-ly,** *adv.;* **-ness,** *n.*
un′re·solv′a·ble, *adj.*
un′re·solved′, *adj.*
un′re·solv′ing, *adj.*
un·res′o·nant, *adj.;* **-ly,** *adv.*
un·res′o·nat′ing, *adj.*
un′re·sound′ed, *adj.*
un′re·source′ful, *adj.;* **-ly,** *adv.;* **-ness,** *n.*
un′re·spect′a·bil′i·ty, *n.*
un′re·spect′a·ble, *adj.*
un′re·spect′ed, *adj.*
un′re·spect′ful, *adj.;* **-ly,** *adv.;* **-ness,** *n.*
un′re·spir′a·ble, *adj.*
un′re·spired′, *adj.*
un·res′pit·ed, *adj.*
un′re·splend′ent, *adj.;* **-ly,** *adv.*
un′re·spond′ing, *adj.*
un′re·spon′si·ble, *adj.;* **-ble·ness,** *n.;* **-bly,** *adv.*
un′re·spon′sive, *adj.;* **-ly,** *adv.;* **-ness,** *n.*
un·rest′ed, *adj.*
un·rest′ful, *adj.;* **-ly,** *adv.;* **-ness,** *n.*
un·rest′ing, *adj.*
un·res′ti·tu′tive, *adj.*
un′re·stor′a·ble, *adj.*
un′re·stor′a·tive, *adj.*
un′re·stored′, *adj.*
un′re·strain′a·ble, *adj.*
un′re·strained′, *adj.*
un′re·strain′ed·ly, *adv.*
un′re·strict′a·ble, *adj.*
un′re·strict′ed, *adj.;* **-ly,** *adv.*
un′re·stric′tive, *adj.;* **-ly,** *adv.*
un′re·sumed′, *adj.*
un′re·sump′tive, *adj.*
un′res·ur·rect′ed, *adj.*
un′re·sus′ci·ta·ble, *adj.*
un′re·sus′ci·tat′ed, *adj.*
un′re·sus′ci·tat′ing, *adj.*
un′re·sus′ci·ta′tive, *adj.*
un′re·tain′a·ble, *adj.*
un′re·tained′, *adj.*
un′re·tain′ing, *adj.*
un′re·tal′i·at′ed, *adj.*
un′re·tal′i·at′ing, *adj.*
un′re·tal′i·a′tive, *adj.*
un′re·tal′i·a·to′ry, *adj.*
un′re·tard′a·ble, *adj.*
un′re·tard′ed, *adj.*
un′re·ten′tive, *adj.;* **-ly,** *adv.;* **-ness,** *n.*
un·ret′i·cent, *adj.;* **-ly,** *adv.*
un·ret′i·nued′, *adj.*
un′re·tired′, *adj.*
un′re·tir′ing, *adj.*
un′re·tort′ed, *adj.*
un′re·touched′, *adj.*
un′re·tract′a·ble, *adj.*
un′re·tract′ed, *adj.*
un′re·trac′tive, *adj.*
un′re·treat′ed, *adj.*
un′re·treat′ing, *adj.*
un′re·trench′a·ble, *adj.*
un′re·trenched′, *adj.*
un′re·trib′u·tive, *adj.*
un′re·trib′u·to′ry, *adj.*
un′re·triev′a·ble, *adj.*
un′re·trieved′, *adj.*
un′ret·ro·ac′tive, *adj.;* **-ly,** *adv.*
un′ret′ro·grad′ed, *adj.*
un′ret′ro·grad′ing, *adj.*
un′ret·ro·gres′sive, *adj.;* **-ly,** *adv.*
un·ret′ted, *adj.*
un′re·turn′a·ble, *adj.*
un′re·turned′, *adj.*
un′re·turn′ing, *adj.*
un′re·veal′a·ble, *adj.*
un′re·vealed′, *adj.*
un′re·veal′ing, *adj.;* **-ly,** *adv.*
un′rev·e·la′tion·al, *adj.*
un·rev′el·ing, *adj.*
un′re·venged′, *adj.*
un′re·venge′ful, *adj.;* **-ly,** *adv.;* **-ness,** *n.*
un′re·veng′ing, *adj.*
un′re·ver′ber·ant, *adj.*
un′re·ver′ber·at′ed, *adj.*
un′re·ver′ber·at′ing, *adj.*
un′re·ver′ber·a′tive, *adj.*
un′re·vered′, *adj.*
un·rev′er·enced, *adj.*
un·rev′er·ent, *adj.;* **-ly,** *adv.*
un′rev·er·en′tial, *adj.;* **-ly,** *adv.*
un′re·versed′, *adj.*
un′re·vers′i·ble, *adj.;* **-bly,** *adv.;* **-ble·ness,** *n.*
un′re·vert′ed, *adj.*
un′re·vert′i·ble, *adj.*
un′re·vert′ing, *adj.*
un′re·vet′ted, *adj.*
un′re·view′a·ble, *adj.*
un′re·viewed′, *adj.*
un′re·viled′, *adj.*
un′re·vil′ing, *adj.*
un′re·vised′, *adj.*
un′re·viv′a·ble, *adj.*
un′re·vived′, *adj.*
un·rev′o·ca·ble, *adj.;* **-bly,** *adv.*
un′re·vok′a·ble, *adj.*
un′re·voked′, *adj.*
un′re·volt′ed, *adj.*
un′re·volt′ing, *adj.*
un′rev·o·lu′tion·ar′y, *adj.*
un′rev·o·lu′tion·ized′, *adj.*
un′re·volved′, *adj.*
un′re·volv′ing, *adj.*
un′re·ward′a·ble, *adj.*
un′re·ward′ed, *adj.*
un′re·ward′ing, *adj.*
un′re·word′ed, *adj.*
un′rhap·sod′ic, *adj.*
un′rhap·sod′i·cal, *adj.;* **-ly,** *adv.*
un′rhe·tor′i·cal, *adj.;* **-ly,** *adv.*
un′rheu·mat′ic, *adj.*
un·rhyme′, *v.t.,* **-rhymed, -rhym·ing.**
un·rhyth′mic, *adj.*
un·rhyth′mi·cal, *adj.;* **-ly,** *adv.*
un·ribbed′, *adj.*
un·rib′boned, *adj.*
un·rid′a·ble, *adj.*
un·rid′den, *adj.*
un·rid′ered, *adj.*
un·ridged′, *adj.*
un·rid′i·culed′, *adj.*
un′ri·dic′u·lous, *adj.;* **-ly,** *adv.;* **-ness,** *n.*
un·rife′, *adj.*
un·rif′fled, *adj.*
un·ri′fled, *adj.*
un·rift′ed, *adj.*
un·right′a·ble, *adj.*
un·right′ed, *adj.*
un·right′ful, *adj.;* **-ly,** *adv.;* **-ness,** *n.*
un·rig′id, *adj.;* **-ly,** *adv.;* **-ness,** *n.*
un·rig′or·ous, *adj.;* **-ly,** *adv.;* **-ness,** *n.*
un·rimed′, *adj.*
un·ring′a·ble, *adj.*
un·ring′ing, *adj.*
un·rinsed′, *adj.*
un·ri′ot·ing, *adj.*
un·ri′ot·ous, *adj.;* **-ly,** *adv.;* **-ness,** *n.*
un·ri′pened, *adj.*
un·ri′pen·ing, *adj.*
un·rip′pa·ble, *adj.*
un·rip′pled, *adj.*
un·rip′pling, *adj.;* **-ly,** *adv.*
un·ris′en, *adj.*
un·ris′i·ble, *adj.*
un·ris′ing, *adj.*
un·risk′a·ble, *adj.*
un·risked′, *adj.*
un·risk′y, *adj.*
un·rit′u·al, *adj.;* **-ly,** *adv.*
un′rit·u·al·is′tic, *adj.*
un·ri′val·a·ble, *adj.*
un·ri′val·ing, *adj.*
un·ri′val·ling, *adj.*
un·ri′val·rous, *adj.*
un·rived′, *adj.*
un·riv′en, *adj.*
un·riv′et·ed, *adj.*
un·riv′et·ing, *adj.*
un·roam′ing, *adj.*
un·roast′ed, *adj.*
un·robbed′, *adj.*
un′ro·bust′, *adj.;* **-ly,** *adv.;* **-ness,** *n.*
un·rocked′, *adj.*
un·rock′y, *adj.*
un·rod′ded, *adj.*
un·roiled′, *adj.*
un·roll′a·ble, *adj.*
un′ro·man′tic, *adj.*
un′ro·man′ti·cal·ly, *adv.*

---

3. *Obs.* to strike from a roll or register. —*v.i.* 4. to become unrolled or spread out: *The tightly wound scrolls unroll easily.* 5. to become continuously visible or apparent: *The landscape unrolled before his eyes.* [ME *unroll(en).* See UN-[1], ROLL]

un·roof (un ro͞of′, -ro͝of′), *v.t.* to take off the roof or covering of. [UN-[2] + ROOF]

un·root (un ro͞ot′, -ro͝ot′), *v.t.* 1. to uproot. —*v.i.* 2. to become unrooted. [ME *unroot(en).* See UN-[2], ROOT[2]]

un·root·ed (un ro͞o′tid, -ro͝ot′id), *adj.* 1. not torn up by the roots: *He was glad to find the garden unrooted out.* 2. (of a person) without roots; rootless: *an unrooted wanderer.* [UN-[1] + *rooted,* ptp. of ROOT[1]]

un·round (un round′), *v.t. Phonet.* to articulate (an ordinarily rounded vowel) without rounding the lips; delabialize. Cf. **round**[1] (def. 60), **spread** (def. 14). [UN-[2] + ROUND]

un·round·ed (un roun′did), *adj. Phonet.* (of a vowel) pronounced without rounding the lips, as the vowel of *bit.* Cf. **rounded** (def. 2), **spread** (def. 36). [UN-[1] + ROUNDED]

un·rove (un rōv′), *Naut.* —*v.t., v.i.* 1. pt. and pp. of **unreeve.** —*adj.* 2. withdrawn from a block, thimble, etc.

UNRRA (un′rə), United Nations Relief and Rehabilitation Administration. Also, **U.N.R.R.A.**

un·ruf·fle (un ruf′əl), *v.,* **-fled, -fling.** —*v.t.* 1. to calm (someone). 2. to smooth out (something). —*v.i.* 3. to become calm or smoothed out. [UN-[2] + RUFFLE]

un·ruf·fled (un ruf′əld), *adj.* 1. calm; not emotionally upset or agitated; steady; unflustered: *She became all excited, but he was completely unruffled.* 2. not ruffled, as a garment; smooth. [UNRUFFLE + -ED[2]] —**un·ruf′fled·ness,** *n.*
—**Syn. 1.** unperturbed, tranquil, serene, imperturbable, cool, composed, peaceful, undisturbed.

un·ru·ly (un ro͞o′lē), *adj.,* **-li·er, -li·est.** not submissive or conforming to rule; ungovernable; turbulent; intractable; refractory; lawless: *an unruly man; an unruly wilderness.* [ME *unruely,* equiv. to *un-* UN-[1] + *ruly, ruely* governable, controllable; see RULE, -Y[1]] —**un·ru′li·ness,** *n.*
—**Syn.** disobedient, unmanageable, uncontrollable, stubborn, disorderly, riotous.

un·sad·dle (un sad′əl), *v.,* **-dled, -dling.** —*v.t.* 1. to take the saddle from. 2. to cause to fall or dismount from a saddle; unhorse. —*v.i.* 3. to take the saddle from a horse. [ME; see UN-[2], SADDLE. Cf. D, Flem *ontsadelen,* OHG *intsatalôn*]

un·safe·ty (un sāf′tē), *n.* unsafe state or condition; exposure to danger or risk; insecurity. [UN-[1] + SAFETY] —**un·safe′tied,** *adj.*

un·said[1] (un sed′), *v.* pt. and pp. of **unsay.**

un·said[2] (un sed′), *adj.* not said; thought but not mentioned or discussed; unstated: *It was best left unsaid.* [UN-[1] + SAID]

un·sat·is·fac·to·ry (un′sat is fak′tə rē), *adj.* not satisfactory; not satisfying or meeting one's demands; inadequate. [UN-[1] + SATISFACTORY] —**un′sat·is·fac′to·ri·ly,** *adv.* —**un′sat·is·fac′to·ri·ness,** *n.*
—**Syn.** disappointing, insufficient.

un·sat·u·rat·ed (un sach′ə rā′tid), *adj.* 1. not saturated; having the power to dissolve still more of a substance. 2. *Chem.* (of an organic compound) having a double or triple bond and capable of taking on elements or groups by direct chemical combination without the liberation of other elements or compounds, as ethylene, $CH_2{=}CH_2$. [UN-[1] + SATURATED] —**un·sat·u·rate** (un sach′ər it, -ə rāt′), *n.* —**un′sat·u·ra′tion,** *n.*

un·sa·vor·y (un sā′və rē), *adj.* 1. not savory; tasteless or insipid: *an unsavory meal.* 2. unpleasant in taste or smell; distasteful. 3. unappealing or disagreeable, as a pursuit: *Poor teachers can make education unsavory.* 4. socially or morally objectionable or offensive: *an unsavory past; an unsavory situation; an unsavory person.* Also, *esp. Brit.,* **un·sa′vour·y.** [ME; see UN-[1], SAVORY[1]] —**un·sa′vor·i·ly;** *esp. Brit.,* **un·sa′vour·i·ly,** *adv.* —**un·sa′vor·i·ness;** *esp. Brit.,* **un·sa′vour·i·ness,** *n.*

un·say (un sā′), *v.t.,* **-said, -say·ing.** to retract (something said). [ME *unsayen.* See UN-[2], SAY]

un·scathed (un skāthd′), *adj.* not scathed; unharmed; uninjured: *an unscathed reputation; an unscathed soldier.* [ME; see UN-[1], SCATHED]

un·schooled (un sko͞old′), *adj.* 1. not schooled, taught, or trained: *Though unschooled, he had a grasp of the subject.* 2. not acquired or artificial; natural: *His unschooled talent was considerably underrated.* [UN-[1] + SCHOOL[1] + -ED[2]]

un·sci·en·tif·ic (un′sī ən tif′ik), *adj.* 1. not scientific; not in accordance with the requirements of science: *Although a comprehensive work, it is unscientific.* 2. not conforming to the principles or methods of science: *an unscientific approach to a problem.* 3. lacking scientific knowledge or familiarity with scientific methods: *He was philosophical but almost wholly unscientific.* [UN-[1] + SCIENTIFIC] —**un′sci·en·tif′i·cal·ly,** *adv.*

un·scram·ble (un skram′bəl), *v.t.,* **-bled, -bling.** 1. to bring out of a scrambled condition; reduce to order or intelligibility. 2. to make (a scrambled radio or telephonic message) comprehensible by systematically tuning the receiver to the frequencies used in transmission. [UN-[2] + SCRAMBLE]

un·scram·bler (un skram′blər), *n.* 1. one who or that which unscrambles. 2. an electronic device that makes scrambled telecommunications signals intelligible by systematically tuning the receiver to the frequencies used in transmission. Cf. **scrambler** (def. 2). [UNSCRAMBLE + -ER[1]]

un·screw (un skro͞o′), *v.t.* 1. to draw or loosen a screw or screws from (a hinge, bracket, etc.). 2. to unfasten (something) by withdrawing screws. 3. to open (a jar, bottle, can, etc.) by turning the lid or cover. —*v.i.* 4. to permit of being unscrewed. [UN-[2] + SCREW]

un·scru·pu·lous (un skro͞o′pyə ləs), *adj.* not scrupulous; unrestrained by scruples; conscienceless; unprincipled. [UN-[1] + SCRUPULOUS] —**un·scru′pu·lous·ly,** *adv.* —**un·scru′pu·lous·ness, un·scru·pu·los·i·ty** (un skro͞o′pyə los′i tē), *n.*
—**Syn.** UNSCRUPULOUS, UNPRINCIPLED refer to lack of moral standards or conscience to guide one's conduct. The UNSCRUPULOUS man is without scruples of conscience, and disregards, or has contempt for, laws of right or justice with which he is perfectly well acquainted, and which should restrain him in his actions: *unscrupulous in methods of making money, in taking advantage of the unfortunate.* The UNPRINCIPLED man is without moral principles or ethical standards in his conduct or actions: *an unprincipled rogue; unprincipled conduct.*

un·seal (un sēl′), *v.t.* 1. to break or remove the seal of; open, as something sealed or firmly closed: *to unseal a letter; to unseal a tomb.* 2. to free from constraint, as a person's thought, speech, behavior, etc.: *Their warmth unsealed her vivacity, and she became friendly.* [ME; see UN-[2], SEAL[1]] —**un·seal′a·ble,** *adj.*

un·sealed (un sēld′), *adj.* 1. not sealed; not stamped or marked with a seal: *unsealed cargo.* 2. not shut or closed with or as if with a seal: *an unsealed letter; an unsealed crate.* 3. not verified, certain, or confirmed: *The verdict is unsealed.* [ME *unseled.* See UNSEAL, -ED[2]]

un·seam (un sēm′), *v.t.* to open the seam or seams of; undo; rip apart: *to unseam a dress.* [UN-[2] + SEAM]

un·search·a·ble (un sûr′chə bəl), *adj.* not searchable; not lending itself to research or exploration; not to be understood by searching; hidden; inscrutable; unfathomable; mysterious: *the unsearchable ways of the universe.* [ME *unserchable.* See UN-[1], SEARCHABLE] —**un·search′a·ble·ness,** *n.* —**un·search′a·bly,** *adv.*

un·sea·son·a·ble (un sē′zə nə bəl), *adj.* 1. not seasonable; out of season; unseasonal: *unseasonable weather.* 2. not befitting the occasion; untimely; ill-timed; inopportune; inappropriate: *Their visits were usually unseasonable.* [ME; see UN-[1], SEASONABLE] —**un·sea′son·a·ble·ness,** *n.* —**un·sea′son·a·bly,** *adv.*

un·sea·soned (un sē′zənd), *adj.* 1. (of things) not seasoned; not matured, dried, etc., by due seasoning: *an unseasoned crop.* 2. (of persons) not inured to a climate, work, etc.; inexperienced: *The men, although working hard, were an unseasoned crew.* 3. (of food) not flavored with seasoning: *It was a tasteless, unseasoned meal.* [UN-[1] + SEASON + -ED[2]]

un·seat (un sēt′), *v.t.* 1. to dislodge from a seat, esp. to throw from a saddle, as a rider; unhorse. 2. to remove from political office by an elective process, by force, or by legal action: *The corrupt mayor was finally unseated.* [UN-[2] + SEAT[1]]

un·se·cured (un′si kyo͝ord′), *adj.* 1. not secured, esp. not insured against loss, as by a bond, pledge, etc.: *an unsecured loan.* 2. not made secure, as a door, lock of hair, etc.; unfastened. [UN-[1] + SECURED]

un′ro·man′ti·cised′, *adj.*
un′ro·man′ti·cized′, *adj.*
un·room′y, *adj.*
un·roost′ed, *adj.*
un·roost′ing, *adj.*
un·roped′, *adj.*
un·rosed′, *adj.*
un·ro′ta·ry, *adj.*
un·ro′tat·ed, *adj.*
un·ro′tat·ing, *adj.*
un′ro·ta′tion·al, *adj.*
un·ro′ta·tive, *adj.*
un·ro′ta·to′ry, *adj.*
un·rot′ted, *adj.*
un·rot′ten, *adj.*
un′ro·tund′, *adj.*
un·rouged′, *adj.*
un·rough′ened, *adj.*
un·roused′, *adj.*
un·rous′ing, *adj.*
un·rout′a·ble, *adj.*
un·rout′ed, *adj.*
un′rou·tine′, *adj.;* **-ly,** *adv.*
un·rov′ing, *adj.*
un·row′dy, *adj.*
un·rowed′, *adj.*
un·row′eled, *adj.*
un·row′elled, *adj.*
un·rubbed′, *adj.*
un·ru′bi·fied′, *adj.*
un·ru′bri·cal, *adj.;* **-ly,** *adv.*
un·ru′bri·cat′ed, *adj.*
un·rud′dered, *adj.*
un·rud′dled, *adj.*
un·rude′, *adj.;* **-ly,** *adv.*
un·rued′, *adj.*
un·rue′ful, *adj.;* **-ly,** *adv.;* **-ness,** *n.*
un·ruff′a·ble, *adj.*
un·ruffed′, *adj.*
un·rug′ged, *adj.*
un·ru′in·a·ble, *adj.*
un·ru′in·ous, *adj.;* **-ly,** *adv.;* **-ness,** *n.*
un·ruled′, *adj.*
un·ru′mi·nant, *adj.*
un·ru′mi·nat′ed, *adj.*
un·ru′mi·nat′ing, *adj.;* **-ly,** *adv.*
un·ru′mi·na′tive, *adj.*
un·rum′maged, *adj.*
un·ru′mored, *adj.*
un·ru′moured, *adj.*
un·rum′pled, *adj.*
un·run′, *adj.*
un·rung′, *adj.*
un·rup′tur·a·ble, *adj.*
un·rup′tured, *adj.*
un·ru′ral, *adj.;* **-ly,** *adv.*
un·rushed′, *adj.*
un·rush′ing, *adj.*
un·rust′, *v.t.*
un·rus′tic, *adj.*
un·rus′ti·cal·ly, *adv.*
un·rus′ti·cat′ed, *adj.*
un·rus′tling, *adj.*
un·sa′bered, *adj.*
un·sa′bled, *adj.*
un·sab′o·taged′, *adj.*
un·sa′bred, *adj.*
un·sac′cha·rine, *adj.*
un′sac·er·do′tal, *adj.;* **-ly,** *adv.*
un·sacked′, *adj.*
un′sac·ra·men′tal, *adj.;* **-ly,** *adv.*
un′sac·ra·men·tar′i·an, *adj.*
un·sa′cred, *adj.;* **-ly,** *adv.*
un·sac′ri·fice′a·ble, *adj.*
un·sac′ri·ficed′, *adj.*
un′sac·ri·fi′cial, *adj.;* **-ly,** *adv.*
un·sac′ri·fic′ing, *adj.*
un′sac·ri·le′gious, *adj.;* **-ly,** *adv.;* **-ness,** *n.*
un·sad′, *adj.;* **-ly,** *adv.;* **-ness,** *n.*
un·sad′dened, *adj.*
un′sa·dis′tic, *adj.*
un′sa·dis′ti·cal·ly, *adv.*
un·safe′, *adj.;* **-ly,** *adv.;* **-ness,** *n.*
un′sa·ga′cious, *adj.;* **-ly,** *adv.;* **-ness,** *n.*
un·sage′, *adj.;* **-ly,** *adv.;* **-ness,** *n.*
un·sag′ging, *adj.*
un·sail′a·ble, *adj.*
un·sailed′, *adj.*
un·saint′ed, *adj.*
un·saint′ly, *adj.*
un′sal·a·bil′i·ty, *n.*
un·sal′a·ble, *adj.;* **-bly,** *adv.*
un′sa·la′cious, *adj.;* **-ly,** *adv.;* **-ness,** *n.*
un·sale′a·ble, *adj.;* **-bly,** *adv.*
un·sa′li·ent, *adj.;* **-ly,** *adv.*
un·sa′line, *adj.*
un·sal′i·vat′ed, *adj.*
un·sal′i·vat′ing, *adj.*
un·sal′low, *adj.;* **-ness,** *n.*
un·sal′ly·ing, *adj.*
un·salt′a·ble, *adj.*
un′sal·ta·to′ri·al, *adj.*
un·sal′ta·to′ry, *adj.*
un·salt′ed, *adj.*
un·salt′y, *adj.*
un′sa·lu′bri·ous, *adj.;* **-ly,** *adv.;* **-ness,** *n.*
un·sal′u·tar·y, *adj.*
un′sa·lu′ta·to′ry, *adj.*
un′sa·lut′ed, *adj.*
un′sa·lut′ing, *adj.*
un·sal′vage·a·ble, *adj.*
un·sal′vaged, *adj.*
un·salved′, *adj.*
un·sanc′ti·fied′, *adj.*
un·sanc′ti·fy′ing, *adj.*
un′sanc·ti·mo′ni·ous, *adj.;* **-ly,** *adv.;* **-ness,** *n.*
un·sanc′tion·a·ble, *adj.*
un·sanc′tioned, *adj.*
un·sanc′tion·ing, *adj.*
un·sanc′ti·tude′, *n.*
un·sanc′ti·ty, *n.*
un·san′daled, *adj.*
un·san′dalled, *adj.*
un·sand′ed, *adj.*
un·san′gui·nar′i·ly, *adv.*
un·san′gui·nar′i·ness, *n.*
un·san′gui·nar′y, *adj.*
un·san′guine, *adj.;* **-ly,** *adv.*
un′san·guin′e·ous, *adj.;* **-ly,** *adv.*
un·san′i·tar′y, *adj.*
un·san′i·tized′, *adj.*
un·san′i·ty, *n.*
un·sa′pi·ent, *adj.;* **-ly,** *adv.*
un′sa·pi·en′tial, *adj.;* **-ly,** *adv.*
un′sa·pon′i·fi′a·ble, *adj.*
un′sa·pon′i·fied′, *adj.*
un·sapped′, *adj.*
un′sar·cas′tic, *adj.*
un′sar·cas′ti·cal, *adj.;* **-ly,** *adv.*
un′sar·don′ic, *adj.*
un′sar·don′i·cal·ly, *adv.*
un′sar·to′ri·al, *adj.;* **-ly,** *adv.*
un·sashed′, *adj.*
un·sat′a·ble, *adj.*
un′sa·tan′ic, *adj.*
un′sa·tan′i·cal, *adj.;* **-ly,** *adv.*
un·satch′eled, *adj.*
un·sat′ed, *adj.*
un′sa·ti·a·bil′i·ty, *n.*
un·sa′ti·a·ble, *adj.;* **-ble·ness,** *n.;* **-bly,** *adv.*
un·sa′ti·at′ed, *adj.*
un·sa′ti·at′ing, *adj.*
un·sat′ing, *adj.*
un′sa·tir′ic, *adj.*
un′sa·tir′i·cal, *adj.;* **-ly,** *adv.;* **-ness,** *n.*
un·sat′i·ris′a·ble, *adj.*
un·sat′i·rised′, *adj.*
un·sat′i·riz′a·ble, *adj.*
un·sat′i·rized′, *adj.*
un·sat′is·fi′a·ble, *adj.*
un·sat′is·fied′, *adj.*
un·sat′ur·a·ble, *adj.*
un·sauced′, *adj.*
un·sav′a·ble, *adj.*
un·sav′age, *adj.;* **-ly,** *adv.;* **-ness,** *n.*
un·save′a·ble, *adj.*
un·saved′, *adj.*
un·sav′ing, *adj.;* **-ly,** *adv.*
un·sa′vored, *adj.*
un·sa′voured, *adj.*
un·sawed′, *adj.*
un·sawn′, *adj.*
un·say′a·ble, *adj.*
un·scab′bard, *v.t.*
un·scabbed′, *adj.*
un·sca′brous, *adj.;* **-ly,** *adv.;* **-ness,** *n.*
un·scaf′fold·ed, *adj.*
un·scal′a·ble, *adj.*
un·scald′ed, *adj.*
un·scald′ing, *adj.*
un·scaled′, *adj.*
un·scal′ing, *adj.*
un·scal′loped, *adj.*
un·scal′y, *adj.*
un·scamped′, *adj.*
un·scan′dal·ised′, *adj.*
un·scan′dal·ized′, *adj.*
un·scan′dal·ous, *adj.;* **-ly,** *adv.*
un·scan′na·ble, *adj.*
un·scanned′, *adj.*
un·scant′y, *adj.*
un·scarce′, *adj.;* **-ly,** *adv.;* **-ness,** *n.*
un·scared′, *adj.*
un·scarfed′, *adj.*
un·scar′i·fied′, *adj.*
un·scarred′, *adj.*
un·scarved′, *adj.*
un·scat′tered, *adj.*
un·scav′enged, *adj.*
un·sce′nic, *adj.*
un·sce′ni·cal·ly, *adv.*
un·scent′ed, *adj.*
un·scep′tered, *adj.*
un·scep′ti·cal, *adj.;* **-ly,** *adv.*
un·scep′tred, *adj.*
un·sched′uled, *adj.*
un′sche·mat′ic, *adj.*
un′sche·mat′i·cal·ly, *adv.*
un·sche′ma·tised′, *adj.*
un·sche′ma·tized′, *adj.*
un·schemed′, *adj.*
un·schem′ing, *adj.*
un′schis·mat′ic, *adj.*
un′schis·mat′i·cal, *adj.*
un·schiz′oid, *adj.*
un′schiz·o·phren′ic, *adj.*
un·schol′ar·like′, *adj.*
un·schol′ar·ly, *adv.*
un′scho·las′tic, *adj.*
un′scho·las′ti·cal·ly, *adv.*
un·scin′til·lant, *adj.*
un·scin′til·lat′ing, *adj.*
un·scis′sored, *adj.*
un·scoffed′, *adj.*
un·scoff′ing, *adj.*
un·scold′ed, *adj.*
un·scold′ing, *adj.*
un·sconced′, *adj.*
un·scooped′, *adj.*
un·scorched′, *adj.*
un·scorch′ing, *adj.*
un·scored′, *adj.*
un·sco′ri·fied′, *adj.*
un·scor′ing, *adj.*
un·scorned′, *adj.*
un·scorn′ful, *adj.;* **-ly,** *adv.;* **-ness,** *n.*
un·scotched′, *adj.*
un·scoured′, *adj.*
un·scourged′, *adj.*
un·scourg′ing, *adj.*
un·scour′ing, *adj.*
un·scowl′ing, *adj.;* **-ly,** *adv.*
un·scraped′, *adj.*
un·scrap′ing, *adj.*
un·scratch′a·ble, *adj.*
un·scratched′, *adj.*
un·scratch′ing, *adj.*
un·scrawled′, *adj.*
un·scrawl′ing, *adj.*
un·screen′a·ble, *adj.*
un·screened′, *adj.*
un·scrib′al, *adj.*
un·scrib′bled, *adj.*
un·scribed′, *adj.*
un·scrimped′, *adj.*
un·scrip′tur·al, *adj.;* **-ly,** *adv.*
un·scrubbed′, *adj.*
un·scru′pled, *adj.*
un·scrut′a·ble, *adj.*
un·scru′ti·nised′, *adj.*
un·scru′ti·nis′ing, *adj.;* **-ly,** *adv.*
un·scru′ti·nized′, *adj.*
un·scru′ti·niz′ing, *adj.;* **-ly,** *adv.*
un·sculp′tur·al, *adj.*
un·sculp′tured, *adj.*
un·scummed′, *adj.*
un·searched′, *adj.*
un·search′ing, *adj.;* **-ly,** *adv.*
un·seared′, *adj.*
un·sea′wor′thi·ness, *n.*
un·sea′wor′thy, *adj.*
un′se·ced′ed, *adj.*
un′se·ced′ing, *adj.*
un′se·clud′ed, *adj.;* **-ly,** *adv.*
un′se·clud′ing, *adj.*
un′se·clu′sive, *adj.;* **-ly,** *adv.;* **-ness,** *n.*
un·sec′ond·ed, *adj.*
un′sec·re·tar′i·al, *adj.*
un′se·cret′ed, *adj.*
un′se·cret′ing, *adj.*
un′se·cre′tive, *adj.;* **-ly,** *adv.;* **-ness,** *n.*
un·se′cret·ly, *adv.*
un·sec′tar′i·an, *adj.*
un′sec·tar′i·an·ize′, *v.t.,* **-ized, -iz·ing.**
un·sec′tion·al, *adj.;* **-ly,** *adv.*
un·sec′tion·al·ised′, *adj.*
un·sec′tion·al·ized′, *adj.*
un·sec′tioned, *adj.*
un·sec′u·lar, *adj.;* **-ly,** *adv.*
un·sec′u·lar·ised′, *adj.*
un·sec′u·lar·ized′, *adj.*
un′se·cure′, *adj.;* **-ly,** *adv.;* **-ness,** *n.*

un·se·duced (un′si do͞ost′, -dyo͞ost′), *adj.* not seduced, esp. by the lure of personal gain, power, fame, etc.: *He remained unseduced by the graft offered him.* [UN-[1] + SEDUCED]

un·seem·ly (un sēm′lē), *adj.* **1.** not seemly; not in keeping with established standards of taste or proper form; unbecoming or indecorous in appearance; improper in speech, conduct, etc.; inappropriate for time or place: *in an unseemly manner; an unseemly act; unseemly behavior; an unseemly hour.* —*adv.* **2.** in an unseemly manner. [ME; see UN-[1], SEEMLY] —**un·seem′li·ness,** *n.*
—**Syn. 1.** unbefitting, inappropriate. See **improper.**

un·seen (un sēn′), *adj.* **1.** not seen; unperceived; unobserved; invisible. **2.** recognizing or comprehending without prior study, as a written text or musical score. [UN-[1] + SEEN]

un·seg·re·gat·ed (un seg′rə gā′tid), *adj.* not segregated, esp. not subject to racial division; integrated: *an unsegregated community.* [UN-[1] + SEGREGATED]

un·self·con·scious (un′self kon′shəs), *adj.* not self-conscious; without affectation or pretense: *an unselfconscious manner.* [UN-[1] + SELF-CONSCIOUS] —**un′self·con′scious·ly,** *adv.* —**un′self·con′scious·ness,** *n.*

un·self·ish (un sel′fish), *adj.* not selfish; disinterested; altruistic. [UN-[1] + SELFISH] —**un·self′ish·ly,** *adv.* —**un·self′ish·ness,** *n.*

un·sell (un sel′), *v.t.,* **-sold, -sell·ing.** to dissuade from a belief in the desirability, value, wisdom, or truth of something: *He tried to unsell the public on its faith in rearmament.* [UN-[2] + SELL]

un·set (un set′), *adj.* **1.** not set; not solidified or made firm, as concrete, asphalt, etc. **2.** (of a gemstone) not mounted in a setting; unmounted. [UN-[2] + SET]

un·set·tle (un set′əl), *v.,* **-tled, -tling.** —*v.t.* **1.** to alter from a settled state; cause to be no longer firmly fixed or established; render unstable; disturb: *a rock formation unsettled by the incessant crashing of waves; Mass violence threatened to unsettle the very foundations of government.* **2.** to shake or weaken (beliefs, feelings, etc.); cause doubt or uncertainty; vex or agitate the mind or emotions; upset; discompose. —*v.i.* **3.** to become unfixed or disordered. [UN-[2] + SETTLE[1]] —**un·set′tle·ment,** *n.*

un·set·tled (un set′əld), *adj.* **1.** not settled; not fixed or stable; without established order; unorganized; disorganized: *An unsettled air hovered over the nation while the new regime strove to establish itself. The newlyweds were still unsettled in their new home.* **2.** continuously moving or changing; not situated in one place: *He led an unsettled life.* **3.** wavering or uncertain, as in opinions, behavior, etc.; unstable; erratic: *an unsettled state of mind.* **4.** not populated or settled, as a region: *an unsettled wilderness.* **5.** undetermined, as a point at issue; undecided; doubtful: *After many years the matter was still unsettled.* **6.** not adjusted, closed, or disposed of, as an account, estate, or law case: *An unsettled case annoyed him.* **7.** liable to change; inconstant; variable: *During their hike they met with unsettled weather.* [UN-[1] + SETTLED] —**un·set′tled·ness,** *n.*
—**Syn. 3.** UNSETTLED, UNSTABLE, UNSTEADY imply a lack of fixity, firmness, and dependability. That which is UNSETTLED is not fixed or determined: *unsettled weather; unsettled claims.* That which is UNSTABLE is wavering, changeable; easily moved, shaken, or overthrown: *unstable equilibrium; an unstable decision.* That which is UNSTEADY is infirm or shaky in position or movement: *unsteady on one's feet; unsteady of purpose.* **5.** indeterminate, unsure. **7.** vacillating, fickle, faltering, irresolute. —**Ant. 1, 3.** stable.

un·sew (un sō′), *v.t.,* **-sewed, -sewn** or **-sewed, -sew·ing.** to remove or rip the stitches of (something sewed). [ME *unsouw(en).* See UN-[2], SEW]

un·sex (un seks′), *v.t.* **1.** to deprive of sexual power; render impotent or frigid; spay or castrate. **2.** (esp. of a woman) to deprive (oneself) of the proper or appropriate character and qualities of one's sex, as by unnatural conduct. **3.** to deprive (a person, esp. a woman) of the character and qualities appropriate to one's sex. [UN-[2] + SEX]

un·shack·le (un shak′əl), *v.t.,* **-led, -ling. 1.** to free from shackles; unfetter. **2.** to free from restraint, as conversation. [UN-[2] + SHACKLE]

un·shad·owed (un shad′ōd), *adj.* not shadowed; not darkened or obscured by shadow; free from gloom. [UN-[1] + SHADOW + -ED[2]]

un·shaped (un shāpt′), *adj.* not shaped or definitely formed. [UN-[1] + SHAPED]

un·shap·en (un shā′pən), *adj.* **1.** not shaped or definitely formed; shapeless; formless; indefinite. **2.** not shapely; unpleasing in shape; ill-formed. **3.** misshapen or deformed. [ME; OE *unsceapen.* See UN-[1], SHAPE, -EN[3]]

un·sheathe (un shēth′), *v.t.,* **-sheathed, -sheath·ing. 1.** to draw from a sheath, as a sword, knife, or the like. **2.** to bring or put forth from a covering, threateningly or otherwise. [UN-[2] + SHEATHE]

un·shell (un shel′), *v.t.* to remove or liberate from or as from a shell: *to unshell nuts; to unshell one's secret thoughts.* [UN-[2] + SHELL]

un·ship (un ship′), *v.,* **-shipped, -ship·ping.** —*v.t.* **1.** to put or take off from a ship, as persons or goods. **2.** to remove from the place proper for its use, as an oar, tiller, etc. —*v.i.* **3.** to become unloaded or removed. [ME; see UN-[2], SHIP]

un·shipped (un shipt′), *adj.* **1.** not shipped, as goods. **2.** (of a person) having no ship. **3.** out of position or formation, as a boat or ship. [UN-[1] + SHIPPED]

un·shroud (un shroud′), *v.t.* to divest of a shroud or something which shrouds or hides: *to unshroud a corpse; to unshroud a mystery.* [UN-[2] + SHROUD]

un·sick·er (un sik′ər), *adj. Scot.* unsafe; untrustworthy. [ME *unsiker.* See UN-[1], SICKER] —**un·sick′ered,** *adj.* —**un·sick′er·ly,** *adv.* —**un·sick′er·ness,** *n.*

un·sight (un sīt′), *adj.* without inspection or examination: *to buy a thing unsight, unseen.* [UN-[1] + SIGHT]

un·sight·ly (un sīt′lē), *adj.* distasteful or unpleasant to look at: *an unsightly wound; unsightly disorder.* [UN-[1] + SIGHTLY] —**un·sight′li·ness,** *n.*
—**Syn.** unattractive, ugly, disagreeable, hideous.
—**Ant.** beautiful.

un·skilled (un skild′), *adj.* **1.** of or pertaining to workers who lack technical training or skill. **2.** not demanding special training or skill: *unskilled occupations.* **3.** exhibiting a marked lack of skill or competence: *an unskilled painting; an unskilled writer.* **4.** not skilled or expert: *He was unskilled in the art of rhetoric.* [UN-[1] + SKILLED]

un′skilled la′bor, 1. work that requires practically no training or experience for its adequate or competent performance. **2.** the labor force employed for such work.

un·skill·ful (un skil′fəl), *adj.* not skillful; clumsy or bungling. Also, *esp. Brit.,* **un·skil′ful.** [ME *unskylful.* See UN-[1], SKILLFUL] —**un·skill′ful·ly;** *esp. Brit.,* **un·skil′ful·ly,** *adv.* —**un·skill′ful·ness;** *esp. Brit.,* **un·skil′ful·ness,** *n.*
—**Syn.** clumsy, untrained, maladroit, inept.

un·sling (un sling′), *v.t.* **1.** to remove (something) from a position in which it is slung: *to unsling a rifle from one's shoulder.* **2.** *Naut.* to take off the slings of; release from slings. [UN-[2] + SLING]

---

un′se·date′, *adj.;* **-ly,** *adv.;* **-ness,** *n.*
un·sed′a·tive, *adj.*
un·sed′en·tar′y, *adj.*
un′sed·i·men′tal, *adj.;* **-ly,** *adv.*
un′se·di′tious, *adj.;* **-ly,** *adv.;* **-ness,** *n.*
un′se·duc′i·ble, *adj.;* **-ble·ness,** *n.;* **-bly,** *adv.*
un′se·duc′tive, *adj.;* **-ly,** *adv.;* **-ness,** *n.*
un·sed′u·lous, *adj.;* **-ly,** *adv.;* **-ness,** *n.*
un·see′a·ble, *adj.*
un·seed′ed, *adj.*
un·seed′ing, *adj.*
un·see′ing, *adj.;* **-ly,** *adv.;* **-ness,** *n.*
un·seek′ing, *adj.*
un·seethed′, *adj.*
un·seeth′ing, *adj.*
un′seg·men′tal, *adj.;* **-ly,** *adv.*
un·seg′men·tar′y, *adj.*
un·seg′ment·ed, *adj.*
un·seg′re·ga·ble, *adj.*
un·seg′re·gat′ing, *adj.*
un′seg·re·ga′tion·al, *adj.*
un·seg′re·ga′tive, *adj.*
un·seign′ior·al, *adj.*
un′sei·gno′ri·al, *adj.*
un·seis′mal, *adj.*
un·seis′mic, *adj.*
un·seiz′a·ble, *adj.*
un·seized′, *adj.*
un′se·lect′, *adj.*
un′se·lect′ed, *adj.*
un′se·lec′tive, *adj.*
un′self-cen′tered, *adj.*
un′self-cen′tred, *adj.*
un′self-know′ing, *adj.*
un′self-pos·sessed′, *adj.*
un′self-right′eous, *adj.;* **-ly,** *adv.;* **-ness,** *n.*
un′self-sac′ri·fi′cial, *adj.;* **-ly,** *adv.*
un′self-sac′ri·fic′ing, *adj.*
un′self-suf·fi′cien·cy, *n.*
un′self-suf·fi′cient, *adj.;* **-ly,** *adv.*
un′se·nes′cent, *adj.*
un·se′nile, *adj.*
un·sen′sate, *adj.*
un′sen·sa′tion·al, *adj.;* **-ly,** *adv.*
un·sensed′, *adj.*
un′sen·si·bil′i·ty, *n.*
un·sen′si·ble, *adj.;* **-ble·ness,** *n.;* **-bly,** *adv.*
un·sens′ing, *adj.*
un·sen′si·tise′, *v.t.,* **-tised, -tis·ing.**
un·sen′si·tive, *adj.;* **-ly,** *adv.;* **-ness,** *n.*
un·sen′si·tize′, *v.t.,* **-tized, -tiz·ing.**
un·sen′so·ry, *adj.*
un·sen′su·al, *adj.;* **-ly,** *adv.*
un′sen·su·al·is′tic, *adj.*
un·sen′su·al·ised′, *adj.*
un·sen′su·al·ized′, *adj.*
un·sen′su·ous, *adj.;* **-ly,** *adv.;* **-ness,** *n.*
un·sent′, *adj.*
un·sen′tenced, *adj.*
un′sen·ten′tious, *adj.;* **-ly,** *adv.;* **-ness,** *n.*
un·sen′tient, *adj.;* **-ly,** *adv.*
un′sen·ti·men′tal, *adj.;* **-ly,** *adv.*
un′sen·ti·men′tal·ised′, *adj.*
un′sen·ti·men′tal·ized′, *adj.*
un·sen′ti·neled, *adj.*
un·sen′ti·nelled, *adj.*
un·sep′ar·a·ble, *adj.;* **-ble·ness,** *n.;* **-bly,** *adv.*
un·sep′ar·ate, *adj.;* **-ly,** *adv.;* **-ness,** *n.*
un·sep′ar·at′ed, *adj.*
un·sep′ar·at′ing, *adj.*
un·sep′a·ra′tive, *adj.*
un·sep′ul·cher, *v.t.*
un′se·pul′chral, *adj.;* **-ly,** *adv.*
un·sep′ul·chre, *v.t.,* **-chred, -chring.**
un·sep′ul·tured, *adj.*
un·se′quenced, *adj.*
un·se′quent, *adj.*
un′se·quen′tial, *adj.;* **-ly,** *adv.*
un′se·ques′tered, *adj.*
un′se·raph′ic, *adj.*
un′se·raph′i·cal, *adj.;* **-ly,** *adv.*
un·sere′, *adj.*
un′se·re·nad′ed, *adj.*
un′se·rene′, *adj.;* **-ly,** *adv.;* **-ness,** *n.*
un·se′ri·al·ised′, *adj.*
un·se′ri·al·ized′, *adj.*
un·se′ri·ous, *adj.;* **-ly,** *adv.;* **-ness,** *n.*
un·ser′rate, *adj.*
un·ser′rat·ed, *adj.*
un·ser′ried, *adj.*
un·serv′a·ble, *adj.*
un·served′, *adj.*
un·ser′vice·a·ble, *adj.;* **-ble·ness,** *n.;* **-bly,** *adv.*
un·serv′iced, *adj.*
un·ser′vile, *adj.;* **-ly,** *adv.*
un·serv′ing, *adj.*
un′ses·qui·pe·da′li·an, *adj.*
un·set′ting, *adj.*
un·set′tle·a·ble, *adj.*
un·sev′er·a·ble, *adj.*
un′se·vere′, *adj.;* **-ly,** *adv.;* **-ness,** *n.*
un·sev′ered, *adj.*
un·sex′u·al, *adj.;* **-ly,** *adv.*
un·shab′bi·ly, *adv.*
un·shab′by, *adj.*
un·shade′, *v.t.,* **-shad·ed, -shad·ing.**
un·shad′i·ly, *adv.*
un·shad′i·ness, *n.*
un·shad′ow·a·ble, *adj.*
un·shad′y, *adj.*
un·shaft′ed, *adj.*
un·shak′a·ble, *adj.*
un·shake′a·ble, *adj.*
un·sha′ken, *adj.*
un·shak′ing, *adj.*
un·sham′a·ble, *adj.*
un·shame′a·ble, *adj.*
un·shamed′, *adj.*
un·shammed′, *adj.*
un·shanked′, *adj.*
un·shap′a·ble, *adj.*
un·shape′a·ble, *adj.*
un·shape′li·ness, *n.*
un·shape′ly, *adj.*
un·shap′ing, *adj.*
un·shar′a·ble, *adj.*
un·share′a·ble, *adj.*
un·shared′, *adj.*
un·shar′ing, *adj.*
un·sharp′, *adj.;* **-ly,** *adv.;* **-ness,** *n.*
un·sharped′, *adj.*
un·sharp′ened, *adj.*
un·sharp′en·ing, *adj.*
un·sharp′ing, *adj.*
un·shat′tered, *adj.*
un·shav′a·ble, *adj.*
un·shave′a·ble, *adj.*
un·shaved′, *adj.*
un·sheared′, *adj.*
un·shed′, *adj.*
un·shed′ding, *adj.*
un·sheer′, *adj.;* **-ness,** *n.*
un·sheet′ed, *adj.*
un·sheet′ing, *adj.*
un·shel′tered, *adj.*
un·shel′ter·ing, *adj.*
un·shelved′, *adj.*
un·shep′herd·ed, *adj.*
un·shep′herd·ing, *adj.*
un·shield′a·ble, *adj.*
un·shield′ed, *adj.*
un·shield′ing, *adj.*
un·shift′ed, *adj.*
un·shift′ing, *adj.*
un·shift′y, *adj.*
un·shim′mer·ing, *adj.;* **-ly,** *adv.*
un·shined′, *adj.*
un·shin′gled, *adj.*
un·shin′ing, *adj.*
un·shin′y, *adj.*
un·ship′pa·ble, *adj.*
un·shirked′, *adj.*
un·shirk′ing, *adj.*
un·shirred′, *adj.*
un·shirt′ed, *adj.*
un·shiv′ered, *adj.*
un·shiv′er·ing, *adj.*
un·shock′a·ble, *adj.*
un·shocked′, *adj.*
un·shock′ing, *adj.*
un·shod′, *adj.*
un·shoed′, *adj.*
un·shored′, *adj.*
un·shorn′, *adj.*
un·short′, *adj.*
un·short′en, *adj.*
un·shot′ted, *adj.*
un·shout′ed, *adj.*
un·shout′ing, *adj.*
un·shov′eled, *adj.*
un·shov′elled, *adj.*
un·show′a·ble, *adj.*
un·showed′, *adj.*
un·show′ered, *adj.*
un·show′er·ing, *adj.*
un·show′i·ly, *adv.*
un·show′i·ness, *n.*
un·shown′, *adj.*
un·show′y, *adj.*
un·shred′ded, *adj.*
un·shrewd′, *adj.;* **-ly,** *adv.;* **-ness,** *n.*
un·shrew′ish, *adj.*
un·shrill′, *adj.*
un·shrined′, *adj.*
un′shrink·a·bil′i·ty, *n.*
un·shrink′a·ble, *adj.*
un·shrink′ing, *adj.;* **-ly,** *adv.*
un·shrived′, *adj.*
un·shriv′eled, *adj.*
un·shriv′elled, *adj.*
un·shriv′en, *adj.*
un·shrug′ging, *adj.*
un·shrunk′, *adj.*
un·shrunk′en, *adj.*
un·shud′der·ing, *adj.*
un·shuf′fled, *adj.*
un·shun′na·ble, *adj.*
un·shunned′, *adj.*
un·shunt′ed, *adj.*
un·shut′, *adj.*
un·shut′tered, *adj.*
un·shy′, *adj.;* **-ly,** *adv.;* **-ness,** *n.*
un·sib′i·lant, *adj.*
un·sic′ca·tive, *adj.*
un·sick′, *adj.;* **-ly,** *adv.*
un·sick′ened, *adj.*
un·sid′ed, *adj.*
un′si·de′re·al, *adj.*
un·sid′ing, *adj.*
un·si′dling, *adj.*
un·sieged′, *adj.*
un·sieved′, *adj.*
un·sift′ed, *adj.*
un·sigh′ing, *adj.*
un·sight′ed, *adj.*
un·sign′a·ble, *adj.*
un·sig′naled, *adj.*
un·sig′nal·ized′, *adj.*
un·sig′nalled, *adj.*
un·sig′nal·ised′, *adj.*
un·sig′na·tured, *adj.*
un·signed′, *adj.*
un·sig′net·ed, *adj.*
un·sig′ni·fi′a·ble, *adj.*
un′sig·nif′i·cant, *adj.;* **-ly,** *adv.*
un′sig·nif′i·ca′tive, *adj.*
un·sig′ni·fied′, *adj.*
un·sig′ni·fy′ing, *adj.*
un·si′lenced, *adj.*
un·si′lent, *adj.;* **-ly,** *adv.*
un′sil·hou·et′ted, *adj.*
un·sil′i·cat′ed, *adj.*
un′si·lic′i·fied′, *adj.*
un·sil′ly, *adj.*
un·sil′vered, *adj.*
un·sim′i·lar, *adj.;* **-ly,** *adv.*
un′sim·i·lar′i·ty, *n.*
un·sim′mered, *adj.*
un·sim′mer·ing, *adj.*
un·sim′per·ing, *adj.*
un·sim′ple, *adj.;* **-ple·ness,** *n.;* **-ply,** *adv.*
un·sim′pli·fied′, *adj.*
un·sim′pli·fy′ing, *adj.*
un·sim′u·lar, *adj.*
un·sim′u·lat′ed, *adj.*
un·sim′u·lat′ing, *adj.*
un·sim′u·la′tive, *adj.*
un′si·mul·ta′ne·ous, *adj.;* **-ly,** *adv.;* **-ness,** *n.*
un′sin·cere′, *adj.;* **-ly,** *adv.*
un·sin′ewed, *adj.*
un·sin′ew·ing, *adj.*
un·sin′ew·y, *adj.*
un·sin′ful, *adj.;* **-ly,** *adv.;* **-ness,** *n.*
un·sing′a·ble, *adj.*
un·singed′, *adj.*
un·sin′gle, *adj.*
un·sin′gu·lar, *adj.;* **-ly,** *adv.;* **-ness,** *n.*
un·sin′is·ter, *adj.;* **-ly,** *adv.;* **-ness,** *n.*
un′sink·a·bil′i·ty, *n.*
un·sink′a·ble, *adj.*
un·sink′ing, *adj.*
un·sin′ning, *adj.*
un·sin′u·ate, *adj.;* **-ly,** *adv.*
un·sin′u·at′ed, *adj.*
un·sin′u·ous, *adj.;* **-ly,** *adv.;* **-ness,** *n.*
un·sipped′, *adj.*
un·sis′tered, *adj.*
un·sis′ter·ly, *adj.*
un·sit′u·at′ed, *adj.*
un·siz′a·ble, *adj.*
un·size′a·ble, *adj.*
un·sized′, *adj.*
un·skep′ti·cal, *adj.;* **-ly,** *adv.*
un·sketch′a·ble, *adj.*
un·sketched′, *adj.*
un·skewed′, *adj.*
un·skew′ered, *adj.*
un·skimmed′, *adj.*
un·skinned′, *adj.*
un·skirt′ed, *adj.*
un·slack′, *adj.*
un·slacked′, *adj.*
un·slack′ened, *adj.*
un·slack′en·ing, *adj.*
un·slack′ing, *adj.*
un·slagged′, *adj.*
un·slain′, *adj.*
un·slak′a·ble, *adj.*
un·slake′a·ble, *adj.*
un·slaked′, *adj.*
un·slammed′, *adj.*
un·slan′dered, *adj.*
un·slan′der·ous, *adj.;* **-ly,** *adv.;* **-ness,** *n.*
un·slant′ed, *adj.*
un·slant′ing, *adj.*
un·slapped′, *adj.*
un·slashed′, *adj.*
un·slat′ed, *adj.*
un·slat′ing, *adj.*
un·slat′ted, *adj.*
un·slaugh′tered, *adj.*
un·slay′a·ble, *adj.*
un·sleaved′, *adj.*
un·sleek′, *adj.*
un·sleep′ing, *adj.*
un·sleep′y, *adj.*
un·sleeved′, *adj.*
un·slen′der, *adj.*
un·sliced′, *adj.*
un·slicked′, *adj.*
un·slid′ing, *adj.*
un·slight′ed, *adj.*
un·slim′, *adj.;* **-ly,** *adv.;* **-ness,** *n.*
un·slimmed′, *adj.*
un·slink′ing, *adj.*

un·snap (un snap′), *v.t.*, **-snapped, -snap·ping.** to undo by or as if by opening snap fasteners: *to unsnap a dress.* [UN-² + SNAP]

un·snarl (un snärl′), *v.t.* to bring out of a snarled condition; disentangle. [UN-² + SNARL²]

un·so·cia·ble (un sō′shə bəl), *adj.* **1.** not sociable; having, showing, or marked by a disinclination to friendly social relations; withdrawn. **2.** lacking or preventing social relationships: *an unsociable boarding house.* [UN-¹ + SOCIABLE] —**un′so·cia·bil′i·ty, un·so′cia·ble·ness,** *n.* —**un·so′cia·bly,** *adv.*

un·sol·der (un sod′ər), *v.t.* **1.** to separate (something soldered). **2.** to disunite; sunder: *Carelessly spoken words can sometimes unsolder ties of friendship.* [UN-² + SOLDER]

un·son·sy (un son′sē), *adj. Brit. Dial.* bringing or boding ill luck. [UN-¹ + SONSY]

un·so·phis·ti·cat·ed (un′sə fis′tə kā′tid), *adj.* **1.** not sophisticated; simple; artless. **2.** without complexity or refinements: *a relatively unsophisticated mechanism.* **3.** unadulterated; pure; genuine. [UN-¹ + SOPHISTICATED] —**un′so·phis′ti·cat′ed·ly,** *adv.* —**un′so·phis′ti·cat′ed·ness, un′so·phis′ti·ca′tion,** *n.*
—**Syn. 1.** ingenuous, guileless, naïve.

un·sound (un sound′), *adj.* **1.** not sound; diseased, as the body or mind. **2.** decayed or impaired, as timber, foods, etc.; defective. **3.** not solid or firm, as foundations. **4.** not well-founded or valid; fallacious: *an unsound argument.* **5.** easily broken; light: *unsound slumber.* **6.** not financially strong; unreliable: *an unsound corporation.* [ME; see UN-¹, SOUND²] —**un·sound′ly,** *adv.* —**un·sound′ness,** *n.*
—**Syn. 1.** infirm, sick, ill, unhealthy. **2.** rotten, unwholesome. **4.** false, erroneous, faulty.

un·spar·ing (un spâr′ing), *adj.* **1.** not sparing; liberal or profuse; excessive. **2.** unmerciful; harsh; severe. [UN-¹ + SPARING] —**un·spar′ing·ly,** *adv.* —**un·spar′ing·ness,** *n.*
—**Syn. 1.** generous, lavish, bountiful. **2.** merciless, unrelenting, relentless.

un·speak (un spēk′), *v.t.*, **-spoke, -spo·ken, -speak·ing.** *Obs.* to recant; retract; unsay. [UN-² + SPEAK]

un·speak·a·ble (un spē′kə bəl), *adj.* **1.** not speakable; that may not be spoken. **2.** exceeding the power of speech; unutterable; inexpressible; indescribable. **3.** inexpressibly bad or objectionable. [ME *unspekeabill.* See UN-¹, SPEAKABLE] —**un·speak′a·ble·ness,** *n.* —**un·speak′a·bly,** *adv.*
—**Syn. 2.** ineffable, undescribable.

un·spent (un spent′), *adj.* **1.** not spent or used, as money. **2.** not used up or consumed: *unspent energy.* [ME; see UN-¹, SPENT]

un·sphere (un sfēr′), *v.t.*, **-sphered, -spher·ing.** to remove from its or one's sphere; displace. [UN-² + SPHERE]

un·spo·ken (un spō′kən), *adj.* **1.** implied or understood without being spoken or uttered. **2.** not addressed (usually fol. by *to*). **3.** not talking; silent. [ME *unspokyn.* See UN-¹, SPOKEN]

un·spot·ted (un spot′id), *adj.* **1.** having no spots or stains; without spots; spotless: *an unspotted breed of dog; unspotted trousers.* **2.** having no moral blemish or stigma: *an unspotted heart; an unspotted reputation.* [ME; see UN-¹, SPOTTED] —**un·spot′ted·ness,** *n.*

un·sta·ble (un stā′bəl), *adj.* **1.** not stable; not firm or firmly fixed; unsteady. **2.** liable to fall, change, or cease. **3.** unsteadfast; inconstant; wavering: *unstable convictions.* **4.** marked by emotional instability: *an unstable person.* **5.** irregular in movement: *an unstable heartbeat.* **6.** *Chem.* noting compounds which readily decompose or change into other compounds. [ME; see UN-¹, STABLE²] —**un·sta′ble·ness,** *n.* —**un·sta′bly,** *adv.*
—**Syn. 2.** precarious. **2, 3.** See **unsettled. 3.** vacillating.

un·stain·a·ble (un stā′nə bəl), *adj.* **1.** that cannot be spotted or stained, as garments. **2.** that cannot be morally reprehensible: *an unstainable person.* [UN-¹ + STAINABLE]

un·stained (un stānd′), *adj.* **1.** not stained or spotted; unsoiled. **2.** without moral blemish. [UN-¹ + STAIN + -ED²]

un·stalked (un stôkt′), *adj.* without a stalk or stalks. [UN-¹ + STALK¹ + -ED²]

un·state (un stāt′), *v.t.*, **-stat·ed, -stat·ing. 1.** *Archaic.* to deprive (a person) of office or rank. **2.** *Obs.* to deprive (a nation, government, etc.) of its character or dignity as a state. [UN-² + STATE]

un·stead·y (un sted′ē), *adj., v.,* **-stead·ied, -stead·y·ing.** —*adj.* **1.** not steady or firm; unstable; shaky: *She poured tea with an unsteady hand; an unsteady ladder.* **2.** fluctuating or wavering: *an unsteady flame; an unsteady business market.* **3.** irregular or uneven: *an unsteady development.* —*v.t.* **4.** to make unsteady. [UN-¹ + STEADY] —**un·stead′i·ly,** *adv.* —**un·stead′i·ness,** *n.*
—**Syn. 1.** See **unsettled. 2.** vacillating, flickering.

un·steel (un stēl′), *v.t.* to bring out of a steeled condition; soften. [UN-² + STEEL]

un·step (un step′), *v.t.*, **-stepped, -step·ping.** to lift from its step, as a mast. [UN-² + STEP]

un·stick (un stik′), *v.t.*, **-stuck, -stick·ing.** to free, as one thing stuck to another. [UN-² + STICK²]

un·slipped′, *adj.*
un·slip′pered, *adj.*
un·slip′per·y, *adj.*
un·slip′ping, *adj.*
un·sloped′, *adj.*
un·slop′ing, *adj.*
un·slopped′, *adj.*
un·slot′ted, *adj.*
un·slouched′, *adj.*
un·slouch′ing, *adj.*
un·slouch′y, *adj.*
un·sloughed′, *adj.*
un·slough′ing, *adj.*
un·slow′, *adj.;* **-ly,** *adv.;* **-ness,** *n.*
un·slowed′, *adj.*
un·slug′gish, *adj.;* **-ly,** *adv.;* **-ness,** *n.*
un·sluiced′, *adj.*
un·slum′ber·ing, *adj.*
un·slum′ber·y, *adj.*
un·slum′brous, *adj.*
un·slumped′, *adj.*
un·slump′ing, *adj.*
un·slung′, *adj.*
un·slurred′, *adj.*
un·sly′, *adj.;* **-ly,** *adv.;* **-ness,** *n.*
un·smacked′, *adj.*
un·smart′ing, *adj.*
un·smashed′ *adj.*
un·smeared′, *adj.*
un·smelled′, *adj.*
un·smell′ing, *adj.*
un·smelt′ed, *adj.*
un·smil′ing, *adj.;* **-ly,** *adv.*
un·smirched′, *adj.*
un·smirk′ing, *adj.;* **-ly,** *adv.*
un·smit′ten, *adj.*
un·smocked′, *adj.*
un·smok′a·ble, *adj.*
un·smoke′a·ble, *adj.*
un·smoked′, *adj.*
un·smok′i·ly, *adv.*
un·smok′i·ness, *n.*
un·smok′ing, *adj.*
un·smok′y, *adj.*
un·smol′der·ing, *adj.*
un·smooth′, *adj.;* **-ly,** *adv.;* **-ness,** *n.*
un·smoothed′, *adj.*
un·smooth′ened, *adj.*
un·smoth′er·a·ble, *adj.*
un·smoth′ered, *adj.*
un·smoth′er·ing, *adj.*
un·smoul′der·ing, *adj.;* **-ly,** *adv.*
un·smudged′, *adj.*
un·smug′, *adj.;* **-ly,** *adv.;* **-ness,** *n.*
un·smug′gled, *adj.*
un·smutched′, *adj.*
un·smut′ted, *adj.*
un·smut′ty, *adj.*
un·snaf′fled, *adj.*
un·snagged′, *adj.*
un·snak′y, *adj.*
un·snared′, *adj.*
un·snatched′, *adj.*
un·sneak′ing, *adj.*
un·sneak′y, *adj.*
un·sneer′ing, *adj.;* **-ly,** *adv.*
un·snipped′, *adj.*
un·snob′bish, *adj.;* **-ly,** *adv.;* **-ness,** *n.*
un·snor′ing, *adj.*
un·snout′ed, *adj.*
un·snubbed′, *adj.*
un·snuffed′, *adj.*
un·snug′, *adj.;* **-ly,** *adv.;* **-ness,** *n.*
un·soaked′, *adj.*
un·soaped′, *adj.*
un·soar′a·ble, *adj.*
un·soar′ing, *adj.*
un·so′ber, *adj.;* **-ly,** *adv.;* **-ness,** *n.*
un·so′bered, *adj.*
un·so′ber·ing, *adj.*
un·so′cial, *adj.;* **-ly,** *adv.*
un·so′cial·ised′, *adj.*
un·so′cial·is′ing, *adj.*
un·so′cial·ism, *n.*
un′so·cial·is′tic, *adj.*
un·so′cial·iz′a·ble, *adj.*
un·so′cial·ized′, *adj.*
un·so′cial·iz′ing, *adj.*
un·so′cial·ly, *adv.*
un′so·ci·o·log′i·cal, *adj.;* **-ly,** *adv.*
un·sock′et·ed, *adj.*
un·soft′, *adj.;* **-ly,** *adv.;* **-ness,** *n.*
un·sof′ten·ing, *adj.*
un·sog′gy, *adj.*
un·soiled′, *adj.*
un·soil′ing, *adj.*
un·sol′aced, *adj.*
un·sol′ac·ing, *adj.*
un·so′lar, *adj.*
un·sold′, *adj.*
un·sol′dier·like′, *adj.*
un·sole′, *v.t.,* **-soled, -sol·ing.**
un·sol′emn, *adj.;* **-ly,** *adv.;* **-ness,** *n.*
un′so·lem′ni·fied′, *adj.*
un·sol′em·nised′, *adj.*
un·sol′em·nized′, *adj.*
un′so·lic′i·tat′ed, *adj.*
un′so·lic′it·ed, *adj.*
un′so·lic′i·tous, *adj.;* **-ly,** *adv.;* **-ness,** *n.*
un·sol′id, *adj.;* **-ly,** *adv.;* **-ness,** *n.*
un′sol·i·dar′i·ty, *n.*
un′so·lid′i·fied′, *adj.*
un′so·lid′i·ty, *n.*
un·sol′i·tar′y, *adj.*
un·sol′u·ble, *adj.;* **-ble·ness,** *n.;* **-bly,** *adv.*
un·solv′a·ble, *adj.;* **-ble·ness,** *n.;* **-bly,** *adv.*
un·solved′, *adj.*
un′so·mat′ic, *adj.*
un·som′ber, *adj.;* **-ly,** *adv.;* **-ness,** *n.*
un·som′bre, *adj.;* **-ly,** *adv.;* **-ness,** *n.*
un·som′no·lent, *adj.;* **-ly,** *adv.*
un·so′nant, *adj.*
un′so·nan′tal, *adj.*
un·so′no·rous, *adj.;* **-ly,** *adv.;* **-ness,** *n.*
un·sooth′a·ble, *adj.*
un·soothed′, *adj.*
un·sooth′ing, *adj.;* **-ly,** *adv.*
un·soot′y, *adj.*
un′so·phis′tic, *adj.*
un′so·phis′ti·cal, *adj.;* **-ly,** *adv.*
un′soph·o·mor′ic, *adj.*
un′soph·o·mor′i·cal, *adj.;* **-ly,** *adv.*
un′so·po·rif′er·ous, *adj.;* **-ly,** *adv.;* **-ness,** *n.*
un′so·po·rif′ic, *adj.*
un·sor′did, *adj.;* **-ly,** *adv.;* **-ness,** *n.*
un·sore′, *adj.;* **-ly,** *adv.;* **-ness,** *n.*
un·sor′row·ing, *adj.*
un·sor′ry, *adj.*
un·sort′, *v.t.*
un·sort′a·ble, *adj.*
un·sot′ted, *adj.*
un·sought′, *adj.*
un·soul′ful, *adj.;* **-ly,** *adv.;* **-ness,** *n.*
un·soul′ish, *adj.*
un·sound′a·ble, *adj.*
un·sound′ed, *adj.*
un·sound′ing, *adj.*
un·sour′, *adj.;* **-ly,** *adv.;* **-ness,** *n.*
un·soused′, *adj.*
un·sov′er·eign, *adj.*
un·sowed′, *adj.*
un·sown′, *adj.*
un·spaced′, *adj.*
un·spa′cious, *adj.;* **-ly,** *adv.;* **-ness,** *n.*
un·spad′ed, *adj.*
un·span′, *v.t.,* **-spanned, -span·ning.**
un·span′gled, *adj.*
un·spanked′, *adj.*
un·spanned′, *adj.*
un·spared′, *adj.*
un·sparked′, *adj.*
un·spark′ling, *adj.*
un·sparred′, *adj.*
un·sparse′, *adj.;* **-ly,** *adv.;* **-ness,** *n.*
un·spasmed′, *adj.*
un′spas·mod′ic, *adj.*
un′spas·mod′i·cal, *adj.;* **-ly,** *adv.*
un·spa′tial, *adj.;* **-ly,** *adv.*
un′spa·ti·al′i·ty, *n.*
un·spat′tered, *adj.*
un·spawned′, *adj.*
un·spayed′, *adj.*
un·speared′, *adj.*
un·spe′cial·ised′, *adj.*
un·spe′cial·is′ing *adj.*
un·spe′cial·ized′, *adj.*
un·spe′cial·iz′ing, *adj.*
un·spec′i·fi′a·ble, *adj.*
un′spe·cif′ic, *adj.*
un′spe·cif′i·cal·ly, *adv.*
un·spec′i·fied′, *adj.*
un·spec′i·fy′ing, *adj.*
un·spe′cious, *adj.;* **-ly,** *adv.;* **-ness,** *n.*
un·specked′, *adj.*
un·speck′led, *adj.*
un·spec′ta·cled, *adj.*
un′spec·tac′u·lar, *adj.;* **-ly,** *adv.*
un·spec′u·lat′ing, *adj.*
un·spec′u·la′tive, *adj.*
un·spec′u·la·to′ry, *adj.*
un·speed′i·ly, *adv.*
un·speed′i·ness, *n.*
un·speed′y, *adj.*
un·spell′a·ble, *adj.*
un·spelled′, *adj.*
un·spelt′, *adj.*
un·spend′a·ble, *adj.*
un·spend′ing, *adj.*
un·spent′, *adj.*
un·spewed′, *adj.*
un·spher′i·cal, *adj.*
un·spher′ing, *adj.*
un·spiced′, *adj.*
un·spic′i·ly, *adv.*
un·spic′i·ness, *n.*
un·spic′y, *adj.*
un·spied′, *adj.*
un·spilled′, *adj.*
un·spilt′, *adj.*
un·spin′na·ble, *adj.*
un·spin′ning, *adj.*
un·spi′ral, *adj.;* **-ly,** *adv.*
un·spi′raled, *adj.*
un·spi′ralled, *adj.*
un·spired′, *adj.*
un·spir′ing, *adj.*
un·spir′it·ed, *adj.;* **-ly,** *adv.*
un·spir′it·ing, *adj.*
un·spir′i·tu·al, *adj.;* **-ly,** *adv.*
un′spir·i·tu·al′i·ty, *n.*
un·spir′it·u·al·ised′, *adj.*
un·spir′it·u·al·is′ing, *adj.*
un·spir′it·u·al·ized′, *adj.*
un·spir′it·u·al·iz′ing, *adj.*
un·spir′it·u·ous, *adj.*
un·spit′ed, *adj.*
un·spite′ful, *adj.;* **-ly,** *adv.*
un·spit′ted, *adj.*
un·splashed′, *adj.*
un·splat′tered, *adj.*
un·splayed′, *adj.*
un·spleen′ish, *adj.;* **-ly,** *adv.*
un·splen′did, *adj.;* **-ly,** *adv.;* **-ness,** *n.*
un·splen′dor·ous, *adj.;* **-ly,** *adv.*
un·splen′dour·ous, *adj.;* **-ly,** *adv.*
un′sple·net′ic, *adj.*
un′sple·net′i·cal·ly, *adv.*
un·spliced′, *adj.*
un·splint′ed, *adj.*
un·splin′tered, *adj.*
un·split′, *adj.*
un·split′ta·ble, *adj.*
un·spoil′a·ble, *adj.*
un·spoiled′, *adj.*
un·spoilt′, *adj.*
un·sponged′, *adj.*
un·spong′y, *adj.*
un·spon′sored, *adj.*
un′spon·ta′ne·ous, *adj.;* **-ly,** *adv.;* **-ness,** *n.*
un·sport′ed, *adj.*
un·sport′ful, *adj.*
un·sport′ing, *adj.*
un·spor′tive, *adj.;* **-ly,** *adv.;* **-ness,** *n.*
un·sports′man·like′, *adj.*
un·sports′man·ly, *adj., adv.*
un·spot′light′ed, *adj.*
un·spot′ta·ble, *adj.*
un·spoused′, *adj.*
un·spout′ed, *adj.*
un·sprained′, *adj.*
un·spray′a·ble, *adj.*
un·sprayed′, *adj.*
un·spread′, *adj.*
un·spread′a·ble, *adj.*
un·spread′ing, *adj.*
un·spright′ly, *adj., adv.*
un·spring′ing, *adj.*
un·sprin′kled, *adj.*
un·sprin′klered, *adj.*
un·sprout′ed, *adj.*
un·sprout′ing, *adj.*
un·spruced′, *adj.*
un·sprung′, *adj.*
un·spun′, *adj.*
un·spu′ri·ous, *adj.;* **-ly,** *adv.;* **-ness,** *n.*
un·spurned′, *adj.*
un·spurred′, *adj.*
un·sput′ter·ing, *adj.*
un·spy′ing, *adj.*
un·squab′bling, *adj.*
un·squan′dered, *adj.*
un·squar′a·ble, *adj.*
un·squared′, *adj.*
un·squash′a·ble, *adj.*
un·squashed′, *adj.*
un·squeam′ish, *adj.;* **-ly,** *adv.;* **-ness,** *n.*
un·squeez′a·ble, *adj.*
un·squeezed′, *adj.*
un·squelched′, *adj.*
un·squint′ing, *adj.*
un·squired′, *adj.*
un·squirm′ing, *adj.*
un·squirt′ed, *adj.*
un·stabbed′, *adj.*
un·sta′bi·lised′, *adj.*
un·sta′bi·lis′ing, *adj.*
un·sta′bi·lized′, *adj.*
un·sta′bi·liz′ing, *adj.*
un·sta′bled, *adj.*
un·stack′, *adj.*
un·stacked′, *adj.*
un·staffed′, *adj.*
un·staged′, *adj.*
un·stag′gered, *adj.*
un·stag′ger·ing, *adj.*
un·stag′i·ly, *adv.*
un·stag′i·ness, *n.*
un·stag′nant, *adj.;* **-ly,** *adv.*
un·stag′nat·ing, *adj.*
un·stag′y, *adj.*
un·staid′, *adj.;* **-ly,** *adv.;* **-ness,** *n.*
un·staled′, *adj.*
un·stale′mat′ed, *adj.*
un·stalled′, *adj.*
un·stam′mer·ing, *adj.;* **-ly,** *adv.*
un·stamped′, *adj.*
un′stam·ped′ed, *adj.*
un·stanch′, *adj.*
un·stanch′a·ble, *adj.*
un·stand′ard, *adj.*
un·stand′ard·is′a·ble, *adj.*
un·stand′ard·ised′, *adj.*
un·stand′ard·iz′a·ble, *adj.*
un·stand′ard·ized′, *adj.*
un·stand′ing, *adj.*
un′stan·za′ic, *adj.*
un·sta′pled, *adj.*
un·starched′, *adj.*
un·starred′, *adj.*
un·start′ed, *adj.*
un·start′ing, *adj.*
un·star′tled, *adj.*
un·star′tling, *adj.*
un·starved′, *adj.*
un·stat′a·ble, *adj.*
un·state′a·ble, *adj.*
un·stat′ed, *adj.*
un·states′man·like′, *adj.*
un·stat′ic, *adj.*
un·stat′i·cal, *adj.;* **-ly,** *adv.*
un·sta′tion, *adj.*
un·sta′tion·ar′y, *adj.*
un·sta′tioned, *adj.*
un′sta·tis′tic, *adj.*
un′sta·tis′ti·cal, *adj.;* **-ly,** *adv.*
un·stat′ued, *adj.*
un′stat·u·esque′, *adj.;* **-ly,** *adv.;* **-ness,** *n.*
un·staunch′, *adj.*
un·staunch′a·ble, *adj.*
un·staved′, *adj.*
un·stay′a·ble, *adj.*
un·stay′ing, *adj.*
un·stead′fast′, *adj.;* **-ly,** *adv.;* **-ness,** *n.*
un·stealth′i·ly, *adv.*
un·stealth′i·ness, *n.*
un·stealth′y, *adj.*
un·steamed′, *adj.*
un·steam′ing, *adj.*
un·steeped′, *adj.*
un·stee′pled, *adj.*
un·steered′, *adj.*
un·stemmed′, *adj.*
un′sten·to′ri·an, *adj.*
un′sten·to′ri·ous·ly, *adj.*
un·ster′e·o·typed′, *adj.*
un·ster′ile, *adj.*
un·ster′i·lized′, *adj.*
un·stern′, *adj.;* **-ly,** *adv.;* **-ness,** *n.*
un·steth′o·scoped′, *adj.*
un·stewed′, *adj.*
un·stick′y, *adj.*
un·stiff′, *adj.;* **-ly,** *adv.;* **-ness,** *n.*
un·stiff′ened, *adj.*
un·sti′fled, *adj.*
un·sti′fling, *adj.*
un′stig·mat′ic, *adj.*
un·stig′ma·tised′, *adj.*
un·stig′ma·tized′, *adj.*
un·stilled′, *adj.*
un·stilt′ed, *adj.*
un·stim′u·la·ble, *adj.*
un·stim′u·lat′ed, *adj.*
un·stim′u·lat′ing, *adj.;* **-ly,** *adv.*
un·stim′u·la′tive, *adj.*
un·sting′ing, *adj.;* **-ly,** *adv.*
un·stint′ed, *adj.*
un·stint′ing, *adj.;* **-ly,** *adv.*
un·stip′pled, *adj.*
un·stip′u·lat′ed, *adj.*

CONCISE PRONUNCIATION KEY: *act, āble, dâre, ärt; ebb, ēqual; if, īce; hot, ōver, ôrder, oil, bo͝ok, o͞oze, out; up, ûrge; chief; sing; shoe; thin, that;* zh as in *measure.* ə = *a* as in *alone, e* as in *system, i* as in *easily, o* as in *gallop, u* as in *circus;* ᵊ as in *button* (butᵊn), *fire* (fīᵊr), *cradle* (krādᵊl). See the full key inside the front cover.

un·stop (un stop′), *v.t.*, **-stopped, -stop·ping.** **1.** to remove the stopper from: *to unstop a bottle.* **2.** to free from any obstruction; open: *to unstop a sewer.* **3.** to draw out the stops of (an organ). [ME *unstoppen.* See UN-², STOP] —**un·stop′pa·ble,** *adj.* —**un·stop′pa·bly,** *adv.*

un·stop·per (un stop′ər), *v.t.* to unstop. [UN-² + STOPPER]

un·sto·ried (un stôr′ēd, -stôr′-), *adj.* without a history; not written as history or told as folklore: *an unstoried island.* [UN-¹ + STORIED¹]

un·strained (un strānd′), *adj.* **1.** not under strain or tension: *an easy, unstrained manner.* **2.** not separated or cleared by straining: *unstrained orange juice.* [ME; see UN-, STRAIN¹, -ED²]

un·strap (un strap′), *v.t.*, **-strapped, -strap·ping.** to take off or slacken the strap of. [UN-² + STRAP]

un·strat·i·fied (un strat′ə fīd′), *adj.* not stratified; not arranged in strata or layers: *unstratified rocks.* [UN-¹ + STRATIFIED]

un·stress (un′stres′), *n.* a syllable lacking in phonetic emphasis and having comparatively weak stress. [UN-¹ + STRESS]

un·stressed (un strest′), *adj.* without stress or emphasis, as a syllable in a word. [UN-¹ + STRESS + -ED²]

un·string (un string′), *v.t.*, **-strung, -string·ing.** **1.** to deprive of a string or strings: *to unstring a violin.* **2.** to take from a string: *to unstring beads.* **3.** to loosen the string or strings of: *to unstring a bow.* **4.** to relax the tension of. **5.** to relax unduly, or weaken (the nerves). **6.** to weaken the nerves of. [UN-² + STRING]

un·striped (un strīpt′, -strī′pid), *adj.* not striped; nonstriated, as muscular tissue. [UN-¹ + STRIPED]

un·strung (un strung′), *v.* **1.** pt. and pp. of **unstring.** —*adj.* **2.** having the string or strings loosened or removed, as a bow or harp. **3.** weakened or nervously unhinged, as a person or his nerves; unnerved; discomposed: *The incident left him unstrung.*

un·stuck (un stuk′), *adj.* **1.** freed or loosened from being fastened or stuck: *When firmly pushed, the door became unstuck.* **2.** out of order, control, or coherence, esp. as implying a loss of cohesiveness; undone: *Their well-laid plans came unstuck under pressure.* [UN-¹ + STUCK]

un·stud·ied (un stud′ēd), *adj.* **1.** not studied; not premeditated or labored; natural; unaffected. **2.** not having studied; not possessing knowledge in a specific field; unversed: *He is unstudied in law.* [ME; see UN-¹, STUDIED]

un·sub·stan·tial (un′səb stan′shəl), *adj.* **1.** not substantial; having no foundation in fact; fanciful; insubstantial: *an unsubstantial argument; unsubstantial hopes.* **2.** without material substance: *the unsubstantial air; an unsubstantial ghost.* **3.** lacking material substance; materially paltry: *an unsubstantial dinner of bread and cheese.* **4.** lacking strength or solidity; flimsy: *an unsubstantial wall of cardboard.* [ME; see UN-¹, SUBSTANTIAL] —**un·sub·stan·ti·al·i·ty** (un′səb stan′shē al′i tē), *n.* —**un′sub·stan′tial·ly,** *adv.*

un·suc·cess (un′sək ses′), *n.* lack of success; failure. [UN-¹ + SUCCESS]

un·suc·cess·ful (un′sək ses′fəl), *adj.* not achieving or not attended with success: *an unsuccessful businessman; an unsuccessful venture.* [UN-¹ + SUCCESSFUL] —**un′suc·cess′ful·ly,** *adv.* —**un′suc·cess′ful·ness,** *n.*

un·suit·a·ble (un sōō′tə bəl), *adj.* not suitable; inappropriate; unfitting; unbecoming. [UN-¹ + SUITABLE] —**un′suit·a·bil′i·ty, un·suit′a·ble·ness,** *n.* —**un·suit′a·bly,** *adv.*

un·sung (un sung′), *adj.* **1.** not sung; not uttered or rendered by singing. **2.** not celebrated in song or verse; not praised or acclaimed: *the unsung heroes of the war.* [UN-¹ + SUNG]

un·sus·pect·ed (un′sə spek′tid), *adj.* **1.** not regarded or considered with suspicion: *He was unsuspected of having committed the crime.* **2.** not imagined to exist. [UN-¹ + SUSPECT + -ED²] —**un′sus·pect′ed·ly,** *adv.* —**un′sus·pect′ed·ness,** *n.*

un·sus·tain·a·ble (un′sə stā′nə bəl), *adj.* not sustainable; not to be supported, maintained, upheld, or corroborated. [UN-¹ + SUSTAINABLE]

un·swathe (un swāth′), *v.t.*, **-swathed, -swath·ing.** to free from that which swathes: *The nurse unswathed the badly burned child of his bandages.* [ME; see UN-², SWATHE¹] —**un·swathe′a·ble,** *adj.*

un·swear (un swâr′), *v.t.*, **-swore, -sworn, -swear·ing.** to retract (something sworn or sworn to); recant by a subsequent oath; abjure. [UN-² + SWEAR]

un·tack (un tak′), *v.t.* **1.** to unfasten (something tacked). **2.** to loose or detach by removing a tack or tacks. [UN-² + TACK¹]

un·tan·gle (un tang′gəl), *v.t.*, **-gled, -gling.** **1.** to bring out of a tangled state; disentangle; unsnarl. **2.** to straighten out or clear up (anything confused or perplexing). [UN-² + TANGLE]

---

un·stir′ra·ble, adj.
un·stirred′, adj.
un·stir′ring, adj.
un·stitched′, adj.
un·stitch′ing, adj.
un·stocked′, adj.
un·stock′inged, adj.
un·sto′ic, adj.
un·sto′i·cal, adj.; -ly, adv.
un·stoked′, adj.
un·sto′len, adj.
un·ston′a·ble, adj.
un·stone′a·ble, adj.
un·stoned′, adj.
un·ston′i·ly, adv.
un·ston′i·ness, n.
un·ston′y, adj.
un·stooped′, adj.
un·stoop′ing, adj.
un·stor′a·ble, adj.
un·storm′a·ble, adj.
un·stormed′, adj.
un·storm′i·ly, adv.
un·storm′i·ness, n.
un·storm′y, adj.
un·stout′, adj.; -ly, adv.; -ness, n.
un·strad′dled, adj.
un·strafed′, adj.
un·straight′, adj.; -ness, n.
un·straight′ened, adj.
un′straight·for′ward, adj.
un·strait′ened, adj.
un·strand′ed, adj.
un·strange′, adj.; -ly, adv.; -ness, n.
un·stran′gled, adj.
un·stran′gu·la·ble, adj.
un·stra·te′gic, adj.
un′stra·te′gi·cal, adj.; -ly, adv.
un·stray′ing, adj.
un·streaked′, adj.
un·stream′ing, adj.
un·stream′lined′, adj.
un·strength′ened, adj.
un·strength′en·ing, adj.
un·stren′u·ous, adj.; -ly, adv.; -ness, n.
un·strep′i·tous, adj.
un·stretch′a·ble, adj.
un·stretched′, adj.
un·strewed′, adj.
un·strewn′, adj.
un·stri′at·ed, adj.
un·strick′en, adj.
un·strict′, adj.; -ly, adv.; -ness, n.
un·stri′dent, adj.; -ly, adv.
un·strid′u·lat′ing, adj.
un·strid′u·lous, adj.
un·strik′ing, adj.
un·stringed′, adj.
un·strin′gent, adj.; -ly, adv.
un·stripped′, adj.
un·striv′ing, adj.
un·stroked′, adj.
un·struc′tur·al, adj.; -ly, adv.
un·struc′tured, adj.
un·strug′gling, adj.
un·stubbed′, adj.
un·stub′bled, adj.
un·stub′born, adj.; -ly, adv.; -ness, n.
un·stuc′coed, adj.
un·stud′ded, adj.
un·stu′di·ous, adj.; -ly, adv.; -ness, n.
un·stuffed′, adj.
un·stuff′i·ly, adv.
un·stuff′i·ness, n.
un·stuff′y, adj.
un·stul′ti·fied′, adj.
un·stul′ti·fy′ing, adj.
un·stum′bling, adj.
un·stung′, adj.
un·stunned′, adj.
un·stunt′ed, adj.
un·stu′pe·fied′, adj.
un·stu′pid, adj.; -ly, adv.; -ness, n.
un·stur′di·ly, adv.
un·stur′di·ness, n.
un·stur′dy, adj.
un·stut′tered, adj.
un·stut′ter·ing, adj.
un·styled′, adj.
un·styl′ish, adj.; -ly, adv.; -ness, n.
un·styl′ized, adj.
un′sub·di·vid′ed, adj.
un′sub·du′a·ble, adj.
un′sub·duct′ed, adj.
un′sub·dued′, adj.
un′sub·ject, adj.
un′sub·ject′ed, adj.
un′sub·jec′tive, adj.; -ly, adv.
un·sub′ju·gat′ed, adj.
un·sub′li·mat′ed, adj.
un′sub·limed′, adj.
un′sub·merged′, adj.
un′sub·mer′gi·ble, adj.
un′sub·merg′ing, adj.
un′sub·mer′si·ble, adj.
un′sub·mis′sive, adj.; -ly, adv.; -ness, n.
un′sub·mit′ted, adj.
un′sub·mit′ting, adj.
un′sub·or′di·nate, adj.
un′sub·or′di·nat′ed, adj.
un′sub·or′di·na′tive, adj.
un′sub·orned′, adj.
un′sub·poe′naed, adj.
un·sub′ro·gat′ed, adj.
un′sub·scribed′, adj.
un′sub·scrib′ing, adj.
un′sub·ser′vi·ent, adj.; -ly, adv.
un′sub·sid′ed, adj.
un′sub·sid′i·ar′y, adj.
un′sub·sid′ing, adj.
un·sub′si·dized′, adj.
un′sub·stan′ti·at′ed, adj.
un′sub·stan·tive, adj.
un·sub′sti·tut′ed, adj.
un·sub′sti·tu′tive, adj.
un·sub′tle, adj.; -tle·ness, n.; -tly, adv.
un′sub·tract′ed, adj.
un′sub·trac′tive, adj.
un′sub·ur′ban, adj.
un′sub·urbed, adj.
un′sub·ven′tioned, adj.
un′sub·ven′tion·ized′, adj.
un′sub·ver′sive, adj.; -ly, adv.; -ness, n.
un′sub·vert′ed, adj.
un′suc·ceed′ed, adj.
un′suc·ceed′ing, adj.
un′suc·ces′sive, adj.; -ly, adv.; -ness, n.
un′suc·cinct′, adj.; -ly, adv.
un·suc′cor·a·ble, adj.
un·suc′cored, adj.
un·suc′cu·lent, adj.; -ly, adv.
un′suc·cumb′ing, adj.
un·sucked′, adj.
un·suck′led, adj.
un·sued′, adj.
un·suf′fer·a·ble, adj.; -ble·ness, n.; -bly, adv.
un·suf′fer·ing, adj.
un′suf·fic′ing, adj.
un·suf′fixed, adj.
un·suf′fo·cat′ed, adj.
un·suf′fo·ca′tive, adj.
un′suf·fused′, adj.
un′suf·fu′sive, adj.
un·sug′ared, adj.
un·sug′ar·y, adj.
un′sug·gest′ed, adj.
un′sug·gest′i·ble, adj.
un′sug·gest′ing, adj.
un′sug·ges′tive, adj.; -ly, adv.; -ness, n.
un′su·i·cid′al, adj.; -ly, adv.
un·suit′ed, adj.
un·suit′ing, adj.
un·sul′fo·nat′ed, adj.
un′sul·fu′re·ous, adj.; -ness, n.
un·sul′fu·rized′, adj.
un·sulk′i·ly, adv.
un·sulk′i·ness, n.
un·sulk′y, adj.
un·sul′len, adj.
un·sul′len·ly, adv.
un·sul′li·a·ble, adj.
un·sul′lied, adj.
un·sul′pho·nat′ed, adj.
un′sul·phu′re·ous, adj.; -ness, n.
un·sul′phu·rized′, adj.
un·sul′try, adj.
un·sum′ma·ble, adj.
un·sum′ma·ris′a·ble, adj.
un·sum′ma·rised′, adj.
un·sum′ma·riz′a·ble, adj.
un·sum′ma·rized′, adj.
un·sum′mon·a·ble, adj.
un·sum′moned, adj.
un·sump′tu·ous, adj.; -ly, adv.; -ness, n.
un·sun′burned′, adj.
un·sun′burnt′, adj.
un·sun′dered, adj.
un·sunk′, adj.
un·sunk′en, adj.
un·sun′ny, adj.
un′su·per·cil′i·ous, adj.; -ly, adv.; -ness, n.
un′su·per·fi′cial, adj.; -ly, adv.
un′su·per′flu·ous, adj.; -ly, adv.; -ness, n.
un′su·pe′ri·or, adj.; -ly, adv.
un′su·per′la·tive, adj.; -ly, adv.; -ness, n.
un′su·per·nat′u·ral, adj.; -ly, adv.; -ness, n.
un′su·per·sed′ed, adj.
un′su·per·sed′ing, adj.
un′su·per·scribed′, adj.
un′su·per·sti′tious, adj.; -ly, adv.; -ness, n.
un·su′per·vised′, adj.
un′su·per·vi′so·ry, adj.
un′su·pine′, adj.
un′sup·plant′a·ble, adj.
un′sup·plant′ed, adj.
un·sup′ple, adj.; -ple·ness, n.; -ply, adv.
un′sup·ple·men′tal, adj.
un′sup·ple·men′ta·ry, adj.
un′sup·ple·ment′ed, adj.
un·sup′pli·a·ble, adj.
un·sup′pli·ant, adj.
un·sup′pli·cat′ed, adj.
un·sup′pli·cat′ing, adj.; -ly, adv.
un′sup·plied′, adj.
un′sup·port′a·ble, adj.; -ble·ness, n.; -bly, adv.
un′sup·port′ed, adj.; -ly, adv.
un′sup·port′ing, adj.
un′sup·pos′a·ble, adj.
un′sup·posed′, adj.
un′sup·po·si′tion·al, adj.
un′sup·pos′i·tive, adj.
un′sup·pressed′, adj.
un′sup·press′i·ble, adj.
un′sup·pres′sive, adj.
un·sup′pu·rat′ed, adj.
un·sup′pu·ra′tive, adj.
un′sur·charged′, adj.
un·sure′, adj.; -ly, adv.; -ness, n.
un·sur′faced, adj.
un·sur′feit·ed, adj.
un·sur′feit·ing, adj.
un·sur′gi·cal, adj.; -ly, adv.
un·surg′ing, adj.
un·sur′li·ly, adv.
un·sur′li·ness, n.
un·sur′ly, adj.
un′sur·mised′, adj.
un′sur·mis′ing, adj.
un′sur·mount′a·ble, adj.
un′sur·mount′ed, adj.
un·sur′named′, adj.
un′sur·pass′a·ble, adj.
un′sur·passed′, adj.
un·sur′pliced, adj.
un′sur·prised′, adj.
un′sur·pris′ing, adj.; -ly, adv.
un′sur·re′al·is′tic, adj.
un′sur·re′al·is′ti·cal·ly, adv.
un′sur·ren′dered, adj.
un′sur·ren′der·ing, adj.
un′sur·round′ed, adj.
un′sur·vey′a·ble, adj.
un′sur·veyed′, adj.
un′sur·vived′, adj.
un′sur·viv′ing, adj.
un′sus·cep′ti·bil′i·ty, n.
un′sus·cep′ti·ble, adj. -ble·ness, n.; -bly, adv.
un′sus·cep′tive, adj.
un′sus·pect′ful, adj.; -ly, adv.; -ness, n.
un′sus·pect′ing, adj.; -ly, adv.
un′sus·pend′ed, adj.
un′sus·pend′i·ble, adj.
un′sus·pi′cious, adj.; -ly, adv.; -ness, n.
un′sus·tained′, adj.
un′sus·tain′ing, adj.
un·su′tured, adj.
un·swabbed′, adj.
un·swad′dled, adj.
un·swad′dling, adj.
un·swag′ger·ing, adj.; -ly, adv.
un·swal′low·a·ble, adj.
un·swal′lowed, adj.
un·swamp′y, adj.
un·swapped′, adj.
un·swarm′ing, adj.
un·sway′a·ble, adj.
un·swayed′, adj.
un·sway′ing, adj.
un·sweat′ed, adj.
un·sweat′ing, adj.
un·sweep′a·ble, adj.
un·sweet′ened, adj.
un·swelled′, adj.
un·swell′ing, adj.
un·swel′tered, adj.
un·swel′ter·ing, adj.
un·swept′, adj.
un·swerv′a·ble, adj.
un·swerved′, adj.
un·swerv′ing, adj.; -ly, adv.; -ness, n.
un·swilled′, adj.
un·swin′gled, adj.
un·switched′, adj.
un·swiv′el, v.t., -eled, -el·ing or (esp. Brit.) -elled, -el·ling.
un·swol′len, adj.
un·swoon′ing, adj.
un·swung′, adj.
un′syl·lab′i·cat′ed, adj.
un′syl·lab′i·fied, adj.
un·syl′la·bled, adj.
un′syl·lo·gis′tic, adj.
un′syl·lo·gis′ti·cal, adj.; -ly, adv.
un′sym·bol′ic, adj.
un′sym·bol′i·cal, adj.; -ly, adv.
un·sym′bol·ised′, adj.
un·sym′bol·ized′, adj.
un′sym·met′ri·cal, adj.; -ly, adv.
un·sym′me·trized′, adj.
un′sym·pa·thet′ic, adj.
un′sym·pa·thet′i·cal·ly, adv.
un·sym′pa·thised′, adj.
un·sym′pa·this′ing, adj.; -ly, adv.
un·sym′pa·thized′, adj.
un·sym′pa·thiz′ing, adj.; -ly, adv.
un′sym·pho′ni·ous, adj.; -ly, adv.
un′symp·to·mat′ic, adj.
un′symp·to·mat′i·cal, adj.; -ly, adv.
un·syn′chro·nised′, adj.
un·syn′chro·nized′, adj.
un·syn′chro·nous, adj.; -ly, adv.; -ness, n.
un·syn′co·pat′ed, adj.
un·syn′di·cat′ed, adj.
un′syn·on′y·mous, adj.; -ly, adv.
un′syn·tac′tic, adj.
un′syn·tac′ti·cal, adj.; -ly, adv.
un·syn′the·sised′, adj.
un·syn′the·sized′, adj.
un′syn·thet′ic, adj.
un′syn·thet′i·cal·ly, adv.
un′syr·inged′, adj.
un′sys·tem·at′ic, adj.
un′sys·tem·at′i·cal, adj.; -ly, adv.
un·sys′tem·a·tised′, adj.
un·sys′tem·a·tis′ing, adj.
un·sys′tem·a·tized′, adj.
un·sys′tem·a·tiz′ing, adj.
un·tab′er·nac′led, adj.
un·ta′bled, adj.
un·tab′u·la·ble, adj.
un·tab′u·lat′ed, adj.
un·tac′i·turn′, adj.; -ly, adv.
un·tack′ling, adj.
un·tact′ful, adj.; -ly, adv.
un·tac′ti·cal, adj.; -ly, adv.
un·tac′tile, adj.
un·tac′tu·al, adj.; -ly, adv.
un·tagged′, adj.
un·tailed′, adj.
un·tai′lored, adj.
un·taint′a·ble, adj.
un·taint′ed, adj.
un·taint′ing, adj.
un·tak′a·ble, adj.
un·take′a·ble, adj.
un·tak′ing, adj.
un·tal′ent·ed, adj.
un·talk′a·tive, adj.
un·talk′ing, adj.
un·tal′lied, adj.
un·tal′lowed, adj.
un·tal′oned, adj.
un·tam′a·ble, adj.
un·tame′, adj.; -ly, adv.; -ness, n.
un·tame′a·ble, adj.
un·tamed′, adj.
un·tam′pered, adj.
un′tan·gen′tal, adj.; -ly, adv.
un′tan·gen′tial, adj.; -ly, adv.
un·tan′gi·ble, adj.
un·tanned′, adj.
un·tan′ta·lised′, adj.
un·tan′ta·lis′ing, adj.
un·tan′ta·lized′, adj.
un·tan′ta·liz′ing, adj.
un·taped′, adj.
un·ta′pered, adj.
un·ta′per·ing, adj.
un·tap′es·tried, adj.
un·tap′pa·ble, adj.
un·tapped′, adj.
un·tar′nish·a·ble, adj.
un·tar′nished, adj.
un·tar′nish·ing, adj.
un·tarred′, adj.
un·tar′ried, adj.
un·tar′ry·ing, adj.
un·tar′tar·ized′, adj.
un·tasked′, adj.
un·tas′seled, adj.
un·tas′selled, adj.
un·tast′a·ble, adj.
un·taste′a·ble, adj.
un·tast′ed, adj.
un·taste′ful, adj.; -ly, adv.; -ness, n.
un·tast′ing, adj.
un·tast′i·ly, adv.
un·tast′y, adj.
un·tat′tered, adj.
un′tat·tooed′, adj.

un·taught (un tôt′), *v.* **1.** pt. and pp. of **unteach.** —*adj.* **2.** not taught; not acquired by teaching; natural: *untaught gentleness.* **3.** not instructed or educated; naïve; ignorant. [ME; see UN-¹, TAUGHT]

un·teach (un tēch′), *v.t.*, **-taught, -teach·ing.** **1.** to cause to be forgotten or disbelieved, as by contrary teaching. **2.** to cause to forget or disbelieve something previously taught. [UN-² + TEACH]

un·ten·a·ble (un ten′ə bəl), *adj.* **1.** incapable of being defended, as an argument, thesis, etc.; indefensible. **2.** not fit to be occupied, as an apartment, house, etc. [UN-¹ + TENABLE] —**un/ten·a·bil′i·ty, un·ten′a·ble·ness,** *n.*

Un·ter den Lin·den (*Ger.* ŏŏn′tər den lin′dən), (formerly) a fashionable street in Berlin.

Un·ter·mey·er (un′tər mī′ər), *n.* **Louis,** born 1885, U.S. poet, critic, and editor.

Un·ter·wal·den (*Ger.* ŏŏn′tər väl′dən), *n.* a canton in central Switzerland: divided into demicantons. Cf. **Obwalden, Nidwalden.**

un·thank·ful (un thangk′fəl), *adj.* **1.** not thankful; ungrateful. **2.** not repaid with thanks; thankless: *an unthankful task.* [ME; see UN-¹, THANKFUL] —**un·thank′ful·ly,** *adv.* —**un·thank′ful·ness,** *n.*

un·thatch (un thach′), *v.t.* to remove or throw off the thatch from: *to unthatch a roof.* [UN-² + THATCH]

un·think (un thingk′), *v.*, **-thought, -think·ing.** —*v.i.* **1.** to end one's thought or reverse the process of thought. —*v.t.* **2.** to dispel from the mind: *Unthink your thoughts.* [UN-² + THINK¹]

un·think·a·ble (un thing′kə bəl), *adj.* **1.** inconceivable; unimaginable: *the unthinkable size of the universe.* **2.** not to be considered; out of the question: *Such a suggestion is unthinkable.* —*n.* **3.** Usually, **unthinkables.** things that are unthinkable: *Someday the current unthinkables may become realities.* [ME; see UN-¹, THINKABLE] —**un·think′a·bil′i·ty, un·think′a·ble·ness,** *n.* —**un·think′a·bly,** *adv.*

un·think·ing (un thing′king), *adj.* **1.** thoughtless; heedless; inconsiderate: *Only an unthinking person would make such a tactless remark.* **2.** indicating lack of thought or reflection: *He often has a dull, unthinking expression on his face.* **3.** not endowed with the faculty of thought: *unthinking matter.* **4.** not exercising thought; not given to reflection: *This book will not profit an unthinking person.* **5.** not thinking; unmindful: *Many common things which adults do in an unthinking fashion have to be carefully learned by little children.* [UN-¹ + THINKING] —**un·think′ing·ly,** *adv.* —**un·think′ing·ness,** *n.*

un·thought¹ (un thôt′), *v.* pt. and pp. of **unthink.** [UN-¹ + THOUGHT²]

un·thought² (un thôt′), *adj.* **1.** not thought; not framed in a thought or thoughts: *After uttering this embarrassing remark, she wished that it might have remained unthought.* **2.** not expected; not anticipated (often fol. by *of*): *The roof was an unthought-of place to find our little dog.* [UN-¹ + THOUGHT²]

un·thought³ (un thôt′), *n.* an absence of thought. [UN-¹ + THOUGHT¹]

un·thread (un thred′), *v.t.* **1.** to draw out or take out the thread from: *to unthread a sewing machine.* **2.** to thread one's way through or out of, as a densely wooded forest. **3.** to disentangle; separate out of a raveled or confused condition: *to unthread a mystery; to unthread a person's confused thoughts.* [UN-² + THREAD]

un·throne (un thrōn′), *v.t.*, **-throned, -thron·ing.** to dethrone or remove as if by dethroning. [UN-² + THRONE]

un·ti·dy (un tī′dē), *adj.*, **-di·er, -di·est,** *v.*, **-died, -dy·ing.** —*adj.* **1.** not tidy or neat; slovenly; disordered: *an untidy room; an untidy person.* **2.** not well-organized or carried out: *an untidy plan.* —*v.t.* **3.** to mess up; disorder; disarrange: *The guests untidied the room.* [ME; see UN-¹, TIDY] —**un·ti′di·ly,** *adv.* —**un·ti′di·ness,** *n.*

un·tie (un tī′), *v.*, **-tied, -ty·ing.** —*v.t.* **1.** to loose or unfasten (anything tied); let or set loose by undoing a knot. **2.** to undo the string or cords of. **3.** to undo, as a cord or a knot; unknot. **4.** to free from restraint. **5.** to resolve, as perplexities. —*v.i.* **6.** to become untied. [ME *untye(n)*, OE *untīegan.* See UN-², TIE]

un·til (un til′), *conj.* **1.** up to the time that or when; till: *He read until his guests arrived.* **2.** before (usually used in negative constructions): *He did not come until the meeting was half over.* —*prep.* **3.** onward to or till (a specified time or occurrence): *He worked until 6 P.M. The children sat in class until recess.* **4.** before (usually used in negative constructions): *He did not go until night.* **5.** *Scot. and North Eng.* to; unto. [ME *untill*, equiv. to *un-* (< Scand; cf. OIcel *unz* up to, as far as) + *till* TILL¹]

un·time·ly (un tīm′lē), *adj.* **1.** not timely; not occurring at a suitable time or season; ill-timed or inopportune: *An untimely downpour prevented the game from being completed.* **2.** premature. —*adv.* **3.** unseasonably; prematurely. [ME *untimliche.* See UN-¹, TIMELY] —**un·time′li·ness,** *n.*
—**Syn. 1.** unseasonable, inappropriate.

un·time·ous (un tī′məs), *adj.* *Scot.* untimely.

un·tinged (un tinjd′), *adj.* **1.** not colored, as by paint, the sun, etc. **2.** not biased or partial; objective: *His report was untinged by sentimentality.* [UN-¹ + TINGED]

un·tit·led (un tīt′əld), *adj.* **1.** without a title: *an untitled nobleman; an untitled book.* **2.** having no right or claim. [UN-¹ + TITLED]

un·to (un′tōō; *unstressed* un′tə), *prep.* *Archaic.* **1.** to (in its various uses, except as the accompaniment of the infinitive). **2.** until; till. [ME; modeled on *until*]

un·told (un tōld′), *adj.* **1.** not told; not related; not revealed: *untold thoughts; untold tales.* **2.** not numbered or enumerated; uncounted: *He used untold sheets of paper in writing the book.* **3.** inexpressible; incalculable: *untold suffering.* [ME; OE *unteald.* See UN-¹, TOLD]

un·touch·a·bil·i·ty (un′tuch ə bil′i tē), *n.* *Hinduism.* the quality or condition of being an untouchable, ascribed in the Vedic tradition to persons of low caste or to persons excluded from the caste system. [UNTOUCHABLE + -ITY]

un·touch·a·ble (un tuch′ə bəl), *adj.* **1.** that may not be touched; of a nature such that it cannot be touched; not palpable; intangible. **2.** too distant to be touched. **3.** vile or loathsome to the touch. **4.** beyond criticism, control, or suspicion: *Modern science considers nothing untouchable.* —*n.* **5.** a member of a lower caste in India whose touch is believed to defile a high-caste Hindu. **6.** one who is beyond reproach as to honesty, diligence, etc. [UN-¹ + TOUCHABLE] —**un·touch′a·bly,** *adv.*

un·touched (un tucht′), *adj.* **1.** not touched or handled, as material. **2.** not explored or visited: *untouched lands.* **3.** not eaten or drunk. **4.** remaining in a pristine state; unchanged: *an untouched innocent; an untouched world.* **5.** not injured or hurt; undamaged: *Although the war raged about it, the temple remained untouched.* **6.** not affected or altered: *She was untouched by the life around her.* **7.** emotionally unmoved; indifferent: *It was a pity she was left untouched by the music.* **8.** not mentioned or described, as in conversation, a book, etc.: *It was left untouched in an otherwise comprehensive study.* [ME; see UN-¹, TOUCHED] —**un·touched′ness,** *n.*

un·to·ward (un tōrd′, -tôrd′), *adj.* **1.** unfavorable or unfortunate: *Untoward circumstances forced him into bankruptcy.* **2.** improper: *untoward social behavior.* **3.** *Archaic.* forward; perverse. [UN-¹ + TOWARD] —**un·to′ward·ly,** *adv.* —**un·to′ward·ness,** *n.*

un·trav·eled (un trav′əld), *adj.* **1.** not having traveled, esp. to distant places; not having gained experience by travel. **2.** not traveled through or over; not frequented by travelers: *an untraveled country lane.* Also, *esp. Brit.*, **un·trav′elled.** [UN-¹ + TRAVELED]

un·tread (un tred′), *v.t.*, **-trod, -trod·den** or **-trod, -tread·ing.** to go back through in the same steps. [UN-² + TREAD]

un·tried (un trīd′), *adj.* **1.** not tried; not attempted, proved, or tested. **2.** not yet tried at law. [UN-¹ + TRIED]

un·taunt′ed, *adj.*
un·taunt′ing, *adj.*; -ly, *adv.*
un·taut′, *adj.*; -ly, *adv.*; -ness, *n.*
un′tau·to·log′i·cal, *adj.*; -ly, *adv.*
un·taw′dry, *adj.*
un·tawed′, *adj.*
un·tax′a·ble, *adj.*
un·tax′ied, *adj.*
un·tax′ing, *adj.*
un·teach′a·ble, *adj.*
un·teamed′, *adj.*
un·tear′a·ble, *adj.*
un·teased′, *adj.*
un·tea′seled, *adj.*
un·tea′selled, *adj.*
un·tech′ni·cal, *adj.*; -ly, *adv.*
un·ted′ded, *adj.*
un·te′di·ous, *adj.*; -ly, *adv.*
un·teem′ing, *adj.*
un·tel′e·graphed′, *adj.*
un·tel′e·vised′, *adj.*
un·tel′ic, *adj.*
un·tell′a·ble, *adj.*
un·tell′ing, *adj.*
un·tem′per·a·ble, *adj.*
un′tem·per·a·men′tal, *adj.*; -ly, *adv.*
un·tem′per·ate, *adj.*; -ly, *adv.*; -ness, *n.*
un·tem′pered, *adj.*
un·tem′per·ing, *adj.*
un′tem·pes′tu·ous, *adj.*; -ly, *adv.*; -ness, *n.*
un·tem′pled, *adj.*
un·tem′po·ral, *adj.*; -ly, *adv.*
un·tem′po·rar′y, *adj.*
un·tempt′a·ble, *adj.*
un′tempt′ed, *adj.*
un·tempt′ing, *adj.*; -ly, *adv.*
un′te·na′cious, *adj.*; -ly, *adv.*; -ness, *n.*
un′te·nac′i·ty, *n.*
un·ten′ant·a·ble, *adj.*
un·ten′ant·ed, *adj.*
un·tend′ed, *adj.*
un·ten′dered, *adj.*
un·ten′der·ized′, *adj.*
un·ten′der·ly, *adv.*
un·ten′e·brous, *adj.*
un·tense′, *adj.*; -ly, *adv.*; -ness, *n.*
un′ten·si·bil′i·ty, *n.*
un·ten′si·ble, *adj.*; -bly, *adv.*
un·ten′sile, *adj.*
un·tens′ing, *adj.*
un·ten′ta·cled, *adj.*
un·ten′tered, *adj.*
un·ten′u·ous, *adj.*; -ly, *adv.*; -ness, *n.*
un·ter′mi·nat′ed, *adj.*
un·ter′mi·nat′ing, *adj.*
un′ter·mi·na′tion·al, *adj.*
un·ter′mi·na′tive, *adj.*
un·ter′raced, *adj.*
un·ter·res′tri·al, *adj.*
un·ter′ri·ble, *adj.*
un·ter·rif′ic, *adj.*
un′ter·rif′i·cal·ly, *adv.*
un·ter′ri·fied′, *adj.*
un·ter′ri·fy′ing, *adj.*
un·ter′ror·ized′, *adj.*
un·terse′, *adj.*; -ly, *adv.*; -ness, *n.*
un·tes′sel·lat′ed, *adj.*
un·test′a·ble, *adj.*
un′tes·ta·men′tal, *adj.*
un′tes·ta·men′ta·ry, *adj.*
un·test′ed, *adj.*
un·tes′ti·fy′ing, *adj.*
un·teth′ered, *adj.*
un·teth′er·ing, *adj.*
un·tex′tu·al, *adj.*; -ly, *adv.*
un·tex′tur·al, *adj.*
un·thanked′, *adj.*
un·thank′ing, *adj.*
un·thawed′, *adj.*
un·thaw′ing, *adj.*
un′the·at′ric, *adj.*
un′the·at′ri·cal, *adj.*; -ly, *adv.*
un′the·is′tic, *adj.*
un′the·is′ti·cal, *adj.*; -ly, *adv.*
un′the·mat′ic, *adj.*
un′the·mat′i·cal·ly, *adv.*
un′the·o·log′ic, *adj.*
un′the·o·log′i·cal, *adj.*; -ly, *adv.*
un′the·o·ret′ic, *adj.*
un′the·o·ret′i·cal, *adj.*; -ly, *adv.*
un′ther·a·peu′tic, *adj.*
un′ther·a·peu′ti·cal, *adj.*; -ly, *adv.*
un·thick′, *adj.*; -ly, *adv.*; -ness, *n.*
un·thick′en, *v.t.*
un·thiev′ish, *adj.*; -ly, *adv.*; -ness, *n.*
un·thinned′, *adj.*
un·thin′ning, *adj.*
un·thirst′ing, *adj.*
un·thirst′y, *adj.*
un·thorn′, *v.t.*
un·thorn′y, *adj.*
un·thor′ough, *adj.*; -ly, *adv.*; -ness, *n.*
un·thought′ful, *adj.*; -ly, *adv.*; -ness, *n.*
un·thralled′, *adj.*
un·thrashed′, *adj.*
un·thread′a·ble, *adj.*
un·thread′ed, *adj.*
un·threat′en·ing, *adj.*; -ly, *adv.*
un·threshed′, *adj.*
un·thrift′i·ly, *adv.*
un·thrift′i·ness, *n.*
un·thrift′y, *adj.*
un·thrilled′, *adj.*
un·thrill′ing, *adj.*
un·thriv′ing, *adj.*
un·throat′i·ly, *adv.*
un·throat′y, *adj.*
un·throb′bing, *adj.*
un·thronged′, *adj.*
un·throt′tled, *adj.*
un·throw′a·ble, *adj.*
un·thrown′, *adj.*
un·thrust′, *adj.*
un·thumped′, *adj.*
un·thun′der·ing, *adj.*
un·thwacked′, *adj.*
un·thwart′a·ble, *adj.*
un·thwart′ed, *adj.*
un·thwart′ing, *adj.*
un·tick′et·ed, *adj.*
un·tick′led, *adj.*
un·tid′al, *adj.*
un·tiered′, *adj.*
un·tight′en, *v.t.*
un·tiled′, *adj.*
un·till′a·ble, *adj.*
un·tilled′, *adj.*
un·till′ing, *adj.*
un·tilt′, *v.t.*
un·tim′bered, *adj.*
un·timed′, *adj.*
un·tim′id, *adj.*; -ly, *adv.*; -ness, *n.*
un·tim′or·ous, *adj.*; -ly, *adv.*; -ness, *n.*
un·tinc′tured, *adj.*
un·tin′dered, *adj.*
un·tin′kered, *adj.*
un·tinned′, *adj.*
un·tin′seled, *adj.*
un·tin′selled, *adj.*
un·tint′ed, *adj.*
un·tip′pa·ble, *adj.*
un·tip′pled, *adj.*
un·tired′, *adj.*; -ly, *adv.*
un·tir′ing, *adj.*; -ly, *adv.*
un·tis′sued, *adj.*
un·tith′a·ble, *adj.*
un·tithed′, *adj.*
un·tit′il·lat′ed, *adj.*
un·tit′il·lat′ing, *adj.*
un·tit′ter·ing, *adj.*
un·tit′u·lar, *adj.*; -ly, *adv.*
un·toad′y·ing, *adj.*
un·toast′ed, *adj.*
un·to′gaed, *adj.*
un·toil′ing, *adj.*
un·tol′er·a·ble, *adj.*; -ble·ness, *n.*; -bly, *adv.*
un·tol′er·at′ed, *adj.*
un·tol′er·at′ing, *adj.*
un·tol′er·a′tive, *adj.*
un·tolled′, *adj.*
un·tombed′, *adj.*
un·toned′, *adj.*
un·tongued′, *adj.*
un·ton′sured, *adj.*
un·tooled′, *adj.*
un′top·o·graph′i·cal, *adj.*; -ly, *adv.*
un·top′pa·ble, *adj.*
un·topped′, *adj.*
un·top′ping, *adj.*
un·top′pled, *adj.*
un·tor′ment·ed, *adj.*
un·tor·ment′ing, *adj.*; -ly, *adv.*
un·torn′, *adj.*
un′tor·pe′doed, *adj.*
un·tor′pid, *adj.*; -ly, *adv.*
un·tor·por·if′ic, *adj.*
un·tor′rid, *adj.*; -ly, *adv.*; -ness, *n.*
un′tor·rid′i·ty, *n.*
un·tor′tious, *adj.*; -ly, *adv.*
un·tor′tu·ous, *adj.*; -ly, *adv.*; -ness, *n.*
un·tor′tured, *adj.*
un·tossed′, *adj.*
un·to′taled, *adj.*
un·to′talled, *adj.*
un·tot′ted, *adj.*
un·tot′ter·ing, *adj.*
un·touch′ing, *adj.*
un·tough′, *adj.*; -ly, *adv.*; -ness, *n.*
un·toured′, *adj.*
un·tox′ic, *adj.*
un·tox′i·cal·ly, *adv.*
un·trace′a·ble, *adj.*
un·traced′, *adj.*
un·trac′er·ied, *adj.*
un·tracked′, *adj.*
un′trac·ta·bil′i·ty, *n.*
un·trac′ta·ble, *adj.*; -ble·ness, *n.*; -bly, *adv.*
un·trad′a·ble, *adj.*
un·trade′a·ble, *adj.*
un·trad′ed, *adj.*
un·trad′ing, *adj.*
un′tra·di′tion·al, *adj.*
un′tra·duced′, *adj.*
un·traf′ficked, *adj.*
un·trag′ic, *adj.*
un·trag′i·cal, *adj.*; -ly, *adv.*; -ness, *n.*
un·trailed′, *adj.*
un·trail′ing, *adj.*
un·trail′er·a·ble, *adj.*
un·trail′ered, *adj.*
un·train′a·ble, *adj.*
un·trained′, *adj.*
un·trai′tor·ous, *adj.*; -ly, *adv.*; -ness, *n.*
un·trammed′, *adj.*
un·tram′meled, *adj.*
un·tram′melled, *adj.*
un·tramped′, *adj.*
un·tram′pled, *adj.*
un·tran′quil, *adj.*; -ly, *adv.*; -ness, *n.*
un·tran′quil·ize′, *v.t.*, -ized, -iz·ing.
un·tran′quil·lise′, *v.t.*, -lised, -lis·ing.
un·trans·act′ed, *adj.*
un′tran·scend′ed, *adj.*
un′tran·scend′ent, *adj.*
un′tran·scen·den′tal, *adj.*; -ly, *adv.*
un′tran·scrib′a·ble, *adj.*
un′tran·scribed′, *adj.*
un′trans·fer′a·ble, *adj.*
un′trans·ferred′, *adj.*
un′trans·fer′ring, *adj.*
un′trans·fig′ured, *adj.*
un′trans·fixed′, *adj.*
un′trans·form′a·ble, *adj.*
un′trans·form′a·tive, *adj.*
un′trans·formed′, *adj.*
un′trans·form′ing, *adj.*
un′trans·fused′, *adj.*
un′trans·fus′i·ble, *adj.*
un′trans·gressed′, *adj.*
un·tran′sient, *adj.*; -ly, *adv.*; -ness, *n.*
un′tran·si′tion·al, *adj.*; -ly, *adv.*
un·tran′si·tive, *adj.*; -ly, *adv.*; -ness, *n.*
un·tran′si·to′ri·ly, *adv.*
un·tran′si·to′ri·ness, *n.*
un·tran′si·to′ry, *adj.*
un′trans·lat′a·ble, *adj.*
un′trans·lat′ed, *adj.*
un′trans·mi′grat′ed, *adj.*
un′trans·mis′si·ble, *adj.*
un′trans·mis′sive, *adj.*
un′trans·mit′ted, *adj.*
un′trans·mut′a·bil′i·ty, *n.*
un′trans·mut′a·ble, *adj.*; -ble·ness, *n.*; -bly, *adv.*
un′trans·mut′ed, *adj.*
un′trans·par′ent, *adj.*; -ly, *adv.*; -ness, *n.*
un′tran·spired′, *adj.*
un′tran·spir′ing, *adj.*
un′trans·plant′ed, *adj.*
un′trans·port′a·ble, *adj.*
un′trans·port′ed, *adj.*
un′trans·posed′, *adj.*
un′tran·sub·stan′ti·at′ed, *adj.*
un·trapped′, *adj.*
un·trashed′, *adj.*
un′trau·mat′ic, *adj.*
un·trav′el·ing, *adj.*
un·trav′el·ling, *adj.*
un·trav′ers·a·ble, *adj.*
un·trav′ersed, *adj.*
un·trav′es·tied, *adj.*
un·treach′er·ous, *adj.*; -ly, *adv.*; -ness, *n.*
un·tread′a·ble, *adj.*
un·trea′son·a·ble, *adj.*
un·treas′ur·a·ble, *adj.*
un·treas′ured, *adj.*
un·treat′a·ble, *adj.*
un·treat′ed, *adj.*
un·treed′, *adj.*
un·trekked′, *adj.*
un·trel′lised, *adj.*
un·trem′bling, *adj.*; -ly, *adv.*
un′tre·men′dous, *adj.*; -ly, *adv.*; -ness, *n.*
un·trem′o·lant, *adj.*
un·trem′u·lant, *adj.*
un·trem′u·lent, *adj.*
un·trem′u·lous, *adj.*; -ly, *adv.*; -ness, *n.*
un·trenched′, *adj.*
un′tre·panned′, *adj.*
un·tres′passed, *adj.*
un·tres′pass·ing, *adj.*
un·tressed′, *adj.*
un·tri′a·ble, *adj.*; -ness, *n.*
un·trib′al, *adj.*; -ly, *adv.*
un·trib′u·tar′i·ly, *adv.*
un·trib′u·tar′y, *adj.*
un·triced′, *adj.*
un·trick′a·ble, *adj.*
un·tricked′, *adj.*
un·tri′fling, *adj.*; -ly, *adv.*

un·trimmed (un trimd′), *adj.* **1.** not trimmed. **2.** *Bookbinding.* (of gathered sections of a book) having the bolts untrimmed by a guillotine or plow. Also called, *esp. Brit.,* **uncut.** [UN-[1] + TRIMMED] —**un·trimmed′ness,** *n.*

un·trod (un trod′), *adj.* not trod; not traversed: *the untrod wastes of Antarctica.* Also, **un·trod′den.** [UN-[1] + TROD]

un·true (un tro͞o′), *adj.* **1.** not true, as to a person or a cause, to fact, or to a standard. **2.** unfaithful; false. **3.** incorrect or inaccurate. [UN-[1] + TRUE] —**un·true′ness,** *n.*

un·truss (un trus′), *v.t., v.i. Archaic.* to loose from or as if from a truss. [ME; see UN-[2], TRUSS]

un·truth (un tro͞oth′), *n., pl.* **-truths** (-tro͞othz, -tro͞oths). **1.** state or character of being untrue. **2.** want of veracity; divergence from truth. **3.** something untrue; a falsehood or lie. **4.** *Archaic.* unfaithfulness; disloyalty. [ME; OE *untrēowth.* See UN-[1], TRUTH]
—**Syn. 3.** fiction, story, tale, fable, fabrication, invention. See **falsehood.**

un·truth·ful (un tro͞oth′fəl), *adj.* not truthful; wanting in veracity; diverging from or contrary to the truth; not corresponding with fact or reality. [UN-[1] + TRUTHFUL] —**un·truth′ful·ly,** *adv.* —**un·truth′ful·ness,** *n.*

un·tuck (un tuk′), *v.t.* to release from or bring out of a tucked condition: *She untucked her legs.* [UN-[2] + TUCK[1]]

un·tune (un to͞on′, -tyo͞on′), *v.t.,* **-tuned, -tun·ing.** **1.** to render or cause to become out of tune: *Changes in weather can untune a violin.* **2.** to discompose; upset, as the mind, emotions, etc. [UN-[2] + TUNE]

un·tu·tored (un to͞o′tərd, -tyo͞o′-), *adj.* not tutored; untaught; uninstructed. [UN-[1] + TUTOR + -ED[3]]

un·twine (un twīn′), *v.t., v.i.,* **-twined, -twin·ing.** to bring or come out of a twined condition. [ME; see UN-[2] + TWINE] —**un·twine′a·ble,** *adj.*

un·twist (un twist′), *v.t., v.i.* to bring or come out of a twisted condition. [UN-[2] + TWIST]

U Nu (o͞o no͞o′). See **Nu, U.**

un·used (un yo͞ozd′ *for 1, 2;* un yo͞ost′ *for 3*), *adj.* **1.** not used; not put to use: *His family is so large that not one room in his house is unused.* **2.** never having been used: *an unused postage stamp.* **3.** not accustomed: *Having come from a tropical country, she is unused to our cold winters.* [ME; see UN-[1], USED]

un·u·su·al (un yo͞o′zho͞o əl), *adj.* not usual, common, or ordinary; uncommon in amount or degree; exceptional: *an unusual sound; an unusual hobby; an unusual response.* [UN-[1] + USUAL] —**un·u′su·al·ly,** *adv.* —**un·u′su·al·ness, un·u′su·al′i·ty,** *n.*
—**Syn.** extraordinary, rare, strange, remarkable, singular, curious, queer, odd.

un·ut·ter·a·ble (un ut′ər ə bəl), *adj.* **1.** not utterable; not pronounceable: *an unutterable foreign word.* **2.** not communicable by utterance; unspeakable; beyond expression: *unutterable joy.* [UN-[1] + UTTERABLE] —**un·ut′ter·a·bly,** *adv.*

un·var·nished (un vär′nisht), *adj.* **1.** plain; clear; straightforward; without vagueness or subterfuge; frank: *the unvarnished truth.* **2.** unfinished, as floors, furniture, etc.; not coated with or as if with varnish. [UN-[1] + VARNISH + -ED[3]]

un·veil (un vāl′), *v.t.* **1.** to remove a veil or other covering from; display; reveal: *The woman unveiled herself.* **2.** to reveal or disclose by or as if by removing a veil or covering: *to unveil a monument; to unveil a secret; to unveil a truth.* —*v.i.* **3.** to become revealed by or as if by removing a veil. [UN-[2] + VEIL]

un·veil·ing (un vā′ling), *n.* an instance or act of presenting or putting on display, esp. for the first time: *the unveiling of a new play; the unveiling of a statue; the unveiling of new methods.* [UNVEIL + -ING[1]]

un·ve·sic·u·lat·ed (un′vi sik′yə lā′tid), *adj. Geol.* without vesicles. [UN-[1] + VESICULATED]

un·vo·cal (un vō′kəl), *adj.* **1.** not outspoken; reserved; not eloquent in speech; inarticulate. **2.** not mellifluous, as the speaking voice. **3.** not musical, as a song. [UN-[1] + VOCAL]

un·voice (un vois′), *v.,* **-voiced, -voic·ing.** *Phonet.* —*v.t.* **1.** to deprive (an ordinarily voiced speech sound) of a part or all of its tonal vibration in pronouncing; devoice. —*v.i.* **2.** to unvoice a speech sound. [UN-[2] + VOICE]

un·voiced (un voist′), *adj.* **1.** not voiced; not uttered: *unvoiced complaints.* **2.** *Phonet.* voiceless; without voice; surd. [UN-[1] + VOICED]

un·warped (un wôrpt′), *adj.* **1.** not warped, as a phonograph record, flooring, etc. **2.** impartial; undistorted, as a point of view. [UN-[1] + WARP + -ED[2]]

un·war·y (un wâr′ē), *adj.* not wary; not cautious or watchful, as against danger or undesirable occurrences. [UN-[1] + WARY] —**un·war′i·ly,** *adv.* —**un·war′i·ness,** *n.*
—**Syn.** incautious, indiscreet, rash, heedless.

un·washed (un wosht′, -wôsht′), *adj.* **1.** not cleaned or purified by or as if by washing: *unwashed dishes; the unwashed soul of a sinner.* —*n.* **2.** an ignorant or lower-class group; rabble: *The author claimed that the unwashed would not understand his books.* [UN-[1] + WASHED]

un·wea·ried (un wēr′ēd), *adj.* **1.** not wearied; not fatigued. **2.** indefatigable. [UN-[1] + WEARY + -ED[3]] —**un·wea′ried·ly,** *adv.* —**un·wea′ried·ness,** *n.*

---

un·trig′, *adj.*
un·trig′gered, *adj.*
un′trig·o·no·met′ric, *adj.*
un′trig·o·no·met′ri·cal, *adj.;* **-ly,** *adv.*
un·trim′ma·ble, *adj.*
un·trin·i·tar′i·an, *adj.*
un·tripped′, *adj.*
un·trip′ping, *adj.*
un·trite′, *adj.;* **-ly,** *adv.;* **-ness,** *n.*
un·trit′u·rat′ed, *adj.*
un′tri·um′phant, *adj.;* **-ly,** *adv.*
un·triv′i·al, *adj.;* **-ly,** *adv.*
un′tro·cha′ic, *adj.*
un·trolled′, *adj.*
un·tro′phied, *adj.*
un·trop′ic, *adj.*
un·trop′i·cal, *adj.;* **-ly,** *adv.*
un·trot′ted, *adj.*
un·trou′bled, *adj.*
un·trou′ble·some, *adj.*
un·trounced′, *adj.*
un·tru′ant, *adj.*
un·truck′led, *adj.*
un·truck′ling, *adj.*
un·trumped′, *adj.*
un·trum′pet·ed, *adj.*
un·trump′ing, *adj.*
un·trun′dled, *adj.*
un·trust′a·ble, *adj.*
un·trust′ed, *adj.*
un·trust′ful, *adj.;* **-ly,** *adv.*
un·trust′ing, *adj.*
un·trust′worth·i·ly, *adv.;* **-ness,** *n.*
un·trust′wor′thy, *adj.*
un·try′ing, *adj.*
un·tubbed′, *adj.*
un′tu·ber′cu·lar, *adj.*
un′tu·ber′cu·lous, *adj.*
un·tuft′ed, *adj.*
un·tugged′, *adj.*
un·tum′bled, *adj.*
un·tu′me·fied′, *adj.*
un·tu′mid, *adj.;* **-ly,** *adv.;* **-ness,** *n.*
un′tu·mid′i·ty, *n.*
un′tu·mul′tu·ous, *adj.;* **-ly,** *adv.;* **-ness,** *n.*
un·tun′a·ble, *adj.;* **-ble·ness,** *n.;* **-bly,** *adv.*
un·tune′a·ble, *adj.;* **-ble·ness,** *n.;* **-bly,** *adv.*
un·tune′ful, *adj.;* **-ly,** *adv.*
un·tun′neled, *adj.*
un·tun′nelled, *adj.*
un·tur′baned, *adj.*
un·tur′bid, *adj.;* **-ly,** *adv.*
un·tur′bu·lent, *adj.;* **-ly,** *adv.*
un·turfed′, *adj.*
un·tur′gid, *adj.;* **-ly,** *adv.*
un·turn′a·ble, *adj.*
un·turned′, *adj.*
un·turn′ing, *adj.*
un·tur′pen·tined′, *adj.*
un·tur′ret·ed, *adj.*
un·tusked′, *adj.*
un·tu′te·lar, *adj.*
un·tu′te·lar′y, *adj.*
un·twilled′, *adj.*
un·twin′kled, *adj.*
un·twin′kling, *adj.*
un·twinned′, *adj.*
un·twirled′, *adj.*
un·twirl′ing, *adj.*
un·twist′a·ble, *adj.*
un·twitched′, *adj.*
un·twitch′ing, *adj.*
un·typed′, *adj.*
un·typ′i·cal, *adj.;* **-ly,** *adv.*
un′ty·ran′nic, *adj.*
un′ty·ran′ni·cal, *adj.;* **-ly,** *adv.*
un·tyr′an·nised′, *adj.*
un·tyr′an·nized′, *adj.*
un·ty′rant·like′, *adj.*
un′u·biq′ui·tous, *adj.;* **-ly,** *adv.;* **-ness,** *n.*
un·ul′cer·at′ed, *adj.*
un·ul′cer·a′tive, *adj.*
un·ul′cer·ous, *adj.;* **-ly,** *adv.;* **-ness,** *n.*
un·um′pired, *adj.*
un·u′ni·fi′a·ble, *adj.*
un·u′ni·fied′, *adj.*
un·u′ni·formed′, *adj.*
un·un′ion·ized′, *adj.*
un′u·nique′, *adj.;* **-ly,** *adv.;* **-ness,** *n.*
un′u·nit′a·ble, *adj.*
un′u·nite′a·ble, *adj.*
un′u·nit′ed, *adj.*
un′u·nit′ing, *adj.*
un′up·braid′ed, *adj.*
un′up·braid′ing, *adj.;* **-ly,** *adv.*
un′up·hol′stered, *adj.*
un′up·set′, *adj.*
un′up·set′ta·ble, *adj.*
un·ur′ban, *adj.*
un′ur·bane′, *adj.;* **-ly,** *adv.*
un·ur′ban·ized′, *adj.*
un·urged′, *adj.*
un·ur′gent, *adj.;* **-ly,** *adv.*
un·urg′ing, *adj.*
un·us′a·ble, *adj.;* **-ble·ness,** *n.;* **-bly,** *adv.*
un·use′a·ble, *adj.;* **-ble·ness,** *n.;* **-bly,** *adv.*
un·use′ful, *adj.;* **-ly,** *adv.;* **-ness,** *n.*
un·ush′ered, *adj.*
un′u·su′ri·ous, *adj.;* **-ly,** *adv.;* **-ness,** *n.*
un′u·surped′, *adj.*
un′u·surp′ing, *adj.*
un′u·til′i·tar′i·an, *adj.*
un·u′ti·liz′a·ble, *adj.*
un·u′ti·lized′, *adj.*
un·ut′tered, *adj.*
un′ux·o′ri·ous, *adj.;* **-ly,** *adv.;* **-ness,** *n.*
un·va′cant, *adj.;* **-ly,** *adv.*
un·va′cat·ed, *adj.*
un·vac′ci·nat′ed, *adj.*
un·vac′il·lat·ing, *adj.*
un·vac′u·ous, *adj.;* **-ly,** *adv.;* **-ness,** *n.*
un·va′grant, *adj.;* **-ly,** *adv.;* **-ness,** *n.*
un·vague′, *adj.;* **-ly,** *adv.;* **-ness,** *n.*
un·vain′, *adj.;* **-ly,** *adv.;* **-ness,** *n.*
un·val′et·ed, *adj.*
un·val′iant, *adj.;* **-ly,** *adv.;* **-ness,** *n.*
un·val′i·dat′ed, *adj.*
un·val′i·dat′ing, *adj.*
un·val′or·ous, *adj.;* **-ly,** *adv.;* **-ness,** *n.*
un·val′u·a·ble, *adj.;* **-bly,** *adv.*
un·val′ued, *adj.*
un·vamped′, *adj.*
un·van′ish·ing, *adj.*
un·van′quish·a·ble, *adj.*
un·van′quished, *adj.*
un·van′quish·ing, *adj.*
un·va′por·ized′, *adj.*
un·va·por·os′i·ty, *n.*
un·va′por·ous, *adj.;* **-ly,** *adv.;* **-ness,** *n.*
un·var′i·a·ble, *adj.;* **-ble·ness,** *n.;* **-bly,** *adv.*
un·var′i·ant, *adj.*
un·var′ied, *adj.*
un·var′i·e·gat′ed, *adj.*
un·var′y·ing, *adj.;* **-ly,** *adv.*
un·vas′cu·lar, *adj.;* **-ly,** *adv.*
un·vas′cu·lous, *adj.*
un·vat′ted, *adj.*
un·vault′ed, *adj.*
un·vault′ing, *adj.*
un·vaunt′ed, *adj.*
un·vaunt′ing, *adj.;* **-ly,** *adv.*
un·veer′ing, *adj.*
un·ve′he·ment, *adj.;* **-ly,** *adv.*
un·veined′, *adj.*
un·vel′vet·y, *adj.*
un·ve′nal, *adj.*
un·vend′a·ble, *adj.*
un·vend′ed, *adj.*
un·vend′i·ble, *adj.*
un′ve·neered′, *adj.*
un′ven·er·a·bil′i·ty, *n.*
un·ven′er·a·ble, *adj.;* **-ble·ness,** *n.;* **-bly,** *adv.*
un·ven′er·at′ed, *adj.*
un·ven′er·a′tive, *adj.*
un′ve·ne′re·al, *adj.*
un·venge′ful, *adj.*
un·ve′ni·al, *adj.;* **-ly,** *adv.;* **-ness,** *n.*
un′ve·ni·al′i·ty, *n.*
un·ven′omed, *adj.*
un·ven′om·ous, *adj.;* **-ly,** *adv.;* **-ness,** *n.*
un·vent′a·ble, *adj.*
un·vent′ed, *adj.*
un·ven′ti·lat′ed, *adj.*
un·ven′tured, *adj.*
un·ven′ture·some, *adj.*
un·ven′tur·ous, *adj.;* **-ly,** *adv.;* **-ness,** *n.*
un′ve·ra′cious, *adj.;* **-ly,** *adv.;* **-ness,** *n.*
un·ver′bal, *adj.;* **-ly,** *adv.*
un·ver′bal·ized′, *adj.*
un′ver·bose′, *adj.;* **-ly,** *adv.;* **-ness,** *n.*
un·ver′dant, *adj.;* **-ly,** *adv.*
un·ver′dured, *adj.*
un·ver′dur·ous, *adj.;* **-ness,** *n.*
un′ve·rid′ic, *adj.*
un′ve·rid′i·cal, *adj.;* **-ly,** *adv.*
un·ver′i·fi′a·bil′i·ty, *n.*
un·ver′i·fi′able, *adj.*
un·ver′i·fi·ca′tive, *adj.*
un·ver′i·fied′, *adj.*
un·ver′i·ta·ble, *adj.;* **-ble·ness,** *n.;* **-bly,** *adv.*
un·ver·mic′u·lat′ed, *adj.*
un·ver′min·ous, *adj.;* **-ly,** *adv.;* **-ness,** *n.*
un·ver′sa·tile, *adj.;* **-ly,** *adv.;* **-ness,** *n.*
un′ver·sa·til′i·ty, *n.*
un·versed′, *adj.*
un·ver′si·fied′, *adj.*
un·ver′te·brate′, *adj.*
un·ver′ti·cal, *adj.;* **-ly,** *adv.*
un′ver·tig′i·nous, *adj.;* **-ly,** *adv.;* **-ness,** *n.*
un·ves′seled, *adj.*
un·vest′ed, *adj.*
un·ve′toed, *adj.*
un′vex·a′tious, *adj.;* **-ly,** *adv.;* **-ness,** *n.*
un·vexed′, *adj.*
un·vi′a·ble, *adj.*
un·vi′brant, *adj.;* **-ly,** *adv.*
un·vi′brat·ed, *adj.*
un·vi′brat·ing, *adj.*
un′vi·bra′tion·al, *adj.*
un′vi·car′i·ous, *adj.;* **-ly,** *adv.;* **-ness,** *n.*
un·vi′cious, *adj.;* **-ly,** *adv.;* **-ness,** *n.*
un·vic′tim·ized′, *adj.*
un′-Vic·to′ri·an, *adj.*
un′vic·to′ri·ous, *adj.*
un·vic′tu·aled, *adj.*
un·vic′tualled, *adj.*
un·view′a·ble, *adj.*
un·viewed′, *adj.*
un·vig′i·lant, *adj.;* **-ly,** *adv.*
un·vig′or·ous, *adj.;* **-ly,** *adv.;* **-ness,** *n.*
un·vil′i·fied′, *adj.*
un·vil′lain·ous, *adj.;* **-ly,** *adv.*
un·vin′di·ca·ble, *adj.*
un·vin′di·cat′ed, *adj.*
un′vin·dic′tive, *adj.;* **-ly,** *adv.;* **-ness,** *n.*
un·vi′nous, *adj.*
un·vin′taged, *adj.*
un·vi′o·la·ble, *adj.;* **-ble·ness,** *n.;* **-bly,** *adv.*
un·vi′o·lat′ed, *adj.*
un·vi′o·la′tive, *adj.*
un·vi′o·lent, *adj.;* **-ly,** *adv.*
un·vir′gin, *adj.*
un·vir′gin·al, *adj.*
un·vir′gin·like′, *adj.*
un·vir′ile, *adj.*
un·vir′tu·ous, *adj.;* **-ly,** *adv.;* **-ness,** *n.*
un·vir′u·lent, *adj.;* **-ly,** *adv.*
un·vis′cer·al, *adj.*
un·vis′i·ble, *adj.;* **-ble·ness,** *n.;* **-bly,** *adv.*
un·vi′sion·ar′y, *adj.*
un·vi′sioned, *adj.*
un·vis′it·a·ble, *adj.*
un·vis′it·ed, *adj.*
un·vis′it·ing, *adj.*
un·vi′sored, *adj.*
un·vis′taed, *adj.*
un·vis′u·al, *adj.;* **-ly,** *adv.*
un·vis′u·al·ised′, *adj.*
un·vis′u·al·ized′, *adj.*
un·vi′tal, *adj.;* **-ly,** *adv.;* **-ness,** *n.*
un·vi′tal·ized′, *adj.*
un·vi′tal·iz′ing, *adj.*
un·vi′ti·a·ble, *adj.*
un·vi′ti·at′ed, *adj.*
un·vi′ti·at′ing, *adj.*
un′vi·tre·os′i·ty, *n.*
un·vit′re·ous, *adj.;* **-ly,** *adv.;* **-ness,** *n.*
un′vi·tres′cent, *adj.*
un·vit′ri·fi′a·ble, *adj.*
un·vit′ri·fied′, *adj.*
un·vit′ri·ol·ized′, *adj.*
un′vi·tu′per·at′ed, *adj.*
un′vi·tu′per·a′tive, *adj.;* **-ly,** *adv.;* **-ness,** *n.*
un′vi·va′cious, *adj.;* **-ly,** *adv.;* **-ness,** *n.*
un·viv′id, *adj.;* **-ly,** *adv.;* **-ness,** *n.*
un·viv′i·fied′, *adj.*
un·viz′ard·ed, *adj.*
un·vi′zored, *adj.*
un·vo′ca·ble, *adj.*
un·vo′cal·ised′, *adj.*
un·vo′cal·ized′, *adj.*
un′vo·cif′er·ous, *adj.;* **-ly,** *adv.;* **-ness,** *n.*
un·void′, *adj.;* **-ness,** *n.*
un·void′a·ble, *adj.*
un·void′ed, *adj.*
un·vol′a·tile, *adj.*
un·vol′a·til·ised′, *adj.*
un·vol′a·til·ized′, *adj.*
un′vol·can′ic, *adj.*
un′vol·can′i·cal·ly, *adv.*
un·vo·li′tion·al, *adj.*
un·vol′i·tive, *adj.*
un·vol′u·ble, *adj.;* **-ble·ness,** *n.;* **-bly,** *adv.*
un·vol′umed, *adj.*
un′vo·lu′mi·nous, *adj.;* **-ly,** *adv.;* **-ness,** *n.*
un·vol′un·tar′i·ly, *adv.*
un·vol′un·tar′y, *adj.*
un′vol·un·teer′ing, *adj.*
un′vo·lup′tu·ous, *adj.;* **-ly,** *adv.;* **-ness,** *n.*
un·vom′it·ed, *adj.*
un′vo·ra′cious, *adj.;* **-ly,** *adv.;* **-ness,** *n.*
un·vot′ed, *adj.*
un·vot′ing, *adj.*
un·vouched′, *adj.*
un′vouch·safed′, *adj.*
un′vowed′, *adj.*
un·voy′ag·ing, *adj.*
un·vul′can·ised′, *adj.*
un·vul′can·ized′, *adj.*
un·vul′gar, *adj.;* **-ly,** *adv.;* **-ness,** *n.*
un·vul′gar·ise′, *v.t.,* **-ised, -is·ing.**
un·vul′gar·ize′, *v.t.,* **-ized, -iz·ing.**
un·vul′ner·a·ble, *adj.*
un·vul′tur·ine′, *adj.*
un·vul′tur·ous, *adj.*
un·vy′ing, *adj.*
un·wad′a·ble, *adj.*
un·wad′ded, *adj.*
un·wad′dling, *adj.*
un·wade′a·ble, *adj.*
un·wad′ed, *adj.*
un·wad′ing, *adj.*
un·waft′ed, *adj.*
un·wa′gered, *adj.*
un·wagged′, *adj.*
un·wailed′, *adj.*
un·wail′ing, *adj.*
un·wain′scot·ed, *adj.*
un·wain′scot·ted, *adj.*
un·waived′, *adj.*
un·waked′, *adj.*
un·wake′ful, *adj.;* **-ly,** *adv.;* **-ness,** *n.*
un·wak′ened, *adj.*
un·wak′en·ing, *adj.*
un·wak′ing, *adj.*
un·walked′, *adj.*
un·wall′, *v.t.*
un·wan′der·ing, *adj.;* **-ly,** *adv.*
un·waned′, *adj.*
un·wan′ing, *adj.*
un·want′ed, *adj.*
un·wan′ton, *adj.*
un·war′bled, *adj.*
un·war′like′, *adj.*
un·warm′a·ble, *adj.*
un·warmed′, *adj.*
un·warm′ing, *adj.*
un·warned′, *adj.*
un·warp′a·ble, *adj.*
un·warp′ing, *adj.*
un·war′rant·a·ble, *adj.;* **-bly,** *adv.;* **-ness,** *n.*
un·war′rant·ed, *adj.;* **-ly,** *adv.*
un·wash′a·ble, *adj.*
un·wast′a·ble, *adj.*
un·wast′ed, *adj.*
un·waste′ful, *adj.;* **-ly,** *adv.;* **-ness,** *n.*
un·watch′a·ble, *adj.*
un·watched′, *adj.*
un·watch′ful, *adj.;* **-ly,** *adv.;* **-ness,** *n.*
un·watch′ing, *adj.*
un·wa′tered, *adj.*
un·wa′ter·marked′, *adj.*
un·wa′ter·y, *adj.*
un·wat′tled, *adj.*
un·waved′, *adj.*
un·wa′ver·a·ble, *adj.*
un·wa′vered, *adj.*
un·wa′ver·ing, *adj.;* **-ly,** *adv.*
un·wav′ing, *adj.*
un·waxed′, *adj.*
un·way′ward, *adj.*
un·weak′ened, *adj.*
un·weak′en·ing, *adj.*
un·wealth′y, *adj.*
un·weap′oned, *adj.*
un·wear′a·ble, *adj.*

un·weave (un wēv′), *v.t.*, **-wove, -wo·ven, -weav·ing.** to undo, take apart, or separate (something woven); unravel. [UN-[2] + WEAVE]

un·weighed (un wād′), *adj.* **1.** not weighed, as for poundage. **2.** not carefully thought about, as statements, opinions, etc. [ME; see UN-[1], WEIGH[1], -ED[2]]

un·weight·ed (un wā′tid), *adj.* **1.** not burdened or encumbered with a heavy load or with mental or emotional matters, problems, etc. **2.** not considered important or significant, as one's opinions, sources, etc.: *an unweighted point of view.* [UN-[1] + WEIGHTED]

un·well (un wel′), *adj.* **1.** not well; ailing; ill. **2.** *Informal.* menstruating. [ME; see UN-[1], WELL[1]] —**un·well′ness,** *n.*

un·wept (un wept′), *adj.* **1.** not wept for; unmourned: *an unwept loss.* **2.** not wept or shed, as tears. [UN-[1] + WEPT]

un·whole·some (un hōl′səm), *adj.* **1.** not wholesome; unhealthful; deleterious to health or physical or moral well-being. **2.** not sound in health; unhealthy, esp. in appearance; suggestive of disease: *an unwholesome pallor.* [ME; see UN-[1], WHOLESOME] —**un·whole′some·ly,** *adv.* —**un·whole′some·ness,** *n.*
—**Syn. 1.** insalubrious, noxious, pernicious.

un·wield·y (un wēl′dē), *adj.* not wieldy; wielded with difficulty; not readily handled or managed in use or action, as from size, shape, or weight; awkward; ungainly. Also, **un·wield′ly.** [ME *unweldy.* See UN-[1], WIELDY] —**un·wield′i·ly,** *adv.* —**un·wield′i·ness,** *n.*
—**Syn.** bulky, unmanageable, clumsy.

un·willed (un wild′), *adj.* not willed; involuntary; unintentional: *It was slight comfort to know that the catastrophe was unwilled.* [UN-[1] + WILLED]

un·will·ing (un wil′ing), *adj.* **1.** not willing; reluctant; loath; averse: *He was an unwilling partner in the crime.* **2.** opposed; offering resistance; stubborn or obstinate; refractory: *Though a captive, he remained to the very end an unwilling, unmanageable spirit.* [UN-[1] + WILLING] —**un·will′ing·ly,** *adv.* —**un·will′ing·ness,** *n.*

un·winc·ing (un win′sing), *adj.* that does not wince; unflinching; fearless. [UN-[1] + WINCING]

un·wind (un wīnd′), *v.*, **-wound, -wind·ing.** —*v.t.* **1.** to undo or loosen from or as if from a coiled condition: *to unwind a rolled bandage; to unwind a coiled rope.* **2.** to reduce tension; relax: *to unwind a person with a drink.* **3.** to disentangle or disengage; untwist: *to unwind one's legs from around the stool.* —*v.i.* **4.** to become unwound. [ME; see UN-[2], WIND[2]] —**un·wind′a·ble,** *adj.* —**un·wind′er,** *n.*

un·wis·dom (un wiz′dəm), *n.* lack of wisdom; folly; rashness; recklessness: *In both thought and action, he was the typification of unwisdom.* [ME; OE *unwīsdōm.* See UN-[1], WISDOM]

un·wise (un wīz′), *adj.* not wise; foolish; imprudent; injudicious; lacking in good sense: *an unwise choice; an unwise man.* [ME; OE *unwīs.* See UN-[1], WISE[1]] —**un·wise′ly,** *adv.* —**un·wise′ness,** *n.*

un·wish (un wish′), *v.t.* **1.** to cease to wish for. **2.** *Obs.* to wish away. [UN-[2] + WISH]

un·wished (un wisht′), *adj.* not wished; undesired; unwelcome. [UN-[1] + WISH + -ED[2]]

un·wished-for (un wisht′fôr′), *adj.* undesired; unwelcome; unwanted: *an unwished-for occurrence.*

un·wit (un wit′), *v.t.*, **-wit·ted, -wit·ting.** to render devoid of wit; derange. [UN-[2] + WIT[1]]

un·wit·nessed (un wit′nist), *adj.* **1.** not perceived by the senses; not noticed or observed: *unwitnessed everyday occurrences.* **2.** lacking the signature of a witness: *an unwitnessed legal document.* [ME; see UN-[1], WITNESS, -ED[3]]

un·wit·ting (un wit′ing), *adj.* **1.** not knowing; unaware; ignorant; oblivious; unconscious: *an unwitting person.* **2.** inadvertent; unintentional; accidental: *His cruelty, though unwitting, pained her.* [ME; see UN-[1], WITTING] —**un·wit′ting·ly,** *adv.* —**un·wit′ting·ness,** *n.*

un·wit·ty (un wit′ē), *adj.* not clever or intelligent; silly; nonsensical. [ME, OE. See UN-[1], WITTY]

un·wont·ed (un wōn′tid, -wôn′-, -wun′-), *adj.* **1.** not customary, habitual, or usual; rare: *unwonted kindness.* **2.** *Archaic.* unaccustomed or unused. [UN-[1] + WONTED] —**un·wont′ed·ly,** *adv.* —**un·wont′ed·ness,** *n.*

un·world·ly (un wûrld′lē), *adj.* **1.** not worldly; not seeking material advantage or gain; spiritually minded. **2.** naïve; unsophisticated; provincial. **3.** not terrestrial; unearthly. [UN-[1] + WORLDLY] —**un·world′li·ness,** *n.*

un·wor·thy (un wûr′thē), *adj.*, *n.*, *pl.* **-thies.** —*adj.* **1.** not worthy; lacking worth or excellence. **2.** not commendable or creditable. **3.** not of adequate merit or character. **4.** of a kind not worthy (often fol. by *of*). **5.** beneath the dignity (usually fol. by *of*): *behavior unworthy of a king.* **6.** undeserving. —*n.* **7.** an unworthy person. [ME; see UN-[1], WORTHY] —**un·wor′thi·ly,** *adv.* —**un·wor′thi·ness,** *n.*

un·wound (un wound′), *v.* pt. and pp. of **unwind.**

un·wrap (un rap′), *v.*, **-wrapped, -wrap·ping.** —*v.t.* **1.** to remove or open the wrapping of. **2.** to open (something wrapped): *Sheila unwrapped the Christmas presents quickly.* —*v.i.* **3.** to become unwrapped. [ME; see UN-[2], WRAP]

un·wreathe (un rēth′), *v.t.*, **-wreathed, -wreath·ing.** to bring out of a wreathed condition; untwist; untwine. [UN-[2] + WREATHE]

un·wrin·kle (un ring′kəl), *v.t.*, **-kled, -kling.** to smoothe the wrinkles from. [UN-[2] + WRINKLE[1]]

un·writ·ten (un rit′ən), *adj.* **1.** not written; not put in writing or print; oral: *an unwritten agreement.* **2.** not actually formulated or expressed; customary; traditional. **3.** containing no writing; blank. [ME, OE *unwriten.* See UN-[1], WRITTEN]

unwrit′ten law′, 1. a law which rests for its authority on custom, judicial decision, etc., as distinguished from law originating in written command, statute, or decree. **2. the unwritten law,** the supposed principle of the right of the individual to avenge wrongs against personal or family honor, esp. in cases involving relations between the sexes: sometimes urged in justification of persons guilty of criminal acts of vengeance.

un·yoke (un yōk′), *v.*, **-yoked, -yok·ing.** —*v.t.* **1.** to free from or as from a yoke. **2.** to part or disjoin, as by removing a yoke. —*v.i. Obs.* **3.** to remove a yoke. **4.** to cease work. [ME *unyoke(n),* OE *ungeocian.* See UN-[2], YOKE]

un·zip (un zip′), *v.*, **-zipped, -zip·ping.** —*v.t.* **1.** to open the zipper of. —*v.i.* **2.** to become unzipped. [UN-[2] + ZIP]

U. of S. Afr., Union of South Africa.

up (up), *adv., prep., adj., n., v.,* **upped, up·ping.** —*adv.* **1.** to, toward, or in a more elevated position: *to climb up to the top of a ladder.* **2.** to or in an erect position: *to stand up.* **3.** out of bed: *to get up.* **4.** above the horizon: *The moon is up.* **5.** to or at any point that is considered higher. **6.** to or at a source, origin, center, or the like: *to follow a stream up to its source.* **7.** to or at a higher point or degree, as of rank, size, value, pitch, loudness, brightness, maturity, speed, etc.: *to move up in a firm; to pump up a tire; to turn a lantern up; to grow up; Prices are going up. Speak up! Hurry up!* **8.** to or at a point of equal advance, extent, etc.: *to catch up in a race.* **9.** ahead; in a leading position in a competition: *He managed to get up on his opponent by three points.* **10.** in continuing contact, esp. as reflecting continuing awareness, knowledge, etc.: *He kept up with the latest developments in mathematics.* **11.** into or in activity, operation, etc.: *to set up vibrations.* **12.** in a state of emotional agitation or distress: *His insults left her all worked up.* **13.** into existence, visible form, etc.: *His sample was worked up in the studio.* **14.** into view, prominence, or consideration: *The lost papers have turned up.* **15.** into or in a place of safekeeping, storage, retirement, etc.: *to lay up riches; to put up preserves.* **16.** into or in a state of union, contraction, etc.: *to add up a column of figures; to fold up.* **17.** to the required or final point: *to pay up one's debts; burned up.* **18.** to a state of completion; to an end: *He finished it all up.* **19.** to a halt: *The horsemen reined up and dismounted.* **20.** *Baseball.* being the player or team batting; at bat. **21.** (used as a function word for additional emphasis, sometimes prec. by *it*): *Go wake your father up. What plugged it up? We laughed it up.* **22.** ahead of an opponent or opponents in points, games, etc.: *The golfer was two strokes up on his nearest competitor.* **23.** each; apiece: *The score was seven up in the final quarter.* **24.** *Naut.* toward the wind: *Put the helm up.* **25. all up with,** at or approaching the end; with defeat or ruin imminent: *He realized it was all up with him when the search party began to close in.* **26. up against,** *Informal.* faced or confronted with: *They were up against formidable obstacles.* **27. up against it,** *Informal.* in a difficult situation, esp. in financial straits: *There was no one to help him when he was up against it.* **28. up and around,** recovered from an illness; able to leave one's bed. Also, **up and about. 29. up to, a.** as far as or approaching a certain part, degree, point, etc.: *She went wading up to her knees; I am up to the eighth lesson.* **b.** in full realization of; making full use of: *He could not live up to their expectations.* **c.** as many as; to the limit of: *up to five men; up to eight and no more.* **d.** *Informal.* having adequate powers or ability for; capable of; equal to: *He didn't think she was up to the job.* **e.** *Informal.* having the duty or responsibility; incumbent upon: *It's up to you to break the news to him.* **f.** engaged in; contriving; doing: *What have you been up to lately?*
—*prep.* **30.** to, toward, or at an elevated place on or in: *He is going up the stairs. The cat is up the tree.* **31.** to, toward, or at a high or higher station, condition, or rank on or in: *He is going up the political ladder in his county. He is well up the social ladder.* **32.** at or to a farther point or higher place on or in: *He is up the street. He is going up the street.* **33.** toward the source, origin, etc., of: *up the stream.* **34.** toward a particular direction or in the interior of a region, territory, etc.: *The explorers were up north.* **35.** in a course or direction which is contrary to that of: *to go up wind.*
—*adj.* **36.** moving in or related to a direction which is up or is regarded as up: *to ride the up elevator from the first floor to the fourth; the up train traveling north; the up platform of a railroad station.* **37.** informed; familiar; aware (usually fol. by *on* or *in*): *He is up on current events.* **38.** concluded; ended; finished; terminated: *The game is up. His hour is up.* **39.** going on or happening; taking place; occurring: *What's up over there?* **40.** in a condition, position, or station which is or is considered high: *to be up on the social scale; to be up for a job.* **41.** in an erect, vertical, or raised position: *The gate at the railroad crossing is up and cars may now cross the tracks. The tent is up.* **42.** above the earth or ground: *The corn is up and ready to be harvested.* **43.** in the air; aloft: *The meteorological balloons are up. The airplanes are up for their reconnaissance flights.* **44.** (of heavenly bodies) risen above the horizon: *The sun is up.* **45.** awake or out of bed: *to be up with insomnia.* **46.** mounted on horseback: *He knows which jockeys are up in every race.* **47.** (of water in natural bodies) high with relation to the banks or shore: *The tide is up.* **48.** built; constructed: *The new museum is up and open to the public.* **49.** facing upward: *He is resting and his face is up.* **50.** (of roads, highways, etc.) having the surface broken or removed (usually used in combination): *a torn-up road.* **51.** in revolt, mutiny, or rebellious agitation: *Many territories were up and preparing to send troops against the government.* **52.** in a state of agitation: *Beware of him when his temper is up.* **53.** in a mood of confidence and high spirits: *He is up for a time and then, without warning, despondent again.* **54.** wrong; amiss: *Her nervous manner told me that something was up.* **55.** ready, as by emotional or physical fitness or disposition (usually fol. by *to*): *Since her illness she has not been up to going out much.* **56.** bound; on the way: *She was on a ship up for Australia.* **57.** arrived at an unfavorable or undesired end: *They knew that their game was up.* **58.** higher than formerly in amount, degree, etc.: *The price of meat was up.* **59.** (of age) advanced (usually fol. by *in*): *He is rather spry for a man so up in years.* **60.** active: *The captain wished to set sail as soon as the wind was up.* **61.** in a legal proceeding as defendant: *He is up for murder.* **62.** in operation or ready for use: *The theater's lights are up.* **63.** (of points or other standards used to determine the winner in a competition) ahead; in advance: *He won the game with two points up over his opponent.* **64.** considered or under consideration: *a candidate up for reelection; a bill which is up before Congress.* **65.** wagered; bet: *He won all the money up in the game.* **66.** living or located inland or on elevated ground: *He lives in a village two miles up from the coast.* **67.** (used with a preceding numeral to indicate that a score is tied in a competition): *It was 10 up at the end of the first half.* **68.** ahead of an opponent or opponents: *They scored three times in a row to go two up.* **69. up and doing,** *Informal.* actively engaged; alert; busy: *During her convalescence she longed to be up and doing.*
—*n.* **70.** an upward movement; ascent. **71.** a rise of fortune, mood, etc.: *He had a great many ups and downs in his time.* **72.** an upbound means of public transportation, as a train or bus. **73.** one who or that which is in a favorable position of wealth, fortune, etc.: *Persons who were ups in the business world suffered losses in the economic depression. This period of prosperity is an up for the entire country.* **74.** an upward slope; elevation. **75.** an upward course or rise, as in price or value: *The landlord promised his tenants there would be no further ups in the rent this year.* **76. on the up and up,** *Slang.* frank; honest; sincere: *He seems to be on the up and up.* Also, **on the up-and-up.**

un·wear′ing, *adj.*
un·wea′ri·some, *adj.*
un·wea′ry, *adj.*
un·wea′ry·ing, *adj.*
un·weath′ered, *adj.*
un·webbed′, *adj.*
un·web′bing, *adj.*
un·wed′, *adj.*
un·wed′ded, *adj.*
un·wedge′, *v.t.*, **-wedged, -wedg·ing.**
un·weed′ed, *adj.*
un·weened′, *adj.*
un·weep′ing, *adj.*
un·weigh′a·ble, *adj.*
un·weigh′ing, *adj.*
un·weight′y, *adj.*
un·wel′come, *adj.*
un·wel′comed, *adj.*
un·wel′com·ing, *adj.*
un·weld′a·ble, *adj.*
un·weld′ed, *adj.*
un′well-in·ten′tioned, *adj.*
un·welt′ed, *adj.*
un·west′ern, *adj.*
un·west′ern·ized′, *adj.*
un·wet′, *adj.*
un·wet′ted, *adj.*
un·whee′dled, *adj.*
un·wheel′, *v.t.*
un·whelped′, *adj.*
un·whet′ted, *adj.*
un·whim′per·ing, *adj.*; **-ly,** *adv.*
un·whim′si·cal, *adj.*; **-ly,** *adv.*; **-ness,** *n.*
un·whin′ing, *adj.*; **-ly,** *adv.*
un·whipped′, *adj.*
un·whipt′, *adj.*
un·whirled′, *adj.*
un·whisked′, *adj.*
un·whisk′ered, *adj.*
un·whis′per·a·ble, *adj.*
un·whis′pered, *adj.*
un·whis′per·ing, *adj.*
un·whis′tled, *adj.*
un·white′, *adj.*
un·whit′ed, *adj.*
un·whit′ened, *adj.*
un·white′washed′, *adj.*
un·wick′ed, *adj.*; **-ly,** *adv.*
un·wid′ened, *adj.*
un·wid′owed, *adj.*
un·wield′a·ble, *adj.*
un·wife′like′, *adj.*
un·wife′ly, *adj.*
un·wig′, *v.t.*, **-wigged, -wig·ging.**
un·wild′, *adj.*; **-ly,** *adv.*; **-ness,** *n.*
un·wil′ful, *adj.*; **-ly,** *adv.*; **-ness,** *n.*
un·will′a·ble, *adj.*
un·will′ful, *adj.*; **-ly,** *adv.*; **-ness,** *n.*
un·wilt′ed, *adj.*
un·wilt′ing, *adj.*
un·wil′y, *adj.*
un·wind′ed, *adj.*
un·win′dowed, *adj.*
un·wind′y, *adj.*
un·winged′, *adj.*
un·wink′ing, *adj.*
un·win′na·ble, *adj.*
un·win′ning, *adj.*
un·win′nowed, *adj.*
un·win′some, *adj.*
un·win′try, *adj.*
un·wiped′, *adj.*
un·wir′a·ble, *adj.*
un·wired′, *adj.*
un·wish′ful, *adj.*; **-ly,** *adv.*; **-ness,** *n.*
un·wist′ful, *adj.*; **-ly,** *adv.*; **-ness,** *n.*
un·witched′, *adj.*
un′with·draw′a·ble, *adj.*
un′with·draw′ing, *adj.*
un′with·drawn′, *adj.*
un·with′er·a·ble, *adj.*
un·with′ered, *adj.*
un·with′er·ing, *adj.*
un′with·held′, *adj.*
un′with·hold′ing, *adj.*
un′with·stand′ing, *adj.*
un′with·stood′, *adj.*
un·woe′ful, *adj.*; **-ly,** *adv.*; **-ness,** *n.*
un·wom′an·ish, *adj.*
un·wom′an·like′, *adj.*
un·wom′an·ly, *adj.*, *adv.*
un·womb′, *v.t.*
un·won′, *adj.*
un·won′der·ful, *adj.*; **-ly,** *adv.*
un·won′der·ing, *adj.*
un·wood′ed, *adj.*
un·wooed′, *adj.*
un·word′a·ble, *adj.*; **-bly,** *adv.*
un·work′a·ble, *adj.*
un·worked′, *adj.*
un·work′ing, *adj.*
un·work′man·like′, *adj.*
un·work′man·ly, *adj.*
un·worm′-eat′en, *adj.*
un·worm′i·ness, *n.*
un·worm′y, *adj.*
un·worn′, *adj.*
un·wor′ried, *adj.*
un·wor′shiped, *adj.*
un·wor′ship·ing, *adj.*
un·wor′shipped, *adj.*
un·wor′ship·ping, *adj.*
un·wound′ed, *adj.*
un·wran′gling, *adj.*
un·wrath′ful, *adj.*; **-ly,** *adv.*; **-ness,** *n.*
un·wrecked′, *adj.*
un·wrenched′, *adj.*
un·wrest′ed, *adj.*
un·wrest′ing, *adj.*
un·wres′tled, *adj.*
un·wretched′, *adj.*
un·wrig′gled, *adj.*
un·wrin′kle·a·ble, *adj.*
un·writ′a·ble, *adj.*
un·writ′ing, *adj.*
un·wronged′, *adj.*
un·wrong′ful, *adj.*; **-ly,** *adv.*; **-ness,** *n.*
un·wrought′, *adj.*
un·wrung′, *adj.*
un·yachts′man·like′, *adj.*
un·yearned′, *adj.*
un·yearn′ing, *adj.*
un·yield′ed, *adj.*
un·yield′ing, *adj.*; **-ly,** *adv.*; **-ness,** *n.*
un·youth′ful, *adj.*; **-ly,** *adv.*; **-ness,** *n.*
un·zeal′ous, *adj.*; **-ly,** *adv.*
un·zone′, *v.t.*, **-zoned, -zon·ing.**

—*v.t. Informal.* **77.** to put or take up. **78.** to make larger; step up: *to up output.* **79.** to raise; go better than (a preceding wager).
—*v.i.* **80.** *Informal.* to start up; begin something abruptly (usually fol. by *and* and another verb): *Then he upped and ran away from home.* **81.** (often used imperatively or hortatively) to rise up: *Up, men, and fight until all of the enemy is defeated!* [ME, OE; c. OFris *up,* OS *up,* OIcel *upp,* MD *up, op;* akin to OHG *ūf* (> G *auf*), Goth *iup*]

up-, a combining form of **up:** *upland, upshot, upheaval.* [ME and OE]

up., **1.** underproof (alcohol). **2.** upper. Also, **u.p.**

up·an·chor (up′aŋg′kər, up′aŋg′-), *v.i.* to weigh anchor.

up-and-com·ing (up′ən kum′iŋg), *adj.* likely to succeed; bright and industrious: *an up-and-coming young executive.*

up-and-down (up′ən doun′), *adj.* **1.** moving alternately up and down: *the up-and-down swing of levers; an up-and-down tune.* **2.** having an uneven surface: *up-and-down countryside.* **3.** changeable: *up-and-down luck.* **4.** perpendicular or nearly so: *a straight up-and-down hillside.* —**up′-and-down′ness,** *n.*

up′-and-down′ di′al, a dial on a timepiece showing how far the mainspring is unwound.

U·pan·i·shad (o͞o pan′i shad′, o͞o pä′ni shäd′), *n. Hinduism.* any of a class of speculative treatises, usually in dialogue form, composed between the 8th and 6th centuries B.C. and first written A.D. c1300: they represent a development beyond that of the Vedas, abandoning the Vedic pantheon and having as their principal message the unity of Brahman and Atman. [< Skt, equiv. to *upa* near to + *ni-shad* to sit or lie down]

U·pan·i·shad·ic (o͞o pan′i shad′ik, -pä′ni shä′dik), *adj.* of, pertaining to, or contemporary with the Upanishads. [UPANISHAD + -IC]

u·pas (yo͞o′pəs), *n.* **1.** the poisonous milky sap of a large moraceous tree, *Antiaris toxicaria,* of Java, used for arrow poison. **2.** the tree. [< Malay: poison]

u·pa·ya (o͝o pä′yə), *n. Buddhism.* any device, as a koan, used for purposes of instruction. [< Skt: lit., a nearing, approach]

up·bear (up bâr′), *v.t.,* **-bore, -borne, -bear·ing.** to bear up; raise aloft; sustain or support. [ME *upbere(n).* See UP-, BEAR[1]] —**up·bear′er,** *n.*

up·beat (up′bēt′), *n. Music.* **1.** an unaccented beat, esp. immediately preceding a downbeat. **2.** the upward stroke with which a conductor indicates such a beat. —*adj.* **3.** optimistic; happy; cheerful: *television dramas with relentlessly upbeat endings.* [UP- + BEAT]

up·bound (up′bound′), *adj.* traveling or affording passage toward the north or in a direction regarded as up: *an upbound freighter; the upbound lane of a highway.* [UP- + BOUND[4]]

up-bow (up′bō′), *n.* (in bowing on a stringed instrument) a stroke toward the heel of the bow: indicated in scores by the symbol V (opposed to *down-bow*).

up·braid (up brād′), *v.t.* **1.** to find fault with or reproach severely; censure: *The military tribunal upbraided the soldier for his cowardice.* **2.** (of things) to bring reproach on; serve as a reproach to. —*v.i.* **3.** *Archaic.* to utter reproaches. [ME; OE *upbregd(an).* See UP-, BRAID] —**up·braid′er,** *n.*
—**Syn. 1.** reprove, blame.

up·braid·ing (up brā′diŋg), *n.* **1.** the act or words of one who upbraids; severe reproof or censure: *The child burst into tears upon receiving an upbraiding from his father.* —*adj.* **2.** severely reproachful or reproving; censorious: *upbraiding remarks.* [UPBRAID + -ING[1], -ING[2]] —**up·braid′ing·ly,** *adv.*

up·bring·ing (up′briŋg′iŋg), *n.* the care and training of the young or a particular type of such care and training: *His religious upbringing fitted him to be a missionary.* [ME; see UP-, BRINGING]

up·build (up bild′), *v.t.,* **-built, -build·ing.** to build up, as with the result of establishing, increasing, enlarging, or fortifying. [UP- + BUILD] —**up·build′er,** *n.*

up·burst (up′bûrst′), *n.* a burst upward. [UP- + BURST]

UPC, the series of short black lines of varied thickness on a package that indicate price, product classification, etc., thus expediting electronic checkout, inventory control, etc., as in a supermarket. [U(NIVERSAL) P(RODUCT) C(ODE)]

up·cast (up′kast′, -käst′), *n., adj., v.,* **-cast, -cast·ing.** —*n.* **1.** an act of casting upward. **2.** the state of being cast upward. **3.** that which is cast or thrown up, as soil or earth in digging. **4.** a shaft or passage up which air passes, as from a mine (opposed to *downcast*). —*adj.* **5.** cast up; turned, directed, or thrown upward: *The child looked at her father with upcast eyes.* —*v.t.* **6.** to cast up or upward. [ME *upcast(en).* See UP-, CAST]

up·chuck (up′chuk′), *v.i., v.t. Slang.* to vomit. [UP- + CHUCK[1]]

up·com·ing (up′kum′iŋg), *adj.* coming up; about to take place, appear, or be presented: *the upcoming spring fashions.* [ME; see UP-, COMING]

up·coun·try (up′kun′trē), *adj.* **1.** of, relating to, residing in, or situated in the interior of a region or country; inland: *an upcountry dialect; upcountry political interests; an upcountry girl; an upcountry town.* **2.** *Disparaging.* unsophisticated. —*n.* **3.** the interior of a region or country. —*adv.* **4.** toward, into, or in the interior of a country: *The explorers trekked upcountry until they came to an inhabited region.* [UP- + COUNTRY]

up·crop·ping (up′krop′iŋg), *n.* an act of cropping up; appearance; growth: *an upcropping of corn.* [UP- + CROPPING, after v. phrase *crop up*]

up·date (up dāt′, up′dāt′), *v.t.,* **-dat·ed, -dat·ing.** to bring up to date. [UP- + DATE[1]] —**up·dat′er,** *n.*

Up·dike (up′dīk′), *n.* **John,** born 1932, U.S. novelist and short-story writer.

up·do (up′do͞o′), *n., pl.* **-dos.** an upswept hairdo. [UP(SWEPT + HAIR)DO]

up·draft (up′draft′, -dräft′), *n.* the movement upward of air or other gas. [UP- + DRAFT]

up·end (up end′), *v.t.* **1.** to set on end, as a barrel, ship, etc. **2.** to affect drastically or radically, as tastes, opinions, reputations, systems. **3.** to defeat in competition, as in boxing, business, etc. —*v.i.* **4.** to become upended. [UP- + END[1]]

up·fold (up fōld′), *v.t.* to fold up or together: *Some morning-glories upfold their flowers by noon.* [ME *upfold(en).* See UP-, FOLD[1]]

up·gath·er (up gath′ər), *v.t.* to gather up or together: *to upgather information.* [UP- + GATHER]

up·grade (*n.* up′grād′; *adj., adv.* up′grād′; *v.* up grād′, up′grād′), *n., adj., adv., v.,* **-grad·ed, -grad·ing.** —*n.* **1.** an incline going up in the direction of movement. **2.** an increase or improvement (usually prec. by *on the*): *Production is on the upgrade.* —*adj.* **3.** uphill; of, pertaining to, on, or along an upgrade. —*adv.* **4.** up a slope. —*v.t.* **5.** to augment the grade of, as in rank, position, importance, quality, value, etc.: *to upgrade laborers to managerial positions; to upgrade the importance of strategic materials during wartime; to upgrade land by improving it with new buildings.* [UP- + GRADE] —**up′grad′er,** *n.*

up·growth (up′grōth′), *n.* **1.** the process of growing up; development: *The speedy upgrowth of nuclear science is opening many new fields of employment.* **2.** that which grows up, esp. a normal organic growth or process. [UP- + GROWTH]

up·heav·al (up hē′vəl), *n.* **1.** an act of upheaving, esp. of a part of the earth's crust. **2.** the state of being upheaved. **3.** strong or violent change or disturbance, as in a society: *A third world war will mean global upheaval such as mankind has never known.* **4.** *Geol.* an upward warping of a part of the earth's crust, forcing certain areas into a relatively higher position than before. [UPHEAVE + -AL[2]]

up·heave (up hēv′), *v.,* **-heaved** or **-hove, -heav·ing.** —*v.t.* **1.** to heave or lift up; raise up or aloft. **2.** to force or throw up violently or with much power, as an erupting volcano. **3.** to cause major disturbance or disorder in: *The revolution upheaved the government, causing its leaders to flee the country.* —*v.i.* **4.** to rise upward, esp. extensively or powerfully. [ME *upheve(n).* See UP-, HEAVE]

up·held (up held′), *v.* pt. and pp. of **uphold.**

up·hill (up′hil′), *adv.* **1.** up or as if up the slope of a hill or other incline; upward: *The soldiers marched uphill. Water does not run uphill without assistance.* —*adj.* **2.** going or tending upward on or as if on a hill: *an uphill road.* **3.** at a high place or point: *an uphill village.* **4.** laboriously fatiguing or difficult: *an uphill struggle to become wealthy.* —*n.* **5.** a rising terrain; ascent. [UP- + HILL]

up·hold (up hōld′), *v.t.,* **-held, -hold·ing.** **1.** to lift upward; raise: *The pilgrims upheld their eyes and thanked Heaven for their safe journey.* **2.** to keep up or keep from sinking; support: *Stout columns upheld the building's heavy roof. Her faith upheld her in that time of sadness.* **3.** to support or defend, as against opposition or criticism: *The high court upheld the lower court's judgment of the case. He fought the duel to uphold his family's honor.* **4.** *Brit.* **a.** to upholster. **b.** to maintain in good condition; take care of. [ME *up hold(en).* See UP-, HOLD] —**up·hold′er,** *n.*
—**Syn. 3.** See **support.**

up·hol·ster (up hōl′stər, ə pōl′-), *v.t.* **1.** to provide (chairs, sofas, etc.) with coverings, cushions, stuffing, springs, etc. **2.** to furnish (an interior) with hangings, curtains, carpets, or the like. [back formation from UPHOLSTERER]

up·hol·ster·er (up hōl′stər ər, ə pōl′-), *n.* one whose business it is to furnish and put in place hangings, curtains, carpets, etc., and to cushion and cover furniture or the like. [earlier *upholster* (see UPHOLD, -STER) + -ER[1]]

up·hol·ster·y (up hōl′stə rē, ə pōl′-), *n., pl.* **-ster·ies.** **1.** the fittings or decorations supplied by an upholsterer, as hangings, draperies, cushions, furniture coverings, or the like; material used to cushion and cover furniture. **2.** the business of an upholsterer. [UPHOLSTER + -Y[3]]

u·phroe (yo͞o′frō, yo͞o′vrō), *n. Naut.* euphroe.

UPI, See **United Press International.** Also, **U.P.I.**

Up·ing·ton (up′iŋg tən), *n.* a city in the N Republic of South Africa. 13,303 (1950).

U·pis (o͞o′pis), *n.* (in pre-Hellenic mythology) a goddess of childbirth, later identified with Artemis.

Up·john (up′jon′), *n.* **Richard,** 1802–78, and his son, **Richard Michell,** 1828–1903, U.S. architects, born in England.

up·keep (up′kēp′), *n.* **1.** the process or activity of providing an establishment, machine, person, etc., with necessary or proper maintenance, repairs, support, or the like: *The machine's faulty operation shows that no one has attended to its upkeep. Since the husband was always unemployed he could not pay for his family's upkeep.* **2.** the total sum of the costs or expenses for this. [UP- + KEEP]

up·land (up′lənd, -land′), *n.* **1.** land elevated above other land. **2.** the higher ground of a region or district; an elevated region. **3.** land or an area of land lying above the level where water flows or where flooding occurs. —*adj.* **4.** of or pertaining to uplands or elevated regions. [UP- + LAND] —**up′land·er,** *n.*

Up·land (up′lənd), *n.* **1.** a city in S California. 15,918 (1960). **2.** a town in SE Pennsylvania. 4343 (1960).

up′land cot′ton, cotton grown in the southeastern part of the United States, characterized chiefly by short-staple length. Also, **Upland cotton.** Also called **American cotton, American upland cotton.**

up′land plov′er, a large, field-inhabiting sandpiper, *Bartramia longicauda,* of eastern North America, resembling a plover. Also called **Bartramian sandpiper.**

up·lift (*v.* up lift′; *n.* up′lift′), *v.t.* **1.** to lift up; raise; elevate. **2.** to improve socially, culturally, morally, or the like: *to uplift downtrodden and deprived peoples.* **3.** to exalt emotionally or spiritually. —*v.i.* **4.** to become uplifted. —*n.* **5.** an act of lifting up or raising; elevation. **6.** the process or work of improving, as socially, intellectually, morally, or the like. **7.** emotional or spiritual exaltation. **8.** a brassiere. **9.** *Geol.* an upheaval. [ME *uplift(en).* See UP-, LIFT] —**up·lift′ment,** *n.*

up·lift·ed (up lif′tid), *adj.* **1.** improved, as in mood, spirit, etc. **2.** raised or elevated, as a beam. [ME; see UP-, *lifted,* ptp. of LIFT]

up·lift·er (up lif′tər), *n.* **1.** one who or that which uplifts. **2.** a person engaged in or devoted to social or moral uplift. [UPLIFT + -ER[1]]

up·most (up′mōst′ *or, esp. Brit.,* -məst), *adj.* uppermost. [UP- + -MOST]

U·po·lu (o͞o pō′lo͞o), *n.* an island in Western Samoa, in the S Pacific: the home of Robert Louis Stevenson for the last five years of his life. 61,343 (1951); 430 sq. mi. *Cap.:* Apia.

up·on (ə pon′, ə pôn′), *prep.* **1.** up and on; upward so as to get or be on: *He climbed upon his horse and rode off.* **2.** in an elevated position on: *There is a television antenna upon every house in the neighborhood.* **3.** in or into complete or approximate contact with, as an attacker or an important or pressing occasion: *The enemy was upon us and our soldiers had little time to escape. The Christmas holiday will soon be upon us and we have hardly begun to buy gifts. The time to take action is upon us.* **4.** immediately or very soon after: *She went into mourning upon her husband's death.* **5.** on the occasion of: *She was joyful upon seeing her child take his first steps.* **6.** on (in any of various senses, used as an equivalent of *on* with no added idea of ascent or elevation, and preferred in certain cases only for euphonic or metrical reasons). [ME; see UP (adv.), ON (prep.)]

up·per (up′ər), *adj.* **1.** higher, as in place, position, pitch, or in a scale: *the upper stories of a house; the upper register of a singer's voice; the upper notes of the C-major scale.* **2.** superior, as in rank, dignity, or station: *The Senate is the upper chamber of the Congress of the United States.* **3.** (of places) at a higher level, more northerly, or farther from the sea: *the upper slopes of a mountain; upper New York State.* **4.** (*often cap.*) *Stratig.* denoting a later division of a period, system, or the like: *the Upper Devonian.* —*n.* **5.** the part of a shoe or boot above the sole, comprising the quarter, vamp, counter, and lining. **6.** Often, **uppers.** a log or piece of lumber of the finest grade. **7.** an upper berth. **8.** a gaiter made of cloth. Cf. **gaiter** (def. 1). **9.** Usually, **uppers. a.** an upper dental plate. **b.** an upper tooth. **10.** *Informal.* the higher of two bunks or berths. **11. on one's uppers,** *Informal.* reduced to poverty; without sufficient means: *They are on their uppers but manage to hide the fact from their friends.* [ME; see UP-, -ER[4]]

up′per air′, *Meteorol.* the atmosphere above the lower portion of the troposphere. Cf. **upper atmosphere.**

Up′per Ar′lington, a city in central Ohio, near Columbus. 28,486 (1960).

up′per arm′, the part of the arm between the shoulder and the elbow.

up′per at′mosphere, *Meteorol.* generally, the portion of the atmosphere above the troposphere. Cf. **upper air.**

Up′per Aus′tria, a province in N Austria. 1,131,218 (1961); 4631 sq. mi. *Cap.:* Linz.

up′per bound′, *Math.* an element greater than or equal to all the elements in a given set: 3 and 4 are upper bounds of the set consisting of 1, 2, and 3. Cf. **bound**[3] (def. 4), **greatest lower bound, least upper bound, lower bound.**

Up′per Bur′ma. See under **Burma.**

Up′per Can′ada, a former British province in Canada 1791–1840: now the S part of Ontario province.

Up′per Carbonif′erous, *Geol.* Pennsylvanian (defs. 2, 4).

up′per case′, *Print.* See under **case**[2] (def. 8).

up·per-case (up′ər kās′), *adj., v.,* **-cased, -cas·ing,** *n.* —*adj.* **1.** (of an alphabetical character) capital. **2.** *Print.* pertaining to or belonging in the upper case. —*v.t.* **3.** to print or write with an upper-case letter or letters. —*n.* **4.** a capital letter.

up′per cham′ber. See **upper house.**

Up′per Chinook′, a Chinookan language of the Columbia River valley from the Deschutes River to the estuary.

up·per-class (up′ər klas′, -kläs′), *adj.* relating to or typical of a high-ranking class in society.

up·per·class·man (up′ər klas′mən, -kläs′-), *n., pl.* **-men.** *U.S.* a junior or senior in a secondary school or college. [UPPER + CLASS + MAN]

up′per crust′, **1.** the topmost layer of crust, as of a pie. **2.** *Informal.* the highest social class.

up·per·cut (up′ər kut′), *n., v.,* **-cut, -cut·ting.** —*n.* **1.** a swinging blow directed upward, as to an adversary's chin. **2.** *Bridge.* a play of a higher trump than necessary knowing made it can be overtrumped by an opponent but that if overtrumped will establish one or more trump winners in the hand of one's partner. —*v.t.* **3.** to strike (an opponent) with an uppercut. **4.** *Bridge.* to uppercut declarer. —*v.i.* **5.** to deliver an uppercut. [UPPER + CUT]

Up′per Dar′by, a town in SE Pennsylvania, near Philadelphia. 93,158 (1960).

up′per deck′, *Naut.* **1.** (of a cargo vessel) the uppermost continuous deck that is capable of being made watertight and is regarded as the uppermost strength deck of the hull; freeboard deck: it may have a shelter deck or awning deck above it, as the weather deck of the hull. **2.** the uppermost continuous deck of a hull. **3.** (in the U.S. Navy) a deck in a superstructure or deckhouse amidships above the main deck.

Up′per E′gypt. See under **Egypt.**

up′per hand′, the dominating or controlling position; the advantage: *to fight desperately to get the upper hand.*

up′per house′, one of two branches of a legislature generally smaller and less representative than the lower branch.

Up′per Klam′ath Lake′. See under **Klamath Lakes.**

Up′per Mich′igan. See **Upper Peninsula.**

up·per·most (up′ər mōst′ *or, esp. Brit.,* -məst), *adj.* Also, **upmost. 1.** highest in place, order, rank, power, etc.: *the uppermost peaks of the mountain; the uppermost class of society.* **2.** topmost; predominant: *a subject of uppermost importance and concern.* —*adv.* **3.** in or into the uppermost place, rank, or predominance: *The blossoms grow uppermost on the stems of these flowers. The psychologist asked the patient to utter those thoughts which came uppermost during the course of the interview.* [UPPER + -MOST]

Up′per Palat′inate. See under **Palatinate** (def. 1).

up′per par′tial tone′, *Music.* overtone (def. 1).

Up′per Penin′sula, the peninsula between lakes Superior and Michigan constituting the N part of Michigan. Also called **Upper Michigan, Northern Michigan.**

Up′per Sad′dle Riv′er, a town in NE New Jersey. 3570 (1960).

Up′per Sandus′ky, a town in central Ohio. 4941 (1960).

up′per school′, a scholastic division, esp. in a private school, including the terminal secondary grades.

up′per sem·i-con·tin′u·ous func′tion (sem′ē-kən tin′yo͞o əs), *Math.* (at a given point) a function for which all functional values at points in a neighborhood of the given point are less than the sum of the functional value at the given point and an arbitrarily selected small number. Cf. **lower semi-continuous function.**

Up′per Sile′sia, a highly industrialized region divided between Germany and Poland after World War I.

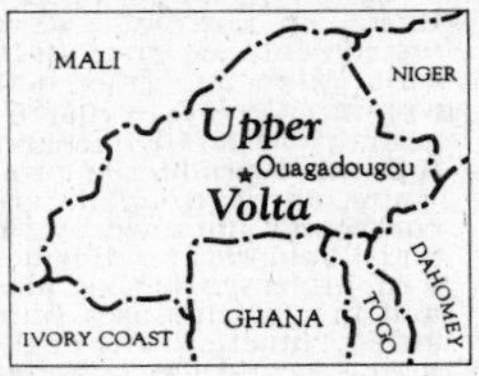

up′per spank′er, *Naut.* See **gaff topsail** (def. 2).

Up′per Tun·gus′ka (to͞on go͞os′kä, -kə, to͞oŋ-), the lower course of the Angara River. Cf. **Angara.**

Up′per Vol′ta, a republic in W Africa: formerly part of French West Africa; renamed Burkina Faso 1984. 4,716,000 (est. 1964); 106,111 sq. mi. *Cap.:* Ouagadougou.

up′per works′, *Naut.* the parts of a ship above the surface of the water when she is loaded for a voyage.

up·pish (up′ish), *adj. Informal.* arrogant; presumptuous; uppity. [UP + -ISH[1]] —**up′pish·ly,** *adv.* —**up′pish·ness,** *n.*

up·pi·ty (up′i tē), *adj. Informal.* affecting an attitude of inflated self-esteem, esp. as a result of being wealthy or pretending to wealth; haughty; snobbish: *The uppity dowager stared superciliously from her limousine.* [prob. UP + *-ity,* extended form of -Y[1]]

Upp·sa·la (up′sä lə, -sə-; *Swed.* o͝op′sä′lä), *n.* a city in SE Sweden. 84,258 (1965). Also, **Upsala.**

up·raise (up rāz′), *v.t.,* **-raised, -rais·ing. 1.** to raise up; lift or elevate. **2.** to raise from a depressed or dejected humor; cheer. [ME *upreise(n).* See UP-, RAISE] —**up·rais′er,** *n.*

up·rear (up rēr′), *v.t.* **1.** to raise up; lift: *The horse upreared its head and whinnied.* **2.** to build; erect: *to uprear a monument in stone.* **3.** to elevate the dignity of; exalt: *God upreared Abraham by making him the father of many nations.* **4.** to bring up; rear: *to uprear children in a good environment.* —*v.i.* **5.** to rise. [ME *uprere(n).* See UP-, REAR[2]]

up·right (up′rīt′, up rīt′), *adj.* **1.** erect or vertical, as in position or posture. **2.** raised or directed vertically or upward. **3.** adhering to rectitude; righteous, honest, or just: *an upright person.* **4.** in accord with what is right: *upright dealings.* —*n.* **5.** the state of being upright or vertical. **6.** something standing erect or vertical, as a piece of timber. **7.** an upright piano. **8.** Usually, **uprights.** *Chiefly Football.* the goal posts. —*adv.* **9.** in an upright position or direction; vertically. —*v.t.* **10.** to render upright. [ME, OE *upriht* (c. G *aufrecht*). See UP, RIGHT] —**up′right′ly,** *adv.* —**up′right′ness,** *n.*
—**Syn. 1.** plumb. UPRIGHT, ERECT, VERTICAL, PERPENDICULAR imply that something is in the posture of being straight upward, not leaning. That which is UPRIGHT is in a position corresponding to that of a man standing up: *A decaying tree no longer standing upright; an upright piano.* ERECT emphasizes the straightness of position or posture: *proud and erect; A flagpole stands erect.* VERTICAL esp. suggests upward direction along the shortest line from the earth to a level above it: *the vertical edge of a door; ornamented by vertical lines.* PERPENDICULAR, a term frequently interchangeable with VERTICAL, is esp. used in mathematics: *the perpendicular side of a right triangle; to erect a perpendicular line from the base of a figure.* **3.** honorable. **6.** pole, prop, pier, pile, column. —**Ant. 1.** leaning, horizontal.

up′right pian′o, a piano with an upright rectangular body and with its strings running vertically. Cf. **spinet** (def. 3).

up·rise (*v.* up rīz′; *n.* up′rīz′), *v.,* **-rose, -ris·en, -ris·ing,** *n.* —*v.i.* **1.** to rise up; get up, as from a lying or sitting posture. **2.** to rise into view: *As we approached the city, the spires of tall buildings uprose as if to greet us.* **3.** to rise in revolt. **4.** to come into existence or prominence: *Many calamities uprose to plague the people during the war. Many geologic changes have occurred since our earth uprose.* **5.** to move upward; mount up; ascend. **6.** to come above the horizon. **7.** to slope upward: *The land uprises from the river to the hills.* **8.** to swell or grow, as a sound: *A blare of trumpets uprose to salute the king.* —*n.* **9.** an act of rising up. [ME *uprise(n).* See UP-, RISE] —**up′ris′er,** *n.*

up·ris·ing (up′rī′ziŋ, up rī′ziŋ), *n.* **1.** an insurrection or revolt. **2.** an act of rising up. **3.** an ascent or acclivity. [ME; see UP-, RISING]
—**Syn. 1.** rebellion.

up·roar (up′rōr′, -rôr′), *n.* **1.** a state of violent and noisy disturbance, as of a multitude; turmoil. **2.** an instance of this. [< D *oproer* tumult; c. MHG *ūfruor,* G *aufruhr;* sense and spelling affected by *roar*]
—**Syn. 1.** tumult, turbulence, commotion, hubbub, furor. See **disorder. 2.** clamor.

up·roar·i·ous (up rōr′ē əs, -rôr′-), *adj.* **1.** characterized by or in a state of uproar; tumultuous. **2.** making an uproar; confused and noisy, as an assembly, person, etc. **3.** very funny, as a person, situation, etc. **4.** very loud, as sounds, utterances, etc. **5.** expressed by or producing uproar. [UPROAR + -IOUS] —**up·roar′i·ous·ly,** *adv.* —**up·roar′i·ous·ness,** *n.*

up·root (up ro͞ot′, -ro͝ot′), *v.t.* **1.** to pull out by or as if by the roots: *The hurricane uprooted many trees and telephone poles.* **2.** to remove violently or tear away from a native place or environment: *During its initial phase the industrial revolution uprooted large segments of the rural population.* **3.** to destroy or eradicate as if by pulling out roots: *By doing away with the nation's culture, the invaders uprooted its most vital traditions.* **4.** to displace, as from a home or country; tear away, as from customs, a way of life, etc.: *to uproot a people.* —*v.i.* **5.** to become uprooted. [UP- + ROOT[2]] —**up·root′ed·ness,** *n.* —**up·root′er,** *n.*

up·rose (up rōz′), *v.* pt. of **uprise.**

up·rouse (up rouz′), *v.t.,* **-roused, -rous·ing.** to rouse up; arouse; awake. [UP- + ROUSE[1]]

Up·sa·la (up′sä lə, -sə-; *Swed.* o͝op′sä′lä′), *n.* Uppsala.

ups′ and downs′, rise and fall of fortune; good and bad times: *Every business has its ups and downs.*

up·set (*v., adj.* up set′; *n.* up′set′), *v.,* **-set, -set·ting,** *n., adj.* —*v.t.* **1.** to overturn: *to upset a pitcher of milk.* **2.** to disturb mentally or emotionally; perturb: *The incident upset her.* **3.** to disturb or derange completely; put out of order; throw into disorder: *to upset a system; to upset a mechanism; to upset an apartment.* **4.** to disturb physically: *It upset his stomach.* **5.** to defeat or overthrow an opponent that is considered more formidable, as in war, politics, sports, etc. **6.** *Metalworking.* to thicken the end of (a piece of heated metal) by hammering on the end against the length of the piece. **7.** to shorten (a strip of metal forming a tire) in the process of resetting it on its wheel. —*v.i.* **8.** to become upset or overturned. —*n.* **9.** an upsetting or instance of being upset; overturn; overthrow. **10.** the defeat of a person or group that is considered more formidable. **11.** a nervous, irritable state of mind. **12.** a disordered or confused arrangement. **13.** *Metalworking.* **a.** a tool used for upsetting. **b.** that which is upset, as a bar end. —*adj.* **14.** overturned: *an upset milk pail.* **15.** disordered; disorganized: *The house is upset.* **16.** distressed; disturbed: *He is emotionally upset. She had an upset stomach.* **17.** *Archaic.* raised up. [ME; see UP-, SET] —**up·set′ta·ble,** *adj.* —**up·set′ter,** *n.* —**up·set′ting·ly,** *adv.*
—**Syn. 1.** UPSET, CAPSIZE, OVERTURN imply a change from an upright or other stable position to a prostrate one. UPSET is a familiar word, applied to simple, everyday actions: *to upset a table, a glass of water.* CAPSIZE is applied especially to the upsetting of a boat or vessel: *to capsize a canoe.* OVERTURN usually suggests violence in upsetting something supposedly stable: *The earthquake overturned houses.* All three are used figuratively, also: *to upset the stock market; to capsize a plan; to overturn a government.* **2.** unnerve, disconcert, fluster. **5.** depose, displace. **11.** perturbation, disturbance. **12.** mess. **16.** concerned, disconcerted, agitated, perturbed, irritated. —**Ant. 2, 3.** steady.

up′set price′, the lowest price at which one is permitted to bid for something being sold at auction.

up·set·ting (up set′iŋ), *adj.* tending to disturb or upset: *an upsetting experience.* [UPSET + -ING[2]]

upset′ting lev′er, *Naval Archit.* the horizontal distance between the center of gravity, acting downward, and the center of buoyancy, acting upward, when they are so placed as to form a couple (**upset′ting cou′ple**) tending to capsize the boat. Cf. **righting lever.**

upset′ting mo′ment, *Naval Archit.* the moment of an upsetting couple. Also called **capsizing moment.**

up·shot (up′shot′), *n.* **1.** the final issue, the conclusion, or the result: *The upshot of the disagreement was a new bylaw.* **2.** the gist, as of an argument or thesis. [UP (in sense of termination) + SHOT[1]]

up·side (up′sīd′), *n.* **1.** the upper side or part. **2. get upsides with,** *Brit.* to get even with. [UP- + SIDE[1]]

up′side down′, **1.** with the upper part undermost. **2.** in or into complete disorder; topsy-turvy: *The burglars turned the house upside down.* —**up′side-down′,** *adj.* —**up′side-down′ness,** *n.*

up′side-down′ cake′, a cake that is baked on a layer of fruit, then turned before serving so that the fruit is on top.

up·si·lon (yo͞op′sə lon′, up′-; *Brit.* yo͞op sī′lən), *n.* **1.** the 20th letter of the Greek alphabet (Υ, υ). **2.** the vowel sound represented by this letter. [< Gk: lit., slender *u*]

up·spring (up spriŋ′), *v.,* **-sprang** or **-sprung, -sprung, -spring·ing,** *n.* —*v.i.* **1.** to spring up. **2.** to come into being or existence; arise: *Only when the war had ended did there upspring the first true prosperity.* —*n. Archaic.* **3.** growth or development. **4.** a coming into existence; origin. [ME *upspring(en).* See UP-, SPRING]

up·stage (up′stāj′), *adv., adj., v.,* **-staged, -stag·ing,** *n.* —*adv.* **1.** on or toward the back of the stage. —*adj.* **2.** of or pertaining to the back of the stage. **3.** haughtily aloof; supercilious. —*v.t.* **4.** to move upstage of (another actor), forcing him to act with back to the audience and thereby overshadowing his performance. **5.** to outdo professionally, socially, etc. **6.** to behave snobbishly toward. —*n.* **7.** the rear half of the stage. **8.** any stage position to the rear of another. [UP- + STAGE]

up·stairs (up′stârz′), *adv., adj., n., pl.* **-stairs.** —*adv.* **1.** up the stairs; to or on an upper floor. **2.** *Informal.* in the mind: *She's a little weak upstairs.* **3.** *Mil. Slang.* at or to a higher level in the air. **4. kick upstairs,** to promote to a higher position that is actually less advantageous in order to be rid of (a person). —*adj.* **5.** Also, **up′stair′.** of, pertaining to, or situated on an upper floor: *an upstairs window; an upstairs apartment.* —*n.* **6.** (*usually construed as sing.*) an upper story or stories; the part of a building or house that is above the ground floor: *The upstairs of this house is entirely rented.* [UP- + STAIRS]

up·stand·ing (up stan′diŋ), *adj.* **1.** standing erect; erect and tall. **2.** of a fine, vigorous type. **3.** upright; honorable; straightforward. [ME; see UP-, STANDING] —**up·stand′ing·ness,** *n.*

up·start (*n., adj.* up′stärt′; *v.* up stärt′), *n.* **1.** one who has risen suddenly from a humble position to wealth, power, or a position of consequence. **2.** a presumptuous and objectionable person who has so risen; parvenu. —*adj.* **3.** being, resembling, or characteristic of an upstart. —*v.i.* **4.** to start up; spring up, as to one's feet. **5.** to spring into existence or into view. —*v.t.* **6.** to cause to start up. [UP- + START] —**up′start′ness,** *n.*

up·state (up′stāt′), *U.S.* —*n.* **1.** the part of a State that is farther north or farther from the chief city, esp. the northerly part of New York State. —*adj.* **2.** of or coming from such an area. [UP- + STATE] —**up′stat′er,** *n.*

up·stream (up′strēm′), *adv.* **1.** toward or in the higher part of a stream; against the current. —*adj.* **2.** directed upstream; situated upstream: *an upstream journey; an upstream hideout.* [UP- + STREAM]

up·stretched (up strecht′), *adj.* stretched upward, as the arms. [UP- + *stretched,* ptp. of STRETCH]

up·stroke (up′strōk′), *n.* an upward stroke, esp. of a pen or pencil, or of a piston in a vertical cylinder. [UP- + STROKE[1]]

up·surge (*v.* up sûrj′; *n.* up′sûrj′), *v.,* **-surged, -surg·ing,** *n.* —*v.i.* **1.** to surge up; increase; rise: *Water upsurged. Crime upsurged.* —*n.* **2.** act of surging up. [UP- + SURGE]

up·sweep (*v.* up swēp′; *n.* up′swēp′), *v.,* **-swept, -sweep·ing,** *n.* —*v.t.* **1.** to sweep upward. —*v.i.* **2.** to be arranged in an upsweep. —*n.* **3.** a sweeping upward, as an increase in elevation or a steep slope. **4.** a hairdo produced by having the hair combed or brushed upward to the top of the head; an upswept hairdo. **5.** a strongly pronounced rise in activity, as in business. **6.** a curved shape of the lower jaw of some animals. [UP- + SWEEP]

up·swell (up swel′), *v.i., v.t.,* **-swelled, -swelled** or **-swol·len, -swell·ing.** to swell up. [ME; see UP-, SWELL]

up·swept (up′swept′), *adj.* **1.** curved or sloped upward: *upswept automobile fenders.* **2.** combed or brushed upward to the top of the head. [ptp. of UPSWEEP]

up·swing (*n.* up′swiŋ′; *v.* up swiŋ′), *n., v.,* **-swung, -swing·ing.** —*n.* **1.** an upward swing or swinging movement, as of a pendulum. **2.** a marked increase or improvement: *an upswing in stock market trading.* —*v.i.* **3.** to make or undergo an upswing. [UP- + SWING[1]]

up·sy-dai·sy (up′sē dā′zē), *interj.* (used to comfort a baby at the moment of lifting him up.) [baby-talk based on UP]

up·take (up′tāk′), *n.* **1.** apprehension; understanding or comprehension; mental grasp: *quick on the uptake; slow on the uptake.* **2.** an act or instance of taking up; a lifting: *the uptake of fertilizer by machines.* **3.** a pipe or passage leading upward from below, as for conducting smoke, a current of air, or the like. [ME; see UP-, TAKE]

up·tear (up târ′), *v.t.,* **-tore, -torn, -tear·ing.** to wrench or tear out by or as if by the roots or foundations; destroy. [UP- + TEAR[2]]

up·throw (*n.* up′thrō′; *v.* up thrō′), *n., v.,* **-threw, -thrown, -throw·ing.** —*n.* **1.** an upheaval, as of the earth's surface. **2.** *Geol.* an upward displacement of rock on one side of a fault. —*v.t.* **3.** to throw or cast up or upward. [UP- + THROW]

up·thrust (up′thrust′), *n.* **1.** a thrust in an upward direction. **2.** *Geol.* an upheaval. [UP- + THRUST]

up·tight (up′tīt′), *adj. Slang.* **1.** tense, nervous, or jittery. **2.** fine, excellent, or perfect. Also, **up′-tight′, up′ tight′.**

up·tilt (up tilt′), *v.t.* to tilt up. [UP- + TILT[1]]

up-to-date (up′tə dāt′), *adj.* **1.** extending to the present time; current; including the latest information or facts: *an up-to-date report.* **2.** in accordance with the latest or newest ideas, standards, techniques, styles etc.; modern. **3.** (of persons, buildings, etc.) keeping up with the times, as in outlook, information, ideas, appearance, style, etc. —**up′-to-date′ly,** *adv.* —**up′-to-date′ness,** *n.*

Up·ton (up′tən), *n.* a boy's given name.

up·torn (up tōrn′), *v.* pp. of **uptear.**

up-to-the-min·ute (up′tə t͟hə min′it), *adj.* extending to the immediate present, as to information, facts, style, etc.: *an up-to-the-minute news report.*

up·town (*adv., n.* up′toun′; *adj.* up′toun′), *adv.* **1.** toward, to, or in the upper part of a town or city: *He rode uptown on the bus.* —*adj.* **2.** moving toward, situated in, or pertaining to the upper part of a town: *an uptown bus.* —*n.* **3.** the uptown section of a town or city: *Uptown is less crowded.* [UP- + TOWN] —**up′town′er,** *n.*

up·trend (up′trend′), *n.* a tendency upward or toward growth, esp. in economic development. [UP- + TREND]

up·turn (*v.* up tûrn′; *n.* up′tûrn′), *v.t.* **1.** to turn up or over: *The farmer upturned clumps of sod with his spade.* **2.** to cause disorder; upheave: *The storm upturned the town.* **3.** to direct or turn upward: *She upturned her face toward Heaven and prayed.* —*v.i.* **4.** to turn up or upward: *Her eyes upturned to see his face.* —*n.* **5.** chaos or extreme disorder, as in society; an upheaval. **6.** an upward turn, or a changing and rising movement, as in prices, business, etc. [UP- + TURN]

up·turned (up tûrnd′), *adj.* **1.** turned or directed upward: *upturned eyes.* **2.** turned over; upside down: *an upturned canoe.* **3.** having a turned-up end: *an upturned nose.* [UP- + TURN + -ED[2]]

UPU, See **Universal Postal Union.**

U.P.W.A., United Packinghouse Workers of America.

up·ward (up′wərd), *adv.* Also, **up′wards. 1.** toward a higher place or position: *The birds flew upward.* **2.** toward a higher or more distinguished condition, rank, level, etc.: *His employer wishes to move him upward in the company.* **3.** more: *fourscore and upward.* **4.** toward a large city, the source or origin of a stream, or the interior of a country or region: *He followed the Thames River upward from the North Sea to London.* **5.** in the upper parts; above. **6. upward** or **upwards of,** more than; above: *His vacation trip cost him upwards of a thousand dollars.* —*adj.* **7.** moving or tending upward; directed at or situated in a higher place or position. [ME; OE *upweard* (c. D *opwaart*). See UP-, -WARD] —**up′ward·ly,** *adv.* —**up′ward·ness,** *n.*

up·whirl (up hwûrl′, -wûrl′), *v.t.* **1.** to cause (something) to whirl upward. —*v.i.* **2.** to be whirled upward. [UP- + WHIRL]

up·wind (*adv., adj.* up′wind′; *n.* up′wind′), *adv.* **1.** toward or against the wind or the direction from which it is blowing: *The hunters stalked upwind. The jumpers could not parachute upwind from the airplane.* —*adj.* **2.** moving or situated toward or in the direction from which the wind is blowing: *an upwind leap; the upwind portions of the aircraft.* —*n.* **3.** a wind that blows against one's course or up a slope. [UP- + WIND[1]]

Ur (ûr), *n.* an ancient Sumerian city on the Euphrates, in S Iraq: extensive excavations, esp. of royal tombs.

ur-[1], var. of **uro-**[1]: *uranalysis.*

ur-[2], var. of **uro-**[2] before a vowel: *urite.*

u·ra·cil (yo͝or′ə sil), *n. Biochem.* a crystalline solid, $C_4H_4N_2O_2$, soluble in hot water, obtained from nucleic acids by hydrolysis: used in biochemical research. [UR-[1] + AC(ETIC) + -IL]

u·rae·mi·a (yo͝o rē′mē ə), *n. Pathol.* uremia. —**u·rae′mic,** *adj.*

u·rae·us (yo͝o rē′əs), *n., pl.* **-us·es.** the sacred asp as represented upon the headdress of divinities and royal personages of ancient Egypt, usually directly over the forehead, as an emblem of supreme power. [< NL < Gk *ouraîos,* repr. Egypt word for cobra, perh. influenced by Gk *ouraîos* of the tail; see -URO[2]]

U, Uraeus

u·ra·ga·wa·ra (o͞o rä′gə wär′ə; *Jap.* o͞o rä′gä wä′rä), *n., pl.* **-ra.** a Japanese scabbard mount protecting an opening for a kozuka. [< Jap]

U·ral (yo͝or′əl), *n.* **1.** a river in the Soviet Union, flowing S from the S Ural Mountains to the Caspian Sea. 1400 mi. long. **2.** a former administrative division comprising a region in the Ural Mountains and its slopes. —*adj.* **3.** of or pertaining to the Ural Mountains or the Ural River.

U·ral-Al·ta·ic (yo͝or′əl al tā′ik), *adj.* **1.** of or pertaining to the Ural Mountains, on the border between the Soviet Union in Europe and Siberia, and the Altai Mountains, in S Siberia and NW Mongolia, or the country or peoples around them. **2.** of or pertaining to Ural-Altaic. **3.** speaking a Ural-Altaic language. —*n.* **4.** a language family consisting of the Uralic and Altaic languages.

U·ra·li·an (yo͝o rā′lē ən), *adj.* **1.** of or pertaining to the Ural Mountains or their inhabitants. **2.** Uralic. [URAL + -IAN]

Ura′lian em′erald, demantoid: not a true emerald.

U·ral·ic (yo͝o ral′ik), *n.* **1.** a family of languages that comprises Finno-Ugric and Samoyed as subfamilies. Hungarian, Finnish, and Estonian belong to Uralic. —*adj.* **2.** Also, **Uralian.** of or pertaining to Uralic. [URAL + -IC]

u·ral·ite (yo͝or′ə līt′), *n.* *Mineral.* hornblende formed by the hydrothermal alteration of pyroxene. [< G *Uralit,* named after URAL MOUNTAINS where found; see -ITE[1]] —**u·ral·it·ic** (yo͝or′ə lit′ik), *adj.*

U′ral Moun′tains, a mountain range in the W Soviet Union, extending N and S from the Arctic Ocean to near the Caspian Sea, forming a natural boundary between Europe and Asia. Highest peak, Mt. Telpos, 5540 ft. Also called **U′rals.**

U·ralsk (o͝o rälsk′), *n.* a city in W Kazakstan, in the W Soviet Union in Asia. 114,000 (est. 1964).

u·ra·nal·y·sis (yo͝or′ə nal′i sis), *n., pl.* **-ses** (-sēz′). urinalysis.

U·ra·ni·a (yo͝o rā′nē ə), *n.* **1.** *Class. Myth.* the Muse of astronomy. **2.** a name of Aphrodite, as representing spiritual love. **3.** a girl's given name.

U·ra·ni·an (yo͝o rā′nē ən), *adj.* pertaining to the planet Uranus. [URAN(US) + -IAN]

u·ran·ic[1] (yo͝o ran′ik), *adj.* *Chem.* **1.** of or containing uranium, esp. in the tetravalent state. **2.** containing uranium in a valence state higher than the corresponding uranous compound. [URAN(IUM) + -IC]

u·ran·ic[2] (yo͝o ran′ik), *adj.* of or pertaining to the heavens; celestial; astronomical: *uranic principles.* [< Gk *ouran(ós)* heaven + -IC]

u·ran·i·nite (yo͝o ran′ə nīt′), *n.* a mineral, probably originally uranium dioxide, UO_2, but altered by radioactive decay, and usually containing more or less uranium trioxide, lead, radium, and helium, occurring in several varieties, including pitchblende: the most important ore of uranium. [URAN(IUM) + -IN[2] + -ITE[1]]

u·ra·nis·cus (yo͝or′ə nis′kəs), *n., pl.* **-nis·ci** (-nis′ī). *Archit.* a starlike ornament, as in a coffer of a ceiling. [< Gk *ouranískos,* equiv. to *ouran(ós)* heaven + *-iskos* adj. suffix]

u·ra·nite (yo͝or′ə nīt′), *n.* *Mineral.* any of the uranium phosphates, as autunite or torbernite. [< G *Uranit.* See URANIUM, -ITE[1]] —**u·ra·nit·ic** (yo͝or′ə nit′ik), *adj.*

u′ranite group′, the mineralogical group including uranites and related minerals.

u·ra·ni·um (yo͝o rā′nē əm), *n.* *Chem.* a white, lustrous, radioactive, metallic element, occurring in pitchblende, and having compounds which are used in photography and in coloring glass. Its uranium-235 isotope is used in atomic and hydrogen bombs and as a nuclear fuel in power reactors. *Symbol:* U; *at. wt.:* 238.03; *at. no.:* 92; *sp. gr.:* 19.07. [< NL; see URAN(US), -IUM]

uranium 235, *Chem.* the radioactive uranium isotope having a mass number of 235 and a half life of 7.07–8.91 $\times 10^8$ years, comprising 0.715 percent of natural uranium. When bombarded with neutrons it undergoes fission with the release of energy. Also called **U-235, U 235**

uranium 238, *Chem.* the radioactive uranium isotope having a mass number 238 and a half life of 4.5 $\times 10^9$ years, comprising 99.28 percent of natural uranium: used chiefly in nuclear reactors as a source of the fissionable isotope plutonium 239. Also called **U-238, U 238**

uranium 239, *Chem.* the uranium isotope with a mass number 239. It is artificially produced by the neutron bombardment of U-238 and undergoes radioactive decay. Also called **U-239, U 239**

Ura′nium Cit′y, a city in NW Saskatchewan, in central Canada, on Lake Athabasca. 3349 (1961).

ura′nium hexaflu′oride, *Chem.* a colorless, water-insoluble, crystalline, volatile solid, UF_6, used in its gaseous state in separating uranium 235 from uranium.

ura′nium se′ries, *Chem.* the radioactive series that starts with uranium 238 and ends with a stable isotope of lead of mass number 206. Also, **u·ra′ni·um-ra′di·um se′ries** (yo͝o rā′nē əm rā′dē əm).

urano-, a learned borrowing from Greek meaning "heavens," used in the formation of compound words: *uranography; uranometry.* [< Gk, comb. form of *ouranós* heavens, heaven]

u·ra·nog·ra·phy (yo͝or′ə nog′rə fē), *n.* the branch of astronomy concerned with the description and mapping of the heavens, and esp. of the fixed stars. Also called **uranology.** [< Gk *ouranographía.* See URANO-, -GRAPHY] —**u′ra·nog′ra·pher, u′ra·nog′ra·phist,** *n.* —**u·ra·no·graph·ic** (yo͝or′ə nə graf′ik), **u′ra·no·graph′i·cal,** *adj.*

u·ra·nol·o·gy (yo͝or′ə nol′ə jē), *n., pl.* **-gies.** *Astron.* **1.** uranography. **2.** a treatise on the celestial bodies. [URANO- + -LOGY] —**u·ra·no·log·i·cal** (yo͝or′ənəloj′i kəl), *adj.*

u·ra·nom·e·try (yo͝or′ə nom′i trē), *n.* *Astron.* **1.** a chart of the positions of the heavenly bodies on the celestial sphere. **2.** the measurement of the positions of heavenly bodies. [< NL *uranometria.* See URANO-, -METRY] —**u·ra·no·met·ri·cal** (yo͝or′ə nə me′tri kəl), *adj.*

u·ra·nos·co·pid (yo͝or′ə nos′kə pid), *n.* **1.** any fish of the family *Uranoscopidae,* comprising the stargazers. —*adj.* **2.** belonging or pertaining to the family *Uranoscopidae.* [< NL *Uranoscopid(ae)* name of the family, equiv. to L *uranoscop(us)* kind of fish (< Gk *ouranoskópos,* lit., observing the heavens; see URANO-, -SCOPE) + *-idae* -ID[2]]

u·ra·nous (yo͝or′ə nəs), *adj.* *Chem.* containing trivalent uranium. [< NL *uranōs(us).* See URANIUM, -OUS]

U·ra·nus (yo͝or′ə nəs, yo͝o rā′-), *n.* **1.** *Class. Myth.* the personification of Heaven and ruler of the world, son and husband of Gaea (Earth) and father of the Titans, the Cyclopes, etc., who confined his children in Tartarus and was dethroned by his son Cronus, youngest of the Titans, at the instigation of Gaea. **2.** *Astron.* the planet seventh in order from the sun, having a diameter of 30,880 miles, a mean distance from the sun of 1,783,000,000 miles, a period of revolution of 84.02 years, and having five satellites.

u·ra·nyl (yo͝or′ə nil), *n.* *Chem.* the bivalent ion, UO_2^{+2}, or group, UO_2, which forms salts with acids. [URA-N(IUM) + -YL] —**u′ra·nyl′ic,** *adj.*

u·ra·ri (yo͝o rär′ē), *n.* curare. [< Carib]

U·rar·ti·an (o͝o rär′tē ən), *adj.* **1.** of or pertaining to Urartu, its people, or their language. —*n.* **2.** a native or inhabitant of Urartu. **3.** the non-Semitic, non-Indo-European language of Urartu, written in a cuneiform syllabic script. [URART(U) + -IAN]

U·rar·tu (o͝o rär′to͞o), *n.* an ancient kingdom, c1270–750 B.C., in E Turkey, on the shore of Lake Van: often invaded by Assyria.

u·rase (yo͝or′ās, -āz), *n.* *Biochem.* urease.

u·rate (yo͝or′āt), *n.* *Chem.* a salt of uric acid. [URO-[1] + -ATE[2]] —**u·rat·ic** (yo͝o rat′ik), *adj.*

ur·ban (ûr′bən), *adj.* **1.** of, pertaining to, or comprising a city or town. **2.** living in a city or cities. **3.** characteristic of or accustomed to cities; citified: *He is an urban type.* [< L *urbān(us),* equiv. to *urb-* (s. of *urbs*) city + *-ānus* -AN]

Ur·ban (ûr′bən), *n.* a boy's given name.

Urban I, Saint, pope A.D. 222–230.

Urban II, (*Odo* or *Otho*) c1042–99, French ecclesiastic: pope 1088–99.

Urban III, (*Uberto Crivelli*) Italian ecclesiastic: pope 1185–87.

Urban IV, (*Jacques Pantaléon*) died 1264, French ecclesiastic: pope 1261–64.

Urban V, (*Guillaume de Grimoard*) c1310–70, French ecclesiastic: pope 1362–70.

Urban VI, (*Bartolomeo Prignano*) c1318–89, Italian ecclesiastic: pope 1378–89.

Urban VII, (*Giovanni Battista Castagna*) 1521–90, Italian ecclesiastic: pope 1590.

Urban VIII, (*Maffeo Barberini*) 1568–1644, Italian ecclesiastic: pope 1623–44.

Ur·ban·a (ûr ban′ə), *n.* a city in E Illinois. 27,294 (1960).

Ur·ban·dale (ûr′bən dāl′), *n.* a town in central Iowa. 5821 (1960).

ur′ban dis′trict, a minor administrative division in England, Wales, and Northern Ireland, with local self-government by a district council, but lacking the charter of a borough.

ur·bane (ûr bān′), *adj.* **1.** having the polish and suavity regarded as characteristic of sophisticated social life in major cities: *an urbane manner.* **2.** reflecting elegance, sophistication, etc., esp. in expression: *He maintained an urbane tone in his letters.* [< L *urbānus.* See URBAN] —**ur·bane′ly,** *adv.* —**ur·bane′ness,** *n.*

ur·ban·ise (ûr′bə nīz′), *v.t.,* **-ised, -is·ing.** *Chiefly Brit.* urbanize. —**ur′ban·i·sa′tion,** *n.*

ur·ban·ism (ûr′bə niz′əm), *n.* **1.** the way of life of persons who live in a large city; urbanization. **2.** See **city planning.** [URBAN + -ISM, modeled on F *urbanisme*]

ur·ban·ist (ûr′bə nist), *n.* one who is a specialist in urban planning. [URBAN + -IST]

ur·ban·is·tic (ûr′bə nis′tik), *adj.* of or pertaining to urbanism. [URBAN(ISM) + -ISTIC] —**ur′ban·is′ti·cal·ly,** *adv.*

ur·ban·ite (ûr′bə nīt′), *n.* a resident of a city; one who lives in an urban community. [URBAN + -ITE[1]]

ur·ban·i·ty (ûr ban′i tē), *n., pl.* **-ties.** **1.** quality of being urbane; refined or elegant courtesy or politeness; suavity: *He was the last word in urbanity.* **2. urbanities,** civilities or amenities: *He lacked the urbanities.* [< L *urbānitās.* See URBANE, -ITY]

ur·ban·ize (ûr′bə nīz′), *v.t.,* **-ized, -iz·ing.** to render urban, as a locality. [URBAN + -IZE] —**ur′ban·i·za′tion,** *n.*

ur′ban renew′al, the art or process of rehabilitating city areas by demolishing, remodeling, or repairing existing structures and building or laying out new housing, public buildings, parks, roadways, and industrial areas on cleared sites in accordance with more or less comprehensive plans. Also called **ur′ban redevel′opment.**

ur′ban sociol′ogy, the sociological study of cities and their role in the development of society.

ur·bi·cul·ture (ûr′bə kul′chər), *n.* the way of life characteristic of cities. [< L *urbi-* (s. of *urbs* city) + CULTURE]

ur·bi et or·bi (o͝or′bē et ôr′bē), *Latin.* to the city (Rome) and the world: the form of address of papal bulls.

ur·ce·o·late (ûr′sē ə lit, -lāt′), *adj.* shaped like a pitcher; swelling out like the body of a pitcher and contracted at the orifice, as a corolla. [< NL *urceolāt(us)* < L *urceol(us),* dim. of *urce(us)* pitcher + *-ātus* -ATE[1]]

ur·chin (ûr′chin), *n.* **1.** a mischievous boy or any small boy or youngster. **2.** See **sea urchin.** **3.** either of two small rollers covered with card clothing used in conjunction with the cylinder in carding. **4.** *Chiefly Brit. Dial.* a hedgehog. **5.** *Obs.* an elf or mischievous sprite. [ME *urchun, urchon* hedgehog < ONF *(h)erichon,* OF *heriçun* < VL **hēriciōn-* (s. of **hēriciō*) < L *ēric(ius)* + *-iōn-* -ION]

urd (o͝ord, ûrd), *n.* the gram, *Phaseolus Mungo.* [< Hindi]

Urd (o͝ord), *n.* *Scand. Myth.* a giantess personifying the past; one of the three Norns that developed from Urdar. Cf. **Skuld, Verdandi.**

Ur·dar (o͝or′där), *n.* *Scand. Myth.* a giantess personifying fate: the original Norn. Cf. **Skuld, Urd, Verdandi.**

Ur·du (o͝or′do͞o, ûr′-, o͝or do͞o′, ûr-), *n.* one of the official languages of Pakistan, a language derived from Hindustani, used by Muslims, and written with Persian-Arabic letters.

ur·dy (ûr′dē), *adj.* *Heraldry.* **1.** noting a crenelated partition line having a pointed termination formed by two diagonal lines at each upward and downward projection. **2.** (of a charge, as an ordinary) having an edge or edges so formed. **3.** (of a cross) pointed, with the ends slightly splayed; cleché: *a cross urdy.* Also, **ur·dé** (ûr′dā, ûr dā′). [perh. misreading of F *vidée* as in *croix vidée* voided cross]

-ure, an abstract-noun suffix of action, result, and instrument, occurring in loan words from French: *pressure; legislature.* [< F *-ure* < L *-ūra*]

u·re·a (yo͝o rē′ə, yo͝or′ē ə), *n.* **1.** *Biochem.* a compound, $CO(NH_2)_2$, occurring in urine and other body fluids as a product of protein metabolism. **2.** *Chem.* a white, cool-tasting, water-soluble powder form of this compound, obtained by the reaction of liquid ammonia and liquid carbon dioxide: used as a fertilizer, animal feed, in the synthesis of plastics, resins, and barbiturates, and in medicine as a diuretic and in the diagnosis of kidney function. Also called **carbamide.** [< NL < F *urée.* See UR-[1], -EE] —**u·re′al, u·re′ic,** *adj.*

u·re′a-form·al′de·hyde res′in (yo͝o rē′ə fôr mal′də hīd′, yo͝or′ē ə-), *Chem.* any of a group of resins formed by the interaction of urea and formaldehyde under conditions that include heat and pH control, the initial condensation product of which is water-soluble and can be applied in solution, and which on further heating becomes water-insoluble: used chiefly in the manufacture of buttons, baking enamels, and for fabric wrinkle resistance.

u·re·ase (yo͝or′ē ās′, -āz′), *n.* *Biochem.* an enzyme that changes urea into ammonium carbonate, found in bacteria, fungi, etc. [URE(A) + -ASE]

u·re·din·i·um (yo͝or′i din′ē əm), *n., pl.* **-din·i·a** (-din′ē ə). *Bot.* (formerly) urediun. [< NL < *ūrēdin-* (s. of L *ūrēdō;* see UREDO) + *-ium* -IUM] —**u′re·din′i·al,** *adj.*

u·re·di·um (yo͝o rē′dē əm), *n., pl.* **-di·a** (-dē ə). *Bot.* the fructification of the rust fungi, bearing uredospores. [< NL; see UREDO, -IUM] —**u·re′di·al,** *adj.*

u·re·do (yo͝o rē′dō), *n.* *Pathol.* a skin irritation; hives; urticaria. [< L *ūrēdō* blast, blight, burning itch, equiv. to *ūr(ere)* to burn + *-ēdō* n. suffix]

u·re·do·so·rus (yo͝o rē′də sôr′əs, -sōr′-), *n., pl.* **-so·ri** (-sôr′ī, -sōr′ī). *Bot.* uredium. [UREDO + SORUS]

u·re·do·spore (yo͝o rē′də spôr′, -spōr′), *n.* *Bot.* the spore of the rust fungi, which appears between the aeciospore and the teliospore, commonly the summer spore. [UREDO + SPORE]

u·re·ide (yo͝or′ē īd′, -id), *n.* *Chem.* any of a group of substances derived from urea in which at least one hydrogen atom has been replaced by an acyl group, as $H_2NCONHCOR$, and of which many cyclic derivatives are sedatives. [URE(A) + -IDE]

u·re·i·do (yə rē′i dō′), *adj.* *Chem.* containing the ureido group. [UREIDE + -O-]

ure′ido group′, *Chem.* the univalent group, H_2NCONH–. Also called **ure′ido rad′ical.**

u·re·mi·a (yo͝o rē′mē ə), *n.* *Pathol.* a condition resulting from the retention in the blood of constituents normally excreted in the urine. Also, **uraemia.** [< NL; see UR-[1], -EMIA]

u·re·mic (yo͝o rē′mik), *adj.* *Pathol.* **1.** pertaining to uremia. **2.** afflicted with uremia. Also, **uraemic.** [< NL; see UREM(IA), -IC]

u·re·na (yo͝o rē′nə), *n.* any tropical, malvaceous herb or shrub of the genus *Urena,* having clusters of small, yellow flowers, esp. *U. lobata,* which yields a useful bast fiber. [< NL < Malay *uren* + L *-a* n. suffix]

-uret, *Chem.* a suffix equivalent to **-ide:** *arseniuret.* [< NL *-urētum*]

u·re·ter (yo͝o rē′tər), *n.* *Anat., Zool.* a muscular duct or tube conveying the urine from a kidney to the bladder or cloaca. See diag. under **kidney.** [< NL < Gk *ourētḗr,* equiv. to *ourē-* (verbid s. of *ourein* to URINATE) + *-tēr* n. suffix] —**u·re′ter·al, u·re·ter·ic** (yo͝or′i ter′ik), *adj.*

uretero-, a combining form of **ureter:** *ureterostomy.*

u·re·ter·o·in·tes·ti·nal (yo͝o rē′tə rō in tes′tə nəl), *adj.* *Anat.* of, pertaining to, or involving the intestine and ureter. [URETERO- + INTESTINAL]

u·re·ter·o·li·thot·o·my (yo͝o rē′tə rō li thot′ə mē), *n., pl.* **-mies.** *Surg.* incision of a ureter for removal of a calculus. [URETERO- + LITHOTOMY]

u·re·ter·os·to·my (yo͝o rē′tə ros′tə mē), *n., pl.* **-mies.** *Surg.* formation of a permanent external opening into the ureter. [URETERO- + -STOMY]

u·re·than (yo͝or′ə than′), *n.* *Chem.* **1.** any derivative of carbamic acid having the formula NH_2COOR. **2.** Also called **ethyl carbamate, ethyl urethane.** a white, crystalline, water-soluble powder, $NH_2COOC_2H_5$, produced by the reaction of urea nitrate with ethyl alcohol or by the reaction of ammonia with either ethyl carbonate or ethyl chloroformate: used chiefly as a solvent, in organic synthesis, as a fungicide and pesticide, and, formerly as a hypnotic. Also, **u·re·thane** (yo͝or′ə thān′, yo͝o reth′ān). [UR(EA) + ETHAN(E)]

urethr-, var. of **urethro-** before a vowel: *urethritis.*

u·re·thra (yo͝o rē′thrə), *n., pl.* **-thrae** (-thrē), **-thras.** *Anat.* the membranous tube that extends from the urinary bladder to the exterior and that in the male conveys semen as well as urine. [< LL < Gk *ourḗthra,* equiv. to *ourē-* (see URETER) + *-thra* n. suffix] —**u·re′thral,** *adj.*

u·re·threc·to·my (yo͝or′ə threk′tə mē), *n., pl.* **-mies.** *Surg.* excision or removal of part or all of the urethra. [URETHR- + -ECTOMY]

u·re·thri·tis (yo͝or′ə thrī′tis), *n.* *Pathol.* inflammation of the urethra. [< NL; see URETHR-, -ITIS] —**u·re·thrit·ic** (yo͝or′ə thrit′ik), *adj.*

urethro-, a combining form of **urethra:** *urethroscope.* Also, *esp. before a vowel,* **urethr-.**

u·re·thro·scope (yo͝o rē′thrə skōp′), *n.* *Med.* an apparatus for observing the urethra. [URETHRO- + -SCOPE] —**u·re·thro·scop·ic** (yo͝o rē′thrə skop′ik), *adj.*

u·re·thros·co·py (yo͝or′ə thros′kə pē), *n.* *Med.* observation of the urethra by a urethroscope. [URETHRO- + -SCOPY]

u·re·thros·to·my (yo͝or′ə thros′tə mē), *n., pl.* **-mies.** *Surg.* the formation of a permanent opening through the perineum into the urethra. [URETHRO- + -STOMY]

u·re·throt·o·my (yo͝or′ə throt′ə mē), *n., pl.* **-mies.** *Surg.* an operation to divide a stricture of the urethra. [URETHRO- + -TOMY]

u·ret·ic (yo͝o ret′ik), *adj.* of, pertaining to, or occurring in the urine. [< LL *ūrēticus* < Gk *ourētikós*, equiv. to *ourē-* (see URETER) + *-tikos* -TIC]

U·rey (yo͝or′ē), *n.* **Harold Clay·ton** (klāt′ən), born 1893, U.S. chemist: Nobel prize 1934.

u·re·yl·ene (yə rē′ə lēn′), *adj.* *Chem.* containing the ureylene group. [URE(A) + -YL + -ENE]

ure′ylene group′, *Chem.* the divalent group, –HNCONH–. Also called **ure′ylene rad′ical.**

Ur·fa (o͝or fä′), *n.* a city in SE Turkey, E of the Euphrates River: on the site of ancient Edessa. 72,873 (1965).

Ur·ga (o͝or′gä), *n.* former name of **Ulan Bator.**

urge (ûrj), *v.,* **urged, urg·ing,** *n.* —*v.t.* **1.** to push or force along; impel with force or vigor: *to urge the cause along.* **2.** to drive with incitement to speed or effort: *to urge dogs on with shouts.* **3.** to press, push, or hasten (the course, activities, etc.): *to urge one's flight.* **4.** to impel, constrain, or move to some action: *urged by necessity.* **5.** to endeavor to induce or persuade, as by entreaties or earnest recommendations; entreat or exhort earnestly: *to urge a person to greater caution.* **6.** to press (something) upon the attention: *to urge a claim.* **7.** to insist on, allege, or assert with earnestness: *to urge the need of haste.* **8.** to press by persuasion or recommendation, as for acceptance, performance, or use; recommend or advocate earnestly: *to urge a plan of action.* —*v.i.* **9.** to exert a driving or impelling force; give an impulse to haste or action: *Hunger urges.* **10.** to make entreaties or earnest recommendations. **11.** to press arguments or allegations, as against a person: *The senator urged against the confirmation of the appointment.* —*n.* **12.** an act of urging; impelling action, influence, or force; impulse. **13.** an involuntary, natural, or instinctive impulse: *the sex urge.* [< L *urg(ēre)* (to) press, force, drive, urge] —**urg′er,** *n.* —**urg′ing·ly,** *adv.*
—**Syn. 4.** incite, goad, stimulate, spur. **7.** aver, asseverate. —**Ant. 1, 2, 3.** deter. **4, 5.** discourage.

Ur·gel (o͝or hel′), *n.* a town in NE Spain, SSW of Andorra. Also called **Seo de Urgel.**

ur·gen·cy (ûr′jən sē), *n., pl.* **-cies. 1.** urgent character; imperativeness; insistence; importunateness. **2. urgencies,** urgent requirements or needs. [< LL *urgentia* pressure, equiv. to L *urgent-* (see URGENT) + *-ia*; see -ENCY]

ur·gent (ûr′jənt), *adj.* **1.** pressing; compelling or requiring immediate action or attention; imperative: *an urgent matter.* **2.** insistent or earnest in solicitation; importunate, as a person: *an urgent pleader.* **3.** expressed with insistence, as requests or appeals: *an urgent tone of voice.* [< L *urgent-* (s. of *urgēns*), equiv. to *urg-* URGE + *-ent-* -ENT] —**ur′gent·ly,** *adv.*

-urgy, an element occurring in loan words from Greek where it meant "work" (*dramaturgy*): on this model, used in the formation of compound words (*metallurgy*). [< Gk *-urgia*, deriv. of *érgon*, c. WORK]

U·ri (o͞o′rē; *Eng.* o͝or′ē), *n.* a canton in central Switzerland. 32,021 (1960); 415 sq. mi. *Cap.:* Altdorf.

-uria, a word element meaning "urine," used in the formation of compound words: *ischuria.* [< Gk *-ouria*. See URO-¹, -IA]

U·ri·ah (yo͝o rī′ə), *n.* **1.** Also, *Douay Bible,* **U·ri·as** (yo͝o rī′əs). the husband of Bathsheba, and an officer in David's army. II Sam. 11. **2.** a boy's given name.

Uri′ah Heep′ (hēp), the hypocritical and villainous clerk in Dickens' *David Copperfield.*

u·ri·al (o͝or′ē əl), *n.* a wild sheep, *Ovis vignei* of southern Asia, having a reddish coat. [< Panjabi *hureāl*]

u·ric (yo͝or′ik), *adj.* of, pertaining to, contained in, or derived from urine. [UR-¹ + -IC]

uric-, var. of **urico-,** esp. before a vowel.

u′ric ac′id, **1.** *Biochem.* a compound, $C_5H_4N_4O_3$, present in human urine, and the principal nitrogenous component of the excrement of reptiles and birds, that in the form of its salts is found in the joints in gout and as the major constituent of kidney stones. **2.** *Chem.* a white, crystalline, odorless, tasteless, very slightly water-soluble powder form of this compound, obtained chiefly from urine or bird excrement or synthesized, used chiefly in organic synthesis. —**u′ric-ac′id,** *adj.*

u·ric·ac·i·de·mi·a (yo͝or′ik as′i dē′mē ə), *n.* *Med.* lithemia. [URIC ACID + -EMIA]

urico-, a combining form of **uric acid:** *uricolytic.* Also, *esp. before a vowel,* **uric-.**

u·ri·col·y·sis (yo͝or′i kol′i sis), *n.* *Biochem.* the decomposition of uric acid. [< NL; see URICO-, -LYSIS] —**u·ri·co·lyt·ic** (yo͝or′i kō lit′ik), *adj.*

U·ri·el (yo͝or′ē əl), *n.* **1.** one of the archangels. II Esdras 4. **2.** a boy's given name.

U·rim and Thum·mim (yo͝or′im; thum′im), *Judaism.* objects, possibly made of metal or precious stones and inscribed with symbols, worn in the breastplate of the high priest and used, perhaps like lots, to determine God's response to a question answerable by "yes" or "no." Ex. 28:30. [part. trans. of Heb *ūrīm wethummīm*]

urin-, var. of **urino-** before a vowel: *urinalysis.*

u·ri·nal (yo͝or′ə nəl), *n.* **1.** a building, an enclosure, or a bathroom fixture where one urinates. **2.** a receptacle to receive the urine of a person with urinary incontinence or that of a bedridden person. [ME < OF < LL < L *ūrīnāl(e)* of urine. See URINE, -AL²]

u·ri·nal·y·sis (yo͝or′ə nal′i sis), *n., pl.* **-ses** (-sēz′). analysis of urine chemically or microscopically. Also, **uranalysis.** [< NL; see URIN-, (AN)ALYSIS]

u·ri·nar·y (yo͝or′ə ner′ē), *adj., n., pl.* **-nar·ies.** —*adj.* **1.** of or pertaining to urine. **2.** pertaining to the organs secreting and discharging urine. —*n. Archaic.* **3.** a reservoir for the reception of urine or the like. **4.** urinal (def. 1). [< NL *ūrīnāri(us).* See URIN-, -ARY]

u′rinary blad′der, *Anat., Zool.* a distensible, muscular and membranous sac, in which the urine is retained until it is discharged from the body.

u′rinary cal′culus, *Pathol.* a calcareous concretion in the urinary tract.

u·ri·nate (yo͝or′ə nāt′), *v.i.,* **-nat·ed, -nat·ing.** to pass or discharge urine. [< ML *ūrīnāt(us),* ptp. of *ūrīn(āre)* < L *ūrīn(a)* URINE + *-ātus* -ATE¹] —**u′ri·na′tion,** *n.* —**u′ri·na′tive,** *adv.*

u·rine (yo͝or′in), *n.* the liquid-to-semisolid waste matter excreted by the kidneys, in man being a yellowish, slightly acid, watery fluid. [ME < OF < L *ūrīn(a)*; akin to Gk *oûron* urine]

u′rine anal′ysis, urinalysis.

u·ri·nif·er·ous (yo͝or′ə nif′ər əs), *adj.* conveying urine. [URIN- + -I- + -FEROUS]

urinif′erous tu′bule, a urine-bearing tubule in a nephron of a kidney.

urino-, a combining form of **urine:** *urinoscopy.* Also, *esp. before a vowel,* **urin-.** [< L < *ūrīn(a)* urine + *-o-* -O-]

u·ri·no·gen·i·tal (yo͝or′ə nō jen′i təl), *adj.* genitourinary. [URINO- + GENITAL]

u·ri·nos·co·py (yo͝or′ə nos′kə pē), *n.* *Med.* uroscopy. [URINO- + -SCOPY]

u·ri·nous (yo͝or′ə nəs), *adj.* of, pertaining to, resembling, or having the odor or qualities of urine. Also, **u·ri·nose** (yo͝or′ə nōs′). [< NL *ūrīnōs(us).* See URIN-, -OUS]

Ur·mi·a (o͝or′mē ə), *n.* **Lake,** a salt lake in NW Iran. ab. 2000 sq. mi. Also called **Lake Urumiyeh.**

urn (ûrn), *n.* **1.** a large or decorative vase, esp. one with an ornamental foot or pedestal. **2.** a vase for holding the ashes of the cremated dead. **3.** a container with a valve, used for making tea or coffee in quantity. **4.** *Bot.* the spore-bearing part of the capsule of a moss, between lid and seta. [ME *urne* < L *ūrna* earthen vessel for ashes, water, etc., deriv. of *ūr(ere)* (to) burn] —**urn′like′,** *adj.*

Ur-Nam·mu (o͝or′nä′mo͞o), *n.* king of the Sumerian city-state of Ur c2000 B.C.

Urn′ Bur′ial, (*Hydriotaphia*) an essay (1658) by Sir Thomas Browne.

urn·field (ûrn′fēld′), *n.* a Bronze Age cemetery in which the ashes of the dead were buried in urns. [URN + FIELD]

uro-¹, a learned borrowing from Greek meaning "urine," used in the formation of compound words: *urology.* Also, *esp. before a vowel,* **ur-.** [< Gk, comb. form of *oûron* urine]

uro-², a learned borrowing from Greek meaning "tail," used in the formation of compound words: *uropod.* Also, *esp. before a vowel,* **ur-.** [comb. form repr. Gk *ourá*]

u·ro·chord (yo͝or′ə kôrd′), *n.* *Zool.* the notochord of an ascidian or tunicate, found mostly in the larva, or more conspicuous in the larva than in the adult, and confined chiefly to the caudal region. [URO-² + CHORD¹] —**u′ro·chor′dal,** *adj.*

u·ro·chrome (yo͝or′ə krōm′), *n.* *Biochem.* a yellow-colored pigment which gives the color to urine. [URO-¹ + CHROME]

Ur′ of the Chaldees′, the city where Abraham was born, sometimes identified with the Sumerian city of Ur. Gen. 11:28, 31; 15:7; Neh. 9:7.

u·ro·gen·i·tal (yo͝or′ō jen′i təl), *adj.* genitourinary. [URO-¹ + GENITAL]

u·rog·e·nous (yo͝o roj′ə nəs), *adj.* *Physiol.* **1.** secreting or producing urine. **2.** contained in urine. [URO-¹ + -GENOUS]

u·ro·gom·phus (yo͝or′ə gom′fəs), *n., pl.* **-phi** (-fī). pseudocercus. [< NL < *ūro-* URO-² + L *gomphus* nail < Gk *gómphos* peg, tooth]

u·ro·lith (yo͝or′ə lith), *n.* *Pathol.* a urinary calculus. [URO-¹ + -LITH] —**u′ro·lith′ic,** *adj.*

u·rol·o·gy (yo͝o rol′ə jē), *n.* the scientific, clinical, and esp. surgical aspects of the study of the urine and the genitourinary tract in health and disease. [URO-¹ + -LOGY] —**u·ro·log·ic** (yo͝or′ə loj′ik), **u′ro·log′i·cal,** *adj.* —**u·rol′o·gist,** *n.*

u·ro·mere (yo͝or′ə mēr′), *n.* any segment of the abdomen of an arthropod. [URO-² + -MERE] —**u·ro·mer·ic** (yo͝or′ə mer′ik), *adj.*

u·ro·pod (yo͝or′ə pod′), *n.* an abdominal limb of an arthropod, esp. one of those on either side of the telson, as in a lobster. [URO-² + -POD] —**u·rop·o·dal** (yo͝o rop′ə dəl), **u·rop′o·dous,** *adj.*

u·ro·pyg·i·al (yo͝or′ə pij′ē əl), *adj.* *Ornith.* of or pertaining to the uropygium. [UROPYGI(UM) + -AL¹]

uropyg′ial gland′, *Ornith.* a gland opening on the back at the base of the tail in most birds that secretes an oily fluid used by the bird in preening its feathers. Also called **oil gland, preen gland.**

u·ro·pyg·i·um (yo͝or′ə pij′ē əm), *n.* *Ornith.* the projecting terminal portion of a bird's body, from which the tail feathers spring. [< NL < Gk *ouropýgion* tail or tail feathers (sp. var. of *orropýgion*), equiv. to *ouro* URO-² + *pyg(ē)* rump, buttocks + L *-ium* -IUM]

u·ros·co·py (yo͝o ros′kə pē), *n.* *Med.* inspection or analysis of the urine as a means of diagnosis. Also, **urinoscopy.** [URO-¹ + -SCOPY] —**u·ro·scop·ic** (yo͝or′ə skop′ik), *adj.* —**u·ros′co·pist,** *n.*

u·ro·some (yo͝or′ə sōm′), *n.* *Zool.* **1.** the tail of a fish, including both the caudal fin and the caudal peduncle. **2.** the abdomen of an arthropod. [URO-² + -SOME³]

u·ro·xan·thin (yo͝or′ə zan′thin), *n.* *Biochem.* a yellow pigment, occurring in normal human urine, that on oxidation is converted to indigo blue. [< G; see URO-¹, -XANTHIN]

Ur·quhart (ûr′kərt), *n.* **Sir Thomas,** 1611–60, Scottish author and translator.

Ur·sa (ûr′sə), *n.* a girl's given name.

Ur·sa Ma·jor (ûr′sə mā′jər), *gen.* **Ur·sae Ma·jor·is** (ûr′sē mə jōr′is, -jôr′-). *Astron.* the Great Bear, the most prominent northern constellation, containing the seven stars that form the Big Dipper.

Ur·sa Mi·nor (ûr′sə mī′nər), *gen.* **Ur·sae Mi·nor·is** (ûr′sē mi nōr′is, -nôr′-). *Astron.* the Little or Lesser Bear, the most northern constellation containing the stars that form the Little Dipper, the outermost of which, at the end of the handle, is Polaris.

ur·si·form (ûr′sə fôrm′), *adj.* having the form of a bear; bear-shaped: *the ursiform koala.* [< L *urs(us)* a bear + -I- + -FORM]

ur·sine (ûr′sīn, -sin), *adj.* **1.** of or pertaining to a bear or bears. **2.** bearlike. [< L *ursīn(us),* equiv. to *urs(us)* a bear + *-īnus* -INE¹]

ur′sine das′yure. See **Tasmanian devil.**

ur′sine howl′er, the red howling monkey, *Alouatta seniculus,* of northern South America.

Ur·spra·che (o͝or′shprä′KHə; *Ger.* o͞or′shprä′KHə), *n.* a hypothetically reconstructed parent language, as Proto-Germanic, the ancestor of the Germanic languages. [< G: original speech]

Ur·su·la (ûr′sə lə, ûrs′yo͝o-), *n.* **1. Saint,** a legendary British princess who, with 11,000 virgins, is said to have been martyred by the Huns at Cologne. **2.** a girl's given name, form of **Ursa.**

Ur·su·line (ûr′sə lin, -līn′, ûrs′yo͝o-), *n.* **1.** *Rom. Cath. Ch.* a member of an order of nuns founded at Brescia, Italy, about 1537, devoted to teaching. —*adj.* **2.** of or pertaining to the Ursulines.

ur·ti·ca·ceous (ûr′tə kā′shəs), *adj.* belonging to the *Urticaceae,* or nettle family of plants. [< NL *urticāc(eae)* name of the genus < L *urtīc(a)* nettle (deriv. of *ūrt-(ere)* (to) burn, sting) + NL *-āceae* -ACEAE + -OUS]

ur·ti·cant (ûr′tə kənt), *adj.* urticating. [< F < ML *urticant-* (s. of *urticāns*), prp. of *urtic(āre)* (to) sting. See URTICATE]

ur·ti·car·i·a (ûr′tə kâr′ē ə), *n.* *Pathol.* a transient condition of the skin, usually caused by an allergic reaction and characterized by pale, irregular, elevated patches and severe itching; nettle rash; hives. [< NL < L *urtīca* nettle + *-āria* -ARIA] —**ur′ti·car′i·al,** *adj.*

ur·ti·cate (ûr′tə kāt′), *v.,* **-cat·ed, -cat·ing.** —*v.t.* **1.** to sting with or as if with nettles. **2.** to whip with nettles, or as if with nettles, esp. so as to produce a stinging sensation; flog; lash. —*v.i.* **3.** to sting in the manner of a nettle. [< ML *urtīcāt(us)* (ptp. of *urtīcāre* to sting), equiv. to L *urtīc(a)* nettle + *-ātus* -ATE¹]

ur·ti·ca·tion (ûr′tə kā′shən), *n.* *Pathol.* the development or eruption of urticaria. [< ML *urtīcātiōn-* (s. of *urtīcātiō*) a stinging, equiv. to *urtīcāt(us)* (see URTICATE) + *-iōn-* -ION]

Uru., Uruguay.

U·ru·gua·ia·na (o͞o′ro͞o gwä yä′nə), *n.* a city in SW Brazil, on the Uruguay River. 51,368 (1960).

U·ru·guay (yo͝or′ə gwā′; *Sp.* o͞o′ro͞o gwī′), *n.* **1.** a republic in SE South America. 2,592,563 (1963); 72,172 sq. mi. *Cap.:* Montevideo. **2.** a river in SE South America, flowing from S Brazil along the boundary of E Argentina into the Río de la Plata. 981 mi. long. —**U·ru·guay·an** (yo͝or′ə gwā′ən, -gwī′ən), *adj., n.*

U·ruk (o͞o′ro͝ok), *n.* an ancient Sumerian city in S Iraq, near the Euphrates: extensive archaeological excavations. Biblical name, **Erech.**

U·rum·chi (o͞o ro͝om′chē), *n.* a city in and the capital of Sinkiang, in NW China. 140,700 (est. 1957). Also, **U·rum·tsi** (o͞o ro͝om′chē). Also called **Tihwa.**

U·ru·mi·yeh (o͞o ro͞o′mē ye), *n.* See **Urmia, Lake.**

U·run·di (o͞o ro͞on′dē), *n.* former name of **Burundi.** Cf. **Ruanda-Urundi.**

u·rus (yo͝or′əs), *n., pl.* **u·rus·es.** the aurochs. [< L *ūrus* a kind of wild ox (c. Gk *oûros*) < Gmc *ūr-*; cf. OE, OHG *ūr*]

u·ru·shi·ol (o͝or′o͞o shē ōl′, -ôl′, -ol′), *n.* a toxic, liquid, catechol derivative, the active irritant principle in several species of the plant genus *Rhus,* as in poison ivy. [< Jap *urushi* lacquer + -OL]

us (us), *pron.* **1.** the objective case of **we:** *They took us to the circus.* **2.** the dative case of **we:** *She asked us the way.* **3.** *Informal.* (used in place of the pronoun *our* in gerundive constructions): *Do you know about us moving to town?* [ME, OE; c. G, Goth *uns*]

U.S., **1.** Uncle Sam. **2.** United Service. **3.** See **United States.**

u.s., **1.** where mentioned above. [< L *ubi supra*] **2.** as above: a formula in judicial acts, directing that what precedes be reviewed. [< L *ut supra*]

USA, United States Army.

U.S.A., **1.** See **United States of America. 2.** United States Army. **3.** Union of South Africa. **4.** (*italics*) a trilogy of novels by John Dos Passos, consisting of *The 42nd Parallel, 1919,* and *The Big Money.*

us·a·ble (yo͞o′zə bəl), *adj.* **1.** that is available for use. **2.** convenient and capable of being used: *His saw is no longer usable.* Also, **useable.** [ME < MF; see USE, -ABLE] —**us′a·bil′i·ty, us′a·ble·ness,** *n.* —**us′a·bly,** *adv.*

U.S.A.F., United States Air Force. Also, **USAF**

USAFI, United States Armed Forces Institute.

us·age (yo͞o′sij, -zij), *n.* **1.** customary way of doing; a custom or practice: *the usages of the last 50 years.* **2.** the customary manner in which a language or a form of a language is spoken or written: *English usage; a grammar based on usage rather than on arbitrary notions of correctness.* **3.** a particular instance of this: *a usage borrowed from French.* **4.** manner of doing or handling something; treatment: *rough usage.* **5.** habitual or customary use; long-continued practice: *immemorial usage.* **6.** an act of using or employing; use. [ME < AF, OF < ML *ūsāticum*), equiv. to L *ūs(us)* (see USE) + *-āticum* -AGE]

us·ance (yo͞o′zəns), *n.* **1.** *Com.* a length of time, exclusive of days of grace and varying in different places, allowed by custom or usage for the payment of foreign bills of exchange. **2.** *Econ.* the income of benefits of every kind derived from the ownership of wealth. **3.** *Archaic.* **a.** use. **b.** custom; habit. **4.** *Obs.* usury. [ME *usaunce* < OF *usance*, prob. < ML *ūsancia*, deriv. of L *ūsant-* (s. of *ūsāns*), prp. of *ūsāre* to USE; see -ANCE]

USAR, United States Army Reserve.

Us·beg (o͝os′beg, us′-), *n., pl.* **-begs,** (*esp. collectively*) **-beg.** Uzbek.

Us·bek (o͝os′bek, us′-), *n., pl.* **-beks,** (*esp. collectively*) **-bek.** Uzbek.

U.S.C., **1.** United States Code. **2.** United States of Colombia. Also, **USC**

U.S.C.A., United States Code Annotated. Also, **USCA**

U.S.C.&G.S., United States Coast and Geodetic Survey.

U.S.C.G., United States Coast Guard. Also, **USCG**

U.S.C. Supp., *Law.* United States Code Supplement.

USDA, United States Department of Agriculture. Also, **U.S.D.A.**

use (*v.* yo͞oz; *n.* yo͞os), *v.,* **used, us·ing,** *n.* —*v.t.* **1.** to employ for some purpose; put into service; make use of: *to use a knife.* **2.** to avail oneself of; apply to one's own purposes: *to use the facilities.* **3.** to expend or consume in use: *We have used the money provided.* **4.** to treat or behave toward: *He did not use his employees with much*

consideration. **5.** to habituate or accustom. **6.** *Archaic.* to practice habitually or customarily; make a practice of. **—v.i. 7.** to be accustomed, wont, or customarily found (used with an infinitive expressed or understood, and, except in archaic use, now only in the past): *He used to go every day.* **8.** *Archaic.* to resort, stay, or dwell customarily. **9. use up, a.** to consume entirely. **b.** to exhaust of vigor or usefulness; finish: *By the end of the war he felt used up and sick of life.*
—n. 10. the act of employing, using, or putting into service: *the use of tools.* **11.** the state of being employed or used. **12.** an instance or way of employing or using something: *proper use of the tool; the painter's use of color.* **13.** a way of being employed or used; a purpose for which something is used: *He was of temporary use. The instrument has different uses.* **14.** the power, right, or privilege of employing or using something: *to lose the use of the right eye; to be denied the use of a library card.* **15.** service or advantage in or for being employed or used; utility or usefulness: *of no practical use.* **16.** help; profit; resulting good: *What's the use?* **17.** occasion or need, as for something to be employed or used: *Have you any use for another calendar?* **18.** continued, habitual, or customary employment or practice; custom; practice: *to follow the prevailing use of such occasions.* **19.** *Law.* **a.** the enjoyment of property, as by the employment, occupation, or exercise of it. **b.** the benefit or profit of lands and tenements in the possession of another who simply holds them for the beneficiary. **c.** the equitable ownership of land to which the legal title is in another; a passive trust. **20.** *Liturgy.* the distinctive form of ritual or of any liturgical observance used in a particular church, diocese, community, etc. **21.** *Metalworking.* **a.** a roughed drop forging. **b.** a piece of an ingot removed for forging. **22.** *Obs.* usual experience. **23. have no use for, a.** to have no occasion or need for: *She appears to have no use for the city.* **b.** to refuse to tolerate; discount: *He had no use for Barry.* **c.** to have a distaste for; dislike: *He has no use for dictators.* **24. make use of,** to use for one's own purposes; employ: *Charitable organizations will make use of your old furniture and clothing.* **25. of no use,** of no advantage or help: *It's of no use to look for that missing earring.* Also, **no use. 26. put to use,** to apply; employ to advantage: *What a shame that no one has put that old deserted mansion to use!* [ME *use(n)* < OF *use(r)* < L *ūs(us),* ptp. of *ūtī* to use]
—Syn. 1. USE, UTILIZE mean to make something serve one's purpose. USE is the general word: *to use a telephone; to use a saw and other tools; to use one's eyes; to use coal or eggs in cooking.* (What is USED often has depreciated or been diminished, sometimes completely consumed: *a used automobile; All the butter has been used.*) As applied to persons, USE implies some selfish or sinister purpose: *to use another to advance oneself.* UTILIZE implies practical or profitable use: *to utilize the means at hand, a modern system of lighting.* **3.** exhaust, waste. **5.** familiarize, inure. **11.** employment, utilization, application, exercise. **12.** handling.

use·a·ble (yo͞o′zə bəl), *adj.* usable. **—use′a·bil′i·ty, use′a·ble·ness,** *n.* **—use′a·bly,** *adv.*

USECC, United States Employees' Compensation Commission.

use·ful (yo͞os′fəl), *adj.* **1.** being of use or service; serving some purpose; serviceable, advantageous, helpful, or of good effect: *a useful member of society.* **2.** of practical use, as for doing work; producing material results; supplying common needs: *the useful arts; useful work.* [USE + -FUL] **—use′ful·ly,** *adv.* **—use′ful·ness,** *n.* **—Syn. 1, 2.** profitable, efficacious, beneficial. **—Ant. 1, 2.** useless.

use·less (yo͞os′lis), *adj.* **1.** of no use; not serving the purpose or any purpose; unavailing or futile: *It is useless to try to reason with him.* **2.** without useful qualities; of no practical good: *a useless person; a useless gadget.* [USE + -LESS] **—use′less·ly,** *adv.* **—use′less·ness,** *n.* **—Syn. 1.** fruitless, profitless, valueless, worthless, inutile. USELESS, FUTILE, INEFFECTUAL, VAIN refer to that which is unavailing. That is USELESS which is unavailing because of the circumstances of the case or some inherent defect: *It is useless to cry over spilt milk.* FUTILE suggests wasted effort and complete failure to attain a desired end: *All attempts were futile.* That is INEFFECTUAL which weakly applies energy in an ill-advised way and does not produce a desired effect: *an ineffectual effort.* That which is VAIN is fruitless or hopeless even after all possible effort: *It is vain to keep on hoping.* **2.** unserviceable, unusable. **—Ant. 1.** effective.

us·er (yo͞o′zər), *n.* **1.** one who or that which uses. **2.** *Law.* **a.** the right to the enjoyment of property. **b.** the exercise of a right to the enjoyment of property. [ME *usere.* See USE, -ER¹]

USES, United States Employment Service. Also, **U.S.E.S.**

U.S.G.A., United States Golf Association. Also, **USGA**

USHA, United States Housing Authority. Also, **U.S.H.A.**

u·shab·ti (yo͞o shab′tē, o͞o-), *n., pl.* **-ti, -tis, -ti·u** (-tē o͞o′). shawabti.

Ush·ant (ush′ənt), *n.* an island off the NW coast of France: naval battles 1778, 1794. 1940 (1962); 4½ mi. long. French, **Ouessant.**

U-shaped (yo͞o′shāpt′), *adj.* being in the form of a U.

Ush·as (o͞osh′əs, o͞o shäs′), *n.* Dawn, a Vedic deity, daughter of Sky and sister of Night. [< Skt]

ush·er (ush′ər), *n.* **1.** one who escorts persons to seats in a church, theater, etc. **2.** an officer or servant having charge of an entrance door; a doorkeeper. **3.** an officer whose business it is to introduce strangers or to walk before a person of rank. **4.** *Brit. Archaic.* a subordinate teacher or an assistant in a school. **—v.t. 5.** to act as an usher to; lead, introduce, or show (usually fol. by *in, into, out,* or *to*): *He ushered the ladies to their seats.* **6.** to attend or bring at the coming or beginning: *They ushered in the new theater season.* **—v.i. 7.** to act as an usher: *He ushered at the banquet.* [ME *uscher* < AF *usser,* OF *(h)uissier* doorman, officer of justice < VL **ustiārius,* equiv. to L *ōsti(um)* door + *-ārius* -ER¹] **—ush′er·ship′,** *n.*

Ush·er (ush′ər), *n.* **James.** See **Ussher, James.**

ush·er·ette (ush′ə ret′), *n.* a female who escorts persons to seats in a church, theater, etc.

USIA, United States Information Agency. Also, **U.S.I.A.**

USIS, United States Information Service. Also, **U.S.I.S.**

Usk (usk), *n.* a river flowing S and SE from SE Wales through SW England into the Severn estuary. 60 mi. long.

Üs·küb (ys kyp′), *n.* Turkish name of **Skoplje.** Also, **Us·küp′.**

Üs·kü·dar (ys ky′där), *n.* Turkish name of **Scutari.**

U.S.L.T.A., United States Lawn Tennis Association. Also, **USLTA**

U.S.M., **1.** United States Mail. **2.** United States Marines. **3.** United States Mint. Also, **USM**

U.S.M.A., United States Military Academy. Also, **USMA**

U.S.M.C., **1.** United States Marine Corps. **2.** United States Maritime Commission. Also, **USMC**

USN, United States Navy. Also, **U.S.N.**

U.S.N.A., **1.** United States National Army. **2.** United States Naval Academy. Also, **USNA**

U.S.N.G., United States National Guard. Also, **USNG**

U.S.N.R., United States Naval Reserve. Also, **USNR**

U.S.N.R.F., United States Naval Reserve Force. Also, **USNRF**

USO, United Service Organizations. Also, **U.S.O.**

U.S.P., United States Pharmacopeia. Also, **U.S. Pharm.**

Us·pal·la′ta Pass′ (o͞os′pä yä′tə; *Sp.* o͞os′pä yä′tä), a mountain pass in S South America, in the Andes, connecting Mendoza, Argentina, and Santiago, Chile. ab. 12,600 ft. high. Also called **La Cumbre.**

U.S.P.H.S., United States Public Health Service. Also, **USPHS**

U.S.P.O., United States Post Office. Also, **USPO**

us·que ad a·ras (o͞os′kwe äd ä′räs; *Eng.* us′kwē ad ā′ras), *Latin.* as far as the altars; accepting everything but what is contrary to religion. Cf. **amicus usque ad aras.**

us·que·baugh (us′kwi bô′, -bä′), *n.* (in Scotland and Ireland) whiskey. [< Ir and ScotGael: lit., water of life]

U.S.R., United States Reserves. Also, **USR**

U.S.R.C., United States Reserve Corps. Also, **USRC**

U.S.S., **1.** United States Senate. **2.** United States Service. **3.** United States Ship. **4.** United States Steamer. **5.** United States Steamship. Also, **USS**

U.S.S.B., United States Shipping Board. Also, **USSB**

U.S.S.Ct., United States Supreme Court.

Ussh·er (ush′ər), *n.* **James,** 1581–1656, Irish prelate and scholar. Also, **Usher.**

U.S.S.R., Union of Soviet Socialist Republics. Also, **USSR**

U.S.S.S., United States Steamship. Also, **USSS**

Us·su·ri (o͞o so͞o′rē), *n.* a river in E Asia, forming part of the boundary between E Manchuria and the SE Soviet Union in Asia, flowing N to the Amur River. 500 mi. long.

Us·su·riisk (o͞o′so͞o rēsk′; *Russ.* o͞o so͞o ryēsk′), *n.* a city in the SE Russian Federation in Asia. 147,000. Formerly, **Voroshilov.**

USTC, United States Tariff Commission.

Ust-Ka·me·no·gorsk (o͞ost′kä men′o gôrsk′), *n.* a city in E Kazakstan, in the W Soviet Union in Asia, on the Irtish River. 198,000 (est. 1964).

us·tu·late (us′chə lit, -lāt′), *adj.* colored or blackened as if scorched. [< L *ustulāt(us)* scorched, burned (ptp. of *ustulāre*), equiv. to *ust(us)* burned (ptp. of *ūrere*) + *-ul-* dim. suffix + *-ātus* -ATE¹]

us·tu·la·tion (us′chə lā′shən), *n.* **1.** the act of scorching or burning. **2.** *Pharm.* the roasting or drying of moist substances so as to prepare them for pulverizing. [< ML *ustulātiōn-* (s. of *ustulātiō*) a scorching, equiv. to L *ustulāt(us)* (see USTULATE) + *-iōn-* -ION]

usu., **1.** usual. **2.** usually.

u·su·al (yo͞o′zho͞o əl, -zhwəl), *adj.* **1.** habitual or customary: *his usual skill.* **2.** commonly met with or observed in experience; ordinary: *the usual January weather.* **3.** commonplace, everyday: *He says the usual things.* **4. as usual,** in the customary or usual manner: *As usual, he forgot her birthday.* **—n. 5.** that which is usual: *He could expect only the usual.* [ME < LL *ūsuāl(is),* equiv. to L *ūs(us)* (see USE) + *-ālis* -AL¹; cf. OF *usuel*] **—u′su·al·ly,** *adv.* **—u′su·al·ness,** *n.*
—Syn. 1. accustomed. USUAL, CUSTOMARY, HABITUAL refer to a settled and constant practice. USUAL indicates that which is to be expected by reason of previous experience, which shows it to occur more often than not: *There were the usual crowds at the celebration.* That which is CUSTOMARY is in accordance with prevailing usage or individual practice: *It is customary to finish up with a bonfire.* That which is HABITUAL has become settled or constant as the result of habit on the part of the individual: *The merchants wore habitual smiles throughout the season.* **2.** general, prevailing, prevalent, everyday, familiar, regular, expected, predictable. **—Ant. 1.** unexpected, extraordinary.

u·su·fruct (yo͞o′zo͞o frukt′, -so͞o-, yo͞oz′yo͞o-, yo͞os′-), *n.* *Roman and Civil Law.* the right of enjoying all the advantages derivable from the use of something which belongs to another, as far as is compatible with the substance of the thing not being destroyed or injured. [< LL *ūsūfrūct(us)* < L *ūsu(s)* (see USE) + *fructus* (see FRUIT)]

u·su·fruc·tu·ar·y (yo͞o′zo͞o fruk′cho͞o er′ē, -so͞o-, yo͞oz′yo͞o-, yo͞os′-), *adj., n., pl.* **-ar·ies.** *Roman and Civil Law.* **—adj. 1.** of, pertaining to, or of the nature of usufruct. **—n. 2.** a person who has a usufruct property. [< LL *ūsūfrūctuārius,* equiv. to *ūsūfrūct(us)* USUFRUCT + *-ārius* -ARY]

U·sum·bu·ra (o͞o′so͞om bo͝or′ə), *n.* a port in and the capital of Burundi, in the W part, on Lake Tanganyika. 47,036 (est. 1960).

u·su·rer (yo͞o′zhər ər), *n.* **1.** one who lends money and charges interest, esp. an exorbitant or unlawful rate; moneylender. **2.** *Obs.* one who lends money at interest. [ME < AF < ML *ūsūrār(ius),* equiv. to *ūsūri(a)* USURY + L *-ārius* -ARY]

u·su·ri·ous (yo͞o zho͝or′ē əs), *adj.* **1.** practicing usury; charging illegal or exorbitant rates of interest for the use of money: *a usurious moneylender.* **2.** constituting or characterized by usury: *usurious rates of interest; a usurious loan.* [USURY + -OUS] **—u·su′ri·ous·ly,** *adv.* **—u·su′ri·ous·ness,** *n.*

u·surp (yo͞o sûrp′, -zûrp′), *v.t.* **1.** to seize and hold (a position, office, power, etc.) by force or without legal right: *The pretender tried to usurp the throne.* **—v.i. 2.** to commit forcible or illegal seizure of an office, power, etc.; encroach. **3.** to use without authority or right; employ wrongfully: *The magazine usurped copyrighted material.* [ME < L *ūsūrp(āre)* (to) take possession through use, equiv. to *ūsū* (abl. of *ūsus* use) + *rapere* to seize] **—u·surp′a·tive,** *adj.* **—u·surp′er,** *n.* **—u·surp′ing·ly,** *adv.*

u·sur·pa·tion (yo͞o′sər pā′shən, -zər-), *n.* **1.** an act of usurping; wrongful or illegal encroachment, infringement, or seizure. **2.** illegal seizure and occupation of a throne. [ME < L *ūsūrpātiōn-* (s. of *ūsūrpātiō*), equiv. to *ūsūrpāt(us)* (ptp. of *ūsūrpāre* (to) USURP) + *-iōn-* -ION] **—u·sur·pa·tive** (yo͞o sûr′pə tiv), **u·sur·pa·to·ry** (yo͞o sûr′pə tôr′ē, -tōr′ē), *adj.*

u·su·ry (yo͞o′zhə rē), *n., pl.* **-ries. 1.** an exorbitant amount or rate of interest, esp. in excess of the legal rate. **2.** the lending or practice of lending money at an exorbitant rate of interest. **3.** *Obs.* interest paid for the use of money. [ME *usurie* < ML *ūsūria* (cf. L *ūsūra*), equiv. to < L *ūs(us)* (see USE) + *-ur-* -URE + *-ia* -Y³]

U.S.V., United States Volunteers. Also, **USV**

usw, **1.** *German.* See **und so weiter. 2.** (*usually cap.*) ultrashort wave. Also, **u.s.w.**

us·ward (us′wərd), *adv.* *Archaic.* toward us. [ME *(to) usward.* See US, -WARD]

ut (ut, o͞ot), *n.* *Music.* the syllable once generally used for the first tone or keynote of a scale and sometimes for the tone C: now commonly superseded by *do.* Cf. **sol-fa.** [see GAMUT]

Ut., Utah.

u.t., universal time.

u·ta (yo͞o′tə), *n.* any of several iguanid lizards of the genus *Uta,* of the western U.S. and northern Mexico. [< NL, named after UTE]

U·tah (yo͞o′tô, yo͞o′tä), *n.* a State in the W United States. 890,627 (1960); 84,916 sq. mi. *Cap.:* Salt Lake City. *Abbr.:* Ut. **—U′tah·an,** *adj., n.*

U·ta·ma·ro (o͞o′tä mä′rō), *n.* **Ki·ta·ga·wa** (kē′tä gä′wä), 1753–1806, Japanese painter, draftsman, and designer of prints.

ut. dict., (in prescriptions) as directed. [< L *ut dictum*]

Ute (yo͞ot, yo͞o′tē), *n., pl.* **Utes,** (*esp. collectively*) **Ute. 1.** a member of an important tribe of the Shoshonean stock of North American Indians, now on reservations in Utah and Colorado. **2.** their language, of the Uto-Aztecan family of languages.

utend., (in prescriptions) to be used. [< L *ūtendum*]

u·ten·sil (yo͞o ten′səl), *n.* **1.** any of the instruments or vessels commonly used in a kitchen, dairy, etc.: *baking utensils.* **2.** any instrument, vessel, or tool serving a useful purpose: *smoking utensils; fishing utensils; farming utensils.* [ME: household articles < MF *utensile* < ML *ūtēnsile* neut. of *ūtēnsilis* useful, deriv. of *ūt(ī)* (to) use] **—Syn. 2.** See **tool.**

uter-, var. of **utero-** before a vowel: *uteralgia.*

u·ter·al·gia (yo͞o′tə ral′jə), *n.* *Med.* pain in or near the womb. [UTER- + -ALGIA]

u·ter·ine (yo͞o′tər in, -tə rīn′), *adj.* **1.** of or pertaining to the uterus or womb. **2.** related through having had the same mother. [late ME < LL *uterīn(us)* of, pertaining to the uterus. See UTER-, -INE¹]

utero-, a combining form of **uterus:** *uterovaginal.* Also, *esp. before a vowel,* **uter-.**

u·ter·us (yo͞o′tər əs), *n., pl.* **u·ter·i** (yo͞o′tə rī′). *Anat., Zool.* the portion of the oviduct in which the fertilized ovum implants itself and develops or rests during prenatal development; the womb of certain mammals. [< L: the womb, matrix; akin to Gk *ustéra*]

Ut·gard (o͞ot′gärd), *n.* *Scand. Myth.* a part of Jotunheim ruled over by Skrymir: sometimes identified with all Jotunheim.

Ut·gard-Lo·ki (o͞ot′gärd lō′kē), *n.* Skrymir.

U Thant (o͞o′ thont′, tont′). See **Thant, U.**

U·ther (yo͞o′thər), *n.* *Arthurian Romance.* king of Britain and father of Arthur. Also called **U′ther Pen·drag′on.**

u·ti (yo͞o′tī), *v.t.* (in prescriptions) to make use of. [< L *ūtī*]

U·ti·ca (yo͞o′ti kə), *n.* **1.** a city in central New York, on the Mohawk River. 100,410 (1960). **2.** an ancient city on the N coast of Africa, NW of Carthage.

u·tile (yo͞o′til), *adj.* *Obs.* useful. [< OF < L *ūtil(is),* equiv. to *ūt(ī)* (to) use + *-ilis* -ILE]

u·ti·le dul·ci (o͞o′ti le do͞ol′kē; *Eng.* yo͞ot′ᵊlē dul′sī), *Latin.* the useful with the pleasant.

u·til·i·dor (yo͞o til′i dôr′), *n.* *Canadian.* an above-ground, insulated network of pipes and cables, used to bring water and electricity to communities situated in areas of permafrost. [UTILI(TY) + *-dor,* as in *thermidor*]

u·ti·lise (yo͞ot′ᵊlīz′), *v.t.,* **-lised, -lis·ing.** *Chiefly Brit.* utilize. **—u′ti·lis′a·ble,** *adj.* **—u′ti·li·sa′tion,** *n.* **—u′ti·lis′er,** *n.*

u·til·i·tar·i·an (yo͞o til′i târ′ē ən), *adj.* **1.** pertaining to or consisting in utility. **2.** having regard to utility or usefulness rather than beauty, ornamentation, etc. **3.** of, pertaining to, or adhering to the doctrine of utilitarianism. **—n. 4.** an adherent of utilitarianism. [UTILIT(Y) + -ARIAN]

u·til·i·tar·i·an·ism (yo͞o til′i târ′ē ə niz′əm), *n.* the ethical doctrine that virtue is based on utility, and that conduct should be directed toward promoting the greatest happiness of the greatest number of persons. [UTILITARIAN + -ISM]

u·til·i·ty (yo͞o til′i tē), *n., pl.* **-ties,** *adj.* —*n.* **1.** state or quality of being useful; usefulness: *This chemical has no utility as an agricultural fertilizer.* **2.** something useful; a useful thing. **3.** a public service, as a streetcar or railroad line, a telephone or electric-light system, or the like. Cf. **public utility** (def. 1). **4.** Often, **utilities.** a useful or advantageous factor or feature: *the relative utilities of a religious or a secular education.* **5.** *Econ.* the capacity of a commodity or a service to satisfy some human want. **6.** the principle and end of utilitarian ethics; well-being or happiness; that which is conducive to the happiness and well-being of the greatest number. **7. utilities,** stocks or bonds of public utilities. —*adj.* **8.** (of domestic animals) raised or kept to constitute an economically profitable product rather than for show or as pets: *utility breeds; utility livestock.* **9.** having or made for a number of useful or practical purposes rather than a single, specialized one: *a utility knife.* **10.** designed chiefly for use or service rather than beauty, high quality, or the like: *a utility vehicle; utility furniture.* [ME *utilite* < OF *utelite* < L *ūtilitāt-* (s. of *ūtilitās*), equiv. to *ūtil(is)* useful (see UTILE) + *-itāt-* -ITY]

util′ity man′, **1.** a worker expected to serve in any capacity when called on. **2.** an actor of miscellaneous small parts. **3.** *Baseball.* a player who is not a regular and whose value lies in his ability to play several positions.

util′ity room′, a room, esp. in a house, reserved for the furnace, washing machine, and other appliances needed for the upkeep of the establishment.

util′ity sash′. See **barn sash.**

u·ti·lize (yo͞ot′ᵊlīz′), *v.t.,* **-lized, -liz·ing.** to put to use; turn to profitable account: *to utilize a stream for driving machinery.* Also, *esp. Brit.,* **utilise.** [< F *utilis(er),* equiv. to *utile* useful (see UTILE) + *-iser* -IZE] —**u′ti·liz′a·ble,** *adj.* —**u′ti·li·za′tion,** *n.* —**u′ti·liz′er,** *n.*
—**Syn.** See **use.**

ut in·fra (o͝ot in′frä; *Eng.* ut in′frə), *Latin.* as (stated or shown) below: used in a book, text, etc.

u·ti pos·si·de·tis (yo͞o′tī pos′i dē′tis), *Internat. Law.* the principle which vests in either of the belligerents at the end of a war all territory actually occupied and controlled by them. [< L: lit., as you possess, as you hold]

ut·most (ut′mōst′ *or, esp. Brit.,* -məst), *adj.* **1.** of the greatest or highest degree, quantity, or the like; greatest: *of the utmost importance.* **2.** being at the farthest point or extremity; farthest: *the utmost reef of the island.* —*n.* **3.** Also, **uttermost.** the greatest degree or amount: *the utmost that can be said; The hotel provides the utmost in comfort.* **4.** the most or best of one's abilities, powers, etc.: *He employed his utmost to benefit mankind.* **5.** the extreme limit or extent: *His patience was taxed to the utmost.* [ME *utmest,* OE *ūtemest.* See OUT, -MOST]

U·to-Az·tec·an (yo͞o′tō az′tek ən), *n.* **1.** an American Indian linguistic stock, widespread from Idaho to the Isthmus of Tehuantepec, and from the Rocky Mountains to the Pacific: this stock includes Hopi, Ute, Shoshone, Comanche, Nahuatl, Pima, and other languages. —*adj.* **2.** of or pertaining to Uto-Aztecan.

U·to·pi·a (yo͞o tō′pē ə), *n.* **1.** an imaginary island described in Sir Thomas More's *Utopia* (1516) as enjoying the utmost perfection in law, politics, etc. **2.** (*usually l.c.*) a place or state of ideal perfection. **3.** (*usually l.c.*) any visionary system of political or social perfection. **4.** an area in the northern hemisphere of Mars. [< NL < Gk *ou* not + *tóp(os)* a place + *-ia* n. suffix]

U·to·pi·an (yo͞o tō′pē ən), *adj.* **1.** of, pertaining to, or resembling Utopia. **2.** (*usually l.c.*) founded upon or involving imaginary or ideal perfection. **3.** (*usually l.c.*) given to dreams or schemes of such perfection. —*n.* **4.** an inhabitant of Utopia. **5.** (*usually l.c.*) an ardent but unpractical political or social reformer; visionary; idealist. [< NL *Utopiān(us).* See UTOPIA, -AN]

u·to·pi·an·ism (yo͞o tō′pē ə niz′əm), *n.* (*sometimes cap.*) the views or habit of mind of a utopian; impracticable schemes of political or social reform. [UTOPIAN + -ISM]

uto′pian so′cialism, (*sometimes cap.*) an economic system based on the premise that if capital voluntarily surrendered its ownership of the means of production to the state or the workers, unemployment and poverty would be abolished. Cf. **socialism.**

U·tra·quist (yo͞o′trə kwist), *n.* Calixtine. [< NL *Utraquist(a),* equiv. to L *utraque* (abl. sing. fem. of *uterque* each, both, equiv. to *uter* either + *-que* and) + *-ista* -IST] —**U′tra·quism,** *n.*

U·trecht (yo͞o′trekt; *Du.* ʏ′trekнt), *n.* **1.** a city in the central Netherlands: treaties ending the War of the Spanish Succession signed here 1714. 261,043 (1962). **2.** a province in the central Netherlands. 677,000 (est. 1960); 511 sq. mi.

u·tri·cle (yo͞o′tri kəl), *n.* **1.** a small sac or baglike body, as an air-filled cavity in a seaweed. **2.** *Bot.* a thin bladderlike pericarp or seed vessel. **3.** *Anat.* the larger of two sacs in the membranous labyrinth of the internal ear. Cf. **saccule** (def. 1). [< L *utricul(us),* dim. of *uter* bag; see -CLE]

u·tric·u·lar (yo͞o trik′yə lər), *adj.* **1.** pertaining to or of the nature of a utricle; baglike. **2.** having a utricle or utricles. [< L *utricul(us)* UTRICLE + -AR[1]]

u·tric·u·late (yo͞o trik′yə lit, -lāt′), *adj. Archaic.* having a utricle; utricular; baglike. [UTRICUL(AR) + -ATE[1]]

u·tric·u·li·tis (yo͞o trik′yə lī′tis), *n. Pathol.* inflammation of the utricle. [< NL; see UTRICLE, -ITIS]

u·tric·u·lus (yo͞o trik′yə ləs), *n., pl.* **-li** (-lī′). utricle.

U·tril·lo (yo͞o tril′ō, o͞o-; *Fr.* ʏ trē yō′), *n.* **Mau·rice** (mô rēs′; *Fr.* mō ʀēs′), 1883–1955, French painter (son of Suzanne Valadon).

U·tsu·no·mi·ya (o͞o tso͞o′nô mē′yä), *n.* a city on central Honshu, in central Japan. 255,748 (1964).

ut su·pra (*Lat.* o͝ot so͞o′prä; *Eng.* ut so͞o′prə). See **u.s.** (def. 2).

Ut·tar Pra·desh (o͝ot′ər prə dāsh′), a state in N India: a former province of British India. 73,746,401 (1961); 113,409 sq. mi. *Cap.:* Lucknow. Formerly, **United Provinces.** Former official name, **United Provinces of Agra and Oudh.**

ut·ter[1] (ut′ər), *v.t.* **1.** to give audible expression to; speak or pronounce: *unable to utter her feelings; The words were uttered in my hearing.* **2.** to give forth (cries, notes, etc.) with the voice: *to utter a sigh.* **3.** *Phonet.* to produce (speech sounds, speechlike sounds, syllables, words, etc.) audibly, with or without reference to formal language. **4.** to express (oneself or itself), esp. in words: *Each writer must utter himself according to his own understanding of life.* **5.** to give forth (a sound) otherwise than with the voice: *The engine uttered a shriek.* **6.** to express by written or printed words. **7.** to make publicly known; publish: *to utter a libel.* **8.** to put into circulation, as coins, notes, etc., and esp. counterfeit money, forged checks, etc. **9.** *Archaic.* to expel; emit. **10.** *Obs.* to publish, as a book. **11.** *Obs.* to sell. —*v.i.* **12.** to employ the faculty of speech; use the voice to talk, make sounds, etc.: *His piety prevented him from uttering on religion.* **13.** to sustain utterance; undergo speaking: *Those ideas are so dishonest they will not utter.* [ME *outre* (see OUT, -ER[6]); c. G *äussern* to declare] —**ut′ter·a·ble,** *adj.* —**ut′ter·er,** *n.* —**ut′ter·less,** *adj.*

ut·ter[2] (ut′ər), *adj.* **1.** complete; total; absolute: *her utter abandonment to grief.* **2.** unconditional; unqualified: *an utter denial.* **3.** extremely strange or unusual; singularly queer: *Her ideas are simply utter.* [ME; OE *uttra, ūtera*] —**ut′ter·ness,** *n.*
—**Syn. 1.** See **absolute.**

ut·ter·ance[1] (ut′ər əns), *n.* **1.** an act of uttering; vocal expression. **2.** manner of speaking; power of speaking: *His very utterance was spellbinding.* **3.** something uttered; a word or words uttered; a cry, animal's call, or the like. **4.** *Ling.* any speech sequence consisting of one or more words and preceded and followed by silence: it may be coextensive with a sentence. **5.** *Obs.* a public sale of goods. [ME; see UTTER[1], -ANCE]

ut·ter·ance[2] (ut′ər əns), *n. Archaic.* the utmost extremity, esp. death. [ME < OF *outrance, oultrance,* equiv. to *oultr(er)* (to) pass beyond (< L *ultrā* beyond) + *-ance* -ANCE]

ut′ter bar′. See **outer bar.**

ut′ter bar′rister. See **outer barrister.**

ut·ter·ing (ut′ər ing), *n. Crim. Law.* the crime of knowingly tendering or showing a forged instrument or counterfeit coin to another with intent to defraud. [UTTER[1] + -ING[1]]

ut·ter·ly (ut′ər lē), *adv.* in an utter manner; completely; absolutely. [ME; see UTTER[2], -LY]

ut·ter·most (ut′ər mōst′ *or, esp. Brit.,* -məst), *adj.* **1.** utmost; most remote or outermost: *the uttermost stars of the galaxy.* **2.** of the greatest or highest degree, quantity, etc.; greatest: *The country's art has reached uttermost perfection.* —*n.* **3.** utmost. [ME; see UTTER[2], -MOST]

U·tu (o͞o′to͞o), *n.* the Sumerian sun god: the counterpart of the Akkadian Shamash.

U.T.W.A., United Textile Workers of America. Also, **UTWA**

UUM, underwater-to air-to underwater missile.

U.V., ultraviolet. Also, **UV**

u·va·la (o͞o′və lə), *n. Geol.* a large sinkhole formed by the coalescence of adjacent sinkholes. [< Serbo-Croatian]

u·va·rov·ite (o͞o vär′ə vīt′, yo͞o-), *n.* a variety of garnet colored emerald-green by the presence of chromium. [< G, named after Count S. S. *Uvarov* (1785–1855), president of St. Petersburg Academy; see -ITE[1]]

u·ve·a (yo͞o′vē ə), *n. Anat.* the vascular tunic of the eye, comprising the iris, choroid coat, and ciliary body. [< ML *ūvea,* var. of L *ūva* the fruit of the vine, a grape] —**u′ve·al, u′ve·ous,** *adj.*

Uve·dale (yo͞od′ᵊl, yo͞ov′dāl), *n.* **Nicholas.** See **Udall.**

u·ve·i·tis (yo͞o′vē ī′tis), *n. Pathol.* inflammation of the uvea. [< NL; see UVEA, -ITIS] —**u·ve·it·ic** (yo͞o′vē it′ik), *adj.*

u·vu·la (yo͞o′vyə lə), *n., pl.* **-las, -lae** (-lē′). *Anat.* the small, fleshy, conical body projecting downward from the middle of the soft palate. See diag. under **mouth.** [< ML *ūvula,* equiv. to L *ūv(a)* grape + *-ula* -ULE]

u·vu·lar (yo͞o′vyə lər), *adj.* **1.** of or pertaining to the uvula. **2.** *Phonet.* articulated with the back of the tongue held close to or touching the uvula, as in the *r*-sound of Parisian French. —*n.* **3.** *Phonet.* a uvular sound. [< NL *ūvulār(is).* See UVULA, -AR[1]] —**u′vu·lar·ly,** *adv.*

u·vu·lat·o·my (yo͞o′vyə lat′ə mē), *n., pl.* **-mies.** *Surg.* uvulotomy.

u·vu·lec·to·my (yo͞o′vyə lek′tə mē), *n., pl.* **-mies.** *Surg.* excision of the uvula. Also called **kionectomy, staphylotomy.** [UVUL(A) + -ECTOMY]

u·vu·li·tis (yo͞o′vyə lī′tis), *n. Pathol.* inflammation of the uvula. [UVUL(A) + -ITIS]

u·vu·lot·o·my (yo͞o′vyə lot′ə mē), *n., pl.* **-mies.** *Surg.* incision or excision of part or all of the uvula. Also, **uvulatomy.** Also called **kionotomy, kiotomy, staphylotomy.** [UVUL(A) + -O- + -TOMY]

U/w, underwriter. Also, **u/w**

ux., wife. [< L *uxor*]

Ux·bridge (uks′brij′), *n.* a town in S Massachusetts. 3377 (1960).

Ux·mal (o͞osн mäl′), *n.* an ancient ruined city in SE Mexico, in Yucatán: a center of later Mayan civilization.

ux·o·ri·al (uk sôr′ē əl, -sōr′-, ug zôr′-, -zōr′-), *adj.* of or pertaining to a wife; typical of or befitting a wife. [< L *ūxor* wife + -IAL] —**ux·o′ri·al·ly,** *adv.*

ux·o·ri·cide (uk sôr′i sīd′, -sōr′-, ug zôr′-, -zōr′-), *n.* **1.** the act of murdering one's wife. **2.** one who murders his wife. [< L *ūxor* wife + -I- + -CIDE] —**ux·o′ri·cid′al,** *adj.*

ux·o·ri·lo·cal (uk sôr′ə lō′kəl, -sōr′-, ug zôr′-, -zōr′-), *adj.* matrilocal. [< L *ūxor* wife + -I- + LOCAL]

ux·o·ri·ous (uk sôr′ē əs, -sōr′-, ug zôr′-, -zōr′-), *adj.* doting upon, foolishly fond of, or affectionately over-submissive toward one's wife. [< L *ūxōrius,* equiv. to *ūxor* wife + *-ius* -IOUS] —**ux·o′ri·ous·ly,** *adv.* —**ux·o′ri·ous·ness,** *n.*

Uz·beg (o͝oz′beg, uz′-), *n., pl.* **-begs,** (*esp. collectively*) **-beg.** Uzbek.

Uz·bek (o͝oz′bek, uz′-), *n., pl.* **-beks,** (*esp. collectively*) **-bek. 1.** a member of a town-dwelling, Turkic people of Turkestan and Uzbekistan. **2.** the Turkic language of the Uzbeks. Also, **Usbeg, Usbek, Uzbeg.**

Uz·bek·i·stan (o͝oz bek′ə stan′, -stän′, uz-), *n.* a republic in S central Asia. 19,906,000; 172,741 sq. mi. *Cap.:* Tashkent. Formerly, **Uz′bek So′viet So′cialist Re·pub′lic.**

Uz·zi·ah (ə zī′ə), *n.* the son and successor of Amaziah as king of Judah, reigned 783?–742? B.C. II Kings 15:13, 30–34. Also, **Azariah.**

V

V, v (vē), *n., pl.* **V's** or **Vs, v's** or **vs. 1.** the 22nd letter of the English alphabet, a consonant. **2.** any spoken sound represented by the letter *V* or *v*, as in *victor, flivver, shove,* etc. **3.** something having the form of a V. **4.** a written or printed representation of the letter *V* or *v*. **5.** a device, as a printer's type, for reproducing the letter *V* or *v*.

V, 1. vagabond. **2.** *Math.* vector. **3.** velocity. **4.** volt.

V, 1. the 22nd in order or in a series, or, when *I* is omitted, the 21st. **2.** (when *i* is eliminated in a series) the 21st in order or in a series. **3.** (*sometimes l.c.*) the Roman numeral for five. Cf. **Roman numerals. 4.** *Chem.* vanadium. **5.** (esp. during World War II) the symbol of allied victory.

v, 1. velocity. **2.** vicinal. **3.** volt.

V., 1. Valve. **2.** Venerable. **3.** Verb. **4.** Verse. **5.** Version. **6.** Versus. **7.** Very. **8.** Vicar. **9.** Vice. **10.** *Vide.* **11.** Village. **12.** Violin. **13.** Virgin. **14.** Viscount. **15.** Vision. **16.** Visual acuity. **17.** Vocative. **18.** Volume.

v., 1. valve. **2.** (in personal names) van. **3.** vector. **4.** vein. **5.** ventral. **6.** verb. **7.** verse. **8.** version. **9.** verso. **10.** versus. **11.** very. **12.** vicar. **13.** vice. **14.** *vide.* **15.** village. **16.** violin. **17.** vision. **18.** vocative. **19.** voice. **20.** volt. **21.** voltage. **22.** volume. **23.** (in personal names) von.

V-1, a robot bomb developed by the Germans in World War II and launched from bases on the ground, chiefly against England. Also, **V-one.**

V-2, a liquid-fueled rocket used as a ballistic missile by the Germans, mainly against London, late in World War II. Also, **V-two.**

V-8. See **V-eight.**

VA, 1. See **Veterans Administration. 2.** Also, **va** volt-ampere.

Va., Virginia.

V.A., 1. Veterans Administration. **2.** Vicar Apostolic. **3.** Vice-Admiral. **4.** (Order of) Victoria and Albert.

v.a., 1. verb active. **2.** verbal adjective.

va·ad (vä′äd, vä äd′), *n., pl.* **va·a·dim** (vä ä dēm′, vä ä′dim). *Hebrew.* a Jewish council charged with the function of furnishing advice on or keeping control over certain community affairs.

Vaal (väl), *n.* a river in S Africa, in the Republic of South Africa, flowing SW from the Transvaal to the Orange River. 700 mi. long.

Vaa·sa (vä′sä), *n.* a seaport in W Finland, on the Gulf of Bothnia. 43,533 (est. 1965).

va·can·cy (vā′kən sē), *n., pl.* **-cies. 1.** state of being vacant; emptiness. **2.** a vacant, empty, or unoccupied place, as untenanted lodgings, office space, etc.: *This building still has several vacancies.* **3.** a gap; opening; breach. **4.** an unoccupied position or office: *to fill a vacancy in the Supreme Court by an appointment.* **5.** lack of thought or intelligence; vacuity: *His face wore a look of utter vacancy.* **6.** *Crystall.* an imperfection in a crystal caused by the presence of an unoccupied lattice position. Cf. **interstitial** (def. 3). **7.** *Archaic.* absence of activity; idleness. [< LL *vacantia.* See VACANT, -ANCY]

va·cant (vā′kənt), *adj.* **1.** having no contents; empty; void: *a vacant niche.* **2.** devoid or destitute (often fol. by *of*): *He was vacant of human sympathy.* **3.** having no occupant; unoccupied: *six vacant chairs; no vacant seats on this train.* **4.** (in real estate law) having no tenant and devoid of furniture, fixtures, etc. (distinguished from *unoccupied*): *a vacant house.* **5.** not in use: *a vacant room.* **6.** free from work, business, activity, etc.: *vacant hours.* **7.** characterized by or proceeding from absence of occupation: *a vacant life.* **8.** devoid of thought or reflection: *a vacant mind.* **9.** characterized by, showing, or proceeding from lack of thought or intelligence: *a vacant answer to a query; a vacant expression on a face.* **10.** not occupied by an incumbent, official, or the like, as a benefice, office, etc. **11.** *Law.* **a.** idle or unutilized; open to any claimant, as land. **b.** without an incumbent; having no heir or claimant; abandoned: *a vacant estate.* [ME < L *vacant-* (s. of *vacāns,* prp. of *vacāre* to be empty); see -ANT] —**va′cant·ly,** *adv.* —**va′cant·ness,** *n.*
—**Syn. 1, 3.** See EMPTY. **9.** blank, vacuous, inane.

va·cate (vā′kāt), *v.,* **-cat·ed, -cat·ing.** —*v.t.* **1.** to cause to be empty or unoccupied; make vacant: *to vacate one's mind of worries.* **2.** to give up possession or occupancy of: *to vacate an apartment.* **3.** to give up or relinquish (an office, position, etc.): *to vacate the presidency of a firm.* **4.** to render inoperative; deprive of validity; void; annul: *to vacate a legal judgment.* —*v.i.* **5.** to withdraw from occupancy; surrender possession: *We will have to vacate when our lease expires.* **6.** to give up or leave a position, office, etc. **7.** *Informal.* to leave; go away. [< L *vacāt(us)* emptied, ptp. of *vacāre* to be empty; see -ATE[1]] —**va′cat·a·ble,** *adj.*

va·ca·tion (vā kā′shən, və-), *n.* **1.** a period of suspension of work, study, or other activity, usually used for rest, recreation, or travel; recess or holiday (often prec. by *on*): *School children are on vacation now.* **2.** a part of the year, regularly set aside, when normal activities of law courts, legislatures, etc., are suspended. **3.** freedom or release from duty, business, or activity. **4.** an act or instance of vacating. —*v.i.* **5.** to take or have a vacation: *Many Americans vacation in the Caribbean.* [< L *vacātiōn-* (s. of *vacātiō* freedom from something; see VACATE, -ION); r. ME *vacacioun* < AF] —**va·ca′tion·less,** *adj.*

Vacation Bible School, a religious school conducted by some churches during the summer for students on vacation.

va·ca·tion·ist (vā kā′shə nist, və-), *n.* a person who is taking a vacation or holiday. Also, **va·ca′tion·er.** [VACATION + -IST]

va·ca·tion·land (vā kā′shən land′, və-), *n.* an area having recreational facilities, historic or picturesque sights, etc., that attract vacationists. [VACATION + LAND]

vac·ci·nal (vak′sə nəl), *adj.* of, pertaining to, or caused by vaccine or vaccination. [VACCIN(ATION) + -AL[1]; cf. F *vaccinal*]

vac·ci·nate (vak′sə nāt′), *v.,* **-nat·ed, -nat·ing.** *Med.* —*v.t.* **1.** to inoculate with the vaccine of cowpox so as to render the subject immune to smallpox. **2.** to inoculate with the modified virus of any of various other diseases, as a preventive measure. —*v.i.* **3.** to perform or practice vaccination. [back formation from VACCINATION]

vac·ci·na·tion (vak′sə nā′shən), *n. Med.* act or practice of vaccinating; inoculation with vaccine. [VACCINE (adj.) + -ATION]

vac·ci·na·tion·ist (vak′sə nā′shə nist), *n. Med.* an advocate of vaccination. [VACCINATION + -IST]

vac·ci·na·tor (vak′sə nā′tər), *n. Med.* **1.** one who vaccinates. **2.** an instrument used in vaccination. [VACCINATE + -OR[2]]

vac·cine (vak sēn′, vak′sēn, -sin), *n.* **1.** the virus of cowpox, used in vaccination, obtained from the vesicles of a cow or person having the disease. **2.** the modified virus of any of various other diseases, used for preventive inoculation. —*adj.* **3.** of or pertaining to vaccination. **4.** of or pertaining to vaccinia. **5.** of, pertaining to, or derived from cows. [< medical L (*variolae*) *vaccīnae* cowpox (in title of Dr. E. Jenner's treatise of 1798), equiv. to *vacc(a)* cow + *-īnae,* fem. pl. of *-īnus* -INE[1]]

vaccine′ point, *Med.* a thin, pointed, vaccine-coated piece of bone or the like, for use in vaccinating.

vac·cin·i·a (vak sin′ē ə), *n.* cowpox. [< NL, equiv. to (*variolae*) *vaccīn(ae)* (see VACCINE) + *-ia* -IA] —**vac·cin′i·al,** *adj.*

vac·cin·i·a·ceous (vak sin′ē ā′shəs), *adj.* belonging to the *Vacciniaceae,* a family of plants usually included in the *Ericaceae,* comprising the blueberry, whortleberry, huckleberry, cranberry, etc. [< L *vaccīni(um)* blueberry + -ACEOUS]

vac·ci·ni·za·tion (vak′sə ni zā′shən), *n. Med.* a vaccination produced by a series of virus inoculations. [VACCINE + -IZATION]

Va·chel (vā′chəl), *n.* a boy's given name.

vac·il·lant (vas′ə lənt), *adj.* wavering; hesitant; indecisive; vacillating. [< L *vacillant-* (s. of *vacillāns*), prp. of *vacillāre* to VACILLATE, see -ANT]

vac·il·late (vas′ə lāt′), *v.i.,* **-lat·ed, -lat·ing. 1.** to sway unsteadily; waver; totter; stagger. **2.** to oscillate or fluctuate. **3.** to waver in mind or opinion; be indecisive, irresolute, or hesitant: *His tendency to vacillate makes him a poor executive.* [< L *vacillāt(us)* (ptp. of *vacillāre* to sway to and fro); see -ATE[1]] —**vac′il·la′tor,** *n.*
—**Syn. 1.** reel. **3.** hesitate. See **waver.**

vac·il·lat·ing (vas′ə lā′ting), *adj.* **1.** not resolute; wavering; indecisive; hesitating: *an ineffectual, vacillating person.* **2.** oscillating; swaying; fluctuating: *a vacillating indicator.* Also, **vacillant.** [VACILLATE + -ING[2]] —**vac′il·lat′ing·ly,** *adv.*

vac·il·la·tion (vas′ə lā′shən), *n.* **1.** act of vacillating; a state of indecision or irresolution. **2.** an instance of vacillating. **3.** unsteady movement; fluctuation. [< L *vacillātiōn-* (s. of *vacillātiō*) a swaying. See VACILLATE, -ION]

vac·il·la·to·ry (vas′ə lə tôr′ē, -tōr′ē), *adj.* marked by or displaying vacillation: *a vacillatory policy of action.* [VACILLATE + -ORY[1]]

vac·u·a (vak′yo͞o ə), *n.* a pl. of **vacuum.**

va·cu·i·ty (va kyo͞o′i tē), *n., pl.* **-ties. 1.** state of being vacuous or without contents; vacancy; emptiness: *the vacuity of the open sea.* **2.** an empty space; void: *a vacuity in the earth formed by erosion.* **3.** a vacuum. **4.** absence or lack of something specified: *a vacuity of feeling.* **5.** a time or state of dullness, lacking in mental or physical action or productivity: *the vacuity of our modern existence.* **6.** absence of thought or intelligence; inanity; blankness: *a pretty face, but a mind of undeniable vacuity.* **7.** something inane, senseless, or stupid: *a conversation full of vacuities.* [< L *vacuitās.* See VACUOUS, -ITY]

Va·cu·na (və kyo͞o′nə), *n.* an ancient Sabine goddess of agriculture eventually identified with Venus and Bellona.

vac·u·o·late (vak′yo͞o ə lit, -lāt′), *adj.* having a vacuole or vacuoles. Also, **vac′u·o·lat′ed.** [VACUOLE + -ATE[1]]

vac·u·o·la·tion (vak′yo͞o ə lā′shən), *n.* **1.** the formation of vacuoles. **2.** state of being vacuolate. **3.** a system of vacuoles. [VACUOLE + -ATION]

vac·u·ole (vak′yo͞o ōl′), *n. Biol.* **1.** a cavity within a cell, often containing a watery liquid or secretion. **2.** a minute cavity or vesicle in organic tissue. [< F < L *vacu(us)* empty + *-olum* dim. suffix] —**vac·u·o·lar** (vak′yo͞o ō′lər, vak′yo͞o ə-, vak′yə lər), *adj.*

vac·u·ous (vak′yo͞o əs), *adj.* **1.** without contents; empty: *the vacuous air.* **2.** lacking in ideas or intelligence: *a vacuous mind.* **3.** expressing or characterized by a lack of ideas or intelligence; inane; stupid: *a vacuous book.* **4.** purposeless; idle: *a vacuous way of life.* [< L *vacuus* empty; see -OUS] —**vac′u·ous·ly,** *adv.* —**vac′u·ous·ness,** *n.*

vac·u·um (vak′yo͞o əm, -yo͞om), *n., pl.* **vac·u·ums** for 1, 2, 4, 5; **vac·u·a** (vak′yo͞o ə) for 1, 2, 4; *adj.; v.* —*n.* **1.** a space entirely devoid of matter. **2.** an enclosed space from which matter, esp. air, has been partially removed so that the matter or gas remaining in the space exerts less pressure than the atmosphere (opposed to *plenum*). **3.** the state or degree of exhaustion in such an enclosed space. **4.** a space not filled or occupied; emptiness; void: *The loss of his beloved left a vacuum in his heart.* **5.** a vacuum cleaner or sweeper. —*adj.* **6.** of, pertaining to, employing, or producing a vacuum. **7.** (of a hollow container) partly exhausted of gas or air. **8.** pertaining to a device or process that makes use of a vacuum to accomplish a desired task. **9.** noting or pertaining to canning or packaging in which air is removed from the container to prevent deterioration of the contents. —*v.t.* **10.** to use a vacuum cleaner on; clean with a vacuum cleaner: *Remember to vacuum the rugs.* **11.** to treat with any vacuum device, as a vacuum drier. —*v.i.* **12.** to use a vacuum cleaner: *After you wash the windows, you can vacuum.* [< neut. of L *vacuus* empty]

vac′uum bot′tle, a bottle or flask having a vacuum liner which prevents the escape of heat from hot contents, usually liquids, or the entrance of heat into cold contents; thermos.

vac′uum clean′er, an electrical apparatus for cleaning carpets, floors, etc., by suction. Also called **vac′uum sweep′er.**

vac′uum cof′fee mak′er, a coffee pot with upper and lower glass units. The upper unit, containing ground coffee, has an open, tubular, filter-stoppered bottom fitting closely into the neck of the lower unit. In the lower unit, water is boiled and rises into the upper unit, where it remains until reduced pressure, resulting from the removal of heat, draws it down into the lower unit again as brewed coffee.

vac′uum con′crete, concrete from which excess moisture and air are sucked to quicken hardening and increase strength.

vac′uum distilla′tion, *Chem.* a process of distillation employing a vacuum that by lowering the pressure on a liquid allows volatilization at a lower temperature than normal.

vac′uum gauge′, a device for measuring pressures below atmospheric pressure in the receiver of an air pump, in steam condensers, and the like.

vac′uum induc′tion fur′nace, *Metall.* an electric furnace operating under a vacuum and utilizing the heat formed by induction.

vac′uum pump′, a pump or device by which a partial vacuum can be produced.

vac′uum tube′, **1.** a sealed glass bulb used in radio and electronics to amplify, detect, or rectify alternating currents, to generate electric oscillations, etc. In its typical form, as a triode, its elements are a heated cathode or filament that emits electrons, a metal plate at a positive potential serving as an electron-receiving plate, and a grid of wire mesh or coil between the cathode and plate which by its potential controls the flow of electrons from cathode to plate. **2.** a sealed glass tube containing a partial vacuum or a highly rarefied gas, in which may be observed the effects of a discharge of electricity passed through the tube between electrodes leading into it. Also called **electron tube;** *esp. Brit.,* **vac′uum valve′, valve;** *Brit.,* **thermionic valve.**

Va·da (vä′də), *n.* a boy's given name.

va·de me·cum (vā′dē mē′kəm, vä′-), *pl.* **va·de me·cums. 1.** something a person carries with him for frequent or regular use. **2.** a book for ready reference; manual; handbook. [< L: lit., go with me]

va·dose (vā′dōs), *adj.* *Geol.* found or located above the water table: *vadose water; vadose zone.* [< L *vadōs(us)* shallow, equiv. to *vad(um)* a shoal, ford + *-ōsus* -OSE[1]]

Vads·ö (väds′œ), *n.* a seaport in NE Norway. 2635 (1950).

Va·duz (vä′dōōts), *n.* a city in and the capital of Liechtenstein, on the upper Rhine. 3514 (est. 1961).

vae vic·tis (wī′ wik′tēs; *Eng.* vē′ vik′tis), *Latin.* woe to the vanquished.

Va·fio (vä′fyō), *n.* Vaphio.

vag·a·bond (vag′ə bond′), *adj.* **1.** wandering from place to place without any settled home; nomadic: *a vagabond tribe.* **2.** leading an unsettled or carefree life. **3.** disreputable; worthless; shiftless. **4.** of, pertaining to, or characteristic of a vagabond: *vagabond habits.* **5.** having an uncertain or irregular course or direction: *a vagabond voyage.* —*n.* **6.** a person, usually without a permanent home, who wanders from place to place; nomad. **7.** an idle wanderer without a permanent home or visible means of support; tramp; vagrant. **8.** a carefree, worthless, or irresponsible person; rogue. [late ME *vagabound* < LL *vagābund(us)*, equiv. to L *vagā(rī)* (to) wander + *-bundus* adj. suffix] —**vag′a·bond′ish,** *adj.*
—**Syn. 7.** hobo, loafer. See **vagrant. 8.** knave, idler.

vag·a·bond·age (vag′ə bon′dij), *n.* **1.** state or condition of being a vagabond; idle wandering. **2.** (collectively) vagabonds. Also called **vag′a·bond′ism.** [VAGABOND + -AGE]

va·gal (vā′gəl), *adj.* of or pertaining to a vagus nerve. [VAG(US) + -AL[1]]

va·gar·i·ous (və gâr′ē əs), *adj.* **1.** characterized by vagaries; erratic; capricious: *the vagarious course of their foreign policy.* **2.** roving; wandering: *vagarious artists.* [VAGARY + -OUS] —**va·gar′i·ous·ly,** *adv.*

va·gar·y (və gâr′ē, vā′gə rē), *n., pl.* **-gar·ies. 1.** an unpredictable, capricious, or erratic action, occurrence, course, or instance: *the vagaries of weather; the vagaries of the economic scene.* **2.** a whimsical, wild, or unusual idea or notion. [appar. < L *vagārī* to wander]
—**Syn. 1.** caprice, whim, quirk, crotchet.

vag·ile (vaj′əl *or, esp. Brit.,* -īl), *adj.* *Biol.* endowed with or having freedom of movement. [< L *vag(us)* wandering + -ILE]

vagin-, var. of **vagino-** before a vowel: *vaginectomy.*

va·gi·na (və jī′nə), *n., pl.* **-nas, -nae** (-nē). **1.** *Anat.* **a.** the passage leading from the uterus to the vulva in certain female mammals. Cf. **oviduct. b.** a sheathlike part or organ. **2.** *Bot.* the sheath formed by the basal part of certain leaves where they embrace the stem. [special use of L *vāgīna* sheath]

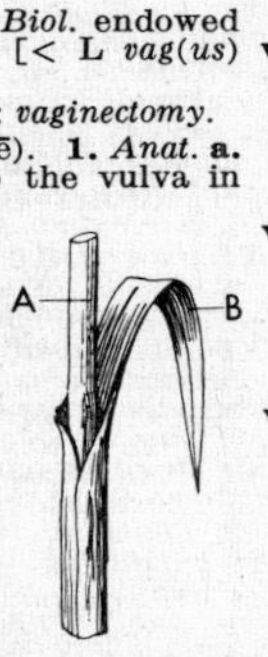

A, Vaginate culm; B, Vaginate leaf

vag·i·nal (vaj′ə nəl), *adj.* **1.** *Anat.* pertaining to the vagina. **2.** pertaining to or resembling a sheath. [VAGIN(A) + -AL[1]]

vag·i·na·lec·to·my (vaj′ə nəlek′tə mē), *n., pl.* **-mies.** *Surg.* vaginectomy (def. 2).

vag·i·nate (vaj′ə nit, -nāt′), *adj.* *Bot.* having a vagina or sheath; sheathed. [< NL *vāgīnāt(us).* See VAGINA, -ATE[1]]

vag·i·nec·to·my (vaj′ə nek′tə mē), *n., pl.* **-mies.** *Surg.* **1.** excision of part or all of the vagina. **2.** Also, **vaginalectomy.** excision of the serous membrane which surrounds the testes. [VAGIN(A) + -ECTOMY]

vag·i·nis·mus (vaj′ə niz′məs), *n.* *Pathol.* a painful spasm of the vagina. [< NL; see VAGINA, -ISM]

vag·i·ni·tis (vaj′ə nī′tis), *n.* *Pathol.* inflammation of the vagina. Also called **colpitis.** [VAGIN(A) + -ITIS]

vagino-, a combining form of **vagina:** *vaginotomy.* Also, *esp. before a vowel,* **vagin-.**

vag·i·no·my·co·sis (vaj′ə nō mī kō′sis), *n.* *Pathol.* a fungous infection of the vagina. [VAGINO- + MYCOSIS]

vag·i·not·o·my (vaj′ə not′ə mē), *n., pl.* **-mies.** *Surg.* colpotomy. [VAGINO- + -TOMY]

va·gran·cy (vā′grən sē), *n., pl.* **-cies. 1.** the state or condition of being a vagrant: *an arrest for vagrancy.* **2.** the conduct of a vagrant. **3.** mental wandering; reverie. [VAGR(ANT) + -ANCY]

va·grant (vā′grənt), *n.* **1.** a person who wanders about idly and has no permanent home or employment; vagabond; tramp. **2.** *Law.* an idle person without visible means of support, as a tramp or beggar. **3.** a person who wanders from place to place; wanderer; rover. —*adj.* **4.** wandering or roaming from place to place; nomadic. **5.** wandering idly without a permanent home or employment; living in vagabondage: *vagrant beggars.* **6.** of, pertaining to, or characteristic of a vagrant: *the vagrant life.* **7.** (of plants) straggling in growth. **8.** not fixed or settled, esp. in course; moving hither and thither: *a vagrant leaf blown by the wind.* [late ME *vag(a)raunt*, equiv. to prp. of AF **vagrer*, perh. < ME **vagren*, b. *vagen* (< L *vagārī* to wander) + **walchren* (> OF *wa(u)crer*), equiv. to *walc-* (see WALK) + *-r-* freq. suffix + *-en* inf. suffix] —**va′grant·ly,** *adv.* —**va′grant·ness,** *n.*
—**Syn. 1.** VAGRANT, VAGABOND describe an idle, disreputable person who lacks a fixed abode. VAGRANT suggests the idea of a tramp, a person with no settled abode or livelihood, an idle and disorderly person: *picked up by police as a vagrant.* VAGABOND especially emphasizes the idea of worthless living, often by trickery, thieving, or other disreputable means: *Actors were once classed with rogues and vagabonds.*

va·grom (vā′grəm), *adj.* *Archaic.* vagrant. [illiterate var. of VAGRANT]

vague (vāg), *adj.,* **va·guer, va·guest. 1.** not clearly or explicitly expressed or stated: *vague promises.* **2.** indefinite or indistinct in nature or character, as ideas, feelings, etc.: *a vague premonition of disaster.* **3.** not clear or distinct to the sight or any other sense; perceptible or recognizable only in an indefinite way: *vague forms in the fog; vague murmurs behind a door.* **4.** not definitely established, determined, confirmed, or known; uncertain: *a vague rumor; The date of his birth is vague.* **5.** (of persons) not clear or definite in thought, understanding, or expression: *He is being vague about his reason for leaving the country. She is rather a vague person.* **6.** (of the eyes, expression, etc.) showing lack of clear perception or understanding: *a vague stare.* [< L *vag(us)* wandering] —**vague′ly,** *adv.* —**vague′ness,** *n.*
—**Syn. 1.** unspecific, imprecise. **3.** obscure, hazy, shadowy.

va·gui·o (vag′ē ō′, vä′gē ō′, väg′yō), *n., pl.* **-os.** baguio.

va·gus (vā′gəs), *n., pl.* **-gi** (-jī). See **vagus nerve.** [< L: wandering] —**va′gal,** *adj.*

va′gus nerve′, *pl.* **vagus nerves.** *Anat.* either one of the tenth pair of cranial nerves, consisting of motor fibers that innervate the muscles of the pharynx, larynx, heart, and thoracic and abdominal viscera, and of sensory fibers that conduct impulses from these structures to the brain.

vail[1] (vāl), *v.t.* **1.** to let sink; lower. **2.** *Archaic.* to take off or doff (one's hat), as in respect or submission. [ME *valen*, aph. var. of *avalen* (now obs.) < MF *avaler* to move down, equiv. to phrase *a val* down (lit., to the valley) (*a* to (< L *ad*) + *val* VALE) + *-er* -ER[3]]

vail[2] (vāl), *Archaic.* —*v.i., v.t.* **1.** to be of use or profit; avail. —*n.* **2.** a tip; gratuity. [late ME; aph. var. of AVAIL]

vail[3] (vāl), *Obs.* —*n.* **1.** a veil. —*v.t.* **2.** to veil.

vain (vān), *adj.* **1.** without real significance, value, or importance; baseless or worthless: *vain pageantry; vain display.* **2.** excessively proud of or concerned about one's own appearance, qualities, achievements, etc.; conceited: *vain of her good figure and fine clothes.* **3.** proceeding from or showing personal vanity: *vain remarks.* **4.** ineffectual or unsuccessful; futile: *a vain attempt to keep the schooner off the reef.* **5.** *Archaic.* senseless or foolish. **6. in vain, a.** without effect or avail; to no purpose: *to please in vain.* **b.** in an improper or irreverent manner: *to take God's name in vain.* [ME < OF < L *vān(us)* empty, vain] —**vain′ly,** *adv.* —**vain′ness,** *n.*
—**Syn. 1.** unimportant, trivial, trifling, nugatory. See **useless. 2.** egotistical, self-complacent, vainglorious, proud, arrogant, overweening. **4.** fruitless, unavailing.
—**Ant. 1.** useful. **2.** humble.

Väi·nä·möi·nen (vai′nä mœi′nen), *n.* *Finnish Legend.* an old magician, the hero of the *Kalevala*, who opposes the magician Joukahainen and the sorceress Louhi.

vain·glo·ri·ous (vān glôr′ē əs, -glōr′-), *adj.* **1.** filled with or given to vainglory: *a vainglorious actor.* **2.** characterized by, showing, or proceeding from vainglory: *a vainglorious estimate of one's ability.* [VAINGLORY + -OUS] —**vain·glo′ri·ous·ly,** *adv.* —**vain·glo′ri·ous·ness,** *n.*

vain·glo·ry (vān′glôr′ē, -glōr′ē, vān glôr′ē, -glōr′ē), *n.* **1.** excessive elation or pride over one's own achievements, abilities, etc.; boastful vanity. **2.** empty pomp or show. [ME *vaineglorie*, trans. of ML *vāna glōria*]
—**Syn. 1.** See **pride. 2.** ostentation. —**Ant. 1.** humility.

vair (vâr), *n.* **1.** a fur much used for lining and trimming garments in the 13th and 14th centuries, generally assumed to have been that of a variety of squirrel with a gray back and white belly. Cf. **miniver** (def. 1). **2.** *Heraldry.* a fur represented by a pattern of escutcheon- or bell-shaped figures, each outlining the adjacent sides of those beside it so that the figures alternate vertically and horizontally both in position and in tinctures, of which argent and azure are common. Cf. **countervair, vair en point.** [ME < OF < L *var(ium)* something particolored; see VARIOUS]

vair en point (vâr′ in point′), *Heraldry.* a fur similar to vair except that forms arranged in pale face the same way but alternate in tincture with each other as well as with the forms on each side. [< F: lit., vair in point]

vair·y (vâr′ē), *adj.* *Heraldry.* having the pattern of vair with specified tinctures other than argent and azure: *vairy sable and or.* [VAIR + -Y[1]]

Väi·sä·lä (vī′sə lə, vā′-), *n.* a ring formation in the second quadrant of the face of the moon, in the libration area and near the North Pole: about 50 miles in diameter.

Vai·she·shi·ka (vī′she shē′kə, vī shā′shə kə), *n.* *Indian Philos.* a school of thought asserting the existence of a universe formed by a god out of atoms of earth, air, fire, and water, as well as out of space, time, ether, mind, and soul, all conceived as substances coexisting eternally with the god. [< Skt *vaiśeṣika*, lit., distinctiveness]

Vaish·na·va (vīsh′nə və), *n.* *Hinduism.* a Bhakti sect devoted to Vishnu. —**Vaish′na·vism,** *n.*

Vais·ya (vīs′yə, vīsh′-), *n.* a member of the Hindu mercantile and professional caste, above the Sudras and below the Kshatriyas. Cf. **Brahman** (def. 1), **Harijan, untouchable** (def. 5). [< Skt *vaiśya* settler]

vai·vode (vī′vōd), *n.* a head of local government in some parts of Slavic Europe. Also, **voivode.** [< NL *vayvoda* << Slav *voj(e)voda*]

vaj·ra (vuj′rə), *n.* *Hinduism.* (in Vedic mythology) the thunderbolt of Indra. [< Skt]

va·keel (və kēl′), *n.* *Anglo-Indian.* a native lawyer. Also, **va·kil′.** [< Hindi *vakīl* < Ar *wakīl*]

Val (val), *n.* **1.** a boy's given name, form of **Valentine. 2.** a girl's given name, form of **Valentina, Valeria,** or **Valerie.**

Val (val), *n.* Valenciennes (def. 2).

val., 1. valentine. **2.** valuation. **3.** value.

Va·la (vä′lə), *n.* *Scand. Myth.* a prophetess.

Va·la·don (VA lA dôN′), *n.* **Su·zanne** (SY ZAN′), 1865–1938, French painter (mother of Maurice Utrillo).

Va·lais (VA le′), *n.* a canton in SW Switzerland. 177,783 (1960); 2021 sq. mi. *Cap.:* Sion.

val·ance (val′əns, vā′ləns), *n.* **1.** a short curtain or piece of drapery that is hung from the edge of a canopy, from the frame of a bed, etc. **2.** a short ornamental piece of drapery placed across the top of a window. [? after VALENCE, French city noted for cloth-making] —**val′anced,** *adj.*

Val·borg (val′bərg), *n.* a boy's or girl's given name.

Val·cour′ Is′land (val kŏŏr′), an island in NE New York, in Lake Champlain: battle 1776.

Val·da (väl′də), *n.* a girl's given name.

Val·dai′ Hills′ (väl dī′), a region of hills and plateaus in the W Soviet Union in Europe, at the source of the Volga River: highest point, 1140 ft.

Val·de·mar I (väl′də mär′). See **Waldemar I.**

Val·dese (val′dez), *n.* a town in central North Carolina. 2941 (1960).

Val·di·via (bäl dē′vyä), *n.* a seaport in S Chile. 57,262 (est. 1959).

Val d'Or (*Fr.* VAL dôR′), a city in SW Quebec, in S Canada. 10,983 (1961).

Val·dos·ta (val dos′tə), *n.* a city in S Georgia. 30,652 (1960).

vale (vāl), *n.* **1.** a valley. **2.** mortal or earthly life. [ME < OF *val* < L *vall(is)* valley]

Va·le (wä′lā; *Eng.* vā′lā, vä′lē), *interj., n.* *Latin.* good-by; farewell.

val·e·dic·tion (val′i dik′shən), *n.* **1.** an act of bidding farewell or taking leave. **2.** an utterance, oration, or the like, given in bidding farewell or taking leave; valedictory. [< L *valediction-* (s. of *valedictiō*), equiv. to *valedict(us)*, ptp. of *valedīcere* (*vale* farewell + *dictus*; see DICTUM) + *-iōn-* -ION]

Valediction Forbidding Mourning, A, a poem (1612) by John Donne.

val·e·dic·to·ri·an (val′i dik tôr′ē ən, -tōr′-), *n.* (in colleges and schools) a student, usually the one ranking highest academically in the graduating class, who delivers the valedictory at the commencement exercises. [VALEDICTORY + -AN]

val·e·dic·to·ry (val′i dik′tə rē), *adj., n., pl.* **-ries.** —*adj.* **1.** bidding good-by; saying farewell: *a valedictory speech.* **2.** of or pertaining to an occasion of leave-taking: *a valedictory ceremony.* —*n.* **3.** an address or oration delivered at the commencement exercises of a college or school on behalf of the graduating class. **4.** any farewell address or oration. [*valedict-* (see VALEDICTION) + -ORY[1]]

va·lence (vā′ləns), *n.* *Chem.* **1.** the quality which determines the number of atoms or groups with which any single atom or group will unite chemically. **2.** the relative combining capacity of an atom or group compared with that of the standard hydrogen atom. The chloride ion, Cl^-, has a valence of one, the capacity to unite with one atom of hydrogen or its equivalent, as in HCl or NaCl. Also, **valency.** [< L *valentia* strength, worth, equiv. to *val-* (root of *valēre* to be strong) + *-entia* -ENCE]

Va·lence (VA läNs′), *n.* a city in and the capital of Drôme, in SE France. 55,023 (1962).

va′lence elec′tron, *Chem.* an electron of an atom that can be transferred to or shared with another atom.

Va·len·ci·a (və len′shē ə, -chə; *Sp.* bä len′thyä), *n.* **1. Guil·ler·mo Le·ón** (gē yer′mô le ôn′), born 1909, Colombian diplomat and statesman: president since 1962. **2.** a region in E Spain: formerly a Moorish kingdom. 1,440,761 (est. 1960); 9085 sq. mi. **3.** a seaport in E Spain. 571,452 (est. 1960). **4.** a city in N Venezuela. 117,667 (est. 1955). **5.** Also, **Va·len′ti·a.** a girl's given name.

Va·len·ci·ennes (və len′sē enz′; *Fr.* VA läN syen′), *n.* **1.** a city in N France, SE of Lille. 46,643 (1962). **2.** Also called **Valen′ciennes′ lace′, Val, Val lace.** *Textiles.* **a.** a flat bobbin lace of linen, worked in one piece with the same thread forming the ground and the motif. **b.** a cotton imitation of it.

va·len·cy (vā′lən sē), *n., pl.* **-cies.** *Chem.* valence.

Va·lens (vā′lənz), *n.* **Fla·vi·us** (flā′vē əs), A.D. c328–378, emperor of the Eastern Roman Empire 364–378.

-valent, a suffix meaning "having worth or value," used esp. in scientific terminology to refer to valence: *quadrivalent.* [< L *valent-* (s. of *valēns*, prp. of *valēre* to be strong), equiv. to *val-* strong + *-ent-* -ENT]

Val·en·ti·na (val′ən tē′nə), *n.* a girl's given name.

val·en·tine (val′ən tīn′), *n.* **1.** a card or message (usually amatory or sentimental but sometimes satirical or comical), or a token or gift sent by one person to another on St. Valentine's Day, sometimes anonymously. **2.** a sweetheart chosen or greeted on St. Valentine's Day. **3.** a written work, message, token, etc., expressing affection for something or someone: *His photographic essay is a valentine to Paris.* [late ME, after the feast of St. *Valentine*]

Val·en·tine (val′ən tīn′), *n.* **1. Saint,** died A.D. c270, Christian martyr at Rome. **2.** Also, **Valentinus.** pope A.D. 827. **3.** a town in N Nebraska. 2875 (1960). **4.** a boy's given name.

Val′entine Day′. See **Saint Valentine's Day.** Also, **Val′entine's Day′.**

Val·en·tin·i·an I (val′ən tin′ē ən), A.D. 321?–375, emperor of Western Roman Empire 364–375. Also, **Val·en·tin·i·a·nus I** (val′ən tin′ē ā′nəs).

Valentinian II, A.D. c371–392, emperor of the Western Roman Empire 375–392. Also, **Valentinianus II.**

Valentinian III, A.D. 419?–455, emperor of the Western Roman Empire 425–455. Also, **Valentinianus III.**

val·en·tin·ite (val′ən ti nīt′, -tē′nīt), *n.* a mineral, antimony trioxide, Sb_2O_3, formed by the oxidation of various minerals containing antimony and occurring in the form of white orthorhombic crystals. [< G *Valentinit,* named after Basil *Valentine* 15th-century German alchemist; see -ITE[1]]

Val·en·ti·no (val′ən tē′nō), *n.* **Rudolph** (*Rodolpho d'Antonguolla*), 1895–1926, U.S. motion-picture actor, born in Italy.

Val·en·ti·nus (val′ən tī′nəs), *n.* Valentine (def. 2).

Va·le·ra (və lâr′ə, -lēr′ə; *for 1 also Irish* vä lā′rə; *for 2 also Sp.* bä le′rä), *n.* **1. Ea·mon De** (ā′mon de). See **De Valera. 2.** a city in W Venezuela. 20,888 (1950).

Va·le·ra y Al·ca·lá Ga·lia·no (bä le′rä ē äl′kä-lä′ gä lyä′nō), **Juan** (hwän), 1824–1905, Spanish novelist, critic, diplomat, and statesman.

Va·le·ri·a (və lēr′ē ə), *n.* a girl's given name. Also, **Val·e·ry** (val′ə rē).

va·le·ri·an (və lēr′ē ən), *n.* **1.** Also called **allheal.** any herb of the genus *Valeriana,* as *V. officinalis,* having white or pink flowers and a root that is used medicinally. **2.** a drug consisting of or made from the root, formerly used as a nerve sedative and antispasmodic. [< ML *valeriān(a)* (herb) of *Valeria* (old Roman province, where plant is said to have been common); see -AN]

Va·le·ri·an (və lēr′ē ən), *n.* (*Publius Licinius Valerianus*) died A.D. c260, Roman emperor 253–260.

va·le·ri·a·na·ceous (və lēr′ē ə nā′shəs), *adj.* belonging to the *Valerianaceae,* a family of plants comprising valerian, spikenard, etc. [VALERIAN + -ACEOUS]

va·ler·ic (və ler′ik, -lēr′-), *adj.* pertaining to or derived from valerian. Also, **va·le·ri·an·ic** (və lēr′ē an′ik). [VALER(IAN) + -IC]

valer′ic ac′id, *Chem.* any of several isomeric organic acids having the formula C_4H_9COOH, the common one being a liquid of pungent odor obtained from valerian roots: used chiefly as an intermediate in perfumery.

Va·le·rie (val′ə rē), *n.* a girl's given name. Also, **Valeria, Valery.**

Va·lé·ry (VA lā RĒ′), *n.* **Paul** (pôl), 1871–1945, French poet and philosopher.

val·et (val′it, val′ā, va lā′; *Fr.* VA le′), *n., v.,* **-et·ed, -et·ing.** —*n.* **1.** a male servant who attends to the personal needs of his employer, as by taking care of clothing or the like; manservant. **2.** a man who is employed for cleaning and pressing, laundering, and similar services for patrons of a hotel, passengers on a ship, etc. **3.** a stand or rack for holding coats, hats, etc. —*v.t., v.i.* **4.** to serve as a valet. [< F; MF *va(s)let* squire, equiv. to *vas-* (< ML *vassus* servant) + *-let* -LET; see VASSAL] —**val′et-less,** *adj.*

va·let de cham·bre (VA le də shän′brə), *pl.* **va·lets de cham·bre** (VA le də shän′brə). *French.* valet (def. 1).

val·e·tu·di·nar·i·an (val′i to͞od′ənâr′ē ən, -tyo͞od′-), *n.* **1.** an invalid. **2.** a person who is excessively concerned about his poor health or ailments. —*adj.* **3.** in poor health; sickly; invalid. **4.** excessively concerned about one's poor health or ailments. **5.** of, pertaining to, or characterized by invalidism. [VALETUDINARY + -AN]

val·e·tu·di·nar·i·an·ism (val′i to͞od′ənâr′ē ə niz′-əm, -tyo͞od′-), *n.* the state, condition, or habits of a valetudinarian. [VALETUDINARIAN + -ISM]

val·e·tu·di·nar·y (val′i to͞od′əner′ē, -tyo͞od′-), *n., pl.* **-nar·ies.** valetudinarian. [< L *valētūdinār(ius)* sickly, equiv. to *valētūdin-* (s. of *valētūdō*) good or bad state of health (*valē(re)* (to) be well + *-tūdō* -TUDE) + *-ārius* -ARY]

val·gus (val′gəs), *n., pl.* **-gus·es.** *Pathol.* —*n.* **1.** an abnormally turned position of a part of the bone structure of a human being, esp. of the leg. —*adj.* **2.** of or in such a position; bowlegged, knock-kneed, or the like. [< L: bow-legged]

Val·hal·la (val hal′ə, väl′häl ə), *n. Teutonic Myth.* the hall of Odin into which the souls of heroes slain in battle and others who had died bravely are received. Also, **Val·hall** (val hal′, väl′häl), **Walhalla, Walhall.** [Latinized form of Icel *valhöll,* equiv. to *val(r) slaughter* (c. OE *wæl*) + *höll* HALL]

val·ian·cy (val′yən sē), *n.* valiant nature or quality; valor; bravery; courage. Also, **val′iance.** [VALI(ANT) + -ANCY]

val·iant (val′yənt), *adj.* **1.** boldly courageous; brave; stout-hearted: *a valiant soldier.* **2.** marked by or showing bravery or valor; heroic: *to make a valiant effort.* **3.** worthy; excellent. [ME *valia(u)nt* < AF (equiv. to MF *vaillant,* prp. of *valoir* to be of worth < L *valēre*), equiv. to *vali-* strong, worthy + *-ant-* -ANT] —**val′iant·ly,** *adv.* —**val′iant·ness,** *n.*
—**Syn. 1.** valorous, dauntless. See **brave.**

val·id (val′id), *adj.* **1.** sound; just; well-founded: *a valid reason; a valid objection.* **2.** producing the desired result; effective: *a valid antidote for gloom; a valid procedure.* **3.** having force, weight, or cogency; authoritative. **4.** legally sound, effective, or binding; having legal force; sustainable in law: *a valid contract.* **5.** *Logic.* (of an argument) containing premises which imply the conclusion. **6.** *Archaic.* robust; well; healthy. [<L *valid(us)* strong, equiv. to *val(ēre)* to be strong + *-idus* -ID[4]] —**val′id·ly,** *adv.* —**val′id·ness,** *n.*
—**Syn. 3.** substantial, cogent. **5.** logical, convincing.

val·i·date (val′i dāt′), *v.t.,* **-dat·ed, -dat·ing. 1.** to make valid; substantiate; confirm: *Time validated our suspicions.* **2.** to give legal force to; legalize. **3.** to give official sanction, confirmation, or approval to, as elected officials, election procedures, documents, etc.: *to validate a passport.* [< ML *validāt(us)* (ptp. of *validāre* to make valid), equiv. to *valid-* (see VALID) + *-ātus* -ATE[1]] —**val′i·da′tion,** *n.* —**val·i·da·to·ry** (val′i də tôr′ē, -tōr′ē), *adj.*
—**Syn. 1.** authenticate, verify. —**Ant. 1.** disprove.

va·lid·i·ty (və lid′i tē), *n.* **1.** the state or quality of being valid: *to question the validity of an intelligence test.* **2.** legal soundness or force. [< LL *validitāt-* (s. of *validitās*), equiv. to L *valid(us)* VALID + *-itāt-* -ITY]

val·ine (val′ēn, -in, vā′lēn, -lin), *n. Biochem.* a white, crystalline, water-soluble amino acid, $(CH_3)_2CHCH(NH_2)COOH$, obtained by the hydrolysis of most plant and animal proteins: used chiefly as a nutrient in medicine and in culture media for certain bacteria. [VAL(ERIC) + -INE[2]]

va·lise (və lēs′ *or, esp. Brit.,* -lēz′), *n.* a small piece of luggage that can be carried by hand, used to hold clothing, toilet articles, etc.; suitcase; traveling bag. [< F (cf. ML *valisia*) < It *valigia* < ?]

Val·kyr·ie (val kēr′ē, -kī′rē, val′kēr ē), *n. Teutonic Myth.* any of the beautiful maidens attendant upon Odin who bring the souls of slain warriors chosen by Odin or Tyr to Valhalla and there wait upon them. Also, **Walkyrie.** [< Icel *valkyrja* chooser of the slain (c. OE *wælcyrie* witch), equiv. to *val(r)* slaughter (c. OE *wæl*) + *kyrja* chooser (c. OE *cyrie*); akin to CHOOSE] —**Val·kyr′i·an,** *adj.*

Val·la (väl′lä), *n.* **Lo·ren·zo** (lô ren′dzō), 1407–57, Italian humanist and critic.

Val′ lace′, Valenciennes (def. 2).

Va·lla·do·lid (bä′lyä dô lēth′), *n.* a city in N Spain, NW of Madrid: Columbus died here 1506. 132,526 (est. 1960).

val·late (val′āt), *adj.* bordered by a ridge, raised edge, or the like. [< LL *vallāt(us)* (ptp. of *vallāre* to surround, border with a wall, rampart), equiv. to *vall(um)* rampart + *-ātus* -ATE[1]]

val·la·tion (və lā′shən), *n. Fort.* **1.** a rampart or entrenchment. **2.** the process or technique of constructing ramparts. [< LL *vallāt(us)* (ptp. of *vallāre* to WALL), equiv. to *vall-* WALL + *-āt(us)* -ATE[1] + *-iōn-* -ION]

val·lec·u·la (və lek′yə lə), *n., pl.* **-lae** (-lē′). *Anat., Bot.* a furrow or depression. [< LL, equiv. to *valle(s)* VALLEY + *-cula* (fem.) -CULE] —**val·lec′u·lar,** adj.

val·lec·u·late (və lek′yə lāt′), *adj.* having a vallecula or valleculae. [VALLECUL(A) + -ATE[1]]

Val·le d'A·o·sta (väl′le dä ô′stä), a region in NW Italy. 99,754 (1961); 1259 sq. mi.

Va·lle de la Pas·cua (bä′ye de lä päs′kwä), a city in N Venezuela. 11,951 (1950).

Va·lle·gran·de (bä′ye grän′de), *n.* a city in central Bolivia. 5094 (1950).

Val·le·jo (və lā′hō; *for 1 also Sp.* bä ye′hō), *n.* **1. Cé·sar** (*Sp.* se′sär), 1895–1938, Peruvian poet. **2.** a city in W California, on San Pablo Bay, NE of San Francisco. 60,877 (1960).

Va·lle·nar (bä′ye när′), *n.* a city in central Chile. 9677 (1952).

Val·let·ta (väl let′tä), *n.* a seaport in and the capital of Malta, on the NE coast: naval station. 18,170 (est. 1962).

val·ley (val′ē), *n., pl.* **-leys. 1.** an elongated depression between uplands, hills, or mountains, esp. one following the course of a stream. **2.** an extensive, more or less flat, and relatively low region drained by a great river system. **3.** any depression or hollow resembling a valley. **4.** a low point or interval in any process, representation, or situation. **5.** any place, period, or situation that is filled with fear, gloom, foreboding, or the like: *the valley of death.* **6.** *Archit.* a depression or angle formed by the meeting of two inclined sides of a roof. **7.** the lower phase of a horizontal wave motion. [ME *valeie, valey* < OF *valee,* equiv. to *val* VALE[1] + *-ee* fem. n. suffix] —**val′ley-like′,** *adj.*

Val·ley (val′ē), *n.* a town in E North Dakota. 7809 (1960).

Val′ley Cen′ter, a town in central Kansas. 2570 (1960).

Val′ley Forge′, a village in SE Pennsylvania: winter quarters of Washington's army 1777–78.

Val′ley of Ten′ Thou′sand Smokes′, a volcanic area in SW Alaska, in Katmai National Monument.

Val′ley of the Kings′, a valley on the west bank of the Nile near the site of Thebes: the necropolis of many of the kings and queens of the 18th and 19th dynasties of ancient Egypt, c1350–c1200 B.C. Also called **Val′ley of the Tombs′.**

Val′ley Park′, a town in E Missouri. 3452 (1960).

Val′ley Stream′, a village on W Long Island, in SE New York. 38,629 (1960).

val′ley wind′ (wind), a wind that ascends a mountain valley during the day. Cf. **mountain wind.**

Val·lom·bro·sa (väl′lôm brô′sä), *n.* a resort in central Italy, near Florence: famous abbey.

Val·mid (val′mid), *n. Pharm., Trademark.* ethinamate.

Val·mi·ki (väl mē′kē), *n.* Hindu poet and reputed author of the Ramayana.

Va·lois (VA lwA′ *for 1, 3;* val′wä *for 2*), *n.* **1.** a member of a ruling family of France which reigned from 1328 to 1589. **2. Dame Ni·nette de** (ni net′). See **de Valois, Dame Ninette. 3.** a county in the Ile de France, which became united to the French crown in 1167 and was established as a duchy in 1406.

Va·lo·na (və lō′nä), *n.* a seaport in SW Albania. 46,905 (est. 1964). Also called **Avlona.**

va·lo·ni·a (və lō′nē ə), *n.* acorn cups of an oak, *Quercus Aegilops,* used in tanning, dyeing, and making ink. [< It *vallonia* < ModGk *balánia,* pl. of *baláni* acorn]

val·or (val′ər), *n.* boldness or determination in facing great danger, esp. in battle; heroic courage; bravery: *He received a medal for valor.* Also, *esp. Brit.,* **val′our.** [ME *valo(u)r* < AF (equiv. to MF *valeur*) < LL *valor* worth, equiv. to L *val(ēre)* (to) be of worth + *-or* -OR[1]]
—**Syn.** intrepidity, spirit. See **courage.** —**Ant.** cowardice.

Va·lo·ra (və lôr′ə, -lōr′ə), *n.* a girl's given name.

val·or·ise (val′ə rīz′), *v.t.,* **-ised, -is·ing.** *Chiefly Brit.* valorize. —**val′or·i·sa′tion,** *n.*

val·or·ize (val′ə rīz′), *v.t.,* **-ized, -iz·ing.** (of a government) to fix and provide for the maintaining of the value or price of (a commercial commodity) by purchasing the commodity at the fixed price. Also, *esp. Brit.,* **valorise.** [VALOR worth + -IZE] —**val′or·i·za′tion,** *n.*

val·or·ous (val′ər əs), *adj.* **1.** having or showing valor; courageous; valiant; brave. **2.** characterized by valor, as actions, exploits, etc. [< ML *valorōs(us)* valiant. See VALOR, -OUS] —**val′or·ous·ly,** *adv.* —**val′-or·ous·ness,** *n.*

Val·pa·rai·so (val′pə rī′sō, -zō), *n.* **1.** Spanish, **Val·pa·ra·í·so** (bäl′pä rä ē′sô). a seaport in central Chile. 259,241 (1960). **2.** a town in NW Florida. 5975 (1960).

valse (VAls), *n., pl.* **valses** (VAls). *French.* waltz.

Valse des To·ré·a·dors, La (*Fr.* lA VAls dā tô rā A-dôr′). See **Waltz of the Toreadors.**

val·u·able (val′yo͞o ə bəl, -yə bəl), *adj.* **1.** having considerable monetary worth; costing or bringing a high price: *a valuable painting; a valuable metal; a valuable crop.* **2.** having qualities worthy of respect, admiration, or esteem: *a valuable friend.* **3.** of considerable use, service, or importance: *a valuable aid; valuable information.* —*n.* **4.** Usually, **valuables.** articles of considerable value, as of personal property or of merchandise, esp. those of relatively small size: *They locked their valuables in the hotel safe.* [VALUE (v.) + -ABLE] —**val′u·a·ble·ness,** *n.* —**val′u·a·bly,** *adv.*
—**Syn. 1.** costly, expensive, rare. VALUABLE, PRECIOUS refer to that which has pecuniary or other value. VALUABLE applies to whatever has value, but esp. to what has considerable monetary value or special usefulness, rarity, etc.: *a valuable watch.* That which is PRECIOUS has a very high intrinsic value or is very dear for its own sake, associations, or the like: *a precious jewel, friendship.* **3.** important, serviceable, useful. —**Ant. 1.** worthless.

val·u·ate (val′yo͞o āt′), *v.t.,* **-at·ed, -at·ing.** to set a value on; appraise. [back formation from VALUATION]

val·u·a·tion (val′yo͞o ā′shən), *n.* **1.** the act of estimating or setting the value of something; appraisal. **2.** an estimated value or worth. **3.** the awareness or acknowledgement of the quality, nature, excellence, or the like, of something: *public valuation of the importance of a college education.* [VALUE (v.) + -ATION; cf. MF *valuation*] —**val′u·a′tion·al,** *adj.* —**val′u·a′tion·al·ly,** *adv.*

val·u·a·tor (val′yo͞o ā′tər), *n.* a person who estimates worth or value; appraiser. [VALUE (v.) + -ATOR]

val·ue (val′yo͞o), *n., v.,* **-ued, -u·ing.** —*n.* **1.** the relative worth, merit, or importance: *the value of a college education; the great value of a queen in chess.* **2.** monetary or material worth, as in commerce or trade: *This piece of land has greatly increased in value.* **3.** the worth of something in terms of the amount of other things for which it can be exchanged or in terms of some medium of exchange. **4.** equivalent worth or return in money, material, services, etc.: *to give value for value received.* **5.** estimated or assigned worth; valuation: *a house with a value of $25,000.* **6.** denomination, as of a monetary issue, postage stamp, etc. **7.** *Math.* **a.** magnitude; quantity; number represented by: *the value of an angle; the value of* **x**; *the value of a sum.* **b.** a point in the range of a function; a point in the range corresponding to a given point in the domain of a function: *The value of* x^2 *at 2 is 4.* **8.** import or meaning; force; significance: *the value of a word.* **9.** liking or affection; favorable regard. **10. values,** *Sociol.* the ideals, customs, institutions, etc., of a society toward which the people of the group have an affective regard. These values may be positive, as cleanliness, freedom, education, etc., or negative, as cruelty, crime, or blasphemy. **11.** *Ethics.* any object or quality desirable as a means or as an end in itself. **12.** *Painting.* degree of lightness or darkness in a color. **13.** *Music.* the relative length or duration of a tone signified by a note. **14.** *Phonet.* **a.** quality. **b.** the phonetic equivalent of a letter, as the sound of *a* in *hat, sang,* etc. —*v.t.* **15.** to calculate or reckon the monetary value of; give a specified material or financial value to; assess; appraise: *They valued their assets at over five million dollars.* **16.** to consider with respect to worth, excellence, usefulness, or importance. **17.** to regard or esteem highly: *He values her friendship.* [ME < OF, n. use of ptp. fem. (c. VALUTA) of *valoir* < L *valēre* to be worth]
—**Syn. 1.** utility. VALUE, WORTH imply intrinsic excellence or desirability. VALUE is that quality of anything which renders it desirable or useful: *the value of sunlight or good books.* WORTH implies esp. spiritual qualities of mind and character, or moral excellence: *Few knew his true worth.* **3.** cost, price. **17.** prize. See **appreciate.**

val·ued (val′yo͞od), *adj.* **1.** highly regarded or esteemed: *a valued speaker on political affairs.* **2.** estimated; appraised: *a loss of jewels valued at $100,000.* **3.** having value of a specified kind: *a many-valued position.* [VALUE + -ED[2]]

val′ue date′, *Banking.* the date on which an entry made on an account becomes effective, used esp. in connection with foreign accounts.

val′ued pol′icy, *Insurance.* a policy in which the company and the policyholder agree to the amount to be paid in the event of total loss of property, regardless of the value of the property.

val′ue judg′ment, an estimate, usually subjective, of the worth, quality, goodness, evil, etc., of something or someone.

val·ue·less (val′yo͞o lis), *adj.* without worth or value; worthless: *valueless stocks; a valueless promise.* [VALUE + -LESS] —**val′ue·less·ness,** *n.*

val·u·er (val′yo͞o ər), *n.* **1.** *Brit.* an appraiser. **2.** a person who values. [VALUE + -ER[1]]

va·lu·ta (və lo͞o′tə), *n.* (in Europe) the value of a currency expressed in terms of its rate of exchange with another currency. [< It < VL **valūta,* n. use of fem. ptp. of L *valēre* to be worth, equiv. to *valu-* (past s. of *valēre*) + *-tus* ptp. suffix]

val·val (val′vəl), *adj.* valvular. [VALVE + -AL[1]]

val·var (val′vər), *adj.* valvular. [VALVE + -AR[1]]

val·vate (val′vāt), *adj.* **1.** furnished with or opening by a valve or valves. **2.** serving as or resembling a valve. **3.** *Bot.* **a.** opening by valves, as certain capsules and anthers. **b.** meeting without overlapping, as the parts of certain buds. **c.** composed of or characterized by such parts. [< L *valvāt(us)* with folding doors. See VALVE, -ATE[1]]

valve (valv), *n.*, *v.*, **valved, valv·ing.** —*n.* **1.** any device for halting or controlling the flow of a liquid, gas, or other material through a passage, pipe, inlet, outlet, etc. **2.** a hinged lid or other movable part which closes or modifies the passage in such a device. **3.** *Anat.* a membranous fold or other structure which controls the flow of a fluid, as one which permits blood to flow in one direction only. **4.** (in musical wind instruments of the trumpet class) a device for changing the length of the air column to alter the pitch of a tone. **5.** *Zool.* **a.** one of the two or more separable pieces composing certain shells. **b.** either half of the silicified shell of a diatom. **6.** *Bot.* **a.** one of the segments into which a capsule dehisces. **b.** a flap or lidlike part of certain anthers. **7.** *Electronics Chiefly Brit.* See **vacuum tube. 8.** *Archaic.* one of the leaves of a double or folding door. —*v.t.* **9.** to provide with a means of controlling the flow of liquid, gas, etc., by inserting a valve. [late ME < L *valva* door-leaf] —**valve′less,** *adj.* —**valve′like′,** *adj.*

Globe valve
A, Wheel
B, Spindle
C, Stuffing nut
D, Disk
E, Valve seat

valved (valvd), *adj.* having or furnished with valves: *a valved trumpet.* [VALVE + -ED[3]]

valve′ gear′, (in a reciprocating engine) the mechanism for opening and closing the valves at certain points in each stroke.

valve′-in-head′ en′gine (valv′in hed′), an engine operating by internal-combustion and having the cylinder head contain the inlet and exhaust valves.

valve·let (valv′lit), *n.* a small valve; valvule. [VALVE + -LET]

valve′ trombone′, a trombone equipped with three or four valves in place of a slide.

val·vu·lar (val′vyə lər), *adj.* **1.** having the form or function of a valve. **2.** operating by a valve or valves. **3.** of or pertaining to a valve or valves, esp. of the heart. Also called **valval, valvar.** [< NL *valvulār(is),* equiv. to *valvul(a)* VALVULE + *-āris* -AR[1]]

val′vular insuffi′ciency, *Pathol.* abnormal closure of a heart valve resulting in failure to prevent regurgitation of blood. Also called **val′vular incom′petence.**

val·vule (val′vyo͞ol), *n.* a small valve or a part resembling a valve. [< NL *valvula.* See VALVE, -ULE]

val·vu·li·tis (val′vyə lī′tis), *n. Pathol.* inflammation of the cardiac-valve leaflets, caused by an acute infectious process, usually rheumatic fever or syphilis. [VALVULE + -ITIS]

val·vu·lot·o·my (val′vyə lot′ə mē), *n., pl.* **-mies.** *Surg.* the opening, slitting, or fracturing of a heart valve along natural lines of cleavage. [*valvulo-* (see VALVULE, -O-) + -TOMY]

vam·brace (vam′brās), *n. Armor.* **1.** a piece of plate armor for the forearm; a lower cannon. Cf. **rerebrace. 2.** plate armor for the whole arm, usually including upper and lower cannons and a couter. [ME *va(u)mbras* < AF *(a)vantbras,* equiv. to *avant-* fore- (see AVAUNT) + *bras* arm (see BRACE)] —**vam′braced,** *adj.*

va·moose (va mo͞os′), *v.,* **-moosed, -moos·ing.** *U.S. Slang.* —*v.i.* **1.** to leave hurriedly or quickly; decamp. —*v.t.* **2.** to leave hurriedly or quickly from; decamp from. [< Sp *vamos* let us go, impv. 1st pers. pl. (< L *vādere* to go fast) of *ir* to go]

va·mose (va mōs′), *v.i., v.t.,* **-mosed, -mos·ing.** *U.S. Slang.* vamoose.

vamp[1] (vamp), *n.* **1.** the portion of a shoe or boot upper that covers the instep and toes. **2.** something patched up or pieced together. **3.** *Jazz.* an accompaniment, usually improvised, consisting of a succession of simple chords. —*v.t.* **4.** to furnish with a vamp, esp. to repair (a shoe or boot) with a new vamp. **5.** to patch up; repair. **6.** to give (something) a new appearance by adding a patch or piece. **7.** to concoct or invent (often fol. by *up*): *He vamped up a few ugly rumors to discredit his enemies.* **8.** *Jazz.* to improvise (an accompaniment or the like). —*v.i.* **9.** *Jazz.* to improvise an accompaniment, tune, etc. [ME *vampe* < AF; MF *avant-pie,* equiv. to *avant-* fore- (see AVAUNT) + *pie* foot (F *pied;* see -PED)] —**vamp′er,** *n.* —**vamp′ish,** *adj.*

vamp[2] (vamp), *n.* **1.** a woman of seductive charm and sensuality who is unscrupulous in her exploitation of men. —*v.t.* **2.** to use one's feminine charms upon; seduce. —*v.i.* **3.** to act as a vamp. [short for VAMPIRE]

vamp·horn (vamp′hôrn′), *n.* a megaphone in use during the 18th and early 19th centuries for public address in church services. [VAMP[1] + HORN; so called for its use in amplifying one voice as an accompaniment in choral singing]

vam·pire (vam′pīər), *n.* **1.** a preternatural being, commonly believed to be the reanimated corpse of a person improperly buried, that is said to suck the blood of sleeping persons at night. **2.** a person who preys ruthlessly upon others; extortionist. **3.** a woman who unscrupulously exploits, ruins, or degrades the men she seduces. **4.** an actress noted for her roles as an unscrupulous seductress: *the vampires of the silent movies.* **5.** Also called **vam′pire bat′.** *Zool.* **a.** any of several Central and South American bats of the genera *Desmodus, Diphylla,* and *Diaemus,* which feed on the blood of man and other vertebrates. **b.** any of several large South American bats of the genera *Phyllostomus* and *Vampyrus,* erroneously believed to feed on blood. **c.** any of various false vampires. [< F < G *Vampir* < Slav; cf. Serbian *vampir,* Russ *upyr*] —**vam·pir·ic** (vam pir′ik), **vam·pir·ish** (vam′pīər ish), *adj.*

vam·pir·ism (vam′pīər iz′əm, -pə riz′-), *n.* **1.** belief in the existence of vampires. **2.** acts or practices of vampires. **3.** unscrupulous exploitation, impoverishment, ruin, or degradation of others. [VAMPIRE + -ISM]

vam·plate (vam′plāt′), *n. Armor.* a metal plate mounted on a lance in front of the grip to protect the hand. [ME *vaunplate* < AF *vaunt-* fore- (see AVAUNT) + *plate* PLATE[1]]

van[1] (van), *n.* **1.** the foremost or front division of an army, a fleet, or any group leading an advance or in position to lead an advance. **2.** those who are in the forefront of a movement or the like. **3.** the forefront in any movement, course of progress, or the like. [short for VANGUARD]

van[2] (van), *n., v.,* **vanned, van·ning.** —*n.* **1.** a covered vehicle, usually a large truck or trailer, used for moving furniture, goods, animals, etc. **2.** *Brit.* **a.** a railway baggage car. **b.** a covered, boxlike railway car, as one used to carry freight or troops. **c.** a small, horse-drawn wagon or truck, as one used by tradesmen to carry light goods. —*v.t.* **3.** to transport or carry in a van. [short for CARAVAN]

van[3] (van; *Du.* vän), *prep.* (*often cap.*) from; of (used in Dutch personal names, originally to indicate place of origin). [c. VON]

van[4] (van), *n. Archaic.* a wing. [var. of FAN[1]]

Van (vän), *n.* **1. Lake,** a salt lake in E Turkey. 1454 sq. mi. **2.** a town on this lake. 42,881 (1960). **3.** a boy's given name.

vanad-, a combining form of **vanadium:** *vanadous.*

van·a·date (van′ə dāt′), *n. Chem.* a salt or ester of a vanadic acid. Also, **va·na·di·ate** (və nā′dē āt′). [VANAD- + -ATE[2]]

va·nad·ic (və nad′ik, -nā′dik), *adj. Chem.* of or containing vanadium, esp. in the trivalent or pentavalent state. [VANAD- + -IC]

vanad′ic ac′id, *Chem.* any of certain acids containing vanadium, esp. one having the formula H_3VO_4.

va·nad·i·nite (və nad′ənīt′), *n.* a mineral, lead chlorovanadate, $Pb_5(VO_4)_3Cl$, occurring in yellow, brown, or greenish crystals: an ore of lead and vanadium. [VANAD- + -IN[2] + -ITE[1]]

va·na·di·ous (və nā′dē əs), *adj. Chem.* vanadous. [VANAD- + -IOUS]

va·na·di·um (və nā′dē əm), *n. Chem.* a rare element occurring in certain minerals and obtained as a light-gray powder with a silvery luster or as a ductile metal: used as an ingredient of steel to toughen it and increase its shock resistance. *Symbol:* V; *at. wt.:* 50.942; *at. no.:* 23; *sp. gr.:* 5.96. [< Icel *Vanad(ís)* epithet of Freya (*Vana,* gen. of VANIR + *dís* goddess) + -IUM]

vana′dium steel′, an alloy steel containing vanadium.

van·a·dous (van′ə dəs), *adj. Chem.* containing divalent or trivalent vanadium. Also, **vanadious.** [VANAD- + -OUS]

Van Al·len (van al′ən), **James Alfred,** born 1914, U.S. physicist.

Van Al′len belt′, *Physics.* either of two regions of high-energy-charged particles surrounding the earth, the inner region centered at an altitude of 2000 miles and the outer region at an altitude between 9000 and 12,000 miles. Also called **Van Al′len radia′tion belt′.** [named after J. A. VAN ALLEN]

Van·brugh (van bro͞o′ *or, esp. Brit.,* van′brə), *n.* **John,** 1664–1726, English dramatist and architect.

Van Bu·ren (van byo͝or′ən), *n.* **1. Martin,** 1782–1862, 8th president of the U.S. 1837–41. **2.** a town in central Arkansas. 6787 (1960). **3.** a town in NE Maine. 3589 (1960). **4.** a boy's given name.

Vance (vans), *n.* a boy's given name.

Van·cou·ver (van ko͞o′vər), *n.* **1. George,** 1758–98, English explorer. **2.** a large island in SW Canada, off the SW coast of British Columbia. 215,003 (1951); 12,408 sq. mi. **3.** a seaport in SW British Columbia, on the Strait of Georgia opposite SE Vancouver island. 384,522 (1961); with suburbs 665,017 (1956). **4.** a city in SW Washington. 32,464 (1960). **5. Mount,** a mountain on the boundary between Alaska and Canada, in the St. Elias Mountains. 15,700 ft.

CANADA
Vancouver Island
Vancouver
Victoria
Seattle
PACIFIC OCEAN
WASHINGTON
OREGON

van·da (van′də), *n.* any of several epiphytic orchids of the genus *Vanda,* of tropical regions of the Eastern Hemisphere, having large white, lilac, blue, or greenish flowers. [< NL < Hindi *vandā* mistletoe < Skt: parasitic plant]

Van·dal (van′dəl), *n.* **1.** a member of a Germanic people who in the 5th century A.D. ravaged Gaul and Spain, settled in Africa, and in A.D. 455 sacked Rome. **2.** (*l.c.*) a person who willfully or ignorantly destroys or mars something beautiful or valuable. —*adj.* **3.** of or pertaining to the Vandals. **4.** (*l.c.*) imbued with or characterized by vandalism. [< LL *Vandal(us),* Latinized tribal name]

Van·da·lia (van dāl′yə), *n.* **1.** a town in W Ohio. 6342 (1960). **2.** a town in central Illinois. 5537 (1960). **3.** a town in central Missouri. 3055 (1960).

Van·dal·ic (van dal′ik), *adj.* **1.** of, pertaining to, or characteristic of the Vandals. **2.** (*l.c.*) of or pertaining to vandalism. [VANDAL + -IC]

van·dal·ism (van′dəliz′əm), *n.* **1.** deliberately mischievous or malicious destruction or damage of property: *The police are attempting to reduce vandalism in our public buildings.* **2.** the conduct or spirit characteristic of the Vandals. **3.** willful or ignorant destruction of artistic or literary treasures. **4.** a vandalic act. [VANDAL + -ISM; cf. F *vandalisme*] —**van′dal·is′tic, van′dal·ish,** *adj.*

van·dal·ize (van′dəlīz′), *v.t.,* **-ized, -iz·ing.** to destroy or deface by vandalism: *The invaders vandalized the museum.* [VANDAL + -IZE]

Van′ de Graaff′ gen′erator (van′ də graf′), *Physics, Elect.* a device for producing high-voltage static electricity, consisting of a hollow, spherical conductor atop a hollow, insulating column through which a movable belt runs between a terminal with high negative potential at the base of the column and a terminal with high positive potential in the spherical conductor, the voltage in the conductor often being used to accelerate particles. Also called **electrostatic generator.** [named after R. J. *Van de Graaff* (1901–66), American physicist]

Van·den·berg (van′dən bûrg′), *n.* **1. Arthur Hendrick** (hen′drik), 1884–1951, U.S. statesman. **2. Hoyt San·ford** (hoit san′fərd), 1899–1954, U.S. general: Chief of Staff of Air Force 1948–53.

Van·der·bilt (van′dər bilt), *n.* **1. Cornelius,** 1794–1877, U.S. financier. **2. Harold Stir·ling** (stûr′ling), born 1884, U.S. business executive.

Van·der·grift (van′dər grift), *n.* a town in central Pennsylvania. 8742 (1960).

Van der Hum (van′ dər ho͞om′; *Du.* vän′ dər hʏm′), a spicy liqueur from South Africa, flavored with tangerine and herbs.

van der Roh·e (van dər rō′ə; *Ger.* fän dεr rō′ə), **Lud·wig Mi·es** (lud′wig; *Ger.* lo͞ot′viкн, lo͞od′-). See **Mies van der Rohe, Ludwig.**

van′ der Waals′ equa′tion (van′ dər wôlz′, wôlz′; *Du.* vän′ dər väls′), *Thermodynamics.* an equation relating the pressure, volume, and absolute temperature of a gas with reference to the finite size of the molecules and the attractive force between them. Also, **van′ der Waals′ equa′tion.** [named after J. D. *van der Waals* (1837–1923), Dutch scientist]

van′ der Waals′ forc′es, *Physical Chem.* weak, nonspecific forces between molecules. Also, **van′ der Waals′ forc′es.** [see VAN DER WAALS' EQUATION]

Van De·van·ter (van′ di van′tər), **Willis,** 1859–1941, U.S. jurist: associate justice of the U.S. Supreme Court 1910–37.

Van Die′men's Land′ (van dē′mənz), former name of **Tasmania.**

Van Dine (van dīn′), **S. S.** See **Wright, Willard Huntington.**

Van Do·ren (van dôr′ən, dôr′-), **Carl,** 1885–1950, U.S. writer, and his brother **Mark,** born 1894, U.S. writer and critic.

Van Dru·ten (van dro͞ot′ən), **John William,** 1901–57, U.S. playwright, born in England.

Van Dyck (van dīk′; *Flem.* vän dīk′), **Sir Anthony,** 1599–1641, Flemish painter. Also, **Vandyke.**

Van·dyke (van dīk′), *n.* **1. Sir Anthony.** See **Van Dyck, Sir Anthony. 2.** (*sometimes l.c.*) See **Vandyke beard. 3.** (*sometimes l.c.*) See **Vandyke collar. 4.** *Print.* a proof having white lines on a brown ground or vice versa, made from a negative for a plate.

Vandyke′ beard′, a short, pointed beard. Also called **Vandyke, vandyke.**

Vandyke′ brown′, **1.** a medium brown color. **2.** any of several dark-brown pigments consisting of iron oxide mixed with lampblack or similar materials.

Vandyke beard

Vandyke′ col′lar, a wide collar of lace and linen with the edge formed into scallops or deep points. Also, **vandyke′ col′lar.** Also called **Vandyke, vandyke.**

vane (vān), *n.* **1.** Also called **weather vane, wind vane.** a device, as a flat piece of metal, fastened to a spire or other elevated object so as to move freely with the wind and indicate its direction. **2.** a similar piece, or sail, in the wheel of a windmill, to be moved by the air. **3.** any of a number of blades or plates attached radially to a rotating drum or cylinder, as in a turbine or pump, which move or are moved by a fluid, as steam, water, hot gases, or air. **4.** a person who is readily changeable or fickle. **5.** *Rocketry.* **a.** any fixed or movable plane surface on the outside of a rocket or guided missile, providing directional control while the missile is within the atmosphere. **b.** a similar plane surface located in the exhaust jet of a reaction engine, providing directional control while the engine is firing. **6.** *Ornith.* the web of a feather. **7.** *Navig., Survey.* either of two fixed projections for sighting an alidade or the like. **8.** *Archery.* feather (def. 8). [ME; OE *fana* flag; c. G *Fahne* flag, Goth *fana* segment of cloth; see GONFALON] —**vaned,** *adj.* —**vane′less,** *adj.*

Vane (vān), *n.* **Sir Henry** (*Sir Harry Vane*), 1613–62, British statesman and author.

Vä·nern (ve′nərn; *Swed.* ve′nərn), *n.* a lake in SW Sweden. 2141 sq. mi. Also, **Vä·ner** (ven′ər), **Vener.**

Va·nes·sa (və nes′ə), *n.* a girl's given name.

Va·neth·a (və neth′ə), *n.* a girl's given name.

Van Fleet (van flēt′), **James Al·ward** (al′wərd), born 1892, U.S. army general.

vang (vang), *n. Naut.* a rope extending from the peak of a gaff to the ship's rail or to a mast, used to steady the gaff. [dial. var. of FANG[1], but perh. < D cognate *vang*]

Van Gogh (van gō′, gôкн′; *Du.* vän кнôкн′), **Vin·cent** (vin′sənt; *Du.* vin sent′). See **Gogh, Vincent van.**

van·guard (van′gärd′), *n.* **1.** the foremost division or the front part of an army; advance guard; van. **2.** the forefront in any movement, field, activity, or the like. **3.** the leaders of any intellectual or political movement. **4.** (*cap.*) *U.S.* a three-stage, satellite-launching rocket, the first two stages powered by liquid-propellant engines and the last stage powered by a solid-propellant engine. [late ME *van(d)gard(e)* < MF *avangarde,* var. of *avant-garde;* see AVAUNT, GUARD]

van·guard·ism (van′gär diz′əm), *n.* the beliefs and activities of persons who consider themselves to be leaders in a particular field or school of thought. [VANGUARD + -ISM] —**van′guard·ist,** *n.*

Va·nier (*Fr.* va nyā′), *n.* **Georges P.** (*Fr.* zhôrzh), 1888–1967, Canadian soldier and diplomat: governor-general 1959–67.

va·nil·la (və nil′ə), *n.* **1.** any tropical, climbing orchid of the genus *Vanilla,* esp. *V. planifolia,* bearing podlike fruit yielding an extract used in flavoring food, in perfumery, etc. **2.** Also called **vanil′la bean′.** the fruit or bean of this orchid. **3.** the extract of this fruit. [< NL < Sp *vainilla* little pod, equiv. to *vain(a)* a sheath (< L *vāgīna* sheath) + *-illa* dim. suffix (< LL *-illa*)]

Vanilla, *Vanilla planifolia*
A, Flowering branch;
B, Fruit
(Length to 10 in.)

vanil′la grass′, holy grass, *Hierochloë odorata,* the shoots of which are used for making baskets, mats, etc. Also called **Seneca grass, sweet grass.**

vanil′la leaf′. See **Carolina vanilla.**

va·nil·lic (və nil′ik), *adj.* pertaining to, derived from, or resembling vanilla or vanillin. [VANILL(A) + -IC]

va·nil·lin (van′əlin, və nil′in), *n.* *Chem.* a white, crystalline, water-insoluble, alcohol-soluble solid, $(CH_3O)(OH)C_6H_3CHO$, obtained by extraction from the vanilla bean or prepared synthetically: used chiefly as a flavoring agent and in perfumery. Also, **van·il·line** (van′əlin, -ə lēn′, və nil′in, -ēn). Also called **vanil′lic al′dehyde.** [VANILL(A) + -IN²]

Va·nir (vä′nir), *n.pl.* (*often l.c.*) *Scand. Myth.* a race of gods, of whom Niord, Frey, and Freya were members, often in conflict with the Aesir.

van·ish (van′ish), *v.i.* **1.** to disappear from sight, esp. quickly; become invisible: *The frost vanished when the sun came out.* **2.** to go away, esp. furtively or mysteriously; disappear by quick departure: *By the time the burglary was discovered, the culprit had vanished.* **3.** to disappear by ceasing to exist; come to an end: *His headache vanished after he took an aspirin.* **4.** *Math.* (of a number, quantity, or function) to become zero. —*v.t.* **5.** to cause to disappear. —*n.* **6.** *Phonet.* the last part of a vowel sound when it differs noticeably in quality from the main sound, as the faint (ē) at the end of the (ā) in the pronunciation of *pain.* [ME *vanisshe(n), vanissen* < MF *(e)vaniss-* (s. of *e(s)vanir*) < L *ex-* EX- + *vānēsce(re)* (to) pass away, equiv. to *vān(us)* VAIN + *-ēscere* inceptive suffix] —**van′ish·er,** *n.* —**van′ish·ing·ly,** *adv.* —**van′ish·ment,** *n.*
—**Syn. 1.** evanesce. See **disappear.** —**Ant. 1.** appear.

van′ishing cream′, a cosmetic similar to cold cream, applied usually to the face as a base for powder.

van′ishing point′, 1. a point of disappearance, cessation, or extinction: *His patience had reached the vanishing point.* **2.** (in the study of perspective in art) that point toward which receding parallel lines appear to converge.

va·ni·tas va·ni·ta·tum (wä′ni täs wä′ni tä′tum; *Eng.* van′i tas′ van′i tā′təm), *Latin.* vanity of vanities.

van·i·ty (van′i tē), *n., pl.* **-ties. 1.** excessive pride in one's appearance, qualities, abilities, achievements, etc.; character or quality of being vain; conceit: *Failure to be elected was a great blow to his vanity.* **2.** an instance or display of this quality or feeling. **3.** something about which one is vain. **4.** lack of real value; hollowness; worthlessness: *the vanity of a selfish life.* **5.** something worthless, trivial, or pointless. **6.** See **vanity case. 7.** See **dressing table. 8.** compact¹ (def. 12). [ME *vanite* < OF < L *vānitāt-* (s. of *vānitās*), equiv. to *vān-* (see VAIN) + *-itāt-* -ITY] —**van′i·tied,** *adj.*
—**Syn. 1.** egotism, complacency, vainglory, ostentation. See **pride. 4.** emptiness, sham, unreality, folly, triviality, futility. —**Ant. 1.** humility.

van′ity case′, a small luggage bag or case for holding cosmetics or toiletries, used or carried by women. Also called **van′ity bag′, van′ity box′.**

Van′ity Fair′, 1. (in Bunyan's *Pilgrim's Progress*) a fair which goes on perpetually in the town of Vanity and symbolizes worldly ostentation and frivolity. **2.** (*often l.c.*) any place or group, as the world, fashionable society, etc., characterized by or displaying a preoccupation with idle pleasures or ostentation. **3.** (*italics*) a novel (1847–48) by Thackeray.

van′ity press′, a printing house that specializes in publishing books for which the authors pay all or most of the costs. Also called **van′ity pub′lisher.**

van Ley·den (vän līd′ən). See **Leyden, Lucas van.**

van′ line′, *U.S.* a transportation company that uses large motor vans for the long-distance moving of household effects.

Van Loon (van lōōn′, lōn′), **Hen·drik Wil·lem** (hen′drik vil′əm), 1882–1944, U.S. author, born in the Netherlands.

van·man (van′man′, -mən), *n., pl.* **-men** (-men′, -mən). a man who works on a van, esp. the driver. [VAN² + MAN¹]

Vannes (van), *n.* a city in and the capital of Morbihan, in NW France. 34,107 (1962).

Van Paas·sen (van pä′sən), **Pi·erre** (pē âr′), (*Pieter Anthonie Laurusse*), born 1895, U.S. journalist, author, and clergyman; born in the Netherlands.

van·quish (vang′kwish, van′-), *v.t.* **1.** to conquer or subdue by superior force, as in battle. **2.** to defeat in any contest or conflict; be victorious over: *to vanquish one's opponent in an argument.* **3.** to overcome or overpower: *He vanquished all his fears.* [ME *vencusche(n), -quisshe(n)* < OF *vencus* ptp. and *venquis* pt. of *veintre* < L *vincere* to overcome] —**van′quish·a·ble,** *adj.* —**van′quish·er,** *n.* —**van′quish·ment,** *n.*
—**Syn. 1.** subjugate, suppress, crush, quell.

Van Rens·se·laer (van ren′sə lər, -lēr′), **Stephen** (*"the Patroon"*), 1765–1839, U.S. political leader and major general.

Van·sit·tart (van sit′ərt), **Sir Robert Gilbert, 1st Baron Vansittart of Denham,** 1881–1957, British statesman and diplomat.

Van·sit·tart·ism (van sit′ər tiz′əm), *n.* a doctrine holding that the militaristic and aggressive policies of German leaders since the time of the Franco-Prussian war have had the support of the German people and that Germany should undergo a program of demilitarization and corrective education to prevent similar action in the future. [VANSITTART + -ISM]

van·tage (van′tij, vän′-), *n.* **1.** a position, condition, or place affording some advantage, as for action: *a point of vantage.* **2.** an advantage or superiority: *the vantage of wisdom that often comes with age.* **3.** *Tennis Obs.* advantage (def. 5). [ME < AF, aph. var. of *avantage* ADVANTAGE]

van′tage ground′, a position or place which gives one an advantage, as for action, view, or defense.

van′tage point′, a position or place which affords a wide or advantageous perspective or view: *to survey a valley from the vantage point of a high hill.*

van't Hoff (vänt hof′), **Ja·co·bus Hen·dri·cus** (yä kō′bœs hen drē′kœs), 1852–1911, Dutch chemist: Nobel prize 1901.

Va·nu·a Le·vu (vä nōō′ä le′vōō), an island in the S Pacific, one of the Fiji Islands. 39,958 (1946); 2137 sq. mi.

Van Vech·ten (van vek′tən), **Carl,** 1880–1964, U.S. author.

van·ward (van′wərd), *adj., adv.* toward or in the van or front. [VAN¹ + -WARD]

Van Zee·land (vän zā′länt), **Paul** (poul), born 1893, Belgian statesman: premier 1935–37.

Van·zet·ti (van zet′ē; *It.* vän dzet′tē), *n.* **Bar·to·lo·me·o** (bär′tô lô me′ô), 1888–1927, Italian anarchist, in the U.S. after 1908. Cf. **Sacco, Nicola.**

Va·phio (vä′fyô), *n.* an archaeological site in S Greece, in Peloponnesus. Also, **Vafio.**

vap·id (vap′id), *adj.* **1.** lacking or having lost life, sharpness, or flavor; insipid; flat: *vapid tea.* **2.** without liveliness or spirit; dull or tedious: *a vapid party; vapid conversation.* [< L *vapid(us)*; akin to VAPOR] —**va·pid′i·ty, vap′id·ness,** *n.* —**vap′id·ly,** *adv.*
—**Syn. 1.** lifeless, flavorless. **2.** spiritless, unanimated, tiresome, prosaic. —**Ant. 1.** pungent. **2.** stimulating.

va·por (vā′pər), *n.* **1.** a visible exhalation, as fog, mist, steam, smoke, etc., diffused through or suspended in the air: *the vapors rising from the bogs.* **2.** *Physics.* a gas at a temperature below its critical temperature. **3.** a substance converted into vapor for technical or medicinal uses. **4.** a combination of a vaporized substance and air. **5.** gaseous particles of drugs that can be inhaled as a therapeutic agent. **6.** an invisible exhalation, as of moisture, noxious gases, etc. **7.** a strange, senseless, or fantastic notion. **8.** *Archaic.* something insubstantial or transitory. **9. vapors,** *Archaic.* **a.** mental depression, hypochondria, or low spirits. **b.** injurious exhalations formerly supposed to be produced within the body, esp. in the stomach. —*v.t.* **10.** to cause to rise or pass off in, or as in, vapor; vaporize. **11.** *Archaic.* to affect with vapors; depress. —*v.i.* **12.** to rise or pass off in the form of vapor. **13.** to emit vapor or exhalations. **14.** to talk or act grandiloquently, pompously, or boastfully; bluster. Also, *esp. Brit.,* **vapour.** [late ME < L *vapor* steam] —**va′por·a·bil′i·ty,** *n.* —**va′por·a·ble,** *adj.* —**va′por·er,** *n.* —**va′por·less,** *adj.* —**va′por·like′,** *adj.*

va·por·es·cence (vā′pə res′əns), *n.* production or formation of vapor. Also, *esp. Brit.,* **vapourescence.** [VAPOR + -ESCENCE] —**va′por·es′cent,** *adj.*

va·po·ret·to (vap′ə ret′ō; *It.* vä′pô ret′tô), *n., pl.* **-tos,** *It.* **-ti** (-tē). a small steamboat used as a passenger bus along a canal, esp. in Venice, Italy. [< It, equiv. to *vapor(e)* steamboat + *-etto* -ET]

vapori-, a combining form of **vapor:** *vaporimeter.* Also, *esp. Brit.,* **vapouri-.**

va·por·if·ic (vā′pə rif′ik), *adj.* **1.** producing vapor; tending or causing to form vapor. **2.** of, pertaining to, or of the nature of vapor; vaporous. Also, *esp. Brit.,* **vapourific.** [VAPORI- + -FIC]

va·por·im·e·ter (vā′pə rim′i tər), *n.* an instrument for measuring vapor pressure or volume. Also, *esp. Brit.,* **vapourimeter.** [VAPORI- + -METER]

va·por·ing (vā′pər ing), *adj.* **1.** that gives forth vapor. **2.** boastful; bragging. —*n.* **3.** act or instance of bragging or blustering; boastful talk. Also, *esp. Brit.,* **vapouring.** [VAPOR + -ING², -ING¹] —**va′por·ing·ly,** *adv.*

va·por·ise (vā′pə rīz′), *v.t., v.i.,* **-ised, -is·ing.** *Chiefly Brit.* vaporize. —**va′por·is′a·ble,** *adj.*

va·por·is·er (vā′pə rī′zər), *n.* *Chiefly Brit.* vaporizer.

va·por·ish (vā′pər ish), *adj.* **1.** of the nature of or resembling vapor: *a vaporish chiffon dress.* **2.** abounding in vapor: *vaporish autumn mornings in the country.* **3.** inclined to or affected by depression or low spirits; depressed. Also, *esp. Brit.,* **vapourish.** [VAPOR + -ISH¹] —**va′por·ish·ness,** *n.*

va·por·i·za·tion (vā′pər i zā′shən), *n.* **1.** the act of vaporizing. **2.** the state of being vaporized. **3.** the rapid change of water into steam, esp. in a boiler. **4.** *Med.* a vapor therapy. Also, *esp. Brit.,* **vaporization, va′por·i·sa′tion, vapourisation.** [VAPOR + -IZATION]

va·por·ize (vā′pə rīz′), *v.,* **-ized, -iz·ing.** —*v.t.* **1.** to cause to change into vapor. —*v.i.* **2.** to become converted into vapor. **3.** to indulge in boastful talk; speak braggingly. Also, *esp. Brit.,* **vapourize, vaporise, vapourise.** [VAPOR + -IZE] —**va′por·iz′a·ble,** *adj.*

va·por·iz·er (vā′pə rī′zər), *n.* **1.** one who or that which vaporizes. **2.** a device for turning liquid into vapor, as an atomizer, esp. one that converts a medicinal substance into a vapor that is inhaled for respiratory relief. Also, *esp. Brit.,* **vapourizer, vaporiser, vapouriser.** [VAPORIZE + -ER¹]

va′por lock′, an obstruction to the flow of fuel to a gasoline engine, caused by the formation of bubbles in the gasoline as a result of overheating.

va·por·ous (vā′pər əs), *adj.* **1.** having the form or characteristics of vapor: *a vaporous cloud.* **2.** full of or abounding in vapor; foggy; misty: *A light shone dimly in the vaporous twilight.* **3.** producing or giving off vapor: *a vaporous bog.* **4.** dimmed or obscured with vapor: *a low valley surrounded by vaporous mountains.* **5.** unsubstantial; diaphanous; airy: *vaporous fabrics; vaporous breezes.* **6.** vaguely formed, fanciful, or unreliable: *vaporous plans; vaporous promises.* Also, *esp. Brit.,* **vapourous.** [VAPOR + -OUS] —**va′por·ous·ly,** *adv.* —**va′por·ous·ness, va·por·os·i·ty** (vā′pə ros′i tē), *n.*

va′por pres′sure, the pressure exerted by the molecules of a vapor, esp. that part of the total pressure exerted by vapor in a mixture of gases, as by water vapor in air.

Va·pors (vā′pərz), *n.* **Sea of.** See **Mare Vaporum.**

va′por ten′sion, 1. See **vapor pressure. 2.** the maximum vapor pressure possible, at a given temperature, in a system composed of a liquid or solid substance in contact with the vapor of that substance.

va′por trail′, contrail.

Va·po·rum (vä pōr′əm, -pôr′-), *n.* **Mare.** See **Mare Vaporum.**

va·por·y (vā′pə rē), *adj.* **1.** vaporous. **2.** vaporish. Also, *esp. Brit.,* **vapoury.** [VAPOR + -Y¹]

va·pour (vā′pər), *n., v.t., v.i.* *Chiefly Brit.* vapor. —**va′pour·a·bil′i·ty,** *n.* —**va′pour·a·ble,** *adj.* —**va′pour·er,** *n.* —**va′pour·less,** *adj.* —**va′pour·like′,** *adj.*

va·pour·es·cence (vā′pə res′əns), *n.* *Chiefly Brit.* vaporescence. —**va′pour·es′cent,** *adj.*

vapouri-, *Chiefly Brit.* vapori-.

va·pour·if·ic (vā′pə rif′ik), *adj.* *Chiefly Brit.* vaporific.

va·pour·im·e·ter (vā′pə rim′i tər), *n.* *Chiefly Brit.* vaporimeter.

va·pour·ing (vā′pər ing), *adj., n.* *Chiefly Brit.* vaporing. —**va′pour·ing·ly,** *adv.*

va·pour·ise (vā′pə rīz′), *v.t., v.i.,* **-ised, -is·ing.** *Chiefly Brit.* vaporize. —**va′pour·is′a·ble,** *adj.*

va·pour·is·er (vā′pə rī′zər), *n.* *Chiefly Brit.* vaporizer.

va·pour·ish (vā′pər ish), *adj.* *Chiefly Brit.* vaporish. —**va′pour·ish·ness,** *n.*

va·pour·i·za·tion (vā′pər i zā′shən), *n.* *Chiefly Brit.* vaporization. Also, **va′pour·i·sa′tion.**

va·pour·ize (vā′pə rīz′), *v.t., v.i.,* **-ized, -iz·ing.** *Chiefly Brit.* vaporize. Also, **vapourise.** —**va′pour·iz′a·ble,** *adj.*

va·pour·iz·er (vā′pə rī′zər), *n.,* *Chiefly Brit.* vaporizer.

va·pour·ous (vā′pər əs), *adj.* *Chiefly Brit.* vaporous. —**va′pour·ous·ly,** *adv.* —**va′pour·ous·ness, va·pour·os·i·ty** (vā′pə ros′i tē), *n.*

va·pour·y (vā′pə rē), *adj.* *Chiefly Brit.* vapory.

va·que·ro (vä kâr′ō; *Sp.* bä ke′rô), *n., pl.* **-que·ros** (-kâr′ōz; *Sp.* -ke′rôs). *Southwestern U.S.* a cowboy or herdsman. [< Sp, equiv. to *vac(a)* cow + *-ero* -ARY]

Var (var), *n.* a department in SE France. 469,557 (1962); 2326 sq. mi. *Cap.:* Draguignan.

VAR, visual aural range.

var., 1. variant. **2.** variation. **3.** variety. **4.** variometer. **5.** various.

va·ra (vär′ə; *Sp.* bä′rä; *Port.* vä′rə), *n., pl.* **va·ras** (vär′əz; *Sp.* bä′räs; *Port.* vä′rəsh). **1.** a unit of length in Spanish- and Portuguese-speaking countries, varying from about 32 inches to about 43 inches. **2.** the square vara, used as a unit of area. [< Sp < L *vāra* forked pole, n. use of fem. of *vārus* crooked, bent]

Va·ra·na·si (və rä′nə sē), *n.* Benares.

va·ran·gi·an (və ran′jē ən), *n.* *European Furniture.* a three-legged armchair of the 16th and 17th centuries, composed of turned uprights and spindles with a triangular seat: known in American furniture as a **Harvard chair.** [so called because believed to have been introduced into Europe by the Varangians]

Va·ran·gi·an (və ran′jē ən), *n.* **1.** one of the Northmen who, under Rurik, established a dynasty in Russia in the 9th century. **2.** a member of the bodyguard **(Varan′gian guard′)** of the Byzantine emperors, esp. in the 11th and 12th centuries, made up of Northmen, Anglo-Saxons, and other northern Europeans. —*adj.* **3.** of or pertaining to the Varangians.

Var·dar (vär′där), *n.* a river in S Europe, flowing from NW Macedonia through N Greece into the Gulf of Salonika. 200 mi. long.

Var·dha·ma·na (vär′də mä′nə), *n.* *Jainism.* a semi-legendary teacher, presently believed to have died c480 B.C., who reformed older doctrines to establish Jainism in its present form: regarded as the twenty-fourth and latest Tirthankara. Also called **Vardhama′-na Mahavi′ra, Mahavira.**

Va·re·se (vä re′se), *n.* a city in N Italy, NW of Milan. 67,043 (1961).

Va·rèse (vä rez′), *n.* **Ed·gard** (ed gar′), 1885–1965, U.S. composer, born in France.

Var·gas (vär′gəs), *n.* **Ge·tu·lio Dor·nel·les** (zhə-tōō′lyōō dôr ne′lis), 1883–1954, Brazilian statesman.

Var·gi·nha (vər zhē′nyə), *n.* a city in E Brazil. 24,944 (1960).

var·gue·no (vär gān′yō), *n., pl.* **-nos.** *Sp. Furniture.* a fall-front desk of the 16th, 17th, and early 18th centuries, having the form of a chest upon a small table. [< Sp *bargueño* (work) of Bargas (small town near Toledo)]

var·i·a (vâr′ē ə), *n.pl.* miscellaneous items, esp. a miscellany of literary works. [< NL, L, neut. pl. of *vari(us)* VARIOUS]

var·i·a·ble (vâr′ē ə bəl), *adj.* **1.** apt or liable to vary or change; changeable: *variable weather; variable moods.* **2.** capable of being varied or changed; alterable: *a variable time limit for completion of a book.* **3.** inconstant; fickle: *a variable lover.* **4.** having much variation or diversity. **5.** *Biol.* deviating from the usual type, as a species or a specific character. **6.** *Astron.* (of a star) changing in brightness. **7.** *Meteorol.* (of wind) tending to change in direction. **8.** *Math.* having the nature or characteristics of a variable. —*n.* **9.** something that may or does vary; a variable feature, factor, or the like. **10.** *Math.* **a.** a quantity or function that may assume any given value or set of values. **b.** a symbol that represents this. **11.** *Logic.* (in the functional calculus) a symbol for an unspecified member of a class of things or statements. Cf. **bound variable, free variable. 12.** *Astron.* See **variable star. 13.** *Meteorol.* a shifting wind, esp. as distinguished from a trade wind. **14. variables,** a region where shifting winds, as distinguished from trade winds, are found. [late ME < L *variābil(is),* equiv. to *vari(us)* VARIOUS + *-ābilis* -ABLE] —**var′i·a·bil′i·ty, var′i·a·ble·ness,** *n.* —**var′i·a·bly,** *adv.*
—**Syn. 3.** vacillating, wavering, fluctuating, unsteady. —**Ant. 1, 3.** constant.

var′iable annu′ity, an annuity in which the premiums are invested chiefly in common stocks or other securities, the annuitant receiving payments based on the yield of the investments instead of in fixed amounts.

var′iable con′trast pa′per, *Photog.* printing paper in which the contrast of the image is controlled by the color of the printing light.

var·i·a·ble-pitch (vâr′ē ə bəl pich′), *adj.* *Aeron., Naut.* (of a propeller) controllable-pitch.

var′iable star′, *Astron.* a star that varies markedly in brightness from time to time. Also called **variable.**

var′iable time′ fuze′. See **proximity fuze.**

Var′iable Zone′. See **Temperate Zone.**

va·ri·a lec·ti·o (wä′ri ä′ lek′ti ō′; *Eng.* vâr′ē ə lek′shē ō′), *pl.* **va·ri·ae lec·ti·o·nes** (wä′ri ī′ lek′ti-ō′nās; *Eng.* vâr′ē ē′ lek′shē ō′nēz). *Latin.* a variant reading. [L]

var·i·ance (vâr′ē əns), *n.* **1.** the state, quality, or fact of being variable, divergent, different, or deviate. **2.** an instance of varying; difference; discrepancy. **3.** *Statistics.* the square of the standard deviation. **4.** *Physics, Chem.* the number of degrees of freedom of a system. **5.** *Law.* **a.** a difference or discrepancy, as between two statements or documents in law which should agree. **b.** a departure from the cause of action originally stated in the complaint. **6.** an official permit to do something normally forbidden by regulations, esp. by building in a way or for a purpose normally forbidden by a zoning law or a building code. **7.** a disagreement, dispute, or quarrel. **8. at variance, a.** (of things) in a state of difference or disagreement. **b.** (of persons) in a state of controversy or dissension: *at variance with one's superiors.* [ME < L *variantia*, equiv. to *vari-* (base of *variāre* to VARY) + *-āntia* -ANCE]

var/iance anal/ysis, *Statistics.* See **analysis of variance.**

var·i·ant (vâr/ē ənt), *adj.* **1.** tending to change or alter; exhibiting variety or diversity; varying: *variant shades of color.* **2.** not agreeing or conforming; differing, esp. from something of the same general kind. **3.** not universally accepted. —*n.* **4.** one who or that which varies. **5.** a different spelling, pronunciation, or form of the same word: *"Vehemency" is a variant of "vehemence."* **6.** a different version or reading of something, as a passage in a translation. [late ME < L *variant-* (s. of *variāns*, prp. of *variāre*), equiv. to *vari-* (see VARY) + *-ant-* -ANT]

var·i·ate (vâr/ē it), *n.* **1.** *Statistics.* a variable quantity associated with a probability distribution; random variable. **2.** variant. [< L *variāt(us)* (ptp. of *variāre* to VARY), equiv. to *vari-* (see VARY) + *-ātus* -ATE[1]]

var·i·a·tion (vâr/ē ā/shən), *n.* **1.** the act, process, or accident of varying in condition, character, or degree: *Prices are subject to variation.* **2.** an instance of this: *There is a variation in the quality of fabrics in this shipment.* **3.** amount, rate, extent, or degree of change: *a temperature variation of 40° in a particular climate.* **4.** a different form of something; variant. **5.** *Music.* **a.** the transformation of a melody or theme with changes or elaborations in harmony, rhythm, and melody. **b.** a varied form of a melody or theme, esp. one of a series of such forms developing the capacities of the subject. **6.** *Ballet.* a solo dance, esp. one forming a section of a pas de deux. **7.** *Astron.* **a.** any deviation from the mean orbit of a heavenly body, esp. of a planetary or satellite orbit. **b.** an inequality in the moon's motion, having a period of one-half synodic month. **8.** Also called **magnetic declination, magnetic variation.** *Navig.* the angle between the geographic and the magnetic meridian at a given point, expressed in plus degrees east or minus degrees west of true north. Cf. **deviation** (def. 4). **9.** *Biol.* **a.** a deviation in the structure or character of an organism from that of others of the same species or group, or that of the parents. **b.** an organism exhibiting such deviation; variety. **10.** *Math.* the least upper bound of the sums of the oscillations of a given function at each subinterval of a specified interval, considered for all possible partitions of the interval. Cf. **bounded** (def. 2c). [< L *variātiōn-* (s. of *variātiō*), equiv. to *variāt(us)* (see VARIATE) + *-iōn-* -ION; r. ME *variacioun* < AF] —**var/i·a/tion·al, var·i·a·tive** (vâr/ē ā/tiv), *adj.* —**var/i·a/tion·al·ly, var/i·a/tive·ly,** *adv.*
—**Syn. 1.** mutation, alteration, modification; deviation, divergence, difference. —**Ant. 1.** sameness.

varia/tion chart/, a chart showing the variations in the declination of the magnetic field on a certain portion of the earth's surface by means of isogonal lines; magnetic chart.

varia/tion of param/eters, *Math.* a method of solving a linear differential equation in which the sum of the terms containing derivatives is equated to a function of the independent variable, involving the solution of the equation in which the sum is equated to zero and using the result to solve the given equation.

varic-, var. of **varico-** before a vowel.

var·i·cel·la (var/i sel/ə), *n.* *Pathol.* See **chicken pox.** [< NL, equiv. to *vari(ola)* VARIOLA + *-cella* dim. suffix] —**var/i·cel/lar,** *adj.*

var·i·cel·late (var/i sel/it, -āt), *adj.* having small varices, as certain shells. [< NL *varicell(a)* (r. L *varicula*, dim. of *varix* varicose vein) + -ATE[1]]

var·i·cel·la·tion (var/i sə lā/shən), *n.* inoculation of a person with chicken pox virus. [VARICELL(A) + -ATION]

var·i·cel·loid (var/i sel/oid), *adj.* resembling varicella. [VARICELL(A) + -OID]

var·i·ces (var/i sēz/), *n.* pl. of **varix.**

varico-, a word element meaning "varicose veins," used in the formation of compound words: *varicocele.* Also, *esp. before a vowel,* **varic-.** [< L *varic-* (s. of *varix*) + -o-. See VARIX]

var·i·co·cele (var/ə kō sēl/), *n.* *Pathol.* a varicose condition of the spermatic veins of the scrotum. [VARICO- + -CELE[1]]

var·i·col·ored (vâr/i kul/ərd), *adj.* having various colors; variegated; motley: *a varicolored print.* Also, *esp. Brit.,* **var/i·col/oured.** [VARI(OUS) + COLORED]

var·i·cose (var/ə kōs/, vâr/-), *adj.* **1.** abnormally or unusually enlarged or swollen: *a varicose vein.* **2.** pertaining to or affected with varices (varicose veins), which often affect the superficial portions of the lower limbs. [< L *varicōs(us).* See VARIC-, -OSE[1]]

var·i·co·sis (var/ə kō/sis), *n.* *Pathol.* **1.** the formation of varices. **2.** varicosity. [VARIC- + -OSIS]

var·i·cos·i·ty (var/ə kos/i tē), *n., pl.* **-ties.** *Pathol.* **1.** state or condition of being varicose. **2.** varix (def. 1). [VARICOSE + -ITY]

var·i·cot·o·my (var/ə kot/ə mē), *n., pl.* **-mies.** *Surg.* an operation for treating varicose veins by subcutaneous incision. [VARICO- + -TOMY]

Var·i·dase (vâr/i dās/), *n.* *Pharm., Trademark.* a combination of streptokinase and streptodornase, used chiefly as an agent for the breakdown of blood clots and of fibrinous or purulent matter resulting from injury or infection.

var·ied (vâr/ēd), *adj.* **1.** characterized by or exhibiting variety; various; diverse; diversified: *varied backgrounds; varied hobbies.* **2.** changed; altered: *a varied estimate.* **3.** having several different colors; variegated. [VARY + -ED[2]] —**var/ied·ly,** *adv.* —**var/ied·ness,** *n.*

var/ied thrush/, a plump, robinlike thrush, *Ixoreus naevius*, of western North America, having black and gray upper parts and orange-tan underparts, with a dark band across the chest. Also called **var/ied rob/in.**

var·i·e·gate (vâr/ē ə gāt/, vâr/ə gāt/), *v.t.,* **-gat·ed, -gat·ing. 1.** to make varied in appearance, as by adding different colors. **2.** to give variety to; diversify. [< LL *variegāt(us)* (ptp. of *variegāre* to make (something) look varied), equiv. to L *vari(us)* VARIOUS + *-eg-* (var. of *-ag-*, root of *agere* to do; see AGENT) + *-ātus* -ATE] —**var/i·e·ga/tor,** *n.*

var·i·e·gat·ed (vâr/ē ə gā/tid, vâr/ə gā/-), *adj.* **1.** varied in appearance or color; marked with patches or spots of different colors. **2.** varied; diversified; diverse. [VARIEGATE + -ED[2]]

var·i·e·ga·tion (vâr/ē ə gā/shən, vâr/ə gā/-), *n.* **1.** the act of variegating. **2.** the state or condition of being variegated; varied coloration. [VARIEGATE + -ION]

var·i·er (vâr/ē ər), *n.* one who or that which varies.

va·ri·e·tal (və rī/i tᵊl), *adj.* **1.** of, pertaining to, designating, or characteristic of a variety. **2.** constituting a variety. [VARIET(Y) + -AL[1]] —**va·ri/e·tal·ly,** *adv.*

va·ri·e·ty (və rī/i tē), *n., pl.* **-ties,** *adj.* —*n.* **1.** the state of being varied or diversified: *to give variety to a diet.* **2.** difference; discrepancy. **3.** a number of different types of things, esp. ones in the same general category: *a large variety of fruits.* **4.** a kind or sort. **5.** a different form, condition, or phase of something: *varieties of pastry; a variety of economic reforms.* **6.** a category within a species, based on some hereditary difference. **7.** a type of animal or plant produced by artificial selection. **8.** *Philately.* a stamp differing from others of the same issue through an accident other than an error of an artist or printer. Cf. **error** (def. 7), **freak**[1] (def. 5). **9.** Also called **vari/ety show/.** *Theat.* entertainment of mixed character, consisting of a number of individual performances or acts, as of singing, dancing, acrobatic exhibitions, playlets, etc. Cf. **vaudeville** (def. 1). —*adj.* **10.** *Theat.* of, pertaining to, or characteristic of a variety: *a variety theater; a variety performer.* [< L *varietās.* See VARIOUS, -ITY]
—**Syn. 1.** diversity, multiplicity. **3.** assortment, collection, group. **5.** kind, sort, class, species. —**Ant. 1.** sameness.

vari/ety meat/, edible meat other than the usual flesh, esp. organs, as tongue, liver, etc.

vari/ety store/, a retail store, as a five-and-ten, carrying a large variety of goods, esp. low-priced articles.

var·i·form (vâr/ə fôrm/), *adj.* varied in form; having various forms. [VARI(OUS) + -FORM] —**var/i·form/ly,** *adv.*

var·in·dor (vâr/in dər), *n.* *Elect.* an inductor having inductance that varies greatly with an applied current. [VAR(IABLE) + IND(UCT)OR]

va·ri·o (vär/ē ō/, vär/yō), *n., pl.* **-os.** baguio.

var·i·o·cou·pler (vâr/ē ō kup/lər), *n.* *Elect.* a transformer having coils with a self-impedance that is essentially constant but a mutual impedance that can be varied by moving one coil with respect to the other. [VARI(ABLE) + -O- + COUPLER]

va·ri·o·la (və rī/ə lə), *n.* *Pathol.* smallpox. [< ML, equiv. to *vari(us)* speckled (see VARIOUS) + *-ola* dim. suffix]

va·ri·o·lar (və rī/ə lər), *adj.* variolous. [VARIOL(A) + -AR[1]]

var·i·o·late (vâr/ē ə lāt/, -lit), *adj.* *Pathol.* resembling smallpox, as a lesion. [VARIOL(A) + -ATE[1]]

var·i·o·la·tion (vâr/ē ə lā/shən), *n.* inoculation of a person with smallpox virus. [VARIOL(A) + -ATION]

var·i·ole (vâr/ē ōl/), *n.* **1.** a shallow pit or depression like the mark left by a smallpox pustule; foveola. **2.** *Petrog.* any of the spherules of variolite. [< F *variole* smallpox < ML *variola* VARIOLA]

var·i·o·lite (vâr/ē ə līt/), *n.* *Petrog.* any of certain fine-grained, basic igneous rocks containing light-colored spherules that give them a pock-marked appearance, esp. on weathered surfaces. [VARIOL(A) + -ITE[1]]

var·i·o·lit·ic (vâr/ē ə lit/ik), *adj.* **1.** *Petrog.* of or resembling variolite, esp. in texture. **2.** spotted; speckled. [VARIOLITE + -IC]

var·i·o·loid (vâr/ē ə loid/), *adj.* **1.** resembling smallpox. **2.** of or pertaining to a mild case of smallpox. —*n.* **3.** a mild smallpox, esp. as occurring in persons who have been vaccinated or have previously had smallpox. [VARIOL(A) + -OID]

var·i·o·loss·er (vâr/ē ə lô/sər), *n.* *Elect.* a device having a power loss that can be controlled by an electromotive force or a current. [VARI(ABLE) + -O- + *losser* (LOSS + -ER[1] on model of *loser*)]

va·ri·o·lous (və rī/ə ləs), *adj.* **1.** of or pertaining to smallpox. **2.** affected with smallpox. **3.** having pits like those left by smallpox. Also, **variolar.** [VARIOL(A) + -OUS]

var·i·om·e·ter (vâr/ē om/i tər), *n.* **1.** *Elect.* an instrument for measuring inductance, consisting essentially of an inductor with two or more coils whose relative position may be changed to vary the inductance. **2.** an instrument for indicating a change in a component of a magnetic field vector, esp. one related to the earth's magnetic field. [*vari-* (see VARIOUS) + -O- + -METER]

var·i·o·rum (vâr/ē ôr/əm, -ōr/-), *adj.* **1.** containing different versions of the text by various editors: *a variorum edition of Shakespeare.* **2.** containing many notes and commentaries by a number of scholars or critics: *a variorum text of Cicero.* —*n.* **3.** a variorum edition or text. [short for L *ēditiō cum notīs variōrum* edition with the notes of various persons]

var·i·ous (vâr/ē əs), *adj.* **1.** of different kinds, as two or more things; differing one from another: *Various experiments have failed to prove his theory.* **2.** marked by or exhibiting variety or diversity: *houses of various designs.* **3.** presenting or having many different qualities or aspects: *a man of various talent.* **4.** having a variety of colors; varicolored. **5.** different from each other; dissimilar. **6.** variant. **7.** numerous; many: *living at various hotels in Florida.* **8.** individual (in a group, class, kind, etc.); separate: *permission from the various officials in Washington.* [< L *varius* manifold, diversified, diverse; see -OUS] —**var/i·ous·ly,** *adv.* —**var/i·ous·ness,** *n.*
—**Syn. 1.** VARIOUS, DIFFERENT, DISTINCT, DIVERSE refer to things which are sufficiently unlike to be perceivably of more than one kind. VARIOUS implies that there are several kinds of the same general thing: *various types of seaweed.* DIFFERENT is applied either to a single thing differing in identity or character from another, or to two or more things differing thus from one another: *two different stories concerning an event.* DISTINCT implies want of connection between things, which, however, may possibly be alike or similar: *two distinct accounts which coincide.* DIVERSE commonly implies a number or assortment of things or parts differing one from another: *three completely diverse proposals for preventing inflation.* **2.** sundry. **3.** diversified, variegated, varied. —**Ant. 1.** identical, same, uniform, similar.

var·is·cite (var/i sīt/), *n.* a mineral, hydrated phosphate of aluminum, $Al(PO_4)\cdot 2H_2O$, occurring mainly in Utah in the form of massive, bluish-green nodules: sometimes used as a gem. [< G *Variscit*, named after *Variscia* Latinized German district name; see -ITE[1]]

var·is·tor (va ris/tər, və-), *n.* *Elect.* a resistor whose resistance automatically varies in proportion to the voltage of the current through it. [VARI(ABLE) + (RESI)STOR]

Var·i·type (vâr/i tīp/), *v.,* **-typed, -typ·ing.** —*v.i.* **1.** to operate a Varityper. —*v.t.* **2.** to set (type) on a Varityper. [back formation from VARITYPER]

Var·i·typ·er (vâr/i tī/pər), *n.* *Trademark.* a typewriterlike machine with interchangeable typefaces, for composing justified matter. —**var/i·typ/ist,** *n.*

va·ri·um et mu·ta·bi·le sem·per fe·mi·na (wä/rē ŏŏm/ et mōō tä/bi lā sem/per fā/mi nä/; *Eng.* vâr/ē əm et myōō tab/ə lē/ sem/pər fem/ə nə), *Latin.* woman is ever fickle and changeable.

var·ix (vâr/iks), *n., pl.* **var·i·ces** (vâr/i sēz/). **1.** Also called **varicosity.** *Pathol.* a permanent abnormal dilation and lengthening of a vein, usually accompanied by some tortuosity; a varicose vein. **2.** *Zool.* a mark or scar on the surface of a shell at a former position of the lip of the aperture. [< L: varicose vein]

Varl (värl), *n.* a boy's given name.

var·let (vär/lit), *n.* *Archaic.* **1.** an attendant or servant. **2.** a page who serves a knight. **3.** a knavish person; rascal. [late ME < MF; var. of VALET]

var·let·ry (vär/li trē), *n.* *Archaic.* **1.** varlets collectively. **2.** the mob or rabble. [VARLET + -RY]

Var/ley loop/ (vär/lē), *Elect.* a device containing a Wheatstone bridge, for comparing resistances and for locating faults in circuits. [named after C. F. *Varley* (1828–83), English electrical engineer]

var·man·nie (vär mä/nē), *n.* (in india) a method of self-defense similar to jujitsu. [?]

var·mint (vär/mənt), *n.* **1.** *Dial.* vermin. **2.** an objectionable or undesirable animal, usually predatory, as a coyote, bobcat, etc. **3.** a despicable, obnoxious, or annoying person. Also, **var/ment.**

var·na (vär/nə, vur/-), *n.* any of the four main Hindu social classes; caste. [< Skt *varṇa:* lit., class]

Var·na (vär/nə), *n.* a seaport in NE Bulgaria, on the Black Sea. 161,800 (est. 1963). Formerly, **Stalin.**

var·nish (vär/nish), *n.* **1.** a preparation consisting of resinous matter, as copal, lac, etc., dissolved in an oil (**oil varnish**) or in alcohol (**spirit varnish**) or other volatile liquid. When applied to the surface of wood, metal, etc., it dries and leaves a hard, more or less glossy, usually transparent coating. **2.** the sap of certain trees, used for the same purpose (**natural varnish**). **3.** any of various other preparations similarly used, as one having India rubber, pyroxylin, or asphalt as its chief constituent. **4.** a coating or surface of varnish. **5.** something resembling or suggesting a coat of varnish; gloss. **6.** superficial polish or external show, esp. to conceal some defect or inadequacy: *The play has a varnish of witty dialogue but lacks a coherent plot.* **7. varnishes,** *Railroads Slang.* a passenger car or train. **8.** *Brit.* nail polish. —*v.t.* **9.** to apply varnish to; coat or cover with varnish. **10.** to give a glossy appearance to. **11.** to give an improved appearance to; embellish; adorn. **12.** to give a superficially pleasing appearance to, esp. in order to deceive: *to varnish the truth.* [ME *varnisch* < MF *vernis, verniz* < ML *vernicium* sandarac < MGk *berníkē*, syncopated var. of Gk *Bereníkē*, city in Cyrenaica] —**var/nish·er,** *n.* —**var/nish·y,** *adj.*

var/nish tree/, **1.** any of various trees yielding sap or other substances used for varnish, as *Rhus verniciflua*, of Japan. **2.** pride-of-India.

Var·ro (var/ō), *n.* **Marcus Te·ren·ti·us** (tə ren/shē əs), c116–27? B.C., Roman scholar and author.

var·si·ty (vär/si tē), *n., pl.* **-ties. 1.** any first-string team, esp. in sports, that represents a school, college, university, or the like: *He is on the varsity in tennis and in debating.* **2.** *Chiefly Brit. Informal.* university. [var. of (UNI)VERSITY]

Var·u·na (vur/ŏŏ nə, vär ə/), *n.* *Hinduism.* the Vedic god of natural and moral law, probably a sky god originally.

var·us (vâr/əs), *n.* *Pathol.* abnormal angulation of a bone or joint, with the angle pointing away from the midline. [< L: crooked, bent]

varve (värv), *n.* (in certain geological formations) an annual deposit usually consisting of two layers, one of fine materials and the other of coarse. [< Sw *varv* a round, (complete) turn]

varve-count (värv/kount/), *n.* a system for determining the age of certain geological formations, based on the number of varves.

var·y (vâr/ē), *v.,* **var·ied, var·y·ing.** —*v.t.* **1.** to change or alter, as in form, appearance, character, substance, etc.: *to vary one's methods.* **2.** to cause to be different from something else: *The orchestra varied last night's program with one new selection.* **3.** to relieve from uniformity or monotony; diversify: *to vary one's diet.* **4.** *Music.* to alter (a melody or theme) by modification or embellishments without changing its identity. —*v.i.* **5.** to show diversity; be different: *The age at which children are ready to read varies.* **6.** to undergo change in appearance, form, substance, character, etc.: *The landscape begins to vary as one drives south.* **7.** to change in succession; follow alternately: *Demand for certain products varies with the seasons.* **8.** to diverge; depart; deviate (usually fol. by *from*): *to vary from a rule; to vary from the norm.* **9.** *Math.* to be subject to change. **10.** *Biol.* to exhibit variation. [ME *varie(n)* < L *variāre*, equiv. to *vari(us)* diverse + *-āre* inf. suffix] —**var/i·er,** *n.* —**var/y·ing·ly,** *adv.*
—**Syn. 1.** modify, mutate. **7.** differ, deviate.

vas (vas), *n., pl.* **va·sa** (vā/sə). *Anat., Zool., Bot.* a vessel or duct. [< L: vessel]

vas-, var. of **vaso-** before a vowel: *vasectomy.*

va·sa mur·rhi·na (vā/sə mə rī/nə, -rē/-), an American art glass, consisting of colored glass dusted with flakes or grains of metal and flashed with clear glass. [< NL: lit., murrhine vessel]

Va·sa·ri (və zär′ē, -sâr′ē; *It.* vä zä′rē), *n.* **Gior·gio** (jôr′jō), 1511–74, Italian painter, architect, and art historian.

Vas·co da Ga·ma (väs′kō də gam′ə, gä′mə; *Port.* vāsh′ko͞o də gä′mə). See **Gama, Vasco da.**

vas·cu·lar (vas′kyə lər), *adj.* *Biol.* pertaining to, composed of, or provided with vessels or ducts which convey fluids, as blood, lymph, or sap. Also, **vas·cu·lose** (vas′kyə lōs′), **vas·cu·lous** (vas′kyə ləs). [< NL *vāsculār(is).* See VASCULUM, -AR[1]] —**vas′cu·lar′i·ty,** *n.* —**vas′cu·lar·ly,** *adv.*

vas′cular bun′dle, bundle (def. 4).

vas′cular plant′, a plant having a vascular system.

vas′cular ray′, *Bot.* a radiate band of parenchyma in the secondary xylem extending into the secondary phloem of the stems of certain vascular plants, formed by the cambium and serving for the storage of food and the conduction of nutriments.

vas′cular tis′sue, *Bot.* plant tissue consisting of ducts or vessels, that, in the higher plants, forms the system **(vas′cular sys′tem)** by which sap is conveyed through the plant.

vas·cu·lum (vas′kyə ləm), *n., pl.* **-la** (-lə), **-lums.** a kind of case or box used by botanists for carrying specimens as they are collected. [< L: little vessel. See VAS, -CULE]

vas de·fe·rens (vas def′ə renz′), *pl.* **va·sa de·fe·ren·ti·a** (vā′sə def′ə ren′shē ə). *Anat., Zool.* the deferent duct of the testis which transports the sperm from the epididymus to the penis. [< NL, L *vās* vessel + *dēferēns* carrying off. See VASE, DEFERENT[2]]

vase (vās, vāz *or, esp. Brit.,* väz), *n.* a hollow container, as of glass, porcelain, earthenware, or metal, usually higher than it is wide, used chiefly to hold cut flowers or for decoration. [< F < L *vās* vessel] —**vase′like′,** *adj.*

vas·ec·to·mise (va sek′tə mīz′, -zek′-, vā-), *v.t.,* **-mised, -mis·ing.** *Chiefly Brit.* vasectomize.

vas·ec·to·mize (va sek′tə mīz′, -zek′-, vā-), *v.t.,* **-mized, -miz·ing.** *Surg.* to perform a vasectomy on. [VASECTOM(Y) + -IZE]

vas·ec·to·my (va sek′tə mē), *n., pl.* **-mies.** *Surg.* excision of the vas deferens, or of a portion of it. [VAS + -ECTOMY]

Vas·e·line (vas′ə lēn′, vas′ə lēn′), *n.* *Trademark.* petrolatum. Also, **vaseline.**

Vash·ti (vash′tī), *n.* the queen of Ahasuerus who was banished for refusing to appear before the king's guests. Esther 1:9–22. Also, *Douay Bible,* **Vasthi.**

vaso-, a learned borrowing from Latin meaning "vessel," used in the formation of compound words: *vasoconstrictor.* Also, *esp. before a vowel,* **vas-.** [< L *vās* vessel + -o-]

vas·o·con·stric·tion (vas′ō kən strik′shən), *n.* *Physiol.* constriction of the blood vessels, as by the action of a nerve. [VASO- + CONSTRICTION]

vas·o·con·stric·tive (vas′ō kən strik′tiv), *adj.* *Physiol.* causing vasoconstriction. [VASO- + CONSTRICTIVE]

vas·o·con·stric·tor (vas′ō kən strik′tər), *Physiol.* —*adj.* **1.** causing the constriction of blood vessels. —*n.* **2.** a nerve or drug that causes vasoconstriction. [VASO- + CONSTRICTOR]

vas·o·de·pres·sor (vas′ō di pres′ər), *adj., n.* *Physiol.* vasodilator. [VASO- + DEPRESSOR]

vas·o·dil·a·ta·tion (vas′ō dil′ə tā′shən, -dī′lə-), *n.* *Physiol.* dilatation of the blood vessels, as by the action of a nerve. Also, **vas·o·di·la·tion** (vas′ō dī lā′shən, -di-). [VASO- + DILATION]

vas·o·di·la·tor (vas′ō dī lā′tər, -di-), *Physiol.* —*adj.* **1.** causing the dilatation or relaxation of blood vessels. —*n.* **2.** a nerve or drug that causes vasodilatation. [VASO- + DILATOR]

vas·o·in·hib·i·tor (vas′ō in hib′i tər), *n.* an agent, as a drug, that inhibits the action of the vasomotor nerves. [VASO- + INHIBITOR] —**vas·o·in·hib·i·to·ry** (vas′ō in hib′i tôr′ē, -tōr′ē), *adj.*

vas·o·li·ga·tion (vas′ō li gā′shən), *n.* *Surg.* ligation of the vas deferens. Also, **vasoligature.** [VASO- + LIGATION]

vas·o·lig·a·ture (vas′ō lig′ə chər), *n.* *Surg.* vasoligation. [VASO- + LIGATURE]

vas·o·mo·tion (vas′ō mō′shən), *n.* *Physiol.* the change in diameter of a blood vessel. [VASO- + MOTION]

vas·o·mo·tor (vas′ō mō′tər), *adj.* *Physiol.* regulating the diameter of blood vessels, as certain nerves. [VASO- + MOTOR]

va·so·pres·sor (vas′ō pres′ər), *n.* a chemical substance, as adrenalin, that raises the blood pressure by causing contraction of the arteriole muscles, narrowing the arteriole passage. [VASO- + PRESSOR]

vas·o·stim·u·lant (vas′ō stim′yə lənt), *adj.* **1.** stimulating the action of the vasomotor nerves. —*n.* **2.** a vasostimulant agent, as a drug. [VASO- + STIMULANT]

vas·ot·o·my (va sot′ə mē), *n., pl.* **-mies.** *Surg.* incision or opening of the vas deferens. [VASO- + -TOMY]

vas·o·ton·ic (vas′ō ton′ik), *adj.* *Physiol.* pertaining to or regulating the tone of the blood vessels. [VASO- + TONIC]

vas·o·tribe (vas′ə trīb′), *n.* *Surg.* angiotribe. [VASO- + Gk *trīb(ein)* (to) crush]

vas·sal (vas′əl), *n.* **1.** (in the feudal system) a person granted the use of land, in return for which he rendered homage, fealty, and usually military service or its equivalent to his lord or other superior; feudal tenant. **2.** a person holding some similar relation to a superior; a subject, subordinate, follower, or retainer. **3.** a servant or slave. —*adj.* **4.** of, pertaining to, or characteristic of a vassal. **5.** having the status or position of a vassal. [ME < MF < ML *vassall(us),* equiv. to *vass(us)* servant (< Celt; cf. OBreton *uuas,* Welsh *gwas* young man, Ir *foss* servant) + *-allus* n. suffix] —**vas′sal·less,** *adj.*

vas·sal·age (vas′ə lij), *n.* **1.** the state or condition of a vassal. **2.** homage or service required of a vassal. **3.** a territory held by a vassal. **4.** *Hist.* (collectively) vassals. **5.** dependence, subjection, or servitude. [ME < MF; see VASSAL, -AGE]

vas·sal·ic (va sal′ik), *adj.* of, pertaining to, or resembling a vassal or vassalage. [VASSAL + -IC]

Vas·sar (vas′ər), a town in E Michigan. 2680 (1960).

vast (vast, väst), *adj.* **1.** of very great area or extent; immense: *the vast reaches of outer space.* **2.** of very great size or proportions; huge; enormous: *vast piles of rubble left in the wake of the war.* **3.** very great in number, quantity, amount, etc.: *vast sums of money; vast mineral resources.* **4.** very great in degree, intensity, etc.: *of vast importance; a workman of vast skill.* —*n.* **5.** *Archaic or Poetic.* an immense or boundless expanse or space. [< L *vast(us)* empty; immense] —**vast′ly,** *adv.* —**vast′ness,** *n.*
—**Syn. 1.** measureless, boundless, gigantic, colossal, stupendous. —**Ant. 1.** small.

Väs·ter·ås (ves′tər ôs′), *n.* a city in central Sweden. 85,054 (1965).

Vas·thi (vas′thī), *n.* *Douay Bible.* Vashti.

vas·ti·tude (vas′ti to͞od′, -tyo͞od′, vä′sti-), *n.* **1.** vastness; immensity: *the vastitude of his love for all mankind.* **2.** a vast expanse or space: *the ocean vastitude.* [< L *vastitūdō.* See VAST, -I-, -TUDE]

vas·ti·ty[1] (vas′ti tē, vä′sti-), *n.* *Archaic.* immensity; vastness. [< L *vastitās.* See VAST, -ITY]

vas·ti·ty[2] (vas′ti tē), *n.* *Archaic.* wasteness; desolation. [< MF *vastite* < L *vastitāt-* (s. of *vastitās*); see VASTITY[1]]

vas·tus (vas′təs), *n., pl.* **-ti** (-tī). *Anat.* any of several muscles in the front part of the thigh constituting part of the quadriceps muscle, the action of which assists in extending the leg. [< L: huge, big]

vast·y (vas′tē, vä′stē), *adj.,* **vast·i·er, vast·i·est.** *Archaic.* vast; immense. [VAST + -Y[1]]

vat (vat), *n., v.,* **vat·ted, vat·ting.** —*n.* **1.** a large container, as a tub, tank, etc., used for storing or holding liquids: *a wine vat.* **2.** *Chem.* **a.** a preparation containing an insoluble dye converted by reduction into a soluble leuco base. **b.** a vessel containing such a preparation. —*v.t.* **3.** to put into or treat in a vat. [ME (south); OE *fæt* vessel; c. Icel *fat* vessel, G *Fass* keg]

Vat., Vatican.

vat′ dye′, *Chem.* any of the class of insoluble dyes impregnated into textile fibers by reduction into soluble leuco bases that regenerate the insoluble dye on oxidation.

vat·ic (vat′ik), *adj.* of, pertaining to, or characteristic of a prophet. Also, **vat′i·cal.** [< L *vāt(ēs)* seer + -IC]

Vat·i·can (vat′i kən), *n.* **1.** Also called **Vat′ican Pal′ace.** the chief residence of the popes in Vatican City. It now also includes a library, archives, art museum, apartments, and administrative offices. **2.** the authority and government of the pope (distinguished from the *quirinal*). [< L *vāticān(us)* (*mons*) Vatican (hill)]

Vat′ican Cit′y, an independent state within the city of Rome, on the right bank of the Tiber. Established in 1929, it is ruled by the Pope and includes St. Peter's Church and the Vatican. ab. 1000 (est. 1954); 109 acres. Italian, **Città del Vaticano.**

Vat′ican Coun′cil, the ecumenical council, convoked in Rome, 1869–70, by Pope Pius IX, that declared the dogma of papal infallibility.

Vat·i·can·ism (vat′i kə niz′əm), *n.* *Usually Derogatory.* the doctrine of the absolute supremacy of the pope. [VATICAN + -ISM] —**Vat′i·can·ist,** *n.*

Vat′ican Swin′dle, The. See **Lafcadio's Adventures.**

Vat·i·can·us (vat′i kan′əs, -kā′nəs), *n.* the Greek uncial codex, dating from the 4th century A.D., that contains most of the text of the Bible. Cf. **codex** (def. 2). [< ML: lit., of the Vatican (library)]

vat·i·cide (vat′i sīd′), *n.* **1.** a person who murders a prophet. **2.** the act of killing a prophet. [< L *vāti-* (s. of *vātes* seer) + -CIDE]

va·tic·i·nal (və tis′ə nəl), *adj.* of, pertaining to, or characterized by prophecy; prophetic. [< L *vāticin(us)* prophetic (*vāticin(ārī)* (to) prophesy + *-us* adj. suffix) + -AL[1]]

va·tic·i·nate (və tis′ə nāt′), *v.t., v.i.,* **-nat·ed, -nat·ing.** to prophesy. [< L *vāticināt(us)* (ptp. of *vāticinārī* to prophesy), equiv. to *vāti-* (s. of *vātes* seer) + *-cin-* (var. of *can-,* root of *canere* to sing, prophesy) + *-ātus* -ATE[1]] —**va·tic′i·na′tor,** *n.*

vat·i·ci·na·tion (vat′i sə nā′shən), *n.* **1.** act of prophesying. **2.** a prophecy. [< L *vāticinātiōn-* (s. of *vāticinātiō*). See VATICINATE, -ION]

vat·man (vat′mən), *n., pl.* **-men.** *Papermaking.* the craftsman who shakes the pulp onto the wire. [VAT + MAN[1]]

Vat·tel (*Ger.* fät′əl), *n.* **Em·me·rich** (*Ger.* em′ə rikh), 1714–67, Swiss jurist and diplomat.

Vät·ter (vet′tər), *n.* a lake in S Sweden. 80 mi. long; 733 sq. mi. Also, **Vät′tern** (vet′tərn), **Vetter.**

Vau·ban (vō bäN′), *n.* **Sé·bas·tien le Pres·tre de** (sā bas tyaN′ lə pre′trə də), 1633–1707, French military engineer and marshal.

Vau·cluse (vō klyz′), *n.* a department in SE France. 303,536 (1962); 1382 sq. mi. *Cap.:* Avignon.

Vaud (vō), *n.* a canton in W Switzerland. 429,512 (1960); 1239 sq. mi. *Cap.:* Lausanne. German, **Waadt.**

vaude·ville (vōd′vil, vōd′-, vō′də-), *n.* **1.** *Chiefly U.S.* theatrical entertainment consisting of a number of individual performances, acts, or mixed numbers, as of singing, dancing, gymnastic exhibitions, etc. Cf. **variety** (def. 9). **2.** a theatrical piece of light or amusing character, interspersed with songs and dances. **3.** a satirical cabaret song. [< F, shortened alter. of MF, *chanson du vau de Vire* song of the VALE[1] of VIRE, a valley of Calvados, France, noted for satirical folksong]

vaude·vil·lian (vôd vil′yən, vōd-, vō′də-), *n.* **1.** Also, **vaude′vil·list.** a person who writes for or performs in vaudeville. —*adj.* **2.** of, pertaining to, or characteristic of vaudeville. [VAUDEVILLE + -IAN]

Vau·dois (vō dwä′), *n., pl.* **-dois.** **1.** a native or inhabitant of Vaud. **2.** the dialect of French spoken in Vaud. [< F; MF *Vaudeis.* See VAUD, -ESE]

Vau·dois (vō dwä′), *n.* (*construed as sing.*) Waldenses.

Vaughan (vôn), *n.* **1. Henry,** 1622–95, English poet and mystic. **2.** a boy's given name.

Vaughan Wil·liams (vôn wil′yəmz), **Ralph,** 1872–1958, English composer.

Vaughn (vôn), *n.* a boy's or girl's given name.

vault[1] (vôlt), *n.* **1.** an arched structure, usually made of stones, concrete, or bricks, forming a ceiling or roof over a hall, room, sewer, or other wholly or partially enclosed construction. **2.** an imitation of such a structure, constructed for aesthetic reasons. **3.** an arched space, chamber, or passage, esp. one located underground. **4.** an underground chamber, as a cellar or a division of a cellar. **5.** a room, often built of or lined with steel, reserved for the storage and safekeeping of valuables, esp. such a room in a bank. **6.** a strong metal cabinet, usually fireproof and burglarproof, for the storage and safekeeping of valuables, important papers, etc. **7.** a burial chamber. **8.** *Anat.* an arched roof of a cavity. **9.** something resembling an arched roof: *the vault of heaven.* —*v.t.* **10.** to construct or cover with a vault. **11.** to make in the form of a vault; arch. **12.** to extend or stretch over in the manner of an arch; overarch: *An arbor vaulted the path.* —*v.i.* **13.** to curve or bend in the form of a vault. [alter. of late ME *vout(e)* < MF *voute, volte* < VL **volta* a turn (cf. It *volta*), n. use of fem. ptp. **vol(vi)ta* (r. L *volūta*) of L *volvere* to turn; see REVOLVE] —**vault′like′,** *adj.*

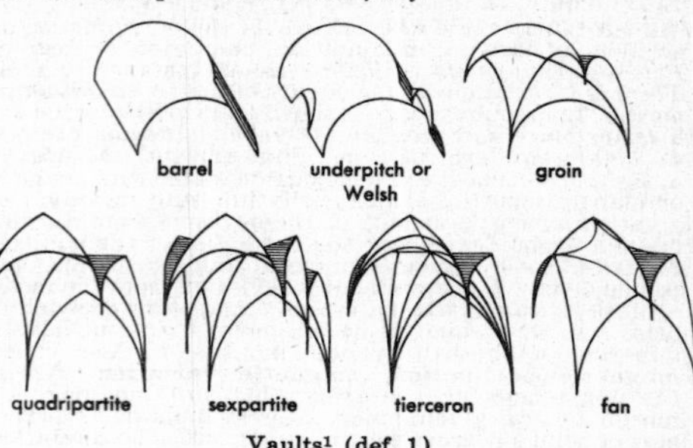

Vaults[1] (def. 1)

vault[2] (vôlt), *v.i.* **1.** to leap or spring, as to or from a position or over something: *He vaulted over the net after the tennis match.* **2.** to leap with the hands supported on something, as on a pole. **3.** to arrive at or achieve something as if by a spring or leap: *to vault into prominence.* —*v.t.* **4.** to leap or spring over: *to vault a fence.* —*n.* **5.** act of vaulting. **6.** a leap of a horse; curvet. [< MF *vol(ter)* (to) leap, turn < OIt *voltare* to turn, deriv. of *volta* a turn (see VAULT[1])] —**vault′er,** *n.*
—**Syn. 1.** See **jump.**

vault·ed (vôl′tid), *adj.* **1.** constructed or covered with a vault, as a building, chamber, etc. **2.** provided with a vault or vaults. **3.** resembling an arched roof: *the vaulted sky.* [VAULT[1] + -ED[2]]

vault·ing[1] (vôl′ting), *n.* **1.** act or process of constructing vaults. **2.** the structure forming a vault or vaults. **3.** a vault, vaulted ceiling, etc., or such structures collectively. [VAULT[1] + -ING[1]]

vault·ing[2] (vôl′ting), *adj.* **1.** leaping up or over. **2.** used in vaulting: *a vaulting pole.* **3.** exaggerated; highflown: *vaulting ambition; vaulting pride.* [VAULT[2] + -ING[2]]

vault′ light′, a windowlike structure set in a pavement or the like to light areas beneath, consisting of thick glass blocks set in a metal frame. Also called **pavement light.**

vault·y (vôl′tē), *adj.* having the appearance or characteristics of a vault; arching: *the vaulty rows of elm trees.* [VAULT[1] + -Y[1]]

vaunt (vônt, vänt), *v.t.* **1.** to speak vaingloriously of; boast of: *to vaunt one's achievements.* —*v.i.* **2.** *Archaic.* to speak vaingloriously or boastfully; brag. —*n.* **3.** a boastful action or utterance. [ME *vaunte(n)* < MF *vanter* to boast < LL *vānitāre,* freq. of **vānāre,* deriv. of *vānus* VAIN. See VANITY] —**vaunt′er,** *n.* —**vaunt′ing·ly,** *adv.*

vaunt-cour·i·er (vônt′ko͝or′ē ər, vänt′-), *n.* *Archaic.* a person who goes in advance, as a herald. [< F *avant-courrier* fore runner, herald. See AVAUNT, COURIER]

vaunt·ed (vôn′tid, vän′-), *adj.* praised boastfully or excessively: *the vaunted beauties of Paris.* [VAUNT + -ED[2]]

vaunt·ing (vôn′ting, vän′-), *adj.* **1.** having a boastfully proud disposition: *a vaunting dictator.* **2.** marked by boastful pride: *a vaunting air of superiority.*

vaunt·y (vôn′tē, vän′-), *adj.* *Scot.* boastful; vain. [VAUNT + Y[1]]

v. aux., auxiliary verb.

vav (väv, vôv), *n.* **1.** the sixth letter of the Hebrew alphabet. **2.** any of the sounds represented by this letter. [< Heb *wāw* a hook]

vav·a·sor (vav′ə sôr′, -sōr′), *n.* (in the feudal system) a vassal, or feudal tenant, holding of a great lord other than the sovereign. Also, **vav·a·sour** (vav′ə so͞or′). [ME *vavasour* < OF, perh. < ML *va(ssus) vassōr(um)* vassal of vassals; see VASSAL]

vav·a·so·ry (vav′ə sôr′ē, -sōr′ē), *n., pl.* **-ries.** **1.** the tenure of a fee held by a vavasor. **2.** lands held by a vavasor. [< ML *vavasoria* < MF *vavasso(u)rie.* See VAVASOR, -Y[3]]

va·ward (vä′wôrd′, vou′ərd), *n.* *Archaic.* vanguard. [late ME var. of *va(u)mwarde* < AF *van(t)warde,* equiv. to *avant* (see AVAUNT) + *warde* < OE *weard* WARD]

vb., **1.** verb. **2.** verbal.

V block, a block having a precise V-shaped groove for checking the roundness or concentricity of a machine part or the like, or for holding cylindrical pieces of work.

VC, Vietcong. Also, **V.C.**

V.C., **1.** Veterinary Corps. **2.** Vice-Chairman. **3.** Vice-Chancellor. **4.** Vice-Consul. **5.** Victoria Cross.

VCR, See **videocassette recorder.**

V.D., venereal disease. Also, **VD**

v.d., various dates.

V-Day (vē′dā′), *n.* a day of final military victory. Cf. **V-E Day, V-J Day.** [short for *Victory Day*]

V.D.M., Minister of the Word of God. [< L *Verbi Dei Minister*]

Ve (ve), *n.* *Scand. Myth.* a brother of Odin.

've, contraction of *have: I've got it. We've been there before.*

Ve·a·dar (vē′ə där′; *Heb.* vē ä där′), *n.* an intercalary month of the Jewish calendar. Also called **Adar Sheni.** Cf. **Jewish calendar.** [< Heb *we* and, additional + ADAR]

veal (vēl), *n.* **1.** Also, **veal·er** (vē′lər). a calf raised for its meat, usually a milk-fed animal less than three months old. **2.** the flesh of the calf as used for food. [ME *ve(e)l* < AF *vel* (OF *veel, veal*) < L *vitellus,* dim. of *vitulus* calf]

veal′ cut′let, a thin slice of veal dipped in egg and a mixture of bread crumbs or flour and seasonings, and sautéed, broiled, or baked.

Veb·len (veb′lən), *n.* **1. Oswald,** 1880–1960, U.S. mathematician. **2. Thor·stein** (thôr′stīn, -stən), 1857–1929, U.S. economist and sociologist.

Veb·le·ni·an (ve blē′nē ən), *n.* **1.** Also called **Veb·len·ite** (veb′lə nīt′). a person who adheres to the economic or sociological theories of Thorstein Veblen. —*adj.* **2.** of, pertaining to, or suggesting the theories of Thorstein Veblen. [VEBLEN + -IAN]

Veb·len·ism (veb′lə niz′əm), *n.* the economic or social theories originated by Thorstein Veblen. [VEBLEN + -ISM]

vec·tion (vek′shən), *n. Med.* the transference of a disease from one person to another. [< L *vectiōn-* (s. of *vectiō* a carrying). See VECTOR, -ION]

vec·to·graph (vek′tə graf′, -gräf′), *n.* a stereoscopic photograph consisting of two superimposed images polarized at 90° to each other and viewed through polarizing eyeglasses for a three-dimensional effect. [VECT(ION) + -O- + -GRAPH]

vec·tor (vek′tər), *n.* **1.** *Math.* **a.** a quantity possessing both magnitude and direction, represented by an arrow the direction of which indicates the direction of the quantity and the length of which is proportional to the magnitude. Cf. **scalar** (def. 3). **b.** any generalization of this quantity. **2.** the direction or course followed by an airplane, missile, or the like. **3.** *Biol.* an insect or other organism that transmits a pathogenic fungus, virus, bacterium, etc. [< L *vect(us)* (ptp. of *vehere* to carry), equiv. to *vec-* (ptp. s. of *vehere*) + *-tus* ptp. suffix + *-or* -OR²] —**vec·to·ri·al** (vek tōr′ē əl, -tôr′-), *adj.* —**vec·to′ri·al·ly,** *adv.*

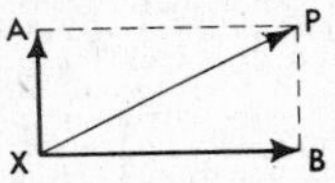

A P X B
XA, XB, Vectors
XP, Resultant

vec′tor addi′tion, *Math.* the process of finding one vector that is equivalent to the result of the successive application of two or more given vectors.

vec′tor anal′ysis, the branch of calculus that deals with vectors and processes involving vectors.

vec·tor·car·di·o·gram (vek′tər kär′dē ə gram′), *n.* the graphic record produced by vectorcardiography. [VECTOR + CARDIOGRAM]

vec·tor·car·di·og·ra·phy (vek′tər kär′dē og′rə fē), *n.* a method of determining the direction and magnitude of the electrical forces of the heart. [VECTOR + CARDIOGRAPHY] —**vec·tor·car·di·o·graph·ic** (vek′tər kär′dē ə graf′ik), *adj.*

vec′tor field′, *Math., Physics.* a region, domain, set, etc., with a vector assigned at each point; vector function.

vec′tor func′tion, *Math.* a function that assigns a vector to each point in a given set.

vec′tor prod′uct. See **cross product.**

vec′tor space′, *Math.* an additive group in which addition is commutative and with which is associated a field of scalars, as the field of real numbers, such that the product of a scalar and an element of the group or a vector is defined, the product of two scalars times a vector is associative, one times a vector is the vector, and two distributive laws hold. Also called **linear space.**

vec′tor sum′, *Math.* the vector, obtained by vector addition, that is equivalent in magnitude and direction to two or more given vectors.

Ve·da (vā′də, vē′-), *n. Hinduism.* **1.** Sometimes, **Vedas.** the entire body of Hindu sacred writings, chief among which are four books, the Rig-Veda, the Sama-Veda, the Atharva-Veda, and the Yajur-Veda. **2.** Also called **Samhita.** each of these four books. **3. Vedas,** these four books, along with the Brahmanas and Upanishads. [< Skt: knowledge] —**Ve·da·ic** (vi dā′ik), *adj.* —**Ve′da·ism** (vā′də iz′əm, vē′-), *n.*

Ve·da (vā′də, vē′-), *n.* a girl's given name.

ve·da·lia (vi dāl′yə, -dā′lē ə), *n.* a ladybug, *Rodolia cardinalis,* introduced into California from Australia, which preys on the cottony-cushion scale. [< NL]

Ve·dan·ta (vi dän′tə, -dan′-), *n.* the chief Hindu philosophy, dealing mainly with the Upanishadic doctrine of the identity of Brahman and Atman, that reached its highest development A.D. c800 through the philosopher Shankara. Cf. **Advaita, dvaita** (def. 2). [< Skt, equiv. to *vēd(a)* VEDA + *-anta* END¹] —**Ve·dan′tic,** *adj.* —**Ve·dan′tism,** *n.* —**Ve·dan′tist,** *n.*

V-E Day, May 8, 1945, the day of victory in Europe for the Allies in World War II.

Ved·da (ved′ə), *n.* a Ceylonese aborigine. Also, **Ved′dah.** [< Singhalese: bowman, hunter]

Ved·der (ved′ər), *n.* a boy's given name.

ve·dette (və det′), *n.* **1.** Also called **vedette′ boat′.** a small naval launch used for scouting. **2.** a mounted sentry in advance of the outposts of an army. Also, **vidette.** [< F < It *vedetta* outlook where a sentinel is posted, equiv. to *ved(ere)* (to) see (< L *vidēre*) + *-etta* -ETTE]

Ve·dic (vā′dik, vē′-), *adj.* **1.** of or pertaining to the Veda or Vedas. **2.** of or pertaining to the Aryans who settled in India c1500 B.C., or to their literature or religion. —*n.* **3.** Also called **Ve′dic San′skrit.** the language of the Veda, closely related to classical Sanskrit. [VED(A) + -IC]

vee (vē), *adj.* **1.** shaped like the letter *V: a vee neckline.* —*n.* **2.** *Slang.* a five-dollar bill. **3.** anything shaped like or suggesting a *V.*

Vee (vē), *n.* a girl's given name.

veep (vēp), *n. Informal.* a vice-president. Also called **vee′pee′.** [from V.P.]

veer¹ (vēr), *v.i.* **1.** to change direction or turn about or aside; shift, turn, or change from one course, position, inclination, etc., to another: *The speaker kept veering from his main topic. The car veered off the road.* **2.** (of the wind) **a.** to change direction clockwise (opposed to *back*). **b.** *Naut.* to shift to a direction more nearly astern (opposed to *haul*). —*v.t.* **3.** to alter the direction or course of; turn. **4.** *Naut.* to turn (a vessel) away from the wind; wear. —*n.* **5.** a change of direction, position, course, etc.: *The falling tree took a veer in an unexpected direction and fell on the house.* [< MF *virer* to turn] —**veer′ing·ly,** *adv.*
—**Syn. 1.** deviate, swerve, diverge.

veer² (vēr), *v.t. Naut.* to slacken or let out: *to veer chain.* [late ME *vere* < MD *viere(n)* to let out; c. MLG *vīren* to slacken, OHG *fieren* to give direction to]

veer·y (vēr′ē), *n., pl.* **veer·ies.** a thrush, *Hylocichla fuscescens,* common in the eastern U.S., noted for its song. Also called **Wilson's thrush.** [? from its flight]

veg (vej), *n., pl.* **veg.** *Brit. Informal.* a vegetable or dish of vegetables: *a dinner with two veg.* [by shortening]

Ve·ga (vē′gə), *n.* **1.** *Astron.* a star of the first magnitude in the constellation Lyra. **2.** a crater in the fourth quadrant of the face of the moon: about 50 miles in diameter. [< ML < Ar *wāki′* falling]

Ve·ga (vā′gə; *Sp.* be′gä), *n.* **1. Lo·pe de** (lô′pe de), (*Lope Félix de Vega Carpio*), 1562–1635, Spanish dramatist and poet. **2.** See **Garcilaso de la Vega.**

veg·e·ta·ble (vej′tə bəl, vej′i tə-), *n.* **1.** any herbaceous plant whose fruit, seeds, roots, tubers, bulbs, stems, leaves, or flower parts are used as food, as the tomato, bean, beet, potato, asparagus, cabbage, etc. **2.** the edible part of such a plant, as the fruit of the tomato or the tuber of the potato. **3.** any member of the vegetable kingdom; plant. **4.** a dull, spiritless, and uninteresting person. —*adj.* **5.** of, consisting of, or made from edible vegetables: *a vegetable diet; a vegetable dinner.* **6.** of, pertaining to, or characteristic of plants: *vegetable life; the vegetable kingdom.* **7.** derived from plants or some part of plants: *vegetable fiber; vegetable oils.* **8.** consisting of, comprising, or containing the substance or remains of plants: *decaying vegetable matter; a vegetable organism.* **9.** of the nature of or resembling a plant: *the vegetable forms of Art Nouveau ornament.* **10.** uneventful; dull: *a vegetable existence.* [late ME (adj.) < LL *vegetābil(is)* able to live and grow, equiv. to *veget(āre)* (to) quicken (see VEGETATE) + *-ābilis* -ABLE]

veg′etable but′ter, any of various fixed vegetable fats that are solid at ordinary temperatures but usually melt at or below body temperature.

veg′etable gold′, saffron (def. 1).

veg′etable i′vory, ivory (def. 9).

veg′etable king′dom. See **plant kingdom.**

veg′etable mar′row, any of various summer squashes, as the cocozelle and zucchini.

veg′etable oil′, any of a large group of oils that are esters of fatty acids and glycerol, obtained from the leaves, fruit, or seeds of plants.

veg′etable oys′ter, salsify.

veg′etable silk′, a fine, glossy fiber, similar to silk cotton, from the seeds of a spiny, Brazilian tree, *Chorisia speciosa.*

veg′etable sponge′, luffa (def. 2).

veg′etable tal′low, any of several tallowlike substances of vegetable origin, used in making candles, soap, etc., and as lubricants.

veg′etable tan′ning, the act or process of tanning hide by the infusion of plant extract.

veg′etable wax′, a wax, or a substance resembling wax, obtained from various plants, as the wax palm.

veg′etable wool′. See under **wool** (def. 6).

veg·e·ta·bly (vej′tə blē, vej′i tə-), *adv.* in the manner of a vegetable: *existing vegetably without hobbies, interests, or friends.* [VEGETABLE + -LY]

veg·e·tal (vej′i tᵊl), *adj.* **1.** of, pertaining to, or of the nature of plants or vegetables. **2.** vegetative (def. 3). [late ME < LL *veget(āre)* to quicken (see VEGETATE) + -AL¹]

veg′etal pole′, *Biol.* the relatively inactive part of an ovum opposite the animal pole, containing much yolk and little cytoplasm. Cf. **animal pole.**

veg·e·tar·i·an (vej′i târ′ē ən), *n.* **1.** a person who, on the basis of moral principles or nutritional theory, refuses to eat meat, fish, fowl, or, in some cases, any food derived from animal life, subsisting on vegetables, fruits, nuts, grain, etc. —*adj.* **2.** of or pertaining to vegetarianism or vegetarians. **3.** devoted to or advocating this practice. **4.** consisting solely of vegetables: *vegetarian vegetable soup.* [VEGET(ABLE) + -ARIAN]

veg·e·tar·i·an·ism (vej′i târ′ē ə niz′əm), *n.* the beliefs or practices of a vegetarian. [VEGETARIAN + -ISM]

veg·e·tate (vej′i tāt′), *v.i.,* **-tat·ed, -tat·ing.** **1.** to grow in, or as in, the manner of a plant. **2.** to live in an inactive, passive, or unthinking way: *vegetating in a stagnant society; to lie on the beach and just vegetate.* **3.** *Pathol.* to grow, or increase by growth, as an excrescence. [< LL *vegetāt(us)* (ptp. of *vegetāre* to quicken, enliven), equiv. to L *veget(us)* lively (*vege-,* s. of *vegere* to excite + *-tus* adj. suffix) + *-ātus* -ATE¹]

veg·e·ta·tion (vej′i tā′shən), *n.* **1.** all the plants or plant life of a place, taken as a whole: *to chop one's way through vegetation; the vegetation of the Nile valley.* **2.** the act or process of vegetating. **3.** a dull existence; life devoid of mental or social activity or of any enlivening stimulation. **4.** *Pathol.* a morbid growth, or excrescence. [< ML *vegetātiōn-* (s. of *vegetātiō*), equiv. to *vegetāt-* (see VEGETATE) + *-iōn-* -ION] —**veg′e·ta′tion·al,** *adj.* —**veg′e·ta′tion·less,** *adj.*

veg·e·ta·tive (vej′i tā′tiv), *adj.* **1.** growing or developing as or like plants; vegetating. **2.** of, pertaining to, or concerned with vegetation or vegetable growth. **3.** of or pertaining to the plant kingdom. **4.** noting the parts of a plant not specialized for reproduction. **5.** (of reproduction) asexual. **6.** denoting or pertaining to those bodily functions that are performed unconsciously or involuntarily. **7.** having the power to produce or support growth in plants: *vegetative mold.* **8.** inactive or passive: *a vegetative existence.* Also, **veg·e·tive** (vej′i tiv). [late ME < ML *vegetātīv(us).* See VEGETATE, -IVE] —**veg′e·ta′tive·ly,** *adv.* —**veg′e·ta′tive·ness,** *n.*

ve·he·mence (vē′ə məns), *n.* **1.** the quality of being vehement; ardor; fervor. **2.** vigorous impetuosity; violence; fury: *the vehemence of his attack.* Also, **ve′he·men·cy.** [< L *vehementia,* equiv. to *vehement-* VEHEMENT + *-ia* -Y³ (L *-entia* > -ENCE)]
—**Syn. 1.** eagerness, verve, zeal, enthusiasm, fervency. **2.** passion. —**Ant. 1, 2.** apathy.

ve·he·ment (vē′ə mənt), *adj.* **1.** zealous; ardent; impassioned: *a vehement defense; vehement enthusiasm.* **2.** characterized by rancor or anger; violent: *vehement hostility; a vehement objection to a law.* **3.** strongly emotional; intense or passionate: *vehement desire; vehement dislike.* **4.** marked by great energy or exertion; strenuous: *vehement clapping; vehement gestures.* [late ME < L *vehement-* (s. of *vehemēns*), var. of *vēment-,* equiv. to *vē-* without + *ment-* (s. of *mēns* mind); see MENTAL¹] —**ve′he·ment·ly,** *adv.*
—**Syn. 1.** earnest, fervent, fervid. **2.** burning, fiery. —**Ant. 1, 2.** dispassionate.

ve·hi·cle (vē′i kəl), *n.* **1.** any means in or by which someone travels or something is carried or conveyed; a means of conveyance or transport: *a motor vehicle; space vehicles.* **2.** a conveyance moving on wheels, runners, tracks, or the like, as a cart, sled, automobile, tractor, etc. **3.** a means of transmission or passage: *Air is the vehicle of sound.* **4.** a carrier, as of infection. **5.** a medium of communication, expression, or display: *The novel is the most fitting vehicle for his talents. Language is the vehicle by which thoughts are transmitted.* **6.** a means of accomplishing a purpose: *The college is a vehicle stimulating good citizenship.* **7.** *Rhet.* the thing or idea to which the subject of a metaphor is compared, as "rose" in "she is a rose." Cf. **tenor** (def. 3). **8.** *Pharm.* a substance, usually fluid, possessing little or no medicinal action, used as a medium for active remedies. **9.** *Painting.* a liquid, as oil, in which a pigment is mixed before being applied to a surface. [< L *vehicul(um),* equiv. to *vehe(re)* to convey + *-culum* -CLE]

ve·hic·u·lar (vē hik′yə lər), *adj.* **1.** of, pertaining to, or for vehicles: *a vehicular tunnel.* **2.** serving as a vehicle. **3.** caused by a vehicle or vehicles; attributed or attributable to vehicles: *vehicular deaths; vehicular homicide.* **4.** carried on or transported by means of a vehicle: *vehicular recording units.* [< LL *vehiculār(is).* See VEHICLE, -AR¹]

ve·hic·u·lum (vē hik′yŏŏ ləm), *n., pl.* **-la** (-lə). (in prescriptions) a vehicle. [< L]

Vehm·ge·richt (fām′gə rıKHt′), *n., pl.* **-rich·te** (-rıKH′tə). *German.* any of the late medieval, informally constituted tribunals in Germany, esp. in Westphalia, in which civil cases were tried openly: serious crimes, as witchcraft and murder, however, were tried in secret. [lit., secret court]

V-eight (vē′āt′), *adj.* noting an internal-combustion engine having two opposed blocks of four cylinders, each inclined so that the axes of the cylinders form an acute angle as seen from the end of the engine. Also, **V-8.**

Ve·ii (vē′yī), *n.* an ancient city in central Italy, in Etruria, near Rome: Etruscan city destroyed by the Romans 396 B.C.

veil (vāl), *n.* **1.** a piece of opaque or transparent material worn over the face for concealment, for protection from the elements, or to enhance the appearance. **2.** a piece of material worn so as to fall over the head and shoulders on each side of the face, forming a part of the headdress of a nun. **3.** the life accepted or the vows made by a woman, when she makes either her novice's vows and takes the white veil, or her irrevocable vows and takes the black veil of a nun. **4.** something that covers, separates, screens, or conceals: *a veil of smoke; the veil of death.* **5.** a mask, disguise, or pretense: *The truth was hidden under a veil of uneasy silence.* **6.** *Bot., Anat., Zool.* a velum. **7.** *Dial.* a caul. **8. take the veil,** to become a nun. —*v.t.* **9.** to cover or conceal with or as with a veil: *She veiled her face in black. A heavy fog veiled the shoreline.* **10.** to hide the real nature of; mask; disguise: *to veil one's intentions.* —*v.i.* **11.** to don or wear a veil: *In Islamic countries many women still veil.* [ME *veile* < AF < VL *vēla,* fem. sing. (orig. neut. pl.) of L *vēlum* covering] —**veil′less,** *adj.* —**veil′like′,** *adj.*

veiled (vāld), *adj.* **1.** having a veil: *a cute little veiled hat.* **2.** covered or concealed by, or as if by, a veil: *a veiled woman; a veiled body.* **3.** not openly or directly expressed; masked; disguised; hidden; obscure: *a veiled threat.* **4.** lacking clarity or distinctness: *veiled sounds; a veiled voice; a veiled image.* [VEIL + -ED³] —**veil·ed·ly** (vā′lid lē), *adv.*

veil·ing (vā′ling), *n.* **1.** act of covering with or as with a veil. **2.** a veil. **3.** a thin net for veils. [VEIL + -ING¹]

veil·leuse (ve yœz′), *n., pl.* **veil·leuses** (ve yœz′). *Fr. Furniture.* a sofa having a low and a high end, with a back that slopes from one end to the other. [< F: lit., female watcher (opposed to sleeper), equiv. to *veill(er)* (to) watch (< L *vigilāre;* see VIGIL) + *-euse,* fem. of *-eur* -OR²]

Veil·lo·nel·la (vā′ə nel′ə, vä′yə-), *n. Bacteriol.* a genus of spherical, anaerobic bacteria, found as parasites in the mouth, intestines, and genitourinary and respiratory tracts of man and animals.

vein (vān), *n.* **1.** one of the system of branching vessels or tubes conveying blood from various parts of the body to the heart. **2.** (loosely) any blood vessel: *The blood of kings flowed in his veins.* **3.** one of the riblike thickenings that form the framework of the wing of an insect. **4.** one of the strands or bundles of vascular tissue forming the principal framework of a leaf. **5.** any body or stratum of ore, coal, etc., clearly separated or defined: *a rich vein of coal.* **6.** a body or mass of igneous rock, deposited mineral, or the like, occupying a crevice or fissure in rock; lode. **7.** a natural channel or watercourse beneath the surface of the earth. **8.** the water running through such a channel. **9.** a streak or marking, as of a different shade or color, running through marble, wood, etc. **10.** a condition, mood, or temper: *conversation in a serious vein; a vein of pessimism.* **11.** a tendency, quality, or strain traceable in character, conduct, writing, etc.; manner or style: *to write in a poetic vein.* —*v.t.* **12.** to furnish with veins. **13.** to mark with lines or streaks suggesting veins. **14.** to extend over or through in the manner of veins: *Broad new highways vein the countryside.* [ME *veine* < OF < L *vēna* vein] —**vein′al,** *adj.* —**vein′less,** *adj.* —**vein′like′,** *adj.*

vein·ing (vā′ning), *n.* **1.** act or process of forming veins or an arrangement or marking resembling veins. **2.** a vein or a pattern of veins or markings suggesting veins. [VEIN + -ING¹]

vein·let (vān′lit), *n.* a small vein. [VEIN + -LET]

vein·stone (vān′stōn′), *n.* gangue. [VEIN + STONE]

vein·ule (vān′yo͞ol), *n.* venule. Also, **vein·u·let** (vān′yə lit). [VEIN + -ULE]

vein·y (vā′nē), *adj.,* **vein·i·er, vein·i·est.** full of veins; veined: *a veiny hand.* [VEIN + -Y¹]

Ve·io·vis (vē yō′vis), *n.* *Rom. Religion.* a god of the dead, sometimes believed to be of Etruscan origin.

vel (vel), *conj.* (in prescriptions) or. [< L]

vel., vellum.

ve·la (vē′lə), *n.* pl. of **velum.**

Ve·la (vē′lə), *n., gen.* **Ve·lo·rum** (vē lōr′əm, -lôr′-). *Astron.* the Sail, a southern constellation: one of the subordinate constellations into which Argo is divided. [< L, pl. of *vēlum* sail]

Vel·a-Ho·tel (vel′ə hō tel′), *n.* *U.S.* a satellite system for detection of nuclear explosions in space.

ve·la·men (və lā′min), *n., pl.* **-lam·i·na** (-lam′ə nə). **1.** *Anat.* a membranous covering; velum. **2.** *Bot.* the thick, spongy integument or epidermis covering the aerial roots of epiphytic orchids. [< L, equiv. to *vēlā(re)* (to) cover + *-men* n. suffix]

ve·lar (vē′lər), *adj.* **1.** of or pertaining to a velum, esp. the soft palate. **2.** *Phonet.* articulated with the back of the tongue held close to or touching the soft palate. —*n.* **3.** *Phonet.* a velar sound. [< L *vēlār(is).* See VELUM, -AR[1]]

ve·lar·i·um (və lâr′ē əm), *n., pl.* **-lar·i·a** (-lâr′ē ə). *Rom. Antiq.* an awning drawn over a theater or amphitheater as a protection from rain or the sun. [< L, equiv. to *vēl(um)* awning + *-ārium* -ARY]

ve·lar·ize (vē′lə rīz′), *v.t.,* **-ized, -iz·ing.** *Phonet.* to pronounce with velar articulation. [VELAR + -IZE] —**ve′lar·i·za′tion,** *n.*

ve·lar·ized (vē′lə rīzd′), *adj.* *Phonet.* pronounced with velar articulation. [VELARIZE + -ED[2]]

Ve·lás·quez (və läs′kās, -kəs; *Sp.* be läs′keth), *n.* Velázquez.

ve·late (*adj.* vē′lit, -lāt; *v.* vē′lāt), *adj., v.,* **-lat·ed, -lat·ing.** —*adj.* **1.** *Bot., Zool.* having a velum. —*v.t.* **2.** *Phonet.* to velarize. [< NL *vēlāt(us).* See VELLUM, -ATE[1]]

ve·la·tion (vē lā′shən), *n.* *Phonet.* pronunciation with velar articulation. [VELATE + -ION]

Ve·láz·quez (və läs′kās, -kəs; *Sp.* be läth′keth), *n.* **Die·go Ro·drí·guez de Sil·va y** (dye′gô rô dhrē′geth de sēl′vä ē), 1599–1660, Spanish painter. Also, **Velásquez.**

veld (velt, felt), *n.* the open country, bearing grass, bushes, or shrubs, or thinly forested, characteristic of parts of S Africa. Also, **veldt.** [< SAfrD: FIELD]

Ve·lel·la (və lel′ə), *n.* a genus of bluish siphonophores, having a flattened float with a vertical crest that is used as a sail. [< NL, equiv. to L *vēl(um)* sail + *-ella* fem. dim. suffix] —**ve·lel′li·dous,** *adj.*

ve′lic point′ (vē′lik), *Naval Archit.* See **center of effort.** [VEL(UM) + -IC]

ve·li·ger (vē′li jər), *n.* a larval stage of certain mollusks, intermediate between the trochophore and the adult form. [< NL; see VELUM, -I-, -GEROUS]

vel·i·ta·tion (vel′i tā′shən), *n.* a minor dispute or encounter. [< L *vēlitātiōn-* (s. of *vēlitātiō*), equiv. to *vēlitāt(us)* (ptp. of *vēlitārī* to skirmish; see VELITES, -ATE[1]) + *-iōn-* -ION]

ve·li·tes (vē′li tēz′), *n.pl.* lightly-armed foot soldiers of ancient Rome. [< L, pl. of *vēlēs* light-armed infantryman, skirmisher]

vel·le·i·ty (və lē′i tē), *n., pl.* **-ties. 1.** volition in its weakest form. **2.** a mere wish, unaccompanied by an effort to obtain it. [< ML *velleitās,* equiv. to L *velle* to be willing + *-itās* -ITY]

vel·li·cate (vel′ə kāt′), *v.,* **-cat·ed, -cat·ing.** —*v.t.* **1.** to pluck; twitch. **2.** to nip, pinch, or the like. **3.** to cause to twitch. —*v.i.* **4.** to move with spasmodic convulsions; twitch. [< L *vellicāt(us),* ptp. of *vellicāre,* freq. of *vellere* to pull, twitch; see -ATE[1]] —**vel′li·ca′tion,** *n.* —**vel′li·ca′tive,** *adj.*

vel·lum (vel′əm), *n.* **1.** calfskin, lambskin, kidskin, etc., treated for use as a writing surface. **2.** a manuscript or the like on vellum. **3.** a texture of paper or cloth resembling vellum. —*adj.* **4.** made of or resembling vellum. **5.** bound in vellum. [late ME *velum, velim* < MF *ve(e)lin* of calf. See VEAL, -IN[1]]

Vel·ma (vel′mə), *n.* a girl's given name, form of **Wilhelmina.** Also, **Vilma.**

ve·lo·ce (ve lô′che), *adj.* played at a fast tempo (used as a musical direction). [< It < L *vēlōci-,* s. of *vēlox* quick]

ve·loc·i·pede (və los′ə pēd′), *n.* **1.** a vehicle, usually having two or three wheels, that is propelled by the rider. **2.** an early kind of bicycle or tricycle. **3.** a light, pedal-driven vehicle used for carrying one person on a railroad track. [< F *vélocipède* bicycle, equiv. to *véloci-* (< L, s. of *vēlox* quick) + *-pède* -PED] —**ve·loc′i·ped′ist,** *n.*

ve·loc·i·ty (və los′i tē), *n., pl.* **-ties. 1.** rapidity of motion or operation; swiftness; speed: *to measure the velocity of the wind.* **2.** *Mech.* the time rate of change of position of a body in reference to a specified direction. **3.** the rate of speed with which something happens; rapidity of action or reaction. [< L *vēlōcitās* speed. See VELOCIPEDE, -TY[2]]
—**Syn. 1.** See **speed.**

veloc′ity mi′crophone, a microphone in which the output varies according to the instantaneous velocity of the air molecules in the incident sound waves.

veloc′ity of circula′tion, the average number of times during a period of time that a monetary unit, as the dollar, is circulated in exchange for goods or services. Also called **veloc′ity of mon′ey.**

ve·lo·drome (vē′lə drōm′, vel′-), *n.* a sports arena equipped with a banked track for cycling. [< F; see VELOCIPEDE, -DROME]

ve·lour (və lo͝or′), *n.* **1.** a velvetlike fabric of rayon, wool, or any of several other natural or synthetic fibers, used for outerwear and upholstery. **2.** a velvety fur felt, as of beaver, for hats. Also, **velours** (və lo͝or′; *Fr.* və lo͞or′). [< F, MF *velour(s),* OF *velo(u)s* < OPr *velos* velvet < L *villōsus* hairy. See VILLUS, -OSE[1]]

ve·lou·té (və lo͞o tā′), *n.* a smooth white sauce made with meat, poultry, or fish stock. Also called **velouté sauce′.** [< F, equiv. to *velout-* (cf. ML *velūtum* velvet) + *-é* -ATE[1]]

Ve·lox (vē′loks), *n.* *Trademark.* a photographic print that has been screened for reproduction as a line cut.

Vel·sen (vel′sən), *n.* a seaport in the W Netherlands. 66,913 (1962).

ve·lum (vē′ləm), *n., pl.* **-la** (-lə), for 1, 2, **-lum** for 3. **1.** *Biol.* any of various veillike or curtainlike membranous partitions. **2.** *Anat.* the soft palate. See under **palate** (def. 1). **3.** a thin cloud, large in horizontal area, that is draped over or penetrated by cumuliform clouds. [< L: sail, covering]

ve·lure (və lo͝or′), *n., v.,* **-lured, -lur·ing.** —*n.* **1.** velvet or a substance resembling it. **2.** a hatter's pad of velvet, plush, or the like, for smoothing or dressing silk hats. —*v.t.* **3.** to smooth or dress (a hat) with a velure. [by alter. < MF *velour* VELOUR; see -URE]

ve·lu·ti·nous (və lo͞ot′ənəs), *adj.* having a soft, velvety surface, as certain plants. [< NL *velūtinus,* lit., velvety. See VELVET, -INE[1], -OUS]

vel·vet (vel′vit), *n.* **1.** a fabric of silk, nylon, acetate, rayon, etc., sometimes having a cotton backing, with a thick, soft pile formed of loops of the warp thread either cut at the outer end or left uncut. **2.** something likened to the fabric velvet, as in softness, texture, etc.: *the velvet of her touch; the velvet of the lawn.* **3.** the soft, deciduous covering of a growing antler. **4.** *Informal.* a very pleasant, luxurious, desirable situation. **5.** *Slang.* **a.** money gained through gambling. **b.** winnings. **c.** clear gain or profit. —*adj.* **5.** Also, **vel′vet·ed.** made of velvet or covered with velvet. **6.** Also, **vel′vet·like′.** resembling velvet; smooth; soft: *a velvet night; a cat's velvet fur.* [ME < ML *velvet(um),* var. of *velūtum,* n. use of neut. of **velūtus* shaggy, equiv. to *vel-* (see VILLUS) + *-ūtus* adj. suffix]

vel′vet ant′, any of several often brightly colored pubescent wasps of the family *Mutillidae,* the wingless, antlike female of which inflicts a severe sting.

vel′vet bent′. See **brown bent.**

vel′vet car′pet, a carpet or rug of pile weave resembling Wilton.

vel·vet·een (vel′vi tēn′), *n.* **1.** a cotton pile fabric with short pile. **2. velveteens,** trousers of this fabric. —*adj.* **3.** made of velveteen: *a velveteen jumper.* [VELVET + *-een* -INE[2]]

vel′vet glove′, an outwardly gentle or friendly manner used to disguise one's firm or ruthless determination.

vel′vet plant′, mullein (def. 1).

vel′vet sponge′, a large commercial sponge, *Hippospongia gossypina,* of the West Indies.

vel·vet·y (vel′vi tē), *adj.* **1.** suggestive of or resembling velvet; smooth; soft: *a velvety voice; a velvety cream sauce.* **2.** (of liquor) smooth-tasting; mild; mellow: *a velvety Scotch.* **3.** gentle and smooth to the touch: *velvety suede; velvety rose petals.* [VELVET + -Y[1]] —**vel′vet·i·ness,** *n.*

Ven., 1. Venerable. **2.** Venice.

ve·na (vē′nə), *n., pl.* **-nae** (-nē). *Anat.* a vein. [late ME < L *vēna* VEIN]

ve·na ca·va (vē′nə kā′və), *pl.* **ve·nae ca·vae** (vē′nē kā′vē). *Anat.* either of two large veins discharging blood into the right atrium of the heart, one (**superior vena cava**) conveying blood from the head, chest, and upper extremities, and the other (**inferior vena cava**) conveying blood from all parts below the diaphragm. See diag. under **heart.** [< L: hollow vein]

ve·na con·trac·ta (vē′nə kən trak′tə), *pl.* **ve·nae con·trac·tae** (vē′nē kən trak′tē). *Hydraul.* any of the locations in a jet of fluid emerging from an orifice where the cross section of the jet is at a minimum, esp. the location of minimum cross section nearest the orifice. [< NL: contracted vein]

ve·nal (vēn′əl), *adj.* **1.** willing to betray one's trust by improper use of authority or influence, esp. in return for a bribe; corruptly open to bribery: *a venal judge.* **2.** able to be purchased, as things not properly offered for sale: *venal acquittals; the venal awarding of contracts.* **3.** associated with or characterized by bribery: *venal administration; venal agreements.* [< L *vēnāl(is),* equiv. to *vēn(um)* for sale (see VEND) + *-ālis* -AL[1]] —**ve′nal·ly,** *adv.*
—**Syn. 1.** bribable, mercenary, corruptible. See **corrupt.** —**Ant. 1.** incorruptible.

ve·nal·i·ty (vē nal′i tē, və-), *n.* the condition or quality of being venal; openness to bribery or corruption. [< LL *vēnālitāt-* (s. of *vēnālitas*). See VENAL, -ITY]

ve·nat·ic (vē nat′ik), *adj.* of or pertaining to hunting. Also, **ve·nat′i·cal.** [< L *vēnātic(us),* equiv. to *vēnāt(us)* (see VENATION) + *-icus* -IC] —**ve·nat′i·cal·ly,** *adv.*

ve·na·tion (vē nā′shən, və-), *n.* **1.** the arrangement of veins, as in a leaf or in the wing of an insect. **2.** these veins collectively. [< L *vēnātiōn-* (s. of *vēnātiō*), equiv. to *vēnāt(us)* (ptp. of *vēnārī* to hunt; see -ATE[1]) + *-iōn-* -ION] —**ve·na′tion·al,** *adj.*

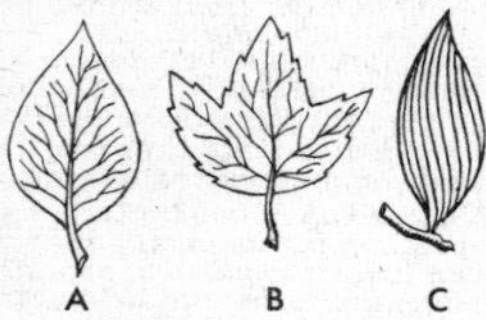

Venations of leaves
A, Pinnate; B, Palmate; C, Parallel

vend (vend), *v.t.* **1.** to sell as one's business or occupation, esp. by peddling: *to vend flowers at a sidewalk stand.* **2.** to give utterance to (opinions, ideas, etc.); publish. —*v.i.* **3.** to engage in the sale of merchandise. **4.** to be disposed of by sale. [< L *vend(ere)* (to) sell, equiv. to *vēnum* (or *vēno*) *dare* offer for sale; see VENAL]

ven·dace (ven′dis, -dās), *n., pl.* **-dac·es,** (*esp. collectively*) **-dace.** a whitefish, *Coregonus vandesius,* found in several lakes in Scotland and England. [? *ven* white (< Celt; cf. OIr *fin(d)* white) + DACE]

Ven·de·an (ven dē′ən), *adj.* **1.** of or pertaining to the Vendée or its inhabitants. —*n.* **2.** a native or inhabitant of the Vendée, esp. one who participated in the royalist revolt in 1793. [VENDÉE + -AN]

vend·ee (ven dē′), *n.* *Chiefly Law.* the person to whom a thing is sold. [VEND + -EE]

Ven·dée (väɴ dā′), *n.* a department in W France, on the Atlantic: royalist revolt 1793–95. 408,928 (1962); 2709 sq. mi. *Cap.:* La Roche-sur-Yon.

Ven·del·i·nus (ven del′ə nəs), *n.* an elliptical walled plain in the fourth quadrant of the face of the moon: about 100 miles long.

Ven·dé·miaire (väɴ dā myer′), *n.* (in the French Revolutionary calendar) the first month of the year, extending from September 22 to October 21. [< F, equiv. to *vendémi-* (< L *vindēmia* vintage) + *-aire* -ARY]

vend·er (ven′dər), *n.* vendor. [VEND + -ER[1]]

ven·det·ta (ven det′ə), *n.* **1.** a private feud in which the members of the family of a murdered person seek to avenge the murder by killing the slayer or one of his relatives, esp. such vengeance as once practiced in Corsica and parts of Italy. **2.** any prolonged and bitter feud, rivalry, contention, or the like: *a political vendetta.* [< It < L *vindicta* vengeance; see VINDICTIVE] —**ven·det′tist,** *n.*

vend·i·ble (ven′də bəl), *adj.* **1.** capable of being vended; salable: *vendible commodities.* **2.** *Obs.* mercenary; venal. —*n.* **3.** Usually, **vendibles.** vendible articles. [late ME < L *vendibil(is).* See VEND, -IBLE] —**vend′i·bil′i·ty, vend′i·ble·ness,** *n.* —**vend′i·bly,** *adv.*

Ven·di·dad (ven dē′däd), *n.* *Zoroastrianism.* a book of formulas to be used against demons. Also called **Videvdat.**

vend′ing machine′, a coin-operated machine for selling small articles, beverages, etc.

ven·di·tion (ven dish′ən), *n.* act of vending; sale. [< L *venditiōn-* (s. of *venditiō*), equiv. to *vendit(us)* (ptp. of *vendere* to VEND; see -ITE[2]) + *-iōn-* -ION]

Ven·dôme (väɴ dōm′), *n.* **Louis Jo·seph de** (lwē zhō zef′ də), 1654–1712, French general and marshal.

ven·dor (ven′dər, ven dôr′), *n.* **1.** a person or agency that sells. **2.** See **vending machine.** Also, **vender.** [< AF *vendo(u)r* < L *venditor.* See VEND, -OR[2]]

ven·due (ven do͞o′, -dyo͞o′), *n.* a public auction. [< D *vendu* < MF *vendue* sale, n. use of fem. of *vendu,* ptp. of *vendre* to sell; see VEND]

ve·neer (və nēr′), *n.* **1.** a very thin layer of wood or other material for facing or inlaying wood. **2.** any of the thin layers of wood glued together to form plywood. **3.** *Building Trades.* a facing of a certain material applied to a different one or to a type of construction not ordinarily associated with it, as a facing of brick applied to a frame house. **4.** a superficially valuable or pleasing appearance: *He hid his gambling operations beneath a veneer of respectability.* —*v.t.* **5.** to overlay or face (wood) with thin sheets of some material, as a fine wood, ivory, tortoise shell, etc. **6.** to face or cover (an object) with any material that is more pleasing, more durable, more readily cleaned, or otherwise more desirable as a surface material than the basic material of the object; revet. **7.** to cement (layers of wood veneer) to form plywood. **8.** to give a superficially valuable or pleasing appearance to. [earlier *fineer* by dissimilation < G *furni(e)ren* to FURNISH] —**ve·neer′er,** *n.*

ve·neer·ing (və nēr′ing), *n.* **1.** the process, act, or craft of applying veneers. **2.** material applied as a veneer. **3.** the surface formed by the application of veneers. **4.** a superficial covering, display, or appearance: *a veneering of civilization.* [VENEER + -ING[1]]

veneer′ patch′, a patch made in one of the veneers of a sheet of plywood before layup. Cf. **panel patch.**

ve·nene (və nēn′), *n.* *Biochem.* venin.

ven·e·nose (ven′ə nōs′), *adj.* *Archaic.* poisonous. [< LL *venēnōs(us),* equiv. to L *venēn(um)* drug, poison + *-ōsus* -OSE[1]]

ven·e·no·sus (ven′ə nō′səs), *adj., n., pl.* **-si** (-sī). (in prescriptions) —*adj.* **1.** poisonous. —*n.* **2.** a poison. [< L]

ven·e·punc·ture (ven′ə pungk′chər, vē′nə-), *n.* *Med.* venipuncture. [< ML *vēnē* (L *vēnae*), gen. sing. of *vēna* VEIN + PUNCTURE]

Ve·ner (ven′ər), *n.* Vänern.

ven·er·a·ble (ven′ər ə bəl), *adj.* **1.** commanding respect because of great age or impressive dignity; worthy of veneration or reverence, as because of high office or noble character: *a venerable member of Congress.* **2.** (of places, buildings, etc.) hallowed by religious, historic, or other lofty associations: *the venerable halls of the Abbey.* **3.** impressive or interesting because of age, antique appearance, etc.: *a venerable oak tree.* **4.** (in ironical use) extremely old or obsolete; ancient: *a venerable automobile.* —*n.* **5.** a venerable person. [late ME < L *venerābil(is),* equiv. to *venerā(rī)* (to) VENERATE + *-bilis* -BLE] —**ven′er·a·bil′i·ty, ven′er·a·ble·ness,** *n.* —**ven′er·a·bly,** *adv.*

ven·er·ate (ven′ə rāt′), *v.t.,* **-at·ed, -at·ing.** to regard or treat with reverence; revere. [< L *venerāt(us)* (ptp. of *venerārī* to worship, revere), equiv. to *vener-* (s. of *venus*) loveliness + *-ātus* -ATE[1]] —**ven′er·a′tor,** *n.*

ven·er·a·tion (ven′ə rā′shən), *n.* **1.** the act of venerating. **2.** the state of being venerated. **3.** the feeling of one who venerates; a feeling of awe, respect, etc.; reverence: *They were filled with veneration for their priests.* **4.** an expression of this feeling: *A memorial was erected in veneration of the dead of both world wars.* [late ME < L *venerātiōn-* (s. of *venerātiō*), equiv. to *venerāt(us)* (see VENERATE) + *-iōn-* -ION] —**ven′er·a′tion·al, ven′er·a′tive,** *adj.* —**ven′er·a′tive·ly,** *adv.* —**ven′er·a′tive·ness,** *n.*
—**Syn. 3.** awe. See **respect.** —**Ant. 3.** disrespect.

ve·ne·re·al (və nēr′ē əl), *adj.* **1.** arising from, connected with, or transmitted through sexual intercourse, as an infection, disease, etc. **2.** pertaining to diseases so arising. **3.** infected with or suffering from venereal disease: *a venereal patient.* **4.** adapted to the cure of such disease: *a venereal remedy.* **5.** of or pertaining to sexual desire or intercourse. **6.** serving or tending to excite sexual desire; aphrodisiac. [late ME < L *venere(us)* of sexual love (see VENUS) + -AL[1]]

vene′real disease′, *Pathol.* any disease characteristically transmitted by sexual intercourse. Cf. **gonorrhea, syphilis, vibriosis.**

ve·ne·re·ol·o·gy (və nēr′ē ol′ə jē), *n.* the branch of medicine dealing with the study and treatment of venereal disease. Also, **ven·er·ol·o·gy** (ven′ə rol′ə jē). [< L *venere(us)* VENEREAL + -O- + -LOGY] —**ve·ne′re·ol′o·gist,** *n.*

ven·er·er (ven′ər ər), *n.* *Archaic.* a huntsman. [VENER(Y)[2] + -ER[1]]

ven·er·y[1] (ven′ə rē), *n.* *Archaic.* the gratification of sexual desire. [< L *vener-* (see VENUS) + -Y[3]]

ven·er·y[2] (ven′ə rē), *n.* *Archaic.* the practice or sport of hunting; the chase. [ME *venerie* hunting < MF, equiv. to *ven(er)* to hunt + *-erie* -ERY]

ven·e·sec·tion (ven′i sek′shən, vē′ni-), *n.* *Surg.* phlebotomy. Also, **venisection.** [< ML *vēnē* (see VENEPUNCTURE) + SECTION]

Ve·ne·ti·a (və nē′shē ə, -shə), *n.* **1.** an ancient district in NE Italy: later a Roman province bounded by the Alps, the Po River, and the Adriatic Sea. **2.** Venezia (def. 1). **3.** a girl's given name.

Ve·ne·tian (və nē′shən), *adj.* **1.** of or pertaining to Venice or its inhabitants. **2.** pertaining to or designating a style of painting developed in Venice principally during the 15th and 16th centuries, characterized chiefly by rich, often warm colors and the illusion of deep space. **3.** in or in imitation of the style typical of Venice: *Venetian architecture.* —*n.* **4.** a native or inhabitant of Venice. **5.** (*l.c.*) *Informal.* See **Venetian blind. 6. Venetians,** a tape or braid for supporting the slats of a Venetian blind. **7.** Also called **Vene′tian cloth′.** *Textiles.* **a.** a wool or worsted fabric made in satin or twill weave and sometimes napped, used in the manufacture of lightweight coats, suits, skirts, and dresses. **b.** a cotton fabric constructed in satin or twill weave and usually mercerized or schreinerized, used chiefly for linings. [< ML *Venetiān(us),* equiv. to *Veneti(a)* Venice + *-ānus* -AN; r. ME *Venicien* < MF]

Vene′tian ball′, a small glass ball containing colorful objects or pieces, used chiefly as a paperweight.

Vene′tian blind′, a blind, as for a window, having overlapping horizontal slats that may be opened or closed, esp. one in which the slats may be raised and drawn together above the window by pulling a cord. —**Ve·ne′tianed,** *adj.*

Vene′tian den′til, *Archit.* (on an archivolt or molding) one of a series of small rectangular blocks having chamfers at alternate edges.

Vene′tian door′, a doorway having a form similar to that of a Palladian window.

Vene′tian glass′, ornamental glassware of the type made at Venice, esp. that from the island of Murano.

Vene′tian red′, 1. a red pigment, originally prepared from a natural oxide of iron, now usually made by calcining a mixture of lime and ferrous sulfate. **2.** a dark shade of orangish red.

Vene′tian su′mac. See **smoke tree** (def. 1).

Vene′tian win′dow. See **Palladian window.**

Ve·net·ic (və net′ik), *n.* an Italic language of NE Italy, known from inscriptions from the 4th to 2nd centuries B.C. [< L *veneticus,* equiv. to *Ve-net(i)* name of the tribe + *-icus* -IC]

Ve·ne·to (*It.* ve′ne tô), *n.* Venezia (def. 1).

Venez., Venezuela.

Ve·ne·zia (ve ne′tsyä), *n.* **1.** Also, **Venetia.** Also called **Veneto.** a region in NE Italy. 3,833,837 (1961); 7095 sq. mi. **2.** Italian name of **Venice.**

Ve·ne·zia Giu·lia (ve-ne′tsyä jōō′lyä), a former region of NE Italy, at the N end of the Adriatic: now mainly in Croatia and Slovenia. The larger part, including the area surrounding the Free Territory of Trieste, was ceded to Yugoslavia 1947; the part remaining in Italy merged with Udine to form Friuli-Venezia Giulia.

Vene′zia Tri·den·ti′na (trē′den tē′nä), a former department in N Italy, now forming the greater part of the region of Trentino-Alto Adige.

Ven·e·zue·la (ven′i zwā′lə, -zwē′-; *Sp.* be′ne swe′lä), *n.* a republic in N South America. 8,772,212 (est. 1965); 352,143 sq. mi. *Cap.:* Caracas. —**Ven′e·zue′lan,** *adj., n.*

venge (venj), *v.t.,* **venged, veng·ing.** *Archaic.* to avenge. [ME *venge(n)* < OF *veng(i)er* < L *vindicāre;* see VINDICATE]

venge·ance (ven′jəns), *n.* **1.** infliction of trouble, as pain, injury, humiliation, or annoyance, on a person or persons who have been a source of injury or annoyance to one: *But have you the right to vengeance?* **2.** an act or opportunity of inflicting such trouble: *a terrible vengeance; to take one's vengeance.* **3. with a vengeance, a.** with force or violence. **b.** greatly; extremely. **c.** to an unreasonable, excessive, or surprising degree: *This was negligence, and with a vengeance.* [ME < OF, equiv. to *vengi(er)* to avenge (see VENGE) + *-ance* -ANCE]
—**Syn. 1.** requital, retaliation. See **revenge.**

venge·ful (venj′fəl), *adj.* **1.** desiring or seeking vengeance; vindictive: *She has a vengeful nature.* **2.** characterized by or showing a vindictive spirit: *a vengeful act; vengeful intentions.* **3.** serving to inflict vengeance: *a vengeful killing.* [(RE)VENGEFUL] —**venge′ful·ly,** *adv.* —**venge′ful·ness,** *n.*
—**Syn. 1.** revengeful, spiteful.

ve·ni·al (vē′nē əl, vēn′yəl), *adj.* **1.** able to be forgiven or pardoned; not seriously wrong, as a sin (opposed to *mortal*). **2.** excusable; trifling; minor: *a venial error; a venial offense.* [ME < ML *veniāl(is),* equiv. to L *veni(a)* grace, favor, indulgence (*ven(us)* love + *-ia* -Y³) + *-ālis* -AL¹] —**ve′ni·al′i·ty, ve′ni·al·ness,** *n.* —**ve′ni·al·ly,** *adv.*

ve′nial sin′, *Rom. Cath. Ch.* a transgression against the law of God, committed without full consent of the will or full awareness of its seriousness, that does not deprive the soul of divine grace. Cf. **mortal sin.**

Ven·ice (ven′is), *n.* **1.** Italian, **Venezia.** a seaport in NE Italy, built on numerous small islands in an inlet of the Gulf of Venice (**Lagoon of Venice**). 336,184 (1961). **2. Gulf of,** the N arm of the Adriatic Sea. **3.** a town in SW Illinois. 5380 (1960). **4.** a town in SW Florida. 3444 (1960).

ven·in (ven′in, vē′nin), *n. Biochem.* any of several poisonous substances found in snake venom. Also, **venene, ven·ine** (ven′ēn). [< F, taken as VEN(OM) + -IN²]

ven·i·punc·ture (ven′ə pungk′chər, vē′nə-), *n. Med.* the puncture of a vein for surgical or therapeutic purposes or for collecting blood specimens for analysis. Also, **venepuncture.** [var. of VENEPUNCTURE]

ve·ni·re fa·ci·as (vi nī′rē fā′shē as′), *Law.* a writ or precept directed to the sheriff, requiring him to summon qualified citizens to act as jurors in the trial of cases. Also called **ve·ni′re.** [< L: lit., make come]

ve·ni·re·man (vi nī′rē mən), *n., pl.* **-men.** *Law.* a person summoned under a venire facias. [*venire* (see VENIRE FACIAS) + MAN¹]

ven·i·sec·tion (ven′i sek′shən, vē′nə-), *n. Surg.* phlebotomy. Also, **venesection.** [VEN(A) + -I- + SECTION]

ven·i·son (ven′i sən, -zen *or, esp. Brit.,* ven′zən), *n.* the flesh of a deer or similar animal as used for food. [ME *ven(a)ison* < OF *veneison, venaison* < L *vēnātiōn-* (see VENATION)]

Ve·nite (vi nī′tē), *n.* **1.** the 95th Psalm (94th in the Vulgate and Douay), used as a canticle at matins or morning prayers. **2.** a musical setting of this psalm. [< L: come ye; so called from the first word of Vulgate text]

ve·ni, vi·di, vi·ci (wā′nē, wē′dē, wē′kē; *Eng.* vē′nī, vī′dī, vī′sī, ven′ē, vē′dē, vē′chē, -sē), *Latin.* I came, I saw, I conquered.

Ve·ni·ze·los (ve′nē ze′lôs), *n.* **E·leu·the·rios** (e′lef-the′ryôs), 1864–1936, prime minister of Greece 1910–15, 1917–20, 1928–33.

Ven·lo (ven′lō), *n.* a city in the SE Netherlands. 57,705 (1962). Also, **Ven·loo** (ven′lō).

Venn′ di′agram (ven), *Math., Symbolic Logic.* a diagram which uses circles to represent sets and their relationships. [named after John Venn (1834–1923), English logician]

Ve·no·li·a (və nō′lē ə), *n.* a girl's given name.

ven·om (ven′əm), *n.* **1.** the poisonous fluid which some animals, as certain snakes, spiders, etc., secrete and introduce into the bodies of their victims by biting, stinging, etc. **2.** something resembling or suggesting poison in its effect; spite; malice: *the venom of jealousy.* **3.** *Archaic.* poison in general. —*v.t.* **4.** *Archaic.* to make venomous; envenom. [var. of ME *venim* < AF; OF *venim, venin* < VL **venimen,* by metathesis, etc. for L *venēnum* poison, love-potion, equiv. to *ven(us)* love (see VENUS) + *-ēnum,* neut. of *-ēnus* -ENE] —**ven′om·less,** *adj.*
—**Syn. 1.** See **poison. 2.** malignity, acrimony, bitterness, acerbity, gall, spleen, hate.

ven·om·ous (ven′ə məs), *adj.* **1.** (of an animal) having a gland or glands for secreting venom; inflicting a poisoned bite, sting, or wound: *a venomous snake.* **2.** full of or containing venom; poisonous: *a venomous wound; a venomous potion.* **3.** spiteful; malignant: *a venomous attack; a venomous tongue.* [ME *venim(o)us* < AF *venimus* (OF *venimeux*). See VENOM, -OUS] —**ven′om·ous·ly,** *adv.* —**ven′om·ous·ness, ven′om·ness,** *n.*

ve·nose (vē′nōs), *adj.* **1.** having many or prominent veins. **2.** venous. [< L *vēnōs(us),* equiv. to *vēn(a)* VEIN + *-ōsus* -OSE¹]

ve·nos·i·ty (vi nos′i tē), *n. Physiol.* the state or quality of being venous. [VENOSE + -ITY]

ve·nous (vē′nəs), *adj.* **1.** of, pertaining to, or of the nature of a vein or veins. **2.** having, characterized by, or composed of veins. **3.** pertaining to the blood in the pulmonary artery, right side of the heart, and most veins, that has become deoxygenated and charged with carbon dioxide during its passage through the body and that in man is normally dark red. [var. of VENOSE; see -OUS] —**ve′nous·ly,** *adv.* —**ve′nous·ness,** *n.*

vent¹ (vent), *n.* **1.** an opening, as in a wall, serving as an outlet for air, smoke, fumes, or the like. **2.** the small opening at the breech of a gun by which fire is communicated to the charge. **3.** *Zool.* the anal or excretory opening of animals, esp. of those below mammals, as birds and reptiles. **4.** a means of exit or escape; an outlet, as from confinement. [prob. VENT² + VENT³] —**vent′less,** *adj.*

vent² (vent), *n.* **1.** expression; utterance: *to give vent to one's emotions.* **2.** *Obs.* the act or fact of venting; emission or discharge. —*v.t.* **3.** to give free play or expression to (an emotion, passion, etc.): *She vented her rage on her associates.* **4.** to give public utterance to: *to vent one's opinions.* **5.** to relieve by giving expression to something: *He vented his disappointment by attacking the character of his successor.* **6.** to release or discharge (liquid, smoke, etc.). **7.** to furnish or provide with a vent or vents. —*v.i.* **8.** to be relieved of pressure or discharged by means of a vent. **9.** (of an otter or other animal) to rise to the surface of the water to breathe. [late ME *vente(n),* by aphesis < MF *e(s)venter,* equiv. to *es-* EX- + *venter* to blow, deriv. of *vent* < L *ventus* WIND¹]

vent³ (vent), *n.* a slit in the back or sometimes at the side of a coat or jacket. [late ME *vente;* r. ME *fente* < MF, deriv. of *fendre* to slit < L *findere* to split]

vent·age (ven′tij), *n.* a small hole or vent, as one of the fingerholes of a flute. [VENT¹ + -AGE]

ven·tail (ven′tāl), *n.* **1.** the pivoted middle element of a face defense of a close helmet. **2.** a flap of mail attached to a coif and fastened across the lower part of the face during combat. Also, **aventail.** [ME < MF *ventaille,* equiv. to *vent* (< L *ventus* WIND¹) + *-aille* -AL²]

ven·ter (ven′tər), *n.* **1.** *Anat., Zool.* **a.** the abdomen or belly. **b.** a bellylike cavity or concavity. **c.** a bellylike protuberance. **2.** *Law.* the womb, or a wife or mother, as a source of offspring. [< L *venter* belly, womb]

ven·ti·duct (ven′ti dukt′), *n.* a duct, pipe, or passage for wind or air, as for ventilating apartments. [*venti-* (comb. form of L *ventus* WIND¹) + DUCT]

ven·ti·late (ven′təlāt′), *v.t.,* **-lat·ed, -lat·ing. 1.** to provide (a room, mine, etc.) with fresh air in place of air that has been used or contaminated. **2.** to expose (blood) to air in the lungs or gills in respiration; oxygenate. **3.** (of air or wind) to circulate through or blow on, so as to cool or freshen the air of: *Even in the hottest days of summer, cool breezes ventilated the house by the sea.* **4.** to expose to the action of air or wind: *to ventilate floor timbers.* **5.** to submit (a question, problem, etc.) to open, full examination and discussion. **6.** to give utterance or expression to (an opinion, complaint, etc.). **7.** to furnish with a vent or opening, as for the escape of air or gas. [< L *ventilāt(us)* (ptp. of *ventilāre* to fan), equiv. to **ventil(us),* var. of *ventulus* mild breeze (*vent(us)* wind + *-ulus* dim. suffix) + *-ātus* -ATE¹] —**ven′ti·la·ble,** *adj.*

ven·ti·la·tion (ven′təlā′shən), *n.* **1.** the act of ventilating. **2.** the state of being ventilated. **3.** facilities or equipment for providing ventilation. [< L *ventilātiōn-* (s. of *ventilātiō*), equiv. to *ventilāt(us)* (see VENTILATE) + *-iōn-* -ION]

ven·ti·la·tive (ven′təlā′tiv), *adj.* **1.** promoting or producing ventilation. **2.** of or pertaining to ventilation. [VENTILATE + -IVE]

ven·ti·la·tor (ven′təlā′tər), *n.* **1.** one who or that which ventilates. **2.** a contrivance or opening used for replacing foul or stagnant air with fresh air. [VENTILATE + -OR²]

ven·ti·la·to·ry (ven′tələ tôr′ē, -tōr′ē), *adj.* of or pertaining to ventilation. [VENTILATE + -ORY¹]

Vent′nor Cit′y (vent′nər), a town in SE New Jersey. 8688 (1960).

ven·tose (ven′tōs), *adj. Archaic.* given to empty talk; windy; flatulent. [< L *ventōs(us)* windy, equiv. to *vent(us)* wind + *-ōsus* -OSE¹] —**ven·tos·i·ty** (ven tos′i tē), *n.*

Ven·tôse (vän tōz′), *n.* (in the French Revolutionary calendar) the sixth month of the year, extending from February 19 to March 20. [< F < L *ventōsus;* see VENTOSE¹]

ventr-, var. of **ventro-** before a vowel.

ven·trad (ven′trad), *adv. Anat., Zool.* toward the ventral side; ventrally. [VENTR- + L *ad* to, towards]

ven·tral (ven′trəl), *adj.* **1.** of or pertaining to the venter or belly; abdominal. **2.** situated on the abdominal side of the body. **3.** of, pertaining to, or situated on the anterior or lower side or surface, as of an organ or part. **4.** *Bot.* of or designating the lower or inner surface, as of a petal, leaf, etc. —*n.* **5.** See **pelvic fin.** [< L *ventrāl(is),* equiv. to *vent(e)r* VENTER + *-ālis* -AL¹] —**ven′tral·ly,** *adv.*

ven′tral fin′. See **pelvic fin.**

ventri-, var. of **ventro-.** Also, **ventr-.**

ven·tri·cle (ven′tri kəl), *n.* **1.** any of various hollow organs or parts in an animal body. **2.** *Anat.* **a.** either of the two lower chambers on each side of the heart that receive blood from the atria and in turn force it into the arteries. See diag. under **heart. b.** one of a series of connecting cavities of the brain. [< L *ventricul(us)* (little) belly, ventricle. See VENTRI-, -CLE]

ven·tri·cose (ven′trə kōs′), *adj.* **1.** swollen, esp. on one side or unequally; protuberant. **2.** having a large abdomen. [< NL *ventricōs(us).* See VENTRI-, -IC, -OSE¹, -OUS] —**ven·tri·cos·i·ty** (ven′trə kos′i tē), *n.*

ven·tric·u·lar (ven trik′yə lər), *adj.* **1.** of, pertaining to, or of the nature of a ventricle. **2.** of or pertaining to a belly or to something resembling one. [< L *ventricul(us)* (see VENTRICLE) + -AR¹]

ventriculo-, a combining form of **ventricle,** used in the formation of compound words: *ventriculogram.* [< L *ventricul(us)* + -O-]

ven·tric·u·lo·gram (ven trik′yə lə gram′), *n.* an x-ray photograph of the ventricles of the brain, usually after the injection of air or gas as a contrast medium. [VENTRICUL(US) + -O- + -GRAM¹]

ven·tric·u·log·ra·phy (ven trik′yə log′rə fē), *n.* the production of ventriculograms following replacement of the fluid in the ventricles with air or a radiopaque substance. [VENTRICULO- + -GRAPHY]

ven·tric·u·lo·punc·ture (ven trik′yə lō pungk′chər), *n. Surg.* the puncture of a ventricle of the brain with a needle. [VENTRICULO- + PUNCTURE]

ven·tric·u·los·to·my (ven trik′yə los′tə mē), *n., pl.* **-mies.** *Surg.* the formation of a drain for cerebrospinal fluid from the ventricles of the brain. [VENTRICULO- + -STOMY]

ven·tric·u·lus (ven trik′yə ləs), *n., pl.* **-li** (-lī′). **1.** the stomach of an insect; that part of the food tract within which digestion and absorption take place. **2.** the muscular portion of a bird's stomach; gizzard. [< L; see VENTRICLE]

ven·tri·lo·qui·al (ven′trə lō′kwē əl), *adj.* of, pertaining to, or using ventriloquism. Also, **ven·tril·o·qual** (ven tril′ə kwəl). [VENTRILOQUY + -AL¹] —**ven′tri·lo′qui·al·ly,** *adv.*

ven·tril·o·quise (ven tril′ə kwīz′), *v.i., v.t.,* **-quised, -quis·ing.** *Chiefly Brit.* ventriloquize.

ven·tril·o·quism (ven tril′ə kwiz′əm), *n.* the art or practice of speaking, with little or no lip movement, in such a manner that the voice does not appear to come from the speaker but from another source, as from a mechanical dummy. Also called **ven·tril′o·quy.** [VENTRILOQU(Y) + -ISM]

ven·tril·o·quist (ven tril′ə kwist), *n.* a person who performs or is skilled in ventriloquism. [VENTRILOQU(Y) + -IST] —**ven·tril′o·quis′tic,** *adj.*

ven·tril·o·quize (ven tril′ə kwīz′), *v.i., v.t.,* **-quized, -quiz·ing.** to speak or produce sounds in the manner of a ventriloquist. Also, *esp. Brit.,* **ventriloquise.** [VENTRILOQU(Y) + -IZE]

ven·tril·o·quy (ven tril′ə kwē), *n.* ventriloquism. [< ML *ventriloqui(um),* equiv. to LL *ventriloqu(us)* belly speaker (*ventri-* VENTRI- + *loquus,* deriv. of *loquī* to speak) + *-ium* -Y³]

Ven·tris (ven′tris), *n.* **Michael George Francis,** 1922–56, English architect and linguist.

ventro-, a learned borrowing from Latin meaning "abdomen," used in the formation of compound words: *ventrotomy.* Also, **ventr-, ventri-.** [comb. form of NL *venter* VENTER]

ven·trot·o·my (ven trot′ə mē), *n., pl.* **-mies.** *Surg.* laparotomy. [VENTRO- + -TOMY]

ven·ture (ven′chər), *n., v.,* **-tured, -tur·ing.** —*n.* **1.** an undertaking involving uncertainty as to the outcome, esp. a risky or dangerous one: *His latest mountain-climbing venture has been unsuccessful.* **2.** a business enterprise or speculation in which loss is risked in the hope of profit; a commercial or other speculation. **3.** the money, ship, cargo, merchandise, or the like, on which risk is taken in a business enterprise or speculation. **4.** *Obs.* hazard or risk. **5. at a venture,** according to chance; at random: *A successor was chosen at a venture.* —*v.t.* **6.** to expose to hazard; risk: *to venture one's fortune; to venture one's life.* **7.** to take the risk of; brave the dangers of: *to venture a voyage into uncharted seas.* **8.** to undertake to express, as when opposition or resistance appears likely to follow; be bold enough; dare: *I venture to say that you are behaving foolishly.* **9.** *Archaic.* to take the risk of sending. —*v.i.* **10.** to make a venture; risk: *He traveled deeper into the country than any explorer before him had dared to venture.* **11.** to take a risk; dare; presume (often fol. by *on, upon,* or an infinitive): *to venture upon an ambitious program of reform.* [late ME, aph. var. of *aventure* ADVENTURE] —**ven′tur·er,** *n.*
—**Syn. 6.** endanger, imperil, jeopardize. **11.** See **dare.**

ven′ture cap′ital, money invested in stocks, esp. in issues of a new corporation. Also called **risk capital.**

ven·ture·some (ven′chər səm), *adj.* **1.** having or showing a disposition to undertake risky or dangerous activities; daring: *a venturesome businessman; a venturesome explorer.* **2.** attended with risk; hazardous: *Auto racing is a venturesome sport.* [VENTURE + -SOME¹] —**ven′ture·some·ly,** *adv.* —**ven′ture·some·ness,** *n.*

Ventu′ri tube′ (ven to͝or′ē), a device for measuring the flow of a fluid, consisting of a tube with a short, narrow center section and widened, tapered ends, so that a fluid flowing through the center section at a higher velocity than through an end section creates a pressure differential that is a measure of the flow of the fluid. [named after G. B. *Venturi* (1746–1822), Italian physicist whose work led to its invention]

ven·tur·ous (ven′chər əs), *adj.* **1.** ready or inclined to face risky situations; bold; daring; adventurous. **2.** hazardous; risky; dangerous: *their venturous voyage.* [VENTURE + -OUS; see ADVENTUROUS] —**ven′tur·ous·ly,** *adv.* —**ven′tur·ous·ness,** *n.*
—**Syn. 1.** enterprising, rash. **2.** perilous. —**Ant. 1.** cautious.

ven·ue (ven′o͞o, ven′yo͞o), *n.* **1.** *Law.* **a.** the place of a crime or cause of action. **b.** the county or place where the jury is gathered and the cause tried. **c.** the designation, in the pleading, of the jurisdiction where a trial will be held. **d.** the statement naming the place and person before whom an affidavit was sworn. **2.** the scene or locale of any action or event. **3.** the position taken by a person engaged in argument or debate; ground. [ME *venue* an attack < MF (lit., a coming), OF *venue* (ptp. fem. of *venir* < L *venīre* to come) < VL **venūta* (r. L *venta*), equiv. to *venu-* VL ptp. s. + *-ta* VL, L fem. ptp. suffix]

ven·ule (ven′yo͞ol), *n.* **1.** a small vein. **2.** one of the branches of a vein in the wing of an insect. Also, **veinule, veinulet.** [< L *vēnula* little vein. See VEIN, -ULE] —**ven′u·lar,** *adj.*

ven·u·lose (ven′yə lōs′), *adj.* having venules. Also, **ven·u·lous** (ven′yə ləs). [VENULE + -OSE¹]

Ve·nus (vē′nəs), *n., pl.* **-us·es** for 2. **1.** an ancient Italian goddess of gardens and spring, identified by the Romans with Aphrodite as the goddess of love and beauty. **2.** an exceptionally beautiful woman. **3.** *Astron.* the planet second in order from the sun, having a diameter of 7700 miles, a mean distance from the sun of 67,000,000 miles, a period of revolution of 225 days, and having no satellites. It is the most brilliant planet in the solar system. **4.** *Chem. Obs.* copper.

Ve′nus and Adon′is, a narrative poem (1593) by Shakespeare.

Ve·nus·berg (vē′nəs bûrg′; *Ger.* vā′no͝os berkн′), *n.* a mountain in central Germany in the caverns of which, according to medieval legend, Venus held court.

Ve′nus de Mi′lo (də mē′lō, mī′-), a Greek statue of Venus in marble, of c200 B.C., found 1820 on Melos and now in the Louvre, Paris. Also, **Ve′nus of Me′los.** Also called **Aphrodite of Melos.**

Ve′nus hair′stone (hâr′stōn′), a quartz crystal containing long, fine needles of rutile, used as a gemstone.

Ve·nu·si·an (və no͞o′sē ən, -shē ən, -shən, -nyo͞o′-), *adj.* **1.** of or pertaining to the planet Venus. —*n.* **2.** a supposed being inhabiting or coming from Venus. [VENUS + -IAN]

Ve′nus of Wil′lendorf. See under **Willendorf.**

Ve′nus's flow′er bas′ket, a glass sponge of the genus *Euplectella*, found in deep waters off the Philippines and Japan, having a cylindrical skeleton formed of an intricate latticework of siliceous spicules.

Venus's flower basket (Length 1 ft.)

Ve·nus's-fly·trap (vē′nə siz flī′trap′), *n.* a plant, *Dionaea muscipula*, native to North and South Carolina, having leaves with two lobes which close like a trap when certain delicate hairs on them are irritated, as by a fly.

Ve′nus's gir′dle, an iridescent blue and green ctenophore, *Cestum veneris*, having a ribbon-shaped, gelatinous body.

Ve·nus's-hair (vē′nə siz hâr′), *n.* a delicate maidenhair fern, *Adiantum Capillus-Veneris.*

Ve′nus's look′ing-glass (lo͝ok′ing glas′, -gläs′), any of several campanulaceous herbs of the genus *Specularia*, esp. *S. Speculum-Veneris*, having blue or white flowers with a rotate corolla.

Venus's—flytrap (Height about 1 ft.)

ver., **1.** verse; verses. **2.** version.

ver·a (ver′ə, var′ə), *adj., adv. Scot.* very.

Ve·ra (vēr′ə), *n.* a girl's given name.

ve·ra·cious (və rā′shəs), *adj.* **1.** habitually speaking the truth; truthful; honest: *a veracious witness.* **2.** characterized by truthfulness; true, accurate, or honest in content: *a veracious statement; a veracious account.* [VERACI(TY) + -OUS] —**ve·ra′cious·ly,** *adv.* —**ve·ra′cious·ness,** *n.*
—**Ant. 1, 2.** mendacious.

ve·rac·i·ty (və ras′i tē), *n., pl.* **-ties.** **1.** habitual observance of truth in speech or statement; truthfulness: *He was not noted for his veracity.* **2.** conformity to truth or fact; accuracy: *Several discrepancies in the story made us question its veracity.* **3.** correctness or accuracy, as of the senses, a scientific instrument, etc. **4.** something veracious; a truth. [< ML *vērācitāt-* (s. of *vērācitās*), equiv. to L *vērāci-* (s. of *vērax*) true + *-tāt-* -TY²]
—**Syn. 1.** honesty.

Ver·a·cruz (ver′ə kro͞oz′; *Sp.* be′rä kro͞os′), *n.* **1.** a state in E Mexico, on the Gulf of Mexico. 2,727,899 (1960); 27,759 sq. mi. *Cap.:* Jalapa. **2.** a seaport in this state: the chief port of Mexico. 137,413 (1960). Formerly, **Ver′a Cruz′.**

Ver·a·lyn (vēr′ə lin′), *n.* a girl's given name.

ve·ran·da (və ran′də), *n.* an open porch, usually roofed and sometimes partly enclosed, attached to the outside of a house or other building; a piazza, portico, or gallery. Also, **ve·ran′dah.** [< Pg *varanda* railing < Hindi; ? akin to L *vārus* crooked (see VARA)] —**ve·ran′daed, ve·ran′dahed,** *adj.*

ve·rat·ric (və ra′trik), *adj. Chem.* of or derived from veratric acid. [< L *vērātr(um)* hellebore + -IC]

verat′ric ac′id, *Chem.* a white, crystalline solid, $(CH_3O)_2C_6H_3COOH$, obtained from the decomposition of veratrine or the like, and synthesized.

ve·rat·ri·dine (və ra′tri dēn′, -din), *n. Chem.* a yellowish-white, amorphous, water-soluble, poisonous alkaloid, $C_{36}H_{51}NO_{11}$, occurring with veratrine in the seeds of the sabadilla. [< L *vērātr(um)* hellebore + -ID³ + -INE²]

ver·a·trine (ver′i trēn′, -trin), *n. Chem.* a white or grayish-white, slightly water-soluble, poisonous mixture of alkaloids obtained by extraction from the seeds of the sabadilla: formerly used in medicine as a counterirritant in the treatment of rheumatism and neuralgia. Also, **ve·ra·tri·a** (və rā′trē ə, -ra′-), **ver·a·trin** (ver′ə trin), **ver·a·tri·na** (ver′ə trī′nə). [< F < L *vērātr(um)* hellebore + F *-ine* -INE²]

verb (vûrb), *n.* any member of a class of words that are formally distinguished in many languages, as in English by the past ending in *-ed*, that function as the main elements of predicates, that typically express action, state, or a relation between two things, and that (when inflected) may be inflected for tense, aspect, voice, mood, and to show agreement with their subject or object. [late ME < L *verb(um)* verb, word]

ver·bal (vûr′bəl), *adj.* **1.** of or pertaining to words: *verbal ability.* **2.** consisting of or in the form of words: *verbal imagery.* **3.** expressed in spoken words; oral rather than written: *verbal communication; verbal agreement.* **4.** pertaining to or concerned with words only, rather than with ideas, facts, or realities: *a purely verbal distinction between two concepts.* **5.** corresponding word for word; verbatim: *a verbal translation.* **6.** using words: *verbal facility.* **7.** consisting of words (as opposed to action): *a merely verbal protest.* **8.** based on the use of words (as opposed to other activity): *a verbal score in a test; verbal I.Q.* **9.** *Gram.* **a.** of, pertaining to, or derived from a verb. **b.** used in a sentence as or like a verb, as participles and infinitives. —*n.* **10.** *Gram.* a word, particularly a noun or adjective, derived from a verb. [late ME < L *verbāl(is)*, equiv. to *verb(um)* VERB + *-ālis* -AL¹] —**ver′bal·ly,** *adv.*
—**Syn. 3.** spoken. See **oral.**

ver′bal auxil′iary, an auxiliary verb, esp. when considered as a member of a separate class of words used with verbs rather than as a special subclass of verbs.

ver·bal·ise (vûr′bə līz′), *v.t., v.i.,* **-ised, -is·ing.** *Chiefly Brit.* verbalize. —**ver′bal·i·sa′tion,** *n.* —**ver′bal·is′er,** *n.*

ver·bal·ism (vûr′bə liz′əm), *n.* **1.** a verbal expression, as a word or phrase. **2.** the way in which something is worded; choice of words; phrasing. **3.** a phrase or sentence having little or no meaning. **4.** words considered as predominating over or obscuring ideas or reality; verbiage. [VERBAL + -ISM]

ver·bal·ist (vûr′bə list), *n.* **1.** a person skilled in the use of words. **2.** a person who concerns himself more with words than with ideas or reality. [VERBAL + -IST] —**ver′bal·is′tic,** *adj.*

ver·bal·i·ty (vər bal′i tē), *n., pl.* **-ties.** **1.** wordiness; verbal diffuseness: *Though impressive at first, the speech did not progress beyond mere verbality.* **2.** a verbal expression of an idea or thought. **3.** the quality or character of a verb. [VERBAL + -ITY]

ver·bal·ize (vûr′bə līz′), *v.,* **-ized, -iz·ing.** —*v.t.* **1.** to express in words: *He couldn't verbalize his feelings.* **2.** *Gram.* to convert into a verb: *to verbalize "butter" into "to butter."* —*v.i.* **3.** to use many words; be verbose. **4.** to express something verbally. Also, *esp. Brit.,* **verbalise.** [VERBAL + -IZE; cf. F *verbaliser*] —**ver′bal·i·za′tion,** *n.* —**ver′bal·iz′er,** *n.*

ver′bal noun′, *Gram.* a noun derived from a verb, esp. by a process applicable to most or all verbs, as, in English, the *-ing* form of *Eating is fun* or of *Smoking is forbidden.*

ver·ba·tim (vər bā′tim), *adv.* **1.** in exactly the same words; word for word: *to repeat something verbatim.* —*adj.* **2.** corresponding word for word to the original source or text: *a verbatim record of the proceedings.* **3.** skilled at recording or noting down speeches, proceedings, etc., with word-for-word accuracy: *a verbatim stenographer.* [late ME < ML, equiv. to *verb(um)* word + *-ātim* adv. suffix]

ver·ba·tim et li·te·ra·tim (wer bä′tim et lē′te-rä′tim; *Eng.* vər bā′tim et lit′ə rā′tim), *Latin.* word for word and letter for letter; in exactly the same words.

ver·be·na (vər bē′nə), *n.* any plant of the genus *Verbena*, comprising the vervains. [< ML; see VERVAIN]

Ver·be·na (vər bē′nə), *n.* a girl's given name.

ver·be·na·ceous (vûr′bə nā′shəs), *adj.* belonging to the *Verbenaceae*, or verbena family of plants, comprising also the lantana, teak, etc. [VERBEN(A) + -ACEOUS]

ver·bi·age (vûr′bē ij), *n.* **1.** overabundance or superfluity of words, as in writing or speech; wordiness; verbosity. **2.** manner or style of expressing something in words; wording: *a manual of official verbiage.* [< F < MF *verbi(er)* (to) gabble (< L *verbium* wording) + *-age* -AGE]

ver·bid (vûr′bid), *n. Gram.* a nonfinite verb form; an infinitive or participle. [VERB + -ID²]

ver·bi·fy (vûr′bə fī′), *v.t.,* **-fied, -fy·ing.** to change into or employ as a verb, as a noun. [VERB + -IFY] —**verb′i·fi·ca′tion,** *n.*

verb·less (vûrb′lis), *adj.* without a verb or verbs: *a verbless phrase.* [VERB + -LESS]

ver·bose (vər bōs′), *adj.* expressed in or characterized by the use of many or too many words; wordy: *a verbose report.* [< L *verbōs(us)*, equiv. to *verb(um)* word + *-ōsus* -OSE¹] —**ver·bose′ly,** *adv.* —**ver·bose′ness,** *n.*
—**Syn.** prolix; tedious, inflated, turgid, bombastic; voluble, talkative, loquacious. —**Ant.** laconic.

ver·bos·i·ty (vər bos′i tē), *n.* the state or quality of being verbose; superfluity of words; wordiness: *His speeches were always marred by verbosity.* [< LL *verbōsitās.* See VERBOSE, -ITY]
—**Syn.** prolixity, redundancy, turgidity. —**Ant.** reticence.

ver·bo·ten (fər bōt′ən; *Eng.* vər bōt′ən), *German.* forbidden, as by law; prohibited.

verb′ phrase′, *Gram.* a group of words including a verb and its complements, objects, or other modifiers that functions syntactically as a verb. In English a verb phrase combines with a noun or noun phrase acting as subject to form a simple sentence.

ver·bum sap (vûr′bəm sap′), a word to the wise is sufficient; no more need be said. Also, **verb. sap.** (vûrb′ sap′), **verbum sat** (vûr′bəm sat′). [short for L *verbum sapienti sat est*]

Ver·cel·li (ver chel′lē), *n.* a city in NW Italy, WSW of Milan. 47,945 (1958).

Vercel′li Book′, a codex of Old English poems and sermons found in the chapter house at Vercelli.

Ver·cin·get·o·rix (vûr′sin jet′ə riks, -get′-), *n.* died 45? B.C., Gallic chieftain conquered by Caesar.

Ver·dan·di (ver′dän dē), *n. Scand. Myth.* an elf personifying the present; one of the three Norns that developed from Urdar. Cf. **Skuld, Urd.** [< Icel *verthandi*, prp. of *vertha* to become; see WORTH²]

ver·dant (vûr′dənt), *adj.* **1.** green with vegetation; covered with growing plants or grass: *a verdant oasis.* **2.** of the color green: *a verdant lawn.* **3.** inexperienced; unsophisticated: *verdant college freshmen.* [VERD(URE) + -ANT] —**ver′dan·cy,** *n.* —**ver′dant·ly,** *adv.*

verd′ antique′ (vûrd), **1.** a green, mottled or impure serpentine, sold as a marble and much used for decorative purposes. **2.** any of various similar green stones. **3.** *Mineral.* andesite porphyry containing crystals of feldspar. Also, **verde′ antique′.** [< F < It *verde antico* green of old. See VERDURE, ANTIQUE]

Verde (vûrd), *n.* **Cape,** a cape in Senegal, near Dakar: the westernmost point of Africa.

ver·der·er (vûr′dər ər), *n. Eng. Forest Law.* a judicial officer in the royal forests having charge esp. of the vert, or trees and undergrowth. Also, **ver′de·ror.** [< AF *verderer*, equiv. to *verder* (< L *viridārium* garden, equiv. to *virid(is)* green + *-ārium* -ER²) + *-er* < -ER¹] —**ver′der·er·ship′,** *n.*

Ver·di (vâr′dē; *It.* ver′dē), *n.* **Giu·sep·pe** (jo͞o zep′pe), 1813–1901, Italian composer.

ver·dict (vûr′dikt), *n.* **1.** *Law.* the finding or answer of a jury given to the court concerning a matter submitted to their judgment: *The jury's verdict was that he was guilty.* **2.** a judgment; decision: *the verdict of the critics.* [ME < ML *vērdict(um)*, var. of *vērēdictum*, lit., something said truly; r. ME *verdit* < AF < L *vērum dictum* true word]

ver·di·gris (vûr′də grēs′, -gris), *n.* a green or bluish patina formed on copper, brass, or bronze surfaces exposed to the atmosphere for long periods of time, consisting principally of basic copper sulfate. Also called **aerugo.** [< MF *ver(t) de gris*; r. ME *ver(t) de Gres* < AF, OF *ver(t) de Grece* green of Greece] —**ver′di·gris′y,** *adj.*

ver·din (vûr′din), *n.* a small, yellow-headed titmouse, *Auriparus flaviceps*, of arid regions of the southwestern U.S. and Mexico, which builds a compact, spherical nest of thorny twigs. [< F *verdin* yellowhammer]

ver·dite (vûr′dīt), *n.* a rock composed mainly of fuchsite and clay, occurring in South Africa in the form of large boulders. [?]

ver·di·ter (vûr′di tər), *n.* either of two pigments, consisting usually of carbonate of copper prepared by grinding either azurite **(blue verditer)** or malachite **(green verditer).** [< MF *verd de terre* (*vert de terre*) green of earth]

Ver·dun (vâr dun′, vûr-; *Fr.* ver dœn′), *n.* **1.** a fortress city in NE France, on the Meuse River. A German offensive was stopped here in 1916 in the bloodiest fighting of World War I. 25,238 (1962). **2.** a city in S Quebec, in SE Canada. 78,317 (1961).

ver·dure (vûr′jər), *n.* **1.** greenness, esp. of fresh, flourishing vegetation. **2.** green vegetation, esp. grass or herbage. **3.** freshness in general; flourishing condition; vigor. [late ME < MF, equiv. to *verd* green (see VERT) + *-ure* -URE] —**ver′dured,** *adj.* —**ver′dure·less,** *adj.*

ver·dur·ous (vûr′jər əs), *adj.* **1.** rich in verdure; freshly green; verdant. **2.** covered with verdure, as places. **3.** consisting of verdure. **4.** of, pertaining to, or characteristic of verdure. [VERDURE + -OUS] —**ver′dur·ous·ness,** *n.*

ver·e·cund (ver′ə kund′), *adj. Archaic.* bashful; modest. [< L *verēcund(us)*, equiv. to *verē(rī)* (to) fear + *-cundus* adj. suffix]

Ve·ree·ni·ging (fə rē′ni king), *n.* a city in the E Republic of South Africa, S of Johannesburg. 74,574 (1960).

Ver·ein (fer īn′; *Eng.* və rīn′), *n., pl.* **-ein·e** (-ī′nə), *Eng.* **-eins.** *German.* a union, association, or society.

Ve·rel (və rel′), *n. Trademark.* a woollike acrylic fiber

Ve·re·na (və rē′nə), *n.* a girl's given name.

Ve·resh·cha·gin (ve resh chä′gin), *n.* **Va·si·li Va·sil·ie·vich** (vä sē′li vä sēl′yə vich), 1842–1904, Russian painter.

verge¹ (vûrj), *n., v.,* **verged, verg·ing.** —*n.* **1.** the edge, rim, or margin of something: *the verge of a desert; to operate on the verge of fraud.* **2.** the limit or point beyond which something begins or occurs; brink: *on the verge of a nervous breakdown; on the verge of a solution to a problem.* **3.** a limiting belt, strip, or border of something. **4.** a narrow strip of turf bordering on a pathway, sidewalk, roadway, etc. **5.** a decorative border, as on or around an object, structural part, etc. **6.** limited room or scope for something: *an action within the verge of one's abilities.* **7.** an area or district subject to a particular jurisdiction. **8.** *Hist.* an area or district in England embracing the royal palace, being the jurisdiction of the Marshalsea Court. **9.** the part of a sloping roof that projects beyond the gable wall. **10.** *Archit.* the shaft of a column or colonette. **11.** a rod, wand, or staff, esp. one carried as an emblem of authority or ensign of office of a bishop, dean, or the like. **12.** *Print.* a triggerlike device for releasing the matrices of a Linotype machine. **13.** *Horol.* **a.** a palletlike lever formerly used in inexpensive pendulum clocks. **b.** See under **verge escapement.** **14.** *Obs.* a stick or wand held in the hand of a person swearing fealty to the lord on being admitted as a tenant. —*v.i.* **15.** to be on the edge or margin; border: *Our property verges on theirs.* **16.** to come close to, approach, or be in transition to some state, quality, etc. (usually fol. by *on*): *a statesman who verged on greatness;*

a situation that verged on disaster. —*v.t.* **17.** to serve as the verge or boundary of: *a high hedge verging the yard.* [late ME < MF < L *virga* rod]
—**Syn. 1.** brim, lip, brink.

verge² (vûrj), *v.i.,* **verged, verg·ing. 1.** to incline; tend (usually fol. by *to* or *toward*): *The economy verges toward inflation.* **2.** to slope or sink. [< L *verge(re)* to turn, bend, be inclined]

verge·board (vûrj′bōrd′, -bôrd′), *n.* bargeboard. [VERGE¹ + BOARD]

verge′ escape′ment, a clock escapement, formerly in use, having for an escape wheel a crown wheel fixed to a horizontal arbor, engaged and released at opposite sides by two pallets fixed to a vertically mounted, horizontally oscillating rod **(verge)** that has a horizontal, weighted crosspiece **(foliot)** fixed to it as a balance.

ver·ger (vûr′jər), *n.* **1.** *Chiefly Brit.* a church official who serves as sacristan, caretaker, usher, and general attendant. **2.** *Brit.* an official who carries the verge or other symbol of office before a bishop, dean, or other dignitary. [late ME; see VERGE¹, -ER¹]

Ver·gil (vûr′jil), *n.* (*Publius Vergilius Maro*) 70–19 B.C., Roman poet: author of *The Aeneid.* **2.** a boy's given name. Also, **Virgil.**

Ver·gil·i·an (vər jil′ē ən, -jil′yən), *adj.* pertaining to or characteristic of the poet Vergil. Also, **Virgilian.** [< L *Virgiliān(us)*; see -AN]

ver·glas (ver glä′), *n., pl.* **-glases** (-glä′, -gläz′). glaze (def. 17). [< F, MF; OF *verre-glaz,* lit., glass-ice, equiv. to *verre* glass (< L *vitrum*) + *glaz* ice (< LL *glacia* ice; see GLACIAL)]

ve·rid·i·cal (və rid′i kəl), *adj.* **1.** truthful; veracious. **2.** corresponding to facts; not illusory; real; actual; genuine. Also, **ve·rid′ic.** [< L *vēridic(us)* (*vēr(us)* true + *-i-* -I- + *-dicus* speaking) + -AL¹] —**ve·rid′i·cal′i·ty,** *n.* —**ve·rid′i·cal·ly,** *adv.*

ver·i·est (ver′ē ist), *adj.* **1.** utmost; most complete: *the veriest stupidity.* **2.** superlative of **very.** [VERY + -EST]

ver·i·fi·ca·tion (ver′ə fə kā′shən), *n.* **1.** the act of verifying. **2.** the state of being verified. **3.** evidence that establishes or confirms the accuracy or truth of: *We could find no verification for his fantastic claims.* **4.** a formal assertion of the truth of something, as by oath, affidavit, etc. **5.** the process of research, examination, etc., required to prove or establish authenticity or validity. **6.** *Law.* a short confirmatory affidavit at the end of a pleading or petition. [< ML *vērificātiōn-* (s. of *vērificātiō*), equiv. to *vērificāt(us)* (ptp. of *vērificāre;* see VERIFY, -ATE¹) + *-iōn-* -ION] —**ver′i·fi·ca′tive, ver′i·fi·ca′to·ry,** *adj.*

ver·i·fied (ver′ə fīd′), *adj.* confirmed as to accuracy or truth by acceptable evidence, action, etc. [VERIFY + -ED²]

ver·i·fy (ver′ə fī′), *v.t.,* **-fied, -fy·ing. 1.** to prove the truth of, as by evidence or testimony; confirm; substantiate: *Events verified his prediction.* **2.** to ascertain the truth or correctness of, as by examination, research, or comparison: *to verify a spelling.* **3.** to act as ultimate proof or evidence of; serve to confirm. **4.** *Law.* **a.** to prove or confirm (an allegation). **b.** to state to be true, esp. in legal use, formally or upon oath. [ME *verifie(n)* < MF *verifier* < LL *vērificāre.* See VERIDICAL, -FY] —**ver′i·fi′a·bil′i·ty, ver′i·fi′a·ble·ness,** *n.* —**ver′i·fi′a·ble,** *adj.* —**ver′i·fi′er,** *n.*
—**Syn. 2.** authenticate, validate.

ver·i·ly (ver′ə lē), *adv.* *Archaic.* in truth; really; indeed. [ME; see VERY, -LY]

Ver·is (ver′is), *n.* **Mare.** See **Mare Veris.**

ver·i·sim·i·lar (ver′i sim′ə lər), *adj.* having the appearance of truth; likely; probable: *a verisimilar tale.* [< L *vērīsimil(is)* (*vērī-,* gen. sing. of *vērus* true, + *similis* like) + -AR¹] —**ver′i·sim′i·lar·ly,** *adv.*

ver·i·si·mil·i·tude (ver′i si mil′i to͞od′, -tyo͞od′), *n.* **1.** the appearance or semblance of truth; likelihood; probability. **2.** something having merely the appearance of truth. [< L *vērīsimilitūdō,* equiv. to *vērī-* (gen. sing. of *vērus* true) + *similitūdō* SIMILITUDE]

ver·ism (vēr′iz əm, ver-), *n.* the theory that rigid representation of truth and reality is essential to art and literature, and therefore the ugly and vulgar must be included. [< L *vēr(us)* true + -ISM] —**ver′ist,** *n., adj.* —**ve·ris′tic,** *adj.*

ver·i·ta·ble (ver′i tə bəl), *adj.* **1.** being truly or very much so: *a veritable triumph; a veritable Rembrandt.* **2.** *Obs.* true, as a statement or tale. [late ME < AF, MF. See VERITY, -ABLE] —**ver′i·ta·ble·ness,** *n.* —**ver′i·ta·bly,** *adv.*

ve·ri·tas (wā′ʀi täs′; *Eng.* ver′i tas′), *n.* *Latin.* truth.

ve·ri·tas vos li·be·ra·bit (wā′ʀi täs′ wōs lē′be rä′bit; *Eng.* ver′i tas′ vōs lib′ə rā′bit), *Latin.* truth will liberate you; the truth shall make you free.

ve·ri·té sans peur (vā ʀē tā′ säɴ pœʀ′), *French.* truth without fear.

ver·i·ty (ver′i tē), *n., pl.* **-ties. 1.** the state or quality of being true; accordance with fact or reality: *to question the verity of a statement.* **2.** something that is true, as a principle, belief, idea, statement, or the like: *the eternal verities.* [late ME < L *vēritās.* See VERI-, -ITY²]

ver·juice (vûr′jo͞os′), *n.* **1.** an acid liquor made from the sour juice of crab apples, unripe grapes, etc., formerly much used for culinary and other purposes. **2.** sourness, as of temper or expression. —*adj.* Also, **ver′juiced′. 3.** of or pertaining to verjuice. **4.** sour in temper, expression, etc. [ME *verjuis* < MF *ver(t)jus,* equiv. to *vert* green (< L *viridis*) + *jus* JUICE]

Ver·laine (veʀ len′), *n.* **Paul** (pôl), 1844–96, French poet.

Ver·li·a (vûr′lē ə), *n.* a girl's given name.

Ver·meer (vər mēr′; *Du.* vəʀ māʀ′), *n.* **Jan** (yän), (*Jan van der Meer van Delft*), 1632–75, Dutch painter.

ver·meil (vûr′mil), *n.* **1.** vermilion red. **2.** metal, as silver or bronze, which has been gilded. —*adj.* **3.** of the color vermilion. [late ME < MF < LL *vermicul(us)* kermes (insect and dye) < L *vermiculus* VERMICULE]

Ver·melle (vər mel′), *n.* a girl's given name.

vermi-, a learned borrowing from Latin meaning "worm," used in the formation of compound words: *vermifuge.* [comb. form of L *vermis* worm]

ver·mi·cel·li (vûr′mi sel′ē, -chel′ē), *n.* a kind of pasta in the form of long, slender, solid threads, resembling spaghetti but thinner. Cf. **macaroni** (def. 1). [< It, pl. of *vermicello* little worm, equiv. to *vermi-* VERMI- + *-cello* dim. suffix]

ver·mi·cide (vûr′mi sīd′), *n.* a substance or agent used to kill worms, esp. a drug used to kill parasitic intestinal worms. [VERMI- + -CIDE] —**ver′mi·cid′al,** *adj.*

ver·mic·u·lar (vər mik′yə lər), *adj.* **1.** of, pertaining to, or done by worms. **2.** consisting of or characterized by sinuous or wavy outlines or markings resembling the form or tracks of a worm. [< ML *vermiculār(is),* equiv. to L *vermicul(us)* VERMICULE + *-āris* -AR¹] —**ver·mic′u·lar·ly,** *adv.*

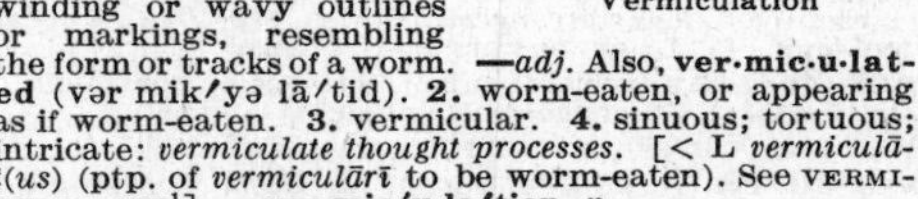

Vermiculation

ver·mic·u·late (*v.* vər mik′yə lāt′; *adj.* vər mik′yə lit, -lāt′), *v.,* **-lat·ed, -lat·ing,** *adj.* —*v.t.* **1.** to work or ornament with winding or wavy outlines or markings, resembling the form or tracks of a worm. —*adj.* Also, **ver·mic·u·lat·ed** (vər mik′yə lā′tid). **2.** worm-eaten, or appearing as if worm-eaten. **3.** vermicular. **4.** sinuous; tortuous; intricate: *vermiculate thought processes.* [< L *vermiculā-t(us)* (ptp. of *vermiculārī* to be worm-eaten). See VERMICULE, -ATE¹] —**ver·mic′u·la′tion,** *n.*

ver·mi·cule (vûr′mə kyo͞ol′), *n.* *Zool.* a small, motile, wormlike structure in the reproduction of certain sporozoans. [< L *vermiculus.* See VERMI-, -CULE]

ver·mic·u·lite (vər mik′yə līt′), *n.* any of a group of platy minerals, hydrous silicates of aluminum, magnesium, and iron, that expand markedly on being heated: used in the expanded state for heat insulation. [VERMICUL(AR) + -ITE¹]

ver·mi·form (vûr′mə fôrm′), *adj.* resembling a worm in shape; long and slender. [< ML *vermiform(is).* See VERMI-, -FORM]

ver′miform appen′dix, *Anat., Zool.* a narrow, blind tube protruding from the cecum, having no known useful function, in man being three to four inches long and situated in the lower right-hand part of the abdomen. See diag. under **intestine.**

ver′miform proc′ess, 1. See **vermiform appendix. 2.** the vermis.

ver·mi·fuge (vûr′mə fyo͞oj′), *adj.* **1.** serving to expel worms or other animal parasites from the intestines, as a medicine. —*n.* **2.** a vermifuge medicine or agent. [VERMI- + -FUGE]

ver·mil·ion (vər mil′yən), *n.* **1.** a brilliant scarlet red. **2.** a bright-red, water-insoluble pigment consisting of mercuric sulfide, once obtained from cinnabar, now usually produced by the reaction of mercury and sulfur. —*adj.* **3.** of the color vermilion. —*v.t.* **4.** to color with or as with vermilion. [ME *vermilioun, vermillon* < AF, MF *verm(e)illon,* equiv. to *vermeil* VERMEIL + *-on* aug. suffix]

Ver·mil·ion (vər mil′yən), *n.* a town in N Ohio. 4785 (1960).

vermil′ion rock′fish, a scarlet-red rockfish, *Sebastodes miniatus,* found along the Pacific coast of North America. Also called **rasher.**

Ver·mil·lion (vər mil′yən), *n.* a town in SE South Dakota. 6102 (1960).

ver·min (vûr′min), *n., pl.* **ver·min.** (*usually construed as pl.*) **1.** noxious, objectionable, or disgusting animals collectively, esp. those of small size which appear commonly and are difficult to control, as flies, lice, bedbugs, cockroaches, mice, rats, etc. **2.** an objectionable or obnoxious person, or a number of such persons. **3.** animals that prey upon game, as coyotes, weasels, etc. [ME *vermyne* < AF, MF *vermin(e)* < VL **verminum,* neut. of **verminus* wormy, equiv. to L *vermi(s)* worm + *-nus* adj. suffix]

ver·mi·na·tion (vûr′mə nā′shən), *n.* **1.** the condition of being infested with vermin, esp. parasitic vermin. **2.** the breeding of vermin. [< L *verminātiōn-* (s. of *verminātiō*), equiv. to *vermināt(us)* (ptp. of *vermināre* to have worms; see VERMIN, -ATE¹) + *-iōn-* -ION]

ver·min·ous (vûr′mə nəs), *adj.* **1.** of the nature of or resembling vermin. **2.** of, pertaining to, or caused by vermin: *verminous diseases.* **3.** infested with vermin, esp. parasitic vermin: *verminous slums.* [< L *verminōs(us).* See VERMIN, -OSE¹, -OUS] —**ver′min·ous·ly,** *adv.* —**ver′min·ous·ness,** *n.*

ver·mis (vûr′mis), *n., pl.* **-mes** (-mēz). *Anat.* the median lobe or division of the cerebellum. [< NL < L: worm]

Ver·mont (vər mont′), *n.* a State of the NE United States: a part of New England. 389,881 (1960); 9609 sq. mi. *Cap.:* Montpelier. *Abbr.:* Vt.

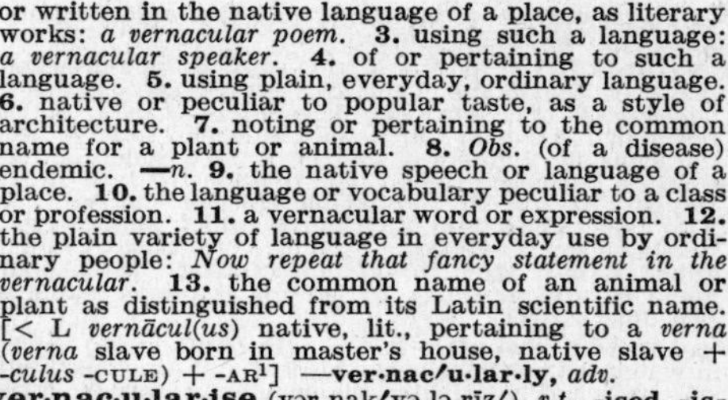

Ver·mont·er (vər mon′tər), *n.* a native or inhabitant of Vermont. [VERMONT + -ER¹]

ver·mouth (vər mo͞oth′; *Fr.* veʀ mo͞ot′), *n.* an aromatized white wine in which herbs, roots, barks, bitters, and other flavorings have been steeped. [< F (now *vermout*) < G *Wermuth* (now *Wermut*) absinthe, WORMWOOD]

vermouth′ cassis′, a mixed drink made with dry vermouth, crème de cassis, soda or mineral water, and cracked ice. [< F; see VERMOUTH, CRÈME DE CASSIS]

Vern (vûrn), *n.* a boy's given name, form of **Vernon.** Also, **Verne.**

Ver·na (vûr′nə), *n.* a girl's given name.

ver·nac·u·lar (vər nak′yə lər), *adj.* **1.** native or originating in the place of its occurrence or use (often considered nonstandard, as opposed to *literary* or *learned* language): *the vernacular language.* **2.** expressed or written in the native language of a place, as literary works: *a vernacular poem.* **3.** using such a language: *a vernacular speaker.* **4.** of or pertaining to such a language. **5.** using plain, everyday, ordinary language. **6.** native or peculiar to popular taste, as a style of architecture. **7.** noting or pertaining to the common name for a plant or animal. **8.** *Obs.* (of a disease) endemic. —*n.* **9.** the native speech or language of a place. **10.** the language or vocabulary peculiar to a class or profession. **11.** a vernacular word or expression. **12.** the plain variety of language in everyday use by ordinary people: *Now repeat that fancy statement in the vernacular.* **13.** the common name of an animal or plant as distinguished from its Latin scientific name. [< L *vernācul(us)* native, lit., pertaining to a *verna* (*verna* slave born in master's house, native slave + *-culus* -CULE) + -AR¹] —**ver·nac′u·lar·ly,** *adv.*

ver·nac·u·lar·ise (vər nak′yə lə rīz′), *v.t.,* **-ised, -is·ing.** *Chiefly Brit.* vernacularize. —**ver·nac′u·lar·i·sa′tion,** *n.*

ver·nac·u·lar·ism (vər nak′yə lə riz′əm), *n.* **1.** a vernacular word or expression. **2.** the use of the vernacular. [VERNACULAR + -ISM]

ver·nac·u·lar·ize (vər nak′yə lə rīz′), *v.t.,* **-ized, -iz·ing.** to translate into the natural pattern of speech peculiar to a people. Also, *esp. Brit.,* **vernacularise.** [VERNACULAR + -IZE] —**ver·nac′u·lar·i·za′tion,** *n.*

ver·nal (vûr′nəl), *adj.* **1.** of or pertaining to spring: *vernal sunshine.* **2.** appearing or occurring in spring: *vernal migratory movements.* **3.** appropriate to or suggesting spring; springlike: *vernal greenery.* **4.** belonging to or characteristic of youth: *vernal longings.* [< L *vernāl(is),* equiv. to *vern(us)* of spring (*vēr* spring, c. Icel *vār,* + *-nus* adj. suffix) + *-ālis* -AL¹] —**ver′nal·ly,** *adv.*

Ver·nal (vûr′nəl), *n.* a town in NE Utah. 3655 (1960).

ver′nal e′quinox, 1. See under **equinox** (def. 1). **2.** Also called **ver′nal point′.** the position of the sun at the time of the vernal equinox.

ver·nal·ise (vûr′nəlīz′), *v.t.,* **-ised, -is·ing.** *Chiefly Brit.* vernalize. —**ver′nal·i·sa′tion,** *n.*

ver·nal·ize (vûr′nəlīz′), *v.t.,* **-ized, -iz·ing.** to shorten the growth period before the blossoming and fruit or seed bearing of (a plant) by chilling its seed or bulb. [VERNAL + -IZE] —**ver′nal·i·za′tion,** *n.*

ver·na·tion (vər nā′shən), *n.* *Bot.* the arrangement of the foliage leaves within the bud. [< NL *vernātiōn-* (s. of *vernātiō*), equiv. to L *vernāt(us)* (ptp. of *vernāre* to be verdant; see VERNAL, -ATE¹) + *-iōn-* -ION]

Verne (vûrn; *Fr.* veʀn), *n.* **Jules** (jo͞olz; *Fr.* zhʏl), 1828–1905, French novelist.

Ver·nell (vər nel′, vûr′nəl), *n.* a girl's given name.

Ver·ner (veʀ′nəʀ; *Dan.* veʀ′nəʀ), *n.* **1. Karl A·dolph** (käʀl ä′dolf), 1846–96, Danish linguist. **2.** a boy's given name, form of **Warner.**

Ver′ner's law′, *Ling.* the statement by K. Verner of a regularity behind some apparent exceptions in the Germanic languages to Grimm's law, namely, that Proto-Germanic noninitial, voiceless fricatives became voiced when between voiced sounds if the immediately following vowel was accented in Proto-Indo-European.

Ver·net (veʀ ne′), *n.* **1. Claude Jo·seph** (klōd zhō zef′), 1714–89, French painter. **2.** his grandson **(É·mile Jean) Hor·ace** (ā mēl′ zhäɴ ô ʀas′), 1789–1863, French painter.

Ver·neuil′ proc′ess (vûr noi′; *Fr.* veʀ nœ′yə), a process for making synthetic rubies, sapphires, spinels, etc., by the fusion at high temperatures of powdered compounds. Also called **flame-fusion process.** [named after A.V.L. *Verneuil,* 19th-century French mineralogist]

ver·ni·cle (vûr′ni kəl), *n.* (*sometimes cap.*) veronica¹ (def. 2). [ME < AF < ML *veronica*]

ver·ni·er (vûr′nē ər), *n.* **1.** Also, **ver′nier scale′.** a small, movable, graduated scale running parallel to the fixed graduated scale of a sextant, theodolite, barometer, or other graduated instrument, and used for measuring a fractional part of one of the divisions of the fixed scale. **2.** *Mach.* an auxiliary device for giving a piece of apparatus a higher adjustment accuracy. —*adj.* **3.** equipped with a vernier: *a vernier barometer.* [named after Pierre VERNIER]

Ver·nier (vûr′nē ər; *Fr.* veʀ nyā′), *n.* **Pierre** (pyeʀ), 1580–1637, French mathematician and inventor.

ver′nier cal′iper, a caliper formed of two pieces sliding across one another, one having a graduated scale and the other a vernier, for measuring the outside dimensions of objects. Also called **ver′nier microm′eter.**

ver′nier com′pass, *Survey.* a compass on a transit **(ver′nier tran′sit)** having a vernier for adjusting magnetic bearings to read as true bearings.

ver′nier en′gine, *Rocketry.* a small, low-thrust rocket engine for correcting the heading and velocity of a long-range ballistic missile.

ver·nis mar·tin (ver nē′ mär tan′; *Fr.* ver nē maʀ taɴ′), a finish for furniture, invented in France in the 18th century in imitation of Chinese lacquer. Also, **vernis′ Martin′.** [< F: lit., Martin varnish, named after the brothers *Martin,* 18th-century French craftsmen]

ver·nix ca·se·o·sa (vûr′niks kas′ē ō′sə), *Med.* the fatty matter, consisting chiefly of dead epidermal cells and sebaceous secretions, covering the skin of a fetus. [< NL: cheeselike varnish]

Ver·no·le·ninsk (*Russ.* veʀ′no le nēnsk′), *n.* former name of **Nikolaev.**

Ver·non (vûr′nən), *n.* **1. Edward** ("*Old Grog*"), 1684–1757, British admiral. **2.** a boy's given name.

Ver′non Val′ley, a town on N Long Island, in SE New York. 5998 (1960).

Ve′ro Beach′ (vēr′ō), a town in central Florida. 8849 (1960).

Ve·ro·na (və rō′nə; *for 1 also It.* ve rô′nä), *n.* **1.** a city in N Italy, on the Adige River. 221,138 (1961). **2.** a town in SW Pennsylvania. 4032 (1960). **3.** a town in NE New Jersey. 13,782 (1960).

Ver·o·nal (ver′ə nəl), *n.* *Pharm., Trademark.* barbital.

Ver·o·nese (ver′ə nēz′, -nēs′), *adj., n., pl.* **-nese.** —*adj.* **1.** of or pertaining to the city or town of Verona. —*n.* **2.** a native or inhabitant of Verona. [VERON(A) + -ESE]

Ve·ro·ne·se (ve′rô ne′ze), *n.* **Paul** (*Paulo Cagliari*), 1528–88, Venetian painter.

ve·ron·i·ca[1] (və ron′ə kə), *n.* **1.** any scrophulariaceous plant of the genus *Veronica*, as the speedwell. **2.** (*sometimes cap.*) Also called **vernicle.** *Eccles.* **a.** the image of the face of Christ, said in legend to have been miraculously impressed on the handkerchief or veil that St. Veronica gave to Him to wipe His face on the way to Calvary. **b.** the handkerchief or veil itself. **c.** Also called **sudarium.** any handkerchief, veil, or cloth bearing a representation of the face of Christ. [< ML, appar. named after St. *Veronica* (but cf. MGk plant name *berenīkion*, equiv. to *Berenīk*(ē) proper name + -*ion* dim. suffix)]

ve·ron·i·ca[2] (və ron′ə kə), *n.* (in bullfighting) a pass in which the matador keeps his feet and legs absolutely still while slowly swinging the open cape away from the charging bull. [special use of VERONICA]

Ve·ron·i·ca (və ron′ə kə), *n.* a girl's given name. Also, **Ve·ron′i·ka.**

Ver·ra·za·no (ver′ə zä′nō; *It.* veʀ′rä tsä′nô), *n.* **Gio·van·ni da** (jô vän′nē dä), c1480–1527?, Italian navigator and explorer. Also, **Ver·raz·za·no** (veʀ′rät tsä′nô), **Ver·ra·za·ni** (veʀ′rä tsä′nē).

Ver′ra·za′no-Nar′rows Bridge′ (ver′ə zä′nō nar′ōz, -dzä′-), a suspension bridge connecting Brooklyn and Staten Island in New York City. 4260-ft. center span, the longest in the world.

ver·ri·ère (ver′ē âr′; *Fr.* ve ʀyeʀ′), *n., pl.* **ver·ri·ères** (ver′ē ârz′; *Fr.* ve ʀyeʀ′). a French bowl similar to a monteith in form and use. [< F: glass stand, frame]

Ver·roc·chio (və rō′kē ō′; *It.* ver rôk′kyô), *n.* **An·dre·a del** (än dre′ä del), 1435–88, Italian goldsmith, sculptor, and painter.

ver·ru·ca (və rōō′kə, ve-), *n., pl.* **-cae** (-sē). **1.** *Med.* a wart. **2.** *Zool.* a small, flattish, wartlike prominence. [< L]

ver·ru·cose (ver′ə kōs′), *adj.* studded with wartlike excrescences or elevations. [VERRUC(A) + -OSE[1]] —**ver·ru·cos·i·ty** (ver′ə kos′i tē), **ver′ru·cose′ness,** *n.*

ver·ru·cous (ver′ə kəs), *adj.* of, pertaining to, marked by, or like a wart or warts. [var. of VERRUCOSE; see -OUS]

vers., *Trig.* See **versed sine.** [by shortening]

Ver·sailles (vər sī′, sālz′; *for 1 also Fr.* ver-sä′yᵊ), *n.* **1.** a city in and the capital of Seine-et-Oise, in N France, about 12 mi. SW of Paris: palace of the French kings; peace treaty between the Allies and Germany 1919. 95,149 (1962). **2.** a town in central Kentucky. 4060 (1960).

ver·sant (vûr′sənt), *n.* **1.** a slope of a mountain or mountain chain. **2.** the general slope of a country or region. [< F, n. use of prp. of *verser* to turn < L *versāre.* See REVERSE, -ANT]

ver·sa·tile (vûr′sə til *or, esp. Brit.,* -tīl′), *adj.* **1.** capable of or adapted for turning easily from one to another of various tasks, fields of endeavor, etc.: *a versatile writer; a versatile musician.* **2.** having or capable of many uses: *a versatile tool; a versatile new plastic.* **3.** *Bot.* attached at or near the middle so as to swing freely, as an anther. **4.** *Zool.* turning either forward or backward: *a versatile toe.* **5.** variable or changeable, as in feeling, purpose, policy, etc.: *versatile moods; versatile enthusiasms.* [< L *versātile,* neut. of *versātilis* revolving, many-sided, equiv. to *versāt(us)* (ptp. of *versāre,* freq. of *vertere* to turn; see REVERSE, -ATE[1]) + -*ilis* -ILE] —**ver′sa·tile·ly,** *adv.* —**ver′sa·til′i·ty, ver′sa·tile·ness,** *n.* —**Syn. 1.** adaptable, all-round, handy.

Versatile (def. 3)
A, Versatile anthers

vers de so·cié·té (veʀ də sô syā tā′; *Eng.* ver′ di sō′sē i tā′), *French.* humorous light verse dealing with fashions and foibles of the time.

verse (vûrs), *n.* **1.** (not in technical use) a stanza. **2.** a succession of metrical feet written, printed, or orally composed as one line; one of the lines of a poem. **3.** a particular type of metrical line: *a hexameter verse.* **4.** a poem, or piece of poetry. **5.** metrical composition; poetry, esp. as involving metrical form. **6.** metrical writing distinguished from poetry because of its inferior quality: *He is a writer of verse, not poetry.* **7.** a particular type of metrical composition: *iambic verse; elegiac verse.* **8.** the collective poetry of an author, period, nation, etc.: *Miltonian verse; Elizabethan verse; American verse.* **9.** a short division of a chapter in the Bible, usually consisting of one sentence or part of a long sentence. **10.** *Music.* **a.** that part of a song following the introduction and preceding the chorus. **b.** a part of a song designed to be sung by a solo voice. **11.** *Rare.* a line of prose, esp. a sentence, or part of a sentence, written as one line; stich. **12.** *Rare.* a subdivision in any literary work. —*adj.* **13.** of, pertaining to, or written in verse: *a verse play; several verse forms.* [ME, OE *vers* < L *versus* a row, line (of poetry), lit., a turning, equiv. to *vers-* (ptp. s. of *vertere* to turn) + -*us* n. suffix (4th decl.)]
—**Syn. 1.** VERSE, STANZA, STROPHE, STAVE are terms for a metrical grouping in poetic composition. VERSE is often mistakenly used for STANZA, but is properly only a single metrical line. A STANZA is a succession of lines (verses) commonly bound together by a rhyme scheme, and usually forming one of a series of similar groups which constitute a poem: *The four-line stanza is the one most frequently used in English.* STROPHE (originally the section of a Greek choral ode sung while the chorus was moving from right to left) is in English poetry practically equivalent to "section"; a STROPHE may be unrhymed or without strict form, but may be a stanza: *Strophes are divisions of odes.* STAVE is a word (now seldom used) which meant a stanza set to music or intended to be sung: *a stave of a hymn; a stave of a drinking song.* **5.** meter, numbers.

versed (vûrst), *adj.* experienced; practiced; skilled; learned (usually fol. by *in*): *He was well versed in Greek and Latin.* [< L *versāt(us)* busied, engaged (see VERSATILE) with -ED[2] for L -*ātus*]

versed′ co′sine. See **coversed sine.**

versed′ sine′, *Trig.* one minus the cosine of a given angle or arc. *Abbr.:* vers. Also called **versine, versin.**

vers·et (vûr′sit), *n.* **1.** *Pros.* a brief verse, esp. from scriptures. **2.** *Music.* a brief piece for pipe organ, formerly used as part of the music for the Catholic Mass. **3.** *Archaic.* versicle. [ME < OF. See VERSE, -ET]

ver·si·cle (vûr′si kəl), *n.* **1.** a little verse. **2.** *Eccles.* one of a series of short sentences, or parts of sentences, usually from the Psalms, said or sung by the officiant, as distinguished from the response of the choir or congregation. Cf. **response** (def. 3a). [late ME < L *versicul(us).* See VERSE, -I-, -CLE]

ver·si·col·or (vûr′si kul′ər), *adj.* **1.** changeable in color: *versicolor skies.* **2.** of various colors; parti-colored: *a versicolor flower arrangement.* Also, *esp. Brit.,* **ver′si·col′our.** [< L; see REVERSE, -I-, COLOR]

ver·sic·u·lar (vər sik′yə lər), *adj.* of or consisting of verses. [< L *versicul(us)* VERSICLE + -AR[1]]

Ver·sie (vûr′sē), *n.* a girl's given name.

ver·sie·ra (vers yâr′ə, vûrs-), *n. Geom.* See **witch of Agnesi.** [< It: witch]

ver·si·fi·ca·tion (vûr′sə fə kā′shən), *n.* **1.** the act of versifying. **2.** verse form; metrical structure. **3.** a metrical version of something. **4.** the art or practice of composing verses. [< L *versificātiōn-* (s. of *versificātiō*), equiv. to *versificāt(us)* (ptp. of *versificāre* to VERSIFY; see -ATE[1]) + -*iōn-* -ION]

ver·si·fy (vûr′sə fī′), *v.,* **-fied, -fy·ing.** —*v.t.* **1.** to relate, describe, or treat (something) in verse. **2.** to convert (prose or other writing) into metrical form. —*v.i.* **3.** to compose verses. [late ME *versifie(n)* < OF *versifier* < L *versificāre.* See VERSE, -IFY] —**ver′si·fi′er,** *n.*

ver·sine (vûr′sīn), *n. Trig.* See **versed sine.** Also, **ver′sin.**

ver·sion (vûr′zhən, -shən), *n.* **1.** a translation. **2.** (*often cap.*) a translation of the Bible or a part of it. **3.** a particular account of some matter, as from one person or source, contrasted with some other account or accounts: *two very different versions of the accident.* **4.** a particular form or variant of something: *a modern version of an antique lamp.* **5.** *Med.* the act of turning a child in the uterus so as to bring it into a more favorable position for delivery. **6.** *Pathol.* an abnormal direction of the axis of the uterus or other organ. [< L *versiōn-* (s. of *versiō* a turning), equiv. to *vers(us)* (ptp. of *vertere* to turn) + -*iōn-* -ION] —**ver′sion·al,** *adj.*
—**Syn. 1.** See **translation. 3.** story, impression.

vers li·bre (veʀ lē′bʀᵊ), *French.* See **free verse.**

vers-li·brist (vâr lē′brist), *n.* a person who writes free verse. [alter. of VERS-LIBRISTE]

vers-li·briste (vâr′lē brēst′; *Fr.* veʀ lē bʀēst′), *n., pl.* **-li·bristes** (-lē brēsts′; *Fr.* -lē bʀēst′). vers-librist. [< F; see VERS LIBRE, -IST]

ver·so (vûr′sō), *n., pl.* **-sos.** *Print.* a left-hand page of a book or manuscript (opposed to *recto*). [short for L *versō foliō* on the turned leaf]

verst (vûrst, verst), *n.* a Russian measure of distance equivalent to 3500 feet or 0.6629 miles or 1.067 kilometers. Also, **verste, werste.** [< Russ *versta* (in part through F *verste* and G *Werst*) line, linear measure; akin to VERSE etc.]

ver·sus (vûr′səs), *prep.* **1.** against (used esp. to indicate an action brought by one party against another in a court of law, or to denote competing teams or players in a sports contest): *Smith versus Jones; Army versus Navy.* **2.** as compared to or as one of two choices; in contrast with: *traveling by plane versus traveling by train.* *Abbr.:* v., vs. [< L: towards, i.e., turned so as to face (something), opposite, over against; see VERSE]

vert (vûrt), *n.* **1.** *Eng. Forest Law.* **a.** vegetation bearing green leaves in a forest and capable of serving as a cover for deer. **b.** the right to cut such trees or shrubs. **2.** *Heraldry.* the tincture, or color, green. —*adj.* **3.** *Heraldry.* of the tincture, or color, green: *a lion vert.* [ME *verte* < AF, MF *vert, verd* < L *viridis* green, equiv. to *vir-* (root of *virēre* to be green) + -*idis* adj. suffix]

vert., vertical.

vertebr-, a combining form of **vertebra:** *vertebral.*

ver·te·bra (vûr′tə brə), *n., pl.* **-brae** (-brē′), **-bras.** *Anat., Zool.* any of the bones or segments composing the spinal column, in man and higher animals consisting typically of a cylindrical body and an arch with various processes, forming a foramen through which the spinal cord passes. [< L: (spinal) joint, equiv. to *verte(re)* (to) turn + -*bra* n. suffix]

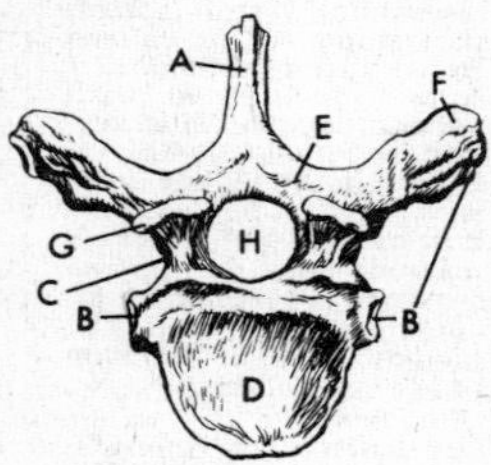

Vertebra
A, Spine; B, Facet of rib; C, Pedicel; D, Body; E, Lamina; F, Transverse process; G, Articular process; H, Spinal canal

ver·te·bral (vûr′tə brəl), *adj.* **1.** of or pertaining to a vertebra or the vertebrae; spinal. **2.** resembling a vertebra. **3.** composed of or having vertebrae. [VERTEBR(A) + -AL[1]] —**ver′te·bral·ly,** *adv.*

ver′tebral col′umn. See **spinal column.**

Ver·te·bra·ta (vûr′tə brā′tə, -brä′-), *n.* the subphylum comprising the vertebrate animals. [< NL, neut. pl. of *vertebrāt(us)* VERTEBRATE]

ver·te·brate (vûr′tə brāt′, -brit), *adj.* **1.** having vertebrae; having a backbone or spinal column. **2.** belonging or pertaining to the *Vertebrata* (or *Craniata*), a subphylum of chordate animals, comprising those having a brain enclosed in a skull or cranium and a segmented spinal column, including mammals, birds, reptiles, amphibians, and fishes. —*n.* **3.** a vertebrate animal. [< L *vertebrāt(us)* jointed. See VERTEBRA, -ATE[1]]

ver·te·brat·ed (vûr′tə brā′tid), *adj.* **1.** having vertebrae; vertebral; vertebrate. **2.** composed of or having segments resembling vertebrae. [VERTEBRATE + -ED[2]]

ver·te·bra·tion (vûr′tə brā′shən), *n.* vertebrate formation. [VERTEBRATE + -ION]

ver·te·bra·tus (vûr′tə brā′təs), *adj. Meteorol.* (of a cloud) having elements arranged in a riblike pattern. [< NL; see VERTEBRATE]

ver·tex (vûr′teks), *n., pl.* **-tex·es, -ti·ces** (-ti sēz′). **1.** the highest point of something; apex; summit; top: *the vertex of a mountain.* **2.** *Anat., Zool.* the crown or top of the head. **3.** *Craniom.* the highest point on the midsagittal plane of the skull or head viewed from the left side when the skull or head is in the Frankfurt Horizontal. **4.** *Astron.* a point in the celestial sphere toward which or from which the common motion of a group of stars is directed. **5.** *Math.* **a.** the point farthest from the base. **b.** a point in a geometrical solid common to three or more sides. **c.** the intersection of two sides of a plane figure. [< L: a whirl; top (of the head), equiv. to *vert(ere)* (to) turn + -*ex,* var. of -*ecs,* equiv. to -*ic* suffix + -*s* ending]

ver·ti·cal (vûr′ti kəl), *adj.* **1.** being in a position or direction perpendicular to the plane of the horizon; upright; plumb. **2.** of, pertaining to, or situated at the vertex. **3.** of or pertaining to the cranial vertex. **4.** *Bot.* **a.** (of a leaf) having the blade in a perpendicular plane, so that neither of the surfaces can be called upper or lower. **b.** being in the same direction as the axis; lengthwise. **4.** of or pertaining to the consolidation of businesses or industries that are closely related in the manufacture or sale of a certain commodity. Cf. **vertical combination. 5.** of, pertaining to, or noting a stratified society, nation, etc. —*n.* **6.** something vertical, as a line, plane, or the like. **7.** a vertical or upright position. **8.** a vertical structural member in a truss. [< L *verticāl(is),* equiv. to *vertic-* (s. of *vertex*) VERTEX + -*ālis* -AL[1]] —**ver′ti·cal′i·ty, ver′ti·cal·ness, ver′ti·cal·ism,** *n.* —**ver′ti·cal·ly,** *adv.*
—**Syn. 1.** See **upright.** —**Ant. 1.** horizontal.

ver′tical an′gle, *Geom.* one of two opposite and equal angles formed by the intersection of two lines.

vertical arc of the 22° parhelion. See **arc of Lowitz.**

ver′tical cir′cle, *Astron.* a great circle on the celestial sphere passing through the zenith.

ver′tical combina′tion, the coordination under one management of individual businesses working separately in related phases of production and sale of a product. Also called **ver′tical integra′tion.**

ver′tical envel′opment, *Mil.* envelopment of an enemy accomplished by parachuting and landing airborne troops at the rear of the enemy's position.

ver′tical mobil′ity, *Sociol.* **1.** movement from one social level to another, as in changing jobs or social status. **2.** cultural diffusion from one social level to another, as the adoption by one economic class of the fashions current or formerly current in another class. Cf. **horizontal mobility.**

ver′tical sta′bilizer, *Aeron.* the fixed vertical surface of an aircraft empennage, to which the rudder is hinged. Also called **ver′tical fin′.**

ver′tical un′ion. See **industrial union.**

ver·ti·ces (vûr′ti sēz′), *n.* a pl. of **vertex.**

ver·ti·cil (vûr′ti sil), *n. Bot., Zool.* a whorl or circle, as of leaves, hairs, etc., arranged round a point on an axis. [< L *verticill(us),* equiv. to *vertic-* (s. of *vertex*) VERTEX + -*illus* dim. suffix]

Verticils

ver·ti·cil·las·ter (vûr′ti si las′tər), *n. Bot.* an inflorescence in which the flowers are arranged in a seeming whorl, consisting in fact of a pair of opposite axillary, usually sessile, cymes, as in many mints. [< L *verticill(us)* VERTICIL + -ASTER[1]] —**ver·ti·cil·las·trate** (vûr′ti si las′trāt, -trit), *adj.*

ver·tic·il·late (vər tis′ə lit, -lāt′, vûr′ti sil′āt), *adj.* *Bot., Zool.* **1.** disposed in or forming verticils or whorls, as flowers, hairs, etc. **2.** having flowers, hairs, etc., so arranged or disposed. Also, **ver·tic′il·lat′ed.** [< L *verticill(us)* VERTICIL + -ATE[1]] —**ver·tic′il·la′tion,** *n.*

ver·tic·i·ty (vər tis′i tē), *n. Physics Rare.* the tendency of a magnetic object to align itself with an external magnetic field. [< NL *verticitās,* equiv. to *vertic-* (s. of *vertex*) VERTEX + -*itās* -ITY]

ver·tig·i·nous (vər tij′ə nəs), *adj.* **1.** whirling; spinning; rotary: *the vertiginous action of a top; vertiginous currents of air.* **2.** affected with vertigo; dizzy. **3.** liable or threatening to cause vertigo: *a vertiginous staircase.* **4.** apt to change quickly; unstable: *a vertiginous economy.* [< L *vertīginōs(us)* dizzy, equiv. to *vertīgin-* (s. of *vertigo*) VERTIGO + -*ōsus* -OUS] —**ver·tig′i·nous·ly,** *adv.* —**ver·tig′i·nous·ness,** *n.*

ver·ti·go (vûr′tə gō′), *n., pl.* **ver·ti·goes, ver·tig·i·nes** (vər tij′ə nēz′). *Pathol.* a disordered condition in which a person or his surroundings seem to be whirling about. [< L: a turning or whirling round, equiv. to *vert(ere)* (to) turn + -*īgo* (gen. -*īginis*) n. suffix]

ver·tu (vər tōō′, vûr′tōō), *n.* virtu.

Ver·tum·nus (vər tum′nəs), *n.* the ancient Roman god of gardens, orchards, and the changing seasons. Also, **Vortumnus.** [< L, equiv. to *vert(ere)* (to) turn, change + -*umnus* n. suffix (< Etruscan)]

Ver·u·la·mi·an (ver′yŏŏ lā′mē ən), *adj.* of or pertaining to Francis Bacon, Baron Verulam. [VERULAM(IUM) + -AN]

Ver·u·la·mi·um (ver′yŏŏ lā′mē əm), *n.* ancient name of **St. Albans.**

ve·rus (vēr′əs), *adj.* (in prescriptions) true; genuine. [< L]

ver·vain (vûr′vān), *n.* any plant of the genus *Verbena,* having elongated or flattened spikes of sessile flowers. [late ME *vervaine* < AF, MF *verveine* < L *verbēna* holy bough carried by priests]

ver′vain mal′low, a perennial herb, *Malva alcea,* of Europe, having pink or white flowers. Also called **European mallow.**

verve (vûrv), *n.* **1.** enthusiasm or vigor, as in literary or artistic work; spirit: *Her latest novel lacks verve.* **2.** vivaciousness; liveliness; animation: *I like a girl with* *plenty of verve.* 3. *Archaic.* talent. [< F: enthusiasm, fancy < L *verba* mere words, talk, pl. of *verbum* word; see VERB]

ver·velle (vûr vel′), *n. Armor.* any of a number of staples riveted along the base of a basinet to hold an aventail. [< Obs. F, MF, OF; *vervelle,* ring on a hawk's leash, perh. alter. of *vertevelle* < LL *vertibul(um)* joint, deriv. of L *vertebra* VERTEBRA]

ver·vet (vûr′vit), *n.* an African monkey, *Cercopithecus aethiops pygerythrus,* allied to the green monkey and the grivet, but distinguished by a rusty patch at the root of the tail. [< F, equiv. to *ver(t)* green (see VERT) + *(gri)vet* GRIVET]

Ver·wand·lung, Die (dē fər vänt′lo͝ong). See **Metamorphosis, The.**

Ver·woerd (fər vo͞ort′), *n.* **Hen·drik Frensch** (hen′drik frens), 1901–66, South African political leader, born in the Netherlands: prime minister 1958–1966.

ver·y (ver′ē), *adv., adj.,* **ver·i·er, ver·i·est.** —*adv.* **1.** in a high degree; extremely; exceedingly: *It is very gracious of you to do this.* **2.** (used as an intensive emphasizing superlatives or stressing identity or oppositeness): *the very best thing to be done; in the very same place as before.* —*adj.* **3.** precise; particular: *That is the very item we have been looking for.* **4.** mere: *The very thought of it is distressing.* **5.** sheer; utter: *She wept from the very joy of knowing he was safe.* **6.** actual: *He was caught in the very act of stealing.* **7.** being such in the true or fullest sense of the term; extreme: *the very heart of the matter.* **8.** true; genuine; worthy of being called such: *the very God; a very fool.* **9.** *Obs.* rightful or legitimate. [ME < AF, OF *verai* (F *vrai*) < VL **vērācus,* alter. of L *vērax* truthful, equiv. to *vēr(us)* true (c. OE *wǣr,* G *wahr* true, correct) + *-āc-, -ax* adj. suffix]

ver′y high′ fre′quency, designed for the production or reproduction of frequencies ranging from 30 to 300 megacycles. *Abbr.:* VHF —**ver′y-high′-fre′quen·cy,** *adj.*

Ver′y lights′ (ver′ē), a variety of colored signal flares, fired from a special pistol (**Very pistol**). [named after E. W. *Very* (1847–1907), American inventor]

ver′y low′ fre′quency, *Radio.* any frequency between 10 and 30 kilocycles per second. *Abbr.:* VLF

Ver′y pis′tol. See under **Very lights.**

Ve·sa·li·us (vi sā′lē əs), *n.* **An·dre·as** (än drā′äs), 1514–64, Flemish anatomist.

ve·si·ca (və sī′kə), *n., pl.* **-cae** (-sē). **1.** *Anat.* a bladder. **2.** See **vesica piscis.** [< L: bladder, blister]

ves·i·cal (ves′i kəl), *adj.* **1.** of or pertaining to a vesica or bladder, esp. the urinary bladder. **2.** resembling a bladder, as in shape or form; elliptical. [< ML *vēsīcāl(is),* equiv. to L *vēsīc(a)* bladder + *-ālis* -AL[1]]

ves·i·cant (ves′ə kənt), *adj.* **1.** producing a blister or blisters, as a medicinal substance; vesicating. —*n.* **2.** a vesicant agent or substance. **3.** *Chemical Warfare.* a chemical agent that causes burns and destruction of tissue both internally and externally. [< NL *vēsīcant-* (s. of *vēsīcāns,* prp. of *vēsīcāre* to VESICATE); see -ANT]

Vesica piscis

ve·si·ca pis·cis (və sī′kə pis′is, pī′sis; və sē′kə pis′kis, pē′sis, ves′i kə), *Fine Arts.* an elliptical figure in pointed form, usually one made by the intersection of two arcs and used, esp. in Early Christian art, as an emblem of Christ; mandorla. [< NL: lit., bladder of a fish]

ves·i·cate (ves′ə kāt′), *v.t.,* **-cat·ed, -cat·ing.** to raise vesicles or blisters on; blister. [< NL *vēsīcāt(us)* (ptp. of *vēsīcāre* to blister), equiv. to *vēsīc-* (see VESICA) + *-ātus* -ATE[1]] —**ves′i·ca′tion,** *n.*

ves·i·ca·to·ry (ves′ə kə tôr′ē, -tōr′ē, və sik′ə-), *adj., n., pl.* **-ries.** vesicant. [< NL *vēsīcātōri(us).* See VESICATE, -ORY[1]]

ves·i·cle (ves′i kəl), *n.* **1.** a small sac or cyst. **2.** *Anat., Zool.* a small bladderlike cavity, esp. one filled with fluid. **3.** *Pathol.* a circumscribed elevation of the epidermis containing serous fluid; blister. **4.** *Bot.* a small bladder, or bladderlike air cavity. **5.** *Geol.* a small, usually spherical cavity in a rock or mineral, due to gas or vapor. [< L *vēsīcula* little bladder. See VESICA, -ULE]

vesico-, a combining form of **vesica:** *vesicotomy.*

ves·i·cot·o·my (ves′ə kot′ə mē), *n. Surg.* incision of the urinary bladder; cystotomy. [VESICO- + -TOMY]

ve·sic·u·lar (və sik′yə lər), *adj.* **1.** of or pertaining to a vesicle or vesicles. **2.** having the form of a vesicle. **3.** characterized by or consisting of vesicles. [< NL *vēsīculār(is),* equiv. to L *vēsīcul(a)* VESICLE + *-āris* -AR[1]] —**ve·sic′u·lar·ly,** *adv.*

vesic′ular exanthe′ma, *Vet. Pathol.* an infectious viral disease of swine, closely resembling foot-and-mouth disease.

vesic′ular stomati′tis, *Vet. Pathol.* a disease of horses, swine, and cattle, communicable to man, caused by a filterable virus. Similar in its symptoms to foot-and-mouth disease, it is characterized by blisters on the lips, snout, and esp. on the tongue and mucous membranes of the mouth.

ve·sic·u·late (*adj.* və sik′yə lit, -lāt′; *v.* və sik′yə lāt′), *adj., v.,* **-lat·ed, -lat·ing.** —*adj.* **1.** characterized by or covered with vesicles. **2.** of the nature of a vesicle. —*v.t., v.i.* **3.** to make or become vesicular. [< NL *vēsīculāt(us),* equiv. to L *vēsīcul(a)* VESICLE + *-ātus* -ATE[1]] —**ve·sic′u·la′tion,** *n.*

vesp., (in prescriptions) evening. [< L *vesper*]

Ves·pa·si·an (ve spā′zhē ən, -zhən), *n.* (*Titus Flavius Sabinus Vespasianus*) A.D. 9–79, Roman emperor 70–79.

ves·per (ves′pər), *n.* **1.** (*cap.*) the evening star, esp. Venus; Hesper. **2.** a bell rung at evening; vesper bell. **3. vespers,** (*sometimes cap.*) *Eccles.* **a.** a religious service in the late afternoon or the evening. **b.** the sixth of the seven canonical hours, or the service for it, occurring in the late afternoon or the evening. **c.** *Rom. Cath. Ch.* a part of the office to be said in the evening by those in major orders, frequently made a public ceremony in the afternoons or evenings of Sundays and holy days. **d.** evensong. **4.** *Archaic.* evening. —*adj.* **5.** of, pertaining to, appearing in, or proper to the evening. **6.** of or pertaining to vespers. [late ME < L: evening (star); c. Gk *hésperos;* akin to WEST]

ves·per·al (ves′pər əl), *n. Eccles.* **1.** the part of an antiphonary containing the chants for vespers. **2.** a cloth used between offices to cover the altar cloth. [< LL *vesperāl(is).* See VESPER, -AL[1]]

ves′per mouse′. See **white-footed mouse.**

ves′per spar′row, a common finch, *Pooecetes gramineus,* of fields and pastures in North America.

ves·per·tide (ves′pər tīd′), *n.* the period of vespers; evening. [VESPER + TIDE[1]]

ves·per·til·i·o·nine (ves′pər til′ē ə nīn′, -nin), *adj.* of or pertaining to the bats of the subfamily *Vespertilioninae,* common in temperate regions and including many well-known species. [< L *vespertiliōn-* (s. of *vespertīliō*) bat, equiv. to **vespertīl(is)* of the evening (see VESPERTINE, -ILE) + *-iōn-* -ION + -INE[1]] —**ves·per·til·i·o·nid** (ves′pər til′ē ə nid), *n., adj.*

ves·per·tine (ves′pər tin, -tīn′), *adj.* **1.** of, pertaining to, or occurring in the evening: *vespertine stillness.* **2.** *Bot.* opening or expanding in the evening, as certain flowers. **3.** *Zool.* appearing or flying in the early evening; crepuscular. Also, **ves·per·ti·nal** (ves′pər tīn′əl). [< L *vespertīn(us),* equiv. to *vesper* VESPER + formative *-t-* + *-īnus* -INE[1]]

ves·pi·ar·y (ves′pē er′ē), *n., pl.* **-ar·ies.** a nest of social wasps. [< L *vesp(a)* WASP + (AP)IARY]

ves·pid (ves′pid), *n.* **1.** any of numerous hymenopterous insects of the family *Vespidae,* comprising social and solitary wasps, as the yellowjackets, hornets, and mason wasps. —*adj.* **2.** belonging or pertaining to the family *Vespidae.* [< NL *Vespid(ae),* equiv. to L *vesp(a)* WASP + *-idae* -ID[2]]

ves·pine (ves′pīn, -pin), *adj.* **1.** of or pertaining to a wasp or wasps. **2.** resembling a wasp. [< L *vesp(a)* WASP + -INE[1]]

Ves·puc·ci (ve spo͞o′chē, -spyo͞o′-; *It.* ves po͞ot′chē), *n.* **A·me·ri·go** (ə mer′ə gō′; *It.* ä′me rē′gō), (*Americus Vespucius*), 1451–1512, Italian merchant, adventurer, and explorer after whom America was named.

ves·sel (ves′əl), *n.* **1.** a craft for traveling on water, now usually one larger than an ordinary rowboat; a ship or boat. **2.** an airship. **3.** a hollow or concave utensil, as a cup, bowl, pitcher, vase, or the like, used for holding liquids or other contents. **4.** *Anat., Zool.* a tube or duct, as an artery, vein, or the like, containing or conveying blood or some other body fluid. **5.** *Bot.* a duct formed in the xylem, composed of connected cells that have lost their intervening partitions, that conducts water and mineral nutrients. Cf. **tracheid.** **6.** a person regarded as a holder or receiver of something, esp. something nonmaterial: *a vessel of grace; a vessel of wrath.* [ME < AF, OF *vessel, va(i)ssel* < L *vascell(um),* equiv. to *vās* (see VASE) + *-cellum* dim. suffix] —**ves′seled;** *esp. Brit.,* **ves′selled,** *adj.*

vest (vest), *n.* **1.** a close-fitting, waist-length, sleeveless garment for men that buttons down the front, designed to be worn under a jacket. **2.** a similar garment, or a part or trimming simulating the front of such a garment, worn by women. Cf. **dickey** (def. 2), **vestee.** **3.** *Brit.* an undervest or undershirt. **4.** a long garment resembling a cassock, worn by men in the time of Charles II. **5.** *Archaic.* **a.** dress; apparel. **b.** an outer garment, robe, or gown. **c.** an ecclesiastical vestment. **6. to play it close to the vest,** *Informal.* to avoid taking unnecessary risks. [< It *veste* robe, dress < L *vestis* garment] —*v.t.* **7.** to clothe; dress; robe. **8.** to dress in ecclesiastical vestments: *to vest a bishop.* **9.** to cover or drape (an altar). **10.** to place or settle (something, esp. property, rights, powers, etc.) in the possession or control of a person or persons (usually fol. by *in*): *to vest authority in a new official.* **11.** to invest or endow (a person, group, committee, etc.) with something, esp. with powers or functions: *to vest the board with power to increase production.* —*v.i.* **12.** to put on vestments. **13.** to become vested in a person or persons, as a right. **14.** to devolve upon a person as possessor; pass into possession or ownership. [late ME < MF *vest(ir)* < L *vestīre* to clothe, equiv. to *vest(is)* garment + *-īre* inf. suffix] —**vest′less,** *adj.* —**vest′-like′,** *adj.*

Ves·ta (ves′tə), *n.* **1.** the ancient Roman goddess of the hearth, worshiped in a temple containing an altar on which a sacred fire was kept burning under the care of vestal virgins: identified with the Greek Hestia. **2.** *Astron.* the third largest and one of the four brightest asteroids. **3.** (*l.c.*) *Brit.* a short friction match with a wood or wax shank. **4.** a girl's given name. [akin to Gk *hestía* hearth, household]

ves·tal (ves′təl), *adj.* **1.** of or pertaining to the goddess Vesta. **2.** of, pertaining to, or characteristic of a vestal virgin; chaste; pure. —*n.* **3.** See **vestal virgin.** **4.** a chaste unmarried woman; virgin. **5.** a nun. [< L *vestāl(is).* See VESTA, -AL[1]]

Ves·ta·li·a (ve stā′lē ə, -stāl′yə), *n.* (*sometimes construed as pl.*) the annual ancient Roman festival of Vesta. [< L; see VESTAL, -IA]

ves′tal vir′gin, (in ancient Rome) one of four, later six, virgins consecrated to Vesta and to the service of tending the sacred fire kept burning perpetually on her altar.

vest·ed (ves′tid), *adj.* **1.** held completely, permanently, and inalienably: *the vested rights of all citizens.* **2.** protected or established by law, commitment, tradition, ownership, etc.: *a vested interest in a company.* **3.** clothed or robed, esp. in ecclesiastical vestments: *a vested priest.* [VEST + -ED[2]]

vest′ed in′terest, **1.** a special interest in an existing system, arrangement, or institution for particular personal reasons. **2.** a permanent right given to an employee under a pension plan. **3. vested interests,** the persons, groups, etc., who dominate the business or financial activities of a nation.

vest·ee (ves tē′), *n.* a decorative front piece worn under a woman's jacket or blouse and visible between its open edges. Cf. **dickey** (def. 2), **vest** (def. 2). [VEST (n.) + *-ee* dim. suffix]

ves·ti·ar·y (ves′tē er′ē), *adj.* of or pertaining to garments or vestments. [ME *vestiarie* < ML *vestiāri-(us).* See VEST (n.), -ARY]

ves·tib·u·lar (ve stib′yə lər), *adj.* of, pertaining to, or resembling a vestibule. [VESTIBULE + -AR[1]]

ves·ti·bule (ves′tə byo͞ol′), *n., v.,* **-buled, -bul·ing.** —*n.* **1.** a passage, hall, or antechamber between the outer door and the interior parts of a house or building. **2.** *Railroads.* an enclosed space at the end of a passenger car, serving as a sheltered entrance to the car from another car or from outside the train. **3.** *Anat., Zool.* any of various cavities or hollows regarded as forming an approach or entrance to another cavity or space, as that of the internal ear. —*v.t.* **4.** to provide with a vestibule or vestibules. [< L *vestibul(um)* forecourt, entrance]

ves′tibule car′, a railroad car having vestibules.

ves′tibule school′, a school in an industrial establishment where new employees are given specific training in the jobs they are to perform.

ves′tibule train′, a railroad train composed of vestibule cars.

Ves·tie (ves′tē), *n.* a girl's given name, form of **Vesta.** Also, **Vesty.**

ves·tige (ves′tij), *n.* **1.** a mark, trace, or visible evidence of something that is no longer present or in existence: *A few columns were the last vestiges of a Greek temple.* **2.** a surviving evidence or remainder of some condition, practice, etc.: *These superstitions are vestiges of an ancient religion.* **3.** a very slight trace or amount of something: *There was not a vestige left of her former beauty.* **4.** *Biol.* a degenerate or imperfectly developed organ or structure having little or no utility, but which in an earlier stage of the individual or in preceding organisms performed a useful function. **5.** *Archaic.* a footprint; track. [< F *vestige* < L *vestigium* footprint]
—**Syn. 1.** token. See **trace. 3.** hint, suggestion.

ves·tig·i·al (ve stij′ē əl), *adj.* of, pertaining to, or of the nature of a vestige: *a vestigial tail.* [VESTIGI(UM) + -AL[1]] —**ves·tig′i·al·ly,** *adv.*

ves·tig·i·um (ve stij′ē əm), *n., pl.* **ves·tig·i·a** (ve-stij′ē ə). *Anat.* a vestigial structure of any kind; vestige. [< L: footprint, trace]

vest·ing (ves′ting), *n.* cloth that is usually of medium or heavy weight and has figures or ridges, as piqué or Bedford cord: used originally for decorative vests and now also for a variety of other garments. [VEST (n.) + -ING[1]]

vest·ment (vest′mənt), *n.* **1.** a garment, esp. an outer garment. **2. vestments,** *Chiefly Literary.* attire; clothing. **3.** an official or ceremonial robe. **4.** *Eccles.* **a.** one of the garments worn by the clergy and their assistants, choristers, etc., during divine service and on other occasions. **b.** one of the garments worn by the celebrant, deacon, and subdeacon during the celebration of the Eucharist. **5.** something that clothes or covers like a garment: *a mountaintop with a vestment of clouds.* [syncopated var. of ME *vestiment* < ML *vestīment(um)* priestly robe, L: garment. See VEST (n.), -MENT] —**vest′ment·al,** *adj.* —**vest′-ment·ed,** *adj.*

vest-pock·et (vest′pok′it), *adj.* **1.** designed to be carried in the pocket of the vest, in a purse, or in a similarly small space; miniature: *a vest-pocket dictionary.* **2.** very small: *a vest-pocket version of the palace at Versailles.*

ves·try (ves′trē), *n., pl.* **-tries.** **1.** a room in or a building attached to a church, in which the vestments, and sometimes liturgical objects, are kept; sacristy. **2.** (in some churches) a room in or a building attached to a church, used as a chapel, for prayer meetings, for the Sunday school, etc. **3.** *Prot. Episc. Ch.* a committee elected by members of a congregation to serve with the churchwardens in managing the temporal affairs of the church. **4.** *Ch. of Eng.* a meeting attended by all the parishioners or by a committee of parishioners during which the official business of the church is discussed. [late ME *vestrie, vestrye.* See VEST (v.), -ERY] —**ves′tral,** *adj.*

ves·try·man (ves′trē mən), *n., pl.* **-men.** a member of a church vestry. [VESTRY + MAN[1]]

ves·ture (ves′chər), *n., v.,* **-tured, -tur·ing.** —*n.* **1.** *Law.* **a.** everything growing on and covering the land, with the exception of trees. **b.** any such product, as grass or wheat. **2.** *Archaic.* **a.** clothing; garments. **b.** something that covers like a garment; covering. —*v.t.* **3.** *Archaic.* to clothe or cover. [late ME < AF; OF *vest(e)ure* < VL **vestītūra,* equiv. to L *vestīt(us),* ptp. of *vestīre* (see VEST, V.) + *-ūra* -URE] —**ves′tur·al,** *adj.*

Ve·su·vi·an (və so͞o′vē ən), *adj.* **1.** of, pertaining to, or resembling Mount Vesuvius; volcanic. —*n.* **2.** (*l.c.*) a type of match formerly used for lighting cigars; fusee. **3.** (*l.c.*) vesuvianite. [VESUVI(US) + -AN]

ve·su·vi·an·ite (və so͞o′vē ə nīt′), *n.* a mineral, chiefly a hydrous silicate of calcium and aluminum, commonly in tetragonal crystals and usually of a brown to green color; idocrase. Also, **vesuvian.** [VESUVIAN + -ITE[1]]

vesu′vianite jade′, a green variety of vesuvianite, used as a gem: not a true jade. Also, **vesu′vian jade′.** Also called **californite.**

Ve·su·vi·us (və so͞o′vē əs), *n.* **Mount,** an active volcano in SW Italy, near Naples. Its eruption destroyed the ancient cities of Pompeii and Herculaneum A.D. 79. ab. 3900 ft.

vet[1] (vet), *n., v.,* **vet·ted, vet·ting.** *Informal.* —*n.* **1.** veterinarian. —*v.t.* **2.** to examine or treat as a veterinarian or a doctor does. **3.** to appraise, verify, or check for accuracy, authenticity, etc.: *An expert vetted the manuscript before publication.* —*v.i.* **4.** to work as a veterinarian. [short for VETERINARIAN]

vet[2] (vet), *n., adj. Informal.* veteran. [short form]

vet., **1.** veteran. **2.** veterinarian. **3.** veterinary.

Ve·ta (vē′tə), *n.* a girl's given name.

vetch (vech), *n.* **1.** any of several mostly climbing, leguminous herbs of the genus *Vicia,* as *V. sativa,* cultivated for forage and soil improvement. **2.** any of various allied plants, as *Lathyrus sativus,* of Europe, cultivated for its edible seeds and as a forage plant. **3.** the beanlike seed or fruit of any such plant. [ME *ve(c)che* < AF, OF *vecce* (F *vesce*) < L *vicia* name of plant] —**vetch′like′,** *adj.*

CONCISE PRONUNCIATION KEY: *act, āble, dâre, ärt; ebb, ēqual; if, īce; hot, ōver, ôrder, oil, bo͝ok, o͞oze, out; up, ûrge; chief; sing; shoe; thin, that;* zh *as in measure.* ə = *a* as in *alone, e* as in *system, i* as in *easily, o* as in *gallop, u* as in *circus;* ə as in *button* (but′ən), *fire* (fīər), *cradle* (krād′əl). See the full key inside the front cover.

vetch·ling (vech′ling), *n.* any leguminous plant of the genus *Lathyrus.* [VETCH + -LING[1]]

veter., veterinary.

vet·er·an (vet′ər ən, ve′trən), *n.* **1.** a person who has had long service or experience in an occupation or office: *a veteran of the police force; a political veteran; a veteran of many sports competitions.* **2.** a person who has served in a military force, esp. one who has fought for his country in a war: *a veteran of World War II.* —*adj.* **3.** (of soldiers) having had service or experience in warfare: *veteran troops.* **4.** experienced through long service or practice; having served for a long period: *a veteran member of Congress.* **5.** of, pertaining to, or characteristic of veterans. [< L *veterān(us)* old (soldier), equiv. to *veter-* (s. of *vetus*) old + *-ānus* -AN]

Vet′erans Administra′tion, *U.S.* the federal agency charged with administering benefits provided by law for veterans of the armed forces. *Abbr.:* VA, V.A.

Vet′erans Day′, November 11, a legal holiday in the U.S. in commemoration of the end of World Wars I and II and in honor of veterans of the armed services: now officially observed on the fourth Monday in October. Formerly, **Armistice Day.**

Vet′erans of For′eign Wars′ of the Unit′ed States′. See **V.F.W.**

vet·er·i·nar·i·an (vet′ər ə nâr′ē ən, ve′trə-), *n.* a person who practices veterinary medicine or surgery. [< L *veterīnāri(us)* VETERINARY + -AN]

vet·er·i·nar·y (vet′ər ə ner′ē, ve′trə-), *n., pl.* **-nar·ies,** *adj.* —*n.* **1.** a veterinarian. —*adj.* **2.** of or pertaining to the medical and surgical treatment of animals, esp. domesticated animals. [< L *veterīnāri(us),* equiv. to *veterīn(ae)* beasts of burden (pl. of *veterīnus,* adj. pertaining to such beasts, equiv. to *veter-,* s. of *vetus* old, i.e., grown, able to take a load + *-īnus* -INE[1]) + *-ārius* -ARY]

vet′erinary med′icine, the branch of medicine dealing with the study, prevention, and treatment of animal diseases, esp. in domesticated animals.

vet·i·ver (vet′ə vər), *n.* **1.** the long, fibrous, aromatic roots of an East Indian grass, *Vetiveria zizanoides,* used for making hangings and screens and yielding an oil used in perfumery. **2.** Also called **khus-khus.** the grass itself. [< Tamil *vetti-vēr* cuscus-root]

vet. med., veterinary medicine.

ve·to (vē′tō), *n., pl.* **-toes,** *v.,* **-toed, -to·ing.** —*n.* **1.** the power or right vested in one branch of a government to cancel or postpone the decisions, enactments, etc., of another branch, esp., the right of a President, governor, or other chief executive to reject bills passed by the legislature. **2.** the exercise of this right. **3.** Also called **ve′to mes′sage.** a document exercising such right and setting forth the reasons for such action. **4.** a nonconcurring vote by which one of the five permanent members of the Security Council can overrule the actions or decisions of the meeting on matters other than procedural. **5.** an emphatic prohibition of any sort. —*v.t.* **6.** to reject (a proposed bill or enactment) by exercising a veto. **7.** to prohibit emphatically. Also called **ve′to pow′er** (for defs. 1, 4). [< L: I forbid] —**ve′to·er,** *n.*

vet. sci., veterinary science.

Vet·ter (vet′ər), *n.* Vätter.

vex (veks), *v.t.* **1.** to irritate; annoy; provoke: *His noisy neighbors often vexed him.* **2.** to torment; trouble; distress; plague; worry: *Lack of money vexes many.* **3.** to discuss or debate (a subject, question, etc.) with vigor or at great length: *to vex a question endlessly without agreeing.* **4.** *Archaic.* to disturb by motion; stir up; toss about. **5.** *Archaic.* to afflict with physical pain. [late ME *vexe(n)* < OF *vexer* < L *vexāre* to shake, jolt, harass, annoy, freq. of *vehere* to carry, convey] —**vex′er,** *n.* —**vex′ing·ly,** *adv.*
—**Syn. 1.** anger, irk, fret, nettle. **2.** hector, harry, harass. —**Ant. 1.** delight.

vex·a·tion (vek sā′shən), *n.* **1.** the act of vexing. **2.** the state of being vexed; irritation; annoyance: *To our vexation, we missed the last bus.* **3.** something that vexes; a cause of annoyance; affliction; nuisance: *The creeping pace of rush-hour traffic was a daily vexation.* [< L *vexātiōn-* (s. of *vexātiō*), equiv. to *vexāt(us)* (ptp. of *vexāre* to VEX; see -ATE[1]) + *-iōn-* -ION]

vex·a·tious (vek sā′shəs), *adj.* **1.** causing vexation; troublesome; annoying: *a vexatious situation.* **2.** *Law.* (of legal actions) instituted without sufficient grounds and serving only to cause annoyance to the defendant. **3.** disorderly; confused; troubled. [VEXATI(ON) + -OUS] —**vex·a′tious·ly,** *adv.* —**vex·a′tious·ness,** *n.*
—**Syn. 1.** disturbing, provoking, irritating. —**Ant. 1.** delightful.

vexed (vekst), *adj.* **1.** irritated; annoyed: *She was vexed at the indifference of the salesclerks.* **2.** much discussed or disputed: *a vexed question.* **3.** tossed about, as waves. [late ME; see VEX, -ED[2]] —**vex·ed·ly** (vek′sid lē), *adv.* —**vex′ed·ness,** *n.*

vex·il·lar·y (vek′sə ler′ē), *n., pl.* **-lar·ies,** *adj.* —*n.* **1.** (in ancient Rome) one of a class of veteran soldiers who served under a special banner. —*adj.* **2.** of or pertaining to a vexillum. [< L *vexillāri(us)* standard-bearer. See VEXILLUM, -ARY]

vex·il·late (vek′sə lit, -lāt′), *adj.* having a vexillum or vexilla. [VEXILL(UM) + -ATE[1]]

vex·il·lum (vek sil′əm), *n., pl.* **vex·il·la** (vek sil′ə). **1.** a military standard or flag carried by ancient Roman troops. **2.** a group of men serving under such a standard. **3.** Also, **vex·il** (vek′sil). *Bot.* the large upper petal of a papilionaceous flower. See diag. under **papilionaceous.** **4.** *Ornith. Rare.* the web or vane of a feather. [< L: standard, flag < ?]

VF, **1.** video frequency. **2.** voice frequency.

V.F.W., *U.S.* Veterans of Foreign Wars: a society composed of veterans of the armed forces who have served overseas during wartime. Also, **VFW**

V.G., Vicar-General.

v.g., for example. [< L *verbi gratia*]

VHF, See **very high frequency.** Also, **vhf, V.H.F.**

Vi, *Chem.* virginium.

V.I., **1.** Vancouver Island. **2.** Virgin Islands.

v.i., **1.** verb intransitive. **2.** see below. [< L *vide infra*]

vi·a (vī′ə, vē′ə), *prep.* **1.** by a route that touches or passes through; by way of: *to fly to Japan via the North Pole.* **2.** by the agency or instrumentality of: *to arrive at a solution via scientific investigation.* —*n.* **3.** *Archit.* a space between two mutules. [< L *viā,* abl. of *via* way]

vi·a·ble (vī′ə bəl), *adj.* **1.** capable of living. **2.** *Physiol.* **a.** physically fitted to live. **b.** (of a fetus) having reached such a stage of development as to be capable of living, under normal conditions, outside the uterus. **3.** *Bot.* able to live and grow. **4.** vivid; real; stimulating, as to the intellect, imagination, or senses: *a period of history that few teachers can make viable.* **5.** practicable; workable: *an alternative plan that seemed more viable.* **6.** having the ability to grow, expand, develop, etc.: *a new and viable country.* [< F, equiv. to *vie* life (< L *vīta*) + *-able* -ABLE] —**vi′a·bil′i·ty,** *n.*

vi′a dol·o·ro′sa (dol′ə rō′sə, dō′lə-), **1.** Christ's route to Golgotha. **2.** a trying, painful, or sorrowful course or series of experiences. [< L: lit., sorrowful road]

vi·a·duct (vī′ə dukt′), *n.* a bridge for carrying a road, railroad, etc., over a valley or the like, consisting of a number of short spans. [< L *via* way + (AQUE)DUCT]

vi·al (vī′əl, vīl), *n., v.,* **-aled, -al·ing** or (*esp. Brit.*) **-alled, -al·ling.** —*n.* **1.** Also, **phial.** a small container, as of glass, for holding liquids: *a vial of rare perfume; a vial of medicine.* **2. pour out vials of wrath,** to wreak vengeance or express anger: *In her preface she pours out vials of wrath on her detractors.* —*v.t.* **3.** to put into or keep in a vial. [late ME *viole,* var. of *fiole* PHIAL]

vi·a me·di·a (wē′ä me′di ä′; *Eng.* vī′ə mē′dē ə), *Latin.* a middle way; a mean between two extremes.

vi·and (vī′ənd), *n.* **1.** an article of food. **2. viands,** articles or dishes of food, now usually of a choice or delicate kind. [late ME *viaunde* < MF *viande* < VL **vīvanda,* var. of L *vīvenda* things to be lived on, ger. neut. pl. of *vīvere* to live]

vi′ ap′ple (vē). See **Otaheite apple.** [*vi* < Tahitian]

vi·at·i·cum (vī at′ə kəm), *n., pl.* **-ca** (-kə), **-cums.** **1.** *Eccles.* the Eucharist or Communion as given to a person dying or in danger of death. **2.** (among the ancient Romans) a provision or allowance for traveling, originally of transportation and supplies, later of money, made to officials on public missions. **3.** money or necessities for any journey. [< L, neut. of *viāticus,* equiv. to *viāt(us)* (ptp. of *viāre* to travel; see VIA, -ATE[1]) + *-icus* -IC]

vi·a·tor (vī ā′tôr), *n., pl.* **vi·a·to·res** (vī′ə tôr′ēz, -tōr′-). a wayfarer; traveler. [< L, equiv. to *viāt(us)* (see VIATICUM) + *-or* -OR[2]]

vibes[1] (vībz), *n.pl. Informal.* vibraharp. [short form] —**vib′ist,** *n.*

vibes[2] (vībz), *n. Slang.* vibration (def. 6). [short form]

Vi·borg (vē′bôr′yᵊ), *n.* Swedish name of **Vyborg.**

vi·brac·u·lum (vī brak′yə ləm), *n., pl.* **-la** (-lə). one of the modified polyps of certain bryozoans, having a long, whiplike appendage. [< NL, equiv. to L *vibrā(re)* (to) shake + *-culum* -CULE] —**vi·brac′u·lar,** *adj.* —**vi·brac′u·loid′,** *adj.*

Vibracula

vi·bra·harp (vī′brə härp′), *n.* a musical percussion instrument that resembles a marimba and is played with mallets, but that has metal instead of wooden bars and has a set of electrically powered resonators for sustaining the tone or creating a vibrato. [< L *vibrā(re)* (to) shake + HARP]

vi·brant (vī′brənt), *adj.* **1.** moving to and fro rapidly; vibrating. **2.** vibrating so as to produce sound, as a string. **3.** (of sounds) characterized by perceptible vibration; resonant; resounding. **4.** pulsating with vigor and energy: *the vibrant life of a large city.* **5.** vigorous; energetic; vital: *a vibrant personality.* **6.** exciting; stimulating; lively: *vibrant colors; a vibrant performance.* **7.** *Phonet.* made with tonal vibration of the vocal cords; voiced. —*n.* **8.** *Phonet.* a vibrant sound (opposed to *surd*). [< L *vibrant-* (s. of *vibrāns,* prp. of *vibrāre* to shake, move to and fro); see -ANT] —**vi′bran·cy, vi′brance,** *n.* —**vi′brant·ly,** *adv.*

vi·bra·phone (vī′brə fōn′), *n.* vibraharp. [< L *vibrā(re)* (to) shake + -PHONE] —**vi·bra·phon·ist** (vī′brə fō′nist, vī brof′ə-), *n.*

vi·brate (vī′brāt), *v.,* **-brat·ed, -brat·ing.** —*v.i.* **1.** to move rhythmically and steadily to and fro, as a pendulum; oscillate. **2.** to move to and fro or up and down quickly and repeatedly; quiver; tremble. **3.** (of sounds) to produce or have a quivering or vibratory effect; resound. **4.** to thrill, as in emotional response. **5.** to move between alternatives or extremes; fluctuate; vacillate. —*v.t.* **6.** to cause to move rhythmically and steadily to and fro, swing, or oscillate. **7.** to cause to move to and fro or up and down quickly and repeatedly; cause to quiver or tremble. **8.** to give forth or emit by, or as by, vibration. **9.** to measure or indicate by vibration or oscillation: *a pendulum vibrating seconds.* [< L *vibrāt(us)* (ptp. of *vibrāre* to move to and fro); see -ATE[1]] —**vi′brat·ing·ly,** *adv.*
—**Syn. 2.** See **shake.** **3.** echo.

vi·bra·tile (vī′brə til, -tīl′), *adj.* **1.** capable of vibrating or of being vibrated. **2.** having a vibratory motion. **3.** of, pertaining to, or of the nature of vibration. [VIBRATE + -ILE] —**vi·bra·til·i·ty** (vī′brə til′i tē), *n.*

vi·bra·tion (vī brā′shən), *n.* **1.** the act of vibrating. **2.** the state of being vibrated. **3.** *Physics.* **a.** the oscillating, reciprocating, or other periodic motion of a rigid or elastic body or medium forced from a position or state of equilibrium. **b.** the analogous motion of the particles of a mass of air or the like, whose state of equilibrium has been disturbed, as in transmitting sound. **4.** an instance of vibratory motion; oscillation; quiver; tremor. **5.** a supernatural emanation, bearing good or ill, that is sensed by or revealed to those attuned to the occult. **6. vibrations,** *Slang.* general emotional feelings one has from another person, a place, situation, etc. [< L *vibrātiōn-* (s. of *vibrātiō*). See VIBRATE, -ION] —**vi·bra′tion·al,** *adj.* —**vi·bra′tion·less,** *adj.*

vi·bra·tive (vī′brə tiv), *adj.* vibratory. [VIBRATE + -IVE]

vi·bra·to (vi brä′tō, vī-), *n., pl.* **-tos.** *Music.* a pulsating effect, produced in singing by the rapid reiteration of emphasis on a tone, and on bowed instruments by a rapid change of pitch corresponding to the vocal tremolo. [< It < L *vibrātus* (ptp.); see VIBRATE]

vi·bra·tor (vī′brā tər), *n.* **1.** one who or that which vibrates. **2.** any of various machines or devices causing a vibratory motion or action. **3.** an appliance with a rubber or other tip of variable shape, made to oscillate very rapidly and used in vibratory massage. **4.** *Elect.* **a.** a device in which, by continually repeated impulses, a steady current is changed into an oscillating current. **b.** a device for producing electric oscillations. [VIBRATE + -OR[2]]

vi·bra·to·ry (vī′brə tôr′ē, -tōr′ē), *adj.* **1.** capable of or producing vibration. **2.** vibrating. **3.** of the nature of or consisting in vibration. **4.** of or pertaining to vibration. Also, **vibrative.** [VIBRATE + -ORY[1]]

vib·ri·o (vib′rē ō′), *n., pl.* **-ri·os.** *Bacteriol.* any of several comma- or S-shaped bacteria of the genus *Vibrio,* certain species of which are pathogenic for man and animals. [< NL, equiv. to *vibr(āre)* (to) shake + *-iō* -ION] —**vib·ri·oid** (vib′rē oid′), *adj.*

vib·ri·on·ic (vib′rē on′ik), *adj.* of or pertaining to an infection by a bacterium of the genus *Vibrio.* [< NL *Vibriōn-* (s. of *Vibriō*) VIBRIO + -IC]

vib′rion′ic abor′tion, *Vet. Pathol.* abortion caused by vibriosis.

vib·ri·o·sis (vib′rē ō′sis), *n. Vet. Pathol.* a venereal disease of cattle and sheep, caused by the organism *Vibrio fetus,* that is characterized by delayed female fertility and by abortion. [< NL; see VIBRIO, -OSIS]

vi·bris·sa (vī bris′ə), *n., pl.* **-bris·sae** (-bris′ē). **1.** one of the stiff, bristly hairs growing about the mouth of certain animals, as a whisker of a cat. **2.** one of the long, slender, bristlelike feathers growing along the side of the mouth in many birds. [< L, equiv. to *vibr(āre)* (to) shake + *-issa* -ESS] —**vi·bris′sal,** *adj.*

vibro-, a prefix meaning "vibration," used in the formation of compound words: *vibrometer.* [< L *vibr(āre)* (to) shake, move to and fro + -o-]

vi·bro·graph (vī′brə graf′, -gräf′), *n.* a device for recording mechanical vibrations. [VIBRO- + -GRAPH]

vi·brom·e·ter (vī brom′i tər), *n.* vibrograph. [VIBRO- + METER]

vi·bur·num (vī bûr′nəm), *n.* **1.** any caprifoliaceous shrub or tree of the genus *Viburnum,* certain species of which, as the cranberry bush, *V. Opulus,* or snowball, are cultivated for ornament. **2.** the dried bark of various species of *Viburnum,* used in medicine. [< L: wayfaring-tree]

Vic (vik), *n.* a boy's given name, form of **Victor.** Also, **Vick.**

Vic., **1.** Vicar. **2.** Vicarage. **3.** Victoria.

vic·ar (vik′ər), *n.* **1.** *Ch. of Eng.* **a.** a person acting as priest of a parish in place of the rector, or as representative of a religious community to which tithes belong. **b.** the priest of a parish the tithes of which are impropriated and who receives only the smaller tithes or a salary. **2.** *Prot. Episc. Ch.* **a.** a clergyman whose sole or chief charge is a chapel dependent on the church of a parish. **b.** a bishop's assistant in charge of a church or mission. **3.** *Rom. Cath. Ch.* an ecclesiastic representing the pope or a bishop. **4.** one who acts in place of another; substitute. **5.** a person who is authorized to perform the functions of another; deputy: *God's vicar on earth.* [ME < AF *vicare,* equiv. to OF *vicaire* < L *vicār(ius)* a substitute, n. use of adj.; see VICARIOUS] —**vic′ar·ship′,** *n.*

vic·ar·age (vik′ər ij), *n.* **1.** the residence of a vicar. **2.** the benefice of a vicar. **3.** the office or duties of a vicar. [late ME; see VICAR, -AGE]

vic′ar apostol′ic, *pl.* **vicars apostolic.** **1.** *Rom. Cath. Ch.* a titular bishop serving either in a district where no episcopal see has been established, or in one where the succession of bishops has been interrupted. **2.** *Eccles. Hist.* an archbishop, bishop, or other ecclesiastic to whom the pope delegated a portion of his jurisdiction.

vic·ar·ate (vik′ər it, -ə rāt′), *n.* vicariate. [VICAR + ATE[1]]

vic′ar capit′ular, *pl.* **vicars capitular.** *Rom. Cath. Ch.* a cleric chosen by a cathedral chapter to manage a bishopric during a vacancy.

vic′ar cho′ral, *pl.* **vicars choral.** *Anglican Ch.* a clergyman or layman in a cathedral who sings certain parts of the service.

vic′ar fo·rane′ (fō rān′, fô-), *pl.* **vicars forane.** *Rom. Cath. Ch.* dean[1] (def. 2b). [*forane* < L *forāne(us)* living away; see FOREIGN]

vic·ar-gen·er·al (vik′ər jen′ər əl), *n., pl.* **vic·ars-gen·er·al.** **1.** *Rom. Cath. Ch.* a priest deputized by a bishop to assist him in the administration of a diocese. **2.** *Ch. of Eng.* an ecclesiastical officer, usually a layman, who assists a bishop or an archbishop in the discharge of his judicial or administrative duties. **3.** a deputy with extensive power or jurisdiction, as Thomas Cromwell when serving as vicegerent of Henry VIII. [ME] —**vic′ar-gen′er·al·ship′,** *n.*

vi·car·i·al (vī kâr′ē əl), *adj.* **1.** of or pertaining to a vicar or vicars. **2.** acting as or holding the office of a vicar. **3.** delegated or vicarious: *vicarial powers.* [< L *vicāri(us)* VICAR + -AL[1]]

vi·car·i·ate (vī kâr′ē it, -āt′, vi-), *n.* **1.** the office or authority of a vicar. **2.** the district presided over by a vicar. Also, **vicarate.** [< ML *vicāriāt(us)* < L *vicāri(us)* VICAR + *-ātus* -ATE[1]]

vicar′iate apostol′ic, *pl.* **vicariates apostolic.** *Rom. Cath. Ch.* a district under the jurisdiction of a vicar apostolic.

vi·car·i·ous (vī kâr′ē əs, vi-), *adj.* **1.** performed, exercised, received, or suffered in place of another: *vicarious punishment.* **2.** taking the place of another person or thing; acting or serving as a substitute. **3.** felt or enjoyed through imagined participation in the experience of others: *a vicarious thrill.* **4.** *Physiol.* noting or pertaining to the performance by one organ of part of the functions normally performed by another. [< L *vicārius* substituting, equiv. to *vic-,* akin to **vicis* (inter-) change (see VICE[3]), + *-ārius* -ARIOUS] —**vi·car′i·ous·ly,** *adv.* —**vi·car′i·ous·ness, vi·car′i·ism,** *n.*

vic·ar·ly (vik′ər lē), *adj.* of, pertaining to, suggesting, or resembling a vicar: *vicarly duties; a vicarly manner.* [VICAR + -LY]

Vic′ar of Christ′, *Rom. Cath. Ch.* the pope, with reference to his claim to stand in the place of Jesus Christ and possess His authority in the church. Also, **Vic′ar of Je′sus Christ′.**

Vic′ar of Wake′field, The, a novel (1766) by Goldsmith.

vice[1] (vīs), *n.* **1.** an immoral or evil habit or practice. **2.** immoral conduct; depraved or degrading behavior: *a life of crime and vice.* **3.** sexual immorality, esp. prostitution. **4.** a particular form of depravity. **5.** a fault, defect, shortcoming, or imperfection: *a minor vice in his literary style.* **6.** a physical defect, flaw, or infirmity: *a constitutional vice.* **7.** a bad habit, as in a horse. **8.** (*cap.*) a character in the English morality plays, a personification of general vice or of a particular vice, serving as the buffoon. [ME < AF, OF < L *vitium* a fault, defect, vice] —**Syn. 1.** See **fault. 2.** depravity, sin, iniquity, wickedness, corruption. **5.** blemish. —**Ant. 1, 2.** virtue.

vice[2] (vīs), *n., v.t.,* **viced, vic·ing.** vise.

vi·ce[3] (vī′sē), *prep.* instead of; in the place of. [< L: instead of, abl. of *vicis (inter)change]

vice-, a learned borrowing from Latin meaning "deputy," used in the formation of compound words: *viceroyalty; vice-chancellor.* [ME << L *vice* VICE[3]]

vice-ad·mi·ral (vīs′ad′mər əl), *n.* a naval officer next in rank below an admiral. —**vice′-ad′mi·ral·ty,** *n.*

vice-chair·man (vīs′châr′mən), *n., pl.* **-men.** a member of a committee, board, group, etc., designated as immediately subordinate to a chairman and serving as such in the latter's absence; a person who acts for and assists a chairman.

vice-chan·cel·lor (vīs′chan′sə lər, -chän′-), *n.* **1.** a substitute, deputy, or subordinate chancellor. **2.** a chancery judge acting in place of a chancellor. **3.** the chief administrator of certain British universities. Cf. **chancellor** (def. 6). [late ME] —**vice′-chan′cel·lor·ship′,** *n.*

vice-con·sul (vīs′kon′səl), *n.* a consular officer of a grade below that of consul. Also, **vice′ con′sul.** —**vice′-con′su·lar,** *adj.* —**vice′-con′su·late,** *n.* —**vice′-con′sul·ship′,** *n.*

vice·ge·ral (vīs jēr′əl), *adj.* of or pertaining to a vicegerent or his position. [VICEGER(ENT) + -AL[1]]

vice·ge·ren·cy (vīs jēr′ən sē), *n., pl.* **-cies. 1.** the position, government, or office of a vicegerent. **2.** the territory or district under a vicegerent. [VICEGER(ENT) + -ENCY]

vice·ge·rent (vīs jēr′ənt), *n.* **1.** an officer appointed by a sovereign or supreme chief as his deputy. **2.** a deputy in general. —*adj.* **3.** exercising delegated powers. **4.** characterized by delegation of powers. [< NL *vicegerent-* (s. of *vicegerēns* managing instead of), equiv. to L *vice* (see VICE[3]) + *gerent-* (s. of *gerēns,* prp. of *gerere* to carry on, conduct); see -ENT]

vice·less (vīs′lis), *adj.* free from vices. [VICE[1] + -LESS]

vic·e·nar·y (vis′ə ner′ē), *adj.* of, pertaining to, or consisting of twenty. [< L *vīcēnāri(us)* *vīcēn(ī)* twenty each + *-ārius* -ARY]

vi·cen·ni·al (vī sen′ē əl), *adj.* **1.** of or for twenty years. **2.** occurring every twenty years. [< L *vīcenni(um)* twenty-year period, equiv. to *vīc(ēnī)* twenty each + *-enni(um)* yearly period (deriv. of *annus* year) + -AL[1]]

Vi·cen·za (vē chen′dzä), *n.* a city in central Venezia, in NE Italy. 97,617 (1961).

vice-pres., vice-president. Also, **Vice-Pres.**

vice-pres·i·dent (vīs′prez′i dənt), *n.* **1.** an officer next in rank to a president, serving, in his absence or during the illness of the president, in his place. **2.** Also, **Vice′-Pres′i·dent.** *U.S. Govt.* the officer of this rank who is elected at the same time as the President and who succeeds to the presidency on the resignation, removal, death, or disability of the President. Also, **vice′pres′ident.** —**vice′-pres′i·den·cy,** *n.* —**vice′-pres·i·den′tial,** *adj.*

vice·re·gal (vīs rē′gəl), *adj.* of or pertaining to a viceroy. [VICE- + REGAL] —**vice·re′gal·ly,** *adv.*

vice-re·gent (*n.* vīs′rē′jənt; *adj.* vīs rē′jənt), *n.* **1.** a deputy regent; a person who acts in the place of a ruler, governor, or sovereign. —*adj.* **2.** of, pertaining to, or occupying the position of a vice-regent. —**vice′-re′gen·cy,** *n.*

vice·reine (vīs′rān), *n.* the wife of a viceroy. [< F, equiv. to *vice-* VICE- + *reine* < L *rēgīna* queen (*rēg-,* base of *rex* king, + *-īna* fem. n. suffix)]

vice·roy (vīs′roi), *n.* **1.** a person appointed to rule a country or province as the deputy of the sovereign: *the viceroy of India.* **2.** an American butterfly, *Limenitis archippus,* closely mimicking the monarch butterfly in coloration. [< MF, equiv. to *vice-* VICE- + *roy* < L *rēgi-,* s. of *rex* king] —**vice′roy·ship′,** *n.*

vice·roy·al·ty (vīs roi′əl tē, vīs′roi′-), *n., pl.* **-ties. 1.** the dignity, office, or period of office of a viceroy. **2.** a country or province ruled by a viceroy. [VICE- + ROYALTY, modeled on F *vice-royauté*]

vice′ squad′, a police squad charged with enforcing laws dealing with gambling, prostitution, and other forms of vice.

vi·ce ver·sa (vī′sə vûr′sə, vī′sē, vīs′), in reverse order from that of a preceding statement; conversely: *She dislikes me, and vice versa.* [< L, equiv. to *vice,* abl. sing. of *vicis change + *versā,* abl. sing. fem. of *versus,* ptp. of *vertere* to turn]

Vi·chy (vish′ē; *Fr.* vē shē′), *n.* a city in central France: provisional capital of unoccupied France 1940–44; hot springs. 31,322 (1962).

Vi·chy·ite (vish′ē īt′, vē′shē-), *n.* a member or adherent of the government established 1940 at Vichy by Marshal Henri Pétain. [VICHY + -ITE[1]]

vi·chy·ssoise (vish′ē swäz′), *n.* a cream soup of potatoes and leeks, usually served chilled and often garnished with chopped chives. [< F, equiv. to VICHY + *-ss-* (< ?) + *-oise,* fem. of *-ois* -ESE]

vi′chy wa′ter (vish′ē), **1.** a natural mineral water from springs at Vichy, containing sodium bicarbonate, other alkaline salts, etc., used in the treatment of digestive disturbances, gout, etc. **2.** a water of similar composition, either natural or artificial. Also, **Vi′chy wa′ter, vi′chy, Vi′chy.**

vic·i·nage (vis′ə nij), *n.* **1.** the region near or about a place; vicinity. **2.** a particular neighborhood or district, or the people belonging to it. **3.** proximity. [< L *vīcīn(us)* near (see VICINITY) + -AGE; r. ME *vesinage* < MF]

vic·i·nal (vis′ə nəl), *adj.* **1.** of, pertaining to, or belonging to a neighborhood or district. **2.** neighboring; adjacent. **3.** *Crystall.* noting a plane the position of which varies very little from that of a fundamental plane of the form. [< L *vīcīnāl(is),* equiv. to *vīcīn(us)* near + *-ālis* -AL[1]; see VICINITY]

vi·cin·i·ty (vi sin′i tē), *n., pl.* **-ties. 1.** the area or region near or about a place; surrounding district; neighborhood: *There are no stores in the vicinity of our house.* **2.** state or fact of being near; proximity; propinquity: *He was troubled by the vicinity of the nuclear testing area.* [< L *vīcīnitās,* equiv. to *vīcīn(us)* near (*vīc(us)* village + *-īnus* -INE[1]) + *-itās* -ITY]

vi·cious (vish′əs), *adj.* **1.** addicted to or characterized by vice; grossly immoral; depraved; profligate: *a vicious life.* **2.** given or readily disposed to evil: *a vicious criminal.* **3.** reprehensible; blameworthy; wrong: *a vicious deception.* **4.** spiteful; malicious: *vicious gossip; a vicious attack.* **5.** unpleasantly severe: *a vicious headache.* **6.** characterized or marred by faults or defects; faulty; unsound: *vicious reasoning.* **7.** savage; ferocious: *They all feared his vicious temper.* **8.** (of an animal) having bad habits or a cruel or fierce disposition: *a vicious bull.* **9.** *Obs.* morbid, foul, or noxious. [ME (< AF) < L *vitiōsus,* equiv. to *viti(um)* fault, vice + *-ōsus* -OSE[1], -OUS] —**vi′cious·ly,** *adv.* —**vi′cious·ness,** *n.* —**Syn. 1.** abandoned, corrupt, iniquitous, sinful. **4.** malevolent. —**Ant. 1.** moral.

vi′cious cir′cle, 1. *Logic.* **a.** (in demonstration) the use of each of two propositions to establish the other. **b.** (in definition) the use of each of two terms to define the other. **2.** *Med.* a series of unhealthy changes in which the first change produces the second which in turn affects the first. **3.** a situation in which effort to solve one problem merely results in the creation of a new problem and in increased difficulty: *a vicious circle where the more I give her, the more she expects.*

vi·cis·si·tude (vi sis′i to͞od′, -tyo͞od′), *n.* **1.** a change or variation occurring in the course of something. **2.** interchange or alternation, as of states or things. **3. vicissitudes,** successive, alternating, or changing phases or conditions, as of life or fortune; ups and downs: *They remained friends through the vicissitudes of 40 years.* **4.** regular change or succession of one state or thing to another. **5.** change; mutation; mutability. [< L *vicissitūdō,* equiv. to *vicissi-* (comb. form of *vicis a turn) + *-tūdō* -TUDE] —**vi·cis·si·tu·di·nar·y** (vi sis′i to͞od′ənər′ē, -tyo͞od′-), **vi·cis′si·tu′di·nous,** *adj.*

Vick (vik), *n.* a boy's given name, form of **Victor.** Also, **Vic.**

Vick′ers num′ber (vik′ərz), *Metall.* a numerical expression of the hardness of a metal as determined by a test (**Vick′ers test′**) in which the sample is indented under a known pressure by a diamond in the form of a square pyramid, after which the surface area of the indentation in square millimeters is divided into the pressure in kilograms. [after *Vickers* Armstrong Ltd., British steel firm]

Vicks·burg (viks′bûrg), *n.* a city in W Mississippi, on the Mississippi River: important Civil War siege and Confederate surrender 1863. 29,130 (1960).

Vick·y (vik′ē), *n.* a girl's given name, form of **Victoria.** Also, **Vick′ie, Viki, Vikki.**

Vi·co (vik′ō; *It.* vē′kô), *n.* **Gio·van·ni Bat·tis·ta** (jô vän′nē bät tēs′tä), 1668–1744, Italian philosopher and jurist. —**Vi·co·ni·an** (vi kō′nē ən), *adj.*

vi·comte (vē kônt′), *n., pl.* **-comtes** (-kônt′). a French viscount. [see VISCOUNT]

vi·com·tesse (vē kôn tes′), *n., pl.* **-tesses** (-tes′). the wife or widow of a vicomte; a French viscountess. [< F, equiv. to *vicomte* VISCOUNT + *-esse* -ESS]

vi·con·ti·el (vī kon′tē əl), *adj. Early Eng. Law.* pertaining to the sheriff or viscount. [< AF *vicontiel,* equiv. to *viconti-* VISCOUNTY + *-el* -AL[1]]

Vict., 1. Victoria. **2.** Victorian.

vic·tim (vik′tim), *n.* **1.** a person who suffers from a destructive or injurious action or agency: *a victim of an automobile accident.* **2.** a person who is deceived or cheated, as by his own emotions or ignorance, by the dishonesty of others, or by some impersonal agency: *a victim of misplaced confidence; the victim of a swindler; a victim of an optical illusion.* **3.** a person or animal sacrificed, or regarded as sacrificed: *war victims.* **4.** a living creature sacrificed in religious rites. [< L *victim(a)* sacrificial beast] —**vic′tim·hood′,** *n.*

vic·tim·ise (vik′tə mīz′), *v.t.,* **-ised, -is·ing.** *Chiefly Brit.* victimize. —**vic′tim·i·sa′tion,** *n.* —**vic′tim·is′er,** *n.*

vic·tim·ize (vik′tə mīz′), *v.t.,* **-ized, -iz·ing. 1.** to make a victim of. **2.** to dupe, swindle, or cheat: *to victimize poor widows.* **3.** to slay as or like a sacrificial victim. [VICTIM + -IZE] —**vic′tim·i·za′tion,** *n.* —**vic′tim·iz′er,** *n.* —**Syn. 2.** defraud, fool, hoodwink, beguile. See **cheat.**

Vic·toire (vēk twar′), *n.* a girl's given name, French form of **Victoria.**

vic·tor (vik′tər), *n.* **1.** a person who has overcome or defeated an adversary; conqueror. **2.** a winner in any struggle or contest. **3.** a word used in communications to represent the letter *V.* [ME < L, equiv. to *vict(us)* (ptp. of *vincere*) + *-or* -OR[2]]

Vic·tor (vik′tər), *n.* **1.** an ancient Roman epithet variously applied to Jupiter, Mars, and Hercules. **2.** a boy's given name.

Victor I, Saint, pope A.D. 189–198.

Victor II, (*Gebhard*) 1018–57, German ecclesiastic: pope 1055–57.

Victor III, (*Dauferius*) 1027–87, Italian ecclesiastic: pope 1086–87.

Victor Em·man·u·el I (i man′yo͞o əl), 1759–1824, king of Sardinia 1802–21.

Victor Emmanuel II, 1820–78, king of Sardinia 1849–78; first king of Italy 1861–78.

Victor Emmanuel III, 1869–1947, king of Italy 1900–46.

Vic·to·ri·a (vik tôr′ē ə, -tōr′-), *n.* **1.** 1819–1901, queen of Great Britain 1837–1901; empress of India 1876–1901. **2.** the ancient Roman goddess of victory, identified with the Greek goddess Nike. **3.** a state in SE Australia. 2,930,113 (1961); 87,884 sq. mi. *Cap.:* Melbourne. **4.** Also called **Hong Kong.** a seaport in and the capital of Hong Kong colony, on the SE coast of China. 663,138 (1961). **5.** a seaport in and the capital of British Columbia, on Vancouver Island, in SW Canada. 54,941 with suburbs, 154,152 (1961). **6.** a city in S Texas. 33,047 (1960). **7. Lake.** Also called **Victoria Nyanza.** a lake in E Africa, in Uganda, Tanganyika, and Kenya: second largest fresh-water lake in the world. 26,828 sq. mi. **8. Mount,** a mountain in SE New Guinea, in the Owen Stanley Range. 13,240 ft. **9.** a girl's given name. **10.** (*l.c.*) a low, light, four-wheeled carriage with a calash top, a seat for two passengers, and a perch in front for the driver. **11.** (*l.c.*) an open touring car having a folding top that usually covers only the rear seat. **12.** (*l.c.*) a water lily, *Victoria regia* (or *amazonica*), of still waters from Paraguay to Venezuela, having leaves often over 6 feet in diameter, and white to rose, nocturnal flowers 12 to 18 inches across.

Victoria (def. 10)

Victo′ria Cross′, a British decoration awarded to soldiers and sailors for acts of conspicuous bravery in the presence of the enemy.

Victo′ria Day′, (in Canada) the first Monday preceding May 25, observed as a national holiday.

Victo′ria Des′ert. See **Great Victoria Desert.**

Victo′ria Falls′, 1. falls of the Zambezi River in S Africa, between Zambia and Southern Rhodesia, near Livingstone. 420 ft. high; more than a mile wide. **2.** See **Iguassú Falls.**

Victo′ria Is′land, an island off the coast of N Canada, in the Arctic Ocean. 80,340 sq. mi.

Victo′ria Land′, a region in Antarctica, bordering on the Ross Sea, mainly in Ross Dependency.

Vic·to·ri·an (vik tôr′ē ən, -tōr′-), *adj.* **1.** of or pertaining to Queen Victoria or the period of her reign: *Victorian poets.* **2.** having the characteristics usually attributed to the Victorians, esp. prudishness and observance of the conventionalities. **3.** *Archit.* **a.** noting or pertaining to the architecture, furnishings, and decoration of English-speaking countries between c1840–c1900, characterized by rapid changes of style as a consequence of aesthetic and philosophical controversy, technological innovations, and changes of fashion, by the frequent presence of ostentation and bad workmanship, and by an overall trend from classicism at the start to romanticism and eclecticism at the middle of the period and thence to classicism again, with attempts at stylistic innovation occurring from time to time. **b.** noting or pertaining to the massive, elaborate work characteristic esp. of the period c1855–80, derived mainly from the Baroque and Gothic styles and characterized by the frequent presence of heavy carved ornament, elaborate moldings, etc., by the use of strong and generally dark colors, by the frequent use of dark varnished woodwork, by the emphasis on geometrical form rather than on textural effects, and frequently by an effect of harshness. —*n.* **4.** a person who lived during the Victorian period. [VICTORI(A) + -AN]

Victorian sideboard

Victo′rian box′, a tree, *Pittosporum undulatum,* of Australia, having shiny, wavy-margined leaves and fragrant clusters of white flowers. Also called **cheesewood.**

Vic·to·ri·an·ism (vik tôr′ē ə niz′əm, -tōr′-), *n.* **1.** the distinctive character, thought, tendencies, etc., of the Victorian period. **2.** an instance or example of such thought, tendencies, etc. [VICTORIAN + -ISM]

Victo′ria Ny·an′za (nī an′zə, nyän′zä), Victoria (def. 7).

vic·to·ri·ate (vik tôr′ē it, -āt′, -tōr′-), *n.* a silver coin of ancient Rome, first issued in the late 3rd century B.C., having a figure of Victory on the reverse. [< L *victōriāt(us),* equiv. to *victōri(a)* VICTORY + *-ātus* -ATE[1]]

vic·to·rine (vik′tə rēn′), *n.* a fur tippet with long tabs at the ends. [prob. after Queen VICTORIA; see -INE[2]]

Vic·to·rine (vik′tə rēn′), *n.* a canon regular of the Order of St. Victor, founded in Paris, France, in 1110, which was famous for its learning and influence in the Middle Ages, and which became extinct during the French Revolution. [< F *Victorin*]

vic·to·ri·ous (vik tôr′ē əs, -tōr′-), *adj.* **1.** having achieved a victory; conquering; triumphant: *our victorious army.* **2.** of, pertaining to, or characterized by victory. [late ME; see VICTORY, -OUS] —**vic·to′ri·ous·ly,** *adv.* —**vic·to′ri·ous·ness,** *n.*

vic·to·ry (vik′tə rē), *n., pl.* **-ries. 1.** a success or triumph over an enemy in battle or war. **2.** an engagement ending in such triumph: *American victories in the Pacific were won at great cost.* **3.** the ultimate and decisive superiority in any battle or contest: *The new vaccine effected a victory over poliomyelitis.* **4.** a success or superior position achieved against any opponent, opposition, difficulty, etc.: *a moral victory.* [ME *victorie* < L *victōria*, equiv. to *victor* VICTOR + *-ia* -Y³] —**vic′to·ry·less,** *adj.*

—**Syn. 3.** VICTORY, CONQUEST, TRIUMPH refer to a successful outcome of a struggle. VICTORY suggests the decisive defeat of an opponent in a contest of any kind: *victory in battle; a football victory.* CONQUEST implies the taking over of control by the victor, and the obedience of the conquered: *a war of conquest; the conquest of Peru.* TRIUMPH implies a particularly outstanding victory: *the triumph of a righteous cause; the triumph of justice.* —**Ant. 3.** defeat.

vic′tory gar′den, (during World War II) a vegetable garden cultivated to increase food production. Also, **Vic′tory gar′den.**

Vic′tory Heights′, a town in S New York. 2528 (1960).

Vic′tory Med′al, 1. a round bronze medal awarded to all those who served in the armed forces of the U.S. during World War I. **2.** a similar medal awarded after World War II.

Vic′tory of Sam′othrace. See **Winged Victory.**

Vic′tory ship′, a fast, turbine-powered cargo ship of World War II, having a capacity of about 11,000 dead-weight tons.

vic·tress (vik′tris), *n.* a female victor. Also, **victrix.** [VICT(O)R + -ESS]

vic·trix (vik′triks), *n., pl.* **vic·tri·ces** (vik′tri sēz′), victress. [< L; see VICTOR, -TRIX]

Vic·trix (vik′triks), *n.* an ancient Roman epithet variously applied to Venus, Diana, and other goddesses.

Vic·tro·la (vik trō′lə), *n.* *Trademark.* a phonograph.

vict·ual (vit′əl), *n., v.,* **-ualed, -ual·ing** or (*esp. Brit.*) **-ualled, -ual·ling.** —*n.* **1. victuals,** food supplies; provisions. **2.** food or provisions for human beings. —*v.t.* **3.** to supply with victuals. —*v.i.* **4.** to take or obtain victuals. **5.** *Archaic.* to eat or feed. Also, **vittle.** [ME *vitaille* < AF, MF *vitail(l)e,* OF *vituaille* < LL *victuālia* provisions, n. use of neut. pl. of L *victuālis* pertaining to food, equiv. to *victu(s)* nourishment, way of living (*vict-,* ptp. s. of *vivere* to live + *-us* 4th decl. n. suffix + *-ālis* -AL¹); mod. sp. < L] —**vict′ual·less,** *adj.*

vict·ual·age (vit′əlij), *n.* food; provisions; victuals. [VICTUAL + -AGE]

vict·ual·er (vit′ələr), *n.* **1.** one who furnishes victuals, esp. a sutler. **2.** a supply ship. **3.** Also called **licensed victualler.** *Brit.* the keeper of an inn or tavern, esp. one licensed to sell liquor. Also, *esp. Brit.,* **vict′ual·ler.** [late ME *vitailler* < AF, equiv. to MF *vitail(l)ier.* See VICTUAL, -ER²]

vi·cu·ña (vī kōō′nə, -kyōō′-, və-, və kōō′nyə), *n.* **1.** a wild South American ruminant, *Lama vicugna,* of the Andes, related to the guanaco but smaller, and yielding a soft, delicate wool. **2.** a fabric of this wool or of some substitute, usually twilled and finished with a soft nap. **3.** a garment, esp. an overcoat, of vicuña. Also, **vicuna.** [< Sp *vicuña* < Quechuan *wikūña*]

Vicuña (2½ ft. high at shoulder; length 5½ ft.)

vid., vide.

Vi·da Es Sue·ño, La (*Sp.* lä bē′dä es swe′nyō). See **Life Is a Dream.**

Vi·dal·ia (vi dāl′yə), *n.* **1.** a town in central Georgia. 10,393. **2.** a town in central Louisiana. 5936.

Vi·dar (vē′där), *n.* *Scand. Myth.* a son of Odin, who will survive Ragnarok after killing Fenrir.

vi·de (wē′de; *Eng.* vī′dē), *v.* *Latin.* see (used esp. to refer a reader to parts of a text).

vi·de an·te (wē′de än′te; *Eng.* vī′dē an′tē), *Latin.* see before (used esp. to refer a reader to parts of a text).

vi·de in·fra (wē′de in′frä; *Eng.* vī′dē in′frə), *Latin.* see below (used esp. to refer a reader to parts of a text).

vi·de·li·cet (wi dā′li ket′; *Eng.* vi del′i sit), *adv.* *Latin.* that is to say; namely (used esp. to introduce examples, details, etc.). *Abbr.:* viz.

vid·e·o (vid′ē ō′), *n.* **1.** the elements of television, as in a program or script, pertaining to the transmission or reception of the image (distinguished from *audio*). **2.** television: *He is a star of stage and video.* —*adj.* **3.** of or pertaining to television, esp. the visual elements. [< L *vidē(re)* (to) see + *-o* as in *audio*]

vid·e·o·cas·sette (vid′ē ō′kə set′, -ka-), *n.* cassette (def. 2).

vid′eocassette′ record′er, an electronic apparatus for connecting to a television set to record television programs on videotape cassettes for later playing. Also called **videorecorder, VCR.**

vid·e·o·disc (vid′ē ō disk′), *n.* a disk on which motion pictures and sound are recorded for later reproduction on a player, esp. on an ordinary television screen. Also, **vid′e·o·disk′.**

vid′eo game′, any of various electronic games that involve moving or movable images controlled by the player on a TV screen.

vid·e·o·gen·ic (vid′ē ō jen′ik), *adj.* telegenic. [VIDEO + -GENIC]

vid·e·o·tape (vid′ē ō tāp′), *n., v.,* **-taped, -tap·ing.** —*n.* **1.** electromagnetic tape on which the electronic impulses produced by the video and audio portions of a television program, motion picture, etc., are recorded by special equipment. —*v.t.* **2.** to record on videotape. Also, **vid′e·o·tape′.**

vi·de post (wē′de pōst; *Eng.* vī′dē pōst′), *Latin.* see after or further (used esp. to refer a reader to parts of a text).

vi·de su·pra (wē′de sōō′prä; *Eng.* vī′dē sōō′prə), *Latin.* see above (used esp. to refer a reader to parts of a text).

vi·dette (vi det′), *n.* vedette.

vi·de ut su·pra (wē′de ōōt sōō′prä; *Eng.* vī′dē ut sōō′prə), *Latin.* see as (stated) above (used esp. to refer a reader to parts of a text).

Vi·dev·dat (vi dāv′dät), *n.* *Zoroastrianism.* Vendidad.

vid·i·con (vid′ə kon′), *n.* *Television.* a camera tube in which a charge-density pattern is formed on a photoconductive surface scanned by a beam of low-velocity electrons for transmission as signals. [b. VID(EO) and ICON(OSCOPE)]

Vi·dor (vī′dôr, -dōr), *n.* **1. King (Wallis),** 1894–1982, U.S. motion-picture director and producer. **2.** a town in SE Texas. 4938 (1960).

vi·du·i·ty (vi dōō′i tē, -dyōō′-), *n.* quality, state, or period of being a widow. [late ME (Scot) *viduite* < L *viduitās,* equiv. to *vidu(a)* WIDOW + *-itās* -ITY]

vid·ya (vid′yä), *n.* *Hinduism, Buddhism.* transcendental knowledge leading toward Brahman. Cf. **avidya.** [< Skt *vidyā* knowledge]

vie (vī), *v.,* **vied, vy·ing.** —*v.i.* **1.** to strive in competition or rivalry with another; contend for superiority: *Swimmers from many nations were vying for the title.* —*v.t.* **2.** *Archaic.* to put forward in competition or rivalry. **3.** *Obs.* to stake in card playing. [by aphesis < MF *envier* to raise the stake (at cards), OF: to challenge, provoke < L *invītāre* to INVITE] —**vi′er,** *n.*

Vi·en·na (vē en′ə), *n.* **1.** a port in and the capital of Austria, in the NE part, on the Danube. 1,627,034 (1961). German, **Wien. 2.** a town in W West Virginia. 9381 (1960).

Vien′na Interna′tional, a socialist organization formed in Vienna in 1921 and merged in 1923 with the Second International to form the Labor and Socialist International. Cf. **international** (def. 6).

Vien′na sau′sage, a small frankfurter, often served as an hors d'oeuvre.

Vienne (vyen), *n.* **1.** a city in SE France, on the Rhone River, S of Lyons: Roman ruins. 28,163 (1962). **2.** a department in W France. 331,619 (1962); 2720 sq. mi. *Cap.:* Poitiers.

Vi·en·nese (vē′ə nēz′, -nēs′), *adj., n., pl.* **-nese.** —*adj.* **1.** of, pertaining to, or characteristic of Vienna: *a Viennese waltz; a Viennese café.* —*n.* **2.** a native or inhabitant of Vienna. [VIENN(A) + -ESE]

Vien·tiane (vyen tyän′), *n.* a city in NW Laos, on the Mekong River: administrative capital. 60,000 (est. 1960). Cf. **Luang Prabang.**

Vie·reck (vēr′ek), *n.* **Peter,** born 1916, U.S. poet and historian.

Vie′ren·deel truss′ (vir′ən dāl′), a frame or beam having rigid joints between the verticals and the chords and no diagonal members. Also called **Vie′rendeel gird′er.** [named after M. *Vierendeel,* 19th-century Belgian engineer]

Vi·et (vē et′, vyet), *Informal.* —*n.* **1.** Vietnam. —*adj.* **2.** Vietnamese.

Vie·ta (vyā′tə), *n.* a crater in the third quadrant of the face of the moon: about 50 miles in diameter.

vi et ar·mis (wē′ et är′mēs; *Eng.* vī′ et är′mis), *Latin.* with force and with arms.

Vi·et·cong (vē′et kông′, vē et′-, vyet′-), *n., pl.* **-cong,** *adj.* —*n.* **1.** a Communist-led army and guerrilla force in South Vietnam during the Vietnam War, supported largely by North Vietnam. **2.** a member or supporter of this force. —*adj.* **3.** of or pertaining to this force or one of its members or supporters. Also, **Vi′et Cong′.** [short for Vietnamese *Viet Nam Cong San* Vietnamese Communist]

Vi·et·minh (vē′et min′, vē et′-, vyet′-), *n.* **1.** a Vietnamese, Communist-led organization whose forces fought against the Japanese and esp. against the French in Indochina: officially in existence 1941–51. **2.** (*construed as pl.*) the leaders, supporters, and fighters of this organization. —*adj.* **3.** of or pertaining to the Vietminh. Also, **Vi′et Minh′.** [short for Vietnamese *Viet Nam Doc Lap Dong Minh Hoi* Vietnam Independence League]

Vi·et·nam (vē′et näm′, -nam′, vē et′-, vyet′-), *n.* a country in SE Asia, comprising the former states of Annam, Tonkin, and Cochin-China: formerly part of French Indochina; divided into North Vietnam and South Vietnam during the Vietnam War but now reunified. 47,500,000 (est. 1977); 126,104 sq. mi. *Cap.:* Hanoi. Also, **Vi′et Nam′.**

Vi·et·nam·ese (vē et′nä mēz′, -mēs′, -nə-, vyet′-), *n., pl.* **-ese,** *adj.* —*n.* **1.** a native or inhabitant of Vietnam. **2.** Formerly, **Annamese, Annamite.** an Austroasiatic language that is the official language of Vietnam. —*adj.* **3.** of or pertaining to Vietnam or its inhabitants. [VIETNAM + -ESE]

Vi′etnam′ War′, a conflict, from 1954 to 1975, between South Vietnam (aided by the U.S., South Korea, Australia, the Philippines, Thailand, and New Zealand) and the Vietcong and North Vietnam (aided by Communist China, the U.S.S.R., and other nations).

Vi·ë·tor (fē′ā tôr′), *n.* **Wil·helm** (vil′helm), 1850–1918, German philologist and phonetician.

Vieux·temps (*Fr.* vyœ tän′), *n.* **Hen·ri Fran·çois Jo·seph** (*Fr.* än rē′ frän swa′ zhô zef′), 1820–81, Belgian violinist and composer.

view (vyōō), *n.* **1.** an instance of seeing or beholding; visual inspection. **2.** sight; vision. **3.** range of sight or vision: *Several running deer came into the view of the hunters.* **4.** a sight or prospect of a landscape, the sea, etc.: *His apartment affords a view of the park.* **5.** a picture or photograph of something: *The postcard bears a view of Mt. Vesuvius.* **6.** a particular aspect of something: *As seen from a practical view, the situation presents several problems.* **7.** mental contemplation, examination, or survey: *a view of existing commitments.* **8.** contemplation or consideration of a matter with reference to action: *a project in view.* **9.** aim, intention, or purpose. **10.** prospect; expectation: *The view for the future in his occupation is gloomy.* **11.** a sight afforded of something from a position stated or qualified: *a bird's-eye view.* **12.** a general account or description of a subject. **13.** a particular way of regarding something: *to take a cheerful view.* **14.** a conception of a thing; opinion; theory: *His view was not supported by the facts.* **15.** a survey; inspection: *a view of the Restoration comedy.* **16. in view, a.** within range of vision. **b.** under consideration. **c.** as an end sought: *She went over the material with the scholarship examination in view.* **17. in view of,** in consideration of; on account of: *In view of the circumstances, it seems best to wait until tomorrow to call.* **18. on view,** in a place for public inspection; on exhibition: *The latest models of automobiles are now on view.* **19. with a view to, a.** with the aim or intention of. **b.** with the expectation or hope of: *They saved their money with a view to being able to buy a house someday.* —*v.t.* **20.** to see; behold: *to view a movie; to view a body.* **21.** to look at; survey; inspect: *to view the construction of a road.* **22.** to contemplate mentally; consider: *to view the repercussions of a decision.* **23.** to regard in a particular light or as specified: *She views every minor setback as a disaster.* **24.** *Fox Hunting.* to sight (a fox). [late ME *v(i)ewe* < AF, equiv. to MF *veue* sight < VL **vidūta,* n. use of fem. of **vidūtus,* r. L *vīsus,* ptp. of *vidēre* to see]

—**Syn. 4.** VIEW, PROSPECT, SCENE, VISTA refer to a landscape or perspective. VIEW is a general word, referring to whatever lies open to sight: *a fine view of the surrounding country.* PROSPECT suggests a sweeping and often distant view, as from a place of vantage: *a beautiful prospect to the south.* SCENE suggests an organic unity in the details such as is to be found in a picture: *a woodland scene.* VISTA suggests a long narrow view, as along an avenue between rows of trees: *a pleasant vista.* **9.** object, design, end, intent. **14.** belief, judgment, estimation, assessment, impression, valuation. See **opinion. 20.** witness, contemplate, regard.

view·a·ble (vyōō′ə bəl), *adj.* **1.** capable of being viewed; visible. **2.** having sufficient interest to warrant being seen; worthy of being viewed: *a viewable movie.* [VIEW + -ABLE]

view′ cam′era, a camera equipped with a lens mount and film holder that can be raised or set at an angle, a bellows that can be additionally extended, and a back that has a ground glass for focusing, used especially for portraits and landscapes.

view·er (vyōō′ər), *n.* **1.** a person or thing that views. **2.** a person who watches television, esp. a devotee of television or of a particular kind of television program: *a weekly show aimed at teenage viewers.* **3.** any of various optical devices to facilitate viewing, esp. one that is small and boxlike with a magnifying lens, and sometimes a light source, in which a photographic transparency may be viewed. **4.** *Informal.* an eyepiece or viewfinder. **5.** an official inspector of property, public works, or the like. [VIEW + -ER¹]

view·find·er (vyōō′fīn′dər), *n.* *Photog.* finder (def. 2). [VIEW + FINDER]

view′ halloa′, *Fox Hunting.* the shout made by a hunter on seeing a fox break cover.

view·less (vyōō′lis), *adj.* **1.** that cannot be seen; invisible. **2.** without an opinion or opinions. [VIEW + -LESS] —**view′less·ly,** *adv.*

view′ mark′, a mark stamped on antique armor or metalwork to indicate inspection and approval by the guild or by officials at the place of manufacture.

view·point (vyōō′point′), *n.* **1.** a place affording a view of something; position of observation: *to sketch a river from the viewpoint of a bluff.* **2.** an attitude of mind, or the circumstances of an individual that conduce to such an attitude: *new marketing techniques seen from the consumer's viewpoint.* [alter. of *point of view,* modeled on *standpoint*]

Views of Mt. Fuji, a series of wood-block prints by Hokusai.

view·y (vyōō′ē), *adj.,* **view·i·er, view·i·est.** *Informal.* **1.** having impractical views; speculative; visionary. **2.** eye-catching; showy. [VIEW + -Y¹]

Vi·gée-Le·brun (vē zhā lə brœn′), *n.* **(Ma·rie Anne) É·li·sa·beth** (ma rē′ an ā lē za bet′), 1755–1842, French painter.

vi·ges·i·mal (vī jes′ə məl), *adj.* **1.** of, pertaining to, or based on twenty. **2.** twentieth. **3.** proceeding by twenties. [< L *vīgēsim(us),* var. (with *g* of *vīgintī* twenty) of *vīcēsimus, vīcensimus* twentieth + -AL¹]

vi·ges·i·mo (vī jes′ə mō′), *n., pl.* **-mos,** *adj.* twentymo. [< L]

vi·ges·i·mo-quar·to (vī jes′ə mō kwôr′tō), *n., pl.* **-tos,** *adj.* *Bookbinding.* twenty-fourmo.

vi·gi·a (vi jē′ə; *Sp.* bē hē′ä), *n., pl.* **-gi·as** (-jē′əz; *Sp.* -hē′äs). **1.** a warning mark made on a navigational chart, indicating a hazard the exact location of which is unknown or the existence of which is uncertain. **2.** an unknown object or phenomenon sighted in the water and regarded as a possible navigational hazard. [< Sp *vigía* lookout, reef, prob. < Pg *vigia,* back formation from *vigiar* < L *vigilāre* to watch; see VIGILANT]

vig·il (vij′əl), *n.* **1.** wakefulness maintained for any reason during the normal hours for sleeping. **2.** a watch or a period of watchful attention maintained at night or at other times: *The nurse kept her vigil at the bedside of the dying man.* **3.** a period of wakefulness from inability to sleep. **4.** *Eccles.* **a.** a devotional watching, or keeping awake, during the customary hours of sleep. **b.** Sometimes, **vigils.** a nocturnal devotional exercise or service, esp. on the eve before a church festival. **c.** the eve, or day and night, before a church festival, esp. an eve which is a fast. [ME *vigil(i)e* < AF < ML *vigilia* eve of a holy day, special use of L *vigilia* watchfulness, equiv. to *vigil-* watchful + *-ia* -Y³]

vig·i·lance (vij′ə ləns), *n.* **1.** state or quality of being vigilant; watchfulness: *Vigilance is required in the event of treachery.* **2.** *Pathol.* insomnia. [alter. (-ANCE for -ANCY) of obs. *vigilancy,* equiv. to *vigil-* (base of *vigilāre* to be watchful) + *-entia* -ANCY]

vig′ilance commit′tee, *U.S.* **1.** an unauthorized committee of citizens organized for the maintenance of order and the summary punishment of crime in the absence of regular or efficient courts. **2.** *Hist.* (in the South) an organization of citizens using extralegal means to control or intimidate Negroes and abolitionists, and, during the Civil War, to suppress loyalty to the Union.

vig·i·lant (vij′ə lənt), *adj.* **1.** keenly watchful to detect danger; wary: *a vigilant policeman.* **2.** ever awake and alert; sleeplessly watchful. [< L *vigilant-* (s. of *vigilāns*), prp. of *vigilāre* to be watchful. See VIGIL, -ANT] —**vig′i·lant·ly,** *adv.* —**vig′i·lant·ness,** *n.*

—**Syn. 2.** awake, sleepless. See **alert.** —**Ant. 1.** careless.

vig·i·lan·te (vij′ə lan′tē), *n.* *U.S.* a member of a vigilance committee. [< Sp: vigilant]

vig·i·lan·tism (vij′ə lən tiz′əm), *n.* a form of conduct or set of attitudes characteristic of or suggestive of vigilantes, esp. in being militant and full of suspicions. [VIGILANT(E) + -ISM]

Vi·gil·i·us (vi jil′ē əs), *n.* died A.D. 555, pope 537–555.

vi·gin·til·lion (vī′jin til′yən), *n., pl.* **-lions,** (*as after a numeral*) **-lion,** *adj.* —*n.* **1.** a cardinal number represented in the United States and France by one followed by 63 zeros and in Great Britain and Germany by one followed by 120 zeros. —*adj.* **2.** amounting to one vigintillion in number. [< L *vīgint(ī)* twenty + (M)ILLION] —**vi/gin·til/lionth,** *adj.*

vi·gnette (vin yet′), *n., v.,* **-gnet·ted, -gnet·ting.** —*n.* **1.** a decorative design or small illustration used on the title page of a book or at the beginning or end of a chapter. **2.** an engraving, drawing, photograph, or the like that is shaded off gradually at the edges so as to leave no definite line at the border. **3.** a decorative design representing branches, leaves, grapes, or the like, as in a manuscript. **4.** any small, pleasing picture or view. **5.** a small, graceful literary sketch. —*v.t.* **6.** *Photog.* to finish (a picture, photograph, etc.) in the manner of a vignette. [< F: lit., little vine (see VINE, -ETTE); so called from vinelike decorations in early books] —**vi·gnett/ist,** *n.*

vi·gnett·er (vin yet′ər), *n. Photog.* a device for blurring the edges of a photographic image so as to fade them into a plain surrounding area. [VIGNETTE + -ER[1]]

Vi·gno·la (vē nyô′lä), *n.* **Gia·co·mo da** (jä′kô mô dä), (*Giacomo Barocchio* or *Barozzi*), 1507–73, Italian architect.

Vi·gny (vē nyē′), *n.* **Al·fred Vic·tor de** (al fred′ vēk tôr′ də), 1797–1863, French poet, novelist, and dramatist.

Vi·go (vē′gō; *Sp.* bē′gô), **1. Bay of,** an inlet of the Atlantic, in NW Spain. 19 mi. long. **2.** a seaport on this bay: naval battle 1702. 146,320 (est. 1960).

vig·or (vig′ər), *n.* **1.** active strength or force. **2.** healthy physical or mental energy or power; vitality. **3.** energetic activity; energy; intensity: *The economic recovery has given the country a new vigor. The dance began again with renewed vigor.* **4.** force of healthy growth in any living matter or organism, as a plant. **5.** active or effective force, esp. legal validity. Also, *esp. Brit.,* **vig/our.** [late ME *vigo(u)r* < AF (equiv. to MF *vigeur*) < L *vigor* force, energy, equiv. to *vig(ēre)* (to) be vigorous, thrive + *-or* -OR[1]] —**vig/or·less,** *adj.*

vig·or·ish (vig′ər ish), *n. Slang.* **1.** a charge paid on a bet, as to a bookie. **2.** interest paid to a moneylender, esp. a usurer. [?]

vi·go·ro·so (vig′ə rō′sō; *It.* vē′gô rô′zô), *adj.* (a musical direction) vigorous or spirited in manner. [< It; c. VIGOROUS]

vig·or·ous (vig′ər əs), *adj.* **1.** full of or characterized by vigor: *to make a vigorous effort.* **2.** strong; active; robust: *a vigorous youngster.* **3.** energetic; forceful: *vigorous steps; a vigorous personality.* **4.** powerful in action or effect: *vigorous law enforcement.* **5.** growing well, as a plant. [ME < OF < ML *vigorōs(us).* See VIGOR, -OUS] —**vig/or·ous·ly,** *adv.* —**vig/or·ous·ness,** *n.*
—**Syn. 2.** sturdy, sound, healthy. See **active. 3.** powerful, forceful. —**Ant. 1–5.** weak.

vi·gou·reux (vig′ə rōō′; *Fr.* vē gōō rœ′), *n.* a fabric having a dark and light pattern produced by the vigoureux printing method.

vigoureux/ print/ing, a printing method in which worsted fibers are printed with the desired color while in sliver form and then processed into yarn, producing a mixed color in the spun yarn and woven fabric. [named after *Vigoureux,* 19th-century French inventor]

Vi·grid (vē′grid), *n. Scand. Myth.* the field on which the last battle between the gods and their enemies is destined to be fought at the time of Ragnarok.

vi·ha·ra (vi här′ə), *n.* **1.** a meeting place of Buddhist monks. **2.** a Buddhist monastery. **3.** (*cap.*) Also called **Brahma Vihara.** one of the four states of mind, namely love, compassion, sympathetic gladness, and equanimity, to be developed by every Buddhist. [< Skt: lit., pastime place]

Vii·pu·ri (vē′pōō rē′), *n.* former name of **Vyborg.**

Vik·i (vik′ē), *n.* a girl's given name, form of **Victoria.** Also, **Vickie, Vicky, Vik/ki.**

Vi·king (vī′king), *n.* **1.** any of the Scandinavian pirates who plundered the northern and western coasts of Europe from the 8th to 10th centuries. **2.** a sea-roving bandit; pirate. Also, **vi/king.** [< Scand; cf. Icel *víkingr;* r. OE *wīcing* pirate; etym. disputed]

vil., village.

vi·la·yet (vē′lä yet′), *n.* a province or main administrative division of Turkey. Also, **eyalet.** [< Turk < Ar *welāyet,* lit., headship, equiv. to *walīy* head + *-et* -ship]

vile (vīl), *adj.,* **vil·er, vil·est. 1.** wretchedly bad: *vile weather; a vile humor.* **2.** highly offensive, unpleasant, or objectionable: *vile slander.* **3.** repulsive or disgusting, as to the senses or feelings: *a vile odor.* **4.** morally debased, depraved, or despicable: *vile thoughts; vile deeds.* **5.** foul; filthy: *vile language.* **6.** poor; wretched: *a vile existence; vile workmanship.* **7.** of mean or low condition: *a vile beggar.* **8.** menial; lowly: *vile tasks.* **9.** degraded; ignominious: *vile servitude.* **10.** of little value or account; paltry: *a vile recompense.* [ME *vil* < OF < L *vīlis* of little worth, base, cheap] —**vile/ly,** *adv.* —**vile/ness,** *n.*
—**Syn. 1.** See **mean**[2]. **3.** repellent. **4.** vicious, evil, iniquitous. **5.** vulgar, obscene. **9, 10.** contemptible. **10.** trivial, trifling. —**Ant. 1.** good. **4.** elevated.

Vi·li (vil′ē), *n. Scand. Myth.* a brother of Odin.

vil·i·fy (vil′ə fī′), *v.t.,* **-fied, -fy·ing. 1.** to speak ill of; defame; slander. **2.** *Obs.* to make vile. [late ME < LL *vīlificāre.* See VILE, -FY] —**vil/i·fi·ca/tion,** *n.* —**vil/i·fi/er,** *n.* —**vil/i·fy/ing·ly,** *adv.*
—**Syn. 1.** depreciate, disparage, slander, calumniate, malign, abuse, asperse, blacken. —**Ant. 1.** commend.

vil·i·pend (vil′ə pend′), *v.t.* **1.** to regard or treat as of little value or account. **2.** to vilify; depreciate. [< LL *vīlipend(ere),* equiv. to L *vīli(s)* cheap (see VILE) + *pendere* to consider (see PEND)] —**vil/i·pend/er,** *n.*

vil·la (vil′ə), *n.* **1.** a country residence or estate, esp. one that is large and imposing. **2.** any imposing or pretentious residence, esp. one in the country or suburbs maintained as a second residence by a wealthy person. **3.** *Brit.* a detached or semidetached dwelling house, usually suburban. [< It or L: a country house, farm, dim. of *vīcus* WICK[3]] —**vil/la·like/,** *adj.*

Vil·la (vē′ə; *Sp.* bē′yä), *n.* **Fran·cis·co** (frän sēs′kô), (*Doroteo Arango, "Pancho Villa"*), 1877–1923, Mexican general and revolutionist.

Vi·lla Cis·ne·ros (bē′lyä thēs ne′rôs, bē′yä sēs ne′rôs), a town in and the capital of Río de Oro, in Spanish Sahara, on the NW coast of Africa. 1011 (1950).

vil·la·dom (vil′ə dəm), *n. Brit.* **1.** villas collectively. **2.** suburban life and society; suburbia. [VILLA + -DOM]

vil·lage (vil′ij), *n.* **1.** a small community or group of houses in a rural area, larger than a hamlet and usually smaller than a town, and sometimes (as in parts of the U.S.) incorporated as a municipality. **2.** the inhabitants of such a community collectively. **3.** a group of animal dwellings resembling a village: *a gopher village.* —*adj.* **4.** of, pertaining to, or characteristic of a village: *village life.* [late ME < MF << L *villāticum.* See VILLA, -AGE] —**vil/lage·less,** *adj.* —**vil/lage·y, vil/lag·y,** *adj.*
—**Syn 1.** See **community.**

vil/lage commu/nity, an early form of community organization in which land belonged to the village, the arable land being allotted to the members or households of the community by more or less permanent arrangements and the waste or excess land remaining undivided.

vil·lag·er (vil′i jər), *n.* an inhabitant of a village. [VILLAGE + -ER[1]]

Vil·la·her·mo·sa (bē′yä er mô′sä), *n.* a city in and the capital of Tabasco, in E Mexico. 52,262 (1960).

vil·lain (vil′ən), *n.* **1.** a cruelly malicious person who is involved in or devoted to wickedness or crime; scoundrel. **2.** a character in a play, novel, or the like, who constitutes an important evil agency in the plot. **3.** villein. [ME *vilein, vilain* < MF < LL *villān(us)* a farm servant. See VILLA, -AN]
—**Syn. 1.** knave, rascal, rapscallion, rogue, scamp.

vil·lain·age (vil′ə nij), *n.* villeinage. Also, **vil/lanage.**

vil·lain·ess (vil′ə nis), *n.* a female villain. [VILLAIN + -ESS]

vil·lain·ous (vil′ə nəs), *adj.* **1.** having a cruel, wicked, malicious nature or character. **2.** of, pertaining to, or befitting a villain: *villainous treachery.* **3.** outrageously base, wicked, or vile: *a villainous attack on someone's character.* **4.** very objectionable or unpleasant; bad; wretched: *a villainous storm.* [late ME; see VILLAIN, -OUS] —**vil/lain·ous·ly,** *adv.* —**vil/lain·ous·ness,** *n.*

vil·lain·y (vil′ə nē), *n., pl.* **-lain·ies. 1.** the actions or conduct of a villain; outrageous wickedness. **2.** a villainous act or deed. **3.** *Obs.* villeinage. [ME *vile(i)nie, vilainie* < OF. See VILLAIN, -Y[3]]

Vil·la-Lo·bos (vē′lä lō′bôs, -bōs, vil′ə; *Port.* vē′lyä lô′bōōsh, -bōōs), *n.* **Hei·tor** (ā′tōōr), 1881–1959, Brazilian composer.

vil·la·nel·la (vil′ə nel′ə; *It.* vēl′lä nel′lä), *n., pl.* **-nel·le** (-nel′ē; *It.* -nel′le). a rustic Italian part song without accompaniment. [< It, fem. of *villanello* rural, rustic, equiv. to *villan(a)* peasant, boor (see VILLAIN) + *-ello* -ish]

vil·la·nelle (vil′ə nel′), *n. Pros.* a short poem of fixed form, written in tercets, usually five in number, followed by a final quatrain, all being based on two rhymes. [< F < It; see VILLANELLA]

Vil·la·no·van (vil′ə nō′vən), *adj.* **1.** Also, **Vil/la·no/va.** of or pertaining to the early Iron Age culture of northern Italy, characterized by lake dwellings. —*n.* **2.** a member of this people. [after *Villanova,* a town in NE Italy; see -AN]

Vil/la Park/ (vil′ə), a city in NE Illinois, near Chicago. 20,391 (1960).

Vil·lard (vi lär′, -lärd′), *n.* **Oswald Garrison,** 1872–1949, U.S. journalist and author.

Vil·la Ri·ca (vil′ə rik′ə), a town in W Georgia. 3450 (1960).

Vil·la/ri effect/ (vi lär′ē), *Physics.* the change in magnetic induction that takes place in certain substances when subjected to longitudinal stress. [named after E. *Villari,* 19th-century Italian physicist]

Vil·lars (vē lar′), *n.* **Claude Louis Hec·tor de** (klōd lwē ek tôr′ də), 1653–1734, marshal of France.

vil·lat·ic (vi lat′ik), *adj.* of or pertaining to the country or to a farm; rural. [< L *villātic(us).* See VILLA, -ATE[1], -IC]

Vil·la·vi·cen·cio (bē′yä vē sen′syô), *n.* a city in central Colombia. 43,000 (1962).

Vil·le·da Mo·ra·les (bē ye′thä mô rä′les), *n.* **Ramón** (rä môn′), born 1909?, Honduran diplomat and statesman: president 1957–63.

vil·lein (vil′ən), *n.* a member of a class of partially free persons under the feudal system who were serfs with respect to their lord but had the rights and privileges of freemen with respect to others. Also, **villain.** [ME; see VILLAIN]

vil·lein·age (vil′ə nij), *n.* **1.** the tenure by which a villein held land and tenements from his lord. **2.** the condition or status of a villein. Also, **villainage, villanage, vil/len·age.** [ME *vilenage* < AF, OF. See VILLEIN, -AGE]

vil/lein soc/age, land held by a tenant who rendered to his feudal lord specified duties of a servile nature. Cf. **free socage.**

Ville·neuve (vēl nœv′), *n.* **Pierre Charles Jean Bap·tiste Sil·ves·tre de** (pyer sharl zhäN ba tēst′ sēl ves′trᵊ də), 1763–1806, French admiral.

Ville Platte (vēl′ plat′), a town in central Louisiana. 7512 (1960).

Ville·ur·banne (vēl yr ban′), *n.* a city in E France, near Lyons. 107,630 (1962).

Vil·liers (vil′ərz, vil′yərz), *n.* **1. Frederic,** 1852–1922, English artist and war correspondent. **2. George.** See **Buckingham, 1st Duke of. 3. George.** See **Buckingham, 2nd Duke of.**

vil·li·form (vil′ə fôrm′), *adj.* **1.** having the form of a villus. **2.** shaped and set so as to resemble the pile of velvet, as the teeth of certain fishes. [< NL *villiform(is).* See VILLUS, -FORM]

Vil·lon (vē yôN′), *n.* **1. Fran·çois** (fräN swa′), 1431–63?, French poet. **2. Jacques** (zhäk), (*Gaston Duchamp*), 1875–1963, French painter.

vil·lose (vil′ōs), *adj.* villous. [< L *villōs(us)* shaggy. See VILLUS, -OSE[1]]

vil·los·i·ty (vi los′i tē), *n., pl.* **-ties. 1.** a villous surface or coating. **2.** a number of villi together. **3.** a villus. [VILLOSE + -ITY]

vil·lous (vil′əs), *adj.* **1.** covered with or of the nature of villi. **2.** having villiform processes. **3.** *Bot.* pubescent with long and soft hairs which are not interwoven. [var. of VILLOSE; see -OUS] —**vil/lous·ly,** *adv.*

vil·lus (vil′əs), *n., pl.* **vil·li** (vil′ī). **1.** *Anat.* one of the minute, wormlike, vascular processes on certain membranes, esp. on the mucous membrane of the small intestine, where they serve in absorbing nutriment. **2.** *Bot.* one of the long, soft, straight hairs covering the fruit, flowers, and other parts of certain plants. [< L: shaggy hair]

Vil·ma (vil′mə), *n.* a girl's given name, form of **Wilhelmina.** Also, **Velma.**

Vil·ni·us (vil′nē ōōs′), *n.* a city in and the capital of Lithuania, in the SE part: formerly in the Soviet Union and earlier in Poland. 582,000. Polish, **Wilno.** Russian, **Vil·na** (vyēl′nə; *Eng.* vil′nə).

vim (vim), *n.* lively or energetic spirit; enthusiasm; vitality. [< L, acc. of *vīs* energy, force]

vi·ma·na (vi mä′nə), *n.* a sanctuary of a Brahman temple. [< Skt *vimāna,* lit., a marking out, akin to *vimāti* he marks out, equiv. to *vi-* apart + *māti* he measures]

vi·men (vī′men), *n., pl.* **vim·i·na** (vim′ə nə). *Bot.* a long, flexible shoot of a plant. [< L: osier, withe, twig] —**vim·i·nal** (vim′ə nᵊl), *adj.*

Vim·i·nal (vim′ə nᵊl), *n.* one of the seven hills on which ancient Rome was built.

vi·min·e·ous (vi min′ē əs), *adj. Bot.* **1.** of, like, or producing long, flexible shoots. **2.** of or made of twigs. [< L *vīmineus* made of osiers, equiv. to *vīmin-* (s. of *vīmen*) osier + *-eus* -EOUS]

v. imp., verb impersonal.

vim·pa (vim′pə), *n. Rom. Cath. Ch.* a silk veil worn over the shoulders and extending down the arms and over the hands, worn by acolytes who carry the miter and crosier at a Pontifical Mass. [< ML < Gmc; see WIMPLE]

Vi·my (vē mē′), *n.* a town in N France, N of Arras: battle 1917. 3009 (1962).

vin (vaN), *n., pl.* **vins** (vaN). *French.* wine.

Vin (vin), *n.* a boy's given name, form of **Vincent.**

vin., (in prescriptions) wine. [< L *vīnum*]

vin-, var. of **vini-,** esp. before a vowel.

vi·na (vē′nä), *n.* a musical stringed instrument of India, consisting of a long, hollow, fretted stick to which one, two, or three gourds are attached to increase the resonance. [< Skt; cf. Hindi *bīṇā*]

Vina

vi·na·ceous (vī nā′shəs), *adj.* **1.** of, pertaining to, or resembling wine or grapes. **2.** of the color of red wine. [< L *vīnāceus.* See WINE, -ACEOUS]

Vi·ña del Mar (bē′nyä del mär′), a city in central Chile, near Valparaiso: seaside resort. 126,460 (1960).

vi·naigre (vē ne′grᵊ), *n. French.* vinegar.

vin·ai·grette (vin′ə gret′), *n.* **1.** Also, **vinegarette.** a small, ornamental bottle or box for holding aromatic vinegar, smelling salts, or the like. —*adj.* **2.** (of a food, as asparagus or artichoke) served with a sauce made with vinegar or with vinaigrette sauce. [< F, equiv. to *vinaigre* VINEGAR + *-ette* -ETTE]

vinaigrette/ sauce/, a tart sauce of oil, vinegar, and seasonings, sometimes including chopped capers, pickles, etc., usually served cold with salads.

vi·nasse (vi nas′), *n. Distilling.* the residuum in a still after distillation; slop. [< F < Pr *vinassa* < L *vīnācea,* fem. of *vīnāceus* VINACEOUS]

Vin/a·ya Pit/aka (vin′ə yə), *Buddhism.* See under **Pali Canon.**

vin blanc (vaN bläN′), *pl.* **vins blancs** (vaN bläN′). *French.* See **white wine.**

Vin·ca (ving′kə), *n.* the genus of plants comprising the periwinkles. [< NL, shortened from L *pervinca* periwinkle]

Vince (vins), *n.* a boy's given name, form of **Vincent.**

Vin·cennes (vin senz′; *for 2 also Fr.* vaN sen′), *n.* **1.** a city in SW Indiana, on the Wabash: the first permanent settlement in Indiana, 1702. 18,046 (1960). **2.** a city in N France, near Paris. 50,499 (1962).

Vin·cent (vin′sənt), *n.* **1. Saint,** died A.D. 304, Spanish martyr: patron saint of winegrowers. **2.** a boy's given name.

Vin·cent de Paul (vin′sənt də pôl′; *Fr.* vaN säN′ də pôl′), **Saint,** 1576–1660, French Roman Catholic priest and reformer.

Vin·cen·tian (vin sen′shən), *Rom. Cath. Ch.* —*n.* **1.** Also called **Lazarist.** a member of the "Congregation of the Mission," founded in France in 1625, engaged chiefly in conducting missions and clerical seminaries. —*adj.* **2.** of or pertaining to St. Vincent de Paul or the Vincentians. [VINCENT (DE PAUL) + -IAN]

Vin/cent's angi/na, *Pathol.* a disease characterized by ulceration of the mucosa of the tonsils, pharynx, and mouth, and by the development of a membrane, caused by a bacillus and spirillum. Also called **Vin/cent's infec/tion, trench mouth.** [named after J. H. *Vincent* (1862–1950), French physician]

Vin·ci (vin′chē; *It.* vēn′chē), *n.* **Le·o·nar·do da** (lē′ə när′dō də, lā′-; *It.* le′ô när′dô dä), 1452–1519, Italian painter, sculptor, architect, musician, engineer, mathematician, and scientist.

vin·ci·ble (vin′sə bəl), *adj.* capable of being conquered or overcome: *vincible fears.* [< L *vincibil(is),* equiv. to *vinc(ere)* (to) overcome + *-ibilis* -IBLE] —**vin/ci·bil/i·ty, vin/ci·ble·ness,** *n.*

vin·cit om·ni·a ve·ri·tas (wing′kit ōm′ni ä′ wē′ri täs′; *Eng.* vin′sit om′nē ə ver′i tas′), *Latin.* truth conquers all things.

vin·cu·lum (ving′kyə ləm), *n., pl.* **-la** (-lə). **1.** a bond signifying union or unity; tie. **2.** *Math.* a stroke or brace drawn over a quantity consisting of several members or terms, as $\overline{a+b}$, in order to show that they are to be considered together. [< L: fetter]

vin·cu·lum ma·tri·mo·ni·i (wing′kōō lōōm′ mä′tri mō′ni ē′; *Eng.* ving′kyə ləm ma′tri mō′nē ī′), *Latin.* the bond of matrimony.

Vin/dhya Hills/ (vind′yä), a mountain range in central India, N of the Narbada River.

Vin′dhya Pra′desh (prä′desh), a former state in central India: now part of Madhya Pradesh.

vin·di·ca·ble (vin′də kə bəl), *adj.* capable of being vindicated: *a vindicable expedient.* [< LL *vindicābil(is),* equiv. to L *vindicā(re)* (see VINDICATE) + *-bilis* -BLE] —**vin′di·ca·bil′i·ty,** *n.*

vin·di·cate (vin′də kāt′), *v.t.,* **-cat·ed, -cat·ing. 1.** to clear, as from an accusation, imputation, suspicion, or the like: *to vindicate someone's honor.* **2.** to afford justification for; justify: *Subsequent events vindicated his policy.* **3.** to uphold or justify by argument or evidence: *to vindicate a claim.* **4.** to assert, maintain, or defend (a right, cause, etc.) against opposition. **5.** to claim for oneself or another. **6.** *Roman and Civil Law.* to regain possession, under claim of title of property through legal procedure, or to assert one's right to possession. **7.** to get revenge for; avenge. **8.** *Obs.* to deliver from; liberate. **9.** *Obs.* to punish. [< L *vindicāt(us)* (ptp. of *vindicāre* to lay legal claim to (property), to free (someone) from servitude (by claiming him as free), to protect, avenge, punish), equiv. to *vindic-* (s. of *vindex* claimant, protector, avenger) + *-ātus* -ATE[1]] —**vin′di·ca′tor,** *n.*
—**Syn. 1.** exonerate. **3, 4.** support.

vin·di·ca·tion (vin′də kā′shən), *n.* **1.** the act of vindicating. **2.** the state of being vindicated. **3.** defense; excuse; justification: *He claimed poverty as a vindication for his thievery.* **4.** something that vindicates: *The subsequent happenings were his vindication.* [< L *vindicātiōn-* (s. of *vindicātiō*), equiv. to *vindicāt(us)* (see VINDICATE) + *-iōn-* -ION]

vin·di·ca·to·ry (vin′də kə tōr′ē, -tôr′ē), *adj.* **1.** tending or serving to vindicate. **2.** punitive; retributive: *vindicatory killings.* Also, **vin·dic·a·tive** (vin dik′ə tiv, vin′də kā′-). [VINDICATE + -ORY[1]]

vin·dic·tive (vin dik′tiv), *adj.* **1.** disposed or inclined to revenge; vengeful: *a vindictive person.* **2.** proceeding from or showing a revengeful spirit: *vindictive rumors.* [< L *vindict(a)* vengeance, fem. of **vindictus* (ptp. of **vindīcere* for *vindicāre;* see VINDICATE) + -IVE] —**vin·dic′tive·ly,** *adv.* —**vin·dic′tive·ness,** *n.*
—**Syn. 1.** unforgiving. See **spiteful.** —**Ant. 1.** forgiving.

vin du pays (vaN dy pā ē′), *French.* wine of the country or region; local wine.

vine (vīn), *n.* **1.** any plant having a long, slender stem that trails or creeps on the ground or climbs by winding itself about a support or holding fast with tendrils or claspers. **2.** the stem of any such plant. **3.** a grape plant. [ME < OF *vi(g)ne* < L *vīnea* vine(yard), equiv. to *vīn(um)* WINE + *-ea,* fem. of *-eus* -EOUS] —**vine′less,** *adj.* —**vine′like′,** *adj.*

vine′ bow′er (bou′ər), a slender, woody vine *Clematis viticella,* of Eurasia, having rose-purple or violet-colored flowers with yellow stamens.

vine′ cac′tus, the ocotillo, *Fouquieria splendens.*

vined (vīnd), *adj.* covered or decorated with vines or representations of vines: *a vined brick wall; vined wallpaper.* [VINE + -ED[3]]

vine·dress·er (vīn′dres′ər), *n.* a person who tends or cultivates vines, esp. grapevines. [VINE + DRESSER[1]]

vin·e·gar (vin′ə gər), *n.* **1.** a sour liquid consisting of dilute and impure acetic acid, obtained by acetous fermentation from wine, cider, beer, ale, or the like: used as a condiment, preservative, etc. **2.** *Pharm.* a solution of a medicinal substance in dilute acetic acid, or vinegar. **3.** sour or irritable speech, manner, or countenance: *His retort was delivered with a strong note of vinegar.* **4.** *Informal.* vigor; high spirits; vim. [ME *vinegre* < OF, equiv. to *vin* WINE + *egre, aigre* sour (see EAGER)] —**vin′e·gar·like′,** *adj.*

vin′egar eel′, a minute nematode worm, *Anguillula aceti,* found in vinegar, fermenting paste, etc. Also called **vin′egar worm′.**

vin·e·gar·ette (vin′ə gə ret′), *n.* vinaigrette (def. 1).

vin′egar fly′, any fly of the family *Drosophilidae,* the larvae of which feed on fruit and decaying vegetation. Also called **fruit fly.**

vin·e·gar·ish (vin′ə gər ish), *adj.* resembling vinegar, as in sourness or acidity: *a vinegarish odor; a vinegarish disposition.* [VINEGAR + -ISH[1]]

vin·e·gar·roon (vin′ə gə ro͞on′), *n.* a large whip scorpion, *Mastigoproctus giganteus,* of the southern U.S. and Mexico, which, when disturbed, emits a volatile fluid having a vinegary odor. [< MexSp *vinagrón,* equiv. to Sp *vinagr(e)* vinegar (< F *vinaigre* VINEGAR) + *-ón* aug. suffix]

Vinegarroon (Length 2½ in.)

vin·e·gar·weed (vin′ə gər wēd′), *n.* an herb, *Trichostema lanceolatum,* of the western coast of the U.S. having blue flowers and growing in dry, sandy soil. Also called **camphorweed.** [VINEGAR + WEED[1]]

vin·e·gar·y (vin′ə gə rē), *adj.* **1.** of the nature of or resembling vinegar; sour; acid: *a vinegary taste.* **2.** having a disagreeable character or manner; crabbed; ill-tempered: *a vinegary person.* [VINEGAR + -Y[1]]

vine·land (vīn′land′), *n.* land particularly suited to the growing of vines. [VINE + LAND]

Vine·land (vīn′lənd), *n.* **1.** a city in S New Jersey. 37,685 (1960). **2.** Vinland.

vine′ ma′ple, a maple, *Acer circinatum,* of the western coast of North America, often having vinelike or prostrate stems that form dense thickets.

vin·er·y (vī′nə rē), *n., pl.* **-er·ies. 1.** a place or enclosure in which vines, esp. grapevines, are grown. **2.** vines collectively. [VINE + -ERY, r. ME *vinary* < ML *vīnāri(um),* n. use of neut. of L *vīnārius* of WINE; see -ARY]

vine′ snake′, any of several slender, arboreal colubrid snakes of the genus *Oxybelis,* ranging from southern Arizona to northern Argentina.

Vin·e·thene (vin′ə thēn′), *n. Pharm., Trademark.* See **vinyl ether.**

vine·yard (vin′yərd), *n.* **1.** a plantation of grapevines, esp. one producing grapes for wine-making. **2.** a sphere of activity, esp. on a high spiritual plane. [ME (see VINE, YARD[2]; r. *win(e)yard,* OE *wīngeard*] —**vine′yard·ist,** *n.*

vingt-et-un (*Fr.* vaN tā œN′), *n. Cards.* blackjack (def. 7b). [< F: lit., twenty-one]

vini-, a learned borrowing from Latin meaning "wine," used in the formation of compound words: *viniculture.* Also, **vin-, vino-.** [< L, comb. form of *vīnum*]

vi·nic (vī′nik, vin′ik), *adj.* of, pertaining to, found in, or derived from wine: *a vinic odor.* [< L *vīn(um)* WINE + -IC]

vin·i·cul·ture (vin′ə kul′chər), *n.* the science or study of making wines. [VINI- + CULTURE] —**vin′i·cul′tur·al,** *adj.* —**vin′i·cul′tur·ist,** *n.*

Vi·nie (vī′nē), *n.* a girl's given name. Also, **Viny.**

vi·nif·er·a (vī nif′ər ə), *adj.* **1.** of, pertaining to, or derived from a European grape, *Vitis vinifera,* cultivated in the western U.S. for table use and for making wine and raisins. —*n.* **2.** a vinifera grape. [< NL, fem. of L *vīnifer* wine-producing. See VINI-, -FER]

vi·nif·er·ous (vī nif′ər əs), *adj.* suitable for or productive of wine: *a viniferous variety of grape.* [< L *vīnifer* (see VINIFERA) + -OUS]

vin·i·fi·ca·tor (vin′ə fə kā′tər), *n.* a condenser for alcohol vapors escaping from fermenting wine. [VINI- + L *-ficātor* maker (see -FIC, -ATE[1], -OR[2])]

Vi·ni·ta (vi nē′tə), *n.* a town in NE Oklahoma. 6027 (1960).

Vin·land (vin′lənd), *n.* a region in E North America variously identified as a place between Newfoundland and Virginia: visited and described by Norsemen ab. A.D. 1000. Also, **Vineland.**

Vin·nie (vin′ē), *n.* a boy's given name, form of Vincent. Also, **Vinny.**

Vin·ni·tsa (vēn′i tsä), *n.* a city in the central Ukraine, in the SW Soviet Union in Europe, on the Bug River. 144,000 (est. 1964).

Vin·ny (vin′ē), *n.* a boy's given name, form of **Vincent.** Also, **Vinnie.**

vi·no (vē′nō), *n., pl.* **-nos.** *Informal.* wine; specifically, red Italian wine, as chianti. [< It]

vino-, var. of **vini-.**

vi·no de pas·to (vē′nō də päs′tō; *Sp.* bē′nō de päs′tō), a pale, dry sherry of Spain. [< Sp: lit., everyday (table) wine]

vin·om·e·ter (vi nom′i tər, vī-), *n.* a hydrometer for measuring the percentage of alcohol in wine. [VINO- + -METER]

vin or·di·naire (vaN ôr dē ner′), *pl.* **vins or·di·naires** (vaN zôr dē ner′). *French.* inexpensive table wine. [lit., ordinary wine]

vi·nos·i·ty (vī nos′i tē), *n.* the collective characteristics of a wine. [< L *vīnōsitās,* equiv. to *vīnōs(us)* VINOUS + *-itās* -ITY]

vi·nous (vī′nəs), *adj.* **1.** of the nature of or resembling wine. **2.** of, pertaining to, or characteristic of wine: *a vinous fragrance.* **3.** produced by, indicative of, or given to indulgence in wine. **4.** wine red; wine-colored: *a vinous hue.* [< L *vīnōs(us),* equiv. to *vīn(um)* WINE + *-ōsus* -OSE[1], -OUS]

vin rouge (vaN ro͞ozh′), *French.* See **red wine.**

Vin·son (vin′sən), *n.* **Frederick Moore,** 1890–1953, U.S. jurist: Chief Justice of the U.S. 1946–53.

vin·tage (vin′tij), *n., adj., v.,* **-taged, -tag·ing.** —*n.* **1.** the wine from a particular harvest or crop. **2.** the annual produce of the grape harvest, esp. with reference to the wine obtained. **3.** an exceptionally fine wine from the crop of a good year, designated and sold as the produce of that year. **4.** act of gathering ripe grapes. **5.** the season of gathering grapes, or of winemaking. **6.** act or process of producing wine; winemaking. **7.** wine, esp. good wine. **8.** the output of a particular time, or the style of something produced then: *a hat of last year's vintage.* **9.** degree of maturity; age: *a man of 50 years' vintage.* —*adj.* **10.** of or pertaining to wines or winemaking. **11.** being of a specified vintage: *Vintage wines are usually more expensive than nonvintage wines.* **12.** being or having the best of a particular quality, workmanship, etc.: *They praised the play as vintage O'Neill.* **13.** being of a past era; representing the high quality of another time: *vintage cars; the nostalgia evoked by vintage movies.* **14.** old-fashioned; obsolete; outdated: *a vintage style of acting that seems laughable today.* —*v.t.* **15.** to gather or harvest (grapes) for wine-making: *The muscats were vintaged too early.* **16.** to make (wine) from grapes: *a region that vintages a truly great champagne.* —*v.i.* **17.** to harvest grapes for wine-making: *They had vintaged too late in the season.* [late ME < AF, equiv. to *vint(er)* VINTNER + *-age* -AGE; r. ME *vindage, vendage* < AF, by dissimilation of OF *vendange* < L *vindēmia* grape-gathering, equiv. to *vīn(um)* grape, WINE + *-dēmia* a taking away (*dēm(ere)* (to) take from, equiv. to *dē-* DE- + *em(ere)* (to) buy (see REDEEM) + *-ia* -Y[3])]

vin·tag·er (vin′tə jər), *n.* a person who helps in the harvest of grapes for winemaking. [VINTAGE + -ER[1]]

vin′tage wine′, a wine, usually of superior quality, made from selected grapes of a certain type, region, and year, then dated and usually stored for aging.

vin′tage year′, the year of production of a vintage wine.

vint·ner (vint′nər), *n.* **1.** a person who makes wine. **2.** the owner of a winery. **3.** *Chiefly Brit.* a wine merchant or dealer. [ME *vint(e)ner,* deriv. of *vin(e)ter* < AF; OF *vinetier* < ML *vīnetārius,* equiv. to L *vīnēt(um)* vineyard (*vīn(um)* WINE + *-ētum* collective suffix) + *-ārius* -ARY]

Vin·ton (vin′tən), *n.* **1.** a town in central Iowa. 4781 (1960). **2.** a town in SW Virginia. 3432 (1960). **3.** a town in SW Louisiana. 2987 (1960). **4.** a boy's given name.

vi·num (vī′nəm), *n.* (in prescriptions) a solution of a medicinal substance in wine. [< L: wine]

vin·y (vī′nē), *adj.,* **vin·i·er, vin·i·est. 1.** of, pertaining to, of the nature of, or resembling vines: *viny tendrils.* **2.** abounding in or producing vines: *a viny region.* [VINE + -Y[1]]

Vi·ny (vī′nē), *n.* a girl's given name. Also, **Vinie.**

vi·nyl (vī′nil, vīn′əl, vin′il, vin′əl), *adj.* **1.** *Chem.* containing the vinyl group. —*n.* **2.** any resin formed by polymerization of compounds containing the vinyl group or plastics made from such resins. [< L *vīn(um)* WINE + -YL]

vi′nyl ac′etate, *Chem.* a colorless, easily polymerized, water-insoluble liquid, $CH_3COOCH{=}CH_2$, produced by the reaction of acetylene and acetic acid: used chiefly in the manufacture of plastics, films, paints, and adhesives.

vi·nyl·a·cet·y·lene (vī′nil ə set′əlēn′, vīn′əl-, vin′il-, vin′əl-), *n. Chem.* a colorless, volatile liquid, $H_2C{=}CHC{\equiv}CH$, used chiefly as an intermediate in the manufacture of the synthetic rubber neoprene. [VINYL + ACETYLENE]

vi·nyl·ate (vīn′əlāt′, vin′-), *v.t.,* **-at·ed, -at·ing.** *Chem.* to subject to vinylation. [back formation from VINYLATION]

vi·nyl·a·tion (vīn′əlā′shən, vin′-), *n. Chem.* the process of introducing the vinyl group into a compound by reaction with acetylene. [VINYL + -ATION]

vi·nyl·ben·zene (vī′nil ben′zēn, -ben zēn′, vīn′əl-, vin′il-, vin′əl-), *n. Chem.* styrene. [VINYL + BENZENE]

vi′nyl chlo′ride, *Chem.* a colorless, easily liquefied, flammable, slightly water-soluble gas, $CH_2{=}CHCl$, having a pleasant, etherlike odor, produced by the reaction of acetylene and hydrochloric acid, or obtained from ethylene dichloride: used in the manufacture of plastics, as a refrigerant, and in the synthesis of polyvinyl chloride and other organic compounds. Also called **chloroethylene, chloroethene.**

vi′nyl e′ther, *Pharm.* a colorless, flammable, slightly water-soluble liquid, $H_2C{=}CHOCH{=}CH_2$, used as an inhalation anesthetic. Also called **divinyl ether.**

vi·nyl·eth·yl·ene (vī′nil eth′ə lēn′, vīn′əl-, vin′il-, vin′əl-), *n. Chem.* butadiene. [VINYL + ETHYLENE]

vi′nyl group′, *Chem.* the univalent group, $CH_2{=}CH{-}$, derived from ethylene. Also called **vi′nyl rad′ical.**

vi·nyl·i·dene (vī nil′i dēn′), *adj. Chem.* containing the vinylidene group. [VINYL + -ID[3] + -ENE]

vinyl′idene chlo′ride, *Chem.* a colorless, volatile, flammable liquid, $CH_2{=}CCl_2$, that is copolymerized chiefly with vinyl chloride to form saran.

vinyl′idene group′, *Chem.* the bivalent group, $H_2C{=}C{=}$, derived from ethylene. Also, **vinyl′idene rad′ical.**

vinyl′idene res′in, *Chem.* See **polyvinylidene resin.**

Vi·nyl·ite (vīn′əlīt′, vin′-), *n. Trademark.* any of a series of thermoplastic, nontoxic, acid-resistant, vinyl resins or plastics: used in coatings, adhesives, film, molded ware, and phonograph records.

vi′nyl pol′ymer, *Chem.* any of a group of compounds derived by polymerization from vinyl compounds, as vinyl acetate, styrene, etc.

vi′nyl res′in, *Chem.* See **polyvinyl resin.**

vi·ol (vī′əl), *n.* a bowed musical instrument, differing from the violin in having deeper ribs, sloping shoulders, a greater number of strings, usually six, and frets: common in the 16th and 17th centuries in various sizes from the treble viol to the bass viol. [< MF *viole* < OPr *viola, viula* (see VIOLA[1]); r. ME *viele* < AF (OF *viel(l)e*) < late OE *fithele* fiddle (with southern *v* for *f*)]

vi·o·la[1] (vē ō′lə, vī-), *n.* **1.** a four-stringed musical instrument of the violin class, slightly larger than the violin; a tenor or alto violin. **2.** a labial organ stop of eight-foot or four-foot pitch, giving tones of a penetrating stringlike quality. [< It *viola,* prob. < OPr *viola, viula* of uncert. orig.; cf. ML *vidula, vitula,* perh. connected with L *vītulārī* to be joyful, celebrate a festival]

vi·o·la[2] (vī′ə lə, vī ō′-), *n.* **1.** any plant of the genus *Viola,* esp. a cultivated variety. Cf. **pansy** (def. 1), **violet** (defs. 1, 2). **2.** a pansy, *V. cornuta,* cultivated as a garden plant. [< L: violet]

Vi·o·la (vī′ə lə, vē′-; vī ō′lə, vē-), *n.* a girl's given name.

vi·o·la·ble (vī′ə lə bəl), *adj.* capable of being violated: *a violable precept.* [< L *violābil(is),* equiv. to *violā(re)* (to) VIOLATE + *-bilis* -BLE] —**vi′o·la·bil′i·ty, vi′o·la·ble·ness,** *n.* —**vi′o·la·bly,** *adv.*

vi·o·la·ceous (vī′ə lā′shəs), *adj.* **1.** belonging to the *Violaceae,* or violet family of plants. **2.** of a violet color; bluish-purple. [< L *violāceus* violet-colored. See VIOLA[2], -ACEOUS] —**vi′o·la′ceous·ly,** *adv.*

vio′la clef′, *Music.* See **alto clef.**

vi·o·la da brac·cio (vē ō′lə də brä′chō, vī-), *pl.* **viola da brac·cios.** an old musical instrument of the viol family, held against the shoulder like a violin: superseded by the modern viola. [< It: lit., viola for the arm]

vi·o·la da gam·ba (vē ō′lə də gäm′bə, -gam′-, vī-), *pl.* **viola da gambas. 1.** an old musical instrument of the viol family, held on or between the knees: superseded by the modern violoncello; bass viol. **2.** an organ stop of eight-foot pitch giving a stringlike tone. [< It: lit., viol for the leg]

Viola da gamba

vi·o·la d'a·mo·re (vē ō′lə dä mōr′ā, -môr′ā, vī-), *pl.* **viola d'amores.** a viol with numerous sympathetic strings and several gut strings, producing a resonant sound. [< It: lit., viol of love]

vi·o·late (vī′ə lāt′), *v.t.,* **-lat·ed, -lat·ing. 1.** to break, infringe, or transgress (a law, rule, agreement, promise, instructions, etc.). **2.** to break in upon or disturb rudely; interfere thoughtlessly with: *to violate the silence of a library reading room.* **3.** to break through or pass by force or without right: *to violate a frontier.* **4.** to treat irreverently or disrespectfully; desecrate; profane: *to violate a church; violate a human right.* **5.** to rape (a woman). [late ME < L *violāt(us)* (ptp. of *violāre* to treat with violence), equiv. to *viol(entus)* VIOLENT + *-ātus* -ATE[1]] —**vi′o·la′tor, vi′o·lat′er,** *n.*

vi·o·la·tion (vī′ə lā′shən), *n.* **1.** the act of violating. **2.** the state of being violated. **3.** a breach, infringement, or transgression, as of a law, rule, promise, etc.: *He was fined for a traffic violation.* **4.** desecration; profanation: *the violation of a cemetery.* **5.** rape; ravishment. **6.** a distortion of meaning or fact. [late ME < L *violātiōn-* (s. of *violātiō*), equiv. to *violāt(us)* (see VIOLATE) + *-iōn-* -ION] —**vi′o·la′tion·al,** *adj.*

vi·o·la·tive (vī′ə lā′tiv, vī′ə lə tiv), *adj.* pertaining to or involving violation. [VIOLATE + -IVE]

vi·o·lence (vī′ə ləns), *n.* **1.** swift and intense force: *the violence of a storm.* **2.** rough or injurious physical force, action, or treatment: *to die by violence.* **3.** an unjust or unwarranted exertion of force or power, as against rights, laws, etc.: *to take over a government by* *violence.* **4.** a violent act or proceeding. **5.** rough or immoderate vehemence, as of feeling or language: *the violence of his hatred.* **6.** injury, as from distortion of meaning or fact: *to do violence to a translation.* [ME < AF, OF < L *violentia,* equiv. to *violent(us)* VIOLENT + *-ia* -Y³; see -ENCE]

vi·o·lent (vī′ə lənt), *adj.* **1.** acting with or characterized by uncontrolled, strong, rough force: *a violent blow; a violent earthquake.* **2.** acting with, characterized by, or caused by injurious or destructive force: *a violent death; violent measures.* **3.** intense in force, effect, etc.; severe; extreme: *violent pain; violent cold.* **4.** roughly or immoderately vehement or ardent: *violent passions.* **5.** furious in impetuosity, energy, etc.: *violent haste.* **6.** of, pertaining to, or constituting a distortion of meaning or fact. [ME < L *violent(us)* appar. equiv. to *vio-* (comb. form of *vīs* force) + *-lentus* adj. suffix] —**vi′o·lent·ly,** *adv.* —**vi′o·lent·ness,** *n.*

vi·o·les·cent (vī′ə les′ənt), *adj.* tending to a violet color: *a violescent twilight sky.* [< L *viol(a)* violet + -ESCENT]

vi·o·let (vī′ə lit), *n.* **1.** any chiefly low, stemless or leafy-stemmed herb of the genus *Viola,* having purple, blue, yellow, white, or variegated flowers. **2.** any such plant except the pansy and the viola. **3.** the flower of any native, wild species of violet, as distinguished from the pansy: the State flower of Illinois, New Jersey, and Rhode Island. **4.** any of various similar plants of other genera. **5.** bluish purple. —*adj.* **6.** of the color violet; bluish-purple: *a violet glass pitcher.* [ME < OF, equiv. to *viole* (< L *viola* violet) + *-ete* -ET] —**vi′o·let·like′, vi′o·let·y,** *adj.*

Vi·o·let (vī′ə lit), *n.* a girl's given name.

vi′olet i′ris, an iris, *Iris verna,* of the eastern U.S., having solitary, violet-blue flowers.

vi′olet ray′, light of the shortest visible wavelength.

vi′olet sage′, a much-branched, perennial herb, *Salvia nemorosa,* of Europe and western Asia, having leaves that are hairy on the underside and purplish-violet flowers.

Vi·o·lette (vī′ə let′, vī′ə lit), *n.* a girl's given name, form of **Violet.** Also, **Vi·o·let·ta** (vī′ə let′ə).

vi′olet wood′, kingwood.

vi′olet wood′ sor′rel, a perennial, woodland herb, *Oxalis violacea,* found throughout most of the area east of the Rocky Mountains having rose-purple or pinkish-white flowers. Also called **purple wood sorrel.**

Violin

vi·o·lin (vī′ə lin′), *n.* **1.** the treble instrument of the family of modern bowed instruments, held nearly horizontal by the player's arm and with the lower part supported against the collarbone or shoulder. **2.** a violinist: *The quartet lacks a violin.* [< It *violino,* equiv. to *viol(a)* (see VIOLA¹) + *-ino* dim. suffix] —**vi′o·lin·is′tic,** *adj.* —**vi′o·lin·is′ti·cal·ly,** *adv.* —**vi′o·lin′less,** *adj.*

violin′ clef′, *Music.* See **treble clef.**

vi·o·lin·ist (vī′ə lin′ist), *n.* a person who plays the violin. [< It *violinist(a).* See VIOLIN, -IST]

vi·o·lin·mak·er (vī′ə lin′mā′kər), *n.* a person who designs and constructs violins, esp. professionally. [VIOLIN + MAKER]

vi·ol·ist¹ (vī′ə list), *n.* a person who plays the viol. [VIOL + -IST]

vi·o·list² (vē ō′list, vī-), *n.* a person who plays the viola. [VIOL(A)¹ + -IST]

Violle (vyôl), *n. Optics.* a unit of luminous intensity, equal to that of one square centimeter of platinum at its temperature of solidification (1773.5°C): equivalent to about 20.17 candles. [named after Jules *Violle* (1841–1923), French physicist]

Viol·let-le-Duc (vyô le′lə dʏk′), *n.* **Eu·gène Em·ma·nu·el** (œ zhen′ e mᴀ nʏ el′), 1814–79, French architect and writer.

vi·o·lon·cel·list (vē′ə lən chel′ist), *n.* cellist. [VIOLONCELL(O) + -IST]

vi·o·lon·cel·lo (vē′ə lən chel′ō), *n., pl.* **-los.** cello. [< It, equiv. to *violon(e)* VIOLONE + *-cello* dim. suffix]

vi·o·lo·ne (vē′ə lō′nā), *n.* **1.** a double bass. **2.** an organ pedal stop of 16-foot pitch, giving a tone resembling the violoncello. [< It, equiv. to *viol(a)* bass-viol + *-one* aug. suffix]

vi·os·ter·ol (vī os′tə rōl′, -rôl′, -rol′), *n. Biochem.* a vitamin D preparation produced by the irradiation of ergosterol. [(ULTRA)VI(OLET) + (ERG)OSTEROL]

VIP, *Informal.* very important person. Also, **V.I.P.**

vi·per (vī′pər), *n.* **1.** any of several venomous Old World snakes of the genus *Vipera,* esp. *V. berus,* a small snake common in northern Eurasia. **2.** any venomous, Old World snake of the family *Viperidae,* characterized by erectile, venom-conducting fangs. **3.** See **pit viper.** **4.** any of various venomous or supposedly venomous snakes. **5.** a malignant or spiteful person. **6.** a false or treacherous person. **7. to nourish a viper in one's bosom,** to protect or encourage a person who proves to be treacherous. [ME, OE *vīpere* < L *vīpera* haplological var. of **vī(vi)pera;* the ancients thought it was VIVIPAROUS] —**vi′per·like′,** *adj.*

vi·per·fish (vī′pər fish′), *n., pl.* (*esp. collectively*) **-fish,** (*esp. referring to two or more kinds or species*) **-fish·es.** any of several deep-sea fishes of the family *Chauliodontidae,* having a large mouth and fanglike teeth. [VIPER + FISH]

vi·per·ine (vī′pər in, -pə rīn′), *adj.* of, pertaining to, or resembling a viper; venomous: *That woman has the most viperine tongue!* [< L *vīperīn(us).* See VIPER, -INE¹]

vi·per·ish (vī′pər ish), *adj.* viperous. [VIPER + -ISH¹] —**vi′per·ish·ly,** *adv.*

vi·per·ous (vī′pər əs), *adj.* **1.** of the nature of or resembling a viper: *a viperous movement.* **2.** of or pertaining to vipers. **3.** characteristic of vipers. **4.** venomous; malignant; spiteful. [VIPER + -OUS] —**vi′per·ous·ly,** *adv.*

vi′per's bu′gloss, the blueweed.

Vi′per's Tan′gle, The, a novel (1932) by François Mauriac. French, **Le Noeud de Vipères.**

vi·ra·go (vi rā′gō, vī-), *n., pl.* **-goes, -gos.** **1.** a violent, loud-voiced, ill-tempered, scolding woman; shrew. **2.** *Archaic.* a woman of masculine strength or spirit. [ME, OE < L, equiv. to *vir* man + *-āgo* suffix expressing association of some kind, here resemblance]

vi·ral (vī′rəl), *adj.* of, pertaining to, or caused by a virus. [VIR(US) + -AL¹]

Vi·ra Sai·va (vir′ə sī′və), *n. Hinduism.* Lingayata. [< Skt, equiv. to *vira* man + *saiva* votary of Shiva]

Vir·bi·us (vûr′bē əs), *n.* an ancient Roman god of the forest and hunting, worshiped with Diana and identified with Hippolytus.

Vir·chow (fir′ᴋʜō), *n.* **Ru·dolf** (ʀo͞o′dôlf), 1821–1902, German pathologist, anthropologist, and political leader.

Vir·den (vûr′dən), *n.* a town in central Illinois. 3309 (1960).

vir·e·lay (vir′ə lā′), *n. Pros.* **1.** an old French form of short poem, composed of short lines running on two rhymes and having two opening lines recurring at intervals. **2.** any of various similar or other forms of poem, as one consisting of stanzas made up of longer and shorter lines, the lines of each kind rhyming together in each stanza, and having the rhyme of the shorter lines of one stanza forming the rhyme of the longer lines of the next stanza. **3.** a medieval song form providing a musical setting for a virelay but having a formal structure different from that of the poem. Also, **vir′e·lai′.** [late ME < OF *virelai,* alter. (see LAY⁴) of *vireli, virli* jingle used as the refrain of a song]

vi·re·mi·a (vī rē′mē ə), *n. Pathol.* the presence in the blood of a virus. [< NL; see VIRUS, -EMIA] —**vi·re′mic,** *adj.*

vir·e·o (vir′ē ō′), *n., pl.* **vir·e·os.** any of several small, insectivorous, American birds of the family *Vireonidae,* having the plumage usually olive-green or gray above and white or yellow below. [< L: ? greenfinch; cf. *virēre* to be green]

Red-eyed vireo, *Vireo olivaceus* (Length 6 in.)

vi·res (wi′rās; *Eng.* vī′rēz), *n. Latin.* pl. of **vis.**

vi·res·cence (vī res′əns), *n. Bot.* state of becoming somewhat, though usually not totally, green, due to the abnormal presence of chlorophyll. [VIRESC(ENT) + -ENCE]

vi·res·cent (vī res′ənt), *adj.* **1.** turning green. **2.** tending to a green color; slightly greenish. [< L *virescent-* (s. of *virescēns,* prp. of *virescere* to become green), equiv. to *vir-* green (see VIREO) + *-escent-* -ESCENT]

Virg., Virginia.

vir·ga (vûr′gə), *n.* (*construed as sing. or pl.*) *Meteorol.* streaks of water drops or ice particles falling out of a cloud and evaporating before reaching the ground (distinguished from *praecipitatio*). [< L: rod, streak]

vir·gate¹ (vûr′git, -gāt), *adj.* shaped like a rod or wand; long, slender, and straight. [< L *virgāt(us);* see VIRGATE²]

vir·gate² (vûr′git, -gāt), *n.* an early English measure of land of varying extent, generally regarded as having been equivalent to a quarter of a hide, or about 30 acres. [< ML *virgāta (terrae)* measure (of land), fem. of L *virgātus* pertaining to a rod, equiv. to *virg(a)* rod + *-ātus* -ATE¹; trans. OE *gierd landes* yard-measure of land]

Vir·gil (vûr′jəl), *n.* **1.** Vergil. **2.** Also, **Vergil.** a boy's given name.

Vir·gil·i·an (vər jil′ē ən, -jil′yən), *adj.* Vergilian.

vir·gin (vûr′jin), *n.* **1.** a girl or woman who has never had sexual intercourse. **2.** an unmarried girl or woman. **3.** *Eccles.* an unmarried, religious woman, esp. a saint. **4. the Virgin,** Mary, the mother of Christ. **5.** a female animal that has never copulated. **6.** a boy or man who has never had sexual intercourse. **7.** an unfertilized insect. **8.** (*cap.*) *Astron., Astrol.* the constellation or sign of Virgo. —*adj.* **9.** being a virgin: *a virgin martyr; a virgin queen.* **10.** consisting of virgins. **11.** of, pertaining to, characteristic of, or befitting a virgin: *virgin modesty.* **12.** pure; unsullied; undefiled: *virgin snow.* **13.** first: *the new Congressman's virgin speech.* **14.** without admixture, alloy, or modification: *virgin gold.* **15.** not previously exploited, cultivated, tapped, or used: *virgin soil; virgin sales territory; virgin timberlands.* **16.** previously unused; used for the first time: *virgin wool.* **17.** without experience of; not previously exposed to: *a mind virgin to the knowledge that such things exist.* **18.** *Zool.* unfertilized. **19.** (of a metal) made directly from ore by smelting, rather than from scrap. **20.** noting the oil obtained, as from olives, by the first pressing without the application of heat. [ME *virgine* < AF, OF < L *virgine(m),* acc. of *virgō* maiden, virgin] —**Syn. 2.** maid, maiden. **12.** chaste, unpolluted. **14.** unalloyed, unadulterated. **15.** fresh, new, maiden. —**Ant. 1, 2.** defiled. **14.** mixed, adulterated.

vir·gin·al¹ (vûr′jə nᵊl), *adj.* **1.** of, pertaining to, characteristic of, or befitting a virgin: *virginal purity.* **2.** continuing in a state of virginity. **3.** pure; unsullied; untouched: *a virginal mountain stream.* **4.** *Zool.* unfertilized. [late ME < L *virgināl(is),* equiv. to *virgin-* VIRGIN + *-ālis* -AL¹] —**vir′gin·al·ly,** *adv.*

vir·gin·al² (vûr′jə nᵊl), *n.* Often, **virginals.** a rectangular harpsichord with the strings stretched parallel to the keyboard, the earlier types placed on a table, popular in the 16th and 17th centuries. [appar. special use of VIRGINAL¹] —**vir′gin·al·ist,** *n.*

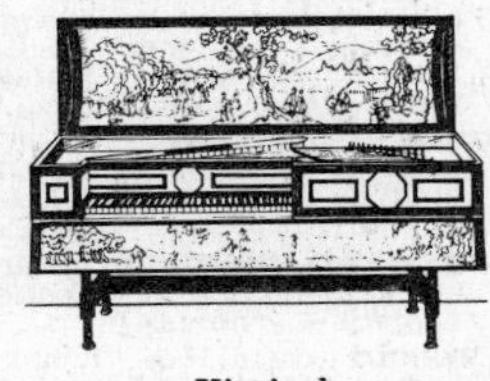

Virginal

vir′gin birth′, **1.** *Theol.* the doctrine or dogma that, by the miraculous agency of God, the birth of Christ did not impair or prejudice the virginity of Mary. Cf. **Immaculate Conception.** **2.** *Zool.* parthenogenesis; parturition by a female who has not copulated.

Vir·gin·ia (vər jin′yə), *n.* **1.** a State in the E United States, on the Atlantic coast: part of the historical South. 3,966,949 (1960); 40,815 sq. mi. *Cap.:* Richmond. *Abbr.:* Va. **2.** a girl's given name.

OHIO PENNSYLVANIA N.J. MD. DEL. W. VA. KY. APPALACHIAN MTS. Roanoke Lynchburg Richmond James Norfolk Virginia TENN. NORTH CAROLINA Portsmouth MILES 0 50 100 150 200

Virgin′ia Beach′, a town in SE Virginia. 8091 (1960).

Virgin′ia bis′tort. See under **bistort** (def. 2).

Virgin′ia blue′bell. See **Virginia cowslip.**

Virgin′ia Cit′y, a mining town in W Nevada: famous for the discovery of the rich Comstock silver lode 1859.

Virgin′ia cow′slip, a wild, boraginaceous herb, *Mertensia virginica,* of the eastern U.S., grown as a garden perennial for its handsome clustered blue flowers. Also called **Virginia bluebell, American lungwort, Roanoke bells, tree lungwort.**

Virgin′ia creep′er, a climbing, vitaceous plant, *Parthenocissus quinquefolia,* of North America, having palmate leaves, usually with five leaflets, and bluish-black berries. Also called **American ivy, ivy vine.**

Virgin′ia deer′, **1.** the common white-tailed deer, *Odocoileus virginianus,* of eastern North America. **2.** any related variety of white-tailed deer.

Virgin′ia fence′. See **snake fence.** Also called **Virgin′ia rail′ fence′.**

Virgin′ia ham′, a ham from a razorback hog, cured in hickory smoke.

Virgin′ia log′ canoe′, cunner².

Vir·gin·ian (vər jin′yən, -ē ən), *adj.* **1.** of or pertaining to the State of Virginia. —*n.* **2.** a native or inhabitant of Virginia. [VIRGINI(A) + AN]

Virgin′ia plan′, *Amer. Hist.* a plan, unsuccessfully proposed at the Constitutional Convention, providing for a legislature of two houses with proportional representation in each house and executive and judicial branches to be chosen by the legislature. Cf. **Connecticut Compromise, New Jersey plan.**

Virgin′ia rail′, a long-billed, American rail, *Rallus limicola,* having blackish and reddish-brown plumage.

Virgin′ia reel′, an American country dance in which the partners start by facing each other in two lines.

Virgin′ia snake′root. See under **snakeroot** (def. 1).

Virgin′ia stock′, a low, spreading, herb, *Malcomia maritima,* of the Mediterranean region, having reddish or white flowers.

Virgin′ia trum′pet flow′er. See **trumpet creeper.**

Virgin′ia wil′low, a shrub, *Itea virginica,* of the eastern and southern U.S., having showy, fragrant, white flowers. Also called **sweet spire.**

vir·gin·i·bus pu·er·is·que (wiʀ gin′i bo͞os′ po͞o′eʀ ēs′kwe; *Eng.* vər jin′ə bəs pyo͞o′ə ris′kwē), *Latin.* for girls and boys.

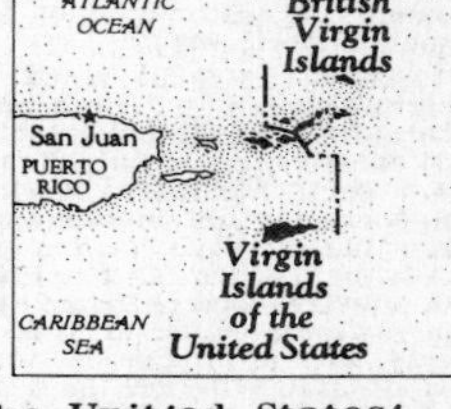

Vir′gin Is′lands, a group of islands in the West Indies, E of Puerto Rico: comprises the Virgin Islands of the United States and the British Virgin Islands.

Vir′gin Is′lands of the Unit′ed States′, a group of islands in the West Indies, including St. Thomas, St. John, and St. Croix: purchased from Denmark 1917. 32,099 (1960); 133 sq. mi. *Cap.:* Charlotte Amalie. Formerly, **Danish West Indies.**

vir·gin·i·ty (vər jin′i tē), *n.* **1.** the state or condition of being a virgin. **2.** the state or condition of being pure, fresh, or unused. [ME *virginite* < AF, OF < L *virginitāt-* (s. of *virginitās*). See VIRGIN, -ITY]

vir·gin·i·um (vər jin′ē əm), *n. Chem.* (formerly) francium. *Symbol:* Vi [VIRGINI(A) + -IUM]

Vir′gin Mar′y, Mary (def. 1).

Vir′gin Queen′, Queen Elizabeth I of England.

Vir′gin Soil′, a novel (1876) by Turgenev.

vir·gin's-bow·er (vûr′jinz bou′ər), any of several climbing varieties of clematis having small, white flowers in large panicles, as *Clematis Vitalba,* of Europe, or *C. virginiana,* of the U.S.

Vir·go (vûr′gō), *n., gen.* **Vir·gi·nis** (vûr′jə nis), for 1. **1.** *Astron.* the Virgin, a zodiacal constellation between Leo and Libra, containing the bright star Spica. **2.** *Astrol.* the sixth sign of the zodiac. See illus. under **zodiac.** [< L: maiden]

vir·gu·late (vûr′gyə lit, -lāt′), *adj.* rod-shaped; virgate. [< L *virgul(a)* (*virg(a)* rod + *-ula* -ULE) + -ATE¹]

vir·gule (vûr′gyo͞ol), *n. Print.* **1.** a short oblique stroke (/) between two words indicating that whichever is appropriate may be chosen to complete the sense of the text in which they occur: *The defendant and/or his attorney must appear in court.* **2.** a dividing line, as in dates, fractions, a run-in passage of poetry to show verse division, etc.: *3/21/27; 3/4; Sweetest love I do not go/For weariness of thee.* Also called **diagonal, separatrix, shilling mark, slant, slash, solidus.** [< F *virgule* comma, little rod < L *virgula;* see VIRGULATE]

vir·i·al (vir′ē əl), *n. Physics.* a quantity that for a system of particles, each of which is located by a vector from the origin of the system and acted upon by a resultant force, is equal to −½ times the sum of the products of this vector and force for each particle. [< G < L *vīri-* (comb. form of *vīres,* pl. of *vis* force) + *-al* -AL¹]

vir·i·des·cent (vir′i des′ənt), *adj.* slightly green; greenish: *a viridescent wall, tinged with moss.* [< LL *viridescent-* (s. of *viridescēns,* prp. of *viridescere* to become green), equiv. to *virid-* green + *-escent-* -ESCENT] —**vir′i·des′cence,** *n.*

vi·rid·i·an (və rid′ē ən), *n.* a long-lasting, bluish-green pigment, consisting of a hydrated oxide of chromium. [< L *viridi(s)* green + -AN]

vi·rid·i·ty (və rid′i tē), *n.* **1.** greenness; verdancy; verdure. **2.** youth; innocence; inexperience. [late ME < L *viriditāt-* (s. of *viriditās*), equiv. to *viridi(s)* green + *-tāt-* -TY[2]]

vir·ile (vir′əl *or, esp. Brit.,* -īl), *adj.* **1.** of, pertaining to, characteristic of, or befitting a man; masculine; manly: *virile strength.* **2.** having or exhibiting masculine energy, forcefulness, or strength in a marked degree. **3.** characterized by a vigorous, masculine spirit: *a virile literary style.* **4.** of, pertaining to, or capable of procreation. [< L *virīle*, neut. of *virīlis* manly, equiv. to *vir* man + *-īlis* -ILE]
—**Syn. 2.** vigorous. See **male.** —**Ant. 1–3.** effeminate.

vir·i·lism (vir′ə liz′əm), *n.* a female disorder in which there is development of secondary male sexual characteristics, as hirsutism and lowered voice, resulting from various, often endocrinopathic, causes; pseudohermaphroditism. [VIRILE + -ISM]

vi·ril·i·ty (və ril′i tē), *n.* **1.** the state or quality of being virile; manly character, vigor, or spirit; masculinity. **2.** the power of procreation. [< L *virilitās*, equiv. to *virīli(s)* VIRILE + *-tās* -TY[2]]

vir·i·lo·cal (vir′ə lō′kəl), *adj.* patrilocal. [< L *viri-* (comb. form of *vir* man) + LOCAL] —**vir′i·lo′cal·ly,** *adv.*

virl (vûrl), *n. Scot.* ferrule (def. 1). [syncopated var. of ME *virole* FERRULE] —**virled,** *adj.*

vi·rol·o·gy (vī rol′ə jē, vi-), *n.* the science dealing with the study of viruses and the diseases caused by them. [*viro-* (comb. form of VIRUS) + -LOGY] —**vi·ro·log·i·cal** (vī′rə loj′i kəl), *adj.* —**vi·rol′o·gist,** *n.*

Vi·ron (vī′rən), *n.* a boy's given name.

Vi·ro·qua (və rō′kwə), *n.* a town in SW Wisconsin. 3926 (1960).

vi·ro·sis (vī rō′sis), *n. Med., Plant Pathol.* infection with a virus. [VIR(US) + -OSIS]

v. irr., irregular verb.

Vir·ta·nen (vir′tä nen), *n.* **Art·tu·ri Il·ma·ri** (ärt′tōō ri il′mä ri), born 1895, Finnish biochemist: Nobel prize 1945.

vir·tu (vər tōō′, vûr′tōō), *n.* **1.** excellence or merit in objects of art, curios, and the like. **2.** (*construed as pl.*) such objects or articles collectively. **3.** a taste for or knowledge of such objects. Also, **vertu.** [< It *virtù* VIRTUE]

vir·tu·al (vûr′chōō əl), *adj.* **1.** being such in power, force, or effect, though not actually or expressly such: *They have been reduced to virtual dependence on his charity.* **2.** *Optics.* **a.** noting an image formed by the apparent convergence of rays geometrically, but not actually, prolonged, as the image formed by a mirror (opposed to *real*). **b.** noting a focus of a system forming virtual images. **3.** *Archaic.* having the inherent power to produce certain effects. [late ME < ML *virtuāl(is)*, equiv. to L *virtu(s)* VIRTUE + *-ālis* -AL[1]] —**vir′tu·al′i·ty,** *n.*

vir·tu·al·ly (vûr′chōō ə lē), *adv.* **1.** for the most part; almost wholly; just about: *The job was virtually completed by the end of the week. He is virtually unknown.* **2.** *Obs.* essentially, although not formally or actually. [ME; see VIRTUAL, -LY]

vir·tue (vûr′chōō), *n.* **1.** moral excellence; goodness; righteousness. **2.** conformity of one's life and conduct to moral and ethical principles; uprightness; rectitude. **3.** chastity, esp. in a girl or woman: *to lose one's virtue.* **4.** a particular moral excellence. Cf. **cardinal virtues, natural virtue, theological virtue. 5.** a good or admirable quality, as of a person or some aspect of a personality: *He has the virtue of knowing his weaknesses.* **6.** effective force; efficacy; power: *a charm with the virtue of removing warts.* **7.** a worthwhile attribute or property, as of a thing or substance: *This finish has the virtue of durability as well as beauty.* **8.** inherent power to produce effects; potency. **9. virtues,** an order of angels. Cf. **angel** (def. 1). **10.** *Archaic.* manly excellence; valor. **11. by** or **in virtue of,** by reason of; because of: *to act by virtue of one's legitimate authority.* **12. make a virtue of necessity,** to do what one is compelled to do without complaint; make the best of a difficult or unsatisfactory situation: *We made a virtue of necessity and worked indoors until the snow stopped.* [alter. (with *i* < L) of ME *vertu* < AF, OF < L *virtūt-* (s. of *virtus*) maleness, worth, virtue, equiv. to *vir* man + *-tūt-* -ness] —**vir′tue·less,** *adj.* —**vir′tue·less·ness,** *n.*
—**Syn. 1.** See **goodness. 2.** probity, integrity. **3.** virginity, purity. **6.** potency. —**Ant. 1.** vice.

vir·tu·o·sic (vûr′chōō os′ik, -ō′sik), *adj.* virtuoso. [VIRTUOS(O) + -IC]

vir·tu·os·i·ty (vûr′chōō os′i tē), *n.* **1.** the character, ability, or skill of a virtuoso. **2.** a fondness for or interest in virtu. [VIRTUOS(O) + -ITY]

vir·tu·o·so (vûr′chōō ō′sō), *n., pl.* **-sos, -si** (-sē), *adj.* —*n.* **1.** a person who has special knowledge or skill in a field. **2.** a person who excels in musical technique or execution. **3.** a person who has a cultivated appreciation of artistic excellence, as a connoisseur or collector of objects of art, curios, antiques, etc. **4.** *Obs.* a person who has special interest or knowledge in the arts and sciences; scientist; scholar. —*adj.* **5.** Also, **virtuosic.** of, pertaining to, or characteristic of a virtuoso: *a virtuoso performance.* [< It: versed, skilled < ML *virtuōsus* VIRTUOUS]

vir·tu·ous (vûr′chōō əs), *adj.* **1.** conforming to moral and ethical principles; morally excellent; upright: *Lead a virtuous life.* **2.** chaste: *a virtuous young woman.* **3.** *Archaic.* able to produce effects; potent. [alter. (with *i* < L) of ME *vertuous* < AF < ML *virtuōsus*, equiv. to L *virtu(s)* VIRTUE + *-ōsus* -OUS] —**vir′tu·ous·ly,** *adv.* —**vir′tu·ous·ness,** *n.*
—**Syn. 1.** good, pure. —**Ant. 1.** vicious.

Vir·tus (vûr′təs), *n.* the ancient Roman personification of courage.

vir·tu·te et ar·mis (wir tōō′te et är′mēs; *Eng.* vər tōō′tē et är′mis, vər tyōō′tē), *Latin.* by virtue and arms: motto of Mississippi.

vi·ru·cide (vī′rə sīd′), *n.* a substance or preparation for killing viruses. [VIRU(S) + -I- + -CIDE] —**vi′ru·cid′al,** *adj.*

vir·u·lence (vir′yə ləns, vir′ə-), *n.* **1.** quality of being virulent. **2.** *Bacteriol.* **a.** the relative ability of a microorganism to cause disease; degree of pathogenicity. **b.** the capability of a microorganism to cause disease. **3.** venomous hostility. **4.** intense sharpness of temper. Also, **vir′u·len·cy.** [< L *vīrulentia*, equiv. to *vīrulent-* VIRULENT + *-ia* -Y[3]; see -ENCE]

vir·u·lent (vir′yə lənt, vir′ə-), *adj.* **1.** actively poisonous; intensely noxious: *a virulent insect bite.* **2.** *Med.* highly infective; malignant or deadly. **3.** *Bacteriol.* of the nature of an organism causing specific or general clinical symptoms. **4.** violently or spitefully hostile. **5.** intensely bitter, spiteful, or malicious: *a virulent accusation.* [< L *vīrulent(us)*, equiv. to *vīru(s)* poison (see VIRUS) + *-lentus* adj. suffix] —**vir′u·lent·ly,** *adv.*
—**Syn. 1.** venomous. **5.** vicious, acerb. —**Ant. 1.** harmless.

vi·rus (vī′rəs), *n., pl.* **-rus·es. 1.** an infectious agent, esp. any of a group of ultramicroscopic, infectious agents that reproduce only in living cells. **2.** See **virus disease. 3.** the liquid excretions from cowpox blisters, used in smallpox vaccinations. **4.** the venom of a poisonous animal. **5.** a corrupting influence on morals or the intellect; poison: *the virus of intolerance.* [< L: slime, poison; akin to OOZE[2]] —**vi′rus·like′,** *adj.*
—**Syn. 1.** See **poison.**

vi′rus disease′, any disease caused by a virus, occurring in man, plants, and animals.

vis (vēs), *n., pl.* **vis.** vise (def. 2).

vis (wēs; *Eng.* vis), *n., pl.* **vi·res** (wē′rēs; *Eng.* vī′rēz). *Latin.* strength; force; power.

Vis., **1.** Viscount. **2.** Viscountess.

vi·sa (vē′zə), *n., pl.* **-sas,** *v.,* **-saed, -sa·ing.** —*n.* **1.** *Govt.* an endorsement made by an authorized representative of a country upon a passport of another country, testifying that the passport has been examined and found in order and permitting entry into or transit through the country making the endorsement. —*v.t.* **2.** to examine and endorse. **3.** to give a visa to; approve a visa for. **4.** to put a visa on (a passport). Also, **visé.** [< F, short for L *carta vīsa* the document (has been) examined; *vīsa* ptp. fem. of *vīsere* to look into, see to, freq. of *vidēre* to see]

vis·age (viz′ij), *n.* **1.** the face, esp. of a human being, usually with reference to shape, features, expression, etc.; countenance. **2.** aspect; appearance. [ME < AF, OF < LL, L *vīs(us)* (LL: face L: sight, appearance, n. use of *vīsus*, ptp. of *vidēre* to see) + F *-age* -AGE] —**vis′aged,** *adj.*
—**Syn. 1.** physiognomy. See **face.**

Vi·sa·kha·pat·nam (vi sä′kə put′nəm), *n.* a seaport in E India, on the Bay of Bengal. 182,000 (1961).

Vi·sa·lia (vi sāl′yə), *n.* a city in central California. 15,791 (1960).

vis·ard (viz′ərd), *n.* vizard.

vis-à-vis (vē′zə vē′; *Fr.* vē za vē′), *adv., adj., prep., n., pl.* **-vis.** —*adv., adj.* **1.** face to face: *They were sitting vis-à-vis at the banquet table. He had a vis-à-vis encounter with his opponent.* **2.** *Numis.* (of a coin) having two portraits facing one another. —*prep.* **3.** in relation to; compared with: *his ambitions vis-à-vis a realistic appraisal of his capabilities.* **4.** facing; opposite: *They were now vis-à-vis the most famous painting in the Louvre.* —*n.* **5.** a person face to face with or situated opposite to another: *He offered a cigarette to his vis-à-vis.* **6.** a person's partner or date at a social affair: *He introduced his vis-à-vis to the hostess.* **7.** a person having or occupying a position, office, etc., of equal authority, rank, or the like: *You'll have to see my vis-à-vis in the Louisville office.* **8.** a carriage in which the occupants sit face to face. **9.** *Furniture.* tête-à-tête (def. 3). [< F; see VIS-AGE]

Vi·sa·yan (vi sī′ən), *n., pl.* **-yans,** (*esp. collectively*) **-yan. 1.** one of a Malay people, the most numerous native race of the Philippines. **2.** the language of this people, an Indonesian language of the Malayo-Polynesian family. Also, **Bisayan.**

Visa′yan Is′lands, a group of islands in the central Philippines, including Panay, Negros, Cebú, Bohol, Leyte, Samar, Masbate, and smaller islands. Spanish, **Bisayas.**

Vis·by (vēs′bY), *n.* a seaport on the Swedish island of Gotland, in the Baltic: an important member of the Hanseatic League. 53,662 (1964). German, **Wisby.**

Visc., **1.** Viscount. **2.** Viscountess.

vis·ca·cha (vis kä′chə), *n.* **1.** a burrowing rodent, *Lagostomus trichodactylus*, about the size of a ground hog, inhabiting the pampas of Paraguay and Argentina, allied to the chinchilla. **2.** Also called **mountain viscacha.** a related rodent of the genus *Lagidium*, of the Andes, about the size of a squirrel, having long, rabbitlike ears and a squirrellike tail. Also, **vizcacha.** [< Sp < Quechuan *wiskácha*]

vis·cer·a (vis′ər ə), *n.pl., sing.* **vis·cus** (vis′kəs). **1.** *Anat., Zool.* the organs in the cavities of the body, esp. those in the abdominal cavity. **2.** (not used scientifically) the intestines; bowels. [< L: internal organs, pl. of *viscus* flesh]

vis·cer·al (vis′ər əl), *adj.* **1.** of or pertaining to the viscera. **2.** affecting the viscera. **3.** of the nature of or resembling viscera. **4.** characterized by or proceeding from instinctive rather than intellectual motivation: *a visceral personality.* **5.** characterized by or dealing with coarse or base emotions; earthy; crude: *This is a rather visceral literary style.* [< ML *viscerāl(is)*, equiv. to *viscer-* VISCERA + *-ālis* -AL] —**vis′cer·al·ly,** *adv.*

vis′ceral leishmani′asis, *Pathol.* kala-azar.

vis·cer·o·to·ni·a (vis′ər ə tō′nē ə), *n. Psychol.* a personality pattern accompanying the endomorphic body type and characterized by extroversion, conviviality, and love of comfort. Cf. **cerebrotonia, somatotonia.** [< NL, equiv. to LL *viscero-* (comb. form of L *viscer(a)* VISCERA) + *ton(us)* + *-ia* -IA] —**vis·cer·o·ton·ic** (vis′ər ə ton′ik), *adj.*

vis·cer·o·trop·ic (vis′ər ə trop′ik, -trō′pik), *adj.* (esp. of viruses) attracted toward or affecting the viscera. [*viscero-* (comb. form repr. L *viscera* VISCERA) + -TROPIC]

vis·cer·o·tro·pism (vis′ər ə trō′piz əm), *n.* viscerotropic attraction or infection. [*viscero-* (see VISCEROTROPIC) + -TROPISM]

vis·cid (vis′id), *adj.* **1.** having a glutinous consistency; sticky; adhesive; viscous. **2.** *Bot.* covered by a sticky substance, as a leaf. [< LL *viscid(us)*, equiv. to *visc(um)* birdlime + *-idus* -ID[4]; see VISCOUS] —**vis·cid′i·ty, vis′cid·ness,** *n.* —**vis′cid·ly,** *adv.*

vis·co·e·las·tic (vis′kō i las′tik), *adj. Physics.* pertaining to a substance having both viscous and elastic properties. [VISCO(US) + ELASTIC]

vis·coid (vis′koid), *adj.* somewhat viscous. Also, **vis·coi′dal.** [VISC(OUS) + -OID]

vis·com·e·ter (vi skom′i tər), *n.* a device for measuring viscosity. Also, **viscosimeter.** [syncopated var. of VISCOSIMETER] —**vis·co·met·ric** (vis′kə me′trik), *adj.* —**vis′co·met′ri·cal·ly,** *adv.* —**vis·com′e·try,** *n.*

vis co·mi·ca (wēs′ kō′mi kä′; *Eng.* vis′ kom′ə kə), *Latin.* comic power.

Vis·con·ti (vēs kôn′tē), *n.* an Italian family that ruled Milan and Lombardy from 1277 to 1447.

vis·cose (vis′kōs), *n.* **1.** a viscous solution prepared by treating cellulose with caustic soda and carbon bisulfide: used in manufacturing regenerated cellulose fibers, sheets, or tubes, as rayon or cellophane. —*adj.* **2.** of, pertaining to, or made from viscose. [< L *viscōs(us)* VISCOUS]

vis·co·sim·e·ter (vis′kō sim′i tər), *n.* viscometer. [VISCOSI(TY) + -METER] —**vis·co·si·met·ric** (vis′kō si me′trik, vi skos′i-), *adj.*

vis·cos·i·ty (vi skos′i tē), *n., pl.* **-ties. 1.** state or quality of being viscous. **2.** *Physics.* **a.** the property of a fluid that resists the force tending to cause the fluid to flow. **b.** the measure of the extent to which a fluid possesses this property. [late ME < ML *viscōsitāt-* (s. of *viscōsitās*), equiv. to L *viscōs(us)* VISCOSE + *-itāt-* -ITY]

vis·count (vī′kount′), *n.* **1.** a nobleman next below an earl or count and next above a baron. **2.** *Hist.* a deputy of a count or earl. **3.** (in England) a sheriff. [late ME *viscounte* < AF (equiv. to OF *visconte*), equiv. to *vis* VICE[3] + *counte* COUNT[2], trans. ML *vicecomes*]

vis·count·cy (vī′kount′sē), *n.* the rank or station of a viscount. Also, **vis′count·ship′.** [VISCOUNT + -CY]

vis·count·ess (vī′koun′tis), *n.* **1.** the wife or widow of a viscount. **2.** a woman holding in her own right a rank equivalent to that of a viscount. [VISCOUNT + -ESS]

vis·count·y (vī′koun′tē), *n., pl.* **-count·ies. 1.** viscountcy. **2.** *Hist.* the jurisdiction of a viscount or the territory under his authority. [VISCOUNT + -Y[3]]

vis·cous (vis′kəs), *adj.* **1.** of a glutinous nature or consistency; sticky; thick; adhesive. **2.** having the property of viscosity. [late ME < L *viscōs(us)*, equiv. to *visc(um)* mistletoe, birdlime (made with mistletoe berries) + *-ōsus* -OUS] —**vis′cous·ly,** *adv.* —**vis′cous·ness,** *n.*

Visct., **1.** Viscount. **2.** Viscountess.

vis·cus (vis′kəs), *n.* sing. of **viscera.**

vise (vīs), *n., v.,* **vised, vis·ing.** —*n.* **1.** any of various devices, usually having two jaws which may be brought together or separated by means of a screw, lever, or the like, used to hold an object firmly while work is being done on it. **2.** Also, **vis.** a winding staircase. —*v.t.* **3.** to hold, press, or squeeze with or as with a vise. Also, **vice.** [ME *vis* < OF *vis* a screw < L *vītis* vine (spiral form gave rise to later meaning)] —**vise′like′,** *adj.*

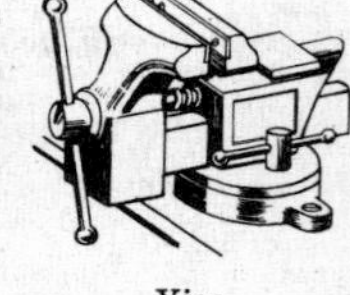

Vise

vi·sé (vē′zā, vē zā′), *n., v.t.,* **vi·séed, vi·sé·ing.** visa. [< F, ptp. of *viser* to inspect, check; see VISA]

Vi·shin·sky (vi shin′skē; *Russ.* vi shin′ski), *n.* **Andrei Ya·nu·ar·ie·vich** (än drā′ yä nōō är′yə vich), 1883–1954, Soviet statesman. Also, **Vyshinsky.**

Vish·nu (vish′nōō), *n. Hinduism.* **1.** "The Pervader," one of a half-dozen solar deities in the Rig-Veda, daily traversing the sky in three strides, morning, afternoon, and night. **2.** (in popular Hinduism) a deity believed to have descended from heaven to earth in several incarnations, or avatars, varying in number from nine to twenty-two, but always including animals. His most important human incarnation is the Krishna of the Bhagavad-Gita. **3.** (in later Hinduism) "the Preserver," the second member of the Trimurti, along with Brahma the Creator and Shiva the Destroyer. [< Skt: lit., the everywhere-active one] —**Vish′nu·ism,** *n.*

vis·i·bil·i·ty (viz′ə bil′i tē), *n., pl.* **-ties** for 6. **1.** the state or fact of being visible. **2.** the relative ability to be seen under given conditions of distance, light, atmosphere, etc.: *The pilot made an instrument landing because of low visibility.* **3.** Also called **visual range.** *Meteorol.* the distance at which a given standard object can be seen and identified with the unaided eye. **4.** the ability to give a relatively large range of unobstructed vision: *a windshield with good visibility.* **5.** *Typography.* legibility (def. 2). **6.** *Archaic.* something visible; a visible thing. [< LL *vīsibilitāt-* (s. of *vīsibilitās*), equiv. to L *vīsibili(s)* VISIBLE + *-tāt-* -TY[2]]

visibil′ity me′ter, any instrument for measuring the visual range through the atmosphere, as a transmissometer.

vis·i·ble (viz′ə bəl), *adj.* **1.** that can be seen; perceptible to the eye: *At dawn the distant mountains became visible.* **2.** capable of being perceived by the mind: *There seems to be no visible solution to the problem.* **3.** apparent; manifest; obvious: *a man with no visible means of support; He has shown a visible dislike for work of any kind.* **4.** conspicuous. **5.** prepared or converted for visual presentation; represented visually. [ME < L *vīsibil(is)*, equiv. to *vīs-* (see VISION) + *-ibilis* -IBLE] —**vis′i·ble·ness,** *n.* —**vis′i·bly,** *adv.*
—**Syn. 1, 2.** discernible. **2.** perceptible. **3.** evident, open, clear, patent, palpable, observable, unmistakable.

vis′ible hori′zon, horizon (def. 1).

vis′ible spec′trum, *Physics.* the range of electromagnetic radiations that are normally visible, having wavelengths of between 3800 and 7600 angstrom units.

vis′ible speech′, *Phonet.* **1.** the representation in graphic or pictorial form of characteristics of speech, as by means of sound spectrograms. **2.** the system of handwritten phonetic symbols invented by Melville Bell in 1867 to provide a visually comprehensible rendition of speech sounds.

Vis·i·goth (viz′ə goth′), *n.* a member of the westerly division of the Goths, which formed a monarchy about A.D. 418, maintaining it in southern France until 507 and in Spain until 711. Cf. **Ostrogoth.** —**Vis′i·goth′ic,** *adj.*

Vi·sine (vī′zēn), *n. Pharm., Trademark.* tetrahydrozoline.

vi·sion (vizh′ən), *n.* **1.** the act or power of sensing with the eyes; sight. **2.** the act or power of anticipating that which will or may come to be: *prophetic vision; the vision of an entrepreneur.* **3.** an experience, generally regarded as beneficent or meaningful, in which a personage, thing, or event appears vividly or credibly to the mind, although not actually present, under the influence of a divine or otherwise spiritual agency or under the influence of a psychological or physiological condition: *a vision of the Apocalypse.* Cf. **hallucination** (def. 1). **4.** something seen or otherwise perceived during such an experience: *The Holy Grail appeared to him in the form of a vision.* **5.** a vivid, imaginative conception or anticipation: *to have visions of wealth and glory.* **6.** something seen; an object of sight. **7.** a sight that resembles something seen in a vision, dream, etc.: *She was a vision of loveliness.* **8.** a scene, person, etc., of extraordinary beauty: *The sky was a vision of red and pink.* —*v.t.* **9.** to exhibit, perceive, or imagine in or as in a vision; envision: *He tried to vision himself in a past century.* [ME < L *vīsiōn-* (s. of *vīsiō*) a seeing, view, equiv. to *vīs(us),* ptp. of *vidēre* to see + *-iōn-* -ION] —**vi′sion·less,** *adj.*

—**Syn. 2.** perception, discernment. **4.** apparition, phantasm, chimera. See **dream.**

vi·sion·al (vizh′ə nᵊl), *adj.* **1.** of or pertaining to visions. **2.** belonging to or seen in a vision. [VISION + -AL[1]] —**vi′sion·al·ly,** *adv.*

vi·sion·ar·y (vizh′ə ner′ē), *adj., n., pl.* **-ar·ies.** —*adj.* **1.** given to or characterized by fanciful, not presently workable, or unpractical ideas, views, or schemes: *a visionary enthusiast.* **2.** given to or concerned with seeing visions. **3.** belonging to or seen in a vision. **4.** unreal; imaginary: *visionary evils.* **5.** purely idealistic or speculative; impractical; unrealizable: *a visionary scheme.* **6.** of, pertaining to, or proper to a vision or visions. —*n.* **7.** a person who sees visions. **8.** a person who is given to audacious, highly speculative, or impractical ideas or schemes; dreamer. [VISION + -ARY] —**vi′sion·ar′i·ness,** *n.*

—**Syn. 1.** impractical, impracticable. **4.** fancied, illusory, chimerical. **5.** romantic. —**Ant. 1.** practical.

vi′sion cloth′, *Theat.* a curtain with an inset scrim behind which a lighted scene appears, as a vision, dream, or the like.

Vi′sion of Judg′ment, The, a satirical poem (1822) by Byron.

vis·it (viz′it), *v.t.* **1.** to go to and stay with (a person or family) or at (a place) for a short time for reasons of sociability, politeness, business, curiosity, etc.: *to visit a friend; to visit clients; to visit Colonial Williamsburg.* **2.** to stay with as a guest. **3.** to come or go to: *to visit a church for a few minutes of prayer.* **4.** to go to for the purpose of official inspection or examination: *a school principal visiting classes; a general visiting his troops.* **5.** to come to in order to comfort or aid: *to visit the sick.* **6.** to come upon; assail; afflict: *The plague visited London in 1665.* **7.** to cause trouble, suffering, etc., to come to: *to visit Job with boils.* **8.** to inflict, as punishment, vengeance, etc. (often fol. by *on* or *upon*). —*v.i.* **9.** to make a visit or visits. **10.** to talk or chat casually: *I met Mary on the street, and we stopped to visit for a moment.* **11.** to inflict punishment. —*n.* **12.** an instance of visiting: *a nice, long visit.* **13.** the act of calling upon a person, place, etc.: *to make a visit.* **14.** a call paid to a person, family, etc. **15.** a stay or sojourn as a guest. **16.** the act of going to a place to make an official inspection or examination. **17.** the act of an officer of a belligerent nation in boarding a vessel in order to ascertain the nature of its cargo, its nationality, etc.: *the right of visit and search.* [ME *visite(n)* (cf. OF *visiter*) < L *vīsitāre,* freq. of *vīsere* to go to see, freq. of *vidēre* to see]

Visit, The, a play (1956) by Friedrich Dürrenmatt.

vis·it·a·ble (viz′i tə bəl), *adj.* **1.** capable of, suitable for, or worthy of being visited: *a visitable island; a visitable museum.* **2.** liable or subject to official visitation. [VISIT + -ABLE]

vis·i·tant (viz′i tənt), *n.* **1.** a temporary resident; visitor; guest. **2.** a visitor to a place of religious or sightseeing interest; pilgrim. **3.** a being believed to come from the spirit world: *a ghostly visitant.* **4.** something, as a mood, feeling, emotion, etc., that overtakes a person from time to time: *Melancholy is an occasional visitant to all men.* **5.** a migratory bird which comes to and stays in a place or region for a temporary period. —*adj.* **6.** *Archaic.* visiting; paying a visit. [< L *vīsitant-* (s. of *vīsitāns*). See VISIT, -ANT]

—**Syn. 1.** See **visitor.**

vis·i·ta·tion (viz′i tā′shən), *n.* **1.** the act of visiting. **2.** a visit for the purpose of making an official examination or inspection. **3.** (*usually cap.*) the visit of the Virgin Mary to her cousin Elizabeth. Luke 1:36–56. **4.** (*cap.*) a church festival, held on July 2, in commemoration of this visit. **5.** the administration of comfort or aid, or of affliction or punishment: *a visitation of the plague.* **6.** a special dispensation, either of favor or of affliction, considered as coming from God. **7.** an experience or event, esp. an unpleasant one, considered as occurring by divine dispensation. **8.** an affliction or punishment, as from God. **9.** the appearance or coming of a supernatural influence or spirit; a supernatural emanation: *The medium promises that tonight I shall have a visitation.* [< L *vīsitātiōn-* (s. of *vīsitātiō*), equiv. to *vīsitāt(us)* (ptp. of *vīsitāre;* see VISIT, -ATE[1]) + *-iōn-* -ION; r. ME *visitacioun* < AF] —**vis′it·a′tion·al,** *adj.*

vis·it·a·to·ri·al (viz′i tə tôr′ē əl, -tōr′-), *adj.* **1.** of or pertaining to an official visitor or official visitation. **2.** having the power of visitation. [< ML *vīsitātōri(us)* (see VISITATION, -ORY[1]) + -AL[1]]

vis′iting card′. See **calling card.**

vis′iting fire′man, 1. an official, dignitary, or otherwise influential person accorded special treatment while visiting an organization, industry, city, etc., esp. one whom it might prove advantageous to impress with special tours or entertainment. **2.** a visitor, as a tourist or vacationer, in a city, presumed to be a big spender.

vis′iting nurse′, a registered nurse employed by a social service agency to give medical care to the sick in their homes or to implement other public health programs.

vis′iting profes′sor, a professor invited to teach at a university or college other than his own for a limited period, usually for a semester or one academic year.

vis′iting teach′er, a teacher in a public school system, assigned to give home instruction to sick or disabled pupils, to investigate truancy, and to aid the harmonious relationship of the family and school.

vis·i·tor (viz′i tər), *n.* a person who visits, as for reasons of friendship, business, duty, travel, or the like: *During the summer the streets are filled with visitors from out of town and abroad.* [late ME *visitour* < AF; OF *visiteor* < LL *vīsitātor,* equiv. to L *vīsitāt(us)* (ptp. of *vīsitāre* to VISIT) + *-or* -OR[2]]

—**Syn.** VISITOR, CALLER, GUEST, VISITANT are terms for one who comes to spend time with or stay with others, or in a place. A VISITOR often stays some time, for social pleasure, for business, sightseeing, etc.: *a visitor at our neighbor's house, in San Francisco.* A CALLER comes for a brief (usually) formal visit: *The caller merely left her card.* A GUEST is anyone receiving hospitality, and the word has been extended to include anyone who pays for meals and lodging: *a welcome guest; a paying guest.* VISITANT applies to a migratory bird or to a supernatural being: *a warbler as a visitant.*

vis·i·to·ri·al (viz′i tôr′ē əl, -tōr′-), *adj.* of or pertaining to a visitor; visitatorial. [VISITOR + -IAL]

vis ma·jor (vis mā′jər), *Law.* See **force majeure.** [< L: lit., greater force]

vi·sor (vī′zər, viz′ər), *n.* **1.** *Armor.* **a.** (on a close helmet) a piece having slits or holes for vision, situated above and pivoted with a beaver or a ventail and beaver. **b.** a similar piece of plate having holes or slits for vision and breathing, attached to or used with any of various other helmets, as the armet, sallet, basinet, or helm. **2.** the projecting front brim of a cap, as a baseball player's cap, used for shading the eyes from the sun. **3.** a rigid flap of opaque material on a frame that can be swung down close to the eyes of a driver of an automobile to shield his eyes from direct sunlight or glare. **4.** a means of concealment; disguise. —*v.t.* **5.** to protect or mask with a visor; shield. Also, **vizor.** [ME *viser* < AF (cf. OF *visiere*), equiv. to *vis* face (see VISAGE) + *-er* -ER[2]] —**vi′sor·less,** *adj.*

vis·ta (vis′tə), *n.* **1.** a view or prospect, esp. one seen through a long, narrow avenue or passage, as between rows of trees, houses, or the like. **2.** such an avenue or passage, esp. when formally planned. **3.** a far-reaching intellectual view: *the vistas of human knowledge.* **4.** a mental view extending over a long period of time or embracing many remembrances or anticipated experiences: *the vistas of one's youth; the vistas of the future.* [< It: a view, n. use of fem. of *visto* (ptp. of *vedere* < L *vidēre* to see) < L *vīs(us)* (ptp. of *vidēre*) + It *-to* < L *-tus* ptp. suffix] —**vis·taed** (vis′təd), *adj.* —**vis′ta·less,** *adj.*

—**Syn. 1.** See **view.**

VISTA (vis′tə), *n.* *U.S.* a national program, sponsored by the Office of Economic Opportunity, for sending volunteers into poor areas to teach various job skills. [V(olunteers) i(n) S(ervice) t(o) A(merica)]

Vis·tu·la (vis′cho͝o lə), *n.* a river in Poland, flowing N from the Carpathian Mountains past Warsaw into the Baltic near Danzig. ab. 650 mi. long. Polish, **Wisła.** German, **Weichsel.**

vis·u·al (vizh′o͞o əl), *adj.* **1.** of or pertaining to seeing or sight: *a visual image.* **2.** used in seeing: *the visual sense.* **3.** optical. **4.** perceptible by the sense of sight; visible: *a visual beauty and harmony.* **5.** perceptible by the mind; of the nature of a mental vision: *a visual impression captured in a line of verse.* —*n.* **6.** a rough, preliminary sketch of an advertising layout, showing possible arrangements of material. Cf. **comprehensive** (def. 5). [late ME < LL *vīsuāl(is),* equiv. to *vīsu(s)* sight (see VISION) + *-ālis* -AL[1]]

vis′ual acu′ity, *Ophthalm.* acuteness of the vision as determined by a comparison with the normal ability to define certain optical letters at a given distance, usually 20 feet. *Abbr.:* V.

vis′ual aid′, any of various materials depending on the sense of sight, as films, slides, photographs, etc., used as aids in teaching.

vis′ual bi′nary, *Astron.* a binary star having components that are sufficiently separated to be resolved by a telescope. Cf. **spectroscopic binary.**

vis′ual field′. See **field of vision.**

vis·u·al·ise (vizh′o͞o ə līz′), *v.i., v.t.,* **-ised, -is·ing.** *Chiefly Brit.* visualize. —**vis′u·al·is′a·ble,** *adj.* —**vis′u·al·i·sa′tion,** *n.* —**vis′u·al·is′er,** *n.*

vis·u·al·ize (vizh′o͞o ə līz′), *v.,* **-ized, -iz·ing.** —*v.i.* **1.** to recall or form mental images or pictures. —*v.t.* **2.** to make visual or visible. **3.** to form a mental image of. **4.** to make perceptible to the mind or imagination. Also, *esp. Brit.,* **visualise.** [VISUAL + -IZE] —**vis′u·al·iz′a·ble,** *adj.* —**vis′u·al·i·za′tion,** *n.* —**vis′u·al·iz′er, vis′u·al·ist,** *n.*

vis·u·al·ly (vizh′o͞o ə lē), *adv.* in a visual manner; with respect to sight; by sight. [VISUAL + -LY]

vis′ual pur′ple, *Biochem.* rhodopsin.

vis′ual range′, visibility (def. 3).

vi·ta (vī′tə; *Lat.* wē′tä), *n., pl.* **vi·tae** (vī′tē; *Lat.* wē′tī). See **curriculum vitae** (def. 1). Also, **vi·tae** (vī′tē). [< L: life]

Vi·ta (vē′tə), *n.* a girl's given name, form of **Davida.**

vi·ta·ceous (vī tā′shəs), *adj.* belonging to the *Vitaceae,* or grape family of plants, also comprising the ampelopsis, Japanese ivy, Virginia creeper, etc. [< NL *Vīt(is)* genus name (< L *vītis* vine) + -ACEOUS]

vi·tal (vīt′ᵊl), *adj.* **1.** of or pertaining to life: *vital processes.* **2.** having remarkable energy, liveliness, or force of personality: *a vital leader.* **3.** being the seat or source of life: *the vital organs.* **4.** necessary to life: *vital fluids.* **5.** necessary to the existence, continuance, or well-being of something; indispensable; essential: *a vital necessity for a healthy society.* **6.** affecting the existence, well-being, truth, etc., of something: *a vital error.* **7.** of critical importance: *vital decisions.* **8.** imparting vigor; vitalizing; invigorating: *The vital rains came at last.* **9.** destructive to life; deadly: *a vital wound.* [late ME < L *vītāl(is),* equiv. to *vīt(a)* life + *-ālis* -AL[1]] —**vi′tal·ly,** *adv.* —**vi′tal·ness,** *n.*

—**Syn. 5.** important, critical. —**Ant. 5.** unimportant.

vi′tal force′, the force that animates and perpetuates living beings and organisms. Also called **vital principle.**

vi′tal func′tion, *Biol., Physiol.* any function of the body that is essential for life.

Vi·tal·ian (vi tāl′yən, -tā′lē ən), *n.* died A.D. 672, pope 657–672.

vi·tal·ise (vīt′ᵊlīz′), *v.t.,* **-ised, -is·ing.** *Chiefly Brit.* vitalize. —**vi′tal·i·sa′tion,** *n.* —**vi′tal·is′er,** *n.*

vi·tal·ism (vīt′ᵊliz′əm), *n.* **1.** the doctrine that phenomena are only partly controlled by mechanical forces, and are in some measure self-determining. Cf. **dynamism** (def. 1) **mechanism** (def. 8). **2.** *Biol.* the doctrine that ascribes the functions of a living organism to a vital principle distinct from chemical and physical forces. [VITAL + -ISM] —**vi′tal·ist,** *n., adj.* —**vi′tal·is′tic,** *adj.* —**vi′tal·is′ti·cal·ly,** *adv.*

vi·tal·i·ty (vī tal′i tē), *n., pl.* **-ties. 1.** exuberant physical strength or mental vigor: *a person of great vitality.* **2.** capacity for survival or for the continuation of a meaningful or purposeful existence: *the vitality of an institution.* **3.** power to live or grow: *the vitality of a language.* **4.** vital force or principle. **5.** something having vital force. [< L *vītālitāt-* (s. of *vītālitās*), equiv. to *vītāli(s)* VITAL + *-tāt-* -TY[2]]

vi·tal·ize (vīt′ᵊlīz′), *v.t.,* **-ized, -iz·ing. 1.** to give life to; make vital. **2.** to give vitality or vigor to; animate. Also, *esp. Brit.,* **vitalise.** [VITAL + -IZE] —**vi′tal·i·za′tion,** *n.* —**vi′tal·iz′er,** *n.*

Vi·tal·li·um (vī tal′ē əm), *n.* *Trademark.* an alloy of cobalt, chromium, and molybdenum, having various dental and surgical applications.

vi′tal prin′ciple. See **vital force.**

vi·tals (vī′tᵊlz), *n.pl.* **1.** those bodily organs that are essential to life, as the brain, heart, liver, lungs, and stomach. **2.** the essential parts of something: *the vitals of a democracy.* [trans. of L *vītālia;* see VITAL]

vi′tal statis′tics, 1. statistics concerning human life or the conditions affecting human life and the maintenance of population. **2.** *Facetious.* the measurements of a woman's figure, esp. the bust, waist, and hips: *Suzanne's vital statistics are 38–22–38.*

vi·ta·mer (vī′tə mər), *n.* *Biochem.* any of several substances similar in chemical structure and metabolic function to vitamins. [VITA(MIN) + (ISO)MER] —**vi·ta·mer·ic** (vī′tə mer′ik), *adj.*

vi·tam im·pen·de·re ve·ro (wē′täm im pen′de re′ wā′rō; *Eng.* vī′tam im pen′də rē vir′ō), *Latin.* to consecrate one's life to truth. Juvenal, *Satires* IV, 91. Motto chosen by J. J. Rousseau.

vi·ta·min (vī′tə min), *n.* *Biochem.* any of a group of organic substances essential in small quantities to normal metabolism, found in minute amounts in natural foodstuffs or sometimes produced synthetically. Deficiencies of vitamins produce specific disorders. Also, **vi·ta·mine** (vī′tə min, -mēn′). [< L *vīt(a)* life + AMIN(E); coined by C. Funk, who thought they were amines] —**vi′ta·min′ic,** *adj.*

vitamin A, *Biochem.* a yellow, fat-soluble, solid terpene alcohol, obtained from carotene and found in green and yellow vegetables, egg yolk, etc.: essential to growth, the protection of epithelial tissue, and the prevention of night blindness.

vitamin A_2, *Biochem.* a vitamin similar to vitamin A, derived from liver oils of fresh-water fish.

vitamin B_1, *Biochem.* thiamine.

vitamin B_2, *Biochem.* riboflavin.

vitamin B_6, *Biochem.* pyridoxine.

vitamin B_{12}, *Biochem.* a deep-red crystalline, water-soluble solid, $C_{63}H_{90}N_{14}O_{14}PCo$, obtained from liver, milk, eggs, fish, oysters, and clams: used chiefly in the treatment of pernicious anemia and sprue, and as a growth factor for hogs, dogs, and chickens. Also called **cyanocobalamin, antipernicious anemia factor.**

vitamin B_c, *Biochem.* See **folic acid.**

vitamin B complex, *Biochem.* an important group of water-soluble vitamins containing vitamin B_1, vitamin B_2, etc.

vitamin C, *Biochem.* See **ascorbic acid.**

vitamin D, *Biochem.* any of the several fat-soluble, antirachitic vitamins D_1, D_2, D_3, found in milk and fish-liver oils, esp. cod and halibut, or obtained by irradiating provitamin D with ultraviolet light.

vitamin D_1, *Biochem.* a mixture of lumisterol and calciferol, obtained by ultraviolet irradiation of ergosterol.

vitamin D_2, *Biochem.* calciferol.

vitamin D_3, *Biochem.* the naturally occurring D vitamin, $C_{27}H_{43}OH$, found in fish-liver oils, differing from vitamin D_2 by slight structural differences in the molecule. Also called **cholecalciferol.**

vitamin E, *Biochem.* a pale-yellow viscous fluid, found in wheat-germ oil, that promotes fertility, prevents abortion, and is active in maintaining the involuntary nervous system, vascular system, and involuntary muscles. Cf. **tocopherol.**

vitamin G, *Biochem.* riboflavin.

vitamin H, *Biochem.* biotin.

vitamin K_1, *Biochem.* a yellowish, oily, viscous liquid, $C_{31}H_{46}O_2$, occurring in leafy vegetables, rice, bran, hog liver, etc., that is obtained esp. from alfalfa or putrefied sardine meat, or synthesized. It promotes blood clotting by increasing the prothrombin content of the blood. Also called **phylloquinone, phytonadione.**

vitamin K_2, *Biochem.* a light-yellow, crystalline solid, $C_{41}H_{56}O_2$, having properties similar to those of vitamin K_1.

vitamin M, *Biochem.* See **folic acid.**

vitamin P, *Biochem.* a water-soluble vitamin, present in citrus fruits, rose hips, and paprika, that maintains the resistance of cell and capillary walls to permeation and change of pressure; citrin.

vitamin X, *Biochem. Obs.* See **vitamin P.**

Vi·ta Nuo·va (*It.* vē′tä nwô′vä), a work in verse and prose (1291?) by Dante.

vi·ta·scope (vī′tə skōp′), *n.* one of the first motion-picture projectors, developed by Thomas Edison. [< L *vīt(a)* life + -SCOPE] —**vi·ta·scop·ic** (vī′tə skop′ik), *adj.*

vite (vēt), *adv.* *Music.* briskly; lively. [< F: rapid, quickly]

Vi·tebsk (vē′tepsk), *n.* a city in NE Byelorussia, in the W Soviet Union, on the Dvina River. 181,000 (est. 1964).

vi·tel·lin (vi tel′in, vī-), *n.* *Biochem.* a phosphoprotein in the yolk of eggs. Also called **ovovitellin.** [VITELL(US) + -IN[2]]

vi·tel·line (vi tel′in, vī-), *adj.* **1.** of or pertaining to the egg yolk. **2.** having a yellow color resembling that of an egg yolk. [late ME < ML *vitellīn(us).* See VITELLUS, -INE¹]

vitel′line mem′brane, the membrane surrounding the egg yolk.

Vi·tel·lo (vi tel′ō), *n.* a crater in the third quadrant of the face of the moon: about 30 miles in diameter.

vi·tel·lus (vi tel′əs, vī-), *n., pl.* **-lus·es.** the yolk of an egg. [< L, equiv. to *vit(ulus)* calf + *-ellus* dim. suffix]

vi·ti·a·ble (vish′ē ə bəl), *adj.* capable of being vitiated. [VITI(ATE) + -ABLE]

vi·ti·ate (vish′ē āt′), *v.t.,* **-at·ed, -at·ing.** **1.** to impair the quality of; make faulty; spoil; mar. **2.** to debase; corrupt; pervert. **3.** to make legally defective or invalid; invalidate: *to vitiate a claim.* [< L *vitiāt(us)* (ptp. of *vitiāre* to spoil), equiv. to *viti(um)* defect, blemish + *-ātus* -ATE¹] **—vi′ti·a′tion,** *n.* **—vi′ti·a′tor,** *n.*

vi·ti·at·ed (vish′ē ā′tid), *adj.* **1.** spoiled; marred. **2.** perverted; corrupted. **3.** rendered invalid. [VITIATE + -ED²]

vi·ti·ce·tum (vit′i sē′təm), *n., pl.* **-tums, -ta** (-tə). a place where vines, esp. grapevines, are cultivated. [< L *vīti(s)* vine (influenced by *vitic-* (s. of *vitex*) chaste tree + *-ētum* (n. suffix) garden, type of plant]

vit·i·cul·ture (vit′ə kul′chər, vī′tə-), *n.* **1.** the culture or cultivation of grapevines; grape-growing. **2.** the study or science of grapes and their culture. [< L *vīti(s)* VINE + CULTURE] **—vit′i·cul′tur·al,** *adj.* **—vit′i·cul′tur·er, vit′i·cul′tur·ist,** *n.*

Vi·ti Le·vu (vē′tē le′vōō), the largest of the Fiji Islands, in the S Pacific. 176,822 (1946); 4053 sq. mi. *Cap.:* Suva.

vit·i·li·go (vit′əlē′gō), *n. Pathol.* a skin disease characterized by smooth, white patches on various parts of the body, caused by the loss of the natural pigment. Also called **leukoderma, piebald skin.** [< L: tetter, appar. equiv. to **vitil(is)* defective (*vit(ium)* blemish + *-ilis* -ILE) + *-īgo* n. suffix] **—vit·i·lig·i·nous** (vit′əlij′ə nəs), *adj.* **—vit′i·li′goid,** *adj.*

Vi·to (vē′tō), *n.* a boy's given name.

Vi·to·ria (vi tôr′ē ə, -tōr′-; *Sp.* bē tô′ryä), *n.* **1. Fran·cis·co de** (fräN thēs′kô de), c1480–1546, Spanish scholar and theologian. **2.** a city in N Spain: decisive defeat of the French forces in Spain 1813. 80,223 (est. 1963).

Vi·tó·ri·a (vi tôr′ē ə, -tōr′-; *Port.* vē tô′ryə), *n.* a seaport in and the capital of Espírito Santo, in E Brazil. 83,900 (1960).

vit·rain (vi′trān), *n.* the friable, vitreous layers in banded bituminous coal. Cf. **clarain, durain.** [< L *vitr(um)* glass + *-ain,* as in *clarain*]

vit·re·ous (vi′trē əs), *adj.* **1.** of the nature of or resembling glass, as in transparency, brittleness, hardness, glossiness, etc.: *vitreous china.* **2.** of or pertaining to glass. **3.** obtained from or containing glass. [< L *vitreus,* equiv. to *vitr(um)* glass + *-eus* -EOUS] **—vit′re·ous·ly,** *adv.* **—vit′re·ous·ness, vit·re·os·i·ty** (vi′trē os′i tē), *n.*

vit′reous electric′ity. See **positive electricity.**

vit′reous hu′mor, *Anat.* the transparent gelatinous substance filling the eyeball behind the crystalline lens. Also called **vit′reous bod′y.** See diag. under **eye.**

vi·tres·cent (vi tres′ənt), *adj.* **1.** becoming glass. **2.** tending to become glass. **3.** capable of being formed into glass. [< L *vitr(um)* glass + -ESCENT] **—vi·tres′cence,** *n.*

vi·tres·ci·ble (vi tres′ə bəl), *adj.* capable of being formed into or of becoming glass; vitrifiable. [VITRESC(ENT) + -IBLE]

vit·re·um (vi′trē əm), *adj.* (in prescriptions) glass. [< L]

vitri-, a learned borrowing from Latin meaning "glass," used in the formation of compound words: *vitriform.* [comb. form of L *vitrum*]

vit·ric (vi′trik), *adj.* **1.** of or pertaining to glass. **2.** of the nature of or resembling glass. [< L *vitr(um)* + -IC]

vit·rics (vi′triks), *n.* **1.** (*construed as sing.*) the art and technology of making glass products. **2.** (*construed as pl.*) articles of glass or other vitreous materials. [see VITRIC, -ICS]

vit·ri·fi·ca·tion (vi′trə fə kā′shən), *n.* **1.** act or process of vitrifying; state of being vitrified. **2.** something vitrified. Also, **vit·ri·fac·tion** (vi′trə fak′shən). [VITRI- + -FICATION]

vit·ri·form (vi′trə fôrm′), *adj.* having the form or appearance of glass. [VITRI- + -FORM]

vit·ri·fy (vi′trə fī′), *v.t., v.i.,* **-fied, -fy·ing.** **1.** to convert or be converted into glass. **2.** to make or become vitreous. [VITRI- + -FY; cf. F *vitrifier*] **—vit′ri·fi′a·bil′i·ty,** *n.* **—vit′ri·fi′a·ble,** *adj.*

vi·trine (vi trēn′), *n.* a display cabinet, wholly glazed on the front and often on the sides and top. [< F, equiv. to *vitre* pane of glass + *-ine* -INE²]

vit·ri·ol (vi′trē əl), *n., v.,* **-oled, -ol·ing** or (*esp. Brit.*) **-olled, -ol·ling.** **—***n.* **1.** *Chem.* any of certain metallic sulfates of glassy appearance, as copper sulfate or blue vitriol, iron sulfate or green vitriol, zinc sulfate or white vitriol, etc. **2.** oil of vitriol; sulfuric acid. **3.** something highly caustic or severe in effect, as criticism. **—***v.t.* **4.** to treat with or as with vitriol, esp. sulfuric acid. [late ME < ML *vitriol(um),* equiv. to *vitri-* VITRI- + *-olum,* neut. of *-olus* adj. suffix]

vit·ri·ol·ic (vi′trē ol′ik), *adj.* **1.** of, pertaining to, or resembling vitriol. **2.** obtained from vitriol. **3.** severely caustic; scathing: *vitriolic criticism.* [VITRIOL + -IC] **—Syn. 3.** acid, bitter. **—Ant. 3.** bland, mild.

vit·ri·ol·ise (vi′trē ə līz′), *v.t.,* **-ised, -is·ing.** *Chiefly Brit.* vitriolize. **—vit′ri·ol·i·sa′tion,** *n.*

vit·ri·o·lize (vi′trē ə līz′), *v.t.,* **-ized, -iz·ing.** **1.** to treat with or change into vitriol. **2.** to injure or burn with sulfuric acid. [VITRIOL + -IZE] **—vit′ri·ol·i·za′tion,** *n.*

vit·rum (vi′trəm), *n., pl.* **vit·ra** (vi′trə). (in prescriptions) glass. [< L]

Vitru′vian scroll′, a scroll forming a stylized wave pattern. Also called **running dog, Vitru′vian wave′, wave scroll.** [named after VITRUVIUS POLLIO]

Vi·tru·vi·us (vi trōō′vē əs), *n.* a walled plain in the first quadrant of the face of the moon, having a dark floor: about 20 miles in diameter.

Vitru′vius Pol′li·o (pol′ē ō′), **Marcus,** fl. 1st century B.C., Roman architect, engineer, and author. **—Vi·tru′vi·an,** *adj.*

Vi·try (vē trē′), *n.* **Phi·lippe de** (fē lēp′ də), 1290?–1361, French music theorist, composer, and poet.

vit·ta (vit′ə), *n., pl.* **vit·tae** (vit′ē). **1.** *Bot.* a tube or receptacle for oil, found in the fruits of most umbelliferous plants. **2.** *Zool., Bot.* a streak or stripe, as of color. [< L: ribbon, fillet, akin to *viēre* to weave together]

vit·tate (vit′āt), *adj.* **1.** provided with or having a vitta or vittae. **2.** striped longitudinally. [< L *vittāt(us),* equiv. to *vitt(a)* fillet + *-ātus* -ATE¹]

vit·tle (vit′əl), *n., v.t., v.i.* victual.

Vit·to·ri·a (vēt tô′rē ä′), *n.* a girl's given name, Italian form of **Victoria.**

vit·u·line (vich′ə lin′, -lin), *adj.* of, pertaining to, or resembling a calf or veal. [< L *vitulīn(us),* equiv. to *vitul(us)* calf + *-īnus* -INE¹]

vi·tu·per·ate (vī tōō′pə rāt′, -tyōō′, vi-), *v.t.,* **-at·ed, -at·ing.** **1.** to find fault with; censure harshly or abusively. **2.** to address harsh or abusive language to; revile. [< L *vituperāt(us)* (ptp. of *vituperāre* to spoil, blame), equiv. to *vituper-* (*vitu-,* var. of *viti-,* s. of *vitium* blemish + *-per-,* var. of *-par-,* root of *parāre;* see PREPARE) + *-ātus* -ATE¹] **—vi·tu′per·a′tor,** *n.*
—Syn. 2. censure, vilify, berate. **—Ant. 2.** praise, commend.

vi·tu·per·a·tion (vī tōō′pə rā′shən, -tyōō′-, vi-), *n.* **1.** the act of vituperating. **2.** verbal abuse or castigation; violent denunciation or condemnation. [< L *vituperātiōn-* (s. of *vituperātio*), equiv. to *vituperāt(us)* (see VITUPERATE) + *-iōn-* -ION]
—Syn. 2. censure, vilification, spite, scolding, defamation, aspersion. **—Ant. 1, 2.** praise.

vi·tu·per·a·tive (vī tōō′pə rā′tiv, -pər ə tiv, -tyōō′-, vi-), *adj.* characterized by or of the nature of vituperation: *vituperative remarks.* [VITUPERATE + -IVE] **—vi·tu′per·a′tive·ly,** *adv.*

vi·va¹ (vē′və, -vä), *interj.* **1.** (*italics*) *Italian, Spanish.* (as an exclamation of acclaim or approval) Long live (the person named)! **—***n.* **2.** a shout of "*viva.*" [lit.: may he live! 3rd pers. sing. pres. subj. of It *vivere,* Sp *vivir* < L *vīvere* to live; see REVIVE]

vi·va² (vī′və), *n.* (in British universities) an oral examination; viva voce. [shortened form]

vi·va·ce (vi vä′chā; *It.* vē vä′che), *adj.* (a musical direction) vivacious; lively. [< It < L *vīvax, -ācis* long-lived, lively; see VIVACITY]

vi·va·cious (vi vā′shəs, vī-), *adj.* **1.** lively; animated; sprightly; gay: *a vivacious girl; a vivacious folk dance.* **2.** *Archaic.* long-lived, or tenacious of life. [VIVACI(TY) + -OUS] **—vi·va′cious·ly,** *adv.* **—vi·va′cious·ness,** *n.*
—Syn. 1. spirited, brisk. **—Ant. 1.** languid.

vi·vac·i·ty (vi vas′i tē, vī-), *n., pl.* **-ties.** **1.** the quality or state of being vivacious. **2.** liveliness; animation; sprightliness: *a people noted for their vivacity.* **3.** a vivacious act or statement. [late ME < L *vīvācitāt-* (s. of *vīvācitās*), equiv. to *vīvāci-* (s. of *vīvax* long-lived, lively, equiv. to *vīv(us)* alive + *-āci-* adj. suffix) + *-tāt-* -TY²]

Vi·val·di (vi väl′dē; *It.* vē väl′dē), *n.* **An·to·nio** (an tō′nē ō′; *It.* än tô′nyô), c1675–1741, Italian violinist and composer.

vi·van·dière (vē väN dyer′), *n., pl.* **-dières** (-dyer′). *French.* a woman who formerly accompanied a French or other Continental army to sell provisions and liquor to the soldiers.

vi·var·i·um (vī vâr′ē əm), *n., pl.* **-var·i·ums, -var·i·a** (-vâr′ē ə). a place, such as a laboratory, where animals are kept alive under conditions simulating their natural state. [< L, equiv. to *vīv(us)* living + *-ārium* -ARY]

vi·va vo·ce (vī′və vō′sē), **1.** by word of mouth; orally. **2.** (in British universities) the oral part of an examination. [< ML: with living voice < L, abl. of *vīva vox*] **—vi′va-vo′ce,** *adj.*

vive (vēv), *interj. French.* (used as an exclamation of acclaim or approval) Long live (the person or notion named)!: *Vive l'amour!*

Vi·ve·ka·nan·da (vē′ve kə nun′də), *n.* (*Narendranath Datta*) 1863–1902, Hindu religious leader and teacher.

vive la ba·ga·telle (vēv lA bA gA tel′), *French.* Long live frivolity!

vive l'a·mour (vēv lA mōōr′), *French.* Long live love!

vive la ré·pu·blique (vēv lA rā py blēk′), *French.* Long live the republic!

vive le roi (vēv lə rwA′), *French.* Long live the king!

vi·ver·rine (vī ver′in, -in, vi-), *adj.* **1.** of or pertaining to the *Viverridae,* a family of small carnivorous mammals including the civets, genets, palm cats, etc. **—***n.* **2.** a viverrine animal. [< NL *viverrīn(us),* equiv. to L *viverr(a)* ferret + *-īnus* -INE¹]

vi·vers (vē′vərz), *n.pl. Chiefly Scot.* victuals; foodstuffs. [< MF *vivres,* pl. of *vivre* food, n. use of *vivre* to live < L *vīvere;* see VIAND]

vives (vīvz), *n.* (*construed as sing.*) *Vet. Pathol.* inflammation and swelling of the submaxillary gland in horses. [< MF *(a)vives* < Sp *adiba(s)* < Ar *adh-dhība* she-wolf]

vi·ve va·le·que (wē′we wä le′kwe; *Eng.* vī′vē vəlē′kwē), *Latin.* live and keep well (used at the end of letters).

vivi-, a learned borrowing from Latin meaning "living," "alive," used in the formation of compound words: *vivisection.* [< L *vīvi-,* comb. form of *vīvus*]

Viv·i·an (viv′ē ən), *n.* **1.** Also, **Vivien.** *Arthurian Romance.* an enchantress, the mistress of Merlin: known as the Lady of the Lake. **2.** a town in NW Louisiana. 2624 (1960). **3.** Also, **Vivien, Vivienne, Vivyan, Vyvyan.** a boy's or girl's given name.

Vi·vi·a·ni (vē vyA nē′), *n.* **Re·né** (rə nā′), 1863–1925, French statesman: premier of France 1911–15.

viv·i·an·ite (viv′ē ə nīt′), *n.* a rare mineral, hydrous ferrous phosphate, $Fe_3(PO_4)_2{\cdot}8H_2O$, occurring in the form of pale blue crystals or powder. [named after J. G. *Vivian,* 19th-century English mineralogist, the finder; see -ITE¹]

viv·id (viv′id), *adj.* **1.** strikingly bright or intense, as color, light, etc.: *The house was painted a vivid green.* **2.** full of life; lively; animated: *a vivid personality.* **3.** presenting the appearance, freshness, spirit, etc., of life; realistic: *a vivid painting; a vivid street scene.* **4.** strong, distinct, or clearly perceptible: *a vivid impression; a vivid recollection.* **5.** forming distinct and striking mental images: *a vivid imagination.* [< L *vīvid(us)* lively, equiv. to *vīv(ere)* to live + *-idus* -ID⁴] **—viv′id·ly,** *adv.* **—viv′id·ness, vi·vid′i·ty,** *n.*
—Syn. 1. bright, brilliant, intense. **2.** spirited, vivacious, intense. **3.** See **picturesque. 4.** discernible, apparent.

Viv·i·en (viv′ē ən), *n.* **1.** Also, **Vivian, Vivienne, Vivyan, Vyvyan.** a boy's or girl's given name. **2.** Vivian (def. 1).

Viv·i·enne (viv′ē ən), *n.* a boy's or girl's given name. Also, **Vivian, Vivien, Vivyan, Vyvyan.**

viv·i·fy (viv′ə fī′), *v.t.,* **-fied, -fy·ing.** **1.** to give life to; animate; quicken. **2.** to enliven; brighten; sharpen. [alter. (with *-fy* for *-ficate*) of late ME *vivificate* < L *vīvificāt(us)* (ptp. of *vīvificāre*). See VIVI-, -FICATE] **—viv′i·fi·ca′tion,** *n.* **—viv′i·fi′er,** *n.*

vi·vip·a·ra (vi vip′ər ə), *n.pl.* viviparous animals. [< L, fem. of *vīviparus* VIVIPAROUS]

vi·vip·ar·ous (vi vip′ər əs), *adj.* **1.** *Zool.* bringing forth living young rather than eggs, as most mammals and some reptiles and fishes. **2.** *Bot.* producing seeds that germinate on the plant. [< L *vīviparus* bringing forth living young. See VIVI-, -PAROUS] **—viv·i·par′a·rism,** *n.* **—viv·i·par·i·ty** (viv′ə par′i tē), **vi·vip′a·rous·ness,** *n.* **—vi·vip′a·rous·ly,** *adv.*

viv·i·sect (viv′i sekt′, viv′i sekt′), *v.t.* **1.** to dissect the living body of (an animal). **—***v.i.* **2.** to practice vivisection. [back formation from VIVISECTION] **—viv′i·sect′i·ble,** *adj.* **—viv′i·sec′tor,** *n.*

viv·i·sec·tion (viv′i sek′shən), *n.* **1.** the action of cutting into or dissecting a living body. **2.** the practice of subjecting living animals to cutting operations, esp. in order to advance physiological and pathological knowledge. [VIVI- + SECTION] **—viv′i·sec′tion·al,** *adj.* **—viv′i·sec′tion·al·ly,** *adv.*

viv·i·sec·tion·ist (viv′i sek′shə nist), *n.* **1.** a person who vivisects. **2.** a person who favors or defends the practice of vivisection. [VIVISECTION + -IST]

Viv·yan (viv′yən), *n.* a boy's or girl's given name. Also, **Vivian, Vivien, Vivienne, Vyvyan.**

vix·en (vik′sən), *n.* **1.** an ill-tempered or quarrelsome woman. **2.** a female fox. [dial. var. of ME *fixen* she-fox, equiv. to OE *fyxen* (adj.) pertaining to a fox (by confusion of suffixes: adj. suffix *-en* was taken to be fem. suffix *-en*] **—vix′en·ish, vix′en·ly,** *adj.* **—vix′en·ish·ly,** *adv.* **—vix′en·ish·ness,** *n.*

Vi·yel·la (vi yel′ə), *Trademark.* a fabric made of cotton and wool in twill weave. Also called **Viyel′la flan′nel.**

viz., videlicet.

viz·ard (viz′ərd), *n.* **1.** a mask. **2.** *Obs.* a visor of a helmet. Also, **visard.** [var. of VISOR; see -ARD] **—viz′ard·ed,** *adj.*

viz·ca·cha (vis kä′chə), *n.* viscacha.

vi·zier (vi zēr′, viz′yər), *n.* **1.** a high official in certain Muslim countries. **2.** a minister of state. Also, **vi·zir′.** [< Turk *vezīr* < Ar *wazīr* burden-bearer, deriv. of *wazara* to carry, bear burdens] **—vi·zier·ate, vi·zir·ate** (vi zēr′it, -āt, viz′yər it, -yə rāt′), **vi·zier′ship, vi·zir′ship,** *n.* **—vi·zier′i·al, vi·zir′i·al,** *adj.*

vi·zor (vī′zər, viz′ər), *n., v.t.* visor. **—vi′zor·less,** *adj.*

V-J Day, August 15, 1945, the day Japan accepted the Allied surrender terms in World War II. [V-J: victory over Japan]

V joint, *Masonry.* an angular, hollow mortar joint.

VL, Vulgar Latin.

v.l., varia lectio.

Vlaar·ding·en (vlär′diŋ ən), *n.* a city in the W Netherlands, at the mouth of the Rhine. 70,404 (1962).

Vlacq (vläk), *n.* a walled plain in the fourth quadrant of the face of the moon: about 56 miles in diameter.

Vla·di·kav·kaz (vlä′di käf käs′), *n.* former name of **Ordzhonikidze.**

Vlad·i·mir (vlad′ə mir′; *Russ.* vlä dē′mir), *n.* **1. Saint.** Also, **Vladimir I, Wladimir.** (*Vladimir the Great*) A.D. c956–1015, first Christian grand prince of Russia 980–1015. **2.** a city in the W RSFSR, in the central part of the Soviet Union in Europe, E of Moscow. 188,000 (est. 1964). **3.** a boy's given name.

Vla·di·vos·tok (vlad′ə vos′tok; *Russ.* vlä di vos tôk′), *n.* a seaport in the SE RSFSR, in the SE Soviet Union in Asia, on the Sea of Japan: eastern terminus of the Trans-Siberian Railroad. 353,000 (est. 1964).

Vla·minck (vlA maNk′), *n.* **Mau·rice de** (mō rēs′ də), 1876–1958, French painter.

VLF, See **very low frequency.** Also, **vlf**

Vlis·sing·en (vlis′iŋ ən), *n.* Dutch name of **Flushing.**

Vl·ta·va (vul′tə və), *n.* a river in the W Czech Republic, flowing N to the Elbe. 270 mi. long. German, **Moldau.**

V-mail (vē′māl′), *n.* a mail system, used by U.S. armed forces during World War II, in which a microfilm of a letter was forwarded for printing in full size on photographic paper before delivery. [V: victory]

V.M.D., Doctor of Veterinary Medicine. [< L *Veterinariae Medicinae Doctor*]

v.n., verb neuter.

V neck, a neckline V-shaped in front.

vo., verso.

VOA, **1.** Voice of America. **2.** Volunteers of America.

voc., vocative.

vocab., vocabulary.

vo·ca·ble (vō′kə bəl), *n.* **1.** a word; term; name. **2.** a word considered only as a combination of certain sounds or letters, without regard to meaning. **—***adj.* **3.** capable of being spoken. [< L *vocābul(um)* a word, a name, equiv. to *vocā(re)* to call + *-bulum* dim. suffix] **—vo′ca·bly,** *adv.*

vo·cab·u·lar·y (vō kab′yə ler′ē), *n., pl.* **-lar·ies.** **1.** the stock of words used by a particular people, class, person, member of an occupation or profession, etc.: *His French vocabulary is rather limited. The scientific vocabulary is constantly growing.* **2.** a list or collection of the words or phrases of a language, branch of science, or the like, usually arranged in alphabetical order and defined: *Study the vocabulary in the fourth chapter.* **3.** the words of a language. **4.** any collection of signs or symbols constituting a means or system of nonverbal communication: *vocabulary of a computer.* **5.** any more or less specific group of forms characteristic of an artist, a style of art, architecture, or the like, etc. [< ML *vocābulārius*, neut. of *vocābulārius* of words, equiv. to L *vocābul(um)* VOCABLE + *-ārius* -ARY] —**vo·cab′u·lar′ied,** *adj.*

vocab′ulary en′try, (in dictionaries) a word, phrase, abbreviation, symbol, affix, name, etc., listed with its definition or explanation in alphabetical order or listed for identification after the word from which it is derived or to which it is related.

vo·cal (vō′kəl), *adj.* **1.** of, pertaining to, or uttered with the voice: *the vocal mechanism; vocal criticism.* **2.** rendered by or intended for singing: *vocal music.* **3.** having a voice: *An animal is a vocal, but not a verbal, being.* **4.** giving forth sound with or as with a voice. **5.** inclined to express oneself in words, esp. copiously or insistently: *a vocal advocate of reform.* **6.** *Phonet.* **a.** vocalic (def. 1). **b.** voiced. —*n.* **7.** a vocal sound. **8.** a musical piece for a singer, usually with instrumental accompaniment. Cf. **instrumental** (def. 9). [late ME < L *vōcāl(is)*, equiv. to *vōc-* (s. of *vox*) + *-ālis* -AL¹] —**vo·cal·i·ty** (vō kal′i tē), **vo′cal·ness,** *n.* —**vo′cal·ly,** *adv.*
—**Syn. 5.** vociferous.

vo′cal cords′, *Anat.* either of the two pairs of folds of mucous membrane projecting into the cavity of the larynx. Cf. **true vocal cords, false vocal cords.**

vo′cal folds′. See **true vocal cord.**

vo·cal·ic (vō kal′ik), *adj.* **1.** of, pertaining to, or resembling a vowel or vowels. **2.** consisting of, characterized by, or containing vowels. [VOCAL + -IC]

vocal′ic allitera′tion. See under **alliteration** (def. 1).

vo·cal·ise (vō′kə līz′), *v.t., v.i.,* **-ised, -is·ing.** *Chiefly Brit.* vocalize. —**vo′cal·i·sa′tion,** *n.* —**vo′cal·is′er,** *n.*

vo·cal·ism (vō′kə liz′əm), *n.* **1.** *Phonet.* **a.** the nature of one or more given vowels. **b.** the system of vowels of a particular language. **2.** the use of the voice, as in speech or song. **3.** the act, principles, or art of singing. [VOCAL + -ISM]

vo·cal·ist (vō′kə list), *n.* a singer. [VOCAL + -IST]

vo·cal·ize (vō′kə līz′), *v.,* **-ized, -iz·ing.** —*v.t.* **1.** to make vocal; utter; articulate; sing. **2.** to endow with a voice; cause to utter. **3.** *Phonet.* **a.** to voice. **b.** to change into a vowel (contrasted with *consonantalize*). **4.** (of Hebrew, Arabic, and other writing systems that do not usually indicate vowels) to furnish with vowel points. —*v.i.* **5.** to use the voice, as in speech or song. **6.** to sing without uttering words, esp. to warm up the voice, practice vowel sounds, etc., before a performance. **7.** to sing scales, arpeggios, trills, or the like, usually to a solmization syllable or a vowel sound. **8.** *Phonet.* to become changed into a vowel. Also, *esp. Brit.,* **vocalise.** [VOCAL + -IZE] —**vo′cal·i·za′tion,** *n.* —**vo′cal·iz′er,** *n.*

Vo′cal Mem′non, one of the two seated figures of the Colossus of Memnon: so called because it once emitted sounds when struck by the rays of the rising sun.

vocat., vocative.

vo·ca·tion (vō kā′shən), *n.* **1.** a particular occupation, business, or profession; calling. **2.** a strong impulse or inclination to follow a particular activity or career. **3.** a divine call to God's service or to the Christian life. **4.** a function or station in life to which one is called by God: *the religious vocation; the vocation of marriage.* [late ME *vocacio(u)n* < L *vocātiōn-* (s. of *vocātiō*) a call, summons, equiv. to *vocāt(us)* ptp. (*voc-*, root of *vocāre* to call + *-ātus* -ATE¹) + *-iōn-* -ION]
—**Syn. 1.** employment, pursuit.

vo·ca·tion·al (vō kā′shə nᵊl), *adj.* **1.** of, pertaining to, or connected with a vocation or occupation: *a vocational aptitude; a vocational school.* **2.** of, pertaining to, or noting instruction or guidance in an occupation or profession chosen as a career or in the choice of a career: *a vocational counselor; vocational training.* [VOCATION + -AL¹] —**vo·ca′tion·al·ly,** *adv.*

voca′tional educa′tion, educational training that provides a student with practical experience in a particular occupational field, as agriculture, home economics, or industry.

voc·a·tive (vok′ə tiv), *adj.* **1.** *Gram.* (in certain inflected languages, as Latin) noting or pertaining to a case used to indicate that a noun refers to a person or thing being addressed. **2.** of, pertaining to, or used in calling, specifying, or addressing. —*n. Gram.* **3.** the vocative case. **4.** a word in the vocative, as Latin *Paule* "O Paul." [late ME < L *vocātīv(us)* (*cāsus*) calling (case), equiv. to *vocāt(us)* (see VOCATION) + *-īvus* -IVE] —**voc′a·tive·ly,** *adv.*

vo·cif·er·ance (vō sif′ər əns), *n.* vociferant utterance; vociferation. [VOCIFER(ANT) + -ANCE]

vo·cif·er·ant (vō sif′ər ənt), *adj.* **1.** vociferating; noisy. —*n.* **2.** one who vociferates. [< L *vōciferant-* (s. of *vōciferāns*), equiv. to *vōcifer-* (see VOCIFERATE) + *-ant-* -ANT]

vo·cif·er·ate (vō sif′ə rāt′), *v.i., v.t.,* **-at·ed, -at·ing.** to speak or cry out loudly or noisily; shout; bawl. [< L *vōciferāt(us)* (ptp. of *vōciferārī* to shout), equiv. to *vōcifer-* (*vōci-*, s. of *vox* voice + *-fer-*, root of *ferre* to bring forth) + *-ātus* -ATE¹] —**vo·cif′er·a′tor,** *n.*

vo·cif·er·a·tion (vō sif′ə rā′shən), *n.* noisy outcry; clamor. [late ME < L *vōciferātiōn-* (s. of *vōciferātiō*), equiv. to *vōciferāt(us)* (see VOCIFERATE) + *-iōn-* -ION]

vo·cif·er·ous (vō sif′ər əs), *adj.* **1.** crying out noisily; clamorous. **2.** characterized by or uttered with vociferation: *a vociferous manner of expression.* [VOCIFER(ANT) + -OUS] —**vo·cif′er·ous·ly,** *adv.* —**vo·cif′er·ous·ness,** *n.*
—**Syn. 1.** loud, noisy, vocal, uproarious, boisterous.

vo·coid (vō′koid), *Phonet.* —*adj.* **1.** vowellike. —*n.* **2.** a vowellike sound. Cf. **contoid.** [VOC(AL) + -OID]

vod·ka (vod′kə), *n.* an unaged, colorless, distilled spirit, originally made in Russia. [< Russ, equiv. to *vod(a)* WATER + *-ka* hypocoristic suffix]

vo·dun (vō do͞on′), *n.* voodoo (def. 1). [< Haitian F < some African tongue; see VOODOO]

Vo·gel (vō′gəl), *n.* **Sir Julius,** 1835–99, New Zealand statesman, born in England: prime minister 1873–75, 1876.

vo·ge·site (vō′gə sīt′), *n. Mineral.* a lamprophyric rock composed of either hornblende or augite and either orthoclase or sanidine. [< L *Voges(us)* VOSGES + -ITE¹]

vo·gie (vō′gē, vog′ē), *adj. Scot.* **1.** conceited; proud. **2.** cheerful; merry. [?]

vogue (vōg), *n.* **1.** the fashion, as at a particular time: *During the twenties, short skirts and short hairdos were the vogue.* **2.** popular currency, acceptance, or favor; popularity: *The book in its day had a great vogue.* [< MF: wave or course of success < OIt *voga* a rowing, deriv. of *vogare* to row, sail (lit., to make waves) < MHG *wagen*, deriv. of *woge* wave]
—**Syn. 1.** mode. See **fashion.**

Vo·gul (vō′go͝ol), *n.* a Finno-Ugric language of the Ugric group, spoken E of the Ural Mountains.

voice (vois), *n., v.,* **voiced, voic·ing.** —*n.* **1.** the sound or sounds uttered through the mouth of living creatures, esp. of human beings in speaking, shouting, singing, etc. **2.** the distinctive range of sounds naturally or characteristically uttered by an individual: *I thought I recognized your voice.* **3.** such sounds considered with reference to their character or quality: *a masculine voice; a sweet voice.* **4.** the condition or effectiveness of the voice for speaking or singing: *The soprano is in poor voice tonight.* **5.** a sound likened to or resembling vocal utterance: *the voice of the wind; the voices of frogs in spring.* **6.** something likened to speech as conveying impressions to the mind: *the voice of nature; the voice of hope.* **7.** the faculty of uttering sounds through the mouth, esp. articulate sounds; speech: *to lose one's voice.* **8.** expression in spoken or written words, or by other means: *to give voice to one's disapproval by a letter.* **9.** expressed opinion or choice: *His voice was for compromise.* **10.** the right to express an opinion or choice: *We were given no voice in the election of officers.* **11.** expressed wish or injunction: *obedient to the voice of God.* **12.** the person or other agency through which something is expressed or revealed: *a warning that proved to be the voice of prophecy.* **13.** musical tone created by the vibration of the vocal cords and amplified by oral and other throat cavities; tone produced in singing. **14.** *Phonet.* the audible result of phonation and resonance. **15.** *Gram.* **a.** a set of categories for which the verb is inflected in some languages, as Latin, and which is typically used to indicate the relation of the verbal action to the subject as performer, undergoer, or beneficiary of its action. **b.** a set of syntactic devices in some languages, as English, that is similar to this set in function. **c.** any of the categories of these sets: *the English passive voice; the Greek middle voice.* **16.** the finer regulation, as of intensity and color, in tuning, esp. of a piano or organ. **17.** a singer: *a score for fifty voices.* **18.** a voice part or parts: *a composition for voice and orchestra.* **19.** a specific range of tones sung by one performer; register: *a piece for alto and tenor voices.* **20.** *Obs.* **a.** rumor. **b.** reputation; fame. **21. the still, small voice,** the conscience: *He was only occasionally troubled by the still, small voice.* **22. with one voice,** in accord; unanimously: *They arose and with one voice acclaimed the new president.* —*v.t.* **23.** to give utterance or expression to; declare; proclaim: *to voice one's discontent.* **24.** *Music.* **a.** to regulate the tone of, as the pipes of an organ. **b.** to write the voice parts for (music). **25.** to utter with the voice. **26.** *Phonet.* to pronounce with glottal vibration. [ME < AF *voiz, voice* (OF *voiz, vois*) < L *vōci-, vōce-*, s. of *vox* VOX] —**voic′er,** *n.*
—**Syn. 5.** cry, call. **6.** sound, language, speech, tongue. **11.** order, command. **12.** mouthpiece, organ. **23.** reveal, disclose, publish.

voice′ box′, the larynx.

voice′ coil′, *Elect.* a moving coil that drives the diaphragm of a sound reproduction system, as a loudspeaker, by the interaction of a changing magnetic field that is produced by a current in the coil and a fixed magnetic field that is produced by permanent magnets.

voiced (voist), *adj.* **1.** having a voice of a specified kind (usually used in combination): *gruff-voiced; shrill-voiced.* **2.** expressed vocally: *his voiced opinion.* **3.** *Phonet.* pronounced with glottal vibrations; phonated (contrasted with *voiceless*): *"b," "v," and "z" are voiced.* [VOICE + -ED³] —**voic·ed·ness** (voi′sid nis, voist′nis), *n.*

voice·ful (vois′fəl), *adj.* having a voice, esp. a loud voice; sounding; sonorous. [VOICE + -FUL] —**voice′ful·ness,** *n.*

voice·less (vois′lis), *adj.* **1.** having no voice; mute; dumb. **2.** uttering no words; silent. **3.** having an unmusical voice. **4.** unspoken; unuttered: *voiceless sympathy.* **5.** *Phonet.* (of a speech sound) **a.** without voice; unvoiced; surd; aphonic (contrasted with *voiced*): *"p," "f," and "s" are voiceless.* **b.** uttered without phonation. **6.** having no vote or right of choice. [VOICE + -LESS] —**voice′less·ly,** *adv.* —**voice′less·ness,** *n.*
—**Syn. 1.** See **dumb.**

voice′ part′, *Music.* the melody or succession of tones for one of the voices or instruments in a harmonic or concerted composition.

voice′ vote′, a vote based on estimation of the relative strength of ayes and noes called out rather than on a counting of individual ballots, a roll call, or a division.

void (void), *adj.* **1.** *Law.* having no legal force or effect; not legally binding or enforceable. **2.** useless; ineffectual; vain. **3.** devoid; destitute (usually fol. by *of*): *a heart void of love; a life void of meaning.* **4.** without contents; empty. **5.** without an incumbent, as an office. **6.** *Math.* (of a set) null. —*n.* **7.** an empty space; emptiness: *He disappeared into the void of the darkness.* **8.** something experienced as a loss or privation: *His death left a great void in her life.* **9.** a gap or opening, as in a wall. **10.** a vacancy; vacuum. **11.** *Typography.* counter³ (def. 8). —*v.t.* **12.** to make ineffectual; invalidate; nullify: *to void a check.* **13.** to empty; discharge; evacuate: *to void excrement.* **14.** to clear or empty (often fol. by *of*): *to void a chamber of occupants.* **15.** *Archaic.* to depart from; vacate. **16.** *Obs.* **a.** to avoid. **b.** to send away; dismiss; expell. —*v.i.* **17.** to defecate. [ME *void(e)* < AF, OF < VL **vocīta*, fem. of **vocītus*, dissimilated var. of L *vocīvus*, var. of *vac(ī)vus* empty; see VACUUM] —**void′ness,** *n.*
—**Syn. 3, 4.** See **empty. 5.** vacant, unoccupied. **7.** vacuum.

void·a·ble (voi′də bəl), *adj.* **1.** capable of being nullified or invalidated. **2.** *Law.* capable of being made or adjudged void. [VOID + -ABLE] —**void′a·ble·ness,** *n.*

void·ance (void′ᵊns), *n.* **1.** the act of voiding. **2.** annulment, as of a contract. **3.** vacancy, as of a benefice. [aph. var. of AVOIDANCE]

void·ed (voi′did), *adj.* **1.** having a void. **2.** having been made void: *a voided contract.* **3.** *Heraldry.* (of a charge) depicted as if the center had been removed so as to leave only an outline: *an inescutcheon voided.* [VOID + -ED²]

void·er (voi′dər), *n.* **1.** one who or that which voids. **2.** *Armor.* gusset (def. 3a). [ME; see VOID, -ER¹]

voi·là (vwa lä′), *interj. French.* There it is! Look! See! (usually used interjectionally to express success or satisfaction).

voi·là tout (vwa la to͞o′), *French.* That's all.

voile (voil; *Fr.* vwal), *n.* a dress fabric of wool, silk, rayon, or cotton, with an open, canvaslike weave. [< F, equiv. to AF *veile* VEIL]

voir dire (vwär′ dēr′; *Fr.* vwar dēr′), *Law.* **1.** an oath administered to a proposed witness or juror by which he is sworn to speak the truth in an examination to ascertain his competence. **2.** the examination itself. [< AF, equiv. to OF *voir* true, truly + *dire* to say]

voi·ture (*Fr.* vwa tyr′), *n., pl.* **-tures** (*Fr.* -tyr′). a carriage, wagon, or other wheeled vehicle. [< F < L *vectūra*, equiv. to *vect-* (ptp. s. of *vehere* to carry) + *-ūra* -URE]

voi·vode (voi′vōd), *n.* vaivode.

voix cé·leste (vwä sā lest′), an organ stop having for each note two pipes tuned to slightly different pitches and producing a wavering, gentle tone. [< F: heavenly voice]

vol., **1.** volcano. **2.** volume. **3.** volunteer.

Vo·lans (vō′lanz), *n., gen.* **Vo·lan·tis** (vō lan′tis). *Astron.* the Flying Fish, a southern constellation between Carina and Hydrus. [< L, prp. of *volāre* to fly]

vo·lant (vō′lənt), *adj.* **1.** engaged in or having the power of flight. **2.** moving lightly; nimble. **3.** *Heraldry.* (of a bird or the like) represented as flying. —*n.* **4.** Also called **vo′lant piece′.** *Armor.* a reinforcing piece for the brow of a helmet. [< F, prp. of *voler* < L *volāre* to fly; see -ANT]

vo·lan·te (vō län′tā; *It.* vô län′te), *adv., adj. Music.* moving lightly and quickly. [< It, equiv. to *vol-* root of *volare* to fly (< L *volāre*) + *-ante* -ANT]

Vo·la·pük (vō′lə pyk′), *n.* one of the earliest of the artificially constructed international auxiliary languages, invented about 1879. Also, **Vol·a·puk** (vō′ə po͝ok′). [*vol*, repr. WO(R)L(D) + *-a-* + *pük*, repr. (S)PEAK] —**Vo′la·puk′ist,** *n.*

vo·lar¹ (vō′lər), *adj.* of or pertaining to the palm of the hand or the sole of the foot. [< L *vol(a)* palm of hand, sole of foot + -AR¹]

vo·lar² (vō′lər), *adj.* pertaining to or used for flight. [< L *vol(āre)* to fly + -AR¹]

vo·la·ry (vō′lə rē, vol′ə-), *n., pl.* **-ries.** *Rare.* **1.** a large cage for confining birds; aviary. **2.** the birds in such a cage. **3.** a flight or flock of birds. [< L *vol(āre)* (to) fly + -ARY]

vol·a·tile (vol′ə til, -tᵊl *or, esp. Brit.,* -tīl′), *adj.* **1.** evaporating rapidly; passing off readily in the form of vapor: *Acetone is a volatile solvent.* **2.** tending or threatening to break out into open violence; explosive: *a volatile political situation; a probable clash of two volatile tempers.* **3.** changeable; mercurial; flighty: *a volatile disposition; volatile affections.* **4.** fleeting; transient: *volatile beauty.* **5.** *Archaic.* able or accustomed to fly, as winged creatures. [ME < L *volātile*, neut. of *volātilis*, equiv. to *volāt(us)* (ptp. of *volāre* to fly; see -ATE¹) + *-ilis* -ILE] —**vol·a·til·i·ty** (vol′ə til′i tē), **vol′a·tile·ness,** *n.*

vol′atile oil′, a distilled oil, esp. one obtained from plant tissue, as distinguished from glyceride oils by their volatility and failure to saponify.

vol′atile salt′, **1.** See **ammonium carbonate. 2.** See **sal volatile** (def. 2).

vol·a·til·ise (vol′ə tᵊlīz′), *v.i., v.t.,* **-ised, -is·ing.** *Chiefly Brit.* volatilize. —**vol′a·til·is′a·ble,** *adj.* —**vol′a·til·i·sa′tion,** *n.* —**vol′a·til·is′er,** *n.*

vol·a·til·ize (vol′ə tᵊlīz′), *v.,* **-ized, -iz·ing.** —*v.i.* **1.** to become volatile; pass off as vapor. —*v.t.* **2.** to make volatile; cause to pass off in the form of vapor. [VOLATILE + -IZE] —**vol′a·til·iz′a·ble,** *adj.* —**vol′a·til·i·za′tion,** *n.* —**vol′a·til·iz′er,** *n.*

vol-au-vent (vō lō väN′), *n. Cookery.* a large shell of light, flaky pastry for filling with vegetable, fish, or meat mixtures, usually with a sauce. [< F: lit., flight on the wind]

vol·can·ic (vol kan′ik), *adj.* **1.** of or pertaining to a volcano or volcanoes: *a volcanic eruption.* **2.** discharged from or produced by volcanoes: *volcanic mud.* **3.** characterized by the presence of volcanoes: *a volcanic island.* **4.** suggestive of or resembling a volcano; potentially explosive; volatile: *a volcanic temper.* [VOLCAN(O) + -IC; cf. F *volcanique*] —**vol·can′i·cal·ly,** *adv.* —**vol·can·ic·i·ty** (vol′kə nis′i tē), *n.*

volcan′ic glass′, a natural glass produced when molten lava cools very rapidly; obsidian.

volcan′ic tuff′, tuff¹.

vol·can·ism (vol′kə niz′əm), *n.* the phenomena connected with volcanoes and volcanic activity. [VOLCAN(O) + -ISM]

vol·ca·no (vol kā′nō), *n., pl.* **-noes, -nos. 1.** a vent in the earth's crust through which lava, steam, ashes, etc., are expelled, either continuously or at irregular intervals. **2.** a mountain or hill, usually having a cuplike crater at the summit, formed around such a vent from the ash and lava expelled through it. [< It *volcano* < L *Vulcānus*, var. of *Vulcānus* VULCAN]

Volca′no Is′lands, three islands in the W Pacific, belonging to Japan. Cf. **Iwo Jima.**

vol·can·ol·o·gy (vol′kə nol′ə jē), *n.* the scientific study of volcanoes and volcanic phenomena. Also, **vulcanology.** [VOLCANO + -LOGY] —**vol·can·o·log·i·cal** (vol′kə nᵊloj′i kəl), **vol′can·o·log′ic,** *adj.* —**vol′can·ol′o·gist,** *n.*

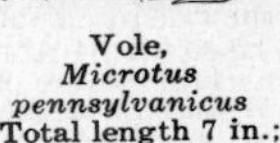

Vole, *Microtus pennsylvanicus* (Total length 7 in.; tail 2 in.)

vole¹ (vōl), *n.* any of several small mouselike or ratlike rodents of the genus *Microtus* and related genera, having short limbs and a short tail. [short for *volemouse* field mouse; *vole* < Norw *voll* field; see WOLD¹]

vole[2] (vōl), *n.* **1.** *Cards.* the winning by one player of all the tricks of a deal. **2. go the vole, a.** to venture everything on the chance of great rewards. **b.** to try one after another, as a variety of occupations: *He went the vole and finally settled on watch-making.* [< F *vol(er)* (to) fly < L *volāre*]

Vol·ga (vol′gə; *Russ.* vôl′gä), *n.* a river flowing from the Valdai Hills in the W Soviet Union E and then S to the Caspian Sea: the longest river in Europe. 2325 mi.

Vol·go·grad (vol′gə grad′; *Russ.* vôl′go grät′), *n.* a city in the SW RSFSR, in the S Soviet Union in Europe, on the Volga River: battles in World War II, September 1942–February 1943. 701,000 (1965). Formerly, **Stalingrad, Tsaritsyn.**

vol·i·tant (vol′i tənt), *adj.* **1.** engaged in or having the power of flight. **2.** active; moving. [< L *volitant-* (s. of *volitāns*, prp. of *volitāre* to flutter), equiv. to *vol-* root of *volāre* to fly + *-it-* freq. suffix + *-ant-* -ANT]

vol·i·ta·tion (vol′i tā′shən), *n.* the act or power of flying. [< ML *volitātiōn-* (s. of *volitātiō*), equiv. to L *volitāt(us)* (ptp. of *volitāre* to flutter; see VOLITANT, -ATE[1]) + *-iōn-* -ION] —**vol′i·ta′tion·al,** *adj.*

vo·li·tion (vō lish′ən), *n.* **1.** the act of willing, choosing, or resolving; exercise of willing: *He offered to help us of his own volition.* **2.** a choice or decision made by the will. **3.** the power of willing; will. [< ML *volitiōn-* (s. of *volitiō*), equiv. to *vol-* (root of L *volō* I will) + *-itiōn-* -ITION] —**vo·li′tion·al, vo·li·tion·ar·y** (vō lish′ə ner′ē), *adj.* —**vo·li′tion·al·ly,** *adv.* —**vo·li′tion·less,** *adj.*
—**Syn. 1.** discretion, choice. See **will**[2].

vol·i·tive (vol′i tiv), *adj.* **1.** of, pertaining to, or characterized by volition. **2.** *Gram.* expressing a wish or permission: *a volitive construction.* [VOLIT(ION) + -IVE]

Volk (fôlk), *n., pl.* **Völk·er** (fœl′kər). *German.* a people; nation.

Volks·deut·scher (fōlks′doi′chər), *n., pl.* **-deut·sche** (-doi′chə). *German.* a member of the German people, esp. one living outside of Germany, usually in central or eastern Europe.

Volks·lied (fôlks′lēt′), *n., pl.* **-lied·er** (-lē′dər). *German.* a folksong.

Volks·sturm (fôlks′shtōōrm), *n. German.* a territorial army formed by the Germans in the latter part of World War II, consisting of men and boys unfit for regular military service. [lit., folk-storm]

vol·ley (vol′ē), *n., pl.* **-leys,** *v.,* **-leyed, -ley·ing.** —*n.* **1.** the flight of a number of missiles together. **2.** the simultaneous discharge of a number of missiles or firearms. **3.** a burst or outpouring of many things at once or in quick succession: *a volley of protests.* **4.** *Tennis.* **a.** the flight of the ball before it hits the ground. **b.** the return of the ball before it hits the ground. **5.** *Soccer.* a kick of the football before it bounces on the ground. **6.** *Cricket.* a ball so bowled that it hits the wicket before it touches the ground. **7.** *Mining.* the explosion of several blasts in the rock at one time. —*v.t.* **8.** to discharge in or as in a volley. **9.** *Tennis.* to return (the ball) before it hits the ground. **10.** *Soccer.* to kick (the ball) before it bounces on the ground. **11.** *Cricket.* to bowl (a ball) in such a manner that it is pitched near the top of the wicket. —*v.i.* **12.** to fly or be discharged together, as missiles. **13.** to move or proceed with great rapidity, as in a volley. **14.** to fire a volley; sound together, as firearms. **15.** to emit or produce loud sounds simultaneously or continuously. [< MF *volee* flight < VL **volāta*, n. use of fem. of L *volātus*, ptp. of *volāre* to fly] —**vol′ley·er,** *n.*

vol·ley·ball (vol′ē bôl′), *n.* **1.** a game, usually played in a gymnasium, the object of which is to keep a large ball in motion, from side to side over a high net, by striking it with the hands before it touches the ground. **2.** the ball used in this game. [VOLLEY + BALL[1]]

Vol·ney (vōl′nē), *n.* a boy's given name.

Vo·log·da (vô′log dä), *n.* a city in the W RSFSR, in the central Soviet Union in Europe, NNE of Moscow. 156,000 (est. 1964).

Vo·los (vô′lôs), *n.* a seaport in E Thessaly, in E Greece: ancient ruins. 49,221 (1961).

vo·lost (vō′lost), *n.* **1.** (formerly) a small administrative peasant division in Russia. **2.** a rural soviet. [< Russ]

vol·plane (vol′plān′), *v.,* **-planed, -plan·ing,** *n.* —*v.i.* **1.** to glide toward the earth in an airplane, with no motor power or with the power shut off. —*n.* **2.** a glide in an airplane. [< F *vol plané* glided flight, equiv. to *vol* flight (back formation from *voler* < L *volāre* to fly) + *plané*, ptp. of *planer* to glide (see PLANE[1])] —**vol′plan·ist,** *n.*

Vol·po·ne (vol pō′nē), *n.* (*or The Fox*) a comedy (1606) by Ben Jonson.

vols., volumes.

Vol·sci (vol′sī), *n.pl.* an ancient people of Latium who were conquered by the Romans in the last part of the 4th century B.C.

Vol·scian (vol′shən), *adj.* **1.** of or pertaining to the Volsci or to their language. —*n.* **2.** one of the Volsci. [< L *Volsc(us)* of the VOLSCI + -IAN]

Vol·stead (vol′sted), *n.* **Andrew Joseph,** 1860–1946, U.S. legislator.

Vol′stead Act′, an act of Congress, introduced in 1919 by Andrew J. Volstead to implement the Eighteenth Amendment of the Constitution, which forbade the sale of alcoholic beverages.

Vol·stead·i·an (vol sted′ē ən, vôl-, vōl-), *adj.* of or pertaining to prohibition or to Volsteadism. [A. J. VOLSTEAD or the VOLSTEAD ACT + -IAN]

Vol·stead·ism (vol′sted iz′əm), *n.* **1.** the policy of prohibiting the sale of liquor to be used as or for a beverage. **2.** the enforcement of this policy. [VOLSTEAD (ACT) + -ISM]

Vol·sung (vol′sŏŏng), *n.* (in the *Volsunga Saga*) **1.** a grandson of Odin and the father of Sigmund and Signy. **2.** any of his family.

Vol·sun·ga Sa·ga (vol′sŏŏng gə sä′gə), an Icelandic saga of the late 13th century, concerning the family of the Volsungs, the theft of the cursed treasure of Andvari, the adventures of Sigurd, his wooing of Brynhild, his enchantment and marriage to Gudrun, and his eventual murder. Also, **Vol′sun·ga·sa′ga.** Cf. **Nibelungenlied.**

volt[1] (vōlt), *n. Elect.* the meter-kilogram-second unit of electromotive force or potential difference, equal to the electromotive force or potential difference that will cause a current of one ampere to flow through a conductor with a resistance of one ohm. *Abbr.:* V, v [named after Alessandro VOLTA]

volt[2] (vōlt), *n.* **1.** *Manège.* **a.** a circular or turning movement of a horse. **b.** a gait in which a horse going sideways turns around a center, with the head turned outward. **2.** *Fencing Obs.* a sudden movement or leap to avoid a thrust. [< F *volte* < It *volta* < VL **volvita* a turn; see VAULT[1]]

vol·ta (vol′tə; *It.* vôl′tä), *n., pl.* **-te** (-tā; *It.* -te). *Music.* turn; time (used in phrases): *una volta* ("once"); *duo volte* ("twice"); *prima volta* ("first time"), etc. [< It: a turn; see VOLT[2]]

Vol·ta (vōl′tə *or, It.,* vôl′tä *for 1;* vol′tä *for 2*), *n.* **1. Count A·les·san·dro** (ä′les sän′drô), 1745–1827, Italian physicist. **2.** a river in W Africa, in Ghana, formed by the confluence of the Black Volta and the White Volta and flowing S into the Bight of Benin. ab. 250 mi. long; with branches ab. 1240 mi. long.

volta-, a combining form of **voltaic:** *voltameter.*

Vol′ta effect′ (vōl′tə), *Elect.* See **contact potential.** [named after A. VOLTA]

volt·age (vōl′tij), *n. Elect.* electromotive force or potential difference expressed in volts. [VOLT[1] + -AGE]

volt′age divid′er, *Elect.* a resistor or series of resistors connected to a voltage source and used to provide voltages which are fractions of that of the source. Also called **potential divider.**

vol·ta·ic (vol tā′ik), *adj.* **1.** *Elect.* noting or pertaining to electricity or electric currents, esp. when produced by chemical action, as in a cell; galvanic. **2.** (*cap.*) of or pertaining to Alessandro Volta. [named after A. VOLTA; see -IC]

volta′ic bat′tery, *Elect.* an electric battery consisting of several voltaic cells connected together. Also called **galvanic battery.**

volta′ic cell′, *Elect.* a cell consisting of two electrodes of different metals immersed in a solution such that chemical action produces an electromotive force.

volta′ic cou′ple, *Elect.* a pair of substances, as two different metals, which when placed in a proper solution produces an electromotive force by chemical action.

volta′ic electric′ity, electric current; moving electric charges.

volta′ic pile′, *Elect.* a cell that consists of several metal disks, each made of one of two dissimilar metals, arranged in an alternating series, and separated by pads moistened with an electrolyte. Also called **galvanic pile, pile, Volta's pile.**

Vol·taire (vol târ′, vōl-; *Fr.* vôl ter′), *n.* (*François Marie Arouet*), 1694–1778, French philosopher, historian, dramatist, and essayist. —**Vol·tair′e·an, Vol·tair′i·an,** *adj., n.*

vol·ta·ism (vol′tə iz′əm), *n.* the branch of electrical science that deals with the production of electricity or electric currents by chemical action. [named after A. VOLTA; see -ISM]

vol·tam·e·ter (vol tam′i tər), *n.* a device for measuring the quantity of electricity passing through a conductor by the amount of electrolytic decomposition it produces, or for measuring the strength of a current by the amount of such decomposition in a given time. Also called **coulometer.** [VOLTA- + -METER] —**vol·ta·met·ric** (vol′tə me′trik), *adj.*

volt·am·me·ter (vōlt′am′mē′tər), *n.* an instrument for measuring voltage or amperage. [VOLT-AM(PERE) + -METER]

volt-am·pere (vōlt′am′pēr), *n. Elect.* an electric measurement unit, equal to the product of one volt and one ampere, equivalent to one watt for direct current systems and a unit of apparent power for alternating current systems. *Abbr.:* Va, va

Vol′ta's pile′ (vōl′təz), *Elect.* See **voltaic pile.** [named after A. VOLTA]

volt-cou·lomb (vōlt′kōō′lom, -kōō lom′), *n. Elect.* a unit of electric energy, equivalent to one joule and equal to the energy produced by the transfer of one coulomb of charge across a potential difference of one volt.

volte-face (volt fäs′; *Fr.* vôltə fas′), *n., pl.* **volte-face.** a turnabout, esp. a reversal of opinion or policy. [< F < It *voltafaccia*, equiv. to *volta* turn (see VOLT[2]) + *faccia* FACE]

vol·ti (vôl′tē), *v. imperative. Music.* turn; turn over: a direction to turn the page. [< It]

volt·me·ter (vōlt′mē′tər), *n. Elect.* a calibrated instrument for measuring the potential difference between two points. [VOLT[1] + -METER]

Vol·tur·no (vôl tōōr′nô), *n.* a river in S central Italy, flowing from the Apennines into the Tyrrhenian Sea. 110 mi. long.

Vol·tur·nus (vol tûr′nəs), *n.* the ancient Roman personification of the east or southeast wind. Cf. **Eurus.**

vol·u·ble (vol′yə bəl), *adj.* characterized by a ready and continuous flow of words; fluent; glib; talkative: *a voluble spokesman for expanded trade relations.* [< L *volūbil(is)* which turns easily, hence rapid (of speech), equiv. to *volū(tus)* ptp. of *volvere* to turn + *-bilis* -BLE] —**vol′u·bil′i·ty, vol′u·ble·ness,** *n.* —**vol′u·bly,** *adv.*
—**Syn.** talkative, loquacious. See **fluent.** —**Ant.** taciturn.

vol·ume (vol′yōōm, -yəm), *n.* **1.** a collection of written or printed sheets bound together and constituting a book. **2.** one book of a related set or series. **3.** *Hist.* a roll of papyrus, parchment, or the like, or of manuscript. **4.** the amount of space, measured in cubic units, that an object or substance occupies. **5.** a mass or quantity, esp. a large quantity, of something: *a volume of mail; volumes of abuse.* **6.** amount; total: *the volume of travel; the volume of sales.* **7.** the degree of sound intensity or audibility; loudness: *to turn up the volume on a radio; noise increasing in volume.* **8.** fullness or quantity of tone. **9. speak volumes, a.** to be very evident or significant: *His testimony spoke volumes.* **b.** to be expressive or meaningful: *Her eyes speak volumes.* [late ME *volum(e)* < MF < L *volūmen* roll (of sheets), equiv. to *volū(tus)* (ptp. of *volvere* to roll) + *-men* n. suffix]
—**Syn. 4.** See **size**[1].

vol·umed (vol′yōōmd, -yəmd), *adj.* **1.** consisting of a volume or volumes (usually used in combination): *a many-volumed work.* **2.** in volumes of rolling or rounded masses, as smoke. [VOLUME + -ED[3]]

vo·lu·me·ter (və lōō′mi tər), *n.* any of various instruments or devices for measuring volume, as of gases, liquids, or solids. [VOLU(ME) + -METER]

vol·u·met·ric (vol′yə me′trik), *adj.* of or pertaining to measurement by volume. Also, **vol′u·met′ri·cal.** [VOLU(ME) + -METRIC[2]] —**vol′u·met′ri·cal·ly,** *adv.* —**vo·lu·me·try** (və lōō′mi trē), *n.*

volumet′ric anal′ysis, *Chem.* **1.** analysis by volume, esp. by titration. **2.** determination of the volume of gases or changes in their volume during combination. Cf. **gravimetric analysis.**

vol′ume veloc′ity, *Physics.* the movement caused by a sound wave of a unit volume of a sound-transmitting medium through a unit area per unit of time.

vo·lu·mi·nous (və lōō′mə nəs), *adj.* **1.** forming, filling, or writing a large volume or many volumes: *His voluminous writings are being assembled for publication in a standard edition.* **2.** sufficient to fill a volume or volumes: *a voluminous correspondence.* **3.** of great volume, size, or extent: *a voluminous flow of lava; voluminous records.* **4.** of ample size, extent, or fullness: *voluminous petticoats.* **5.** *Archaic.* having many coils, convolutions, or windings. [< LL *volūminōs(us)* full of folds, equiv. to L *volūmin-* (s. of *volūmen*) VOLUME + *-ōsus* -OUS] —**vo·lu′mi·nous·ly,** *adv.* —**vo·lu′mi·nous·ness, vo·lu·mi·nos·i·ty** (və lōō′mə nos′i tē), *n.*

Vö·lund (vœ′lŏŏnd), *n. Scand. Myth.* Wayland.

vol·un·ta·rism (vol′ən tə riz′əm), *n.* **1.** *Philos.* any theory that regards the will rather than the intellect as the fundamental agency or principle. **2.** voluntaryism. [VOLUNTAR(Y) + -ISM] —**vol′un·ta·rist,** *n., adj.* —**vol′un·ta·ris′tic,** *adj.*

vol·un·tar·y (vol′ən ter′ē), *adj., n., pl.* **-tar·ies.** —*adj.* **1.** done, made, brought about, undertaken, etc., of one's own accord or by free choice: *a voluntary contribution.* **2.** of, pertaining to, or acting in accord with the will: *voluntary cooperation; voluntary actions.* **3.** of, pertaining to, or depending on voluntary action: *voluntary schools; voluntary hospitals.* **4.** *Law.* **a.** acting or done without compulsion or obligation. **b.** done by intention, and not by accident: *voluntary manslaughter.* **c.** made without valuable consideration: *a voluntary conveyance or settlement.* **5.** *Physiol.* subject to or controlled by the will: *voluntary muscles.* **6.** having the power of willing or choosing: *a voluntary agent.* **7.** proceeding from a natural impulse; spontaneous: *voluntary laughter.* —*n.* **8.** something done voluntarily. **9.** a piece of music, frequently spontaneous and improvised, performed as a prelude to a larger work, esp. a piece of organ music performed before, during, or after an office of the church. [late ME < L *voluntāri(us)*, equiv. to *volunt(ās)* willingness, inclination + *-ārius* -ARY] —**vol·un·tar·i·ly** (vol′ən ter′ə lē, vol′ən târ′-), *adv.* —**vol′un·tar′i·ness,** *n.*
—**Syn. 1.** considered, purposeful, planned, intended, designed. See **deliberate. 7.** free, unforced, natural, unconstrained. VOLUNTARY, SPONTANEOUS agree in applying to something which is a natural outgrowth or natural expression arising from circumstances and conditions. VOLUNTARY implies having given previous consideration, or having exercised judgment: *a voluntary confession; a voluntary movement; The offer was a voluntary one.* That which is SPONTANEOUS arises as if by itself from the nature of the circumstances or condition: *spontaneous applause, combustion, expression of admiration.*

vol′untary associa′tion, a group of individuals joined together on the basis of mutual interest or common objectives, esp. a business group that is not organized or constituted as a legal entity.

vol·un·tar·y·ism (vol′ən ter′ē iz′əm), *n.* the principle or system of supporting churches, schools, etc., by voluntary contributions or aid, independently of the state. Also, **voluntarism.** [VOLUNTARY + -ISM] —**vol′un·tar′y·ist,** *n.*

vol·un·teer (vol′ən tēr′), *n.* **1.** a person who voluntarily offers himself for a service or undertaking; a person who performs a service of his own free will. **2.** *Mil.* a person who enters the service voluntarily rather than through conscription or draft, esp. for special or temporary service rather than as a member of the regular or permanent army. **3.** *Law.* **a.** a person whose actions are not founded on any legal obligation so to act. **b.** one to whom a conveyance is made or promise given without valuable consideration. **4.** *Agric.* a volunteer plant. **5.** (*cap.*) a native or inhabitant of Tennessee (the **Volunteer State**) (used as a nickname). —*adj.* **6.** of, pertaining to, or being a volunteer or volunteers: *a volunteer fireman; volunteer services.* **7.** *Agric.* growing without being seeded, planted, or cultivated by a person; springing up spontaneously. —*v.i.* **8.** to offer oneself for some service or undertaking. **9.** to enter service or enlist as a volunteer. —*v.t.* **10.** to offer (oneself or one's services) for some undertaking or purpose. **11.** to give, bestow, or perform without being asked: *to volunteer a song.* **12.** to say, tell, or communicate voluntarily: *to volunteer an explanation.* **13.** *Archaic.* to offer to undertake or undergo: *to volunteer a dangerous assignment.* [< F *volontaire* < L *voluntāri(us)* VOLUNTARY, with -EER for F *-aire*]

Volunteers′ in Ser′vice to America. See **VISTA.**

Vol′unteers′ of Amer′ica, a religious reform and relief organization, similar to the Salvation Army, founded in New York City in 1896 by Ballington Booth, son of William Booth, the founder of the Salvation Army. *Abbr.:* VOA

Vol′unteer′ State′, Tennessee (used as a nickname).

Vo·lup·tas (və lup′təs), *n.* the ancient Roman goddess of pleasure.

vo·lup·tu·ar·y (və lup′chōō er′ē), *n., pl.* **-ar·ies,** *adj.* —*n.* **1.** a person whose life is devoted to the pursuit and enjoyment of luxury and sensual pleasure. —*adj.* **2.** of, pertaining to, or characterized by preoccupation with luxury and sensual pleasure: *voluptuary tastes.* [< LL *voluptuāri(us)* (r. L *voluptārius*) pertaining to (sensual) pleasure, equiv. to *volupt(ās)* pleasure + *-u-* (see VOLUPTUOUS) + *-ārius* -ARY]

vo·lup·tu·ous (və lup′cho͞o əs), *adj.* **1.** full of, characterized by, or ministering to indulgence in luxury, pleasure, and sensuous enjoyment: *a voluptuous life.* **2.** derived from gratification of the senses: *voluptuous pleasure.* **3.** directed toward or concerned with sensuous enjoyment or sensual pleasure: *voluptuous desires.* **4.** given or inclined to sensuous enjoyment or sensual pleasure: *His writings reveal him as a man of voluptuous tastes.* **5.** suggestive of an inclination to sensuality: *a voluptuous mouth.* **6.** sensuously pleasing or delightful: *voluptuous beauty.* [late ME < L *voluptuōsus,* equiv. to *volupt(ās)* pleasure + *-u-* (< ?) + *-ōsus* -OUS] —**vo·lup′tu·ous·ly,** *adv.* —**vo·lup′tu·ous·ness, vo·lup·tu·os·i·ty** (və lup′cho͞o os′i tē), *n.*
—**Syn. 1.** See **sensual.**

vo·lute (və lo͞ot′), *n.* **1.** a spiral or twisted formation or object. **2.** *Archit.* a spiral ornament, found esp. in the capitals of the Ionic, Corinthian, and Composite orders. **3.** *Carpentry.* a horizontal scrolled termination to the handrail of a stair. **4.** *Zool.* **a.** a turn or whorl of a spiral shell. **b.** any tropical marine gastropod of the family *Volutidae,* many species of which have shells prized for their beautiful coloration. **5.** the spiral casing surrounding the impeller of a volute pump. —*adj.* **6.** having a volute or rolled-up form. **7.** *Mach.* **a.** spirally shaped or having a part so shaped. **b.** moving in a circular way, esp. if combined with a lateral motion. [< L *volūta,* fem. of *volūtus* turned, rolled, ptp. of *volvere.* See REVOLVE] —**vo·lut′ed,** *adj.* —**vo·lu′tion,** *n.*

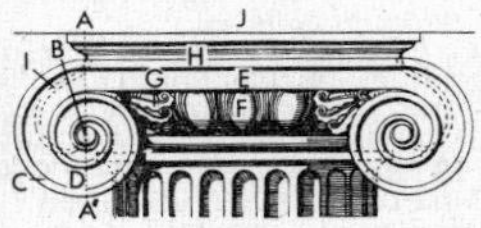

Volute on an Ionic capital
A and A[1], Cathetus;
B, Eye of volute;
C, Hem; D, Volute;
E, Balteus; F, Echinus;
G, Palmette masking intersection of echinus and volute; H, Abacus; I, Typical section of pulvinar; J, Lowermost fascia of architrave

volute′ pump′, a centrifugal pump with an impeller that is surrounded by a spiral casing.

volute′ spring′, a coil spring, conical in shape, extending in the direction of the axis of the coil. See illus. under **spring.**

vol·va (vol′və), *n. Bot.* the membranous envelope which encloses various immature or button mushrooms. See diag. under **mushroom.** [< L: covering, akin to *volvere* to roll, wrap] —**vol·vate** (vol′vit, -vāt), *adj.*

vol·velle (vol′vel), *n. Astron.* a medieval instrument consisting of a series of concentric rotating disks, used to compute the phases of the moon and its position in relation to that of the sun. [late ME < ML *volvella,* equiv. to L *volv(ere)* to turn + *-ella* dim. suffix]

vol·vent (vol′vənt), *n. Zool.* a small, pear-shaped nematocyst discharging a thread that entangles its prey. [< L *volvent-* (s. of *volvēns*), prp. of *volvere* to turn, twist; see -ENT]

vol·vox (vol′voks), *n.* any colonial, fresh-water flagellate of the genus *Volvox* that forms a hollow, greenish sphere of flagellated cells, and is usually considered to be a green alga. [< NL, equiv. to L *volv(ere)* to turn, roll + *-ox* (as in *ferox*)]

vol·vu·lus (vol′vyə ləs), *n., pl.* **-lus·es.** *Pathol.* a torsion, or twisting, of the intestine, causing intestinal obstruction. [< ML, equiv. to L *volv(ere)* to turn, twist + *-ulus* -ULE]

vo·mer (vō′mər), *n. Anat.* a bone of the skull in most vertebrates, in man forming a large part of the septum between the right and left cavities of the nose. [< L: plowshare] —**vo·mer·ine** (vō′mə rīn′, -mər in, vom′ə-rīn′, -ər in), *adj.*

vom·i·ca (vom′ə kə), *n., pl.* **-i·cae** (-i sē′). *Pathol.* **1.** a cavity, usually in the lungs, containing pus. **2.** the pus content of such a cavity. [< L: a boil, ulcer, equiv. to *vom(ere)* to discharge (see VOMIT) + *-ica,* fem. of *-icus* -IC]

vom·it (vom′it), *v.i.* **1.** to eject the contents of the stomach through the mouth; regurgitate; throw up. **2.** to be ejected or come out with force or violence. —*v.t.* **3.** to eject from the stomach through the mouth; spew. **4.** to cast out or eject as if in vomiting; send out forcefully or violently: *The volcano vomited flames and molten rock.* **5.** to cause (a person) to vomit. —*n.* **6.** the act of vomiting. **7.** the matter ejected in vomiting. [late ME *vomite(n)* < L *vomitāre,* freq. of *vomere* to discharge, vomit] —**vom′it·er,** *n.* —**vom′i·tive, vom′i·tous,** *adj.* —**vom′i·tous·ly,** *adv.*

vom·i·to (vom′i tō′, vō′mi-), *n. Pathol.* the black vomit of yellow fever. Also called **vom·i·to ne·gro** (vom′i tō′ nē′grō, nā′-, vō′mi-). [< Sp *vómito* < L *vomitus* (see VOMITUS)]

vom·i·to·ri·um (vom′i tôr′ē əm, -tōr′-), *n., pl.* **-to·ri·a** (-tôr′ē ə, -tōr′-). vomitory (def. 5). [< LL]

vom·i·to·ry (vom′i tôr′ē, -tōr′ē), *adj., n., pl.* **-ries.** —*adj.* **1.** inducing vomiting; emetic. **2.** of or pertaining to vomiting. —*n.* **3.** an emetic. **4.** an opening through which something is ejected or discharged. **5.** Also called **vomitorium.** an opening, as in a stadium or theater, permitting large numbers of people to enter or leave. [< L *vomitōri(us),* equiv. to *vomit(us)* ptp. of *vomere* to vomit + *-ōrius* -ORY[1]]

vom·i·tu·ri·tion (vom′i cho͝o rish′ən), *n. Med.* **1.** ineffectual efforts to vomit. **2.** the vomiting of small amounts of matter. **3.** *Obs.* vomiting with little effort. [< ML *vomituritiōn-* (s. of *vomituritiō*) nausea, alter. of L *vomitiōn-* (s. of *vomitiō*) a vomiting by inserting *-turi-,* desiderative infix; L *vomitiōn-,* equiv. to *vomit(us)* (ptp. of *vomere* to discharge) + *-iōn-* -ION]

vom·i·tus (vom′i təs), *n., pl.* **-tus·es.** *Med.* **1.** the act of vomiting. **2.** vomited matter. [< L (4th decl.): a vomiting; see VOMIT]

von (von; *Ger.* fôn, *unstressed* fən), *prep.* from; of (used in German and Austrian personal names, originally to indicate place of origin and later to indicate nobility): *Paul von Hindenburg.*

Von Bé·ké·sy (von bā′ke shē), *n.* **Ge·org** (gā′ôrg), born 1899, U.S. physicist, born in Hungary: Nobel prize for medicine 1961.

von Braun (von broun′; *Ger.* fən broun′). See **Braun, Wernher von.**

Von Kár·mán (von kär′män, -mən), **Theodore,** 1881–1963, U.S. scientist and aeronautical engineer, born in Hungary.

Von Neu·mann (von noi′män, -mən), **John,** 1903–57, U.S. mathematician, born in Hungary.

Von Stro·heim (von strō′hīm, shtrō′-; *Ger.* fən shtrō′hīm), **E·rich** (er′ik; *Ger.* e′rikh), 1885–1957, U.S. actor and director, born in Austria.

voo·doo (vo͞o′do͞o), *n., pl.* **-doos,** *adj., v.,* **-dooed, -doo·ing.** —*n.* **1.** Also, **vodun.** a polytheistic religion practiced chiefly by West-Indian Negroes, deriving principally from African cult worship and containing elements borrowed from the Catholic religion. **2.** a person who practices this religion. **3.** a fetish or other object of voodoo worship. **4.** a group of magical and ecstatic rites associated with voodoo. **5.** (not in technical use) black magic; sorcery. —*adj.* **6.** of, pertaining to, associated with, or practicing voodoo. —*v.t.* **7.** to affect by voodoo sorcery or conjuration. [< Creole F *voudou* << some WAfr tongue; cf. Ewe *vodu* demon]

voo·doo·ism (vo͞o′do͞o iz′əm), *n.* the voodoo rites, practices, sorcery, or superstition. [VOODOO + -ISM] —**voo′doo·ist,** *n.* —**voo′doo·is′tic,** *adj.*

VOR, *Navig.* omnirange. [*v(ery high frequency) o(mni) r(ange)*]

-vora, a combination of **-vore** and **-a,** used as a final element esp. in names of zoological orders: *Carnivora.* [< L, neut. pl. of *-vorus* -VOROUS]

vo·ra·cious (vō rā′shəs, vô-, və-), *adj.* **1.** craving or consuming large quantities of food: *a voracious teenager; a voracious appetite.* **2.** eager to absorb, obtain, possess, or consume, esp. to excess; insatiable: *voracious readers; a voracious dictator; a voracious collector.* [VORACI(TY) + -OUS] —**vo·ra′cious·ly,** *adv.* —**vo·ra′cious·ness,** *n.*
—**Syn. 1.** See **ravenous. 2.** rapacious.

vo·rac·i·ty (vō ras′i tē, vô-, və-), *n.* the condition or quality of being voracious. [< L *vorācitās,* equiv. to *vorāci-* (s. of *vorax*) gluttonous + *-tās* -TY[2]]

vo·rant (vōr′ənt, vôr′-), *adj. Heraldry.* (of an animal) represented as devouring, esp. another animal: *a serpent vorant a toad.* [< L *vorant-* (s. of *vorāns*), prp. of *vorāre* to swallow up; see -ANT]

Vor·arl·berg (fōr′ärl′berkh′), *n.* a province in W Austria. 226,323 (1961); 1004 sq. mi. *Cap.:* Bregenz.

-vore, a learned borrowing from Latin meaning "eating," used in the formation of compound words: *carnivore.* Cf. **-vora, -vorous.** [< F < L *-vora,* neut. pl. of *-vorus* -VOROUS]

Vor·la·ge (fōr′lä′gə), *n., pl.* **-ge.** *German.* a position in which a skier leans forward but keeps his heels in contact with the skis.

Vo·ro·nezh (vo rô′nesh), *n.* a city in the SW RSFSR, in the central Soviet Union in Europe. 577,000 (1965).

Vo·ro·noff (vo rô′nof, vô′ro-), *n.* **Serge** (serzh), 1866–1951, Russian physician.

Vo·ro·nov (vô′ro nof), *n.* **Gen·na·di** (ge nä′di), born 1910, Russian government official: alternate member of the Presidium.

Vo·ro·shi·lov (vôr′ə shē′ləf; *Russ.* və ru shi′ləf), *n.* **1. Kli·ment E·fre·mo·vich** (klyi myent′ yi frye′mə vyich), 1881–1969, Soviet general: president of the Soviet Union 1953–60. **2.** former name of **Ussuriisk.**

Vo·ro·shi·lov·grad (vo ro shē′lof grät′), *n.* former name of **Lugansk.**

Vo·ro·shi·lovsk (vo ro shē′lofsk), *n.* former name of **Stavropol.**

-vorous, a combination of **-vore** and **-ous,** used in the formation of adjectives from nouns with stems in **-vora** and **-vore:** *carnivorous.* [< L *-vorus* devouring]

vor·spiel (fōr′shpēl, fôr′-), *n.* an introductory movement to a musical work, esp. a prelude or overture. [< G: lit., fore-play]

Vor·ster (fôr′stər), *n.* **Balthazar Johannes,** born 1915, South African political leader: prime minister since 1966.

vor·tex (vôr′teks), *n., pl.* **-tex·es, -ti·ces** (-ti sēz′). **1.** a whirling mass of water, esp. one in which a force of suction operates, as a whirlpool. **2.** a whirling mass of air, esp. one in the form of a visible column or spiral, as a tornado. **3.** a whirling mass of fire, flame, etc. **4.** a state of affairs likened to a whirlpool for violent activity, irresistible force, etc. **5.** something regarded as drawing into its powerful current everything that surrounds it: *the vortex of war.* **6.** (in Cartesian philosophy) a rapid rotatory movement of cosmic matter about a center, regarded as accounting for the origin or phenomena of bodies or systems of bodies in space. [< L, var. of *vertex* VERTEX]

vor·ti·cal (vôr′ti kəl), *adj.* **1.** of or pertaining to a vortex. **2.** suggesting or resembling a vortex. **3.** moving in a vortex. [< L *vortic-* (s. of *vortex*) + -AL[1]] —**vor′ti·cal·ly,** *adv.*

vor·ti·cel·la (vôr′ti sel′ə), *n., pl.* **-cel·lae** (-sel′ē), **-cel·las.** any ciliate protozoan of the genus *Vorticella,* having a transparent, bell-shaped body with a retractile stalk. [< NL; see VORTICAL, -ELLA]

vor·ti·ces (vôr′ti sēz′), *n.* a pl. of **vortex.**

vor·tic·i·ty (vôr tis′i tē), *n., pl.* **-ties.** *Mech.* a measure of the circulation of a fluid: a quantity equal to twice the angular momentum of a particle of the fluid around which there is circulation. [< L *vortic-* (s. of *vortex;* see VORTEX) + -ITY]

vor·ti·cose (vôr′tə kōs′), *adj.* vortical; whirling. [< L *verticōs(us)* eddying. See VORTICAL, -OSE[1]] —**vor′ti·cose′ly,** *adv.*

vor·tig·i·nous (vôr tij′ə nəs), *adj.* resembling a vortex; whirling; vortical. [var. of VERTIGINOUS]

Vor·tum·nus (vôr tum′nəs), *n.* Vertumnus.

Vosges (vōzh), *n.* **1.** a range of low mountains in NE France: highest peak, 4668 ft. **2.** a department in NE France. 380,676 (1962); 2279 sq. mi. *Cap.:* Épinal.

Vos·tok (vô′stok), *n.* one of a series of manned satellites orbited by the Soviet Union.

vot·a·ble (vō′tə bəl), *adj.* capable of being voted upon; subject to a vote: *a votable issue.* Also, **voteable.**

vo·ta·ry (vō′tə rē), *n., pl.* **-ries,** *adj.* —*n.* Also, **vo′ta·rist;** *referring to a woman,* **vo·ta·ress** (vō′tər is). **1.** a person who is bound by solemn religious vows, as a monk or a nun. **2.** an adherent of a religion or cult; a worshiper of a particular deity or sacred personage. **3.** a person who is devoted or addicted to some subject or pursuit: *a votary of jazz.* **4.** a devoted follower or admirer. —*adj.* **5.** consecrated by a vow. **6.** of or pertaining to a vow. [< L *vōt(um)* a vow + -ARY]

vote (vōt), *n., v.,* **vot·ed, vot·ing.** —*n.* **1.** a formal expression of opinion or choice, either positive or negative, made by an individual or body of individuals. **2.** the means by which such expression is made, as a ballot, ticket, etc. **3.** the right to such expression: *to give women the vote.* **4.** the decision reached by voting, as by a majority of ballots cast: *Was the vote for or against the resolution?* **5.** a collective expression of will as inferred from a number of votes: *the labor vote; the farm vote.* **6.** an expression of approval, agreement, or judgment: *to give someone a vote of confidence; an action that constitutes a vote for increased aid to education.* **7.** *Obs.* **a.** an ardent wish or prayer. **b.** a vow. —*v.i.* **8.** to express or signify will or choice in a matter, as by casting a ballot: *For whom will you vote for president?* —*v.t.* **9.** to enact, establish, or determine by vote: *to vote down a proposed amendment; to vote an incompetent mayor out of office.* **10.** to support by one's vote: *to vote the Republican ticket.* **11.** to advocate by or as by one's vote: *to vote that the report be accepted.* **12.** to declare or decide by general consent: *They voted the trip a success.* [late ME < L *vōt(um)* a vow]

vote·a·ble (vō′tə bəl), *adj.* votable.

vote·less (vōt′lis), *adj.* **1.** lacking or without a vote. **2.** denied the right to vote, esp. in political elections. [VOTE + -LESS]

vot·er (vō′tər), *n.* **1.** a person who votes. **2.** a person who has a right to vote; elector. [VOTE (v.) + -ER[1]]

vot′ing machine′, a mechanical apparatus used in a polling place to register and count the votes.

vot′ing pa′per, *Brit.* a ballot.

vo·tive (vō′tiv), *adj.* **1.** offered, given, dedicated, etc., in accordance with a vow: *a votive offering.* **2.** performed, undertaken, etc., in consequence of a vow. **3.** of the nature of or expressive of a wish or desire. [< L *vōtīv(us),* equiv. to *vōt(um)* a vow + *-īvus* -IVE] —**vo′tive·ly,** *adv.* —**vo′tive·ness,** *n.*

vo′tive Mass′, *Rom. Cath. Ch.* a Mass which does not correspond with the office of the day but is said, as for a special intention, at the choice of the celebrant.

vo·tress (vō′tris), *n. Archaic.* a female votary; votaress. [var. of VOTARESS]

Vo·ty·ak (vō′tē ak′), *n.* a Uralic language of the Permian branch.

vouch (vouch), *v.i.* **1.** to support as being true, certain, reliable, etc. (usually fol. by *for*): *His record in office vouches for his integrity.* **2.** to attest; guarantee; certify (usually fol. by *for*): *to vouch for someone in a business transaction.* —*v.t.* **3.** to warrant; attest; confirm. **4.** to sustain or uphold by, or as by, practical proof or demonstration. **5.** to affirm or declare as with warrant; vouch for. **6.** to adduce or quote in support, as extracts from a book or author; cite in warrant or justification, as authority, instances, facts, etc. **7.** to support or authenticate with vouchers. **8.** (formerly) to call or summon (a person) into court to make good a warranty of title. **9.** *Obs.* to call or take as a witness. —*n. Obs.* **10.** a vouching; an assertion. **11.** a formal attestation; a supporting warrant. [ME *vouche(n)* < AF, MF *vo(u)cher,* OF *(a)vochier* < L *(ad)vocare;* see ADVOCATE]

vouch·er (vou′chər), *n.* **1.** one who or that which vouches. **2.** a document, receipt, stamp, or the like, which gives evidence of an expenditure. **3.** *Early Eng. Law.* **a.** one called into court to warrant another's title. **b.** the act of vouching another person to make good a warranty. [< AF *voucher* to vouch; orig. F inf. used as n. but now taken as VOUCH + -ER[1]] —**vouch′er·a·ble,** *adj.*

vouch·safe (vouch sāf′), *v.,* **-safed, -saf·ing.** —*v.t.* **1.** to grant or give, as by favor, graciousness, or condescension: *to vouchsafe a reply to a question.* **2.** to allow or permit, as by favor or graciousness: *They vouchsafed his return to his own country.* —*v.i.* **3.** to have the graciousness (to do something); condescend; deign. [ME phrase *vouche sauf.* See VOUCH, SAFE] —**vouch·safe′ment,** *n.*
—**Syn. 1.** bestow, confer, accord.

vouge (vo͞ozh), *n.* an axlike, shafted weapon having a curved blade tapering to a point at the top, used by foot soldiers in the 14th century and after. [< F < Celt; cf. Welsh *gwyddif* scythe, equiv. to ML *vidubium*]

vous·soir (vo͞o swär′), *n. Archit.* any of the pieces, in the shape of a truncated wedge, which form an arch or vault. See diag. under **arch.** [< F; r. ME *vousor(i)e* < AF, equiv. to OF *volsoir* < VL **volsōr(ium),* equiv. to *vols(us)* (r. L *volūtus,* ptp. of *volvere* to turn) + *-ōrium* -ORY[2]]

Vou·vray (vo͞ov rā′; *Fr.* vo͞o vre′), *n.* **1.** a town in W central France, E of Tours: noted for fine wines. 2753 (1962). **2.** a medium dry, white wine of this region.

vow (vou), *n.* **1.** a solemn promise, pledge, or personal commitment: *marriage vows; a vow of secrecy.* **2.** a solemn, religiously binding promise made to God or to any deity or saint, as to perform some act, make some offering or gift, or enter some service or condition. **3.** a solemn or earnest declaration. **4. take vows,** to enter a religious order or house. —*v.t.* **5.** to make a vow of; promise by a vow, as to God or a saint: *to vow a crusade or a pilgrimage.* **6.** to pledge or resolve solemnly to do, make, give, observe, etc.: *They vowed revenge.* **7.** to declare solemnly or earnestly; assert emphatically (often fol. by a clause as object): *She vowed that she would take the matter to court.* **8.** to dedicate or devote by a vow: *to vow oneself to the service of God.* —*v.i.* **9.** to make a vow. **10.** to make a solemn or earnest declaration. [ME < AF, OF *vo(u)* < L *vōtum,* neut. of *vōtus,* ptp. of *vovēre* to vow] —**vow′er,** *n.* —**vow′less,** *adj.*

vow·el (vou′əl), *n.* **1.** *Phonet.* **a.** (in English articulation) a speech sound produced without occluding, diverting, or obstructing the flow of air from the lungs (opposed to *consonant*). **b.** (in a syllable) the sound of greatest sonority, as *i* in *grill.* Cf. **consonant** (def. 1b). **c.** (in linguistic function) a concept empirically determined as a phonological element in structural contrast with consonant, as the (ē) of *be* (bē), *we* (wē), and *yeast* (yēst). **2.** a letter representing or usually representing a vowel, as, in English, *a, e, i, o, u, w, y.* —*adj.* **3.** of or pertaining to a vowel or vowels. [ME < OF *vouel* < L *vōcāl(is)* adj.; see VOCAL] —**vow′el·less,** *adj.* —**vow′el·like′,** *adj.* —**vow′el·y, vow′el·ly,** *adv.*

vow·el·ize (vou′ə līz′), *v.t.,* **-ized, -iz·ing.** to provide (a Hebrew, Arabic, etc., text) with vowel points. [VOWEL + -IZE] —**vow′el·i·za′tion,** *n.*

vow′el point′, any of a group of auxiliary symbols, as small lines and dots, placed above or below consonant symbols to indicate vowels in a writing system, as that of Hebrew or Arabic, in which vowels are otherwise not written.

vow′el sys′tem, *Ling.* the vowel sounds of a language, esp. when considered as forming an interrelated and interacting group. Cf. **consonant system.**

vox an·gel·i·ca (voks′ an jel′i kə), a pipe-organ stop producing delicate tones and having two pipes for each digital, one of which is tuned slightly sharp, so that by their dissonance a wavy effect is produced. Also called **vox′ cae·les′tis** (si les′tis). [< L: angelic voice]

vox bar·ba·ra (voks′ bär′bər ə), a questionably unconventional word or term; barbarism: applied esp. to neo-Latin terms in botany, zoology, etc., which are formed from elements that are neither Latin nor Greek. [< L: foreign voice]

vox, et prae·te·re·a ni·hil (wōks′, et prī te′re-ä′ ni′hil; *Eng.* voks′, et pri ter′ē ə nī′hil), *Latin.* a voice, and nothing more.

vox hu·ma·na (voks′ hyo͞o mā′nə), a pipe-organ stop designed to produce tones resembling those of the human voice. [< L: human voice]

vox pop., vox populi.

vox po·pu·li (voks′ pop′yə lī′), the voice of the people. [< L]

vox po·pu·li, vox De·i (wōks pō′po͝o lē′, wōks de′ē; *Eng.* voks pop′yə lī′, voks dē′ī), *Latin.* the voice of the people (is) the voice of God.

voy·age (voi′ij), *n., v.,* **-aged, -ag·ing.** —*n.* **1.** a course of travel or passage, esp. a long journey by water to a distant place. **2.** a passage through air or space, as a flight in an airplane or space vehicle. **3.** a journey or expedition from one place to another by land. **4.** Often, **voyages.** a series of journeys or travels as the subject of a written account, or the account itself: *the voyages of Marco Polo.* **5.** *Obs.* an enterprise or undertaking. —*v.i.* **6.** to make or take a voyage; travel; journey. —*v.t.* **7.** to traverse by a voyage: *to voyage the seven seas.* [ME *ve(i)age, viage, voyage* < AF, OF < L *viāticum* travel-money; see VIATICUM] —**voy′ag·er,** *n.*
—**Syn. 1.** cruise. See **trip.**

vo·ya·geur (vwä′yä zhûr′, voi ə-; *Fr.* vwa ya-zhœr′), *n., pl.* **-geurs** (-zhûrz′; *Fr.* -zhœr′). (in Canada) a man who is an expert woodsman, boatman, and guide in remote regions, esp. one employed by fur companies to transport supplies to and from their distant stations. [< F: traveler, equiv. to *voyag(er)* (to) travel (deriv. of *voyage* journey; see VOYAGE) + *-eur* -OR[2]]

vo·yeur (vwä yûr′, voi-; *Fr.* vwa yœr′), *n., pl.* **-yeurs** (-yûrz′; *Fr.* -yœr′). a person who engages in voyeurism. [< F, equiv. to *voi(r)* (to) see (< L *vidēre*) + *-eur* -OR[2]]

vo·yeur·ism (vwä yûr′iz əm, voi-), *n.* the practice of obtaining sexual gratification by looking at sexual objects or acts, esp. secretively. [VOYEUR + -ISM]

voy·eur·is·tic (vwä′yə ris′tic, voi′ə-), *adj.* of, pertaining to, or characteristic of a voyeur or of voyeurism. [VOYEUR + -IST + -IC] —**voy′eur·is′ti·cal·ly,** *adv.*

voy·euse (vwa yœz′), *n., pl.* **voy·euses** (vwa yœz′). *Fr. Furniture.* a chair of the 18th century used at game tables, having a padded top rail on which spectators could lean. [< F; fem. of VOYEUR]

Voyt (voit), *n.* a boy's given name.

V.P., Vice-President. Also, **V. Pres.**

v.p., verb passive.

V.R., Queen Victoria. [< L *Victoria Regina*]

v.r., verb reflexive.

vrai·sem·blance (vre sän bläns′), *n.* *French.* appearance of truth; verisimilitude.

V. Rev., Very Reverend.

Vries (vrēs), *n.* **Hu·go de** (hy′gō də). See **De Vries, Hugo.**

vrille (vril), *n., v.,* **vrilled, vrill·ing.** *Aeron.* —*n.* **1.** a maneuver involving the spinning, head-first descent of an aircraft. —*v.i.* **2.** to execute such a maneuver. [< F: lit., tendril, equiv. to *vir(er)* (to) wind, turn (< ?) + *-ille* < L *-icula* dim. suffix]

Vri·ta (vrit′ə), *n.* *Hinduism.* (in Vedic mythology) the personification of evil and leader of the Danavas.

vrouw (frou; *Eng.* vrou), *Dutch.* **1.** a woman; wife; lady. **2.** (used as a title before the name of a married woman) Mrs.

vs., **1.** verse. **2.** versus.

V.S., Veterinary Surgeon.

v.s., vide supra.

V-shaped (vē′shāpt′), *adj.* having the shape of the letter V: *a V-shaped flying formation.*

V sign, 1. a symbol of victory formed by the raised index and middle fingers. **2.** this sign used as an indication of approval.

vss., versions.

V/STOL (vē′stōl′), Vertical Short Take-Off and Landing.

Vt., Vermont.

v.t., verb transitive.

V.T.C., 1. Volunteer Training Corps. **2.** voting trust certificate.

Vte., Vicomte.

Vtesse., Vicomtesse.

VT fuze, a variable time fuze.

VTO, *Aeron.* vertical take-off.

VTOL (vē′tōl′), *n.* *Aeron.* **1.** vertical take-off and landing. **2.** an airplane capable of taking off and landing vertically, having forward speeds comparable to those of conventional aircraft.

V′-type en′gine (vē′tīp′), *Auto.* an engine having the cylinders aligned in two banks at an angle to each other, forming a V.

Vuel·ta A·ba·jo (vwel′tə ə bä′hō; *Sp.* bwel′tä ä vä′hō), a region in W Cuba.

vug (vug, vo͝og), *n.* *Mining.* a small cavity in a rock or lode, often lined with crystals. Also, **vugg, vugh.** [< Cornish *vooga* cave; cf. L *fovea* pit, pitfall] —**vug′gy,** *adj.*

Vuil·lard (vwē yar′), *n.* **(Jean) É·dou·ard** (zhän ā dwar′), 1868–1940, French painter.

Vul., Vulgate.

Vul·can (vul′kən), *n.* the ancient Roman god of fire and metalworking, identified with the Greek Hephaestus. [< L *Vulcān(us)*]

Vul·ca·na·li·a (vul′kə nā′lē ə, -nāl′yə), *n.* (*sometimes construed as pl.*) an ancient Roman festival, in honor of Vulcan.

Vul·ca·ni·an (vul kā′nē ən), *adj.* **1.** of, pertaining to, or associated with Vulcan. **2.** (*l.c.*) volcanic. **3.** (*l.c.*) of or pertaining to metalworking. [< L *Vulcāni(us)* of Vulcan + -AN]

vul·can·ise (vul′kə nīz′), *v.t.,* **-ised, -is·ing.** *Chiefly Brit.* vulcanize. —**vul′can·is′a·ble,** *adj.* —**vul′can·i·sa′tion,** *n.* —**vul′can·is′er,** *n.*

vul·can·ism (vul′kə niz′əm), *n.* *Geol.* the series of phenomena connected with the origin and movement of molten rock material, both volcanic and plutonic. [var. of VOLCANISM] —**vul′can·ist,** *n.*

vul·can·ite (vul′kə nīt′), *n.* a hard, readily cut and polished rubber, obtained by vulcanizing rubber with a large amount of sulfur, used in the manufacture of combs, buttons, and for electric insulation; ebonite. [VULCAN + -ITE[1]]

vul·can·i·zate (vul′kə ni zāt′), *n.* a vulcanized substance. [VULCANIZE + -ATE[1]]

vul·can·ize (vul′kə nīz′), *v.t.,* **-ized, -iz·ing. 1.** to treat (rubber) with sulfur or some compound of sulfur while under a moderate heat (110°–140°C), in order to render it nonplastic and give greater elasticity, durability, etc.: sometimes a large amount of sulfur and a more extensive heat treatment are employed, in order to make it very hard, as in the case of vulcanite. **2.** to treat (rubber) similarly with sulfur or sulfur compounds, but without heat, with only superficial results. **3.** to subject (a substance other than rubber) to some analogous process, as to harden it. Also, *esp. Brit.,* **vulcanise.** [VULCAN + -IZE] —**vul′can·iz′a·ble,** *adj.* —**vul′can·i·za′tion,** *n.* —**vul′can·iz′er,** *n.*

vul′canized fi′ber, a leatherlike substance made by compression of layers of paper or cloth which have been treated with acids or zinc chloride, used chiefly for electric insulation.

vul·can·ol·o·gy (vul′kə nol′ə jē), *n.* volcanology. [*vulcan-* (var. of *volcan-* as in VOLCANIC) + -o- + -LOGY] —**vul·can·o·log·i·cal** (vul′kə nᵊloj′i kəl), *adj.* —**vul′can·ol′o·gist,** *n.*

Vulg., Vulgate.

vulg., 1. vulgar. **2.** vulgarly.

vul·gar (vul′gər), *adj.* **1.** characterized by ignorance of or lack of good breeding or taste: *vulgar ostentation.* **2.** indecent; obscene; lewd: *a vulgar work; a vulgar gesture.* **3.** crude; coarse; unrefined: *a vulgar peasant.* **4.** of, pertaining to, or constituting the ordinary people in a society: *the vulgar masses.* **5.** current; popular; common: *vulgar idols; a vulgar success; vulgar beliefs.* **6.** spoken by, or being in the language spoken by, the people generally; vernacular: *a vulgar translation of the Greek text of the New Testament.* **7.** lacking in distinction, aesthetic value, or charm; banal; ordinary: *a vulgar painting; vulgar architecture.* —*n.* **8.** *Archaic.* the common people. **9.** *Obs.* the vernacular. [late ME < L *vulgār(is),* equiv. to *vulg(us)* the general public + *-āris* -AR[1]] —**vul′gar·ly,** *adv.* —**vul′gar·ness,** *n.*
—**Syn. 1.** unrefined, inelegant, low, coarse, ribald. See **common. 3.** boorish, rude. **6.** colloquial.

vul′gar frac′tion. See **common fraction.**

vul·gar·i·an (vul gâr′ē ən), *n.* a vulgar person, esp. one whose vulgarity is the more conspicuous for his wealth, prominence, or pretensions to good breeding. [VULGAR + -IAN]

vul·gar·ise (vul′gə rīz′), *v.t.,* **-ised, -is·ing.** *Chiefly Brit.* vulgarize. —**vul′gar·i·sa′tion,** *n.* —**vul′gar·is′er,** *n.*

vul·gar·ism (vul′gə riz′əm), *n.* **1.** vulgar behavior or character; vulgarity. **2.** a vulgar expression; a word or phrase used only in common colloquial, and esp. in coarse speech. [VULGAR + -ISM]

vul·gar·i·ty (vul gar′i tē), *n., pl.* **-ties. 1.** the state or quality of being vulgar: *She chose to ignore the vulgarity of his remark.* **2.** something vulgar, as an act or expression. [< LL *vulgāritās* the common herd. See VULGAR, -ITY]

vul·gar·ize (vul′gə rīz′), *v.t.,* **-ized, -iz·ing.** to make vulgar; lower; debase: *to vulgarize standards of etiquette.* Also, *esp. Brit.,* **vulgarise.** [VULGAR + -IZE] —**vul′gar·i·za′tion,** *n.* —**vul′gar·iz′er,** *n.*

Vul′gar Lat′in, popular Latin, as distinguished from literary or standard Latin, esp. those spoken forms of Latin from which the Romance languages developed.

Vul·gate (vul′gāt, -git), *n.* **1.** the Latin version of the Bible, prepared chiefly by St. Jerome at the end of the 4th century A.D., and used as the authorized version in liturgical services of the Roman Catholic Church. **2.** (*l.c.*) any commonly recognized text or version of a work. —*adj.* **3.** of or pertaining to the Vulgate. **4.** (*l.c.*) commonly used or accepted; common. [< L *vulgāta* (*editiō*) popular edition (of the Bible); *vulgāta* fem. ptp. of *vulgāre* to make common, publish, deriv. of *vulgus* the public. See VULGAR, -ATE[1]]

vul·gus (vul′gəs), *n., pl.* **-gus·es** for 2. **1.** the common people; masses. **2.** an exercise in Latin formerly required of English public-school pupils. [< L]

vulned (vulnd), *adj.* *Heraldry.* (of a man, beast, or bird) represented as wounded, with drops of blood depicted: *a lion or, vulned gules.* [< L *vuln(us)* a wound + -ED[3]]

vul·ner·a·ble (vul′nər ə bəl), *adj.* **1.** capable of or susceptible to being wounded or hurt, as by a weapon: *a vulnerable part of the body.* **2.** open to moral attack, criticism, temptation, etc.: *an argument vulnerable to refutation; He has proved himself vulnerable to bribery.* **3.** (of a place) open to attack or assault; difficult to defend: *a vulnerable bridge.* **4.** *Bridge.* having won one of the games of a rubber. [< LL *vulnerābil(is),* equiv. to *vulnerā(re)* to wound + *-bilis* -BLE; see VULNERARY] —**vul′ner·a·bil′i·ty, vul′ner·a·ble·ness,** *n.* —**vul′ner·a·bly,** *adv.*

vul·ne·rant om·nes, ul·ti·ma ne·cat (wo͞ol′ne-ränt′ ōm′nās, o͞ol′ti mä′ ne′kät; *Eng.* vul′nə rant′ om′nēz, ul′tə mə nē′kat), *Latin.* all (hours) wound, the last (one) kills: inscription used on dials of clocks in churches or on public monuments.

vul·ner·ar·y (vul′nə rer′ē), *adj., n., pl.* **-ar·ies.** —*adj.* **1.** used to promote the healing of wounds, as herbs or other remedies. —*n.* **2.** a remedy for wounds. [< L *vulnerāri(us),* equiv. to *vulner-* (s. of *vulnus*) wound + *-ārius* -ARY]

Vul·pec·u·la (vul pek′yə lə), *n., gen.* **-lae** (-lē′). *Astron.* the Little Fox, a northern constellation between Cygnus and Aquila. [< L, equiv. to *vulpē(s)* fox + *-cula,* fem. of *-culus* -CULE]

vul·pec·u·lar (vul pek′yə lər), *adj.* pertaining to or resembling a fox; vulpine. [< LL *vulpēculār(is).* See VULPECULA, -AR[1]]

vul·pi·cide (vul′pi sīd′), *n.* *Brit.* **1.** the act of killing a fox other than by hunting it with hounds. **2.** a person who kills a fox by means other than hunting it with hounds. Also, **vul′pe·cide′.** [< L *vulpi-* (s. of *vulpēs*) fox + -CIDE] —**vul′pi·cid′al,** *adv.* —**vul′pi·cid·ism,** *n.*

vul·pine (vul′pīn, -pin), *adj.* pertaining to, like, or characteristic of a fox. [< L *vulpīn(us),* equiv. to *vulp(i)-* (s. of *vulpēs* fox) + *-īnus* -INE[1]]

vul·pi·nite (vul′pə nīt′), *n.* *Mineral.* a variety of anhydrite, occurring at Vulpino, Italy, in granular, scaly masses: used as an ornamental stone. [named after *Vulpin(o)*; see -ITE[1]]

vul·si·nite (vul′sə nīt′), *n.* a trachytic rock, composed chiefly of andesine, sanidine, mica, and horneblende. [named after *Vulsini* (now Bolseno), Etruscan town near which the rock was found; see -ITE[1]]

vul·ture (vul′chər), *n.* **1.** any of several large, primarily carrion-eating Old World birds of prey of the family *Accipitridae,* often having a naked head and less powerful feet than those of the related hawks and eagles. **2.** any of several superficially similar New World birds of the family *Cathartidae.* **3.** one who or that which preys, esp. greedily or unscrupulously: *That vulture would sell out his best friend.* [late ME < L *vultur*] —**vul′ture·like′,** *adj.*

Turkey vulture, *Cathartes aura* (Length 2½ ft.; wingspread to 6 ft.)

vul·tur·ine (vul′chə rīn′, -chər in), *adj.* **1.** of, pertaining to, or characteristic of a vulture or vultures. **2.** resembling a vulture, esp. in rapacious or predatory qualities: *a vulturine critic.* Also, **vul·tur·ous** (vul′chər əs). [< L *vulturīn(us).* See VULTURE, -INE[1]]

vulv-, a combining form of **vulva:** *vulvitis.*

vul·va (vul′və), *n., pl.* **-vae** (-vē), **-vas.** *Anat.* the external female genitalia. [< L: covering] —**vul′val, vul′var,** *adj.* —**vul·vi·form** (vul′və fôrm′), **vul·vate** (vul′vāt, -vit), *adj.*

vul·vi·tis (vul vī′tis), *n.* *Pathol.* inflammation of the vulva. [< NL; see VULV-, -ITIS]

vv., 1. verses. **2.** violins.

v.v., vice versa.

vv.ll., variae lectiones.

V.W., Very Worshipful.

Vyat·ka (vyät′kä), *n.* former name of **Kirov.**

Vy·borg (vē′bôrg), *n.* a seaport in the NW RSFSR, in the NW Soviet Union in Europe, on the Gulf of Finland: formerly in Finland. 51,000 (1959). Swedish, **Viborg.** Formerly, **Viipuri.**

Vy·cor (vī′kôr), *n.* *Trademark.* a durable, highly heat-resistant glass containing approximately 96 percent silica, used chiefly for making laboratory vessels, as beakers, crucibles, flasks, etc.

Vyer·nyi (vyer′nē), *n.* former name of **Alma-Ata.**

vy·ing (vī′ing), *adj.* **1.** competing; contending: *All vying swimmers come to the judge's desk.* —*v.* **2.** ppr. of **vie.** [VIE + -ING[2]] —**vy′ing·ly,** *adv.*

Vy·rene (vī′rēn, vī rēn′), *n.* a boy's given name.

Vy·shin·sky (vi shin′skē; *Russ.* vi shin′ski), *n.* **Andrei Yanuarievich.** See **Vishinsky, Andrei Yanuarievich.**

Vyv·yan (viv′yən), *n.* a boy's or girl's given name. Also, **Vivian, Vivien, Vivienne, Vivyan.**

W, w (dub′əl yōō′), *n., pl.* **W's** or **Ws, w's** or **ws. 1.** the 23rd letter of the English alphabet, a semivowel. **2.** any spoken sound represented by the letter *W* or *w,* as in *way, glower, row,* etc. **3.** something having the shape of a W. **4.** a written or printed representation of the letter *W* or *w.* **5.** a device, as a printer's type, for reproducing the letter *W* or *w.*

W, 1. watt; watts. **2.** West. **3.** Western. **4.** withdrawn; withdrew. **5.** withheld.

W, 1. the 23rd in order or in a series, or, when *I* is omitted, the 22nd. **2.** *Chem.* tungsten. **3.** wolfram. **4.** wolframium.

w, 1. watt; watts. **2.** withdrawn; withdrew. **3.** withheld.

W., 1. Wales. **2.** warden. **3.** warehouse. **4.** Washington. **5.** watt; watts. **6.** Wednesday. **7.** weight. **8.** Welsh. **9.** West. **10.** Western. **11.** width. **12.** *Physics.* work.

w., 1. warden. **2.** warehouse. **3.** watt; watts. **4.** week; weeks. **5.** weight. **6.** west. **7.** western. **8.** wide. **9.** width. **10.** wife. **11.** with. **12.** won. **13.** *Physics.* work.

w/, with.

wa' (wô, wä), *n. Scot.* wall.

W.A., 1. West Africa. **2.** Western Australia.

WAA, War Assets Administration.

WAAC (wak), *n.* **1.** *U.S.* **a.** Women's Army Auxiliary Corps: founded during World War II. **b.** a member of the Women's Army Auxiliary Corps. Cf. **Wac. 2.** *Brit.* **a.** Women's Army Auxiliary Corps: founded in 1917. **b.** a member of the Women's Army Auxiliary Corps. Cf. **WRAC.** Also, **W.A.A.C.**

Waadt (vät), *n.* German name of **Vaud.**

Waaf (waf), *n. Brit.* **1.** Women's Auxiliary Air Force: formed during World War II as an auxiliary of the Royal Air Force. **2.** a member of the Women's Auxiliary Air Force. Also, **W.A.A.F.**

Waal (väl), *n.* a river in the central Netherlands, flowing W to the Meuse River: the center branch of the lower Rhine. 52 mi. long.

Waals (väls), *n.* **Jo·han·nes Di·de·rick van der** (yō hä′nəs dē′də rik vän dər), 1837–1923, Dutch physicist: Nobel prize 1910.

wab (wäb), *n. Scot. and North Eng.* web. [OE *wæbb,* var. of *webb* WEB]

Wa·bash (wô′bash), *n.* a river flowing from W Ohio through Indiana, along part of the boundary between Indiana and Illinois, into the Ohio River. 475 mi. long.

Wa·ba·sha (wô′bə shô′), *n.* a town in SE Minnesota. 2500 (1960).

wab·ble[1] (wob′əl), *v.i., v.t.,* **-bled, -bling.** wobble. —**wab′bler,** *n.* —**wab′bling·ly,** *adv.*

wab·ble[2] (wob′əl), *n.* the larva of a botfly, *Cuterebra emasculator,* that infests squirrels and other rodents. [var. of WARBLE[2]]

wab′ble saw′. See **drunken saw.**

wab·bly (wob′lē), *adj.,* **-bli·er, -bli·est.** wobbly. —**wab′bli·ness,** *n.*

Wac (wak), *n.* a member of the Women's Army Corps, an auxiliary of the U.S. Army.

Wace (wäs, wās; *Fr.* was), *n.* **Ro·bert** (rob′ərt; *Fr.* rô ber′), ("*Wace of Jersey*"), c1100–c1180, Anglo-Norman poet born on the Channel Island of Jersey.

wack (wak), *n. Slang.* an eccentric, strange, or odd person. [prob. back formation from WACKY]

wack·e (wak′ə), *n.* a soft rock of fine texture, derived from disintegrated basaltic rocks. [< G: a kind of stone]

wack·y (wak′ē), *adj.,* **wack·i·er, wack·i·est.** *Slang.* odd or irrational; crazy: *She's awfully nice, even if she is a little wacky.* Also, **whacky.** [nonsense formation; cf. *icky* not a member of the group; prob. akin to WHACK] —**wack′i·ly,** *adv.* —**wack′i·ness,** *n.*

Wa·co (wā′kō), *n.* a city in central Texas, on the Brazos River. 97,808 (1960).

wad[1] (wod), *n., v.,* **wad·ded, wad·ding.** —*n.* **1.** a small mass, lump, or ball of something: *a wad of paper; a wad of tobacco.* **2.** a small mass of cotton, wool, or other fibrous or soft material, used for stuffing, padding, packing, etc. **3.** a roll of something, esp. of bank notes. **4.** *Slang.* a comparatively large stock or quantity of something, esp. money: *He's got a healthy wad salted away.* **5.** a plug of cloth, tow, paper, or the like, used to hold the powder or shot, or both, in place in a gun or cartridge. **6.** *Brit. Dial.* a bundle, esp. a small one, of hay, straw, etc. —*v.t.* **7.** to form (material) into a wad. **8.** to roll tightly (often fol. by *up*): *He wadded his cap into his pocket.* **9.** to hold in place by a wad: *They rammed and wadded the shot into their muskets.* **10.** to put a wad into; stuff with a wad. **11.** to fill out with or as with wadding; stuff; pad: *to wad a quilt; to wad a speech with useless information.* [? < Scand; cf. Sw *vadd* padding, c. G *Watte*] —**wad′der,** *n.*

wad[2] (wod), *n.* a soft, earthy, black to dark-brown mass of manganese oxide minerals. [?]

wad[3] (wäd, wəd), *auxiliary verb. Scot.* would.

wad[4] (wod), *Scot. Law.* —*n.* **1.** a legal pledge; security. **2. in wad,** pledged; held as security. [OE *wædd,* var. of *wedd* pledge; see WED]

Wa·dai (wä dī′), *n.* a former independent sultanate of the Sudan, in N central Africa: now part of the Republic of Chad.

wad·ding (wod′ing), *n.* **1.** any fibrous or soft material for stuffing, padding, packing, etc., esp. carded cotton in specially prepared sheets. **2.** material used as wads for guns, cartridges, etc. **3.** a wad or lump. [WAD[1] + -ING[1]]

wad·dle (wod′əl), *v.,* **-dled, -dling,** *n.* —*v.i.* **1.** to walk with short steps, swaying or rocking from side to side, as a duck. **2.** to move in any similar, slow, rocking manner; wobble: *The ship waddled into port.* —*n.* **3.** the act or an instance of waddling, esp. a waddling gait. [WADE + -LE; c. G *watteln*] —**wad′dler,** *n.* —**wad′dling·ly,** *adv.* —**wad′dly,** *adj.*

wad·dy (wod′ē), *n., pl.* **-dies,** *v.,* **-died, -dy·ing.** *Australian.* —*n.* **1.** a heavy wooden war club of the Australian aborigines. —*v.t.* **2.** to beat or strike with a waddy. [< native Austral]

Wad·dy (wod′ē), *n.* a boy's given name, form of **Wadsworth.**

wade (wād), *v.,* **wad·ed, wad·ing,** *n.* —*v.i.* **1.** to walk through water, snow, sand, or any other substance that impedes free motion or offers resistance to movement: *to wade through the mud.* **2.** to walk in water, when partially immersed: *He wasn't swimming; he was wading.* **3.** to play in water: *The children were wading in the pool most of the afternoon.* **4.** to make one's way slowly or laboriously: *to wade through a dull book.* **5.** *Obs.* to go or proceed. —*v.t.* **6.** to pass through or cross by wading; ford: *to wade a stream.* **7. wade in** or **into,** *Informal.* **a.** to begin energetically. **b.** to attack strongly: *to wade into a thoughtless husband; to wade into a mob of rioters.* —*n.* **8.** the act or an instance of wading: *We went for a wade in the shallows.* [ME; OE *wadan* to go; c. Icel *vatha,* G *waten;* akin to OE *wæd* ford, sea, L *vadum* shoal, ford, *vādere* to go, rush] —**wad′a·ble, wade′a·ble,** *adj.*

Wade (wād), *n.* a boy's given name.

Wa·de·na (wo dē′nə), *n.* a town in central Minnesota. 4381 (1960).

wad·er (wā′dər), *n.* **1.** one who or that which wades. **2.** any of various long-legged birds, as cranes, herons, storks, sandpipers, plovers, etc., that wade in water in search of food. **3. waders,** high, waterproof boots used for wading, as by fishermen, duck hunters, laborers, etc. [WADE + -ER[1]]

Wades·bor·o (wādz′bûr ō, -bur ō), *n.* a town in S North Carolina. 3744 (1960).

wa·di (wä′dē), *n., pl.* **-dis.** (in Arabia, Syria, northern Africa, etc.) **1.** the channel of a watercourse which is dry except during periods of rainfall. **2.** such a stream or watercourse itself. **3.** an oasis. Also, **wady.** [< Ar *wādī*]

Wa·di Hal·fa (wä′dē häl′fə), a town in the N Sudan, on the Nile. 11,006 (1956).

wad′ing bird′, wader (def. 2).

wad·mal (wod′məl), *n.* a bulky woolen fabric woven of coarse yarn and heavily napped, formerly much used in England and Scandinavia for the manufacture of durable winter garments. Also, **wad′maal, wad′mel wad′mol, wad′moll.** [late ME < Scand; cf. Icel *vathmāl* kind of cloth, equiv. to *vath-* (< ?) + *māl* (see PIECEMEAL)]

Wad Me·da·ni (wäd mə dä′nē, med′ənē), a city in the E Sudan, on the Blue Nile. 47,677 (1956).

wad·na (wad′nə), *Scot.* contraction of *would not.* [WAD[3] + NA]

wad·set (wod′set), *n., v.t.,* **-set·ted, -set·ting.** *Scot. Law.* mortgage. [var. of ME *wedset,* OE *tō wedde settan* set for pledge; see WAD[4]]

wad·set·ter (wod′set ər), *n. Scot. Law.* a person who mortgages his land; mortgagor. [WADSET + -ER[1]]

Wads·worth (wodz′wərth), *n.* a boy's given name.

wa·dy (wä′dē), *n., pl.* **-dies.** wadi.

wae (wā), *n. Scot. and North Eng.* woe. [OE *wā* WOE]

wae·sucks (wā′suks), *interj. Scot.* alas. Also, **waesuck** (wā′suk). [WAE + *sucks,* var. of SAKE[2]]

waf (waf, wäf), *adj., n. Scot.* waff[2].

Waf (waf), *n.* a member of the Women in the Air Force, an auxiliary of the U.S. Air Force.

Wafd (woft), *n.* the nationalist party in the United Arab Republic. [< Ar: lit., deputation] —**Wafd′ist,** *n., adj.*

wa·fer (wā′fər), *n.* **1.** a thin, crisp cake or biscuit, often sweetened and flavored. **2.** a thin disk of unleavened bread, used in the Eucharist, as in the Roman Catholic Church. **3.** a thin disk of dried paste, gelatin, adhesive paper, or the like, used for sealing letters, attaching papers, etc. **4.** *Med.* a thin, circular sheet of dry paste or the like, or a pair of such sheets, for moistening and using to wrap about or enclose a powder to be swallowed. **5.** any small, thin disk, as a washer, piece of insulation, etc. —*v.t.* **6.** to seal, close, or attach by means of a wafer or wafers: *to wafer a letter.* [late ME *wafre* < MD *wafer,* var. of *wafel* WAFFLE[1]; cf. F *gaufre* (OF *walfre*)] —**wa′fer·like′, wa′fer·y,** *adj.*

wa·fer-thin (wā′fər thin′), *adj.* very thin: *a wafer-thin slice.*

waff[1] (waf, wäf), *n. Scot. and North Eng.* **1.** a puff or blast of air, wind, etc. **2.** a brief view; glance. [*waff* (v.), var. of WAVE]

waff[2] (waf, wäf), *Scot.* —*adj.* **1.** worthless. **2.** solitary; without companions. —*n.* **3.** a vagrant or vagabond. Also, **waf, wauf.** [var. of WAIF] —**waff′ness,** *n.*

waf·fie (wä′fē), *n. Scot.* a worthless person, esp. a vagrant or vagabond. Also, **waufie.** [WAFF[2] + -IE]

waf·fle[1] (wof′əl), *n.* **1.** a batter cake with a pattern of deep indentations on each side, formed by the gridlike design on each of the two hinged parts of the metal appliance (**waf′fle i′ron**) in which the cake is baked, which are closed during baking. —*adj.* **2.** Also, **waf′fled.** having a gridlike or indented lattice shape or design: *a waffle weave.* [< D *wafel,* equiv. to *waf-* (cf. OHG *waba* honeycomb) + *-el* n. suffix; akin to WEB]

waf·fle[2] (wof′əl), *v.i.* **-fled, -fling.** *Brit.* to talk foolishly or without purpose; idle away time talking. [*waff* to yelp (obs.; cf. WAFF[1]) + -LE]

waf′fle cloth′, honeycomb (def. 5a).

W. Afr., 1. West Africa. **2.** West African.

WAFS, Women's Auxiliary Ferrying Squadron. Also, **W.A.F.S.**

waft[1] (waft, wäft), *v.t.* **1.** to carry lightly and smoothly through the air or over water: *The gentle breeze wafted the sound of music to our ears.* **2.** to send or convey lightly, as if in flight: *The actress wafted kisses to her admirers in the audience.* **3.** *Obs.* to signal to, summon, or direct by waving. —*v.i.* **4.** to float or be carried, esp. through the air: *The sound wafted on the breeze. The music wafted across the lake.* —*n.* **5.** a sound, odor, etc., faintly perceived: *a waft of perfume.* **6.** a wafting movement; light current or gust: *a waft of air.* **7.** the act of wafting. **8.** *Naut.* waif (def. 4). [back formation from obs. *wafter,* late ME *waughter* armed escort vessel < D or LG *wachter* guard; in some senses confused with WAFF[1]] —**waft′er,** *n.*

waft[2] (waft, wäft), *n.* *Scot.* weft[1]. [OE *gewæf*, var. of *gewef* WEFT[1]]

waft·age (waf′tij, wäf′-), *n.* *Archaic.* **1.** the act of wafting. **2.** the state of being wafted. [WAFT[1] + -AGE]

waf·ture (waf′chər, wäf′-), *n.* **1.** the act of wafting. **2.** something wafted: *waftures of incense.* [WAFT[1] + -URE]

wag (wag), *v.*, **wagged, wag·ging,** *n.* —*v.t.* **1.** to move from side to side, forward and backward, or up and down, esp. rapidly and repeatedly: *a dog wagging his tail.* **2.** to move (the tongue), as in idle or indiscreet chatter. **3.** to shake (a finger) at someone, as in reproach. **4.** to move or nod (the head). —*v.i.* **5.** to be moved from side to side or one way and the other, esp. rapidly and repeatedly, as the head or the tail. **6.** to move constantly, esp. in idle or indiscreet chatter: *Her behavior set local tongues wagging.* **7.** to get along; travel; proceed: *Let the world wag how it will.* **8.** to totter or sway. **9.** *Brit. Slang.* to play truant; play hooky. —*n.* **10.** the act of wagging: *a friendly wag of the tail.* **11.** a person given to droll, roguish, or mischievous humor; wit. [ME *wagge* < Scand; cf. Icel *vagga* to rock; see WAGGLE] —**wag′ger,** *n.*

wage (wāj), *n.*, *v.*, **waged, wag·ing.** —*n.* **1.** Often, **wages.** money that is paid or received for work or services, as by the hour, day, or week. Cf. **living wage, minimum wage. 2.** Usually, **wages.** *Econ.* the share of the products of industry received by labor for its work (as distinct from the share going to capital). **3.** Usually, **wages.** (*construed as sing. or pl.*) recompense or return: *The wages of sin is death.* **4.** *Obs.* a pledge or security. —*v.t.* **5.** to carry on (a battle, war, conflict, argument, etc.): *to wage war against a nation.* **6.** *Chiefly Brit. Dial.* to hire. **7.** *Obs.* **a.** to stake or wager. **b.** to pledge. —*v.i.* **8.** *Obs.* to contend; struggle. [ME < AF, equiv. to OF *guage* GAGE[1] < VL **wadium* < Gmc; see WED] —**wage′less,** *adj.* —**wage′less·ness,** *n.*
—**Syn. 1.** earnings, emolument, compensation, remuneration. See **pay. 5.** undertake.

wage′ earn′er, a person who works for wages.

wa·ger (wā′jər), *n.* **1.** something risked or staked on an uncertain event; bet: *to place a wager on a soccer match.* **2.** the act of betting. **3.** the subject or terms of a bet. **4.** *Early Eng. Law.* a pledge to make good one's cause by the supporting oaths of others or by battle. —*v.t.* **5.** to risk (something) on the issue of a contest or any uncertain event or matter; bet. **6.** *Hist.* to pledge oneself to (battle) for the decision of a case. —*v.i.* **7.** to make or offer a wager; bet. [ME *wajour, wager* < AF *wageure*, equiv. to *wage(r)* to pledge (see WAGE) + *-ure* -URE] —**wa′ger·er,** *n.*
—**Syn. 1.** stake, hazard, risk, venture. **5.** stake, venture.

wage′ scale′, 1. a schedule of wages paid workers performing related tasks in an industry or shop. **2.** a particular employer's wage schedule.

wage′ slave′, a person who works for a wage, esp. at disagreeable tasks or with total and immediate dependency on the income derived from such labor.

wage·work·er (wāj′wûr′kər), *n.* a member of the laboring class; wage earner. [WAGE + WORKER] —**wage′work′ing,** *adj.*, *n.*

Wag·ga Wag·ga (wog′ə wog′ə), a city in central New South Wales, in SE Australia. 22,092 (1961).

wag·ger·y (wag′ə rē), *n.*, *pl.* **-ger·ies. 1.** the action, spirit, or language of a wag; roguish or droll humor: *the waggery of Shakespeare's clowns.* **2.** a waggish act; jest or joke. [WAG + -ERY]

wag·gish (wag′ish), *adj.* **1.** like a wag; roguish in merriment and good humor; jocular: *Fielding and Sterne are waggish writers.* **2.** characteristic of or befitting a wag: *waggish humor.* [WAG + -ISH[1]] —**wag′gish·ly,** *adv.* —**wag′gish·ness,** *n.*
—**Syn. 1.** roguish, jocund, mischievous, merry, jocose, droll, comical, funny. See **humorous.**

wag·gle (wag′əl), *v.*, **-gled, -gling,** *n.* —*v.i.* **1.** to wobble or shake, esp. while in motion: *the ball waggled slowly to a stop. The leaves of the tree waggled in the wind.* —*v.t.* **2.** to move up and down or from side to side in a short, rapid manner; wag: *to waggle one's head.* **3.** *Golf.* to make a waggle with (a golf club). —*n.* **4.** a waggling motion. **5.** *Golf.* a swinging movement made with a golf club to and fro over the ball prior to a stroke. [WAG + -LE] —**wag′gling·ly,** *adv.*

wag·gly (wag′lē), *adj.* waggling; unsteady. [WAGGLE + -Y[1]]

wag·gon (wag′ən), *n.*, *v.t.*, *v.i.* *Chiefly Brit.* wagon.

wag·gon·age (wag′ə nij), *n.* *Chiefly Brit.* wagonage.

wag·gon·er (wag′ə nər), *n.* *Chiefly Brit.* waggoner.

wag·gon·ette (wag′ə net′), *n.* *Chiefly Brit.* wagonette.

wag·gon-head·ed (wag′ən hed′id), *adj.* *Chiefly Brit.* wagon-headed.

wag·gon·load (wag′ən lōd′), *n.* *Chiefly Brit.* wagonload.

Wag·ner (wag′nər *for 1, 4, 5;* väg′nər *or Ger.* väg′nəʀ *for 2, 3*), *n.* **1. Ho·nus** (hō′nəs), (*John Peter*), 1874–1955, U.S. baseball player. **2. Ot·to** (ot′ō; *Ger.* ôt′ō), 1841–1918, Austrian architect. **3. Rich·ard** (rich′ərd; *Ger.* ʀiᴋʜ′ärt), 1813–83, German composer. **4. Robert F(erdinand),** 1877–1953, U.S. politician. **5.** his son, **Robert F(erdinand), Jr.,** born 1910, U.S. politician: mayor of New York City 1954–65.

Wag·ne·ri·an (väg nēr′ē ən), *adj.* **1.** of, pertaining to, or characteristic of Richard Wagner or his works: *Wagnerian grandeur; a Wagnerian soprano.* —*n.* **2.** Also, **Wag·ner·ite** (väg′nə rīt′). a follower or admirer of the music or theories of Richard Wagner. [WAGNER + -IAN]

Wag·ner·ism (väg′nə riz′əm), *n.* **1.** Richard Wagner's theory or practice of music drama, differing from earlier, esp. Italian, operatic theory or practice chiefly in its concentration on continuous musical and dramatic flow, increased emphasis on the orchestra, and extensive use of the leitmotif. **2.** the study, imitation, or influence of the music of Richard Wagner. [WAGNER + -ISM] —**Wag′ner·ist,** *n.*

Wag·ner-Jau·regg (väg′nəʀ you′ʀek), *n.* **Ju·li·us** (yo͞o′lē o͝os′), 1857–1940, Austrian psychiatrist: Nobel prize for medicine 1927.

wag·on (wag′ən), *n.* **1.** any of various kinds of four-wheeled vehicles designed to be pulled or having its own motor and ranging from a child's toy to a commercial vehicle for the transport of heavy loads, delivery, etc. **2.** *Brit.* a railway freight car or flatcar. **3.** (*cap.*) *Astron.* See **Charles's Wain. 4.** a police van for transporting prisoners; patrol wagon: *The fight broke up before the wagon arrived.* **5.** a baby carriage. **6.** See **station wagon. 7.** *Obs.* a chariot. **8. hitch one's wagon to a star,** to have a high ambition, ideal, or purpose: *It is better to hitch one's wagon to a star than to wander aimlessly through life.* **9. on the wagon,** *Slang.* abstaining from alcoholic beverages. Also, **on the water wagon.** Also, *Brit.*, **on the water cart.** —*v.t.* **10.** to transport or convey by wagon. —*v.i.* **11.** to proceed or haul goods by wagon: *It was strenuous to wagon up the hill.* Also, *esp. Brit.*, **waggon.** [< D *wagen;* c. OE *wægn* WAIN] —**wag′on·less,** *adj.*
—**Syn. 1.** cart, van, wain, truck, dray, lorry.

wag·on·age (wag′ə nij), *n.* *Archaic.* **1.** transportation or conveyance by wagon. **2.** money paid for this. **3.** a group of wagons; wagon train. Also, *esp. Brit.*, **waggonage.** [WAGON + -AGE]

wag′on boss′, a man in charge of a wagon train.

wag·on·er (wag′ə nər), *n.* **1.** a person who drives a wagon. **2.** (*cap.*) *Astron.* the northern constellation Aurigo. **3.** *Obs.* a charioteer. Also, *esp. Brit.*, **waggoner.** [WAGON + -ER[1]]

Wag·on·er (wag′ə nər), *n.* a town in E Oklahoma. 4469 (1960).

wag·on·ette (wag′ə net′), *n.* a light, four-wheeled carriage, with or without a top, having a crosswise seat in front and two lengthwise seats facing each other at the back. Also, *esp. Brit.*, **waggonette.** [WAGON + -ETTE]

wag·on-head·ed (wag′ən hed′id), *adj.* *Archit.* of the form of a round arch or a semicylinder, like the cover of a wagon when stretched over the bows, as a ceiling, roof, etc. Also, *esp. Brit.*, **waggon-headed.**

wag′on job′ber. See **truck jobber.**

wa·gon-lit (*Fr.* vA gôN lē′), *n.*, *pl.* **wa·gons-lits** (vA-gôN lē′). (in continental European usage) a railroad sleeping car. [< F: lit., bed car, equiv. to *wagon* railway coach (< E) + *lit* bed (< L *lectus*)]

wag·on·load (wag′ən lōd′), *n.* the load carried by a wagon. Also, *esp. Brit.*, **waggonload.** [WAGON + LOAD]

wag′on roof′. See **barrel vault.**

wag′on seat′, *U.S. Furniture.* a plain, unupholstered settee, usually with a slat back, for use either indoors or in a wagon. Also called **rumble seat.**

wag′on sol′dier, *Mil. Slang.* a field-artillery soldier.

wag′on-spring clock′ (wag′ən spring′), an early American clock driven by a leaf spring at the bottom of the case.

wag·on-the-wall (wag′on thə wôl′, -ôn-), *n.* (in New England, c1800) the dial and works of a pendulum clock, sold with a hood but without the whole case.

wag′on train′, a train of wagons and horses, as one carrying military supplies.

wag′on vault′. See **barrel vault.**

Wa·gram (vä′gʀäm), *n.* a village in NE Austria: Napoleon defeated the Austrians here in 1809.

wag·tail (wag′tāl′), *n.* **1.** any of numerous small, chiefly Old World birds of the family *Motacillidae*, having a slender body with a long, narrow tail that is habitually wagged up and down. **2.** any of several similar birds, as the water thrushes of the genus *Seiurus.* [WAG + TAIL[1]]

Wah·ha·bi (wə hä′bē, wä-), *n.*, *pl.* **-bis.** *Islam.* a follower of Abd-al-Wahhab, opposing all practices not sanctioned by the Koran. Wahhabis, the most conservative Muslim group, are today found mainly in Saudi Arabia. Also, **Wa·ha′bi, Wa·ha·bite** (wä hä′bīt), **Wah·ha′bee, Wah·ha′bite.** [< Ar, equiv. to *Wahhāb* (see def.) + -ī suffix of appurtenance]

Wah·ha·bism (wə hä′biz əm, wä-), *n.* the group of doctrines or practices of the Wahhabis. Also, **Wah·ha·bi·ism** (wə hä′bē iz′əm, wä-), **Wa·ha′bism.** [WAHHAB(I) + -ISM]

Wa·hi·a·wa (wä′hē ə wä′), *n.* a city on central Oahu, in Hawaii. 15,512 (1960).

wa·hoo[1] (wä ho͞o′, wä′ho͞o), *n.*, *pl.* **-hoos.** any of various American shrubs or small trees, as an elm, *Ulmus alata*, or a linden, *Tilia heterophylla.* [< Creek *uhawhu* kind of elm]

wa·hoo[2] (wä′ho͞o′, wä′ho͞o), *n.*, *pl.* **-hoos.** a shrub or small tree, *Euonymus atropurpureus*, of North America, having pendulous capsules which in dehiscing reveal the bright-scarlet arils of the seeds. [< Dakota *wāhu* arrowwood]

wa·hoo[3] (wä ho͞o′, wä′ho͞o), *n.*, *pl.* **-hoos,** (*esp. collectively*) **-hoo.** a large, swift game fish, *Acanthocybium solandri*, of the high seas. Also called **peto.** [?]

Wa·hoo (wä′ho͞o), *n.* a town in E Nebraska. 3610 (1960).

Wah·pe·ton (wô′pi tən), *n.* a town in SE North Dakota. 5876 (1960).

Wai·a·lu·a (wī′ä lo͞o′ä), *n.* a town in NW Oahu, in central Hawaii. 2689 (1960).

Wai·chow (wī′jō′), *n.* a city in S Kwangtung, in SE China, E of Canton. ab. 35,000. Also called **Waiyeung, Huichou.**

waif (wāf), *n.* **1.** a person who has no home or friends, esp. a child. **2.** something found, the owner of which is not known, esp. a stray animal. **3.** a stray item or article: *to gather waifs of gossip.* **4.** Also, **waft, weft.** *Naut.* a signaling, or a signal given, by a flag rolled and stopped or fastened. [ME < AF, orig. adj., lost, stray, unclaimed (equiv. to OF *guaif* stray beast) < Scand; cf. Icel *veif* movement to and fro; see WAIVE[1]]

Wai·ki·ki (wī′kē kē′, wī′kē kē′), *n.* a beach on SE Oahu, in Hawaii; part of Honolulu.

wail (wāl), *v.i.* **1.** to utter a prolonged, inarticulate, mournful cry, usually high pitched or clear sounding, as in grief or suffering: *to wail with pain.* **2.** to make mournful sounds, as music, the wind, etc. **3.** to lament or mourn bitterly. **4.** *Jazz.* to perform exceptionally well. **5.** *Slang.* to express emotion musically or verbally in an exciting, satisfying way. —*v.t.* **6.** to express deep sorrow for; mourn; lament; bewail: *to wail the dead; to wail one's fate.* **7.** to express in wailing; cry or say in lamentation: *to wail one's grief.* —*n.* **8.** act of wailing. **9.** a wailing cry, as of grief, pain, despair, etc. **10.** any similar mournful sound: *the wail of an old tune.* [ME *weile;* perh. deriv. of OE *weilā(wei)* WELLAWAY; cf. OE *wǣlan* to torment, Icel *vǣla* to wail] —**wail′er,** *n.* —**wail′ing·ly,** *adv.*

wail·ful (wāl′fəl), *adj.* mournful; plaintive. [WAIL + -FUL] —**wail′ful·ly,** *adv.*

Wail′ing Wall′, a wall in Jerusalem where Jews, on certain occasions, assemble for prayer and lamentation. It is traditionally believed to be the remains of the west wall of the Temple which was built by Herod and destroyed by Titus in 70 A.D. Also called **Wail′ing Wall′ of the Jews′.**

wail·some (wāl′səm), *adj.* *Archaic.* wailful. [WAIL + -SOME[1]]

Wai·lu·ku (wī lo͞o′ko͞o), *n.* a town on NW Maui, in central Hawaii. 6969 (1960).

Wai·ma·na·lo (wī′mä nä′lō), *n.* a town in SE Oahu, in central Hawaii. 3011 (1960).

wain (wān), *n.* **1.** (*cap.*) *Astron.* See **Charles's Wain. 2.** a farm wagon or cart. **3.** *Archaic.* a chariot. [ME, OE *wægn;* c. G *Wagen*, D *wagen.* See WEIGH]

wain·a·ble (wā′nə bəl), *adj.* *Old. Eng. Law.* capable of being cultivated or plowed; tillable. [< AL *wainābil(is)*, equiv. to *wain-* (s. of AF *wai(g)ner* to till; see GAIN[1]) + *-ābilis* -ABLE]

wain·age (wā′nij), *n.* *Old Eng. Law.* the aggregate of equipment and implements considered as essential to husbandry. [< AL *waināg(ium)*, equiv. to *wain-* (see WAINABLE) + *-āgium* -AGE]

wain·rope (wān′rōp′), *n.* *Obs.* a rope or trace for drawing a wain. [WAIN + ROPE]

wain·scot (wān′skət, -skot), *n.*, *v.*, **-scot·ed, -scot·ing** or (*esp. Brit.*) **-scot·ted, -scot·ting.** —*n.* **1.** wood, esp. oak and usually in the form of paneling, for lining interior walls. **2.** the lining itself, esp. as covering the lower portion of a wall. **3.** a dado, esp. of wood, lining an interior wall. **4.** *Brit.* oak of superior quality and cut, imported from the Baltic countries for fine woodwork. —*v.t.* **5.** to line the walls of (a room, hallway, etc.) with or as with woodwork: *a room wainscoted in oak.* [ME < MLG or MD *wagenschot*, equiv. to *wagen* WAIN + *schot* (?)]

wain′scot chair′, *Eng. Furniture.* an armchair of the 17th century, made of oak and having a solid paneled back.

wain·scot·ing (wān′skō ting), *n.* **1.** paneling or woodwork with which rooms, hallways, etc., are wainscoted. **2.** wainscots collectively. Also, *esp. Brit.*, **wain·scot·ting** (wān′skət ing, -skot′-). [WAINSCOT + -ING[1]]

wain·wright (wān′rīt′), *n.* a wagon maker. [WAIN + WRIGHT]

Wain·wright (wān′rīt′), *n.* **Jonathan May·hew** (mā′hyo͞o), 1883–1953, U.S. general.

wair (wâʀ), *v.t.* *Chiefly Scot.* ware[3].

waist (wāst), *n.* **1.** the part of the body in man between the ribs and the hips, usually the narrowest part of the torso. **2.** the part of a garment covering this part of the body. **3.** blouse (def. 1). **4.** the part of a one-piece garment covering the body from the neck or shoulders more or less to the waistline, esp. this part of a woman's or child's garment. **5.** a child's undergarment to which other articles of apparel may be attached. **6.** the part of an object, esp. a central or middle part, which resembles or is analogous to the human waist: *the waist of a violin.* **7.** *Naut.* the central part of a ship; that part of the deck between the forecastle and the quarterdeck. **8.** the constricted portion of the abdomen of certain insects, as a wasp. [late ME *wast*, apocopated var. of *wastum*, OE *wæstm* growth, form figure; akin to WAX[2]] —**waist′less,** *adj.*

waist·band (wāst′band′, -bənd), *n.* a band encircling the waist, esp. as a part of a skirt, pair of trousers, etc. [WAIST + BAND[2]]

waist·cloth (wāst′klôth′, -kloth′), *n.*, *pl.* **-cloths** (-klôthz′, -klothz′, -klôths′, -kloths′). a loincloth. [WAIST + CLOTH]

waist·coat (wes′kət, wāst′kōt′), *n.* **1.** *Chiefly Brit.* vest (def. 1). **2.** a garment for women which is similar to a man's vest. **3.** a body garment for men, formerly worn under the doublet. [WAIST + COAT] —**waist′coat·ed,** *adj.*

waist·coat·ing (wes′kə ting, wāst′kō′ting), *n.* a fabric for making waistcoats. [WAISTCOAT + -ING[1]]

waist-deep (wāst′dēp′), *adj.* being at or rising to the the level of the waist.

waist·ed (wā′stid), *adj.* **1.** having a waist of a specified kind (usually used in combination): *long-waisted; high-waisted.* **2.** (of an object, a container, etc.) shaped like a waist; having concave sides: *a waisted vase.* [WAIST + -ED[3]]

waist·er (wā′stər), *n.* a seaman stationed in the waist of a warship or whaler, usually a disabled, old seaman or a young, inexperienced one. [WAIST + -ER[1]]

waist-high (wāst′hī′), *adj.* extending as high as the waist: *a waist-high hedge.*

waist·line (wāst′līn′), *n.* **1.** the encircling boundary of the narrowest part of the waist. **2.** the juncture point of the skirt and waist of a garment, as a dress. [WAIST + LINE[1]]

waist′ oar′, *Naut.* See **midship oar.**

wait (wāt), *v.i.* **1.** to stay or rest in expectation; remain in a state of repose or inaction, as until something expected happens (often fol. by *for, till,* or *until*): *to wait for someone to leave.* **2.** (of things) to be available or in readiness: *A letter is waiting for you.* **3.** to remain neglected for a time: *a matter that can wait.* **4.** to postpone or delay something or to be postponed or delayed: *We waited a week and then bought the house. Your vacation will have to wait until next month.* **5.** to look forward to eagerly: *I'm just waiting for the day somebody knocks him down.* —*v.t.* **6.** to continue stationary or inactive in expectation of; await: *to wait one's turn at a telephone booth.* **7.** (of things) to be in readiness for; be reserved for; await: *Glory waits thee.* **8.** to postpone or delay in expectation: *Don't wait supper for me. Wait a better time to ask for a raise.* **9.** *Archaic.* to attend upon or escort, esp. as a sign of respect. **10. wait on, a.** to perform the duties of an attendant or servant for. **b.** to supply the wants of a person, as serving a meal or serving a customer in a store. **c.** to call upon or visit (a person, esp. a superior): *to wait on Her Majesty at the palace.* **d.** *Falconry.* (of a hawk) to soar over ground until prey appears. **e.** *Dial.* to wait for; await. **11. wait table.** See **table** (def. 20). **12. wait up,** *Informal.* **a.**

to postpone going to bed to await someone's arrival. **b.** to halt and wait for another to join one, as in running or walking: *Don't go so fast! Wait up for me!* **—n. 13.** the act or an instance of waiting or awaiting; delay; halt: *a wait at the border.* **14.** a period or interval of waiting: *There will be a long wait between trains.* **15.** *Theat.* **a.** the time between two acts or the like. **b.** See **stage wait. 16.** *Brit.* **a. waits,** (formerly) a band of musicians employed by a city or town to play music in parades, for official functions, etc. **b.** a street musician, esp. a singer. **c.** one of a band of carolers. **d.** a piece sung by carolers, esp. a Christmas carol. **17.** *Obs.* a watchman. **18. lie in wait,** to wait in ambush: *The army lay in wait in the forest.* [early ME *waite(n)* < AF *waitie(r)* (OF *guaitier*) < OHG *wahtēn* to watch, deriv. of *wahta* a watch]
—Syn. 1. await, linger, remain, abide, delay. WAIT, TARRY imply pausing to linger and thereby putting off further activity until later. WAIT usually implies staying for a limited time and for a definite purpose, that is, for something expected: *to wait for a train.* TARRY is a somewhat archaic word for WAIT but it suggests lingering, perhaps aimlessly delaying, or pausing (briefly) in a journey: *to tarry on the way home; to tarry overnight at an inn.*

wait-a-bit (wāt′ə bit′), *n.* any of various plants bearing thorns or prickly appendages, as a procumbent herb, *Harpagophytum procumbens,* of southern Africa, or the greenbrier. [trans. of SAfrD *wacht-een-beetje*]

Waite (wāt), *n.* **1. Morrison Rem·ick** (rem′ik), 1816–88, U.S. jurist: Chief Justice of the U.S. 1874–88. **2.** a boy's given name.

wait·er (wā′tər), *n.* **1.** a man who waits on table, as in a restaurant. **2.** a tray for carrying dishes, a tea service, etc.; salver. **3.** a person who waits or awaits. **4.** *Obs.* an attendant. [ME; see WAIT, -ER[1]] **—wait′er·less,** *adj.*

wait·ing (wā′ting), *n.* **1.** a period of waiting: *Never had I experienced such waiting.* **2. in waiting, a.** in attendance, as upon a royal personage. **b.** *Brit. Mil.* being next due for some obligation or privilege. **—adj. 3.** serving, or being in attendance: *waiting man; waiting maid; waiting woman.* [ME (n.); see WAIT, -ING[1], -ING[2]] **—wait′ing·ly,** *adv.*

Wait′ing for Go·dot′ (gə dō′), a play (1952) by Samuel Beckett.

wait′ing game′, a stratagem in which action on a matter is reserved for or postponed to a later time, allowing one to wait for a more advantageous time to act or to see what develops in the meantime.

wait′ing list′, a list of persons waiting, as for reservations, appointments, living accommodations, etc.

wait′ing pe′riod, 1. a specified delay, required by law, between officially stating an intention and acting on it, as between securing a wedding license and getting married. **2.** *Insurance.* the required delay between the date of inception of a claim and the date on which the indemnity becomes payable, as in workmen's compensation insurance, unemployment insurance, etc.

wait′ing room′, a room for the use of persons waiting, as in a railroad station, a physician's office, etc.

wait·list (wāt′list′), *v.t.* to place on a waiting list, esp. for a seat on an airplane: *All they could do was to waitlist us for the afternoon flight.* [v. formed from n. phrase *waiting list*]

wait·ress (wā′tris), *n.* a woman who waits on table, as in a restaurant. [WAIT(E)R + -ESS] **—wait′ress·less,** *adj.*

waive[1] (wāv), *v.t.,* **waived, waiv·ing. 1.** to refrain from claiming or insisting on; relinquish; forgo: *to waive one's right; to waive one's rank; to waive honors.* **2.** *Law.* to relinquish (a known right, interest, etc.) intentionally. **3.** to put aside for the time; defer; postpone; dispense with: *to waive formalities.* **4.** to put aside or dismiss from consideration or discussion: *waiving my attempts to explain.* [ME *weyve(n)* < AF *weyve(r)* (to) make a WAIF (of someone) by forsaking or outlawing (him)]
—Syn. 1. resign, renounce, surrender, remit, demit, give up. **—Ant. 1.** demand.

waive[2] (wāv), *v.t., v.i.,* **waived, waiv·ing.** *Obs.* to wave.

waiv·er (wā′vər), *n. Law.* **1.** an intentional relinquishment of some right, interest, or the like. **2.** an express or written statement of such relinquishment. [< AF *weyver* to WAIVE[1] used as n.; see -ER[3]]

waiv′er of pre′mium, *Insurance.* a provision in a policy establishing specific conditions under which the policy will be kept in force without the policyholder's being required to continue to pay premiums.

Wai·yeung (wī′yōōng′), *n.* Waichow.

wa·ka (wä′kə), *n., pl.* **-ka, -kas.** a Japanese poem consisting of alternating five-syllable and seven-syllable lines, and concluding with an additional seven-syllable line. [< Jap]

Wa·kash·an (wä kash′ən, wô′kə shan′), *n.* a family of American Indian languages spoken in British Columbia and Washington and including esp. Kwakiutl and Nootka. [< Nootka *Wa(u)kash* (lit., good) + -AN]

Wa·ka·ya·ma (wä′kä yä′mä), *n.* a seaport on S Honshu, in S Japan. 312,000 (est. 1963).

wake[1] (wāk), *v.,* **waked** or **woke, waked** or **wok·en, wak·ing,** *n.* **—v.i. 1.** to become roused from sleep; awake; awaken; waken (often fol. by *up*). **2.** to be or continue to be awake: *Whether I wake or sleep, I think of you.* **3.** to remain awake for some purpose, duty, etc.: *I will wake until you return.* **4.** to become roused from a tranquil or inactive state; awaken; waken: *to wake from one's daydreams.* **5.** to become cognizant or aware of something; awaken; waken: *to wake to the true situation.* **6.** *Dial.* to hold a wake over a corpse. **7.** *Chiefly Dial.* to keep watch or vigil. **—v.t. 8.** to rouse from sleep; awake; awaken; waken (often fol. by *up*): *Don't wake me for breakfast. Wake me up at six o'clock.* **9.** to rouse from inactivity, lethargy, apathy, etc. (often fol. by *up*): *The tragedy woke us up to the need for safety precautions.* **10.** to hold a wake over (a corpse). **11.** *Chiefly Dial.* to keep watch or vigil over. **—n. 12.** a watching, or a watch kept, esp. for some solemn or ceremonial purpose. **13.** a watch or vigil by the body of a dead person before burial, sometimes accompanied by feasting or merrymaking. **14.** a local annual festival in England, formerly held in honor of the patron saint or on the anniversary of the dedication of a church but now usually having little or no religious significance. **15.** the state of being awake: *between sleep and wake.* [ME *wake(n)* to watch, be or become awake, OE *wacian;* ME *wakede* (past tense), OE *wacode;* ME *wook* (past tense), OE *wōc,* past of *wæcnan* to WAKEN; akin to D *waken,* G *wachen,* Icel *vaka*] **—wak′er,** *n.*
—Syn. 8. arouse. **9.** stimulate, activate, animate, kindle, provoke. **—Ant. 1.** sleep.

wake[2] (wāk), *n.* **1.** the track of waves left by a ship or other object moving through the water: *The wake of the boat glowed in the darkness.* **2.** the path or course of anything that has passed or preceded: *The tornado left ruin in its wake.* **3. in the wake of, a.** as a result of: *An investigation followed in the wake of the scandal.* **b.** succeeding; following: *in the wake of the pioneers.* [< Scand; cf. Icel *vök* hole in the ice]

Wa·kee·ney (wô′kē nē), *n.* a town in central Kansas. 2808 (1960).

Wake·field (wāk′fēld′), *n.* **1.** a city in S Yorkshire, in N England: battle 1460. 61,591 (1961). **2.** a town in E Massachusetts, near Boston. 24,295 (1960). **3.** a town in NW Michigan, in the Upper Peninsula. 3231 (1960). **4.** an estate in E Virginia, on the Potomac River: birthplace of George Washington; restored as a national monument in 1932. **5.** a boy's given name.

Wake′ For′est, a town in central North Carolina. 2664 (1960).

wake·ful (wāk′fəl), *adj.* **1.** unable to sleep; not sleeping; indisposed to sleep: *Excitement made the children wakeful.* **2.** characterized by absence of sleep: *a wakeful night.* **3.** watchful; alert; vigilant: *a wakeful foe.* [WAKE[1] + -FUL] **—wake′ful·ly,** *adv.* **—wake′ful·ness,** *n.*
—Syn. 1. sleepless, awake, insomnious, restless. **3.** wary, observant. **—Ant. 1, 2.** sleepy.

Wake′ Is′land, an island in the N Pacific, belonging to the U.S.: air base. 3 sq. mi.

wake·less (wāk′lis), *adj.* (of sleep) sound; deep; undisturbed: *He lay in wakeless sleep.* [WAKE[1] + -LESS]

wak·en (wā′kən), *v.t.* **1.** to rouse from sleep; wake; awake; awaken. **2.** to rouse from inactivity; stir up or excite; arouse; awaken: *to waken the reader's interest.* **—v.i. 3.** to wake, or become awake; awaken. [ME; OE *wæcnan;* c. Icel *vakna;* cf. WAKE[1]] **—wak′en·er,** *n.*
—Syn. 1. arouse.

wak·en·ing (wā′kə ning), *n.* **1.** awakening. **2.** *Scots Law.* a revival of a legal action or the process by which this is done. [ME; see WAKEN, -ING[1]]

wake·rife (wāk′rīf′), *adj. Scot. and North Eng.* wakeful. [WAKE[1] + RIFE] **—wake′rife′ness,** *n.*

wake-rob·in (wāk′rob′in), *n.* **1.** the cuckoopint. **2.** any of various other arums or araceous plants, as the jack-in-the-pulpit. **3.** *U.S.* any of various liliaceous plants of the genus *Trillium,* as *T. erectum,* having rank-smelling, purple, pink, or white flowers.

wake-up (wāk′up′), *n. U.S. Dial.* flicker[2].

wa·ki·za·shi (wä kē′zä shē′), *n., pl.* **-shi.** a short Japanese sword carried by a samurai, usually equipped with a matching kogai and kozuka: used for fighting and for suicide. Cf. **katana.** [< Jap]

Waks·man (waks′mən), *n.* **Sel·man Abraham** (sel′mən), 1888–1973, U.S. microbiologist: Nobel prize for medicine 1952.

Wal., 1. Wallachian. **2.** Walloon.

Wa·la·chi·a (wo lā′kē ə), *n.* Wallachia. **—Wa·la′chi·an,** *adj., n.*

Wal·ays (wol′is), *n.* **Sir William.** See **Wallace, Sir William.**

Wał·brzych (väl′bzhikh), *n.* a city in SW Poland, in Silesia. 122,000 (est. 1963). German, **Waldenburg.**

Wal·bur·ga (väl bōōr′gä), *n.* Walpurgis.

Wal·che·ren (väl′khə rən), *n.* an island in the SW Netherlands: part of Zeeland province. 77,839 (est. 1956); 82 sq. mi.

Wal·cott (wôl′kət, -kot), *n.* **Joe** (*Arnold Cream*) ("*Jersey Joe*"), born 1914, U.S. boxer: world heavyweight champion 1951–52.

Wald (wôld), *n.* **Lillian,** 1867–1940, U.S. social worker.

Wal·de·mar I (väl′də mär′), ("*the Great*") 1131–82, king of Denmark 1157–82. Also, **Valdemar I.**

Wal·den (wôl′dᵊn), *n.* a town in SE New York. 4851.

Wal·den·burg (väl′dən bōōrk′), *n.* German name of **Walbrzych.**

Wal′den, or Life′ in the Woods′ (wôl′dən), a book of philosophical observations (1854) by Thoreau.

Wal·den·ses (wol den′sēz), *n.* (*construed as sing.*) a Christian sect which arose after 1170 in southern France, under the leadership of Pierre Waldo, a merchant of Lyons, and joined the Reformation movement in the 16th century. [pl. of ME *Waldensis* < ML, trans. of F *Vaudois;* see -ESE] **—Wal·den·si·an** (wol den′sē ən, -shən), *adj., n.*

wald·glas (väld′gläs′), *n.* common medieval and Renaissance glassware, made from unrefined materials and characterized by a green color. [< G: lit., forest glass (so called from its being produced by glassmakers of the German forests)]

wald·grave (wôld′grāv), *n.* (in the Holy Roman Empire) an officer having jurisdiction over a royal forest. [< G *Waldgraf* (*Wald* forest + *Graf* count)]

Wald·heim (wôld′hīm′; *Ger.* vält′hīm′), *n.* **Kurt** (kûrt; *Ger.* kōōrt), Austrian diplomat: secretary-general of the United Nations 1972–82; president of Austria since 1986.

Wal′dorf sal′ad (wôl′dôrf), a salad of celery, diced apples, nuts, and mayonnaise. [named after *Waldorf-Astoria* Hotel in New York City]

Wald·stein (*Ger.* vält′shtīn′), *n.* **Al·brecht von** (*Ger.* äl′brekht fən). See **Wallenstein, Albrecht Wenzel Eusebius von.**

wale[1] (wāl), *n., v.,* **waled, wal·ing. —n. 1.** a streak, stripe, or ridge produced on the skin by the stroke of a rod or whip; welt. **2.** the vertical rib in knit goods or a chain of loops running lengthwise in knit fabric (opposed to *course*). **3.** the texture or weave of a fabric. **4.** *Naut.* **a.** any of certain strakes of thick outside planking on the sides of a wooden ship. **b.** gunwale. **5.** Also, **wa·ler** (wā′lər), **whaler.** Also called **breast timber, ranger.** *Engineering, Building Trades.* a horizontal timber or other support for reinforcing various upright members, as sheet piling, concrete form boards, etc., or for retaining earth at the edge of an excavation. **6.** a ridge on the outside of a horse collar. **—v.t. 7.** to mark with wales. **8.** to weave with wales. **9.** *Engineering, Building Trades.* to reinforce or fasten with a wale or wales. [ME; OE *walu* ridge, rib, weal; c. Icel *vǫlr,* Goth *walus* rod, wand]

wale[2] (wāl), *n., v.,* **waled, wal·ing.** *Scot. and North Eng.* **—n. 1.** that which is selected as the best; choice. **—v.t. 2.** to choose; select. [ME *wal(e)* < Scand; cf. Icel *val* choice; c. G *Wahl;* cf. VALHALLA]

Wa·ler (wā′lər), *n.* a horse bred in New South Wales, Australia, as a military saddle horse; exported in the 19th century to India. [after New South *Wales;* see -ER[1]]

Wales (wālz), *n.* a division of the United Kingdom, in SW Great Britain. 2,766,800; 8016 sq. mi. Medieval, **Cambria.**

Dublin
IRELAND
IRISH SEA
Liverpool
Wales
ENGLAND
Cardiff
London
ENGLISH CHANNEL

Wa·łę·sa (və wen′sə), *n.* **Lech** (lek), born 1943, Polish labor leader; Nobel peace prize 1983.

Wal′fish Bay′ (wôl′fish). See **Walvis Bay.**

Wal·hal·la (wal hal′ə, val-, wäl hä′lə, väl-), *n.* Valhalla. Also, **Wal·hall** (wal hal′, wal′hal).

Wal·hal·la (wôl hal′ə), *n.* a town in NW South Carolina. 3431 (1960).

wal·ing (wā′ling), *n. Engineering, Building Trades.* **1.** a number of wales, taken as a whole. **2.** timber for use as wales. **3.** wale[1] (def. 5). [WALE[1] + -ING[1]]

walk (wôk), *v.i.* **1.** to go or travel on foot at a moderate speed or pace; proceed by steps; move by advancing the feet alternately so that there is always one foot on the ground in bipedal locomotion and two or more feet on the ground in quadrupedal locomotion. **2.** to go about or travel on foot for exercise or pleasure: *We can walk in the park after lunch.* **3.** to go about on the earth, or appear to living persons, as a ghost: *to believe that spirits walk at night.* **4.** (of things) to move in a manner suggestive of walking, as through repeated vibrations or the effect of alternate expansion and contraction: *He typed so hard that the lamp walked right off the desk.* **5.** to conduct oneself in a particular manner; pursue a particular course of life: *to walk humbly with thy God.* **6.** *Baseball.* to receive a base on balls. **7.** *Basketball.* (of a player in possession of the ball) to take more than two steps without dribbling or passing the ball. **8.** *Obs.* to be in motion or action. **—v.t. 9.** to proceed through, over, or upon at a moderate pace on foot: *walking London streets by night; walking the floor all night.* **10.** to spend or pass (time) in walking (often fol. by *away*): *We walked the morning away along the beach.* **11.** to cause or accomplish by walking: *We saw them walking guard over the chain gang.* **12.** to cause to walk; lead, drive, or ride at a walk, as an animal: *We walked our horses the last quarter of a mile.* **13.** to force or help to walk, as a person: *They were walking him around the room soon after his operation.* **14.** to conduct or accompany on a walk: *He walked them about the park.* **15.** to move (a box, trunk, or other object) in a manner suggestive of walking, as by a rocking motion. **16.** *Baseball.* (of a pitcher) to give a base on balls to (a batter). **17.** *Basketball.* to advance (the ball) by taking more than two steps without dribbling or passing. **18.** to examine, measure, etc., by traversing on foot: *to walk a track; to walk the boundaries of the property.* **19. walk off,** to get rid of by walking: *to walk off a headache.* **20. walk off with, a.** to remove illegally; steal. **b.** to win or attain, as in a competition: *to walk off with the first prize for flower arrangements.* **c.** to surpass one's competitors; win easily; be outstanding: *to walk off with the fight.* **21. walk out,** *Informal.* **a.** to go on strike. **b.** to leave in protest: *to walk out of a committee meeting.* **22. walk out on,** *Informal.* to leave unceremoniously; desert; forsake: *to walk out on one's family.* **23. walk out with,** *Brit.* to court or be courted by: *Cook is walking out with the chauffeur.* **24. walk Spanish, a.** to be forced by another to walk on tiptoe. **b.** to walk cautiously. **c.** to be discharged or dismissed. **d.** to discharge or dismiss (someone). **25. walk the plank.** See **plank** (def. 5). **26. walk through,** *Theat.* **a.** to act in a first rehearsal. **b.** to perform or read a script in a perfunctory manner. **c.** to make little or no effort in performing one's role: *He didn't like the script and walked through his part.* **—n. 27.** the act or an instance of walking or going on foot. **28.** a period of walking for exercise or pleasure: *to go for a walk.* **29.** a distance walked or to be walked, often in terms of the time required: *not more than ten minutes' walk from town.* **30.** the gait or pace of a person or an animal that walks. **31.** a characteristic or individual manner of walking: *It was impossible to mistake her walk.* **32.** a department or branch of activity, or a particular line of work: *They found every walk of life closed against them.* **33.** *Baseball.* See **base on balls. 34.** *Sports.* a walking race. **35.** a path or way for pedestrians at the side of a street or road; sidewalk. **36.** a place prepared or set apart for walking. **37.** a path in a garden or the like. **38.** a passage between rows of trees. **39.** an enclosed yard, pen, or the like where domestic animals are fed and left to exercise. **40.** a sheepwalk. **41.** a ropewalk. **42.** (in the West Indies) a plantation of trees, esp. coffee trees. **43.** a group, company, or congregation, esp. of snipes. **44.** *Brit.* **a.** the route of a street vender, tradesman, or the like. **b.** the district or area in which such a route is located. **c.** a tract of forest land under the charge of one forester or keeper. **45.** *Archaic.* manner of behavior; conduct; course of life. **46.** *Obs.* a haunt or resort. [ME; OE *wealc(an)* (to) roll, toss, *gewealcan* to go; c. D, G *walken* to full (cloth), Icel *válka* to toss]
—Syn. 1. step, stride, stroll, saunter, ambulate, perambulate, promenade, pace, march, tramp, hike, tread. **28.** stroll, promenade, march, tramp, hike, constitutional. **30.** step, carriage. **32.** sphere, area, field, career, course. **36, 37.** path, passage, footpath, alley.

walk·a·ble (wô′kə bəl), *adj.* **1.** capable of being traveled, crossed, or covered by walking: *a walkable road; a walkable distance.* **2.** suited to or adapted for walking: *walkable shoes.* [WALK + -ABLE]

walk·a·bout (wôk′ə bout′), *n.* **1.** *Brit.* a walking tour. **2.** *Australian.* **a.** a brief, informal leave from work, taken by an aborigine to wander the bush, visit relatives, or return to native life. **b.** absence from work. [WALK + ABOUT]

walk·a·way (wôk′ə wā′), *n.* an easy victory or conquest. [n. use of v. phrase *walk away*]

walk-down (wôk′doun′), *n.* **1.** a store, living quarters, etc., located below the street level and approached by a flight of steps: *It was a dimly-lit walk-down optimistically called a garden apartment.* —*adj.* **2.** (of a store, restaurant, apartment, etc.) located below the level of the sidewalk: *a little walk-down bierstube in Greenwich Village.* [n., adj. use of v. phrase *walk down*]

walk·er (wô′kər), *n.* **1.** an enclosing framework on casters or wheels for supporting a baby who is learning to walk. **2.** a similar lightweight structure, sometimes having wheels or gliders and arm supports, used by invalids, the handicapped, or the aged in walking. **3.** one who or that which walks or likes to walk: *He's a great walker.* [ME; see WALK, -ER[1]]

Walk·er (wô′kər), *n.* a boy's given name.

Walk′er hound′, an American foxhound having a black, tan, and white, or, sometimes, a tan and white coat. Also called **Walk′er fox′hound.**

walk·ie-talk·ie (wô′kē tô′kē), *n.* *Radio.* a combined transmitter and receiver light enough to be carried by one man: developed originally for military use in World War II. [see WALK, TALK, -IE]

walk-in (wôk′in′), *adj.* **1.** of or pertaining to persons who walk into a place from the street, esp. irregularly or without an appointment: *walk-in customers; walk-in sales; a walk-in patient.* **2.** large enough to be walked into. —*n.* **3.** something large enough to be walked into, as a closet. **4.** an assured victory in an election or other contest. [adj., n. use of v. phrase *walk in*]

walk′-in apart′ment, a ground-floor apartment having a private entrance directly from the street, rather than through a hallway of the building.

walk′-in clos′et, a closet that is large enough to permit one to enter by walking.

walk·ing (wô′king), *adj.* **1.** considered as one who can or does walk or that which walks: *The hospital contained six walking patients. He's walking proof that people can lose weight quickly.* **2.** used for or as an aid in walking: *She put on her walking shoes and went out.* **3.** suitable for, characterized by, or consisting of walking: *True sightseeing is a walking affair. We took a walking tour of Spain.* **4.** of or pertaining to an implement or machine drawn by a draft animal and operated or controlled by a person on foot: *a walking plow.* **5.** of or pertaining to a mechanical part that moves back and forth. —*n.* **6.** the act or action of one who or that which walks: *Walking was the best exercise for him.* **7.** the manner or way in which one walks. **8.** the state or condition of that on which or through which one walks: *The walking is dry over here.* [ME; see WALK, -ING[2], -ING[1]]

walk′ing bass′ (bās), (in jazz piano) a left-hand accompaniment consisting of a continuous rhythm of four beats to the measure, usually with a repetitive melodic pattern.

walk′ing beam′, an overhead oscillating lever, pivoted at the middle, for transmitting force from a vertical connecting rod below one end to a vertical connecting rod, pump rod, etc., below the other end. Also called **working beam.**

walk′ing del′egate, (formerly) an official appointed by a trade union to go from place to place to investigate conditions, to ascertain whether union contracts were being fulfilled, and, sometimes, to negotiate contracts between employers and the union.

walk′ing fern′, a fern, *Camptosorus rhizophyllus,* having simple fronds tapering into a prolongation which often takes root at the apex. Also called **walking leaf.**

walk′ing fish′, any of various fishes able to survive and move about on land, as the mudskipper or climbing perch.

walk′ing gen′tleman, a person who has a small role in a theatrical production, as a walk-on or supernumerary. Also, *referring to a woman,* **walk′ing la′dy.**

Walk′ing Horse′. See **Tennessee Walking Horse.**

walk′ing leaf′, **1.** See **leaf insect.** **2.** See **walking fern.**

walk′ing line′, a line on the plan of a curving staircase on which all treads are of a uniform width and which is considered to be the ordinary path taken by persons on the stair.

walk′ing pa′pers, *Informal.* a notification of dismissal: *They gave him his walking papers yesterday.*

walk′ing stick′, **1.** a stick held in the hand and used to help support oneself while walking. **2.** Also called **stick insect.** any of several orthopterous insects of the family *Phasmidae,* having a long, slender, twiglike body.

Walking stick, *Diapheromera femorata* (Length 2 to 3 in.)

walk′ing tick′et, *Informal.* See **walking papers.**

walk′-in refrig′erator, a refrigerated storage room, as at a butcher shop.

walk-on (wôk′on′, -ôn′), *n.* **1.** Also called **walk′ing part′.** a small part in a play or other entertainment, esp. one without speaking lines. Cf. **bit[2]** (def. 4). **2.** an entertainer or actor who plays such a part. [n. use of v. phrase *walk on*]

walk·out (wôk′out′), *n.* **1.** a strike by workers. **2.** the act of leaving or being absent from a meeting, esp. as an expression of protest. [n. use of v. phrase *walk out*]

walk·o·ver (wôk′ō′vər), *n.* **1.** *Racing.* a walking or trotting over the course by a contestant who is the only starter. **2.** an unopposed or easy victory. **3.** any task easily done. [n. use of v. phrase *walk over*]

walk-through (wôk′thro͞o′), *n.* **1.** *Theat.* **a.** a rehearsal in which physical action is combined with reading the lines of a play. **b.** a perfunctory performance of a script. **2.** *Television.* a rehearsal without cameras. [n. use of v. phrase *walk through*]

walk-up (wôk′up′), *U.S. Informal.* —*n.* **1.** an apartment above the ground floor in a building that has no elevator. **2.** a building, esp. an apartment house, that has no elevator. —*adj.* **3.** located above the ground floor in a building that has no elevator. **4.** having no elevator. [n., adj. use of v. phrase *walk up*]

Wal·kü·re, Die (*Ger.* dē väl ky′rə). See **Ring of the Nibelung.**

walk·way (wôk′wā′), *n.* **1.** any passage for walking, esp. one connecting the various areas of a ship, factory, park, etc. **2.** a garden path or walk. **3.** the front walk of a house, leading from the door to the sidewalk or road. [WALK + WAY]

Wal·kyr·ie (wal kēr′ē, val-), *n.* Valkyrie.

walk·y-talk·y (wô′kē tô′kē), *n., pl.* **-talk·ies.** walkie-talkie.

wall (wôl), *n.* **1.** any of various permanent upright constructions having a length much greater than the thickness and presenting a continuous surface except where pierced by doors, windows, etc.: used for shelter, protection, or privacy, or to subdivide interior space, to support floors, roofs, or the like, to retain earth, to fence in an area, etc. **2.** Usually, **walls.** a rampart raised for defensive purposes. **3.** an immaterial or intangible barrier, obstruction, etc., suggesting a wall: *a wall of prejudice.* **4.** a wall-like, enclosing part, thing, mass, etc.: *a wall of fire; a wall of troops.* **5.** an embankment to prevent flooding, as a levee, sea wall, or the like. **6.** the outermost film or layer of structural material protecting, surrounding, and defining the physical limits of an object: *the wall of a blood cell.* **7. drive** or **push to the wall,** to force into a desperate situation; humiliate or ruin completely: *Not content with merely winning the match, they used every opportunity to push the inferior team to the wall.* **8. go over the wall,** *Slang.* to break out of prison: *Roadblocks have been set up in an effort to capture several convicts who went over the wall.* **9. go to the wall, a.** to be defeated in a conflict or competition; yield. **b.** to fail in business, esp. to become bankrupt. **c.** to be put aside or forgotten. —*adj.* **10.** of or pertaining to a wall: *wall space.* **11.** growing against or on a wall: *wall plants; wall cress.* **12.** situated, placed, or installed in or on a wall: *wall hangings; a wall safe.* —*v.t.* **13.** to enclose, shut off, divide, protect, border, etc., with or as with a wall (often fol. by *in* or *off*): *to wall the yard; to wall in the play area; He is walled in by lack of opportunity.* **14.** to seal or fill (a doorway or other opening) with a wall: *to wall an unused entrance.* **15.** to seal or entomb (something or someone) within a wall (usually fol. by *up*): *The workmen had walled up the cat quite by mistake.* [ME, OE < L *vall(um)* palisade, deriv. of *vallus* stake, post; see WALE[1]] —**wall′-less,** *adj.* —**wall′-like′,** *adj.*
—**Syn. 2.** battlement, breastwork, bulwark, barrier, bunker, bastion. **3.** obstruction. **5.** dike. **15.** immure.

wal·la (wä′lä), *n.* wallah.

wal·la·ba (wol′ə bə), *n.* **1.** any of several leguminous trees of the genus *Eperua,* of the Guianas and northern Brazil. **2.** the hard, heavy wood of any of these trees, used in the construction of buildings. [< Arawak]

wal·la·by (wol′ə bē), *n., pl.* **-bies,** (*esp. collectively*) **-by.** any of various small and medium-sized kangaroos of the genera *Macropus, Thylogale, Petrogale,* etc., some of which are no larger than rabbits. [< native Austral *wolabā*]

Wallaby, *Wallabia agilis* (Height 2½ ft.; tail 2 ft.)

Wal·lace (wol′is, wô′lis), *n.* **1. Alfred Russel,** 1823–1913, English naturalist, explorer, and author. **2. Henry (A·gard)** (ā′gärd) 1888–1965, U.S. agriculturalist, author, and statesman: Secretary of Agriculture 1933–40; vice-president of the U.S. 1941–45; Secretary of Commerce 1945–46. **3. Lewis** ("*Lew*"), 1827–1905, U.S. general and novelist. **4. Sir William.** Also, **Walays, Wallensis.** 1272?–1305, Scottish military leader and patriot. **5.** a boy's given name.

Wal′lace's line′, *Zoogeog.* an imaginary line that separates the Oriental and Australian zoogeographical regions and passes between Bali and Lombok, west of Celebes, and east of the Philippines. [named after Alfred Russel WALLACE]

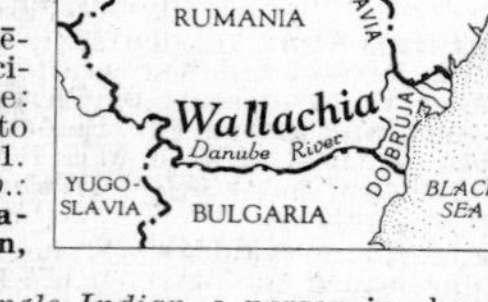

Wal·lach (väl′äкн), *n.* **Ot·to** (ôt′ō), 1847–1931, German chemist: Nobel prize 1910.

Wal·la·chi·a (wo lā′kē ə), *n.* a former principality in SE Europe: united with Moldavia to form Rumania in 1861. 29,569 sq. mi. *Cap.:* Bucharest. Also, **Walachia.** —**Wal·la′chi·an,** *adj., n.*

wal·lah (wä′lä), *n.* *Anglo-Indian.* a person in charge of, employed at, or concerned with a particular thing: *a book wallah; a ticket wallah.* Also, **walla.** [< Hindi *-wālā* suffix of relation]

wal·la·roo (wol′ə ro͞o′), *n., pl.* **-roos,** (*esp. collectively*) **-roo.** any of several large kangaroos of the genus *Osphranter,* of the grassy plains of Australia. [< native Austral *wolarū*]

Wal·la·sey (wol′ə sē), *n.* a city in NW Cheshire, in NW England, on the Mersey estuary, near Liverpool. 103,213 (1961).

Wal·la Wal·la (wol′ə wol′ə), a city in SE Washington. 24,536 (1960).

wall·board (wôl′bōrd′, -bôrd′), *n.* an artificial material manufactured in large sheets for use in making or covering walls, ceilings, etc., as a substitute for wooden boards or plaster. [WALL + BOARD]

wall′ box′, *Building Trades.* an enclosed iron or steel socket built into a masonry wall to support the end of a wooden beam.

wall′ creep′er, a small, gray and crimson, Old World bird, *Tichodroma muraria,* which inhabits cliffs in mountainous areas.

wall′ cress′, a perennial herb, *Arabis albida,* of the Caucasus Mountains, having tufted, white foliage and fragrant, white flowers.

Walled′ Lake′, a town in SE Michigan. 3550 (1960).

walled′ plain′, a circular or almost circular area on the moon, sometimes with a floor that is depressed, usually partially enclosed by walls that rise to varying heights and that are usually lower than those of a crater; ring; ring formation. Also called **ringed plain.**

Wal·len·sis (wo len′sis), *n.* **Sir William.** See **Wallace, Sir William.**

Wal·len·stein (wol′ən stīn′; *for 1, 3 also Ger.* väl′ənshtīn′), *n.* **1.** Also, **Waldstein. Al·brecht Wen·zel Eu·se·bi·us von** (äl′brekнt ven′tsəl oi zā′bē o͝os′ fən), **Duke of Fried·land** (frēd′land′, -lənd; *Ger.* frēt′länt′), 1583–1634, born in Bohemia, Austrian general. **2. Alfred,** born 1898, U.S. cellist and conductor. **3.** (*italics*) a three-part historical tragedy (1799) by Schiller, including *Wallenstein's Camp, The Piccolomini,* and *Wallenstein's Death.*

Wal·ler (wol′ər, wô′lər), *n.* **1. Edmund,** 1607–87, English poet. **2. Thomas** ("*Fats*"), 1904–43, U.S. jazz pianist.

wal·let (wol′it, wô′lit), *n.* **1.** a flat, folding pocketbook, esp. one large enough to hold paper money, credit cards, driver's license, etc. **2.** *Chiefly Brit.* a bag for carrying food, clothing, toilet articles, etc., during a journey; knapsack or rucksack. [ME *walet* < ?]

wall·eye (wôl′ī), *n., pl.* **-eyes,** (*esp. collectively for 1, 2*) **-eye. 1.** a large game fish, *Stizostedion vitreum,* found in the lakes and rivers of northeastern North America; pikeperch. **2.** any of various other fishes having large, staring eyes. **3.** an eye characteristic of a walleyed person or animal. [back formation from WALLEYED]

wall·eyed (wôl′īd′), *adj.* **1.** having eyes in which there is an abnormal amount of the white showing, because of divergent strabismus. **2.** having an eye or the eyes presenting little or no color, as the result of a light-colored or white iris or of white opacity of the cornea. **3.** having large, staring eyes, as some fishes. **4.** marked by excited or agitated staring of the eyes, as in fear, rage, frenzy, or the like: *He stood there in walleyed astonishment.* [alter. of OE *waldenige,* equiv. to *wal(e)de* streaked (see WALE[1], -ED[3]) + *-n-* (< ?) + *-ige* -eyed (see EYE); cf. ME *wawileghed,* Icel *vagleygr* (*vagl* film + *eygr* eyed)]

wall′eye pol′lack, a cod, *Theragra chalcogrammus,* found in the northern Pacific, that is related to and resembles the pollack.

wall′ fern′, the polypody, *Polypodium vulgare* or *P. virginianum.*

wall·flow·er (wôl′flou′ər), *n.* **1.** a European plant, *Cheiranthus Cheiri,* which, when growing wild on walls, cliffs, etc., has sweet-scented, usually yellow or orange flowers, but when cultivated has flowers varying in color from pale yellow to brown-red or purple. **2.** any brassicaceous plant of the genera *Cheiranthus* and *Erysimum.* **3.** someone, esp. a young woman, who remains at the side at a party or dance because she is shy, unpopular, or has no partner. [WALL + FLOWER]

wal·lie (wol′ē), *adj., adv., n.* *Scot.* wally[1].

Wal·lie (wol′ē), *n.* **1.** a boy's given name, form of **Wallace** or **Walter. 2.** a girl's given name, form of **Wallis.** Also, **Wally.**

Wal·ling·ford (wol′ing fərd), *n.* a town in S Connecticut. 29,920 (1960).

Wal·ling·ton (wol′ing tən), *n.* a town in NE New Jersey. 9261 (1960).

wall′ i′ron, (on the exterior of a wall) a metal bracket supporting a downspout, lightning rod, etc.

Wal·lis (wol′is, wô′lis), *n.* **1. John,** 1616–1703, English mathematician. **2.** a boy's given name, form of **Wallace. 3.** a girl's given name.

wall′ mold′ing. See **back molding.**

Wal·loon (wo lo͞on′), *n.* **1.** one of a people inhabiting chiefly the southern and southeastern parts of Belgium and adjacent regions in France. **2.** the French dialect of Belgium, esp. southeast. —*adj.* **3.** of or pertaining to the Walloons or their language. [< F *Wallon,* equiv. to *wall* (<< Gmc **walh-* foreign(er); see WALNUT) + *-on* n. suffix]

Walloon′ sword′, pappenheimer.

wal·lop (wol′əp), *v.t.* *Informal.* **1.** to beat soundly; thrash. **2.** to strike with a vigorous blow; belt; sock: *Mantle walloped the ball out of the park.* **3.** to defeat thoroughly, as in a game. **4.** *Chiefly Scot.* to flutter, wobble, or flop about. —*v.i.* **5.** *Informal.* to move violently and clumsily: *The puppy walloped down the walk.* **6.** (of a liquid) to boil violently. **7.** *Obs.* to gallop. —*n.* **8.** *Informal.* **a.** a vigorous blow. **b.** the ability to deliver vigorous blows, as in boxing: *That fist of his packs a wallop.* **c.** the ability to effect a forceful impression; punch: *That ad packs a wallop.* **d.** a pleasurable thrill; kick: *The joke gave them all a wallop.* **9.** *Informal.* a violent, clumsy movement; lurch. **10.** *Obs.* a gallop. [ME *wal(l)op* (n.), late ME *walopen* (v.) < AF < ?; see GALLOP]

wal·lop·er (wol′ə pər), *n.* **1.** *Informal.* one who or that which wallops. **2.** *Brit. Dial.* something extraordinarily big or unbelievable; whopper. [WALLOP + -ER[1]]

wal·lop·ing (wol′ə ping), *Informal.* —*n.* **1.** a sound beating or thrashing. **2.** a thorough defeat. —*adj.* **3.** impressively big or good; whopping. [ME; see WALLOP, -ING[1], -ING[2]]

wal·low (wol′ō), *v.i.* **1.** to roll about or lie in water, snow, mud, dust, or the like, as for refreshment: *Goats wallowed in the dust.* **2.** to live self-indulgently; luxuriate; revel: *to wallow in luxury; to wallow in sentimentality.* **3.** to flounder about; move along or proceed clumsily or with difficulty: *A gunboat wallowed toward port.* **4.** to surge up or billow forth, as smoke, heat, etc.: *Waves of black smoke wallowed into the room.* —*n.* **5.** the act or an instance of wallowing. **6.** a place in which animals wallow: *hog wallow; an elephant wallow.* **7.** the indentation produced by animal wallowing: *a series of wallows across the farmyard.* [ME *walwe,* OE *wealwian* to roll; c. Goth *walwjan,* L *volvere*]
—**Syn. 1.** welter.

wal·low·er (wol′ō ər), *n.* **1.** one who or that which wallows. **2.** (in a windmill) a horizontal gear driven off the brake wheel. [WALLOW + -ER[1]; from way the wheel moves]

wall·pa·per (wôl′pā′pər), *n.* **1.** paper, usually with printed decorative patterns in color, for pasting on and covering the walls or ceilings of rooms, hallways, etc. —*v.t.* **2.** to put wallpaper on (a wall, ceiling, etc.) or to furnish (a room, house, etc.) with wallpaper. [WALL + PAPER]

wall′ pel′li·to·ry, a small, bushy, Old World urticaceous plant, *Parietaria officinalis,* growing on walls, and said to be a diuretic and refrigerant.

wall-piece (wôl′pēs′), *n.* (formerly) a small cannon or heavy firearm attached to a swivel and mounted on a wall or the rail of a ship for defense.

wall′ plate′, 1. *Building Trades.* a horizontal member built into or laid along the top of a wall to support and distribute the pressure from joists, rafters, etc. **2.** *Mach.* a vertical metal plate secured against a wall, as to attach a bracket. **3.** *Mining.* one of the longer members of a set. Cf. **end plate.**

wall′ pock′et, *Theat.* a stage pocket set into a stage wall.

wall′ rock′, *Mining.* the rock forming the walls of a vein.

wall′ rock′et, a European, cruciferous plant, *Diplotaxis tenuifolia,* growing along walls, fences, etc.

wall′ rue′, a small delicate fern, *Asplenium Ruta-muraria,* growing on walls and cliffs.

Walls·end (wôlz′end′), *n.* **1.** a city in SE Northumberland, NE England, on the Tyne. 49,785 (1961). **2.** a type of coal widely used in Great Britain, esp. for domestic purposes.

wall′ sock′et, socket (def. 2b).

Wall′ Street′, 1. a street in New York City, in S Manhattan: the major financial center of the U.S. **2.** the money market or the financiers of the U.S.

wal·ly[1] (wā′lē), *adj., adv., n., pl.* **-lies.** *Scot.* **—*adj.*** **1.** fine; splendid. **2.** handsome. **3.** ample; strong; large. **—*adv.*** **4.** finely; wonderfully. **—*n.*** **5.** a toy; bauble; gewgaw. Also, **wallie, waly.** [WALE[2] + -Y[1]]

wal·ly[2] (wā′lē), *interj. Scot. and North Eng.* waly[1].

Wal·ly (wol′ē), *n.* **1.** a boy's given name, form of **Wallace** or **Walter. 2.** a girl's given name, form of **Wallis.** Also, **Wallie.**

wal·ly·drag (wā′lē dʀag′, -dʀäg′, wol′ē-), *n. Scot.* a feeble, dwarfed animal or person. Also called **wal·ly·drai·gle** (wā′lē dʀā′gəl, wol′ē-). [? *wally* (var. of WALLOW) + DRAG]

wal·nut (wôl′nut′, -nət), *n.* **1.** the edible nut of trees of the genus *Juglans,* of the North Temperate zone. **2.** a tree bearing this nut. **3.** the wood of such a tree. **4.** *Northeastern U.S.* the hickory nut. **5.** any of various fruits or trees resembling the walnut. **6.** a somewhat reddish shade of brown, as that of the heartwood of the black walnut tree. [ME; OE *wealh-hnutu,* lit., foreign nut; see WELSH, NUT]

Wal′nut Creek′, a town in W California. 9903 (1960).

Wal′nut Heights′, a town in W California. 5080 (1960).

Wal′nut Ridge′, a town in NE Arkansas. 3547 (1960).

Wal·pole (wôl′pōl′, wol′-), *n.* **1. Horace, 4th Earl of Or·ford** (ôr′fərd), (*Horatio Walpole*), 1717–97, English novelist and essayist (son of Sir Robert Walpole). **2. Sir Hugh Seymour,** 1884–1941, English novelist, born in New Zealand. **3. Sir Robert, 1st Earl of Or·ford** (ôr′fərd), 1676–1745, British statesman: prime minister 1715–17; 1721–42.

Wal′pole tea′. See **New Jersey tea.**

Wal·pur·gis (väl po͝or′gis), *n.* **Saint,** A.D. c710–780, English missionary and abbess in Germany: feast day May 1st. Also, **Wal·bur·ga** (väl bo͝or′gä), **Wal·pur·ga** (väl po͝or′gä).

Wal·pur·gis·nacht (väl po͝oʀ′gis näKHt′), *n. German.* See **Walpurgis Night.**

Walpur′gis Night′, the evening preceding the feast day of St. Walpurgis, on which, according to a formerly popular German superstition, witches held a sabbath, esp. on Brocken peak. German, **Walpurgisnacht.**

Wal·ras (VAL RA′), *n.* **(Ma·rie Es·prit) Lé·on** (MA ʀē′ es pʀē′ lā ôN′), 1834–1910, French economist.

wal·rus (wôl′rəs, wol′-), *n., pl.* **-rus·es** (*esp. collectively*) **-rus.** either of two large marine mammals of the genus *Odobenus,* of arctic seas, related to the seals, and having flippers, a pair of large tusks, and a thick, tough skin. [< D: lit., WHALE HORSE; c. G *Walross,* Dan *hvalros;* cf. OE *horshwæl* horse-whale]

Atlantic walrus,
Odobenus rosmarus
(Tusks to 3 ft.; length to 11 ft.)

wal′rus mustache′, a thick, shaggy mustache hanging down loosely at both ends.

Wal·sall (wôl′sôl), *n.* a city in S Staffordshire, in central England, near Birmingham. 117,836 (1961).

Wal·sen·burg (wôl′sən bûrg′), *n.* a town in S Colorado. 5071 (1960).

Walsh (wôlsh), *n.* a boy's given name, form of **Wallace.**

Wal·sing·ham (wôl′sing əm), *n.* **Sir Francis,** c1530–90, English statesman: Secretary of State 1573–90.

Walt (wôlt), *n.* a boy's given name, form of **Walter.**

Wal·ter (väl′tər *for 1;* wôl′tər *for 2–4*), *n.* **1. Bru·no** (bro͞o′nō), (*Bruno Schlesinger*), 1876–1962, German opera and symphony conductor, in U.S. after 1939. **2. Thomas U·stick** (yo͞o′stik), 1804–87, U.S. architect. **3.** a walled plain in the southern hemisphere of the face of the moon at the border of the third and fourth quadrants: about 90 miles in diameter. **4.** a boy's given name.

Wal·ter·bor·o (wôl′tər bûr′ō, -bur′ō), *n.* a town in S South Carolina. 5417 (1960).

Wal·te·rene (wôl′tə rēn′), *n.* a girl's given name.

Wal·ters (wôl′tərz), *n.* a town in S Oklahoma. 2825 (1960).

Wal·tham (wôl′thəm), *n.* a city in E Massachusetts. 55,413 (1960).

Wal·tham·stow (wôl′təm stō′, -thəm-), *n.* a city in SW Essex, in SE England, near London. 108,788 (1961).

Wal·ther von der Vo·gel·wei·de (väl′tər fôn dər fō′gəl vī′də), c1170–c1230, German minnesinger and poet.

Wal·ton (wôl′tᵊn), *n.* **1. Ernest Thomas Sin·ton** (sin′tᵊn), born 1903, Irish physicist: Nobel prize 1951. **2. I·zaak** (ī′zək), 1593–1683, English writer. **3. Sir William Turner,** born 1902, English composer. **4.** a town in S New York. 3855 (1960). **—Wal·to·ni·an** (wôl tō′nē ən), *n., adj.*

waltz (wôlts), *n.* **1.** a ballroom dance, in moderately fast triple meter, in which the dancers revolve in perpetual circles, taking one step to each beat. **2.** a piece of music for, or in the rhythm of, this dance. **—*adj.*** **3.** of, pertaining to, or characteristic of the waltz, as music, rhythm, or dance: *waltz tempo.* **—*v.i.*** **4.** to dance or move in a waltz step or rhythm: *an invitation to waltz.* **5.** *Informal.* **a.** to move breezily or casually: *to waltz in late for dinner.* **b.** to progress easily or successfully (often fol. by *through*): *to waltz through an exam.* **—*v.t.*** **6.** to lead (a partner) in dancing a waltz. **7.** *Informal.* to move or lead briskly: *He waltzed us right into the governor's office.* [back formation from G *Walzer* (taken as *walz* + -ER[1]), deriv. of *walzen* to roll, dance; cf. obs. E *walt* unsteady and dial. *walter* to roll] **—waltz′er,** *n.* **—waltz′like′,** *adj.*

Waltz′ of the Tor′eadors, a comedy (1932) by Jean Anouilh. French, **La Valse des Toréadors.**

waltz′ time′. See **three-quarter time.**

Wal′vis Bay′ (wôl′vis), **1.** a bay in S Africa, on the coast of South-West Africa. **2.** a seaport on this bay. **3.** an enclave of the Republic of South Africa around this bay: administered by South-West Africa. 2421 (1951); 347 sq. mi. Also, **Walfish Bay.**

wal·y[1] (wā′lē, wô′-), *interj. Scot. and North Eng.* (an exclamation of sorrow or woe) alas! Also, **wally.** [appar. short form of OE *wālāwā* alas!; see WELLAWAY]

wal·y[2] (wā′lē), *adj., adv., n., pl.* **wal·ies.** *Scot.* wally[1].

wam·ble (wom′əl, wam′-), *v.,* **-bled, -bling,** *n.* **—*v.i.*** **1.** *Chiefly Dial.* **a.** to move unsteadily. **b.** to roll or twist one's body. **2.** *Obs.* **a.** to feel nausea. **b.** (of the stomach) to turn over in nausea. **—*n.*** *Chiefly Dial.* **3.** an unsteady or rolling movement. **4.** a feeling of nausea. [ME *wamle,* nasalized var. of WOBBLE; cf. Norw *vamla* to stagger] **—wam′bli·ness,** *n.* **—wam′bling·ly,** *adv.* **—wam′bly,** *adj.*

wame (wām), *n. Scot. and North Eng.* **1.** the abdomen; belly. **2.** *Obs.* womb; uterus. [var. of WOMB]

wame·fou (wām′fo͞o), *n. Scot. and North Eng.* a bellyful of food. Also, **wame′fu, wame·ful, wame·full** (wām′fo͝ol). [WAME + *-fou,* Scot var. of -FUL]

wam·mus (wom′əs), *n., pl.* **-mus·es.** wamus (def. 2).

Wam·pa·no·ag (wäm′pə nō′ag), *n., pl.* **-ags,** (*esp. collectively*) **-ag. 1.** a member of an American Indian people of the region around Narragansett Bay, in Rhode Island. **2.** the speech of the Wampanoag Indians, a dialect of the Massachusett language. [< Natick, equiv. to *wampan* shiny, east + *-o-* (cf. *ohke* earth) + *-ag* pl. suffix]

wamp·ish (wam′pish, wäm′-), *v.i. Scot.* to wave about or flop to and fro. [? phonesthemic]

wam·pum (wom′pəm, wôm′-), *n.* **1.** Also called **peag, seawan, sewan.** cylindrical beads made from shells, pierced and strung, used by North American Indians as money and for ornaments, esp. such beads when white, but also including the more valuable black or dark purple varieties. **2.** *Slang.* money. [short for WAMPUMPEAG]

wam·pum·peag (wom′pəm pēg′, wôm′-), *n.* wampum, esp. of the black or the dark purple variety. [< Narraganset, equiv. to *wamp(an)* shiny + *anpi* string of beads + *-ag* pl. suffix]

wam·pus (wom′pəs), *n., pl.* **-pus·es. 1.** *Chiefly Dial.* a strange or objectionable person; lout. **2.** wamus (def. 2). [see WAMUS]

wa·mus (wô′məs, wom′əs), *n., pl.* **-mus·es.** *U.S.* **1.** a heavy cardigan jacket, loosely knit and belted. **2.** Also, **wammus, wampus.** a durable, coarse, outer jacket. [< D *wammes* (equiv. to G *Wams* vest, undershirt), MD *wambuis* < dial. OF *wambois* < OHG *wamb(a)* belly (see WOMB) + F *-ois* -ESE; see GAMBESON]

wan (won), *adj.,* **wan·ner, wan·nest,** *v.,* **wanned, wan·ning. —*adj.*** **1.** of an unnatural or sickly pallor; pallid; lacking color: *His wan face suddenly flushed.* **2.** showing or suggesting ill health, fatigue, unhappiness, etc.: *a wan look; a wan smile.* **3.** lacking in forcefulness, competence, or effectiveness: *his wan attempts to organize the alumni.* **4.** *Archaic.* **a.** dark or gloomy. **b.** pale in color or hue. **—*v.i., v.t.*** **5.** *Archaic.* to become or make wan. [ME; OE *wann* dark, gloomy; c. G *Wahn* madness] **—wan′ly,** *adv.* **—wan′ness,** *n.*
—Syn. 1. ashen. See **pale**[1]. **—Ant. 1.** ruddy.

Wan·a·ma·ker (won′ə mā′kər), *n.* **John,** 1838–1922, U.S. merchant and philanthropist.

Wan·a·mas·sa (won′ə mas′ə), *n.* a town in E New Jersey. 3928 (1960).

Wan·a·que (won′ə kyo͞o′, -kē′), *n.* a town in NE New Jersey. 7126 (1960).

wan·chanc·y (won chan′sē), *adj. Scot.* unlucky; ill-fated. [*wanchance* misfortune (ME *wan-* un- + CHANCE) + -Y[1]]

Wan·chüan (wän′chyän′), *n.* a city in NW Hopeh, in NE China: capital of the former Chahar province. 229,300 (est. 1957). Formerly, **Kalgan.**

wand (wond), *n.* **1.** a slender stick or rod, esp. one used by a magician, conjurer, or diviner. **2.** a rod or staff carried as an emblem of one's office or authority. **3.** a slender shoot, stem, or branch of a shrub or tree: *She was lissome as a hazel wand.* **4.** *U.S. Archery.* a slat 6 feet by 2 inches placed at a distance of 100 yards for men and 60 yards for women, and used as a target. [ME, prob. < Scand; cf. Icel *vöndr,* c. Goth *wandus;* akin to WEND] **—wand′like′,** *adj.*

Wan·da (won′də), *n.* a girl's given name.

wan·der (won′dər), *v.i.* **1.** to ramble without a definite purpose or objective; roam, rove, or stray: *to wander over the earth.* **2.** to go aimlessly, indirectly, or casually; meander: *The river wanders among the rocks.* **3.** to extend in an irregular course or direction: *Foothills wandered off to the south.* **4.** to move, pass, or turn idly, as the hand, the eyes, a pen, etc. **5.** (of the mind, thoughts, desires, etc.) to take one direction or another without conscious intent or control: *His attention wandered as the speaker droned on.* **6.** to stray from a path, place, companions, etc.: *During the storm the ship wandered from its course.* **7.** to deviate in conduct, belief, etc.; err; go astray: *Let me not wander from Thy Commandments.* **8.** to think or speak confusedly or incoherently: *As she is very old, she occasionally wanders.* **—*v.t.*** **9.** to travel about, on, or through: *He wandered the streets.* **—*n.*** **10.** *Mech.* the drift of a gyroscope or a similar device. [ME *wandre(n),* OE *wandrian* (c. G *wandern*), freq. of *wendan* to WEND; see -ER[6]] **—wan′der·er,** *n.*
—Syn. 1. range, stroll. **2.** saunter. **6.** stray, swerve, veer. **8.** ramble, rave.

Wan·der·er (won′dər ər), *n. Scot. Hist.* a Covenanter persecuted by Charles II and James II, esp. one who fled home to follow rebellious Presbyterian ministers who refused to accept episcopacy.

wan·der·ing (won′dər ing), *adj.* **1.** moving from place to place without a fixed plan; roaming; rambling: *wandering tourists.* **2.** having no permanent residence; nomadic: *a wandering tribe of Indians.* **3.** meandering; winding: *a wandering river; a wandering path.* **—*n.*** **4.** an aimless roving about; leisurely traveling from place to place: *a period of delightful wandering through Italy.* **5.** Usually, **wanderings. a.** aimless travels; meanderings: *His wanderings took him all over the world.* **b.** disordered thoughts or utterances; incoherencies: *mental wanderings; the wanderings of delirium.* [ME (n., adj.), OE *wandringende* (adj.). See WANDER, -ING[2], -ING[1]] **—wan′der·ing·ly,** *adv.* **—wan′der·ing·ness,** *n.*

wan′dering al′batross, a large albatross, *Diomedea exulans,* of southern waters, having the plumage mostly white with dark markings on the upper parts. See illus. under **albatross.**

Wan′dering Jew′, 1. a legendary character condemned to roam without rest because he struck Christ on the day of Crucifixion. **2.** Also, **wan′dering Jew′, Wan′dering-jew′.** any of various trailing or creeping plants, as *Zebrina pendula* or *Tradescantia fluminensis.*

Wan·der·jahr (vän′dəʀ yär′), *n., pl.* **-jah·re** (-yä′ʀə). *German.* **1.** a year or period of travel, wandering, absence from one's work, etc. **2.** (formerly) a year in which an apprentice traveled and improved his skills before settling down to the practice of his trade.

wan·der·lust (won′dər lust′; *Ger.* vän′dəʀ lo͝ost′), *n.* an instinctive impulse or a great desire to rove or travel about. [< G, equiv. to *wander(n)* to WANDER + *Lust* desire, LUST]

wan·der·oo (won′də ro͞o′), *n., pl.* **-der·oos. 1.** any of several langurs, of Ceylon. **2.** a macaque, *Macacus silenus,* of southern India. [< Sinhalese *wanduru* (pl.) < Skt *vānara* monkey]

W. & f., (in shipping) water and feed.

wan·dle (won′dᵊl, won′ᵊl), *adj. Scot. and North Eng.* supple; lithe. [cf. OE *wandlung* vacillation, equiv. to **wandol* changeable + *-ung* -ING[1]]

Wan·do·ro·bo (wän′də rō′bō), *n., pl.* **-bos,** (*esp. collectively*) **-bo.** Dorobo.

Wands·worth (wonz′wərth), *n.* a borough of SW London, England. 347,209 (1961).

wane (wān), *v.,* **waned, wan·ing,** *n.* **—*v.i.*** **1.** (of the moon) to decrease periodically in the extent of its illuminated portion after the full moon. Cf. **wax**[2] (def. 2). **2.** to decline in power, importance, prosperity, etc.: *Colonialism is waning.* **3.** to decrease in strength, intensity, etc.: *Daylight waned, and night came on. His enthusiasm for the cause is waning.* **4.** to draw to a close; approach an end: *Summer is waning.* **—*n.*** **5.** a gradual decrease or decline in strength, intensity, power, etc. **6.** the drawing to a close of life, an era, a period, etc. **7.** the waning of the moon. **8.** a period of waning. **9.** a defect in a plank or board characterized by bark or insufficient wood at a corner or along an edge, due to the curvature of the log. **10. on the wane,** decreasing; diminishing: *The popularity of that song is on the wane.* [ME; OE *wanian* to lessen; c. MD, MHG *wanen,* Icel *vana*] **—Syn. 2, 3.** diminish, fail, sink. **5.** diminution; failure, decay.

wane·y (wā′nē), *adj.,* **wan·i·er, wan·i·est. 1.** wany (def. 1). **2.** (of a timber) having a wane or wanes.

Wang·chuk (wäng′cho͝ok), *n.* **Jig·me Dor·ji** (jig′mä dôr′jē), born 1929, king of Bhutan since 1952.

wan·gle (wang′gəl), *v.,* **-gled, -gling,** *n. Informal.* **—*v.t.*** **1.** to bring about, accomplish, or obtain by contrivance, scheming, or underhanded methods: *to wangle an invitation.* **2.** to falsify or manipulate for dishonest ends: *to wangle business records.* **—*v.i.*** **3.** to use contrivance, scheming, or underhanded methods to obtain some goal or result. **4.** to manipulate something for dishonest ends. **—*n.*** **5.** the act or an instance of wangling. [b. WAG (the tongue) and DANGLE (about someone, i.e., hang around him, court his favor)] **—wan′gler,** *n.*

Wan·hsien (wän′shyen′), *n.* a city in E Szechwan, in central China, on the Yangtze. 110,000 (est. 1950).

wan·i·gan (won′ə gən), *n.* (in the Pacific Northwest) **1.** a lumberjack's trunk. **2.** a lumber camp's supply chest. **3.** a small house on wheels or tractor treads, used as an office or shelter in temporary lumber camps. Also, **wan·gan, wan·gun** (wang′gən), **wan′ni·gan.** [< Algonquian]

wan′ing moon′, the moon at any time after full moon and before new moon (so called because its illuminated area is decreasing). Cf. **waxing moon.** See diag. under **moon.**

wan·ion (won′yən), *n. Archaic.* curse; vengeance. [ME *waniand,* prp. of *wanien* to WANE]

wan·na·be (won′ə bē′, wô′nə-), *n., pl.* **-bes.** *Informal.* one who aspires, often vainly, to emulate another's success or attain eminence in some area.

Wan·ne-Eick·el (vä′nə ī′kəl), *n.* a city in W West Germany. 107,800 (1963).

wan·nish (won′ish), *adj.* somewhat wan. [ME; see WAN, -ISH[1]]

want (wont, wônt), *v.t.* **1.** to feel a need or a desire for; wish for: *to want one's dinner; always wanting something new.* **2.** to wish, need, crave, demand, or desire (often fol. by an infinitive): *I want to see you. He wants to be notified.* **3.** to be without or be deficient in: *to want judgment; to want knowledge.* **4.** to fall short by (a specified amount): *The sum collected wants but a few dollars of the desired amount.* **5.** to require or need: *The house wants painting.* **—*v.i.*** **6.** to feel inclined; wish; like (often fol. by *to*): *We can stay home if you want.* **7.** to be deficient by the absence of some part or thing, or to feel or have a need (sometimes fol. by *for*): *He did not want for abilities.* **8.** to have need (usually fol. by *for*): *If you want for anything, let him know.* **9.** to be in a state of destitution, need, or poverty: *He would never allow*

his parents to want. **10.** to be lacking or absent, as a part or thing necessary to completeness: *All that wants is his signature.* **11. want in** or **out, a.** *Informal.* to desire to enter or leave: *The cat wants in.* **b.** *Slang.* to desire acceptance in or release from (something specified): *I talked with Louie about our plan, and he wants in.* —*n.* **12.** something wanted or needed; necessity: *My wants are few.* **13.** something desired, demanded, or required: *a woman of childish, capricious wants.* **14.** absence or deficiency of something desirable or requisite; lack: *plants dying for want of rain.* **15.** the state of being without something desired or needed; need: *to be in want of an assistant.* **16.** state of being without the necessaries of life; destitution; poverty: *a country where want is virtually unknown.* **17.** a sense of lack or need of something: *to feel a vague want.* [ME *wante* < Scand; cf. Icel *vanta* to lack] —**want′er,** *n.* —**want′less,** *adj.* —**want′less·ness,** *n.*
—**Syn. 1.** require, need. See **wish. 3.** lack, need. **12.** desideratum. **14.** dearth, scarcity, scarceness, inadequacy, insufficiency, paucity, meagerness. **16.** privation, penury, indigence, straits. See **poverty.**

want′ ad′. See **classified ad.**

want·age (won′tij, wôn′-), *n.* that which or an amount which is lacking, desired, or needed. [WANT + -AGE]

Wan·tagh (won′tô), *n.* a town on S Long Island, in SE New York. 34,172 (1960).

want·ing (won′ting, wôn′-), *adj.* **1.** lacking or absent: *a motor with some of the parts wanting.* **2.** deficient in some part, thing, or respect: *to be wanting in courtesy.* —*prep.* **3.** lacking; without: *a box wanting a lid.* **4.** less; minus: *a century wanting three years.* [ME; see WANT, -ING[2]]

want′ list′, a list of desired items circulated among dealers by a hobbyist, museum, collector, etc., in the hopes of locating and purchasing them.

wan·ton (won′tᵊn), *adj.* **1.** done, shown, used, etc., maliciously or unjustifiably: *a wanton attack; wanton cruelty.* **2.** deliberate and without motive or provocation; uncalled-for; headstrong; willful: *Why jeopardize your career in such a wanton way?* **3.** without regard for what is right, just, humane, etc.; careless; reckless: *a wanton attacker of men's religious convictions.* **4.** sexually lawless or unrestrained; loose; lascivious; lewd. **5.** extravagantly or excessively luxurious, as a person, manner of living, style, etc. **6.** *Archaic.* **a.** luxuriant, as vegetation. **b.** sportive or frolicsome, as children, young animals, etc. **c.** having free play: *wanton breezes; a wanton brook.* —*n.* **7.** a wanton or lascivious person, esp. a woman. —*v.i.* **8.** to behave in a wanton manner; become wanton. —*v.t.* **9.** to squander, esp. in pleasure (often fol. by *away*): *to wanton away one's inheritance.* [ME *wantowen,* lit., undisciplined, ill-reared, OE *wan-* not + *togen* disciplined, reared, ptp. of *teen* to draw, train, deriv. of *tēon,* c. G *ziehen,* L *dūcere* to lead; akin to TOW[1]] —**wan′ton·ly,** *adv.* —**wan′ton·ness,** *n.*
—**Syn. 1.** malicious. **2.** calculated. **3.** heedless, inconsiderate. **4.** licentious, dissolute, immoral, libidinous, concupiscent, lustful. **5.** lavish. **9.** waste. —**Ant. 3.** careful, considerate. **4, 5.** restrained.

wan·y (wā′nē), *adj.,* **wan·i·er, wan·i·est. 1.** Also, **waney.** waning; decreasing; diminished in part. **2.** waney (def. 2). [WANE + -Y[1]]

wap[1] (wop, wap), *v.t., v.i.,* **wapped, wap·ping,** *n.* whop.

wap[2] (wap, wop), *v.,* **wapped, wap·ping,** *n. Brit. Dial.* —*v.t.* **1.** to wrap. —*n.* **2.** something that wraps, as a turn of string. [late ME *wappe(n)* < ?]

Wap·a·ko·net·a (wop′ə kə net′ə), *n.* a town in W Ohio. 6756 (1960).

Wap·a·to (wop′ə tō′), *n.* a town in S Washington. 3137 (1960).

wap·a·too (wop′ə to͞o′), *n., pl.* **-toos.** an arrowhead plant, *Sagittaria latifolia.* [< Cree]

wap·en·take (wop′ən tāk′, wap′-), *n.* (formerly in N England and the Midlands) a subdivision of a shire or county corresponding to a hundred. [ME < Scand; cf. Icel *vāpnatak* (OE *wǣpen-getæc*) show of weapons at public voting, equiv. to *vāpna* (gen. pl. of *vāpn* WEAPON) + *tak* taking; see TAKE]

wap·in·schaw (wop′ən shô′, wap′-), *n.* wappenshaw.

wap·i·ti (wop′i tē), *n., pl.* **-tis,** (*esp. collectively*) **-ti.** the elk of North America. [< Shawnee: lit., white rump]

wap·pen·shaw (wop′ən shô′, wap′-), *n.* a periodic muster or review of troops or persons under arms, formerly held in certain districts of Scotland to satisfy military chiefs that their men were properly armed and faithful to the local lord or chieftain. Also, **wapinschaw, wap′pen·shaw′ing, weaponshaw.** [short for *wappenshawing* (Scot), equiv. to *wappen* (OE *wǣpna,* gen. pl. of *wǣp(e)n* WEAPON) + *shawing* showing (see SHOW); cf. D *wapenschouwing*]

wap·per·jaw (wop′ər jô′), *n.* **1.** *U.S. Informal.* a projecting underjaw. **2.** *Brit. Dial.* a crooked mouth. [*wapper* (< ?) + JAW] —**wap′per·jawed′,** *adj.*

Wap′pin·gers Falls′ (wop′in jərz), a town in SE New York. 4447 (1960).

war[1] (wôr), *n., v.,* **warred, war·ring,** *adj.* —*n.* **1.** a conflict carried on by force of arms, as between nations or between parties within a nation; warfare, as by land, sea, or air. **2.** a state or period of armed hostility or active military operations: *The two nations were at war with each other.* **3.** a contest carried on by force of arms, as in a series of battles or campaigns: *the War of 1812.* **4.** active hostility or contention; conflict; contest: *a war of words.* **5.** armed fighting, as a science, profession, activity, art, etc.; methods or principles of waging armed conflict: *War is the soldier's business.* **6.** *Cards.* **a.** a game for two or more persons, played with a 52-card pack evenly divided between the players, in which each player turns up one card at a time with the higher card taking the lower, and in which, when both turned up cards match, each player lays one card face down and turns up another, the player with the higher card of the second turn taking all the cards laid down. **b.** an occasion in this game when both turned up cards match. **7.** *Archaic.* a battle. —*v.i.* **8.** to make or carry on war; fight: *to war with a neighboring nation.* **9.** to carry on active hostility or contention: *Throughout his life he warred with sin and corruption.* **10.** to be in conflict or in a state of strong opposition: *The temptation warred with his conscience.* —*adj.* **11.** of, belonging to, used in, or due to war: *war preparations; war hysteria.* [ME, late OE *werre* < OF (Norman dial.) < OHG *werra* strife; akin to WAR[2]] —**war′less,** *adj.* —**war′less·ly,** *adv.* —**war′less·ness,** *n.*

war[2] (wär), *adj., adv. Scot. and North Eng.* worse. Also, **waur.** [ME *werre* < Scand; cf. Icel *verri* WORSE]

War (wôr), *n.* a town in S West Virginia. 3006 (1960).

War′ and Peace′, a novel (1862–69) by Leo Tolstoy.

war′ ba′by, 1. a child born or conceived in wartime. **2.** an illegitimate child born in wartime of a father in the armed forces.

War·beck (wôr′bek), *n.* **Per·kin** (pûr′kin), 1474–99, Flemish imposter who pretended to the throne of England.

War′ Between′ the States′, the American Civil War: used esp. in the former Confederate States.

war·bird (wôr′bûrd′), *n.* a military aircraft. [WAR[1] + BIRD]

war·ble[1] (wôr′bəl), *v.,* **-bled, -bling,** *n.* —*v.i.* **1.** to sing or whistle with trills, quavers, or melodic embellishments: *The canary warbled most of the day.* **2.** *U.S.* to yodel. **3.** (of electronic equipment) to produce a continuous sound varying regularly in pitch and frequency. —*v.t.* **4.** to sing (an aria or other selection) with trills, quavers, or melodious turns. **5.** to express or celebrate in or as if in song; carol. —*n.* **6.** a warbled song or succession of melodic trills, quavers, etc. **7.** the act of warbling. [late ME *werble* a tune < MF (northeast dial.) < OHG *werbel* something that turns, equiv. to *werb-* (c. OE *hweorf-* in *hweorfan* to turn) + *-el* n. suffix]

war·ble[2] (wôr′bəl), *n. Vet. Pathol.* **1.** a small, hard tumor on a horse's back, produced by the galling of the saddle. **2.** a lump in the skin of an animal's back, containing the larva of a warble fly. [?; cf. obs. Sw *varbulde* boil] —**war′bled,** *adj.*

war′ble fly′, any of several dipterous insects of the family *Hypodermatidae,* the larvae of which produce warbles in cattle and other animals.

war·bler (wôr′blər), *n.* **1.** one who or that which warbles. **2.** any of several small, chiefly Old World songbirds of the family *Sylviidae.* Cf. **blackcap** (def. 1), **reed warbler. 3.** Also called **wood warbler.** any of numerous small, insectivorous, New World birds of the family *Parulidae,* many species of which are brightly colored. Cf. **yellow warbler.** [WARBLE[1] + -ER[1]]

war′bling vir′eo, a grayish-green, American vireo, *Vireo gilvus,* characterized by its melodious warble.

war′ bon′net, an American Indian headdress consisting of a headband with a tail of ornamental feathers.

war′ bride′, 1. a girl or woman who marries a serviceman during wartime, esp. a soldier, sailor, etc., about to go overseas. **2.** a foreign girl or woman who marries a serviceman who is overseas and goes to live in his country.

War·burg (vär′bo͝orᴋʜ; *Eng.* wôr′bərg), *n.* **Ot·to Hein·rich** (ôt′ō hīn′rɪᴋʜ), born 1883, German physiologist: Nobel prize for medicine 1931.

war′ chest′, money set aside or scheduled for a particular purpose or activity, as for a political campaign or organizational drive.

war′ cloud′, something that threatens war; a harbinger of conflict.

war′ correspon′dent, a reporter or commentator assigned to send news or opinions directly from battle areas.

war′ crime′, Usually, **war crimes.** crimes committed against an enemy, captives, or subjects in wartime which violate international agreements or, as in the case of genocide, are offenses against humanity. —**war′ crim′inal.**

war′ cry′, 1. a cry, word, phrase, etc., shouted in charging or in rallying to attack; battle cry. **2.** a slogan, phrase, or motto used to unite a political party, rally support for a cause, etc.

ward (wôrd), *n.* **1.** a division or district of a city or town, as for administrative or political purposes. **2.** one of the districts into which certain English and Scottish boroughs are divided. **3.** a division, floor, or room of a hospital for a particular class or group of patients: *a convalescent ward; a critical ward.* **4.** any of the separate divisions of a prison. **5.** *Mormon Ch.* one of the subdivisions of a stake, presided over by a bishop. **6.** *Fort.* an open space within or between the walls of a castle or fortified place: *the castle's lower ward.* **7.** *Law.* **a.** a person, esp. a minor, who has been legally placed under the care of a guardian or a court. **b.** the state of being under the care or control of a legal guardian. **c.** guardianship over a minor or some other person legally incapable of managing his own affairs. **8.** the state of being under restraining guard or in custody. **9.** a person who is under the protection or control of another. **10.** a movement or posture of defense, as in fencing. **11.** a curved ridge of metal inside a lock, forming an obstacle to the passage of a key which does not have a corresponding notch. **12.** the notch or slot in the bit of a key, into which such a ridge fits. **13.** the act of keeping guard or protective watch: *watch and ward.* **14.** *Archaic.* a company of guards or a garrison. [ME *warde,* OE *weard*] —*v.t.* **15.** to avert, repel, or turn aside (danger, harm, an attack, an assailant, etc.) (usually fol. by *off*): *to ward off a blow; to ward off evil.* **16.** to place in a ward, as of a hospital or prison. **17.** *Archaic.* to protect; guard. [OE *weardian;* c. MD *waerden,* G *warten;* cf. GUARD (v.)] —**ward′less,** *adj.*
—**Syn. 1.** precinct. **9.** protégé. **15.** parry, prevent.

Ward (wôrd), *n.* **1. Ar·te·mas** (är′tə məs), 1727–1800, American general in American Revolution. **2. Ar·te·mus** (är′tə məs), (*Charles Farrar Browne*), 1834–67, U.S. humorist. **3. Barbara.** See **Jackson, Lady Barbara. 4. Mrs. Humphry** (*Mary Augusta Arnold*), 1851–1920, English novelist, born in Tasmania. **5. Sir Joseph George,** 1856–1930, New Zealand statesman, born in Australia: Prime Minister 1906–12, 1928–30. **6. Lester Frank,** 1841–1913, U.S. sociologist. **7. Nathaniel** ("*Theodore de la Guard*"), 1578?–1652, English clergyman, lawyer, and author in America. **8.** a boy's given name.

-ward, a native English suffix indicating spatial or temporal direction: *toward; seaward; afterward; backward.* Also, **-wards.** [ME; OE *-weard* towards; c. G *-wärts*]

war′ dance′, (among primitive peoples) a dance preliminary to a warlike excursion or in celebration of a victory.

ward·ed (wôr′did), *adj.* having notches, slots, or wards, as in locks and keys. [WARD (v.) + -ED[2]]

ward′ eight′, a mixed drink containing whiskey, lemon juice, grenadine, and often soda water, served in a tall glass with crushed ice and sometimes garnished with an orange slice and a cherry.

war·den (wôr′dᵊn), *n.* **1.** a person charged with the care or custody of persons, animals, or things; keeper. **2.** the chief administrative officer in charge of a prison. **3.** any of various public officials charged with superintendence, as over a port, wildlife, etc. **4.** See **air raid warden. 5.** See **fire warden. 6.** (in Connecticut) the chief executive officer of a borough. **7.** (formerly) the principal official in a region, town, etc. **8.** *Brit.* **a.** (*cap.*) (traditionally, in certain titles) the president or governor of specific schools and colleges: *Warden of Merton College.* **b.** a member of a livery company of the City of London. **9.** *Canadian.* the head of certain county or local councils. **10.** a member of the governing body of a guild. **11.** a churchwarden. **12.** *Archaic.* a gatekeeper. [ME *wardein* < OF (northeast dial.), equiv. to *ward-* (root of *warder* to GUARD) + *-ein,* var. of *-ien, -enc* < G *-ing* -ING[1]] —**ward′en·ship′,** *n.*
—**Syn. 1.** warder, guardian, guard, custodian, caretaker superintendent.

Ward·en (wôr′dᵊn), *n.* **1.** *Brit.* any of several pears having a crisp, firm flesh, used in cookery. **2.** a boy's given name, form of **Ward.**

Warden, The, a novel (1855) by Anthony Trollope.

ward·en·ry (wôr′dᵊn rē), *n., pl.* **-ries.** the office, jurisdiction, or district of a warden. [WARDEN + -RY]

ward·er[1] (wôr′dər), *n.* **1.** a person who guards something, as a watchman, caretaker, etc. **2.** a soldier or other person set to guard an entrance. **3.** *Chiefly Brit.* an official having charge of prisoners in a jail. [late ME *warder(e)* (see WARD, -ER[1]); cf. AF *wardere* < ME] —**ward′er·ship′,** *n.*

ward·er[2] (wôr′dər), *n.* a truncheon or staff of office or authority, used in giving signals. [late ME < ?]

ward′ heel′er, *U.S.* a minor politician who canvasses voters and does other chores for a political machine or party boss.

Ward′i·an case′ (wôr′dē ən), a type of terrarium having a top and sides of glass, used esp. for transporting living plants. [named after Nathaniel B. *Ward* (1791–1868), English botanist; see -IAN]

ward′ing file′, a thin file for doing fine metalwork, as cutting keys or the wards of locks.

ward·ress (wôr′dris), *n. Chiefly Brit.* a female warder. [WARD(E)R[1] + -ESS]

ward·robe (wôr′drōb), *n.* **1.** a stock of clothes or costumes, as of a person or of a theatrical company. **2.** a piece of furniture for holding clothes, now usually a tall, upright case fitted with hooks, shelves, etc. **3.** a room or place in which to keep clothes or costumes. **4.** the department of a royal or other great household charged with the care of wearing apparel. [late ME *warderobe* < AF, OF (northeast dial). See WARD, ROBE]

ward′robe trunk′, a large, upright trunk, usually with space on one side for hanging clothes and drawers or compartments on the other for small articles, shoes, etc.

ward·room (wôrd′ro͞om′, -ro͝om′), *n.* (on a warship) **1.** the area serving as the living quarters for all commissioned officers except the commanding officer. **2.** the dining saloon and lounge for these officers. **3.** these officers collectively. [WARD + ROOM]

-wards, var. of **-ward:** *towards; afterwards.* [ME; OE *-weardes,* equiv. to *-weard* toward + *-es* -S[1]]

ward·ship (wôrd′ship), *n.* **1.** guardianship; custody. **2.** *Law.* the guardianship over a minor or ward. [WARD + -SHIP]

ware[1] (wâr), *n.* **1.** Usually, **wares. a.** articles of merchandise or manufacture; goods: *a peddler selling his wares.* **b.** any intangible items, as services or products of artistic or intellectual creativity, that are salable: *an architect displaying his wares on the drawing board; an actor's wares.* **2.** a specified kind or class of merchandise or of manufactured article (usually used in combination): *silverware; glassware.* **3.** pottery, or a particular kind of pottery: *Delft ware.* **4.** *Archaeol.* a group of ceramic types classified according to surface characteristics, as glaze and hardness, rather than shape and color. [ME; OE *waru;* c. G *Ware*]

ware[2] (wâr), *adj., v.,* **wared, war·ing.** *Archaic.* —*adj.* **1.** watchful, wary, or cautious. **2.** aware; conscious. —*v.t.* **3.** to beware of (usually used in the imperative). [ME; OE *wær;* c. G *(ge)wahr* aware, Icel *varr*]

ware[3] (wâr), *v.t.,* **wared, war·ing.** *Scot. and North Eng.* to spend or expend (money, time, worry, etc.). Also, *esp. Scot.,* **wair.** [ME < Scand; cf. Icel *verja* to spend, invest; c. OE *werian* to WEAR]

ware[4] (wâr), *n. Scot. and North Eng.* the first season in the year; spring. [ME < ON *vār* spring; cf. L *vēr* (see VERNAL), Gk *ēar* spring]

Ware (wâr), *n.* a town in central Massachusetts. 6650 (1960).

ware·house (*n.* wâr′hous′; *v.* wâr′houz′, -hous′), *n., pl.* **-hous·es** (-hou′ziz), *v.,* **-housed, -hous·ing.** —*n.* **1.** a building, or a part of one, for the storage of goods, merchandise, etc. **2.** *Brit.* a large retail store. **3.** a building, or a part of one, in which wholesalers keep large stocks of merchandise, which they display and sell to retailers. —*v.t.* **4.** to place, deposit, or store in a warehouse. **5.** to place in a government or bonded warehouse, to be kept until duties are paid. [WARE[1] + HOUSE]

ware·house·man (wâr′hous′mən), *n., pl.* **-men. 1.** a person who stores goods for others for pay. **2.** a person who is employed in or who manages a warehouse. [WAREHOUSE + MAN[1]]

ware′house receipt′, a receipt for goods placed in a warehouse, either negotiable or nonnegotiable.

ware·room (wâr′ro͞om′, -ro͝om′), *n.* a room in which goods are stored or are displayed for sale. [WARE[1] + ROOM]

Ware′ Shoals′, a town in NW South Carolina. 2671 (1960).

war·fare (wôr′fâr′), *n.* **1.** the process of military struggle between two nations or groups of nations, political groups, or the like; war. **2.** armed conflict between two massed enemies. **3.** a military operation, esp. an attack, against an enemy. [WAR[1] + FARE: a faring forth to war]

war·fa·rin (wôr′fə rin), *n. Chem.* a colorless, crystalline, water-insoluble, poisonous solid, $C_{19}H_{16}O_4$, used chiefly for killing rodents. [*W*(*isconsin*) *A*(*lumni*) *R*(*esearch*) *F*(*oundation*) (owners of patent) + (COU-M)ARIN]

War·field (wôr′fēld′), *n.* **David,** 1866–1951, U.S. actor.

war′ foot′ing, the condition or status of a military force or other organization when operating under a state of war or as if a state of war existed.

war′ game′, *Mil.* a simulated military operation, carried out to test the validity of a war plan or operational concept: in its simplest form, two opposing teams of officers take part, and when necessary, military units of the required strength are employed.

War·gen·tin (wär gen′tᵊn, -tən), *n.* a walled plain in the third quadrant of the face of the moon: about 55 miles in diameter.

war′ ham′mer. See **pole hammer.**

war′ hat′, *Armor.* See **chapel de fer.**

war·head (wôr′hed′), *n.* the forward section of a self-propelled missile, bomb, torpedo, or the like, containing the explosive, chemical, or atomic charge. [WAR¹ + HEAD]

War·hol (wôr′hôl, -hol), *n.* **Andy,** 1930?–87, U.S. pop artist.

war·horse (wôr′hôrs′), *n.* **1.** a horse used in war; charger. **2.** *Informal.* a veteran, as a soldier or politician, of many struggles and conflicts. **3.** a musical composition, play, etc., which has been seen, heard, or performed excessively. [WAR¹ + HORSE]

war·i·ly (wâr′ə lē), *adv.* in a wary manner. [WARY + -LY]

war·i·ness (wâr′ē nis), *n.* the state or quality of being wary. [WARY + -NESS]

war·i·son (war′i sən), *n.* a note sounded as a signal for assault. [ME < AF, OF (northeast dial.): defense, possessions, equiv. to *waris-* (s. of *warir* to defend, possess < Gmc; cf. OE *warian* to defend, possess) + *-on* n. suffix]

wark (wärk), *n., v.i. Brit. Dial.* **1.** pain; ache. **2.** work. [ME *warke,* OE *wærc;* c. Icel *verkr*]

War′ La′bor Board′. See **National War Labor Board.**

war·like (wôr′līk′), *adj.* **1.** fit, qualified, or ready for war; martial: *a warlike fleet; warlike tribes.* **2.** threatening or indicating war: *a warlike tone.* **3.** of or pertaining to war: *a warlike expedition.* [ME; see WAR¹, -LIKE]
—**Syn. 2.** bellicose, belligerent, hostile; inimical, unfriendly. —**Ant. 2.** peaceful.

war·lock (wôr′lok′), *n.* **1.** a man aided by the Devil in practicing magic arts; sorcerer. **2.** a fortuneteller or conjurer. [ME *warloghe, -lach,* OE *wǣrloga* oath-breaker, devil, equiv. to *wǣr* covenant + *-loga* betrayer (deriv. of *l*(*ē*)*ogan* to lie)]

war′ lord′, **1.** a military leader, esp. of a warlike nation. **2.** a military commander who has seized power, esp. in one section of a country. **3.** tuchun. Also, **war-lord** (wôr′lôrd′).

warm (wôrm), *adj.* **1.** having or giving out a moderate degree of heat, as perceived by the senses: *a warm bath.* **2.** of or at a moderately high temperature; characterized by comparatively high temperature: *a warm oven; a warm climate; a warm summer.* **3.** having a sensation of bodily heat: *to be warm from fast walking.* **4.** conserving or maintaining warmth or heat: *warm clothes.* **5.** (of colors) suggestive of warmth; inclining toward red or orange, rather than toward green or blue. **6.** characterized by or showing lively feelings, passions, emotions, sympathies, etc.: *a warm heart; warm interest.* **7.** strongly attached; intimate: *warm friends.* **8.** cordial or hearty: *a warm welcome.* **9.** heated, irritated, or angry: *to become warm when contradicted.* **10.** animated, lively, brisk, or vigorous: *a warm debate.* **11.** strong or fresh: *a warm scent.* **12.** *Informal.* close to something sought, as in a game. **13.** *Informal.* uncomfortable or unpleasant: *His opponents made things so warm that he decided to quit.* **14.** *Brit. Informal.* well off; in easy circumstances. —*v.t.* **15.** to make warm; heat (often fol. by *up*): *to warm one's hands; to warm up a room.* **16.** to heat or cook (something) for reuse, as leftovers (usually fol. by *over* or *up*): *to warm up yesterday's stew.* **17.** to excite enthusiasm, ardor, cheerfulness, or vitality in (someone): *The wine soon warmed the company.* **18.** to inspire with kindly feeling; affect with lively pleasure: *It warms my soul.* **19.** to fill (a person, crowd, etc.) with strong feelings, as hatred, resentment, anger, zeal, etc.: *Restrictions had warmed the crew to the point of mutiny.* **20. warm the bench,** *Sports.* to serve as a substitute who rarely plays in a game: *The young outfielder warmed the bench for the Yankees last season.* —*v.i.* **21.** to become warm or warmer (often fol. by *up*): *The room will warm up when the fire gets going.* **22.** to become ardent, enthusiastic, animated, etc. (often fol. by *up* or *to*): *The speaker quickly warmed to his subject.* **23.** to grow kindly, friendly, or sympathetically disposed (often fol. by *to* or *toward*): *My heart warms toward him.* **24. warm up, a.** to prepare for a game, sports contest, dance, etc., by practice or exercise beforehand. **b.** to increase in excitement, intensity, violence, etc.: *The racial situation was warming up.* **c.** to become friendlier or more receptive: *No matter how hard I tried, I just couldn't warm up to that proposal.* —*n.* **25.** *Informal.* a warming: *Sit at the fire and have a warm.* [ME; OE *wearm;* c. G *warm,* Icel *varmr,* Gk *thermós* hot, L *formus* warm] —**warm′er,** *n.* —**warm′ish,** *adj.* —**warm′ly,** *adv.* —**warm′ness,** *n.*
—**Syn. 1.** lukewarm, tepid, heated. **6.** hearty, enthusiastic, zealous, fervent, fervid, emotional, ardent. **7.** friendly, close. **8.** fervent. **9.** annoyed, vexed, irate, furious. **10.** vehement. **17.** animate, excite, waken, stir, rouse, arouse. —**Ant. 1.** cool.

War′ Man′power Commis′sion, *U.S. Govt.* the board (1942–45) that regulated the most efficient use of labor during World War II. *Abbr.:* WMC

warm-blood·ed (wôrm′blud′id), *adj.* **1.** designating or pertaining to animals, as mammals and birds, whose blood ranges in temperatures from about 98° to 112°F, and remains relatively constant, irrespective of the temperature of the surrounding medium; poikilothermic. **2.** ardent, impetuous, or passionate: *young and warm-blooded valor.* —**warm′-blood′ed·ness,** *n.*

warmed-o·ver (wôrmd′ō′vər), *adj.* **1.** (of cooked foods) heated again: *warmed-over stew.* **2.** reworked or repeated without enthusiasm or introduction of new ideas; stale: *a warmed-over version of an old show.*

warmed-up (wôrmd′up′), *adj.* warmed-over (def. 1).

warm′ front′, *Meteorol.* a transition zone between a mass of warm air and the colder air it is replacing.

warm-heart·ed (wôrm′här′tid), *adj.* having or showing sympathy, affection, cordiality, etc.: *a warm-hearted welcome.* Also, **warm′heart′ed.** —**warm′-heart′ed·ly, warm′heart′ed·ly,** *adv.* —**warm′-heart′ed·ness, warm′heart′ed·ness,** *n.*
—**Syn.** sympathetic, compassionate, kind.

warm′ing pan′, a long-handled, covered pan, usually of brass, filled with live coals, hot water, etc., formerly used for warming beds.

war′min·ster broom′ (wôr′minz tər, -min stər), a shrub, *Cytisus praecox,* of western Asia and the Mediterranean region, having yellowish-white or yellow, pealike flowers. [after *Warminster,* England]

war·mong·er (wôr′mung′gər, -mong′-), *n.* a person who advocates, wants, or tries to precipitate war. [WAR¹ + MONGER]

war·mon·ger·ing (wôr′mung′gər ing, -mong′-), *n.* the practices and principles of a warmonger. [WARMONGER + -ING¹]

war·mouth (wôr′mouth′), *n., pl.* **-mouths** (-mouthz′, -mouths′), (*esp. collectively*) **-mouth.** a fresh-water sunfish, *Chaenobryttus gulosus,* found in the eastern U.S., having a patch of small teeth on its tongue. [?]

warm′ sec′tor, *Meteorol.* the region bounded by the cold and warm fronts of a cyclone.

warm′ spring′, a thermal spring having a temperature less than 98°F. Cf. **hot spring.**

Warm′ Springs′, a town in W Georgia: resort; site of foundation for treatment of poliomyelitis. 538 (1960).

warmth (wôrmth), *n.* **1.** the quality or state of being warm; moderate or gentle heat. **2.** the sensation of moderate heat. **3.** liveliness of feelings, emotions, or sympathies; ardor or fervor; enthusiasm or zeal: *She spoke her mind with great warmth. There was warmth in his greeting and in his handshake.* **4.** the quality of being intimate and attached: *Every child needs warmth and affection from his family.* **5.** an effect of brightness, cheerfulness, coziness, etc., achieved by the use of warm colors: *The room has warmth since it was redecorated.* **6.** the means or ability to produce a sensation of heat: *a jacket with little warmth.* **7.** slight anger or irritation: *His denial betrayed some warmth.* [ME *wermth.* See WARM, -TH¹] —**warmth′less,** *adj.* —**warmth′less·ness,** *n.*

warm-up (wôrm′up′), *n.* the act or an instance of warming up: *The spectators came early to watch the players go through their warm-ups. The dancers went through a quick warm-up.* [n. use of v. phrase *warm up*]

warn (wôrn), *v.t.* **1.** to give notice, advice, or intimation to (a person, group, etc.) of danger, impending evil, possible harm, or anything else unfavorable: *They warned him of a plot against him. He was warned that his life was in danger.* **2.** to urge or advise to be careful; caution: *to warn a careless driver.* **3.** to admonish or exhort, as to action or conduct: *He warned his employees to be on time.* **4.** to notify, apprise, or inform: *to warn a person of an intended visit.* **5.** to give notice to (a person, group, etc.) to go, keep at a distance, etc. (often fol. by *away, off,* etc.): *A sign warns trespassers off private grounds. A marker warned boats away from the dock.* **6.** to give authoritative or formal notice to (someone); order; summon: *to warn a person to appear in court.* —*v.i.* **7.** to give a warning; caution: *to warn of further disasters.* [ME; OE *warn*(*ian*); c. G *warnen.* Cf. WARE²] —**warn′er,** *n.*
—**Syn. 1.** forewarn. WARN, CAUTION, ADMONISH imply attempting to prevent another from running into danger or getting into unpleasant or undesirable circumstances. To WARN is to speak plainly and usually in strong terms: *to warn him about danger and possible penalties.* To CAUTION is to advise about necessary precautions, to put one on his guard about or against some circumstance or condition (usually less serious): *to caution him against trying to go,* thus emphasizing avoidance of penalties. ADMONISH suggests giving earnest, authoritative advice, exhortation, with only tacit references to danger or penalty: *to admonish one for neglecting duties.*

War·ner (wôr′nər), *n.* **Charles Dud·ley** (dud′lē), 1829–1900, U.S. editor and essayist.

War′ner Rob′ins, a city in central Georgia. 18,633 (1960).

warn·ing (wôr′ning), *n.* **1.** the act or utterance of one who warns or the existence, appearance, sound, etc., of that which warns. **2.** that which serves to warn, give notice, or caution: *We fired a warning at the intruders.* —*adj.* **3.** serving to warn, advise, caution: *a warning bell.* [ME (n.); OE *war*(*e*)*nung* (n.). See WARN, -ING¹, -ING²] —**warn′ing·ly,** *adv.*
—**Syn. 2.** caution, admonition, advice; omen, sign, portent, augury, presage.

warn′ing pe′riod, *Horol.* a brief period before the striking of a timepiece in which the striking mechanism is prepared for release.

war′ nose′, the explosive forward section of a projectile, as of a torpedo, shell, etc.; warhead.

War′ of Amer′ican Independ′ence, *Brit.* See **American Revolution.**

War of 1812, a war between the United States and Great Britain from 1812 to 1815.

War′ of Independ′ence. See **American Revolution.**

war′ of nerves′, a conflict using psychological techniques, such as propaganda, threats, and false rumors, rather than direct violence, in order to confuse, thwart, or intimidate an enemy.

War′ of Seces′sion. See **American Civil War.**

War′ of the Aus′trian Succes′sion, the war (1740–48) in which Austria, England, and Holland opposed Prussia, France, and Spain over the selection of rulers for territories within the Austrian Empire. Cf. **King George's War.**

War′ of the Grand′ Alli′ance, the war (1689–97) in which England, Holland, Spain, and the Holy Roman Empire opposed France. Cf. **King William's War.**

War′ of the Na′tions. See **World War I.**

War′ of the Rebel′lion. See **American Civil War.**

War′ of the Span′ish Succes′sion, a war (1701–1714) fought by Austria, England, the Netherlands, and Prussia against France and Spain, arising from disputes about the succession in Spain after the death of Charles II of Spain.

warp (wôrp), *v.t.* **1.** to bend or twist out of shape, esp. from a straight or flat form, as timbers, flooring, etc. **2.** to bend or turn from the natural or true direction or course. **3.** to distort or cause to distort from the truth, fact, true meaning, etc.; bias, falsify: *Prejudice warps the mind.* **4.** *Aeron.* to curve or bend (a wing or other airfoil) at the end or ends to promote equilibrium or to secure lateral control. **5.** *Naut.* to move (a vessel) into a desired place or position by hauling on a rope that has been fastened to something fixed, as a buoy, anchor, or the like. **6.** *Agric.* to fertilize (land) by inundation with water that deposits alluvial matter. —*v.i.* **7.** to become bent or twisted out of shape, esp. out of a straight or flat form: *The wood has warped in drying.* **8.** to be or become biased; hold or change an opinion due to prejudice, external influence, or the like. **9.** *Naut.* **a.** to warp a ship or boat into position. **b.** (of a ship or boat) to move by being warped. **10.** (of a strata in the earth's crust) to bend slightly, to a degree that no fold or fault results. [ME *werpe*(*n*), OE *weorpan* to throw; c. G *werfen,* Icel *verpa,* Goth *wairpan*] —*n.* **11.** a bend, twist, or variation from a straight or flat form in something, as in wood that has dried unevenly. **12.** a mental twist, bias, or quirk, or a biased or twisted attitude or judgment. **13.** the set of yarns placed lengthwise in the loom, crossed by and interlaced with the weft, and forming the lengthwise threads in a woven fabric. See diag. under **weave. 14.** Also called **spring, spring line.** *Naut.* a rope for warping or hauling a ship or boat along or into position. **15.** alluvial matter deposited by water, esp. water let in to inundate low land so as to enrich it. [ME *warpe,* OE *wearp;* c. G *Warf,* Icel *varp*] —**warp′age,** *n.*
—**Syn. 1.** turn, contort, distort, spring. **2.** swerve, deviate. —**Ant. 1, 7.** straighten.

war′ paint′, **1.** paint applied by American Indians to their faces and bodies before going to war. **2.** *Informal.* make-up; cosmetics. **3.** *Informal.* full dress; regalia.

war·path (wôr′path′, -päth′), *n., pl.* **-paths** (-pathz′, -päthz′). **1.** the path or course taken by American Indians on a warlike expedition. **2. on the warpath, a.** seeking, preparing for, or engaged in war. **b.** in a state of anger or indignation; hostile: *The police are on the warpath because the suspect is at large.* [WAR¹ + PATH]

warp′ beam′, a roller, located at the back of the loom, on which the warp ends are wound in preparation for weaving. Also called **warp roll.**

warp·er (wôr′pər), *n.* **1.** one who or that which warps. **2.** *Textiles.* a machine used to wind warp ends in preparation for weaving. [OE *weorpere.* See WARP, -ER¹]

warp′ing bridge′. See **docking bridge.**

warp·ing-frame (wôr′ping frām′), *n.* a wooden frame containing evenly spaced pegs on which the warp is wound in preparation for weaving.

warp′ knit′, a fabric or garment so constructed that runs do not occur: knitted from a warp beam that feeds yarn to the knitting frame.

warp-knit·ted (wôrp′nit′id), *adj.* designating a fabric made by warp knitting.

warp′ knit′ting, a knitting process in which the yarn is knitted vertically in a flat form. Cf. **weft knitting.**

war·plane (wôr′plān′), *n.* an airplane designed for, or used in, warfare. [WAR¹ + PLANE¹]

War′ Produc′tion Board′, *U.S. Govt.* the board (1942–45) that supervised and regulated the production and sale of matériel essential to the logistics of World War II. *Abbr.:* WPB

warp′ roll′. See **warp beam.**

warp·wise (wôrp′wīz′), *adv. Textiles.* in a vertical direction; at right angles to the filling; lengthwise. [WARP + -WISE]

Warr′ A′cres (wôr), a town in central Oklahoma. 7135 (1960).

war·ra·gal (wôr′ə gəl), *n., adj. Australian.* warrigal.

war·rant (wôr′ənt, wor′-), *n.* **1.** authorization, sanction, or justification. **2.** that which serves to give reliable or formal assurance of something; guarantee, pledge, or security. **3.** something considered as having the force of a guarantee, or being positive assurance of a thing: *The cavalry and artillery were considered sure warrants of success.* **4.** a writing or document certifying or authorizing something, as a receipt, license, or commission. **5.** *Law.* an instrument, issued by a magistrate, authorizing an officer to make an arrest, seize property, make a search, or carry a judgment into execution. **6.** the certificate of authority or appointment issued to an officer of the armed forces below the rank of a commissioned officer. **7.** a warehouse receipt. **8.** a written authorization for the payment or receipt of money: *a treasury warrant.* —*v.t.* **9.** to give authority to; authorize. **10.** to give reason or sanction for; justify: *The circumstances warrant such measures.* **11.** to give one's word for; vouch for (often used with a clause to emphasize something asserted): *I'll warrant he did!* **12.** to give a formal assurance, or a guarantee or promise, to or for; guarantee: *to warrant someone honorable treatment; to warrant payment; to warrant safe delivery.* **13.** to guarantee the quantity, quality, and other representations of (an article, product, etc.), as to a purchaser. **14.** to guarantee or secure title to (the purchaser of goods); assure indemnification against loss to. **15.** *Law.* to guarantee title of an estate or other granted property (to a grantee). [ME *warant* < AF (var. of OF *guarant*) < G; cf. MLG *warend, -ent* warranty, n. use of prp. of *waren* to warrant; see GUARANTY] —**war′rant·less,** *adj.*
—**Syn. 2.** warranty, surety. **4.** permit, voucher, writ, order, chit. **11.** guarantee, attest.

war·rant·a·ble (wôr′ən tə bəl, wor′-), *adj.* **1.** capable of being warranted. **2.** (of deer) of a legal age for hunting. [WARRANT + -ABLE] —**war′rant·a·ble·ness,** *n.*

war·ran·tee (wôr′ən tē′, wor′-), *n.* one to whom a warranty is made. [WARRANT(Y) or WARRANT(OR) + -EE]

war·rant·er (wôr′ən tər, wor′-), *n.* warrantor. [WARRANT + -ER¹]

war′rant of′ficer, **1.** (in the U.S. Armed Forces) an officer of one of four grades ranking above enlisted men and below commissioned officers. **2.** a similar officer in other countries.

war·ran·tor (wôr′ən tôr′, wor′-), *n.* one who warrants or makes a warranty. [WARRANT + -OR²]

war·ran·ty (wôr′ən tē, wor′-), *n., pl.* **-ties. 1.** the act or an instance of warranting; assurance; authorization; warrant. **2.** *Law.* **a.** an engagement, express or implied, in assurance of some particular in connection with a contract, as of sale: *an express warranty of the quality of goods.* **b.** Also called **covenant of warranty.** a covenant in a deed to land by which the party conveying assures the grantee that he will enjoy the premises free from interference by any person claiming under a superior title. Cf. **quitclaim deed, warranty deed. c.** (in the law of insurance) a statement or promise, made by the party insured, and included as an essential part of the contract, falsity or nonfulfillment of which renders the policy void. **d.** a judicial document, as a warrant or writ. **3.** a written guarantee given to the purchaser of a new appliance, automobile, or other item by the manufacturer or dealer, usually specifying that the manufacturer will make any repairs or replace defective parts free of charge for a stated period of time. [ME *warantie* < AF (var. of OF *guarantie*). See WARRANT, -Y[3]]

war′ranty deed′, *Law.* a deed containing a covenant of warranty. Cf. **quitclaim deed.**

war·ren (wôr′ən, wor′-), *n.* **1.** a place where rabbits breed or abound. **2.** a building, tenement, district, etc., containing many tenants in limited or crowded quarters. [late ME *warenne* < AF (var. of OF *g(u)arenne*) < OG **warinne* game park, equiv. to *war-* (root of OHG *warjan* to defend) + *-inne* fem. n. suffix]

War·ren (wôr′ən, wor′-), *n.* **1. Earl,** born 1891, U.S. lawyer and political leader: Chief Justice of the U.S. since 1953. **2. Joseph,** 1741–75, American physician, statesman, and patriot. **3. Robert Penn,** born 1905, U.S. novelist and poet. **4.** a city in SE Michigan, near Detroit. 89,246 (1960). **5.** a city in NE Ohio, NW of Youngstown. 59,648 (1960). **6.** a town in S Arkansas. 6752 (1960). **7.** a boy's given name.

war·ren·er (wôr′ə nər, wor′-), *n.* the keeper of a rabbit warren. [ME; see WARREN, -ER[1]]

War·rens·burg (wor′inz bûrg′), *n.* a town in central Missouri. 9689 (1960).

War·ren·ton (wor′ən tən), *n.* a town in N Virginia. 3522 (1960).

War′ren truss′, a truss for a bridge, girder, etc., having alternating, inclined tension and compression members dividing the web into similar triangular panels: sometimes found in combination with vertical posts or a crossing set of diagonals. See illus. under **truss.** [named after Russell *Warren* (1783–1860), American architect]

War·ren·ville (wor′ən vil), *n.* a town in NE Illinois. 3134 (1960).

war·ri·gal (wôr′ə gəl), *Australian.* —*n.* **1.** dingo. **2.** any large or ferocious dog. **3.** a wild horse. —*adj.* **4.** wild; ferocious; savage. Also, **warragal.** [< native Austral *warragul* ferocious]

War·ring·ton (wôr′ing tən, wor′-), *n.* **1.** a city in S Lancashire, in NW England, on the Mersey River. 75,533 (1961). **2.** a town in W Florida, on the Gulf of Mexico. 16,752 (1960).

war·ri·or (wôr′ē ər, wor′yər, wor′ē ər, wor′yər), *n.* **1.** a man engaged or experienced in warfare; soldier. **2.** a person who has shown great vigor, courage, or aggressiveness, as in politics. [early ME *werreieor* < AF (equiv. to OF *guerreieor*, etc.), equiv. to *werr(e)* WAR[1] + *-ei-* v. suffix + *-eor* -OR[2]] —**war′ri·or·like′,** *adj.*

war′ risk′ insur′ance, life insurance for members of the armed forces.

warrty., warranty.

war·saw (wôr′sô), *n.* **1.** Also, **war′saw group′er.** a large grouper, *Epinephelus nigritus*, found in the warmer waters of the Atlantic Ocean. **2.** the jewfish, *Epinephelus itajara*, found off both coasts of tropical America. [< Sp *guasa*, imperfectly reproduced in E]

War·saw (wôr′sô), *n.* **1.** Polish, **War·sza·wa** (vär shä′vä). a city in and the capital of Poland, in the E central part, on the Vistula River. 1,203,000 (est. 1963). **2.** a town in N Indiana. 7234 (1960). **3.** a town in W New York. 3653 (1960).

War′saw Conven′tion, a multilateral treaty on aviation set up chiefly to limit air carriers' liability to passengers and shippers on international flights in the event of an accident.

War′saw Pact′, an organization formed in Warsaw, Poland (1955), comprising Albania, Bulgaria, Czechoslovakia, East Germany, Hungary, Poland, Rumania, and the U.S.S.R., for collective defense under a joint military command. Also called **War′saw Trea′ty Organiza′tion.** Cf. **NATO.**

war·ship (wôr′ship′), *n.* a ship built or armed for combat purposes. Also called **war vessel.** [WAR[1] + SHIP]

war·sle (wär′səl), *v.i., v.t.,* **-sled, -sling,** *n. Chiefly Scot.* wrestle. [ME; OE **wǣrstlian*, metathetic var. (cf. OE *wǣrstlic* of wrestling) of *wrǣstlian* to WRESTLE] —**war′sler,** *n.*

Wars′ of the Ros′es, *Eng. Hist.* the civil struggle between the royal house of Lancaster, whose emblem was a red rose, and the royal house of York, whose emblem was a white rose, beginning in 1455 and ending with the accession of Henry VII in 1485 and the union of the two houses.

war·stle (wär′səl), *v.i., v.t.,* **-stled, -stling,** *n. Chiefly Scot.* wrestle. [var. of WARSLE] —**war′stler,** *n.*

war′ sur′plus, equipment, supplies, etc., originally used by or manufactured for the armed forces, but disposed of cheaply as surplus or obsolete: *He made his fortune in war surplus.*

wart (wôrt), *n.* **1.** a small, usually hard, abnormal elevation on the skin, caused by a filterable virus. **2.** any small protuberance, as on the surface of certain plants, the skin of certain animals, etc. [ME; OE *wearte*; c. G *Warze*, Icel *varta*; akin to L *verrūca* wart] —**wart′ed,** *adj.* —**wart′less,** *adj.* —**wart′like′,** *adj.*

Wart hog (2½ ft. high at shoulder; total length 6 ft.; tail 1½ ft.)

War·ta (vär′tä), *n.* a river in Poland, flowing NW and W into the Oder. 445 mi. long. German, **War·the** (vär′tə).

Wart·burg (värt′bo͝orkh), *n.* a castle in East Germany, in Thuringia, near Eisenach: Luther translated the New Testament here 1521–22.

wart′ hog′, an African wild swine, *Phacochoerus aethiopicus*, having large tusks and warty excrescences on the face.

war·time (wôr′tīm′), *n.* **1.** a time or period of war: *Strict travel regulations apply only in wartime.* —*adj.* **2.** caused by, characteristic of, or occurring during war: *wartime shortages.* [WAR[1] + TIME]

wart′ snake′, either of two stout, nonvenomous colubrid snakes of the subfamily *Acrochordinae*, found from southeastern Asia to northern Australia, and having the skin covered with wartlike, three-pointed scales.

wart·y (wôr′tē), *adj.,* **wart·i·er, wart·i·est. 1.** having warts; covered with or as with warts. **2.** resembling a wart. [WART + -Y[1]]

war′ ves′sel, warship.

war-wea·ry (wôr′wēr′ē), *adj.* **1.** utterly exhausted and dejected by war, esp. after a prolonged conflict. **2.** (of an airplane) damaged beyond use except as scrap or as a source of salvageable spare parts. —**war′-wea′ri·ness,** *n.*

war′ whoop′, a yell uttered in making an attack: *The war whoop of the American Indian was bloodcurdling.*

War·wick (wôr′ik, wor′- *or, for* 2, 5, 6, wôr′wik), *n.* **1. Earl of Salisbury and of** (*Richard Neville*) (*"the Kingmaker"*), 1428–71, English military leader and statesman. **2.** a city in E Rhode Island. 68,504 (1960). **3.** a town in and the county seat of Warwickshire in central England: castle. 16,032 (1961). **4.** Warwickshire. **5.** a town in SE New York. 3218 (1960). **6.** a boy's given name.

War·wick·shire (wôr′ik shēr′, -shər, wor′-), *n.* a county in central England. 2,023,289 (1961); 983 sq. mi. *Co. seat:* Warwick. Also called **Warwick.**

war·y (wâr′ē), *adj.,* **war·i·er, war·i·est. 1.** watchful, or on one's guard, esp. habitually; on the alert, as to avoid danger; cautious; careful: *He was wary of grammatical errors.* **2.** arising from or characterized by caution: *to give someone a wary look.* [WARE[2] + -Y[1]] —**war′i·ly,** *adv.* —**war′i·ness,** *n.*

—**Syn. 1.** alert, vigilant, guarded, circumspect, prudent. See **careful.**

war′ zone′, (during wartime) a combat area in which the rights of neutrals are suspended, esp. such an area on the high seas, where ships flying a neutral flag are subject to attack.

was (wuz, woz; *unstressed* wəz), *v.* 1st and 3rd pers. sing. pt. indic. of **be.** [ME; OE *wæs*, past tense sing. of *wesan* to be; c. Goth, OHG, OFris *was*, Icel *var*; see WASSAIL]

wa·sa·bi (wä′sə bē), *n.* **1.** a cruciferous plant, *Eutrema wasabi*, of Asia. **2.** the pungent, greenish root of this plant, which is grated and used as a condiment. [< Jap]

Wa′satch Range′ (wô′sach), a mountain range in N Utah and SE Idaho. Highest peak, Mt. Timpanogos, 12,008 ft.

Was·co (wos′kō), *n.* a town in central California. 6841 (1960).

wase (wāz), *n. Brit. Dial.* a wisp, bundle, or pad of straw. [ME; c. MSw *vasi* bundle of straws, LG *wase* bundle of sticks, pad for head]

Wa·se·ca (wo sē′kə), *n.* a town in S Minnesota. 5898 (1960).

wash (wosh, wôsh), *v.t.* **1.** to apply water or some other liquid to (something or someone) for the purpose of cleansing; cleanse by dipping, rubbing, or scrubbing in water or some other liquid. **2.** to remove (dirt, stains, paint, or any matter) by or as by the action of water (usually fol. by *out, off,* etc.): *to wash grime out of clothing.* **3.** to free from ceremonial defilement or from sin, guilt, etc.: *to be washed whiter than the snow.* **4.** to bathe, wet, or moisten with water or other liquid: *a meadow newly washed with morning dew.* **5.** to flow through, over, or against: *a shore or cliff washed by waves.* **6.** to carry, bring, remove, or deposit (something) by means of water or any liquid, or as the water or liquid does (often fol. by *up, down,* or *along*): *The storm washed the boat up on the shore. Wash the chicken down with a little white wine. A sailor was washed overboard.* **7.** to wear or diminish, as water does by flowing over or against a surface (often fol. by *out* or *away*): *The rain had washed away the lettering on the stone.* **8.** (of flowing water) to form a channel, stream, etc.: *The flood had washed a new channel through the bottom lands.* **9.** *Mining.* **a.** to subject (earth or ore) to the action or force of water in order to separate valuable material. **b.** to separate (valuable material) in this way. **10.** to purify (a gas or gaseous mixture) by passage through or over a liquid. **11.** to cover with a watery or thin coat of color. **12.** to overlay with a thin coat or deposit of metal: *to wash brass with gold.* —*v.i.* **13.** to wash oneself: *After using the insecticide spray they washed completely.* **14.** to wash clothes: *Monday is the day we wash.* **15.** to cleanse anything with or in water or other liquid. **16.** to undergo washing without injury, esp. shrinking or fading: *fabrics guaranteed to wash.* **17.** *Chiefly Brit. Informal.* to be found true, valid, or real when tested or closely scrutinized; stand being put to the proof: *His honesty won't wash.* **18.** to be carried or driven by water (often fol. by *along* or *ashore*): *The boat had washed ashore in the night.* **19.** to flow or beat with a lapping sound, as waves on a shore. **20.** to move along in or as in waves, or with a rushing movement, as water. **21.** to be eroded, as by a stream, rainfall, etc.: *a hillside that washes frequently.* **22.** to be removed by the action of water (often fol. by *away*): *Much of the topsoil washes away each spring.* **23. wash down,** to clean completely by washing: *to wash down a car.* **24. wash one's hands of.** See **hand** (def. 74). **25. wash out, a.** to rid of something by washing: *to wash out stains.* **b.** to damage or demolish by the action of water: *The embankment was washed out by the storm.* **c.** *Slang.* to fail to qualify or continue; be eliminated: *to wash out of graduate school.* **26. wash up, a.** to wash one's face and hands: *Aren't you going to wash up? Dinner is almost ready.* **b.** to wash (dishes, flatware, pots, etc.): *I'll wash up the dishes, don't bother. We had someone in to wash up after the party.* **c.** to end, esp. ignominiously (usually in the passive): *After that performance, he's all washed up as a singer.* —*n.* **27.** the act or process of washing with water or other liquid: *to give the car a wash.* **28.** a quantity of clothes, linens, etc., washed, or to be washed, at one time: *a heavy wash.* **29.** a liquid with which something is washed, wetted, colored, overspread, etc.: *He gave the building a wash of pale blue.* **30.** the flow, sweep, dash, or breaking of water: *The wash of the waves had drenched us.* **31.** the sound made by this: *listening to the wash of the Atlantic.* **32.** water moving along in waves or with a rushing movement: *the wash of the incoming tide.* **33.** the rough or broken water left behind a moving ship, boat, etc.; wake: *The little boats tossed about in the wash from the liner's propellers.* **34.** *Aeron.* the disturbance in the air left behind by a moving airplane or any of its parts: *wing wash.* **35.** any of various liquids for grooming or cosmetic purposes: *a hair wash.* **36.** a lotion or other liquid having medicinal properties, as an antiseptic solution or the like (often used in combination): *to apply wash to a skinned knee; mouthwash; eyewash.* **37.** *Mining.* minerals from which valuable material can be extracted by washing. **38.** the wearing away of the shore by breaking waves. **39.** a tract of land washed by the action of the sea or a river. **40.** a marsh, fen, or bog. **41.** a small stream or shallow pool. **42.** a shallow arm of the sea or a shallow part of a river. **43.** a depression or channel formed by flowing water. **44.** *Geol.* alluvial matter transferred and deposited by flowing water. **45.** Also called **dry wash.** *Western U.S.* the dry bed of an intermittent stream. **46.** a broad, thin layer of color applied by a continuous movement of the brush, as in water-color painting. **47.** Also called **watershed, weathering.** *Archit.* **a.** an upper surface so inclined as to shed rain water from a building. **b.** any member of a building having such a surface. **48.** a thin coat of metal applied in liquid form: *a gold wash.* **49.** waste liquid matter, refuse food, etc., from the kitchen, as for hogs; swill (often used in combination): *hogwash.* **50.** washy or weak liquor or liquid food. **51.** the fermented wort from which the spirit is extracted in distilling. **52. come out in the wash, a.** to have a good or satisfactory result; turn out eventually: *The situation may look hopeless now, but it will all come out in the wash.* **b.** to be revealed; become known. —*adj.* **53.** capable of being washed without shrinking, fading, etc.; washable: *a wash dress.* [ME; OE *wasc(an)* (c. D *wasschen*, G *waschen*, Icel *vaska*) < Gmc **watskan*, equiv. to *wat-* (see WATER) + *-sk-* v. suffix + *-an* inf. suffix]

—**Syn. 1.** clean, lave, rinse, launder, scrub, mop, swab. **4.** bedew. **5.** bathe. **27.** ablution, cleansing, bathing. **40.** swamp, morass.

Wash (wosh, wôsh), *n.* **1. The,** a shallow bay of the North Sea, on the coast of E England. 20 mi. long; 15 mi. wide. **2.** a boy's given name, form of **Washburn** or **Washington.**

Wash., Washington (defs. 4, 5).

wash·a·ble (wosh′ə bəl, wô′shə-), *adj.* capable of being washed without shrinking, fading, or the like. [WASH + -ABLE] —**wash′a·bil′i·ty,** *n.*

wash′ and wear′, noting or pertaining to a garment that can be washed, that dries quickly, and that requires little or no ironing; drip-dry.

wash·board (wosh′bōrd′, -bôrd′, wôsh′-), *n.* **1.** a rectangular board or frame, typically with a corrugated metallic surface, on which clothes are rubbed in the process of washing. **2.** a baseboard around the walls of a room. **3.** Also called **splashboard.** *Naut.* **a.** a thin, broad plank fastened to and projecting above the gunwale or side of a boat to keep out the spray and sea. **b.** a similar board on the sill of a port. [WASH + BOARD]

wash·bowl (wosh′bōl′, wôsh′-), *n.* a large bowl or basin used for washing one's hands and face, small articles of clothing, etc. Also called **wash·ba·sin** (wosh′bā′sin, wôsh′-). [WASH + BOWL[1]]

Wash·burn (wosh′bûrn, wôsh′-), *n.* a boy's given name.

wash·cloth (wosh′klôth′, -kloth′, wôsh′-), *n., pl.* **-cloths** (-klôthz′, -klothz′, -klôths′, -kloths′). a small cloth for washing one's face or body. [WASH + CLOTH]

wash·day (wosh′dā′, wôsh′-), *n.* the day set apart in a household for washing clothes: *Monday is always washday at our house.* [WASH + DAY]

washed-out (wosht′out′, wôsht′-), *adj.* **1.** faded, esp. from washing. **2.** *Informal.* **a.** weary; exhausted. **b.** tired-looking; wan. [adj. use of v. phrase *wash out*]

washed-up (wosht′up′, wôsht′-), *adj. Informal.* done for; having failed completely. [adj. use of v. phrase *wash up*]

wash·er (wosh′ər, wô′shər), *n.* **1.** one who or that which washes. **2.** a machine or apparatus for washing something. **3.** a flat ring or perforated piece of leather, rubber, metal, etc., used to give tightness to a joint, to prevent leakage, to distribute pressure, etc., as under the head of a nut or bolt. [ME; see WASH, -ER[1]] —**wash′er·less,** *adj.*

wash·er·man (wosh′ər mən, wô′shər-), *n., pl.* **-men. 1.** a man who washes clothes, linens, etc., for hire; laundryman. **2.** a man who operates a machine for washing, as in a phase of a manufacturing process. [WASHER + MAN[1]]

wash·er·wom·an (wosh′ər wo͝om′ən, wô′shər-), *n., pl.* **-wom·en.** a woman who washes clothes, linens, etc., for hire; laundress. [WASHER + WOMAN]

wash·er·y (wosh′ə rē, wô′shə-), *n., pl.* **-er·ies.** *Mining.* the area at a mine where minerals are sorted, washed, and delivered for shipment. [WASH + -ERY]

wash′ goods′, textiles that will not fade or become weakened by washing.

wash·in (wosh′in′, wôsh′-), *n. Aeron.* a warp in an airfoil which gives an increase in the angle of attack toward the tip. Also, **wash′-in′.** Cf. **washout** (def. 3). [n. use of v. phrase *wash in*]

wash·i·ness (wosh′ē nis, wô′shē-), *n.* the state or quality of being washy. [WASHY + -NESS]

wash·ing (wosh′ing, wô′shing), *n.* **1.** the act of one who or that which washes; ablution. **2.** clothes, linens, etc., washed or to be washed, esp. those washed at one time; wash. **3.** Often, **washings.** any liquid that has been used to wash something. **4.** matter removed or carried off in washing something or by the force of water: *The washings from numerous spring floods had clogged the mouth of the river.* **5.** material, as gold dust, obtained by washing earth, gravel, etc. 6. a placer or other superficial deposit which has been washed by prospectors or miners. 7. a thin coating or covering applied in liquid form: *a washing of gold on the Capitol dome.* 8. the act of making a wash sale. [ME *wasschunge.* See WASH, -ING[1]]

wash′ing machine′, an apparatus, esp. a household appliance, for washing clothing, linens, etc.

wash′ing so′da. See **sodium carbonate** (def. 2).

Wash·ing·ton (wosh′ing tən, wôsh′ing-), *n.* **1. Boo·ker T(al·ia·ferro)** (bo͝ok′ər tol′ə vər), 1856–1915, U.S. reformer, educator, author, and lecturer. **2. George,** 1732–99, 1st president of the U.S. 1789–97. **3. Martha** (*Martha Dandridge*), 1732–1802, wife of George. **4.** Also called **Washington, D.C.** the capital of the United States, on the Potomac between Maryland and Virginia: coextensive with the District of Columbia. 637,651. *Abbr.:* Wash. **5.** Also called **Washington State.** a State in the NW United States, on the Pacific coast. 2,853,214 (1960); 68,192 sq. mi. *Cap.:* Olympia. *Abbr.:* Wash. **6.** a city in SW Pennsylvania. 23,545 (1960). **7.** a town in E North Carolina. 9939 (1960). **8.** a town in central Missouri. 7961 (1960). **9.** a town in SE Iowa. 6037 (1960). **10.** a town in central Illinois. 5919 (1960). **11.** a town in NW New Jersey. 5723 (1960). **12.** a town in NE Georgia. 4440 (1960). **13. Mount,** a mountain in N New Hampshire, in the White Mountains: highest peak in the NE United States. 6293 ft. **14. Lake,** a lake in W Washington, near Seattle. 20 mi. long. **15.** a boy's given name.

Wash·ing·to·ni·an (wosh′ing tō′nē ən, wôsh′ing-), *adj.* **1.** living in or coming from Washington, D.C., or the State of Washington. —*n.* **2.** a native or inhabitant of Washington, D.C., or the State of Washington. [WASHINGTON + -IAN]

Wash′ington lil′y, a bulbous herb, *Lilium washingtonianum,* of the western coast of the U.S., having fragrant, purple-spotted, white flowers.

Wash′ington palm′, either of two fan palms, *Washingtonia filifera* or *W. gracilis* (*robusta*), of southern California and adjacent regions.

Wash′ington Park′, a town in SW Illinois. 6601 (1960).

Wash′ington pie′, a Boston cream pie, with raspberry jam instead of custard between the layers.

Wash′ington's Birth′day, February 22, the date of birth of George Washington, observed as a legal holiday in most States of the U.S.

Wash′ington Square′, a short novel (1881) by Henry James.

Wash′ington State′, the State of Washington, esp. as distinguished from Washington, D.C.

Wash′ington Ter′race, a town in N Utah. 6441 (1960).

Wash′ington thorn′, a dense tree, *Crataegus phaenopyrum,* of the eastern coast of the U.S., having triangular leaves, small clusters of white flowers, and bright red fruit.

Wash′ington West′, a town in SW Pennsylvania. 3951 (1960).

wash′ing tub′, *Chiefly Brit.* washtub.

Wash·i·ta (wosh′i tô′, wôsh′i-), *n., pl.* **-tas,** (*esp. collectively*) **-ta.** Ouachita.

wash-leath·er (wosh′leth′ər, wôsh′-), *n.* a soft leather, usually sheepskin, dressed in imitation of chamois. Also, **wash′leath′er.**

Wa·shou·gal (wo sho͞o′gəl), *n.* a town in SW Washington. 2672 (1960).

wash·out (wosh′out′, wôsh′-), *n.* **1.** a washing out of earth, gravel, etc., by water, as from an embankment or a roadway by heavy rain, a flash flood, etc. **2.** the hole, break, or erosion produced by such a washing out. **3.** Also, **wash′-out′.** *Aeron.* a warp in an airfoil which gives a decrease in the angle of attack towards the tip. Cf. **washin. 4.** *Informal.* an utter failure. [n. use of v. phrase *wash out*]

wash·rag (wosh′rag′, wôsh′-), *n.* washcloth. [WASH + RAG[1]]

wash·room (wosh′ro͞om′, -ro͝om′, wôsh′-), *n.* a room having washbowls and other toilet facilities. [WASH + ROOM]

wash′ sale′, an illegal sale on the stock exchange in which securities appear to (but do not actually) change ownership, effected by simultaneous purchases and sales through different agents or between accomplices in order to give the appearance of wide market activity and interest in a stock.

wash·stand (wosh′stand′, wôsh′-), *n.* **1.** a piece of furniture holding a basin, pitcher, etc., for use in washing one's hands and face. **2.** a stationary fixture having faucets with running water, for the same purpose. [WASH + STAND]

wash·tub (wosh′tub′, wôsh′-), *n.* a tub for use in washing clothes, linens, etc. Also, *Brit.,* **washing tub.** [WASH + TUB]

wash-up (wosh′up′, wôsh′-), *n.* **1.** act of washing: *Allow five minutes for wash-up.* **2.** a place, as a bathroom, for washing: *The maid called from the wash-up.* [n. use of v. phrase *wash up*]

wash·wom·an (wosh′wo͝om′ən, wôsh′-), *n., pl.* **-wom·en** (-wim′ən). washerwoman. [WASH + WOMAN]

wash·y (wosh′ē, wô′shē), *adj.,* **wash·i·er, wash·i·est. 1.** diluted too much; weak: *washy coffee.* **2.** pale, thin, or weak, as if from excessive dilution; pallid: *washy coloring.* [WASH + -Y[1]]

was·n't (wuz′ənt, woz′-), contraction of *was not.*

wasp (wosp), *n.* **1.** any of numerous social or solitary, hymenopterous insects of *Vespidae, Sphecidae,* and allied families, generally having a long, slender body and narrow waist. **2.** a person who is snappish or petulant. [ME *waspe,* OE *wæsp,* metathetic var. of *wæps,* deriv. of *wæfs* (by dissimilation), equiv. to *wæf-* (see WEAVE) + suffixal *-s;* akin to D *wesp,* G *Wespe,* L *vespa*] —**wasp′like′,** *adj.*

Wasp, *Eumenes fraternus* (Length ½ in.)

WASP (wosp), *n.* **1.** a member of the Women's Airforce Service Pilots, an organization disbanded in 1944. **2.** *Often Disparaging.* a white Anglo-Saxon Protestant (as considered by minority groups to be a dominant type in American society that maintains an inflexibly clannish solidarity).

wasp·ish (wos′pish), *adj.* **1.** like or suggesting a wasp, esp. in behavior. **2.** quick to resent a trifling affront or injury; snappish. **3.** irascibly or petulantly spiteful: *waspish writing.* **4.** having a slight or slender build. [WASP + -ISH[1]] —**wasp′ish·ly,** *adv.* —**wasp′ish·ness,** *n.*
—**Syn. 2.** resentful. **3.** testy, touchy.

Wasps, The, a satirical comedy (422 B.C.) by Aristophanes.

wasp′ waist′, a woman's slender waistline, esp. when the result of tight corseting. —**wasp′-waist′ed,** *adj.*

wasp·y (wos′pē), *adj.,* **wasp·i·er, wasp·i·est.** resembling a wasp; waspish. [WASP + -Y[1]] —**wasp′i·ly,** *adv.* —**wasp′i·ness,** *n.*

was·sail (wos′əl, -āl, was′-, wo sāl′), *n.* **1.** a salutation wishing health to a person, used in England in early times when presenting a cup of drink or when drinking to the person. **2.** a festivity or revel with drinking of healths. **3.** liquor for drinking healths on festive occasions, esp. spiced ale, as on Christmas Eve and Twelfth-night. **4.** *Archaic.* a song sung in wassailing. —*v.i.* **5.** to drink healths; revel with drinking. —*v.t.* **6.** to drink to the health or success of; toast. [ME *was-hail,* equiv. to *was* be (OE *wæs,* var. of *wes,* impv. of *wesan* to be) + *hail* HALE[1] (i.e., in good health) < Scand; cf. Icel *heill* hale; r. OE *wæs hāl* be hale or whole. See WHOLE, HEAL] —**was′sail·er,** *n.*

Was·ser·mann (wä′sər mən; *Ger.* väs′ər män′), *n.* **1. Au·gust von** (ou′go͝ost fən), 1866–1925, German physician and bacteriologist. **2. Ja·kob** (yä′kôp), 1873–1934, German novelist.

Was′sermann reac′tion, a diagnostic test for syphilis using the fixation of a complement by the serum of a syphilitic individual. Also called **Was′sermann test′.** [named after A. von WASSERMANN]

wast (wost; *unstressed* wəst), *v. Archaic.* a 2nd pers. sing. pt. indic. of **be.**

Wast (väst), *n.* **Hugo,** pen name of Gustavo Martínez Zuviría.

wast·age (wā′stij), *n.* **1.** loss by use, wear, decay, etc. **2.** loss or losses as the result of wastefulness: *The annual wastage of time due to illness is appalling.* **3.** the action or process of wasting: *the steady wastage of erosion.* **4.** that which is wasted; waste or waste materials: *The river was befouled by factory wastage.* [WASTE + -AGE]

waste (wāst), *v.,* **wast·ed, wast·ing,** *n., adj.* —*v.t.* **1.** to consume, spend, or employ uselessly or without adequate return; use to no avail; squander: *to waste money; to waste words.* **2.** to fail or neglect to use: *to waste an opportunity.* **3.** to destroy or consume gradually; wear away: *The waves waste the rock of the shore.* **4.** to wear down or reduce in bodily substance, health, or strength; emaciate; enfeeble: *to be wasted by disease or hunger.* **5.** to destroy, devastate, or ruin: *a country wasted by a long and futile war.*
—*v.i.* **6.** to be consumed, spent, or employed uselessly or without giving full value or being fully utilized or appreciated. **7.** to become gradually consumed, used up, or worn away: *A candle wastes in burning.* **8.** to become physically worn; lose flesh or strength; become emaciated or enfeebled. **9.** to diminish gradually; dwindle, as wealth, power, etc.: *The might of England is wasting.* **10.** to pass gradually, as time.
—*n.* **11.** useless consumption or expenditure; use without adequate return; the act or an instance of wasting: *The project was a waste of material, money, time, and energy.* **12.** neglect, instead of use: *waste of opportunity.* **13.** gradual destruction, impairment, or decay: *the waste and repair of bodily tissue.* **14.** devastation or ruin, as from war, fire, etc. **15.** a region or place devastated or ruined: *The forest fire left a blackened waste.* **16.** anything unused, unproductive, or not properly utilized. **17.** an uncultivated tract of land. **18.** a wild region or tract of land; desolate country, desert, or the like. **19.** an empty, desolate, or dreary tract or extent: *a waste of snow.* **20.** anything left over or superfluous, as excess material, by-products, etc., not of use for the work in hand: *a fortune made in salvaging factory wastes.* **21.** remnants, as from the working of cotton, used for wiping machinery, absorbing oil, etc. **22.** *Phys. Geog.* material derived by mechanical and chemical disintegration of rock, as the detritus transported by streams, rivers, etc. **23.** garbage; refuse. **24. wastes,** excrement. **25. go to waste,** to fail to be used or consumed; be wasted: *She hates to see good food go to waste.* **26. lay waste,** to devastate; destroy; ruin: *Forest fires lay waste thousands of acres yearly.*
—*adj.* **27.** not used or in use: *waste energy; waste talents.* **28.** (of land, regions, etc.) wild, desolate, barren, or uninhabited; desert. **29.** (of regions, towns, etc.) in a state of desolation and ruin, as from devastation or decay. **30.** left over or superfluous: *to utilize waste products of manufacture.* **31.** having served or fulfilled a purpose; no longer of use. **32.** rejected as useless or worthless; refuse: *to salvage waste products.* **33.** *Physiol.* pertaining to material unused by or unusable to the organism. **34.** designed or used to receive, hold, or carry away excess, superfluous, used, or useless material (often in combination): *a waste pipe; waste container.* **35.** *Obs.* excessive; needless. [ME *wast* < AF (equiv. to OF *guast*) < OHG *wuosti* (the *-a-* < L *vastus* empty, waste)] —**wast′a·ble,** *adj.* —**waste′less,** *adj.*
—**Syn. 1.** misspend, dissipate, fritter away, expend. **3.** erode. **5.** ravage, pillage, plunder, sack, spoil, despoil. **9.** decline, perish, wane, decay. **11.** dissipation. **13.** diminution, decline, emaciation, consumption. **14.** spoliation, desolation. **18.** See **desert**[1]. **23.** rubbish, trash. **26.** See **ravage. 29.** ruined, ghostly, destroyed. **30.** unused, useless, superfluous, extra.
—**Ant. 1.** save.

waste·bas·ket (wāst′bas′kit, -bä′skit), *n.* a basket for wastepaper, small items of trash, etc., to be disposed of as refuse. Also called **wastepaper basket.** [WASTE + BASKET]

waste′ book′, *Bookkeeping Brit.* a daybook.

waste·ful (wāst′fəl), *adj.* **1.** given to or characterized by useless consumption or expenditure: *wasteful methods; a wasteful way of life.* **2.** grossly extravagant; prodigal: *a wasteful party.* **3.** devastating or destructive: *wasteful war.* [late ME; see WASTE, -FUL] —**waste′ful·ly,** *adv.* —**waste′ful·ness,** *n.*

waste·land (wāst′land′), *n.* **1.** land that is uncultivated or barren. **2.** an area which is devastated, as by flood, storm, war, etc. **3.** something, as a period of history, phase of existence, locality, etc., which is spiritually or intellectually barren: *Some New Yorkers tend to regard the rest of the country as a wasteland.* [WASTE + LAND]

Waste′ Land′, The, a poem (1922) by T. S. Eliot.

waste·lot (wāst′lot′), *n. Chiefly Canadian.* a vacant lot, esp. one overgrown with weeds or covered with rubbish. [WASTE + LOT]

waste·ness (wāst′nis), *n.* the state or condition of being waste, desolate, or the like. [late ME; see WASTE, -NESS]

waste·pa·per (wāst′pā′pər), *n.* paper thrown away as useless. [WASTE + PAPER]

waste′paper bas′ket, wastebasket.

waste·pile (wāst′pīl′), *n. Solitaire.* a pile of cards with each card turned face up, consisting of cards drawn from the stock that at the time drawn were not able to be played and that are unavailable for play temporarily or permanently. Also called **talon.** [WASTE + PILE[1]]

waste′ pipe′, **1.** a pipe for draining liquid waste or excess liquids. **2.** *Plumbing.* a pipe for draining away the wastes of a building other than those from water closets. Cf. **soil pipe.**

waste′ prod′uct, **1.** material discarded as useless in the process of producing something. **2.** feces, urine, and other material excreted in the life process.

wast·er (wā′stər), *n.* **1.** one who or that which wastes time, money, etc. **2.** a piece of ceramic ware warped, cracked, or melted during firing. **3.** a spendthrift or wastrel. **4.** a destroyer: *The Vandals were wasters of cities.* **5.** *Chiefly Brit.* wastrel (def. 2). [ME < AF *wastere.* See WASTE, -ER[1]]

waste·ry (wā′strē), *n. Scot. and North Eng.* wastry.

waste′ waste′, tin plate too defective to be acceptable, even after recoating.

waste′ well′. See **absorbing well.**

wast·ing (wā′sting), *adj.* **1.** gradually reducing the fullness and strength of the body: *a wasting disease.* **2.** laying waste; devastating; despoiling: *the ravages of a wasting war.* [ME; see WASTE, -ING[2]] —**wast′ing·ly,** *adv.* —**wast′ing·ness,** *n.*

wast·rel (wā′strəl), *n.* **1.** a wasteful person; spendthrift. **2.** *Chiefly Brit.* **a.** refuse; waste. **b.** a waif; abandoned child. **c.** an idler or good-for-nothing. [WASTE + -REL]

wast·ry (wā′strē), *n. Scot. and North Eng.* wastefulness; reckless extravagance. Also, **wastery, wast′rie.** [WASTE + -RY]

wat[1] (wat, wot), *Scot.* —*adj., n.* **1.** wet. **2.** pt. of **wet.**

wat[2] (wät), *n.* a Buddhist temple or monastery in Thailand or Cambodia. [< Thai < Skt *vāṭa* enclosure]

Wat (wot), *n.* a boy's given name, form of **Walter** or **Watkins.**

watch (woch), *v.i.* **1.** to be alertly on the lookout, look attentively, or observe, as to see what comes, is done, happens, etc.: *to watch while an experiment is performed.* **2.** to look or wait attentively and expectantly (usually fol. by *for*): *to watch for a signal; to watch for an opportunity.* **3.** to be careful or cautious: *Watch when you cross the street.* **4.** to keep awake, esp. for a purpose; remain vigilant, as for protection or safekeeping: *to watch with a sick person.* **5.** to keep vigil, as for devotional purposes. **6.** to keep guard: *He was assigned to watch at the door.* —*v.t.* **7.** to keep under attentive view or observation, as in order to see or learn something; view attentively or with interest: *to watch a play; to watch a football game.* **8.** to contemplate or regard mentally: *to watch his progress.* **9.** to look or wait attentively and expectantly for: *to watch one's opportunity.* **10.** to guard, tend, or oversee, esp. for protection or safekeeping: *to watch the baby.* **11. watch out,** to be on one's guard; be cautious: *Watch out for cars when you cross the road.* **12. watch over,** to guard for protection or safekeeping: *She watched over us like a mother hen over her brood.* —*n.* **13.** close, continuous observation for the purpose of seeing or discovering something: *Their watch for the birds was unrewarding.* **14.** vigilant guard, as for protection, restraint, etc.: *to keep watch for prowlers.* **15.** a keeping awake for some special purpose: *a watch beside a sickbed.* **16.** a period of time for watching or keeping guard: *to stand the first watch.* **17.** a small, portable timepiece. **18.** a chronometer. **19.** *Naut.* **a.** a period of time, usually four hours, during which one part of a ship's crew is on duty, taking turns with another part. **b.** a certain part, usually a half, of a vessel's officers and crew who together attend to the working of the vessel for an allotted period of time. **20.** one of the periods, usually three or four, into which the night was divided in ancient times, as by the Greeks or Hebrews: *the fourth watch of the night.* **21.** one who or those who watch, as a lookout, watchman, or body of watchmen: *A watch was posted at sunset. The watch in the crow's-nest gave the alarm.* **22.** a flock of nightingales. **23. on the watch,** vigilant; alert: *The hunter was on the watch for moving objects.* **24. watch and watch,** *Naut.* noting a system of watches stood by two groups of men in alternation. [ME *wacche,* OE *wæccan,* doublet of *wacian* to wake]
—**Syn. 1.** WATCH, LOOK, SEE imply being aware of things around one by perceiving them through the eyes. To WATCH is to be a spectator, to look on or observe, or to fix the attention upon during passage of time: *to watch while a procession passes.* To LOOK is to direct the gaze with the intention of seeing, to use the eyesight with attention: *to look for violets in the spring; to look at articles displayed for sale.* To SEE is to perceive with the eyes, to obtain a visual impression, with or without fixing the attention: *animals able to see in the dark.* **9.** await. **10.** protect. **13.** inspection, attention. **14.** vigil. **21.** sentry, sentinel, guard.

watch′ and ward′, a continuous watch or vigil, by or as by night and by day, esp. for the purpose of guarding: *He established a watch and ward society to guard the community's morals.*

watch·band (woch′band′), *n.* a metal, fabric, or leather bracelet or strap attached to a wrist watch to hold it on the wrist. [WATCH + BAND[2]]

watch′ cap′, *U.S. Navy.* a knitted woolen cap worn by enlisted men on duty in cold weather.

watch·case (woch′kās′), *n.* the case or outer covering for the works of a watch. [WATCH + CASE[2]]

watch′ chain′, a chain, frequently of gold or silver, often attached to a pocket watch, serving as an ornament and, when passed through a buttonhole in the vest, as a guard against loss or theft of the watch.

watch·cry (woch′krī′), *n., pl.* **-cries.** watchword.

watch·dog (woch′dôg′, -dog′), *n.* **1.** a dog kept to guard property. **2.** a watchful guardian: *a self-appointed watchdog of the public morals.* [WATCH + DOG]

watch·er (woch′ər), *n.* **1.** a person who watches or who keeps watch. **2.** See **poll watcher.** [WATCH + -ER[1]]

watch′ fire′, a fire maintained during the night as a signal and for providing light and warmth for guards.

watch·ful (woch′fəl), *adj.* **1.** vigilant or alert; closely observant: *The sentry remained watchful throughout the night.* **2.** characterized by vigilance or alertness: *The scientist has a sharp and watchful eye.* **3.** *Archaic.* wakeful. [WATCH + -FUL] —**watch′ful·ly,** *adv.* —**watch′ful·ness,** *n.*
—**Syn. 1.** attentive, heedful, careful, circumspect, cautious, wary. See **alert.**

watch′ guard′, a short chain, cord, or ribbon for securing a watch when worn on the person.

watch·less (woch′lis), *adj.* **1.** not watchful or alert; lacking in vigilance: *an irresponsible and watchless sentry.* **2.** having no watchman; without guards or sentries: *We welcomed the watchless nights of peacetime.* [WATCH + -LESS] —**watch′less·ness,** *n.*

watch·mak·er (woch′mā′kər), *n.* a person whose occupation it is to make and repair watches. [WATCH + MAKER] —**watch′mak′ing,** *n.*

watch·man (woch′mən), *n., pl.* **-men. 1.** a person who keeps guard over a building at night, to protect it from fire or thieves. **2.** (formerly) a person who guards or patrols the streets at night. [late ME; see WATCH, MAN[1]] —**watch′man·ly,** *adj.*

watch′ meet′ing, a religious meeting or service on watch night, terminating on the arrival of the new year. Also called **watch′-night serv′ice** (woch′nīt′).

watch′ night′, **1.** the last night of the year, observed in a watch meeting. **2.** See **watch meeting.**

watch·out (woch′out′), *n.* the act of looking out for or anticipating something; lookout: *Keep a watchout for dishonest behavior.* [n. use of v. phrase *watch out*]

watch′ pock′et, a small pocket in a garment, as in a vest or trousers, for holding a pocket watch, change, etc. Cf. **fob**[1] (def. 1).

watch′ tack′le, a small tackle used for hauling, as a luff tackle, esp. on the decks of vessels.

watch·tow·er (woch′tou′ər), *n.* a tower on which a sentinel keeps watch. [WATCH + TOWER]

Wat·chung (wä chung′, wä′chung), *n.* a town in central New Jersey. 3312 (1960).

watch·word (woch′wûrd′), *n.* **1.** a word or short phrase to be communicated, on challenge, to a sentinel or guard; password or countersign. **2.** a word or phrase expressive of a principle or rule of action; slogan: *Conservation has been our watchword.* **3.** a rallying cry of a party, club, team, etc. [late ME; see WATCH, WORD]
—**Syn. 1, 2.** shibboleth. **3.** motto.

wa·ter (wô′tər, wot′ər), *n.* **1.** a transparent, odorless, tasteless liquid, a compound of hydrogen and oxygen, H_2O, freezing at 32°F or 0°C and boiling at 212°F or 100°C, which in a more or less impure state constitutes rain, oceans, lakes, rivers, etc.: it contains 11.188 percent hydrogen and 88.812 percent oxygen, by weight. **2.** a special form or variety of this liquid, as rain. **3.** Often, **waters.** this liquid in an impure state as obtained from a mineral spring: *Last year we went to Marienbad for the waters.* **4.** the liquid content of a river, inlet, etc., with reference to its relative height esp. as dependent on tide: *a difference of 20 feet between high and low water.* **5.** that which enters a vessel through leaks or over the side: *The ship was taking water at an alarming rate.* **6.** the surface of a stream, river, lake, ocean, etc.: *above, below, or on the water.* **7. waters, a.** flowing water, or water moving in waves: *The river's mighty waters.* **b.** the sea or seas bordering a particular country or continent or located in a particular part of the world: *We left San Diego and sailed south for Mexican waters.* **8.** a liquid solution or preparation, esp. one used for cosmetic purposes: *lavender water; lemon water.* **9.** any of various solutions of volatile or gaseous substances in water: *ammonia water.* **10.** any liquid or aqueous organic secretion, exudation, humor, or the like, as tears, perspiration, urine, the amniotic fluids, etc. **11.** *Finance.* fictitious assets or the inflated values they give to the stock of a corporation. **12.** a wavy, lustrous pattern or marking, as on silk fabrics, metal surfaces, etc. **13.** *Jewelry.* the degree of transparency and brilliancy of a diamond or other precious stone. **14. above water,** out of embarrassment or trouble, esp. of a financial nature: *His wife had extravagant tastes, and they never seemed to be able to get above water.* **15. break water, a.** any object emerging from water, as a fish, anchor, or submarine. **b.** *Swimming.* to break the surface of the water with the feet, esp. in swimming the breast stroke doing the frog kick. **c.** to break the amniotic sac prior to parturition. **16. by water,** by ship or boat: *It was much less expensive to send the goods by water.* **17. hold water, a.** to be logical, defensible, or valid: *That accusation won't hold any water.* **b.** to check the movement of a rowboat by keeping the oars steady with the blades vertical. **18. in deep water,** *Slang.* in great distress or difficulty; in a dangerous situation: *Their marriage has been in deep water for some time.* **19. in hot water.** See **hot water. 20. like water,** lavishly; abundantly; freely: *The champagne flowed like water.* **21. make water, a.** (of a boat) to allow water to enter; leak. **b.** to urinate.
—*v.t.* **22.** to sprinkle, moisten, or drench with water: *to water the flowers; to water a street.* **23.** to supply (animals) with water for drinking. **24.** to furnish with a supply of water, as a ship. **25.** to furnish water to (a region), as by streams; supply (land) with water, as by irrigation: *The valley is watered by a branch of the Colorado River. Our land is watered by the All-American Canal.* **26.** to dilute, weaken, soften, or adulterate with, or as with, water (often fol. by *down*): *to water soup; to water down an unfavorable report.* **27.** *Finance.* to issue or increase the par value of (shares of stock) without having the assets to warrant doing so (often fol. by *down*). **28.** to produce a wavy, lustrous pattern, marking, or finish on (fabrics, metals, etc.): *watered silk.*
—*v.i.* **29.** to discharge, fill with, or secrete water or liquid, as the eyes when irritated, or as the mouth at the sight or thought of tempting food. **30.** to drink water, as an animal. **31.** to take in a supply of water, as a ship: *Our ship will water at Savannah.* **32. make (someone's) mouth water,** to excite a desire or appetite for something: *The roasting turkey made our mouths water.*
—*adj.* **33.** of or pertaining to water in any way: *a water journey.* **34.** holding, or designed to hold, water: *a water jug.* **35.** worked or powered by water: *a water turbine.* **36.** heating, pumping, or circulating water (often used in combination): *hot-water furnace; city waterworks.* **37.** used in or on water: *water skis.* **38.** containing or prepared with water, as for hardening, dilution, etc.: *water mortar.* **39.** located or occurring on, in, or by water: *water music; water frontage.* **40.** residing by or in, or ruling over, water: *water people; water deities.* [ME; OE *wæter;* c. G *Wasser,* D *water;* akin to Icel *vatn,* Goth *wato*] —**wa′ter·er,** *n.* —**wa′ter·less,** *adj.* —**wa′ter·less·ly,** *adv.* —**wa′ter·less·ness,** *n.* —**wa′ter·like′,** *adj.*

wa·ter·age (wô′tər ij, wot′ər-), *n.* *Brit.* **1.** the shipping of freight over water routes; transportation of freight by water. **2.** the cost of such shipping; freight charges. [WATER + -AGE]

wa′ter ar′um, an aquatic herb, *Calla palustris,* of the North Temperate Zone, having minute, green flowers and red berries. Also called **wild calla.**

wa′ter back′, a reservoir or arrangement of tubing at the back of certain stoves or fireplaces for containing water to be heated by the fire.

wa′ter ballet′, a series of synchronized movements, patterns, and other visual effects performed in the water by swimmers before an audience, usually to a musical accompaniment.

wa′ter bath′, **1.** a system for the control of temperature in which a vessel containing the material to be heated is set into one containing water and receiving the heat directly. **2.** a bath of water.

Wa′ter Bear′er, *Astron., Astrol.* Aquarius. [ME *waterberere,* OE *wæterberere*] —**wa′ter-bear′ing,** *adj.*

wa′ter·bed (wô′tər bed′, wot′ər-), *n.* a vinyl mattress-shaped bag filled with water and placed on a bedframe, for making the surface conform to the sleeper's body in any position.

Water beetle; ***Captotomus interrogatus*** **(Length ½ in.)**

wa′ter bee′tle, any of various aquatic beetles, as a predaceous diving beetle.

wa′ter bench′, a Pennsylvania Dutch dresser having a lower portion closed with doors for milk pails, an open shelf for water pails, and an upper section with shallow drawers. Also called **bucket bench, milk bench.**

wa′ter bird′, an aquatic bird; a swimming or wading bird.

wa′ter bis′cuit, a crackerlike biscuit prepared from flour and water.

wa′ter blis′ter, a blister which contains a clear, serous fluid, as distinguished from a blood blister in which the fluid is sanguineous.

wa′ter boat′, a vessel for supplying ships with fresh water.

wa′ter boat′man, any of numerous aquatic insects of the family *Corixidae* that have paddlelike hind legs. Also called **boat bug.**

wa′ter bomb′, a paper bag filled with water for dropping from a height, as from the window of the upper story of a house, upon a passer-by below.

wa·ter·borne (wô′tər bōrn′, -bôrn′, wot′ər-), *adj.* **1.** floating or moving on water; supported by water: *The ship was waterborne ten months after the keel was laid.* **2.** transported by ship or boat: *waterborne commerce.* **3.** communicated by water, esp. drinking water: *waterborne diseases.* [WATER + BORNE]

wa′ter bot′tle, *Chiefly Brit.* canteen (def. 1).

wa′ter bou′get (bo͞o′jit), **1.** (formerly) a leather bag suspended at each end of a pole or yoke and used for carrying water. **2.** Also, **wa′ter budg′et.** *Heraldry.* a representation of a pair of these joined by a yoke, used as a charge. [*bouget,* var. of BUDGET]

wa′ter boy′, **1.** a person who carries a canteen or bucket of drinking water to those too occupied to fetch it, as to soldiers, laborers, football players, etc. **2.** a person who sees that livestock is supplied with water, as by filling water troughs.

wa·ter·brain (wô′tər brān′, wot′ər-), *n.* *Vet. Pathol.* gid, in sheep. [WATER + BRAIN]

Waterbuck, ***Kobus ellipsiprymnus*** **(4 ft. high at shoulder; horns 2½ ft.; total length 6 ft.; tail 10 in.)**

wa′ter brash′, *Pathol.* heartburn (def. 1).

wa·ter·buck (wô′tər buk′, wot′ər-), *n.* any of several large African antelopes of the genus *Kobus* frequenting marshes and reedy places, esp. *K. ellipsiprymnus,* of southern and central Africa. [WATER + BUCK[1]]

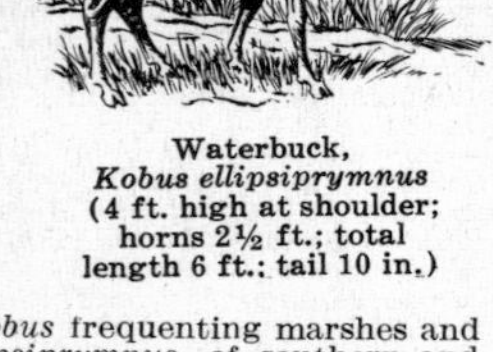

Water buffalo (5½ ft. high at shoulder; length 9 ft.)

wa′ter buf′falo, a buffalo, *Bubalus bubalis,* of the Old World tropics, having large, flattened, curved horns. Also called **water ox.**

wa′ter bug′, **1.** any of various aquatic hemipterous insects, as of the family *Belostomatidae* **(giant water bug). 2.** (loosely) a cockroach.

Wa·ter·bur·y (wô′tər ber′ē, -bə rē, wot′ər-), *n.* **1.** a city in W Connecticut. 107,130 (1960). **2.** a town in central Vermont. 2984 (1960).

wa′ter chest′nut, **1.** any aquatic plant of the genus *Trapa,* bearing an edible, nutlike fruit, esp. *T. natans,* of the Old World. **2.** the fruit itself. Also called **wa′ter cal′trop.**

wa′ter chin′quapin, **1.** an American lotus, *Nelumbo lutea,* having pale-yellow flowers and an edible seed. **2.** the seed itself, similar in flavor to the chinquapin.

wa′ter clock′, a device, as a clepsydra, for measuring time by the flow of water.

wa′ter clos′et, **1.** *Chiefly Brit.* an enclosed room or compartment containing a toilet bowl fitted with a mechanism for flushing. **2.** *Dial.* a privy or bathroom.

wa·ter·col·or (wô′tər kul′ər, wot′ər-), *n.* **1.** a pigment for which water and not oil is used as a vehicle. **2.** the art or technique of painting with such pigments. **3.** a painting or design executed in such pigments by this technique. Also, *esp. Brit.,* **wa′ter·col′our.** [WATER + COLOR] —**wa′ter-col′or;** *esp. Brit.,* **wa′ter-col′our,** *adj.* —**wa′ter·col′or·ist;** *esp. Brit.,* **wa′ter-col′our·ist,** *n.*

wa·ter-cool (wô′tər ko͞ol′, wot′ər-), *v.t.* to cool by means of water, esp. by water circulating in pipes or a water jacket, as an engine, machine gun, etc.

wa′ter cool′er, **1.** a bottle or other container for holding drinking water which is cooled, as by ice, and drawn off for use by a faucet or spigot. **2.** a drinking fountain in which water is cooled by mechanical refrigeration.

wa·ter·course (wô′tər kōrs′, -kôrs′, wot′ər-), *n.* **1.** a stream of water, as a river or brook. **2.** the bed of a stream which flows only seasonally. **3.** a natural channel conveying water. **4.** a channel or canal made for the conveyance of water. [WATER + COURSE]

wa·ter·craft (wô′tər kraft′, -kräft′, wot′ər-), *n.* **1.** skill in boating and water sports. **2.** any boat or ship. **3.** boats and ships collectively. [WATER + CRAFT]

wa′ter crake′, **1.** *Brit.* the spotted crake. **2.** *Brit. Dial.* the water ouzel, *Cinclus aquaticus.*

wa·ter·cress (wô′tər kres′, wot′ər-), *n.* **1.** a perennial cress, *Rorippa Nasturtium officinale,* usually growing in clear, running water, and having pungent leaves. **2.** the leaves, used for salads, soups, and as a garnish. [ME; c. MD, MLG *waterkerse.* See WATER, CRESS]

wa′ter cure′, **1.** hydropathy; hydrotherapy. **2.** a method of torture in which the victim is forced to drink great quantities of water.

wa′ter cur′tain, a sheet of water from a series of sprinklers for protecting the walls and roof of a building from fires outside the building.

wa′ter dog′, **1.** a dog that swims well or is trained to retrieve waterfowl in hunting. **2.** *Informal.* a person who feels at home in or on the water.

wa·ter·dog (wô′tər dôg′, -dog′, wot′ər-), *n.* any of several large salamanders, as a mudpuppy or hellbender. [WATER + DOG]

wa·tered-down (wô′tərd doun′, wot′ərd-), *adj.* made weaker or less effective from or as from dilution with water: *a watered-down cocktail; Spectators saw a watered-down version of the famous opera.*

wa′tered steel′, hand-wrought steel, made in various Asian countries, from parts of a bloom of heterogeneous composition, repeatedly folded over and welded and finally etched to reveal the resulting grain: used esp. for sword blades. Also called **Damascus steel, damask, damask steel.**

Wa·ter·ee (wô′tə rē′, wot′ə-), *n.* a river flowing from W North Carolina into South Carolina, joining the Congaree River to form the Santee River. Cf. **Catawba** (def. 4).

wa·ter·fall (wô′tər fôl′, wot′ər-), *n.* **1.** a steep fall or flow of water in a watercourse from a height, as over a precipice; cascade. **2.** a manner of arranging women's hair, as in long, loose waves. [ME; OE *wætergefeall.* See WATER, FALL]

wa·ter-fast (wô′tər fast′, -fäst′, wot′ər-), *adj.* (of a color or dye) resistant to the effects caused by water; not changed or faded by the action of water.

wa′ter feath′er, **1.** a water milfoil, *Myriophyllum proserpinacoides.* **2.** a North American featherfoil, *Hottonia inflata.*

wa·ter·find·er (wô′tər fīn′dər, wot′ər-), *n.* a person who uses a divining rod to discover a source of water in the ground; dowser or water witch. [WATER + FINDER]

wa′ter flag′, a European iris, *Iris pseudacorus,* naturalized throughout eastern North America, having bluish-green leaves and violet-veined, yellow flowers, and growing in moist places. Also called **yellow flag.**

wa′ter flea′, any of various small crustaceans which move about in the water like fleas, as *Daphnia.*

Wa·ter·ford (wô′tər fərd, wot′ər-), *n.* **1.** a county in Munster province, in the S Republic of Ireland. 71,439 (1961); 710 sq. mi. **2.** its county seat: a seaport. 28,216 (1961). **3.** a town in E New York. 2915 (1960).

wa′ter foun′tain, a drinking fountain, water cooler, or other apparatus supplying drinking water.

wa·ter·fowl (wô′tər foul′, wot′ər-), *n., pl.* **-fowls,** (*esp. collectively*) **-fowl. 1.** a water bird, esp. a swimming bird. **2.** such birds taken collectively, esp. the swans, geese, and ducks. [ME; c. G *Wasservogel.* See WATER, FOWL]

wa′ter frame′, an early spinning machine driven by water power.

wa·ter·front (wô′tər frunt′, wot′ər-), *n.* **1.** land on the edge of a body of water. **2.** a part of a city or town on such land; wharf or dock section. **3.** a container placed before a stove to heat water. [WATER + FRONT]

wa′ter gap′, a transverse gap in a mountain ridge, cut by and giving passage to a stream.

wa′ter gas′, a toxic gaseous mixture consisting chiefly of carbon monoxide and hydrogen, prepared from steam and incandescent coke: used as an illuminant, fuel, and in organic synthesis. Also called **blue gas.** —**wa′ter-gas′,** *adj.*

wa′ter gate′, **1.** a gate for halting or controlling the flow of water in a watercourse; floodgate. **2.** a gateway leading to the edge of a body of water, as at a landing. [late ME]

Wa·ter·gate (wô′tər gāt′, wot′ər-), *n.* **1.** a political scandal involving the break-in in 1972 at Democratic party headquarters in Washington, D.C., by men connected with the Republican reelection campaign for President Nixon, and other illegal activities including attempts to cover up evidence related to the break-in, which resulted in Nixon's resignation in 1974. **2.** any political scandal involving improper use of governmental office for partisan or personal advantage, usually by bribery, special-interest deals, and other illegal or unethical activities. [from the name of the building in which the break-in occurred]

wa′ter gauge′, any device for indicating the height of water in a reservoir, tank, boiler, or other vessel.

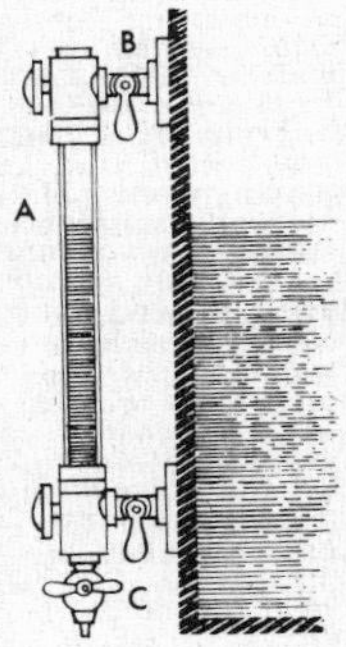

wa′ter glass′, **1.** a drinking glass; tumbler. **2.** a glass container for holding water, as for growing bulbs, plants, or the like. **3.** a glass tube used to indicate water level, as in a boiler. **4.** a device for observing objects beneath the surface of the water, consisting essentially of an open tube or box with a glass bottom. **5.** See **sodium silicate.** Also, **wa′ter-glass′.**

wa′terglass paint′ing, stereochromy.

wa′ter gum′, **1.** (in the U.S.) a tupelo, *Nyssa sylvatica biflora,* of the southern States. **2.** (in Australia) any of several myrtaceous trees growing near water.

wa′ter gun′. See **water pistol.**

wa′ter ham′mer, **1.** the concussion which results when a moving volume of water in a pipe is suddenly stopped. **2.** a tube or other container partially filled with water and exhausted of air, the shaking of which causes the water to strike the sides of the container and to produce a sound similar to that produced by a hammer.

Water gauge for boiler
A, Water level
B, Upper cock
C, Lower cock

wa′ter haw′thorn. See **Cape pondweed.**

wa′ter heat′er, a household appliance consisting of a gas or electric heating unit under a tank in which water is heated and stored.

wa′ter hem′lock, any poisonous, umbelliferous plant of the genus *Cicuta,* as *C. virosa* of Europe, and *C. maculata* of North America, growing in swamps and marshy places.

wa′ter hen′, **1.** the moorhen or gallinule, *Gallinula chlorpus,* of Europe. **2.** the coot, *Fulica americana.*

wa′ter hole′, **1.** a depression in the surface of the ground, containing water. **2.** a source of drinking water, as a spring, well, etc., in the desert. **3.** a pond; pool. **4.** a cavity containing water in the dry bed of a river. **5.** a hole in the frozen surface of a lake, pond, stream, etc.

wa′ter hol′ly. See **Oregon grape** (def. 3).

wa′ter hy′acinth, a tropical, floating aquatic plant, *Eichornia crassipes,* that grows so prolifically it often hinders passage of boats by blanketing the surface of the water.

wa′ter ice′, **1.** ice formed by direct freezing of fresh or salt water, and not by compacting of snow. **2.** a frozen dessert, similar to sherbet, made of water, sweetener, and fruit syrup or other flavorings.

wa·ter-inch (wô′tər inch′, wot′ər-), *n. Hydraulics.* the quantity of water (approx. 500 cubic feet) discharged in 24 hours through a circular opening of 1 inch diameter leading from a reservoir in which the water is constantly only high enough to cover the orifice.

wa·ter·i·ness (wô′tə rē nis, wot′ə-), *n.* the state or condition of being watery or diluted. [WATERY + -NESS]

wa·ter·ing (wô′tər ing, wot′ər-), *n.* **1.** the act of one who or that which waters. **2.** a watered appearance on silk or other fabric. —*adj.* **3.** supplying water or used to water. **4.** pertaining to medicinal springs or to a seabathing resort. [ME (n.); OE *wæterung.* See WATER, -ING¹, -ING²]

wa′tering can′. See **watering pot.**

wa′tering place′, **1.** *Brit.* a seaside or lakeside vacation resort featuring bathing, boating, etc. **2.** *Chiefly Brit.* a health resort near mineral springs, a lake, or the sea, featuring therapeutic baths, water cures, or the like. **3.** a place where drinking water may be obtained by men or animals, as a spring, water hole, etc. [late ME *watrynge place*]

wa′tering pot′, a container for water, typically of metal and having a spout with a perforated nozzle, for watering or sprinkling plants, flowers, etc. Also called **watering can, sprinkling can.**

wa·ter·ish (wô′tər ish, wot′ər-), *adj.* somewhat, or tending to be, watery. [WATER + -ISH¹] —**wa′ter·ish·ly,** *adv.* —**wa′ter·ish·ness,** *n.*

wa′ter jack′et, a casing or compartment containing water, placed about something to keep it cool or otherwise regulate its temperature, as around the cylinder or cylinders of an internal-combustion engine.

wa·ter-jack·et (wô′tər jak′it, wot′ər-), *v.t.* to surround or fit with a water jacket.

wa′ter jump′, any small body of water which a horse must jump over, as in a steeplechase.

wa·ter-laid (wô′tər lād′, wot′ər-), *adj. Ropemaking.* noting a rope laid left-handed from three or four plain-laid ropes, in the making of which water was used to wet the fibers instead of the more customary oil or tallow.

wa′ter lance′, *Mach.* a lance using water.

wa·ter-lance (wô′tər lans′, -läns′, wot′ər-), *v.t.,* **-lanced, -lanc·ing.** to clean with a water lance.

wa′ter leaf′, **1.** *Papermaking.* paper before sizing, when still water-absorbent. **2.** Also called **Lesbian leaf.** (in Greek architecture and sculpture) a motif of heart-shaped leaves having a conspicuous midrib.

wa·ter·leaf (wô′tər lēf′, wot′ər-), *n., pl.* **-leafs, -leaves. 1.** an herb, *Hydrophyllum canadense,* of eastern North America, having white flowers. **2.** Also called **Indian salad, Shawnee salad.** a related perennial herb, *H. virginianum,* of eastern North America, having white or violet-purple flowers. [WATER + LEAF]

wa′ter lem′on. See **yellow granadilla.**

wa·ter·less (wô′tər lis, wot′ər-), *adj.* **1.** devoid of water; dry. **2.** needing no water, as for cooking. [ME *waterlees,* OE *wæterlēas.* See WATER, -LESS] —**wa′ter·less·ly,** *adv.* —**wa′ter·less·ness,** *n.*

wa′terless cook′er, **1.** a tight-lidded kitchen utensil in which food can be cooked using only a small amount of water or only the juices emitted while cooking. **2.** See **pressure cooker.**

wa′ter let′tuce, a floating, aquatic plant, *Pistia Stratiotes,* having a rosette of thick, spongy leaves.

wa′ter lev′el, **1.** the surface level of any body of water. **2.** the level to which a vessel is immersed; water line.

wa′ter light′, *Naut.* a signal attached to a life buoy, consisting of a can filled with a chemical composition that ignites upon contact with the water.

wa′ter lil′y, **1.** any aquatic plant of the genus *Nymphaea,* species of which have large, disklike, floating leaves and showy, fragrant flowers, esp. *N. odorata,* of America or *N. alba,* of Europe. **2.** any plant of the genus *Nuphar.* **3.** a nymphaeaceous plant. **4.** the flower of any such plant.

Water lily, *Nymphaea odorata*

wa′ter lil′y tu′lip, a showy tulip, *Tulipa kaufmanniana,* of Turkestan, having spreading, white or pale-yellow flowers with red-marked, yellow centers.

wa′ter line′, **1.** *Naut.* **a.** the part of the outside of a ship's hull that is just at the water level. **b.** See **load line. 2.** *Naval Archit.* any of a series of lines on the hull plans of a vessel representing the intersection of a series of parallel horizontal planes with the form of the hull, usually taken as the inner surface of the shell: appears on the sheer plan as a straight line parallel to some base line, as the level to which the vessel is immersed or the bottom of the keel, on the half-breadth plan as a curved or angular form, and on the body plan as a horizontal straight or slightly curved line. **3.** the line in which water at its surface borders upon a floating body. **4.** See **water level** (def. 1). **5.** Also called **watermark.** a line indicating the former level or passage of water: *A water line all around the cellar served as a reminder of the flood.* **6.** a pipe, hose, tube, or other line for conveying water. Also, **wa′ter-line′.**

wa·ter·locked (wô′tər lokt′, wot′ər-), *adj.* enclosed entirely, or almost entirely, by water: *a waterlocked nation.* [WATER + *locked* (ptp. of LOCK¹)]

wa′ter lo′cust, a tree, *Gleditsia aquatica,* of the southeastern coastal U.S., having long-stalked, thin pods. Also called **swamp locust.**

wa·ter·log (wô′tər lôg′, -log′, wot′ər-), *v.t.,* **-logged, -log·ging. 1.** to cause (a boat, ship, etc.) to become uncontrollable as a result of flooding. **2.** to soak, fill, or saturate with water so as to make soggy or useless. —*v.i.* **3.** to become saturated with water. [back formation from WATERLOGGED]

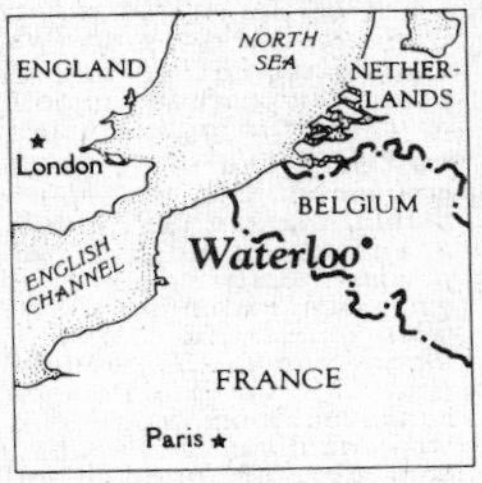

wa·ter·logged (wô′tər lôgd′, -logd′, wot′ər-), *adj.* **1.** so filled or flooded with water as to be heavy or unmanageable, as a ship. **2.** excessively saturated with or as if with water: *waterlogged ground; waterlogged with fatigue.* [WATER + LOGGED]

Wa·ter·loo (wô′tər lo͞o′, wot′ər-, wô′tər lo͞o′, wot′ər-; *for 1 also Flem.* vä′tər lō′), *n.* **1.** a village in central Belgium, south of Brussels: Napoleon decisively defeated here on June 18, 1815. **2.** a decisive or crushing defeat: *The candidate met his Waterloo in the national elections.* **3.** a city in E Iowa. 71,755 (1960). **4.** a town in central New York. 5098 (1960). **5.** a town in SW Illinois. 3739 (1960).

wa′ter loss′, evapotranspiration (def. 2).

wa′ter main′, a main pipe or conduit in a system for conveying water.

wa·ter·man (wô′tər mən, wot′ər-), *n., pl.* **-men. 1.** a man who manages or works on a boat; boatman. **2.** a person skilled in rowing or boating. [late ME; see WATER, MAN¹]

wa·ter·man·ship (wô′tər mən ship′, wot′ər-), *n.* **1.** the skill, duties, business, etc., of a waterman. **2.** skill in rowing or boating. [WATERMAN + -SHIP]

wa′ter mar′igold, an aquatic, composite plant, *Bidens Beckii,* of North America, having golden-yellow flowers.

wa·ter·mark (wô′tər märk′, wot′ər-), *n.* **1.** a mark indicating the height to which water rises or has risen, as in a river, inlet, etc. **2.** See **water line** (def. 5). **3.** a figure or design impressed in some paper during manufacture, visible when the paper is held to the light. —*v.t.* **4.** to mark (paper) with a watermark. **5.** to impress (a design, pattern, etc.), as a watermark. [WATER + MARK¹]

wa′ter mead′ow, a meadow kept fertile by flooding.

wa·ter·mel·on (wô′tər mel′ən, wot′ər-), *n.* **1.** the large, roundish or elongated fruit of a trailing cucurbitaceous vine, *Citrullus vulgaris,* having a hard, green rind and a sweet, juicy, usually pink or red pulp. **2.** the plant or vine. [WATER + MELON]

wa′ter me′ter, a device for measuring and registering the quantity of water that passes through a pipe or other outlet.

wa′ter mil′foil, any of various aquatic plants, chiefly of the genus *Myriophyllum,* the submersed leaves of which are very finely divided.

wa′ter mill′, a mill with machinery driven by water. [late ME]

wa′ter moc′casin, **1.** cottonmouth. **2.** any of various similar but harmless snakes, as a water snake of the genus *Natrix.*

wa′ter mo′tor, any form of prime mover or motor that is operated by the kinetic energy, pressure, or weight of water, esp. a small turbine or water wheel fitted to a pipe supplying water.

wa′ter nymph′, **1.** a nymph of the water, as a naiad, a Nereid, or an Oceanid. **2.** See **water lily. 3.** any aquatic plant of the genus *Najas.* [late ME]

wa′ter oak′, **1.** an oak, *Quercus nigra,* of the southern U.S., growing chiefly along streams and swamps. **2.** any of several other American oaks.

wa′ter oats′. See **wild rice.**

wa′ter of crystalliza′tion, *Chem.* water of hydration, formerly thought necessary to crystallization: now usually regarded as affecting crystallization only as it forms new molecular combinations.

wa′ter of hydra′tion, *Chem.* the portion of a hydrate which is represented as, or can be expelled as, water: now usually regarded as being in true molecular combination with the other atoms of the compound, and not existing in the compound as water.

wa′ter o′leander. See **swamp loosestrife.**

wa′ter opos′sum, yapok.

wa′ter ou′zel, any of several stocky, aquatic birds of the family *Cinclidae,* related to the thrushes, esp. *Cinclus aquaticus,* of Europe, and *C. mexicanus,* of western North America, having dense, oily plumage, and noted for the habit of jerking the body when perching and walking.

wa′ter ox′. See **water buffalo.**

wa′ter paint′, a pigment, as watercolor, in which water is used as the vehicle.

wa′ter part′ing, a watershed or divide.

wa′ter pep′per, any of several polygonaceous plants of the genus *Polygonum,* growing in wet places, esp. the smartweed, *P. Hydropiper.*

wa′ter pim′pernel, **1.** the brookweed. **2.** the pimpernel, *Anagallis arvensis.*

wa′ter pipe′, **1.** a pipe for conveying water. **2.** a smoking apparatus, as a hookah or narghile, in which the smoke is drawn through a container of water and cooled before reaching the mouth. [late ME]

wa′ter pip′it, a common pipit, *Anthus spinoletta,* of the Northern Hemisphere.

wa′ter pis′tol, a toy gun that shoots a stream of liquid. Also called **water gun, squirt gun.**

wa′ter plane′, *Naval Archit.* the plane bound by the water line of a hull at a given draft.

wa′ter plant′, a plant that grows in water.

wa′ter plan′tain, any aquatic herb of the genus *Alisma,* esp. *A. Plantago-aquatica,* growing in shallow water and having leaves suggesting those of the common plantain.

wa′ter plat′ter, **1.** See **Santa Cruz water lily. 2.** See **royal water lily.**

wa′ter plug′, a fireplug; hydrant.

wa′ter pock′et, **1.** a cavity at the foot of a cliff formed by the falling action of an intermittent stream. **2.** a plunge basin.

wa′ter po′lo, an aquatic game played by two teams of seven swimmers each, the object being to score goals by pushing, carrying, or passing an inflated ball across the opponent's goal line.

wa′ter pop′py, a Brazilian, aquatic herb, *Hydrocleis nymphoides,* having yellow, poppylike flowers.

wa′ter pow′er, **1.** the power of water used, or capable of being used, to drive machinery, turbines, etc. **2.** a waterfall or descent in a watercourse capable of being so used. **3.** a water right possessed by a mill. Also, **wa′ter·pow′er.**

wa′ter pox′, *Pathol.* **1.** See **chicken pox. 2.** See **ground itch.**

wa·ter·proof (wô′tər pro͞of′, wot′ər-), *adj.* **1.** impervious to water. **2.** rendered impervious to water by some special process, as coating, treating with rubber, or the like: *a waterproof hat.* —*n.* **3.** *Chiefly Brit.* a raincoat or other outer coat impervious to water. **4.** any of several coated or rubberized fabrics which are impervious to water. —*v.t.* **5.** to make waterproof. [WATER + -PROOF] —**wa′ter·proof′er,** *n.* —**wa′ter·proof′ness,** *n.*

wa·ter·proof·ing (wô′tər pro͞o′fing, -pro͞o′-, wot′ər-), *n.* **1.** a substance by which something is made waterproof. **2.** act or process of making something waterproof. [WATERPROOF + -ING¹]

wa′terproofing salt′, *Chem.* any of several metallic salts, specifically aluminum acetate, used in waterproofing textiles.

wa′ter purs′lane, any of various marsh plants somewhat resembling purslane, as a lythraceous plant, *Didiplis diandra,* of North America.

wa′ter rail′, an Old World rail, *Rallus aquaticus,* having olive-brown plumage marked with black and a long, red bill.

wa′ter rat′, **1.** any of various rodents having aquatic habits. **2.** the muskrat, *Ondatra zibethica.* **3.** (in Australia and New Guinea) any of the aquatic rats of the subfamily *Hydromyinae,* esp. of the genus *Hydromys.* **4.** *Slang.* a vagrant or thief who frequents a waterfront.

wa·ter-re·pel·lent (wô′tər ri pel′ənt, wot′ər-), *adj.* having a finish which resists but is not impervious to water.

wa·ter-re·sist·ant (wô′tər ri zis′tənt, -zis′-, wot′ər-), *adj.* resisting though not entirely preventing the penetration of water.

wa′ter rice′. See **wild rice.**

wa′ter right′, the right to make use of the water from a particular stream, lake, or irrigation canal.

wa′ter sail′, *Naut.* **1.** a triangular sail set fore-and-aft beneath a bowsprit. **2.** a shallow sail laced to the boom of a schooner mainsail; save-all. **3.** a sail set beneath a boom of a lower studding sail.

wa′ter sap′phire, a transparent variety of cordierite, found in Ceylon, Madagascar, and elsewhere, sometimes used as a gem.

wa·ter·scape (wô′tər skāp′, wot′ər-), *n.* a picture or view of the sea or other body of water. [WATER + (LAND)SCAPE]

wa′ter scor′pion, any of several aquatic hemipterous insects of the family *Nepidae,* having raptorial front legs and a long respiratory tube at the rear of the abdomen.

wa·ter·shed (wô′tər shed′, wot′ər-), *n.* **1.** *Chiefly Brit.* the ridge or crest line dividing two drainage areas; water parting; divide. **2.** the region or area drained by a river, stream, etc.; drainage area. **3.** *Archit.* wash (def. 47). **4.** *Naut.* eyebrow (def. 5). **5.** a point of division between two phases, conditions, etc.: *The treaty to ban most atomic tests may prove to be one of history's great watersheds.* [WATER + SHED²]

wa′ter shield′, **1.** Also called **water target.** an aquatic plant, *Brasenia Schreberi,* having purple flowers, floating leaves, and a jellylike coating on the underwater stems and roots. **2.** a fanwort, esp. *Cabomba caroliniana.* See illus. under **dimorphism.**

wa·ter-sick (wô′tər sik′, wot′ər-), *adj. Agric.* excessively watered, esp. by irrigation, so that tilling and planting cannot be done. [OE *wæter seoc* dropsical]

wa·ter·side (wô′tər sīd′, wot′ər-), *n.* **1.** the margin, bank, or shore of a river, lake, ocean, etc. —*adj.* **2.** of, pertaining to, or situated at the waterside: *waterside insects; waterside resort.* **3.** working by the waterside: *waterside police.* [late ME; see WATER, SIDE[1]]

wa′ter ski′, a ski on which to water-ski, designed to plane over water: it is shorter and broader than the ski used on snow.

wa·ter-ski (wô′tər skē′, wot′ər-), *v.i.*, **-skied, -ski·ing.** to plane over water on water skis or a water ski by grasping a towing rope pulled by a speedboat. —**wa′ter-ski′er,** *n.*

wa′ter smoke′. See **steam fog.**

wa′ter snail′. See **Archimedes' screw.**

wa′ter snake′, **1.** any of numerous and widely distributed harmless, colubrid snakes of the genus *Natrix,* found in or near fresh water. **2.** any of various other snakes living in or frequenting water. **3.** (*cap.*) *Astron.* the constellation Hydrus.

wa′ter snow′flake, a tropical, floating, aquatic plant, *Nymphoides indicum,* having round leaves and white flowers with yellowish centers.

wa·ter-soak (wô′tər sōk′, wot′ər-), *v.t.* to soak or saturate with water.

wa′ter sof′tener, any of a group of substances which when added to water containing calcium and magnesium ions cause their precipitation or change their usual properties: used in the purification of water for the laboratory, and for giving water more efficient sudsing ability with soap.

wa·ter-sol·u·ble (wô′tər sol′yə bəl, wot′ər-), *adj.* capable of dissolving in water, as certain vitamins: *water-soluble B and C.*

wa′ter span′iel, one of either of two breeds of spaniels, used for retrieving waterfowl. Cf. **American water spaniel, Irish water spaniel.**

Irish water spaniel (2 ft. high at shoulder)

wa′ter speed′well, a speedwell, *Veronica Anagallis-aquatica,* found esp. in marshes, brooks, and ditches.

wa·ter·spout (wô′tər spout′, wot′ər-), *n.* **1.** a pipe running down the side of a house or other building to carry away water from the gutter of the roof. **2.** a spout, duct, or the like, from which water is discharged. **3.** a funnel-shaped or tubular portion of a cloud over the ocean or other body of water which, laden with mist and spray, resembles a solid column of water reaching upward to the cloud from which it hangs. Cf. **tornado** (def. 1). [late ME; see WATER, SPOUT]

wa′ter sprite′, a sprite or spirit inhabiting the water, as an undine.

wa′ter star′wort, any aquatic herb of the genus *Callitriche.*

wa′ter strid′er, any of several hemipterous insects of the family *Gerridae,* having long, slender legs fringed with hairs, enabling them to dart about on the surface of water.

wa·ter-struck (wô′tər struk′, wot′ər-), *adj.* (of bricks) made with a mold wetted to permit freeing.

wa′ter supply′, **1.** the supply of purified water available to a community. **2.** the facilities for storing and supplying this water, as reservoirs, pipe lines, etc. —**wa′ter-sup·ply′,** *adj.*

wa′ter sys′tem, **1.** a river and all its branches. **2.** a system of supplying water, as throughout a metropolitan area.

wa′ter ta′ble, **1.** the depth below which the ground is saturated with water. **2.** *Archit.* a projecting stringcourse or similar structural member placed so as to divert rain water from a building. [late ME]

wa′ter tar′get. See **water shield** (def. 1).

wa′ter thrush′, **1.** either of two North American warblers, *Seirus noveboracensis* or *S. motacilla,* usually found near streams. **2.** *Brit.* the water ouzel, *Cinclus aquaticus.*

wa′ter ti′ger, the larva of a predaceous diving beetle.

wa·ter·tight (wô′tər tīt′, wot′ər-), *adj.* **1.** constructed or fitted so tightly as to be impervious to water: *The ship had six watertight compartments.* **2.** so devised or planned as to be impossible to defeat, evade, or nullify: *a watertight contract; a watertight alibi.* [late ME; see WATER, TIGHT] —**wa′ter·tight′ness,** *n.*

wa′ter ton′, a unit of volume equal to 224 British imperial gallons.

Wa′ter·ton Lakes′ Na′tional Park′ (wô′tər-tən, wot′ər-), a national park in W Canada, in S Alberta. 220 sq. mi.

wa′ter tow′er, **1.** a vertical pipe or tower into which water is pumped to obtain a required height above a given level; standpipe. **2.** a fire-extinguishing apparatus for throwing a stream of water on the upper parts of a tall burning building.

Wa·ter·town (wô′tər toun′, wot′ər-), *n.* **1.** a town in E Massachusetts, on the Charles River, near Boston: U.S. arsenal. 39,092 (1960). **2.** a city in N New York. 33,306 (1960). **3.** a city in E South Dakota. 14,077 (1960).

wa′ter trap′, *Golf.* a pond, stream, or the like serving as a trap in a golf course.

wa·ter-tube boil′er (wô′tər to͞ob′, -tyo͞ob′, wot′ər-), a boiler for generating steam by passing water in tubes (**wa′ter tubes′**) through flames and hot gases. Cf. **fire-tube boiler.**

wa′ter tur′bine, a turbine driven by the momentum or reactive force of water.

wa′ter tur′key, the snakebird, *Anhinga anhinga.*

Wa′ter Val′ley, a town in central Mississippi. 3206 (1960).

wa′ter va′por, gaseous water, esp. when diffused and below its boiling point, as distinguished from steam.

Wa·ter·ville (wô′tər vil′, wot′ər-), *n.* a city in SW Maine. 18,695 (1960).

Wa·ter·vliet (wô′tər vlēt′, wot′ər-), *n.* a city in E New York, on the Hudson: oldest U.S. arsenal. 13,917 (1960).

wa′ter wag′on, **1.** a wagon used to transport water, as in military field operations, a construction site, etc. **2. on the water wagon.** See **wagon** (def. 9).

wa·ter·ward (wô′tər wərd, wot′ər-), *adv.* in the direction of water or a body of water. Also, **wa′ter-wards.** [ME; see WATER, -WARD]

wa′ter wave′, **1.** a wave on the surface of a body of water. **2.** a wave that is set into lotioned hair with combs and then allowed to dry by the application of heat from a drier.

wa·ter-wave (wô′tər wāv′, wot′ər-), *v.t.*, **-waved, -wav·ing.** to set (hair) in a water wave.

wa·ter·way (wô′tər wā′, wot′ər-), *n.* **1.** a river, canal, or other body of water as a route or way of travel or transport. **2.** *Shipbuilding.* **a.** (in a wooden vessel) a thick strake of planking forming a raised margin for the deck planking inside the bulwarks. **b.** (in a steel or iron vessel) a depressed gutter at the edge of the deck inside the bulwarks, used esp. when the decking is wooden. **3.** a channel for vessels, as a fairway in a harbor. [ME; OE *wæterweg.* See WATER, WAY]

wa′terway plank′, *Naut.* See **margin plank.**

wa·ter·weed (wô′tər wēd′, wot′ər-), *n.* **1.** an aquatic plant without special use or beauty. **2.** Also called **ditch-moss.** a plant, *Anacharis* (*Elodea*) *canadensis,* of North America, common in fresh-water streams and ponds. [WATER + WEED[1]]

wa′ter wheel′, **1.** a wheel or turbine turned by the weight or momentum of water and used to operate machinery. **2.** a wheel with buckets for raising or drawing water, as a noria. **3.** the paddle wheel of a steamboat. [late ME]

wa′ter wil′low. **1.** See **swamp loosestrife. 2.** any of several acanthaceous herbs of the genus *Justica,* growing in water or wet places, esp. *J. americana,* of North America, having pale violet to white flowers.

wa′ter wings′, a fabric contrivance shaped like a pair of wings and inflated with air, usually worn under the arms to keep the body afloat while one learns to swim.

wa′ter witch′, **1.** Also, **wa′ter witch′er.** a person skilled at water witching; dowser. **2.** a witch believed to haunt lakes, ponds, etc.

wa′ter witch′ing, the supposed discovering of subterranean streams by means of a divining rod.

wa·ter·works (wô′tər wûrks′, wot′ər-), *n.*, *pl.* **-works. 1.** (*construed as sing. or pl.*) a complete system of reservoirs, pipelines, conduits, etc., by which water is collected, purified, stored, and pumped to urban users. **2.** (*construed as sing.*) a pumping station or a purifying station of such a system. **3.** (*usually construed as pl.*) Sometimes, **waterwork.** a spectacular display of water, mechanically produced, as for a pageant. **4.** *Slang.* tears, or the source of tears: *to turn on the waterworks.* **5.** *Slang.* the kidneys. [WATER + WORKS]

wa·ter·worn (wô′tər wōrn′, wot′ər-), *adj.* worn by the action of water; smoothed by the force or movement of water. [WATER + WORN]

wa·ter·y (wô′tə rē, wot′ə-), *adj.* **1.** pertaining to or connected with water: *watery Neptune.* **2.** full of or abounding in water, as soil, a region, etc.; soggy; boggy. **3.** containing much or too much water: *a watery paste; a watery batter.* **4.** soft, soggy, tasteless, etc., due to excessive water or overcooking: *watery vegetables; a watery stew.* **5.** tearful. **6.** of the nature of water: *watery vapor.* **7.** resembling water in appearance or color: *eyes of a watery blue.* **8.** resembling water in consistency or viscosity: *a watery fluid.* **9.** of poor or weak quality; thin, washy, or vapid: *watery writing.* **10.** consisting of water: *a watery grave.* **11.** discharging, filled with, or secreting a waterlike morbid substance. [OE *wæterig.* See WATER, -Y[1]] —**wa′ter·i·ly,** *adv.*

Wa·then (wä′thən), *n.* a boy's given name.

Wat·kins (wot′kinz), *n.* a boy's given name.

Wat′kins Glen′, a village in W New York, on Seneca Lake: gorge and cascades. 2,813 (1960).

Wat′ling Is′land (wot′ling). See **San Salvador** (def. 1).

Wa·ton·ga (wə tong′gə), *n.* a town in central Oklahoma. 3252 (1960).

Wat·se·ka (wot sē′kə), *n.* a town in E Illinois. 5219 (1960).

Wat·son (wot′sən), *n.* **1. James Dewey,** born 1928, U.S. biologist: Nobel prize for medicine 1962. **2. John** ("*Ian Maclaren*"), 1850–1907, Scottish clergyman and novelist. **3. John Broa·dus** (brō′dəs), 1878–1958, U.S. psychologist. **4. John Christian,** 1867–1941, Australian statesman, born in Chile: prime minister 1904. **5. Thomas John,** 1874–1956, U.S. industrialist. **6. Sir William,** 1858–1935, English poet. **7.** a boy's given name.

Wat′son and the Shark′, a painting (1778) by John Singleton Copley.

Wat·son-Went·worth (wot′sən went′wûrth′), *n.* **Charles, 2nd Marquis of Rock·ing·ham** (rok′ing əm), 1730–82, British statesman: prime minister 1765–66, 1782.

watt (wot), *n.* the meter-kilogram-second unit of power, equivalent to one joule per second and equal to the power in a circuit in which a current of one ampere flows across a potential difference of one volt. *Abbr.:* W; w; W.; w. [named after James WATT]

Watt (wot), *n.* **1. James,** 1736–1819, Scottish engineer and inventor. **2. Sir Robert Alexander Watson,** born 1892, Scottish physicist. **3.** one of two adjoining, elliptical walled plains in the fourth quadrant of the face of the moon, the other being Steinheil: about 41 miles long and 30 miles wide.

watt·age (wot′ij), *n.* **1.** power, as measured in watts. **2.** the amount of power required to operate an electrical appliance or device. [WATT + -AGE]

Wat·teau (wo tō′; *Fr.* VA tō′; *adj. also* wot′ō), *n.* **1. Jean An·toine** (zhäN äN twAN′), 1684–1721, French painter. —*adj.* **2.** pertaining to or in the style of Watteau: *a Watteau shepherdess.*

Wat′teau back′, a loose, full back of a woman's gown, held in, in folds, at the neck and slightly below.

Wat·ter·son (wot′ər sən), *n.* **Henry** ("*Marse Henry*"), 1840–1921, U.S. journalist and political leader.

watt-hour (wot′our′, -ou′ər), *n.* a unit of work equal to the power of one watt operating for one hour, equivalent to 3600 joules. *Abbr.:* Wh Also, **watt′hour′.**

wat·tle (wot′əl), *n.*, *v.*, **-tled, -tling,** *adj.* —*n.* **1.** Often, **wattles.** *Chiefly Brit.* a number of rods or stakes interwoven with twigs or tree branches for making fences, walls, etc. **2. wattles,** a number of poles laid on a roof to hold thatch. **3.** (in Australia) any of various acacias whose shoots and branches were used by the early colonists for wattles, now valued esp. for their bark, which is used in tanning. **4.** *Brit. Dial.* **a.** a twig, stick, rod, or wand. **b.** a hurdle. **5.** *Ornith.* a fleshy lobe or appendage hanging down from the throat or chin of certain birds, as the domestic fowl, the turkey, etc. —*v.t.* **6.** to bind, wall, fence, etc., with wattle or wattles. **7.** to roof or frame with or as with wattles. **8.** to form into a basketwork; interweave; interlace. **9.** to make or construct by interweaving twigs or branches: *to wattle a fence.* —*adj.* **10.** built or roofed with wattle or wattles. [ME *wattel,* OE *watul* covering, var. of *wætla* bandage; see WAD[1]]

wat′tle and daub′, **1.** Also, **wat′tle and dab′.** Also called **stud and mud.** a building technique employing wattles plastered with clay and mud. **2.** a form of wall construction consisting of upright posts or stakes interwoven with twigs or tree branches and plastered with a mixture of clay and straw.

wat·tle·bird (wot′əl bûrd′), *n.* an Australian honey eater, *Anthochaera paradoxa,* having a pendulous wattle on each side of the throat. [WATTLE + BIRD]

watt·less (wot′lis), *adj. Elect.* without watts or power, as an alternating current which differs in phase by 90 degrees from the applied electromotive force or an electromotive force which differs in phase by 90 degrees from the current. [WATT + -LESS]

watt·me·ter (wot′mē′tər), *n. Elect.* a calibrated instrument for measuring electric power in watts. [WATT + -METER]

Watts (wots), *n.* **1. George Frederick,** 1817–1904, English painter and sculptor. **2. Isaac,** 1674–1748, English theologian and hymnist.

Watts-Dun·ton (wots′dun′tᵊn), *n.* **(Walter) Theodore** (*Walter Theodore Watts*), 1832–1914, English poet, novelist, and critic.

watt-sec·ond (wot′sek′ənd), *n.* a unit of work equal to the energy of one watt acting for one second; the equivalent of one joule. Also, **watt′sec′ond.**

Wa·tu·si (wä to͞o′sē), *n.*, *pl.* **-sis,** (*esp. collectively*) **-si. 1.** a member of a tall, slender, partly Caucasoid people of Rwanda and Burundi. **2.** (*usually l.c.*) a dance that is a modification of the frug. —*v.i.* **3.** to dance the watusi.

waucht (*Scot.* wäKHt, wôKHt; *Eng. Dial.* wäft), *n.*, *v.t.*, *v.i. Scot. and North Eng.* waught.

Wau·chu·la (wô cho͞o′lə), *n.* a town in central Florida. 3411 (1960).

Wau·con·da (wô kon′də), *n.* a town in NE Illinois. 3227 (1960).

wauf (wof), *adj.*, *n. Scot.* waff[2].

wauf·ie (wof′ē), *n. Scot.* waffie.

waugh (wôf), *adj. Scot. and North Eng.* **1.** tasteless; insipid. **2.** unpleasant to taste. **3.** unpleasant to smell. **4.** (of tastes, smells, sounds, etc.) weak; faint. [OE *wealg* nauseous ?]

Waugh (wô), *n.* **1. Alec** (*Alexander Raban*), born 1898, English novelist, traveler, and lecturer (son of Arthur, brother of Evelyn). **2. Arthur,** 1866–1943, English literary critic, publisher, and editor (father of Alec and Evelyn). **3. Evelyn (Arthur St. John),** 1903–66, English novelist, satirist, biographer, and author of books on travel (son of Arthur, brother of Alec). **5. Frederick Judd** (jud), 1861–1940, U.S. painter and illustrator.

waught (*Scot.* wäKHt, wôKHt; *Eng. Dial.* wäft), *Scot. and North Eng.* —*n.* **1.** a copious draft. —*v.t.*, *v.i.* **2.** to drink fully. Also, **waucht.** [?]

wauk (wôk, wäk), *v.i.*, *v.t.*, *n. Scot.* wake[1].

Wau·ke·gan (wô kē′gən), *n.* a city in NE Illinois, on Lake Michigan, N of Chicago. 55,719 (1960).

Wau·ke·sha (wô′ki shô′), *n.* a city in SE Wisconsin, W of Milwaukee. 30,004 (1960).

Wau·kon (wô kon′), *n.* a town in NE Iowa. 3639 (1960).

wauk·rife (wôk′rīf′, wäk′-), *adj. Scot.* wakerife.

waul (wôl), *v.i.* to cry like a cat or a newborn infant; squall. Also, **wawl.** [? < Scand; cf. Icel *vāla* to wail. See CATERWAUL]

Wau·pac·a (wô pak′ə), *n.* a town in central Wisconsin. 3984 (1960).

Wau·pun (wô pon′), *n.* a town in central Wisconsin. 7935 (1960).

waur (wôR, wäR), *adj.*, *adv. Scot. and North Eng.* worse. [var. of WAR[2]]

Wau·sau (wô′sô), *n.* a city in central Wisconsin. 31,943 (1960).

Wau·se·on (wô′sē on′), *n.* a town in NW Ohio. 4311 (1960).

Wau·wa·to·sa (wô′wə tō′sə), *n.* a city in SE Wisconsin, near Milwaukee. 56,923 (1960).

wave (wāv), *n.*, *v.*, **waved, wav·ing.** —*n.* **1.** a disturbance on the surface of a liquid body, as the sea or a lake, in the form of a moving ridge or swell. **2.** any surging or progressing movement or part resembling a wave of the sea: *a wave of the pulse.* **3.** a swell, surge, or rush, as of feeling, excitement, prosperity, etc.: *a wave of disgust sweeping over a person; a wave of cholera throughout the country.* **4.** a widespread feeling, opinion, tendency, etc.: *a wave of anti-intellectualism; the new wave of installment buying.* **5.** a mass movement, as of troops, settlers, migrating birds, etc. **6.** an outward curve, or one of a series of such curves, in a surface or line; undulation. **7.** the act or an instance of waving, as a flag or the hand. **8.** a fluttering sign or signal made with the hand, a flag, etc.: *a farewell wave.* **9.** natural waviness of the hair, or a special treatment to impart waviness: *to have a wave in one's hair; to get a shampoo and a wave.* **10.** a period or spell of unusually hot or cold weather. **11.** *Physics.* a progressive disturbance propagated from point to point in a medium or space without progress or advance by the points themselves, as in the transmission of sound or light. **12.** *Archaic.* **a.** water. **b.** a body of water. **c.** the sea. —*v.i.* **13.** to move freely and gently back and forth or up and down, as by the action of air currents, sea swells, etc.: *The flags were waving in the wind.* **14.** to curve alternately in opposite directions; have an undulating form: *The road waved along the valley.* **15.** to bend or sway up and down or to and fro, as branches or plants in the wind. **16.** to be moved, esp. alternately in opposite directions: *The lady's handkerchief waved in encouragement.* **17.** to give a signal by fluttering or flapping something: *She waved to me with her hand.* —*v.t.* **18.** to cause to flutter or have a waving motion in: *A night wind waves the tattered banners.* **19.** to cause to bend or sway up and down or to and fro: *The storm waved the heavy branches of the elm.* **20.** to give an undulating form to; cause to curve up and down or in and out. **21.** to give a wavy appearance or pattern to, as silk. **22.** to impart a wave to (the hair). **23.** to move, esp. alternately in opposite directions: *to wave the hand.* **24.** to signal to by waving a flag or the like; direct by a waving movement: *to wave a train to a halt; to wave traffic around an obstacle.* **25.** to signify or express by a waving movement: *to wave a last good-by.* [ME; OE *wafian;* c. MHG *waben.* See WAVER¹] —**wave′less,** *adj.* —**wave′less·ly,** *adv.* —**wav′ing·ly,** *adv.* —**wave′-like′,** *adj.*

—**Syn. 1.** undulation, sea. WAVE, RIPPLE, BREAKER, SURF refer to a ridge or swell on the surface of water. WAVE is the general word: *waves in a high wind.* A RIPPLE is the smallest kind of wave, such as is caused by a stone thrown into a pool: *ripples in a brook.* A BREAKER is a wave breaking, or about to break, upon the shore or upon rocks: *the roar of breakers.* SURF is the collective name for breakers: *Heavy surf makes bathing dangerous.* **13.** undulate, fluctuate, flutter, float, sway, rock.

Wave (wāv), *n.* an enlisted member of the Waves. Also, **WAVE.** [see WAVES]

wave′ cy′clone, *Meteorol.* a cyclone that forms on a front and, in maturing, produces an increasingly sharp, wavelike deformation of the front.

waved (wāvd), *adj.* having a form, outline, or appearance resembling waves; undulating. [WAVE + -ED³]

wave′ drag′. See **aerodynamic wave drag.**

wave′ equa′tion, 1. *Math., Physics.* an equation describing wave motion, $\nabla^2\phi = \frac{1}{c^2}\frac{\delta^2\phi}{\delta t^2}$ where ∇ is the Laplace operator, ϕ is a wave function, c is the velocity of propagation, and t is the time. **2.** *Physics.* See **Schrödinger wave equation.**

wave-form (wāv′fôrm′), *n.* *Physics.* the shape of a wave, a graph obtained by plotting the instantaneous values of a periodic quantity against the time.

wave′ front′, *Physics.* a surface, real or imaginary, that is the locus of all adjacent points at which the phase of oscillation is the same.

wave′ func′tion, *Physics.* **1.** a solution of a wave equation. **2.** the solution of the Schrödinger wave equation: the square of the absolute value of its amplitude represents the probability of finding a given particle in a given element of volume.

wave′ guide′, *Electronics.* a piece of hollow, conducting tubing, usually rectangular or circular in cross section, used as a conductor or directional transmitter for microwaves propagated through its interior.

wave·length (wāv′length′), *n.* *Physics.* the distance, measured in the direction of propagation of a wave, between two successive points in the wave that are characterized by the same phase of oscillation. Also, **wave′ length′.** [WAVE + LENGTH]

wave·let (wāv′lit), *n.* a small wave; ripple. [WAVE + -LET]

Wa·vell (wā′vəl), *n.* **Archibald Percival, 1st Earl,** 1883–1950, British field marshal and author: viceroy of India 1943–47.

wa·vell·ite (wā′və līt′), *n.* a hydrous aluminum fluophosphate occurring as a white to yellowish-green or brown mineral, often in radiating fibers. [named after W. *Wavell* (d. 1829), English physician, the finder; see -ITE¹]

wave′ mechan′ics, *Physics.* the part of quantum mechanics that describes elementary particles by means of their wavelike properties.

wave·me·ter (wāv′mē′tər), *n.* a device for measuring the wave length or frequency of a radio wave. [WAVE + -METER]

wave′ mold′ing, any architectural member, as a stringcourse, having a Vitruvian scroll in low relief.

wave′ num′ber, the number of waves in one centimeter of light in a given wavelength.

wa·ver¹ (wā′vər), *v.i.* **1.** to sway to and fro; flutter: *Foliage wavers in the breeze.* **2.** to flicker or quiver, as light: *A distant beam wavered and then disappeared.* **3.** become unsteady; begin to fail or give way: *When she heard the news her senses wavered.* **4.** to shake or tremble, as the hands, voice, etc.: *Her voice wavered.* **5.** to feel or show doubt, indecision, etc.; vacillate: *He wavered in his determination.* **6.** (of things) to fluctuate or vary: *Prices wavered.* **7.** to totter or reel: *The earth quaked and the tower wavered.* —*n.* **8.** an act of wavering, fluttering, or vacillating. [ME (see WAVE, -ER⁶); c. dial. G *wabern* to move about, Icel *vafra* to toddle] —**wa′ver·er,** *n.* —**wa′ver·ing·ly,** *adv.*

—**Syn. 4.** quiver. **5.** WAVER, FLUCTUATE, VACILLATE refer to an alternation or hesitation between one direction and another. WAVER means to hesitate between choices: *to waver as to what course to pursue.* FLUCTUATE suggests irregular change from one side to the other or up and down: *The prices of stocks fluctuate when there is bad news followed by good.* VACILLATE is to make up one's mind and change it again suddenly; to be undecided as to what to do: *We must not vacillate but must set a day.*

wav·er² (wā′vər), *n.* **1.** a person who waves or causes something to flutter or have a waving motion: *Election time brings out the wavers of flags and haranguers of mobs.* **2.** a person who specializes in waving hair. **3.** something, as a curling iron, used for waving hair. [WAVE + -ER¹]

Wa·ver·ley (wā′vər lē), *n.* (or *'Tis Sixty Years Since*) a historical novel (1814) by Sir Walter Scott: the first of the Waverley Novels.

Wa′verley Nov′els, a group of novels written by Sir Walter Scott.

Wa·ver·ly (wā′vər lē), *n.* **1.** a town in NE Iowa. 6357 (1960). **2.** a town in S New York. 5950 (1960). **3.** a town in S Ohio. 3830 (1960). **4.** a town in central Tennessee. 2891 (1960).

Waves (wāvz), *n.*, **Sea of.** See **Mare Undarum.**

Waves (wāvz), *n.* (*construed as sing. or pl.*) Women's Reserve, U.S. Naval Reserve. Also, **WAVES.** [*W*(*omen's*) *A*(*ppointed*) *V*(*olunteer*) *E*(*mergency*) *S*(*ervice*)]

wave′ scroll′. See **Vitruvian scroll.**

wave·son (wāv′sən), *n.* *Old Eng. Law.* goods from a ship wrecked at sea that are found floating on the water. [WAVE + *-son* (formed after AF *floteson* FLOTSAM)]

wave′ the′ory, *Physics.* the theory that light is transmitted as a wave, similar to oscillations in magnetic and electric fields. Also called **undulatory theory.** Cf. **corpuscular theory.**

wave′ train′, *Physics.* a series of successive waves spaced at regular intervals.

wa·vey (wā′vē), *n., pl.* **-veys.** *U.S. and Canada Dial.* any of various wild geese. [< Algonquian]

wav·y¹ (wā′vē), *adj.,* **wav·i·er, wav·i·est. 1.** curving alternately in opposite directions; undulating: *a wavy course; wavy hair.* **2.** abounding or characterized by waves: *the wavy sea.* **3.** resembling or suggesting waves: *a cotton material with a wavy pattern.* **4.** *Bot.* **a.** bending with successive curves in opposite directions, as a margin. **b.** having such a margin, as a leaf. **5.** *Heraldry.* noting a partition line or ordinary formed in a series of S-curves. Cf. **undé. 6.** vibrating or tremulous; unsteady; wavering. [WAVE + -Y¹] —**wav′i·ly,** *adv.* —**wav′i·ness,** *n.*

wa·vy² (wā′vē), *n., pl.* **-vies.** *Chiefly Canadian.* wavey.

wāw (wou), *n.* the 27th letter of the Arabic alphabet. [< Ar]

wawl (wôl), *v.i.* *Chiefly Scot.* waul.

wax¹ (waks), *n.* **1.** Also called **beeswax.** a solid, yellowish, nonglycerine substance allied to fats and oils, secreted by bees, plastic when warm and melting at about 145°F, variously employed in making candles, models, casts, ointments, etc., and used by bees in constructing their honeycomb. **2.** any of various similar substances, as spermaceti, the secretions of certain insects, and the secretions of certain plants. Cf. **vegetable wax, wax insect. 3.** any of a group of substances composed of hydrocarbons, alcohols, fatty acids, and esters that are solid at ordinary temperatures. **4.** cerumen; earwax. **5.** a resinous substance used by shoemakers for rubbing thread. **6.** See **sealing wax. 7.** a person or object suggesting wax, as in manageability, malleability, etc.: *She was helpless wax in their hands.* —*v.t.* **8.** to rub, smear, stiffen, polish, etc., with wax: *to wax the floor.* **9.** to fill crevices (in ornamental marble) with colored material. **10.** *Informal.* to make a phonograph recording of. —*adj.* **11.** made of, pertaining to, or resembling wax: *a wax doll; a wax candle.* [ME; OE *weax;* c. D *was,* G *Wachs,* Icel *vax*] —**wax′er,** *n.* —**wax′like′,** *adj.*

wax² (waks), *v.i.,* **waxed; waxed** or (*Poetic*) **wax·en; wax·ing. 1.** to increase in extent, quantity, intensity, power, etc.: *Discord waxed at an alarming rate.* **2.** (of the moon) to increase in the extent of its illuminated portion before the full moon. Cf. **wane** (def. 1). **3.** to grow or become: *He waxed angry at the insinuation.* [ME; OE *weaxan;* c. G *wachsen;* akin to WAIST]

—**Syn. 1.** extend, grow, lengthen, enlarge, dilate.

wax³ (waks), *n.* *Chiefly Brit.* a fit of anger; rage. [? special use of WAX²]

wax′ bean′, 1. a variety of string bean bearing yellowish, waxy pods. **2.** the pod of this plant, used for food.

wax·ber·ry (waks′ber′ē, -bə rē), *n., pl.* **-ries. 1.** the wax myrtle, or the bayberry. **2.** the snowberry. [WAX¹ + BERRY]

wax·bill (waks′bil′), *n.* any of several Old World weaverbirds, esp. of the genus *Estrilda,* having white, pink, or red bills of waxy appearance, often kept as pets. [WAX¹ + BILL²]

waxed′ pa′per. See **wax paper.**

waxed′ tab′let. See **wax tablet.**

wax·en (wak′sən), *adj.* **1.** made of or covered, polished, or treated with wax. **2.** resembling or suggesting wax: *Illness gave his face a waxen appearance.* **3.** weak, manageable, or impressionable, as a person or his characteristics: *The minds of young children are waxen.* —*v.* **4.** *Archaic.* pp. of **wax². [ME; OE *weaxen.* See WAX¹, -EN²]

wax′ flow′er. See **Madagascar jasmine.**

wax′ gourd′, 1. a vine, *Benincasa hispida,* of tropical Asia, having a brown, hairy stem, large, solitary, yellow flowers, and melonlike fruit. **2.** the fruit itself. Also called **Chinese watermelon, tunka, white gourd.**

wax′ing moon′, the moon at any time after new moon and before full moon, so called because its illuminated area is increasing. Cf. **waning moon.** See diag. under **moon.**

wax′ in′sect, any of several homopterous insects that secrete a waxy substance, esp. a Chinese scale insect, *Ericerus pe-la.*

wax′ jack′, an illuminating device consisting of a reel holding a waxed wick which is fed upward through a pierced plate. Also called **taper jack.**

wax′ moth′. See **bee moth.**

wax′ myr′tle, a shrub or tree of the genus *Myrica,* as *M. cerifera,* bearing small berries coated with wax which is sometimes used in making candles. Also called **tallow-shrub.**

wax′ palm′, 1. a tall, pinnate-leaved palm, *Ceroxylon andicola,* of the Andes, whose stem and leaves yield a resinous wax. **2.** Also called **carnauba.** a palmate-leaved palm, *Copernicia cerifera,* of Brazil, having leaves coated with a hard wax.

wax′ pa′per, a whitish, translucent wrapping paper made moistureproof by a paraffin coating. Also, **waxed paper.**

wax′ pink′. See **rose moss.**

wax·plant (waks′plant′, -plänt′), *n.* any climbing or trailing, asclepiadaceous plant of the genus *Hoya,* of tropical Asia and Australia, having glossy leaves and umbels of pink, white, or yellowish, waxy flowers. [WAX¹ + PLANT]

wax′ priv′et, an evergreen shrub, *Ligustrum japonicum,* of Japan and Korea, having leathery leaves and white flower clusters.

wax′ tab′let, a tablet made of bone, wood, etc., and covered with wax, used by ancients for writing with a stylus. Also called **waxed tablet.**

wax·weed (waks′wēd′), *n.* an American, lythraceous herb, *Cuphea* (or *Parsonsia*) *petiolata,* having a viscid pubescence and purple flowers. [WAX¹ + WEED¹]

wax·wing (waks′wing′), *n.* any of several passerine birds of the family *Bombycillidae,* having a showy crest and secondaries tipped with a red, waxy material, as *Bombycilla garrulus* (**Bohemian waxwing**), of the Northern Hemisphere. [WAX¹ + WING]

wax·work (waks′wûrk′), *n.* **1.** an artistic object made of wax, as a figure, ornament, etc. **2.** an object, esp. the life-size effigy of a person, made of wax. **3.** the bittersweet, *Celastrus scandens.* [WAX¹ + WORK]

wax·works (waks′wûrks′), *n., pl.* **-works.** (*usually construed as sing.*) an exhibition of or a museum for displaying wax figures, ornaments, etc. [WAX¹ + WORKS]

wax·y¹ (wak′sē), *adj.,* **wax·i·er, wax·i·est. 1.** resembling wax in appearance or characteristics: *His face had a waxy shine.* **2.** abounding in, covered with, or made of wax: *Be careful! The floor is waxy.* **3.** *Pathol.* pertaining to or suffering from a degeneration caused by deposits of an insoluble waxlike material in an organ. **4.** pliable, yielding, or impressionable: *a waxy personality.* [WAX¹ + -Y¹] —**wax′i·ly,** *adv.* —**wax′i·ness,** *n.*

wax·y² (wak′sē), *adj.,* **wax·i·er, wax·i·est.** *Chiefly Brit.* angry. [WAX³ + -Y¹]

way¹ (wā), *n.* **1.** manner, mode, or fashion: *a new way of looking at a matter; to reply in a polite way.* **2.** characteristic or habitual manner: *He has many strange ways.* **3.** a method, plan, or means for attaining a goal: *to find a way to reduce costs.* **4.** a respect or particular: *The plan is defective in several ways.* **5.** a direction or vicinity: *Look this way. We're having a drought out our way.* **6.** passage or progress on a course: *to make one's way on foot; to lead the way.* **7.** distance: *They've come a long way.* **8.** a path or course leading from one place to another: *What's the shortest way to town?* **9.** *Brit.* an old Roman road: *Icknield Way.* **10.** *Brit.* a minor street in a town: *He lives in Stepney Way.* **11.** a road, route, passage, or channel (usually used in combination): *highway; waterway; doorway.* **12.** *Law.* a right of way. **13.** any line of passage or travel, used or available: *to blaze a way through dense woods.* **14.** space for passing or advancing: *to clear a way through the crowd.* **15.** Often, **ways.** a habit or custom: *I don't like his ways at all. The grandmother lived by the ways of the old country.* **16.** course or mode of procedure that one chooses or wills (sometimes fol. by *with*): *She always has her own way. It was another of those stories in which the villain has his way with the heroine.* **17.** condition, as to health, prosperity, or the like: *to be in a bad way.* **18.** range or extent of experience or notice: *the best device that ever came in my way.* **19.** a course of life, action, or experience: *The way of transgressors is hard.* **20.** *Informal.* business: *to be in the haberdashery way.* **21.** *Naut.* **ways,** two or more groundways down which a hull slides in being launched. **22.** *Mach.* a longitudinal strip, as in a planer, guiding a moving part along a surface. **23.** *Naut.* movement or passage through the water. **24. by the way,** in the course of one's remarks; incidentally: *By the way, have you received that letter yet?* **25. by way of, a.** by the route of; through; via. **b.** as a method or means of: *to number articles by way of distinguishing them.* **c.** *Brit.* in the state or position of; ostensibly (being, doing, etc.): *He is by way of being an authority on the subject.* **26. come one's way,** to come to one; befall one: *A bit of good fortune came my way.* **27. give way, a.** to withdraw or retreat: *The army gave way before the advance of the enemy.* **b.** to collapse; yield; break down: *If he keeps up as he is doing, he will surely give way under the strain.* **28. give way to, a.** to yield to: *He gave way to their entreaties.* **b.** to become unrestrained or uninhibited; lose control of (one's temper, emotions, etc.): *She gave way to tears and said she was quitting.* **29. go out of one's way,** to do something that inconveniences one; make an unusual effort: *Please don't go out of your way on my account.* **30. have way on,** *Naut.* (of a vessel) to be in motion in the direction in which it is headed. **31. in a family way,** *Informal.* pregnant. **32. in a way,** after a fashion; to some extent: *In a way, she's the nicest person I know.* **33. in someone's way,** forming a hindrance, impediment, or obstruction: *He might have succeeded in his ambition, had not circumstances been in his way. She protested, when invited to stay for dinner, that she would be in our way.* Also, **in the way. 34. in way of,** *Naut.* adjacent to; beside. **35. lead the way, a.** to go along a course in advance of others, as a guide. **b.** to take the initiative; be first or most prominent: *In fashion she has always led the way.* **36. make one's way, a.** to go forward; proceed: *to make one's way through the mud.* **b.** to achieve recognition or success; advance: *to make one's way in the world.* **37. make way, a.** to allow to pass; clear the way: *Make way for the king!* **b.** to relinquish to another; withdraw: *He resigned to make way for a younger man.* **38. out of the way, a.** in a state or condition so as not to obstruct or hinder. **b.** dealt with; disposed of: *I feel better, now that problem is out of the way.* **c.** murdered: *to have a person put out of the way.* **d.** out of the frequented way; at a distance from the usual route. **e.** improper; amiss: *There was something decidedly out of the way about his perfunctory apology.* **f.** extraordinary; unusual: *Such behavior was out of the way for him.* **39. pave the way to** or **for.** See **pave** (def. 2). **40. see one's way clear,** to regard as suitable or possible; consider seriously: *We couldn't see our way clear to spending so much money at once.* Also, **see one's way. 41. take one's way,** to start out; travel; go: *He took his way across the park and headed uptown.* **42. under way, a.** in motion, as a ship that has weighed anchor. **b.** in progress, as an enterprise [ME; OE *weg;* c. D, G *Weg,* Icel *vegr,* Goth *wigs*] —**way′less,** *adj.*

—**Syn. 3.** scheme, device. See **method. 4.** detail, part. **7.** space, interval. **11.** track. **15.** usage, practice, wont.

way² (wā), *adv.* **1.** Also, **'way.** away; from this or that place: *Go way.* **2.** to a great degree or at quite a distance; far: *way too heavy; way down the road.* [ME, aph. var. of AWAY]

way·bill (wā′bil′), *n.* **1.** a list of goods sent by a common carrier, as a railroad, with shipping directions. **2.** See **air waybill.** [WAY + BILL¹]

Way·cross (wā′krôs′, -kros′), *n.* a city in SE Georgia. 20,944 (1960).

way·far·er (wā′fâr′ər), *n.* a traveler, esp. on foot. [ME *weyfarere.* See WAY, FARE, -ER[1]]

way·far·ing (wā′fâr′ing), *adj., n.* traveling, esp. on foot. [ME; OE *wegfarende,* equiv. to *weg* (see WAY) + *farende,* prp. of *faran* to FARE]

way′faring tree′, **1.** a Eurasian shrub, *Viburnum Lantana,* having cymes of white flowers, found along roadsides and grown as an ornamental in the U.S. **2.** the hobblebush. [short for *wayfaring man's tree*]

way·go·ing (wā′gō′ing), *Chiefly Scot. and North Eng.* —*adj.* **1.** going away; departing. **2.** of or pertaining to one who goes away. —*n.* **3.** act of leaving; departure; leavetaking. [WAY + GOING]

way′going crop′, *Law.* See **away-going crop.**

way·laid (wā lād′), *v.* pt. and pp. of **waylay.**

Way·land (wā′lənd), *n.* (in N European folklore) the king of the elves, a smith and artificer: known in Scandinavia as Völund and in Germany as Wieland.

way·lay (wā lā′), *v.t.,* **-laid, -lay·ing.** **1.** to intercept or attack from ambush, as in order to rob, seize, or slay. **2.** to await and accost unexpectedly: *The actor was waylaid by a swarm of admirers.* [WAY + LAY[1], after MLG, MD *wegelagen* to lie in wait, deriv. of *wegelage* a lying in wait] —**way·lay′er,** *n.*

way·leave (wā′lēv′), *n. Law.* a right of way over or under another's ground or property, as for transporting coals from a colliery. [late ME *waylefe.* See WAY, LEAVE[2]]

way·less (wā′lis), *adj.* lacking a way, road, or path; trackless: *wayless countryside.* [ME; OE *weglēas.* See WAY, -LESS]

Wayne (wān), *n.* **1. Anthony** ("*Mad Anthony*"), 1745–96, American Revolutionary War general. **2.** a town in N New Jersey. 29,353 (1960). **3.** a city in SE Michigan, near Detroit. 16,034 (1960). **4.** a town in NE Nebraska. 4217 (1960). **5.** a boy's given name.

Waynes·bor·o (wānz′bûr ō, -bur ō), *n.* **1.** a city in N Virginia. 15,694 (1960). **2.** a town in E Georgia. 5359 (1960). **3.** a town in SE Mississippi. 3892 (1960).

Waynes·burg (wānz′bûrg), *n.* a town in SW Pennsylvania. 5188 (1960).

Waynes·ville (wānz′vil), *n.* a town in W North Carolina. 6159 (1960).

Way′ of All Flesh′, The, a novel (1903) by Samuel Butler.

Way′ of The World′, The, a comedy of manners (1700) by William Congreve.

way′ out′, *Brit.* an exit or exit door, as in a theater.

way-out (wā′out′), *adj. Informal.* **1.** advanced in style or technique: *way-out jazz.* **2.** exotic or esoteric in character: *way-out coffeehouses and poetry readings.* [(A)WAY + OUT]

way′ point′, **1.** a place or point between major points on a route. **2.** See **way station.**

ways (wāz), *n.* (*construed as sing.*) way (defs. 7, 15, 21). [ME *weyes,* OE *weges,* gen. sing. of *weg* WAY]

-ways, a suffix appearing in native English adverbs: *always; sideways.* [ME, comb. form of *weyes* WAYS]

ways′ and means′, **1.** legislation, methods, and means of raising revenue for the use of the government. **2.** methods and means of accomplishing or paying for something. [late ME]

way·side (wā′sīd′), *n.* **1.** the side of the way; land immediately adjacent to a road, highway, path, etc.; roadside. —*adj.* **2.** being, situated, or found at or along the wayside: *a wayside inn.* [late ME; see WAY, SIDE[1]]

way′ sta′tion, *U.S.* a station intermediate between principal stations, as on a railroad.

way′ train′, a train that stops at every station along a route; local train.

way·ward (wā′wərd), *adj.* **1.** turned or turning away from what is right or proper; willful; disobedient: *a wayward son; wayward behavior.* **2.** swayed or prompted by caprice; capricious: *wayward fancy; a wayward impulse; to be wayward in one's affections.* **3.** turning or changing irregularly; irregular: *a wayward stream; a wayward breeze.* [ME; aph. var. of *awayward.* See AWAY, -WARD] —**way′ward·ly,** *adv.* —**way′ward·ness,** *n.*
—**Syn. 1.** contrary, headstrong, stubborn, obstinate, disobedient, unruly, refractory, intractable. See **willful. 3.** unsteady, inconstant, changeable.

way·worn (wā′wōrn′, -wôrn′), *adj.* worn or wearied by travel: *She was wayworn after the long trip.* [WAY + WORN]

Way·za·ta (wī zet′ə, -zā′tə), *n.* a town in E Minnesota. 3219 (1960).

Wa·zir·a·bad (wə zēr′ä bäd′), *n.* Balkh.

Wa·zir·i·stan (wä zēr′i stän′), *n.* a mountainous region in Pakistan, in NW West Pakistan province.

Wb, weber; webers.

W/B, waybill. Also, **W.B.**

w.b., **1.** warehouse book. **2.** water ballast. **3.** waybill. **4.** westbound.

WbN, See **west by north.**

WbS, See **west by south.**

W.C., West Central (postal district in London, England).

w.c., **1.** *Chiefly Brit.* water closet. **2.** without charge.

W.C.T.U., Woman's Christian Temperance Union.

wd., **1.** ward. **2.** word.

W.D., War Department.

WDC, War Damage Corporation.

we (wē), *pron. pl.; possessive* **our** or **ours,** *objective* **us. 1.** nominative pl. of **I. 2.** (used by a speaker or writer to denote himself and another person or persons): *We have two children. In this block we all own our own houses.* **3.** (used to denote people in general): *the marvels of science which we take for granted.* **4.** (used to indicate a particular profession, nationality, political party, etc., which includes the speaker or writer): *We in the medical profession have moral responsibilities.* **5.** Also called **the royal "we."** (used by a sovereign, or by other high officials and dignitaries, in place of "I" in formal speech): *We do not wear this crown without humility.* **6.** Also called **the editorial "we."** (used by editors and other writers as a circumlocution for the repetitive and too personal "I"): *As for this column, we will have nothing to do with shady politicians.* **7.** you (used familiarly, often with the implication of mild condescension or sarcasm, as in addressing a child, a patient, a poseur, etc.): *We know that's naughty, don't we? It's time we took our medicine. Aren't we testy?* **8.** (used in the predicate following a copulative verb): *It is we who should thank you.* **9.** (used in apposition with a noun, esp. for emphasis): *We Americans are a sturdy lot.* [ME, OE; c. D *wij,* G *wir,* Icel *vēr,* Goth *weis*]

weak (wēk), *adj.* **1.** not strong; liable to yield, break, or collapse under pressure or strain; fragile; frail: *a weak fortress; a weak spot in armor.* **2.** lacking in bodily strength or healthy vigor, as from age, sickness, etc.; feeble; infirm: *a weak old man; weak eyes.* **3.** not having much political strength, governing power, or authority: *a weak nation; a weak ruler.* **4.** lacking in force, potency, or efficacy; impotent, ineffectual, or inadequate: *weak sunlight; a weak wind.* **5.** lacking in rhetorical or creative force or effectiveness: *a weak reply to the charges; one of the author's weakest novels.* **6.** lacking in logical or legal force or soundness: *a weak argument.* **7.** deficient in mental power, intelligence, or judgment: *a weak mind.* **8.** not having much moral strength or firmness, resolution, or force of character: *to prove weak under temptation; weak compliance.* **9.** deficient in amount, volume, loudness, intensity, etc.; faint; slight: *weak vibrations; a weak current of electricity; a weak pulse.* **10.** deficient, lacking, or poor in something specified: *a hand weak in trumps; I'm weak in spelling.* **11.** deficient in the essential or desirable properties or ingredients: *weak tea; a weak infusion.* **12.** unstressed, as a syllable, vowel, or word. **13.** (of Germanic verbs) inflected with suffixes, without inherited change of the root vowel, as English *work, worked,* and having a preterit ending in a dental, as English *bring, brought.* **14.** (of Germanic nouns and adjectives) inflected with endings originally appropriate to stems terminating in *-n,* as *Alte* in German *der alte Mann* ("the old man") is a weak adjective. **15.** (of wheat or flour) having a low gluten content or having a poor quality of gluten. **16.** *Photog.* thin; not dense. **17.** *Com.* characterized by a decline in prices: *The market was weak in the morning but rallied in the afternoon.* [ME *weik* < Scand (cf. Icel *veikr*); c. OE *wāc,* D *week,* G *weich;* akin to OE *wīcan* to yield, give way, Icel *vīkja* to move, turn, draw back, G *weichen* to yield] —**weak′ish,** *adj.* —**weak′ish·ly,** *adv.* —**weak′ish·ness,** *n.*
—**Syn. 1.** breakable, delicate. **2.** senile, sickly, unwell, invalid. WEAK, DECREPIT, FEEBLE, WEAKLY imply a lack of strength or of good health. WEAK means not physically strong, because of extreme youth, old age, illness, etc.: *weak after an attack of fever.* DECREPIT means old and broken in health to a marked degree: *decrepit and barely able to walk.* FEEBLE denotes much the same as WEAK, but connotes being pitiable or inferior: *feeble and almost senile.* WEAKLY suggests a long-standing sickly condition, a state of chronic bad health: *A weakly child may become a strong man.* **4.** ineffective. **6.** unsound, ineffective, inadequate, illogical, inconclusive, unsustained, unsatisfactory, lame, vague. **7.** unintelligent, simple, foolish, stupid, senseless, silly. **8.** vacillating, wavering, unstable, irresolute, fluctuating, undecided, weak-kneed. **9.** slender, slim, inconsiderable, flimsy, poor, trifling, trivial. **11.** wanting, short, lacking. —**Ant. 1.** strong.

weak′ accumula′tion point′, *Math.* See **accumulation point.**

weak′ derived′ set′, *Math.* See **derived set.**

weak·en (wē′kən), *v.t., v.i.* to make or become weak or weaker. [WEAK + -EN[1]] —**weak′en·er,** *n.*
—**Syn.** enfeeble, debilitate, enervate, undermine, sap, exhaust, deplete, lessen, diminish, lower, reduce, impair, minimize, invalidate. —**Ant.** strengthen.

weak′ end′ing, *Pros.* a verse ending in which the metrical stress falls on a word or syllable which would not be stressed in natural utterance, as a preposition, the object of which is carried over to the next line.

weak′er sex′, the female sex; women.

weak·fish (wēk′fish′), *n., pl.* (*esp. collectively*) **-fish,** (*esp. referring to two or more kinds or species*) **-fish·es.** any sciaenoid food fish of the genus *Cynoscion,* as *C. regalis,* found along the Atlantic and Gulf coasts of the U.S. [< D *weekvis* (obs.), equiv. to *week* soft + *vis* FISH]

weak·hand·ed (wēk′han′did), *adj.* **1.** having weak hands. **2.** having insufficient help; shorthanded: *The flu epidemic didn't help the already weakhanded office.* [WEAK + HANDED]

weak-head·ed (wēk′hed′id), *adj.* **1.** easily intoxicated by alcoholic beverages. **2.** prone to dizziness or giddiness. **3.** weak-minded. —**weak′-head′ed·ly,** *adv.* —**weak′-head′ed·ness,** *n.*

weak·heart·ed (wēk′här′tid), *adj.* without courage or fortitude; fainthearted. [WEAK + HEARTED] —**weak′heart′ed·ly,** *adv.* —**weak′heart′ed·ness,** *n.*

weak-kneed (wēk′nēd′), *adj.* yielding readily to opposition, pressure, intimidation, etc. —**weak′-kneed′ly,** *adv.* —**weak′-kneed′ness,** *n.*

weak·ling (wēk′ling), *n.* **1.** a person who is physically or morally weak. —*adj.* **2.** weak; not strong. [WEAK + -LING[1]]

weak·ly (wēk′lē), *adj.,* **-li·er, -li·est,** *adv.* —*adj.* **1.** weak or feeble in constitution; not robust; sickly. —*adv.* **2.** in a weak manner. [ME *weekely.* See WEAK, -LY] —**weak′li·ness,** *n.*
—**Syn. 1.** See **weak.**

weak-mind·ed (wēk′mīn′did), *adj.* **1.** having or showing a lack of mental firmness; irresolute; vacillating. **2.** having or showing mental feebleness; foolish. —**weak′-mind′ed·ly,** *adv.* —**weak′-mind′ed·ness,** *n.*

weak·ness (wēk′nis), *n.* **1.** the state or quality of being weak; lack of strength, firmness, vigor, or the like; feebleness. **2.** an inadequate or defective quality, as in a person's character; slight fault or defect: *to show great sympathy for human weaknesses.* **3.** a self-indulgent liking or special fondness, as for a particular object: *I've always had a weakness for the opera.* **4.** an object of special desire; something very difficult to resist: *Chocolates were her weakness.* [ME *weikenes.* See WEAK, -NESS]
—**Syn. 1.** fragility. **2.** flaw. See **fault.** —**Ant. 1.** strength.

weak′ sis′ter, *Slang.* **1.** a vacillating person; coward. **2.** a part or element that undermines the whole of something; a weak link: *The weak sisters in the class found the assignments too difficult.*

weak-willed (wēk′wild′), *adj.* having or showing a want of firmness of will; easily swayed; pliable.

weal[1] (wēl), *n.* **1.** *Archaic.* well-being, prosperity, or happiness: *the public weal; weal and woe.* **2.** *Obs.* wealth or riches. **3.** *Obs.* the body politic; the state. [ME *wele,* OE *wela;* cf. WELL[1]]

weal[2] (wēl), *n.* wheal (def. 2). [var. of WALE[1], with *ea* of WHEAL]

weald (wēld), *n.* wooded or uncultivated country. [ME *weeld,* OE *weald* forest; c. G *Wald;* cf. WOLD[1]]

Weald (wēld), *n.* **The,** a region in SE England, in Kent, Surrey, and Essex counties: once a forest area; now an agricultural region.

wealth (welth), *n.* **1.** a great quantity or store of money, valuable possessions, property, or other riches: *the wealth of a city.* **2.** a rich abundance or profusion of anything; a plentiful amount: *a wealth of imagery.* **3.** *Econ.* **a.** all things that have a value in money, in exchange, or in use. **b.** anything that has utility and is capable of being appropriated or exchanged. **4.** rich or valuable contents or produce: *the wealth of the soil.* **5.** the state of being rich; prosperity; affluence: *persons of wealth and standing.* **6.** *Obs.* happiness. [ME *welth* (see WELL[1], -TH[1]); modeled on *health*] —**wealth′less,** *adj.*
—**Syn. 3a.** possessions, assets, goods, property, money. **5.** opulence, fortune. —**Ant. 5.** poverty.

wealth·y (wel′thē), *adj.,* **wealth·i·er, wealth·i·est. 1.** having great wealth; rich; affluent: *a wealthy person; a wealthy nation.* **2.** characterized by, pertaining to, or suggestive of wealth: *a wealthy appearance.* **3.** rich in character, quality, or amount; abundant or ample: *a novel that is wealthy in its psychological insights.* [late ME; see WEALTH, -Y[1]] —**wealth′i·ly,** *adv.* —**wealth′i·ness,** *n.*
—**Syn. 1.** prosperous, well-to-do, moneyed. See **rich. 3.** copious. —**Ant. 1.** poor. **3.** scanty.

Wealth·y (wel′thē), *n.* a variety of red apple, grown in the U.S., ripening in early autumn. [?]

wean[1] (wēn), *v.t.* **1.** to accustom (a child or young animal) to food other than its mother's milk; cause to stop the need to suckle or depend on the mother for food. **2.** to withdraw (a person, the affections, one's dependency, etc.) from some object, habit, form of enjoyment, or the like: *The need to reduce had weaned us from rich desserts.* [ME *wene,* OE *wenian;* c. D *wennen,* G (*ge*)*wöhnen,* Icel *venja* to accustom] —**wean·ed·ness** (wē′nid nis, wēnd′-), *n.*

wean[2] (wēn), *n. Scot.* a child. [contr. of *wee ane* little one]

wean·er (wē′nər), *n. Stockbreeding.* a device placed over the mouth of an animal that is being weaned, to keep it from suckling. [WEAN[1] + -ER[1]]

wean·ling (wēn′ling), *n.* **1.** a child or animal newly weaned. —*adj.* **2.** newly weaned. [WEAN + -LING[1]]

weap·on (wep′ən), *n.* **1.** any instrument or device for use in attack or defense in combat, fighting, or war, as a sword, rifle, cannon, etc. **2.** anything used against an opponent, adversary, or victim: *the deadly weapon of satire.* **3.** *Zool.* any part or organ serving for attack or defense, as claws, horns, teeth, stings, etc. [ME *wepen,* OE *wǣpen;* c. Icel *vāpn,* Goth *wepna* (pl.), G *Waffe*] —**weap′oned,** *adj.* —**weap′on·less,** *adj.*

weap·on·eer (wep′ə nēr′), *n.* **1.** *Mil.* a person who prepares an atomic bomb for detonation. **2.** a person who designs nuclear weapons. [WEAPON + -EER; modeled (inexactly) on *bombardier*]

weap·on·ry (wep′ən rē), *n.* **1.** weapons or weaponlike instruments collectively. **2.** the invention and production of weapons. [WEAPON + -RY]

weap·on·shaw (wep′ən shô′), *n.* wappenshaw. Also, **weap·schaw·ing** (wep′shô ing), **weap·on·show** (wep′ən shō′).

wear (wâr), *v.,* **wore, worn, wear·ing,** *n.* —*v.t.* **1.** to carry or have on the body or about the person as a covering, equipment, ornament, or the like: *to wear a coat; to wear a saber; to wear a disguise.* **2.** to have or use on the person habitually: *to wear a wig.* **3.** to bear or have in one's aspect or appearance: *to wear a smile; to wear an air of triumph.* **4.** to cause (garments, linens, etc.) to deteriorate or change by wear: *Hard use has worn these gloves.* **5.** to impair, deteriorate, or consume gradually by use or any continued process (often used in combination): *a well-worn volume.* **6.** to waste or diminish gradually by rubbing, scraping, washing, etc.: *rocks worn by the waves.* **7.** to make (a hole, channel, way, etc.) by such action. **8.** to bring about or cause a specified condition in (a person or thing) by use, deterioration, or gradual change: *to wear clothes to rags; to wear a person to a shadow.* **9.** to weary; fatigue; exhaust: *Toil and care soon wear the spirit.* **10.** to pass (time) gradually or tediously (usually fol. by *away* or *out*): *We wore the afternoon away in arguing.* **11.** *Naut.* to bring (a vessel) on another tack by turning her head away from the wind until the wind is on her stern, and then bringing her head up toward the wind on the other side. **12.** *Brit. Dial.* to gather and herd (sheep or cattle) to a pen or pasture. —*v.i.* **13.** to undergo gradual impairment, diminution, reduction, etc., from wear, use, attrition, or other causes (often fol. by *away, down, out,* or *off*). **14.** to retain shape, color, usefulness, value, etc., under wear, use, or any continued strain: *a strong material that will wear; colors that wear well.* **15.** to become or grow gradually by use or trial: *My patience is wearing thin.* **16.** (of time) to pass, esp. slowly or tediously (often fol. by *on* or *away*): *As the day wore on, we had less and less to talk about.* **17.** to have the quality of being easy (or difficult) to tolerate, esp. after a relatively long association: *It's hard to get to know him, but he wears well. That idea won't wear.* **18.** *Naut.* (of a vessel) to come round on another tack by turning away from the wind. **19.** *Obs.* to be commonly worn; to be in fashion. **20. wear down, a.** to reduce or impair by long wearing: *to wear down the heels of one's shoes.* **b.** to weary; tire: *His constant talking wears me down.* **c.** to prevail by persistence; overcome: *to wear down the opposition.* **21. wear off,** to diminish slowly or gradually or to diminish in effect; disappear: *The drug began to wear off.* **22. wear out, a.** to make or become unfit or useless through hard or extended use: *to wear out clothes.* **b.** to expend or consume, esp. slowly or gradually. **c.** to exhaust, as by continued strain; weary: *to wear out one's patience.* —*n.* **23.** the act of wearing; use, as of a garment: *articles for winter wear; I've had a lot of wear out of this coat.* **24.** the state of being worn, as on the person. **25.** clothing, garments, or other articles for wearing, esp. when fashionable or appropriate for a articular function (often used in combination): *travel wear; sportswear.* **26.** gradual impairment, wasting, iminution, etc., as from use: *The carpet shows wear.* **7.** the quality of resisting deterioration with use; urability. **28.** *Naut.* the maneuver of wearing a vessel. ME *were,* OE *wer(ian);* c. Icel *verja,* Goth *wasjan* to lothe] **—wear′er,** *n.*

ear·a·bil·i·ty (wâr′ə bil′i tē), *n.* the durability of lothing under normal wear. [WEARABLE + -ITY]

ear·a·ble (wâr′ə bəl), *adj.* **1.** capable of being worn; appropriate, suitable, or ready for wearing. **—n. 2.** Usually, **wearables.** that which may be worn; lothing. [WEAR + -ABLE]

ear′ and tear′ (târ), damage or deterioration esulting from ordinary use; normal depreciation.

ea·ri·ful (wēr′ē fəl), *adj.* **1.** full of weariness; atigued; exhausted. **2.** causing weariness or fatigue; edious; tiresome; annoying. [late ME; see WEARY, FUL] **—wea′ri·ful·ly,** *adv.* **—wea′ri·ful·ness,** *n.*

ea·ri·less (wēr′ē lis), *adj.* unwearying; tireless: *a eariless vigil.* [late ME; see WEARY, -LESS] **—wea′-i·less·ly,** *adv.*

ear·ing (wâr′ing), *adj.* **1.** relating to or made for ear. **2.** gradually impairing or wasting: *Reading small rint can be wearing on the eyes.* **3.** wearying or exhaust-ig: *a wearing task.* [WEAR + -ING[2]] **—wear′ing·ly,** *dv.*

ear′ing appar′el, clothing; garments.

ear·ish (wēr′ish), *adj.* *Brit. Dial.* **1.** tasteless; in-ipid. **2.** sickly; feeble. **3.** stupid. [ME *werishe.* See EARY, -ISH[1]]

ea·ri·some (wēr′ē səm), *adj.* **1.** causing weariness; atiguing: *a difficult and wearisome march.* **2.** tiresome r tedious: *a wearisome person; a wearisome book.* ate ME *werysom.* See WEARY, -SOME[1]] **—wea′ri·some-y,** *adv.* **—wea′ri·some·ness,** *n.*
—Syn. 1. tiring. **2.** boring, monotonous, humdrum, ull, prosy, prosaic. **—Ant. 2.** interesting.

ear′ land′, *Mech.* either of the areas of two atched or fitted surfaces which show signs of wear or olishing from rubbing against one another.

ear·proof (wâr′pro͞of′), *adj.* resistant to damage r deterioration by normal use or wear. [WEAR + PROOF]

ea·ry (wēr′ē), *adj.,* **-ri·er, -ri·est,** *v.,* **-ried, -ry·ing.** *—adj.* **1.** physically or mentally exhausted by hard work, xertion, strain, etc.; fatigued; tired: *weary eyes; a eary brain.* **2.** characterized by or causing fatigue: *weary journey.* **3.** impatient or dissatisfied with omething (often fol. by *of*): *weary of excuses.* **4.** char-cterized by or causing impatience or dissatisfaction; edious; irksome: *a weary wait.* —*v.t., v.i.* **5.** to make or ecome weary; fatigue or tire: *The long hours of work ave wearied me.* **6.** to make or grow impatient or issatisfied with something or at having too much of omething (often fol. by *of*): *We had quickly wearied at uch witless entertainment. The long drive had wearied us f desert scenery.* [ME *wery,* OE *wērig;* OS *-wōrig;* kin to OE *wōrian* to crumble, break down, totter] **—wea′ri·ly,** *adv.* **—wea′ri·ness,** *n.* **—wea′ry·ing-y,** *adv.*
—Syn. 1. spent. See **tired**[1]. **4.** tiresome, wearisome. . exhaust. **6.** irk; jade. **—Ant. 1.** energetic. **4.** in-eresting. **6.** interest.

ea·sand (wē′zənd), *n.* *Archaic.* **1.** throat. **2.** sophagus; gullet. **3.** trachea; windpipe. Also, *esp. Scot.,* **weason, weazand, wessand.** [ME *wesand,* OE *wǣsend,* var. of *wāsend* gullet; c. OFris *wāsande* vindpipe]

ea·sel (wē′zəl), *n., pl.* **-sels,** (*esp. collectively*) **-sel,** *v.* —*n.* **1.** any small carnivore of the genus *Mustela,* of the amily *Mustelidae,* having long, slender body and eeding chiefly on small odents. **2.** any of vari-us similar animals of the amily *Mustelidae.* **3.** a unning, sneaky person. . a tracked vehicle used n snow, resembling a ractor. **5.** *Slang.* an nformer; stool pigeon. *—v.i.* **6.** to evade an bligation, duty, or the ike; renege (often fol. by ut): *That's one invitation I'd like to weasel out of.* **7.** to use weasel words; be mbiguous; mislead: *Upon cross-examination the witness egan to weasel.* **8.** *Slang.* to inform. [ME *wesele,* OE *wesle, weosule;* c. OHG *wisula,* G *Wiesel*]

Weasel,
Mustela frenata
(Total length 16 in.; tail 6 in.)

ea·sel·ly (wē′zə lē), *adj.* resembling a weasel, esp. n features or manner: *a weaselly little man with furtive yes.* [WEASEL + -Y[1]]

ea·sel-word·ed (wē′zəl wûr′did), *adj.* stated in n intentionally ambiguous or evasive way: *His inept studying resulted in a final essay full of weasel-worded eneralizations.*

wea′sel words′, statements that are evasive, in-direct, or intentionally misleading or ambiguous.

wea·son (wē′zən), *n.* *Chiefly Scot.* weasand.

weath·er (weŧħ′ər), *n.* **1.** the state of the atmosphere with respect to wind, temperature, cloudiness, moisture, pressure, etc. **2.** a strong wind or storm or strong winds and storms collectively: *We've had some real weather this spring.* **3.** Usually, **weathers.** changes or vicissi-tudes in one's lot or fortunes: *He remained a good friend in all weathers.* **4. keep one's weather eye open,** *Informal.* to be on one's guard; be watchful: *A serious investor keeps his weather eye open to anticipate changes in the market.* **5. under the weather,** *Informal.* **a.** somewhat indisposed; ailing; ill. **b.** suffering from a hangover. **c.** more or less drunk: *Many accidents are caused by drivers who are under the weather.* —*v.t.* **6.** to expose to the weather; dry, season, or otherwise affect by exposure to the air or atmosphere: *to weather lumber before marketing it.* **7.** to discolor, disintegrate, or affect injuriously, as by the effects of weather: *These crumbling stones have been weathered by the centuries.* **8.** to bear up against and come safely through (a storm, danger, trouble, etc.). **9.** *Naut.* (of a ship, mariner, etc.) to pass or sail to the windward of: *to weather a cape.* **10.** *Archit.* to cause to slope, so as to shed water. —*v.i.* **11.** to undergo change, esp. discoloration or disintegration, as the result of exposure to atmospheric conditions. **12.** to endure or resist exposure to the weather: *a coat that weathers well.* **13.** to go or come safely through a storm, danger, trouble, etc. (usually fol. by *through*): *It was a difficult time for her, but she weathered through beautifully.* [ME, OE *weder;* c. D *weder,* G *Wetter,* Icel *vethr*] **—weath′er·a·bil′i·ty,** *n.* **—weath′er·er,** *n.*

weath′er back′, an application of weatherproof material to the inner side of a wall facing.

weath·er-beat·en (weŧħ′ər bēt′ən), *adj.* **1.** bearing evidences of wear or damage as a result of exposure to the weather. **2.** tanned, hardened, or otherwise affected by exposure to weather: *a weatherbeaten face.*

weath·er·board (weŧħ′ər bōrd′, -bôrd′), *n.* **1.** *U.S.* an early type of board used as a siding for a building, having parallel faces with a rabbet in the upper edge and so laid that the lower edge of each board overlaps the upper edge of the board below and fits within the rabbet. **2.** *Chiefly Brit.* any of various forms of board used as a siding for a building. **3.** *Naut.* the side of a vessel toward the wind. —*v.t.* **4.** to cover or furnish with weatherboards. [WEATHER + BOARD]

weath·er·board·ing (weŧħ′ər bōr′ding, -bôr′-), *n.* **1.** a covering or facing of weatherboards. **2.** weatherboards collectively. [WEATHERBOARD + -ING[1]]

weath·er-bound (weŧħ′ər bound′), *adj.* delayed or shut in by bad weather.

Weath′er Bu′reau, a bureau of the U.S. Department of Commerce that gathers meteorological information, makes weather forecasts, issues storm and flood warnings, etc.

weath·er·cock (weŧħ′ər kok′), *n.* **1.** a weather vane in the shape of a cock. **2.** (loosely) any weather vane. **3.** a person who readily adopts the latest fads, opinions, etc.: *The countess is the weathercock of the jet set.* —*v.t.* **4.** to equip with a weathercock: *to weathercock the foremast.* —*v.i.* **5.** *Rocketry.* (of an airplane or missile) to tend to turn in the direction of the wind. [ME *wedercoc.* See WEATHER, COCK[1]]

weath′er deck′, (of a ship) the uppermost continuous deck exposed to the weather.

weath·ered (weŧħ′ərd), *adj.* **1.** seasoned or otherwise affected by exposure to the weather. **2.** (of wood) artificially treated to seem discolored or stained by the action of air, rain, etc. **3.** (of rocks) worn, disintegrated, or changed in color or composition by the action of the weather. **4.** *Archit.* made sloping or inclined, as a window sill, to prevent the lodgment of water. [WEATHER + -ED[2]]

weath′er eye′, **1.** sensitivity and alertness to signs of change in the weather. **2.** a steady and astute watch, esp. close observation and alertness to change, as in circumstance, condition, status, etc.: *He kept a weather eye out for new political developments.*

weath·er·fish (weŧħ′ər fish′), *n., pl.* (*esp. collectively*) **-fish,** (*esp. referring to two or more kinds or species*) **-fish·es.** any of several loaches of the genus *Misgurnus,* esp. the European *M. fossilis,* which shows increased activity in response to changes in barometric pressure. [WEATHER + FISH]

Weatherfish
Misgurnus fossilis
(Length 10 in.)

Weath·er·ford (weŧħ′ər fərd), *n.* **1.** a town in N Texas. 9759 (1960). **2.** a town in W Oklahoma. 4499 (1960).

weath′er gauge′, **1.** *Naut.* See under **gauge** (def. 17). **2.** the position of advantage; upper hand: *Having bought out his competitors, he now has the weather gauge in the industry.*

weath·er·glass (weŧħ′ər glas′, -gläs′), *n.* any of various instruments, as a barometer or a hygroscope, designed to indicate the state of the atmosphere. [WEATHER + GLASS]

weath·er·ing (weŧħ′ər ing), *n.* **1.** wash (def. 47). **2.** material used as a weather strip. [ME *wedering,* OE *wederung.* See WEATHER, -ING[1]]

weath′er joint′, a mortar joint having a downward and outward slope. Also called **weath′ered joint′.**

weath·er·ly (weŧħ′ər lē), *adj.* *Naut.* (of a ship or boat) making very little leeway when close-hauled. [WEATHER + -LY] **—weath′er·li·ness,** *n.*

Weath·er·ly (weŧħ′ər lē), *n.* a town in central Pennsylvania. 2591 (1960).

weath·er·man (weŧħ′ər man′), *n., pl.* **-men. 1.** a person who reports and forecasts the weather. **2.** an employee or officer of the U.S. Weather Bureau. [WEATHER + MAN[1]]

weath′er map′, a map or chart showing weather conditions over a wide area at a particular time, compiled from simultaneous observations at different places.

weath·er·proof (weŧħ′ər pro͞of′), *adj.* **1.** able to withstand exposure to all kinds of weather. —*v.t.* **2.** to make (something) weatherproof. [WEATHER + -PROOF] **—weath′er·proof′ness,** *n.*

weath′er ra′dar, radar designed or suitable for use in detecting clouds and precipitation.

weath′er report′, a summary of weather conditions, often including predicted conditions, for an area.

weath′er sig′nal, a visual signal, as a light or flag, indicating a weather forecast.

weath′er sta′tion, an installation equipped and used for the making of meteorological observations.

weath′er strip′, a narrow strip of metal, wood, rubber, etc., placed between a door or window sash and its frame to exclude rain, air, etc.

weath·er-strip (weŧħ′ər strip′), *v.t.,* **-stripped, -strip·ping.** to apply weather stripping to (something).

weath′er strip′ping, **1.** See **weather strip. 2.** a number of weather strips, taken collectively.

weath′er tide′, *Naut.* a tide moving against the direction of the wind.

weath·er·tight (weŧħ′ər tīt′), *adj.* secure against wind, rain, etc. [WEATHER + TIGHT] **—weath′er-tight′ness,** *n.*

weath′er vane′, vane (def. 1).

weath·er-wise (weŧħ′ər wīz′), *adj.* **1.** skillful in predicting weather. **2.** skillful in predicting reactions, opinions, etc.: *weather-wise political experts.* [late ME *wederwise.* See WEATHER, WISE[1]]

weath·er·worn (weŧħ′ər wōrn′, -wôrn′), *adj.* weather-beaten. [WEATHER + WORN]

weave (wēv), *v.,* **wove** or (*Rare*) **weaved; wo·ven** or **wove; weav·ing;** *n.* —*v.t.* **1.** to interlace (threads, yarns, strips, fibrous material, etc.) so as to form a fabric or material. **2.** to form by interlacing threads, yarns, strands, or strips of some material: *to weave a basket; to weave cloth.* **3.** to form by combining various elements or details into a connected whole: *to weave a tale; to weave a plan.* **4.** to introduce as an element or detail into a connected whole (usually fol. by *in* or *into*): *to weave a melody into a musical composition.* **5.** to move (someone or something) along in a winding or zigzag course; move from side to side, esp. to avoid obstructions: *to weave one's way through traffic.* —*v.i.* **6.** to form or construct fabric or a material by interlacing threads, yarns, strips, etc. **7.** to compose a connected whole by combining various elements or details. **8.** to be or become formed or composed from the interlacing of materials or the combining of various elements: *The yarn wove into a beautiful fabric.* **9.** to move or proceed from side to side: *dancers weaving in time to the music.* —*n.* **10.** a pattern of or method for interlacing yarns. [ME *weve,* OE *wefan;* c. Icel *vefa,* G *weben;* see WEB]
—Syn. 3. contrive, fabricate, construct, compose. **4.** insert, intermix, intermingle.

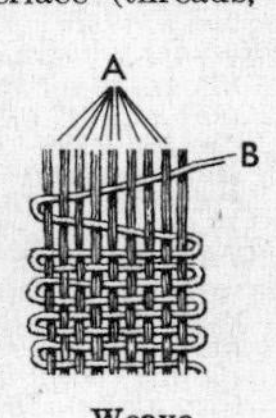

Weave
A, Warp
B, Filling

weave′ bead′, *Welding.* See under **bead** (def. 12).

weav·er (wē′vər), *n.* **1.** a person who weaves. **2.** a person whose occupation is weaving. **3.** a weaverbird. [late ME *wevere.* See WEAVE, -ER[1]]

Wea·ver (wē′vər), *n.* **1. Robert Clifton,** born 1907, U.S. economist and government official: first Secretary of Housing and Urban Development, 1966–68. **2.** a boy's given name.

weav·er·bird (wē′vər bûrd′), *n.* any of numerous, chiefly African and Asian, passerine birds of the family *Ploceidae,* that are related to the finches and that build elaborately woven nests. Also called **weav′er finch′.** [WEAVER + BIRD]

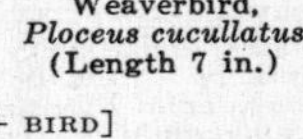

Weaverbird,
Ploceus cucullatus
(Length 7 in.)

Weavers, The, a play (1892) by Gerhart Hauptmann.

wea′ver's hitch′. See **sheet bend.** Also called **weav′er's knot′.**

wea·zand (wē′zənd), *n.* *Chiefly Scot.* weasand.

web (web), *n., v.,* **webbed, web·bing.** —*n.* **1.** something formed by or as by weaving or interweaving. **2.** a thin silken fabric spun by spiders and by the larvae of some insects, as the webworms, tent caterpillars, etc.; cobweb. **3.** a woven fabric, esp. a whole piece of cloth in the course of being woven or after it comes from the loom. **4.** something resembling woven material, esp. something having an interlaced or latticelike appearance: *He looked up at the web of branches of the old tree. His hands were covered with a web of dirt and grime.* **5.** webbing. **6.** *Zool.* **a.** a membrane which connects the digits of an animal. **b.** that which connects the toes of aquatic birds and aquatic mammals. **7.** *Ornith.* **a.** the series of barbs on each side of the shaft of a feather. **b.** the series on both sides, collectively. **8.** an integral or separate part of a beam, rail, truss, or the like, that forms a continuous, flat, narrow, rigid connection between two stronger, broader parallel parts, as the flanges of a structural shape, the head and foot of a rail, or the upper and lower chords of a truss. **9.** *Mach.* an arm of a crank, usually one of a pair, holding one end of a crankpin at its outer end. **10.** *Metalworking.* a thin piece of superfluous metal at the edge of a forging; fin. **11.** *Archit.* (in a vault) any surface framed by ribbing. **12.** the flat woven strip, without pile, often found at one or both ends of an Oriental rug. **13.** *Rocketry.* a block of solid propellant having holes cut out in a symmetrical pattern, used in a rocket or missile. **14.** a large roll of paper, as for continuous feeding of a press. **15.** *Informal.* a network of radio or television broadcasting stations. **16.** an intricate set or pattern of circumstances, facts, evidence, etc.: *The thief was convicted by a web of evidence. Who can understand the web of life?* **17.** a network of interlinked stations, services, communications, etc., covering a region or country. —*v.t.* **18.** to cover with or as with a web; envelop. **19.** to ensnare or entrap. —*v.i.* **20.** to make or form a web. [ME, OE; c. D, LG *webbe,* Icel *vefr;* akin to WEAVE] **—web′less,** *adj.* **—web′like′,** *adj.*

Web of spider

Webb (web), *n.* **(Martha) Beatrice (Potter),** 1858–1943, and her husband **Sidney (James), 1st Baron Pass·field** (pas′fēld′), 1859–1947, English economists, social reformers, authors, and socialists.

Webb (web), *n.* a crater in the fourth quadrant of the face of the moon: about 18 miles in diameter.

Webb′ Cit′y, a town in SW Missouri. 6740 (1960).

webbed (webd), *adj.* **1.** having the fingers or toes connected by a web or membrane: *the webbed foot of a duck or beaver.* **2.** connected or joined by a web, as the fingers or toes. **3.** formed like or with a web: *a webbed roof.* [WEB + -ED[3]]

Web·be She·be·li (web′ā shi bā′lē). See **Webi Shebeli.** Also, **Web′be Shi·be′li.**

web·bing (web′ing), *n.* **1.** a strong, woven material of hemp, cotton, or jute, in bands of various widths, used for belts, carrying straps, harness, etc. **2.** such woven bands nailed on furniture under springs or upholstery, for support. **3.** *Zool.* the membrane forming a web or webs. **4.** something resembling this, as the leather thongs or piece connecting the sections for the thumb and forefinger in a baseball glove or mitt. **5.** any material or part formed from interlaced threads, thongs, branches, etc., or having a latticelike appearance, as the face of a tennis racket. [late ME; see WEB, -ING[1]]

web·by (web′ē), *adj.*, **-bi·er, -bi·est.** **1.** pertaining to, of the nature of, or resembling a web. **2.** webbed. [WEB + -Y[1]]

we·ber (vā′bər, wē′-, web′ər), *n. Elect.* the meter-kilogram-second unit of magnetic flux and magnetic pole strength, equal to a flux that produces an electromotive force of one volt in a single turn of wire when the flux is uniformly reduced to zero in a period of one second; 10^8 maxwells. *Abbr.:* Wb [named after W. E. WEBER]

We·ber (vā′bər; *Ger.* vā′bər), *n.* **1. Ernst Hein·rich** (ernst hīn′rikh), 1795–1878, German physiologist. **2. Baron Karl Ma·ri·a Frie·drich Ernst von** (kärl mä rē′ä frē′drikh ernst fən), 1786–1878, German pianist, conductor, and composer. **3. Max** (maks; *Ger.* mäks), 1864–1920, German sociologist and political economist. **4. Wil·helm E·du·ard** (vil′helm ā′doo-ärt′), 1804–91, German physicist (brother of Ernst).

We·be′ri·an apparat′us (vā bēr′ē ən), *n.* (in certain fishes) a chain of small bones connecting the inner ear with the air bladder. [named after E. H. WEBER; see -IAN]

We·bern (vā′bərn; *Ger.* vā′bərn), *n.* **An·ton von** (än′tōn fən), 1883–1945, Austrian composer.

web-fed (web′fed′), *adj.* (of a printing press) fed by and designed to print a continuous roll of paper. Cf. **sheet-fed.**

web′ foot′, *Furniture.* a pad foot having the appearance of toes joined by a web. Also called **duck foot.**

web·foot (web′fo͝ot′), *n., pl.* **-feet.** **1.** a foot with the toes joined by a web. **2.** (*cap.*) a native or inhabitant of Oregon (the **Webfoot State**) (used as a nickname). **3.** an animal with webfeet. [WEB + FOOT] —**web′ foot′-ed,** *adj.*

Web′foot State′, Oregon (used as a nickname).

web′ frame′, *Naut.* a deep transverse frame reinforcing the hull of a ship. Also called **transverse.**

We·bi She·be·li (wā′bi shi bā′lē), a river in E Africa, flowing SE from central Ethiopia to the Juba River, in Somalia. ab. 700 mi. long. Also, **Webbe Shebeli, Webbe Shibeli, We′bi Shibe′li.**

web′ mem′ber, *Civ. Eng.* any of the structural members of a truss between the chords.

web′ press′, *Print.* a press into which paper is fed automatically from a large roll. Also, **web′-fed′ press′.**

web′ spin′ner, any of several elongated slender insects of the order *Embioptera* that nest in silken webs spun by organs in the enlarged front tarsi. Also called **embiid.**

web·ster (web′stər), *n. Archaic.* a weaver. [ME; OE *webbestre.* See WEB, -STER]

Web·ster (web′stər), *n.* **1. Daniel,** 1782–1852, U.S. statesman and orator. **2. John,** c1580–1625?, English dramatist. **3. Noah,** 1758–1843, U.S. lexicographer and essayist. **4.** a town in SW Maine. 4747 (1960). **5.** a town in W New York. 3060 (1960).

Web′ster-Ash′bur·ton Trea′ty (web′stər ash′-bûr tən), an agreement between the U.S. and England in 1842 fixing the boundary line between Canada and the State of Maine. [named after Daniel WEBSTER and Alexander BARING, 1st Baron *Ashburton,* who negotiated it]

Web′ster Cit′y, a town in central Iowa. 8520 (1960).

Web′ster Groves′, a city in E Missouri, near St. Louis. 28,990 (1960).

Web·ste·ri·an (web stēr′ē ən), *adj.* **1.** pertaining to or characteristic of Daniel Webster, his political theories, or his oratory. **2.** pertaining to or characteristic of Noah Webster or his dictionary. [WEBSTER + -IAN]

web·ster·ite (web′stə rīt′), *n.* aluminite. [named after T. *Webster,* 19th-century Englishman; see -ITE[1]]

web-toed (web′tōd′), *adj.* web-footed.

web·worm (web′wûrm′), *n.* the larva of any of several pyralid moths, as *Hyphantria cunea* **(fall webworm)** or *Loxostege similalis* **(garden webworm),** which spins a web over the foliage on which it feeds. [WEB + WORM]

Wechs′ler-Belle′vue Scale′ (weks′lər bel′vyo͞o), *Psychol.* a series of tests for measuring intelligence, adapted for both adults and children. [named after Dr. David *Wechsler* (b. 1896), American psychologist and *Bellevue* Hospital]

wecht (wekht), *n. Scot.* weight.

wecht·y (wekh′tē), *adj. Scot.* weighty.

wed (wed), *v.,* **wed·ded** or **wed, wed·ding.** —*v.t.* **1.** to marry (another person) in a formal ceremony; take as one's husband or wife. **2.** to unite (a couple) in marriage or wedlock; marry. **3.** to bind by close or lasting ties; attach firmly: *He wedded himself to the cause of the poor.* **4.** to blend together or unite inseparably: *It is the perfect novel which weds style and content.* —*v.i.* **5.** to contract marriage; marry. **6.** to become united or to blend: *a building that will wed with the landscape.* [ME *wedde,* OE *weddian* to pledge; c. G *wetten* to bet, Icel *vethja* pledge; cf. WADSET]

we'd (wēd), contraction of *we had, we should,* or *we would.*

Wed., Wednesday.

wed·ded (wed′id), *adj.* **1.** united in matrimony; married: *the wedded couple; a wedded woman.* **2.** of or pertaining to marriage or to those married: *the wedded state; wedded happiness.* **3.** attached or dedicated, esp. obstinately or unshakably: *a fearless man wedded to a just cause.* **4.** associated or bound together inseparably: *form and substance in wedded harmony.* [ME; OE *geweddodan.* See WED, -ED[2]]

Wed′dell Sea′ (wed′əl), an arm of the Atlantic, E of Antarctic Peninsula.

wed·ding (wed′ing), *n.* **1.** the act or ceremony of marrying; marriage; nuptials. **2.** the anniversary of a marriage, or its celebration: *They invited guests to their silver wedding.* **3.** the act or an instance of blending or joining, esp. opposite or contrasting elements: *a perfect wedding of conservatism and liberalism.* [ME; OE *weddung.* See WED, -ING[1]] —**Syn. 1.** See **marriage.**

wed′ding cake′, **1.** a white cake, traditionally in tiered layers, covered with white icing and decorated. **2.** (in England) a fruit cake, similar in appearance.

wed′ding chest′, an ornamented chest for a trousseau.

wed′ding day′, **1.** the day of a wedding. **2.** the anniversary of a wedding.

wed′ding march′, a musical composition played during a wedding procession.

wed′ding ring′, **1.** a ring, usually of gold, platinum, or silver, given to the bride by the groom during a marriage ceremony. **2.** a ring similarly given to the groom by the bride. [ME]

We·de·kind (vā′də kint), *n.* **Frank** (fränk), 1864–1918, German poet and dramatist.

we·deln (vād′əln), *n.* a skiing technique first developed in Austria in the 1950's that consists of high-speed turns made in succession with both skis parallel while not noticeably setting the ski edges on a slope. [< G: lit., wagging (the tail)]

wedge (wej), *n., v.,* **wedged, wedg·ing.** —*n.* **1.** a piece of hard material with two principal faces meeting in a sharply acute angle, for raising, holding, or splitting objects by applying a pounding or driving force, as from a hammer. Cf. **machine** (def. 4b). **2.** a piece of anything of like shape: *a wedge of pie.* **3.** a cuneiform character or stroke of this shape. **4.** *Meteorol.* (formerly) an elongated area of relatively high pressure. **5.** something that serves to part, split, divide, etc.: *a wedge was driven into the party organization.* **6.** *Mil.* (formerly) a tactical formation generally in the form of a V with the point toward the enemy. **7.** *Golf.* a club with an iron head the face of which is nearly horizontal, for lofting the ball, esp. out of sand traps and high grass. **8.** *Metalworking.* a forming tool used in spinning metal. —*v.t.* **9.** to separate or split with or as with a wedge (often fol. by *open, apart,* etc.): *to wedge open a log.* **10.** to pack or fix tightly by driving in a wedge or wedges. **11.** to thrust, drive, fix, etc., like a wedge: *He wedged himself through the narrow opening.* **12.** *Ceram.* to pound (clay) in order to remove air bubbles. **13.** to fell or direct the fall of (a tree) by driving wedges into the cut made by the saw. —*v.i.* **14.** to force a way like a wedge (usually fol. by *in, into, through,* etc.): *The box won't wedge into such a narrow space.* [ME *wegge,* OE *wecg;* c. dial. G *Weck* (OHG *wecki*), Icel *veggr*] —**wedge′like′,** *adj.*

Wedge

wedged (wejd), *adj.* having the shape of a wedge. [WEDGE + -ED[3]]

wedge′ heel′, a heel formed by a roughly triangular or wedgelike piece that extends from the front to the back of the sole, used on women's shoes.

Wedg·ie (wej′ē), *n. Trademark.* a shoe having a wedge heel.

Wedg·wood (wej′wo͝od′), *n.* **1. Josiah,** 1730–95, English potter. **2.** *Trademark* ceramic ware of Josiah Wedgwood and his successors.

wedg·y (wej′ē), *adj.,* **wedg·i·er, wedg·i·est.** resembling a wedge; wedgelike. [WEDGE + -Y[1]]

wed·lock (wed′lok), *n.* the state of marriage; matrimony. [ME *wedlok,* OE *wedlāc,* lit., a pledging, equiv. to *wed* pledge (see WED) + *-lāc* verbal n. suffix] —**Syn.** nuptials, espousal.

Wednes·day (wenz′dē, -dā), *n.* the fourth day of the week, following Tuesday. [ME *Wednesdai,* OE **Wēdnesdæg,* mutated var. of *Wōdnesdæg* Woden's day; c. D *Woensdag,* Dan *onsdag;* trans. of L *Mercurii dies* day of Mercury]

Wednes·days (wenz′dēz, -dāz), *adv.* on or during Wednesdays; every Wednesday.

wee (wē), *adj.,* **we·er, we·est,** *n.* —*adj.* **1.** little; very small. **2.** very early: *in the wee hours of the morning.* —*n.* **3.** *Scot.* **a.** a little bit. **b.** a short space of time. [ME *we,* var. of *wei* (small) quantity, OE *wēg,* var. of *wǣge* weight, akin to *wegan* to WEIGH[1]] —**Syn. 1.** tiny, diminutive; minuscule.

weed[1] (wēd), *n.* **1.** a valueless plant growing wild, esp. one that grows on cultivated ground to the exclusion or injury of the desired crop. **2.** any useless, troublesome, or noxious plant, esp. one that grows profusely: *The vacant lot was covered with weeds.* **3.** *Slang.* **a.** a cigarette or cigar. **b.** a marijuana cigarette. **4.** a thin, ungainly person or animal. **5.** a wretched or useless animal, esp. a horse unfit for racing or breeding purposes. **6. the weed, a.** *Informal.* tobacco. **b.** *Slang.* marijuana. —*v.t.* **7.** to free from weeds or troublesome plants; to root out weeds from: *to weed a garden.* **8.** to root out or remove (a weed or weeds), as from a garden (often fol. by *out*): *to weed out crab grass from a lawn.* **9.** to remove as being undesirable, inefficient, or superfluous (often fol. by *out*): *to weed out inexperienced players.* **10.** to rid (something) of undesirable or superfluous elements. —*v.i.* **11.** to remove weeds or the like. [ME *wede,* OE *wēod;* c. OS *wiod* weed, MD *wiet* fern] —**weed′less,** *adj.* —**weed′like′,** *adj.*

weed[2] (wēd), *n.* **1. weeds,** mourning garments: *widow's weeds.* **2.** a mourning band of black crepe or cloth, as worn on a man's hat or coat sleeve. **3.** *Archaic.* **a.** a garment: *clad in rustic weeds.* **b.** clothing. [ME *wede,* OE *wǣd,* (*ge*)*wǣde* garment, clothing; c. OS *wād, gewādi,* OHG *wāt, gewāti* clothing; cf. WADMAL]

Weed (wēd), *n.* **1. Thur·low** (thûr′lō), 1797–1882, U.S. journalist and politician. **2.** a town in N California. 3223 (1960).

Wee·da (wē′də), *n.* a girl's given name, form of **Ouida.**

weed·er (wē′dər), *n.* **1.** a person who removes weeds, as from a garden or lawn. **2.** a device, as a tool or machine, for removing weeds. [late ME; see WEED[1], -ER[1]]

weed-kill·er (wēd′kil′ər), *n.* an herbicide.

weed·y (wē′dē), *adj.,* **weed·i·er, weed·i·est.** **1.** full of or abounding in weeds. **2.** consisting of or pertaining to weeds. **3.** (of a plant, flower, etc.) growing poorly or in a straggling manner. **4.** (of a person or animal) thin, ungainly, or scrawny. [late ME; see WEED[1], -Y[1]] —**weed′i·ly,** *adv.* —**weed′i·ness,** *n.*

week (wēk), *n.* **1.** a period of seven successive days, usually understood as beginning with Sunday and ending with Saturday. **2.** a period of seven successive days that begins with or includes an indicated day: *the week of June 3; Christmas week.* **3.** a period of seven successive days devoted to a particular celebration, honor, cause, etc.: *National Book Week.* **4.** the working days or working portion of the seven-day period; workweek: *A 35-hour week is now a commonplace.* —*adv.* **5.** *Brit.* seven days before or after a specified day: *I shall come Tuesday week. He left yesterday week.* [ME *weke,* OE *wice;* c. D *week,* Icel *vika* week, Goth *wiko* turn, L *vicis* change]

week·day (wēk′dā′), *n.* **1.** any day of the week except the Sabbath. —*adj.* **2.** of or on a weekday: *weekday occupations.* [ME; OE *wicdæg.* See WEEK, DAY]

week·days (wēk′dāz′), *adv.* every day, esp. Monday through Friday, during the workweek: *Weekdays we're open from nine till five.* [WEEK + DAYS]

week·end (wēk′end′), *n.* **1.** the end of a week, esp. the period of time between Friday evening and Monday morning: *We spent the weekend at Virginia Beach.* —*adj.* **2.** of, for, or on a weekend: *a weekend pass; a weekend excursion.* —*v.i.* **3.** to pass the weekend, as at a place: *They weekended at their country place.* [WEEK + END[1]]

week·end·er (wēk′en′dər), *n.* **1.** a person who goes on a weekend vacation. **2.** a weekend guest. **3.** a traveling bag large enough to carry the clothing and personal articles needed for a weekend trip. **4.** a small pleasure boat, esp. a sailboat, equipped to accommodate usually not more than four persons for a weekend cruise. [WEEKEND + -ER[1]]

week·ends (wēk′endz′), *adv.* every weekend; on or during weekends: *We go fishing weekends.* [WEEK + END[1] + -S[3]]

week′end war′rior, *U.S. Military Slang.* a reservist who attends weekend meetings of his unit in order to fulfill his military obligations.

Week·ley (wēk′lē), *n.* **Ernest,** 1865–1954, English etymologist and lexicographer.

week·ly (wēk′lē), *adj., adv., n., pl.* **-lies.** —*adj.* **1.** done, happening, appearing, etc., once a week, or every week: *a weekly appointment with an analyst.* **2.** computed or determined by the week: *a special weekly rate.* **3.** of or pertaining to a week or the working days in a week: *a day of respite from our weekly labors.* —*adv.* **4.** once a week; by the week: *to visit someone weekly; to pay rent weekly.* —*n.* **5.** a periodical appearing once a week. [late ME; see WEEK, -LY]

Weems (wēmz), *n.* **Mason Locke,** 1759–1825, U.S. clergyman and biographer.

ween (wēn), *v.t., v.i. Archaic.* **1.** to think; suppose. **2.** to expect, hope, or intend. [ME *wene(n),* OE *wēnan* to expect; c. Goth *wenjan,* Icel *væna* to hope, expect, G *wähnen* to imagine]

wee·nie (wē′nē), *n. Informal.* a wiener. Also, **weeny, wienie.**

wee·ny (wē′nē), *n., pl.* **-nies.** *Informal.* weenie.

weep[1] (wēp), *v.,* **wept, weep·ing,** *n.* —*v.i.* **1.** to express grief, sorrow, or any overpowering emotion by shedding tears; shed tears; cry: *to weep for joy; to weep with rage.* **2.** to let fall drops of water or other liquid; drip; leak: *The old water tank was weeping at the seams.* **3.** to exude water or liquid, as soil, rock, a plant stem, a sore, etc. —*v.t.* **4.** to weep for (someone or something); mourn with tears or other expression of sorrow: *He wept his dead brother.* **5.** to shed (tears); pour forth in weeping: *to weep tears of gratitude.* **6.** to let fall or give forth in drops: *trees weeping an odorous gum.* **7.** to pass, bring, put, etc., with the shedding of tears (usually fol. by *away, out,* etc.): *to weep one's eyes out; to weep oneself to sleep.* —*n.* **8.** *Informal.* weeping, or a fit of weeping. **9.** exudation of water or liquid. [ME *wepe(n),* OE *wēpan* to wail; c. Goth *wopjan* to call, Icel *æpa* to cry out] —**Syn. 1.** sob; wail, lament. **4.** bewail, bemoan, lament. —**Ant. 1.** laugh, rejoice.

weep[2] (wēp), *n. Brit. Dial.* the lapwing, *Vanellus vanellus,* of Europe, so called from its cries.

weep·er (wē′pər), *n.* **1.** a person who weeps. **2.** (formerly) a hired mourner at a funeral. **3.** something worn as a badge of mourning, as a widow's black veil. **4.** a wine bottle that has lost some of its contents through the cork. **5.** any of various loose-hanging, streamerlike objects, as a long, hanging hatband, a tendril of moss hanging from a tree, etc. [late ME; see WEEP[1], -ER[1]]

weep′ hole′, *Building Trades.* a hole for draining off accumulated moisture, as from condensation or seepage. [alter. of *weeping-hole*]

weep·ing (wē′ping), *adj.* **1.** expressing grief, sorrow, or any overwhelming emotion by shedding tears: *weeping multitudes.* **2.** tearful; weepy: *a weeping fit.* **3.** tending or liable to cry; given to crying. **4.** dripping or oozing liquid. **5.** (of trees, shrubs, etc.) having slender, drooping branches. [ME; OE *wepende.* See WEEP[1], -ING[2]] —**weep′ing·ly,** *adv.*

weep′ing gold′en bell′, a shrub, *Forsythia suspensa,* of China, which has long, arching, pendulous, hollow branches which root at the tip in age, and golden-yellow flowers.

weep′ing my′all. See under **myall.**

weep′ing wil′low, an Asian willow, *Salix babylonica,* characterized by the drooping habit of its branches: grown as an ornamental.

weep·y (wē′pē), *adj.,* **weep·i·er, weep·i·est.** **1.** of or like weeping; tearful. **2.** easily moved to tears. **3.** exuding water or other moisture; leaky; seepy. [WEEP[1] + -Y[1]] —**weep′i·ness,** *n.*

wee·ver (wē′vər), *n.* **1.** either of two small, European, marine fishes of the genus *Trachinus, T. draco* **(greater weever)** or *T. vipera* **(lesser weever),** having highly poisonous dorsal spines. **2.** any fish of the same family, *Trachinidae.* [? ME **wever,* OE *wifer* arrow (c. Icel *vifr* sword); modern meaning by assoc. with obs. *wiver* viper; see WIVERN]

wee·vil (wē′vəl), *n.* **1.** Also called **snout beetle.** any of numerous beetles of the family *Curculionidae,* which have the head prolonged into a snout, and which are destructive to nuts, grain, fruit, etc. **2.** any of several related beetles of the family *Mylabridae,* the larvae of which live and feed in seeds, esp. those of legumes. [ME *wevel,* OE *wifel;* c. OHG *wibil* beetle; akin to WAVE]

wee·vil·y (wē′və lē), *adj.* infested with weevils. Also, **wee′vil·ly, wee·viled, wee·villed** (wē′vəld). [WEEVIL + -LY]

wee·wee (wē′wē′), *n., v.,* **-weed, -weeing.** *Baby Talk.* —*n.* **1.** urine. —*v.i.* **2.** to urinate.

weft[1] (weft), *n.* **1.** *Textiles.* filling (def. 4). **2.** a woven fabric or garment. [ME, OE; see WEAVE]

weft[2] (weft), *n.* *Naut.* waif (def. 4).

weft-knit·ted (weft′nit′id), *adj.* noting or pertaining to a fabric made by weft knitting. Also, **weft′-knit′.**

weft′ knit′ting, a knitting process in which the yarn is knitted horizontally and in a circular form. Also called **filling knitting.** Cf. **warp knitting.**

weft·wise (weft′wīz′), *adv.* *Textiles.* in a horizontal direction; from selvage to selvage; crosswise. [WEFT[1] + -WISE]

Wehr·macht (vâr′mäkht′), *n.* the German armed forces of the years prior to and during World War II. [< G, equiv. to *Wehr* defense + *Macht* force]

Wei (wā), *n.* any of several dynasties that ruled in China, esp. one ruling A.D. 64–220, and one ruling A.D. 386–534.

Weich·sel (vīk′səl), *n.* German name of the **Vistula.**

Weid·man (wīd′mən), *n.* **1. Charles,** born 1901, U.S. dancer, choreographer, and teacher. **2. Jerome,** born 1913, U.S. author.

Wei·er·strass (vī′ər sträs′, -shträs′; *Ger.* vī′ər-shträs′), *n.* **Karl The·o·dor** (kärl tā′ō dôr′), 1815–97, German mathematician.

Wei′erstrass approxima′tion the′orem, *Math.* the theorem that for any continuous function on a closed interval, there is a polynomial such that the difference in values of the function and the polynomial at each point in the interval is less in absolute value than some positive number. [named after K. T. WEIERSTRASS]

Wei·gel (wī′gəl), *n.* a crater in the third quadrant of the face of the moon: about 20 miles in diameter.

wei·ge·la (wī gē′lə, -jē′-, wī′gə lə), *n.* any of various shrubby, caprifoliaceous plants of the genus *Weigela*, of eastern Asia, having funnel-shaped, white, pink, or crimson flowers. Also, **wei·ge·li·a** (wī gē′lē ə, -jē′-). [< NL, named after C. E. *Weigel* (1748–1831), German physician]

weigh (wā), *v.t.* **1.** to determine or ascertain the force which gravitation exerts upon (a person or thing) by use of a balance, scale, or other mechanical device: *to weigh oneself; to weigh potatoes; to weigh gases.* **2.** to hold up or balance, as in the hand, in order to estimate the weight. **3.** to measure, separate, or apportion (a certain quantity of something) according to weight (usually fol. by *out*): *to weigh out five pounds of sugar.* **4.** to make heavy; increase the weight or bulk of; weight: *We weighed the drapes to make them hang properly.* **5.** to evaluate in the mind; consider carefully in order to reach an opinion, decision, or choice: *to weigh the facts; to weigh a proposal.* **6.** *Archaic.* to raise, lift, or hoist (something). **7.** *Obs.* to think important; esteem. —*v.i.* **8.** to have weight or a specified amount of weight: *to weigh less; to weigh a ton.* **9.** to have importance, moment, or consequence: *Your recommendation weighs heavily in his favor.* **10.** to bear down as a weight or burden (usually fol. by *on* or *upon*): *Responsibility weighed upon him.* **11.** to consider carefully or judicially: *to weigh well before deciding.* **12.** (of a ship) to raise the anchor and get under way: *The ship weighed early and escaped in the fog.* **13. weigh anchor,** *Naut.* to heave up a ship's anchor in preparation for getting under way. **14. weigh down, a.** to be or cause to become bowed under a weight: *trees weighed down by snow and ice.* **b.** to lower the spirits of; burden; depress: *weighed down with care.* **15. weigh in,** *Sports.* **a.** (of a boxer or wrestler) to be weighed by a medical examiner on the day of a bout. **b.** to be of the weight determined by such a weighing: *He weighed in at 170 pounds.* **c.** (of a jockey) to be weighed with the saddle and weights after a race. **16. weigh one's words.** See **word** (def. 25). **17. weigh out,** *Horse Racing.* (of a jockey) **a.** to be weighed with the saddle and weights before a race. **b.** to be of the weight determined by such a weighing. [ME *weghe,* OE *wegan* to carry, weigh; c. D *wegen,* G *wägen,* Icel *vega,* L *vehere*] —**weigh′a·ble,** *adj.* —**weigh′er,** *n.*
—**Syn. 5.** ponder, contemplate. See **study.**

weigh·bridge (wā′brij′), *n.* a platform scale that stands flush with a road and is used for weighing trucks, livestock, etc. [WEIGH + BRIDGE[1]]

weigh-in (wā′in′), *n.* *Sports.* the act or an instance of weighing in: *After the weigh-in the fighters posed for photographers.* [n. use of v. phrase *weigh in*]

weigh·man (wā′mən), *n., pl.* **-men. 1.** one whose occupation is weighing goods, produce, etc. **2.** *Mining.* one who weighs coal extracted from a mine, esp. in mines where miners are paid according to the weight of the coal they dig. Cf. **checkweighman.** [WEIGH + MAN[1]]

weight (wāt), *n.* **1.** the amount or quantity of heaviness or mass; amount a thing weighs. **2.** *Physics.* the force which gravitation exerts upon a body, equal to the mass of the body times the local acceleration of gravity: commonly taken, in a region of constant gravitational acceleration, as a measure of mass. **3.** a system of units for expressing heaviness or mass: *avoirdupois weight.* **4.** a unit of heaviness or mass: *The pound is a common weight in English-speaking countries.* **5.** a body of determinate mass, as of metal, for using on a balance or scale in weighing objects, substances, etc. **6.** a specific quantity of a substance which is determined by weighing or which weighs a fixed amount: *a half-ounce weight of gold dust.* **7.** any heavy load, mass, or object: *Put down that weight and rest your arms.* **8.** an object used or useful solely because of its heaviness: *the weights of a clock. A weight held the door open.* **9.** a mental or moral burden, as of care, sorrow, or responsibility: *the weight of cares; Knowing you are safe takes a weight off my mind.* **10.** importance, moment, consequence, or effective influence: *an opinion of great weight.* **11.** *Statistics.* a measure of the relative importance of an item in a statistical population. **12.** (of clothing, textiles, etc.) **a.** relative heaviness or thickness as related to warmth, or to seasonal use (often used in combination): *a winter-weight jacket.* **b.** relative heaviness or thickness as related to use: *a bolt of coat-weight woolen cloth.* **13.** *Print.* (of type) the degree of blackness or boldness. **14.** (in boxing and wrestling) a division or class to which a contestant belongs according to how much he weighs: *Cassius Clay has a brother who fights in the same weight.* **15.** the total amount the jockey, saddle, and leads must weigh on a racehorse during a race, according to the conditions of the race: *Jacinto has a weight of 122 pounds in the seventh race.* **16.** the stress or accent value given a sound, syllable, or word. **17. by weight,** according to measurement of heaviness or mass: *Rates are determined by weight.* **18. carry weight,** to have importance or significance; influence: *His opinion is certain to carry weight.* **19. pull one's weight,** to contribute one's rightful share of work to a project or job: *They will finish in time if everyone pulls his weight.* Also, **pull one's own weight. 20. throw one's weight around** or **about,** to use one's power and influence, esp. beyond the bounds of propriety to secure some personal gain: *After the boss started throwing his weight around, he managed to get a new car from the company.* —*v.t.* **21.** to add weight to; load with additional weight: *to weight sacks before dumping them overboard.* **22.** to load (fabrics, threads, etc.) with mineral or other matter to increase the weight or bulk. **23.** to burden with or as with weight: *to be weighted with years.* **24.** *Statistics.* to give a statistical weight to. **25.** to bias or slant toward a particular goal or direction; manipulate: *The teacher weighted the test so students who had read both books would make the highest marks.* **26.** to assign (a racehorse) a specific weight to carry in a race: *The handicapper weighted Dapper Dan with 128 pounds.* [ME; OE *wiht* (c. D *wicht,* G *(Ge)wicht*), equiv. to *wih-* (see WEIGH) + *-t* -TH[1]] —**weight′er,** *n.*
—**Syn. 10.** effect, power, efficacy, import, significance.

weight′ den′sity, the weight per unit volume of a substance or object.

weight·ed (wā′tid), *adj.* **1.** burdened; loaded; having additional weight. **2.** adjusted or adapted to a representative value, esp. in determining the value of a legislator's vote as proportionate to the population of his constituency. [WEIGHT + -ED[2]] —**weight′ed·ly,** *adv.* —**weight′ed·ness,** *n.*

weight′ for age′, *Horse Racing.* the poundage assigned to be borne by a horse in a race, based on the age of the horse.

weight·less (wāt′lis), *adj.* being without apparent weight, as a body accelerated by gravitation or acted upon by a force that neutralizes gravitation. [WEIGHT + -LESS] —**weight′less·ly,** *adv.* —**weight′less·ness,** *n.*

weight′ lift′ing, the act, art, or sport of lifting barbells of given poundages in a prescribed manner, as a competitive event or conditioning exercise. —**weight′ lift′er.**

weight·y (wā′tē), *adj.,* **weight·i·er, weight·i·est. 1.** having considerable weight; heavy; ponderous: *a weighty bundle.* **2.** burdensome or troublesome: *the weightier cares of sovereignty.* **3.** important or momentous: *weighty negotiations.* **4.** having or exerting influence, power, etc.; influential: *a weighty merchant of Boston.* [late ME; see WEIGHT, -Y[1]] —**weight′i·ly,** *adv.* —**weight′i·ness,** *n.*
—**Syn. 3.** significant, serious, grave, consequential. See **heavy.** —**Ant. 1, 3.** light. **3.** unimportant.

Wei·hai·wei (wā′hī′wā′), *n.* a seaport in NE Shantung, in NE China: district leased to Great Britain 1898–1930. 175,000 (est. 1950); 285 sq. mi.

Weill (wīl; *Ger.* vīl), *n.* **Kurt** (kûrt; *Ger.* ko͝ort), 1900–50, German composer, in the U.S. after 1935.

Weil's′ disease′ (vīlz, wīlz), *Med.* a type of leptospirosis in man, characterized by fever, jaundice, muscular pain, and inflammation of the liver, caused by the spirochete *Leptospira icterohaemorrhagiae.* [named after Adolf *Weil* (1848–1916), German physician]

Wei·mar (vī′mär), *n.* a city in SW East Germany. 66,675 (est. 1955). —**Wei·mar′i·an,** *adj., n.*

Wei·mar·an·er (vī′mə rä′nər, wī′mə rä′-), *n.* one of a German breed of hunting dogs having a smooth silver-gray to dark-gray coat, a cropped tail, and blue-gray or amber eyes. [< G, after WEIMAR; see -AN, -ER[1]]

Wei′mar Repub′lic, the German republic (1919–33), founded at Weimar.

Wein·ber·ger (wīn′bûr gər), *n.* **Ja·ro·mir** (yär′ə-mēr′), born 1896, Czech composer, in the U.S.

Wei·nek (wī′nek), *n.* a crater in the fourth quadrant of the face of the moon: about 18 miles in diameter.

Wein·gart·ner (vīn′gärt′nər), *n.* **(Paul) Fe·lix (Edler von Münz·berg)** (poul fā′liks ād′lər fən myntsʹ-berkh′), 1863–1942, Austrian composer, conductor, and writer.

weir (wēr), *n.* **1.** a small dam in a river or stream. **2.** an obstruction placed across a stream to cause the water to pass through a particular opening or notch, for measuring the quantity flowing. **3.** a fence, as of brush or narrow boards, or a net set in a stream, channel, etc., for catching fish. **4.** *Brit. Dial.* an embankment or levee built to hold a river or stream in its course or to divert it into a new course. [ME, OE, deriv. of root of OE *werian* to defend, dam up] —**weir′less,** *adj.*

weird (wērd), *adj.* **1.** involving or suggesting the supernatural; unearthly or uncanny: *a weird sound; weird lights.* **2.** fantastic; bizarre: *a weird getup.* **3.** *Archaic.* concerned with or controlling fate or destiny. —*n.* *Chiefly Scot.* **4.** fate; destiny. **5.** fate (def. 6). [ME *werd,* OE *wyrd;* akin to WORTH[2]] —**weird′li·ness,** *n.* —**weird′ly,** *adv.* —**weird′ness,** *n.*
—**Syn. 1.** unnatural, preternatural. WEIRD, EERIE, UNEARTHLY, UNCANNY refer to that which is mysterious and apparently outside natural law. That is WEIRD which is suggestive of the fateful intervention of supernatural influences in human affairs: *the weird adventures of a group lost in the jungle.* That is EERIE which, by suggesting the ghostly, makes one's flesh creep: *an eerie moaning from a deserted house.* That is UNEARTHLY which seems by its nature to belong to another world: *an unearthly light which preceded the storm.* That is UNCANNY which is mysterious because of its apparent defiance of the laws established by experience: *an uncanny ability to recall numbers.* —**Ant. 1.** natural.

weird·o (wēr′dō), *n., pl.* **weird·os.** *Slang.* weirdy.

weird′ sis′ters, 1. the Fates. **2.** *Scand. Myth.* the Norns.

weird·y (wēr′dē), *n., pl.* **weird·ies.** *Slang.* a mysteriously odd, eccentric, or abnormal person or thing. Also, **weird′ie, weirdo.** [WEIRD + -Y[2]]

Weir·ton (wēr′tᵊn), *n.* a city in N West Virginia, on the Ohio River. 28,201 (1960).

weis·en·heim·er (wī′zən hī′mər), *n.* wisenheimer.

Wei·ser (wē′sər), *n.* a town in W Idaho. 4208 (1960).

Weis·gall (vīs′gäl, wīs′-), *n.* **Hugo,** born 1912, U.S. composer and conductor, born in Czechoslovakia.

Weis·mann (vīs′män′), *n.* **Au·gust** (ou′go͞ost), 1834–1914, German biologist. —**Weis′mann·i·an,** *adj., n.*

Weis·mann·ism (vīs′män iz′əm), *n.* *Biol.* the theories of heredity as expounded by Weismann, esp. the theory that all inheritable characters are carried in the germ plasm which passes from one generation to another and which is isolated from the soma, and that acquired characters are not and cannot be inherited. [WEISMANN + -ISM]

Weiss (wīs), *n.* a walled plain in the third quadrant of the face of the moon: about 39 miles in diameter.

weiss′ beer′ (vīs, wīs), a light-colored, highly effervescent beer prepared largely from malted wheat. [< G *Weissbier* white beer]

Weiss·horn (vīs′hôrn′), *n.* a mountain in S Switzerland, in the Alps. 14,804 ft.

Weiz·mann (vīts′män′; *Eng.* wīts′mən, wīz′-), *n.* **Cha·im** (khī′im), 1874–1952, Israeli chemist and Zionist leader, born in Russia: 1st president of Israel 1948–52.

we·jack (wē′jak), *n.* fisher (def. 3). [< Algonquian]

we·ka (wā′kä, wē′kə), *n.* any of several large, flightless, New Zealand rails of the genus *Gallirallus.* [< Maori]

welch (welch, welsh), *v.i.* *Slang.* welsh. —**welch′er,** *n.*

Welch (welch, welsh), *adj., n.* Welsh.

Welch (welch *or, for 1,* welsh), *n.* **1. Robert, Jr.,** born 1889, retired U.S. candy manufacturer: founder of the John Birch Society. **2.** a town in S West Virginia. 5313 (1960).

Welch·man (welch′mən, welsh′-), *n., pl.* **-men.** Welshman.

wel·come (wel′kəm), *interj., n., v.,* **-comed, -com·ing,** *adj.* —*interj.* **1.** (a word of kindly greeting, as to one whose arrival gives pleasure): *Welcome, stranger!* —*n.* **2.** a kindly greeting or reception, as to one whose arrival gives pleasure: *to give someone a warm welcome.* **3. wear out one's welcome,** to make one's visits so frequent or of such long duration that they become offensive: *Your cousins have long since worn out their welcome.* —*v.t.* **4.** to greet the arrival of (a person, guests, etc.) with pleasure or kindly courtesy. **5.** to receive or accept with pleasure; regard as pleasant or good: *to welcome a change.* **6.** to meet, accept, or counter (an arrival, action, challenge, etc.) with a strong or violent response: *They welcomed him with hisses and catcalls. I welcome your challenge and will fight you any time.* —*adj.* **7.** gladly received, as one whose arrival gives pleasure: *a welcome visitor.* **8.** agreeable, as something arriving, occurring, or experienced: *a welcome letter; a welcome rest.* **9.** given full right by the cordial consent of others: *He is welcome to try it.* **10.** without obligation for the courtesy or favor received (used as a conventional response to expressions of thanks): *You're quite welcome.* [ME < Scand; cf. Icel *velkominn,* equiv. to *vel* WELL[1] + *kominn* COME (ptp.); r. OE *wilcuma,* equiv. to *wil-* welcome (see WILL[2]) + *cuma* comer] —**wel′come·less,** *adj.* —**wel′come·ly,** *adv.* —**wel′come·ness,** *n.* —**wel′com·er,** *n.*

wel′come wag′on, 1. a vehicle which carries information about the community, gifts, and sample products of local merchants to newcomers in an area. **2.** (*often cap.*) the group sponsoring such a service.

weld[1] (weld), *v.t.* **1.** to unite or fuse, as pieces of metal, by hammering, compressing, or the like, esp. after rendering soft or pasty by heat, and sometimes with the addition of fusible material like or unlike the pieces to be united. **2.** to bring into complete union, harmony, agreement, etc. —*v.i.* **3.** to undergo welding; be capable of being welded: *a metal that welds easily.* —*n.* **4.** a welded junction or joint. **5.** the act of welding or the state of being welded. [var. of WELL[2] in obs. sense] —**weld′a·bil′i·ty,** *n.* —**weld′a·ble,** *adj.* —**weld′er, weld′dor,** *n.* —**weld′less,** *adj.*

weld[2] (weld), *n.* **1.** a mignonette, *Reseda Luteola,* of southern Europe, yielding a yellow dye. **2.** the dye. Also, **wold, woald, would.** [ME *welde;* c. MLG *walde,* MD *woude*]

weld·ment (weld′mənt), *n.* a welded assembly. [WELD[1] + -MENT]

wel·fare (wel′fâr′), *n.* **1.** the state or condition with regard to good fortune, health, happiness, prosperity, etc.; well-being: *to look after a child's welfare; the physical or moral welfare of society.* **2.** See **welfare work. 3. on welfare,** receiving financial aid from the government or from a private organization because of hardship and need. [ME, from phrase *wel fare.* See WELL[1], FARE]
—**Syn. 1.** success, weal, benefit, profit, advantage.

wel′fare econom′ics, a branch of economics concerned with improving human welfare and social conditions chiefly through the optimum distribution of wealth, the relief or reduction of unemployment, etc.

wel′fare fund′, a fund set up by a union or employer, providing benefits to workers during a period of unemployment or disablement, as salary continuance while ill.

Wel′fare Is′land, an island in the East River, in New York City: hospitals. Formerly, **Blackwells Island.**

wel′fare state′, a state in which the welfare of the people in such matters as social security, health and education, housing, and working conditions is the responsibility of the government.

wel′fare work′, the efforts or programs of an agency, community, business organization, etc., to improve living conditions, increase job opportunities, secure hospitalization, and the like, for needy persons within its jurisdiction. —**wel′fare work′er.**

wel·far·ism (wel′fâr′iz əm, -fä riz′-), *n.* the set of attitudes and policies characterizing or tending toward the establishment of a welfare state. [WELFARE + -ISM]

wel·kin (wel′kin), *n.* *Chiefly Literary.* the sky; the vault of heaven. [ME *welken(e),* OE *welcn,* var. of *wolcen* cloud, sky; c. G *Wolke;* akin to OE *wlaco* tepid]

well[1] (wel), *adv., adj., compar.* **bet·ter,** *superl.* **best,** *interj., n.* —*adv.* **1.** in a satisfactory, favorable, prosperous, or advantageous manner; fortunately; happily: *Business is going well. We are well supplied with magazines.* **2.** in a good, moral, or proper manner: *to do well in school; to behave well.* **3.** commendably, meritoriously, or excellently: *to write well and reason well; a difficult task well done.* **4.** with propriety, justice, or reason: *I could not well refuse.* **5.** in satisfactory or good measure; adequately or sufficiently: *Think well before you act.* **6.** thoroughly, carefully, or soundly: *to shake well before using; listen well.* **7.** to a considerable extent or degree: *a sum well over the amount fixed; to dilute the acid well.* **8.** personally; to a great degree of intimacy: *to know a person well.* **9.** certainly; without doubt: *I anger easily, as you well know.* **10.** with good nature; without rancor: *He took the joke well.* **11. as well, a.** in addition; also; too: *She insisted on having* *her hair cut, dyed, and set, and on a manicure as well.* **b.** equally: *The town grew as well because of its location as because of its superb climate.* **12. as well as,** as much or as truly as; equally as: *She was good as well as beautiful.* —*adj.* **13.** in good health; sound in body and mind: *Are you well? He is not a well man.* **14.** satisfactory, pleasing, or good: *All is well with us.* **15.** proper, fitting, or gratifying: *It is well that you didn't go.* **16.** in a satisfactory position; well-off: *I am very well as I am.* —*interj.* **17.** (used to express surprise, reproof, etc.): *Well! There's no need to shout.* **18.** (used to introduce a sentence, resume a conversation, etc.): *Well, who would have thought he could do it?* —*n.* **19.** well-being; good fortune; success: *to wish well to someone.* **20. leave well enough alone,** avoid changing something that is satisfactory. [ME, OE *wel(l)*; c. D *wel*, G *wohl*, Icel *vel*, Goth *waila*] —**well′ness,** *n.*

—**Syn. 2.** properly, correctly, skillfully, adeptly, accurately, efficiently. **4.** suitably. **5.** fully, amply, abundantly. **7.** rather, quite. **13.** healthy, hale, sound, hearty. **14.** fine. **15.** suitable, befitting, appropriate. **16.** fortunate, happy. —**Ant. 2.** poorly, badly. **13.** ill, sick.

—**Usage.** See **good.**

well[2] (wel), *n.* **1.** a hole drilled or bored into the earth to obtain water, petroleum, natural gas, brine, or sulfur. **2.** a spring or natural source of water. **3.** an apparent reservoir or a source of human feelings, emotions, energy, etc.: *He was a well of gentleness and courtesy.* **4.** a container, receptacle, or reservoir for a liquid: *the well of ink in a fountain pen.* **5.** any sunken or deep, enclosed space, as a shaft for air or light, stairs, elevator, etc., extending vertically through the floors of a building. **6.** *Naut.* **a.** a part of a weather deck between two superstructures, extending from one side of a vessel to the other. **b.** a compartment or enclosure around a ship's pumps to make them easily accessible and protect them from being damaged by the cargo. **7.** a hollow compartment, recessed area, or depression for holding a specific item or items, as to hold fish in the bottom of a boat, the retracted wheels of an airplane in flight, etc. **8.** any shaft dug or bored into the earth, as for storage space, a mine, etc. **9.** a depression or opening in the surface of a table or desk top. [ME, OE; c. G *Welle* wave] —*v.i.* **10.** to rise, spring, or gush, as water, from the earth or some other source (often fol. by *up, out,* or *forth*): *Tears welled up in her eyes.* —*v.t.* **11.** to send welling up or forth: *a fountain welling its pure water.* —*adj.* **12.** like, of, resembling, or used in connection with a well. [ME *welle(n)*, OE *wellan* (c. D *wellen*, Icel *vella*), var. of *wiellan*, causative of *weallan* to boil]

we'll (wēl), contraction of *we will.*

well-ad·vised (wel′advīzd′), *adj.* **1.** acting with caution, care, or wisdom: *He would be well-advised to sell the stock now.* **2.** based on or showing wise consideration: *There was a well-advised delay in carrying out the plan.* [ME *well avysed*]

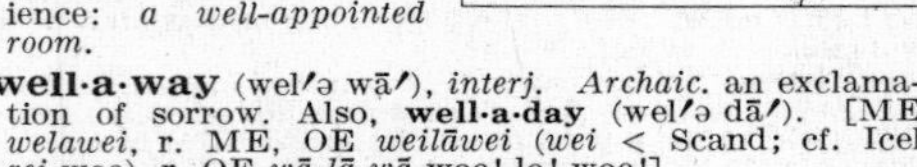

Wel′land Canal′ (wel′ənd), a ship canal in S Canada, in Ontario, connecting lakes Erie and Ontario: 8 locks. 25 mi. long.

well-ap·point·ed (wel′ə poin′tid), *adj.* attractively equipped, arranged, or furnished, esp. for comfort or convenience: *a well-appointed room.*

well·a·way (wel′ə wā′), *interj. Archaic.* an exclamation of sorrow. Also, **well·a·day** (wel′ə dā′). [ME *welawei*, r. ME, OE *weilāwei* (*wei* < Scand; cf. Icel *vei* woe), r. OE *wā lā wā* woe! lo! woe!]

well-bal·anced (wel′bal′ənst), *adj.* **1.** rightly balanced, adjusted, or regulated: *a well-balanced diet.* **2.** sensible; sane: *a well-balanced mind; a well-balanced disposition.*

well-be·ing (wel′bē′ing), *n.* a good or satisfactory condition of existence; a state characterized by health, happiness, and prosperity; welfare: *to look after the well-being of one's children; to influence the well-being of the nation.*

well-be·lov·ed (wel′bi luv′id, -luvd′), *adj.* **1.** loved deeply and sincerely: *my well-beloved fiancé.* **2.** highly respected and honored: *our well-beloved speaker.* —*n.* **3.** a person who is loved dearly: *in respect for the well-beloved.* [ME *wel biloved*]

well·born (wel′bôrn′), *adj.* born of a good, noble, or highly esteemed family. [ME; OE *welboren.* See WELL[1], BORN]

well-bred (wel′bred′), *adj.* **1.** well brought up; properly trained and educated: *a well-bred boy.* **2.** showing good breeding, as in behavior, manners, etc. **3.** (of animals) of a desirable breed or pedigree.

well′ car′, *Railroads.* a car having a floor depressed between the trucks to permit the carrying of excessively high objects.

well-chos·en (wel′chō′zən), *adj.* chosen with care, as for suitability, preciseness, etc.: *He entered at a well-chosen moment. She told him in a few well-chosen words.*

well′ deck′, *Naut.* a partial weather deck below the level of the main weather deck of a vessel. —**well′-decked′,** *adj.*

well-de·fined (wel′di fīnd′), *adj.* sharply or clearly stated, outlined, described, etc.: *a well-defined character; a well-defined boundary.*

well-dis·posed (wel′di spōzd′), *adj.* **1.** favorably, sympathetically, or kindly disposed: *The sponsors are well-disposed toward our plan.* **2.** of good disposition: *Our children are all well-disposed.* [ME]

well·do·er (wel′dōō′ər), *n. Obs.* **1.** a person who does well or acts rightly. **2.** a doer of good deeds. [late ME; see WELL[1], DOER]

well·do·ing (wel′dōō′ing), *n.* **1.** good conduct or action. —*adj.* **2.** kind-hearted, diligent, or willing and constant in effort: *an industrious, welldoing woman; a welldoing steed.* [late ME; see WELL[1], DOING]

well-done (wel′dun′), *adj.* **1.** performed accurately and diligently; executed with skill and efficiency. **2.** (of meat) thoroughly cooked, esp. until all redness is gone. [late ME]

well-dressed (wel′drest′), *adj.* attired in clothing that is of good quality, is properly fitted, and is appropriate and becoming.

well-dress·ing (wel′dres′ing), *n.* (in parts of rural Britain) a traditional ceremony of decorating wells with flowers in thanks for the blessing of an abundant supply of pure water. —**well′dress′er,** *n.*

Wel·ler (wel′ər), *n.* **Thomas Huck·le** (huk′əl), born 1915, U.S. physician: Nobel prize 1954.

Welles (welz), *n.* **1. (George) Orson,** 1915–85, U.S. actor, director, and producer. **2. Gideon,** 1802–78, U.S. journalist, legislator, and government official: Secretary of the Navy 1861–69. **3. Sumner,** 1892–1961, U.S. diplomat and government official.

Welles·ley (welz′lē), *n.* **1. Arthur.** See **Wellington, 1st Duke of. 2.** his brother **Robert Col·ley** (kol′ē), **1st Marquis,** 1760–1842, British statesman and administrator, born in Ireland: governor general of India 1797–1805. **3.** a city in E Massachusetts, near Boston. 26,071 (1960).

well-es·tab·lished (wel′e stab′lisht), *adj.* permanently founded; settled; firmly set: *a well-established business; a well-established habit.*

Wel·lesz (vel′es), *n.* **E·gon** (ā′gōn), born 1885, Austrian musicologist and composer.

well′-a·bol′ished, *adj.*
well′-a·bound′ing, *adj.*
well′-ab·sorbed′, *adj.*
well′-ac′cent·ed, *adj.*
well′-ac·cen′tu·at′ed, *adj.*
well′-ac·cept′ed, *adj.*
well′-ac·com′mo·dat′ed, *adj.*
well′-ac·com′pa·nied, *adj.*
well′-ac·com′plished, *adj.*
well′-ac·cord′ed, *adj.*
well′-ac·cred′it·ed, *adj.*
well′-ac·cu′mu·lat′ed, *adj.*
well′-ac·cus′tomed, *adj.*
well′-a·chieved′, *adj.*
well′-ac·knowl′edged, *adj.*
well′-ac·quaint′ed, *adj.*
well′-ac·quired′, *adj.*
well′-act′ed, *adj.*
well′-a·dapt′ed, *adj.*
well′-ad·dict′ed, *adj.*
well′-ad·dressed′, *adj.*
well′-ad·just′ed, *adj.*
well′-ad·min′is·tered, *adj.*
well′-ad·mit′ted, *adj.*
well′-a·dopt′ed, *adj.*
well′-a·dorned′, *adj.*
well′-ad·vanced′, *adj.*
well′-ad′ver·tised′, *adj.*
well′-ad′vo·cat′ed, *adj.*
well′-af·fect′ed, *adj.*
well′-aged′, *adj.*
well′-aimed′, *adj.*
well′-aired′, *adj.*
well′-al·lied′, *adj.*
well′-al·lot′ted, *adj.*
well′-al′tered, *adj.*
well′-a·mend′ed, *adj.*
well′-a·mused′, *adj.*
well′-an′a·lysed′, *adj.*
well′-an′a·lyzed′, *adj.*
well′-an′chored, *adj.*
well′-an′no·tat′ed, *adj.*
well′-an·nounced′, *adj.*
well′-a·noint′ed, *adj.*
well′-an′swered, *adj.*
well′-an·tic′i·pat′ed, *adj.*
well′-ap·par′eled, *adj.*
well′-ap·par′elled, *adj.*
well′-ap·pear′ing, *adj.*
well′-ap·plaud′ed, *adj.*
well′-ap·plied′, *adj.*
well′-ap·pre′ci·at′ed, *adj.*
well′-ap·proached′, *adj.*
well′-ap·pro′pri·at′ed, *adj.*
well′-ap·proved′, *adj.*
well′-ar′bi·trat′ed, *adj.*
well′-ar′gued, *adj.*
well′-armed′, *adj.*
well′-ar′mored, *adj.*
well′-ar′moured, *adj.*
well′-a·roused′, *adj.*
well′-ar·ranged′, *adj.*
well′-ar·rayed′, *adj.*
well′-ar·tic′u·lat′ed, *adj.*
well′-as′cer·tained′, *adj.*
well′-as·sem′bled, *adj.*
well′-as·sert′ed, *adj.*
well′-as·sessed′, *adj.*
well′-as·signed′, *adj.*
well′-as·sim′i·lat′ed, *adj.*
well′-as·sist′ed, *adj.*
well′-as·so′ci·at′ed, *adj.*
well′-as·sort′ed, *adj.*
well′-as·sumed′, *adj.*
well′-as·sured′, *adj.*
well′-at·tached′, *adj.*
well′-at·tained′, *adj.*
well′-at·tempt′ed, *adj.*
well′-at·tend′ed, *adj.*
well′-at·tend′ing, *adj.*
well′-at·test′ed, *adj.*
well′-at·tired′, *adj.*
well′-at·trib′ut·ed, *adj.*
well′-au′dit·ed, *adj.*
well′-au·then′ti·cat′ed, *adj.*
well′-au′thor·ized′, *adj.*
well′-av′er·aged, *adj.*
well′-a·wak′ened, *adj.*
well′-a·ward′ed, *adj.*
well′-a·ware′, *adj.*
well′-backed′, *adj.*
well′-baked′, *adj.*
well′-baled′, *adj.*
well′-band′aged, *adj.*
well′-banked′, *adj.*
well′-bar′bered, *adj.*
well′-based′, *adj.*
well′-bathed′, *adj.*
well′-beat′en, *adj.*
well′-be·com′ing, *adj.*
well′-be·fit′ting, *adj.*
well′-be·got′ten, *adj.*
well′-be·gun′, *adj.*
well′-be·haved′, *adj.*
well′-be·known′, *adj.*
well′-be·lieved′, *adj.*
well′-bent′, *adj.*
well′-be·spo′ken, *adj.*
well′-be·stowed′, *adj.*
well′-blacked′, *adj.*
well′-blend′ed, *adj.*
well′-blessed′, *adj.*
well′-blood′ed, *adj.*
well′-bod′ing, *adj.*
well′-boiled′, *adj.*
well′-bond′ed, *adj.*
well′-boned′, *adj.*
well′-boot′ed, *adj.*
well′-bored′, *adj.*
well′-borne′, *adj.*
well′-bot′tled, *adj.*
well′-bought′, *adj.*
well′-bound′, *adj.*
well′-bowled′, *adj.*
well′-boxed′, *adj.*
well′-braced′, *adj.*
well′-braid′ed, *adj.*
well′-branched′, *adj.*
well′-brand′ed, *adj.*
well′-brewed′, *adj.*
well′-bro′ken, *adj.*
well′-browned′, *adj.*
well′-brushed′, *adj.*
well′-built′, *adj.*
well′-bur′ied, *adj.*
well′-burned′, *adj.*
well′-burnt′, *adj.*
well′-bus′ied, *adj.*
well′-but′toned, *adj.*
well′-cal′cu·lat′ed, *adj.*
well′-called′, *adj.*
well′-cam′ou·flaged′, *adj.*
well′-caned′, *adj.*
well′-can′vassed, *adj.*
well′-car′pet·ed, *adj.*
well′-carved′, *adj.*
well′-cased′, *adj.*
well′-cast′, *adj.*
well′-caught′, *adj.*
well′-cau′tioned, *adj.*
well′-cel′e·brat′ed, *adj.*
well′-ce·ment′ed, *adj.*
well′-cen′tered, *adj.*
well′-cen′tred, *adj.*
well′-cer′ti·fied′, *adj.*
well′-changed′, *adj.*
well′-chap′er·oned′, *adj.*
well′-char′ac·ter·ized′, *adj.*
well′-charged′, *adj.*
well′-chart′ed, *adj.*
well′-chauf′feured, *adj.*
well′-checked′, *adj.*
well′-cheered′, *adj.*
well′-cher′ished, *adj.*
well′-chewed′, *adj.*
well′-chilled′, *adj.*
well′-chopped′, *adj.*
well′-churned′, *adj.*
well′-cir′cu·lat′ed, *adj.*
well′-cir′cum·stanced′, *adj.*
well′-civ′i·lized′, *adj.*
well′-clad′, *adj.*
well′-classed′, *adj.*
well′-clas′si·fied′, *adj.*
well′-cleansed′, *adj.*
well′-cleared′, *adj.*
well′-cloaked′, *adj.*
well′-clois′tered, *adj.*
well′-closed′, *adj.*
well′-clothed′, *adj.*
well′-coached′, *adj.*
well′-coat′ed, *adj.*
well′-coined′, *adj.*
well′-col·lect′ed, *adj.*
well′-col′o·nized′, *adj.*
well′-col′ored, *adj.*
well′-col′oured, *adj.*
well′-combed′, *adj.*
well′-com·bined′, *adj.*
well′-com·mand′ed, *adj.*
well′-com·menced′, *adj.*
well′-com·mend′ed, *adj.*
well′-com·mit′ted, *adj.*
well′-com·mu′ni·cat′ed, *adj.*
well′-com·pact′ed, *adj.*
well′-com·pared′, *adj.*
well′-com′pen·sat′ed, *adj.*
well′-com·piled′, *adj.*
well′-com·plet′ed, *adj.*
well′-com·plex′ioned, *adj.*
well′-com·posed′, *adj.*
well′-com·pre·hend′ed, *adj.*
well′-con·cealed′, *adj.*
well′-con·ced′ed, *adj.*
well′-con·ceived′, *adj.*
well′-con′cen·trat′ed, *adj.*
well′-con·cert′ed, *adj.*
well′-con·clud′ed, *adj.*
well′-con·coct′ed, *adj.*
well′-con·cord′ed, *adj.*
well′-con·densed′, *adj.*
well′-con·di′tioned, *adj.*
well′-con·ferred′, *adj.*
well′-con·fid′ed, *adj.*
well′-con·firmed′, *adj.*
well′-con·nect′ed, *adj.*
well′-con·served′, *adj.*
well′-con·sid′ered, *adj.*
well′-con′sti·tut′ed, *adj.*
well′-con·strict′ed, *adj.*
well′-con·struct′ed, *adj.*
well′-con·tained′, *adj.*
well′-con·tent′ed, *adj.*
well′-con·test′ed, *adj.*
well′-con·tin′ued, *adj.*
well′-con·tract′ed, *adj.*
well′-con·trast′ed, *adj.*
well′-con·trived′, *adj.*
well′-con·trolled′, *adj.*
well′-con·veyed′, *adj.*
well′-con·vinced′, *adj.*
well′-cooked′, *adj.*
well′-cooled′, *adj.*
well′-cop′ied, *adj.*
well′-corked′, *adj.*
well′-cor·rect′ed, *adj.*
well′-cor′set·ed, *adj.*
well′-cos′tumed, *adj.*
well′-couched′, *adj.*
well′-coun′seled, *adj.*
well′-coun′selled, *adj.*
well′-cou′pled, *adj.*
well′-court′ed, *adj.*
well′-cov′ered, *adj.*
well′-crammed′, *adj.*
well′-cred′it·ed, *adj.*
well′-crit′i·cized′, *adj.*
well′-cro·cheted′, *adj.*
well′-cropped′, *adj.*
well′-crossed′, *adj.*
well′-crushed′, *adj.*
well′-cul′ti·vat′ed, *adj.*
well′-cul′tured, *adj.*
well′-cured′, *adj.*
well′-curled′, *adj.*
well′-cur′ried, *adj.*
well′-curved′, *adj.*
well′-cush′ioned, *adj.*
well′-cut′, *adj.*
well′-danced′, *adj.*
well′-dark′ened, *adj.*
well′-darned′, *adj.*
well′-de·bat′ed, *adj.*
well′-de·ceived′, *adj.*
well′-de·cid′ed, *adj.*
well′-dec′o·rat′ed, *adj.*
well′-de·creed′, *adj.*
well′-de·fend′ed, *adj.*
well′-de·ferred′, *adj.*
well′-de·layed′, *adj.*
well′-de·lib′er·at′ed, *adj.*
well′-de·lin′e·at′ed, *adj.*
well′-de·liv′ered, *adj.*
well′-dem′on·strat′ed, *adj.*
well′-de·pict′ed, *adj.*
well′-de·rived′, *adj.*
well′-de·scribed′, *adj.*
well′-de·served′, *adj.*; **-ly,** *adv.*
well′-des′ig·nat′ed, *adj.*
well′-de·signed′, *adj.*
well′-de·sign′ing, *adj.*
well′-de·sired′, *adj.*
well′-de·stroyed′, *adj.*
well′-de·vel′oped, *adj.*
well′-de·vised′, *adj.*
well′-di′ag·nosed′, *adj.*
well′-dif·fused′, *adj.*
well′-di·gest′ed, *adj.*
well′-di·rect′ed, *adj.*
well′-dis·bursed′, *adj.*
well′-dis′ci·plined, *adj.*
well′-dis·cussed′, *adj.*
well′-dis·guised′, *adj.*
well′-dis·persed′, *adj.*
well′-dis·played′, *adj.*
well′-dis·put′ed, *adj.*
well′-dis·sect′ed, *adj.*
well′-dis·sem′bled, *adj.*
well′-dis′si·pat′ed, *adj.*
well′-dis·tin′guished, *adj.*
well′-dis·trib′ut·ed, *adj.*
well′-di·ver′si·fied, *adj.*
well′-di·vid′ed, *adj.*
well′-doc′u·ment′ed, *adj.*
well′-do·mes′ti·cat′ed, *adj.*
well′-dom′i·nat′ed, *adj.*
well′-dosed′, *adj.*
well′-drained′, *adj.*
well′-dram′a·tized′, *adj.*
well′-drawn′, *adj.*
well′-dried′, *adj.*
well′-drilled′, *adj.*
well′-driv′en, *adj.*
well′-dust′ed, *adj.*
well′-earned′, *adj.*
well′-eased′, *adj.*
well′-ed′it·ed, *adj.*
well′-ed′u·cat′ed, *adj.*
well′-ef·fect′ed, *adj.*
well′-e·lab′o·rat′ed, *adj.*
well′-el′e·vat′ed, *adj.*
well′-e·lim′i·nat′ed, *adj.*
well′-em·bod′ied, *adj.*
well′-em′pha·sized′, *adj.*
well′-em·ployed′, *adj.*
well′-en·act′ed, *adj.*
well′-en·cour′aged, *adj.*
well′-end′ed, *adj.*
well′-en·dorsed′, *adj.*
well′-en·dowed′, *adj.*
well′-en·forced′, *adj.*
well′-en′gi·neered′, *adj.*
well′-en·graved′, *adj.*
well′-en·light′ened, *adj.*
well′-en′tered, *adj.*
well′-en·ter·tained′, *adj.*
well′-en·ti′tled, *adj.*
well′-e·nu′mer·at′ed, *adj.*
well′-e·quipped′, *adj.*
well′-e·rect′ed, *adj.*
well′-es·cort′ed, *adj.*
well′-es·sayed′, *adj.*
well′-es·teemed′, *adj.*
well′-es′ti·mat′ed, *adj.*

ell-fa·vored (wel′fā′vərd), *adj.* of pleasing appearance; good-looking; pretty or handsome. Also, *sp. Brit.*, **well′-fa′voured.** [late ME] —**well′-a′vored·ness;** *esp. Brit.*, **well′-fa′voured·ness,** *n.*

ell-fed (wel′fed′), *adj.* fat; plump. [ME *wel edde*]

ell-fixed (wel′fikst′), *adj. Informal.* wealthy; prosperous; well-to-do; well-heeled.

ell-found (wel′found′), *adj.* well-furnished with upplies, necessaries, etc.: *a well-found ship.*

ell-found·ed (wel′foun′did), *adj.* having a foun-ation in fact; based on good reasons, information, tc.: *well-founded suspicions.* [late ME]

ell-groomed (wel′gro͞omd′), *adj.* **1.** having the hair, kin, etc., well cared for; well-dressed, clean, and neat: *well-groomed young man.* **2.** (of an animal) tended, leaned, combed, etc., with great care. **3.** carefully ared for; neat; tidy: *a well-groomed lawn.*

ell-ground·ed (wel′groun′did), *adj.* **1.** based on ood reasons; well-founded: *His opposition to the cheme is well-grounded.* **2.** well or thoroughly instructed n the basic principles of a subject: *He is well-grounded n mathematics.* [late ME]

ell-han·dled (wel′han′dəld), *adj.* **1.** having been andled or used much: *a sale of well-handled goods.* **2.** nanaged, directed, or completed with efficiency: *a ell-handled political campaign.* **3.** treated with taste, iscretion, etc.: *a delicate but well-handled subject.*

ell·head (wel′hed′), *n.* **1.** a fountainhead; source. **.** Also called **wellhouse.** a shelter for a well. [ME *velleheved.* See WELL², HEAD]

ell-heeled (wel′hēld′), *adj. Informal.* well-off; ich.

ell·hole (wel′hōl′), *n.* **1.** the shaft of a well. **2.** a all, narrow opening surrounded by walls, as a stairwell. WELL² + HOLE]

ell·house (wel′hous′), *n., pl.* **-hous·es** (-hou′ziz). vellhead (def. 2). [WELL² + HOUSE]

ell-in·formed (wel′in fôrmd′), *adj.* having ex-ensive knowledge or information, as in one particular ubject or in a variety of subjects: *Eric is very well-nformed in art history.* [late ME]

el·ling·ton (wel′ing tən), *n.* **1. 1st Duke of** *Arthur Wellesley*) (*"the Iron Duke"*), 1769–1852, British eneral and statesman, born in Ireland: prime minister 1828–30. **2.** See **Wellington boot. 3.** a seaport in and the capital of New Zealand, on S North Island. 123,969 (1961). **4.** a town in S Kansas. 8809 (1960). **5.** a town in N Ohio. 3599 (1960). **6.** a town in N Texas. 3137 (1960).

Wel′lington boot′, 1. a leather boot with the front part of the top extending above the knee. **2.** See **half Wellington.** Also, **wel′lington boot′.** Also called **Wellington, wellington.**

well-in·ten·tioned (wel′in ten′shənd), *adj.* well-meaning.

well-knit (wel′nit′), *adj.* closely joined together or related; firmly constructed: *a well-knit society; a well-knit plot; a muscular, well-knit body.* [late ME]

well-known (wel′nōn′), *adj.* **1.** clearly or fully known: *The well-known reasons are obvious.* **2.** familiarly known; familiar: *a well-known face.* **3.** generally or widely known: *a well-known painting.* [late ME]

well′-made play′ (wel′mād′), a play characterized by an emphasis on the construction of a conventional and sometimes contrived plot. [*well-made* late ME]

well-man·nered (wel′man′ərd), *adj.* polite; courte-ous.

well-mean·ing (wel′mē′ning), *adj.* **1.** meaning or intending well; having good intentions: *a well-meaning but tactless person.* **2.** Also, **well-meant** (wel′ment′). proceeding from good intentions: *Her well-meaning words were received in frosty silence.* [late ME] —**well′-mean′er,** *n.*

well-met (wel′met′), *adj. Archaic.* (used as a saluta-tion or part of a salutation in indicating pleasure at seeing someone). Also, **well′ met′.** Cf. **hail-fellow.** [WELL¹ + MET]

well-nigh (wel′nī′), *adv.* very nearly; almost: *It's well-nigh bedtime.* [ME *wel ne(i)h,* OE *wel nēah.* See WELL¹, NIGH]

well-off (wel′ôf′, -of′), *adj.* **1.** in a satisfactory, favorable, or good position or condition: *If a person has his health, he is well-off.* **2.** having sufficient money for comfortable living; well-to-do. **3.** adequately provided.

well-oiled (wel′oild′), *adj.* **1.** *Slang.* drunk. **2.** oper-ating with efficiency: *a well-oiled department.*

well-or·dered (wel′ôr′dərd), *adj.* arranged, planned, or occurring in a desirable way, sequence, etc.

well′-or′dered set′, *Math.* a totally ordered set in which every nonempty subset has an element having the property that there is no element in the subset less than the given element. Cf. **partially ordered set, totally ordered set.**

well′-or′der·ing the′orem (wel′ôr′dər ing), *Math.* the theorem of set theory that every set can be made a well-ordered set.

well·point (wel′point′), *n. Engineering, Building Trades.* a perforated tube driven into the ground to collect water from the surrounding area so that it can be pumped away, as to prevent an excavation from filling with ground water. [WELL² + POINT]

well-pre·served (wel′pri zûrvd′), *adj.* having been maintained in good condition; preserving a new or youthful appearance: *a well-preserved manuscript; a well-preserved elderly couple.*

well-read (wel′red′), *adj.* having read extensively (sometimes fol. by *in*): *a pleasure to talk with such a well-read person; to be well-read in oceanography.*

Wells (welz), *n.* **1. H(erbert) G(eorge),** 1866–1946, English novelist and historian. **2.** a historic town in E Somersetshire, in SW England: famous cathedral. 6691 (1961). **3.** a town in S Minnesota. 2897 (1960).

Wells·bor·o (welz′bûr ō, -bur ō), *n.* a town in N Pennsylvania. 4369 (1960).

Wells·burg (welz′bûrg), *n* a town in NW West Virginia. 5514 (1960).

wells·ite (wel′zīt), *n.* a mineral, hydrous silicate of calcium, barium, potassium, sodium, and aluminum, occurring in colorless or white crystals. [named after H. L. *Wells* (1855–1924), American chemist; see -ITE¹]

well′ smack′, *Naut.* a fishing smack having a well for keeping the catch alive.

well-spo·ken (wel′spō′kən), *adj.* **1.** speaking well, fittingly, or pleasingly: *The new chairwoman was very well-spoken.* **2.** polite in speech: *a well-spoken gentleman.* **3.** spoken in an apt, fitting, or pleasing manner: *a few well-spoken words on civic pride.* [late ME]

well·spring (wel′spring′), *n.* **1.** the head or source of a spring, stream, river, etc.; fountainhead. **2.** a source or supply of anything, esp. when considered inexhausti-ble: *a wellspring of affection.* [ME, OE; see WELL², SPRING]

Wells·ton (wel′stən), *n.* **1.** a town in E Missouri. 7979 (1960). **2.** a town in S Ohio. 5728 (1960).

ell′-ev′i·denced, *adj.*
ell′-ex·am′ined, *adj.*
ell′-ex′e·cut′ed, *adj.*
ell′-ex·em′pli·fied′, *adj.*
ell′-ex′er·cised′, *adj.*
ell′-ex·ert′ed, *adj.*
ell′-ex·hib′it·ed, *adj.*
ell′-ex·pend′ed, *adj.*
ell′-ex·pe′ri·enced, *adj.*
ell′-ex·plained′, *adj.*
ell′-ex′pli·cat′ed, *adj.*
ell′-ex·posed′, *adj.*
ell′-ex·pressed′, *adj.*
ell′-fab′ri·cat′ed, *adj.*
ell′-fad′ed, *adj.*
ell′-farmed′, *adj.*
ell′-fash′ioned, *adj.*
ell′-fas′tened, *adj.*
ell′-fea′tured, *adj.*
ell′-fenced′, *adj.*
ell′-fer·ment′ed, *adj.*
ell′-filled′, *adj.*
ell′-filmed′, *adj.*
ell′-fil′tered, *adj.*
ell′-fi·nanced′, *adj.*
ell′-fin′ished, *adj.*
ell′-fit′ted, *adj.*
ell′-fit′ting, *adj.*
ell′-flanked′, *adj.*
ell′-fla′vored, *adj.*
ell′-fla′voured, *adj.*
ell′-flood′ed, *adj.*
ell′-fo′cused, *adj.*
ell′-fo′cussed, *adj.*
ell′-fold′ed, *adj.*
ell′-fol′lowed, *adj.*
ell′-fooled′, *adj.*
ell′-fore·seen′, *adj.*
ell′-for′est·ed, *adj.*
ell′-fore·warned′, *adj.*
ell′-forged′, *adj.*
ell′-for·got′ten, *adj.*
ell′-formed′, *adj.*
ell′-for′mu·lat′ed, *adj.*
ell′-for′ti·fied′, *adj.*
ell′-fought′, *adj.*
ell′-framed′, *adj.*
ell′-freck′led, *adj.*
ell′-fre·quent′ed, *adj.*
ell′-fright′ened, *adj.*
ell′-fu′eled, *adj.*
ell′-fu′elled, *adj.*
ell′-func′tion·ing, *adj.*
ell′-fur′nished, *adj.*
ell′-gained′, *adj.*
ell′-gait′ed, *adj.*
ell′-gar′dened, *adj.*
ell′-gar′ment·ed, *adj.*
ell′-gar′nished, *adj.*
ell′-gath′ered, *adj.*
ell′-geared′, *adj.*
ell′-gift′ed, *adj.*
ell′-got′ten, *adj.*
ell′-gov′erned, *adj.*
ell′-grad′ed, *adj.*
ell′-grained′, *adj.*
ell′-grat′i·fied′, *adj.*
ell′-grav′eled, *adj.*
ell′-grav′elled, *adj.*
ell′-grav′en, *adj.*
ell′-greased′, *adj.*
ell′-greet′ed, *adj.*
ell′-guard′ed, *adj.*
ell′-guid′ed, *adj.*
well′-ham′mered, *adj.*
well′-hard′ened, *adj.*
well′-har′nessed, *adj.*
well′-hatched′, *adj.*
well′-haz′ard·ed, *adj.*
well′-head′ed, *adj.*
well′-heard′, *adj.*
well′-healed′, *adj.*
well′-heat′ed, *adj.*
well′-hedged′, *adj.*
well′-heeled′, *adj.*
well′-helped′, *adj.*
well′-hemmed′, *adj.*
well′-hewn′, *adj.*
well′-hid′den, *adj.*
well′-hinged′, *adj.*
well′-hit′, *adj.*
well′-housed′, *adj.*
well′-hu′mored, *adj.*
well′-hu′moured, *adj.*
well′-hung′, *adj.*
well′-iced′, *adj.*
well′-i·den′ti·fied′, *adj.*
well′-ig·nored′, *adj.*
well′-il′lus·trat′ed, *adj.*
well′-i·mag′ined, *adj.*
well′-im′i·tat′ed, *adj.*
well′-im·mersed′, *adj.*
well′-im·plied′, *adj.*
well′-im·posed′, *adj.*
well′-im·pressed′, *adj.*
well′-im·proved′, *adj.*
well′-im′pro·vised′, *adj.*
well′-in·au′gu·rat′ed, *adj.*
well′-in·clined′, *adj.*
well′-in′dexed, *adj.*
well′-in′di·cat′ed, *adj.*
well′-in·hab′it·ed, *adj.*
well′-in·i′ti·at′ed, *adj.*
well′-in·spect′ed, *adj.*
well′-in·stalled′, *adj.*
well′-in′sti·tut′ed, *adj.*
well′-in·struct′ed, *adj.*
well′-in′su·lat′ed, *adj.*
well′-in·sured′, *adj.*
well′-in′te·grat′ed, *adj.*
well′-in′ter·est·ed, *adj.*
well′-in·ter′pret·ed, *adj.*
well′-in·tro·duced′, *adj.*
well′-in·vent′ed, *adj.*
well′-in·vest′ed, *adj.*
well′-in·ves′ti·gat′ed, *adj.*
well′-i′roned, *adj.*
well′-ir′ri·gat′ed, *adj.*
well′-i′tem·ized′, *adj.*
well′-joined′, *adj.*
well′-judged′, *adj.*
well′-jus′ti·fied′, *adj.*
well′-kept′, *adj.*
well′-kin′dled, *adj.*
well′-knit′, *adj.*
well′-knit′ted, *adj.*
well′-knot′ted, *adj.*
well′-la′bored, *adj.*
well′-la′boured, *adj.*
well′-laced′, *adj.*
well′-laid′, *adj.*
well′-lard′ed, *adj.*
well′-launched′, *adj.*
well′-laun′dered, *adj.*
well′-learned′, *adj.*
well′-leased′, *adj.*
well′-led′, *adj.*
well′-lent′, *adj.*
well′-let′tered, *adj.*
well′-lev′eled, *adj.*
well′-lev′elled, *adj.*
well′-light′ed, *adj.*
well′-liked′, *adj.*
well′-lined′, *adj.*
well′-linked′, *adj.*
well′-lit′, *adj.*
well′-load′ed, *adj.*
well′-locked′, *adj.*
well′-lodged′, *adj.*
well′-loft′ed, *adj.*
well′-loved′, *adj.*
well′-main·tained′, *adj.*
well′-man′aged, *adj.*
well′-manned′, *adj.*
well′-man′u·fac′tured, *adj.*
well′-ma·nured′, *adj.*
well′-mapped′, *adj.*
well′-marked′, *adj.*
well′-mar′ket·ed, *adj.*
well′-mar′ried, *adj.*
well′-masked′, *adj.*
well′-mas′tered, *adj.*
well′-matched′, *adj.*
well′-ma·tured′, *adj.*
well′-meas′ured, *adj.*
well′-mend′ed, *adj.*
well′-mer′it·ed, *adj.*
well′-meth′od·ized′, *adj.*
well′-milked′, *adj.*
well′-min′gled, *adj.*
well′-mixed′, *adj.*
well′-mod′u·lat′ed, *adj.*
well′-mo′ti·vat′ed, *adj.*
well′-mo′tived, *adj.*
well′-mount′ed, *adj.*
well′-named′, *adj.*
well′-nar′rat·ed, *adj.*
well′-nav′i·gat′ed, *adj.*
well′-need′ed, *adj.*
well′-ne·go′ti·at′ed, *adj.*
well′-not′ed, *adj.*
well′-nour′ished, *adj.*
well′-nursed′, *adj.*
well′-nur′tured, *adj.*
well′-o·beyed′, *adj.*
well′-ob·served′, *adj.*
well′-oc′cu·pied′, *adj.*
well′-op′er·at′ed, *adj.*
well′-or′gan·ised′, *adj.*
well′-or′gan·ized′, *adj.*
well′-o′ri·ent′ed, *adj.*
well′-out′lined′, *adj.*
well′-packed′, *adj.*
well′-paid′, *adj.*
well′-paint′ed, *adj.*
well′-paired′, *adj.*
well′-par′a·graphed′, *adj.*
well′-parked′, *adj.*
well′-patched′, *adj.*
well′-pa·trolled′, *adj.*
well′-pa′tron·ised′, *adj.*
well′-pa′tron·ized′, *adj.*
well′-paved′, *adj.*
well′-pay′ing, *adj.*
well′-pen′sioned, *adj.*
well′-peo′pled, *adj.*
well′-per·ceived′, *adj.*
well′-per·formed′, *adj.*
well′-per·suad′ed, *adj.*
well′-phi·los′o·phized′, *adj.*
well′-pho′to·graphed′, *adj.*
well′-picked′, *adj.*
well′-pi′lot·ed, *adj.*
well′-pitched′, *adj.*
well′-placed′, *adj.*
well′-planned′, *adj.*
well′-plant′ed, *adj.*
well′-played′, *adj.*
well′-pleased′, *adj.*
well′-plot′ted, *adj.*
well′-plowed′, *adj.*
well′-plucked′, *adj.*
well′-point′ed, *adj.*
well′-po·liced′, *adj.*
well′-pol′ished, *adj.*
well′-polled′, *adj.*
well′-pon′dered, *adj.*
well′-posed′, *adj.*
well′-po·si′tioned, *adj.*
well′-post′ed, *adj.*
well′-post·poned′, *adj.*
well′-prac′ticed, *adj.*
well′-pre·pared′, *adj.*
well′-pressed′, *adj.*
well′-priced′, *adj.*
well′-primed′, *adj.*
well′-prin′ci·pled, *adj.*
well′-print′ed, *adj.*
well′-prized′, *adj.*
well′-pro·longed′, *adj.*
well′-pro·nounced′, *adj.*
well′-pro·por′tioned, *adj.*
well′-pros′e·cut′ed, *adj.*
well′-pro·tect′ed, *adj.*
well′-proved′, *adj.*
well′-prov′en, *adj.*
well′-pro·vid′ed, *adj.*
well′-pub′lished, *adj.*
well′-pun′ished, *adj.*
well′-put′, *adj.*
well′-qual′i·fied′, *adj.*
well′-raised′, *adj.*
well′-rat′ed, *adj.*
well′-reared′, *adj.*
well′-rea′soned, *adj.*
well′-re·ceived′, *adj.*
well′-re·cit′ed, *adj.*
well′-rec′og·nised′, *adj.*
well′-rec′og·nized′, *adj.*
well′-rec′om·mend′ed, *adj.*
well′-re·cord′ed, *adj.*
well′-re·cov′ered, *adj.*
well′-re·ferred′, *adj.*
well′-re·fined′, *adj.*
well′-re·flect′ed, *adj.*
well′-re·freshed′, *adj.*
well′-re·gard′ed, *adj.*
well′-reg′u·lat′ed, *adj.*
well′-re·hearsed′, *adj.*
well′-re·marked′, *adj.*
well′-re·mem′bered, *adj.*
well′-ren′dered, *adj.*
well′-re·paid′, *adj.*
well′-re·paired′, *adj.*
well′-re·placed′, *adj.*
well′-re·plen′ished, *adj.*
well′-re·port′ed, *adj.*
well′-rep′re·sent′ed, *adj.*
well′-re·put′ed, *adj.*
well′-re·solved′, *adj.*
well′-re·spect′ed, *adj.*
well′-rest′ed, *adj.*
well′-re·stored′, *adj.*
well′-re·viewed′, *adj.*
well′-re·vised′, *adj.*
well′-re·ward′ed, *adj.*
well′-rhymed′, *adj.*
well′-rid′den, *adj.*
well′-ri′pened, *adj.*
well′-roast′ed, *adj.*
well′-rolled′, *adj.*
well′-root′ed, *adj.*
well′-round′ed, *adj.*
well′-rubbed′, *adj.*
well′-ruled′, *adj.*
well′-run′, *adj.*
well′-run′ning, *adj.*
well′-sac′ri·ficed′, *adj.*
well′-sail′ing, *adj.*
well′-salt′ed, *adj.*
well′-sanc′tioned, *adj.*
well′-sand′ed, *adj.*
well′-sat′is·fied′, *adj.*
well′-scat′tered, *adj.*
well′-scent′ed, *adj.*
well′-sched′uled, *adj.*
well′-schooled′, *adj.*
well′-scorched′, *adj.*
well′-scored′, *adj.*
well′-screened′, *adj.*
well′-scrubbed′, *adj.*
well′-sealed′, *adj.*
well′-searched′, *adj.*
well′-sea′soned, *adj.*
well′-seat′ed, *adj.*
well′-se·clud′ed, *adj.*
well′-se·cured′, *adj.*
well′-seed′ed, *adj.*
well′-se·lect′ed, *adj.*
well′-sep′a·rat′ed, *adj.*
well′-served′, *adj.*
well′-set′tled, *adj.*
well′-sewn′, *adj.*
well′-shad′ed, *adj.*
well′-shak′en, *adj.*
well′-shaped′, *adj.*
well′-sharp′ened, *adj.*
well′-shaved′, *adj.*
well′-shel′tered, *adj.*
well′-shod′, *adj.*
well′-shot′, *adj.*
well′-show′ered, *adj.*
well′-shown′, *adj.*
well′-sim′u·lat′ed, *adj.*
well′-sit′u·at′ed, *adj.*
well′-sized′, *adj.*
well′-sketched′, *adj.*
well′-skilled′, *adj.*
well′-soaked′, *adj.*
well′-sold′, *adj.*
well′-solved′, *adj.*
well′-sort′ed, *adj.*
well′-sound′ing, *adj.*
well′-spaced′, *adj.*
well′-speak′ing, *adj.*
well′-spent′, *adj.*
well′-spiced′, *adj.*
well′-sprayed′, *adj.*
well′-spun′, *adj.*
well′-stacked′, *adj.*
well′-staffed′, *adj.*
well′-staged′, *adj.*
well′-stained′, *adj.*
well′-stat′ed, *adj.*
well′-stirred′, *adj.*
well′-stitched′, *adj.*
well′-stocked′, *adj.*

Wells·ville (welz′vil), *n.* **1.** a town in E Ohio. 7117 (1960). **2.** a town in W New York. 5967 (1960).

well′ sweep′, sweep (def. 30).

well-thought-of (wel′thôt′uv′, -ov′), *adj.* highly esteemed; of good reputation: *He is a well-thought-of man. This new book is well-thought-of.*

well-timed (wel′tīmd′), *adj.* fittingly or appropriately timed; opportune; timely: *a well-timed demand for new legislation.*

well-to-do (wel′tə do͞o′), *adj.* **1.** prosperous; well-off. **2.** characterized by or indicating prosperity: *well-to-do circumstances; a city with a well-to-do appearance.* —**Syn. 1.** rich, comfortable; affluent, moneyed.

well-turned (wel′tûrnd′), *adj.* **1.** smoothly or gracefully shaped; well-formed: *a well-turned tower; a well-turned ankle.* **2.** gracefully and concisely expressed: *a well-turned phrase.*

well-wish·er (wel′wish′ər), *n.* a person who wishes well to another person, a cause, etc. —**well′-wish′ing,** *adj., n.*

well-worn (wel′wōrn′, -wôrn′), *adj.* **1.** showing the effects of extensive use or wear: *well-worn carpets; a well-worn volume of favorite poems.* **2.** trite, hackneyed, or stale: *a well-worn saying; to hear a well-worn tune.* **3.** fittingly or becomingly worn or borne: *a well-worn reserve that never seems haughty.*

Wels′bach burn′er (welz′bak, -bäk; *Ger.* vels′bäKH), *Trademark.* a gaslight consisting essentially of a Bunsen burner on which an incombustible mantle (**Wels′bach man′tle**) composed of thoria and some ceria becomes brilliantly incandescent when affected by flame.

welsh (welsh, welch), *v.i. Slang.* **1.** to cheat by failing to pay a gambling debt: *You aren't going to welsh on me, are you?* **2.** to fail deliberately to meet one's obligations: *He welshed on his promise to help in the campaign.* Also, **welch.** [? special use of WELSH] —**welsh′er,** *n.*

Welsh (welsh, welch), *adj.* **1.** of or pertaining to Wales, its people, or their language. —*n.* **2.** the inhabitants of Wales and their descendants elsewhere. **3.** Also called **Cymric, Kymric.** the Celtic language of Wales. Also, **Welch.** [ME *Welische,* OE *Welisc,* deriv. of *Walh* Briton, foreigner (cf. L *Volcae* a Gallic tribe); c. G *welsch* foreign, Italian]

Welsh (welsh), *n.* a town in SW Louisiana. 3332 (1960).

Welsh′ cor′gi (kôr′gē), one of either of two Welsh breeds of dogs having short legs, erect ears, and a foxlike head. Cf. **Cardigan** (def. 2), **Pembroke** (def. 3).

Welsh corgi, Cardigan (1 ft. high at shoulder)

Welsh′ dress′er, *Eng. Furniture.* a sideboard having drawers or compartments below and open, shallow shelves above.

Welsh·man (welsh′mən, welch′-), *n., pl.* **-men.** a native or inhabitant of Wales. Also, **Welchman.** [ME, OE; see WELSH, MAN[1]]

Welsh′ po′ny, one of a breed of small, sturdy ponies raised originally in Wales.

Welsh′ pop′py, a perennial herb, *Meconopsis cambrica,* of western Europe, having pale green, slightly hairy foliage and pale-yellow flowers.

Welsh′ proc′ess, an obsolete process for smelting and refining copper in which sulfide ores were roasted repeatedly to remove iron and sulfur.

Welsh′ rab′bit, a dish consisting of melted cheese, usually mixed with ale or beer, milk, and spices, served over toast. [prob. of jocular orig.]

Welsh′ rare′bit. See **Welsh rabbit.**

Welsh′ spring′er span′iel, one of a Welsh breed of springer spaniels having a red and white coat.

Welsh′ ter′rier, one of a Welsh breed of terriers having a wiry, black-and-tan coat, resembling an Airedale but smaller.

Welsh terrier (15 in. high at shoulder)

Welsh′ vault′. See **underpitch vault.**

Welsh·wom·an (welsh′wo͝om′ən, welch′-), *n., pl.* **-wom·en.** a woman who is a native or inhabitant of Wales. [late ME; see WELSH, WOMAN]

welt (welt), *n.* **1.** a ridge or wale on the surface of the body, as from a blow of a stick or whip. **2.** a blow producing such a ridge or wale. **3.** *Shoemaking.* **a.** a strip, as of leather, set in between the outsole of a shoe and the edges of its insole and upper, through which these parts are joined by stitching or stapling. **b.** a strip, usually of leather, which ornaments a shoe. **4.** a strengthening or ornamental finish along a seam, the edge of a garment, etc. **5.** a seam in which one edge is cut close to the stitching line and covered by the other edge, which is stitched over it. —*v.t.* **6.** to beat soundly, as with a stick or whip. **7.** to furnish or supply (a shoe or garment) with a welt or welts; to sew a welt on to. [late ME *welte, walt* shoemaker's welt, OE *wælt* (thigh) sinew, var. of *weald* groin (basic meaning: that which holds things together)]

Welt·an·schau·ung (velt′än′shou′o͝ong), *n. German.* **1.** the philosophy of an individual or a group, esp. a race, with an interpretation of world history or civilization. **2.** a comprehensive conception or image of the universe and of man's relation to it. [lit., manner of looking at the world]

Welt·an·sicht (velt′än′ziKHt), *n. German.* a world view; an attitude toward, or interpretation of, reality.

wel·ter[1] (wel′tər), *v.i.* **1.** to roll, toss, or heave, as waves, the sea, etc. **2.** to roll, writhe, or tumble about; wallow, as animals (often fol. by *about*): *pigs weltering about happily in the mud.* **3.** to lie bathed in or be drenched in something, esp. blood. **4.** to become deeply or extensively involved, associated, entangled, etc.: *to welter in setbacks, confusion, and despair.* —*n.* **5.** a confused mass; a jumble or muddle: *a welter of anxious faces; a vast welter of conflicting opinions.* **6.** a state of commotion, turmoil, or upheaval: *the welter which followed the surprise attack.* **7.** a rolling, tossing, or tumbling about, as or as if by the sea, waves, wind, etc.: *He fought his way to shore through the mighty welter.* [ME, freq. (see -ER[6]) of obs. *welt* to roll, OE *weltan;* c. MD *welteren,* LG *weltern* to roll]

wel·ter[2] (wel′tər), *n.* **1.** *Informal.* a welterweight boxer or wrestler. —*adj.* **2.** (of a steeplechase or hurdle race) pertaining to, or noting a race in which the horses bear welterweights. [WELT + -ER[1]]

wel·ter·weight (wel′tər wāt′), *n.* **1.** a boxer or other contestant intermediate in weight between a lightweight and a middleweight, esp. a professional boxer weighing up to 147 pounds. **2.** (in a steeplechase or hurdle race) a weight of 28 pounds that is assigned to a horse in addition to the poundage assigned based on the age of the horse. **3.** a rider of steeplechase or hurdle-race horses who, though acting as a jockey, is of comparatively average weight and not small or light-weight as a professional jockey; heavyweight rider. [WELTER[2] + WEIGHT]

Welt·po·li·tik (velt′pō li tēk′), *n. German.* the policy of a nation with respect to the world. [lit., world politics]

Welt·schmerz (velt′shmerts′), *n. German.* sorrow which one feels and accepts as his necessary portion in life; sentimental pessimism. [lit., world-pain]

Wel·ty (wel′tē), *n.* **Eu·do·ra** (yo͞o dōr′ə, -dôr′ə), born 1909, U.S. short-story writer and novelist.

Wem·bley (wem′blē), *n.* a city in E Middlesex, in SE England, near London. 124,843 (1961).

Wemyss (wēmz), *n.* a parish in central Fife, in E Scotland, on the Firth of Forth: castle. 28,465 (1951).

wen[1] (wen), *n.* **1.** *Pathol.* a benign encysted tumor of the skin, esp. on the scalp, containing sebaceous matter; a sebaceous cyst. **2.** *Brit. Slang.* a large, crowded city or a crowded urban district: *London is the great wen of England.* [ME, OE *wenn;* c. D *wen*]

wen[2] (wen), *n.* wyn.

We·natch·ee (wə nach′ē), *n.* a city in central Washington. 16,726 (1960).

Wen·ces·laus (wen′sis lôs′), *n.* **1.** Also, **Wen′ces·las′.** 1361–1419, emperor of the Holy Roman Empire 1378–1400; as Wenceslaus IV, king of Bohemia 1378–1419. **2. Saint** (*"Good King Wenceslaus"*), A.D. 903?–c935, duke of Bohemia 928–935. German, **Wenzel.**

wench (wench), *n.* **1.** a girl or young woman. **2.** a country lass or working girl: *The milkmaid was a healthy wench.* **3.** *Archaic.* a strumpet. —*v.i.* **4.** to associate, esp. habitually, with promiscuous women. [ME, back formation from *wenchel,* OE *wencel* child, akin to *wancol* tottering, said of child learning to walk; akin to G *wankeln* to totter] —**wench′er,** *n.*

wench·man (wench′mən), *n., pl.* **-men.** *Ichthyol.* a snapper, *Pristipomoides andersoni,* found in the Atlantic Ocean. [? *wench angler's reel (see WINCH[1]) + MAN[1]]

Wen·chow (wen′chou′; *Chin.* wun′jō′), *n.* former name of **Yungkia.**

wend (wend), *v.,* **wend·ed** or (*Archaic*) **went; wend·ing.** —*v.t.* **1.** to pursue or direct (one's way). —*v.i.* **2.** *Archaic.* to proceed or go. [ME; OE *wend(an);* c. D, G *wenden,* Goth *wandjan,* causative of *windan* to wind]

Wend (wend), *n.* a member of a Slavic people in Saxony and adjoining parts of Prussia; Sorb. [< G *Wende;* c. OE *Winedas* (pl.); cf. L *Venedī* Slavs < Gmc (basic sense: dwellers in a watery, swampy region)]

Wen·dell (wen′d^{ə}l), *n.* a boy's given name.

Wend·ish (wen′dish), *adj.* **1.** of or pertaining to the Wends or their language; Sorbian. —*n.* **2.** Sorbian (def. 2). [< G *wendisch,* equiv. to *Wende* WEND + *-isch* -ISH[1]]

Wen·dy (wen′dē), *n.* a girl's given name. Also, **Wen′dey, Wen′die.**

wen·ny (wen′ē), *adj.,* **-ni·er, -ni·est.** **1.** of the nature of or resembling a wen. **2.** having a wen or wens. [WEN[1] + -Y[1]]

We·no·nah (wi nō′nə), *n.* a girl's given name. Also, **We·no′na, Winona.**

Wens·ley·dale (wenz′lē dāl′), *n.* a rich, medium-hard, white cheese with blue veins, somewhat strong in flavor. Also called **Wens′leydale cheese′.** [after *Wensleydale,* Yorkshire, England, where it is made]

went (went), *v.* **1.** pt. of **go. 2.** *Archaic.* a pt. and pp. of **wend.**

wen·tle·trap (wen′t^{ə}l trap′), *n.* any of several marine gastropods of the family *Scalariidae,* having a whitish, spiraled shell. [< D *wenteltrap* winding stairway, spiral shell, equiv. to *wentel,* earlier *wendel* (akin to OE *windel* winding staircase; see WIND[2]) + *trap* tread, step, stair, akin to OE *treppan* to tread]

Went·worth (went′wûrth′), *n.* **1. Thomas, 1st Earl of Strafford.** See **Strafford, 1st Earl of. 2. William Charles,** 1793–1872, Australian political leader, author, and journalist.

Wentz·ville (wents′vil), *n.* a town in E Missouri. 2742 (1960).

Wen·zel (*Ger.* ven′tsəl), *n.* Wenceslaus.

wept (wept), *v.* pt. and pp. of **weep**[1].

were (wûr *or, esp. Brit.,* wâr; *unstressed* wər), *v.* a 2nd pers. sing. pt. indic., pl. pt. indic., and pt. subj. of **be.** [ME; OE *wǣre* past subj., *wǣre* past ind. 2nd pers. sing. and *wǣron* past ind. pl. of *wesan* to be; c. D, G *waren,* Dan *var,* etc. See WAS]

we're (wēr), contraction of *we are.*

were·gild (wûr′gild′, wer′gild′), *n.* wergild.

were·n't (wûrnt, wûr′ənt), contraction of *were not.*

were·wolf (wēr′wo͝olf′, wûr′-, wâr′-), *n., pl.* **-wolves** (-wo͝olvz′). (in folklore and superstition) a human being that has changed or been changed into a wolf, or is capable of assuming the form of a wolf, while retaining human intelligence. Also, **werwolf.** [ME *werwolf,* OE *werwulf,* equiv. to *wer* man (c. Goth *wair,* L *vir*) + *wulf* WOLF; c. MD *weerwolf,* OHG *werwolf*]

Wer·fel (*Ger.* veR′fəl), *n.* **Franz** (*Ger.* fRänts), 1890–1945, Austrian novelist, poet, and dramatist, born in Czechoslovakia; in the U.S. after 1939.

wer·gild (wûr′gild, wer′-), *n.* (in Anglo-Saxon England and other Germanic countries) **1.** money paid to the relatives of a murder victim in compensation for loss and to prevent a blood feud. **2.** the amount of money fixed as compensation for the murder or disablement of a person, computed on the basis of rank. Also, **wer′geld, weregild.** [ME (Scot) *weregylt,* OE *wer(e)gild,* equiv. to *wer* man (c. Goth *wair,* L *vir*) + *gild* GELD[2]; c. MD *weergelt,* OHG *wergelt;* see YIELD]

Wer·ner (wûr′nər; *for 1 also Ger.* veR′nəR), *n.* **1. Al·fred** (al′fred, -frid; *Ger.* äl′fRāt), 1866–1919, Swiss chemist: Nobel prize 1913. **2.** a crater in the fourth quadrant of the face of the moon: about 45 miles in diameter. **3.** a boy's given name, form of **Warner.**

Wer·ne·ri·an (wər nēr′ē ən, ver-), *adj.* pertaining to or characteristic of the views or the classificatory system of Alfred Werner. [WERNER + -IAN]

wer·ner·ite (wûr′nə rīt′), *n.* a variety of scapolite. [named after A. G. *Werner* (1750–1817), German mineralogist; see -ITE[1]]

wersh (wersh), *adj. Scot.* wearish.

werste (vûrst), *n.* verst.

wert (wûrt; *unstressed* wərt), *v. Archaic.* a 2nd pers. sing. pt. indic. and subj. of **be.**

Wert′heim effect′ (vert′hīm), *Elect.* the electromotive force occurring in a ferromagnetic wire when it is twisted in a longitudinal magnetic field. [after proper name]

Wer·the·ri·an (ver tēr′ē ən), *adj.* of, pertaining to, or characteristic of Werther, the morbidly sentimental hero of *The Sorrows of Werther,* who kills himself for unrequited love of the wife of a friend. [*Werther* + -IAN]

wer·wolf (wēr′wo͝olf′, wûr′-, wâr′-), *n., pl.* **-wolves** (-wo͝olvz′). werewolf.

Wes (wes), *n.* a boy's given name, form of **Wesley.**

We·ser (vā′zər), *n.* a river flowing through N West Germany into the North Sea. ab. 300 mi. long.

We·ser·mün·de (*Ger.* vā′zəR myn′də), *n.* former name of **Bremerhaven.**

wes·kit (wes′kit), *n.* a vest or waistcoat, esp. one worn by women. [alter. of WAISTCOAT]

Wes·la·co (wes′lə kō′), *n.* a city in S Texas. 15,649 (1960).

Wes·ley (wes′lē *or, esp. Brit.,* wez′-), *n.* **1. Charles,** 1707–88, English evangelist and hymnist. **2.** his brother **John,** 1703–91, English theologian and evangelist: founder of Methodism. **3.** a boy's given name.

Wes·ley·an (wes′lē ən *or, esp. Brit.,* wez′-), *adj.* **1.** of or pertaining to John Wesley, founder of Methodism. **2.** pertaining to Methodism. —*n.* **3.** a follower of John Wesley. **4.** *Chiefly Brit.* a member of the denomination founded by him; Methodist. [WESLEY + -AN]

Wes·ley·an·ism (wes′lē ə niz′əm *or, esp. Brit.,* wez′-), *n.* the evangelical principles taught by John Wesley; Methodism. Also, **Wes′ley·ism.** [WESLEYAN + -ISM]

Wes′leyan Meth′odist, a member of any of the churches founded on the evangelical principles of John Wesley.

Wes·ley·ville (wes′lē vil), *n.* a town in NW Pennsylvania. 3534 (1960).

wes·sand (wē′zənd), *n. Chiefly Scot.* weasand.

Wes·sex (wes′iks), *n.* **1.** (in the Middle Ages) a kingdom, later an earldom, in S England. *Cap.:* Winchester. See map under **Mercia. 2.** the fictional region of the novels of Thomas Hardy, principally identifiable with Dorsetshire. [OE *Westseaxe, -seaxan* West Saxons or their kingdom]

well′-stored′, *adj.*
well′-straight′ened, *adj.*
well′-strained′, *adj.*
well′-strapped′, *adj.*
well′-stressed′, *adj.*
well′-stretched′, *adj.*
well′-stroked′, *adj.*
well′-strung′, *adj.*
well′-stud′ied, *adj.*
well′-stuffed′, *adj.*
well′-styled′, *adj.*
well′-sug′ared, *adj.*
well′-suit′ed, *adj.*
well′-sum′ma·rised′, *adj.*
well′-sum′ma·rized′, *adj.*
well′-sun′burned′, *adj.*
well′-sung′, *adj.*
well′-su′per·vised′, *adj.*
well′-sup′ple·ment′ed, *adj.*
well′-sup·plied′, *adj.*
well′-sup·port′ed, *adj.*
well′-sup·pressed′, *adj.*
well′-sus·tained′, *adj.*
well′-sys′tem·a·tised′, *adj.*
well′-sys′tem·a·tized′, *adj.*
well′-tai′lored, *adj.*
well′-tamed′, *adj.*
well′-tanned′, *adj.*
well′-taught′, *adj.*
well′-taxed′, *adj.*
well′-tend′ed, *adj.*
well′-test′ed, *adj.*
well′-thought′, *adj.*
well′-thought′-out′, *adj.*
well′-thrashed′, *adj.*
well′-thrown′, *adj.*
well′-tied′, *adj.*
well′-tilled′, *adj.*
well′-tint′ed, *adj.*
well′-toast′ed, *adj.*
well′-told′, *adj.*
well′-toned′, *adj.*
well′-trained′, *adj.*
well′-trans·lat′ed, *adj.*
well′-trav′eled, *adj.*
well′-trav′elled, *adj.*
well′-treat′ed, *adj.*
well′-trod′, *adj.*
well′-trod′den, *adj.*
well′-trust′ed, *adj.*
well′-tuned′, *adj.*
well′-tu′tored, *adj.*
well′-typed′, *adj.*
well′-un′der·stood′, *adj.*
well′-u·nit′ed, *adj.*
well′-used′, *adj.*
well′-u′ti·lized′, *adj.*
well′-var′ied, *adj.*
well′-var′nished, *adj.*
well′-veiled′, *adj.*
well′-ven′ti·lat′ed, *adj.*
well′-ver′i·fied′, *adj.*
well′-vis′u·al·ised′, *adj.*
well′-vis′u·al·ized′, *adj.*
well′-voiced′, *adj.*
well′-vouched′, *adj.*
well′-warmed′, *adj.*
well′-warned′, *adj.*
well′-war′rant·ed, *adj.*
well′-washed′, *adj.*
well′-watched′, *adj.*
well′-wa′tered, *adj.*
well′-weighed′, *adj.*
well′-whipped′, *adj.*
well′-wind′ed, *adj.*
well′-win′dowed, *adj.*
well′-wired′, *adj.*
well′-wit′nessed, *adj.*
well′-won′, *adj.*
well′-wood′ed, *adj.*
well′-word′ed, *adj.*
well′-worked′, *adj.*
well′-wo′ven, *adj.*
well′-writ′ten, *adj.*
well′-wrought′, *adj.*
well′-yoked′, *adj.*

CONCISE ETYMOLOGY KEY: <, descended or derived from; >, whence; b., blend of, blended; c., cognate with; deriv., derivative; equiv., equivalent; imit., imitative; m., modification of; obl., oblique; r., replacing; s., stem; sp., spelling; trans., translation; ?, origin unknown, perhaps; *, hypothetical. See the full key inside the front cover.

west (west), *n.* **1.** a cardinal point of the compass, 90° to the left when facing north, corresponding to the point where the sun is seen to set. **2.** the direction in which this point lies. **3.** (*usually cap.*) a region or territory situated in this direction, esp. the western part of the U.S., as distinguished from the East: *a vacation trip through the West.* **4.** (*cap.*) the western part of the world, as distinguished from the East or Orient; the Occident. **5.** (*cap.*) the noncommunist countries of Western Europe and the Americas. —*adj.* **6.** directed or proceeding toward the west. **7.** coming from the west, as wind. **8.** lying toward or situated in the west. **9.** *Eccles.* designating, lying toward, or in that part of a church opposite to and farthest from the altar. —*adv.* **10.** to, toward, or in the west: *They moved west after the war. The car headed west.* **11. go west,** *Informal.* **a.** to die. **b.** to become useless; decline; fail: *Our fondest hopes have gone west. Abbr.:* W, W., w. [ME, OE; c. D, G *west,* Icel *vestr;* cf. F *ouest* < OE]

West (west), *n.* **1. Benjamin,** 1738–1820, U.S. painter, in England after 1763. **2. Mae,** 1892–1980, U.S. actress. **3. Nathanael** (*Nathan Wallenstein Weinstein*), 1902–40, U.S. novelist. **4. Dame Rebecca** (*Cicily Isabel Fairfield Andrews*), 1892–1983, English novelist, journalist, and critic, born in Ireland.

West., western. Also, **west.**

West′ Al′lis (al′is), a city in SE Wisconsin, near Milwaukee. 68,159 (1960).

West′ Atlan′tic, a group of languages of W Africa spoken mostly in Senegal, constituting a branch of the Niger-Congo subfamily of languages, and including Fulani and Wolof.

West′ Bel′mar, a town in E New Jersey. 2511 (1960).

West′ Bend′, a town in SE Wisconsin. 9969 (1960).

West′ Bengal′, a state in E India: formerly part of the province of Bengal. 34,926,279 (1961); 33,805 sq. mi. *Cap.:* Calcutta. Cf. **Bengal** (def. 1).

West′ Berlin′. See under **Berlin** (def. 2).

West·bor·ough (west′bûr′ō, -bur′ō), *n.* a town in central Massachusetts. 4011 (1960).

west·bound (west′bound′), *adj.* proceeding or headed west. [WEST + -BOUND[2]]

West′ Brom′wich (brum′ij, -ich, brom′-), a city in S Staffordshire, in central England, near Birmingham. 95,909 (1961).

West·brook (west′brŏŏk′), *n.* a boy's given name.

West′ Bur′lington, a town in SE Iowa. 2560 (1960).

west′ by north′, *Navig., Survey.* a point on the compass 11°15′ north of west. *Abbr.:* WbN

west′ by south′, *Navig., Survey.* a point on the compass 11°15′ south of west. *Abbr.:* WbS

West′ Cald′well, a town in NE New Jersey. 8314 (1960).

West′ Car′rollton, a town in W Ohio. 4749 (1960).

West′ Ches′ter, a city in SE Pennsylvania. 15,705 (1960).

West·ches·ter (west′ches tər), *n.* a city in NE Illinois, near Chicago. 18,092 (1960).

West′ Chica′go, a town in NE Illinois. 6854 (1960).

West′ Colum′bia, 1. a town in central South Carolina. 6410 (1960). **2.** a town in S Texas. 2947 (1960).

West′ Con′cord, a town in SW North Carolina. 5510 (1960).

West′ Covi′na, a city in SW California, E of Los Angeles. 50,645 (1960).

West′ Der′ry (der′ē), a town in SE New Hampshire. 4468 (1960).

West′ Dundee′, a town in NE Illinois. 2530 (1960).

West′ Elmi′ra, a town in S New York. 5763 (1960).

West′ End′, 1. a fashionable residential section of London, England: noted for theaters. **2.** a town in central Florida. 3124 (1960).

West′ End′ An′niston, a town in E Alabama. 5485 (1960).

west·er[1] (wes′tər), *n.* a wind or storm coming from the west. [WEST + -ER[1]]

west·er[2] (wes′tər), *v.i.* **1.** (of heavenly bodies) to move or tend westward. **2.** to shift or veer toward the west. [late ME; see WEST, -ER[6]]

west·er·ing (wes′tər ing), *adj.* moving or shifting toward the west: *the westering sun; a westering wind.* [WESTER[2] + -ING[2]]

west·er·ly (wes′tər lē), *adj., adv., n., pl.* **-lies.** —*adj.* **1.** moving, directed, or situated toward the west: *clouds drifting in a westerly direction.* **2.** (esp. of a wind) coming from the west: *a westerly gale.* —*adv.* **3.** toward the west: *to escape westerly.* **4.** from the west: *a sharp wind blowing westerly.* —*n.* **5.** a wind that blows from the west: *an occasional westerly that pommeled the island.* [WESTER[1] + -LY] —**west′er·li·ness,** *n.*

Wes·ter·ly (wes′tər lē) *n.* a town in SW Rhode Island. 9698 (1960).

Wes·ter·mark (wes′tər märk′; *Fin.* ves′tər märk′), *n.* **Ed·ward Al·ex·an·der** (ed′wərd al′ig zan′dər; *Fin.* ed′värd ä′lek sän′dər), 1862–1939, Finnish sociologist.

west·ern (wes′tərn) *adj.* **1.** lying toward or situated in the west: *our company's western office.* **2.** directed or proceeding toward the west: *a western migration.* **3.** coming or originating from the west, as a wind. **4.** (*often cap.*) of, pertaining to, living in, or characteristic of the West, esp. the western U.S.: *a Western ranch; a Western cowboy.* **5.** (*usually cap.*) Occidental: *to adopt Western dress.* **6.** (*usually cap.*) of or pertaining to the noncommunist countries of Europe and the Americas: *Western trade agreements.* **7.** (*cap.*) of or pertaining to the Western Church. —*n.* **8.** one living in a western region or country. **9.** (*often cap.*) a story, movie, or radio or television play about the U.S. West of the 19th century. **10.** See **western sandwich.** [ME, OE *westerne,* equiv. to *west* WEST + *-erne* -ERN]

West′ern Austral′ia, a state in W Australia. 736,629 (1961); 975,920 sq. mi. *Cap.:* Perth. —**West′ern Austral′ian.**

West′ern Church′, 1. the Roman Catholic Church, sometimes with the Anglican Church, or, more broadly, the Christian churches of western Europe and those churches elsewhere which are connected with or have sprung from them. **2.** the Christian church in the countries once comprised in the Western Empire and in countries evangelized from these countries, or that part of the Christian church which acknowledged the Roman Catholic popes after the Great Schism of 1054.

west′ern dia′mondback rat′tlesnake, an extremely venomous diamondback rattlesnake, *Crotalus atrox,* of the southwestern U.S. and Mexico.

West′ern Em′pire. See **Western Roman Empire.**

West·ern·er (wes′tər nər), *n.* (*sometimes l.c.*) a native or inhabitant of the West, esp. of the western U.S. [WESTERN + -ER[1]]

west′ern frame′. See **platform frame.**

West′ern Ghats′, a low mountain range in W India, along the W margin of the Deccan plateau and bordering on the Arabian Sea. ab. 1000 mi. long.

West′ern Han′. See **Earlier Han.**

West′ern Hem′isphere, 1. the western part of the terrestrial globe, including North and South America, their islands, and the surrounding waters. **2.** that half of the earth traversed in passing westward from the prime meridian to 180° longitude.

west′ern hem′lock, a hemlock, *Tsuga heterophylla,* of western North America: the State tree of Washington.

West′ern Hin′di, the vernacular of the western half of the Hindi-speaking area in India: the basis of Hindustani and hence of literary Hindi and Urdu.

West′ern In′dia States′, a former group of associated states in W India, largely on Kathiawar peninsula.

west·ern·ise (wes′tər nīz′), *v.t.,* **-ised, -is·ing.** *Chiefly Brit.* westernize. —**west′ern·i·sa′tion,** *n.*

West′ern Is′lands, Hebrides.

west·ern·ism (wes′tər niz′əm), *n.* (*often cap.*) a word, idiom, or practice characteristic of people of the Occident or of the western U.S. [WESTERN + -ISM]

west·ern·ize (wes′tər nīz′), *v.t.,* **-ized, -iz·ing.** to influence with ideas, customs, practices, etc., characteristic of the Occident or of the western U.S. Also, *esp. Brit.,* **westernise.** [WESTERN + -IZE] —**west′ern·i·za′tion,** *n.*

west′ern ju′niper. See **yellow cedar** (def. 2).

west·ern·most (wes′tərn mōst′ *or, esp. Brit.,* -məst), *adj.* most western or westerly; farthest west. [WESTERN + -MOST]

west′ern moun′tain ash′, a mountain ash, *Sorbus sitchensis,* of western North America.

West′ern O′cean, *Naut.* the North Atlantic Ocean.

west′ern om′elet, an omelet prepared with diced green peppers, onions, and ham.

west′ern pa′per birch′, a variety of paper birch, *Betula papyrifera subcordata,* of western North America.

West·ern·port (wes′tərn pōrt′, -pôrt′), *n.* a town in NW Maryland. 3559 (1960).

west′ern red′ ce′dar, 1. an arborvitae, *Thuja plicata,* of western North America, grown as an ornamental. **2.** the soft, fragrant, reddish wood of this tree, used in the construction of houses, in shipbuilding, for making boxes, etc. **3.** the Rocky Mountain juniper, *Juniperus Scopulorum.*

West′ern Reserve′, a tract of land in NE Ohio reserved by Connecticut (1786) when its rights to other land in the western U.S. were ceded to the federal government: relinquished in 1800.

West′ern Ro′man Em′pire, the western portion of the Roman Empire after its division, A.D. 395, which became extinct A.D. 476. Also called **Western Empire.**

West′ern sad′dle, a heavy, often elaborately decorated saddle used by cowboys and characterized by a deep seat, high cantle and pommel, pommel horn, wide leather flaps for protecting the rider's legs, numerous rings and saddle strings by or to which equipment may be attached, and little padding. See illus. under **saddle.** Also called **stock saddle.**

West′ern Samo′a, an independent state comprising the W part of Samoa: formerly a trust territory of New Zealand. 110,000 (est. 1962); 1133 sq. mi. *Cap.:* Apia. Cf. **Samoa, American Samoa.** —**West′ern Samo′an.**

west′ern sand′wich, a sandwich with a western omelet for a filling.

West′ern Slavs′. See under **Slav** (def. 1).

west′ern tan′ager, a tanager, *Piranga ludoviciana,* of western North America, the male of which is yellow, black, and orange-red.

West′ern Thrace′. See under **Thrace** (def. 2).

west′ern wool′. See **territory wool.**

west′ern yel′low pine′. See **ponderosa pine.**

Wes·ter·ville (wes′tər vil), *n.* a town in central Ohio. 7011 (1960).

West·fa·len (vest fä′lən), *n.* German name of **Westphalia.**

West·field (west′fēld′), *n.* **1.** a city in NE New Jersey. 31,447 (1960). **2.** a city in S Massachusetts. 26,302 (1960). **3.** a town in W New York. 3878 (1960).

West′ Flan′ders, a province in W Belgium. 1,021,081 (est. 1964); 1249 sq. mi. *Cap.:* Bruges.

West′ Flem′ish, Flemish as used in West Flanders. *Abbr.:* WFlem

West′ Frank′fort, a town in S Illinois. 9027 (1960).

West′ Fri′sian, Frisian as used in the western part of Friesland. *Abbr.:* WFris

West′ German′ic, 1. a subbranch of Germanic that includes English, Frisian, Flemish, Dutch, Plattdeutsch, Yiddish, and German. **2.** of or pertaining to this subbranch of Germanic.

West′ Ger′many, a former republic in central Europe: created in 1949 by the coalescing of the British, French, and U.S. zones of occupied Germany established in 1945. 62,080,000; 96,025 sq. mi. *Cap.:* Bonn. Official name, **Federal Republic of Germany.** Cf. **Germany.** —**West′ Ger′man.**

West′ Glens′ Falls′, a town in E New York. 2725 (1960).

West′ Goth′, a Visigoth. [(erroneous) trans. of VISIGOTH]

west′ Green′land cur′rent, an ocean current flowing northward along the west coast of Greenland.

West′ Gulf′port, a town in SE Mississippi. 3323 (1960).

West′ Ham′ (ham), a city in SW Essex, in SE England, near London. 157,186 (1961).

West′ Hart′ford, a town in central Connecticut. 62,382 (1960).

West′ Har′tle·pool (här′tᵊl po͞ol′), a seaport in E Durham, in NE England, at the mouth of the Tees. 77,073 (1961).

West′ Ha′ven, a town in S Connecticut, near New Haven. 43,002 (1960).

West′ Hav′erstraw, a town in SE New York. 5020 (1960).

West′ Ha′zleton, a town in central Pennsylvania. 6278 (1960).

West′ Hel′e·na (hel′ə nə), a town in E Arkansas. 8385 (1960).

West′ Home′stead, a town in SW Pennsylvania. 4155 (1960).

West′ In′dian ce′dar. See **Spanish cedar.**

West′ In′dian gher′kin, gherkin (def. 2).

West′ In′dian kale′, malanga.

West′ In′dies, 1. Also called **the Indies.** an archipelago in the N Atlantic between North and South America, comprising the Greater Antilles, the Lesser Antilles, and the Bahamas. **2.** Also called **West′ In′dies Federa′tion. Federation of,** a former federation 1958–62 of the British islands in the Caribbean, comprising Barbados, Jamaica, Trinidad, Tobago, and the Windward and Leeward island colonies. —**West′ In′dian.**

West′ In′dies Asso′ciated States′, a former group (1967–81) of territorial islands in the West Indies in association with the United Kingdom: original members included Antigua, Dominica, Grenada, St. Kitts-Nevis-Anguilla, St. Lucia, St. Vincent, and adjacent islands. All member islands now independent except Anguilla

west·ing (wes′ting), *n.* **1.** *Navig.* the distance due west made good on any course tending westward; westerly departure. **2.** *Survey.* a distance west from a north-south reference line. [WEST + -ING[1]]

West·ing·house (wes′ting hous′), *n.* **George,** 1846–1914, U.S. inventor and manufacturer.

West′inghouse brake′, a railroad air brake operated by compressed air. [named after George WESTINGHOUSE, its inventor]

West′ I′ri·an (ēr′ē än′), the W part of the island of New Guinea, formerly a Dutch territory: a province of Indonesia since 1963. 700,000 (est. 1964); ab. 159,000 sq. mi. Also called **West New Guinea.** Formerly, **Netherlands New Guinea, Dutch New Guinea.**

West′ Kankakee′, a town in NE Illinois. 3197 (1960).

west·lin (west′lin), *adj. Scot.* western; westerly. Also, **west·ling** (west′ling). [var. of WESTLINS]

West′ Linn′, a town in NW Oregon. 3933 (1960).

west·lins (west′linz), *adv. Scot.* westwards; to the west. Also, **west·lings** (west′linz, -lingz). [WEST + *-lins* (Scot), var. of *-lings* (-LING[2] + -S[1])]

West′ Long′ Branch′, a town in E New Jersey. 5337 (1960).

West′ Lo′thi·an (lō′thē ən), a county in S Scotland. 92,764 (1961); 120 sq. mi. *Co. seat:* Linlithgow. Formerly, **Linlithgow.**

Westm., Westminster.

West·meath (west′mēth′, -mēth′), *n.* a county in Leinster in the N central Republic of Ireland. 52,861 (1961). 681 sq. mi. *Co. seat:* Mullingar.

West′ Mem′phis, a city in E Arkansas, on the Mississippi. 19,374 (1960).

West′ Miam′i, a town in S Florida. 5296 (1960).

West′ Miff′lin, a city in W Pennsylvania, on the Monongahela River. 27,289 (1960).

West′ Milwau′kee, a town in SE Wisconsin. 5043 (1960).

West·min·ster (west′min′stər), *n.* **1.** a central borough (officially a city) of London, England: Westminster Abbey, Houses of Parliament, Buckingham Palace. 85,223 (1961). **2.** a town in N Maryland. 6123 (1960).

West′minster Ab′bey, a Gothic church in London, England.

West′minster Assem′bly, a convocation which met at Westminster, London, 1643–49, and formulated the articles of faith (**West′minster Confes′sion of Faith′**) which are accepted as authoritative by most Presbyterian churches.

West′ Monroe′, a city in N Louisiana. 15,215 (1960).

West·mont (west′mont), *n.* **1.** a town in central Pennsylvania. 6573 (1960). **2.** a town in NE Illinois. 5997 (1960).

West·more·land (west′mōr′lənd, -môr-), *n.* **William Childs,** born 1914, U.S. army officer: commander of U.S. forces in Vietnam and Thailand 1964–68.

West·mor·land (west′mōr′lənd, -môr′-; *Brit.* west′mər lənd), *n.* a county in NW England, partially in the Lake District. 67,222 (196)1; 789 sq. mi. *Co. seat:* Appleby.

west·most (west′mōst′ *or, esp. Brit.,* -məst), *adj.* westernmost. [ME; r. ME, OE *westmest;* see -MOST]

West′ Mys′tic, a town in SE Connecticut. 3268.

West′ New′ Guin′ea. See **West Irian.**

West′ New′ton, a town in SW Pennsylvania. 3982 (1960).

West′ New′ York′, a town in NE New Jersey, across the Hudson from New York City. 35,547 (1960).

West′ Nor′ri·ton (nor′i tən), a town in SE Pennsylvania. 8342 (1960).

west-north·west (west′nôrth′west′; *Naut.* west′nôr′west′), *Navig., Survey.* —*n.* **1.** a point on the compass midway between west and northwest. —*adj.* **2.** coming from this point: *a west-northwest wind.* **3.** directed toward this point: *a west-northwest course.* —*adv.* **4.** from this point: *The wind is blowing west-northwest.* **5.** toward this point: *sailing west-northwest. Abbr.:* WNW

west-north·west·ward (west′nôrth′west′wərd; *Naut.* west′nôr′west′wərd), *Naut.* —*adj.* **1.** moving, bearing, facing or situated toward the west-northwest. —*adv.* **2.** toward the west-northwest. Also, **west′-north′west′ward·ly.**

Wes·ton (wes′tən), *n.* a town in central West Virginia. 8754 (1960).

Wes′ton cell′, *Trademark.* a cell that consists of a mercury and a cadmium electrode in an electrolyte of a cadmium sulfate solution and produces a nearly constant voltage of 1.0188 used as a reference for measurement purposes. Also called **Wes′ton stand′ard cell′.**

West′ Or′ange, **1.** a town in NE New Jersey, near Newark. 28,605 (1960). **2.** a town in SE Texas. 4848 (1960).

West·o·ver (west′ō vər), *n.* a town in N West Virginia. 4749 (1960).

West′ Pak′istan, former name (1947–71) of Pakistan, when it was the W section of a divided country. Cf. **Bangladesh.**

West′ Palm′ Beach′, a city in SE Florida: winter resort. 56,208 (1960).

West′ Pat′erson, a town in NE New Jersey. 7602 (1960).

West·pha·li·a (west fā′lē ə, -fāl′yə), *n.* a former province in NW Germany, now a part of North Rhine-Westphalia: treaty ending the Thirty Years' War 1648. German, **Westfalen.** —**West·pha′li·an,** *adj., n.*

West′ Pitts′ton, a town in NE Pennsylvania. 6998 (1960).

West′ Plains′, a town in S Missouri. 5836 (1960).

West′ Point′, **1.** a military reservation in SE New York, on the Hudson: U.S. Military Academy. **2.** a town in E Mississippi. 8550 (1960). **3.** a town in W Georgia. 4610 (1960). **4.** a town in E Nebraska. 2921 (1960).

West·port (west′pōrt′, -pôrt′), *n.* **1.** a town in SW Connecticut. 20,955 (1960). **2.** a seaport on the NW coast on South Island, in W New Zealand. 5505 (1957).

West′ Ports′mouth, a town in S Ohio. 3100 (1960).

West′ Prus′sia, a former province of Prussia, now in Poland. German, **West·preus·sen** (vest′proi′sən). —**West′ Prus′sian.**

West′ Punjab′, a region in E Pakistan, formerly part of the Indian province of Punjab.

West′ Read′ing, a town in central Pennsylvania. 4938 (1960).

West′ Rid′ing (rī′ding), an administrative division of Yorkshire, England. 3,641,228 (1961); 2790 sq. mi. *Co. seat:* Wakefield.

West′ Sax′on, **1.** the Old English dialect of the West Saxon kingdom, dominant after A.D. c850 and the medium of nearly all the literary remains of Old English. **2.** any of the Englishmen of the period before the Norman Conquest who lived in the region south of the Thames and west of Surrey and Sussex. **3.** a person whose native tongue was West Saxon. **4.** of or pertaining to the West Saxons or their dialect. [late ME alter. of OE *Westseaxan* WESSEX; see WEST, SAXON]

west-south·west (west′south′west′), *Navig., Survey.* —*n.* **1.** a point on the compass midway between west and southwest. —*adj.* **2.** coming from this point: *a west-southwest wind.* **3.** directed toward this point: *a west-southwest course.* —*adv.* **4.** from this point: *The wind is blowing west-southwest.* **5.** toward this point: *sailing west-southwest. Abbr.:* WSW

west-south·west·ward (west′south′west′wərd; *Naut.* west′sou′west′wərd), *Naut.* —*adj.* **1.** moving, bearing, facing, or situated toward the west-southwest. —*adv.* **2.** toward the west-southwest. Also, **west′-south′west′ward·ly.**

West′ Suf′folk, an administrative division of Suffolk, in E England. 129,969 (1961); 611 sq. mi. *Co. seat:* Bury St. Edmonds.

West′ Sus′sex, an administrative division of Sussex, in SE England. 411,224 (1961); 628 sq. mi. *Co. seat:* Chichester.

West′ Ter′re Haute′, a town in W Indiana. 3006 (1960).

West′ Un′ion, a town in NE Iowa. 2551 (1960).

West′ View′, a town in SW Pennsylvania. 8079 (1960).

West′ View′ Park′, a town in NE Tennessee. 4722 (1960).

West·ville (west′vil), *n.* **1.** a town in SW New Jersey. 4951 (1960). **2.** a town in E Illinois. 3497 (1960).

West′ Virgin′ia, a State in the E United States. 1,860,421 (1960); 24,181 sq. mi. *Cap.:* Charleston. *Abbr.:* W.Va. —**West′ Virgin′ian.**

West·wall (west′wôl′; *Ger.* vest′väl′), *n.* See **Siegfried line.** [WEST + WALL]

west·ward (west′wərd), *adj.* **1.** moving, bearing, facing, or situated toward the west: *a westward migration of farm workers.* —*adv.* **2.** Also, **west′wards.** toward the west; west: *a train moving westward.* —*n.* **3.** the westward part, direction, or point: *The wind had veered to the westward.* [ME; OE *westweard.* See WEST, -WARD]

West′ward, Ho!′, a historical novel (1855) by Charles Kingsley.

west·ward·ly (west′wərd lē), *adj.* **1.** having a westward direction or situation: *the westwardly migration of the 1850's.* —*adv.* **2.** toward the west. [WESTWARD + -LY]

West′ War′wick, a town in E Rhode Island, near Providence. 21,414 (1960).

West·we·go (west wē′gō), *n.* a town in SE Louisiana. 9815 (1960).

West′ Wenatch′ee, a town in central Washington. 2518 (1960).

west′ wind′ drift′ (wind). See **antarctic circumpolar current.**

West′ Win′ter Ha′ven, a town in central Florida. 5050 (1960).

West·wood (west′wŏŏd′), *n.* a town in NE New Jersey. 9046 (1960).

west·work (west′wûrk′), *n.* (in German Romanesque architecture) a monumental western front to a church, treated as a tower or combination of towers containing an entrance and vestibule below and a chapel above. [WEST + WORK]

West·worth (west′wûrth′), *n.* a town in N Texas. 3321 (1960).

West′ Wyo′ming, a town in central Pennsylvania. 3166 (1960).

West′ York′, a town in S Pennsylvania. 5526 (1960).

West′ Yu′ma, a town in SW Arizona. 2781 (1960).

wet (wet), *adj.,* **wet·ter, wet·test,** *n., v.,* **wet** or **wet·ted, wet·ting.** —*adj.* **1.** moistened, covered, or soaked, wholly or in part, with water or some other liquid: *wet hands; a wet sponge.* **2.** moist or damp; not dry: *wet ink; wet paint.* **3.** characterized by the presence or use of water or other liquid. **4.** moistened or dampened with rain; rainy: *Wet streets make driving hazardous.* **5.** *U.S.* allowing or favoring allowance of the manufacture and sale of alcoholic beverages: *a wet town.* **6.** preserved in a liquid, as food in syrup, a specimen in alcohol, etc. **7.** of or having frequent heavy rains: *the wet season; a wet country.* **8.** laden with a comparatively high percent of moisture or vapor, esp. water vapor: *There was a wet breeze from the west.* **9.** *Slang.* **a.** intoxicated. **b.** marked by drinking: *a wet night.* **10.** using water or done in or under water, as certain chemical, mining, and manufacturing processes. **11. all wet,** *Slang.* completely mistaken; in error: *He insisted that our assumptions were all wet.* **12. wet behind the ears,** *Informal.* immature; naïve; green: *She was too wet behind the ears to bear such responsibilities.* —*n.* **13.** that which is or makes wet, as water or other liquid; moisture: *The wet from the earth had made the basement unlivable.* **14.** damp weather; rain: *Stay out of the wet as much as possible.* **15.** *U.S.* one in favor of allowing the manufacture and sale of alcoholic beverages. —*v.t.* **16.** to make (something) wet, as by moistening or soaking: *Wet your hands before soaping them.* **17.** to urinate on or in: *The dog had wet the carpet. The baby wet his diapers.* —*v.i.* **18.** to become wet (sometimes fol. by *through*): *Dampness may cause plastered walls to wet. My jacket has wet through.* **19.** (of animals and children) to urinate. **20. wet one's whistle.** See **whistle** (def. 14). [ME *wett,* ptp. of *wete(n),* OE *wǣtan* to wet; r. ME *weet,* OE *wǣt,* c. OFris *wēt,* Icel *vātr;* see WATER] —**wet′ly,** *adv.* —**wet′ness,** *n.* —**wet′ter,** *n.* —**wet′tish,** *adj.*

—**Syn. 1.** damped, drenched. **2.** dank. **4.** misty, drizzling. **8.** humid. **13.** wetness, humidity, dampness, dankness. **14.** drizzle. **16.** WET, DRENCH, SATURATE, SOAK imply moistening something thoroughly. To WET is to moisten in any manner with water or other liquid: *to wet or dampen a cloth.* DRENCH suggests wetting completely as by a downpour: *A heavy rain drenched the fields.* SATURATE implies wetting to the limit of absorption: *to saturate a sponge.* To SOAK is to keep covered or partially covered by a liquid for a time: *to soak beans before baking.* —**Ant. 1.** dry.

wet·back (wet′bak′), *n.* *Often Disparaging.* a Mexican laborer who enters the U.S. illegally, as by wading the Rio Grande. [WET + BACK[1]]

wet′ blan′ket, **1.** a blanket dampened with water so as to extinguish a fire. **2.** a person or thing that dampens enthusiasm or enjoyment or has a discouraging or depressing effect: *Nobody ever asks her out because she's such a wet blanket.*

wet-blan·ket (wet′blang′kit), *v.t.* **1.** to extinguish (a fire) with a wet blanket. **2.** to dampen the enthusiasm or enjoyment of (a person, group, etc.).

wet′ bulb′, a thermometer bulb which is kept moistened when humidity determinations are being made with a psychrometer.

wet′ cell′, *Elect.* a cell whose electrolyte is in liquid form and free to flow.

wet′ chinook′. See under **Chinook** (def. 4).

wet′ com′pass, *Navig.* a compass having a compass card floating in a liquid. Also called **liquid compass.** Cf. **dry compass.**

wet′ con′tact, *Elect.* a contact through which direct current flows.

wet′ dock′, *Naut.* a dock accessible only around the time of high tide and entered through locks or gates.

wet′ fly′, *Angling.* an artificial fly designed for use under water. Cf. **dry fly.**

weth·er (weth′ər), *n.* **1.** a castrated male sheep. **2.** See **wether wool.** [OE; c. OS *withar,* OHG *widar,* Icel *vethr,* Goth *withrus*]

Weth·ers·field (weth′ərz fēld′), *n.* a town in central Connecticut. 20,561 (1960).

weth′er wool′, wool from previously shorn sheep. Also called **wether.**

wet·land (wet′land′), *n.* Usually, **wetlands.** a tract of land having wet and spongy soil, as a marsh, swamp, or bog. [WET + LAND]

wet′ machine′, *Papermaking.* a machine for dewatering pulp.

wet′ nurse′, a woman hired to suckle another's infant.

wet-nurse (wet′nûrs′), *v.t.,* **-nursed, -nurs·ing.** **1.** to act as a wet nurse to (an infant). **2.** to give excessive care or attention to; to treat as if helpless: *The warden is accused of wet-nursing his prisoners.*

wet′ pack′, *Med.* a type of bath in which wet sheets are applied to the patient.

wet·proof (wet′prōōf′), *adj.* waterproof. [WET + -PROOF]

wet′ pud′dling, *Metall.* puddling on a hearth rich in iron oxide so that carbon monoxide is generated, giving the iron the appearance of boiling. Also called **pig boiling.** Cf. **dry puddling.**

wet′ strength′, *Papermaking.* the relative resistance of paper to tearing when wet, resulting from the addition of resins during manufacture.

wet·ta·bil·i·ty (wet′ə bil′i tē), *n.* **1.** the condition of being wettable. **2.** the degree or extent to which something absorbs or can be made to absorb moisture. [WETTABLE + -ITY]

wet·ta·ble (wet′ə bəl), *adj.* **1.** able to be wetted. **2.** made soluble or receptive to moisture, as by the addition of a chemical agent. [WET + -ABLE]

Wet·ter·horn (vet′ər hôrn′), *n.* a mountain in S Switzerland, in the Bernese Alps. 12,149 ft.

wet′ting a′gent, *Chem.* any admixture to a liquid for increasing its ability to penetrate, or spread over the surface of, a given material, esp. cloth, paper, or leather.

We·tump·ka (wi tump′kə), *n.* a town in central Alabama. 3672 (1960).

wet′ wash′, laundry that has been washed but not dried or ironed. Cf. **dry wash** (def. 1).

we've (wēv), contraction of *we have.*

We·wo·ka (wə wō′kə), *n.* a town in central Oklahoma. 5954 (1960).

Wex·ford (weks′fərd), *n.* **1.** a county in Leinster province, in the SE Republic of Ireland. 83,308 (1961); 908 sq. mi. **2.** its county seat: a seaport. 11,328 (1961).

wey (wā), *n., pl.* **weys.** **1.** an old British unit of weight of various values, esp., 16 stones of 16 pounds each, or 256 pounds. **2.** an old Scotch-Irish unit of capacity equal to 40 U.S. bushels. [ME; OE *wǣge* weight. See WEIGH]

Wey·den (vīd′ən), *n.* **Roger** or **Ro·gier** (*Flem.* rô gēr′) **van der** (van dər; *Flem.* vän dər), 1400?–64, Flemish painter.

Wey·gand (vā gän′), *n.* **Ma·xime** (mak sēm′), 1867–1965, French general.

Weyl (vīl), *n.* **Her·mann** (hûr′mən; *Ger.* her′män′), 1885–1955, German mathematician, in the U.S. after 1933.

Wey·mouth (wā′məth), *n.* a town in E Massachusetts, S of Boston. 48,177 (1960).

wf, *Print.* See **wrong font.** Also, **w.f.**

WFlem, West Flemish.

WFris, West Frisian.

WFTU, World Federation of Trade Unions. Also, **W.F.T.U.**

W.G., **1.** water gauge. **2.** weight guaranteed. **3.** wire gauge. Also, **w.g.**

W. Ger., **1.** West Germanic. **2.** West Germany.

W. Gmc., West Germanic. Also, **WGmc.**

Wh, watt-hour. Also, **wh, whr**

whack (hwak, wak), *v.t.* **1.** *Informal.* to strike with a smart, resounding blow or blows. **2.** *Slang.* to divide into or take in shares: *Whack the loot between us two.* —*v.i.* **3.** *Informal.* to strike a smart, resounding blow or blows. —*n.* **4.** *Informal.* a smart, resounding blow: *a whack with his hand.* **5.** *Informal.* a trial or attempt: *to take a whack at a job.* **6.** *Slang.* a portion or share. **7.** *Slang.* condition; good condition; order: *My stomach's out of whack.* [var. of THWACK] —**whack′er,** *n.*

whack·ing (hwak′ing, wak′ing), *adj.* *Chiefly Brit. Informal.* large. [WHACK + -ING[2]]

whack·y (hwak′ē, wak′ē), *adj.,* **whack·i·er, whack·i·est.** wacky.

whale[1] (hwāl, wāl), *n., pl.* **whales,** (*esp. collectively*) **whale,** *v.,* **whaled, whal·ing.** —*n.* **1.** any of the larger marine mammals of the order *Cetacea,* esp. as distinguished from the smaller dolphins and porpoises, having a fishlike body, forelimbs modified into flippers, and a head that is horizontally flattened. **2.** *Slang.* something extraordinarily big, great, or fine of its kind: *a whale of a lot of money; a whale of a tale.* **3.** (*cap.*) *Astron.* the constellation Cetus. —*v.i.* **4.** to engage in whaling or whale fishing. [ME; OE *hwæl;* c. G *Wal(fisch),* Icel *hvalr;* akin to L *squalus* kind of fish, equiv. to movable *s-* + *-qualus*] —**whale′like′,** *adj.*

Bowhead whale,
Balaena mysticetus
(Length to 65 ft.)

whale[2] (hwāl, wāl), *v.,* **whaled, whal·ing,** *n.* —*v.t.* **1.** *Informal.* to hit, thrash, or beat soundly. —*n.* **2.** *Engineering, Building Trades.* wale[1] (def. 5).

whale·back (hwāl′bak′, wāl′-), *n.* *Naut.* **1.** a cargo vessel having a hull with a convex deck continuing the tumble home of the topsides, used esp. on the Great Lakes in early 1900's. **2.** a deck or cover curving upward; turtleback. **3.** something shaped like the back of a whale, as a rounded hill or an ocean wave. [WHALE[1] + BACK[1]]

whale·boat (hwāl′bōt′, wāl′-), *n.* a long, narrow boat designed for quick turning and use in rough seas: formerly used in whaling, now mainly for sea rescue. [WHALE[1] + BOAT]

whale·bone (hwāl′bōn′, wāl′-), *n.* **1.** an elastic, horny substance growing in place of teeth in the upper jaw of certain whales, and forming a series of thin, parallel plates on each side of the palate; baleen. **2.** a thin strip of this substance, for stiffening a corset. [WHALE[1] + BONE[1]]

whale′bone whale′, any whale of the suborder *Mysticeti,* having plates of whalebone on the sides of the upper jaw for filtering plankton from the water. Also called **baleen whale.** Cf. **toothed whale.**

whale·man (hwāl′mən, wāl′-), *n., pl.* **-men.** a man whose occupation is whaling; whaler. [WHALE[1] + MAN[1]]

whal·er[1] (hwā′lər, wā′-), *n.* a person or vessel employed in whaling. [WHALE[1] + -ER[1]]

whal·er[2] (hwā′lər, wā′-), *n.* wale[1] (def. 5). [WHALE[2] + -ER[1]]

Whales (hwālz, wālz), *n.* **Bay of,** an inlet of the Ross Sea, in Antarctica: location of Little America.

whale·suck·er (hwāl′suk′ər, wāl′-), *n.* a large, blue remora, *Remilegia australis,* which attaches itself to whales and dolphins. [WHALE[1] + SUCKER]

whal·ing (hwā′ling, wā′-), *n.* the work or industry of capturing and rendering whales; whale fishing. [WHALE[1] + -ING[1]]

whal′ing port′, a home port for whaling vessels.

wham (hwam, wam), *n., v.,* **whammed, wham·ming,** *adv.* —*n.* **1.** a loud sound produced by an explosion or sharp impact: *the wham of a pile driver.* **2.** a forcible impact. —*v.t., v.i.* **3.** to hit or make a forcible impact, esp. one producing a loud sound: *The boat whammed into the dock. He whammed the door shut.* —*adv.* **4.** Also, **wham·mo** (hwam′ō, wam′ō). abruptly; with startling suddenness: *The car ran wham up against the building.* [imit.]

wham·my (hwam′ē, wam′ē), *n., pl.* **-mies.** *Slang.* the evil eye; jinx. [WHAM + -Y[2], one of the methods of putting a whammy on someone being to strike the fist into the palm]

whang (hwang, wang), *n.* **1.** *Informal.* a resounding blow. **2.** *Informal.* the sound produced by such a blow: *the whang of gongs and cymbals.* **3.** *Dial.* **a.** a

CONCISE ETYMOLOGY KEY: <, descended or derived from; >, whence; b., blend of, blended; c., cognate with; deriv., derivative; equiv., equivalent; imit., imitative; m., modification of; obl., oblique; r., replacing; s., stem; sp., spelling; trans., translation; ?, origin unknown, perhaps; *, hypothetical. See the full key inside the front cover.

thong, esp. of leather. **b.** Also called **thong leather.** leather used to make thongs, lacing, etc.; rawhide. —*v.t.* **4.** *Informal.* to strike with a resounding blow. —*v.i.* **5.** *Informal.* to resound with such a blow. [alter. of *thwang,* early form of THONG; cf. WHITTLE, WHACK]

whang·doo·dle (hwaŋ′do͞od′əl, waŋ′-), *n. Slang.* a fanciful creature of undefined nature. [nonsense formation; see WHANG, DOODLE]

whang·ee (hwaŋ ē′, waŋ ē′), *n.* **1.** a bamboo of the genus *Phyllostachys,* of China. **2.** a walking stick or cane made from the stem of this plant. [< Chin *huang* hard bamboo + *-ee* < ?]

whap (hwop, wop), *v.t., v.i.,* **whapped, whap·ping,** *n.* whop.

whap·per (hwop′ər, wop′-), *n.* whopper.

whap·ping (hwop′iŋ, wop′-), *adj.* whopping.

wharf (hwôrf, wôrf), *n., pl.* **wharves** (hwôrvz, wôrvz), **wharfs,** *v.* —*n.* **1.** a structure built on the shore of or projecting into a harbor, stream, etc., so that vessels may be moored alongside to load or unload or to lie at rest; quay; pier. **2.** *Obs.* **a.** a river bank. **b.** the shore of the sea. —*v.t.* **3.** to provide with a wharf or wharves. **4.** to place or store on a wharf: *The schedule allowed little time to wharf the cargo.* **5.** to accommodate at or bring to a wharf: *The new structure will wharf several vessels. The skipper wharfed his boat with ease.* —*v.i.* **6.** to tie up at a wharf; dock: *The ship wharfed in the early morning.* [ME; OE *hwearf* embankment; c. MLG *warf;* akin to G *Werf* pier] —**wharf′less,** *adj.*

wharf·age (hwôr′fij, wôr′-), *n.* **1.** the use of a wharf: *to charge higher rates for wharfage.* **2.** storage of goods at a wharf: *conditions that make wharfage hazardous.* **3.** the charge or payment for the use of a wharf: *to pay one's wharfage monthly.* **4.** wharves collectively, esp. the number of wharves in a particular port. [WHARF + -AGE]

wharf·in·ger (hwôr′fin jər, wôr′-), *n.* one who owns or has charge of a wharf. [WHARFAGE + -ER[1], with *-n-* as in *passenger, messenger,* etc.]

wharf′ rat′, **1.** a large brown rat that is commonly found on wharves. **2.** a person who lives or loiters near wharves, often existing by pilfering from ships or warehouses.

Whar·ton (hwôr′tən, wôr′-), *n.* **1. Edith** (*Edith Newbold Jones*), 1862–1937, U.S. novelist. **2.** a town in S Texas. 5734 (1960). **3.** a town in central New Jersey. 5006 (1960).

wharve (hwôrv, wôrv), *n. Spinning.* a wheel or round piece of wood on a spindle, serving as a flywheel or as a pulley. [ME *wherve,* OE *hweorfa;* deriv. of *hwerfan* to revolve]

wharves (hwôrvz, wôrvz), *n.* a pl. of **wharf.**

what (hwut, hwot, wut, wot; *unstressed* hwət, wət), *pron., pl.* **what,** *n., adj., adv., interj., conj.* —*pron.* **1.** (used interrogatively as a request for specific information): *What is the matter? What is your name?* **2.** (used interrogatively to inquire about the character, occupation, etc., of a person): *What does he do? What does she take me for?* **3.** (used interrogatively to inquire as to the origin, identity, etc., of something): *What is that bird?* **4.** (used interrogatively to inquire as to the worth, usefulness, force, or importance of something): *What is wealth without friends?* **5.** (used interrogatively to request a repetition of words or information not fully understood, usually used in elliptical constructions): *You need what?* **6.** (used interrogatively to inquire the reason or purpose of something, usually used in elliptical constructions): *What of it? What for?* **7.** (used relatively to indicate that which): *This is what he says. I will send what was promised.* **8.** whatever; anything that: *Say what you please. Come what may.* **9.** how much?: *What does it cost?* **10.** the kind of thing or person that: *He said what everyone expected he would. She is just what I was expecting.* **11.** as much as; as many as: *Everyone should give what he can.* **12.** the thing or fact that (used in parenthetic clauses): *He went to the meeting and, what was worse, insisted on speaking.* **13.** (used to indicate more to follow, additional possibilities, alternatives, etc.): *You know what? Shall we go or what?* **14.** *Brit.* don't you agree?: *An unusual chap, what?* **15.** (used as an intensifier in exclamatory phrases, often fol. by an indefinite article): *What luck! What an idea!* **16.** *Chiefly Nonstandard.* that; which; who: *She's the one what told me.* **17. so what?** *Informal.* (an expression of disinterest, disinclination, or contempt.) **18. what have you,** *Informal.* and other things of the same kind; and so forth: *money, jewels, stocks, and what have you.* **19. what if,** what would be the outcome if; suppose that: *What if everyone who was invited comes?* **20. what it takes,** *Informal.* that which enables one to achieve success or attain a desired end, as good looks, ability, money, etc.: *There's a young man who has what it takes to get along in the world.* **21. what's what,** *Informal.* the true situation; all the facts: *Ask someone who knows what's what.* —*n.* **22.** the true nature or identity of something, or the sum of its characteristics: *a lecture on the what and how of crop rotation.* —*adj.* **23.** (used interrogatively before nouns and pronouns): *What news? What clothes shall I pack?* **24.** whatever: *Take what supplies you need.* —*adv.* **25.** to what extent or degree?; how much?: *What does it matter?* **26.** (used to introduce a prepositional phrase beginning with *with*): *What with storms and all, his return was delayed.* **27.** *Archaic.* in what respect? how?: *What can I help you?* **28.** *Obs.* for what reason or purpose? why? —*interj.* **29.** (used in exclamatory expressions, often fol. by a question): *What, no salt?* —*conj.* **30.** *Dial.* as much as; as far as: *He helps me what he can.* **31. but what,** but that; but who; who or that . . . not: *Who knows but what the sun may still shine.* [ME; OE *hwæt;* c. G *was,* D *wat,* Icel *hvat,* Goth *hwa,* L *quod,* etc.]

what'd (hwut′id, hwot′-, wut′-, wot′-), contraction of *what did: What'd you say?*

what·e'er (hwut âr′, hwot-, wut-, wot-, hwət-, wət-), *pron., adj. Poetic.* whatever.

what·ev·er (hwut ev′ər, hwot-, wut-, wot-, hwət-, wət-), *pron.* **1.** anything that (usually used in relative clauses): *Do whatever you like. Whatever you say is all right with me.* **2.** (used relatively to indicate a quantity of a specified or implied antecedent): *Take whatever you like of these apples.* **3.** no matter what: *Do it, whatever happens.* **4.** any or any one of a number of things whether specifically known or not: *papers, magazines, or whatever.* **5.** what (used interrogatively): *Whatever do you mean?* —*adj.* **6.** in any amount; to any extent: *whatever merit the work has.* **7.** no matter what: *whatever rebuffs he might receive.* **8.** being what or who it may be: *Whatever the reason, he refuses to go.* **9.** of any kind (used as an intensifier following the noun or pronoun it modifies): *any person whatever.* [ME; see WHAT, EVER]

What′ Ev′ery Wom′an Knows′, a comedy (1908) by Sir James M. Barrie.

what'll (hwut′əl, hwot′-, wut′-, wot′-), contraction of *what shall* or *what will: What'll I do and what'll she say?*

what·not (hwut′not′, hwot′-, wut′-, wot′-), *n.* **1.** a stand with shelves for bric-a-brac, books, etc. **2.** something or anything of the same or similar kind: *sheets, pillowcases, towels, napkins, and whatnot.* [from the phrase *what not?*]

what's (hwuts, hwots, wuts, wots; *unstressed* hwəts, wəts), **1.** contraction of *what is* or *what has.* **2.** *Informal.* contraction of *what does: What's the man say?*

what·so·e'er (hwut′sō âr′, hwot′-, wut′-, wot′-), *pron., adj. Poetic.* whatsoever.

what·so·ev·er (hwut′sō ev′ər, hwot′-, wut′-, wot′-), *pron., adj.* (an intensive form of **whatever**): *whatsoever it be; in any place whatsoever.* [ME, equiv. to *what so* (OE *swā hwæt swā*) + *ever* EVER]

what've (hwut′əv, hwot′-, wut′-, wot′-), contraction of **what have:** *What've you done with the money?*

whaup (hwäp, hwôp, wäp, wôp), *n. Scot.* the curlew, *Numenius arquata.* [earlier **whalp,* akin (by gradation) to OE *hwilpe* plover]

wheal (hwēl, wēl), *n.* **1.** a small, burning or itching swelling on the skin, as from a mosquito bite or from hives. **2.** Also, **weal.** a wale or welt. [akin to WHELK[2] and to obs. *wheal* (v.), OE *hwelian* to suppurate, develop weals]

wheat (hwēt, wēt), *n.* **1.** the grain of any cereal grass of the genus *Triticum,* esp. *T. aestivum* (*T. sativum*), used in the form of flour for white bread, cakes, pastry, etc. **2.** the plant, which bears the edible grain in dense spikes. [ME *whete,* OE *hwǣte;* c. Icel *hveiti,* Goth *hwaiteis,* G *Weizen*] —**wheat′less,** *adj.*

wheat′ cake′, a pancake made of wheat flour.

wheat·ear (hwēt′ēr′, wēt′-), *n.* any of several small, chiefly Old World thrushes of the genus *Oenanthe,* having a distinctive white rump, esp. *O. oenanthe,* of Eurasia and North America. [back formation from *wheatears,* equiv. to **whiters* white rump. See WHITE, ARSE]

wheat·en (hwēt′ən, wēt′-), *adj.* **1.** made of wheat flour or grain. **2.** of or pertaining to wheat. [ME *wheten,* OE *hwǣten.* See WHEAT, -EN[2]]

wheat′ germ′, the embryo or nucleus of the wheat kernel, used in or on foods as a concentrated source of vitamins.

wheat·grass (hwēt′gras′, -gräs′, wēt′-), *n.* any of several wheatlike grasses of the genus *Agropyron,* grown for forage in the western U.S. [WHEAT + GRASS]

Wheat·ley (hwēt′lē, wēt′-), *n.* **Phil·lis** (fil′is), 1753?–84, American poet, born in Africa.

Whea·ton (hwēt′ən, wēt′-), *n.* **1.** a town in central Maryland. 54,635 (1960). **2.** a city in NE Illinois, W of Chicago. 24,312 (1960).

Wheat′ Ridge′, a town in central Colorado, near Denver. 21,619 (1960).

wheat′ rust′, *Plant Pathol.* any of several diseases of wheat caused by several rust fungi of the genus *Puccinia.*

Wheat·stone (hwēt′stōn′, wēt′- *or, esp. Brit.,* hwēt′stən, wēt′-), *n.* **Sir Charles,** 1802–75, English physicist and inventor.

Wheat′stone bridge′, *Elect.* a bridge for measuring an unknown resistance by comparing it with a known resistance. Also, **Wheat′stone's bridge′.** Cf. **bridge** (def. 11). [named after C. WHEATSTONE]

wheat·worm (hwēt′wûrm′, wēt′-), *n.* a small nematode worm, *Tylenchus tritici,* causing earcockle in wheat. [WHEAT + WORM]

whee·dle (hwēd′əl, wēd′-), *v.,* **-dled, -dling.** —*v.t.* **1.** to endeavor to influence (a person) by smooth, flattering, or beguiling words or acts: *Though she wheedled him incessantly, he would not consent.* **2.** to persuade (a person) by such words or acts: *She wheedled him into going to the theater with her.* **3.** to obtain (something) by artful persuasions: *She wheedled a new car out of her father.* —*v.i.* **4.** to use beguiling or artful persuasions: *There's no need to wheedle if you really need something.* [? aspirated var. of **weedle,* OE *wǣdlian* to beg, deriv. of *wǣdle* beggar equiv. to *wǣth-* wandering + *-la* masc. n. suffix] —**whee′dler,** *n.* —**whee′dling·ly,** *adv.*

—**Syn. 1.** mollify, flatter, cajole. **2, 3.** coax, tease, beguile, inveigle.

wheel (hwēl, wēl), *n.* **1.** a circular frame or disk arranged to revolve on an axis, as on or in vehicles, machinery, etc. **2.** any machine, apparatus, instrument, etc., shaped like this or having a circular frame, disk, or revolving drum as an essential feature: *a potter's wheel; roulette wheel; steering wheel.* **3.** a circular frame with an axle connecting to the rudder of a ship, for steering: *He took the wheel during the storm.* **4.** *Informal.* a bicycle. **5.** an old instrument of torture in the form of a circular frame on which the victim was stretched until disjointed. **6.** a round object, decoration, etc.: *a wheel of cheese; a design of red wheels and blue squares.* **7.** a circular firework which revolves rapidly while burning; pinwheel. **8.** a rotating instrument which Fortune is represented as turning in order to bring about changes or reverses in human affairs. **9. wheels,** moving, propelling, or animating agencies: *the wheels of commerce; the wheels of thought.* **10.** a cycle, recurring action, or steady progression: *the wheel of days and nights.* **11.** a wheeling or circular movement: *the intricate wheels of the folk dances.* **12.** (formerly) a movement of troops, ships, etc., drawn up in line, as if turning on a pivot. **13.** *Naut.* **a.** a paddle wheel. **b.** a propeller. **14.** *Slang.* someone active and influential, as in business, politics, etc.; an important person: *a big wheel.* **15. at the wheel, a.** at the steering wheel of a ship, motor vehicle, etc. **b.** in command or control: *His ambition is to be at the wheel of a large corporation by the age of forty.* **16. wheels within wheels,** an involved interaction of motives or agencies operating to produce the final result: *Government agencies are a study of wheels within wheels.* —*v.t.* **17.** to cause to turn, rotate, or revolve, as on an axis. **18.** to perform (a movement) in a circular or curving direction. **19.** to move, roll, or convey on wheels, casters, etc.: *The servants wheel out the tables.* **20.** to provide (a vehicle, machine, etc.) with a wheel or wheels. —*v.i.* **21.** to turn on or as on an axis or about a center; revolve, rotate, or pivot. **22.** *Brit. Mil.* to turn: *Right wheel!* **23.** to move in a circular or curving course: *pigeons wheeling above.* **24.** to turn so as to face in a different direction (often fol. by *about* or *around*): *He wheeled about and faced his opponent squarely.* **25.** to change one's opinion or procedure (often fol. by *about* or *around*): *He wheeled around and argued for the opposition.* **26.** to roll along on or as on wheels; travel along smoothly: *The car wheeled along the highway.* **27. wheel and deal,** *Slang.* to exert domination or great influence in one's sphere of activity; operate independently and without restraint. [ME, OE *hwēol, hweohl;* c. D *wiel,* Icel *hjōl,* Gk *kýklos;* see CYCLE] —**wheel′less,** *adj.*

wheel·a·brate (hwēl′ə brāt′, wēl′-), *v.t.,* **-brat·ed, -brat·ing.** to harden the surface of (steel) by bombarding it with a Wheelabrator. [back formation from WHEELABRATOR]

Wheel·a·bra·tor (hwēl′ə brā′tər, wēl′-), *n. Trademark.* a device for shot-peening steel by throwing shot from a rotor by centrifugal force.

wheel′ and ax′le, a simple machine consisting, in its typical form, of a cylindrical drum to which a wheel concentric with the drum is firmly fastened: ropes are so applied that as one unwinds from the wheel, another rope is wound on to the drum.

wheel′ an′imalcule, a rotifer.

wheel′ back′, a chair back having the form of a circle or oval with spindles or bars meeting at the center.

wheel·bar·row (hwēl′bar′ō, wēl′-), *n.* **1.** a frame or box for conveying a load, usually supported at one end by a wheel and at the other by two vertical legs above which are two horizontal shafts used in lifting the legs from the ground when the vehicle is pushed or pulled. **2.** a similar vehicle with more than one wheel. —*v.t.* **3.** to move or convey in a wheelbarrow. [ME; see WHEEL, BARROW[1]] —**wheel′bar′row·er,** *n.*

wheel′barrow race′, a novelty race between a number of paired contestants in which one member of each pair walks on his hands while his legs are supported by his partner.

wheel·base (hwēl′bās′, wēl′-), *n. Auto.* the distance measured in inches from the center of the front-wheel spindle to the center of the rear-wheel axle. [WHEEL + BASE[1]]

wheel′ bug′, an assassin bug, *Arilus cristatus,* which has a toothed, semicircular crest on the pronotum, and which preys on other insects.

wheel·chair (hwēl′châr′, wēl′-), *n.* a chair mounted on large wheels for use by invalids and convalescents. [WHEEL + CHAIR]

wheeled (hwēld, wēld), *adj.* **1.** equipped with or having wheels (often used in combination): *a wheeled vehicle; a four-wheeled carriage.* **2.** moving or traveling on wheels: *wheeled transportation.* [WHEEL + -ED[3]]

wheel·er (hwē′lər, wē′-), *n.* **1.** one who or that which wheels. **2.** a person who makes wheels; wheelwright. **3.** something provided with a wheel or wheels (usually used in combination): *a four-wheeler; a stern-wheeler.* **4.** See **wheel horse** (def. 1). [WHEEL + -ER[1]]

Wheel·er (hwē′lər, wē′-), *n.* **1. Burton Kendall,** born 1882, U.S. political leader. **2. Joseph,** 1836–1906, U.S. soldier and political leader. **3. William Al·mon** (al′mən, ôl′-), 1819–1887, vice-president of the U.S. 1877–81.

wheel·er-deal·er (hwē′lər dē′lər, wē′-), *n. Slang.* a person who wheels and deals. Also, **wheel′er and deal′er.**

Wheel·ers·burg (hwē′lərz bûrg′, wē′-), *n.* a town in S Ohio. 2682 (1960).

wheel′ horse′, **1.** a horse, or one of the horses, harnessed behind others and nearest the front wheels of a vehicle. **2.** a reliable, diligent, and strong worker.

wheel·house (hwēl′hous′, wēl′-), *n., pl.* **-hous·es** (-hou′ziz). pilothouse. [WHEEL + HOUSE]

wheel·ing (hwē′liŋ, wē′-), *n.* **1.** the act of one who moves, travels, conveys, etc., on or as on wheels, esp. cycling. **2.** a rotating or circular motion: *the wheeling of birds.* **3.** the condition of a road for travel by wheeled vehicles: *A state highway is usually good wheeling.* [WHEEL + -ING[1]]

Wheel·ing (hwē′liŋ, wē′-), *n.* **1.** a city in N West Virginia, on the Ohio River. 53,400 (1960). **2.** a town in NE Illinois. 7169 (1960).

wheel′ lock′, **1.** an old type of gunlock in which sparks are produced by the friction of a small steel wheel against a piece of iron pyrites. **2.** a gun having such a gunlock.

wheel·man (hwēl′mən, wēl′-), *n., pl.* **-men. 1.** Also, **wheelsman.** a helmsman or steersman. **2.** a rider of a bicycle, tricycle, or the like. [WHEEL + MAN[1]]

wheel′ of for′tune, **1.** wheel (def. 8). **2.** a wheel-like gambling device that is rotated or spun to determine the winner or winners of certain prizes.

wheel′ of life′, *Buddhism.* **1.** the symbol of the cycle of birth, death, and reincarnation. **2.** a pictorial representation of this.

wheel′ ore′, bournonite.

wheels·man (hwēlz′mən, wēlz′-), *n., pl.* **-men.** wheelman (def. 1). [WHEEL + 's[1] + MAN[1]]

wheel′ stat′ic, noise in an automobile radio induced by wheel rotation.

wheel′ win′dow, a rose window having prominent radiating mullions. Also called **Catherine wheel, marigold window.**

wheel·work (hwēl′wûrk′, wēl′-), *n.,* a train of gears, as in a timepiece. [WHEEL + WORK]

wheel·wright (hwēl′rīt′, wēl′-), *n.* one whose trade it is to make or repair wheels, wheeled carriages, etc. [ME; see WHEEL, WRIGHT]

Wheel·wright (hwēl′rīt′, wēl′-), *n.* **John,** 1592?–1679, English clergyman in America.

wheen (hwēn, wēn), *adj. Scot. and North Eng.* few. [ME (north) *quheyn,* OE *hwēne,* instr. case of *hwōn* few, a few]

wheeze (hwēz, wēz), *v.*, **wheezed, wheez·ing,** *n.* **—***v.i.* **1.** to breathe with difficulty and with a whistling sound: *His asthma was causing him to wheeze.* **2.** to make a sound resembling difficult breathing: *The old locomotive wheezed into the station.* **—***n.* **3.** a wheezing breath or sound. **4.** an old and frequently used gag or joke, esp. one used by entertainers: *that classic wheeze about the chicken crossing the road.* **5.** a trite saying, story, etc.: *one of Aesop's wheezes.* [late ME *whese,* OE *hwǣsan to blow (whence *hwǣst* blowing); c. Icel *hvǣsa* to hiss] **—wheez′er,** *n.* **—wheez′ing·ly,** *adv.*

wheez·y (hwē′zē, wē′-), *adj.*, **wheez·i·er, wheez·i·est.** afflicted with or characterized by wheezing: *wheezy breathing.* [WHEEZE + -Y[1]] **—wheez′i·ly,** *adv.* **—wheez′i·ness,** *n.*

whelk[1] (hwelk, welk), *n.* any of several large, spiral-shelled, marine gastropods of the family *Buccinidae,* esp. *Buccinum undatum,* which is used for food in Europe. [aspirated var. of ME *welk,* OE *weoloc*]

Whelk, ***Buccinum undatum*** **(Length 3 in.)**

whelk[2] (hwelk, welk), *n.* a pimple or pustule. [ME *whelke,* OE *hwylca, hwelca;* see WHEAL]

whelked (hwelkt, welkt), *adj.* ridged like the shell of a snail: *a whelked horn.* [WHELK[1] + -ED[2]]

whelm (hwelm, welm), *v.t.* **1.** to submerge; engulf. **2.** to overcome utterly; overwhelm: *whelmed by misfortune.* [ME *whelme,* appar. b. (now dial.) *whelve* (OE *gehwelfan* to bend over) + HELM[2] (v.) (OE *helmian* to cover)]

whelp (hwelp, welp), *n.* **1.** the young of the dog, or of the wolf, bear, lion, tiger, seal, etc. **2.** *Contemptuous.* a youth. **3.** *Mach.* **a.** any of a series of longitudinal projections or ridges on the barrel of a capstan, windlass, etc. **b.** any of the teeth of a sprocket wheel. [ME; OE *hwelp;* c. G *Welf*] **—***v.t., v.i.* **4.** (of a female dog, lion, etc.) to give birth to (young). [ME *whelpen,* OE *hwelpian*] **—whelp′less,** *adj.*

when (hwen, wen), *adv.* **1.** at what time or period?; how long ago?; how soon?: *When are they to arrive? When did the Roman Empire exist?* **2.** under what circumstances?; upon what occasion?: *When is a letter of condolence in order? When did you ever see such a crowd?* **—***conj.* **3.** at what time: *to know when to be silent.* **4.** at the time or in the event that: *when we were young; when the noise stops.* **5.** at any time; whenever: *He is impatient when he is kept waiting.* **6.** upon or after which; and then: *We had just fallen asleep when the bell rang.* **7.** while on the contrary; considering that; whereas: *Why are you here when you should be in school?* **—***pron.* **8.** what time: *Since when is that allowed? Till when is the store open?* **9.** which time: *They left on Monday, since when we have heard nothing.* **—***n.* **10.** the time of anything: *the when and the where of an act.* [ME *when(ne),* OE *hwenne;* c. G *wann* when, *wenn* (cf. Goth *hwan* when, how); akin to WHO, WHAT]
—Usage. See **where.**

when·as (hwen az′, wen-), *conj.* **1.** *Archaic.* **a.** when. **b.** inasmuch as. **2.** *Obs.* whereas. [late ME; see WHEN, AS[1]]

whence (hwens, wens), *adv.* **1.** from what place?: *Whence comest thou?* **2.** from what source, origin, or cause?: *Whence has he wisdom?* **—***conj.* **3.** from what place, source, cause, etc.: *He told whence he came.* [ME *whennes, whannes,* equiv. to *whanne* (by syncope from OE *hwanone* whence) + *-s* -S[1]]
—Usage. Since WHENCE means "from what place?" it should not be preceded by "from" in careful speech and writing: *Whence did he come?* (not *From whence did he come?*)

whence·so·ev·er (hwens′sō ev′ər, wens′-), *adv., conj.* from whatsoever place, source, or cause. [modeled on WHERESOEVER]

when·e'er (hwen âr′, wen-), *conj. Poetic.* whenever (def. 1).

when·ev·er (hwen ev′ər, wen-), *conj.* **1.** at whatever time; at any time when: *Come whenever you like.* **2.** when? (used emphatically): *Whenever did he say that?* [late ME; see WHEN, EVER]

when-is·sued (hwen′ish′o͞od *or, esp. Brit.,* -is′yo͞od, wen′-), *adj.* of, pertaining to, or noting an agreement to buy securities which will be paid for at the time of delivery. *Abbr.:* W.I. or w.i.

when·so·ev·er (hwen′sō ev′ər, wen′-), *adv., conj.* at whatsoever time. [ME, equiv. to *whenso* (modeled on *whereso*) + *ever* EVER]

where (hwâr, wâr), *adv.* **1.** in or at what place?: *Where is he? Where do you live?* **2.** in what position or circumstances?: *Where do you stand on this question? Without money, where are you?* **3.** in what particular respect, way, etc.?: *Where does this affect us?* **4.** to what place, point, or end; whither?: *Where are you going?* **5.** from what source; whence?: *Where did you get such a notion?* **—***conj.* **6.** in or at what place, part, point, etc.: *Find where he is. Find where the trouble is.* **7.** in or at the place, part, point, etc., in or at which: *The book is where you left it.* **8.** in a position, case, etc., in which: *Where ignorance is bliss, 'tis folly to be wise.* **9.** in any place, position, case, etc., in which; wherever: *Use the ointment where pain is felt.* **10.** to what or whatever place; to the place or any place to which: *Go where? I will go where you go.* **11.** in or at which place; and there: *They came to the town, where they lodged for the night.* **—***pron.* **12.** what place?: *Where did you come from?* **13.** the place in which; point at which: *This is where the boat docks. That was where the phone rang.* **—***n.* **14.** a place; that place in which something is located or occurs: *the wheres and hows of job hunting.* [ME *whēn,* OE *hwǣr;* c. D *waar,* OHG *hwār;* akin to Icel *hvar,* Goth *hwar*]
—Usage. In careful English, WHERE is not used in place of WHEN: *A holiday is when we have time off* should be rewritten as: *A holiday is an occasion when we have time off.* WHERE should not be used to replace THAT: *I see by the papers that* (not *where*) *he has retired.* The phrases WHERE AT and WHERE TO are generally considered too informal to be used in good writing, and are likewise avoided in speech: *Where is she?* (not *Where is she at?*); *Where are you going?* (not *Where are you going to?*).

where·a·bout (hwâr′ə bout′, wâr′-), *adv. Rare.* whereabouts.

where·a·bouts (hwâr′ə bouts′, wâr′-), *adv.* **1.** about where? where? **—***conj.* **2.** near or in what place: *trying to find whereabouts in the world we were.* **—***n.* **3.** (*construed as sing. or pl.*) the place where a person or thing is; the locality of a person or thing: *no clue as to his whereabouts.* [late ME *wheraboutes,* equiv. to ME *wheraboute* (see WHERE, ABOUT) + *-s* -S[1]]

where·as (hwâr az′, wâr-), *conj., n., pl.* **where·as·es.** **—***conj.* **1.** while on the contrary: *One came promptly, whereas the others hung back.* **2.** it being the case that, or considering that (used esp. in formal preambles). **—***n.* **3.** a qualifying or introductory statement, esp. one having "whereas" as the first word: *to read the whereases in the will.* [ME *wheras* WHERE; see AS[1]]

where·at (hwâr at′, wâr-), *adv., conj.* **1.** at which: *a reception whereat many were present.* **2.** to which, or in reference to which; whereupon: *a remark whereat he quickly angered; Whereat we shamed him for his foolishness.* [ME *wherat.* See WHERE, AT]

where·by (hwâr bī′, wâr-), *conj., adv.* **1.** by what or by which. **2.** *Obs.* by what? how? [ME *wherby.* See WHERE, BY]

where'd (hwârd, wârd), contraction of *where did: Where'd you go on your holiday?*

wher·e'er (hwâr âr′, wâr-), *conj., adv. Archaic.* wherever.

where·fore (hwâr′fôr, -fōr, wâr′-), *adv.* **1.** for what? why? **—***conj.* **2.** for what or which cause or reason: *Wherefore let us be grateful.* **—***n.* **3.** the cause or reason: *to study the whys and wherefores of a situation.* [ME; see WHERE, FOR]
—Syn. 2. See **therefore.**

where·from (hwâr frum′, -from′, wâr-), *conj., adv.* from which; whence. [WHERE + FROM]

where·in (hwâr in′, wâr-), *conj.* **1.** in what or in which. **—***adv.* **2.** in what way or respect? [ME *wherin.* See WHERE, IN]

where·in·to (hwâr in′to͞o, wâr-; hwâr′in to͞o′, wâr′-), *conj.* into which. [WHERE + INTO]

where'll (hwârl, wârl), contraction of *where shall* or *where will: Where'll I be ten years from now?*

where·of (hwâr uv′, -ov′, wâr-), *adv., conj.* of what, which, or whom. [ME *wherof.* See WHERE, OF]

where·on (hwâr on′, -ôn′, wâr-), *conj.* **1.** on what or which. **—***adv.* **2.** *Archaic.* on what? [ME *wheron.* See WHERE, ON]

where're (hwâr′ər, wâr′-, hwâr, wâr), contraction of *where are: Where're you going?*

where's (hwârz, wârz), **1.** contraction of *where is: Where's my share?* **2.** *Informal.* contraction of *where has: Where's he been all night?*

where·so·e'er (hwâr′sō âr′, wâr′-), *conj. Poetic.* wheresoever.

where·so·ev·er (hwâr′sō ev′ər, wâr′-), *conj. Archaic.* in or to whatsoever place; wherever. [ME *wheresoever,* equiv. to *whereso* (OE (*swā*) *hwǣr swā*) + *ever* EVER]

where·through (hwâr thro͞o′, wâr-), *conj.* through, during, or because of which. [ME *hwerthrough.* See WHERE, THROUGH]

where·to (hwâr to͞o′, wâr-), *conj., adv.* **1.** to what or what place or end. **2.** to which. [ME *wherto.* See WHERE, TO]

where·up·on (hwâr′ə pon′, -pôn′, wâr′-), *conj.* **1.** upon what or upon which. **2.** at or after which. **3.** *Archaic.* upon what? [ME *wherupon.* See WHERE, UPON]

where've (hwârv, wârv, hwâr′əv, wâr′-), contraction of *where have: Where've you seen this before?*

wher·ev·er (hwâr ev′ər, wâr-), *conj.* **1.** in, at, or to whatever place. **2.** in any case or condition: *wherever it is heard of.* **—***adv.* **3.** where? (used emphatically): *Wherever did you find that?* [ME; OE *hwǣr ǣfre.* See WHERE, EVER]

where·with (hwâr with′, -with′, wâr-), *adv.* **1.** with which; by means of which. **2.** *Archaic.* **a.** with what? **b.** because of which; by reason of which. **c.** whereupon; at which. **—***pron.* **3.** that by which; that with which. **—***n.* **4.** *Rare.* wherewithal. [ME *wherwith.* See WHERE, WITH]

where·with·al (hwâr′with ôl′, wâr′-), *n.* **1.** that wherewith to do something; means or supplies for the purpose or need, esp. money: *the wherewithal to pay my rent.* **—***adv.* **2.** by means of which; out of which. **3.** *Archaic.* wherewith. **—***pron.* **4.** wherewith. [WHERE + WITHAL]

wher·ry (hwer′ē, wer′ē), *n., pl.* **-ries,** *v.,* **-ried, -ry·ing.** **—***n.* **1.** a light rowboat for one person; skiff. **2.** any of various barges, fishing vessels, etc., used locally in England. **3.** (in England) a light rowboat used for carrying passengers and goods on rivers. **—***v.t., v.i.* **4.** to use, or transport in, a wherry. [late ME *whery* < ?]

whet (hwet, wet), *v.,* **whet·ted, whet·ting,** *n.* **—***v.t.* **1.** to sharpen (a knife, tool, etc.) by grinding or friction. **2.** to make keen or eager; stimulate: *to whet the appetite; to whet the curiosity.* **—***n.* **3.** the act of whetting. **4.** something that whets; appetizer. **5.** *Dial.* **a.** a spell of work. **b.** a while: *to talk a whet.* [ME *whette,* OE *hwettan* (deriv. of *hwæt* bold); c. G *wetzen,* Icel *hvetja,* Goth *gahwatjan* to incite] **—whet′ter,** *n.*

wheth·er (hweth′ər, weth′-), *conj.* **1.** (used to introduce the first of two or more alternatives, and sometimes repeated before the second or later alternative, usually with the correlative *or*): *It matters little whether we go or stay. Whether we go or whether we stay, the result is the same.* **2.** (used to introduce a single alternative, the other being implied or understood, or some clause or element not involving alternatives): *See whether he has come. I doubt whether we can do any better.* **3. whether or no,** under whatever circumstances; regardless: *He threatens to go whether or no.* **—***pron. Archaic.* **4.** which (of two)? **5.** (used to introduce a question presenting alternatives, usually with the correlative *or*). [ME; OE *hwether, hwæther,* equiv. to *hwe-, hwa-* (see WHO) + *-ther* comp. suffix; c. Icel *hvatharr,* Goth *hwathar*]
—Usage. See **if.**

whet·stone (hwet′stōn′, wet′-), *n.* **1.** a stone for sharpening cutlery or tools by friction. **2.** anything that sharpens: *a whetstone for dull wits.* [ME *whetston,* OE *hwetstān.* See WHET, STONE]

whet·ter (hwet′ər, wet′-), *n.* one who or that which whets: *a peripatetic whetter of knives and axes; a whetter for the most obstinate appetite.* [WHET + -ER[1]]

whew (hwyo͞o), *interj.* **1.** (a whistling exclamation or sound expressing astonishment, dismay, relief, etc.) **—***n.* **2.** an utterance of "whew." [imit.]

Whe·well (wā′wəl, hyo͞o′əl), *n.* a crater in the first quadrant of the face of the moon: about 5 miles in diameter.

whey (hwā, wā), *n.* a milk serum, separating as a watery liquid from the curd after coagulation, as in the making of cheese. [ME *wheye,* OE *hwǣg;* c. D, LG *wei*] **—whey′ish·ness,** *n.* **—whey′like′,** *adj.*

whey·ey (hwā′ē, wā′ē), *adj.* of, like, or containing whey. [WHEY + -EY[1]]

whey·face (hwā′fās′, wā′-), *n.* a face that or a person who is pallid, as from fear. [WHEY + FACE] **—whey′faced′,** *adj.*

whey·ish (hwā′ish, wā′-), *adj.* rather like whey: *a mottled, wheyish complexion.* [WHEY + -ISH[1]]

whf., wharf.

which (hwich, wich), *pron.* **1.** (of a certain number or group mentioned or implied) what one?: *Which of these do you want? Which do you want?* **2.** whichever: *Choose which appeals to you.* **3.** (used relatively in restrictive and nonrestrictive clauses to represent a specified antecedent, the antecedent being a thing, concept, body of persons, or, archaically, one person): *The book, which I read last night, was exciting. The socialism which Owen preached was unpalatable to many. The lawyer represented five families, of which the Costello family was the largest.* **4.** (used relatively in restrictive clauses having *that* as the antecedent): *Damaged goods constituted part of that which was sold at the auction.* **5.** (used after a preposition to represent a specified antecedent): *the horse on which I rode.* **6.** (used relatively to represent a specified or implied antecedent) the one that; a particular one that: *You may choose which you like from this assortment.* **7.** (used in parenthetic clauses) the thing or fact that: *He hung around for hours and, which was worse, kept me from doing my work.* **—***adj.* **8.** what one of (a certain number or group mentioned or implied)?: *Which book do you want?* **9.** no matter what; any that: *Go which way you please, you'll end up here.* **10.** whichever: *Use which method you prefer.* **11.** being previously mentioned: *It stormed all day, during which time the ship broke up.* [ME; OE *hwilc,* equiv. to *hwi-* (see WHO) + *-līc* body, shape, kind (see LIKE[1]); c. D *welk,* G *welch,* Goth *hwileiks,* lit., of what form]
—Usage. Teachers of English and many good writers and stylists have long maintained that the distinction between WHICH and THAT in relative clauses is a useful one that should be kept. The traditional rule is that THAT is used to introduce restrictive relative clauses and WHICH to introduce nonrestrictive relative clauses. In *The house that has green shutters has been sold,* the relative clause is restrictive, hence is introduced by THAT. (That is, "It was the house with green shutters, not the one with red or other shutters, that was sold.") In *The house, which has green shutters, has been sold,* the relative clause is descriptive or parenthetical, hence is introduced by WHICH. In practice, however, this distinction is made more often in careful writing than in ordinary speech—where stress can often serve to express the restrictiveness or nonrestrictiveness of a clause—and many excellent writers regularly fail to treat THAT and WHICH differently.
On the other hand, WHICH is used regularly in referring to inanimate objects and, usually, animals and never to people, while THAT can be used for either. WHO, in its various forms, is used only in referring to people and, sometimes to animals, especially pets: *The house that is on the hill is white. The house, which is on the hill, is white. The man whom* (or *that*) *you saw is my father.* Note that WHO can be either restrictive or nonrestrictive.

which·ev·er (hwich ev′ər, wich-), *pron.* **1.** (of a certain number or group specified or implied) any one that: *Take whichever you like.* **2.** no matter which: *Whichever you choose, the others will be offended.* **—***adj.* **3.** (of an indicated number) no matter which: *whichever day; whichever ones you choose.* [late ME; see WHICH, EVER]

which·so·ev·er (hwich′sō ev′ər, wich′-), *pron., adj.* whichever. [late ME, equiv. to *whichso* (modeled on *whatso*) + *ever* EVER]

whick·er (hwik′ər, wik′-), *v.i.* **1.** to whinny; neigh. **—***n.* **2.** a whinny; neigh. [*whick-* (as in OE *hwicung* squeaking, said of mice) + -ER[6]; akin to G *wiehern* to neigh]

whid (hwid, hwud, wid, wud), *v.,* **whid·ded, whid·ding,** *n. Scot.* **—***v.i.* **1.** to move quickly and quietly. **—***n.* **2.** a quick, noiseless movement. [appar. akin to OE *hwitha* akin to breeze; c. Icel *hvitha* gust]

whid·ah (hwid′ə, wid′ə), *n.* whydah.

whiff[1] (hwif, wif), *n.* **1.** a slight gust or puff of wind, air, vapor, smoke, or the like: *a whiff of fresh air.* **2.** a slight trace of odor or smell: *a whiff of onions.* **3.** a single inhalation or exhalation of air, tobacco smoke, or the like. **4.** a slight outburst: *a little whiff of temper.* **—***v.i.* **5.** to blow or come in whiffs or puffs, as wind, smoke, etc. **6.** to inhale or exhale whiffs, as in smoking tobacco. **7.** *Baseball Slang.* (of a batter) to strike out by swinging at and missing the pitch charged as the third strike. **—***v.t.* **8.** to blow or drive with a whiff or puff, as the wind does. **9.** to inhale or exhale (air, tobacco smoke, etc.) in whiffs. **10.** to smoke (a pipe, cigar, etc.). **11.** *Baseball Slang.* (of a pitcher) to cause (a batter) to whiff. [aspirated var. of ME *weffe* whiff (of steam or vapor)] **—whiff′er,** *n.*

whiff[2] (hwif, wif), *n.* any of several flatfishes having both eyes on the left side of the head, of the genus *Citharichthys,* as *C. cornutus* **(horned whiff),** found from New England to Brazil. Cf. **left-eyed flounder.** [?]

whif·fet (hwif′it, wif′-), *n.* **1.** a small dog. **2.** *U.S. Informal.* an insignificant person; whippersnapper. **3.** a little whiff. [WHIFF[1] + -ET, modeled on *whippet*]

whif·fle (hwif′əl, wif′-), *v.,* **-fled, -fling.** **—***v.i.* **1.** to blow in light or shifting gusts or puffs, as the wind; veer or toss about irregularly. **2.** to shift about; vacillate; be fickle. **—***v.t.* **3.** to blow with light, shifting gusts. [WHIFF + -LE]

whif·fler[1] (hwif′lər, wif′-), *n.* **1.** a person who frequently shifts his opinions, attitudes, interests, etc. **2.** a person who is vacillating or evasive in an argument. [WHIFFLE + -ER[1]]

whif·fler[2] (hwif′lər, wif′-), *n. Hist.* an attendant, usually bearing a staff, battle-ax, or sword, employed to clear the way for a procession. [earlier *wiffler* armed attendant, equiv. to *wiffle* (var. of ME *wifle,* OE *wifel* battle-ax) + -ER[1]]

W, Whiffletrees

hif·fle·tree (hwif′əl trē′, wif′-), *n.* a crossbar, pivoted at the middle, to which the traces of a harness are fastened for pulling a cart, carriage, plow, etc. Also called **whippletree, singletree, swingletree.** Cf. **doubletree.** [var. of WHIPPLETREE]

hiff′ of grape′shot, a violent means of suppressing a riot, demonstration, or other form of popular revolt or protest.

hig (hwig, wig), *v.i.*, **whigged, whig·ging.** *Scot.* to move along briskly. [? See WHIG, with reference to the march of the *whiggamores*]

hig (hwig, wig), *n.* **1.** *Amer. Hist.* **a.** a member of the patriotic party during the Revolutionary period; supporter of the Revolution. **b.** a member of a political party (c1834–1855) which was formed in opposition to the Democratic party, and favored a loose construction of the Constitution and a high protective tariff. **2.** *Brit. Politics.* **a.** a member of a major political party in Great Britain which, in general, held liberal principles and favored reforms: later called the Liberal party. **b.** (in later use) one of the more conservative members of the Liberal party. —*adj.* **3.** being a Whig. **4.** of, pertaining to, or characteristic of the Whigs. [short for *whiggamore* (member of band of Scottish rebels that marched on Edinburgh in 1648), equiv. to *whig* to + (BLACK)AMOOR; first element *whig* akin to WHEY, one of its meanings]

Whig·ger·y (hwig′ə rē, wig′-), *n.*, Whiggism. [WHIG + -ERY]

hig·gish (hwig′ish, wig′-), *adj.* **1.** of, pertaining to, or characteristic of Whigs or Whiggism. **2.** inclined to Whiggism. [WHIG + -ISH[1]] —**Whig′gish·ly,** *adv.* —**Whig′gish·ness,** *n.*

hig·gism (hwig′iz əm, wig′-), *n.* the principles or practices of Whigs. [WHIG + -ISM]

whig·ma·lee·rie (hwig′mə lēr′ē, wig′-), *n.* **1.** a whim; notion. **2.** a whimsical or fanciful ornament or contrivance; gimmick. [?]

whig·ma·lee·ry (hwig′mə lēr′ē, wig′-), *n.*, *pl.* **-ries.** whigmaleerie.

while (hwīl, wīl), *n.*, *conj.*, *prep.*, *v.*, **whiled, whil·ing.** —*n.* **1.** a period or interval of time: *to wait a long while; He arrived a short while ago.* **2.** *Archaic.* a particular time or occasion. **3. all the while,** at or during this time; all along: *She realized all the while that the cake would fall.* **4. worth one's while,** worth one's time, trouble, or expense: *The art exhibition that opened yesterday isn't worth your while.* —*conj.* **5.** during or in the time that. **6.** throughout the time that; as long as. **7.** at the same time that (implying opposition or contrast); whereas; although: *While he appreciated the honor, he could not accept the position.* **8.** at the same time that (showing an analogous or corresponding action): *The floor was strewn with books, while magazines covered the tables.* —*prep.* **9.** *Archaic.* until. —*v.t.* **10.** to cause (time) to pass, esp. in some easy or pleasant manner (usually fol. by *away*). [ME; OE *hwīl*; c. D *wijl*, G *weile*, Goth *hweila*, Icel *hvīla*]

whiles (hwīlz, wīlz), *adv.* **1.** *Chiefly Scot.* at times. **2.** *Obs.* in the meantime. —*conj.* **3.** *Archaic.* while. [ME; see WHILE, -S[1]]

whil·li·kers (hwil′ə kərz, wil′-), *interj.* *Informal.* (used as an intensive after *gee* or *golly* to express astonishment, delight, etc.) Also, **whil·li·kins** (hwil′ə kinz, wil′-). [?]

whi·lom (hwī′ləm, wī′-), *adj.* **1.** former; erstwhile: *whilom friends.* —*adv.* **2.** *Archaic.* at one time. [ME; OE *hwīlum* at times, dat. pl. of *hwīl* WHILE (n.)]

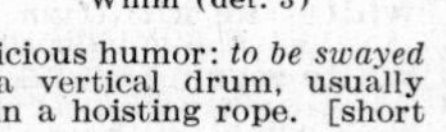
Whim (def. 3)

whilst (hwīlst, wīlst), *conj.* *Chiefly Brit.* while. [late ME *whilest.* See WHILES; inorganic *-t*, as in *amongst, amidst*, etc.]

whim (hwim, wim), *n.* **1.** an odd or capricious idea, notion, or desire; a sudden or freakish fancy: *He had a sudden whim to take a midnight walk.* **2.** capricious humor: *to be swayed by whim.* **3.** *Mining Obs.* a vertical drum, usually horse-operated, for winding in a hoisting rope. [short for WHIM-WHAM]
—**Syn. 1.** whimsy, humor, caprice, vagary, quirk, crotchet, chimera.

whim·brel (hwim′brəl, wim′-), *n.* a curlew, *Numenius phaeopus*, of both the New and Old Worlds. [*whim* (? imit.) + -REL]

whim·per (hwim′pər, wim′-), *v.i.* **1.** to cry with low, plaintive, broken sounds, as a child, an adult, or a dog. —*v.t.* **2.** to utter in a whimper. —*n.* **3.** a whimpering cry or sound. [obs. *whimp* to whine + -ER[6]] —**whim′per·er,** *n.* —**whim′per·ing·ly,** *adv.*
—**Syn. 1.** whine, weep, sob. **3.** whine, sob.

whim·sey (hwim′zē, wim′-), *n.*, *pl.* **-seys.** whimsy.

whim·si·cal (hwim′zi kəl, wim′-), *adj.* **1.** given to whimsy or fanciful notions; capricious: *a pixyish, whimsical sprite of a fellow.* **2.** of the nature of or proceeding from whimsy, as thoughts, actions, etc.: *Her writing showed whimsical notions of human behavior.* **3.** erratic; unpredictable: *He was so whimsical with regard to the project that I stopped relying on him.* [WHIMS(Y) + -ICAL] —**whim′si·cal·ly,** *adv.*
—**Syn. 1.** notional, changeable, crotchety, freakish.

whim·si·cal·i·ty (hwim′zi kal′i tē, wim′-), *n.*, *pl.* **-ties. 1.** Also, **whim′si·cal·ness.** whimsical quality or character. **2.** a whimsical notion, speech, or act. [WHIMSICAL + -ITY]

whim·sy (hwim′zē, wim′-), *n.*, *pl.* **-sies. 1.** capricious humor or disposition; extravagant, fanciful, or excessively playful expression: *a play likely to please those with a strong tolerance for whimsy.* **2.** an odd or fanciful notion. **3.** anything odd or fanciful; a product of playful or capricious fancy: *a whimsy from an otherwise thoughtful writer.* Also, **whimsey.** [WHIM(-WHAM + FANTA)SY]
—**Syn. 2.** caprice, whim, humor, quirk, vagary. **3.** fantasy, make-believe.

whim-wham (hwim′hwam′, wim′wam′), *n.* **1.** any odd or fanciful object or thing; a gimcrack. **2. whim-whams,** *Informal.* nervousness; jitters: *He had a bad case of the whim-whams after the accident.* [repetitive compound with gradation; cf. *flimflam, jim-jam*, etc.]

whin[1] (hwin, win), *n.* *Chiefly Brit.* any thorny or prickly shrub, esp. furze or gorse. [late ME *whynne*, appar. < Scand; cf. Icel *hvingras* bent grass] —**whin′ny,** *adj.*

whin[2] (hwin, win), *n.* **1.** whinstone. **2.** any of various other hard, dark-colored rocks. [?]

whin·chat (hwin′chat′, win′-), *n.* a small, Old World thrush, *Saxicola rubetra*, having a buff-colored breast and white at the base of the tail. [WHIN[1] + CHAT[1]]

whine (hwīn, wīn), *v.*, **whined, whin·ing,** *n.* —*v.i.* **1.** to utter a low, usually nasal, complaining cry or sound, as from uneasiness, discontent, peevishness, etc.: *The puppies were whining from hunger.* **2.** to snivel or complain in a peevish, self-pitying way: *He is always whining about his problems.* —*v.t.* **3.** to utter with or as if with a whine: *She whined her litany of complaints, which he serenely ignored.* —*n.* **4.** a whining utterance, sound, or tone. **5.** a feeble, peevish complaint. [ME; OE *hwīnan* (to) whiz; c. Icel *hvīna*] —**whin′er,** *n.* —**whin′ing·ly,** *adv.*
—**Syn. 1.** moan, whimper. **2.** See **complain.**

whin·ny (hwin′ē, win′ē), *v.*, **-nied, -ny·ing,** *n.* —*v.i.* **1.** to utter the characteristic cry of a horse; neigh. —*v.t.* **2.** to express by whinnying. —*n.* **3.** a neigh. [imit.; cf. earlier *whrinny*, L *hinnīre*]

whin·stone (hwin′stōn′, win′-), *n.* any of the dark-colored, fine-grained rocks such as dolerite and basalt trap. [WHIN[2] + STONE]

whin·y (hwī′nē, wī′-), *adj.*, **whin·i·er, whin·i·est.** complaining; fretful; cranky: *He's whiny because he missed his nap.* Also, **whin′ey.** [WHINE + -Y[1]]

whip (hwip, wip), *v.*, **whipped** or **whipt, whip·ping,** *n.* —*v.t.* **1.** to strike with quick, repeated strokes of something slender and flexible; lash: *He impatiently whipped his leg with his riding crop.* **2.** to beat with a strap, lash, rod, or the like, esp. by way of punishment or chastisement; flog; thrash: *Criminals used to be whipped for minor offenses.* **3.** to lash or castigate with words. **4.** to drive with lashes; urge or force on with, or as with, a lash, rod, etc. **5.** to unite, bring together, bring into line, etc., as a party whip does: *The sergeant was ordered to whip the troops into line.* **6.** *Informal.* to outdo or defeat decisively, as in an athletic contest. **7.** to hoist or haul by means of a whip. **8.** to move quickly and suddenly; pull, jerk, seize, or the like, with a sudden movement (often fol. by *out, in, into*, etc.): *He whipped his gun out of its holster.* **9.** to fish (a stream, lake, etc.) with rod and line, esp. by making repeated casts: *I whipped the stream all day and caught nothing.* **10.** to overlay or cover (cord, rope, etc.) with cord, thread, or the like wound about it: *to whip the end of a hawser.* **11.** to wind (cord, twine, thread, etc.) about something: *The tailor whipped the seams with heavy thread.* **12.** to use a light overcasting stitch in sewing. **13.** to beat (eggs, cream, etc.) to a froth with an eggbeater, whisk, fork, or other implement in order to mix in air and cause them to expand. —*v.i.* **14.** to move or go quickly and suddenly (usually fol. by *around, into, off*, etc.); dart; whisk: *She whipped into the store for a bottle of milk.* **15.** to beat or lash about, as a pennant in the wind. **16.** to fish with rod and line, esp. by casting the line frequently. **17. whip in,** *Hunting.* to prevent from wandering, as hounds. **18. whip off,** *Informal.* to write hurriedly: *He whipped off three new songs last night.* **19. whip up,** *Informal.* **a.** to plan or assemble quickly: *to whip up a delicious dinner.* **b.** to incite; arouse; stir: *The crowd was whipped up to a frenzy.* —*n.* **20.** an instrument for striking, as in driving animals or in punishing, typically consisting of a lash or other flexible part with a more rigid handle. **21.** a whipping or lashing stroke or motion. **22.** a windmill vane. **23.** *Chiefly Brit.* one who uses a whip as part of his work, as a driver of horses, a coachman, or the like. **24.** *Hunting.* a whipper-in. **25.** *Politics.* **a.** a party manager in a legislative body who secures attendance for voting and directs other members. **b.** *Eng.* a written call made on members of a party to be in attendance for voting. **26.** a tackle consisting of a fall rove through a single standing block **(single whip)** so as to change the direction of hauling with no mechanical advantage, or consisting of a fall secured at one end and rove through a single running and a single standing block **(double whip)** so as to change the direction of hauling with a mechanical advantage of two, neglecting friction. Cf. **gun tackle. 27.** the wrapping around the end of a whipped cord or the like. **28.** a dish made of cream or egg whites whipped to a froth with flavoring, often with fruit pulp or the like: *prune whip.* **29.** Also called **whirl.** *Mach.* eccentric rotation of a shaft having its center line slightly curved between supporting bearings. [ME *whippe*, aspirated var. of *wippe(n)*; c. D *wippen* to swing, oscillate; cf. LG *wip(pe)* quick movement] —**whip′like′,** *adj.* —**whip′per,** *n.*
—**Syn. 2.** scourge, flagellate, switch, punish, chastise. **6.** overcome, conquer. **8, 13.** whisk. **20.** switch, scourge.

whip·cord (hwip′kôrd′, wip′-), *n.* **1.** a cotton, woolen, or worsted fabric with a steep, diagonally ribbed surface. **2.** a strong, hard-twisted cord, sometimes used for the lashes of whips. **3.** a cord made from the intestines of animals; catgut. [ME *wyppe-cord.* See WHIP, CORD]

whip-crack·er (hwip′krak′ər, wip′-), *n.* **1.** one who cracks a whip. **2.** one who exerts authority, esp. excessively or ostentatiously.

whip′ graft′, a graft prepared by cutting both the scion and the stock in a sloping direction and inserting a tongue in the scion into a slit in the stock. Also called **tongue graft.**

whip′ hand′, 1. the hand that holds the whip, in driving. **2.** an advantageous or controlling position: *He had the whip hand throughout the debate.*

whip·lash (hwip′lash′, wip′-), *n.* **1.** the lash of a whip. **2.** Also, **whip′lash in′jury.** a neck injury caused by a sudden jerking backward, forward, or both, of the head: *Whiplash resulted when his car was struck from behind.* [WHIP + LASH[1]]

whipped (hwipt, wipt), *adj.* **1.** having received a whipping. **2.** subdued or defeated as though by whipping: *the puzzled, whipped look of the migrant workers.* **3.** beaten into a froth: *whipped cream for the gingerbread.* [WHIP + -ED[2]]

Whippet (22 in. high at shoulder)

whip·per-in (hwip′ər in′, wip′-), *n.*, *pl.* **whip·pers-in. 1.** *Fox Hunting.* a professional or honorary member of a hunt staff who assists the huntsman with the hounds. **2.** *Brit.* whip (def. 23).

whip·per·snap·per (hwip′ər snap′ər, wip′-), *n.* an unimportant but offensively presumptuous person, esp. a young one. [jingling extension of *whipsnapper* a cracker of whips]

whip·pet (whip′it, wip′-), *n.* **1.** one of a breed of small, swift dogs resembling a greyhound, used for hunting rabbits and for racing. **2.** Also called **whip′pet tank′,** a fast, light tank used by the British in World War I. [? alter. of phrase *whip it* move briskly]

whip·ping (hwip′ing, wip′-), *n.* **1.** a beating or flogging, esp. one administered with a whip or the like in punishment. **2.** an arrangement of cord, twine, or the like, whipped or wound about a thing, as to bind parts together or prevent unraveling, as at the end of a rope. [WHIP + -ING[1]]

whip′ping boy′, 1. a person who is made to bear the blame for another's mistake; scapegoat. **2.** (formerly) a boy educated along with and taking punishment in place of a young prince or nobleman.

whip′ping cream′, *Cookery.* cream that contains enough butterfat to allow it to be made into whipped cream.

whip′ping post′, a post to which persons are tied to undergo whipping as a legal penalty.

Whip·ple (hwip′əl, wip′-), *n.* **George Hoyt** (hoit), born 1878, U.S. pathologist: Nobel prize for medicine 1934.

whip·ple·tree (hwip′əl trē′, wip′-), *n.* whiffletree. [*whipple* (see WHIP, -LE) + TREE]

Whip′ple truss′, a truss having vertical compression members and diagonal tension members which cross two panels. Cf. **Pratt truss.** [named after Squire *Whipple* (1804–88), American civil engineer]

whip·poor·will (hwip′ər wil′, wip′-, hwip′ər wil′, wip′-), *n.* a nocturnal, North American goatsucker, *Caprimulgus vociferus*, having a variegated plumage of gray, black, white, and tawny. [imit.]

whip·ray (hwip′rā′, wip′-), *n.* any ray having a long, whiplike tail, esp. a stingray. [WHIP + RAY[2]]

whip′ roll′, *Textiles.* a roller, located at the back of a loom, that guides the warp ends as they come up from the warp beam on their way to the harness.

whip·saw (hwip′sô′, wip′-), *n.*, *v.*, **-sawed, -sawed** or **-sawn, -saw·ing.** —*n.* **1.** a saw for cutting small curves, as a compass or key saw, esp. one having a blade in a frame. **2.** a saw for two persons, as a pitsaw, used to divide timbers lengthwise. —*v.t.* **3.** to cut with a whipsaw. **4.** to win two bets from (a person) at one turn or play, as at faro. **5.** to defeat or worst in two ways at once. [WHIP + SAW[1]]

whip′ scor′pion, any of numerous arachnids of the order *Pedipalpi*, of tropical and warm temperate regions, resembling a scorpion but having an abdomen that ends in a slender, nonvenomous whip.

whip·snake (hwip′snāk′, wip′-), *n.* **1.** any of several long, slender New World snakes of the genus *Masticophis*, the tail of which resembles a whip. **2.** any of various similar colubrid snakes. Also, **whip′ snake′.** [WHIP + SNAKE]

whip·staff (hwip′staf′, -stäf′, wip′-), *n.*, *pl.* **-staves, -staffs.** *Naut.* a lever for controlling a tiller: used esp. in the 17th century. [WHIP + STAFF[1]]

whip·stall (hwip′stôl′, wip′-), *Aeron.* —*n.* **1.** a stall during a vertical climb in which the nose of the airplane falls forward and downward in a whiplike movement. —*v.t.* **2.** to cause (an aircraft) to undergo whipstall. —*v.i.* **3.** to whipstall an aircraft. [WHIP + STALL[1]]

whip·stitch (hwip′stich′, wip′-), *v.t.* **1.** to sew with stitches passing over an edge, in joining, finishing, or gathering. —*n.* **2.** one such stitch. **3.** *Informal.* a little while; instant: *She drops in to see us every whipstitch.* [WHIP + STITCH[1]]

whip·stock (hwip′stok′, wip′-), *n.* the handle of a whip. [WHIP + STOCK]

whip·tail (hwip′tāl′, wip′-), *n.* **1.** any of several whip-tailed American lizards of the genus *Cnemidophorus*, characterized by great agility and alertness. **2.** any of various other whip-tailed animals, as the whip scorpion. [WHIP + TAIL[1]]

whip-tailed (hwip′tāld′, wip′-), *adj.* having a long, slender tail like a whiplash. [WHIPTAIL + -ED[3]]

whip′-tailed ray′, a whipray.

whip·worm (hwip′wûrm′, wip′-), *n.* any of several parasitic nematodes of the genus *Trichuris*, having a long, slender, whiplike anterior end. [WHIP + WORM]

whir (hwûr, wûr), *v.*, **whirred, whir·ring,** *n.* —*v.i.* **1.** to go, fly, dart, revolve, or otherwise move quickly with a humming or buzzing sound: *An electric fan whirred softly in the corner.* —*v.t.* **2.** to move or transport (a thing, person, etc.) with a whirring sound: *The plane whirred them away into the night.* —*n.* **3.** act or sound of whirring: *the whir of wings.* Also, **whirr.** [ME *quirre* (Scot) < Scand; cf. Dan *hvirre*, Norw *kvirra.* See WHIRL]

whirl (hwûrl, wûrl), *v.i.* **1.** to turn around, spin, or rotate rapidly: *The merry-go-round whirled noisily.* **2.** to turn about or aside quickly: *He whirled and faced his pursuers.* **3.** to move, travel, or be carried rapidly along on wheels or otherwise: *He whirled along the freeway in his new car.* **4.** to feel as though spinning rapidly; reel as from dizziness: *My head began to whirl.* —*v.t.* **5.** to cause to turn around, spin, or rotate rapidly. **6.** to send, drive, or carry in a circular or curving course. **7.** to drive, send, or carry along with great or dizzying rapidity. **8.** *Obs.* to hurl. —*n.* **9.** act of whirling; rapid rotation or gyration. **10.** a whirling movement; quick turn or swing. **11.** a short drive, run, walk, or the like; spin. **12.** something that whirls; a whirling current or mass. **13.** a rapid round of events, affairs, etc.: *Her life was a whirl of cocktail parties and dinner dates.* **14.** a state marked by a dizzying succession or mingling of feelings, thoughts, etc. **15.** an attempt or trial, esp. one undertaken tentatively or experimentally: *Even if you don't agree with my plan, won't you give it a whirl?* **16.** *Mach.* whip (def. 29). **17.** *Metalworking.* a rotating

arrangement of dies for straightening wire. [ME *whirle* < Scand; cf. Icel *hvirfla* to whirl, akin to OE *hwyrflung* turning, revolving, *hwyrfel* circuit, etc. See WHORL] —**whirl/er,** *n.* —**whirl/ing·ly,** *adv.*
—**Syn. 1.** gyrate, pirouette. **1, 5.** revolve, twirl, wheel. **9.** spin, revolution.

whirl·a·bout (hwûrl/ə bout/, wûrl/-), *n.* **1.** a whirling about. **2.** a whirligig. —*adj.* **3.** whirling about. [WHIRL + ABOUT]

whirl/ gate/, *Foundry.* a gate designed to reduce turbulence in metal entering a mold.

whirl·i·cote (hwûr/lə kōt/, wûr/-), *n.* a large, heavy coach or carriage. [appar. miswritten (by John Stow) for late ME *whirlecole,* equiv. to *whirle* WHIRL + *-cole* -CULE]

whirl·i·gig (hwûr/lə gig, wûr/-), *n.* **1.** something that whirls, revolves, or goes around; an apparatus that whirls or revolves. **2.** a whirling or revolving motion or course; continuous round or succession; revolving cycle: *the whirligig of fashion.* **3.** a giddy or flighty person. **4.** a merry-go-round or carrousel. **5.** a toy for whirling or spinning, as a top. [late ME *whirlegigge.* See WHIRL, GIG[1]]

whirl/igig bee/tle, any of numerous aquatic beetles of the family *Gyrinidae,* commonly seen circling rapidly about in large numbers on the surface of the water.

whirl/ing der/vish, *Islam.* a dervish whose actions include ecstatic whirling, dancing, chanting, etc.

whirl·pool (hwûrl/pōōl/, wûrl/-), *n.* **1.** a whirling eddy or current, as in a river or the sea, produced by irregularity in the channel or stream banks, by the meeting of opposing currents, by the interaction of winds and tides, etc.; a vortex of water. **2.** *Heraldry.* gurge (def. 2). [WHIRL + POOL; cf. OE *hwyrfepōl*]

whirl/pool bath/, a therapeutic bath in which a part or parts of the body are immersed in whirling hot water.

whirl·wind (hwûrl/wind/, wûrl/-), *n.* **1.** any of several relatively small masses of air rotating rapidly round a more or less vertical axis and advancing simultaneously over land or sea, as the dust devil, tornado, or waterspout. **2.** anything resembling a whirlwind, as in violent action, destructive force, etc. **3.** any circling rush or violent onward course. **4. reap the whirlwind,** to suffer the penalties for one's misdeeds. Hos. 8:7. [ME < Scand; cf. Icel *hvirfilvindr;* c. G *Wirbelwind*]

whirl·y (hwûr/lē, wûr/-), *n., pl.* **whirl·ies.** a violent whirlwind carrying snow, occurring in Antarctica. [WHIRL + -Y[2]]

whirl·y·bird (hwûr/lē bûrd/, wûr/-), *n.* *Informal.* helicopter. [*whirly* (see WHIRL, -Y[1]) + BIRD]

whirr (hwûr, wûr), *v.i., v.t., n.* whir.

whir·ry (hwûr/ē, wûr/ē), *v.,* **-ried, -ry·ing.** *Scot.* —*v.i.* **1.** to hurry; go rapidly. —*v.t.* **2.** to carry (something) or drive (cattle) swiftly. [perh. b. WHIR and (HUR)RY]

whish (hwish, wish), *v.i.* **1.** to make, or move with, a whiz or swish. —*n.* **2.** a whishing sound. [imit.]

whisht (hwist, wist, hwisht, wisht), *interj., adj., n., v.i., v.t.* whist[2]. [cf. OE *hwiscettung* squeaking (said of mice)]

whisk[1] (hwisk, wisk), *v.t.* **1.** to sweep (dust, crumbs, etc., or a surface) with a whisk broom, brush, or the like. **2.** to move with a rapid, sweeping stroke: *She whisked everything off the table with her arm.* **3.** to draw, snatch, carry, etc., lightly and rapidly: *He whisked the money into his pocket.* —*v.i.* **4.** to sweep, pass, or go lightly and rapidly. —*n.* **5.** act of whisking. **6.** a rapid, sweeping stroke; light, rapid movement. [late ME *quhiske* (Scot) < Scand (aspiration from E); cf. Dan *viske* to wipe, c. G *wischen*]

whisk[2] (hwisk, wisk), *v.t.* **1.** to whip (eggs, cream, etc.) to a froth with a whisk or beating implement. —*n.* **2.** a small bunch of grass, straw, hair, or the like, esp. for use in brushing. **3.** See **whisk broom. 4.** an implement, usually a bunch of wire loops held together in a handle, for beating or whipping eggs, cream, etc. [aspirated var. of ME *wisk* < Scand; cf. Icel *visk* wisp, c. G *Wisch* wisp of straw]

whisk/ broom/, a small short-handled broom used chiefly to brush clothes.

whisk·er (hwis/kər, wis/-), *n.* **1.** Usually, **whiskers.** the hair growing on the side of a man's face, esp. when worn long and with the chin clean-shaven. **2. whiskers,** the beard generally. **3.** a single hair of the beard. **4.** *Archaic.* a mustache. **5.** one of the long, stiff, bristly hairs growing about the mouth of certain animals, as the cat, rat, etc.; vibrissa. **6.** Also called **whisk/er boom/, whisk/er pole/.** *Naut.* any spar for extending the clew or clews of a sail so that it can catch more wind. **7.** *Electronics.* See **cat whisker** (def. 2). **8.** *Crystall.* a thin filament of a crystal, usually several millimeters long and one to two microns in diameter, having unusually great strength. [late ME; see WHISK[1], -ER[1]] —**whisk/er·less,** *adj.* —**whisk/er·y,** *adj.*

whisk·ered (hwis/kərd, wis/-), *adj.* having, wearing, or covered with whiskers. [WHISKER + -ED[3]]

whis·key (hwis/kē, wis/-), *n., pl.* **-keys,** *adj.* —*n.* **1.** a distilled alcoholic liquor made from grain, as barley, rye, corn, etc., usually containing from 43 to 50 percent of alcohol. **2.** a drink of whiskey. **3.** a word used in communications to represent the letter W. —*adj.* **4.** made of, relating to, or resembling whiskey. Also, **whisky.** [short for *whiskybae* < Gael *uisgebeatha* USQUEBAUGH]

whis/key jack/. See **Canada jay.** [formerly *whiskey-john,* popular version of Algonquian *wiskatjân*]

whis/key sour/, a cocktail made with whiskey, lemon juice, and sugar.

whis·ky (hwis/kē, wis/-), *n., pl.* **-kies,** *adj.* whiskey, esp. Scotch or Canadian whisky.

whis·per (hwis/pər, wis/pər), *v.i.* **1.** to speak with soft, hushed sounds, using the breath, lips, etc., but with no vibration of the vocal cords. **2.** *Phonet.* to produce utterance substituting breath for phonation. **3.** to talk softly and privately (often implying gossip, slander, plotting, or the like): *The king knew that the courtiers were whispering.* **4.** (of trees, water, breezes, etc.) to make a soft, rustling sound like that of whispering. —*v.t.* **5.** to utter with soft, low sounds, using the breath, lips, etc.: *He whispered endearments to her.* **6.** *Phonet.* to utter (speech sounds) substituting breath for phonation. **7.** to say or tell in a whisper; to tell privately. **8.** to speak to or tell (a person) in a whisper, or privately. —*n.* **9.** the mode of utterance, or the voice, of one who whispers: *He spoke in a whisper.* **10.** a sound, word, remark, or the like, uttered by whispering; something said or repeated privately: *He heard of the whispers and acted to disprove them.* **11.** a soft, rustling sound like a whisper: *the whisper of leaves in the wind.* [ME *whispere(n),* OE *hwisprian;* c. G *wispern;* akin to Icel *hviskra* to whisper, *hvísla* to whistle. See WHINE]

whis·per·er (hwis/pər ər, wis/-), *n.* **1.** one who or that which whispers. **2.** a gossip, talebearer, rumormonger, or the like. [WHISPER + -ER[1]]

whis·per·ing (hwis/pər ing, wis/-), *n.* **1.** whispered talk or conversation. **2.** rumor, hearsay, or gossip. **3.** a whispered sound. —*adj.* **4.** that whispers; making a sound like a whisper. **5.** like a whisper. **6.** given to whispering; gossipy. **7.** conversing in whispers. [ME (n.), OE *hvisprunge* (n.). See WHISPER, -ING[2], -ING[1]] —**whis/per·ing·ly,** *adv.*

whis/pering campaign/, the organized spreading by word of mouth of insinuations, rumors, or charges meant to destroy the reputation of a person, organization, cause, etc.

whis/pering gal/lery, a space or gallery beneath a dome or broad arch in which low sounds produced at any of certain points are clearly audible at certain other distant points.

whis·per·ous (hwis/pər əs, wis/-), *adj.* whispery. [WHISPER + -OUS] —**whis/per·ous·ly,** *adv.*

whis·per·y (hwis/pə rē, wis/-), *adj.* **1.** like a whisper: *a soft, whispery voice.* **2.** abounding in whispers or other quiet, mysterious sounds: *dark, whispery streets.* [WHISPER + -Y[1]]

whist[1] (hwist, wist), *n.* a card game played by four players, two against two, with 52 cards. [special use of WHIST[2]; r. *whisk* earlier name of game < ?]

whist[2] (hwist, wist), *interj.* **1.** hush! silence! be still! —*adj.* **2.** *Archaic.* hushed; silent; still. —*n.* **3.** *Chiefly Irish.* silence: *Hold your whist.* —*v.i.* **4.** *Archaic.* to be or become silent. —*v.t.* **5.** *Obs.* to silence. Also, **whisht.** [imit.; cf. SHH, SHUSH, etc.]

whis·tle (hwis/əl, wis/-), *v.,* **-tled, -tling,** *n.* —*v.i.* **1.** to make a clear musical sound, a series of such sounds, or a high-pitched, warbling sound by the forcible expulsion of the breath through a small opening formed by contracting the lips, or through the teeth, with the aid of the tongue. **2.** to make such a sound or series of sounds otherwise, as by blowing on some device. **3.** (of a device) to produce a similar sound when actuated by steam or the like: *This teakettle will whistle when it boils.* **4.** to emit similar sounds from the mouth, as birds do. **5.** to move, go, pass, etc., with a whistling or whizzing sound, as a bullet, the wind, etc. —*v.t.* **6.** to produce by whistling: *He can whistle any tune.* **7.** to call, direct, or signal by or as by whistling: *He whistled his dog over.* **8.** to send with a whistling or whizzing sound. **9. whistle for,** to demand or expect without success; fail to obtain: *After promising to pay, he told us we could whistle for our money.* —*n.* **10.** an instrument for producing whistling sounds by means of the breath, steam, etc., as a small wooden or tin tube, a pipe, or a similar device with an air chamber containing a small ball which oscillates when air is forced through an opening, producing a high-pitched, warbling tone. **11.** a sound produced by whistling: *a prolonged whistle of astonishment.* **12.** a simple fipple flute. **13. blow the whistle on,** *Slang.* to stop (a person, organization, etc., from continuing a specific activity): *As a buyer, he used to get a lot of Christmas gifts from manufacturers until the management blew the whistle on him. The government blew the whistle on the missile project.* **14. wet one's whistle,** *Informal.* to take a drink. [ME; OE *hwistlian;* akin to Icel *hvísla* to whistle, *hviskra* to whisper. See WHINE] —**whis/tle·a·ble,** *adj.* —**whis/tly,** *adj.*

whis·tler (hwis/lər, wis/-), *n.* **1.** one who or that which whistles. **2.** something that makes a sound like a whistle: *The windstorm was a 60-mile-an-hour whistler.* **3.** any of various birds whose wings whistle in flight, esp. the goldeneye and European widgeon. **4.** thickhead (def. 2). **5.** a large marmot, *Marmota caligata,* of mountainous northwestern North America, closely related to the woodchuck. **6.** a horse afflicted with whistling. [ME; OE *hwistlere.* See WHISTLE, -ER[1]]

Whis·tler (hwis/lər, wis/-), *n.* **James (Abbott) McNeill** (mək nēl/), 1834–1903, U.S. painter and etcher, in France and England after 1855. —**Whis·tle·ri·an** (hwis lēr/ē ən, wis-), *adj.*

Whis/tler's Moth/er, a painting (1871) by James McNeill Whistler. Also called **The Artist's Mother, Arrangement in Black and Gray.**

whis/tle stop/, **1.** a small, unimportant town, esp. one along a railroad line. **2.** a short talk from the rear platform of a train, esp. during a political campaign. **3.** a brief appearance, single performance, or the like, in a small town, as during a political campaign, theatrical tour, etc.

whis·tle-stop (hwis/əl stop/, wis/-), *v.i.,* **-stopped, -stop·ping.** to campaign for political office by traveling around the country, originally by train, stopping at small communities to reach voters in small groups.

whis·tling (hwis/ling, wis/-), *n.* **1.** act of one who or that which whistles. **2.** the sound produced. **3.** *Vet. Med.* a form of roaring characterized by a peculiarly shrill sound. [ME; OE *hwistlung.* See WHISTLE, -ING[1]] —**whis/tling·ly,** *adv.*

whis/tling buoy/, *Naut.* a buoy having a whistle operated by air trapped and compressed in an open-bottomed chamber by the rising and falling water level caused by natural wave action.

whis/tling duck/. See **tree duck.**

whis/tling swan/, a large, white, North American swan, *Olor columbianus,* having black feet and a small yellow spot at the base of the black bill, noted for its whistling cry.

whit (hwit, wit), *n.* a particle; bit; jot (used esp. in negative phrases): *not a whit better.* [appar. scribal metathetic var. of ME, OE *wiht* WIGHT[1]]

Whit (hwit, wit), *n.* a boy's given name, form of **Whitcomb** or **Whitfield** or **Whitaker.**

Whit·a·ker (hwit/ə kər, wit/-), *n.* **1.** a crater in the fourth quadrant of the face of the moon, in the libration area: about 70 miles in diameter. **2.** Also, **Whittaker.** a boy's given name.

Whit·by (hwit/bē, wit/-), *n.* a seaport in NE Yorkshire, in NE England: ruins of an abbey; church council A.D. 664. 11,662 (1961).

Whit·comb (hwit/kəm, -kōm, wit/-), *n.* a boy's given name.

white (hwīt, wīt), *adj.,* **whit·er, whit·est,** *n., v.,* **whit·ed, whit·ing.** —*adj.* **1.** of the color of pure snow, of the margins of this page, etc.; reflecting nearly all the rays of sunlight or a similar light: *Her white dress was dazzling in the sun.* **2.** light or comparatively light in color. **3.** (of human beings) marked by slight pigmentation of the skin, esp. Caucasoid. **4.** dominated by or including only members of the white race: *a white club; a white school.* **5.** pallid or pale, as from fear or other strong emotion: *He turned white with rage.* **6.** (in music) lacking color, resonance, warmth, etc.: *the white tones of the soprano's upper register.* **7.** silvery, gray, or hoary: *white hair.* **8.** characterized by snow; snowy: *Do you think we'll have a white Christmas?* **9.** lacking color; transparent. **10.** (politically) radically conservative. **11.** *Archaic.* blond or fair. **12.** blank, as an unoccupied space in printed matter: *Fill in the white space below.* **13.** (of silverware) not burnished. **14.** *Armor.* composed entirely of polished steel plates without fabric or other covering; alwite. **15.** wearing white clothing: *a white friar.* **16.** *Slang.* honest; dependable: *That's very white of you.* **17.** auspicious or fortunate. **18.** free from spot or stain. **19.** morally pure; innocent. **20.** without malice; harmless: *white magic.* **21.** (of wines) light-colored or yellowish, as opposed to red. **22.** *Brit. Informal.* (of coffee) containing milk. **23. bleed white,** *Informal.* to be or cause to be deprived of all one's resources: *Dishonesty is bleeding the union white.* —*n.* **24.** a color without hue at one extreme end of the scale of grays, opposite to black. A white surface reflects light of all hues completely and diffusely. Most so-called whites are very light grays: fresh snow, for example, reflects about 80 percent of the incident light, but to be strictly white, snow would have to reflect 100 percent of the incident light. It is the ultimate limit of a series of shades of any color. **25.** a hue completely desaturated by admixture with white, the highest value possible. **26.** quality or state of being white. **27.** lightness of skin pigment. **28.** a white material or substance. **29.** the white part of something. **30.** *Biol.* a pellucid viscous fluid which surrounds the yolk of an egg; albumen. **31.** the white part of the eyeball: *He has a speck in the white of his eye.* **32. whites, a.** (*construed as sing.*) *Pathol.* leukorrhea. **b.** white or nearly white clothing. **c.** top-grade white flour. **33.** white wine: *You drink the red, and I'll drink the white. Graves is a good white.* **34.** a type or breed which is white in color. **35.** Usually, **whites.** a blank space in printing. **36.** (*cap.*) a hog of any of several breeds having a white coat, as a Chester White. **37.** *Entomol.* any of several white-winged butterflies of the family *Pieridae,* as the common cabbage butterflies. **38.** white fabric. **39.** *Archery.* **a.** the outermost ring of the butt. **b.** an arrow that hits this portion of the butt. **c.** the central part of the butt or target, formerly painted white but now painted gold or yellow. **d.** *Archaic.* a target painted white. **40.** *Chess, Checkers.* the men or pieces which are light-colored. **41.** (*often cap.*) a member of a royalist, conservative, or reactionary political party. **42. in the white,** in an unfinished state or condition, as furniture wood which has not been stained or varnished. —*v.t.* **43.** *Print.* **a.** to make white by leaving blank spaces (often fol. by *out*). **b.** to whiten (areas of artwork) in retouching preparatory to photoengraving (often fol. by *out*). **44.** *Archaic.* to make white; whiten. [ME *whit(e),* OE *hwīt;* c. G *weiss,* Icel *hvītr,* Goth *hweits*]

White (hwīt, wīt), *n.* **1. Byron R(aymond)** ("*Whizzer*"), born 1917, U.S. lawyer and jurist: associate justice of the U.S. Supreme Court since 1962. **2. E(l·wyn) B(rooks)** (el/win), born 1899, U.S. humorist and poet. **3. Edward Douglass,** 1845–1921, U.S. jurist: Chief Justice of the U.S. 1910–21. **4. Gilbert,** 1720–93, English clergyman, naturalist, and writer. **5. Stan·ford** (stan/fərd), 1853–1906, U.S. architect. **6. Stewart Edward,** 1873–1946, U.S. novelist. **7. T(erence) H(an·bur·y)** (han/bə rē), 1896–1964, English novelist. **8. William A(l·an·son)** (al/ən sən), 1870–1937, U.S. neurologist, psychiatrist, and writer. **9. William Allen,** 1868–1944, U.S. journalist.

white/ ac/id, *Chem.* a mixture of hydrofluoric acid and ammonium bifluoride, used in etching glass.

white·a·cre (hwīt/ā/kər, wīt/-), *n.* a fanciful designation for a hypothetical piece of land, esp. as distinguished from blackacre; formerly used in lawbooks for illustrative purposes. [WHITE + ACRE]

white/ ad/miral. See under **purple** (def. 6).

white/ alert/, **1.** (in military or civilian defense) an all-clear signal, directive, etc., indicating that the danger of air raid no longer exists. **2.** a return to normal conditions following an attack or a threat of attack. Cf. **blue alert, red alert, yellow alert.**

white/ al/kali, **1.** *Agric.* a whitish layer of mineral salts, esp. sodium sulfate, sodium chloride, and magnesium sulfate, often found on top of soils under low rainfall. **2.** refined soda ash.

white/ ant/, termite.

white/ ash/. See under **ash**[2] (def. 1).

white/ as/pen. See under **aspen** (def. 1).

white·bait (hwīt/bāt/, wīt/-), *n., pl.* **-bait.** any small, delicate fish cooked whole without being cleaned, in Europe, esp. the sprat. [so called from use as bait]

white/ bass/ (bas), an edible, fresh-water serranid fish, *Roccus chrysops,* of the Great Lakes and Mississippi River drainage, silvery with yellow below and having the sides streaked with blackish lines. Also called **silver bass.**

white/ bay/. See **sweet bay** (def. 2).

white·beam (hwīt/bēm/, wīt/-), *n.* a tree, *Sorbus Aria,* of Europe, having leathery leaves, showy, white flowers, and mealy, orange-red or scarlet fruit. [WHITE + BEAM]

white/ bear/. See **polar bear.**

white·beard (hwīt/bērd/, wīt/-), *n.* an old man, esp. one with a white or gray beard. [late ME; see WHITE, BEARD]

white/ belt/, *Judo.* a white belt worn on the costume and indicating that the player is a beginner. Cf. **black belt** (def. 3), **brown belt, green belt** (def. 2). —**white/-belt/,** *adj.*

white′ birch′, 1. the European birch, *Betula pendula,* yielding a hard wood. 2. See **paper birch.**

white′ blood′ cell′, a leukocyte. Also called **white′ blood′ cor′puscle.**

white′ book′, an official report issued by a government, usually bound in white.

White·boys (hwīt′boiz′, wīt′-), *n.* (*construed as sing.*) a secret agrarian peasant organization, active in Ireland during the early 1760's, whose members wore white shirts for recognition on their night raids to destroy crops, barns, and other property in redressing grievances against landlords and protesting the paying of tithes. [WHITE + BOY + -S[3]]

white′ bread′, any white or light-colored bread made from finely ground, usually bleached, flour. [ME *whit bre(e)d;* r. OE *hwitehlāf.* See WHITE, LOAF[1]]

white′ bronze′, bronze containing a very high proportion of tin.

white′ bry′ony, a European bryony, *Bryonia alba.*

white′ cam′pion. See **evening campion.**

white·cap (hwīt′kap′, wīt′-), *n.* 1. a wave with a broken and foaming white crest. 2. (*cap.*) *U.S.* one who wears a white hood, esp. a member of a group that, by terrorism or lynching, seeks to control or drive away persons deemed harmful to the community. [WHITE + CAP[1]]

white′ cast′ i′ron. See **white iron.**

white′ ce′dar, 1. a coniferous tree, *Chamaecyparis thyoides,* of the swamps of the eastern U.S. 2. the wood of this tree, used in the construction of boxes, crates, wooden utensils, etc. 3. the arborvitae, *Thuja occidentalis.* 4. the incense cedar, *Libocedrus decurrens.* 5. See **macnab cypress.** 6. an evergreen tree, *Tabebuia pallida,* of central and northern South America and the West Indies, having showy pink flowers. 7. Also called **Oregon cedar, Port Orford cedar.** a pinaceous tree, *Chamaecyparis lawsoniana,* of the western U.S. and Europe, grown for its timber and as an ornamental.

White·chap·el (hwīt′chap′əl, wīt′-), *n.* a district in E London, England.

white′ clo′ver, a clover, *Trifolium repens,* having white flowers, common in pastures and meadows. See illus. under **clover.** [ME *white clovere* (*clavere*), OE *hwītclǣfre.* See WHITE, CLOVER]

white′ coal′, water, as of a stream, used for power.

white-col·lar (hwīt′kol′ər, wīt′-), *adj.* belonging or pertaining to the salaried or professional workers whose jobs generally do not involve manual labor. Cf. **blue-collar.**

white′ crab′. See **ghost crab.**

white′ crap′pie. See under **crappie.**

white′-crowned spar′row (hwīt′kround′, wīt′-), a North American sparrow, *Zonotrichia leucophrys,* having black and white stripes on the head.

white·cup (hwīt′kup′, wīt′-), *n.* a creeping, perennial herb, *Nierembergia rivularis,* of Argentina, having bell-shaped, rose- or blue-tinged, cream-white flowers. [WHITE + CUP]

whit·ed (hwī′tid, wī′-), *adj.* 1. made white; bleached; blanched. 2. covered with whitewash, whiting, or the like. [ME; see WHITE, -ED[3]]

white′ dai′sy, an herb, *Layia glandulosa,* found from British Columbia to the southwestern U.S., having a sticky-hairy stem and white or pinkish-rose ray flowers.

white′ damp′, a poisonous coal-mine gas composed chiefly of carbon monoxide.

white′ dew′, dew that has become frozen.

whit′ed sep′ulcher, an evil person who feigns goodness; hypocrite. Matt. 23:27.

white′ dwarf′, *Astron.* a star of average mass and very small volume of which the density may be a ton per cubic inch, as the companion of Sirius.

white′ ear′drop, Dutchman's-breeches.

white′ el′ephant, 1. an abnormally whitish or pale elephant, usually found in Thailand; an albino elephant. 2. a possession entailing great expense out of proportion to its usefulness or value to the owner: *When he bought the mansion he didn't know it was going to be such a white elephant.* 3. a possession unwanted by the owner but difficult to dispose of: *His Victorian bric-a-brac and furniture were white elephants.*

white′ en′sign, the British naval ensign, consisting of the red cross of St. George on a white field, with the British union occupying the upper quarter along the hoist.

white-eye (hwīt′ī′, wīt′-), *n., pl.* **-eyes.** any of numerous small, chiefly tropical, Old World songbirds of the family *Zosteropidae,* most species of which have a ring of white feathers around the eye. Also called **silver-eye.**

white′-eyed vir′eo (hwīt′īd′, wīt′-), a vireo, *Vireo griseus,* of eastern North America, having olive, yellow, and white plumage, a yellow ring around each eye, and white irises.

white·face (hwīt′fās′, wīt′-), *n.* 1. a Hereford. 2. *Theat.* a performer, as a clown, who appears in clown white. [WHITE + FACE]

white-faced (hwīt′fāst′, wīt′-), *adj.* 1. having a white or pale face. 2. marked with white on the front of the head, as a horse. 3. having a white front or surface.

white′-faced hor′net. See under **hornet.**

white′ feath′er, 1. a symbol of cowardice. 2. **show the white feather,** to behave in a cowardly manner. [orig. from a white feather in a gamecock's tail, taken as a sign of inferior breeding and hence of poor fighting qualities]

White·field (hwit′fēld′, wit′-), *n.* **George,** 1714–70, English Methodist evangelist. —**White′field′i·an, White′field·ite′,** *n.*

white′ fir′, 1. a fir, *Abies concolor,* of western North America, yielding a soft wood used for lumber, pulp, boxes, etc. 2. the wood of this tree. 3. any of various similar firs of western North America, or their wood.

white·fish (hwīt′fish′, wīt′-), *n., pl.* (*esp. collectively*) **-fish,** (*esp. referring to two or more kinds or species*) **-fish·es.** 1. any of several fishes of the family *Coregonidae,* found in northern waters of North America and Eurasia, similar to the trout but having a smaller mouth and larger scales. Cf. **lake whitefish, round whitefish.** 2. a marine food fish of California, *Caulolatilus princeps.* 3. any of various silvery fishes of the minnow or carp family. 4. the beluga, *Delphinapterus leucas.* [late ME; see WHITE, FISH]

White·fish (hwīt′fish′, wīt′-), *n.* a town in NW Montana. 2965 (1960).

White′fish Bay′, a city in SE Wisconsin, N of Milwaukee. 18,390 (1960).

white′ flag′, 1. an all-white flag or piece of cloth, used as a symbol of surrender or truce. 2. **hoist, show,** or **wave the white flag,** to give up; weaken; yield.

white′ flax′, gold-of-pleasure.

white·fly (hwīt′flī′, wīt′-), *n., pl.* **-flies.** any of several plant-sucking, homopterous insects of the family *Aleyrodidae,* having the body and wings dusted with a white, powdery wax, and often being serious crop pests. [WHITE + FLY[2]]

white′-foot·ed mouse′ (hwīt′fo͝ot′id, wīt′-), any of several North American, woodland mice of the genus *Peromyscus,* esp. *P. leucopus,* having white feet and undersides. Also called **deer mouse, vesper mouse, wood mouse.**

white′ fox′. See **arctic fox.**

White′ Fri′ar, a Carmelite friar: so called from the distinctive white cloak worn. [late ME]

White·fri·ars (hwīt′frī′ərz, wīt′-), *n.* a district in central London, England.

white′-front·ed goose′ (hwīt′frun′tid, wīt′-), a grayish-brown wild goose, *Anser albifrons,* of Eurasia and western North America, having a white patch on the front of the face.

white′ frost′, a heavy coating of frost.

white′ globe′ lil′y, a bulbous herb, *Calochortus albus,* of California, having globe-shaped, white flowers with a purplish base.

white′ gold′, any of several gold alloys colored white by the presence of nickel or platinum.

white′ gold′enrod, silverrod.

white′ goods′, 1. bleached goods, esp. cotton or linen fabrics. 2. household goods, as bed sheets, tablecloths, towels, etc., formerly bleached and finished in white but now often patterned and colored. 3. large household appliances, as refrigerators, stoves, washing machines, etc.

white′ gourd′. See **wax gourd.**

white′ grape′. See **riverbank grape.**

white-ground (hwīt′ground′, wīt′-), *adj.* pertaining to or designating a style of vase painting developed in Greece from the 6th to the 4th centuries B.C., characterized chiefly by a white background of slip onto which were painted polychromatic figures.

white′ gum′, any of various Australian eucalyptuses having a whitish bark.

white′ gyr′falcon. See under **gyrfalcon.**

white-haired (hwīt′hârd′, wīt′-), *adj.* 1. having white hair. 2. *Informal.* favorite; fair-haired: *Our engineer is the white-haired boy of the missile division.* [late ME; see WHITE, HAIR, -ED[3]]

white′ hake′, a food fish, *Urophycis tenuis,* found esp. off the North Atlantic coast of the U.S.

White′ Hall′, a town in central Illinois. 3012 (1960).

White·hall (hwīt′hôl′, wīt′-), *n.* 1. Also called **White′hall Pal′ace.** a former palace in central London, England, originally built in the reign of Henry III: execution of Charles I, 1649. 2. the main thoroughfare in London, England, between Trafalgar Square and the Houses of Parliament. 3. the British government or its policies. 4. a city in central Ohio, near Columbus. 20,818 (1960). 5. a city in W Pennsylvania, near Pittsburgh. 16,075 (1960). 6. a town in E New York. 4016 (1960). 7. a town in SW Michigan. 2590 (1960).

White′hall boat′, a rowboat formerly used along the coasts of the U.S., rowed by from one to six persons and used as a pleasure boat, yacht tender, and for transportation inside harbors.

White·head (hwīt′hed′, wīt′-), *n.* **Alfred North,** 1861–1947, English philosopher and mathematician, in the U.S. after 1924.

white-head·ed (hwīt′hed′id, wīt′-), *adj.* 1. white-haired. 2. having fair or flaxen hair.

white′ heat′, 1. a stage of intense activity, excitement, feeling, etc.: *The sales campaign is at white heat. He's working at a white heat to finish the job.* 2. an intense heat at which a substance glows with white light.

white′ hole′, pigeonhole (def. 3).

white′ hope′, 1. one whose accomplishments are expected to bring fame, prestige, or distinction to his profession, country, school, etc.: *In his youth he was touted as the white hope of the American theater.* 2. *Sports.* (formerly) a white man who had a good chance of winning the heavyweight boxing championship from a Negro.

white′ horse′, a white-topped wave; whitecap.

White·horse (hwīt′hôrs′, wīt′-), *n.* a town in and the capital of the Yukon Territory, in NW Canada. 5031 (1961).

white-hot (hwīt′hot′, wīt′-), *adj.* 1. extremely hot. 2. showing white heat. 3. exceedingly enthusiastic, ardent, angry, devoted, etc.; impassioned; perfervid: *He shouted his fierce, white-hot loyalty to the king.*

White′ House′, the, 1. Also called **Executive Mansion.** the official residence of the President of the United States, at Washington, D.C.: a large, two-story, freestone building painted white. 2. *U.S.* the executive branch of the federal government.

white′ i′ron, cast iron having most or all of its carbon in the form of cementite and exhibiting a silvery fracture. Also called **white cast iron.**

white′ i′ron py′rites, *Mineral.* marcasite (def. 1).

white′ lead′ (led), 1. a white, heavy powder, basic lead carbonate, $2PbCO_3 \cdot Pb(OH)_2$, used as a pigment, in putty, and in medicinal ointments for burns. 2. the putty made from this substance in oil. 3. white lead ore; cerussite. [late ME]

white′ lead′ ore′, *Mineral.* cerussite.

white′ leath′er, leather treated with chemicals, as alum, salt, etc.; tawed leather. Also, **whitleather.**

white′ leg′, *Pathol.* See **milk leg.**

white′ lie′, a minor lie uttered from polite, amiable, or pardonable motives; polite or harmless fib.

white′ line′, 1. any blank or white part or margin. 2. a white layer in a horse's hoof. 3. a solid or uninterrupted stripe of paint, tiles, or the like, down the center of a road for controlling traffic.

white·line (hwīt′līn′, wīt′-), *n.* *Naut.* codline. [WHITE + LINE[1]]

white′ liq′uor, (in making wood pulp for paper) the chemicals used to digest the wood, basically sodium hydroxide and sodium hyposulfite. Cf. **black liquor.**

white′ list′, 1. a list of individuals, organizations, etc., having security clearance from government officials. 2. a list of persons thought by a business concern to be qualified or otherwise suitable for employment. 3. a list of novels, motion pictures, etc., deemed suitable for juveniles, members of a particular faith, or other specified groups of individuals. 4. a list of business establishments approved for patronage because of hiring practices, religious or political affiliations, etc. 5. a list kept by a labor union, containing the names of employers who maintain working conditions approved by the union. Cf. **blacklist.**

white-liv·ered (hwīt′liv′ərd, wīt′-), *adj.* 1. lacking courage; cowardly; lily-livered. 2. lacking in vitality or spirit; pale; unhealthy.

white′ lo′tus. See under **Egyptian lotus** (def. 1).

white′ lu′pine. See under **lupine**[1].

white·ly (hwīt′lē, wīt′-), *adv.* with a white hue or color: *The sun shone whitely.* [late ME; see WHITE, -LY]

white′ mahog′any, 1. an Australian eucalyptus, *Eucalyptus acmenioides.* 2. the hard, heavy wood of this tree, used for making railroad ties, posts, etc. 3. primavera (def. 2).

White·man (hwīt′mən, wīt′-), *n.* **Paul** ("*Pops*"), born 1891, U.S. orchestra conductor.

white′ man's′ bur′den, the alleged duty of the white race to care for subject peoples of other races in its colonial possessions. [from the title of a poem by Rudyard Kipling]

white′ Maripo′sa, a Mariposa lily, *Calochortus venustus,* having white or pale lilac flowers.

white′ mar′lin, a small marlin, *Tetrapterus albidus,* found in the western Atlantic Ocean, pale blue above and silvery below.

white′ mat′ter, *Anat.* nerve tissue, esp. of the brain and spinal cord, which contains fibers only and is nearly white in color. Cf. **gray matter** (def. 1).

white′ meat′, 1. any light-colored flesh meat, as veal, the breast of chicken, etc. (distinguished from *red meat*). 2. meat that is light-colored before cooking, as veal or breast of chicken or of turkey (distinguished from *dark meat*). 3. *Archaic.* food made from milk. Also called **light meat** (for defs. 1, 2). [late ME]

white′ mel′ilot, a Eurasian, biennial herb, *Melilotus alba,* naturalized in the U.S., having white flowers. Also called **Bokhara clover.**

white′ met′al, any of various light-colored alloys, as Babbitt metal, Britannia metal, etc.

White′ Moun′tains, a mountain range in N New Hampshire, part of the Appalachian Mountains. Highest peak, Mt. Washington, 6293 ft.

white′ mul′berry. See under **mulberry** (def. 2).

white′ mus′tard. See under **mustard** (def. 2).

whit·en (hwīt′ən, wīt′-), *v.t., v.i.* to make or become white. [ME; see WHITE, -EN[1]]
—**Syn.** WHITEN, BLANCH, BLEACH mean to make or become white. To WHITEN implies giving a white color or appearance by putting a substance of some kind on the outside: *to whiten shoes.* To BLANCH implies taking away natural or original color throughout: *to blanch celery by growing it in the dark.* To BLEACH implies making white by placing in (sun) light or by using chemicals: *to bleach linen, hair.* —**Ant.** blacken.

whit·en·er (hwīt′ənər, wīt′-), *n.* 1. one who or that which whitens. 2. a preparation for making something white, as a bleach, dye, polish, or the like: *a bottle of shoe whitener.* 3. one who applies whitener, as in a manufacturing process. [WHITEN + -ER[1]]

white·ness (hwīt′nis, wīt′-), *n.* 1. quality or state of being white. 2. paleness. 3. purity. 4. a white substance. [ME *whitenes,* OE *hwītnes.* See WHITE, -NESS]

White′ Nile′, the part of the Nile above Khartoum. ab. 500 mi. long. Cf. **Nile.**

whit·en·ing (hwīt′əning, wīt′-), *n.* 1. act or process of making or turning white. 2. a preparation for making something white; whiting. [WHITEN + -ING[1]]

white′ oak′, 1. an oak, *Quercus alba,* of eastern North America, having a light-gray to white bark and yielding a hard, durable wood: the State tree of Connecticut and Maryland. 2. an oak, *Quercus petraea,* of England. 3. any of several other species of oak, as *Q. Garryana* or *Q. lobata,* of western North America, or *Q. Robur,* of Great Britain. 4. the wood of any of these trees.

White′ Oak′, a town in W Pennsylvania. 9047 (1960).

white′ o′sier. See **pepper bush.**

white′ pa′per, 1. paper bleached white. 2. an official governmental report. 3. *Brit.* a special publication of the House of Commons on a specific subject, usually reporting results of a recent investigation or summarizing policy. Cf. **blue book** (def. 3), **white book.**

White′ Pass′, a mountain pass in SE Alaska, near Skagway. 2888 ft. high.

white′ pa′ternoster, an incantation for warding off evil spirits. Cf. **black paternoster.**

white′ pep′per, a condiment prepared from the husked dried berries of the pepper plant, used either whole or ground.

white′ perch′, 1. a small game fish, *Morone americana,* found in streams along the Atlantic coast of the U.S. 2. See **fresh-water drum.** 3. See **silver perch** (def. 2).

white′ pine′, 1. a pine, *Pinus Strobus,* of eastern North America, yielding a light-colored, soft, light wood of great commercial importance. 2. the wood itself. 3. any of various other similar species of pine.

white′-pine′ wee′vil (hwīt′pīn′, wīt′-), a brown beetle, *Pissodes strobi,* the larvae of which feed on the terminal buds and shoots of white pine and other conifers.

white′ plague′, *Pathol.* tuberculosis, esp. pulmonary tuberculosis.

White′ Plains′, a city in SE New York, near New York City: battle 1776. 50,485 (1960).

white′ pop′lar, 1. an Old World poplar, *Populus alba,* widely cultivated in the U.S., having the underside

of the leaves covered with a dense silvery-white down. **2.** the soft, straight-grained wood of the tulip tree.
white′ pota′to, potato (def. 1).
white′ pri′mary, *U.S.* (formerly) a direct primary of the Democratic party in southern States in which only white persons were permitted to vote.
white′ race′, (loosely) Caucasoid peoples.
white′ rain′bow, fogbow.
white′ rat′, an albino variety of the Norway rat, *Rattus norvegicus,* used in biological experiments.
White′ Riv′er, a river flowing SE from NW Arkansas into the Mississippi River. 690 mi. long.
White′ Riv′er Junc′tion, a town in E Vermont. 2546 (1960).
white-robed (hwīt′rōbd′, wīt′-), *adj.* clothed in a white robe or robes: *the white-robed figure of Father Time.*
White′ Rock′, one of a variety of white Plymouth Rock chickens.
white′ room′, a room in which precision equipment is assembled under dust-free conditions at a controlled temperature.
white′ rose′, *Eng. Hist.* the emblem of the royal house of York. Cf. **red rose, Wars of the Roses.**
white′ rose′ mal′low, an herb, *Hibiscus oculiroseus,* found in marshes along the northeastern coast of the U.S., having white or pink flowers with red eyes.
White′ Rus′sia, Byelorussia.
White′ Rus′sian, **1.** Byelorussian (def. 2). **2.** a Russian who fought against the Bolsheviks in the Russian civil war. **3.** Byelorussian (def. 3).
White′ Rus′sian So′viet So′cialist Repub′lic, Byelorussia (def. 1).
white′ rust′, **1.** *Plant Pathol.* a disease of plants, characterized by pustules of white spores on affected parts that become yellow and malformed, caused by fungi of the genus *Albugo.* **2.** any fungus causing this disease.
white′ sage′, a perennial, shrubby, herb, *Audibertia polystachya,* of California, having white-hairy foliage and white flowers. Also called **greasewood.**
white′ sale′, a sale of sheets, pillowcases, and other white goods.
white′ salm′on, the yellowtail, *Seriola dorsalis.*
white′ san′dalwood. See under **sandalwood** (def. 2).
white′ sa·po′te (sə pō′tē), a tree, *Casimiroa edulis,* of tropical America, having greenish, inconspicuous flowers and tomatolike, fleshy fruit, yellow on the inside and gray or yellowish-green on the outside. Also called **Mexican apple.** [*sapote* < Sp *zapote* a kind of fruit tree]
white′ sap′phire, *Mineral.* a colorless variety of corundum, used as a gemstone.
white′ sauce′, a sauce made of butter, flour, seasonings, and milk or sometimes chicken or veal stock; béchamel.
White′ Sea′, an arm of the Arctic Ocean, in the NW Soviet Union in Europe. ab. 36,000 sq. mi.
white′ shark′. See **great white shark.**
white′ slave′, **1.** a girl or woman who is sold or forced into prostitution. **2.** a white person held as a slave or in some condition resembling slavery. —**white′-slave′,** *adj.*
White′ Slave′ Act′. See **Mann Act.**
white′ slav′er, a person engaged in white-slave traffic or business.
white′ slav′ery, the condition of or traffic in white slaves.
white-slav·ing (hwīt′slā′ving, wīt′-), *n.* traffic in white slaves.
white·smith (hwīt′smith′, wīt′-), *n.* a tinsmith. [ME, modeled on *blacksmith*]
white′ snake′root, a North American boneset, *Eupatorium rugosum,* that has heads of white flowers and causes trembles and milk sickness. Also called **Indian sanicle, richweed.**
white′ space′, the unprinted area of a piece of printing, as of a poster or newspaper page, or of a portion of a piece of printing, as of an advertisement; blank space: *White space is as important to an effective layout as type. Leave plenty of white space between the illustrations.*
white′ spruce′, **1.** a spruce, *Picea glauca,* of northern North America, having bluish-green leaves and silvery-brown bark. **2.** the light, soft wood of this tree, used for pulp and in the construction of boxes, crates, etc.
white′ squall′, *Naut.* a whirlwind or violent disturbance of small radius, not accompanied by the usual clouds but indicated merely by the whitecaps and turbulent water beneath it.
white′ stork′, a large, Eurasian stork, *Ciconia ciconia,* having white plumage with black in the wings and a red bill: the bird in legend that delivers newborn babies. See illus. under **stork.**
white′ stur′geon, a dark gray sturgeon, *Acipenser transmontanus,* found in marine and fresh waters along the northwestern coast of North America. Also called **Pacific sturgeon.**
White′ Sul′phur Springs′, a town in SE West Virginia. 2676 (1960).
white′ suprem′acist, one who advocates or supports the theory of white supremacy.
white′ suprem′acy, the belief, theory, or doctrine that the white man has a natural superiority over the Negro and must keep him subordinated.
white′ swamp′ azal′ea, a shrub, *Azalea viscosa,* of the central U.S., having clustered, glandular, hairy, fragrant, white or pinkish flowers. Also called **swamp honeysuckle.**
white′-tailed deer′ (hwīt′tāld′, wīt′-), a common North American deer, *Odocoileus virginianus,* having a tail with a white underside. Also, **white′tail deer′, white′tail′.**
white′-tailed kite′, an American kite, *Elanus leucurus,* having gray plumage with a white head, breast, and tail.
white′-tailed sea′ ea′gle. See **gray sea eagle.**
white′ tas′sel flow′er, a perennial herb, *Petalostemon candidum,* of the midwestern U.S., having slender spikes of white flowers.
white·thorn (hwīt′thôrn′, wīt′-), *n.* the hawthorn, *Crataegus Oxyacantha.* [ME, trans. of L *alba spīna*]
white·throat (hwīt′thrōt′, wīt′-), *n.* **1.** any of several small songbirds having white throats, esp. an Old World warbler, *Sylvia communis.* **2.** See **white-throated sparrow.** [WHITE + THROAT]
white′-throat·ed spar′row (hwīt′thrō′tid, wīt′-), a common, North American finch, *Zonotrichia albicollis,* having a white patch on the throat and a black and white striped crown. Also called **whitethroat.**
white′ tie′, **1.** a white bow tie for men, worn with formal evening dress. **2.** formal evening dress for men (distinguished from *black tie*).
white′ ti′ti. See under **titi**[2].
white′ trash′, *Derogatory.* **1.** a member of the class of poor whites, esp. in the southern U.S. **2.** poor whites collectively.
white′ trum′pet lil′y, a bulbous herb, *Lilium longiflorum,* of Japan, having fragrant, pure white, trumpet-shaped flowers nearly seven inches long.
white′ trum′pet narcis′sus, a narcissus, *Narcissus moschatus,* having cream-white flowers.
white′ tur′nip, the turnip, *Brassica Rapa.*
white′ up′land as′ter, a perennial herb, *Aster ptarmicoides,* of North America, having white ray flowers in branching clusters.
White·ville (hwīt′vil, wīt′-), *n.* a town in S North Carolina. 4683 (1960).
white′ vit′riol. See **zinc sulfate.**
White′ Vol′ta, a river in W Africa, in Ghana: a branch of the Volta River. ab. 550 mi. long. Cf. **Volta** (def. 2).
white·wall (hwīt′wôl′, wīt′-), *n.* a rubber tire for an automobile, bicycle, etc., having a sidewall partly white and partly black. Also called **white′wall tire′.** [WHITE + (SIDE)WALL]
white′ wal′nut, butternut (def. 1).
white·wash (hwīt′wosh′, -wôsh′, wīt′-), *n.* **1.** a composition, as of lime and water or of whiting, size, and water, used for whitening walls, woodwork, etc. **2.** anything used to cover up defects, gloss over faults or errors, or give a specious semblance of respectability, honesty, etc.: *The report was a whitewash of the scandal.* **3.** *Informal.* (in sports) a defeat in which the loser fails to score. —*v.t.* **4.** to whiten with whitewash. **5.** to cover up or gloss over the defects, faults, or errors of. **6.** *Informal.* (in sports) to defeat by keeping the opponent from scoring at all: *The Yankees whitewashed the visitors eight to nothing.* [WHITE + WASH] —**white′wash′er,** *n.*
white′ wa′ter, **1.** frothy water, as in whitecaps, rapids, etc. **2.** light-colored sea water over a shoal, sandy bottom, etc.
White·wa·ter (hwīt′wô′tər, -wot′ər, wīt′-), *n.* a town in SE Wisconsin. 6380 (1960).
white′ wa′ter lil′y, any water lily of the genus *Nymphaea,* esp. *N. odorata,* having fragrant, white flowers.
white′ wax′, a yellowish-white, somewhat translucent, tasteless solid, prepared by bleaching beeswax, used chiefly in pharmacy.
white′ whale′, beluga (def. 2).
white′ wine′, wine having a yellowish to amber color derived from the light-colored grapes used in production, or from dark grapes with the skins, pulp, and seeds removed. [ME; cf. F *vin blanc*]
white·wing (hwīt′wing′, wīt′-), *n.* one who wears a white uniform, esp. a public street cleaner. [WHITE + WING]
white′-winged dove′ (hwīt′wingd′, wīt′-), a common dove, *Zenaida asiatica,* of the southwestern U.S. and Mexico.
white′-winged sco′ter, a blackish North American duck, *Melanitta deglandi,* having a white patch on each wing. Also called **white′-winged coot′.**
white·wood (hwīt′wŏŏd′, wīt′-), *n.* **1.** any of numerous trees, as the tulip tree or the linden, yielding a white or light-colored wood. **2.** the wood. **3.** a cottonwood of the genus *Populus.* [WHITE + WOOD[1]]
white′ wood′ as′ter, a perennial herb, *Aster divaricatus,* of North America, having white ray flowers and growing in dry woods.
whit·ey (hwī′tē, wī′-), *n.* *American Negro Slang, Disparaging.* a white person or white people collectively. Also, **White′y, whity.**
Whit·field (hwit′fēld′, wit′-), *n.* a boy's given name.
whith·er (hwith′ər, with′-), *Archaic.* —*adv.* **1.** to what place?; where? **2.** to what end, point, action, or the like?; to what? —*conj.* **3.** to which place. [ME, var. of ME, OE *hwider,* alter. of *hwæder* (c. Goth *hwadre*), modeled on *hider* HITHER]
whith·er·so·ev·er (hwith′ər sō ev′ər, with′-), *conj.* to whatsoever place. [ME, equiv. to *whitherso* (OE *swā hwider swā*) + *ever* EVER]
whith·er·ward (hwith′ər wərd, with′-), *adv.* *Archaic.* toward what place; in what direction. Also, **whith′er·wards.** [ME; see WHITHER, -WARD]
whit·ing[1] (hwī′ting, wī′-), *n., pl.* (*esp. collectively*) **-ing,** (*esp. referring to two or more kinds or species*) **-ings.** **1.** a slender food fish of the genus *Menticirrhus,* of the croaker family, found along the Atlantic coast of North America. **2.** the hake, *Merluccius bilinearis.* **3.** any of several European fishes of the cod family, esp. *Merlangus merlangus.* [late ME, perh. alter. of OE *hwītling* kind of fish; cf. MD *witinc,* of which the E may be a trans.: *whit-* for *wit-*, *-ing* for *-inc*]
whit·ing[2] (hwī′ting, wī′-), *n.* pure-white chalk (calcium carbonate) which has been ground and washed, used in making putty, whitewash, silver polish, etc. [ME; OE *hwīting-* (in *hwītingmelu;* see MEAL[2]). See WHITE, -ING[1]]
Whit·ing (hwī′ting, wī′-), *n.* a town in NW Indiana. 8137 (1960).
Whit·ins·ville (hwī′tinz vil, wī′-), *n.* a town in S Massachusetts. 5102 (1960).
whit·ish (hwī′tish, wī′-), *adj.* somewhat white; tending to white. [late ME; see WHITE, -ISH[1]] —**whit′ish·ness,** *n.*
whit·leath·er (hwit′leth′ər, wit′-), *n.* See **white leather.** [late ME *whitlether.* See WHITE, LEATHER]
whit·low (hwit′lō, wit′-), *n.* *Pathol.* an inflammation of the deeper tissues of a finger or toe, esp. of the terminal phalanx, usually terminating in suppuration. Also called **agnail.** [ME *whit(f)lowe, whitflawe.* See WHITE, FLAW[1]]
whit′low grass′, a cruciferous herb, *Draba verna,* of Europe and North America, having leaves in a basal rosette. [so called because believed to cure whitlows]
whit·low·wort (hwit′lō wûrt′, wit′-), *n.* any of several herbs of the genus *Paronychia,* of temperate and warm regions. [WHITLOW + WORT[2]]
Whit·man (hwit′mən, wit′-), *n.* **1. Marcus,** 1802–47, U.S. missionary and pioneer. **2. Walt(er),** 1819–92, U.S. poet. **3.** a boy's given name. 
Whit·mire (hwit′mīər), *n.* a town in central South Carolina. 2663 (1960).
Whit·mon·day (hwit′mun′dē, -dā, wit′-), *n.* the Monday following Whitsunday. [modeled on WHITSUNDAY]
Whit·ney (hwit′nē, wit′-), *n.* **1. Eli,** 1765–1825, U.S. manufacturer and inventor. **2. John Hay,** born 1904, U.S. diplomat and newspaper publisher. **3. William Dwight,** 1827–94, U.S. philologist and lexicographer. **4. Mount,** a mountain in E California, in the Sierra Nevada Mountains. 14,495 ft. **5.** a town in NW South Carolina. 2502 (1960). **6.** a boy's given name.
whit·rack (hwit′rak′, wit′-), *n.* *Brit. Dial.* a weasel; ermine or stoat. Also, **whit·ret** (hwit′rət, wit′-), **whitterick.** [dissimilated var. of ME *whitrat.* See WHITE, RAT]
Whit·sun (hwit′sən, wit′-), *adj.* **1.** of or pertaining to Whitsunday or Whitsuntide. —*n.* **2.** Whitsunday or Whitsuntide. [ME *Whitsone(n),* deriv. of *Whitsonenday* by apocope. See WHITSUNDAY]
Whit·sun·day (hwit′sun′dē, -dā, wit′-; hwit′sən-dā′, wit′-), *n.* the seventh Sunday after Easter, celebrated as a festival in commemoration of the descent of the Holy Spirit on the day of Pentecost. [ME *whitsonenday,* OE *Hwīta Sunnandæg* white Sunday; generally thought to come from the white baptismal robes worn on that day]
Whit·sun·tide (hwit′sən tīd′, wit′-), *n.* the week beginning with Whitsunday, esp. the first three days of this week. Also called **Whit Week.** [ME *whitsone(n)-tide.* See WHITSUN, TIDE[1]]
Whit·ta·ker (hwit′ə kər, wit′-), *n.* **1. Charles Evans,** born 1901, U.S. jurist: associate justice of the U.S. Supreme Court 1957–62. **2.** Also, **Whitaker.** a boy's given name.
whit·ter·ick (hwit′ər ik, wit′-), *n.* *Brit. Dial.* whitrack.
Whit·ti·er (hwit′ē ər, wit′-), *n.* **1. John Green·leaf** (grēn′lēf′), 1807–92, U.S. poet. **2.** a city in SW California, E of Los Angeles. 33,663 (1960).
Whit·ting·ton (hwit′ing tən, wit′-), *n.* **Richard** ("*Dick Whittington*"), 1358?–1423, English merchant and philanthropist: Lord Mayor of London 1398, 1406–07, 1419–20.
whit·tle (hwit′əl, wit′-), *v.,* **-tled, -tling,** *n.* —*v.t.* **1.** to cut, trim, or shape (a stick, piece of wood, etc.) by taking off bits with a knife: *He whittled the wood into a rough figure.* **2.** to cut off (a bit or bits). **3.** to reduce the amount of, as if by whittling; pare down; take away by degrees (usually fol. by *down, away,* etc.): *to whittle down expenses; to whittle away a large sum of money.* —*v.i.* **4.** to cut bits or chips from wood or the like with a knife, as in shaping something or as a mere aimless diversion: *The porch where they were whittling was strewn with chips and shavings.* **5.** *Dial.* to tire oneself or another by worrying or fussing. —*n.* **6.** *Brit. Dial.* a knife, esp. a large one as a carving knife or a butcher knife. [late ME, alter. of *thwitel* knife, OE *thwīt(an)* (to) cut + *-el* -LE] —**whit′tler,** *n.*
Whit·tle (hwit′əl, wit′-), *n.* **Sir Frank,** born 1907, English engineer and inventor.
whit·tling (hwit′ling, wit′-), *n.* **1.** act of one who whittles. **2.** Often, **whittlings.** a bit or chip whittled off. [WHITTLE + -ING[1]]
Whit·tues·day (hwit′tōōz′dē, -dā, -tyōōz′-, wit′-), *n.* the day following Whitmonday. [modeled on WHITSUNDAY]
Whit′ Week′, Whitsuntide. [modeled on WHITSUNDAY]
whit·y (hwī′tē, wī′-), *adj.,* **whit·i·er, whit·i·est,** *n.* —*adj.* **1.** whitish. —*n.* **2.** *Slang.* whitey. [WHITE + -Y[1]]
whiz[1] (hwiz, wiz), *v.,* **whizzed, whiz·zing,** *n.* —*v.i.* **1.** to make a humming, buzzing, or hissing sound, as an object passing rapidly through the air. **2.** to move or rush with such a sound: *The angry hornets whizzed by in a cloud.* —*v.t.* **3.** to cause to whiz. **4.** to treat with a whizzer. —*n.* **5.** the sound of a whizzing object. **6.** a swift movement producing such a sound. **7.** *Informal.* one who is quite good at a particular activity, in a certain field, etc.: *He's a whiz at math.* Also, **whizz.** [imit.; cf. FIZZ] —**whiz′zing·ly,** *adv.*
whiz[2] (hwiz, wiz), *n.* wizard (def. 3).
whiz-bang (*n.* hwiz′bang′, wiz′-; *adj.* hwiz′bang′, wiz′-), —*n.* **1.** *Mil.* a small, high-speed shell whose sound as it flies through the air arrives almost at the same instant as its explosion. **2.** a firecracker with a similar effect. —*adj.* **3.** *Informal.* excellent; first-rate; topnotch: *a whiz-bang navigator.* Also, **whizz′-bang′.** [orig. imit.]
Whiz′ Kid′, *Slang.* a youthful and exceptionally intelligent, successful, or influential executive, agent, or advisor. Also, **whiz′ kid′.**
whiz·zer (hwiz′ər, wiz′-), *n.* **1.** something that whizzes. **2.** a centrifugal machine for drying sugar, grain, clothes, etc. [WHIZZ + -ER[1]]
whiz·zo (hwiz′ō, wiz′ō), *Brit. Slang.* —*adj.* **1.** absolutely first-rate; superb; excellent. —*interj.* **2.** an exclamation of approval, wonder, or pleasure. [formed on WHIZ[1]]
who (hōō), *pron.; possessive* **whose;** *objective* **whom.** **1.** what person?: *Who did it? Whose is this? To whom*

did you write? **2.** (of a person) of what character, origin, position, importance, etc.: *Who does she think she is?* **3.** the person that or any person that (used relatively to represent a specified or implied antecedent): *It was who you thought. Ask whom you like.* **4.** (used relatively in restrictive and nonrestrictive clauses to represent a specified antecedent, the antecedent being a person or sometimes an animal or personified thing): *Any boy who wants to can learn to swim. Mrs. Johnson, of whom I spoke yesterday, came to tea today.* **5.** *Archaic.* the person or persons who. **6. as who should say,** *Archaic.* in a manner of speaking; so to say. [ME; OE *hwā*; c. Goth *hwas*, OHG *hwer*, L *quis*, etc.]
—Usage. See **which.**

WHO, See **World Health Organization.**

whoa (hwō, wō), *interj.* stop! (used esp. to horses). [dial. var. of HO]

who'd (ho͞od), contraction of *who would: Who'd have thought it!*

who·dun·it (ho͞o dun′it), *n. Informal.* a narrative dealing with a murder or a series of murders and the detection of the criminal; detective story. [jocular formation from question *Who done it?*, equiv. to standard E *Who did it?*]

who·e'er (ho͞o âr′), *pron. Poetic.* whoever.

who·ev·er (ho͞o ev′ər), *pron.; possessive* **whos·ev·er;** *objective* **whom·ev·er. 1.** whatever person; anyone that: *Whoever did it should be proud. Tell it to whomever you like.* **2.** no matter who: *I won't do it, whoever asks.* **3.** who?; what person? (used to express astonishment, disbelief, disdain, etc.): *Whover is that? Whoever told you such a thing?* [ME; see WHO, EVER]

whole (hōl), *adj.* **1.** comprising the full quantity, amount, extent, number, etc., without diminution or exception; entire, full, or total: *He ate the whole pie? They ran the whole distance.* **2.** containing all the elements properly belonging; complete: *She has a whole set of antique china.* **3.** undivided; in one piece: *to swallow a thing whole.* **4.** *Math.* integral, or not fractional. **5.** uninjured, undamaged, or unbroken; sound; intact: *He was surprised to find himself whole after the accident.* **6.** being fully or entirely as specified: *He has a whole sister and two half sisters.* **7.** pertaining to all aspects of human nature, esp. one's physical, intellectual, and spiritual development: *education for the whole man.* **8. out of whole cloth,** without foundation in fact; fictitious: *a story made out of whole cloth.* **—n. 9.** the whole assemblage of parts or elements belonging to a thing; the entire quantity, account, extent, or number: *He accepted some of the parts but rejected the whole.* **10.** a thing complete in itself, or comprising all its parts or elements. **11.** an assemblage of parts associated or viewed together as one thing; a unitary system. **12. as a whole,** all things included or considered; altogether: *As a whole, the relocation seems to have been beneficial.* **13. on** or **upon the whole, a.** in view of all the circumstances; after consideration. **b.** disregarding exceptions; in general: *I would have to say that, upon the whole, the neighborhood is improving.* [ME *hole, hool*, OE *hāl*; c. D *heel*, G *heil*, Icel *heill*; see HALE¹, HEAL; sp. with *w* reflects dial. speech] **—whole′ness,** *n.*
—Syn. 1. undiminished, undivided, integral, complete, unbroken, unimpaired, uninjured, undamaged, perfect, sound, intact. **9.** totality, aggregate. WHOLE, TOTAL mean the entire or complete sum or amount. The WHOLE is all there is; every part, member, aspect; the complete sum, amount, quantity of anything, not divided; the entirety: *the whole of one's property, family.* TOTAL also means whole, complete amount, or number, but conveys the idea of something added together or added up: *The total of his gains amounted to millions.* **—Ant. 1.** partial. **9.** part.

whole′ blood′, 1. blood directly from the body, from which none of the elements have been removed, used in transfusions. **2.** relationship between persons through both parents. Cf. **half blood.** [ME]

whole′ broth′er, a brother whose parents are the same as one's own.

whole′ gale′, *Meteorol.* (on the Beaufort scale) a wind of 55–63 miles per hour.

whole·heart·ed (hōl′här′tid), *adj.* fully or completely sincere, enthusiastic, energetic, etc.; hearty; earnest: *a wholehearted attempt to comply.* [WHOLE + HEARTED] **—whole′heart′ed·ly,** *adv.* **—whole′heart′ed·ness,** *n.*

whole′ hog′, *Slang.* **1.** the furthest extent; everything: *With them it was the whole hog or nothing.* **2. go whole hog,** to do something completely or thoroughly: *The townspeople went whole hog and had bands and a welcoming committee to greet the returning hero.* Also, **go the whole hog.**

whole-length (hōl′lengkth′, -length′), *adj.* **1.** extended to or having its entire length; not shortened or abridged: *a whole-length report.* **2.** portraying, reflecting, or accommodating the full length of the human figure: *a whole-length sofa; a whole-length portrait of the general.* **—n. 3.** a portrait or statue showing the full length of its subject: *The painting gallery had a roomful of whole-lengths.*

whole′ life′ insur′ance. See **ordinary life insurance.**

whole′ milk′, milk containing all its constituents as received from the cow or other milk-giving animal.

whole′ note′, *Music.* a note equivalent in duration to four quarter notes. See illus. under **note.**

whole′ num′ber, an integral.

whole′ rest′, *Music.* a rest equivalent in duration to a whole note.

whole·sale (hōl′sāl′), *n., adj., adv., v.,* **-saled, -sal·ing. —n. 1.** the sale of goods in large amounts, as to retailers or jobbers rather than to consumers directly (opposed to *retail*). **2. by wholesale, a.** in large quantities, as in the sale of commodities. **b.** on a large scale without discrimination: *The big resorts offer recreation by wholesale.* **—adj. 3.** of, pertaining to, or engaged in sale by wholesale. **4.** extensive; broadly indiscriminate: *wholesale discharge of workers.* **—adv. 5.** in a wholesale way; on wholesale terms: *I can get it for you wholesale.* **—v.t., v.i. 6.** to sell by wholesale. [late ME, from the phrase *(by) hole sale* in gross] **—whole′sal′er,** *n.*
—Syn. 4. far-reaching, comprehensive, thorough, inclusive, undiscriminating, promiscuous.

whole′ sis′ter, a sister whose parents are the same as one's own.

whole′ snipe′, the common snipe. See under **snipe** (def. 1).

whole·some (hōl′səm), *adj.* **1.** conducive to moral or general well-being; salutary; beneficial: *wholesome recreation; wholesome environment.* **2.** conducive to bodily health; healthful; salubrious: *wholesome food; wholesome air; wholesome exercise.* **3.** suggestive of physical or moral health, esp. in appearance. **4.** healthy or sound. [ME *ho(o)lsom*, OE **hālsum* (see WHOLE, -SOME¹); c. Icel *heilsamr*, OHG *heilsam*] **—whole′some·ly,** *adv.* **—whole′some·ness,** *n.*
—Syn. 1. helpful; good. **2.** nourishing, nutritious. **2, 3.** See **healthy.**

whole-souled (hōl′sōld′), *adj.* wholehearted; hearty.

whole′ step′, *Music.* an interval of two semitones, as A–B or B–C♯; a major second. Also called **whole′ tone′.**

whole′-tone scale′ (hōl′tōn′), *Music.* a scale progressing entirely by whole tones, as C, D, E, F♯, G♯, A♯, C.

whole-wheat (hōl′hwēt′, -wēt′), *adj.* prepared with the complete wheat kernel.

who·lism (hō′liz əm), *n.* holism. **—who·lis′tic,** *adj.*

who'll (ho͞ol), contraction of *who will* or *who shall.*

whol·ly (hō′lē, hōl′lē), *adv.* **1.** entirely; totally; altogether; quite. **2.** to the whole amount, extent, etc. **3.** so as to comprise or involve all. [ME *holliche*, OE **hāllīche.* See WHOLE, -LY]

whom (ho͞om), *pron.* **1.** the objective case of **who:** *Whom did you call? Of whom are you speaking? With whom did you stay?* **2.** the dative case of **who:** *You gave whom the book?* [ME; OE *hwām*, dat. of *hwā* WHO]

whom·ev·er (ho͞om ev′ər), *pron.* the objective case of **whoever:** *She invited whomever she met. Whomever she spoke to, she was invariably polite.* [ME; see WHOM, EVER]

whomp (hwomp, womp), *Informal.* **—n. 1.** a loud, heavy blow, slap, bang, or the like: *He fell on the floor with an awful whomp.* **—v.t. 2.** to defeat (a person, opposing team, etc.) decisively: *The Cards whomped the Yankees.* **3.** to slap or strike: *He would whomp the kids at the slightest provocation.* **—v.i. 4.** to make a banging or slapping noise: *Guns whomped in the distance.* [imit.]

whom·so·ev·er (ho͞om′sō ev′ər), *pron.* the objective case of **whosoever:** *Ask whomsoever you like. Inquire of whomsoever you meet.* [late ME, equiv. to *whomso* (early ME *(swā) hwām swā*; see WHOM, SO¹) + *-ever* EVER]

whoop (ho͞op, hwo͞op, wo͞op), *n.* **1.** a cry or shout, as of hunters, warriors, etc. **2.** the whooping sound characteristic of whooping cough. **3. not worth a whoop,** *Informal.* to be worthless: *Her promises aren't worth a whoop.* **—v.i. 4.** to utter a loud cry or shout in expressing enthusiasm, excitement, etc. **5.** to cry as an owl, crane, or certain other birds. **6.** to make the characteristic sound accompanying the deep intake of air following a series of coughs in whooping cough. **—v.t. 7.** to utter with or as with a whoop or whoops. **8.** to whoop to or at. **9.** to call, urge, pursue, or drive with whoops: *to whoop dogs on.* **10. whoop it up,** *Slang.* **a.** to raise a disturbance, as to celebrate noisily: *They whooped it up after winning the big game.* **b.** to arouse enthusiasm for; promote: *Every spring they whoop it up for the circus.* **—interj. 11.** a cry to attract attention from afar, or to show excitement, encouragement, enthusiasm, etc. [ME *whope(n)*, OE *hwōpan* to threaten (see WAR WHOOP); c. Goth *hwopan* to boast]

whoop-de-do (wo͞op′dē do͞o′, -do͞o′, hwo͞op′-, wo͞op′-), *n., pl.* **-dos.** *Informal.* **1.** lively and noisy festivities; merrymaking; conviviality: *New Year's Eve whoop-de-do.* **2.** heated discussion or debate, esp. in public: *a whoop-de-do over the new tax bill.* **3.** extravagant publicity or fanfare: *the whoop-de-do of a movie premiere.* Also, **whoop′-de-doo′.** [irreg.; see WHOOP]

whoop·ee (*n.* hwo͞op′ē, wo͞op′ē, hwo͞o′pē, wo͞o′-; *interj.* hwo͞op′ē′, wo͞op′ē′, hwo͞o′pē′, wo͞o′-), *Informal.* **—n. 1. make whoopee,** to engage in uproarious merrymaking: *He was making whoopee at the local bars.* **—interj. 2.** a shout of exuberant joy. [WHOOP + *-ee* intensive suffix]

whoop′ee cup′, *Informal.* a paper cup or similar receptacle for airplane passengers to vomit into should they become airsick.

whoop·er (ho͞o′pər, hwo͞o′-, wo͞o′-), *n.* **1.** one who or that which whoops. **2.** See **whooper swan.** [WHOOP + -ER¹]

whoop′er swan′, a common, Old World swan, *Olor cygnus*, noted for its whooping cry.

whoop′ing cough′ (ho͞o′ping, ho͝op′ing), *Pathol.* an infectious disease of the respiratory mucous membrane, esp. of children, characterized by a series of short, convulsive coughs followed by a deep inspiration accompanied by a whooping sound. Also called **chincough, pertussis.**

whoop′ing crane′, a large, white, nearly extinct, North American crane, *Grus americana*, having a loud, whooping call. See illus. under **crane.**

whoops (hwo͝ops, hwo͞ops, wo͝ops, wo͞ops), *interj.* (used to express surprise, mild embarrassment, etc., or as a casual apology.) [WHOOP + *-s* intensive suffix]

whoosh (hwo͞osh, wo͞osh, hwo͝osh, wo͝osh), *n.* **1.** a loud, rushing noise, as of air or water: *There was a great whoosh of air as the door opened.* **—v.i. 2.** to move swiftly with a gushing or hissing noise: *gusts of wind whooshing through the pine trees.* **—v.t. 3.** to move (an object, a person, etc.) with a whooshing motion or sound: *The storm was whooshing the waves up over the road.* Also, **woosh.** [imit.]

whoo·sis (ho͞o′zis), *n., pl.* **-sis·es.** *Informal.* **1.** an object or person whose name is not known or cannot be recalled: *It's the whoosis next to the volume control.* **2.** a person or thing considered typical or illustrative: *the usual paragraph about the party given by Mme. Whoosis.* Also, **whoosy, whosis.** [? alter. of phrase *who's this*]

whoo·sy (ho͞o′zē), *n., pl.* **-sies.** *Informal.* whoosis.

whop (hwop, wop), *v.,* **whopped, whop·ping,** *n. Informal.* **—v.t. 1.** to strike forcibly. **2.** to defeat soundly, as in a contest. **3.** to put or pull violently; whip: *to whop out a book.* **—v.i. 4.** *U.S.* to plump suddenly down; flop. **—n. 5.** a forcible blow. **6.** the sound made by it. **7.** a bump; heavy fall. Also, **whap, wap.** [late ME, aspirated form of WAP]

whop·per (hwop′ər, wop′-), *n. Informal.* **1.** something uncommonly large of its kind. **2.** a big lie. Also, **whapper.** [WHOP + -ER¹]

whop·ping (hwop′ing, wop′-), *adj. Informal.* very large of its kind; thumping: *We caught four whopping trout.* Also, **whapping.** [WHOP + -ING²]

whore (hōr, hôr *or, often,* ho͝or), *n., v.,* **whored, whor·ing. —n. 1.** a woman who engages in promiscuous sexual intercourse, usually for money; prostitute; harlot; strumpet. **—v.i. 2.** to act as a whore. **3.** to consort with whores. **—v.t. 4.** *Obs.* to make a whore of; corrupt; debauch. [ME, OE *hōre*; c. Icel *hōra*, G *Hure*, Goth *hors* harlot, L *cārus* dear]

who're (ho͞o′ər), contraction of *who are.*

whore·dom (hōr′dəm, hôr′- *or, often,* ho͝or′-), *n.* **1.** the activity or state of whoring. **2.** *Bible.* idolatry. [ME *hordom*, equiv. to OE *hōr* adultery + *-dōm* -DOM; cf. Icel *hōrdōmr*]

whore·house (hōr′hous′, hôr′- *or, often,* ho͝or′-), *n., pl.* **-hous·es** (-hou′ziz). a house or apartment in which prostitutes are available for hire; house of prostitution; brothel. [ME *hoore-hows.* See WHORE, HOUSE]

whore′house cut′, *Cards.* a cut in which a pack is divided into two parts each of which is divided again before the pack is reassembled.

whore·mong·er (hōr′mung′gər, -mong′-, hôr′- *or often,* ho͝or′-), *n.* one who consorts with whores; a lecher or pander. Also called **whore·mas·ter** (hōr′mas′tər, -mä′stər, hôr′- *or, often,* ho͝or′-). [WHORE + MONGER] **—whore′mon′ger·ing, whore′mas′ter·y,** *n.*

whore·son (hōr′sən, hôr′- *or, often,* ho͝or′-), *Archaic.* **—n. 1.** a bastard. **2.** wretch; scoundrel. **—adj. 3.** wretched; scurvy. [ME *horeson* SON of a WHORE; cf. Icel *hōruson(r)*]

whor·ish (hōr′ish, hôr′- *or, often,* ho͝or′-), *adj.* having the character of a whore; lewd; unchaste. [WHORE + -ISH¹] **—whore′ish·ly,** *adv.* **—whore′ish·ness,** *n.*

whorl (hwûrl, hwôrl, wûrl, wôrl), *n.* **1.** a circular arrangement of like parts, as leaves, flowers, etc., round a point on an axis; verticil. **2.** one of the turns or volutions of a spiral shell. **3.** anything shaped like a coil. **4.** one of the central ridges of a fingerprint, forming at least one complete circle. **5.** *Textiles.* a flywheel or pulley, as for a spindle. [late ME *whorle, whorvil*, etc., OE *hwyrfel*, equiv. to *hweorfa* whorl of a spindle + *-el* n. suffix]

Whorls of ammonite

whorled (hwûrld, hwôrld, wûrld, wôrld), *adj.* **1.** having a whorl or whorls. **2.** disposed in the form of a whorl, as leaves. [WHORL + -ED³]

whorled′ loose′strife. See under **loosestrife** (def. 1).

whorled′ milk′weed, a leafy herb, *Asclepias verticillata*, of central and eastern North America, having leaves in whorls and greenish-white flowers, growing in dry places.

whorl′ foot′, *Furniture.* See **French foot** (def. 1).

whort (hwûrt, wûrt), *n.* the whortleberry. Also, **whor·tle** (hwûr′tᵊl, wûr′-), **wort.** [dial. var. of ME *hurte*, OE *horte* WHORTLEBERRY]

whor·tle·ber·ry (hwûr′tᵊl ber′ē, wûr′-), *n., pl.* **-ries. 1.** the edible, black berry of an ericaceous shrub, *Vaccinium Myrtillus*, of Europe and Siberia. **2.** the shrub itself. Also, **hurtleberry.** [dial. var. of ME *hurtilberye*, equiv. to *hurte* (see WHORT) + *-l* (< ?) + *berye* BERRY]

who's (ho͞oz), **1.** contraction of *who is: Who's there?* **2.** contraction of *who has: Who's seen it?*

whose (ho͞oz), *pron.* **1.** (the possessive case of **who** used as an adjective): *Whose umbrella did I take? Whose is this one?* **2.** (the possessive case of **which** used as an adjective): *a word whose meaning escapes me; an animal whose fur changes color.* **3.** the one or ones belonging to what person: *Whose won the third prize?* [ME *whos*, early ME *hwās*; r. *hwas*, OE *hwæs*, gen. of *hwā* WHO]

whose·so·ev·er (ho͞oz′sō ev′ər), *pron.* **1.** (the possessive case of **whosoever** used as an attributive adjective): *Whosesoever books are overdue will be fined.* **2.** the one or ones belonging to whomsoever: *Whosesoever are left here will be confiscated.* [earlier *whoseso* (see WHOSE, SO¹) + EVER]

whos·ev·er (ho͞oz ev′ər), *pron.* **1.** (the possessive case of **whoever** used as an adjective): *Whosever wagon this is, get it out of here. Whosever is this ridiculous hat?* **2.** the one or ones belonging to whomever: *Whosever will win, do you think?* [WHOSE + EVER]

who·sis (ho͞o′zis), *n.* whoosis.

who·so (ho͞o′sō), *pron.* whosoever; whoever. [ME, early ME *hwa swa*, OE *(swā) hwā swā.* See WHO, SO¹]

who·so·ev·er (ho͞o′sō ev′ər), *pron.; possessive* **whose·so·ev·er;** *objective* **whom·so·ev·er.** whoever; whatever person: *Whosoever wants to apply should write to the bureau.* [ME; see WHOSO, EVER]

who's′ who′, 1. a reference work containing short biographical entries on the outstanding persons in a country, industry, profession, etc.: *a who's who in automotive engineering.* **2.** the outstanding or influential persons in a community, industry, profession, or other group: *The who's who of racing will be there.*

whr., watt-hour.

whr. m., watt-hour meter.

whse., warehouse.

whsle., wholesale.

whs. stk., warehouse stock.

why (hwī, wī), *adv., conj., n., pl.* **whys,** *interj.* **—adv. 1.** for what; for what reason, cause, or purpose?: *Why did you behave so badly?* **—conj. 2.** for what cause or reason: *I don't know why he is leaving.* **3.** for which; on account of which (usually after *reason* to introduce a relative clause): *the reason why he refused to go.* **4.** the reason for which: *That is why he returned.* **—n. 5.** a question concerning the cause or reason for which something is done, achieved, etc.: *a child's unending hows and whys.* **6.** the cause or reason: *the whys and wherefores of a troublesome situation.* **—interj. 7.** (an expression of surprise, hesitation, etc., or sometimes a mere expletive): *Why, it's all gone!* [ME; OE *hwī, hwȳ*, instr. case of *hwæt* WHAT; c. OIcel *hvī*]

Why·al·la (hwī al′ə, wī-), *n.* a city in S Australia. 13,711 (1961).

whyd·ah (hwid′ə, wid′ə), *n.* **1.** any of several small, African weaverbirds of the subfamily *Viduinae,* the males of which have elongated, drooping tail feathers during the breeding season. **2.** any of several unrelated weaverbirds of the genera *Coliuspasser, Drepanoplectes,* or *Diatropura,* the males of which have long tails. Also, **whidah.** Also called **widow bird.** [alter. of WIDOW (BIRD) to make name agree with that of a town in Dahomey, West Africa, one of its haunts]

W.I., 1. West Indian. **2.** West Indies.

w.i., when issued: used to indicate a transaction to be completed when the security is issued at a later date.

Wi·ak (wē yäk′), *n.* Biak.

Wich·i·ta (wich′i tô′), *n.* a city in S Kansas, on the Arkansas River. 254,698 (1960).

Wich′ita Falls′, a city in N Texas. 101,724 (1960).

Wich·man (wik′mən, vik′män), *n.* a crater in the third quadrant of the face of the moon: about 8 miles in diameter.

wick[1] (wik), *n.* a bundle or loose twist or braid of soft threads, or a woven strip or tube, as of cotton or asbestos, which in a candle, lamp, oil stove, cigarette lighter, or the like, serves to draw up the melted tallow or wax or the oil or other flammable liquid to be burned. [ME *wicke, weke,* OE *wice, wēoc(e)*; c. OHG *wiohha* lint, wick (G *Wieke* lint), MD *wiecke,* MLG *wēke;* akin to OE *wōci(g)e,* Skt *vāgurā* noose] **—wick′less,** *adj.*

wick[2] (wik), *n.* *Curling.* a narrow opening in the field, bounded by other players' stones. [?]

wick[3] (wik), *n.* **1.** *Brit. Dial.* a farm, esp. a dairy farm. **2.** *Archaic.* a village; hamlet. [ME *wik, wich,* OE *wīc* house, village (equiv. to OS *wīc,* OHG *wich*) < L *vīcus* village, estate, c. Gk *oikos* house; see ECOLOGY, ECONOMY]

Wick (wik), *n.* a town in and the county seat of Caithness, in N Scotland: herring fisheries. 7545 (est. 1964)

wick·ed (wik′id), *adj.* **1.** evil or morally bad in principle or practice; sinful; vicious; iniquitous: *wicked people; wicked habits.* **2.** mischievous or playfully malicious: *These wicked kittens upset everything.* **3.** distressingly severe, as a storm, wound, or cold: *This has been a wicked winter.* **4.** unjustifiable; dreadful; beastly: *wicked prices; a wicked exam.* **5.** ill-natured; vicious: *a wicked horse; a wicked tongue.* **6.** extremely troublesome or dangerous: *wicked roads.* **7.** unpleasant; foul: *a wicked odor.* **8.** *Slang.* excellent; masterly: *He plays a wicked trumpet. He's a wicked man on bass.* [ME *wikked,* equiv. to *wikke* bad (? OE *wicca* wizard, used as adj.) + *-ed* (*-ede* -ED[3]). See WITCH] **—wick′ed·ly,** *adv.*

—Syn. 1. unrighteous, ungodly, godless, impious, profane, blasphemous; unprincipled; immoral, profligate, corrupt, depraved, dissolute; heinous; infamous, amoral, vile, flagitious, atrocious, villainous. See **bad**[1]. **—Ant. 1.** good.

wick·ed·ness (wik′id nis), *n.* **1.** quality or state of being wicked. **2.** wicked conduct or practices. **3.** a wicked act or thing. [ME; see WICKED, -NESS]

wick·er (wik′ər), *n.* **1.** a slender, pliant twig; osier; withe. **2.** plaited or woven twigs or osiers as the material of baskets, chairs, etc.; wickerwork. **3.** something made of wickerwork, as a basket. **—***adj.* **4.** consisting or made of wicker: *a wicker basket.* **5.** covered with wicker: *a wicker jug.* [ME < Scand; cf. dial. Sw *vikker* willow. See WEAK]

wick·er·work (wik′ər wûrk′), *n.* work consisting of plaited or woven twigs or osiers; articles made of wicker. [WICKER + WORK]

wick·et (wik′it), *n.* **1.** a small door or gate, esp. one beside, or forming part of, a larger one. **2.** a window or opening, often closed by a grating or the like, as in a door, or forming a place of communication in a ticket office, a teller's cage in a bank, etc. **3.** a small gate by which a canal lock is emptied. **4.** a gate by which a flow of water is regulated, as to a water wheel. **5.** *Cricket.* **a.** either of the two frameworks, each consisting of three stumps with two bails in grooves across the tops, at which the bowler aims the ball. **b.** the area between the wickets; the playing field. **c.** one batsman's turn at the wicket. **d.** the period during which two men bat together. **e.** a batsman's inning that is not completed or not begun. **6.** *Croquet.* a hoop or arch. **7.** a turnstile in an entrance. **8. to be on, have, or bat a sticky wicket,** *Brit. Slang.* to be at or have a disadvantage. [ME *wiket* < AF (equiv. to OF *guischet*) < Gmc; cf. MD *wiket* wicket, equiv. to *wik-* (akin to OE *wīcan* to yield; see WEAK) + *-et* n. suffix]

wick·et·keep·er (wik′it kē′pər), *n.* *Cricket.* the player on the fielding side who stands immediately behind the wicket to stop balls that pass it. [WICKET + KEEPER]

Wick·ford (wik′fərd), *n.* a town in central Rhode Island. 2934 (1960).

wick·ing (wik′ing), *n.* material for wicks. [WICK[1] + -ING[1]]

wick·i·up (wik′ē up′), *n.* **1.** (in Nevada, Arizona, etc.) an American Indian hut made of brushwood or covered with mats. **2.** *Western U.S.* any rude hut. Also, **wick′y·up′, wikiup.** [prob. < Algonquian (Sac-Fox-Kickapoo) *wikiyapi* lodge, dwelling. See WIGWAM]

Wick·liffe (wik′lif), *n.* **1. John.** Also, **Wic′lif.** See **Wycliffe, John. 2.** a city in NE Ohio, near Cleveland. 15,760 (1960).

Wick·low (wik′lō), *n.* a county in Leinster province, in the E Republic of Ireland. 58,473 (1961); 782 sq. mi. *Co. seat:* Wicklow.

wic·o·py (wik′ə pē), *n., pl.* **-pies. 1.** the leatherwood, *Dirca palustris.* **2.** any of various willow herbs, as *Chamaenerion angustifolium.* **3.** basswood. **4.** staggerbush. [< Algonquian *wik′pi, wighebi,* etc., inner bark]

wid·der (wid′ər), *n.* *Dial.* widow.

wid·der·shins (wid′ər shinz′), *adv.* *Chiefly Scot.* withershins.

wid·dy[1] (wid′ē), *n., pl.* **-dies.** *Chiefly Scot.* **1.** a band or rope, traditionally, one made from intertwined willow twigs. **2.** a hangman's rope; noose. Also, **wid′die, woody.** [late ME (north), var. of WITHY]

wid·dy[2] (wid′ē), *n., pl.* **-dies.** *Dial.* widow.

wide (wīd), *adj.,* **wid·er, wid·est,** *adv., n.* **—***adj.* **1.** having considerable or great extent from side to side; broad: *a wide boulevard.* **2.** having a certain or specified extent from side to side: *three feet wide.* **3.** of great horizontal extent; extensive; vast; spacious: *the wide plains of the West.* **4.** of great range or scope; embracing a great number or variety of subjects, cases, etc.: *wide reading; wide experience.* **5.** open to the full or a great extent; expanded; distended: *to stare with wide eyes.* **6.** full, ample, or roomy, as clothing: *He wore wide, flowing robes.* **7.** apart or remote from a specified point or object: *a guess wide of the truth.* **8.** *Phonet.* lax (def. 7). **9.** too far or too much to one side: *a shot wide of the mark.* **10.** *Baseball Informal.* outside (def. 11): *The pitch was wide of the plate.* **11.** *Brit. Slang.* shrewd; wary. **—***adv.* **12.** to a great, or relatively great, extent from side to side: *The river runs wide here.* **13.** over an extensive space or region, or far abroad: *scattered far and wide.* **14.** to the full extent of opening: *Open your mouth wide.* **15.** to the utmost, or fully: *to be wide awake.* **16.** away from or to one side of a point, mark, purpose, or the like; aside; astray: *The shot went wide.* **—***n.* **17.** *Cricket.* a bowled ball that goes wide of the wicket, and counts as a run for the side batting. **18.** *Archaic.* a wide space or expanse. [ME; OE *wīd;* c. D *wijd,* G *weit,* Icel *vīthr*] **—wide′ness,** *n.*

—Syn. 1. WIDE, BROAD refer to dimensions. They are often interchangeable, but WIDE especially applies to things of which the length is much greater than the width: *a wide road, piece of ribbon.* BROAD is more emphatic, and applies to things of considerable or great width, esp. to surfaces extending laterally: *a broad valley.* **3.** boundless; comprehensive; ample. **—Ant. 1.** narrow.

wide-an·gle (wīd′ang′gəl), *adj.* *Photo.* **1.** noting or pertaining to a lens having an angle of view of 60° or more, and a focal length of less than the diagonal of the film used with it. **2.** employing, or made with, a wide-angle lens: *a wide-angle camera; a wide-angle shot.*

wide-a·wake (wīd′ə wāk′), *adj.* **1.** fully awake; with the eyes wide open. **2.** alert, keen, or knowing: *a wide-awake young man.* **—***n.* **3.** Also called **wide′-awake hat′.** a soft, low-crowned felt hat. **4.** *Informal.* the sooty tern. **—wide′-a·wake′ness,** *n.*

—Syn. 2. watchful, vigilant; sharp, quick, astute.

wide-eyed (wīd′īd′), *adj.* with the eyes open wide, as in amazement, innocence, sleeplessness, etc.

wide·ly (wīd′lē), *adv.* **1.** to a wide extent. **2.** over a wide space or area: *a widely distributed plant.* **3.** by or among a large number of persons: *a man who is widely known.* **4.** in many or various subjects, cases, etc.: *to be widely read.* **5.** greatly, very much, or very: *two widely differing accounts of an incident.* [WIDE + -LY]

wide′mouth blind′cat (wīd′mouth′). See under **blindcat.** [WIDE + MOUTH]

wide·mouthed (wīd′mouthd′, -moutht′), *adj.* **1.** (of a person, object, body of water, etc.) having a wide mouth: *a widemouthed river.* **2.** (of a person) having the mouth opened wide, as in astonishment, horror, etc.: *He stared widemouthed in amazement.* [WIDE + MOUTH + -ED[3]]

wid·en (wīd′ən), *v.t., v.i.* to make or become wide or wider; broaden; expand. [WIDE + -EN[1]] **—wid′en·er,** *n.*

wide-o·pen (wīd′ō′pən), *adj.* **1.** opened to the full extent: *a wide-open window.* **2.** having loose or irregular enforcement or nonenforcement or lack of laws concerning liquor, vice, gambling, etc.: *a wide-open town.* [late ME]

wide-rang·ing (wīd′rān′jing), *adj.* extending over a large area; extensive or diversified in scope: *wide-ranging lands; a wide-ranging discussion.*

wide-screen (wīd′skrēn′), *adj.* of or pertaining to motion pictures projected on a screen having greater width than height, usually in a ratio of 1 to 2.5.

wide·spread (wīd′spred′), *adj.* **1.** spread over or open, or occupying a wide space. **2.** distributed over a wide region, or occurring in many places or among many persons or individuals: *widespread poverty.* [WIDE + SPREAD]

wide-spread·ing (wīd′spred′ing), *adj.* **1.** spreading over or covering a large area: *wide-spreading showers; wide-spreading ivy.* **2.** affecting or reaching a large area: *a wide-spreading infection.*

widg·eon (wij′ən), *n., pl.* **-eons,** (*esp. collectively*) **-eon** for 1. **1.** any of several fresh-water ducks between the mallard and teal in size, as *Anas penelope,* of the Old World, having a reddish-brown head with a buff crown. Cf. **baldpate** (def. 2). **2.** *Obs.* a fool. Also, **wigeon.** [? < AF *wigeon, var. of F *vigeon* < VL; cf. ML *vipio* kind of crane (deriv. of *wip-* imit. of bird's cry)]

widg·et (wij′it), *n.* **1.** a small mechanical device, as a knob, switch, etc., esp. one whose name is not known or cannot be recalled; gadget: *a row of widgets on the instrument panel.* **2.** something considered typical or representative, as of a manufacturer's products: *the widgets coming off the assembly line.* [alter. of GADGET]

wid·ish (wī′dish), *adj.* rather wide: *a widish bookcase; widish hips.* [WIDE + -ISH[1]]

wid·ow (wid′ō), *n.* **1.** a woman who has lost her husband by death and has not married again. **2.** *Cards.* an additional hand or part of a hand, as one dealt to the table. **3.** *Print.* a short last line of a paragraph, esp. one less than half of the full measure. **4.** a woman often left alone because her husband devotes his free time to a hobby or sport (used in combination). Cf. **golf widow.** **—***v.t.* **5.** to make (someone) a widow: *She was widowed by the war.* **6.** to deprive of anything cherished or needed: *A surprise attack widowed the army of its supplies.* **7.** *Obs.* **a.** to endow with a widow's right. **b.** to survive as the widow of. [ME *wid(e)we,* OE *widuwe;* c. Goth *widuwo,* G *Witwe,* L *vidua* (fem. of *viduus* bereaved), Skt *vidhavā* widow. See DIVIDE] **—wid′ow·ly,** *adj.*

wid′ow bird′, whydah. [trans. of NL *Vidua* name of the genus (L: lit., widow). See WHYDAH]

wid·ow·er (wid′ō ər), *n.* a man who has lost his wife by death and has not married again. [late ME (see WIDOW, -ER[1]); r. *widow* (now dial.), OE *widuwa*] **—wid′ow·ered,** *adj.* **—wid′ow·er·hood′,** *n.*

wid·ow·hood (wid′ō ho͝od′), *n.* state or period of being a widow or, sometimes, a widower. [ME *wid(e)wehood,* OE *widuwanhād,* equiv. to *widuwan,* gen. sing. of *widuwe* WIDOW + *hād* -HOOD]

wid·ow's-cross (wid′ōz krôs′, -kros′), *n.* an evergreen shrub, *Sedum pulchellum,* of the southeastern U.S., having purplish flowers. Also called **flowering moss.**

wid′ow's cruse′, an inexhaustible supply of something: in allusion to the miracle of the cruse of oil in I Kings 17:10–16 and II Kings 4:1–7.

wid′ow's mite′, a small contribution given cheerfully by one who can ill afford it. Mark 12:41–44.

wid′ow's peak′, a point formed in the hairline in the middle of the forehead.

wid′ow's walk′, a platform or walk atop a roof, as on certain coastal New England houses of the 18th and early 19th centuries: often used as a lookout for incoming ships.

width (width *or, often,* with), *n.* **1.** extent from side to side; breadth; wideness. **2.** a piece of the full wideness, as of cloth. [WID(E) + -TH[1], modeled on *breadth*]

width·wise (width′wīz′ *or, often,* with′-), *adv.* in the direction of the width. Also, **width·ways** (width′wāz′ *or, often,* with′-). [WIDTH + -WISE]

Wi·du·kind (vē′do͞o kint′), *n.* Wittekind.

wie geht's (vē gāts′), *German.* how are you?

Wie·land (vē′länt), *n.* **1. Chris·toph Mar·tin** (kris′tôf mär′tēn), 1733–1813, German poet, novelist, and critic. **2. Hein·rich** (hīn′riKH), 1877–1957, German chemist: Nobel prize 1927.

Wie·land (vē′länt), *n.* *German Myth.* Wayland.

wield (wēld), *v.t.* **1.** to exercise (power, authority, influence, etc.), as in ruling or dominating: *He wielded his power justly.* **2.** to use (a weapon, instrument, etc.) effectively; to handle or employ actively. **3.** *Archaic.* to guide or direct. **4.** *Obs.* to govern. [ME *welde(n),* OE *wieldan* to control, deriv. of *wealdan* to rule; c. G *walten,* Icel *valda,* Goth *waldan;* akin to L *valēre* to be strong, prevail] **—wield′a·ble,** *adj.* **—wield′er,** *n.*

—Syn. 2. manipulate, control.

wield·y (wēl′dē), *adj.,* **wield·i·er, wield·i·est.** readily wielded or managed, as in use or action. [late ME; see WIELD, -Y[1]]

Wien (vēn), *n.* **1. Wil·helm** (vil′helm), 1864–1928, German physicist: Nobel prize 1911. **2.** German name of **Vienna.**

wie·ner (wē′nər), *n.* *U.S.* **1.** frankfurter. **2.** See **Vienna sausage.** Also, **wie·ner·wurst** (wē′nər wûrst′). [< G, short for *Wiener Wurst* Viennese sausage]

Wie·ner (wē′nər), *n.* **Nor·bert** (nôr′bərt), 1874–1964, U.S. mathematician.

Wie·ner schnit·zel (vē′nər shnit′səl, shnit′səl), a breaded veal cutlet, variously seasoned or garnished. [< G, equiv. to *Wiener* Viennese + *Schnitzel* cutlet, chop]

wie·nie (wē′nē), *n.* weenie.

Wies·ba·den (vēs′bäd′ən), *n.* a city in W West Germany: health resort; mineral springs. 258,000 (est. 1963).

wife (wīf), *n., pl.* **wives** (wīvz), *v.,* **wifed, wif·ing.** **—***n.* **1.** a woman joined in marriage to a man; a woman considered in relation to her husband; spouse. **2.** a woman (*archaic or dial.,* except in combination): *housewife; midwife; fishwife.* **3. take to wife,** to marry (a particular woman): *He took an heiress to wife and was regarded with suspicion by her family.* **—***v.i., v.t.* **4.** *Rare.* wive. [ME, OE *wīf* woman; c. D *wijf,* G *Weib,* Icel *vīf*] **—wife′dom,** *n.* **—wife′less,** *adj.* **—wife′less·ness,** *n.*

wife·hood (wīf′ho͝od), *n.* **1.** state of being a wife. **2.** wifely character or quality; wifeliness. [ME *wifhood,* OE *wīfhād.* See WIFE, -HOOD]

wife·like (wīf′līk′), *adj.* **1.** wifely. **—***adv.* **2.** in a manner befitting a wife. [WIFE + -LIKE]

wife·ly (wīf′lē), *adj.,* **-li·er, -li·est.** of, like, or befitting a wife. Also, **wifelike.** [ME *wifly,* OE *wīflīc.* See WIFE, -LY] **—wife′li·ness,** *n.*

wig (wig), *n., v.,* **wigged, wig·ging.** **—***n.* **1.** an artificial covering of hair for the head, worn formerly as an ordinary hair covering and now to conceal baldness, as part of official attire, for disguise, ornament, etc. **2.** *Brit. Informal.* a wigging. **—***v.t.* **3.** to furnish with a wig or wigs. **4.** *Brit. Informal.* to reprimand or reprove severely. **—***v.t.* **5.** *Brit. Informal.* to scold. [short for PERIWIG] **—wig′less,** *adj.* **—wig′like′,** *adj.*

wig·an (wig′ən), *n.* a stiff, canvaslike fabric for stiffening parts of garments. [after WIGAN, where originally produced]

Wig·an (wig′ən), *n.* a city in S Lancashire, in W England. 78,702 (1961).

wig·eon (wij′ən), *n., pl.* **-eons,** (*esp. collectively*) **-eon.** widgeon.

wig·ger·y (wig′ə rē), *n., pl.* **-ger·ies. 1.** wigs or a wig; false hair. **2.** the wearing of wigs. [WIG + -ERY]

Wig·gin (wig′in), *n.* **Kate Douglas,** 1856–1923, U.S. writer.

wig·ging (wig′ing), *n.* *Brit. Informal.* a scolding or reproof. [WIG + -ING[1]]

wig·gle (wig′əl), *v.,* **-gled, -gling,** *n.* **—***v.i.* **1.** to move or go with short, quick, irregular movements from side to side: *The puppies wiggled with delight.* **—***v.t.* **2.** to cause to wiggle; move quickly and irregularly from side to side. **—***n.* **3.** a wiggling movement or course. **4.** a wiggly line. **5.** a dish of creamed fish or shellfish, and peas. [ME *wigle(n),* freq. of dial. *wig* to wag; akin to OE *wegan* to move, *wēg* motion, *wicga* insect; cf. Norw *vigla* to totter, freq. of *vigga* to rock oneself, D, LG *wiggelen*]

wig′gle nail′, a fastener consisting of a piece of corrugated sheet steel with one wavy edge sharpened, for uniting two pieces of wood, as in a miter joint.

wig·gler (wig′lər), *n.* **1.** one who or that which wiggles. **2.** wriggler (def. 2). [WIGGLE + -ER[1]]

Wig·gles·worth (wig′əlz wûrth′), *n.* **Michael,** 1631–1705, U.S. theologian and author, born in England.

wig·gle-tail (wig′əl tāl′), *n.* wriggler (def. 2).

wig·gly (wig′lē), *adj.,* **-gli·er, -gli·est. 1.** wiggling: *a wiggly child.* **2.** undulating; wavy: *a wiggly line.* [WIGGL(E) + -Y[1]]

wight[1] (wīt), *n.* **1.** *Archaic.* **a.** a human being. **b.** a supernatural being, as a witch or sprite. **2.** *Obs.* any living being; a creature. [ME, OE *wiht;* c. G *Wicht,* Icel *vættr,* Goth *waiht*]

wight[2] (wīt), *adj.* *Brit. Dial.* **1.** strong and brave, esp. in war. **2.** active; nimble. [ME < Scand; cf. Icel *vīgt,* neut. of *vīgr* able to fight]

Wight (wīt), *n.* **Isle of,** an island off the S coast of England, forming an administrative division of Hampshire. 95,479 (1961); 147 sq. mi. *Co. seat:* Newport.

wig·mak·er (wig′mā′kər), *n.* one who makes or sells wigs. [WIG + MAKER]

Wig·ner (wig′nər), *n.* **Eugene Paul,** born 1902, U.S. physicist, born in Hungary: Enrico Fermi Award 1958; Nobel prize 1963.

Wig·town (wig′tən, -toun′), *n.* a county in SW Scotland. 29,107 (est. 1959); 487 sq. mi. *Co. seat:* Wigtown. Also called **Wig·town·shire** (wig′tən shēr′, -shər, -toun′-).

wig·wag (wig′wag′), *v.*, **-wagged, -wag·ging,** *n.* —*v.t., v.i.* **1.** to move to and fro. **2.** *Naut.* to signal by movements of two flags or the like waved according to a code. —*n.* **3.** *Naut.* the act or process of sending messages by the movements of two flags or the like waved according to a code. **4.** a message so signaled. [*wig* to wag (now dial.; see WIGGLE) + WAG; repetitive compound with gradation, parallel to ZIGZAG, etc.] —**wig′wag′ger,** *n.*

wig·wam (wig′wom, -wôm), *n.* **1.** an American Indian hut or lodge, usually of rounded or oval shape, formed of poles overlaid with bark, mats, or skins. **2.** *U.S. Slang.* a large, often temporary structure used by a political party, esp. for a convention. **3. the Wigwam.** See **Tammany Hall** (def. 2). [< Abnaki (Algonquian): their abode]

Wigwam

wik·i·up (wik′ē up′), *n.* wickiup.

Wil·ber·force (wil′bər fōrs′, -fôrs′), *n.* **William,** 1759–1833, British statesman, philanthropist, and writer.

Wil·bur (wil′bər), *n.* **1. Richard,** born 1921, U.S. poet. **2.** Also, **Wil′ber.** a boy's given name.

Wil·bur·ite (wil′bə rīt′), *n.* a member of a conservative body of Quakers formed in 1845 in protest against the evangelicalism of the Gurneyites. [after John *Wilbur* (1774–1856), American Quaker preacher; see -ITE[1]]

wil·co (wil′kō), *interj.* (esp. in radio transmission) an indication that the message just received will be complied with. [short for *will comply*]

Wil·cox (wil′koks), *n.* **Ella Wheeler,** 1850–1919, U.S. poet.

wild (wīld), *adj.* **1.** living in a state of nature; not tamed or domesticated: *a wild animal; wild geese.* **2.** growing or produced without cultivation or the care of man, as plants, flowers, fruit, honey, etc.: *wild cherries.* **3.** uncultivated, uninhabited, or waste: *wild land; This is still wild country.* **4.** uncivilized or barbarous: *wild tribes; wild savages.* **5.** of unrestrained violence, fury, intensity, etc.; violent; furious: *wild strife; wild storms.* **6.** characterized by or indicating violent feelings or excitement, as actions, a person's appearance, etc. **7.** frantic; distracted, crazy, or mad: *to drive someone wild.* **8.** violently or uncontrollably affected: *wild with rage; wild with pain.* **9.** undisciplined, unruly, lawless, or turbulent: *a gang of wild boys; a wild crew.* **10.** unrestrained, untrammeled, or unbridled: *wild hilarity; wild enthusiasm.* **11.** disregardful of moral restraints as to pleasurable indulgence: *He repented his wild youth.* **12.** unrestrained by reason or prudence: *wild schemes; a wild idea.* **13.** extravagant or fantastic: *wild fancies.* **14.** disorderly or disheveled: *wild hair.* **15.** wide of the mark: *He scored on a wild throw.* **16.** *Informal.* intensely eager or enthusiastic: *wild to get started; wild about the new styles.* **17.** *Cards.* (of a card) having its value decided by the wishes of the players. **18.** *Metall.* (of molten metal) generating large amounts of gas during cooling, so as to cause violent bubbling. —*adv.* **19.** in a wild manner; wildly. **20. run wild, a.** to grow unchecked: *The rambler roses are running wild.* **b.** to show lack of restraint or control: *Those children are allowed to run wild.* —*n.* **21.** Often, **wilds.** an uncultivated, uninhabited, or desolate region or tract; waste; wilderness; desert: *a cabin in the storm-swept wild; a safari to the wilds of Africa.* **22. the wild,** the wilderness; uncultivated areas: *the lure of the wild.* [ME, OE *wilde;* c. D, G *wild,* Goth *wiltheis,* Icel *villr,* Sw *vild*] —**wild′ly,** *adv.* —**wild′ness,** *n.*

—**Syn. 1.** undomesticated, untamed, feral, ferine, savage, unbroken, ferocious. **4.** barbarian. **5.** tempestuous, stormy, frenzied, turbulent, boisterous. **7.** insane. **9.** self-willed, ungoverned, riotous, unrestrained, wayward. **10.** uncontrolled. **12.** reckless, rash, extravagant, impracticable. **13.** grotesque, bizarre, strange, fanciful. **14.** unkempt. —**Ant. 1.** tame.

Wil·da (wil′də), *n.* a girl's given name, form of **Wilhelmina.** Also, **Willa.**

wild′ all′spice, the spicebush.

wild′ bean′, groundnut.

wild′ ber′gamot, a perennial herb, *Monardo fistulosa,* of eastern North America, having lilac-colored or purple flowers, growing in dry places.

wild′ bleed′ing-heart, an herb, *Dicentra eximia,* of the eastern coast of the U.S., having branched clusters of rose-colored or pink flowers.

wild′ boar′, a wild, Old World swine, *Sus scrofa,* from which most of the domestic hogs are believed to be derived.

Wild boar (3 ft. high at shoulder; total length 4½ ft.; tail 6 in.)

wild′ bri′er, 1. the dog rose, *Rosa canina.* **2.** the sweetbrier, *Rosa Eglanteria.* **3.** any other brier growing wild.

wild′ cal′la. See **water arum.**

wild′ car′rot, an umbelliferous weed, *Daucus carota,* having a thin and woody root, common in fields and waste places: the wild form of the cultivated carrot.

wild·cat (wīld′kat′), *n., pl.,* for 1–4, **-cats,** (*esp. collectively*) **-cat,** *adj., v.,* **-cat·ted, -cat·ting.** —*n.* **1.** any of several North American felines of the genus *Lynx.* Cf. **lynx. 2.** a yellowish-gray, black-striped, European feline, *Felis sylvestris,* resembling and closely related to the domestic cat with which it interbreeds freely. **3.** a similar feline, *Felis libyca,* of northern Africa, believed to be the chief ancestor of the domestic cat. **4.** any of several other of the smaller felines, as the serval, ocelot, etc. **5.** a quick-tempered or savage person. **6.** *U.S. Slang.* a single locomotive operating without a train, as one switching cars. **7.** an exploratory well drilled in an effort to discover deposits of oil or gas; a prospect well. **8.** a reckless or unsound enterprise, business, etc. **9.** *Naut.* a shaped drum on a windlass, engaging with the links of an anchor chain. —*adj.* **10.** characterized by or proceeding from reckless or unsafe business methods: *wildcat companies; wildcat stocks.* **11.** of or pertaining to an illicit enterprise or product. **12.** running without control or regulation, as a locomotive, or apart from the regular schedule, as a train. —*v.i.* **13.** to search an area of unknown or doubtful productivity for oil, ore, or the like, esp. as an independent prospector. —*v.t.* **14.** to search (an area of unknown or doubtful productivity) for oil, ore, or the like. [late ME *wilde cat;* cf. MLG *wildkatte*]

wild′cat bank′, *U.S. Informal.* a bank which issued notes without adequate security in the period before the establishment of the national banking system in 1864.

wild′cat strike′, a labor strike that has not been called or sanctioned by the officials of the union. Also called **outlaw strike, quickie strike.**

wild·cat·ter (wīld′kat′ər), *n.* *Informal.* **1.** an oil prospector. **2.** one who promotes risky or unsound business ventures. [WILDCAT + -ER[1]]

wild′ cel′ery. See **tape grass.**

wild′ cher′vil, a honewort, *Cryptotaenia canadensis,* of North America.

wild′ clove′, bayberry (def. 3).

wild′ corn′, dog-plum.

wild′ date′, a feather palm, *Phoenix sylvestris,* of India, having drooping, bluish-green or grayish leaves and small, orange-yellow fruit.

Wild′ Duck′, The, a play (1884) by Henrik Ibsen.

Wilde (wīld), *n.* **Oscar (Fin·gal O'Fla·her·tie Wills)** (fing′gəl ō flā′hər tē wilz, ō flâr′tē), ("*Sebastian Melmoth*"), 1854–1900, Irish poet, dramatist, novelist, essayist, and critic.

wil·de·beest (wil′də bēst′; *Du.* vil′də bāst′), *n., pl.* **-beests,** (*esp. collectively*) **-beest,** *Du.* **-bees·te** (-bās′tə). gnu. [< SAfrD: lit., wild beast]

wil·der (wil′dər), *Archaic.* —*v.t.* **1.** to cause to lose one's way. **2.** to bewilder. —*v.i.* **3.** to lose one's way. **4.** to be bewildered. [cf. Icel *villr* astray, *villst* to go astray] —**wil′der·ment,** *n.*

Wil·der (wīl′dər), *n.* **1. Billy,** born 1906, U.S. motion-picture director, producer, and writer; born in Austria. **2. Thorn·ton (Niv·en)** (thôrn′tᵊn niv′ən), born 1897, U.S. novelist and playwright.

wil·der·ness (wil′dər nis), *n.* **1.** a wild and uncultivated region, as of forest or desert, uninhabited or inhabited only by wild animals; a tract of wasteland. **2.** any desolate tract, as of open sea. **3.** a part of a garden set apart for plants growing with unchecked luxuriance. **4.** a bewildering mass or collection. [ME, OE *wilder(en)* wild (*wildor, wilder* wild beast + *-en* -EN[1]) + -NESS, the n. suffix r. adj. one] —**Syn. 1.** See **desert**[1].

Wil·der·ness (wil′dər nis), *n.* a wooded area in NE Virginia: several battles fought here in 1864 between Grant and Lee.

wild-eyed (wīld′īd′), *adj.* **1.** having an angry, insane, or distressed expression in the eyes. **2.** extremely irrational, senseless, or radical: *He favors a wild-eyed plan to irrigate the Sahara Desert.*

wild′ fig′, the caprifig.

wild·fire (wīld′fīᵊr′), *n.* **1.** a highly flammable composition, as Greek fire, difficult to extinguish when ignited, formerly used in warfare. **2.** sheet lightning, unaccompanied by thunder. **3.** the ignis fatuus or a similar light. **4.** *Plant Pathol.* a disease of tobacco and soybeans, characterized by brown, necrotic spots, each surrounded by a yellow band, on the leaves, caused by a bacterium, *Pseudomonas tabaci.* **5.** *Pathol. Obs.* erysipelas or some similar disease. [ME *wildefire,* OE *wildfȳr.* See WILD, FIRE]

wild′ flax′, 1. the gold-of-pleasure. **2.** the common toadflax, *Linaria vulgaris.*

wild′ flow′er, 1. the flower of a plant that normally grows in fields, forests, etc., without deliberate cultivation. **2.** the plant itself. Also, **wild′flow′er.**

wild·fowl (wīld′foul′), *n.* a game bird, esp. a duck, goose, or swan. [ME *wilde foul,* OE *wildefugl.* See WILD, FOWL]

wild′ gera′nium, a crane's-bill, *Geranium maculatum,* of the eastern U.S., having rose-purple flowers.

wild′ goose′, any undomesticated goose, esp. the graylag or Canada goose. [ME *wilde gos,* OE *wildgōs.* See WILD, GOOSE]

wild′-goose′ chase′ (wīld′gōōs′), **1.** a wild or absurd search for something nonexistent or unobtainable: *The building had been demolished, but we wasted the whole afternoon on a wild-goose chase looking for it.* **2.** any senseless pursuit of an object or end; a hopeless enterprise: *Her scheme of being a movie star is a wild-goose chase.*

wild-head·ed (wīld′hed′id), *adj.* given to wild or exorbitant ideas.

wild′ hol′lyhock, checkerbloom.

wild′ hon′eysuckle. See **pinxster flower.**

Wild′ Hunt′, (in northern European legend) a phantom hunt, conducted either in the sky or in forests.

Wild′ Hunts′man, the leader of the Wild Hunt, often associated with Odin.

wild′ hy′acinth, 1. a camass, *Camassia scilloides,* of eastern North America. **2.** the harebell, *Scilla nonscripta,* of Europe.

wild′ hydran′gea, a shrub, *Hydrangea arborescens,* found throughout the eastern half of the U.S., having white flowers. Also called **sevenbark.**

wild′ in′digo, any American, leguminous plant of the genus *Baptisia,* esp. *B. tinctoria,* having yellow flowers.

wild·ing (wīl′ding), *n.* **1.** a wild apple tree. **2.** its fruit. **3.** any plant that grows wild. **4.** a plant, originally cultivated, that now grows wild; an escape. **5.** a wild animal. —*adj.* **6.** *Archaic.* not cultivated or domesticated; wild. [WILD + -ING[1]]

wild′ ip′ecac, 1. See **spreading dogbane. 2.** See **horse gentian.**

wild′ let′tuce, any of various uncultivated species of lettuce, growing as weeds in fields and waste places, esp. an English species, *Lactuca scariola,* or a North American species, *L. canadensis.*

wild·life (wīld′līf′), *n.* wild animals, esp. those hunted for food or sport. [WILD + LIFE]

wild′ lil′y-of-the-val′ley, bead-ruby.

wild·ling (wīld′ling), *n.* a wild plant, flower, or animal. [WILD + -LING[1]]

wild′ mad′der, 1. madder[1] (defs. 1, 2). **2.** either of two bedstraws, *Galium Mollugo* or *G. tinctorium.*

wild′ man′, 1. one who is uncivilized; a savage. **2.** a man of violent temper, erratic behavior, etc. **3.** a man of extreme or outrageous political opinions. [ME]

wild′ man′drake, the May apple, *Podophyllum peltatum.*

wild′ mar′joram. See **pot marjoram.**

wild′ monks′hood, a perennial herb, *Aconitum uncinatum,* of the eastern central U.S., having blue flowers, growing in rich, moist soil.

wild′ mul′berry, a West Indian herb, *Morinda Royoc,* naturalized in southern Florida, having white flowers and fleshy, yellow fruit. Also called **yawweed.**

wild′ mus′tard, the charlock.

wild′ oat′, 1. any uncultivated species of *Avena,* esp. a common weedy grass, *A. fatua,* resembling the cultivated oat. **2. sow one's wild oats,** to lead a dissolute life in one's youth, esp. to be promiscuous before marriage.

wild′ oats′, a hardy, perennial herb, *Uvularia sessilifolia,* of eastern North America, having deep green, hairy leaves and greenish-yellow, tube-shaped flowers.

wild′ o′leander. See **swamp loosestrife.**

wild′ o′leaster, the buffalo berry, *Shepherdia argentea.*

wild′ ol′ive, any tree resembling the olive in structure or fruit.

wild′ or′ange. See **laurel cherry.**

wild′ pan′sy, any uncultivated or wild form of the common pansy, *Viola tricolor.*

wild′ pars′ley, any of several umbelliferous plants resembling the parsley in shape and structure.

wild′ pars′nip, an umbelliferous weed, *Pastinaca sativa,* having an inedible acrid root, common in fields and waste places: the wild form of the cultivated parsnip.

wild′ pas′sion flow′er, the maypop, *Passiflora incarnata.*

wild′ pennyroy′al. See **corn mint.**

wild′ pink′, an American catchfly, *Silene pennsylvanica.*

wild′ pitch′, *Baseball.* a pitched ball that the catcher misses and could not be expected to catch, resulting in a base runner's or runners' advancing one or more bases or the batter's reaching first base safely. Cf. **passed ball.**

wild′ pota′to, 1. man-of-the-earth. **2.** the groundnut, *Apios tuberosa.* **3.** the spring beauty, *Claytonia virginica.*

wild′ pump′kin, calabazilla.

wild′ rice′, 1. a tall, aquatic grass, *Zizania aquatica,* of northeastern North America. **2.** the grain of this plant, used for food. Also called **water oats, water rice.**

wild′ rose′, any native species of rose, usually having a single flower with the corolla consisting of one circle of roundish, spreading petals.

wild′ rose′mary, a bog shrub, *Ledum palustre,* found from the North Temperate Zone to the Arctic Circle, having leaves which are rusty-hairy beneath with rolled margins, and white flowers. Also called **crystal tea.**

wild′ rub′ber, rubber obtained from trees growing wild.

wild′ rye′, any grass of the genus *Elymus,* somewhat resembling rye.

wild′ sage′. See **mountain sage.**

wild′ sarsaparil′la, a low herb, *Aralia nudicaulis,* of eastern North America, having a single, long-stalked, compound leaf and a ball-like cluster of greenish-yellow flowers.

wild′ sen′na, a subshrubby senna, *Cassia marilandica,* of the eastern U.S., having yellow flowers. Also called **American senna.**

wild′ serv′ice tree′. See under **service tree** (def. 1).

wild′ silk′, tussah.

wild′ spike′nard, a perennial herb, *Smilacina racemosa,* of shady areas in North America, having greenish-white flowers in clusters and pinkish-red berries. Also called **treacleberry.**

wild′ spin′ach, any of various plants of the genus *Chenopodium,* sometimes used in place of spinach.

wild′ sun′flower. See **giant sunflower.**

wild′ sweet′ pea′, goat's-rue.

wild′ sweet′ pota′to, man-of-the-earth.

wild′ sweet′ wil′liam, 1. See **blue phlox. 2.** an herb, *Phlox maculata,* of eastern North America, having purple-spotted stems and pink or purple flowers.

wild′ thyme′, mother-of-thyme.

wild′ vanil′la, a composite plant, *Trilisa odoratissima,* of the southeastern U.S., having leaves with a persistent, vanillalike fragrance.

Wild′ West′, the western frontier region of the U.S., before the establishment of stable government.

Wild′ West′ show′, an entertainment, often as part of a circus, representing scenes and events from the early history of the western U.S. and displaying feats of marksmanship, horseback riding, rope twirling, and the like.

wild·wood (wīld′wŏŏd′), *n.* a wood growing in the wild or natural state; forest. [ME *wilde wode,* OE *wilde wudu.* See WILD, WOOD[1]]

Wild·wood (wīld′wŏŏd′), *n.* a town in S New Jersey. 4690 (1960).

Wild′wood Crest′, a town in S New Jersey. 3011 (1960).

wild′ worm′wood. See **sea wormwood.**

wild′ yam′, any of several uncultivated yams, esp. *Dioscorea villosa,* of the U.S., having a woody, tuberous root.

wile (wīl), *n.*, *v.*, **wiled, wil·ing.** —*n.* **1.** a trick, artifice, or stratagem meant to fool, trap, or entice. **2. wiles,** artful or beguiling behavior. **3.** deceitful cunning; trickery. —*v.t.* **4.** to beguile, entice, or lure (*away, from, into,* etc.): *The music wiled him from his study.* **5. wile away,** to spend or pass (time), esp. in a leisurely or pleasurable fashion: *to wile away the long winter nights.* [ME, OE *wigle* divination; cf. Icel *vēl* artifice, equiv. to **wihl-*, c. (by Verner's law) OE *wigl-*. See GUILE]
—**Syn. 1, 2.** deception, contrivance, maneuver, device. See **trick. 3.** chicanery, fraud.

Wi·ley (wī′lē), *n.* a boy's given name, form of **William.**

Wil·fred (wil′frid), *n.* a boy's given name. Also, **Wil′frid.**

wil·ful (wil′fəl), *adj.* willful. —**wil′ful·ly,** *adv.* —**wil′ful·ness,** *n.*

Wil·helm (vil′helm; *Eng.* wil′helm), *n.* **1.** Also called **Wilhelm I,** a walled plain in the third quadrant of the face of the moon: about 60 miles in diameter. **2.** a boy's given name, German form of **William.**

Wilhelm I, 1. See **William I** (def. 3). **2.** *Astron.* Wilhelm.

Wilhelm II. See **William II** (def. 2).

Wil·hel·mi·na (wil′ə mē′nə, wil′hel-; *Du.* vil′hel-mē′nä), *n.* **1. Mount,** a mountain in central West Irian, in the Orange Mountains. 15,584 ft. **2.** a girl's given name.

Wilhelmina I, (*Wilhelmina Helena Pauline Maria of Orange-Nassau*) 1880–1962, queen of the Netherlands 1890–1948 (mother of Juliana).

Wil·helm Meis·ter (vil′helm mī′stər), a novel (1795–1829) by Goethe, concerning the education of a young man.

Wil·helms·ha·ven (vil′helms hä′fən), *n.* a seaport in N West Germany, on the North Sea. 100,400 (1963).

Wil·helm·stras·se (vil′helm shträ′sə), *n.* **1.** a street in the center of Berlin, Germany: former location of the German foreign office and other government buildings. **2.** (formerly) the foreign office and policies of the German government.

Wil·helm Tell (vil′helm tel′), a drama (1804) by Schiller, based on the legendary Swiss patriot William Tell.

Wilkes (wilks), *n.* **1. Charles,** 1798–1877, U.S. rear admiral and explorer. **2. John,** 1727–97, English political leader and journalist. **3.** a boy's given name, form of **William.**

Wilkes-Bar·re (wilks′bar′ē, -bar′ə, -bâr′), *n.* **1.** a city in E Pennsylvania, on the Susquehanna River. 63,551 (1960). **2.** a town in central Pennsylvania. 4319 (1960).

Wilkes′ Land′, a coastal region of Antarctica, S of Australia.

Wil·kie (wil′kē), *n.* a boy's given name, form of **William.**

Wil·kins (wil′kinz), *n.* **1. Sir George Hubert,** 1888–1958, Australian antarctic explorer, aviator, and aerial navigator. **2. Mary Eleanor.** See **Freeman, Mary Eleanor. 3. Maurice Hugh Frederick,** born 1916, English biophysicist born in New Zealand: Nobel prize for medicine 1962. **4. Roy,** 1901–81, U.S. journalist and civil rights leader: executive secretary of the NAACP 1955–76. **5.** a town in SW Pennsylvania. 8272 (1960). **6.** a walled plain in the fourth quadrant of the face of the moon: about 40 miles in diameter.

Wil·kins·burg (wil′kinz bûrg′), *n.* a borough in SW Pennsylvania, near Pittsburgh. 30,066 (1960).

will[1] (wil), *v.* and *auxiliary v.*, *pres. sing. 1st pers.* **will,** *2nd* **will** or (*Archaic*) **wilt,** *3rd* **will,** *pres. pl.* **will;** *past sing. 1st pers.* **would,** *2nd* **would** or (*Archaic*) **wouldst,** *3rd* **would,** *past pl.* **would;** *past part.* (*Obs.*) **wold** or **would;** *imperative, infinitive, and pres. participle lacking.* —*auxiliary verb.* **1.** am (is, are, etc.) about or going to (in future constructions, sometimes noting in the first person promise or determination, in the second and third persons mere futurity): *I will be there tomorrow. She will see you at dinner.* **2.** am (is, are, etc.) disposed or willing to: *People will do right.* **3.** am (is, are, etc.) expected or required to: *You will report to the principal at once.* **4.** may be expected or supposed to: *You will not have forgotten him. This will be right.* **5.** am (is, are, etc.) determined or sure to (used emphatically): *You would do it. People will talk.* **6.** am (is, are, etc.) accustomed to, or do usually or often: *You will often see him sitting there. He would write for hours at a time.* **7.** am (is, are, etc.) habitually disposed or inclined to: *Boys will be boys. After dinner he would smoke his pipe.* **8.** am (is, are, etc.) capable of; can: *This tree will live without water for three months.* **9.** am (is, are, etc.) going to: *I will bid you "Good night"!* —*v.t., v.i.* **10.** to wish; desire; like: *Go where you will. Ask, if you will, who the owner is.* [ME; OE *wyllan;* c. D *willen,* G *wollen,* Icel *vilja,* Goth *wiljan,* L *velle* to wish]
—**Usage.** See **shall.**

will[2] (wil), *n.*, *v.*, **willed, will·ing.** —*n.* **1.** the faculty of conscious and especially of deliberate action; the power of control the mind has over its own actions: *the freedom of the will.* **2.** power of choosing one's own actions: *to have a strong or a weak will.* **3.** the act or process of using or asserting one's choice; volition: *My hands are obedient to my will.* **4.** wish or desire: *to submit against one's will.* **5.** purpose or determination, often hearty or stubborn determination; willfulness: *to have the will to succeed.* **6.** the wish or purpose as carried out, or to be carried out: *to work one's will.* **7.** disposition, whether good or ill, toward another. **8.** *Law.* **a.** a legal declaration of a person's wishes as to the disposition of his property or estate after his death, usually written and signed by the testator and attested by witnesses. **b.** the document containing such a declaration. **9. at will, a.** at one's discretion or pleasure; as one desires: *to wander at will through the countryside.* **b.** at one's disposal or command. —*v.t.* **10.** to decide, bring about, or attempt to effect or bring about by act of will: *He can walk if he wills it.* **11.** to purpose, determine on, or elect, by act of will: *If he wills success, he can find it.* **12.** to give by will or testament; bequeath or devise. **13.** to influence by exerting will power: *She was willed to walk the tightrope by the hypnotist.* —*v.i.* **14.** to exercise the will: *To will is not enough; one must do.* **15.** to decide or determine: *Others debate, but the king wills.* [ME, OE (also ME *wille,* OE *willa*); c. D *Wille,* G *Wille,* Icel *vili,* Goth *wilja;* v. OE *willian*] —**will′er,** *n.*
—**Syn. 3.** choice. **4.** pleasure, disposition, inclination. **5.** resolution, decision. WILL, VOLITION refer to conscious choice as to action or thought. WILL denotes fixed and persistent intent or purpose: *Where there's a will there's a way.* VOLITION is the power of forming an intention or the incentive for using the will: *to exercise one's volition in making a decision.* **10.** determine. **12.** leave.

Will (wil), *n.* a boy's given name, form of **William.**

Wil·la (wil′ə), *n.* a girl's given name, form of **Wilhelmina.** Also, **Wilda.**

Wil·la·bel (wil′ə bel′), *n.* a girl's given name. Also, **Wil′la·belle′.**

will·a·ble (wil′ə bəl), *adj.* capable of being willed or fixed by will. [late ME; see WILL[2], -ABLE]

Wil·laert (wil′ärt, vil′-), *n.* **A·dri·an** (ā′drē ən, ä′-drē än′), c1480–1562, Flemish composer.

Wil·lam·ette (wi lam′it), *n.* a river flowing N through NW Oregon into the Columbia River at Portland. ab. 290 mi. long.

Wil·lard (wil′ərd), *n.* **1. Emma (Hart),** 1787–1870, U.S. educator and poet. **2. Frances Elizabeth Caroline,** 1839–98, U.S. educator, reformer, and author. **3. Jess,** 1883–1968, U.S. boxer: world heavyweight champion 1915–19. **4.** a town in N Ohio. 5457 (1960). **5.** a boy's given name.

will-call (wil′kôl′), *adj.* noting a department in a store where goods ordered by a customer are held until called for. [from the phrase (*the buyer*) *will call*]

will′ con′test, legal proceedings to contest the authenticity or validity of a will.

willed (wild), *adj.* having a will (usually used in combination): *strong-willed; weak-willed.* [ME; see WILL[2], -ED[3]]

Wil·lem I (vil′əm). See **William I** (def. 2).

wil·lem·ite (wil′ə mīt′), *n.* a mineral, a zinc silicate, Zn_2SiO_4, sometimes containing manganese, occurring in prismatic crystals or granular masses, usually greenish, sometimes white, brown, or red: a minor ore of zinc. [named after King WILLEM I; see -ITE[1]]

Wil·lem·stad (wil′əm stät′), *n.* a seaport on the island of Curaçao, in the S West Indies: capital of the Netherlands Antilles. 46,899 (est. 1956).

Wil·len·dorf (vil′ən dôrf′), *n.* a village in NE Austria, near Krems: site of an Aurignacian settlement where a 4½ in. limestone statuette (**Venus of Willendorf**) was found.

Wil·lene (wi lēn′), *n.* a girl's given name.

Willes·den (wilz′dən), *n.* a city in E Middlesex, in SE England, near London. 170,835 (1961).

wil·let (wil′it), *n.*, *pl.* **-lets,** (*esp. collectively*) **-let.** a large, North American shorebird, *Catoptrophorus semipalmatus,* having a striking black and white wing pattern. [short for *pill-will-willet,* conventional imit. of bird's cry]

Wil·let (wil′it), *n.* a boy's given name, form of **William.**

Wil·lette (wi let′), *n.* a girl's given name. Also, **Wil·let·ta** (wi let′ə).

will′ for pow′er. See **will to power.**

will·ful (wil′fəl), *adj.* **1.** deliberate, voluntary, or intentional: *The coroner ruled it willful murder.* **2.** perversely obstinate; unreasonably stubborn or headstrong: *He castigated his willful son.* Also, **wilful.** [ME; OE *wilful* willing. See WILL[2], -FUL] —**will′ful·ly,** *adv.* —**will′ful·ness,** *n.*
—**Syn. 1.** volitional. **2.** intransigent; contrary, refractory, pig-headed, inflexible, obdurate, adamant. WILLFUL, HEADSTRONG, PERVERSE, WAYWARD refer to one who stubbornly insists upon doing as he pleases. WILLFUL suggests a stubborn persistence in doing what one wishes, esp. in opposition to those whose wishes or commands ought to be respected or obeyed: *a willful child who disregarded his parents' advice.* One who is HEADSTRONG is often foolishly, and sometimes violently, self-willed: *reckless and headstrong youths.* The PERVERSE person is unreasonably or obstinately intractable or contrary, often with the express intention of being disagreeable: *perverse out of sheer spite.* WAYWARD in this sense has the connotation of rash wrong-headedness which gets one into trouble: *a reform school for wayward girls.* —**Ant. 2.** obedient, tractable.

Wil·liam (wil′yəm), *n.* **1.** a word formerly used in communications to represent the letter W. **2.** a boy's given name.

William I, 1. ("*the Conqueror*") 1027–87, duke of Normandy 1035–87; king of England 1066–87 (son of Robert I, duke of Normandy). **2.** Also, **Willem I.** (*William I of Orange*) ("*the Silent*") 1533–84, Dutch leader, statesman and revolutionary leader born in Germany: prince of Orange 1544–84; count of Nassau 1559–84; 1st stadholder of the United Provinces of the Netherlands 1578–84. **3.** Also, **Wilhelm I.** (*Wilhelm Friedrich Ludwig*) 1797–1888, King of Prussia 1861–88; emperor of Germany 1871–88 (brother of Frederick William IV).

William II, 1. (*William Rufus*) ("*the Red*") 1056?–1100, King of England 1087–1100 (son of William I, duke of Normandy). **2.** Also, **Wilhelm II.** (*Frederick Wilhem Viktor Albert*) 1859–1941, king of Prussia and emperor of Germany 1888–1918.

William III, (*William III of Orange*) 1650–1702, stadholder of the United Provinces of the Netherlands 1672–1702; king of England 1689–1702, joint ruler with his wife Mary II.

William IV, ("*the Sailor-King*") 1765–1837, king of Great Britain and Ireland 1830–37 (brother of George IV).

Wil′liam of Malmes′bur·y (mämz′ber′ē, -bə rē, -brē), c1090–1143?, English historian.

Wil·liams (wil′yəmz), *n.* **1. Ben Ames** (āmz), 1889–1953, U.S. novelist and short-story writer. **2. Em·lyn** (em′lin), born 1905, Welsh playwright and actor. **3. G. Mennen,** born 1911, U.S. politician and diplomat. **4. Ralph Vaughan.** See **Vaughan Williams, Ralph. 5. Roger,** 1603?–83, English clergyman in America: founder of Rhode Island colony 1636. **6. Tennessee** (*Thomas Lanier Williams*), 1914–83, U.S. dramatist. **7. Theodore Samuel** (*Ted*), born 1918, U.S. baseball player. **8. William,** 1731–1811, U.S. merchant and revolutionary statesman. **9. William Car·los** (kär′lōs), 1883–1963, U.S. poet, novelist, and physician. **10.** a town in central Arizona. 3559 (1960). **11.** a walled plain in the first quadrant of the face of the moon: about 22 miles in diameter.

Wil·liams·burg (wil′yəmz bûrg′), *n.* **1.** a city in SE Virginia: colonial capital of Virginia; now restored to its original pre-Revolutionary style. 6832 (1960). **2.** a town in SE Kentucky. 3478 (1960).

Wil·liam·son (wil′yəm sən), *n.* a town in SW West Virginia. 6746 (1960).

Wil·liams·port (wil′yəmz pōrt′, -pôrt′), *n.* a city in central Pennsylvania, on the Susquehanna River. 41,967 (1960).

Wil·liams·ton (wil′yəm stən), *n.* **1.** a town in E North Carolina. 6924 (1960). **2.** a town in NW South Carolina. 3721 (1960).

Wil·liams·town (wil′yəmz toun′), *n.* **1.** a town in NW Massachusetts. 5428 (1960). **2.** a town in SW New Jersey. 2722 (1960). **3.** a town in W West Virginia. 2632 (1960).

Wil·liams·ville (wil′yəmz vil), *n.* a town in W New York. 6316 (1960).

Wil′liam Tell′, a legendary Swiss patriot forced by the Austrian governor to shoot an apple off his son's head with bow and arrow. German, **Wilhelm Tell.**

Wil′liam the Con′queror. See **William I** (def. 1).

Wil·lie (wil′ē), *n.* **1.** a boy's given name, form of **William. 2.** a girl's given name. Also, **Willy.**

wil·lies (wil′ēz), *n.pl. Slang.* nervousness or fright; jitters; creeps (usually prec. by *the*): *That horror movie gave me the willies.* [?]

will·ing (wil′ing), *adj.* **1.** disposed or consenting; inclined: *I am willing to go despite her attitude.* **2.** cheerfully consenting or ready: *He is a willing worker.* **3.** done, given, borne, used, etc., with cheerful readiness. [ME; OE *willende*. See WILL[2], -ING[2]] —**will′ing·ly,** *adv.* —**will′ing·ness,** *n.*
—**Syn. 1.** minded.

Wil·lis (wil′is), *n.* a boy's given name, form of **William.**

Wil·lis·ton (wil′i stən), *n.* **1.** a city in NW North Dakota, on the Missouri River. 11,866 (1960). **2.** a town in W South Carolina. 2722 (1960).

Wil′liston Park′, a town on W Long Island, in SE New York. 8255 (1960).

Wil·lits (wil′its), *n.* a town in NW California. 3410 (1960).

wil·li·waw (wil′ə wô′), *n.* a violent squall that blows in the Strait of Magellan. Also, **wil′lie-wa′, wil′li·wau′, willy-waa, willywaw.** [var. of WILLY-WILLY]

Will·kie (wil′kē), *n.* **Wen·dell Lewis** (wen′dᵊl), 1892–1944, U.S. executive, lawyer, and political leader.

will-less (wil′lis), *adj.* **1.** having or exerting no will: *a timid, will-less little man.* **2.** done or occurring without the will; involuntary: *They showed a will-less compliance with the order.* **3.** leaving no will; intestate: *to die will-less.* —**will′-less·ly,** *adv.* —**will′-less·ness,** *n.*

will-o'-the-wisp (wil′ə thə wisp′), *n.* **1.** See **ignis fatuus** (def. 1). **2.** anything that deludes or misleads by luring on. [orig. *Will* (i.e. William) *with the wisp;* see WISP] —**will′o'-the-wisp′ish;** *esp. Brit.,* **will′o'-the-wisp′y,** *adj.*

Wil·lough·by (wil′ə bē), *n.* **1.** a city in NE Ohio, near Cleveland. 15,058 (1960). **2.** a boy's given name.

Wil′loughby Hills′, a town in NE Ohio. 4241 (1960).

wil·low (wil′ō), *n.* **1.** any tree or shrub of the genus *Salix,* many species of which have tough, pliable twigs or branches used for wickerwork, etc. **2.** the wood of any of these trees. **3.** *Informal.* something, esp. a cricket bat, made of willow wood. **4.** Also called **willower.** a machine consisting essentially of a cylinder armed with spikes revolving within a spiked casing, for opening and cleaning cotton or other fiber. —*v.t.* **5.** to treat (textile fibers) with a willow. [ME *wilwe,* var. of *wilghe,* OE *welig;* c. D *wilg,* LG *wilge,* Gk *helíkē* (aspirated var. of *elíkē* convolution < prehistoric **welikā*)] —**wil′low-like′,** *adj.* —**wil′low·ish,** *adj.*

wil·low·er (wil′ō ər), *n.* **1.** a person or a thing that willows. **2.** willow (def. 4). [alter. of *willyer;* see WILLY, -ER[1]]

wil′low herb′, 1. an onagraceous plant, *Epilobium* (*Chamaenerion*) *angustifolium,* having narrow, willowlike leaves and racemes of purple flowers. **2.** any plant of this genus. **3.** the purple loosestrife, *Lythrum Salicaria.*

Wil·lo·wick (wil′ə wik), *n.* a city in NE Ohio, near Cleveland. 18,749 (1960).

wil′low-leaved jas′mine (wil′ō lēvd′), a shrub, *Cestrum parqui,* of Chile, having willowlike leaves and clustered, whitish or yellowish flowers that are very fragrant at night.

wil′low myr′tle, a myrtaceous tree *Agonis flexuosa,* of Australia, having willowlike leaves and white flowers.

wil′low oak′, an oak, *Quercus Phellos,* of the southwestern U.S., having entire, lanceolate leaves, yielding a hard, heavy wood used in the construction of buildings.

wil′low pat′tern, a decorative design in English ceramics, depicting chiefly a willow tree, small bridge, and two birds, derived from Chinese sources and introduced in approximately 1780: often executed in blue and white but sometimes in red and white.

Wil′low Run′, a suburban area W of Detroit, Michigan, near Ypsilanti: airport.

Wil·lows (wil′ōz), *n.* a town in central California. 4139 (1960).

wil′low war′bler, any of several usually grayish-green leaf warblers, esp. *Phylloscopus trochilus,* of Europe.

wil·low·ware (wil′ō wâr′), *n.* china using the willow pattern. [WILLOW + WARE[1]]

wil·low-wort (wil′ō wûrt′), *n.* See **golden loosestrife.**

wil·low·y (wil′ō ē), *adj.* **1.** pliant; lithe. **2.** gracefully slender and supple. **3.** abounding with willows. [WILLOW + -Y[1]]

will′ pow′er, control of one's impulses and actions; self-control.

Wills (wilz), *n.* **Helen New·ing·ton** (no͞o′ing tən, nyo͞o′-), born 1906, U.S. tennis player.

Will·stät·ter (vil′shtet′ər), *n.* **Rich·ard** (rikн′ärt), 1872–1942, German chemist: Nobel prize 1915.

will′ to pow′er, (in the philosophy of Nietzche) the self-assertive drive in all individuals to live and to attain power, regarded as the supreme quality of the superman. Also called **will for power.**

wil·ly (wil′ē), *n.*, *pl.* **-lies,** *v.*, **-lied, -ly·ing.** —*n.* **1.** willow (def. 4). —*v.t.* **2.** to willow (cotton). [special use of dial. *willy,* OE *wilige* basket (orig. one made of willow twigs); akin to WILLOW]

ʼil·ly (wil′ē), *n.* **1.** a boy's given name, form of **William.** **2.** a girl's given name. Also, **Willie.**

ʼill·yard (wil′yərd), *adj. Scot. and North Eng.* obstinate; willful. Also, **will·yart** (wil′yərt). [? *willyar,* orig. basket-maker (whence surname *Willier*) but taken as derived from WILL² + *-d* -ED³; see WILLY, WILLOWER]

ʼil·ly-nil·ly (wil′ē nil′ē), *adv.* **1.** willingly or unwillingly: *He'll have to do it willy-nilly.* —*adj.* **2.** shilly-shallying; vacillating. [from the phrase *will ye, nill ye.* See WILL¹, NILL]

ʼil·ly-waa (wil′ē wô′), *n.* williwaw. Also, **wil′ly-waw′.**

ʼil·ly-wil·ly (wil′ē wil′ē), *n., pl.* **-lies.** *Australian.* a severe tropical cyclone. [< native Austral]

ʼil·ma (wil′mə), *n.* a girl's given name.

ʼil·mer (wil′mər), *n.* a boy's given name.

ʼil·mer·ding (wil′mər ding), *n.* a town in SW Pennsylvania. 4349 (1960).

ʼil·mette (wil met′), *n.* a city in NE Illinois, near Chicago. 28,268 (1960).

ʼil·ming·ton (wil′ming tən), *n.* **1.** a seaport in N Delaware, on the Delaware River. 95,827 (1960). **2.** a seaport in SE North Carolina, on the Cape Fear River. 44,013 (1960). **3.** a town in SW Ohio. 8915 (1960). **4.** a town in NE Illinois. 4210 (1960). —**Wil·ming·to·ni·an** (wil′ming tō′nē ən), *n.*

ʼil·more (wil′mōr, -môr), *n.* a town in central Kentucky. 2773 (1960).

ʼil′mot Provi′so (wil′mət), an amendment to a bill introduced into Congress in 1846, passed by the House of Representatives but rejected by the Senate, prohibiting slavery in territory purchased by the U.S. from Mexico.

ʼil·no (vēl′nô), *n.* Polish name of **Vilna.**

ʼil·son (wil′sən), *n.* **1. Angus Frank Johnstone,** born 1913, English writer. **2. Charles Thom·son Rees** (tom′sən rēs), 1869–1959, Scottish physicist: Nobel prize 1927. **3. Edmund,** 1895–1972, U.S. literary and social critic. **4. Henry** (*Jeremiah Jones Colbath*), 1812–1875, U.S. politician: vice-president of the U.S. 1873–75. **5. (James) Harold,** born 1916, British statesman: prime minister 1964–70, 1974–76. **6. John** ("*Christopher North*"), 1785–1854, Scottish poet, journalist, and critic. **7. (Thomas) Wood·row** (wŏŏd′rō), 1856–1924, 28th president of the U.S. 1913–21: Nobel peace prize 1919. **8. Sloan,** born 1920, U.S. journalist and novelist. **9. Mount,** a mountain in SW California, near Pasadena: observatory. 5710 ft. **10.** a city in E North Carolina. 28,753 (1960). **11.** a town in E Pennsylvania. 8465 (1960). **12.** a crater in the third quadrant of the face of the moon: about 40 miles in diameter. **13.** a boy's given name.

Wil′son cloud′ cham′ber, *Physics.* See **cloud chamber.** Also called **Wil′son cham′ber.** [named after Charles T. R. WILSON]

Wil′son Dam′, a dam on the Tennessee River, in NW Alabama, at Muscle Shoals: a part of the Tennessee Valley Authority. 4862 ft. long; 137 ft. high.

Wil·so·ni·an (wil sō′nē ən), *adj.* of, pertaining to, or characteristic of Woodrow Wilson. [WILSON + -IAN]

Wil·son·ism (wil′sə niz′əm), *n.* the theories, methods, or practices of Woodrow Wilson. Also, **Wil·so·ni·an·ism** (wil sō′nē ə niz′əm). [WILSON + -ISM]

Wils′on's black′cap. See **Wilson's warbler.**

Wil′son's pet′rel, a small petrel, *Oceanites oceanicus,* which breeds in the Southern Hemisphere but ranges into the North Atlantic and Pacific. [named after Alexander *Wilson* (1766–1813), Scottish-American ornithologist]

Wil′son's phal′arope, a phalarope, *Steganopus tricolor,* which breeds in the prairie regions of North America and winters in Argentina and Chile. [see WILSON'S PETREL]

Wil′son's snipe′, an American snipe, *Capella delicata,* having reddish-brown, black, and white plumage. See illus. under **snipe.** [see WILSON'S PETREL]

Wil′son's thrush′, veery. [see WILSON'S PETREL]

Wil′son's war′bler, a North American warbler, *Wilsonia pusilla,* having yellow plumage and a black patch on top of the head. Also called **Wilson's blackcap.** [see WILSON'S PETREL]

wilt¹ (wilt), *v.i.* **1.** to become limp and drooping, as a fading flower; wither. **2.** to lose strength, vigor, assurance, etc.: *The boy scouts wilted by the end of the hike.* —*v.t.* **3.** to cause to wilt. —*n.* **4.** act of wilting; state of being wilted: *There was a sudden wilt of interest in the discussion.* [dial. var. of *wilk* to wither, itself a var. of *welk,* ME *welke(n)* < MD; akin to WELKIN, G *welk* faded (orig., moist)]

wilt² (wilt), *v. Archaic.* second pers. sing. pres. ind. of **will**¹.

wilt³ (wilt), *n.* **1.** *Plant Pathol.* **a.** the drying out, drooping, and withering of the leaves of a plant due to inadequate water supply, excessive transpiration, or vascular disease. **b.** a disease so characterized. **2.** a virus disease of various caterpillars, characterized by the liquefaction of body tissues. Also, **wilt′ disease′** (for defs. 1b, 2). [special use of WILT¹]

Wilt (wilt), *n.* a boy's given name, form of **Wilton.**

Wil·ton (wil′tᵊn), *n.* Also called **Wil′ton car′pet, Wil′ton rug′.** a carpet woven like Brussels carpet, on a Jacquard loom but having the loops cut to form a velvet pile. [named after *Wilton,* town of Wiltshire, England]

Wil·ton (wil′tᵊn), *n.* a boy's given name.

Wil′ton Man′or, a town in S Florida. 8257 (1960).

Wilt·shire (wilt′shēr, -shər), *n.* **1.** Also, **Wilts** (wilts). a country in S England. 422,753 (1961); 1345 sq. mi. *Co. seat:* Salisbury. **2.** one of an English breed of white sheep having long, spiral horns. **3.** Also called **Wilt′shire cheese′.** a cylindrical, semihard cheese, moister and flakier than Cheddar.

wi·ly (wī′lē), *adj.,* **wil·i·er, wil·i·est.** full of, marked by, or proceeding from wiles; crafty; cunning. [ME; see WILE, -Y¹] —**wil′i·ly,** *adv.* —**wil′i·ness,** *n.*
—**Syn.** artful, sly, designing, intriguing, tricky, foxy, deceitful, treacherous. —**Ant.** straightforward, open.

wim·ble (wim′bəl), *n., v.,* **-bled, -bling.** —*n.* **1.** a device used in mining or the like for extracting the rubbish from a bored hole. **2.** a marbleworker's brace for drilling. **3.** any of various other instruments for boring. —*v.t.* **4.** to bore or perforate with or as with a wimble. [ME < MD or MLG *wimmel* auger; see GIMLET]

Wim·ble·don (wim′bəl dən), *n.* a city in N Surrey, in SE England, near London: international tennis tournaments. 56,994 (1961).

wim·min (wim′in), *n.pl. Eye Dialect.* women.

wimp (wimp), *n.* a weak, shy, ineffectual person. [orig. uncert.; cf. WHIMPER]

wim·ple (wim′pəl), *n., v.,* **-pled, -pling.** —*n.* **1.** a woman's headcloth drawn in folds about the chin, formerly worn out of doors, and still in use by nuns. **2.** *Chiefly Scot.* **a.** a fold or wrinkle, as in cloth. **b.** a curve, bend, or turn, as in a road or river. —*v.t.* **3.** to cover or muffle with or as with a wimple. **4.** to cause to ripple or undulate, as water. **5.** *Archaic.* to veil or enwrap. —*v.i.* **6.** to ripple, as water. **7.** *Archaic.* to lie in folds, as a veil. **8.** *Chiefly Scot.* to follow a curving course, as a road or river. [ME, var. of ME, OE *wimpel;* c. D, LG *wimpel,* Icel *vimpill*]

Wimple

Wims′hurst machine′ (wimz′hûrst), *Elect.* a device for the production of electric charges by electrostatic action, consisting of two discs revolving in opposite directions such that the friction between them generates the electricity. Also called **Wims′hurst gen′erator.** [named after J. *Wimshurst* (d. 1903), English engineer]

win¹ (win), *v.,* **won** or (*Obs.*) **wan; won; win·ning;** *n.* —*v.i.* **1.** to finish first in a race, contest, or the like. **2.** to succeed by striving or effort (sometimes fol. by *out*): *He applied for a scholarship and won. His finer nature won out.* **3.** to gain the victory; overcome an adversary: *The home team won.* —*v.t.* **4.** to succeed in reaching (a place, condition, etc.), esp. by great effort: *They won the shore through a violent storm.* **5.** to get by effort, as through labor, competition, or conquest: *He won his post after years of striving.* **6.** to gain (a prize, fame, etc.): *He won the prize by being the first to finish the race.* **7.** to be successful in (a game, battle, etc.). **8.** to make (one's way), as by effort, ability, etc. **9.** to attain or reach (a point, goal, etc.). **10.** to gain (favor, love, consent, etc.) as by qualities or influence. **11.** to gain the favor, regard, or adherence of. **12.** to gain the consent or support of; persuade (often fol. by *over*): *The speech won him over to our side.* **13.** to persuade to marry; gain in marriage. **14.** *Brit. Mining.* **a.** to obtain (ore, coal, etc.). **b.** to prepare (a vein, bed, mine, etc.) for working, by means of shafts or the like. —*n.* **15.** a victory, as in a game or horse race. **16.** *U.S.* the position of the competitor who comes in first in a horse race, harness race, etc. Cf. **place** (def. 30b), **show** (def. 33). [ME *winne(n),* OE *winnan* to work, fight, bear; c. G *(ge)winnen,* Goth *winnan,* Icel *vinna*] —**win′na·ble,** *adj.*
—**Syn. 5.** obtain, secure, acquire, achieve, reach, procure. See **gain**¹. **12.** convince.

win² (win), *v.,* **winned, win·ning.** *Scot. and North Eng.* —*v.i.* **1.** to reside; dwell. —*v.t.* **2.** to dry (hay, wood, etc.) by exposure to air and sun. [? var. of WINNOW]

Win (win), *n.* a boy's given name, form of **Winchell** or **Winston.**

wince¹ (wins), *v.,* **winced, winc·ing,** *n.* —*v.i.* **1.** to shrink, as in pain or from a blow; start; flinch. —*n.* **2.** a wincing or shrinking movement; a slight start. [ME *winse(n),* var. of *winche(n), wenche(n)* (to) kick < AF **wenc(h)ier* (equiv. to OF *guenc(h)ier*) < Gmc (? OE). Cf. WENCH, WINCH¹] —**winc′er,** *n.* —**winc′ing·ly,** *adv.* —**winc′ing·ness,** *n.*
—**Syn. 1.** blench, quail, avoid.

wince² (wins), *n.* winch¹ (def. 4).

winch¹ (winch), *n.* **1.** the crank or handle of a revolving machine. **2.** a windlass turned by a crank, for hoisting or hauling. **3.** any of various devices for cranking. **4.** Also, **wince.** *Textiles.* **a.** any machine equipped with rollers that guide cloth through a dye or finishing solution in an open vat. **b.** a roller between two dyeing vats for passing cloth from one vat to another. —*v.t.* **5.** to hoist or haul by means of a winch. [ME *winche,* OE *wince* pulley; akin to WENCH, WINCE¹, WINK¹] —**winch′er,** *n.*

winch² (winch), *v.i., n. Archaic.* wince¹.

Win·chell (win′chəl), *n.* a boy's given name.

Win·ches·ter (win′ches′tər, -chi stər), *n.* **1.** a city in and the county seat of Hampshire, in S England: cathedral; capital of the early Wessex kingdom and of medieval England. 46,230 (1961). **2.** a city in N Virginia: Civil War battles 1862, 1864. 15,110 (1960). **3.** a town in E Massachusetts, near Boston. 19,376 (1960). **4.** a town in E Indiana. 5742 (1960). **5.** a town in S Tennessee. 4760 (1960). **6.** See **Winchester rifle.**

Win′chester bush′el. See under **bushel**¹ (def. 1). [named after WINCHESTER, England]

Win′chester ri′fle, a type of magazine rifle, first made in about 1866. [named after D. F. *Winchester* (1810–80), American manufacturer]

Winck·el·mann (ving′kəl män′), *n.* **Jo·hann Jo·a·chim** (yō′hän yō′ä кнim), 1717–68, German archaeologist and art historian.

wind¹ (*n.* wind, *Poetic* wīnd; *v.* wind), *n.* **1.** air in natural motion, as along the earth's surface. **2.** a gale; storm; hurricane. **3.** any stream of air, as that produced by a bellows, fan, etc. **4.** air that is blown or forced to produce a musical sound in singing or playing an instrument. **5.** See **wind instrument.** **6.** wind instruments collectively. **7. the winds,** the members of an orchestra or band who play the wind instruments. **8.** breath or breathing: *to catch one's wind.* **9.** the power of breathing freely, as during continued exertion: *Smoking affected his wind.* **10.** any influential force or trend: *strong winds of public opinion.* **11.** a hint or intimation: *to catch wind of a stock split.* **12.** air carrying an animal's odor or scent. **13.** empty talk; mere words. **14.** vanity; conceitedness. **15.** gas generated in the stomach and intestines. **16.** *Boxing Slang.* the pit of the stomach where a blow may cause a temporary shortness of breath; solar plexus. **17.** any direction of the compass. **18.** a state of unconcern, recklessness, or abandon: *to throw all caution to the winds.* **19. between wind and water, a.** (of a ship) at or near the water line. **b.** in a vulnerable or precarious spot: *In his profession one is always between wind and water.* **20. break wind,** to expel gas from the stomach and bowels through the anus. **21. how the wind blows** or **lies,** what the tendency or probability is: *Try to find out how the wind blows.* Also, **which way the wind blows.** **22. in the teeth of the wind,** sailing directly into the wind; against the wind. Also, **in the eye of the wind, in the wind's eye.** **23. in the wind,** about to occur; imminent; impending: *There's good news in the wind.* **24. off the wind, a.** away from the wind; with the wind at one's back. **b.** (of a sailing vessel) headed into the wind with sails shaking or aback. **25. on the wind,** as close as possible to the wind. Also, **on a wind.** **26. sail close to the wind, a.** Also, **sail close on a wind.** to sail as nearly as possible in the direction from which the wind is blowing. **b.** to practice economy in the management of one's affairs. **c.** to verge on a breach of propriety or decency. **d.** to escape (punishment, detection, etc.) by a narrow margin; take a risk. **27. take the wind out of one's sails,** to destroy a person's self-assurance, as by unexpectedly disproving his argument; disconcert; deflate; frustrate: *Foreign competition for a time nearly took the wind out of the sails of the auto industry.* —*v.t.* **28.** to expose to wind or air. **29.** to follow by the scent. **30.** to make short of wind or breath, as by vigorous exercise. **31.** to let recover breath, as by resting after exertion. —*v.i.* **32.** to catch the scent or odor of game. [ME, OE; c. D, G *Wind,* Icel *vindr,* Goth *winds,* L *ventus*]
—**Syn. 1.** WIND, AIR, ZEPHYR, BREEZE, BLAST, GUST refer to a quantity of air set in motion naturally. WIND applies to any such air in motion, blowing with whatever degree of gentleness or violence. AIR, usually poetical, applies to a very gentle motion of the air. ZEPHYR, also poetical, refers to an air characterized by its soft, mild quality. A BREEZE is usually a cool, light wind. BLAST and GUST apply to quick, forceful winds of short duration; BLAST implies a violent rush of air, often a cold one, whereas a GUST is little more than a flurry. **15.** flatulence.

wind² (wīnd), *v.,* **wound** or (*Rare*) **wind·ed; wind·ing;** *n.* —*v.i.* **1.** to change direction; bend; turn; take a frequently bending course; meander: *The river winds through the forest.* **2.** to have a circular or spiral course or direction. **3.** to coil or twine about something: *The ivy winds around the house.* **4.** to be twisted or warped, as a board. **5.** to proceed circuitously or indirectly. **6.** to undergo winding, or winding up. —*v.t.* **7.** to encircle or wreathe, as with something twined, wrapped, or placed about. **8.** to roll or coil (thread, string, etc.) into a ball, on a spool, or the like (often fol. by *up*). **9.** to remove or take off by unwinding (usually fol. by *off* or *from*): *She wound the thread off the bobbin.* **10.** to twine, fold, wrap, or place about something. **11.** to adjust (a mechanism) for operation by some turning or coiling process (often fol. by *up*): *to wind a clock.* **12.** to haul or hoist by means of a winch, windlass, or the like (often fol. by *up*). **13.** to make (one's or its way) in a winding or frequently bending course: *The stream winds its way through the woods.* **14.** to make (one's or its way) by indirect, stealthy, or devious procedure: *to wind one's way into another's confidence; a doubt that winds its way into one's consciousness.* **15. wind up, a.** to bring to a state of great tension; excite: *He was all wound up before the game.* **b.** to bring or come to an end; conclude: *to wind up the campaign.* **c.** to settle or arrange in order to conclude: *to wind up one's affairs.* **d.** *Baseball.* (of a pitcher) to execute a windup. —*n.* **16.** act of winding. **17.** a single turn, twist, or bend of something wound: *If you give it another wind, you'll break the mainspring.* **18.** a twist producing an uneven surface. **19. out of wind,** (of boards, plasterwork, etc.) flat and true. [ME; OE *wind(an);* c. D, G *winden,* Icel *vinda,* Goth *-windan;* akin to WEND, WANDER]

wind³ (wīnd, wind), *v.t.,* **wind·ed** or **wound, wind·ing.** **1.** to blow (a horn, a blast, etc.). **2.** to sound by blowing. **3.** to signal or direct by blasts of the horn or the like. [special use of WIND¹]

wind·a·ble (wīn′də bəl), *adj.* that can be wound. [WIND² + -ABLE]

wind·age (win′dij), *n.* **1.** the influence of the wind in deflecting a missile. **2.** the amount of such deflection. **3.** the degree to which a gunsight must be adjusted to correct for windage. **4.** a difference between the diameter of a projectile and that of the gun bore, for the escape of gas and the prevention of friction. **5.** *Naut.* that portion of a vessel's surface upon which the wind acts. **6.** *Mach.* friction between a rotor and the air within its casing, as in an electric generator. **7.** *Elect.* the resisting influence of air against the rotating armature of a dynamo, creating a power loss. [WIND¹ + -AGE]

Win·daus (vin′dous), *n.* **A·dolf** (ä′dôlf), 1876–1959, German chemist: Nobel prize 1928.

wind·bag (wind′bag′), *n.* **1.** *Slang.* an empty, voluble, pretentious talker. **2.** the bag of a bagpipe. [late ME; see WIND¹, BAG] —**wind′bag′ger·y,** *n.*

wind-bell (wind′bel′), *n.* **1.** a bell sounded by the action of the wind. **2.** Usually, **wind-bells.** a group of small pieces of glass, metal, etc., hanging freely in proximity and sounded by the action of the wind.

Wind·ber (wind′bər), *n.* a town in central Pennsylvania. 6994 (1960).

wind·blown (wind′blōn′), *adj.* **1.** blown by the wind: *windblown hair.* **2.** (of trees) growing in a certain shape because of strong prevailing winds. **3.** (of a hair style) bobbed short, with the ends combed toward the forehead. [WIND¹ + BLOWN¹]

wind-borne (wind′bōrn′, -bôrn′), *adj.* carried by the wind, as pollen or seed.

wind·bound (wind′bound′), *adj.* (of a sailing ship, sailboat, or the like) kept from sailing by a wind from the wrong direction or one of too high velocity. [WIND¹ + -BOUND¹]

wind·break (wind′brāk′), *n.* a growth of trees, a structure of boards, or the like, serving as a shelter from the wind. [WIND¹ + BREAK]

Wind·break·er (wind′brā′kər), *n. Trademark.* a waist-length or slightly longer jacket of suede or chamois leather or like material, with a close-fitting elastic hip band and cuffs, often having a collar, for sports or other outdoor wear.

wind-bro·ken (wind′brō′kən), *adj. Vet. Med.* (of horses) having the breathing impaired; affected with heaves.

wind·burn (wind′bûrn′), *n.* an inflammation of the skin, esp. that of the face and hands, caused by overexposure to the wind. [WIND¹ + BURN¹] —**wind′-burned′,** *adj.*

Wind′ Cave′ Na′tional Park′ (wind), a national park in SW South Dakota. 41½ sq. mi.

wind·cheat·er (wind′chē′tər), *n.* *Chiefly Brit.* a lightweight jacket for sports or other outdoor wear. [WIND¹ + CHEATER]

wind·chest (wind′chest′), *n.* a chamber containing the air supply for the reeds or pipes of an organ. [WIND¹ + CHEST]

wind′ chill′, the coldness felt on the exposed human flesh by a combination of temperature and wind velocity. Also called **wind′-chill fac′tor.**

wind′ col′ic (wind), *Vet. Med.* (esp. in horses) flatulence caused by gases that result from the eating of fermenting vegetation; bloat.

wind′ cone′ (wind), windsock.

wind·ed (win′did), *adj.* **1.** having wind or breath of a specified kind (usually used in combination): *short-winded; broken-winded.* **2.** out of breath. [late ME; see WIND¹, -ED³] —**wind′ed·ness,** *n.*

wind·er (wīn′dər), *n.* **1.** one who or that which winds. **2.** a staircase step for changing direction. Cf. **flier** (def. 7). **3.** a plant that coils or twines itself about something. **4.** an instrument or a machine for winding thread or the like. [WIND² + -ER¹]

Win·der (wīn′dər), *n.* a town in central Georgia. 5555 (1960).

Win·der·mere (win′dər mēr′), *n.* **Lake,** a lake in NW England, between Westmorland and Lancashire: the largest lake in England. 10½ mi. long; 5⅔ sq. mi.

wind′ ero′sion (wind), the erosion, transportation, and deposition of topsoil by the wind, esp. in dust storms.

wind·fall (wind′fôl′), *n.* **1.** something blown down by the wind, as fruit. **2.** an unexpected gain, piece of good fortune, or the like. [late ME; see WIND¹, FALL]

wind·flaw (wind′flô′), *n.* flaw² (def. 1). [WIND¹ + FLAW²]

wind·flow·er (wind′flou′ər), *n.* any plant of the genus *Anemone.* [trans. of ANEMONE]

wind·gall (wind′gôl′), *n.* *Vet. Med.* a puffy distention of the synovial bursa at the fetlock joint. [WIND¹ + GALL²] —**wind′galled′,** *adj.*

wind′ gap′ (wind), a cut that indents only the upper part of a mountain ridge.

wind′ gauge′ (wind), **1.** anemometer. **2.** a scale on the rear sight of a rifle by which the sight is adjusted to correct for windage.

Wind·ham (win′dəm), *n.* a town in NE Ohio. 3777 (1960).

wind′ harp′ (wind). See **aeolian harp.**

Wind·hoek (*Du.* vint′ho͝ok′), *n.* a city in and the capital of South-West Africa, in the central part. 36,016 (1960).

wind·hov·er (wind′huv′ər, -hov-), *n.* the kestrel, *Fako tinnunculus.* [WIND¹ + HOVER; from its hovering flight, head to the wind]

wind′ in′dicator (wind), a large weathervane used at airports to indicate wind direction.

wind·ing (wīn′ding), *n.* **1.** act of one who or that which winds. **2.** a bend, turn, or flexure. **3.** a coiling, folding, or wrapping, as of one thing about another. **4.** something that is wound or coiled, or a single round of it. **5.** *Elect.* **a.** a symmetrically laid, electrically conducting current path in any device. **b.** the manner of such coiling: *a series winding.* —*adj.* **6.** bending or turning; sinuous. **7.** spiral, as stairs. [ME (n.), OE *windung* (n.), equiv. to *wind-* WIND² + *-ung*, gradative var. of -ING¹; see -ING²] —**wind′ing·ly,** *adv.* —**wind′ing·ness,** *n.*

wind′ing frame′, a machine on which yarn or thread is wound.

wind′ing num′ber, *Math.* the number of times a closed curve winds around a point not on the curve. Also called **index.**

wind′ing sheet′, **1.** a sheet in which a corpse is wrapped for burial. **2.** a mass of tallow or wax that has run down and hardened on the side of a candle, sometimes considered an omen of misfortune. [late ME; see WINDING, SHEET¹]

wind′ in′strument (wind), a musical instrument sounded by the breath or other air current, as the trumpet, trombone, clarinet, flute, etc.

wind·jam·mer (wind′jam′ər, win′-), *n.* *Informal.* **1.** (formerly) a merchant ship propelled by sails. **2.** any large sailing ship. **3.** a member of its crew. **4.** *Slang.* a long-winded person; a great talker. [WIND¹ + *jammer* (see JAM¹, -ER¹); so called in contempt]

wind·lass (wind′ləs), *n.* **1.** a device for raising or hauling objects, usually consisting of a horizontal cylinder or barrel turned by a crank, lever, motor, or the like, upon which a cable, rope, or chain winds, the outer end of the cable being attached directly or indirectly to the weight to be raised or the thing to be hauled or pulled; winch. —*v.t.* **2.** to raise, haul, or move by means of a windlass. [ME *windelas*, equiv. to *windel(en)*, freq. of *winden* to WIND², + *-as* pole (< Scand; cf. Icel *āss* beam, pole)]

Windlass (Hand operated)

wind′lass bitt′. See **carrick bitt.**

win·dle (win′dᵊl, win′ᵊl), *n.* *Scot. and North Eng.* a measure of corn, wheat, or other commodities equal to approximately three bushels, but varying in different regions. [ME *wyndel*, OE *windel* box, basket; akin to WIND²]

wind·less (wind′lis), *adj.* **1.** free from wind; calm: *a windless day.* **2.** out of breath. [late ME; see WIND¹, -LESS] —**wind′less·ly,** *adv.* —**wind′less·ness,** *n.*

win·dle·straw (win′dᵊl strô′, win′ᵊl-), *n.* *Brit. Dial.* **1.** a withered stalk of any of various grasses. **2.** any of various long-stalked species of grass. **3.** any tall, thin person. **4.** any light or flimsy material or object. Also, *esp. Scot.,* **winlestrae.** [OE *windelstrēaw.* See WINDLE, STRAW]

wind·mill (wind′mil′), *n.* **1.** any of various machines for grinding, pumping, etc., driven by the force of the wind acting upon a number of vanes or sails. **2.** *Aeron.* a small air turbine with blades, like those of an airplane propeller, exposed on a moving aircraft and driven by the air, used to operate gasoline pumps, radio apparatus, etc. **3.** an imaginary opponent, wrong, etc. (in allusion to Cervantes' *Don Quixote*): *to fight windmills; to tilt at windmills.* —*v.t.* **4.** *Aeron.* (of a propeller engine or turbojet engine) to rotate solely under the force of a passing airstream. [ME; see WIND¹, MILL¹]

wind of 120 days (wind), Seistan.

Win·dom (win′dəm), *n.* a town in SW Minnesota. 3691 (1960).

Windmill

win·dow (win′dō), *n.* **1.** an opening in the wall of a building, the side of a vehicle, etc., for the admission of air or light, or both, commonly fitted with a frame in which are set movable sashes containing panes of glass. **2.** such an opening with the frame, sashes, and panes of glass, or any other device, by which it is closed. **3.** the frame, sashes, and panes of glass, or the like, intended to fit such an opening: *Finally the builders put in the windows.* **4.** a windowpane. **5.** anything likened to a window in appearance or function, as a transparent section in an envelope, displaying the address. **6.** metal strips, wires, or bars dropped from aircraft or ejected from missiles to confuse hostile radar detectors; chaff. —*v.t.* **7.** to furnish with a window or windows. **8.** *Obs.* to display, place, or put in a window. [ME *windoge, windowe* < Scand; cf. Icel *vindauga*, equiv. to *vindr* wind + *auga* eye] —**win′dow·less,** *adj.* —**win′dow·y,** *adj.*

win′dow back′, woodwork, esp. paneling, beneath the stool of a window.

win′dow box′, **1.** a box for growing plants, placed at or in a window. **2.** a hollow space in a window frame for a sash weight.

win′dow dress′er, a person employed to decorate the display windows of a store, usually with merchandise offered for sale.

win′dow dress′ing, **1.** the art, act, or technique of decorating the display windows of a store. **2.** misrepresentation of facts, as of one's financial condition, so as to give a more favorable impression.

win′dowless mon′ad, (in the philosophy of Leibnitz) a monad having no direct causal or perceptual relation with any other monad.

win·dow·light (win′dō līt′), *n.* windowpane (def. 1). [WINDOW + LIGHT¹]

win·dow·pane (win′dō pān′), *n.* **1.** a plate of glass for filling a window sash within the frame. **2.** a flounder, *Scophthalmus aquosus,* found along the Atlantic coast of North America, characterized by the thinness and translucency of its body. [WINDOW + PANE]

win′dow sash′, the frame holding the pane or panes of a window.

win′dow seat′, **1.** a seat built beneath the sill of a recessed or other window. **2.** a bench having two arms and no back.

win′dow shade′, a shade or blind for a window, usually a sheet of sturdy, sized cloth or paper on a spring roller.

win·dow-shop (win′dō shop′), *v.i.,* **-shopped, -shop·ping.** to look at articles in the windows of stores without making any purchases. —**win′dow-shop′per,** *n.*

win′dow sill′, the sill under a window.

wind·pipe (wind′pīp′), *n.* the trachea of an air-breathing vertebrate. [WIND¹ + PIPE¹]

wind-pol·li·nat·ed (wind′pol′ə nā′tid), *adj.* *Bot.* being pollinated by air-borne pollen. —**wind′-pol′li·na′tion,** *n.*

wind′ pop′py (wind), an annual herb, *Meconopsis heterophylla,* of western North America, having satiny, brick-red flowers with purple centers.

wind·proof (wind′pro͞of′), *adj.* resisting wind, as fabric, a jacket, coat, etc. [WIND¹ + -PROOF]

wind′ pump′ (wind), a pump driven by a windmill.

Wind′ Riv′er Range′ (wind), a mountain range in W Wyoming, part of the Rocky Mountains. Highest peak, Gannett Peak, 13,785 ft.

wind·rode (wind′rōd′), *adj.* *Naut.* (of a moored vessel) riding with the force of the wind. Cf. **tiderode.** [WIND¹ + RODE]

wind′ rose′ (wind), **1.** a map symbol showing, for a given locality or area, the frequency and strength of the wind from various directions. **2.** a diagram showing the relation of wind direction to other weather conditions at a given location.

wind·row (wind′rō′, win′-), *n.* **1.** a row or line of hay raked together to dry before being made into cocks or heaps. **2.** any similar row, as of sheaves of grain, made for the purpose of drying. **3.** a row of dry leaves, dust, etc., swept together by the wind. —*v.t.* **4.** to arrange in a windrow or windrows. [WIND¹ + ROW²] —**wind′row′er,** *n.*

wind′ sail′ (wind), *Naut.* a sail rigged over a hatchway, ventilator, or the like, to divert moving air downward into the vessel.

wind′ scale′ (wind), a numerical scale, as the Beaufort scale, for designating relative wind intensities.

wind·screen (wind′skrēn′, win′-), *n.* *Chiefly Brit.* windshield.

wind′ shaft′ (wind), the shaft driven by the sails of a windmill.

wind′ shake′ (wind), **1.** a flaw in wood supposed to be caused by the action of strong winds upon the trunk of the tree. **2.** such flaws collectively. Also called **cup shake.**

wind·shak·en (wind′shā′kən), *adj.* **1.** affected by windshake. **2.** shaken by the wind.

wind′ shear′ (wind), **1.** the rate at which the wind's velocity changes from point to point in any direction. **2.** a condition in which the speed or direction of the wind changes abruptly, thereby endangering aircraft.

wind′ shelf′ (wind). See **smoke shelf.**

wind·shield (wind′shēld′, win′-), *n.* a shield of glass, in one or more sections, projecting above and across the dashboard of an automobile. Also called, *esp. Brit.,* **wind-screen.** [WIND¹ + SHIELD]

wind′shield wip′er, an automatic device consisting of a squeegee connected to a mechanical arm attached to a windshield, used to maintain clarity of vision by wiping off rain, snow, etc.

wind′ ship′ (wind), a large sailing vessel.

wind′ sleeve′ (wind), windsock.

wind·sock (wind′sok′), *n.* a tapered, tubular cloth vane, open at both ends and having at the larger end a fixed ring pivoted to swing freely at the top of a pole or stanchion to catch the wind, installed at airports or elsewhere to indicate wind direction and approximate intensity. Also called **air sock, wind cone, wind sleeve.** [WIND¹ + SOCK¹]

Wind·sor (win′zər), *n.* **1.** a member of the royal family that has ruled England since 1917. **2. Duke of.** See **Edward VIII.** **3.** Also called **New Windsor.** a city in E Berkshire, in S England, on the Thames: the site of the residence **(Wind′sor Cas′tle)** of English sovereigns since William the Conqueror. 27,126 (1961). **4.** a city in S Ontario, in SE Canada, opposite Detroit, Michigan. 114,367 (1961). **5.** a town in E Vermont. 3256 (1960). **6.** a town in central Missouri. 2714 (1960).

Wind′sor bench′, a bench similar in construction to a Windsor chair. Also called **Wind′sor settee′.**

Wind′sor chair′, (*sometimes l.c.*) a wooden chair of many varieties, having a spindle back and legs slanting outward: common in 18th-century England and in the American colonies.

Windsor chairs

Wind′sor Heights′, a town in central Iowa 5906 (1960).

Wind′sor knot′, a wide, triangular knot for tying a four-in-hand necktie.

Wind′sor tie′, a wide, soft necktie of black silk, tied at the neck in a loose bow.

wind′ star′ (wind), *Navig.* a diagram illustrating wind velocities and directions determined by the double drift method.

wind·storm (wind′stôrm′), *n.* a storm with heavy wind, but little or no precipitation. [WIND¹ + STORM]

wind·suck·er (wind′suk′ər), *n.* *Vet. Med.* a horse afflicted with cribbing. [WIND¹ + SUCKER]

wind·suck·ing (wind′suk′ing), *n.* *Vet. Med.* cribbing (def. 1).

wind·surf·ing (wind′sûr′fing), *n.* a form of sailing in which a flexible sail is mounted on a surfboard and the craft is guided while standing up. [WIND¹ + SURF + -ING¹] —**wind′surf′er,** *n.*

wind-swept (wind′swept′), *adj.* open or exposed to the wind: *a wind-swept beach.*

wind′ tee′ (wind), a large, T-shaped weather vane on or near an airfield. Also called **air tee, landing tee.**

wind·tight (wind′tīt′), *adj.* so tight as to prevent passage of wind or air. [WIND¹ + TIGHT]

wind′ tun′nel (wind), *Aeron.* a tube in which a steady current of air can be maintained at a controlled velocity, equipped with devices for measuring and recording forces and moments on scale models of complete aircraft or of their parts or, sometimes, on full-scale aircraft or their parts.

wind·up (wīnd′up′), *n.* **1.** the conclusion of any action, activity, etc.; the end or close. **2.** a final act or part. **3.** *Baseball.* the preparatory movements of the arm before pitching a ball. Cf. **stretch** (def. 22). [n. use of v. phrase *wind up*]

wind′ vane′ (wind), vane (def. 1).

wind·ward (wind′wərd), *adv.* **1.** toward the wind; toward the point from which the wind blows. —*adj.* **2.** pertaining to, situated in, or moving toward the quarter from which the wind blows (opposed to *leeward*). —*n.* **3.** the point or quarter from which the wind blows. **4.** the side toward the wind. **5. to windward,** in a position of vantage: *We got to windward of the difficulty.* Also, **to the windward.** [WIND¹ + -WARD] —**wind′ward·ness,** *n.*

Wind′ward Is′lands, **1.** a group of islands in the SE West Indies, consisting of the S part of the Lesser Antilles: includes British and French territories. **2.** a group of British islands in the SE West Indies, consisting of Dominica, St. Lucia, Grenada, and St. Vincent, and their dependencies. 314,295 (1960); 821 sq. mi.

Wind′ward Pas′sage, a strait in the West Indies, between Cuba and Haiti. 50 mi. wide.

wind·way (wind′wā′), *n.* **1.** a passage for air. **2.** *Music.* flue¹ (def. 4b). [WIND¹ + WAY]

wind·y (win′dē), *adj.,* **wind·i·er, wind·i·est.** **1.** accompanied or characterized by wind: *a windy day.* **2.** exposed to or swept by the wind: *a windy hill.* **3.** consisting of or resembling wind: *a windy tempest of activity.* **4.** toward the wind; windward. **5.** unsubstantial or empty. **6.** of the nature of, characterized by, or given to prolonged, empty talk; voluble; verbose; bombastic. **7.** characterized by or causing flatulence. **8.** *Chiefly Scot.* boastful. [ME; OE *windig.* See WIND¹, -Y¹] —**wind′i·ly,** *adv.* —**wind′i·ness,** *n.*

Wind′y Cit′y, **1.** Chicago, Ill. (usually prec. by *the*): *We spent a wonderful weekend in the Windy City.* **2.** of or pertaining to Chicago: *taking a fling at Windy City politics.*

windz (winz), *n.* winze.

wine (wīn), *n., adj., v.,* **wined, win·ing.** —*n.* **1.** fermented juice of the grape, made in many varieties such as red, white, sweet, dry, still, and sparkling, for use as a beverage, in cookery, religious rites, etc., and usually having an alcoholic content of 14 percent or less. **2.** a particular variety of such fermented grape juice: *port and sherry wines.* **3.** the juice, fermented or unfermented, of various other fruits or plants, used as a beverage, sauce, etc.: *gooseberry wine; currant wine.* **4.** a dark reddish color, as of red wines. **5.** *Pharm.* vinum. **6.** something that invigorates, cheers, or intoxicates like wine. **7.** *Brit.* **a.** a social gathering at which wine is the major beverage. **b.** a party, esp. one held by university students, for drinking wine. **8.** *Obs.* intoxication due to the drinking of wine. **9. new wine in old bottles,** something new placed in or superimposed on an old or existing form, system, etc. Matt. 9:17. —*adj.* **10.** dark red in color. —*v.t.* **11.** to supply with wine: *He wined his cellar with rare vintages.* —*v.i.* **12.** to drink wine. **13. wine and dine,** to entertain lavishly: *They wined and dined him in order to get him to sign the new contract.* [ME, OE *wīn* (c. G *Wein,* D *wijn,* Icel *vīn,* Goth *wein*) << L *vīnum,* c. Gk *oinos* < ?] —**wine′less,** *adj.* —**win′ish,** *adj.*

wine·ber·ry (wīn′ber′ē, -bə rē), *n., pl.* **-ries. 1.** a prickly shrub, *Rubus phoenicolasius,* of China and Japan, having pinkish or white flowers and small, red fruits. **2.** the fruit of this plant. [ME *winberie,* OE *wīnberige* grape. See WINE, BERRY]

wine·bib·ber (wīn′bib′ər), *n.* one who drinks much wine. [WINE + BIBBER] —**wine′bib′bing,** *n., adj.*

wine′ cel′lar, 1. a cellar for the storage of wine. **2.** the wine stored there; a store or stock of wines.

wine-col·ored (wīn′kul′ərd), *adj.* of the color of wine; dark red.

wine-cool·er (wīn′ko͞o′lər), *n.* a bucket for holding ice to chill a bottle of wine.

wine′ gal′lon, a former English gallon of 231 cubic inches: equal to the present U.S. standard gallon.

wine·glass (wīn′glas′, -gläs′), *n.* **1.** a drinking glass, as a goblet, having a foot and a stem and used specifically for serving wine. **2.** *Naut.* a transverse section amidships of a hull, as that of a keeled sailboat, resembling a wineglass in silhouette. [WINE + GLASS]

wine·glass·ful (wīn′glas′fo͝ol′, -gläs′-), *n., pl.* **-fuls.** the capacity of a wineglass, commonly considered as equal to 2 fluid ounces or ¼ cup. [WINEGLASS + -FUL]

wine·grow·er (wīn′grō′ər), *n.* one who owns or works in a vineyard and winery. [WINE + GROWER]

wine·grow·ing (wīn′grō′ing), *n.* **1.** the work or business of a winegrower. **2.** the industry of producing wine. [WINE + GROWING]

wine′ meas′ure, a former English system of measures for wine, in which the wine gallon was equal to 231 cubic inches, and which was smaller than the gallon for beer.

wine′ palm′, any of various palms yielding toddy. Cf. **toddy** (def. 2).

wine′ press′, a machine in which the juice is pressed from grapes for wine. Also, **wine′ press′er.**

win·er·y (wī′nə rē), *n., pl.* **-er·ies.** an establishment for making wine. [WINE + -ERY]

Wine·sap (wīn′sap′), *n.* **1.** a red variety of apple that ripens in the autumn. **2.** the tree bearing this fruit. [WINE + SAP[1]]

Wines′burg, Ohi′o (wīnz′bûrg), a cycle of short stories (1919) by Sherwood Anderson.

wine·shop (wīn′shop′), *n.* a shop where wine is sold. [WINE + SHOP]

wine·skin (wīn′skin′), *n.* a vessel made of the nearly complete skin of a goat or the like, used, esp. in the East, for holding wine. [WINE + SKIN]

wine′ ta′ble, a horseshoe-shaped serving table.

Win·field (win′fēld′), *n.* **1.** a town in NW Alabama. 2907 (1960). **2.** a boy's given name.

Win·fred (win′frid), *n.* a boy's given name.

wing (wing), *n.* **1.** either of the two anterior extremities or appendages of the scapular arch or shoulder girdle of most birds and of bats, which constitute the forelimbs and correspond to the human arms and are adapted for flight. **2.** either of two corresponding parts in flightless birds, which may be rudimentary, as in certain ratite birds, or adapted for swimming, as in penguins. **3.** any of certain other winglike structures of other animals, as the patagium of a flying squirrel. **4.** one of the paired, thin, lateral extensions of the body wall of an insect, located on the mesothorax and the metathorax, by means of which it flies. **5.** a similar structure with which gods, angels, demons, etc., are conceived to be provided for the purpose of flying. **6.** *Informal.* an arm of a human being, esp. a baseball player's pitching or throwing arm. **7.** a means or instrument of flight, travel, or progress. **8.** the act or manner of flying. **9.** something resembling or likened to a bird's wing, as a vane or sail of a windmill. **10.** *Aeron.* **a.** that portion of a main supporting surface confined to one side of an airplane. **b.** both portions taken collectively. **11.** *Archit.* a part of a building projecting on one side of, or subordinate to, a central or main part. **12.** *Furniture.* either of two forward extensions of the sides of the back of an easy chair. **13.** *Mil., Navy.* either of the two side portions of an army or fleet, usually called right wing and left wing, and distinguished from the center; flank units. **14.** *U.S.* an administrative and tactical unit of the Air Force consisting of two or more groups, headquarters, and certain supporting and service units. **15.** (in flight formation) noting a position to the side and just to the rear of another airplane. **16.** *Fort.* either of the longer sides of a crownwork, uniting it to the main work. **17.** *Sports.* **a.** (in some team games) any one of the positions, or a player in such a position, on the far side of the center position, known as the left and right wings with reference to the direction of the opposite goal. **b.** such a position or player in the first line of a team. **18.** *Theat.* **a.** the platform or space on the right or left of the stage proper. **b.** See **wing flat. 19.** *Anat.* an ala: *the wings of the sphenoid.* **20.** *Bot.* **a.** any leaflike expansion, as of a samara. **b.** one of the two side petals of a papilionaceous flower. See diag. under **papilionaceous. 21.** *Brit.* a fender of an automobile, truck, bicycle, or other vehicle. **22.** either of the parts of a double door, screen, etc. **23.** the feather of an arrow. **24.** a group within a political party: *conflict between the right wing and the left wing.* **25.** *Naut.* one of the far side areas of the hold of a merchant vessel. **26. on the wing, a.** in flight, or flying: *a bird on the wing.* **b.** in motion; traveling; active: *Talent scouts are on the wing in search of a new leading lady.* **27. take wing, a.** to begin to fly; take to the air. **b.** to leave in haste; depart: *When she saw the beautiful dress, her resolution to save money swiftly took wing.* **28. under one's wing,** under one's protection, care, or patronage: *My aunt is always taking stray dogs and cats under her wing.* —*v.t.* **29.** to equip with wings. **30.** to enable to fly, move rapidly, etc.; lend speed or celerity to. **31.** to supply with a winglike part, a side structure, etc. **32.** to transport on or as on wings. **33.** to perform or accomplish by wings. **34.** to traverse in flight. **35.** to wound or disable in the wing: *to wing a bird.* **36.** to wound (a person) in an arm or other nonvital part. **37.** to bring down (as a flying bird) by a shot. **38.** to brush or clean with a wing. **39.** *Theat.* to perform (a part, role, etc.) relying on prompters in the wings. —*v.i.* **40.** to travel on or as on wings; fly; soar: *They are winging to the coast.* [ME *wenge* (pl.) < Scand; cf. Icel *vængir* (pl.)] —**wing′like′,** *adj.*

wing′ and wing′, *Naut.* with a sail extended on each side, as with the foresail out on one side and the mainsail out on the other.

wing·back (wing′bak′), *n.* *Football.* **1.** an offensive back who lines up outside of an end. **2.** the position played by this back. [WING + BACK[1]]

wing′back forma′tion, *Football.* **1.** See **single wingback formation. 2.** See **double wingback formation.**

wing′ bit′, a flat bit projecting to one side near the end of a key.

wing′ bolt′, a bolt with a head like a wing nut.

wing′ bow′ (bō), (of poultry) the distinctively colored feathers on the shoulder or bend of the wing of a bird.

wing′ case′, *Entomol.* elytron. Also called **wing′ cov′er.**

wing′ chair′, a large upholstered chair having a back with wings. Also, **winged′ chair′.**

Wing chair

wing′ col′lar, a stand-up collar having the front edges or corners folded down, worn by men for formal or evening dress.

wing′ command′er, 1. *Brit.* an officer in the Royal Air Force equivalent in rank to a lieutenant colonel in the U.S. Air Force. **2.** an officer of the U.S. Navy or Air Force who commands a wing.

wing′ cov′erts, *Ornith.* the feathers which cover the bases of the quill feathers of the wing in birds, divided into greater, middle, and primary coverts.

wing′ dam′, a jetty for diverting the current of a stream. Also called **spur, spur dike.**

wing-ding (wing′ding′), *n.* *Slang.* **1.** a fit, either induced by drugs or feigned. **2.** a fit of anger; a rage. **3.** a noisy, exciting celebration or party. [nonsense formation, var. of *whing-ding*]

winged (wingd *or, esp. Poetic,* wing′id), *adj.* **1.** having wings. **2.** having a winglike part or parts: *a winged bone; a winged seed.* **3.** abounding with wings or winged creatures. **4.** moving or passing on or as if on wings: *winged words.* **5.** rapid or swift. **6.** elevated or lofty: *winged sentiments.* **7.** disabled in the wing, as a bird. **8.** wounded in an arm or other nonvital part. [late ME; see WING, -ED[3]] —**wing′ed·ly,** *adv.* —**wing′ed·ness,** *n.*

winged′ aca′cia, a prickly, hairy shrub, *Acacia alata,* of Australia, having light yellow flower heads.

winged′ everlast′ing, a bushy herb, *Ammobium alatum,* of Australia, having winged branches and javelin-shaped leaves.

Winged′ Horse′, *Astron.* the constellation Pegasus.

winged′ pea′, a prostrate, annual herb, *Lotus Tetragonolobus,* of southern Europe, having purplish-red flowers and edible pods and seed.

winged′ spin′dle tree′, a stiff, spreading shrub, *Euonymus alatus,* of eastern Asia, having corky-winged twigs, yellowish flowers, and purplish fruit.

Winged′ Vic′tory, a Greek marble statue (c200 B.C.) of Nike found at Samothrace and now in the Louvre, Paris. Also called **Nike of Samothrace, Victory of Samothrace, Winged′ Vic′tory of Sam′othrace.**

wing·er (wing′ər), *n.* (in Rugby, soccer, etc.) one who plays a wing position. [WING + -ER[1]]

wing′ flat′, *Theat.* a flat, esp. a two-fold, usually forming part of a unit of four panels of painted scenery. Also called **coulisse.**

wing-foot·ed (wing′fo͝ot′id), *adj.* **1.** having winged feet. **2.** swift.

wing·less (wing′lis), *adj.* **1.** having no wings. **2.** having only rudimentary wings, as an apteryx. [WING + -LESS] —**wing′less·ness,** *n.*

wing·let (wing′lit), *n.* **1.** a little wing. **2.** *Zool.* alula. [WING + -LET]

wing′ load′ing, *Aeron.* See under **loading** (def. 4).

wing′ nut′, a nut having two flat, widely projecting pieces such that it can be readily tightened with the thumb and forefinger.

wing·o·ver (wing′ō′vər), *n.* *Aeron.* an airplane maneuver involving a steep, climbing turn to a near stall, then a sharp drop of the nose, a removal of bank, and a final leveling off in the opposite direction. [WING + OVER]

wings (wingz), *n.* **1.** *Mil. Informal.* a badge bearing the image of a spread pair of bird's wings with a distinctive center design, awarded to an aircrewman on completion of certain requirements. Also called **aviation badge. 2.** a gold-embroidered green badge in the shape of a spread pair of bird wings worn by junior and cadette girl scouts to indicate previous membership in a Brownie troop.

wing′ shoot′ing, *Hunting.* act or practice of shooting at birds moving through the air.

wing′ shot′, *Hunting.* **1.** a shot taken at a bird moving through the air. **2.** an expert in shooting birds moving through the air.

wing′ skid′, *Aeron.* a skid attached to the wing tip of an airplane to prevent it from touching the ground.

Wings′ of the Dove′, The (duv), a novel (1902) by Henry James.

wing·span (wing′span′), *n.* the distance between the wing tips of an airplane. [WING + SPAN[1]]

wing·spread (wing′spred′), *n.* (of a winged creature or object) the distance between the most outward tips of the wings when they are extended as possible. [WING + SPREAD]

wing′ tip′, 1. the extreme outer edge of an airplane wing. **2.** a toecap, often with a perforated pattern, having a point at the center and a piece at each side extending back along the top and sides. **3.** a style of shoe with such a toe.

wing-wea·ry (wing′wēr′ē), *adj.* tired from flying or traveling.

wing·y (wing′ē), *adj.,* **wing·i·er, wing·i·est. 1.** having wings. **2.** rapid; swift. [WING + -Y[1]]

Win·i·fred (win′ə frid), *n.* a girl's given name.

wink[1] (wingk), *v.i.* **1.** to close and open the eyes quickly. **2.** to close and open one eye quickly as a hint or signal or with some sly meaning (often fol. by *at*): *He winked at a girl across the room.* **3.** (of the eyes) to close and open thus; blink. **4.** to shine with little flashes of light; twinkle: *The city lights winked in the distance.* —*v.t.* **5.** to close and open (the eyes or an eye) quickly; execute or give (a wink). **6.** to drive or force by winking (usually fol. by *back* or *away*): *She attempted to wink back the tears.* **7.** to signal or convey by a wink. **8. wink at,** to ignore deliberately, as to avoid the necessity of taking action: *It is time for public-spirited citizens to stop winking at the misappropriation of tax money.* —*n.* **9.** act of winking. **10.** a winking movement, esp. of one eye as in giving a hint or signal. **11.** a hint or signal given by winking. **12.** the time required for winking once; an instant or twinkling: *I'll be there in a wink.* **13.** a little flash of light; a twinkle. **14.** the least bit: *I didn't sleep a wink last night because of the thunderstorm.* [ME *winke(n),* OE *wincian;* c. G *winken* to wave, signal] —**wink′ing·ly,** *adv.*

—**Syn. 1.** WINK, BLINK refer to rapid motions of the eyelid. To WINK is to close and open either one or both eyelids with a rapid motion. To BLINK suggests a sleepy, dazed, or dazzled condition in which it is difficult to focus the eyes or see clearly: *Bright sun makes one blink.* **4.** sparkle.

wink[2] (wingk), *n.* *Games.* a disk or similar small object used in tiddlywinks. [(TIDDLY)WINK(S)]

Win·kel·ried (*Ger.* ving′kəl rēt′), *n.* **Ar·nold von** (*Ger.* är′nôlt fən), died 1386?, Swiss hero in the battle of Sempach, 1386.

wink·er (wing′kər), *n.* **1.** one who or that which winks. **2.** a blinker or blinder for a horse. **3.** *Informal.* an eyelash or an eye. [WINK[1] + -ER[1]]

win·kle (wing′kəl), *n., v.,* **-kled, -kling.** *Brit.* —*n.* **1.** any of various marine gastropods; periwinkle. —*v.t.* **2.** *Informal.* to pry (something) out of a place, as winkle meat is dug out of its shell with a pin (usually fol. by *out*). [short for PERIWINKLE]

win·kle·hawk (wing′kəl hôk′), *n.* an L-shaped tear in fabric. [< G *Winkel* angle, corner + *Hak(en)* hook]

win·le·strae (win′əl strā′), *n.* *Chiefly Scot.* windlestraw.

Win·ne·ba·go (win′ə bā′gō), *n., pl.* **-gos,** (*esp. collectively*) **-go. 1.** a member of a North American Indian tribe speaking a Siouan language closely related to Assiniboin, Teton, and Mandan, formerly located in Green Bay, Wisconsin, now living in Green Bay and NE Nebraska. **2. Lake,** a lake in E Wisconsin. 30 mi. long.

Win·ne·muc·ca (win′ə muk′ə), *n.* a town in N Nevada. 3453 (1960).

Win·ne·pe·sau·kee (win′ə pə sô′kē), *n.* **Lake,** a lake in central New Hampshire: summer resort. 25 mi. long.

win·ner (win′ər), *n.* one who or that which wins; victor. [ME; see WIN, -ER[1]]

Win·ner (win′ər), *n.* a town in S South Dakota. 3705 (1960).

win′ner's cir′cle, a small, usually circular area or enclosure at a race track where awards are bestowed on winning mounts and their jockeys.

Winn·field (win′fēld′), *n.* a town in central Louisiana. 7022 (1960).

Win·nie (win′ē), *n.* **1.** a boy's given name, form of **Winston. 2.** a girl's given name, form of **Winifred.** Also, **Winny.**

Win·nie-the-Pooh (win′ē thə po͞o′), *n.* a collection of children's stories (1926) by A. A. Milne.

win·ning (win′ing), *n.* **1.** the act of one who or that which wins. **2.** Usually, **winnings.** that which is won, esp. money. **3.** *Mining.* **a.** any opening by which coal is being or has been extracted. **b.** a bed of coal ready for mining. —*adj.* **4.** that wins; successful or victorious, as in a contest: *the winning team.* **5.** charming; engaging; pleasing: *a winning child; a winning smile.* [ME; see WIN, -ING[1], -ING[2]] —**win′ning·ly,** *adv.* —**win′ning·ness,** *n.*

—**Syn. 5.** captivating, attractive, winsome. —**Ant. 1, 4.** losing. **5.** repulsive.

win′ning gal′lery, *Court Tennis.* a winning opening on the hazard side, below the penthouse and farthest from the dedans. Cf. **dedans** (def. 1), **grille** (def. 3).

win′ning haz′ard. See under **hazard** (def. 10).

win′ning o′pening, *Court Tennis.* the dedans, winning gallery, or grille.

win′ning post′, a post on a race track, marking the goal of a race.

Win·ni·peg (win′ə peg′), *n.* **1.** a city in and the capital of Manitoba, in S Canada, on the Red River. 265,429 (1961). **2. Lake,** a lake in S Canada, in Manitoba. ab. 260 mi. long; ab. 9300 sq. mi. **3.** a river in S Canada, flowing NW from the Lake of the Woods to Lake Winnipeg. ab. 200 mi. long. —**Win′ni·peg′ger,** *n.*

Win·ni·pe·go·sis (win′ə pə gō′sis), *n.* **Lake,** a lake in S Canada, in W Manitoba, W of Lake Winnipeg. 2086 sq. mi.

win·nock (win′ək), *n.* *Scot.* window. [ME *windok,* Scot var. of *windog(e)* WINDOW]

win·now (win′ō), *v.t.* **1.** to free (grain) from the lighter particles of chaff, dirt, etc., esp. by throwing it into the air and allowing the wind or a forced current of air to blow away impurities. **2.** to drive or blow (chaff, dirt, etc.) away by fanning. **3.** to blow upon; fan. **4.** to subject to some process of separating or distinguishing; analyze critically; sift: *to winnow a mass of statements.* **5.** to separate or distinguish (valuable from worthless parts) (sometimes fol. by *out*): *to winnow falsehood from truth.* **6.** to pursue (a course) with flapping wings in flying. **7.** *Archaic.* to fan or stir (the air) as with the wings in flying. —*v.i.* **8.** to free grain from chaff by wind or driven air. **9.** to fly with flapping wings; flutter. —*n.* **10.** a device or contrivance used for winnowing. **11.** act of winnowing. [ME *win(d)we(n),* OE *windwian* (see WIND[1]); cf. L *ventilāre,* deriv. of *vent(us)* wind] —**win′now·er,** *n.*

Winns·bor·o (winz′bûr ō, -bur ō), *n.* **1.** a town in NE Louisiana. 4437 (1960). **2.** a town in central South Carolina. 3479 (1960). **3.** a town in NE Texas. 2675 (1960).

Win·ny (win′ē), *n.* **1.** a boy's given name, form of **Winston. 2.** a girl's given name, form of **Winifred.** Also, **Winnie.**

win·o (wī′nō), *n., pl.* **win·os.** *Slang.* a person, usually a derelict, who keeps himself intoxicated on cheap wine. [WINE + -*o* suffix of association]

Wi·no·na (wi nō′nə), *n.* **1.** a city in SE Minnesota, on the Mississippi. 24,895 (1960). **2.** a town in central Mississippi. 4282 (1960). **3.** Also, **Wenona, Wenonah.** a girl's given name.

Wi·noos·ki (wi no͞o′skē, -no͝os′kē), *n.* a town in NW Vermont. 7420 (1960).

Wins·low (winz′lō), *n.* **1. Edward,** 1595–1655, English colonist and author in America: governor of the Plymouth colony 1633, 1639, 1644. **2.** a town in central Arizona. 8862 (1960). **3.** a town in S Maine. 3640 (1960). **4.** a boy's given name.

win·some (win′səm), *adj.* winning, engaging, or charming: *a winsome smile.* [ME *winsom,* OE *wynsum,* equiv. to *wyn* joy + -*sum* -SOME[1]] —**win′some·ly,** *adv.* —**win′some·ness,** *n.*

Win·some (win′səm), *n.* a girl's given name.

Win·sor (win′zər), *n.* **Justin,** 1831–97, U.S. librarian and historian.

Win·sted (win′stid), *n.* a town in NW Connecticut. 8136 (1960).

Win·ston (win′stən), *n.* **1.** a town in central Florida. 3323 (1960). **2.** a boy's given name.

Win·ston-Sa·lem (win′stən sā′ləm), *n.* a city in N North Carolina. 111,135 (1960).

win·ter (win′tər), *n.* **1.** the cold season between autumn and spring in northern latitudes (in the Northern Hemisphere from the winter solstice to the vernal equinox; in the Southern Hemisphere from the summer solstice to the autumnal equinox). **2.** the months of December, January, and February in the U.S., and of November, December, and January in Great Britain. **3.** cold weather: *a touch of winter in northern Florida.* **4.** the colder half of the year (opposed to *summer*). **5.** a whole year as represented by this season: *a man of sixty winters.* **6.** a period like winter, as the last or final period of life, a period of decline, decay, inertia, dreariness, or adversity: *the winter of our discontent.* —*adj.* **7.** of, pertaining to, or characteristic of winter: *There was a beautiful winter sunset.* **8.** (of fruit and vegetables) of a kind that may be kept for use during the winter. —*v.i.* **9.** to spend or pass the winter: *We plan to winter in Italy.* **10.** to keep, feed, or manage during the winter, as plants or cattle: *The cows are wintering in the barn.* [ME, OE; c. G *Winter,* Icel *vetr,* Goth *wintrus;* akin to WET, WATER] —**win′ter·er,** *n.* —**win′ter·ish,** *adj.* —**win′ter·ish·ly,** *adv.* —**win′ter·less,** *adj.*

win′ter ac′onite, a small, ranunculaceous herb, *Eranthis hyemalis,* of the Old World, often cultivated for its bright-yellow flowers, which appear very early in the spring.

win′ter bar′ley, barley that is planted in the autumn to be harvested in the spring or early summer.

win·ter·ber·ry (win′tər ber′ē), *n., pl.* **-ries. 1.** any of several North American hollies of the genus *Ilex,* having red berries that are persistent through the winter. **2.** See **black alder** (def. 1). [WINTER + BERRY]

win·ter·bourne (win′tər bōrn′, -bo͝orn′), *n.* **1.** a channel filled only at a time of excessive rainfall. **2.** (*cap.*) **Frederick,** the narrator of Henry James's short novel, *Daisy Miller.* [OE *winterburna.* See WINTER, BURN[2]]

win′ter cher′ry, 1. Also called **Chinese lantern plant.** a Eurasian ground cherry, *Physalis Alkengi,* bearing fruit enclosed in a showy, orange-red, inflated calyx. **2.** the red, berrylike fruit of this plant.

win′ter cress′, any cress of the genus *Barbarea,* having lyrate leaves and yellow flowers.

win′ter crook′neck, any of several winter varieties of squash, *Cucurbita moschata,* having elongated, curved necks.

win·ter·feed (win′tər fēd′), *v.,* **-fed, -feed·ing,** *n.* —*v.t.* **1.** to feed (cattle, sheep, etc.) during the winter when pasturage is not available: *He winterfed the animals.* **2.** to supply (grain, hay, etc.) to livestock in winter: *We winterfed corn and oats to the animals.* —*v.i.* **3.** to provide feed for livestock in winter: *We were obliged to winterfeed through April this year.* —*n.* **4.** the feed given to livestock during the winter. [WINTER + FEED]

win′ter floun′der, a flounder, *Pseudopleuronectes americanus,* found along the Atlantic coast of North America, used as food, esp. in winter. Also called **blackback flounder.**

Win′ter Gar′den, a town in central Florida. 5513 (1960).

win·ter·green (win′tər grēn′), *n.* **1.** a small, creeping, evergreen, ericaceous shrub, *Gaultheria procumbens,* common in eastern North America, having white, bell-shaped flowers, a bright-red, berrylike fruit, and aromatic leaves which yield a volatile oil. **2.** the oil of this shrub; wintergreen oil; methyl salicylate. **3.** the flavor of oil of wintergreen or something flavored with it. **4.** any of various other plants of the same genus. **5.** any of various small evergreen herbs of the genera *Pyrola* and *Chimaphila.* [trans. of D *wintergroen* or G *Wintergrün*]

win′tergreen bar′berry, an evergreen shrub, *Berberis julianae,* of central China, having spiny leaves, dark green above, pale beneath, bluish-black fruit, and clustered, yellow flowers.

win′tergreen oil′. See **methyl salicylate.**

win·ter-har·dy (win′tər här′dē), *adj.* (esp. of plants, shrubs, or the like) able to survive the effects of cold weather.

Win′ter Ha′ven, a city in central Florida. 16,227 (1960).

win′ter he′liotrope, an evergreen, *Petasites fragrans,* of the Mediterranean region, having small, fragrant, off-white to purple flowers. Also called **sweet coltsfoot.**

win·ter·ize (win′tə rīz′), *v.t.,* **-ized, -iz·ing.** to prepare (an automobile, house, etc.) for cold weather by (in automobiles) adding antifreeze and changing weight of oil, (in houses) adding insulation, heating units, etc. [WINTER + -IZE] —**win′ter·i·za′tion,** *n.*

win′ter jas′mine, a shrub, *Jasminum nudiflorum,* of China, having winter-blooming, yellow flowers.

win·ter·kill (win′tər kil′), *v.t., v.i.* *U.S.* to kill by or die from exposure to the cold of winter, as wheat. [WINTER + KILL[1]] —**win′ter·kill′ing,** *adj., n.*

win′ter lamb′, a lamb born in the fall or early winter and sold for slaughter prior to May 20.

win′ter mel′on, a variety of late-keeping muskmelon, *Cucumis melo inodorus,* having a sweet, edible flesh.

win′ter oats′, oats that are planted in the autumn to be harvested in the spring or early summer.

Win′ter Park′, a city in E Florida. 17,162 (1960).

win′ter purs′lane, an annual herb, *Montia perfoliata,* of western North America, having small, white flowers. Also called **Indian lettuce, miner's lettuce.**

Win·ter·rei·se, Die (*Ger.* dē vin′tə rī′zə), a song cycle (1827) by Franz Schubert, consisting of 24 songs set to poems of Wilhelm Müller.

Win·ters (win′tərz), *n.* **1. Y·vor** (ī′vôr), born 1900, U.S. poet and critic. **2.** a town in central Texas. 3266 (1960).

win′ter sa′vory. See under **savory**[2].

Win′ter's bark′, (*sometimes l.c.*) an evergreen tree, *Drimys winteri,* ranging from Mexico to Cape Horn, having aromatic leaves and jasmine-scented flowers. [named after William *Winter,* 16th-century English captain]

Win′ter Sea′. See **Mare Hiemis.**

Win·ter·set (win′tər set′), *n.* **1.** (*italics*) a drama in verse (1935) by Maxwell Anderson. **2.** a town in central Iowa. 3639 (1960).

win′ter sol′stice, *Astron.* the solstice on or about December 21st that marks the beginning of winter in the Northern Hemisphere.

win′ter squash′, any of several squashes of the varieties *Cucurbita maxima* or *C. moschata* that mature in late autumn and are used, when ripe, as a vegetable.

Win′ter's Tale′, The, a drama (1610–11?) by Shakespeare.

Win·ters·ville (win′tərz vil), *n.* a town in E Ohio. 3597 (1960).

win·ter·tide (win′tər tīd′), *n.* *Poetic.* wintertime. [ME; OE *wintertīd.* See WINTER, TIDE[1]]

win·ter·time (win′tər tīm′), *n.* the season of winter. [ME; r. ME, OE *wintertīd* WINTERTIDE]

win′ter vetch′, a hardy, hairy, climbing herb, *Vicia villosa,* of Eurasia, having numerous, violet-blue flowers.

win′ter wheat′, wheat that is planted in the autumn to be harvested in the spring or early summer.

win′ter wren′, (in the Western Hemisphere) the wren, *Troglodytes troglodytes.*

win·ter·y (win′tə rē), *adj.,* **-ter·i·er, -ter·i·est.** wintry.

win′ter yel′lowlegs, *Dial.* the greater yellowlegs. See under **yellowlegs.**

Win·throp (win′thrəp), *n.* **1. John,** 1588–1649, English colonist in America: 1st governor of the Massachusetts Bay colony 1629–33, 1637–40, 1642–44, 1646–49. **2.** his son, **John,** 1606–76, English colonist in America: colonial governor of Connecticut 1657, 1659–76. **3. John** or **Fitz-John** (fits′jon′), 1638–1707, American soldier and statesman: colonial governor of Connecticut 1698–1707 (son of the younger John Winthrop). **4. Robert Charles,** 1809–94, U.S. politician: Speaker of the House 1847–49. **5.** a town in E Massachusetts, near Boston. 20,303 (1960). **6.** a boy's given name.

Win′throp desk′. See **Governor Winthrop desk.**

Win′throp Har′bor, a town in NE Illinois. 3848 (1960).

win·tle (win′tᵊl), *n., v.i.,* **-tled, -tling.** *Scot.* —*n.* **1.** a rolling or staggering motion. —*v.i.* **2.** to roll or swing back and forth. **3.** to tumble over; capsize. [< D or Flem; cf. MD *wentelen,* Flem *windtelen* to roll; appar. freq. of *winden* to WIND[2]]

Win·ton (win′tən), *n.* a town in NE Pennsylvania. 5456 (1960).

win·try (win′trē), *adj.,* **-tri·er, -tri·est. 1.** of or characteristic of winter: *wintry blasts; wintry skies.* **2.** resembling winter weather; having snow, frost, cold, storms, etc.: *We had wintry weather well into May last year.* **3.** suggestive of winter, as in lack of warmth or cheer: *a wintry manner.* Also, **wintery.** [OE *wint(e)rig;* see WINTER, -Y[1]] —**win′tri·ly,** *adv.* —**win′tri·ness,** *n.*

win·y (wī′nē), *adj.,* **win·i·er, win·i·est. 1.** of, like, or characteristic of wine. **2.** affected by wine. [WINE + -Y[1]]

winze[1] (winz), *n.* *Mining.* a vertical or inclined shaft driven downward from a drift into an orebody. Also, **windz.** [earlier *winds,* appar. WIND[1]]

winze[2] (winz), *n.* *Scot.* a curse. [< MD *wens(ch)* WISH]

wipe (wīp), *v.,* **wiped, wip·ing,** *n.* —*v.t.* **1.** to rub lightly with or on a cloth, towel, paper, the hand, etc., in order to clean or dry the surface of: *He wiped the furniture with a damp cloth.* **2.** to remove by rubbing with or on something (usually fol. by *away, off, out,* etc.): *Wipe the dirt off your shoes. Wipe the dust from the pictures.* **3.** to remove as if by rubbing (usually fol. by *away, off,* etc.): *Wipe that smile off your face!* **4.** to erase, as from existence or memory (often fol. by *from*): *to wipe a thought from one's mind.* **5.** to rub or draw (something) over a surface, as in cleaning or drying. **6.** *Plumbing.* **a.** to apply (solder in a semifluid state) by spreading with leather or cloth over the part to be soldered. **b.** to form (a joint) in this manner. **7.** *Mach.* (of a rotating shaft or the like) to melt the brasses of (a bearing) through friction. **8.** *Naut.* to move an electrically charged cable that is wrapped around a ship's hull up and down (the hull) to reduce the magnetic field of the hull; to degauss (the hull of a ship). **9. wipe out, a.** to destroy completely; demolish: *The entire city was wiped out.* **b.** *Informal.* to murder; kill: *They wiped him out to keep him from appearing as a witness.* —*n.* **10.** act of wiping: *She gave a few quick wipes to the furniture.* **11.** a rub, as of one thing over another. **12.** Also called **wipe′-off′.** *Motion Pictures.* a technique in film editing by which the projected image of a scene appears to be pushed or wiped off the screen by the image that follows. **13.** a sweeping stroke or blow. **14.** a gibe. **15.** *Mach.* a wiper. **16.** *Slang.* a handkerchief. [ME; OE *wīp(ian);* c. OHG *wīfan* to wind round, Goth *weipan* to crown, L *vibrāre* to move to and fro]

wip·er (wī′pər), *n.* **1.** one who or that which wipes. **2.** that with which something is wiped, as a towel, handkerchief, squeegee, etc. **3.** *Elect.* that portion of a selector or other similar device which makes contact with the terminals of a bank. **4.** *Mach.* a projection or partial cam, as on a rotating shaft, moving to lift or dislodge another part, esp. so as to let it drop when released. [WIPE + -ER[1]]

wire (wīər), *n., adj., v.,* **wired, wir·ing.** —*n.* **1.** a slender, stringlike piece or filament of relatively rigid or flexible metal, usually circular in section, manufactured in a great variety of diameters and metals depending on its application. **2.** such pieces as a material. **3.** a length of such material, consisting either of a single filament or of several filaments woven or twisted together and usually insulated with a dielectric material, used as a conductor of electricity. **4.** a cross wire or a cross hair. **5.** a barbed-wire fence. **6.** a long wire or cable used in cable, telegraph, or telephone systems. **7.** *Naut.* a wire rope. **8.** a telegram. **9.** *Informal.* the telegraphic system: *to send a message by wire.* **10. wires,** a system of wires by which puppets are moved. **11.** a metallic string of a musical instrument. **12.** *Horse Racing.* a wire stretched across and above the track at the finish line, under which the horses pass. **13.** *Ornith.* one of the extremely long, slender, wirelike filaments or shafts of the plumage of various birds. **14.** a metal device for snaring rabbits and other small game. **15.** *Papermaking.* the woven wire mesh over which the wet pulp is spread in a papermaking machine. **16. pull wires,** *Informal.* to use one's position or influence to obtain a desired result: *to pull wires to get someone a job.* **17. the wire,** the telephone: *There's someone on the wire for you.* **18. under the wire,** just within the limit or deadline; scarcely; barely: *to get an application in under the wire.* —*adj.* **19.** made of wire; consisting of or constructed with wires. **20.** resembling wire; wirelike. —*v.t.* **21.** to furnish with a wire or wires. **22.** to install an electric system of wiring, as for lighting, etc. **23.** to fasten or bind with wire: *He wired the halves together.* **24.** to put on a wire, as beads. **25.** *Informal.* to send by telegraph, as a message: *Please wire the money at once.* **26.** *Informal.* to send a telegraphic message to: *She wired him to come at once.* **27.** to snare by means of a wire or wires. **28.** *Croquet.* to block (a ball) by placing it behind the wire of an arch. —*v.i.* **29.** *Informal.* to send a telegraphic message; telegraph: *Don't write; wire.* [ME, OE *wīr;* c. LG *wīr,* Icel *vīra-* wire, OHG *wiara* fine gold work, Gk *iris* (deriv. of **wiris*) rainbow; akin to L *vi(ēre)* (to) weave together] —**wir′a·ble,** *adj.* —**wire′like′,** *adj.*

wire′ a′gency. See **wire service.**

wire′ cloth′, a material of wires of moderate fineness, used for making strainers, manufacturing paper, etc. —**wire′-cloth′,** *adj.*

wire′ cut′ter, any of various devices designed to cut wire.

wired (wīərd), *adj.* **1.** equipped with wires, as for electricity, telephone service, etc. **2.** made of wire; consisting of or constructed with wires: *a wired barrier.* **3.** tied or secured with wires: *wired bales of wastepaper.* **4.** strengthened or supported with wires: *a sculpture of wired papier-maché.* [late ME; see WIRE, -ED[3]]

wire·danc·er (wīər′dan′sər, -dän′-), *n.* one who dances or performs other feats on a high wire. [WIRE + DANCER] —**wire′danc′ing,** *n.*

wire·draw (wīər′drô′), *v.t.,* **-drew, -drawn, -draw·ing. 1.** to draw (metal) out into wire, esp. by pulling forcibly through a series of holes of gradually decreasing diameter in a succession of dies. **2.** to draw out to great length, in quantity or time; stretch out to excess. **3.** to strain unwarrantably, as in meaning. [back formation from *wiredrawer;* see WIRE, DRAWER] —**wire′draw′er,** *n.*

wire·drawn (wīər′drôn′), *adj.* **1.** drawn out long and thin like a wire. **2.** (of ideas, comparisons, etc.) finely spun; extremely intricate; minute. [WIRE + DRAWN]

wired′ tel′evision. See **closed-circuit television.**

wire′ entan′glement, a barbed-wire obstacle, usually mounted on posts and zigzagged back and forth along a front, designed to channel, delay, or halt an advance by enemy foot soldiers.

wire′ gauge′, a gauge calibrated for determining the diameter of wire.

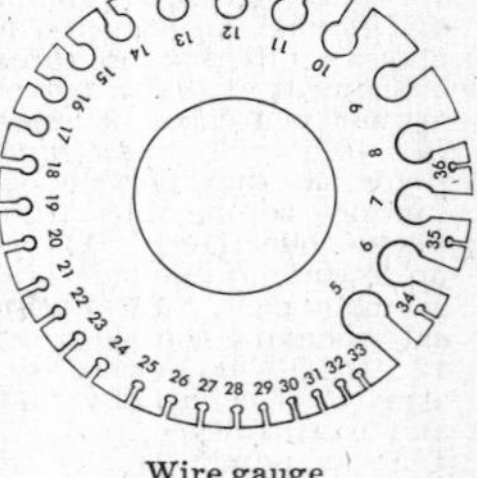
Wire gauge

wire′ gauze′, a gauzelike fabric woven of very fine wires.

wire′ glass′, a pane or sheet of glass having a network of wire embedded within it as a reinforcement.

wire′ grass′, 1. *U.S.* a widely distributed southern grass, *Cynodon Dactylon,* used for pasture and turf. **2.** any of various similar grasses with spreading habit, that may be a pest in cultivated fields. **3.** See **Canada bluegrass.**

wire·hair (wīər′hâr′), *n.* a fox terrier having a wiry coat. Also called **wire′-haired ter′rier.** [WIRE + HAIR]

wire-haired (wīər′hârd′), *adj.* having coarse, stiff, wirelike hair.

wire′-haired point′ing grif′fon, griffon[2] (def. 2).

wire′ house′, *Stock Exchange.* a brokerage firm with branch offices connected with their main office by a private system of telephone, telegraph, and teletype wires.

Wirehair (15½ in. high at shoulder)

wire·less (wīər′lis), *adj.* **1.** having no wire. **2.** noting or pertaining to any of various devices which are operated with or actuated by electromagnetic waves. **3.** *Chiefly Brit.* radio. —*n.* **4.** wireless telegraphy or telephony. **5.** a wireless telegraph or telephone, or the like. **6.** a wireless message. **7.** *Chiefly Brit.* **a.** a radio receiving set. **b.** a radio broadcast or program. —*v.t., v.i.* **8.** to telegraph or telephone by wireless. [WIRE + -LESS] —**wire′less·ly,** *adv.* —**wire′less·ness,** *n.*

wire′less tel′egraph, radiotelegraph.

wire′less teleg′raphy, radiotelegraphy.

wire′less tel′ephone, radiotelephone.

CONCISE ETYMOLOGY KEY: <, descended or derived from; >, whence; b., blend of, blended; c., cognate with; deriv., derivative; equiv., equivalent; imit., imitative; m., modification of; obl., oblique; r., replacing; s., stem; sp., spelling; trans., translation; ?, origin unknown, perhaps; *, hypothetical. See the full key inside the front cover.

wire′less teleph′ony, radiotelephony.

wire′ loop′ bind′ing, a method of loose-leaf binding in which the sheets are kept together by a connected series of rings of light wire.

wire·man (wīər′mən), *n., pl.* **-men.** one who installs and maintains electric wiring. [WIRE + MAN[1]]

wire′ pack′, *Mining.* a circular support for a roof, made of rubble bound with wire mesh.

Wire·pho·to (wīər′fō′tō), *n., pl.* **-tos,** *v.,* **-toed, -to·ing.** —*n.* **1.** *Trademark.* a device for transmitting photographs over distances by wire, consisting essentially of a photosensitive element that scans the picture and converts lights and shadows into electric impulses which are transmitted to a receiver where they actuate a point light source that scans areas of a photosensitive paper to reproduce the original image. **2.** a photograph so transmitted. —*v.t.* **3.** (*l.c.*) to transmit (a photograph) by means of a Wirephoto.

wire·pull·er (wīər′po͝ol′ər), *n.* **1.** one who or that which pulls wires. **2.** one who uses secret means to direct and control the actions of others, esp. for selfish ends; an intriguer. **3.** snake (def. 3b). [WIRE + PULLER]

wire·pull·ing (wīər′po͝ol′ing), *n.* **1.** act of pulling wires. **2.** the use of influence to manipulate persons or organizations, as political organizations, for one's own ends. [WIRE + PULLING]

wir·er (wīər′ər), *n.* **1.** one who wires. **2.** one who uses wire to snare game. [WIRE + -ER[1]]

wire′ record′er, a device for recording sound on a steel wire by magnetizing the wire as it passes an electromagnet, the sound being reproduced by the motion of the wire past a receiver.

wire′ record′ing, **1.** the process or technique of recording on wire as it is being magnetized. **2.** a recording made by such a process.

wire′ room′, a bookmaking establishment, esp. one disguised as a lawful business.

wire′ rope′, a rope made of or containing strands of wire twisted together.

wire′ serv′ice, a press association that syndicates news by wire to its subscribers or members. Also called **wire agency.** Cf. **news service.**

wire′ side′, the wrong side of a sheet of paper; the side against the wire during manufacture. Cf. **felt side.**

wire·sonde (wīər′sond′), *n. Meteorol.* an instrument carried aloft by a captive balloon and sending, by means of a wire cable, temperature and humidity data. [WIRE + SONDE]

wire·spun (wīər′spun′), *adj.* **1.** drawn out as wire is. **2.** overly subtle; obscure. **3.** having too little substance. [WIRE + SPUN]

wire-stitch (wīər′stich′), *v.t. Bookbinding.* to stitch (the backs of gathered sections) by means of a machine that automatically forms staples from a continuous reel of wire. —**wire′-stitch′er,** *n.*

wire·tap (wīər′tap′), *n., v.,* **-tapped, -tap·ping,** *adj.* —*n.* **1.** act or technique of tapping telephone or telegraph wires for evidence or other information. —*v.t.* **2.** to obtain (information, evidence, etc.) by tapping telephone or telegraph wires: *to wiretap conversations.* **3.** to listen in on by means of a wiretap: *to wiretap a telephone; to wiretap a conversation.* —*v.i.* **4.** to tap telephone or telegraph wires for evidence, information, etc. —*adj.* **5.** pertaining to or obtained by wiretap. [back formation from WIRETAPPER]

wire·tap·per (wīər′tap′ər), *n.* **1.** one who taps wires to learn the nature of messages passing over them. **2.** a swindler who professes to have betting tips or other information from tapped telephone wires. [WIRE + TAPPER[1]]

wire′ vine′, a twining vine, *Muehlenbeckia complexa,* of New Zealand, having wirelike stems and circular leaves. Also called **maidenhair-vine.**

wire wheel (wīər′ hwēl′, wēl′ *for 1;* wīər′ hwēl′, wēl′ *for 2*), **1.** a wheellike brush having stiff wire bristles and used esp. for finishing or cleaning metal. **2.** a wheel, as on a sports car, having wire spokes.

wire·work (wīər′wûrk′), *n.* **1.** work consisting of wire. **2.** fabrics or articles made of wire. [WIRE + WORK]

wire·works (wīər′wûrks′), *n., pl.* **-works.** (*construed as sing. or pl.*) an establishment where wire is made or put to some industrial use. [WIRE + WORKS] —**wire′-work′er,** *n.*

wire·worm (wīər′wûrm′), *n.* **1.** any of the slender, hard-bodied larvae of click beetles, many of which live underground and feed on the roots of plants. **2.** any of various small myriapods. **3.** See **stomach worm.** [WIRE + WORM]

wire′-wound resis′tor (wīər′wound′), *Elect.* a resistor consisting of a wire with a high resistance wound in a coil around a cylindrical core of insulating material. Also, **wire′wound resis′tor.**

wire-wove (wīər′wōv′), *adj.* **1.** made of woven wire. **2.** noting fine glazed paper used esp. as letter paper. [WIRE + WOVE]

wir·ing (wīər′ing), *n.* **1.** act of one who wires. **2.** *Elect.* the aggregate of wires in a lighting system, switchboard, radio, etc. —*adj.* **3.** that installs or is used in wiring. [WIRE + -ING[1], -ING[2]]

wir·ra (wir′ə), *interj. Irish Eng.* an exclamation of sorrow or lament. [short for Ir *a Muire* O Mary, a call to the Virgin]

Wirtz (wûrts), *n.* **William Willard,** born 1912, U.S. lawyer and government official: Secretary of Labor since 1962.

wir·y (wīər′ē), *adj.,* **wir·i·er, wir·i·est.** **1.** made of wire. **2.** in the form of wire. **3.** resembling wire, as in form, stiffness, etc.: *wiry grass.* **4.** lean and sinewy; vigorous; strong: *a wiry little man.* **5.** produced by or resembling the sound of a vibrating wire: *wiry tones.* [WIRE + -Y[1]] —**wir′i·ly,** *adv.* —**wir′i·ness,** *n.*

wis (wis), *v.t., v.i. Archaic.* to know. [by false analysis of IWIS as *I wis* I know; see WIT[2]]

Wis., Wisconsin. Also, **Wisc.**

Wis·by (viz′bē; *Eng.* wiz′bē), *n.* German name of **Visby.**

Wis·con·sin (wis kon′sən), *n.* **1.** a State in the N central United States: a part of the Midwest. 3,951,777 (1960); 56,154 sq. mi. *Cap.:* Madison. *Abbr.:* Wis., Wisc. **2.** a river flowing SW from N Wisconsin to the Mississippi. 430 mi. long. **3.** the fourth stage of the glaciation of North America during the Pleistocene. Cf. **Würm.** —**Wis·con′-sin·ite′,** *n.*

Wiscon′sin Rap′ids, a city in central Wisconsin. 15,042 (1960).

Wisd., Wisdom of Solomon.

wis·dom (wiz′dəm), *n.* **1.** quality or state of being wise; knowledge of what is true or right coupled with just judgment as to action; sagacity, discernment, or insight. **2.** scholarly knowledge or learning: *the wisdom of the schools.* **3.** wise sayings or teachings. **4.** a wise act or saying. **5.** (*cap.*) *Douay Bible.* See **Wisdom of Solomon.** [ME, OE; c. Icel. *vīsdōmr,* G *Weistum.* See WISE[1], -DOM] —**wis′dom·less,** *adj.*

—**Syn. 1.** discretion, judgment, understanding. **2.** sapience, erudition, enlightenment. See **information.** —**Ant. 1, 2.** stupidity.

Wis′dom of Je′sus, Son′ of Si′rach (sī′rak), Ecclesiasticus.

Wis′dom of Sol′omon, a book of the Apocrypha. Also called, *Douay Bible,* **Wisdom.**

wis′dom tooth′, **1.** the third molar on each side of the upper and lower jaws: the last tooth to erupt. **2.** **cut one's wisdom teeth,** to attain maturity or discretion: *It is unlikely that he will ever cut his wisdom teeth, since he is over forty and still behaves like a child.*

wise[1] (wīz), *adj.,* **wis·er, wis·est,** *v.,* **wised, wis·ing.** —*adj.* **1.** having the power of discerning and judging properly as to what is true or right; possessing discernment, judgment, or discretion. **2.** characterized by or showing such power; judicious or prudent: *a wise decision.* **3.** possessed of or characterized by scholarly knowledge or learning; learned; erudite: *wise in the law.* **4.** having knowledge or information as to facts, circumstances, etc.: *We are wiser for his explanations.* **5.** *Slang.* informed; in the know: *You're wise, so why not give us the low-down?* **6. be** or **get wise to,** *Slang.* to be or become cognizant of; learn: *to get wise to a fraud.* **7. get wise,** *Slang.* **a.** to become informed. **b.** to be or become presumptuous or impertinent: *Don't get wise with me, young man!* **8. put someone wise,** *U.S. Slang.* to inform a person; let a person in on a secret or generally unknown fact: *He used to work hard until some of the others put him wise to what was going on.* —*v.t.* **9.** *Slang.* to make wise or aware: *I'll wise you, kid.* **10.** *Archaic.* having knowledge of magic or witchcraft. **11. wise up,** *U.S. Slang.* to make or become aware of a secret or generally unknown fact, situation, attitude, etc.: *They wised him up on how to shirk his work. He never wised up to the fact that the joke was on him.* [ME, OE *wīs;* c. D *wijs,* G *weise,* Icel *vīss,* Goth *-weis;* akin to WIT[1]] —**wise′ly,** *adv.*

—**Syn. 1, 2.** discerning, sage, sensible, sagacious, intelligent, penetrating. —**Ant. 1, 2.** foolish.

wise[2] (wīz), *n.* way of proceeding; manner; fashion (usually used in combination or in certain phrases): *otherwise; lengthwise; in any wise; in no wise.* [ME, OE: way, manner, etc.; melody (OE); c. D *wijze,* G *Weise* manner, melody, Icel *vīsa* short poem, Dan *vise* ballad]

wise[3] (wīz), *v.t.,* **wised, wis·ing.** **1.** *Chiefly Scot.* **a.** to instruct. **b.** to induce or advise. **c.** to show the way to; guide. **2.** *Scot.* to direct the course of; cause to turn. [ME *wise(n),* OE *wīsian* to show the way, guide, direct, deriv. of *wīs* WISE[1]; c. OHG *wīsan,* Icel *vīsa* in same sense]

Wise (wīz), *n.* **1. Stephen Samuel,** 1874–1949, U.S. rabbi, theologian, and Zionist leader; born in Hungary. **2.** a town in SW Virginia. 2614 (1960).

-wise, a suffixal use of **wise[2]** in adverbs denoting manner, position, direction, reference, etc.: *clockwise; nowise; timewise; marketwise; edgewise; sidewise.* Cf. **-ways.**

wise·a·cre (wīz′ā′kər), *n.* **1.** *Usually Humorous or Disparaging.* one who possesses or affects to possess great wisdom. **2.** See **wise guy.** [< MD *wijssegher* soothsayer]

wise·crack (wīz′krak′), *Informal.* —*n.* **1.** a smart or facetious remark. —*v.i.* **2.** to make wisecracks. —*v.t.* **3.** to say as a wisecrack. [WISE[1] + CRACK] —**wise′-crack′er,** *n.*

—**Syn. 1.** jest, witticism, quip.

wise′ guy′, a cocksure, conceited, and often insolent person; smart aleck: *He has a reputation for being a wise guy.* Also called **wiseacre.**

Wise·man (wīz′mən), *n.* **Nicholas Patrick Stephen,** 1802–65, Irish cardinal and author, born in Spain.

wis·en·heim·er (wī′zən hī′mər), *n.* a wiseacre or smart aleck. Also, **weisenheimer.** [WISE[2] + *-enheimer* (abstracted from names of German origin, such as *Oppenheimer*)]

wi·sent (vē′zənt), *n.* bison (def. 2). [< G; OHG *wisunt;* cf. OE *wesend, weosend,* OIcel *v-ī-sundr,* OPruss *wissambrs*]

wish (wish), *v.t.* **1.** to want; desire; long for (usually fol. by an infinitive or a clause): *I wish to travel. I wish that it were morning.* **2.** to desire (a person or thing) to be (as specified): *to wish the problem settled.* **3.** to entertain wishes, favorably or otherwise, for: *to wish one well; to wish one ill.* **4.** to bid, as in greeting or leave-taking: *to wish one a good morning.* **5.** to command: *I wish him to come.* **6.** to entertain (wishes), favorably or otherwise (usually fol. by *to*): *to wish well to a person or a cause.* —*v.i.* **7.** to desire; long; yearn (often fol. by *for*): *Mother says I may go if I wish. I wished for a book.* **8.** to make a wish: *She wished so much she believed her dreams would come true.* **9. wish on, a.** to force or impose: *I wouldn't wish that awful job on my worst enemy.* **b.** Also, **wish upon.** to make a wish using some object as a magical talisman: *to wish on a star.* —*n.* **10.** a distinct mental inclination toward the doing, obtaining, attaining, etc., of something; a desire felt or expressed: *to disregard the wishes of others.* **11.** an expression of a wish, often one of a kindly or courteous nature: *to send one's best wishes.* **12.** that which is wished: *He got his wish, a new car.* [ME *wisshe(n),* OE *wȳscan;* c. G *wünschen,* Icel *æskja;* akin to OE *wynn* joy, L *venus* loveliness] —**wish′er,** *n.* —**wish′-less,** *adj.*

—**Syn. 1.** crave. WISH, DESIRE, WANT indicate a longing for something. To WISH is to feel an impulse toward attainment or possession of something; the strength of the feeling may be of greater or less intensity: *I wish I could go home.* DESIRE, a more formal word, suggests a strong wish: *They desire a new regime.* WANT, usually colloquial in use, suggests a feeling of lack or need which imperatively demands fulfillment: *People all over the world want peace.* **5.** direct, order. **8.** will, want.

wish·bone (wish′bōn′), *n.* **1.** a forked bone, formed by the fusion of the two clavicles, in front of the breastbone in most birds; furcula. **2.** Also called **double sprit, split sprit, wish′bone gaff′.** *Naut.* a sprit composed of two slightly curved pieces of wood, pivoted to a mast by a gooseneck and joined at the outer ends by a crosspiece: used to hold out the clew of a wishbone trysail, which passes between the pieces. [WISH + BONE[1]]

wish′bone rig′, *Naut.* a rig used on schooners and ketches, including a jib-headed mainsail (**wish′bone try′sail**) having a greatly elevated clew held out by a wishbone. Also called **main-trysail rig.**

wish·ful (wish′fəl), *adj.* having or showing a wish; desirous; longing. [WISH + -FUL] —**wish′ful·ly,** *adv.* —**wish′ful·ness,** *n.*

wish′ful think′ing, interpretation of facts, actions, words, etc., as one would like them to be rather than as they really are. —**wish′ful think′er.**

wish-wash (wish′wosh′, -wôsh′), *n.* a drink that is thin and weak. [abstracted from WISHY-WASHY]

wish·y-wash·y (wish′ē wosh′ē, -wô′shē), *adj.* **1.** washy or watery, as a liquid; thin and weak. **2.** lacking in decisiveness; without strength or character; feeble. [gradational compound based on WASHY] —**wish′y-wash′i·ly,** *adv.* —**wish′y-wash′i·ness,** *n.*

Wi·sła (vē′swä), *n.* Polish name of the **Vistula.**

Wis·mar (vis′mär), *n.* a seaport in N East Germany, on the Baltic. 54,834 (est. 1955).

wisp (wisp), *n.* **1.** a handful or small bundle of straw, hay, or the like. **2.** any small or thin tuft, lock, mass, etc.: *wisps of hair.* **3.** a person or thing that is small, delicate, or barely discernible: *a mere wisp of a girl; a wisp of a frown.* **4.** *Archaic.* a whisk broom. **5.** *Chiefly Brit. Dial.* **a.** a pad or twist of straw, as used to rub down a horse. **b.** a twisted bit of straw used as a torch. **6.** a will-o'-the-wisp or ignis fatuus. —*v.t.* **7.** to twist into a wisp. [ME *wisp, wips;* akin to WIPE] —**wisp′like′,** *adj.*

wisp·y (wis′pē), *adj.,* **wisp·i·er, wisp·i·est.** being a wisp or in wisps; wisplike: *a wispy plant.* Also, **wisp′ish.** [WISP + -Y[1]] —**wisp′i·ly,** *adv.* —**wisp′i·ness,** *n.*

Wiss·ler (wis′lər), *n.* **Clark,** 1870–1947, U.S. anthropologist.

wist (wist), *v.* pt. and pp. of **wit[2].**

Wis·ter (wis′tər), *n.* **Owen,** 1860–1938, U.S. novelist.

wis·te·ri·a (wi stēr′ē ə), *n.* any climbing, leguminous shrub of the genus *Wisteria,* having showy, pendent racemes of blue-violet, white, purple, or rose flowers. Also, **wis·tar·i·a** (wi stēr′ē ə, -stâr′-). [named after C. *Wistar* (1761–1818), American anatomist]

wist·ful (wist′fəl), *adj.* **1.** characterized by melancholy; longing; yearning. **2.** pensive, esp. in a melancholy way. [obs. *wist* quiet, silent, attentive (var. of WHIST[2]) + -FUL] —**wist′ful·ly,** *adv.* —**wist′ful·ness,** *n.*

wit[1] (wit), *n.* **1.** the keen perception and cleverly apt expression of those connections between ideas which awaken amusement and pleasure. **2.** speech or writing showing such perception and expression. **3.** a person having or noted for such perception and expression. **4.** understanding, intelligence, or sagacity: *He doesn't have wit enough to come in out of the rain.* **5.** Usually, **wits. a.** mental abilities, or powers of intelligent observation, keen perception, ingenious contrivance, etc.: *using one's wits to get ahead.* **b.** mental faculties; senses: *to lose one's wits.* **6. at one's wit's end.** See **end[1]** (def. 23). **7. keep** or **have one's wits about one,** to remain alert and observant; be prepared for or equal to anything: *It pays to keep your wits about you if you plan to drive at night.* **8. live by one's wits,** to provide for oneself by employing ingenuity or cunning; live precariously: *He traveled around the world, living by his wits.* [ME, OE; c. G *Witz,* Icel *vit;* akin to WIT[2]]

—**Syn. 1.** drollery, facetiousness, waggishness, repartee. See **humor.** **4.** wisdom, sense, mind.

wit[2] (wit), *v.t., v.i., pres. sing. 1st pers.* **wot,** *2nd* **wost,** *3rd* **wot,** *pres. pl.* **wit** or **wite;** *past and past part.* **wist;** *pres. part.* **wit·ting.** **1.** *Archaic.* to know. **2. to wit,** that is to say; namely: *It was the time of the vernal equinox, to wit, the beginning of spring.* [ME *wit(en),* OE *witan;* c. D *weten,* G *wissen,* Icel *vita,* Goth *witan* to know, L *vidēre,* Gk *idein* to see. See WOT]

wit·an (wit′ən), *n. Early Eng. Hist.* **1.** the members of the national council or witenagemot. **2.** (*construed as sing.*) the witenagemot. [OE, pl. of *wita* one who knows, councilor; see WIT[2]]

witch (wich), *n.* **1.** a person, now esp. a woman, who professes or is supposed to practice magic, esp. black magic or the black art; sorceress. Cf. **warlock.** **2.** an ugly or malignant woman; hag: *She's a real old witch.* **3.** one who uses a divining rod; dowser. —*v.t.* **4.** to affect by or as by witchcraft; bewitch; charm. **5.** to bring by or as by witchcraft (often fol. by *into, to,* etc.): *She witched him into going.* —*adj.* **6.** of, pertaining to, or designed as protection against witches. —*v.i.* **7.** to prospect with a divining rod; dowse. [ME *wicche,* OE *wicce.* See WICKED] —**witch′hood,** *n.*

witch′ ball′, **1.** a decorated blown glass ball. **2.** a ball covered with pieces of flat mirrors suspended from the ceiling of a ballroom and rotated so that bright lights directed at it cause it to sparkle.

witch·craft (wich′kraft′, -kräft′), *n.* **1.** the art or practices of a witch; sorcery; magic. **2.** magical influence; witchery. [ME *wicchecraft,* OE *wiccecræft.* See WITCH, CRAFT]

—**Syn. 1.** See **magic.**

witch′ doc′tor, a man in some primitive societies who attempts to cure sickness and to exorcise evil spirits by the use of magic.

witch-elm (wich′elm′), *n.* wych-elm.

witch·er·y (wich′ə rē), *n., pl.* **-er·ies.** **1.** witchcraft; magic. **2.** magical influence; fascination; charm: *the witchery of her beauty.* [WITCH + -ERY]

witch·es′-be·som (wich′iz bē′zəm), *n. Plant Pathol.* witches'-broom.

witch·es′-broom (wich′iz broom′, -brŏŏm′), *n. Plant Pathol.* an abnormal, brushlike growth of small thin branches on woody plants, caused esp. by fungi, viruses, and mistletoes.

witch′es′ Sab′bath, *Demonology.* Sabbat.

witch′ grass′, a panic grass, *Panicum capillare,* having a bushlike compound panicle, common as a weed in North America. [see QUITCH GRASS]

witch′ ha′zel, **1.** a shrub, *Hamamelis virginiana,* of eastern North America. **2.** a liquid extraction from the leaves or bark of this plant, containing water and alcohol, used externally as an embrocation for inflammations and bruises and as an astringent. Also, **wych-hazel.** [*witch,* var. of *wych* (see WYCH-ELM)]

witch′ hob′ble, the hobblebush.

witch′ hunt′, an intensive effort to discover and expose disloyalty, subversion, dishonesty, or the like, usually based on slight, doubtful, or irrelevant evidence. Also, **witch′-hunt′.** —**witch′ hunt′er.** —**witch′-hunt′ing.**

witch·ing (wich′ing), *n.* **1.** the use or practice of witchcraft. **2.** fascination; charm; enchantment. —*adj.* **3.** of, characterized by, or suitable for sorcery, black magic, or other such activities: *a witching potion.* **4.** enchanting; fascinating. [late ME, deriv. of obs. *witch* to use witchcraft, OE *wiccian*). See WITCH -ING[1], -ING[2]] —**witch′ing·ly,** *adv.*

witch′ing hour′, midnight: *a rendezvous at the witching hour.*

witch′ moth′, any of several large noctuid moths of the genus *Erebus,* esp. the blackish *E. odora* (**black witch**).

witch′ of A·gne′si (ä nyā′zē), *Geom.* a plane curve symmetrical about the *y*-axis and asymptotic to the *x*-axis, generated by the locus of the point of intersection of a line drawn parallel to the *x*-axis through the point where the circumference of a fixed circle of radius *r,* tangent to the *x*-axis at the origin, is cut by a radius vector drawn from the origin, and a line drawn parallel to the *y*-axis through the point where the radius vector intersects a line drawn parallel to the *x*-axis at 2*r.* Equation: $x^2y=4r^2(2r-y)$. [named after Maria Gaetana *Agnesi* (1718–99), Italian mathematician and philosopher]

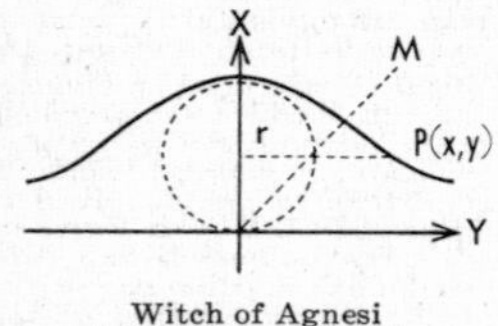

Witch of Agnesi
MQ:MP :: OM:OA

witch′'s mark′. See **devil's mark.**

witch·y (wich′ē), *adj.,* **witch·i·er, witch·i·est.** **1.** accomplished by or as if by witchcraft: *strange, witchy sounds.* **2.** similar to or characteristic of a witch; witchlike: *a witchy enjoyment of mischief-making.* [WITCH + -Y[1]]

wite[1] (wīt), *n., v.,* **wit·ed, wit·ing.** —*n.* **1.** (in Anglo-Saxon law) **a.** a fine imposed by a king or lord on a subject who committed a serious crime. **b.** a fee demanded for granting a special privilege. **2.** *Chiefly Scot.* responsibility for a crime, fault, or misfortune; blame. —*v.t.* **3.** *Chiefly Scot.* to blame for; declare guilty of. Also, **wyte.** [ME, OE: penalty; c. OHG *wīzi,* Icel *vīti;* akin to OE *wītan* to blame]

wite[2] (wīt), *v.* a pres. pl. of **wit**[2].

wit·e·na·ge·mot (wit′ənə gə mōt′), *n. Early Eng. Hist.* the assembly of the witan; the national council attended by the king, aldermen, bishops, and nobles. [OE, equiv. to *witena,* gen. pl. of *wita* councilor (see WITAN) + *gemōt* MOOT]

with[1] (with, wiŧh), *prep.* **1.** accompanied by; accompanying: *I will go with you. He fought with his brother against the enemy.* **2.** in some particular relation to (esp. implying interaction, company, association, conjunction, or connection): *I dealt with the problem. She agreed with me.* **3.** characterized by or having: *a man with initiative.* **4.** (of means or instrument) by the use of: *to line a coat with silk; to cut with a knife.* **5.** (of manner) using or showing: *to work with diligence.* **6.** in correspondence, comparison, or proportion to: *Their power increased with their number. How does their plan compare with ours?* **7.** in regard to: *to be pleased with a gift.* **8.** (of cause) owing to: *to die with pneumonia; to pale with fear.* **9.** in the region, sphere, or view of: *It is day with us while it is night with the Chinese.* **10.** (of separation) from: *to part with a thing.* **11.** against, as in opposition or competition: *He fought with his brother over the inheritance.* **12.** in the keeping or service of: *to leave something with a friend.* **13.** in affecting the judgment, estimation, or consideration of: *Her argument carried a lot of weight with the trustees.* **14.** at the same time as or immediately after; upon: *And with that last remark, she turned and left.* **15.** of the same opinion or conviction as: *Are you with me or against me?* **16.** in the same locality or vicinity as: *He can't live with her, and he can't live without her.* **17. in with.** See **in** (def. 22). **18. with child,** pregnant. **19. with that,** that (def. 28). [ME, OE (c. Icel *vith*), appar. short var. of OE *wither* against; c. OS *withar,* OHG *widar,* Icel *vithr,* Goth *withra,* equiv. to *wi-* + comp. suffix (see FARTHER)]
—**Syn. 4.** See **by.**

with[2] (with), *n.* withe (def. 4).

with-, a combining form of **with,** having a separative or opposing force: *withstand; withdraw.* [ME, OE. See WITH[1]]

with·al (wiŧh ôl′, with-), *Archaic.* —*adv.* **1.** with it all; as well; besides. **2.** in spite of all; nevertheless. **3.** with that; therewith. —*prep.* **4.** with (used after its object). [ME phrase *with al(le);* r. OE *mid ealle, mid eallum.* See WITH[1], ALL]

with·am·ite (wiŧh′ə mīt′), *n. Mineral.* a member of the epidote group, containing manganese and similar to piedmontite. [named after H. *Witham,* 19th-century Englishman; see -ITE[1]]

with·draw (wiŧh drô′, with-), *v.,* **-drew, -drawn, -draw·ing.** —*v.t.* **1.** to draw back, away, or aside; take back; remove: *She withdrew her hand from his. He withdrew his savings from the bank.* **2.** to retract or recall: *to withdraw a remark; to withdraw an untrue charge.* —*v.i.* **3.** to go or move back, away, or aside; retire; retreat: *to withdraw from reality; The others tactfully withdrew.* **4.** to remove oneself from some activity, competition, etc.: *He withdrew before I could nominate him.* **5.** to cease using or consuming an addictive narcotic (fol. by *from*): *to withdraw from heroin.* **6.** *Parl. Proc.* to remove an amendment, motion, etc., from consideration. [ME *withdrawe(n).* See WITH-, DRAW] —**with·draw′a·ble,** *adj.* —**with·draw′er,** *n.* —**with·draw′ing·ness,** *n.*
—**Syn. 1.** subtract. **2.** revoke, rescind, disavow. **3.** See **depart.**

with·draw·al (wiŧh drô′əl, with-), *n.* act or condition of withdrawing. Also, **with·draw′ment.** [WITHDRAW + -AL[2]]

withdraw′al symp′tom, any of a number of physical and psychological disturbances, as sweating and depression, experienced by a narcotic addict deprived of a required drug dosage.

withdraw′ing room′, *Archaic.* a room to withdraw or retire to; drawing room.

with·drawn (wiŧh drôn′, with-), *v.* **1.** pp. of **withdraw.** —*adj.* **2.** removed from circulation, contact, competition, etc. **3.** shy; retiring; reticent. —**with·drawn′ness,** *n.*

with·drew (wiŧh drōō′, with-), *v.* pt. of **withdraw.**

withe (with, wiŧh, wīŧh), *n., v.,* **withed, with·ing.** —*n.* **1.** a willow twig or osier. **2.** any tough, flexible twig or stem suitable for binding things together. **3.** an elastic handle for a tool, to lessen shock occurring in use. **4.** Also, **with, wythe.** a partition dividing flues of a chimney. —*v.t.* **5.** to bind with withes. [ME, OE *withthe;* akin to Icel *vith* WITHY, Goth *(kuna)wida* chain, L *viēre* (to) weave together]

with·er (wiŧh′ər), *v.i.* **1.** to shrivel; fade; decay: *The grapes had withered on the vine.* **2.** to lose the freshness of youth, as from age (often fol. by *away*): *She could see her beauty withering away.* —*v.t.* **3.** to make flaccid, shrunken, or dry, as from loss of moisture; cause to lose freshness, bloom, vigor, etc.: *The drought withered the buds.* **4.** to affect harmfully: *Reputations were withered by the scandal.* **5.** to abash, as by a scathing glance: *He gave her a look that withered her.* [ME; ? var. of WEATHER (v.)] —**with′ered·ness,** *n.* —**with′er·er,** *n.* —**with′er·ing·ly,** *adv.*
—**Syn. 1.** wrinkle, shrink, dry, decline, languish, droop, waste. WITHER, SHRIVEL imply a shrinking, wilting, and wrinkling. WITHER (of plants and flowers) is to dry up, shrink, wilt, fade, whether as a natural process or as the result of exposure to excessive heat or drought: *Plants withered in the hot sun.* SHRIVEL, used of thin, flat objects and substances, such as leaves, the skin, etc., means to curl, roll up, become wrinkled: *The leaves shrivel in cold weather. Paper shrivels in fire.*

With·er (wiŧh′ər), *n.* **George,** 1588–1667, English poet and pamphleteer. Also, **Withers** (wiŧh′ərz).

with·er·ite (wiŧh′ə rīt′), *n.* a white to grayish mineral, barium carbonate, $BaCO_3$, occurring in crystals and masses: a minor ore of barium. [named after W. *Withering,* (1741–99), who first described it; see -ITE[1]]

withe′ rod′, either of two North American viburnums, *Viburnum cassinoides* or *V. nudum,* having tough, osierlike shoots.

with·ers (wiŧh′ərz), *n.* (*construed as pl.*) **1.** the highest part of the back at the base of the neck of a horse, cow, sheep, etc. See diag. under **dog, horse. 2. wring one's withers,** to cause one anxiety or trouble: *The long, involved lawsuit is wringing his withers.* [?]

with·er·shins (wiŧh′ər shinz′), *adv. Chiefly Scot.* in a direction contrary to the natural one, esp. contrary to the apparent course of the sun, counterclockwise, or the like: considered as unlucky or causing disaster. Also, **widdershins.** [OE *withersynes* backwards, equiv. to *wither* opposite (see WITH[1]) + *-syn-* (? akin to OE *sīth* motion, deriv. of **sinth;* see SEND) + *-es* -S[1]]

With·er·spoon (wiŧh′ər spōōn′), *n.* **John,** 1723–94, U.S. theologian and statesman, born in Scotland.

with·hold (with hōld′, wiŧh-), *v.,* **-held, -hold·ing.** —*v.t.* **1.** to hold back; restrain or check. **2.** to refrain from giving or granting: *to withhold payment.* —*v.i.* **3.** to hold back; refrain. [ME *withholde(n).* See WITH-, HOLD[1]] —**with·hold′er,** *n.*
—**Syn. 1, 2.** suppress, repress. See **keep.** —**Ant. 1, 2.** advance.

withhold′ing tax′, that part of an employee's tax liability withheld by the employer from wages or salary and paid directly to the government. Also called **withholding.**

with·in (wiŧh in′, with-), *adv.* **1.** in or into the interior or inner part; inside. **2.** in or into a house, building, etc.; indoors: *The fire was burning on the hearth within.* **3.** on or as regards the inside; internally. **4.** inside an enclosed place, area, room, etc.: *He was startled by a cry from within.* **5.** in the mind, heart, or soul; inwardly. —*prep.* **6.** in or into the interior of or the parts or space enclosed by: *within a city or its walls.* **7.** inside of; in. **8.** in the compass or limits of; not beyond: *within view; to live within one's income.* **9.** at or to some point not beyond, as in length or distance; not farther than: *within a radius of a mile.* **10.** at or to some amount or degree not exceeding: *within two degrees of freezing.* **11.** in the course or period of, as in time: *within one's lifetime; within one's memory; within three minutes.* **12.** inside of the limits fixed or required by; not transgressing: *within the law; within reason.* **13.** in the field, sphere, or scope of: *within the family; within one's power.* —*n.* **14.** the inside of a place, space, or building. [ME *withinne,* OE *withinnan,* equiv. to *with* WITH[1] + *innan* (from) within, equiv. to *in* IN + *-an* suffix of motion from]

with·in·doors (wiŧh in′dōrz′, -dôrz′, with-), *adv.* into or inside the house. [WITHIN + DOOR + -S[1]]

with·in-named (wiŧh in′nāmd′, with-), *adj.* that is named herein.

with·out (wiŧh out′, with-), *prep.* **1.** with the absence, omission, or avoidance of; not with; with no or none of; lacking: *without help; without shoes; without her helping me; without him to help.* **2.** free from; excluding: *a world without hunger.* **3.** at, on, or to the outside of; outside of: *both within and without the house or the city.* **4.** beyond the compass, limits, range, or scope of (now used chiefly in opposition to *within*): *whether within or without the law.* —*adv.* **5.** in or into an exterior or outer place; outside. **6.** outside a house, building, etc.: *The carriage awaits without.* **7.** lacking something implied or understood: *We must take this or go without.* **8.** as regards the outside; externally. —*n.* **9.** outside of a place, region, area, room, etc.: *We heard a cry from the without.* —*conj.* **10.** *Chiefly Dial.* unless. [ME *without(e)(n),* OE *withūtan,* equiv. to *with* WITH[1] + *-ūtan* (from) without, equiv. to *ūt* OUT + *-an* suffix of motion from]

with·out·doors (wiŧh out′dōrz′, -dôrz′, with-), *adv. Archaic.* out of doors. [WITHOUT + DOOR + -S[1]]

with·stand (with stand′, wiŧh-), *v.,* **-stood, -stand·ing.** —*v.t.* **1.** to stand or hold out against; resist or oppose, esp. successfully: *to withstand rust; to withstand the invaders; to withstand temptation.* —*v.i.* **2.** to stand in opposition. [ME *withstande(n),* OE *withstandan* (see WITH-, STAND); c. Icel *vithstanda;* akin to G *widerstehen*] —**with·stand′er,** *n.* —**with·stand′ing·ness,** *n.*
—**Syn. 1.** confront, face. See **oppose.**

with·y (wiŧh′ē, with′ē), *n., pl.* **with·ies,** *adj.,* **with·i·er, with·i·est.** *Chiefly Brit.* —*n.* **1.** a willow. **2.** a pliable branch or twig, esp. a withe. **3.** a band, loop, halter, or rope of slender twigs; widdy. —*adj.* **4.** made of pliable branches or twigs, esp. of withes. **5.** flexible; pliable. [ME; OE *wīthig* (see WITHE); akin to Icel *vīth(i)r,* OHG *wīda,* Gk *eitea* (deriv. of **weitea*) willow, L *vītis* vine]

with·y·wind (wiŧh′ē wind′, with′-), *n.* traveler's-joy. [WITHY + WIND[2]; r. *withwind,* ME, OE *withewinde,* equiv. to *withe-* (? *withthe* WITHE) + *winde* (? deriv. of *windan* to WIND[2])]

wit·less (wit′lis), *adj.* lacking wit or intelligence; stupid; foolish. [ME; OE *witlēas.* See WIT[1], -LESS] —**wit′less·ly,** *adv.* —**wit′less·ness,** *n.*

wit·ling (wit′ling), *n.* a person who affects wittiness. [WIT[1] + -LING[1]]

wit·loof (wit′lōf), *n.* See **French endive.** Also called **wit′loof chic′ory.** [< D: lit., white foliage; see WHITE, LEAF]

wit·ness (wit′nis), *v.t.* **1.** to see or know by personal presence and perception: *to witness an accident.* **2.** to be present at (an occurrence) as a formal witness, spectator, bystander, etc.: *She witnessed our wedding.* **3.** to bear witness to; testify to; give or afford evidence of. **4.** to attest by one's signature: *He witnessed her will.* —*v.i.* **5.** to bear witness; testify; give or afford evidence. —*n.* **6.** one who, being present, personally sees or perceives a thing; a beholder, spectator, or eyewitness. **7.** a person or thing that affords evidence. **8.** one who gives testimony, as in a court of law. **9.** one who signs a document in attestation of the genuineness of its execution. **10.** testimony or evidence: *to bear witness to the truth of a statement.* **11.** (*cap.*) a member of the Jehovah's Witnesses. [ME, OE *witnes.* See WIT[1], -NESS] —**wit′ness·a·ble,** *adj.* —**wit′ness·er,** *n.*
—**Syn. 1.** perceive, watch, mark, notice, note. See **observe.**

wit·ness-box (wit′nis boks′), *n. Chiefly Brit.* See **witness stand.**

wit′ness cor′ner, *Survey.* a point, marked by a monument, situated at a known distance from and bearing relative to a corner which is used as a reference point but on which it is impossible to place a monument.

wit′ness mark′, a mark or stake set to identify a property corner or a survey point.

wit′ness stand′, the place occupied by one giving testimony in a court.

Witt (wit), *n.* a boy's given name.

Wit·te (vit′ə), *n.* **Ser·gei Yul·ie·vich** (ser gā′ yōōl′yə vich), 1849–1915, Russian statesman.

wit·ted (wit′id), *adj.* having wit or wits (usually used in combination): *quick-witted; slow-witted; dull-witted.* [late ME; see WIT[1], -ED[3]] —**wit′ted·ness,** *n.*

Wit·te·kind (vit′ə kint), *n.* died A.D. 807?, Westphalian chief: leader of the Saxons against Charlemagne. Also, **Widukind.**

Wit·ten·berg (wit′ən bûrg′; *Ger.* vit′ən berkh′), *n.* a city in central East Germany, on the Elbe: Luther taught in the university here; beginnings of the Reformation 1517. 48,132 (est. 1955).

Wit·ter (wit′ər), *n.* a boy's given name.

Witt·gen·stein (vit′gən shtīn′, -stīn), *n.* **Lud·wig (Jo·sef Jo·hann)** (lōōt′vikh yō′zef yō′hän, lōōd′-), 1889–1951, Austrian philosopher. —**Witt′gen·stein′i·an,** *adj., n.*

wit·ti·cism (wit′i siz′əm), *n.* a witty remark or sentence. [deriv. of WITTY, modeled on *criticism*]
—**Syn.** joke, jest, quip, sally, wisecrack.

wit·ting (wit′ing), *adj.* **1.** knowing; aware; conscious. —*n.* **2.** *Chiefly Dial.* knowledge. [late ME *witing.* See WIT[2], -ING[2], -ING[1]] —**wit′ting·ly,** *adv.*

wit·tol (wit′əl), *n. Archaic.* a man who knows of and tolerates his wife's infidelity. [ME *wetewold,* equiv. to *wete* WIT[2] + *-wold,* modeled on *cokewold* CUCKOLD]

wit·ty (wit′ē), *adj.,* **-ti·er, -ti·est.** **1.** possessing wit in speech or writing; amusingly clever in perception and expression: *a witty writer.* **2.** characterized by wit: *a witty remark.* **3.** *Brit. Dial.* intelligent; clever. [ME; OE *wittig.* See WIT[1], -Y[1]] —**wit′ti·ly,** *adv.* —**wit′ti·ness,** *n.*
—**Syn. 1, 2.** droll, funny, original, sparkling, brilliant. See **humorous.** —**Ant. 1, 2.** dull, stupid.

Wit·wa·ters·rand (wit wô′tərz rand′, -wot′ərz-), *n.* a rocky ridge in S Africa, in the Republic of South Africa, near Johannesburg. Also called **The Rand.**

wive (wīv), *v.,* **wived, wiv·ing.** —*v.i.* **1.** to take a wife; marry. —*v.t.* **2.** to take as wife; marry. **3.** to provide with a wife. [ME; OE *wīfian;* see WIFE]

wi·vern (wī′vərn), *n. Heraldry.* wyvern.

wives (wīvz), *n.* pl. of **wife.**

wiz·ard (wiz′ərd), *n.* **1.** one who professes to practice magic; a magician or sorcerer. **2.** a conjurer or juggler. **3.** Also, **whiz, wiz** (wiz). *Informal.* a person of amazing skill or accomplishment: *a wizard at chemistry.* —*adj.* **4.** of or pertaining to a wizard. **5.** magic. **6.** *Brit. Slang.* superb; excellent; wonderful: *That's wizard!* [late ME *wisard.* See WISE[1], -ARD] —**wiz′ard·like′,** *adj.*
—**Syn. 1.** enchanter, necromancer, thaumaturge, diviner.

wiz·ard·ly (wiz′ərd lē), *adj.* of, like, or befitting a wizard. [WIZARD + -LY]

wiz·ard·ry (wiz′ər drē), *n.* the art or practices of a wizard; sorcery; magic. [WIZARD + -RY]

wiz·en (wiz′ən; *Dial.* wē′zən), *Brit. Dial.* —*v.i., v.t.* **1.** to wither; shrivel; dry up. —*adj.* **2.** wizened. [ME *wisen,* OE *wisnian;* c. Icel *visna* to wither]

wiz·ened (wiz′ənd; *Dial.* wē′zənd), *adj.* withered; shriveled: *a wizened old man; wizened features.* [WIZEN + -ED²]

wk., **1.** week. **2.** work.

wkly., weekly.

w.l., **1.** water line. **2.** wave length.

Wla·di·mir (vlad′ə mēr′; *Russ.* vlä dē′mir), *n.* Vladimir.

WLB, War Labor Board.

w. long., west longitude.

Wm., William.

w/m, (in shipping) weight and/or measurement.

WMC, War Manpower Commission.

wmk., watermark.

WMO, World Meteorological Organization.

WNW, west-northwest.

wo (wō), *n., pl.* **wos,** *interj.* *Archaic.* woe.

W.O., **1.** wait order. **2.** War Office. **3.** warrant officer.

w/o, without.

woad (wōd), *n.* **1.** a European, brassicaceous plant, *Isatis tinctoria,* formerly cultivated for a blue dye extracted from its leaves. **2.** the dye extracted from this plant. [ME *wode,* OE *wād* (c. G *Waid*); akin to F *guède,* ML *waizda* < Gmc]

woad·ed (wō′did), *adj.* dyed or colored blue with woad. [WOAD + -ED³]

woad·wax·en (wōd′wak′sən), *n.* an ornamental, leguminous shrub, *Genista tinctoria,* whose flowers yield a yellow dye formerly used with woad to make a permanent green dye. Also, **woad′wax′, woodwaxen, woodwax.** Also called **dyer's-broom, dyer's furze, dyer's greenweed, dyer's greenwood.** [ME *wodewaxen,* equiv. to *wode* WOOD¹ + *waxen* grown (ptp. of *waxen* to WAX²); r. ME *wodewax,* OE *wuduweax* (see WOOD¹, WAX²)]

woald (wōld), *n.* weld².

w.o.b., (in shipping) washed overboard.

wob·be·gong (wob′ē gong′), *n.* *Australian.* the carpet shark. [native Austral]

wob·ble (wob′əl), *v.,* **-bled, -bling,** *n.* —*v.i.* **1.** to incline to one side and to the other alternately, as a wheel, top, or other rotating body when not properly balanced. **2.** to move unsteadily from side to side: *The table wobbled on its uneven legs.* **3.** to show unsteadiness; tremble; quaver: *His voice wobbled.* **4.** to vacillate; waver. —*v.t.* **5.** to cause to wobble. —*n.* **6.** a wobbling movement. Also, **wabble.** [< LG *wabbel(n);* akin to Icel *vafla* to toddle, MHG *wabelen* to waver, OE *wæflian* to speak incoherently] —**wob′bler,** *n.*

wob′ble pump′, *Aeron.* an auxiliary hand pump for supplying fuel to the carburetor of an aircraft engine when the automatic pumping mechanism fails.

wob′ble saw′. See **drunken saw.**

wob·bling (wob′ling), *adj.* that wobbles or causes to wobble. Also, **wabbling.** [WOBBLE + -ING²] —**wob′bling·ly,** *adv.*

wob·bly (wob′lē), *adj.,* **-bli·er, -bli·est.** shaky; unsteady. Also, **wabbly.** [WOBBLE + -Y¹]

Wob·bly (wob′lē), *n., pl.* **-blies.** *Informal.* a member of the Industrial Workers of the World. [akin to Canadian *Wobby* in same sense: ? *Wob* (alter. of *W.O.W.,* abbr. of *Workers of the World*) + -y²]

wo·be·gone (wō′bi gôn′, -gon′), *adj.* *Archaic.* woebegone.

Wo·burn (wō′bərn, wo͞o′-), *n.* a city in E Massachusetts, N of Boston. 31,214 (1960).

w.o.c., without compensation.

Wode·house (wo͝od′hous′), *n.* **P(el·ham) G(ren·ville)** (pel′əm), 1881–1975, U.S. novelist and humorist, born in England.

Wo·den (wōd′ən), *n.* the chief god of the pagan Anglo-Saxons, identified with the Scandinavian Odin. Also, **Wo′dan.** [ME, OE (c. G *Wotan,* Icel *Othinn*), equiv. to *wōd* WOOD² + *-en* n. suffix marking headship; Woden was the leader of the Wild Hunt]

wodge (woj), *n.* *Brit. Informal.* **1.** a lump, chunk, or wad. **2.** an object having a lumpy, bulgy shape. [? alter. of WEDGE] —**wodg′y,** *adj.*

woe (wō), *n.* **1.** grievous distress, affliction, or trouble: *His woe was almost beyond description.* **2.** an affliction: *She suffered a fall, among her other woes.* —*interj.* **3.** an exclamation of grief, distress, or lamentation. [ME *wo,* OE *wā,* interj. (cf. WELLAWAY); c. G *Weh,* D *wee,* Icel *vei,* L *vae*]

—**Syn. 1.** anguish, tribulation, trial, wretchedness, melancholy. See **sorrow.** —**Ant. 1.** joy.

woe·be·gone (wō′bi gôn′, -gon′), *adj.* **1.** beset with woe; affected by woe, esp. in appearance. **2.** showing or indicating woe: *He always had a woebegone look on his face.* [ME *wo begon* woe (has or had) surrounded (someone), *wo* WOE + *begon,* equiv. to ptp. of *bego,* OE *begān* to surround, besiege (see BE-, GO¹)] —**woe′be·gone′ness,** *n.*

woe·ful (wō′fəl), *adj.* **1.** full of woe; wretched; unhappy: *Hers is a woeful situation.* **2.** affected with, characterized by, or indicating woe: *Her poetry is a conglomeration of woeful ditties.* **3.** of wretched quality; sorry; poor: *a woeful collection of paintings.* Also, **wo′ful.** [ME; see WOE, -FUL] —**woe′ful·ly, wo′ful·ly,** *adv.* —**woe′ful·ness, wo′ful·ness,** *n.*

woe·some (wō′səm), *adj.* *Archaic.* woeful. [WOE + -SOME¹]

Wof·fing·ton (wof′ing tən), *n.* **Margaret** ("*Peg Woffington*"), 1714–60, Irish actress in England.

Wöh·ler (vûr′lər, vûr′-; *Ger.* vœ′lər), *n.* **1. Frie·drich** (frē′drikh), 1800–82, German chemist. **2.** a crater in the fourth quadrant of the face of the moon: about 16 miles in diameter.

wok (wok), *n.* a large, bowl-shaped metal pan widely used in cooking Chinese food. [< Chin]

woke (wōk), *v.* a pt. of **wake.**

wok·en (wō′kən), *v.* a pp. of **wake.**

wold¹ (wōld), *n.* **1.** an elevated tract of open country. **2.** Often, **wolds.** an open, hilly district, esp. in England, as in Yorkshire or Lincolnshire. [ME; OE *w(e)ald* forest; c. G *Wald;* akin to Icel *vǫllr* plain, and to WILD]

wold² (wōld), *n.* weld².

wold³ (wôld), *v.* *Obs.* a pp. of **will¹.**

wolf (wo͝olf), *n., pl.* **wolves** (wo͝olvz), *v.* —*n.* **1.** any of several large, carnivorous mammals of the genus *Canis,* of the family *Canidae,* esp. *C. lupus,* usually hunting in packs, formerly distributed throughout the Northern Hemisphere but now chiefly restricted to the more unpopulated parts of its range. **2.** the fur of such an animal. **3.** any of various wolflike animals of different families, as the thylacine. **4.** (*cap.*) *Astron.* the constellation Lupus. **5.** the larva of any of various small insects infesting granaries. **6.** a cruelly rapacious person. **7.** *Informal.* a man who is direct in making amorous advances to many women. **8.** *Music.* **a.** the harsh discord heard in certain chords of keyboard instruments, esp. the organ, when tuned on some system of unequal temperament. **b.** a chord or interval in which such a discord appears. **c.** (in bowed instruments) a discordant or false vibration in a string due to a defect in structure or adjustment of the instrument. **9. cry wolf,** to give a false alarm: *Is she really sick or is she just crying wolf?* **10. keep the wolf from the door,** to avert poverty or starvation; provide sufficiently for: *Grandma didn't leave us much, children, but it should keep the wolf from the door.* **11. wolf in sheep's clothing,** one who conceals his true evil intentions or character beneath an innocent exterior. —*v.t.* **12.** *Informal.* to devour voraciously (often fol. by *down*): *The tramp wolfed down the scraps in a moment.* —*v.i.* **13.** to hunt for wolves. [ME; OE *wulf;* c. G *Wolf,* Icel *ulfr,* Goth *wulfs,* L *lupus,* Gk *lýkos,* Skt *vrka*] —**wolf′like′,** *adj.*

Wolf, *Canis lupus* (3 ft. high at shoulder; total length 5½ ft.; tail 1½ ft.)

Wolf (vôlf), *n.* **1. Frie·drich Au·gust** (frē′drikh ou′go͞ost), 1759–1824, German classical scholar. **2. Hu·go** (ho͞o′gō), 1860–1903, Austrian composer. **3. Baron Christian von.** See **Wolff, Baron Christian von. 4.** a boy's given name.

wolf·ber·ry (wo͝olf′ber′ē, -bə rē), *n., pl.* **-ries. 1.** a caprifoliaceous shrub, *Symphoricarpos occidentalis,* of northern North America, bearing white berries. **2.** silverberry. Also called **buckbrush.** [WOLF + BERRY]

wolf-boy (wo͝olf′boi′), *n.* a boy whose origin is unknown and whose generally feral behavior and habits give the impression that he was reared by or among wolves.

wolf′ call′, a whistle, shout, or the like, uttered by a male in admiration of a female's appearance.

wolf-child (wo͝olf′chīld′), *n., pl.* **-chil·dren.** a child, esp. a boy, who is thought to have been suckled or nurtured by wolves.

wolf′ cub′, *Brit.* a member of the junior division, for boys from 8 to 11, of the Boy Scouts; cub scout.

wolf′ dog′, **1.** any dog used in hunting wolves. **2.** a cross between a wolf and a domestic dog. **3.** an Eskimo dog.

Wolfe (wo͝olf), *n.* **1. Charles,** 1791–1823, Irish poet. **2. James,** 1727–59, English general. **3. Thomas (Clay·ton)** (klāt′ən), 1900–38, U.S. novelist. **4.** a boy's given name.

wolf-eel (wo͝olf′ēl′), *n.* a large, eellike fish, *Anarrhichthys ocellatus,* found along the Pacific coast of North America.

Wol·fert (wo͝ol′fərt), *n.* **Ira,** born 1908, U.S. journalist and novelist.

Wolff (vôlf; *Eng.* wo͝olf), *n.* **1. Chris·ti·an von** (kris′tē än′ fən), **Baron.** Also, **Wolf.** 1679–1754, German philosopher and mathematician. **2. Kas·par Frie·drich** (käs′pär frē′drikh), 1733–94, German anatomist and physiologist. —**Wolff′i·an,** *adj.*

Wolf-Fer·ra·ri (vôlf′fer rä′rē), *n.* **Er·man·no** (er män′nō), 1876–1948, Italian composer.

Wolff′ian bod′y, *Embryol.* the mesonephros. [named after Kaspar Friedrich WOLFF; see -IAN]

wolf·fish (wo͝olf′fish′), *n., pl.* (*esp. collectively*) **-fish,** (*esp. referring to two or more kinds or species*) **-fish·es. 1.** a large acanthopterygian fish of the genus *Anarrhichas,* as *A. lupus* of the northern Atlantic, allied to the blenny, and noted for its ferocious appearance and habits. **2.** lancetfish. [WOLF + FISH]

Wolf·gang (wo͝olf′gang; *Ger.* vôlf′gäng), *n.* a boy's given name.

wolf′ her′ring, a voracious clupeoid fish, *Chirocentrus dorab,* found in the tropical Indian and Pacific oceans. Also called **dorab.**

wolf·hound (wo͝olf′hound′), *n.* any of several large dogs used in hunting wolves. Cf. **borzoi, Irish wolfhound.** [WOLF + HOUND¹]

wolf·ish (wo͝ol′fish), *adj.* **1.** resembling a wolf, as in form or characteristics. **2.** characteristic of or befitting a wolf; fiercely rapacious. [WOLF + -ISH¹] —**wolf′ish·ly,** *adv.* —**wolf′ish·ness,** *n.*

Wolf′ Lake′, a town in SW Michigan. 2525 (1960).

wolf·man (wo͝olf′man′), *n., pl.* **-men.** *Folklore.* a man who assumes the appearance of a wolf on certain occasions, as at the time of the full moon; werewolf. [WOLF + MAN¹]

wolf′ note′, wolf (defs. 8a, c).

wolf′ pack′, **1.** a group of submarines operating together in hunting down and attacking enemy convoys. **2.** a group of wolves hunting together. [WOLF + PACK¹ (trans. of G *Rudel* pack)]

Wolf′ Point′, a town in NE Montana. 3585 (1960).

wolf·ram (wo͝ol′frəm), *n.* **1.** *Chem.* tungsten. **2.** *Mineral.* wolframite. [< G; orig. man's name, equiv. to *Wolf* WOLF + *Ram(n)* RAVEN¹]

wolf·ram·ate (wo͝ol′frə māt′), *n.* *Chem.* tungstate. [WOLFRAM + -ATE²]

wolf·ram·ic (wo͝ol fram′ik), *adj.* *Chem.* tungstic. [WOLFRAM + -IC]

wolf·ram·ite (wo͝ol′frə mīt′, vôl′-), *n.* a mineral, iron manganese tungstate, $(Fe,Mn)WO_4$, occurring in heavy grayish-black to brownish-black tabular or bladed crystals: an important ore of tungsten. Also, **wolfram.** [WOLFRAM + -ITE¹]

wolf·ra·mi·um (wo͝ol frā′mē əm, vôl-), *n.* tungsten. [WOLFRAM + -IUM]

Wolf·ram von Esch·en·bach (vôl′främ fən esh′ən bäkh′), c1170–c1220, German poet.

wolfs·bane (wo͝olfs′bān′), *n.* any of several plants of the genus *Aconitum,* esp. *A. lycoctonum,* having yellow flowers. [WOLF + 's¹ + BANE]

wolf′ spi′der, any of numerous spiders of the family *Lycosidae,* that hunt their prey instead of snaring it in a web.

wolf′ whis′tle, a wolf call made by whistling, often characterized by a sliding sound from a high to a low note.

Wol·las·ton (wol′ə stən *or, esp. Brit.,* wo͝ol′-), *n.* a crater in the second quadrant of the face of the moon: about 8 miles in diameter.

wol·las·ton·ite (wo͝ol′ə stə nīt′), *n.* a mineral, calcium silicate, $CaSiO_3$, occurring usually in fibrous white masses. [named after W. H. *Wollaston* (1766–1828), English chemist; see -ITE¹]

Wol′las·ton wire′ (wo͝ol′ə stən), extremely fine wire formed by a process (**Wol′laston proc′ess**) in which the metal, drawn as an ordinary wire, is encased in another metal and the two drawn together as ordinary wire, after which the outer metal is stripped off or dissolved. [see WOLLASTONITE]

Wol·lon·gong (wo͝ol′ən gông′, -gong′), *n.* a seaport in E New South Wales, in E Australia. 131,754 (1961).

Wo·lof (wō′lof), *n.* a language of Senegal, a Niger-Congo language closely related to Fulani.

Wolse·ley (wo͝olz′lē), *n.* **Gar·net Joseph** (gär′nit), **1st viscount,** 1833–1913, British field marshal.

Wol·sey (wo͝ol′zē), *n.* **Thomas,** 1475?–1530, English cardinal and statesman.

wolv·er (wo͝ol′vər), *n.* one who hunts for wolves. [WOLVE(S) + -ER¹]

Wol·ver·hamp·ton (wo͝ol′vər hamp′tən), *n.* a city in S Staffordshire, in W England. 150,385 (1961).

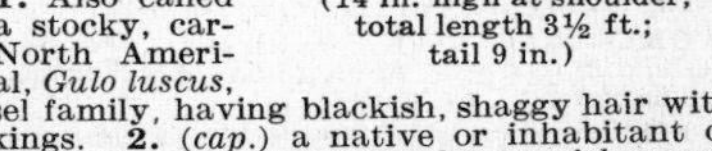

Wolverine (14 in. high at shoulder; total length 3½ ft.; tail 9 in.)

wol·ver·ine (wo͝ol′və rēn′), *n.* **1.** Also called **carcajou.** a stocky, carnivorous, North American mammal, *Gulo luscus,* of the weasel family, having blackish, shaggy hair with white markings. **2.** (*cap.*) a native or inhabitant of Michigan (the Wolverine State) (used as a nickname). [*wolvering* (with -INE² for -ING¹), equiv. to *wolver* wolf-like creature (*wolv-* + *-er* < ?) + -ING¹]

Wol′verine State′, Michigan (used as a nickname).

wolves (wo͝olvz), *n.* pl. of **wolf.**

wom·an (wo͝om′ən), *n., pl.* **wom·en** (wim′in), *v., adj.* —*n.* **1.** the female human being (distinguished from *man*). **2.** an adult female person. **3.** a female attendant to a lady of rank. **4.** a wife. **5.** feminine nature, characteristics, or feelings: *There's not much of the woman about her.* **6.** a sweetheart or paramour; mistress. **7.** a female person who cleans house, cooks, etc.; housekeeper: *The woman will be in to clean today.* **8.** women collectively: *Woman is fickle.* —*v.t.* **9.** to call (one) "woman," esp. rudely or condescendingly. **10.** to put into the company of a woman. **11.** to equip or staff with women: *The office is now fully womaned with servicemen's wives.* **12.** *Obs.* to cause to act or yield like a woman. —*adj.* **13.** of women; womanly. **14.** female: *a woman plumber.* [ME *womman, wimman,* OE *wīfman,* equiv. to *wīf* female + *man* human being; see WOMEN] —**wom′an·less,** *adj.*

—**Syn. 1.** WOMAN, FEMALE, LADY apply to the adult of the human race correlative with man. WOMAN is the general term: *a woman nearing middle age.* FEMALE refers esp. to sex. It was formerly used interchangeably with WOMAN, but now sometimes has a contemptuous implication: *a strong-minded female.* LADY formerly implied family or social position, but is now used conventionally for any woman (esp. as a courteous term for one engaged in menial tasks): *a scrub lady; a highborn lady; the appearance of a lady.* —**Ant. 1.** man.

wom·an-chas·er (wo͝om′ən chā′sər), *n.* a man who is excessively attentive to women in hope of receiving their attention, affection, etc.

wom·an-hat·er (wo͝om′ən hā′tər), *n.* a person, esp. a man, who dislikes women; misogynist.

wom·an·hood (wo͝om′ən ho͝od′), *n.* **1.** state of being a woman; womanly character or qualities. **2.** women collectively: *It's an insult to American womanhood.* [late ME; see WOMAN, -HOOD]

wom·an·ise (wo͝om′ə nīz′), *v.t., v.i.,* **-ised, -is·ing.** *Chiefly Brit.* womanize.

wom·an·ish (wo͝om′ə nish), *adj.* **1.** womanlike or feminine. **2.** weakly feminine; effeminate. [late ME; see WOMAN, -ISH¹] —**wom′an·ish·ly,** *adv.* —**wom′an·ish·ness,** *n.*

—**Syn. 2.** See **womanly.**

wom·an·ize (wo͝om′ə nīz′), *v.,* **-ized, -iz·ing.** —*v.t.* **1.** to make effeminate. —*v.i.* **2.** to pursue or court women habitually. Also, *esp. Brit.,* **womanise.** [WOMAN + -IZE]

wom·an·iz·er (wo͝om′ə nī′zər), *n.* woman-chaser, esp. a philanderer. [WOMANIZE + -ER¹]

wom·an·kind (wo͝om′ən kīnd′), *n.* women, as distinguished from men; the female sex. [late ME; see WOMAN, KIND²]

wom·an·like (wo͝om′ən līk′), *adj.* like a woman; womanly. [late ME; see WOMAN, -LIKE]

—**Syn.** See **womanly.**

wom·an·ly (wo͝om′ən lē), *adj.* **1.** like or befitting a woman; feminine; not masculine or girlish. —*adv.* **2.** in the manner of, or befitting, a woman. [ME *wommanlich(e).* See WOMAN, -LY] —**wom′an·li·ness, wom′an·ness,** *n.*

—**Syn. 1.** ladylike. WOMANLY, WOMANLIKE, WOMANISH mean resembling a woman. WOMANLY implies resemblance in appropriate, fitting ways: *womanly decorum, modesty.* WOMANLIKE, a neutral synonym, may suggest mild disapproval or, more rarely, disgust: *Womanlike, she (he) burst into tears.* WOMANISH usually implies an inappropriate resemblance and suggests weakness or effeminacy: *womanish petulance.*

wom′an of the house′. See **lady of the house.**

wo′man of the streets′, a prostitute; a streetwalker. Also, **wom′an of the street′.**

wom′an of the world′, a woman experienced and sophisticated in the ways and manners of the world, esp. the world of society.

wom·an·pow·er (wo͝om′ən pou′ər), *n.* potential or actual power from the endeavors of women: *the utilization of womanpower during a great national emergency.* [WOMAN + POWER]

wom′an's rights′. See **women's rights.**

wom′an suf′frage, the right of women to vote; female suffrage. —**wom′an-suf′frage,** *adj.* —**wom′an-suf′fra·gist,** *n.*

womb (wo͞om), *n.* **1.** the uterus of the human female and certain higher mammals. **2.** the place in which anything is formed or produced: *the womb of time.* **3.** the interior of anything. **4.** *Obs.* the belly. [ME, OE: belly, womb; c. D *wam,* G *Wamme,* Goth *wamba* belly; cf. WAMUS] —**wombed,** *adj.*

Wombat,
Vombatus hirsutus
(Length 3 ft.)

wom·bat (wom′bat), *n.* any of several burrowing, herbivorous marsupials of the family *Vombatidae,* of Australia, about the size of a badger. [< native Austral]

wom·en (wim′in), *n.* pl. of **woman.**

Wom′en at Point′ Sur′, The (sûr), a narrative poem (1927) by Robinson Jeffers.

wom·en·folk (wim′in fōk′), *n.* (*construed as pl.*) **1.** women in general; all women. **2.** a particular group of women. Also, **wom′en·folks′.** [WOMEN + FOLK]

Wom′en in Love′, a novel (1920) by D. H. Lawrence.

wom′en's rights′, the rights claimed for women, equal to those of men, with respect to suffrage, property, the professional fields, etc. Also, **woman's rights.**

wom′en's room′. See **ladies' room.**

wom·er·a (wom′ər ə), *n.* a device used by Australian aborigines for propelling spears or darts. Also, **woomera.** [< native Austral]

wom·mer·a (wom′ər ə), *n.* *Australian.* boomerang. [< native Austral]

won[1] (wun), *v.* a pt. and pp. of **win.**

won[2] (wun, wo͝on, wōn), *v.i.,* **wonned, won·ning.** *Archaic.* to dwell; abide; stay. [ME *wone,* OE *wunian;* c. G *wohnen;* see WONT]

won[3] (won), *n., pl.* **won.** a paper money and monetary unit of South Korea, equal to 100 chon and equivalent to about .0038 of a U.S. dollar: replaced the hwan in 1962.

won·der (wun′dər), *v.i.* **1.** to think or speculate curiously: *to wonder about the origin of the solar system.* **2.** to be filled with admiration, amazement, or awe; marvel (often fol. by *at*): *He wondered at her composure in such a crisis.* **3.** to doubt: *I wonder if she'll really get here.* —*v.t.* **4.** to speculate curiously or be curious about; be curious to know: *to wonder what happened.* **5.** to feel wonder at: *I wonder that you went.* —*n.* **6.** something strange and surprising; a cause of surprise, astonishment, or admiration: *the seven wonders of the world; It is a wonder he declined such an offer.* **7.** the emotion excited by what is strange and surprising; a feeling of surprised or puzzled interest, sometimes tinged with admiration: *He felt wonder mingled with awe at the Grand Canyon.* **8.** a miracle; miraculous deed or event. **9. for a wonder,** as the reverse of what might be expected; surprisingly: *She came on time, for a wonder, and worked hard all day.* [ME; OE *wundor;* c. D *wonder,* G *Wunder,* Icel *undr*] —**won′der·er,** *n.* —**won′der·less,** *adj.*
—**Syn. 1.** conjecture, meditate, ponder, question. **7.** surprise, astonishment, amazement, bewilderment, awe.

won·der·ber·ry (wun′dər ber′ē), *n., pl.* **-ries.** the black, edible fruit of an improved garden variety of the black nightshade. Also called **sunberry.** [WONDER + BERRY]

won′der boy′, a young man who is unusually successful in business or especially popular in his social contacts.

won′der child′, an unusually intelligent or talented child.

won′der drug′, a drug, usually recently discovered or developed, noted for its startling curative effect, as an antibiotic or sulfa drug. Also called **miracle drug.**

won·der·ful (wun′dər fəl), *adj.* of a kind to excite wonder; marvelous; extraordinary; remarkable. [ME; OE *wundorful* (see WONDER, -FUL); c. G *wundervoll*] —**won′der·ful·ly,** *adv.* —**won′der·ful·ness,** *n.*
—**Syn.** awesome, wondrous, miraculous, prodigious, astonishing, amazing, astounding, phenomenal, unique, curious, strange. —**Ant.** ordinary.

won·der·ing (wun′dər ing), *adj.* expressing admiration or amazement; marveling. [WONDER + -ING[2]] —**won′der·ing·ly,** *adv.*

Won′der Lake′, a town in NE Illinois. 3543 (1960).

won·der·land (wun′dər land′), *n.* **1.** a land of wonders or marvels. **2.** a wonderful country or region: *a wonderland of snow; a winter wonderland.* [WONDER + LAND]

won·der·ment (wun′dər mənt), *n.* **1.** wondering or wonder. **2.** a cause or occasion of wonder. [WONDER + -MENT]

won·der-strick·en (wun′dər strik′ən), *adj.* struck or affected with wonder. Also, **won·der-struck** (wun′dər struk′).

won·der·work (wun′dər wûrk′), *n.* a wonderful work; marvel; miracle. [OE *wundorweorc.* See WONDER, WORK]

won·der-work·er (wun′dər wûr′kər), *n.* a worker or performer of wonders or marvels. —**won′der-work′ing,** *adj.*

won·drous (wun′drəs), *adj.* **1.** *Literary.* wonderful; remarkable. —*adv.* **2.** *Archaic.* wonderfully; remarkably. [metathetic var. of ME *wonders* (gen. of WONDER) wonderful; sp. conformed to -OUS; c. G *Wunders*] —**won′drous·ly,** *adv.* —**won′drous·ness,** *n.*

wong·a-wong·a (wong′ə wong′ə), *n.* a woody vine, *Pandorea pandorana,* of Australia, having white or yellowish-white flowers in showy clusters. [< native Austral]

won·ky (wong′kē), *adj. Brit. Slang.* **1.** shaky; wobbly. **2.** unreliable; not trustworthy. [var. of dial. *wanky,* equiv. to *wank(le)* (ME *wankel,* OE *wancol;* see WENCH) + -Y[1]]

won·na (wun′nə), *Scot.* contraction of *will not.*

Wön·san (wœn′sän′), *n.* a seaport in E North Korea. 112,952 (1949). Japanese, **Gensan.**

wont (wônt, wōnt, wunt), *adj., n., v.,* **wont, wont** or **wont·ed, wont·ing.** *Archaic.* —*adj.* **1.** accustomed; used (usually fol. by an infinitive): *He was wont to rise at dawn.* —*n.* **2.** custom; habit; practice: *It was her wont to lie abed till noon.* —*v.t.* **3.** to accustom (a person), as to a thing. **4.** to render (a thing) customary or usual (usually used passively). —*v.i.* **5.** *Archaic.* to be wont; to be accustomed. [ME *woned,* OE *(ge)wunod,* ptp. of *(ge)wunian* to be used to (see WON[2]); c. G *(ge)wöhnt*] —**wont′less,** *adj.*
—**Syn. 1.** habituated, wonted. **2.** use. —**Ant. 1.** unaccustomed.

won't (wōnt, wunt), contraction of *will not.*

wont·ed (wôn′tid, wōn′-, wun′-), *adj.* **1.** accustomed; habituated; used. **2.** customary, habitual, or usual: *He took his wonted place in the library.* [WONT + -ED[3]] —**wont′ed·ly,** *adv.* —**wont′ed·ness,** *n.*
—**Syn. 1.** wont.

won ton (won′ ton′), **1.** (in Chinese cooking) a dumpling filled with minced pork and spices, usually boiled in and served with soup, but sometimes fried as a side dish. **2.** a soup containing won tons. [< Chin (Cantonese dial.) *wan t'an,* lit., pastry]

woo (wo͞o), *v.t.* **1.** to seek the favor, affection, or love of, esp. with a view to marriage. **2.** to seek to win: *to woo fame.* **3.** to invite (consequences, whether good or bad) by one's own action: *to woo one's own destruction.* **4.** to seek to persuade (a person, group, etc.), as to do something; solicit; importune. —*v.i.* **5.** to make love to a woman; court: *He went wooing.* **6.** to solicit favor or approval; entreat: *Further attempts to woo proved useless.* [ME *wowe,* OE *wōgian*] —**woo′ing·ly,** *adv.*

wood[1] (wo͝od), *n.* **1.** the hard, fibrous substance composing most of the stem and branches of a tree or shrub, and lying beneath the bark; the xylem. **2.** the trunks or main stems of trees as suitable for architectural and other purposes; timber or lumber. **3.** firewood. **4.** the cask, barrel, or keg, as distinguished from the bottle: *aged in the wood.* **5.** See **wood block** (def. 1). **6.** *Music.* **a.** a wooden wind instrument. **b.** such instruments collectively in a band or orchestra. **c. the woods,** the members of an orchestra or band who play the wooden wind instruments. **7.** Usually, **woods.** a large and thick collection of growing trees; a grove or forest: *They picnicked in the woods.* **8.** *Golf.* a club with a wooden head, as a driver, brassie, or spoon, for hitting long shots. Cf. **iron** (def. 5). **9. out of the woods,** out of a dangerous, perplexing, or difficult situation; secure; safe. —*adj.* **10.** made of wood; wooden. **11.** used to store, carve, or carry wood: *a wood chisel.* **12.** dwelling or growing in woods: *wood bird.* —*v.t.* **13.** to cover or plant with trees. **14.** to supply with wood; get supplies of wood for. —*v.i.* **15.** to take in or get supplies of wood (often fol. by *up*): *to wood up before the approach of winter.* [ME; OE *wudu,* earlier *widu;* c. Icel *vithr,* OHG *witu,* OIr *fid*] —**wood′less,** *adj.* —**Syn. 7.** See **forest.**

wood[2] (wo͝od), *adj. Archaic.* **1.** wild, as with rage or excitement. **2.** mad; insane. [ME; OE *wōd;* c. Icel *ōthr;* akin to G *Wut,* rage, OE *wōth* song, L *vātes* seer]

Wood (wo͝od), *n.* **1. Grant,** 1892–1942, U.S. painter. **2. Leonard,** 1860–1927, U.S. military doctor and political administrator.

wood′ al′cohol. See **methyl alcohol.**

wood′ anem′one, any of several anemones, esp. *Anemone nemorosa,* of the Old World, or *A. quinquefolia,* of the U.S.

wood′ bet′ony, 1. a betony. **2.** a scrophylariaceous herb, *Pedicularis canadensis,* of eastern North America.

wood·bin (wo͝od′bin′), *n.* a box for wood fuel. Also called **wood′box′.** [WOOD[1] + BIN]

wood·bine (wo͝od′bīn′), *n.* **1.** a European honeysuckle, *Lonicera Periclymenum.* **2.** any of various other honeysuckles, as *L. Caprifolium* **(American woodbine). 3.** *U.S.* the Virginia creeper, *Parthenocissus quinquefolia.* [ME *wodebinde,* OE *wudubind,* equiv. to *wudu* WOOD[1] + *bind* binding; see BIND]

Wood·bine (wo͝od′bīn), *n.* a town in SE New Jersey. 2823 (1960).

wood′ block′, 1. a block of wood engraved in relief, for printing from; woodcut. **2.** a print or impression from such a block. **3.** a hollow block of hard wood struck with a wooden stick or mallet and used in the percussion section of an orchestra. —**wood′-block′,** *adj.*

wood·bor·er (wo͝od′bôr′ər, -bōr′-), *n.* **1.** a tool, operated by compressed air, for boring wood. **2.** *Entomol.* borer (def. 3). **3.** *Zool.* borer (def. 4). [WOOD[1] + BORER]

wood·box (wo͝od′boks′), *n.* a box, bin, or the like, for holding firewood; woodbin. [WOOD[1] + BOX[1]]

Wood·bridge (wo͝od′brij′), *n.* a town in NE New Jersey. 78,846 (1960).

Wood·burn (wo͝od′bərn), *n.* a town in NW Oregon. 3120 (1960).

Wood·bur·y (wo͝od′ber′ē, -bə rē), *n.* a town in W Connecticut. 3910 (1960).

wood-carv·er (wo͝od′kär′vər), *n.* one whose occupation is wood carving.

wood′ carv′ing, 1. the art or technique of carving objects by hand from wood or of carving decorations into wood. **2.** something made or decorated in such a manner.

wood·chat (wo͝od′chat′), *n.* **1.** Also, **wood′chat shrike′.** a shrike, *Lanius senator,* of Europe and northern Africa, having a black forehead and a chestnut crown, nape, and mantle. **2.** *Rare.* any of various Asiatic thrushes, esp. of the genus *Larvivora.* [WOOD[1] + CHAT[2]]

Woodchuck
(Total length 2 ft.;
tail 7 in.)

wood·chuck (wo͝od′chuk′), *n.* a stocky, burrowing, North American marmot, *Marmota monax,* that hibernates in the winter. Also called **ground hog.** [alter. of Cree *wuchak* fisher, marten, weasel]

wood′ clamp′. See **hand screw** (def. 2).

Wood′cliff Lake′ (wo͝od′klif′), a town in NE New Jersey. 2742 (1960).

wood′ coal′, 1. brown coal; lignite. **2.** charcoal.

wood·cock (wo͝od′kok′), *n., pl.* **-cocks,** (*esp. collectively*) **-cock. 1.** an Old World, snipelike game bird, *Scolopax rusticola,* having a long bill, short legs, and large eyes placed far back on the head. **2.** a similar and closely related but smaller bird, *Philohela minor,* of eastern North America. **3.** *Archaic.* a simpleton. [ME *wodecok,* OE *wuducoc.* See WOOD[1], COCK[1]]

wood·craft (wo͝od′kraft′, -kräft′), *n.* **1.** skill in anything which pertains to the woods or forest, esp. in making one's way through the woods, or in hunting, trapping, etc. **2.** forestry (defs. 1, 2). **3.** the art of making or carving wooden objects. [late ME; see WOOD[1], CRAFT]

wood·crafts·man (wo͝od′krafts′mən, -kräfts′-), *n., pl.* **-men.** one who is skilled in woodcraft. [WOOD[1] + CRAFTSMAN]

wood·creep·er (wo͝od′krē′pər), *n.* woodhewer, [WOOD[1] + CREEPER]

wood′ cud′weed, a weedy, perennial herb, *Gnaphalium sylvaticum,* of the North Temperate Zone, having woolly foliage and numerous, dirty-white flowerheads in a leafy spike. Also called **chafeweed, owl's-crown.**

wood·cut (wo͝od′kut′), *n.* **1.** a carved block of wood from which prints are made. **2.** a print or impression from such a block. [WOOD[1] + CUT]

wood·cut·ter (wo͝od′kut′ər), *n.* **1.** one who cuts down trees for firewood. **2.** one who makes woodcuts. [WOOD[1] + CUTTER] —**wood′cut′ting,** *n.*

wood′ daf′fodil, strawflower (def. 2).

Wood′ Dale′, a town in NE Illinois. 3071 (1960).

Wood duck
(Length 1½ ft.)

wood′ duck′, a North American duck, *Aix sponsa,* which nests in trees, the male of which has a long crest and black, chestnut, green, purple, and white plumage.

wood·ed (wo͝od′id), *adj.* **1.** covered with or abounding in woods or trees. **2.** having wood (often used in combination): *a hard-wooded tree.* [WOOD[1] + -ED[3]]

wood·en (wo͝od′ən), *adj.* **1.** Also, **wood.** consisting or made of wood: *a wooden ship.* **2.** stiff, ungainly, or awkward: *to walk with a wooden gait.* **3.** without spirit, animation, or awareness: *a wooden stare.* **4.** dull or stupid: *wooden wits.* **5.** indicating the fifth event of a series, as a wedding anniversary. [WOOD[1] + -EN[2]] —**wood′en·ly,** *adv.* —**wood′en·ness,** *n.*

wood′ engrav′ing, 1. the art or process of engraving designs in relief with a burin on the end grain of wood, for printing. **2.** a block of wood so engraved. **3.** a print or impression from it. —**wood′ engrav′er.**

wood·en·head (wo͝od′ən hed′), *n.* *Informal.* a stupid person; blockhead. [WOODEN + HEAD]

wood·en-head·ed (wo͝od′ən hed′id), *adj.* *Informal.* thick-headed, dull; stupid. —**wood′en-head′ed·ness,** *n.*

Wood′en Horse′. See **Trojan Horse** (def. 1).

wood′en In′dian, 1. a carved wooden statue of a standing American Indian, formerly placed before a cigar store as an advertisement. **2.** (*often l.c.*) *Informal.* a person who appears emotionless and unresponsive; a poker face.

wood′en nick′el, a small wooden disk, souvenir token, or the like, having a value of five cents, or no value: *Don't take any wooden nickels.*

wood′en shoe′, sabot (def. 1).

wood′en tongue′, *Vet. Med.* actinobacillosis.

wood·en·ware (wo͝od′ən wâr′), *n.* vessels, utensils, etc., made of wood. [WOODEN + WARE[1]]

wood′en wed′ding, the fifth wedding anniversary.

wood′ fern′, any of several shield ferns of the genus *Dryopteris.*

Wood·ford (wo͝od′fərd), *n.* a boy's given name.

wood′ frog′, a reddish-brown or yellowish-brown frog, *Rana sylvatica,* found in moist woodlands of eastern North America, having a dark, masklike marking on the head.

wood′ grouse′, the capercaillie.

wood·hew·er (wo͝od′hyo͞o′ər), *n.* any of numerous New World, tropical, passerine birds of the family *Dendrocolaptidae,* having stiffened tail feathers and creeperlike habits. Also called **woodcreeper.** [WOOD[1] + HEWER]

wood′ hoo′poe, any of several tropical, African birds of the family *Phoeniculidae,* having metallic, blackish plumage and slender, curved bills.

wood·house (wo͝od′hous′), *n., pl.* **-hous·es** (-hou′ziz). a house or shed in which wood is stored. [late ME; see WOOD[1], HOUSE]

wood′ hy′acinth, an Old World squill, *Scilla nonscripta,* having drooping flowers.

Wood ibis,
Mycteria americana
(Length 4 ft.)

wood′ i′bis, any of several storks of the subfamily *Mycteriinae,* having chiefly white plumage and a featherless head and resembling the true ibises in having curved bills, esp. *Mycteria americana,* of the warm parts of America, and *Ibis ibis,* of Africa.

Wood·lake (wo͝od′lāk′), *n.* a town in central California. 2623 (1960).

wood·land (*n.* wo͝od′land′, -lənd; *adj.* wo͝od′lənd), *n.* **1.** land covered with woods or trees. —*adj.* **2.** of, pertaining to, or inhabiting the woods; sylvan: *a woodland nymph.* [OE *wuduland.* See WOOD[1], LAND]

wood·land·er (wo͝od′lən dər), *n.* an inhabitant of the woods. [WOODLAND + -ER[1]]

wood·lark (wo͝od′lärk′), *n.* a small, European songbird, *Lullula arborea,* noted for its song in flight. [ME *wodelarke.* See WOOD[1], LARK[1]]

CONCISE ETYMOLOGY KEY: <, descended or derived from; >, whence; b., blend of, blended; c., cognate with; deriv., derivative; equiv., equivalent; imit., imitative; m., modification of; obl., oblique; r., replacing; s., stem; sp., spelling; trans., translation; ?, origin unknown, perhaps; *, hypothetical. See the full key inside the front cover.

Wood·lawn (wŏŏd′lôn′), *n.* a town in SW Ohio. 3007 (1960).

wood′ lil′y, a lily, *Lilium philadelphicum,* of eastern North America, having orange-red flowers.

wood′ lot′, a tract, esp. on a farm, set aside for trees.

wood′ louse′, *Zool.* any of certain small, terrestrial isopod crustaceans of the genera *Oniscus, Armadillidium,* etc., having a flattened, elliptical body some of which are capable of being rolled up into a ball.

Wood-Lynne (wood′lin), *n.* a town in SW New Jersey. 3128 (1960).

wood·man (wŏŏd′mən), *n., pl.* **-men. 1.** woodsman (def. 1). **2.** one who fells timber, esp. for fuel. **3.** *Brit.* **a.** a forester having charge of the king's woods. **b.** a woodcutter. **c.** a dealer in wood, esp. one who sells kindling wood. **4.** *Obs.* a hunter of forest game. [ME *wodeman,* OE *wudumann.* See WOOD[1], MAN[1]] —**wood·man·craft** (wŏŏd′mən kraft′, -kräft′), *n.*

wood′ mead′ow grass′, a coarse, spreading, perennial grass, *Poa nemoralis,* of Eurasia, having flowers in long, narrow clusters.

wood′ mouse′, 1. any of various mice living in woodlands. **2.** See **white-footed mouse.**

wood·note (wŏŏd′nōt′), *n.* a wild or natural musical tone, as that of a forest bird. [WOOD[1] + NOTE]

wood′ nymph′, 1. (esp. in legend) a nymph of the woods; dryad. **2.** a brown satyr butterfly, *Minois alope,* having a broad yellow band across each front wing marked with black and white eyespots. **3.** any of several Central and South American hummingbirds, esp. of the genus *Thalurania.*

wood·peck·er (wŏŏd′pek′ər), *n.* any of numerous scansorial birds of the family *Picidae,* having a hard, chisellike bill which it hammers repeatedly into wood after insects, stiff tail feathers to assist in climbing, and usually more or less boldly patterned plumage. [WOOD[1] + PECKER]

wood′ pe′wee, a small American flycatcher, *Contopus virens.*

wood′ pig′eon, 1. ringdove (def. 1). **2.** See **band-tailed pigeon.**

wood·pile (wŏŏd′pīl′), *n.* a pile or stack of firewood. [WOOD[1] + PILE[1]]

wood′ pitch′, the final product of the destructive distillation of wood.

wood·print (wŏŏd′print′), *n.* woodcut. [WOOD[1] + PRINT]

wood′ pulp′, wood reduced to pulp through mechanical and chemical treatment for use in the manufacture of certain kinds of paper.

wood′ puss′y, *U.S. Dial.* **1.** a skunk. **2.** a polecat.

wood′ rab′bit, a cottontail.

wood′ rat′. See **pack rat** (def. 1).

wood′ ray′. See **xylem ray.**

Wood-Ridge (wŏŏd′rij′), *n.* a town in NE New Jersey. 7964 (1960).

Wood·row (wŏŏd′rō), *n.* a boy's given name.

wood·ruff (wŏŏd′rəf, -ruf′), *n.* a low, aromatic, rubiaceous herb, *Asperula odorata,* of the Old World, having small, sweet-scented, white flowers. [ME *woderove,* OE *wudurōfe,* equiv. to *wudu* WOOD[1] + *rōfe,* var. of *rīfe* (deriv. of **rȳfe*), c. G *Rübe* carrot]

Wood·ruff (wŏŏd′rəf), *n.* a town in NW South Carolina. 3679 (1960).

Wood′ruff key′, *Mach.* a key having the form of a nearly semicircular disk fitting into a recess in a shaft. [appar. after the proper name]

Woods (wŏŏdz), *n.* **Lake of the.** See **Lake of the Woods.**

wood′ sage′, a perennial herb, *Teucrium canadense,* of eastern North America, having hairy leaves and purple flowers.

wood′ screw′, any of various screws that have a slotted head and a gimlet point that permit them to be driven into wood with a screwdriver.

Woods·field (wŏŏdz′fēld′), *n.* a town in E Ohio. 2956 (1960).

wood·shed (wŏŏd′shed′), *n., v.,* **-shed·ded, -shed·ding.** —*n.* **1.** a shed for keeping wood for fuel. —*v.i.* **2.** *Slang.* to practice a musical instrument assiduously and with a specific goal in mind: *He's woodshedding for next week's show.* [WOOD[1] + SHED[1]]

wood·si·a (wŏŏd′zē ə), *n.* any rock-inhabiting fern of the genus *Woodsia,* of temperate and cold regions. [named after J. *Woods* (d. 1864), English botanist]

Wood·side (wŏŏd′sīd′), *n.* a town in W California. 3592 (1960).

woods·man (wŏŏdz′mən), *n., pl.* **-men. 1.** Also, **woodman.** one accustomed to life in the woods and skilled in the arts of the woods, as hunting, trapping, etc. **2.** a lumberman. [WOOD[1] + -S[3] + MAN[1]]

Wood′son Ter′race (wŏŏd′sən), *n.* a town in E Missouri. 6048 (1960).

wood′ sor′rel, any of numerous herbs of the genus *Oxalis,* esp. *O. Acetosella,* of Europe and North America, having heart-shaped, trifoliolate leaves, and white, pink-veined flowers. [WOOD[1] + SORREL[2] (after F *sorrel de bois*), r. *woodsour;* so called from sour taste of the leaves]

wood′ spir′it, 1. See **methyl alcohol. 2.** (esp. in legend) a supernatural, incorporeal being believed to inhabit the forest.

Wood·stock (wŏŏd′stok′), *n.* a town in NE Illinois. 8897 (1960).

wood′ stork′. See **wood ibis.**

Woods·town (wŏŏdz′toun′), *n.* a town in SW New Jersey. 2942 (1960).

wood′ sug′ar, *Chem.* a white, crystalline, water-soluble powder, $C_5H_{10}O_5$, the dextrorotatory form of xylose: used chiefly in dyeing and tanning.

wood-swal·low (wŏŏd′swol′ō), *n.* any of several passerine birds of the family *Artamidae,* of southeastern Asia, Australia, and New Guinea, having long wings and noted for their powers of flight.

woods·y (wŏŏd′zē), *adj.,* **woods·i·er, woods·i·est.** *U.S.* of, or characteristic or suggestive of, the woods: *a woodsy fragrance.* [WOOD[1] + -S[3] + -Y[1]]

wood′ tar′, a dark viscid product obtained from wood by distillation or by slow burning without flame, used in its natural state to preserve timber, rope, etc., or subjected to further distillation to yield creosote, oils, and a final residuum, wood pitch.

Wood Tech., Wood Technologist.

wood′ thrush′, a large thrush, *Hylocichla mustelina,* common in woodlands of eastern North America. See illust. under **thrush**[1].

wood·turn·er (wŏŏd′tûr′nər), *n.* a person whose occupation is wood turning. [WOOD[1] + TURNER[1]]

wood′ turn′ing, the forming of wood articles upon a lathe. —**wood′-turn′ing,** *adj.*

wood′ vin′egar. See **pyroligneous acid.**

wood′ war′bler, warbler (def. 3).

Wood·ward (wŏŏd′wərd), *n.* **1. Robert Burns,** born 1917, U.S. chemist: Nobel prize 1965. **2.** a town in NW Oklahoma. 7747 (1960.)

wood·wax·en (wŏŏd′wak′sən), *n.* woadwaxen. Also called **wood·wax** (wŏŏd′waks′).

wood·wind (wŏŏd′wind′), *n.* **1.** a musical wind instrument of the group comprising the flutes, clarinets, oboes, bassoons, and occasionally, the saxophones. **2. woodwinds,** the section of an orchestra or band comprising the woodwind instruments. —*adj.* **3.** of, relating to, or composed of woodwinds. [WOOD[1] + WIND[3]]

wood-wool (wŏŏd′wŏŏl′), *n.* fine wood shavings, usually of pine, or chemically-treated wood fibers: used for surgical dressings, as an insulating material, as a binder in plaster, for packing and protecting breakable objects, etc.

wood·work (wŏŏd′wûrk′), *n.* **1.** objects or parts made of wood. **2.** the interior wooden fittings, esp. of a house, as doors, stairways, moldings, etc. [WOOD[1] + WORK]

wood·work·er (wŏŏd′wûr′kər), *n.* a worker in wood, as a carpenter, joiner, or cabinetmaker. [WOOD[1] + WORKER]

wood·work·ing (wŏŏd′wûr′king), *n.* **1.** act or art of one who works in wood. —*adj.* **2.** pertaining to or used for shaping wood: *woodworking tools.* [WOOD[1] + WORKING]

wood·worm (wŏŏd′wûrm′), *n.* a worm or larva that breeds in or bores in wood. [WOOD[1] + WORM]

wood·y[1] (wŏŏd′ē), *adj.,* **wood·i·er, wood·i·est. 1.** abounding with woods; wooded. **2.** belonging or pertaining to the woods; sylvan. **3.** consisting of or containing wood; ligneous. **4.** resembling wood, as in appearance, texture, toughness, etc.: *What a woody vegetable the parsnip is!* [late ME; see WOOD[1], -Y[1]] —**wood′i·ness,** *n.*

wood·y[2] (wud′ē, wōō′dē), *n., pl.* **wood·ies,** *adj.,* **wood·i·er, wood·i·est.** *Chiefly Scot.* widdy[1].

Wood·y (wŏŏd′ē), *n.* a boy's given name, form of **Woodrow.**

wood′y night′shade, bittersweet (def. 1).

woo·er (wōō′ər), *n.* a person who woos, as a suitor or lover. [ME *wowere, wower,* OE *wōgere.* See WOO, -ER[1]]

woof (wŏŏf, wōōf), *n.* **1.** filling (def. 4). **2.** *Brit.* warp (def. 13). **3.** texture; fabric. [ME *oof, owf,* OE *ōwef, āwef* (cf. *gewef*), equiv. to *ō-, ā-* (< ?) + *wef* (akin to WEB, etc.); modern *w-* from WEFT, WARP, etc.]

woof·er (wŏŏf′ər), *n.* a loudspeaker designed for the reproduction of low-frequency sounds. [*woof,* imit. of dog's bark + -ER[1]]

wool (wŏŏl), *n.* **1.** the fine, soft, curly hair that forms the fleece of sheep and certain other animals, characterized by minute, overlapping surface scales which give it its felting property. **2.** fabrics and garments of sheep's wool. **3.** woolen yarn used for knitting, crocheting, ornamental needlework, etc.; worsted. **4.** any of various substances used commercially as substitutes for the wool of sheep or other animals. **5.** a woollike yarn or material made from cellulose by a process similar to that used in manufacturing rayon or artificial silk. **6.** any of certain vegetable fibers, as cotton, flax, etc., used as wool, esp. after preparation by special process **(vegetable wool). 7.** any finely fibrous or filamentous matter suggestive of the wool of sheep: *glass wool; steel wool.* **8.** any coating of short, fine hairs or hairlike processes, as on a caterpillar or a plant; pubescence. **9.** *Informal.* the human hair, esp. when short, thick, and crisp. **10. all wool and a yard wide,** genuine; excellent; sincere: *He was a real friend, all wool and a yard wide.* **11. dyed in the wool,** inveterate; confirmed: *a sinner who was dyed in the wool.* **12. pull the wool over someone's eyes,** to deceive or delude one: *The boy thought that by hiding the broken dish he would be able to pull the wool over his mother's eyes.* [ME *wolle,* OE *wull(e),* c. D *wol,* G *Wolle,* Icel *ull,* Goth *wulla;* akin to L *vellus* fleece, Gk *oûlos* woolly, etc.] —**wool′-like′,** *adj.*

wool′ clip′, the total yield of wool shorn during one season from the sheep of a particular region.

wool·en (wŏŏl′ən), *n.* **1.** any cloth of carded wool yarn of which the fibers vary in length: bulkier, looser, less regular, and of greater twist than worsted. **2. woolens,** wool cloth or clothing. —*adj.* **3.** made or consisting of wool: *woolen cloth.* **4.** of or pertaining to wool or woolen fabrics. Also, *esp. Brit.,* **woollen.** [ME *wollen,* OE *wullen,* var. of *wyllen.* See WOOL, -EN[2]]

wool·er (wŏŏl′ər), *n.* a domestic animal raised for its wool. [WOOL + -ER[1]]

Woolf (wŏŏlf), *n.* **Virginia** (*Adeline Virginia Stephen Woolf*), 1882–1941, English novelist, essayist, and critic.

wool′ fat′, lanolin.

wool·fell (wŏŏl′fel′), *n.* the skin of a wool-bearing animal with the fleece still on it. [ME *wolle fell.* See WOOL, FELL[4]]

wool·gath·er·ing (wŏŏl′gath′ər ing), *n.* **1.** indulgence in idle fancies and in daydreaming; absent-mindedness: *His woolgathering was a handicap in school. Instead of concentrating, he would go woolgathering.* **2.** gathering of the tufts of wool shed by sheep and caught on bushes. [WOOL + GATHERING] —**wool′gath′er·er,** *n.*

wool·grow·er (wŏŏl′grō′ər), *n.* one who raises sheep or other wool-bearing animals for the production of wool. [WOOL + GROWER] —**wool′grow′ing,** *n.*

Wooll·cott (wŏŏl′kət), *n.* **Alexander,** 1887–1943, U.S. essayist and journalist.

wool·len (wŏŏl′ən), *n., adj. Chiefly Brit.* woolen.

Wool·ley (wŏŏl′ē), *n.* **Sir (Charles) Leonard,** 1880–1960, English archaeologist and explorer.

wool·ly (wŏŏl′ē), *adj.,* **-li·er, -li·est,** *n., pl.* **-lies.** —*adj.* **1.** consisting of wool: *a woolly fleece.* **2.** resembling wool: *woolly hair; a woolly sweater.* **3.** clothed or covered with wool or something resembling it: *a woolly caterpillar.* **4.** *Bot.* covered with a pubescence of soft hairs resembling wool. **5.** *Informal.* like the rough, vigorous atmosphere of the early West in America: *wild and woolly.* **6.** fuzzy; unclear; disorganized: *woolly thinking.* —*n.* **7.** *Western U.S.* a woolbearing animal; sheep. **8.** Usually, **woollies.** *Informal.* a knitted undergarment of wool or other fiber. **9.** *Informal.* any woolen garment, as a sweater. Also, **wooly.** [WOOL + -Y[1]] —**wool′li·ness,** *n.*

wool′ly bear′, the caterpillar of any of several moths, as a tiger moth, having a dense coat of woolly hairs.

wool·ly-head·ed (wŏŏl′ē hed′id), *adj.* **1.** having hair of a woolly texture or appearance. **2.** marked by fuzzy thinking; muddleheaded; dim-witted. —**wool′ly-head′ed·ness,** *n.*

wool′ly man′zanita, a tree or shrub, *Arctostaphylos tomentosa,* found from British Columbia to California, having broad leaves with the underside covered with white hairs, and pink or white flowers.

wool·man (wŏŏl′mən), *n., pl.* **-men.** a person who buys and sells wool; wool dealer. [WOOL + MAN[1]]

wool·pack (wŏŏl′pak′), *n.* **1.** the package in which wool was formerly done up, as for transportation. **2.** something resembling such a package, as a fleecy cloud. **3.** *Meteorol.* a cumulus cloud of fleecy appearance with a horizontal base. [WOOL + PACK[1]]

wool·sack (wŏŏl′sak′), *n.* **1.** a sack or bag of wool. **2.** *Brit.* **a.** (in the House of Lords) one of a number of cloth-covered seats or divans stuffed with wool, for the use of judges, esp. one for the Lord Chancellor. **b.** the Lord Chancellor's office. [WOOL + SACK[1]]

wool·shed (wŏŏl′shed′), *n.* a building in which sheep are sheared and wool is gathered and prepared for market. [WOOL + SHED[1]]

wool′sort·ers′ disease′ (wŏŏl′sôr′tərz), *Pathol.* pulmonary anthrax in man, caused by inhaling the spores of *Bacillus anthracis.* [WOOL + SORTER + 'S[1]]

wool′ sponge′, a commercial sponge, *Hippiospongia lachne,* of Florida and the West Indies, the surface of which resembles the fleece of a sheep. Also called **sheepswool sponge.**

wool′ sta′pler, 1. a dealer in wool. **2.** one who sorts wool, according to the staple or fiber. —**wool′-sta′pling,** *adj.*

Wool·wich (wŏŏl′ij, -ich), *n.* a borough of E London, England: royal military academy and arsenal. 146,397 (1961).

Wool·worth (wŏŏl′wûrth′), *n.* **Frank Win·field** (win′fēld′), 1852–1919, U.S. merchant.

wool·y (wŏŏl′ē), *adj.,* **wool·i·er, wool·i·est,** *n., pl.* **wool·ies.** woolly. —**wool′i·ness,** *n.*

woo·mer·a (wōō′mər ə), *n.* womera.

woom·er·ang (wōō′mə rang′), *n. Australian Obs.* boomerang.

Woon·sock·et (wōōn sok′it), *n.* a city in NE Rhode Island. 47,080 (1960).

woo·ra·li (wŏŏ rä′lē), *n.* curare.

woosh (wōōsh, wŏŏsh), *n., v.i., v.t.* whoosh.

Woos·ter (wŏŏs′tər), *n.* **1. David,** 1711–77, American Revolutionary War general. **2.** a city in N Ohio. 17,046 (1960).

wootz (wōōts), *n.* cast crucible steel made in India by primitive methods. [*wook* (appar. by misprint) < Kanarese *(w)ukku* steel]

wooz·y (wōō′zē, wŏŏz′ē), *adj.,* **wooz·i·er, wooz·i·est.** *Informal.* **1.** stupidly confused; muddled: *woozy from a blow on the head.* **2.** physically out of sorts, as with dizziness, faintness, or slight nausea: *He felt woozy after the flu.* **3.** drunken. [? short for *boozy-woozy,* rhyming compound based on BOOZY] —**wooz′i·ly,** *adv.* —**wooz′i·ness,** *n.*

wop (wop), *n. Disparaging and Offensive.* an Italian or a person of Italian descent. [? It (south) *guappo* dandy]

Worces·ter (wŏŏs′tər), *n.* **1. Joseph Emerson,** 1784–1865, U.S. lexicographer. **2.** a city in central Massachusetts. 186,587 (1960). **3.** a city in and the county seat of Worcestershire, in W England, on the Severn: cathedral; Cromwell's defeat of the Scots 1651. 65,865 (1961). **4.** Worcestershire.

Worces′ter chi′na, a soft-paste porcelain containing very little clay or none at all, made at Worcester, England, since 1751. Also called **Royal Worcester, Worces′ter por′celain.**

Worces·ter·shire (wŏŏs′tər shēr′, -shər), *n.* a county in W central England. 568,642 (1961); 699 sq. mi. *Co. seat:* Worcester. Also called **Worcester.**

Worces′tershire sauce′, a sharp sauce made with soy, vinegar, spices, etc., originally made in Worcester, England.

word (wûrd), *n.* **1.** a unit of language, consisting of one or more spoken sounds or their written representation, that can stand as a complete utterance or can be separated from the elements that accompany it in an utterance by other such units. Words are composed of one or more morphemes with relative freedom to enter into syntactic constructions, and are either the smallest units susceptible of independent use or consist of two or three such units combined under certain linking conditions, as with the loss of primary accent which distinguishes *black′bird′* from *black′ bird′.* Words are typically thought of as representing an indivisible concept, action, or feeling, or as having a single referent, are usually separated by spaces in writing, and are distinguished phonologically, as by accent, in many languages. **2. words, a.** speech or talk, esp. insincere or vacuous speech: *Words, words, words! Words mean little when action is called for.* **b.** the text or lyrics of a song as distinguished from the music. **c.** contentious or angry speech; a quarrel: *We had words and she walked out on me.* **3.** a short talk or conversation: *Marston, I'd like a word with you.* **4.** an expression or utterance: *a word of praise or of warning.* **5.** warrant, assurance, or promise: *to give one's word; to keep one's word.* **6.** news; tidings; information: *We received word of his death.* **7.** a verbal signal, as a password, watchword,

or countersign. **8.** an authoritative utterance, or command: *His word was law.* **9.** *Computer Technol.* See **machine word. 10.** (*cap.*) Also called **the Word, the Word of God. a.** the Scriptures; the Bible. **b.** the Logos. **c.** the message of the gospel of Christ. **11.** *Archaic.* a proverb or motto. **12. at a word,** in immediate response to an order or request; in an instant: *At a word he came to take the situation in hand.* **13. be as good as one's word,** to hold to one's promises; be dependable: *She said she would finish the dress today, and was as good as her word.* **14. eat one's words,** to retract one's statement: *They told him he would never succeed at anything, but he made them eat their words.* **15. have a word with,** to talk briefly with; discuss: *Tell your aunt that I would like to have a word with her.* **16. have no words for,** to be unable to describe: *She had no words for the sights she had witnessed.* **17. in a word,** in summary; in short: *In a word, there was no comparison.* Also, **in one word. 18. in so many words, a.** in a few words; tersely. **b.** in unequivocal terms; explicitly: *He told them in so many words to get out.* **19. man** or **woman of one's word,** a person who can be trusted to keep a promise; a reliable person: *As a woman of her word, she pledged to come to our assistance if we needed her.* **20. of few words,** laconic; taciturn: *He is a man of few words but of profound thoughts.* **21. of many words,** talkative; loquacious; wordy: *She is a woman of many words but of little wit.* **22. put in a good word for,** to speak favorably of; commend: *In his position of influence, he was often asked to put in a good word for this one and that one.* Also, **put in a word for. 23. take one at one's word,** to take a statement to be literal and true: *She should know better than to take him at his word in view of his past behavior.* **24. take the words out of one's mouth,** to say exactly what another person was about to say. **25. weigh one's words,** to choose one's words carefully in speaking or writing: *It was an important message, and he was weighing his words.* **26. word of mouth.** See **mouth** (def. 14.) Also, **by word of mouth.**
—*v.t.* **27.** to express in words; put into words; select words to express; phrase: *to word a contract with great care; He words his thoughts badly.*
—*interj.* **28. my word!** or **upon my word!** *Chiefly Brit.* (used as an exclamation of surprise or astonishment.) [ME, OE; c. D *woord,* G *Wort,* Icel *orth,* Goth *waurd;* akin to OPruss *wirds,* L *verbum* word, Lith *vardas* name]
—**Syn. 4.** statement, assertion, declaration. **5.** pledge. **6.** message, report, account, advice. **7.** catchword, shibboleth. **8.** order.

word′ ac′cent, *Phonet.* See **word stress.**

word·age (wûr′dij), *n.* **1.** words collectively. **2.** quantity or amount of words: *The wordage of the document exceeds a million.* **3.** verbiage; wordiness. **4.** choice of words; wording: *His wordage betrayed his lack of knowledge on the subject.* [WORD + -AGE]

word′ associa′tion, stimulation of an associative pattern by a word.

word′ associa′tion test′, *Psychol.* a technique for determining a subject's associative pattern by providing a verbal stimulus to which a verbal response is required.

word-blind (wûrd′blīnd′), *adj.* having alexia.

word′ blind′ness, alexia.

word·book (wûrd′bŏŏk′), *n.* **1.** a book of words, usually with definitions, explanations, etc.; a dictionary. **2.** the libretto of an opera. [WORD + BOOK]

word′ class′, *Gram.* a group of words all of which are members of the same form class or part of speech.

word′ deaf′ness, *Pathol.* inability to comprehend the meanings of words though they are heard, caused by lesions of the auditory center of the brain. Also called **mind deafness, psychic deafness.** —**word′-deaf′,** *adj.*

word-for-word (wûrd′fər wûrd′), *adj.* **1.** in exactly the same words; verbatim. **2.** one word at a time, without regard for the sense of the whole: *a word-for-word translation.*

word′ game′, any game or contest involving skill in using, forming, guessing, or changing words or expressions, such as anagrams or Scrabble.

word·ing (wûr′ding), *n.* **1.** the act or manner of expressing in words; phrasing. **2.** the form of words in which a thing is expressed: *He liked the thought but not the wording.* [WORD + -ING[1]]
—**Syn.** See **diction.**

word·less (wûrd′lis), *adj.* **1.** speechless, silent, or mute. **2.** not put into words; unexpressed. [ME; see WORD, -LESS] —**word′less·ly,** *adv.* —**word′less·ness,** *n.*

word-lore (wûrd′lōr′, -lôr′), *n.* **1.** a study of words and their derivations. **2.** the vocabulary of a particular language and the history of the words in this vocabulary. Also, **word′lore′.**

word′ of hon′or, a pledge of one's honor that a specified condition, bargain, etc., will be fulfilled; oath; promise.

word-of-mouth (wûrd′əv mouth′), *adj.* spread or made known by verbal communication: *The producers rely on word-of-mouth advertising.*

word′ or′der, the way in which words are arranged in sequence in a sentence or smaller construction: *In Latin, word order is freer than in English.*

word′ paint′ing, 1. an effective verbal description. **2.** See **tone painting.** —**word′ paint′er.**

word′ pic′ture, a description in words, esp. one that is unusually vivid: *He drew a word picture of a South Pacific sunset.*

word·play (wûrd′plā′), *n.* **1.** clever or subtle repartee; verbal wit. **2.** a play on words; pun. [WORD + PLAY]

word′ proc′essing, a computerized system programmed for rapid, efficient production and editing of letters, reports, business records, etc., usually including a keyboard, a video display, memory storage on tapes or disks, and a high-speed printer. —**word′ proc′essor.**

S A T E D
A T O N E
T O A S T
E N S U E
D E T E R

Word square

word·smith (wûrd′smith′), *n.* an expert in the use of words. [WORD + SMITH]

word′ square′, a set of words such that when arranged one beneath another in the form of a square they read alike horizontally and vertically.

word′ stress′, the stress pattern or patterns associated with the words of a particular language when they are considered in isolation. Also called **word accent.** Cf. **sentence stress.**

Words·worth (wûrdz′wûrth′), *n.* **William,** 1770–1850, English poet: poet laureate 1843–50. —**Words·worth′i·an,** *adj., n.* —**Words·worth′i·an·ism,** *n.*

word′ time′, *Computer Technol.* the time required to transfer a machine word, esp. one stored serially, from one memory unit to another. Cf. **access time.**

word·y (wûr′dē), *adj.,* **word·i·er, word·i·est. 1.** characterized by or given to the use of many, or too many, words; verbose: *She grew impatient at his wordy reply.* **2.** pertaining to or consisting of words; verbal. [ME; OE *wordig.* See WORD, -Y[1]] —**word′i·ly,** *adv.* —**word′i·ness,** *n.*
—**Syn. 1.** prolix, talkative, loquacious, voluble.

wore (wōr, wôr), *v.* pt. of **wear.**

work (wûrk), *n., adj., v.,* **worked** or **wrought, work·ing.** —*n.* **1.** exertion or effort directed to produce or accomplish something; labor; toil. **2.** that on which exertion or labor is expended; something to be made or done; a task or undertaking: *The students finished their work in class.* **3.** productive or operative activity. **4.** employment, as in some form of industry, esp. as a means of earning one's livelihood: *to be without work; to look for work.* **5.** materials, things, etc., on which one is working or is to work. **6.** the result of exertion, labor, or activity; a deed or performance. **7.** a product of exertion, labor, or activity: *a work of art; literary works; musical works.* **8.** an engineering structure, as a building, bridge, dock, or the like. **9.** a building, wall, trench, or the like, constructed or made as a means of fortification. **10. works, a.** (*construed as sing. or pl.*) a place or establishment for carrying on some form of labor or industry: *iron works.* **b.** the working parts of a mechanical contrivance: *the works of a watch.* **c.** *Theol.* acts performed in obedience to the law of God; righteous deeds. **11.** *Physics.* force times the distance through which it acts; specifically, the transference of energy equal to the product of the component of a force that acts in the direction of the motion of the point of application of the force and the distance through which the point of application moves. **12.** the piece being cut, formed, ground, or otherwise processed in a machine tool, grinder, punch press, etc. **13. at work, a.** working, as at one's job: *Don't phone him at work.* **b.** in action or operation: *We were taken on a tour of a book manufacturing plant to see the machines at work.* **14. get the works,** *Slang.* to suffer cruel treatment; be victimized: *He got the works from his business partner.* **15. give someone the works,** *Slang.* **a.** to treat cruelly or roughly; abuse. **b.** to murder: *Someone had given him the works and thrown his body into the river.* **16. gum up the works,** *Slang.* to spoil something, as through blundering or stupidity: *The surprise party was all arranged, but her little brother gummed up the works and told her.* **17. make short work of,** to finish or dispose of quickly: *We made short work of the chocolate layer cake.* **18. out of work,** unemployed; jobless: *Many men in the area were out of work.* **19. shoot the works,** *Slang.* to make an intense or unsparing effort, spend all one's resources, etc.: *Let's shoot the works and order the crêpes suzette.*
—*adj.* **20.** of, for, or concerning work: *work clothes.* **21.** working (def. 17). [ME *worke,* OE *worc;* r. ME *werk,* OE *weorc;* c. G *Werk,* Icel *verk,* Gk *érgon*]
—*v.i.* **22.** to do work; labor. **23.** to be employed, as in some industry, esp. as a means of earning one's livelihood: *He hasn't worked for six weeks.* **24.** to be in operation, as a machine: *Stay away from the machine when it's working.* **25.** to act or operate effectively: *The pump will not work. The plan works.* **26.** to attain a specified condition, as by continuous effort (often fol. by *up, round, loose,* etc.): *The nails worked loose.* **27.** to have an effect or influence, as on a person or on the mind or feelings of a person. **28.** to move in agitation, as the features under strong emotion. **29.** to make way with effort or under stress: *The ship works to windward.* **30.** *Naut.* to give slightly at the joints, as a vessel under strain at sea. **31.** *Mach.* to move improperly, as from defective fitting of parts or from wear. **32.** to undergo treatment by labor in a given way: *This dough works slowly.* **33.** to ferment, as a liquid.
—*v.t.* **34.** to use or manage (an apparatus, contrivance, etc.) in operation: *She can work many business machines.* **35.** to bring about (any result) by or as by work or effort; effect, accomplish, cause, or do: *to work a change.* **36.** to expend work on; manipulate or treat by labor: *to work butter.* **37.** to put into effective operation. **38.** to operate (a mine, farm, etc.) for productive purposes: *to work a coal mine.* **39.** to carry on operations in (a district or region). **40.** to make, fashion, or execute by work. **41.** to achieve or win by work or effort: *to work one's passage.* **42.** to keep (a person, a horse, etc.) at work: *She works her men hard.* **43.** to influence or persuade, esp. insidiously: *to work a crowd into a frenzy.* **44.** *Informal.* **a.** to use guile or trickery on (a person or persons); obtain some favor or profit: *See if you can work your uncle for a new car. The swindler worked the whole town.* **b.** to put into use guilefully or insidiously for one's own ends: *to work one's poise and charm in landing a new job.* **45.** to make or decorate by needlework or embroidery: *She worked a needlepoint cushion.* **46.** to cause fermentation in. **47. work in** or **into, a.** to bring or put in, esp. to insert subtly or indirectly: *The tailor worked in the patch skillfully.* **b.** to arrange a time for: *The dentist was very busy, but said he would be able to work me in late in the afternoon.* **48. work off, a.** to lose or dispose of, as by exercise or labor: *We decided to work off the effects of a heavy supper by walking for an hour.* **b.** to pay or fulfill by working: *He worked off his debt by doing odd jobs.* **49. work on** or **upon,** to exercise influence on; persuade; affect: *She says she will never date him, but I'll work on her, and maybe she'll change her mind.* **50. work out, a.** to bring about by work, effort, or action. **b.** to solve, as a problem. **c.** to arrive at by or as by calculation. **d.** to pay (a debt) by working instead of paying money. **e.** to exhaust, as a mine. **f.** to issue in a result. **g.** to evolve; elaborate. **h.** to amount to (a total or specified figure); add up (to): *The total works out to 3,176.* **i.** to put into effect or operation; prove feasible: *I hope this works out.* **j.** to practice, exercise, or train, esp. in order to become proficient in an athletic sport: *The boxers are working out at the gym.* **51. work over, a.** to study or examine thoroughly: *For my term paper I worked over 30 volumes of Roman history.* **b.** *Slang.* to beat unsparingly, esp. in order to obtain something or out of revenge: *They threatened to work him over until he talked.* **52. work up, a.** to move or stir the feelings; excite. **b.** to prepare; elaborate: *Work up some plans.* **c.** to increase in efficiency or skill: *She worked up her typing speed to seventy words a minute.* **53. work up to,** rise to a higher position; advance: *He worked up to the presidency.* [ME *worke,* (v. use of *worke* (n.); r. ME *wyrche,* OE *wyrcean;* c. G *wirken,* Icel *verkja,* Goth *waurkjan*] —**work′less,** *adj.* —**work′less·ness,** *n.*
—**Syn. 1.** WORK, DRUDGERY, LABOR, TOIL refer to exertion of body or mind in performing or accomplishing something. WORK is the general word, and may apply to exertion which is either easy or hard: *heavy work; part-time work; outdoor work.* DRUDGERY suggests continuous, dreary, and dispiriting work, esp. of a menial or servile kind: *the drudgery of household tasks.* LABOR particularly denotes hard manual work: *labor on a farm, in a steel mill.* TOIL suggests wearying or exhausting labor: *toil which breaks down the worker's health.* **2.** enterprise, project, job, responsibility. **3.** industry, occupation, business. **4.** trade, calling, vocation, profession. **6.** product, achievement, feat. **22.** toil, moil, drudge. **34.** operate, manipulate, handle. **35.** perform, execute, produce, achieve. **40.** finish, form, shape. **43.** move.
—**Ant. 1.** play, rest.

work·a·ble (wûr′kə bəl), *adj.* **1.** practicable or feasible: *He needs a workable arrangement of his time.* **2.** capable of or suitable for being worked. [WORK + -ABLE] —**work′a·bil′i·ty, work′a·ble·ness,** *n.*

work·a·day (wûr′kə dā′), *adj.* **1.** of or befitting working days; characteristic of a workday and its occupations. **2.** ordinary; commonplace; humdrum; everyday; prosaic. [ME *werkeday* < Scand; cf. Icel *virkidagr* working day, weekday]

work·a·hol·ic (wûr′kə hô′lik, -hol′ik), *n. Informal.* a person obsessively occupied with work at the expense of normal leisure, human relationships, etc. [WORK + A(LCO)HOLIC] —**work′a·hol′ism,** *n.*

work-and-tum·ble (wûrk′ən tum′bəl), *adj. Print.* noting a method of imposition by which pages for both sides of a sheet are so arranged in one form that after a sheet has been printed on one side it can be turned over from left to right, printed on the reverse, and cut in two to form two complete sheets. Cf. **work-and-turn, work-and-twist.**

work-and-turn (wûrk′ən tûrn′), *adj. Print.* noting a method of imposition by which pages for both sides of a sheet are so arranged in one form that after a sheet has been printed on one side it can be turned over end over end, printed on the reverse, and cut in two to form two complete sheets. Cf. **work-and-tumble, work-and-twist.**

work-and-twist (wûrk′ən twist′), *adj. Print.* noting a method of imposition, esp. for narrow columns with cross-lines, by which the form for part of the matter is locked up head to head or side to side, the two to be combined by pivoting the sheet 180° after the first impression and overprinting the one on the other. Also called **work-and-whirl** (wûrk′ən hwûrl′, -wûrl′). Cf. **work-and-tumble, work-and-turn.**

work·bag (wûrk′bag′), *n.* a bag for holding implements and materials for work, esp. needlework. [WORK + BAG]

work·bench (wûrk′bench′), *n.* a sturdy table at which an artisan works. [WORK + BENCH]

work·book (wûrk′bŏŏk′), *n.* **1.** a manual of operating instructions. **2.** a book designed to guide the work of a student by inclusion of some instructional material, and usually providing questions, exercises, etc. **3.** a book in which a record is kept of work completed or planned. [WORK + BOOK]

work·box (wûrk′boks′), *n.* a box to hold instruments and materials for work, esp. needlework. [WORK + BOX[1]]

work′ camp′, a camp for prisoners sentenced to labor, esp. to outdoor labor such as roadbuilding, farming, etc.

work·day (wûrk′dā′), *n.* **1.** a day on which work is done; working day. **2.** the part of a day during which one works. **3.** the length of time during a day on which one works: *He has a seven-hour workday five days a week.* —*adj.* **4.** workaday. [ME *werkday,* OE *weorcdæg.* See WORK, DAY]

worked (wûrkt), *adj.* that has undergone working. [WORK + -ED[2]]
—**Syn.** WORKED, WROUGHT both apply to something on which effort has been applied. WORKED implies expended effort of almost any kind: *a worked silver mine.* WROUGHT implies fashioning, molding, or making, esp., by hand: *a wrought iron railing.*

worked-up (wûrkt′up′), *adj.* wrought-up.

work·er (wûr′kər), *n.* **1.** one who or that which works. **2.** a laborer or employee: *steel workers.* **3.** a person engaged in a particular field, activity, or cause: *a worker in psychological research; a worker for the Republican party.* **4.** (in the Soviet Union) a citizen, excluding the peasants and members of the army or navy. **5.** *Entomol.* a sterile or infertile female ant, bee, wasp, or termite. **6.** *Print.* one of a set of electrotyped plates used to print from, as contrasted with a set of molders. **7.** any of several rollers covered with card clothing that work in combination with the stripper rollers and the cylinder in the carding of fibers. [late ME *werker, worcher.* See WORK, -ER[1]] —**work′er·less,** *adj.*

work′ farm′, a farm to which juvenile offenders are sent for a period to work, for disciplinary purposes or rehabilitation.

work·folk (wûrk′fōk′), *n.pl.* people who work for a wage, salary, commission, etc., esp. rural or agricultural employees. Also, **work′folks′.** [late ME; see WORK, FOLK]

work′ force′, 1. the total number of workers in a specific undertaking: *a holiday for the company's work force.* **2.** the total number of persons employed or employable: *a sharp increase in the nation's work force.*

work′ func′tion, 1. *Physics.* the least energy necessary to free an electron from a metal surface. **2.** *Thermodynamics.* See **Helmholtz free energy.**

work·horse (wûrk′hôrs′), *n.* **1.** a horse used for plowing, hauling, and other heavy labor, as distinguished from a riding horse, race horse, etc. 2. a person who works tirelessly at a task, assumes extra duties, etc. [WORK + HORSE]

work·house (wûrk′hous′), *n., pl.* **-hous·es** (-hou′-ziz). 1. *U.S.* a house of correction. 2. *Brit.* (formerly) a house or institution, supported by public, parish, or union funds, in which paupers were fed and lodged and set to work; a poorhouse in which paupers were given work. 3. *Obs.* a workshop. [ME *werkhous,* OE *weorchūs* workshop. See WORK, HOUSE]

work·ing (wûr′king), *n.* 1. act of a person or thing that works. 2. operation; action: *the involuted workings of his mind.* 3. the process of molding something skillfully into a shape: *The working of clay is easy when it's damp.* 4. act of manufacturing or building a thing. 5. (of a problem) act of solving. 6. Usually, **workings.** a part of a mine, quarry, or the like, in which work is being or has been carried on. 7. the process of fermenting, as of yeasts. 8. a slow advance involving exertion. 9. disturbed or twisting motions: *The working of his limbs revealed his disease.* —*adj.* 10. that works. 11. doing some form of work or labor, esp. manual, mechanical, or industrial work, as for a living: *a working man.* 12. operating; producing effects, results, etc. 13. pertaining to, connected with, or used in operating or working. 14. serving for the purposes of working. 15. large enough for working or being worked: *a working sample.* 16. that moves with sudden jerks, esp. from deep emotion. 17. Also, **work.** (of a face or edge, as of a timber or a metal casting) shaped and planed as a reference for further shaping and planing. [ME *werking.* See WORK, -ING[1], -ING[2]]

work′ing as′set, *Accounting.* invested capital which is comparatively liquid.

work′ing beam′. See **walking beam.**

work′ing cap′ital, 1. the amount of capital needed to carry on a business. 2. *Accounting.* current assets minus current liabilities. 3. liquid capital assets as distinguished from fixed capital assets.

work′ing-cap·i·tal fund′ (wûr′king kap′i tᵊl), a fund established to finance operating activities in an industrial enterprise.

work′ing class′, 1. those persons working for wages, esp. in manual labor. 2. the social or economic class composed of these workers.

work·ing-class (wûr′king klas′, -kläs′), *adj.* of, pertaining to, or characteristic of the working class.

work′ing day′, 1. the amount of time that a worker must work for an agreed daily wage. 2. a day ordinarily given to working (distinguished from *holiday*). 3. the daily period of hours for working.

work·ing-day (wûr′king dā′), *adj.* workaday; everyday.

work′ing draw′ing, an accurately measured and detailed drawing of a structure, machine, etc., or of any part of one, used as a guide to workmen in constructing it.

work′ing flu′id, *Mech.* a liquid or gaseous working substance.

work′ing girl′, 1. a woman who works. 2. *U.S. Slang.* a prostitute.

work′ing hypoth′esis. See under **hypothesis** (def. 1).

work·ing·man (wûr′king man′), *n., pl.* **-men.** a man of the working class; a man, whether skilled or unskilled, who earns his living at some manual or industrial work. [WORKING + MAN[1]]

work′ing or′der, the condition of a mechanism when it is functioning properly: *The stove hasn't been in working order since we moved in.*

work′ing pa′pers, legal papers giving information often required for employment.

work′ing rail′. See **fly rail** (def. 2).

work′ing sub′stance, a substance, usually a fluid, that undergoes changes in pressure, temperature, volume, or form as part of a process for accomplishing work.

work·ing·wom·an (wûr′king wŏŏm′ən), *n., pl.* **-wom·en.** a female worker; woman of the working class. [WORKING + WOMAN]

work′ load′, the amount of work that a machine, employee, or group of employees can be or is expected to perform.

work·man (wûrk′mən), *n., pl.* **-men.** 1. a man employed or skilled in some form of manual, mechanical, or industrial work. 2. a male worker. [ME *werkman,* OE *weorcman.* See WORK, MAN[1]] —**work′man·less,** *adj.*

work·man·like (wûrk′mən līk′), *adj.* 1. like or befitting a workman. 2. skillful; well executed: *a workmanlike piece of writing.* 3. *Usually Disparaging.* showing or giving evidence of little more than technical proficiency: *The composer has also provided a workmanlike overture.* Also, **work′man·ly.** [late ME *werkmanlike.* See WORKMAN, -LIKE]

work·man·ship (wûrk′mən ship′), *n.* 1. the art or skill of a workman; skill in working or execution. 2. quality or mode of execution, as of a thing made. 3. the product or result of the labor and skill of a workman; work executed. [late ME *werkmanschipe.* See WORKMAN, -SHIP]

work′men's compensa′tion insur′ance, insurance required by law from employers for the protection of employees while engaged in the employer's business. The amount of the claim is stipulated by law (**work′men's compensa′tion law′**).

work′ of art′, 1. a piece of creative work in the arts, esp. a painting or a piece of sculpture. 2. a process or product that has or can be perceived as having aesthetic value, esp. an act or thing that can be judged separately from any utilitarian considerations.

work·out (wûrk′out′), *n.* 1. a trial or practice session in athletics, as in running, boxing, or football. 2. physical exercise: *He goes to the gym for a workout twice a week.* 3. any trial or practice session. [n. use of v. phrase *work out*]

work·peo·ple (wûrk′pē′pəl), *n.pl.* people employed at work or labor; workers; employees. [WORK + PEOPLE]

work·piece (wûrk′pēs′), *n.* a piece of work being machined. [WORK + PIECE]

Work′ Pro′jects Administra′tion. See **WPA.**

work·room (wûrk′rōōm′, -rŏŏm′), *n.* a room in which work is carried on. [WORK + ROOM]

Works′ and Days′, a didactic poem (8th century? B.C.) by Hesiod.

works′ coun′cil, *Chiefly Brit.* 1. an elected body of employee representatives which deals with management regarding grievances, working conditions, wages, etc., and which is consulted by management in regard to labor matters. 2. a joint council or committee representing employer and employees which discusses working conditions, wages, etc., within a plant or business.

work′ sheet′, 1. a sheet of paper on which work schedules, working time, special instructions, etc., are recorded. 2. a piece or scrap of paper on which problems, ideas, or the like, are set down in tentative form. 3. *Accounting.* a sheet of paper on which is printed a series of columns and into which tentative figures are entered as a preliminary step in preparing the adjusted or final statement.

work·shop (wûrk′shop′), *n.* 1. a room, group of rooms, or building in which work, esp. mechanical work, is carried on. 2. a seminar, discussion group, or the like, which emphasizes exchange of ideas and the demonstration and application of techniques, skills, etc.: *a theater workshop.* [WORK + SHOP]

Works′ Prog′ress Administra′tion. See **WPA.**

work′ sta′tion, a work or office area for one person, usually equipped with a computer terminal or other electronic equipment.

work·ta·ble (wûrk′tā′bəl), *n.* a table for working at, often with drawers or receptacles for materials, tools, etc., as for sewing. [WORK + TABLE]

work′ train′, a train which transports railroad workers, building materials, etc., to construction or maintenance assignments on the railroad.

work-up (wûrk′up′), *n. Print.* an undesirable deposit of ink on a surface being printed, caused by the forcing into type-high position of quads or other spacing material. [n. use of v. phrase *work up*]

work·week (wûrk′wēk′), *n.* the total number of regular working hours or days in a week. [WORK + WEEK]

work·wom·an (wûrk′wŏŏm′ən), *n., pl.* **-wom·en.** 1. a female worker. 2. a woman employed or skilled in some manual, mechanical, or industrial work. [WORK + WOMAN]

world (wûrld), *n.* 1. the earth or globe, considered as a planet. 2. a particular division of the earth: *the New World.* 3. the earth, with its inhabitants, affairs, etc., during a particular period: *the ancient world.* 4. mankind; the human race; humanity: *The world must eliminate war and poverty.* 5. the public generally: *The whole world knows it.* 6. the class of persons devoted to the affairs, interests, or pursuits of this life: *The world worships success.* 7. society; secular, social, or fashionable life, with its ways and interests: *He withdrew from the world to practice his art.* 8. a particular class of mankind, with common interests, aims, etc.: *the fashionable world.* 9. any sphere, realm, or domain, with all pertaining to it: *woman's world; the world of dreams; the insect world.* 10. the entire system of created things; the universe; the macrocosm. 11. any complex whole conceived as resembling the universe: *A microcosm may be thought of as a world in miniature.* 12. one of the three general groupings of physical nature: *animal world; mineral world; vegetable world.* 13. any period, state, or sphere of existence: *this world; the world to come.* 14. a very great quantity or extent: *to do a world of good.* 15. any indefinitely great expanse. 16. any heavenly body: *the starry worlds.* 17. **bring into the world, a.** to give birth to; bear: *My grandmother brought nine children into the world.* **b.** to deliver or assist in the delivery of (a baby): *In his 40 years of practice the doctor had brought many children into the world.* 18. **come into the world,** to be born; come into being: *Her first child came into the world in the middle of a blizzard.* 19. **for all the world, a.** for any consideration, however great: *She wouldn't come to visit us for all the world.* **b.** in every respect; precisely: *You look for all the world like my Aunt Mary.* 20. **in the world, a.** at all; ever: *I never in the world would have believed such an obvious lie.* **b.** from among all possibilities: *Where in the world did you find that hat?* 21. **on top of the world.** See **top**[1] (def. 25). 22. **out of this** or **the world,** *Informal.* exceptional; fine: *She bakes an apple pie that is out of this world.* 23. **set the world on fire,** (used chiefly in negative constructions) to achieve great success: *He didn't seem to be the type to set the world on fire.* 24. **think the world of,** to like or admire greatly: *His co-workers think the world of him.* 25. **world without end,** for all eternity; for always: *forever and ever, world without end.* [ME, OE, var. of OE *weorold;* c. D *wereld,* G *Welt,* Icel, *veröld,* all < Gmc **wer-ald-,* lit., man-era] —**Syn.** 1. See **earth.**

World′ Bank′, an international bank established in 1944 to assist in the reconstruction and development of member nations, esp. through the guaranteeing of loans. Official name, **International Bank for Reconstruction and Development.**

world-beat·er (wûrld′bē′tər), *n.* a person or thing that surpasses all others of like kind, as in quality, ability, endurance, etc.

World′ Commun′ion Sun′day, the first Sunday in October, during which members of ecumenical churches throughout the world celebrate Holy Communion, esp. to affirm their unity in Christ.

World′ Coun′cil of Church′es, an ecumenical organization formed in 1948 in Amsterdam, The Netherlands, comprising more than 160 Protestant and Eastern churches in over 48 countries, for the purpose of cooperative, coordinated action in theological, ecclesiastical, and secular matters.

World′ Court′. See **Permanent Court of International Justice.**

World′ Day′ of Prayer′ (prâr), the first Friday in Lent, during which Christians belonging to ecumenical communions pray for foreign missions.

world′ fed′eralism, 1. federalism on a world-wide level. 2. (*caps.*) the movement, doctrines, and aims of World Federalists.

world′ fed′eralist, 1. a promoter or supporter of world federalism. 2. (*caps.*) a member of a movement, active since 1947, proposing a world government on a federal basis, having powers of maintaining order and peace among the nations.

World′ Health′ Organiza′tion, an agency of the United Nations, established in 1948, concerned with improving the health of the world's people and preventing or controlling communicable diseases on a worldwide basis through various technical projects and programs. *Abbr.:* WHO

world·ling (wûrld′ling), *n.* one devoted to the interests and pleasures of this world; a worldly person. [WORLD + -LING[1]]

world·ly (wûrld′lē), *adj.,* **-li·er, -li·est,** *adv.* —*adj.* 1. of or pertaining to this world as contrasted with heaven, spiritual life, etc.; earthly; mundane. 2. devoted to, directed toward, or connected with the affairs, interests, or pleasures of this world. 3. of or pertaining to the people or laity; secular; not ecclesiastical, religious, etc. 4. *Obs.* of, pertaining to, or existing on earth: *ants, flies, and other worldly insects.* —*adv.* 5. in a worldly manner (archaic except in combination): *worldly-wise; worldly-minded.* [ME; OE *wor(u)ldlic.* See WORLD, -LY] —**world′li·ness,** *n.*
—**Syn.** 1. temporal. See **earthly.** 2. urbane, cosmopolitan. —**Ant.** 1. spiritual.

world·ly-mind·ed (wûrld′lē mīn′did), *adj.* having or showing a worldly mind or devotion to the affairs and interests of this world. —**world′ly-mind′ed·ness,** *n.*

world·ly-wise (wûrld′lē wīz′), *adj.* wise as to the affairs of this world. [late ME]

world′ pow′er, a nation, organization, or institution so powerful that it is capable of influencing or changing the course of world events.

world′ proc′ess, *Philos.* 1. change within time, regarded as meaningful in relation to a transcendent principle or plan. 2. *Hegelianism.* change, regarded as the temporal expression and fulfillment of the absolute idea.

World′ Se′ries, *Baseball.* an annual series of games played in the fall between the winning teams of the two major leagues, the first team to win four games being declared the professional champions of the U.S. Also, **World's′ Se′ries.**

world's′ fair′, a large fair or international exposition in which various nations participate with exhibitions of their arts, crafts, industrial and agricultural products, scientific achievements, etc.

world-shak·er (wûrld′shā′kər), *n.* something of sufficient importance or magnitude to affect the entire world (often used negatively): *The book is no world-shaker, but it's pleasant reading.*

world-shak·ing (wûrld′shā′king), *adj.* of sufficient size, importance, or magnitude to affect the entire world: *the world-shaking effects of an international clash.*

world's′ old′est profes′sion, prostitution.

world′ soul′, a supposed soul of the world or universe.

world′ spir′it, God; the moving force in the universe.

world′ war′, a war that is waged in many parts of the world and involves most of the principal nations of the world.

World War I, the war fought mainly in Europe and the Middle East, with the Central Powers of Germany, Austria-Hungary, Turkey, and Bulgaria on the one side and on the other the Triple Entente of Great Britain, France, and Russia, aided by the U.S., Belgium, Serbia, Japan, and others, beginning on July 28, 1914, and ending on November 11, 1918, with the collapse of the Central Powers. Also called **Great War, War of the Nations.**

World War II, the war between the Axis (mainly Germany, Italy, and Japan) and the Allies (mainly Great Britain, France, the Soviet Union, and the United States), beginning on September 1, 1939, with the German invasion of Poland and ending with the surrender of Germany on May 8, 1945, and of Japan on August 14, 1945.

world-wea·ry (wûrld′wēr′ē), *adj.* weary of the world; bored with existence, material pleasures, etc. —**world′-wea′ri·ness,** *n.*

world-wide (wûrld′wīd′), *adj.* extending or spread throughout the world.

worm (wûrm), *n.* 1. *Zool.* any of numerous long, slender, soft-bodied, legless, bilateral invertebrates including the flatworms, roundworms, acanthocephalans, nemerteans, gordiaceans, and annelids. 2. (loosely) any of numerous small creeping animals with more or less slender, elongated bodies, and without limbs or with very short ones, including individuals of widely differing kinds, as earthworms, tapeworms, insect larvae, adult forms of some insects, etc. 3. something resembling or suggesting a worm in appearance, movement, etc. 4. a groveling, abject, or contemptible person. 5. the spiral pipe in which the vapor is condensed in a still. 6. (not in technical use) See **screw thread.** 7. See **screw conveyor.** 8. a rotating cylinder or shaft, cut with one or more helical threads, that engages with and drives a worm wheel. 9. something that penetrates, injures, or consumes slowly or insidiously, like a gnawing worm. 10. **worms, a.** (*construed as sing.*) *Pathol., Vet. Pathol.* any disease or disorder arising from the presence of parasitic worms in the intestines or other tissues. **b.** (*construed as pl.*) *Metall.* irregularities visible on the surfaces of some metals subject to plastic deformation. 11. the lytta of a dog or other carnivorous animal. 12. *Metall.* an outbreak of molten metal forced through a crust of solidified metal by gas pressure. 13. **a worm may** or **will turn,** even the humble and weak will finally rebel against abuse: *He may be a coward, but even a worm will turn.* —*v.i.* 14. to move or act like a worm; creep, crawl, or advance slowly or stealthily. 15. to get by insidious procedure (usually fol. by *into*): *to worm into another's favor.* 16. *Metall.* craze (def. 8a). —*v.t.* 17. to make, cause, bring, etc., along by creeping or crawling, or by stealthy or devious advances. 18. to get by persistent, insidious efforts (usually fol. by *out* or *from*): *to worm a secret out of a person.* 19. to free from worms: *He wormed the puppies.* 20. *Naut.* to wind yarn or the like spirally round (a rope) so as to fill the spaces between the strands and render the surface smooth. [ME; OE *wyrm,* worm, serpent; c. D *worm,* G *Wurm,* Icel *ormr,* L *vermis;* cf. VERMIN, VARMINT] —**worm′er,** *n.* —**worm′less,** *adj.* —**worm′like′, worm′ish,** *adj.*

worm′ drive′, *Mach.* a drive mechanism utilizing a worm gear.

worm-eat·en (wûrm′ēt′ᵊn), *adj.* 1. eaten into or gnawed by worms. 2. impaired by time, decayed, or antiquated. [late ME *wormeten* (see WORM, EAT); r. ME *wormete,* OE *wyrmǣte* worm-eaten (state)]

worm′ fence′. See **snake fence.**

worm·fish (wûrm′fish′), *n., pl. (esp. collectively)* **-fish,** *(esp. referring to two or more kinds or species)* **-fish·es.** any of several small, slender fishes of the family *Microdesmidae*, found in tropical, marine waters. [WORM + FISH]

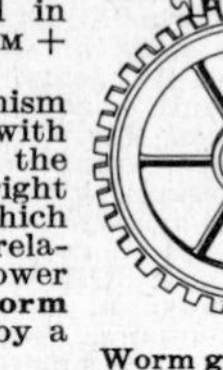

Worm gear (def. 2)

worm′ gear′, **1.** a mechanism consisting of a worm engaging with and driving a worm wheel, the two axes usually being at right angles, used in instances in which a relatively low speed and a relatively large amplification of power are desired. **2.** Also called **worm wheel.** a gear wheel driven by a worm. Also, **worm′gear′.**

worm′ grass′, **1.** a creeping evergreen, *Sedum album*, of the Mediterranean region, having fleshy leaves and white flowers in terminal branching clusters. **2.** the pinkroot, *Spigelia marilandica.*

worm·hole (wûrm′hōl′), *n.* a hole made by a burrowing or gnawing worm, as in timber, nuts, etc. [WORM + HOLE]

wor·mil (wôr′mil), *n. Vet. Pathol.* warble[2] (def. 2). [alter. of *warnel*, OE *wernægel*, lit., man-nail (i.e., horny place made by man). See WEREWOLF, NAIL]

worm′ liz′ard, any of numerous burrowing, legless lizards of the family *Amphisbaenidae*, that are found chiefly in Africa and South America and that resemble an earthworm in shape and habits.

worm·root (wûrm′ro͞ot′, -ro͝ot′), *n.* pinkroot. [WORM + ROOT[1]]

Worms (wûrmz; *Ger.* vôrms), *n.* **1.** a city in E Rhineland-Palatinate, in W West Germany. 63,100 (1963). **2. Diet of,** the council or diet held here (1521) at which Luther was condemned as a heretic.

worm·seed (wûrm′sēd′), *n.* **1.** the dried, unexpanded flower heads of a wormwood, *Artemisia Cina* (**Levant wormseed**), or the fruit of certain goosefoots, esp. *Chenopodium anthelminticum*, the Mexican tea or American wormseed, used as an anthelmintic drug. **2.** any of these plants. [late ME *wyrmsed.* See WORM, SEED]

worm′seed oil′, *Chem.* See **chenopodium oil.**

worm′ snake′, **1.** any of several small, wormlike snakes, esp. *Carphophis amoenus*, of the eastern and central U.S. **2.** See **blind snake.**

worm′ wheel′. See **worm gear** (def. 2). —**worm′-wheel′,** *adj.*

worm·wood (wûrm′wo͝od′), *n.* **1.** any composite herb or low shrub of the genus *Artemisia*. **2.** a bitter, aromatic herb, *A. Absinthium*, of the Old World, once used as a vermifuge and a tonic, but more recently chiefly in making absinthe. **3.** something bitter, grievous, or extremely unpleasant; bitterness. [late ME *wormwode* (see WORM, WOOD[1]); r. ME *wermode*, OE *wermōd*, c. G *Wermut;* see VERMOUTH]

worm′wood sage′. See **mountain sage.**

worm·y (wûr′mē), *adj.,* **worm·i·er, worm·i·est.** **1.** containing a worm or worms; contaminated with worms. **2.** damaged or bored into by worms; worm-eaten. **3.** wormlike; groveling; low. [late ME; see WORM, -Y[1]] —**worm′i·ness,** *n.*

worn (wōrn, wôrn), *v.* **1.** pp. of **wear.** —*adj.* **2.** diminished in value or usefulness through wear, use, handling, etc.: *worn clothing; worn tires.* **3.** wearied; exhausted. —**worn′ness,** *n.*

worn-out (wōrn′out′, wôrn′-), *adj.* **1.** worn or used until no longer fit for use. **2.** depleted of energy, strength, enthusiasm, or the like; exhausted; fatigued. —**worn′-out′ness,** *n.*

wor·ried (wûr′ēd, wur′-), *adj.* **1.** having or characterized by worry; concerned; anxious: *His worried parents called the police.* **2.** indicating, expressing, or attended by worry: *worried looks.* [WORRY + -ED[2]] —**wor′ried·ly,** *adv.*

wor·ri·ment (wûr′ē mənt, wur′-), *n. Informal.* **1.** trouble; annoyance. **2.** worry; anxiety. [WORRY + -MENT]

wor·ri·some (wûr′ē səm, wur′-), *adj.* **1.** worrying, annoying, or disturbing; causing worry: *a worrisome problem.* **2.** inclined to worry. [WORRY + -SOME[1]] —**wor′ri·some·ly,** *adv.*

wor·ry (wûr′ē, wur′ē), *v.,* **-ried, -ry·ing,** *n., pl.* **-ries.** —*v.i.* **1.** to feel uneasy or anxious; fret; torment oneself with or suffer from disturbing thoughts. **2.** to move with effort: *an old car worrying up hill.* —*v.t.* **3.** to make uneasy or anxious; trouble; torment with annoyances, cares, anxieties, etc.; plague, pester, or bother: *His debts worried him.* **4.** to seize, esp. by the throat, with the teeth and shake or mangle, as one animal does another. **5.** to harass by repeated biting, snapping, etc. **6. worry along** or **through,** *Informal.* to progress or succeed by constant effort, despite difficulty: *To others the situation seemed intolerable, but with luck and persistence she worried through.* —*n.* **7.** worried condition or feeling; uneasiness or anxiety. **8.** a cause of uneasiness or anxiety; trouble. **9.** act of worrying. **10.** *Fox Hunting.* the action of the hounds in tearing to pieces the carcass of a fox. [ME *wory*, var. of *wery, wiry*, OE *wyrgan* to strangle; c. G *würgen*] —**wor′ri·er,** *n.* —**wor′ri·less,** *adj.* —**wor′ry·ing·ly,** *adv.*

—**Syn. 1.** chafe, fidget. **3.** tease, harry, hector, badger, disquiet. WORRY, ANNOY, HARASS all mean to disturb or interfere with someone's comfort or peace of mind. To WORRY is to cause anxiety, apprehension, or care: *to worry one's parents.* To ANNOY is to vex or irritate by continued repetition of interferences: *to annoy the neighbors.* HARASS implies long-continued worry and annoyance: *Cares of office harass a president.* **7.** apprehension, solicitude, disquiet, misgiving, fear. See **concern.**

wor·ry·wart (wûr′ē wôrt′, wur′-), *n.* a person who tends to worry habitually and often needlessly; pessimist; fussbudget. [WORRY + WART]

worse (wûrs), *adj., comparative of* **bad** *and* **ill.** **1.** bad or ill in a greater or higher degree; inferior in excellence, quality, or character. **2.** more unfavorable or injurious. **3.** in less good condition; in poorer health. —*n.* **4.** that which is worse. —*adv.* **5.** in a more evil, wicked, severe, or disadvantageous manner. **6.** with more severity, intensity, etc.; in a greater degree. [ME; OE *wiersa;* c. Icel *verri*, Goth *wairsiza;* see WAR[2]] —**worse′ness,** *n.*

wors·en (wûr′sən), *v.t., v.i.* to make or become worse. [ME *worsene(n).* See WORSE, -EN[1]]

wors·er (wûr′sər), *adj., adv. Dial.* worse.

wor·set (wûr′sit), *n., adj. Brit. Dial.* worsted. Also, **worssett.**

wor·ship (wûr′ship), *n., v.,* **-shiped, -ship·ing** or *(esp. Brit.)* **-shipped, -ship·ping.** —*n.* **1.** reverent honor and homage paid to God or a sacred personage, or to any object regarded as sacred. **2.** formal or ceremonious rendering of such honor and homage: *They attended worship this morning.* **3.** adoring reverence or regard: *excessive worship of business success.* **4.** the object of adoring reverence or regard. **5.** *(sometimes cap.) Chiefly Brit.* a title of honor used in addressing or mentioning certain magistrates and others of high rank or station (usually prec. by *his* or *your*). **6.** *Archaic.* honorable character or standing: *men of worship.* —*v.t.* **7.** to render religious reverence and homage to. **8.** to feel an adoring reverence or regard for (any person or thing). —*v.i.* **9.** to render religious reverence and homage, as to a deity. **10.** to attend services of divine worship. **11.** to feel an adoring reverence or regard. [ME *wors(c)hipe*, OE *worthscipe*, var. of *weorthscipe.* See WORTH, -SHIP] —**wor′ship·a·ble,** *adj.* —**wor′ship·er;** *esp. Brit.,* **wor′ship·per,** *n.* —**wor′ship·ing·ly;** *esp. Brit.,* **wor′ship·ping·ly,** *adv.* —**wor′ship·less,** *adj.*

—**Syn. 1.** See **reverence. 3.** honor, homage, adoration, idolatry. **8.** honor, venerate, revere, adore, glorify, idolize, adulate. —**Ant. 8.** detest.

wor·ship·ful (wûr′ship fəl), *adj.* **1.** given to the worship of something. **2.** *(sometimes cap.) Chiefly Brit.* a formal title of honor used in announcing or mentioning certain highly regarded or respected persons or groups (usually prec. by *the*). [ME; see WORSHIP, -FUL] —**wor′ship·ful·ly,** *adv.* —**wor′ship·ful·ness,** *n.*

wors·sett (wûr′sit), *n., adj. Brit. Dial.* worset.

worst (wûrst), *adj., superlative of* **bad** *and* **ill.** **1.** bad or ill in the highest, greatest, or most extreme degree: *the worst person.* **2.** most faulty, unsatisfactory, or objectionable: *the worst paper submitted.* **3.** most unfavorable or injurious. **4.** in the poorest condition: *the worst house on the block.* **5.** most unpleasant, unattractive, or disagreeable: *the worst personality I've ever known.* **6.** most lacking in skill; least skilled: *the worst typist in the group.* **7. in the worst way,** *Informal.* in an extreme degree; very much: *She wanted a doll for Christmas in the worst way.* Also, **the worst way.** —*n.* **8.** that which is worst. **9. at worst,** if the worst happens; under the worst conditions: *He will be expelled from school, at worst.* Also, **at the worst. 10. get the worst of something,** to be defeated; lose: *to get the worst of a fight.* **11. if worst comes to worst,** if the very worst happens: *If worst comes to worst, we still have some money in reserve.* —*adv.* **12.** in the most evil, wicked, severe, or disadvantageous manner. **13.** with the most severity, intensity, etc.; in the greatest degree. —*v.t.* **14.** to give (one) the worst of a contest or struggle; defeat; beat: *He worsted him easily.* [ME *worste*, OE *wur(re)sta*, var. of *wyr(re)sta, wer(re)sta;* c. Icel *verstr*]

wor·sted (wo͝os′tid, wûr′stid), *n.* **1.** firmly twisted yarn or thread spun from combed, stapled wool fibers of the same length, for weaving, knitting, etc. Cf. **woolen. 2.** wool cloth woven from such yarns, having a hard, smooth surface and no nap. —*adj.* **3.** consisting or made of worsted. [ME *worsted(e)* special use of *Worstede* (OE *Wurthestede*, now *Worstead*), name of parish in Norfolk (England) where the cloth was made]

wort[1] (wûrt), *n.* the unfermented or fermenting infusion of malt which after fermentation becomes beer or mash. [ME; OE *wyrt* root, plant; c. G *Würze* spice; see WORT[2]]

wort[2] (wûrt), *n.* a plant; herb; vegetable (usually used in combination). [ME; OE *wyrt* root, plant; c. OHG *wurz*, Icel *urt* herb, Goth *waurts* root; akin to ROOT[1]]

wort[3] (wûrt), *n.* whort.

worth[1] (wûrth), *prep.* **1.** good or important enough to justify (what is specified): *advice worth taking; a place worth visiting.* **2.** having a value of, or equal in value to, as in money: *This vase is worth twelve dollars.* **3.** having property to the value or amount of: *He is worth millions.* —*n.* **4.** excellence of character or quality as commanding esteem: *men of worth.* **5.** usefulness or importance, as to the world, to a person, or for a purpose: *His worth to the world is inestimable.* **6.** value, as in money. **7.** a quantity of something of a specified value: *ten cents' worth of candy.* **8.** wealth; riches; property or possessions: *net worth.* **9. for all one is worth,** *Informal.* with one's best effort; to the utmost: *He ran for all he was worth.* **10. put in one's two cents worth,** *Slang.* to offer one's opinion in a dispute or discussion. Also, **put in one's two cents.** [ME; OE *w(e)orth;* c. G *Wert* (OHG *werd*), Icel *verthr*, Goth *wairths*]

—**Syn. 1.** deserving, meriting, justifying. **4.** See **merit. 6.** See **value.**

worth[2] (wûrth), *v.i. Archaic.* to happen or betide: *woe worth the day.* [ME *worthe(n)*, OE *wurthan, weorthan;* c. Icel *vertha*, G *werden*, Goth *wairthan* to become, L *vertere* to turn]

Worth (wûrth), *n.* a town in NE Illinois. 8196 (1960).

Wor·thing·ton (wûr′thing tən), *n.* **1.** a town in central Ohio. 9239 (1960). **2.** a town in SW Minnesota. 9015 (1960).

worth·less (wûrth′lis), *adj.* without worth; of no use, importance, or value; good-for-nothing; useless; valueless: *a worthless person; a worthless contract.* [WORTH[1] + -LESS] —**worth′less·ly,** *adv.* —**worth′less·ness,** *n.*

worth·while (wûrth′hwīl′, -wīl′), *adj.* such as to repay one's time, attention, interest, work, trouble, etc.: *a worthwhile book.* Also, *esp. Brit.,* **worth′-while′.** [WORTH[1] + WHILE] —**worth′while′ness;** *esp. Brit.,* **worth′-while′ness,** *n.*

wor·thy (wûr′thē), *adj.,* **-thi·er, -thi·est,** *n., pl.* **-thies.** —*adj.* **1.** having adequate or great merit, character, or value: *a worthy successor.* **2.** of commendable excellence or merit; deserving (often fol. by *of* or an infinitive): *a book worthy of praise; a man worthy to lead.* —*n.* **3.** a person of eminent worth, merit, or position: *The town worthies included the doctor and the lawyer.* **4.** any person (usually used ironically or facetiously): *gamblers, racketeers, and other worthies.* [ME; see WORTH[1], -Y[1]] —**wor′thi·ly,** *adv.* —**wor′thi·ness,** *n.*

—**Syn. 2.** meritorious, worthwhile, estimable, excellent, exemplary, righteous, upright, honest.

wot (wot), *v. Archaic.* first and third pers. sing. pres. of **wit**[2]. [ME *woot*, OE *wāt;* c. Icel *veit*, G *weiss*, Goth *wait*, Gk *oida*, Skt *veda;* see WIT[2]]

Wo·tan (vō′tän, vō′-), a Germanic god corresponding to the Scandinavian Odin.

Wot·ton (wot′ən), *n.* **Henry,** 1568–1639, English poet and diplomat.

Wouk (wōk), *n.* **Herman,** born 1915, U.S. novelist.

would[1] (wo͝od; *unstressed* wəd), *v.* **1.** a pt. and pp. of **will**[1]. **2.** (used to express a wish): *I would it were true. Would he were here!* **3.** (used in place of *will*, to make a statement or form a question less direct or blunt): *That would scarcely be fair. Would you be so kind?* [ME, OE *wolde.* See WILL[1]]

would[2] (wōld), *n.* weld[2].

would-be (wo͝od′bē′), *adj.* **1.** wishing or pretending to be: *a would-be wit.* **2.** intended to be: *a would-be kindness.*

would·n't (wo͝od′ənt), contraction of *would not.*

wouldst (wo͝odst), *v. Archaic.* second pers. sing. pt. of **will**[1].

wound[1] (wo͞ond; *Archaic and Literary* wound), *n.* **1.** an injury to an organism, usually one involving division of tissue or rupture of the integument or mucous membrane, due to external violence or some mechanical agency rather than disease. **2.** a similar injury to the tissue of a plant. **3.** an injury or hurt to feelings, sensibilities, reputation, etc. —*v.t.* **4.** to inflict a wound upon; injure; hurt. —*v.i.* **5.** to inflict a wound or wounds. [ME; OE *wund;* c. OHG *wunta*, Icel *und*, Goth *wunds*] —**wound′ed·ly,** *adv.* —**wound′ing·ly,** *adv.* —**wound′less,** *adj.*

—**Syn. 1.** cut, stab, laceration, lesion, trauma. See **injury. 3.** insult, pain, grief, anguish. **4.** harm, damage, cut, stab, lacerate.

wound[2] (wound), *v.* a pt. and pp. of **wind**[2] and **wind**[3].

wound·ed (wo͞on′did), *adj.* **1.** suffering injury or bodily harm, as a laceration, bullet wound, or the like: *to bandage a wounded hand.* **2.** marred; impaired; damaged: *a wounded reputation.* —*n.* **3.** wounded persons collectively (often prec. by *the*): *emergency treatment for the wounded.* [ME, OE *gewundode.* See WOUND[1], -ED[2]]

wound·fin (wo͞ond′fin′), *n.* a slender, scaleless cyprinid fish, *Plagopterus argentissimus*, found in the tributaries of the Colorado River system, having a sharp spine in front of the dorsal fin and each pelvic fin. [WOUND[1] + FIN]

wound·wort (wo͞ond′wûrt′), *n.* See **kidney vetch.** [WOUND[1] + WORT[2]]

wou·ra·li (wo͞o rä′lē), *n.* curare.

wove (wōv), *v.* a pt. and pp. of **weave.**

wo·ven (wō′vən), *v.* a pp. of **weave.**

wove′ pa′per, paper that exhibits a pattern of fine mesh when held up to the light. Cf. **laid paper.**

wow[1] (wou), *v.t.* **1.** *Slang.* to gain an enthusiastic response from; to thrill. —*n.* **2.** *Slang.* an extraordinary success: *His act is a real wow. She's a wow in the new part.* —*interj.* **3.** *Informal.* (an exclamation of surprise, wonder, pleasure, or the like): *Wow! Look at that!*

wow[2] (wou, wō), *n.* **1.** a slow variation or distortion in the pitch fidelity of reproduced sound, caused by fluctuations in the speed of a component in the sound-reproducing system. **2.** *Brit. Dial.* a howl, wail, bark, whine, or mew. —*v.i.* **3.** *Brit. Dial.* to howl, wail, bark, whine, or mew. [imit.]

wow·ser (wou′zər), *n. Australian.* an excessively puritanical person. [?]

Woz·zeck (vô′tsek), *n.* an opera (1925) by Alban Berg.

W.P., **1.** weather permitting. **2.** wire payment. **3.** working pressure. Also, **WP, w.p.**

wp., *Baseball*, wild pitch; wild pitches.

WPA, Work Projects Administration: the former federal agency (1935–43) charged with instituting and administering public works in order to relieve national unemployment. Originally, **Works Progress Administration.**

WPB, War Production Board. Also, **W.P.B.**

wpm, words per minute.

w.r., **1.** warehouse receipt. **2.** *Insurance.* war risk.

WRA, War Relocation Authority.

WRAC, *Brit.* Women's Royal Army Corps. Also, **W.R.A.C.**

wrack[1] (rak), *n.* **1.** wreck or wreckage. **2.** ruin or destruction: *gone to wrack and ruin.* **3.** a vestige, fragment, or trace of something that has been destroyed: *leaving not a wrack behind.* **4.** seaweed or other marine vegetation cast on the shore. [ME *wrak;* OE *wræc* vengeance, misery, akin to *wracu* vengeance, misery, *wrecan* to WREAK]

wrack[2] (rak), *n., v.i.* rack[4].

WRAF (raf), *Brit.* Women's Royal Air Force. Also, **W.R.A.F.**

wraith (rāth), *n.* **1.** an apparition of a living person supposed to portend his death. **2.** a visible spirit. [?] —**wraith′like′,** *adj.*

Wran·gel (rang′gəl; *Russ.* vrän gel′yə), *n.* a Russian island in the Arctic Ocean, off the coast of the NE Soviet Union in Asia: meteorological station. ab. 2000 sq. mi.

Wran·gell (rang′gəl), *n.* **1. Mount,** an active volcano in SE Alaska, in the Wrangell Mountains. 14,006 ft. **2.** a town in SE Alaska. 1315 (1960).

Wran′gell Moun′tains, a mountain range in SE Alaska. Highest peak, Mt. Bona, 16,420 ft.

wran·gle (rang′gəl), *v.,* **-gled, -gling,** *n.* —*v.i.* **1.** to argue or dispute, esp. in a noisy or angry manner. —*v.t.* **2.** to argue or dispute. **3.** *U.S.* to tend or round up (cattle, horses, or other livestock). —*n.* **4.** a noisy or angry dispute; controversy; altercation. [late ME, appar. < LG *wrangeln*, freq. of *wrangen* to struggle, make uproar; akin to WRING]

—**Syn. 1.** quarrel, bicker, brawl. **4.** argument, quarrel, brawl.

wran·gler (rang′glər), *n.* **1.** one who wrangles or disputes. **2.** (at Cambridge University, England) one placed in the first class in the mathematics tripos: *Robert ranked first and was senior wrangler. Tommy* ranked second and was junior wrangler. Four others were also wranglers. [WRANGLE + -ER[1]]

wrap (rap), *v.*, **wrapped, wrap·ping,** *n.* —*v.t.* **1.** to enclose, envelop, or muffle in something wound or folded about (often fol. by *up*): *She wrapped her head in a scarf.* **2.** to enclose and make fast (an article, bundle, etc.) within a covering of paper or the like (often fol. by *up*): *He wrapped up the package in brown paper.* **3.** to wind, fold, or bind (something) about as a covering. **4.** to protect with coverings, outer garments, etc. (usually fol. by *up*). **5.** to surround, envelop, shroud, or hide. **6.** to fold or roll up. —*v.i.* **7.** to wrap oneself (usually fol. by *up*). **8.** to become wrapped, as about something; fold. **9. wrapped up in, a.** intensely absorbed in; engrossed in: *wrapped up in one's work.* **b.** involved in; bound up with: *Peace is wrapped up in mutual willingness to compromise.* **10. wrap up, a.** *Informal.* to conclude (an activity): *Now that we've wrapped up that project, we can go on to another.* **b.** *Slang.* to damage severely: *He wrapped up his car the other night.* —*n.* **11.** something to be wrapped about the person, esp. in addition to the usual indoor clothing, as a shawl, scarf, or mantle: *evening wrap.* **12. wraps,** outdoor garments; coverings, furs, etc. [ME, b. obs. *wry* (OE *wrēon* to cover, clothe, hide) and LAP[2]; cf. ME var. *wlappe,* with only *w* of *wry*]

wrap·a·round (rap′ə round′), *adj.* **1.** overlapping or appearing to overlap another part, as a skirt that wraps around the body and overlaps at a full-length opening: *a wraparound dress; a wraparound robe; wraparound sunglasses; a wraparound windshield.* —*n.* **2.** a wraparound object. **3.** outsert. **4.** *Print.* a thin metal, plastic, or rubber plate made flat and then wrapped around a cylinder for printing on a rotary press. **5.** *Brit.* See **book jacket.** Also, **wrap′-a-round′.** [WRAP + AROUND]

wrap·per (rap′ər), *n.* **1.** one who or that which wraps. **2.** that in which something is wrapped; a covering or cover. **3.** a long, loose outer garment. **4.** a woman's loose bathrobe; negligee. **5.** *Brit.* See **book jacket.** **6.** the tobacco leaf used for covering a cigar. **7.** *Armor.* a supplementary beaver reinforcing the chin and mouth area of an armet of the 15th century. [late ME; see WRAP, -ER[1]]

wrap·ping (rap′ing), *n.* Often, **wrappings.** that in which something is wrapped. [late ME; see WRAP, -ING[1]]

wrap′ping pa′per, heavy paper used for wrapping packages, parcels, etc.

wrapt (rapt), *v.* a pt. and pp. of **wrap.**

wrap-up (rap′up′), *n.* a report, esp. a final report, which gives a summary or the highlights of what has been presented previously: *He gave a wrap-up of the evening news.* [n. use of v. phrase *wrap up*]

wrasse (ras), *n.* any of various marine fishes of the family *Labridae,* esp. of the genus *Labrus,* having thick, fleshy lips, powerful teeth, and usually a brilliant color, certain species being valued as food fishes. [< Cornish *wrach,* lenited form of *gwrach*]

wras·tle (ras′əl), *v.i., v.t.,* **-tled, -tling,** *n. Dial.* wrestle. Also, **rassle, rastle.** [ME *wrastle(n)* to WRESTLE; see WARSLE]

wrath (rath, räth *or, esp. Brit.,* rôth), *n.* **1.** strong, stern, or fierce anger; deeply resentful indignation; ire. **2.** vengeance or punishment as the consequence of anger. —*adj.* **3.** *Archaic.* wroth. [ME *wraththe,* OE *wrǣththo,* equiv. to *wrāth* WROTH + *-tho* -TH[1]] —**wrath′less,** *adj.*
—**Syn. 1.** rage, resentment, dudgeon, fury, choler, passion. —**Ant. 1.** equanimity, pleasure.

wrath·ful (rath′fəl, räth′- *or, esp. Brit.,* rôth′-), *adj.* **1.** very angry; ireful; full of wrath: *They trembled before the wrathful queen.* **2.** characterized by or showing wrath: *wrathful words.* [ME; see WRATH, -FUL] —**wrath′ful·ly,** *adv.* —**wrath′ful·ness,** *n.*
—**Syn. 1.** irate, furious, raging, incensed, resentful, indignant, enraged. —**Ant. 1.** equable, pleased.

wrath·y (rath′ē, rä′thē *or, esp. Brit.,* rô′thē), *adj.,* **wrath·i·er, wrath·i·est.** *Informal.* wrathful; angry. [WRATH + -Y[1]] —**wrath′i·ly,** *adv.* —**wrath′i·ness,** *n.*

wreak (rēk), *v.t.* **1.** to inflict or execute (punishment, vengeance, etc.): *They wreaked havoc on the enemy.* **2.** to carry out the promptings of (one's rage, ill humor, will, desire, etc.), as on a victim or object: *He wreaked his anger on the workmen.* [ME *wreke(n),* OE *wrecan;* c. G *rächen* to avenge, Icel *reka* to drive, avenge, Goth *wrikan* to persecute, L *urgēre* to drive, push] —**wreak′er,** *n.*

wreath (rēth), *n., pl.* **wreaths** (rēthz), *v.* —*n.* **1.** something twisted or bent into a circular form; a circular band of flowers, foliage, or any ornamental work, for adorning the head or for any decorative purpose; a garland or chaplet. **2.** any ringlike, curving, or curling mass or formation: *a wreath of clouds.* **3.** (in stair building) **a.** a curved section of a handrail. **b.** Also called **wreath′ piece′.** a curved section of a string. **4.** *Heraldry.* torse. —*v.t., v.i.* **5.** to wreathe. [ME *wrethe,* OE *wrǣth* (equiv. to *wrǣd*), cf. *writha* thong, collar and see WRITHE] —**wreath′less,** *adj.* —**wreath′like′,** *adj.*

wreathe (rēth), *v.,* **wreathed, wreathed** or (*Archaic*) **wreath·en; wreath·ing.** —*v.t.* **1.** to encircle or adorn with or as with a wreath or wreaths. **2.** to form as a wreath by twisting, twining, or otherwise. **3.** to surround in curving or curling masses or form. **4.** to envelop: *a face wreathed in smiles.* —*v.i.* **5.** to take the form of a wreath or wreaths. **6.** to move in curving or curling masses, as smoke. [WREATH; in some senses, back formation from late ME *wrethen* (*wrethe* WREATH + *-en* -EN[2])] —**wreath′er,** *n.*

wreathed′ col′umn, a column having a twisted or spiral form.

wreath′ gold′enrod, a bluish-green herb, *Solidago caesia,* of eastern and southern North America, having leafy, yellow flower clusters.

wreck (rek), *n.* **1.** any building, structure, or thing reduced to a state of ruin. **2.** wreckage, goods, etc., remaining above water after a shipwreck, esp. when cast ashore. **3.** the ruin or destruction of a vessel in the course of navigation; shipwreck. **4.** a vessel in a state of ruin from disaster at sea, on rocks, etc. **5.** the ruin or destruction of anything: *the wreck of one's hopes.* **6.** a person of ruined health; someone in bad shape physically or mentally: *The strain of his work left him a complete wreck.* —*v.t.* **7.** to cause the wreck of (a vessel), as in navigation; shipwreck. **8.** to involve in a wreck. **9.** to cause the ruin or destruction of: *to wreck a car.* —*v.i.* **10.** to be involved in a wreck; become wrecked: *The trains wrecked at the crossing.* **11.** to act as a wrecker; engage in wrecking. [ME *wrek* < Scand; cf. Icel *rek* deriv. of *wrek (AF *wrec* < ME)]
—**Syn. 5.** devastation, desolation. **9.** destroy, devastate, shatter. See **spoil.** —**Ant. 9.** create.

wreck·age (rek′ij), *n.* **1.** act of wrecking; state of being wrecked. **2.** remains or fragments of something that has been wrecked: *They searched the wreckage for survivors.* [WRECK + -AGE]

wreck·er (rek′ər), *n.* **1.** one who or that which wrecks. **2.** a person, car, or train employed in removing wreckage, debris, etc., as from railroad tracks. **3.** Also called **tow car, tow truck.** a vehicle equipped with a mechanical apparatus for hoisting and pulling, used to tow wrecked, disabled, or stalled automobiles. **4.** Also called **housewrecker.** a person whose business it is to demolish and remove houses or other buildings, as in clearing sites for other use. **5.** a person or vessel employed in recovering wrecked or disabled vessels, or their equipment and contents, as for the owners or underwriters. **6.** one who plunders wrecks, esp. after exhibiting false signals in order to cause shipwrecks. [WRECK + -ER[1]]

wreck·fish (rek′fish′), *n., pl.* **-fish·es,** (*esp. collectively*) **-fish.** a large, brown serranid fish, *Polyprion americanus,* of the Mediterranean Sea and tropical Atlantic Ocean, often found near wrecks. Also called **stone bass.** [WRECK + FISH]

wreck·ful (rek′fəl), *adj. Archaic.* causing wreckage. [WRECK + -FUL]

wreck′ing bar′. See **pinch bar.**

wreck′ing car′, a car that is equipped as a wrecker. Cf. **wrecker** (def. 2).

wreck′ing crane′, *Railroads.* a crane for lifting and removing wrecked rolling stock.

wren (ren), *n.* **1.** any of numerous small, active, passerine birds of the family *Troglodytidae,* esp. *Troglodytes troglodytes,* of the Northern Hemisphere, having dark brown plumage barred with black. Cf. **house wren, marsh wren, rock wren, winter wren.** **2.** any of various similar, unrelated birds, esp. any of several Old World warblers. [ME, OE *wrenne;* cf. OHG *wrendilo,* Icel *rindill*]

House wren, ***Troglodytes aedon*** **(Length 5 in.)**

Wren (ren), *n.* **1. Sir Christopher,** 1632–1723, English architect. **2. Percival Christopher,** 1885–1941, English novelist.

Wren (ren), *n.* (*sometimes l.c.*) *Chiefly Brit. Informal.* a member of the Wrens.

wrench (rench), *v.t.* **1.** to twist suddenly and forcibly; pull, jerk, or force by a violent twist: *He wrenched the prisoner's wrist.* **2.** to overstrain or injure (the ankle, knee, etc.) by a sudden, violent twist: *When she fell, she wrenched her ankle.* **3.** to affect distressingly as if by a wrench. **4.** to wrest, as from the right use or meaning: *He tried to wrench the facts from their proper significance.* —*v.i.* **5.** to twist, turn, or move suddenly aside. **6.** to give a wrench or twist at something. —*n.* **7.** a wrenching movement; a sudden, violent twist: *He wrenched away.* **8.** a painful, straining twist, as of the ankle or wrist. **9.** a sharp, distressing strain, as to the feelings. **10.** a twisting or distortion, as of meaning. **11.** a tool for gripping and turning or twisting the head of a bolt, a nut, a pipe, or the like, commonly consisting of a bar of metal with fixed or adjustable jaws. [ME *wrenche(n),* OE *wrencan* to twist, turn; c. G *renken*] —**wrench′er,** *n.* —**wrench′ing·ly,** *adv.*

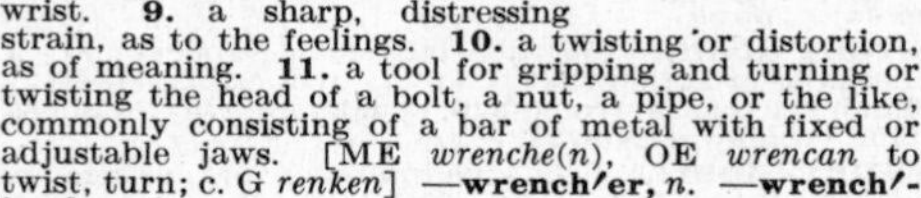

Wrenches (def. 11)
A, Box wrench
B, Open end wrench
C, Socket wrench
D, Allen wrench

Wrens (renz), *n.* (*construed as sing. or pl.*) *Chiefly Brit. Informal.* the Women's Royal Naval Service: established in 1917 as an auxiliary to the Royal Navy. [*WRNS,* with *E* put in to give the sequence a vowel]

wren-thrush (ren′thrush′), *n.* an oscine bird, *Zeledonia coronata,* of the high mountains of Costa Rica and Panama.

wren-tit (ren′tit′), *n.* a small, brown bird, *Chamaea fasciata,* of the western U.S., resembling a wren and a titmouse, and having a long, tapered, barred tail.

wrest (rest), *v.t.* **1.** to twist or turn; pull, jerk, or force by a violent twist. **2.** to take away by force: *to wrest a knife from a child.* **3.** to get by effort: *to wrest a living from the soil.* **4.** to twist or turn from the proper course, application, use, meaning, or the like. —*n.* **5.** a wresting; a twist or wrench. **6.** a key or small wrench for tuning stringed musical instruments, as the harp or piano, by turning the pins to which the strings are fastened. [ME *wreste(n),* OE *wrǣstan;* c. Icel *reista;* akin to WRIST] —**wrest′er,** *n.*
—**Syn. 1, 3.** wring. **3.** See **extract.** **4.** wrench.

wres·tle (res′əl), *v.,* **-tled, -tling,** *n.* —*v.i.* **1.** to engage in wrestling. **2.** to contend, as in a struggle for mastery; grapple: *to wrestle with a problem; to wrestle with one's conscience.* —*v.t.* **3.** to contend with in wrestling. **4.** to force by or as if by wrestling. **5.** *U.S.* to throw (a calf or other animal) for branding. —*n.* **6.** an act of or a bout at wrestling. **7.** a struggle. [ME, OE *wrǣstlian (cf. OE *wrǣstlere* wrestler), freq. of *wrǣstan* to WREST] —**wres′tler,** *n.*

wres·tling (res′ling), *n.* **1.** a sport in which two opponents struggle hand to hand in order to pin or press each other's shoulders to the mat or ground, with the style, rules, and regulations differing widely in amateur and professional matches. Cf. **catch-as-catch-can** (def. 1), **Greco-Roman** (def. 3). **2.** act of one who wrestles. [ME; OE *wrǣstlung.* See WRESTLE, -ING[1]]

wrest′ pin′, peg (def. 5).

wretch (rech), *n.* **1.** a deplorably unfortunate or unhappy person. **2.** a person of despicable or base character. [ME *wrecche,* OE *wrecca* exile, adventurer; c. G *Recke* warrior, hero, Icel *rekkr* man; akin to WREAK]

wretch·ed (rech′id), *adj.* **1.** very unfortunate in condition or circumstances; miserable; pitiable. **2.** characterized by or attended with misery and sorrow. **3.** despicable, contemptible, or mean: *He's a wretched little miser.* **4.** poor, sorry, or pitiful; worthless: *a wretched job of sewing.* [ME *wrecchede.* See WRETCH, -ED[3]] —**wretch′ed·ly,** *adv.* —**wretch′ed·ness,** *n.*
—**Syn. 1.** dejected, distressed, afflicted, woeful, woebegone, forlorn, unhappy. **2.** WRETCHED, MISERABLE, SORRY refer to that which is unhappy, afflicted, or distressed. WRETCHED refers to a condition of extreme affliction or distress, esp. as outwardly apparent: *wretched hovels.* MISERABLE refers more to the inward feeling of unhappiness or distress: *a miserable life.* SORRY applies to distressed, often poverty-stricken outward circumstances; but it has connotations of unworthiness, incongruousness, or the like, so that the beholder feels more contempt than pity: *in a sorry plight.* **3.** base, vile, worthless, bad. —**Ant. 1.** comfortable, happy, enviable.

wrick (rik), *v.t., v.i., n.* wrench; strain. [ME *wrikke(n)* to make abrupt movements; perh. akin to WRINKLE, WRENCH]

wri·er (rī′ər), *adj.* comparative of **wry.**

wri·est (rī′ist), *adj.* superlative of **wry.**

wrig·gle (rig′əl), *v.,* **-gled, -gling,** *n.* —*v.i.* **1.** to twist to and fro; writhe; squirm. **2.** to move along by twisting and turning the body, as a worm or snake. **3.** to make one's way by shifts or expedients (often fol. by *out*): *to wriggle out of a difficulty.* —*v.t.* **4.** to cause to wriggle: *to wriggle one's hips.* **5.** to bring, get, make, etc., by wriggling: *to wriggle one's way through a narrow opening.* —*n.* **6.** act of wriggling; a wriggling movement. [< MLG *wriggelen* (c. D *wriggelen*), freq. of *wriggen to twist, turn, akin to OE *wrīgian* to twist; see WRY] —**wrig′gling·ly,** *adv.*

wrig·gler (rig′lər), *n.* **1.** one who or that which wriggles. **2.** Also called **wiggler, wiggle-tail.** the larva of a mosquito. [WRIGGLE + -ER[1]]

wrig·gle·work (rig′əl wûrk′), *n.* decorative engraving of a metal surface with repeated zigzags. [WRIGGLE + WORK]

wrig·gly (rig′lē), *adj.,* **-gli·er, -gli·est.** **1.** twisting; writhing; squirming: *a wriggly caterpillar.* **2.** evasive; shifty: *wriggly behavior; a wriggly character.* [WRIGGLE + -Y[1]]

wright (rīt), *n.* a workman, esp. a constructive workman (used chiefly in combination): *a wheelwright; a playwright.* [ME; OE *wryhta,* metathetic var. of *wyrhta* worker; see WORK]

Wright (rīt), *n.* **1. Fanny** (*Francis Wright Darusmont*), 1795–1852, U.S. abolitionist and social reformer, born in Scotland. **2. Frank Lloyd,** 1869–1959, U.S. architect. **3. Joseph,** 1855–1935, English philologist and lexicographer. **4. Joseph** ("*Wright of Derby*"), 1734–97, English painter. **5. Or·ville** (ôr′vil), 1871–1948, and his brother **Wilbur,** 1867–1912, U.S. aeronautical inventors. **6. Richard,** 1908–60, U.S. novelist. **7. Russel,** born 1904, U.S. industrial designer. **8. Willard Huntington** ("*S. S. Van Dine*"), 1888–1939, U.S. journalist, critic, and author. **9.** a boy's given name.

Wrights·town (rīts′toun′), *n.* a town in central New Jersey. 4846 (1960).

wring (ring), *v.,* **wrung** or (*Rare*) **wringed; wring·ing;** *n.* —*v.t.* **1.** to twist forcibly: *Grandpa caught the chicken and wrung its neck in a second.* **2.** to twist and compress, or compress without twisting, in order to force out water or other liquid (often fol. by *out*): *to wring clothes.* **3.** to extract or expel by twisting or compression (usually fol. by *out* or *from*). **4.** to affect painfully by or as if by some contorting or compressing action; pain, distress, or torment. **5.** to clasp tightly with or without twisting: *to wring one's hands in pain.* **6.** to force (usually fol. by *off*) by twisting. **7.** to extract or extort as if by twisting. —*v.i.* **8.** to perform the action of wringing something. **9.** to writhe, as in anguish. —*n.* **10.** a wringing; forcible twist or squeeze. [ME; OE *wringan;* c. G *ringen* to wrestle; base *wring-* nasalized var. of *wrig-;* see WRIGGLE]
—**Syn. 6, 7.** wrest.

wring·er (ring′ər), *n.* **1.** one who or that which wrings. **2.** an apparatus or machine which by pressure forces water or the like out of anything wet. **3.** an experience, occurrence, happening, or the like, which leaves a person emotionally and physically depleted; an ordeal (usually prec. by *through the*): *His child's illness really put him through the wringer.* [ME; see WRING, -ER[1]]

wrin·kle[1] (ring′kəl), *n., v.,* **-kled, -kling.** —*n.* **1.** a ridge or furrow on a surface, due to contraction, folding, rumpling, or the like; corrugation; slight fold; crease: *The wrinkles on her face revealed her age.* —*v.t.* **2.** to form a wrinkle or wrinkles in; corrugate; crease: *Don't wrinkle your dress.* —*v.i.* **3.** to become contracted into wrinkles; become wrinkled. [late ME, back formation from *wrinkled,* OE *gewrinclod,* ptp. of *gewrinclian* to wind round; perh. akin to WRICK, WRENCH] —**wrin′kle·a·ble,** *adj.* —**wrin′kled·ness,** *n.* —**wrin′kle·less,** *adj.*

wrin·kle[2] (ring′kəl), *n. Informal.* an ingenious trick or device; a clever innovation: *a new advertising wrinkle.* [late ME, equiv. to *wrinc* trick (OE *wrenc;* see WRENCH) + -LE]

wrin·kly (ringk′lē), *adj.,* **-kli·er, -kli·est.** having wrinkles or tending to wrinkle; creased; puckery: *a wrinkly material impossible to keep pressed.* [WRINKLE + -Y[1]]

wrist (rist), *n.* **1.** the carpus or lower part of the forearm where it joins the hand. **2.** the joint or articulation between the forearm and the hand. **3.** the part of an article of clothing that fits around the wrist. **4.** *Mach.* See **wrist pin.** [ME, OE; c. G *Rist* back of hand, Icel *rist* instep; akin to WRITHE]

wrist·band (rist′band′), *n.* the band of a sleeve, esp. that of a shirt sleeve, which covers the wrist. [WRIST + BAND[2]]

wrist′ drop′, *Pathol.* paralysis of the extensor muscles of the hand causing it to droop, due to injuries or some poisons, as lead or arsenic. Also, **wrist′-drop′.**

wrist·let (rist′lit), *n.* **1.** a band worn around the wrist, esp. to protect it from cold. **2.** a bracelet. **3.** *Slang.* a handcuff. [WRIST + -LET]

wrist·lock (rist′lok′), *n. Wrestling.* a hold in which an opponent's wrist is grasped and twisted. [WRIST + LOCK[1]]

wrist′ pin′, *Mach.* a pin joining the end of a connecting rod to a trunk piston or the end of a piston rod.

wrist′ plate′, *Mach.* a platelike part of a mechanism, oscillating in its own plane, to which links or rods are attached by pins.

wrist′ watch′, a watch attached to a strap or band worn about the wrist. Also, **wrist′watch′.**

writ[1] (rit), *n.* **1.** *Law.* **a.** a formal order under seal, issued in the name of a sovereign, government, court, or other competent authority, enjoining the officer or other person to whom it is issued or addressed to do or refrain from some specified act. **b.** (in early English law) any formal document in letter form, under seal, and in the sovereign's name. **2.** something written; a writing: *sacred writ.* [ME, OE; c. Icel *rit* writing, Goth *writs* letter. See WRITE]

writ[2] (rit), *v. Archaic.* a pt. and pp. of **write.**

write (rīt), *v.,* **wrote** or (*Archaic*) **writ; writ·ten** or (*Archaic*) **writ; writ·ing.** —*v.t.* **1.** to trace or form (characters, letters, words, etc.) on the surface of some material, as with a pen, pencil, or other instrument or means; inscribe: *Write your name on the board.* **2.** to express or communicate in writing; give a written account of. **3.** to fill in the blank spaces of (a printed form) with writing: *to write a check.* **4.** to execute or produce by setting down words, figures, etc.: *to write two copies of a letter.* **5.** to compose and produce in words or characters duly set down: *to write a letter to a friend.* **6.** to produce as author or composer: *to write a sonnet; to write a symphony.* **7.** to trace significant characters on, or mark or cover with writing. **8.** to impress the marks or indications of: *Honesty is written on his face.* **9.** *Computer Technol.* **a.** to put or place (information) into a memory unit. **b.** to record (information) in a memory unit. **10.** to underwrite. —*v.i.* **11.** to trace or form characters, words, etc., with a pen, pencil, or other instrument or means, or as a pen or the like does: *He writes with a pen.* **12.** to write as a profession or occupation: *He writes for the* Daily Inquirer. *He used to write for the musical theater.* **13.** to express ideas in writing. **14.** to write a letter or letters, or communicate by letter: *Write if you get work.* **15.** to compose or work as a writer or author. **16.** *Computer Technol.* to write into a memory unit. **17.** to be useful for writing; serve as an implement for writing: *This pen does not write.* **18. write down, a.** to set down in writing; record; note. **b.** to depreciate, as in writing against; injure; disparage. **c.** to direct one's efforts in writing to a lower level, as to a less intelligent reader or audience: *He writes down to the public.* **19. write off, a.** to cancel an entry in an account, as an unpaid and uncollectable debt. **b.** to regard as worthless, lost, obsolete, etc.; decide to forget: *They decided to write off their attempt at pioneering and return to civilization.* **c.** to amortize: *The new equipment was written off in three years.* **20. write out, a.** to put into writing. **b.** to write in full form; state completely. **c.** to exhaust the capacity or resources of by excessive writing: *He's just another author who has written himself out.* **21. write up, a.** to put into writing, esp. in full detail: *Write up a report.* **b.** to bring up to date in writing; add the latest facts to. **c.** to present to public notice in a written description or account. **d.** to commend to the public by a favorable description or account. **e.** *Accounting.* to make an excessive valuation of (an asset). [ME; OE *wrītan;* c. G. *reissen* to tear, draw, Icel *rīta* to write] —**writ′a·ble,** *adj.*

write-down (rīt′doun′), *n. Accounting.* **1.** a reduction of the entered value of an asset account. **2.** the procedure of reducing the recorded value of an asset, either by estimate or as a plan. [n. use of v. phrase *write down*]

write-in (rīt′in′), *adj.* **1.** written onto the ballot by the voter: *a write-in vote; a write-in candidate.* —*n.* **2.** a candidate or vote for a candidate not listed on the printed ballot: *Write-ins may swing the election.* [adj., n. use of v. phrase *write in*]

write-off (rīt′ôf′, -of′), *n.* **1.** a cancellation from the accounts as a loss. **2.** an uncollectable account. **3.** a reduction in book value; depreciation. [n. use of v. phrase *write off*]

writ·er (rī′tər), *n.* **1.** a person engaged in writing books, articles, stories, etc., esp. as an occupation or profession; an author or journalist. **2.** a clerk, scribe, or the like. **3.** one who commits his thoughts, ideas, etc., to writing: *an expert letter writer.* **4.** (in a piece of writing) the author (used as a circumlocution for "I," "me," "my," etc.): *The writer wishes to state. It is known to the writer.* **5.** one who writes or is able to write: *a writer in script; one who reads well but is deficient as a writer.* **6.** *Scot.* a lawyer or solicitor. [ME, OE *writere.* See WRITE, -ER[1]]

writ′er's cramp′, *Pathol.* spasmodic contractions of the muscles of the thumb and forefinger during writing, sometimes accompanied by pain.

write-up (rīt′up′), *n.* **1.** a written description or account, sometimes one favorable to the subject, as in a newspaper or magazine: *This movie really got a write-up. The play got a terrible write-up.* **2.** *Accounting.* an increase in the book value of a corporation which is not warranted by the true assets of the corporation. [n. use of v. phrase *write up*]

writhe (rīth), *v.,* **writhed, writh·ing,** *n.* —*v.i.* **1.** to twist the body about, or squirm, as in pain, violent effort, etc. **2.** to shrink mentally, as in acute discomfort. —*v.t.* **3.** to twist or bend out of shape or position; distort; contort. **4.** to twist (oneself, the body, etc.) about, as in pain. —*n.* **5.** a writhing movement; a twisting of the body, as in pain. [ME; OE *wrīthan* to twist, wind; c. Icel *rītha* to knit, twist; akin to WREATH, WRY] —**writh′er,** *n.* —**writh′ing·ly,** *adv.*

writh·en (rith′ən), *adj. Archaic.* twisted. [ME; see WRITHE, -EN[3]]

writ·ing (rī′ting), *n.* **1.** act of one who or that which writes. **2.** state of being written; written form: *to commit one's thoughts to writing.* **3.** that which is written; characters or matter written with a pen or the like: *His writing is illegible.* **4.** such characters or matter with respect to style, kind, quality, etc. **5.** an inscription. **6.** a letter. **7.** any written or printed paper, as a document, deed, or the like. **8.** literary or musical style, form, quality, technique, etc.: *His writing shows a keen knowledge of history. The writing fails to utilize the resources of the orchestra.* **9.** a literary composition or production. **10.** the profession of a writer: *He turned to writing at an early age.* **11. the Writings,** Hagiographa. **12. writing on the wall.** See **handwriting** (def. 4). [ME, OE; see WRITE, -ING[1]]

writ′ing desk′, **1.** a piece of furniture with a surface for writing upon, usually with drawers and pigeonholes to hold writing materials, etc. **2.** a portable case that holds writing materials and provides, when opened, a surface on which to write.

writ′ing pa′per, **1.** paper on which to write. **2.** stationery; notepaper.

writ′ of assist′ance, *Amer. Hist.* a writ issued by a superior colonial court authorizing officers of the British crown to summon aid and enter and search any premises.

writ′ of elec′tion, a writ by an executive authority requiring the holding of an election, esp. one issued by a governor to require a special election for filling a vacancy in the representation from a State.

writ′ of er′ror, *Law.* a writ issued by an appellate court to the court of record where a case was tried, requiring that the record of the trial be sent to the appellate court for examination of alleged errors.

writ′ of extent′, *Eng. Law.* extent (def. 4a).

writ′ of prohibi′tion, *Law.* a command by a higher court that a lower court shall not exercise jurisdiction in a particular case.

writ′ of right′, **1.** *Eng. Law.* (formerly) a writ directed to a person who presides over a feudal court, directing him to render justice between his vassals in a dispute as to ownership of land: usually led to a trial in a royal court if feudal ownership was involved. **2.** *Law.* a common-law writ to restore land to its rightful owner or tenants.

writ·ten (rit′ən), *v., adj.* —*v.* **1.** a pp. of **write.** —*adj.* **2.** expressed in writing (distinguished from *spoken*).

W.R.N.S., *Brit.* Women's Royal Naval Service.

wrnt., warrant.

Wroc·law (vrôts′läf), *n.* Polish name of **Breslau.**

wrong (rông, rong), *adj.* **1.** not in accordance with what is morally right or good: *a wrong deed.* **2.** deviating from truth or fact; erroneous: *a wrong answer.* **3.** not correct in action, judgment, opinion, method, etc., as a person; in error: *You are wrong to blame him.* **4.** not proper or usual; not in accordance with requirements or recommended practice: *the wrong way to hold a golf club.* **5.** out of order; awry; amiss: *Something is wrong with the machine.* **6.** not suitable or appropriate: *He always says the wrong thing.* **7.** that should be worn or kept inward or under: *You're wearing the sweater wrong side out.* —*n.* **8.** that which is wrong, or not in accordance with morality, goodness, justice, truth, or the like; evil: *He committed many wrongs. The wrongs they suffered aged them.* **9.** *Law.* **a.** an invasion of another's right, to his damage. **b.** a tort. **10. get in wrong,** *Slang.* to cause to come into disfavor: *He is forever getting in wrong with the people next door.* **11. in the wrong,** to blame; in error: *He knew he was in the wrong, but refused to concede the point.* —*adv.* **12.** in a wrong manner; not rightly; awry; amiss: *You did it wrong again.* **13. go wrong, a.** to go amiss; fail: *Everything is going wrong today.* **b.** to pursue an immoral course; become depraved: *It is sad that one so young should go wrong.* —*v.t.* **14.** to do wrong to; treat unfairly or unjustly; injure or harm. **15.** to impute evil to (someone) unjustly; malign. [ME, OE perh. < Scand; cf. Dan *vrang* wrong, Icel *rangr* awry; c. D *wrang* acid, tart; akin to WRING] —**wrong′er,** *n.* —**wrong′ly,** *adv.* —**wrong′ness,** *n.*
—**Syn. 1.** bad, evil, wicked, sinful, immoral, iniquitous, reprehensible, unjust, crooked. **2.** inaccurate, incorrect, false, untrue, mistaken. **6.** improper, unsuitable. **8.** misdoing, wickedness, sin, vice. **14.** maltreat, abuse, oppress, cheat, defraud, dishonor.

wrong·do·er (rông′dōō′ər, -dōō′-, rong′-), *n.* one who does wrong, esp. a sinner or transgressor. [late ME; see WRONG, DOER]

wrong·do·ing (rông′dōō′ing, -dōō′-, rong′-), *n.* **1.** behavior or action that is wrong, evil, or blameworthy. **2.** an act that is wrong, evil, or blameworthy; misdeed; sin. [WRONG + DOING]

wrong′ font′, *Print.* the improper font, or size and style of type, for its place. *Abbr.:* wf, w.f.

wrong·ful (rông′fəl, rong′-), *adj.* **1.** full of or characterized by wrong; unjust or unfair: *a wrongful act; a wrongful charge.* **2.** having no legal right; unlawful: *The court ruled it was a wrongful diversion of trust income.* [ME; see WRONG, -FUL] —**wrong′ful·ly,** *adv.* —**wrong′ful·ness,** *n.*

wrong-head·ed (rông′hed′id, rong′-), *adj.* wrong in judgment or opinion; misguided and stubborn; perverse. Also, **wrong′head′ed.** —**wrong′-head′ed·ly, wrong′head′ed·ly,** *adv.* —**wrong′-head′ed·ness, wrong′head′ed·ness,** *n.*

Wron·ski·an (ränz′kē ən, vränz′-, rän′skē-, vrän′-), *n. Math.* the determinant of order *n* associated with a set of *n* functions, in which the first row consists of the functions, the second row consists of the first derivatives of the functions, the third row consists of their second derivatives, and so on. [named after Jozef *Wronski* (1778–1853), Polish mathematician; see -AN]

wrote (rōt), *v.* a pt. of **write.**

wroth (rôth, roth *or, esp. Brit.,* rōth), *adj.* **1.** angry; wrathful (usually used predicatively): *He was wroth to see the damage to his home.* **2.** stormy; violent; turbulent: *the wroth sea; wroth weather.* [ME; OE *wrāth;* c. D *wreed* cruel, Icel *reithr* angry. See WRITHE]

Wrot·tes·ley (rots′lē), *n.* a crater in the fourth quadrant of the face of the moon: about 37 miles in diameter.

wrought (rôt), *v.* **1.** a pt. and pp. of **work.** —*adj.* **2.** worked. **3.** elaborated; embellished. **4.** not rough or crude. **5.** produced or shaped by beating with a hammer as iron or silver articles.
—**Syn. 2.** See **worked.**

wrought′ i′ron, a comparatively pure form of iron, almost entirely free of carbon and having a fibrous structure including a uniformly distributed slag content, that is readily forged and welded. —**wrought′-i′ron,** *adj.*

wrought′ i′ron cast′ing, **1.** the act or process of casting with mitis metal. **2.** a casting made from mitis metal.

wrought-up (rôt′up′), *adj.* excited; perturbed: *She's all wrought-up about nothing.* Also called **worked-up.**

W.R.S.S.R., White Russian Soviet Socialist Republic.

wrung (rung), *v.* a pt. and pp. of **wring.**

wry (rī), *adj.,* **wri·er, wri·est.** **1.** produced by a distortion or lopsidedness of the facial features: *a wry grin.* **2.** abnormally bent or turned to one side; twisted; crooked; distorted: *a wry mouth; a wry nose.* **3.** devious in course or purpose; misdirected. **4.** contrary; perverse. **5.** distorted or perverted, as in meaning. **6.** bitterly or disdainfully ironic or amusing: *wry remarks about Congress.* [adj. use of *wry* (v.), ME *wryen*(n), OE *wrīgian* to go forward, swerve; c. D *wrijgen* to twist; akin to OE *wrigels,* L *rīcula* veil, Gk *rhoikós* crooked] —**wry′ly,** *adv.* —**wry′ness,** *n.*
—**Syn. 2.** awry, askew. —**Ant. 2.** straight.

wry·mouth (rī′mouth′), *n., pl.* (*esp. collectively*) **-mouth,** (*esp. referring to two or more kinds or species*) **-mouths** (-mouthz′). **1.** any blennioid fish of the family *Cryptacanthodidae,* having a large, upturned mouth, esp. *Cryptacanthodes maculatus,* found in the Atlantic Ocean. **2.** any of several related fishes. Also called **ghostfish.** [WRY + MOUTH]

wry·neck (rī′nek′), *n.* **1.** *Informal.* **a.** torticollis. **b.** a person having torticollis. **2.** any of several small, Old World, scansorial birds of the subfamily *Jynginae,* of the woodpecker family, noted for the peculiar habit of twisting the head and neck. [WRY + NECK]

wry-necked (rī′nekt′), *adj. Informal.* afflicted with wryneck. Also, **wry′necked′.**

W.S., West Saxon.

WSA, War Shipping Administration.

WSW, west-southwest. Also, **W.S.W.**

wt., weight.

Wu·chang (wōō′chäng′), *n.* a city in E China at the junction of the Han and Yangtze rivers. 205,000 (est. 1950). Cf. **Wuhan.**

wud (wŏŏd), *adj. Chiefly Scot.* wood; mad. [see WOOD[2]]

Wu·han (wōō′hän′), *n.* the three cities of Hankow, Hanyang, and Wuchang in E China at the junction of the Han and Yangtze rivers, actually forming one extensive metropolitan area. 2,146,000 (est. 1957). Also called **Han Cities.**

Wu·hsien (wōō′shyen′), *n.* a city in S Kiangsu, in E China. 381,000 (est. 1950). Formerly, **Soochow.**

Wu·hu (wōō′hōō′), *n.* a port in E Anhwei, in E China, on the Yangtze River. 242,100 (est. 1957).

wul·fen·ite (wŏŏl′fə nīt′), *n.* a mineral consisting of lead molybdate, occurring usually in tabular crystals, and varying in color from grayish to bright-yellow or red; yellow lead ore. [named after F. X. von *Wulfen* (1728–1805), Austrian scientist]

Wul·fi·la (wŏŏl′fə lə), *n.* Ulfilas.

Wun·der·kind (vŏŏn′dər kint′; *Eng.* vŏŏn′dər-kind′, wun′-), *n., pl.* **-kin·der** (-kin′dər), *Eng.* **-kinds.** *German.* **1.** a wonder child or child prodigy. **2.** one who succeeds, esp. in business, at a comparatively early age: *At 28 he was the* Wunderkind *of the movie industry.*

Wundt (vŏŏnt), *n.* **Wil·helm Max** (vil′helm mäks), 1832–1920, German physiologist and psychologist. —**Wundt′i·an,** *adj.*

Wup·per·tal (vŏŏp′ər täl′), *n.* a city in W West Germany, in the Ruhr Valley: formed by the union of Barmen, Elberfeld, and smaller communities 1929. 422,900 (1963).

wur·ley (wûr′lē), *n., pl.* **-leys, -lies.** *Australian.* **1.** an aborigine's shelter, made of branches and leaves. **2.** a nest, esp. a rat's nest. [< native Austral]

Würm (vŏŏrm, wŏŏrm, wûrm; *Ger.* VYRM), *n.* the fourth stage of the glaciation of Eurasia during the Pleistocene. Cf. **Wisconsin** (def. 3). [after a district in the Alps; name chosen by A. Peuck, as *Würm* is representative of the last stage of extreme cold]

wurst (wûrst, wŏŏrst), *n.* sausage (def. 1). [< G: lit., mixture; akin to WORSE]

Würt·tem·berg (wûr′təm bûrg′; *Ger.* VYR′təm-BERKH′), *n.* a former state in SW West Germany: now part of Baden-Württemberg.

wurtz·i·lite (wûrt′sə līt′), *n.* a massive black bituminous substance, similar to asphalt but having a high degree of elasticity. [named after Henry *Wurtz* (d. 1910), American mineralogist; see -I-, -LITE]

wurtz·ite (wûrt′sīt), *n. Mineral.* a dimorph of sphalerite, zinc sulfide, ZnS, similar in structure to greenockite and brownish-black in color. [< F, named after Charles *Wurtz* (1817–84), French chemist; see -ITE[1]] —**wurtz·it·ic** (wərt sit′ik), *adj.*

Würz·burg (wûrts′bûrg; *Ger.* VYRTS′bŏŏrkh′), *n.* a city in NW Bavaria, in S West Germany, on the Main River. 119,700 (1963).

Wur·zel·bau·er (wûrt′səl bou′ər), *n.* a walled plain in the third quadrant of the face of the moon: about 50 miles in diameter.

Wu·sih (wōō′sē′, -shē′), *n.* a city in S Kiangsu, in E China. 613,000 (est. 1957).

Wuth′er·ing Heights′ (wuth′ər ing), a novel (1846) by Emily Brontë.

wu-wei (wōō′wā′), *n.* (in philosophical Taoism) action accomplishing its purpose in accordance with the natures of things and events. Cf. **yu-wei.** [< Chin (Mandarin dial.): lit., without action]

W.Va., West Virginia.

W.V.S., *Brit.* Women's Voluntary Service.

WW, World War.

Wy., Wyoming.

Wy·an·dot (wī′ən dot′), *n., pl.* **-dots,** (*esp. collectively*) **-dot** for **1.** **1.** an Indian of the former Huron confederacy. **2.** a dialect of the Huron language, esp. as used by those elements of the Huron tribe regrouped in Oklahoma. Also, **Wyandotte.**

Wy·an·dotte (wī′ən dot′), *n., pl.* **-dottes** for 2, 3; (*esp. collectively for 3*) **-dotte.** **1.** a city in SE Michigan, on the Detroit River. 43,519 (1960). **2.** one of an American breed of chickens, raised for meat and eggs. **3.** Wyandot.

Wy·att (wī′ət), *n.* **1. James,** 1746–1813, English architect. **2. Sir Thomas,** 1503?–42, English poet and diplomat. **3.** a boy's given name. Also, **Wy′at.**

wych-elm (wich′elm′), *n.* an elm, *Ulmus glabra,* of northern and western Europe. Also, **witch-elm.** [*wych* (ME *wyche,* OE *wice* wych-elm) + ELM]

Wych·er·ley (wich′ər lē), *n.* **William,** c1640–1716, English dramatist and poet.

wych-ha·zel (wich′hā′zəl), *n.* See **witch hazel.**

Wyc·liffe (wik′lif), *n.* **John,** c1320–84, English theologian, religious reformer, and Biblical translator. Also, **Wyc′lif, Wickliffe, Wiclif.** —**Wyc′liff·ism, Wyc′lif·ism,** *n.*

Wyc·lif·fite (wik′li fīt′), *adj.* **1.** of or pertaining to Wycliffe or the Wycliffites. —*n.* **2.** a follower of John Wycliffe; Lollard. Also, **Wyc′lif·ite′.** [< ML *Wyclefita.* See WYCLIFFE, -ITE¹]

wye (wī), *n., pl.* **wyes. 1.** the letter Y, or something having a similar shape. **2.** *Elect.* a three-phase, Y-shaped, circuit arrangement. **3.** *Railroads.* a Y-shaped track arrangement for reversing the direction of trains.

Wye (wī), *n.* a river flowing from central Wales through SW England into the Severn estuary. 130 mi. long.

wye′ lev′el, *Survey.* an instrument, consisting of a spirit level mounted under and parallel to a telescope, which can be rotated in its Y-shaped supports for adjustment.

Wy·eth (wī′əth), *n.* **1. Andrew New·ell** (no͞o′əl, nyo͞o′-), born 1917, U.S. painter. **2.** his father **Newell Con·vers** (kon′vərz), 1882–1945, U.S. illustrator and painter.

Wyld (wīld), *n.* **Henry Cecil Kennedy,** 1870–1945, English lexicographer and linguist.

Wy·lie (wī′lē), *n.* **1. Elinor** (*Elinor Morton Hoyt*), 1885–1928, U.S. poet and novelist. **2. Philip,** born 1902, U.S. novelist and critic.

wy·lie·coat (wī′lē kōt′), *n. Scot. and North Eng.* **1.** a woolen or flannel undergarment, as a warm undershirt. **2.** a petticoat. [ME (Scot) *wyle cot,* equiv. to *wyle* (< ?) + *cot* COAT]

wynd (wīnd), *n. Chiefly Scot.* a narrow street or alley. [ME (Scot) *wynde,* OE *gewind* winding path. See WIND²]

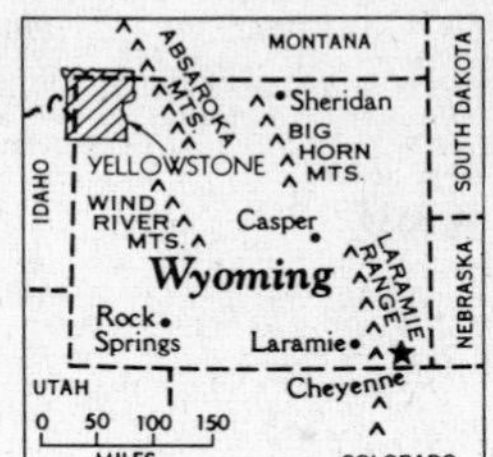

wynn (win), *n.* the rune for *w.* Also, **wen.** [OE: lit., joy]

Wynne (win), *n.* a town in E Arkansas. 4922 (1960).

Wyn·ne·wood (win′i-wo͝od′), *n.* a town in central Oklahoma. 2509 (1960).

Wyo., Wyoming.

Wy·o·ming (wī ō′ming), *n.* **1.** a State in the NW United States. 330,066 (1960); 97,914 sq. mi. *Cap.:* Cheyenne. *Abbr.:* Wyo., Wy. **2.** a city in W Michigan, near Grand Rapids. 45,829 (1960). **3.** a town in SW Ohio. 7736 (1960). **4.** a town in NE Pennsylvania. 4127 (1960). —**Wy·o·ming·ite** (wī ō′ming īt′), *n.*

Wyo′ming Val′ley, a valley in NE Pennsylvania, along the Susquehanna River: Indian massacre 1778.

Wy·o·mis·sing (wī′ə mis′ing), *n.* a town in central Pennsylvania. 5044 (1960).

wyte (wīt), *v.,* **wyt·ed, wyt·ing,** *n. Chiefly Scot.* wite¹.

wythe (with, with, with), *n.* withe (def. 4).

Wythe (with), *n.* **George,** 1729–1806, U.S. jurist and statesman.

Wythe·ville (with′vil), *n.* a town in SW Virginia. 5634 (1960).

wy·vern (wī′vərn), *n. Heraldry.* a two-legged winged dragon having the hinder part of a serpent with a barbed tail. Also, **wivern.** [ME *wyvre* < AF *wivre* (OF *guivre*) << OHG *wīpera* < L *vīpera* VIPER; modern *-n* unexplained]

Wyvern

X

X, x (eks), *n., pl.* **X's** or **Xs, x's** or **xs. 1.** the 24th letter of the English alphabet, a consonant. **2.** any spoken sound represented by the letter *X* or *x*, as in *xylene, box, Xerxes*, etc. **3.** something having the shape of an X. **4.** a written or printed representation of the letter *X* or *x*. **5.** a device, as a printer's type, for reproducing the letter *X* or *x*.

X, 1. the 24th in order or in a series, or, when *I* is omitted, the 23rd. **2.** (*sometimes l.c.*) the Roman numeral for 10. Cf. **Roman numerals. 3.** Christ. **4.** Christian. **5.** *Elect.* reactance. **6.** *U.S. Slang.* a ten-dollar bill. **7.** a rating for a film recommended for adults only. **8.** *Chem. Obs.* xenon.

x, 1. an unknown quantity or a variable. **2.** ex[1] (def. 1). **3.** experimental. **4.** a sign used at the end of letters, telegrams, etc., to indicate a kiss. **5.** a sign indicating multiplication; times: $8 \times 8 = 64$. **6.** a sign used between figures indicating dimensions: 3″ × 4″ (read: "three by four inches"); 3″ × 4″ × 5″ (read: "three by four by five inches"). **7.** power of magnification: *50x telescope.* **8.** (used as a signature by an illiterate person.) **9.** crossed with. **10.** out of; foaled by: *a colt by Flag-a-way x Merrylegs.* **11.** (used to indicate choice, as on a ballot, examination, etc.) **12.** (used to indicate an error or incorrect answer, as on a test.) **13.** *Math.* (in Cartesian coordinates) the *x*-axis. **14.** *Chess.* captures. **15.** a person, thing, agency, factor, etc., of unknown identity.

x (eks), *v.t.*, **x-ed** or **x'd** (ekst), **x-ing** or **x'ing** (ek′sing). **1.** to cross out or mark with or as if with an *x* (often fol. by *out*): *to x out an error.* **2.** to indicate choice, as on a ballot, examination, etc. (often fol. by *in*): *to x in the man of your choice.*

xa·lo·stock·ite (sä′lō stō′kīt), *n. Mineral.* a pale variety of grossularite, occurring in white marble found at Xalostoc, Mexico. [named after *Xalostoc;* see -ITE[1]]

xanth-, var. of **xantho-** before a vowel: *xanthate; xanthous.*

xan·thate (zan′thāt), *n. Chem.* a salt or ester of xanthic acid. [XANTH- + -ATE[2]] **—xan·tha′tion,** *n.*

Xan·the (zan′thē), *n.* a girl's given name.

xan·the·in (zan′thē in), *n.* the part of the coloring matter in yellow flowers that is soluble in water. [< F *xanthéine,* equiv. to *xanth-* XANTH- + *-éine* n. suffix to distinguish it from F *xanthine* XANTHIN]

Xan·thi·an (zan′thē ən), *adj.* of or pertaining to the ancient city of Xanthus. [XANTH(US) + -IAN]

xan·thic (zan′thik), *adj.* **1.** of or pertaining to a yellow or yellowish color. **2.** *Bot.* yellow. **3.** *Chem.* of or derived from xanthine or xanthic acid. [< F *xanthique.* See XANTH-, -IC]

xan′thic ac′id, *Chem.* an unstable organic acid with the type formula ROCSSH where R is a group, the methyl and ethyl esters of which are colorless, oily liquids with a penetrating odor. Its copper salts are bright yellow.

xan·thin (zan′thin), *n.* **1.** the part of the coloring matter in yellow flowers which is insoluble. Cf. **xanthein. 2.** a yellow coloring matter in madder. [< F *xanthine,* or < G *Xanthin.* See XANTH-, -IN[2]]

xan·thine (zan′thēn, -thin), *n. Biochem., Chem.* **1.** a crystalline nitrogenous compound, $C_5H_4N_4O_2$, related to uric acid, found in urine, blood, and certain animal and vegetable tissues. **2.** any derivative of this compound. [< F; see XANTH-, -INE[2]]

Xan·thip·pe (zan tip′ē), *n.* **1.** fl. late 5th century B.C., wife of Socrates. **2.** a scolding or ill-tempered wife; a shrewish woman. Also, **Xantippe.**

xantho-, a learned borrowing from Greek meaning "yellow," used in the formation of compound words: *xanthophyll.* Also, *esp. before a vowel,* **xanth-.** [comb. form of Gk *xanthós*]

xan·tho·chroid (zan′thə kroid′), *Ethnol.* **—***adj.* **1.** belonging to or pertaining to the light-complexioned or light-haired peoples of the white race. **—***n.* **2.** a person having xanthochroid characteristics. [< NL *xanthochr(oi)* yellow-pale ones < Gk *xanth-* XANTH- + *ōchroí* (pl. of *ōchrós* pale) + -OID]

xan·tho·phyll (zan′thə fil), *n. Biochem.* lutein (def. 1). Also, **xan′tho·phyl.** [< F *xanthophylle.* See XANTHO-, -PHYLL] **—xan′tho·phyll′ous,** *adj.*

xan′tho·pro·te′ic ac′id (zan′thə prō tē′ik, zan′-), *Chem.* a yellow substance of unknown structure formed by the action of nitric acid on proteins. [XANTHO- + PROTE(IN) + -IC]

xan·tho·sid·er·ite (zan′thə sid′ə rīt′), *n.* a mineral, hydrous iron oxide, $Fe_2O_3{\cdot}2H_2O$. [XANTHO- + SIDER- ITE]

xan·thous (zan′thəs), *adj.* **1.** yellow. **2.** yellowish. [XANTH- + -OUS]

Xan·thus (zan′thəs), *n.* **1.** an ancient city of Lycia, in SW Asia Minor, near the mouth of the Xanthus River: valuable archaeological remains have been found in the ruins. **2.** (in the *Iliad*) **a.** one of two immortal horses of Achilles that wept when Patroclus was killed by Hector. Cf. **Balius. b.** a Trojan warrior slain by Diomedes. **c.** the name given to the river god Scamander by the gods.

Xan·tip·pe (zan tip′ē), *n.* Xanthippe.

xat (KHät), *n.* a carved totem pole of various North American Indian peoples. [< Haida]

Xa·vi·er (zā′vē ər, zav′ē-, zā′vyər), *n.* **1. Saint Francis** (*Francisco Javier*) ("*the Apostle of the Indies*"), 1506–52, Spanish Jesuit missionary, esp. in India and Japan. **2.** a boy's given name. **—Xa·ve·ri·an** (zā vēr′ē ən, za-), *adj.*

x-ax·is (eks′ak′sis), *n., pl.* **x-ax·es** (eks′ak′sēz). *Math.* **1.** Also called **axis of abscissas.** (in a plane Cartesian coordinate system) the axis, usually horizontal, along which the abscissa is measured and from which the ordinate is measured. See diag. under **abscissa. 2.** (in a three-dimensional Cartesian coordinate system) the axis along which values of *x* are measured and at which both *y* and *z* equal zero.

xc, *Stock Exchange.* without coupon. Also, **xcp** [x (def. 2) + *c*(*oupon*)]

X chromosome, *Biol.* a sex chromosome that carries genes for femaleness in humans and most mammals and that usually occurs in pairs in a female and singly in males. Cf. **Y chromosome.**

xcl, *Insurance.* excess current liabilities.

xd, *Stock Exchange.* without dividends. Also, **xdiv.**

x-dis·ease (eks′di zēz′), *n. Vet. Pathol.* **1.** hyperkeratosis (def. 2). **2.** See **blue comb.**

Xe, *Chem.* xenon.

xe·bec (zē′bek), *n.* a small three-masted vessel of the Mediterranean, formerly much used by corsairs, now employed to some extent in commerce. Also, **chebeck, zebec, zebeck.** [< Catalan *xabec* or Sp *xabeque* (now *jabeque*), both < Ar *shabbāk;* first *e* < var. *chebec* < F]

Xebec

xen-, var. of **xeno-** before a vowel: *xenia.*

xe·ni·a (zē′nē ə), *n. Bot.* the immediate influence or effect of the pollen on structures, as the seed or fruit, other than the embryo. [< NL < Gk *xenía.* See XEN-, -IA] **—xe′ni·al,** *adj.*

Xe·ni·a (zē′nē ə *or, for 1, 2,* zēn′yə), *n.* **1.** a city in W Ohio. 20,445 (1960). **2.** *Class. Myth.* an epithet of Athena, meaning "hospitable." **3.** Also, **Zenia.** a girl's given name.

xeno-, a learned borrowing from Greek meaning "alien," "strange," "guest," used in the formation of compound words: *xenogamy, xenolith.* Also, *esp. before a vowel,* **xen-.** [comb. form of Gk *xénos* stranger, guest (n.); alien, foreign, strange (adj.)]

Xe·no·cle·a (zē′nə klē′ə), *n. Class. Myth.* a priestess at Delphi who refused to prophesy for Hercules because he had not been purified after killing Iphitus.

Xe·noc·ra·tes (zə nok′rə tēz′), *n.* 396–314 B.C., Greek philosopher. **—Xen·o·crat·ic** (zen′ə krat′ik), **Xe·noc′ra·te′an,** *adj.*

xen·o·cryst (zen′ə krist), *n. Mineral.* a rock or crystal surrounded by magma and retained as an inclusion in the resulting igneous rock. [XENO- + CRYST(AL)] **—xen′o·crys′tic,** *adj.*

xen·o·di·ag·no·sis (zen′ə dī′əg nō′sis), *n. Med.* a method of diagnosing certain diseases caused by insects, ticks, or other vectors, by feeding uninfected vectors on the patient and later examining them for infections. [XENO- + DIAGNOSIS] **—xen·o·di·ag·nos·tic** (zen′ə-dī′əg nos′tik), *adj.*

xen·o·do·che·ion (zen′ə də kē′yon, -kī′on), *n., pl.* **-che·ia** (-kē′yə, -kī′ə). xenodochium.

xen·o·do·che·um (zen′ə də kē′əm), *n., pl.* **-che·a** (-kē′ə). xenodochium.

xen·o·do·chi·um (zen′ə də kī′əm), *n., pl.* **-chi·a** (-kī′ə). an ancient Greek or Roman inn. [< NL < MGk *xenodocheîon* hotel, equiv. to Gk *xeno-* XENO- + *docheîon* holder]

xe·nog·a·my (zə nog′ə mē), *n. Bot.* pollination of the stigma of a flower by pollen from a flower on another plant. Cf. **geitonogamy.** [XENO- + -GAMY]

xen·o·gen·e·sis (zen′ə jen′i sis), *n. Biol.* **1.** the supposed generation of offspring completely and permanently different from the parent. **2.** heterogenesis (def. 1). Also, **xe·nog·e·ny** (zə noj′ə nē). [XENO- + GENESIS] **—xen·o·ge·net·ic** (zen′ō jə net′ik), **xen′o·gen′ic,** *adj.*

xen·o·lith (zen′əlith), *n. Petrog.* a rock fragment foreign to the igneous rock in which it is embedded. [XENO- + -LITH] **—xen′o·lith′ic,** *adj.*

xen·o·mor·phic (zen′ə môr′fik), *adj.* **1.** Also called **allotriomorphic.** *Petrog.* noting or pertaining to a mineral constituent of a rock, which does not have its characteristic crystalline form, but one forced upon it by other constituents of the rock; anhedral. **2.** in an unusual form; having a strange form. [XENO- + -MORPHIC] **—xen′o·mor′phi·cal·ly,** *adv.*

xe·non (zē′non, zen′on), *n. Chem.* a heavy, colorless, chemically inactive, monatomic gaseous element present in the atmosphere in the proportion of one volume in 170,000,000 volumes of air: used for filling radio, television, and luminescent tubes. *Symbol:* Xe; *at. wt.:* 131.30; *at. no.:* 54. [< Gk *xénon,* neut. of *xénos* strange]

Xe·noph·a·nes (zə nof′ə nēz′), *n.* **1.** c570–c480 B.C., Greek philosopher and poet. **2.** a walled plain in the second quadrant of the face of the moon, in the libration area: about 67 miles in diameter. **—Xe·noph′a·ne′an,** *adj.*

xen·o·phobe (zen′ə fōb′), *n.* one who fears or hates foreigners, strange customs, etc. [XENO- + -PHOBE]

xen·o·pho·bi·a (zen′ə fō′bē ə), *n.* an unreasonable fear or hatred of foreigners or strangers or of that which is foreign or strange. [XENO- + -PHOBIA] **—xen′o·pho′bic,** *adj.*

Xen·o·phon (zen′ə fən, -fon′), *n.* **1.** 434?–355? B.C., Greek historian and essayist. **2.** a boy's given name. **—Xen·o·phon·te·an** (zen′ə fon′tē ən, -fon tē′-), **Xen·o·phon·ti·an** (zen′ə fon′tē ən), **Xen·o·phon·tine** (zen′ə-fon′tin, -tən), *adj.*

xer-, var. of **xero-** before a vowel: *xerophthalmia.*

xe·rarch (zēr′ärk), *adj. Ecol.* (of a sere) originating in a dry habitat. [XER- + -ARCH]

Xe·res (*Sp.* he′res, *older* she′res), *n.* former name of **Jerez.**

xe·ric (zēr′ik), *adj.* of, pertaining to, or adapted to a dry environment. [XER- + -IC[1]] **—xe′ri·cal·ly,** *adv.*

xero-, a learned borrowing from Greek meaning "dry," used in the formation of compound words: *xerophyte.* Also, *esp. before a vowel,* **xer-.** [comb. form of Gk *xērós* dry]

xe·ro·der·ma (zēr′ə dûr′mə), *n. Pathol.* a disease in which the skin becomes dry and hard and usually scaly. [XERO- + DERMA]

xe·rog·ra·phy (zi rog′rə fē), *n.* a process for making copies of printed, written, or pictorial material from film or paper, in which areas on a sheet of plain paper corresponding to those areas on the original that are to be reproduced are sensitized with a charge of static

CONCISE ETYMOLOGY KEY: <, descended or derived from; >, whence; b., blend of, blended; c., cognate with; deriv., derivative; equiv., equivalent; imit., imitative; m., modification of; obl., oblique; r., replacing; s., stem; sp., spelling; trans., translation; ?, origin unknown, perhaps; *, hypothetical. See the full key inside the front cover.

electricity so that, when powdered with a colored resin carrying an opposite charge, only the charged areas retain the resin, which is then fused to the paper to make it permanent. [XERO- + -GRAPHY] **—xe·ro·graph·ic** (zēr′ə graf′ik), *adj.* **—xe′ro·graph′i·cal·ly,** *adv.*

xe·roph·a·gy (zi rof′ə jē), *n., pl.* **-gies.** a Lenten fast observed esp. during Holy Week, constituting the strictest fast in the Eastern Church. Also, **xe·ro·pha·gia** (zēr′ə fā′jə, -jē ə). [< LL *xerophagia* < Gk *xērophagía,* deriv. of *xērophagein* to eat dry food. See XERO-, -PHAGY]

xe·roph·i·lous (zi rof′ə ləs), *adj.* **1.** *Bot.* growing in or adapted to dry, esp. dry and hot, regions. **2.** *Zool.* living in dry situations. [XERO- + -PHILOUS] **—xe·roph′i·ly,** *n.*

xe·roph·thal·mi·a (zēr′of thal′mē ə), *n. Ophthalm.* abnormal dryness of the eyeball characterized by conjunctivitis, caused by a deficiency of tears and attributed to a lack of vitamin A. [XER- + OPHTHALMIA] **—xe′roph·thal′mic,** *adj.*

xe·ro·phyte (zēr′ə fīt′), *n.* a plant adapted for growth under dry conditions. [XERO- + -PHYTE] **—xe·ro·phyt·ic** (zēr′ə fit′ik), *adj.* **—xe′ro·phyt′i·cal·ly,** *adv.* **—xe·ro·phyt·ism** (zēr′ə fī′tiz əm, -fi tiz′-), *n.*

xe·ro·sere (zēr′ə sēr′), *n. Ecol.* a sere originating on dry soil. [XERO- + SERE²]

xe·ro·sis (zi rō′sis), *n. Med.* **1.** abnormal dryness, as of the eye or skin. **2.** normal sclerosis of the tissue in an aged person. [XER- + -OSIS] **—xe·rot·ic** (zi rot′ik), *adj.*

Xer·ox (zēr′oks), *n. Trademark.* **1.** a process for reproducing printed, written, or pictorial matter by xerography. **—***v.t., v.i.* **2.** (*l.c.*) to print or reproduce by xerography.

Xerx·es (zûrk′sēz), *n.* a boy's given name.

Xerxes I, 519?–465 B.C., king of Persia 486?–465 (son of Darius I).

x-height (eks′hīt′), *n. Typography.* the height of a lower-case x.

x-high (eks′hī′), *adj. Typography.* (of a type character) equal in height to a lower-case x of the same face and size.

Xho·sa (kō′sə, -zə, kô′-), *n., pl.* **-sas,** (*esp. collectively*) **-sa** for 2. **1.** a Bantu language spoken in Cape Province in the Republic of South Africa. **2.** a member of a people speaking this language. **—Xho′san,** *adj.*

xi (zī, sī; *Gk.* ksē), *n., pl.* **xis. 1.** the 14th letter of the Greek alphabet (Ξ, ξ). **2.** the group of consonant sounds represented by this letter.

Xi·me·nes (hē me′neth), *n.* See **Jiménez de Cisneros.**

x in, *Stock Exchange.* without interest. Also, **x in, x-i., x.i., xint, x-int., x. int.**

Xin·gú (shing gōō′), *n.* a river flowing N through central Brazil to the Amazon. 1300 mi. long.

-xion, *Chiefly Brit.* var. of **-tion:** *connexion; inflexion.*

Xi′ par′ticle, *Physics.* hyperon.

Xi·pe (hē′pā), *n.* the Aztec god of sowing or planting. Also called **Xi′pe To·tec′** (tō tek′).

xiph·i·stér·num (zif′i stûr′nəm), *n., pl.* **-na** (-nə). *Anat.* the lowermost of the three segments of the sternum. Cf. **gladiolus** (def. 2), **manubrium** (def. 2a). [< NL *xiphi-* (comb. form of Gk *xíphos* sword) + STERNUM] **—xiph′i·ster′nal,** *adj.*

xiph·oid (zif′oid), *adj.* **1.** *Anat., Zool.* sword-shaped; ensiform. **—***n.* **2.** the xiphisternum. [< NL *xiphoīd(ēs)* < Gk *xiphoeidḗs* swordlike, equiv. to *xípho(s)* sword + *-eidēs* -OID]

xiph·o·su·ran (zif′ə sŏŏr′ən), *adj.* **1.** belonging or pertaining to the order *Xiphosura,* comprising the horseshoe crabs. **—***n.* **2.** an arthropod of the order *Xiphosura;* a horseshoe crab. [< NL *xiphosūr(a)* (< Gk *xíphos* sword + *ourá* tail) + -AN]

XL, extra large.

x-line (eks′līn′), *n. Print.* See **mean line.**

Xmas, Christmas.

Xn., Christian.

Xnty., Christianity.

xo·a·non (zō′ə non′), *n., pl.* **-na** (-nə). *Gk. Antiq.* a simple, carved image, esp. one in which the original block of either stone or wood is readily apparent. [< Gk, akin to *xŷein* to scrape, carve. See XYSTER]

X·o·graph (ek′sə graf′, -gräf′), *n. Trademark.* **1.** a specially printed reproduction of a photograph or drawing that gives a three-dimensional effect created in the printing process. **2.** the special photographic and printing methods used for making such a reproduction.

XP (kī′rō′, kē′rō′), *n.* the Christian monogram made from the first two letters of the Greek word for Christ. [< Gk XP(ΙΣΤΟΣ) CHRIST]

x pr, *Stock Exchange.* without privileges.

XQ., cross question. Also, **xq**

xr, *Stock Exchange.* without rights. Also, **x rts**

X-rat·ed (eks′rā′tid), *adj.* **1.** (of a motion picture) rated X; suitable for adults only. **2.** obscene or sexually explicit: *an X-rated subject.*

x-ray (eks′rā′), *n.* **1.** Often, **x-rays.** a form of electromagnetic radiation, similar to light but of shorter wavelength and capable of penetrating solids and of ionizing gases. **2.** a radiograph made by x-rays. **3.** a word in communications to represent the letter *X.* **—***v.t.* **4.** to examine by means of x-rays. **5.** to make an x-ray radiograph of. **6.** to treat with x-rays. **—***adj.* **7.** of or pertaining to x-rays. Also, **X′-ray′.** [trans. of G *X-strahl*]

x′-ray pho′tograph, a radiograph made with x-rays. **—x′-ray photog′raphy.**

x′-ray ther′apy, *Med.* treatment of a disease, such as cancer, using controlled quantities of x-rays.

x′-ray tube′, an electronic tube for producing x-rays, essentially a cathode-ray tube in which a metal target is bombarded with high-energy electrons.

x-stretch·er (eks′strech′ər), *n. Furniture.* a stretcher having the form of an X.

Xt., Christ.

Xtian., Christian.

Xty., Christianity.

x-u·nit (eks′yōō′nit), *n.* a unit used to express the wavelength of x-rays or gamma rays, equal to approximately 10^{-11} cm or 10^{-3} angstrom. *Abbr.:* Xu, XU

Xu·thus (zōō′thəs), *n. Class. Myth.* a son of Hellen and Orseïs, and the husband of Creusa.

xw, *Stock Exchange.* without warrant.

X-wave (eks′wāv′), *n. Radio.* See **extraordinary wave.**

xyl-, var. of **xylo-** before a vowel: *xylic.*

xy·lan (zī′lan), *n. Chem.* the pentosan occurring in woody tissue which hydrolyzes to xylose: used as the source of furfural. [XYL- + -AN]

xy·lem (zī′ləm, -lem), *n. Bot.* the part of a vascular bundle consisting of tracheids, vessels, parenchyma cells, and fibers, and forming the woody tissue of a plant. See diag. under **stem.** [XYL- + *-em* -EME]

xy′lem ray′, a vascular ray extending into or located entirely within the secondary xylem. Also called **wood ray.** See diag. under **stem.**

xy·lene (zī′lēn), *n. Chem.* any of three oily, colorless, water-insoluble, flammable, toxic, isomeric liquids having the formula $C_6H_4(CH_3)_2$, of the benzene series, obtained mostly from coal tar: used chiefly in the manufacture of dyes. Also, **xylol.** Also called **dimethylbenzene.** [XYL- + -ENE]

xy·lic (zī′lik), *adj. Chem.* of or derived from xylic acid. [XYL- + -IC]

xy′lic ac′id, *Chem.* any of six colorless, crystalline, isomeric acids having the formula $(CH_3)_2C_6H_3COOH$, derived from xylene.

xy·li·dine (zī′li dēn′, -din, zil′i-), *n.* **1.** any of six isomeric compounds that have the formula $(CH_3)_2C_6H_3NH_2$, derivatives of xylene, resembling aniline: used in dye manufacture. **2.** an oily liquid consisting of a mixture of certain of these compounds, used commercially in making dyes. [XYL- + -ID² + -INE²]

xylo-, a learned borrowing from Greek meaning "wood," used in the formation of compound words: *xylotomy.* Also, *esp. before a vowel,* **xyl-.** [comb. form of Gk *xýlon*]

xy·lo·graph (zī′lə graf′, -gräf′), *n.* an engraving on wood. [XYLO- + -GRAPH]

xy·log·ra·phy (zī log′rə fē), *n.* the art of engraving on wood, or of printing from such engravings. [< F *xylographie.* See XYLO-, -GRAPHY] **—xy·log′ra·pher,** *n.* **—xy·lo·graph·ic** (zī′lə graf′ik), **xy′lo·graph′i·cal,** *adj.* **—xy′lo·graph′i·cal·ly,** *adv.*

xy·loid (zī′loid), *adj.* resembling wood; ligneous. [XYL- + -OID]

xy·lol (zī′lōl, -lol), *n.* xylene. [XYL- + -OL¹]

xy·lon′ic ac′id (zī lon′ik), *Chem.* a viscous liquid, $CH_2OH(CHOH)_3COOH$, obtained from xylose by oxidation. [< Gk *xýlon* wood + -IC]

xy·lo·phage (zī′lə fāj′), *n. Rare.* a wood-eating insect. [XYLO- + -PHAGE]

xy·loph·a·gous (zī lof′ə gəs), *adj.* **1.** feeding on wood, as the larvae of certain insects. **2.** perforating or destroying timber, as certain mollusks, crustaceans, and fungi. [< Gk *xylophágos.* See XYLO, -PHAGOUS]

xy·lo·phone (zī′lə fōn′), *n.* a musical instrument consisting of a graduated series of wooden bars, usually sounded by striking with small wooden hammers. [XYLO- + -PHONE] **—xy·lo·phon·ic** (zī′lə fon′ik), *adj.* **—xy·lo·phon·ist** (zī′lə fō′nist, zī lof′ə nist, zi-), *n.*

Xylophone

xy·lose (zī′lōs), *n. Chem.* a colorless, crystalline aldopentose, $C_5H_{10}O_5$, derived from xylan, straw, corn cobs, etc., by treating with heated dilute sulfuric acid, and dehydrating to furfural if stronger acid is used. [XYL- + -OSE²]

xy·lo·stro·ma (zī′lə strō′mə), *n., pl.* **-ma·ta** (-mə tə). *Bot.* the felted, blackish stroma of some species of wood-destroying fungi. [< NL; see XYLO-, STROMA] **—xy′lo·stro′ma·toid′,** *adj.*

xy·lot·o·mous (zī lot′ə məs), *adj.* boring into or cutting wood, as certain insects. [XYLO- + -TOMOUS]

xy·lot·o·my (zī lot′ə mē), *n.* the art of cutting sections of wood, as with a microtome, for microscopic examination. [XYLO- + -TOMY] **—xy·lot′o·mist,** *n.*

xyst (zist), *n.* **1.** (in ancient Greek and Roman architecture) a covered portico, as a promenade. **2.** (in an ancient Roman villa) a garden walk planted with trees. [< L *xyst(us)* garden terrace, shaded walk < Gk *xystós* a covered colonnade]

xys·ter (zis′tər), *n.* a surgical instrument for scraping bones. [< NL < Gk *xystḗr* scraping tool, equiv. to *xys-* (s. of *xŷein* to scrape) + *-tēr* instrument or agent n. suffix]

xys·tum (zis′təm), *n., pl.* **-ta** (-tə). xyst.

xys·tus (zis′təs), *n., pl.* **-ti** (-tī). xyst.

Xys·tus I (zis′təs). See **Sixtus I.**

Xystus II. See **Sixtus II.**

Xystus III. See **Sixtus III.**

Y

Y, y (wī), *n., pl.* **Y's** or **Ys, y's** or **ys.** **1.** the 25th letter of the English alphabet, a semivowel. **2.** any spoken sound represented by the letter *Y* or *y*, as in *yet, city, rhythm,* etc. **3.** something having the shape of a Y. **4.** a written or printed representation of the letter *Y* or *y*. **5.** a device, as a printer's type, for reproducing the letter *Y* or *y*.

Y, **1.** the 25th in order or in a series, or, when *I* is omitted, the 24th. **2.** (*sometimes l.c.*) the medieval Roman numeral for 150. Cf. **Roman numerals.** **3.** (*sometimes l.c.*) *Elect.* admittance. **4.** yen[1]. **5.** *Chem.* yttrium.

y, *Math.* **1.** a symbol frequently used to indicate an unknown quantity. **2.** *Math.* (in Cartesian coordinates) the *y*-axis.

y-, an inflective prefix occurring in certain obsolete words (*ywis*) and esp. in archaic past participles: *yclad.* [ME *y-, i-,* OE *ge-* prefix of uncertain meaning, sometimes of perfective or intensifying force; c. OFris, OS *ge-, gi-,* Goth *ga-,* G *ge-,* perh. L *com-* together]

-y[1], a native English suffix of adjectives meaning "characterized by or inclined to" the substance or action of the word or stem to which the suffix is attached: *juicy; grouchy; rumbly; dreamy.* Also, **-ey**[1]. [OE *-ig;* c. G *-ig,* perh. L *-ic(us),* Gk *-ik(os)*]

-y[2], a hypocoristic suffix common in names: *pussy; Billy; Whitey.* Also, **-ey**[2], **-ie.** [ME; often through Scot influence]

-y[3], a suffix of various origins used in the formation of action nouns from verbs (*inquiry*), also found in other abstract nouns: *carpentry, infamy.* [repr. L *-ia, -ium;* Gk *-ia, -eia, -ion;* F *-ie;* G *-ie*]

Y., **1.** Young Men's Christian Association. **2.** Young Men's Hebrew Association. **3.** Young Women's Christian Association. **4.** Young Women's Hebrew Association.

y., **1.** yard; yards. **2.** year; years.

ya (yə), *pron. Eye Dialect.* **1.** you: *Hey! ya dope!* **2.** your: *Ya father's moustache!*

yā (yä), *n.* the 28th letter of the Arabic alphabet. [< Ar]

yab·ber (yab′ər), *n. Australian.* jabber. [< native Austral *yabba* language, akin to *ya* to speak]

Ya·blo·noi′ Moun′tains (yä′blo noi′), a mountain range in the SE Soviet Union in Asia, E of Lake Baikal. Also called **Ya·blo·no·voi** (yä′blo no voi′).

yacht (yot), *n.* **1.** a vessel used for private cruising, racing, or other noncommercial purposes. —*v.i.* **2.** to sail, voyage, or race in a yacht. [var. of *yaught* < early D *jaght* (short for *jaghtschip* ship for chasing), equiv. to *jag(en)* (to) chase (c. G *jagen* to hunt) + *-t* n. suffix] —**yacht′y,** *adj.*

yacht′ chair′, a folding armchair consisting of a wooden frame across which are stretched strips of canvas to form the seat and back.

yacht′ club′, an organization of yachtsmen, for the purpose of encouraging and directing the sport of yachting.

yacht·ing (yot′ing), *n.* the practice or sport of sailing or voyaging in a yacht. [YACHT + -ING[1]]

yachts·man (yots′mən), *n., pl.* **-men.** one who owns or sails a yacht. [YACHT + 'S[1] + MAN[1]] —**yachts′man·ship′, yacht′man·ship′,** *n.*

yachts·wom·an (yots′wo͝om′ən), *n., pl.* **-wom·en.** a woman who owns or sails a yacht, or who is devoted to yachting. [YACHT + 'S[1] + WOMAN]

yack·e·ty-yak (yak′i tē yak′), *n., v.,* **-yakked, -yak·king.** *Slang.* —*n.* **1.** uninterrupted, often idle or gossipy, talk. —*v.i.* **2.** to talk, esp. pointlessly and uninterruptedly; yak: *They yackety-yakked for an hour or more.* Also, **yack′ety-yack′, yakety-yak, yakity-yak.** [? imit.]

Ya·cui·ba (yä kwē′bä), *n.* a city in SE Bolivia. 5027 (1950).

yad (yäd; *Eng.* yôd), *n., pl.* **ya·dim** (yä dēm′; *Eng.* yô′dim). *Hebrew.* a tapered, usually ornamented rod, usually of silver, with the tip of the tapered part forming a fist with the index finger extended, used by the reader of a scroll of the Torah to indicate his place. [lit., hand]

Yad·kin (yad′kin), *n.* a part of the Pee Dee River which flows SE through central North Carolina.

yaff (yaf), *v.i. Scot. and North Eng.* to bark; yelp. [? b. *waff* bark and YAP or YAWP]

ya·ger (yä′gər), *n.* jaeger (defs. 2, 3).

Ya′gi anten′na (yä′gē, yag′ē), *Radio.* a sharply directional antenna array, consisting of one or two dipoles connected to the transmitting or receiving circuit, and several insulated dipoles all parallel and about equally spaced in a line. [named after Hidetsugu *Yagi* (b. 1886), Japanese electrical engineer]

yah (yä, yâ), *interj.* an exclamation of impatience or derision.

Ya·ha·ta (yä′hä tä′), *n.* Yawata.

Yah·gan (yä′gən), *n., pl.* **-gans,** (*esp. collectively*) **-gan.** a member of an Indian people of the southern coast of Tierra del Fuego and adjacent islands. [*Yahg(a)* a place in Tierra del Fuego + -AN]

Ya·hoo (yä′ho͞o, yā′-, yä ho͞o′), *n., pl.* **-hoos.** **1.** (in Swift's *Gulliver's Travels*) one of a race of brutes, having the form of man and all his vices, who are subject to the Houyhnhnms. **2.** (*l.c.*) a rough, coarse, or uncouth person. **3.** (*l.c.*) *U.S.* a yokel; lout. [name coined by Swift] —**ya′hoo·ism,** *n.*

Yahr·zeit (yär′tsīt), *n. Judaism.* the anniversary of the death of a parent, brother, or other close relative, observed by lighting a memorial lamp or candle the night before and reciting the *Kaddish* at the evening service of the day before and at the morning and afternoon services of the day itself. Also, **Jahrzeit.** [< Yiddish, special use of MHG *jārzīt* anniversary (lit., year-time). See YEAR, TIDE[1]]

Yah·weh (yä′we), *n.* a name of God, transliterated by scholars from the Tetragrammaton and commonly rendered Jehovah. Also, **Yah′we, Yah·veh, Yah·ve** (yä′ve), **Jahveh, Jahve, Jahweh, Jahwe.** [< Heb]

Yah·wism (yä′wiz əm), *n.* the worship of Yahweh or the religious system based on such worship. Also, **Yah·vism** (yä′viz əm), **Jahvism, Jahwism.** [YAHW(EH) + -ISM]

Yah·wist (yä′wist), *n.* the writer of the earliest major source of the Hexateuch, in which God is characteristically referred to as Yahweh rather than Elohim. Also, **Yah·vist** (yä′vist), **Jahvist, Jahwist.** Cf. **Elohist.** [YAHW(EH) + -IST]

Yah·wis·tic (yä wis′tik), *adj.* of, pertaining to, or characteristic of the Yahwist. Also, **Yah·vis·tic** (yä-vis′tik), **Jahvistic, Jahwistic.** [YAHWIST + -IC]

Yaj·ur-Ve·da (yuj′o͝or vā′də, -vē′-), *n. Hinduism.* a Samhita, containing a collection of sacrificial formulas. Cf. **Veda.** [< Skt *yajur* sacred, holy (c. HAGIO-) + *veda* VEDA]

yak[1] (yak), *n.* **1.** a stocky, shaggy-haired wild ox, *Poephagus grunniens,* of the Tibetan highlands. **2.** a domesticated variety of this animal. [< Tibetan *gyag*]

Yak,
Poephagus grunniens
(6 ft. high at shoulder;
total length to 14 ft.;
tail 3 ft.)

yak[2] (yak), *n., v.i.,* **yakked, yak·king.** *Slang.* yackety-yak. [prob. imit.]

yak·e·ty-yak (yak′i-tē yak′), *n., v.i.,* **-yakked, -yak·king.** yackety-yak. Also, **yak′ity-yak′.**

Yak·i·ma (yak′ə mə), *n.* a city in S Washington. 43,284 (1960).

yak·ka (yak′ə), *n. Australian.* work, esp. hard work. [from native (Queensland) word]

Ya·kut (yä ko͝ot′), *n.* a Turkic language of northeastern Siberia.

Yakut′ Auton′omous Repub′lic, an autonomous republic in the NE Russian Federation in Asia. 1,081,000; 1,198,146 sq. mi. *Cap.:* Yakutsk.

Ya·kutsk (yä kutsk′), *n.* a city in E RSFSR, in the NE Soviet Union in Asia, on the Lena River. 74,000 (1959).

Yale (yāl), *n.* **1.** **El·i·hu** (el′ə hyo͞o′), 1648–1721, English colonial official, born in America: governor of Madras 1687–92; principal benefactor of the Collegiate School at Saybrook, Connecticut (now Yale University). **2.** a boy's given name.

y'all (yôl), *pron.* **you-all.**

Yal·ta (yôl′tə; *Russ.* yäl′tä), *n.* a seaport in the S Ukraine, in the SW Soviet Union in Europe, on the Black Sea: wartime conference of Roosevelt, Churchill, and Stalin February 4–12, 1945. 47,100 (1959).

Ya·lu (yä′lo͞o′; *Chin.* yä′lʏ′), *n.* a river in E Asia, forming part of the boundary between Manchuria and North Korea and flowing SW to the Yellow Sea. 300 mi. long.

yam (yam), *n.* **1.** the starchy, tuberous root of any of various climbing vines of the genus *Dioscorea,* cultivated for food in the warmer regions in the Eastern and Western hemispheres. **2.** any of these plants. **3.** *Southern U.S.* the sweet potato. **4.** *Scot.* potato (def. 1). [prob. < Pg *inhame* or Sp *(i)ñame* << WAfr; akin to Senegal *nyami* to eat]

Ya·ma (yum′ə), *n. Hindu Myth.* the Vedic god presiding over the underworld. [< Skt, name of the male twin of *Yami* (orig., twin)]

Ya·ma·ga·ta (yä′mä gä′tä), *n.* **Prince A·ri·to·mo** (ä′rē tô′mô), 1838–1922, Japanese field marshal and statesman.

Ya·ma·mo·to (yä′mä mô′tô), *n.* **I·so·ro·ku** (ē′sô-rô′ko͞o), 1884–1943, Japanese naval officer.

Ya·ma·shi·ta (yä′mä shē′tä), *n.* **To·mo·yu·ki** (tô′-mô yo͞o′kē), ("*the Tiger of Malaya*"), 1885–1946, Japanese general.

Ya·ma·to-e (yä′mä tō e′), *n. Japanese.* a narrative style of painting developed from the 12th to 14th centuries, characterized chiefly by continuous illustrations often executed on long scrolls.

yam′ bean′, either of two species of tropical, leguminous vines of the genus *Pachyrhizus,* having edible pods and edible, turniplike roots.

ya·men (yä′mən), *n.* (in the Chinese Empire) the residence or office of a public official. [var. of *yamun* < Chin *ya* office + *mên* gate]

Ya·mé·o·go (yä mā′ō gō′), *n.* **Maurice,** born 1921, African statesman: president of the Republic of Upper Volta 1960–66.

Ya·mi (yä′mē), *n., pl.* **-mis,** (*esp. collectively*) **-mi.** a member of an Indonesian people of Hungtow Island, off the southeastern coast of Taiwan.

yam·mer (yam′ər), *Informal.* —*v.i.* **1.** to whine or complain. **2.** to make an outcry or clamor; talk loudly and persistently. —*v.t.* **3.** to utter clamorously or in complaint: *They yammered their complaints until she let them see the movie.* —*n.* **4.** the act or noise of yammering. [late ME *yamur, yamer* < MD *jammer(en);* r. ME *yomer,* OE *geōmr(ian)* (to) complain, deriv. of *geōmor* sad; akin to G *Jammer* lamentation] —**yam′-mer·er,** *n.*

yam·pee (yam′pē), *n.* a herbaceous vine, *Dioscorea trifida,* of South America, having edible tubers. Also called **cush-cush.** [< AmerInd; perh. alter. of word akin to Ute *yámpă*]

Ya·na (yä′nə), *n.* an extinct language that was spoken in northern California on the western slopes of Lassen Peak and is best known for a complex, systematic difference between men's and women's speech.

Yan·cey (yan′sē), *n.* a boy's given name.

Yang (yäng, yang), *n.* See under **Yin and Yang.**

Yang (yäng), *n.* **Chen Ning** (chen ning), born 1922, Chinese physicist in the U.S.: Nobel prize 1957.

Yang·kü (*Chin.* yäng′kʏ′), *n.* Taiyüan.

Yang·tze (yaṉg′sē; *Chin.* yäṉg′tse′), *n.* a river in E Asia, flowing from the Tibetan plateau through central China to the East China Sea. ab. 3200 mi. long. Also called **Yang·tze-Kiang** (yaṉg′sē-kyaṉg′; *Chin.* yäṉg′tse′-gyäṉg′).

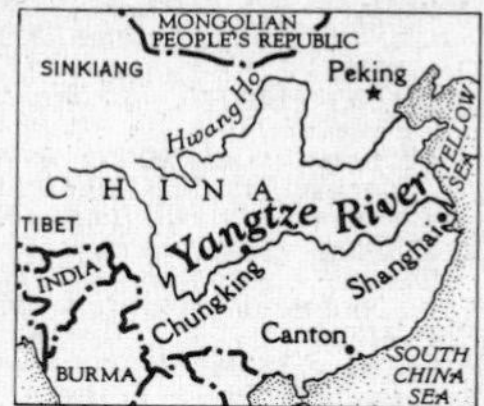

Ya·ni·na (yä′nē nä′), *n.* Serbian name of **Ioannina.** Also, **Yan′ni·na′.**

yank (yaṉgk), *v.t., v.i.* **1.** to pull or remove abruptly and vigorously: *Yank down on the bell rope. Yank him out of school.* —*n.* **2.** an abrupt, vigorous pull; jerk. [?]

Yank (yaṉgk), *n., adj. Slang.* Yankee. [shortened form]

Yan·kee (yaṉg′kē), *n.* **1.** a native or inhabitant of New England. **2.** a native or inhabitant of a northern State, esp. of one of the northeastern States which sided with the Union in the American Civil War. **3.** a native or inhabitant of the United States. **4.** a federal or Northern soldier in the American Civil War. **5.** a word used in communications to represent the letter *Y.* **6.** (*l.c.*) *Naut.* a large staysail used by yachtsmen as a jib in a light breeze. —*adj.* **7.** of, pertaining to, or characteristic of a Yankee or Yankees: *Yankee ingenuity.* [? back formation from D *Jan Kees* John Cheese, nickname (mistaken for plural) applied by the Dutch of colonial New York to English settlers in Connecticut]

Yan·kee·dom (yaṉg′kē dəm), *n.* **1.** the region inhabited by Yankees. **2.** Yankees collectively. [YANKEE + -DOM]

Yan′kee Doo′dle (do͞od′ᵊl), a song with a melody of apparent British origin, popular with American troops during the Revolutionary War. [YANKEE + DOODLE (? *doodle* fool or *doodle* to pipe)]

Yan·kee·fy (yaṉg′kē fī′, -ki-), *v.t.*, **-fied, -fy·ing.** to cause to acquire Yankee traits or characteristics: *She was afraid that a year in a Connecticut college had Yankeefied her speech.* [YANKEE + -FY]

Yan·kee·ism (yaṉg′kē iz′əm), *n.* **1.** Yankee character or characteristics. **2.** a Yankee peculiarity, as of speech. [YANKEE + -ISM]

Yan·kee·land (yaṉg′kē land′), *n.* **1.** *Chiefly Southern U.S.* the northern states of the U.S. **2.** *Chiefly Brit.* the U.S. **3.** *Chiefly Northern U.S.* New England. [YANKEE + LAND]

Yank·ton (yaṉgk′tən), *n.* a town in SE South Dakota. 9279 (1960).

yan·qui (yäṉg′kē), *n., pl.* **-quis** (-kēs). (*often cap.*) *Spanish.* (in Latin America) Yankee; a citizen of the U.S.

Yao (you), *n.* a legendary emperor of China who, with his successor **(Shun),** was a paragon of good government.

Ya·oun·dé (*Fr.* YA o͞on dā′), *n.* a city in and the capital of Cameroon, in the SW part. 58,099 (1957). Also, **Yaunde.**

yap (yap), *v.,* **yapped, yap·ping,** *n.* —*v.i.* **1.** to bark snappishly; yelp. **2.** *Slang.* to talk snappishly, noisily, or foolishly. —*v.t.* **3.** to utter by yapping. —*n.* **4.** a snappish bark; a yelp. **5.** *Slang.* **a.** snappish, noisy, or foolish talk. **b.** the mouth: *Keep your yap shut.* **6.** *Slang.* **a.** a hoodlum. **b.** a bumpkin; fool. [imit.] —**yap′per,** *n.* —**yap′ping·ly,** *adv.*

Yap (yäp, yap), *n.* one of the Caroline Islands, in the W Pacific: U.S. cable station. 5108 including adjacent islands (est. 1955); 83 sq. mi.

ya·pok (yə pok′), *n.* an aquatic, Central and South American opossum, *Chironectes variegatus* (or *minimus*), having webbed hind feet and a grayish coat. Also called **water opossum.** [after *Oyapok,* a river forming the border between French Guiana and N Brazil]

ya·pon (yô′pon), *n.* yaupon.

yapp (yap), *n.* See **circuit binding.** Also called **yapp′ bin′ding.** [named after William *Yapp,* 19th-century English bookseller]

Ya·pu·rá (*Sp.* yä′po͞o rä′), *n.* Japurá.

Ya·qui (yä′kē), *n., pl.* **-quis,** (*esp. collectively*) **-qui** for 1. **1.** a member of a Pima Indian people of Sonora, Mexico. **2.** the language of the Yaqui Indians. **3.** a river in NW Mexico, flowing into the Gulf of California. 420 mi. long.

yar (yâr), *n.* yare (defs. 1, 2).

yar·ak (yar′ak), *n. Falconry.* a state of prime fitness in a hawk. [? < Pers *yārakī* strength]

Yar·bor·ough (yär′bûr′ō, -bur′ō *or, esp. Brit.,* -bər ə), *n. Whist, Bridge.* a hand none of the cards of which are higher than a nine. [named after the 2nd Earl of *Yarborough,* (d. 1897)]

yard[1] (yärd), *n.* **1.** a common unit of linear measure in English speaking countries, equal to 3 feet or 36 inches, and equivalent to 0.9144 meter. **2.** *Naut.* a long spar, supported more or less at its center, to which the head of a square sail, lateen sail, or lugsail is bent. **3.** yard-of-ale. [ME *yerd(e),* OE (Anglian) *gerd;* c. D *gard,* G *Gerte* rod]

yard[2] (yärd), *n.* **1.** the ground which immediately adjoins or surrounds a house, public building, or other structure. **2.** an enclosed area outdoors, often paved and surrounded by or adjacent to a building; a court. **3.** an outdoor enclosure designed for the exercise of students, inmates, etc.: *a prison yard.* **4.** an outdoor space surrounded by a group of buildings, as on a college campus: *a pep rally in the college yard.* **5.** a pen or other enclosure for livestock. **6.** an enclosure within which any work or business is carried on (often used in combination): *navy yard; a brickyard.* **7.** an outside area used for storage, assembly, or the like. **8.** *Railroads.* a system of parallel tracks, crossovers, switches, etc., where cars are switched and made up into trains, and where cars, locomotives, and other rolling stock are kept when not in use or awaiting repairs. **9.** a piece of ground set aside for cultivation; garden; field. **10.** the winter pasture or browsing ground of moose and deer. **11. the Yard,** *Brit.* See **Scotland Yard** (def. 2). —*v.t.* **12.** to put into or enclose in a yard. [ME *yerd,* OE *geard* enclosure; c. D *gaard* garden, Icel *garthr* yard, Goth *gards* house (OSlav *grad,* Russ *gorod* town, prob. < Gmc), L *hortus* garden, OIr *gort* field; akin to GARDEN]

yard·age[1] (yär′dij), *n.* measurement, or the amount measured in yards. [YARD[1] + -AGE]

yard·age[2] (yär′dij), *n.* **1.** the use of a yard or enclosure, as in loading or unloading cattle or other livestock at a railroad station. **2.** the charge for such use. [YARD[2] + -AGE]

yar·dang (yär′däṉg), *n. Geol.* an irregular ridge formed on the surface of sand, silt, etc., by the action of the wind, usually parallel to the prevailing wind direction. [< Turk, abl. of *yar* cliff, precipice]

yard·arm (yärd′ärm′), *n. Naut.* either of the outer portions of the yard of a square sail. [YARD[1] + ARM[1]]

yard′ goods′. See **piece goods.**

yard′ grass′, a coarse annual grass, *Eleusine indica,* of the Old World, common in dooryards and fields.

yard′-long bean′ (yärd′lôṉg′, -loṉg′). See **asparagus bean.**

yard·man[1] (yärd′mən), *n., pl.* **-men.** *Naut.* a sailor assigned to the yards of a vessel. [YARD[1] + MAN[1]]

yard·man[2] (yärd′mən), *n., pl.* **-men.** a man who works in a railroad yard, boatyard, or the like. [YARD[2] + MAN[1]]

yard·mas·ter (yärd′mas′tər, -mä′stər), *n.* a person who superintends all or part of a railroad yard. [YARD[2] + MASTER]

yard-of-ale (yärd′əv āl′), *n.* a trumpet-shaped glass about three feet long with a bulb at the closed end, for serving ale or beer. Also called **aleyard, yard.**

yard·stick (yärd′stik′), *n.* **1.** a stick a yard long, commonly marked with subdivisions, used for measuring. **2.** any standard of measurement or judgment: *Advancement of educational opportunity must be the yardstick of national progress.* [YARD[1] + STICK[1]]

yare (yâr *or, esp. for 1, 2,* yär), *adj.,* **yar·er, yar·est. 1.** quick; agile; lively. **2.** (of a ship) quick to the helm; easily handled or maneuvered. **3.** *Archaic.* **a.** ready; prepared. **b.** nimble; quick. Also, **yar** (for defs. 1, 2). [ME; OE *gearu, gearo,* equiv. to *ge-* Y- + *earu* ready; c. D *gaar,* G *gar* done, dressed (as meat)] —**yare′ly,** *adv.*

Yar·kand (yär′känd′), *n.* Soche.

Yar·mouth (yär′məth), *n.* **1.** a seaport in SW Nova Scotia, in SE Canada: summer resort. 8636 (1961). **2.** a town in SW Maine. 2913 (1960). **3. Great.** See **Great Yarmouth.**

Yar·muk (yär mo͝ok′), *n.* a river in NW Jordan, flowing W into the Jordan River. 50 mi. long.

yar·mul·ke (yär′məl kə, yä′məl-), *n. Judaism.* a skullcap worn, esp. during prayer and religious study, by Jewish males, esp. those adhering to Orthodox or Conservative tradition. Also, **yar′mel·ke.** [< Yiddish]

yarn (yärn), *n.* **1.** thread made of natural or synthetic fibers, and used for knitting and weaving. **2.** a continuous strand or thread made from glass, metal, plastic, etc. **3.** the thread, in the form of a loosely twisted aggregate of fibers, as of hemp, of which rope is made **(rope yarn). 4.** *Informal.* a tale, esp. a long story of adventure or incredible happenings: *He spun a yarn that outdid any I had ever heard.* —*v.t.* **5.** to calk (a pipe joint) with oakum or the like. —*v.i.* **6.** *Informal.* to spin a yarn; tell stories. [ME; OE *gearn;* c. G *Garn;* akin to Icel *görn* gut, Gk *chordḗ* intestine, chord, Lith *žarnà* entrails, L *hernia* a rupture, Skt *hira* vein]

yarn-dyed (yärn′dīd′), *adj.* (of fabrics) woven from yarns previously dyed (opposed to *piece-dyed*).

Ya·ro·slavl (yä ʀo släv′lᵊ), *n.* a city in the W RSFSR, in the central Soviet Union in Europe, on the Volga. 467,000 (est. 1964).

yar·o·vize (yär′ə vīz′), *v.t.,* **-vized, -viz·ing.** jarovize. —**yar′o·vi·za′tion,** *n.*

yar·ra·man (yar′ə mən), *n., pl.* **-men.** *Australian Archaic.* horse. [< native Austral]

yar·row (yar′ō), *n.* **1.** an asteraceous plant, *Achillea millefolium,* of Europe and America, having finely divided leaves and whitish flowers, sometimes used in medicine as a tonic and astringent. **2.** any of various other plants of the genus *Achillea.* [ME *yar(o)we,* OE *gearwe;* c. G *Garbe* sheaf]

Yar·row (yar′ō), *n.* a river in SE Scotland, flowing into the Tweed. 14 mi. long.

yash·mak (yäsh mäk′, yash′mak), *n.* the veil worn by Muslim women in public. Also, **yash·mac′.** [< Turk *yaşmak*]

Yasht (yasht, yusht), *n. Zoroastrianism.* **1.** a hymn to a deity. **2. Yashts,** hymns to various deities, forming part of the Avesta. [< Avestan *yashtay*]

Yas·na (yus′nə), *n. Zoroastrianism.* a part of the Avesta including the Gathas and other liturgical texts. —**Yas·ni·an** (yus′nē ən), *adj.*

Yas·sy (yä′sē), *n.* Jassy.

yat·a·ghan (yat′ə gan′, -gən; *Turk.* yä′tä gän′), *n.* a Turkish saber having a doubly curved blade, concave toward the hilt, and a hilt with a prominent pommel and no guard. Also, **ataghan, yat′a·gan′.** [< Turk *yātāghan*]

Yataghan (Turkish)

ya·ta·ta (yä′tə tə, yat′ə tə), *n. U.S. Slang.* empty conversation. [imit.]

yat·ter (yat′ər), *Chiefly Brit.* —*v.i.* **1.** to chatter or jabber. —*n.* **2.** chatter; idle talk. [? YA(P + CHA)TTER]

yaud (yôd, yäd), *n. Scot. and North Eng.* a mare, esp. an old, worn-out one. [< Icel *jalda* mare]

yauld (yôd, yôld, yäd, yäld), *adj. Scot. and North Eng.* active; vigorous. [?]

Yaun·de (youn′dā), *n.* Yaoundé.

yaup (yôp, yäp), *v.i., n.* yawp. —**yaup′er,** *n.*

yau·pon (yô′pən), *n.* a holly shrub or small tree, *Ilex vomitoria,* of the southern U.S., having leaves which are sometimes used as a substitute for tea. Also, **yapon.** [< Catawba *yopun,* equiv. to *yop* shrub, bush, tree + *-un* dim. suffix]

yau·ti·a (you tē′ə), *n.* a stemless, araceous plant, *Xanthosoma sagittaefolium,* cultivated in tropical America for its tuberous, starchy root: cooked and eaten like potatoes [< AmerSp < Taino]

yaw[1] (yô), *v.i.* **1.** to deviate temporarily from a straight course, as a vessel. **2.** (of an aircraft) to have a motion about its vertical axis. **3.** (of a rocket or guided missile) to deviate from a stable flight attitude by oscillation of the longitudinal axis in the horizontal plane. —*v.t.* **4.** to cause to yaw. —*n.* **5.** a movement of deviation from the direct course, as of a vessel. **6.** a motion of an aircraft about its vertical axis. **7.** an angle, to the right or left, determined by the direction of motion of an aircraft or spacecraft and its vertical and longitudinal plane of symmetry. **8.** (of a rocket or guided missile) **a.** act of yawing. **b.** the angular displacement of the longitudinal axis due to yawing. [?]

yaw[2] (yô), *n. Pathol.* one of the lesions of yaws. [back formation from YAWS]

Yawl[1] (def. 2)

Ya·wa·ta (yä′wä tä′), *n.* a city on N Kyushu, in SW Japan: steel industry. 332,163 (1964). Also, **Yahata.**

yaw·ey (yô′ē), *adj.* of or pertaining to yaws. [YAW[2] + -EY[1]]

yawl[1] (yôl), *n.* **1.** a ship's small boat, manned by four or six oarsmen. **2.** a two-masted, fore-and-aft-rigged sailing vessel having a large mainmast and a smaller jiggermast or mizzenmast stepped abaft the sternpost. Cf. **ketch.** [< D *jol* kind of boat < ?]

yawl[2] (yôl), *n., v.i., v.t. Brit. Dial.* yowl; howl. [akin to YOWL]

yawl-rigged (yôl′rigd′), *adj.* rigged in the manner of a yawl.

yaw·me·ter (yô′mē′tər), *n. Aeron.* an instrument that measures the yaw of an aircraft. [YAW[1] + -METER]

yawn (yôn), *v.i.* **1.** to open the mouth involuntarily with a prolonged, deep inhalation of air, as from drowsiness or weariness. **2.** to open wide like a mouth. **3.** to extend or stretch wide, as an open and deep space. —*v.t.* **4.** to say with a yawn. **5.** *Archaic.* to open wide, or lay open, as if by yawning. —*n.* **6.** act of yawning. **7.** an opening; open space; chasm. [ME *yane(n), yone(n),* OE *geonian,* akin to OE *gānian, gīnan,* Icel *gīna,* G *gähnen,* L *hiāre* to gape] —**yawn′er,** *n.* —**Syn. 1.** gape.

yawn·ful (yôn′fəl), *adj.* causing or arousing yawns, esp. as the result of boredom, tedium, or the like: *a yawnful story about her childhood.* [YAWN + -FUL] —**yawn′ful·ly,** *adv.*

yawn·ing (yô′niṉg), *adj.* **1.** being or standing wide open; gaping: *the yawning mouth of a cave.* **2.** indicating by yawns one's weariness or indifference: *The lecturer was oblivious to his yawning audience.* [ME; OE *geniendum.* See YAWN, -ING[2]] —**yawn′ing·ly,** *adv.*

yawn·y (yô′nē), *adj.,* **yawn·i·er, yawn·i·est.** emitting or causing yawns: *yawny spectators; a yawny book.* [YAWN + -Y[1]]

yawp (yôp, yäp), *v.i.* **1.** *Informal.* to utter a loud, harsh cry; to yelp, squawk, or bawl. **2.** *Slang.* to talk noisily and foolishly. —*n.* **3.** *Informal.* **a.** a harsh cry. **b.** raucous or querulous speech. **4.** *Slang.* a noisy, foolish utterance. Also, **yaup.** [ME *yolpen;* akin to YELP] —**yawp′er,** *n.*

yaws (yôz), *n.* (*construed as sing.*) *Pathol.* a disease occurring in certain tropical regions, caused by the organism *Treponema pertenue,* and characterized by an eruption of raspberrylike excrescences on the skin. Also called **frambesia, pian.** Cf. **mother yaw.** [< Carib. dial.]

yaw·weed (yô′wēd′), *n.* See **wild mulberry.** [YAW(S) + WEED[1], from the belief that it could cure yaws]

y-ax·is (wī′ak′sis), *n., pl.* **y-ax·es** (wī′ak′sēz). *Math.* **1.** Also called **axis of ordinates.** (in a plane Cartesian coordinate system) the axis, usually vertical, along which the ordinate is measured and from which the abscissa is measured. See diag. under **ordinate. 2.** (in a three-dimensional Cartesian coordinate system) the axis along which values of y are measured and at which both x and z equal zero.

ya·za·ta (yä zä′tä), *n.* any of the lesser ancient Iranian gods. [< Avestan: beneficent one]

Yazd (yäzd), *n.* Yezd.

Yaz·oo (yaz′o͞o), *n.* a river flowing SW from N Mississippi into the Mississippi River at Vicksburg. 188 mi. long.

Yaz′oo-type riv′er (yaz′o͞o tīp′), *Geol.* a tributary stream which flows for a long distance parallel to a river with a high natural levee.

Yb, *Chem.* ytterbium.

Y.B., yearbook.

y-blen·ny (wī′blen′ē), *n., pl.* **-nies,** (*esp. collectively*) **-ny.** a small, elongated blenny, *Allolumpenus hypochromus,* found in the northeastern Pacific Ocean.

Y chromosome, *Biol.* a sex chromosome carrying genes that produce male characteristics in man and most mammals and that occurs singly, in males only. Cf. **X chromosome.**

Y.C.L., Young Communist League.

y·clad (ē klad′), *v. Archaic.* pp. of **clothe.** [ME; see Y-, CLAD]

y·clept (ē klept′), *v.* a pp. of **clepe.** Also, **y·cleped′.** [ME *ycleped,* OE *geclypod,* ptp. of *clypian, cleopian,* to CLEPE]

yd., yard; yards.

yds., yards.

ye[1] (yē), *pron.* **1.** *Archaic* (*except in some elevated or ecclesiastical prose*), *Literary, or Brit. Dial.* **a.** (used nominatively as the plural of **thou,** esp. in rhetorical, didactic, or poetic contexts, in addressing a group of persons or things): *O ye of little faith; ye brooks and hills.* **b.** (used nominatively for the second person singular, esp. in polite address): *Do ye not know me?* **c.** (used objectively in the second person singular or plural): *I have something to tell ye. Arise, the enemy is upon ye!* **2.** (used with mock seriousness in an invocation, mild oath, or the like): *Ye gods and little fishes!* [ME; OE *gē;* c. D *gij,* G *ihr,* Icel *ér,* Goth *jus*]

ye[2] (t͟hē; *spelling pron.* yē), *definite article. Archaic.* the[1].

yea (yā), *adv.* **1.** yes (used in affirmation or assent). **2.** *Archaic.* **a.** indeed: *Yea, and he did come.* **b.** not only this but even: *a good, yea, a noble man.* **—***n.* **3.** an affirmation; an affirmative reply or vote. **4.** one who votes in the affirmative. [ME *ye, ya,* OE *gēa;* c. D, G, Icel, Goth *ja*]

yeah (yâ), *adv. Informal.* yes. [var. of YEA or YES]

yeah-yeah (yâ′yâ′), *adj.* yé-yé.

yeal·ing (yē′lin), *n. Scot.* a person of the same age as oneself. [? E(VEN) + *eil(d)ing* age]

yean (yēn), *v.i.* (of a sheep or goat) to bring forth young. [ME *yene(n),* OE *geēanian* to bring forth young; akin to EWE]

yean·ling (yēn′ling), *n.* **1.** the young of a sheep or a goat; a lamb or a kid. **—***adj.* **2.** just born; infant. [YEAN + -LING[1]]

year (yēr), *n.* **1.** a period of 365 or 366 days, in the Gregorian calendar, divided into 12 calendar months, now reckoned as beginning Jan. 1 and ending Dec. 31 **(calendar year).** Cf. **common year, leap year. 2.** a period of approximately the same length in other calendars. **3.** a space of 12 calendar months calculated from any point: *This should have been finished a year ago.* **4.** *Astron.* **a.** Also called **lunar year.** a division of time equal to 12 lunar months. **b.** Also called **astronomical year, equinoctial year, solar year, tropical year.** a division of time equal to about 365 days, 5 hours, 48 minutes, and 46 seconds, representing the interval between one vernal equinox and the next. **c.** Also called **sidereal year.** a division of time equal to the equinoctial year plus 20 minutes, representing the time required for the earth to complete one revolution around the sun, measured with relation to the fixed stars. Cf. **anomalistic year. 5.** the time in which any planet completes a revolution round the sun: *the Martian year.* **6.** a full round of the seasons. **7.** a period out of every 12 months, devoted to a certain pursuit, activity, or the like: *the academic year.* **8. years, a.** age. **b.** old age: *a man of years.* **c.** time, esp. a long time: *the years of hardship and frustration.* **9. a year and a day,** a period specified as the limit of time in various legal matters, as in determining a right or a liability, to allow for a full year by any way of counting. **10. year in and year out,** regularly through the years; continuously: *Year in and year out they went to Florida for the winter.* Also, **year in, year out.** [ME *yeer,* OE *gēar;* c. D *jaar,* G *Jahr,* Icel *ār,* Goth *jēr,* Gk *hôros* a year, *hōra* a season of the year, part of a day, hour]

year-a·round (yēr′ə round′), *adj.* year-round.

year·book (yēr′bŏŏk′), *n.* a book published annually, containing information, statistics, etc., about the year: *a college yearbook; an encyclopedia yearbook.* [YEAR + BOOK]

year-end (yēr′end′), *n.* **1.** year's end; the end of a calendar year. **—***adj.* **2.** taking place or done at the year-end: *a year-end sale; a year-end audit.*

year·ling (yēr′ling), *n.* **1.** an animal in its second year. **2.** a horse one year old, dating from January 1 of the year after the year of foaling. **—***adj.* **3.** a year old. **4.** of a year's duration or standing: *a yearling bride.* [late ME (see YEAR, -LING[1]); c. G *Jährling*]

year·long (yēr′lông′, -long′), *adj.* lasting for a year. [YEAR + LONG[1]]

year·ly (yēr′lē), *adj., adv., n., pl.* **-lies.** **—***adj.* **1.** pertaining to a year or to each year. **2.** done, made, happening, appearing, coming, etc., once a year or every year: *a yearly medical examination.* **3.** continuing for a year. **4.** lasting but a year. **—***adv.* **5.** once a year; annually. **—***n.* **6.** a publication appearing once a year. [ME *yeerly,* OE *gēarlīc.* See YEAR, -LY]

yearn (yûrn), *v.i.* **1.** to have an earnest or strong desire; *to yearn for a long vacation.* **2.** to feel tenderness; be moved or attracted: *They yearned over their delicate child.* [ME *yerne(n),* OE *giernan* deriv. of *georn* eager; akin to Icel *girna* to desire (perh. L *hortārī* to urge), OIr *(to)-gairim* I desire; Gk *chaír(ein)* to rejoice, Skt *háryati* he desires] **—yearn′er,** *n.*
—Syn. 1. aspire.

yearn·ing (yûr′ning), *n.* **1.** deep longing, esp. when accompanied by tenderness or sadness: *a widower's yearning for his wife.* **2.** an instance of such longing. [ME; OE *gierninge.* See YEARN, -ING[1]] **—yearn′ing·ly,** *adv.*
—Syn. 1. See **desire.**

Year′ of Confu′sion, (in ancient Rome) the year of 445 days preceding the introduction, in 46 B.C., of the Julian calendar: lengthened to compensate for the cumulative errors of the Roman calendar.

year′ of grace′, a specified year of the Christian era: *this year of grace; the year of grace 1970.*

year-round (yēr′round′), *adj.* continuing, active, operating, etc., throughout the year: *a year-round vacation spot.* Also, **year-around.**

year's′ mind′, a Requiem Mass said one year after a person's death or burial.

yeast (yēst), *n.* **1.** a yellowish, somewhat viscid, semifluid froth or sediment consisting of the cells of certain minute fungi, occurring in fruit juices, malt worts, and other saccharine liquids, and used to induce fermentation in the manufacture of alcoholic liquors, esp. beer, as a leaven in dough to render it light and spongy, and in medicine. Cf. **bottom yeast, top yeast. 2.** any minute, unicellular, ascomycetous fungus of the genus *Saccharomyces,* and related genera. **3.** spume; foam. **4.** ferment; agitation. **—***v.i.* **5.** to ferment. **6.** to be covered with froth. [ME *ye(e)st,* OE *gist, gyst;* c. D *gist,* G *Gischt* yeast, foam, Icel *jöstr, jastr* yeast, Gk *zestós* boiled, Skt *yāsati* it boils] **—yeast′less,** *adj.* **—yeast′like′,** *adj.*

yeast′ cake′, 1. a small cake of compacted yeast for baking or the like. **2.** a cake or sweet bread containing yeast as a leavening agent.

yeast′ nucle′ic ac′id, *Biochem.* See **RNA.**

yeast′ plant′, yeast (def. 2).

yeast·y (yē′stē), *adj.,* **yeast·i·er, yeast·i·est. 1.** of, containing, or resembling yeast. **2.** frothy; foamy. **3.** youthful; exuberant; ebullient. **4.** trifling; frivolous. **5.** characterized by agitation, excitement, etc.: *the yeasty years immediately following college.* [YEAST + -Y[1]] **—yeast′i·ly,** *adv.* **—yeast′i·ness,** *n.*

Yeats (yāts), *n.* **William Butler,** 1856–1939, Irish dramatist, poet, and essayist: Nobel prize 1923. **—Yeats′i·an,** *adj.*

Yed·do (yed′dō′), *n.* former name of **Tokyo.** Also, **Ye′do′.**

yed′do haw′thorn (yed′ō), a shrub, *Raphiolepis umbellata,* of Japan, having thick leaves and dense, hairy clusters of white, fragrant flowers.

Ye·fre·mov (*Russ.* ye fre′mof), *n.* **Le·o·nid Ni·ko·la·ye·vich** (*Russ.* le o nēt′ ni ko lä′yə vich). See **Efremov, Leonid Nikolayevich.**

yegg (yeg), *n. Slang.* **1.** an itinerant burglar, esp. one whose thefts are insignificant. **2.** a thug. [? var. of *yekk* beggar, a term once popular in California Chinatowns; ? the surname of an American burglar]

yegg·man (yeg′mən), *n., pl.* **-men.** yegg. [YEGG + MAN[1]]

Yeisk (āsk), *n.* a seaport in the SW RSFSR, in the SW Soviet Union in Europe, on the Sea of Azov. 55,000 (1959). Also, **Eisk, Eysk.**

yeld (yeld), *adj. Scot.* eild (def. 1). [ME; OE *gelde;* c. G *Gelt;* akin to GELD[1]]

yel·dring (yel′drin), *n. Scot. and North Eng.* yoldring.

yelk (yelk), *n. Dial.* yolk.

yell (yel), *v.i.* **1.** to cry out with a strong, loud, clear sound: *He always yells when he is angry.* **2.** to scream with pain, fright, etc. **—***v.t.* **3.** to utter or tell by yelling: *to yell an order to the troops.* **—***n.* **4.** a cry uttered by yelling. **5.** *U.S.* a cheer or shout of fixed words or syllables, as one adopted by a school or college. [ME *yelle(n),* OE *gellan, giellan;* c. G *gellen* to resound, D *gillen;* akin to OE *galan* to sing >> (NIGHTIN)GALE]

yel·low (yel′ō), *adj.* **1.** of a bright color like that of butter, lemon, etc.; between green and orange in the spectrum. **2.** having the yellowish skin characteristic of Mongoloid peoples. **3.** denoting or pertaining to the Mongoloid race. **4.** *Often Disparaging.* having the yellowish skin of a mulatto or dark-skinned quadroon. **5.** of sallow complexion. **6.** *Informal.* cowardly. **7.** (of journalism, a newspaper, etc.) **a.** sensational, esp. morbidly or offensively so: *That yellow rag carried all the gory details.* **b.** dishonest in editorial comment and the presentation of news, esp. in sacrificing truth for sensationalism: *Objective reporting isn't always a match for yellow journalism.* **8.** jealous; envious. **—***n.* **9.** a hue between green and orange in the spectrum. **10.** the yolk of an egg. **11.** a yellow pigment or dye. **—***v.t., v.i.* **12.** to make or become yellow: *Yellow the sheets with dye. The white stationery yellows with age.* [ME *yelou,* OE *geolo, geolu;* c. G *gelb,* D *geel,* L *helvus* pale-yellow; akin to Icel *gulr*] **—yel′low·ly,** *adv.* **—yel′low·ness,** *n.*

yel′low alert′, 1. (in military or civilian defense) the first alert given when enemy aircraft are discovered approaching a military installation, city, coastline, etc. **2.** the signal or alarm sounded for this alert. Cf. **blue alert, red alert, white alert.**

yel′low arch′angel, a weedy, perennial herb, *Lamium Galeobdolon,* of Europe, having yellow flowers.

yel′low av′ens. See **herb bennet.**

yel·low·back (yel′ō bak′), *n.* **1.** (formerly) an inexpensive, often lurid, novel bound in yellow cloth or paper. **2.** a gold certificate. Cf. **certificate** (def. 4b). [YELLOW + BACK[1]]

yel′low bell′, a woody vine or shrub, *Allamanda neriifolia,* of Brazil, having golden-yellow, bell-like flowers, striped brownish-red inside.

yel·low-bel·lied (yel′ō bel′ēd), *adj. Slang.* cowardly; lily-livered.

yel′low-bellied sap′sucker, a sapsucker, *Sphyrapicus varius,* of eastern North America, having a red patch on the forehead and black and white plumage with a pale-yellow abdomen. Also called **yel′low-bellied wood′pecker.**

yel·low·bel·ly (yel′ō bel′ē), *n., pl.* **-lies.** one who is without courage, fortitude, or nerve; coward. [YELLOW + BELLY]

yel′low bile′, *Old Physiol.* a humor regarded as causing anger; choler.

yel′low-billed cuck′oo (yel′ō bild′), a North American cuckoo, *Coccyzus americanus,* which has a yellow bill and which, unlike many cuckoos, constructs its own nest and rears its own young.

yel′low-billed mag′pie. See under magpie (def. 1).

yel′low birch′, 1. a North American birch, *Betula lutea,* having yellowish or silvery gray bark. **2.** the hard, light, reddish-brown wood of this tree, used for making furniture, in the construction of buildings, boxes, etc. Also called **silver birch.**

yel·low·bird (yel′ō bûrd′), *n.* **1.** *Brit. Dial.* any of various yellow or golden birds, as the golden oriole of Europe. **2.** *U.S. Dial.* **a.** any of several American goldfinches. **b.** See **yellow warbler.** [YELLOW + BIRD]

yel′low brass′, an alloy of about 65 percent copper and 35 percent zinc, with traces of lead and iron.

yel′low-breast·ed chat′ (yel′ō bres′tid), an American warbler, *Icteria virens,* having a yellow throat and breast and greenish-brown upper parts.

yel′low bush′, a shrub or small tree, *Rhamnus caroliniana,* found from the southeastern U.S. to Texas and Nebraska, having red fruit that turns black. Also called **Indian cherry.**

yel′low cal′la lil′y. See **golden calla lily.**

yel′low cam′omile. See **golden marguerite.**

yel′low ce′dar, 1. See **Alaska cedar. 2.** Also called **western juniper.** a round-headed tree, *Juniperus occidentalis,* of the western coast of the U.S., having scalelike leaves with a gland on the back and oval, blue-black fruit.

yel′low cop′per ore′, chalcopyrite.

yel′low-crowned night′ her′on (yel′ō kround′). See under **night heron.**

yel′low cy′press. See **Alaska cedar.**

yel′low dai′sy, the black-eyed Susan, *Rudbeckia hirta.*

yel′low dog′, a cowardly, despicable person; a craven.

yel′low-dog′ con′tract (yel′ō dôg′, -dog′), a contract between a worker and an employer in which, as a condition of employment, the worker agrees not to remain in or join a union.

Yel′low Em′peror. See **Huang Ti.**

yel′low fe′ver, *Pathol.* an acute, often fatal, infectious, febrile disease of warm climates, caused by a filterable virus transmitted by a mosquito, *Aedes aegypti,* and characterized by jaundice, vomiting, hemorrhages, etc. Also called **yellow jack.**

yel′low-fe′ver mosqui′to (yel′ō fē′vər), a mosquito, *Aedes aegypti,* that transmits yellow fever and dengue.

yel′low·fin tu′na (yel′ō fin′), an important food fish, *Thunnus albacares,* found in warm seas. [YELLOW + FIN]

yel′low flag′, 1. *Naut.* See **quarantine flag. 2.** See **water flag.**

yel′low fox′glove, a hairy herb, *Digitalis ambigua,* of Eurasia, having finger-shaped, brown-marked, yellow flowers nearly two inches long.

yel′low gen′tian, a perennial herb, *Gentiana lutea,* of Europe and Asia Minor, having yellow flowers, the rootstock yielding a bitter tonic. Also called **bitterwort.**

yel′low goat′fish, a goatfish, *Mulloidichthys martinicus,* found in the Atlantic Ocean from Florida to Panama.

yel′low granadil′la, a climbing vine, *Passiflora laurifolia,* of tropical America, having red-spotted white flowers nearly four inches wide, with a white and violet-colored crown, and edible, yellow fruit. Also called **Jamaica honeysuckle, water lemon.**

yel′low grass′, the bog asphodel, *Narthecium americanum.*

yel·low-green (yel′ō grēn′), *n.* **1.** a color containing both yellow and green. **—***adj.* **2.** of the color yellow-green.

yel′low-green al′ga, an alga of the phylum *Chrysophyta,* in which the chlorophyll is masked by a brown or yellow pigment.

yel′low gum′, 1. any of several Australian eucalyptuses, as *Eucalypti melliodora,* having yellowish bark. **2.** the black gum, *Nyssa sylvatica.*

yel·low·ham·mer (yel′ō ham′ər), *n.* **1.** a common European bunting, *Emberiza citrinella,* the male of which is marked with bright yellow. **2.** *U.S. Dial.* the flicker, *Colaptes auratus.* [b. earlier *yellow-ham* (OE *geolu* YELLOW + *hama* covering; i.e., yellow-feathered bird) and *yelambre* (OE *geolu* + *amore;* c. G *Ammer* bunting)]

Yel′low Hats′, (in Tibet) the sect of Buddhist monks established after religious reforms in the 14th century. Also called **Gelugpa.** Cf. **Red Hats.**

yel′low-head·ed black′bird (yel′ō hed′id), a North American blackbird, *Xanthocephalus xanthocephalus,* having a yellow head.

yel′low hon′eysuckle, a spreading, twining vine, *Lonicera flava,* of the southern and eastern U.S., having leaves that are blue-green on the underside and fragrant, tubular, orange-yellow flowers.

yel·low·ish (yel′ō ish), *adj.* somewhat yellow; tending to yellow; tinged with yellow. [ME; see YELLOW, -ISH[1]]

yel′low jack′, 1. *Informal.* See **quarantine flag. 2.** *Pathol.* See **yellow fever. 3.** any carangoid fish, esp. a Caribbean food fish, *Caranx bartholomaei.* **4.** *(caps., italics)* a play (1934) by Sidney Howard.

Yellowjacket, *Vespula maculifrons* **(Length ¾ in.)**

yel·low·jack·et (yel′ō jak′it), *n.* any of several paper wasps of the family *Vespidae,* having a black body with bright yellow markings. [YELLOW + JACKET]

yel′low jas′mine. See **Carolina jessamine.** Also, **yel′low jes′samine.**

Yel·low·knife (yel′ō nīf′), *n.* a city in the central Northwest Territories, in N central Canada, on Great Slave Lake. 3245 (1961).

yel′low la′dy's-slipper, a showy orchid, *Cypripedium Calceolus,* of eastern North America, having purple-tinged, yellow flowers two inches wide.

yel′low lead′ ore′ (led), wulfenite.

yel·low·legs (yel′ō legz′), *n.* (*construed as sing.*) either of two American shore birds having yellow legs, *Totanus melanoleucus* **(greater yellowlegs),** or *T. flavipes* **(lesser yellowlegs).** [YELLOW + LEGS]

yel′low light′, a traffic light, usually preceding a signal halting traffic in a particular direction.

yel′low lo′cust. See **black locust.**

yel′low loose′strife. See under **loosestrife** (def. 1).

yel′low mel′ilot, a perennial herb, *Melilotus officinalis,* of Eurasia, having yellow flowers. Also called **king's clover.**

yel′low mercu′ric ox′ide. See under **mercuric oxide.**

yel′low met′al, 1. a yellow alloy of about 60 percent copper and about 40 percent zinc; naval brass. **2.** gold.

yel′low mom·bin′ (mōm bēn′), a tropical tree, *Spondias Mombin,* having purplish-green flowers and yellow, fleshy, egg-shaped, edible fruit. Also called **hog plum.**

Yel′low New′town, 1. a variety of yellow apple that ripens in the autumn. **2.** the tree bearing this fruit. Also called **Newtown Pippin.**

yel′low pag′es, *U.S.* the classified section of a telephone directory, listing subscribers by the type of business or service they offer.

yel′low perch′. See under **perch**[2] (def. 1).

yel′low per′il, 1. the alleged danger of a predominance of the yellow race, with its enormous numbers, over the white race and Western civilization generally. **2.** the yellow race, regarded as presenting such a danger.

yel′low peril′la. See **Canada moonseed.**

yel′low pike′perch (pīk′pûrch′), the walleye, *Stizostedion vitreum.*

yel′low pine′, 1. any of several North American pines yielding a strong, yellowish wood. **2.** the wood of any such tree.

yel′low pitch′er plant′, trumpets.

yel′low pop′lar, the tulip tree, *Liriondendron Tulipifera.*

yel′low prus′siate of pot′ash. See **potassium ferrocyanide.**

yel′low puccoon′, a perennial herb, *Lithospermum incisum,* of central and western North America, having numerous branches and bright or pale yellow flowers.

Yel′low Riv′er. See **Hwang Ho.**

yel′low rust′, *Plant Pathol.* See **stripe rust.**

yel·lows (yel′ōz), *n.* (*construed as sing.*) **1.** *Plant Pathol.* a disease of plants, characterized by the loss of green pigments in and the stunting of affected parts, caused by a fungus or a virus. **2.** *Vet. Pathol.* jaundice. **3.** *Obs.* jealousy. [YELLOW (n.) + -S[3]]

yel′low sage′. See **red sage.**

Yel′low Sea′, an arm of the Pacific N of the East China Sea, between China and Korea. Chinese, **Hwang Hai.**

yel′low spot′, *Anat.* a small, circular, yellowish area on the retina, opposite the pupil.

Yel′low Springs′, a town in Ohio. 4167 (1960).

yel′low star′. See **false sunflower.**

Yel·low·stone (yel′ō stōn′), *n.* a river flowing from NW Wyoming through Yellowstone Lake and NE through Montana into the Missouri River in W North Dakota. 671 mi. long.

yel′low stone′crop, a creeping evergreen, *Sedum reflexum,* of Europe, having golden-yellow flowers.

Yel′lowstone Falls′, two waterfalls of the Yellowstone River, in Yellowstone National Park: upper falls, 109 ft. high; lower falls, 308 ft. high.

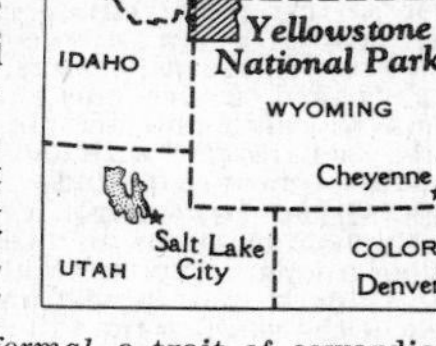

Yel′lowstone Lake′, a lake in NW Wyoming, in Yellowstone National Park. 20 mi. long; 140 sq. mi.

Yel′lowstone Na′tional Park′, a park in NW Wyoming and adjacent parts of Montana and Idaho: geysers, hot springs, falls, canyon. 3458 sq. mi.

yel′low streak′, *Informal.* a trait of cowardice in one's character.

yel·low·tail (yel′ō tāl′), *n., pl.* **-tails,** (*esp. collectively*) **-tail.** **1.** a game fish, *Seriola dorsalis,* of California. **2.** Also called **yel′lowtail snap′per.** a small, West Indian snapper, *Ocyurus chrysurus.* **3.** See **yellowtail flounder.** **4.** any of several other fishes with a yellow caudal fin. [YELLOW + TAIL[1]]

yel′lowtail floun′der, a right-eyed flounder, *Limanda ferruginea,* found along the Atlantic coast of North America, having a yellowish tail fin and rusty-red spots on the body. Also called **rusty dab.**

yel·low·throat (yel′ō thrōt′), *n.* any of several American warblers of the genus *Geothlypis,* having a yellow throat, esp. *B. trichas* (**Maryland yellowthroat**). [YELLOW + THROAT]

yel′low-throat·ed vir′eo (yel′ō thrō′tid), an olive-green vireo, *Vireo flavifrons,* of eastern North America, having a bright yellow throat and breast.

yel′low tril′lium, a hardy, perennial herb, *Trillium viride luteum,* of the central U.S., having mottled, stalkless leaves and lemon-scented, yellow or greenish-yellow flowers.

yel′low tuft′, a perennial herb, *Alyssum argenteum,* of Europe, having headlike clusters of deep yellow flowers.

yel′low war′bler, a small, American warbler, *Dendroica petechia,* the male of which has yellow plumage streaked with brown on the underparts. Also called **golden warbler.**

yel′low wa′ter lil′y, any of several water lilies, as a spatterdock or *Nymphaea mexicana,* having yellow flowers.

yel·low·weed (yel′ō wēd′), *n.* **1.** *U.S. Dial.* any of certain coarse species of goldenrod. **2.** the European ragwort, *Senecio Jacobaea.* [YELLOW + WEED[1]]

yel·low·wood (yel′ō wŏŏd′), *n.* **1.** the hard, yellow wood of a fabaceous tree, *Cladrastis lutea,* of the southern U.S. **2.** the tree itself, having showy, white flowers and yielding a yellow dye. **3.** any of various other yellow woods, as that of a small tree, *Schaefferia frutescens,* of southern Florida and neighboring regions. **4.** any of the trees yielding these woods. [YELLOW + WOOD[1]]

yel·low·y (yel′ō ē), *adj.* somewhat yellow. [YELLOW + -Y[1]]

yelp (yelp), *v.i.* **1.** to give a quick, sharp, shrill cry, as dogs, foxes, etc. **2.** to call or cry out sharply: *The boy yelped in pain when the horse stepped on his foot.* —*v.t.* **3.** to utter or express by or as by yelping. —*n.* **4.** a quick, sharp bark or cry. [ME *yelpe(n),* OE *gelpan* to boast; c. LG *galpen* to croak] —**yelp′er,** *n.*

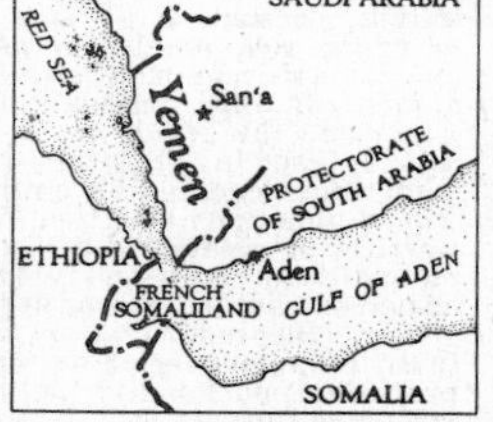

Yem·en (yem′ən), *n.* a republic in SW Arabia: with the United Arab Republic, formerly constituted the United Arab States. 5,834,000 (est. 1965); ab. 75,000 sq. mi. *Cap.:* San'a.

Yem·en·ite (yem′ə nīt′), *n.* **1.** a native or inhabitant of Yemen. —*adj.* **2.** of or pertaining to Yemen or its people. Also, **Yem·e·ni** (yem′ə nē). [YEMEN + -ITE[1]]

yen[1] (yen), *n., pl.* **yen.** **1.** an aluminum coin and monetary unit of Japan, equal to 100 sen or 1000 rin, and equivalent to about .0028 of a U.S. dollar. *Abbr.:* ¥, Y **2.** a former silver coin of Japan. [< Jap < Chin *yüan* a round thing, a dollar]

yen[2] (yen), *n., v.,* **yenned, yen·ning.** *Informal.* —*n.* **1.** desire; craving: *He had a yen for apple pie.* —*v.i.* **2.** to have a craving; yearn. [? < Chin (slang) *yan* craving]

Yen·an (yen′än′), *n.* a city in N Shensi, in NE China: the capital of Communist China prior to the capture of the city by Nationalist forces in 1947. Also called **Fushih.**

Ye·ni·se·i (yen′i sā′; *Russ.* ye ni sā′yᵊ), *n.* a river in the Soviet Union in Asia, flowing N from Tuva Republic to the Arctic Ocean. 2800 mi. long.

yen·ta (yen′tə), *n. Slang.* a disagreeable, gossipy, annoying woman. [< Yiddish]

Yen·tai (yen′tī′), *n.* Chefoo.

yeo., yeomanry.

yeo·man (yō′mən), *n., pl.* **-men,** *adj.* —*n.* **1.** a petty officer in a navy, having chiefly clerical duties in the U.S. Navy. **2.** *Brit.* a farmer who cultivates his own land. **3.** *Archaic.* **a.** a servant, attendant, or subordinate official in a royal or other great household. **b.** a subordinate or assistant, as of a sheriff or other official or in a craft or trade. **4.** *Archaic or Hist.* one of a class of lesser freeholders, below the gentry, who cultivated their own land, early admitted in England to political rights. —*adj.* **5.** of, pertaining to, composed of, or characteristic of yeomen: *the yeoman class.* **6.** performed or rendered in a workmanlike manner, esp. in situations that involve a great deal of effort or labor: *He did a yeoman job on the problem.* [ME *yeman, yoman,* equiv. to *ye, yo* (?, deriv. of *geng, gong,* variants of *young*) + *man* MAN[1]]

yeo·man·ly (yō′mən lē), *adj.* **1.** of the condition or rank of a yeoman. **2.** pertaining to or befitting a yeoman. —*adv.* **3.** like or as befits a yeoman. [ME *yemanly.* See YEOMAN, -LY]

yeo′man of the guard′, a member of the bodyguard of the English sovereign, instituted in 1485, which now consists of 100 men, including officers, having purely ceremonial duties. Also called **Yeo′man of the Roy′al Guard′.**

yeo·man·ry (yō′mən rē), *n.* **1.** yeomen collectively. **2.** a British volunteer cavalry force, originally composed largely of yeomen, that became part of the British Territorial Army. [ME; see YEOMAN, -RY]

yeo′man's serv′ice, good, useful, or workmanlike service: *His trusty sword did him yeoman's service.* Also, **yeo′man serv′ice.**

yep (yep), *adv. Informal.* yes.

-yer, var. of **-er**[2] after *w: lawyer; sawyer.*

Yer·ba Bue·na (yâr′bə bwā′nə, yûr′bə), **1.** an island in San Francisco Bay between Oakland and San Francisco, California: a 500 ft. two-story tunnel across this island connects the two spans of the San Francisco-Oakland bridge. **2.** (*l.c.*) a labiate herb, *Satureia Douglasii,* of the Pacific coast of North America, used formerly in medicine as an anthelmintic and emmenagogue. **3.** (*l.c.*) a trailing, perennial herb, *Micromeria chamissonis,* of the western coast of North America, having hairy leaves, solitary white flowers, and branches that root at the tips.

Ye·re·van (yer′ə vän′; *Russ.* yi ʀyi vän′), *n.* a city in and the capital of Armenia, in the W part. 1,199,000. Also, **Erevan, Erivan.**

yerk (yûrk), *Chiefly Brit. Dial.* —*v.t.* **1.** to strike or whip. **2.** to stir up; arouse; excite. **3.** to jerk. **4.** to move (a part of one's body) with a jerk. **5.** to pull (stitches) tight or bind tightly. —*v.i.* **6.** to kick. **7.** to rise suddenly. **8.** to enter into eagerly. —*n.* **9.** a kick or jerk. **10.** a thud or blow, as from a stick. [late ME < ?]

yes (yes), *adv., n., pl.* **yes·es.** —*adv.* **1.** (used to express affirmation or assent or to mark the addition of something emphasizing and amplifying a previous statement): *Do you want that? Yes, I do.* **2.** (used to express an emphatic contradiction of a previously negative statement or command): *Don't do that! Oh, yes I will!* **3.** (used, usually interrogatively, to express hesitation, uncertainty, curiosity, etc.): *"Yes?" he said as he opened the door. That was a marvelous show! Yes?* **4.** (used to express polite or minimal interest or attention.) —*n.* **5.** an affirmative reply. [ME *yes, yis,* OE *gēse,* prob., equiv. to *gēa* YEA + *sī* be it (pres. subj. sing. of *bēon* to be)]

ye′se (yēs), *Scot. Archaic.* contraction of *ye shall.*

Ye·se·nin (ye se′nin), *n.* **Ser·gey A·lek·san·dro·vich** (seʀ gā′ ä′le ksän′dʀo vich), 1895–1925, Russian poet. Also, **Esenin.**

ye·shi·va (yə shē′və; *Heb.* yə shē′vä), *n., pl.* **-vahs, -voth** (-vōt). **1.** an Orthodox Jewish school for the religious and secular education of children of elementary school age. **2.** an Orthodox Jewish school of higher instruction in Jewish learning, chiefly for students preparing to enter the rabbinate. [< Heb: academy, orig., sitting (i.e., a place to sit)]

ye·shi·vah (yə shē′və; *Heb.* yə shē′vä), *n., pl.* **-vahs, -voth** (-vōt). yeshiva.

Ye·sil·koy (ye′shēl koi′), *n.* a town in Turkey, near Istanbul. Formerly, **San Stefano.**

yes′ man′, *Informal.* one who always agrees with his superior; a sycophant.

yes·ter (yes′tər), *adj. Archaic.* of or pertaining to yesterday. [back formation from YESTERDAY, etc.]

yester-, a native English prefix indicating the previous occurrence of the time referred to by the word to which the prefix is attached: *yesterday; yesterweek; yesterevening.* [comb. form repr. OE *geostran, giestron;* c. G *gestern,* D *gisteren,* L *hesternus*]

yes·ter·day (yes′tər dē, -dā′), *adv.* **1.** on the day preceding this day. **2.** a short time ago: *Yesterday your money went further.* —*n.* **3.** the day preceding this day. **4.** time in the immediate past. —*adj.* **5.** belonging or pertaining to the day before or to a time in the immediate past: *yesterday morning.* [ME; OE *geostran dæg.* See YESTER-, DAY] —**yes′ter·day·ness,** *n.*

yes·ter·eve (yes′tər ēv′), *n., adv. Archaic.* yesterevening. [YESTER- + EVE]

yes·ter·eve·ning (yes′tər ēv′ning), *Archaic.* —*n.* **1.** yesterday evening. —*adv.* **2.** during yesterday evening. [YESTER- + EVENING]

yes·ter·morn·ing (yes′tər môr′ning), *Archaic.* —*n.* **1.** yesterday morning. —*adv.* **2.** during yesterday morning. [YESTER- + MORNING]

yes·tern (yes′tərn), *adj. Archaic.* yester.

yes·ter·night (yes′tər nīt′), *Archaic.* —*n.* **1.** last night. —*adv.* **2.** during last night. [ME; OE *gystran niht.* See YESTER-, NIGHT]

yes·ter·noon (yes′tər nōōn′), *Archaic* —*n.* **1.** yesterday noon. —*adv.* **2.** at noon yesterday. [YESTER- + NOON]

yes·ter·week (yes′tər wēk′), *Archaic.* —*n.* **1.** last week. —*adv.* **2.** during last week. [YESTER- + WEEK]

yes·ter·year (yes′tər yēr′), *n.* **1.** last year; time not long past. —*adv.* **2.** during time not long past. [YESTER- + YEAR]

yes·treen (ye strēn′), *adv. Scot.* yesterday evening; last evening. [YEST(E)R- + E(V)EN[2]]

yet (yet), *adv.* **1.** at the present time; now: *Don't go yet. Are they here yet?* **2.** up to a particular time; thus far: *He had not yet come.* **3.** in the time still remaining; before all is done: *There is yet time.* **4.** from the preceding time; as previously; still: *He came here on a vacation 20 years ago, and he is here yet.* **5.** in addition; again: *The mail brought yet another reply.* **6.** moreover: *I've never read it nor yet intend to.* **7.** even; still (used to emphasize a comparative): *a yet milder tone; yet greater power.* **8.** though the case be such; nevertheless: *strange and yet very true.* **9. as yet.** See **as**[1] (def. 23). —*conj.* **10.** though; still; nevertheless: *It is good, yet it could be improved.* [ME *yet(e)* < OE *gīet(a);* c. MHG *ieze* yet, now > G *jetzt* now]
—**Syn. 1–10.** See **but**[1].

yet·i (yet′ē), *n.* (*sometimes cap.*) See **Abominable Snowman.** [< Tibetan]

yett (yet), *n. Chiefly Scot.* gate. [dial. var., ME; OE *geat*]

Yet·ta (yet′ə), *n.* a girl's given name.

yeuk (yōōk), *Scot.* —*v.i.* **1.** to itch. —*n.* **2.** an itching sensation. [late ME *yuke* < MD *jeuken* to itch; r. ME (north) *yeke, yike* ITCH] —**yeuk′y,** *adj.*

Yev·tu·shen·ko (yev′tōō sheng′kō; *Russ.* yef tōō-shen′ko), *n.* **Yev·ge·ny A·le·xan·dro·vich** (yev ge′nē ä′le ksän′dro vich), born 1933, Russian poet. Also, **Evtushenko.**

yew[1] (yōō), *n.* **1.** any of several evergreen, coniferous trees and shrubs of the genus *Taxus,* of the Old World, North America, and Japan. **2.** the fine-grained, elastic wood of any of these trees. **3.** an archer's bow made of this wood. **4.** this tree or its branches as a symbol of sorrow, death, or resurrection. [ME *ew(e),* OE *ēow, ī(o)w;* c. Icel *ȳr,* OHG *īga, īwa* (MHG *iwe,* G *Eibe*), OIr *ibar* (MIr *eo*)]

yew[2] (yōō, *unstressed* yŏŏ), *pron. Eye Dialect.* you.

yé-yé (ye′ye′), *adj. Informal.* **1.** of, pertaining to, or characteristic of young sophisticates. **2.** youthful, lively, and sophisticated, as young adults who influence the trends of fashion, entertainment, etc. **3.** of, pertaining to, or characteristic of teen-agers. **4.** having exuberance, optimism, and enthusiasm for current fads, as a teen-ager or young adult. Also, **yeah-yeah.** [< F: transliteration of YEAH-YEAH]

Yezd (yezd), *n.* a city in central Iran. 66,484 (1956). Also, **Yazd.**

Ye·zo (ye′zō), *n.* former name of **Hokkaido.**

Y·gerne (ē gern′), *n. Arthurian Romance.* Igraine.

Ygg·dra·sil (ig′drə sil, yg′-), *n. Scand. Myth.* an evergreen ash tree, the three roots of which bind together Asgard, Midgard, and Niflheim. Also, **Yg′dra·sil, Iggdrasil, Igdrasil.**

YHA, Youth Hostels Association.

YHVH, a transliteration of the Tetragrammaton. Also, **YHWH, JHVH, JHWH** [< Heb]

yi (yē), *n.* (in Chinese philosophy) faithful performance of one's specified duties to society. [< Chin]

yid (yid), *n. Contemptuous and Offensive.* a Jew. [YID(DISH)]

Yid·dish (yid′ish), *n.* **1.** a language consisting of a group of closely similar High German dialects, with vocabulary admixture from Hebrew and Slavic, written in Hebrew letters, spoken mainly by Jews in countries E of Germany and by Jewish emigrants from these regions, and now the official language of Birobizhan, an autonomous Jewish region in the SE Soviet Union in Asia. —*adj.* **2.** of, pertaining to, or characteristic of Yiddish. [< G *jüdisch* Jewish]

yield (yēld), *v.t.* **1.** to give forth or produce by a natural process or in return for cultivation: *This farm yields enough fruit to meet all our needs.* **2.** to produce or furnish (payment, profit, or interest): *She has a trust fund which yields four percent interest annually. That investment will yield a handsome return.* **3.** to give up, as to superior power or authority: *They yielded the fort to the enemy.* **4.** to give up or surrender (oneself): *He yielded himself to temptation.* **5.** to give up or over; relinquish or resign: *to yield the floor to the Senator from Ohio.* **6.** to give as due or required: *to yield obedience or thanks; to yield the right of way to an ambulance.* **7.** to cause; give rise to: *The play yielded only one good laugh.* —*v.i.* **8.** to give a return, as for labor expended; produce; bear. **9.** to surrender or submit, as to superior power: *The rebels yielded after a week.* **10.** to give way to influence, entreaty, argument, or the like: *Don't yield to her outrageous demands.* **11.** to give place or precedence (usually fol. by *to*): *to yield to another; Will the Senator from New York yield?* **12.** to give way to force, pressure, etc., so as to move, bend, collapse, or the like. —*n.* **13.** act of yielding or producing. **14.** that which is yielded. **15.** the quantity or amount yielded. **16.** *Chem.* the quantity of product formed by the interaction of two or more substances, generally expressed as a percentage of the quantity obtained to that theoretically obtainable. **17.** the income produced by a financial investment, usually shown as a percentage of cost. [ME *yelde(n),* OE *g(i)eldan* to pay; c. G *gelten* to be worth, apply to] —**yield′a·ble,** *adj.* —**yield′er,** *n.*
—**Syn. 1.** furnish, supply, render, bear. **3.** abandon, abdicate, waive, forgo. YIELD, SUBMIT, SURRENDER mean to give way or give up to someone or something. To YIELD is to concede under some degree of pressure, but not necessarily to surrender totally: *to yield ground to an enemy.* To SUBMIT is to give up more completely to authority, superior force, etc., and to cease opposition, although usually with reluctance: *to submit to control.* To SURRENDER is to give up complete possession of, relinquish, and cease claim to: *to surrender a fortress, one's freedom, rights.* **6.** impart, bestow. **10.** relax, bend, bow. **14.** fruit. See **crop.** —**Ant. 4.** resist.

yield·ing (yēl′ding), *adj.* **1.** inclined to give in; submissive; compliant: *a timid, yielding man.* **2.** tending to give way, esp. under pressure; flexible; supple; pliable: *a yielding mattress; yielding toys of inflated plastic.* **3.** (of a crop, soil, etc.) producing a yield; productive. [ME; see YIELD, -ING[2]] —**yield′ing·ly,** *adv.* —**yield′ing·ness,** *n.*

yield′ing prop′, *Mining.* a prop designed to shorten when loaded in excess of a certain weight.

yield′ strength′, *Physics.* the stress necessary to produce a given inelastic strain, usually two percent.

Yig·dal (yig däl′), *n. Judaism.* a liturgical prayer or hymn expressing the faith of Israel in God, usually sung responsively by the cantor and congregation at the close of the evening service on the Sabbath and festivals. [< Heb: lit., becomes great]

yill (yil), *n. Scot.* ale.

Yi·ma (yē′mä), *n.* *Zoroastrianism.* a legendary king who, having reigned under the protection of Ahura Mazda in perfect happiness, sinned and lost for the world the immortality it had enjoyed.

yin (yin), *adj., n., pron.* *Scot.* one.

Yin (yin), *n.* **1.** Shang. **2.** See under **Yin and Yang.**

Yin and Yang (yin′ ənd yäng′, yang′), (in Chinese philosophy and religion) two principles, one negative, dark, and feminine **(Yin),** and one positive, bright, and masculine **(Yang),** whose interaction influences the destinies of creatures and things.

Yin and Yang

Ying·kow (ying′kou′), *n.* a port in NE China, near the Gulf of Liaotung: the major port of Manchuria. 131,400 (1953). Also called **Newchwang.**

Yin′-Yang′ School′ (yin′yäng′, -yang′), a school of ancient Chinese philosophers who interpreted history in terms of the influence of the seasons and of five elements, earth, wood, metal, fire, and water. Also called **Five-Elements School.**

yip (yip), *v.,* **yipped, yip·ping,** *n.* —*v.i.* **1.** to bark sharply, as a young dog. —*n.* **2.** a sharp bark; yelp. [late ME *yippe,* ? alter. of *yilpe* YELP (making word more imit. of bird's cheep)]

yipe (yīp), *interj.* (an expression or exclamation of fright, surprise, pain, etc.) [? var. of YAP]

yip·pee (yip′ē), *interj.* (an exclamation used to express joy, exultation, or the like.)

yip·pie (yip′ē), *n.* a member of an antiwar group of young, politically active hippies. Also, **Yip′pie.** [*Youth International Party;* modeled on HIPPIE]

yird (yûrd), *n.* *Scot. and North Eng.* earth.

yirr (yûr), *Scot.* —*v.i.* **1.** to snarl or growl, as a dog does. —*n.* **2.** a growl or snarl, as of a dog. [? OE *georr(an)* to make a harsh sound]

Yiz·kor (yēz kôr′; *Eng.* yis′kər), *n.* *Hebrew.* the Jewish service for commemorating the dead, held on Yom Kippur, Shemini Atzereth, the second day of Shabuoth, and the last day of Passover. [lit., be mindful]

-yl, *Chem.* a suffix used in the names of radicals: *ethyl.* [comb. form repr. Gk *hýlē* matter, wood, substance]

y·lang-y·lang (ē′läng ē′läng), *n.* **1.** an aromatic tree, *Carangium odoratum* (or *Cananga odorata*), of the Philippines, Java, etc., having fragrant, drooping flowers which yield a volatile oil used in perfumery. **2.** the oil or perfume. Also, **ilang-ilang.** [< Tagalog *álang-ilang*]

y·lem (ī′ləm), *n.* the initial substance of the universe from which all matter is said to be derived. [ME < ML, L *hȳlem,* acc. of *hȳlē* < Gk *hýlē* matter, wood]

Y.M.C.A., Young Men's Christian Association.

Y.M.Cath.A., Young Men's Catholic Association.

Y.M.H.A., Young Men's Hebrew Association.

Y·mir (ē′mir, ʏ′mir), *n.* *Scand. Myth.* the earliest being and the progenitor of the giants, killed by Odin and his brothers. From his flesh the earth was made, from his blood the waters, and from his skull the heavens. Also, **Y·mer** (ē′mər).

yo (yō), *interj.* (used as an exclamation to express excitement, get someone's attention, etc.)

y.o., **1.** year old. **2.** years old.

Yoa·kum (yō′kəm), *n.* a town in S Texas. 5761 (1960).

yod (yōōd; *Heb.* yôd), *n.* **1.** the 10th letter of the Hebrew alphabet. **2.** any of the sounds represented by this letter. [< Heb *yod* hand]

yo·del (yōd′əl), *v.,* **-deled, -del·ing,** or (*esp. Brit.*) **-delled, -del·ling,** *n.* —*v.t., v.i.* **1.** to sing with frequent changes from the ordinary voice to falsetto and back again, in the manner of the Swiss and Tyrolean mountaineers. **2.** to call or shout in a similar fashion. —*n.* **3.** a song, refrain, etc., so sung. **4.** a call or shout so uttered. Also, **yodle.** [< G *jodeln*] —**yo′del·er;** *esp. Brit.,* **yo′del·ler,** *n.*

yo·dle (yōd′əl), *v.t., v.i.,* **-dled, -dling,** *n.* yodel. —**yo′dler,** *n.*

Yo·ga (yō′gə), *n.* **1.** (*sometimes l.c.*) union of the self with the supreme being or ultimate principle. **2.** (*sometimes l.c.*) any of the methods or disciplines by which such union is attained, identified as those of karma, bhakti, etc. **3.** a school of Hindu philosophy advocating and prescribing a course of physical and mental disciplines for attaining such union. [< Hind < Skt *yoga* union; akin to YOKE[1]] —**Yo·gic** (yō′gik), *adj.* —**Yo′gism,** *n.*

yogh (yōᴋʜ), *n.* the letter ȝ used in the writing of Middle English to represent a palatal fricative, as in *ȝung* (Modern English "young") or a velar fricative, as in *liȝtliche* (Modern English "lightly"). [ME]

yo·ghurt (yō′gərt), *n.* yogurt. Also, **yo′ghourt.**

yo·gi (yō′gē), *n., pl.* **-gis** (-gēz). one who practices Yoga. Also, **yo·gin** (yō′gin). [< Hind *yogī* < Skt *yogin,* deriv. of *yoga* YOGA]

yo·gi·ni (yō′gə nē), *n.* a woman who practices Yoga. [< Hind *yogin*]

yo·gurt (yō′gərt), *n.* a prepared food having the consistency of custard, made from milk curdled by the action of cultures, sometimes sweetened or flavored. Also, **yoghurt.** [< Turk *yoğhurt*]

yo-heave-ho (yō′hēv′hō′), *interj.* (a chant formerly shouted by sailors when hauling something together.)

yo-ho (yō hō′), *interj., v.,* **-hoed, -ho·ing.** —*interj.* **1.** (used as a call or shout to attract attention, accompany effort, etc.) —*v.i.* **2.** to shout "yo-ho!"

yoicks (hīk; *spelling pron.* yoiks), *interj.* *Rare.* huic. [cf. HOICKS]

yoke[1] (yōk), *n., pl.* **yokes** for 1, 3–18, **yoke** for 2; *v.,* **yoked, yok·ing.** —*n.* **1.** a contrivance for joining together a pair of draft animals, esp. oxen, usually consisting of a crosspiece with two bow-shaped pieces, each enclosing the head of an animal. Cf. **harness** (def. 1). **2.** a pair of draft animals fastened together by a yoke: *five yoke of oxen.* **3.** something resembling a yoke or a bow of a yoke in form or use. **4.** a frame fitting the neck and shoulders of a person, for carrying a pair of buckets or the like, one at each end. **5.** *Mach.* a viselike piece gripping two parts firmly together. **6.** Also called **fork.** a forklike termination, for a rod or shaft, inside which another part is secured; spade handle. **7.** a crosshead attached to the upper piston of an opposed piston engine with rods to transmit power to the crankshaft. **8.** (in an airplane) a double handle, somewhat like a steering wheel in form, by which the elevators are controlled. **9.** *Naut.* a crossbar on the head of the rudder of a small boat, having lines or chains attached to the ends so as to permit the steering of the boat from forward. **10.** a fitting for the neck of a draft animal for suspending the tongue of a cart, carriage, etc., from a harness. **11.** See **spreader beam.** **12.** a shaped piece in a garment, fitted about or below the neck and shoulders or about the hips, from which the rest of the garment hangs. **13.** an emblem or symbol of subjection, servitude, slavery, etc., as an archway under which prisoners of war were compelled to pass by the ancient Romans and others. **14.** a horizontal piece forming the top of a window frame. **15.** a Y-shaped piece connecting branch pipes with a main soil pipe. **16.** something that couples or binds together; a bond or tie. **17.** *Brit. Dial.* (esp. in Kent) **a.** the time during which a plowman and his team work without stopping; a period of plowing. **b.** a measure or area of land equal to over 50 but less than 60 acres. **18.** a word formerly used in communications to represent the letter *Y.* —*v.t.* **19.** to put a yoke on; join or couple by means of a yoke. **20.** to attach (a draft animal) to a plow or vehicle; harness a draft animal to (a plow or vehicle): *to yoke oxen; to yoke a wagon.* **21.** to join, couple, link, or unite. **22.** *Obs.* to bring into subjection or servitude. —*v.i.* **23.** to be or become joined, linked, or united. [ME *yok(e),* OE *geoc;* c. D *juk,* G *Joch,* Icel *ok,* L *jugum,* Gk *zygón,* Hittite *yugan,* Skt *yuga*] —**yoke′less,** *adj.* —**Syn. 2.** See **pair.**

Y, Yoke

yoke[2] (yōk), *n.* yolk.

yoke·fel·low (yōk′fel′ō), *n.* **1.** an intimate associate; a partner. **2.** a spouse. Also, **yoke·mate** (yōk′māt′). [YOKE[1] + FELLOW, trans. of Gk *sýzygos*]

yoke′ front′. See **oxbow front.**

yo·kel (yō′kəl), *n.* a rustic; a country bumpkin. [?] —**yo′kel·ish,** *adj.*

Yok·ka·i·chi (yō′kä ē′chē), *n.* a city on W central Honshu, in S Japan. 210,359 (1964).

Yo·ko·ha·ma (yō′kə hä′mə; *Jap.* yō′kô hä′mä), *n.* a seaport on SE Honshu, in central Japan, on Tokyo Bay: destructive earthquake 1923. 1,639,307 (1964).

Yokoha′ma bean′, a vine, *Stizolobium Hasjoo,* of Japan, having dark purple flowers and white-hairy pods.

Yo·ko·su·ka (yō′kə sōō′kə, yə kōōs′kə; *Jap.* yō′kô-sōō′kä), *n.* a seaport on SE Honshu, in central Japan, on Tokyo Bay: naval base. 310,229 (1964).

Yo·kuts (yō′kuts), *n., pl.* **-kuts.** **1.** a member of a North American Indian group of small tribes speaking related dialects and occupying the San Joaquin Valley of California and the adjoining eastern foothill regions. Nearly all the Valley Yokuts are extinct; some foothill groups remain. **2.** a Penutian family of languages spoken by the Yokuts.

Yo·lan·de (yō lan′də; *Fr.* yô länd′), *n.* a girl's given name. Also, **Eolande, Yo·lan·da** (yō lan′də).

yol·dring (yol′drin, yōl′-), *n.* *Scot. and North Eng.* a yellowhammer. Also, **yeldring.** [earlier *yowlring,* equiv. to *yowl* (OE *geolu* YELLOW) + RING[1]]

yolk (yōk, yōlk), *n.* **1.** the yellow and principal substance of an egg, as distinguished from the white. **2.** *Biol.* the part of the contents of the egg of an animal that enters directly into the formation of the embryo, together with any material that nourishes the embryo during its formation. **3.** the essential part; the inner core. **4.** a natural grease exuded from the skin of sheep. Also, **yoke.** [ME *yolke, yelke,* OE *geoloca* (*geolu* yellow + *-ca* n. suffix)] —**yolk′less,** *adj.* —**yolk′y,** *adj.*

Yom Kip·pur (yôm kip′ər; *Heb.* yôm′ kē pōōr′), a Jewish high holy day observed on the 10th day of the month of Tishri by abstinence from food and drink and by the daylong recitation of prayers of repentance in the synagogue. Also called **Day of Atonement.** [< Heb, equiv. to *yōm* day + *kippur* atonement]

yom tob (*Yiddish* yôn′ təv, təf; *Heb.* yôm′ tôv′), *pl.* *Yiddish* **yom tobs** (yôn′ təvz, təfs), *Heb.* **yo·mim to·vim** (yä mēm′ tô vēm′). *Hebrew.* See **yom tov.**

yom tov (*Yiddish* yôn′ təv, təf; *Heb.* yôm′ tôv′), *pl.* *Yiddish* **yom tovs** (yôn′ təvz, təfs), *Heb.* **yo·mim to·vim** (yä mēm′ tô vēm′). *Yiddish.* holiday. [lit., good day]

yon (yon), *Chiefly Dial.* —*adj., adv.* **1.** yonder. —*pron.* **2.** that or those yonder. [ME; OE *geon;* akin to D *gene,* G *jener,* Goth *jains* that, Icel *enn, inn* the]

yond (yond), *adv., adj.* *Archaic.* yonder. [ME; OE *geond;* akin to D *ginds,* Goth *jaind.* See YON]

yon·der (yon′dər), *adj.* **1.** being the more distant or farther: *Yonder stream is deeper and fresher than this one.* **2.** being in that place or over there; being that or those over there: *That road yonder is the one to take.* —*adv.* **3.** at, in, or to that place (specified or more or less distant); over there. [ME *yonder, yender* (with *-er* as in HITHER, THITHER); akin to D *ginder,* Goth *jaindre*]

yo·ni (yō′nē), *n.* (in Shaktism) the external female genitals regarded as the symbol of Shakti. Cf. **linga** (def. 2). [< Skt]

Yon·kers (yong′kərz), *n.* a city in SE New York, on the Hudson, near New York City. 190,634 (1960). —**Yon′kers·ite′,** *n.*

Yonne (yôn), *n.* a department in central France. 269,826 (1962); 2881 sq. mi. *Cap.:* Auxerre.

yoo-hoo (yōō′hōō′), *interj.* **1.** (used as an exclamation to get someone's attention, in calling to another person, or the like.) —*v.i.* **2.** to get or attempt to get someone's attention by or as if by calling "yoo-hoo": *yoo-hooing across the back fence.* [imit.]

yore (yōr, yôr), *n.* **1.** *Chiefly Literary.* time past: *knights of yore.* —*adv.* **2.** *Obs.* of old; long ago. [ME; OE *geāra,* appar. akin to *gēar* YEAR]

York (yôrk), *n.* **1.** a member of the royal house of England which ruled from 1461 to 1485. **2.** **1st Duke of** (*Edmund of Langley*), 1341–1402, progenitor of the house of York (son of Edward III). **3.** **Alvin Cullum** (*Sergeant*), 1887–1964, U.S. soldier. **4.** Yorkshire (def. 1). **5.** Ancient, **Eboracum.** a city and the county seat of Yorkshire, in NE England, on the Ouse: the capital of Roman Britain; cathedral. 104,468 (1961). **6.** a city in SE Pennsylvania: meeting of the Continental Congress 1777–78. 54,504 (1960). **7.** an estuary in E Virginia, flowing SE into Chesapeake Bay. 40 mi. long. **8. Cape,** a cape at the NE extremity of Australia. **9.** a town in SE Nebraska. 6173 (1960). **10.** a town in N South Carolina. 4758 (1960). **11.** a town in W Alabama. 2932 (1960).

York′ boat′, (*sometimes l.c.*) *Canadian.* a large rowboat or heavy canoe used for transporting supplies, esp. by fur trappers in the Canadian Northwest. [after *York,* Manitoba, Canada, where it was originally built as a canoe by the Hudson's Bay Company]

York·ist (yôr′kist), *n.* **1.** an adherent or member of the royal family of York, esp. in the Wars of the Roses. —*adj.* **2.** belonging or pertaining to the English royal family of York. **3.** of or pertaining to the Yorkists. [YORK + -IST]

York′ rite′, one of the two advanced divisions of Masonic membership, leading to the Knights Templar degree. Cf. **Scottish rite.**

York·shire (yôrk′shēr, -shər), *n.* **1.** Also called **York, Yorks** (yôrks). a county in N England, comprised of the administrative counties of East Riding, North Riding, and West Riding. 3,722,561 (1961); 6089 sq. mi. *Co. seat:* York. **2.** one of an English breed of white hogs having erect ears.

York′shire bond′. See **flying bond.**

York′shire chair′. See **Derbyshire chair.**

York′shire clock′, a broad tall-case clock of the late 18th and early 19th centuries.

York′shire pud′ding, a pudding made of an unsweetened batter of flour, salt, eggs, and milk, baked under meat as it roasts to catch the drippings or baked separately with a small amount of meat drippings.

York′shire ter′rier, one of an English breed of toy terriers having a long, silky, straight coat that is dark steel blue from the back of the skull to the tail and tan on the head, chest, and legs.

Yorkshire terrier (8 in. high at shoulder)

York·ton (yôrk′tən), *n.* a city in SE Saskatchewan, in S Canada. 9995 (1961).

York·town (yôrk′toun′), *n.* **1.** a village in SE Virginia: surrender (October 19, 1781) of Cornwallis to Washington in the American Revolution. **2.** a town in S Texas. 2527 (1960).

York·ville (yôrk′vil), *n.* a town in central New York. 3749 (1960).

Yo·ru·ba (yor′ōō bə, -bä′, yôr′-), *n., pl.* **-bas,** (*esp. collectively*) **-ba** for 1. **1.** a member of a numerous West African coastal Negro people and linguistic stock. **2.** the language of the Yoruba; a Kwa language. —**Yo′ru·ban,** *adj.*

Yo·ru·ba·land (yō′rōō bä land′), *n.* a former kingdom in W Africa, in the E part of the Slave Coast: now a region in SW Nigeria.

Yo·sem·i·te (yō sem′i tē), *n.* a valley in E California, in the Sierra Nevada Mountains: a part of Yosemite National Park. 7 mi. long.

Yosem′ite Falls′, a series of falls in Yosemite National Park: upper falls, 1436 ft. high; middle, 626 ft. high; lower, 320 ft. high. Total height (including rapids), 2526 ft.

Yosem′ite Na′tional Park′, a national park in E California. 1182 sq. mi.

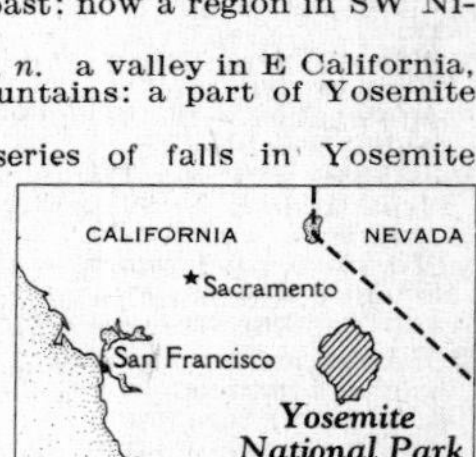

Yo·shi·hi·to (yō′shə hē′tō; *Jap.* yō′shē hē′tô), *n.* 1879–1926, emperor of Japan 1912–26 (son of Mutsuhito).

Yosh·kar-O·la (*Russ.* yosh kär′o lä′), *n.* Ioshkar-Ola.

you (yōō; *unstressed* yŏŏ), *pron., possessive* **your** or **yours** *dative* and *objective* **you,** *n., pl.* **yous.** —*pron.* **1.** the pronoun of the second person singular or plural, used of the person or persons being addressed: *I'm sure he called you, not me or him.* **2.** (used nominatively as the subject of a sentence): *You are the highest bidder.* **3.** one; anyone; people in general: *a garden you would be proud of; a tiny animal you can't even see.* **4.** (used in apposition with the subject of a sentence, sometimes repeated for emphasis following the subject): *You children pay attention. You rascal, you!* **5.** (used by a writer or speaker in direct address): *if you will permit me to digress.* **6.** (used rhetorically in addressing a person or persons not present or in personifying an object): *May you rest in peace. You are a monument to our faith.* **7.** (used by a speaker or writer in referring to a particular profession, nationality, political party, etc.): *As doctors, you know this as well as I.* **8.** (used in the predicate following a copulative verb): *It is you who are to blame.* **9.** (used as the direct object of a verb): *We cannot help you.* **10.** (used as the object of a preposition): *This package came for you.* **11.** (used as an indirect object): *Did he give you the book?* **12.** *Informal.* (used in place of the pronoun *your* with a gerund): *There's no sense in you getting upset. I heard about you being elected.* **13.** *Archaic.* **a.** yourself; yourselves: *Get you home. Make you ready.* **b.** a pl. form of the pronoun *ye.* —*n.* **14.** something or someone closely identified with or resembling the person addressed: *Let's face it, my dear, that evening dress is you. It was like seeing another you.* **15.** the nature or character of the person addressed: *Try to discover the hidden you.* [ME; OE *ēow* (dat., acc. of *gē* YE[1]); c. D *u,* OG *iu*] —**Usage. 12.** See **me.**

you-all (yōō ôl′, yôl), *pron.* *Chiefly Southern U.S.* (used in direct address to two or more persons, or to one person who represents a family, organization, etc.): *You-all come back now, hear? Tell your mother it's time you-all came to visit us.*

You′ Can′t′ Go′ Home′ Again′, a novel (1940) by Thomas Wolfe.

You' Can't' Take' It With' You', a comedy (1936) by George S. Kaufman and Moss Hart.

you'd (yo͞od), contraction of *you had* or *you would.*

you'll (yo͞ol; *unstressed* yo͝ol), contraction of *you will* or *you shall.*

You·lou (yo͞o'lo͞o), *n.* **Ful·bert** (fo͝ol'bərt), born 1917, African political leader: president of the Republic of Congo 1959–63.

young (yung), *adj.* **young·er** (yung'gər), **young·est** (yung'gist), *n.* —*adj.* **1.** being in the first or early stage of life or growth; youthful; not old: *a young girl.* **2.** having the appearance, freshness, vigor, or other qualities of youth. **3.** of or pertaining to youth: *in one's young days.* **4.** inexperienced. **5.** not far advanced in years in comparison with another or others. **6.** junior, as applied to the younger of two persons having the same name: *the young Mr. Smith.* **7.** being in an early stage generally, as of existence, progress, operation, etc.; new; early: *It is a young company, not yet firmly established.* **8.** representing or advocating recent or progressive tendencies, policies, or the like. —*n.* **9.** those who have youth; young persons collectively: *the educated young of today; a game for young and old.* **10.** young offspring: *a mother hen protecting her young.* **11. with young,** pregnant. [ME *yong(e),* OE *geong;* c. D *jong,* G *jung,* Icel *ungr,* Goth *jungs;* akin to L *juvenis*]
—**Syn. 1.** growing. YOUNG, YOUTHFUL, JUVENILE all refer to lack of age. YOUNG is the general word for that which is undeveloped, immature, and in process of growth: *a young colt, child; young shoots of wheat.* YOUTHFUL has connotations suggesting the favorable characteristics of youth, such as vigor, enthusiasm, and hopefulness: *youthful sports, energy, outlook.* JUVENILE may suggest less desirable characteristics, such as childishness, petulance, idleness, selfishness, or heedlessness (*juvenile behavior*), or it may refer simply to the years, up to the later teens, before legal responsibility: *juvenile delinquency; juvenile court; juvenile books.* —**Ant. 1.** mature, old.

Young (yung), *n.* **1. Art(hur Henry),** 1866–1944, U.S. cartoonist and author. **2. Brig·ham** (brig'əm), 1801–77, U.S. Mormon leader. **3. Denton T.** (*Cy*), 1867–1955, U.S. baseball player. **4. Edward,** 1683–1765, English poet. **5. Ella,** 1867–1956, Irish poet and mythologist in the U.S. **6. Owen D.,** 1874–1962, U.S. lawyer, industrialist, government administrator, and financier. **7. Stark** (stärk), 1881–1963, U.S. drama critic, novelist, and playwright. **8. Thomas,** 1773–1829, English physician, physicist, mathematician, and Egyptologist. **9. Whitney M., Jr.,** 1921–71, U.S. social worker and educator: executive director of the National Urban League 1961–71. **10.** An elliptical crater in the fourth quadrant of the face of the moon: about 40 miles long and 34 miles wide.

young·ber·ry (yung'ber'ē, -bə rē), *n., pl.* **-ries.** *Hort.* the large, dark-purple, sweet fruit of a trailing blackberry in the southwest U.S., a cross between several blackberries. [named after B. M. *Young,* American hybridizer, who developed it c1900]

young' blood', youthful people, ideas, practices, etc.

Young'er Ed'da. See under **Edda.**

young-eyed (yung'īd'), *adj.* **1.** clear-eyed; bright-eyed. **2.** having a youthful outlook; enthusiastic; fresh.

young' fus'tic, 1. fustet (def. 2). **2.** the dye obtained from dyewood of the fustet.

young' hy'son. See under **hyson.**

Young' It'aly, a secret society in Italy, founded by Mazzini in 1831 to replace the Carbonari.

young' la'dy, 1. a young, usually unmarried woman of refinement, grace, breeding, etc. **2.** a girl friend; sweetheart; fiancée: *Stuart brought his young lady to meet the family.* [late ME]

young·ling (yung'ling), *n.* **1.** a young person. **2.** anything young, as a young animal. **3.** a novice; a beginner. —*adj.* **4.** young; youthful. [ME *yongling,* OE *geongling;* c. D *jongeling,* G *Jüngling.* See YOUNG, -LING[1]]

Young' Lon'igan, a novel (1932) by James T. Farrell. Cf. **Studs Lonigan.**

young' man', 1. a male in early manhood. **2.** a boy friend; sweetheart; fiancé: *She introduced us to her young man.* [ME *yongmon*]

Young' Man'hood of Studs' Lon'igan, The, a novel (1934) by James T. Farrell. Cf. **Studs Lonigan.**

young one (yung' ən, wən), a child or offspring: *They have five young ones and another on the way.*

Young' plan', a plan, reducing the reparations provided by the Dawes plan, devised by an international committee headed by Owen D. Young, and put into effect in 1929.

Young' Pretend'er. See **Stuart, Charles Edward**

Young's' mod'ulus, *Physics.* a coefficient of elasticity of a substance, expressing the ratio between a stress that acts to change the length of a body and the fractional change in length caused by this force. [named after Thomas YOUNG, who derived it]

young·ster (yung'stər), *n.* **1.** a child. **2.** a young person. **3.** a young horse or other animal. **4.** *Brit. Navy Informal.* a midshipman of less than four years' standing. **5.** (in the U.S. Naval Academy) a midshipman in his second year. [YOUNG + -STER]
—**Syn. 2.** youth, lad, stripling, boy; girl.

Youngs·town (yungz'toun'), *n.* a city in NE Ohio. 166,689 (1960).

young' thing', 1. a young person, esp. a girl: *She's a young thing and cannot leave her mother.* **2.** a young animal.

Young' Turk', 1. a member of a Turkish reformist and nationalist party that was founded in the latter part of the 19th century and was the dominant political party in Turkey in the period 1908–18. **2.** an insurgent in a political party, esp. one belonging to a group or faction that supports liberal or progressive policies: *The leadership of the party passed from the cautious old-line conservatives to the zealous Young Turks.* **3.** Also, **young' Turk'.** any person aggressively advocating reform within an organization.

Young·wood (yung'wo͝od'), *n.* a town in SW Pennsylvania. 2813 (1960).

youn·ker (yung'kər), *n.* **1.** a youngster. **2.** *Obs.* a young noble or gentleman. [< MD *jonckher,* equiv. to *jonc* YOUNG + *hēre* lord; c. G *Junker*]

your (yo͝or, yōr, yôr; *unstressed* yər), *pron.* **1.** (a form of the possessive case of **you** used as an attributive adjective): *Your jacket is in that closet. I like your idea.* Cf. **yours. 2.** (used informally to indicate all members of a group, occupation, etc., or things of a particular type): *Take your factory worker, for instance. Your power brakes don't need that much servicing.* **3.** (used to indicate that one belonging to oneself or to any person): *The consulate is your best source of information. As you go down the hill, the library is on your left.* [ME; OE *ēower* (gen. of *gē* YE[1]); c. G *euer*]
—**Usage.** See **me.**

you're (yo͝or; *unstressed* yər), contraction of *you are.*

your'n (yo͝orn, yōrn, yôrn), *pron. Dial.* yours. Also, **yourn.** [YOUR + *-n* as in MINE[1]]

yours (yo͝orz, yōrz, yôrz), *pron.* **1.** (a form of the possessive case of **you** used as a predicate adjective): *Which cup is yours? Is she a friend of yours?* **2.** that which belongs to you: *Yours was the first face I recognized.* [YOUR + *-s* as in HIS]

your·self (yo͝or self', yōr-, yôr-, yər-), *n., pl.* **-selves** (-selvz'). **1.** (an emphatic appositive of **you** or **ye**): *a letter you yourself wrote.* **2.** (a reflexive form of **you**): *Did you ever ask yourself "why"?* **3.** (used as the object of a preposition or as the direct or indirect object of a verb): *People like yourself often feel that way. I wanted to see Jane and yourself before I left.* **4.** your normal or customary self: *You'll soon be yourself again.* **5.** oneself: *The surest way is to do it yourself.* [from phrase *your self.* See YOUR, SELF]
—**Usage.** See **myself.**

yours' tru'ly, 1. a conventional phrase used at the end of a letter. **2.** *Informal.* I; myself; me: *I'm only in business to profit yours truly.*

yous[1] (yo͞oz), *n.* pl. of **you.**

yous[2] (yo͞oz; *unstressed* yəz), *pron.* youse.

youse (yo͞oz; *unstressed* yəz), *pron. Nonstandard.* you (usually used in addressing two or more people).

youth (yo͞oth), *n., pl.* **youths** (yo͞oths, yo͞othz), (*collectively*) **youth. 1.** the condition of being young. **2.** the appearance, freshness, vigor, spirit, etc., characteristic of one who is young. **3.** the time of being young; early life: *His youth was spent at the farm.* **4.** the period of life from puberty to the attainment of full growth; adolescence. **5.** the first or early period of anything: *The business, even in its youth, showed great potentiality.* **6.** young persons collectively. **7.** a young person, esp. a young man. [ME *youthe,* OE *geoguth;* c. D *jeugd,* G *Jugend*] —**youth'less,** *adj.*
—**Syn. 3.** minority, immaturity. **7.** youngster, teenager, adolescent, stripling, lad, boy. —**Ant. 3.** maturity.

youth-and-old-age (yo͞oth'ən ōld'āj'), *n.* a stiff-growing, erect, annual herb, *Zinnia elegans,* of Mexico, having solitary flowers nearly 4½ inches wide, the disks yellow or orange, the rays purple or reddish-lilac.

youth·en (yo͞o'thən), *v.t.* **1.** to make youthful; to restore youth to (someone or something). —*v.i.* **2.** to become youthful. [YOUTH + -EN[1]]

youth·ful (yo͞oth'fəl), *adj.* **1.** characterized by youth; young. **2.** of, pertaining to, or befitting youth: *refreshing youthful attitudes.* **3.** having the appearance, freshness, vigor, etc., of youth: *She is 60 but her optimism has kept her youthful.* **4.** early in time. **5.** *Phys. Geog.* (of topographical features) having undergone erosion to a slight extent only. [YOUTH + -FUL] —**youth'ful·ly,** *adv.* —**youth'ful·ness,** *n.*
—**Syn. 3.** See **young.**

youth' group', an organization of young people, as for social purposes, usually under the sponsorship of a church, political organization, or the like.

youth'ful offend'er, a young delinquent, esp. a first offender, usually from 14 to 21 years old, whom the court tries to correct and guide rather than to punish as a criminal. Also, **youth' offend'er.**

youth' hos'tel, hostel (def. 1).

youth' hos'teler, a person who stays at youth hostels during travels.

you've (yo͞ov; *unstressed* yo͝ov), contraction of *you have.*

yow (you), *interj., n.* (an exclamation or shout of pain, dismay, etc.) [imit.]

yowl (youl), *v.i.* **1.** to utter a long distressful or dismal cry, as an animal or a person; howl. —*n.* **2.** a yowling cry; a howl. [ME *yuhele, yule, youle,* appar. from a cry of pain or distress *yuhele.* Cf. OE *geoh-* (in *geohthu* grief), *wā lā* alas]

yowl·er (you'lər), *n.* **1.** one who yowls; a howler. **2.** See **ocean pout.** [YOWL + -ER[1]]

Yo-Yo (yō'yō), *n., pl.* **-Yos.** *Trademark.* a toy, consisting of two round, flat-sided blocks of wood, plastic, or metal connected by a dowel pin in the center, around which a string is wound. The Yo-Yo is spun out and reeled in by the string, one end of which remains looped around the player's finger.

y·per·ite (ē'pə rīt'), *n. Chem.* See **mustard gas.** [< F *ypérite,* named after YPRES; see -ITE[1]]

Y potential, *Elect.* the potential difference between the terminal in a three-phase armature and the neutral point of the circuit.

Y·pres (*Fr.* ē'prᵊ; *Brit. or facetious* wī'pərz), *n.* a town in W Belgium: battles 1914–18. 18,358 (est. 1964). Flemish, **Ieper.**

Y.P.S.C.E., Young People's Society of Christian Endeavor.

Yp·si·lan·ti (ip'sə lan'tē), *n.* **1. Alexander,** 1792–1828, Greek patriot and revolutionary leader. **2.** his brother **De·me·tri·os** (di mē'trē əs; *Gk.* the mē'trē ôs), 1793–1832, Greek patriot and revolutionary leader. **3.** a city in SE Michigan, W of Detroit. 20,957 (1960). Also, **Yp·si·lan·tis, Yp·se·lan·tes** (*Gk.* ē'psē län'dēs) (for defs. 1, 2).

Y·quem (ē kem'), *n.* See **Château d'Yquem.**

yr., 1. year; years. **2.** your.

Y·re'ka Cit'y (wī rē'kə), a town in N California. 4759 (1960).

yrs., 1. years. **2.** yours.

Y·ser (*Fr.* ē zer'), *n.* a river flowing from N France through NW Belgium into the North Sea: battles 1914–18. 55 mi. long.

Y·seult (i so͞olt'), *n.* **1.** German, **Y·sol·de** (ē zôl'də). Iseult. **2.** a girl's given name, form of **Iseult.**

Ys·pa·da·den Pen·kawr (ys pa dad'ᵊn pen'kour), *Welsh Legend.* the father of Olwen.

Yt, *Chem.* yttrium.

Y.T., Yukon Territory.

yt·ter·bi·a (i tûr'bē ə), *n. Chem.* a colorless mass, Yb_2O_3, which forms colorless salts: used in certain alloys and ceramics. Also called **ytter'bium ox'ide.** [< NL, named after *Ytterby* a quarry near Stockholm, Sweden, where found; see -IA]

yt·ter·bite (i tûr'bīt), *n.* gadolinite. [*Ytterb(y)* (see YTTERBIA); see -ITE[1]]

yt·ter·bi·um (i tûr'bē əm), *n. Chem.* a rare metallic element found in the mineral gadolinite, and forming compounds resembling those of yttrium. *Symbol:* Yb; *at. wt.:* 173.04; *at. no.:* 70; *sp. gr.:* 6.96. [< NL; see YTTERBITE, -IUM] —**yt·ter'bic, yt·ter'bous,** *adj.*

ytter'bium met'al, *Chem.* See **yttrium metal.**

yt·tri·a (i'trē ə), *n. Chem.* a white, water-insoluble powder, Y_2O_3, used chiefly in incandescent gas and acetylene mantles. Also called **yt'trium ox'ide.** [< NL, named after *Ytt(e)r(by).* See YTTERBIA]

yt·trif·er·ous (i trif'ər əs), *adj.* yielding or containing yttrium. [YTTRI(UM) + -FEROUS]

yt·tri·um (i'trē əm), *n. Chem.* a rare trivalent metallic element, found in gadolinite and other minerals. *Symbol:* Y, Yt; *at. wt.:* 88.905; *at. no.:* 39; *sp. gr.:* 4.47. Cf. **rare-earth element.** [< NL, named after *Ytt(e)r(by).* See YTTERBIA, -IUM] —**yt'tric,** *adj.*

yt'trium met'al, *Chem.* any of a subgroup of rare-earth metals, of which the cerium and terbium metals comprise the other two subgroups. Cf. **rare-earth element.**

yt·tro·tan·ta·lite (i'trō tan'tᵊlīt'), *n.* a mineral, tantalite and niobate of yttrium and various elements, as iron, and cerium, occurring in the form of brown-black crystals. [*yttro-* (comb. form of YTTRIUM) + TANTALITE]

Yü (yʏ), *n.* a legendary Chinese emperor who drained the land and made the mountains.

yu·an (yo͞o än'; *Chin.* yʏän), *n., pl.* **-an.** Also called **yuan' dol'lar.** a copper coin of Nationalist China, equal to 100 cents and equivalent to about .025 of a U.S. dollar; dollar. [< Chin]

Yü·an (yo͞o än'; *Chin.* yʏän), *n.* (*sometimes l.c.*) (in the Republic of China) a department of government; council.

Yü·an (yo͞o än'; *Chin.* yʏän), *n.* **1.** a Mongol dynasty in China, 1260–1368, founded by Kublai Khan. **2.** Yüen.

Yüan Shih-kai (yʏän' shē'kī'), 1859–1916, president of China 1912–16.

Yu·ca·tán (yo͞o'kə tan'; *Sp.* yo͞o'kä tän'), *n.* **1.** a peninsula in SE Mexico and N Central America comprising parts of SE Mexico, N Guatemala, and British Honduras. **2.** a state in SE Mexico, in N Yucatán Peninsula. 614,049 (1960); 14,868 sq. mi. *Cap.:* Mérida. Also, **Yu·ca·tan** (yo͞o'kə tan').

GULF OF MEXICO
BAY OF CAMPECHE
Yucatán Peninsula
CARIBBEAN SEA
MEXICO
BRITISH HONDURAS
GUATEMALA
HONDURAS

Yu·ca·tec (yo͞o'kə tek'), *n., pl.* **-tecs,** (*esp. collectively*) **-tec. 1.** a member of an American Indian people of Yucatán, Mexico. **2.** the Mayan dialect of these people. **3.** a native or inhabitant of Yucatán, Mexico. —**Yu'ca·tec'an,** *adj.*

yuc·ca (yuk'ə), *n.* any liliaceous plant of the genus *Yucca,* of the warmer regions of America, having pointed, usually rigid leaves and panicles of white, waxy flowers: the State flower of New Mexico. [< Sp *yuca* tropical plant < Taino]

yuc'ca moth', any of several white moths of the genus *Tegeticula* that pollinate the yucca plant, the larvae of which develop in the ovary of the plant, consuming some of the seeds.

Yucca, *Yucca gloriosa* (Height about 8 ft.)

yuck·y (yuk'ē), *adj.,* **yuck·i·er, yuck·i·est.** *Slang.* thoroughly unappetizing, disgusting, or repugnant: *a yucky mixture of Brussels sprouts, raisins, and stewed tomatoes.*

Yü·en (yo͞o en'; *Chin.* yʏen), *n.* a river in S China, flowing NE to Tungting. 540 mi. long. Also, **Yüan.**

Yu·ga (yo͝og'ə), *n. Hinduism.* **1.** an age of time. **2.** any of four ages, the Satya, the Treta, the Dvapara, and the Kali, each worse than the last, forming a cycle due to begin again when the Kali has come to an end.

Yugo., Yugoslavia.

Yu·go·slav (yo͞o'gō släv', -slav'), *n.* **1.** a native or inhabitant of Yugoslavia. **2.** a southern Slav; a member of the southern group of Slavic peoples. Cf. **Slav.** —*adj.* **3.** of or pertaining to the Yugoslavs. Also, **Yu'go-Slav', Jugoslav, Jugo-Slav.**

Yu·go·sla·vi·a (yo͞o'gō slä'vē ə), *n.* **1.** a federal republic in SE Europe: since 1992 composed of Serbia and Montenegro. 10,392,000; 39,449 sq. mi. *Cap.:* Belgrade. **2.** Formerly (1918–29), **Kingdom of the Serbs, Croats, and Slovenes.** a republic in S Europe on the Adriatic: formed 1918 from the kingdoms of Serbia and Montenegro and part of Austria-Hungary; a federal republic 1945–91 composed of Bosnia and Herzegovina, Croatia, Macedonia, Serbia, and Slovenia. Also, **Jugoslavia.** —**Yu'go·sla'vi·an,** *adj., n.* —**Yu'go·slav'ic,** *adj.*

yuk (yuk), *n.* **1.** yak[2]. —*interj.* **2.** (used in repetition to indicate one's pleasure or contempt at what has been said, done, etc.)

Yu·ka·ghir (yo͞o'kə gēr'), *n., pl.* **-ghirs,** (*esp. collectively*) **-ghir** for 1. **1.** a member of a Mongoloid people of northeastern Siberia. **2.** the language of the Yukaghir, of known relationship only to two obscure languages of the region.

Yu·ka·gir (yo͞o'kə gēr'), *n., pl.* **-girs,** (*esp. collectively*) **-gir.** Yukaghir.

Yu·ka·wa (yo͞o'kä wä), *n.* **Hi·de·ki** (hē'de kē), born 1907, Japanese physicist: Nobel prize 1949.

Yu·kon (yo͞o'kon), *n.* **1.** a river flowing NW and then SW from NW Canada through Alaska to the Bering Sea. ab. 2000 mi. long. **2.** a territory in NW Canada. 14,628 (1961); 207,076 sq. mi. *Cap.:* Whitehorse. **3.** a town in central Oklahoma. 3076 (1960). —**Yu'kon·er,** *n.*

Yu′kon time′. See under **standard time.**

yu·lan (yo͞o′lan; *Chin.* yʏ′län′), *n.* a tree, *Magnolia denudata,* of central China, having large, cup-shaped, fragrant, fleshy, white flowers and cylindrical, brownish fruit. [< Chin, equiv. to *yü* jade + *lan* orchid]

yule (yo͞ol), *n.* Christmas, or the Christmas season. [ME *yole,* OE *geōl(a)* Christmastide; c. Icel *jōl;* akin to Goth *jiuleis*]

yule′ log′, a large log of wood which traditionally formed the backlog of the fire at Christmas. Also called **yule′ block′, yule′ clog′.**

yule·tide (yo͞ol′tīd′), *n.* **1.** the Christmas season. —*adj.* **2.** of or pertaining to the Christmas season. [YULE + TIDE[1]]

Yu·ma (yo͞o′mə), *n., pl.* **-mas** (*esp. collectively*) **-ma** for 1. **1.** a member of an American Indian people of Arizona. **2.** the Yuman dialect of the Yuma Indians, mutually intelligible with the dialect of the Mohave Indians. **3.** a city in SW Arizona, on the Colorado River. 23,974 (1960).

Yu·man (yo͞o′mən), *n.* **1.** a group comprising the language shared by the Yuma and Mohave Indians and several other languages of the lower valley of the Colorado River. —*adj.* **2.** of or pertaining to Yuman.

yum·my (yum′ē), *adj.,* **-mi·er, -mi·est.** *Informal.* **1.** pleasing to the senses, esp. to the taste; delicious: *The waiter brought the ladies a tray of yummy desserts.* **2.** beautiful; luxurious; extremely attractive: *a yummy new gown.* [*yum* exclamation of pleasure + -Y[1]]

Yung·kia (yo͝ong′kyä′), *n.* a seaport in SE Chekiang, in E China. 201,600 (est. 1957). Formerly, **Wenchow.**

Yün·nan (yo͞o nan′; *Chin.* yʏn′nän′), *n.* **1.** a province in SW China. 19,100,000 (est. 1957); 168,417 sq. mi. *Cap.:* Kunming. **2.** Kunming.

yup·pie (yup′ē), *n.* (*sometimes cap.*) a young, well-educated city-dweller having an affluent lifestyle. [*y*(*oung*) *u*(*rban*) *p*(*rofessional*) + -IE]

yu·quil·la (yo͞o kē′ə; *Sp.* yo͞o kē′yä), *n., pl.* **-quil·las** (-kē′əz; *Sp.* -kē′yäs). a tree, *Manihot carthaginensis,* of Central America, having greenish-yellow flowers in small clusters, yielding an inferior rubber. [< Sp, equiv. to *yuc*(*a*) YUCCA + *-illa* n. suffix]

Yur·ev (yo͝or′yef), *n.* Russian name of **Tartu.**

Yu·ri·ma·guas (yo͞o′rē mä′gwäs), *n.* a city in N Peru. 5918 (1952).

yurt (yo͝ort), *n.* a circular, portable dwelling used by Mongol and Turkic peoples of central Asia. [< Turkic: dwelling]

yu-wei (yo͞o′wā′), *n.* (in philosophical Taoism) action of an artificial or arbitrary kind. Cf. **wu-wei.** [< Chin: lit., some action]

Yu·zov·ka (*Russ.* yo͞o′zof kä′), *n.* former name of **Donetsk.**

Y·vette (i vet′, ē vet′), *n.* a girl's given name, form of **Yvonne.**

Y·vonne (i von′, ē von′; *Fr.* ē vôn′), *n.* a girl's given name.

Y.W.C.A., Young Women's Christian Association.

Y.W.H.A., Young Women's Hebrew Association.

y·wis (i wis′), *adv. Archaic.* iwis.

Z

Z, z (zē or, *esp. Brit.*, zed; *Archaic* iz′ərd), *n., pl.* **Z's** or **Zs, z's** or **zs.** **1.** the 26th letter of the English alphabet, a consonant. **2.** any spoken sound represented by the letter *Z* or *z*, as in *zero, zigzag, buzzer*, etc. **3.** something having the shape of a Z. **4.** a written or printed representation of the letter *Z* or *z*. **5.** a device, as a printer's type, for reproducing the letter *Z* or *z*.

Z, 1. *Astron.* zenith distance. **2.** Zone.

Z, 1. the 26th in order or in a series, or, when *I* is omitted, the 25th. **2.** (*sometimes l.c.*) the medieval Roman numeral for 2000. Cf. **Roman numerals. 3.** *Chem.* atomic number. **4.** *Elect.* impedance.

z, 1. an unknown quantity or variable. **2.** zone. **3.** *Math.* (in Cartesian coordinates) the *z*-axis.

Z., 1. zero. **2.** zinc.

zā (zä), *n.* the 11th letter of the Arabic alphabet. [< Ar *zā(y)*]

ẓā (zä), *n.* the 17th letter of the Arabic alphabet. [< Ar]

za·ba·glio·ne (zä′bəl yō′nē; *It.* dzä′bä lyô′ne), *n.* *Italian Cookery.* a foamy, custardlike mixture of egg yolks, sugar, and Marsala wine, usually served hot or chilled, as a dessert. Also, **za·ba·io·ne, za·ba·jo·ne** (zä′bə yō′nē; *It.* dzä′bä yô′ne). Also called **sabayon.** [< It, var. of *zabaione*, perh. < LL *sabai(a)* an Illyrian drink + It *-one* aug. suffix]

Zab·rze (zäb′zhe), *n.* a city in SW Poland: formerly in Germany. 198,000 (est. 1963). German, **Hindenburg.**

Zab·u·lon (zab′yo͝o lən, zə byo͞o′lən), *n.* *Douay Bible.* Zebulun.

Za·ca·te·cas (sä′kä te′käs), *n.* **1.** a state in central Mexico. 817,831 (1960); 28,125 sq. mi. **2.** the capital of this state. 28,473 (1960).

za·ca·tón (zak′ə tōn′, sak′-; *Sp.* sä′kä tôn′), *n.* a grass, *Epicampes* (*Muhlenbergia*) *macroura*, used in papermaking. [< MexSp. See SACATON]

Zach (zak), *n.* a boy's given name, form of **Zachariah.** Also, **Zack.**

Zach·a·ri·ah (zak′ə rī′ə), *n.* **1.** the father of John the Baptist. Luke 1:5. **2.** a man referred to as a martyr by Jesus. Matt. 23:35; Luke 11:51. **3.** a boy's given name. Also, **Zacharias;** *Douay Bible,* **Zachary** (for defs. 1, 2).

Zach·a·ri·as (zak′ə rī′əs), *n.* **1.** *Douay Bible.* Zechariah. **2. Saint.** Also, **Zachary.** died 752, Greek ecclesiastic, born in Italy: pope 741–752. **3.** Zachariah (defs. 1, 2). **4.** a boy's given name, form of **Zachariah.**

Zach·a·ry (zak′ə rē), *n.* **1.** a town in central Louisiana. 3268 (1960). **2.** *Douay Bible.* Zachariah (defs. 1, 2). **3.** Zacharias (def. 2).

zack (zak), *n.* *Australian.* a coin worth sixpence. [?]

Zack (zak), *n.* a boy's given name, form of **Zachariah** or **Zackary.** Also, **Zach.**

Za·cyn·thus (zə kin′thəs, -sin′-), *n.* Latin name of **Zante.**

Za·dar (zä′där), a seaport in W Croatia, on the Adriatic: formerly, with surrounding territory, an exclave of Italy. 116,174. Formerly, **Zara.**

zad·dik (tsä dēk′; *Eng.* tsä′dik), *n., pl.* **zad·di·kim** (tsä dē kēm′; *Eng.* tsä dik′im). *Hebrew.* **1.** a person of outstanding virtue and piety. **2.** the leader of a Hasidic group. Also, **tzaddik.** [lit., righteous]

Zad·kine (zäd kēn′), *n.* **Os·sip** (o sēp′), 1890–1967, Russian sculptor, in France.

Za·dok (zā′dok), *n.* **1.** Also, *Douay Bible,* **Sadoc.** a priest at the time of David and Solomon. I Sam. 15:34–37; I Kings 1:7, 8. **2.** a boy's given name.

zaf·fer (zaf′ər), *n.* an artificial mixture, resembling smalt, containing cobalt oxide and, usually, silica, used to produce a blue color in glass and in ceramic glazes. Also, **zaf′fre.** [< It *zaffera*, ? < L *sapphīra* SAPPHIRE]

zaf·tig (zäf′tik), *adj.* **1.** (of a woman) having a plump and sexually attractive figure. **2.** full-bodied; well-proportioned. [< Yiddish]

zag (zag), *v.i.*, **zagged, zag·ging.** *U.S. Facetious.* to move in one of the two directions followed in a zigzag course: *First we zigged, then we zagged, trying to avoid the bull.* [clipped form of ZIGZAG]

Zag·a·zig (zäg′ä zēg′), *n.* a city in the NE United Arab Republic, on the Nile delta. 123,200 (1959). Also, **Zaqaziq.**

Zagh·lul Pa·sha (zäg′lo͞ol pä′shä), **Saad** (säd), c1860–1927, prime minister of Egypt 1924–27.

Za·greb (zä′greb), *n.* a city in and the capital of Croatia, in the NW part. 1,174,512. German, **Agram.**

Zag·re·us (zag′rē əs), *n.* a child deity in Orphic mythology, later identified with Dionysus, whom Hera ordered the Titans to slay.

Zag′ros Moun′tains (zag′rəs), a mountain range in S and SW Iran, extending along parts of the borders of Turkey and Iraq. Highest peak, Zardeh Kuh, 14,912 ft.

Zag·ut (zag′ət), *n.* a walled plain in the fourth quadrant of the face of the moon: about 50 miles in diameter.

Za·he·dan (zä′hē dän′), *n.* a city in E Iran. 5000 (1961). Also, **Za′hi·dan′.**

zai·bat·su (zī′bät so͞o′), *n.* (*construed as sing. or pl.*) *Japanese.* the great industrial or financial combinations of Japan. [lit., wealth-family]

Zai·di (zī′dē), *n.* *Islam.* a member of a Shiite sect prominent in Yemen. [< Ar *Zaid* an imam of 8th century + *-i* n. suffix of membership]

za·ire (zä ēr′, zä′ēr), *n., pl.* **za·ire.** a paper money and monetary unit of Zaire, equal to 100 makuta.

Za·ire (zä ēr′, zä′ēr), *n.* Formerly, **Belgian Congo, Democratic Republic of the Congo.** a republic in central Africa: a former Belgian colony. 17,400,000 (est. 1970); 905,328 sq. mi. *Cap.:* Kinshasa. —**Za·ir′e·an,** *n., adj.*

za·kah (zə kä′), *n.* *Islam.* a tax, supposedly 40 percent of personal income of every kind, levied for the relief of the poor. [var. of *zakat* < Ar]

za·kat (zä′kät), *n.* *Islam.* **1.** zakah. **2.** sadaqat.

za·kus·ka (zə ko͞os′kə), *n., pl.* **-ki** (-kē), **-ka.** *Russian Cookery.* See **hors d'oeuvre.** [< Russ, equiv. to *za-* besides (prefix) + *kus* morsel + *-ka* dim. suffix]

Za·kyn·thos (zä′kēn thôs′; *Eng.* zə kin′thəs), *n.* Greek name of **Zante.**

Za·ma (zā′mə, zä′mä), *n.* an ancient town in N Africa, SW of Carthage: the Romans defeated Hannibal near here in the final battle of the second Punic War, 202 B.C.

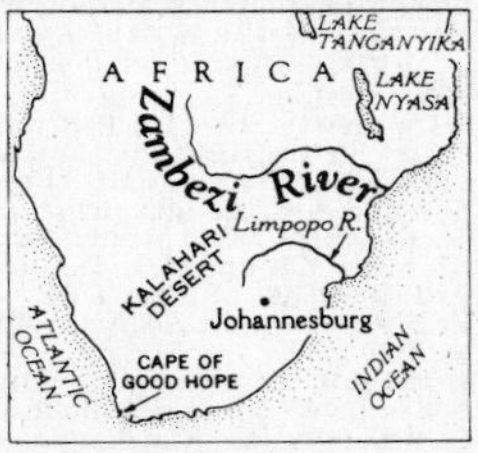

za·mar·ra (zə mär′ə), *n.* a sheepskin coat of the kind worn by shepherds in Spain. [< Sp < Basque *zamar* sheepskin]

Zam·bac (zam′bak), *n.* See **Arabian jasmine.**

Zam·be·zi (zam bē′zē), *n.* a river in S Africa, flowing S from Zambia through E Angola and then E along the border between Zambia and Zimbabwe and then SE through central Mozambique to the Indian Ocean: Victoria Falls. 1650 mi. long. —**Zam·be′zi·an,** *adj.*

Zam·bi·a (zam′bē ə, zäm′-), *n.* a republic in S Africa: a former British protectorate and part of the Federation of Rhodesia and Nyasaland; gained independence October 24, 1964; a member of the British Commonwealth of Nations. 3,650,000 (est. 1964); 288,130 sq. mi. *Cap.:* Lusaka. Formerly, **Northern Rhodesia.**

Zam·bo·an·ga (säm′bō äng′gä), *n.* a seaport on SW Mindanao, in the Philippines. 128,981 (est. 1960).

za·mi·a (zā′mē ə), *n.* any cycadaceous plant of the genus *Zamia*, chiefly of tropical and subtropical America, having a short, tuberous stem and a crown of palmlike pinnate leaves. [< NL, special use of L *zamiae* (pl.), misreading of Pliny's (*nucēs*) *azāniae* pine (nuts)]

za·min·dar (zə mēn där′), *n.* *Hist.* (in India) **1.** a landlord required to pay a land tax to the British government. **2.** (under Mogul rule) a collector of farm revenue, who paid a fixed sum on the district assigned to him. Also, **zemindar.** [< Hindi < Pers *zamīndār* landholder, equiv. to *zamīn* earth, land + *-dār* holding, possession]

Za·mo·ra (thä mô′rä), *n.* **Al·ca·lá** (äl′kä lä′), (*Niceto Alcalá Zamora y Torres*), 1877–1949, Spanish statesman: 1st president of the Republic 1931–36.

zan·der (zan′dər), *n., pl.* **-ders,** (*esp. collectively*) **-der.** a pikeperch, *Stizostedion lucioperca*, found in the fresh waters of central Europe. [< G, perh. < Slav]

Zane (zān), *n.* a boy's given name, form of **John.**

Zanes·ville (zānz′vil), *n.* a city in SE Ohio. 39,077 (1960).

Zang·will (zang′wil), *n.* **Israel,** 1865–1926, English novelist and playwright.

Zan·te (zän′tē, -tā, zan′-), *n.* **1.** a Greek island, off the W coast of Greece: southernmost of the Ionian Islands. 35,509 (1961); 157 sq. mi. **2.** a seaport on and the capital of this island. 11,209 (1951). Greek, **Zakynthos.** Latin, **Zacynthus.**

zan·thox·y·lum (zan thok′sə ləm), *n.* the bark of any of several shrubs or trees of the genus *Zanthoxylum*, esp. *Z. americanum*, the prickly ash, and *Z. Clava-Herculis*, the Hercules'-club, used in medicine. [< NL < Gk *xantho-* XANTHO- + *xýlon*; see XYL-]

Zan·uck (zan′ək), *n.* **Dar·ryl F(rancis)** (dar′əl), 1902–79, U.S. motion-picture producer.

za·ny (zā′nē), *adj.*, **-ni·er, -ni·est,** *n., pl.* **-nies.** —*adj.* **1.** ludicrously or whimsically comical; clownishly crazy. —*n.* **2.** an apish buffoon; clown. **3.** a silly person; simpleton. **4.** a secondary, stock character in old comedies who mimicked his master. **5.** one who plays the clown or makes a fool of himself in order to amuse others. [< It *zan(n)i*, Venetian and Lombardic var. of *Gianni* for *Giovanni* John] —**za′ni·ly,** *adv.* —**za′ni·ness, za′ny·ism,** *n.* —**za′ny·ish,** *adj.*

Zan·zi·bar (zan′zə bär′, zan′zə bär′), *n.* **1.** an island off the E coast of Africa: with Pemba and adjacent small islands that formerly comprised a British protectorate which became independent in 1963; now part of Tanzania. 165,253 (1958); 640 sq. mi. **2.** a seaport on W Zanzibar. 57,923 (1958). —**Zan′zi·ba′ri,** *adj., n.*

zap (zap), *v.t., v.i.*, **zapped, zap·ping.** *Slang.* **1.** to kill or shoot. **2.** to attack, defeat, or destroy. [imit. of the sound of gunfire]

Za·pa·ta (sä pä′tä), *n.* **E·mi·lia·no** (e′mē lyä′nô), 1877?–1919, Mexican revolutionist and agrarian reformer: guerrilla leader 1911–16.

za·pa·te·a·do (zä′pə te ä′dō; *Sp.* sä′pä te ä′thō), *n., pl.* **-dos** (-dōz; *Sp.* -thôs). a Spanish dance for a solo performer, marked by rhythmic tapping of the heels. [< Sp: clog or shoe dance, n. use of ptp. of *zapatear* to strike with the shoe, tap, deriv. of *zapato* shoe. See SABOT, -ADE[1]]

Za·po·rozh·e (zä′po rôzh′ye), *n.* a city in the SE Ukraine, in the SW Soviet Union in Europe, on the Dnieper River. 550,000 (1965). Formerly, **Aleksandrovsk.**

zap·ti·ah (zup tē′ä), *n.* a Turkish policeman. Also, **zap·ti·eh** (zup tē′e). [< Turk *daptiyah* < Ar *ḍābiṭiyah*, lit., government official, deriv. of *ḍabṭ*]

Za·qa·ziq (zä′kä zēk′), *n.* Zagazig.

Za·ra (zä′rä; *It.* dzä′rä), *n.* former name of **Zadar.**

Za·ra·go·za (thä′rä gô′thä, sä′rä gô′sä), *n.* Spanish name of **Saragossa.**

Zar·a·thus·tra (zar′ə tho͞o′strə), *n.* Zoroaster. —**Zar·a·thus·tri·an** (zar′ə tho͞o′strē ən), *adj., n.* —**Zar′a·thus′tric,** *adj.*

zar·a·tite (zar′ə tīt′), *n.* a mineral, hydrated basic nickel carbonate, occurring in the form of emerald-green incrustations on chromite and magnetite. [< Sp *zaratita*, named after *Zarate* Spanish surname; see -ITE[1]]

Zar·deh Kuh (zär′də ko͞o′), a mountain in W Iran: the highest peak of the Zagros Mountains, 14,921 ft. Also, **Zard Kuh** (zärd′ ko͞o′).

za·re·ba (zə rē′bə), *n.* (in the Sudan and adjoining regions) a protective enclosure, as of thorn bushes. Also, **za·ree′ba.** [< Ar *zarībah* pen]

zarf (zärf), *n.* (in the Levant) a holder, usually of ornamental metal, for a coffee cup without a handle. [< Ar *ẓarf* vessel, sheath]

Z, Zarf

zar·zue·la (zär zwā′lə, -zwē′-; *Sp.* thär thwe′lä, sär swe′), *n., pl.* **-las** (-ləz; *Sp.* -läs). a Spanish opera having spoken dialogue and often a satirically treated, topical theme. [< Sp, after *La Zarzuela,* palace near Madrid where first performance took place (1629)]

zas·tru·ga (zas′trə gə, zä′strə-, zastro͞o′-, zə-), *n., pl.* **-gi** (-gē). sastruga.

Zau·ber·berg, Der (*Ger.* deʀ tsou′bəʀ berk′). See **Magic Mountain, The.**

Zau·ber·flö·te, Die (*Ger.* dē tsou′bəʀ flœ′tə). See **Magic Flute, The.**

zax (zaks), *n.* a hatchetlike tool for cutting and punching nail holes in slate. [dial. var. of *sax,* OE *seax* dagger, short sword; c. Icel *sax* sword; akin to SAW[1]]

z-ax·is (zē′ak′sis), *n., pl.* **z-ax·es** (zē′ak′sēz). *Math.* (in a three-dimensional Cartesian coordinate system) the axis along which values of *z* are measured and at which both *x* and *y* equal zero.

za·yin (zä′yin), *n.* **1.** the seventh letter of the Hebrew alphabet. **2.** the consonant sound represented by this letter. [< Heb]

za-zen (zä′zen′), *n. Zen.* meditation in a prescribed, cross-legged posture. [< Jap; see ZEN]

z.B., zum Beispiel.

Z-bar (zē′bär′), *n.* a metal bar with a Z-shaped section. Also called **zee.**

Ze·a (zē′ä, zē′ə), *n.* **1.** Keos. **2.** a girl's given name.

zeal (zēl), *n.* fervor for a person, cause, or object; eager desire or endeavor; enthusiastic diligence; ardor. [late ME *zele* < L *zēl(us)* < Gk *zēlos*] —**zeal′less,** *adj.*
—**Syn.** intensity, passion. —**Ant.** apathy.

Zea·land (zē′lənd), *n.* the largest island of Denmark: Copenhagen is located here. 1,771,557 (1960). 2709 sq. mi. Also, **Seeland.** Danish, **Sjaelland.** —**Zea′land·er,** *n.*

zeal·ot (zel′ət), *n.* **1.** a person who shows zeal. **2.** an excessively zealous person; fanatic. **3.** (*cap.*) *Judaism.* a member of a radical, warlike, ardently patriotic group in Judea, particularly prominent from A.D. 69 to 81, advocating the violent overthrow of Roman rule and vigorously resisting the efforts of the Romans and their supporters to heathenize the Jews and Judaism. [< LL *zēlōtēs* < Gk, equiv. to *zēlō-* (var. s. of *zēloûn* to be zealous; see ZEAL) + *-tēs* agent suffix]
—**Syn.** bigot.

zeal·ot·ry (zel′ə trē), *n.* undue or excessive zeal; fanaticism. [ZEALOT + -RY]

zeal·ous (zel′əs), *adj.* full of, characterized by, or due to zeal; ardently active, devoted, or diligent. [< L *zēlōs(us).* See ZEAL, -OUS] —**zeal′ous·ly,** *adv.* —**zeal′ous·ness,** *n.*
—**Syn.** enthusiastic, eager, fervid, fervent, intense, passionate, warm.

ze·bec (zē′bek), *n.* xebec. Also, **ze′beck.**

Zeb·e·dee (zeb′i dē′), *n.* the father of the apostles James and John. Matt. 4:21.

Ze·bo·im (zi bō′əm), *n.* one of the cities that were destroyed along with Sodom and Gomorrah. Deut. 29: 23. Also, *Douay Bible,* **Seboim.**

ze·bra (zē′brə), *n., pl.* **-bras,** (*esp. collectively*) **-bra. 1.** any of several horselike, African animals of the genus *Equus,* having a characteristic pattern of black or dark-brown stripes on a whitish background. **2.** Also, **ze′bra but′ter·fly.** a nymphalid butterfly, *Heliconius charithonius,* having black wings barred with yellow. **3.** a word formerly used in communications to represent the letter Z. [< Pg < OSp: wild ass < ?] —**ze′bra·like′, ze·bra·ic** (zi brā′ik), *adj.* —**ze·brine** (zē′brin, -brīn), *adj.*

Zebra, *Equus burchelli* (4 ft. high at shoulder; total length 8½ ft.; tail 1½ ft.)

ze′bra cross′ing, a street crossing marked with white stripes.

ze·bra·fish (zē′brə fish′), *n., pl.* **-fish·es,** (*esp. collectively*) **-fish.** an oviparous fish, *Brachydanio rerio,* having zebralike stripes, often kept in aquariums. [ZEBRA + FISH]

ze·bra-plant (zē′brə plant′), *n.* a foliage plant, *Calathea zebrina,* of Brazil, having leaves which are striped with yellow-green and olive-green.

ze·brass (zē′bras), *n.* the offspring of a zebra and an ass. [ZEBR(A) + ASS[1]]

ze′bra swal′lowtail, a swallowtail butterfly, *Papilio marcellus,* having black and greenish-white stripes on the wings.

ze′bra-tailed liz′ard (zē′brə tāld′), a lizard, *Callisaurus draconoides,* found in sandy deserts of Mexico and the southwestern U.S., having a long tail marked with black bands. Also called **gridiron-tailed lizard.**

ze·bra·wood (zē′brə wo͝od′), *n.* **1.** any of several trees, esp. *Connarus guianensis,* of tropical America, yielding a striped, hard wood used for making furniture. **2.** the wood of any of these trees. [ZEBRA + WOOD[1]]

ze·bru·la (zē′bro͞o lə), *n.* the offspring of a female horse and a male zebra. Also, **ze·brule** (zē′bro͞ol). [ZEBR(A) + L (*m*)*ūla* MULE]

ze·bu (zē′byo͞o), *n.* a domesticated, Asiatic, bovine animal, *Bos indicus,* having a large hump over the shoulders and a large dewlap. [< F *zébu,* perh. < Tibetan]

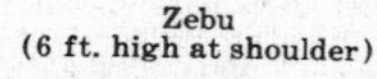

Zebu (6 ft. high at shoulder)

Zeb·u·lon (zeb′yə lon′), *n.* a boy's given name.

Zeb·u·lun (zeb′yo͞o lən, zə byo͞o′lən), *n.* **1.** a son of Jacob and Leah. Gen. 30:20. **2.** one of the 12 tribes of Israel. Also, *Douay Bible,* **Zabulon.**

Zeb·u·lun·ite (zeb′yə lə nīt′), *n.* a member of the tribe of Zebulun. Num. 26:27. [ZEBULUN + -ITE[1]]

zec·chi·no (zə kē′nō; *It.* tsek kē′nō), *n., pl.* **-ni** (-nē). sequin (defs. 2, 4). Also, **zech·in** (zek′in). [< It. See SEQUIN]

Zech., Zechariah.

Zech·a·ri·ah (zek′ə rī′ə), *n.* **1.** a Minor Prophet of the 6th century B.C. **2.** a book of the Bible bearing his name. Also, *Douay Bible,* **Zacharias.**

zed (zed), *n.* **1.** *Chiefly Brit.* the letter *Z* or *z.* **2.** a Z-bar. [ME < MF *zede* < L *zēta* < Gk]

Zed (zed), *n.* a boy's given name, form of **Zedekiah.**

Ze·da·kah (tsə dä kä′; *Eng.* tsə dō′kə), *n. Hebrew.* tzedakah.

zed-bar (zed′bär′), *n. Brit.* See **Z-bar.**

Zed·e·ki·ah (zed′ə kī′ə), *n.* **1.** Also, **Zidkijah;** *Douay Bible,* **Sedecias.** the last king of Judah. II Kings 24, 25; Jer. 52:1–11. **2.** a boy's given name.

zed·o·a·ry (zed′ō er′ē), *n.* an East Indian drug consisting of the rhizome of either of two species of curcuma, *Curcuma zedoaria* or *C. aromatica,* used as a stimulant. [late ME *zeduarye* < ML *zeduāria* < Ar *zedwār* + L *-ia* -Y[3]]

zee (zē), *n.* **1.** *Chiefly U.S.* the letter *Z* or *z.* **2.** See **Z-bar.**

Zee·brug·ge (zē′bro͝og′ə; *Flemish.* zā′bʀœᴋʜ′ə), *n.* a seaport in NW Belgium: part of the city of Bruges; German submarine base in World War I.

Zee·land (zē′lənd; *Du.* zā′länt), *n.* **1.** a province in the SW Netherlands, consisting largely of islands. 283,721 (est. 1960); 1041 sq. mi. *Cap.:* Middelburg. **2.** a town in SW Michigan. 3702 (1960). —**Zee′land·er,** *n.*

Zee·man (zā′män′), *n.* **Pie·ter** (pē′təʀ), 1865–1943, Dutch physicist: Nobel prize 1902.

Zee′man effect′, *Physics, Optics.* the dividing of a spectral line or lines as a result of placing a radiation source in a magnetic field. The division consists of three equally spaced lines **(normal Zeeman effect)** in systems for which the spin quantum number is zero, or of three or more unequally spaced lines **(anomalous Zeeman effect)** in systems for which the spin quantum number is not zero. Cf. **Paschen-Back effect.** [named after P. ZEEMAN]

ze·in (zē′in), *n.* **1.** *Biochem.* a soft, yellow powder obtained from corn, used chiefly in the manufacture of textile fibers, plastics, and paper coatings. **2.** a man-made fiber produced from this protein. [< NL *zē(a)* maize (L *zēa* spelt < Gk *zeiá* barley, wheat; c. Skt *yávas* grain) + -IN[2]]

Zeist (zīst), *n.* a city in the central Netherlands. 54,011 (1962).

Zeit·geist (tsīt′gīst′), *n. German.* the spirit of the time; general trend of thought or feeling characteristic of a particular period of time.

Zeke (zēk), *n.* a boy's given name, form of **Ezekiel.**

Zel·da (zel′də), *n.* a girl's given name, form of **Griselda.**

Ze·li·e·no·ple (zē′lē ə nō′pəl, zēl′yə-), *n.* a town in W Pennsylvania. 3284 (1960).

Ze·lig (zē′lig, zel′ig; *Ger.* tse′liᴋʜ), *n.* a boy's given name. Also, **Selig.**

Zel·la (zel′ə), *n.* a girl's given name. Also, **Zel′le.**

Zel·mi·ra (zel mī′rə), *n.* a girl's given name.

Zel·la·mae (zel′ə mā′), *n.* a girl's given name.

Ze·los (zel′os), *n.* the ancient Greek personification of zeal or emulation: the son of the Titan Pallas and of Styx, and the brother of Bia, Cratus, and Nike.

ze·min·dar (zə mēn där′), *n.* zamindar.

ze·mi·roth (zə mē ʀōt′), *n.pl. Hebrew.* traditional songs of a religious character that are sung by Jews during the evening meal on Friday and the afternoon meal on Saturday. [lit., song]

Zem·strom (zem′strəm), *n. U.S.S.R.* an elective assembly of a local district or of a province, having the supervision and regulation of affairs within its territory. [< Russ, deriv. of *zemlya* band]

zem·stvo (zemst′vō; *Russ.* zyem′stfo), *n., pl.* **zemstvos** (zemst′vōz; *Russ.* zyem′stfoz). *Russ. Hist.* a county council, founded in 1864 by Alexander II to replace the abolished authority of the nobles, that became the core of the liberal movement from 1905 to 1917. [< Russ, deriv. of *zemlya* land, earth]

Zen (zen), *n.* **1.** *Buddhism.* a Mahayana movement, introduced into China in the 6th century A.D. and into Japan in the 12th century, the emphasis of which was upon enlightenment for the student by the most direct possible means, accepting formal studies and observances only when they formed part of such means. Chinese, **Ch'an.** Cf. **koan, mondo. 2.** the discipline and practice of this sect. [< Jap < Chin *ch'an* < Pali *jhāna* < Skt *dhyāna* religious meditation] —**Zen′ic,** *adj.*

ze·na·na (ze nä′nə), *n.* (in India) **1.** the part of the house in which the women and girls of a family are secluded. **2.** its occupants collectively. —*adj.* **3.** of or pertaining to the zenana or its occupants. [< Hindi < Pers *zanāna,* deriv. of *zan* woman; c. Skt *jani* woman, wife, Gk *gynḗ,* OSlav *žena,* OE *cwēn* woman, wife; see QUEEN]

Zend (zend), *n.* **1.** *Zoroastrianism.* a translation and exposition of the Avesta in Pahlavi. **2.** *Archaic.* Avestan (def. 1). [< Pers: interpretation, commentary] —**Zend′ic,** *adj.*

Zend-A·ves·ta (zend′ə ves′tə), *n. Zoroastrianism.* the Avesta together with the Zend. [< Parsee, var. of *Avesta'-va-zend* AVESTA with commentary]

zen·do (zen′dō), *n., pl.* **-dos.** the meditation room of a Zen monastery. [< Jap: meditation place]

Zeng·er (zeng′ər, -gər), *n.* **John Peter,** 1697–1746, American journalist, printer, and publisher, born in Germany.

Ze·ni·a (zē′nē ə), *n.* a girl's given name. Also, **Xenia.**

Zen·ist (zen′ist), *n.* one who advocates or practices Zen. [ZEN + -IST]

ze·nith (zē′nith *or, esp. Brit.,* zen′ith), *n.* **1.** the point on the celestial sphere vertically above a given position or observer. Cf. **nadir. 2.** highest point or state; culmination. [ME *cenith* < ML *cenit* < Ar *samt* road, incorrectly read as *senit* by medieval scribes (cf. Ar *samt ar-rās* road above (over) one's head, the opposite of *nadir*)]
—**Syn. 2.** apex, summit. —**Ant. 1, 2.** nadir.

ze·nith·al (zē′nə thəl *or, esp. Brit.,* zen′ə-), *adj.* **1.** of or pertaining to the zenith; situated at or near the zenith. **2.** (of a map) drawn to indicate the actual direction of any point from the center point. [ZENITH + -AL[1]]

ze′nithal equidis′tant projec′tion. See **azimuthal equidistant projection.**

ze′nith dis′tance, *Astron.* the angular distance from the zenith of a point on the celestial sphere to the sphere, measured along a great circle that is perpendicular to the horizon; the complement of the altitude.

ze′nith tube′, *Astron.* a telescope mounted to point only at the zenith, used at the U.S. Naval and other observatories for measuring time by the stars.

Ze·no (zē′nō), *n.* an elliptical walled plain in the first quadrant of the moon: about 41 miles long and 34 miles wide.

Ze·no·bi·a (zə nō′bē ə), *n.* **1.** (*Septimia Bathzabbai*) died after A.D. 272, queen of Palmyra in Syria A.D. 267–272. **2.** a girl's given name.

Ze·no of Ci·ti·um (zē′nō əv sish′ē əm), c340–c265 B.C., Greek philosopher, born in Cyprus. Also called **Ze′no, Ze′no the Sto′ic.**

Ze′no of E′lea, c490–c430 B.C., Greek philosopher.

zen·o·pho·bi·a (zen′ə fō′bē ə), *n.* xenophobia.

ze·o·lite (zē′ə līt′), *n.* any of a group of hydrated silicates of aluminum with alkali metals, commonly occurring as secondary minerals in cavities in basic igneous volcanic rocks. [< Gk *ze(în)* (to) boil + -o- + -LITE] —**ze·o·lit·ic** (zē′ə lit′ik), *adj.*

Zeph., Zephaniah.

Zeph·a·ni·ah (zef′ə nī′ə), *n.* **1.** a Minor Prophet of the 7th century B.C. **2.** a book of the Bible bearing his name. Also, *Douay Bible,* **Sophonias.**

Zeph·i·ran (zef′ə ran′), *n. Trademark.* See **benzalkonium chloride.**

zeph·yr (zef′ər), *n.* **1.** a gentle, mild breeze. **2.** (*cap.*) *Literary.* the west wind personified. **3.** any of various things of fine, light quality, as fabric, yarn, etc. [< L *zephyr(us)* < Gk *zéphyros* the west wind]
—**Syn. 1.** See **wind**[1].

zeph′yr cloth′, a lightweight worsted cloth.

zeph·yr·e·an (zef′ə rē′ən), *adj.* of, pertaining to, or like a zephyr; full of or containing light breezes. Also, **ze·phyr·i·an** (zi fēr′ē ən), **zeph·yr·ous** (zef′ər əs). [ZEPHYR + -EAN]

Zeph·yr·hills (zef′ər hilz′), *n.* a town in central Florida. 2887 (1960).

Zeph·y·ri·nus (zef′ə rī′nəs), *n.* **Saint,** pope A.D. 198?–217.

zeph′yr lil′y, a bulbous herb, *Zephyranthes grandiflora,* of tropical America, having red or pink flowers nearly three inches long.

Zeph·y·rus (zef′ər əs), *n. Class. Myth.* the west wind personified.

zeph′yr wor′sted, lightweight worsted yarn.

zeph′yr yarn′, any of various soft, lightweight yarns, often of silk, rayon, or a combination of natural and synthetic fibers, for woven and knit goods.

Zep·pe·lin (zep′ə lin), *n.* **1.** a large dirigible balloon consisting of a long, cylindrical, covered framework containing compartments or cells filled with gas, and of various structures for holding the engines, passengers, etc. **2.** (*often l.c.*) any rigid airship or dirigible.

Zep·pe·lin (tsep′ə lēn′), *n.* **Count Fer·di·nand von** (feʀ′di nänt′ fən), 1838–1917, German general and aeronaut: designer and manufacturer of the Zeppelin.

Zer·matt (tseʀ mät′), *n.* a village in S Switzerland, near the Matterhorn: resort. 2731 (1960). 5315 ft. above sea level.

Zer′me·lo's ax′iom (tser′mə lōz′), *Math.* See **axiom of choice.**

Zer·ni·ke (zâr′nə kə, zûr′-; *Du.* zeʀ′ni ke), *n.* **Frits** (frits; *Du.* fʀets), 1888–1966, Dutch physicist: Nobel prize 1953.

ze·ro (zēr′ō), *n., pl.* **-ros, -roes,** *v.,* **-roed, -ro·ing,** *adj.* —*n.* **1.** the figure or symbol 0, which stands for the absence of quantity in the Arabic notation for numbers; a cipher. **2.** the origin of any kind of measurement; line or point from which all divisions of a scale, as a thermometer, are measured in either a positive or a negative direction. **3.** a mathematical value intermediate between positive and negative values. **4.** naught; nothing. **5.** the lowest point or degree. **6.** *Ling.* the absence of a linguistic element, as a phoneme or morpheme in a position in which one previously existed or might by analogy be expected to exist: *Inflectional endings were reduced to zero. The alternant of the plural morpheme in "sheep" is zero.* **7.** *Ordn.* a sight setting for both elevation and windage on any particular range causing a projectile to strike the center of the target on a normal day, under favorable light conditions, with no wind blowing. **8.** *Math.* **a.** the identity element of a group in which the operation is addition. **b.** (of a function, esp. of a function of a complex variable) a point at which a given function, usually a function of a complex variable, has the value zero; a root. **9.** (*cap.*) a single-engine Japanese fighter plane used in World War II. —*v.t.* **10.** to adjust (an instrument or apparatus) to a zero point or to an arbitrary reading from which all other readings are to be measured. **11. zero in,** to adjust the sight settings of (a rifle) by calibrated firing on a standard range with no wind blowing. —*adj.* **12.** *Ling.* noting a hypothetical morphological element that is posited as existing by analogy with a regular pattern of inflection or derivation in a language, but which is not represented by any sequence of phonological elements: *the zero allomorph of "-ed" in "cut"; "Deer" has a zero plural.* **13.** *Meteorol.* **a.** (of an atmospheric ceiling) pertaining to or limiting vertical visibility to 50 feet or less. **b.** of, pertaining to, or limiting horizontal visibility to 165 feet or less. [< It < ML *zephirum* < Ar *ṣifr* CIPHER]

ze′ro-base′ budg′eting (zēr′ō bās′), a process in government and corporate finance of justifying an overall budget each fiscal year or each review period rather than dealing only with proposed changes from a previous budget. Also, **ze′ro-based′ budg′eting.**

ze·ro-di·vi·sor (zēr′ō di vī′zər), *n. Math.* a nonzero element of a ring such that its product with some other nonzero element of the ring equals zero.

ze′ro grav′ity, *Physics.* the condition in which the apparent effect of gravity is zero, as in a body in free fall or in orbit.

ze′ro hour′, 1. *Mil.* (esp. in World War I) the time set for the beginning of an attack. **2.** *Informal.* a decisive or critical time.

CONCISE ETYMOLOGY KEY: <, descended or derived from; >, whence; b., blend of, blended; c., cognate with; deriv., derivative; equiv., equivalent; imit., imitative; m., modification of; obl., oblique; r., replacing; s., stem; sp., spelling; trans., translation; ?, origin unknown, perhaps; *, hypothetical. See the full key inside the front cover.

Ze′rol gear′ (zēr′ōl), *Mach., Trademark.* a bevel gear with teeth that intersect the pitch cone in circular arcs so that the ends lie in the same plane.

ze′ro-point en′ergy (zēr′ō point′), *Physics.* energy in a substance at the temperature of absolute zero.

ze′roth law′ of thermodynam′ics (zēr′ōth), the principle that any two systems in thermal equilibrium with a third system are in thermal equilibrium with each other. Cf. **law of thermodynamics** (def. 1). [ZERO + -TH[2]]

ze′ro vec′tor, *Math.* a vector of which all the components are zero.

ze·ro-ze·ro (zēr′ō zēr′ō), *adj.* *Meteorol.* (of atmospheric conditions) having or characterized by zero visibility in both horizontal and vertical directions.

Ze·rub·ba·bel (zə rub′ə bəl), *n.* a leader of the Jews on their return from Jerusalem after the Babylonian captivity. Ezra 2:1, 2; 3:2–13. Also, *Douay Bible,* **Zorobabel.**

Zer·van (zûr′vən), *n.* Zurvan.

Zer·van·ism (zûr′və niz′əm), *n.* Zurvanism. —**Zer′·van·ite′,** *n.*

zest (zest), *n.* **1.** anything added to impart flavor, cause relish, etc. **2.** an agreeable or piquant flavor imparted to something. **3.** piquancy; interest; charm. **4.** keen relish; hearty enjoyment; gusto. —*v.t.* **5.** to give zest, relish, or piquancy to. [< F *zest* (now *zeste*) orange or lemon peel used for flavoring < ?] —**zest′less,** *adj.* —**zest′y,** *adj.*
—**Syn. 3.** spice, tang.

zest·ful (zest′fəl), *adj.* **1.** full of zest. **2.** characterized by keen relish, hearty enjoyment, etc. [ZEST + -FUL] —**zest′ful·ly,** *adv.* —**zest′ful·ness,** *n.*

ze·ta (zā′tə, zē′-), *n.* **1.** the sixth letter of the Greek alphabet (Z, ζ). **2.** the consonant sound represented by this letter. [< Gk *zêta* < Sem; cf. Heb *ṣādhē*]

ze′ta func′tion, *Math.* the function defined for each real number *x* by the limit as *n* tends to infinity of the series $1 + \frac{1}{2^x} + \frac{1}{3^x} + \ldots + \frac{1}{n^x}$. Also called **Riemann zeta function.**

Ze·tes (zē′tēz), *n.* *Class. Myth.* a son of Boreas and Orithyia, and an Argonaut.

Ze·thar (zē′thär), *n.* one of the seven eunuchs who served in the court of King Ahasuerus. Esther 1:10.

Ze·thus (zē′thəs), *n.* *Class. Myth.* a son of Zeus and Antiope and twin brother of Amphion, whom he assisted in building the walls of Thebes.

Zet·land (zet′lənd), *n.* See **Shetland Islands.**

zeug·ma (zo͞og′mə), *n.* *Gram., Rhet.* the use of a verb with two subjects or objects, or of an adjective with two nouns, although appropriate to only one of the two, as in *to wage war and peace.* [< Gk: a yoking, equiv. to *zeug(nýnai)* (to) yoke + *-ma* n. suffix] —**zeug·mat·ic** (zo͞og mat′ik), *adj.* —**zeug·mat′i·cal·ly,** *adv.*

Zeus (zo͞os), *n.* the supreme deity of the ancient Greeks, a son of Cronus and Rhea, brother of Demeter, Hades, Hera, Hestia, and Poseidon, and father of a number of gods, demigods, and mortals; the god of the heavens, identified by the Romans with Jupiter. [< Gk (gen. *Diós*). See TUESDAY]

Zeux·is (zo͞ok′sis), *n.* fl. c430–c400 B.C., Greek painter.

Zhda·nov (zhdä′nəf), *n.* a city in the SE Ukraine, in the SW Soviet Union in Europe, on the Sea of Azov. 320,000 (est. 1962). Formerly, **Mariupol.**

Zhi·to·mir (zhi tô′mir), *n.* a city in the central Ukraine, in the SW Soviet Union, WSW of Kiev. 124,000 (est. 1964).

Zhiv·kov (zhiv kôf′), *n.* **To·dor** (tô′dor), born 1911, Bulgarian political leader: prime minister since 1962.

Zhu·kov (zho͞o′kof), *n.* **Gri·go·ri Kon·stan·ti·no·vich** (gri gô′ri kon′stän tē′no vich), 1896–1974, Russian marshal.

ZI, *Mil.* Zone of the Interior.

zib·el·ine (zib′ə līn′, -lin), *adj.* **1.** of or pertaining to the sable. —*n.* **2.** the fur of the sable. **3.** a thick woolen cloth with a flattened hairy nap. Also, **zib′el·line′.** [< MF < It *zibellino,* equiv. to *zibel-* (<< Slav; see SABLE) + *-ino* n. suffix; r. *sibelin* < OF]

zib·et (zib′it), *n.* a civet, *Viverra zibetha,* of India, the Malay Peninsula, etc. [< ML *zibethum* or It *zibetto* < Ar *zabād*]

Zid·ki·jah (zid kī′jə), *n.* Zedekiah (def. 1). Neh. 10:1.

Zieg·feld (zig′feld), *n.* **Flor·enz** (flôr′ənz, flor′-), 1867–1932, U.S. theatrical producer.

Zie·gler (zē′glər; *Ger.* tsē′glər), *n.* **Carl** (kärl; *Ger.* kärl), 1897–1973, German chemist: Nobel prize 1963.

Zif (zif), *n.* *Chiefly Biblical.* the month of the Jewish calendar equivalent to Iyar. I Kings 6:1. [< Heb]

zig (zig), *v.i.,* **zigged, zig·ging.** *U.S. Facetious.* to move in one of the two directions followed in a zigzag course: *He zigged when he should have zagged.* [back formation from ZIGZAG]

zig·gu·rat (zig′o͝o rat′), *n.* (among the ancient Babylonians and Assyrians) a temple of Sumerian origin in the form of a pyramidal tower, consisting of a number of stories and having about the outside a broad ascent winding round the structure, presenting the appearance of a series of terraces. Also, **zik·ku·rat, zik·u·rat** (zik′o͝o rat′). [< Assyrian *ziqqurratu* height]

Zi·guin·chor (*Fr.* zē gan shôr′), *n.* a seaport in SW Senegal. 15,100 (1954).

zig·zag (zig′zag′), *n., adj., adv., v.,* **-zagged, -zag·ging.** —*n.* **1.** a line, course, or progression characterized by sharp turns first to one side and then to the other. **2.** one of a series of such turns, as in a line or path. —*adj.* **3.** proceeding or formed in a zigzag. —*adv.* **4.** with frequent sharp turns from side to side; in a zigzag manner: *The child ran zigzag along the beach.* —*v.t.* **5.** to make (something) zigzag, as in form or course; move or maneuver (something) in a zigzag direction: *They zigzagged their course to confuse the enemy. He zigzagged his car back and forth across the highway.* —*v.i.* **6.** to proceed in a zigzag line or course. [< F; r. earlier *ziczac* < F < G *zickzack,* gradational compound based on *Zacke* TACK[1]] —**zig′zag′ged·ness,** *n.*

zig·zag·ger (zig′zag′ər), *n.* **1.** one who or that which zigzags. **2.** an attachment on a sewing machine for making zigzag stitches. [ZIGZAG + -ER[1]]

zig′zag rule′, a folding rule composed of light strips of wood joined by rivets and hinged so as to be stiff when fully opened, all the opening and closing being in parallel planes.

zilch (zilch), *Slang.* zero; nothing: *They were left with zilch.* [perh. continuous with earlier *zilch* snafu, *Mr. Zilch* a character in *Ballyhoo,* a humor magazine first published in 1931]

zil·lah (zil′ə), *n.* (in British India) formerly, any of the districts into which a province was divided for administrative purposes. [< Hindi *ḍilah* < Ar *ḍil'* part]

Zil·lah (zil′ə), *n.* one of the two wives of Lamech. Gen. 4:19. Also, *Douay Bible,* **Sella.**

zil·lion (zil′yən), *n., pl.* **-lions,** (*as after a numeral*) **-lion,** *adj.* *Informal.* —*n.* **1.** an extremely large, indeterminate number. —*adj.* **2.** of, pertaining to, or amounting to a zillion. [*z* + *-illion,* modeled on *million*]

Zil·pah (zil′pə), *n.* the mother of Gad and Asher. Gen. 30:10–13.

zi·mar·ra (zi mär′ə), *n.* *Rom. Cath. Ch.* a cassock with a small cape attached. Also called **simar.** [< It; see SIMAR]

Zim·bab·we (zim bä′bwā), *n.* **1.** Formerly, **Southern Rhodesia, Rhodesia.** a republic in S Africa. 7,500,000 (est. 1980); 150,338 sq. mi. *Cap.:* Salisbury. **2.** the site of ruins, discovered c1870, in Rhodesia, probably built by a Bantu people, consisting of a main group of ruins (**Great Zimbabwe**) and a smaller group (**Little Zimbabwe**) 8 miles away, variously dated as originating in the 9th century A.D. or as late as the 14th or 15th century.

Zim·ba·list (zim′bə list; *Russ.* zim bä lēst′), *n.* **Efrem** (ef′rəm; *Russ.* i frem′), 1889–1970, U.S. violinist and composer, born in Russia.

zinc (zingk), *n., v.,* **zincked** or **zinced** (zingkt), **zinck·ing** or **zinc·ing** (zing′king). —*n.* **1.** *Chem.* a bluish-white metallic element occurring as a sulfide, oxide, carbonate, silicate, etc., resembling magnesium in its chemical relations: used in making galvanized iron, alloys such as brass and die-casting metal, as an element in voltaic cells, and, when rolled out into sheets, as a protective covering for roofs, etc. *Symbol:* Zn; *at. wt.:* 65.37; *at. no.:* 30; *sp. gr.:* 7.14 at 20°C. **2.** a piece of this metal used as an element in a voltaic cell. —*v.t.* **3.** to coat or cover with zinc. [< G *Zink,* perh. deriv. of *Zinn* TIN] —**zinck′y, zinc′y, zink′y,** *adj.* —**zinc′oid,** *adj.*

zinc·ate (zing′kāt), *n.* *Chem.* a salt derived from H_2ZnO_2, the acid form of amphoteric zinc hydroxide. [ZINC + -ATE[2]]

zinc′ blende′, *Mineral.* sphalerite.

zinc′ chlo′ride, *Chem.* a white, crystalline, deliquescent, water-soluble, poisonous solid, $ZnCl_2$, used chiefly as a wood preservative, as a disinfectant and antiseptic, and in the manufacture of vulcanized fiber, parchment paper, and soldering fluxes.

zinc′ green′. See **cobalt green** (def. 2).

zinc·ic (zing′kik), *adj.* pertaining to or containing zinc. [ZINC + -IC]

zinc·if·er·ous (zing kif′ər əs, zin sif′-), *adj.* yielding or containing zinc. [ZINC + -I- + -FEROUS]

zinc·i·fy (zing′kə fī′), *v.t.,* **-fied, -fy·ing.** to cover or impregnate with zinc. [ZINC + -I- + -FY] —**zinc′i·fi·ca′tion,** *n.*

zinc·ite (zing′kīt), *n.* a brittle, deep-red to orange-yellow mineral, native zinc oxide, ZnO, usually massive or granular: an important ore of zinc. [ZINC + -ITE[1]]

zinck·en·ite (zing′kə nīt′), *n.* *Mineral.* zinkenite.

zin·co·graph (zing′kə graf′, -gräf′), *n.* **1.** *Obs.* a zinc plate produced by zincography. **2.** a print from such a plate. [ZINC + -O- + -GRAPH]

zin·cog·ra·phy (zing kog′rə fē), *n.* the art or process of producing a printing surface on a zinc plate, esp. of producing one in relief by etching away unprotected parts with acid. [ZINC + -O- + -GRAPHY] —**zin·cog′ra·pher,** *n.* —**zin·co·graph·ic** (zing′kə graf′ik), **zin′co·graph′i·cal,** *adj.*

zinc′ oint′ment, *Pharm.* an ointment composed of paraffin, white petroleum, and 20 percent of zinc oxide, used in medicine chiefly in the treatment of skin conditions.

zinc·ous (zing′kəs), *adj.* zincic. [ZINC + -OUS]

zinc′ ox′ide, *Chem., Pharm.* a white or yellowish-white, amorphous, odorless, water-insoluble powder, ZnO, used chiefly as a paint pigment, in cosmetics, dental cements, matches, white printing inks, opaque glass, and in medicine as an astringent and antiseptic in the treatment of certain skin conditions. Also called **flowers of zinc, philosopher's wool, zinc white.**

zinc′ phos′phide, *Chem.* a dark-gray, gritty, water-insoluble, poisonous powder, Zn_3P_2, used chiefly as a rat poison.

zinc′ ste′arate, *Chem.* a white, fine, soft, water-insoluble powder, $Zn(C_{18}H_{35}O_2)_2$, used in the manufacture of cosmetics, ointments, and lacquers, as a drying agent for rubber, and as a waterproofing agent for textiles, paper, etc.

zinc′ sul′fate, *Chem.* a colorless, crystalline, water-soluble powder, $ZnSO_4 \cdot 7H_2O$, used for preserving skins and wood, electrodeposition of zinc, in the bleaching of paper, as a mordant in calico printing, and in medicine as an astringent, styptic, and emetic. Also called **white vitriol, zinc′ vit′riol.**

zinc′ white′. See **zinc oxide.**

Zin·der (zin′dər), *n.* a city in S Niger. 13,200 (1954).

zin·fan·del (zin′fən del′), *n.* **1.** a black vinifera grape, grown in California. **2.** a dry red wine made from this grape in California. [?]

zing (zing), *n.* **1.** enthusiasm; vitality; animation: *a pretty coed with lots of zing.* **2.** a quality or characteristic that excites the interest, enthusiasm, etc.: *a tourist town with lots of zing.* **3.** a sharp, singing or whining noise, as of a bullet passing through the air. —*interj.* **4.** (used to imitate the rapid movement of an object through the air.) —*v.i.* **5.** to move or proceed with a sharp, singing or whining noise: *The cars zinged down the highway.* —*v.t.* **6.** to make move with or as with a sharp, singing or whining noise: *He zinged a slider right over the plate.* [dial. var. of SING] —**zing′y,** *adj.*

zin·gi·ber·a·ceous (zin′jə bə rā′shəs), *adj.* belonging to the *Zingiberaceae,* or ginger family of plants. Also, **zinziberaceous.** [< NL *zingiber* genus name (see GINGER) + -ACEOUS]

Zin·jan·thro·pus (zin jan′thrə pəs), *n.* a tentative genus of Australopithecines based on a skull and other skeletal remains found at the Olduvai Gorge in Tanganyika. [< NL < Ar *Zinj* East Africa + Gk *ánthrōpos* man]

zin·ken·ite (zing′kə nīt′), *n.* a steel-gray mineral with metallic luster, lead antimony sulfide, $PbSb_2S_4$. Also, **zinckenite.** [< G *Zinkenit,* named after J. K. L. *Zincken* (1790–1862), German mineralogist and mining director; see -ITE[1]]

zin·ni·a (zin′ē ə), *n.* **1.** any composite plant of the genus *Zinnia* (*Crassina*), found in Mexico and the U.S. **2.** a zinnia, *Z. elegans:* the State flower of Indiana. [< NL, named after J. G. *Zinn* (1727–59), German botanist; see -IA]

zinn·wald·ite (tsin′väl tīt′), *n.* *Mineral.* a yellow-brown variety of mica containing iron, found with tin ores. [named after *Zinnwald,* village in Czechoslovakia where first found; see -ITE[1]]

Zi·nov·iev (zi nôf′yəf), *n.* **Gri·go·ri Ev·se·e·vich** (gri gô′ri ef se′yə vich), 1883–1936, Russian political leader.

Zi·nov·ievsk (zi nôf′yəfsk), *n.* former name of **Kirovograd.**

Zins·ser (zin′sər), *n.* **Hans** (hanz, hänz), 1878–1940, U.S. bacteriologist.

Zin·zen·dorf (tsin′tsən dorf′), *n.* **Count Ni·ko·la·us Lud·wig von** (nē′kô lä′o͝os lo͞ot′vikh fən, lo͞od′-), 1700–60, German religious leader: reformer and organizer of the Moravian Church.

zin·zi·ber·a·ceous (zin′zə bə rā′shəs), *adj.* zingiberaceous.

Zi·on (zī′ən), *n.* **1.** a hill in Jerusalem, on which the Temple was built. **2.** the Jewish people. **3.** Palestine as the Jewish homeland and symbol of Judaism. **4.** heaven as the final gathering place of true believers. Also, **Sion.** [< Heb *tsiyōn* (*z* repr. *ts* as in G); r. ME, OE *Sion* < LL (Vulgate) < Gk (Septuagint) < Heb, as above]

Zi·on·ism (zī′ə niz′əm), *n.* a world-wide Jewish movement for the establishment in Palestine of a national homeland for the Jews. [ZION + -ISM] —**Zi′on·ist,** *n., adj.* —**Zi′on·is′tic,** *adj.* —**Zi·on·ite** (zī′ə nīt′), *n.*

Zi′on Na′tional Park′, a park in SW Utah. 148 sq. mi.

zip[1] (zip), *n., v.,* **zipped, zip·ping.** —*n.* *Informal.* **1.** a sudden, brief hissing sound, as of a bullet. **2.** energy; vim; vigor. —*v.i.* **3.** to move with a zipping sound. **4.** *Informal.* to act or move with speed or energy: *I'll just zip upstairs.* —*v.t. Informal.* **5.** to convey with speed and energy: *I'll zip you downtown in no time.* **6.** to add vitality or zest to (usually fol. by *up*): *A little garlic will zip up the salad.* [imit.]

zip[2] (zip), *v.,* **zipped, zip·ping.** —*v.t.* **1.** to fasten or unfasten with a zipper: *Zip up your jacket before you catch cold. Zip open the traveling case.* **2.** to enclose or free by doing up or undoing a zipper: *Zip this money into your wallet. Zip me out of my dress.* —*v.i.* **3.** to become fastened or unfastened by means of a zipper: *a handy purse that zips shut.* **4.** to do up or undo a zipper. [back formation from ZIPPER]

Zi·pan·gu (zi pang′go͞o), *n.* Marco Polo's name for Japan.

zip′ code′, *U.S.* a system to facilitate the delivery of mail, consisting of a five-digit code written directly after the address, the first three digits indicating the State and place of delivery, the last two digits the post office or postal zone. Also, **ZIP code, Zip code.** [*Z*(*one*) *i*(*mprovement*) *p*(*rogram*)]

zip′ fas′tener, *Brit.* a zipper.

zip′ gun′, a homemade pistol, typically consisting of a metal tube taped to a wooden stock and firing a .22-caliber bullet.

zip·per (zip′ər), *n.* **1.** one who or that which zips. **2.** Also called **slide fastener.** a device, usually of metal but sometimes of plastic, used for fastening clothing, valises, etc., consisting of two toothed tracks or spiral metal or plastic coils, each bordering one of two facing parts, and a piece that either interlocks or separates them when pulled. **3.** a rubber and fabric boot or overshoe fastened up the leg by a slide fastener. —*v.t., v.i.* **4.** zip[2]. [formerly trademark]

zip·pered (zip′ərd), *adj.* fastened or fitted with a zipper or zippers: *zippered slipcovers.* [ZIPPER + -ED[2]]

Zip·po·rah (zi pōr′ə, -pôr′ə, zip′ər ə), *n.* the daughter of Jethro and the wife of Moses. Ex. 2:21. Also, *Douay Bible,* **Sephora.**

zip·py (zip′ē), *adj.,* **-pi·er, -pi·est.** *Informal.* lively; peppy. [ZIP[1] + -Y[1]]

zir·con (zûr′kon), *n.* **a common mineral, zirconium silicate, $ZrSiO_4$, occurring in small tetragonal crystals or grains of various colors, usually opaque: used as a refractory when opaque and as a gem when transparent. [< G *Zirkon;* r. JARGON[2]]**

zir·con·ate (zûr′kə nāt′), *n.* *Chem.* a salt of the acid form of zirconium hydroxide. [ZIRCON + -ATE[2]]

zir·co·ni·a (zər kō′nē ə), *n.* *Chem.* a white, heavy, amorphous, odorless and tasteless, infusible, water-insoluble powder, ZrO_2, used chiefly as a pigment for paints, an abrasive, and in the manufacture of refractory crucibles. Also called **zirco′nium ox′ide, zirco′nium diox′ide.** [< NL; see ZIRCON, -IA]

zir·co·ni·um (zər kō′nē əm), *n.* *Chem.* a metallic element found combined in zircon, baddeleyite, etc., resembling titanium chemically: used in steel metallurgy, as a scavenger, as a refractory, and as an opacifier in vitreous enamels. *Symbol:* Zr; *at. wt.:* 91.22; *at. no.:* 40; *sp. gr.:* 6.49 at 20°C. [< NL; see ZIRCON, -IUM] —**zir·con·ic** (zər kon′ik), *adj.*

zir·co·nyl (zûr′kə nil), *adj.* *Chem.* containing the group, ZrO=, as zirconyl bromide, $ZrOBr_2$. [ZIRCON + -YL]

zisch·äg·ge (tsish′eg′ə), *n.* *Armor.* a German and eastern European burgonet of the 16th and 17th centuries, having a fixed fall, a sliding nasal, and cheek pieces separated from the neck guard. [< G: lit., slip-peak]

Zis·ka (zis′kə), *n.* **Jan** (yän), c1370–1424, Bohemian general. Also, **Žižka.**

zith·er (zith′ər), *n.* a musical instrument, consisting of a flat sounding box with numerous strings stretched over it, which is placed on a horizontal surface and played with a plectrum and the fingertips. [< G < L *cithara* < Gk *kithára*] —**zith′er·ist,** *n.*

zith·ern (zith′ərn), *n.* **1.** cittern. **2.** zither.

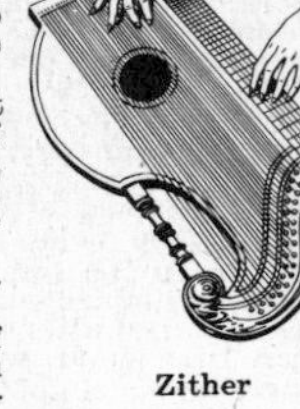
Zither

zit·tern (zit′ərn), *n.* cittern.

Zi·u·su·dra (zē′o͞o so͞o′drə), *n.* a legendary Sumerian king who built a boat in which to escape the Deluge. Cf. **Atrahasis.**

Zi·wiye (zē′wē), *n.* an ancient city in W Iran: large collection of ivory, gold, and bronze artifacts, dating from c675 to c600 B.C., found here in 1946. Also, **Zi·wi·yè** (zē′wē yə).

zi·zith (tsit′sis; *Heb.* tsē tsēt′, tsi′tsis), *n.* (*construed as sing. or pl.*) *Judaism.* the fringes or tassels of entwined threads formerly worn at the corners of the outer garment and now worn at the four corners of the tallith and the *arba kanfoth.* Also, **tzitzith.** [< Heb]

Žiž·ka (zhish′kä), *n.* **Jo·hann** (yō′hän). See **Ziska, Jan.**

zizz (ziz), *n.* *Brit. Informal.* a catnap.

Zl., zloty.

Zla·to·ust (zlä to o͞ost′), *n.* a city in the W RSFSR, in the W Soviet Union in Asia, in the Ural Mountains. 167,000 (est. 1962).

zlo·ty (zlô′tē), *n., pl.* **-tys,** (*collectively*) **-ty.** a nickel coin and monetary unit of Poland, equal to 100 groszy and equivalent to about .04 of a U.S. dollar. *Abbr.:* Zl. [< Pol: golden]

Zn, *Chem.* zinc.

Zna·nie·cki (znä nyets′kē), *n.* **Flo·ri·an** (flô rē′än), 1882–1958, Polish sociologist.

zo-, var. of **zoo-** before a vowel: *zooid.*

zo·a (zō′ə), *n.* pl. of **zoon.**

-zoa, a plural combining form occurring as the final element in names of zoological groups: *Protozoa.* [pl. comb. form of NL *zōon* < Gk *zôion* animal]

Zo·an (zō′an), *n.* Biblical name of **Tanis.**

zo·an·thro·py (zō an′thrə pē), *n.* *Psychiatry.* a mental disorder in which one believes himself to be an animal. [ZO- + ANTHROP- + -Y[3]]

Zo·ar (zō′ər), *n.* the city where Lot and his family took refuge during the destruction of Sodom and Gomorrah. Gen. 19:20–30. Also, *Douay Bible,* **Segor.**

zod., zodiac.

zo·di·ac (zō′dē ak′), *n.* **1.** an imaginary belt of the heavens, extending about 8° on each side of the ecliptic, within which are the apparent paths of the sun, moon, and principal planets. It contains twelve constellations and hence twelve divisions called signs of the zodiac. Each division, however, because of the precession of the equinoxes, now contains the constellation west of the one from which it took its name. **2.** a circular or elliptical diagram representing this belt, and usually containing pictures of the animals, human figures, etc., which are associated with the constellations and signs. **3.** a circuit or round. [< L *zōdiac(us)* < Gk *zōidiakós* (*kýklos*) signal (circle), equiv. to *zōidi(on)* animal sign (*zôi(on)* animal + *-dion* dim. suffix) + *-akos* -AC] —**zo·di·a·cal** (zō dī′ə kəl), *adj.*

Zodiac

zodi′acal light′, a luminous tract in the sky, seen in the west after sunset or in the east before sunrise and thought to be the light reflected from a cloud of meteoric matter revolving round the sun.

Zo·e (zō′ē, zō), *n.* a girl's given name. Also, **Zo′ë.**

zo·e·trope (zō′ē trōp′), *n.* a device for giving an illusion of motion, consisting of a slitted drum which, when whirled, shows a succession of images placed opposite the slits within the drum as one moving image. [< Gk *zōḗ* life + *tropḗ* turn]

Zog I (zōg), (*Ahmed Bey Zogu*) 1895–1961, king of Albania 1928–39. Also, **Zog·u I** (zōg′wə; *Eng.* zō′go͞o).

zo·gan (zō′gän; *Jap.* zô′gän), *n.* decorative Japanese inlay work in metal, as on sword mounts. [< Jap]

Zo·har (zō′här), *n.* a theosophical work, consisting chiefly of mystical interpretations of and commentaries on the Pentateuch.

zois·ite (zoi′sīt), *n.* a mineral, hydrous calcium aluminum silicate, $Ca_2Al_3O(SiO_4)(Si_2O_7)(OH)$: a variety of epidote nearly free of iron. [named after Baron S. *Zois* von Edelstein (1747–1819), Slovenian nobleman who discovered it; see -ITE[1]]

Zo·la (zō′lə; *Fr.* zô lȧ′), *n.* **É·mile** (ā mēl′), 1840–1902, French novelist. —**Zo′la·esque′,** *adj.*

Zöll·ner (zol′nər), *n.* an elliptical walled plain in the fourth quadrant of the face of the moon: about 28 miles long and 20 miles wide.

Zoll′ner illu′sion (tsul′nər; *Ger.* tsœ′nər), *Psychol.* a spatial illusion in which parallel lines intersected by short oblique lines are perceived as converging or diverging. [named after J. K. F. *Zöllner,* 19th-century German physicist]

Zollner illusion

Zoll·ver·ein (tsôl′fer īn′), *n.* **1.** (in the 19th century) a union of German states for the maintenance of a uniform tariff on imports from other countries, and of free trading among themselves. **2.** any similar union or arrangement between a number of states; a customs union. [< G, equiv. to *Zoll* custom, duty, tariff + *Verein* union]

Zom·ba (zom′bə), *n.* a city in and the capital of Malawi, in the S part. 6600 (est. 1956).

zom·bi (zom′bē), *n., pl.* **-bis. 1.** the python god among certain West Africans. **2.** the snake god worshiped in the voodoo ceremonies in the West Indies and certain parts of the southern U.S. **3.** a supernatural force which brings a corpse to physical life. **4.** *Canadian Slang.* an army conscript assigned to home defense. **5.** zombie. Also, **zombie** (for defs. 1–4). [< WAfr: fetish] —**zom′bi·ism,** *n.*

zom·bie (zom′bē), *n.* **1.** the body of a dead person given the semblance of life by a supernatural force, usually for some evil purpose. **2.** a tall drink made typically with several kinds of rum, citrus juice, and often apricot liqueur. **3.** *Slang.* someone little smarter or livelier than a corpse; dummy; oaf. **4.** *Slang.* an eccentric or peculiar person. **5.** zombi. Also, **zombi** (for defs. 1–4). [var. of ZOMBI]

zon·al (zōn′əl), *adj.* **1.** of or pertaining to a zone or zones. **2.** of the nature of a zone. Also, **zon·a·ry** (zō′nə rē). [ZONE + -AL[1]] —**zon′al·ly,** *adv.*

zo·na pel·lu·ci·da (zō′nə pə lo͞o′si də, pel yo͞o′-), *pl.* **zo·nae pel·lu·ci·dae** (zō′nē pə lo͞o′si dē′, pel yo͞o′-). *Anat.* the transparent, noncellular layer, often having radial striations, surrounding the ovum of mammals. [< NL; see ZONE, PELLUCID]

zon·ate (zō′nāt), *adj.* **1.** marked with a zone or zones, as of color, texture, or the like. **2.** arranged in a zone or zones. Also, **zo′nat·ed.** [ZONE + -ATE[1]]

zo·na·tion (zō nā′shən), *n.* **1.** state or condition of being zonate. **2.** arrangement or distribution in zones. [ZONE + -ATION]

zon·da (zon′də; *Sp.* sôn′dä), *n.* (in the Argentine pampas) a hot, oppressive wind. [< AmerSp]

zone (zōn), *n., v.,* **zoned, zon·ing.** —*n.* **1.** any continuous tract or area, usually circular, which differs in some respect, or is distinguished for some purpose, from adjoining tracts or areas, or within which certain distinctive circumstances exist or are established. **2.** *Geog.* any of five great divisions of the earth's surface, bounded by lines parallel to the equator, and named according to the prevailing temperature. Cf. **North Frigid Zone, North Temperate Zone, South Frigid Zone, South Temperate Zone, Torrid Zone.** See illus. in next column. **3.** *Biogeog.* an area characterized by a particular set of organisms, whose presence is determined by environmental conditions, as an altitudinal belt on a mountain. **4.** *Geol.* a horizon. **5.** *Geom.* a part of the surface of a sphere included between two parallel planes. **6.** a specific district, area, etc., within which a uniform charge is made for transportation or some similar service. **7.** the total number of available railroad terminals within a given circumference around a given shipping center. **8.** an area or district in a city or town under special restrictions as to the type of buildings that may be erected. **9.** See **time zone. 10.** Also called **postal delivery zone.** (in the U.S. postal system) any of the numbered districts into which a city or metropolitan area is divided for expediting the sorting and delivery of mail. **11.** *Sports.* a particular portion of a playing area: *The wing was trapped with the puck in his own defensive zone.* **12.** *Archaic.* a girdle or belt; cincture. —*v.t.* **13.** to mark with zones or bands. **14.** to divide into zones, tracts, areas, etc., as according to existing characteristics or as distinguished for some purpose. **15.** to divide (a city, town, neighborhood, etc.) into areas subject to special restrictions as to the type of buildings that may be erected. **16.** to encircle or surround with a zone, girdle, belt, or the like. —*v.i.* **17.** to be formed into a zone or zones. [< L *zōna* < Gk *zṓnē* belt] —**zone′less,** *adj.*
—**Syn. 1.** region. See **belt. 16.** gird, band.

zone′ defense′, *Sports.* a method of defense, esp. in basketball and football, in which each member of the defensive team guards a specified portion of the playing area. Cf. **man-to-man defense.**

zone′ line′, *Ice Hockey.* See **blue line.**

zone′ melt′ing, a process of purifying any of various metals and other materials, as germanium or silicon, by passing it in bar form through an induction coil in such a way that each part of the bar melts within the coil momentarily, causing the impurities to be driven from the molten area toward the end of the bar that has not passed through the coil. Also called **zone′ refin′ing.** Cf. **cage zone melting.**

zone′ of fire′, *Mil.* the area within which a unit is prepared to place its fire.

zone′ of inte′rior, the part of a theater of war not included in the theater of operations.

Zon·i·an (zō′nē ən), *n.* **1.** a U.S. citizen living in the Canal Zone. —*adj.* **2.** of or pertaining to the Zonians. [ZONE + -IAN]

zon·ing (zō′ning), *adj.* (esp. in city planning) of or pertaining to the division of an area into zones: *The city fathers planned to revise the zoning laws.* [ZONE + -ING[2]]

zo·nite (zō′nīt), *n.* a body segment of a diplopod. [ZONE + -ITE[1]]

Zon′ta Club′ (zon′tə), one of an organization of service clubs composed of business and professional women, founded in 1919 and being a member of a worldwide organization **(Zon′ta Interna′tional)** dedicated to promoting world peace and fellowship. [< Siouan *zonta* to be trusted]

Zon·ti·an (zon′tē ən), *n.* **1.** a member of a Zonta Club. —*adj.* **2.** of or pertaining to a Zonta Club or its members. [ZONT(A) + -IAN]

zon·ule (zōn′yo͞ol), *n.* a little zone, belt, band, etc. [< NL *zōnula.* See ZONE, -ULE] —**zon·u·lar** (zōn′yə lər), *adj.*

zoo (zo͞o), *n., pl.* **zoos.** See **zoological garden.** [first two syllables of ZOOLOGICAL GARDEN taken as one syllable]

zoo-, a learned borrowing from Greek meaning "living being," "animal," used in the formation of compound words: *zoometry; zooplankton.* Also, *esp. before a vowel,* **zo-.** [comb. form repr. Gk *zôion* animal]

zoochem., zoochemistry.

zo·o·chem·is·try (zō′ə kem′i strē), *n.* the branch of chemistry dealing with the constituents of the animal body; animal chemistry. Also, **zo′ö·chem′is·try.** [ZOO- + CHEMISTRY] —**zo·o·chem·i·cal, zo·ö·chem·i·cal** (zō′ə kem′i kəl), *adj.*

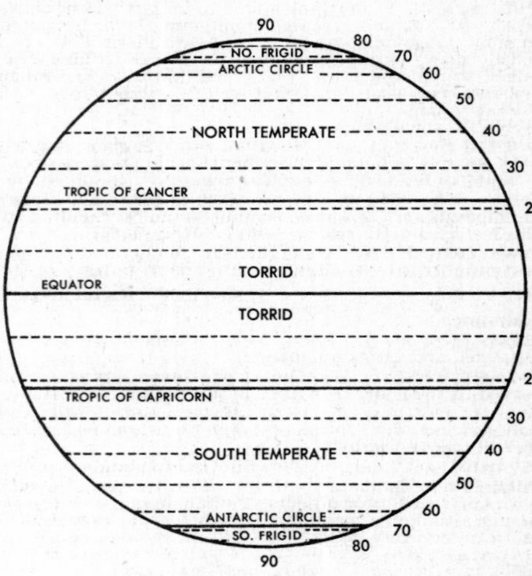

Terrestial zones

zo·o·chore (zō′ə kōr′, -kôr′), *n.* *Bot.* a plant whose structure adapts it for dispersion by animals. Also, **zo′ö·chore′.** [ZOO- + Gk *chōr(ein)* (to) spread]

zoogeog., zoogeography. Also, **zoögeog.**

zo·o·ge·og·ra·phy (zō′ə jē og′rə fē), *n.* **1.** the science dealing with the geographical distribution of animals. **2.** the study of the causes, effects, and other relations involved in such distributions. Also, **zo′ö·ge·og′ra·phy.** [ZOO- + GEOGRAPHY] —**zo′o·ge·og′ra·pher, zo′ö·ge·og′ra·pher,** *n.* —**zo·o·ge·o·graph·ic, zo·ö·ge·o·graph·ic** (zō′ə jē′ə graf′ik), **zo′o·ge′o·graph′i·cal, zo′ö·ge′o·graph′i·cal,** *adj.* —**zo′o·ge′o·graph′i·cal·ly, zo′ö·ge′o·graph′i·cal·ly,** *adv.*

zo·o·gloe·a (zō′ə glē′ə), *n.* *Bacteriol.* a jellylike mass of microorganisms. Also, **zo′ö·gloe′a.** [ZOO- + NL *gloea* gum < Gk *gloía* glue] —**zo′o·gloe′al, zo′ö·gloe′al, zo′o·gle′al, zo′ö·gle′al,** *adj.*

zo·o·graft·ing (zō′ə graf′ting, -gräf′-), *n.* zooplasty. Also, **zo′ö·graft′ing.** [ZOO- + GRAFTING]

zo·og·ra·phy (zō og′rə fē), *n.* the branch of zoology dealing with the description of animals. Also, **zo·ög′ra·phy.** [ZOO- + -GRAPHY] —**zo·og′ra·pher, zo·ög′ra·pher,** *n.* —**zo·o·graph·ic, zo·ö·graph·ic** (zō′ə graf′ik), **zo′o·graph′i·cal, zo′ö·graph′i·cal,** *adj.*

zo·oid (zō′oid), *n.* **1.** *Biol.* any organic body or cell capable of spontaneous movement and of an existence more or less apart from or independent of the parent organism. **2.** *Zool.* **a.** any animal organism or individual capable of separate existence, and produced by fission, gemmation, or some method other than direct sexual reproduction. **b.** one of the individuals, as certain free-swimming medusas, which intervene in the alternation of generations between the products of proper sexual reproduction. **c.** any one of the recognizably distinct individuals or elements of a compound or colonial animal, whether detached, detachable, or not. —*adj.* **3.** Also, **zo·oi′dal, zo·öi′dal.** pertaining to, resembling, or of the nature of an animal. Also, **zo′öid.** [ZO- + -OID]

zooks (zo͝oks, zo͞oks), *interj.* (used in exclamatory phrases as a mild oath.) [short for *gadsooks,* lit., God's hooks. See GAD, HOOK]

zool., **1.** zoological. **2.** zoologist. **3.** zoology. Also, **zoöl.**

zo·ol·a·try (zō ol′ə trē), *n.* the worship of or excessive attention to animals. Also, **zo·öl′a·try.** [ZOO- + -LATRY] —**zo·ol′a·ter, zo·öl′a·ter,** *n.* —**zo·ol′a·trous, zo·öl′a·trous,** *adj.*

zo·o·log·i·cal (zō′ə loj′i kəl), *adj.* **1.** of or pertaining to zoology. **2.** relating to or concerned with animals. Also, **zo′ö·log′i·cal, zo′o·log′ic, zo′ö·log′ic.** [ZOOLOG(Y) + -ICAL] —**zo′o·log′i·cal·ly, zo′ö·log′i·cal·ly,** *adv.*

zo′olog′ical gar′den, a park or other large enclosure inwhich live animals are kept for public exhibition. Also, **zoo.**

zo·ol·o·gist (zō ol′ə jist), *n.* a specialist in zoology. Also, **zo·öl′o·gist.** [ZOOLOG(Y) + -IST]

zo·ol·o·gy (zō ol′ə jē), *n., pl.* **-gies. 1.** the science or branch of biology dealing with animals. **2.** a treatise on zoology. **3.** the animal life of a particular region. Also, **zo·öl′o·gy.** [ZOO- + -LOGY]

zoom (zo͞om), *v.i.* **1.** to move quickly or suddenly with a loud humming or buzzing sound: *cars zooming by on the freeway.* **2.** to fly an airplane suddenly and sharply upward at great speed for a short distance, as in regaining altitude, clearing an obstacle, signaling, etc. **3.** *Photog.* to magnify or reduce an image by adjusting a zoom lens. **4.** *Motion Pictures, Television.* to change rapidly from a long shot to a close-up while maintaining the subject or scene in focus. —*v.t.* **5.** to cause (an airplane) to zoom. **6.** to fly over (an obstacle) by zooming. **7.** *Photog.* to adjust (a zoom lens) in order to magnify or reduce an image. —*n.* **8.** act or process of zooming. **9.** a zooming sound. [imit.]

zo·om·e·try (zō om′i trē), *n.* measurement of the proportionate lengths or sizes of the parts of animals. Also, **zo·öm′e·try.** [ZOO- + -METRY] —**zo·o·met·ric, zo·ö·met·ric** (zō′ə me′trik), **zo′o·met′ri·cal, zo′ö·met′ri·cal,** *adj.*

zoom′ lens′, (in a camera or motion-picture projector) a lens assembly whose focal length can be continuously adjusted to provide various degrees of magnification without any loss of focus, thus combining the features of wide-angle, normal, and telephoto lenses.

zo·o·mor·phic (zō′ə môr′fik), *adj.* **1.** ascribing animal form or attributes to beings or things not animal, esp. to a deity in the form of an animal. **2.** characterized by a highly stylized or conventionalized representation of animal forms. **3.** representing or using animal forms. Also, **zo′ö·mor′phic.** [ZOO- + -MORPHIC] —**zo′o·morph′, zo′ö·morph′,** *n.*

zo·o·mor·phism (zō′ə môr′fiz əm), *n.* **1.** zoomorphic representation, as in ornament. **2.** zoomorphic conception, as of a deity. Also, **zo′ö·mor′phism.** [ZOO-MORPH(IC) + -ISM]

zo·on (zō′on), *n., pl.* **zo·a** (zō′ə). *Zool.* any of the individuals of a compound organism. Also, **zo′ön.** [< NL *zōon* < Gk *zôion* animal] —**zo·on′al, zo·ön′al,** *adj.*

-zoon, a combining form of **zoon:** *ptychozoon.*

zo·on·o·sis (zō on′ə sis, zō′ə nō′sis), *n.* *Pathol.* a disease of animals communicable to man. Also, **zo·ön′o·sis.** [ZOON + -OSIS]

zo·oph·i·lous (zō of′ə ləs), *adj.* **1.** *Bot.* adapted to pollination by the agency of animals. **2.** having an affinity for animals. Also, **zo·öph′i·lous, zo·o·phil·ic, zo·ö·phil·ic** (zō′ə fil′ik). [ZOO- + -PHILOUS]

zo·o·pho·bi·a (zō′ə fō′bē ə), *n.* abnormal fear of animals. Also, **zo′ö·pho′bi·a.** [ZOO- + -PHOBIA] —**zo·oph·o·bous, zo·öph·o·bous** (zō of′ə bəs), *adj.*

zo·oph·o·rus (zō of′ər əs), *n., pl* **-o·ri** (-ə rī′). zophorus. Also, **zo·öph′o·rus.** [< L < Gk *zōiophóros.* See ZOO-, -PHORE] —**zo·o·phor·ic, zo·ö·phor·ic** (zō′ə fôr′ik, -for′-), *adj.*

zo·o·phyte (zō′ə fīt′), *n.* any of various invertebrate animals resembling a plant, as a coral, a sea anemone, etc. Also, **zo′ö·phyte′.** [< NL *zōophyton* < Gk *zōióphyton.* See ZOO-, -PHYTE] —**zo·o·phyt·ic, zo·ö·phyt·ic** (zō′ə fit′ik), **zo′o·phyt′i·cal, zo′ö·phyt′i·cal,** *adj.*

zo·o·plank·ton (zō′ə plangk′tən), *n.* the animal organisms in plankton. Also, **zo′ö·plank′ton.** Cf. **phytoplankton.** [ZOO- + PLANKTON]

zo·o·plas·ty (zō′ə plas′tē), *n.* *Surg.* the transplantation of living tissue from a lower animal to the human body. Also, **zo′ö·plas′ty.** Also called **zoografting.** [ZOO- + -PLASTY] —**zo′o·plas′tic, zo′ö·plas′tic,** *adj.*

zo·o·sperm (zō′ə spûrm′), *n.* *Bot. Obs.* zoospore. Also, **zo′ö·sperm′.** [ZOO- + -SPERM] —**zo·o·sper·mat·ic, zo·ö·sper·mat·ic** (zō′ə spər mat′ik), *adj.*

zo·o·spo·ran·gi·um (zō′ə spə ran′jē əm), *n., pl.* **-gi·a** (-jē ə). *Bot.* a sporangium or spore case in which zoospores are produced. Also, **zo′ö·spo·ran′gi·um.** [ZOO- + SPORANGIUM] —**zo′o·spo·ran′gi·al, zo′ö·spo·ran′gi·al,** *adj.*

zo·o·spore (zō′ə spōr′, -spôr′), *n.* **1.** *Bot.* an asexual spore produced by certain algae and some fungi, capable of moving about by means of flagella. **2.** *Zool.* any of the minute motile flagelliform or amoeboid bodies which issue from the sporocyst of certain protozoans. Also, **zo′ö·spore′.** [ZOO- + SPORE] —**zo·o·spor·ic, zo·ö·spor·ic** (zō′ə spôr′ik, -spor′-), **zo·os·por·ous, zo·ös·por·ous** (zō os′pər əs, zō′ə spōr′-, -spôr′-), *adj.*

zo·ot·o·my (zō ot′ə mē), *n.* the dissection or the anatomy of animals. Also, **zo·öt′o·my.** [< NL *zōotomia.* See ZOO-, -TOMY] —**zo·o·tom·ic, zo·ö·tom·ic** (zō′ə tom′ik), **zo′o·tom′i·cal, zo′ö·tom′i·cal,** *adj.* —**zo′o·tom′i·cal·ly, zo′ö·tom′i·cal·ly,** *adv.* —**zo·ot′o·mist, zo·öt′o·mist,** *n.*

zo·o·tox·in (zō′ə tok′sin), *n.* any toxin of animal origin, as a snake or scorpion venom, or serum produced by means of such toxin. Also, **zo′ö·tox′in.** [ZOO- + TOXIN]

zoot′ suit′, a suit with baggy, tight-cuffed pants and an oversized coat. [rhyming compound based on SUIT]

zoot′ suit′er, a person who wears a zoot suit.

zoot·y (zōō′tē), *adj.* *Slang.* characteristic of a zoot-suiter; extreme or flamboyant in style or appearance: *a zooty new convertible.* [ZOOT (SUIT) + -Y[1]]

Zo·phar (zō′fər), *n.* a friend of Job. Job. 2:11. Also, *Douay Bible,* **Sophar.**

zo·pho·rus (zō′fər əs), *n., pl.* **-pho·ri** (-fə rī′). a frieze having representations of men or animals. Also, **zoophorus.** [< L < Gk *zōiphóros.* See ZO-, -PHORE]

Zo·ra (zōr′ə, zôr′ə), *n.* a girl's given name.

Zo·ra·bell (zōr′ə bel′, zôr′-), *n.* a girl's given name.

Zo·ran·a (zō ran′ə, zō-), *n.* a girl's given name.

zo·rap·ter·an (zō rap′tər ən), *n.* any of the small, superficially termitelike insects of the order *Zygoptera* that live in clusters or groups in decaying wood. [< NL *zōrapter(a)* (< Gk *zōr(ós)* pure + *áptera,* neut. pl. of *ápteros* APTEROUS) + -AN]

zo·ri (zôr′ē), *n., pl.* **zo·ri.** a low Japanese sandal consisting of a flat sole fastened to the foot by thongs passing between the big toe and the toe beside it. [< Jap]

zor·il (zôr′il, zor′-), *n.* a weasellike, African animal, *Ictonyx striatus,* resembling a skunk in coloration and habits. Also, **zo·ril·la** (zə ril′ə), **zo·rille** (zə ril′). [var. of *zorille* < F < Sp *zorilla, -o,* equiv. to *zorra, -o* fox + *-illa, -o* dim. suffix]

Zorn (sôrn), *n.* **An·ders Le·on·hard** (än′dərs lā′ô-närd′), 1860–1920, Swedish painter, etcher, and sculptor.

Zorn′s′ lem′ma (zôrnz), *Math.* a theorem of set theory that if every totally ordered subset of a nonempty partially ordered set has an upper bound, then there is an element in the set such that the set contains no element greater than the specified given element.

Zo·ro·as·ter (zōr′ō as′tər, zôr′-), *n.* fl. 6th century B.C., Persian religious teacher. Also called **Zarathustra.**

Zo·ro·as·tri·an (zōr′ō as′trē ən, zôr′-), *adj.* **1.** of or pertaining to Zoroaster or to Zoroastrianism. —*n.* **2.** one of the adherents of Zoroastrianism, now chiefly represented by the Gabars of Iran and the Parsees of India.

Zo·ro·as·tri·an·ism (zōr′ō as′trē ə niz′əm, zôr′-), *n.* an Iranian religion, supposedly founded c600 B.C. by Zoroaster, the principal beliefs of which were in the existence of a supreme deity, Ahura Mazda, and in a cosmic struggle between a spirit of good, Spenta Mainyu, and a spirit of evil, Angra Mainyu. Also, **Zo′ro·as′trism.** Also called **Mazdaism.**

Zo·rob·a·bel (zō rob′ə bəl, zô-), *n.* *Douay Bible.* Zerubbabel.

Zor·ri·lla y Mo·ral (thôr rē′lyä ē mô räl′), **Jo·sé** (hô se′), 1817–93, Spanish poet and dramatist.

Zo·ser (zō′sər), *n.* fl. c2800 B.C., Egyptian ruler of the 3rd dynasty.

Zo·si·mus (zō′sə məs), *n.* **Saint,** pope 417–418.

zos·ter (zos′tər), *n.* **1.** *Pathol.* shingles. **2.** *Gk. Antiq.* a belt or girdle. [< L < Gk *zōstḗr* girdle]

Zos·te·ri·a (zo stēr′ē ə), *n.* *Class. Myth.* an epithet of Athena, meaning "one who girds with armor."

Zou·ave (zōō äv′, zwäv), *n.* **1.** (*sometimes l.c.*) one of a body of infantry in the French army, composed originally of Algerians, distinguished for their dash, hardiness, and picturesque Oriental uniform. **2.** a member of any body of soldiers adopting a similar dress and drill, esp. a soldier serving in any of certain volunteer regiments in the American Civil War. [< F < *Zwāwa* Kabyle tribal name]

zouk (zōōk), *n.* a style of dance music that originated in Guadeloupe and Martinique, featuring Caribbean rhythms over a disco beat and played with electric guitars and synthesizers. [appar. < Lesser Antillean Creole French; said to mean lit. "place to dance, party"]

zounds (zoundz), *interj.* *Archaic.* (used as a mild oath). [(*God*)'*s* (*w*)*ounds*]

zow·ie (zou′ē), *interj.* (used to express keen pleasure, surprise, approval, etc.)

Zr, *Chem.* zirconium.

Zsig·mon·dy (zhig′môn dē), *n.* **Rich·ard** (riKH′ärt), 1865–1929, German chemist, born in Austria: Nobel prize 1925.

Z twist, a direction of the twist in yarns, from top right to bottom left, resembling the long stroke of the letter *Z.* Cf. **S twist.**

Zuc·ca·ri (tsōōk′kä rē′), *n.* **Fre·de·ri·go** (fre′de-rē′gō), 1543?–1609, and his brother **Tad·de·o** (täd de′-ô), 1529–66, Italian painters. Also, **Zuc·ca·ro** (tsōōk′-kä rô′), **Zuc·che·ro** (tsōōk′ke rô′).

zuc·chet·to (zōō ket′ō; *It.* tsōōk ket′tô), *n., pl.* **-tos,** *It.* **-ti** (-tē). a small, round skullcap worn by Roman Catholic ecclesiastics, a priest's being black, a bishop's violet, a cardinal's red, and the Pope's white; calotte. [< It, var. of *zucchetta,* equiv. to *zucc(a)* gourd, head (var. of *cucuzza;* cf. L *cucurbita*) + *-etta* -ETTE]

zuc·chi·ni (zōō kē′nē), *n., pl.* **-ni, -nis. 1.** a variety of summer squash that is shaped like a cucumber and that has a smooth, dark-green skin. **2.** the plant bearing this fruit. [< It, pl. of *zucchino,* equiv. to *zucc(a)* gourd (see ZUCCHETTO) + *-ino* dim. suffix]

Zuc·chi·us (zōō′kē əs, zōō kē′-), *n.* a crater in the SE quadrant of the face of the moon: about 50 miles in diameter.

Zug (tsōōKH), *n.* **1.** a canton in central Switzerland. 52,489 (1960). 92 sq. mi. **2.** the capital of this canton. 19,489 (1960).

zug·zwang (tsōōk′tsfäng), *n.* *Chess.* a situation in which a player is limited to moves that cost him pieces or have some other damaging effect on his position. [< G: lit., move compulsion]

Zui·der Zee (zī′dər zē′; *Du.* zœi′dər zā′), a former shallow inlet of the North Sea in central Netherlands: now IJssel Lake. Also, **Zuyder Zee.**

Zu'l·hij·jah (zōōl hij′ä), *n.* the 12th month of the Islamic calendar.

Zu'l·ka·dah (zōōl′kə dä′), *n.* the 11th month of the Islamic calendar.

Zu·lo·a·ga (thōō′lô ä′gä), *n.* **Ig·na·cio** (ēg nä′thyô), 1870–1945, Spanish painter.

Zu·lu (zōō′lōō), *n., pl.* **-lus,** (*esp. collectively*) **-lu,** *adj.* —*n.* **1.** a people of SE Africa, inhabiting the coastal region between Natal and Lourenço Marques. **2.** a member of the Zulu people. **3.** the language of the Zulus, a Bantu language. **4.** a word used in communications to represent the letter *Z.* —*adj.* **5.** of or pertaining to the Zulus or their language.

Zu·lu·land (zōō′lōō land′), *n.* a territory in NE Natal, in the Republic of South Africa.

Zu·ñi (zōō′nyē, -nē, sōō′-), *n., pl.* **-ñis,** (*esp. collectively*) **-ñi** for 1. **1.** a member of a tribe of North American Indians inhabiting the largest of the Indian pueblos, in western New Mexico. **2.** the language of the Zuñi tribe, of uncertain linguistic affinity, though inclusion in Uto-Aztecan has been suggested. [< Sp < Keresan *Sú̄nyitsa*] —**Zu′ñi·an,** *adj., n.*

Zu′ñi Pueb′lo, a town in W New Mexico. 3585 (1960).

zun·yite (zōōn′yīt), *n.* a rare mineral, basic silicate of aluminum with fluorine and chlorine. [ZUÑ(I) + -ITE[1]]

Zu·pus (zōō′pəs), *n.* a crater in the third quadrant of the face of the moon: about 20 miles in diameter.

Zur·ba·rán (thōōr′bä rän′), *n.* **Fran·cis·co de** (frän thēs′kô the), 1598–1663?, Spanish painter.

Zu·rich (zŏŏr′ik), *n.* **1.** a canton in N Switzerland. 952,304 (1960); 668 sq. mi. **2.** the capital of this canton, on the Lake of Zurich. 440,170 (1960). **3. Lake of,** a lake in N Switzerland. 25 mi. long; 34 sq. mi. German, **Zü·rich** (tsY′riKH) (for defs. 1, 2).

Zur·van (zûr′vən), *n.* the ancient Iranian god of time and fate. Also, **Zervan.** Cf. **Zurvanism.**

Zur·van·ism (zûr′və niz′əm), *n.* an ancient Iranian religion, probably related to Zoroastrianism, centered around the worship of Zurvan as the father of Ahura Mazda. Also, **Zervanism.** [ZURVAN + -ISM]

Zuy·der Zee (zī′dər zē′; *Du.* zœi′dər zā′). See **Zuider Zee.**

Zweig (zwīg, swīg; *Ger.* tsvīKH), *n.* **1. Ar·nold** (är′-nəld; *Ger.* är′nôlt), 1887–1968, German novelist, essayist, and dramatist. **2. Ste·fan** (stef′ən, -än; *Ger.* shte′fän), 1881–1942, Austrian dramatist, critic, biographer, and novelist.

Zwick·au (tsvik′ou), *n.* a city in W Saxony, in S East Germany. 129,394 (est. 1959).

Zwick·y (tsvik′ē), *n.* **Fritz** (frits), born 1898, Swiss astrophysicist, born in Bulgaria, in the U.S. since 1925.

zwie·back (zwī′bak′, -bäk′, zwē′-, swī′-; *Ger.* tsvē′-bäk′), *n.* a special egg bread made into rusks. [< G: twice-baked, equiv. to *zwie* twice + *backen* to bake. See TWI-, BAKE[1], and cf. BISCUIT]

Zwing·li (zwing′lē, swing′-; *Ger.* tsving′lē), *n.* **Ul·rich** (ōōl′riKH) or **Hul·dreich** (hōōl′driKH), 1484–1531, Swiss Protestant reformer.

Zwing·li·an (zwing′glē ən, swing′-, tsving′lē-), *adj.* **1.** of or pertaining to Ulrich Zwingli or his doctrines, which largely agreed with those of Luther and which offered a distinctive interpretation of the Lord's Supper. —*n.* **2.** a follower of Zwingli. [ZWINGLI + -AN] —**Zwing′li·an·ism,** *n.* —**Zwing′li·an·ist,** *n., adj.*

zwit·ter·i·on (tsvit′ər ī′ən), *n.* *Physical Chem.* an ion with both a positive and a negative charge. Also, **zwit′ter-i′on.** [< G *Zwitter* half-breed + -ION] —**zwit·ter·i·on·ic** (tsvit′ər ī on′ik), *adj.*

Zwol·le (zwôl′ə), *n.* a city in the central Netherlands. 56,779 (1962).

Zwor·y·kin (zwôr′ə kin; *Russ.* zvôr′yə kin), *n.* **Vlad·i·mir Kos·ma** (vlad′ə mēr′ koz′mə; *Russ.* vlä dē′mir kôz mä′), born 1889, U.S. physicist and engineer born in Russia.

zyg·a·poph·y·sis (zig′ə pof′i sis, zī′gə-), *n., pl.* **-ses** (-sēz′). *Anat., Zool.* one of the articular processes upon the neural arch of a vertebra, usually occurring in two pairs, one anterior and the other posterior, and serving to interlock each vertebra with the ones above and below. [ZYG- + APOPHYSIS] —**zyg·ap·o·phys·e·al, zyg·ap·o·phys·i·al** (zig′ap ə fiz′ē əl), *adj.*

zygo-, a learned borrowing from Greek meaning "yoke," "yoked," "yoke-shaped," used in the formation of compound words: *zygomorphic.* Also, *esp. before a vowel,* **zyg-.** [comb. form of Gk *zygón* YOKE]

zy·go·dac·tyl (zī′gə dak′til, zig′ə-), *adj.* **1.** Also, **zy·go·dac·ty·lous** (zī′gə-dak′tī ləs, zig′ə-). (of a bird) having the toes of each foot arranged in pairs, with two toes in front and two behind. —*n.* **2.** a zygodactyl bird. [ZYGO- + DACTYL] —**zy′go·dac′tyl·ism,** *n.*

Zygodactyl foot

zy·go·gen·e·sis (zī′gō jen′i sis, zig′-ō-), *n.* *Biol.* **1.** the formation of a zygote. **2.** reproduction by means of gametes. [ZYGO- + GENESIS] —**zy·go·ge·net·ic** (zī′gō jə net′ik), *adj.*

zy·go·ma (zī gō′mə, zi-), *n., pl.* **-ma·ta** (-mə tə). *Anat.* **1.** See **zygomatic arch. 2.** the zygomatic process of the temporal bone. **3.** See **zygomatic bone.** [< NL < Gk, equiv. to *zygo(ún)* (to) yoke (see ZYGO-) + *-ma* n. suffix]

zy·go·mat·ic (zī′gə mat′ik, zig′ə-), *Anat.* —*adj.* **1.** of, pertaining to, or situated near the zygoma. —*n.* **2.** See **zygomatic bone.** [*zygomat-* (comb. form of ZYGOMA) + -IC]

zy′gomat′ic arch′, *Anat.* the bony arch below the orbit of the skull that is formed by the union of the zygomatic process of the temporal bone and the temporal process of the zygomatic bone. See diag. under **skull.**

zy′gomat′ic bone′, *Anat.* a bone on each side of the face below the eye, forming the prominence of the cheek and part of the orbit. Also called **malar, malar bone, cheekbone.** See diag. under **skull.**

zy′gomat′ic proc′ess, *Anat.* any of several bony processes that articulate with the zygomatic bone.

zy·go·mor·phic (zī′gə môr′fik, zig′ə-), *adj.* **1.** *Biol.* having bilateral symmetry; monosymmetric. **2.** *Bot.* divisible into similar or symmetrical halves by one plane only, as a flower. Also, **zy′go·mor′phous.** [ZYGO- + -MORPHIC] —**zy′go·mor′phism, zy′go·mor′phy,** *n.*

zy·go·phore (zī′gə fōr′, -fôr′), *n.* (in certain fungi) any of several specialized branches of hyphae, bearing the isogametes that unite to produce a zygospore. [ZYGO- + -PHORE] —**zy·go·phor·ic** (zī′gə fôr′ik, -for′-, zig′ə-), *adj.*

zy·go·phyl·la·ceous (zī′gō fə lā′shəs, zig′ō-), *adj.* belonging to the *Zygophyllaceae,* or bean caper family of plants. [< NL *zygophyll(um)* genus name (see ZYGO-, -PHYLL) + -ACEOUS]

zy·go·phyte (zī′gə fīt′, zig′ə-), *n.* a plant which reproduces by means of zygospores. [ZYGO- + -PHYTE]

zy·gop·ter·an (zī gop′tər ən), *adj.* belonging or pertaining to the suborder *Zygoptera,* comprising the damsel flies. [ZYGO- + Gk *pter(ón)* wing + -AN]

zy·go·sis (zī gō′sis, zi-), *n.* *Biol.* the union of two gametes; conjugation. [< NL < Gk: a yoking. See ZYG-, -OSIS] —**zy·gose** (zī′gōs, zig′ōs), *adj.*

zy·go·spore (zī′gə spōr′, -spôr′, zig′ə-), *n.* *Bot.* a cell formed by fusion of two similar gametes, as in certain algae and fungi. [ZYGO- + SPORE] —**zy·go·spor·ic** (zī′gə spôr′ik, -spor′-, zig′ə-), *adj.*

zy·gote (zī′gōt, zig′ōt), *n.* *Biol.* **1.** the cell produced by the union of two gametes. **2.** the individual developing from such a cell. [< Gk *zygōtós* yoked] —**zy·got·ic** (zī got′ik, zi-), *adj.* —**zy·got′i·cal·ly,** *adv.*

zy·go·tene (zī′gə tēn′, zig′ə-), *n.* *Biol.* the synaptic stage in meiosis, during which homologous chromosomes conjugate. [< F *zygotène,* equiv. to *zygo-* ZYGO- + *-tène* < L *taenia* < Gk *tainía* fillet]

zy·mase (zī′mās), *n.* *Biochem.* an enzyme in yeast that causes the decomposition of sugar into alcohol and carbon dioxide, obtainable in the form of an extract. [ZYM- + -ASE]

zyme (zīm), *n.* *Obs.* the specific principle regarded as the cause of a zymotic disease. Cf. **zymosis.** [< Gk *zýmē* leaven]

zymo-, a learned borrowing from Greek meaning "ferment," "leaven," used in the formation of compound words: *zymology*. Also, *esp. before a vowel*, **zym-**. [comb. form repr. Gk *zȳmē* leaven]

zy·mo·gen (zī′mə jən), *n. Biochem.* any of various substances that may change into an enzyme because of some internal change. Also called **proenzyme, proferment.** [< G; see ZYMO-, -GEN]

zy·mo·gen·e·sis (zī′mə jen′i sis), *n. Biochem.* the change of a zymogen into an enzyme. [ZYMO- + GENESIS]

zy·mo·gen·ic (zī′mə jen′ik), *adj. Biochem.* **1.** of or pertaining to a zymogen. **2.** causing fermentation. Also, **zy·mog·e·nous** (zī moj′ə nəs). [ZYMO- + -GENIC]

zy·mol·o·gy (zī mol′ə jē), *n. Biochem.* the science dealing with fermentation and the action of enzymes; enzymology. [ZYMO- + -LOGY] —**zy·mo·log·ic** (zī′mə-loj′ik), *adj.* —**zy·mol′o·gist,** *n.*

zy·mol·y·sis (zī mol′i sis), *n. Biochem.* **1.** the digestive and fermentative action of enzymes. **2.** fermentation or other hydrolytic reactions produced by an enzyme. [ZYMO- + -LYSIS] —**zy·mo·lyt·ic** (zī′mə lit′ik), *adj.*

zy·mom·e·ter (zī mom′i tər), *n.* an instrument for ascertaining the degree of fermentation. [ZYMO- + -METER]

zy·mo·plas·tic (zī′mō plas′tik), *adj.* producing enzymes. [ZYMO- + -PLASTIC]

zy·mo·sis (zī mō′sis), *n., pl.* **-ses** (-sēz). **1.** an infectious or contagious disease. **2.** *Obs.* a process analogous to fermentation, by which certain infectious and contagious diseases were supposed to be produced. [< NL < Gk. See ZYM-, -OSIS]

zy·mos·then·ic (zī′məs then′ik), *adj.* increasing the activity of an enzyme. [ZYMO- + STHENIC]

zy·mot·ic (zī mot′ik), *adj.* **1.** pertaining to or caused by, or as if by, fermentation. **2.** of or pertaining to zymosis or to zymotic diseases. [< Gk *zymōtik(ós)* causing fermentation] —**zy·mot′i·cal·ly,** *adv.*

zymot′ic disease′, *Obs.* an infectious disease, as smallpox, typhoid fever, etc., which was regarded as due to the presence in the body of a morbific principle acting in a manner analogous to fermentation.

zy·mur·gy (zī′mûr jē), *n.* the branch of chemistry dealing with fermentation, as in winemaking, brewing, distilling, the preparation of yeast, etc. [ZYM- + -URGY]

Zyr·i·an (zir′ē ən), *n.* a Uralic language belonging to the Permian branch and having written documents from the 14th century to the present. Also called **Komi.**

ZZ, zigzag approach.

zZ, at the time; acting. Also, **z.Z.** [< G *zur Zeit*]

zz, zigzag.

Zz., ginger. Also, **zz.** [< L *zingiber*]

zZt, at this time. [< G *zu Zeit*] Also, **z.Zt.**

ZZZ, (used to represent the sound of a person snoring.)

PRESIDENTS OF THE UNITED STATES

Name	Born	Died	Birthplace	Residence	Religious Affiliation	Party	Dates in Office	Wife's Name	Wife's Dates	Children
1. George Washington	Feb. 22, 1732	Dec. 14, 1799	Westmoreland Co., Va.	Va.	Episcopalian	Fed.	1789–1797	Martha Dandridge Custis	1732–1802	0
2. John Adams	Oct. 30, 1735	July 4, 1826	Quincy, Mass.	Mass.	Unitarian	Fed.	1797–1801	Abigail Smith	1744–1818	5
3. Thomas Jefferson	Apr. 13, 1743	July 4, 1826	Shadwell, Va.	Va.	Episcopalian	Rep.*	1801–1809	Martha Wayles Skelton	1748–1782	6
4. James Madison	Mar. 16, 1751	June 28, 1836	Port Conway, Va.	Va.	Episcopalian	Rep.*	1809–1817	Dolly Payne Todd	1768–1849	0
5. James Monroe	Apr. 28, 1758	July 4, 1831	Westmoreland Co., Va.	Va.	Episcopalian	Rep.*	1817–1825	Elizabeth Kortwright	1768–1830	2
6. John Quincy Adams	July 11, 1767	Feb. 23, 1848	Quincy, Mass.	Mass.	Unitarian	Rep.*	1825–1829	Louise Catherine Johnson	1775–1852	4
7. Andrew Jackson	Mar. 15, 1767	June 8, 1845	New Lancaster Co., S.C.	Tenn.	Presbyterian	Dem.	1829–1837	Rachel Donelson Robards	1767–1828	0
8. Martin Van Buren	Dec. 5, 1782	July 24, 1862	Kinderhook, N.Y.	N.Y.	Reformed Dutch	Dem.	1837–1841	Hannah Hoes	1783–1819	4
9. William Henry Harrison†	Feb. 9, 1773	Apr. 4, 1841	Berkeley, Va.	Ohio	Episcopalian	Whig	1841	Anna Symmes	1775–1864	10
10. John Tyler	Mar. 29, 1790	Jan. 18, 1862	Greenway, Va.	Va.	Episcopalian	Whig	1841–1845	[1] Letitia Christian	1790–1842	7
								[2] Julia Gardiner	1820–1889	7
11. James Knox Polk	Nov. 2, 1795	June 15, 1849	Mecklenburg Co., N.C.	Tenn.	Methodist	Dem.	1845–1849	Sarah Childress	1803–1891	0
12. Zachary Taylor†	Nov. 24, 1784	July 9, 1850	Orange Co., Va.	La.	Episcopalian	Whig	1849–1850	Margaret Smith	1788–1852	6
13. Millard Fillmore	Jan. 7, 1800	Mar. 8, 1874	Cayuga Co., N.Y.	N.Y.	Unitarian	Whig	1850–1853	[1] Abigail Powers	1798–1853	2
								[2] Caroline Carmichael McIntosh	1813–1881	0
14. Franklin Pierce	Nov. 23, 1804	Oct. 8, 1869	Hillsboro, N.H.	N.H.	Episcopalian	Dem.	1853–1857	Jane Means Appleton	1806–1863	3
15. James Buchanan	Apr. 23, 1791	June 1, 1868	Mercersburg, Pa.	Pa.	Presbyterian	Dem.	1857–1861	*none*		0
16. Abraham Lincoln†	Feb. 12, 1809	Apr. 15, 1865	Hardin Co., Ky.	Ill.	Nonmember	Rep.‡	1861–1865	Mary Todd	1818–1882	4
17. Andrew Johnson	Dec. 29, 1808	July 31, 1875	Raleigh, N.C.	Tenn.	Nonmember	Dem.‡	1865–1869	Eliza McCardle	1810–1876	5
18. Ulysses Simpson Grant	Apr. 27, 1822	July 23, 1885	Point Pleasant, Ohio	Ill.	Methodist	Rep.	1869–1877	Julia Dent	1826–1902	4
19. Rutherford Birchard Hayes	Oct. 4, 1822	Jan. 17, 1893	Delaware, Ohio	Ohio	Nonmember	Rep.	1877–1881	Lucy Ward Webb	1831–1889	8
20. James Abram Garfield†	Nov. 19, 1831	Sept. 19, 1881	Orange, Ohio	Ohio	Disciples of Christ	Rep.	1881	Lucretia Rudolph	1832–1918	7
21. Chester Alan Arthur	Oct. 5, 1830	Nov. 18, 1886	Fairfield, Vt.	N.Y.	Episcopalian	Rep.	1881–1885	Ellen Lewis Herndon	1837–1880	3
22. Grover Cleveland	Mar. 18, 1837	June 24, 1908	Caldwell, N.J.	N.Y.	Presbyterian	Dem.	1885–1889	Frances Folsom	1864–1947	5
23. Benjamin Harrison	Aug. 20, 1833	Mar. 13, 1901	North Bend, Ohio	Ind.	Presbyterian	Rep.	1889–1893	[1] Caroline Lavinia Scott	1832–1892	2
								[2] Mary Scott Lord Dimmock	1858–1948	1
24. Grover Cleveland	See number 22						1893–1897			
25. William McKinley†	Jan. 29, 1843	Sept. 6, 1901	Niles, Ohio	Ohio	Methodist	Rep.	1897–1901	Ida Saxton	1847–1907	2
26. Theodore Roosevelt	Oct. 27, 1858	Jan. 6, 1919	New York, N.Y.	N.Y.	Reformed Dutch	Rep.	1901–1909	[1] Alice Hathaway Lee	1861–1884	1
								[2] Edith Kermit Carow	1861–1948	5
27. William Howard Taft	Sept. 15, 1857	Mar. 8, 1930	Cincinnati, Ohio	Ohio	Unitarian	Rep.	1909–1913	Helen Herron	1861–1943	3
28. Woodrow Wilson	Dec. 28, 1856	Feb. 3, 1924	Staunton, Va.	N.J.	Presbyterian	Dem.	1913–1921	[1] Ellen Louise Axson	1860–1914	3
								[2] Edith Bolling Galt	1872–1961	0
29. Warren Gamaliel Harding†	Nov. 2, 1865	Aug. 2, 1923	Bloomington Grove, Ohio	Ohio	Baptist	Rep.	1921–1923	Florence Kling De Wolfe	1860–1924	0
30. Calvin Coolidge	July 4, 1872	Jan. 5, 1933	Plymouth, Vt.	Mass.	Congregational	Rep.	1923–1929	Grace A. Goodhue	1879–1957	2
31. Herbert Clark Hoover	Aug. 10, 1874	Oct. 20, 1964	West Branch, Iowa	Calif.	Society of Friends	Rep.	1929–1933	Lou Henry	1875–1944	2
32. Franklin Delano Roosevelt†	Jan. 30, 1882	Apr. 12, 1945	Hyde Park, N.Y.	N.Y.	Episcopalian	Dem.	1933–1945	Anna Eleanor Roosevelt	1884–1962	6
33. Harry S. Truman	May 8, 1884	Dec. 26, 1972	Lamar, Mo.	Mo.	Baptist	Dem.	1945–1953	Elizabeth Virginia Wallace	1885–1982	1
34. Dwight David Eisenhower	Oct. 14, 1890	Mar. 28, 1969	Denison, Tex.	N.Y.	Presbyterian	Rep.	1953–1961	Mamie Geneva Doud	1896–1979	2
35. John Fitzgerald Kennedy†	May 29, 1917	Nov. 22, 1963	Brookline, Mass.	Mass.	Roman Catholic	Dem.	1961–1963	Jacqueline Bouvier	1929–	3
36. Lyndon Baines Johnson	Aug. 27, 1908	Jan. 22, 1973	Johnson City, Tex.	Tex.	Disciples of Christ	Dem.	1963–1969	Claudia Alta Taylor	1912–	2
37. Richard Milhous Nixon§	Jan. 9, 1913		Yorba Linda, Calif.	Calif.	Society of Friends	Rep.	1969–1974	Thelma Patricia Ryan	1913–	2
38. Gerald Rudolph Ford	July 14, 1913		Omaha, Neb.	Mich.	Episcopalian	Rep.	1974–1977	Elizabeth Bloomer	1918–	4
39. James Earl Carter, Jr.	Oct. 1, 1924		Plains, Ga.	Ga.	Baptist	Dem.	1977–1981	Rosalynn Smith	1927–	4
40. Ronald Wilson Reagan	Feb. 6, 1911		Tampico, Ill.	Calif.	Presbyterian	Rep.	1981–1989	[1] Jane Wyman	1914–	2
								[2] Nancy Davis	1923–	2
41. George Herbert Walker Bush	June 12, 1924		Milton, Mass.	Tex.	Episcopalian	Rep.	1989–1993	Barbara Pierce	1925–	6
42. William Clinton	Aug. 19, 1946		Hope, Ark.	Ark.	Baptist	Dem.	1993–	Hillary Rodham	1947–	1

*Now the Democratic party †Died in office ‡Elected on the Union party ticket §Resigned

VICE PRESIDENTS OF THE UNITED STATES

	Name	Born	Died	Birthplace	Residence	Party	Dates in Office	Wife's Name	Children
1.	John Adams	Oct. 30, 1735	July 4, 1826	Quincy, Mass.	Mass.	Fed.	1789–1797	Abigail Smith	5
2.	Thomas Jefferson	Apr. 13, 1743	July 4, 1826	Shadwell, Va.	Va.	Rep.	1797–1801	Martha Wayles Skelton	6
3.	Aaron Burr	Feb. 6, 1756	Sept. 14, 1836	Newark, N.J.	N.Y.	Rep.	1801–1805	Theodosia Bartow Prevost	1
4.	George Clinton†	July 26, 1739	Apr. 20, 1812	Ulster Co., N.Y.	N.Y.	Rep.	1805–1812	Cornelia Tappen	6
5.	Elbridge Gerry†	June 17, 1744	Nov. 23, 1814	Marblehead, Mass.	Mass.	Rep.	1813–1814	Ann Thompson	7
6.	Daniel D. Tompkins	June 21, 1774	June 11, 1825	Scarsdale, N.Y.	N.Y.	Rep.	1817–1825	Hannah Minthorne	7
7.	John C. Calhoun	Mar. 18, 1782	Mar. 31, 1850	Abbeville, S.C.	S.C.	Rep.	1825–1832	Floride Calhoun	9
8.	Martin Van Buren	Dec. 5, 1782	July 24, 1862	Kinderhook, N.Y.	N.Y.	Dem.	1833–1837	Hannah Hoes	4
9.	Richard M. Johnson	Oct. 17, 1781	Nov. 19, 1850	Louisville, Ky.	Ky.	Dem.	1837–1841	*none*	0
10.	John Tyler*	Mar. 29, 1790	Jan. 18, 1862	Greenway, Va.	Va.	Whig	1841	[1] Letitia Christian [2] Julia Gardiner	7, 7
11.	George M. Dallas	July 10, 1792	Dec. 31, 1864	Philadelphia, Pa.	Pa.	Dem.	1845–1849	Sophia Nicklin	0
12.	Millard Fillmore*	Jan. 7, 1800	Mar. 8, 1874	Cayuga Co., N.Y.	N.Y.	Whig	1849–1850	[1] Abigail Powers	2
								[2] Caroline Carmichael McIntosh	0
13.	William R. King†	Apr. 7, 1786	Apr. 18, 1853	Sampson Co., N.C.	Ala.	Dem.	1853	*none*	0
14.	John C. Breckinridge	Jan. 21, 1821	May 17, 1875	Lexington, Ky.	Ky.	Dem.	1857–1861	Mary C. Burch	0
15.	Hannibal Hamlin	Aug. 27, 1809	July 4, 1891	Paris, Me.	Me.	Rep.	1861–1865	[1] Sarah Jane Emery [2] Ellen Vesta Emery	0, 1
16.	Andrew Johnson*	Dec. 29, 1808	July 31, 1875	Raleigh, N.C.	Tenn.	Dem.‡	1865	Eliza McCardle	5
17.	Schuyler Colfax	Mar. 23, 1823	Jan. 13, 1885	New York, N.Y.	Ind.	Rep.	1869–1873	[1] Evelyn Clark [2] Ellen W. Wade	0, 0
18.	Henry Wilson†	Feb. 16, 1812	Nov. 22, 1875	Farmington, N.H.	Mass.	Rep.	1873–1875	Harriet Malvina Howe	1
19.	William A. Wheeler	June 30, 1819	June 4, 1887	Malone, N.Y.	N.Y.	Rep.	1877–1881	Mary King	0
20.	Chester A. Arthur*	Oct. 5, 1830	Nov. 18, 1886	Fairfield, Vt.	N.Y.	Rep.	1881	Ellen Lewis Herndon	3
21.	Thomas A. Hendricks†	Sept. 7, 1819	Nov. 25, 1885	Muskingham Co., Ohio	Ind.	Dem.	1885	Eliza C. Margan	1
22.	Levi P. Morton	May 16, 1824	May 16, 1920	Shoreham, Vt.	N.Y.	Rep.	1889–1893	[1] Lucy Young Kimball	0
								[2] Anna Livingston Read Street	5
23.	Adlai E. Stevenson	Oct. 23, 1835	June 15, 1914	Christian Co., Ky.	Ill.	Dem.	1893–1897	Letitia Green	1
24.	Garret A. Hobart†	June 3, 1844	Nov. 21, 1899	Long Branch, N.J.	N.J.	Rep.	1897–1899	Jennie Tuttle	2
25.	Theodore Roosevelt*	Oct. 27, 1858	Jan. 6, 1919	New York, N.Y.	N.Y.	Rep.	1901	[1] Alice Hathaway Lee	1
								[2] Edith Kermit Carow	5
26.	Charles W. Fairbanks	May 11, 1852	June 4, 1918	Unionville Centre, Ohio	Ind.	Rep.	1905–1909	Cornelia Cole	0
27.	James S. Sherman†	Oct. 24, 1855	Oct. 30, 1912	Utica, N.Y.	N.Y.	Rep.	1909–1912	Carrie Babcock	3
28.	Thomas R. Marshall	Mar. 14, 1854	June 1, 1925	N. Manchester, Ind.	Ind.	Dem.	1913–1921	Lois I. Kimsey	0
29.	Calvin Coolidge*	July 4, 1872	Jan. 5, 1933	Plymouth, Vt.	Mass.	Rep.	1921–1923	Grace A. Goodhue	2
30.	Charles G. Dawes	Aug. 27, 1865	Apr. 23, 1951	Marietta, Ohio	Ill.	Rep.	1925–1929	Caro D. Blymer	4
31.	Charles Curtis	Jan. 25, 1860	Feb. 8, 1936	Topeka, Kan.	Kan.	Rep.	1929–1933	Anna E. Baird	3
32.	John Nance Garner	Nov. 22, 1868	Nov. 7, 1967	Red River Co., Tex.	Tex.	Dem.	1933–1941	Ettie Rheiner	0
33.	Henry Agard Wallace	Oct. 7, 1888	Nov. 18, 1965	Adair Co., Iowa	Iowa	Dem.	1941–1945	Ilo Browne	3
34.	Harry S. Truman*	May 8, 1884	Dec. 26, 1972	Lamar, Mo.	Mo.	Dem.	1945	Elizabeth Virginia Wallace	1
35.	Alben W. Barkley	Nov. 24, 1877	Apr. 30, 1956	Graves Co., Ky.	Ky.	Dem.	1949–1953	[1] Dorothy Brower [2] Jane Hadley	3, 0
36.	Richard M. Nixon	Jan. 9, 1913		Yorba Linda, Calif.	Calif.	Rep.	1953–1961	Thelma Patricia Ryan	2
37.	Lyndon B. Johnson*	Aug. 27, 1908	Jan. 22, 1973	Johnson City, Tex.	Tex.	Dem.	1961–1963	Claudia Alta Taylor	2
38.	Hubert H. Humphrey	May 27, 1911	Jan. 13, 1978	Wallace, S. Dak.	Minn.	Dem.	1965–1969	Muriel Fay Buck	4
39.	Spiro T. Agnew§	Nov. 9, 1918		Baltimore, Md.	Md.	Rep.	1969–1973	Elinor Isobel Judefind	4
40.	Gerald R. Ford‖	July 14, 1913		Omaha, Neb.	Mich.	Rep.	1973–1974	Elizabeth Bloomer	4
41.	Nelson A. Rockefeller¶	July 8, 1908	Jan. 26, 1979	Bar Harbor, Me.	N.Y.	Rep.	1974–1977	[1] Mary Todhunter Clark	5
								[2] Margaretta Fitler Murphy	2
42.	Walter F. Mondale	Jan. 5, 1928		Ceylon, Minn.	Minn.	Dem.	1977–1981	Joan Adams	3
43.	George H. W. Bush*	June 12, 1924		Milton, Mass.	Tex.	Rep.	1981–1989	Barbara Pierce	6
44.	J. Danforth Quayle	Feb. 4, 1947		Indianapolis, Ind.	Ind.	Rep.	1989–1993	Marylin Tucker	3
45.	Albert A. Gore, Jr.	Mar. 31, 1948		Washington, D.C.	Tenn.	Dem.	1993–	Mary Elizabeth ("Tipper") Aitcheson	4

*Succeeded to Presidency †Died in office ‡Elected on the Union party ticket §Resigned ‖Nominated by R. M. Nixon, whom he later succeeded as President ¶Nominated by G. R. Ford

THE DECLARATION OF INDEPENDENCE

IN CONGRESS, JULY 4, 1776.

A DECLARATION BY THE REPRESENTATIVES OF THE UNITED STATES OF AMERICA.

IN GENERAL CONGRESS ASSEMBLED.

When in the Course of human Events, it becomes necessary for one People to dissolve the Political Bands which have connected them with another, and to assume among the Powers of the Earth, the separate and equal Station to which the Laws of Nature and of Nature's God entitle them, a decent Respect to the Opinions of Mankind requires that they should declare the causes which impel them to the Separation.

We hold these Truths to be self-evident, that all Men are created equal, that they are endowed by their Creator with certain unalienable Rights, that among these are Life, Liberty, and the Pursuit of Happiness—That to secure these Rights, Governments are instituted among Men, deriving their just Powers from the Consent of the Governed, that whenever any Form of Government becomes destructive of these Ends, it is the Right of the People to alter or to abolish it, and to institute new Government, laying its Foundation on such Principles, and organizing its Powers in such Form, as to them shall seem most likely to effect their Safety and Happiness. Prudence, indeed, will dictate that Governments long established should not be changed for light and transient Causes; and accordingly all Experience hath shewn, that Mankind are more disposed to suffer, while Evils are sufferable, than to right themselves by abolishing the Forms to which they are accustomed. But when a long Train of Abuses and Usurpations, pursuing invariably the same Object, evinces a Design to reduce them under absolute Despotism, it is their Right, it is their Duty, to throw off such Government, and to provide new Guards for their future Security. Such has been the patient Sufferance of these Colonies; and such is now the Necessity which constrains them to alter their former Systems of Government. The History of the present King of Great-Britain is a History of repeated Injuries and Usurpations, all having in direct Object the Establishment of an absolute Tyranny over these States. To prove this, let Facts be submitted to a candid World.

He has refused his Assent to Laws, the most wholesome and necessary for the public Good.

He has forbidden his Governors to pass Laws of immediate and pressing Importance, unless suspended in their Operation till his Assent should be obtained; and when so suspended, he has utterly neglected to attend to them.

He has refused to pass other Laws for the Accommodation of large Districts of People, unless those People would relinquish the Right of Representation in the Legislature, a Right inestimable to them, and formidable to Tyrants only.

He has called together Legislative Bodies at Places unusual, uncomfortable, and distant from the Depository of their public Records, for the sole Purpose of fatiguing them into Compliance with his Measures.

He has dissolved Representative Houses repeatedly, for opposing with manly Firmness his Invasions on the Rights of the People.

He has refused for a long Time, after such Dissolutions, to cause others to be elected; whereby the Legislative Powers, incapable of Annihilation, have returned to the People at large for their exercise; the State remaining in the mean time exposed to all the Dangers of Invasion from without, and Convulsions within.

He has endeavoured to prevent the Population of these States; for that Purpose obstructing the Laws for Naturalization of Foreigners; refusing to pass others to encourage their Migrations hither, and raising the Conditions of new Appropriations of Lands.

He has obstructed the Administration of Justice, by refusing his Assent to Laws for establishing Judiciary Powers.

He has made Judges dependent on his Will alone, for the Tenure of their Offices, and the Amount and Payment of their Salaries.

He has erected a Multitude of new Offices, and sent hither Swarms of Officers to harrass our People, and eat out their Substance.

He has kept among us, in Times of Peace, Standing Armies, without the consent of our Legislatures.

He has affected to render the Military independent of and superior to the Civil Power.

He has combined with others to subject us to a Jurisdiction foreign to our Constitution, and unacknowledged by our Laws; giving his Assent to their Acts of pretended Legislation:

For quartering large Bodies of Armed Troops among us:

For protecting them, by a mock Trial, from Punishment for any Murders which they should commit on the Inhabitants of these States:

For cutting off our Trade with all Parts of the World:

For imposing Taxes on us without our Consent:

For depriving us, in many Cases, of the Benefits of Trial by Jury:

For transporting us beyond Seas to be tried for pretended Offences:

For abolishing the free System of English Laws in a neighbouring Province, establishing therein an arbitrary Government, and enlarging its Boundaries, so as to render it at once an Example and fit Instrument for introducing the same absolute Rule into these Colonies:

For taking away our Charters, abolishing our most valuable Laws, and altering fundamentally the Forms of our Governments:

For suspending our own Legislatures, and declaring themselves invested with Power to legislate for us in all Cases whatsoever.

He has abdicated Government here, by declaring us out of his Protection and waging War against us.

He has plundered our Seas, ravaged our Coasts, burnt our Towns, and destroyed the Lives of our People.

He is, at this Time, transporting large Armies of foreign Mercenaries to compleat the Works of Death, Desolation, and Tyranny, already begun with circumstances of Cruelty and Perfidy, scarcely paralleled in the most barbarous Ages, and totally unworthy the Head of a civilized Nation.

He has constrained our fellow Citizens taken Captive on the high Seas to bear Arms against their Country, to become the Executioners of their Friends and Brethren, or to fall themselves by their Hands.

He has excited domestic Insurrections amongst us, and has endeavoured to bring on the Inhabitants of our Frontiers, the merciless Indian Savages, whose known Rule of Warfare, is an undistinguished Destruction, of all Ages, Sexes and Conditions.

In every stage of these Oppressions we have Petitioned for Redress in the most humble Terms: Our repeated Petitions have been answered only by repeated Injury. A Prince, whose Character is thus marked by every act which may define a Tyrant, is unfit to be the Ruler of a free People.

Nor have we been wanting in Attentions to our British Brethren. We have warned them from Time to Time of Attempts by their Legislature to extend an unwarrantable Jurisdiction over us. We have reminded them of the Circumstances of our Emigration and Settlement here. We have appealed to their native Justice and Magnanimity, and we have conjured them by the Ties of our common Kindred to disavow these Usurpations, which, would inevitably interrupt our Connections and Correspondence. They too have been deaf to the Voice of Justice and of Consanguinity. We must, therefore, acquiesce in the Necessity, which denounces our Separation, and hold them, as we hold the rest of Mankind, Enemies in War, in Peace, Friends.

We, therefore, the Representatives of the United States of America, in General Congress, Assembled, appealing to the Supreme Judge of the World for the Rectitude of our Intentions, do, in the Name, and by Authority of the good People of these Colonies, solemnly Publish and Declare, That these United Colonies are, and of Right ought to be, Free and Independent States; that they are absolved from all Allegiance to the British Crown, and that all political Connection between them and the State of Great-Britain, is and ought to be totally dissolved; and that as Free and Independent States, they have full Power to levy War, conclude Peace, contract Alliances, establish Commerce, and to do all other Acts and Things which Independent States may of right do. And for the support of this Declaration, with a firm Reliance on the Protection of divine Providence, we mutually pledge to each other our Lives, our Fortunes, and our sacred Honor.

Signed by Order and in Behalf *of the* Congress,
JOHN HANCOCK, President.

Attest.
CHARLES THOMSON, Secretary.

[Signers of the Declaration of Independence[1]]

John Hancock

NEW-HAMPSHIRE. *Josiah Bartlett, Wm. Whipple, Matthew Thornton.*[2]

MASSACHUSETTS-BAY. *Saml. Adams, John Adams, Robt. Treat Paine, Elbridge Gerry.*

RHODE-ISLAND AND PROVIDENCE, &C. *Step. Hopkins, William Ellery.*

CONNECTICUT. *Roger Sherman, Saml. Huntington, Wm. Williams, Oliver Wolcott.*

NEW-YORK. *Wm. Floyd, Phil. Livingston, Frans. Lewis, Lewis Morris.*

NEW-JERSEY. *Richd. Stockton, Jno. Witherspoon, Fras. Hopkinson, John Hart, Abra. Clark.*

PENNSYLVANIA. *Robt. Morris, Benjamin Rush, Benja. Franklin, John Morton, Geo. Clymer, Jas. Smith, Geo. Taylor, James Wilson, Geo. Ross.*

DELAWARE. *Cæsar Rodney, Geo. Read, (Tho M:Kean.)*[3]

MARYLAND. *Samuel Chase, Wm. Paca, Thos. Stone, Charles Carroll, of Carrollton.*

VIRGINIA. *George Wythe, Richard Henry Lee, Th. Jefferson, Benja. Harrison, Thos. Nelson, jr. Francis Lightfoot Lee, Carter Braxton.*

NORTH-CAROLINA. *Wm. Hooper, Joseph Hewes, John Penn.*

SOUTH-CAROLINA. *Edward Rutledge, Thos. Heyward, junr. Thomas Lynch, junr. Arthur Middleton.*

GEORGIA. *Button Gwinnett, Lyman Hall, Geo. Walton.*

1. Based upon the authenticated list printed by order of Congress on January 18, 1777.
2. Matthew Thornton's name was signed on the engrossed copy following the Connecticut Members, but was transferred in the printed copy to its proper place with the other New Hampshire Members.
3. Thomas KcKean's name was not included in the list of signers printed by order of Congress on January 18, 1977, as he did not sign the engrossed copy until some time thereafter, probably in 1781.

THE CONSTITUTION OF THE UNITED STATES

We, the People of the United States, in order to form a more perfect union, establish justice, insure domestic tranquility, provide for the common defence, promote the general welfare, and secure the blessings of liberty to ourselves and our posterity, do ordain and establish this Constitution for the United States of America.

ARTICLE I.

Sect. 1. ALL legislative powers herein granted shall be vested in a Congress of the United States, which shall consist of a Senate and House of Representatives.

Sect. 2. The House of Representatives shall be composed of members chosen every second year by the people of the several states, and the electors in each state shall have the qualifications requisite for electors of the most numerous branch of the state legislature.

No person shall be a representative who shall not have attained to the age of twenty-five years, and been seven years a citizen of the United States, and who shall not, when elected, be an inhabitant of that state in which he shall be chosen.

[Representatives and direct taxes shall be apportioned among the several states which may be included within this Union, according to their respective numbers, which shall be determined by adding to the whole number of free persons, including those bound to service for a term of years, and excluding Indians not taxed, three-fifths of all other persons.][1] The actual enumeration shall be made within three years after the first meeting of the Congress of the United States, and within every subsequent term of ten years, in such manner as they shall by law direct. The number of representatives shall not exceed one for every thirty thousand, but each state shall have at least one representative; and until such enumeration shall be made, the state of New-Hampshire shall be entitled to chuse three, Massachusetts eight, Rhode-Island and Providence Plantations one, Connecticut five, New-York six, New-Jersey four, Pennsylvania eight, Delaware one, Maryland six, Virginia ten, North-Carolina five, South-Carolina five, and Georgia three.

When vacancies happen in the representation from any state, the Executive authority thereof shall issue writs of election to fill such vacancies.

The House of Representatives shall chuse their Speaker and other officers; and shall have the sole power of impeachment.

Sect. 3. The Senate of the United States shall be composed of two senators from each state, [chosen by the legislature thereof,][2] for six years; and each senator shall have one vote.

Immediately after they shall be assembled in consequence of the first election, they shall be divided as equally as may be into three classes. The seats of the senators of the first class shall be vacated at the expiration of the second year, of the second class at the expiration of the fourth year, and of the third class at the expiration of the sixth year, so that one-third may be chosen every second year; [and if vacancies happen by resignation, or otherwise, during the recess of the Legislature of any state, the Executive thereof may make temporary appointments until the next meeting of the Legislature, which shall then fill such vacancies.][3]

No person shall be a senator who shall not have attained to the age of thirty years, and been nine years a citizen of the United States, and who shall not, when elected, be an inhabitant of that state for which he shall be chosen.

The Vice-President of the United States shall be President of the senate, but shall have no vote, unless they be equally divided.

The Senate shall chuse their other officers, and also a President pro tempore, in the absence of the Vice-President, or when he shall exercise the office of President of the United States.

The Senate shall have the sole power to try all impeachments. When sitting for that purpose, they shall be on oath or affirmation. When the President of the United States is tried, the Chief Justice shall preside: And no person shall be convicted without the concurrence of two-thirds of the members present.

Judgment in cases of impeachment shall not extend further than to removal from office, and disqualification to hold and enjoy any office of honor, trust or profit under the United States; but the party convicted shall nevertheless be liable and subject to indictment, trial, judgment and punishment, according to law.

Sect. 4. The times, places and manner of holding elections for senators and representatives, shall be prescribed in each state by the legislature thereof; but the Congress may at any time by law make or alter such regulations, except as to the places of chusing Senators.

The Congress shall assemble at least once in every year, and such meeting shall [be on the first Monday in December,][4] unless they shall by law appoint a different day.

Sect. 5. Each house shall be the judge of the elections, returns and qualifications of its own members, and a majority of each shall constitute a quorum to do business; but a smaller number may adjourn from day to day, and may be authorized to compel the attendance of absent members, in such manner, and under such penalties as each house may provide.

Each house may determine the rules of its proceedings, punish its members for disorderly behaviour, and, with the concurrence of two-thirds, expel a member.

Each house shall keep a journal of its proceedings, and from time to time publish the same, excepting such parts as may in their judgment require secrecy; and the yeas and nays of the members of either house on any question shall, at the desire of one-fifth of those present, be entered on the journal.

Neither house, during the session of Congress, shall, without the consent of the other, adjourn for more than three days, nor to any other place than that in which the two houses shall be sitting.

Sect. 6. The senators and representatives shall receive a compensation for their services, to be ascertained by law, and paid out of the treasury of the United States. They shall in all cases, except treason, felony and breach of the peace, be privileged from arrest during their attendance at the session of their respective houses, and in going to and returning from the same; and for any speech or debate in either house, they shall not be questioned in any other place.

No senator or representative shall, during the time for which he was elected, be appointed to any civil office under the authority of the United States, which shall have been created, or the emoluments whereof shall have been encreased during such time; and no person holding any office under the United States, shall be a member of either house during his continuance in office.

Sect. 7. All bills for raising revenue shall originate in the house of representatives; but the senate may propose or concur with amendments as on other bills.

Every bill which shall have passed the house of representatives and the senate, shall, before it become a law, be presented to the president of the United States; if he approve he shall sign it, but if not he shall return it, with his objections to that house in which it shall have originated, who shall enter the objections at large on their journal, and proceed to reconsider it. If after such reconsideration two-thirds of that house shall agree to pass the bill, it shall be sent, together with the objections, to the other house, by which it shall likewise be reconsidered, and if approved by two-thirds of that house, it shall become a law. But in all such cases the votes of both houses shall be determined by yeas and nays, and the names of the persons voting for and against the bill shall be entered on the journal of each house respectively. If any bill shall not be returned by the President within ten days (Sundays excepted) after it shall have been presented to him, the same shall be a law, in like manner as if he had signed it, unless the Congress by their adjournment prevent its return, in which case it shall not be a law.

Every order, resolution, or vote to which the concurrence of the Senate and House of Representatives may be necessary (except on a question of adjournment) shall be presented to the President of the United States; and before the same shall take effect, shall be approved by him, or, being disapproved by him, shall be repassed by two-thirds of the Senate and House of Representatives, according to the rules and limitations prescribed in the case of a bill.

Sect. 8. The Congress shall have power

To lay and collect taxes, duties, imposts and excises, to pay the debts and provide for the common defence and general welfare of the United States; but all duties, imposts and excises shall be uniform throughout the United States;

To borrow money on the credit of the United States;

To regulate commerce with foreign nations, and among the several states, and with the Indian tribes;

To establish an uniform rule of naturalization, and uniform laws on the subject of bankruptcies throughout the United States;

To coin money, regulate the value thereof, and of foreign coin, and fix the standard of weights and measures;

To provide for the punishment of counterfeiting the securities and current coin of the United States;

To establish post offices and post roads;

To promote the progress of science and useful arts, by securing for limited times to authors and inventors the exclusive right to their respective writings and discoveries;

To constitute tribunals inferior to the supreme court;

To define and punish piracies and felonies committed on the high seas, and offences against the law of nations;

To declare war, grant letters of marque and reprisal, and make rules concerning captures on land and water;

To raise and support armies, but no appropriation of money to that use shall be for a longer term than two years;

To provide and maintain a navy;

To make rules for the government and regulation of the land and naval forces;

To provide for calling forth the militia to execute the laws of the union, suppress insurrections and repel invasions;

To provide for organizing, arming, and disciplining, the militia, and for governing such part of them as may be employed in the service of the United States, reserving to the States respectively, the appointment of the officers, and the authority of training the militia according to the discipline prescribed by Congress;

To exercise exclusive legislation in all cases whatsoever, over such district (not exceeding ten miles square) as may, by cession of particular States, and the acceptance of Congress, become the seat of the government of the United States, and to exercise like authority over all places purchased by the consent of the legislature of the state in which the same shall be, for the erection of forts, magazines, arsenals, dock-yards, and other needful buildings;—And

To make all laws which shall be necessary and proper for carrying into execution the foregoing powers, and all other powers vested by this constitution in the government of the United States, or in any department or officer thereof.

Sect. 9. The migration or importation of such persons as any of the states now existing shall think proper to admit, shall not be prohibited by the Congress prior to the year one thousand eight hundred and eight, but a tax or duty may be imposed on such importation, not exceeding ten dollars for each person.

The privilege of the writ of habeas corpus shall not be suspended, unless when in cases of rebellion or invasion the public safety may require it.

No bill of attainder or ex post facto law shall be passed.

No capitation, or other direct, tax shall be laid, unless in proportion to the census or enumeration herein before directed to be taken.[5]

No tax or duty shall be laid on articles exported from any state. No preference shall be given any regulation of commerce or revenue to the ports of one state over those of another: nor shall vessels bound to, or from, one state, be obliged to enter, clear, or pay duties in another.

No money shall be drawn from the treasury, but in consequence of appropriations made by law; and a regular statement and account of the receipts and expenditures of all public money shall be published from time to time.

No title of nobility shall be granted by the United States:—And no person holding any office of profit or trust under them, shall, without the consent of the Congress, accept of any present, emolument, office, or title, of any kind whatever, from any king, prince, or foreign state.

Sect. 10. No state shall enter into any treaty, alliance, or confederation; grant letters of marque and reprisal; coin money; emit bills of credit; make any thing but gold and silver coin a tender in payment of debts; pass any bill of attainder, ex post facto law, or law impairing the obligation of contracts, or grant any title of nobility.

No state shall, without the consent of the Congress, lay any imposts or duties on imports or exports, except what may be absolutely necessary for executing its inspection laws; and the net produce of all duties and imposts, laid by any state on imports or exports, shall be for the use of the Treasury of the United States; and all such laws shall be subject to the revision and controul of the Congress. No state shall, without the consent of Congress, lay any duty of tonnage, keep troops, or ships of war in time of peace, enter into any agreement or compact with another state, or with a foreign power, or engage in war, unless actually invaded, or in such imminent danger as will not admit of delay.

II.

Sect. 1. The executive power shall be vested in a president of the United States of America. He shall hold his office during the term of four years, and, together with the vice-president, chosen for the same term, be elected as follows.

1. The part enclosed by brackets was changed by section 2 of Amendment XIV.
2. The clause enclosed by brackets was changed by clause 1 of Amendment XVII.
3. The part enclosed by brackets was changed by clause 2 of Amendment XVII.
4. The clause enclosed by brackets was changed by section 2 of Amendment XX.
5. *See also* Amendment XVI.

Each state shall appoint, in such manner as the legislature therof may direct, a number of electors, equal to the whole number of senators and representatives to which the state may be entitled in the Congress: but no senator or representative, or person holding an office of trust or profit under the United States, shall be appointed an elector.

[The electors shall meet in their respective states, and vote by ballot for two persons, of whom one at least shall not be an inhabitant of the same state with themselves. And they shall make a list of all the presons voted for, and of the number of votes for each; which list they shall sign and certify, and transmit sealed to the seat of the government of the United States, directed to the president of the senate. The president of the senate shall, in the presence of the senate and house of representatives, open all the certificates, and the votes shall then be counted. The person having the greatest number of votes shall be the president, if such number be a majority of the whole number of electors appointed; and if there be more than one who have such majority, and have an equal number of votes, then the house of representatives shall immediately chuse by ballot one of them for president; and if no person have a majority, then from the five highest on the list the said house shall in like manner chuse the president. But in chusing the president, the votes shall be taken by states, the representation from each state having one vote; a quorum for this purpose shall consist of a member or members from two-thirds of the states and a majority of all the states shall be necessary to a choice. In every case, after the choice of the president, the person having the greatest number of votes of the electors shall be the vice-president. But if there should remain two or more who have equal votes, the senate shall chuse from them by ballot the vice-president.][6]

The Congress may determine the time of chusing the electors, and the day on which they shall give their votes; which day shall be the same throughout the United States.

No person except a natural born citizen, or a citizen of the United States, at the time of the adoption of this constitution, shall be eligible to the office of president; neither shall any person be eligible to that office who shall not have attained to the age of thirty-five years, and been fourteen years a resident within the United States.

In case of the removal of the president from office, or of his death, resignation, or inability to discharge the powers and duties of the said office, the same shall devolve on the vice-president and the Congress may by law provide for the case of removal, death, resignation or inability, both of the president and vice-president, declaring what officer shall then act as president, and such officer shall act accordingly, until the disability be removed, or a president shall be elected.

The president shall, at stated times, receive for his services, a compensation, which shall neither be encreased nor diminished during the period for which he shall have been elected, and he shall not receive within that period any other emolument from the United States, or any of them.

Before he enter on the execution of his office, he shall take the following oath or affirmation:

"I do solemnly swear (or affirm) that I will faithfully execute the office of president of the United States, and will to the best of my ability, preserve, protect and defend the constitution of the United States."

Sect. 2. The president shall be commander in chief of the army and navy of the United States, and of the militia of the several States, when called into the actual service of the United States; he may require the opinion, in writing, of the principal officer in each of the executive departments, upon any subject relating to the duties of their respective offices, and he shall have power to grant reprieves and pardons for offences against the United States, except in cases of impeachment.

He shall have power, by and with the advice and consent of the senate, to make treaties, provided two-thirds of the senators present concur; and he shall nominate, and by and with the advice and consent of the senate, shall appoint ambassadors, other public ministers and consuls, judges of the supreme court, and all other officers of the United States, whose appointments are not herein otherwise provided for, and which shall be established by law. But the Congress may by law vest the appointment of such inferior officers, as they think proper, in the president alone, in the courts of law, or in the heads of departments.

The president shall have power to fill up all vacancies that may happen during the recess of the senate, by granting commissions which shall expire at the end of their next session.

Sect. 3. He shall from time to time give to the Congress information of the state of the union, and recommend to their consideration such measures as he shall judge necessary and expedient; he may, on extraordinary occasions, convene both houses, or either of them, and in case of disagreement between them, with respect to the time of adjournment, he may adjourn them to such time as he shall think proper; he shall receive ambassadors and other public ministers; he shall take care that the laws be faithfully executed, and shall commission all the officers of the United States.

Sect. 4. The president, vice-president and all civil officers of the United States, shall be removed from office on impeachment for, and conviction of, treason, bribery, or other high crimes and misdemeanors.

III.

Sect. 1. The judicial power of the United States, shall be vested in one supreme court, and in such inferior courts as the Congress may from time to time ordain and establish. The judges, both of the supreme and inferior courts, shall hold their offices during good behaviour, and shall, at stated times, receive for their services, a compensation, which shall not be diminished during their continuance in office.

Sect. 2. The judicial power shall extend to all cases, in law and equity, arising under this constitution, the laws of the United States, and treaties made, or which shall be made, under their authority; to all cases affecting ambassadors, other public ministers and consuls; to all cases of admiralty and maritime jurisdiction; to controversies to which the United States shall be a party; to controversies between two or more States, between a state and citizens of another state,[7] between citizens of different States, between citizens of the same state claiming lands under grants of different States, and between a state, or the citizens thereof, and foreign States, citizens or subjects.

In all cases affecting ambassadors, other public ministers and consuls, and those in which a state shall be party, the supreme court shall have original jurisdiction. In all the other cases before mentioned, the supreme court shall have appellate jurisdiction, both as to law and fact, with such exceptions, and under such regulations as the Congress shall make.

The trial of all crimes, except in cases of impeachment, shall be by jury; and such trial shall be held in the state where the said crimes shall have been committed; but when not committed within any state, the trial shall be at such place or places as the Congress may by law have directed.

Sect. 3. Treason against the United States, shall consist only in levying war against them, or in adhering to their enemies, giving them aid and comfort. No person shall be convicted of treason unless on the testimony of two witnesses to the same overt act, or on confession in open court.

The Congress shall have power to declare the punishment of treason, but no attainder of treason shall work corruption of blood, or forfeiture except during the life of the person attainted.

IV.

Sect. 1. Full faith and credit shall be given in each state to the public acts, records, and judicial proceedings of every other state. And the Congress may by general laws prescribe the manner in which such acts, records and proceedings shall be proved, and the effect thereof.

Sect. 2. The citizens of each state shall be entitled to all privileges and immunities of citizens in the several states.

A person charged in any state with treason, felony, or other crime, who shall flee from justice and be found in another state, shall, on demand of the executive authority of the state from which he fled, be delivered up, to be removed to the state having jurisdiction of the crime.

[No person held to service or labour in one state, under the laws thereof, escaping into another, shall, in consequence of any law or regulation therein, be discharged from such service or labour, but shall be delivered up on claim of the party to whom such service or labour may be due.][8]

Sect. 3. New states may be admitted by the Congress into this union; but no new state shall be formed or erected within the jurisdiction of any other state; nor any state be formed by the junction of two or more states, or parts of states, without the consent of the legislatures of the states concerned as well as of the Congress.

The Congress shall have power to dispose of and make all needful rules and regulations respecting the territory or other property belonging to the United States; and nothing in this Constitution shall be so construed as to prejudice any claims of the United States, or of any particular state.

Sect. 4. The United States shall guarantee to every state in this union a Republican form of government, and shall protect each of them against invasion; and on application of the legislature, or of the executive (when the legislature cannot be convened) against domestic violence.

V.

The Congress, whenever two-thirds of both houses shall deem it necessary, shall propose amendments to this constitution, or, on the application of the legislatures of two-thirds of the several states, shall call a convention for proposing amendments, which, in either case, shall be valid to all intents and purposes, as part of this constitution, when ratified by the legislatures of three-fourths of the several states, or by conventions in three-fourths thereof, as the one or the other mode of ratification may be proposed by the Congress; Provided, that no amendment which may be made prior to the year one thousand eight[9] hundred and eight shall in any manner affect the first and fourth clauses in the ninth section of the first article; and that no state, without its consent, shall be deprived of its equal suffrage in the senate.

VI.

All debts contracted and engagements entered into, before the adoption of this Constitution, shall be as valid against the United States under this Constitution, as under the confederation.

This constitution, and the laws of the United States which shall be made in pursuance thereof; and all treaties made, or which shall be made, under the authority of the United States, shall be the supreme law of the land; and the judges in every state shall be bound thereby, any thing in the constitution or laws of any state to the contrary notwithstanding.

The senators and representatives beforementioned, and the members of the several state legislatures, and all executive and judicial officers, both of the United States and of the several States, shall be bound by oath or affirmation, to support this constitution; but no religious test shall ever be required as a qualification to any office or public trust under the United States.

VII.

The ratification of the conventions of nine States, shall be sufficient for the establishment of this constitution between the States so ratifying the same.

Done in Convention, by the unanimous consent of the States present, the seventeenth day of September, in the year of our Lord one thousand seven hundred and eighty-seven, and of the Independence of the United States of America the twelfth. In witness whereof we have hereunto subscribed our Names.

George Washington, President,
And Deputy from Virginia.

NEW-HAMPSHIRE. *John Langdon, Nicholas Gilman.*

MASSACHUSETTS. *Nathaniel Gorham, Rufus King.*

CONNECTICUT. *William Samuel Johnson, Roger Sherman.*

NEW-YORK. *Alexander Hamilton.*

NEW-JERSEY *William Livingston, David Brearley, William Paterson, Jonathan Dayton.*

PENNSYLVANIA. *Benjamin Franklin, Thomas Mifflin, Robert Morris, George Clymer, Thomas Fitzsimons, Jared Ingersoll, James Wilson, Gouverneur Morris.*

DELAWARE. *George Read, Gunning Bedford, Junior, John Dickinson, Richard Bassett, Jacob Broom.*

MARYLAND. *James M'Henry, Daniel of St. Tho. Jenifer, Daniel Carrol.*

VIRGINIA. *John Blair, James Madison, Junior.*

NORTH-CAROLINA. *William Blount, Richard Dobbs Spaight, Hugh Williamson.*

SOUTH-CAROLINA. *John Rutledge, Charles Cotesworth Pinckney, Charles Pinckney, Pierce Butler.*

GEORGIA. *William Few, Abraham Baldwin.*

Attest, *William Jackson,* SECRETARY.

6. This paragraph has been superseded by Amendment XII.
7. This clause has been affected by Amendment XI.
8. This paragraph has been superseded by Amendment XIII.
9. Misprinted "seven" in the original broadside of September 17, 1787, when the figures of the preceding draft were spelled out. Corrected by Dunlap & Claypoole in their Pennsylvania Packet reprint of September 19, 1787. It was the only error of text in the original print. Correct in engrossed copy.

Articles in addition to, and Amendment of the Constitution of the United States of America, proposed by Congress, and ratified by the Legislatures[10] *of the several States, pursuant to the fifth Article of the original Constitution.*

ARTICLE [I][11]

Congress shall make no law respecting an establishment of religion, or prohibiting the free exercise thereof; or abridging the freedom of speech, or of the press; or the right of the people peaceably to assemble, and to petition the Government for a redress of grievances.

ARTICLE [II]

A well regulated Militia, being necessary to the sceurity of a free State, the right of the people to keep and bear Arms, shall not be infringed.

ARTICLE [III]

No Soldier shall, in time of peace be quartered in any house, without the consent of the Owner, nor in time of war, but in a manner to be prescribed by law.

ARTICLE [IV]

The right of the people to be secure in their persons, houses, papers, and effects, against unreasonable searches and seizures, shall not be violated, and no Warrants shall issue, but upon probable cause, supported by Oath or affirmation, and particularly describing the place to be searched, and the persons or things to be seized.

ARTICLE [V]

No person shall be held to answer for a capital, or otherwise infamous crime, unless on a presentment or indictment of a Grand Jury, except in cases arising in the land or naval forces, or in the Militia, when in actual service in time of War or public danger; nor shall any person be subject for the same offence to be twice put in jeopardy of life or limb; nor shall be compelled in any criminal case to be a witness against himself, nor be deprived of life, liberty, or property, without due process of law; nor shall private property be taken for public use, without just compensation.

ARTICLE [VI]

In all criminal prosecutions, the accused shall enjoy the right to a speedy and public trial, by an impartial jury of the State and district wherein the crime shall have been committed, which district shall have been previously ascertained by law, and to be informed of the nature and cause of the accusation; to be confronted with the witnesses against him; to have compulsory process for obtaining witnesses in his favor, and to have the Assistance of Counsel for his defence.

ARTICLE [VII]

In Suits at common law, where the value in controversy shall exceed twenty dollars, the right of trial by jury shall be preserved, and no fact tried by a jury, shall be otherwise reexamined in any Court of the United States, than according to the rules of the common law.

ARTICLE [VIII]

Excessive bail shall not be required, nor excessive fines imposed, nor cruel and unusual punishments inflicted.

ARTICLE [IX]

The enumeration in the Constitution, of certain rights, shall not be construed to deny or disparage others retained by the people.

ARTICLE [X]

The powers not delegated to the United States by the Constitution, nor prohibited by it to the States, are reserved to the States respectively, or to the people.

ARTICLE [XI][12]

The judicial power of the United States shall not be construed to extend to any suit in law or equity, commenced or prosecuted against one of the United States by Citizens of another State, or by Citizens or Subjects of any Foreign State.

ARTICLE [XII][13]

The Electors shall meet in their respective states, and vote by ballot for President and Vice-President, one of whom, at least, shall not be an inhabitant of the same state with themselves; they shall name in their ballots the person voted for as President, and in distinct ballots the person voted for as Vice-President, and they shall make distinct lists of all persons voted for as President, and of all persons voted for as Vice-President, and of the number of votes for each, which lists they shall sign and certify, and transmit sealed to the seat of the government of the United States, directed to the President of the Senate;—The President of the Senate shall, in the presence of the Senate and House of Representatives, open all the certificates and the votes shall then be counted;—The person having the greatest number of votes for President, shall be the President, if such number be a majority of the whole number of Electors appointed; and if no person have such majority, then from the persons having the highest numbers not exceeding three on the list of those voted for as President, the House of Representatives shall choose immediately, by ballot, the President. But in choosing the President, the votes shall be taken by states, the representation from each state having one vote; a quorum for this purpose shall consist of a member or members from two-thirds of the states, and a majority of all the states shall be necessary to a choice. [And if the House of Representatives shall not choose a President whenever the right of choice shall devolve upon them, before the fourth day of March next following, then the Vice-President shall act as President, as in the case of the death or other constitutional disability of the President.]—[14] The person having the greatest number of votes as Vice-President, shall be the Vice-President, if such number be a majority of the whole number of Electors appointed, and if no person have a majority, then from the two highest numbers on the list, the Senate shall choose the Vice-President; a quorum for the purpose shall consist of two-thirds of the whole number of Senators, and a majority of the whole number shall be necessary to a choice. But no person constitutionally ineligible to the office of President shall be eligible to that of Vice-President of the United States.

ARTICLE XIII[15]

Section 1. Neither slavery nor involuntary servitude, except as a punishment for crime whereof the party shall have been duly convicted, shall exist within the United States, or any place subject to their jurisdiction.

Section 2. Congress shall have power to enforce this article by appropriate legislation.

ARTICLE XIV[16]

Section 1. All persons born or naturalized in the United States, and subject to the jurisdiction thereof, are citizens of the United States and of the State wherein they reside. No State shall make or enforce any law which shall abridge the privileges or immunities of citizens of the United States; nor shall any State deprive any person of life, liberty, or property, without the due process of law; nor deny to any person within its jurisdiction the equal protection of the laws.

Section 2. Representatives shall be apportioned among the several States according to their respective numbers, counting the whole number of persons in each State, excluding Indians not taxed. But when the right to vote at any election for the choice of electors for President and Vice President of the United States, Representatives in Congress, the Executive and Judicial officers of a State, or the members of the Legislature thereof, is denied to any of the male inhabitants of such State, being twenty-one years of age, and citizens of the United States, or in any way abridged, except for participation in rebellion, or other crime, the basis of representation therein shall be reduced in the proportion which the number of such male citizens shall bear to the whole number of male citizens twenty-one years of age in such State.

Section 3. No person shall be a Senator or Representative in Congress, or elector of President and Vice President, or hold any office, civil or military, under the United States, or under any State, who, having previously taken an oath, as a member of Congress, or as an officer of the United States, or as a member of any State legislature, or as an executive or judicial officer of any State, to support the Constitution of the United States, shall have engaged in insurrection or rebellion against the same, or given aid or comfort to the enemies thereof. But Congress may by a vote of two-thirds of each House, remove such disability.

Section 4. The validity of the public debt of the United States, authorized by law, including debts incurred for payment of pensions and bounties for services in suppressing insurrection or rebellion, shall not be questioned. But neither the United States nor any State shall assume or pay any debt or obligation incurred in aid of insurrection or rebellion against the United States, or any claim for the loss or emancipation of any slave; but all such debts, obligations and claims shall be held illegal and void.

Section 5. The Congress shall have power to enforce, by appropriate legislation, the provisions of this article.

ARTICLE XV[17]

Section 1. The right of citizens of the United States to vote shall not be denied or abridged by the United States or by any State on account of race, color, or previous condition of servitude.

Section 2. The Congress shall have power to enforce this article by appropriate legislation.

ARTICLE XVI[18]

The Congress shall have power to lay and collect taxes on incomes, from whatever source derived, without apportionment among the several States, and without regard to any census or enumeration.

ARTICLE [XVII][19]

The Senate of the United States shall be composed of two Senators from each State, elected by the people thereof, for six years; and each Senator shall have one vote. The electors in each State shall have the qualifications requisite for electors of the most numerous branch of the State legislatures.

When vacancies happen in the representation of any State in the Senate, the executive authority of such State shall issue writs of election to fill such vacancies: *Provided*, That the legislature of any State may empower the executive thereof to make temporary appointments until the people fill the vacancies by election as the legislature may direct.

This amendment shall not be so construed as to affect the election or term of any Senator chosen before it becomes valid as part of the Constitution.

ARTICLE [XVIII][20]

[Section 1. After one year from the ratification of this article the manufacture, sale, or transportation of intoxicating liquors within, the importation thereof into, or the exportation therof from the United States and all territory subject to the jurisdiction thereof for beverage purposes is hereby prohibited.

[Sec. 2. The Congress and the several States shall have concurrent power to enforce this article by appropriate legislation.

[Sec. 3. This article shall be inoperative unless it shall have been ratified as an amendment to the Constitution by the legislatures of the several States, as provided in the Constitution, within seven years from the date of the submission hereof to the States by the Congress.]

---

10. The first 20 amendments and the Twenty-second, Twenty-third, and Twenty-fourth Amendments were ratified by State Legislatures. The Twenty-first Amendment, by its terms, was ratified by "conventions in the several States."
11. The first 10 amendments (termed articles), together with 2 others that failed of ratification, were proposed to the several States by resolution of Congress on September 25, 1789. The ratifications were transmitted by the Governors to the President and by him communicated to Congress from time to time. The first 10 amendments were ratified by 11 of the 14 States. Virginia completed the required three fourths by ratification on December 15, 1791, and its action was communicated to Congress by the President on December 30, 1791. The legislatures of Massachusetts, Georgia and Connecticut ratified them on March 2, 1939, March 24, 1939, and April 19, 1939, respectively.
12. The Eleventh Amendment was proposed by resolution of Congress on March 4, 1794. It was declared by the President, in a message to Congress dated January 8, 1798, to have been ratified by three fourths of the several States. Records of the Department of State show that the 11th Amendment was ratified by 13 of the 16 States and rejected by New Jersey and Pennsylvania.
13. The Twelfth Amendment was proposed in lieu of the original third paragraph of section 1 of article II, by resolution of Congress on December 8, 1803. It was declared in a proclamation of the Secretary of State, dated September 25, 1804, to have been ratified by three fourths of the States. Records of the Department of State show that the 12th Amendment was ratified by 12 of the 17 States and rejected by Connecticut and Delaware.
14. The part enclosed by brackets has been superseded by section 3 of Amendment XX.
15. The Thirteenth Amendment was proposed by resolution of Congress which the President approved on February, 1, 1865. It was declared in a proclamation of the Secretary of State, dated December 18, 1865, to have been ratified by 27 States. Subsequent records of the Department of State show that the 13th Amendment was ratified by 7 additional States. It was rejected by Mississippi.
16. The Fourteenth Amendment was proposed by resolution of Congress on June 13, 1866. By a concurrent resolution of Congress adopted July 21, 1868, it was declared to have been ratified by "three fourths and more of the several States of the Union," and the Secretary of State was required duly to promulgate the amendment as a part of the Constitution. He accordingly issued a proclamation, dated July 28, 1868, declaring the amendment to have been ratified by 30 States, "being more than three fourths." Records of the Department of the State show that the 14th Amendment was subsequently ratified by 3 more of the States. It was rejected by Kentucky and New Jersey.
17. The Fifteenth Amendment was proposed by resolution of Congress on February 26, 1869. It was declared in a proclamation of the Secretary of State, dated March 30, 1870, to have been ratified by 29 States, which "constitute three fourths." Records of the Department of State show that the 15th Amendment was subsequently ratified by 6 more of the States. It was rejected by Kentucky and Tennessee.
18. The Sixteenth Amendment was proposed by resolution of Congress on July 12, 1909. It was declared in a proclamation of the Secretary of State, dated February 25, 1913, to have been ratified by 38 States, which "constitute three fourths." Subsequent records of the Department of State show that the 16th Amendment was ratified by 4 more of the States. It was rejected by Connecticut, Rhode Island, and Utah.
19. The Seventeenth Amendment was proposed by resolution of Congress on May 13, 1912. It was declared a proclamation of the Secretary of State, dated May 31, 1913, to have been ratified by 36 States, which "constitute three fourths." Records of the Department of State show that the 17th Amendment was subsequently ratified by 1 more of the States. It was rejected by Utah and Delaware.
20. The Eighteenth Amendment was proposed by resolution of Congress on December 18, 1917. It was declared in a proclamation of the Acting Secretary of State, dated January 29, 1919, to have been ratified by 36 States, which "constitute three fourths." Subsequent records of the Department of State show that the 18th Amendment was ratified by 10 more of the 48 States. It was rejected by Rhode Island. By its own terms the 18th Amendment became effective one year after its ratification, which was consummated on January 16, 1919, and therefore went into effect on January 16, 1920.

    Repeal of the 18th Amendment on December 5, 1933, was proclaimed by the President in his proclamation of that date, when the ratification of the 21st Amendment was certified by the Acting Secretary of State.

ARTICLE [XIX][21]

The right of citizens of the United States to vote shall not be denied or abridged by the United States or by any State on account of sex.

Congress shall have power to enforce this article by appropriate legislation.

ARTICLE [XX][22]

Section 1. The terms of the President and Vice President shall end at noon on the 20th day of January, and the terms of Senators and Representatives at noon on the 3d day of January, of the years in which such terms would have ended if this article had not been ratified; and the terms of their successors shall then begin.

Sec. 2. The Congress shall assemble at least once in every year, and such meeting shall begin at noon on the 3d day of January, unless they shall by law appoint a different day.

Sec. 3. If, at the time fixed for the beginning of the term of the President, the President elect shall have died, the Vice President elect shall become President. If a President shall not have been chosen before the time fixed for the beginning of his term, or if the President elect shall have failed to qualify, then the Vice President elect shall act as President until a President shall have qualified; and the Congress may by law provide for the case wherein neither a President elect nor a Vice President elect shall have qualified, declaring who shall then act as President, or the manner in which one who is to act shall be selected, and such person shall act accordingly until a President or Vice President shall have qualified.

Sec. 4. The Congress may by law provide for the case of the death of any of the persons from whom the House of Representatives may choose a President whenever the right of choice shall have devolved upon them, and for the case of the death of any of the persons from whom the Senate may choose a Vice President whenever the right of choice shall have devolved upon them.

Sec. 5. Sections 1 and 2 shall take effect on the 15th day of October following the ratification of this article.

Sec. 6. This article shall be inoperative unless it shall have been ratified as an amendment to the Constitution by the legislatures of three-fourths of the several States within seven years from the date of its submission.

ARTICLE [XXI][23]

Section 1. The eighteenth article of amendment to the Constitution of the United States is hereby repealed.

Sec. 2. The transportation or importation into any State, Territory, or possession of the United States for delivery or use therein of intoxicating liquors, in violation of the laws thereof, is hereby prohibited.

Sec. 3. This article shall be inoperative unless it shall have been ratified as an amendment to the Constitution by conventions in the several States, as provided in the Constitution, within seven years from the date of the submission hereof to the States by the Congress.

ARTICLE [XXII][24]

Section 1. No person shall be elected to the office of the President more than twice, and no person who has held the office of President, or acted as President, for more than two years of a term to which some other person was elected President shall be elected to the office of the President more than once. But this Article shall not apply to any person holding the office of President when this Article was proposed by the Congress, and shall not prevent any person who may be holding the office of President, or acting as President, during the term within which this Article becomes operative from holding the office of President or acting as President during the remainder of such term.

Sec. 2. This article shall be inoperative unless it shall have been ratified as an amendment to the Constitution by the legislatures of three-fourths of the several States within seven years from the date of its submission to the States by the Congress.

ARTICLE [XXIII][25]

Section 1. The District constituting the seat of Government of the United States shall appoint in such manner as the Congress may direct:

A number of electors of President and Vice President equal to the whole number of Senators and Representatives in Congress to which the District would be entitled if it were a State, but in no event more than the least populous State; they shall be in addition to those appointed by the States, but they shall be considered, for the purposes of the election of President and Vice President, to be electors appointed by a State; and they shall meet in the District and perform such duties as provided by the twelfth article of amendment.

Section 2. The Congress shall have power to enforce this article by appropriate legislation.

ARTICLE [XXIV][26]

Section 1. The right of citizens of the United States to vote in any primary or other election for President or Vice President, for electors for President or Vice President, or for Senator or Representative in Congress, shall not be denied or abridged by the United States or any State by reason of failure to pay any poll tax or other tax.

Section 2. The Congress shall have power to enforce this article by appropriate legislation.

ARTICLE [XXV][27]

Section 1. In case of the removal of the President from office or his death or resignation, the Vice President shall become President.

Section 2. Whenever there is a vacancy in the office of the Vice President, the President shall nominate a Vice President who shall take the office upon confirmation by a majority vote of both houses of Congress.

Section 3. Whenever the President transmits to the President pro tempore of the Senate and the Speaker of the House of Representatives his written declaration that he is unable to discharge the powers and duties of his office, and until he transmits to them a written declaration to the contrary, such powers and duties shall be discharged by the Vice President as Acting President.

Section 4. Whenever the Vice President and a majority of either the principal officers of the executive departments or of such other body as Congress may by law provide, transmit to the President pro tempore of the Senate and the Speaker of the House of Representatives their written declaration that the President is unable to discharge the powers and duties of his office, the Vice President shall immediately assume the powers and duties of the office as acting President.

Thereafter, when the President transmits to the President pro tempore of the Senate and the Speaker of the House of Representatives his written declaration that no inability exists, he shall resume the powers and duties of his office unless the Vice President and a majority of either the principal officers of the executive department or of such other body as Congress may by law provide, transmit within four days to the President pro tempore of the Senate and the Speaker of the House of Representatives their written declaration that the President is unable to discharge the powers and duties of his office. Thereupon Congress shall decide the issue, assembling within 48 hours for that purpose if not in session. If the Congress, within 21 days after receipt of the latter written declaration, or, if Congress is not in session, within 21 days after Congress is required to assemble, determines by two-thirds vote of both houses that the President is unable to discharge the powers and duties of his office, the Vice President shall continue to discharge the same as Acting President; otherwise, the President shall resume the powers and duties of his office.

ARTICLE [XXVI][28]

Section 1. The right of citizens of the United States, who are eighteen years of age or older, to vote shall not be denied or abridged by the United States or by any State on account of age.

Section 2. The Congress shall have the power to enforce this article by appropriate legislation.

---

21. The Nineteenth Amendment was proposed by resolution of Congress on June 4, 1919. It was declared in a proclamation of the Secretary of State, dated August 26, 1920, to have been ratified by 36 States, which "constitute three fourths." Subsequent records of the Department of State show that the 19th Amendment was ratified by 2 more of the 48 States. It was rejected by Georgia, South Carolina, Delaware, Mississippi, Louisiana and Virginia.
22. The Twentieth Amendment was proposed by resolution of Congress on March 2, 1932. It was declared in a proclamation of the Secretary of State, dated February 6, 1933, to have been ratified by 39 States, which "constitute more than the requisite three fourths." Subsequent records of the Department of State show that the 20th Amendment was ratified by all of the 48 States before sections 1 and 2 became effective on October 15, 1933. The other sections of the amendment became effective on Janury 23, 1933, when its ratification was consummated by three fourths of the States.
23. The Twenty-first Amendment was proposed by resolution of Congress on February 20, 1933. It was certified in a proclamation of the Acting Secretary of State dated December 5, 1933, to have been ratified by conventions of 36 States, which "constitute the requisite three fourths of the whole number of States." Subsequent records of the Department of State show that the 21st Amendment was ratified by 1 more State. It was rejected by the convention of South Carolina. North Carolina voted against holding a convention.
24. The Twenty-second Amendment was proposed by resolution of Congress on March 24, 1947. Ratification was completed on February 27, 1951, when the thirty-sixth State (Minnesota) approved the amendment. On March 1, 1951, the Administrator of General Services certified that "the States whose Legislatures have so ratified the said proposed Amendment constitute the requisite three-fourths of the whole number of States in the United States." Records of the General Services Administration show that the 22nd Amendment was subsequently ratified by 5 additional States.
25. The Twenty-third Amendment was proposed by resolution of Congress on June 16, 1960. The Administrator of General Services certified the ratification and adoption of the amendment by three-fourths of the States on April 3, 1961. It was rejected by Arkansas.
26. The Twenty-fourth Amendment was proposed by resolution of Congress on August 27, 1962. It was declared in a Proclamation of the Administrator of General Services dated February 4, 1964, to have been ratified by three fourths of the States. It was rejected by the legislature of Mississippi on December 20, 1962.
27. The Twenty-fifth Amendment to the Constitution was proposed by the Congress on July 6, 1965. It was declared in a certificate of the Administrator of General Services, dated February 23, 1967, to have been ratified by the legislatures of 39 of the 50 States. Ratification was completed on February 10, 1967. The amendment was subsequently ratified by Connecticut, Montana, South Dakota, Ohio, Alabama, North Carolina, Illinois, and Texas.
28. The Twenty-sixth Amendment to the Constitution was proposed by the Ninety-second Congress by Senate Joint Resolution No. 7, which was approved by the Senate on March 10, 1971, and by the House of Representatives on March 23, 1971. It was declared by the Administrator of General Services on July 5, 1971, to have been ratified by the legislatures of 39 of the 50 States.

A MANUAL OF STYLE

FOREWORD

A Manual of Style is based on the rules for grammar and copy presentation recommended and developed by the United States Government Printing Office. Following these principles of good usage and editorial custom, the *Manual* provides a set of formal rules regularly imposed on manuscripts of varying content and composition to give them a common shape and style. Although simple rules of grammar may be—and are in fact—prescribed, the English language itself is infinitely flexible. Not every alternative usage could be included in the *Manual,* but it may easily be used for clarity and confidence in writing of all kinds.

PROOFREADER'S MARKS

Proofreader's marks are indicated as follows:

Mark	Meaning
⊙	Insert period
^	Insert comma
:	Insert colon
;	Insert semicolon
?	Insert question mark
!	Insert exclamation mark
=/	Insert hyphen
∨	Insert apostrophe
	Insert quotation marks
	Insert 1-en dash
	Insert 1-em dash
#	Insert space
ld>	Insert ( ) points of space
shill	Insert shilling
∨	Superior
∧	Inferior
(/)	Parentheses
[/]	Brackets
□	Indent 1 em
	Indent 2 ems
¶	Paragraph
no ¶	No paragraph
tr	Transpose[1]—used in margin
∽	Transpose[2]—used in text
sp	Spell out
ital	Italic—used in margin
———	Italic—used in text
b.f.	Boldface—used in margin
~~	Boldface—used in text
s.c.	Small caps—used in margin
═══	Small caps—used in text
rom.	Roman type
caps.	Caps—used in margin
≡	Caps—used in text
c+sc	Caps & small caps—used in margin
═	Caps & small caps—used in text
l.c.	Lowercase—used in margin
/	Used in text to show deletion or substitution
	Delete
	Delete and close up
w.f.	Wrong font
⁀	Close up
⊐	Move right
⊏	Move left
⊓	Move up
⊔	Move down
‖	Align vertically
=	Align horizontally
][	Center horizontally
	Center vertically
eq.#	Equalize space—used in margin
∨∨∨	Equalize space—used in text
....	Let it stand—used in text
stet.	Let it stand—used in margin
⊗	Letter(s) not clear
run over	Carry over to next line
run back	Carry back to preceding line
out, see copy	Something omitted—see copy
?/?	Question to author to delete[3]
∧	Caret—General indicator used to mark position of error.

[1]In lieu of the traditional mark "tr" used to indicate letter or number transpositions, the striking out of the incorrect letters or numbers and the placement of the correct matter in the margin of the proof is the preferred method of indicating transposition corrections.

[2]Corrections involving more than two characters should be marked by striking out the entire word or number and placing the correct form in the margin. This mark should be reserved to show transposition of words.

[3]The form of any query carried should be such that an answer may be given simply by crossing out the complete query if a negative decision is made or the right-hand (question mark) portion to indicate an affirmative answer.

TYPOGRAPHICAL ERRORS

It does not appear that the earliest printers had any method of correcting errors before the form was on the press. The learned The learned correctors of the first two centuries of printing were notproofreaders in our sense, they where rather what we should term office editors. Their labors were chiefly to see that the proof corresponded to the copy, but that the printed page was correct in its latinity—that the words were there, and that the sense was right. They cared but little about orthography, bad letters, or purely printers errors, and when the text seemed to them wrong they consulted fresh authorities or altered it on their own responsibility. Good proofs in the modern sense, were impossible until professional readers were employed men who had first a printer's education, and then spent many years in the correction of proof. The orthography of English, which for the past century has undergone little change, was very fluctuating until after the publication of Johnson's Dictionary, and capitals, which have been used with considerable regularity for the past 80 years, were previously used on the miss or hit plan. The approach to regularity, so far as we have, may be attributed to the growth of a class of professional proofreaders, and it is to them that we owe the correctness of modern printing. More er ors have been found in the Bible than in any other one work. For many generations it was frequently the case that Bibles were brought out stealthily, from fear of governmental interference. They were frequently printed from imperfect texts, and were often modified to meet the views of those who publised themThe story is related that a certain woman in Germany, who was the wife of a Printer, and had become disgusted with the continual assertions of the superiority of man over woman which she had heard, hurried into the composing room while her husband was at supper and altered a sentence in the Bible, which he was printing, so that it read Narr, instead of Herr, thus making the verse read "And he shall be thy fool" instead of "and he shall be thy lord." The word not was omitted by Barker, the king's printer in England in 1632, in printing the seventh commandment He was fined £3000 on this account.

NOTE.—The system of marking proofs can be made easier by the use of an imaginary vertical line through the center of the type area. The placement of corrections in the left-hand margin for those errors found in the left-hand portion of the proof and in the right-hand margin for right-side errors prevents overcrowding of marks and facilitates corrections.

PUNCTUATION

Punctuation is a device used to clarify the meaning of written or printed language. Well-planned word order requires a minimum of punctuation. The trend toward less punctuation calls for skillful phrasing to avoid ambiguity and to ensure exact interpretation. The *Manual* can only offer general rules of text treatment. A rigid design or pattern of punctuation cannot be laid down, except in broad terms. The adopted style, however, must be consistent and be based on sentence structure.

The general principles governing the use of punctuation are (1) that if it does not clarify the text it should be omitted, and (2) that in the choice and placing of punctuation marks the sole aim should be to bring out more clearly the author's thought. Punctuation should aid in reading and prevent misreading.

Apostrophes and possessives

The possessive case of a singular or plural noun not ending in *s* is formed by adding an apostrophe and *s*. The possessive case of a singular or plural noun ending in *s* or with an *s* sound is formed by adding an apostrophe only.

man's, men's
prince's, princes'
Essex's, Essexes'
Co.'s, Cos.'
hostess', hostesses'
princess', princesses'
Jones', Joneses'
Jesus'
Mars'
Dumas'
Schmitz'

In compound nouns, the *'s* is added to the element nearest the object possessed.

comptroller general's decision
attorneys general's appointments
Mr. Brown of New York's motion
attorney at law's fee
John White, Jr.'s (no comma) account

Joint possession is indicated by placing an apostrophe on the last element of a series, while individual or alternative possession requires the use of an apostrophe on each element of a series.

soldiers and sailors' home
Brown & Nelson's store
men's, women's, and children's clothing
St. Michael's Men's Club
editor's or proofreader's opinion
Carter's or Reagan's administration
Mrs. Smith's and Mrs. Allen's children
the Army's and the Navy's work
master's and doctor's degrees

In the use of an apostrophe in geographic names, firm names, the names of organizations and institutions, and the titles of books, the authentic form is to be followed. (Note use of "St.")

Harpers Ferry; Hells Canyon
Masters, Mates & Pilots' Association
Dentists' Supply Co. of New York
International Ladies' Garment Workers' Union
Freedmen's Hospital
Court of St. James's
St. Peter's Church
St. Elizabeths Hospital
Johns Hopkins University
Hinds' Precedents
but Martha's Vineyard

Generally the apostrophe should not be used after names of countries and other organized bodies ending in *s*, or after words more descriptive than possessive (not indicating personal possession), except when plural does not end in *s*.

United States control
United Nations meeting
Southern States industries
Massachusetts laws
Bureau of Ships report
Actors Equity Association
House of Representatives session
Teamsters Union
editors handbook
syrup producers manual
technicians guide
teachers college
merchants exchange
children's hospital
Young Men's Christian Association
but Veterans' Administration (in conformity with enabling statute)
Congress' attitude

Possessive pronouns do not take an apostrophe.

its ours theirs

Possessive indefinite or impersonal pronouns require an apostrophe.

each other's books
one's home
someone's pen
but somebody else's proposal

The singular possessive case is used in such general terms as the following:

arm's length
attorney's fees
author's alterations
confectioner's sugar
cow's milk
distiller's grain
fuller's earth
miner's inch
printer's ink
traveler's checks
writer's cramp

In addition to illustrating possession, an apostrophe is used to indicate contractions, the omission of figures or letters, and the coined plurals of letters, figures, and symbols.

don't
I've
ne'er
it's (it is) (it has)
class of '92
spirit of '76
three R's
4-H'ers
49'ers
TV'ers
the 1920's *or* the twenties; *not* the '20's *nor* 20's
but age: in her seventies
Btu's
OK's
MC'ing
RIF'ing
RIF'd
RIF's
YMCA's
ABC's
a's; ¶'s; 7's
T's, Y's
2 by 4's (lumber)
but 10s (yarn and thread)
4½s (bonds)
3s (golf)

The apostrophe is omitted in abbreviations, and also in shortened forms of certain other words.

Danl., *not* Dan'l
Sgt., *not* Sg't
phone
coon
possum
Frisco
Halloween
copter
but ma'am

The plural of spelled-out numbers, of words referred to as words, and of words already containing an apostrophe is formed by adding *s* or *es;* but *'s* is added to indicate the plural of words used as words if the omission of the apostrophe would cause difficulty in reading.

twos, threes, sevens
ands, ifs, and buts
ins and outs
ups and downs
whereases and wherefores
yeses and noes
but do's and don'ts
which's and that's

The possessive case is often used in lieu of an objective phrase even though ownership is not involved.

1 day's labor (labor for 1 day)
2 hours' traveltime
a stone's throw
2 weeks' pay
5 or 10 billion dollars' worth
for charity's sake
for pity's sake

The possessive case is not used in such expressions as the following, in which one noun modifies another.

day labor (labor by the day)
quartermaster stores
State prison
State rights

For euphony, nouns ending in *s* or *ce* and followed by a word beginning with *s* form the possessive by adding an apostrophe only.

for goodness' sake
Mr. Hughes' service
for old times' sake
for acquaintance' sake
for conscience' sake

A possessive noun used in an adjective sense requires the addition of *'s.*

He is a friend of John's
Stern's is running a sale

A noun preceding a gerund should be in the possessive case.

in the event of Mary's leaving
the ship's hovering nearby

Brace

The brace is used to show the relation of one line or group of lines to another group of lines. The point of the brace is placed toward the fewer number of lines; or if the number of lines is the same, toward the single group.

Supervision of timber sales.	1-hour jobs	District 1	1½ hours' travel	Sales conducted monthly from May to July.
		District 7		
		District 6		
	2-hour jobs	District 4	1 hour's travel	
	3-hour jobs	District 2	2 hours' travel	
		District 3		
		District 5		

Brackets

Brackets, in pairs, are used—

In transcripts, congressional hearings, testimony in courtwork, etc., to enclose interpolations that are not specifically a part of the original quotation, corrections, explanations, omissions, editorial comments, or a caution that an error is reproduced literally.

We found this to be true at the Government Printing Office [GPO].
He came on the 3d [2d] of July.
Our conference [lasted] 2 hours.
The general [Washington] ordered him to leave.
The paper was as follows [reads]:
I do not know. [Continues reading:]
[Chorus of "Mr. Chairman."]
They fooled only themselves. [Laughter.]
Our party will always serve the people [applause] in spite of the opposition [loud applause]. (If more than one bracketed interpolation, both are included within the sentence.)
The WITNESS. He did it that way [indicating].
Q. Do you know these men [handing witness a list]?
The bill had *not* been paid. [Italic added.] *or* [Emphasis added.]
The statue [sic] was on the statute books.
The WITNESS. This matter is classified. [Deleted.]
[Deleted.]
Mr. JONES. Hold up your hands. [Show of hands.]
Answer [after examining list]. Yes; I do.
Q. [Continuing.]
A. [Reads:]
A. [Interrupting.]
[Discussion off the record.]
[Pause.]
The WITNESS [interrupting]. It is known—
Mr. JONES [continuing]. Now let us take the next item.
Mr. SMITH [presiding]. Do you mean that literally?
Mr. JONES [interposing]. Absolutely.
[The matter referred to is as follows:]
The CHAIRMAN [to Mr. Smith].

The CHAIRMAN [reading]:
Mr. KELLEY [to the chairman]. From 15 to 25 percent.
[Objected to.]
[Mr. Smith nods.]
[Mr. Smith aside.]
[Mr. Smith makes further statement off the record.]
Mr. JONES [for Mr. Smith].
A VOICE FROM AUDIENCE. Speak up.
SEVERAL VOICES. Quiet!

In bills, contracts, etc., to indicate matter that is to be omitted.

In mathematics, to denote that enclosed matter is to be treated as a unit.

When matter in brackets makes more than one paragraph, start each paragraph with a bracket and place the closing bracket at end of last paragraph.

Colon

The colon is used—

Before a final clause that extends or amplifies preceding matter.

Give up conveniences; do not demand special privileges; do not stop work: these are necessary while we are at war.
Railroading is not a variety of outdoor sport: it is service.

To introduce formally any matter that forms a complete sentence, question, or quotation.

The following question came up for discussion: What policy should be adopted?
He said: [If direct quotation of more than a few words follows].
There are three factors, as follows: First, military preparation; second, industrial mobilization; and third, manpower.

After a salutation.

MY DEAR SIR:
Ladies and Gentlemen:
To Whom It May Concern:

In expressing clock time.

2:40 p.m.

After introductory lines in lists, tables, and leaderwork, if subentries follow.

Seward Peninsula:
Council district:
Northern Light Mining Co.
Wild Goose Trading Co.
Fairhaven district: Alaska Dredging Association (single subitem runs in).
Seward Peninsula: Council district (single subitem runs in):
Northern Light Mining Co.
Wild Goose Trading Co.

In Biblical and other citations.

Luke 4:3.
I Corinthians xiii:13.
Journal of Education 3:342–358.

In bibliographic references, between place of publication and name of publisher.

Congressional Directory. Washington: U.S. Government Printing Office.

To separate book titles and subtitles.

Financial Aid for College Students: Graduate
Germany Revisited: Education in the Federal Republic

In imprints before the year (en space each side of colon).

U.S. Government Printing Office
Washington : 1984

In proportions.

Concrete mixed 5:3:1
but 5-2-1 (when so in copy)

In double colon as ratio sign.

1:2::3:6

Comma

The comma is used—

To separate two words or figures that might otherwise be misunderstood.

Instead of hundreds, thousands came.
Instead of 20, 50 came.
February 10, 1929.
In 1930, 400 men were dismissed.
To John, Smith was very kind.
What the difficulty is, is not known.
but He suggested that that committee be appointed.

Before a direct quotation of only a few words following an introductory phrase.

He said, "Now or never."

To indicate the omission of a word or words.

Then we had much; now, nothing.

After each of a series of coordinate qualifying words.

short, swift streams; *but* short tributary streams

Between an introductory modifying phrase and the subject modified.

Beset by the enemy, they retreated.

Before and after *Jr., Sr., Esq., Ph.D., F.R.S., Inc.*, etc., within a sentence except where possession is indicated.

Henry Smith, Jr., chairman
Peter Johns, F.R.S., London
Washington, DC, schools
Motorola, Inc., factory
Alexandria, VA's waterfront
Brown, A.H., Jr. (*not* Brown, Jr., A.H.)
but John Smith 2d (*or* II); Smith, John, II
Mr. Smith, Junior, also spoke (where only last name is used)

To set off parenthetic words, phrases, or clauses.

Mr. Jefferson, who was then Secretary of State, favored the location of the National Capital at Washington.
It must be remembered, however, that the Government had no guarantee.
It is obvious, therefore, that this office cannot function.
The atom bomb, which was developed at the Manhattan project, was first used in World War II.
Their high morale might, he suggested, have caused them to put success of the team above the reputation of the college.
The restriction is laid down in title IX, chapter 8, section 15, of the code.
but:
The man who fell [restrictive clause] broke his back.
The dam that gave way [restrictive clause] was poorly constructed.
He therefore gave up the search.

To set off words or phrases in apposition or in contrast.

Mr. Green, the lawyer, spoke for the defense.
Mr. Jones, attorney for the plaintiff, signed the petition.
Mr. Smith, not Mr. Black, was elected.
James Roosevelt, Democrat, of California.

After each member within a series of three or more words, phrases, letters, or figures used with *and, or,* or *nor.*

red, white, and blue
horses, mules, and cattle; *but* horses and mules and cattle
by the bolt, by the yard, or in remnants
a, b, and c
neither snow, rain, nor heat
2 days, 3 hours, and 4 minutes (series); *but* 2 days 3 hours 4 minutes (age)

Before the conjunction in a compound sentence.

Fish, mollusks, and crustaceans were plentiful in the lakes, and turtles frequented the shores.
The boy went home alone, and his sister remained with the crowd.

After a noun or phrase in direct address.

Senator, will the measure be defeated?
Mr. Chairman, I will reply to the gentleman later.
but Yes, sir; he did see it.
No, sir; I do not recall.

After an interrogative clause, followed by a direct question.

You are sure, are you not?
You will go, will you not?

Between title of person and name of organization in the absence of the words *of* or *of the.*

Chief, Division of Finance
chairman, Committee on Appropriations
colonel, 7th Cavalry
president, Yale University

Inside closing quotation mark.

He said "four," not "five."
"Freedom is an inherent right," he insisted.
Items marked "A," "B," and "C," inclusive, were listed.

To separate thousands, millions, etc., in numbers of four or more digits.

4,230 50,491 1,250,000

After year in complete dates within sentence.

The reported dates of September 11, 1943, to June 12, 1944, were erroneous.
This was reflected in the June 13, 1959, report.
but Production for June 1950 was normal. The 10 February 1980 deadline passed.

The comma is omitted—

Between superior figures or letters in footnote references.

Numerous instances may be cited.[1 2]
Data are based on October production.[a b]

Before ZIP (zone improvement plan) Code postal-delivery number.

Government Printing Office, Washington, DC 20401
Thornburg, VA 22565-0120

Between month, holiday, or season and year in dates.

June 1938; 22d of May 1938; February and March 1938; January, February, and March 1938; January 24 A.D. 1938; 15th of June A.D. 1938; 150 B.C.; Labor Day 1966; Easter Sunday 1966; 5 January 1944 (military usage); spring 1929

Between the name and number of an organization.

Columbia Typographical Union No. 101
General U.S. Grant Post No. 25

In fractions, in decimals, and in serial numbers, except patent numbers.

$\frac{1}{2500}$
1.0947
page 2632
202–275–2303 (telephone number)
1721–1727 St. Clair Avenue
Executive Order 11242
motor No. 189463
1450 kilocycles; 1100 meters (no comma unless more than four figures, radio only)

Between two nouns one of which identifies the other.

The Children's Bureau's booklet "Infant Care" is a bestseller.

Before ampersand (&).

Brown, Wilson & Co.
Mine, Mill & Smelter Workers

Before abbreviations of compass directions.

6430 Princeton Dr. SW.

In bibliographies, between name of publication and volume or similar number.

American Library Association Bulletin 34:238, April 1940.

Wherever possible without danger of ambiguity.

$2 gold
$2.50 U.S. currency
$3.50 Mexican
Executive Order No. 21
General Order No. 12; *but* General Orders, No. 12
Public Law 85-1
He graduates in the year 2000 (*not* 2,000)
My age is 30 years 6 months 12 days.
John Lewis 2d (*or* II)
Murphy of Illinois; Murphy of New York
Carroll of Carrollton; Henry of Navarre (places closely identified with the persons); *but* Clyde Downs, of Maryland; President Hadley, of Yale University
James Bros. et al.; *but* James Bros., Nelson Co., et al. (last element of series)

Dash

The em dash is used—

To mark a sudden break or abrupt change in thought.

He said—and no one contradicted him—"The battle is lost."
If the bill should pass—which God forbid!—the service will be wrecked.
The auditor—shall we call him a knave or a fool?—approved an inaccurate statement.

To indicate an interruption or an unfinished word or sentence. A 2-em dash will be used when the interruption is by a person other than the speaker, and a 1-em dash will show self-interruption.

"Such an idea can scarcely be——"
"The word 'donation'——"
"The word 'dona——'"
"He said: 'Give me lib——'"
"The bill reads 'repeal,' not 'am——'"
Q. Did you see——A. No, sir.
Mr. Brown [reading]:
The report goes on to say that—
Observe this closely—
during the fiscal year * * *

Instead of commas or parentheses, if the meaning may thus be clarified.

These are shore deposits—gravel, sand, and clay—but marine sediments underlie them.

Before a final clause that summarizes a series of ideas.

Freedom of speech, freedom of worship, freedom from want, freedom from fear—these are the fundamentals of moral world order.

After an introductory phrase reading into the following lines and indicating repetition of such phrase.

I recommend—
That we accept the rules;
That we also publish them; and
That we submit them for review.

With a preceding question mark, in lieu of a colon.

How can you explain this?—"Fee paid, $5."

To precede a credit line or a run-in credit or signature.

Still achieving, still pursuing,
Learn to labor and to wait.
—*Longfellow.*

Every man's work shall be made manifest.
—I Corinthians 3:13.
This statement is open to question.—Gerald H. Forsythe.

After a run-in sidehead.

To separate run-in questions and answers in testimony.

Q. Did he go?—A. No.

The em dash is not used—

At the beginning of any line of type, except as shown previously for credit lines.

Immediately after a comma, colon, or semicolon.

A 3-em dash is used—

In bibliographies to indicate repetition.

Powell James W., Jr., Hunting in Virginia's lowlands. 1972. 200 pp.
——— Fishing off Delmarva. 1972. 28 pp.

The en dash is used—

In a combination of (1) figures, (2) capital letters, or (3) figures and capital letters. (An en dash, not a hyphen, is used, even when such terms are adjectival modifiers.)

exhibit 6–A
5–20 bonds
DC–14; *but* Convair 340
Public Law 85–1, *but* Public Laws 85–1—85–20 (note em dash between two elements with en dashes)
301–942–8367 (telephone number including area code)
section 12 (a)–(f)
I–95 (interstate)
WTOP–AM–FM–TV
4–H Club
LK–66–A(2)–74
$15–$20
CBS–TV network
AFL–CIO merger
but ACF-Brill Motors Co.
loran-C
Mig-21

In the absence of the word *to* when denoting a period of time.

1935–37
January–June
Monday–Friday

The en dash is not used—

For *to* when the word *from* precedes the first of two related figures or expressions.

From January 1 to June 30, 1951; *not* from January 1–June 30, 1951.

For *and* when the word *between* precedes the first of two related figures or expressions.

Between 1923 and 1929; *not* between 1923–29

Ellipses

Three asterisks (preferred form) or three periods, separated by en quads, are used to denote an ellipsis within a sentence, at the beginning or end of a sentence, or in two or more consecutive sentences. To achieve faithful reproduction of excerpt material, editors using period ellipses should indicate placement of terminal period in relation to an ellipsis at the end of a sentence.

He called * * * and left. * * * When he returned the * * *.
* * * called * * * and left. * * * he returned the * * *.
He called * * * and * * *. When he returned the * * *.
He called * * * and * * * he returned the * * *. [Two or more consecutive sentences, including intervening punctuation]

Ellipses are not overrun alone at the end of a paragraph.

When both asterisks and periods for ellipsis occur in the copy and periods are not specifically requested, use asterisks throughout.

A line of asterisks (or periods) indicates an omission of one or more entire paragraphs. In 26½-pica or wider measure, a line of "stars" means seven asterisks indented 2 ems at each end of the line, with the remaining space divided evenly between the asterisks. In measures less than 26½ picas, five asterisks are used. Quotation marks are not used on line of asterisks or periods in quoted matter. Where line of asterisks ends complete quotation, no closing quote is used.

* * * * *

Indented matter in 26½-pica or wider measure also requires a seven-asterisk line to indicate the omission of one or more entire paragraphs.

An extra indention is added in indented matter; except where there are too many varying indentions, then all the asterisks (or periods) have the same alignment.

If an omission occurs in the last part of a paragraph immediately before a line of asterisks, three asterisks are used, in addition to the line of asterisks, to indicate such an omission.

If two or more sizes of type are used on a page, 10-point asterisks are indented 2 ems, 8-point and 6-point asterisks being aligned with the 10-point asterisks.

Equalize spacing above and below an ellipsis line.

Exclamation point

The exclamation point is used to mark surprise, incredulity, admiration, appeal, or other strong emotion, which may be expressed even in a declarative or interrogative sentence.

He acknowledged the error!
How beautiful!
"Great!" he shouted. [Note omission of comma.]
What!
Who shouted, "All aboard!" [Note omission of question mark.]

In direct address, either to a person or a personified object, *O* is used without an exclamation point, or other punctuation; but if strong feeling is expressed, an exclamation point is placed at the end of the statement.

O my friend, let us consider this subject impartially.
O Lord, save Thy people!

In exclamations without direct address or appeal, *oh* is used instead of *O*, and the exclamation point is omitted.

Oh, but the gentleman is mistaken.
Oh dear; the time is so short.

Hyphen

The hyphen (a punctuation mark, not an element in the spelling of words) is used—

To connect the elements of certain compound words.

To indicate continuation of a word divided at end of a line.

Between the letters of a spelled word.

The Style Board changed the spelling a-l-i-n-e to a-l-i-g-n.
Note the adoption of g-a-u-g-e to replace g-a-g-e and the addition of e-n-s-u-r-e.

To separate elements of chemical formulas.

The hyphen, as an element, may be used—

To represent letters deleted or illegible words in copy.

d - - n h - ll Leroy Joseph B - - -

Parentheses

Parentheses are used—

To set off matter not intended to be part of the main statement or not a grammatical element of the sentence, yet important enough to be included. In colloquy, brackets must be used.

This case (124 U.S. 329) is not relevant.
The result (see fig. 2) is most surprising.
The United States is the principal purchaser (by value) of these exports (23 percent in 1955 and 19 percent in 1956).

To enclose a parenthetic clause where the interruption is too great to be indicated by commas.

You can find it neither in French dictionaries (at any rate, not in Littré) nor in English.

To enclose an explanatory word not part of a written or printed statement.

the Erie (PA) News; *but* the News of Erie, PA
Portland (OR) Chamber of Commerce; *but* Washington, DC, schools.

To enclose letters or numbers designating items in a series, either at beginning of paragraphs or within a paragraph.

The order of delivery will be: (*a*) Food, (*b*) clothing, and (*c*) tents and other housing equipment.
You will observe that the sword is (1) old fashioned, (2) still sharp, and (3) unusually light for its use.
Paragraph 7(B)(1)(*a*) will be found on page 6. (Note parentheses closed up.)

To enclose a figure inserted to confirm a written or printed statement given in words if double form is specifically requested.

This contract shall be completed in sixty (60) days.

A reference in parentheses at the end of a sentence is placed before the period, unless it is a complete sentence in itself.

The specimen exhibits both phases (pl. 14, *A*, *B*).
The individual cavities show great variation. (See pl. 4.)

If a sentence contains more than one parenthetic reference, the one at the end is placed before the period.

This sandstone (see pl. 6) occurs in every county of the State (see pl. 1).

When a figure is followed by a letter in parentheses, no space is used between the figure and the opening parenthesis; but if the letter is not in parentheses and the figure is repeated with each letter, the letter is closed up with the figure.

15(*a*). Classes, grades, and sizes.
15*a*. Classes, grades, and sizes.

If both a figure and a letter in parentheses are used before each paragraph, a period and an en space are used after the closing parenthesis; if the figure is not repeated before each letter in parenthesis but is used only before the first, the period is placed after the figure.

15(*a*). When the figure is used before the letter in each paragraph—
15(*b*). The period is placed after the closing parenthesis.
15. (*a*) When the figure is used before letter in first paragraph but not repeated with subsequent letters—
(*b*) The period is used after the figure only.
Sec. 12 (a) If no period is used and a letter in parentheses appears after a numbered item—
(b) Space must be used after the number if at least one other lettered subsection is shown.

Note position of period relative to closing parenthesis:

The vending stand sells a variety of items (sandwiches, beverages, cakes, etc.).
The vending stand sells a variety of items (sandwiches, beverages, cakes, etc. (sometimes ice cream)).
The vending stand sells a variety of items. (These include sandwiches, beverages, cakes, etc. (6).)

To enclose bylines in congressional work.

(By Sylvia Porter, staff writer)

When matter in parentheses makes more than one paragraph, start each paragraph with a parenthesis and place the closing parenthesis at end of last paragraph.

Period

The period is used—

After a declarative sentence that is not exclamatory or after an imperative sentence.

Stars are suns.
He was employed by Sampson & Co.
Do not be late.
On with the dance.

After an indirect question or after a question intended as a suggestion and not requiring an answer.

Tell me how he did it.
May we hear from you.
May we ask prompt payment.

In place of a parenthesis after a letter or number denoting a series.

a. Bread well baked.
b. Meat cooked rare.
c. Cubed apples stewed.

1. Punctuate freely.
2. Compound sparingly.
3. Index thoroughly.

Sometimes to indicate ellipsis.
After a run-in sidehead.

Conditional subjunctive.—The conditional subjunctive is required for all unreal and doubtful conditions.
2. Peacetime preparation.—*a.* The Chairman of the National Security Resources Board, etc.
2. *Peacetime preparation—Industrial mobilization plans.*—The Chairman of the National Security Resources Board, etc.
2. Peacetime preparation.—*Industrial mobilization.*—The Chairman of the National Security Resources Board, etc.
62. *Determination of types.—a. Statement of characteristics.*—Before types of equipment, etc.
Steps in planning for procurement.—(1) *Determination of needs.*—To plan for the procurement of such arms, etc.
62. *Determination of types.—(a) Statement of characteristics.*—Before, etc.
DETERMINATION OF TYPES.—Statement of characteristics.—Before types of, etc.
NOTE.—The source material was furnished.
but Source: U.S. Department of Commerce, Bureau of the Census.

Paragraphs and subparagraphs may be arranged according to the scheme below. The sequence is not fixed, and variations, in addition to the use of center and side heads or indented paragraphs, may be adopted, depending on the number of parts.

I. (Roman numeral)	(1)
A.	(*a*)
1.	(i) (lowercase Roman numeral)
a.	(*aa*)

To separate integers from decimals in a single expression.

3.75 percent $3.50 1.25 meters

In continental European languages, to indicate thousands.

1.317 72.190.175

After abbreviations, unless otherwise specified.

Apr.	RR.
fig.	*but* m (meter)
Ph.D.	kc (kilocycle)
NE. (Northeast)	NY (New York)

After legends and explanatory matter beneath illustrations. Legends without descriptive language do not receive periods.

FIGURE 1.—Schematic drawing.
FIGURE 1.—Continued.
but FIGURE 1 (no period)

After *Article 1, Section 1,* etc., at beginning of paragraphs. An en space is used after such terms.

A center period is sometimes used—

To indicate multiplication. (Multiplication sign preferable.)

$a \cdot b$ $(a \times b)$

The period is omitted—

After—

Lines in title pages.
Center, side, and running heads.
Continued lines.
Boxheads of tables.
Scientific, chemical, or other symbols.

This rule does not apply to abbreviation periods.

After a quotation mark that is preceded by a period.

He said, "Now or never."

After letters used as names without specific designation.

Officer B; Subject A, etc.
A said to B that all is well.
Mr. A told Mr. B that the case was closed.
Mr. X (for unknown or censored name)
but Mr. A. [for Mr. Andrews]. I do not want to go.
Mr. K. [for Mr. King]. The meeting is adjourned.

After a middle initial which is merely a letter and not an abbreviation of a name.

Daniel D Tompkins	*but* Harry S. Truman
Ross T McIntire	(his preference)

After a short name which is not an abbreviation of the longer form.

Alex Ed Sam

After Roman numerals used as ordinals.

King George V
Apollo XII insigne
Super Bowl XVII

After words and incomplete statements listed in columns. Full-measure matter is not to be regarded as a column.

After explanatory matter set in 6 point under leaders or rules.

....
(Name) (Address) (Position)

Immediately before leaders, even if an abbreviation precedes the leaders.

Question mark

The question mark is used—

To indicate a direct query, even if not in the form of a question.

Did he do it?
He did what?
Can the money be raised? is the question.
Who asked, "Why?" (Note single question mark)
"Did you hurt yourself, my son?" she asked.

To express more than one query in the same sentence.

Can he do it? or you? or anyone?

To express doubt.

He said the boy was 8(?) feet tall. (No space before question mark)
The statue(?) was on the statute books.
The scientific identification *Dorothia?* was noted.

Quotation marks

Quotation marks are used—

To enclose direct quotations. (Each part of an interrupted quotation begins and ends with quotation marks.)

The answer is "No."
He said, "John said, 'No.'"
"John," said Henry, "why do you go?"

To enclose any matter following such terms as *entitled, the word, the term, marked, designated, classified, named, endorsed, cited as, referred to as,* or *signed;* but are not used to enclose expressions following the terms *known as, called, so-called,* etc., unless such expressions are misnomers or slang.

Congress passed the act entitled "An act * * *."
After the word "treaty," insert a comma.
Of what does the item "Miscellaneous debts" consist?
The column "Imports from foreign countries" was not * * *.
The document will be marked "Exhibit No. 21"; *but* The document may be made exhibit No. 2.
The check was endorsed "John Adamson."
It was signed "John."
Beryllium is known as glucinium in some European countries.
It was called profit and loss.
The so-called investigating body.

To enclose titles of addresses, articles, books, captions, chapter and part headings, editorials, essays, headings, headlines, hearings, motion pictures and plays (including television and radio programs), papers, short poems, reports, songs, studies, subheadings, subjects, and themes. All principal words are to be capitalized.

An address on "Uranium-235 in the Atomic Age"
The article "Germany Revisited" appeared in the last issue.
"The Conquest of Mexico," a published work (book)
Under the caption "Long-Term Treasury's Rise"
The subject was discussed in "Courtwork." (chapter heading)
It will be found in "Part XI: Early Thought."
The editorial "Haphazard Budgeting"
"Compensation," by Emerson (essay)
"United States To Appoint Representative to U.N." (heading for headline)
In "Search for Paradise" (motion picture); "South Pacific" (play)
A paper on "Constant-Pressure Combustion" was read.
"O Captain! My Captain!" (short poem)
The report "Atomic Energy: What It Means to the Nation"; *but* annual report of the Public Printer
This was followed by the singing of "The Star-Spangled Banner."
Under the subhead "Sixty Days of Turmoil" will be found * * *.
The subject (or theme) of the conference is "Peaceful Uses of Atomic Energy."
also Account 5, "Management fees."
Under the heading "Management and Operation."
Under the appropriation "Building of ships, Navy."

The lines of a poem should range on the left, those that rhyme taking the same indention. Poems are usually centered on the longest line; overs 3 ems; 6 points of space betwen stanzas.

We care not whence they came,
  Dear in their lifeless clay.
Whether unknown or known to fame,
Their cause and country still the same,
  They died—and wore the gray.

At the beginning of each paragraph of a quotation, but at the end of the last paragraph only.

To enclose a letter or communication, which bears both date and signature, within a letter.

To enclose misnomers, slang expressions, sobriquets, coined words, or ordinary words used in an arbitrary way.

His report was "bunk."
It was a "gentlemen's agreement."
The "invisible government" is responsible.
George Herman "Babe" Ruth.
but He voted for the lameduck amendment.

Quotation marks will not be borne off from adjacent characters except when they precede a fraction or an apostrophe or precede or follow a superior figure or letter, in which case a thin space will be used. A thin space will also be used to separate double and single quotation marks.

Quotation marks are not used—

To enclose titles of works of art: paintings, statuary, etc.

To enclose names of newspapers or magazines.

To enclose complete letters having date and signature.

To enclose extracts that are indented or set in smaller type, or solid extracts in leaded matter; but indented matter in text that is already quoted carries quotation marks.

In indirect quotations.

Tell her yes.
He could not say no.

Before a display initial which begins a quoted paragraph.

The comma and the final period will be placed inside the quotation marks. Other punctuation marks should be placed inside the quotation marks only if they are a part of the matter quoted.

Ruth said, "I think so."
"The President," he said, "will veto the bill."
The trainman shouted, "All aboard!"
Who asked, "Why?"
The President suggests that "an early occasion be sought * * *."
Why call it a "gentlemen's agreement"?

In congressional and certain other classes of work showing amendments, and in courtwork with quoted language, punctuation marks are printed after the quotation marks when not a part of the quoted matter.

Insert the words "growth", "production", and "manufacture".
To be inserted immediately after the words "cadets, U.S. Coast Guard;".
Change "February 1, 1983", to "June 30, 1983".
"Insert in lieu thereof 'July 1, 1983,'."

When occurring together, quotation marks should precede the footnote reference number.

The commissioner claimed that the award was "unjustified."[1]
His exact words were: "The facts in the case prove otherwise."[2]

Quotation marks should be limited, if possible, to three sets (double, single, double).

"The question in the report is, 'Can a person who obtains his certificate of naturalization by fraud be considered a "bona fide" citizen of the United States?'"

Semicolon

The semicolon is used—

To separate clauses containing commas.

Donald A. Peters, president of the First National Bank, was also a director of New York Central; Harvey D. Jones was a director of Oregon Steel Co. and New York Central; Thomas W. Harrison, chairman of the board of McBride & Co., was also on the board of Oregon Steel Co.
Reptiles, amphibians, and predatory mammals swallow their prey whole or in large pieces, bones included; waterfowl habitually take shellfish entire; and gallinaceous birds are provided with gizzards that grind up the hardest seeds.
Yes, sir; he did see it.
No, sir; I do not recall.

To separate statements that are too closely related in meaning to be written as separate sentences, and also statements of contrast.

Yes; that is right.
No; we received one-third.
It is true in peace; it is true in war.
War is destructive; peace, constructive.

To set off explanatory abbreviations or words which summarize or explain preceding matter.

The industry is related to groups that produce finished goods; i.e., electrical machinery and transportation equipment.
There were involved three metal producers; namely, Jones & Laughlin, Armco, and Kennecott.

The semicolon is not used—

Where a comma will suffice.

Regional offices are located in New York, NY, Chicago, IL, and Dallas, TX.

Single punctuation

Single punctuation is used wherever possible without ambiguity.

124 U.S. 321 (no comma)
SIR: (no dash)
Joseph replied, "It is a worthwhile effort." (no outside period)

Type

All punctuation marks, including parentheses, brackets, and superior reference figures, are set to match the type of the words which they adjoin. A lightface dash is used after a run-in boldface sidehead followed by lightface matter. Lightface brackets, parentheses, or quotation marks shall be used when both boldface and lightface matter are enclosed.

Charts: C&GS 5101 (N.O. 18320), page **282 (see above);** N.O. **93491 (Plan);** page 271.

CAPITALIZATION

It is impossible to give rules that will cover every conceivable problem in capitalization; but by considering the purpose to be served and the underlying principles, it is possible to attain a considerable degree of uniformity. The correct usage with respect to any term not included can be determined by analogy or by application of the rules.

Proper names

Proper names are capitalized.

Rome	John Macadam	Italy
Brussels	Macadam family	Anglo-Saxon

Derivatives of proper names

Derivatives of proper names used with a proper meaning are capitalized.

Roman (of Rome)	Johannean	Italian

Derivatives of proper names used with acquired independent common meaning, or no longer identified with such names, are lowercased. Since this depends upon general and long-continued usage, a more definite and all-inclusive rule cannot be formulated in advance.

roman (type)	watt (electric unit)
brussels sprouts	plaster of paris
venetian blinds	italicize
macadam (crushed rock)	anglicize
	pasteurize

Common nouns and adjectives in proper names

A common noun or adjective forming an essential part of a proper name is capitalized; the common noun used alone as a substitute for the name of a place or thing is not capitalized.

Massachusetts Avenue; the avenue
Washington Monument; the monument
Statue of Liberty; the statue
Hoover Dam; the dam
Boston Light; the light
Modoc National Forest; the national forest
Panama Canal; the canal
Soldiers' Home of Ohio; the soldiers' home
Johnson House (hotel); Johnson house (residence)
Crow Reservation; the reservation
Federal Express; the express
Cape of Good Hope; the cape
Jersey City; *also* Washington City; *but* city of Washington; the city
Cook County; the county
Great Lakes; the lakes
Lake of the Woods; the lake
North Platee River; the river
Lower California; *but* lower Mississippi
Charles the First; Charles I
Seventeenth Census; the 1960 census

If a common noun or adjective forming an essential part of a name becomes separated from the rest of the name by an intervening common noun or adjective, the entire expression is no longer a proper noun and is therefore not capitalized.

Union Station: union passenger station
Eastern States: eastern farming States
Western States: western farming States

A common noun used alone as a well-known short form of a specific proper name is capitalized.

the Capitol (at Washington); *but* State capitol (building)
the Channel (English Channel)
the District (District of Columbia)
the Soldiers' Home (District of Columbia only)

The plural form of a common noun capitalized as part of a proper name is also capitalized.

Seventh and I Streets
Lakes Erie and Ontario
Potomac and James Rivers
State and Treasury Departments
British and French Governments
Presidents Washington and Adams

A common noun used with a date, number, or letter, merely to denote time or sequence, or for the purpose of reference, record, or temporary convenience, does not form a proper name and is therefore not capitalized.

abstract B	mile 7.5
act of 1928	page 2
amendment 5	paragraph 4
apartment 2	part I
appendix C	phase 3
article 1	plate IV
book II	region 3
chapter III	room A722
chart B	rule 8
class I	schedule K
collection 6	section 3
column 2	signature 4
drawing 6	spring 1926
exhibit D	State route 236
figure 7	station 27
first district (not congressional)	table 4
form 4	title IV
graph 8	treaty of 1919
group 7	volume X
history 3	war of 1914
interstate 95	ward 2

The following terms are lowercased, even with a name or number.

aqueduct	lock
breakwater	pier
buoy	reclamation project
chute	ship canal
dam (*but* capitalize with proper name)	shipway
	slip
dike	spillway
dock	tunnel (*but* capitalize with proper name)
drydock	
irrigation project	watershed
jetty	weir
levee	wharf

Definite article in proper place names

To achieve greater distinction or to adhere to the authorized form, the word *the* (or its equivalent in a foreign language) used as a part of an official name or title is capitalized. When such name or title is used adjectively, *the* is not capitalized, nor is it supplied at any time when not in copy.

British Consul v. *The Mermaid* (title of legal case)
The Dalles (OR); The Weirs (NH); *but* the Dalles region; the Weirs streets
The Hague; *but* the Hague Court; the Second Hague Conference
El Salvador; Las Cruces; L'Esterel
The Mall (Washington, DC)
The Gambia
The Netherlands
but the Congo, the Sudan

In common practice, the above rule is disregarded in references to newspapers, periodicals, vessels, airships, trains, firm names, etc.

the Times	the *Los Angeles*
the Atlantic Monthly	the *U-3*
the Washington Post	the Federal Express
the *Mermaid*	the National Photo Co.

Particles in names of persons

In foreign names, such particles as *d', da, de, della, den, du, van,* and *von* are capitalized unless preceded by a forename or title. Individual usage, if ascertainable, should be followed.

Da Ponte; Cardinal da Ponte
Den Uyl; Johannes den Uyl; Prime Minister den Uyl
Du Pont; E.I. du Pont de Nemours & Co.
Van Renesselaer; Stephen van Rensselaer
Von Braun; Wernher von Braun
but d'Orbigny; Alcide d'Orbigny; de la Madrid; Miguel de la Madrid

In anglicized names such particles are usually capitalized, even if preceded by a forename or title, but individual usage, if ascertainable, should be followed.

Justice Van Devanter; Reginald De Koven
Thomas De Quincey; William De Morgan
Henry van Dyke (his usage)
Samuel F. Du Pont (his usage); Irénée du Pont

If copy is not clear as to the form of such a name (for example, *La Forge* or *Laforge*), the two-word form should be used.

De Kalb County (AL, GA, IL, IN);
but DeKalb County (TN)

In names set in capitals, *de, von,* etc., are also capitalized.

Names of organized bodies

The full names of existing or proposed organized bodies and their shortened names are capitalized; other substitutes, which are most often regarded as common nouns, are capitalized only in certain specified instances to indicate preeminence or distinction.

National governmental units:
U.S. Congress: 98th Congress; the Congress; Congress; the Senate; the House; Committee of the Whole, the Committee; *but* committee (all other congressional committees)
Department of Agriculture: the Department; Division of Publications, the Division; *similarly* all departmental units; *but* legislative, executive, and judicial departments
Bureau of the Census: the Census Bureau, the Bureau; *but* the agency
Geological Survey: the Survey
Interstate Commerce Commission: the Commission
Government Printing Office: the Printing Office, the Office
American Embassy, British Embassy: the Embassy; *but* the consulate; the consulate general
Treasury of the United States: General Treasury; National Treasury; Public Treasury; the Treasury; Treasury notes; New York Subtreasury, the subtreasury
Department of Defense:
Military Establishment; Armed Forces; All-Volunteer Forces; *but* armed services
U.S. Army: the Army; All-Volunteer Army; the Infantry; 81st Regiment; Army Establishment: the Army Band; Army officer; Regular Army officer; Reserve officer; Volunteer officer; *but* army shoe; Grant's army; Robinson's brigade; the brigade; the corps; the regiment; infantryman
U.S. Navy: the Navy; the Marine Corps; Navy (Naval) Establishment; Navy officer; *but* naval shipyard; naval officer; naval station
U.S. Air Force: the Air Force
U.S. Coast Guard: the Coast Guard
French Ministry of Foreign Affairs; the Ministry; French Army; British Navy
International organizations:
United Nations: the Council; the Assembly; the Secretariat
Permanent Court of Arbitration: the Court; the Tribunal (only in the proceedings of a specific arbitration tribunal)
Hague Peace Conference of 1907: the Hague Conference; the Peace Conference; the Conference
Common-noun substitutes:
Virginia Assembly: the assembly; the senate; the house of delegates
California State Highway Commission: Highway Commission of California; the highway commission; the commission
Montgomery County Board of Health: the Board of Health, Montgomery County; the board of health; the board
Common Council of the City of Pittsburgh: the common council; the council
Buffalo Consumers' League: the consumers' league; the league
Republican Party: the party
Southern Railroad Co.: the Southern Railroad; Southern Co.; Southern Road; the railroad company; the company
Riggs National Bank: the Riggs Bank; the bank
Metropolitan Club: the club
Yale School of Law: Yale University School of Law; School of Law, Yale University; school of law

The names of members and adherents of organized bodies are capitalized to distinguish them from the same words used merely in a descriptive sense.

a Representative (U.S. Congress)	a Socialist
	an Odd Fellow
a Republican	a Communist
an Elk	a Boy Scout
a Liberal	a Knight (K.C., K.P., etc.)
a Shriner	

Names of countries, domains, and administrative divisions

The official designations of countries, national domains, and their principal administrative divisions are capitalized only if used as part of proper names, as proper names, or as proper adjectives.

United States: the Republic; the Nation; the Union; the Government; *also* Federal, Federal Government; *but* republic (when not referring specifically to one such entity); republican (in general sense); a nation devoted to peace

New York State: the State, a State (a definite political subdivision of first rank); State of Veracruz; Balkan States; six States of Australia; State rights; *but* state (referring to a federal government, the body politic); foreign states; church and state; statehood; state's evidence
Territory (Canada): Yukon, Northwest Territories; the Territory(ies), Territorial; *but* territory of American Samoa, Guam, Virgin Islands
Dominion of Canada: the Dominion; *but* dominion (in general sense)
Ontario Province, Province of Ontario: the Province, Provincial; *but* province, provincial (in general sense)
Crown Colony of Hong Kong, Cyprus: the colony, crown colony

The similar designations *commonwealth, confederation (federal), government, nation (national), powers, republic,* etc., are capitalized only if used as part of proper names, as proper names, or as proper adjectives.

British Commonwealth, Commonwealth of Virginia: the Commonwealth: *but* a commonwealth government (general sense)
Swiss Confederation: the Confederation; the Federal Council; the Federal Government; *but* confederation, federal (in general sense)
French Government: the Government; French and Italian Governments; Soviet Government; the Governments; *but* government (in general sense); the Churchill government; European governments
Cherokee Nation: the nation; *but* Greek nation; American nations
National Government (of any specific nation); *but* national customs
Allied Powers, Allies (in World Wars I and II); *but* our allies, weaker allies; Central Powers (in World War I); *but* the powers; European powers
Republic of South Africa: the Republic; *but* republic (in general sense)

Names of regions, localities, and geographic features

A descriptive term used to denote a definite region, locality, or geographic feature is a proper name and is therefore capitalized; also for temporary distinction a coined name of a region is capitalized.

the North Atlantic States; the Gulf States; the Central States; the Pacific Coast States; the Lake States; East North Central States; Eastern North Central States; Far Western States; Eastern United States
the West; the Midwest; the Middle West; Far West
the Eastern Shore (Chesapeake Bay)
the Badlands (SD and NE)
the Continental Divide (Rocky Mountains)
Deep South; Midsouth
the Occident; the Orient
the Far East
Far Eastern; the East
Middle East, Middle Eastern, Mideast, Mideastern (Asia)
Near East (Balkans, etc.)
the Promised Land
the Continent (continental Europe)
the Western Hemisphere
the North Pole; the North and South Poles
the Temperate Zone; the Torrid Zone
the East Side, Lower East Side (sections of a city)
Western Germany; Western Europe (political entities)
but lower 48 (States); the Northeast corridor

A descriptive term used to denote mere direction or position is not a proper name and is therefore not capitalized.

north; south; east; west
northerly; northern; northward
eastern; oriental; occidental
east Pennsylvania; southern California
northern Virginia
west Florida; *but* West Florida (1763–1819)
eastern region; western region
north-central region
east coast; eastern seaboard
central Europe; south Germany; southern France
but East Germany; West Germany (political entities)

Names of calendar divisions

The names of divisions are capitalized.

January; February; March; etc.
Monday; Tuesday; Wednesday; etc.
but spring; summer; autumn (fall); winter

Names of historic events, etc.

The names of holidays, ecclesiastic feast and fast days, and historic events are capitalized.

Battle of Bunker Hill
Christian Era; Middle Ages; *but* 20th century
Feast of the Passover; the Passover
Fourth of July; the Fourth
Reformation
Renaissance
Veterans Day
War of 1812; World War II; *but* war of 1914; Korean war

Trade names

Trade names, variety names, and names of market grades and brands are capitalized. Common nouns following such names are not capitalized.

Foamite (trade name)
Plexiglas (trade name)
Snow Crop (trade name)
Choice lamb (market grade)
Yellow Stained cotton (market grade)
Red Radiance rose (variety)

Scientific names

The name of a phylum, class, order, family, or genus is capitalized; the name of a species is not capitalized, even though derived from a proper name.

Arthropoda (phylum), Crustacea (class), Hypoparia (order), Agnostidae (family), *Agnostus* (genus)
Agnostus canadensis; Aconitum wilsoni; Epigaea repens (genus and species)

In scientific descriptions coined terms derived from proper names are not capitalized.

aviculoid menodontine

A plural formed by adding *s* to a Latin generic name is capitalized.

Rhynchonellas Spirifers

In soil science the 24 soil classifications are capitalized.

Alpine Meadow Bog Brown

Capitalize the names of the celestial bodies Sun and Moon, as well as the planets Earth, Mercury, Venus, Mars, Jupiter, Saturn, Uranus, Neptune, and Pluto. Lowercase the word *moon* in such expressions as "the moons of Jupiter."

Fanciful appellations

A fanciful appellation used with or for a proper name is capitalized.

Big Four	New Deal
Dust Bowl	New Federalism
Great Society	New Frontier
Holocaust	Prohibition
Hub (Boston)	Great Depression
Keystone State	Third World

Personification

A vivid personification is capitalized.

The Chair recognized the gentleman from New York.
For Nature wields her scepter mercilessly.

All are architects of Fate,
Working in these walls of Time.

Religious terms

Words denoting the Deity except *who, whose,* and *whom;* names for the Bible and other sacred writings and their parts; and names of confessions of faith and of religious bodies and their adherents and words specifically denoting Satan are all capitalized.

Heavenly Father; the Almighty; Lord; Thee; Thou; He; Him; *but* himself; [God's] fatherhood
Mass; red Mass; Communion
Divine Father; *but* divine providence; divine guidance; divine service
Son of Man; Jesus' sonship; the Messiah; *but* a messiah; messiahship; messianic; messianize; christology; christological
Bible, Holy Scriptures, Scriptures, Word; Koran; *also* Biblical; Scriptural; Koranic
New Testament; Ten Commandments
Gospel (memoir of Christ); *but* gospel truth
Apostles' Creed; Augsburg Confession; Thirty-nine Articles
Episcopal Church; an Episcopalian; Catholicism; a Protestant
Christian; *also* Christendom; Christianity; Christianize
Black Friars; Brother(s); King's Daughters; Daughter(s); Ursuline Sisters; Sister(s)
Satan; His Satanic Majesty; Father of Lies; the Devil; *but* a devil; the devils; devil's advocate

Titles of persons

Civil, religious, military, and professional titles, as well as those of nobility, immediately preceding a name are capitalized.

President Reagan	Examiner Jones (law)
King George	Vice-Presidential candidate White
Ambassador Gibson	*but* baseball player Jones
Lieutenant Fowler	maintenance man Smith
Chairman Smith	
Dr. Bellinger	
Nurse Cavell	
Professor Leverett	

To indicate preeminence or distinction in certain specified instances, a common-noun title immediately following the name of a person or used alone as a substitute for it is capitalized.

Title of a head or assistant head of state:
Ronald W. Reagan, President of the United States: the President; the President-elect; the Executive; the Chief Magistrate; the Commander in Chief; ex-President Carter: former President Truman; *similarly* the Vice President; the Vice-President-elect; ex-Vice-President Mondale
Charles Robb, Governor of Virginia: the Governor of Virginia; the Governor; *similarly* the Lieutenant Governor; *but* secretary of state of Idaho; attorney general of Maine
Title of a head or assistant head of an existing or proposed National governmental unit:
George P. Shultz, Secretary of State: the Secretary; *similarly* the Acting Secretary; the Under Secretary; the Assistant Secretary; the Director; the Chief or Assistant Chief; the Chief Clerk; etc.; *but* Secretaries of the military departments; secretaryship
Titles of the military:
General of the Army(ies): United States only; Supreme Allied Commander; Gen. John W. Vessey, Chairman, Joint Chiefs of Staff; Joint Chiefs of Staff; Chief of Staff, U.S. Air Force; the Chief of Staff; *but* the commanding general; general (military title standing alone not capitalized)
Titles of members of diplomatic corps:
Walter S. Gifford, Ambassador Extraordinary and Plenipotentiary: the American Ambassador; the British Ambassador; the Ambassador; the Senior Ambassador; His Excellency; *similarly* the Envoy Extraordinary and Minister Plenipotentiary; the Envoy; the Minister; the Chargé d'Affaires; the Chargé; Ambassador at Large; Minister Without Portfolio; *but* the consul general; the consul; the attaché; etc.
Title of a ruler or prince:
Elizabeth II, Queen of England: the Queen; the Crown; Her Most Gracious Majesty; Her Majesty; *similarly* the Emperor; the Sultan; etc.
Charles, Prince of Wales: the Prince; His Royal Highness
Titles not capitalized:
Charles F. Hughes, rear admiral, U.S. Navy: the rear admiral

Lloyd H. Elliott, president of George Washington University: the president
C.H. Eckles, professor of dairy husbandry: the professor
Patricia Rowles, chairwoman of the committee; the chairman; the chairperson; the chair

In formal lists of delegates and representatives of governments, all titles and descriptive designations immediately following the names should be capitalized if any one is capitalized.

A title in the second person is capitalized.

Your Excellency	Mr. Secretary
Your Highness	Not salutation:
Your Honor	my dear General
Mr. Chairman	my dear sir
Madam Chairman	

Titles of publications, papers, documents, acts, laws, etc.

In the full or short English titles of periodicals, series of publications, annual reports, historic documents, and works of art, the first word and all important words are capitalized.

Statutes at Large; Revised Statues; District Code; Bancroft's History; Journal (House or Senate) (short titles); *but* the code; the statutes
Atlantic Charter; Balfour Declaration; *but* British white paper
Chicago's American; *but* Chicago American Publishing Co.
Reader's Digest; *but* New York Times Magazine; Newsweek magazine
Monograph 55; Research Paper 123; Bulletin 420; Circular A; Article 15: Uniform Code of Military Justice; Senate Document 70; House Resolution 45; Presidential Proclamation No. 24; Executive Order No. 24; Royal Decree No. 24; Public Law 89–1; Private and Union Calendars; Calendar No. 80; Calendar Wednesday; Committee Print No. 32, committee print; *but* Senate bill 416; House bill 61
Annual Report of the Public Printer, 1966; *but* seventh annual report, 19th annual report
Declaration of Independence; the Declaration
Constitution (United States or with name of country); constitutional; *but* New York State constitution: first amendment, 12th amendment
Kellogg Pact; North Atlantic Pact; Atlantic Pact; Treaty of Versailles; Jay Treaty; *but* treaty of peace, the treaty (descriptive designations); treaty of 1919
United States v. *Four Hundred Twenty-two Casks of Wine* (law)
The Blue Boy, Excalibur, Whistler's Mother (paintings)

All principal words are capitalized in titles of addresses, articles, books, captions, chapter and part headings, editorials, essays, headings, headlines, motion pictures and plays (including television and radio programs), papers, short poems, reports, songs, subheadings, subjects, and themes. The foregoing are also quoted.

In the short or popular titles of acts (Federal, State, or foreign) the first word and all important words are capitalized.

Revenue Act; Walsh-Healey Act; Freedom of Information Act; Classification Act; *but* the act; Harrison narcotic law; Harrison narcotic bill; interstate commerce law; sunset law

The capitalization of the titles of books, etc., written in a foreign language is to conform to national practice in that language.

First words

The first word of a sentence, of an independent clause or phrase, of a direct quotation, of a formally introduced series of items or phrases following a comma or colon, or of a line of poetry, is capitalized.

The question is, Shall the bill pass?
He asked, "And where are you going?"
The vote was as follows: In the affirmative, 23; in the negative, 11; not voting, 3.

Lives of great men all remind us
We can make our lives sublime.

The first word of a fragmentary quotation is not capitalized.

He objected "to the phraseology, not to the ideas."

The first word following a colon, an exclamation point, or a question mark is not capitalized if the matter following is merely a supplementary remark making the meaning clearer.

Revolutions are not made: they come.
Intelligence is not replaced by mechanism: even the televox must be guided by its master's voice.
But two months dead! nay, not so much; not two.

What is this?
Your knees to me? to your corrected son?

The first word following *Whereas* in resolutions, contracts, etc., is not capitalized; the first word following an enacting or resolving clause is capitalized.

Whereas the Constitution provides * * *; and
Whereas Congress has passed a law * * *;
Whereas, moreover, * * *: Therefore be it
Whereas the Senate provided for the * * *: Now, therefore, be it
Resolved, That * * *; and be it further
Resolved (jointly), That * * *
Resolved by the House of Representatives (the Senate concurring), That * * *. (Concurrent resolution, Federal Government.)
Resolved by the Senate of Oklahoma (the House of Representatives concurring therein), That * * *. (Concurrent resolution, using name of State.)
Resolved by the senate (the house of representatives concurring therein), That * * *. (Concurrent resolution, not using name of State.)
Resolved by the Assembly and Senate of the State of California (jointly), That * * *. (Joint resolution, using name of State.)
Resolved by the Washington Board of Trade, That * * *
Provided, That * * *
Provided further, That * * *
Provided, however, That * * *
And provided further, That * * *
Ordered, That * * *
Be it enacted, That * * *

Center and side heads

Unless otherwise marked, (1) centerheads are set in capitals, and (2) sideheads are set in lowercase and only the first word and proper names are capitalized. In centerheads making two lines, wordbreaks should be avoided. The first line should be centered and set as full as possible.

Except as indicated elsewhere, everything in a cap heading is set in caps; in a cap and small-cap heading, in caps and small caps; and in a small-cap heading, in small caps, including, if available, parentheses, brackets, and figures.

In heads set in caps, a small-cap *c* or *ac,* if available, is used in such names as *McLean* or *MacLeod;* otherwise a lowercase *c* or *ac* is used. In heads set in small caps, a space is used after the *c* or the *ac.*

In such names as *LeRoy, DeHostis, LaFollette,* etc. (one-word forms only), set in caps, the second letter of the particle is made a small cap, if available; otherwise lowercase is used. In heads set in small caps, a space is used.

In matter set in caps and small caps or caps and lowercase, capitalize all principal words, including parts of compounds which would be capitalized standing alone. The articles *a, an,* and *the;* the prepositions *at, by, for, in, of, on, to,* and *up;* the conjunctions *a, but, if, or,* and *nor;* and the second element of a compound numeral are not capitalized.

World en Route to All-Out War
Curfew To Be Set at 10 o'Clock
Man Hit With 2-Inch Pipe
No-Par-Value Stock for Sale
Yankees May Be Winners in Zig-Zag Race
Ex-Senator Is To Be Admitted
Notice of Filing and Order on Exemption From Requirements
but Building on Twenty-first Street (if spelled)
One Hundred and Twenty-three Years (if spelled)
Only One-tenth of Shipping Was Idle
Many 35-Millimeter Films in Production
Built-Up Stockpiles Are Necessary (*Up* is an adverb here)
His Per Diem Was Increased (*Per Diem* is used as a noun here); Lower Taxes per Person (*per* is a preposition here)

If a normally lowercased short word is used in juxtaposition with a capitalized word of like significance, it should also be capitalized.

Buildings In and Near Minneapolis

In a heading set in caps and lowercase or in caps and small caps, a normally lowercased last word, if it is the only lowercased word in the heading, should also be capitalized.

All Returns Are In

The first element of an infinitive is capitalized.

Controls To Be Applied; *but* Aid Sent to Disaster Area

In matter set in caps and small caps, such abbreviations as *etc., et al.,* and *p.m.* are set in small caps; in matter set in caps and lowercase, these abbreviations are set in lowercase.

PLANES, GUNS, SHIPS, ETC.
JAMES BROS. ET AL. (no comma)
IN RE THE 8 P.M. MEETING
Planes, Guns, Ships, etc.
James Bros. et al.
In re the 8 p.m. Meeting

Accents in cap lines should be omitted even if the same words carry accents in text.

Paragraph series letters in parentheses appearing in heads set in caps, caps and small caps, small caps, or in caps and lowercase are to be set as in copy.

SECTION 1.580 (f)(1)

Addresses, salutations, and signatures

The first word and all principal words in addresses, salutations, and signatures are capitalized.

Interjections

The interjection *O* is always capitalized; within a sentence other interjections are not capitalized.

Sail on, O Ship of State!
For lo! the days are hastening on.
But, oh, how fortunate!

Historic or documentary accuracy

Where historic, documentary, technical, or scientific accuracy is required, capitalization and other features of style of the original text should be followed.

Where strict adherence to a rule on capitalization in headings detracts from an intended meaning or effect, the supervisor in the markup section must be consulted.

COMPOUND WORDS

A compound word is a union of two or more words, either with or without a hyphen. It conveys a unit idea that is not as clearly or quickly conveyed by the component words in unconnected succession. The hyphen in a compound is a mark of punctuation that not only unites but separates the component words, and thus facilitates understanding, aids readability, and ensures correct pronunciation.

In applying the following rules and in using the Guide to Compounding, the living fluidity of our language should be kept in mind. Word forms constantly undergo modification. Two-word forms often acquire the hyphen first, are printed as one word later, and not infrequently the transition is from the two- to the one-word form, bypassing the hyphen stage.

The rules as laid down cannot be applied inflexibly. Exceptions must necessarily be allowed, so that general good form will not be offended. However, current language trends point definitely to closing up words which, through frequent use, have become associated in the reader's mind as units of thought. The tendency to amalgamate words, particularly two short words, assures easier continuity, and is a natural progression from the older and less flexible treatment of words.

General rules

In general, omit the hyphen when words appear in regular order and the omission causes no ambiguity in sense or sound.

banking hours	living costs
blood pressure	palm oil
book value	patent right
census taker	real estate
day laborer	rock candy
eye opener	training ship
fellow citizen	violin teacher

Words are usually combined to express a literal or nonliteral (figurative) unit idea that would not be as clearly expressed in unconnected succession.

afterglow	gentleman
bookkeeping	newsprint
cupboard	right-of-way
forget-me-not	whitewash

Unless otherwise indicated, a derivative of a compound retains the solid or hyphenated form of the original compound.

coldbloodedness	praiseworthiness
footnoting	railroader
ill-advisedly	Y-shaped
outlawry	

Except after the short prefixes *co, de, pre, pro,* and *re,* which are generally printed solid, a hyphen is used to avoid doubling a vowel or tripling a consonant.

cooperation	brass-smith
deemphasis	Inverness-shire
preexisting	thimble-eye
anti-inflation	ultra-atomic
micro-organism	shell-like
semi-independent	hull-less
	but co-occupant

Solid compounds

Print solid two nouns that form a third when the compound has only one primary accent, especially when the prefixed noun consists of only one syllable or when one of the elements loses its original accent.

airship	fishmonger
bathroom	footnote
bookseller	locksmith
cupboard	workman
dressmaker	

Print solid a noun consisting of a short verb and an adverb as its second element, except when the use of the solid form would interfere with comprehension.

blowout	hangover
breakdown	holdup
flareback	makeready
giveaway	markoff
pickup	tradeoff
runoff	*but* cut-in
setup	run-in
showdown	tie-in
throwaway	

Compounds beginning with the following nouns are usually printed solid.

book	school
eye	shop
horse	snow
house	way
mill	wood
play	work

Compounds ending in the following are usually printed solid, especially when prefixed word consists of one syllable.

berry	monger
bird	over
blossom	owner
board	*but* #ownership
boat	person
book	picker
borne	picking
bound	piece
box	plane
boy	power
brained	proof
bug	roach
bush	room
craft	shop
field	site
fish	skin
flower	smith
fly	stone
girl	store
grower	tail
headed	tight
hearted	time (not clock)
holder	ward
hopper	ware
house	water
keeper	way
keeping	wear
land	weed
light	wide
like	wise
line	woman
load	wood
maid	work
maker	worker
making	working
man	worm
master	worthy
mate	writer
mill	writing
mistress	yard

Print solid *any, every, no,* and *some* when combined with *body, thing,* and *where;* when *one* is the second element, print as two words if meaning a single or particular person or thing; to avoid mispronunciation, print *no one* as two words at all times.

anybody	nobody
anything	nothing
anywhere	nowhere
anyone	no one
everybody	somebody
everything	something
everywhere	somewhere
everyone	someone

but any one of us may stay; every one of the pilots is responsible.

Print compound personal pronouns as one word.

herself	oneself	thyself
himself	ourselves	yourself
itself	themselves	yourselves
myself		

Print as one word compass directions consisting of two points, but use a hyphen after the first point when three points are combined.

northeast	north-northeast
southwest	south-southwest

Unit modifiers

Print a hyphen between words, or abbreviations and words, combined to form a unit modifier immediately preceding the word modified, except as indicated in the following rule and elsewhere throughout this section. This applies particularly to combinations in which one element is a present or past participle.

agreed-upon standards
Baltimore-Washington road
collective-bargaining talks
contested-election case
contract-bar rule
cost-of-living increase
drought-stricken area
English-speaking nation
fire-tested material
Federal-State-local cooperation
German-English descent
guided-missile program
hard-of-hearing class
high-speed line
large-scale project
law-abiding citizen
long-term loan
long-term-payment loan
lump-sum payment
most-favored-nation clause
multiple-purpose uses
no-par-value stock
part-time personnel
rust-resistant covering
service-connected disability
state-of-the-art technology
tool-and-die maker
up-or-down vote
U.S.-owned property; U.S.-flag ship
1-inch diameter; 2-inch-diameter pipe
10-word telegram
a 4-percent increase, the 10-percent rise
but 4 percent citric acid, 4 percent interest[1]

Where meaning is clear and readability is not aided, it is not necessary to use a hyphen to form a temporary or made compound. Restraint should be exercised in forming unnecessary combinations of words used in normal sequence.

atomic energy power
bituminous coal industry
child welfare plan
civil rights case
civil service examination
durable goods industry
flood control study
free enterprise system
high school student; elementary school grade
income tax form
interstate commerce law
land bank loan
land use program
life insurance company
mutual security funds
national defense appropriation
natural gas company
per capita expenditure
Portland cement plant
production credit loan
public utility plant
real estate tax
small businessman
social security pension
soil conservation measures
special delivery mail; parcel post delivery
speech correction class
but no-hyphen rule (readability aided); *not* no hyphen rule

Print without a hyphen a compound predicate adjective or predicate noun the second element of which is a present participle.

The duties were price fixing.
The effects were far reaching.
The shale was oil bearing.
The area was used for beet raising.

[1]Note the absence of an article: *a, an,* or *the.* The word *of* is understood here.

Print without a hyphen a compound predicate adjective the second element of which is a past participle; also, omit the hyphen in a predicate modifier of comparative or superlative degree.

The area is drought stricken.
The paper is fine grained.
Moderately fine grained wood.
The boy is freckle faced.
This material is fire tested.
The cars are higher priced.
The reporters are best informed.

Print without a hyphen a two-word modifier the first element of which is a comparative or superlative.

better drained soil
best liked books
higher level decision
highest priced apartment
larger sized dress
better paying job
lower income group
but uppercrust society
lowercase, uppercase type (printing)
undercoverman
upperclassman
bestseller (noun)
lighter-than-air craft
higher-than-market price

Do not use a hyphen in a two-word unit modifier the first element of which is an adverb ending in *ly,* nor use hyphens in a three-word unit modifier the first two elements of which are adverbs.

eagerly awaited moment
wholly owned subsidiary
unusually well preserved specimen
very well defined usage
longer than usual lunch period
very well worth reading
not too distant future
often heard phrase
but ever-normal granary
ever-rising flood
still-new car
still-lingering doubt
well-known lawyer
well-kept farm

Proper nouns used as unit modifiers, either in their basic or derived form, retain their original form; but the hyphen is printed when combining forms.

Latin American countries
North Carolina roads
a Mexican-American
South American trade
Spanish-American pride
Winston-Salem festival
Afro-American program
Anglo-Saxon period
Franco-Prussian War
but Minneapolis-St. Paul region
North American-South American sphere
French-English descent
Washington-Wilkes-Barre route

Do not confuse a modifier with the word it modifies. In some instances clarity can be achieved by the writer by using such terms as businessperson, shoe repairer, worker, etc.

elderly clothesman
competent shoemaker
field canning factory
gallant serviceman
light blue hat (weight)
average taxpayer
American flagship
well-trained schoolteacher
preschool children (kindergarten)
but common stockholder
stock ownership
small businessman
working men and women
steam powerplant site
meat packinghouse owner
old-clothes man
wooden-shoe maker
tomato-canning factory
service men and women
light-blue hat (color)
income-tax payer
American-flag ship
elementary school teacher
pre-school children (before school)

Where two or more hyphenated compounds have a common basic element and this element is omitted in all but the last term, the hyphens are retained.

2- or 3-em quads, *not* 2 or 3-em quads; 2- to 3- and 4- to 5-ton trucks
2- by 4-inch boards, *but* 2 to 6 inches wide
8-, 10-, and 16-foot boards
6.4-, 3.1-, and 2-percent pay raises
moss- and ivy-covered walls, *not* moss and ivy-covered walls
long- and short-term money rates, *not* long and short-term money rates
but twofold or threefold, *not* two or threefold
goat, sheep, and calf skins, *not* goat, sheep, and calfskins
intrastate and intracity, *not* intra-state and -city
American owned and managed companies
preoperative and postoperative examination

Do not use a hyphen in a unit modifier consisting of a foreign phrase.

ante bellum days
bona fide transaction
ex officio member
per capita tax
per diem employee
prima facie evidence

Do not print a hyphen in a unit modifier containing a letter or a numeral as its second element.

abstract B pages
article 3 provisions
class II railroad
grade A milk
point 4 program
ward D beds

Do not use a hyphen in a unit modifier enclosed in quotation marks unless it is normally a hyphenated term, but quotation marks are not to be used in lieu of a hyphen.

"blue sky" law
"good neighbor" policy
"tie-in" sale
but right-to-work law

Print combination color terms as separate words, but use a hyphen when such color terms are unit modifiers.

bluish green
dark green
orange red
bluish-green feathers
iron-gray sink
silver-gray body

Do not use a hyphen between independent adjectives preceding a noun.

big gray cat
a fine old southern gentleman

Prefixes, suffixes, and combining forms

Print solid combining forms and prefixes, except as indicated elsewhere.

*after*birth
*Anglo*mania
*ante*date
*anti*slavery
*bi*weekly
*by*law
*circum*navigation
*cis*alpine
*co*operate
*contra*position
*counter*case
*de*energize
*demi*tasse
*ex*communicate
*extra*curricular
*fore*tell
*heroi*comic
*hyper*sensitive
*hypo*acid
*in*bound
*infra*red
*inter*view
*intra*spinal
*intro*vert
*iso*metric
*macro*analysis
*meso*thorax
*meta*genesis
*micro*phone
*mis*state
*mono*gram
*multi*color
*neo*phyte
*non*neutral
*off*set
*out*bake
*over*active
*pan*cosmic
*para*centric
*parti*coated
*peri*patetic
*plano*convex
*poly*nodal
*post*script
*pre*exist
*pro*consul
*pseudo*scholastic
*re*enact
*retro*spect
*semi*official
*step*father
*sub*secretary
*super*market
*thermo*couple
*tran*sonic
*trans*ship
*tri*color
*ultra*violet
*un*necessary
*under*flow

Print solid combining forms and suffixes, except as indicated elsewhere.

port*able*
cover*age*
oper*ate*
plebis*cite*
twenty*fold*
spoon*ful*
kilo*gram*
geo*graphy*
man*hood*
self*ish*
pump*kin*
meat*less*
out*let*
wave*like*
procure*ment*
inner*most*
partner*ship*
lone*some*
home*stead*
north*ward*
clock*wise*

Print solid words ending in *like,* but use a hyphen to avoid tripling a consonant or when the first element is a proper name.

lifelike
lilylike
bell-like
girllike
Scotland-like
MacArthur-like

Use a hyphen or hyphens to prevent mispronunciation, to insure a definite accent on each element of the compound, or to avoid ambiguity.

anti-hog-cholera serum
co-op
multi-ply (several plies)
non-civil-service position
non-tumor-bearing tissue
pre-position (before)
re-cover (cover again)
re-sorting (sort again)
re-treat (treat again)
un-ionized
un-uniformity
but rereferred

Use a hyphen to join duplicated prefixes.

re-redirect
sub-subcommittee
super-superlative

Print with a hyphen the prefixes *ex, self,* and *quasi.*

ex-governor
ex-serviceman
ex-trader
ex-vice-president[2]
self-control
self-educated
but selfhood
selfsame
quasi-academic
quasi-argument
quasi-corporation
quasi-young

Unless usage demands otherwise, use a hyphen to join a prefix or combining form to a capitalized word. (The hyphen is retained in words of this class set in caps.)

anti-Arab
pro-British
un-American
non-Government
post-World War II *or* post-Second World War
non-Federal
but nongovernmental
overanglicize
prezeppelin
transatlantic

[2] In official usage, the title of Vice President of the United States is written without a hyphen; the hyphen is also omitted in all like titles, such as vice admiral, vice consul, etc.

Numerical compounds

Print a hyphen between the elements of compound numbers from twenty-one to ninety-nine and in adjective compounds with a numerical first element.

twenty-one
twenty-first
6-footer
24-in ruler
3-week vacation
8-hour day
10-minute delay
20th-century progress
3-to-1 ratio
5-to-4 vote
.22-caliber cartridge
2-cent-per-pound tax
four-in-hand tie
three-and-twenty
two-sided question
multimillion-dollar fund
10-dollar-per-car tax
thirty- (30-) day period
second grade children
but one hundred and twenty-one
100-odd
foursome
threescore
foursquare
$20 million airfield

Print without a hyphen a modifier consisting of a possessive noun preceded by a numeral.

1 month's layoff	2 hours' work
1 week's pay	3 weeks' vacation

Print a hyphen between the elements of a fraction, but omit it between the numerator and the denominator when the hyphen appears in either or in both.

one-thousandth
two-thirds
two one-thousandths
twenty-three thirtieths
twenty-one thirty-seconds
three-fourths of an inch

A unit modifier following and reading back to the word or words modified takes a hyphen and is always printed in the singular.

motor, alternating-current, 3-phase, 60-cycle, 115-volt
glass jars: 5-gallon, 2-gallon, 1-quart
belts: 2-inch, 1¼-inch, ½-inch, ¼-inch

Civil and military titles

Do not hyphenate a civil or military title denoting a single office, but print a double title with a hyphen.

ambassador at large
assistant attorney general
commander in chief
comptroller general
Congressman at Large
major general
sergeant at arms
notary public
secretary general
under secretary; *but* under-secretaryship
vice president,[2] *but* vice-presidency
secretary-treasurer
treasurer-manager

The adjectives *elect* and *designate,* as the last element of a title, require a hyphen.

President-elect
Vice-President-elect
ambassador-designate
minister-designate

Scientific and technical terms

Do not print a hyphen in scientific terms (names of chemicals, diseases, animals, insects, plants) used as unit modifiers if no hyphen appears in their original form.

carbon monoxide poisoning
guinea pig raising
hog cholera serum
methyl bromide solution
stem rust control
equivalent uranium content
whooping cough remedy
but Russian-olive plantings
Douglas-fir tree

Chemical elements used in combination with figures use a hyphen, except with superior figures.

polonium-210
uranium-235; *but* U^{235}; Sr^{90}; ${}_{92}U^{234}$
Freon-12

Note use of hyphens and closeup punctuation in chemical formulas.

9-nitroanthra (1,9,4,10)bis(1)oxathiazone-2,7-bisdioxide
Cr-Ni-Mo
2,4-D

Print a hyphen between the elements of technical compound units of measurement.

candela-hour	light-year
crop-year	passenger-mile
horsepower-hour	staff-hour
	but kilowatthour

Improvised compounds

Print with a hyphen the elements of an improvised compound.

blue-pencil (v.)
18-year-old (n., u.m.)
know-it-all (n.)
know-how (n.)
lick-the-finger-and-test-the-wind economics
make-believe (n.)
one-man-one-vote principle
roll-on/roll-off ship
stick-in-the-mud (n.)
let-George-do-it attitude
how-to-be-beautiful course
hard-and-fast rule
penny-wise and pound-foolish policy
first-come-first-served basis
but a basis of first come, first served
easy come, easy go

Use hyphens in a prepositional-phrase compound noun consisting of three or more words.

cat-o'-nine-tails
government-in-exile
grant-in-aid
jack-in-the-box
man-of-war
mother-in-law
mother-of-pearl
patent-in-fee
but coat of arms
heir at law
next of kin
officer in charge

When the corresponding noun form is printed as separate words, the verb form is always hyphenated.

cold-shoulder	blue-pencil	cross-brace

Print a hyphen in a compound formed of repetitive or conflicting terms and in a compound naming the same thing under two aspects.

boogie-woogie	pitter-patter
comedy-ballet	razzle-dazzle
dead-alive	walkie-talkie
devil-devil	willy-nilly
even-stephen	young-old
farce-melodrama	*but* bowwow
murder-suicide	dillydally
nitty-gritty	riffraff

Use a hyphen in a nonliteral compound expression containing an apostrophe in its first element.

asses'-eyes
ass's-foot
bull's-eye
cat's-paw
crow's-nest
but The cat's paw is soft.
There is the crow's nest.

Use a hyphen to join a single capital letter to a noun or a participle.

H-bomb	V-necked	*but* x ray
I-beam	S-iron	x raying
T-shaped	T-square	
U-boat	X-ed out	

Print idiomatic phrases without hyphens.

come by	insofar as	nowadays
inasmuch as	Monday week	

ABBREVIATIONS

Abbreviations are used to save space and to avoid distracting the mind of the reader by a needless spelling out of repetitious words or phrases.

The nature of the publication governs the extent to which abbreviations are used. In text of technical and legal publications, and in parentheses, brackets, footnotes, sidenotes, tables, leaderwork, and bibliographies, many words are frequently abbreviated. Cut-in sideheads, legends, tables of contents, and indexes follow the style of the text.

Internal and terminal punctuation in units of measure are to be omitted to conform with practice adopted by scientific, technical, and industrial groups, nationally and internationally. Where omission of terminal punctuation causes confusion; e.g., the symbol *in* (inch) mistaken for the preposition *in,* the abbreviation should be spelled out.

Standard and easily understood forms are preferable, and they should be uniform throughout a job. Abbreviations not generally known should be followed in the text by the spelled-out forms in parentheses the first time they occur; in tables and leaderwork such explanatory matter should be supplied in a footnote. As the printer cannot rewrite the copy, the author should supply these explanatory forms.

In technical matter, abbreviations for units of measure should be used only with figures; similarly, many other abbreviations should not appear in isolation; for example, energy is measured in foot-pounds, *not* energy is measured in ft·lb.

Capitals, hyphens, periods, and spacing

In general, an abbreviation follows the capitalization and hyphening of the word or words abbreviated. It is followed by a period unless otherwise indicated.

c.o.d. St. *but* ft·lb

Abbreviations and initials of a personal name with points are set without spaces. However, abbreviations composed of contractions and initials or numbers, will retain space.

U.S.
U.S.S.R.
U.N.
U.S.C. (*but* Rev. Stat.)
B.S., LL.D., Ph.D., B.Sc.
H.R. 116 (*but* S. 116, S. Con. Res. 116)
C.A.D.C. (*but* App. D.C.)
A.B. Secrest, D.D.S.
A.F. of L.-CIO (*or* AFL-CIO preferred)
AT&T
Texas A&M
R&D
A.D., B.C.
e.s.t.
i.e., e.g. (*but* op. cit.)
J.F.K.
L.B.J.

Except as otherwise designated, points and spaces are omitted after initials used as shortened names of governmental agencies and of other organized bodies. "Other organized bodies" shall be interpreted to mean organized bodies that have become popularly identified with a symbol, such as MIT (Massachusetts Institute of Technology), GM (General Motors), GMAC (General Motors Acceptance Corp.), etc. Symbols, when they appear in copy, may be used for acts of Congress. Example: ARA (Area Redevelopment Act).

MIT	TVA	ARC
NLRB	AFL-CIO	ASTM

Geographic terms

U.S. (for United States) will be used when preceding the word *Government* or the name of a Government organization, except in formal writing (treaties, Executive orders, proclamations, etc.); congressional bills; legal citations and courtwork; covers and title pages unless abbreviation is requested; and in association with name or names of other countries.

U.S. Government
U.S. Congress
U.S. Department of Health and Human Resources
U.S. district court
U.S. Supreme Court (*but* Supreme Court of the United States)
U.S. Army (*but* Army of the United States)
U.S. monitor *Nantucket*
U.S.-NATO assistance
U.S.-U.S.S.R. meeting
U.S. Government efforts to control inflation must be successful if the United States is to have a stable economy.
but British, French, and United States Governments; United States-British talks

With the exceptions in the above rule, the abbreviation *U.S.* is used in the adjective position, but is spelled out when used as a noun.

U.S. foreign policy
U.S. farm-support program
U.S. attorney
U.S. citizen
but Foreign policy of the United States
United States Code (official title)
United States Steel Corp. (legal title)

The names of foreign countries, except U.S.S.R. (to avoid too long a name), are not abbreviated.

In other than formal usage, all States of the United States, the Canal Zone, Puerto Rico, and the Virgin Islands are abbreviated immediately following any capitalized geographic term, including armory, arsenal, airbase, airport, barracks, depot, fort, Indian agency, military camp, national cemetery (also forest, historic site, memorial, seashore, monument, park), naval shipyard, proving ground, reservation (forest, Indian, or military), and reserve or station (military or naval).

Prince George County, VA
Mount Rainier National Forest, WA
Stone Mountain, GA
National Naval Medical Center, Bethesda, MD
Mark Twain National Wildlife Refuge, IL-IA-MO (note use of hyphens here)
Richmond, VA
Arlington National Cemetery, VA
Aberdeen Proving Ground, MD
Friendship Airport, MD
Redstone Arsenal, AL
but Leavenworth freight yards, Kansas Altoona sidetrack, Wisconsin

The Postal Service style of two-letter State and Province abbreviations is to be used.

UNITED STATES

AL	Alabama	MD	Maryland
AK	Alaska	MA	Massachusetts
AZ	Arizona	MI	Michigan
AR	Arkansas	MN	Minnesota
CA	California	MS	Mississippi
CO	Colorado	MO	Missouri
CT	Connecticut	MT	Montana
DE	Delaware	NE	Nebraska
FL	Florida	NV	Nevada
GA	Georgia	NH	New Hampshire
HI	Hawaii	NJ	New Jersey
ID	Idaho	NM	New Mexico
IL	Illinois	NY	New York
IN	Indiana	NC	North Carolina
IA	Iowa	ND	North Dakota
KS	Kansas	OH	Ohio
KY	Kentucky	OK	Oklahoma
LA	Louisiana	OR	Oregon
ME	Maine	PA	Pennsylvania

RI	Rhode Island	WV	West Virginia
SC	South Carolina	WI	Wisconsin
SD	South Dakota	WY	Wyoming
TN	Tennessee	CZ	Canal Zone
TX	Texas	DC	District of Columbia
UT	Utah	GU	Guam
VT	Vermont	PR	Puerto Rico
VA	Virginia	VI	Virgin Islands
WA	Washington		

CANADA

AB	Alberta	NS	Nova Scotia
BC	British Columbia	ON	Ontario
LB	Labrador	PE	Prince Edward Island
MB	Manitoba	PQ	Quebec
NB	New Brunswick	SK	Saskatchewan
NF	Newfoundland	UT	Yukon Territory
NT	Northwest Territories		

The names of other insular possessions, trust territories, and *Long Island, Staten Island,* etc., are not abbreviated.

The names of Canadian Provinces and other foreign political subdivisions are not abbreviated except as noted above.

Addresses

The words *street, avenue, place, road, square, boulevard, terrace, drive, court,* and *building,* following name or number, are abbreviated in footnotes, sidenotes, tables, leaderwork, and lists.

In addresses, a single period is used with the abbreviations *NW., SW., NE., SE.* (indicating sectional divisions of cities) following name or number. *North, South, East,* and *West* are spelled out at all times.

The word *Street* or *Avenue* as part of a name is not abbreviated even in parentheses, footnotes, sidenotes, tables, and leaderwork.

14th Street Bridge   Ninth Avenue Bldg.

The words *county, fort, mount, point,* and *port* are not abbreviated. *Saint (St.)* and *Sainte (Ste.)* should be abbreviated.

Descriptions of tracts of land

If fractions are spelled out in land descriptions, *half* and *quarter* are used (not *one-half* nor *one-quarter*).

south half of T. 47 N., R. 64E.

In the description of tracts of public land the following abbreviations are used (periods are omitted after abbreviated compass directions that immediately precede and close up on figures):

SE¼NW¼ sec. 4, T. 12 S., R. 15 E., of the Boise Meridian
lot 6, NE¼ sec. 4, T. 6 N., R. 1 W.
N½ sec. 20, T. 7 N., R. 2 W., sixth principal meridian
Tps. 9, 10, 11, and 12 S., Rs. 12 and 13 W.
T. 2 S., Rs. 8, 9, and 10 E., sec. 26
T. 3 S., R. 1 E., sec. 34, W½E½, W½, and W½SE¼SE¼
sec. 32 (with or without a township number)

In case of an unavoidable break in a land-description symbol group at end of a line, use no hyphen and break after fraction.

Names and titles

The following forms are not always abbreviations, and copy should be followed as to periods:

Al   Ed   Will
Alex   Fred
Ben   Sam

In signatures the exact form used by the signer must be retained.

George Wythe   Geo. Taylor

In company and other formal names, if it is not necessary to preserve the full legal title, the forms *Bro., Bros., Co., Corp., Inc., Ltd.,* and *&* are used. *Association* and *Manufacturing* are not abbreviated.

Radio Corp. of America
Aluminum Co. of America
Standard Oil Co. of New Jersey
Ronald G. Brown & Bro.
Jones Bros. & Co.
American Telephone & Telegraph Co.
Norbert J. Schackmar Investment Corp.
Vic Sport Shop, Inc.
Maryland Steamship Co., Ltd.
Chesapeake & Delaware Canal
Fairmount Building & Loan Association
Electronics Manufacturing Co.
Texas College of Arts & Industries
National Barrel & Drum Association
Robert Wilson & Associates, Inc.
U.S. News & World Report
Baltimore & Ohio Railroad
Mine, Mill & Smelter Workers
but Little Theater Company
Senate Banking, Housing, and Urban Affairs Committee
Federal Savings and Loan Insurance Corporation (Federal unit)

Company and *Corporation* are not abbreviated in names of Federal Government units.

Panama Railroad Company
Commodity Credit Corporation

In parentheses, footnotes, sidenotes, tables, and leaderwork, abbreviate the words *railroad* and *railway* (*RR.* and *Ry.*), except in such names as "Washington Railway & Electric Co." and "Florida Railroad & Navigation Corp." *SS* for *steamship, MS* for *motorship,* etc., preceding name are used at all times.

In the names of informal companionships the word *and* is spelled out.

Gilbert and Sullivan   Currier and Ives

In other than formal usage, a civil, military, or naval title preceding a name is abbreviated if followed by Christian or given name or initial; but *Mr., Mrs., Miss, Ms., M., MM., Messrs., Mlle., Mme.,* and *Dr.* are abbreviated with or without Christian or given name or initial.

Adj.	Maj. Gen.
Adj. Gen.	M. Sgt.
Adm. (admiral)	Orderly Sgt.
A1c. (airman, first class)	Ord. Sgt. (ordnance sergeant)
Asst. Surg.	Passed Asst. Surg.
Brig. Gen.	Pfc. (private first class)
Bvt. (brevet)	PO (petty officer)
Capt.	Prof.
Col.	Pvt.
Comdr.	Q.M. Gen.
Cpl.	Q.M. Sgt.
CWO (chief warrant officer)	Rdm3c. (radarman, third class)
En1c. (engineman, first class)	Rear Adm.
Ens.	S1c. (seaman, first class)
1st Lt.	2d Lt.
1st Sgt.	Sfc. (sergeant, first class)
Gen.	Sgt.
Gov.	Sgt. Maj.
Hosp. Corpsman 3c.	Sp3c. (specialist, third class)
Hosp. Sgt.	S. Sgt.
Hosp. Steward	Supt.
Insp. Gen.	Surg.
Judge Adv. Gen.	Surg. Gen.
Lt.	T2g. (technician, second grade)
Lt. Col.	T. Sgt.
Lt. Comdr.	Vice Adm.
Lt. Gen.	WO (warrant officer)
Lt. Gov.	WO (jg.)
Lt. (jg.)	
Maj.	

If requested, the following military abbreviations will be used:

ADM, admiral
BG, brigadier general
CDR, commander
COL, colonel
CPL, corporal
CAPT, captain
CPT, captain
CWO4, chief warrant officer (W-4)
ENS, ensign
LCDR, lieutenant commander
LT, lieutenant
LTC, lieutenant commander
LTG, lieutenant general
LTJG, lieutenant junior grade
2LT, second lieutenant
MAJ, major
PFC, private first class
PVT, private
RADM, radarman
SFC, sergeant first class
S4, specialist four
SGT, sergeant
VADM, vice admiral
WO1, warrant officer

Spell *Senator, Representative, commodore,* and *commandant.*

Unless preceded by *the,* abbreviate *honorable, reverend,* and *monsignor* when followed by the first name, initials, or title.

Hon. Elihu Root; the Honorable Elihu Root; the Honorable Mr. Root
the Honorables William H. Rehnquist, Lewis F. Powell, Jr., and Harry A. Blackmun
Rev. Martin Luther King, Jr.; the Reverend Dr. King; Rev. Dr. King; Reverend King (*not* Rev. King, *nor* the Reverend King)
Rt. Rev. James E. Freeman; the Right Reverend James E. Freeman; Very Rev. Henry Boyd; the Very Reverend Henry Boyd
Rt. Rev. Msgr. John Bird; the Right Reverend Monsignor John Bird

The following and similar forms are used after a name:

Esq., Jr., Sr.
2d, 3d (*or* II, III) (not preceded by comma)
Degrees: LL.D., M.A., Ph.D., etc.
Fellowships, orders, etc.: F.R.S., K.C.B., C.P.A., etc.

The abbreviation *Esq.* and other titles such as *Mr., Mrs.,* and *Dr.,* should not appear with any other title or with abbreviations indicating scholastic degrees.

John L. Smith, Esq., *not* Mr. John L. Smith, Esq., *nor* John L. Smith, Esq., A.M.; *but* James A. Jones, Jr., Esq.
Ford Maddox, A.B., Ph.D., *not* Mr. Ford Maddox, A.B., Ph.D.
George Gray, M.D., *not* Mr. George Gray, M.D., *nor* Dr. George Gray, M.D.
Dwight A. Bellinger, D.V.M.

Sr. and *Jr.* should not be used without Christian or given name or initials, but may be used in combination with any title.

A.K. Jones, Jr., or Mr. Jones, Junior, *not* Jones, Jr., *or* Jones, Junior.
President J.B. Nelson, Jr.

When name is followed by abbreviations designating religious and fraternal orders and scholastic and honorary degrees, their sequence is as follows: Orders, religious first; theological degrees; academic degrees earned in course; and honorary degrees in order of bestowal.

Henry L. Brown, D.D., A.M., D.Lit.
T.E. Holt, C.S.C., S.T.Lr., LL.D., Ph.D.
Samuel J. Deckelbaum, P.M.

Academic degrees standing alone may be abbreviated.

John was graduated with a B.A. degree; *but* bachelor of arts degree (lowercase if spelled out).
He earned his Ph.D. by hard work.

In addresses, signatures, and lists of names, including leaderwork but not in tables or in centerheads, *Mr., Mrs.,* and other titles preceding a name, and *Esq., Jr., Sr., 2d,* and *3d* folwing a name, are set in roman caps and lowcase if the name is in caps and small caps. If e name is in caps, they are set in caps and nall caps, if small caps are available—otherwise in caps and lowercase.

arts of publications

For parts of publications mentioned in arentheses, brackets, footnotes, sidenotes, list references, synonymies, tables, and leaderork, and followed by figures, letters, or oman numerals, the following abbreviations e used:

app., apps. (appendix, appendixes)
art., arts. (article, articles)
bull., bulls. (bulletin, bulletins)
ch., chs. (chapter, chapters)
col., cols. (column, columns)
ed., eds. (edition, editions)
fig., figs. (figure, figures)
No., Nos. (number, numbers)
p., pp. (page, pages)
par., pars. (paragraph, paragraphs)
pl., pls. (plate, plates)
pt., pts. (part, parts)
sec., secs. (section, sections)
subch., subchs. (subchapter, subchapters)
subpar., subpars. (subparagraph, subparagraphs)
subpt., subpts. (subpart, subparts)
subsec., subsecs. (subsection, subsections)
supp., supps. (supplement, supplements)
vol., vols. (volume, volumes)

The word *article* and the word *section* are bbreviated when appearing at the beginning f a paragraph and set in caps and small caps ollowed by a period and an en space, except hat the first of a series is spelled out.

ART. 2; SEC. 2; etc.; *but* ARTICLE 1; SECTION 1
ART. II; SEC. II; etc.; *but* ARTICLE I; SECTION I

At the beginning of a legend, the word *figure* receding the legend number is not abbreviated.

FIGURE 4.—Landscape.

Terms relating to Congress

The words *Congress* and *session,* when accompanied by a numerical reference, are abbreviated in parentheses, brackets, and text footnotes. In sidenotes, lists of references, synonymies, tables, leaderwork, and footnotes to tables and leaderwork, the following abbreviations are used:

92d Cong., 1st sess.	Public Law 84, 92d Cong.
1st sess., 92d Cong.	Private Law 68, 92d Cong.

In references to bills, resolutions, documents, and reports in parentheses, brackets, footnotes, sidenotes, tables, and leaderwork, the following abbreviations are used:

H.R. 416 (House bill)
S. 116 (Senate bill)
The above two examples may be used in either abbreviated or spelled-out form in text.
H. Res. 5 (House resolution)
H. Con. Res. 10 (House concurrent resolution)
H.J. Res. 21 (House joint resolution)
S. Res. 50 (Senate resolution)
S. Con. Res. 17 (Senate concurrent resolution)
S.J. Res. 45 (Senate joint resolution)
H. Conf. Rept. 10 (House conference report)
H. Doc. 35 (House document)
S. Doc. 62 (Senate document)
H. Rept. 214 (House report)
S. Rept. 410 (Senate report)
Ex. Doc. B (Executive document)
Ex. F (92d Cong., 2d sess.)
Ex. Rept. 9 (92d Cong., 1st sess.)
Misc. Doc. 16 (miscellaneous document)
Public Res. 47

References to statutes in parentheses, footnotes, sidenotes, tables, leaderwork, and congressional work are abbreviated as follows:

Rev. Stat. (Revised Statutes); 43 Rev. Stat. 801; 18 U.S.C. 38
Supp. Rev. Stat. (Supplement to the Revised Statutes)
Stat. L. (Statutes at Large)
but Public Law 85–1

Calendar divisions

Names of months followed by the day, or day and year, are abbreviated in footnotes, tables, leaderwork, and sidenotes, and in bibliographies. *May, June,* and *July* are always spelled out. In narrow columns in tables, however, the names of months may be abbreviated even if standing alone. Preferred forms follow:

Jan.	Apr.	Oct.
Feb.	Aug.	Nov.
Mar.	Sept.	Dec.

In text only, dates as part of a citation or reference within parentheses or brackets are also abbreviated.

(Op. Atty. Gen., Dec. 4, 1985)
(Congressional Record, Sept. 25, 1981)
[From the *New York Times,* Mar. 4, 1978]
[From the Mar. 4 issue]
On Jan. 25 (we had commenced on Dec. 26, 1977) the work was finished. (In footnotes, tables, leaderwork, and sidenotes)
On January 25, a decision was reached (Op. Atty. Gen., Dec. 4, 1975). (Text, but with citation in parentheses)
but On January 25 (we had commenced on December 26, 1967) the work was finished. (Not a citation or reference in text)

Weekdays are not abbreviated, but the following forms are used, if necessary, in lists or in narrow columns in tables:

Sun.	Wed.	Fri.
Mon.	Thurs.	Sat.
Tues.		

The following forms are to be used when abbreviating names of time zones:

A.s.t, Atlantic standard time
A.t., Atlantic time
c.s.t., central standard time
c.t., central time
d.s.t., daylight saving (no "s") time
e.d.t., eastern daylight time
e.s.t., eastern standard time
e.t., eastern time
G.c.t., Greenwich civil time
G.m.a.t., Greenwich mean astronomical time
G.m.t., Greenwich mean time
l.s.t., local standard time
m., noon (meridies)
m.s.t., mountain standard time
m.t., mountain time
P.s.t., Pacific standard time
P.t., Pacific time
u.t., universal time

Coined words and symbols

To obtain uniform treatment in the formation of coined words and symbols, the following formula, which conforms to current usage, should be applied:

When only first letter of each word or selected words is used to make up symbol, use all caps:
APPR (Army package power reactor)
MAG (Military Advisory Group)
MIRV (multiple independently targetable reentry vehicle)
SALT (strategic arms limitation talks)
STEP (supplemental training and employment program)

Where first letters of prefixes and/or suffixes are utilized as part of established expressions, use all caps:
CPR (*cardio*p*ulmonary* r*esuscitation*)
ESP (*extras*ensory p*erception*)
FLIR (*f*orward-*l*ooking *i*nfra*r*ed)

Where an acronym or abbreviated form is copyrighted or established by law, copy must be followed:
ACTION (agency of Government; not an acronym)
MarAd (*Mar*itime *Ad*ministration)
NACo (*N*ational *A*ssociation of *Co*unties)
MEDLARS (*Med*ical *L*iterature *A*nalysis and *R*etrieval *S*ystem)

When proper names are used in shortened form any word of which uses more than first letter of each word, use caps and lowercase:
Conrail (Consolidated Rail Corporation)
Vepco (Virginia Electric Power Co.)
Inco (International Nickel Co.)
Aramco (Arabian-American Oil Co.)

In common-noun combinations made up of more than first letter of lowercased words, use lowercase:
loran (*lo*ng-*ra*nge *n*avigation)
sonar (*so*und *na*vigation *r*anging)
secant (*se*paration *c*ontrol of *a*ircraft by *n*onsynchronous *t*echniques)

The words *infra* and *supra* are not abbreviated.

Terms of measure

Compass directions are abbreviated as follows:

N.	S.	10° N. 25° W.
NE.	NNW.	NW. by N. ¼ W.
E.	W.	
SW.	ESE.	

The words *latitude* and *longitude,* followed by figures, are abbreviated in parentheses, brackets, footnotes, sidenotes, tables, and leaderwork, and the figures are always closed up.

lat. 52°33′05″ N. long. 13°21′10″ E.

Avoid breaking latitude and longitude figures at end of line; space out line instead. In case of an unavoidable break at end of line, use hyphen.

Temperature and gravity are expressed in figures. When using the degree mark bump to cap letters, not against figures. Note the following abbreviations and letter symbols:

abs, absolute	API, American Petroleum Institute
Bé, Baumé	Twad, Twaddell
°C,[1] degree Celsius[2]	100 °C
°F, degree Fahrenheit	212 °F[1]
°R, degree Rankine	671.67 °R
K, kelvin	273.15 K
°API	18 °API

References to meridian in statements of time are abbreviated as follows:

10 a.m.	12 m. (noon)
2:30 p.m.	12 p.m. (midnight)

The word *o'clock* is not used with abbreviations of time.

Metric unit letter symbols are set lowercase roman unless the unit name has been derived from a proper name, in which case the first letter of the symbol is capitalized (for example Pa for pascal and W for watt). The exception is the letter L for liter. The same form is used for singular and plural. The preferred symbol for *cubic centimeter* is cm^3; use *cc* only when requested.

A space is used between a figure and a unit symbol except in the case of the symbols for degree, minute, and second of plane angle.

3 m 25 °C *but* 33°15′21″

Prefixes for multiples and submultiples

E	exa (10^{18})	d	deci (10^{-1})
P	peta (10^{15})	c	centi (10^{-2})
T	tera (10^{12})	m	milli (10^{-3})
G	giga (10^{9})	μ	micro (10^{-8})
M	mega (10^{6})	n	nano (10^{-9})
k	kilo (10^{3})	p	pico (10^{-12})
h	hecto (10^{2})	f	femto (10^{-15})
da	deka (10)	a	atto (10^{-18})

[1] Without figures preceding it, *°C* or *°F* should be used only in boxheads and over figure columns in tables.
[2] Preferred form (superseding Centigrade) approved by Ninth General Conference on Weights and Measures, October 1948.

Metric units

m, meter (for length)
g, gram (for weight or mass)
L, liter (for capacity)

Length

km	kilometer	dm	decimeter
hm	hectometer	cm	centimeter
dam	dekameter	mm	millimeter
m	meter		

Area

km^2	square kilometer
hm^2	square hectometer
dam^2	square dekameter
m^2	square meter
dm^2	square decimeter
cm^2	square centimeter
mm^2	square millimeter

Volume

km^3	cubic kilometer
hm^3	cubic hectometer
dam^3	cubic dekameter
m^3	cubic meter
dm^3	cubic decimeter
cm^3	cubic centimeter
mm^3	cubic millimeter

Weight

kg	kilogram	dg	decigram
hg	hectogram	cg	centigram
dag	dekagram	mg	milligram
g	gram	μg	microgram

Land area

ha	hectare
a	are

Capacity of containers

kL	kiloliter	dL	deciliter
hL	hectoliter	cL	centiliter
daL	dekaliter	mL	milliliter
L	liter		

A similar plan of abbreviation applies to any unit of the metric system.

A	ampere	kV	kilovolt
VA	voltampere	kVA	kilovoltampere
c	cycle (radio)	kW	kilowatt
F	farad	mF	millifarad
H	henry	mH	millihenry
J	joule	μF	microfarad (one-millionth of a farad)
V	volt		
W	watt		
kc	kilocycle		

The following forms are used when units of English weight and measure and units of time are abbreviated, the same form of abbreviation being used for both singular and plural:

Length	*Area and volume*
in, inch	in^2, square inch
ft, foot	in^3, cubic inch
yd, yard	mi^2, square mile
mi, mile (statute)	ft^3, cubic foot

Time

yr, year	h, hour
mo, month	min, minute
d, day	s, second

Weight

gr, grain
dr, dram
oz, ounce
lb, pound
cwt, hundredweight
dwt, pennyweight
ton(s), not abbreviated
but t, metric ton (tonne)

Capacity

gill(s), not abbreviated	
pt, pint	pk, peck
qt, quart	bu, bushel
gal, gallon	bbl, barrel

In astrophysical and similar scientific matter, magnitudes and units of time may be expressed as follows, if so written in copy.

$2\overset{\mathrm{M}}{\bullet}3$ $5^{h}3^{m}9^{s}$ 4.5^{h}

Money

The following are some of the abbreviations and symbols used for indicating money:

$, dol. (dollar)	₱ (peso)
c, ct, ¢ (cent, cents)	£ (pound)
LT175 (Turkish)	s (shilling)
US$15,000	d (pence)
Mex$2,650	£12 16s 8d (*not* 12/16/8)

Use "US$" if omission, in relatively rare instances, would result in confusion.

ITALIC

Italic is sometimes used to differentiate or to give greater prominence to words, phrases, etc. However, an excessive amount of italic defeats this purpose, and its use in general work should be restricted as indicated.

Emphasis, foreign words, titles of publications

Italic is not used for mere emphasis, foreign words, or the titles of publications unless it is specially requested and the copy is edited therefor.

In nonlegal work, *ante, post, infra,* and *supra* are italicized only when part of a legal citation. Otherwise these terms, as well as the abbreviations *id, ibid., op. cit., et seq.,* and other foreign words, phrases, and their abbreviations, are printed in roman.

When "emphasis supplied," "emphasis added," or "emphasis ours" appears in copy, it should not be changed; but "underscore supplied" should be changed to "italic supplied."

When copy is submitted with instructions to set "all roman (no italic)," these instructions will not apply to *Ordered, Resolved, Be it enacted,* etc.; titles following signatures or addresses; or the parts of datelines which are always set in italic.

Names of aircraft and vessels

The names of aircraft, vessels, and spacecraft are italicized unless otherwise indicated. In lists set in columns and in stubs and reading columns of tables consisting entirely of such names they will be set in roman. Missiles and rockets will be caps and lowercase and will not be italicized.

SS *America;* the liner *America*
the *Friendship*
the Bermuda *Clipper*
U.S.S. *Nautilus* (submarine)
U.S.S. *Wisconsin*
ex-U.S.S. *Savannah*
USCGS (U.S. Coast and Geodetic Survey) ship *Pathfinder*
C.S.N. *Virginia*
CG cutter *Thetus*
the *U-7*
destroyer *31*
H.M.S. *Hornet*
HS (hydrofoil ship) *Denison*
MS (motorship) *Richard*
FPV (free piston vessel) *James*
GTS (gas turbine ship) *Alexander*
NS (nuclear ship) *Savannah*
MV (motor vessel) *Havtroll*
Freedom 7; Friendship 7 (U.S. spaceships)
West Virginia class or type
the *Missouri's* (roman "s") turret
the *U-7's* (roman "s") deck
F-18 *Hornet*
F-15 *Eagle*
but Air Force One (President's plane)
B-50 (type of plane)
DD-882
LST-1155
Mig; Mig-21
PT-109

Names of vessels are quoted in matter printed in other than lowercase roman.

Sinking of the "Lusitania"
Sinking of the "Lusitania"
SINKING OF THE "LUSITANIA" (caps and small caps)
SINKING OF THE "LUSITANIA"

Names of legal cases

The names of legal cases are italicized, except the *v.* When requested, the names of such cases may be set in roman with italic *v.* In matter set in italic, legal cases are set in roman with the *v.* being set roman.

"The Hornet" and "The Hood," 124 F.2d 45
Smith v. *Brown et al.*
Smith Bros. case (172 App. Div. 149)
Smith Bros. case, *supra*
Smith Bros. case
As cited in *Smith Bros.*
John Doe v. *Richard Roe*
but John Doe against Richard Roe, the *Cement* case
SMITH *v.* BROWN ET AL. (heading)
SMITH v. BROWN ET AL. (heading)
Durham rule
Brown decision

Scientific names

The scientific names of genera, subgenera, species, and subspecies (varieties) are italicized, but are set in roman in italic matter; the names of groups of higher rank than genera (phyla, classes, orders, families, tribes, etc.) are printed in roman.

A.s. perpallidus
Dorothia? sp. (roman "?")
Tsuga canadensis
Cypripedium parviflorum var. *pubescens*
the genera *Quercus* and *Liriodendron*
the family Leguminosae; the family Nessiteras rhombopteryx
Measurements of specimens of Cyanoderma erythroptera neocara

Quotation marks should be used in place of italic for scientific names appearing in lines set in caps, caps and small caps, or boldface, even if there is italic type available in the series.

NUMERALS

Most rules for the use of numerals are based on the general principle that the reader comprehends numerals more readily than numerical word expressions, particularly in technical, scientific, or statistical matter. However, for special reasons numbers are spelled out in indicated instances.

The following rules cover the most common conditions that require a choice between the use of numerals and words. Some of them, however, are based on typographic appearance rather than on the general principle stated above.

Arabic numerals are generally preferable to Roman numerals.

Numbers expressed in figures

A figure is used for a single number of *10* or more with the exception of the first word of the sentence.

50 ballots	nearly 10 miles
10 guns	about 40 men
24 horses	10 times as large

Numbers and numbers in series

When 2 or more numbers appear in a sentence and 1 of them is *10* or more, figures are used for each number. See supporting rule for units of time, measurement, or money.

Each of 15 major commodities (9 metal and 6 nonmetal) was in supply.
but Each of nine major commodities (five metal and four nonmetal) was in supply.

Petroleum came from 16 fields, of which 8 were
discovered in 1956.

but Petroleum came from nine fields, of which eight
were discovered in 1956.

That man has 3 suits, 2 pairs of shoes, and 12
pairs of socks.

but That man has three suits, two pairs of shoes, and
four hats.

Of the 13 engine producers, 6 were farm equip
ment manufacturers, 6 were principally en
gaged in the production of other types o
machinery, and 1 was not classified in th
machinery industry.

but Only nine of these were among the large manu
facturing companies, and only three wer
among the largest concerns.

There were three 6-room houses, five 4-room
houses, and three 2-room cottages, and the
were built by 20 men.

There were three six-room houses, five four
room houses, and three two-room cottage
and they were built by nine men.

Only 4 companies in the metals group appear o
the list, whereas the 1947 census shows at leas
4,400 establishments.

but If two columns of sums of money add or subtrac
one into the other and one carries points an
ciphers, the other should also carry points an
ciphers.

At the hearing, only one Senator and one Co
gressman testified.

There are four or five things that can be done.

A unit of measurement, time, or mone
which is always expressed in figures, does n
affect the use of figures for other numeric
expressions within a sentence.

Each of the five girls earned 75 cents an hour.
Each of the 15 girls earned 75 cents an hour.
A team of four men ran the 1-mile relay in
minutes 20 seconds.
This usually requires from two to five wash
and a total time of 2 to 4 hours.
This usually requires 9 to 12 washes and a to
time of 2 to 4 hours.
The contractor, one engineer, and one survey
inspected the 1-mile road.

but There were two six-room houses, three fo
room houses, and four two-room cottages, a
they were built by nine men in thirty 5-d
weeks.

Figures are used for serial numbers.

Bulletin 725
Document 71
pages 352–57
lines 5 and 6
paragraph 1
chapter 2
290 U.S. 325
Genesis 39:20
202–275–2348 (telephone number)
the year 1931
1721–1727 St. Clair Avenue

but Letters Patent No. 2,189,463

A colon preceding figures does not af
their use.

The result was as follows: 12 voted yea, 4
dissented.
The result was as follows: nine voted yea, fou
dissented.

Measurement and time

Units of measurement and time, actua
implied, are expressed in figures.

a. Age:
6 years old
52 years 10 months 6 days
a 3-year-old
at the age of 3 (*years* implied)

b. Clock time (see also Time):
4:30 p.m.
10 o'clock *or* 10 p.m. (*not* 10 o'clock p.m.; 2
in the afternoon; 10:00 p.m.); 12 m. (noon
p.m. (midnight); this p.m.; in the p.m.
half past 4
4ʰ30ᵐ *or* 4.5ʰ, in scientific work, if so written in copy
0025, 2359 (astronomical and military time)
08:31:04 (stopwatch reading)

c. Dates:
June 1985 (*not* June, 1985); June 29, 1985 (*not* June 29th, 1985)
March 6 to April 15, 1935 (*not* March 6, 1935, to April 15, 1935)
May, June, and July 1965 (*but* June and July 1965)
15 April 1951 (military)
4th of July (*but* Fourth of July, meaning the holiday)
the 1st [day] of the month (*but* the last of April or the first [part] of May, not referring to specific days)
in the year 2000 (*not* 2,000)

In referring to a fiscal year, consecutive years, or a continuous period of 2 years or more, when contracted, the forms 1900–11, 1906–38, 1931–32, 1801–2, 1875–79 are used (*but* upon change of century, 1895–1914 and to avoid three ciphers together, 1900–1901). For two or more separate years not representing a continuous period, a comma is used instead of a dash (1875, 1879); if the word *from* precedes the year or the word *inclusive* follows it, the second year is not shortened and the word *to* is used in lieu of the dash (from 1933 to 1936; 1935 to 1936, inclusive).

In dates, *A.D.* precedes the year (A.D. 937); *B.C.* follows the year (254 B.C.).

d. Decimals: In text a cipher should be supplied before a decimal point if there is no unit, and ciphers should be omitted after a decimal point unless they indicate exact measurement.

0.25 inch; 1.25 inches
silver 0.900 fine
specific gravity 0.9547
gauge height 10.0 feet

but .30 caliber (meaning 0.30 inch, bore of small arms); 30 calibers (length)

e. Degrees, etc. (spaces omitted):
longitude 77°04′06″ E.
latitude 49°26′14″ N.
35°30′; 35°30′ N.
a polariscopic test of 85°
an angle of 57°
strike N. 16° E.
dip 47° W. *or* 47° N. 31° W.
25.5′ (preferred); *also* 25′.5 *or* 25.′5, as in copy

but two degrees of justice;
12 degrees of freedom
32d degree Mason
150 million degrees Fahrenheit

f. Game scores:
1 up (golf)
3 to 2 (baseball)
7 to 6 (football), etc.
2 all (tie)

g. Market quotations:
4½ percent bonds
Treasury bonds sell at 95
Metropolitan Railroad, 109
gold is 109
wheat at 2.30
sugar, .03; *not* 0.03

h. Mathematical expressions:
multiplied by 3 divided by 6 a factor of 2

i. Measurements:
7 meters
about 10 yards
8 by 12 inches
8- by 12-inch page
2 feet by 1 foot 8 inches by 1 foot 3 inches
2 by 4 (lumber) (*not* 2 x 4 or 2 × 4)
1½ miles
6 acres
9 bushels
1 gallon
3 ems
20/20 (vision)
30/30 (rifle)
12 gauge shotgun
2,500 horsepower
15 cubic yards
6-pounder
80 foot-pounds
10s (for yarns and threads)
f/2.5 (camera focal length)

but tenpenny nail; fourfold; three-ply; five votes; six bales; two dozen; one gross; zero miles; seven-story building

j. Money:
$3.65; $0.75; 75 cents; 0.5 cent
$3 (*not* $3.00) per 200 pounds
75 cents apiece
Rs32,25,644 (Indian rupees)
2.5 francs *or* fr2.5
£2 4s. 6d.
T£175
65 yen
₱265

but two pennies, three quarters, one half, six bits, etc.

k. Percentage:
12 percent; 25.5 percent; 0.5 percent (*or* one-half of 1 percent)
3.65 bonds; 3.65s; 5–20 bonds; 5–20s; 4⅛s; 3s
50–50 (colloquial expression)
5 percentage points
an 1100-percent rise

l. Proportion:
1 to 4 1–3–5 1:62,500

m. Time (see also Clock time):
6 hours 8 minutes 20 seconds
10 years 3 months 29 days
7 minutes
8 days
4 weeks
1 month
3 fiscal years
1 calendar year

but four centuries; three decades;
three quarters (9 months)
statistics of any one year
in a year or two
four afternoons
one-half hour

n. Unit modifiers:
5-day week
8-year-old wine
8-hour day
10-foot pole
½-inch pipe
5-foot-wide entrance
10-million-peso loan
a 5-percent increase
20th-century progress

but two-story house
five-man board
$20 million airfield

o. Vitamins B_{12}, B_T, A_1, etc.

Ordinal numbers

Except as indicated below, and also for day preceding month, figures are used in text and footnotes to text for serial ordinal numbers beginning with *10th.* In tables, leaderwork, footnotes to tables and leaderwork, and in sidenotes, figures are used at all times. Military units are expressed in figures at all times when not the beginning of sentence, except *Corps.*

29th of May, *but* May 29
First Congress; 82d Congress
ninth century; 20th century
Second Congressional District;
20th Congressional District
seventh region; 17th region
eighth parallel; 38th parallel
fifth ward; 12th ward
ninth birthday; 66th birthday
first grade; 11th grade
1st Army
1st Calvary Division
323d Fighter Wing
12th Regiment
9th Naval District
7th Fleet
7th Air Force
7th Task Force

but XII Corps (Army usage)
Court of Appeals for the Tenth Circuit
Seventeenth Decennial Census (title)

When ordinals appear in juxtaposition and one of them is *10th* or more, figures are used for such ordinal numbers.

This legislation was passed in the 1st session of the 92d Congress.
He served in the 9th and 10th Congresses.
From the 1st to the 92d Congress.
He represented the 1st, 4th, and 13th wards.
We read the 8th and 12th chapters.
but The district comprised the first and second precincts.
He represented the first, third, and fourth regions.
The report was the sixth in a series of 14.

Ordinals and numerals appearing in a sentence are treated according to the separate rules dealing with ordinals and numerals standing alone or in a group.

The fourth group contained three items.
The fourth group contained 12 items.
The 8th and 10th groups contained three and four items, respectively.
The eighth and ninth groups contained 9 and 12 items, respectively.

Beginning with *10th,* figures are used in text matter for numbered streets, avenues, etc., but in tables, leaderwork, footnotes to tables and leaderwork, and sidenotes, figures are used at all times and *street, avenue,* etc., are abbreviated.

First Street NW.; *also* in parentheses: (Fifth Street) (13th Street); 810 West 12th Street; North First Street; 1021 121st Street; 2031 18th Street North; 711 Fifth Avenue; 518 10th Avenue; 51–35 61st Avenue

Punctuation

The comma is used in a number containing four or more digits, except in serial numbers, common and decimal fractions, astronomical and military time, and kilocycles and meters of not more than four figures pertaining to radio.

Chemical formulas

In chemical formulas full-sized figures are used before the symbol or group of symbols to which they relate, and inferior figures are used after the symbol.

$$6PbS\cdot(Ag,Cu)_2S\cdot 2As_2S_3O_4$$

Numbers spelled out

Numerals are spelled out at the beginning of a sentence or head. Rephrase a sentence or head to avoid beginning with figures.

Five years ago***; *not* 5 years ago***
Five hundred and fifty men are employed***; *not* 550 men are employed***
"Five-Year Plan Announced"; not "5-Year Plan Announced" (head)
Although 1965 may seem far off, it***; *not* 1965 may seem far off, but it***
Employees numbering 207,843***; *not* 207,843 employees***
Benefits amounting to $69,603,566***; *not* $69,603,566 worth of benefits***

1958 REPORT *change to* THE 1958 REPORT

$3,000 BUDGETED *change to* THE SUM OF $3,000 BUDGETED

4 MILLION JOBLESS *change to* JOBLESS NUMBER 4 MILLION

In testimony, hearings, transcripts, and Q. and A. matter, figures are used immediately following Q. and A. or name of interrogator or witness for years (e.g., 1958), sums of money, decimals, street numbers, and for numerical expressions beginning with *101.*

Mr. BIRCH, Junior. 1977 was a good year.
Mr. BELL. $1 per share was the return. Two dollars in 1956 was the alltime high. Nineteen hundred and seventy-eight may be another story.
Colonel DAVIS. 92 cents.
Mr. SMITH. 12.8 people.
Mr. JONES. 1240 Pennsylvania Avenue NW., Washington, DC 20004.
Mr. SMITH. Ninety-eight persons.
Q. 101 years? *But* Q. One hundred years?
A. 200 years.
Mr. SMITH. Ten-year average would be how much?

A spelled-out number should not be repeated in figures, except in legal documents. In such instances use these forms:

five (5) dollars, *not* five dollars (5)
ten dollars ($10), *not* ten ($10) dollars

Numbers appearing as part of proper names or mentioned in connection with serious and dignified subjects such as Executive orders, legal proclamations, and in formal writing are spelled out.

Three Rivers, PA, Fifteenmile Creek, etc.
the Thirteen Original States
in the year nineteen hundred and eighty-four
the Ninety-eighth Congress
millions for defense but not one cent for tribute
threescore years and ten
Ten Commandments
Air Force One (Presidential plane)

Numbers larger than *1,000,* if spelled out, should be in the following form:

two thousand and twenty
one thousand eight hundred and fifty
one hundred and fifty-two thousand three hundred and five
eighteen hundred and fifty (serial number)

Numbers of less than *100* preceding a compound modifier containing a figure are spelled out.

two ¾-inch boards
twelve 6-inch guns
but 120 8-inch boards
three four-room houses

Indefinite expressions are spelled out.

the seventies; the early seventies; *but* the early 1870s *or* 1970s
in his eighties, *not* his '80s *or* 80s
midthirties (age, years, money)
a thousand and one reasons
between two and three hundred horses[1]
twelvefold; thirteenfold; fortyfold; hundredfold; twentyfold to thirtyfold
but 1 to 3 million
mid-1971; mid-1970s
40-odd people; nine-odd people
40-plus people
100-odd people
3½-fold; 250-fold; 2.5-fold/41-fold

The use of such words as *nearly, about, around, approximately,* etc., do not constitute indefinite expressions.

The bass weighed about 6 pounds.
She was nearly 80 years old.

Except as indicated previously, a number less than *10* is spelled out within a sentence.

six horses — *but* 3½ cans
five wells — 2½ times *or* 2.5 times
eight times as large

For typographic appearance and easy grasp of large numbers beginning with *million,* the word *million* or *billion* is used.

The following are guides to treatment of figures as submitted in copy. If copy reads—

$12,000,000, *change to* $12 million
2,750,000 dollars, *change to* $2.75 million
2.7 million dollars, *change to* $2.7 million
2⅜ million dollars, *change to* $2⅜ million
two and one-half million dollars, *change to* $2½ million
a hundred cows, *change to* 100 cows
a thousand dollars, *change to* $1,000
a million and a half, *change to* 1½ million
two thousand million dollars, *change to* $2,000 million
less than a million dollars, *change to* less than $1 million
t $2,700,000, *do not change to* $2.7 million
so $10 to $20 million; 10 or 20 million; between 10 and 20 million
4 millions of assets
amounting to 4 millions
$1,270,000
$1,270,200,000
$2¾ billion; $2.75 billion; $2,750 million
$500,000 to $1 million
300,000; *not* 300 thousand
$½ billion to $1¼ billion (note full figure with second fraction); $1¼ to $1½ billion
three-quarters of a billion dollars
5 or 10 billion dollars' worth

[1]Better: Between 200 and 300 horses.

Related numbers appearing at the beginning a sentence, separated by no more than three ›rds, are treated alike.

Fifty or sixty more miles away is snowclad Mount McKinley.
Sixty and, quite often, seventy listeners responded.
Fifty or, in some instances, almost 60 applications were filed.

ıctions

Fractions standing alone, or if followed by *of* ›r *of an,* are generally spelled out.

three-fourths of an inch; *not* ¾ inch *or* ¾ of an inch
one-half inch
one-half of a farm; *not* ½ of a farm
one-fourth inch
seventh-tenths of 1 percent
if copy so reads:
three-quarters of an inch
half an inch
a quarter of an inch
one-tenth
one-hundredth
two one-hundredths
one-thousandth
five one-thousandths
thirty-five one-thousandths
½ to 1¾ pages
½-inch pipe
½-inch-diameter pipe
3½ cans; 2½ times

ractions (¼, ½, ¾, ⅜, ⅝, ⅞, 1⁄2954) or the shilling k with full-sized figures (1/4, 1/2954) may ʟsed only when either is specifically re-sted. A comma should not be used in any ȷof a built-up fraction of four or more digits ɑ decimals.

ractions are used in a unit modifier.

ınch pipe; *not* one-half-inch pipe
mile run
point rise

ɪan numerals

repeated letter repeats its value; a letter ɛd after one of greater value adds to it; a lɛ placed before one of greater value subts from it; a dashline over a letter denotes nıplied by 1,000.

I	1	LXX	70
II	2	LXXV	75
II	3	LXXIX	79
I	4	LXXX	80
V	5	LXXXV	85
V	6	LXXXIX	89
V	7	XC	90
V	8	XCV	95
I	9	XCIX	99
X	10	C	100
X	15	CL	150
X	19	CC	200
X	20	CCC	300
X	25	CD	400
X	29	D	500
X	30	DC	600
X	35	DCC	700
XX	39	DCCC	800
XI	40	CM	900

XLV	45	M	1,000
XLIX	49	MD	1,500
L	50	MM	2,000
LV	55	MMM	3,000
LIX	59	MMMM or MV̄	4,000
LX	60	V̄	5,000
LXV	65	M̄	1,000,000
LXIX	69		

Dates

MDC	1600	MCMXXX	1930
MDCC	1700	MCMXL	1940
MDCCC	1800	MCML	1950
MCM or MDCCCC	1900	MCMLX	1960
MCMX	1910	MCMLXX	1970
MCMXX	1920	MCMLXXX	1980

FOOTNOTES, INDEXES, AND CONTENTS

Footnotes and reference marks

Except as noted under "Abbreviations," footnotes to text follow the style of text.

In a publication divided into chapters, sections, or articles, each beginning a new page, text footnotes begin with 1 in each such division. In a publication without such divisional grouping, footnotes are numbered consecutively from 1 to 99, and then begin with 1 again. However, in supplemental sections, such as appendixes or bibliographies, which are not parts of the publication proper, footnotes begin with 1.

Copy preparers must see that references and footnotes are plainly marked and must also indicate the measure if footnotes are to be doubled up.

On a job that is not completed, the last footnote number must be given to the supervisor, who will record it so that there will be no question as to the next footnote number.

If a reference is repeated on another page, it should carry the original footnote; but to avoid repetition of a long note, the copy preparer may use the words "See footnote 3 (6, etc.) on p.—" instead of the entire footnote.

Unless copy is otherwise marked: (1) Footnotes to 12-point text (except 12-point briefs) are set in 8 point; (2) footnotes to 11-point text are set in 8 point, except in Supreme Court reports, in which they are set in 9 point; (3) footnotes to 10- and 8-point text are set in 7 point.

Footnotes are set as paragraphs at the bottom of the page and are separated from the text by a 50-point rule, flush on the left, with no less than 2 points of space above and below the rule.

Footnotes to indented matter (other than excerpt footnotes) are set full measure.

To achieve faithful reproduction of indented excerpt material (particularly legal work) containing original footnotes, these footnotes are also indented and placed at the bottom of the excerpt, separated by 6 points of space. No side dash is used. Reference numbers are not changed to fit the numbering sequence of text footnotes.

Footnotes must always begin on the page carrying the reference. The breaking over of a footnote from one page to the next should be avoided.[1]

Footnotes to charts, graphs, and other illustrations should be placed immediately beneath such illustrative material.

A cutoff dash is not required between the chart or graph and the footnotes.

For reference marks use: (1) Roman superior figures, (2) italic superior letters, and (3) symbols. Superior figures (preferred), letters, and symbols are separated from the words to which they apply by thin spaces, unless immediately preceded by periods or commas.

Where reference figures might lead to ambiguity (for example, in matter containing exponents), asterisks, daggers, etc., or italic superior letters may be used.

When symbols or signs are used for footnote reference marks, their sequence should be (*) asterisk, (†) dagger, (‡) double dagger, and (§) section mark. Should more symbols be needed, these may be doubled or tripled, but for simplicity and greater readability, it is preferable to extend the assortment by adding other single-character symbols.

Symbols with commonly established other meanings likely to produce confusion, such as the percent mark (%) and the number mark (#), should not be used.

To avoid possible confusion with numerals and letters frequently occurring in charts and graphs, it is preferable in such instances to use symbols as reference marks.

When items carry several reference marks, the superior-figure reference precedes an asterisk, dagger, or similar character used for reference.

A superior reference mark follows all punctuation marks except a dash but falls inside a closing parenthesis or bracket if applying only to matter within the parentheses or brackets.

Two or more superior footnote references occurring together are separated by thin spaces.

Indexes and tables of contents

Indexes and tables of contents are set in the same style as the text, except that *See* and *see also* are set in italic.

Page, section, paragraph, etc., over figure columns are set in roman, flush on right.

454 ANNUAL REPORT OF THE SECRETARY OF THE TREASURY

Notes—Continued
  Treasury:
    Marketable: Page
      Exchanges 459

456 ANNUAL REPORT OF THE SECRETARY OF THE TREASURY

Notes—Continued Page
  Treasury 459

Where a word occurs in an index page column, either alone or with a figure, it is set flush on the right. If the word extends back into the leaders, it is preceded by an en space.

Page
Explanatory diagram .... Frontispiece
General instructions VIII
Capitalization (*see also* Abbreviations) 16
Correct imposition (diagram) .... Facing 34
Explanatory diagram .... Frontispiece
Legends. (*See* miscellaneous rules.)
Appendixes A, B, C, and D, maps, illustrations, and excerpts .... In supplemental volume

For better appearance, Roman numerals should be set in small caps in the figure columns of tables of contents and indexes.

In indexes set with leaders, if the page numbers will not fit in the leader line, the first number only is set in that line and the other numbers are overrun. If the entry makes three or more lines and the last line of figures is not full, do not use a period at the end.

If page folios overrun due to an excessive amount of figures use this form 220, 224, 227, 230, 240
And this way when overrun folios make two or more lines 220, 224–25, 230–40, 245, 246, 250–55, 258, 300, 320, 330, 350, 360, 370, 380, 390, 400, 410–500, 510, 520, 530, 540, 550, 560, 570, 580, 590, 600–20, 630, 640, 650, 660, 670,680, 690, 700

Overrun page numbers are indented 3½ ems in measures not over 20 picas and 7 ems in wider measures, more than one line being used if necessary. These indentions are increased as necessary to not less than 2 ems more than the line immediately above or below.

When copy specifies that all turnovers are to be a certain number of ems, the turnovers of the figure column shall be held in 2 ems more than the specified indention.

Examples of block-type indexes:

Example 1

Medical officer, radiological defense, 3
Medicolegal dosage, 44
Military Liaison Committee, 4
Monitoring, 58
  Air, 62
  Personnel, 59
    Civilian, 60
    Military, 59
  Sea, 61
  Ship, 61
Monitors, radiological defense, 3

NEPA, 29
NEPS; project, 30
Neutron(s), 16
  Flux, 41
Nuclear binding energy, 22
Nuclear energy, release of, 23

Example 2

Brazil—Continued
  Exchange restrictions—Continued
    Williams mission (*see also* Williams, John H., special mission), efforts in connection with exchange control situation, 586–88
  Trade agreement with United States, proposed:
    Draft text, 558–67
    Proposals for:
      Inclusion of clauses relating to exchange control operation, 550, 551, 557
      Joint United States-Brazilian declaration of policy: Brazilian attitude, 553, 569, 570, 572–74; information concerning, 550, 551, 552

In index entries the following forms are used:

Brown, A.H., Jr. (*not* Brown, Jr., A.H.)
Brown, A.H., & Sons (*not* Brown & Sons, A.H.)
Brown, A.H., Co. (*not* Brown Co., A.H.)
Brown, A.H., & Sons Co. (*not* Brown & Sons Co., A.H.)

In a table of contents, where *chapter, plate,* or *figure* is followed by a number and period, an en space is used after the period. The periods are aligned on the right.

Chapter Page
I. Introduction 1
II. Summary 1
VI. Conclusions 7

Subheads in indexes and tables of contents are centered in the full measure.

In contents set in combination of two sizes of lightface type, or in combination of boldface and lightface type, all leaders and page numbers will be set in lightface roman type. Contents set entirely in boldface will use boldface page numbers. All page numbers will be set in the predominant size.

Page
PART I. MAINTENANCE OF PEACE AND SECURITY 5
  Disarmament 6
  Peaceful Uses of Atomic Energy 7
Part I. Maintenance of Peace and Security 5
  Disarmament 6
  Peaceful Uses of Atomic Energy 7
Part I. Maintenance of Peace and Security 5
  Disarmament 6
  Peaceful Uses of Atomic Energy 7

When a footnote breaks from an odd (right-hand) page to an n (left-hand) page, the word (*Continued*) will be placed flush t below the last line where the break occurs. The usual 50-nt dash is used above each part. Where break occurs on fac- pages; i.e., from even page to odd page, do not use (*Contin-*) lines.